CHILTON'S
AUTO REPAIR MANUAL
1992-1996

Publisher & Editor-In-Chief	Kerry A. Freeman, S.A.E.
Executive Editors	Dean F. Morgantini, S.A.E., W. Calvin Settle, Jr., S.A.E.
Managing Editor	Nicholas L. D'Andrea
Senior Editors	Debra Gaffney, Jacques Gordon, Michael L. Grady, Kevin M. G. Maher, Richard J. Rivele, S.A.E., Richard T. Smith, Jim Taylor, Ron Webb
Special Products Managers	Eric O. Cole, Kenneth J. Grabowski, A.S.E., S.A.E.
Project Managers	Larry Braun, S.A.E., A.S.C., Thomas P. Browne III, Joseph DeFrancesco, Robert E. Doughten, Benjamin E. Greisler, S.A.E., Martin J. Gunther, Craig P. Nangle, A.S.E., Richard Schwartz
Editorial Staff	Jaffer A. Ahmad, Chris Armenti, Bradley Bower, James Carr, Robert A. Chabot, William C. Cottman, A.S.E., Leonard Davis, A.S.E., Michael DiFurio Jr., S.A.E., Robert F. Dougherty Jr., John J. Ferraro, A.S.E., S.A.E., Sam Fiorani, Matthew E. Frederick, William C. Friedauer, Edward J. Giacomucci, A.S.E., S.A.E., Al Gibbs, Herbert Guie Jr, Dawn M. Hoch, David E. Jester, Lori Johnson, A.S.E., William Kessler, Kenneth F. Konzelman, Neil J. Leonard, A.S.E., James R. Marotta, Robert McAnally, Raymond K. Moore, Norman D. Norville, A.S.E., Christine L. Nuckowski, Eric S. Peterson, A.S.E., Ernest H. Ralph, A.S.E., Charles Ramsey, A.S.E., Roy Ripple, A.S.E., Don Schnell, A.S.E., S.A.E., Paul Shanahan, Larry E. Stiles, Gordon L. Tobias, Anthony Tortorici, A.S.E., S.A.E., Albert A. Wood, A.S.E.
Manager, Product Systems Development	Robert E. Maxey
Production Manager	Andrea M. Steiger
Assistant Production Manager	Marsha Park Herman
Production Specialists	Christina Davis, Kimberly T. Hayes, Joseph C. McGinty, Elizabeth E. Thompson
Director of Manufacturing	Mike D'Imperio
Asst. Manufacturing Manager	Robin Norman
President, Chilton Enterprises	David S. Loewith
Senior Vice President	Ronald A. Hoxter

CHILTON BOOK COMPANY
ONE OF THE **DIVERSIFIED PUBLISHING COMPANIES,**
A PART OF **CAPITAL CITIES/ABC, INC.**

Manufactured in
© 1995 Chilton Book Company
Chilton Way, Radnor, PA 19089
ISBN 0-8019-7916-1
ISSN 0069-3634

1234567890 4321098765

CAR MODELS

Table of Contents

Car Sections

HOW TO USE THIS MANUAL

HOW TO USE THIS MANUAL

Car Section

Car sections are grouped by manufacturer and arranged in alphabetical order. The text and illustrations that comprise the service procedures in each Car Section are arranged in the following order of systems and components: Engine Mechanical, Engine Lubrication, Engine Cooling, Engine Electrical, Emission Controls, Fuel System, Drive Axle, Manual Transmission/Transaxle, Clutch, Automatic Transmission/Transaxle, Front Suspension, Rear Suspension, Steering, Brakes, Chassis Electrical.

Specification charts are always located at the front of each section. All illustrations are located as close as possible to the pertinent text. Procedures are for all models in the particular section unless specifically noted otherwise.

Locating Information

The Table of Contents, at the front of the book, lists the beginning of each Car Section in the manual.

To find where a particular Car Section is located in the book, you need only look in the Table of Contents. Once you have found the proper section, you may wish to find where specific procedures are located in that section. Turn to the Index at the front of the section. At the upper left-hand side is a listing of the main topics within the section and the page number they will be found on. Following the main topics is an alphabetical listing of all the procedures within the section and their page numbers.

Safety Notice

Proper service and repair procedures are vital to the safe, reliable operation of all motor vehicles, as well as the personal safety of those performing repairs. This manual outlines procedures for servicing and repairing vehicles using safe effective methods. The procedures contain many NOTES and CAUTIONS which should be followed along with standard safety procedures to eliminate the possibility of personal injury or improper service which could damage the vehicle or compromise its safety.

It is important to note that repair procedures and techniques, tools and parts for servicing motor vehicles, as well as the skill and experience of the individual performing the work vary widely. It is not possible to anticipate all of the conceivable ways or conditions under which vehicles may be serviced, or to provide cautions as to all of the possible hazards that may result. Standard and accepted safety precautions and equipment should be used when handling toxic or flammable fluids, and safety goggles or other protection should be used during cutting, grinding, chiseling, prying, or any other process that can cause material removal or projectiles.

Some procedures require the use of tools specially designed for a specific purpose. Before substituting another tool or procedure, you must be completely satisfied that neither your personal safety, nor the performance of the vehicle will be endangered.

Part Numbers

Part numbers listed in this book are not recommendations by Chilton for any product by brand name. They are references that can be used with interchange manuals and aftermarket supplier catalogs to locate each brand supplier's discrete part number.

Although information in this manual is based on industry sources and is as complete as possible at the time of publication, the possibility exists that some car manufacturers made later changes which could not be included here. Information on very late models may not be available in some circumstances. While striving for total accuracy, Chilton Book Company cannot assume responsibility for any errors, changes, or omissions that may occur in the compilation of this data.

Copyright Notice

CHRYSLER CORPORATION

EAGLE—Summit, Summit Wagon, Talon **DODGE**—Stealth **PLYMOUTH**—Laser

FIRING ORDERS

NOTE: To avoid confusion, always replace spark plug wires one at a time.

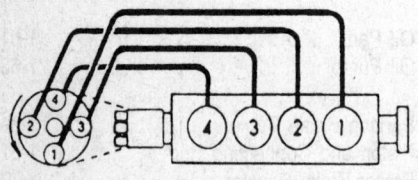

84701001

1.8L and 1993–96 2.4L Engines
Engine Firing Order: 1–3–4–2
Distributor Rotation: Counterclockwise

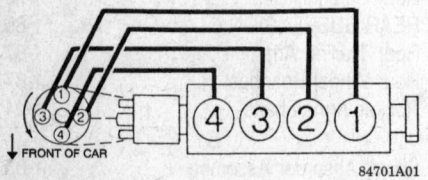

84701A01

1.5L Engine
Engine Firing Order: 1–3–4–2
Distributor Rotation: Counterclockwise

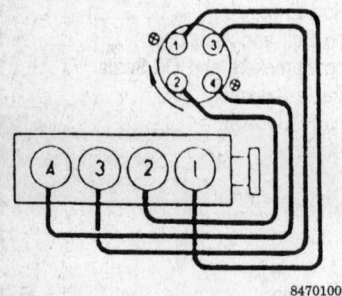

84701002

1.8L and 1992 2.4L Engines
Engine Firing Order: 1–3–4–2
Distributor Rotation: Clockwise

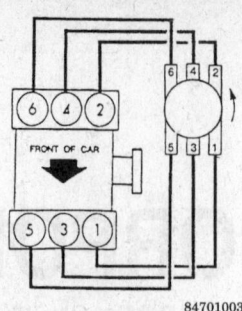

FRONT OF CAR

84701003

3.0L SOHC Engine
Engine Firing Order:
1–2–3–4–5–6
Distributor Rotation:
Counterclockwise

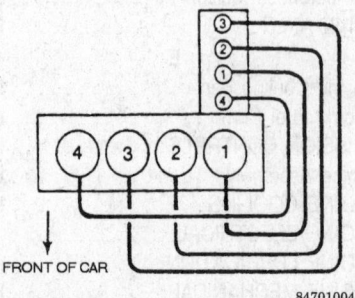

FRONT OF CAR

84701004

2.0L Engine
Engine Firing Order: 1–3–4–2
Distributorless Ignition System

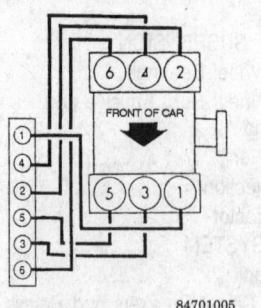

FRONT OF CAR

84701005

3.0L DOHC Engine
Engine Firing Order:
1–2–3–4–5–6
Distributorless Ignition System

ENGINE ELECTRICAL

NOTE: Disconnecting the negative battery cable on some vehicles may interfere with the functions of the on board computer systems and may require the computer to undergo a relearning process, once the negative battery cable is reconnected.

Distributor

REMOVAL

1. Disconnect the negative battery cable. Remove the ignition wire cover, if equipped.
2. Disconnect the distributor harness electrical connectors.
3. Unscrew the distributor cap hold-down screws or release the clips and lift off the distributor cap with all ignition wires connected. Remove the coil wire, if necessary.
4. Matchmark the rotor to the distributor housing and the distributor housing to the engine.

NOTE: Do not crank the engine during this procedure. If the engine is cranked, the matchmark must be disregarded.

5. Remove the hold-down nut.
6. Carefully remove the distributor from the engine.

INSTALLATION

NOTE: Some engines may be sensitive to the routing of the distributor sensor wires. If routed near the high-voltage coil wire or the spark plug wires, the electromagnetic field surrounding the high voltage wires could generate an occasional disruption of the ignition system operation.

Timing Not Disturbed

1. Install a new distributor housing O-ring and lubricate the distributor drive gear and O-ring with clean oil.
2. Install the distributor in the engine so the rotor is aligned with the matchmark on the housing and the housing is aligned with the matchmark on the engine. Make sure the distributor is fully seated and the distributor shaft is fully engaged.
3. Install the hold-down.
4. Connect the distributor harness connectors.
5. Make sure the sealing O-ring is in place, install the distributor cap and tighten the screws or secure the clips.
6. Connect the negative battery cable.
7. Adjust the ignition timing and tighten the hold-down nut to 7–9 ft. lbs. (10–13 Nm).

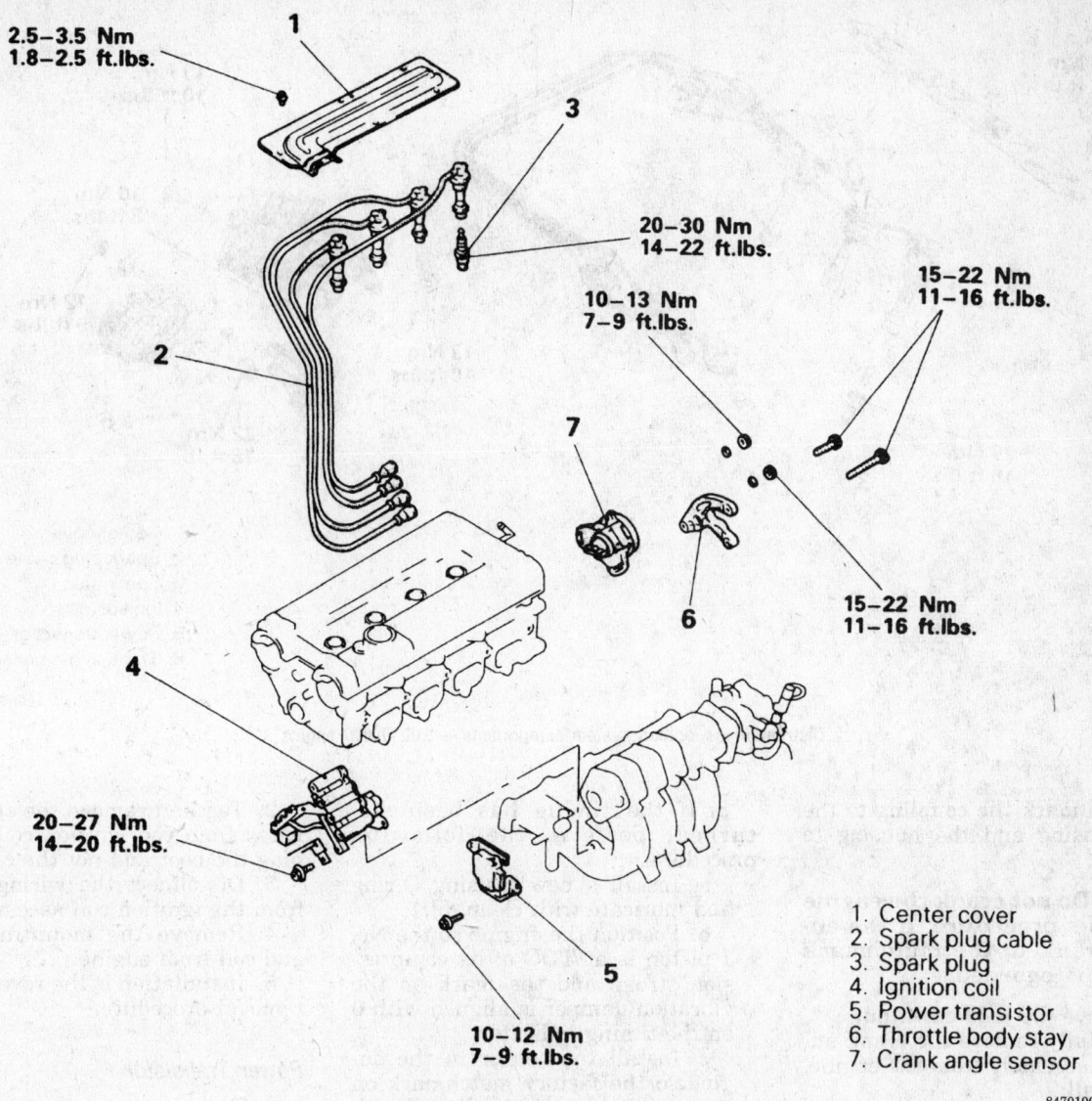

1. Center cover
2. Spark plug cable
3. Spark plug
4. Ignition coil
5. Power transistor
6. Throttle body stay
7. Crank angle sensor

84701008

Distributorless ignition system components — 2.0L engines

Timing Disturbed

1. Install a new distributor housing O-ring and lubricate with clean oil.

2. Position the engine so the No. 1 piston is at TDC of its compression stroke and the mark on the vibration damper is aligned with **0** on the timing indicator.

3. Align the distributor housing and gear mating marks. Install the distributor in engine so the slot or groove of the distributor's installation flange aligns with the distributor installation stud in the engine block. Make sure the distributor is fully seated. Inspect alignment of the dis-

tributor rotor making sure the rotor is aligned with the position of the No. 1 ignition wire in the distributor cap.

NOTE: Make sure the rotor is pointing to where the No. 1 terminal originates inside the cap, if equipped, and not where the No. 1 ignition wire plugs into the cap.

4. Install the hold-down nut.
5. Connect the distributor harness connectors.
6. Make sure the sealing O-ring is in place, install the distributor cap and tighten the screws or secure the clips.
7. Connect the negative battery cable.

8. Adjust the ignition timing and tighten the hold-down bolt to 7–9 ft. lbs. (10–13 Nm).

Distributorless Ignition

REMOVAL AND INSTALLATION

Crank Angle Sensor

1. Disconnect the negative battery cable.
2. Disconnect the sensor harness connector.
3. Unscrew the cap hold-down screws and lift off the cap.

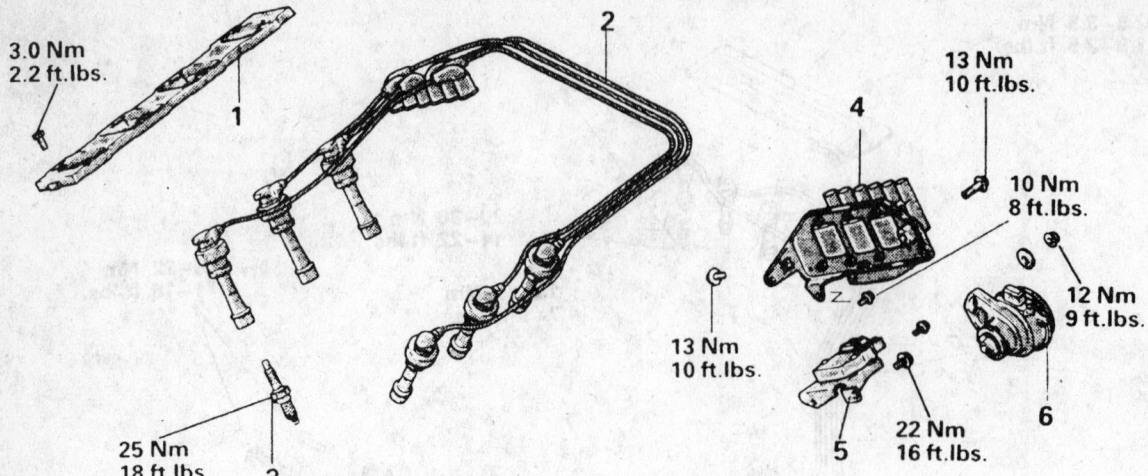

1. Center cover
2. Spark plug cable
3. Spark plug
4. Ignition coil
5. Power transistor
6. Crank angle sensor

84701010

Distributorless ignition system components — 3.0L DOHC engine

4. Matchmark the coupling to the sensor housing and the housing to the engine.

NOTE: Do not crank the engine during this procedure. If the engine is cranked, the matchmark must be disregarded.

5. Remove the hold-down nut.
6. Carefully remove the crank angle sensor assembly from the engine.

To install:

7. If the timing is not disturbed, perform the following procedures:

a. Install a new housing O-ring and lubricate with clean oil.

b. Install the assembly in the engine so the coupling is aligned with the matchmark on the housing and the housing is aligned with the matchmark on the engine. Make sure the sensor assembly is fully seated and the shaft is fully engaged.

c. Install the hold-down nut.

d. Connect the harness connector.

e. Make sure the sealing O-ring is in place, install the cap and tighten the screws.

f. Connect the negative battery cable.

g. Adjust the ignition timing, if applicable, and tighten the hold-down nut to 7–9 ft. lbs. (10–13 Nm).

8. If the timing has been disturbed, perform the following procedures:

a. Install a new housing O-ring and lubricate with clean oil.

b. Position the engine so the No. 1 piston is at TDC of its compression stroke and the mark on the vibration damper is aligned with **0** on the timing indicator.

c. Install the sensor in the engine so the factory matchmark on the coupling (notch) is aligned with the matchmark on the housing (punch mark) and the housing is aligned with the matchmark on the engine. Make sure the sensor assembly is fully seated and the shaft is fully engaged.

d. Install the hold-down nut.

e. Connect the harness connector.

f. Make sure the sealing O-ring is in place, install the cap and tighten the screws.

g. Connect the negative battery cable.

h. Adjust the ignition timing, if applicable, and tighten the hold-down nut to 7–9 ft. lbs. (10–13 Nm)

Ignition Coil

1. Disconnect the negative battery cable.

2. Tag and remove the spark plug wires from the ignition coil by gripping the boot and not the cable.

3. Disconnect the wiring harness from the ignition coil assembly.

4. Remove the mounting screws and coil from engine.

5. Installation is the reverse of the removal procedure.

Power Transistor

1. Disconnect the negative battery cable.

2. Tag and disconnect the wires from the power transistor.

3. Remove the retaining screw and lift the power transistor from the engine.

4. Installation is the reverse of the removal procedure.

Ignition Timing

ADJUSTMENT

1. Set the parking brake, start and run the engine until normal operating temperature is obtained. Keep all lights and accessories OFF and the front wheels straight-ahead. Place the transaxle in **P** or automatic tran-

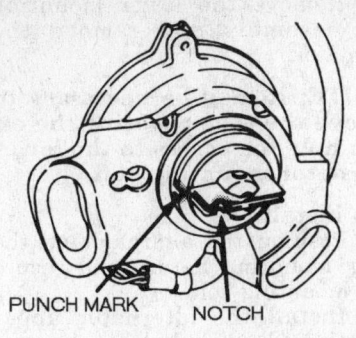

PUNCH MARK   NOTCH

84701011

Crank angle sensor alignment marks

saxle or neutral for manual transaxle.

NOTE: On Canadian vehicles the lights will remain on when the vehicle is running, this will not be a problem.

2. Locate the wire connector on the ignition coil connector. Insert a paper clip behind the TACH terminal connector to act as a tachometer adapter. Connect a tachometer to the paper clip. If not at specification, set the idle speed at the correct level.

3. Turn the engine **OFF** and remove the water-proof cover from the ignition timing adjusting connector. This connector is located near the center of the firewall on Summit and Summit Wagon or on the firewall just behind the battery on Laser, Talon and Stealth. Connect a jumper wire from this terminal to a good ground.

4. Connect a conventional power timing light to the No. 1 cylinder spark plug wire. Start the engine and run at idle.

5. Aim the timing light at the timing scale located near the crankshaft pulley.

6. Loosen the distributor or crank angle sensor hold-down nut just enough so the housing can be rotated.

7. Turn the housing in the proper direction until the specified timing is reached. Tighten the hold-down nut and recheck the timing. Turn the engine **OFF**.

8. Remove the jumper wire from the ignition timing adjusting terminal and install the water-proof cover.

9. Start the engine and check the actual timing without the terminal grounded. This reading should be approximately 5 degrees more than the basic timing. Actual timing may increase according to altitude. Also, actual timing may fluctuate because of slight variation accomplished by the

ECU. As long as the basic timing is correct, the engine is timed correctly.

10. Turn the engine **OFF**. Disconnect the timing equipment and tachometer.

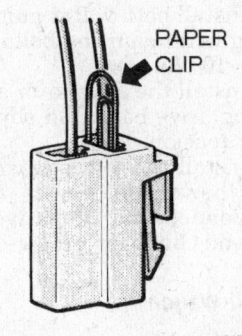

PAPER CLIP

84701012

Insert paper clip into connector as shown

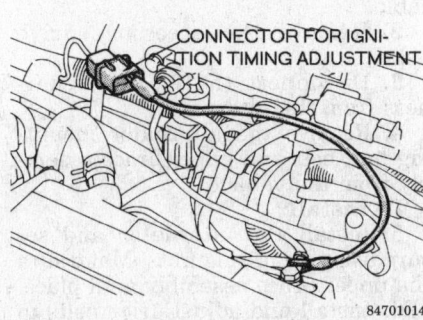

CONNECTOR FOR IGNITION TIMING ADJUSTMENT

84701014

Ignition timing adjustment harness connection — except Stealth

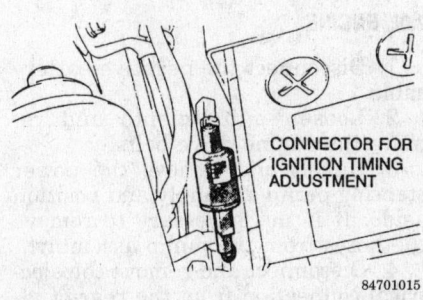

CONNECTOR FOR IGNITION TIMING ADJUSTMENT

84701015

Ignition timing adjustment harness connector — Stealth

Alternator

PRECAUTIONS

Several precautions must be observed with alternator-equipped vehicles to avoid damage to the unit.

• If the battery is removed for any reason, make sure it is reconnected with the correct polarity. Reversing the battery connections may result in damage to the 1-way rectifiers or the battery.

• When utilizing a booster battery as a starting aid, always connect the positive to positive terminals and the negative terminal from the booster battery to a good engine ground on the vehicle being started.

• Never use a fast charger as a booster to start vehicles.

• Disconnect the battery cables when charging the battery with a fast charger.

• Never attempt to polarize the alternator.

• Do not use test lamps of more than 12 volts when checking diode continuity.

• Do not short across or ground any of the alternator terminals.

• The polarity of the battery, alternator and regulator must be matched and considered before making any electrical connections within the system.

• Never separate the alternator on an open circuit. Make sure all connections within the circuit are clean and tight.

• Disconnect the battery ground terminal when performing any service on electrical components.

• Disconnect the battery if arc welding is to be done on the vehicle.

BELT TENSION ADJUSTMENT

1. Place a straightedge along the top edge of the belt and across 2 pulleys. Allow both ends of the straightedge to rest on top of each pulley for support.

2. Measure the deflection of the belt from the straightedge with a force of about 22 lbs. applied midway between the 2 pulleys. Deflection should be:

   a. Summit: 0.22–0.35 in. (5.5–9.0mm)

   b. Summit Wagon: 0.34–0.47 in. (8.5–12mm).

   c. Laser with 1.8L engine: 0.32–0.43 in. (8.0–11.0mm)

   d. Laser and Talon with 2.0L engine: 0.35–0.45 in. (9.0–11.5mm)

e. Stealth with 3.0L SOHC engine: 0.24–0.35 in. (6.0–9.0mm)

f. Stealth with 3.0L DOHC engine: 0.16–0.22 in. (4.0–5.5mm)

3. Belt tension can also be checked with a tension gauge. The desired value should be 55–110 lbs. (250–500 N).

4. Loosen the adjusting bolt or fixing bolt locknut on the alternator, alternator bracket or tension pulley. Then move the alternator or turn the adjusting bolt to adjust belt tension. Secure the bolt or locknut when finished.

REMOVAL AND INSTALLATION

Summit and Summit Wagon

1.5L AND 2.4L ENGINES

1. Disconnect the negative battery cable.
2. On Summit, remove the left side cover panel under the vehicle.
3. Remove the drive belts.
4. Remove both water pump pulleys.
5. Remove the alternator upper bracket/brace.
6. Disconnect the alternator electrical connectors and remove alternator.

To install:
7. Position the alternator on the lower mounting fixture and install the lower mounting bolt and nut. Tighten nut just enough to allow for movement of the alternator.
8. Install the alternator upper bracket/brace and connect the alternator electrical harness.
9. Install the water pump pulleys.
10. Install the drive belts and adjust to the proper tension.
11. Install the left side cover panel under the vehicle as required.
12. Connect the negative battery cable and check for proper operation.

1.6L ENGINE

1. Disconnect the negative battery cable.
2. Remove the left side cover panel under the vehicle.
3. Remove the alternator and power steering drive belts and both water pump pulleys.
4. Remove the alternator adjuster brace.
5. Disconnect the alternator electrical connection.
6. Remove the battery, windshield washer tank and battery tray.
7. Remove the attaching bolts at the top of the radiator and gently lift the radiator to provide clearance for

removing the alternator from the vehicle. Do not disconnect the radiator hoses.
8. Unbolt and remove the alternator from the vehicle.

To install:
9. While lifting the radiator, position the alternator on the engine mounting fixture. Lower the radiator and reinstall the upper attaching bolts.
10. Install the lower mounting bolt and nut. Tighten nut just enough to allow movement of the alternator.
11. Install the battery, windshield washer tank and battery tray.
12. Connect the alternator electrical connections.
13. Install the alternator adjuster brace.
14. Install both water pump pulleys and tighten mounting bolts to 6–7 ft. lbs. (8–10 Nm).
15. Install the alternator and power steering drive belts and adjust to the proper tension.
16. Install the left side cover panel under the vehicle.
17. Connect the negative battery cable and check for proper operation.

Summit Wagon

1.8L ENGINE

1. Disconnect negative battery cable.
2. Remove the accessory drive belts.
3. Disconnect the electrical harness from the alternator.
4. Remove the alternator mounting nut, bolt and upper brace assembly from the vehicle.

To install:
5. Install the alternator and secure using mounting nuts. Make sure the upper brace assembly is in place.
6. Install and adjust drive belts to the proper tension. Secure all mounting hardware.
7. Reconnect the negative battery cable and check system operation.

2.0L ENGINE

1. Disconnect the negative battery cable.
2. Loosen adjustments and remove the engine drive belts.
3. Unbolt and remove the power steering pump assembly and position aside. It is not necessary to remove the hoses from the pump assembly.
4. Disconnect and remove the electrical connection from the rear of alternator assembly.
5. Unbolt and remove the upper support adjusting bracket.

6. Remove the lower mounting bolt assembly and remove the alternator.

NOTE: It may be necessary to remove the tape covering the escape hole for access to the lower alternator mounting bolt.

To install:
7. Position the alternator on the lower mounting fixture and secure with mounting bolt.
8. Install the alternator upper mounting/adjusting bracket, be sure to install spacer and lockwashers.
9. Connect wiring harness connections to alternator.
10. Install the drive belts, adjust and tighten all mounting brackets.
11. Connect the battery terminal, run engine and test charging system.

Laser and Talon

1. Disconnect the negative battery cable. Remove the left side undercover from the vehicle.
2. If equipped with air conditioning, remove the condenser electric fan motor and shroud assembly.
3. Remove alternator, power steering, water pump and air conditioner compressor drive belts.
4. Remove both water pump pulleys and the alternator top support brace.
5. Disconnect the alternator wiring harness.
6. Remove the lower mounting bolt and remove the alternator from the vehicle.

To install:
7. Position alternator on the lower mounting fixture and secure with mounting bolt.
8. Connect wiring harness to the rear of the alternator.
9. Install water pump pulleys and tighten bolts.
10. Install top alternator support bracket and fan belts. Adjust belts and tighten all support brackets.
11. If equipped with air conditioning, install the condenser electric fan motor and shroud assembly.
12. Connect the negative battery terminal, run engine and test charging system.

Stealth

3.0L SOHC ENGINE

1. Disconnect the negative battery cable.
2. Loosen the tensioner pulley and remove the alternator drive belt.
3. Remove the accelerator cable from the intake plenum extension.

4. Remove the brake booster vacuum hose.

5. On California models equipped with an EGR valve, unbolt the valve and remove it.

6. Disconnect the alternator wiring harness connectors.

7. Remove the alternator upper and lower mounting bolts. Remove the alternator from behind the surge tank at the center of the vehicle.

To install:

8. Position the alternator on the lower mounting fixture and install and tighten the bolts.

9. Install the EGR valve using a new gasket, if removed. Connect the vacuum hose connection at the brake booster.

10. Install the accelerator cable to the intake plenum extension. Check the accelerator cable adjustment as follows:

   a. Turn the ignition key **ON** but do not start the engine. With the ignition left in this condition wait 15 seconds.

   b. Check to insure that the throttle lever is in contact with the fixed Speed Adjusting Screw (SAS).

   c. Check that the inner cable play is within specifications. For manual transaxle, the desired value is 0.04–0.08 in. (1–2mm). If equipped with automatic transaxle, the desired value is 0.12–0.20 in. (3–5mm).

   d. If not within the desired value, loosen the adjusting bolts and slide plate so play at the inner cable will fall within the desired value. Retighten the adjusting bolts.

11. Reinstall the drive belt and adjust the tensioner until the proper belt tension is achieved.

12. Connect the negative battery cable and check the charging system for proper operation.

3.0L DOHC ENGINE

1. Disconnect the negative battery cable.

2. On turbocharged models, remove the air intake pipe and hoses.

3. If equipped with air conditioning, remove the clamp nut that secures the air conditioning hose.

4. Raise the air conditioning suction hose and suspend it from the engine hood using a cord.

5. Loosen the tensioner pulley and remove the alternator drive belt.

6. Disconnect the oxygen sensor connector.

7. Disconnect the alternator wiring harness.

8. Remove the alternator bracket to engine block mounting bolts and remove the bracket and alternator as an assembly.

9. Separate the alternator from the mounting bracket on a workbench.

To install:

10. Install the alternator onto the bracket and install bracket assembly to the engine.

11. Connect the oxygen sensor connector.

12. Connect wiring harness to the rear of the alternator.

13. Install the drive belt and adjust to proper tension using the tensioner pulley.

14. Install air conditioning suction hose to its original position and secure using clamp nut.

15. Install the air intake delivery hoses and air pipe.

16. Reconnect the negative battery cable and check the charging system for proper operation.

Starter

REMOVAL AND INSTALLATION

Summit and Summit Wagon

1. Disconnect the negative battery cable.

2. Disconnect the air-flow sensor assembly connector and remove the breather hose. Remove the resonator retaining nuts and remove the air intake hose and resonator assembly as required.

NOTE: Use care when removing the air cleaner cover because the air-flow sensor is attached and is a sensitive component.

3. Remove the heat shield from under the intake manifold on the 1.5L engine.

4. Disconnect the starter motor electrical connections.

5. Remove the starter motor mounting bolts and remove the starter.

6. The installation is the reverse of the removal procedure.

7. Tighten starter mounting bolts to 20–25 ft. lbs. (27–34 Nm.)

8. Connect the negative battery cable and check the starter for proper operation.

Laser and Talon

1. Remove the battery and battery tray from the engine compartment.

2. Disconnect the speedometer cable connector at the transaxle end.

3. If equipped with 1.8L engine, remove the bracket on the lower side if the intake manifold.

4. Disconnect the starter motor electrical connections.

5. Remove the starter motor mounting bolts and remove the starter.

6. The installation is the reverse of the removal procedure.

7. Tighten starter mounting bolts to 20–25 ft. lbs. (27–34 Nm.)

8. Connect the negative battery cable and check the starter for proper operation.

Stealth

1. Disconnect the negative battery cable.

2. Raise the vehicle and support safely.

3. Remove the engine undercover.

4. Disconnect the wiring from the starter.

5. Remove the mounting bolts and remove the starter from the vehicle.

6. The installation is the reverse of the removal procedure.

7. Tighten starter mounting bolts to 20–25 ft. lbs. (27–34 Nm.)

8. Connect the negative battery cable and check the starter for proper operation.

CHASSIS ELECTRICAL

Air Bag

DISARMING

1. Position the front wheels in the straight-ahead position and place the key in the **LOCK** position. Remove the key from the ignition lock cylinder.

2. Disconnect the negative battery cable and insulate the cable end with high-quality electrical tape or similar non-conductive wrapping.

3. Wait at least 1 minute before working on the vehicle. The air bag system is designed to retain enough voltage to deploy the air bag for a short period of time even after the battery has been disconnected.

Heater Blower Motor

REMOVAL AND INSTALLATION

Summit and Summit Wagon

1. Disconnect the negative battery cable.
2. Remove the glove box assembly and pry off the speaker cover to the lower right of the glove box.
3. Remove the passenger side lower cowl side trim kick panel.
4. Remove the passenger side knee protector which is the panel surrounding in the glove box opening.
5. Remove the glove frame along top of glove box opening.
6. Remove the lap heater duct. This is a small piece on vehicles without a rear heater and much larger on vehicles with a rear heater.
7. Disconnect the electrical connector from the blower motor.
8. Remove the cooling tube from the blower assembly.
9. On Summit, remove the Multi-Point Injection (MPI) control unit from the lower side of the cowl.
10. Remove the blower motor assembly.
11. Separate the blower assembly case and packing seal from the blower motor flange.
12. Remove the fan retaining nut and fan in order to renew the motor.
   To install:
13. Check that the blower motor shaft is not bent and that the packing and blower case are in good condition.
14. Assemble the fan and motor. Install the blower assembly and connect the wiring and cooling tube.
15. Install the MPI control unit as required. Install the lap heater duct.
16. Install the glove box frame, interior trim pieces and glove box assembly.
17. Connect the negative battery cable and check the entire climate control system for proper operation.

Laser and Talon

1. Disconnect the negative battery cable.

   NOTE: If equipped with an air bag, be sure to disarm it before working on the vehicle. Failure to disarm an air bag could result in personal injury or death.

2. Remove the right side duct, if equipped. Remove the cooling tube from the blower assembly.
3. Remove the blower motor assembly. Remove the packing seal.

4. Remove the fan retaining nut and fan in order to renew the motor.
   To install:
5. Check that the blower motor shaft is not bent and the packing is in good condition.
6. Assemble the motor and fan. Install the blower motor and connect the wiring harness connector.
7. Install the cooling tube. Install the right side duct, if equipped.
8. Connect the negative cable and check the entire climate control system for proper operation.

Stealth

1. Disconnect the negative battery cable.

   NOTE: If equipped with an air bag, be sure to disarm it before working on the vehicle. Failure to disarm an air bag could result in personal injury or death.

2. Remove the glove box, glove box outer case and the instrument panel undercover.
3. Remove the lower and side glove box frames from the instrument panel. If equipped with air conditioning, remove the lower evaporator mounting nut and bolt.
4. Disconnect the air selection wire attached to the blower case.
5. Disconnect the electrical harness from the blower motor. Remove the blower motor assembly.
6. Remove the packing seal. Remove the fan retaining nut and fan in order to renew the motor.
   To install:
7. Check that the blower motor shaft is not bent and that the packing in in good condition.
8. Assemble the motor and fan. Install the blower motor and connect the wiring harness connector.
9. Connect the air selection wire to the blower case.
10. Install the lower evaporator mounting nut and bolt, if removed. Install the lower and side glove box frames to the instrument panel.
11. Install glove box, glove box outer case and the instrument panel undercover.
12. Reconnect the negative battery cable. Check the entire climate control system for proper operation.

Windshield Wiper Motor

REMOVAL AND INSTALLATION

Summit and Summit Wagon

FRONT

1. Disconnect the negative battery cable.
2. Remove the windshield wiper arms by unscrewing the cap nuts and lifting the arms from the linkage posts.
3. Remove the front deck garnish panel.
4. Remove both windshield holders.
5. Remove the clips that hold the deck cover. If they are the pin type, they may be removed using the following procedure:
   a. Remove the clip by pressing down on the center pin with a suitable blunt pointed tool. Press down a little more than $1/16$ in. (2mm). This releases the clip. Pull the clip outward to remove it.
   b. Do not push the pin inward more than necessary because it may damage the grommet or if pushed too far, the pin may fall in. Once the clips are removed, use a plastic trim stick to pry the deck cover loose.
6. On Summit remove the air intake screen.
7. Loosen the wiper motor assembly mounting bolts and remove the windshield wiper motor. Disconnect the linkage from the motor assembly. If necessary, remove the linkage from the vehicle.

   NOTE: The installation angle of the crank arm and motor has been factory set, do not remove them unless it is necessary to do so. If arm must be removed, remove them only after marking their mounting positions.

   To install:
8. Install the windshield wiper motor and connect the linkage. Connect the electrical harness to the motor.
9. When installing the trim and garnish pieces and reusing pin type clips, use the following procedure:
   a. With the pin pulled out, insert the trim clip into the hole in the trim.
   b. Push the pin inward until the pin's head is flush with the grommet.
   c. Check that the trim is secure.
10. Install the wiper arms and tighten nuts to 17 ft. lbs. (24 Nm).

1. Glove box assembly
2. Speaker cover
3. Right kickpanel
4. Right knee protector
5. Glove box frame
6. Lap heater duct
7. Electrical connector
8. Hose
9. MPI control unit
10. Blower motor assembly
11. Blower case
12. Packing seal
13. Fan
14. Blower motor

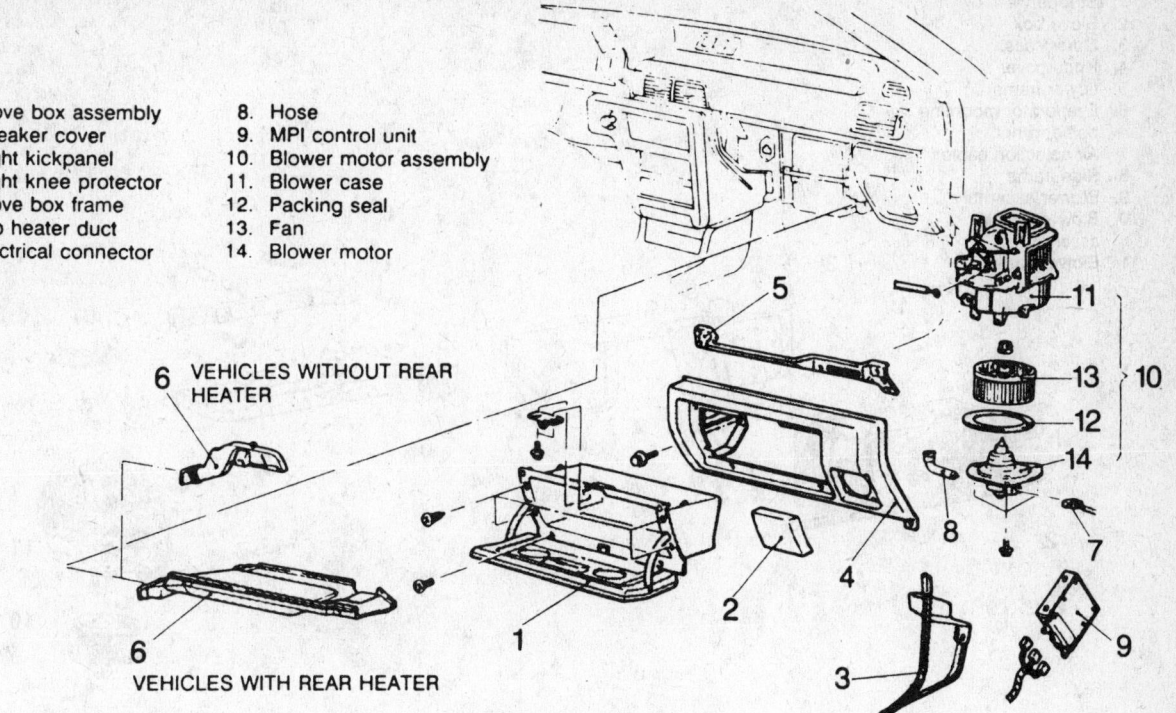

85691002

Blower motor assembly — Summit

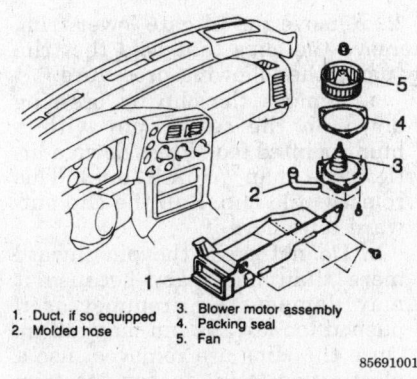

1. Duct, if so equipped
2. Molded hose
3. Blower motor assembly
4. Packing seal
5. Fan

85691001

Blower motor assembly — Laser and Talon

11. Connect the negative battery cable and check the wiper system for proper operation.

REAR

1. Disconnect the negative battery cable.

2. Remove the rear wiper arm by removing the cap nut cover, unscrewing the cap nut and lifting the arm from the linkage post.

3. Remove the large interior trim panel. Use a plastic trim stick to unhook the trim clips of the liftgate trim. There will be a row of metal liftgate clips across the top. There will be 2 rows of trim clips that retain the rest of the panel.

4. Disconnect the electrical harness at the wiper motor. Remove the rear wiper assembly. Do not loosen the grommet for the wiper post.

To install:

5. Install the motor and grommet. Mount the grommet so the arrow on the grommet is pointing downward.

6. Install the wiper arm.

7. Connect the negative battery cable and check rear wiper system for proper operation.

8. If operation is satisfactory, fit the tabs on the upper part of the liftgate trim into the liftgate clips and secure the liftgate trim.

Laser and Talon

FRONT

1. Disconnect the negative battery cable.

2. Remove the windshield wiper arms by unscrewing the cap nuts and lifting the arms from the linkage posts.

3. Remove the front garnish panel.

4. Remove the air inlet trim pieces.

5. Remove the hole cover.

6. Remove the wiper motor by loosening the mounting bolts, removing the motor assembly, then disconnecting the linkage.

NOTE: The installation angle of the crank arm and motor has been factory set; do not remove them unless it is necessary to do so. If they must be removed, remove them only after marking their mounting positions.

To install:

7. Install the windshield wiper motor and connect the linkage.

8. Reinstall all trim pieces.

9. Reinstall the wiper blades. Note that the driver's side wiper arm should be marked **D** or **Dr** and the passenger's side wiper arm should be marked **A** or **As**. The identification marks should be located at the base of the arm, near the pivot. Install the arms so the blades are 1 inch from the garnish molding when in the parked position.

10. Connect the negative battery cable and check the wiper system for proper operation.

REAR

1. Disconnect the negative battery cable.

2. Remove the rear wiper arm by removing the cover, unscrewing the nut and lifting the arm from the linkage post.

1. Stopper
2. Blove box
3. Outer case
4. Undercover
5. Lower frame
6. Evaporator mounting bolt and nut
7. Air selection cable
8. Side frame
9. Blower assembly
10. Blower motor assembly
11. Blower case

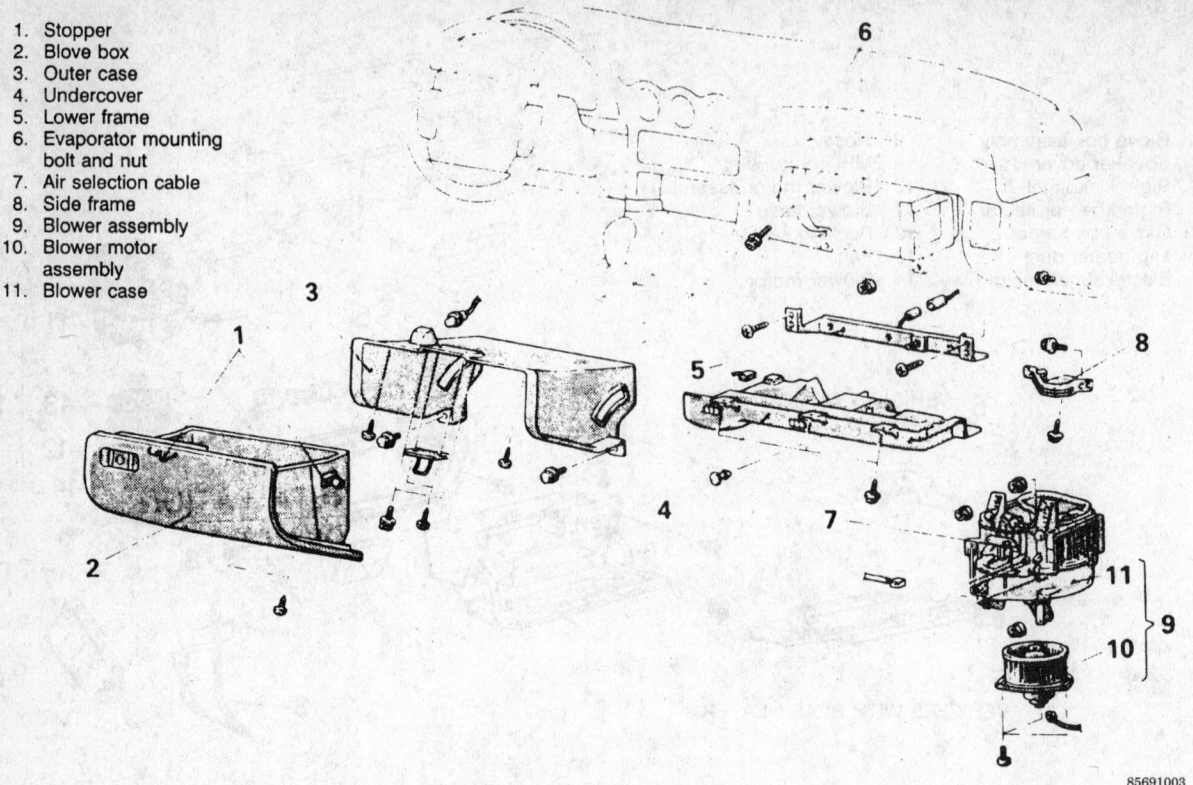

85691003

Blower motor assembly — Stealth

3. Remove the large interior trim panel. Use a plastic trim stick to unhook the trim clips of the liftgate trim.

4. If equipped with rear air spoiler, remove the wiper grommet.

5. Remove the rear wiper assembly. Do not loosen the grommet for the wiper post.

To install:

6. Install the motor and grommet. Mount the grommet so the arrow on the grommet is pointing upward.

7. Install the wiper arm.

8. Connect the negative battery cable and check the rear wiper for proper operation.

9. If operation is satisfactory, fit the tabs on the upper part of the liftgate trim into the liftgate clips and secure the liftgate trim.

Stealth

FRONT

1. Disconnect the negative battery cable.

2. Remove the windshield wiper arms by unscrewing the cap nuts and lifting the arms from the linkage posts.

3. Remove the front deck garnish assembly.

4. Remove the air inlet cover.

5. Remove the access hole cover.

6. Remove the wiper motor mounting bolts.

7. Detach the motor crank arm from the wiper linkage and remove the motor.

NOTE: The installation angle of the crank arm and motor has been factory set; do not remove them unless it is necessary to do so. If they must be removed, remove them only after marking their mounting positions.

To install:

8. Install the windshield wiper motor and connect the linkage.

9. Install the access hole cover.

10. Reinstall the wiper blades. Note that the driver's side wiper arm should be marked **D** and the passenger's side wiper arm should be marked **A**. The identification marks should be located at the base of the arm, near the pivot. Install the arms so the blades are parallel to the garnish molding when parked.

11. Connect the negative battery cable and check the wiper system for proper operation.

REAR

1. Disconnect the negative battery cable.

2. Remove the liftgate lower trim. Remove the clips that hold the trim by using the following procedure:

a. Remove the clip by pressing down on the center pin with a blunt pointed tool. Press down a little more than $1/16$ in. (2mm). This releases the clip. Pull the clip outward to remove it.

b. Do not push the pin inward more than necessary because it may damage the grommet or if pushed too far, the pin may fall in. Once the clips are removed, use a plastic trim stick to pry the trim cover loose.

3. Remove the rear spoiler, center brace and center brake light.

4. Lift the small cover, remove the retaining nut and remove the wiper arm and spacer.

5. Remove the mounting bolts and remove the wiper motor.

To install:

6. Install the motor and install the retaining bolts.

7. Install the spacer, wiper arm and retaining nut. The arm should be positioned so the upper tip points to the upper left corner of the rear window when parked. Connect the battery and check the operation of the motor before proceeding. If satisfactory, disconnect the cable and proceed.

8. Install the rear spoiler and related parts.

9. Install the interior trim piece.

10. Connect the negative battery cable and recheck the system for proper operation.

Windshield Wiper Switch

REMOVAL AND INSTALLATION

Stealth

1. Disconnect the negative battery cable.

2. If equipped with an air bag, disarm as follows:

a. Position the front wheels in the straight-ahead position and place the key in the **LOCK** position. Remove the key from the ignition lock cylinder.

b. Disconnect the negative battery cable and insulate the cable end with high-quality electrical tape or similar non-conductive wrapping.

c. Wait at least 1 minute before working on the vehicle. The air bag system is designed to retain enough voltage to deploy the air bag for a short period of time even after the battery has been disconnected.

3. Remove the steering wheel as follows:

a. Remove the air bag module mounting nut from behind the steering wheel.

b. To disconnect the connector of the clockspring from the air bag module, press the air bag's lock toward the module to spread the lock open. While holding lock in this position, use a small tipped prying tool to gently pry the connector from the module.

c. Store the air bag module in a clean, dry place with the pad cover facing up.

d. Remove the steering wheel retaining nut and use a steering wheel puller to remove the wheel. Do not use a hammer or the collapsible mechanism in the column could be damaged.

4. Remove the hood lock release handle.

5. Remove the switches from the knee protector below the steering column and remove the exposed retaining screws. Then remove the knee protector.

6. Remove the column upper and lower covers.

7. Remove necessary duct work and disconnect the windshield wiper switch connectors.

8. Remove the retaining screws and remove the windshield wiper switch assembly from the steering column.

To install:

9. Install the wiper switch to the steering column and connect the connectors.

10. Install any removed duct work.

11. Install the upper and lower column covers.

12. Install the knee protector and switches.

13. Install the hood release handle.

14. Confirm that the front wheels are in a straight-ahead position. Center the clockspring by aligning the **NEUTRAL** mark on the clockspring with the mating mark on the casing. Then install the steering wheel and torque the retaining nut to 29 ft. lbs. (40 Nm).

15. Connect the negative battery cable and check the windshield wiper and washer for proper operation.

Rear Wiper Switch

REMOVAL AND INSTALLATION

All Models

1. Remove the rear wiper/washer switch from the instrument panel by using a plastic trim stick.

2. Carefully pry the switch from the dash panel and disconnect electrical harness.

3. Installation is reverse of removal.

Instrument Cluster

REMOVAL AND INSTALLATION

Summit

1992

1. Disconnect the negative battery cable. Remove the center trim panel.

2. Remove the knee protector. If pin type clips are used, they may be removed using the following procedure:

a. This type of clip is removed by pressing down on the center pin with a suitable blunt pointed tool. Press down a little more than $1/16$ in. (2mm). This releases the clip. Pull the clip outward to remove it.

b. Do not push the pin inward more than necessary because it may damage the grommet or the pin may fall in, if pushed in too far. Once the clips are removed, use a plastic trim stick, if necessary, to pry the knee protector loose.

3. Remove the instrument cluster bezel.

4. Remove the instrument cluster. Disassemble and remove gauges or the speedometer, as required.

NOTE: If the speedometer cable adapter requires service, disconnect the cable at the transaxle end. Pull the cable slightly toward the vehicle interior, release the lock by turning the adapter to the right or left and remove the adapter.

To install:

5. Install the speedometer head into the instrument cluster.

6. Install the instrument cluster into the dash panel and install the cluster bezel.

7. Install the knee protector and secure.

8. Connect the negative battery cable and check all cluster-related items for proper operation.

1993–96

1. Disconnect negative battery terminal.

2. Remove the lower knee protector and lower instrument panel.

3. Remove the instrument panel trim or bezel.

4. Remove the bolts from the steering column and lower for clearance.

5. Remove the instrument cluster from the dash panel and disconnect the speedometer cable by releasing the locking clip.

To install:

6. Install the instrument cluster into the dash panel and connect the speedometer cable during installation. Be sure the locking clip of the cable is secured.

7. Secure the steering column and tighten bolts to 8 ft. lbs. (12 Nm).

8. Replace the instrument cluster bezel or trim.

9. Replace the lower instrument panel and replace the knee protector.

10. Connect the negative battery cable and check instrument panel operation.

Summit Wagon

1. Disconnect negative battery cable.

2. Remove the 2 retainer screws on the lower surface of the meter hood.

3. Remove the retainer screws from the under side top portion of the meter hood.

4. Carefully remove the meter hood from the face of the combination meter.

5. Remove the 4 retainer screws and the combination meter assembly with the bezel attached. Remove the front bezel and remove gauges or the speedometer as required.

NOTE: If the speedometer cable adapter requires service, disconnect the cable at the transaxle end. Pull the cable slightly toward the vehicle interior, release the lock by turning the adapter to the right or left and remove the adapter.

6. Assemble instrument cluster and attach front bezel or face trim using retaining screws.

7. Install the combination meter, secure with 4 retaining screws and attach the speedometer cable.

8. Install 2 retaining screws to the meter hood.

9. Connect the negative battery cable and check all cluster-related items for proper operation.

Laser and Talon

1. Disconnect the negative battery cable.

NOTE: If equipped with an air bag, be sure to disarm it before entering the vehicle.

2. Remove the screw cover on the side of the cluster panel assembly.

3. Remove the front instrument cluster bezel.

4. Remove the instrument cluster. Disassemble and remove gauges or the speedometer as required.

NOTE: If the speedometer cable adapter requires service, disconnect the cable at the transaxle end. Pull the cable slightly toward the vehicle interior, release the lock by turning the adapter to the right or left and remove the adapter.

5. The installation is the reverse of the removal procedure. Use care not to damage the printed circuit board or any gauge components.

6. Connect the negative battery cable and check all cluster-related items for proper operation.

Stealth

1. Disconnect the negative battery cable.

NOTE: If equipped with an air bag, be sure to disarm it before entering the vehicle.

2. Remove the hood lock release handle and switches from the knee protector below the steering column. Then remove the exposed retaining

screws and remove the knee protector.

3. Remove the upper and the lower steering column covers. Use care not to break internal alignment tabs of upper and lower column covers.

4. Remove the instrument cluster bezel or faceplate.

5. On vehicles with mechanical type speedometer drive, disconnect the speedometer cable at the transaxle.

6. Remove the instrument cluster while pulling the speedometer cable slightly toward the interior for access.

7. Release the speedometer cable lock by turning adaptor to the left or right and then remove the adapter.

8. Disconnect harness connections and remove cluster from vehicle.

9. Disassemble instrument cluster and remove gauges or the speedometer as required.

To install:

10. The installation is the reverse of the removal procedure. Use care not to damage the printed circuit board or any gauge components.

11. Connect the negative battery cable and check all cluster-related items for proper operation.

Concealed Headlights

MANUAL OPERATION

If the headlight covers will not raise electrically, remove the fusible link from the relay box, then remove the boot on the rear area of the pop-up motor and turn the manual knob clockwise until the headlight cover is open. Perform this procedure on both the left and right sides.

Combination Switch

REMOVAL AND INSTALLATION

Summit and Summit Wagon

NOTE: The headlights, turn signals, dimmer switch, horn switch, windshield wiper/washer, intermittent wiper switch and on some models, the cruise control function are all built into 1 multi-function combination switch that is mounted on the steering column.

1. Disconnect the negative battery cable.

2. Remove the knee protector panel under the steering column,

then the upper and lower column covers. On Summit Wagon, remove the instrument panel under cover.

3. Remove the horn pad by pulling the lower end outward.

4. Matchmark and remove the steering wheel with a steering wheel puller. Do not hammer on the steering wheel to remove it or the collapsible mechanism may be damaged.

5. On Summit Wagon, remove the instrument panel hood to gain clearance between the combination switch and the instrument panel, if required.

6. Disconnect all connectors, remove the wiring clip and remove the column switch assembly.

To install:

7. Install the switch assembly and secure all harness connectors with clips if needed Make sure the wires are not pinched or out of place.

8. Install the instrument panel meter hood, if removed.

9. Install the steering wheel. Torque the steering wheel-to-column nut to 29 ft. lbs. (40 Nm).

10. Install the column covers and knee protector.

11. Connect the negative battery cable and check all functions of the combination switch for proper operation.

Laser and Talon

NOTE: The headlights, turn signals, dimmer switch, windshield/washer and, on some models, the cruise control function are all built into 1 multi-function combination switch that is mounted on the steering column.

1. Disconnect the negative battery cable.

2. Remove the knee protector panel under the steering column, then the upper and lower column covers.

3. Remove the horn pad attaching screw on the under side of the steering wheel and remove the horn pad by pushing the pad upward.

4. Matchmark and remove the steering wheel with a steering wheel puller. Do not hammer on the steering wheel to remove it or the collapsible mechanism may be damaged.

5. Locate the rectangular plugs in the knee protector on either side of the steering column. Pry these plugs out and remove the screws. Remove the screws from the hood lock release lever and remove the knee protector.

6. Remove the upper and lower column covers.

7. Remove the lap cooler ducts.

8. Remove the band retaining the switch wiring.

9. Disconnect all connectors, remove the wiring clip and remove the column switch assembly.

To install:

10. Install the switch assembly and secure the clip. Make sure no wires are pinched or out of place.

11. Install the lap cooler ducts.

12. Install the column covers and knee protector.

13. Install the steering wheel. Torque the steering wheel-to-column nut to 29 ft. lbs. (40 Nm).

14. Connect the negative battery cable and check all functions of the combination switch for proper operation.

Stealth

NOTE: The headlights, turn signals and dimmer switch are all built into 1 multi-function combination switch that is mounted on the left side of the steering column.

1. Disconnect the negative battery cable.

2. If equipped with an air bag, disarm as follows:

a. Position the front wheels in the straight-ahead position and place the key in the **LOCK** position. Remove the key from the ignition lock cylinder.

b. Disconnect the negative battery cable and insulate the cable end with high-quality electrical tape or similar non-conductive wrapping.

c. Wait at least 1 minute before working on the vehicle. The air bag system is designed to retain enough voltage to deploy the air bag for a short period of time even after the battery has been disconnected.

NOTE: If equipped with an air bag, be sure to disarm it before entering the vehicle. Failure to do so could result in personal injury or death.

3. Remove the steering wheel as follows:

a. Remove the air bag module mounting nut from behind the steering wheel.

b. To disconnect the connector of the clockspring from the air bag module, press the air bag's lock toward the module to spread the lock open. While holding lock in this position, use a small tipped prying

tool to gently pry the connector from the module.

c. Store the air bag module in a clean, dry place with the pad cover facing up.

d. Remove the steering wheel retaining nut and use a steering wheel puller to remove the wheel. Do not use a hammer or the collapsible mechanism in the column could be damaged.

4. Remove the hood lock release handle.

5. Remove the switches from the knee protector below the steering column and remove the exposed retaining screws. Then remove the knee protector.

6. Remove the steering column upper and lower covers.

7. Remove lap cooler and foot shower duct work as necessary. Gently disconnect the combination switch connectors.

8. Remove the retaining screws from the combination switch and remove the combination switch assembly from the steering column.

To install:

9. Install the switch to the steering column and connect the harness connections.

10. Install any removed duct work.

11. Install the column covers.

12. Install the knee protector and switches.

13. Install the hood release handle.

14. Confirm that the front wheels are in a straight-ahead position. Center the clockspring by aligning the **NEUTRAL** mark on the clockspring with the mating mark on the casing. Then install the steering wheel and torque the retaining nut to 29 ft. lbs. (40 Nm).

15. Attach air bag module wiring connector to clockspring connection. Install air bag module and tighten mounting nuts to 43 inch lbs. (5 Nm).

16. Connect the negative battery cable and check all functions of the combination switch for proper operation.

Ignition Lock/Switch

REMOVAL AND INSTALLATION

Summit, Summit Wagon, Laser and Talon

1. Disconnect the negative battery cable. Remove the hood lock release lever from the lower panel.

2. Remove the lower instrument panel knee protector.

3. On Laser/Talon, remove ductwork with lower knee panel and remove the steering wheel assembly.

NOTE: Use proper steering wheel puller equipment when removing the steering wheel. The use of a hammer for removal could damage the collapsible mechanism within the column.

4. Remove the lower steering column cover. On Summit Wagon, remove the instrument panel hood.

5. Remove the upper steering column cover.

6. Remove the clip that holds the wiring harness against the steering column.

7. Insert the key into the steering lock cylinder and turn to the **ACC** position.

8. With a small pointed tool, push the lock pin of the steering lock cylinder inward and pull the lock cylinder out.

9. Remove the key reminder switch, if equipped.

10. Unplug the ignition switch harness connector. Remove the ignition switch mounting screws and pull the switch from the steering lock cylinder.

NOTE: When equipped with automatic transaxle, Laser and Talon have safety-lock systems and will have a key interlock cable installed in a slide lever on the side of the key cylinder. Carefully unhook the interlock cable from the lock cylinder while withdrawing cylinder from lock housing.

To install:

11. With the ignition key removed, install the slide lever and the interlock cable to the steering lock cylinder. Apply grease to the interlock cable and install cylinder into the lock housing. Check for normal operation of the interlock system.

12. Install the ignition switch into the rear of the lock cylinder housing. Be sure to align the keyway of the ignition switch with interlock cylinder.

13. Connect harness connections and install the wiring clip.

14. Install the steering column upper and lower covers. On Summit Wagon, install the instrument panel hood.

15. Install the knee protector.

16. Connect the negative battery cable and check the ignition switch and lock for proper operation.

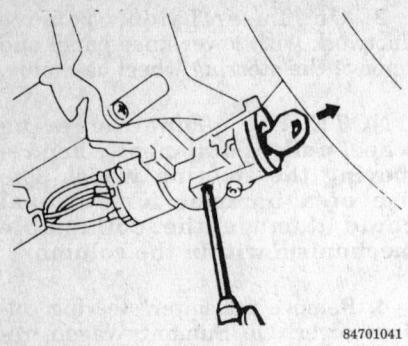

84701041

Steering interlock cylinder pin release — Laser/Talon

Stealth

NOTE: If equipped with an air bag, be sure to disarm it before starting any repairs on the vehicle.

1. Disconnect the negative battery cable.

2. If equipped with an air bag, disarm as follows:

a. Position the front wheels in the straight-ahead position and place the key in the **LOCK** position. Remove the key from the ignition lock cylinder.

b. Disconnect the negative battery cable and insulate the cable end with high-quality electrical tape or similar non-conductive wrapping.

c. Wait at least 1 minute before working on the vehicle. The air bag system is designed to retain enough voltage to deploy the air bag for a short period of time even after the battery has been disconnected.

3. If equipped with an air bag, remove the air bag module as follows:

a. Remove the air bag module mounting nut from behind the steering wheel.

b. To disconnect the connector of the clockspring from the air bag module, press the air bag's lock towards the module to spread the lock open. While holding lock in this position, use a small tipped prying tool to gently pry the connector from the module.

c. Store the air bag module in a clean, dry place with the pad cover facing up.

4. Remove the steering wheel retaining nut and use a steering wheel puller to remove the wheel. Do not use a hammer or the collapsible mechanism in the column could be damaged.

5. Remove the hood lock release handle.

6. Remove the switches from the knee protector below the steering column and remove the exposed retaining screws. Then remove the knee protector.

7. Remove the steering column upper and lower covers. Use care removing covers to prevent breakage of alignment tabs.

8. Remove lap cooler and foot shower duct work. Disconnect the windshield wiper, combination switch and ignition switch harness connectors.

9. Remove the retaining screws and remove the entire column switch/clockspring assembly from the left side of the steering column.

10. Remove mounting screws from the ignition switch and pull switch from interlock cylinder.

11. To remove the lock cylinder, insert the key and place in the **ACC** position. With a small pointed tool, push the lock pin of the steering lock cylinder inward and pull the lock cylinder out.

To install:

12. Install the lock cylinder into the interlock housing. Be sure the lock pin snaps into place.

13. Install ignition switch into interlock housing. Align keyway of ignition switch with lock cylinder and secure with mounting screws.

14. Install the column switch/clockspring assembly to the steering column and connect the harness connections.

15. Install lap cooler and foot shower duct work.

16. Install the upper and lower steering column covers.

17. Install the knee protector and switches.

18. Install the hood release handle.

19. Center the clockspring by aligning the **NEUTRAL** mark on the clockspring with the mating mark on the casing. Then install the steering wheel and torque the retaining nut to 29 ft. lbs. (40 Nm).

20. Attach air bag module wiring connector to clockspring connection. Install air bag module and tighten mounting nuts to 43 inch lbs. (5 Nm).

21. Connect the negative battery cable and check all functions of column-mounted switches and the ignition switch for proper operation.

Brake Light Switch

ADJUSTMENT

1. Disconnect the negative battery cable.

NOTE: If equipped with an air bag, be sure to disarm it before entering the vehicle.

2. The brake light switch works off the brake pedal lever. To adjust, disconnect the electrical connection and loosen the switch locknut.

3. Screw the switch inward until it contacts the stop on the brake pedal arm. Back out the switch 1/2–1 full turn. The distance between the end of the switch plunger bore and the brake lever stop should be 0.020–0.040 in. (0.5–1.0mm).

4. Tighten the locknut and connect the wires.

5. Connect the negative battery cable.

6. Make sure the brake light turn ON when the brake pedal is depressed and go out when the pedal is released. Also, make sure the cruise control system operates properly.

REMOVAL AND INSTALLATION

1. Disconnect the negative battery cable.

NOTE: If equipped with an air bag, be sure to disarm it before starting any repairs on the vehicle.

2. Locate the brake light switch above the brake pedal lever.

3. Disconnect the wiring connectors from the switch and unscrew the switch.

To install:

4. Thread the brake light switch into the switch holding bracket. Adjust the switch to achieve correct operation.

5. Connect the brake light wires.

6. Connect the negative battery cable.

7. Make sure the brake lights turn ON when the brake pedal is depressed and go out when the pedal is released. Also, make sure the cruise control system operates properly.

Clutch Switch

ADJUSTMENT

The clutch interlock switch is located at the top of the clutch pedal arm. Note that there may be 2 switches; 1

will be a cruise control cut-out switch.

1. Clutch interlock switch adjustment is made with the pedal fully depressed.

2. Measure the gap between the switch plunger and the arm stop. The gap should be 0.140 in. (3.5mm).

3. If adjustment is necessary, loosen the locknut and rotate the switch until the desired clearance is obtained. Tighten locknut to lock switch in place.

4. After completing the adjustment, check that the pedal free-play measured at the face of the pedal pad is 0.240–0.510 in. (6–13mm). The distance between the pedal pad and the firewall when the clutch is disengaged (applied) should be 2.20 in. (55mm) or more for Summit and Stealth, 1.77 in. (45mm) or more on Summit Wagon and 2.80 in. (71mm) or more for Laser and Talon. If these dimensions are not correct, the hydraulic clutch system may need further servicing.

REMOVAL AND INSTALLATION

1. Disconnect the negative battery cable.

NOTE: If equipped with an air bag, be sure to disarm it before starting any repairs on vehicle

2. Locate the interlock switch above the clutch pedal lever.

3. Disconnect the wiring connectors from the switch and unscrew the switch.

To install:

4. Thread the switch into the mounting bracket and adjust to 0.140 in. (3.5mm) clearance with the pedal depressed.

5. Reconnect the interlock wires.

6. Make sure the engine will not start unless the clutch pedal is depressed. Also, make sure the cruise control system operates properly.

Neutral Safety Switch

ADJUSTMENT

1. Disconnect the negative battery cable and locate the neutral safety switch on the top of the transaxle.

NOTE: Apply parking brake and chock wheels before placing transaxle into the N position

2. At the transmission, loosen the shift cable adjustment nut and inside the vehicle place the gearshift selector lever in **N**.

3. Place the manual shift control lever in **N**.

4. Loosen neutral safety switch mounting screws and rotate switch body so the manual control lever 0.20 in. (5mm) hole and the switch body 0.20 in. (5mm) holes are aligned.

5. Tighten switch body mounting bolts to 7–9 ft. lbs. (10–12 Nm).

6. At the shift cable adjusting nut, gently pull cable to remove any slack. Tighten locknut to 7–10 ft. lbs. 10–14 Nm).

7. Verify that the switch lever moves to positions corresponding to each position of the selector lever. Connect the negative battery terminal.

8. Make sure the engine only starts in the **P** and **N** positions. Also make sure the reverse lights operate only in the **N** selection.

REMOVAL AND INSTALLATION

1. Disconnect the negative battery cable.

2. Disconnect the selector cable from the lever.

3. Remove the 2 retaining screws and lift off the switch.

4. The installation is the reverse of the removal procedure. Do not tighten the bolts until the switch is adjusted.

5. After installation and adjustment make sure the engine only starts in the **P** and **N** selections. Also check that the reverse lights operate only in the **N** selection.

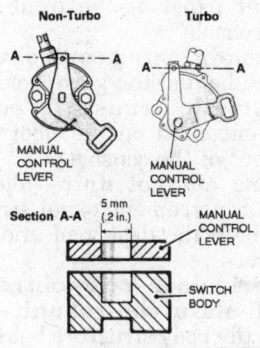

84701122

Neutral safety switch — Laser and Talon

Fuses, Circuit Breakers and Relays

LOCATION

Summit and Summit Wagon

FUSES AND FUSIBLE LINKS

Main fuse panel — passenger's side, under the hood, just behind the battery.

Main relay bank — passenger's side, under the hood, just behind the battery.

Fuse links — passenger's side, under the hood, just behind the battery.

Air conditioning control relay center — passenger's side, under the hood, up front behind the headlight.

Multi-purpose fuse block — inside the vehicle, on the left side behind the driver's knee protector.

RELAYS

Headlight relay, power window relay, radiator fan motor relay and alternator relay — passenger's side, under the hood, just behind the battery.

Air conditioner compressor relay, the condenser fan motor relay and the condenser fan motor control relay — under the hood, up front behind the headlight.

Intermittent wiper relay — incorporated into the column switch.

Seat belt warning timer relay — behind the instrument panel to the right of the center air conditioning outlets.

Multi-Point Injection control relay — inside the passenger compartment behind the right kick panel on Summit Wagon or behind the forward part of the console, on the left side on Summit.

Starter relay — right side of the vehicle in the relay box.

Defogger relay — under the driver's left side knee protector.

Door lock relay — behind the driver's side kick panel, at the bottom.

Heater relay, the turn signal and hazard flasher unit and the defogger timer — located in the multi-purpose fuse panel located under the driver's left side knee protector.

Automatic seatbelt motor relay — located in the driver's side windshield post on Summit hatchback, and inside the trim panel on the driver;s side rear quarter panel, just behind the front door post on Summit Sedan and Summit Wagon.

Laser and Talon

FUSES AND FUSIBLE LINKS

MPI circuit — 20 amp fuse link — under the hood in a centralized junction with the battery positive cable clamp.

Radiator fan motor circuit — 30 amp fuse link — under the hood in a centralized junction with the battery positive cable clamp.

Ignition switch circuit — 30 amp fuse link — under the hood in a centralized junction with the battery positive cable clamp.

Secondary fuse panel — located on the passenger side, under the hood, just forward of the strut tower.

Secondary fuse panel — driver's side, under the hood, back against the firewall.

Multi-purpose fuse block — located inside the vehicle, on the left side behind the driver's knee protector.

RELAYS

Taillight relay, headlight relay, radiator fan motor relay, pop-up (retractable light) motor relay, power window relay, alternator relay and fog light relay — passenger side of vehicle, under the hood, just forward of the strut tower.

Air conditioning condenser fan relays and air conditioning compressor clutch relay — driver's side of vehicle, under the hood, just forward of the strut tower.

Door lock relay, starter relay defogger timer — interior relay box inside the vehicle passenger compartment.

Stealth

FUSES AND FUSIBLE LINKS

Main fuse panel — located on the passenger side, under the hood, just forward of the air flow box. This panel also contains several fusible links.

Multi-purpose fuse block — located under the instrument panel, on the left side behind the driver's knee protector.

RELAYS

Radiator fan relay, air conditioning system relays — centralized fuse/relay panel on the driver side, under the hood just forward of the strut tower.

Taillight relay, headlight relay, pop-up (retractable light) motor relay, horn relay, alternator relay and fog light relay — engine compartment in front of the air flow box.

Blower motor and theft alarm horn — inside the vehicle above the fuse box.

Computers

LOCATION

Summit and Summit Wagon

Multi-Point Injection (MPI) control unit — located under the instrument panel at the top of the passenger side kick panel next to the blower motor.

Air conditioning control unit — mounted behind the glove box.

Automatic transaxle control unit — mounted on the floor at the very front of the console.

Cruise control unit — under the instrument panel behind the driver's side knee protector.

Electric door lock control unit — fastened to the body structure behind the driver's side kick panel.

Automatic seat belt control unit — under the console next to hand brake handle.

ELC 4-speed automatic transaxle control unit — under the console next to hand brake handle.

Anti-lock Braking System (ABS) control unit — under the instrument panel at center of dash.

Laser and Talon

Multi-Point Injection (MPI) control unit — located under the instrument panel at the front of the center console.

Air conditioning control unit — mounted behind the glove box.

Automatic transaxle control unit — mounted on the floor at the very front of the console.

Cruise control unit — mounted at top of instrument panel structure near where the dash pad and windshield meet.

Electric door lock control unit or theft-alarm control unit — fastened to the body structure behind the passenger's side kick panel.

Automatic seat belt control unit — fastened to the body structure under the trim panel at the base of the driver's side door latch pillar.

Anti-Lock Brake control unit — mounted behind the right side rear quarter trim panel.

Stealth

Multi-Point Injection (MPI) control unit — located under the instrument panel at the front of the center console.

Automatic transaxle control unit — mounted on the floor at the very front of the console.

Air conditioning control unit — mounted at the front of the center console just above the MPI control unit.

Air conditioner compressor lock controller — mounted on the bottom of the heater core housing under the right side of the instrument panel.

Cruise control unit — located behind the right side kick panel.

Electronic Timing and Control System (ETACS) unit — located just to the left of the steering column.

Air bag diagnosis unit — located under the arm rest in the console.

Electronic Suspension Control (ESC) control unit — mounted behind the right rear trim panel behind an access door.

Anti-Lock Brake control unit — mounted behind the right side rear quarter trim panel.

Active exhaust control unit — located in the rear luggage compartment, behind the left side trim panel.

Flashers

LOCATION

Summit, Summit Wagon, Laser and Talon

Turn signal and hazard flasher unit — located in the multi-purpose fuse panel located under the driver's left side knee protector.

Cruise Control

ADJUSTMENT

Before starting adjustments, turn air conditioner and lights **OFF**. Warm engine until the idle is stable and the rpm is correct. Stop engine and set the ignition switch to **OFF**. On 1.5L engine and Laser equipped with 1.8L engine, turn the ignition switch to the **ON** position, without starting the engine. Leave in the position for approximately 15 seconds. Confirm there are no sharp bends in the accelerator, throttle and cruise control cables. Check the inner cables for correct slack. If too loose or too tight, adjust with the following procedure:

1. Remove the air cleaner. If equipped with a protective cover over the actuator, remove it.

2. First, adjust the accelerator cable on the throttle valve side. After loosening the adjustment bolts at the air intake plenum side and freeing the inner cable, use the adjusting bolts that secure the plate so the free-play of the inner cable becomes

0.040–0.080 in (1–2mm). If there is excessive play of the accelerator cable, when climbing a hill the vehicle speed will drop substantially. If there is no play, the idling speed will increase.

3. After adjusting the accelerator cable, confirm that the throttle lever touches the idle position switch.

4. Next, adjust the accelerator cable on the accelerator pedal side. Loosen the adjusting bolt or locknut. While keeping the intermediate link of the actuator in close contact with the stop, adjust the inner cable play of accelerator cable **A** to 0–0.040 in.

(0–1mm) for manual transaxle vehicles or 0.080–0.120 in. (2–3mm) for automatic transaxle vehicles

5. After making the adjustment of the cable, make sure the throttle lever at the engine side moves 0.040–0.080 in (1–2mm) when the actuator link is turned. If the throttle lever movement is incorrect, adjust by turning adjusting nut **B**.

6. Confirm that the throttle valve fully opens and closes by operating the accelerator pedal.

7. Install the air cleaner.

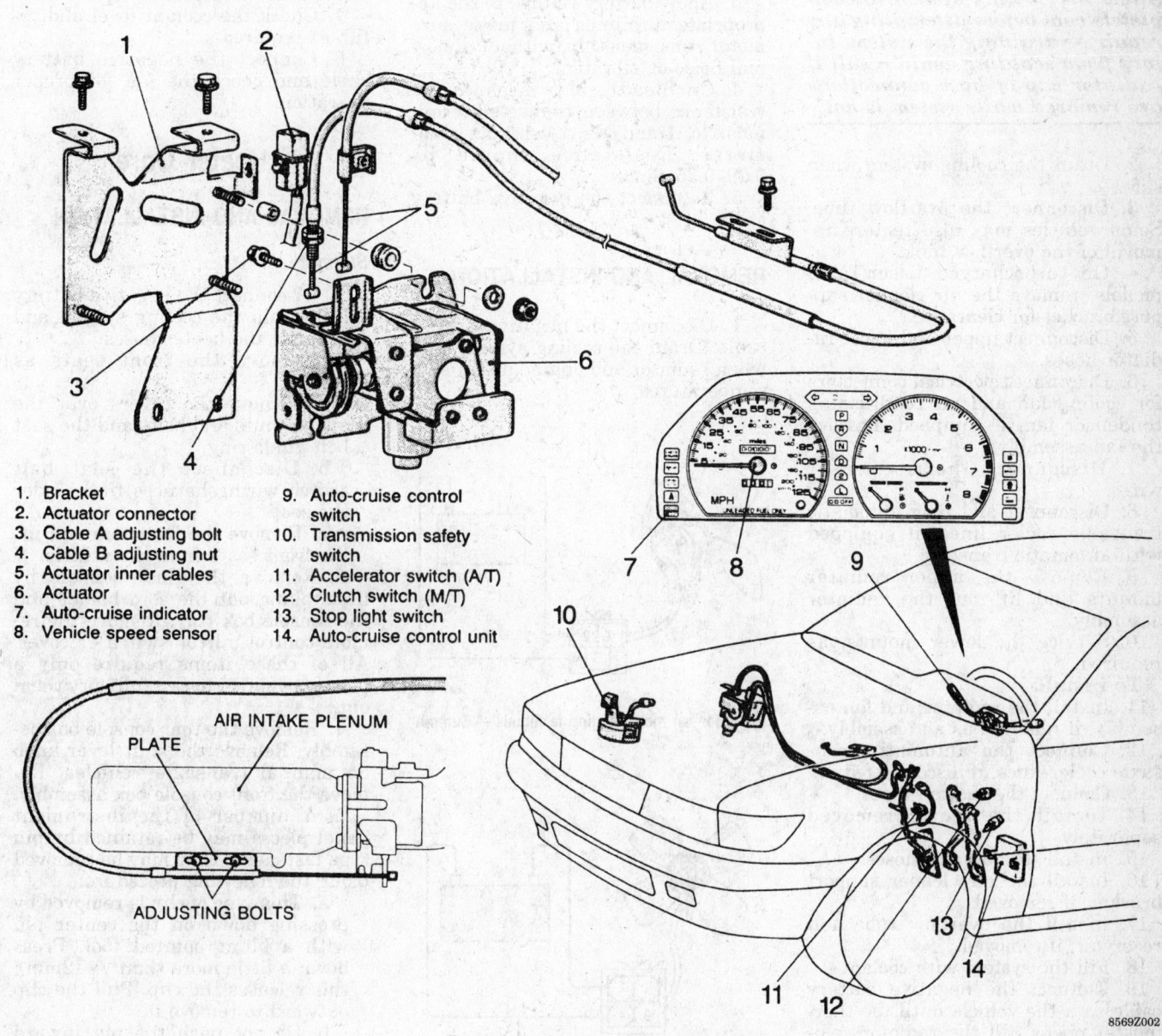

1. Bracket
2. Actuator connector
3. Cable A adjusting bolt
4. Cable B adjusting nut
5. Actuator inner cables
6. Actuator
7. Auto-cruise indicator
8. Vehicle speed sensor
9. Auto-cruise control switch
10. Transmission safety switch
11. Accelerator switch (A/T)
12. Clutch switch (M/T)
13. Stop light switch
14. Auto-cruise control unit

AIR INTAKE PLENUM

PLATE

ADJUSTING BOLTS

8569Z002

Main cruise control components — Summit

ENGINE COOLING

Radiator

REMOVAL AND INSTALLATION

1. Disconnect the negative battery cable.

— CAUTION —
Allow the cooling system to completely cool before attempting any repair or draining the system. Injury from scalding could result if radiator cap or hose connections are removed while system is hot.

2. Drain the cooling system when safe.
3. Disconnect the overflow tube. Some vehicles may also require removal of the overflow tank.
4. On turbocharged Laser/Talon models, remove the air cleaner support bracket for clearance.
5. Disconnect upper and lower radiator hoses.
6. Disconnect electrical connectors for cooling fan and air conditioning condenser fan, if equipped. Remove the fan assembly.
7. Disconnect thermo sensor wires.
8. Disconnect and plug automatic transaxle cooler lines, if equipped with automatic transaxle.
9. Remove the upper radiator mounts and lift out the radiator assembly.
10. Service the lower mounts, as required.
To install:
11. Install the radiator and fan assembly, if removed as an assembly.
12. Connect the automatic transaxle cooler lines, if disconnected.
13. Connect the thermo wires.
14. Install the fan if removed separately.
15. Install the radiator hoses.
16. Install the air cleaner support bracket, if removed.
17. Install the overflow tube and reservoir, if removed.
18. Fill the system with coolant.
19. Connect the negative battery cable, run the vehicle until the thermostat opens, fill the radiator completely and check the automatic transaxle fluid level, if equipped.
20. Once the vehicle has cooled, recheck the coolant level.

Electric Cooling Fan

TESTING

— CAUTION —
Make sure the key is in the OFF position when checking the electric cooling fan. If not, the fan could turn ON at any time, causing serious personal injury.

1. Disconnect the negative battery cable.
2. Disconnect the electrical plug from the fan motor harness.
3. Apply battery voltage to the appropriate terminals and make sure motor runs smoothly, without abnormal noise or vibration.
4. On Stealth, also measure the resistance between connector terminals No. 1 and No. 4 using an ohmmeter. Resistance should be 0.29–0.35 ohms.
5. Reconnect the negative battery cable.

REMOVAL AND INSTALLATION

1. Disconnect the negative battery cable. Drain the cooling system only when radiator and engine are at safe temperatures.

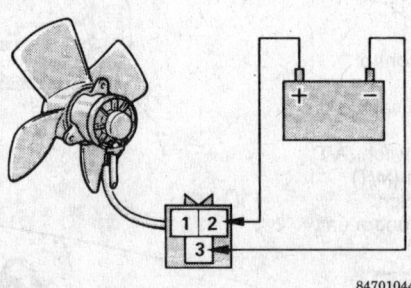

Radiator fan motor testing terminals — Summit

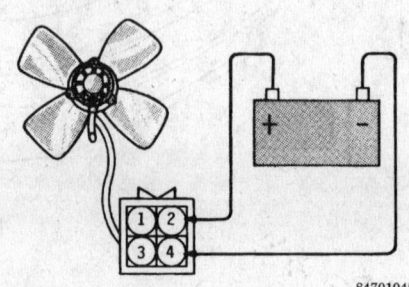

Radiator fan motor testing terminals — Summit Wagon and Laser/Talon

2. Unplug the cooling fan and radiator sensor connector(s). Most of these connectors employ a waterproof connector. When disconnecting, make sure all parts of the connector remain intact.
3. Disconnect the upper radiator hose from the radiator and remove overflow tank.
4. Remove the fan mounting screws. The radiator and condenser cooling fans are separately removable.
5. Remove the fan assembly and disassemble as required.
6. The installation is the reverse of the removal procedure.
7. Check the coolant level and refill, as required.
8. Connect the negative battery cable and check the fan for proper operation.

Heater Core

REMOVAL AND INSTALLATION

Summit

1. Disconnect the negative battery cable. Drain the cooling system and disconnect the heater hoses.
2. Remove the front seats as follows:
    a. Remove the covers over the anchor nuts and bolts and the seat belt guide ring.
    b. Disconnect the seat belt switch wiring harness from under the seat.
    c. Remove the fasteners and lift the front seats from the vehicle.
3. Remove the floor console by first taking out the coin holder and the console box tray. Remove the remote control mirror switch or cover. All of these items require only a plastic trim tool to carefully pry them out.
4. Remove the rear console box assembly. Remove the shift lever knob on manual transaxle vehicles. Remove the front console box assembly.
5. A number of the instrument panel pieces may be retained by pin type fasteners. They may be removed using the following procedure:
    a. This type of clip is removed by pressing down on the center pin with a blunt pointed tool. Press down a little more than $1/16$ (2mm); this releases the clip. Pull the clip outward to remove it.
    b. Do not push the pin inward more than necessary because it may damage the grommet of the pin may fall in, if pushed in too far. Once the clips are removed, use a

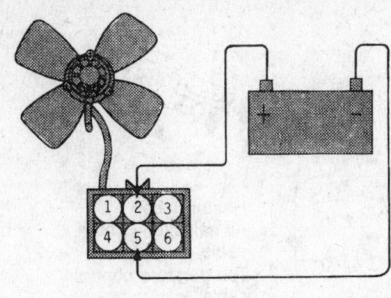

84701046

Radiator fan motor testing terminals — Stealth

plastic trim stick to pry the piece loose.

6. Remove both lower cowl trim panels (kick panels). Remove the ashtray. Remove the center panel around the radio.

7. Remove the sunglass pocket at the upper left side of panel and the side panel into which it mounts.

8. Remove the hood release handle and the driver's side knee protector. Remove the steering column top and bottom covers. Remove the radio.

9. Remove the glove box assembly and striker. Remove the instrument panel lower cover, by pulling forward. Remove the heater control assembly screw.

10. Remove the instrument cluster bezel and pull out the gauge assembly.

11. Remove the speedometer adapter by disconnecting the speedometer cable at the transaxle pulling the cable slightly towards the vehicle interior and giving a slight twist on the adapter to release it.

12. Insert a small flat-tipped tool to open the tab on the gauge cluster connector. Remove the harness connectors.

13. Remove, by prying with a plastic trim tool, the right side speaker cover and the speaker, the upper side defroster grilles and the clock or plug to gain access to some of the instrument panel mounting bolts.

14. Lower the steering column by removing the bolt and nut. Remove the instrument panel bolts and the instrument panel.

15. Disconnect the air selection, temperature and mode selection control cables from the heater box and remove the heater control assembly.

16. Remove the connector for the ECI control relay. Remove both stamped steel instrument panel supports. Remove the heater duct work.

17. Remove the heater box mounting nuts. Remove the automatic transaxle ELC control box. Remove the evaporator mounting nuts and clips.

18. With the evaporator pulled toward the vehicle interior, remove the heater unit. Be careful not to damage the heater tubes or to spill coolant inside the vehicle.

19. Remove the cover plate around the heater tubes and the core fastener clips. Pull the heater core from the heater box, being careful not to damage the fins or tank ends.

To install:

20. Thoroughly clean and dry the inside of the case. Install the heater core to the heater box. Install the clips and cover.

21. Install the heater unit into position on the vehicle while pulling outward on the evaporator.

22. Install the evaporator and heater unit mounting nuts and clips. Install the automatic transaxle ELC box.

23. Connect the air selection, temperature and mode selection control cables from the heater box and install the heater control assembly.

24. Install both stamped steel instrument panel supports. Connect the connector for the ECI control relay.

25. Install the remaining instrument panel components reversing the removal procedure.

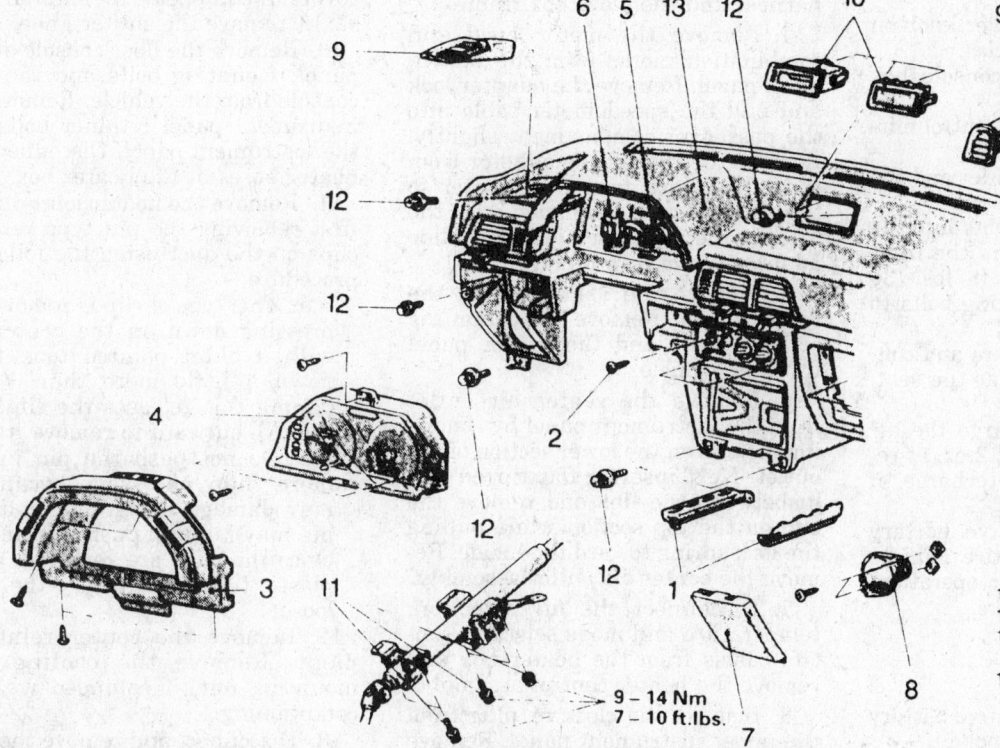

1. Lower cover
2. Screw
3. Cluster bezel
4. Instrument cluster
5. Speedometer cable adaptor
6. Wiring harness
7. Speaker garnish
8. Speaker
9. Side defroster grille
10. Clock or plug
11. Mounting bolts
12. Instrument panel mounting bolts
13. Instrument panel

9 – 14 Nm
7 – 10 ft.lbs.

85691004

Instrument panel and related parts — Summit

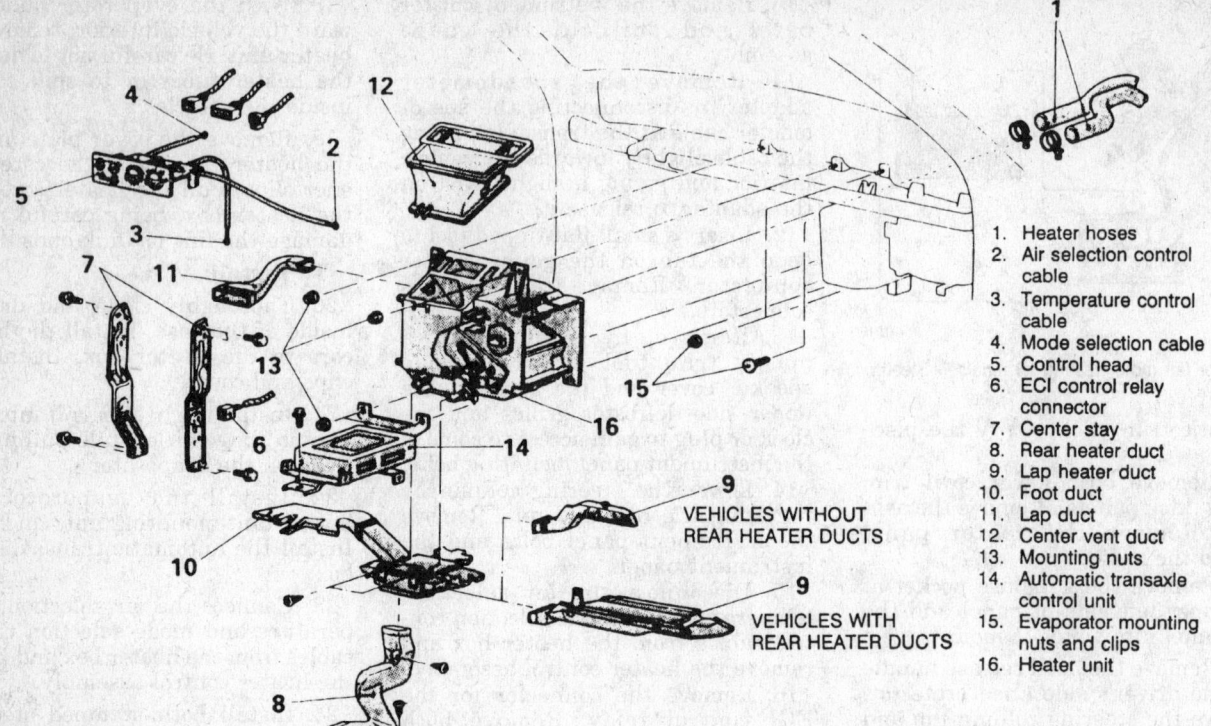

1. Heater hoses
2. Air selection control cable
3. Temperature control cable
4. Mode selection cable
5. Control head
6. ECI control relay connector
7. Center stay
8. Rear heater duct
9. Lap heater duct
10. Foot duct
11. Lap duct
12. Center vent duct
13. Mounting nuts
14. Automatic transaxle control unit
15. Evaporator mounting nuts and clips
16. Heater unit

VEHICLES WITHOUT REAR HEATER DUCTS

VEHICLES WITH REAR HEATER DUCTS

85691005

Heater case and related parts — Summit

26. Install the center console as follows:

a. Install the front console box assembly.

b. Install the shift lever knob on manual transaxle vehicles.

c. Install the rear console box assembly.

d. Install the remote control mirror switch or cover.

e. Install the coin holder and the console box tray.

27. Position the front seats into the vehicle. Install and torque the front seat retainer nuts to 25 ft. lbs. (36 Nm) and the rear mounting bolts to 25–40 ft. lbs. (35–55 Nm).

28. Install fastener covers and connect the wiring harness at the seat. Refill the cooling system.

29. Evacuate and recharge the air conditioning system. Add 2 oz. of refrigerant oil during the recharge, if evaporator was replaced.

30. Connect the negative battery cable and check the entire climate control system for proper operation. Check the system for leaks.

Summit Wagon

1. Disconnect the negative battery cable. Drain the engine coolant.

2. Remove the hood lock release handle, instrument panel under-cover, lower frame, foot duct, lap duct and the lap heater duct.

3. Remove the glove box speaker harness and the glove box frame.

4. Remove the meter hood and combination meter from the instrument panel. Remove the adapter lock and pull the speedometer cable into the passenger compartment slightly. Remove the rear of the adapter from the cable. Next, turn the adapter so the notch section is aligned with the tab on the cable section and slide adapter outward to remove.

5. Remove the ashtray from the center panel. Remove the mounting screws, radio and the center panel from the vehicle.

6. Remove the center air outlet from the instrument panel by removing the clip on the lower section of the outlet. Next insert a flat tipped tool in between the fins and remove the clip on the top section while pulling the lock spring toward the inside. Remove the center air outlet assembly.

7. Disconnect the air selection, temperature and mode selection control cables from the heater box and remove the heater control assembly.

8. Remove the clock or plug from the upper instrument panel. Remove the instrument panel retaining bolt under the plug.

9. Lower the steering column by removing the bolt and nut under the column. Remove the floor console side covers. If equipped with manual transaxle, remove the shifter knob.

10. Remove the floor console switch panel, mounting bolts and the floor console from the vehicle. Remove the instrument panel retainer bolts and the instrument panel. Disconnect the heater hoses at the heater box.

11. Remove the heater joint duct by first removing the pin type retainer clips on the duct using the following procedure:

a. This type of clip is removed by pressing down on the center pin with a blunt pointed tool. Press down a little more than 1/16 in. (2mm); this releases the clip. Pull the clip outward to remove it.

b. Do not push the pin inward more than necessary because it may damage the grommet or the pin may fall in if pushed in too far. Once the clips are removed, use a plastic trim stick to pry the piece loose.

12. Remove the center reinforcement. Remove the cooling unit mounting nut, if equipped with air conditioning.

13. Disconnect and remove the ABS control unit and the automatic transmission ELC control unit.

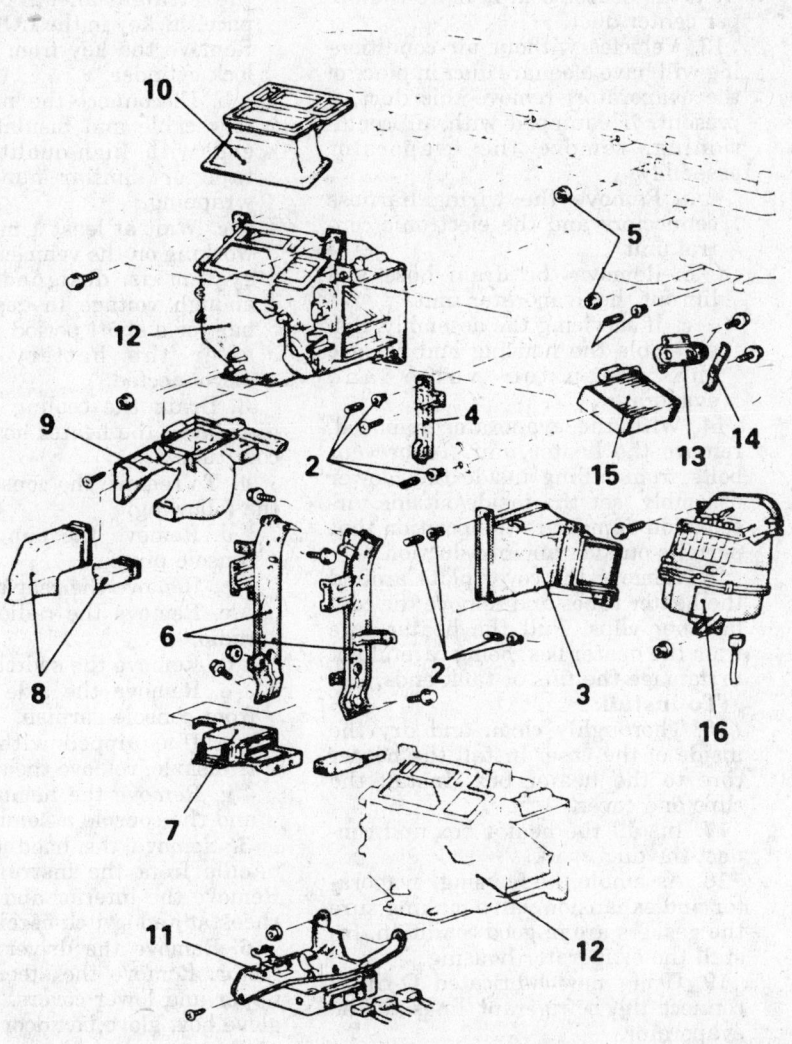

1. Heater hose connection
2. Retainer clips
3. Joint duct
4. Plate sub-assembly (vehicles with air conditioning)
5. Cooling unit installation nut (vehicles with air conditioning)
6. Center reinforcement
7. ABS Control unit assembly
8. Rear heater duct connection
9. Foot distribution duct
10. Center ventilation duct assembly
11. Automatic transaxle control unit
12. Heater unit
13. Plate
14. Clamp
15. Heater core

85691006

Heater case and related parts — Summit Wagon

14. Remove the foot distribution duct and disconnect the rear heater duct connection. Remove both stamped steel instrument panel supports.

15. Remove the mounting bolts and the heater unit from the vehicle. Be careful not to damage the heater tubes or to spill coolant inside the vehicle.

16. Remove the cover plate around the heater tubes and the core fastener clips. Pull the heater core from the heater box, being careful not to damage the fins or tank ends.

To install:

17. Thoroughly clean and dry the inside of the case. Install the heater core to the heater box. Install the clips and cover.

18. Install the heater unit into position on the vehicle and install the evaporator and heater unit mounting nuts and clips.

19. Install the automatic transaxle ELC box and the ABS control unit.

20. Connect the air selection, temperature and mode selection control cables from the heater box and install the heater control assembly.

21. Install both stamped steel instrument panel supports. Connect the connector for the ECI control relay. Install the remaining instrument panel components reversing the removal procedure.

22. Install the center console as follows:

   a. Install the front console box assembly.

   b. Install the shift lever knob on manual transaxle vehicles.

   c. Install the rear console box assembly.

   d. Install the floor console switch panel.

   e. Install the coin holder and the console box tray.

23. Refill the cooling system. Evacuate and recharge the air conditioning system. Add 2 oz. of refrigerant oil during the recharge, if the evaporator was replaced.

24. Connect the negative battery cable and check the entire climate control system for proper operation. Check the system for leaks.

Laser and Talon

1. Disconnect the negative battery cable.

2. Drain the cooling system and discharge the air conditioning system. Disconnect the refrigerant lines from the evaporator, if equipped. Cover the exposed ends of the lines to minimize contamination.

3. Remove the floor console by first removing the plugs, then the screws retaining the side covers and the small cover piece in front of the shifter. Remove the shifter knob, if equipped with manual transmission, and the cup holder. Remove both small pieces of upholstery to gain access to retainer screws. Disconnect both electrical connectors at the front of the console. Remove the shoulder harness guide plates and the console assembly.

4. Locate the rectangular plugs in the knee protector on either side of the steering column. Pry these plugs out and remove the screws. Remove the screws from the hood lock release lever and the knee protector.

5. Remove the upper and lower column covers. Remove the narrow panel covering the instrument cluster cover screws and remove the cover. Remove the radio panel and the radio.

6. Remove the center air outlet assembly by reaching through the grille and pushing the side clips out with a small flat-tipped tool while carefully prying the outlet free.

7. Pull the heater control knobs off and remove the heater control panel assembly. Open the glove box, remove the plugs from the sides and the glove box assembly.

8. Remove the instrument gauge cluster and the speedometer adapter by disconnecting the speedometer cable at the transaxle, pulling the cable slightly towards the vehicle interior, then giving a slight twist on the adapter to release it.

9. Remove the left and right speaker covers from the top of the instrument panel. Remove the center plate below the heater controls.

10. Remove the heater control assembly retaining screws. Remove the lower air duct. Lower the steering column by removing the support bolts.

11. Remove the instrument panel mounting screws, bolts and the instrument panel assembly. Remove

both stamped steel reinforcement pieces.

12. Remove the lower duct work from the heater box. Remove the upper center duct.

13. Vehicles without air conditioning will have a square duct in place of the evaporator; remove this duct, if present. If equipped with air conditioning, remove the evaporator assembly:

a. Remove the wiring harness connectors and the electronic control unit.

b. Remove the drain hose and lift out the evaporator unit.

c. If servicing the assembly, disassemble the housing and remove the expansion valve and evaporator.

14. With the evaporator removed, remove the heater unit. To prevent bolts from falling inside the blower assembly, set the inside/outside air-selection damper to the position that permits outside air introduction.

15. Remove the cover plate around the heater tubes and remove the core fastener clips. Pull the heater core from the heater box, being careful not to damage the fins or tank ends.

To install:

16. Thoroughly clean and dry the inside of the case. Install the heater core to the heater box. Install the clips and cover.

17. Install the heater box and connect the duct work.

18. Assemble the housing, evaporator and expansion valve making sure the gaskets are in good condition. Install the evaporator housing.

19. Using new lubricated O-rings, connect the refrigerant lines to the evaporator.

20. Install the electronic transaxle ELC box. Connect all wires and control cables.

21. Install the instrument panel assembly and the console by reversing their removal procedures.

22. Evacuate and recharge the air conditioning system. It the evaporator was replaced, add 2 oz. of refrigerant oil during the recharge.

23. Connect the negative battery cable and check the entire climate control system for proper operation. Check the system for leaks.

Stealth

NOTE: If equipped with an air bag, be sure to disarm it before starting any repairs on the vehicle.

1. Disconnect the negative battery cable.

2. If equipped with an air bag, disarm as follows:

a. Position the front wheels in the straight-ahead position and pace the key in the **LOCK** position. Remove the key from the ignition lock cylinder.

b. Disconnect the negative battery cable and insulate the cable end with high-quality electrical tape or similar non-conductive wrapping.

c. Wait at least 1 minute before working on the vehicle. The air bag system is designed to retain enough voltage to deploy the air bag for a short period of time even after the battery has been disconnected.

3. Drain the cooling system and disconnect the heater hoses from the core tubes.

4. To remove the console, perform the following:

a. Remove the cup holder and console plug.

b. Remove the rear console.

c. Remove the radio bezels and radio.

d. Remove the switch bezel.

e. Remove the side covers and front console garnish.

f. If equipped with a manual transaxle, remove the shifter knob.

g. Remove the mounting screws and the console assembly.

5. Remove the hood lock release handle from the instrument panel. Remove the interior and dash lights rheostat and switch bezel to its right.

6. Remove the driver's knee protector. Remove the steering column upper and lower covers. Remove the glove box, glove box door striker and cover.

7. Remove the center air outlet assembly and the climate control switch assembly. Remove the instrument cluster bezel and cluster.

8. If equipped with front speakers, remove them; if not, remove the plug in their place. Disconnect the wiring harnesses on the right side of the instrument panel.

9. Remove the steering shaft support bolts and lower the steering column. Remove the instrument panel mounting hardware and remove the instrument panel from the vehicle.

10. Remove the center reinforcement. Remove the foot warmer ducts and lap duct.

11. If equipped with air conditioning, remove the evaporator case mounting bolt and nut to allow clearance for heater unit removal.

12. Remove the center duct above the heater unit. Remove the heater

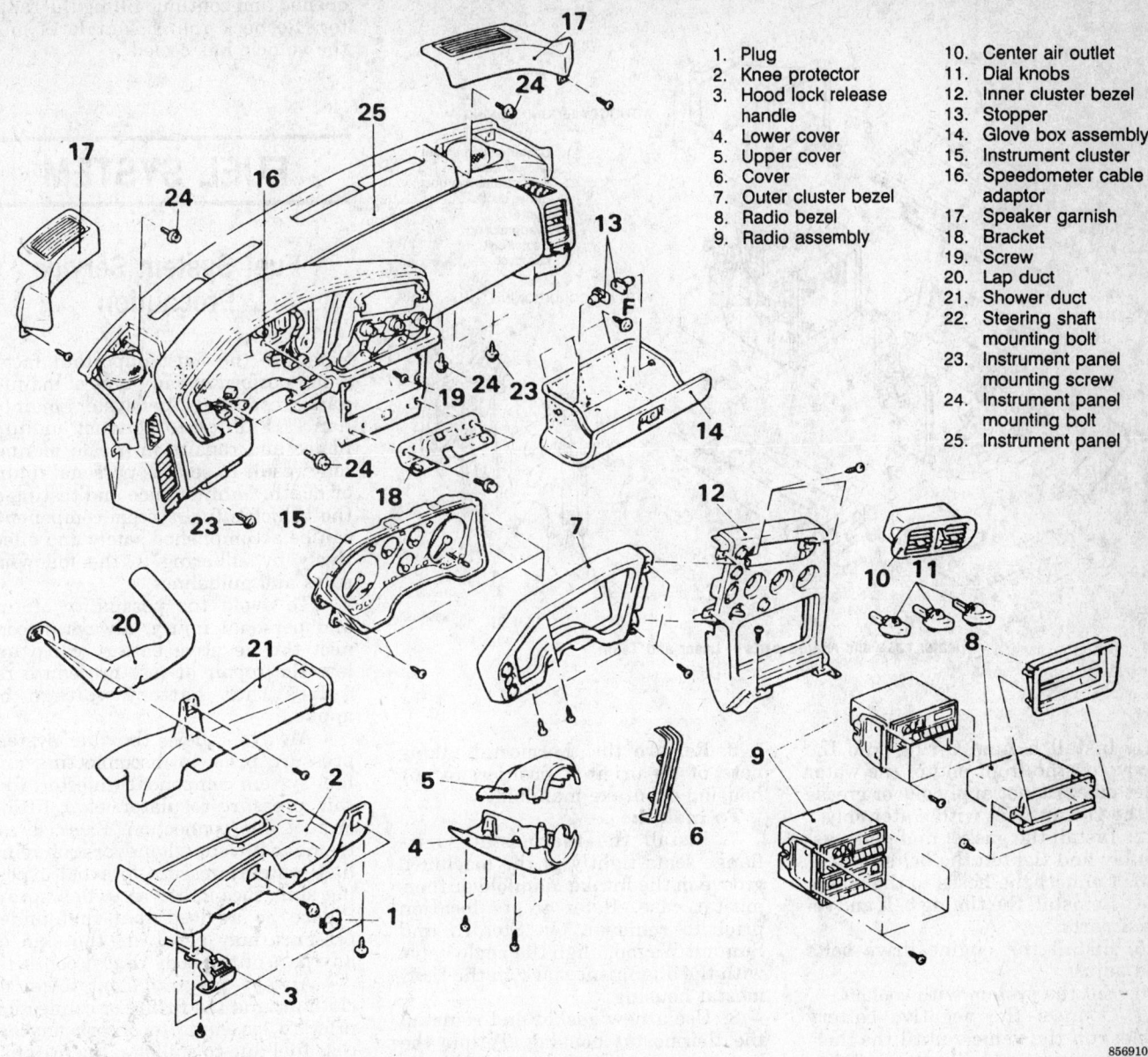

1. Plug
2. Knee protector
3. Hood lock release handle
4. Lower cover
5. Upper cover
6. Cover
7. Outer cluster bezel
8. Radio bezel
9. Radio assembly
10. Center air outlet
11. Dial knobs
12. Inner cluster bezel
13. Stopper
14. Glove box assembly
15. Instrument cluster
16. Speedometer cable adaptor
17. Speaker garnish
18. Bracket
19. Screw
20. Lap duct
21. Shower duct
22. Steering shaft mounting bolt
23. Instrument panel mounting screw
24. Instrument panel mounting bolt
25. Instrument panel

85691007

Instrument panel and related parts — Laser and Talon

unit and disassemble on the workbench. Remove the heater core from the heater case.

To install:

13. Thoroughly clean and dry the inside of the case and install the heater core and all related parts. Install the heater unit to the vehicle and install the mounting screws.

14. Install the center duct above the unit. Secure the evaporator case with the bolt and nut.

15. Install the lap duct and foot warmer ducts. Install the center reinforcement. Install the instrument panel by reversing its removal procedures.

16. Install the hood lock release cable handle. Install the console. Fill the cooling system.

17. Connect the negative battery cable and check the entire climate control system for proper operation and leaks.

Water Pump

REMOVAL AND INSTALLATION

1. Disconnect the negative battery cable.

2. Drain the cooling system.

3. Remove the engine undercover.

4. Disconnect the clamp bolt from the power steering hose.

5. Support the engine with the appropriate equipment and remove the engine mount bracket.

6. Remove the timing belt(s) from the front of the engine.

7. Disconnect the coolant hoses from the pump, if equipped.

8. Remove the alternator brace.

9. Remove the water pump, gasket and O-ring where the water inlet pipe(s) joins the pump.

To install:

10. Thoroughly clean and dry both gasket surfaces of the water pump and block.

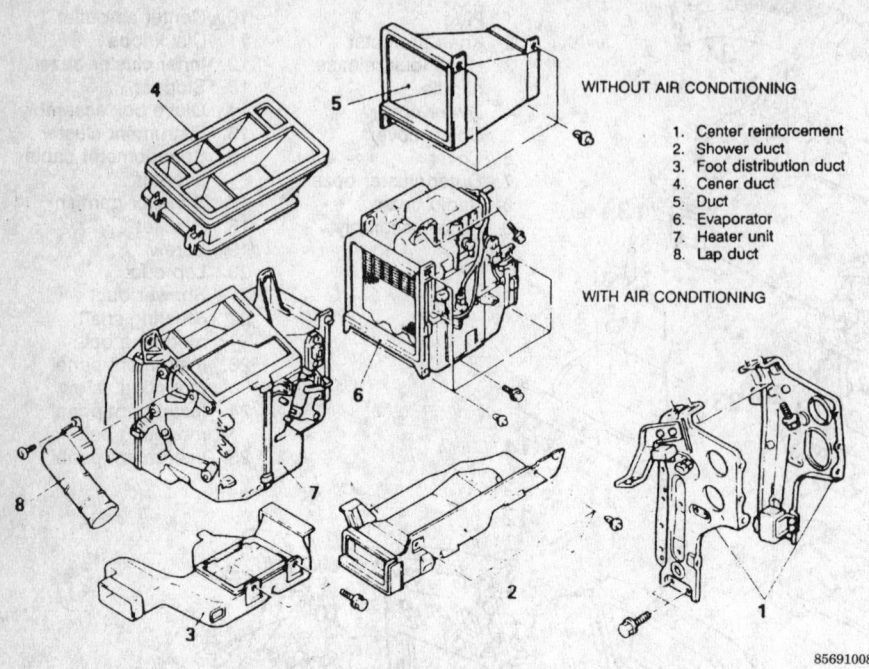

WITHOUT AIR CONDITIONING

1. Center reinforcement
2. Shower duct
3. Foot distribution duct
4. Cener duct
5. Duct
6. Evaporator
7. Heater unit
8. Lap duct

WITH AIR CONDITIONING

85691008

Heater case and related parts — Laser and Talon

11. Install a new O-ring into the groove on the front end of the water inlet pipe. Do not apply oils or grease to the O-ring. Wet with water only.

12. Install the gasket and pump assembly and tighten the bolts.

13. Connect the hoses to the pump.

14. Reinstall the timing belt and related parts.

15. Install the engine drive belts and adjust.

16. Fill the system with coolant.

17. Connect the negative battery cable, run the vehicle until the thermostat opens and fill the radiator completely.

18. Once the vehicle has cooled, recheck the coolant level.

Thermostat

REMOVAL AND INSTALLATION

1. Disconnect the negative battery cable.

2. Drain the cooling system.

3. On Stealth, remove necessary air intake plumbing.

4. Disconnect the upper radiator hose and overflow hose from the thermostat housing.

5. Remove the thermostat housing and gasket.

6. Remove the thermostat taking note of its original position in the housing or intake manifold.

To install:

7. Install the thermostat so its flange seats tightly in the machined groove in the intake manifold or thermostat case. Refer to its location prior to removal. On Stealth and Summit Wagon, align the jiggle valve with the alignment mark on the thermostat housing.

8. Use a new gasket and reinstall the thermostat housing. Torque the housing mounting bolts to 12–14 ft. lbs. (17–20 Nm).

9. Fill the system with coolant.

10. Install removed air intake plumbing.

11. Connect the negative battery cable, run the vehicle until the thermostat opens and fill the radiator completely.

12. Once the vehicle has cooled, recheck the coolant level.

Cooling System Bleeding

All vehicles are equipped with a self-bleeding thermostat. Slowly fill the cooling system in the conventional manner; air will vent through the jiggle valve in the thermostat. Run the vehicle until the thermostat has opened and continue filling the radiator. Recheck the coolant level after the vehicle has cooled.

FUEL SYSTEM

Fuel System Service Precaution

Safety is the most important factor when performing any type of maintenance, especially fuel system maintenance. Failure to conduct maintenance and repairs in a safe manner may result in serious personal injury or death. Maintenance and testing of the vehicle's fuel system components can be accomplished safely and effectively by adhering to the following rules and guidelines.

• To avoid the possibility of fire and personal injury, always disconnect the negative battery cable unless the repair or test procedure requires that battery voltage be applied.

• Always relieve the fuel system pressure prior to disconnecting any fuel system component (injector, fuel rail, pressure regulator, etc.), fitting or fuel line connection. Exercise extreme caution whenever relieving fuel system pressure to avoid exposing skin, face and eyes to fuel spray. Please be advised that fuel under pressure may penetrate the skin or any part of the body that it contacts.

• Always place a shop towel or cloth around the fitting or connection prior to loosening to absorb any excess fuel due to spillage. Ensure that all fuel spillage (should it occur) is quickly removed from engine surfaces. Ensure that all fuel soaked cloths or towels are deposited into a suitable waste container.

• Always keep a dry chemical (Class B) fire extinguisher near the work area.

• Do not allow fuel spray or fuel vapors to come into contact with a spark or open flame.

• Always use a backup wrench when loosening and tightening fuel line connection fittings. This will prevent unnecessary stress and torsion to fuel line piping. Always follow the proper torque specifications.

• Always replace worn fuel fitting O-rings with new. Do not substitute fuel hose or equivalent where fuel pipe is installed.

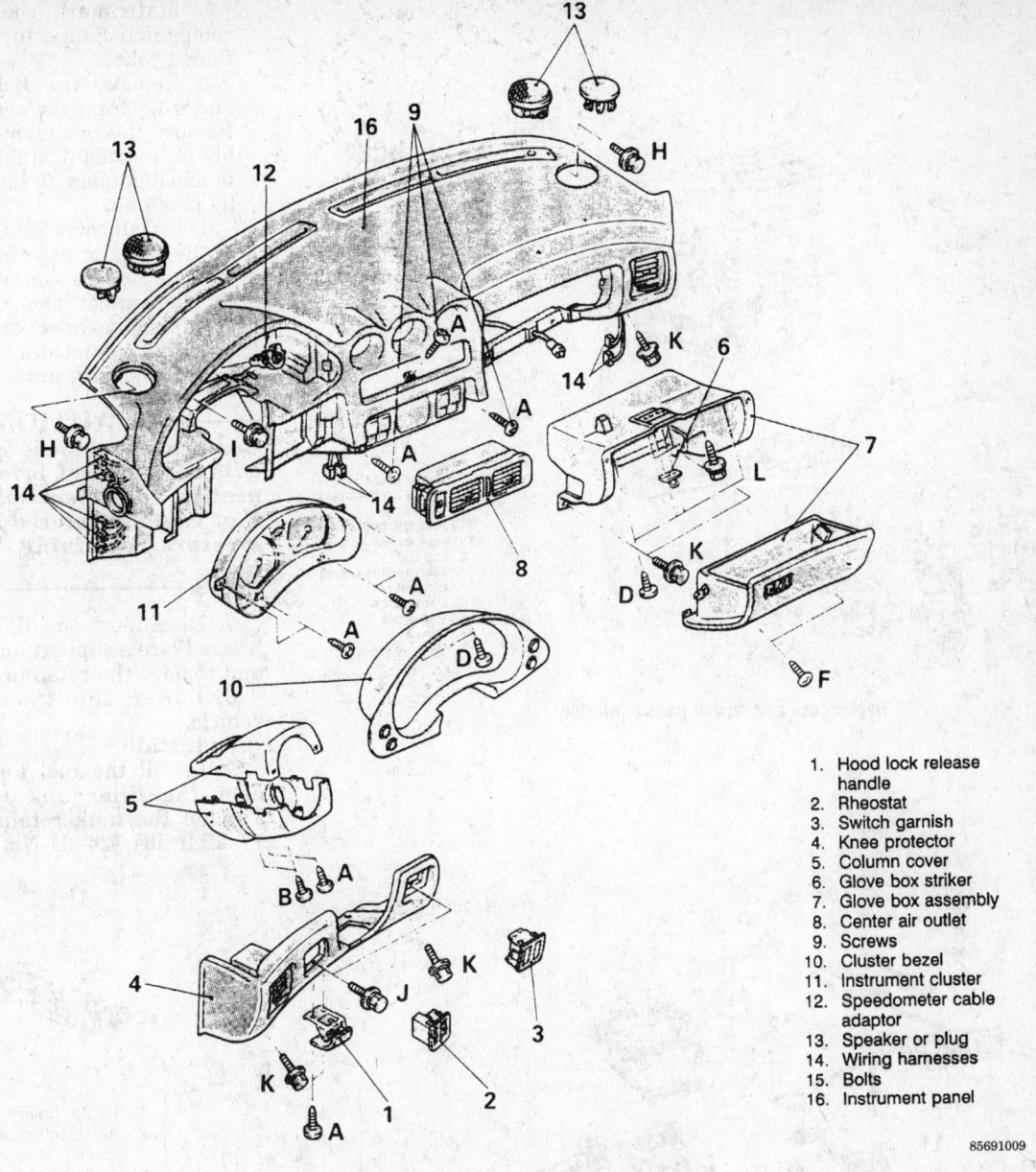

1. Hood lock release
   handle
2. Rheostat
3. Switch garnish
4. Knee protector
5. Column cover
6. Glove box striker
7. Glove box assembly
8. Center air outlet
9. Screws
10. Cluster bezel
11. Instrument cluster
12. Speedometer cable
    adaptor
13. Speaker or plug
14. Wiring harnesses
15. Bolts
16. Instrument panel

85691009

Instrument panel and related parts — Stealth

RELIEVING FUEL SYSTEM PRESSURE

1. Loosen the fuel filler cap to release fuel tank pressure.
2. Disconnect the fuel pump harness connector:

   a. Summit — remove the rear seat cushion to gain access to the connector.

   b. Summit Wagon — remove the rubber grommet on the underside of the floor panel, in front of the fuel tank, to gain access to the connector.

   c. Laser and Talon — the connector is located at the rear of the fuel tank.

   d. Stealth — remove the fuel system access cover in the luggage compartment to gain access to the connector.

3. Start the vehicle and allow it to run until it stalls from lack of fuel. Turn the key to the **OFF** position.
4. Disconnect the negative battery cable, then reconnect the fuel pump connector.
5. Wrap shop towels around the fitting that is being disconnected to absorb residual fuel in the lines.
6. Place shop towels into proper safety container.

Fuel Tank

REMOVAL AND INSTALLATION

1. Relieve fuel system pressure.
2. Disconnect the negative battery cable.
3. Raise the vehicle and support safely.
4. Drain the fuel from the fuel tank into an approved container.
5. On Summit Wagon equipped with AWD, remove the propeller shaft as follows:

   a. Remove the center exhaust pipe bracket.

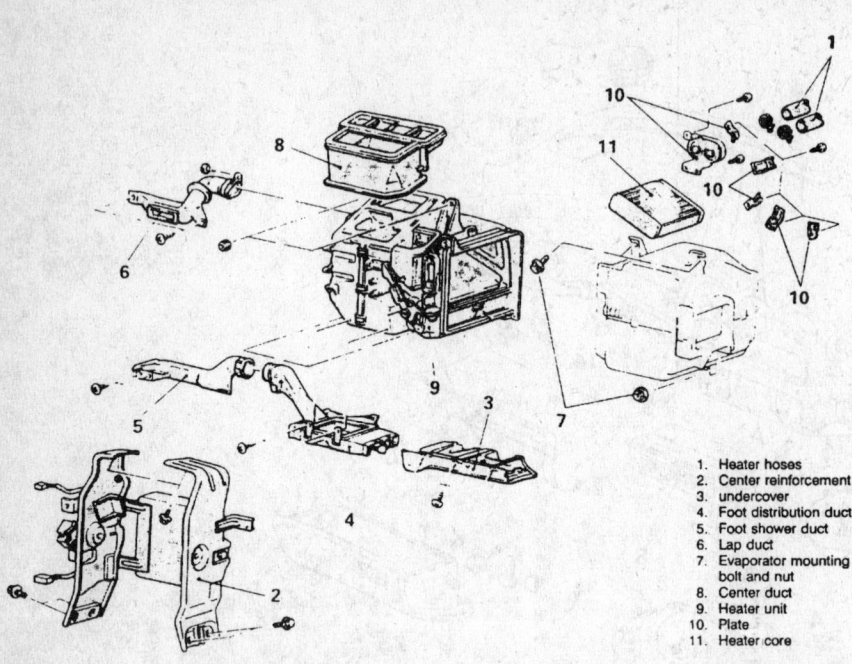

1. Heater hoses
2. Center reinforcement
3. undercover
4. Foot distribution duct
5. Foot shower duct
6. Lap duct
7. Evaporator mounting bolt and nut
8. Center duct
9. Heater unit
10. Plate
11. Heater core

85691010

Heater case and related parts — Stealth

b. Matchmark the differential companion flange to the propeller flange yoke.

c. Remove the bolts, washers and nuts from the center support. Remove the propeller shaft assembly in a straight and level manner to avoid damage to the boot caused by pinching.

d. Install cover into the rear end of the transfer case to prevent the entry of foreign materials.

6. Disconnect the return hose, high pressure hose and all other hoses and connectors connected to the pump/sending unit.

— **CAUTION** —
Cover all fuel hose connections with a shop towel, prior to disconnecting, to prevent splash of fuel that could be caused by residual pressure remaining in the fuel line.

7. Disconnect the filler and vent hoses. Place a support under the tank and remove the retaining nuts.

8. Lower the tank from the vehicle.

To install:

9. Install the fuel tank and connect the filler and vent hoses. Tighten the tank retaining nuts to 17–22 ft. lbs. (24–31 Nm).

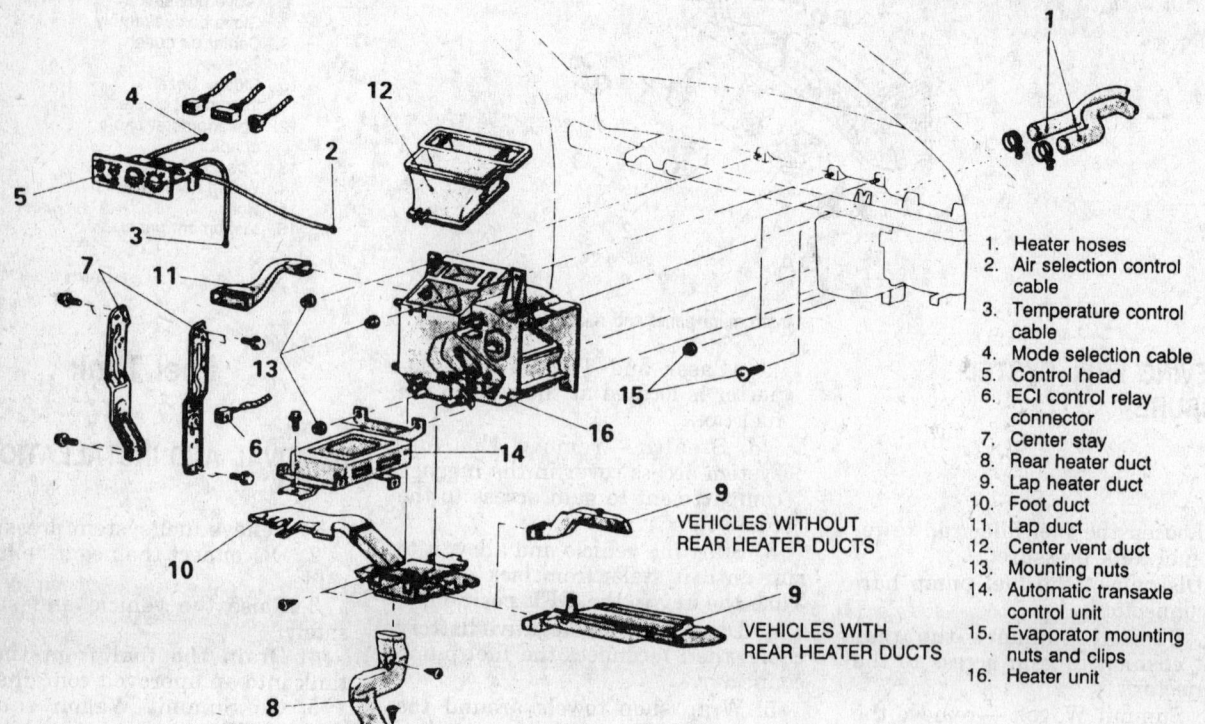

VEHICLES WITHOUT REAR HEATER DUCTS

VEHICLES WITH REAR HEATER DUCTS

1. Heater hoses
2. Air selection control cable
3. Temperature control cable
4. Mode selection cable
5. Control head
6. ECI control relay connector
7. Center stay
8. Rear heater duct
9. Lap heater duct
10. Foot duct
11. Lap duct
12. Center vent duct
13. Mounting nuts
14. Automatic transaxle control unit
15. Evaporator mounting nuts and clips
16. Heater unit

85691005

Instrument panel fastener identification — Summit

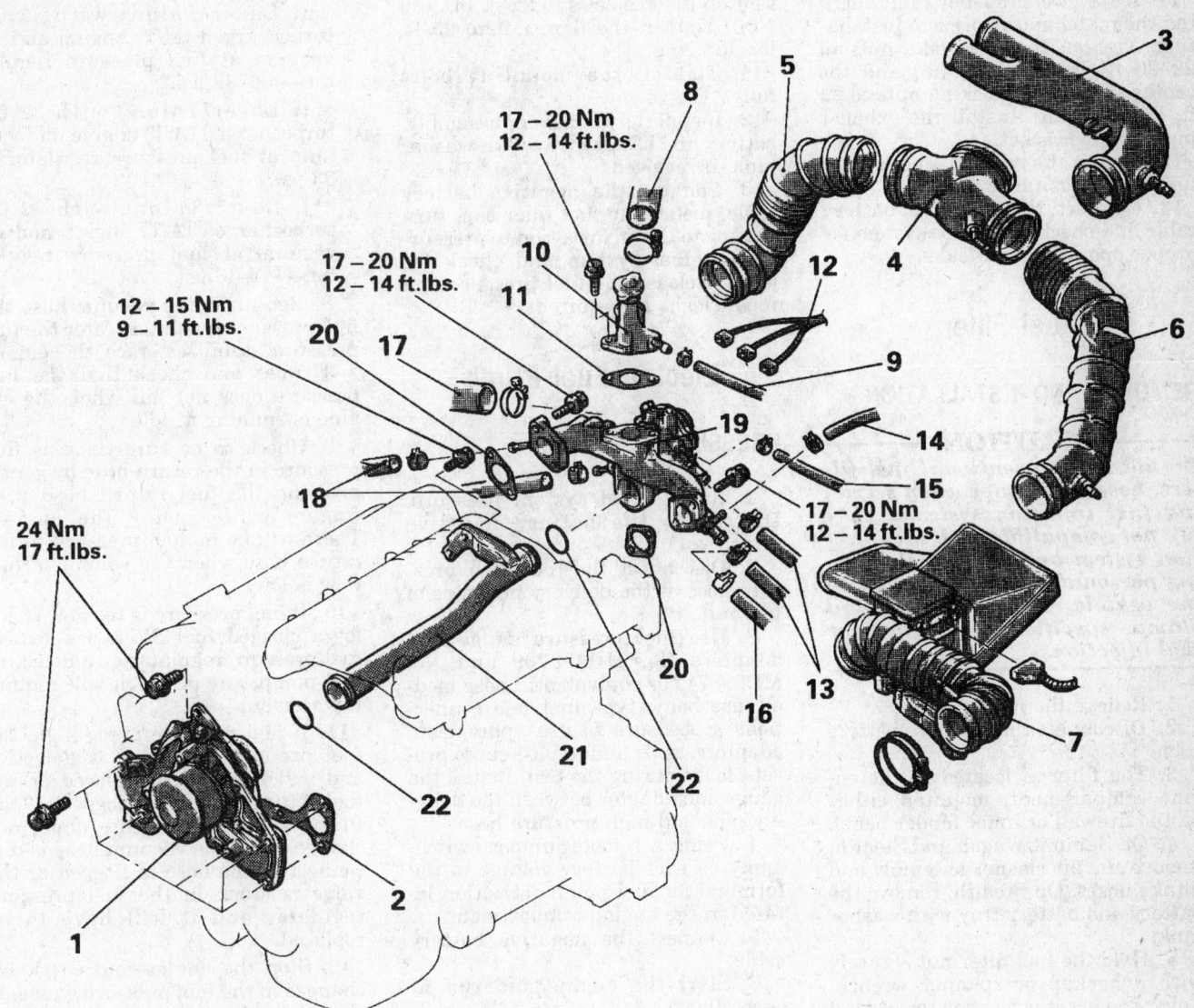

17 – 20 Nm
12 – 14 ft.lbs.

17 – 20 Nm
12 – 14 ft.lbs.

12 – 15 Nm
9 – 11 ft.lbs.

24 Nm
17 ft.lbs.

17 – 20 Nm
12 – 14 ft.lbs.

1. Water pump
2. Gasket
3. Air hose A (Turbo)
4. Air intake hose A (Turbo)
5. Air intake hose B (Turbo)
6. Air intake hose C (Turbo)
7. Air intake hose (Non-Turbo)
8. Connection of radiator upper hose
9. Connection of water hose (Turbo)
10. Water outlet fitting
11. Gasket

12. Connection of harness
13. Connection of heater hose
14. Connection of water hose A
15. Connection of water hose
16. Connection of water hose (Turbo)
17. Connection of radiator lower hose
18. Connection of water hose (Turbo)
19. Thermostat housing
20. Gasket
21. Inlet water pipe
22. O-ring

84701055

Water pump assembly — 3.0L DOHC engine

10. Connect the return hose, high pressure hose and all other hoses and connectors connected to the pump/sending unit.

11. Install the propeller shaft aligning the matchmarks prior to installation. Tighten the rear yoke nuts to 22–25 ft. lbs. (30–35 Nm) and the center support self-locking nuts to 22 ft. lbs. (30 Nm). Install the exhaust pipe center bracket.

12. Lower the vehicle and return fuel to the gas tank.

13. Connect the negative battery cable and check the entire system for proper operation and leaks.

Fuel Filter

REMOVAL AND INSTALLATION

——————— CAUTION ———————
Do not use conventional fuel filters, hoses or clamps when servicing fuel injection systems. They are not compatible with the injection system and could fail, causing personal injury or damage to the vehicle. Use only hoses and clamps specifically designed for fuel injection.

1. Relieve the fuel pressure.
2. Disconnect the negative battery cable.
3. The filter is located in the engine compartment, mounted either on the firewall or inner fender panel.
4. On Summit Wagon and Stealth, remove the air cleaner assembly and intake hoses. On Stealth, remove the battery and battery tray with washer tank.
5. Hold the fuel filter nut securely with a backup or spanner wrench. Cover the hoses with shop towels and remove the eye bolt. Discard the gaskets.
6. On Stealth, the high pressure hose connection is accomplished with another eye bolt connection; first separate the flare nut connection at the line, then repeat Step 5. Otherwise, separate the flare nut connection at the filter. Discard the gaskets.
7. Remove the mounting bolts and remove the fuel filter from the vehicle.

To install:
8. Install a new O-rings whenever fuel connections have been disassembled.
9. Install the filter to its bracket only finger-tight. Movement of the filter will ease attachment of the fuel lines.

10. Install new O-rings and connect the high pressure hose and eye bolt, then the main pipe and eye bolt. While holding the fuel filter nut, tighten the eye bolts to 22 ft. lbs. (30 Nm). Tighten the flare nut to 25 ft. lbs. (35 Nm).

11. Tighten the mounting bolts fully.

12. Install the air cleaner assembly, battery and battery tray with washer tank, if removed.

13. Connect the negative battery cable, install the fuel filler cap, turn the key to the **ON** position to pressurize the fuel system and check for leaks. Release the fuel pressure and repair leaks as required.

Electric Fuel Pump

PRESSURE TESTING

1. Relieve fuel system pressure. Disconnect the battery negative cable.
2. Disconnect the fuel high pressure hose at the delivery pipe side of fuel rail.
3. Use fuel pressure gauge and adapters No. MD998709 and No. MD998742 or equivalent. These models use banjo type fuel line connections so be sure to use appropriate adaptors, seals and/or gaskets to prevent leaks during the test. Install the gauge and adapter between the delivery pipe and high pressure hose.
4. Using a remote jumper switch, apply positive battery voltage to the terminal for fuel pump activation located in the engine compartment.
5. Connect the negative battery cable.
6. Start the engine and run at curb idle speed.
7. Measure the fuel pressure and compare to specifications:
   a. Summit and Summit Wagon with vacuum at fuel pressure regulator — 38 psi.
   b. Summit and Summit Wagon with no vacuum at fuel pressure regulator — 47–50 psi.
   c. Laser/Talon with 1.8L engine and vacuum at fuel pressure regulator — 38 psi.
   d. Laser/Talon with 1.8L engine and no vacuum at fuel pressure regulator — 47–50 psi.
   e. Laser/Talon with 2.0L engine and vacuum at fuel pressure regulator — 38 psi.
   f. Laser/Talon with 2.0L engine and no vacuum at fuel pressure regulator — 47–50 psi.

   g. Laser/Talon with 2.0L turbocharged (M/T) engine and vacuum at fuel pressure regulator — 27 psi.
   h. Laser/Talon with 2.0L turbocharged (M/T) engine and no vacuum at fuel pressure regulator — 36–38 psi.
   i. Laser/Talon with 2.0L turbocharged (A/T) engine and vacuum at fuel pressure regulator — 33 psi.
   j. Laser/Talon with 2.0L turbocharged (A/T) engine and no vacuum at fuel pressure regulator — 41–46 psi.

8. Reconnect the vacuum hose the fuel pressure regulator. After the fuel pressure stabilizes, race the engine 2–3 times and check that the fuel pressure does not fall when the engine is running at idle.

9. Check to be sure there is fuel pressure in the return hose by gently pressing the fuel return hose with fingers while racing the engine. There will be no fuel pressure in the return hose when the volume of fuel flow is low.

10. If fuel pressure is too low, check for a clogged fuel filter, a defective fuel pressure regulator or a defective fuel pump, any of which will require replacement.

11. If fuel pressure is too high, the fuel pressure regulator is defective and will have to be replaced or the fuel return is bent or clogged. If the fuel pressure reading does not change when the vacuum hose is disconnected, the hose is clogged or the valve is stuck in the fuel pressure regulator and it will have to be replaced.

12. Stop the engine and check for changes in the fuel pressure gauge. It should not drop. If the gauge reading does drop, watch the rate of drop. If fuel pressure drops slowly, the likely cause is a leaking injector which will require replacement. If the fuel pressure drops immediately after the engine is stopped, the check valve in the fuel pump isn't closing and the fuel pump will have to be replaced.

13. Relieve fuel system pressure.

14. Disconnect the high pressure hose and remove the fuel pressure gauge from the delivery pipe.

15. Install a new O-ring in the groove of the high pressure hose. Connect the hose to the delivery pipe and tighten the screws. After installation, apply battery voltage to the terminal for fuel pump activation to run the fuel pump. Check for leaks.

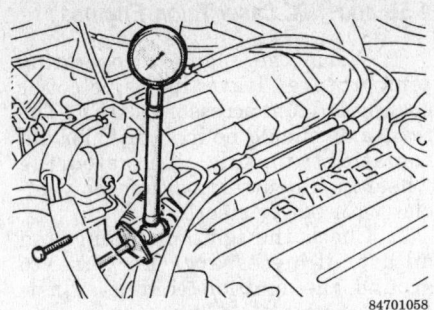

Fuel pressure gauge installation at high pressure hose

84701058

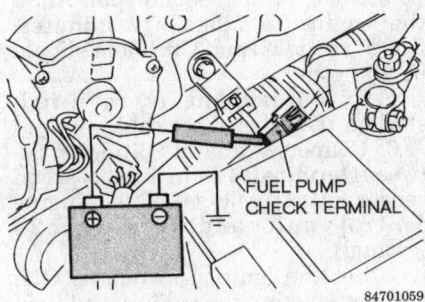

FUEL PUMP CHECK TERMINAL

84701059

Fuel pump activation test terminal

REMOVAL AND INSTALLATION

Summit and Summit Wagon

1. Relieve fuel system pressure. Remove the fuel filler cap.

2. Disconnect the negative battery cable.

3. Raise and safely support the vehicle.

4. The fuel pump is located in the fuel tank. Drain the fuel from the fuel tank.

5. On Summit Wagon equipped with AWD, remove the rear propeller shaft from the vehicle as follows:

　a. Remove the center exhaust pipe bracket.

　b. Matchmark the differential companion flange to the propeller flange yoke.

　c. Remove the bolts, washers and nuts from the center support. Remove the propeller shaft assembly in a straight and level manner to avoid damage to the boot caused by pinching.

　d. Install cover into the rear end of the transfer case to prevent the entry of foreign materials.

6. Disconnect the return hose, high pressure hose and all other hoses and connectors connected to the pump and sending unit.

7. Disconnect the filler and vent hoses. Place a support under the tank and remove the retaining nuts. Lower the tank from vehicle.

8. Remove retaining nuts and remove the fuel pump assembly from tank.

To install:

9. Install the replacement pump using a new gasket. Be certain the pump is installed in the same location, facing the same direction as before.

10. Install the fuel tank and secure the retainer nuts. Connect all electrical harness connectors. Reconnect all vent hoses, fuel supply and fuel return hoses securing with the proper clamps.

11. On Summit Wagon equipped with AWD, install the propeller shaft aligning the matchmarks prior to installation. Tighten the rear yoke nuts to 22–25 ft. lbs. (30–35 Nm) and the center support self-locking nuts to 22 ft. lbs. (30 Nm).

12. Install the exhaust pipe center bracket. Check that electrical connectors are properly installed and all fuel hose connections are tight.

13. Connect the negative battery cable and check the entire fuel system for proper operation and leaks. If repairing of a fuel leak is required, release the fuel system pressure prior to repairing system.

Laser and Talon

WITH FWD

1. Relieve fuel system pressure. Remove the fuel filler cap.

2. Disconnect the negative battery cable.

3. Raise and safely support the vehicle.

4. Drain the fuel from the fuel tank.

5. Remove the electrical connector from the fuel pump.

6. Remove the high pressure fuel hose connector.

7. Loosen self-locking nuts on tank support straps to the end of the stud bolts.

8. Remove the right side lateral rod attaching bolt and disconnect the arm from the right body coupling. Lower the lateral rod and suspend from the axle beam.

9. Remove the holding bolt and gasket from the base of the tank and remove the fuel pump assembly.

To install:

10. Align the 3 projections on packing with the holes on the fuel pump and the nipples on the pump facing the same direction as before removal.

11. Install the holding bolt through the bottom of the tank. Make sure the gasket on the bolt is replaced and is not pinched during installation.

12. Install the right side lateral rod and attaching bolt into the right body coupling.

13. Tighten self-locking nuts on tank support straps. Install the high pressure fuel hose connector.

14. Install the electrical connector to the fuel pump assembly.

15. Connect the negative battery cable and check the entire system for proper operation and leaks.

WITH AWD

1. Relieve fuel system pressure. Remove the fuel filler cap.

2. Disconnect the negative battery cable.

3. The fuel pump is located in the fuel tank. Remove the hole cover located in the rear floor pan.

4. Remove the electrical connector from the fuel pump. Remove the overfill limiter (two-way valve).

5. Cover the hose connection with a shop towel to prevent any splash of fuel due to residual pressure in the fuel pipe. Remove the high pressure fuel hose connectors.

6. Remove the fuel pump and gauge assembly from the tank.

To install:

7. Align the 3 projections on the packing with the holes on the fuel pump and the nipples on the pump facing the same direction as before removal.

8. Install the high pressure hose connections.

9. Install the overfill limiter (two-way valve) and the electrical connector to the fuel pump.

10. Reconnect the negative battery cable and check the entire system for leaks.

11. Install MOPAR Rope Caulk Sealer part 4026044 or equivalent, to the rear floor pan and install the cover into place.

STEALTH

1. Relieve fuel system pressure. Remove the fuel filler cap.

2. Disconnect the negative battery cable.

3. The fuel pump is located in the fuel tank. Drain the fuel from the fuel tank.

4. Remove the fuel gauge cover located in the rear floor pan.

5. Remove the fuel pump and gauge electrical connector. Remove the overfill limiter (two-way valve).

6. Disconnect both sides of the high pressure fuel hose. When disconnecting the fuel pump side of the

hose, hold the pump side nut with a wrench while turning the nut on the hose side. This will prevent any damage that will occur to the fittings and the hoses if 2 wrenches are not used.

7. Remove the fuel pump and gauge assembly from the tank.

To install:

8. Align the 3 projections on the packing with the holes on the fuel pump and the nipples on the pump facing the same direction as before removal.

9. Temporarily tighten the flare nut on the high pressure hose by hand. Making sure the hose does not twist, tighten body side nut to 22 ft. lbs. (30 Nm) and the fuel pump side nut to 25 ft. lbs. (35 Nm).

10. Install the overfill limiter (2-way valve) with the long shouldered side of the valve facing the canister.

11. Connect the electrical connector to the pump assembly.

12. Reconnect the negative battery cable and check the entire system for leaks.

13. Install MOPAR Rope Caulk Sealer part 4026044 of equivalent, to the rear floor pan and install the cover into place.

Fuel Injection

IDLE SPEED ADJUSTMENT

NOTE: The idle speed is controlled electronically and adjustment is usually unnecessary. However, the idle speed may be checked using the following procedures.

Summit and Summit Wagon

1.8L AND 2.4L ENGINES

1. Warm the engine to operating temperature, leave lights, electric cooling fan and accessories **OFF**. The transaxle should be in **N** or **P** for automatic transaxle. The steering wheel in a neutral position for vehicles with power steering.

2. Insert the paper clip into the single terminal rpm connector in the engine compartment, and connect the primary voltage detection type tachometer to the paper clip.

3. Ground the self-diagnostic control terminal of the diagnostic connector with a jumper wire.

4. Remove the waterproof female connector from the ignition timing adjustment connector. Ground the ignition timing adjustment terminal.

5. Start the engine and run at idle. Check the basic idle speed, the desired value is 700–800 rpm.

6. If the value is not within specifications, turn the Speed Adjusting Screw (SAS) to make the necessary adjustment.

NOTE: If the idle speed is higher than the standard value, inspect the SAS screw for evidence of movement. If there is evidence that the SAS screw has been adjusted, readjust to the proper setting. If the screw does not look as though it has been adjusted, it is possible that there is leakage as a result of deterioration of the Fast Idle Air Valve (FIAV) and, if so the throttle body should be replaced.

7. Turn the ignition **OFF**. Disconnect and remove the jumper wires from the diagnosis control terminal and the ignition timing adjustment terminal.

8. Start the engine and let run at idle speed for about 10 minutes, check to be sure the idling condition is normal.

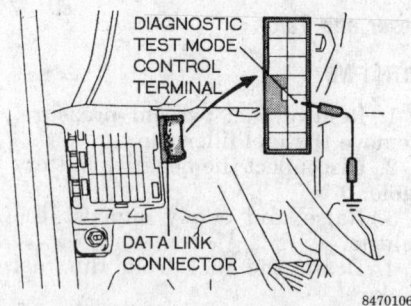

Grounding the diagnostic terminal — Summit Wagon

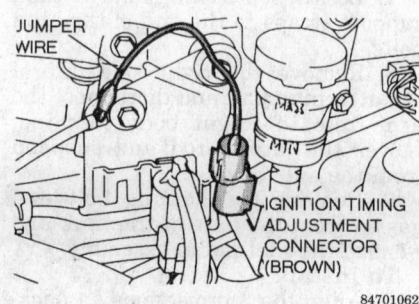

Grounding the ignition timing adjustment terminal — Summit Wagon

1.5L and 1.8L Laser/Talon Engines

1. Warm the engine to operating temperature, leave lights, electric cooling fan and accessories **OFF**. The transaxle should be in **N** or **P** for automatic transaxle. The steering wheel in a neutral position for vehicles with power steering.

2. Check the ignition timing and adjust, if necessary. Be sure to ground the ignition timing adjustment terminal.

3. Connect a tachometer to the CRC filter connector. Use a paper clip for a tach adapter.

4. Run the engine for more than 10 seconds at 2000–3000 rpm. Allow the engine to idle for 2 minutes. Check the idle rpm. Curb idle should be 750 rpm.

5. If adjustment is required, slacken the accelerator cable.

6. Connect a digital voltmeter between terminal **19** throttle position sensor output voltage) of the engine control unit and terminal **24** (ground).

7. Set the ignition switch to **ON**, without starting the engine, and hold it in that position for 15 seconds or more. Turn the ignition switch **OFF**.

8. Disconnect the connectors of the idle speed control servo and lock the idle speed control plunger at the initial position. Back out the fixed Speed Adjusting Screw (SAS).

9. Start the engine and allow to idle. Basic idle speed should be at specification. A new engine may idle a little lower. If the vehicle stalls or has a very low idle speed, suspect a deposit buildup on the throttle valve which must be cleaned.

10. If the idle speed is wrong, adjust with the idle speed control adjusting screw. Use a hexagon wrench if possible. Turn in the fixed SAS until the engine speed rises. Then back out the fixed SAS until the Touch Point where the engine speed does not fall any longer, is found. Back out the fixed SAS an additional ½ turn from the touch point.

11. Stop the engine. Turn the ignition switch to **ON** but do not start engine. Check that the output voltage from the throttle position sensor is 0.48–0.52 volts. If it is out of specification, adjust by loosening the throttle position sensor mounting screws and rotating the throttle position sensor. Turning the throttle position sensor clockwise increases the output voltage. After adjustment, tighten screws firmly.

12. Turn the ignition switch **OFF**.

13. Adjust the free-play of the accelerator cable, reconnect the connectors

of the idle speed control servo and remove the voltmeter.

14. Start the engine and check the curb idle. It should be 700 rpm.

15. Turn the ignition switch to **OFF**, disconnect the negative battery cable for more than 10 seconds and reconnect. This clears any trouble codes introduced during testing.

16. Restart the engine, allow to run for 5 minutes and check for good idle quality.

1.6L, 2.0L and 3.0L Engines

1. Warm the engine to operating temperature, leave lights, electric

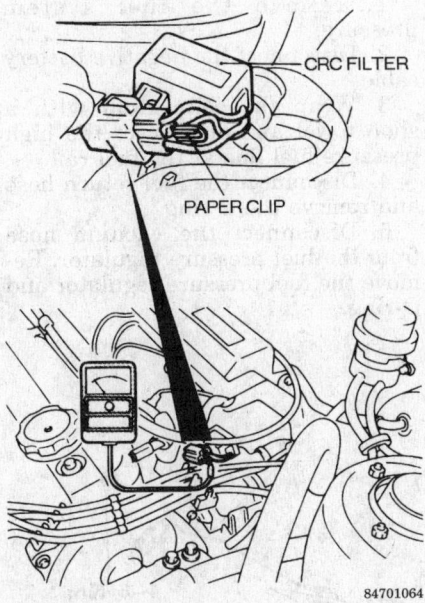

Harness for tachometer connection — Laser/Talon 1.8L Engine

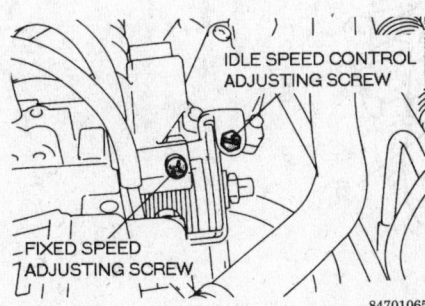

Adjustment points for idle speed — Laser/Talon 1.8L Engine

cooling fan and accessories **OFF**. The transaxle should be in **N**. The steering wheel in a neutral position for vehicles with power steering.

2. Check the ignition timing and adjust, if necessary. Be sure to ground ignition timing adjustment connector.

3. Connect a tachometer to the single pin connector terminal under the hood.

4. Run the engine for more than 10 seconds at 2000–3000 rpm. Allow the engine to idle for 2 minutes. Check the idle rpm. Curb idle should be 750 rpm.

5. If adjustment is required, disconnect the waterproof female connector used for ignition timing adjustment. Connect this terminal to ground using a jumper wire.

6. Locate the self-diagnosis terminal under the dashboard and connect terminal No. **10** to ground with a jumper wire.

7. Start the engine and allow to idle. Check that the basic idle speed is at specification. On Stealth, the tachometer reading will be 1/3 of the actual engine speed. Multiply the reading by 3 to figure the actual engine speed. If the idle speed deviates from this speed, check the following:

   a. A new engine will idle more slowly. Break-in should take approximately 300 miles.

   b. If the vehicle stalls or has a very low idle speed, suspect a deposit buildup on the throttle valve which must be cleaned.

   c. If the idle speed is high even though the speed adjusting screw is fully closed, check that the idle position switch (fixed speed adjusting screw) position has changed. If so, adjust the idle position switch.

   d. If after all these checks the idle is still out of specification, it is probable that there is leakage resulting from deterioration of the Fast-Idle Air Valve (FIAV) and the throttle body will need to be replaced.

8. Turn the ignition switch **OFF** and stop the engine. Disconnect the jumper wire from the diagnosis connector, disconnect the jumper wire from the ignition timing connector and reconnect the waterproof connector. Disconnect the tachometer.

9. Restart the engine, allow to run for 5 minutes and check for good idle quality.

Fuel Injector

REMOVAL AND INSTALLATION

1.5L and 1.8L Laser/Talon Engines

1. Relieve the fuel system pressure.

2. Disconnect the negative battery cable. Remove the air breather hose, as required.

3. Disconnect the vacuum connections and the fuel return hose. Cover the connection with shop cloths in case of any residual pressure and to avoid fuel spillage.

4. Remove the fuel pressure regulator and O-ring.

5. Wrap the connection with a shop towel and disconnect the high pressure fuel line at the fuel rail.

6. Remove the accelerator cable clamp as required. Remove the connection for the control harness.

7. Disconnect the electrical harness from each injector connector.

8. Remove the injector rail retaining bolts. Make sure the rubber mounting bushings do not get lost.

9. Lift the rail assembly up and away from engine.

10. Remove the injectors from the rail by pulling gently. Discard the lower insulator. Check the resistance through the injector. The specification is 13–16 ohms at 70°F (20°C).

To install:

11. Install a new grommet and O-ring to the injector. Coat the O-ring with light weight oil.

12. Install the injector to the fuel rail.

13. Install the fuel rail and injectors to the manifold. Make sure the rubber bushings are in place before tightening the mounting bolts.

14. Tighten the retaining bolts to 72 inch lbs. (11 Nm).

15. Connect the electrical connectors to the injectors.

16. Replace the O-ring on the fuel pressure regulator, lightly lubricate and insert on delivery pipe.

17. Connect the fuel return hose.

18. Replace the O-ring on high pressure fuel line, lightly lubricate it and connect to delivery pipe.

19. Connect the negative battery cable and check the entire system for proper operation and leaks.

1.8L Summit Wagon and 2.4L Engines

1. Relieve the fuel system pressure.

2. Disconnect the negative battery cable.

3. Disconnect and remove the air intake hoses, as required.

Grounding of self-diagnostic harness connector — 1.6L and 2.0L engines

84701066

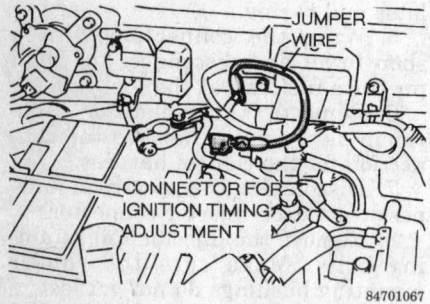

Ignition timing adjustment connector — 1.6L and 2.0L engines

84701067

4. Wrap the connection with a shop towel and disconnect the high pressure fuel line at the fuel rail.

5. Disconnect the fuel return hose and remove the O-ring.

6. Disconnect the accelerator cable connection from the throttle body and position aside.

7. Disconnect the vacuum connection from the fuel pressure regulator.

8. Disconnect the electrical harness connector from each fuel injector.

9. Remove the injector rail retaining bolts. Make sure the rubber mounting insulators do not get lost.

10. Lift the rail assembly up and away from engine.

11. Remove the injectors from the rail by pulling gently. Discard the lower insulator. Check the resistance through the injector. The specification is 13–16 ohms at 70°F (20°C).

To install:

12. Install a new grommet and O-ring to the injector. Coat the O-ring with light weight oil.

13. Install the injector to the fuel rail.

14. Install the fuel rail and injectors to the manifold. Make sure the rubber bushings are in place before tightening the mounting bolts.

15. Tighten the retaining bolts to 8.7 ft. lbs. (12 Nm).

16. Connect the electrical connectors to the injectors.

17. Replace the O-ring on the fuel pressure regulator, lightly lubricate and install on the delivery pipe. Connect the vacuum hose to the fuel pressure regulator.

18. Connect the fuel return hose.

19. Replace the O-ring on high pressure fuel line, lightly lubricate it and connect to delivery pipe.

20. Reconnect the accelerator cable to the throttler body and adjust to specifications.

21. Connect the negative battery cable and check the entire system for proper operation and leaks.

1.6L and 2.0L DOHC Engines

1. Relieve the fuel system pressure.

2. Disconnect the negative battery cable.

3. Wrap the connection with a shop towel and disconnect the high pressure fuel line at the fuel rail.

4. Disconnect the fuel return hose and remove the O-ring.

5. Disconnect the vacuum hose from the fuel pressure regulator. Remove the fuel pressure regulator and O-ring.

1. Connection for breather hose
2. Connection for PCV hose
3. Connection for high pressure fuel hose
4. O-ring
5. Connection for vacuum hose
6. Connection for fuel return hose
7. Fuel pressure regulator
8. O-ring
9. Connection for control harness
10. Fuel rail
11. Insulator
12. Insulator
13. Injector
14. O-ring
15. Grommet

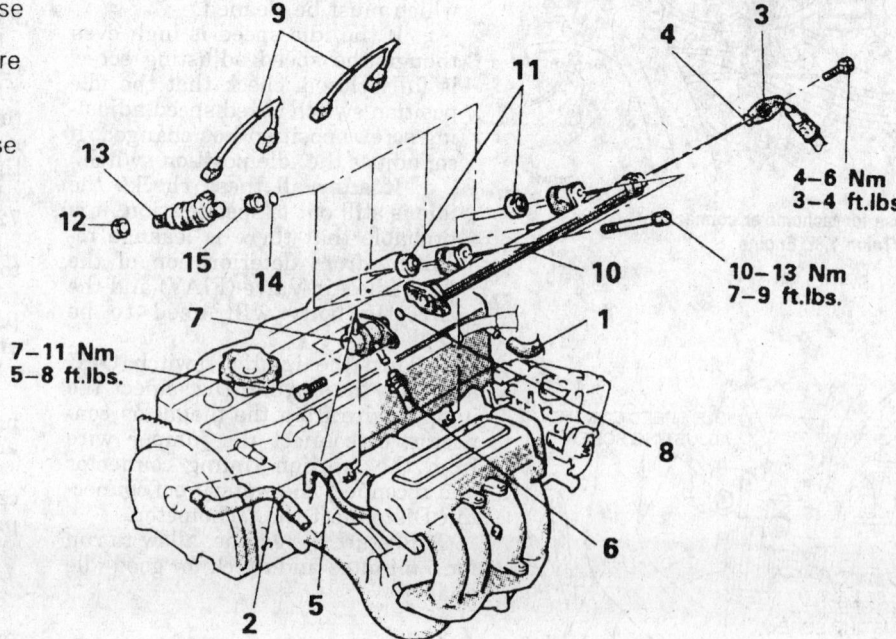

84701068

Fuel rail and injector assembly — 1.5L and 1.8L engines

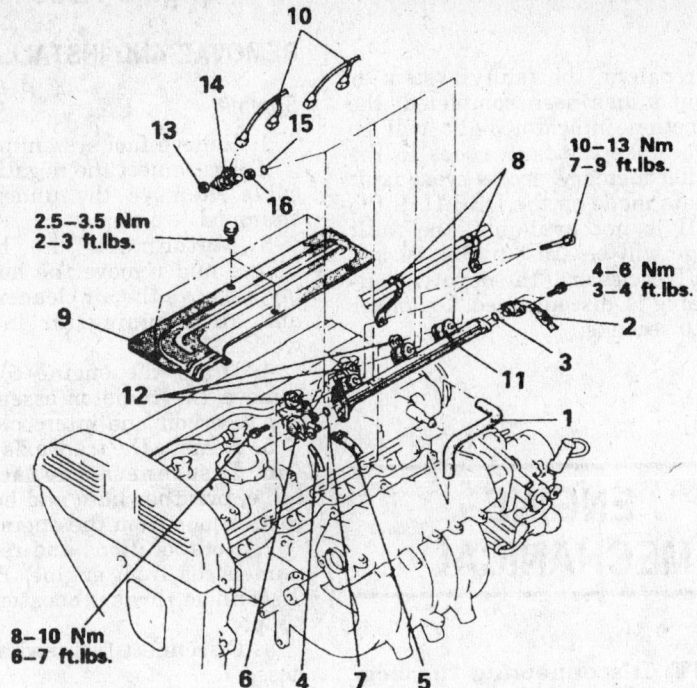

1. Connection for PCV hose
2. Connection for high pressure fuel hose
3. O-ring
4. Connection for vacuum hose
5. Connection for fuel return hose
6. Fuel pressure regulator
7. O-ring
8. Accelerator cable clamp
9. Center cover
10. Connection for control harness
11. Fuel rail
12. Insulator
13. Insulator
14. Injector
15. O-ring
16. Grommet

10–13 Nm
7–9 ft.lbs.

4–6 Nm
3–4 ft.lbs.

2.5–3.5 Nm
2–3 ft.lbs.

8–10 Nm
6–7 ft.lbs.

84701069

Fuel rail and injector assembly — 1.6L and 2.0L engines

6. Disconnect the PCV hose. On Laser and Talon, remove the center cover.

7. Label and disconnect the electrical connectors from each injector.

8. Remove the injector rail retaining bolts. Make sure the rubber mounting bushings do not get misplaced.

9. Lift the rail assembly up and away from the engine.

10. Remove the injectors from the rail by pulling gently. Discard the lower insulator. Check the resistance through the injector. The specification for 2.0L turbocharged engine is 2–3 ohms at 70°F (20°C). The specification for the others is 13–15 ohms at 70°F (20°C).

To install:

11. Install a new grommet and O-ring to the injector. Coat the O-ring with light oil.

12. Install the injector to the fuel rail.

13. Replace the seats in the intake manifold. Install the fuel rail and injectors to the manifold. Make sure the rubber bushings are in place before tightening the mounting bolts. Tighten the retaining bolts to 72 inch lbs. (11 Nm).

14. Tighten the retaining bolts to 72 inch lbs. (11 Nm).

15. Connect the connectors to the injectors and install the center cover. Connect the PCV hose.

16. Replace the O-ring, lightly lubricate it and connect the fuel pressure regulator.

17. Connect the fuel return hose.

18. Replace the O-ring, lightly lubricate it and connect the high pressure fuel line.

19. Connect the negative battery cable and check the entire system for proper operation and leaks.

3.0L Engine

1. Relieve the fuel system pressure.
2. Disconnect the negative battery cable.
3. Drain the cooling system.
4. Disconnect all components from the air intake plenum and remove the plenum from the intake manifold. Discard the gaskets.
5. Wrap the connection with a shop towel and disconnect the high pressure fuel line at the fuel rail.
6. Disconnect the fuel return hose and remove the O-ring.
7. Disconnect the vacuum hose from the fuel pressure regulator. Remove the fuel pressure regulator and O-ring.
8. Disconnect the electrical connectors from each injector.
9. Remove the fuel pipe connecting the fuel rails. Remove the injector

rail retaining bolts. Make sure the rubber mounting bushings do not get lost.

10. Lift the rail assemblies up and away from the engine.

11. Remove the injectors from the rail by pulling gently. Discard the lower insulator. Check the resistance through the injector. The specification for 3.0L turbocharged engine is 2–3 ohms at 68°F (20°C). The specification for non-turbocharged 3.0L engine is 13–15 ohms at 68°F (20°C).

To install:

12. Install a new grommet and O-ring to the injector. Coat the O-ring with light oil.

13. Install the injector to the fuel rail.

14. Replace the seats in the intake manifold. Install the fuel rails and injectors to the manifold. Make sure the rubber bushings are in place before tightening the mounting bolts.

15. Tighten the retaining bolts to 72 inch lbs. (11 Nm). Install the fuel pipe with new gasket.

16. Connect the electrical connectors to the injectors.

17. Replace the O-ring, lightly lubricate it and connect the fuel pressure regulator.

18. Connect the fuel return hose.

19. Replace the O-ring, lightly lubricate it and connect the high pressure fuel line.

20. Using new gaskets, install the intake plenum and all related items. Torque the plenum mounting bolts to 13 ft. lbs. (18 Nm).

21. Fill the cooling system.

22. Connect the negative battery cable and check the entire system for proper operation and leaks.

EMISSION CONTROLS

Emission Warning Lamp

The malfunction indicator light will come **ON** each time the ignition key is turned **ON** and stays on for 5 seconds as a bulb test. If the ECU receives an incorrect signal or no signal from a checked sensor, the check engine light on the instrument panel is illuminated and repair of the vehicle is required.

RESETTING

Once repair of the faulty system or component has been completed, the malfunction indicator light will go out. To erase the fault codes in the controller memory, access erase fault code data mode on the DRB II. If the DRB II is not available, the fault message will be erased after 50 key ON/OFF cycles or if the negative battery cable is disconnected for longer than 10 seconds.

ENGINE MECHANICAL

NOTE: Disconnecting the negative battery cable on some vehicles may interfere with the functions of the on board computer systems and may require the computer to undergo a relearning process, once the negative battery cable is reconnected.

Engine Assembly

REMOVAL AND INSTALLATION

Summit

1. Relieve fuel system pressure.

2. Disconnect the negative battery cable. Remove the under cover if equipped.

3. Matchmark the hood and hinges and remove the hood assembly. Remove the air cleaner assembly and all adjoining air intake duct work.

4. Drain the engine coolant and remove the radiator assembly, coolant reservoir and intercooler.

5. Remove the transaxle assembly.

6. Disconnect the accelerator cable, breather hose and heater hose connections from the engine.

7. Note locations and remove vacuum hoses from engine. Be sure to disconnect brake booster vacuum supply.

8. Disconnect fuel feed and return hoses.

9. Disconnect oxygen sensor connection, coolant temperature gauge and coolant temperature sensor connections.

10. On models with automatic transmissions, disconnect the thermo switch.

1. Connection of high pressure fuel hose
2. Connection of fuel return hose
3. Connection of vacuum hose
4. Fuel pressure regulator
5. Connection of control harness
6. Fuel pipe
7. Fuel rail
8. Insulator
9. Injector support
10. Injector
11. Insulator
12. O-ring
13. Grommet

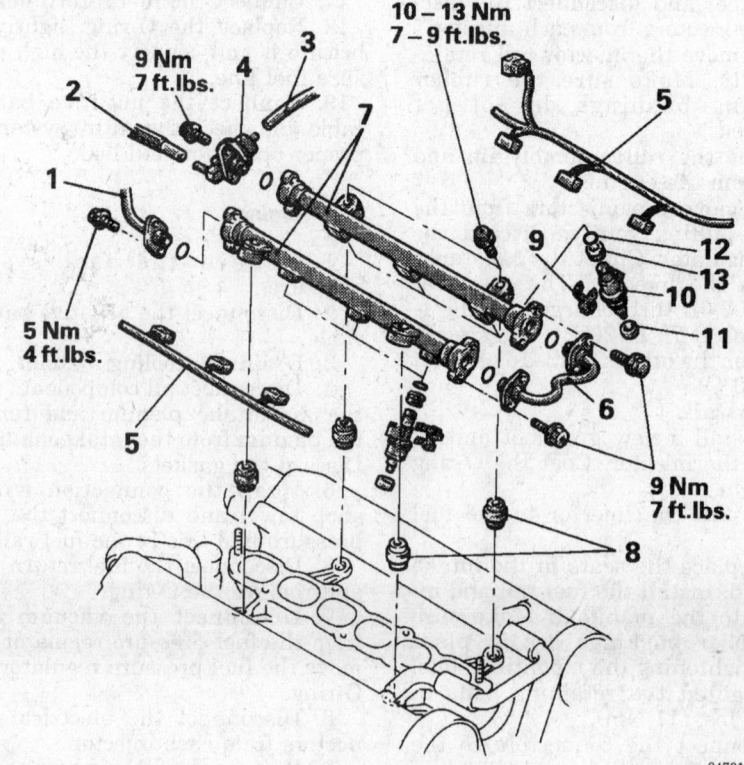

Fuel rail and injector assembly — 3.0L engine

11. Disconnect harness connections for the idle speed control, motor position sensor and throttle position sensor.

12. Disconnect EGR temperature sensor (California).

13. Note locations for reassembly and disconnect injector connections.

14. Disconnect power transistor, ignition coil and noise filter connections.

15. Disconnect alternator and power steering switch wiring.

16. Remove the air conditioner drive belt and the air conditioning compressor. Leave the hoses attached. Do not discharge the system. Wire the compressor aside.

17. Remove the power steering pump and wire aside.

18. Remove the starter and alternator harness clamp (1.8L engine).

19. Remove the exhaust manifold to head pipe nuts. Discard the gasket.

20. Attach a hoist to the engine and support the engine weight. Remove the engine mount bracket. Remove any torque control brackets (roll stoppers).

21. Remove the engine assembly from the vehicle.

To install:

22. Install the engine and secure in position. The front lower mount through bolt nut should not be tightened until the full weight of the engine is on the mount. Tighten through bolt to 72 ft. lbs. (100 Nm) and bracket mounting bolts to 42 ft. lbs. (58 Nm).

23. Using a new gasket, position exhaust pipe onto the manifold and tighten 3 hole flange nuts to 22–29 ft. lbs. (30–40 Nm) or 36 ft. lbs. (50 Nm) for 2 hole flange.

24. Install power steering pump, alternator and air conditioner compressor. Install and adjust drive belts, tighten all mounting bolts.

25. Connect alternator and power steering wiring.

26. Secure alternator and starter harness clamp.

27. Connect noise filter, ignition coil and power transistor connections.

28. Connect fuel injector harness connections.

29. On California models, connect EGR temperature sensor plug

30. Connect wiring for idle speed control, motor position sensor and throttle position sensor.

31. On automatic transmission models, connect the thermo switch.

32. Connect oxygen sensor, coolant temperature gauge and coolant temperature sensor.

33. Using new O-rings, connect fuel feed and return hoses and tighten bolts to 3–4 ft. lbs. (4–6 Nm).

34. Connect noted vacuum hoses and connect brake booster vacuum supply.

35. Connect breather hose, heater hoses and accelerator cable. Inspect accelerator cable for proper adjustment.

36. Install the transaxle assembly.

37. Install radiator assembly and refill the cooling system, engine oil and transmission oil.

38. Install air cleaner and hood assembly.

39. Connect negative battery cable and run engine.

40. Inspect all connections and check all fluid levels.

Summit Wagon

1. Relieve fuel system pressure.

2. Disconnect the negative battery cable. Remove the under cover if equipped.

3. Matchmark the hood and hinges and remove the hood assembly. Remove the air cleaner assembly and all adjoining air intake duct work.

4. Drain the engine coolant and remove the radiator assembly, coolant reservoir and intercooler.

5. Remove the transaxle assembly.

6. Disconnect the accelerator cable, breather hose and heater hose connections from the engine.

7. Note locations and remove vacuum hoses from engine. Be sure to disconnect brake booster vacuum supply.

8. Disconnect fuel feed and return hoses.

9. Disconnect oxygen sensor connection, coolant temperature gauge and coolant temperature sensor connections.

10. On models with automatic transmissions, disconnect the thermo switch.

11. Disconnect harness connections for the idle speed control, motor position sensor and throttle position sensor.

12. Disconnect EGR temperature sensor (California).

13. Note locations for reassembly and disconnect injector connections.

14. Disconnect power transistor, ignition coil and noise filter connections.

15. Disconnect alternator and power steering switch wiring.

16. Remove the air conditioner drive belt and the air conditioning compressor. Leave the hoses attached

and do not discharge the system. Wire the compressor aside.

17. Remove the power steering pump and wire aside.

18. Remove the starter and alternator harness clamp (1.8L engine).

19. Remove the exhaust manifold to head pipe nuts. Discard the gasket.

20. Attach a hoist to the engine and support the engine weight. Remove the engine mount brackets.

21. Remove the engine assembly from the vehicle.

To install:

22. Install the engine and secure into position. Secure the front engine mount bracket to block and tighten bolts to 29–36 ft. lbs. (39–49 Nm). Install through bolt and tighten bolt to 51 ft. lbs. (70 Nm).

23. Using a new gasket, attach head pipe to exhaust manifold.

24. On 1.8L engines, install the starter motor and attach the alternator wiring harness clamp.

25. Install the power steering pump and air conditioner assemblies.

26. Install engine drive belts and adjust as necessary. Tighten all mounting and adjusting bolts.

27. Connect wiring for power steering switch and alternator.

28. Connect power transistor, ignition coil and noise filter wiring.

29. Connect fuel injector wiring harness connections.

30. On California model vehicles, connect the EGR temperature sensor connection.

31. Connect harness connections for the idle speed control, motor position sensor and throttle position sensor.

32. On models with automatic transmissions, connect the thermo switch.

33. Connect oxygen sensor connection, coolant temperature gauge and coolant temperature sensor connections.

34. Connect fuel feed and return hoses.

35. Connect vacuum hoses to engine and be sure to connect brake booster vacuum supply.

36. Connect the accelerator cable, breather hose and heater hose connections to the engine.

37. Install the transaxle assembly.

38. Install the radiator and overflow assembly. Refill the cooling system.

39. Install the hood assembly, air cleaner assembly and all adjoining air intake duct work.

40. Connect negative battery cable and run engine.

41. Inspect all connections and check all fluid levels.

Laser and Talon

1. Relieve fuel system pressure.
2. Disconnect the negative battery cable. Remove the under cover if equipped.
3. Matchmark the hood and hinges and remove the hood assembly. Remove the air cleaner assembly and all adjoining air intake duct work.
4. Drain the engine coolant and remove the radiator assembly, coolant reservoir and intercooler.
5. Remove the transaxle assembly.
6. Disconnect the accelerator cable, breather hose and heater hose connections from the engine
7. Note locations and remove vacuum hoses from engine. Be sure to disconnect brake booster vacuum supply.
8. Disconnect fuel feed and return hoses.
9. Disconnect oxygen sensor connection, coolant temperature gauge and coolant temperature sensor connections.
10. On turbocharged models, disconnect the following:
   a. Connection for solenoid valve.
   b. Solenoid valve bracket.
   c. Connection for knock sensor.
11. Disconnect harness connections for the idle speed control, motor position sensor and throttle position sensor.
12. Disconnect EGR temperature sensor (California).
13. Note locations for reassembly and disconnect injector connections.
14. Disconnect ignition power transistor and ignition coil connections.
15. Disconnect control wiring harness and ground cable from engine.
16. Disconnect alternator and power steering switch wiring.
17. Disconnect alternator harness clamp and wiring for oil pressure switch.
18. Remove the air conditioner and power steering belts.
19. Remove the air conditioning compressor. Leave the hoses attached and do not discharge the system. Wire the compressor aside.
20. Remove the power steering pump and wire aside without disconnecting the fluid hoses.
21. Remove the exhaust manifold to head pipe nuts. Discard the gasket.
22. Attach a hoist to the engine and support the engine weight. Remove the engine mount bolts and brackets.
23. Remove the engine assembly from the vehicle.

To install:

24. Install the engine and secure into position. Secure the front engine mount bracket to block and tighten bolts to 36–47 ft. lbs. (50–65 Nm). Install through bolt and tighten bolt to 43–58 ft. lbs. (60–80 Nm).
25. Using a new gasket, attach head pipe to exhaust manifold. Tighten nuts to 22–29 ft. lbs. (30–40 Nm) for non-turbo models or 29–43 ft. lbs. (40–60 Nm) for turbocharged models.
26. Install the power steering pump and air conditioner assemblies.
27. Install engine drive belts and adjust as necessary. Tighten all mounting and adjusting bolts.
28. Connect wiring for power steering switch and alternator.
29. Connect power transistor, ignition coil and noise filter wiring.
30. Connect fuel injector wiring harness connections.
31. On California model vehicles, connect the EGR temperature sensor connection.
32. Connect harness connections for the idle speed control, motor position sensor and throttle position sensor.
33. Connect oxygen sensor, coolant temperature gauge and coolant temperature sensor connections.
34. On turbocharged models connect the following:
   a. Connection for solenoid valve.
   b. Solenoid valve bracket.
   c. Connection for knock sensor.
35. Connect fuel feed and return hoses.
36. Connect vacuum hose and brake booster connections.
37. Connect the accelerator cable, breather hose and heater hose connections.
38. Install the transaxle assembly.
39. Install the radiator assembly, intercooler and coolant reservoir, fill system.
40. Install the hood assembly, air cleaner assembly and all adjoining air intake duct work.
41. Connect negative battery cable and run engine.
42. Inspect all connections and check all fluid levels.

Stealth

1. Relieve fuel system pressure.
2. Matchmark the hood and hinges and remove the hood assembly. Remove the air cleaner assembly and all adjoining air intake duct work.
3. Disconnect and remove cruise control linkage and actuator assemblies.
4. Drain the engine coolant and remove the radiator assembly, coolant reservoir and intercooler.
5. Disconnect the heated oxygen sensor connection at the front exhaust pipe.
6. Unbolt and remove the front exhaust pipe assembly, discard gaskets.
7. Remove the transaxle assembly.
8. Disconnect the accelerator cable, breather hose and heater hose connections from the engine
9. Note locations and remove vacuum hoses from engine. Be sure to disconnect brake booster vacuum supply.
10. Disconnect fuel feed and return hoses.
11. Remove the solenoid valve assembly and disconnect ground cable.
12. Disconnect purge hose and EGR temperature sensor, if equipped.
13. Remove the air conditioning and power steering drive belts.
14. Unbolt and remove the air conditioning compressor and the power steering pump assemblies.

NOTE: When removing the power steering pump and a/c compressor, it is not necessary to disconnect the hoses. Position the units aside and use rope or wire to secure.

15. Disconnect harness connections for the idle speed control, motor position sensor and throttle position sensor.
16. Disconnect EGR temperature sensor (California).
17. On turbocharged models, disconnect the following:
   a. Connection for booster vacuum hose.
   b. Connections for oil cooler lines and discard the sealing rings.
   c. Connection for oxygen sensor.
18. Disconnect wiring at the oil pressure switch and oil pressure gauge unit.
19. Disconnect fuel injection wiring harness plug.
20. Disconnect wiring from the knock sensor and the crankshaft angle sensor.
21. Disconnect coolant temperature switch, coolant temperature sensor and coolant temperature gauge unit connections.
22. Disconnect wiring to ignition coil, condenser and power transistor.
23. Disconnect variable induction motor connection.
24. Open the cover of relay box and disconnect alternator wiring.
25. Attach a hoist to the engine and support the engine weight. Remove the engine mount bracket.

26. Remove the front and rear roll stopper bracket mounting bolts.

27. Remove the engine assembly from the vehicle.

To install:

28. Install the engine and secure into position. Secure the engine mount bracket to block and tighten bolts to 72–87 ft. lbs. (100–120 Nm). Install through bolt and tighten bolt to 51 ft. lbs. (70 Nm).

29. Install the front and rear roll stopper through bolt and tighten to 36–43 ft. lbs. (50–60 Nm).

30. Open the cover of relay box and connect alternator wiring.

31. Connect variable induction motor connection.

32. Connect fuel feed and return hoses. Using a new sealing ring, tighten pressure hose connection to 4 ft. lbs. (5 Nm).

33. Connect wiring to ignition coil, condenser and power transistor.

34. Connect coolant temperature switch, coolant temperature sensor and coolant temperature gauge unit connections.

35. Connect wiring from the knock sensor and the crankshaft angle sensor.

36. Connect fuel injection wiring harness plug.

37. Connect wiring at the oil pressure switch and oil pressure gauge unit.

38. On turbocharged models, connect the following:

   a. Connection for booster vacuum hose.

   b. Connections for oil cooler lines using new sealing rings. Tighten fittings to 29–33 ft. lbs. (40–49 Nm).

   c. Connection for oxygen sensor.

39. Connect EGR temperature sensor (California).

40. Connect harness connections for the idle speed control, motor position sensor and throttle position sensor.

41. Install the air conditioning compressor and the power steering pump assemblies.

42. Install engine drive belts.

43. Connect purge hose and EGR temperature sensor, if equipped.

44. Install the solenoid valve assembly and connect ground cable to engine block.

45. Reconnect vacuum hoses to engine. Be sure to connect brake booster vacuum supply.

46. Connect the accelerator cable, breather hose and heater hose connections to the engine.

47. Install the transaxle assembly.

48. Install the front exhaust pipe assembly, using new gaskets. Tighten manifold mounting bolts to 36 ft. lbs. (50 Nm).

49. Connect the heated oxygen sensor connection at the front exhaust pipe.

50. Replace the radiator assembly, coolant reservoir and intercooler. Refill the cooling system.

51. Install and connect cruise control linkage and actuator assemblies.

52. Install the hood assembly, air cleaner assembly and all adjoining air intake duct work.

53. Connect negative battery cable and run engine.

54. Inspect all connections and check all fluid levels.

Engine Mounts

REMOVAL AND INSTALLATION

1. Disconnect the negative battery cable. Remove the air cleaner and all necessary air duct work.

2. Raise and safely support the engine so it is not resting on the engine mount. One suggested way is a block of wood between a floor jack and the oil pan. Use care not to bend or damage any components.

3. Remove the retainer bolt from the clamp securing the power steering pressure hose and the air conditioning low pressure hose.

4. Remove the engine mount bracket and body connection through bolt. Take note of the position of the arrow on the oval shaped mounting stopper plate. This is important.

5. Remove the engine mounting bracket and stopper plate.

6. Lower mounts (roll stoppers) are removed by removing the through bolt, then the frame bolts. On Stealth, the condenser fan assembly and front catalytic converter must first be removed to gain access to the front mount.

To install:

7. Install the engine mounting bracket and stopper plate. Note the arrows on the stopper plates and make sure they are installed properly. On most engines the arrows will face the towards the center of the engine.

8. Install the lower front roll stopper so the part of the bracket with the hole in it is facing the front of the vehicle.

9. The front lower mount through bolt nut should not be tightened until the full weight of the engine is on the

mount. Torque specifications are as follows:

Summit

1992 — Upper mount to engine nuts and bolts — 36–47 ft. lbs. (50–65 Nm)

1992 — Upper mount through bolt nut — 65–80 ft. lbs. (90–110 Nm)

1992 — Lower mount through bolt nut — 33–43 ft. lbs. (45–60 Nm)

1993–96 — Upper mount to engine nuts and bolts — 42 ft. lbs. (57 Nm)

1993–96 — Upper mount through bolt nut — 51 ft. lbs. (69 Nm)

1993–95 — Lower mount through bolt nut — 42 ft. lbs. (58 Nm)

Summit Wagon

Upper mount to engine nuts and bolts — 42 ft. lbs. (58 Nm)

Upper mount through bolt nut — 51 ft. lbs. (70 Nm)

Lower mount through bolt nut — 42 ft. lbs. (58 Nm)

Laser and Talon

Upper mount to engine nuts and bolts — 36–47 ft. lbs. (50–65 Nm)

Upper mount through bolt nut — 43–58 ft. lbs. (60–80 Nm)

Lower mount through bolt nut — 36–47 ft. lbs. (50–65 Nm)

Stealth

Upper mount to engine nuts and bolts — 72–87 ft. lbs. (100–120 Nm)

Upper mount through bolt nut — 51 ft. lbs. (70 Nm)

Lower mount through bolt nut — 36–43 ft. lbs. (47–60 Nm).

Cylinder Head

REMOVAL AND INSTALLATION

1.5L (Summit) and 1.8L (Laser/Talon) Engines

1. Relieve the fuel system pressure. Disconnect the negative battery cable.

2. Drain the cooling system.

3. Remove the air intake hose and the breather hose.

4. Disconnect the accelerator cable. There will be 2 cables, if equipped with cruise control.

5. Place a shop towel around the high pressure fuel line to absorb any residual fuel remaining in the system. Disconnect the high pressure fuel line.

6. Remove the upper radiator hose, the water breather hose, the

water bypass hose and the heater hose.

7. Disconnect the PCV hose.

8. Remove the spark plug cables.

9. Disconnect and plug the fuel return line.

10. Disconnect the vacuum line for the brake booster.

11. Disconnect the electrical connections for the oxygen sensor, engine coolant temperature gauge unit and the water temperature sensor.

12. Disconnect the electrical connections for the idle speed control motor, throttle position sensor and motor position sensor.

13. Disconnect wiring connectors for ignition distributor, fuel injectors, EGR temperature sensor (California vehicles), power transistor, condenser and ground cable.

14. Disconnect the engine control wiring harness.

15. Remove the clamp that holds the power steering pressure hose to the engine mounting bracket.

16. Place a jack and wood block under the oil pan and carefully lift just enough to take the weight off the engine mounting bracket, remove the bracket.

17. Remove the valve cover, gasket and half-round seal.

18. Remove the timing belt front upper cover.

19. Rotate the crankshaft clockwise and align the timing marks. Remove the sprocket bolt and remove the sprocket with the timing belt attached. Remove the timing belt rear upper cover.

———— CAUTION ————
The crankshaft must always be rotated clockwise. Do not rotate engine by turning the camshaft.

20. Remove the exhaust pipe self-locking nuts and separate the exhaust pipe from the exhaust manifold. Discard the gasket.

21. Loosen the cylinder head mounting bolts in 3 Steps, starting from the outside and working inward. Lift off the cylinder head assembly and remove the head gasket.

To install:

22. Thoroughly clean and dry the mating surfaces of the head and block. Check the cylinder head for cracks, damage or engine coolant leakage. Remove scale, sealing compound and carbon. Clean oil passages thoroughly. Check the head for flatness. End to end, the head should be within 0.002 in. normally with 0.008 in. the maximum allowed out of true. The total thickness allowed to be re-

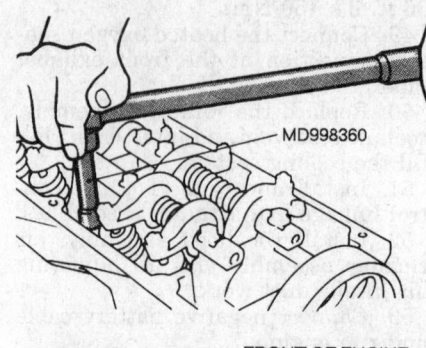

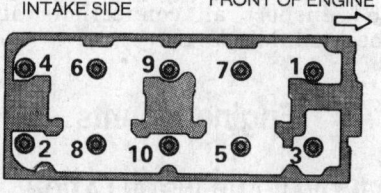

Cylinder head bolt removal sequence — Summit 1.5L and Laser/Talon 1.8L engines

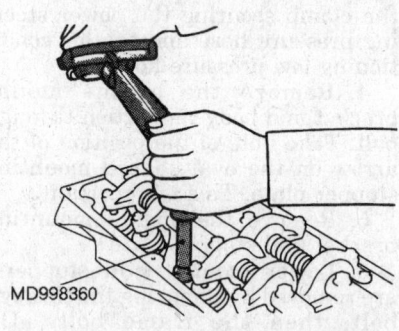

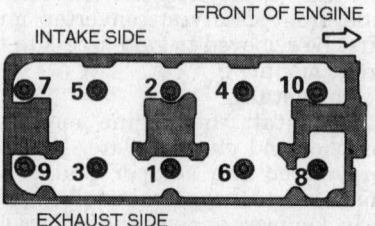

Cylinder head bolt installation sequence — Summit 1.5L and Laser/Talon 1.8L engines

moved from the head and block is 0.008 in. maximum.

23. Place a new head gasket on the cylinder block with the identification marks facing upward. Make sure the gasket has the proper identification mark for the engine. Do not use sealer on the gasket.

24. Carefully install the cylinder head on the block. Using 3 even Steps, torque the head bolts in sequence, to 51–54 ft. lbs. (70–75 Nm).

25. Install a new exhaust pipe gasket and connect the exhaust pipe to the manifold. Install the upper rear timing cover.

26. Align the timing marks and install the cam sprocket. Torque the retaining bolt to 47–54 ft. lbs. (65–75 Nm) on 1.5L engine or 58–72 ft. lbs. (80–100 Nm) on 1.8L engine. Check the belt tension and adjust, if necessary. Install the outer timing cover.

27. Apply sealer to the perimeter of the half-round seal. Install a new valve cover gasket. Install the valve cover.

28. Install the engine mount bracket. Once secure, remove the jack.

29. Install the clamp that holds the power steering pressure hose to the engine mounting bracket.

30. Connect or install all previously disconnected hoses, cables and electrical connections. Adjust the throttle cable(s).

31. Replace the O-rings and connect the fuel lines.

32. Install the air intake hose. Connect the breather hose.

33. Change the engine oil and oil filter.

34. Fill the system with coolant.

35. Connect the negative battery cable, run the vehicle until the thermostat opens, fill the radiator completely.

36. Check and adjust the idle speed and ignition timing.

37. Once the vehicle has cooled, recheck the coolant level.

Summit Wagon

1.8L ENGINE

1. Relieve fuel system pressure. Disconnect the negative battery cable.

2. Drain the cooling system. Disconnect the brake booster vacuum hose and PVC valve connection.

3. Remove the upper radiator hose, overflow tube and the water hose from the thermostat to the throttle body.

4. Disconnect the air flow sensor connector. Remove the air cleaner case cover and the air intake hose.

5. Wrap the connection with a shop towel and disconnect the high pressure fuel line at the fuel rail.

6. Disconnect the fuel return hose and remove the O-ring.

7. Disconnect the accelerator cable connection from the throttle body and position aside.

8. Disconnect the electrical harnesses at the oil pressure switch, oxygen sensor, water temperature sensor connector and distributor.

9. Disconnect the wiring from condenser, idle speed control, throttle position sensor and knock sensor.

10. Note harness plug connections for reassembly and disconnect fuel injectors.

11. Disconnect the spark plug cables from each spark plug.

12. Unbolt the control harness assembly and position aside.

13. Remove the thermostat housing, thermostat and the thermostat case with O-ring from the engine.

14. Remove the rocker cover.

15. Remove the timing belt upper cover.

16. Rotate the crankshaft in the clockwise direction to align the camshaft timing marks. Matchmark the camshaft sprocket and the timing belt. Tie the camshaft sprocket and the timing belt together so the sprocket will not move with respect to the timing belt.

17. While holding the camshaft sprocket in position using the appropriate wrench, remove the camshaft sprocket and with the belt attached. Wire the sprocket and belt aside making sure constant tension is maintained on the belt. Do not allow the belt to slacken or engine timing may be altered.

NOTE: When removing the camshaft sprocket, do not allow the crankshaft to rotate. If crankshaft rotation did occur, the engine timing may have been changed. Confirm proper engine timing during installation.

18. Loosen the cylinder head bolts in 2 or 3 Steps in the appropriate order and remove from the cylinder head.

19. Remove the cylinder head from the engine.

——— CAUTION ———
When removing the cylinder head, take care not to bend or damage the plug guide. The plug guide can not be replaced.

20. Remove the cylinder head gasket from the block.

To install:

21. Thoroughly clean and dry the mating surfaces of the head and block. Check the cylinder head for cracks, damage or engine coolant leakage. Remove scale, sealing compound and carbon. Clean oil passages thoroughly. Check the head for flatness. End to end, the head should be within 0.002 in. normally with 0.008 in. the maximum allowed out of true. The total thickness allowed to be removed from the head and block is 0.008 in. maximum.

22. Place a new head gasket on the cylinder block with the identification

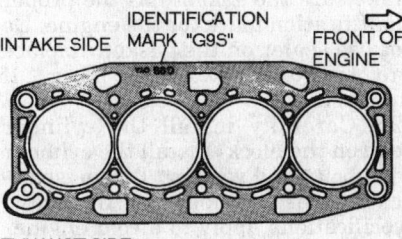

Cylinder head bolt removal sequence — Summit Wagon 1.8L engine

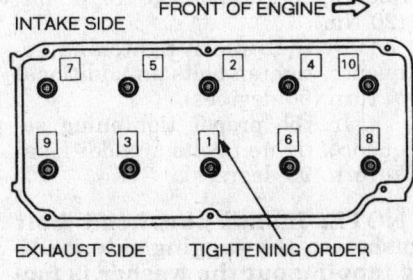

Cylinder head gasket identification — Summit Wagon 1.8L engine

FRONT OF ENGINE ⇨

INTAKE SIDE

[7] [5] [2] [4] [10]

[9] [3] [1] [6] [8]

EXHAUST SIDE   TIGHTENING ORDER

84701075

Cylinder head bolt installation sequence — Summit Wagon 1.8L engine

marks facing upward. Make sure the gasket has the proper identification mark for the engine. Do not use sealer on the gasket.

23. Carefully install the cylinder head on the block. Inspect the cylinder head bolt prior to installation, the length below the head of the bolts should be below the limit of 3.795 in. (96.4mm). If bolt shank length exceeds limit, bolt must be replaced.

24. Apply a small amount of engine oil to the thread section and the washer of the cylinder head bolt and install so the sagging side made by tapping out the washer is facing upward. (chamfer edge faces up).

25. Tighten the cylinder head bolts in the proper order as follows:

a. In the proper tightening sequence, torque bolts to 54 ft. lbs. (75 Nm).

b. In the reverse order of the tightening sequence, fully loosen bolts.

c. In the proper tightening sequence, torque bolts to 14 ft. lbs. (20 Nm).

d. In the proper tightening sequence, tighten bolts an additional ¼turn (90 degrees).

e. In the proper tightening sequence, tighten bolts an additional ¼turn (90 degrees).

26. Install the camshaft sprocket and tighten bolt to 65 ft. lbs. (90 Nm), while holding the sprocket in place using the appropriate wrench. Confirm proper timing mark alignment.

27. Install the upper timing belt cover and rocker cover.

28. Loosen the water pipe mounting bolt.

29. Apply a thin bead of sealant MD970389 or equivalent, to the water tube connection on the thermostat case.

30. Apply a small amount of water to the O-ring of the water inlet pipe and press the thermostat case assembly onto the water inlet pipe. Install the thermostat case assembly mounting bolt tightening to 16 ft. lbs. (22 Nm).

31. Tighten the water pipe mounting bolt.

32. Install the thermostat into the housing so the jiggle valve is located at the top. Tighten the housing bolts to 10 ft. lbs. (14 Nm).

33. Connect the upper radiator hose to the thermostat housing.

34. Connect or install all previously disconnected hoses, cables and electrical connections. Adjust the throttle cable(s).

35. Replace the O-rings and reconnect the fuel lines.

36. Install the air intake hose. Connect the breather hose, air cleaner case cover and air flow sensor connector.

37. Change the engine oil and oil filter. Reconnect the brake booster and the PCV vacuum hoses.

38. Fill the system with coolant.

39. Connect the negative battery cable, run the vehicle until the thermostat opens, fill the radiator completely.

40. Check and adjust the idle speed and ignition timing.

41. Check all systems for leaks. Allow the engine to cool and recheck the coolant level.

2.4L ENGINE

1. Relieve fuel system pressure. Disconnect the negative battery cable.

2. Drain the cooling system.

3. Disconnect the accelerator cable.

4. Disconnect the air flow sensor connector and the air intake hose. Remove the air cleaner cover.

5. Disconnect the PCV hose and brake booster hose connection.

6. Disconnect the water hose connection at the throttle body to water inlet pipe.

7. Disconnect the water hose connection at the throttle body to thermostat hose.

8. Wrap the connection with a shop towel and disconnect the high pressure fuel line at the fuel rail.

9. Disconnect the fuel return hose and remove the O-ring.

10. Disconnect the accelerator cables connection at the throttle body.

11. Disconnect the spark plug cables from the spark plugs.

12. Disconnect the electrical connectors from the oxygen sensor, water temperature gauge unit, engine coolant temperature sensor and throttle position sensor.

13. Disconnect wiring for the power transistor connector, ignition coil, distributor, and air conditioner compressor.

14. Label prior to disconnecting and remove the fuel injector wiring harness connections.

15. Remove the bolt retaining the power steering hose and air conditioner hose clamp.

16. Remove the bolt holding the ground wire to the manifold.

17. Remove the upper and lower radiator hose connections at the engine.

18. Remove the exhaust pipe to manifold nuts and discard the gasket.

19. Remove the timing belt upper cover.

20. Remove the valve cover, gasket and half-round seal.

21. Rotate the crankshaft clockwise until the timing marks are aligned. Matchmark the timing sprocket to the belt.

22. Remove the sprocket bolt and remove the sprocket with the timing belt attached. Attach a flexible cord to the hood and suspend the sprocket so it cannot turn and there is no slack in the belt. Remove the timing belt rear upper cover.

23. Loosen the head bolts in the correct sequence in 2 or 3 steps. Remove the cylinder head bolts and head assembly from the block.

To install:

24. Thoroughly clean and dry the mating surfaces of the head and block. Check the cylinder head for cracks, damage or engine coolant leakage. Remove scale, sealing compound and carbon. Clean oil passages thoroughly. Check the head for flatness. End to end, the head should be within 0.002 in. normally with 0.008 in. the maximum allowed out of true. The total thickness allowed to be removed from the head and block is 0.008 in. maximum.

25. Place a new head gasket on the cylinder block with the identification marks at the top (upward) position. Make sure the gasket has the proper identification mark for the engine. Do not use sealer on the gasket. Replace the turbo gasket and ring, if equipped.

26. Carefully install the cylinder head on the block. Install the cylinder head bolts and washer. Torque specifications are as follows. All torque specifications apply to a cold engine.

a. In the proper tightening sequence, torque bolts to 54 ft. lbs. (75 Nm).

b. In the reverse order of the tightening sequence, fully loosen bolts.

c. In the proper tightening sequence, torque bolts to 14 ft. lbs. (20 Nm).

d. In the proper tightening sequence, tighten bolts an additional 1/4 turn (90 degrees).

e. In the proper tightening sequence, tighten bolts an additional 1/4 turn (90 degrees).

NOTE: Install the head bolt washer so the sagging side made by tapping out the washer is facing upward.

27. Install the camshaft sprocket and tighten bolt to 65 ft. lbs. (90 Nm),

while holding the sprocket in place using the appropriate wrench. Confirm proper timing mark alignment.

28. Apply sealer to the perimeter of the half-round seal and to the lower edges of the half-round portions of the belt-side of the new gasket. Install the valve cover and tighten bolts to 26.5–30 inch lbs. (3–3.5 Nm).

29. Install the power steering and air conditioning compressor hose clamp in position and secure with the retainer bolt. Tighten the bolt to 9 ft. lbs. (12 Nm).

30. Connect the exhaust pipe to the manifold using new self-locking nuts and replace gasket. Tighten nuts to 29–36 ft. lbs. (40–50 Nm).

31. Reconnect fuel injector harness connections.

32. Attach the upper and lower radiator hose connections at the engine.

33. Connect wiring for the power transistor connector, ignition coil, distributor, and air conditioner compressor.

34. Connect the electrical connectors from the oxygen sensor, water temperature gauge unit, engine coolant temperature sensor and throttle position sensor.

35. Connect the spark plug cables to the spark plugs.

36. Connect the accelerator cables connection at the throttle body.

37. Connect the fuel feed and return hoses, replace O-rings.

38. Connect the water hose connection at the throttle body to water inlet pipe.

39. Connect the water hose connection at the throttle body to thermostat hose.

40. Connect the PCV hose and brake booster hose connection.

41. Connect the air flow sensor connector and the air intake hose. Install the air cleaner cover.

42. Connect the ground wire to the manifold.

43. Fill the system with coolant. Adjust the accelerator cable.

44. Firmly set the parking brake. Start the engine and allow to idle until the thermostat opens, add coolant as required to fill system to the appropriate level.

45. Check all systems for leaks. Allow the engine to cool and recheck the coolant level.

Laser and Talon

2.0L ENGINE

1. Relieve fuel system pressure. Disconnect the negative battery cable.

2. Drain the cooling system.

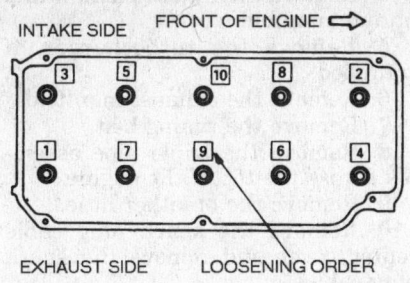

Cylinder head bolt removal sequence — Summit Wagon 2.4L and Laser/Talon 2.0L engines

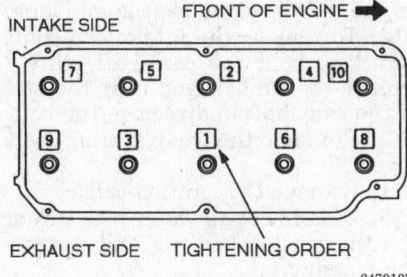

Cylinder head bolt installation sequence — Summit Wagon 2.4L and Laser/Talon 2.0L engines

3. Disconnect the accelerator cable. There will be 2 cables if equipped with cruise-control.

4. Remove the air cleaner with the air intake hose.

5. Disconnect the oxygen sensor, engine coolant temperature sensor, the engine coolant temperature gauge unit and the engine coolant temperature switch.

6. Disconnect the idle speed control motor, throttle position sensor and crankshaft angle sensor electrical connections.

7. Disconnect wiring for the ignition coil, power transistor and noise filter.

8. Disconnect the EGR temperature sensor (California vehicles).

9. Note connections and remove fuel injector harness plug.

10. Disconnect the ground cable and engine control wiring harness.

11. Remove the upper radiator hose and the overflow tube.

12. Remove the spark plug cable center cover and remove the spark plug cables.

13. Remove the air intake hose and breather hose.

14. Disconnect and plug the high pressure fuel line. Use a shop towel to absorb any excess fuel and discard sealing ring.

15. Disconnect the small vacuum hoses.

16. Remove the heater hose and water bypass hose.

17. Remove the PCV hose.

18. If turbocharged, remove the vacuum hoses, water line and eyebolt connection for the oil line for the turbo.

19. Disconnect and plug the fuel return hose.

20. Disconnect the brake booster vacuum hose.

21. Remove the timing belt.

22. Remove the valve cover and the half-round seal.

23. On non-turbocharged engines, remove the exhaust pipe self-locking nuts and separate the exhaust pipe from the exhaust manifold. Discard the gasket.

24. On turbocharged engines, remove the sheetmetal heat protector and remove the bolts that attach the turbocharger to the exhaust manifold.

25. Loosen the cylinder head mounting bolts in 3 steps, starting from the outside and working inward. Lift off the cylinder head assembly and remove the head gasket.

To install:

26. Thoroughly clean and dry the mating surfaces of the head and block. Check the cylinder head for cracks, damage or engine coolant leakage. Remove scale, sealing compound and carbon. Clean oil passages thoroughly. Check the head for flatness. End to end, the head should be within 0.002 in. normally with 0.008 in. the maximum allowed out of true. The total thickness allowed to be removed from the head and block is 0.008 in. maximum.

27. Place a new head gasket on the cylinder block with the identification marks at the front top (upward) position. Make sure the gasket has the proper identification mark for the engine. Do not use sealer on the gasket. Replace the turbo gasket and ring, if equipped.

28. Carefully install the cylinder head on the block. Using 3 even steps, torque the head bolts in sequence to 65–72 ft. lbs. (90–100 Nm) for 1992 vehicles. For 1993–96 model years torque specifications are as follows. All torque specifications apply to a cold engine.

   a. In the proper tightening sequence, torque bolts to 54 ft. lbs. (75 Nm).

   b. In the reverse order of the tightening sequence, fully loosen bolts.

   c. In the proper tightening sequence, torque bolts to 14 ft. lbs. (20 Nm).

   d. In the proper tightening sequence, tighten bolts an additional ¼ turn (90 degrees).

   e. In the proper tightening sequence, tighten bolts an additional ¼ turn (90 degrees).

29. On turbocharged engine, tighten turbocharger to exhaust manifold bolts to 40–47 ft. lbs. (50–65 Nm). Install a new exhaust pipe gasket and connect the exhaust pipe. Tighten nuts to 22–29 ft. lbs. (30–40 Nm) on non-turbo engines or 29–43 ft. lbs. (40–60 Nm) on turbocharged engines.

30. Apply sealer to the perimeter of the half-round seal and to the lower edges of the half-round portions of the belt-side of the new gasket. Install the valve cover and tighten bolts to 24–36 inch lbs. (2.5–3.5 Nm).

31. Install the timing belt assembly.

32. Connect the brake booster vacuum supply and PCV hose.

33. Connect the fuel feed and return hoses using new O-rings.

34. If turbocharged, install the vacuum hoses, water line and eyebolt connection for the turbocharger oil supply line. Tighten the oil line fitting bolt to 10–14 ft. lbs. (14–19 Nm), always use new sealing rings.

35. Connect heater and bypass hose connections.

36. Connect the air intake hose and breather hose.

37. Connect the spark plug wires and install the center wire cover.

38. Install the upper radiator hose and the overflow tube.

39. Connect the ground cable and engine control wiring harness.

40. Connect the fuel injector electrical connections.

41. Connect wiring for the ignition coil, power transistor and noise filter.

42. Connect the EGR temperature sensor (California vehicles).

43. Connect the idle speed control motor, throttle position sensor and crankshaft angle sensor electrical connections.

44. Connect the oxygen sensor, engine coolant temperature sensor, the engine coolant temperature gauge unit and the engine coolant temperature switch wiring.

45. Install the air cleaner with the air intake hose.

46. Connect and adjust the accelerator cable. There will be 2 cables if equipped with cruise-control.

47. Change the engine oil and oil filter.

48. Fill the system with coolant.

49. Connect the negative battery cable, run the vehicle until the thermostat opens, fill the radiator completely.

50. Check and adjust the idle speed and ignition timing.

51. Once the vehicle has cooled, recheck the coolant level.

Stealth

3.0L SOHC ENGINE

1. Relieve fuel system pressure. Disconnect the negative battery cable.

2. Drain the cooling system.

3. Remove the air intake hose.

4. Remove the exhaust manifold.

5. Remove the air intake plenum and intake manifold.

6. Remove the timing belt.

7. Remove the camshaft sprocket and rear timing belt cover.

8. Remove the power steering pump bracket. If removing the rear head, remove the alternator brace.

9. Disconnect the water inlet pipe.

10. Remove the purge pipe assembly.

11. Remove the valve cover.

12. Loosen the cylinder head mounting bolts in 3 steps, starting from the outside and working inward. Lift off the cylinder head assembly and remove the head gasket.

To install:

13. Thoroughly clean and dry the mating surfaces of the head and block. Check the cylinder head for cracks, damage or engine coolant leakage. Remove scale, sealing compound and carbon. Clean oil passages thoroughly. Check the head for flatness. End to end, the head should be within 0.002 in. normally with 0.008 in. the maximum allowed out of true. The total thickness allowed to be removed from the head and block is 0.008 in. maximum.

14. Place a new head gasket on the cylinder block making sure the identification mark on the cylinder head gasket is in the front top (upward) location. Do not use sealer on the gasket. Make sure the gasket has the proper identification mark for the engine.

15. Carefully install the cylinder head on the block. Make sure the head bolt washers are installed with the chamfered edge upward. Using 3 even steps, torque the head bolts in sequence, to 76–83 ft. lbs. (105–115 Nm). This torque specifications assumes the engine is cold.

16. Apply sealer to the lower edges of the half-round portions of the belt-side of the new gasket and install the valve cover. Tighten valve cover bolts to 7–9 ft. lbs. (12–15 Nm).

17. Install the purge pipe assembly.

18. Connect the water inlet pipe.

19. Install the power steering pump bracket and alternator brace.

20. Install the rear timing belt cover and cam sprocket. Torque the retaining bolt to 65 ft. lbs. (90 Nm).

21. Install the timing belt and all related items.

22. Using all new gaskets, install the intake manifold, air intake plenum and exhaust manifold, following the proper torque sequences.

23. Install the air intake hose.

24. Change the engine oil and oil filter.

25. Fill the system with coolant.

26. Connect the negative battery cable, run the vehicle until the thermostat opens, fill the radiator completely.

27. Check and adjust the idle speed and ignition timing.

28. Once the vehicle has cooled, recheck the coolant level.

3.0L DOHC ENGINE

1. Relieve fuel system pressure. Disconnect the negative battery cable.

2. Drain the cooling system.

3. Remove the air intake hoses.

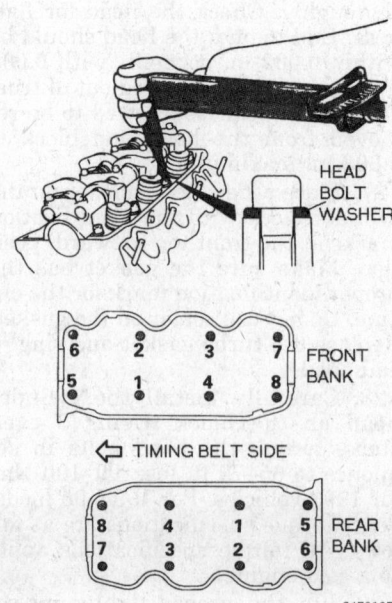

Cylinder head bolt installation sequence — Stealth 3.0L SOHC engine

4. Remove air intake plenum and intake manifold.

5. Remove the turbocharger, if equipped.

6. Remove the exhaust manifold.

7. Remove the timing belt.

8. Remove the triple pipe assembly across the top of the engine.

9. Remove the breather hose.

10. Remove the spark plug cable center cover and remove the spark plug cables.

11. When removing the valve cover, note that bolts for the front head are black and bolts for the rear head are green. Also, all bolts are 10mm long except the 1 closest to the sprockets on the rear head which is 20mm long.

12. To remove the intake camshaft sprocket, hold the camshaft with a wrench on the hexagon near the end of the camshaft and remove the bolt.

13. Remove the rear timing belt cover.

14. Remove the ignition coil.

15. Disconnect all water hoses from the thermostat housing and remove the housing.

16. Disconnect the water inlet from the front head and discard O-ring.

17. Loosen the cylinder head mounting bolts in 3 steps, starting from the outside and working inward. Lift off the cylinder head assembly and remove the head gasket.

To install:

18. Thoroughly clean and dry the mating surfaces of the head and block. Check the cylinder head for cracks, damage or engine coolant leakage. Remove scale, sealing compound and carbon. Clean oil passages thoroughly. Check the head for flatness. End to end, the head should be within 0.002 in. normally with 0.008 in. the maximum allowed out of true. The total thickness allowed to be removed from the head and block is 0.008 in. maximum.

19. Place a new head gasket on the cylinder block with the identification marks in the front top (upward) position. Do not use sealer on the gasket.

20. Carefully install the cylinder head on the block. Make sure the head bolt washers are installed with the chamfered edge upward. Using 3 even steps, torque the head bolts in sequence to 76–83 ft. lbs. (105–115 Nm) for non-turbocharged cold engine or 87–94 ft. lbs. (120–130 Nm) for turbocharged cold engine.

21. On turbocharged models, loosen all cylinder head bolts and retighten in sequence to 87–94 ft. lbs. (120–130 Nm).

22. Install new O-ring and connect the water inlet to the front head.

23. Replace the gaskets and install the thermostat housing and connect the hoses.

24. Install the ignition coil and center rear timing belt cover.

25. Install the intake camshaft sprocket. Use hex flange on camshaft to secure and torque the retaining bolt to 65 ft. lbs. (90 Nm).

26. Apply sealer to the lower edges of the half-round portions of the belt-side of the new gasket and install the valve cover. Make sure green bolts are installed on the rear head and black bolts are installed on the front head. Also, make sure the longest bolt is installed in its proper location closest to the sprockets on the rear head. Tighten the bolts in the proper sequence to 26 inch lbs. (3 Nm). Then retighten bolts No. 1–6 to 35 inch lbs. (4 Nm).

27. Connect the spark plug cables and install the center cover.

28. Install the breather hose.

29. Install the triple pipe assembly across the top of the engine and torque the retaining bolts to 7 ft. lbs. (10 Nm).

30. Install the timing belt and all related items.

31. Using all new gaskets, install the intake manifold, air intake plenum, turbocharger and exhaust manifold, following the proper torque sequences.

32. Install the air intake hoses.

33. Change the engine oil and oil filter.

34. Fill the system with coolant.

35. Connect the negative battery cable, run the vehicle until the thermostat opens, fill the radiator completely.

36. Adjust the accelerator cable. Check and adjust the idle speed and ignition timing.

37. Once the vehicle has cooled, recheck the coolant level.

Valve Lifters

REMOVAL AND INSTALLATION

1.6L and 2.0L Engines

1. Release the fuel system pressure. Disconnect the negative battery cable.

2. Disconnect the accelerator cable, PCV hoses, breather hoses, spark plug cables and the remove the valve cover.

3. Rotate the crankshaft clockwise and align the timing marks so No. 1 piston will be at TDC of the compression stroke. At this time the timing

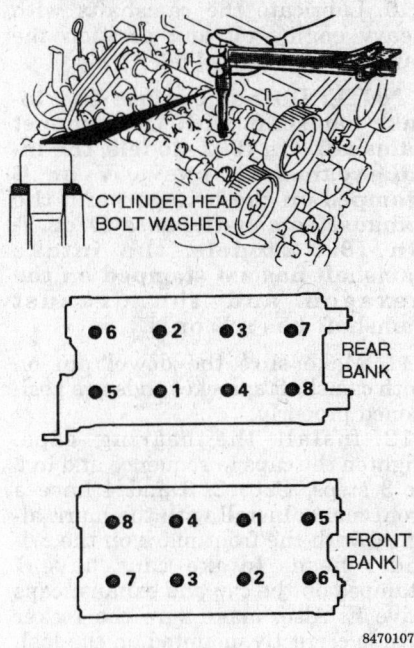

CYLINDER HEAD BOLT WASHER

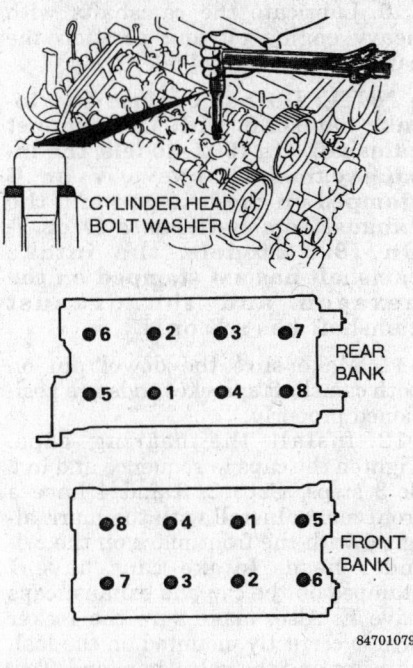

Cylinder head bolt torque sequence — Stealth 3.0L DOHC engine

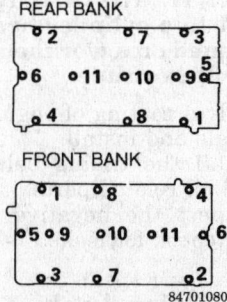

Valve cover bolt torque sequence — Stealth 3.0L DOHC engine

marks on the camshaft sprocket and the upper surface of the cylinder head should coincide, and the dowel pin of the camshaft sprocket should be at the upper side.

NOTE: Always rotate the crankshaft in a clockwise direction. Make a mark on the back of the timing belt indicating the direction of rotation so it may be reassembled in the same direction if it is to be reused.

4. Remove the timing belt upper and lower covers.

5. Remove the timing belt.

6. Remove the crank angle sensor.

7. Remove the camshafts. Be sure to position or mark bearing caps for proper reinstallation.

8. Visually inspect the rocker arm roller and replace if damage or seizure is evident. Check the roller for smooth rotation. Replace if excess play or binding is present. Also, inspect valve contact surface for possible damage or seizure. It is recommended that all rocker arms and lash adjusters be replaced together.

9. Remove the valve lifters from the cylinder head.

To install:

10. Install the lash adjusters and rocker arms into the cylinder head. Lubricate lightly with clean oil prior to installation.

11. Apply engine oil to the lobes and journals of each camshaft. Install the camshafts into the cylinder head taking care not to confuse the intake and the exhaust camshaft; the intake camshaft has a slit on its rear end for driving the crank angle sensor. Align shafts so dowel pins on camshaft sprocket end are located on the top.

12. Install and tighten the camshaft bearing caps in the proper sequence, torquing to 14–15 ft. lbs. (19–21 Nm) in 3 even progressions.

13. Replace the camshaft oil seals and install the sprockets. Torque camshaft sprocket bolt to 58–72 ft. lbs. (80–100 Nm).

14. Locate the dowel pin on the sprocket end of the intake camshaft at the top position, if not already done.

15. Align the punch mark on the crank angle sensor housing with the notch on the sensor plate. Install the crank angle sensor into the cylinder head.

16. Install the timing belt, covers and related components.

17. Install the valve cover using new gasket. Reconnect all related components.

18. Reconnect the negative battery cable.

1.8L, 2.4L (1992) and 3.0L SOHC Engines

1. Disconnect the negative battery cable.

2. Remove the valve cover. Install lash adjuster retainer tools MD998443 or equivalent, to prevent the auto-lash adjuster from falling out of the rocker arm.

3. Remove the distributor adapter housing on 3.0L engines.

4. Rotate the engine clockwise and position at TDC compression stroke.

5. Remove the timing belt assembly.

6. Loosen rocker arm and shaft assembly evenly in several steps. Remove the rocker arm and shaft assembly as a complete unit.

7. Remove the lifters from the rocker arms. It is recommended that all lash adjusters and rockers be replaced as a complete set.

To install:

8. Immerse the lash adjusters in clean diesel fuel. Using a small wire, move the plunger of the lash adjuster up and down 4 or 5 times while pushing down lightly on the check ball in order to bleed out the air. Install the lash adjusters in the rocker arms.

9. Lubricate the camshaft and rocker shaft with heavy engine oil and position on the cylinder head.

10. Apply a drop of sealant to the rear edges of the end caps.

11. Install the assembly into the front bearing cap making sure the notches in the rocker shafts are facing up. Insert the installation bolt but do not tighten at this point.

12. Install the remaining cap bolts and tighten evenly and gradually to 15 ft. lbs. (20 Nm). Tighten the front cap retaining bolts to 17 ft. lbs. (24 Nm). Remove the lash adjuster retainers.

13. Install the distributor extension, if removed.

14. Install the valve cover with a new gasket and tighten to 4–5 ft. lbs. (5–7 Nm).

15. Connect the negative battery cable.

3.0L DOHC Engine

1. Relieve the fuel system pressure.

2. Disconnect battery negative cable.

3. Remove the timing belt cover and timing belt.

4. Remove the center cover, breather and PCV hoses, and spark plug cables.

5. Remove the rocker cover, semicircular packing, throttle body stay, both camshaft sprockets, and oil seals.

6. Remove the crank angle sensor and adaptor.

7. Remove the intake and exhaust camshafts.

8. Remove rocker arms and lash adjusters from the head. It is recommended that all lash adjusters and rockers be replaced as a complete set.

To install:

9. Immerse the lash adjusters in clean diesel fuel. Using a small wire, move the plunger of the lash adjuster up and down 4 or 5 times while pushing down lightly on the check ball in

order to bleed out the air. Install the lash adjusters in the cylinder head.

10. Lubricate the camshafts with heavy engine oil and position the camshafts on the cylinder head.

NOTE: Do not confuse the intake camshaft with the exhaust camshaft. On 1992 models, the intake camshaft has a V or B stamped on the hexagon and the exhaust camshaft has a D or F. On 1993 models, the intake camshaft has a J stamped on the hexagon and the exhaust camshaft has a K or N.

11. Make sure the dowel pin on both camshaft sprocket ends are positioned properly.

12. Install the bearing caps. Tighten the caps in sequence and in 2 or 3 steps. Caps 2, 3 and 4 have a front mark. Install with the mark aligned with the front mark on the cylinder head. Intake caps have **I** stamped on the cap and exhaust caps have **E**. Also, make sure the rocker arm is correctly mounted on the lash adjuster and the valve stem end. Torque the front and rear retaining cap bolts to 15 ft. lbs. (20 Nm) and tighten the center 3 retaining cap bolts to 8 ft. lbs. (11 Nm).

NOTE: If installing the camshaft to a cylinder head that is positioned on a workbench, the valves will protrude.

13. Apply a coating of engine oil to the oil seals and install.

14. Install the timing belt, valve cover and all related parts.

15. Connect the negative battery cable and check for leaks.

Valve Lash

ADJUSTMENT

Summit and Summit Wagon

1.5L AND 1.8L ENGINES

NOTE: Incorrect valve clearances will cause unsteady engine operation, excessive noise and reduced engine output. Check the valve clearances and adjust as required while the engine is hot.

1. Warm the engine to operating temperature, turn **OFF** and disconnect the negative battery cable.

2. Remove all spark plugs so engine can be easily turned by hand.

3. Remove the valve cover.

4. Turn the crankshaft clockwise to position the engine at Top Dead

Center (TDC). The notch on the crankshaft pulley will be aligned with the **T** mark on the timing belt lower cover. This brings both No. 1 and No. 4 cylinder pistons to TDC.

5. Check the valve lash at cylinder No. 1 intake, cylinder No. 1 exhaust, cylinder No. 2 intake and cylinder No. 3 exhaust valves.

6. Rotate the crankshaft clockwise 1 complete turn. Check the valve lash at cylinder No. 2 exhaust, cylinder No. 3 intake and cylinder No. 4 intake and exhaust valves.

7. Valve lash specifications are as follows:

1.5L Summit engine: Exhaust–0.010 in. (0.25mm) hot or 0.007 in. (0.17mm) cold; Intake–0.006 in. (0.15mm) hot or 0.003 in. (0.07mm) cold.

1.8L Summit Wagon engine: Intake–0.004 in. (0.09mm) cold: Exhaust–0.008 in. (0.20mm) cold.

8. If the valve clearances are out of specification, loosen the rocker arm locknut and adjust the clearance using a feeler gauge while turning the adjusting screw. Be sure to hold the screw to prevent it from turning when tightening the locknut.

9. After adjusting the valves, install the valve cover and spark plugs, and connect the negative battery cable.

Rocker Arms/Shafts

REMOVAL AND INSTALLATION

Summit Wagon

1.5L AND 1.8L ENGINES

1. Disconnect the negative battery cable.

2. Remove the valve cover and discard the gasket.

3. Remove the rocker shaft hold-down bolts gradually and evenly and remove the rocker shaft/arm assemblies.

4. If disassembly is required, keep all parts in the exact order of removal. Inspect the roller surfaces of the rockers. Replace if there are any signs of damage or if the roller does not turn smoothly. Check the inside bore of the rockers and the adjuster tip for wear.

To install:

5. Lubricate the rocker shaft with clean engine oil and install the rockers and springs in their proper places.

6. Install the rocker shaft assemblies on the engine and tighten the bolts gradually and evenly. On 1.5L

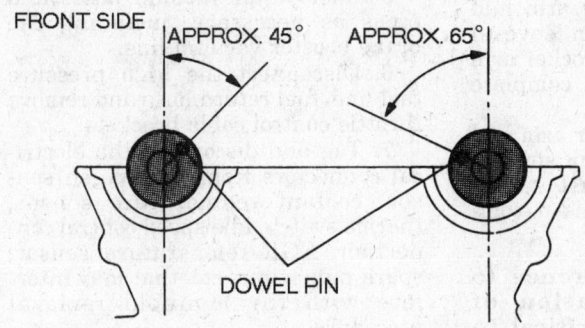
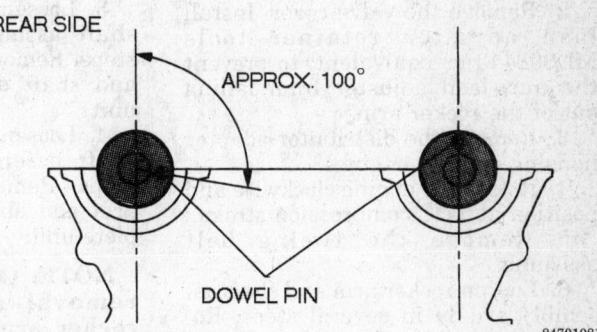

Camshaft dowel pin positioning — Stealth 3.0L DOHC engine

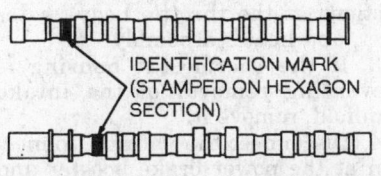

Camshaft identification — Stealth 3.0L DOHC engine

engine, torque to 21–25 ft. lbs. (29–35 Nm). On Summit Wagon equipped with 1.8L engine, torque the rocker shaft bolts to 23 ft. lbs. (32 Nm).

7. Install the valve cover with a new gasket.

8. Connect the negative battery cable.

Summit and Laser/Talon

1.6L AND 2.0L ENGINES

1. Release the fuel system pressure. Disconnect the negative battery cable.

2. Disconnect the accelerator cable, PCV hoses, breather hoses,

spark plug cables and the remove the valve cover.

3. Rotate the crankshaft clockwise and align the timing marks so No. 1 piston will be at TDC of the compression stroke. At this time the timing marks on the camshaft sprocket and the upper surface of the cylinder head should coincide, and the dowel pin of the camshaft sprocket should be at the upper side.

NOTE: Always rotate the crankshaft in a clockwise direction. Make a mark on the back of the timing belt indicating the direction of rotation so it may be reassembled in the same direction if it is to be reused.

4. Remove the timing belt upper and lower covers.

5. Remove the timing belt.

6. Remove the crank angle sensor.

7. Remove the camshafts. Be sure to position or mark bearing caps for proper reinstallation.

8. Visually inspect the rocker arm roller and replace if damage or seizure is evident. Check the roller for smooth rotation. Replace if excess play or binding is present. Also, inspect valve contact surface for possible damage or seizure. It is recommended that all rocker arms and lash adjusters be replaced together.

To install:

9. Install the rocker arms and lubricate lightly with clean oil prior to installation.

10. Apply engine oil to the lobes and journals of each camshaft. Install the camshafts into the cylinder head taking care not to confuse the intake and the exhaust camshaft; the intake camshaft has a slit on its rear end for driving the crank angle sensor. Align shafts so dowel pins on camshaft sprocket end are located on the top.

11. Install and tighten the camshaft bearing caps in the proper sequence, torquing to 14–15 ft. lbs. (19–21 Nm) in 3 even progressions.

12. Replace the camshaft oil seals and install the sprockets. Torque camshaft sprocket bolt to 58–72 ft. lbs. (80–100 Nm).

13. Locate the dowel pin on the sprocket end of the intake camshaft at the top position, if not already done.

14. Align the punch mark on the crank angle sensor housing with the notch on the sensor plate. Install the crank angle sensor into the cylinder head.

15. Install the timing belt, covers and related components.

16. Install the valve cover using new gasket. Reconnect all related components.

1-45

1.8L, 2.4L and 3.0L SOHC Engines

EXCEPT 1993–96 2.4L ENGINE

1. Disconnect the negative battery cable.

2. Remove the valve cover. Install lash adjuster retainer tools MD998443 or equivalent, to prevent the auto-lash adjuster from falling out of the rocker arm.

3. Remove the distributor adapter housing on 3.0L engines.

4. Rotate the engine clockwise and position at TDC compression stroke.

5. Remove the timing belt assembly.

6. Loosen rocker arm and shaft assembly evenly in several steps. Remove the rocker arm and shaft assembly as a complete unit.

7. Remove the rear camshaft bearing cap and slide rocker arms, springs and washers from shaft. Note location and positioning of all rocker shaft components.

8. Visually inspect the rocker arm roller and replace if damage or seizure is evident. Check the roller for smooth rotation. Replace if excess play or binding is present. Also, inspect valve contact surface for possible damage or seizure. It is recommended that all rocker arms and lash adjusters be replaced together.

To install:

9. Immerse the lash adjusters in clean diesel fuel. Using a small wire, move the plunger of the lash adjuster up and down 4 or 5 times while pushing down lightly on the check ball in order to bleed out the air. Install the lash adjusters in the rocker arms.

10. Lubricate the camshaft and rocker shaft with heavy engine oil and position on the cylinder head.

11. Apply a drop of sealant to the rear edges of the end caps.

12. Install the assembly into the front bearing cap making sure the notches in the rocker shafts are facing up. Insert the installation bolt but do not tighten at this point.

13. Install the remaining cap bolts and tighten evenly and gradually to 15 ft. lbs. (20 Nm). Tighten the front cap retaining bolts to 17 ft. lbs. (24 Nm). Remove the lash adjuster retainers.

14. Install the distributor extension, if removed.

15. Install the valve cover with a new gasket and tighten to 4–5 ft. lbs. (5–7 Nm).

16. Connect the negative battery cable.

1993–96 2.4L Engine

1. Disconnect the negative battery cable.

2. Remove the valve cover. Install lash adjuster retainer tools MD998443 or equivalent, to prevent the auto-lash adjuster from falling out of the rocker arm.

3. Loosen intake rocker arm and shaft assembly evenly in several steps. Remove the intake rocker arm and shaft assembly as a complete unit.

4. Loosen exhaust rocker arm and shaft assembly evenly in several steps. Remove the exhaust rocker arm and shaft assembly as a complete unit.

NOTE: Order in reference to removal and installation of rocker arm shafts is critical to prevent damage.

5. Visually inspect the rocker arm roller and replace if damage or seizure is evident. Check the roller for smooth rotation. Replace if excess play or binding is present. Also, inspect valve contact surface for possible damage or seizure. It is recommended that all rocker arms and lash adjusters be replaced together.

—— WARNING ——
Do not disassemble the rocker arm and shaft assembly.

6. Install the exhaust rocker arm and shaft assembly as a complete unit. Tighten the exhaust rocker arm and shaft assembly evenly in several steps to 21–25 ft. lbs. (28–34 Nm).

7. Install the intake rocker arm and shaft assembly as a complete unit. Tighten the intake rocker arm and shaft assembly evenly in several steps to 21–25 ft. lbs. (28–34 Nm).

8. Remove the lash adjuster retainers and confirm that notches of rocker arm shafts are positioned toward the outside of the cylinder head.

9. Install the valve cover with a new gasket and tighten to 26–30 inch lbs. (3.0–3.5 Nm).

10. Connect the negative battery cable.

Air Intake Plenum and Intake Manifold

REMOVAL AND INSTALLATION

Except 3.0L Engine

1. Relieve the fuel system pressure.

2. Disconnect battery negative cable and drain the cooling system.

3. Disconnect the accelerator cable, breather hose and air intake hose.

4. Disconnect the upper radiator hose, heater hose and water bypass hose.

5. Remove all vacuum hoses and pipes as necessary, including the brake booster vacuum line.

6. Disconnect the high pressure fuel line, fuel return hose and remove throttle control cable brackets.

7. Tag and disconnect the electrical connectors from the oxygen sensor, coolant temperature sensor, thermo switch, idle speed control connection, EGR temperature sensor, spark plug wires, etc. that may interfere with the manifold removal procedure.

8. Remove the fuel rail, fuel injectors, pressure regulator and insulators.

9. Remove the fuel delivery pipe, injectors and pressure regulator from the engine.

10. Distributor removal is necessary on the 1992 2.4L engine. Match-mark the distributor shaft to the housing and the housing to the head or nearest accessory prior to removal.

11. Remove the intake manifold bracket.

12. Disconnect the water hose connections at the throttle body, water inlet, and heater assembly.

13. If the thermostat housing is preventing removal of the intake manifold, remove it.

14. Disconnect the vacuum connection at the power brake booster and the PCV valve if still connected.

15. Remove the intake manifold mounting bolts and remove the intake manifold assembly. Disassemble manifold from the intake plenum on a work bench as required.

To install:

16. Assemble the intake manifold assembly using all new gaskets. Torque air intake plenum bolts to 11–14 ft. lbs. (15–19 Nm).

17. Clean all gasket material from the cylinder head intake mounting surface and intake manifold assembly. Check both surfaces for cracks or other damage. Check the intake manifold water passages and jet air passages for clogging. Clean if necessary.

18. Install a new intake manifold gasket to the head and install the manifold. Torque the manifold in a criss-cross pattern, starting from the inside and working outwards to 11–14 ft. lbs. (15–19 Nm).

19. Install the fuel delivery pipe, injectors and pressure regulator from the engine. Torque the retaining bolts to 7–9 ft. lbs. (10–13 Nm).

20. Install the thermostat housing, intake manifold brace bracket, distributor and throttle body stay bracket.

21. Connect or install all hoses, cables and electrical connectors that were removed or disconnected during the removal procedure.

22. Fill the system with coolant.

23. Connect the negative battery cable, run the vehicle until the thermostat opens, fill the radiator completely.

24. Adjust the accelerator cable. Check and adjust the idle speed and ignition timing.

25. Once the vehicle has cooled, recheck the coolant level.

3.0L Engine

1. Relieve the fuel system pressure.

2. Disconnect battery negative cable and drain the cooling system.

3. Remove the air intake hose(s).

4. Disconnect the accelerator control cables from the throttle body.

5. Matchmark and disconnect the vacuum hoses including the brake booster hose.

6. Disconnect the clutch booster vacuum hose connection, if equipped.

7. Disconnect all harness connectors.

8. Disconnect EGR components on California vehicles.

9. Remove the plenum retaining bracket.

10. Remove the plenum retaining nuts and bolts and remove the air intake plenum. Discard the gasket.

11. Disconnect the high pressure and return fuel hoses.

12. Matchmark and disconnect the vacuum hoses.

13. Disconnect the wire harness connectors.

14. Remove the fuel rail with the injectors attached.

15. On SOHC engines, disconnect the water hoses. On DOHC engines, remove the timing belt upper cover.

16. Remove the intake manifold mounting nuts; turbocharged engines have cone disc springs under some of the nuts which should be removed. Remove the intake manifold and discard the gaskets.

To install:

17. Check all items for cracks, clogging and warpage. Maximum warpage is 0.008 in. (0.2mm). Replace all questionable parts.

18. Thoroughly clean and dry the mating surfaces of the heads, intake manifold and air intake plenum.

19. Install new intake manifold gaskets to the heads with the adhesive side facing up.

20. Place the manifold on the heads and install the cone disc springs and/or lock washers.

21. Lubricate the studs lightly with oil, then install the nuts following this procedure:

    a. Tighten the nuts on the front bank to 26–43 inch lbs. (3–5 Nm).

    b. Tighten the nuts on the rear bank to 9–11 ft. lbs. (12–15 Nm).

    c. Tighten the nuts on the front bank to 9–11 ft. lbs. (12–15 Nm).

    d. Repeat Steps B and C.

    e. On non-turbocharged engines only, tighten the nuts to a final torque of 13–14 ft. lbs. (18–19 Nm).

22. On SOHC engines, connect the water hoses. On DOHC engines, install the timing belt upper cover.

23. Install the fuel rail assembly.

24. Connect the harness connector and vacuum hoses.

25. Replace the O-ring and connect the fuel hoses.

26. Install a new intake air plenum gasket and install the plenum. Tighten the retaining nuts and bolts evenly and gradually to 13 ft. lbs. (18 Nm).

27. Install the retaining bracket.

28. Connect EGR components on California vehicles.

29. Connect the harness connectors and vacuum hoses.

30. Connect and adjust the accelerator cables.

31. Install the air intake hose(s).

32. Fill the system with coolant.

33. Connect the negative battery cable, run the vehicle until the thermostat opens, fill the radiator completely.

34. Check and adjust the idle speed and ignition timing.

35. Once the vehicle has cooled, recheck the coolant level.

Exhaust Manifold

REMOVAL AND INSTALLATION

Non-Turbocharged Engines

1. Disconnect battery negative cable.

2. Raise the vehicle and support safely.

3. Remove the exhaust pipe to exhaust manifold nuts and separate exhaust pipe. Discard gasket.

4. Lower vehicle.

5. Remove electric cooling fan assembly, if necessary. If removing the front manifold on 3.0L engine, remove the dipstick tube. If removing the front manifold from 3.0L DOHC engine, remove the alternator.

6. Disconnect necessary EGR components.

7. On all except 3.0L engine, remove outer exhaust manifold heat shield and engine hanger. Disconnect the electrical connector and remove the oxygen sensor.

8. Remove the exhaust manifold mounting bolts, the inner heat shield and the exhaust manifold.

To install:

9. Clean all gasket material from the mating surfaces and check the manifold for damage.

10. Install a new gasket and install the manifold. Tighten the nuts to in a criss-cross pattern to:

SOHC engines — 11–14 ft. lbs. (15–20 Nm).

1.6L and 2.0L engines — 18–22 ft. lbs. (25–30 Nm).

3.0L DOHC engine — 22 ft. lbs. (30 Nm).

11. Install the heat shields.

12. Connect EGR components.

13. Install the electric cooling fan assembly, dipstick tube and alternator, as required.

14. Install a new flange gasket and connect the exhaust pipe.

15. Connect the negative battery cable and check for exhaust leaks.

1.6L and 2.0L Turbocharged Engines

1. Disconnect the battery negative cable. Drain the cooling system.

2. Remove the condenser cooling fan and power steering pump and bracket as required.

3. Disconnect the oxygen sensor.

4. Raise the vehicle and support safely.

5. On 2.0L engine, drain the oil from the crankcase and remove the oil level indicator and tube.

6. Remove the exhaust pipe to turbocharger nuts and separate the exhaust pipe. Discard the gasket.

7. Lower vehicle. Remove air intake and vacuum hose connections.

8. Remove the upper exhaust manifold and turbocharger heat shields. Remove the exhaust manifold to turbocharger attaching bolts and nut.

9. Remove the engine hanger, water and oil lines from the turbo.

10. Remove the exhaust manifold mounting nuts. Remove the exhaust manifold and gasket.

To install:

11. Clean all gasket material from the mating surfaces and check the manifold for damage.

12. Install new gaskets and install the manifold. Tighten the manifold to head nuts in a criss-cross pattern to 18–22 ft. lbs. (25–30 Nm). Tighten the manifold to turbo nut and bolts to 40–47 ft. lbs. (55–65 Nm).

13. Install the engine hanger, water and oil lines to the turbocharger.

14. Install the heat shields.

15. Install the new gasket and connect the exhaust pipe.

16. Install the condenser cooling fan and power steering pump. Connect the oxygen sensor harness.

17. Install the oil level indicator and tube replacing O-ring as required.

18. Fill the crankcase with clean oil and refill the cooling system.

19. Connect the negative battery cable and check for exhaust leaks.

3.0L Turbocharged Engine

1. Disconnect the negative battery cable.

2. Drain the engine coolant.

3. Remove the turbocharger assembly.

4. Remove the heat shield.

5. Remove the mounting nuts and remove the exhaust manifold. Note that cone disc springs are installed at all lower mounting points.

To install:

6. Clean all gasket material from the mating surfaces and check the manifold for damage.

7. Install new gaskets and install the manifold. Make sure all cone disc springs are in their original locations with the grooved side facing the nut. Tighten the manifold nuts using the following procedure:

 a. Tighten all but the outer 2 nuts to 22 ft. lbs. (30 Nm).

 b. Tighten the outer 2 nuts to 34–38 ft. lbs. (47–53 Nm).

 c. Loosen the outer 2 nuts, then torque them to 22 ft. lbs. (30 Nm).

8. Install the heat shield.

9. Install the turbocharger assembly.

10. Fill the cooling system.

11. Connect the negative battery cable and check for exhaust leaks.

Turbocharger

Many turbocharger failures are due to oil supply problems. Heat soak after hot shutdown can cause the engine oil in the turbocharger and oil lines to coke. Often the oil feed lines will become partially or completely blocked with hardened particles of carbon, blocking oil flow. Check the oil feed pipe and oil return line for clogging. Clean these tubes well. Always use new gaskets above and below the oil feed eyebolt fitting. Do not allow particles of dirt or old gasket material to enter the oil passage hole and that no portion of the new gasket blocks the passage.

REMOVAL AND INSTALLATION

1.6L and 2.0L Engines

1. Disconnect the negative battery cable.

2. Drain the engine oil, cooling system and remove the radiator. On Laser and Talon with air conditioning, remove the condenser fan assembly with the radiator.

3. Disconnect the oxygen sensor connector and remove the sensor.

4. Remove the oil dipstick and tube on Laser and Talon.

5. Remove the air intake bellows hose, the wastegate vacuum hose, the connections for the air outlet hose, and the upper and lower heat shields.

6. On Laser and Talon, unbolt the power steering pump and bracket assembly and leaving the hoses connected, wire it aside.

7. Remove the self-locking exhaust manifold nuts, the triangular engine hanger bracket, the eyebolt and gaskets that connect the oil feed line to the turbo center section, and the water cooling lines. The water line under the turbo has a threaded connection.

8. Remove the exhaust pipe nuts and gasket and lift off the exhaust manifold. Discard the gasket.

9. Remove the 2 through bolts and 2 nuts that hold the exhaust manifold to the turbocharger.

10. Remove the 2 capscrews from the oil return line (under the turbo). Discard the gasket. Separate the turbo from the exhaust manifold. The 2 water pipes and oil feed line can still be attached.

11. Visually check the turbine wheel (hot side) and compressor wheel (cold side) for cracking or other damage. Check whether the turbine wheel and the compressor wheel can be easily turned by hand. Check for oil leakage. Check whether or not the wastegate valve remains open. If any problem is found, replace the part. Inspect oil passages for restriction or deposits and clean as required.

12. The wastegate can be checked with a pressure tester. Apply approximately 9 psi to the actuator and make sure the rod moves. Do not apply more than 10.3 psi or the diaphragm in the wastegate may be damaged. Vacuum applied to the wastegate actuator should be maintained, replace if leaks vacuum. Do not attempt to adjust the wastegate valve.

To install:

13. Prime the oil return line with clean engine oil. Replace all locking nuts. Before installing the threaded connection for the water inlet pipe, apply light oil to the inner surface of the pipe flange. Assemble the turbocharger and exhaust manifold.

14. Install the exhaust manifold using a new gasket.

15. Connect the water cooling lines, oil feed line and engine hanger.

16. If removed, install the power steering pump and bracket.

17. Install the heat shields, air outlet hose, wastegate hose and air intake bellows.

18. Install the oil dipstick tube and dipstick. Install the oxygen sensor.

19. Install the radiator assembly.

20. Fill the engine with oil, fill the cooling system and reconnect the negative battery cable.

3.0L Engine

RIGHT SIDE (FRONT) TURBOCHARGER

1. Disconnect the negative battery cable.

2. Remove the radiator.

3. Remove the right side transaxle bracket.

4. Remove the front exhaust pipe.

5. Carefully matchmark, diagram or photograph all air intake hoses and pipes along the front of the engine. It is imperative that all of these pieces are installed in the exact same positions when assembling. Remove the hoses and pipes and keep covered in a clean area.

6. Remove the alternator.

7. Remove the oil dipstick tube.

8. Remove the turbocharger heat protector.

9. Remove the water feed pipes.

10. Remove the oxygen sensor.

11. Remove the oil return line.

12. Remove the exhaust extension fitting and bracket.

13. Remove all air conditioning components preventing removal of the turbocharger.

14. Remove the oil feed tube.

15. Remove the turbocharger to exhaust manifold bolts and remove the turbocharger assembly.

To install:

16. Visually check the turbine wheel (hot side) and compressor wheel (cold side) for cracking or other

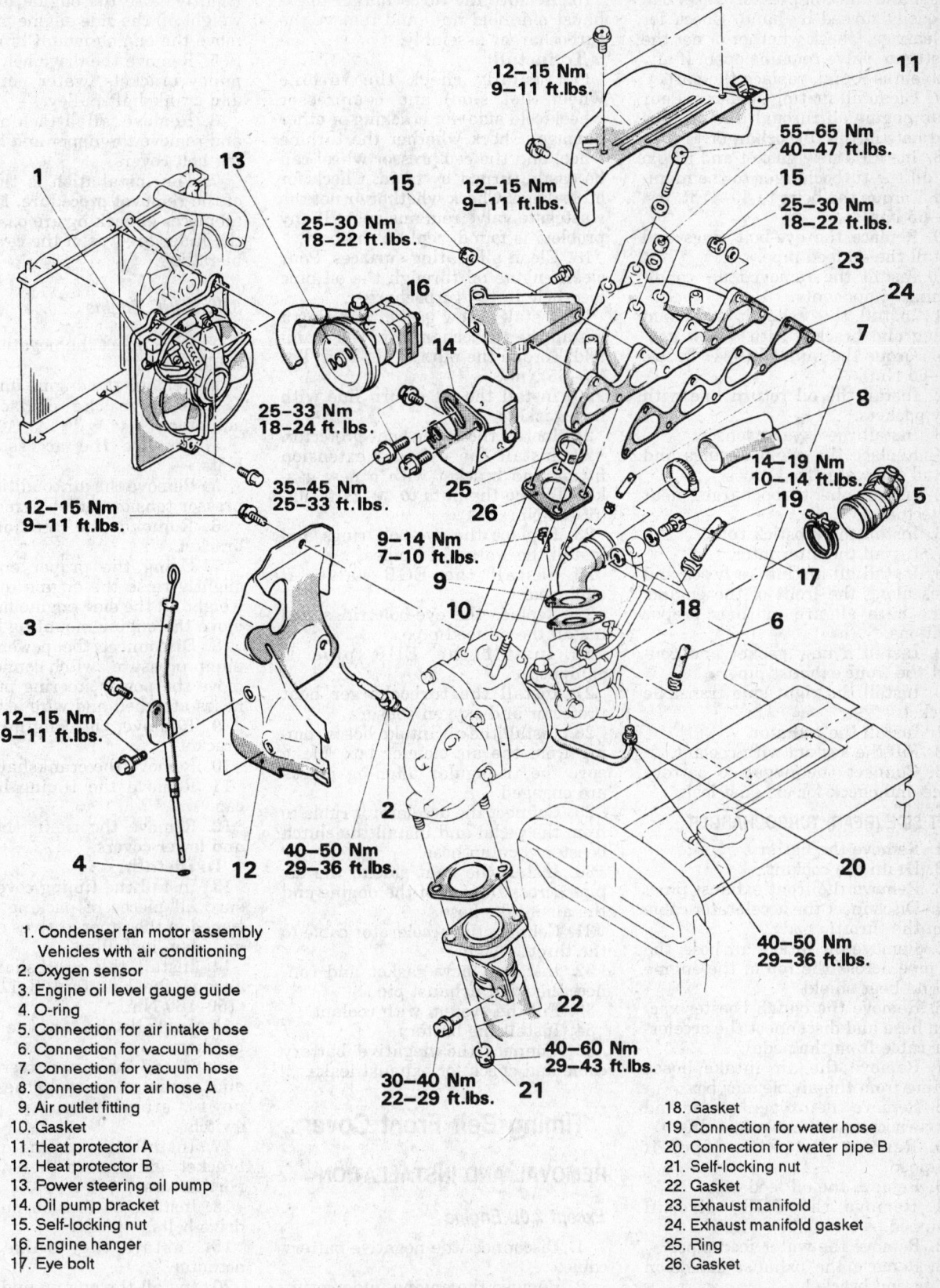

12–15 Nm
9–11 ft.lbs.

11

55–65 Nm
40–47 ft.lbs.

12–15 Nm
9–11 ft.lbs.

15

25–30 Nm
18–22 ft.lbs.

13

15

25–30 Nm
18–22 ft.lbs.

1

16

23

14

24

7

8

25–33 Nm
18–24 ft.lbs.

14–19 Nm
10–14 ft.lbs.

5

25

19

35–45 Nm
25–33 ft.lbs.

12–15 Nm
9–11 ft.lbs.

26

9–14 Nm
7–10 ft.lbs.

17

9

18

3

10

6

12–15 Nm
9–11 ft.lbs.

20

2

4

12

40–50 Nm
29–36 ft.lbs.

40–50 Nm
29–36 ft.lbs.

22

40–60 Nm
29–43 ft.lbs.

30–40 Nm
22–29 ft.lbs.

21

1. Condenser fan motor assembly
   Vehicles with air conditioning
2. Oxygen sensor
3. Engine oil level gauge guide
4. O-ring
5. Connection for air intake hose
6. Connection for vacuum hose
7. Connection for vacuum hose
8. Connection for air hose A
9. Air outlet fitting
10. Gasket
11. Heat protector A
12. Heat protector B
13. Power steering oil pump
14. Oil pump bracket
15. Self-locking nut
16. Engine hanger
17. Eye bolt

18. Gasket
19. Connection for water hose
20. Connection for water pipe B
21. Self-locking nut
22. Gasket
23. Exhaust manifold
24. Exhaust manifold gasket
25. Ring
26. Gasket

84701084

Turbocharger assembly — 2.0L engine

damage. Check whether the turbine wheel and the compressor wheel can be easily turned by hand. Check for oil leakage. Check whether or not the wastegate valve remains open. If any problem is found, replace the part.

17. Clean all mating surfaces. Pour clean engine oil through the oil pipe feed hole in the turbocharger.

18. Install a new gasket and ring a install the turbocharger to the manifold. Torque the bolts to 40–47 ft. lbs. (55–65 Nm).

19. Replace the eye-bolt rings and install the oil feed pipe.

20. Install the removed air conditioning components.

21. Install the exhaust extension fitting and bracket with a new gasket. Torque the nuts to 40–47 ft. lbs. (55–65 Nm).

22. Install the oil return line with new gaskets.

23. Install the oxygen sensor.

24. Replace the eye-bolt rings and install the water feed pipes.

25. Install the turbocharger heat protector.

26. Install the dipstick tube.

27. Install the alternator.

28. Install all air intake hoses and pipes along the front of the engine. Make sure all are in their proper positions.

29. Install a new gasket and connect the front exhaust pipe.

30. Install the right side transaxle bracket.

31. Install the radiator.

32. Fill the system with coolant.

33. Connect the negative battery cable and check for exhaust leaks.

LEFT SIDE (REAR) TURBOCHARGER

1. Remove the battery.
2. Drain the coolant.
3. Remove the front exhaust pipe.
4. Disconnect the accelerator cable from the throttle body.
5. Remove the intake air hose, the air pipe across the top of the engine and its heat shield.
6. Remove the clutch booster vacuum hose and disconnect the accelerator cable from the pedal.
7. Remove the air intake hoses coming from the air cleaner box.
8. Remove the oxygen sensor and the turbocharger heat protector.
9. Remove the EGR pipe, if equipped.
10. Remove the oil feed pipe.
11. Remove the EGR valve, if equipped.
12. Remove the water feed pipes.
13. Remove the exhaust extension fitting and bracket.
14. Remove the inner heat protector.

15. Remove the oil return tube.
16. Remove the turbocharger to exhaust manifold nuts and remove the turbocharger assembly.

To install:
17. Visually check the turbine wheel (hot side) and compressor wheel (cold side) for cracking or other damage. Check whether the turbine wheel and the compressor wheel can be easily turned by hand. Check for oil leakage. Check whether or not the wastegate valve remains open. If any problem is found, replace the part.

18. Clean all mating surfaces. Pour clean engine oil through the oil pipe feed hole in the turbocharger.

19. Install a new gasket and ring a install the turbocharger to the manifold. Torque the nuts to 40–47 ft. lbs. (55–65 Nm).

20. Install the oil return line with new gaskets.

21. Install the inner heat protector.

22. Install the exhaust extension fitting and bracket with a new gasket. Torque the nuts to 40–47 ft. lbs. (55–65 Nm).

23. Replace the eye-bolt rings and install the water feed pipes.

24. Install the EGR valve, if equipped.

25. Replace the eye-bolt rings and install the oil feed pipe.

26. Install the EGR pipe if equipped.

27. Install the turbocharger heat protector and oxygen sensor.

28. Install the air intake hoses coming from the air cleaner box. Make sure the triangular aligning marks are engaged.

29. Connect the accelerator cable to from the pedal and install the clutch booster vacuum hose.

30. Install the heat shield, the air pipe across the top of the engine and the air intake hose.

31. Connect the accelerator cable to the throttle body.

32. Install a new gasket and connect the front exhaust pipe.

33. Fill the system with coolant.

34. Install the battery.

35. Connect the negative battery cable and check for exhaust leaks.

Timing Belt Front Cover

REMOVAL AND INSTALLATION

Except 3.0L Engine

1. Disconnect the negative battery cable.
2. Remove the engine undercover.
3. On Summit Wagon, remove the coolant reservoir.

4. Using the proper equipment, slightly raise the engine to take the weight off the side engine mount. Remove the engine mount bracket.

5. Remove the drive belts, tension pulley brackets, water pump pulley and crankshaft pulley.

6. Remove all attaching screws and remove the upper and lower timing belt covers.

7. The installation is the reverse of the removal procedure. Make sure all pieces of packing are positioned in the inner grooves of the covers when installing.

3.0L SOHC Engine

1. Disconnect the negative battery cable.
2. Remove the engine undercover.
3. Remove the cruise control actuator.
4. Remove the accessory drive belts.
5. Remove the air conditioner compressor tension pulley assembly.
6. Remove the tension pulley bracket.
7. Using the proper equipment, slightly raise the engine to take the weight off the side engine mount. Remove the engine mounting bracket.
8. Disconnect the power steering pump pressure switch connector. Remove the power steering pump with hoses attached and wire aside.
9. Remove the engine support bracket.
10. Remove the crankshaft pulley.
11. Remove the timing belt cover cap.
12. Remove the timing belt upper and lower covers.

To install:
13. Install the timing covers. Make sure all pieces of packing are positioned in the inner grooves of the covers when installing.

14. Install the crankshaft pulley. Torque the bolt to 108–116 ft. lbs. (150–160 Nm).

15. Install the engine support bracket.

16. Install the power steering pump and reconnect wire harness at the power steering pump pressure switch.

17. Install the engine mounting bracket and remove the engine support fixture.

18. Install the tension pulleys and drive belts.

19. Install the cruise control actuator.

20. Install the engine undercover.

21. Connect the negative battery cable.

3.0L DOHC Engine

1. Disconnect the negative battery cable.

2. Remove the engine undercover.

3. Remove the cruise control actuator.

4. Remove the alternator. Remove the air hose and pipe.

5. Remove the belt tensioner assembly and the power steering belt.

6. Remove the crankshaft pulley.

7. Disconnect the brake fluid level sensor.

8. Remove the timing belt upper cover.

9. Using the proper equipment, slightly raise the engine to take the weight off the side engine mount. Remove the engine mount bracket.

10. Remove the alternator/air conditioner idler pulley.

11. Remove the engine support bracket. The mounting bolts are different lengths; mark them for proper installation.

12. Remove the timing belt lower cover. Timing bolt cover mounting bolts are different in length, note their position during removal.

To install:

13. Make sure all pieces of packing are positioned in the inner grooves of the lower cover, position cover on engine and install mounting bolts in their original location.

14. Install the engine support bracket and secure using mounting bolts in their original location. Lubricate the reaming area of the reamer bolt and tighten slowly.

15. Install the idler pulley.

16. Install the engine mount bracket. Remove the engine support fixture.

17. Make sure all pieces of packing are positioned in the inner grooves of the upper cover and install.

18. Connect the brake fluid level sensor.

19. Install the crankshaft pulley. Torque the bolt to 130–137 ft. lbs. (180–190 Nm).

20. Install the belt tensioner assembly and the power steering belt.

21. Install the air hose and pipe.

22. Install the alternator.

23. Install the cruise control actuator.

24. Install the engine undercover.

25. Connect the negative battery cable.

Timing Belt and Tensioner

ADJUSTMENT

1.5L (Summit) and 1.8L (Laser/Talon) Engines

1. Disconnect the negative battery cable.

2. Remove the timing belt covers.

3. On 1.8L engine, adjust the silent shaft (inner) belt tension first. Loosen the idler pulley center bolt so the pulley can be moved.

4. Move the pulley by hand so the long side of the belt deflects about 1/4 in.

5. Hold the pulley tightly so the pulley cannot rotate when the bolt is tightened. Tighten the bolt to 15 ft. lbs. (20 Nm) and recheck the deflection amount.

6. To adjust the timing (outer) belt, first loosen the pivot side tensioner bolt and then the slot side bolt. Allow the spring to remove the slack.

7. Tighten the slot side tensioner bolt and then the pivot side bolt. If the pivot side bolt is tightened first, the tensioner could turn with bolt, causing over tension.

8. Turn the crankshaft clockwise. Loosen the pivot side tensioner bolt and then the slot side bolt. Tighten the slot bolt and then the pivot side bolt.

9. Check the belt tension on 1.5L engine by holding the tensioner and timing belt together by hand and give the belt a slight thumb pressure at a point level with tensioner center. Make sure the belt cog crest comes as deep as about 1/4 of the width of the slot side tensioner bolt head. On 1.8L engine, the deflection of the longest span of the belt should be about 0.40 in. Do not manually overtighten the belt or it will howl.

10. Install the timing belt covers and all related items.

11. Connect the negative battery cable.

Summit Wagon

1.8L AND 2.4L ENGINES (EXCEPT 1993–96 2.4L ENGINES)

1. Disconnect negative battery cable.

2. Remove the timing belt covers.

3. On 2.4L engine, adjust the silent shaft (inner) belt tension first as follows:

a. Loosen the idler pulley center bolt so the pulley can be moved.

b. Move the pulley by hand so the long side of the belt deflects about 1/4 in.

c. Hold the pulley tightly so the pulley cannot rotate when the bolt is tightened. Tighten the bolt to 15 ft. lbs. (20 Nm) and recheck the deflection amount.

4. To adjust the timing (outer) belt, first loosen the pivot side tensioner bolt and then the slot side bolt. Allow the spring to remove the slack.

5. Check to make sure the timing marks on each sprocket are aligned. Turn the crankshaft in clockwise direction, by 2 teeth of the crankshaft sprocket.

NOTE: The purpose of Step 5 is to apply the proper amount of tension to the tension side of the timing belt, be sure not to turn the crankshaft in the opposite direction (counterclockwise).

6. Tighten the slot side tensioner bolt and then the pivot side bolt. If the pivot side bolt is tightened first, the tensioner could turn with bolt, causing over tension.

7. Lightly clamp the center of the span between the camshaft sprocket and the water pump sprocket on the belt tension side with your thumb and forefinger. Check to be sure the clearance between the reverse surface of the belt and the inside of the undercover seal line is at the standard value.

a. 1.8L engine — 1.18 in. (30mm).

b. 2.4L engine — 0.55 in. (14mm).

8. Install the timing belt covers and all related items.

9. Connect the negative battery cable.

1993–96 2.4L Engine

The 1993–96 2.4L engine incorporates the use of an auto-tensioner to control tension of the timing belt. The following procedure refers to adjustment of new belts. This engine also uses a second timing belt to drive a silent shaft.

1. Disconnect the negative battery cable.

2. Remove the timing belt covers.

3. Adjust the silent shaft (inner) belt tension first. Loosen the idler pulley center bolt so the pulley can be moved.

4. Move the pulley by hand so the long side of the belt deflects 0.20–0.28 in. (5–7mm).

5. Hold the pulley tightly so the pulley cannot rotate when the bolt is tightened. Tighten the bolt to 15 ft. lbs. (20 Nm) and recheck tension.

6. To adjust the timing (outer) belt, turn the crankshaft clockwise

and position No. 1 cylinder to TDC of compression stroke.

7. Loosen the center bolt of tensioner pulley and unbolt auto-tensioner assembly. The auto-tensioner assembly must be reset to correctly adjust belt tension.

8. Remove and position the auto-tensioner into a vise with soft jaws. The plug at the rear of tensioner protrudes, be sure to use a washer as a spacer, to protect the plug from contacting vise jaws.

9. Slowly push the rod into the tensioner until the set hole in rod is aligned with set hole in the auto-tensioner.

10. Insert a 0.055 in. (1.4mm) wire into the aligned set holes. Unclamp the tensioner from vise and install to vehicle. Tighten tensioner to 14–20 ft. lbs. (20–27 Nm).

11. Align all timing marks and raise tensioner against belt to remove slack, snug tensioner bolt.

12. Loosen the center bolt. Using tool No. MD998752 or equivalent and a torque wrench, apply a torque of 22.5–24 inch lbs. (2.6–2.8 Nm). If the body of the vehicle interferes with the special tool and the torque wrench, use a jack and slightly raise the engine assembly.

13. Screw tool MD998738 or exact equivalent into the engine left support bracket until its end makes contact with the tensioner arm.

14. Tighten tensioner pulley to 35 ft. lbs. (48 Nm).

15. Screw tool MD998738 or exact equivalent several more turns so the set wire in the auto-tensioner can be removed. Remove the tool assembly.

16. Rotate the crankshaft 2 complete turns clockwise and let it sit for approximately 15 minutes. Then, measure the auto tensioner protrusion (the distance between the tensioner arm and auto tensioner body) to ensure that it is within 0.15–0.18 in. (3.8–4.5mm). If out of specification, repeat adjustment until the specified value is obtained.

17. If the timing belt tension adjustment is being performed with the engine mounted in the vehicle, and clearance between the tensioner arm and the auto tensioner body cannot be measured, the following alternative method can be used:

   a. Screw in special tool MD998738 or equivalent, until its end makes contact with the tensioner arm.

   b. After the special tool makes contact with the arm, screw it in some more to retract the auto tensioner pushrod while counting the number of turns the tool makes until the tensioner arm is brought into contact with the auto tensioner body. Make sure the number of turns the special tool makes conforms with the standard value of 2.5–3 turns.

   c. Install the rubber plug to the timing belt rear cover.

18. Install the timing belt covers and all related items.

19. Connect the negative battery cable.

1.6L and 2.0L Engines

1. Disconnect the negative battery cable.

2. Remove the timing belt covers.

3. Adjust the silent shaft (inner) belt tension first. Loosen the idler pulley center bolt so the pulley can be moved.

4. Move the pulley by hand so the long side of the belt deflects 0.20–0.28 in. (5–7mm).

5. Hold the pulley tightly so the pulley cannot rotate when the bolt is tightened. Tighten the bolt to 15 ft. lbs. (20 Nm) and recheck tension.

6. To adjust the timing (outer) belt, turn the crankshaft clockwise and position No. 1 cylinder to TDC of compression stroke.

7. Loosen the center bolt of tensioner pulley and unbolt auto-tensioner assembly. The auto-tensioner assembly must be reset to correctly adjust belt tension.

8. Remove and position the auto-tensioner into a vise with soft jaws. The plug at the rear of tensioner protrudes, be sure to use a washer as a spacer, to protect the plug from contacting vise jaws.

9. Slowly push the rod into the tensioner until the set hole in rod is aligned with set hole in the auto-tensioner.

10. Insert a 0.055 in. (1.4mm) wire into the aligned set holes. Unclamp the tensioner from vise and install to vehicle. Tighten tensioner to 14–20 ft. lbs. (20–27 Nm).

11. Align all timing marks and raise tensioner against belt to remove slack, snug tensioner bolt.

12. Loosen the tensioner center bolt. Using tool No. MD998752 or equivalent and a torque wrench, apply a torque of 22.5–24 inch lbs. (2.6–2.8 Nm). If the body of the vehicle interferes with the special tool and the torque wrench, use a jack and slightly raise the engine assembly.

13. Screw tool MD998738 or exact equivalent into the engine left sup-

port bracket until its end makes contact with the tensioner arm.

14. Tighten tensioner pulley to 35 ft. lbs. (48 Nm).

15. Screw tool MD998738 or exact equivalent several more turns so the set wire in the auto-tensioner can be removed. Remove the tool assembly.

16. Rotate the crankshaft 2 complete turns clockwise and let it sit for approximately 15 minutes. Then, measure the auto tensioner protrusion (the distance between the tensioner arm and auto tensioner body) to ensure that it is within 0.15–0.18 in. (3.8–4.5mm). If out of specification, repeat adjustment until the specified value is obtained.

17. If the timing belt tension adjustment is being performed with the engine mounted in the vehicle, and clearance between the tensioner arm and the auto tensioner body cannot be measured, the following alternative method can be used:

   a. Screw in special tool MD998738 or equivalent, until its end makes contact with the tensioner arm.

   b. After the special tool makes contact with the arm, screw it in some more to retract the auto tensioner pushrod while counting the number of turns the tool makes until the tensioner arm is brought into contact with the auto tensioner body. Make sure the number of turns the special tool makes conforms with the standard value of 2.5–3 turns.

   c. Install the rubber plug to the timing belt rear cover.

18. Install the timing belt covers and all related items.

19. Connect the negative battery cable.

3.0L SOHC Engine

1. Disconnect the negative battery cable.

2. Remove the timing belt covers.

3. Loosen the bolt that holds the tensioner in place and allow the spring to automatically apply tension to the belt.

4. Rotate the crankshaft smoothly, 2 engine revolutions clockwise. Tighten the tensioner bolt to 20 ft. lbs. (25 Nm). Do not turn the engine counterclockwise.

5. Measure the belt tension between the rear camshaft sprocket and the crankshaft with belt tension gauge. The specification is 46–68 lbs. (210–310 N).

6. Install the timing belt covers and all related items.

7. Connect the negative battery cable.

3.0L DOHC Engine

1. Disconnect the negative battery cable.

2. Remove the timing belt covers.

3. To adjust the timing belt, turn the crankshaft clockwise and position No. 1 cylinder to TDC of compression stroke.

4. Loosen the center bolt of tensioner pulley and unbolt auto-tensioner assembly. The auto-tensioner assembly must be reset to correctly adjust belt tension.

5. Remove and position the auto-tensioner into a vise with soft jaws. The plug at the rear of tensioner protrudes, be sure to use a washer as a spacer to protect the plug from contacting vise jaws.

6. Slowly push the rod into the tensioner until the set hole in rod is aligned with set hole in the auto-tensioner.

7. Insert a 0.055 in. (1.4mm) wire into the aligned set holes. Unclamp the tensioner from vise and install to vehicle. Tighten tensioner to 17 ft. lbs. (24 Nm).

8. Align all timing marks and raise tensioner pulley against belt to remove slack, snug tensioner bolt.

9. Loosen the center bolt on the tensioner pulley. Using tool MD998767 or equivalent and a torque wrench, apply a torque of 7.2 ft. lbs. (10 Nm). Tighten the tensioner bolt to 42 ft. lbs. (58 Nm) and make sure the tensioner does not rotate with the bolt.

10. Remove the set wire attached to the auto tensioner.

11. Rotate the crankshaft 2 complete turns clockwise and let it sit for approximately 5 minutes. Then, check that the set pin can easily be inserted and removed from the hole in the auto tensioner.

NOTE: Even if the set pin can not be easily inserted, the auto tensioner is normal if its rod protrusion is within specification.

12. Measure the auto tensioner protrusion (the distance between the tensioner arm and auto tensioner body) to ensure that it is within 0.15–0.18 in. (3.8–4.5mm). If out of specification, repeat adjustment procedure until the specified value is obtained.

13. Check again that the timing marks on all sprockets are in proper alignment.

14. Install the timing belt covers and all related items.

15. Connect the negative battery cable.

REMOVAL AND INSTALLATION

1.5L (Summit) and 1.8L (Summit Wagon) Engines

1. Disconnect the negative battery cable. Remove the engine under cover.

2. Rotate crankshaft clockwise and position engine at TDC compression stroke.

3. Raise and safely support the weight of the engine using the appropriate equipment. Remove the front engine mount bracket and accessory drive belts.

4. On Summit Wagon, remove the coolant reservoir tank.

5. Remove timing belt upper and lower covers.

6. Make a mark on the back of the timing belt indicating the direction of rotation so it may be reassembled in the same direction if it is to be reused. Loosen the timing belt tensioner and remove the timing belt.

NOTE: If coolant or engine oil comes in contact with the timing belt, they will drastically shorten its life. Also, do not allow engine oil or coolant to contact the timing belt sprockets or tensioner assembly.

7. Remove the tensioner spacer, tensioner spring and tensioner assembly.

8. Inspect the timing belt for cracks on back surface, sides, bottom and check for separated canvas. Check the tensioner pulley for smooth rotation.

To install:

9. Position the tensioner, tensioner spring and tensioner spacer on engine block.

10. Align the timing marks on the camshaft sprocket and crankshaft sprocket. This will position No. 1 piston on TDC on the compression stroke.

11. Position the timing belt on the crankshaft sprocket and keeping the tension side of the belt tight, set it on the camshaft sprocket.

12. Apply counterclockwise force to the camshaft sprocket to give tension to the belt and make sure all timing marks are aligned.

13. Loosen the pivot side tensioner bolt and the slot side bolt. Allow the spring to remove the slack.

14. Tighten the slot side tensioner bolt and then the pivot side bolt. If the pivot side bolt is tightened first,

the tensioner could turn with bolt, causing over tension.

15. Turn the crankshaft clockwise. Loosen the pivot side tensioner bolt and then the slot side bolt to allow the spring to take up any remaining slack. On 1.8L engine, tighten the adjuster bolt to 18 ft. lbs. (24 Nm). On 1.5L engine, tighten the slot bolt and then the pivot side bolt to 14–20 ft. lbs. (20–27 Nm).

16. Install the timing belt covers and all related items.

17. Connect the negative battery cable.

1.6L and 2.0L Engines

NOTE: The 1.6L engine is not equipped with silent shafts. Disregard all instructions pertaining to silent shafts if working on that engine.

1. Disconnect the negative battery cable.

2. Remove the timing belt upper and lower covers.

3. Rotate the crankshaft clockwise and align the timing marks so No. 1 piston will be at TDC of the compression stroke. At this time the timing marks on the camshaft sprocket and the upper surface of the cylinder head should coincide, and the dowel pin of the camshaft sprocket should be at the upper side.

NOTE: Always rotate the crankshaft in a clockwise direction. Make a mark on the back of the timing belt indicating the direction of rotation so it may be reassembled in the same direction if it is to be reused.

4. Remove the auto tensioner and remove the outermost timing belt.

5. Remove the timing belt tensioner pulley, tensioner arm, idler pulley.

6. Locate the access plug on the side of block. Remove the plug and install a phillips screwdriver. Remove the oil pump sprocket nut, oil pump sprocket, special washer, flange and spacer.

7. Remove the silent shaft (inner) belt tensioner and remove the belt.

To install:

8. Align the timing marks on the crankshaft sprocket and the silent shaft sprocket.

9. Fit the inner timing belt over the crankshaft and silent shaft sprocket. Ensure that there is no slack in the belt.

10. While holding the inner timing belt tensioner with your fingers, adjust the timing belt tension by applying a force towards the center of the

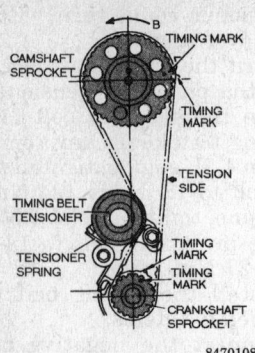

Timing alignment marks — 1.5L engine

84701087

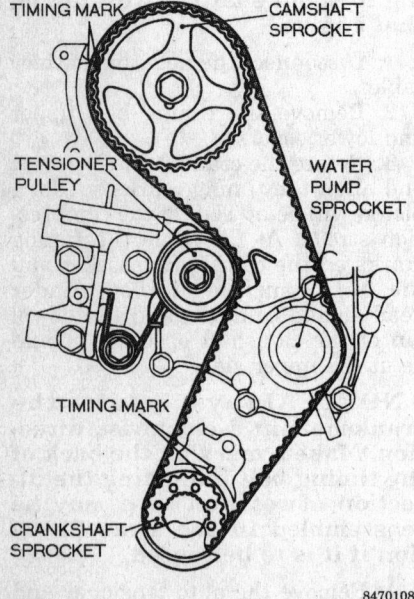

Timing alignment marks — 1.8L Summit Wagon engine

84701088

belt, until the tension side of the belt is taut. Tighten the tensioner bolt.

NOTE: When tightening the bolt of the tensioner, ensure that the tensioner pulley shaft does not rotate with the bolt. Allowing it to rotate with the bolt can cause excessive tension on the belt.

11. Check belt for proper tension by depressing the belt on long side with your finger and noting the belt deflection. The desired reading is 0.20–0.28 in. (5–7mm). If tension is not correct, readjust and check belt deflection.

12. Install the flange, crankshaft and washer to the crankshaft. The flange on the crankshaft sprocket must be installed towards the inner timing belt sprocket. Tighten bolt to 80–94 ft. lbs. (110–130 Nm).

NOTE: There is a possibility to align all timing marks and have the oil pump sprocket out of time, causing an engine vibration during operation. If the following step is not followed exactly, there is a 50 percent chance that the oil pump shaft alignment will be 180 degrees off.

13. Before installing the timing belt, ensure that the oil pump sprocket shaft is in the correct position as follows:
   a. Remove the plug from the rear side of the block and insert a phillips screwdriver with shaft diameter of 0.31 in. (8mm) into the hole.
   b. With the timing marks still aligned, the shaft of the screwdriver must be able to go in at least 2.36 in. (60mm). If the tool can only go in 0.79–0.98 in. (20–25mm), the shaft is not in the correct orientation and will cause a vibration during engine operation. Remove the tool from the hole and turn the oil pump sprocket 1 complete revolution. Realign the timing marks and insert the tool. The shaft of the tool must go in at least 2.36 in. (60mm).
   c. Recheck and realign the timing marks.
   d. Leave the tool in place to hold the oil pump silent shaft while continuing.
14. To install the oil pump sprocket and tighten the nut to 36–43 ft. lbs. (50–60 Nm).
15. Position the auto-tensioner into a vise with soft jaws. The plug at the rear of tensioner protrudes, be sure to use a washer as a spacer to protect the plug from contacting vise jaws.
16. Slowly push the rod into the tensioner until the set hole in rod is aligned with set hole in the auto-tensioner.
17. Insert a 0.055 in. (1.4mm) wire into the aligned set holes. Unclamp the tensioner from vise and install to vehicle. Tighten tensioner to 17 ft. lbs. (24 Nm).
18. When installing the timing belt, turn the 2 camshaft sprockets so their dowel pins are located on top. Align the timing marks facing each other with the top surface of the cylinder head. When you let go of the exhaust camshaft sprocket, it will rotate 1 tooth in the counterclockwise direction. This should be taken into account when installing the timing belts on the sprocket.

NOTE: The same sprockets are used for the intake and exhaust camshafts and are provided with 2 timing marks. When the sprocket is mounted on the exhaust camshaft, use the timing mark on the right with the dowel pin hole on top. For the intake camshaft sprocket, the timing mark is on the left with the dowel pin hole on top.

19. Align the crankshaft sprocket and oil pump sprocket timing marks.
20. After alignment of the oil pump sprocket timing marks, remove the plug on the cylinder block and insert a Phillips screwdriver with a shaft diameter of 0.31 in. (8mm) through the hole. If the shaft can be inserted 2.4 in. deep, the silent shaft is in the correct position. If the shaft of the tool can only be inserted 0.8–1.0 in. (20–25mm) deep, turn the oil pump sprocket 1 turn and realign the marks. Reinsert the tool making sure it is inserted 2.4 in. deep. Keep the tool inserted in hole for the remainder of this procedure.

NOTE: The above step assures that the oil pump socket is in correct orientation to the silent shafts. This step must not be skipped or a vibration may develope during engine operation.

21. Install the timing belt as follows:
   a. Install the timing belt around the intake camshaft sprocket and retain it with 2 spring clips or binder clips.
   b. Install the timing belt around the exhaust sprocket, aligning the timing marks with the cylinder head top surface using 2 wrenches. Retain the belt with 2 spring clips.
   c. Install the timing belt around the idler pulley, oil pump sprocket, crankshaft sprocket and the tensioner pulley. Remove the 2 spring clips.
   d. Lift upward on the tensioner pulley in a clockwise direction and tighten the center bolt. Make sure all timing marks are aligned.
   e. Rotate the crankshaft ¼ turn counterclockwise. Then, turn in clockwise until the timing marks are aligned again.
22. To adjust the timing (outer) belt, turn the crankshaft ¼ turn counterclockwise, then turn it clockwise to move No. 1 cylinder to TDC.
23. Loosen the center bolt. Using tool MD998738 or equivalent and a torque wrench, apply a torque of

1.88–2.03 ft. lbs. (2.6–2.8 Nm). Tighten the center bolt.

24. Screw the special tool into the engine left support bracket until its end makes contact with the tensioner arm. At this point, screw the special tool in some more and remove the set wire attached to the auto tensioner, if the wire was not previously removed. Then remove the special tool.

25. Rotate the crankshaft 2 complete turns clockwise and let it sit for approximately 15 minutes. Then, measure the auto tensioner protrusion (the distance between the tensioner arm and auto tensioner body) to ensure that it is within 0.15–0.18 in. (3.8–4.5mm). If out of specification, repeat belt adjustment procedure until the specified value is obtained.

26. If the timing belt tension adjustment is being performed with the engine mounted in the vehicle, and clearance between the tensioner arm and the auto tensioner body cannot be measured, the following alternative method can be used:

  a. Screw in special tool MD998738 or equivalent, until its end makes contact with the tensioner arm.

  b. After the special tool makes contact with the arm, screw it in some more to retract the auto tensioner pushrod while counting the number of turns the tool makes until the tensioner arm is brought into contact with the auto tensioner body. Make sure the number of turns the special tool makes conforms with the standard value of 2.5–3 turns.

  c. Install the rubber plug to the timing belt rear cover.

27. Install the timing belt covers and all related items.

28. Connect the negative battery cable.

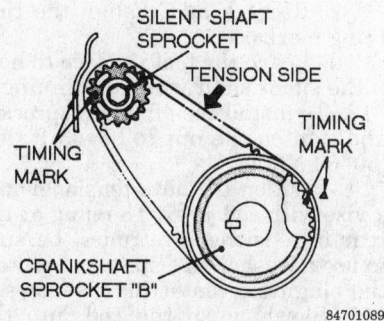

Silent shaft alignment marks — 2.0L DOHC Laser/Talon engine

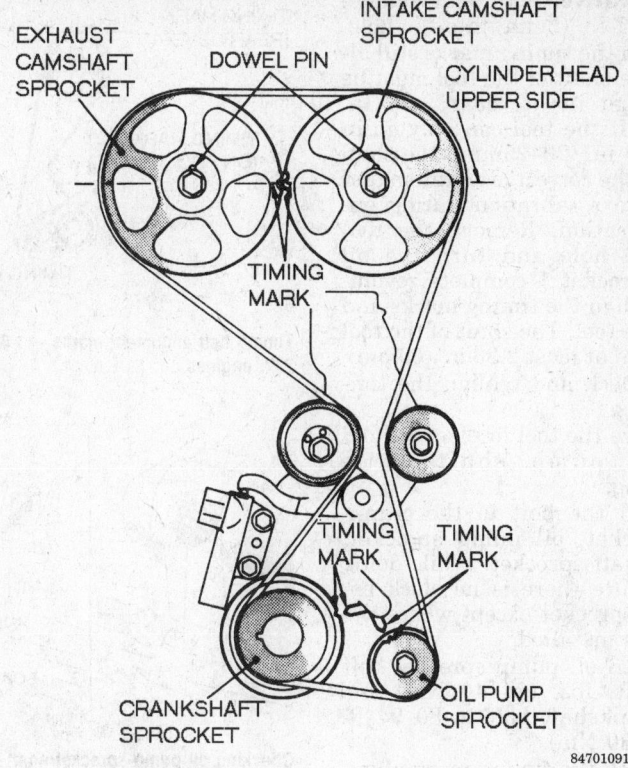

Timing belt alignment marks — 2.0L DOHC Laser/Talon engine

1.8L (Laser/Talon) and 2.4L Engines

EXCEPT 1993–96 2.4L ENGINES

1. Position the engine so the No. 1 piston is at TDC of compression stroke.
2. Disconnect the negative battery cable. On Summit Wagon with 2.4L engine, remove the coolant reservoir and the power steering and air conditioner hose clamp bolt.
3. Remove the timing belt covers.
4. Remove the timing belt tensioner pulley, tensioner arm, idler pulley.
5. Locate the access plug on the side of block. Remove the plug and install a phillips screwdriver. Remove the oil pump sprocket nut, oil pump sprocket, special washer, flange and spacer.
6. Remove the outer crankshaft sprocket and flange.
7. Remove the silent shaft (inner) belt tensioner and remove the belt.

To install:

8. Align the timing marks of the silent shaft sprockets and the crankshaft sprocket with the timing marks on the front case. Wrap the timing belt around the sprockets so there is no slack in the upper span of the belt and the timing marks are still aligned.

9. Install the tensioner pulley and move the pulley by hand so the long side of the belt deflects 0.20–0.28 in. (5–7mm).

10. Hold the pulley tightly so the pulley cannot rotate when the bolt is tightened. Tighten the bolt to 15 ft. lbs. (20 Nm) and recheck the deflection amount.

11. Install the timing belt tensioner fully toward the water pump and tighten the bolts. Place the upper end of the spring against the water pump body.

12. Align the timing marks of the camshaft, crankshaft and oil pump sprockets with their corresponding marks on the front case or rear cover.

NOTE: There is a possibility to align all timing marks and have the oil pump sprocket out of time, causing an engine vibration during operation. If the following step is not followed exactly, there is a 50 percent chance that the oil pump shaft alignment will be 180 degrees off.

13. Before installing the timing belt, ensure that the oil pump sprocket is in the correct position as follows:

  a. Remove the plug from the rear side of the block and insert a phillips screwdriver with shaft diameter of 0.31 in. (8mm) into the hole.

b. With the timing marks still aligned, the shaft of the tool must be able to go in at least 2.36 in. (60mm). If the tool can only go in 0.79–0.98 in. (20–25mm), the shaft is not in the correct orientation and will cause a vibration during engine operation. Remove the tool from the hole and turn the oil pump sprocket 1 complete revolution. Realign the timing marks and insert the tool. The shaft of the tool must go in at least 2.36 in. (60mm).

c. Recheck and realign the timing marks.

d. Leave the tool in place to hold the oil pump shaft while continuing.

14. Install the belt to the crankshaft sprocket, oil pump sprocket, then camshaft sprocket. While doing so, make sure there is no slack between the sprocket except where the tensioner is installed.

15. Tighten oil pump sprocket bolt to 26–29 ft. lbs. (34–40 Nm) and tighten crankshaft bolt to 80–94 ft. lbs. (110–130 Nm).

16. Recheck the timing mark alignment. If all are aligned, loosen the tensioner mounting bolt and allow the tensioner to apply tension to the belt.

17. Remove the tool that is holding the silent shaft and rotate the crankshaft a distance equal to 2 teeth on the camshaft sprocket. This will allow the tensioner to automatically apply the proper tension on the belt. Do not manually overtighten the belt or it will howl.

18. Tighten the lower mounting bolt first, then the upper spacer bolt.

19. To verify correct belt tension, check that the deflection at the longest span of the belt has 0.40 in. (12mm) clearance from the belt cover.

20. Install the timing belt covers and all related items.

21. Connect the negative battery cable.

1993–96 2.4L Engine

1. Disconnect the negative battery cable.

2. Remove the timing belt upper and lower covers.

3. Rotate the crankshaft clockwise and align the timing marks so No. 1 piston will be at TDC of the compression stroke. At this time the timing marks on the camshaft sprocket and the upper surface of the cylinder head should coincide, and the dowel

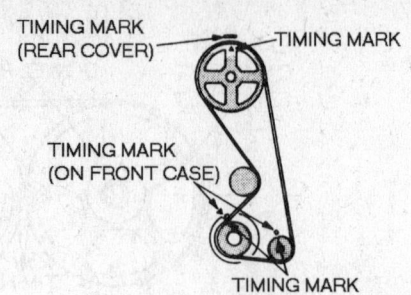

Timing belt alignment marks — 1.8L and 1992 2.4L engines

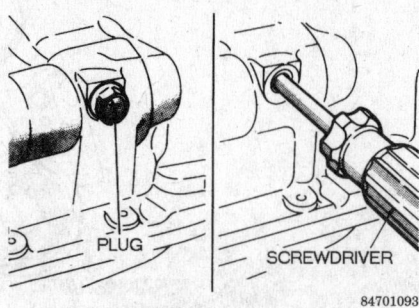

Checking oil pump sprocket shaft — 1.8L and 1992 2.4L engines

pin of the camshaft sprocket should be at the upper side.

NOTE: Always rotate the crankshaft in a clockwise direction. Make a mark on the back of the timing belt indicating the direction of rotation so it may be reassembled in the same direction if it is to be reused.

4. Remove the auto tensioner and remove the outermost timing belt.

5. Remove the timing belt tensioner pulley, tensioner arm, idler pulley.

6. Locate the access plug on the side of block. Remove the plug and install a phillips screwdriver. Remove the oil pump sprocket nut, oil pump sprocket, special washer, flange and spacer.

7. Remove the silent shaft (inner) belt tensioner and remove the belt.

To install:

8. Align the timing marks on the crankshaft sprocket and the silent shaft sprocket. Fit the inner timing belt over the crankshaft and silent shaft sprocket. Ensure that there is no slack in the belt.

9. While holding the inner timing belt tensioner with your fingers, adjust the timing belt tension by applying a force towards the center of the

belt, until the tension side of the belt is taut. Tighten the tensioner bolt.

NOTE: When tightening the bolt of the tensioner, ensure that the tensioner pulley shaft does not rotate with the bolt. Allowing it to rotate with the bolt can cause excessive tension on the belt.

10. Check belt for proper tension by depressing the belt on long side with your finger and noting the belt deflection. The desired reading is 0.20–0.28 in. (5–7mm). If tension is not correct, readjust and check belt deflection.

11. Install the flange, crankshaft and washer to the crankshaft. The flange on the crankshaft sprocket must be installed towards the inner timing belt sprocket. Tighten bolt to 80–94 ft. lbs. (110–130 Nm).

NOTE: There is a possibility to align all timing marks and have the oil pump sprocket out of time, causing an engine vibration during operation. If the following step is not followed exactly, there is a 50 percent chance that the oil pump shaft alignment will be 180 degrees off.

12. Before installing the timing belt, ensure that the oil pump sprocket is in the correct position as follows:

a. Remove the plug from the rear side of the block and insert a phillips screwdriver with shaft diameter of 0.31 in. (8mm) into the hole.

b. With the timing marks still aligned, the shaft of the tool must be able to go in at least 2.36 in. (60mm). If the tool can only go in 0.79–0.98 in. (20–25mm), the shaft is not in the correct orientation and will cause a vibration during engine operation. Remove the tool from the hole and turn the oil pump sprocket 1 complete revolution. Realign the timing marks and insert the tool. The shaft of the tool must go in at least 2.36 in. (60mm).

c. Recheck and realign the timing marks.

d. Leave the tool in place to hold the silent shaft while continuing.

13. To install the oil pump sprocket and tighten the nut to 36–43 ft. lbs. (50–60 Nm).

14. Position the auto-tensioner into a vise with soft jaws. The plug at the rear of tensioner protrudes, be sure to use a washer as a spacer to protect the plug from contacting vise jaws.

15. Slowly push the rod into the tensioner until the set hole in rod is aligned with set hole in the auto-tensioner.

16. Insert a 0.055 in. (1.4mm) wire into the aligned set holes. Unclamp the tensioner from vise and install to vehicle. Tighten tensioner to 17 ft. lbs. (24 Nm).

17. When installing timing belt, the camshaft sprocket dowel pin should be located on top. Align all timing marks.

18. Align the crankshaft sprocket, camshaft sprocket and oil pump sprocket timing marks.

19. Install the timing belt as follows:

    a. Install the timing belt around the idler pulley, oil pump sprocket, crankshaft sprocket, camshaft and the tensioner pulley.

    b. Lift upward on the tensioner pulley in a clockwise direction and tighten the center bolt. Make sure all timing marks are aligned.

    c. Rotate the crankshaft ¼ turn counterclockwise. Then, turn in clockwise until the timing marks are aligned again.

20. Loosen the center bolt. Using tool No. MD998752 or equivalent and a torque wrench, apply a torque of 1.88–2.03 ft. lbs. (2.6–2.8 Nm). Tighten the center bolt.

21. Screw the tool No. MD998738 into the engine left support bracket until its end makes contact with the tensioner arm and tighten tensioner pulley to 35 ft. lbs. (48 Nm). At this point, screw the special tool in some more and remove the set wire attached to the auto tensioner. Then remove the special tool.

22. Rotate the crankshaft 2 complete turns clockwise and let it sit for approximately 15 minutes. Then, measure the auto tensioner protrusion (the distance between the tensioner arm and auto tensioner body) to ensure that it is within 0.15–0.18 in. (3.8–4.5mm). If out of specification, repeat belt adjustment procedure until the specified value is obtained.

23. If the timing belt tension adjustment is being performed with the engine mounted in the vehicle, and clearance between the tensioner arm and the auto tensioner body cannot be measured, the following alternative method can be used:

    a. Screw in tool No. MD998738 or equivalent, until its end makes contact with the tensioner arm.

    b. After the tool makes contact with the arm, screw it in some more to retract the auto tensioner pushrod while counting the number of turns the tool makes until the tensioner arm is brought into contact with the auto tensioner body. Make sure the number of turns the tool makes conforms with the standard value of 2.5–3 turns.

    c. Install the rubber plug to the timing belt rear cover.

24. Install the timing belt covers and all related items.

25. Connect the negative battery cable.

3.0L SOHC Engine

1. Position the engine so the No. 1 cylinder is at TDC of its compression stroke. Disconnect the negative bat-

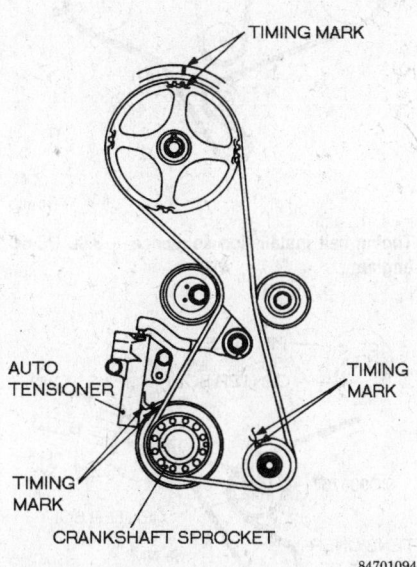

Timing belt alignment marks — 1993–96 2.4L engines

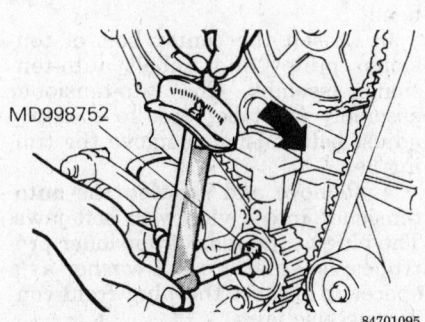

Timing belt adjusting tool No. MD998752 — 1993–96 2.4L engines

tery cable. Remove the timing covers from the engine.

2. If the same timing belt will be reused, mark the direction of the timing belt's rotation for installation in the same direction. Make sure the engine is positioned so the No. 1 cylinder is at the TDC of its compression stroke and the timing marks are aligned with the engine's timing mark indicators.

3. Loosen the timing belt tensioner bolt and remove the belt. If the tensioner is not being removed, position it as far away from the center of the engine as possible and tighten the bolt.

4. If the tensioner is being removed, paint the outside of the spring to ensure that it is not installed backwards. Unbolt the tensioner and remove it along with the spring.

To install:

5. Install the tensioner, if removed, and hook the upper end of the spring to the water pump pin and the lower end to the tensioner in exactly the same position as originally installed. If not already done, position both camshafts so the marks align with those on the rear. Rotate the crankshaft so the timing mark aligns with the mark on the front cover.

6. Install the timing belt on the crankshaft sprocket and while keeping the belt tight on the tension side, install the belt on the front camshaft sprocket.

7. Install the belt on the water pump pulley, then the rear camshaft sprocket and the tensioner.

8. Rotate the front camshaft counterclockwise to tension the belt between the front camshaft and the crankshaft. If the timing marks became misaligned, repeat the procedure.

9. Install the crankshaft sprocket flange.

10. Loosen the tensioner bolt and allow the spring to apply tension to the belt.

11. Turn the crankshaft 2 full turns in the clockwise direction until the timing marks align again. Now that the belt is properly tensioned, torque the tensioner lock bolt to 21 ft. lbs. (29 Nm). Measure the belt tension between the rear camshaft sprocket and the crankshaft with belt tension gauge. The specification is 46–68 lbs. (210–310 N).

12. Install the timing belt covers and all related parts.

13. Connect the negative battery cable and road test the vehicle.

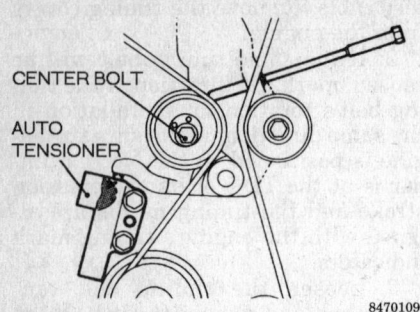

Timing belt adjusting tool No. MD998738 — 1993–96 2.4L engines

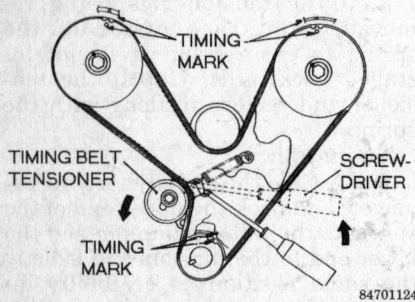

Timing belt alignment marks — 3.0L SOHC engine

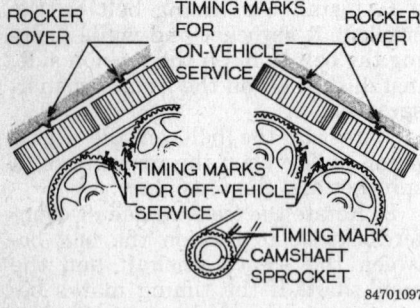

Timing belt alignment marks — 3.0L DOHC engine

3.0L DOHC Engine

1. Position the engine so the No. 1 cylinder is at TDC of its compression stroke. Disconnect the negative battery cable. Remove the timing covers from the engine.

2. If the same timing belt will be reused, mark the direction of the timing belt's rotation for installation in the same direction. Make sure the engine is positioned so the No. 1 cylinder is at the TDC of its compression stroke and the timing marks are aligned with the engine's timing mark

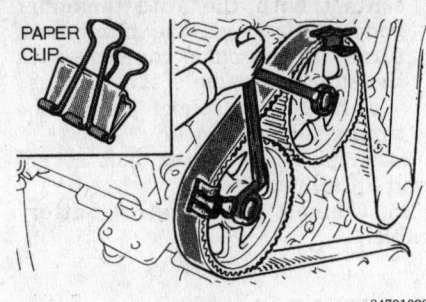

Securing camshafts for timing belt installation — 3.0L DOHC engine

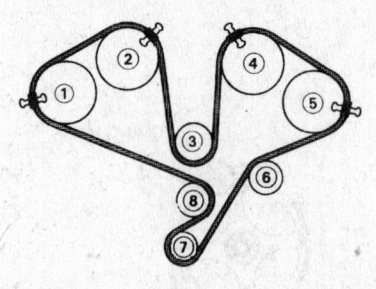

Timing belt installation sequence — 3.0L DOHC engine

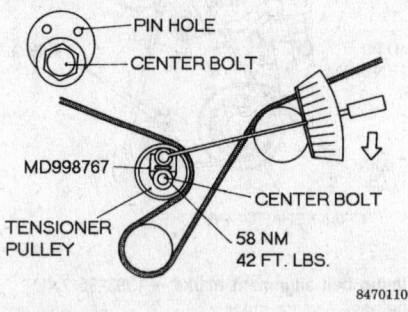

Timing belt tension adjustment — 3.0L DOHC engine

indicators on the valve covers or head.

3. Loosen the center bolt of tensioner pulley and unbolt auto-tensioner assembly. The auto-tensioner assembly must be reset to correctly adjust belt tension. Remove the timing belt.

4. Remove and position the auto-tensioner into a vise with soft jaws. The plug at the rear of tensioner protrudes, be sure to use a washer as a spacer to protect the plug from contacting vise jaws.

5. Slowly push the rod into the tensioner until the set hole in rod is

aligned with set hole in the auto-tensioner.

6. Insert a 0.055 in. (1.4mm) wire into the aligned set holes. Unclamp the tensioner from vise and install to vehicle. Tighten tensioner to 17 ft. lbs. (24 Nm).

7. Clean and inspect both auto tensioner mounting bolts. Coat the threads of the old bolts with Mopar thread sealer 4318034 or equivalent. If new bolts are installed, inspect the heads of the new bolts. If there is white paint on the bolt head, no sealer is required. If there is no paint on the head of the bolt, apply a coat of thread sealer to the bolt. Install both bolts and torque to 17 ft. lbs. (24 Nm).

To install:

WARNING
Turning the camshaft sprocket when the timing belt is removed could cause the valves to interfere with the pistons.

8. Align the mark on the crankshaft sprocket with the mark on the front case. Then move the sprocket 3 teeth clockwise to lower the piston so the valves do not touch the piston if the camshafts are being moved.

9. Turn each camshaft sprocket 1 at a time to align the timing marks with the mark on the valve cover or head. If the intake and exhaust valves of the same cylinder are opened simultaneously, they could interfere with each other. Therefore, if any resistance is felt, turn the other camshaft to move the valve.

10. Using paper clips to secure the timing belt to sprockets, install the timing belt in the following order. Be sure camshafts to cylinder heads and crankshaft to front cover timing marks are aligned.
   a. Exhaust camshaft sprocket (front bank).
   b. Intake camshaft sprocket (front bank).
   c. Water pump pulley.
   d. Intake camshaft sprocket (rear bank).
   e. Exhaust camshaft sprocket (rear bank).
   f. Idler pulley.
   g. Crankshaft pulley.
   h. Tensioner pulley.

NOTE: Since the camshaft sprockets turn easily, secure them with box wrenches to install timing belt.

11. Align all timing marks and raise tensioner pulley against belt to remove slack, snug tensioner bolt.

12. Loosen the center bolt on the tensioner pulley. Using tool MD998767 or equivalent and a torque wrench, apply a torque of 7.2 ft. lbs. (10 Nm). Tighten the tensioner bolt to 42 ft. lbs. (58 Nm) and make sure the tensioner does not rotate with the bolt.

13. Remove the set wire attached to the auto tensioner.

14. Rotate the crankshaft 2 complete turns clockwise and let it sit for approximately 5 minutes. Then, check that the set pin can easily be inserted and removed from the hole in the auto tensioner.

NOTE: Even if the set pin cannot be easily inserted, the auto tensioner is normal if its rod protrusion is within specification.

15. Measure the auto tensioner protrusion (the distance between the tensioner arm and auto tensioner body) to ensure that it is within 0.15–0.18 in. (3.8–4.5mm). If out of specification, repeat adjustment procedure until the specified value is obtained.

16. Check again that the timing marks on all sprockets are in proper alignment.

17. Install the timing belt covers and all related items.

18. Connect the negative battery cable.

Timing Sprockets and Oil Seals

REMOVAL AND INSTALLATION

1. Disconnect the negative battery cable.

2. Remove the valve cover(s) and timing belt(s).

3. Remove the crankshaft pulley retainer bolts and remove the pulley.

4. Remove the crankshaft sprocket retainer bolt and washer from the sprocket, if used, and remove sprocket. If sprocket is difficult to remove, the appropriate puller may be used. If no bolts are used on the sprocket, use the appropriate puller to remove.

5. Hold the camshaft stationary using the hexagon cast between journals No. 2 and 3 and remove the retainer bolt. Remove the sprocket from the camshaft. If the camshaft does not have a hexagon cast between journals No. 2 and 3, use the appropriate spanner wrench to hold the shaft in position while removing the bolt.

6. Pry the seals from the bores and replace using the proper installation tools.

7. Install the sprockets to their shafts. Install the retainer bolts and torque the camshaft sprocket bolt to 47–54 ft. lbs. (65–75 Nm) on 1.5L engine, 65 ft. lbs. (90 Nm) on Summit Wagon and 1992–93 Stealth or 58–72 ft. lbs. (80–100 Nm) on the remaining engines.

8. Torque the crankshaft sprocket retaining bolt to 80–94 ft. lbs. (110–130 Nm) on 1.6L, 1.8L, 2.0L and 2.4L engines or 51–72 ft. lbs. (70–100 Nm) on 1.5L engine. On V-6 3.0L SOHC engines, tighten the crankshaft retaining bolt to 108–116 ft. lbs. (150–160 Nm) or 130–137 ft. lbs. (180–190 Nm) for 3.0L DOHC engines.

9. Install the timing belt(s) and valve cover(s).

10. Connect the negative battery cable and check for leaks.

Camshaft

REMOVAL AND INSTALLATION

1.5L Engine

1. Disconnect the negative battery cable.

2. Rotate the engine to bring No. 1 piston to TDC of its compression stroke. Remove the timing belt and valve cover.

3. Remove the camshaft sprocket and oil seal.

4. Loosen both rocker arm assemblies gradually and evenly and remove.

5. Remove the camshaft from the head.

6. Carefully check all parts for damage and wear.

To install:

7. Lubricate the camshaft with heavy engine oil and slide it into the head.

8. If equipped, insert the camshaft thrust case in cylinder head with the threaded hole facing upward and align the threaded hole with the bolt hole in the cylinder head. Install and firmly tighten the attaching bolt.

9. Check the camshaft endplay between the thrust case and camshaft. The camshaft endplay should be 0.0020–0.0080 in. (0.05–0.20mm). If the endplay is not within specification, replace the camshaft thrust bearing.

10. Install the rocker shaft assemblies. Torque the bolts gradually and evenly to 21–25 ft. lbs. (29–35 Nm).

11. When installing the oil seal, coat the external surface with engine oil. Position the seal on the camshaft end and drive it into place.

12. Install the camshaft sprocket, timing belt and valve cover with new gasket.

13. Connect the negative battery cable and check for leaks.

1.6L and 2.0L Engines

1. Relieve the fuel system pressure.

2. Disconnect battery negative cable.

3. Disconnect the accelerator cable.

4. Remove the timing belt cover and timing belt.

5. Remove the center cover, breather and PCV hoses, and spark plug cables.

6. Remove the rocker cover, semicircular packing, throttle body stay, crankshaft angle sensor, both camshaft sprockets, and oil seals.

7. Loosen the bearing cap bolts in 2–3 steps. Label and remove all camshaft bearing caps.

NOTE: If the bearing caps are difficult to remove, use a plastic hammer to gently tap the rear part of the camshaft.

8. Remove the intake and exhaust camshafts.

9. Check the camshaft journals for wear or damage. Check the cam lobes for damage. Also, check the cylinder head oil holes for clogging.

To install:

10. Lubricate the camshafts with heavy engine oil and position the camshafts on the cylinder head.

NOTE: Do not confuse the intake camshaft with the exhaust camshaft. The intake camshaft has a split on its rear end for driving the crank angle sensor.

11. Make sure the dowel pin on both camshaft sprocket ends are located on the top.

12. Install the bearing caps. Tighten the caps in sequence and in 2 or 3 steps. No. 2 and 5 caps are of the same shape. Check the markings on the caps to identify the cap number and intake/exhaust symbol. Only **L** (intake) or **R** (exhaust) is stamped on No. 1 bearing cap. Also, make sure the rocker arm is correctly mounted on the lash adjuster and the valve stem end. Torque the retaining bolts to 15 ft. lbs. (20 Nm).

13. Apply a coating of engine oil to the oil seal. Using tool MD998307 or

equivalent, press-fit the seal into the cylinder head.

14. Align the punch mark on the crank angle sensor housing with the notch in the plate. With the dowel pin on the sprocket side of the intake camshaft at top, install the crank angle sensor on the cylinder head.

NOTE: Do not position the crank angle sensor with the punch mark positioned opposite the notch; this position will result in incorrect fuel injection and ignition timing.

15. Install the timing belt, valve cover and all related parts.
16. Connect the negative battery cable and check for leaks.

1.8L and 2.4L Engines

SUMMIT WAGON

1. Disconnect the negative battery cable.
2. On 1.8L engine, remove the battery and battery cover. Disconnect the air flow sensor connector and remove the air cleaner case cover.
3. Remove the breather hose. Disconnect the PCV hose.
4. Label and disconnect the spark plug cables.
5. On 1.8L engine, remove the distributor assembly.
6. Remove the rocker cover and the timing belt assembly.
7. Remove the camshaft sprocket retainer bolt while holding shaft stationary with appropriate spanner wrench. Remove the sprocket from the shaft.
8. Remove the camshaft oil seal.
9. Install lash adjuster retainers on 2.4L engine. Remove both rocker arm shaft assemblies from the head. Do not disassembly rocker arms and rocker arm shaft assemblies.
10. Remove the camshaft from the cylinder.
11. Inspect the bearing journals on the camshaft, cylinder head, and bearing caps.
   To install:
12. Lubricate the camshaft journals and camshaft with clean engine oil and install the camshaft in the cylinder head.
13. Install the rocker arm and shaft assemblies. On 1.8L engine, tighten the rocker arm shaft retainer bolts to 21–25 ft. lbs. (29–35 Nm). On 2.4L engine, tighten the rocker arm, bearing caps and shaft assembly to 14 ft. lbs. (20 Nm).
14. Remove the lash adjuster retainers. Install new camshaft oil seal.

15. Install camshaft sprocket and retainer bolt torquing to 65 ft. lbs. (90 Nm).
16. Install the timing belt.
17. On 1.8L engine, install the distributor.
18. On 1.8L engine, check the valve lash adjustment using specifications for a cold engine.
19. Install the rocker cover using new gasket material on mating surfaces.
20. Connect the spark plug cables.
21. Install the breather hose and connect the PCV hose.
22. Connect the air flow sensor connector and install the air cleaner case cover.
23. On 1.8L engine, install the battery and battery cover.
24. Connect the negative battery cable. Run the engine at idle until normal operating temperature is reached. Check idle speed and ignition timing and adjust as required.

1.8L (Laser/Talon) and 3.0L SOHC Engines

1. Disconnect the negative battery cable. Remove the valve covers and timing belt.
2. Install auto lash adjuster retainer tools MD998443 or equivalent, on the rocker arms.
3. If removing the right side (front) camshaft on 3.0L engine, remove the distributor extension.
4. Remove the camshaft bearing caps but do not remove the bolts from the caps.
5. Remove the rocker arms, rocker shafts and bearing caps, as an assembly.
6. Remove the camshaft from the cylinder head.
7. Inspect the bearing journals on the camshaft, cylinder head, and bearing caps.
   To install:
8. Lubricate the camshaft journals and camshaft with clean engine oil and install the camshaft in the cylinder head.
9. Align the camshaft bearing caps with the arrow mark depending on cylinder numbers and install in numerical order.
10. Apply sealer at the ends of the bearing caps and install the assembly.
11. Torque the bearing cap bolts in the following sequence: No. 3, No. 2, No. 1 and No. 4 to 85 inch lbs. (10 Nm).
12. Repeat the sequence increasing the torque to 15 ft. lbs. (20 Nm).
13. Install the distributor extension if it was removed.

14. Install the timing belt, valve cover and all related parts.
15. Connect the negative battery cable and check for leaks.

3.0L DOHC Engine

1. Relieve the fuel system pressure.
2. Disconnect battery negative cable.
3. Remove the timing belt cover and timing belt.
4. Remove the center cover, breather and PCV hoses, and spark plug cables.
5. Remove the rocker cover, semicircular packing, throttle body stay, crankshaft angle sensor, both camshaft sprockets, and oil seals.
6. Remove the crank angle sensor and adaptor.
7. Loosen the bearing cap bolts in 2–3 steps. Label and remove all camshaft bearing caps.

NOTE: If the bearing caps are difficult to remove, use a plastic hammer to gently tap the rear part of the camshaft.

8. Remove the intake and exhaust camshafts.
9. Check the camshaft journals for wear or damage. Check the cam lobes for damage. Also, check the cylinder head oil holes for clogging.
   To install:
10. Lubricate the camshafts with heavy engine oil and position the camshafts on the cylinder head.

NOTE: Do not confuse the intake camshaft with the exhaust camshaft. The intake camshaft has a V or B stamped on the hexagon depending on the application. The exhaust camshaft has a C, D or F stamped on the hexagon depending on application.

11. Make sure the dowel pin on both camshaft sprocket ends are located.
12. Install the bearing caps. Tighten the caps in sequence and in 2 or 3 steps. Caps 2, 3 and 4 have a front mark. Install with the mark aligned with the front mark on the cylinder head. Intake caps have **I** stamped on the cap and exhaust caps have **E**. Also, make sure the rocker arm is correctly mounted on the lash adjuster and the valve stem end. Torque the retaining bolts to 15 ft. lbs. (20 Nm).
13. Apply a coating of engine oil to the oil seals and install.
14. Install the timing belt, valve cover and all related parts.

15. Connect the negative battery cable and check for leaks.

Silent Shaft

REMOVAL AND INSTALLATION

1.8L Laser/Talon and 2.4L Engines

1. Disconnect the negative battery cable.
2. Remove the oil filter, oil pressure switch, oil gauge sending unit, oil filter mounting bracket and gasket.
3. Raise and safely support the vehicle. Drain engine oil. Remove engine oil pan, oil screen and gasket.
4. Lower the vehicle. Remove the timing belts.
5. Remove the front engine cover which is also the oil pump cover. Different length bolts are used. Take note of their locations. On 1.8L engine, if the cover sticks to the block, look for a special slot provided and pry with a flat edge tool. Discard the shaft seal and gasket.
6. Remove the oil pump driven gear flange bolt. When loosening this bolt, first insert a tool approximately ⅜ in. diameter into the plug hole on the left side of the cylinder block to hold the silent shaft. Remove the oil pump gears and remove the front case assembly. Remove the threaded plug, the oil pressure relief spring and plunger.
7. Remove the silent shaft oil seals, the crankshaft oil seal and front case gasket.
8. Remove the silent shafts.
To install:
9. Carefully install the silent shafts to the block.
10. Install the oil pump components.
11. Install new seals and install the front case with a new gasket.
12. Install the timing belts and all related items. Make sure the orientation of the silent shafts is correct using alignment tool as specified in the timing belt section of this chapter.

NOTE: The timing of the oil pump sprocket and connected silent shaft can be incorrect, even with the timing mark aligned. Incorrect orientation of the silent shaft will result in engine vibration during operation. Follow the alignment procedure in the timing belt section of this chapter.

13. Install the oil pan, oil filter mounting bracket, oil switches oil filter and oil.

14. Connect the negative battery cable and check for leaks.

Piston and Connecting Rod

POSITIONING

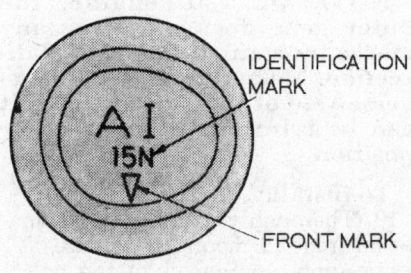

Piston identification marks — 1.5L engine

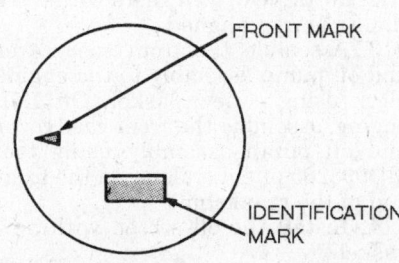

Piston identification marks — 1.6L, 1.8L Summit Wagon and 2.0L engines

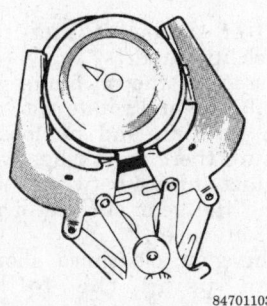

Piston identification marks — 1.8L, 2.0L Summit Wagon and 2.4L engines

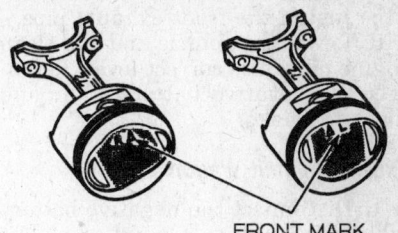

Piston identification marks — 3.0L engine

ENGINE LUBRICATION

Oil Pan

REMOVAL AND INSTALLATION

Summit Wagon

1. Disconnect negative battery cable.
2. Raise and safely support the vehicle.
3. Remove the front exhaust pipe and gasket.
4. If equipped with AWD, remove the transfer assembly with the propeller shaft still installed.
5. Remove the bell housing cover.
6. If equipped with 2.4L engine and FWD, remove the front left driveshaft from the transaxle.
7. Remove the oil pan mounting bolts and nuts. Remove the oil pan using tool MD998727 or equivalent, and a brass bar. Take care not to deform the pan flange during removal.
To install:
8. Thoroughly clean and dry the oil pan, cylinder block bolts and bolt holes.
9. Apply a thin bead of sealer around the flange surface of the oil pan. Make sure the bead of sealer is on the area between the bolt holes and the inside of the pan, and in the shallow groove around the flange of the oil pan.
10. Assemble the oil pan to the cylinder block within 15 minutes after applying the sealant.
11. Install the oil pan mounting bolts and nuts and tighten to 5 ft. lbs. (7 Nm).
12. Install the bellhousing cover.

13. Install the front driveshaft.

14. Install the transfer assembly.

15. Install the front exhaust pipe.

16. Lower the vehicle and add clean engine oil to the correct level. Reconnect the negative battery cable and check for leaks.

Except Summit Wagon

1. Disconnect the negative battery cable.

2. Raise the vehicle and support safely.

3. Remove the oil pan drain plug and drain the engine oil. On 1.6L engine equipped with turbocharger, remove the oil return pipe and gasket.

4. On 1.8L engine, disconnect and lower the exhaust pipe.

5. On Stealth equipped with AWD, remove the transfer assembly.

6. On 2.0L engine, remove the crossmember, disconnect and lower the exhaust pipe and on turbocharged engines, disconnect the return pipe for the turbocharger from the side of the oil pan.

7. Remove the oil pan mounting bolts, separate and remove the engine oil pan.

To install:

8. Thoroughly clean and dry the oil pan, cylinder block bolts and bolt holes.

9. Apply a thin bead of sealer around the surface of the oil pan.

10. Assemble the oil pan to the cylinder block within 15 minutes after applying the sealant.

11. Install the oil pan mounting bolts and torque to 4–6 ft. lbs. (6–8 Nm). On 1.6L engine equipped with turbocharger, install the oil return pipe using a new gasket.

12. Fill the engine with the proper amount of oil.

13. Connect the negative battery cable and check for leaks.

Oil Pump

REMOVAL AND INSTALLATION

NOTE: Whenever the oil pump is disassembled or the cover removed, the gear cavity must be filled with petroleum jelly for priming purposes. Do not use grease.

1. Disconnect the negative battery cable.

2. Remove the front engine mount bracket and accessory drive belts.

3. Remove timing belt upper and lower covers.

4. Remove the timing belt and crankshaft sprocket.

5. Remove the oil pan.

6. Remove the oil screen and gasket.

7. Remove and tag the front cover mounting bolts. Note the lengths of the mounting bolts as they are removed for proper installation.

8. On 1.6L engine, remove the plug cap using tool MD998162 or equivalent, and remove the oil pressure switch.

9. Remove the front case cover and oil pump assembly. If necessary, the silent shaft can come out with the assembly. Disassemble as required.

NOTE: On 1.5L engine, the outer gear does not have any marks indicating its installed direction. Make a mark on the reverse side of the outer gear so it can be reinstalled in its proper position.

To install:

10. Thoroughly clean all gasket material from all mounting surfaces.

11. Apply engine oil to the entire surface of the gears or rotors. On 1.5L engine, make sure the outer gear is installed in the same direction as before according to the mark made at the time of removal.

12. On engines with silent shafts and 1.8L (Summit Wagon) engine, install the drive/driven gears with the 2 timing marks aligned.

13. Assemble the front case cover and oil pump assembly to the engine block using a new gasket. On 1.6L engine, assemble the front case cover and oil pump assembly using tool MD998285 or equivalent, on the front end of the crankshaft.

14. Install the oil screen with new gasket.

15. Install the oil pan and timing belts.

16. Connect the negative battery cable and check for adequate oil pressure.

CHECKING

1. After disassembling the oil pump, clean all parts.

2. Assemble the oil pump gear to the front case and rotate it to ensure smooth rotation and no looseness. Make sure there is no ridge wear on the contact surface between the front case and the gear surface of the oil pump front cover.

3. The gear clearance should be checked using the following procedure:

a. On 1.5L engine, check the outer ring shaped gear. The distance between the outer circumference and the front case should be 0.0039–0.0079 in. The outer gear's side clearance be 0.0016–0.0039 in. The tip clearance or clearance between the outer and inner gear teeth with the inner gear teeth meshed, should be 0.0024–0.0071 in. with a maximum limit of 0.0138 in.

b. On 1.6L and 2.4L engines, with the drive and driven gears installed in the front case, measure the tip clearance of the gears. The distance between the tips of the drive gear's teeth and the case should be 0.0063–0.0083 in. with a limit of 0.0098 in. The distance between the tips of the driven gear's teeth and the case should be 0.0051–0.0071 in. with a limit of 0.0098 in. The endplay is checked by placing a straight-edge across the machined cover surface and measuring with a feeler gauge. The endplay for the drive gear should be 0.0031–0.0055 in. with a limit of 0.0098 in. The endplay for the driven gear on 1.6L engine is 0.0024–0.0047 in. with a limit of 0.0098 in. and 0.0051–0.0071 in. with a limit of 0.0098 in.

c. On 1.8L (Laser) engine, with the drive and driven gears installed in the front case, measure the tip clearance of the gears. The distance between the tips of the drive gear's teeth and the case should be 0.0024–0.0047 in. with a limit of 0.079 in. The distance between the tips of the driven gear's teeth and the case should be 0.0039–0.0079 in. with a limit of 0.071 in. The endplay is checked by placing a straight-edge across the machined cover surface and measuring with a feeler gauge. The endplay for the drive gear should be 0.0039–0.0063 in. with a limit of 0.008 in. The endplay for the driven gear is 0.0008–0.0020 in. with a limit of 0.006 in.

d. On 1.8L (Summit Wagon) engine, with the drive and driven gears installed in the front case, measure the tip clearance of the gears. The distance between the tips of the inner gear's teeth and the case should be 0.0016–0.0039 in. (0.06–0.18mm). The distance between the outer gear and the case should be 0.0039–0.0071 in. (0.10–0.18mm). The distance between the upper portion of the inner gear teeth and the teeth of the outer gear is 0.0024–0.0071 in. (0.06–0.18mm).

e. On 2.0L engine, with the drive and driven gears installed in the front case, measure the tip clearance of the gears. The distance between the tips of the drive gear's teeth and the case should be 0.0063–0.0083 in. with a limit of 0.0098 in. The distance between the tips of the driven gear's teeth and the case should be 0.0051–0.0071 in. with a limit of 0.0098 in. The endplay is checked by placing a straight-edge across the machined cover surface and measuring with a feeler gauge. The endplay for the drive gear should be 0.0031–0.0055 in. with a limit of 0.0098 in. The endplay for the driven gear is 0.0024–0.0047 in. with a limit of 0.0098 in.

f. On 3.0L engine, assemble the rotors on the pump housing and check the clearance between the rotors and the housing. The clearance specification is 0.0039–0.0071 in. The side clearance is checked by placing a straight-edge across the machined cover surface and measuring with a feeler gauge. This specification is 0.0016–0.0037 in.

4. If any measurement is beyond specification, replace the entire pump assembly.

Rear Main Bearing Oil Seal

REMOVAL AND INSTALLATION

1. Disconnect the negative battery cable.
2. Remove the transaxle from the vehicle.
3. Remove the flywheel/ring gear assembly.
4. Remove the rear engine plate and the bellhousing cover.
5. If the crankshaft rear oil seal case is leaking, remove it. Otherwise, just remove the oil seal. Some engines have a separator that should also be removed.
To install:
6. Lubricate the inner diameter of the new seal with clean engine oil.
7. Install the oil seal in the crankshaft rear oil seal case using tool MD998376 or equivalent. Press the seal all the way in without tilting it. Force the oil separator into the oil seal case so the oil hole in the separator is downward.
8. Install the seal case with a new gasket.
9. Install the flywheel and transaxle.
10. Connect the negative battery cable and check for leaks.

MANUAL TRANSAXLE

Transaxle Assembly

NOTE: If the vehicle is going to be rolled while the halfshafts are out of the vehicle, obtain 2 outer CV-joints or proper equivalent tools and install to the hubs. If the vehicle is rolled without the proper torque applied to the front wheel bearings, the bearings will no longer be usable.

REMOVAL AND INSTALLATION

Summit

1. Disconnect the negative battery cable.
2. Remove the battery and battery tray.
3. Remove the air cleaner assembly and vacuum hoses.
4. Raise the vehicle and support safely.
5. Drain the transaxle oil.
6. If equipped with 1.6L engine, remove the tension rod.
7. Disconnect the shifter cables.
8. Remove the clutch release cylinder and clutch oil line bracket and secure to the body. Do not disconnect the fluid lines. Disconnect the clutch cable, if equipped with cable controlled clutch system.
9. Disconnect the backup lamp switch connector, speedometer cable connection and remove the starter motor.
10. Remove the transaxle mounting bolts and bracket.
11. Remove the sheetmetal undercover.
12. Disconnect the tie rod ends and the lower ball joint connections.
13. Remove the halfshafts by inserting a prybar between the transaxle case and the driveshaft and prying the shaft from the transaxle. Do not pull on the driveshaft. Doing so damages the inboard joint. Use the prybar. Do not insert the prybar so far the oil seal in the case is damaged. Remove the right side shaft as just described. The left side shaft can be removed by tapping with a plastic hammer. Remove the shaft with the hub and knuckle as an assembly. Don't tap on the center bearing or it will be damaged. Tie the shafts aside. Note the circle clip on the end of the inboard shafts. These should not be reused.

14. Remove the bellhousing lower cover. Remove the transaxle to engine bolts and lower the transaxle from the vehicle.
To install:
15. Install the transaxle to the engine and install the mounting bolts.
16. When installing the halfshafts, use new circlips on the axle ends. Take care to get the inboard joint parts straight, not bent relative to the axle. Care must be taken to ensure that the oil seal lip of the transaxle is not damaged by the serrated part of the driveshaft.
17. Install the undercover.
18. Install the mounting brackets.
19. Install the starter making sure to fasten the ground wire with the upper fastener and the harness fastener with the lower fastener.
20. Connect the backup light switch connector and speedometer cable.
21. Install the clutch and shifter actuation components. If the hydraulic system was opened, it should be bled after installation.
22. Install the tension rod.
23. Install the air cleaner and battery.
24. Make sure the vehicle is level when refilling the transaxle. Use Hypoid gear oil or equivalent, GL-4 or higher.
25. Connect the negative battery cable and check the transaxle for proper operation. Make sure the reverse lights come ON when in reverse.

Summit Wagon

1. Disconnect negative battery cable. Support the weight of the engine using the appropriate fixture.
2. Remove the air cleaner assembly. Remove the transaxle upper coupling bolts.
3. Raise and safely support the vehicle.
4. Disconnect the control cable connection from the transaxle.
5. Disconnect the reverse light switch connection.
6. Disconnect the speedometer cable from the transaxle.
7. Remove the starter motor leaving the harness connected and secure aside.
8. Disconnect the tie rod end from the steering knuckle. Disconnect the stabilizer bar.
9. Remove the right side under cover. Drain the transaxle fluid.
10. Insert a prybar between the transaxle case and the driveshaft and pry the shaft from the transaxle. Turn the driveshaft and suspend with a wire so there are no sharp

bends in any of the joints. Turn the right side shaft 90 degrees towards the front of the vehicle so it will not be a hindrance.

NOTE: When removing the shaft, use a prybar. Do not pull on the driveshaft; doing so will damage the inboard joint. Do not insert the prybar so deep as to damage the oil seal.

11. Remove the clutch oil line bracket bolt and remove the release cylinder. Suspend cylinder out of the way leaving the oil lines connected.

12. On AWD models, remove the front exhaust pipe and transfer assembly.

13. Remove the center support member.

14. Remove the bellhousing cover. Support the transaxle using a transmission jack.

15. Remove the transaxle mount bolt.

16. Remove the transaxle assembly lower part coupling bolts.

17. Slide the transaxle assembly away from the engine and remove from the vehicle.

To install:

18. Position the transaxle assembly against the engine. Install the transaxle assembly lower part coupling bolts.

19. Install the transaxle mount bolt and tighten nut to 51 ft. lbs. (70 Nm).

20. On 1.8L engine, install the center support member.

21. Remove the transaxle jack. Install the bellhousing cover.

22. Install the clutch oil line bracket bolt and release cylinder.

23. Install the front driveshafts so the inboard joint part of the shaft is straight in relation to the transaxle. Care must be taken to ensure that the oil seal lip part of the transaxle is not damaged by the serrated part of the driveshaft.

24. Connect the tie rod end from the steering knuckle. Disconnect the stabilizer bar.

25. Install the right side under cover. Install the starter motor.

26. Connect the tie rod ends to the steering knuckle and secure using new cotter pin.

27. Reconnect the speedometer cable, backup switch connector and the control cable connector.

28. Refill the transaxle assembly with Hypoid gear oil or equivalent, GL-4 or higher. Install the air cleaner assembly.

29. Connect the negative battery cable and check the transaxle and transfer case for proper operation.

Make sure the reverse lights come ON when in reverse.

Laser and Talon

1. Remove the battery.

2. Remove the auto-cruise actuator and bracket underhood, on the passenger side inner fender wall.

3. Drain the transaxle and transfer case.

4. Remove the air intake hose.

5. Remove the cotter pin securing the select and shift cables and remove the cable ends from the transaxle.

6. Remove the connection for the clutch release cylinder and without disconnecting the hydraulic line, secure aside.

7. Disconnect the backup light switch and the speedometer cable.

8. Disconnect the starter electrical connections and remove the starter motor.

9. Remove the transaxle mount bracket.

10. Raise the vehicle and support safely. Remove the undercover.

11. Remove the cotter pin and disconnect the tie rod end from the steering knuckle.

12. Remove the self-locking nut and remove the lower arm ball joint.

13. Remove the halfshafts by inserting a prybar between the transaxle case and the driveshaft and prying the shaft from the transaxle. Do not pull on the driveshaft. Doing so damages the inboard joint. Use the prybar. Do not insert the prybar so far the oil seal in the case is damaged. On AWD, remove the right side shaft as just described. The left side shaft can be removed by tapping the axle case with a plastic hammer and removing the shaft with the hub and knuckle as an assembly. Don't tap on the center bearing or it will be damaged. Tie the shafts aside. Note the circle clip on the end of the inboard shafts. These should not be reused.

14. On AWD vehicle, disconnect the front exhaust pipe.

15. On AWD vehicle, remove the transfer case by removing the attaching bolts, moving the transfer case to the left and lowering the front side. Remove it from the rear driveshaft. Be careful of the oil seal. Do not allow the prop shaft to hang; tie it up. Cover the transfer case openings to keep out dirt.

16. Remove the underpan from the transaxle bellhousing. On AWD, also remove the crossmember and the triangular gusset.

17. Remove the transaxle lower coupling bolt. It is just above the half-

shaft opening on 2WD or transfer case opening on AWD.

18. Remove the transaxle assembly. On turbocharged vehicle, take care to prevent damaging the lower radiator hose with the transaxle housing. Wind tape around the lower hose and put tape on the transaxle housing. Support the transaxle assembly using the proper jack, move the transaxle to the right and lower it.

To install:

19. Install the transaxle to the engine and install the mounting bolts.

20. Install the transaxle lower coupling bolt.

21. Install the underpan, crossmember and the triangular gusset.

22. Install the transfer case on AWD vehicles and connect the exhaust pipe.

23. When installing the halfshafts, use new circlips on the axle ends. Take care to get the inboard joint parts straight, not bent relative to the axle. Care must be taken to ensure that the oil seal lip of the transaxle is not damaged by the serrated part of the driveshaft.

24. Connect the tie rod and ball joint to the steering knuckle.

25. Install the transaxle mount bracket.

26. Install the starter motor.

27. Connect the backup light switch and the speedometer cable.

28. Install the clutch release cylinder.

29. Connect the select and shift cables and install new cotter pins.

30. Install the air intake hose.

31. Install the auto-cruise actuator and bracket underhood, on the passenger side inner fender wall.

32. Install the battery.

33. Make sure the vehicle is level when refilling the transaxle. Use Hypoid gear oil or equivalent, GL-4 or higher.

34. Connect the negative battery cable and check the transaxle and transfer case for proper operation. Make sure the reverse lights come on when in reverse.

Stealth

1. Remove the battery and battery tray. Raise the vehicle and support safely. Drain the transaxle oil and the oil from the transfer case.

2. If equipped with AWD, disconnect the exhaust pipe. Remove the mounting bolts and lower the transfer case from the vehicle.

3. Remove the left side splash shield and engine under cover.

4. Remove the air cleaner assembly and all adjoining duct work.

5. Disconnect the shifter control cables and speedometer connector.

6. Remove the clutch release cylinder.

7. Disconnect the reverse light switch.

8. Support the weight of the transaxle and remove the transaxle mount through bolt. Remove the access plug, remove the bolts for the bracket and remove the brackets.

9. Disconnect the transaxle ground cable.

10. Disconnect the tie rod end and ball joint from the steering knuckle.

11. Remove the right frame member.

12. Remove the starter motor.

13. Remove the halfshafts by inserting a prybar between the transaxle case and the driveshaft and prying the shaft from the transaxle. Do not pull on the driveshaft. Doing so damages the inboard joint. Use the prybar. Do not insert the prybar so far the oil seal in the case is damaged. On AWD, remove the right side shaft as just described. The left side shaft can be removed by tapping with a plastic hammer. Remove the shaft with the hub and knuckle as an assembly. Don't tap on the center bearing or it will be damaged. Tie the shafts aside. Note the circle clip on the end of the inboard shafts. These should not be reused.

14. Remove the transaxle brackets.

15. Remove the transaxle assembly. On turbocharged vehicles, take care to prevent damaging the lower radiator hose with the transaxle housing. Wind tape around the lower hose and put tape on the transaxle housing. Support the transaxle assembly using the proper jack, move the transaxle away from the engine and lower it.

   To install:

16. Install the transaxle to the engine and install the mounting bolts.

17. When installing the halfshafts, use new circlips on the axle ends. Take care to get the inboard joint parts straight, not bent relative to the axle. Care must be taken to ensure that the oil seal lip of the transaxle is not damaged by the serrated part of the driveshaft.

18. Install the starter motor and cover.

19. Install the right side frame member.

20. Install the ball joint and tie rod to the steering knuckle.

21. Connect the transaxle ground cable.

22. Install the side mount brackets and install the access plug.

23. Connect the reverse light switch.

24. Install the clutch release cylinder.

25. Connect the shifter control cables and speedometer connector.

26. Install the transfer case and related items on AWD vehicles.

27. Install the air cleaner assembly and all adjoining duct work.

28. Install the left side splash shield.

29. Install the battery tray and battery.

30. Make sure the vehicle is level when refilling the transaxle. Use Hypoid gear oil or equivalent, GL-4 or higher.

31. Connect the negative battery cable and check the transaxle and transfer case for proper operation. Make sure the reverse lamps come ON when in reverse.

LINKAGE ADJUSTMENT

There are 2 cables, the select cable and the shift cable.

1. On the transaxle, put select lever in **N** and move the transaxle shift lever to put it in **4th** gear. Depress the clutch, if necessary, to shift.

2. Move the shift lever in the vehicle to the **4th** gear position until it contacts the stop.

3. Turn the adjuster turn buckle so the shift cable eye aligns with the eye in the gear shift lever. When installing the cable eye, make sure the flange side of the plastic bushing at the shift cable end is on the cotter pin side.

4. The cables should be adjusted so the clearance between the shift lever and the 2 stoppers are equal when the shift lever is moved to 3rd and 4th gear. Move the shift lever to each position and check that the shifting is smooth.

CLUTCH

Clutch Assembly

REMOVAL AND INSTALLATION

1. Disconnect the negative battery cable. Raise and safely support the vehicle.

2. Remove the transaxle assembly from the vehicle.

3. Remove the pressure plate attaching bolts. If the pressure plate is to be reused, loosen the bolts in succession, 1 or 2 turns at a time to prevent warping the the cover flange.

4. Remove the pressure plate release bearing assembly and the clutch disc. Do not use solvent to clean the bearing.

5. Inspect the condition of the clutch components and replace any worn parts.

   To install:

6. Inspect the flywheel for heat damage or cracks. Resurface or replace the flywheel as required, using new bolts.

7. Using the proper alignment tool, install the clutch disc to the flywheel. Install the pressure plate assembly and tighten the pressure plate bolts evenly to 14–16 ft. lbs. (19–22 Nm). Remove the alignment tool.

8. Apply a very light coat of high temperature grease to the clutch fork at the ball pivot and where the fork contacts the bearing. Also a little bit of grease can be applied to end of the release cylinder's pushrod and to the pushrod hole on the fork. Apply a light coat of grease on the transaxle input shaft splines.

9. Install a new clutch release bearing. Pack its inner surface with high temperature grease.

10. Install the transaxle assembly and check for proper clutch operation.

PEDAL HEIGHT/FREE-PLAY ADJUSTMENT

1. Measure the clutch pedal height from the face of the pedal pad to the firewall. The desired distances are as follows:

   a. Summit — 6.61–6.8 in. (168–171mm)

   b. Laser and Talon — 6.93–7.17 in. (176–182mm)

   c. Stealth with FWD — 6.93–7.17 in. (176–182mm)

   d. Stealth with AWD — 7.2–7.4 in. (183–188mm)

   e. Summit Wagon — 7.68–7.87 in. (195–200mm)

2. Measure the clutch pedal clevis pin play at the face of the pedal pad. The standard values are as follows:

   a. Summit — 0.04–0.12 in. (1–3mm)

   b. Laser and Talon — 0.04–0.12 in. (1–3mm)

   c. Stealth with FWD — 0.24–0.51 in. (6–13mm)

   d. Stealth with AWD — 0.49–0.79 in. (12–20mm)

   e. Summit Wagon — 0.04–0.12 in. (1–3mm)

3. If the clutch pedal height or clevis pin play are not within the standard values, adjust as follows:

a. For vehicles without cruise control, turn and adjust the bolt so the pedal height is the standard value, then tighten the locknut.

b. Vehicles with auto-cruise control system, disconnect the clutch switch connector and turn the switch to obtain the standard clutch pedal height. Then, lock with the locknut.

c. Turn the pushrod to adjust the clutch pedal clevis pin play to agree with the standard value and secure the pushrod with the locknut.

NOTE: When adjusting the clutch pedal height or the clutch pedal clevis pin play, be careful not to push the pushrod toward the master cylinder.

d. Check that when the clutch pedal is depressed all the way, the interlock switch switches over from ON to OFF.

Clutch Cable

ADJUSTMENT

To adjust the clutch cable, turn the adjusting wheel at the firewall to obtain the proper free-play of about 1 inch.

REMOVAL AND INSTALLATION

1. Disconnect the negative battery cable.
2. Remove the cable retaining clamps.
3. Remove the cotter pin from the clutch actuating arm at the transaxle and disconnect the cable.
4. Rotate the adjusting wheel counterclockwise to loosen the cable. Disconnect the cable at the pedal and remove the cable from the vehicle.
5. The installation is the reverse of the removal procedure.
6. Lubricate all pivot points. Adjust the cable to achieve proper free-play.

Clutch Master Cylinder

REMOVAL AND INSTALLATION

1. Disconnect the negative battery cable.
2. Remove necessary underhood components in order to gain access to the clutch master cylinder.

3. Loosen the line at the cylinder and allow the fluid to drain. Use care; brake fluid damages paint.
4. On Summit, Summit Wagon, Laser, Talon and FWD Stealth, remove the clevis pin retainer at the clutch pedal and remove the washer and clevis pin. AWD Stealth has a clutch pedal booster which directly activates the master cylinder.
5. Remove the 2 nuts and pull the cylinder from the firewall. A seal should be between the mounting flange and firewall. This seal should be replaced.
6. The installation is the reverse of the removal procedure.
7. Lubricate all pivot points with grease.
8. Bleed the system at the slave cylinder using DOT 3 brake fluid and check the adjustment of the clutch pedal.

Clutch Release Cylinder

REMOVAL AND INSTALLATION

1. Disconnect the negative battery cable. Remove necessary underhood components in order to gain access to the clutch release cylinder.
2. Remove the hydraulic line and allow the system to drain.
3. Remove the bolts and pull the cylinder from the transaxle housing. On some 1.5L engines, instead of a pushrod bearing against the clutch arm, a clevis pin and yoke is used. Simply remove the circlip, pull out the clevis pin and remove the cylinder.
4. The installation is the reverse of the removal procedure.
5. Lubricate all pivot points with grease.
6. Bleed the system using DOT 3 brake fluid.

Hydraulic Clutch System Bleeding

1. Fill the reservoir with brake fluid.
2. Loosen the bleed screw, have the clutch pedal pressed to the floor.
3. Tighten the bleed screw and release the clutch pedal.
4. Repeat the procedure until the fluid is free of air bubbles.

NOTE: It is suggested to attach a hose to the bleeder and place the other end into a container at least ½ full of brake fluid during

the bleeding operation. Do not allow the reservoir to run out of fluid during bleeding.

AUTOMATIC TRANSAXLE

Transaxle Assembly

NOTE: If the vehicle is going to be rolled while the halfshafts are out of the vehicle, obtain 2 outer CV-joints or proper equivalent tools and install to the hubs. If the vehicle is rolled without the proper torque applied to the front wheel bearings, the bearings will no longer be usable.

REMOVAL AND INSTALLATION

Summit

1. Disconnect the negative battery cable.
2. Remove the battery and battery tray.
3. Remove the air pipe and air hose.
4. Raise the vehicle and support safely.
5. Drain the transaxle oil.
6. If equipped with 1.6L engine, remove the tension rod.
7. Disconnect the control cable and cooler lines.
8. Disconnect the throttle control cable on 3-speed transaxle.
9. Disconnect the shift control solenoid valve connector on 4 speed transaxle.
10. Disconnect the inhibitor switch and kickdown servo switch on 4 speed transaxle.
11. Disconnect the pulse generator and oil temperature sensor on 4 speed transaxle.
12. Disconnect the speedometer cable and remove the starter.
13. Remove the transaxle mounting bolts and bracket.
14. Remove the under guard pan.
15. Disconnect the steering tie rod end and the ball joint from the steering arm.
16. Remove the halfshafts at the inboard side from the transaxle. Tie the joint assembly aside.
17. Remove the bellhousing cover and remove the driveplate bolts.
18. Remove the transaxle assembly lower connecting bolt, located just over the halfshaft opening.

19. Properly support the transaxle assembly and lower it moving it to the right for clearance.

To install:

20. After the torque converter has been mounted on the transaxle, install the transaxle assembly on the engine. Tighten the driveplate bolts to 34–38 ft. lbs. (46–53 Nm). Install the bellhousing cover.

21. Replace the circlips and install the halfshafts to the transaxle.

22. Install the tie rods and ball joint to the steering arm.

23. Install the underguard and the mounting brackets.

24. Install the starter.

25. Connect the speedometer cable.

26. Connect the control cables, oil cooler lines and electrical connections.

27. Install the tension rod.

28. Install the air pipe and hose, battery tray and battery.

29. Refill with Dexron® II, Mopar ATF Plus type 7176 or equivalent, automatic transaxle fluid.

30. Start the engine and allow to idle for 2 minutes. Apply parking brake and move selector through each gear position, ending in **N**. Recheck fluid level and add if necessary. Fluid level should be between the marks in the **HOT** range.

Summit Wagon

1. Disconnect negative battery cable.

2. Remove the air cleaner assembly.

3. Disconnect the transaxle control lever. Disconnect and plug the oil cooler lines.

4. Disconnect the pulse generator connector, oil temperature connector, kickdown servo switch connector, inhibitor switch connector and solenoid valve connection.

5. Disconnect the speedometer cable connection. Remove the oil level dipstick and tube.

6. Install holding fixture to the top of the engine to support engine weight.

7. Remove the top transaxle upper coupling bolts. Raise and safely support the vehicle.

8. Remove the starter motor leaving wire harness attached.

9. Remove the right side under cover. Drain the transaxle fluid.

10. Disconnect the tie rod ends, stabilizer bar and lower ball joints.

11. If equipped with AWD, it will be necessary to remove the right driveshaft from the vehicle.

12. Except AWD vehicles, remove the driveshafts from the transfer

case, insert a prybar between the driveshaft and the transaxle case and pry the shaft from the transaxle housing. Swing the shafts out of the way keeping the joints straight and suspend using wire. Turn the right shaft 90 degrees toward the front of the vehicle so it will not be a hindrance.

NOTE: Do not pull on the shaft during removal from the transaxle; doing so will damage the inboard joint. Do not insert the prybar so deep as to damage the oil seal.

13. Remove the lower bellhousing cover. Scribe a mark on the driveplate and transaxle converter face using chalk. Remove the driveplate connecting bolts while turning the crankshaft.

14. Support the transaxle using a transmission jack. Remove the center support.

15. Remove the transaxle mount bolt and bracket.

16. If equipped with AWD, disconnect the front exhaust pipe and remove the transfer assembly.

17. Remove the lower transaxle case coupling bolts, press the torque converter towards the transfer case to prevent separation during removal and lower the transfer case from the vehicle.

To install:

18. Install the transaxle into the vehicle and secure using the lower case coupling bolts.

19. Install the transaxle mount bolt and bracket, torque through bolt nut to 51 ft. lbs. (70 Nm).

20. Align the scribe marks on the converter and the driveplate. Install the driveplate connecting bolts torquing to 33–38 ft. lbs. (46–53 Nm).

21. Install the transfer assembly and the center crossmember. Remove the transmission jack.

22. Install the center exhaust pipe.

23. Install the drive axles into the transfer case taking care not to damage the oil seal lip part of the transaxle with the serrated part of the driveshaft.

24. Connect the tie rod ends, stabilizer bar and lower ball joints.

25. Install the right side under cover.

26. Lower the vehicle. Install the upper transaxle coupling bolts.

27. Connect the speedometer cable and the electrical harness connectors disconnected during the removal procedure.

28. Install the starter motor torquing the retainer bolts to 35 ft. lbs. (49 Nm).

29. Connect the transaxle cooler hoses and the connections for the manual controls.

30. Install the air cleaner assembly and the oil level dipstick and tube.

31. Refill with Dexron® II, Mopar ATF Plus type 7176 or equivalent, automatic transaxle fluid.

32. Start the engine and allow to idle for 2 minutes. Apply parking brake and move selector through each gear position, ending in **N**. Recheck fluid level and add if necessary. Fluid level should be between the marks in the **HOT** range. Check operation of all gauges and meters.

Laser and Talon

1. Remove the battery and battery tray.

2. Drain the transaxle fluid.

3. Remove the air cleaner assembly, intercooler and air hose.

4. Remove the adjusting nut and disconnect the shift cable.

5. Disconnect and tag the electrical connectors for the solenoid, neutral safety switch (inhibitor switch), the pulse generator kickdown servo switch and oil temperature sensor.

6. Disconnect the speedometer cable and oil cooler lines.

7. Disconnect the wires to the starter motor and remove the starter.

8. Remove the upper transaxle to engine bolts.

9. Support the transaxle and remove the transaxle mounting bracket.

10. Raise the vehicle and support safely. Remove the sheetmetal under guard.

11. Remove the tie rod ends and the ball joints from the steering knuckle.

12. Remove the halfshafts by inserting a prybar between the transaxle case and the driveshaft and prying the shaft from the transaxle. Do not pull on the driveshaft. Doing so damages the inboard joint. Use the prybar. Do not insert the prybar so far the oil seal in the case is damaged. Tie the halfshafts aside.

13. On AWD, disconnect the exhaust pipe, remove the frame pieces, and remove the transfer case.

14. Remove the lower bellhousing cover and remove the special bolts holding the flexplate to the torque converter. To remove, turn the engine crankshaft with a box wrench and bring the bolts into position appropriate for removal, 1 at a time. After removing the bolts, push the torque converter toward the transaxle so it doesn't stay on the engine allowing oil to pour out the converter

hub or cause damage to the converter.

15. Remove the lower transaxle to engine bolts and remove the transaxle assembly.

To install:

16. After the torque converter has been mounted on the transaxle, install the transaxle assembly on the engine. Tighten the driveplate bolts to 34–38 ft. lbs. (46–53 Nm). Install the bellhousing cover.

17. On AWD, install the transfer case and frame pieces. Connect the exhaust pipe using a new gasket.

18. Replace the circlips and install the halfshafts to the transaxle.

19. Install the tie rods and ball joint to the steering arm.

20. Install the transaxle mounting bracket.

21. Install the under guard.

22. Install the starter.

23. Connect the speedometer cable and oil cooler lines.

24. Connect the solenoid, neutral safety switch (inhibitor switch), the pulse generator kickdown servo switch and oil temperature sensor.

25. Install the shift control cable.

26. Install the air hose, intercooler and air cleaner assembly.

27. If equipped with auto-cruise, install the control actuator and bracket.

28. Refill with Dexron® II, Mopar ATF Plus type 7176 or equivalent, automatic transaxle fluid.

29. Start the engine and allow to idle for 2 minutes. Apply parking brake and move selector through each gear position, ending in **N**. Recheck fluid level and add if necessary. Fluid level should be between the marks in the **HOT** range.

Stealth

1. Disarm the air bag, if equipped. Remove the battery, battery tray and washer tank.

2. Remove the air cleaner assembly and adjoining duct work.

3. Disconnect the shifter control cable.

4. Disconnect and plug the oil cooler hoses.

5. Disconnect the inhibitor switch, kickdown servo switch, pulse generator, oil temperature sensor, shift control solenoid valve, and ground cable.

6. Disconnect the speedometer cable.

7. Raise the vehicle and support safely. Remove the undercovers.

8. Support the weight of the transaxle and remove the mount bracket. Remove the upper bellhousing bolts.

9. Disconnect the tie rod end and ball joint from the steering knuckle.

10. Remove the right frame member.

11. Remove the starter.

12. Remove the halfshafts by inserting a prybar between the transaxle case and the driveshaft and prying the shaft from the transaxle. Do not pull on the driveshaft. Doing so damages the inboard joint. Use the prybar. Do not insert the prybar so far the oil seal in the case is damaged. Tie the halfshafts aside.

13. Remove the remaining mounting brackets.

14. Remove the bellhousing cover plate.

15. Remove the special bolts holding the flexplate to the torque converter.

16. After removing the bolts, push the torque converter toward the transaxle so it doesn't stay on the engine side and allow oil to pour out the converter hub.

17. Remove the lower transaxle to engine bolts and remove the transaxle assembly.

To install:

18. After the torque converter has been mounted on the transaxle, install the transaxle assembly on the engine. Tighten the driveplate bolts to 34–38 ft. lbs. (46–53 Nm). Install the bellhousing cover.

19. Install the mounting brackets.

20. Replace the circlips and install the halfshafts to the transaxle.

21. Install the starter and frame member.

22. Install the tie rods and ball joint to the steering arm.

23. Install the upper bellhousing bolts.

24. Install the transaxle mounting bracket.

25. Install the undercovers.

26. Connect the speedometer cable.

27. Connect the inhibitor switch, kickdown servo switch, pulse generator, oil temperature sensor, shift control solenoid valve, and ground cable.

28. Connect the oil cooler hoses.

29. Connect the shifter control cable.

30. Install the air cleaner assembly and adjoining duct work.

31. Install the washer tank, battery tray and battery.

32. Refill with Dexron® II, Mopar ATF Plus type 7176 or equivalent, automatic transaxle fluid.

33. Start the engine and allow to idle for 2 minutes. Apply parking brake and move selector through each gear position, ending in **N**. Recheck fluid level and add if necessary. Fluid level should be between the marks in the **HOT** range.

SHIFTER CONTROL CABLE ADJUSTMENT

1. The shifter cable adjustment is done at the neutral safety switch (inhibitor switch). Locate the switch on the transaxle and note the alignment holes in the arm and the body of the switch. Place the selector lever in **N**. Place the manual lever of the transaxle in the **N** position.

2. Check alignment of the hole in the manual control lever to the hole in the inhibitor switch body. If the holes do not align, adjustment is required.

3. To adjust, loosen the nut on the cable end and pull the cable end by hand until the alignment holes match. Tighten the nut. Check that the transaxle shifts and conforms to the positions of the selector lever.

THROTTLE CONTROL CABLE ADJUSTMENT

Some vehicles do not use a throttle linkage. Instead, the throttle position sensor provides an electric signal to the transaxle, so no linkage adjustment is required.

1. Check that the throttle lever is in the curb idle position, with the engine **OFF** but at normal operating temperature.

2. At the lower cable bracket, raise the cone shaped cover to uncover a small fitting on the cable. By loosening the locknut and adjuster nut, make the distance between the fitting on the cable and the lower collar is 0.020–0.060 in.

3. With the throttle in the wide open position, check that the cable does not bind.

TRANSFER CASE

Transfer Case Assembly

REMOVAL AND INSTALLATION

Laser, Talon and Stealth

1. Disconnect the battery negative cable.

2. Raise the vehicle and support safely. Drain the transfer oil.

3. On Stealth, remove necessary front bumper components.

4. Disconnect the front exhaust pipe.

5. Unbolt the transfer case assembly and remove by sliding it off the rear driveshaft. Be careful not to damage the oil seal in the transfer case output housing. Do not let the rear driveshaft hang; suspend it from a frame piece. Cover the opening in the transaxle and transfer case to keep oil from dripping and to keep dirt out.

To install:

6. Lubricate the driveshaft sleeve yoke and oil seal lip on the transfer extension housing. Install the transfer case assembly to the transaxle. Use care when installing the rear driveshaft to the transfer case output shaft.

7. Tighten the transfer case to transaxle bolts to 40–43 ft. lbs. (55–60 Nm) on Laser and Talon with manual transaxle; 43–58 ft. lbs. (60–80 Nm) on Laser and Talon with automatic transaxle or 64 ft. lbs. (88 Nm) on Stealth.

8. Install the exhaust pipe using a new gasket. Install removed bumper components.

9. Refill the transfer case and check oil levels in transaxle and transfer case.

Summit Wagon

1. Disconnect the battery negative cable.

2. Raise the vehicle and support safely. Drain the oil from the transfer assembly.

3. Disconnect the front exhaust pipe.

4. Make mating marks on the differential companion flange and the flange yoke. Remove the propeller shaft.

NOTE: Remove the propeller shaft in a straight and level manner so as to ensure that the boot is not damaged through pinching. Damage can be avoided if a piece of cloth or similar material is inserted into the boot. Cover the opening of the transfer assembly to prevent dirt from entering the transfer assembly.

5. Remove the transfer assembly mounting bolts and the transfer assembly from the vehicle.

To install:

6. Position the transfer assembly into the vehicle and secure using the mounting bolts, tightened to 51 ft. lbs. (70 Nm).

7. Align the mating marks and install propeller shaft.

8. Attach the front exhaust pipe using new gasket.

9. Reconnect the negative battery and lower the vehicle. Refill the transfer case and check oil levels in transaxle and transfer case.

DRIVE AXLE

Halfshaft

REMOVAL AND INSTALLATION

NOTE: If the vehicle is going to be rolled while the halfshafts are out of the vehicle, obtain 2 outer CV-joints or proper equivalent tools and install to the hubs. If the vehicle is rolled without the proper torque applied to the front wheel bearings, the bearings will no longer be usable.

1. Disconnect the negative battery cable.

2. Remove the cotter pin, halfshaft nut and washer.

3. Raise the vehicle and support safely. Remove the lower ball joint and the tie rod end from the steering knuckle.

4. On vehicles with an inner shaft, remove the center support bearing bracket bolts and washers.

5. On vehicles with an inner shaft, remove the halfshaft by setting up a puller on the outside wheel hub and pushing the halfshaft from the front hub. Then tap the shaft union at the joint case with a plastic hammer to remove the halfshaft shaft and inner shaft from the transaxle.

6. On vehicles without an inner shaft, remove the halfshaft by setting up a puller on the outside wheel hub and pushing the halfshaft from the front hub. After pressing the outer shaft, insert a prybar between the transaxle case and the halfshaft and pry the shaft from the transaxle. Do not pull on the shaft; doing so damages the inboard joint. Do not insert the prybar too far or the oil seal in the case may be damaged.

To install:

7. Inspect the halfshaft boot for damage or deterioration. Check the ball joints and splines for wear.

8. Replace the circlips on the ends of the halfshafts.

9. Insert the halfshaft into the transaxle. Make sure it is fully seated.

10. Pull the strut assembly out and install the other end to the hub.

11. Install the center bearing bracket bolts and tighten to 33 ft. lbs. (45 Nm).

12. Install the washer so the chamfered edge faces outward. Install the nut and tighten temporarily.

13. Install the tie rod end and ball joint.

14. Install the wheel and lower the vehicle to the floor. Tighten the axle nut with the brakes applied. Tighten the nut to a maximum torque of 188 ft. lbs. (260 Nm). Install the cotter pin and bend to secure.

CV-Boot

DESCRIPTION

The vehicles use several different types of joints. Engine size, transaxle type, whether the joint is an inboard or outboard joint, even which side of the vehicle is being serviced could make a difference in joint type. Be sure to properly identify the joint before attempting joint or boot replacement. Look for identification numbers at the large end of the boots and/or on the end of the metal retainer bands.

The 4 types of joints used are the Birfield Joint, (B.J.), the Tripod Joint (T.J.), the Double Off-set Joint (D.O.J.) and the Rzeppa Joint (R.J.). In addition, some left side shafts will have a round dynamic damper installed on the shaft. Special grease is generally used with these joints and is often supplied with the replacement joint and/or boot. Do not use regular chassis grease.

In most cases, a specification is called out for the distance between the large and small boot bands. This is so the boot will not be installed either too loose or too tight, which could cause early wear and cracking, allowing the grease to get out and water and dirt in, leading to early joint failure.

REMOVAL AND INSTALLATION

Except Double Off-Set Joint

Although joint types vary, the basic procedures are the same, with the exception of the Double Offset Joint. The following is a general procedure which should apply to most applications.

1. Disconnect the negative battery cable. Remove the halfshaft.

2. Remove the snapring next to the tripod joint spider assembly from the halfshaft with snapring pliers and remove the spider assembly from the shaft. Do not disassemble the spider and use care in handling.

3. Side cutter pliers can be used to cut the metal retaining bands.

4. If the boot is be reused, wrap vinyl tape around the spline part of the shaft so the boot will not be damaged when removed. Remove the dynamic damper, if used, and boots from the shaft.

To install:

5. Double check that the correct replacement parts are being installed. Wrap vinyl tape around the splines to protect the boot and install the boots and damper, if used, in the correct order.

6. Fill the inside of the boot with the specified grease. Often the grease supplied in the replacement parts kit is meant to be divided in half, with half being used to lubricate the joint and half being used inside the boot. Keep grease off the rubber part of the dynamic damper (if used).

7. Secure the boot bands with the halfshaft in a horizontal position. Make sure Distance A is set properly according to the chart. T.J. joints on Stealth should have Distance A set to 3.23–3.47 in. (82–88mm). T.J. joints on Summit Wagon should have Distance A set to 3.11–3.35 in. (79–85mm) for 1.8L engine or 3.03–3.27 in. (77–83mm) for 2.4L engines.

8. Install the halfshaft.

Double Off-Set Joint

1. Remove the halfshaft. The Double Off-set Joint (D.O.J.) is bigger than other joints and in these applications, is only used as an inboard joint.

2. Side cutter pliers can be used to cut the metal retaining bands.

3. Locate and remove the large circlip at the base of the joint. Remove the outer race (the body of the joint).

4. Matchmark the shaft, D.O.J. inner race and cage. Remove the joint balls and the small snapring from the shaft. With a brass drift pin, tap lightly and evenly around the inner race to remove the race and the inner cage from the shaft.

5. If the boot is to be reused, wipe the grease from the splines and wrap the splines in vinyl tape before sliding the boot from the shaft.

To install:

6. Be sure to tape the shaft splines before installing the boots. Fill the inside of the boot with the specified grease. Often the grease supplied in the replacement parts kit is meant to be divided in half, with half being used to lubricate the joint and half being used inside the boot.

7. Install the cage onto the halfshaft so the small diameter side of the cage is installed first. Align the matchmarks made at disassembly on the inner race and shaft. With a brass drift pin, tap lightly and evenly around the inner race to install the

race until it comes into contact with the rib of the shaft. Apply the specified grease to the inner race and cage and fit them together aligning the matchmarks. Insert the balls into the cage.

8. Install the outer race (the body of the joint) after filling with the specified grease. The outer race should be filled with this grease.

9. Tighten the boot bands securely. Make sure Distance A is set properly according to the chart.

10. Install the halfshaft.

Driveshaft and U-Joints

REMOVAL AND INSTALLATION

Laser, Talon and Stealth With AWD

1. Disconnect the negative battery cable. Raise the vehicle and support safely.

2. The rear driveshaft is a 3-piece unit, with a front, center and rear propeller shaft. Remove the nuts and insulators from the center support bearing. Work carefully. There will be a number of spacers which will differ from vehicle to vehicle. Check the number of spacers and note their locations for reference during reassembly.

DISTANCE A—SUMMIT		
TRIPOD JOINTS		
1.5L, 1.6L w/A.T.,	LH Shaft—3.15 in. ±.12 in. (80mm±3mm)	
	RH Shaft—3.35 in. ±.12 in. (85mm±3mm)	
1.6L, w/M.T.,	—3.35 in. ±.12 in. (80mm±3mm)	
DOUBLE OFFSET JOINTS		
1.6L Non Turbo	—2.92 in. ±.12 in. (75mm±3mm)	
1.6L Turbo	—3.15 in. ±.12 in. (80mm±3mm)	
DISTANCE A—LASER/TALON		
1.8L from 5-89	LH Shaft—2.95 in. ±.12 in. (75mm±3mm)	
1.8L from 5-89	RH Shaft—3.35 in. ±.12 in. (85mm±3mm)	
2.0L from 5-89	2WD-LH Shaft—3.15 in. ±.12 in. (80mm±3mm)	
2.0L Turbo	2WD LH Shaft—3.15 in. ±.12 in. (80mm±3mm)	
2.0L	2WD RH Shaft—3.15 in. ±.12 in. (80mm±3mm)	
2.0L Turbo	2WD RH Shaft—3.15 in. ±.12 in. (80mm±3mm)	
2.0L	4WD LH Shaft—3.35 in. ±.12 in. (85mm±3mm)	
2.0L	4WD RH Shaft—3.35 in. ±.12 in. (85mm±3mm)	

84701107

CV-joint measurements — installed length

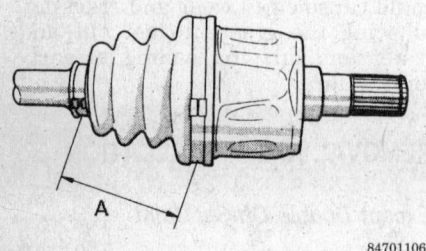

84701106

CV-joint measured distance

3. Matchmark the rear differential companion flange and the rear driveshaft flange yoke. Remove the companion shaft bolts and remove the driveshaft, keeping it as straight as possible so as to ensure that the boot is not damaged or pinched. Use care to keep from damaging the oil seal in the output housing of the transfer case.

NOTE: Damage to the boot can be avoided and work will be easier if a piece of cloth or similar material is inserted in the boot.

4. Do not lower the rear of the vehicle or oil will flow from the transfer case. Cover the opening to keep dirt out.

To install:

5. Install the driveshaft to the vehicle and align the matchmarks at the rear yoke. Install the bolts and torque to 22–25 ft. lbs. (30–35 Nm) on Laser and Talon or 36–43 ft. lbs. (50–60 Nm) on Stealth.

6. Install the center support bearing with all spacers in place. Torque the retaining nuts to 22–25 ft. lbs. (30–35 Nm).

7. Check the fluid levels in the transfer case and rear differential case.

Summit Wagon

1. Disconnect the battery negative cable.
2. Raise the vehicle and support safely. Drain the oil from the transfer assembly.
3. Disconnect the front exhaust pipe.
4. Make mating marks on the differential companion flange and the flange yoke. Remove the locking nut from the center support and remove the propeller shaft. Make note of washers and spacers used so they can be reinstalled in their original location.

NOTE: Remove the propeller shaft in a straight and level manner so as to ensure that the boot is not damaged through pinching. Damage can be avoided if a piece of cloth or similar material is inserted into the boot. Cover the opening of the transfer assembly to prevent dirt from entering the transfer assembly.

5. Installation is the reverse of the removal procedure. Tighten the rear flange bolts and nuts to 22–25 ft. lbs. (30–35 Nm), the locking nuts on the center support to 22 ft. lbs. (30 Nm), refill the transfer assembly and check the fluid level in the transaxle assembly.

Rear Axle Shaft, Bearing and Seal

REMOVAL AND INSTALLATION

Laser, Talon and Stealth With AWD

1. Disconnect the negative battery cable. Raise the vehicle and support safely.
2. Remove the bolts that attach the rear halfshaft to the companion flange.
3. Use a prybar to pry the inner shaft out of the differential case. Don't insert the prybar too far or the seal could be damage.
4. Remove the rear halfshaft from the vehicle.
5. If equipped with ABS, remove the rear wheel speed sensor.
6. Remove the caliper, pads and brake rotor.
7. Hold the axle shaft stationary and remove the axle shaft self-locking nut and washer.
8. Using a slide hammer, separate the axle shaft from the companion flange and remove.
9. Use a vice and gear puller tool to disassemble the axle shaft and companion flange assemblies.

To install:

10. Assemble the axle shaft and companion shaft assemblies using new parts as required.
11. Install the axle shaft to the housing and slide the axle shaft over it. Install the washer and new self-locking nut. Hold the axle shaft stationary and torque the nut to 116–159 ft. lbs. (160–220 Nm) for Laser and Talon. Torque to 188–217 ft. lbs. (260–300 Nm) for Stealth.
12. Install the brake rotor, pads and caliper.
13. Install the ABS rear wheel speed sensor.
14. Replace the circlip and install the rear halfshaft to the differential case. Make sure it snaps in place. Torque the companion flange bolts to 40–47 ft. lbs. (55–65 Nm).
15. Check the fluid level in the rear differential.

Summit Wagon With AWD

1. Disconnect the negative battery cable. Raise the vehicle and support safely.
2. Remove the bolts that attach the rear halfshaft to the rear carrier.

3. Remove the cotter pin, driveshaft nut cover and nut from the rear driveshaft.

NOTE: Do not apply the vehicle weight to the wheel bearing while loosening the driveshaft nut or bearing damage may occur.

4. Separate the shaft from the hub using a puller. Remove the shaft from the flange and lift from the vehicle.
5. Installation is the reverse of the removal procedure. Torque the retainers on the rear carrier to 40–47 ft. lbs. (55–65 Nm) and the shaft end nut to 145–188 ft. lbs. (200–260 Nm).

Front Wheel Hub, Knuckle and Bearing

REMOVAL AND INSTALLATION

1. Disconnect the negative battery cable.
2. Remove the cotter pin, halfshaft nut and washer.
3. Raise the vehicle and support safely. If equipped with ABS, remove the front wheel speed sensor. Remove the ball joint and tie rod end from the steering knuckle.
4. Remove the caliper and brake pads and suspend with a wire.
5. On vehicles with an inner shaft, remove the center support bearing bracket bolts and washers. Remove the halfshaft by setting up a puller on the outside wheel hub and pushing the halfshaft from the front hub. Then tap the joint case with a plastic hammer to remove the halfshaft shaft and inner shaft from the transaxle.
6. On vehicles without an inner shaft, remove the halfshaft by setting up a puller on the outside wheel hub and pushing the halfshaft from the front hub. After pressing the outer shaft, insert a prybar between the transaxle case and the halfshaft and pry the shaft from the transaxle.
7. On Stealth with AWD, the front hub/bearing assembly can be serviced at this point as a unit. If the knuckle is being removed, proceed. All others models require knuckle removal for service.
8. Unbolt the lower end of the strut and remove the hub and steering knuckle assembly.
9. Set up a puller with the knuckle/hub in a vise and pull the hub from the knuckle. Do not use a hammer to accomplish this or the bearing will be damaged.

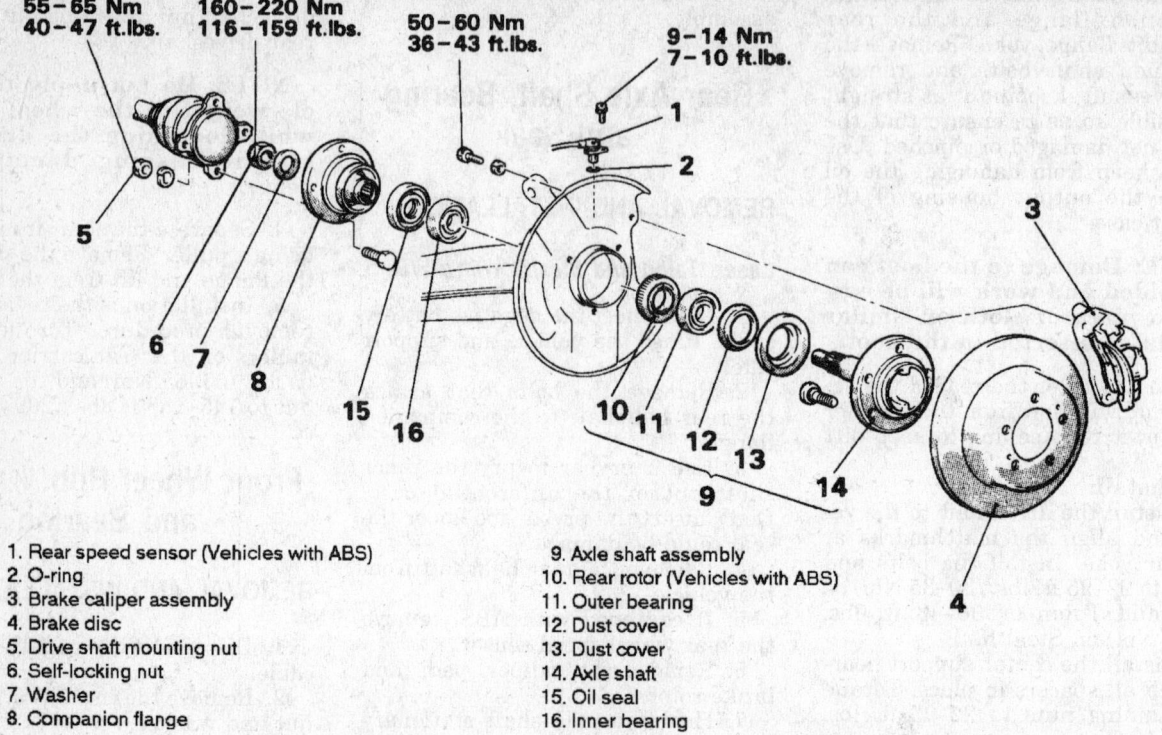

55–65 Nm
40–47 ft.lbs.

160–220 Nm
116–159 ft.lbs.

50–60 Nm
36–43 ft.lbs.

9–14 Nm
7–10 ft.lbs.

1. Rear speed sensor (Vehicles with ABS)
2. O-ring
3. Brake caliper assembly
4. Brake disc
5. Drive shaft mounting nut
6. Self-locking nut
7. Washer
8. Companion flange

9. Axle shaft assembly
10. Rear rotor (Vehicles with ABS)
11. Outer bearing
12. Dust cover
13. Dust cover
14. Axle shaft
15. Oil seal
16. Inner bearing

84701109

Rear axle shaft and hub assembly — Laser, Talon and Stealth

10. Once the hub and outer bearing inner race are removed with a puller, the bearing outer races can be removed by tapping out with a brass drift pin and a hammer.

To install:

11. Assemble the hub/knuckle assembly with pressing tools, using new parts as required.

12. Install the knuckle assembly to the vehicle and install the strut bolts.

13. On AWD Stealth, torque the front hub/bearing assembly nuts to 76 ft. lbs. (105 Nm).

14. Apply a thin coat of grease to the outside of the outer races and install into the hub with a bearing driver.

15. Apply multi-purpose grease to the bearings, inside surface of the hub and the lip of the grease seal. Place the outside bearing into the knuckle and install the seal with a driver.

16. The hub is assembled to the knuckle with a puller. Draw the parts together firmly to seat the bearings. Use a small torque wrench to check the bearing turning torque. It should be 16 inch lbs. or less for Laser, Talon and Stealth or 11 lbs. or less for Summit. Check that the bearings feel smooth when rotated.

17. Apply a thin coat of grease to the lip of the halfshaft side axle seal

and drive into place until it contacts the inner bearing outer race.

18. Replace the circlips on the ends of the halfshafts.

19. Insert the halfshaft into the transaxle. Make sure it is fully seated.

20. Pull the strut assembly out and install the other end to the hub.

21. Install the center bearing bracket bolts and tighten to 33 ft. lbs. (45 Nm).

22. Install the washer so the chamfered edge faces outward. Install the nut and tighten temporarily.

23. Install the tie rod end and ball joint.

24. Install the wheel and lower the vehicle to the floor. Tighten the axle nut with the brakes applied. Tighten the nut to a torque of 145–188 ft. lbs. (200–260 Nm). Install the cotter pin and bend to secure.

Pinion Seal

REMOVAL AND INSTALLATION

Front Differential

1. Disconnect the negative battery cable.
2. Remove the front halfshaft.

3. Using a prying tool, pry the seal from the case.

To install:

4. Apply a thin coat of multi-purpose grease to the seal lip and the seal contact surface.

5. Install the new seal with an appropriate driver.

6. Install the front halfshaft.

Rear Differential

1. Raise the vehicle and support safely.

2. Matchmark the rear propeller shaft and companion flange and remove the shaft. Don't let it hang from the transaxle. Tie it up to the underbody.

3. Hold the companion flange stationary and remove the large self-locking nut in the center of the companion flange.

4. Using a puller, remove the flange. Pry the old seal out.

To install:

5. Apply a thin coat of multi-purpose grease to the seal lip and the companion flange seal contacting surface. Install the new seal with an appropriate driver.

6. Install the companion flange. Install a new locknut and torque to 137 ft. lbs. (190 Nm) on Summit Wagon and 116–160 ft. lbs. (157–220

Nm) on the remaining models. The rotation torque of the drive pinion should be 10 inch lbs. for new bearings and 4 inch lbs. for used bearings.

7. Install the propeller shaft.

Differential Carrier

REMOVAL AND INSTALLATION

Summit Wagon With AWD

1. Raise the vehicle and support safely.

2. Drain the differential gear oil and remove the center exhaust pipe.

3. Remove the rear halfshafts from the carrier and support out of the way.

4. Matchmark the differential companion flange and flange yoke for reference during installation and disconnect the propeller shaft from the carrier. Support shaft out of the way leaving attached to the transfer assembly.

5. Support the rear carrier assembly using the appropriate equipment. Remove the carrier mounting bolts and lower carrier from the vehicle.

To install:

6. Raise the rear carrier into position and torque the side retaining bolts to 72–87 ft. lbs. (100–120 Nm). Tighten the retainer bolts through the rear support member to 69 ft. lbs. (95 Nm).

7. Install the propeller shaft, with matchmarks aligned, and the rear halfshafts to the carrier. Tighten the halfshaft flange nuts to 40–47 ft. lbs. (55–65 Nm).

8. Install the center exhaust pipe using new gasket.

9. With the vehicle level, fill the rear differential.

Laser, Talon and Stealth with AWD

1. Raise the vehicle and support safely.

2. Drain the differential gear oil and remove the center exhaust pipe.

3. Matchmark and remove the rear driveshaft.

4. Remove the rear halfshafts.

5. On Stealth, remove or disconnect the 4 wheel steering oil pump.

6. The large mounting bolts that hold the differential carrier support plate to the underbody may use self-locking nuts. Before removing them, support the rear axle assembly in the middle with a transaxle jack. Remove the nuts, then remove the support plate(s) and the square dynamic damper from the rear of the carrier.

7. Lower the differential carrier and remove from the vehicle.

To install:

8. Install the unit and all mounting brackets. Replace all locknuts.

9. Use new circlips on the inboard joints and install.

10. Install the rear driveshaft, matching up the marks made at disassembly.

11. With the vehicle level, fill the rear differential.

STEERING

Steering Wheel

NOTE: If equipped with an air bag, be sure to disarm it before starting repairs on the vehicle. Failure to do so could result in personal injury or death.

REMOVAL AND INSTALLATION

Summit, Summit Wagon, Laser and Talon

WITHOUT AIR BAG

1. Disconnect the negative battery cable.

2. Remove the horn pad and disconnect horn button connector.

3. Remove steering wheel retaining nut.

4. Matchmark the steering wheel to the shaft.

5. Use a steering wheel puller to remove the steering wheel. Do not hammer on steering wheel to remove it. The collapsible column mechanism may be damaged.

To install:

6. Align the matchmarks and install the steering wheel. Torque the retaining nut to 29 ft. lbs. (40 Nm).

7. Install the steering wheel attaching nut and torque to 33 ft. lbs. (45 Nm).

8. Reconnect the horn connector and install the horn pad.

Stealth

1. Disconnect the negative battery cable.

2. Remove the air bag module mounting nut from behind the steering wheel. Matchmark the steering wheel.

3. Disconnect the connector of the clockspring from the air bag module, press the air bag's lock towards the module to spread the lock open.

While holding lock in this position, use a small tipped prying tool to gently pry the connector from the module.

4. Store the air bag module in a clean, dry place with the pad cover facing up.

5. Remove the steering wheel retaining nut. Matchmark the steering wheel to the shaft. Use a steering wheel puller to remove the wheel. Do not use a hammer or the collapsible mechanism in the column could be damaged.

To install:

6. Confirm that the front wheels are in a straight-ahead position. Center the clockspring by aligning the **NEUTRAL** mark on the clockspring with the mating mark on the casing.

7. Line up and install the steering wheel. Torque the retaining nut to 29 ft. lbs. (40 Nm).

Steering Column

NOTE: If equipped with an air bag, be sure to disarm it before starting any repairs on the vehicle.

REMOVAL AND INSTALLATION

1. Disconnect the negative battery cable.

2. Remove the instrument panel undercover or knee protector.

3. Remove the trim clip, foot shower duct and lap shower duct.

4. Remove the steering wheel and air bag module as required. Remove the column upper and lower cover. Disconnect the key interlock cable if equipped.

5. Disconnect all connector to column-mounted items.

6. Remove the band from the steering joint cover. Remove the joint assembly and gear box connecting bolt.

7. Remove the screws that attach the rubber seal to the firewall.

8. Remove the lower and upper column mounting bolts.

9. Remove the steering column assembly.

To install:

10. Install the column so the splines are inserted around the rack input shaft. Install the pinch bolt.

11. Install the mounting bolts.

12. Install the rubber seal screws.

13. Connect the connectors and interlock cable.

14. Install the column covers.

15. Install the remaining interior pieces.

16. Connect the negative battery cable and check all column-mounted switches for proper operation.

Manual Steering Rack

ADJUSTMENT

1. Remove the rack and pinion assembly.

2. Mount the rack in a vise and with a small torque wrench and an adapter to connect to the input shaft, position the rack at its center. Tighten the rack support cover, the bottom plug, to 11 ft. lbs. In the neutral position, rotate the shaft clockwise 1 turn in 4–6 seconds. Return the rack support cover 30–60 degrees and adjust the total pinion torque to 5–11 inch lbs.

3. When adjusting, set to the higher side of the specification. Make sure there is no ratcheting or catching when operating the rack. If the rack cannot be adjusted to specification, check the rack support cover components or replace. After adjusting, lock the rack support cover with the locking nut.

REMOVAL AND INSTALLATION

Summit

1. Disconnect the battery negative cable. Raise the vehicle and support safely.

2. Remove the pinch bolt holding the lower steering column joint to the rack and pinion input shaft.

3. Remove the cotter pins and disconnect the tie rod ends.

4. Remove the rack and pinion steering assembly and its rubber mounts.

5. The installation is the reverse of the removal procedure.

6. Perform a front end alignment.

Laser and Talon

1. Disconnect the negative battery cable. Raise the vehicle and support safely.

2. Remove the bolt holding lower steering column joint to the rack and pinion input shaft.

3. Remove the cotter pins and disconnect the tie rod ends.

4. Locate the triangular brace near the stabilizer bar brackets on the crossmember and remove both the brace and the stabilizer bar brackets.

5. Remove the through bolt from the round roll stopper and remove the rear bolts from the center crossmember.

6. Disconnect the front exhaust pipe.

7. Remove the rack and pinion steering assembly and its rubber mounts. Move the rack to the right to remove from the crossmember. Use caution to avoid damaging the boots.

To install:

8. Install the rack and mounting bolts, torquing bolts to 43–58 ft. lbs. (60–80 Nm). When installing the rubber rack mounts, align the projection of the mounting rubber with the indentation in the crossmember. Install the pinch bolt.

9. Connect the exhaust pipe.

10. Install the center member mounting bolts and roll stopper through bolt.

11. Install the stabilizer bar brackets and brace.

12. Connect the tie rod ends.

13. Perform a front end alignment.

Power Steering Rack

ADJUSTMENT

1. Disconnect the negative battery cable.

2. Raise the vehicle and support safely.

3. Remove the steering rack assembly from the vehicle.

NOTE: If equipped with air bag, prior to removal of the steering gear box, center the front wheels and remove the ignition key. Failure to do so may damage the SRS clockspring and render SRS system inoperative, risking serious driver injury.

4. Secure the steering rack assembly in a vise. Do not clamp the vise jaws on the steering housing tubes. Clamp the vise jaws only on the housing cast metal.

5. Remove the steering gear housing end plug from the steering gear shaft bore using tool 6103 or equivalent.

6. Remove the preload adjustment cap locknut from the steering gear housing bore using tool 6097 or equivalent.

7. With rack at center position, check torque on the rack support cover to 11 ft. lbs. (15 Nm).

8. With rack at center position, rotate the shaft clockwise 1 turn in 4–6 seconds. Return the rack support cover 30–60 degrees and adjust the total pinion torque to 5–11 inch lbs. Set the standard value at its highest value when adjusting. Assure no ratcheting or catching when operating the rack towards the shaft direction.

9. Secure the preload adjustment cap with a new locknut using tool 6097 or equivalent. Do not allow the adjustment cap to rotate when tightening the locknut.

10. Install the end plug using tool 6103 or equivalent.

REMOVAL AND INSTALLATION

Summit and Summit Wagon

1. Disconnect the battery negative cable. Raise the vehicle and support safely.

2. Remove the pinch bolt holding the lower steering column joint to the rack and pinion input shaft.

3. Remove the cotter pins and disconnect the tie rod ends from the steering knuckle.

4. On Summit Wagon equipped with AWD, remove the transfer case rear bracket.

5. On Summit Wagon equipped with 2.4L engine and FWD, disconnect the stabilizer bar and remove as required.

6. Disconnect the power steering fluid pressure pipe and return hose from the rack fittings.

7. Remove the rack and pinion steering assembly and its rubber mounts.

To install:

8. Install the steering gear into the vehicle and secure using the retainer clamps and bolts.

9. Connect the power steering fluid lines to the rack fittings.

10. Install the stabilizer bar and rear transaxle bracket.

11. Connect the tie rod ends to the steering knuckles.

12. Connect the negative battery cable. Refill the reservoir and bleed the system.

13. Perform a front end alignment.

Laser and Talon

1. Disconnect the negative battery cable. Raise the vehicle and support safely.

2. Remove the bolt holding lower steering column joint to the rack and pinion input shaft.

3. Remove the transfer case, if equipped.

4. Remove the cotter pins and disconnect the tie rod ends.

5. Locate the triangular brace near the stabilizer bar brackets on the crossmember and remove both

the brace and the stabilizer bar brackets.

6. Remove the through bolt from the round roll stopper and remove the rear bolts from the center crossmember.

7. Disconnect the front exhaust pipe.

8. Disconnect the power steering fluid pressure pipe and return hose from the rack fittings.

9. Remove the rack and pinion steering assembly and its rubber mounts. Move the rack to the right to remove from the crossmember. Use caution to avoid damaging the boots.

To install:

10. Install the rack and install the mounting bolts. Torque the mounting bolts to 43–58 ft. lbs. (60–80 Nm). When installing the rubber rack mounts, align the projection of the mounting rubber with the indentation in the crossmember. Install the pinch bolt.

11. Connect the power steering fluid lines to the rack.

12. Connect the exhaust pipe.

13. Install the center member mounting bolts and roll stopper through bolt.

14. Install the stabilizer bar brackets and brace.

15. Connect the tie rod ends.

16. Install the transfer case.

17. Refill the reservoir and bleed the system.

18. Perform a front end alignment.

Stealth

NOTE: If equipped with air bag, prior to removal of the steering gear box, center the front wheels and remove the ignition key. Failure to do so may damage the SRS clockspring and render SRS system inoperative, risking serious driver injury.

1. Disconnect the negative battery cable. Disarm the air bag.

2. Disconnect the front exhaust pipe.

3. If equipped with AWD, remove the transfer case assembly.

4. Remove the bolt holding lower steering column joint to the rack and pinion input shaft.

5. Remove the cotter pins and disconnect the tie rod ends.

6. Remove the left and right frame members.

7. Remove the stabilizer bar bracket.

8. If equipped with 4 wheel steering, disconnect the lines going to the rear pump.

9. Remove the rack and pinion steering assembly and its rubber mounts. Move the rack to the right to remove from the crossmember. Use caution to avoid damaging the boots.

To install:

10. Install the rack and install the mounting bolts, tightening bolts to 51 ft. lbs. (70 Nm). When installing the rubber rack mounts, align the projection of the mounting rubber with the indentation in the crossmember. Install the pinch bolt.

11. Connect the lines going to the 4 wheel steering rear pump and to the rack itself.

12. Install the frame members and torque the bolts to 50 ft. lbs. (68 Nm).

13. Connect the tie rods and instal new cotter pins.

14. Install the transfer case and front exhaust pipe.

15. Refill the reservoir and bleed the system.

16. Perform front end alignment.

Rear Steering Gear

REMOVAL AND INSTALLATION

1. Disconnect the negative battery cable. Raise the vehicle and support safely.

2. Drain the power steering fluid.

3. Remove the main muffler assembly.

4. Remove the rear shock absorber lower mounting bolts.

5. Using the proper equipment, support the weight of the rear differential. Remove the 2 small crossmember brackets.

6. Remove the large self-locking crossmember mounting nuts on the differential side.

7. Remove the oil line clamp bolts.

8. Remove the pressure tubes.

9. Hold the tie rod ends stationary and remove the tie rod end nuts. Remove the tie rod ends from the trailing arms.

10. Remove the mounting bolts and remove the rear steering gear.

To install:

11. Secure the unit to the crossmember tightening the bolts to 30 ft. lbs. (42 Nm). Move the power cylinder piston rod over its full stroke to determine its neutral position.

12. Align the tie rod ends with the holes in the trailing arms and install the nuts. Adjust the length of the tie rods with the nuts if necessary. The difference in length between the 2 tie rod ends should not exceed 0.04 in. (1mm). Tighten tie rod nuts to 42 ft. lbs. (58 Nm).

13. Replace the O-rings and install the pressure tubes. Clamp and secure in place.

14. Install the large self-locking crossmember mounting nuts on the differential side and torque to 80–94 ft. lbs. (110–130 Nm).

15. Install the 2 small crossmember brackets. Remove the support equipment.

16. Install the shock mounting bolts.

17. Install the muffler assembly.

18. Refill the reservoir and bleed the system.

19. To check and see if the system is functioning:

a. Raise the vehicle safely so all 4 wheels turn freely.

b. Run the vehicle at 50 mph.

c. Turn the steering wheel quickly to the left and right and make sure the rear wheels steer in the same direction as the front wheels.

20. Perform a rear alignment.

Power Steering Pump

REMOVAL AND INSTALLATION

Front

1. Disconnect the battery negative cable.

2. Remove the pressure switch connector from the side of the pump.

3. If the alternator is located under the oil pump, cover it with a shop towel to protect it from oil.

4. Disconnect the return fluid line. Remove the reservoir cap and allow the return line to drain the fluid from the reservoir. If the fluid is contaminated, disconnect the ignition high tension cable and crank the engine several times to drain the fluid from the gearbox.

5. On Summit Wagon equipped with 2.4L engine, remove the alternator drive belt and the heat protector.

6. Disconnect the pressure line.

7. Remove the pump drive belt and unbolt the pump from its bracket.

To install:

8. Install the pump, wrap the belt around the pulley and tighten the bolts.

9. Replace the O-rings and connect the pressure line. Connect the pressure line so the notch in the fitting aligns with and contacts the pump's guide bracket.

10. Connect the return line.

11. Connect the pressure switch connector.

12. Adjust the belt tension and tighten the adjusting bolts.

13. Refill the reservoir and bleed the system.

Rear

STEALTH WITH FOUR WHEEL STEERING

1. Disconnect the negative battery cable. Raise the vehicle and support safely.

2. Drain the power steering fluid.

3. Remove the main muffler assembly.

4. Remove the rear shock absorber lower mounting bolts.

5. Using the proper equipment, support the weight of the rear differential. Remove the 2 small crossmember brackets.

6. Remove the large self-locking crossmember mounting nuts on the differential side.

7. Disconnect the pressure and suction hoses from the fittings on the pump.

8. Remove the pump retaining bolt and remove the pump from the rear differential assembly. Do not attempt to disassemble the pump; it is not serviceable.

To install:

9. Replace the O-ring and install the pump assembly to the differential. Make sure the housing is fully seated and the gear is fully engaged. Install the retaining bolt.

10. Replace the O-ring and connect the fluid lines to the pump.

11. Install the large self-locking crossmember mounting nuts on the differential side. Torque to 80–94 ft. lbs. (110–130 Nm).

12. Install the 2 small crossmember brackets. Remove the support equipment.

13. Install the shock mounting bolts.

14. Install the muffler assembly.

15. Refill the reservoir and bleed the system.

16. To check and see if the system is functioning:

    a. Raise the vehicle safely so all 4 wheels turn freely.

    b. Run the vehicle at 50 mph.

    c. Turn the steering wheel quickly to the left and right and make sure the rear wheels steer in the same direction as the front wheels.

BELT ADJUSTMENT

1. Press the belt in about the center between the power steering pump pulley and the pulley it shares, usually the water pump pulley. With reasonable pressure applied (about 22 lbs.) the belt should deflect about $1/4$–$3/8$ in.

2. Adjustment can be made by loosening the 3 bolts that hold the pump. Place a suitable bar or lever between the body of the pump and gently pry to get the desired tension.

3. Retighten the 3 bolts and check again.

SYSTEM BLEEDING

Front

1. Raise the vehicle and support safely.

2. Manually turn the pump pulley a few times.

3. Turn the steering wheel all the way to the left and to the right 5 or 6 times.

4. Disconnect the ignition high tension cable and, while operating the starter motor intermittently, turn the steering wheel all the way to the left and right 5–6 times for 15–20 seconds. During bleeding, make sure the fluid in the reservoir never falls below the lower position of the filter. If bleeding is attempted with the engine running, the air will be absorbed in the fluid. Bleed only while cranking.

5. Connect ignition high tension cable, start engine and allow to idle.

6. Turn the steering wheel left and right until there are no air bubbles in the reservoir. Confirm that the fluid is not milky and the level is up to the specified position on the gauge. Confirm that there is is very little change in the fluid level when the steering wheel is turned. If the fluid level changes more than 0.2 in. the air has not been completely bled. Repeat the process.

Rear

1. Bleed the front system.

2. Start the engine and let it idle. Raise and safely support the vehicle.

3. Loosen the bleeder screw on the left side of the control valve and install special tool MB991230 to the bleeder.

4. Turn the steering wheel all the way to the left, then immediately turn it half way back. Confirm that air has discharged with the fluid.

5. Repeat Step 5 two or three times as required, to remove all air from the rear system. Stop the engine.

6. Loosen the power cylinder (rear steering gear) bleeder screw about $1/8$ turn and install the same special tool with the rotation prevention metal fixtures to prevent the bleeder from opening more. Attach a plastic tube to the bleeder.

7. Start the engine and run to 50 mph to circulate the fluid.

8. Maintain a speed of 20 mph and turn the steering wheel back and forth. Air should be discharged through the tube of the special tool and into the oil reservoir.

9. Repeat until all air is removed from the power cylinder.

NOTE: If air has not been completely bled from the system, the pump will make a humming noise or an unusual noise will come from the flow control valve: this also contributes to shortened pump life.

Tie Rod Ends

REMOVAL AND INSTALLATION

1. Disconnect the battery negative cable.

2. Raise the vehicle and support safely.

3. Wire brush the threads on the tie rod shaft and lubricate with penetrating oil. Loosen the locknut.

4. Remove the cotter pin and nut and press the tie rod end from the steering knuckle.

5. Hold the tie rod shaft with locking pliers and turn the tie rod end off, counting the number of turns for installation.

6. The installation is the reverse of the removal procedure. Install the tie rod end the same number of turns that it took to remove the old tie rod.

7. Perform front end alignment.

BRAKES

Master Cylinder

REMOVAL AND INSTALLATION

1. Disconnect the negative battery cable.

2. Disconnect the fluid level sensor connector.

3. Disconnect the brake lines from the master cylinder. On Laser and Talon, a separate reservoir is used. Plug the lines to prevent drainage.

4. On Stealth, disconnect the low pressure hose.

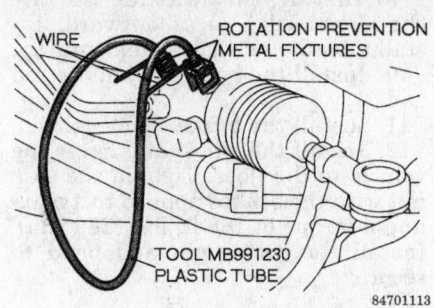

Bleeding rear steering system

5. Remove the 2 nuts securing the master cylinder and lift off. On Summit Wagon, slide the proportioning valve assembly off of the master cylinder mounting studs prior to master cylinder removal.

To install:

6. Bench bleed the master cylinder.

7. Install master cylinder and proportioning valve to the studs and install the nuts. Tighten mounting nuts to 7 ft. lbs. (10 Nm).

8. Install the brake lines to the master cylinder. Bleed brake system starting at the master cylinder. If air remains in the system continue bleeding the entire system.

9. Connect the negative battery cable and check the brakes for proper operation.

Proportioning Valve

REMOVAL AND INSTALLATION

Except Summit, Summit Wagon, Laser and Talon

1. Disconnect the negative battery cable.

2. Locate the proportioning valve, usually below the master cylinder.

3. Tag and disconnect the brake lines from the valve.

4. Remove the proportioning valve from the engine compartment. On Summit Wagon, remove the master cylinder retainer nuts to remove the proportioning valve assembly.

5. The installation is the reverse of the removal procedure.

6. Bleed the brakes in the following order:

Summit and Summit Wagon

1. Left rear wheel cylinder or caliper.

2. Right front cylinder.

3. Right rear wheel cylinder or caliper.

4. Left front caliper.

5. Connect the negative battery cable and check the brakes for proper operation.

Laser and Talon

1. Right rear caliper.

2. Left front caliper.

3. Left rear caliper.

4. Right front caliper.

5. Connect the negative battery cable and check the brakes for proper operation.

Power Brake Booster

REMOVAL AND INSTALLATION

1. Disconnect the negative battery cable. On some models, relocate the relay box and the solenoid valve located at the power brake unit.

2. Disconnect the vacuum hose from the booster. Pull it straight off. Prying off the vacuum hose could damage the check valve installed in the brake booster.

3. Disconnect the brake level sensor connector.

4. Remove the nuts attaching the master cylinder to the booster and remove the master cylinder.

5. From inside the passenger compartment, remove the cotter pin and clevis pin that secures the booster pushrod to the brake pedal.

6. Remove the nuts that attach the booster to the dash panel and remove it from the vehicle.

7. The installation is the reverse of the removal procedure.

8. Connect the negative battery cable, bleed the brakes and check for proper operation.

Brake Caliper

REMOVAL AND INSTALLATION

Front Brakes

1. Disconnect the negative battery cable.

2. Raise the vehicle and support safely. Remove appropriate wheel assembly.

3. To disconnect the front brake hose, hold the nut on the brake hose side and loosen the flared brake line nut.

4. Remove the caliper lock pins and remove the caliper.

5. The installation is the reverse of the removal procedure. Make sure

the brake hose is not twisted after installation. Refill the brake fluid as required and bleed the brakes.

Rear Brakes

SUMMIT, SUMMIT WAGON, LASER AND TALON

1. Disconnect the negative battery cable.

2. Raise the vehicle and support safely. Remove appropriate wheel assembly.

3. Disconnect the parking brake cable from the actuator on the caliper.

4. To disconnect the brake hose, hold the nut on the brake hose side and loosen the flared brake line nut.

5. Remove the retaining bolts and remove rear caliper assembly.

6. The installation is the reverse of the removal procedure. Make sure the brake hose is not twisted after installation.

7. Refill the brake fluid as required and bleed the brakes.

STEALTH

1. Disconnect the negative battery cable.

2. Raise the vehicle and support safely. Remove appropriate wheel assembly.

3. To disconnect the brake hose, hold the nut on the brake hose side and loosen the flared brake line nut.

4. Remove the caliper lock pins and remove the caliper.

5. The installation is the reverse of the removal procedure. Make sure the brake hose is not twisted after installation. Refill the brake fluid as required and bleed the brakes.

Disc Brake Pads

REMOVAL AND INSTALLATION

1. Disconnect the battery negative cable.

2. Raise the vehicle and support safely.

3. Remove appropriate wheel assembly.

4. On the front of AWD Stealth, remove the pad retaining pins and pull the pads out of the caliper body.

5. On others, remove the caliper from its adaptor. Do not allow the caliper to hang by the brake line. On some vehicles, the caliper can be flipped up by leaving the upper pin in place and using it as a pivot point. Take note of the clips, pins, antisqueal shims and other parts for reference at assembly.

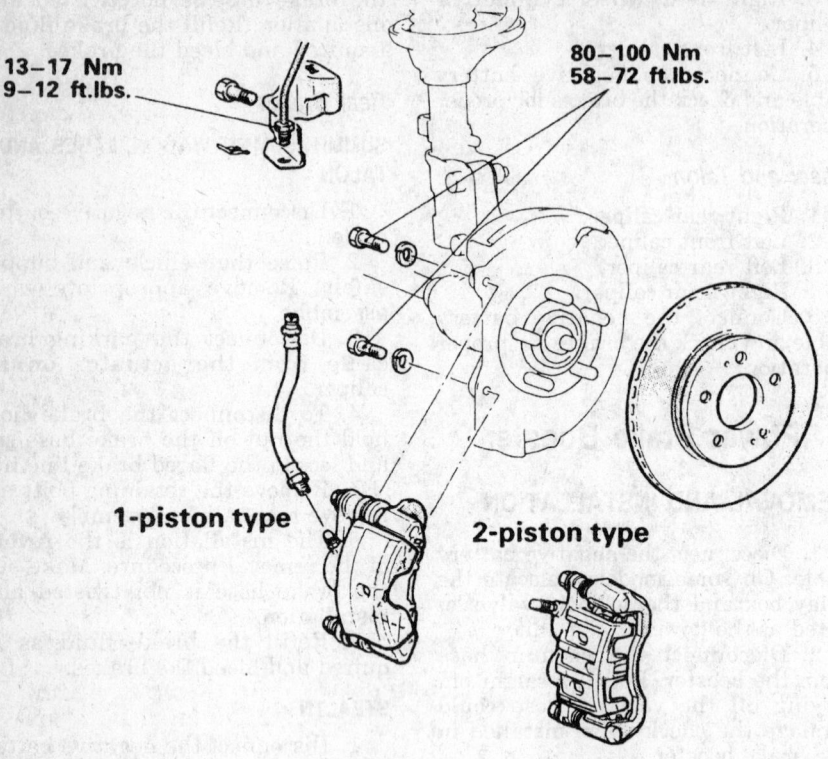

13–17 Nm
9–12 ft.lbs.

80–100 Nm
58–72 ft.lbs.

1-piston type

2-piston type

79161003

Front disc brake caliper removal — Laser and Talon

6. On vehicles with rear disc brakes, it may help to loosen the parking brake cable from inside the vehicle and disconnect the parking brake end from the rear caliper.

To install:

7. Use a large C-clamp to compress the piston(s) back into the caliper bore. On rear disc brakes with the parking brake mechanism incorporated into the caliper, a special tool is needed to turn the piston back into the bore.

8. Install the pads and all other small parts. Note that rear disc pads on calipers with the parking brake mechanism incorporated into the caliper should have a projection on the back side of the shoe that fits into the rear caliper piston.

9. Install the caliper. Make sure the brake hose is not twisted after installation. Connect the parking brake cable if disconnected.

10. Install the tire and wheel assembly and connect the negative battery cable. Pump the brake pedal until firm before putting transaxle in gear or moving vehicle.

Brake Rotor

REMOVAL AND INSTALLATION

Summit Front Rotor

1. Loosen the large driveshaft nut while the vehicle is still on the ground with the brakes applied. Then raise and safely support vehicle. Remove appropriate wheel assembly.

2. Remove the axle end nut and lock washer.

3. Remove the caliper from its bracket. Do not allow the caliper to hang by the brake line. Remove the brake pads.

4. Remove the ball joint and tie rod end from the lower control arm.

5. Use and puller to push the halfshaft through the rotor/hub assembly.

6. Remove the lower strut bolts and remove the assembly from the vehicle.

7. To separate the rotor from the hub assembly, remove the rotor retainer bolts and separate using tool MB991001 or equivalent.

To install:

8. Assemble the rotor and hub. Tighten the nuts to 40 ft. lbs. (54 Nm) and install the assembly to the vehicle.

9. Install the washer so the chamfered edge faces outward. Install the nut and tighten temporarily.

10. Install the ball joint and tie rod end.

11. Install the brake components.

12. Install the wheel and lower the vehicle to the floor. Tighten the axle nut with the brakes applied to a maximum torque of 188 ft. lbs. (260 Nm). Install the cotter pin and bend to secure.

Except Summit Front Rotor

1. Raise the vehicle and support safely. Remove appropriate wheel assembly.

2. Remove the caliper and brake pads.

3. The rotor on most models is held to the hub by 2 small threaded screws. Remove screws, if equipped, and pull off the rotor.

4. Installation is the reverse of the removal process.

Brake Drum

REMOVAL AND INSTALLATION

With Rear Hub Assembly

1. Raise the vehicle and support safely.

2. Remove the wheel and tire assembly.

3. Remove the brake drum from the vehicle.

4. The installation is the reverse of the removal procedure.

Without Rear Hub Assembly

1. Raise the vehicle and support safely.

2. Remove the wheel and tire assembly.

3. Remove the dust cap.

4. Remove the self-locking nut.

5. Remove the outer wheel bearing.

6. Remove the drum with the inner wheel bearing from the spindle. Remove the grease seal.

To install:

7. To determine if the self-locking nut is reusable:

   a. Screw in the self-locking nut until about 1/8 in. of the spindle is showing.

   b. Measure the torque required to turn the self-locking nut counterclockwise.

   c. The lowest allowable torque is 48 inch lbs. (5.5 Nm). If the measured torque is less than the specification, replace the nut.

8. Lubricate and install the inner wheel bearing. Install a new grease seal.

9. Install the drum to the spindle.

10. Lubricate and install the outer wheel bearing.

11. Torque the self-locking nut to 108–145 ft. lbs. (150–200 Nm).

12. Install the grease cap.

Brake Shoes

REMOVAL AND INSTALLATION

1. Raise the vehicle and support safely. Remove appropriate wheel assembly.

2. Remove the brake drum. Remove the shoe to shoe spring.

3. Remove the shoe to lever spring and remove the adjuster assembly.

4. Take note of the springs and clips for proper reassembly. Remove the shoe hold-down clips and remove the shoes. Separate the parking brake cable from the rear brake shoe during removal.

To install:

5. Thoroughly clean and dry the backing plate. To prepare the backing plate, lubricate the bosses, anchor pin and parking brake actuating lever pivot surface lightly with lithium-based grease.

6. Remove, clean and dry all parts still on the old shoes. Lubricate the star wheel shaft threads with anti-sieze lubricant and transfer all parts to their proper locations on the new shoes.

7. Install shoes to the vehicle.

8. Connect the parking brake cable.

9. Adjust the star wheel.

10. To determine if the self-locking nut is reusable:

    a. Screw in the self-locking nut until about ⅛ in. of the spindle is showing.

    b. Measure the torque required to turn the self-locking nut counterclockwise.

    c. The lowest allowable torque is 48 inch lbs. (5.5 Nm). If the measured torque is less than the specification, replace the nut.

11. Remove any grease from the brake linings and install the drum to the spindle.

12. Lubricate and install the outer wheel bearing.

13. Torque the self-locking nut to 108–145 ft. lbs. (150–200 Nm).

14. Install the grease cap.

Wheel Cylinder

REMOVAL AND INSTALLATION

1. Raise the vehicle and support safely.

2. Remove the wheel and the brake drum.

3. Remove the shoe-to-lever spring and the upper shoe-to-shoe spring. Spread the upper portion of the brake shoes slightly.

4. Remove and plug the brake line from the wheel cylinder.

5. Remove the wheel cylinder retaining bolts and remove the cylinder from the backing plate.

To install:

6. Apply a very thin coating of silicone sealer to the cylinder mounting surface, install the cylinder to the backing plate and install the retaining bolts.

7. Connect the brake line to the wheel cylinder.

8. Install brake springs and the brake drum.

9. To determine if the self-locking nut is reusable:

    a. Screw in the self-locking nut until about ⅛ in. of the spindle is showing.

    b. Measure the torque required to turn the self-locking nut counterclockwise.

    c. The lowest allowable torque is 48 inch lbs. (5.5 Nm). If the measured torque is less than the specification, replace the nut.

10. Torque the self-locking nut to 108–145 ft. lbs. (150–200 Nm) if equipped.

11. Install the grease cap.

12. Install the tire and wheel assembly.

13. Fill the system with clean brake fluid and bleed the rear brakes.

Parking Brake Cable

ADJUSTMENT

1. Make sure the parking brake cable is free and is not frozen or sticking. With the engine running, forcefully depress the brake pedal 5–6 times. Check the parking brake stroke. It should be 5–7 notches on Summit, Summit Wagon, Laser and Talon or 3–5 notches on Stealth. If not, adjust using the following procedure.

2. On rear drum brakes, adjust the rear brakes. On rear disc brakes, make sure the parking brake mechanism is not frozen or sticking.

3. On Summit, remove the rear console box. On Laser and Talon, remove the console carpeting. On Stealth, remove the coin holder or cup holder and the underlying plug. This will expose the adjusting nut within the console. On Summit Wagon, remove the floor console.

4. Rotate the adjusting nut to adjust the parking brake stroke to the 5–7 notch setting. After making the adjustment, check there is no looseness between the adjusting nut and the parking brake lever, then tighten the locknut.

NOTE: Do not adjust the parking brake too tight. If the number of notches is less than specification, the cable has been pulled too much and the automatic adjuster will fail or the brakes will drag.

5. After adjusting the lever stroke, raise the rear of the vehicle and safely support. With the parking brake lever in the released position, turn the rear wheels to confirm that the rear brakes are not dragging.

6. Check that the parking brake holds the vehicle on an incline.

REMOVAL AND INSTALLATION

1. Disconnect the negative battery cable.

NOTE: If equipped with an air bag, be sure to disarm it before starting repairs on the vehicle.

2. Remove the floor console by prying out the coin holder, box tray and remote mirror switch, if equipped, or the cover. Remove the small cover around the seat belt from the console side. Remove the screws from the center section and remove the rear part of the console.

NOTE: If equipped with SRS, when removing the floor console, don't allow any impact or shock to the SRS diagnostic unit.

3. On some vehicles, it will be necessary to remove the rear seat cushion.

4. Remove the center cable clamp and grommet.

5. Raise the vehicle and support safely.

6. At the rear wheel, remove the brake drum or disc and disconnect the cable end from the parking brake strut lever or actuator. If necessary, compress the retaining strips to remove the cable from the backing plate.

7. Unfasten any other frame retainers and remove the cables.

8. The installation is the reverse of the removal procedure.

9. Adjust the rear brakes and parking brake cables.

10. Connect the negative battery cable and check the rear wheels to confirm that the rear brakes are not dragging.

11. Check that the parking brake holds the vehicle on an incline.

Brake System Bleeding

NOTE: If using a pressure bleeder, follow the instructions furnished with the unit and choose the correct adaptor for the application. Do not substitute an adapter that almost fits as it will not work and could be dangerous.

MASTER CYLINDER

If the master cylinder is off the vehicle it can be bench bled.

1. Connect 2 short pieces of brake line to the outlet fittings, bend them until the free end is below the fluid level in the master cylinder reservoir.

2. Fill the reservoir with fresh brake fluid. Pump the piston slowly until no more air bubbles appear in the reservoirs.

3. Disconnect the 2 short lines, refill the master cylinder and securely install the cylinder caps.

4. If the master cylinder is on the vehicle, it can still be bled, using a flare nut wrench.

5. Open the brake lines slightly with the flare nut wrench while pressure is applied to the brake pedal by a helper inside the vehicle.

6. Be sure to tighten the line before the brake pedal is released.

7. Repeat the process with both lines until no air bubbles come out.

8. Refill master cylinder and always bleed the complete brake system.

CALIPERS AND WHEEL CYLINDERS

1. Fill the master cylinder with fresh brake fluid. Check the level often during the procedure.

2. Starting with the wheel farthest from the master cylinder, remove the protective cap from the bleeder and place where it will not be lost. Clean the bleeder screw.

— **CAUTION** —

When bleeding the brakes, keep face away from the brake area. Spewing fluid may cause facial and/or visual damage. Do not allow brake fluid to spill on the car's finish; it will remove the paint.

---

3. If the system is empty, the most efficient way to get fluid down to the wheel is to use a pressure bleeder tool. Open the bleeder until brake fluid flows without signs of air bubbles, close bleeder.

NOTE: If the pedal is pumped rapidly, the fluid will churn and create small air bubbles, which are almost impossible to remove from the system. These air bubbles will accumulate and a spongy pedal will result.

4. If the manual procedure is to be used to pump brake fluid to the caliper or wheel cylinder, open the bleed screw and have an assistant press the brake pedal to the floor.

5. Close the bleeder bleeder screw before releasing the brake pedal, have the helper slowly release the pedal. Wait 15 seconds and repeat the procedure until no more air comes out of the bleeder upon application of the brake pedal. Remember to close the bleeder before the pedal is released inside the vehicle each time the bleeder is opened. If not, air will be introduced into the system.

6. Repeat the procedure on remaining wheel cylinders in the following order:

Summit and Summit Wagon
• Left rear wheel cylinder or caliper.
• Right front cylinder.
• Right rear wheel cylinder or caliper.
• Left front caliper.

Laser, Talon and Stealth
• Right rear caliper.
• Left front caliper.
• Left rear caliper.
• Right front caliper.

7. Hydraulic brake systems must be totally flushed if the fluid becomes contaminated with water, dirt or other corrosive chemicals. To flush, bleed the entire system until all fluid has been replaced with the correct type of new fluid.

8. Install the bleeder cap on the bleeder to keep dirt out and refill master cylinder. Always road test the vehicle after brake work of any kind is done.

Anti-lock Brake System Service

PRECAUTIONS

• Certain components within the ABS system are not intended to be serviced or repaired individually. Only those components with REMOVAL AND INSTALLATION procedures should be serviced.

• Do not use rubber hoses or other parts not specifically designed for the ABS system. When using repair kits, replace all parts included in the kit. Partial or incorrect repair may lead to functional problems and require the replacement of components.

• Lubricate rubber parts with clean, fresh brake fluid to ease assembly. Do not use lubricated shop air to clean parts; damage to rubber components may result.

• Use only DOT 3 brake fluid from an unopened container.

• If any hydraulic component or line is removed or replaced, it may be necessary to bleed the entire system.

• A clean repair area is essential. Always clean the reservoir and cap thoroughly before removing the cap. The slightest amount of dirt in the fluid may plug an orifice and impair the system function. Perform repairs after components have been thoroughly cleaned; use only denatured alcohol to clean components. Do not allow ABS components to come into contact with any substance containing mineral oil; this includes used shop rags.

• The Anti-Lock control unit is a microprocessor similar to other computer units in the vehicle. Ensure that the ignition switch is **OFF** before removing or installing controller harnesses. Avoid static electricity discharge at or near the controller.

• If any arc welding is to be done on the vehicle, the ALCU connectors should be disconnected before welding operations begin.

Hydraulic Unit

REMOVAL AND INSTALLATION

Summit Wagon

1. Disconnect the negative battery cable. Remove the splash shield from under the vehicle.

2. Use a syringe or similar device to remove as much fluid as possible from the reservoir. Some fluid will be spilled from lines during removal of

the hydraulic unit; protect adjacent painted surfaces.

3. Remove the dust cover and the oil reservoir.

4. Disconnect the brake lines from the hydraulic unit. Correct reassembly is critical. Label or identify the lines before removal. Plug each line immediately after removal.

5. Disconnect the hydraulic unit electrical harness connectors.

6. Disconnect the hydraulic unit ground strap from the chassis.

7. Remove the 3 nuts holding the hydraulic unit. Remove the unit upwards.

NOTE: The hydraulic unit is heavy; use care when removing it. The unit must remain in the upright position at all times and be protected from impact and shock.

8. Set the unit upright supported by blocks on the workbench. The hydraulic unit must not be tilted or turned upside down. No component of the hydraulic unit should be loosened or disassembled.

9. The bracket assemblies and relays may be removed, if desired.

To install:

10. Install the relays and brackets, if removed.

11. Install the hydraulic unit into the vehicle, keeping it upright at all times.

12. Install the retaining nuts and tighten.

13. Connect the ground strap to the chassis bracket. Connect the hydraulic unit wiring harness.

14. Connect the hydraulic unit electrical harness connectors.

15. Install the dust cover and the oil reservoir.

16. Connect each brake line loosely to the correct port and double check the placement. Tighten each line to 10 ft. lbs. (13.5 Nm).

17. Fill the reservoir to the MAX line with brake fluid.

18. Bleed the master cylinder, then bleed the brake lines. Refill the master cylinder and check for proper operation.

Laser and Talon

1. Disconnect the negative battery cable. Use a syringe or similar device to remove as much fluid as possible from the reservoir. Some fluid will be spilled from the lines during removal or the hydraulic unit; protect adjacent painted surfaces.

2. On turbocharged engine, remove the center intercooler duct. Loosen the clamps and remove the

bolts holding the duct to the air cleaner.

3. Disconnect the brake lines from the hydraulic unit. Correct reassembly is critical. Label or identify the lines before removal. Plug each line immediately after removal.

4. Remove the cover from the relay box. Disconnect the electrical harness to the hydraulic unit.

5. Disconnect the hydraulic unit ground strap from the chassis.

6. Remove the 3 nuts holding the hydraulic unit. Remove the unit upwards.

NOTE: The hydraulic unit is heavy; use care when removing it. The unit must remain in the upright position at all times and be protected from impact and shock.

7. Set the unit upright supported by blocks on the workbench. The hydraulic unit must not be tilted or turned upside down. No component of the hydraulic unit should be loosened or disassembled.

8. The bracket assemblies and relays may be removed, if desired.

To install:

9. Install the relays and brackets, if removed

10. Install the hydraulic unit to the vehicle, keeping it upright at all times.

11. Install the retaining nuts and tighten.

12. Connect the ground strap to the chassis bracket. Connect the hydraulic unit wiring harness.

13. Install the cover on the relay box.

14. Connect each brake line loosely to the correct port and double check the placement. Tighten each line to 10 ft. lbs. (13.5 Nm).

15. Fill the reservoir to the MAX line with brake fluid.

16. Bleed the master cylinder, then bleed the brake lines.

17. If equipped, install the intercooler air duct.

Stealth

1. Disconnect the negative battery cable. Remove the splash shield from beneath the vehicle.

2. Use a syringe or similar device to remove as much fluid as possible from the reservoir. Some fluid will be spilled from lines during removal of the hydraulic unit; protect adjacent painted surfaces.

3. Lift the relay box with the harness attached and position it aside.

4. Remove the air intake duct.

5. Disconnect the brake lines from the hydraulic unit. Correct reassembly is critical. Label or identify the lines before removal. Plug each line immediately after removal. It will be necessary to hold the relay box aside to allow wrench access.

6. Disconnect the wiring harness connections at the hydraulic unit.

7. Disconnect the hydraulic unit ground strap from the chassis.

8. Remove the 3 bolts holding the hydraulic unit bracket. Remove the unit and the bracket.

NOTE: The hydraulic unit is heavy; use care when removing it. The unit must remain in the upright position at all times and be protected from impact and shock.

9. Set the unit upright supported by blocks on the workbench. The hydraulic unit must not be tilted or turned upside down. No component of the hydraulic unit should be loosened or disassembled.

10. Loosen the nut holding the bracket to the hydraulic unit and remove the bracket.

11. Disconnect the external ground wire from the bracket.

To install:

12. Install the bracket, if removed. Connect the ground wire to the bracket.

13. Install the hydraulic unit into the vehicle, keeping it upright at all times.

14. Install the retaining nuts and tighten. Connect the hydraulic unit wiring harness.

15. Connect each brake line loosely to the correct port and double check the placement. Tighten each line to 11 ft. lbs. (15 Nm).

16. Fill the reservoir to the MAX line with brake fluid. Bleed the master cylinder, then bleed the brake lines.

17. Secure the relay box in position and install the air duct. Install the splash shield.

Anti-Lock Control Unit

REMOVAL AND INSTALLATION

Except Summit Wagon

1. Ensure that the ignition switch is **OFF** throughout the procedure.

2. Remove the interior right rear quarter trim panel and rear seat back and/or cushion.

3. Release the lock on the bottom of the connector; disconnect the multi-pin connector from the control

unit. On Laser and Talon, access may be easier if the external ground is disconnected from the bracket.

4. Remove the retaining nuts and remove the control unit from its bracket. The bracket may be removed, if desired.

To install:

5. Place the bracket in position. Install the controller and tighten the retaining nuts.

6. Connect the ground wire to the bracket, if removed. Ensure a proper, tight connection. The ground must be connected before the multi-pin harness is connected.

7. Connect the multi-pin connector and secure the lock. Install the rear quarter trim panel and seat.

Summit Wagon

1. Ensure that the ignition switch is **OFF** throughout the procedure.

2. Remove the cup holder in front of the center console.

3. Remove the console side covers.

4. Disconnect the electrical harness from the control unit.

5. Remove the fasteners and the control unit from the vehicle.

6. Installation is the reverse of the removal procedures.

G-Sensor

The G-Sensor is found only on All Wheel Drive (AWD) vehicles.

REMOVAL AND INSTALLATION

Summit Wagon

1. Disconnect the negative battery cable.

2. Remove the floor console.

3. Disconnect the wiring harness connector from the sensor.

4. Remove the retaining screw and G-sensor from the mounting bracket.

5. Installation is the reverse of the removal procedure.

Laser and Talon

1. Ensure that the ignition switch is **OFF** throughout the procedure.

2. Remove the rear seat cushion. Disconnect the wiring harness to G-sensor.

3. Remove the retaining bolts and remove the sensor.

4. To install, position the sensor, tighten the retaining bolts and connect the harness.

5. Install the rear seat cushion.

Stealth

1. Disconnect the negative battery cable. Remove the rearmost console assembly.

NOTE: If equipped with SRS, when removing the floor console, don't allow any impact or shock to the SRS diagnostic unit.

2. Remove the front console assembly.

3. Disconnect the G-sensor wiring harness.

4. Remove the G-sensor from the bracket. Remove the bracket, if desired.

To install:

5. Reinstall the bracket. Tighten the bolts to 4 ft. lbs. (5 Nm).

6. Install the G-sensor and connect the wiring harness.

7. Install the front and rear console assemblies.

Wheel Speed Sensors

CAUTION

Vehicles equipped with air bag systems will have wiring and system components in the fender or wheel well area. The ABS components must be correctly identified before beginning repairs. Improper work procedures may cause impaired function of the ABS and/or SRS systems.

REMOVAL AND INSTALLATION

1. Disconnect the negative battery cable. Raise and safely support the vehicle.

2. Remove the wheel and tire. Remove the inner fender or splash shield.

3. Beginning at the sensor end, carefully disconnect or release each clip and retainer along the sensor wire. Take careful note of the exact position of each clip; they must be reinstalled in the identical position. Rear wheel sensor harnesses will be held by plastic wire ties; these may be cut away but must be replaced at reassembly.

4. Disconnect the sensor connector at the end of the harness.

5. Remove the 2 bolts holding the speed sensor bracket to the knuckle and remove the assembly from the vehicle.

NOTE: The speed sensor has a pole piece projecting from it. This exposed tip must be protected from impact or scratches.

Do not allow the pole piece to contact the toothed wheel during removal or installation.

6. Remove the sensor from the bracket.

To install:

7. Assemble the sensor onto the bracket and tighten the bolt to 10 ft. lbs. (14 Nm). Note that the brackets are different for the left and right front wheels. Each bracket has identifying letters stamped on it.

8. Temporarily install the speed sensor to the knuckle; tighten the bolts only finger-tight.

9. Route the cable correctly and loosely install the clips and retainers. All clips must be in their original position and the sensor cable must not be twisted. Improper installation may cause cable damage and system failure.

NOTE: The wiring in the harness is easily damaged by twisting and flexing. Use the white stripe on the outer insulation to keep the sensor harness properly placed.

10. Use a brass of other non-magnetic feeler gauge to check the air gap between the tip of the pole piece and the toothed wheel. Correct gap is 0.012–0.035 in. (0.3–0.9mm). Tighten the 2 sensor bracket bolts to 10 ft. lbs. (14 Nm) with the sensor located so the gap is the same at several points on the toothed wheel. If the gap is incorrect, it is likely that the toothed wheel is worn or improperly installed.

11. Tighten the screws and bolts for the cable retaining clips.

12. Install the inner fender or splash shield. Install the wheel and tire. Lower the vehicle to the ground.

Front Toothed Wheel Rings

REMOVAL AND INSTALLATION

1. Disconnect the negative battery cable. Raise and safely support the vehicle.

2. Remove the wheel and tire.

3. Remove the wheel speed sensor and disconnect sufficient harness clips to allow the sensor and wiring to be moved out of the work area.

NOTE: The speed sensor has a pole piece projecting from it. This exposed tip must be protected from impact or scratches. Do not allow the pole piece to contact the toothed wheel during removal or installation.

4. Remove the front hub and knuckle assembly. Remove the hub from the knuckle

5. Support the hub in a vise with protected jaws. Remove the retaining bolts from the toothed wheel and remove the toothed wheel.

To install:

6. Fit the new toothed wheel onto the hub and tighten the retaining bolts to 7 ft. lbs. (10 Nm).

7. Assemble the hub to the knuckle. Install the hub and knuckle assembly to the vehicle.

8. Install the wheel speed sensor. Install the wheel and tire. Lower the vehicle to the ground.

Rear Toothed Wheel Rings

REMOVAL AND INSTALLATION

Front Wheel Drive

1. Disconnect the negative battery cable. Remove the wheel and tire.

2. Remove the wheel speed sensor and disconnect sufficient harness clips to allow the sensor and wiring to be moved out of the work area.

NOTE: The speed sensor has a pole piece projecting from it. This exposed tip must be protected from impact or scratches. Do not allow the pole piece to contact the toothed wheel during removal or installation.

3. Remove the hub assembly.

4. Support the hub in a vise with protected jaws. Remove the retaining bolts from the toothed wheel and remove the toothed wheel.

To install:

5. Fit the new toothed wheel onto the hub and tighten the retaining bolts to 7 ft. lbs. (10 Nm).

6. Install the hub assembly to the vehicle.

7. Install the tounged washer and hub nut. Tighten to 166 ft. lbs. (230 Nm) on Summit Wagon or 166–188 ft. lbs. (230–260 Nm) on the remaining models. Crimp at the indentation and install the grease cap.

8. Install the wheel speed sensor. Install the wheel and tire. Lower the vehicle to the ground.

All Wheel Drive

EXCEPT SUMMIT WAGON

1. Disconnect the negative battery cable. Raise and safely support the vehicle.

2. Remove the wheel and tire. Disconnect the parking brake cable at the caliper or shoes.

3. Remove the speed sensor and its O-ring. Disconnect sufficient clamps and wire ties to allow the sensor to be moved well out of the work area.

NOTE: The speed sensor has a pole piece projecting from it. This exposed tip must be protected from impact or scratches. Do not allow the pole piece to contact the toothed wheel during removal or installation.

4. Remove the brake caliper and brake disc.

5. Remove the 3 retaining nuts and bolts holding the outer end of the driveshaft to the companion flange. Swing the axle shaft away and support it with stiff wire. Do not overextend the joint in the axle; do not allow it to hang of its own weight.

6. Remove the retaining nut and washer on the back of the driveshaft. Use special tool MB990767 or equivalent, to counterhold the hub.

7. Remove the companion flange from the knuckle. Using an axle puller which bolts to the wheel lugs, remove the axle shaft assembly.

8. Fit the shaft assembly in a press with the toothed wheel completely supported by a bearing plate such as special tool MB990560 or equivalent.

9. Press the toothed wheel off the axle shaft.

To install:

10. Press the new toothed wheel onto the shaft with the groove facing the axle shaft flange.

11. Install the axle shaft to the knuckle and fit the companion flange in place.

12. Install the lock washer and a new self-locking nut on the axle shaft. Hold the axle shaft stationary and torque the nut to 116–159 ft. lbs. (160–220 Nm) for Laser and Talon. Torque to 188–217 ft. lbs. (260–300 Nm) for Stealth.

13. Swing the axle assembly into place and install the nuts and bolts. Tighten each to 45 ft. lbs. (61 Nm).

14. Install the brake disc and caliper. Install the wheel speed sensor. Always use a new O-ring.

15. Connect the parking brake cable to the caliper. Install the wheel and tire; lower the vehicle to the ground.

Summit Wagon

1. Disconnect the negative battery cable. Raise and safely support the vehicle. Remove the wheel and tire assembly.

2. Remove the cotter pin cover and driveshaft nut.

3. Remove the speed sensor and its O-ring. Disconnect sufficient clamps and wire ties to allow the sensor to be moved well out of the work area.

NOTE: The speed sensor has a pole piece projecting from it. This exposed tip must be protected from impact or scratches. Do not allow the pole piece to contact the toothed wheel during removal or installation.

4. Remove the rear driveshaft from the vehicle.

5. Fit the shaft assembly in a press with the toothed wheel completely supported by a bearing plate such as special tool MB990560 or equivalent.

6. Press the toothed wheel off the axle shaft.

To install:

7. Press the new toothed wheel onto the shaft with the groove facing the axle shaft flange.

8. Install the axle on the vehicle. Tighten the inner flange retainers to 40–47 ft. lbs. (55–65 Nm).

9. Install the driveshaft nut and torque to 145–188 ft. lbs. (200–260 Nm). Secure using a new cotter pin.

10. Install the speed sensor and secure the wiring harness in its original location. Always use a new O-ring.

11. Install the wheel and tire assembly.

FRONT SUSPENSION

MacPherson Strut

REMOVAL AND INSTALLATION

1. Disconnect the negative battery cable.

2. On Summit Wagon, if removing the right front strut, remove the auto-cruise control actuator.

3. On Summit Wagon, disconnect and remove the daytime running lamp delay and control unit from the mounting bracket located on top of the left strut tower.

4. Raise and safely support vehicle.

5. Remove the brake hose and tube bracket. Do not pry the brake hose and tube clamp away when removing it.

6. If equipped with ABS, disconnect the front speed sensor mounting clamp from the strut.

7. Support the lower arm and remove the strut to knuckle bolts. Use a piece of wire to suspend the knuckle to keep the weight off the brake hose.

8. Before removing the top bolts, make matchmarks on the body and the strut insulator for proper reassembly. If this plate is installed improperly, the wheel alignment will be wrong. Remove the strut upper bolts and remove the strut assembly from the vehicle.

To install:

9. Install the strut to the vehicle and install the top bolts.

10. Connect the ECS connector.

11. Install to the knuckle and install the bolts.

12. Install the brake hose bracket and the ABS clamp.

13. Install the daytime running lamp delay and control unit to the mounting bracket located on top of the left strut tower.

14. Install the auto-cruise control actuator.

15. Install the wheel and tire assembly.

16. Perform a front end alignment.

Strut Cartridge

REPLACEMENT

─── **CAUTION** ───

Use extreme care when disassembling struts. Coil springs must be compressed into a loaded position for strut removal. Never remove the strut cap nut without using proper spring compression tools or equipment.

1. Hold the spring upper seat and loosen the self-locking nut.

─── **CAUTION** ───

The self-locking nut should be loosened only, not removed.

2. Position the strut assembly into spring compression tool No. MB991237/MB991238 or equivalent.

3. Compress spring only enough to free top spring cap. Secure the strut body and remove the self-locking nut.

4. Note position and location when removing the top insulator, upper spring seat with rubber insulator and bump rubber with dust shield.

5. Remove the strut cartridge body and replace only as a complete assembly.

6. Inspect all parts for wear or damage, be sure to check top spring support bearing for smooth operation. Replace any parts found to be worn or defective.

To install:

7. Install strut cartridge body into spring assembly.

8. Install dust boot, spring seat with rubber spring pad and top spring insulator.

9. Install washer and self-locking nut. Tighten nut to 14–18 ft. lbs. (20–25 Nm) for Laser and Stealth or 14–22 ft. lbs. (20–30 Nm) for Summit.

10. Release spring compression tool while seating spring against perch.

Lower Ball Joints

INSPECTION

The lower ball joints on these vehicles are not serviceable. If defective, the entire lower arm must be replaced. The ball joints can be checked using the following procedure:

1. Wiggle the ball joint a few times to make sure it is free.

2. Double-nut the stud and use a torque wrench to measure how much torque is required to turn it. Starting torque should be:

a. Summit: 48 inch lbs. (5.5 Nm) or less.

b. Laser and Talon: 26–87 inch lbs. (3–10 Nm).

c. Stealth: 86–191 inch lbs. (10–22 Nm).

d. Summit Wagon: 17–78 inch lbs. (2–9 Nm).

3. If the stud has more resistance than specified, replace the lower arm assembly. If the resistance is less, it may still be reused unless it has excessive play.

4. A new grease boot can be installed using a large socket for a driver.

Lower Control Arm

REMOVAL AND INSTALLATION

1. Disconnect the negative battery cable.

2. Raise the vehicle and support safely allowing wheels and suspension to hang freely.

3. Remove sway bar links from lower control arm.

4. Disconnect the ball joint stud from the steering knuckle.

5. Remove the inner mounting frame-through bolt and nut.

6. Remove the rear mount bolts. Remove the clamp if equipped.

7. Remove the rear rod bushing if servicing.

To install:

8. Assemble the control arm and bushing.

9. Install the control arm to the vehicle and install the through bolt. Replace the nut and snug temporarily.

10. Install the rear mount clamp, bolts and replacement nuts. Torque the bolts to 43–58 ft. lbs. (60–80 Nm) on Summit, 51 ft. lbs. on Summit Wagon or 72 ft. lbs. (100 Nm) on Laser, Talon and Stealth. Torque the nuts, if equipped, to 30 ft. lbs. (41 Nm).

11. Connect the ball joint stud to the knuckle. Install a new nut and torque to 43–52 ft. lbs. (60–72 Nm).

12. Install the sway bar and links.

13. Lower the vehicle to the floor for the final torquing of the frame mount through bolt.

14. Once the full weight of the vehicle is on the floor, torque the frame mount through bolt nuts to 78 ft. lbs. (108 Nm) on Summit Wagon or 75–90 ft. lbs. (102–122 Nm) on remaining models.

15. Connect the negative battery cable.

Sway Bar

REMOVAL AND INSTALLATION

Summit, Laser and Talon

1. Disconnect the negative battery cable.

2. Raise and safely support vehicle. Remove the front exhaust pipe if necessary.

3. On Summit, remove the tie rod end from the steering knuckle.

4. Remove the center crossmember rear installation bolts.

5. Remove the stabilizer link bolts. On the ball stud type, hold ball stud with a hex wrench and remove the self-locking nut with a box wrench.

6. Remove the stabilizer bar mounts and remove the bar from the vehicle.

7. The installation is the reverse of the removal procedure. Lubricate all rubber parts when installing. Note that the bar brackets are marked left and right.

8. Tighten link bolts with rubber bushings just until the bushings are squashed to the width of the washer.

Summit Wagon

1. Disconnect the negative battery cable.

2. Raise and safely support vehicle. Remove the front exhaust pipe.

3. Remove the stabilizer bar mounting nuts.

4. Remove the bolts from the stabilizer bar mounting fixtures and remove the bar, bushings and fixtures from the vehicle.

5. Installation is the reverse of the removal procedure. Torque the stabilizer fixture mounting fixtures to 16 ft. lbs. (22 Nm), the stabilizer bar link nuts to 29 ft. lbs. (40 Nm) and the exhaust flange nuts to 33 ft. lbs. (45 Nm).

Stealth

1. Disconnect the negative battery cable.

2. Raise the vehicle and support safely.

3. Remove the front exhaust pipe and engine undercover.

4. Remove the left and right frame members.

5. On AWD vehicles with automatic transaxle, remove the transfer case bracket and transfer case.

6. Remove the sway bar link.

7. Remove the sway bar brackets and remove the sway bar from the vehicle.

To install:

8. Note that the bar brackets are marked left and right. Lubricate all rubber parts and install the bushings, the sway bar and brackets.

9. Install the sway bar link.

10. Install the transfer case and bracket.

11. Install the frame members.

12. Install the engine undercover and exhaust pipe.

13. Connect the negative battery cable.

Front Wheel Bearings

All vehicles are front or all-wheel drive. Please refer to the Drive Axle section for bearing information.

REAR SUSPENSION

Shock Absorber Assembly

REMOVAL AND INSTALLATION

1. Disconnect the negative battery cable.

2. Remove the trim cover inside the hatch area for access to the top mounting nuts.

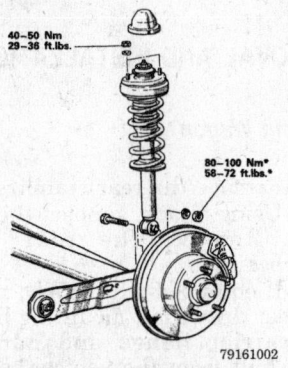

40–50 Nm
29–36 ft.lbs.

80–100 Nm*
58–72 ft.lbs.*

79161002

Shock mounting point on the rear axle

1. Piston rod tightening nut
2. Washer
3. Upper bushing (A)
4. Bracket assembly
5. Upper spring pad
6. Upper bushing (B)
7. Collar
8. Cup assembly
9. Dust cover
10. Bump rubber
11. Coil spring
12. Shock absorber

3. Support the lower arm with a jack and remove the lower mounting nut.

4. Remove the cap from the upper end of the shock.

5. Remove the upper mounting nut and the shock from the vehicle.

To install:

6. Install the shock absorber to the lower arm so the flat mounting boss on the shock absorber is against the lower control arm. Install the lower nut and tighten to 72 ft. lbs. (100 Nm).

7. Install the upper nut and torque to 33 ft. lbs. (45 Nm).

8. Install the cap and trim cover.

9. Lower the arm and remove the jack.

MacPherson Strut

REMOVAL AND INSTALLATION

1. Disconnect the negative battery cable. Remove the trim panel inside the trunk or hatch area for access to the top mounting nuts.

2. Reference mark the top strut cap and remove the top cap and mounting nuts. Do not disconnect the center locknut.

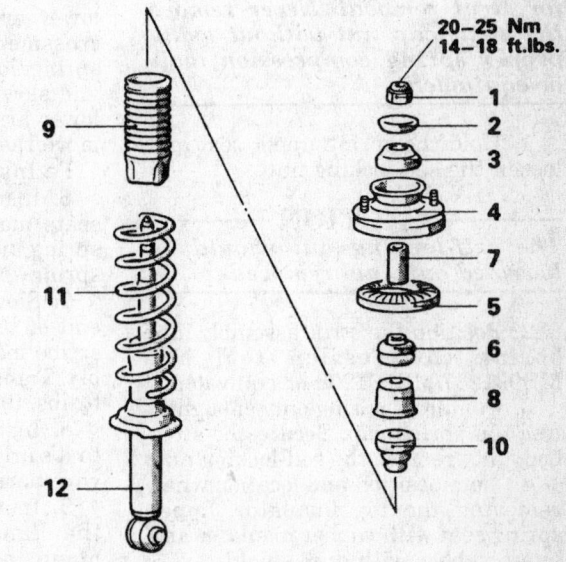

20–25 Nm
14–18 ft.lbs.

79161001

Shock assembly exploded view. Be sure to replace all the parts in the correct order

3. Disconnect the Electronically Controlled Suspension (ECS) harness plug.

4. Remove the brake tube bracket bolt.

5. Raise and safely support torsion axle and arm assembly slightly. Make sure the jack does not contact the lateral rod.

6. Remove the strut lower mounting nut and remove strut from the vehicle.

To install:

7. Install assembled strut, noting cap position and install top cap mounting nuts. Tighten cap mounting bolts to 18–25 ft. lbs. (25–35 Nm) for Summit or 33 ft. lbs. for Laser/Talon and Stealth.

8. Raise rear suspension assembly and install bottom mounting through bolt, tighten to 64 ft. lbs. (89 Nm). Bottom mounting bolt should be tightened with the suspension unloaded.

9. Secure brake tube bracket.

10. Connect the ECS harness plug.

11. Install trunk trim and connect the negative battery cable.

Strut Cartridge

REPLACEMENT

——— CAUTION ———

Use extreme care when disassembling struts. Coil springs must be compressed into a loaded position for strut removal. Never remove the strut cap nut without using proper spring compression tools or equipment.

1. Hold the spring upper seat and loosen the self-locking nut.

——— CAUTION ———

The self-locking nut should be loosened only, not removed.

2. Position the strut assembly into spring compression tool No. MB991237/MB991238 or equivalent.

3. Compress spring only enough to free top spring cap. Secure the strut body and remove the self-locking nut.

4. Note position and location when removing the top insulator, upper spring seat with rubber insulator and bump rubber with dust shield.

5. Remove the strut cartridge body and replace only as a complete assembly.

6. Inspect all parts for wear or damage, be sure to check top spring support bearing for smooth opera-

tion. Replace any parts found to be worn or defective.

To install:

7. Install strut cartridge body into spring assembly.

8. Install dust boot, spring seat with rubber spring pad and top spring insulator.

9. Install washer and self-locking nut. Tighten nut to 14–18 ft. lbs. (20–25 Nm) for Laser and Stealth or 14–22 ft. lbs. (20–30 Nm) for Summit.

10. Release spring compression tool while seating spring against perch.

Coil Springs

REMOVAL AND INSTALLATION

Summit Wagon

1. Remove the rear stabilizer bar.

2. Using a jack, support the lower arm. Remove the rear shock absorber.

3. If equipped with AWD, remove the rear driveshaft mounting bolts at the carrier flange and hang the driveshaft from the vehicle body using wire.

4. If equipped with ABS, remove the speed sensor clamp bolt and relocate out of the way. Do not apply tension to the wire harness of the connector.

5. Scribe mating marks on the lower arm shaft assembly and the crossmember. To remove the coil spring, loosen the shaft assembly nut and slowly lower the rear end of the lower arm. It is not necessary to remove the nut, only to loosen it.

To install:

6. Install the coil spring into the seats making sure both ends of the spring are correctly aligned with the spring seat groove.

7. Slowly raise the rear the rear end of the lower arm and align the scribe marks made during disassembly. Tighten shaft assembly nut to 69 ft. lbs. (95 Nm).

8. Install the speed sensor clamp to it's original location and secure the wire harness making.

9. Install the rear driveshaft to the flange and secure tightening mounting bolts to 40–47 ft. lbs. (55–65 Nm).

10. Reconnect the lower portion of the shock and tighten the retaining bolt to 72 ft. lbs. (100 Nm).

11. Lower the arm and remove the jack.

Rear Control Arms

REMOVAL AND INSTALLATION

Laser and Talon With AWD and Stealth

1. Disconnect the negative battery cable. On FWD Stealth, remove the rear strut assembly. Raise and safely support vehicle. Remove the brake line clamp bolt.

2. Remove the ball joint(s) from the rear trailing arm/steering knuckle.

3. If removing the lower arm, disconnect the sway bar link from the arm.

4. Matchmark and remove the inboard lower arm pivot bolt, if necessary, and remove the arm from the vehicle.

5. Installation is the reverse of the removal procedure. Replace all self-locking nuts. Do not torque the inboard pivot nuts until the full weight of the vehicle is on the ground.

6. On Laser and Talon, torque the lower arm installation nut to 65–80 ft. lbs. (90–110 Nm) and the upper arm installation nut to 101–116 ft. lbs. (140–160 Nm). On Stealth, torque the lower and the upper arm installation nuts to 101–116 ft. lbs. (140–160 Nm).

7. Perform a rear wheel alignment.

Summit Wagon

1. Disconnect negative battery cable.

2. Remove the rear stabilizer bar.

3. If equipped with AWD, remove the rear axle shaft.

4. Remove the rear brake drum.

5. If equipped with ABS, remove the rear caliper assembly and brake disc.

6. Remove the rear hub assembly. If equipped with ABS, take care not to damage the rotor teeth during hub removal.

7. Disconnect the parking brake cable from the rear brake shoe.

8. If equipped with ABS, disconnect and remove the rear wheel sensor.

NOTE: The speed sensor has a pole piece projecting from it. This exposed tip must be protected from impact or damage. Do not allow the pole piece to contact the toothed wheel during removal or installation.

9. Remove the rear shock and coil spring.

10. Remove the brake line and parking brake mounting bolts from the lower control arm.

11. Matchmark and remove the inboard lower arm pivot bolt. Remove the flange bolt and the arm from the vehicle.

To install:

12. Install the arm on the vehicle and secure with the flange bolt, temporarily tighten the nut. Install the arm pivot bolt and temporarily tighten the nut.

13. Install the rear shock and coil spring.

14. Install the brake line and parking brake mounting bolts to the lower control arm.

15. Connect the parking brake cable to the rear brake shoe.

16. Install the rear hub assembly.

17. Install the rear brake drum or, if equipped with ABS, install the rear caliper assembly and brake disc.

18. Install the rear axle shaft.

19. Install and connect the rear wheel speed sensor. Use a brass or other non-magnetic feeler gauge to check the air gap between the tip of the pole piece and the toothed wheel. Correct gap is 0.012–0.035 in. (0.3–0.9mm). Tighten the 2 sensor bracket bolts to 10 ft. lbs. (14 Nm) with the sensor located so the gap is the same at several points on the toothed wheel. If the gap is incorrect, it is likely that the toothed wheel is worn or improperly installed.

20. Lower the vehicle and tighten the lower arm flange bolt nut and the arm pivot bolt to 69 ft. lbs. (95 Nm).

21. Install the rear stabilizer bar and reconnect the negative battery cable.

22. Bleed the brake system if any lines where opened. Adjust the parking brake and perform a rear wheel alignment.

Rear Trailing Arm

REMOVAL AND INSTALLATION

Laser and Talon With AWD and Stealth

1. Disconnect the negative battery cable. Raise and safely support vehicle.

2. Remove the rear caliper from the brake disc and suspend with a wire. Remove the brake disc. Disconnect the parking brake cable and remove the mounting bolts along the trailing arm.

3. Remove the bolt(s) holding the speed sensor bracket to the knuckle and remove the assembly from the vehicle.

NOTE: The speed sensor has a pole piece projecting from it. This exposed tip must be protected from impact or damage. Do not allow the pole piece to contact the toothed wheel during removal or installation.

4. On AWD, remove the rear axle to companion flange bolts and nuts and separate the axle from the companion flange. Remove the self-locking nut and remove the axle hub and companion flange. Remove the dust shield.

5. On FWD Stealth, remove the axle hub unit, parking brake shoes and backing plate. Remove the sway bar link bolt.

6. Remove the lower strut mounting bolt.

7. Remove the control arms from the trailing arm.

8. Remove the trailing arm front mounting nuts and bolts and remove the trailing arm from the vehicle. On AWD, remove the connecting rod at the front of the arm using tool MB991254 or equivalent.

To install:

9. Assemble the trailing arm and connecting rod. Install the trailing arm to the vehicle and install the front mounting nuts and bolts. Complete the final tightening of these when the full weight of the vehicle is on the ground.

10. Install the control arms to the trailing arm, using new self-locking nuts.

11. Install the lower strut bolt.

12. On FWD Stealth, install the sway bar link. Install the parking brake parts and axle hub unit.

13. On AWD, install the dust shield, axle hub and companion flange with a new self-locking nut. Connect the rear axle to the companion flange.

14. Temporarily install the speed sensor to the knuckle; tighten the bolts only finger-tight.

15. Route the cable correctly and loosely install the clips and retainers. All clips must be in their original position and the sensor cable must not be twisted. Improper installation may cause cable damage and system failure.

NOTE: The wiring in the harness is easily damaged by twisting and flexing. Use the white stripe on the outer insulation to keep the sensor harness properly placed.

16. Use a brass or other non-magnetic feeler gauge to check the air gap between the tip of the pole piece and the toothed wheel. Correct gap is 0.012–0.035 inch (0.3–0.9mm). Tighten the 2 sensor bracket bolts to 10 ft. lbs. (14 Nm) with the sensor located so the gap is the same at several points on the toothed wheel. If the gap is incorrect, it is likely that the toothed wheel is worn or improperly installed.

17. Install the brake disc, caliper and connect the parking brake cable, if not already done. Install the mounting clamps bolts.

18. Double check everything for correct routing and installation. Lower the vehicle so its full weight is on the floor.

19. On Laser, Talon and FWD Stealth, torque the front trailing arm/spindle assembly mount nuts to 101–116 ft. lbs. (140–160 Nm). On AWD Stealth, tighten front trailing arm/spindle assembly mount nuts to 145–174 ft. lbs. (200–240 Nm).

20. Perform a rear wheel alignment.

Rear Wheel Bearings

REMOVAL AND INSTALLATION

Summit

1. Raise the vehicle and support safely.

2. Remove the tire and wheel assembly.

3. If equipped with rear disc brakes, remove the caliper from the disc and remove the brake disc.

4. Remove the dust cap and bearing nut. Do not use an air gun to remove the nut.

5. Remove the outer wheel bearing.

6. Remove the drum and/or axle hub with the inner wheel bearing and the grease seal.

7. Remove the grease seal and remove the inner bearing.

To install:

8. Lubricate the inner bearing and install to the drum or hub.

9. Install a new grease seal.

10. To determine if the self-locking nut is reusable:

  a. Screw in the self-locking nut until about ⅛ in. of the spindle is showing.

  b. Measure the torque required to turn the self-locking nut counterclockwise.

  c. The lowest allowable torque is 48 inch lbs. (5.5 Nm). If the measured torque is less than the specification, replace the nut.

11. Install the drum and/or hub to the vehicle.

12. Lubricate and install the outer wheel bearing to the spindle.

13. Torque the self-locking nut to 108–145 ft. lbs. (150–200 Nm).

14. Set up a dial indicator and measure the endplay while moving the hub or drum in and out. If the endplay exceeds 0.008 in. (0.2mm), retorque the nut. If still beyond the limit, replace the bearings.

15. Install the grease cap and wheel assembly.

Summit Wagon

1. Raise the vehicle and support safely. Remove the tire and wheel assembly.

2. If equipped with ABS, remove the caliper assembly, brake disc and rear wheel speed sensor from the adapter. If not equipped with ABS, remove the brake drum.

NOTE: The speed sensor has a pole piece projecting from it. This exposed tip must be protected from impact or damage. Do not allow the pole piece to contact the toothed wheel during removal or installation.

3. Remove the dust cap, nut and tounged washer. Do not use an air gun to remove the nut.

4. Remove the rear hub assembly taking care not to scrape or damage the teeth of the speed rotor, if equipped.

5. Inspect the hub unit bearing for wear or damage. If replacement of the bearing is required, the hub assembly and bearing is to be replaced as a unit. The rear hub unit bearing assembly should should not be dismantled.

6. Installation is the reverse of the removal procedure.

Laser, Talon and Stealth

1. Raise the vehicle and support safely.

2. Remove the tire and wheel assembly.

3. Remove the bolt(s) holding the speed sensor bracket to the knuckle and remove the assembly from the vehicle.

NOTE: The speed sensor has a pole piece projecting from it. This exposed tip must be protected from impact or scratches. Do not allow the pole piece to contact the toothed wheel during removal or installation.

4. Remove the caliper from the brake disc and suspend with a wire.

5. Remove the brake disc.

6. Remove the grease cap, self-locking nut and tounged washer.

7. Remove the rear hub assembly.

NOTE: The rear hub assembly can not be disassembled. If bearing replacement is required, replace the assembly as a unit.

To install:

8. Install the hub assembly.

9. Install the tounged washer and a new self-locking nut. Torque the nut to 144–188 ft. lbs. (200–260 Nm), align with the indentation in the spindle and crimp.

10. Set up a dial indicator and measure the endplay while moving the hub in and out. If the endplay exceeds 0.004 in. (0.1mm) for Laser and Talon or 0.002 in. (0.05mm) for Stealth, retorque the nut. If still beyond the limit, replace the hub unit.

11. Install the grease cap and brake parts.

12. Temporarily install the speed sensor to the knuckle; tighten the bolts only finger-tight.

13. Route the cable correctly and loosely install the clips and retainers. All clips must be in their original position and the sensor cable must not be twisted. Improper installation may cause cable damage and system failure.

NOTE: The wiring in the harness is easily damaged by twisting and flexing. Use the white stripe on the outer insulation to keep the sensor harness properly placed.

14. Use a brass or other non-magnetic feeler gauge to check the air gap between the tip of the pole piece and the toothed wheel. Correct gap is 0.012–0.035 in. (0.3–0.9mm). Tighten the 2 sensor bracket bolts to 10 ft. lbs. (14 Nm) with the sensor located so the gap is the same at several points on the toothed wheel. If the gap is incorrect, it is likely that the toothed wheel is worn or improperly installed.

15. Install the wheel.

Rear Axle Assembly

REMOVAL AND INSTALLATION

Except Summit Wagon

1. Raise the vehicle and support safely.

2. Remove the tire and wheel assembly.

3. If equipped with ABS, remove the bolts holding the speed sensor bracket to the trailing arm and remove the sensor assembly from the vehicle.

NOTE: The speed sensor has a pole piece projecting from it. This exposed tip must be protected from impact or damage. Do not allow the pole piece to contact the toothed wheel during removal or installation.

4. If equipped with rear disc brakes, remove the caliper from the disc and remove the brake disc.

5. Remove the dust cap and bearing nut. Do not use an air gun to remove the nut.

6. Remove the outer wheel bearing.

7. Remove the drum and/or axle hub with the inner wheel bearing and the grease seal.

8. Remove the parking brake cable, brake hose, tube bracket and brake shoes with backing plate from the axle.

9. Remove the lateral rod mounting bolt and nut and secure the lateral rod to the axle beam with a piece of wire.

10. Using the proper equipment, slightly raise the torsion axle and arm assembly. Remove lower strut mounting bolt.

11. Remove the front trailing arm mount bolts and remove the rear axle assembly.

To install:

12. Install the rear axle assembly to the vehicle and install the strut mounting bolts. Install the front mount bolts and lateral rod bolts. Do not tighten these until the full weight of the vehicle is on the ground.

13. Install the backing plate, brake shoes, cable and hose.

14. On Summit, to determine if the self-locking nut is reusable:

   a. Screw in the self-locking nut until about ⅛ in. of the spindle is showing.

   b. Measure the torque required to turn the self-locking nut counterclockwise.

   c. The lowest allowable torque is 48 inch lbs. (5.5 Nm). If the measured torque is less than the specification, replace the nut.

15. Install the drum and/or axle hub. On Summit, lubricate and install the outer wheel bearing to the spindle. Torque the self-locking nut to 108–145 ft. lbs. (150–200 Nm).

16. On Laser and Talon, install the tounged washer and a new self-locking nut. Torque the nut to 144–188 ft.

lbs. (200–260 Nm), align with the indentation in the spindle, and crimp.

17. Install the grease cap and brake parts.

18. Temporarily install the speed sensor to the knuckle; tighten the bolts only finger-tight.

19. Route the cable correctly and loosely install the clips and retainers. All clips must be in their original position and the sensor cable must not be twisted. Improper installation may cause cable damage and system failure.

NOTE: The wiring in the harness is easily damaged by twisting and flexing. Use the white stripe on the outer insulation to keep the sensor harness properly placed.

20. Use a brass or other non-magnetic feeler gauge to check the air gap between the tip of the pole piece and the toothed wheel. Correct gap is 0.012–0.035 in. (0.3–0.9mm). Tighten the 2 sensor bracket bolts to 10 ft. lbs. (14 Nm) with the sensor located so the gap is the same at several points on the toothed wheel. If the gap is incorrect, it is likely that the toothed wheel is worn or improperly installed.

21. Install the wheel.

22. Lower the vehicle so the full weight of the vehicle is on the floor.

23. On Summit, torque the front trailing arm bolt to 94–108 ft. lbs. (130–150 Nm). On Laser and Talon, torque the trailing arm bolt to 72–87 ft. lbs. ((100–120 Nm).

Chrysler Corporation

CHRYSLER—LeBaron **PLYMOUTH**—Acclaim, Sundance **DODGE**—Daytona, Shadow, Spirit

FIRING ORDERS

NOTE: To avoid confusion, always replace spark plug wires one at a time.

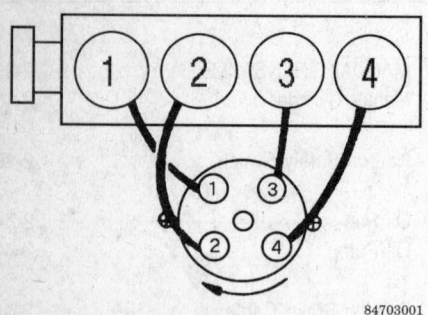

84703001

2.2L and 2.5L Engines (Except Turbo III)
Engine Firing Order: 1–3–4–2
Distributor Rotation: Clockwise

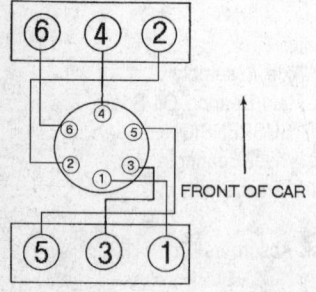

FRONT OF CAR

84703002

3.0L Engine
Engine Firing Order: 1–2–3–4–5–6
Distributor Rotation:
Counterclockwise

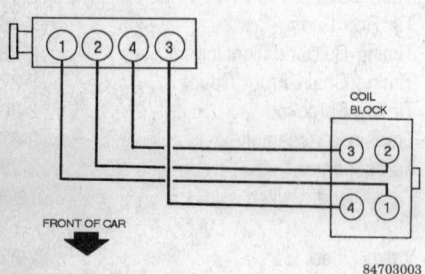

COIL
BLOCK

FRONT OF CAR

84703003

2.2L Turbo III Engines
Engine Firing Order: 1–3–4–2
Distributorless Ignition System

ENGINE ELECTRICAL

NOTE: Disconnecting the negative battery cable on some vehicles may interfere with the functions of the on board computer systems and may require the computers to undergo a relearning process, once the negative battery cable is reconnected.

Distributor

REMOVAL

1. Disconnect the negative battery cable.
2. Disconnect the distributor pickup lead wires. Remove the splash shield, if equipped.
3. Unscrew the distributor cap hold-down screws and lift off the distributor cap with all ignition wires still connected.
4. Remove the coil wire, if necessary.
5. Matchmark the rotor to the distributor housing and the distributor housing to the engine.

NOTE: Do not crank the engine during this procedure. If the engine is cranked, the matchmark must be disregarded.

6. Remove the hold-down bolt and clamp or nut.
7. Remove the distributor from the engine.

INSTALLATION

Timing Not Disturbed

1. Install a new distributor housing O-ring.
2. Install the distributor in the engine so the rotor is aligned with the matchmark on the housing and the housing is aligned with the matchmark on the engine. Make sure the distributor is fully seated and the distributor shaft is fully engaged.
3. Install the hold-down clamp and snug the fastener.
4. Connect the distributor harness connector. Install the splash shield, if equipped.
5. Install the distributor cap and secure retainers.
6. Connect the negative battery cable.
7. Adjust the ignition timing and secure the hold-down.

Timing Disturbed

1. Install a new distributor housing O-ring.
2. Position the engine so the No. 1 piston is at TDC of the compression stroke and the mark on the vibration damper is aligned with 0 on the timing indicator.
3. Install the distributor in the engine so the rotor is aligned with the position of the No. 1 ignition wire on the distributor cap and the housing is aligned with the matchmark on the engine. Make sure the distributor is fully seated and the distributor shaft is fully engaged.

NOTE: There are distributor cap runners inside the cap on 3.0L engine. Make sure the rotor is pointing to where the No. 1 runner originates inside the cap and not where the No. 1 ignition wire plugs into the cap.

4. Install the hold-down clamp and snug retainer.
5. Connect the distributor wire harness connector. Install the splash shield, if equipped.
6. Install the distributor cap and tighten the screws.
7. Connect the negative battery cable.
8. Adjust the ignition timing and tighten the hold-down bolt.

Distributorless Ignition System

REMOVAL AND INSTALLATION

Crankshaft Sensor

1. Disconnect negative battery cable.
2. Remove the inter-cooler to turbocharger air hose.
3. Disconnect the crankshaft sensor wiring harness connector.
4. Remove the timing sensor retaining bolts and lift the sensor straight up and out of the transaxle housing.
   To install:
5. Install the sensor into the transaxle. Apply a downward pressure on the sensor until contact with the transaxle housing is made and secure with the mounting bolt. Tighten bolt to a torque of 105 inch lbs. (12 Nm).
6. Connect the sensor electrical harness and the negative battery cable.
7. Install air inlet hose.
8. Connect the negative battery cable.

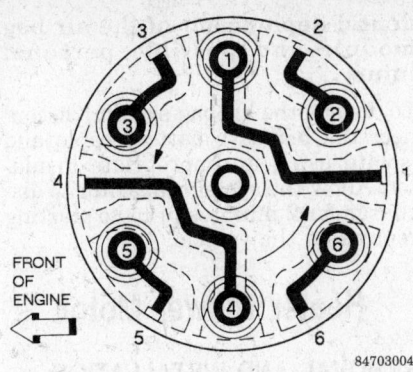

Distributor cap terminal routing — 3.0L engine

84703004

Camshaft Sensor

1. Disconnect negative battery cable.

2. Disconnect the cam reference sensor lead at the wiring harness connector.

3. Remove the sensor retainer bolt and remove the sensor.

4. If installing the original sensor, clean off the old spacer from the sensor face. A new spacer must be installed during installation. If installing a new sensor, confirm that a new paper spacer is installed on the sensor prior to installation.

To install:

5. Install the sensor into the cylinder head and push the sensor downward until contact is made with the camshaft gear. While holding the sensor in this position, install and tighten the retainer bolt to 105 inch lbs. (12 Nm).

6. Connect the sensor wire harness connector and the negative battery cable.

Ignition Coil

1. Remove the ignition cables from the coil pack.

2. Disconnect the harness connector from the coil pack.

3. Remove the ignition coil fasteners and the coil pack from the engine.

4. Installation is the reverse of the removal procedure. Torque the fasteners to 105 inch lbs. (12 Nm).

Ignition Timing

The ignition timing cannot be set or adjusted on the on the 2.2L Turbo III engine.

ADJUSTMENT

1. Start the engine, set the parking brake and run the engine until at normal operating temperature. Be sure to turn all lights and accessories **OFF**.

2. If a magnetic timing unit is available, insert the probe into the receptacle near the timing scale. The scale is located on the top of the bellhousing on 2.2L and 2.5L engines or near the crankshaft pulley on the 3.0L engine.

3. If a magnetic timing unit is not available, connect a conventional power timing light to the No. 1 cylinder spark plug wire.

4. If a Diagnostic Readout Box II (DRB II) is available, access the Basic Timing Mode.

5. If the DRB II is not available, disconnect the coolant sensor. This sensor is located on the side of the thermostat housing on 2.2L and 2.5L engines and between the distributor or thermostat housing on 3.0L engine. The Check Engine light on the instrument panel must be ON.

6. Aim the timing light at the timing scale or read the magnetic timing unit.

7. Loosen the distributor holddown bolt or nut enough so the distributor can be rotated.

8. Turn the distributor in the proper direction until the specified timing according to the VECI label is reached. Tighten the hold-down bolt or nut and recheck the timing.

9. Turn the engine **OFF**. Connect the coolant sensor and check to make sure the Check Engine light does not come ON when the vehicle is restarted. Disconnect the timing apparatus.

10. If the coolant temperature sensor was disconnected, erase the created fault code using the Erase Fault Code mode on the DRB II.

Alternator

PRECAUTIONS

Several precautions must be observed when working with the alternator to avoid damage to the unit.

- If the battery is removed for any reason, make sure it is reconnected with the correct polarity. Reversing the battery connections may result in damage to the one-way rectifiers.
- When utilizing a booster battery as a starting aid, always connect the positive to positive terminals and the negative terminal from the booster battery to a good engine ground on the vehicle being started.
- Never use a fast charger as a booster to start vehicles.

- Disconnect the battery cables when charging the battery with a fast charger.
- Never attempt to polarize the alternator.
- Do not use test lights of more than 12 volts when checking diode continuity.
- Do not short or ground any of the alternator terminals.
- The polarity of the battery, alternator and regulator must be matched and considered before making any electrical connections within the system.
- Disconnect the battery ground terminal when performing any service on electrical components.
- Disconnect the battery if arc welding is to be done on the vehicle.

BELT TENSION ADJUSTMENT

NOTE: The belt tension is automatically adjusted by a dynamic tensioner on the 2.2L Turbo III and 3.0L engines. Periodic adjustment is not necessary.

1. Loosen the pivot bolt slightly.

2. Raise the vehicle and support safely. Remove the splash shield. Loosen the T bolt locknut enough so the alternator can be moved.

3. Tighten the adjusting bolt until the belt deflects about ¼ in. under a 10 lb. load.

4. Tighten the locknut and pivot bolt.

REMOVAL AND INSTALLATION

Except 2.2L Turbo III and 3.0L Engines

1. Disconnect the negative battery cable. Remove the accessory drive belt.

2. If equipped with air conditioning, it may be necessary to remove the air conditioning compressor to gain access to the alternator. Position the compressor aside without disconnecting the refrigerant lines.

3. Remove the oil filter to allow the alternator to be removed from above.

4. Remove all mounting bolts, spacers and adjuster bolt, if equipped, and remove the alternator from the brackets. Note locations and disconnect the wire harness from the rear of the alternator and remove alternator from the vehicle.

To install:

5. Position alternator and and connect the wiring harness.

6. Install mounting through bolts, adjuster and brackets.

7. Install air conditioner compressor assembly.

8. Replace oil filter and check oil level.

9. Install fan drive belts and adjust.

10. Connect the battery terminal, run engine and test alternator for proper operation.

11. When safe, all fluid levels.

2.2L Turbo III Engine

1. Disconnect negative battery cattery cable.

2. Remove the alternator/air conditioning drive belt.

3. Remove the air conditioner compressor mounting bolts and remove compressor from the mounting bracket. Position the compressor aside to allow for alternator removal. It is not necessary to disconnect the refrigerant hoses from the compressor.

4. Remove the alternator mounting bracket bolts and separate the alternator from the mounting bracket. Remove the B+ terminal nut, field terminal nuts and ground wire harness hold-down nuts. Remove the wire harness connectors from the alternator.

5. Remove the alternator from the vehicle.

To install:

6. Install the alternator into position and reattach the wire harness connectors using the appropriate fasteners.

7. Align the mounting ears on the alternator to the mounting bracket and secure using the alternator mounting bolts.

8. Install the air conditioning compressor to the bracket and install the mounting bolts.

9. Install the accessory drive belt.

10. Connect the negative battery cable and check for proper operation of the charging system.

3.0L Engine

1. Disconnect negative battery cable.

2. Release the dynamic belt tensioner using a 1/2 in. breaker bar and remove the alternator drive belt.

3. Remove the alternator mounting bolts and position the alternator so the wire terminals are accessible. Remove the wire connector fasteners, harness and the alternator from the vehicle.

4. Installation is the reverse of the removal procedure. Connect the negative battery cable and check for proper operation of the charging system.

Starter

REMOVAL AND INSTALLATION

1. Disconnect the negative battery cable.

2. On 2.2L and 2.5L engines, remove the attaching nut and bolt at the top of the bellhousing. Raise the vehicle and support safely.

3. Remove the rear mount from the starter, if equipped. If equipped with 2.2L or 2.5L engine, remove the heat shield retainer clip and the shield from the starter.

4. Unbolt the starter and remove from the bellhousing. Position the starter so the wire harness connectors are accessible, remove the retainers and the wire harness from the starter solenoid.

5. Remove the starter motor from the vehicle.

To install:

6. Connect the wire harness to the starter assembly. If equipped with a 2.2L or 2.5L engine, position the heat shield on the starter assembly and secure in place using the shield retainer clip.

7. On the 2.2L and 2.5L engines, install the lower bolt loosely, then lower the vehicle and install the uppermost nut and bolt from above. Torque starter retainer bolts to 40 ft. lbs. (54 Nm). Raise the vehicle again and torque the bottom mounting bolt to the same value. Install the rear mount to the starter as required.

8. On the 3.0L engine, install all mounting bolts and torque to 40 ft. lbs. (54 Nm) evenly.

9. Connect the negative battery cable and check the starter for proper operation.

CHASSIS ELECTRICAL

Air Bag

DISARMING

NOTE: Before attempting any repair procedure that is located in the area of an air bag sensor or wire harness, it is recommended that the air bag system be disarmed. Failure to disarm the air bag system may result in accidental deployment of the air bag module and possible personal injury.

To disarm the air bag system, disconnect the negative battery cable and isolate using an appropriate insulator. Allow the system capacitor to discharge for 2 minutes prior to starting repairs on the vehicle.

Heater Blower Motor

REMOVAL AND INSTALLATION

1. Disconnect the negative battery cable.

2. Remove the glove box assembly, lower right side instrument panel trim cover and right cowl trim panel, as required. Disconnect the blower lead wire connector.

3. If equipped with air conditioning, disconnect the 2 vacuum lines at the recirculating air door actuator.

4. Remove the 2 screws at the top of the blower housing that secure it to the unit cover.

5. Remove the 5 screws from around the blower housing and separate the blower housing from the heater unit.

6. Remove the 3 screws that secure the blower and wheel assembly to the heater or air conditioning housing and remove the assembly from the unit. Remove the fan from the blower motor.

To install:

7. Install the fan onto the blower motor and position motor assembly in housing. Secure motor using 3 mounting screws.

8. Install the blower housing and the heater unit and secure with screws.

9. Connect the 2 vacuum hoses to the recirculating air door actuator as required.

10. Connect the blower lead wire connector.

11. Install the glove box assembly, lower right side instrument panel trim cover and right cowl trim panel, as required.

12. Connect the negative battery cable and check the blower motor for proper operation.

Windshield Wiper Motor

REMOVAL AND INSTALLATION

1. Disconnect the negative battery cable.

2. Remove the wiper arms and the blades. Disconnect hoses from con-

nector at the base of each arm. Remove the cowl top plastic cover and screen.

3. Remove the wiper motor cover, if equipped. Disconnect the motor wiring harness connector.

4. Remove the wiper motor mounting nuts. Remove the wiper motor, pivot and links from the vehicle as an assembly.

To install:

5. Install wiper motor as an assembly with pivot and links.

6. Connect all electrical wiring and install wiper motor covering.

7. Install screen and cowl plastic cover.

8. Connect hoses at the base of each wiper arm and install wiper arms.

9. Connect the negative battery cable and check the wiper motor for proper operation.

Liftgate Wiper Motor

REMOVAL AND INSTALLATION

Daytona

1. Disconnect the negative battery cable.

2. To remove the wiper arm, lift the arm against its spring tension and release the latch. Lift the arm off the motor shaft.

3. Open the liftgate and remove the trim panel. Disconnect the wiring harness connector from the motor.

4. Remove the grommet from the liftgate glass.

5. Remove the screws that fasten the bracket to the liftgate and remove the motor assembly from the vehicle.

To install:

6. Install a new grommet in the liftgate glass.

7. Position the motor to the liftgate and secure, tightening 2 retaining screws to 70 inch lbs. (8 Nm).

8. Connect the electrical harness to the wiper motor.

9. Install the wiper arm onto the wiper motor shaft.

10. Install the interior rear trim panel.

11. Reconnect the negative battery cable and check the rear wiper assembly for proper operation.

Windshield Wiper Switch

REMOVAL AND INSTALLATION

Vehicles With Standard Steering Column

1. Disconnect the negative battery cable and insulate to prevent accidental contact with battery post.

2. Remove the lower steering column cover, if equipped.

3. Straighten the steering wheel so the tires are pointing straight-ahead.

NOTE: If equipped with an airbag, it is imperative that the air bag system be disarmed prior to starting repair procedures and that the steering wheel removal and installation procedure under Steering be followed.

4. Remove the steering wheel.

5. Remove the plastic wiring channel from under the steering column.

6. Disconnect the wiper switch connector, intermittent wipe module connector and cruise control connector, as equipped.

7. Remove the side lock housing cover.

8. Remove the slotted hex-head screw that attaches the wiper switch and turn signal switch assembly, then remove the switch.

9. Remove the control knob from the end of the stalk. Pull the round nylon switch covering up the control stalk and remove the revealed screws that attach the control stalk sleeve to the wiper switch.

10. Rotate the control stalk shaft to the full clockwise position and remove the shaft from the wiper switch by pulling it straight out.

To install:

11. Install the control shaft to the wiper switch, install the screws, nylon switch covering and the control knob.

12. Run the wiring through the opening and down the steering column, position the switch and install the hex-head screw. Make sure the dimmer switch rod is properly engaged.

13. Install the side lock housing cover.

14. Connect the wires and install the wiring channel.

15. Install the steering wheel and torque the nut to 45 ft. lbs. (61 Nm).

16. Install the horn pad and the lower steering column cover.

17. Connect the negative battery cable. Check the wiper and washer,

cruise control, turn signal and dimmer switches for proper operation.

With Tilt Steering Column

1. Disconnect the negative battery cable and insulate to protect against accidental contact with the battery post.

2. Remove the lower steering column cover and remove the plastic wiring channel from the under the steering column.

3. Position the steering wheel so the tires are pointing straight-ahead.

NOTE: If equipped with an airbag, it is imperative that the air bag system be disarmed prior to starting repair procedures and that the steering wheel removal and installation procedure under Steering be followed.

4. Remove the steering wheel.

5. Depress the lockplate with the proper depressing tool, remove the retaining ring from its groove and remove the tool, ring, lockplate, cancelling cam and spring.

6. Remove the switch stalk actuator screw and arm.

7. Remove the hazard switch knob.

8. Disconnect the turn signal switch, wiper switch, intermittent module and cruise control connectors, if equipped.

9. Remove the 3 screws and remove the turn signal switch. Tape the connector to the wires to aid in removal.

10. Remove the ignition key light.

11. Place the key in the **LOCK** position and remove the key. Insert a thin tool into the slot next to the switch mounting screw boss, depress the spring latch at the bottom of the slot releasing the lock. Remove the lock cylinder.

12. Remove the buzzer switch and wedge spring.

13. Remove the 3 housing cover screws and remove the housing cover.

14. Remove the wiper switch pivot pin with a punch and remove the switch.

15. Remove the control knob from the end of the stalk. Pull the round nylon switch covering up the control stalk and remove the revealed screws that attach the control stalk sleeve to the wiper switch.

16. Rotate the control stalk shaft to the full clockwise position and remove the shaft from the wiper switch by pulling it straight out.

To install:

17. Install the control shaft to the wiper switch, install the screws, ny-

lon switch covering and the control knob.

18. Run the wiring through the opening and down the steering column, position the switch and install the wiper switch pivot pin.

19. Install the housing cover.

20. Install the buzzer switch and wedge spring.

21. Install the lock cylinder.

22. Install the ignition key light.

23. Install the turn signal switch, switch stalk actuator arm and hazard switch knob.

24. Install the spring, cancelling cam, lockplate and ring on the steering shaft. Depress the plate with the depressing tool and install the ring securely in the groove. Remove the tool slowly.

25. Connect the turn signal switch, wiper switch, intermittent module and cruise control connectors, if equipped. Install the channel.

26. Install the steering wheel and torque the nut to 45 ft. lbs. (61 Nm).

27. Install the horn pad.

28. Connect the negative battery cable and check the wiper and washer, cruise control, turn signal switch and dimmer switch for proper operation.

29. Install the lower column cover, if equipped.

Daytona and LeBaron

WITH POD MOUNTED SWITCH

1. Disarm the air bag system as follows:

   a. Disconnect the negative battery cable and isolate using an appropriate insulator.

   b. Allow the system capacitor to discharge for 2 minutes prior to starting repairs on the vehicle.

NOTE: Failure to disarm the air bag system may result in accidental deployment of the air bag module and possible personal injury.

2. Remove the panel vent grille above the switch pod assembly and remove the 2 revealed pod mounting screws.

3. If equipped with tilt wheel, position the steering wheel in the lowest position.

4. Remove the 2 remaining screws under the pod and pull the pod from the instrument cluster. Disconnect the wiring harnesses and remove the pod.

5. Unhook the switch linkage from the buttons, remove the switch mounting screws and the switch.

To install:

6. Latch the switch linkage in the up position. Insert the switch into the pod and install the mounting screws. Unlatch the linkage and install onto the push buttons.

7. Operate all switch modes checking for correct operation.

8. Reinstall the inner switch pod panel retainer screws and install the pod assembly into the instrument cluster. Secure pod with the retainer screws.

9. Install the steering wheel, the panel vent grille and connect the negative battery cable. Check for proper operation of the switch.

Instrument Cluster

REMOVAL AND INSTALLATION

Except Daytona and LeBaron

1. Disconnect the negative battery cable. Disarm the air bag system if equipped.

2. Remove the instrument cluster bezel. Cluster removal is not necessary if just removing gauges.

3. When only removing gauge(s) or the speedometer, remove the trip odometer reset knob. If necessary, remove the mask and lens assembly and remove the desired gauge from the cluster. Disconnect the speedometer cable, if equipped, when removing the speedometer.

4. If equipped with automatic transaxle and column shift lever, remove the upper and lower column covers and disconnect the gear indicator cable.

5. Remove the screws attaching the cluster assembly to the instrument panel.

6. Pull the cluster out. Disconnect all harness wiring connectors and the speedometer cable, if equipped. Remove the cluster from the vehicle.

To install:

7. Position the cluster and feed the gear indicator cable through its slot.

8. Connect all wiring and install the speedometer cable to the speedometer, if removed; make sure the cable end is securely clicked in place.

9. Install the cluster retaining screws. Connect the gearshift indicator cable.

10. Install the upper and lower steering column covers and the cluster bezel.

11. Connect the negative battery cable, check all gauges and the speedometer for proper operation. Make sure the gearshift indicator is properly aligned.

Daytona and LeBaron

1. Disconnect the negative battery cable. Disarm the air bag system, if equipped.

2. Remove the panel vent grille above the switch pod assembly and remove the 2 revealed pod mounting screws.

3. Remove the 2 remaining screws under the pod and pull the pod out to disconnect the wiring harnesses. Remove the pod from the instrument panel.

4. Unscrew the tilt column lever, if equipped, remove the screws from under the upper steering column shrouds and remove the shrouds.

5. Pull rearward to disengage the cluster trim bezel retaining clips and remove the bezel.

6. When only removing gauges or the speedometer, remove the mask and lens assembly and remove the desired assembly from the cluster.

7. Remove the screws attaching the cluster to the instrument panel.

8. Pull the cluster out and disconnect all wiring harnesses and the turbo gauge hose, if equipped. Remove the cluster from the vehicle.

To install:

9. Position the cluster and connect all wiring and the turbo hose, if it was disconnected.

10. Install the cluster mounting screws.

11. Install the cluster trim bezel.

12. Install the steering column shrouds and the tilt lever, if equipped.

13. Install the switch pod assembly and panel vent grille.

14. Connect the negative battery cable and check all gauges, switches and the speedometer for proper operation.

Concealed Headlights

MANUAL OPERATION

1. Disconnect the negative battery cable.

2. On the Fifth Avenue and Imperial, locate the manual override knob, which is located under the center of the front bumper fascia and concealed by a cover flap. On the Daytona, lift the hood, look through the sight shield at the headlight and locate the manual override knob.

3. Remove the protective cover boot.

4. Rotate the manual override knob to raise the headlight cover(s). Several revolutions may be required to start movement of the doors.

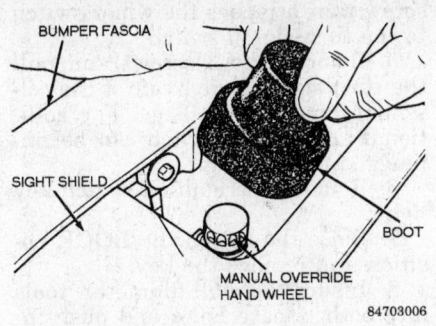

Concealed headlight manual override — Daytona

5. Connect the negative battery cable.

Headlight Switch

REMOVAL AND INSTALLATION

Except Daytona and LeBaron

1. Disconnect the negative battery cable.
2. Remove the headlight switch bezel or cluster bezel, as required.
3. Remove the screws securing the headlight switch mounting plate to the instrument panel. Pull the assembly out and disconnect the connectors from the switch.
4. Depress the spring button and remove the headlight switch knob and stem.
5. Remove the escutcheon, if equipped, and remove the nut that attaches the switch to the mounting plate.
6. The installation is the reverse of the removal procedure.
7. Connect the negative battery cable and check the switch for proper operation.

Daytona and LeBaron

1. Disconnect the negative battery cable.

2. Remove the panel vent grille above the switch pod assembly and remove the 2 revealed pod mounting screws.
3. Remove the 2 remaining screws under the pod and pull the pod out to disconnect the wiring harnesses. Remove the pod from the instrument panel.
4. Remove the turn signal switch lever by pulling it straight out of the pod.
5. Remove the inner panel from the pod. Remove the turn signal switch in order to gain access to the headlight switch retainers.
6. Remove the switch mounting screws.
7. Disconnect the switch linkage from the buttons by pulling the linkage straight up. Remove the switch.

To install:

8. Latch the switch linkage in the up position. Insert the dimmer shaft into the dimmer knob while aligning the switch to the pod assembly.
9. Install the switch attaching screws.
10. Unlatch linkage and install onto push buttons. Operate the switch to assure correct installation.
11. Reconnect the wiring for the turn signal switch, if disconnected, and install switch to its original position. Make sure switch wiring is properly clipped into position.
12. Place together the inner and the outer bezel sections and install the inner switch pod panel retainer screws from underneath the switch pod.
13. Install the turn signal lever by pushing straight into the switch assembly.
14. Install the switch pod assembly into the instrument panel.
15. Reconnect the negative battery terminal and check for proper system function.

Turn Signal Switch

REMOVAL AND INSTALLATION

Vehicles With Standard Column

1. Disconnect the negative battery cable. Disarm the air bag system, if equipped.
2. Remove the lower steering column cover.
3. Position the steering wheel so the tires are pointing straight-ahead.

NOTE: If equipped with an airbag, it is imperative that the steering wheel removal and installation procedure is followed.

4. Remove the steering wheel.
5. Remove the plastic wiring channel from the under the steering column and disconnect the turn signal switch connector.
6. Remove the hazard switch knob. Remove the slotted hex-head screw that attaches the wiper switch to the turn signal switch.
7. Remove the 3 screws and pull the turn signal switch out of the column.

To install:

8. Run the wiring through the opening and down the steering column, position the switch and install the hex-head screw. Make sure the dimmer switch rod is properly engaged.
9. Install the 3 screws and the hazard switch knob.
10. Connect the wires and install the wiring channel.
11. Install the steering wheel and torque the nut to 45 ft. lbs. (61 Nm).
12. Install the horn pad.
13. Connect the negative battery cable and check the turn signal switch and dimmer switch for proper operation.
14. Install the lower column cover, if equipped.

With Tilt Steering Column

1. Disconnect the negative battery cable. Disarm the air bag system, if equipped.
2. Remove the lower steering column cover, if equipped and remove the plastic wiring channel from the under the steering column.
3. Position the steering wheel so the tires are pointing straight-ahead.

NOTE: If equipped with an airbag, it is imperative that the steering wheel removal and installation procedure is followed.

4. Remove the steering wheel.

VIEW FROM BOTTOM

ROTATE THUMB WHEEL

84703007

Concealed headlight manual override — Fifth Avenue and Imperial

5. Depress the lockplate with the proper depressing tool, remove the retaining ring from its groove and remove the tool, ring, lockplate, cancelling cam and spring.

6. Remove the stalk actuator screw and arm.

7. Remove the hazard switch knob.

8. Disconnect the turn signal switch connector.

9. Remove the 3 screws and remove the turn signal switch. Tape the connector to the wires to aid in removal.

To install:

10. Run the wiring through the opening and down the steering column, install the turn signal switch, switch stalk actuator arm and hazard switch knob.

11. Install the spring, cancelling cam, lockplate and ring on the steering shaft. Depress the plate with the depressing tool and install the ring securely in the groove. Remove the tool slowly.

12. Connect the turn signal switch connector and install the channel.

13. Install the steering wheel and torque the nut to 45 ft. lbs. (61 Nm).

14. Install the horn pad.

15. Connect the negative battery cable and check the turn signal switch and dimmer switch for proper operation.

16. Install the lower column cover.

Daytona and LeBaron

REMOTE MOUNTED SWITCH

1. Disconnect the negative battery cable.

2. Remove the panel vent grille above the switch pod assembly and remove the 2 revealed pod mounting screws.

3. Remove the 2 remaining screws under the pod and pull the pod out to disconnect the wiring harnesses. Remove the pod from the instrument panel.

4. Remove the turn signal switch lever by pulling it straight out of the pod.

5. Remove the inner panel from the pod.

6. Remove the turn signal switch mounting screws and slide the switch out of the slot.

7. Unplug the switch harness from the 8-way connector and remove the switch.

To install:

8. Connect the wire connector, install the switch into the switch pod and secure with the switch retainer screws.

9. Install the turn signal control lever into the switch. Install the pod assembly into the instrument panel.

10. Connect the negative battery terminal and check for proper operation of all switch controlled systems.

Combination Switch

REMOVAL AND INSTALLATION

LeBaron Landau, Shadow, Sundance, Spirit and Acclaim

1. Disconnect the negative battery cable. Disarm the air bag system, if equipped.

2. Remove the tilt lever, if equipped.

3. Remove the upper and the lower steering column covers.

4. Remove the combination switch tamper-proof mounting screws. Gently pull the switch away from the steering column and loosen the connector screw; the screw will remain in the connector. Disconnect the connector from the switch.

To install:

5. Install the wiring connector to the switch and tighten the connector to 17 inch lbs. (2 Nm).

6. Mount the combination switch to the column and torque the retainers to 17 inch lbs. (2 Nm).

7. Install both the upper and the lower steering column covers.

8. Install the tilt lever if removed.

9. Connect the negative battery cable and check switch for proper operation.

Ignition Lock

REMOVAL AND INSTALLATION

Standard Column

EXCEPT ACUSTAR COLUMN

NOTE: The Acustar column can be identified by the halo light around the ignition key cylinder.

1. Disconnect the negative battery cable. Disarm the air bag system, if equipped.

2. Position the steering wheel so the tires are pointing straight-ahead.

NOTE: If equipped with an airbag, it is imperative that the steering wheel removal and installation procedure is followed.

3. Remove the steering wheel.

4. Remove the hazard switch knob. Remove the slotted hex-head screw that attaches the wiper switch to the turn signal switch.

5. Remove the 3 screws and pull the turn signal switch out of the column as far as it will go. For additional access, the switch can be unplugged from below.

6. Remove the ignition switch key light.

7. Place the key in the **LOCK** position and remove the key.

8. Insert 2 small-diameter tools into both release holes and push inward to release the spring-loaded lock retainers while simultaneously pulling the key lock cylinder out of its bore.

To install:

9. Install the key cylinder.

10. Install the ignition switch key light.

11. Install the turn signal switch and hazard switch knob, then connect all wiring.

12. Install the steering wheel and torque the nut to 45 ft. lbs. (61 Nm).

13. Install the horn pad.

14. Connect the negative battery cable and check the lock cylinder for proper operation.

15. Install the lower column cover, if equipped.

Tilt Column

EXCEPT ACUSTAR COLUMN

NOTE: The Acustar column can be identified by the halo light around the ignition key cylinder.

1. Disconnect the negative battery cable. Disarm the air bag system if equipped.

2. Position the steering wheel so the tires are pointing straight-ahead.

NOTE: If equipped with an airbag, it is imperative that the steering wheel removal and installation procedure is followed.

3. Remove the steering wheel.

4. Depress the lockplate with the proper depressing tool, remove the retaining ring from its groove, then remove the tool, ring, lockplate, cancelling cam and spring.

5. Remove the stalk actuator screw and arm.

6. Remove the hazard switch knob.

7. Remove the turn signal switch mounting screws and pull the switch out of the column as far as the wires will allow. Unplug harness from below if necessary.

8. Remove the ignition key light.

9. Place the key in the **LOCK** position and remove the key. Insert a thin tool into the slot next to the

switch mounting screw boss, depress the spring latch at the bottom of the slot releasing the lock and remove the lock cylinder.

To install:

10. Install the lock cylinder.

11. Install the ignition key light.

12. Install the turn signal switch, switch stalk actuator arm and hazard switch knob.

13. Install the spring, cancelling cam, lockplate and ring on the steering shaft. Depress the plate with the depressing tool and install the ring securely in the groove. Remove the tool slowly making sure the ring is properly seated in the groove on the shaft.

14. Connect the electrical harness at the base of the steering column if disconnected.

15. Install the steering wheel and torque the nut to 45 ft. lbs. (61 Nm).

16. Install the horn pad.

17. Connect the negative battery cable and check the turn signal switch for proper operation.

18. Install the lower column cover.

Ignition Switch

REMOVAL AND INSTALLATION

Except Acustar Steering Column

NOTE: The Acustar column can be identified by the halo light around the ignition key cylinder.

1. Disconnect the negative battery cable. Disarm the air bag system if equipped.

2. Remove the lower steering column cover.

3. Remove the steering column retaining nuts and lower the steering column so the steering wheel is resting on the driver's seat.

4. Remove the 2 screws that attach the ignition switch to the steering column.

5. Rotate the switch 90 degrees and pull up to disengage it from the ignition switch rod.

To install:

6. Engage the switch with the rod, rotate the switch 90 degrees and push down until fully engaged.

7. Install the mounting screws finger-tight.

8. Place the key in the **LOCK** position and remove the key. Adjust the switch by pushing up gently on the switch to take up all slack in the rod and secure in this position by tightening the mounting screws.

9. Raise the steering column and hand-tighten the mounting nuts. Reconnect the negative battery cable and check the switch for proper operation in all positions.

10. Secure the column mounting nuts to 105 inch lbs. (12 Nm). Install the steering column cover.

Ignition Lock/Switch

REMOVAL AND INSTALLATION

Acustar Steering Column

NOTE: The Acustar column can be identified by the halo light around the ignition key cylinder.

1. Disconnect the negative battery cable. Disarm the air bag, if equipped.

NOTE: Failure to disarm the air bag system may result in accidental deployment of the air bag module and possible personal injury.

2. Remove the tilt lever by turning counterclockwise, if equipped.

3. Remove the 3 Torx® T-20 screws and remove the upper and lower column covers.

4. Remove the 3 ignition switch tamper-resistant screws using Torx® tool APEX 440-TX20H or equivalent.

5. Pull the switch away from the column. Release the connector locks on the 2 wiring connectors and disconnect them from the switch.

6. Remove the key lock cylinder from the ignition switch as follows:

   a. Insert the key and turn the switch to the **LOCK** position. Using a small tool, depress the key cylinder retaining pin until flush with the key cylinder surface.

   b. Rotate the key clockwise to the **OFF** position to unseat the key cylinder from the ignition switch

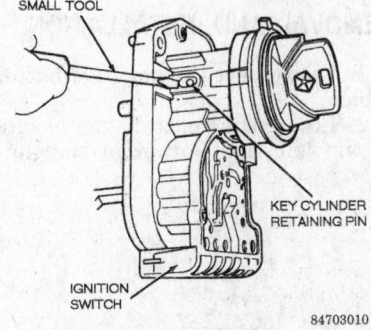

Depressing the cylinder retaining pin — Acustar column

assembly. The cylinder bezel should be about ⅛ in. above the ignition switch halo light ring. Do not attempt to remove the key cylinder at this point.

   c. With the key cylinder unseated, rotate the key and cylinder counterclockwise to the **LOCK** position and remove the key.

   d. Remove the key cylinder from the ignition switch.

To install:

7. If equipped with floor mounted gear shifter, place the selector in the **P** position.

8. Connect the electrical harness to the ignition switch making sure the locking tabs are fully seated in the wiring connectors.

9. Place the gear shift lever in the **P** position. Mount the ignition switch to the column as follows:

   a. Place the ignition switch in the **LOCK** position. The switch is in the lock position when the column lock flag is parallel to the ignition switch terminals.

   b. Position the ignition switch lock dowel pin so it will engage the steering column park lock slider linkage.

   c. Apply a light coat of grease to the column lock flag and the park lock dowel pin. Place the ignition against the lock housing opening on the steering column. Ensure ignition switch park lock dowel pin enters the slot in the park lock slider linkage in the steering column.

   d. Install the ignition switch mounting screws and torque to 17 inch lbs. (2 Nm).

10. Install the steering column covers. If equipped with tilt wheel, install the tilt lever.

11. Install the ignition key to the lock cylinder as follows:

   a. With the key cylinder and ignition switch in the **LOCK** position, key not in cylinder, gently insert the key cylinder into the ignition switch until it bottoms.

   b. Insert the ignition key into the ignition cylinder. Simultaneously, push in on the cylinder and rotate the key to the end of travel. The ignition cylinder should now be fully seated in the ignition switch.

12. Connect the negative battery cable.

13. Check the push-to-lock and park lock functions, halo lighting and all ignition switch positions for proper operation.

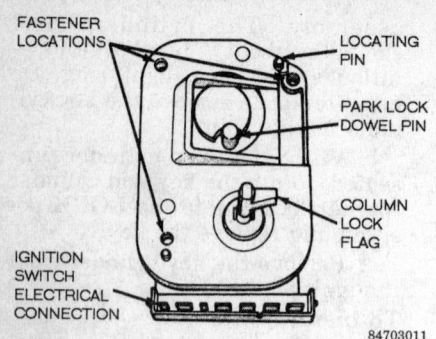

Preparing the ignition switch for installation — Acustar column

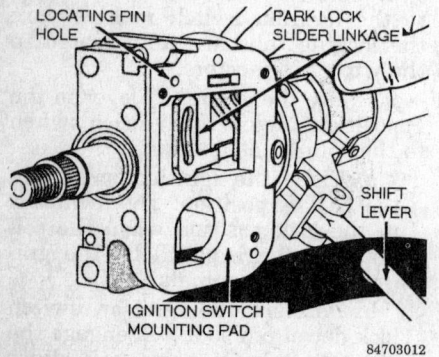

Ignition switch mounting pad — Acustar column

Brake Light Switch

ADJUSTMENT

1. Disconnect the negative battery cable. Disarm the air bag system, if equipped.
2. Remove the lower steering column cover.
3. Push the switch and retainer bracket forward towards the brake pedal as far as it will go. The brake pedal should move forward slightly.
4. Gently pull back on the brake pedal bringing the striker back toward the switch. Continue to pull back on the brake pedal until it will go back no further. This will cause the switch to ratchet backward to the correct position.
5. Connect the negative battery cable.
6. Verify correct adjustment of the brake light switch; with the engine OFF, apply the brake pedal and check to make sure the brake lights are illuminated. If the brake lights do not go ON, readjust the switch.
7. Install the lower steering column cover.

REMOVAL AND INSTALLATION

1. Disconnect the negative battery cable.
2. Unplug the brake light switch connectors above the brake pedal.
3. Remove the brake light switch and bracket assembly from the brake pedal bracket.
4. Remove the switch from its mounting bracket.
5. Installation is the reverse of the removal procedure. After installation, adjustment of the brake light switch is required.

Clutch Switch

NOTE: Some vehicles are equipped with a clutch/starter interlock switch. Otherwise, a clutch switch is installed on vehicles equipped with speed control only. Its function is to cancel the set speed when the clutch is depressed.

REMOVAL AND INSTALLATION

1. Disconnect the negative battery cable.
2. Unplug the switch connectors near the pedals.
3. Remove the switch and bracket assembly from the mounting bracket.
4. Remove the switch from its bracket.
5. The installation is the reverse of the removal procedure.
6. Connect the negative battery cable and check the speed control system for proper operation.

Neutral Safety Switch

REMOVAL AND INSTALLATION

1. Disconnect the negative battery cable.
2. Locate the neutral safety switch at the left rear corner of the automatic transaxle. The neutral safety switch is the black switch located to the right of the PRNDL switch. Unplug the switch harness connector from the switch.
3. Remove the switch from the transaxle. Place a drain pan under the switch to catch any transaxle fluid that may leak out during switch removal.
4. The installation is the reverse of the removal procedure. Torque the switch to 25 ft. lbs. (34 Nm).
5. Connect the negative battery cable and check the switch for proper operation.

Fuses, Circuit Breakers and Relays

LOCATION

Spirit, Acclaim, Shadow and Sundance

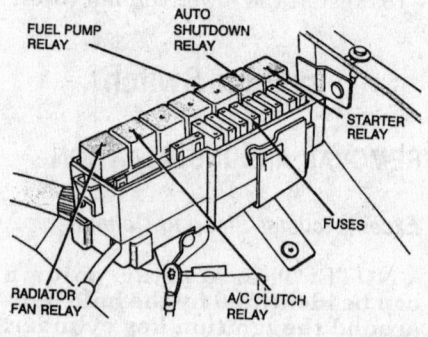

Relay identification — Daytona

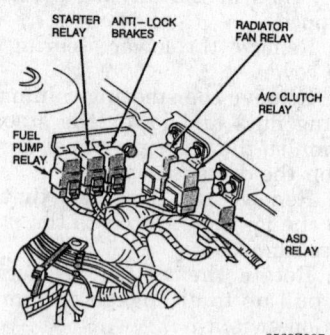

Relay identification — LeBaron, Spirit, Acclaim, Shadow, Sundance

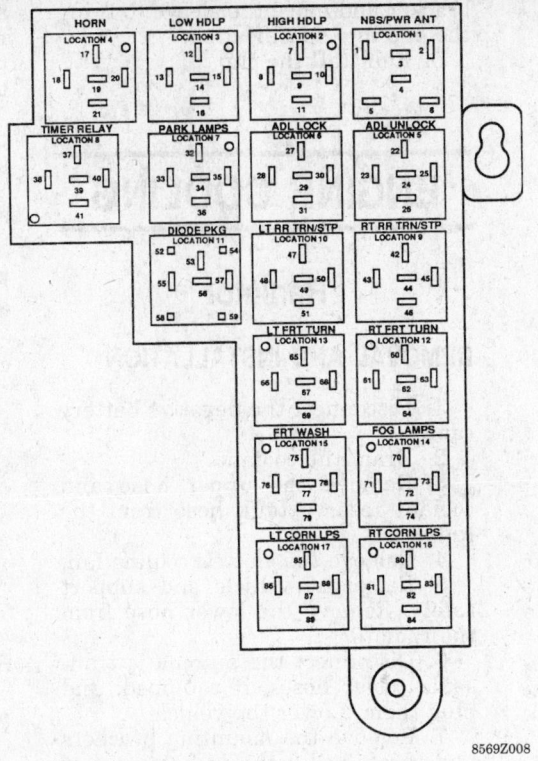

Relay identification — Wire-end view of the relay back on the left side kick panel — Daytona and LeBaron

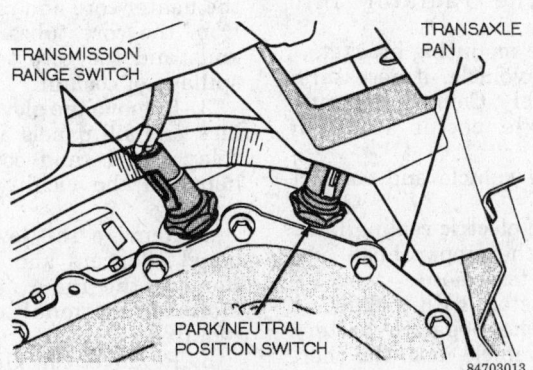

Neutral safety switch location — 4 speed, 41TE automatic transaxle

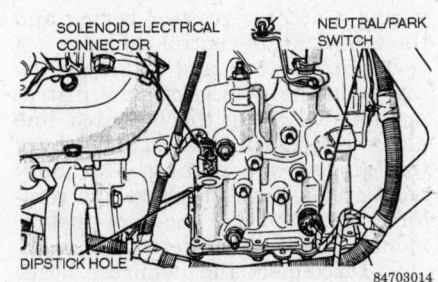

Neutral safety switch location — 3-speed Torqueflight automatic transaxle

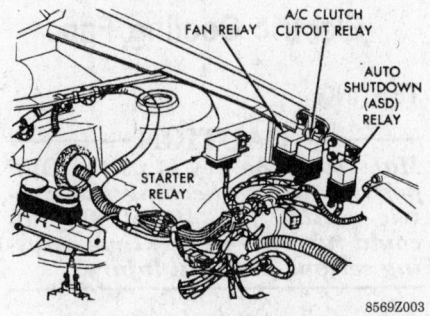

Relay identification — Shadow convertible

The fuse block is located behind the steering column cover, accessible by removing the fuse access panel above the hood latch release lever. The relay and flasher module is located behind an access panel in the glovebox. Included in the module are the hazard and turn signal flashers along with the time delay and horn relays. Additional relays are mounted on the inner fender panel near the battery and strut tower.

Daytona and LeBaron

The fuse block is located behind a removable access panel to the left of the lower portion of the steering column.

On Daytona and LeBaron, a relay bank is located on the left side kick panel. The Power Distribution Center, which contains additional relays and fuses, is located in the engine compartment behind the battery. Each item is identified on the cover.

Flashers

LOCATION

The flasher module is located behind an access panel in the glovebox.

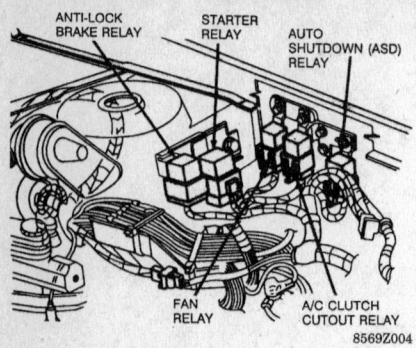

ANTI-LOCK BRAKE RELAY
STARTER RELAY
AUTO SHUTDOWN (ASD) RELAY
FAN RELAY
A/C CLUTCH CUTOUT RELAY

8569Z004

Relay identification — without Power Distribution Center

Computers

LOCATION

Single Board Engine Controller (SBEC) — is located in the engine compartment, to the left of the battery.

Transaxle controller — is located inside the passenger compartment, behind the right side kick panel.

Body controller, if equipped — is located inside the passenger compartment, behind the right side kick panel.

Cruise Control

CABLE ADJUSTMENT

2.2L and 2.5L Engines

1. The clearance between the throttle stud and cable clevis should be 1/16 in.
2. To adjust the cable, remove the retaining clip or loosen the retaining clamp nut at the throttle bracket.
3. Pull all slack out of the cable using a 1/16 in. diameter tool to account for proper clearance. Make sure the curb idle position of the throttle blade is not affected.
4. Reinstall the retaining clip or nut.

3.0L Engine

1. Grip the cable core and lightly push toward the servo.
2. While holding the position, mark the core wire next to the protective sleeve.
3. Pull the core wire away from the servo. There should be a 0.24 in. (6mm) gap between the mark on the core wire and the protective sleeve.
4. If the gap is not correct, remove the adjustment clip from the throttle

bracket and move the sleeve to bring the gap into specification.
5. Reinstall the clip.

ENGINE COOLING

Radiator

REMOVAL AND INSTALLATION

1. Disconnect the negative battery cable.
2. Drain the coolant.
3. Remove the upper hose and coolant reserve tank hose from the radiator.
4. Remove the electric cooling fan.
5. Raise the vehicle and support safely. Remove the lower hose from the radiator.
6. Disconnect the automatic transaxle cooler hoses, if equipped, and plug them. Lower the vehicle.
7. Remove the mounting brackets and carefully lift the radiator out of the engine compartment.
   To install:
8. Lower the radiator into position.
9. Install the mounting brackets.
10. Raise the vehicle, if necessary, and support safely. Connect the automatic transaxle cooler lines, if equipped.
11. Lower the vehicle and connect the lower hose.
12. Install the electric cooling fan.
13. Connect the upper hose and coolant reserve tank hose.
14. Fill the system with coolant.
15. Connect the negative battery cable, run the vehicle until the thermostat opens, fill the radiator completely and check the automatic transaxle fluid level, if equipped.
16. Once the vehicle has cooled, recheck the coolant level.

Electric Cooling Fan

TESTING

— CAUTION —
Make sure the key is in the OFF position when checking the electric cooling fan. If not, the fan could turn ON at any time, causing serious personal injury.

1. Unplug the fan connector.
2. Using a jumper wire, connect the terminals of the fan connector to

a good 12 volt source observing correct polarity. The female terminal on the fan motor is normally the negative terminal.
3. The fan should come ON with the circuit completed and should run smoothly and free of vibrations.
4. If not, the fan is defective and should be replaced.

REMOVAL AND INSTALLATION

1. Disconnect the negative battery cable.
2. Unplug the connector.
3. Remove the mounting screws.
4. Remove the fan assembly from the vehicle.
5. The installation is the reverse of the removal procedure.

Heater Core

REMOVAL AND INSTALLATION

Without Air Conditioning

1. Disconnect the negative battery cable. Drain the cooling system.
2. Clamp off the heater hoses near the heater core and remove the hoses from the core tubes. Plug the hose ends and the core tubes to prevent spillage of coolant.
3. Remove the glove box, right side kick and sill panels and all modules, relay panels and computer components in the vicinity of the heater housing.
4. Remove the lower instrument panel silencers and reinforcements. Remove the radio and other dash-mounted optional equipment, as required.
5. Remove the floor console, if equipped. Remove the floor and defroster distribution ducts.
6. Remove the bolt holding the right side instrument panel to the right cowl.
7. Disconnect the blower motor wiring, antenna, resistor wiring and the temperature control cable.
8. On Daytona and LeBaron, using a cutting device, cut the instrument panel along the indented line along the padded cover to the right of the glove box opening. Cut only plastic, not metal. Remove the reinforcement and the piece of instrument panel that is riveted to it.
9. Disconnect the demister hoses from the top of the housing, if equipped.
10. Disconnect the hanger strap from the package and rotate it aside.

11. Remove the retaining nuts from the package mounting studs at the firewall.

12. Fold the carpeting and insulation back to provide a little more working room and to prevent spillage from staining the carpeting. Pull the right side of the instrument panel out as far as possible.

13. Remove the heater housing from under the dash panel and remove it from the passenger compartment. If the passenger seat is preventing removal, remove it.

14. Disassemble the housing assembly as follows:

   a. Locate and remove the retaining nut from the blend air door pivot shaft.

   b. Remove the crank arm by squeezing the retainer away from the shaft and pulling straight upward.

   c. Disconnect the vacuum lines from the defroster and panel mode vacuum actuator and position them aside.

   d. Remove the heater unit cover attaching screws going upward at the defroster outlet chamber.

   e. Remove the 2 heater unit cover attaching screws going upward at the air inlet plenum.

   f. Remove the remaining heater unit cover attaching screws going downward into the housing and remove the cover.

15. Remove the retaining screw from the heater core and remove the core from the housing assembly.

To install:

16. Remove the temperature control door from the housing and clean the unit out with solvent. Lubricate the lower pivot rod and its well and install. Wrap the heater core with foam tape and place it in position. Secure it with its screw.

17. Assemble the housing, making sure all cover screws were installed.

18. Connect the demister hoses. Install the nuts to the firewall and connect the hanger strap inside the passenger compartment.

19. Fold the carpeting back into position. Install the bolt that attaches the right side of the instrument panel to the cowl.

20. Connect the blower motor wiring, antenna, resistor wiring and the temperature control cable.

21. Install the air distribution ducts. Install the floor console, if equipped. Install the radio and all other dash mounted items that were removed during the disassembly procedure.

22. Install the lower instrument panel reinforcements and silencers. Install all modules, relay panels and computer components that were removed during disassembly.

23. Install the glove box and right side kick and sill panels. Install the passenger seat, if removed.

24. Connect the heater hoses to the heater core tubes. Fill the cooling system.

25. Connect the negative battery cable and check the entire climate control system for proper operation and leakage.

With Air Conditioning

1. Disconnect the negative battery cable. Properly discharge the air conditioning system. Drain the cooling system.

2. Clamp off the heater hoses near the heater core and remove the hoses from the core tubes. Plug the hose ends and the core tubes to prevent spillage of coolant.

3. Disconnect the H-valve connection at the valve and remove the H-valve. Remove the condensation tube.

4. Disconnect the vacuum lines at the brake booster and water valve.

5. Remove the glove box, right side kick, sill panels and all modules, relay panels and computer components in the vicinity of the housing. Remove the blower motor from the housing.

6. Remove the lower instrument panel silencers and reinforcements. Remove the radio, cigar lighter, ashtray receiver and the heater/air conditioning control unit from the instrument panel. If equipped with Automatic Temperature Control (ATC), disconnect the instrument wiring from the rear face of the ATC control unit.

7. Remove the floor console, if equipped. Remove the floor and center air distribution ducts. Remove the bolt holding the right side instrument panel to the right cowl.

8. Disconnect the blower motor wiring, antenna, resistor wiring and the temperature control cable. Disconnect the vacuum harness at the connection at the top of the housing.

9. On Daytona and LeBaron, using a cutting device, cut the instrument panel along the indented line along the padded cover to the right of the glove box opening. Cut only plastic, do not cut through the metal dash support. Remove the reinforcement and the piece of instrument panel that is riveted to it.

10. Disconnect the demister hoses from the top of the housing, if equipped. Disconnect the hanger

strap from the package and rotate it aside. Remove the retaining nuts from the package mounting studs at the firewall.

11. Fold the carpeting and insulation back to provide a little more working room and to prevent spillage from staining the carpeting. Pull the right side of the instrument panel out as far as possible.

12. Remove the air conditioning and heater housing assembly from under the dash panel and remove it from the passenger compartment. Remove the passenger seat if more clearance is required.

13. Disassemble the housing assembly as follows:

   a. Locate and remove the retaining nut from the blend air door pivot shaft.

   b. Remove the crank arm by squeezing the retainer away from the shaft and pulling straight upward.

   c. Disconnect the vacuum lines from the defroster and panel mode vacuum actuators and position them aside.

   d. Remove the heater/air conditioning unit cover attaching screws going upward at the defroster outlet chamber.

   e. Remove the 2 heater/air conditioning unit cover attaching screws going upward at the air inlet plenum.

   f. Remove the remaining air conditioning unit cover attaching screws going downward into the housing and remove the cover.

14. Remove the retaining screw from the heater core and remove the core from the housing assembly.

To install:

15. Remove the temperature control door from the housing and clean the unit out with solvent. Lubricate the lower pivot rod and its well and install. Wrap the heater core with foam tape and place it in position. Secure it with its screw.

16. Assemble the housing, making sure all vacuum tubing is properly routed. Install the crank arm onto the shaft and secure using the retainer clip.

17. Feed the vacuum lines through the hole in the firewall and install the assembly to the vehicle. Connect the vacuum harness and demister hoses. Install the nuts to the firewall and connect the hanger strap inside the passenger compartment.

18. Fold the carpeting and insulation back into position. Install the bolt that attaches the right side of the instrument panel to the cowl.

19. Connect the blower motor wiring, antenna, resistor wiring and temperature control cable. If equipped with ATC, reconnect the wire harness to the rear of the control assembly.

20. Install the center and floor distribution ducts. Install the floor console, if equipped. Install the radio and any other dash mounted items that were removed during the disassembly procedure.

21. Install the lower instrument panel reinforcements and silencers. Install all modules, relay panels and computer components removed during disassembly.

22. Install the glove box and right side kick and sill panels. Install the passenger seat, if removed.

23. Connect the vacuum lines at the brake booster and water valve. Using new gaskets, install the H-valve and condensation tube.

24. Connect the heater hoses to the core tubes at the firewall. Using the proper equipment, evacuate and recharge the air conditioning system. Fill the cooling system.

25. Connect the negative battery cable and check the entire climate control system for proper operation and leakage.

Water Pump

REMOVAL AND INSTALLATION

2.2L and 2.5L Engines

1. Disconnect the negative battery cable.

2. Drain the cooling system.

3. If equipped with air conditioning, remove the compressor from the bracket and position it aside. It is not necessary to discharge the air conditioning system.

4. Remove the alternator and bracket from the engine. Have a drain pan under the side mounting stud because the stud screws into a water jacket and coolant will spill out when it is removed. Remove the pulley and belt from the water pump.

5. Disconnect the lower radiator hose and heater hose from the water pump.

6. Remove the water pump housing attaching screws and remove the assembly from the vehicle. Discard the O-ring. The 2.2L Turbo III engine is equipped with a spacer (coolant deflector) between the pump housing

and block on the lower mounting stud.

NOTE: Use care when removing the coolant deflector because it will be reused.

7. Remove the water pump from the housing. The 2.2L Turbo III engine is equipped with a coolant deflector that will be re-used.

To install:

8. Using a new gasket or silicone sealer, install the water pump to the housing.

9. On 2.2L Turbo III engine, install the coolant deflector to the block and install the spacer to the lower stud. Install a new O-ring to the housing and install to the engine. Torque the 3 upper bolts to 21 ft. lbs. (30 Nm) and the lower nut to 50 ft. lbs. (68 Nm).

10. Install the water pump pulley and torque the bolts to 21 ft. lbs. (30 Nm). Connect the radiator hose and heater hose to the water pump.

11. Install the alternator and compressor bracket to the engine. Install the alternator and the air conditioning compressor. Adjust the accessory drive belts.

12. Remove the hex-head plug on the top of the thermostat housing. Fill the radiator with coolant until the coolant comes out the plug hole. Install the plug and continue to fill the radiator.

13. Connect the negative battery cable, run the vehicle until the thermostat opens, fill the radiator completely and check for leaks.

14. Once engine has cooled, recheck the coolant level and add as required.

3.0L Engine

1. Disconnect the negative battery cable.

2. Drain the cooling system.

3. Remove the timing cover. If the same timing belt will be reused, mark the direction of the timing belt's rotation for installation in the same direction. Make sure the engine is positioned so the No. 1 cylinder is at the TDC of its compression stroke and the sprocket's timing marks are aligned with the engine's timing mark indicators.

4. Loosen the timing belt tensioner bolt and remove the belt. Position the tensioner as far away from the center of the engine as possible and tighten the bolt. Remove the water pump mounting bolts, separate the pump from the water inlet pipe and remove the pump from the engine.

To install:

5. Install the water pump to the engine with new gasket in place. Torque the water pump mounting bolts to 20 ft. lbs. (27 Nm).

6. If not already done, position both camshafts so the marks align with those on the alternator bracket (rear bank) and inner timing cover (front bank). Rotate the crankshaft so the timing mark aligns with the mark on the oil pump.

7. Install the timing belt on the crankshaft sprocket and while keeping the belt tight on the tension side (right side), install the belt on the front camshaft sprocket.

8. Install the belt on the water pump pulley, then the rear camshaft sprocket and the tensioner.

9. Rotate the front camshaft counterclockwise to tension the belt between the front camshaft and the crankshaft. If the timing marks are not aligned, repeat the procedure.

10. Install the crankshaft sprocket flange.

11. Loosen the tensioner bolt and allow the spring to tension the belt.

12. Turn the crankshaft 2 full turns in the clockwise direction only until the timing marks are aligned and torque the tensioner lock bolt to 21 ft. lbs. (29 Nm).

13. Refill the cooling system. This system uses a self-bleeding thermostat, so there is no need to bleed the system. Connect the negative battery cable, road test the vehicle and check for leaks.

Thermostat

REMOVAL AND INSTALLATION

1. Disconnect the negative battery cable. Drain the coolant down to thermostat level or below.

2. Remove the thermostat housing.

3. Remove the thermostat and discard the gasket. Clean the housing mating surfaces and install a new gasket.

To install:

4. Install the thermostat into the housing and position the housing on the engine. Tighten bolts to 21 ft. lbs. (28 Nm) for 2.2L and 2.5L engines or 113 inch lbs. (12 Nm) for 3.0L engines.

5. Add coolant to the proper level.

6. On 2.2L and 2.5L engines, remove the plug on top of the thermostat housing. On 2.2L Turbo III engine, remove the coolant temperature sensor on top of the housing. Fill the

radiator with coolant until the coolant comes out the hole. Install the plug or sensor and continue to fill the radiator. The 3.0L engine thermostat is self-bleeding.

7. Connect the negative battery cable, run the vehicle until the thermostat opens, fill the radiator completely and check for leaks.

8. Once the vehicle has cooled, recheck the coolant level.

COOLING SYSTEM BLEEDING

To bleed air from the 2.2L and 2.5L engines, remove the plug or sensor on the top of the thermostat housing. Fill the radiator with coolant until the coolant comes out the hole. Install the plug and continue to fill the radiator. This will vent all trapped air from the engine.

The thermostat in the 3.0L engine is equipped with a small air vent valve that allows trapped air to bleed from the system during refilling. This valve eliminates the need for cooling system bleeding in those engines.

FUEL SYSTEM

Fuel System Service Precautions

Safety is the most important factor when performing not only fuel system maintenance but any type of maintenance. Failure to conduct maintenance and repairs in a safe manner may result in serious personal injury or death. Maintenance and testing of the vehicle's fuel system components can be accomplished safely and effectively by adhering to the following rules and guidelines.

• To avoid the possibility of fire and personal injury, always disconnect the negative battery cable unless the repair or test procedure requires that battery voltage be applied.

• Always relieve the fuel system pressure prior to disconnecting any fuel system component (injector, fuel rail, pressure regulator, etc.), fitting or fuel line connection. Exercise extreme caution whenever relieving fuel system pressure to avoid exposing skin, face and eyes to fuel spray. Please be advised that fuel under pressure may penetrate the skin or any part of the body that it contacts.

• Always place a shop towel or cloth around the fitting or connection prior to loosening to absorb any excess fuel due to spillage. Ensure that all fuel spillage (should it occur) is quickly removed from engine surfaces. Ensure that all fuel soaked cloths or towels are deposited into a suitable waste container.

• Always keep a dry chemical (Class B) fire extinguisher near the work area.

• Do not allow fuel spray or fuel vapors to come into contact with a spark or open flame.

• Always use a backup wrench when loosening and tightening fuel line connection fittings. This will prevent unnecessary stress and torsion to fuel line piping. Always follow the proper torque specifications.

• Always replace worn fuel fitting O-rings with new. Do not substitute fuel hose or equivalent where fuel pipe is installed.

NOTE: Flexible Fuel Vehicles (FFV) are available in specific model production. Although many of the components are similar they cannot be interchanged. These vehicles can operate on a fuel mixture of gasoline and methanol up to 85 percent methanol. Components for Flexible Fuel Vehicles (FFV) can be identified by a green coloring or have a green label or tag attached.

RELIEVING FUEL SYSTEM PRESSURE

Engines With Test Port on Fuel Rail

1. Disconnect the negative battery terminal.
2. Remove the fuel filler cap.
3. Remove protective cap from the fuel test port on the fuel rail.
4. Place the open end of fuel pressure release hose tool C-4799-1 or equivalent, into an approved safety container.

NOTE: Fuel pressure test gauge tool C-4799-A contains pressure release hose C-4799-A.

5. Connect the other end of release hose to the fuel pressure test port.
6. Fuel pressure will bleed off into safety container.

Engines Without Test Port On Fuel Rail

1. Loosen the fuel filler cap to release fuel tank pressure.
2. Locate and disconnect the fuel injector harness connector.
3. Connect a jumper wire from terminal No. 1 of the appropriate connector to ground.
4. Being careful not to allow contact between the jumper leads, connect a jumper wire to terminal No. 2 of the connector and touch the other end of the jumper to the positive battery post for no longer than 5 seconds. This will relieve fuel pressure.
5. Remove the jumper wires, disconnect the negative battery cable and continue with fuel system service.

Fuel Tank

REMOVAL AND INSTALLATION

1. Disconnect the negative battery cable.
2. Relieve the fuel pressure.
3. Raise the vehicle and support safely.
4. Using the proper equipment, drain the fuel tank.
5. Remove the screws that hold the filler neck to the quarter panel. On some models, it may be necessary to remove the right rear tire assembly to access the filler tube.
6. Disconnect the wiring and hoses from the tank.
7. Place a transmission jack or equivalent under the center of the tank and apply slight pressure. Remove the tank straps.
8. Remove the filler tube from the tank.
9. Lower the tank and disconnect the vapor separator rollover valve hose. Remove the fuel tank from the vehicle.

To install:
10. Raise the tank into position and connect all harnesses and vacuum hoses.
11. Install the tank straps and tighten the retaining nuts.
12. Install the screws that hold the filler neck to the quarter panel.
13. Connect the negative battery cable, start the engine and check for leaks.

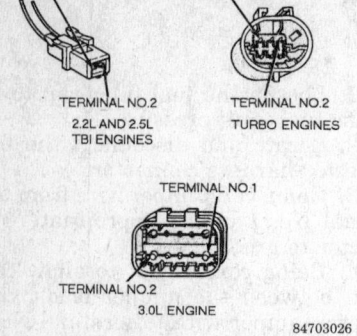

Injector harness connections

Fuel Filter

REMOVAL AND INSTALLATION

CAUTION

Do not use conventional fuel filters, hoses or clamps when servicing this fuel system. They are not compatible with the injection system and could fail, causing personal injury or damage to the vehicle. Use only hoses and clamps specifically designed for fuel injection.

1. Disconnect the negative battery cable.
2. Relieve the fuel pressure.
3. The filter is located on the frame rail toward the rear of the vehicle. Raise the vehicle and support safely. Remove the filter retaining screw and remove the filter assembly from the mounting plate.
4. Disconnect the quick connect fittings at the fuel filter and the fuel supply tube. Wrap a shop towel around the hoses prior to removing to absorb fuel that may leak from the connection. Remove the filter from the vehicle.
To install:
5. Install the inlet hose on the fuel tube and secure. Replace old clamp with new and tighten to 10 inch lbs. (1 Nm).
6. Install the outlet hose on the filter outlet fitting and secure. Tighten new clamp to 10 inch lbs. (1 Nm).
7. Position the filter assembly on the mounting plate and tighten the mounting screw to 75 inch lbs. (8 Nm).
8. Connect the negative battery cable, start the engine and check for leaks.

Electric Fuel Pump

PRESSURE TESTING

1. Relieve the fuel pressure.
2. Properly connect the fuel system pressure tester:
   a. Non-turbocharged engines — special tool C–4799 and adaptor 6539 or equivalent, is installed between the fuel supply hose and the engine fuel line assembly.
   b. Turbocharged engines — special tool C–4799 or equivalent, is installed to the fuel rail service valve.
3. With the key in the **RUN** position, put the DRB II in the Activate Auto Shutdown Relay mode; this will activate the fuel pump and pressurize the system.
4. If the pressure is within specifications, release the fuel system pressure and reinstall the fuel hose.
5. If fuel pressure is below specifications, install the tester with the adaptor in the fuel supply line between the tank and the filter and repeat the test. Release the fuel system pressure prior to opening the fuel system.
6. If the pressure is 5 psi higher than in Step 5, replace the fuel filter. If no change is observed, squeeze the return hose. If pressure increases, replace the pressure regulator. If no change is observed, the problem is either a clogged or restricted in-tank sock filter or a defective pump.
7. If fuel pressure is above specifications, remove the fuel return line hose from the chassis line at the fuel tank and connect a 3 foot piece of fuel hose to the return line. Put the other end into a 2 gallon minimum capacity approved gasoline container. Repeat the test. If pressure is now correct, replace the fuel pump assembly.
8. If fuel pressure is still above specifications, release the fuel system pressure and remove the fuel return line hose from the chassis fuel tubes close to the engine.
9. Attach fuel pressure tester to the fuel return hose, place the other end of the hose into an approved gasoline container and repeat the test.
10. If the pressure is now correct, check for a restricted fuel return line. If the fuel pressure did not change, replace the fuel pressure regulator.

REMOVAL AND INSTALLATION

1. Disconnect the negative battery cable.

2. Relieve the fuel system pressure.
3. Raise the vehicle and support safely.
4. Using the proper equipment, drain the fuel tank.
5. Remove the screws that hold the filler neck to the quarter panel.
6. Disconnect the wiring and hoses from the tank.
7. Place a transmission jack under the center of the tank and apply slight pressure. Remove the tank straps.
8. Remove the filler tube from the tank.
9. Lower the tank and disconnect the vapor separator rollover valve hose. Remove the fuel tank from the vehicle.
10. Using a hammer and a brass drift, tap the lock ring counterclockwise to release the pump.
11. Partially pull the pump assembly out of the tank until the return line hose connection is visible at the of the pump assembly.
12. Disconnect the fuel fitting by pressing in on the ears.
13. Remove the pump from the tank with the O-ring. Discard the O-ring, pump inlet filter and inlet seal. Disassemble as required.
To install:
14. Install a new inlet seal, filter and strainer O-ring onto the pump. When installing strainer onto the pump reservoir body, make sure the locking tabs on the reservoir body lock over the locking tangs on the strainer.
15. Install the pump into the tank so the fuel return hose is not kinked.
16. Install the lock ring with a hammer and brass punch turning the ring clockwise. Overtightening of the lock ring may result in a leak.
17. Install the fuel tank and remaining components into position.
18. Connect the negative battery cable, start the engine and check the fuel system for leaks.

Fuel Injection

IDLE SPEED ADJUSTMENT

The idle speed is controlled by the Idle Air Control motor (IAC). The IAC is controlled by the SMEC or SBEC, which receives data from various sensors and switches in the system and adjusts the engine idle to a predetermined speed. Idle speed specifications can be found on the Vehicle Emission Control Information (VECI) label located in the engine compartment. If the idle speed is not within specifications and there are no problems with the system, the throttle body should be replaced.

IDLE MIXTURE ADJUSTMENT

There is no idle mixture adjustment provided with any Chrysler fuel injection system.

Fuel Injector

REMOVAL AND INSTALLATION

2.2L and 2.5L Non–Turbocharged Engines

1. Disconnect the negative battery cable.
2. Remove the air cleaner assembly.
3. Relieve the fuel pressure.
4. Remove the injector hold-down Torx® screw and the hold-down.
5. Using a pair of small flat-tipped tools, lift the cap off the injector.
6. Gently pry the injector from its pod.
7. Remove the lower O-ring from the pod.
   To install:
8. Install the new lower O-ring on the injector.
9. Align the injector terminal housing with the locating socket in the injector cap.
10. Press the injector cap so the upper O-ring flange is flush with the lower surface of the cap.
11. Spray the inner surfaces of the injector pod with a carburetor parts cleaner to remove residual varnish and gasoline.
12. Lubricate the O-rings sparingly with unmedicated petroleum jelly.
13. Place the injector and cap into the injector pod and align the cap locating pin with the locating hole in the casting.

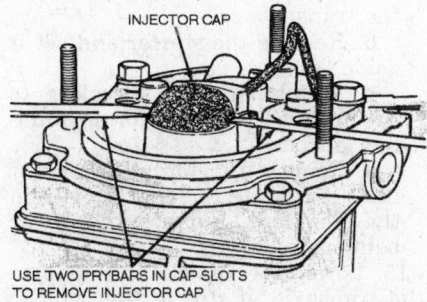

INJECTOR CAP

USE TWO PRYBARS IN CAP SLOTS TO REMOVE INJECTOR CAP

84703027

Removal of injector cap — 2.2L and 2.5L non-turbo engines

14. Press firmly on the injector cap until it is flush with the casting surface.
15. Align the hole in the hold-down with the pin on the cap and install.
16. Push down on the cap, install the screw and torque to 35 inch lbs. (4 Nm).
17. Connect the negative battery cable and check for leaks using the DRB II to activate the fuel pump.
18. Install the air cleaner.

2.2L and 2.5L Turbocharged Engines

1. Disconnect the negative battery cable.
2. Relieve the fuel system pressure.
3. Disconnect the injector wiring connector from the injector.
4. Unbolt the fuel rail from the rear of the engine. Position the fuel rail assembly so the fuel injectors are easily accessible. If necessary, disconnect the hoses from the fuel rail and remove it from the engine.
5. Remove the injector lock clip from the fuel rail and injector. Pull the injector straight out of the fuel rail receiver cup.
6. Check the injector O-ring for damage. If the O-ring is damaged, replace it. If the injector is being reused, install a protective cap on the injector tip to prevent damage.
7. Repeat the procedure for the remaining injectors.
   To install:
8. Before installing an injector the rubber O-ring should be lubricated with a drop of clean engine oil to aid in installation.
9. Install injector top end into fuel rail receiver cup.
10. Install injector clip by sliding the open end into top slot of the injector and onto the receiver cup ridge into the side slots of clip.
11. Repeat the steps for the remaining injectors.

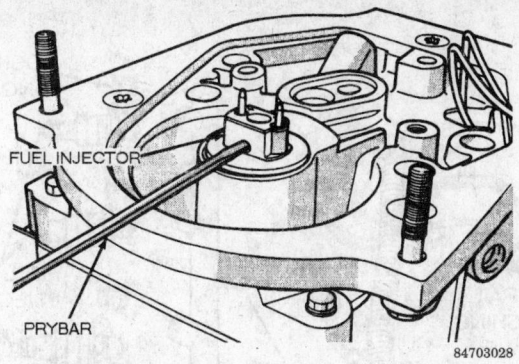

FUEL INJECTOR

PRYBAR

84703028

Removal of fuel injector — 2.2L and 2.5L non-turbo engines

12. Install the fuel rail.
13. Connect the negative battery cable and check for leaks using the DRB II to activate the fuel pump.

3.0L Engine

1. Disconnect the negative battery cable.
2. Relieve the fuel system pressure.
3. Remove the air cleaner to throttle body hose.
4. Disconnect the throttle cable from the throttle body and disconnect the kickdown linkage. Remove the throttle cable bracket attaching bolts.
5. Disconnect the harness connectors from the Idle Air Control (IAC) motor and the Throttle Position Sensor (TPS) on the throttle body.
6. Matchmark and carefully remove the vacuum hoses from the throttle body.
7. Remove the PCV and brake booster hoses from the air intake plenum.
8. Remove the ignition coil from the intake plenum, if mounted there.
9. Remove the EGR tube flange from the intake plenum, if equipped.
10. Unplug the coolant temperature sensor and charge temperature sensor, if equipped.
11. Remove the vacuum connection from the air intake plenum vacuum connector.
12. Remove the fuel hoses from the fuel rail and plug them.
13. Remove the air intake plenum to intake manifold bolts and remove the plenum and gaskets. Cover the intake manifold openings.
14. Remove the vacuum hoses from the fuel rail.
15. Label and disconnect the fuel injector wiring harness from each injector.
16. Remove the fuel rail attaching bolts and remove the fuel rail with the wiring harness from the vehicle.

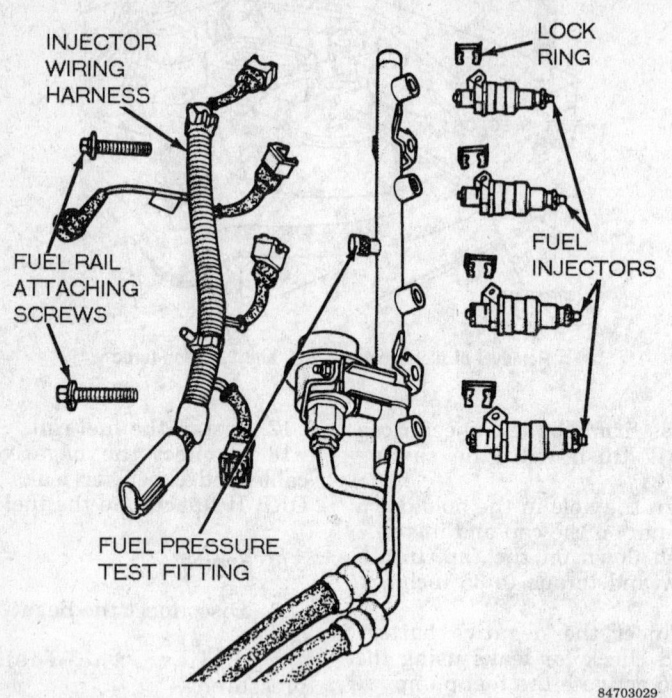

INJECTOR WIRING HARNESS

LOCK RING

FUEL INJECTORS

FUEL RAIL ATTACHING SCREWS

FUEL PRESSURE TEST FITTING

84703029

Fuel rail and injector assembly — 2.2L and 2.5L turbo engines

Position the rail on the bench upside down so the injectors are easily accessible.

17. Remove the retainer clip from the slot on the fuel injector and remove by pulling the injector straight out of the rail.

To install:

18. Lubricate the rubber O-ring with clean oil and install to the rail receiver cap. Install the injector clip to the top slot of the injector, plug in the connector and install the connector clip.

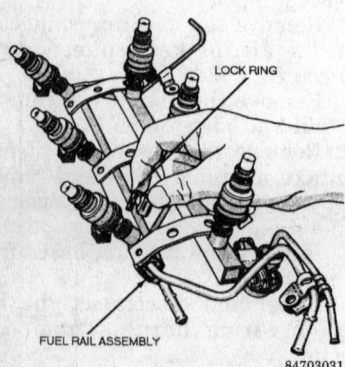

LOCK RING

FUEL RAIL ASSEMBLY

84703031

Fuel rail and injector assembly — 3.0L engine

19. Install the fuel rail to the vehicle and tighten attaching bolts to 115 inch lbs. (13 Nm).

20. Plug in the injector harness and connect the vacuum hoses to the fuel rail.

21. Install new intake plenum gaskets with the beaded sealer side up and install the intake plenum. Torque the attaching bolts and nuts to 115 inch lbs. (13 Nm).

22. Reconnect the EGR tube flange and tighten to 200 inch lbs. (22 Nm).

23. Install the fuel hoses to the fuel rail. Tighten holddown bolts to 95 inch lbs. (10 Nm).

24. Connect remaining items that were attached to the intake plenum and throttle body.

25. Connect the negative battery cable and check for leaks using the DRB II to activate the fuel pump.

ENGINE MECHANICAL

NOTE: Disconnecting the negative battery cable on some vehicles may interfere with the func-

tions of the on-board computer systems and may require the computers to undergo a relearning process, once the negative battery cable is reconnected.

Engine Assembly

REMOVAL AND INSTALLATION

2.2L and 2.5L Engines

1. Disconnect the negative battery cable and all engine ground straps. Relieve the fuel pressure.

2. Mark the hood hinge outline on the hood and remove the hood.

3. Drain the cooling system. Remove the radiator hoses, fan assembly, radiator and intercooler, if equipped.

4. Remove the air cleaner, duct hoses and oil filter.

5. If equipped with air conditioning, unbolt the air conditioning compressor and position it aside. It is not necessary to disconnect the refrigerant lines from the compressor.

6. Remove the power steering pump mounting bolts and position the pump aside, without disconnecting any fluid lines.

7. Label and disconnect all electrical connectors from the engine, alternator and fuel injection system.

8. Disconnect and plug the fuel lines and heater hoses.

9. Disconnect the throttle linkage.

10. Remove the alternator.

11. Raise the vehicle and support safely.

12. Disconnect the exhaust pipe from the manifold. Remove the right inner fender shield.

13. If equipped with a manual transaxle, remove the transaxle.

14. If equipped with an automatic transaxle, perform the following procedures:

a. Remove the lower cover from the transaxle case.

b. Remove the starter and set it aside.

c. Matchmark the flexplate to the torque converter for installation purposes.

d. Remove the torque converter bolts. Separate the converter from the flexplate. Remove the lower bellhousing bolts.

15. Lower the vehicle and support the transaxle, if still in the vehicle, with a floor jack or equivalent. Attach an engine lifting device to the engine.

16. Remove the remaining bellhousing bolts.

NOTE: If removing the insulator-to-rail screws, 1st mark the position of the insulator on the side rail to insure proper alignment during reinstallation.

17. Remove the front engine mount nut/bolt and the left insulator through-bolt or the insulator bracket to transaxle bolts.
18. Lift and remove the engine from the vehicle.

To install:

19. Lower the engine into the engine compartment. Make sure the lifting device is supporting the full weight of the engine and loosely install all of the mounting bolts until all are threaded. Then tighten front mounting bolt to 100 ft. lbs. (133 Nm), left side block-to-engine bolts to 125 ft. lbs. (169 Nm) and right side block-to-engine bolts to 75 ft. lbs. (102 Nm).
20. Remove the lifting device.
21. Raise the vehicle and support safely.
22. If equipped with a manual transaxle, install the transaxle.
23. If equipped with an automatic transaxle, align the mating marks and install the torque converter bolts. Torque bolts to 55 ft. lbs. (75 Nm). Install the torque converter inspection plate and the starter.
24. Connect the exhaust pipe. Lower the vehicle.
25. Install the alternator, power steering pump and air conditioning compressor, if equipped.
26. Connect the fuel lines and heater hoses.
27. Connect the throttle linkage.
28. Connect all remaining electrical connectors.
29. Install the air cleaner assembly and oil filter.
30. Install the radiator, fan assembly, hoses and intercooler, if equipped.
31. Fill the engine with the proper amount of engine oil. Connect the negative battery cable.
32. Refill the cooling system. Start the engine, allow it to reach normal operating temperature. Check for leaks.
33. Check the ignition timing and adjust if necessary.
34. Install the hood aligning the matchmarks made during the removal procedure.

3.0L Engine

1. Disconnect the negative battery cable. Relieve the fuel pressure.

2. Matchmark the hinge-to-hood position and remove the hood.
3. Drain the cooling system. Disconnect and label all engine electrical connections.
4. Remove the coolant hoses from the radiator and engine. Remove the radiator and cooling fan assembly.
5. Remove the air cleaner assembly. Disconnect the fuel lines from the engine. Disconnect the accelerator cable from the throttle body.
6. Raise the vehicle and support safely. Drain the engine oil.
7. Remove the air conditioning compressor mounting bolts, the drive belts and position the compressor aside. Disconnect the exhaust pipe from the exhaust manifold.
8. Remove the transaxle inspection cover, matchmark the converter to the flexplate, and remove the torque converter bolts.
9. Remove the power steering pump mounting bolts and set the pump aside, upright, with the fluid lines attached.
10. Remove the lower bellhousing bolts. Disconnect and label the starter motor wiring and remove the starter motor from the engine.
11. Lower the vehicle. Disconnect and label all electrical connectors from the engine, alternator and fuel injection system, vacuum hoses, and engine ground straps.
12. Support the transaxle with a floor jack or equivalent. Attach an engine lifting device to the engine.
13. Remove the upper transaxle-to-engine bolts.
14. To separate the engine mounts from the insulators, mark the right insulator-to-right frame support and remove the mounting bolts. Remove the front engine mount through bolt. Remove the left insulator through bolt from inside the wheel housing. Remove the insulator bracket-to-transaxle bolts.
15. Lift and remove the engine from the vehicle.

To install:

16. Lower the engine into the engine compartment. Align the engine mounts and install the bolts; do not tighten the bolts until all bolts have been installed. Torque the through bolts to 75 ft. lbs. (102 Nm).
17. Install the upper transaxle-to-engine mounting bolts and torque to 75 ft. lbs. (102 Nm). Remove the engine lifting fixture from the engine.
18. Raise the vehicle and support safely.
19. Align the converter marks, and install the torque converter bolts. Install the transaxle inspection cover.

20. Connect the exhaust pipe to the exhaust manifold. Install the starter motor and connect the wiring.
21. Install the power steering pump and air conditioning compressor. Adjust the drive belt tension, if necessary.
22. Lower the vehicle. Reconnect all vacuum hoses and electrical connections to the engine.
23. Connect the fuel lines and accelerator cable.
24. Install the radiator and fan assembly. Connect the fan motor wiring. Connect the radiator hoses and refill the cooling system.
25. Refill the engine with the proper oil to the correct level.
26. Connect the engine ground straps. Install the hood aligning the matchmarks made during removal. Connect the negative battery cable.
27. Start and run the engine until normal operating temperature is reached. Check for fluid leaks. Adjust the transaxle linkage, if necessary.

Engine Mounts

REMOVAL AND INSTALLATION

2.2L and 2.5L Engines

RIGHT SIDE MOUNT

1. Disconnect the negative battery cable.
2. Matchmark the engine mount to its frame mounting location.
3. Remove the load on the engine motor mounts by carefully supporting the engine and transaxle assembly with a floor jack.
4. Remove the through-bolt from the insulator assembly and remove the insulator.
5. Installation is the reverse of the removal procedure. Make sure the matchmarks are aligned before tightening bolts.
6. Tighten the lower yoke nut 1st, then the through-bolt nut, then the body mounting bolts.

FRONT MOUNT

1. Disconnect the negative battery cable.
2. Matchmark the engine mount to its frame mounting location.
3. Remove the load on the engine motor mounts by carefully supporting the engine and transaxle assembly with a floor jack.
4. Remove the bolt from the insulator and front crossmember bracket.
5. Remove the front engine mount bracket to front crossmember screws

and nuts. Remove the insulator assembly.

6. Installation is the reverse of the removal procedure.

3.0L Engine

1. Raise the vehicle and support safely. Using the proper equipment, support the weight of the engine.

2. Remove all bolts and nuts that attach the mount to the engine strut, transaxle or body and remove the mount assembly from the vehicle.

3. Remove the through-bolt and separate the insulator from the yoke bracket as required.

4. The installation is the reverse of the removal procedure. Make sure the matchmarks are aligned before tightening bolts.

5. Tighten the lower yoke nut 1st, then the through bolt nut, then the body mounting bolts.

Cylinder Head

REMOVAL AND INSTALLATION

2.2L and 2.5L Engines

EXCEPT 2.2L DOHC ENGINE

1. Disconnect the negative battery cable from the battery and cylinder head. Relieve the fuel pressure. Drain the cooling system. Remove the dipstick bracket nut from the thermostat housing and remove the ignition coil from the thermostat housing if installed there.

2. Remove the air cleaner assembly. Remove the upper radiator hose and disconnect the heater hoses.

3. Disconnect and label the vacuum lines, hoses and wiring connectors from the manifold(s), throttle body and from the cylinder head.

4. Disconnect all linkages and the fuel line from the throttle body. Unbolt the cable bracket. Remove the ground strap attaching screw from the firewall.

5. Remove the power steering pump assembly and position aside. It is not necessary to disconnect power steering pump supply and return hoses.

6. If equipped with air conditioning, remove the air conditioning compressor from the mounting bracket and position aside. The factory recommends that the compressor mounting bracket be removed prior to removing the cylinder head, however, if the upper compressor mounting bolts that thread into the cylinder head are removed from the compres-

sor mounting bracket, in most cases, the cylinder head can be removed with the bracket in place. If the bracket is to be removed, perform the following procedure:

    a. Remove the alternator pivot bolt and remove the alternator from the bracket. Turn the alternator so the wire connections are facing up and disconnect the harness connectors from the rear of the alternator.

    b. Remove the air conditioning compressor belt idler.

    c. Remove the right engine mount yoke screw securing engine mount support strut to the engine.

    d. Remove the 5 side mounting bolts retaining the bracket to the front of the engine.

    e. Remove the front mounting nut. Remove the front bolt and strut and rotate the solid mount bracket away from the engine. Slide the bracket on the stud until free of the mounting studs and remove from the engine.

7. Remove the upper timing belt cover. Raise the vehicle and support safely. Disconnect the exhaust pipe from the exhaust manifold. Disconnect the water hose and oil drain from the turbocharger, if equipped.

8. Rotate the engine by hand until the timing marks align. The No. 1 piston should be at TDC of its compression stroke. Lower the vehicle.

9. With the timing marks aligned, remove the camshaft sprocket. The camshaft sprocket can be suspended to keep the timing intact. Remove the spark plug wires from the spark plugs.

10. Remove the valve cover and curtain. Remove the cylinder head bolts and washers, starting from the outside and working inward.

11. Remove the cylinder head from the engine.

12. Clean the cylinder head gasket mating surfaces. Clean and inspect all cylinder head bolt threads for necking or stretching. It is recommended that all head bolts be replaced with new prior to installation of the cylinder head.

To install:

NOTE: Head bolt diameter is 11mm. These bolts are identified with the number 11 on the head of the bolt. The 10mm bolts used on previous vehicles will thread into an 11mm bolt hole, but will permanently damage the cylinder block. Make sure the correct bolts are used when replacing head bolts.

13. Using new gaskets and seals, install the head to the engine.

14. Using new head bolts of the correct diameter, assembled with the old washers, torque the cylinder head bolts in sequence to 45 ft. lbs. (61 Nm). Repeating the sequence, torque the bolts to 65 ft. lbs. (88 Nm). With the bolts at 65 ft. lbs., turn each bolt an additional ¼ turn.

15. Install the timing belt and covers. Install the solid mount compressor bracket, if removed.

16. Install the upper air conditioning compressor mounting bracket bolts, if removed. Install the air conditioning compressor to the mounting bracket and secure with the mounting nuts.

17. Raise and safely support the vehicle. Reconnect the exhaust pipe to the manifold using a new gasket as required.

18. Connect the remaining hoses, linkage and electrical harness connectors disconnected during the removal procedure.

19. Refill the cooling system. Connect the negative battery cable. Start the engine and check for leaks. Adjust the timing, as required.

2.2L Turbo III Engine

1. Disconnect the negative battery cable at the battery terminal and unbolt it from the head. Relieve the fuel pressure. Drain the cooling system.

2. Remove the air cleaner assembly with all ductwork.

3. Remove the timing belt covers. Rotate the engine by hand until the timing marks align (No. 1 piston at TDC). Remove the timing belt.

4. Remove the air conditioning compressor and bracket from the cylinder head.

5. Disconnect the turbocharger coolant lines and separate the intake and exhaust manifolds from the cylinder head.

6. Remove the ignition cable cover and valve covers. Disconnect and label all wiring connectors, hoses and ignition wires from the cylinder head.

7. Remove the cylinder head and gasket from the engine.

8. Clean the cylinder head gasket mating surfaces. Clean and inspect all cylinder head bolt threads for necking. If necking has occurred, the threads on the bolts will not be uniform or straight when held up against a straight edge, and will require replacement. It is recommended that all head bolts be replaced with new prior to installation of the cylinder head.

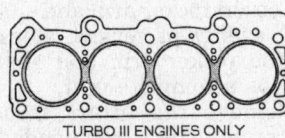

2.2L AND 2.25L NATURAL ASPIRATED AND 2.5L FFV ENGINES

TURBO III ENGINES ONLY

84703032

Cylinder head gasket identification — 2.2L and 2.5L engines

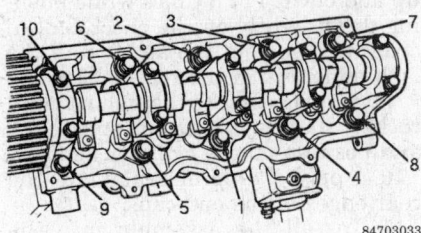

84703033

Cylinder head torque sequence — 2.2L and 2.5L engines

To install:

NOTE: The head gasket used on the Turbo III engine is unique to that engine. Make sure the replacement head gasket is identical to the original gasket before installing. Head bolt diameter is 11mm and the head bolts are unique to this engine. These bolts are identified with the number 11 on the head of the bolt and are not interchangeable with other engines. Make sure the correct bolts are used when replacing head bolts.

9. Using new gaskets and seals, install the head to the engine. Using new head bolts assembled with the old washers, torque the cylinder head bolts in sequence, to 45 ft. lbs. (61 Nm). Repeating the sequence, torque the bolts to 65 ft. lbs. (88 Nm). With the bolts at 65 ft. lbs., turn each bolt an additional ¼ turn. Final torque must be over 90 ft. lbs. (122 Nm).

10. Install the timing belt and all related items.

11. Install the intake and exhaust manifolds.

12. Install the air conditioning compressor and bracket the cylinder head.

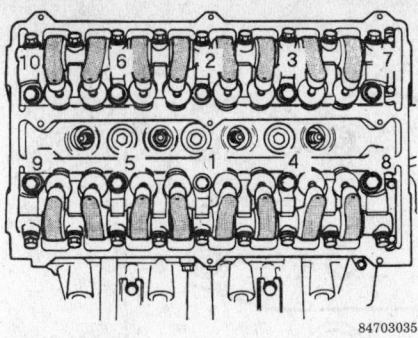

84703035

Cylinder head torque sequence — 2.2L DOHC turbo engine

13. Install the valve covers and torque the bolts to 105 inch lbs. (12 Nm).

14. Install the air cleaner assembly and all ductwork.

15. Refill the cooling system. Connect the negative battery cable. Start the engine and check for leaks.

3.0L Engine

1. Disconnect the negative battery cable. Relieve the fuel pressure. Drain the cooling system.

2. Rotate the engine and position at TDC.

3. Remove the drive belt and the air conditioning compressor from its mount and support it aside. Using a ½ in. drive breaker bar, insert it into the square hole of the serpentine drive belt tensioner, rotate it counterclockwise to reduce the belt tension and remove the belt. Remove the alternator and power steering pump from the brackets and move them aside.

4. Raise the vehicle and support safely. Remove the right front wheel assembly and the right inner splash shield.

5. Remove the crankshaft pulleys and the torsional damper.

6. Lower the vehicle. Using a floor jack and a block of wood positioned under the oil pan, raise the engine slightly. Remove the engine mount bracket from the timing cover end of the engine and the timing belt covers.

7. To remove the timing belt, perform the following procedures:
   a. Rotate the crankshaft to position the No. 1 cylinder on the TDC of its compression stroke if not already done; the crankshaft sprocket timing mark should align with the oil pan timing indicator and the camshaft sprocket's timing marks (triangles) should align with the rear timing belt cover's timing marks.

b. Mark the timing belt in the direction of rotation for reinstallation purposes.

c. Loosen the timing belt tensioner and remove the timing belt.

NOTE: When removing the timing belt from the camshaft sprocket, make sure the belt does not slip off the crankshaft sprocket and opposite side camshaft sprocket.

8. Remove the air cleaner assembly. Label and disconnect the spark plug wires and the vacuum hoses.

9. Remove the valve cover.

10. Install auto lash adjuster retainer tools MD998443 or equivalent, on the rocker arms.

11. If removing the front cylinder head, matchmark the distributor rotor-to-distributor housing and the housing-to-distributor extension locations. Remove the distributor and the distributor extension.

12. Remove the camshaft bearing assembly to cylinder head bolts (do not remove the bolts from the assembly). Remove the rocker arms, rocker shafts and bearing caps as an assembly, as required. Remove the camshafts from the cylinder head and inspect them for damage, if necessary.

13. Remove the intake manifold assembly.

14. Remove the exhaust manifold and crossover.

15. Remove the cylinder head bolts, starting from the outside and working inward. Remove the cylinder head from the engine.

16. Clean the gasket mounting surfaces and check the heads for warpage; the maximum warpage allowed is 0.008 in. (0.20mm).

To install:

17. Install the new cylinder head gaskets over the dowels on the engine block.

18. Install the cylinder heads on the engine and torque the cylinder head bolts in sequence using 3 even steps to 80 ft. lbs. (108 Nm).

19. Install or connect all items removed or disconnected during the removal procedure.

20. When installing the timing belt over the camshaft sprocket, use care not to allow the belt to slip off the opposite camshaft sprocket.

21. Make sure the timing belt is installed on the camshaft sprocket in the same position as when removed.

22. Refill the cooling system. Connect the negative battery cable. Start the engine and check for leaks using the DRB II to activate the fuel pump. Adjust the timing as required.

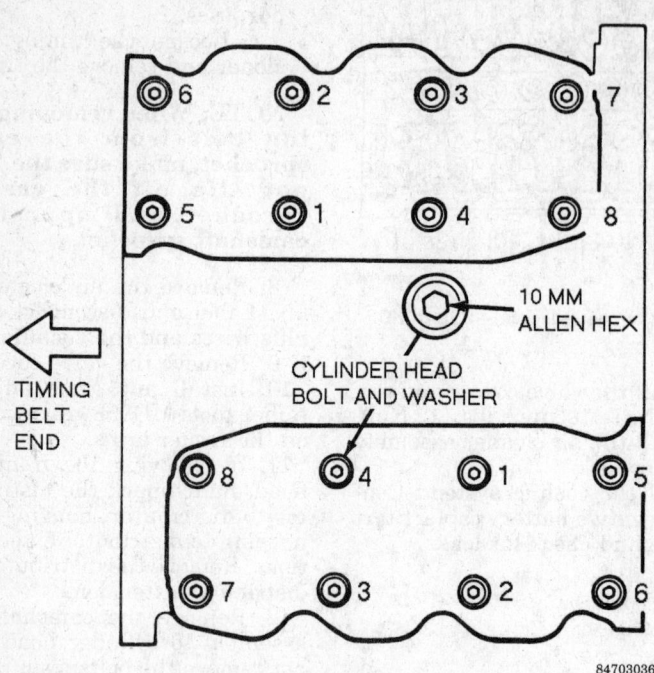

10 MM ALLEN HEX

CYLINDER HEAD BOLT AND WASHER

TIMING BELT END

84703036

Cylinder head torque sequence — 3.0L engine

Valve Lifters

REMOVAL AND INSTALLATION

2.2L and 2.5L Engines

EXCEPT 2.2L DOHC

1. Disconnect the negative battery cable.
2. Remove the valve cover and curtain. If removing all lifters, remove the upper timing belt cover, camshaft and rocker arms.
3. If only removing 1 lifter, rotate the crankshaft until the low point of the desired cam lobe is contacting the rocker arm.
4. Using the special valve spring compressor tool 4682 or equivalent, depress the valve spring without dislodging the keepers and slide the rocker arm out.
5. Remove the valve lifter(s) from the bore(s).
   To install:
6. Lubricate the lifter(s) and their bore(s) with clean engine oil.
7. Install the lifter(s) into the appropriate bore, keeping in the original location, and install the rocker arms.
8. Install the camshaft sprocket and timing belt upper cover, if removed.

9. Apply form-in-place Mopar Silicone Rubber Adhesive Sealant or equivalent gasket material to the rocker cover and replace both cover end seals.
10. Install to rocker cover to the engine and secure with the retainer bolts tightened to 105 inch lbs. (12 Nm).
11. Connect the negative battery cable and check the lifters for proper operation.

2.2L Turbo III Engine

1. Disconnect the negative battery cable.
2. Remove the valve cover(s).
3. Remove the rocker arm shaft(s).
4. Slide the rocker arm(s) off the shaft and remove the lash adjuster from the rocker arm.
5. The installation is the reverse of the removal procedure.
6. Connect the negative battery cable.

3.0L Engine

1. Disconnect the negative battery cable.
2. Remove the valve cover. Install lash adjuster retainer tools MD998443 or equivalent, to prevent the auto-lash adjuster from falling out of the rocker arm.

3. Remove the distributor adapter housing.
4. Rotate the engine clockwise and position cylinder No. 1 at TDC compression stroke.
5. Remove the timing belt assembly.
6. Loosen rocker arm and shaft assembly evenly in several steps. Remove the rocker arm and shaft assembly as a complete unit.
7. Remove the lifters from the rocker arms. It is recommended that all lash adjusters and rockers be replaced as a complete set.
   To install:
8. Immerse the lash adjusters in clean diesel fuel. Using a small wire, move the plunger of the lash adjuster up and down 4 or 5 times while pushing down lightly on the check ball in order to bleed out the air. Install the lash adjusters in the rocker arms.
9. Lubricate the camshaft and rocker shaft with heavy engine oil and position on the cylinder head.
10. Apply a drop of sealant to the rear edges of the end caps.
11. Install the assembly into the front bearing cap, making sure the notches in the rocker shafts are facing up. Insert the installation bolt but do not tighten at this point.
12. Install the remaining cap bolts and tighten evenly and gradually to 15 ft. lbs. (20 Nm). Tighten the front cap retaining bolts to 17 ft. lbs. (24 Nm). Remove the lash adjuster retainers.
13. Install the distributor extension, if removed.
14. Install timing belt.
15. Install the valve cover with a new gasket and tighten to 4–5 ft. lbs. (5–7 Nm).
16. Connect the negative battery cable.

Rocker Arms/Shafts

REMOVAL AND INSTALLATION

2.2L and 2.5L Engines

EXCEPT TURBO III

1. Disconnect the negative battery cable.
2. Remove the valve cover.
3. Rotate the crankshaft until the low point of the desired cam lobe is contacting the rocker arm.
4. Using the special valve spring compressor tool or equivalent, depress the valve spring without dislodging the keepers and slide the rocker arm out.

5. The installation is the reverse of the removal procedure.

2.2L Turbo III Engine

1. Disconnect the negative battery cable.
2. Remove the valve cover(s).
3. Remove the rocker arm retaining bolts in the proper removal sequence.
4. Remove the rocker shaft assembly from the cylinder head.
5. Keep all parts in order and disassemble as required. Inspect the lash adjusters carefully.

To install:
6. Lubricate and assemble the rocker arms to the shaft.
7. Make sure the lash adjusters are at least partially full of oil. This is indicated by little or no plunger travel when depressing. Install to the rocker arms.
8. Install the assembly and tighten the bolts in the proper sequence to 18 ft. lbs. (24 Nm).
9. Install the valve cover(s).
10. Connect the negative battery cable.

3.0L Engine

1. Disconnect the negative battery cable.

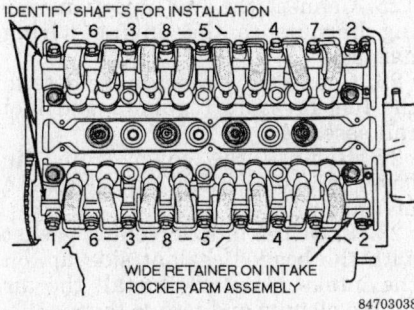

IDENTIFY SHAFTS FOR INSTALLATION

WIDE RETAINER ON INTAKE ROCKER ARM ASSEMBLY

84703038

Rocker shaft retaining bolt removal sequence — 2.2L turbo engine

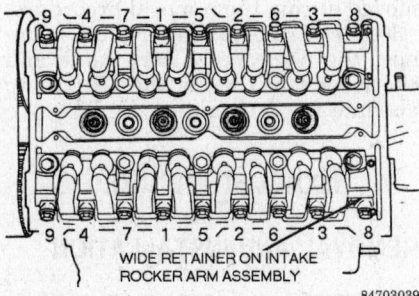

WIDE RETAINER ON INTAKE ROCKER ARM ASSEMBLY

84703039

Rocker shaft retaining bolt installation sequence — 2.2L turbo engine

2. Remove the valve cover. Install lash adjuster retainer tools MD998443 or equivalent, to prevent the auto-lash adjuster from falling out of the rocker arm.
3. Remove the distributor adapter housing.
4. Rotate the engine clockwise and position at TDC compression stroke.
5. Remove the timing belt assembly.
6. Loosen rocker arm and shaft assembly evenly in several steps. Remove the rocker arm and shaft assembly as a complete unit.

To install:
7. Immerse the lash adjusters in clean diesel fuel. Using a small wire, move the plunger of the lash adjuster up and down 4 or 5 times while pushing down lightly on the check ball in order to bleed out the air. Install the lash adjusters in the rocker arms.
8. Lubricate the camshaft and rocker shaft with heavy engine oil and position on the cylinder head.

NOTE: Intake rocker shaft has an extra oil hole at the bottom side of shaft for identification

9. Apply a drop of sealant to the rear edges of the end caps.
10. Install the assembly into the front bearing cap making sure the notches in the rocker shafts are facing up. Insert the installation bolt but do not tighten at this point.
11. Install the remaining cap bolts and tighten evenly and gradually to 15 ft. lbs. (20 Nm). Tighten the front cap retaining bolts to 17 ft. lbs. (24 Nm). Remove the lash adjuster retainers.
12. Install the distributor extension, if removed.
13. Install timing belt.
14. Install the valve cover with a new gasket and tighten to 4–5 ft. lbs. (5–7 Nm).
15. Connect the negative battery cable.

Intake Manifold

REMOVAL AND INSTALLATION

2.2L Turbo III Engine

1. Disconnect the negative battery cable. Relieve the fuel system pressure. Drain the cooling system.
2. Remove the fresh air duct from the air filter housing. Remove the inlet hose from the intercooler.
3. Remove the radiator hose from the thermostat housing.
4. Remove the DIS ignition coil from the intake manifold.

5. Disconnect the throttle and speed control cables from the throttle body.
6. Disconnect the intercooler-to-throttle body outlet hose. Disconnect the vacuum hoses from the throttle body and carefully remove the harness.
7. Disconnect the AIS motor and TPS wiring connectors.
8. Remove the PCV breather/separator box and vacuum harness assembly. Remove the brake booster hose, vacuum vapor harness and fuel pressure regulator from the intake manifold.
9. Disconnect the fuel injector wiring harness and charge temperature sensor.
10. Wrap shop towels around the fittings and disconnect the fuel supply and return fuel lines.
11. Remove the intake manifold retaining bolts and remove the manifold from the cylinder head.

To install:
12. Inspect the manifold for damage of any kind. Thoroughly clean and dry the mating surfaces.
13. Install the new gasket and manifold to the cylinder head. Starting at the center and working outwards, torque the bolts gradually and evenly to 17 ft. lbs. (23 Nm).
14. Lubricate the quick-connect fuel fittings with oil and connect to the chassis tubes. Ensure they are locked by pulling on them.
15. Install the PCV breather/separator box and vacuum harness assembly. Connect the brake booster hose, vacuum vapor harness and fuel pressure regulator to the intake manifold.
16. Connect the fuel injector wiring harness and charge temperature sensor. Connect the AIS motor and TPS wiring connectors.
17. Connect the vacuum hoses from the throttle body and carefully remove the harness. Connect the intercooler-to-throttle body outlet hose.
18. Connect the throttle and speed control cables from the throttle body.
19. Install the DIS ignition coil to the intake manifold.
20. Connect the radiator hose to the thermostat housing.
21. Install the inlet hose to the intercooler. Install the fresh air duct to the air filter housing.
22. Refill and bleed the cooling system. Connect the negative battery cable. Start the engine and check for leaks.

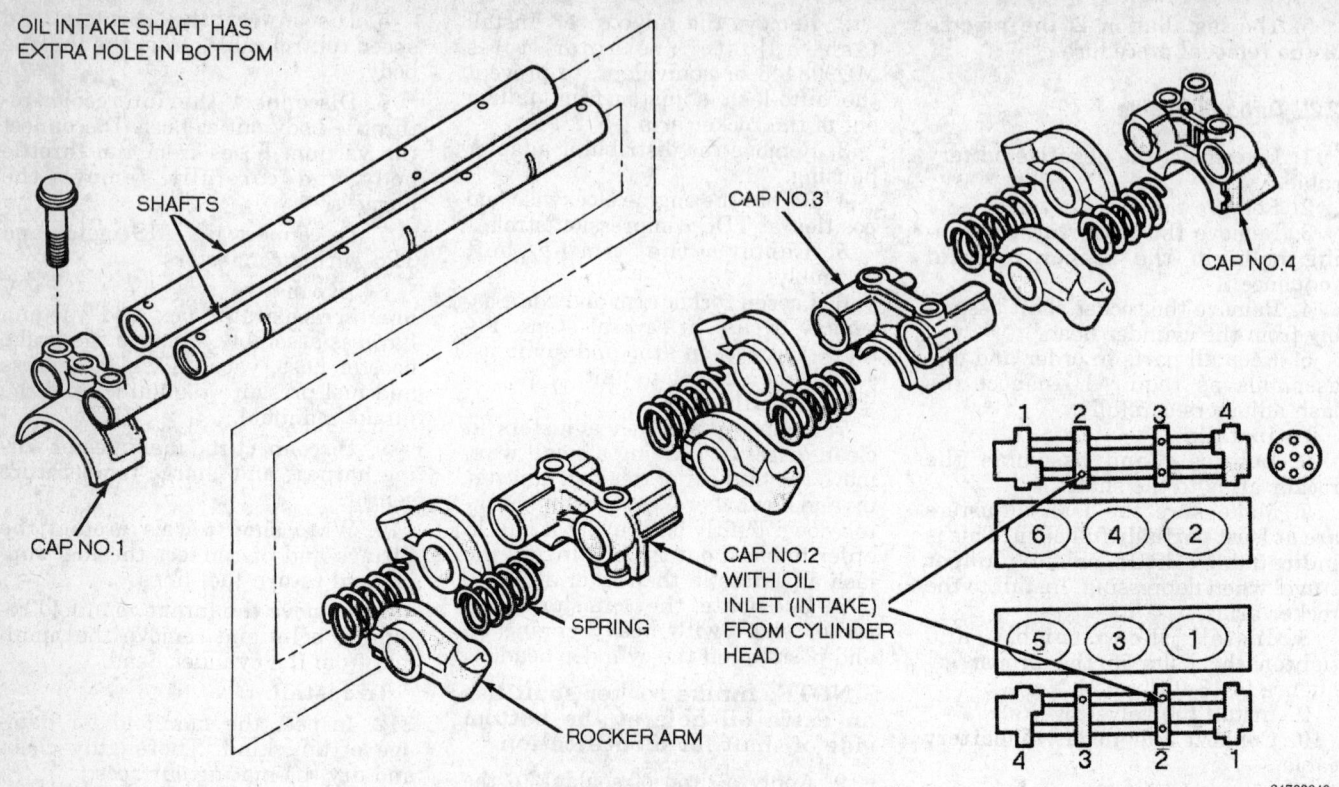

OIL INTAKE SHAFT HAS
EXTRA HOLE IN BOTTOM

SHAFTS

CAP NO.3

CAP NO.4

CAP NO.1

CAP NO.2
WITH OIL
INLET (INTAKE)
FROM CYLINDER
HEAD

SPRING

ROCKER ARM

84703040

Rocker shaft assembly — 3.0L engine

3.0L Engine

1. Disconnect the negative battery cable. Relieve the fuel system pressure.
2. Drain the cooling system.
3. Remove the throttle body to air cleaner hose.
4. Remove the throttle body and transaxle kickdown linkage.
5. Remove the AIS motor and TPS wiring connectors from the throttle body.
6. Remove and label the vacuum hose harness from the throttle body.
7. Remove the PCV and brake booster hoses from the intake plenum. Remove the EGR tube flange from the air intake plenum, if equipped.
8. Disconnect and label the charge and temperature sensor wiring at the intake manifold.
9. Remove the vacuum connections from the air intake plenum vacuum connector.
10. Remove the fuel hoses from the fuel rail.
11. Remove the air intake plenum mounting bolts and remove the plenum.
12. Remove the vacuum hoses from the fuel rail and pressure regulator.

13. Disconnect the fuel injector wiring harness from the engine wiring harness.
14. Remove the fuel pressure regulator mounting bolts and remove the regulator from the fuel rail.
15. Remove the fuel rail mounting bolts and remove the fuel rail from the intake manifold.
16. Separate the radiator hose from the thermostat housing and heater hoses from the heater pipe.
17. Remove the intake manifold mounting bolts and remove the manifold from the engine.
18. Clean the gasket mounting surfaces on the engine and intake manifold.

To install:

19. Using new gaskets, position the intake manifold on the engine and install the mounting nuts and washers.
20. Torque the mounting nuts gradually and evenly, in sequence, to 15 ft. lbs. (20 Nm).
21. Make sure the injector holes are clean. Lubricate the injector O-rings with a drop of clean engine oil and install the injector assembly onto the engine.
22. Install and torque the fuel rail mounting bolts to 10 ft. lbs. (14 Nm).
23. Install the fuel pressure regulator onto the fuel rail.

24. Install the fuel supply and return tube and the vacuum crossover hold-down bolt.
25. Connect the fuel injection wiring harness to the engine wiring harness.
26. Connect the vacuum harness to the fuel pressure regulator and fuel rail assembly.
27. Remove the cover from the lower intake manifold and clean the mating surface.
28. Place the intake plenum gasket with the beaded sealant side up, on the intake manifold. Install the air intake plenum and torque the mounting bolts gradually and evenly, in sequence, to 10 ft. lbs. (14 Nm).
29. Connect or install all remaining items that were disconnected or removed during the removal procedure.
30. Refill the cooling system. Connect the negative battery cable and check for leaks using the DRB II to activate the fuel pump.

Exhaust Manifold

REMOVAL AND INSTALLATION

2.2L DOHC and 2.2L Turbo III Engine

1. Disconnect the negative battery cable.

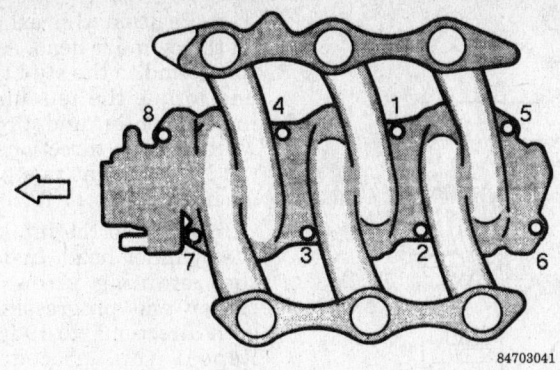

Intake manifold bolt torque sequence — 3.0L engine

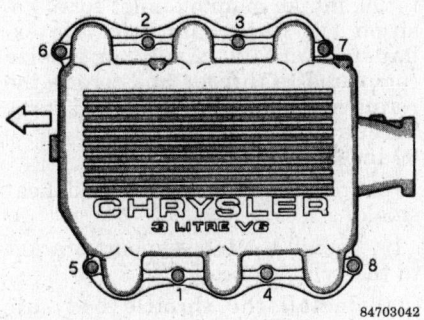

Intake plenum bolt torque sequence — 3.0L engine

2. Remove the turbocharger assembly, if equipped.

3. Remove the coolant tube from the cylinder head.

4. Remove the exhaust manifold retaining nuts and remove the manifold.

5. Clean the gasket mounting surfaces. Inspect the manifolds for cracks, flatness and/or damage.

To install:

6. Install a new exhaust manifold gasket. Do not use sealer of any kind.

7. Position the manifold on the studs and install the retaining nuts. Starting at the center and working outwards, torque the nuts gradually and evenly to 17 ft. lbs. (23 Nm).

8. Using a new gasket, connect the coolant tube to the cylinder head.

9. Install the turbocharger assembly, if removed.

10. Start the engine and check for exhaust leaks.

3.0L Engine

1. Disconnect the negative battery cable. Raise the vehicle and safely support.

2. Disconnect the exhaust pipe from the rear exhaust manifold, at the articulated joint.

3. Disconnect the EGR tube from the rear manifold and disconnect the oxygen sensor wire.

4. Remove the crossover pipe to manifold bolts.

5. Remove the rear manifold to cylinder head nuts and the manifold.

6. Lower the vehicle and remove the heat shield from the manifold.

7. Remove the front manifold to cylinder head nuts and remove the manifold.

8. Clean the gasket mounting surfaces. Inspect the manifolds for cracks, flatness and/or damage.

To install:

9. When installing, the numbers 1–3–5 on the gaskets are used with the rear cylinders and 2–4–6 are on the gasket for the front cylinders. Torque the manifold to cylinder head nuts to 14 ft. lbs. (19 Nm).

10. Install the crossover pipe to the manifold.

11. Connect the EGR tube and oxygen sensor wire.

12. Connect the exhaust pipe to the rear exhaust manifold, at the articulated joint.

13. Connect the negative battery cable and check the manifolds for leaks.

Combination Manifold

REMOVAL AND INSTALLATION

2.2L and 2.5L Engines (Except 2.2L DOHC)

WITHOUT TURBOCHARGER

NOTE: On some vehicles, some of the manifold attaching bolts are not accessible or too heavily sealed from the factory and cannot be removed on the vehicle. Head removal is necessary in these situations.

1. Disconnect the negative battery cable.

2. Relieve the fuel system pressure.

3. Drain the cooling system.

4. Remove the air cleaner and disconnect all vacuum lines, electrical wiring and fuel lines from the throttle body.

5. Disconnect the throttle linkage.

6. Loosen the power steering pump and remove the drive belt.

7. Remove the power brake vacuum hose from the intake manifold.

8. Remove the water hoses from the water crossover.

9. Raise and safely support the vehicle. Disconnect the exhaust pipe from the exhaust manifold.

10. Remove the power steering pump from its mounting bracket and set it aside.

11. Remove the intake manifold support bracket, if equipped.

12. Remove the EGR tube, if equipped.

13. Remove the intake manifold bolts.

14. Lower the vehicle.

15. Remove the intake manifold.

16. Remove the exhaust manifold retainer nuts.

17. Remove the exhaust manifold.

To install:

18. Install a new combination manifold gasket. Coat steel gasket lightly with gasket sealer on the manifold side. Do not coat a compression gasket with sealer.

19. Install the manifold assembly. Starting from the middle and working outwards, install the mounting nuts and torque to 13–17 ft. lbs. (18–23 Nm). Install the heat cowl to the exhaust manifold.

20. Install the intake manifold. Starting from the middle and working outward, torque the bolts to 17 ft. lbs. (23 Nm).

21. Install the EGR tube, if removed.

22. Install the intake support bracket, if equipped.

23. Install the power steering pump.

24. Raise the vehicle and support safely. Install the exhaust pipe to the exhaust manifold.

25. Install the water hoses to the water crossover.

26. Install the power brake vacuum hose to the intake manifold.

27. Connect the throttle linkage.

28. Install all vacuum lines, electrical wiring and fuel lines to the carburetor or throttle body.

29. Install the air cleaner assembly.

30. Refill the cooling system.

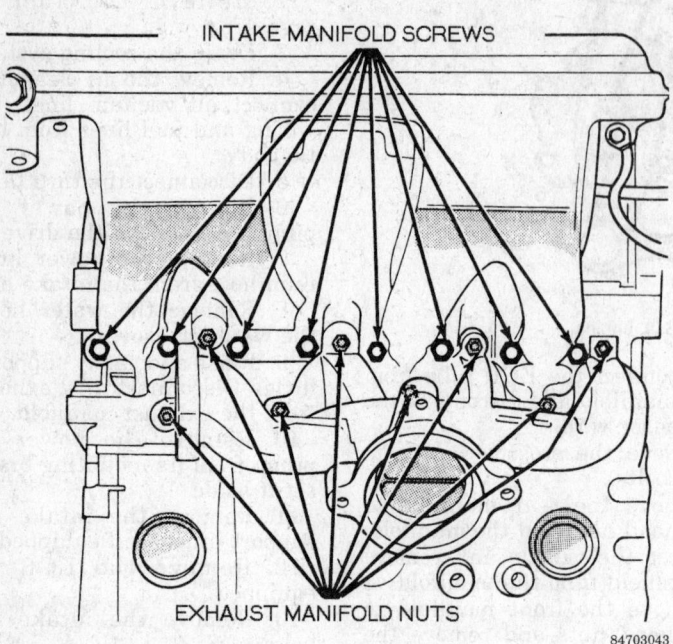

INTAKE MANIFOLD SCREWS

EXHAUST MANIFOLD NUTS

84703043

Combination manifold attaching locations — 2.2L and 2.5L Non-turbo engines

31. Connect the negative battery cable and check the manifolds for leaks.

WITH TURBOCHARGER

NOTE: On some vehicles, some of the manifold attaching bolts are not accessible or too heavily sealed from the factory and cannot be removed from the vehicle. Head removal is necessary in these situations.

1. Disconnect the negative battery cable. Drain the cooling system. Raise and safely support the vehicle.
2. Disconnect the exhaust pipe at the articulated joint. Disconnect the oxygen sensor at the electrical connection.
3. Remove the turbocharger to engine support bracket.
4. Loosen the oil drain back tube connector hose clamps. Move the tube down on the engine block fitting.
5. Disconnect the turbocharger coolant inlet tube from the engine block and disconnect the tube support bracket.
6. Remove the air cleaner assembly, including the throttle body adaptor, hose and air cleaner box with support bracket.

7. Disconnect the accelerator linkage, injector wiring harness, throttle body electrical connector and vacuum hoses.
8. Remove the bracket to intake manifold screws and the bracket to heat shield retainer clips. Remove the heat shield.
9. Remove the fuel return and supply lines at the fuel rail. Cover hose connections with a rag to absorb any fuel spray caused by residual pressure in the lines prior to disconnecting.
10. Remove the fuel rail retaining bolts. Remove the fuel rail from the vehicle, with injectors attached, by pulling straight upward.
11. Disconnect the turbocharger oil feed line at the oil sending unit tee fitting. Remove the turbocharger from the engine.
12. Remove the 8 intake manifold retainer screws and washers and remove the intake manifold.
13. Remove the 8 exhaust manifold retainer nuts and remove the exhaust manifold.
To install:
14. Position a new 2-sided Grafoil intake/exhaust manifold gasket; do not use sealant.

15. Position the exhaust manifold on the cylinder head. Apply anti-seize compound to the stud threads, install and torque the retaining nuts, starting at center and progressing outward in both directions, to 17 ft. lbs. (23 Nm). Repeat this procedure until all nuts are at 17 ft. lbs. (23 Nm).
16. Position the intake manifold on the cylinder head. Install and torque the retaining screws, starting at center and progressing outward in both directions, to 19 ft. lbs. (26 Nm). Repeat this procedure until all screws are at 19 ft. lbs. (26 Nm).
17. Connect the turbocharger outlet to the intake manifold inlet tube. Position the turbocharger on the exhaust manifold. Apply anti-seize compound to threads and torque the retainer nuts to 30 ft. lbs. (41 Nm). Torque the connector tube clamps to 30 inch lbs. (3 Nm).
18. Install the cowl mounted heat shield.
19. Install the tube support bracket to the cylinder head.
20. Install the throttle body air horn into the turbocharger inlet tube. Install and torque the throttle body to intake manifold screws to 21 ft. lbs. (28 Nm). Torque the tube clamp to 30 inch lbs.
21. Reconnect the turbocharger oil feed line to the oil sending unit tee fitting and bearing housing, if disconnected. Torque the tube nuts to 10 ft. lbs. (14 Nm).
22. Install the air cleaner assembly. Connect the vacuum lines and accelerator cables.
23. Install the fuel rail and injectors to the engine and secure with the mounting bolts. Connect the fuel rail supply and return lines.
24. Install the air shield to bracket clips, if not already done.
25. Connect the turbocharger inlet coolant tube to the engine block. Torque the tube nut to 30 ft. lbs. (41 Nm). Install the tube support bracket.
26. Install the turbocharger housing-to-engine block support bracket and the screws hand-tight. Torque the block screw 1st to 40 ft. lbs. (54 Nm). Torque the screw to the turbocharger housing to 20 ft. lbs. (27 Nm).
27. Reposition the drain back hose connector and tighten the hose clamps. Reconnect the exhaust pipe.
28. Refill the cooling system.
29. Connect the negative battery cable and check the manifolds for leaks.

Turbocharger

REMOVAL AND INSTALLATION

1. Disconnect negative battery cable.

NOTE: On some vehicles, some of the turbocharger to exhaust manifold nuts are not accessible enough to loosen and cannot be removed from the vehicle. Head removal is necessary in these situations.

2. From above the vehicle, perform the following removal procedures:

   a. Remove the front engine mount through bolt and rotate the top of the engine forward away from the cowl.

   b. Separate the coolant line from the water box and turbocharger housing.

   c. Separate the oil feed line from the turbocharger housing.

   d. Remove the wastegate rod-to-gate retainer clip. Remove the 3 upper and 1 lower driver's side nuts retaining the turbocharger to the manifold.

   e. Disconnect the vacuum lines at the electrical lead from the oxygen sensor.

3. Raise and safely support the vehicle.

4. Remove the right front wheel and tire assembly.

5. Remove the right halfshaft assembly.

6. Remove the turbocharger to block support bracket. Separate the oil drain back tube fitting from the turbocharger housing and remove the fitting and hose.

7. Remove the remaining turbocharger to manifold retaining nuts.

8. Disconnect the articulated exhaust pipe joint from the turbocharger housing.

9. Remove the lower coolant line and the turbocharger inlet fitting.

10. Lift the turbocharger off the manifold mounting studs and lower assembly from the vehicle.

To install:

11. Position the turbocharger on the exhaust manifold. Apply an antiseize compound, Loctite® 771–64 or equivalent, to the threads and torque the retaining nuts to 40 ft. lbs. (54 Nm). Connect the vacuum hose.

NOTE: Before installing the turbocharger assembly to the engine, be sure it is 1st charged with oil. Failure to do this may cause damage to the turbocharger assembly.

12. Install the lower coolant line. Install the oil drain back tube into the turbocharger housing with new gasket in place.

13. Install and tighten turbocharger to block support bracket finger-tight. First, tighten the block screw to 40 ft. lbs. (54 Nm), then tighten screw to turbocharger housing to 20 ft. lbs. (27 Nm).

14. Reposition exhaust pipe to the manifold and secure with the retainer bolts. Torque the shouldered bolts 20 ft. lbs. (28 Nm).

15. Install the right driveshaft and the wheel and tire assembly to the vehicle.

16. Lower the vehicle and perform the following installation procedures:

   a. Install the 3 turbocharger to manifold retainer nuts torquing to 40 ft. lbs. (54 Nm).

   b. Reconnect the oxygen sensor lead and the vacuum harness if still disconnected.

   c. Attach the oil feed line to the turbocharger bearing housing and tighten fitting to 10 ft. lbs. (14 Nm).

   d. Apply thread sealant to the water box and turbocharger return coolant line end fittings. Install the coolant line fittings and tighten to 30 ft. lbs. (41 Nm).

   e. Align the front engine mount in the crossmember bracket.

   f. Install the through bolt and tighten to 40 ft. lbs. (54 Nm).

17. Refill the cooling system. Connect the negative battery cable and check the turbocharger for proper operation.

Timing Chain Front Cover

REMOVAL AND INSTALLATION

2.2L Turbo III and 2.5L Engines

These engines are equipped with 2 balance shafts installed in a carrier attached to the crankcase. The 2 shafts are driven by a short chain from the crankshaft, to rotate twice the crankshaft speed.

1. Disconnect the negative battery cable. Raise the vehicle and support safely.

2. Remove the timing belt. Remove the oil pan, the oil pickup, the crankshaft belt sprocket and the front crankshaft oil seal retainer.

3. Remove the balance shaft chain cover, the guide and the tensioner.

4. Remove the balance shaft sprocket-to-shaft bolt, the gear cover-to-balance shaft bolt and the crank-

shaft sprocket-to-crankshaft bolts, then the sprockets with the balance shaft chain.

To install:

5. Install the balance chain sprocket and torque the sprocket to crankshaft bolts to 11 ft. lbs. (13 Nm).

6. Rotate the crankshaft to position the No. 1 cylinder on the TDC of the compression stroke; the timing marks on the chain sprocket should align with the parting line on the left side of the No. 1 main bearing cap.

7. Position the balance shaft sprocket into the balance chain so the sprocket (yellow dot) timing mark mates with the yellow link on the chain.

8. Install the balance chain/sprocket assembly onto the crankshaft and the balance shaft.

NOTE: The timing marks on the sprocket, the lower nickel-plated link and the arrow on the side of the gear cover should line up when the balance shafts are correctly timed.

9. Torque the sprocket to shaft bolts to 21 ft. lbs. (28 Nm). If necessary to secure the crankshaft while tightening the bolts, place a block of wood between the crankcase and the crankshaft counterbalance.

10. Loosely install the chain tensioners and place a shim (0.039 in. x 2.75 in.) between the chain and the tensioner. Apply firm pressure, to reduce the chain slack, to the tensioner shoe. Torque the tensioner to front gear cover bolts to 8.5 ft. lbs. (12 Nm).

11. Install the chain cover and the rear cover to the carrier housing and torque the bolts to 8.5 ft. lbs. (12 Nm).

12. Replace the crankshaft retainer seal, apply silicone sealer to the mating surface and install the retainer.

13. Install the oil pickup and oil pan.

14. Install the crankshaft sprocket and the timing belt.

15. Connect the negative battery cable, add fluids to the correct level and road test the vehicle.

Timing Belt Cover

REMOVAL AND INSTALLATION

2.2L and 2.5L Engines

UPPER COVER

1. Disconnect the negative battery cable.

2. Remove the nuts and bolts that attach the upper cover to the valve cover, block or cylinder head.

3. Remove the bolt that attaches the upper cover to the lower cover.

4. Remove the upper cover.

5. Installation is the reverse of the removal procedure.

LOWER COVER

1. Disconnect the negative battery cable.

2. Raise the vehicle and support safely.

3. Remove the right tire and wheel assembly. Remove the right side inner splash shield.

4. Remove the crankshaft pulley, water pump pulley and the accessory drive belt(s).

5. Remove the lower cover attaching bolts and the cover from the engine.

6. The installation is the reverse of the removal procedure.

3.0L Engine

1. Disconnect the negative battery cable.

2. If equipped with air conditioning, remove the air conditioning compressor mounting bolts and position compressor aside. It is not necessary to remove the refrigerant lines from the compressor.

3. Remove the air conditioning compressor bracket mounting screws. Remove the bracket and adjustable drive belt tensioner from the engine block.

4. Remove the power steering/alternator belt tensioner mounting bolt and remove the tensioner.

5. Remove the power steering pump mounting bolts and position the pump assembly aside.

6. Raise the vehicle and safely support. Remove the right inner fender splash shield.

7. Remove the crankshaft pulley bolt and the pulley/damper assembly from the crankshaft.

8. Lower the vehicle and place a floor jack under the engine to support it.

9. Separate the front engine mount insulator from the bracket. Raise the engine slightly and remove the mount bracket.

10. Remove the timing belt cover bolts and the upper and lower covers from the engine.

To install:

11. Install the timing belt covers and retainer bolts to the engine Tighten bolts to 115 inch lbs. (14 Nm).

12. While aligning the engine position and the mount, lower the engine into the front support and secure with the retaining bolts and nuts.

13. Install the crankshaft pulley bolt and the pulley/damper assembly to the crankshaft.

14. With the engine securely in place, install the right inner splash shield.

15. Install the power steering pump, air conditioner compressor mounting bracket, air conditioning compressor and the belt adjuster brackets. Install the accessory drive belts.

16. Connect the negative battery cable.

Timing Belt and Tensioner

ADJUSTMENT

Except 2.2L Turbo and 3.0L Engines

1. Disconnect the negative battery cable.

2. Raise the vehicle and support safely. Remove the right front inner splash shield.

3. Remove the tensioner cover.

4. Place the special tensioning tool C–4703 on the hex of the tensioner so the weight is at about the 10 o'clock position. Loosen the adjuster retainer bolt.

5. The tensioner should drop to the 9 o'clock position. Reposition the tool as required in order to have it end up at the 9 o'clock position (parallel to the ground, hanging toward the rear of the vehicle) ± 15 degrees.

6. Hold the tool in position and tighten the tensioner retainer bolt. Do not pull the tool past the position achieved by the tension adjustment tool or the belt will be too tight, causing a howling noise during operation or possible belt breakage.

7. Install the cover and the splash shield.

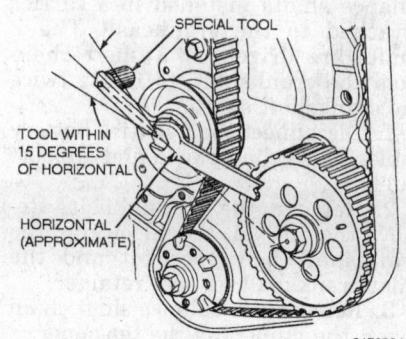

Adjusting timing belt tension — 2.2L and 2.5L engines

2.2L Turbo Engine

1. Disconnect the negative battery cable.

2. Remove the timing covers.

3. Install a belt tension gauge on the timing belt between the camshaft sprockets. For the reading the be accurate, make sure the tension gauge is between the teeth on the belt.

4. Rotate the tensioner clockwise to adjust the belt tension to 110 lbs. (445 N) for new belt or 70 lbs. (311 N) for used belt.

5. Rotate the crankshaft clockwise 2 revolutions and recheck the tension. Adjust as required.

6. Install the timing covers and related components.

3.0L Engines

1. Disconnect the negative battery cable.

2. Remove the timing belt covers.

3. Loosen the bolt that holds the timing belt tensioner in place.

4. Allow the spring only to pull the tensioner in automatically. Do not manually move the tensioner or the belt will be too tight.

5. Tighten the tensioner locking bolt.

6. Install the timing belt covers and all related parts.

REMOVAL AND INSTALLATION

2.2L (SOHC) and 2.5L Engines

1. Disconnect the negative battery cable.

2. Position the engine so the No. 1 piston is at TDC of its compression stroke.

3. Remove the timing belt covers. Remove the timing belt tensioner and allow the belt to hang free.

4. Place a floor jack under the engine and separate the right motor mount.

5. Remove the air conditioning compressor belt idler pulley, if equipped, and remove the mounting stud. Remove the compressor/alternator bracket as follows:

a. Remove the alternator pivot bolt and remove the alternator from the bracket. Turn the alternator so the wire connections are facing up and disconnect the harness connectors from the rear of the alternator.

b. Remove the air conditioning compressor belt idler.

c. Remove the right engine mount yoke screw securing engine mount support strut to the engine.

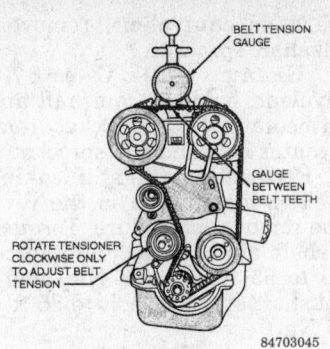

Checking timing belt tension — 2.2L DOHC engine

d. Remove the 5 side mounting bolts retaining the bracket to the front of the engine.

e. Remove the front mounting nut. Remove the front bolt and strut and rotate the solid mount bracket away from the engine. Slide the bracket on the stud until free of the mounting studs and remove from the engine.

f. Remove the timing belt from the vehicle.

To install:

6. Turn the crankshaft sprocket and intermediate shaft sprocket until the marks align. Use a straight-edge from bolt to bolt to confirm alignment.

7. Turn the camshaft until the small hole in the sprocket is at the top and the arrows on the hub align with the camshaft cap to cylinder head mounting lines. When looking through the hole on top of the camshaft sprocket, the uppermost center nipple of the valve cover end seal should be at the center of the hole. Use a mirror to check the alignment of the arrows so it is viewed straight on and not at an angle from above. Install the belt but let it hang free at this point.

8. Install the air conditioning compressor/alternator bracket, idler pulley and motor mount. Remove the floor jack. Raise the vehicle and support safely. Have the tensioner at an arm's reach because the timing belt will have to be held in position with one hand.

9. To properly install the timing belt, reach up and engage it with the camshaft sprocket. Turn the intermediate shaft counterclockwise slightly, then engage the belt with the intermediate shaft sprocket. Hold the belt against the intermediate shaft sprocket and turn clockwise to take up all tension; if the timing marks are out of alignment, repeat until alignment is correct.

10. Using a wrench, turn the crankshaft sprocket counterclockwise slightly and wrap the belt around it. Turn the sprocket clockwise so there is no slack in the belt between sprockets; if the timing marks are out of alignment, repeat until alignment is correct.

NOTE: If the timing marks are in line but slack exists in the belt between either the camshaft and intermediate shaft sprockets or the intermediate and crankshaft sprockets, the timing will be incorrect when the belt is tensioned. All slack must be only between the crankshaft and camshaft sprockets.

11. Install the tensioner and install the mounting bolt loosely. Place the special tensioning tool C–4703 on the hex of the tensioner so the weight is at about the 9 o'clock position (parallel to the ground, hanging toward the rear of the vehicle) ± 15 degrees.

12. Hold the tool in position and tighten the bolt to 45 ft. lbs. (61 Nm). Do not pull the tool past the 9 o'clock position; this will make the belt too tight and will cause it to howl or possibly break.

13. Lower the vehicle and recheck the camshaft sprocket positioning. If it is correct install the timing belt covers and all related parts.

14. Connect the negative battery cable and road test the vehicle.

2.2L Turbo III Engine

1. Disconnect the negative battery cable.

2. Remove the timing belt covers.

3. Install appropriate engine support tool and lift the engine slightly. Separate the right motor mount.

4. Raise the vehicle and support safely. Remove the lower accessory drive belt idler pulley bracket assembly.

5. Loosen the timing belt tensioner and remove the timing belt and idler pulley.

To install:

6. Remove the air cleaner fresh air duct, ignition cable cover, spark plugs and valve covers.

7. Loosen the rocker arm retaining bolts about 3 turns in the proper sequence. Check all lash adjusters and replace any that are damaged.

8. Align and pin both camshaft sprockets with 3/32 in. drill bits or pin punches.

9. Install a dial indicator so the plunger is in the No. 1 spark plug hole. Rotate the crankshaft until the No. 1 piston is at TDC. Matchmark the crankshaft sprocket to the engine block for reference. The intermediate

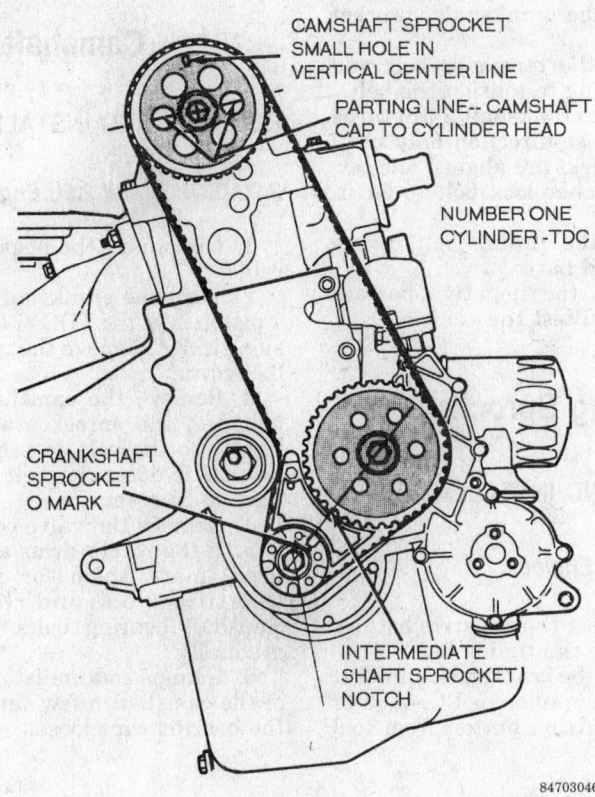

CAMSHAFT SPROCKET SMALL HOLE IN VERTICAL CENTER LINE

PARTING LINE-- CAMSHAFT CAP TO CYLINDER HEAD

NUMBER ONE CYLINDER -TDC

CRANKSHAFT SPROCKET O MARK

INTERMEDIATE SHAFT SPROCKET NOTCH

Timing belt alignment — 2.2L and 2.5L Non-turbo engines

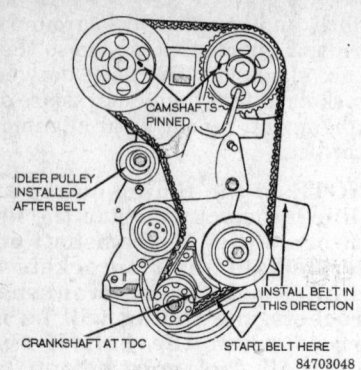

CAMSHAFTS PINNED

IDLER PULLEY INSTALLED AFTER BELT

INSTALL BELT IN THIS DIRECTION

CRANKSHAFT AT TDC

START BELT HERE

84703048

Timing belt installation — 2.2L turbo engine

shaft sprocket does not need to be timed.

10. Install the timing belt and idler pulley starting at the crankshaft and working counterclockwise. Make sure there is no slack between sprockets when installing.

11. Install a belt tension gauge on the timing belt between the camshaft sprockets. Remove the pins from the camshaft sprockets.

12. Rotate the tensioner clockwise to adjust the belt tension to 110 lbs. (445 N) for new belt or 70 lbs. (311 N) for used belt. Torque the tensioner bolt 39 ft. lbs. (53 Nm).

13. Rotate the crankshaft clockwise 2 revolutions and recheck the timing and tension. Adjust as required.

14. Torque the rocker arm bolts in sequence to 18 ft. lbs. (24 Nm).

15. Install engine mount and timing belt covers.

16. Install the spark plugs, valve covers, ignition cable cover and air duct.

17. Connect the negative battery cable.

3.0L Engine

1. If possible, position the engine so the No. 1 cylinder is at TDC of its compression stroke. Disconnect the negative battery cable. Remove the timing covers from the engine.

2. If the same timing belt will be reused, mark the direction of the timing belt's rotation for installation in the same direction. Make sure the engine is positioned so the No. 1 cylinder is at the TDC of its compression stroke and the sprockets timing marks are aligned with the engine's timing mark indicators.

3. Loosen the timing belt tensioner and remove the belt. If not removing the tensioner, position it as far away from the center of the engine as possible and tighten the bolt.

4. If the tensioner is being removed, paint the outside of the spring to ensure it is not installed backwards. Unbolt the tensioner and remove it along with the spring.

To install:

5. Install the tensioner if removed, and hook the upper end of the spring to the water pump pin and the lower end to the tensioner in exactly the same position as originally installed. If not already done, position both camshafts so the marks align with those on the alternator bracket (rear bank) and inner timing cover (front bank). Rotate the crankshaft so the timing mark aligns with the mark on the oil pump.

6. Install the timing belt on the crankshaft sprocket and while keeping the belt tight on the tension side (right side), install the belt on the front camshaft sprocket.

7. Install the belt on the water pump pulley, then the rear camshaft sprocket and the tensioner.

8. Rotate the front camshaft counterclockwise to tension the belt between the front camshaft and the crankshaft. If the timing marks came out of line, repeat the procedure.

9. Install the crankshaft sprocket flange.

10. Loosen the tensioner bolt and allow the spring to tension the belt.

11. Turn the crankshaft 2 full turns in the clockwise direction only until the timing marks are aligned and torque the tensioner lock bolt to 21 ft. lbs. (29 Nm).

12. Install the timing belt covers and all related parts.

13. Connect the negative battery cable and road test the vehicle.

Timing Sprockets

REMOVAL AND INSTALLATION

2.2L and 2.5L Engines

1. Disconnect the negative battery cable. Remove the timing belt.

2. Remove the crankshaft sprocket bolt. Using the puller tool C–4685 or equivalent and the button from tool

L–4524 or equivalent, remove the crankshaft sprocket.

3. Using tool C–4687 or equivalent, hold the camshaft and/or intermediate shaft sprocket, remove the center bolt and the sprocket(s).

4. Replace the seal(s) if leaking.

5. The installation is the reverse of the removal procedure. Torque the camshaft and intermediate sprocket bolts to 65 ft. lbs. (88 Nm) and the crankshaft sprocket bolt to 85 ft. lbs. (115 Nm).

3.0L Engine

1. Disconnect the negative battery cable.

2. Remove the timing belt.

3. To remove the camshaft sprocket, hold the sprocket with tool MB990775 or equivalent, and remove the retaining bolt and washer.

4. To remove the crankshaft sprocket, remove the bolt and remove the sprocket from the crankshaft. Replace any leaking seals.

5. The installation is the reverse of the removal procedure. Torque the camshaft sprocket bolt to 70 ft. lbs. (95 Nm) while holding the sprocket with the holding tool. Torque the crankshaft sprocket bolt. to 110 ft. lbs. (150 Nm).

Camshaft

REMOVAL AND INSTALLATION

2.2L (SOHC) and 2.5L Engines

1. Disconnect the negative battery cable.

2. Turn the crankshaft so the No. 1 piston is at the TDC of the compression stroke. Remove the upper timing belt cover.

3. Remove the camshaft sprocket bolt and the sprocket and suspend tightly so the belt does not lose tension. If it does, the belt timing will have to be reset.

4. Remove the valve cover.

5. If the rocker arms are being reused, mark them for installation identification and loosen the camshaft bearing bolts, evenly and gradually.

6. Using a soft mallet, tap the rear of the camshaft a few times to break the bearing caps loose.

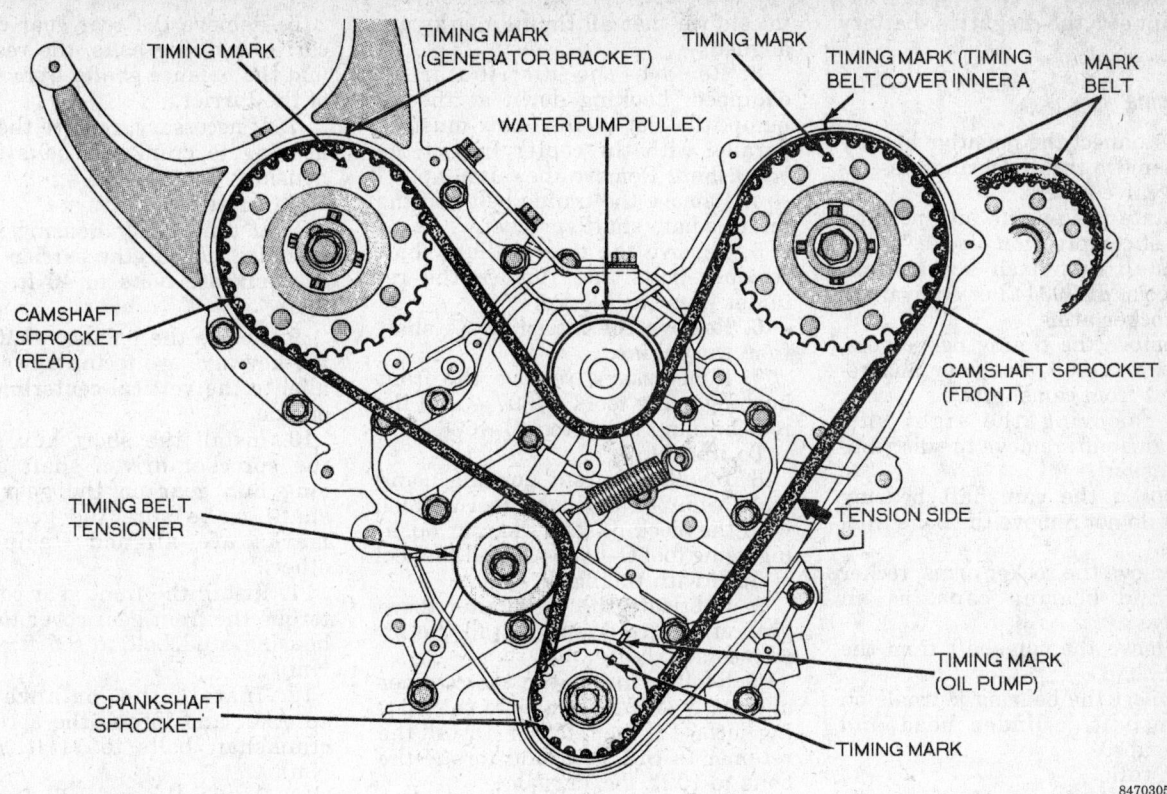

Timing belt installation — 3.0L engines

7. Remove the bolts, bearing caps and the camshaft with seals.

NOTE: Take note of the color of the paint stripe on the rear camshaft seal. These stripes differentiate seal sizes. If a seal with a different color stripe is installed, a severe leak will develop if the seal is too small or the cap will not be able to be fully installed if the seal is too big. Also, oversized components can be identified as follows: the top of the bearing caps are painted green and O/SJ is stamped behind the oil galley plug on the end of the head. The barrel of an oversized camshaft is also painted green and O/SJ is stamped on the end of the shaft. If normal sized parts are installed in place of oversized ones, oil pressure will be significantly reduced.

8. Check the oil passages for blockages and the parts for wear and damage and replace parts, as required. Clean the gasket mounting surfaces.

To install:

9. Transfer the sprocket key to the new camshaft. New rocker arms and a new camshaft sprocket bolt are normally included with the camshaft

package. Install the rocker arms, lubricate the camshaft and install with end seals installed.

10. Place the bearing caps with No. 1 at the timing belt end and No. 5 at the transaxle end. The camshaft bearing caps are numbered and have arrows facing forward. Torque the camshaft bearing bolts evenly and gradually to 18 ft. lbs. (24 Nm).

NOTE: Apply RTV silicone gasket material to the No. 1 and 5 bearing caps. Install the bearing caps before the seals are installed.

11. Mount a dial indicator to the front of the engine and check the camshaft endplay. Play should not exceed 0.020 in.

12. Install the camshaft sprocket and the new bolt.

13. Reinstall timing belt.

14. Install the valve cover with a new gasket.

15. Connect the negative battery cable, run engine, set engine timing and check for leaks.

2.2L Turbo III Engine

1. Disconnect the negative battery cable.

2. Remove the cylinder head.

3. Remove the rocker shaft assemblies.

4. The thrust plates in the rear of the head are not interchangeable; the intake camshaft uses a wider plate. Identify the plates and remove them.

5. To remove the cam seal, push the cam toward the seal end and the seal will be pushed out of its bore in the head.

6. Carefully pull the camshaft from the head. The intake and exhaust camshafts are not interchangeable. If both are being removed, identify them for installation purposes.

To install:

7. Inspect the camshaft for wear and replace any parts that are damaged.

8. Lubricate the journals with fresh engine oil and insert the camshaft into the head.

9. Install the thrust plates and tighten the retaining nuts to 55–70 inch lbs. (6–8 Nm).

10. Install new camshaft seals flush with the head surface using installation tool C–4680 or equivalent.

11. Move the camshaft as far rearward as possible. Use a dial indicator and measure the endplay. Endplay specification is 0.001–0.008 in. (0.026–0.206mm).

12. Install the rocker shaft assemblies.

13. Install the cylinder head.

14. Connect the negative battery cable.

3.0L Engine

1. Disconnect the negative battery cable. Remove the air cleaner assembly and valve covers.

2. Rotate the engine and position at TDC of compression stroke.

3. Install auto lash adjuster retainer tools MD998443 or equivalent, on the rocker arms.

4. Remove the timing belt covers, loosen timing belt tensioner and remove belt from camshafts.

5. If removing the right side (front) camshaft, remove the distributor extension.

6. Loosen the camshaft bearing caps but do not remove the bolts from the caps.

7. Remove the rocker arms, rocker shafts and bearing caps, as an assembly.

8. Remove the camshaft from the cylinder head.

9. Inspect the bearing journals on the camshaft, cylinder head and bearing caps.

To install:

10. Lubricate the camshaft journals and camshaft with clean engine oil and install the camshaft in the cylinder head.

11. Align the camshaft bearing caps with the arrow mark (depending on cylinder numbers) and in numerical order.

12. Apply sealer at the ends of the bearing caps and install the assembly.

13. Torque the bearing cap bolts, in the following sequence: No. 3, No. 2, No. 1 and No. 4 to 85 inch lbs. (10 Nm).

14. Repeat the sequence increasing the torque to 175–180 inch lbs. (18–20 Nm).

15. Install timing belt assembly.

16. Install the distributor extension, if removed.

17. Install the valve cover and all related parts.

18. Connect the negative battery cable.

Intermediate Shaft

REMOVAL AND INSTALLATION

2.2L and 2.5L Engines

1. Disconnect the negative battery cable.

2. Rotate the engine so the No. 1 piston is at TDC of its compression stroke. Remove the timing belt covers

to confirm that all timing marks are aligned.

3. Remove the distributor, if equipped. Looking down at the oil pump, the slot in the shaft must be parallel with the center line of the crankshaft. Remove the oil pump.

4. Remove the timing belt and the intermediate shaft sprocket.

5. Remove the intermediate shaft retainer bolts and remove the retainer from the block.

6. Remove the intermediate shaft from the engine.

7. If necessary, remove the front bushing using tool C–4697–2 and the rear bushing using tool C–4686–2.

To install:

8. Install the front bushing using tool C–4697–1 until the tool is flush with the block. Install the rear bushing using tool C–4686–1 until the tool is flush with the block.

9. Lubricate the distributor drive gear, if equipped, and install the intermediate shaft.

10. Replace the seal in the retainer and apply silicone sealer to the mating surface of the retainer. Install the retainer to the block and torque the bolts to 10 ft. lbs. (12 Nm).

11. Install the intermediate shaft sprocket and the timing belt.

12. With the timing belt properly installed, install the oil pump so the slot is parallel to the center line of the crankshaft. If equipped, install the distributor so the rotor is aligned with the No. 1 spark plug wire tower on the cap.

13. Connect the negative battery cable, check for leaks and adjust the ignition timing, as required.

Balance Shafts

REMOVAL AND INSTALLATION

2.2L Turbo and 2.5L Engines

1. Disconnect the negative battery cable. Raise the vehicle and support safely.

2. Remove the timing belt. Remove the oil pan, the oil pickup, the crankshaft belt sprocket and the front crankshaft oil seal retainer.

3. Remove the balance shaft chain cover, chain guide and the tensioner.

4. Remove the balance shaft sprocket-to-shaft bolt, the gear cover to balance shaft bolt and the crankshaft sprocket-to-crankshaft bolts, then the sprockets with the balance shaft chain.

5. Remove the front gear cover-to-carrier housing stud, the gear cover and the balance shaft drive gears.

6. Remove the rear gear cover-to-carrier housing bolts, the rear cover and the balance shafts from the rear of the carrier.

7. If necessary, remove the carrier housing to crankcase bolts and the housing.

To install:

8. If the carrier housing is being installed, torque the carrier housing to crankcase bolts to 40 ft. lbs. (54 Nm).

9. Rotate the balance shafts until the keyways are facing upward, parallel to the vertical centerline of the engine.

10. Install the short hub gear on the sprocket driven shaft and the long hub gear on the gear driven shaft; make sure the gear timing marks are aligned (facing each other).

11. Install the front gear cover and torque the front gear cover to carrier housing stud bolt to 8.5 ft. lbs. (12 Nm).

12. Install the balance chain sprocket and torque the sprocket to crankshaft bolts to 11 ft. lbs. (13 Nm).

13. Rotate the crankshaft to position the No. 1 cylinder on the TDC of the compression stroke; the timing marks on the chain sprocket should align with the parting line on the left side of the No. 1 main bearing cap.

14. Position the balance shaft sprocket into the balance chain so the sprocket (yellow dot) timing mark mates with the yellow link on the chain.

15. Install the balance chain/sprocket assembly onto the crankshaft and the balance shaft. Torque the sprocket to shaft bolts to 21 ft. lbs. (28 Nm). If necessary to secure the crankshaft while tightening the bolts, place a block of wood between the crankcase and the crankshaft counterbalance.

16. Loosely, install the chain tensioners and place a shim (0.039 in. x 2.75 in.) between the chain and the tensioner. Apply firm pressure, to reduce the chain slack, to the tensioner shoe. Torque the tensioner upper bolt 1st, and then the lower pivot bolt to 8.5 ft. lbs. (12 Nm). Remove the shim from the tensioner.

17. Install the chain cover and the rear cover to the carrier housing and torque the bolts to 8.5 ft. lbs. (12 Nm).

18. Replace the crankshaft retainer seal, apply silicone sealer to the mating surface and install the retainer.

19. Install the oil pickup and oil pan.

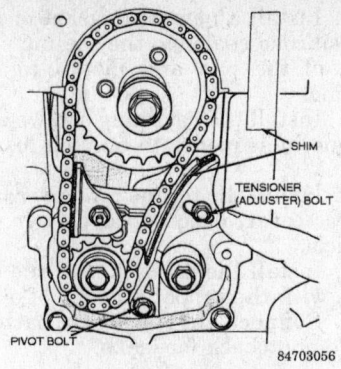

Alignment of balance shaft gear sprockets

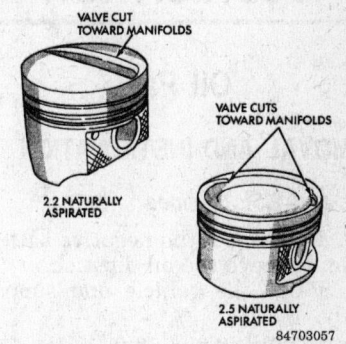

Balance shaft chain tension adjustment

Piston and Connecting Rod

POSITIONING

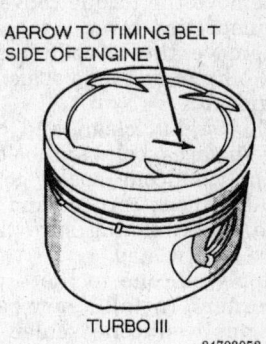

Piston positioning — 2.2L and 2.5L Non-turbo engine

20. Install the crankshaft sprocket, timing belt and related components.

21. Connect the negative battery cable, correct all engine fluid levels and road test the vehicle.

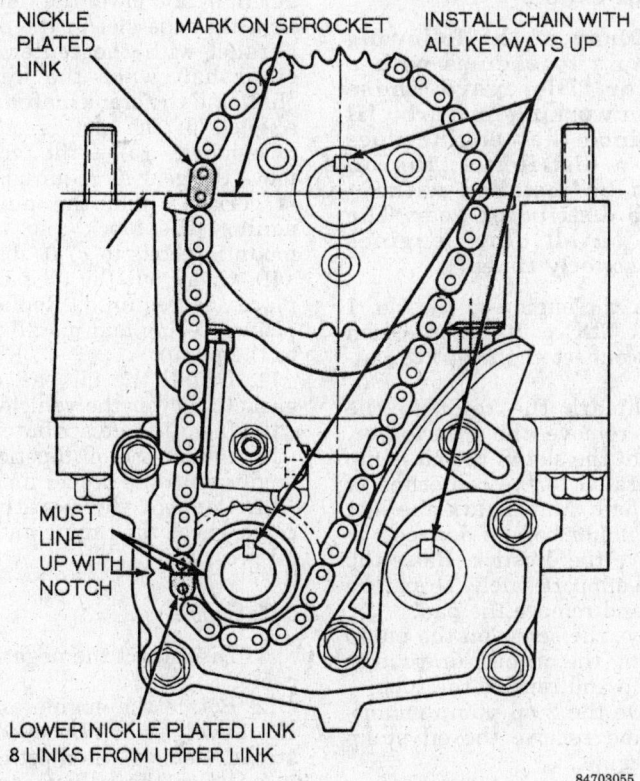

Balance shaft and crankshaft sprocket alignment

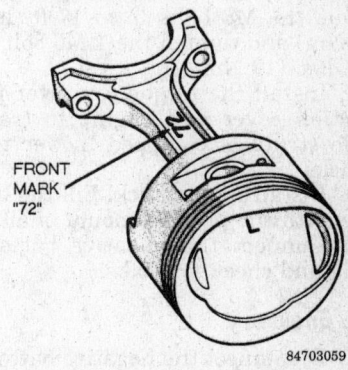

Piston positioning — 2.2L turbo III engine

Piston positioning — 3.0L engine

ENGINE LUBRICATION

Oil Pan

REMOVAL AND INSTALLATION

2.2L and 2.5L Engines

1. Disconnect the negative battery cable. Remove the oil dipstick.
2. Raise the vehicle and support safely.
3. Drain the engine oil.
4. Remove the engine to transaxle struts, if equipped.
5. Remove the torque converter or clutch inspection cover.
6. Remove the oil pan retaining screws, oil pan and side seals.

To install:

7. Thoroughly clean and dry all sealing surfaces, bolts and bolt holes.
8. Apply silicone sealer to the 4 end seal-to-block corners and install the end seals making sure the corners are not twisted.
9. Apply silicone to the 4 pan-to-block corners. Install a new pan gasket or apply silicone sealer to the sealing surface of the pan and install to the engine making sure not to dislodge the end seals.
10. Install the retaining screws and torque the M8 bolts to to 17 ft. lbs. (23 Nm) and tighten the 1 M6 bolt to 9 ft. lbs. (12 Nm).
11. Install the torque converter inspection cover and engine to transaxle struts, if equipped. Lower the vehicle.
12. Install the dipstick. Fill the engine with the proper amount of oil.
13. Connect the negative battery cable and check for leaks.

3.0L Engine

1. Disconnect the negative battery cable.
2. Raise the vehicle and support safely.
3. Remove the torque converter bolt access cover.
4. Drain the engine oil.
5. Remove the oil pan retaining screws and remove the oil pan and gasket.

To install:

6. Thoroughly clean and dry all sealing surfaces, bolts and bolt holes.
7. Apply silicone sealer to the chain cover-to-block mating seam and the rear main seal retainer-to-block seam, if equipped.

8. Install a new pan gasket or apply silicone sealer to the sealing surface of the pan and install to the engine.
9. Install the retaining screws and torque in sequence to 50 inch lbs. (6 Nm).
10. Install the torque converter bolt access cover, if equipped. Lower the vehicle.
11. Install the dipstick. Fill the engine with the proper amount of oil.
12. Connect the negative battery cable and check for leaks.

Oil Pump

REMOVAL AND INSTALLATION

2.2L and 2.5L Engines

NOTE: Many of the following steps pertain to engines with a distributor. Disregard these steps when working on Turbo III engine. Since that engine does not have a distributor, the oil pump can be installed without timing the distributor gear. The oil pump on all other engines must be properly timed.

1. Crank the engine so the No. 1 piston is at TDC of its compression stroke. Disconnect the negative battery cable.
2. Matchmark the rotor to the block and remove the distributor. Confirm that the slot in the oil pump shaft is parallel to the centerline of the crankshaft. Matchmark the slot to the distributor bore, if desired.
3. Remove the dipstick. Raise the vehicle and support safely. Drain the engine oil and remove the pan.
4. Remove the screw on the pump cover holding the oil pick-up tube to the oil pump and remove the tube.
5. Remove the 2 oil pump mounting bolts and remove the oil pump from the engine.

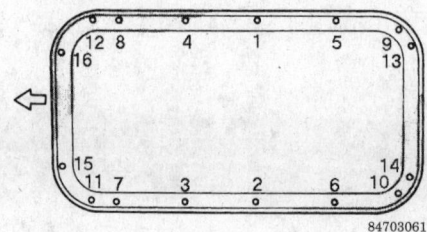

84703061

Oil pan bolt torque sequence — 3.0L engines

To install:

6. Prime the pump by pouring fresh oil into the pump intake and turning the driveshaft until oil comes out of the pressure port. Repeat a few times until no air bubbles are present.
7. Apply Loctite® 515, Mopar Gasket Maker® or equivalent, to the pump body to block machined surface interface. Lubricate the oil pump and distributor driveshaft.
8. Align the timing mark on the intermediate sprocket so it is aligned with the timing mark on the crankshaft sprocket. Install the pump fully and rotate back and forth to ensure proper positioning between the pump mounting surface and the machined surface of the block.
9. Install the mounting bolts finger-tight and lower the vehicle to confirm that the slot in the oil pump is parallel with the centerline of the crankshaft when the intermediate shaft and the crankshaft are properly aligned. If the slot is not properly positioned, raise the vehicle and move the gear as required. If the slot is correct, hold the pump firmly against the block and torque the mounting bolts to 17 ft. lbs. (23 Nm).
10. Clean out the oil pickup or replace, as required. Replace the oil pickup O-ring and install the pickup to the pump.
11. Install the oil pan using new gaskets. Lower the vehicle.
12. Install the distributor.
13. Install the oil dipstick. Fill the engine with the proper amount of oil.
14. Connect the negative battery cable, check the timing and check the oil pressure.

3.0L Engine

1. Disconnect the negative battery cable.
2. Rotate the engine and position No. 1 cylinder at TDC of compression stroke. Remove the dipstick.
3. Raise the vehicle and support safely. Remove the timing belt, drain the engine oil and remove the oil pan from the engine. Remove the oil pickup.
4. Remove the oil pump mounting bolts and remove the pump from the front of the engine. Note the different length bolts and their positions for installation.

To install:

5. Clean the gasket mounting surfaces of the pump and engine block.
6. Prime the pump by packing the inside of the oil pump with non-medicated petroleum jelly. Using a new gasket, install the oil pump on the

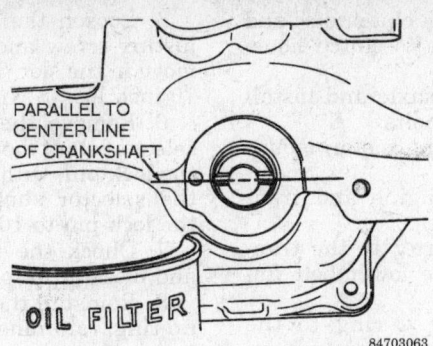

PARALLEL TO CENTER LINE OF CRANKSHAFT

OIL FILTER

84703063

Oil pump shaft alignment as viewed from distributor opening — 2.2L, 2.2L turbo and 2.5L engines

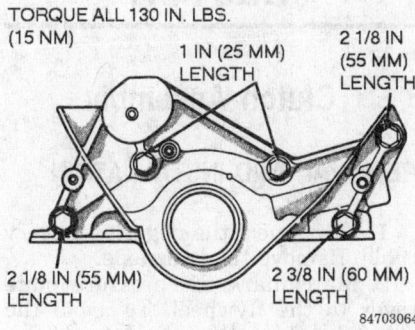

TORQUE ALL 130 IN. LBS. (15 NM)

1 IN (25 MM) LENGTH

2 1/8 IN (55 MM) LENGTH

2 1/8 IN (55 MM) LENGTH

2 3/8 IN (60 MM) LENGTH

84703064

Oil pump bolt location — 3.0L engines

engine and torque all bolts to 130 inch lbs. (15 Nm).

7. Install the balancer and crankshaft sprocket to the end of the crankshaft.

8. Clean out the oil pickup or replace, as required. Replace the oil pickup gasket ring and install the pickup to the pump.

9. Install the timing belt, oil pan and all related parts.

10. Install the dipstick. Fill the engine with the proper amount of oil.

11. Connect the negative battery cable and check the oil pressure.

CHECKING

2.2L and 2.5L Engine

1. Remove the cover from the oil pump.

2. Check endplay of the inner rotor using a feeler gauge and a straight-edge placed across the pump body. The specification is 0.001–0.004 in. (0.03–0.09mm).

3. Measure the clearance between the inner and outer rotors. The maximum clearance is 0.008 in. (0.20mm).

4. Measure the clearance between the outer rotor and the pump body.

The maximum clearance is 0.014 in. (0.35mm).

5. The minimum thickness of the outer rotor is 0.944 in. (23.96mm). The minimum diameter of the outer rotor is 2.77 in. (62.70mm). The minimum thickness of the inner rotor is 0.943 in. (23.95mm).

6. Check the cover for warpage. The maximum allowable is 0.003 in. (0.076mm).

7. Check the pressure relief valve for damage. The spring's free length specification is 1.95 in. (49.50mm).

8. Assemble the outer rotor with the larger chamfered edge in the pump body. Torque the cover screws to 10 ft. lbs. (12 Nm).

3.0L Engine

1. With the oil pump assembly removed from the engine, inspect the case of the pump for damage and remove the rear cover

2. Remove the pump rotors and inspect the case for excessive wear.

3. Measure the diameter of the inner rotor hub that sits in the case. Measure the inside diameter of the inner rotor hub bore. Subtract the 1st measurement from the 2nd; if the result is over 0.006 in. (0.15mm), replace the oil pump assembly.

4. Measure the clearance between the outer rotor and the case. The specification is 0.004–0.007 in. (0.10–0.18mm).

5. Check the side clearance of the rotors using a feeler gauge and a straight-edge placed across the case. The specification is 0.0015–0.0035 in. (0.04–0.09mm).

6. Check the relief plunger and spring for damage and breakage.

7. Install the rear cover to the case.

Rear Main Bearing Oil Seal

REMOVAL AND INSTALLATION

1. Disconnect the negative battery cable.

2. Remove the transaxle. Remove the flywheel or flexplate.

3. If there is leakage coming from the rear seal retainer, drain the engine oil and remove the oil pan. Remove the rear main oil seal retainer.

4. Remove the seal from the retainer.

To install:

5. Lightly coat the seal outer diameter with Loctite® Stud N' Bearing Mount or equivalent.

6. Install the seal to the retainer.

7. If the retainer was removed, thoroughly clean and dry the retainer to block sealing surfaces and install a new gasket or apply silicone sealer and install the retainer. Install the pan, if it was removed.

8. Install the flywheel or flexplate and the transaxle.

9. Connect the negative battery cable, correct all engine fluid levels and check for leaks.

MANUAL TRANSAXLE

Transaxle Assembly

REMOVAL AND INSTALLATION

NOTE: If the vehicle is going to be rolled while the transaxle is out of the vehicle, obtain 2 outer CV-joints to install to the hubs. If the vehicle is rolled without the proper torque applied to the front wheel bearings, the bearings will no longer be usable. Different transaxles are used according to application. It is important to use the round identification tag screwed to the top of the case when obtaining parts for exact parts matching. The tag should be reinstalled for future reference.

1. Disconnect the negative battery cable.

2. Remove the air cleaner assembly with all ducts. Remove the upper bellhousing bolts. Disconnect the reverse light switch and the ground wire.

3. Remove the starter attaching nut and bolt at the top of the bellhousing.

4. Raise the vehicle and support safely. Remove the left front tire and wheel assembly. Remove the left front fender inner skirt. Remove the axle end cotter pins, nut locks, spring washers and axle nuts.

5. Remove the ball joint retaining bolts and pry the control arm from the steering knuckle. Position a drainpan under the transaxle where the axles enter the differential or extension housing. Remove the axles from the transaxle or center bearing. Unbolt the center bearing and remove the intermediate axle from the transaxle, if equipped.

6. Remove the anti-rotation link from the crossmember. Disconnect the shifter cables from the transaxle and unbolt the cable bracket.

7. Remove the speedometer gear adaptor bolt and remove the adaptor from the transaxle.

8. Remove the rear mount from the starter, unbolt the starter and position aside.

9. Using the proper equipment, support the weight of the engine.

10. Remove the front motor mount and bracket.

11. Position a transaxle jack under the transaxle assembly.

12. Remove the lower bellhousing bolts.

13. Remove the left side splash shield. Remove the transaxle mount bolts.

14. Carefully pry the transaxle from the engine.

15. Slide the transaxle rearward until the input shaft clears the clutch disc.

16. Pull the transaxle completely away from the clutch housing and remove it from the vehicle.

17. To prepare the vehicle for rolling, support the engine with a suitable support or reinstall the front motor mount to the engine. Then reinstall the ball joints to the steering knuckle and install the retaining bolt. Install the obtained outer CV-joints to the hubs, install the washers and torque the axle nuts to 180 ft. lbs. (244 Nm). The vehicle may now be safely rolled.

To install:
18. Lubricate the pilot bushing and input shaft splines lightly with high temperature lubricant.

19. Mount the transaxle securely on a jack. Lift it into place until the input shaft is centered in the clutch housing opening. Roll the transaxle forward until the input shaft splines fully engage with the clutch disc and install the transaxle to clutch housing bolts.

20. Raise the transaxle and install the left side mount bolts.

21. Install the front motor mount and bracket.

22. Remove the engine and transaxle support fixtures.

23. Install the starter to the transaxle and install the lower bolt finger-tight.

24. Install a new O-ring to the speedometer cable adaptor and install to the extension housing; make sure it snaps in place. Install the retaining bolt.

25. Install the shift cable bracket and snap the cable ends in place. Install the anti-rotation link.

26. Install the axles and center bearing, if equipped. Install the ball joints to the steering knuckles. Torque the axle nuts to 180 ft. lbs. (244 Nm) and install new cotter pins. Fill the transaxle with SAE 5W-30 engine oil until the level is even with the bottom of the filler hole. Install the splash shield and install the wheels. Lower the vehicle.

27. Install the upper bellhousing bolts.

28. Install the starter attaching nut and bolt at the top of the bellhousing. Raise the vehicle and tighten the starter bolt from under the vehicle. Lower the vehicle.

29. Connect the reverse light switch and the ground wire.

30. Install the air cleaner assembly.

31. Connect the negative battery cable and check the transaxle for proper operation. Make sure the reverse lights are on when the transaxle is in **R**.

CABLE ADJUSTMENT

1. Working over the left front fender, remove the lock pin from the transaxle selector shaft housing.

2. Reverse the lock pin so the long end is down and insert it into the same threaded hole while pushing the selector shaft into the selector housing. A hole in the selector shaft will align with the lock pin, allowing the lock pin to be screwed into the housing. This operation locks the selector shaft in the neutral position between 3rd and 4th gears.

3. Remove the gearshift knob, the retaining nut and the pull-up ring from the gearshift lever.

4. If necessary, remove the shift lever boot and console to expose the gearshift linkage. The selector cable is not adjustable.

5. Loosen the crossover cable adjusting screw and allow the cable to move in the slot. Tighten the screw to 70 inch lbs. (8 Nm).

6. Remove the lock pin from the selector shaft housing and reinstall the lock pin, with the long end up, in the selector shaft housing. Torque the lock pin to 10 ft. lbs. (12 Nm).

7. Check the 1st/reverse shifting and blockout into reverse.

8. Reinstall the console, boot, pull-up ring, retaining nut and knob.

CLUTCH

Clutch Assembly

REMOVAL AND INSTALLATION

1. Disconnect the negative battery cable. Remove the transaxle.

2. Matchmark the pressure plate cover to the flywheel. To avoid the clutch plate falling and becoming damaged during removal, insert a clutch aligning tool into the pressure plate and through the clutch plate and into the pilot bearing.

3. Loosen the flywheel to pressure plate bolts gradually and evenly to avoid warpage.

4. Remove the pressure plate and clutch assembly from the flywheel.

5. Inspect and replace the pilot bearing if necessary.

6. Sand or replace the flywheel if scoring, cracks or heat damage is present.

7. Sparingly apply anti-sieze compound to the pilot bearing, input shaft and clutch disc splines. Install a new release bearing.

To install:
8. Install the clutch disc assembly to the flywheel and, using a clutch disc alignment tool, align the disc on the flywheel and cover. Be sure to position clutch disc so the raised hub of the disc is facing away from the flywheel.

9. Torque the pressure plate/clutch assembly mounting bolts to the flywheel gradually and evenly to 21 ft. lbs. (28 Nm).

10. Install the transaxle to the vehicle.

11. Connect the negative battery cable, correct fluid levels as required and check the clutch operation and reverse lights.

PEDAL FREE-PLAY ADJUSTMENT

All vehicles are equipped with a self-adjusting cable operated mechanism and no adjustment is provided. The mechanism is located above the clutch pedal, where the cable and pivot points may be lubricated.

Clutch Cable

REMOVAL AND INSTALLATION

1. Disconnect the negative battery cable.
2. Remove the retainer from the clutch release lever at the transaxle by pulling on the tail of the ball stud.
3. Pry out the ball end of the cable from the positioner adjuster on the back of the brake pedal and remove the cable, passing it through the hoop in the shock tower mounting bracket.
4. Installation is the reverse of the removal procedure. After installation, push and lift the clutch pedal 2 or 3 times to allow the mechanism to adjust the cable.

AUTOMATIC TRANSAXLE

Transaxle Assembly

REMOVAL AND INSTALLATION

NOTE: If the vehicle is going to be rolled while the transaxle is out of the vehicle, obtain 2 outer CV-joints to install to the hubs. If the vehicle is rolled without the proper torque applied to the front wheel bearings, the bearings will no longer be usable.

1. Disconnect the negative battery cable. If equipped with 3.0L engine, drain the coolant and remove the coolant return extension. Remove the dipstick.
2. Remove the air cleaner assembly if it is preventing access to the upper bellhousing bolts. Remove the upper bellhousing bolts and water tube, where applicable. Note locations and unplug all electrical connectors from the transaxle.
3. If equipped with a 2.2L or 2.5L engine, remove the starter attaching nut and bolt at the top of the bellhousing.

4. Disconnect the transaxle control cable at the transaxle. Raise the vehicle and support safely.
5. Remove the tire and wheel assemblies. Remove the axle end cotter pins, nut locks, spring washers and axle nuts.
6. Remove the ball joint retaining bolts and pry the control arm from the steering knuckle. Position a drain pan under the transaxle where the axles enter the differential or extension housing. Remove the axles from the transaxle or center bearing. Unbolt the center bearing and remove the intermediate axle from the transaxle, if equipped.
7. Drain the transaxle. Disconnect and plug the fluid cooler hoses. If equipped with Direct Ignition System (DIS), disconnect the harness connector and remove the crankshaft position sensor from the transaxle bellhousing.
8. Remove the speedometer cable adaptor bolt and remove the adaptor from the transaxle.
9. Remove the starter. Remove the torque converter inspection cover, matchmark the torque converter to the flexplate and remove the torque converter bolts.
10. Using the proper equipment, support the weight of the engine. Remove the front motor mount and bracket.
11. Position a transaxle jack under the transaxle.
12. Remove the lower bellhousing bolts.
13. Remove the left side splash shield. Remove the transaxle mount bolts.
14. Carefully pry the transaxle from the engine.
15. Slide the transaxle rearward until dowels disengage from the mating holes in the transaxle case.
16. Pull the transaxle completely away from the engine and remove it from the vehicle.
17. To prepare the vehicle for rolling, support the engine with a suitable support or reinstall the front motor mount to the engine. Then reinstall the ball joints to the steering knuckle and install the retaining bolt. Install the obtained outer CV-joints to the hubs, install the washers and torque the axle nuts to 180 ft. lbs. (244 Nm). The vehicle may now be safely rolled.

To install:
18. Install the transaxle securely on transmission jack. Rotate the converter so it will align with the positioning of the flexplate.

19. Apply a coating of high temperature grease to the torque converter pilot hub.
20. Raise the transaxle into place and push it forward until the dowels engage and the bellhousing is flush with the block. Install the transaxle to bellhousing bolts.
21. Raise the transaxle and install the left side mount bolts. Install the torque converter bolts and torque to 55 ft. lbs. (74 Nm).
22. Install the front motor mount and bracket. Remove the engine and transaxle support fixtures.
23. Install the starter to the transaxle. Install the bolt finger-tight if equipped with a 2.2L or 2.5L engine.
24. Install a new O-ring to the speedometer cable adaptor and install to the extension housing; make sure it snaps in place. Install the retaining bolt.
25. Connect the shifter and kickdown linkage to the transaxle, if equipped.
26. Install the axles and center bearing, if equipped. Install the ball joints to the steering knuckles. Torque the axle nuts to 180 ft. lbs. (244 Nm) and install new cotter pins. Install the splash shield and wheels. Lower the vehicle. Install the dipstick.
27. Install the upper bellhousing bolts and water pipe, if removed.
28. If equipped with 2.2L or 2.5L engine, install the starter attaching nut and bolt at the top of the bellhousing. Raise the vehicle again and tighten the starter bolt from under the vehicle. Lower the vehicle.
29. Connect all electrical wiring to the transaxle.
30. Install the air cleaner assembly, if removed. Fill the transaxle with the proper amount of Mopar ATF Plus Type 7176 or conventional Dexron®II.
31. Connect the negative battery cable and check the transaxle for proper operation.

UPSHIFT AND KICKDOWN LEARNING PROCEDURE

A-604 Ultradrive Transaxle

The A-604 4-speed, electronic transaxle is the 1st to use fully adaptive controls. The controls perform their functions based on real time feedback sensor information. Although, the transaxle is conventional in design, functions are controlled by its ECM.

Since the A-604 is equipped with a learning function, each time the battery cable is disconnected, the ECM memory is lost. In operation, the transaxle must be shifted many times for the learned memory to be re-input to the ECM; during this period, the vehicle will experience rough operation. The transaxle must be at normal operating temperature when learning occurs.

1. Maintain constant throttle opening during shifts. Do not move the accelerator pedal during upshifts.
2. Accelerate the vehicle with the throttle ⅛–½ open.
3. Make fifteen to twenty 1–2, 2–3 and 3–4 upshifts. Accelerating from a full stop to 50 mph each time at the aforementioned throttle opening is sufficient.
4. With the vehicle speed below 25 mph, make 5–8 wide open throttle kickdowns to 1st gear from either 2nd or 3rd gear. Allow at least 5 seconds of operation in 2nd or 3rd gear prior to each kickdown.
5. With the vehicle speed greater than 25 mph, make 5 part throttle to wide open throttle kickdowns to either 3rd or 2nd gear from 4th gear. Allow at least 5 seconds of operation in 4th gear, preferably at road load throttle prior to performing the kickdown.

SHIFT LINKAGE ADJUSTMENT

1. Apply the parking brake. Place the shifter in the **P** detent.
2. Loosen the clamp bolt on the gearshift cable bracket.
3. Pull the shift lever all the way to the front detent position and tighten the lock screw.
4. Check for proper neutral safety switch operation.

THROTTLE PRESSURE CABLE ADJUSTMENT

1. Run the engine until it reaches normal operating temperature.
2. Loosen the cable mounting bracket lock screw.
3. Position the bracket so both alignment tabs are touching the transaxle case surface and tighten the lock screws.
4. Release the cross lock on the cable assembly by pulling the cross lock up.
5. To ensure proper adjustment, the cable must be free to slide all the way toward the engine against its stop after the cross lock is released.
6. Move the transaxle throttle control lever fully clockwise and press the cross lock down until it snaps into position.

7. Road test the vehicle and check the shift points.

THROTTLE PRESSURE ROD ADJUSTMENT

1. Run the engine until it reaches normal operating temperature.
2. Loosen the adjustment swivel lock screw.
3. To ensure proper adjustment, the swivel must be free to slide along the flat end of the throttle rod. Disassembly, clean and lubricate as required.
4. Hold the transaxle throttle control lever firmly toward the engine and tighten the swivel screw.
5. Road test the vehicle and check the shift points.

DRIVE AXLE

Halfshaft

REMOVAL AND INSTALLATION

1. Disconnect the negative battery cable.
2. Remove the cotter pin, nut lock and spring washer from the end of the halfshaft. Apply the brakes and loosen the hub nut while the vehicle is on the floor.
3. Raise the vehicle and support safely. Remove the tire and wheel assembly.
4. Remove the axle nut and washer.
5. Remove the ball joint retaining bolt and pry the control arm down to release the ball stud from the steering knuckle.
6. If removing the right halfshaft, remove the speedometer pinion retainer nut from the extension on the right side of the transaxle and remove the pinion.
7. Position a drainpan under the transaxle where the halfshaft enters the differential or extension housing. Remove the halfshaft from the steering knuckle and then the transaxle or center bearing by pulling on the inner joint. Unbolt the center bearing from the block and remove the intermediate shaft from the transaxle, if equipped.

To install:
8. Install the halfshaft or intermediate shaft to the transaxle, being careful not to damage the side seals.

Make sure the inner joint clicks into place inside the differential. Install the center bearing retaining bolts if equipped, then install the outer shaft to the center bearing.
9. Pull the front strut out and insert the outer joint into the front hub.
10. If necessary, turn the ball joint stud to position the bolt retaining indent to the inside of the vehicle. Install the ball joint stud into the steering knuckle. Install the retaining bolt and nut and torque to 70 ft. lbs. (95 Nm). This nut and bolt combination is unique to this application and should not be replaced with conventional hardware. Use original equipment parts if replacing.
11. Install the speedometer pinion to the extension on the transaxle and secure using the mounting bolt.
12. Install the axle nut washer and nut and torque the nut to 180 ft. lbs. (244 Nm). Install the spring washer, nut lock and a new cotter pin.
13. Install the tire and wheel assembly.

CV-Boot

REMOVAL AND INSTALLATION

NOTE: Use only clamps provided with the replacement package when servicing. Plastic wire ties and other straps will not clamp tightly enough and grease will sling out, causing costly damage to the joint.

Inner Joint

1. Remove the halfshaft from the vehicle.
2. If cutting the boot away, mark and note the boot positioning on the shaft relative to the raised shoulders. Remove the boot clamps to gain access to the tripod retention system.
3. Separate the housing from the tripod according to the following:

NOTE: Hold the rollers in place when removing the housing from the tripod or the needle bearings may fall out.

a. A.C.I. — Has retaining tabs integral with the staked boot retaining collar. Hold the housing and lightly compress the CV-joint retention spring while bending the tabs back. Support the housing as the retention spring pushes it from the housing.
b. G.K.N. — Has retaining tabs integral with the housing cover. Hold the housing and lightly compress the CV-joint retention spring

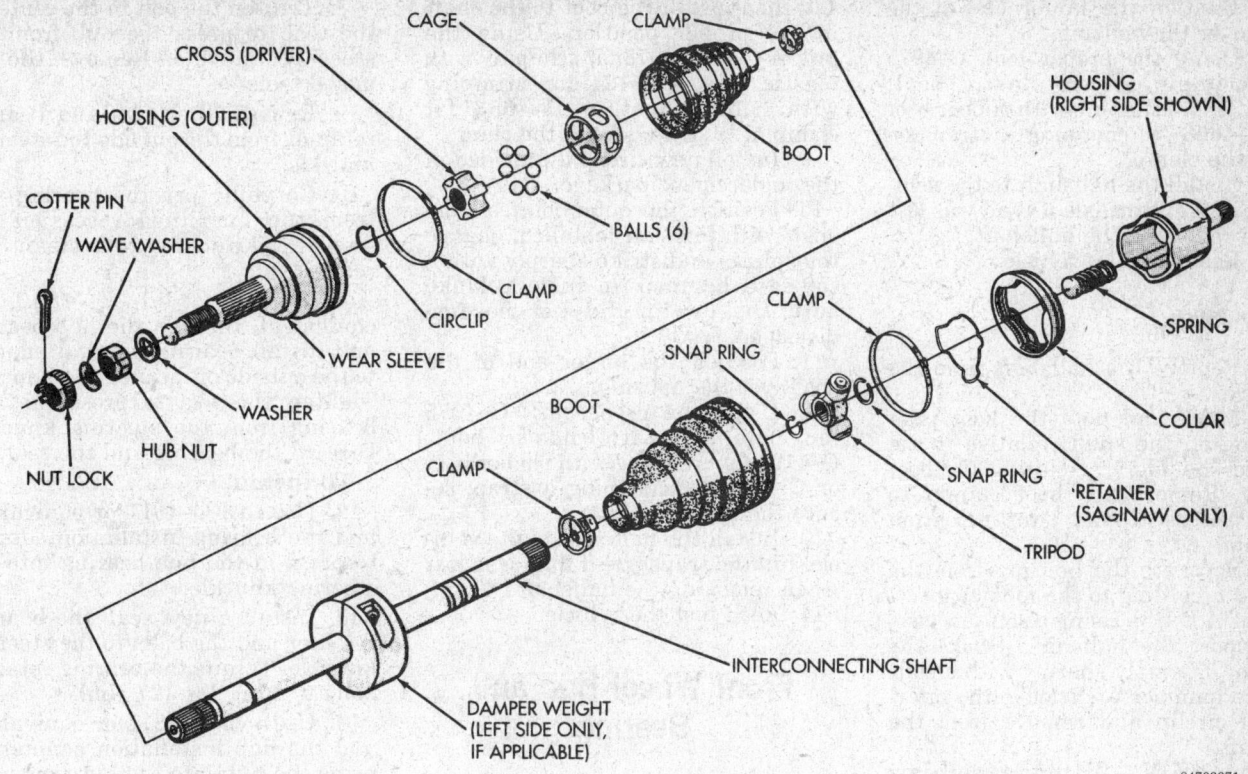

CAGE · CLAMP · CROSS (DRIVER) · HOUSING (OUTER) · BOOT · HOUSING (RIGHT SIDE SHOWN) · COTTER PIN · WAVE WASHER · BALLS (6) · CLAMP · SPRING · CIRCLIP · WEAR SLEEVE · CLAMP · SNAP RING · COLLAR · WASHER · BOOT · SNAP RING · HUB NUT · CLAMP · RETAINER (SAGINAW ONLY) · NUT LOCK · TRIPOD · INTERCONNECTING SHAFT · DAMPER WEIGHT (LEFT SIDE ONLY, IF APPLICABLE)

84703071

Exploded view of halfshaft assembly

while bending the tabs back. Support the housing as the retention spring pushes it from the housing.

c. S.S.G. — Uses a wire ring tripod retainer which expands into a groove around the top of the housing. Pry the wire ring, without damaging it, out of the groove and slide the tripod from the housing.

4. Remove the snapring from the end of the shaft and remove the tripod.

5. If not already done, mark the boot positioning on the shaft relative to the raised shoulders. Remove the boot from the shaft.

6. Remove as much old grease as possible from the joint. Inspect all parts for wear or damage.

NOTE: Do not use petroleum based solvents on the joints, shaft or boot to clean; it will ruin hidden rubber seals within the joint. Use only chlorine based cleaner or hot soapy water to clean the joint, if necessary. Make sure the joint is completely dry before assembling.

To install:

7. On right inner joint of shafts of turbocharged vehicles, slide a new rubber washer seal over the stub shaft and down into the groove provided.

8. If the clamping device is not a straight strap, install it on the shaft 1st, then install the boot to the shaft in the proper position. Using the proper tool, C–4975 for crimping with plastic boot, C–4124 for crimping with rubber boot or C–4653 for clamping a strap, secure the clamp.

9. Slide the tripod on the shaft:

a. A.C.I. — Slide the tripod on the shaft with the non-chamfered edge facing the tripod retainer ring groove.

b. G.K.N. — Slide the tripod on the shaft with the non-chamfered edge facing the tripod retainer ring groove.

c. S.S.G. — Place the wire ring tripod retainer over the shaft, then slide the tripod. The tripod may installed either way; both ends are the same.

10. Install the snapring into its groove on the shaft to lock the tripod in position.

11. Distribute the grease provided in the grease package as follows or according to the instructions in the package:

a. A.C.I. — Distribute 1 of the 2 packets of grease into the boot and the remaining packet into the housing.

b. G.K.N — If equipped with 3 packets of grease, distribute 2 of

the 3 packets into the boot and the remaining packet into the housing. Otherwise, distribute ½ of the packet of grease into the boot and the remaining amount into the housing.

c. S.S.G. — Distribute ½ of the packet of grease into the boot and the remaining amount into the housing.

12. Position the spring in the housing spring pocket with the spring cup attached to the exposed end of the spring. Place a dab of grease on the concave surface of the spring cup.

13. Keeping the spring centered, install the housing to the tripod as follows:

a. A.C.I. — Slip the housing onto the tripod. Do not bend the retaining tabs back into their original position. Instead, secure the boot to hold the housing. The tripod must be reengaged to the housing with the shaft installed on the vehicle.

b. G.K.N — Slip the housing onto the tripod. Bend the retaining tabs back into their original positions. Check for proper retention ability.

c. S.S.G. — Slip the housing onto the tripod and install the tripod wire retaining ring. Check for proper retention ability.

14. Position the larger end of the boot over the housing.

15. Using the proper tool, C–4975 for crimping with plastic boot, C–4124 for crimping with rubber boot or C–4653 for clamping a strap, secure the clamp.

16. Install the halfshaft to the vehicle. Fill the transaxle if fluid was lost when removing the halfshaft.

17. Road test the vehicle.

Outer Joint

1. Remove the halfshaft from the vehicle.

2. Mark and note the boot positioning on the shaft, relative to the raised shoulders, if cutting the boot away. Remove the boot clamps to gain access to the joint retention system.

3. Separate the housing from the tripod according to the following:

a. A.C.I. — Using a soft-jaw vise, support the halfshaft. Strike the joint assembly sharply with a soft-face hammer to dislodge the internal circlip and remove from the shaft.

b. G.K.N — Using a soft-jaw vise, support the halfshaft. Strike the joint assembly sharply with a soft-face hammer to dislodge the internal circlip and remove from the shaft.

c. S.S.G. — Loosen the damper weight bolts and slide it and the boot toward the inner joint. Expand the snapring and slide the joint from the shaft. Reinstall the damper weight and torque the bolts to 21 ft. lbs. (28 Nm).

4. If damaged, remove the wear sleeve from the CV-joint machined ledge.

5. Remove the circlip from the groove.

6. If not already done, mark the boot positioning on the shaft relative to the raised shoulders and remove the boot from the shaft.

7. Remove as much old grease as possible from the joint. Inspect all parts for wear or damage.

NOTE: Do not use petroleum based solvents on the joints, shaft or boot to clean; it will ruin hidden rubber seals within the joint. Use only chlorine based cleaner or hot soapy water to clean the joint, if necessary. Make sure the joint it completely dry before assembling.

To install:

8. If the clamping device is not a straight strap, install it on the shaft

1st, then install the boot to the shaft in the proper position. Using the proper tool, C–4975 for crimping with plastic boot, C–4124 for crimping with rubber boot or C–4653 for clamping a strap, secure the clamp.

9. Install new circlip if provided in the replacement package.

10. Position the outer joint on the shaft with hub nut installed, engage the splines and strike sharply with a soft-face hammer to install. Make sure the circlip did not become dislodged.

11. Position the larger end of the boot over the housing.

12. Using the proper tool C–4975 for crimping with plastic boot, C–4124 for crimping with rubber boot or C–4653 for clamping a strap, secure the clamp.

13. Install the halfshaft to the vehicle. Fill the transaxle if fluid was lost when removing the halfshaft.

14. Road test the vehicle.

Front Wheel Hub and Bearing

REMOVAL AND INSTALLATION

Pressed-In (Two-Piece) Hub and Bearing

NOTE: Some hub and bearing replacement packages include the one-piece unit. If this is the case, follow the installation steps for one-piece unit instead of for the two-piece unit.

1. Loosen the hub nut while the vehicle is on the floor and the brakes are applied. Raise and safely support the vehicle.

2. Remove the tire and wheel assembly. Remove the brake caliper from the adaptor and remove the adaptor. Remove the brake disc.

3. Remove the hub nut and the washer from the stub shaft.

4. Disconnect the tie rod end from the steering arm using the appropriate puller.

5. Remove the clamp bolt securing the ball joint stud into the steering knuckle and separate.

6. Matchmark the lower strut mount to the knuckle. Remove the 2 strut clamp bolts and remove the knuckle from the vehicle.

7. Attach the hub removal tool C–4811 or equivalent, and the triangular adapter, to the 3 rear threaded holes of the steering knuckle housing with the thrust button inside the hub bore.

8. Tighten the bolt in the center of the tool, to press the hub from the steering knuckle. Remove the removal tools.

9. Remove the bolts and bearing retainer from the outside the steering knuckle.

10. Carefully pry the bearing seal from the machined recess of the steering knuckle and clean the recess.

11. Insert tool C–4811 or equivalent, through the hub bearing and install bearing removal adapter to the outside of the steering knuckle. Tighten the tool to press the hub bearing from the steering knuckle. Discard the bearing and the seal.

To install:

12. Use tool C–4811 or equivalent, and the bearing installation adapter to press in the hub bearing into the steering knuckle.

13. Install a new seal, the bearing retainer and the bolts to the steering knuckle. Torque the bearing retainer bolts to 20 ft. lbs. (27 Nm).

14. Use tool C–4811 or equivalent, and the hub installation adapter, to press the hub into the hub bearing.

15. Using the bearing installation tool C–4698 or equivalent, drive the new dust seal into the rear of the steering the hub and bearing from the knuckle as required.

16. Install the steering knuckle onto the vehicle guiding the halfshaft through the hub and install the 2 strut strut bolts. Align the matchmarks made during disassembly and tighten the nuts. The vehicle will require a front end alignment.

17. Install the ball joint stud into the steering knuckle and secure with the original knuckle clamp bolt tightened to 105 ft. lbs. (145 Nm) torque.

18. Install the tie rod end to the steering knuckle. Tighten the attaching nut to 35 ft. lbs. (47 Nm) and install new cotter pin.

19. Install the brake disc and caliper to the knuckle assembly.

20. Clean all foreign material from the threads of the axle stub shaft and install the washer and hub nut. With the brakes applied, torque the nut to 180 ft. lbs. (244 Nm) torque.

21. Install the spring washer, nut lock and new cotter pin. Wrap the prongs of the cotter pin tightly around the nut lock.

22. Install the tire and wheel assembly and tighten the lug nuts to 95 ft. lbs. (129 Nm).

23. Align the front end of the vehicle and road test.

Bolt-In (One-Piece) Hub and Bearing

NOTE: Knuckle removal is not necessary for bearing and hub replacement. If the hub and bearing assembly requires replacement, it is to be replaced as an assembly.

1. Loosen the hub nut while the vehicle is on the floor and the brakes are applied. Raise and safely support the vehicle.

2. Remove the tire and wheel assembly from the vehicle.

3. Remove the hub nut and the washer from the stub shaft.

4. Disconnect the tie rod end from the steering arm using the appropriate puller.

5. Remove the clamp bolt securing the ball joint stud into the steering knuckle and separate.

6. Remove the caliper guide pin bolts and separate the caliper assembly from the braking disc. Support the caliper with wire hook and not by the hydraulic hose.

7. Separate the steering knuckle assembly from the ball joint stud. Pull the knuckle assembly out and away from the halfshaft.

NOTE: Care must be taken when separating the halfshaft from the knuckle, do not sepa-

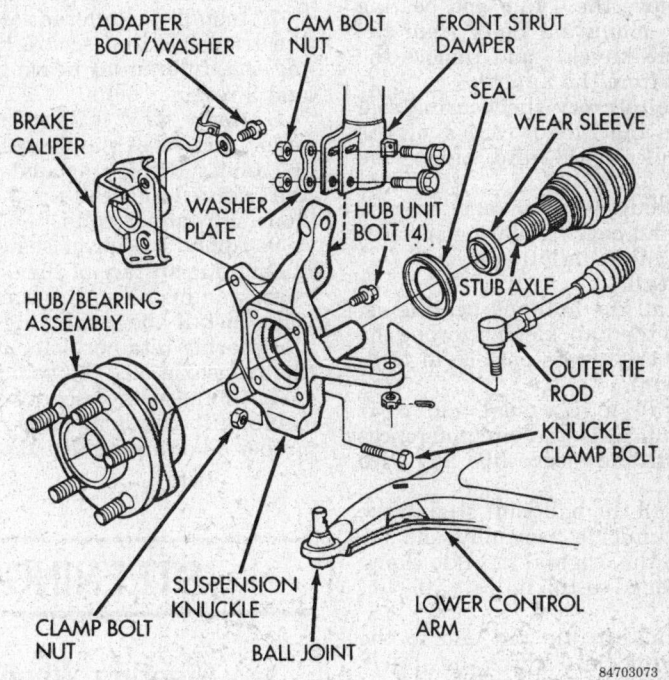

Bolt-In (One-Piece) Hub and Bearing assembly

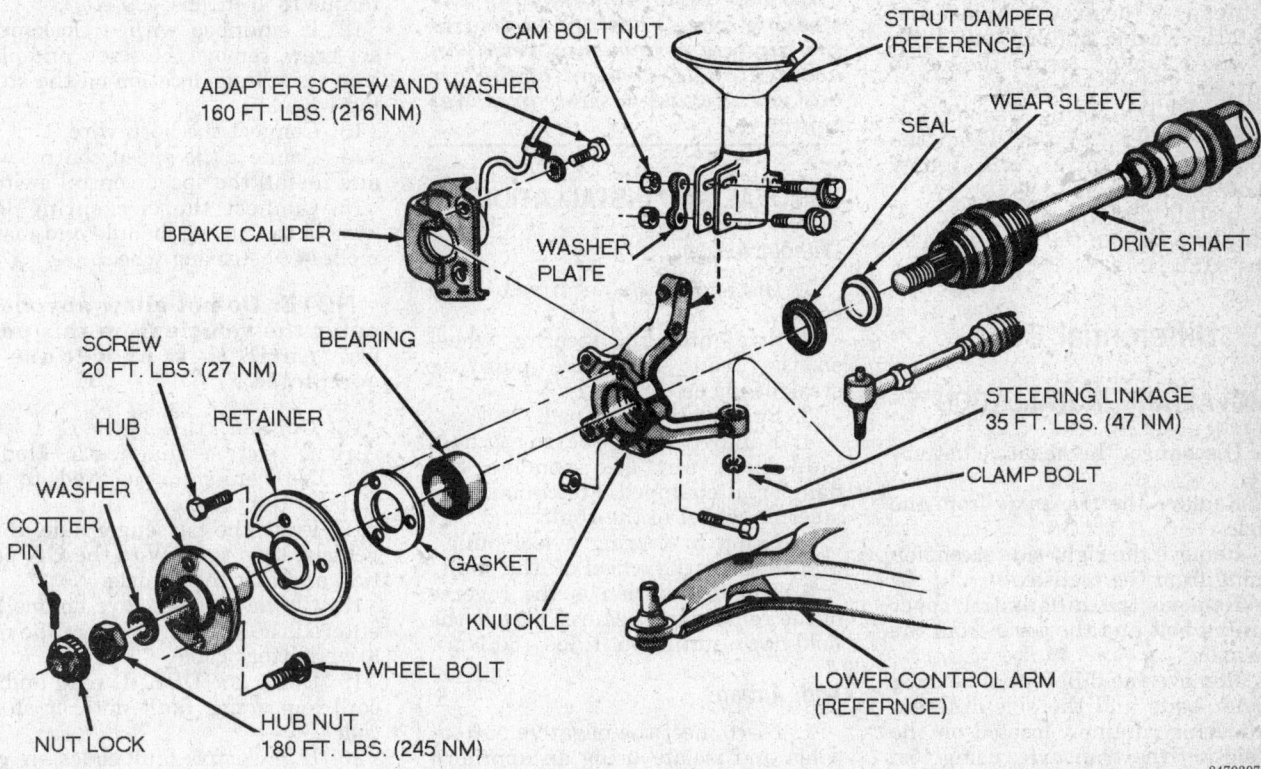

Pressed-In (Two-Piece) Hub and Bearing assembly

rate the inner C/V-joint during this operation. **Do not allow the halfshaft to hang by the inner C/V-joint, it must be supported.**

8. Remove the 4 hub and bearing assembly mounting bolts from the rear of the knuckle and remove the assembly from the knuckle.

9. Carefully pry the bearing seal from the machined recess of the steering knuckle and clean the recess.

10. Thoroughly clean and dry the knuckle and bearing mating surfaces and the seal installation area.

To install:

11. Install the hub and bearing assembly to the knuckle and torque the bolts in a criss-cross pattern to 45 ft. lbs. (65 Nm).

12. Install a new seal and wear sleeve. Lubricate the circumferences of the seal and sleeve liberally with grease.

13. Install the ball joint stud to the steering knuckle assembly and secure with the original knuckle clamp bolt tightened to 105 ft. lbs. (145 Nm) torque.

14. Install the tie rod end to the steering knuckle. Tighten the attaching nut to 35 ft. lbs. (47 Nm) and install new cotter pin.

15. Install the brake disc and caliper to the knuckle assembly.

16. Clean all foreign material from the threads of the axle stub shaft and install the washer and hub nut. With the brakes applied, torque the nut to 180 ft. lbs. (244 Nm) torque.

17. Install the spring washer, nut lock and new cotter pin. Wrap the prongs of the cotter pin tightly around the nut lock.

18. Install the tire and wheel assembly and tighten the lug nuts to 95 ft. lbs. (129 Nm).

Differential Case

REMOVAL AND INSTALLATION

1. Disconnect the negative battery cable.

2. Remove the transaxle from the vehicle.

3. Remove the right side extension housing from the transaxle.

4. Remove the differential cover retaining bolt and the cover from the transaxle.

5. Remove the differential bearing retainer bolts and the side differential bearing retainer, located on the left side of the transaxle, using tool L–4435 or equivalent. Use caution and take note of shims and their posi-

tioning; they can be dislodged during removal.

6. Remove the differential case from the transaxle.

To install:

7. Install the differential case into the transaxle and secure by installing the differential bearing retainer and 3 retainer bolts.

8. Apply RTV sealant around the inner surface of the extension housing under the O-ring and install to the transaxle. Install the 2 extension housing retainer bolts.

9. Apply a bead of sealer around the mating surface of the differential cover and install to the transaxle.

10. Install the remaining differential bearing retainer bolts and install the transaxle into the vehicle.

11. Connect the negative battery cable, fill the transaxle with the proper oil and road test the vehicle.

STEERING

Steering Wheel

—— CAUTION ——
On vehicles equipped with the air bag system, the system must be disarmed prior to removing the steering wheel. Failure to disarm the air bag system may result in accidental deployment of the air bag module and possible personal injury.

REMOVAL AND INSTALLATION

Without Airbag

1. Disconnect the negative battery cable.

2. Straighten the steering wheel so the front tires are pointing straight-ahead.

3. Remove the horn pad.

4. Remove the steering wheel hold-down nut and remove the damper, if equipped. Matchmark the steering wheel to the shaft.

5. Using a steering wheel puller, pull the steering wheel off the shaft.

6. The installation is the reverse of the removal procedure. Torque the hold-down nut to 45 ft. lbs. (60 Nm).

With Airbag

1. Disconnect the negative battery cable and isolate using an appropriate insulator. Allow the system capacitor to discharge for 2 minutes

prior to starting repairs on the vehicle.

2. Straighten the steering wheel so the front tires are pointing straight-ahead.

3. Remove the 4 nuts located on the back side of the steering wheel that attach the airbag module to the steering wheel.

4. Lift the module and disconnect the connectors. Remove the speed control switch, if equipped.

5. If equipped with the setscrew, place it in the clockspring to ensure proper positioning when the steering wheel is removed.

6. Remove the steering wheel hold-down nut and remove the damper, if equipped. Matchmark the steering wheel to the shaft.

7. Using a steering wheel puller, pull the steering wheel off the shaft.

To install:

8. Position the steering wheel on the steering column. Make sure the flats on the hub of the steering wheel are aligned with the formations on the clockspring.

9. Pull the airbag and speed control connectors through the lower, larger hole in the steering wheel and pull the horn wire through the smaller hole at the top. Make sure the wires are not pinched anywhere.

10. Install the damper, if equipped.

11. Install the hold-down nut and torque to 45 ft. lbs. (60 Nm).

12. If equipped with a clockspring setscrew, remove the screw and place it in its storage location on the steering wheel.

13. Connect the horn wire.

14. Connect the speed control wire and install the speed control switch.

15. Connect the clockspring lead wire to the airbag module and install module to steering wheel.

NOTE: Do not allow anyone to enter the vehicle from this point on, until this procedure is completed.

16. Connect the DRB II to the Airbag System Diagnostic Module (ASDM) connector located to the right of the console.

17. From the passenger side of the vehicle, turn the key to the **ON** position and exit the vehicle.

18. Check to make sure no one has entered the vehicle. Connect the negative battery cable.

19. Using the DRB II, read and record any active fault data or stored codes.

20. If any active fault codes are present, perform the proper diagnostic procedures before continuing.

21. If there are no active fault codes, erase the stored fault codes; if there are active codes, the stored codes will not erase.

22. From the passenger side of the vehicle, turn the key **OFF**, then **ON** and observe the instrument cluster airbag warning light. It should come on for 6–8 seconds, then go out, indicating the system is functioning normally. If the warning light either fails to come ON or stays lit, there is a system malfunction and further diagnostics are needed.

Steering Column

CAUTION

On vehicles equipped with the air bag system, the system must be disarmed prior to removing the steering wheel. Failure to disarm the air bag system may result in accidental deployment of the air bag module and possible personal injury.

REMOVAL AND INSTALLATION

Acustar Column

1. Disconnect the negative battery cable. Disarm the air bag system, if equipped.

2. Straighten the steering wheel so the front tires are pointing straight-ahead.

3. Remove the steering wheel hold-down nut and remove the damper, if equipped. Matchmark the steering wheel to the shaft.

4. Using a steering wheel puller, pull the steering wheel off the shaft.

5. If equipped with column shift, disconnect the transaxle shift cable from the steering column by prying it out of the grommet in the shift lever.

6. If equipped with pointer type gear indicator, loosen the setscrew on the lower side of the steering column and remove the pointer needle.

7. If equipped with a cable actuated gear shift indicator, place the gear shift lever in the **N** or **P** position and remove the PRNDL indicator actuation cable from the steering column actuator arm. Swing the lock bar located on the lower portion of the insert upward and squeeze the legs together. Remove the insert from the steering column.

8. Disconnect all wiring connectors from below the instrument panel that lead up into the steering column.

9. Remove the nuts that attach the steering column assembly to the instrument panel support.

10. Remove the retaining pin in the upper to lower steering coupler retaining bolt. Remove the upper to lower steering coupler retaining nut and pinch bolt from the coupling and separate the stub shaft from the steering gear coupling.

11. Remove the column from the vehicle.

To install:

12. Install new cable attaching grommet into the steering column shift lever. Install the steering column into the vehicle. Guide the stub shaft into the steering gear coupling and install the pinch bolt and nut, if equipped.

13. Install the nuts that attach the steering column assembly to the instrument panel support. Torque the steering column assembly to support bracket nuts to 105 inch. lbs. (12 Nm).

14. Connect the wire harness connectors at the base of the steering column.

15. If equipped with a cable actuated gear shift indicator, route the PRNDL actuator assembly under the left column wing and along the left side of the steering column. Insert the flange of the actuator assembly into the steering column jacket. Engage the lock bar to secure the actuator assembly to the housing. Hook the cable to the steering column actuator arm. Move the shifter to **N** and check for proper pointer location. If the pointer is misaligned, adjust the pointer arm using a $\frac{9}{64}$ in. Allen head wrench.

16. If equipped with pointer type gear shift indicator, install the pointer into the indicator housing and the steering column and secure.

17. Connect the transaxle shift cable to the shift lever on the steering column. Readjust the transaxle shift linkage.

18. Install the clockspring, steering wheel and remaining components removed during disassembly.

19. Connect the negative battery cable and check the steering column and all related components for proper operation.

Manual Rack and Pinion Steering Gear

REMOVAL AND INSTALLATION

1. Disconnect the negative battery cable.

2. Raise the vehicle and support safely.

3. Remove front wheel assemblies.

4. Remove the cotter pins, castellated nuts and tie rod ends from the steering knuckles.

5. Support the front crossmember using a transmission jack. Remove the front suspension crossmember attaching bolts and nuts.

6. Lower the crossmember.

7. Remove the tie rod inner boot shields.

8. Remove the steering gear bolts from the front suspension crossmember.

9. Remove the steering gear from the left side of the vehicle.

To install:

10. Transfer the required parts to the new rack, as required.

11. Place the rack on the crossmember and torque the steering gear attaching bolts to 21 ft. lbs. (29 Nm). Attach the boot shields.

12. Have a helper inside the vehicle remove the trim boot and align the stub shaft with the coupling while the crossmember is raised into position. If a helper is not available, the steering column will have to be unbolted so the steering shaft can be inserted into the coupling. The right rear crossmember bolt is a pilot bolt that correctly locates the crossmember; tighten it 1st. Torque the crossmember bolts to 90 ft. lbs. (122 Nm).

13. Install the tie rod ends to the steering knuckle and torque the nut to 45 ft. lbs. (61 Nm). Install a new cotter pin.

14. Insert the stub shaft shim where the stub shaft goes into the coupling.

15. Connect the negative battery cable and check the gear for proper operation.

Power Rack and Pinion Steering Gear

REMOVAL AND INSTALLATION

NOTE: The power steering gear assembly should not be serviced or adjusted. If a malfunction or oil leak should occur, the complete steering gear should be replaced.

1. Disconnect the negative battery cable.

2. Raise the vehicle and support safely.

3. Remove both front wheel assemblies.

4. Remove the cotter pins, castellated nuts and tie rod ends from the steering knuckles.

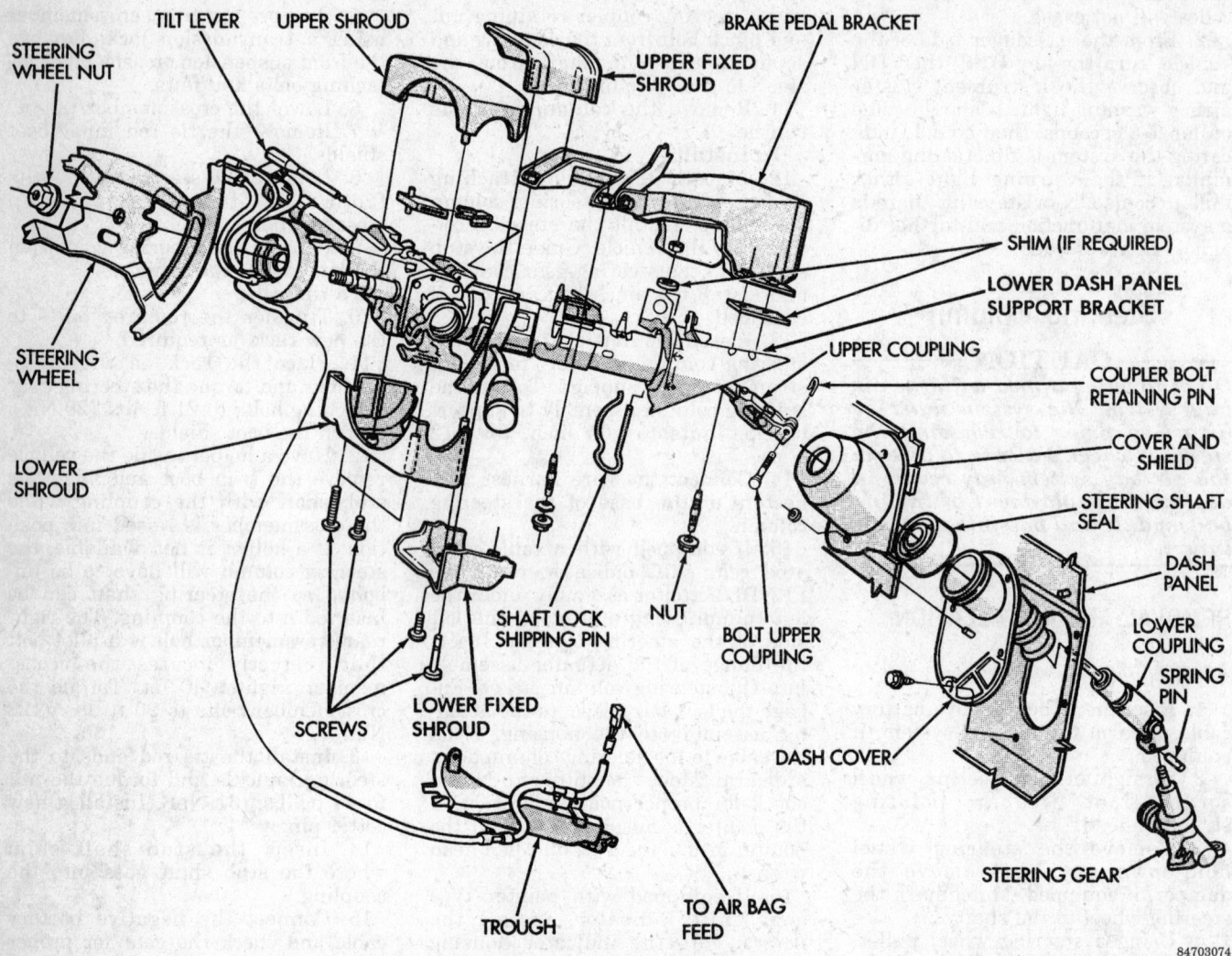

STEERING WHEEL NUT

TILT LEVER

UPPER SHROUD

BRAKE PEDAL BRACKET

UPPER FIXED SHROUD

SHIM (IF REQUIRED)

LOWER DASH PANEL SUPPORT BRACKET

UPPER COUPLING

COUPLER BOLT RETAINING PIN

COVER AND SHIELD

STEERING SHAFT SEAL

DASH PANEL

LOWER COUPLING

SPRING PIN

STEERING WHEEL

LOWER SHROUD

SHAFT LOCK SHIPPING PIN

NUT

BOLT UPPER COUPLING

DASH COVER

STEERING GEAR

SCREWS

LOWER FIXED SHROUD

TROUGH

TO AIR BAG FEED

84703074

Acustar tilt and standard steering column

5. If equipped, remove the anti-rotational link from the crossmember. The lower universal joint is removed with the steering gear.

6. Disconnect and plug the oil pressure line from the rack. Disconnect and plug the return hose from the line coming from the rack.

7. Support the front crossmember using a transmission jack. Remove the front suspension crossmember attaching bolts and nuts.

8. Lower the crossmember.

9. Remove the tie rod inner boot shields.

10. Remove the steering gear bolts from the front suspension crossmember.

11. Remove the steering gear from the left side of the vehicle.

To install:

12. Transfer the required parts to the new rack, as required.

13. Place the rack on the crossmember and torque the steering gear attaching bolts to 50 ft. lbs. (68 Nm). Using new O-rings, attach the fluid lines and the boot shields.

14. Have a helper inside the vehicle remove the trim boot and align the stub shaft with the coupling while the crossmember is raised into position. If a helper is not available, the steering column will have to be unbolted so the steering shaft can be inserted into the coupling. The right

rear crossmember bolt is a pilot bolt that correctly locates the crossmember, tighten it 1st. Torque the crossmember bolts to 90 ft. lbs. (122 Nm).

15. Install the anti-rotational link.

16. Install the tie rod ends to the steering knuckle and torque the nut to 45 ft. lbs. (61 Nm). Install a new cotter pin.

17. Insert the stub shaft shim where the stub shaft goes into the coupling.

18. Refill the power steering pump with the proper type and amount of fluid.

19. Connect the negative battery cable and check the gear for proper operation.

20. Adjust toe-in.

Power Steering Pump

REMOVAL AND INSTALLATION

1. Disconnect the negative battery cable.

2. Position a drain pan under the power steering pump. Raise and safely support the vehicle.

3. Disconnect the fluid hoses from the pump and plug them. On 3.0L engine, remove the tube and dipstick assembly from the pump.

4. Remove the front bracket attaching bolts and remove the belt from the pulley.

5. On 3.0L engine, disconnect the front exhaust pipe from the exhaust manifold and position aside. This is required for clearance to remove the pump.

6. Loosen the rear pump-to-bracket nut. Remove the bolt attaching the pulley side of the power steering pump to the mounting bracket.

7. On 3.0L engine, remove the nut holding the power steering pump rear support bracket to the pump. Remove the the 2 bolts mounting the power steering pump support bracket to the engine and remove the bracket.

8. Lower the vehicle. Remove the remaining retaining bolts and the rear mounting nut. Remove the power steering pump from the vehicle.

9. Remove the pulley from the pump with the proper puller. Install the pulley on the new pump using the special installation tools.

To install:

10. Install the pump to the engine making sure, on 3.0L engine, that the stud on the back of the pump is in the slotted hole in the bracket.

11. Install the mounting screws. Install the tube and dipstick assembly on the pump, if equipped.

12. Install the exhaust pipe to the manifold using a new gasket where required.

13. Install the power steering pump drive belt and adjust the tension as required.

14. Refill the pump using the correct fluid and bleed the system.

BELT ADJUSTMENT

NOTE: The belt tension is automatically adjusted by a dynamic tensioner on the 3.0L engine. Adjustment is not possible.

1. Loosen the bracket mounting bolts.

2. On vehicles with a square drive, use a ½ in. drive breaker bar in the square hole provided in the bracket to move the pump away from the engine. On all other vehicles, tighten the adjusting nut until the pump is in the desired position. Do not pry against the fluid reservoir, damage will result.

3. With the pump moved enough so the belt deflects about ¼–½ in. under a 10 lb. load, tighten the bolts.

SYSTEM BLEEDING

1. Fill the reservoir with power steering fluid. Do not add transmission fluid in the power steering pump.

2. Turn the wheels to the full left turn position and add fluid until the reservoir is full.

3. Start the engine and add fluid to bring the level to the correct level.

4. To purge the system of air, turn the steering wheel from side to side without contacting the stops.

5. Return the wheel to the straight-ahead position and operate the engine for 2 minutes before road testing.

Tie Rod Ends

REMOVAL AND INSTALLATION

1. Raise the vehicle and support safely. Remove the cotter pin and nut from the tie rod end.

2. Using a puller, remove the tie rod from the steering knuckle.

3. Mark the tie rod-to-sleeve location for approximate reassembly.

4. Loosen the sleeve clamp nut and bolt, if equipped, and unscrew the tie rod end from the sleeve or inner tie rod.

5. The installation is the reverse of the removal procedure. Torque the stud nuts to 45 ft. lbs. (61 Nm) and install a new cotter pin.

6. Perform a front end alignment as required.

BRAKES

Master Cylinder

REMOVAL AND INSTALLATION

1. Disconnect the negative battery cable.

2. Disconnect brake lines from the master cylinder and plug master cylinder fluid outlets.

3. Remove the nuts attaching the master cylinder to the power booster.

4. Disconnect the electrical connector from the master cylinder, if equipped. Remove the master cylinder from the mounting studs.

5. Remove the fluid reservoir from the cylinder as required.

To install:

6. Bench bleed the master cylinder as follows:

   a. Mount master cylinder in a vise.

   b. Attach tube to the fluid outlets on the master cylinder and bend tube so the outlet end of the tubes will be below the surface of brake fluid in each reservoir.

   c. Fill both reservoirs with brake fluid conforming to DOT 3 specifications.

   d. Slowly depress the piston and then allow the piston to return to the released position. Repeat this procedure until no bubbles are present in the fluid exiting the tubes.

   e. Remove the tubes from the master cylinder and refill the reservoir with fluid.

7. Install the master cylinder to the mounting studs and install the retainer nuts. Tighten mounting nuts to 250 inch lbs. (28 Nm).

8. Install the brake lines to the master cylinder loosely. Have a helper slowly depress the brake pedal from inside the vehicle. While the pedal is being depressed, tighten the fluid lines to the master cylinder.

9. Connect the negative battery cable and check the brakes for proper operation.

Combination Valve

REMOVAL AND INSTALLATION

1. Disconnect the negative battery cable.

2. Raise the vehicle and support safely.

3. Tag and disconnect the brake lines from the valve.

4. Disconnect the wires to the pressure switch.

5. Remove the combination valve from the frame bracket.

6. The installation is the reverse of the removal procedure.

7. Bleed the brakes in the following order:

    a. Right rear wheel cylinder or caliper

    b. Left rear wheel cylinder or caliper

    c. Right front caliper

    d. Left front caliper

8. Connect the negative battery cable and check the brakes for proper operation.

Power Brake Booster

REMOVAL AND INSTALLATION

1. Disconnect the negative battery cable. Disconnect the vacuum hose(s) from the booster.

2. Remove the nuts attaching the master cylinder to the booster and move the master cylinder aside.

3. From inside the vehicle, remove the clip that secures the booster pushrod to the brake pedal and remove the nuts that attach the booster to the dash panel. Remove the booster from the vehicle.

4. The installation is the reverse of the removal procedure.

5. Connect the negative battery cable and check the brakes for proper operation.

Brake Caliper

REMOVAL AND INSTALLATION

1. Raise the vehicle and support safely.

2. Remove the tire and wheel assembly.

3. Remove the caliper mounting bolts.

4. Lift the caliper off the adapter and away from the disc. Remove the outer pad from the caliper.

5. Remove the brake hose retaining bolt from the caliper.

To install:

6. Install the brake hose to the caliper using new copper washers.

7. Install the outer brake pad to the caliper.

8. Position the caliper over the rotor so the caliper engages the adaptor correctly. Install the mounting bolts. Install the hold-down spring, if equipped.

9. Fill the master cylinder and bleed the brakes. Make sure the brake hose is not twisted after installation.

Disc Brake Pads

REMOVAL AND INSTALLATION

1. Remove some of the fluid from the master cylinder.

2. Raise the vehicle and support safely. Remove the tire and wheel assemblies.

3. Remove the hold-down spring if necessary. Remove the caliper and remove the outer pad from the caliper.

4. Remove the inner pad from the adaptor.

To install:

5. Use a large C-clamp to compress the piston back into the caliper bore.

6. Install the inner pad to the adaptor and install the outer disc brake pad into caliper.

7. Position the caliper over the rotor so the caliper engages the adaptor correctly and install the retainer pin(s).

8. Install the hold-down spring, if removed.

9. Refill the master cylinder.

Brake Rotor

REMOVAL AND INSTALLATION

1. Raise the vehicle and support safely. Remove the tire and wheel assembly.

2. Remove the caliper and brake pads.

3. Remove the factory installed clips, if equipped. It is not necessary to reinstall these clips.

4. Remove the rotor from the hub.

5. The installation is the reverse of the removal procedure.

Brake Drum

REMOVAL AND INSTALLATION

1. Raise the vehicle and support safely.

2. Remove the wheel and tire assembly.

3. Remove the dust cap.

4. Remove the cotter pin and nut lock.

5. Remove the wheel bearing nut and washer from the spindle.

6. Remove the outer wheel bearing.

7. Remove the drum with the inner wheel bearing from the spindle. If the drum is difficult to remove, remove the plug from the rear of the backing plate and push the self adjuster lever away from the star wheel. Rotate the star wheel with an upward motion to retract the shoes and remove the drum. Remove the grease seal.

To install:

8. Lubricate and install the inner wheel bearing. Install a new grease seal.

9. Install the drum to the spindle.

10. Lubricate and install the outer wheel bearing, washer and nut. When the bearing preload is properly set, install the nut lock and a new cotter pin.

11. Install the grease cap.

12. Install the wheel and tire assembly. Adjust the rear brakes as required.

Brake Shoes

REMOVAL AND INSTALLATION

NOTE: Three brake shoe assemblies are used on front wheel drive vehicles. Vehicles will have axle sets of either 200mm or 220mm Kelsey Hayes or Varga brake shoes. The Varga brake shoes are marked for left or right side installation.

1. Raise the vehicle and support safely. Remove the wheel and tire assemblies and the drums.

2. Remove the automatic adjuster spring and lever.

3. Rotate the automatic adjuster star wheel enough so both shoes move out far enough to be free of the wheel cylinder boots.

4. Disconnect the parking brake cable from the actuating lever.

5. Remove the lower shoe to shoe or shoe to anchor spring(s).

6. With the shoes held together by the upper shoe to shoe spring, remove them from the backing plate.

To install:

7. Thoroughly clean and dry the backing plate. To prepare the backing plate, lubricate the bosses, anchor pin and parking brake actuating lever pivot surface lightly with lithium based grease.

8. Remove, clean and dry all parts still on the old shoes. Lubricate the star wheel shaft threads with antisieze lubricant and transfer all parts

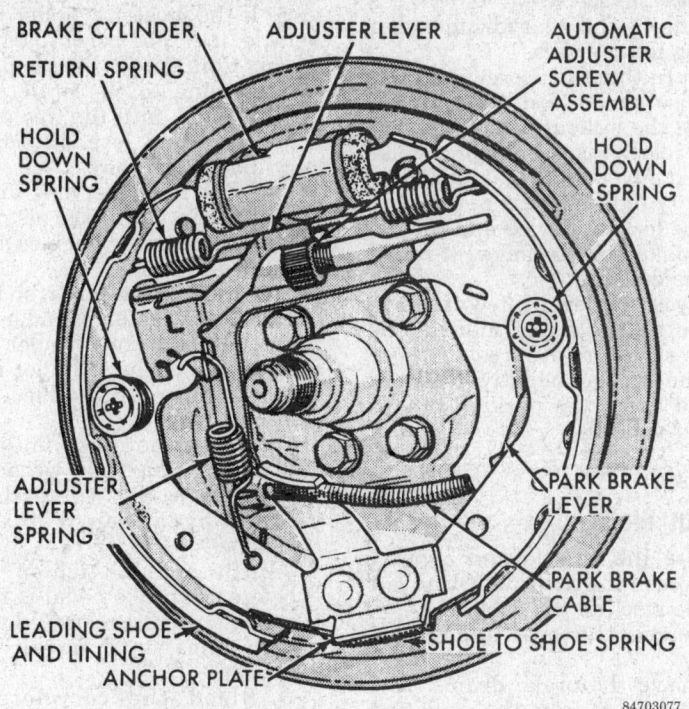

Kelsey Hayes 200mm and 220mm brakes — left rear wheel

84703077

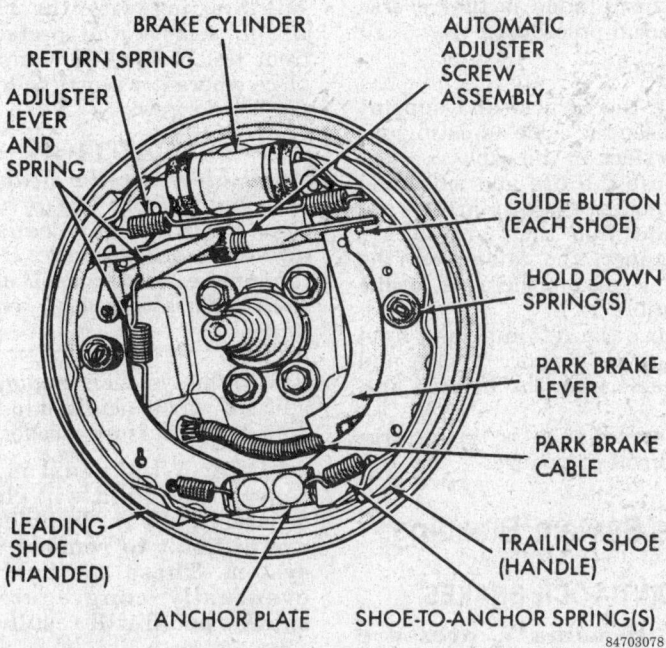

Varga brakes — left rear wheel

84703078

to their proper locations on the new shoes.

9. Install the lower spring(s).

10. Connect the parking brake cable.

11. Install the automatic adjuster lever and spring.

12. Adjust the star wheel.

13. Remove any grease from the linings and install the drum.

14. Complete the brake adjustment with the wheels installed.

Wheel Cylinder

REMOVAL AND INSTALLATION

1. Raise the vehicle and support safely.

2. Remove the wheel, drum and brake shoes.

3. Remove and plug the brake line from the wheel cylinder.

4. Remove the wheel cylinder bolts and remove the cylinder from the backing plate.

To install:

5. Apply a very thin coating of silicone sealer to the cylinder mounting surface, install the cylinder to the backing plate and install the retaining bolts.

6. Connect the brake line to the wheel cylinder.

7. Install all brake parts that were removed.

8. Install the tire and wheel assembly.

9. Bleed the brakes.

Parking Brake Cable

ADJUSTMENT

Except Daytona and LeBaron

1. Release the parking brakes fully.

2. Raise the vehicle and support safely.

3. Adjust the rear brakes.

4. Loosen the adjusting nut until there is slack in all the cables.

5. Rotate the rear wheels and tighten the cable adjusting nut until there is a slight drag at the wheels.

6. Continue to rotate the rear wheels and loosen the nut until all drag is eliminated.

7. Back off the nut an additional 2 turns.

8. Apply and release the parking brake several times. Upon the least release, verify there is no drag at the wheels.

9. To check the operation, make sure the parking brake holds on an incline.

Daytona and LeBaron

The parking brake hand lever contains a self-adjusting loaded clockspring feature. Routine parking brake adjustment is not required.

REMOVAL AND INSTALLATION

Front Cable

EXCEPT DAYTONA AND LEBARON

1. Loosen the adjusting nut from under the vehicle.
2. Lift the carpet and floor matting and remove the floor pan seal.
3. Pull the cable end forward and disconnect from the clevis.
4. Pull the cable through the hole and remove.
5. The installation is the reverse of the removal procedure. Adjust cable as required.
6. Connect the negative battery cable and check the parking brakes for proper operation.

DAYTONA AND LEBARON

———— CAUTION ————
The parking brake hand lever contains a self-adjusting clockspring loaded to about 30 lbs. Care must be taken when handling components in the vicinity of the hand lever or serious personal injury may result.

1. Disconnect the negative battery cable.
2. Disengage the cable from the equalizer bracket in the console.
3. Lift the carpet and floor matting and remove the floor pan seal.
4. Separate the cable from the rear parking brake lever.
5. Pull the cable through the hole and remove.
To install:
6. Install the cable and connect to the rear shoes and equalizer bracket. Install the floor pan seal and position the carpet.
7. To reload, lockout and adjust the system:
   a. Pull on the equalizer output cable with at least 30 lbs. pressure to wind up the spring. Continue until the self-adjuster lockout pawl is positioned about midway between the self-adjuster sector.
   b. Rotate the lockout pawl into the self-adjuster sector by turning the Allen screw clockwise. This ac-

tion requires very little effort; do not force the screw.
   c. Adjust the rear drum-in-hat parking brake shoes.
   d. Turn the Allen screw counterclockwise about 15 degrees. When turning the lockout device, self-adjuster release is a snapping noise followed by a detent that should be felt. Very light effort is required to seat the lockout device into the detent. Make sure to follow through into the detent.
   e. Cycle the lever a few times to complete the adjustment. The wheels should rotate freely.
8. Connect the negative battery cable and check the parking brakes for proper operation.

Rear Cable

REAR DRUM BRAKES

1. Raise the vehicle and support safely. Loosen the cable adjusting nut to provide slack in the cable.
2. Remove the tire and wheel assembly
3. Remove the brake drums. Disconnect the cable from the actuating lever on the rear brake shoe assembly.
4. Remove the retaining clip from the cable at the support bracket and pull the cable from the trailing arm assembly.
5. The installation is the reverse of the removal procedure.

REAR DISC BRAKES

1. Raise the vehicle and support safely. Loosen the cable adjusting nut to provide slack in the cable.
2. Remove the tire and wheel assembly. Remove the disc brake caliper and rotor from the rear hub.
3. Disconnect the cable from the actuating lever on the rear brake shoe assembly.
4. Remove the retaining clip from the cable at the support bracket and pull the cable from the trailing arm assembly.
5. The installation is the reverse of the removal procedure.

Brake System Bleeding

EXCEPT ANTI-LOCK BRAKES

NOTE: If using a pressure bleeder, follow the instructions furnished with the unit and choose the correct adaptor for the application. Do not substitute an adapter that almost fits as it will not work and could be dangerous.

Master Cylinder

1. If the master cylinder is off the vehicle, it can be bench bled.
   a. Connect 2 short pieces of brake line to the outlet fittings, bend them until the free end is below the fluid level in the master cylinder reservoirs.
   b. Fill the reservoir with fresh brake fluid. Pump the piston slowly until no more air bubbles appear in the reservoirs.
   c. Disconnect the 2 short lines, refill the master cylinder and securely install the cylinder caps.
2. If the master cylinder is on the vehicle, it can still be bled, using a flare nut wrench.
   a. Open the brake lines slightly with the flare nut wrench while pressure is applied to the brake pedal by a helper inside the vehicle.
   b. Be sure to tighten the line before the brake pedal is released.
   c. Repeat the procedure with both lines until no air bubbles appear.
3. Bleed the complete brake system.

Calipers and Wheel Cylinders

1. Fill the master cylinder with fresh brake fluid. Check the level often during the procedure.
2. Starting with the right rear wheel, remove the protective cap from the bleeder, if equipped, and place where it will not be lost. Clean the bleed screw.

———— CAUTION ————
When bleeding the brakes, keep face away from the brake area. Spewing fluid may cause facial and/or visual damage. Do not allow brake fluid to spill on the vehicle's finish; it will remove the paint.

3. If the system is empty, the most efficient way to get fluid to the wheel is to use a pressure bleeder.

NOTE: If the pedal is pumped rapidly, the fluid will churn and create small air bubbles, which are difficult to remove from the system. These air bubbles will eventually congregate and a spongy pedal will result.

4. Once fluid has been pumped to the caliper or wheel cylinder, open the bleed screw again, have the helper press the brake pedal to the floor, lock the bleeder and have the helper slowly release the pedal. Wait 15 seconds and repeat the procedure

(including the 15 second wait) until no more air comes out of the bleeder upon application of the brake pedal. Remember to close the bleeder before the pedal is released inside the vehicle each time the bleeder is opened. If not, air will be induced into the system.

5. Repeat the procedure on remaining wheels in order:
   a. Left rear
   b. Right front
   c. Left front

6. Hydraulic brake systems must be totally flushed if the fluid becomes contaminated with water, dirt or other corrosive chemicals. To flush, bleed the entire system until all fluid has been replaced with the correct type of new fluid.

7. Install the bleeder cap(s), if equipped, on the bleeder to keep dirt out. Always road test the vehicle after brake work of any kind is done.

ANTI-LOCK BRAKES

The brake system must be bled any time air is permitted to enter the system through loosened or disconnected lines or hoses, or anytime the modulator is removed. Excessive air within the system will cause a soft or spongy feel in the brake pedal.

When bleeding any part of the system, the reservoir must remain close to FULL at all times. Check the level frequently and top off fluid as needed.

The Bendix 6 Anti-lock brake system must be bled as 2 separate brake systems. Proper procedures must be followed if the system is to work correctly. The normal portion of the brake system is bled in the usual fashion with either pressure or manual bleeding equipment and must be fully and properly bled before bleeding the modulator.

Bleeding the Modulator Assembly

To bleed the ABS unit, the battery must be relocated outside the vehicle and connected to the vehicle with jumper cables. This allows access to the 4 bleeder screws on top of the modulator assembly. Additionally, the DRB II must be connected to the diagnostic plug before bleeding begins; the DRB II is used to activate the system(s) during the procedure. The 4 components to be bled within the modulator are (in order) the secondary sump, the primary sump, the primary accumulator and the secondary accumulator. Use the following procedure to bleed the modulator assembly.

------ **CAUTION** ------
Wear eye protection when bleeding the modulator assembly and always use a hose on the bleed screw to direct the flow of fluid away from painted surfaces. Bleeding the modulator may result in the release of very high pressure fluid.

1. Connect a clear hose to the secondary sump bleeder screw and route the hose to a clear container.
2. Either install and pressurize the pressure bleeding equipment at the master cylinder or have an assistant provide light and constant pressure on the brake pedal.
3. Open the bleeder screw about ½–¾ turn. Use the DRB II to select the ACTUATE VALVES test; actuate the left front build/decay valve.
4. Bleed until the fluid flows free of air bubbles or until the brake pedal bottoms.
5. Tighten the bleeder screw and release the brake pedal if it was being held.
6. Repeat Steps 2 through 5 until the fluid is free of air bubbles. Remember to check the fluid reservoir level periodically.

7. Select and actuate the right rear build/decay valve and perform Steps 2–5 until the fluid flows without air bubbles.
8. Move the bleeder tube to the primary sump bleeder screw.
9. Pressurize the pressure bleeding equipment at the master cylinder or have an assistant provide light and constant pressure on the brake pedal.
10. Open the bleeder screw about ½–¾ turn. Using the DRB II, actuate the right front build/decay valve.
11. Bleed until the fluid flows free of air bubbles or until the brake pedal bottoms.
12. Tighten the bleeder screw and release the brake pedal if it was being held.
13. Repeat Steps 2 through 5 until the fluid is free of air bubbles. Remember to check the fluid reservoir level periodically.
14. Select and actuate the left rear build/decay valve. Perform Steps 2–5 until the fluid runs free of air bubbles.
15. Move the bleeder tube to the primary accumulator bleeder screw.
16. Pressurize the pressure bleeding equipment at the master cylinder or have an assistant provide light and constant pressure on the brake pedal.

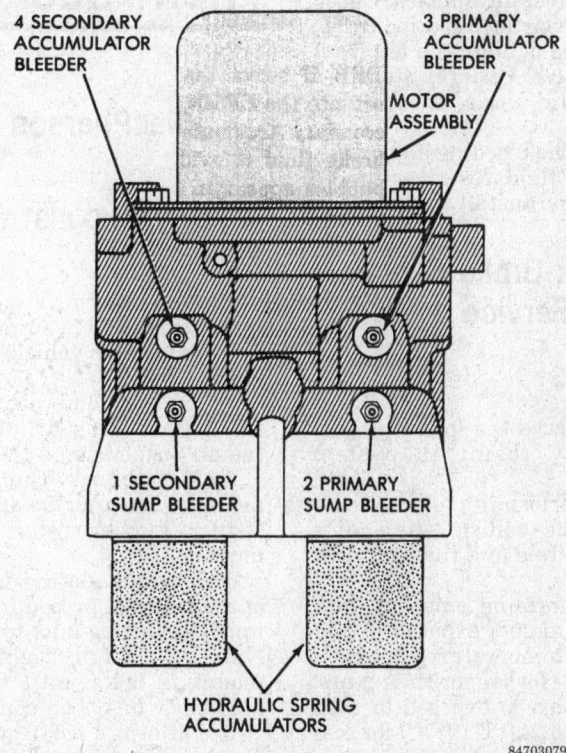

Bleeder locations on ABS modulator assembly — Acclaim, Daytona, LeBaron, Shadow, Spirit and Sundance

17. Open the bleeder screw about 1/2–3/4 turn. Using the DRB II, actuate the right front/left rear isolation valve.

18. Bleed until the fluid flows free of air bubbles or until the brake pedal bottoms.

19. Tighten the bleeder screw and release the brake pedal if it was being held.

20. Repeat Steps 2 through 5 until the fluid is free of air bubbles. Check the fluid reservoir level periodically.

21. Select and actuate the right front build/decay valve. Perform Steps 2–5 until the fluid runs free of air bubbles.

22. Move the bleeder tube to the secondary accumulator bleeder screw.

23. Pressurize the pressure bleeding equipment at the master cylinder or have an assistant provide light and constant pressure on the brake pedal.

24. Open the bleeder screw about 1/2–3/4 turn. Using the DRB II, actuate the left front/right rear isolation valve.

25. Bleed until the fluid flows free of air bubbles or until the brake pedal bottoms.

26. Tighten the bleeder screw and release the brake pedal if it was being held.

27. Repeat Steps 2 through 5 until the fluid is free of air bubbles. Check the fluid reservoir level periodically.

28. Select and actuate the left front build/decay valve. Perform Steps 2–5 until the fluid runs free of air bubbles.

29. Remove the bleeding apparatus; fill the brake fluid reservoir to the correct level and install the cap.

Anti-Lock Brake System Service

PRECAUTIONS

Failure to observe the following precautions may result in system damage.

• Before performing electric arc welding on the vehicle, disconnect the control module and the hydraulic unit connectors.

• When performing painting work on the vehicle, do not expose the control module to temperatures in excess of 185°F (85°C) for longer than 2 hrs. The system may be exposed to temperatures up to 200°F (95°C) for less than 15 min.

• Never disconnect or connect the control module or hydraulic modula-

tor connectors with the ignition switch **ON**.

• Never disassemble any component of the Anti-Lock Brake System (ABS) which is designated non-serviceable; the component must be replaced as an assembly.

• When filling the master cylinder, always use brake fluid which meets DOT-3 specifications; petroleum-based fluid will destroy the rubber parts.

DEPRESSURIZING THE HYDRAULIC ACCUMULATOR

1. With the ignition **OFF**, pump the brake pedal a minimum of 40 times, using approximately 50 lbs. (222 N) pedal force. A noticeable change in pedal feel will occur when the accumulator is discharged.

2. When a definite increase in pedal effort is felt, pump the pedal a few additional times. This should remove all hydraulic pressure from the system.

FRONT SUSPENSION

MacPherson Strut

REMOVAL AND INSTALLATION

1. Remove the 3 mounting nuts from the shock tower under the hood.

2. Raise the vehicle and support safely.

3. Remove the brake hose bracket screw from the strut and disconnect the air suspension hose, if equipped.

4. Matchmark the lower strut mount to the knuckle and remove the strut to knuckle bolts, nuts and nut plate.

5. The installation is the reverse of the removal procedure. Torque the upper mounting nuts to 20 ft. lbs. (27 Nm). Do not fully tighten the lower mounting bolts until the front end alignment has been completed.

6. Perform a front end alignment. Torque the strut to knuckle nuts to final torque of 75 ft. lbs. (100 Nm) plus 1/4 turn.

Strut Cartridge

REPLACEMENT

---------- CAUTION ----------
Use extreme care when disassembling struts. Coil springs must be compressed into a loaded position for strut removal. Never remove the strut cap nut without using proper spring compression tools or equipment.
---

1. Position the strut assembly into spring compression tool C–4838 or equivalent.

2. Compress spring only enough to free top spring cap. Secure the strut body and remove the self-locking nut.

3. Note position and location when removing the top insulator, upper spring seat with rubber insulator and bump rubber with dust shield.

4. Remove the strut cartridge body and replace only as a complete assembly.

5. Inspect all parts for wear or damage, be sure to check top spring support bearing for smooth operation. Replace any parts found to be worn or defective.

To install:

6. Position strut assembly in the vertical position and install strut cartridge body into spring assembly.

7. Install dust boot, spring seat with rubber spring pad and top spring insulator.

8. Install the strut shaft retaining nut. Use tool L–4558 to torque the retaining nut to 55 ft. lbs. (75 Nm) plus 1/4 turn.

9. Release spring compression tool while seating spring against perch.

Lower Ball Joints

INSPECTION

To inspect the ball joints, grasp the grease fitting by hand with the vehicle on the ground. If the grease fitting can be moved at all by hand, the ball joint should be replaced.

REMOVAL AND INSTALLATION

1. Raise the vehicle and support safely. Remove the tire and wheel assembly.

2. Remove the lower control arm from the vehicle.

3. Pry off the ball joint seal. Position the receiver cup tool C–46992 or equivalent, to support the lower control arm while receiving the ball joint assembly.

4. Press against the ball joint upper housing to remove the ball joint from the lower control arm.

To install:

5. By hand, position the ball joint assembly into the bore in the lower control arm. Be sure the ball joint is not cocked in the bore of the control arm.

6. Position arm assembly in press with installer tool C-46992 or equivalent, supporting the control arm.

7. Apply pressure against the ball joint assembly until the joint is fully seated against the bottom of the control arm. Do not apply excessive pressure against the control arm.

8. Position a new seal over the stud of the ball joint so it is against the ball joint housing. Using a 1½ in. socket, press the seal onto ball joint housing until it is seated against the top surface of the control arm.

9. Install the control arm on the vehicle.

10. Install the tire and wheel assembly.

Lower Control Arms

REMOVAL AND INSTALLATION

1. Raise the vehicle and support safely. Remove the tire and wheel assembly.

2. Remove the sway bar to lower control arm retainer on both sides of the vehicle. Rotate the bar down away from the control arm.

3. Remove the ball joint stud retaining bolt and nut.

4. Pry the lower control arm from the steering knuckle.

5. Remove the control arm to crossmember bolts, nuts bushings and retainers.

6. Remove the control arm from the vehicle.

7. Transfer all reusable parts to the new control arm and lubricate.

8. Position the control arm onto the vehicle and install the attaching bolts. Loosely assemble the nuts to the attaching bolts.

9. Install the ball joint to the steering knuckle and tighten the retaining nut and bolt to 105 ft. lbs. (145 Nm).

10. Position the sway bar against the lower control arm and install the retainers, torquing to 50 ft. lbs. (70 Nm). Install the tire and wheel assembly.

11. Lower the vehicle so the suspension is supporting the weight of the vehicle. Tighten the lower cross-

member to control arm mounting bolts to 125 ft. lbs. (169 Nm).

12. Align the front suspension.

Sway Bar

REMOVAL AND INSTALLATION

1. Raise the vehicle and support safely.

2. Remove the front sway bar brackets and retainers.

3. Remove the sway bar support brackets and bushings from the lower control arm. Remove the sway bar from the vehicle.

4. The installation is the reverse of the removal procedure. Lubricate the sway bar bushings liberally with grease before assembling and torque retainers to 50 ft. lbs. (70 Nm).

REAR SUSPENSION

Shock Absorbers

REMOVAL AND INSTALLATION

1. Raise the vehicle and support safely.

2. If equipped with air shocks, disconnect the air lines from the shock.

3. If removing the right rear shock on vehicle equipped with air suspension, disconnect the height sensor connector located on the right rear frame rail.

4. Support the trailing arm and remove the upper and lower shock attaching bolts.

5. Remove the shock from the vehicle.

6. The installation is the reverse of the removal procedure.

7. Tighten shock absorber mounting nuts to 40 ft. lbs. (54 Nm).

Coil Springs

REMOVAL AND INSTALLATION

Except Load Leveling Suspension

1. Raise the vehicle and support safely.

2. Using the proper equipment, support the weight of the rear axle.

3. Remove the bolts that attach the shock to the lower mounting bracket.

4. Lower the axle assembly until the spring and upper isolator can be removed. Do not stretch the brake hose.

5. Remove the 2 screws holding the cup to the rail and remove the assembly.

To install:

6. Position the cup to the rail and install the 2 attaching screws.

7. Install the isolator over the jounce bumper and install the spring.

8. Raise the axle and loosely assemble both shock absorber attaching bolts. Remove the rear axle support and lower the vehicle.

9. With the suspension supporting the weight of the vehicle, tighten both lower shock bolts to 45 ft. lbs. (61 Nm).

Load Leveling Suspension

1. Disconnect negative battery cable.

2. Raise and safely support the vehicle. Remove the wheel and tire assembly.

3. Disconnect the air lines and the electrical connectors from the solenoid. Remove the solenoid.

4. Release the upper air spring retainer clips. Remove the lower spring to axle nut.

5. Pry assembly down to pull the alignment studs through the retaining clips and remove the assembly.

To install:

6. Position assembly lower stud into the axle seat and upper alignment pins through the frame rail adaptor.

7. Install the upper retainer clips.

8. Install the lower spring to axle nut loosely.

9. Install the solenoid and connect the air lines and electrical connector.

10. Connect the negative battery cable.

11. Charge the air spring by activating the spring solenoid and air compressor. Add air for 60 seconds. The compressor is activated by grounding pin S08 to pin X20.

12. After partial air recharge, tighten lower spring the axle nut to 50 ft. lbs. (68 Nm).

13. Install tire and wheel assembly.

Rear Wheel Bearings

REMOVAL AND INSTALLATION

1. Raise the vehicle and support safely.

2. Remove the tire and wheel assembly.

3. If equipped with rear disc brakes, remove the caliper and rotor. Support the caliper out of the way, don't let the caliper hang from the hydraulic hose.

4. Remove the grease cap, cotter pin, nut lock, nut, thrust washer and outer wheel bearing.

5. Carefully slide the hub or drum from the spindle. Using the appropriate tool, remove the grease seal and inner bearing from the drum or hub and replace as required.

6. Coat the stub axle shaft with multi-purpose grade 2 EP grease and slide the hub onto the shaft. Do not drag the seal or inner bearing over the threaded area of the stub axle.

7. Install the outer bearing, thrust washer and nut. Tighten the nut to 20–26 ft. lbs. (27–34 Nm).

8. Back the adjuster nut off ¼ turn, then tighten finger-tight only. Position the nut lock over the nut and install a new cotter pin.

9. Install the grease cap, tire and wheel assembly.

Rear Axle Assembly

REMOVAL AND INSTALLATION

1. Raise the vehicle and support safely.

2. Disconnect the parking brake cable at the connection. Detach the cable housing from the hanger bracket.

3. Disconnect the brake tubes from the hoses and unclip the brake tubes from the axle housing. Disconnect the rear wheel speed sensors, if equipped with anti-lock brakes.

4. Using the proper equipment, support the weight of the axle.

5. Remove the lower bolt from the shock absorbers and remove the track bar to axle pivot bolt. Suspend the track bar with a wire.

6. Lower the axle and remove the springs.

7. Support pivot bushing ends of the trailer arms. Remove the pivot bushing hanger bracket to frame screws. Lower and remove the axle from the vehicle.

To install:

8. Raise and support the axle. Attach the pivot bushing hanger brackets to frame rail. Tighten screws to 45 ft. lbs. (61 Nm).

9. Install the rear spring and insulators. Raise the rear axle and install the shock absorber and track bar through bolts loosely.

10. Reconnect the brake tubes and attach the hose mounting brackets.

11. Connect parking brake cable and speed sensor, if equipped.

12. Install the tire and wheel assembly. Bleed the brake system.

13. With the suspension supporting the weight of the vehicle, tighten the lower shock absorber bolts to 45 ft. lbs. (61 Nm) and the track bar bolt to 70 ft. lbs. (95 Nm).

Chrysler Corporation 3

CHRYSLER—New Yorker Salon, 5th Avenue   **DODGE**—Dynasty, Imperial

FIRING ORDERS

NOTE: To avoid confusion, always replace spark plug wires one at a time.

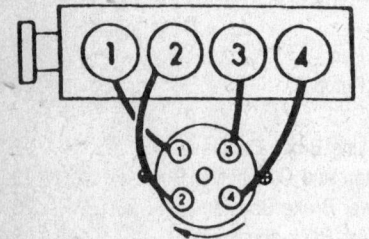

2.5L Engine
Engine Firing Order: 1–3–4–2
Distributor Rotation: Clockwise

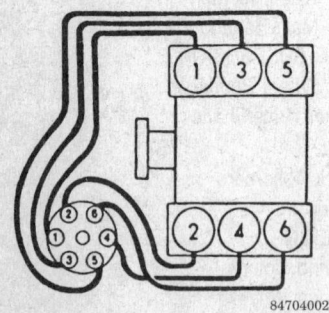

3.0L Engine
Engine Firing Order: 1–2–3–4–5–6
Distributor Rotation: Counterclockwise

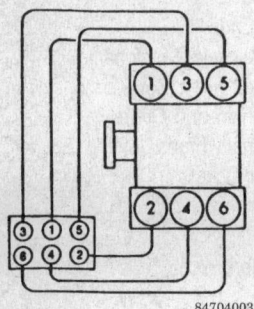

3.3L and 3.8L Engines
Engine Firing Order:
1–2–3–4–5–6
Distributorless Ignition
System

ENGINE ELECTRICAL

NOTE: Disconnecting the negative battery cable on some vehicles may interfere with the functions of the on board computer systems and may require the computer to undergo a relearning process, once the negative battery cable is reconnected.

Distributor

REMOVAL

1. Disconnect the negative battery cable.
2. Disconnect the distributor pickup lead wires. Remove the splash shield, if equipped.
3. Unscrew the distributor cap hold-down screws and lift off the distributor cap with all ignition wires still connected. Remove the coil wire, if necessary.
4. Matchmark the rotor to the distributor housing and the distributor housing to the engine.

NOTE: Do not crank the engine during this procedure. If the engine is cranked, the matchmark must be disregarded.

5. Remove the hold-down bolt and clamp or nut.
6. Remove the distributor from the engine.

INSTALLATION

Timing Not Disturbed

1. Install a new distributor housing O-ring.
2. Install the distributor in the engine so the rotor is aligned with the matchmark on the housing and the housing is aligned with the matchmark on the engine. Make sure the distributor is fully seated and the distributor shaft is fully engaged.
3. Install the hold-down clamp and snug the hold-down bolt or install the nut.
4. Connect the distributor pickup lead wires. Install the splash shield, if equipped.

5. Install the distributor cap and tighten the screws.
6. Connect the negative battery cable.
7. Adjust the ignition timing and tighten the hold-down bolt.

Timing Disturbed

1. Install a new distributor housing O-ring.
2. Position the engine so No. 1 piston is at TDC of the compression stroke and the mark on the vibration damper is aligned with **0** on the timing indicator.
3. Install the distributor in the engine so the rotor is aligned with the position of the No. 1 ignition wire on the distributor cap and the housing is aligned with the matchmark on the engine. Make sure the distributor is fully seated and the distributor shaft is fully engaged.

NOTE: There are distributor cap runners inside the cap on 3.0L engine. Make sure the rotor is pointing to where the No. 1 runner originates inside the cap and not where the No. 1 ignition wire plugs into the cap.

4. Install the hold-down clamp and snug the hold-down bolt or install the nut.
5. Connect the distributor pickup lead wires. Install the splash shield, if equipped.
6. Install the distributor cap and tighten the screws.
7. Connect the negative battery cable.
8. Adjust the ignition timing and tighten the hold-down nut or bolt.

Distributorless Ignition System

REMOVAL AND INSTALLATION

Ignition Coil

1. Disconnect the negative battery cable.
2. Remove the spark plug wires from the coil.
3. Disconnect the electrical connector.
4. Remove the coil mounting screws.
5. Remove the coil from the engine.

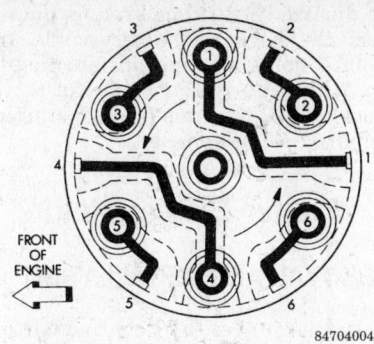

Distributor cap terminal internal routing — 3.0L engine

6. The installation is the reverse of the removal procedure. Torque the fasteners to 105 inch lbs. (12 Nm).

Crankshaft Position Sensor

1. Disconnect the negative battery cable.
2. Remove the inter-cooler to turbocharger air hose.
3. Disconnect the sensor lead at the harness connector.
4. Remove the sensor retaining bolt.
5. Pull the sensor straight up out the transaxle housing.
6. If the sensor is being reinstalled, remove any remains of the old spacer completely and attach a new spacer to the sensor. If a new spacer is not used, the sensor will not function properly. New sensors are packaged with a new spacer.
To install:
7. Install the sensor to the transaxle housing and push the sensor down until it contacts the driveplate.
8. Hold in this position and install the retaining bolt. Torque to 9 ft. lbs. (12 Nm).
9. Install air inlet hose.
10. Connect the sensor lead wire and the negative battery cable.

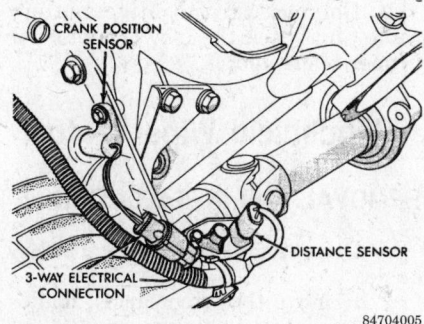

Crankshaft position sensor — 3.3L and 3.8L engines

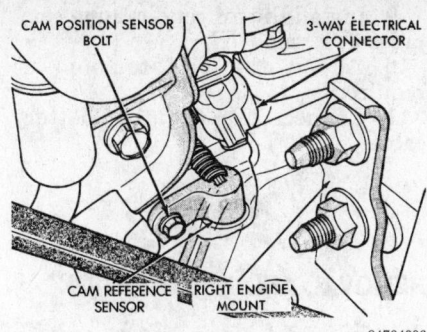

Camshaft position sensor — 3.3L and 3.8L engines

Camshaft Position Sensor

1. Disconnect the negative battery cable.
2. Disconnect the sensor lead at the harness connector.
3. Loosen the sensor retaining bolt sufficiently to allow the slotted mounting surface to slide past the bolt.
4. Pull the sensor straight up and out of the chain case cover. Resistance may be high due to the rubber O-ring.
5. If the sensor is being reinstalled, remove any remains of the old spacer completely and attach a new spacer to the sensor. If a new spacer is not used, the sensor will not function properly. New sensors are packaged with a new spacer.
To install:
6. Inspect the O-ring for damage and replace, if necessary.
7. Lubricate the O-ring with oil. Install the sensor to the chain case cover and push the sensor into its bore until contact is made with the cam timing gear.
8. Hold in this position and tighten the bolt to 9 ft. lbs. (12 Nm).
9. Connect the wire and rout it away from the accessory drive belt.
10. Connect the negative battery cable.

Ignition Timing

ADJUSTMENT

NOTE: The ignition timing on the distributorless 3.3L and 3.8L engines cannot be changed or set.

1. Start the engine, set the parking brake and run the engine until at normal operating temperature. Keep all lights and accessories **OFF**.
2. If a magnetic timing unit is available, insert the probe into the receptacle near the timing scale. The scale is located on the top of the bellhousing on the 2.5L engine and near the crankshaft pulley on the 3.0L engine.
3. If a magnetic timing unit is not available, connect a conventional power timing light to the No. 1 cylinder spark plug wire.
4. Connect the red lead of a tachometer to the negative primary terminal of the coil and connect the black lead to a good ground.
5. Connect the Diagnostic Readout Box II (DRB II) and access the Basic Timing Mode. If the DRB II is not available, disconnect the coolant sensor located near the thermostat housing. The Check Engine light on the instrument panel must be ON.
6. Aim the timing light at the timing scale or read the magnetic timing unit.
7. Loosen the distributor hold-down bolt just enough so the distributor can be rotated.
8. Turn the distributor in the proper direction until the specified timing according to the VECI label is reached. Tighten the hold-down bolt or nut and recheck the timing.
9. Turn the engine **OFF**. Connect the coolant sensor. Make sure the Check Engine light does not come ON when the vehicle is restarted. Disconnect the timing apparatus and tachometer.
10. If the coolant temperature sensor was disconnected, erase the created fault code using the Erase Fault Code mode on the DRB II.

Alternator

PRECAUTIONS

Several precautions must be observed when working with the alternator to avoid damaging the unit.

• If the battery is removed for any reason, make sure it is reconnected with the correct polarity. Reversing the battery connections may result in damage to the one-way rectifiers.
• When utilizing a booster battery as a starting aid, always connect the positive to positive terminals and the negative terminal from the booster battery to a good engine ground on the vehicle being started.
• Never use a fast charger as a booster to start vehicles.
• Disconnect the battery cables when charging the battery with a fast charger.
• Never attempt to polarize the alternator.

• Do not use test lights of more than 12 volts when checking diode continuity.

• Do not short across or ground any of the alternator terminals.

• The polarity of the battery, alternator and regulator must be matched and considered before making any electrical connections within the system.

• Never separate the alternator on an open circuit. Make sure all connections within the circuit are clean and tight.

• Disconnect the battery ground terminal when performing any service on electrical components.

• Disconnect the battery if arc welding is to be done on the vehicle.

BELT TENSION ADJUSTMENT

NOTE: The belt tension is automatically adjusted by a dynamic tensioner on the 3.0L, 3.3L and 3.8L engines. Periodic adjustment is not necessary.

1. Loosen the pivot bolt slightly.
2. Raise the vehicle and support safely. Remove the splash shield. Loosen the "T" bolt locknut enough so the alternator can be moved.
3. Tighten the adjusting bolt until the belt deflects about ¼ in. under a 10 lb. load.
4. Tighten the "T" bolt locknut to 40 ft. lbs. (54 Nm).

REMOVAL AND INSTALLATION

1. Disconnect the negative battery cable.
2. On the 2.5L engine, remove the air conditioning compressor and position it aside.
3. On 3.0L, 3.3L and 3.8L engines, release the dynamic belt tensioner and remove the accessory drive belt. On 2.5L engine, loosen the mounting bolts, move the alternator toward the engine and remove the drive belt(s).
4. Remove the mounting bolts and spacers and remove the alternator from the brackets.
5. Remove the battery positive, field and ground terminals from the rear of the alternator. Remove the wire harness hold-down screw from the alternator, if equipped.
To install:
6. Connect all wiring to the proper terminals on the rear of the alternator and install the wire harness hold-down screw, if equipped.
7. Position the alternator in the mounting brackets.
8. Install the spacers, pivot bolt and adjuster bolt. Install the belt.

9. Install the air conditioning compressor, if removed.
10. Adjust the belt tension, as required.
11. Connect the negative battery cable.

Starter

REMOVAL AND INSTALLATION

1. Disconnect the negative battery cable.
2. On the 2.5L engine, remove the attaching nut and bolt at the top of the bellhousing. Raise the vehicle and support safely.
3. Remove the rear mount and heat shield from the starter, if equipped.
4. Unbolt the starter and remove from the vehicle.
5. Disconnect the solenoid lead wires from the starter.
To install:
6. Connect the solenoid lead wires and install the heat shield, if equipped.
7. On the the 2.5L engine, install the lower bolt loosely, then lower the vehicle and install the nut and bolt from above and torque to 40 ft. lbs. (54 Nm).
8. Raise the vehicle and torque the bottom bolt to the same value. Install the rear mount to the starter.
9. On 3.0L, 3.3L and 3.8L engines, install all mounting bolts and torque to 40 ft. lbs. (54 Nm) evenly.
10. Connect the negative battery cable and check the starter for proper operation.

CHASSIS ELECTRICAL

Air Bag

DISARMING

NOTE: Before attempting any repair procedure that is located in the area of an air bag sensor or wire harness, it is recommended that the air bag system be disarmed. Failure to disarm the air bag system may result in accidental deployment of the air bag module and possible personal injury.

To disarm the air bag system, disconnect the negative battery cable and isolate using an appropriate insulator. Allow the system capacitor to discharge for 2 minutes prior to starting repairs on the vehicle.

Heater Blower Motor

REMOVAL AND INSTALLATION

1. Disconnect the negative battery cable.
2. Remove the glove box assembly, lower the right side instrument panel trim cover and right cowl trim panel, as required. Disconnect the blower lead wire connector.
3. If equipped with air conditioning, disconnect the 2 vacuum lines from the recirculation door actuator and position the actuator to the side.
4. Remove the 2 screws at the top of the blower housing that secure it to the unit cover.
5. Remove the 5 screws from around the blower housing and separate the blower housing from the unit.
6. Remove the 3 screws that secure the blower assembly to the heater or air conditioning housing and remove the assembly from the unit. Remove the fan from the blower motor.
To install:
7. Install the fan onto the blower motor and position motor assembly in housing. Secure motor using 3 mounting screws.
8. Install the blower housing and the heater unit and secure with screws.
9. Connect the 2 vacuum hoses to the recirculating air door actuator as required.
10. Connect the blower lead wire connector.
11. Install the glove box assembly, lower right side instrument panel trim cover and right cowl trim panel, as required.
12. Connect the negative battery cable and check the blower motor for proper operation.

Windshield Wiper Motor

REMOVAL AND INSTALLATION

1. Disconnect the negative battery cable.
2. Remove the wiper arms, blades and the plastic cowl top cover.
3. Remove the attaching screws from each pivot assembly.

4. Remove the motor mounting bracket retainer bolts and disconnect the wiper motor harness connector.

5. Remove the wiper motor, pivot and links from the vehicle as an assembly.

6. Clamp the wiper motor in a vise and remove the nut from the end of the motor shaft. Do not allow the shaft of the motor to turn from the PARK position.

To install:

7. Assemble the linkage to the motor. Make sure the crank fits over the **D** slot on the motor shaft. Tighten the motor shaft nut to 90 inch lbs. (10 Nm).

8. Make sure the motor is still in the PARK position prior to installing the wiper linkage. If not, temporarily connect the motor to the wiring harness and operate the switch to position the motor in the PARK position. Connect the linkage to the motor.

9. Install the wiper motor, pivot and links to the vehicle as an assembly.

10. Secure the mounting bracket retainer bolts to 70 inch. lbs. (8 Nm). Attach the wiper motor harness.

11. Cycle the switch and turn OFF to assure motor is in the PARK position. Install the cowl top plastic cover and wiper arms tightening the retaining nuts to 150 inch lbs. (17 Nm).

12. Connect the negative battery cable and check for proper operation of the wipers.

Windshield Wiper Switch

REMOVAL AND INSTALLATION

NOTE: The windshield wiper switch is part of the combination switch.

Standard Column

1. Disconnect the negative battery cable.

2. Remove the lower steering column cover.

3. Straighten the steering wheel so the tires are pointing straight-ahead.

NOTE: If equipped with an airbag, it is imperative that the steering wheel removal and installation procedure under Steering is followed.

4. Matchmark the steering wheel to shaft and remove the steering wheel.

5. Remove the plastic wiring channel from the underside of the steering column.

6. Disconnect the wiper switch connector, intermittent wipe module connector and cruise control connector, if equipped.

7. Remove the side lock housing cover.

8. Remove the slotted hex-head screw that attaches the wiper switch to the turn signal switch and remove the switch.

9. Remove the control knob from the end of the stalk. Pull the round nylon hider up the control stalk and remove the revealed screws that attach the control stalk sleeve to the wiper switch.

10. Rotate the control stalk shaft to the full clockwise position and remove the shaft from the wiper switch by pulling it straight out.

To install:

11. Install the control shaft to the wiper switch, install the screws, the hider and the control knob.

12. Run the wiring through the opening and down the steering column, position the switch and install the hex-head screw. Make sure the dimmer switch rod is properly engaged.

13. Install the side lock housing cover.

14. Connect the wires and install the wiring channel.

15. Align the matchmark Install the steering wheel and torque the nut to 45 ft. lbs. (61 Nm).

16. Install the horn pad.

17. Connect the negative battery cable and check the wiper and washer, cruise control, turn signal switch and dimmer switch for proper operation.

18. Install the lower column cover.

Tilt Column

1. Disconnect the negative battery cable.

2. Remove the lower steering column cover and remove the plastic wiring channel from the underside of the steering column.

3. Straighten the steering wheel so the tires are pointing straight-ahead.

NOTE: If equipped with an airbag, it is imperative that the steering wheel removal and installation procedure under Steering is followed.

4. Remove the steering wheel.

5. Depress the lock plate with the proper depressing tool, remove the retaining ring from its groove and remove the tool, ring, lock plate, cancelling cam and spring.

6. Remove the switch stalk actuator screw and arm.

7. Remove the hazard switch knob.

8. Disconnect the turn signal switch, wiper switch, intermittent module and cruise control connectors, if equipped.

9. Remove the 3 screws and remove the turn signal switch. Tape the connector to the wires to aid in removal.

10. Remove the ignition key light.

11. Place the key in the **LOCK** position and remove the key. Insert a thin tool into the slot next to the switch mounting screw boss, depress the spring latch at the bottom of the slot releasing the lock. Remove the lock cylinder.

12. Remove the buzzer switch and wedge spring.

13. Remove the 3 housing cover screws and remove the housing cover.

14. Remove the wiper switch pivot pin with a punch and remove the switch.

15. Remove the control knob from the end of the stalk. Pull the round nylon hider up the control stalk and remove the revealed screws that attach the control stalk sleeve to the wiper switch.

16. Rotate the control stalk shaft to the full clockwise position and remove the shaft from the wiper switch by pulling it straight out.

To install:

17. Install the control shaft to the wiper switch, install the screws, the hider and the control knob.

18. Run the wiring through the opening and down the steering column, position the switch and install the wiper switch pivot pin.

19. Install the housing cover.

20. Install the buzzer switch and wedge spring.

21. Install the lock cylinder.

22. Install the ignition key light.

23. Install the turn signal switch, switch stalk actuator arm and hazard switch knob.

24. Install the spring, cancelling cam, lock plate and ring on the steering shaft. Depress the plate with the depressing tool and install the ring securely in the groove. Remove the tool slowly.

25. Connect the turn signal switch, wiper switch, intermittent module and cruise control connectors, if equipped. Install the wiring channel.

26. Install the steering wheel and torque the nut to 45 ft. lbs. (61 Nm).

27. Install the horn pad.

28. Connect the negative battery cable and check the wiper and

washer, cruise control, turn signal switch and dimmer switch for proper operation.
29. Install the lower column cover.

Instrument Cluster

REMOVAL AND INSTALLATION

1. Disconnect the negative battery cable and disarm the air bag system, if equipped. Move the gear selector lever to the lowest position.
2. Remove the 5 screws retaining the upper bezel and 4 screws attaching the lower bezel to the instrument panel. Remove bezels from the instrument panel.
3. When only removing gauge(s) or the speedometer, remove the trip odometer reset knob by pulling straight back. Remove the mask and lens assembly and the desired gauge from the cluster.
4. Disconnect the gear indicator cable. If equipped with PRNDL indicator assembly, disconnect and remove PRNDL as follows:
   a. Move the shifter to the PARK position.
   b. Remove the guide tube from behind the fuse block and disconnect the eyelet from the column actuating arm.
   c. Release the lock lever on the lower end of the column insert and squeeze the legs together.
   d. Remove the insert from the steering column and secure out of the way.
5. Remove the rear window defogger bezel and the radio bezel. Remove the upper steering column cover.
6. Remove the 4 screws attaching the cluster housing to the base panel and pull the cluster out. Disconnect the 2 wiring harnesses and remove the cluster from the vehicle.
To install:
7. Connect the wiring harness. Install cluster assembly and connect the gear indicator cable. If equipped with PRNDL assembly, install as follows:
   a. Route the PRNDL guide tube through the access hole in the base of the panel. Release the guide tube behind the fuse block.
   b. Insert the flange of the column insert into the column, squeeze the legs together with the tabs under column jacket and engage the lock bar to secure the insert.
   c. Hook the eyelet to the steering column actuator and check the

pointer, which should be pointing to **N** position.
   d. If alignment is incorrect, adjust pointer to align with the center of the **N** by turning the adjuster screw located by the cable actuator arm.
8. Install the upper and lower steering column cover, radio bezel, rear window defroster bezel and the cluster bezel.
9. Install the retaining screws.
10. Connect the negative battery cable and check all gauges and the speedometer for proper operation. Make sure the gearshift indicator is properly aligned.

Concealed Headlights

MANUAL OPERATION

1. Disconnect the negative battery cable.
2. Locate the manual override knob located under the center of the front bumper.
3. Rotate the manual override knob to raise the headlight cover(s).
4. Connect the negative battery cable.

Headlight Switch

REMOVAL AND INSTALLATION

1. Disconnect the negative battery cable. Remove the headlight cluster bezel.
2. Remove the screws securing the headlight and heated rear window switch module to the instrument panel. Pull the assembly out to disconnect the connectors from the switch.
3. Depress the spring button and remove the headlight switch knob and stem.
4. Remove the escutcheon and remove the nut that attaches the switch to the mounting plate.
5. The installation is the reverse of the removal procedure.

Combination Switch

REMOVAL AND INSTALLATION

1. Disconnect the negative battery cable.
2. Remove the tilt lever, if equipped.
3. Remove the steering column covers.

4. Remove the combination switch tamper-proof mounting screws and pull the switch away from the steering column.
5. Loosen the connector screw; the screw will remain in the connector.
6. Disconnect the connector from the switch.
To install:
7. Install the wiring connector to the switch and tighten the connector retainer screw to 17 inch lbs. (2 Nm).
8. Mount the combination switch to the column and tighten the retaining screws to 17 inch lbs. (2 Nm).
9. Install the tilt lever to the column, if equipped.
10. Connect the negative battery cable and check for proper operation of all switch functions.

Ignition Lock/Switch

REMOVAL AND INSTALLATION

Acustar Steering Column

NOTE: The Acustar column can be identified by the "halo" light around the ignition key cylinder.

1. Disconnect the negative battery cable.

NOTE: Failure to disarm the air bag system may result in accidental deployment of the air bag module and possible personal injury.

2. Remove the tilt lever by turning counterclockwise, if equipped.
3. Remove the 3 Torx® T-20 screws and remove the upper and lower column covers.
4. Remove the 3 ignition switch tamper resistant screws using Torx® tool No. APEX 440-TX20H or equivalent.
5. Pull the switch away from the column. Release the connector locks on the 2 wiring connectors and disconnect them from the switch.
6. Remove the key lock cylinder from the ignition switch by performing the following:
   a. Insert the key and turn the switch in the **LOCK** position. Using a small tool, depress the key cylinder retaining pin flush with the key cylinder surface.
   b. Rotate the key clockwise to the **OFF** position to unseat the key cylinder from the ignition switch assembly. The cylinder bezel should be about ⅛ in. above the ignition switch halo light ring. Do

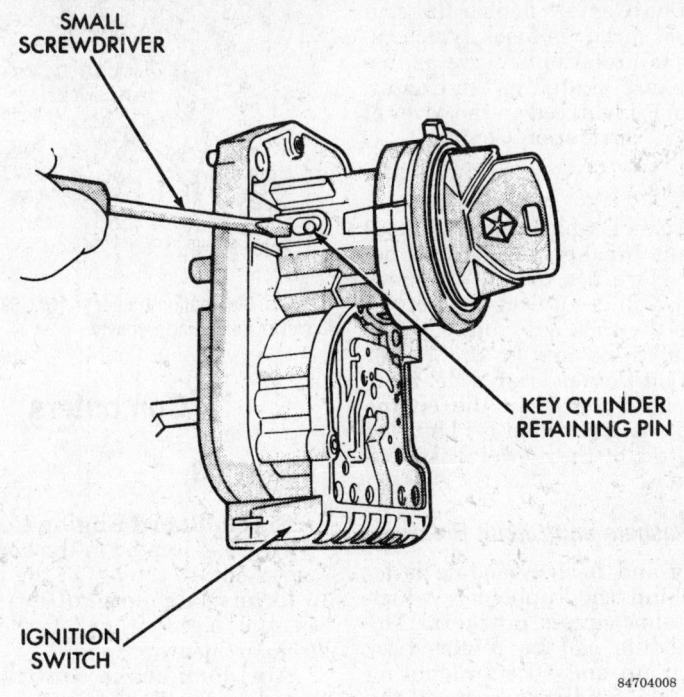

Depressing the cylinder retaining pin — Acustar column

84704008

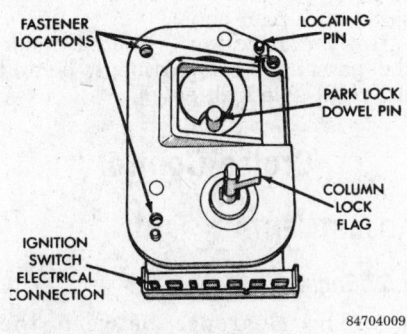

84704009

Preparing the ignition switch for installation — Acustar column

not attempt to remove the key cylinder at this point.

c. With the key cylinder in the unseated position, rotate the key counterclockwise to the **LOCK** position and remove the key.

d. Remove the key cylinder from the ignition switch.

To install:

7. Connect the wiring connectors.

8. Mount ignition switch to the column by performing the following:

a. Position the shifter in **P** position. The park lock dowel pin on the ignition switch assembly must engage with the column park lock slider linkage.

b. Verify that the ignition switch is in the **LOCK** position. The flag should be parallel to the ignition switch terminals. Apply a small amount of grease to the flag and pin.

c. Position the park lock link to mid-travel.

d. Align the locating pin hole and its pin and position the ignition switch against the lock housing face, make sure the pin is inserted into the park lock link contour slot. Torque the retaining screws to 17 inch lbs. (2 Nm).

9. With the key cylinder and ignition switch in the **LOCK** position, key not in cylinder, gently insert the key cylinder into the ignition switch until it bottoms.

10. Insert the key. Simultaneously push in on the cylinder and rotate the key to the **RUN** position. This action should fully seat the cylinder in the ignition switch.

11. Install the column covers and the tilt lever, if equipped.

12. Connect the negative battery cable and check the push-to-lock and park lock functions, halo lighting and all ignition switch positions for proper operation.

Brake Light Switch

ADJUSTMENT

1. Disconnect the negative battery cable. Disarm the air bag system, if equipped.

2. Remove the lower steering column cover.

3. Push the switch and retainer bracket forward towards the brake pedal as far as it will go. The brake pedal should move forward slightly.

4. Gently pull back on the brake pedal bringing the striker back toward the switch. Continue to pull back on the brake pedal until it will go back no further. This will cause the switch to ratchet backward to the correct position.

5. Connect the negative battery cable.

6. Verify correct adjustment of the brake light switch; with the engine **OFF**, apply the brake pedal and check to make sure the brake lights are illuminated. If the brake lights do not go ON, readjust the switch as outlined above.

7. Install the lower steering column cover.

REMOVAL AND INSTALLATION

1. Disconnect the negative battery cable.

2. Unplug the brake light switch connectors near the brake pedal.

3. Remove the switch and bracket assembly from the brake pedal bracket.

4. Remove the switch from its bracket.

To install:

5. Install the switch and bracket assembly to the brake pedal bracket and push the switch forward as far as it will go; the brake pedal should move forward slightly.

6. Pull back on the brake pedal bringing the striker toward the switch until the pedal will not go back any further.

7. This will cause the switch to ratchet backward into position and automatic adjustment is complete.

8. Connect the negative battery cable and check the switch for proper operation. Also, make sure the speed control system functions properly, if equipped.

Neutral Safety Switch

REMOVAL AND INSTALLATION

1. Disconnect the negative battery cable.

2. Locate the neutral safety switch at the left rear corner of the automatic transaxle, in the left front of engine compartment. Do not confuse it with the white PRNDL switch on the A604 automatic transaxle. Unplug the switch connector.

3. Remove the switch from the transaxle.

4. The installation is the reverse of the removal procedure. Torque the switch to 25 ft. lbs. (34 Nm).

5. Connect the negative battery cable and check the switch for proper operation.

Fuses, Circuit Breakers and Relays

LOCATION

Fusible Links

If not equipped with a Power Distribution Center, fusible links are part of the large wiring harness behind the battery. If equipped with a Power Distribution Center, fusible links in the form of cartridge fuses, which resemble small relays but serve as fusible links, are located in the Center. Each item is identified on the cover of the Power Distribution Center.

Fuse Panels

The fuse panel, which contains fuses and circuit breakers, is located behind the glove box door. To remove the panel, pull it out from the bottom and slide the tabs out from the top. Additional fuses are in the Power Distribution Center located near the left side strut tower in the engine compartment. Each item is identified on the cover of the Power Distribution Center.

Relays, Flashers and Circuit Breakers

The relay and flasher module is located behind the cupholder, which also contains circuit breakers. The entire module can be removed by pushing it up and off its mounting bracket. Additional relays are in the Power Distribution Center located near the left side strut tower in the engine compartment. Each item is identified on the cover of the Power Distribution Center.

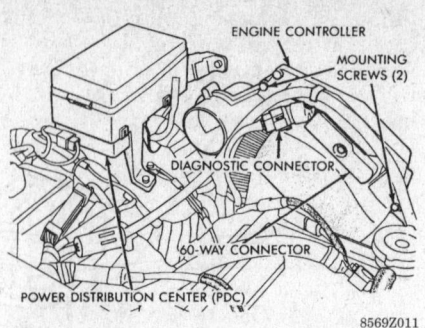

Power Distribution Center — 1992–93 New Yorker Salon and Dynasty

Computers

LOCATION

Single Board Engine Controller (SBEC) — located in the engine compartment, to the left of the battery.

Transaxle controller — located in the right front of the engine compartment.

Anti-lock brake controller — located under the battery tray.

Air suspension controller — if equipped with automatic load leveling or automatic air suspension, the controller is located behind the right side trunk trim panel.

Body controller — located inside the passenger compartment, behind the right side kick panel.

Cruise Control

ADJUSTMENT

2.5L Engine

1. The clearance between the throttle stud and cable clevis should be $1/16$ in.

2. To adjust the cable, remove the retaining clip or loosen the retaining clamp nut at the throttle bracket.

3. Pull all slack out of the cable using a suitable $1/16$ in. diameter tool to account for proper clearance. Make sure the curb idle position of the throttle blade is not affected.

4. Reinstall the retaining clip or nut.

3.0L, 3.3L and 3.8L Engines

1. Grip the cable core and lightly push toward the servo.

2. While holding the position, mark the core wire next to the protective sleeve.

3. Pull the core wire away from the servo. There should be a 0.24 in.

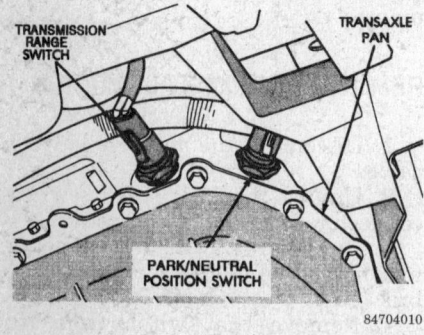

Neutral safety switch identification — A413 automatic transaxle

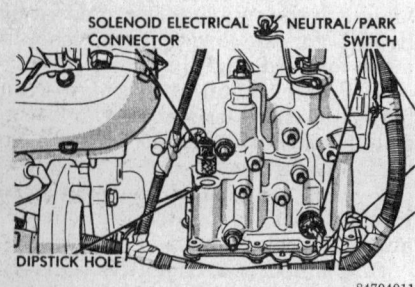

Neutral safety switch identification — A604 automatic transaxle

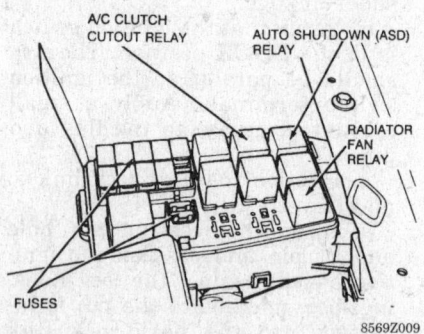

Relays and fuses in the Power Distribution Center

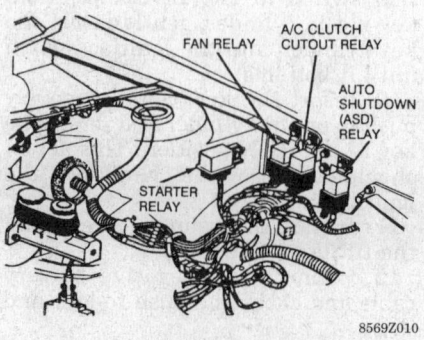

Engine compartment relay identification

(6mm) gap between the mark on the core wire and the protective sleeve.

4. If the gap is not correct, remove the adjustment clip from the throttle bracket and move the sleeve to bring the gap into specification.

5. Reinstall the clip.

ENGINE COOLING

Radiator

REMOVAL AND INSTALLATION

1. Disconnect the negative battery cable.

2. Drain the coolant.

3. Remove the upper hose and coolant reserve tank hose from the radiator.

4. Remove the electric cooling fan.

5. Raise the vehicle and support safely. Remove the lower hose from the radiator.

6. If the cooler is in the radiator, disconnect and plug the automatic transaxle cooler hoses. Lower the vehicle.

7. Remove the mounting brackets and carefully lift the radiator out of the engine compartment.

To install:

8. Lower the radiator into position.

9. Install the mounting brackets.

10. Raise the vehicle and support safely. Connect the automatic transaxle cooler lines, if disconnected.

11. Connect the lower hose. Lower the vehicle.

12. Install the electric cooling fan.

13. Connect the upper hose and coolant reserve tank hose.

14. Fill the system with coolant and bleed.

15. Connect the negative battery cable, run the vehicle until the thermostat opens, fill the radiator completely and check the automatic transaxle fluid level.

16. Once cooled, recheck the coolant level.

Electric Cooling Fan

—— **CAUTION** ——

Make sure the key is in the OFF position when working the electric cooling fan. If not, the fan could turn ON at any time, causing serious personal injury.

TESTING

1. Unplug the fan connector.

2. Using a jumper wire, connect the female terminal of the fan connector to the negative battery terminal.

3. The fan should come ON when the male terminal is connected to the positive battery terminal.

4. If not, the fan is defective and should be replaced.

REMOVAL AND INSTALLATION

1. Disconnect the negative battery cable.

2. Unplug the vehicle harness connector from the fan connector.

3. Remove the mounting screws.

4. Remove the fan assembly from the vehicle.

5. The installation is the reverse of the removal procedure.

Heater Core

REMOVAL AND INSTALLATION

1. Disconnect the negative battery cable. Properly discharge the air conditioning system, Drain the cooling system.

2. Clamp off the heater hoses near the heater core and remove the hoses from the core tubes. Plug the hose ends and the core tubes to prevent spillage of coolant.

3. Disconnect the H-valve connection at the valve and remove the H-valve. Remove the condensation tube.

4. Disconnect the vacuum lines at the brake booster and water valve, if equipped.

5. Remove the right upper and lower under-panel silencers. Remove the steering column cover and ashtray. Remove the left side under-panel silencer. Remove the right side cowl trim piece.

6. Remove the glove box assembly and the right side instrument panel reinforcement. Remove the center distribution and defroster adaptor ducts.

7. Disconnect the relay module, blower motor wiring and 25-way connector bracket and fuse block from the panel. Disconnect the demister hoses from the top of the package.

8. Disconnect the temperature control cable and vacuum harness, if equipped. If equipped with Automatic Temperature Control (ATC), disconnect the instrument panel wiring from the rear of the ATC unit.

9. Disconnect the hanger strap from the package and rotate it out of the way. Remove the retaining nuts from the package mounting studs at the firewall.

10. Fold the carpeting and insulation back to provide a little more working room and to prevent spillage from staining the carpeting. Move the package rearward to clear the mounting studs and lower.

11. Pull the right side of the instrument panel out as far as possible. Rotate the package while removing it from under the instrument panel.

12. To disassemble the housing assembly, remove the vacuum diaphragm, if equipped. Then remove the retaining screws from the cover and the cover.

13. Remove the retaining screw from the heater core and the core from the housing assembly.

To install:

14. Remove the temperature control door from the housing and clean the unit out with solvent. Lubricate the lower pivot rod and its well and install. Wrap the heater core with foam tape and place it in position. Secure it with its screw. Assemble the package, making sure all vacuum tubing is properly routed.

15. If equipped, feed the vacuum lines through the hole in the firewall and install the assembly to the vehicle. Connect the vacuum harness and demister hoses. Install the nuts to the firewall and connect the hanger strap inside the passenger compartment.

16. Fold the carpeting back into position. Connect the wiring to the ATC unit, if equipped. Install the fuse block. Connect the 25-way connector, relay module and blower motor wiring.

17. Install the center distribution and defroster adaptor ducts. Install the right side instrument panel reinforcement and the glove box assembly.

18. Install the right side cowl trim piece, left side under-panel silencer, steering column cover, ashtray and right side under-panel silencers.

19. Connect the vacuum lines at the brake booster and water valve. Using new gaskets, install the H-valve and condensation tube. Connect the heater hoses.

20. Using the proper equipment, evacuate and recharge the air conditioning system. Fill the cooling system.

21. Connect the negative battery cable and check the entire climate

control system for proper operation and leakage.

Water Pump

REMOVAL AND INSTALLATION

2.5L Engine

1. Disconnect the negative battery cable.
2. Drain the cooling system.
3. Remove the air conditioning compressor from the bracket and position it to the side. It is not necessary to remove the refrigerant hoses from the compressor.
4. Remove the alternator and bracket from the engine. Have a drain pan under the side mounting stud because the stud screws into a water jacket, and coolant will spill out when it is removed. Remove the pulley and belt from the water pump.
5. Disconnect the lower radiator hose and heater hose from the water pump.
6. Remove the water pump housing attaching screws and remove the assembly from the vehicle. Discard the O-ring.
7. Remove the water pump from the housing.
To install:
8. Using a new gasket or silicone sealer, install the water pump to the housing.
9. Install a new O-ring to the housing and install to the engine. Torque the bolts to 21 ft. lbs. (30 Nm).
10. Install the water pump pulley and torque the bolts to 21 ft. lbs. (30 Nm). Connect the radiator hose and heater hose to the water pump.
11. Install all items removed to gain access to the water pump, then adjust the belts.
12. Remove the hex-head plug on the top of the thermostat housing. Fill the radiator with coolant until the coolant comes out the plug hole. Install the plug and continue to fill the radiator.
13. Connect the negative battery cable, run the vehicle until the thermostat opens, fill the radiator completely and check for leaks.
14. Once the vehicle has cooled, recheck the coolant level.

3.0L Engine

1. Disconnect the negative battery cable.
2. Drain the cooling system.
3. Rotate the engine to TDC of compression stroke.

4. Remove the timing cover. If the same timing belt will be reused, mark the direction of the timing belt's rotation, for installation in the same direction. Make sure the engine is positioned so the No. 1 cylinder is at the TDC of its compression stroke and the sprockets timing marks are aligned with the engine's timing mark indicators.
5. Loosen the timing belt tensioner bolt and remove the belt. Position the tensioner as far away from the center of the engine as possible and tighten the bolt. Remove the water pump mounting bolts, separate the pump from the water inlet pipe and remove the pump from the engine.
To install:
6. Install the pump with a new gasket to the engine. Torque the water pump mounting bolts to 20 ft. lbs. (27 Nm).
7. If not already done, position both camshafts so the marks line up with those on the alternator bracket (rear bank) and inner timing cover (front bank). Rotate the crankshaft so the timing mark aligns with the mark on the oil pump.
8. Install the timing belt on the crankshaft sprocket and while keeping the belt tight on the tension side (right side), install the belt on the front camshaft sprocket.
9. Install the belt on the water pump pulley, then the rear camshaft sprocket and the tensioner.
10. Rotate the front camshaft counterclockwise to tension the belt between the front camshaft and the crankshaft. If the timing marks became misaligned, repeat the procedure.
11. Install the crankshaft sprocket flange.
12. Loosen the tensioner bolt and allow the spring to tension the belt.
13. Turn the crankshaft 2 full turns in the clockwise direction only until the timing marks align again. Now that the belt is properly tensioned, torque the tensioner lock bolt to 21 ft. lbs. (29 Nm).
14. Refill the cooling system. This system uses a self-bleeding thermostat, so there is no need to bleed the system. Connect the negative battery cable and road test the vehicle.

3.3L and 3.8L Engines

1. Disconnect the negative battery cable.
2. Drain the cooling system.
3. Remove the serpentine belt.
4. Raise the vehicle and support safely. Remove the right front tire

and wheel assembly and lower fender shield.
5. Remove the water pump pulley.
6. Remove the 5 mounting screws and remove the pump from the engine.
7. Discard the O-ring.
To install:
8. Using a new O-ring, install the pump to the engine. Torque the mounting bolts to 9 ft. lbs. (12 Nm).
9. Install the water pump pulley.
10. Install the fender shield, tire and wheel assembly. Lower the vehicle.
11. Install the serpentine belt.
12. Remove the engine temperature sending unit. Fill the radiator with coolant until the coolant comes out the sending unit hole. Install the sending unit and continue to fill the radiator.
13. Connect the negative battery cable, run the vehicle until the thermostat opens, fill the radiator completely and check for leaks.
14. Once cooled, recheck the coolant level.

Thermostat

REMOVAL AND INSTALLATION

1. Disconnect the negative battery cable. Drain the coolant down to thermostat level or below.
2. Remove the thermostat housing retaining bolts and the housing.
3. Remove the thermostat and discard the gasket.
4. Clean the housing mating surfaces and use a new gasket.
To install:
5. Install the thermostat into the housing with new gasket in place and secure using fasteners.
6. Fill the system with coolant as follows:
   a. On the 2.5L engine, remove the hex-head plug on the thermostat housing. Fill the radiator with coolant until the coolant comes out the plug hole. Install the plug and continue to fill the radiator.
   b. The 3.0L engine is equipped with a self-bleeding thermostat; bleeding is not necessary.
   c. On 3.3L and 3.8L engines, remove the engine temperature sending unit. Fill the radiator with coolant until the coolant comes out the sending unit hole. Install the sending unit and continue to fill the radiator.
7. Connect the negative battery cable, run the vehicle until the ther-

mostat opens, fill the radiator completely and check for leaks.

8. Once the vehicle has cooled, recheck the coolant level.

COOLING SYSTEM BLEEDING

To bleed air from the 2.5L engine, remove the plug on the top of the thermostat housing. Fill the radiator with coolant until the coolant comes out the hole. Install the plug and continue to fill the radiator. This will vent all trapped air from the engine.

The thermostat in the 3.0L engine is equipped with a small air vent valve that allows trapped air to bleed from the system during refilling. This valve negates the need for cooling system bleeding in those engines.

On 3.3L and 3.8L engines, remove the engine temperature sending unit. Fill the radiator with coolant until the coolant comes out the hole. Install the switch and continue to fill the radiator. This will vent all trapped air from the engine.

FUEL SYSTEM

Fuel System Service Precautions

Safety is the most important factor when performing not only fuel system maintenance but any type of maintenance. Failure to conduct maintenance and repairs in a safe manner may result in serious personal injury or death. Maintenance and testing of the vehicle's fuel system components can be accomplished

safely and effectively by adhering to the following rules and guidelines.

• To avoid the possibility of fire and personal injury, always disconnect the negative battery cable unless the repair or test procedure requires that battery voltage be applied.

• Always relieve the fuel system pressure prior to disconnecting any fuel system component (injector, fuel rail, pressure regulator, etc.), fitting or fuel line connection. Exercise extreme caution whenever relieving fuel system pressure to avoid exposing skin, face and eyes to fuel spray. Please be advised that fuel under pressure may penetrate the skin or any part of the body that it contacts.

• Always place a shop towel or cloth around the fitting or connection prior to loosening to absorb any excess fuel due to spillage. Ensure that all fuel spillage (should it occur) is quickly removed from engine surfaces. Ensure that all fuel soaked cloths or towels are deposited into a suitable waste container.

• Always keep a dry chemical (Class B) fire extinguisher near the work area.

• Do not allow fuel spray or fuel vapors to come into contact with a spark or open flame.

• Always use a backup wrench when loosening and tightening fuel line connection fittings. This will prevent unnecessary stress and torsion to fuel line piping. Always follow the proper torque specifications.

• Always replace worn fuel fitting O-rings with new. Do not substitute fuel hose or equivalent where fuel pipe is installed.

RELIEVING FUEL SYSTEM PRESSURE

1. Loosen the fuel filler cap to release fuel tank pressure.

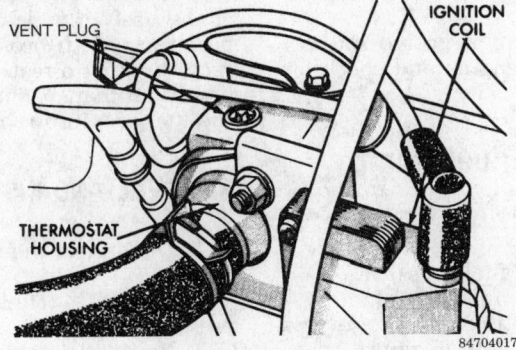

Cooling system bleeding plug — 2.5L engine

2. Locate and disconnect the fuel injector harness connector.

3. Connect a jumper wire from terminal No. 1 of the appropriate connector to ground.

4. Being careful not to allow contact between the jumper leads, connect a jumper wire to terminal No. 2 of the connector and touch the other end of the jumper to the positive battery post for no longer than 5 seconds. This will relieve fuel pressure.

5. Remove the jumper wires and continue with fuel system service.

Engines With Test Port On Fuel Rail

1. Disconnect the negative battery terminal.

2. Remove the fuel filler cap.

3. Remove protective cap from the fuel test port on the fuel rail.

4. Place the open end of fuel pressure release hose tool C-4799-1 or equivalent, into an approved safety container.

NOTE: Fuel pressure test gauge tool C-4799-A contains pressure release hose C-4799-A.

5. Connect the other end of release hose to the fuel pressure test port.

6. Fuel pressure will bleed off into safety container.

Fuel Tank

REMOVAL AND INSTALLATION

1. Disconnect the negative battery cable.

2. Release the fuel system pressure.

3. Raise the vehicle and support safely.

4. Using the proper equipment, drain the fuel tank.

5. Remove the screws that hold the filler neck to the quarter panel.

6. Disconnect the electrical wiring harness and fuel hoses from the tank.

7. Place a transmission jack or equivalent, under the center of the tank and apply slight pressure. Loosen the tank straps, lower the tank slightly and disconnect the hose from the pressure relief rollover valve. Carefully remove the filler tube from the tank.

8. Remove the tank straps and lower the tank from the vehicle.

To install:

9. Raise the tank into position and connect all harnesses, fuel hoses and vacuum hoses.

10. Install the tank straps and tighten the retaining nuts.

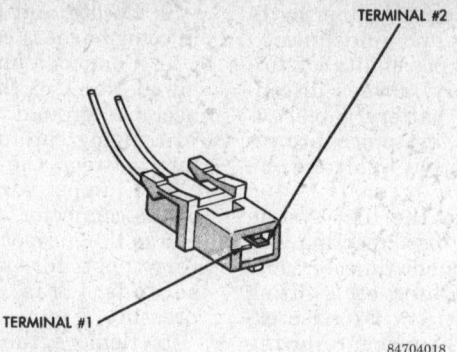

Fuel injector harness identification — 2.5L engines

84704018

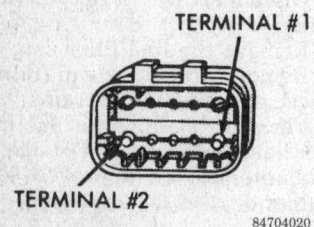

84704020

Fuel injector harness identification — 1992–93 3.0L, 3.3L and 3.8L engines

11. Install the screws that hold the filler neck to the quarter panel.

12. Connect the negative battery cable, start the engine and check for leaks.

Fuel Filter

REMOVAL AND INSTALLATION

--- CAUTION ---

Do not use conventional fuel filters, hoses or clamps when servicing this fuel system. They are not compatible with the injection system and could fail, causing personal injury or damage to the vehicle. Use only hoses and clamps specifically designed for fuel injection.

1. Disconnect the negative battery cable.

2. Release the fuel system pressure.

3. The filter is located on the frame rail toward the rear of the vehicle. Raise the vehicle and support safely. Remove the filter retaining screw and remove the filter assembly from the mounting plate.

4. Wrap a shop towel around the hoses to absorb fuel. Remove the hoses from the filter and fuel tube and discard the clamps and the filter. If equipped with Quick Connect fuel fittings, disconnect as follows:

   a. Remove any loose dirt from the fitting.

   b. Pull back on the fitting while pushing in on the plastic ring.

   c. Separate the connection.

5. Cover open fuel lines to prevent contamination.

To install:

6. Install the inlet hose on the fuel tube and tighten the new clamp to 10 inch lbs. If equipped with Quick Connect fittings, install as follows:

   a. Lubricate the fuel tube nipple with clean 30W engine oil.

   b. Insert the nipple into the Quick Connect fitting. The tube should be locked in place, if the connection is correctly made. If the tube will not lock, inspect the connection making sure the black plastic release is not causing the locking retainer to jam in the release position.

   c. Using the DRB II, actuate the ASD Fuel System Test to pressurize the fuel system. Inspect the Quick Connect fitting for leaks.

7. Install the outlet hose on the filter outlet fitting and tighten the new clamp to 10 inch lbs.

8. Position the filter assembly on the mounting plate and tighten the mounting screw to 75 inch lbs. (8 Nm).

9. Connect the negative battery cable, start the engine and check for leaks.

Electric Fuel Pump

PRESSURE TESTING

1. Relieve the fuel pressure.

2. Properly connect the fuel system pressure tester:

   a. 2.5L and 3.0L engines — special tool C–4799A or equivalent, is installed between the fuel supply hose and the engine fuel line assembly.

   b. 3.3L and 3.8L engines — special tool C–4799A or equivalent, is installed to the fuel rail service valve.

3. With the key in the **RUN** position, place the DRB II in the activate auto shutdown relay mode; this will activate the fuel pump and pressurize the system.

4. Compare pressure with the desired readings listed below:

   2.5L TBI engine — 39 psi
   3.0L MPI engine — 48 psi
   3.3L MPI engine — 48 psi
   3.8L MPI engine — 48 psi

NOTE: The above fuel pressure readings reflect fuel pressures obtained with the vacuum hose disconnected from the fuel pressure regulator.

5. If fuel pressure is below specifications, install the tester in the fuel supply line between the tank and the filter and repeat the test.

6. If the pressure is 5 psi higher than in Step 5, replace the fuel filter. If no change is observed, squeeze the return hose. If pressure increases, replace the pressure regulator. If no change is observed, the problem is either a plugged in-tank sock filter or a defective pump.

7. If fuel pressure is above specifications, remove the fuel return line hose from the chassis line at the fuel tank and connect a 3 foot piece of fuel hose to the return line. Put the other end into a 2 gallon minimum capacity approved gasoline container. Repeat the test. If pressure is now correct, check the in-tank return hose for kinking. Replace the fuel pump assembly if the in-tank reservoir check valve or aspirator jet is obstructed.

8. If pressure is still above specifications, remove the fuel return hose from the throttle body. Connect a substitute hose to the throttle body return nipple and place the other end of the hose in a clean container. Repeat the test. If pressure is now correct, check for a restricted fuel return line. If no change is observed, replace the fuel pressure regulator.

REMOVAL AND INSTALLATION

1. Disconnect the negative battery cable.

2. Release the fuel system pressure.

3. Raise the vehicle and support safely.

4. Using the proper equipment, drain the fuel tank.

5. Remove the fuel tank from the vehicle

6. Using a hammer and a brass drift, tap the lock ring counterclockwise to release the pump.

7. Disconnect the fuel fitting.

8. Remove the pump from the tank with the O-ring. Discard the O-ring, pump inlet filter and inlet seal. Disassemble as required.

To install:

9. Install a new inlet seal and filter on the end of the pump.

10. Install a new O-ring to the pump.

11. Connect the reservoir hose to the pump assembly at the suction end of the pump. Press the female fitting onto the pump assembly male end until the ears snap in place.

12. Install the pump into the tank so the fuel return hose is not kinked.

13. Install the lock ring with a hammer and brass punch turning the ring clockwise.

14. Install the fuel tank into the vehicle.

15. Connect the negative battery cable, start the engine and check for leaks.

Fuel Injection

IDLE SPEED ADJUSTMENT

The idle speed is controlled by the Idle Air Control (IAC) motor. The IAC motor is controlled by the Single Board Engine Controller (SBEC), which receives data from various sensors and switches in the system and adjusts the engine idle to a predetermined speed. Idle speed specifications can be found on the Vehicle Emission Control Information (VECI) label located in the engine compartment. If the idle speed is not within specifications and there are no problems with the system, the throttle body should be suspect and possibly replaced.

IDLE MIXTURE ADJUSTMENT

There is no idle mixture adjustment provided with any Chrysler fuel injection system.

Fuel Injector

REMOVAL AND INSTALLATION

2.5L Engine

1. Disconnect the negative battery cable.

2. Remove the air cleaner assembly.

3. Relieve the fuel pressure.

4. Remove the injector hold-down Torx® screw and the hold-down.

5. Using a small flat-tipped tool, lift the cap off the injector.

6. Using the same tool, gently pry the injector from its pod.

7. Remove the lower O-ring from the pod.

To install:

8. Install the new lower O-ring on the injector. Be sure to align injector wiring terminals.

9. Align the injector terminal housing with the locating socket in the injector cap.

10. Press the injector cap so the upper O-ring flange is flush with the lower surface of the cap.

11. Spray the inner surfaces of the injector pod with carburetor parts cleaner to remove residual varnish and gasoline.

12. Lubricate the O-rings sparingly with clean oil.

13. Place the injector and cap into the injector pod and align the cap locating pin with the locating hole in the casting.

14. Press firmly on the injector cap until it is flush with the casting surface.

15. Align the hole in the hold-down with the pin on the cap and install.

16. Push down on the cap, install the screw and torque to 35 inch lbs. (4 Nm).

17. Connect the negative battery cable and check for leaks using the DRB II to activate the fuel pump.

18. Install the air cleaner.

3.0L Engine

1. Disconnect the negative battery cable.

2. Relieve the fuel pressure.

3. Remove the air cleaner to throttle body hose.

4. Disconnect the throttle cable from the throttle body and disconnect the kickdown linkage. Remove the throttle cable bracket attaching bolts.

5. Disconnect the connectors to the throttle body.

6. Matchmark and carefully remove the vacuum hoses from the throttle body.

7. Remove the PCV and brake booster hoses from the air intake plenum.

8. Remove the ignition coil from the intake plenum, if mounted there.

9. Remove the EGR tube flange from the intake plenum, if equipped.

10. Unplug the coolant temperature sensor and charge temperature sensor, if equipped.

11. Remove the vacuum connection from the air intake plenum vacuum connector.

12. Remove the fuel hoses from the fuel rail and plug them.

13. Remove the air intake plenum to intake manifold bolts and remove the plenum and gaskets. Cover the intake manifold openings.

14. Remove the vacuum hoses from the fuel rail.

15. Disconnect the fuel injector wiring harness.

16. Remove the fuel rail attaching bolts and remove the fuel rail with the wiring harness from the vehicle. Position the rail on the bench upside down so the injectors are easily accessible.

17. Remove the small connector retainer clip and unplug the injector. Remove the injector clip off the fuel rail and injector. Pull the injector straight out of the rail.

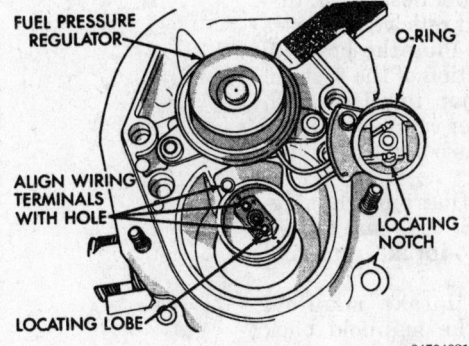

FUEL PRESSURE REGULATOR   O-RING

ALIGN WIRING TERMINALS WITH HOLE

LOCATING NOTCH

LOCATING LOBE

84704021

Installation of fuel injector — 2.5L engine

To install:

18. Lubricate the rubber O-ring with clean oil and install to the rail receiver cap. Install the injector clip to the **TOP** slot of the injector, plug in the connector and install the connector clip.

19. Install the fuel rail to the vehicle and plug in the injector harness. Connect the vacuum hoses to the fuel rail.

20. Install new intake plenum gaskets with the beaded sealer side up and install the intake plenum. Torque the attaching bolts and nuts to 115 inch lbs. (13 Nm).

21. Install the fuel hoses to the fuel rail.

22. Install or connect all items that were removed or disconnected from the intake plenum and throttle body.

23. Connect the negative battery cable and check for leaks using the DRB I or II to activate the fuel pump.

3.3L and 3.8L Engines

1. Disconnect the negative battery cable.

2. Release the fuel system pressure.

3. Remove the air cleaner and hose assembly.

4. Disconnect the throttle cable. Remove the wiring harness from the throttle cable bracket and intake manifold water tube.

5. Remove the vacuum hose harness from the throttle body.

6. Remove the PCV and brake booster hoses from the air intake plenum.

7. Remove the EGR tube flange from the intake plenum, if equipped.

8. Unplug the charge temperature sensor and unplug all vacuum hoses from the intake plenum.

9. Remove the cylinder head to intake plenum strut.

10. Disconnect the MAP sensor and oxygen sensor connector. Remove the engine mounted ground strap.

11. Release the fuel hose quick disconnect fittings and remove the hoses from the fuel rail. Plug the hoses to prevent contamination of the system. Always place a shop towel or cloth around the fitting or connection prior to loosening to absorb any excess fuel due to spillage.

12. Remove the Distributorless Ignition System (DIS) coils and the alternator bracket-to-intake manifold bolt.

13. Remove the intake manifold bolts and rotate the manifold back over the rear valve cover. Cover the intake manifold.

14. Remove the vacuum harness from the pressure regulator.

15. Remove the fuel tube retainer bracket screw and fuel rail attaching bolts. Spread the retainer bracket to allow for clearance when removing the fuel tube.

16. Remove the fuel rail injector wiring clip from the alternator bracket.

17. Disconnect the cam sensor, coolant temperature sensor and engine temperature sensor.

18. Remove the fuel rail from the engine taking care not to damage or drop injectors during removal.

19. Position the rail on a work bench so the injectors are easily accessible.

20. On 1992–93 engines, remove the injectors from the fuel rail by rotating while lightly pulling the injector from the fuel rail. The retainer spring clip will stay on the injector. Inspect the clip, if damaged it will require replacement.

To install:

21. Lubricate the rubber O-ring on the injector with clean oil.

22. On 1991 engines, install the injector to the fuel rail receiver cap and install the clip to the slot in the injector, plug in the connector and install the connector retainer clip.

23. On 1992–93 engines, install the injector retainer clip by sliding the open end into the **TOP SLOT** of the injector. The edge of the receiver cup will slide into the side slots in the clip. Install the injector top end into the fuel rail receiver cup taking care not to damage the O-ring during installation.

24. Install the fuel rail to the engine. Connect the harness connectors to each injector.

25. Connect the cam sensor, coolant temperature sensor and engine temperature sensor.

26. Install the fuel rail injector wiring clip to the alternator bracket.

27. Install the fuel rail attaching bolts and fuel tube retainer bracket screw.

28. Install the vacuum harness to the pressure regulator.

29. Install the intake manifold with a new gasket. Install the bolts only finger-tight. Install the alternator bracket to intake manifold bolt and the cylinder head to intake manifold strut and bolts. Torque the intake manifold mounting bolts to 21 ft. lbs. (28 Nm) starting from the middle and working outward. Torque the bracket and strut bolts to 40 ft. lbs. (54 Nm).

30. Install or connect all items that were removed or disconnected from the intake manifold and throttle body.

31. Connect the fuel hoses to the rail. Push the fittings in until they click in place.

32. Install the air cleaner assembly.

33. Connect the negative battery cable and check for leaks using the DRB II to activate the fuel pump.

EMISSION CONTROLS

Emission Warning Lamps

RESETTING

In order to reset the Emission Warning Lamp, actuate erase fault code data using the DRB II tester connected to the diagnostic connector located in the engine compartment near the engine controller.

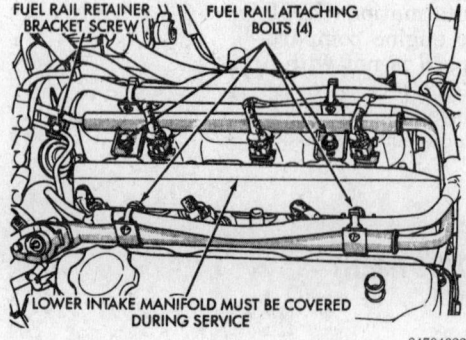

FUEL RAIL RETAINER BRACKET SCREW FUEL RAIL ATTACHING BOLTS (4)

LOWER INTAKE MANIFOLD MUST BE COVERED DURING SERVICE

84704022

Fuel rail and injector assembly — 3.3L and 3.8L engines

ENGINE MECHANICAL

NOTE: Disconnecting the negative battery cable on some vehicles may interfere with the functions of the on board computer systems and may require the computer to undergo a relearning process, once the negative battery cable is reconnected.

Engine Assembly

REMOVAL AND INSTALLATION

2.5L Engine

1. Disconnect the negative battery cable and all engine ground straps. Relieve the fuel pressure.
2. Mark the hood hinge outline on the hood and remove the hood.
3. Drain the cooling system. Remove the radiator hoses, fan assembly and radiator.
4. Remove the air cleaner, duct hoses and oil filter.
5. Unbolt the air conditioning compressor from its mount and position it aside. It is not necessary to disconnect the refrigerant hoses.
6. Remove the power steering pump mounting bolts and position the pump aside. Disconnecting the fluid lines from the pump is not necessary.
7. Label and disconnect all electrical connectors from the engine, alternator and fuel injection system.
8. Disconnect and plug the fuel lines and heater hoses.
9. Disconnect the throttle linkage.
10. Remove the alternator.
11. Raise the vehicle and support safely.
12. Disconnect the exhaust pipe from the manifold.
13. Remove the right inner fender shield. Remove the lower cover from the transaxle case.
14. Remove the starter and set it aside. Matchmark the flexplate to the torque converter for installation purposes. Remove the torque converter bolts. Separate the converter from the flexplate. Remove the lower bellhousing bolts.
15. Lower the vehicle and support the transaxle with a floor jack or equivalent. Attach an engine lifting device to the engine.

16. Remove the remaining belhousing attaching bolts.

NOTE: If removing the insulator-to-rail screws, first mark the position of the insulator on the side rail to ensure proper alignment during reinstallation.

17. Remove the front engine mount nut/bolt and the left insulator through bolt or the insulator bracket to transaxle bolts.
18. Lift the engine from the vehicle and remove.

To install:

19. Lower the engine into the engine compartment. Make sure the lifting device is supporting the full weight of the engine and loosely install all of the mounting bolts until all are threaded. Then tighten all bolts.
20. Remove the lifting device.
21. Raise the vehicle and support safely.
22. If equipped with an automatic transaxle, install the torque converter bolts and torque to 55 ft. lbs. (75 Nm).
23. Install the torque converter inspection plate and starter.
24. Connect the exhaust pipe. Lower the vehicle.
25. Install the alternator, power steering pump and air conditioning compressor.
26. Connect the fuel lines and heater hoses.
27. Connect the throttle linkage.
28. Connect all remaining electrical connectors.
29. Install the air cleaner assembly and oil filter.
30. Install the radiator, fan assembly and hoses.
31. Fill the engine with the proper amount of engine oil. Connect the negative battery cable.
32. Refill the cooling system. Start the engine, allow it to reach normal operating temperature and check all fluids for leaks.
33. Check the ignition timing and adjust if necessary.
34. Install the hood making sure to realign with the marks during disassembly.
35. When the engine is cool, recheck all fluid levels.

3.0L, 3.3L and 3.8L Engines

1. Disconnect the negative battery cable. Release the fuel system pressure.
2. Matchmark the hinge-to-hood position and remove the hood.

3. Drain the cooling system. Disconnect and label all engine electrical connections.
4. Remove the coolant hoses from the radiator and engine. Remove the radiator and cooling fan assembly.
5. Remove the air cleaner assembly. Disconnect the fuel lines from the engine. Disconnect the accelerator cable from the engine.
6. Raise the vehicle and support safely. Drain the engine oil.
7. Remove the air conditioning compressor mounting bolts, the drive belts and position the compressor to the side with lines attached. Disconnect the exhaust pipe from the exhaust manifold.
8. Remove the transaxle inspection cover, matchmark the converter to the flexplate and remove the torque converter bolts.
9. Remove the power steering pump mounting bolts and set the pump aside, upright, with the fluid lines attached.
10. Remove the lower bellhousing bolts. Disconnect and label the starter motor wiring and remove the starter motor from the engine.
11. Lower the vehicle. Disconnect and label the vacuum hoses and engine ground straps.
12. Support the transaxle with a floor jack or equivalent. Attach an engine lifting device to the engine.
13. Remove the upper transaxle-to-engine bolts.
14. To separate the engine mounts from the insulators, mark the right insulator-to-right frame support and remove the mounting bolts. Remove the front engine mount through bolt. Remove the left insulator through bolt, from inside the wheel housing. Remove the insulator bracket-to-transaxle bolts.
15. Lift and remove the engine from the vehicle.

To install:

16. Lower the engine into the engine compartment. Align the engine mounts and install the bolts; do not tighten the bolts until all bolts have been installed. Torque the through bolts to 75 ft. lbs. (102 Nm).
17. Install the upper transaxle-to-engine mounting bolts and torque to 75 ft. lbs. (102 Nm). Remove the engine lifting fixture from the engine.
18. Raise the vehicle and support safely.
19. Align the converter marks, install the torque converter bolts and tightening to 55 ft. lbs. (75 Nm). Install the transaxle inspection cover.

20. Connect the exhaust pipe to the exhaust manifold. Install the starter motor and connect the wiring.

21. Install the power steering pump and air conditioning compressor. Adjust the drive belt tension, if necessary.

22. Lower the vehicle. Reconnect all vacuum hoses and electrical connections to the engine.

23. Connect the fuel lines and accelerator cable.

24. Install the radiator and fan assembly. Connect the fan motor wiring. Connect the radiator hoses and refill the cooling system.

25. Refill the engine with the proper oil to the correct level.

26. Connect the engine ground straps. Install the hood and align the matchmarks. Connect the battery.

27. Start and run the engine until it reaches normal operating temperatures and check for leaks. Adjust the transaxle linkage, if necessary.

Engine Mounts

REMOVAL AND INSTALLATION

2.5L Engine

RIGHT SIDE MOUNT

1. Disconnect the negative battery cable.

2. Matchmark the engine mount to its frame mounting location.

3. Remove the load on the engine motor mounts by carefully supporting the engine and transmission assembly with a floor jack.

4. Remove the through bolt from the insulator assembly and remove the insulator.

To install:

5. Install the insulator to its position and install the retaining bolts loosely.

6. Tighten the lower yoke nut first, then the through bolt nut and then the body mounting bolts. Make sure the matchmarks are aligned before tightening bolts.

FRONT MOUNT

1. Disconnect the negative battery cable.

2. Matchmark the engine mount to its frame mounting location.

3. Remove the load on the engine motor mounts by carefully supporting the engine and transmission assembly with a floor jack so it will rotate.

4. Remove the bolt from the insulator and front crossmember bracket.

5. Remove the front engine mount bracket to front crossmember screws and nuts. Remove the insulator assembly.

To install:

6. Install front engine mount and secure to crossmember. Tighten bolts to 50 ft. lbs. (68 Nm).

7. Install front mount through bolt and tighten to 75 ft. lbs. (102 Nm).

8. Remove the floor jack and connect the negative battery cable.

3.0L, 3.3L and 3.8L Engines

1. Raise the vehicle and support safely, if necessary. Using the proper equipment, support the weight of the engine.

2. Remove all bolts and nuts that attach the mount to the engine strut, transaxle or body and remove the mount assembly from the vehicle.

3. Remove the through bolt and separate the insulator from the yoke bracket as required.

4. The installation is the reverse of the removal procedure. Make sure the matchmarks are aligned before tightening bolts.

5. Tighten the lower yoke nut first, then the through bolt nut, then the body mounting bolts.

Cylinder Head

REMOVAL AND INSTALLATION

2.5L Engine

1. Relieve the fuel pressure. Disconnect the negative battery cable and unbolt it from the head. Drain the cooling system.

2. Rotate the engine and position at TDC of compression stroke.

3. Remove the dipstick bracket nut from the thermostat housing. Remove the ignition coil from the thermostat housing if mounted there.

4. Remove the air cleaner assembly. Remove the upper radiator hose and disconnect the heater hoses.

5. Disconnect and label the vacuum lines, hoses and wiring connectors from the manifolds, throttle body and from the cylinder head.

6. Disconnect the all linkages and the fuel line from the throttle body. Unbolt the cable bracket. Remove the ground strap attaching screw from the firewall.

7. Remove the air conditioning compressor from the mounting bracket. It is not necessary to disconnect the refrigerant hoses from the air compressor.

8. Remove the upper air conditioning compressor/alternator mount bolts that thread into the cylinder head. The cylinder head can be remove with the bracket mounted on the engine.

9. Remove the upper timing belt cover.

10. Raise the vehicle and support safely. Disconnect the exhaust pipe from the exhaust manifold.

11. If not already done, rotate the engine by hand, until the timing marks align. The No. 1 piston should be at TDC of its compression stroke. Lower the vehicle.

12. With the timing marks aligned, remove the camshaft sprocket and disconnect the timing belt. Remove the spark plug wires from the spark plugs.

13. Remove the valve cover and curtain. Remove the cylinder head bolts and washers, starting from the outside and working inward.

14. Remove the cylinder head from the engine.

15. Clean the cylinder head gasket mating surfaces.

To install:

16. Using new gaskets and seals, install the cylinder head to the engine block. Using new head bolts assembled with the old washers, torque the cylinder head bolts in sequence, to 45 ft. lbs. (61 Nm). Repeating the sequence, torque the bolts to 65 ft. lbs. (88 Nm). With the bolts at 65 ft. lbs., turn each bolt an additional 1/4 turn.

17. Install the camshaft sprocket and the timing belt.

18. Raise and safely support the vehicle. Connect the exhaust pipe to the exhaust manifold replacing the gasket as required.

19. Install the air conditioning compressor and the alternator to the mounting bracket and reconnect all electrical connectors.

20. Install the accessory drive belt and adjust tension as required.

21. Apply form-in-place Mopar Silicone Rubber Adhesive Sealant or equivalent gasket material to the rocker cover and replace both cover end seals.

22. Install to rocker cover to the engine and secure with the retainer bolts tightened to 105 inch lbs. (12 Nm).

23. Refill the cooling system. Connect the negative battery cable. Start the engine and check for leaks using the DRB I or II to activate the fuel pump.

24. Adjust the timing as required.

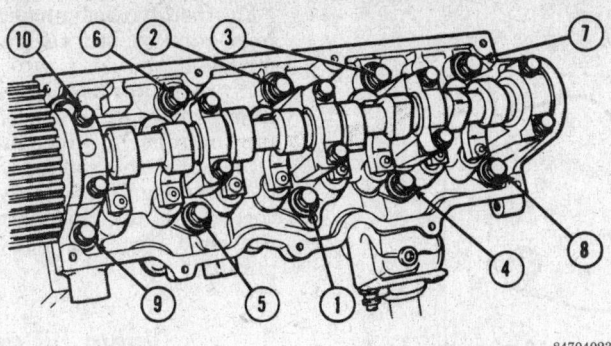

84704023

Cylinder head bolt torque sequence — 2.5L engine

3.0L Engine

1. Release the fuel system pressure. Disconnect the negative battery cable. Drain the cooling system.

2. Remove the compressor drive belt and the air conditioning compressor from its mount and support it aside.

3. Using a ½ in. drive breaker bar, insert it into the square hole of the serpentine drive belt tensioner, rotate it counterclockwise to reduce the belt tension and remove the belt.

4. Remove the alternator and power steering pump from the brackets and position them aside.

5. Raise the vehicle and support safely. Remove the right front wheel and the inner splash shield.

6. Remove the crankshaft pulleys and the torsional damper.

7. Lower the vehicle. Using a floor jack and a block of wood positioned under the oil pan, raise the engine slightly. Remove the engine mount bracket from the timing cover end of the engine.

8. To remove the timing belt, perform the following procedures:

   a. Rotate the crankshaft to position the No. 1 cylinder on the TDC of its compression stroke; the crankshaft sprocket timing mark should align with the oil pan timing indicator and the camshaft sprockets timing marks (triangles) should align with the timing marks on the rear timing belt covers.

   b. Remove the timing belt covers.

   c. Mark the timing belt in the direction of rotation for reinstallation purposes.

   d. Loosen the timing belt tensioner and remove the timing belt.

NOTE: When removing the timing belt from the camshaft sprocket, make sure the belt does not slip off the other camshaft sprocket. Support the belt so it cannot slip off the crankshaft sprocket and opposite side camshaft sprocket.

9. Remove the air cleaner assembly. Label and disconnect the spark plug wires and the vacuum hoses.

10. Remove the valve cover.

11. Install auto lash adjuster retainer tool MD998443 or equivalent, on the rocker arms.

12. If removing the front cylinder head, matchmark the distributor rotor to the distributor housing and the housing to distributor extension locations. Remove the distributor and the distributor extension.

13. Remove the camshaft bearing assembly to cylinder head bolts but do not remove the bolts from the assembly. Remove the rocker arms, rocker shafts and bearing caps as an assembly, as required. Remove the camshafts from the cylinder head and inspect them for damage.

14. Remove the intake manifold assembly.

15. Remove the exhaust manifold.

16. Remove the cylinder head bolts, starting from the outside and working inward. Remove the cylinder head from the engine.

17. Clean the gasket mounting surfaces and check the heads for warpage; maximum warpage is 0.008 in. (0.20mm).

   To install:

18. Install the new cylinder head gasket(s) over the dowels on the engine block.

19. Install the cylinder head(s) on the engine and torque the cylinder head bolts, in sequence, using 3 even steps, to 80 ft. lbs. (108 Nm).

20. Installing the timing belt over the camshaft sprocket, use care not to allow the belt to slip off the opposite camshaft sprocket. Make sure the timing belt is installed on the camshaft sprocket in the same position as when removed.

21. Rotate the engine 2 complete revolutions and check for timing mark alignment.

22. Install the intake and exhaust manifolds to the engine using new gaskets where applicable.

23. Install the engine mounting bolts.

24. Raise and safely support the vehicle. Connect the exhaust pipe to the manifold.

25. Connect the remaining electrical connector disconnected during the cylinder head removal.

26. Refill the cooling system. Connect the negative battery cable. Start the engine and check for leaks using the DRB II to activate the fuel pump.

27. Adjust the timing as required.

3.3L and 3.8L Engines

1. Relieve the fuel pressure. Disconnect the negative battery cable. Drain the cooling system.

2. Remove the intake manifold with the throttle body.

3. Disconnect the coil wires, coolant temperature sending unit wire, heater hoses and bypass hose.

4. Remove the closed ventilation system hoses, evaporation control system hoses and valve cover.

5. Remove the exhaust manifold.

6. Remove the rocker arm and shaft assemblies. Remove the pushrods and identify them in ensure installation in their original positions.

7. Remove the head bolts and remove the cylinder head from the block.

   To install:

8. Clean the gasket mounting surfaces and install a new head gasket to the block.

9. Install the head to the block. Before installing the head bolts, inspect them for stretching at the threads. Hold a straight-edge up to the threads. If the threads are not all even and in alignment, the bolt is stretched and should be replaced.

10. Torque the bolts in sequence to 45 ft. lbs. (61 Nm). Repeat the sequence and torque the bolts to 65 ft. lbs. (88 Nm). With the bolts at 65 ft. lbs., turn each bolt an additional ¼ turn.

NOTE: Cylinder head bolt final torque should be at least 90 ft. lbs. (122 Nm). If this torque is not achieved, the cylinder head bolts are to be replaced.

11. Torque the lone smaller head bolt in the rear of the head to 25 ft. lbs. (33 Nm) after the other 8 bolts have been properly torqued.

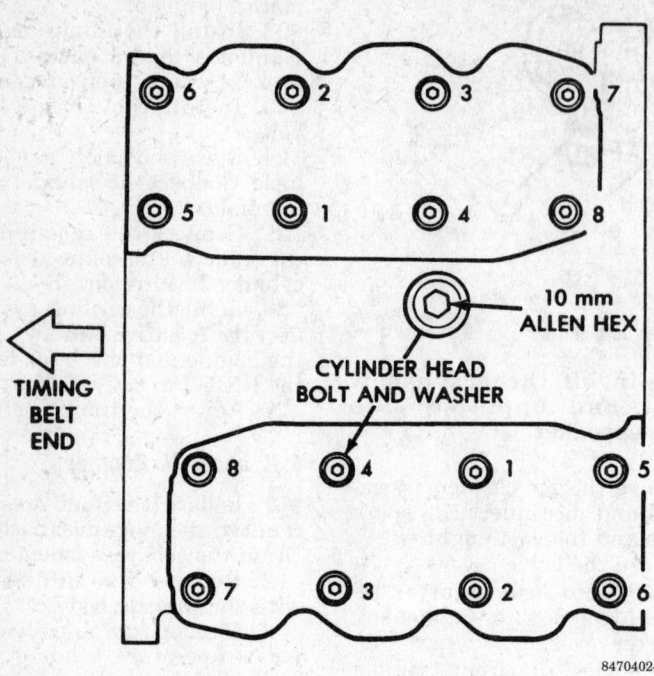

Cylinder head bolt torque sequence — 3.0L engine

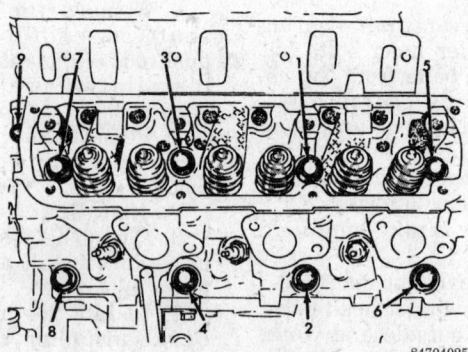

Cylinder head bolt torque sequence — 3.3L and 3.8L engines

12. Install the pushrods, rocker arms and shafts and torque the bolts to 21 ft. lbs. (28 Nm).

13. Place a drop of silicone sealer onto each of the 4 manifold to cylinder head gasket corners.

CAUTION
The intake manifold gasket is composed of very thin and sharp metal. Handle this gasket with care or damage to the gasket or personal injury could result.

14. Install the intake manifold gasket and torque the end retainers to 105 inch lbs. (12 Nm).

15. Install the intake manifold and torque the bolts in sequence to 10 inch lbs. Repeat the sequence increasing the torque to 17 ft. lbs. (23 Nm) and recheck each bolt for 17 ft. lbs. After the bolts are torqued, inspect the seals to ensure that they have not become dislodged.

16. Lubricate the injector O-rings with clean oil and position the fuel rail in place. Install the rail mounting bolts.

17. Install the valve cover with a new gasket. Install the exhaust manifold.

18. Install or connect all remaining items removed or disconnected during the removal procedure.

19. Refill the cooling system. Connect the negative battery cable. Start the engine and check for leaks using the DRB I or II to activate the fuel pump.

Valve Lifters

REMOVAL AND INSTALLATION

2.5L Engine

1. Disconnect the negative battery cable.

2. Remove the valve cover and curtain. If removing all lifters, remove the upper timing belt cover, camshaft and rocker arms.

3. If only removing 1 lifter, rotate the crankshaft until the low point of the desired cam lobe is contacting the rocker arm.

4. Using the special valve spring compressor tool 4682 or equivalent, depress the valve spring without dislodging the keepers and slide the rocker arm out.

5. Remove the valve lifter(s) from the bore(s).

To install:

6. Lubricate the lifter(s) and their bore(s) with clean engine oil.

7. Install the lifter(s) into the appropriate bore, keeping in the original location, and install the rocker arms.

8. Install the camshaft sprocket and timing belt upper cover, if removed.

9. Apply form-in-place Mopar Silicone Rubber Adhesive Sealant or equivalent gasket material to the rocker cover and replace both cover end seals.

10. Install to rocker cover to the engine and secure with the retainer bolts tightened to 105 inch lbs. (12 Nm).

11. Connect the negative battery cable and check the lifters for proper operation.

3.0L Engine

1. Disconnect the negative battery cable.

2. Remove the valve cover. Install lash adjuster retainer tools MD998443 or equivalent, to prevent the auto-lash adjuster from falling out of the rocker arm.

3. Remove the distributor adapter housing.

4. Rotate the engine clockwise and position at TDC compression stroke.

5. Remove the timing belt assembly.

6. Loosen rocker arm and shaft assembly evenly in several steps. Remove the rocker arm and shaft assembly as a complete unit.

7. Remove the lifters from the rocker arms. It is recommended that all lash adjusters and rockers be replaced as a complete set.

To install:

8. Immerse the lash adjusters in clean diesel fuel. Using a small wire, move the plunger of the lash adjuster up and down 4 or 5 times while pushing down lightly on the check ball in order to bleed out the air. Install the lash adjusters in the rocker arms.

9. Lubricate the camshaft and rocker shaft with heavy engine oil and position on the cylinder head.

10. Apply a drop of sealant to the rear edges of the end caps.

11. Install the assembly into the front bearing cap making sure the notches in the rocker shafts are facing up. Insert the installation bolt but do not tighten at this point.

12. Install the remaining cap bolts and tighten evenly and gradually to 15 ft. lbs. (20 Nm). Tighten the front cap retaining bolts to 17 ft. lbs. (24 Nm). Remove the lash adjuster retainers.

13. Install the distributor extension, if removed.

14. Install timing belt.

15. Install the valve cover with a new gasket and tighten to 4–5 ft. lbs. (5–7 Nm).

16. Connect the negative battery cable.

3.3L and 3.8L Engines

1. Disconnect the negative battery cable. Relieve the fuel pressure.

2. Remove the cylinder head(s) to gain access to the valve lifter(s).

3. Remove the yoke retainer and aligning yoke(s).

4. Use an appropriate valve lifter removal tool to remove each lifter from its bore. If reinstalling the tappets, identify each upon removal to ensure installation in the original position. Inspect each lifter and bore for scuffs, wear or damage.

NOTE: If the lifter or bore in the cylinder block is severely scored, it is possible to ream the bore to the next oversize and replace with the oversized tappet.

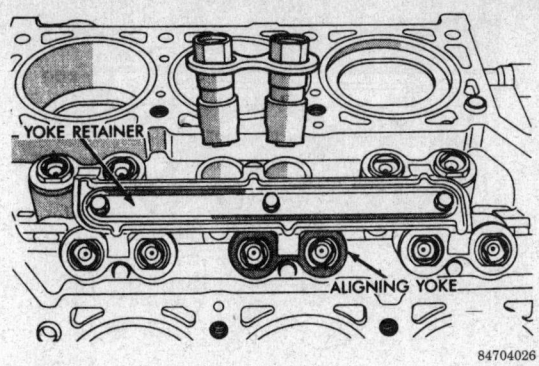

Aligning yoke and yoke retainer for roller lifters — 3.3L and 3.8L engines

To install:

5. Lubricate the lifter(s) and bore(s) and install.

6. Install aligning yoke(s).

7. Install the yoke retainer and torque the bolts to 105 inch lbs. (12 Nm).

8. Install the cylinder head(s) and all related components.

9. Connect the negative battery cable and check the lifters for proper operation.

Rocker Arms/Shafts

REMOVAL AND INSTALLATION

2.5L Engine

1. Disconnect the negative battery cable.

2. Remove the valve cover.

3. Rotate the crankshaft until the low point of the desired cam lobe is contacting the rocker arm.

4. Use special valve spring compressor tool C–4682A or equivalent, to depress the valve spring without dislodging the keepers, and slide the rocker arm out from under the camshaft.

5. The installation is the reverse of the removal procedure.

3.0L Engine

1. Disconnect the negative battery cable.

2. Remove the valve cover. Install lash adjuster retainer tools MD998443 or equivalent, to prevent the auto-lash adjuster from falling out of the rocker arm.

3. Remove the distributor adapter housing.

4. Rotate the engine clockwise and position at TDC compression stroke.

5. Remove the timing belt assembly.

6. Loosen rocker arm and shaft assembly evenly in several steps. Re-

move the rocker arm and shaft assembly as a complete unit.

To install:

7. Immerse the lash adjusters in clean diesel fuel. Using a small wire, move the plunger of the lash adjuster up and down 4 or 5 times while pushing down lightly on the check ball in order to bleed out the air. Install the lash adjusters in the rocker arms.

8. Lubricate the camshaft and rocker shaft with heavy engine oil and position on the cylinder head.

NOTE: Intake rocker shaft has an extra oil hole at the bottom side of shaft for identification

9. Apply a drop of sealant to the rear edges of the end caps.

10. Install the assembly into the front bearing cap making sure the notches in the rocker shafts are facing up. Insert the installation bolt but do not tighten at this point.

11. Install the remaining cap bolts and tighten evenly and gradually to 15 ft. lbs. (20 Nm). Tighten the front cap retaining bolts to 17 ft. lbs. (24 Nm). Remove the lash adjuster retainers.

12. Install the distributor extension, if removed.

13. Install timing belt.

14. Install the valve cover with a new gasket and tighten to 4–5 ft. lbs. (5–7 Nm).

15. Connect the negative battery cable.

3.3L and 3.8L Engines

1. Disconnect the negative battery cable.

2. Remove the upper intake manifold assembly and valve cover.

3. Remove the rocker shaft retaining bolts and retainers.

4. Remove the rocker shaft and arm assembly. Disassemble and repair as required.

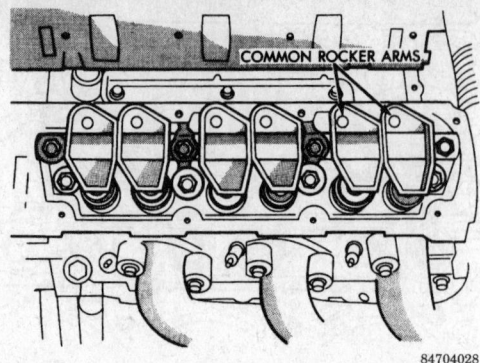

Rocker arm assembly — 3.3L and 3.8L engines

5. The installation is the reverse of the removal procedure. Torque the retaining bolts gradually and evenly to 21 ft. lbs. (28 Nm).

6. Allow 20 minutes tappet-bleed-down time after rocker shaft installation before starting the engine.

Intake Manifold

REMOVAL AND INSTALLATION

3.0L Engine

1. Disconnect the negative battery cable. Relieve the fuel system pressure.

2. Drain the cooling system.

3. Remove the throttle body to air cleaner hose.

4. Remove the throttle body and transaxle kickdown linkage.

5. Remove the AIS motor and TPS wiring connectors from the throttle body.

6. Remove and label the vacuum hose harness from the throttle body.

7. From the air intake plenum, remove the PCV and brake booster hoses and the EGR tube flange.

8. Disconnect and label the remaining electrical sensor connections at the intake manifold.

9. Remove the vacuum connections from the air intake plenum vacuum connector.

10. Remove the fuel hoses from the fuel rail. Always place a shop towel or cloth around the fitting or connection prior to loosening to absorb any excess fuel due to spillage.

11. Remove the air intake plenum mounting bolts and remove the plenum.

12. Remove the vacuum hoses from the fuel rail and pressure regulator.

13. Disconnect the fuel injector wiring harness from the engine wiring harness.

14. Remove the fuel pressure regulator mounting bolts and remove the regulator from the fuel rail.

15. Remove the fuel rail mounting bolts and remove the fuel rail from the intake manifold.

16. Separate the radiator hose from the thermostat housing and heater hoses from the heater pipe.

17. Remove the intake manifold mounting bolts and remove the manifold from the engine.

18. Clean the gasket mounting surfaces on the engine and intake manifold.

To install:

19. Using new gaskets, position the intake manifold on the engine and install the mounting nuts and washers.

20. Torque the mounting nuts gradually and evenly, in sequence, to 15 ft. lbs. (20 Nm).

21. Make sure the injector holes are clean. Lubricate the injector O-rings with clean engine oil and install the injector assembly onto the engine.

22. Install and torque the fuel rail mounting bolts to 10 ft. lbs. (14 Nm).

23. Install the fuel pressure regulator onto the fuel rail.

24. Install the fuel supply and return tube and the vacuum crossover hold-down bolt.

25. Connect the fuel injection wiring harness to the engine wiring harness.

26. Connect the vacuum harness to the fuel pressure regulator and fuel rail assembly.

27. Remove the cover from the lower intake manifold and clean the mating surface.

28. Place the intake plenum gasket with the beaded sealant side up, on the intake manifold. Install the air intake plenum and torque the mounting bolts gradually and evenly, in sequence, to 10 ft. lbs. (14 Nm).

29. Connect or install all remaining items that were disconnected or removed during the removal procedure.

30. Refill the cooling system. Connect the negative battery cable and check for leaks using the DRB II to activate the fuel pump.

3.3L and 3.8L Engines

1. Disconnect the negative battery cable. Relieve the fuel pressure. Drain the cooling system.

2. Remove the air cleaner to throttle body hose assembly.

3. Disconnect the throttle cable and remove the wiring harness from the bracket.

4. Remove AIS motor and TPS wiring connectors from the throttle body.

5. Remove the vacuum hose harness from the throttle body.

6. Remove the PCV and brake booster hoses from the air intake plenum.

7. Disconnect the charge temperature sensor electrical connector. Remove the vacuum harness connectors from the intake plenum.

8. Remove the cylinder head to the intake plenum strut.

9. Disconnect the MAP sensor and oxygen sensor connectors. Remove the engine mounted ground strap.

10. Remove the fuel hoses from the fuel rail and plug them. Always place

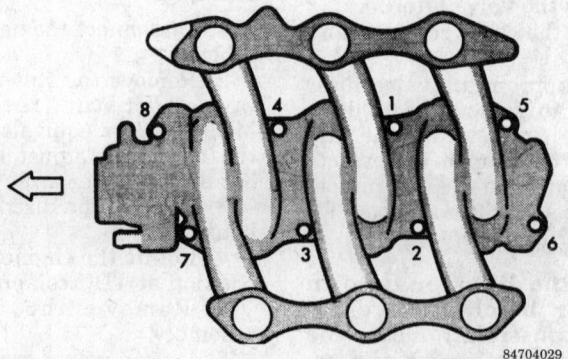

Intake manifold torque sequence — 3.0L engine

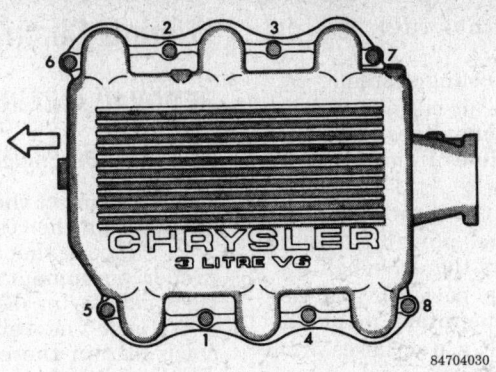

84704030

Intake plenum torque sequence — 3.0L engine

a shop towel or cloth around the fitting or connection prior to loosening to absorb any excess fuel due to spillage.

11. Remove the DIS coils and the alternator bracket to intake manifold bolt.

12. Remove the upper intake manifold attaching bolts and remove the upper manifold.

13. Remove the vacuum harness connector from the fuel pressure regulator.

14. Remove the fuel tube retainer bracket screw and fuel rail attaching bolts. Spread the retainer bracket to allow for clearance when removing the fuel tube.

15. Remove the fuel rail injector wiring clip from the alternator bracket.

16. Disconnect the cam sensor, coolant temperature sensor and engine temperature sensor.

17. Remove the fuel rail.

18. Remove the upper radiator hose, bypass hose and rear intake manifold hose.

19. Remove the intake manifold bolts and remove the manifold from the engine.

20. Remove the intake manifold seal retaining screws and remove the manifold gasket.

21. Clean out clogged end water passages and fuel runners.

To install:

22. Clean and dry all gasket mating surfaces.

23. Place a drop of silicone sealer onto each of the 4 manifold-to-cylinder head gasket corners.

24. Install the intake manifold gasket and torque the end retainers to 10 ft. lbs. (12 Nm).

25. Install the intake manifold and torque the bolts in sequence to 10 inch lbs. Repeat the sequence increasing the torque to 17 ft. lbs. (23 Nm) and recheck each bolt for 17 ft. lbs. of torque. After the bolts are torqued, inspect the seals to ensure that they have not become dislodged.

26. Lubricate the injector O-rings with clean oil and position the fuel rail in place. Install the rail mounting bolts.

27. Connect the cam sensor, coolant temperature sensor and engine temperature sensor.

28. Install the fuel rail injector wiring clip to the alternator bracket.

29. Install the fuel rail attaching bolts and fuel tube retainer bracket screw.

30. Install the vacuum harness to the pressure regulator.

31. Install the upper intake manifold with a new gasket. Install the bolts only finger-tight. Install the alternator bracket to intake manifold bolt and the cylinder head to intake manifold strut and bolts. Torque the intake manifold mounting bolts to 21 ft. lbs. (28 Nm) starting from the middle and working outward. Torque the bracket and strut bolts to 40 ft. lbs. (54 Nm).

32. Install or connect all items that were removed or disconnected from the intake manifold and throttle body.

33. Connect the fuel hoses to the rail. Push the fittings in until they click in place.

34. Install the air cleaner assembly.

35. Connect the negative battery cable and check for leaks using the DRB II to activate the fuel pump.

Exhaust Manifold

REMOVAL AND INSTALLATION

3.0L Engine

1. Disconnect the negative battery cable. Raise the vehicle and support safely.

2. Disconnect the exhaust pipe from the rear exhaust manifold at the articulated joint.

3. Disconnect the EGR tube from the rear manifold and unplug the oxygen sensor wire.

4. Remove the crossover pipe to manifold bolts.

5. Remove the rear manifold to cylinder head nuts and the manifold.

6. Lower the vehicle and remove the heat shield from the manifold.

7. Remove the front manifold to cylinder head nuts and the manifold.

8. Clean the gasket mounting surfaces. Inspect the manifolds for cracks, flatness and/or damage.

To install:

9. When installing, the numbers 1–3–5 on the gaskets are used with the rear cylinders and 2–4–6 are on the gasket for the front cylinders. Torque the manifold to cylinder head nuts to 14–17 ft. lbs. (19–23 Nm).

10. Install the crossover pipe to manifold.

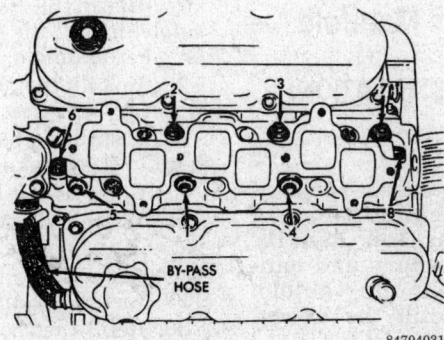

84704031

Intake manifold torque sequence — 3.3L and 3.8L engines

CAUTION

The intake manifold gasket is composed of very thin and sharp metal. Handle this gasket with care or damage to the gasket or personal injury could result.

11. Connect the EGR tube and oxygen sensor wire.

12. Connect the exhaust pipe to the rear exhaust manifold, at the articulated joint.

13. Connect the negative battery cable and check the manifolds for leaks.

3.3L and 3.8L Engines

1. Disconnect the negative battery cable.

2. If removing the rear manifold, raise the vehicle and support safely. Disconnect the exhaust pipe at the articulated joint from the rear exhaust manifold.

3. Separate the EGR tube from the rear manifold and disconnect the oxygen sensor wire.

4. Remove the alternator/power steering support strut.

5. Remove the bolts attaching the crossover pipe to the manifold.

6. Remove the bolts attaching the manifold to the head and remove the manifold.

7. If removing the front manifold, remove the heat shield, bolts attaching the crossover pipe to the manifold and the nuts attaching the manifold to the head.

8. Remove the manifold from the engine.

To install:

9. Install the manifold to the engine and secure using the mounting bolts and nuts tightened to 17 ft. lbs. (23 Nm). Install the heat shield, if removed.

10. Install the crossover pipe to the manifold.

11. Connect the EGR tube and oxygen sensor wire.

12. Connect the exhaust pipe to the rear exhaust manifold, at the articulated joint.

13. Connect the negative battery cable and check the manifolds for leaks.

Combination Manifold

REMOVAL AND INSTALLATION

2.5L Engine

NOTE: In some cases, some of the manifold attaching bolts are not accessible or too heavily sealed from the factory and cannot be removed on the vehicle. Head removal would be necessary in these situations.

1. Disconnect the negative battery cable.

2. Relieve the fuel system pressure.

3. Drain the cooling system.

4. Remove the air cleaner and disconnect all vacuum lines, electrical wiring and fuel lines from the throttle body.

5. Disconnect the throttle linkage.

6. Loosen the power steering pump and remove the drive belt.

7. Remove the power brake vacuum hose from the intake manifold.

8. Remove the water hoses from the water crossover.

9. Raise the vehicle and support safely.

10. Disconnect the exhaust pipe from the exhaust manifold.

11. Remove the power steering pump from its mounting bracket and set it aside. It is not necessary to remove the fluid lines.

12. Remove the EGR tube.

13. Remove the intake manifold bolts.

14. Lower the vehicle.

15. Remove the intake manifold.

16. Remove the exhaust manifold nuts.

17. Remove the exhaust manifold.

To install:

18. Install a new combination manifold gasket.

19. Install the exhaust manifold assembly. Install the mounting nuts and torque to 17 ft. lbs. (23 Nm.) starting from the middle and working outward. Install the heat cowl to the exhaust manifold.

20. Install the intake manifold. Torque the bolts to 17 ft. lbs. (23 Nm.) starting from the middle and working outward.

21. Install the EGR tube, if removed.

22. Install the intake support bracket, if equipped.

23. Install the power steering pump.

24. Raise the vehicle and support safely. Install the exhaust pipe to the exhaust manifold.

25. Install the water hoses to the water crossover.

26. Install the power brake vacuum hose to the intake manifold.

27. Connect the throttle linkage.

28. Install all vacuum lines, electrical wiring and fuel lines to the throttle body.

29. Install the air cleaner assembly.

30. Refill the cooling system.

31. Connect the negative battery cable and check the manifolds for leaks.

Timing Chain Front Cover

REMOVAL AND INSTALLATION

3.3L and 3.8L Engines

1. Disconnect the negative battery cable. Drain the cooling system.

2. Support the engine using the proper equipment and remove the right side motor mount.

3. Raise the vehicle and support safely. Drain the engine oil and remove the oil pan.

4. Remove the right wheel and splash shield.

5. Remove the drive belt.

6. Unbolt the air conditioning compressor and position it to the side. Remove the compressor mounting bracket.

7. Remove the crankshaft pulley bolt and remove the pulley using a puller.

8. Remove the idler pulley from the engine bracket and remove the bracket.

9. Remove the cam sensor from the timing chain cover.

10. Remove the cover mounting bolts and the cover from the engine. Make sure the oil pump inner rotor does not fall out. Remove the 3 O-rings from the coolant passages and the oil pump outlet.

To install:

11. Thoroughly clean and dry the gasket mating surfaces. Install new O-rings to the block.

12. Remove the crankshaft oil seal from the cover. The seal must be removed from the cover when installing to ensure proper oil pump engagement.

13. Using a new gasket, install the chain case cover to the engine.

14. Make certain the oil pump is engaged onto the crankshaft before proceeding or there will be no oil pressure. Install the attaching bolts and torque to 20 ft. lbs. (27 Nm).

15. Use tool C–4992 to install the crankshaft oil seal. Install the crankshaft pulley using a 5.9 in. bolt used with thrust bearing and washer plate L–4524. Make sure the pulley bottoms out on the inner diameter of the crankshaft seal. Install the bolt and torque to 40 ft. lbs. (54 Nm).

16. Install the engine bracket and torque the bolts to 40 ft. lbs. (54 Nm). Install the idler pulley to the engine bracket.

17. To install the cam sensor, perform the following:

   a. Clean off the old spacer from the sensor face completely. A new spacer must be attached to the cam

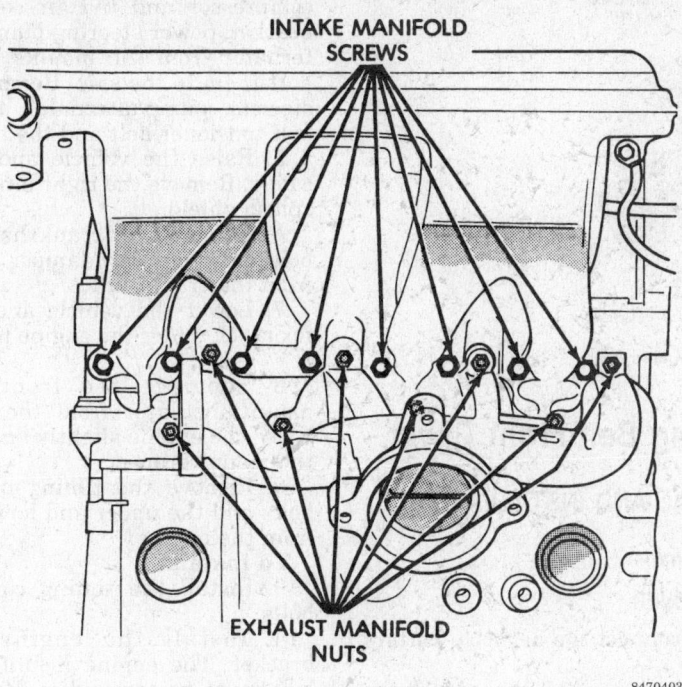

Intake and exhaust manifold attaching points — 2.5L engine

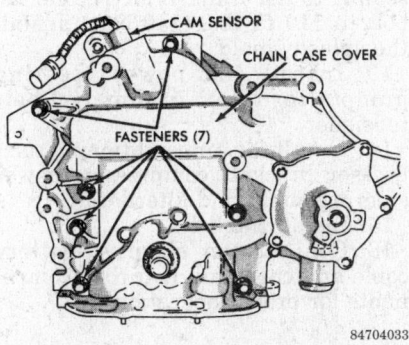

84704033

Timing chain cover — 3.3L and 3.8L engines

sensor prior to installation; if a new spacer is not used, engine performance will be adversely affected.

b. Inspect the O-ring for damage and replace, if necessary. Lubricate the O-ring lightly with oil and push the sensor into its bore in the chain case cover until contact is made with the cam timing gear. Hold in this position and tighten the bolt to 9 ft. lbs. (12 Nm).

18. Install the air conditioning compressor and bracket.

19. Install the drive belt.

20. Install the inner splash shield and wheel.

21. Install the oil pan with a new gasket.

22. Install the motor mount.

23. Remove the engine temperature sensor and fill the cooling system until the level reaches the vacant sensor hole. Install the sensor and continue to fill the radiator. Fill the engine with the proper amount of oil.

24. Connect the negative battery cable and check for leaks.

Front Cover Oil Seal

REPLACEMENT

3.3L and 3.8L Engines

1. Disconnect the negative battery cable.

2. Raise the vehicle and support safely. Remove the right front wheel and the inner splash shield.

3. Remove the drive belt.

4. Remove the crankshaft bolt. Using a puller, remove the crankshaft pulley.

5. Use tool C–4991 to remove the seal.

To install:

6. Clean out the bore. Place the seal with the spring toward the engine. Install the new seal using tool C–4992 until it is flush with the cover.

7. Lubricate the seal and install the crankshaft pulley using a 5.9 in. bolt with thrust bearing and washer plate L–4524. Make sure the pulley bottoms out on the inner diameter of the crankshaft seal. Install the bolt and torque to 40 ft. lbs. (54 Nm).

8. Install the drive belt.

9. Install the splash shield and wheel.

10. Connect the negative battery cable and check for leaks.

Timing Chain and Gears

REMOVAL AND INSTALLATION

3.3L and 3.8L Engines

1. If possible, position the engine so the No. 1 piston is at TDC of its compression stroke. Disconnect the negative battery cable. Drain the coolant.

2. Remove the timing chain case cover.

3. Remove the camshaft sprocket attaching bolt. Remove the camshaft sprocket and timing chain together.

4. Using the appropriate puller, remove the crankshaft sprocket taking care not to damage the crankshaft surface.

To install:

5. Position the new crankshaft sprocket onto the crankshaft using soft mallet and appropriate driver. Be sure to fully seat the sprocket in position.

6. If not already done, rotate the crankshaft so the timing mark is at the 12 o'clock position. Place the timing chain around the camshaft sprocket and place the timing mark to the 6 o'clock position.

7. Place the timing chain around the crankshaft sprocket and install the camshaft sprocket to the engine.

8. Using a straight-edge check the alignment of the timing marks.

9. Install the camshaft bolt and washer and tighten to 35 ft. lbs. (47 Nm).

10. Rotate the crankshaft 2 revolutions and check for proper alignment of the timing marks. If the marks do not align, remove the camshaft sprocket and realign.

11. Check the camshaft endplay. New thrust plate specifications are 0.005–0.012 in. or 0.012 in. for an old thrust plate. Replace the thrust plate if not within specifications.

12. Install the timing chain snubber and tighten the retainer screws to 105 inch lbs. (12 Nm).

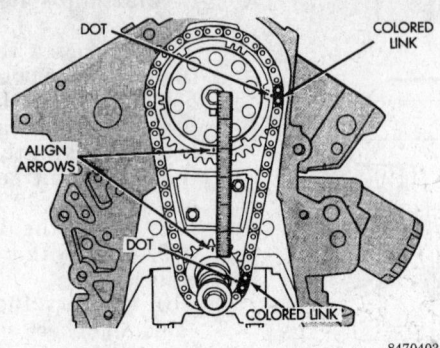

Alignment of timing chain marks — 3.3L and 3.8L engines

13. Thoroughly clean and dry the gasket mating surfaces.

14. Install new O-rings to the block.

15. Remove the crankshaft oil seal from the cover. The seal must be removed from the cover when installing to ensure proper oil pump engagement.

16. Using a new gasket, install the chain case cover to the engine.

17. Make certain that the oil pump is engaged onto the crankshaft before proceeding or severe engine damage will result. Install the attaching bolts and torque to 20 ft. lbs. (27 Nm).

18. Use tool C–4992 to install the crankshaft oil seal. Install the crankshaft pulley using a 5.9 in. suitable bolt and thrust bearing and washer plate L–4524. Make sure the pulley bottoms out on the crankshaft seal diameter. Install the bolt and torque to 40 ft. lbs. (54 Nm).

19. Install all other parts removed during the chain case cover removal procedure.

20. To install the cam sensor, first clean off the old spacer from the sensor face completely. Inspect the O-ring for damage and replace, if necessary. A new spacer must be attached to the cam sensor prior to installation; if a new spacer is not used, engine performance will be adversely affected. Oil the O-ring lightly and push the sensor into its bore in the chain case cover until contact is made with the cam timing gear. Hold in this position and tighten the bolt to 10 ft. lbs. (12 Nm).

21. Refill the cooling system and fill the engine with oil.

22. Connect the negative battery cable, road test the vehicle and check for leaks.

Timing Belt Front Cover

REMOVAL AND INSTALLATION

2.5L Engine

UPPER COVER

1. Disconnect the negative battery cable.

2. Remove the bolt that attach the upper cover to the valve cover.

3. Remove the nuts that attaches the upper cover to the lower cover.

4. Remove the upper cover by lifting upward. Guide the cover front inner lip past the timing belt and valve cover during removal.

5. Installation is the reverse of the removal procedure.

LOWER COVER

1. Disconnect the negative battery cable.

2. Remove the bolt that attaches the upper cover to the lower cover.

3. Raise the vehicle and support safely. Remove the right side splash shield.

4. Remove the crankshaft pulley, water pump pulley and drive belts.

5. Remove the lower cover attaching bolts and remove the lower cover.

6. The installation is the reverse of the removal procedure.

3.0L Engine

1. Disconnect the negative battery cable.

2. To remove the air conditioning compressor belt, loosen the adjustment pulley locknut, turn the screw counterclockwise to reduce the drive belt tension and remove the belt.

3. To remove the serpentine drive belt, insert a ½ in. breaker bar in to the square hole of the tensioner pulley, rotate it counterclockwise to reduce the drive belt tension and remove the belt.

4. Remove the air conditioning compressor and the air compressor bracket, power steering pump and alternator from the mounts and support them to the side. Remove power steering pump/alternator automatic belt tensioner bolt and the tensioner.

5. Raise the vehicle and support safely. Remove the right inner fender splash shield.

6. Remove the crankshaft pulley bolt and the pulley/damper assembly from the crankshaft.

7. Lower the vehicle and place a floor jack under the engine to support it.

8. Separate the front engine mount insulator from the bracket. Raise the engine slightly and remove the mount bracket.

9. Remove the timing belt cover bolts and the upper and lower covers from the engine.

To install:

10. Install the timing covers and bolts.

11. Install the engine mount bracket. The engine mount through bolt must be torqued to 100 ft. lbs. (136 Nm) with the engine support removed and the engine's weight on the mount.

12. Install the pulley damper assembly to the crankshaft. Torque the bolt to 110 ft. lbs. (149 Nm). Install the splash shield.

13. Install the power steering pump/alternator automatic belt tensioner.

14. Install the air conditioning compressor bracket, compressor, power steering pump and alternator.

15. Install the belts.

16. Connect the negative battery cable and check all disturbed components for proper operation.

Timing Belt and Tensioner

ADJUSTMENT

2.5L Engine

1. Disconnect the negative battery cable.

2. Raise the vehicle and support safely. Remove the right front inner splash shield.

3. Remove the tensioner cover.

4. Place the special tensioning tool C–4703 on the hex of the tensioner so the weight is at about the 10 o'clock position, then loosen the bolt.

5. The tensioner should drop to the 9 o'clock position. Reposition the tool as required in order to have it end up at the 9 o'clock position, par-

allel to the ground, hanging toward the rear of the vehicle, ± 15 degrees.

6. Hold the tool in position and tighten the bolt. Do not pull the tool past the 9 o'clock position or the belt will be too tight and will cause howling or possible breakage.

7. Install the cover and the splash shield.

3.0L Engine

1. Disconnect the negative battery cable.

2. Remove the timing belt covers.

3. Loosen the bolt that holds the timing belt tensioner in place.

4. Allow the spring only to pull the tensioner in automatically. Do not manually move the tensioner or the belt will be too tight.

5. Tighten the tensioner locking bolt.

6. Install the timing belt covers and all related parts.

REMOVAL AND INSTALLATION

2.5L Engine

1. If possible, position the engine so the No. 1 piston is at TDC of its compression stroke. Disconnect the negative battery cable.

2. Remove the timing belt covers. Loosen the timing belt tensioner retainer bolt, remove the belt from the tensioner and allow it to hang free.

3. Place a floor jack under the engine so the full weight of the engine is on the jack. Separate the right motor mount.

4. Remove the air conditioning compressor belt idler pulley, if equipped. Remove the air conditioning compressor and alternator from the solid mount bracket.

5. Remove the compressor/alternator mounting bracket from the engine.

6. Remove the timing belt from the camshaft and crankshaft sprockets.

To install:

7. Turn the crankshaft sprocket and intermediate shaft sprocket until the marks are in line. Make sure the elongated hole in the intermediate shaft is at the top side of the sprocket. Position a straight-edge across the timing marks using center of crankshaft and intermediate sprocket retainer bolt heads as a guide for straightness, and confirm alignment.

8. Turn the camshaft until the small hole in the sprocket is at the top and rows on the hub are in line with the camshaft cap to cylinder

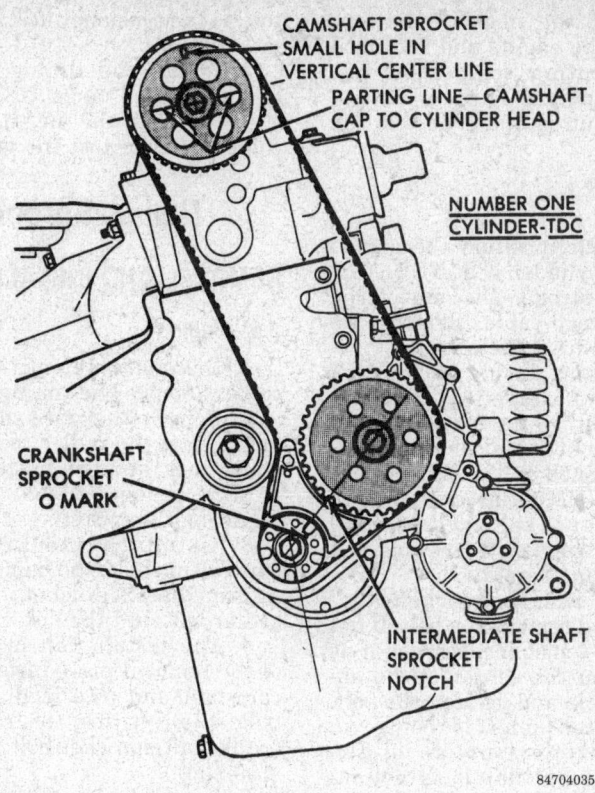

Timing belt alignment — 2.5L engine

head mounting lines. If necessary, use a mirror to see the alignment so it is viewed straight on and not at an angle from above. Install the belt around each timing sprocket in the approximate position of installation.

9. Install the air conditioning compressor/alternator bracket, idler pulley and motor mount. Remove the floor jack. Raise the vehicle and support safely. Have the tensioner at an arm's reach because the timing belt will have to be held in position with one hand.

10. To properly install the timing belt, reach up and position on the camshaft sprocket. Turn the intermediate shaft counterclockwise slightly (1–2 teeth), then engage the belt with the intermediate shaft sprocket. Hold the belt against the intermediate shaft sprocket and turn clockwise to take up all tension; if the timing marks are out of alignment, repeat until alignment is correct.

11. Using a wrench, turn the crankshaft sprocket counterclockwise slightly (1–2 teeth), and position belt on sprocket. Turn the sprocket clockwise so there is no slack in the belt between sprockets; if the timing marks between the crankshaft and the intermediate shaft or the timing marks on the camshaft sprocket are

out of alignment, repeat until alignment is correct.

NOTE: If the timing marks are in line but slack exists in the belt between either the camshaft and intermediate shaft sprockets or the intermediate and crankshaft sprockets, the timing will be incorrect when the belt is tensioned. All slack must only be between the crankshaft and camshaft sprockets at the rear of the engine.

12. Install the tensioner, if removed, and install the mounting bolt loosely. Place the special tensioning tool C–4703 on the hex of the tensioner so the weight is at about the 9 o'clock position, parallel to the ground, hanging toward the rear of the vehicle, ± 15 degrees.

13. Hold the tool in position and tighten the bolt to 45 ft. lbs. (61 Nm). Do not pull the tool past the 9 o'clock position; this will make the belt too tight and will cause it to howl or possibly break.

14. Lower the vehicle and recheck all timing sprockets to assure correct alignment. If correct, install the timing belt covers, crankshaft pulleys and the remaining components removed.

15. Connect the negative battery cable. Start the engine and run until normal operating temperature is reached. Check the ignition timing, adjust as required and road test the vehicle.

3.0L Engine

1. If possible, position the engine so the No. 1 cylinder is at TDC of its compression stroke. Disconnect the negative battery cable. Remove the timing covers from the engine.

2. If the same timing belt will be reused, mark the direction of the timing belt's rotation, for installation in the same direction. Make sure the engine is positioned so the No. 1 cylinder is at the TDC of its compression stroke and the sprockets timing marks are aligned with the engine's timing mark indicators.

3. Loosen the timing belt tensioner bolt and remove the belt. If not removing the tensioner, position it as far away from the center of the engine as possible and tighten the bolt.

4. If the tensioner is being removed, paint the outside of the spring to ensure that it is not installed backwards. Unbolt the tensioner and remove it along with the spring.

To install:

5. Install the tensioner, if removed, and hook the upper end of the spring to the water pump pin and the lower end to the tensioner in exactly the same position as originally installed. If not already done, position both camshafts so the marks align with those on the alternator bracket (rear bank) and inner timing cover (front bank). Rotate the crankshaft so the timing mark aligns with the mark on the oil pump.

6. Install the timing belt on the crankshaft sprocket and while keeping the belt tight on the tension side (right side), install the belt on the front camshaft sprocket.

7. Install the belt on the water pump pulley, then the rear camshaft sprocket and the camshaft.

8. Rotate the front camshaft counterclockwise to tension the belt between the front camshaft and the crankshaft. If the timing marks became misaligned, repeat the procedure.

9. Install the crankshaft sprocket flange.

10. Loosen the tensioner bolt and allow the spring to tension the belt.

11. Turn the crankshaft 2 full turns in the clockwise direction only until the timing marks align again. Now that the belt is properly tensioned,

torque the tensioner lock bolt to 21 ft. lbs. (29 Nm).

12. Install the timing belt covers and all related parts.

13. Connect the negative battery cable and road test the vehicle.

Timing Sprockets

REMOVAL AND INSTALLATION

2.5L Engine

1. Disconnect the negative battery cable. Remove the timing belt.

2. Remove the crankshaft sprocket bolt. Using the puller tool C–4685 or equivalent, and the button from tool L–4524 or equivalent, remove the crankshaft sprocket.

3. Using the tool C–4687 or equivalent, hold the camshaft and/or intermediate sprocket, remove the center bolt and the sprocket(s).

4. The installation is the reverse of the removal procedure. Torque the camshaft and intermediate sprocket bolts to 65 ft. lbs. (88 Nm) and the crankshaft sprocket bolt to 85 ft. lbs. (115 Nm).

5. Connect the negative battery cable and road test the vehicle.

3.0L Engine

1. Disconnect the negative battery cable.

2. Remove the timing belt.

3. To remove the camshaft sprocket, hold the sprocket with tool MB990775 or equivalent, and remove the retaining bolt and washer.

4. To remove the crankshaft sprocket, remove the bolt and remove the sprocket from the crankshaft.

5. The installation is the reverse of the removal procedure. Torque the camshaft sprocket bolt to 70 ft. lbs. (95 Nm) while holding the sprocket with the holding tool. Torque the crankshaft sprocket bolt. to 112 ft. lbs. (151 Nm).

6. Connect the negative battery cable and road test the vehicle.

Camshaft

REMOVAL AND INSTALLATION

2.5L Engine

1. Disconnect the negative battery cable.

2. Turn the crankshaft so the No. 1 piston is at the TDC of its compression stroke. Remove the upper timing belt cover.

3. Remove the valve cover.

4. Remove the camshaft sprocket bolt and the sprocket from the end of the camshaft, taking care not to allow the timing belt to loosen. Suspend the camshaft timing sprocket, with the belt in place tightly so the belt does not lose tension. If it does, the belt timing will have to be reset.

5. If the rocker arms are being reused, mark them so they can be installed in the same position and loosen the camshaft bearing bolts, evenly and gradually.

6. Using a soft mallet, tap the rear of the camshaft a few times to break the bearing caps loose.

7. Remove the bolts, bearing caps and the camshaft with seals. Keep bearing caps in same orientation during removal so they can be installed in the exact location on assembly.

NOTE: Take note of the color of the paint stripe on the rear camshaft seal. These stripes differentiate seal sizes. If a seal with a different color stripe is installed, a severe leak will develop if the seal is too small or the cap will not be able to be fully installed if the seal is too big. Also, oversized components can be identified as follows: the top of the bearing caps are painted green and "O/SJ" is stamped behind the oil galley plug on the end of the head. The barrel of an oversized camshaft is also painted green and "O/SJ" is stamped on the end of the shaft. If normal sized parts are installed in place of oversized ones, oil pressure will be significantly reduced.

8. Check the oil passages for blockages and all parts for wear and damage and replace parts as required. Clean the gasket mounting surfaces.

To install:

9. Transfer the camshaft sprocket key to the new camshaft. New rocker arms and a new camshaft sprocket bolt are normally included with the camshaft package. Install the rocker arms, lubricate the camshaft journals and lobes with clean engine oil and install on the cylinder head.

NOTE: Apply RTV silicone gasket material to the No. 1 and 5 bearing caps. Install the bearing caps before the seals are installed.

10. Install the bearing caps in the same orientation as prior to removal. The bearing cap with No. 1 should be at the timing belt end and No. 5 at the transaxle end. The camshaft

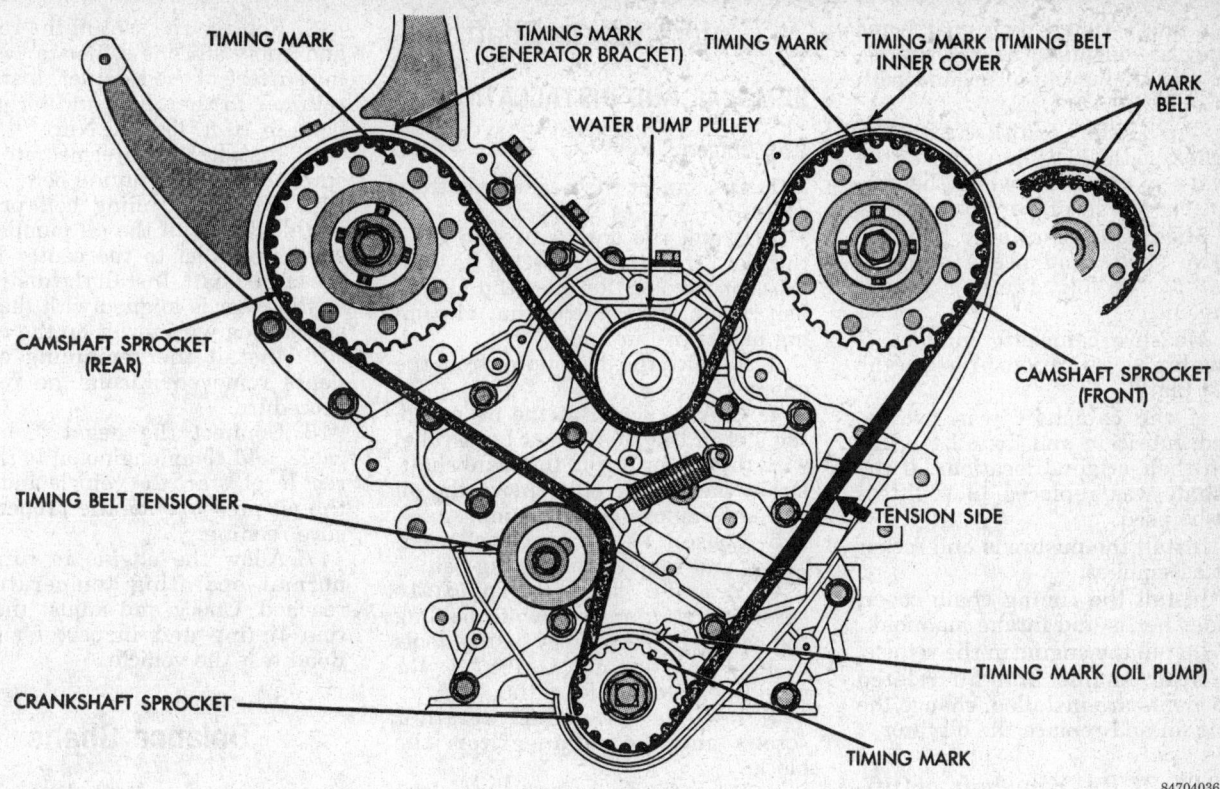

Timing belt alignment — 3.0L engine

bearing caps are numbered and have arrows facing forward. Torque the camshaft bearing bolts evenly and gradually to 18 ft. lbs. (24 Nm).

11. Mount a dial indicator to the front of the engine and check the camshaft endplay. Play should not exceed 0.020 in.

12. Install the front and the rear camshaft end seals into position in the bearing caps using the appropriate driver. Make sure the correct size seals are used or oil leakage will result.

13. Install the camshaft sprocket and belt to the camshaft using the new bolt.

14. Apply form-in-place Mopar Silicone Rubber Adhesive Sealant or equivalent gasket material to the rocker cover and replace both cover end seals.

15. Install to rocker cover to the engine and secure with the retainer bolts tightened to 105 inch lbs. (12 Nm).

16. Connect the negative battery cable and check for leaks.

3.0L Engine

1. Disconnect the negative battery cable. Remove the air cleaner assembly and valve covers.

2. Install auto lash adjuster retainer tools MD998443 or equivalent on the rocker arms.

3. If removing the right side (front) camshaft, remove the distributor extension.

4. Remove the camshaft bearing caps but do not remove the bolts from the caps.

5. Remove the rocker arms, rocker shafts and bearing caps, as an assembly.

6. Remove the camshaft from the cylinder head.

7. Inspect the bearing journals on the camshaft, cylinder head and bearing caps.

To install:

8. Lubricate the camshaft journals and camshaft with clean engine oil and install the camshaft in the cylinder head.

9. Align the camshaft bearing caps with the arrow mark depending on cylinder numbers and install in numerical order.

10. Apply sealer at the ends of the bearing caps and install the assembly.

11. Torque the bearing cap bolts, in the following sequence: No. 3, No. 2, No. 1 and No. 4 to 85 inch lbs. (10 Nm).

12. Repeat the sequence increasing the torque to 175 inch lbs. (18 Nm).

13. Install the distributor extension, if removed.

14. Install the valve cover and all related components.

15. Connect the negative battery cable and road test the vehicle.

3.3L and 3.8L Engines

1. Relieve the fuel pressure. Disconnect the negative battery cable.

2. Remove the engine from the vehicle. Remove the intake manifold, cylinder heads, timing chain cover and timing chain from the engine.

3. Remove the rocker arm and shaft assemblies.

4. Label and remove the pushrods and lifters.

5. Remove the camshaft thrust plate.

6. Install a long bolt into the front of the camshaft to facilitate its removal. Remove the camshaft being careful not to damage the cam bearings with the cam lobes.

To install:

7. Install the camshaft to within 2 in. of its final installation position.

8. Install the camshaft thrust plate and 2 bolts and torque to 10 ft. lbs. (12 Nm).

9. Place both camshaft and crankshaft gears on the bench with the timing marks on the exact imaginary

center line through both gear bores as they are installed on the engine. Place the timing chain around both sprockets.

10. Turn the crankshaft and camshaft so the keys line up with the keyways in the gears when the timing marks are in proper position.

11. Slide both gears over their respective shafts and use a straight-edge to check timing mark alignment.

12. Measure camshaft endplay. If not within specifications, replace the thrust plate.

13. If the camshaft was not replaced, lubricate and install the lifters in their original locations. If the camshaft was replaced, new lifters must be used.

14. Install the pushrods and rocker shaft assemblies.

15. Install the timing chain cover, cylinder heads and intake manifold.

16. Install the engine in the vehicle.

17. After engine and all related components are installed, change the engine oil and replace the oil filter.

NOTE: If the camshaft or lifters have been replaced, add 1 pint of Mopar crankcase conditioner or equivalent, when replenishing the oil to aid break in. This mixture should be left in the engine for a minimum of 500 miles and drained at the next normal oil change.

18. Fill the radiator with coolant.

19. Connect the negative battery cable, set all adjustments to specifications and check for leaks.

Intermediate Shaft

REMOVAL AND INSTALLATION

2.5L Engine

1. Disconnect the negative battery cable.

2. Crank the engine around until the No. 1 piston is at TDC of its compression stroke. Remove the timing belt covers and confirm that all timing marks are in line.

3. Remove the distributor from the engine.

4. Looking down at the oil pump, the slot in the shaft must be parallel with the center line of the crankshaft. Drain the engine oil, remove the oil pan and remove the oil pump.

5. Loosen the timing belt tensioner and remove the timing belt.

6. Remove the intermediate sprocket retainer bolt while holding the sprocket stationary using tools C–4687 and adapter C–4687–1. Remove the sprocket from the shaft.

7. Remove the shaft retainer screws and the retainer from the block.

8. Remove the intermediate shaft from the engine.

9. If necessary, remove the front bushing using tool C–4697–2 and the rear bushing using tool C–4686–2.

To install:

10. Install the front bushing using tool C–4697–1 until the tool is flush with the block. Install the rear bushing using tool C–4686–1 until the tool is flush with the block.

11. Lubricate the distributor drive gear and install the intermediate shaft into the block.

12. Replace the seal in the retainer and apply silicone sealer to the mating surface of the retainer. Install the retainer to the block and torque the bolts to 10 ft. lbs. (12 Nm).

13. Install the intermediate shaft sprocket and the timing belt.

14. With the timing belt properly installed, install the oil pump so the slot is parallel to the center line of the crankshaft. Install the distributor so the rotor is aligned with the No. 1 spark plug wire tower on the cap.

15. Install the remaining components removed during the removal procedure.

16. Connect the negative battery cable, add clean engine oil to the correct level, start the vehicle and check the oil pressure for the proper pressure reading.

17. Allow the engine to run until normal operating temperature is reached. Check and adjust the ignition timing and inspect for leaks. Road test the vehicle.

Balance Shafts

REMOVAL AND INSTALLATION

2.5L Engine

1. Disconnect the negative battery cable. Raise the vehicle and support safely.

2. Remove the timing belt. Remove the oil pan, the oil pickup, the crankshaft belt sprocket and the front crankshaft oil seal retainer.

3. Remove the balance shaft chain cover, the guide and the tensioner.

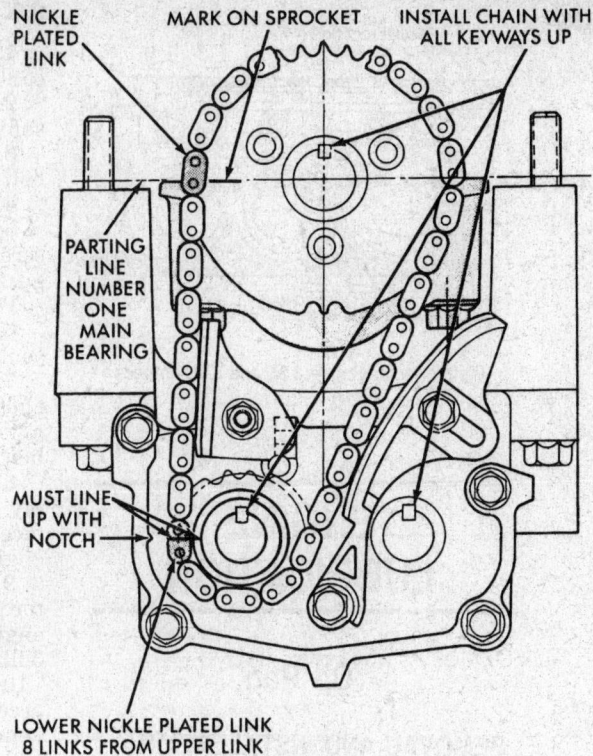

Balance shaft chain alignment — 2.5L engine

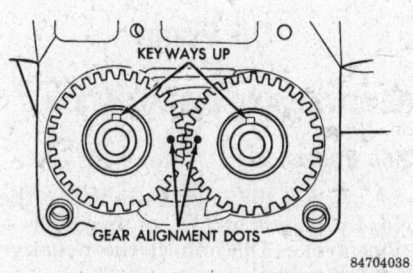

Balance shaft gear alignment — 2.5L engine

4. Remove the balance shaft sprocket-to-shaft bolt, the gear cover-to-balance shaft bolt and the crankshaft sprocket-to-crankshaft bolts, then the sprockets with the balance shaft chain.

5. Remove the front gear cover-to-carrier housing stud, the gear cover and the balance shaft drive gears.

6. Remove the rear gear cover-to-carrier housing bolts, the rear cover and the balance shafts from the rear of the carrier.

7. If necessary, remove the carrier housing-to-crankcase bolts and the housing.

To install:

8. If the carrier housing is being installed, torque the carrier housing-to-crankcase bolts to 40 ft. lbs. (54 Nm).

9. Rotate the balance shafts until the keyways are facing upward, parallel to the vertical centerline of the engine.

10. Install the short hub gear on the sprocket driven shaft and the long hub gear on the gear driven shaft; make sure the gear timing marks are aligned facing each other.

11. Install the front gear cover and torque the front gear cover-to-carrier housing stud bolt to 8.5 ft. lbs. (12 Nm).

12. Install the balance chain sprocket and torque the sprocket-to-crankshaft bolts to 11 ft. lbs. (13 Nm).

13. Rotate the crankshaft to position the No. 1 cylinder on the TDC of its compression stroke; the timing marks on the chain sprocket should align with the parting line on the left side of the No. 1 main bearing cap.

14. Position the balance shaft sprocket into the balance chain so the sprocket (yellow dot) timing mark mates with the yellow link on the chain.

15. Install the balance chain/sprocket assembly onto the crankshaft and the balance shaft. Torque the sprocket-to-shaft bolts to 21 ft. lbs. (28 Nm). If necessary to secure the crankshaft while tightening the bolts, place a block of wood between the crankcase and the crankshaft counterbalance.

16. Loosely install the chain tensioners and place a shim between the chain and the tensioner. In order to reduce the chain slack, apply firm pressure to the tensioner shoe. Torque the tensioner-to-front gear cover bolts to 8.5 ft. lbs. (12 Nm).

17. Install the chain cover and the rear cover to the carrier housing and torque the bolts to 8.5 ft. lbs. (12 Nm).

18. Replace the crankshaft retainer seal, apply silicone sealer to the mating surface and install the retainer.

19. Install the oil pickup and oil pan.

20. Install the crankshaft sprocket and the timing belt.

21. Add clean engine oil to fill the crankcase to the proper level. Connect the negative battery cable, start the vehicle and check for proper oil pressure. Allow the engine to idle until normal operating temperature is reached. Check and adjust the ignition timing as required. Road test the vehicle.

Piston and Connecting Rod

POSITIONING

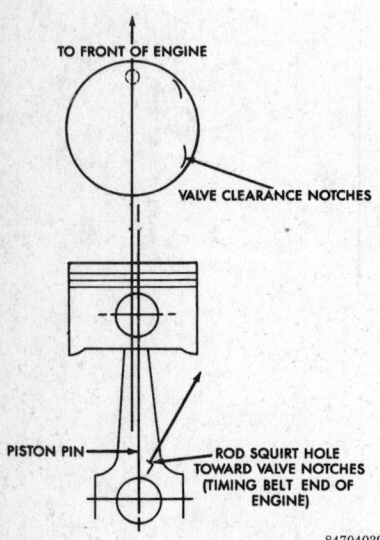

Piston positioning — 2.5L engine

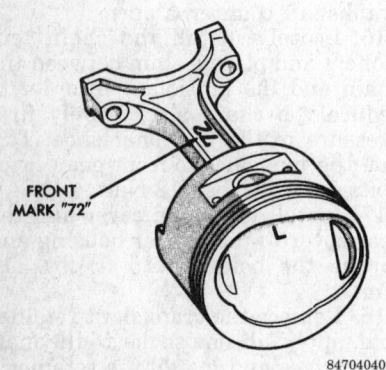

Piston positioning — 3.0L engine

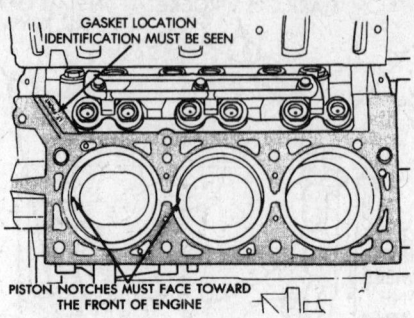

Piston positioning — 3.3L and 3.8L engines

ENGINE LUBRICATION

Oil Pan

REMOVAL AND INSTALLATION

2.5L Engine

1. Disconnect the negative battery cable. Remove the oil dipstick.
2. Raise the vehicle and support safely.
3. Drain the engine oil.
4. Remove the engine to transaxle struts, if equipped.
5. Remove the torque converter or clutch inspection cover.
6. Remove the oil pan retaining screws, oil pan and side seals.
To install:
7. Thoroughly clean and dry all sealing surfaces, bolts and bolt holes.
8. Apply silicone sealer to the 4 end seal-to-block corners and install the end seals making sure the corners are not twisted.
9. Apply silicone to the 4 pan-to-block corners. Install a new pan gasket or apply silicone sealer to the sealing surface of the pan and install to the engine making sure not to dislodge the end seals.
10. Install the retaining screws and torque the M8 bolts to to 17 ft. lbs. (23 Nm) and tighten the one M6 bolt to 9 ft. lbs. (12 Nm).
11. Install the torque converter inspection cover and engine to transaxle struts, if equipped. Lower the vehicle.
12. Install the dipstick. Fill the engine with the proper amount of oil.
13. Connect the negative battery cable and check for leaks.

3.0L, 3.3L and 3.8L Engines

1. Disconnect the negative battery cable.
2. Raise the vehicle and support safely.
3. Remove the torque converter bolt access cover.
4. Drain the engine oil.
5. Remove the oil pan retaining screws and remove the oil pan and gasket.
To install:
6. Thoroughly clean and dry all sealing surfaces, bolts and bolt holes.
7. Apply silicone sealer to the chain cover-to-block mating seam and the rear main seal retainer-to-block seam, if equipped.
8. Install a new pan gasket or apply silicone sealer to the sealing surface of the pan, and install to the engine.
9. Install the retaining screws and torque to 50 inch lbs. (6 Nm) for 3.0L engines or 200 inch lbs. (23 Nm) for 3.3L and 3.8L engines.
10. Install the torque converter bolt access cover, if equipped. Lower the vehicle.
11. Install the dipstick. Fill the engine with the proper amount of clean engine oil.
12. Connect the negative battery cable and check for leaks.

Oil Pump

REMOVAL AND INSTALLATION

2.5L Engine

1. Crank the engine around so the No. 1 piston is at TDC of its compression stroke. Disconnect the negative battery cable.
2. Matchmark the rotor to the block and remove the distributor. Confirm that the slot in the oil pump shaft is parallel to the centerline of the crankshaft. Matchmark the slot to the distributor bore, if desired.
3. Remove the oil dipstick. Raise the vehicle and support safely. Drain the engine oil and remove the pan.
4. Remove the oil pickup.
5. Remove the 2 mounting bolts and remove the oil pump from the engine.
To install:
6. Prime the pump by pouring fresh oil into the pump intake and turning the driveshaft until oil comes out the pressure port. Repeat a few times until no air bubbles are present.
7. Apply Loctite® 515 or equivalent, to the pump body-to-block

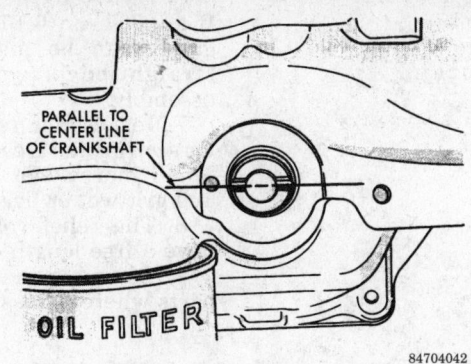

Oil pump shaft alignment — 2.5L engine

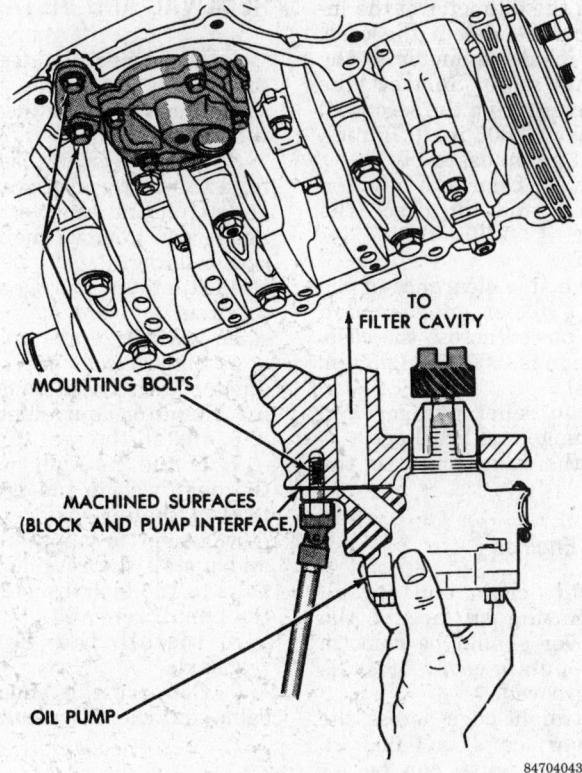

Oil pump installation — 2.5L engine

machined surface interface. Lubricate the oil pump and distributor driveshaft.

8. Align the slot so it will be in the same position as when it was removed. If it is not, the distributor will not be timed correctly. Install the pump fully and rotate back and forth to ensure proper positioning between the pump mounting surface and the machined surface of the block.

9. Install the mounting bolts finger-tight and lower the vehicle to confirm proper slot positioning. If the slot is not properly positioned, raise the vehicle and move the gear, as required. If the slot is correct, hold the

pump firmly against the block and torque the mounting bolts to 17 ft. lbs. (23 Nm).

10. Clean out the oil pickup or replace if necessary. Replace the oil pickup O-ring and install the pickup to the pump.

11. Install the oil pan using new gaskets. Lower the vehicle.

12. Install the distributor.

13. Install the dipstick. Add clean engine oil to fill the crankcase to the proper level.

14. Connect the negative battery cable, start the vehicle and check for proper oil pressure. Allow the engine to idle until normal operating tem-

perature is reached. Check and adjust the ignition timing as required. Road test the vehicle.

3.0L Engine

NOTE: The oil pump assembly is located within the front cover.

1. Disconnect the negative battery cable. Remove the dipstick.

2. Raise the vehicle and support safely. Remove the timing belt, drain the engine oil and remove the oil pan from the engine. Remove the oil pickup.

3. Remove the oil pump mounting bolts and remove the pump from the front of the engine. Note the different length bolts and their position in the pump for installation.

To install:

4. Clean the gasket mounting surfaces of the pump and engine block.

5. Prime the pump by pouring fresh oil into the pump and turning the rotors. Using a new gasket, install the oil pump on the engine and torque all bolts to 130 inch lbs. (15 Nm).

6. Install the balancer and crankshaft sprocket to the end of the crankshaft.

7. Clean out the oil pickup or replace, if necessary. Replace the oil pickup gasket ring and install the pickup to the pump.

8. Install the timing belt, oil pan and all related parts.

9. Install the dipstick. Fill the engine with the proper amount of oil.

10. Connect the negative battery cable and check the oil pressure.

3.3L and 3.8L Engines

NOTE: The oil pump assembly is located within the front timing chain cover.

1. Disconnect the negative battery cable. Remove the dipstick.

2. Raise the vehicle and support safely. Drain the oil and remove the oil pan.

3. Remove the oil pickup.

4. Remove the chain case cover.

5. Disassemble the oil pump and remove its components from the block.

To install:

6. Assemble the pump. Torque the rotor cover screws to 105 inch lbs. (12 Nm).

7. Prime the oil pump by filling the rotor cavity with fresh oil and turning the rotors until oil comes out the pressure port. Repeat a few times until no air bubbles are present.

8. Install the chain case cover and tighten bolts to 20 ft. lbs. (27 Nm).

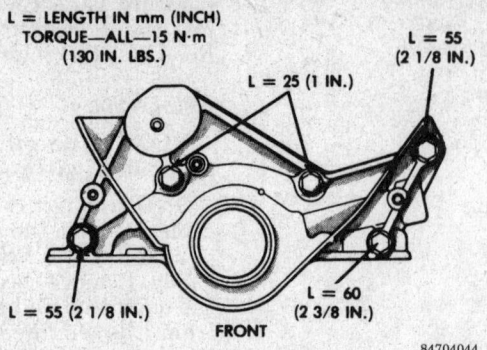

L = LENGTH IN mm (INCH)
TORQUE—ALL—15 N·m
(130 IN. LBS.)

L = 25 (1 IN.)

L = 55
(2 1/8 IN.)

L = 55 (2 1/8 IN.)

L = 60
(2 3/8 IN.)

FRONT

84704044

Oil pump assembly — 3.0L engine

9. Clean out the oil pickup or replace, if necessary. Replace the oil pickup O-ring and install the pickup to the pump. Tighten pickup mounting bolt to 250 inch lbs. (28 Nm).

10. Install the oil pan.

11. Install the dipstick. Fill the engine with the proper amount of oil.

12. Connect the negative battery cable and check the oil pressure.

CHECKING

2.5L Engine

1. Remove the cover from the oil pump.

2. Check endplay of the inner rotor using a feeler gauge and a straight-edge placed across the pump body. The specification is 0.001–0.004 in. (0.03–0.09mm).

3. Measure the clearance between the inner and outer rotors. The maximum clearance is 0.008 in. (0.20mm).

4. Measure the clearance between the outer rotor and the pump body. The maximum clearance is 0.014 in. (0.35mm).

5. The minimum thickness of the outer rotor is 0.944 in. (23.96mm). The minimum diameter of the outer rotor is 2.77 in. (62.70mm). The minimum thickness of the inner rotor is 0.943 in. (23.95mm).

6. Check the cover for warpage. The maximum allowable is 0.003 in. (0.076mm).

7. Check the pressure relief valve for damage. The spring's free length specification is 1.95 in. (49.50mm).

8. Assemble the outer rotor with the larger chamfered edge in the pump body. Torque the cover screws to 10 ft. lbs. (12 Nm).

3.0L Engine

1. Remove the rear cover.

2. Remove the pump rotors and inspect the case for excessive wear.

3. Measure the diameter of the inner rotor hub that sits in the case. Measure the inside diameter of the inner rotor hub bore. Subtract the first measurement from the second; if the result is over 0.006 in. (0.15mm), replace the oil pump assembly.

4. Measure the clearance between the outer rotor and the case. The specification is 0.004–0.007 in. (0.10–0.18mm).

5. Check the side clearance of the rotors using a feeler gauge and a straight-edge placed across the case. The specification is 0.0015–0.0035 in. (0.04–0.09mm).

6. Check the relief plunger and spring for damage and breakage.

7. Install the rear cover to the case.

3.3L and 3.8L Engines

1. Thoroughly clean and dry all parts. The mating surface of the chain case cover should be smooth. Replace the pump cover if it is scratched or grooved.

2. Lay a straight-edge across the pump cover surface. If a 0.003 in. (0.076mm) feeler gauge can be inserted between the cover and straight-edge, the cover should be replaced.

3. The minimum thickness of either rotor is 0.301 in. (7.63mm). The minimum diameter of the outer rotor is 3.14 in. (79.78mm).

4. Install the outer rotor onto the chain case cover, press to one side and measure the clearance between the rotor and case. If the measurement exceeds 0.022 in. (56mm) and the rotor is good, replace the chain case cover.

5. Install the inner rotor to the chain case cover and measure the clearance between the rotors. If the clearance exceeds 0.008 in. (0.203mm), replace both rotors.

6. Place a straight-edge over the chain case cover between bolt holes.

If a 0.004 in. (0.102mm) thick feeler gauge can be inserted under the straight-edge, replace the pump assembly.

7. Inspect the relief valve plunger for scoring and freedom of movement. Small marks may be removed with 400 grit wet or dry sandpaper.

8. The relief valve spring should have a free length of 1.95 in.

9. Assemble the pump using new parts where necessary.

Rear Main Bearing Oil Seal

REMOVAL AND INSTALLATION

1. Disconnect the negative battery cable.

2. Remove the transaxle. Remove the flexplate.

3. If there is any leakage coming from the rear seal retainer, drain the engine oil and remove the oil pan, if necessary. Remove the rear main oil seal retainer.

4. Remove the seal from the retainer.

To install:

5. Lightly coat the seal outer diameter with Loctite® Stud N' Bearing Mount or equivalent.

6. Install the seal to the retainer.

7. If the retainer was removed, thoroughly clean and dry the retainer to block sealing surfaces and install a new gasket or apply silicone sealer and install the retainer and tighten bolts to 105 inch lbs. (12 Nm). Install the pan, if removed.

8. Install the flexplate and transaxle.

9. Connect the negative battery cable and check for leaks.

AUTOMATIC TRANSAXLE

Transaxle Assembly

REMOVAL AND INSTALLATION

NOTE: If the vehicle is going to be rolled while the transaxle is out of the vehicle, obtain 2 outer CV-joints to install to the hubs. If the vehicle is rolled without the proper torque applied to the front wheel bearings, the bearings will no longer be usable.

1. Disconnect the negative battery cable. Drain the coolant. Remove the transaxle fluid dipstick.

2. Remove the air cleaner assembly if it is preventing access to the upper bellhousing bolts. Remove the upper bellhousing bolts and water tube, where applicable. Unplug all electrical connectors from the transaxle.

3. If equipped with 2.5L engine, remove the upper starter attaching nut and bolt at the top of the bellhousing.

4. Raise the vehicle and support safely. Remove the wheels. Remove the axle end cotter pins, nut locks, spring washers and axle nuts.

5. Remove the speedometer cable adaptor bolt and remove the adaptor from the transaxle extension housing.

6. Remove the ball joint retaining bolts and pry the control arm from the steering knuckle.

7. Position a drainpan under the transaxle where the axles enter the differential or extension housing. Remove the axles from the transaxle or center bearing. Unbolt the center bearing and remove the intermediate axle from the transaxle, if equipped.

8. Drain the transaxle. Disconnect and plug the fluid cooler hoses. Disconnect the shifter and kickdown linkage from the transaxle, if equipped.

9. Remove the starter. Remove the torque converter inspection cover, matchmark the torque converter to the flexplate and remove the torque converter bolts.

10. Using the proper equipment, support the weight of the engine.

11. Remove the front motor mount and bracket.

12. Position a transaxle jack under the transaxle and remove the lower bellhousing bolts.

13. Remove the left side splash shield. Remove the transaxle mount bolts.

14. Carefully pry the transaxle from the engine.

15. Slide the transaxle rearward until the dowels disengage from the mating holes in the transaxle case.

16. Pull the transaxle completely away from the engine and remove it from the vehicle.

17. To prepare the vehicle for rolling, support the engine with a support or reinstall the front motor mount to the engine. Then reinstall the ball joints to the steering knuckle and install the retaining bolt. Install the obtained outer CV-joints to the hubs, install the washers and torque

the axle nuts to 180 ft. lbs. (244 Nm). The vehicle may now be safely rolled.

To install:

18. Install the transaxle securely on the jack. Rotate the converter so it will align with the positioning of the flexplate.

19. Apply a light coating of high temperature grease to the torque converter pilot hub.

20. Raise the transaxle into place and push it forward until the dowels engage and the bellhousing is flush with the block. Install the transaxle to bellhousing bolts.

21. Raise the transaxle and install the left side mount bolts. Install the torque converter bolts and torque to 55 ft. lbs. (74 Nm).

22. Install the front motor mount and bracket. Remove the engine and transaxle support fixtures.

23. Install the starter to the transaxle. Install the bolt finger tight, if equipped with 2.5L engine.

24. Install the axles making sure to install new retainer clips at the transaxle end of each shaft. Install the ball joints to the steering knuckles. Torque the axle nuts to 180 ft. lbs. (244 Nm) and install new cotter pins.

25. Connect the shifter and kickdown linkage to the transaxle, if equipped. Install a new O-ring to the speedometer cable adaptor and install to the extension housing; make sure it snaps in place. Install the retaining bolt.

26. Install the splash shield and install the wheels.

27. Install the upper bellhousing bolts and water pipe, if removed.

28. If equipped with 2.5L engine, install the starter attaching nut and bolt at the top of the bellhousing. Raise the vehicle again and tighten the starter bolt from under the vehicle.

29. Connect all electrical wiring to the transaxle. Lower the vehicle. Install the dipstick.

30. Install the air cleaner assembly, if removed. Fill the transaxle with the proper amount of Mopar ATF Plus Type 7176.

31. Connect the negative battery cable and check the transaxle for proper operation.

UPSHIFT AND KICKDOWN LEARNING PROCEDURE

A–604 Ultra-Drive Transaxle

The A–604 4 speed, electronic transaxle was the first to use fully adaptive controls. The controls perform their functions based on real time

feedback sensor information. Although, the transaxle is conventional in design, its functions are controlled by the ECM.

Since the A–604 is equipped with a learning function, each time the battery cable is disconnected, the ECM memory is lost. In operation, the transaxle must be shifted many times for the learned memory to be re-inputed in the ECM; during this period, the vehicle will experience rough operation. The transaxle must be at normal operating temperature when learning occurs.

1. Maintain constant throttle opening during shifts. Do not move the accelerator pedal during upshifts.

2. Accelerate the vehicle with the throttle $1/8$–$1/2$ open.

3. Make fifteen to twenty 1/2, 2/3 and 3/4 upshifts. Accelerating from a full stop to 50 mph each time at the aforementioned throttle opening is sufficient.

4. With the vehicle speed below 25 mph, make 5–8 wide open throttle kickdowns to 1st gear from either 2nd or 3rd gear. Allow at least 5 seconds of operation in 2nd or 3rd gear prior to each kickdown.

5. With the vehicle speed greater than 25 mph, make 5 part throttle to wide open throttle kickdowns to either 3rd or 2nd gear from 4th gear. Allow at least 5 seconds of operation in 4th gear (preferably at road load throttle) prior to performing the kickdown.

SHIFT LINKAGE ADJUSTMENT

1. Place the shifter in the **P** detent.

2. Loosen the clamp bolt on the gearshift cable bracket.

3. Pull the shift lever all the way to the front detent position and tighten the lock screw.

4. Check for proper neutral safety switch operation.

THROTTLE PRESSURE CABLE ADJUSTMENT

1. Run the engine until it reaches normal operating temperature.

2. Loosen the cable mounting bracket lock screw.

3. Position the bracket so both alignment tabs are touching the transaxle case surface and tighten the lock screws.

4. Release the cross lock on the cable assembly by pulling the cross lockup.

5. To ensure proper adjustment, the cable must be free to slide all the

way toward the engine against its stop after the cross lock is released.

6. Move the transaxle throttle control lever fully clockwise and press the cross lock down until it snaps into position.

7. Road test the vehicle and check the shift points.

DRIVE AXLE

Halfshaft

REMOVAL AND INSTALLATION

1. Disconnect the negative battery cable.

2. Raise the vehicle and support safely. Remove the tire and wheel assembly.

3. Remove the cotter pin from the end of the halfshaft. Remove the nut lock, spring washer, axle nut and washer.

4. Remove the speedometer pinion retainer bolt from the extension housing on the transaxle and remove the pinion by pulling upward. The pinion must be removed prior to removing the right side halfshaft or damage to the speedometer pinion may occur.

5. Remove the ball joint retaining bolt and pry the control arm down to release the ball stud from the steering knuckle.

6. Position a drain pan under the transaxle where the halfshaft enters the differential or extension housing.

7. Pull the strut assembly out — be careful of air suspension and ABS components if equipped — and remove the halfshaft from the hub and transaxle or center bearing by pulling on the inner joint. Unbolt the center bearing from the block and remove the intermediate shaft from the transaxle, if equipped.

To install:

8. Install the halfshaft or intermediate shaft to the transaxle, being careful not to damage the side seals. Make sure the inner joint clicks into place inside the differential. Install the center bearing retaining bolts, if equipped. Install the outer shaft to the center bearing, if equipped.

9. Pull the front strut out — be careful of air suspension and ABS components if equipped — and insert the outer joint into the front hub.

10. If necessary, turn the ball joint stud to position the bolt retaining indent to the inside of the vehicle. In-

stall the ball joint stud into the steering knuckle. Install the retaining bolt and nut.

11. Install the axle nut washer and nut and torque the nut to 180 ft. lbs. (244 Nm). Install the spring washer, nut lock and a new cotter pin.

12. Install the tire and wheel assembly.

CV-Boot

REMOVAL AND INSTALLATION

NOTE: Use only clamps provided with the replacement package when servicing. Plastic wire ties and other straps will not clamp tightly enough and grease will sling out causing costly damage to the joint.

Inner Joint

1. Raise the vehicle and support safely. Remove the halfshaft from the vehicle.

2. If cutting the boot away, mark and note the boot positioning on the shaft relative to the raised shoulders. Remove the boot clamps to gain access to the tripod retention system.

NOTE: Always hold the rollers in place when removing the housing from the tripod or the needle bearing may fall out.

3. Separate the housing from the tripod according to the following:

  a. G.K.N. — Has retaining tabs integral with the housing cover. Hold the housing and lightly compress the CV-joint retention spring while bending the tabs back. Support the housing as the retention spring pushes it from the housing.

  b. S.S.G. — Uses a wire ring tripod retainer which expands into a groove around the top of the housing. Use a tool to pry the wire ring, without damaging it, out of the groove and slide the tripod from the housing.

4. Remove the snapring from the end of the shaft and remove the tripod.

5. If not already done, mark the boot positioning on the shaft, relative to the raised shoulders and remove the boot from the shaft.

6. Remove as much old grease as possible from the joint. Inspect all parts for wear or damage.

NOTE: Do not use petroleum-based solvents on the joints, shaft or boot to clean; it will ruin hidden rubber seals within the joint. Use only chlorine-based cleaner

or hot soapy water to clean the joint, if necessary. Make sure the joint is completely dry before assembling.

To install:

7. If equipped, slide a new rubber washer seal over the stub shaft and down into the groove provided.

8. If the clamping device is not a straight strap, install it on the shaft first, then install the boot to the shaft in the proper position. Using the proper tool, C-4975 for crimping with plastic boot, C-4124 for crimping with rubber boot or C-4653 for clamping a strap, secure the clamp.

9. Slide the tripod onto the shaft:

  a. G.K.N — Slide the tripod on the shaft with the non-chamfered edge facing the tripod retainer ring groove.

  b. S.S.G. — Place the wire ring tripod retainer over the shaft, then slide the tripod. The tripod may installed either way; both ends are the same.

10. Install the snapring into its groove on the shaft to lock the tripod in position.

11. Distribute the grease provided in the grease package as follows, or according to the instructions in the package:

  a. G.K.N — If equipped with 3 packets of grease, distribute 2 of the 3 packets into the boot and the remaining packet into the housing. Otherwise, distribute ½ of the packet of grease into the boot and the remaining amount into the housing.

  b. S.S.G. — Distribute ½ of the packet of grease into the boot and the remaining amount into the housing.

12. Position the spring in the housing spring pocket with the spring cup attached to the exposed end of the spring. Place a dab of grease on the concave surface of the spring cup.

13. Keeping the spring centered, install the housing to the tripod as follows:

  a. G.K.N — Slip the housing onto the tripod. Bend the retaining tabs back into their original positions. Check for proper retention ability.

  b. S.S.G. — Slip the housing onto the tripod and install the tripod wire retaining ring. Check for proper retention ability.

14. Position the larger end of the boot over the housing.

15. Using the proper tool, C-4975 for crimping with plastic boot, C-4124 for crimping with rubber boot

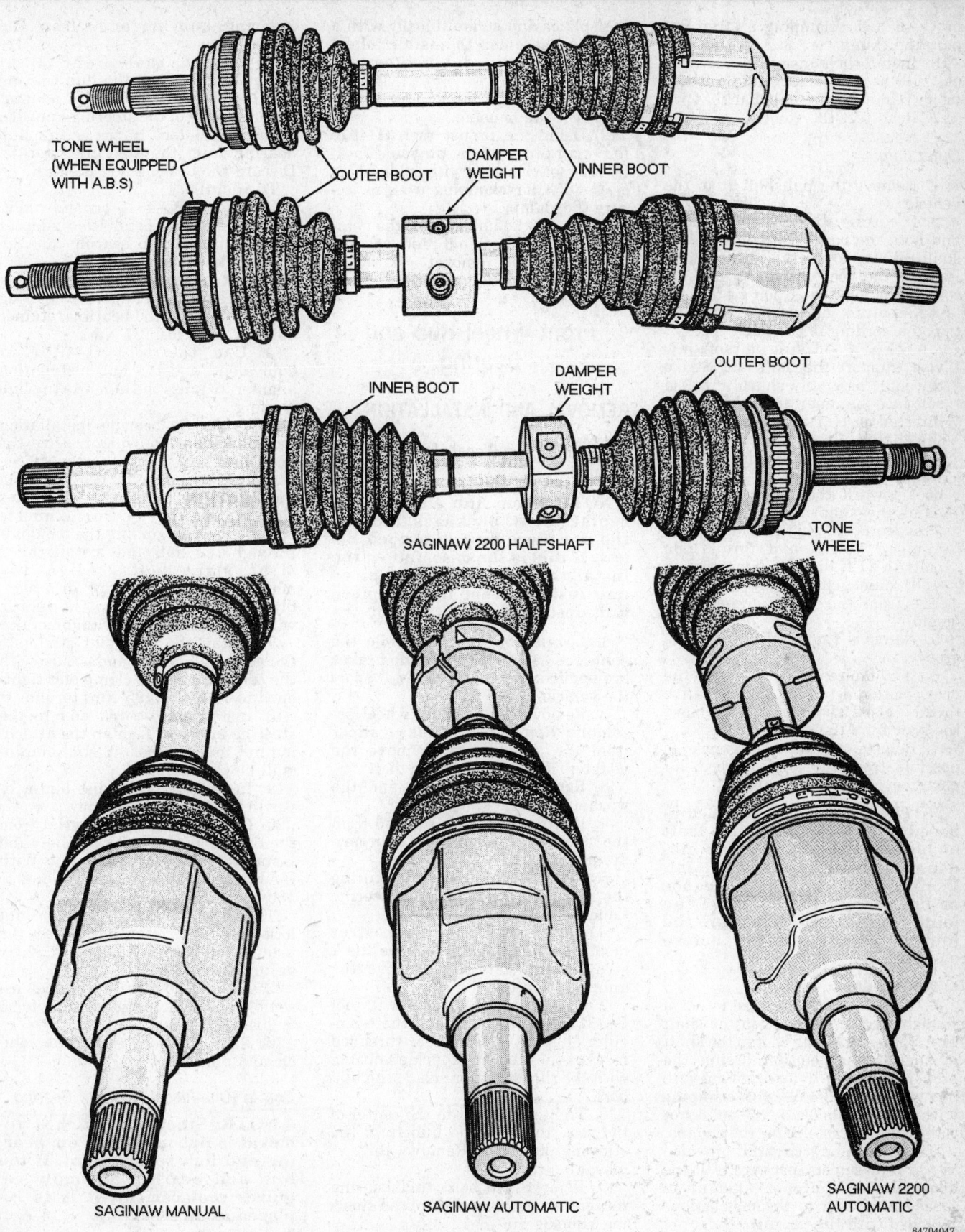

TONE WHEEL
(WHEN EQUIPPED
WITH A.B.S)

OUTER BOOT

DAMPER
WEIGHT

INNER BOOT

INNER BOOT

DAMPER
WEIGHT

OUTER BOOT

TONE
WHEEL

SAGINAW 2200 HALFSHAFT

SAGINAW MANUAL

SAGINAW AUTOMATIC

SAGINAW 2200
AUTOMATIC

84704047

Driveshaft identification (halfshafts)

or C–4653 for clamping a strap, secure the clamp.

16. Install the halfshaft to the vehicle. Fill the transaxle if fluid was lost when removing the halfshaft.

17. Road test the vehicle.

Outer Joint

1. Remove the halfshaft from the vehicle.

2. If cutting the boot away, mark and note the boot positioning on the shaft relative to the raised shoulders. Remove the boot clamps to gain access to the joint retention system.

3. Separate the housing from the tripod according to the following:

   a. G.K.N — Using a soft-jaw vise, support the halfshaft. Strike the joint assembly sharply with a soft-face hammer to dislodge the internal circlip and remove from the shaft.

   b. S.S.G. — Loosen the damper weight bolts and slide it and the boot toward the inner joint. Expand the snapring and slide the joint from the shaft. Reinstall the damper weight and torque the bolts to 21 ft. lbs. (28 Nm).

4. If damaged, remove the wear sleeve from the CV-joint machined ledge.

5. Remove the circlip from the groove.

6. If not already done, mark the boot positioning on the shaft, relative to the raised shoulders and remove the boot from the shaft.

7. Remove as much old grease as possible from the joint. Inspect all parts for wear or damage.

NOTE: Do not use petroleum-based solvents on the joints, shaft or boot to clean; it will ruin hidden rubber seals within the joint. Use only chlorine-based cleaner or hot soapy water to clean the joint, if necessary. Make sure the joint is completely dry before assembling.

To install:

8. If the clamping device is not a straight strap, install it on the shaft first, then install the boot to the shaft in the proper position. Using the proper tool, C–4975 for crimping with plastic boot, C–4124 for crimping with rubber boot or C–4653 for clamping a strap, secure the clamp.

9. Install a new circlip if provided in the replacement package. Fill the boot with the proper amount of grease according to the instructions provided with the package.

10. Position the outer joint on the shaft with hub nut installed, engage the splines and strike sharply with a soft-face hammer to install. Make sure the circlip did not become dislodged.

11. Position the larger end of the boot over the housing.

12. Using the proper tool, C–4975 for crimping with plastic boot, C–4124 for crimping with rubber boot or C–4653 for clamping a strap, secure the clamp.

13. Install the halfshaft to the vehicle. Fill the transaxle if fluid was lost during halfshaft removal.

14. Road test the vehicle.

Front Wheel Hub and Bearing

REMOVAL AND INSTALLATION

Pressed In (Two-Piece) Hub and Bearing

NOTE: Some hub and bearing replacement packages include the one-piece unit described below. If this is the case, follow the installation steps for one-piece unit instead of for the two-piece unit described here.

1. Loosen the hub nut while the vehicle is on the floor and the brakes are applied. Raise and safely support the vehicle.

2. Remove the tire and wheel assembly. Remove the brake caliper from the adaptor and remove the adaptor. Remove the brake disc.

3. Remove the hub nut and the washer from the stub shaft.

4. Disconnect the tie rod end from the steering arm using the appropriate puller.

5. Remove the clamp bolt securing the ball joint stud into the steering knuckle and separate.

6. Matchmark the lower strut mount to the knuckle. Remove the 2 strut clamp bolts and remove the knuckle from the vehicle.

7. Attach the hub removal tool C–4811 or equivalent, and the triangular adapter, to the 3 rear threaded holes of the steering knuckle housing with the thrust button inside the hub bore.

8. Tighten the bolt in the center of the tool, to press the hub from the steering knuckle. Remove the removal tools.

9. Remove the bolts and bearing retainer from the outside of the steering knuckle.

10. Carefully pry the bearing seal from the machined recess of the steering knuckle and clean the recess.

11. Insert tool C–4811 or equivalent, through the hub bearing and install bearing removal adapter to the outside of the steering knuckle. Tighten the tool to press the hub bearing from the steering knuckle. Discard the bearing and the seal.

To install:

12. Use tool C–4811 or equivalent, and the bearing installation adapter to press in the hub bearing into the steering knuckle.

13. Install a new seal, the bearing retainer and the bolts to the steering knuckle. Torque the bearing retainer bolts to 20 ft. lbs. (27 Nm).

14. Use the tool C–4811 or equivalent, and the hub installation adapter, to press the hub into the hub bearing.

15. Using the bearing installation tool C–4698 or equivalent, drive the new dust seal into the rear of the steering the hub and bearing from the knuckle as required.

16. Install the steering knuckle onto the vehicle guiding the halfshaft through the hub and install the 2 strut strut bolts. Align the matchmarks made during disassembly and tighten the nuts. The vehicle will require a front end alignment.

17. Install the ball joint stud into the steering knuckle and secure with the original knuckle clamp bolt tightened to 70 ft. lbs. (95 Nm) torque.

18. Install the tie rod end to the steering knuckle. Tighten the attaching nut to 35 ft. lbs. (47 Nm) and install new cotter pin.

19. Install the brake disc and caliper to the knuckle assembly.

20. Clean all foreign material from the threads of the axle stub shaft and install the washer and hub nut. With the brakes applied, torque the nut to 180 ft. lbs. (244 Nm) torque.

21. Install the spring washer, nut lock and new cotter pin. Wrap the prongs of the cotter pin tightly around the nut lock.

22. Install the tire and wheel assembly and tighten the lug nuts to 95 ft. lbs. (129 Nm).

23. Align the front end of the vehicle and road test.

Bolt In (One-Piece) Hub and Bearing

NOTE: Steering knuckle removal is not necessary for bearing and hub replacement. If the hub and bearing assembly requires replacement, it is to be replaced as an assembly.

1. Loosen the hub nut while the vehicle is on the floor and the brakes

are applied. Raise and safely support the vehicle.

2. Remove the tire and wheel assembly from the vehicle.

3. Remove the hub nut and the washer from the stub shaft.

4. Disconnect the tie rod end from the steering arm using the appropriate puller.

5. Remove the clamp bolt securing the ball joint stud into the steering knuckle and separate.

6. Remove the caliper guide pin bolts and separate the caliper assembly from the braking disc. Support the caliper with wire hook and not by the hydraulic hose.

7. Separate the steering knuckle assembly from the ball joint stud. Pull the knuckle assembly out and away from the halfshaft.

NOTE: Care must be taken when separating the halfshaft from the knuckle, do not separate the inner CV-joint during this operation. Do not allow the halfshaft to hang by the inner CV-joint, it must be supported.

8. Remove the 4 hub and bearing assembly mounting bolts from the rear of the knuckle and remove the assembly from the knuckle.

9. Carefully pry the bearing seal from the machined recess of the steering knuckle and clean the recess.

10. Thoroughly clean and dry the knuckle and bearing mating surfaces and the seal installation area.

To install:

11. Install the hub and bearing assembly to the knuckle and torque the bolts in a criss-cross pattern to 45 ft. lbs. (65 Nm).

12. Install a new seal and wear sleeve. Lubricate the circumferences of the seal and sleeve liberally with grease.

13. Install the ball joint stud to the steering knuckle assembly and secure with the original knuckle clamp bolt tightened to 105 ft. lbs. (145 Nm) torque.

14. Install the tie rod end to the steering knuckle. Tighten the attaching nut to 35 ft. lbs. (47 Nm) and install new cotter pin.

15. Install the brake disc and caliper to the knuckle assembly.

16. Clean all foreign material from the threads of the axle stub shaft and install the washer and hub nut. With the brakes applied, torque the nut to 180 ft. lbs. (244 Nm) torque.

17. Install the spring washer, nut lock and new cotter pin. Wrap the prongs of the cotter pin tightly around the nut lock.

18. Install the tire and wheel assembly and tighten the lug nuts to 95 ft. lbs. (129 Nm). Align the front end as required.

Differential Case

REMOVAL AND INSTALLATION

1. Disconnect the negative battery cable.

2. Remove the transaxle from the vehicle.

3. Remove the right side extension housing from the transaxle.

4. Remove the differential cover retaining bolt and the cover from the transaxle.

5. Remove the differential bearing retainer bolts and the side differential bearing retainer, located on the left side of the transaxle, using tool L–4435 or equivalent. Use caution and take note of shims and their positioning, they can become dislodged during removal.

6. Remove the differential case from the transaxle.

To install:

7. Install the differential case into the transaxle and secure by installing the differential bearing retainer and 3 retainer bolts.

8. Apply RTV sealant around the inner surface of the extension housing under the O-ring and install to the transaxle. Install the 2 extension housing retainer bolts.

9. Apply a bead of sealer around the mating surface of the differential cover and install to the transaxle.

10. Install the remaining differential bearing retainer bolts and install the transaxle into the vehicle.

11. Connect the negative battery cable, fill the transaxle with the proper oil and road test the vehicle.

STEERING

Steering Wheel

---CAUTION---
On vehicles equipped with the air bag system, the system must be disarmed prior to removing the steering wheel. Failure to disarm the air bag system may result in accidental deployment of the air bag module and possible personal injury.

Front suspension components

REMOVAL AND INSTALLATION

Without Airbag

1. Disconnect the negative battery cable.

2. Straighten the steering wheel so the front tires are pointing straight-ahead.

3. Remove the horn pad.

4. Remove the steering wheel hold-down nut and remove the damper, if equipped. Matchmark the steering wheel to the shaft.

5. Using a steering wheel puller, pull the steering wheel off the shaft.

6. The installation is the reverse of the removal procedure. Torque the hold-down nut to 45 ft. lbs. (60 Nm).

With Airbag

1. Disconnect the negative battery cable and isolate using an appropriate insulator. Allow the system capacitor to discharge for 2 minutes prior to starting repairs on the vehicle.

2. Straighten the steering wheel so the front tires are pointing straight forward.

3. Remove the 4 nuts located on the back side of the steering wheel that attach the airbag module to the steering wheel.

4. Lift the module and disconnect the connectors. Remove the speed control switch, if equipped.

NOTE: All columns except Acustar are equipped with a clockspring setscrew held by a plastic tether on the steering wheel. Acustar mounted clocksprings are auto-locking. If the steering column is not an Acustar and is lacking the setscrew, obtain one before proceeding.

5. If equipped with the setscrew, place it in the clockspring to ensure proper positioning when the steering wheel is removed.

6. Remove the steering wheel hold-down nut and damper, if equipped. Matchmark the steering wheel to the shaft.

7. Using a steering wheel puller, pull the steering wheel off the shaft.

To install:

8. Position the steering wheel on the steering column. Make sure the flats on the hub of the steering wheel are aligned with the formations on the clockspring.

9. Pull the airbag and speed control connectors through the lower, larger hole in the steering wheel and pull the horn wire through the smaller hole at the top. Make sure the wires are not pinched anywhere.

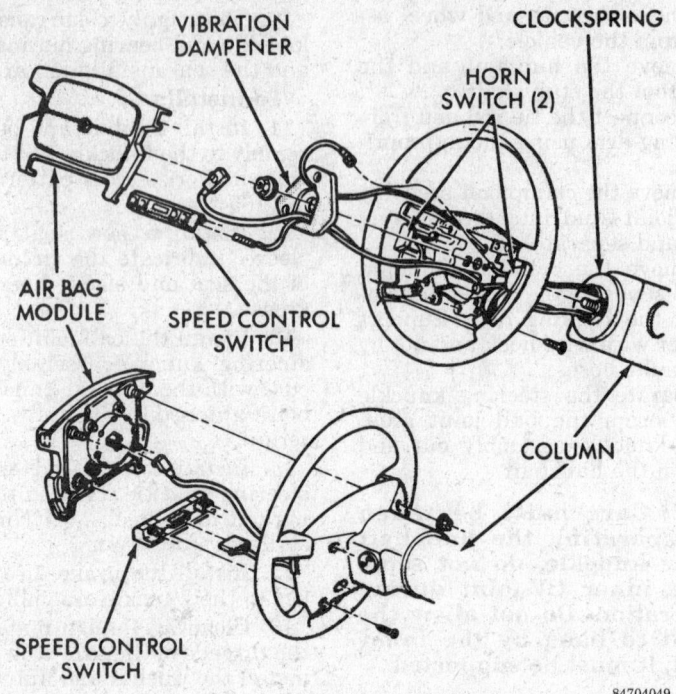

Air bag module and related components

84704049

10. Install the damper, if equipped.

11. Install the hold-down nut and torque to 45 ft. lbs. (60 Nm).

12. If equipped with a clockspring setscrew, remove the screw and place it in its storage location on the steering wheel.

13. Connect the horn wire.

14. Connect the speed control wire and install the speed control switch.

15. Connect the clockspring lead wire to the airbag module and install module to steering wheel.

NOTE: Do not allow anyone to enter the vehicle from this point on, until this procedure is completed.

16. Connect the DRB II to the Airbag System Diagnostic Module (ASDM) connector located to the right of the console.

17. From the passenger side of the vehicle, turn the key to the **ON** position.

18. Check to make sure nobody has entered the vehicle. Connect the negative battery cable.

19. Using the DRB II, read and record any active fault data or stored codes.

20. If any active fault codes are present, perform the proper diagnostic procedures before continuing.

21. If there are no active fault codes, erase the stored fault codes. If there are active codes, the stored codes will not erase.

22. From the passenger side of the vehicle, turn the key **OFF**, then **ON** and observe the instrument cluster airbag warning light. It should come on for 6–8 seconds, then go out, indicating the system is functioning normally. If the warning light either fails to come **ON** or stays lit, there is a system malfunction and the proper diagnostic procedures should be performed.

Steering Column

REMOVAL AND INSTALLATION

Acustar Column

1. Disconnect the negative battery cable. Disarm the air bag system, if equipped.

2. Straighten the steering wheel so the front tires are pointing straight-ahead.

3. Remove the steering wheel hold-down nut and remove the damper, if equipped. Matchmark the steering wheel to the shaft.

4. Using a steering wheel puller, pull the steering wheel off the shaft.

5. If equipped with column shift, disconnect the transaxle shift cable from the steering column by prying it out of the grommet in the shift lever.

6. If equipped with pointer type gear indicator, loosen the setscrew on the lower side of the steering column and remove the pointer needle.

7. If equipped with a cable actuated gear shift indicator, place the gear shift lever in the **N** or **P** position and remove the PRNDL indicator actuation cable from the steering column actuator arm. Swing the lock bar located on the lower portion of the PRNDL insert upward and squeeze the legs together. Remove the insert from the steering column.

8. Disconnect all wiring connectors from below the instrument panel that lead up into the steering column.

9. Remove the nuts that attach the steering column assembly to the instrument panel support.

10. Remove the retaining pin in the upper to lower steering coupler retaining bolt. Remove the upper to lower steering coupler retaining nut and pinch bolt from the coupling and separate the stub shaft from the steering gear coupling.

11. Remove the column from the vehicle.

To install:

12. Install new cable attaching grommet into the steering column shift lever. Install the steering column into the vehicle. Guide the stub shaft into the steering gear coupling and install the pinch bolt and nut, if equipped.

13. Install the nuts that attach the steering column assembly to the instrument panel support. Torque the steering column assembly to support bracket nuts to 105 inch. lbs. (12 Nm).

14. Connect the wire harness connectors at the base of the steering column.

15. If equipped with a cable actuated gear shift indicator, route the PRNDL actuator assembly under the left column wing and along the left side of the steering column. Insert the flange of the actuator assembly into the steering column jacket. Engage the lock bar to secure the actuator assembly to the housing. Hook the cable to the steering column actuator arm. Move the shifter to **N** and check for proper pointer location. If the pointer is misaligned, adjust the pointer arm using a $9/64$ in. Allen wrench.

16. If equipped with pointer type gear shift indicator, install the pointer into the indicator housing and the steering column and secure.

17. Connect the transaxle shift cable to the shift lever on the steering column. Readjust the transaxle shift linkage.

18. Install the clockspring, steering wheel and remaining components removed during disassembly.

19. Connect the negative battery cable and check the steering column and all related components for proper operation.

Power Rack and Pinion

NOTE: The power steering gear should not be serviced. If a malfunction or fluid leak occurs, the complete assembly should be replaced.

REMOVAL AND INSTALLATION

1. Disconnect the negative battery cable.
2. Raise the vehicle and support safely.
3. Remove the front tire and wheel assemblies.
4. Remove the cotter pins, castellated nuts and tie rod ends from the steering knuckles.
5. Disconnect the engine damper strut from the crossmember if equipped.
6. Place a transmission jack under the front crossmember and apply a slight upward pressure on the crossmember. Remove the front suspension crossmember attaching bolts and lower the crossmember using the jack. Disconnect the steering gear from the steering column at the stub shaft while lowering the crossmember from the vehicle.
7. Disconnect and plug the oil pressure line from the rack. Disconnect and plug the return hose from the line coming from the rack.
8. Remove the tie rod inner boot shields.
9. Remove the steering gear bolts from the front suspension crossmember.
10. Remove the steering gear from the left side of the vehicle.

To install:
11. Place the rack on the crossmember and torque the steering gear attaching bolts to 21 ft. lbs. (29 Nm). Attach the fluid lines and the boot shields.
12. Have a helper inside the vehicle remove the trim boot and align the stub shaft with the coupling while the crossmember is raised into position. If a helper is not available, the

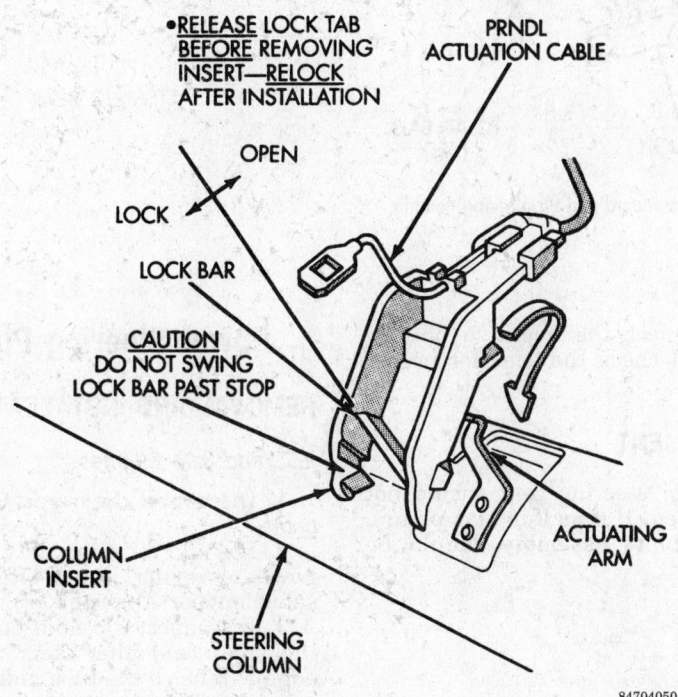

PRNDL cable removal — 1992–93 vehicles

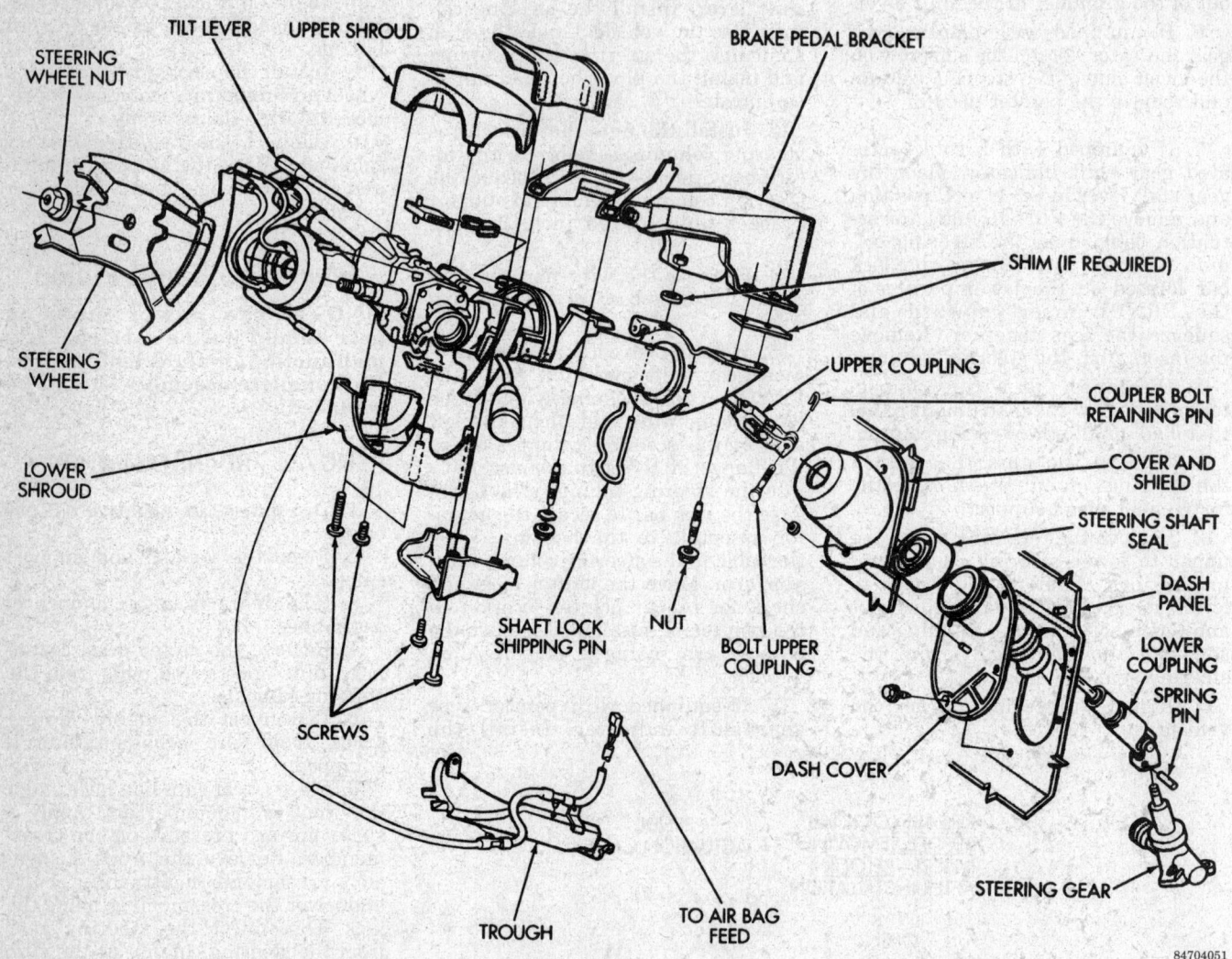

STEERING WHEEL NUT

TILT LEVER

UPPER SHROUD

BRAKE PEDAL BRACKET

STEERING WHEEL

SHIM (IF REQUIRED)

LOWER SHROUD

UPPER COUPLING

COUPLER BOLT RETAINING PIN

COVER AND SHIELD

STEERING SHAFT SEAL

DASH PANEL

LOWER COUPLING

SPRING PIN

SHAFT LOCK SHIPPING PIN

NUT

BOLT UPPER COUPLING

DASH COVER

SCREWS

STEERING GEAR

TROUGH

TO AIR BAG FEED

84704051

Acustar standard and tilt steering column

steering column will have to be un-bolted so the steering shaft can be inserted into the coupling. The right rear crossmember bolt is a pilot bolt that correctly locates the cross-member; tighten it first. Torque the crossmember bolts to 90 ft. lbs. (122 Nm).

13. Install the tie rod ends to the steering knuckle and torque the nut to 45 ft. lbs. (61 Nm). Install a new cotter pin.

14. Insert the stub shaft shim where the stub shaft goes into the coupling.

15. Refill the power steering pump.

16. Connect the negative battery cable and check the gear for proper operation.

ADJUSTMENT

The power steering gear should not be adjusted. If a malfunction occurs, the complete assembly should be replaced.

Power Steering Pump

REMOVAL AND INSTALLATION

2.5L and 3.0L Engines

1. Disconnect the negative battery cable.

2. Position a drain pan under the power steering pump. Raise and safely support the vehicle.

3. Disconnect the fluid hoses from the pump and plug them. On 3.0L engine, remove the tube and dipstick assembly from the pump.

4. Remove the front bracket at-taching bolts and remove the belt from the pulley.

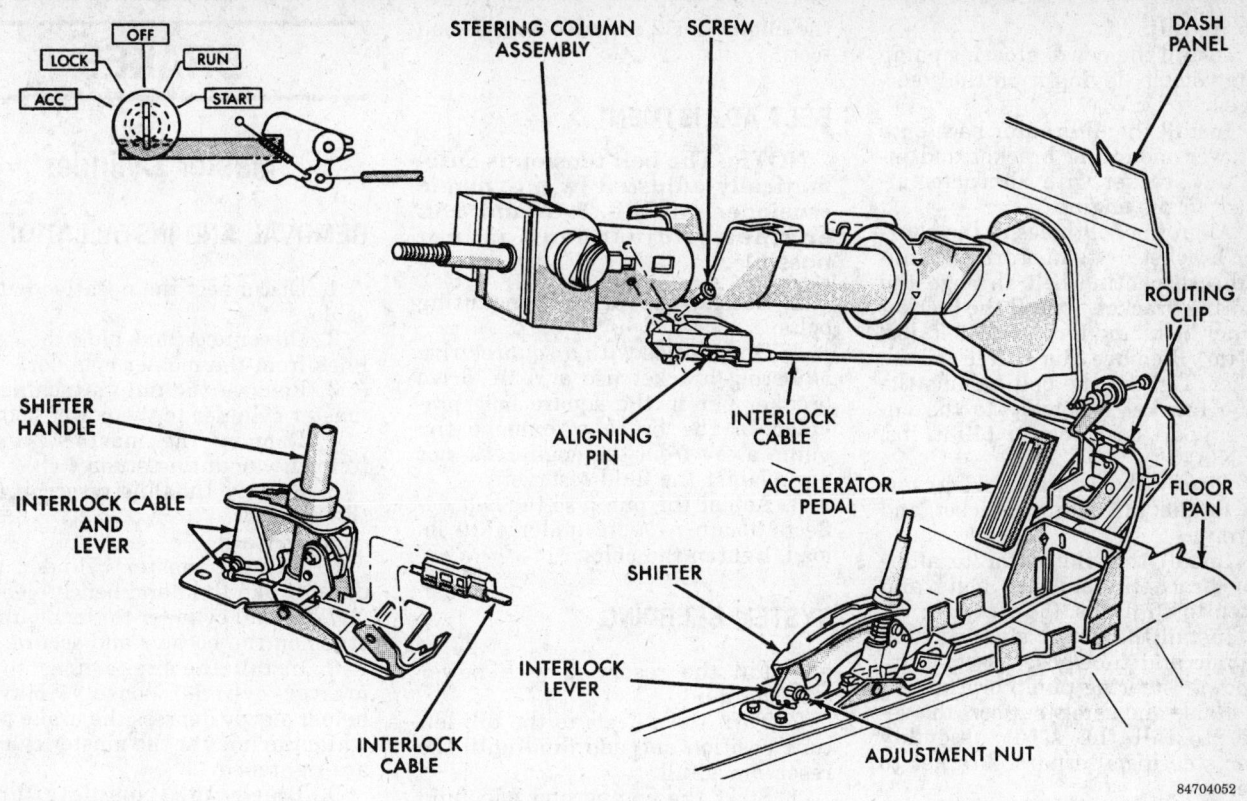

Acustar interlock system components

5. On 3.0L engine, disconnect the front exhaust pipe from the exhaust manifold and position aside. This is required for clearance to remove the pump.

6. Loosen the rear pump-to-bracket nut. Remove the bolt attaching the pulley side of the power steering pump to the mounting bracket.

7. On 3.0L engine, remove the nut holding the power steering pump rear support bracket to the pump. Remove the the 2 bolts mounting the power steering pump support bracket to the engine and remove the bracket.

8. Lower the vehicle. Remove the remaining retaining bolts and the rear mounting nut. Remove the power steering pump from the vehicle.

9. Remove the pulley from the pump with the proper puller. Install the pulley on the new pump using the special installation tools.

To install:

10. Install the pump to the engine making sure, on 3.0L engine, that the stud on the back of the pump is in the slotted hole in the bracket.

11. Install the mounting screws. Install the tube and dipstick assembly on the pump, if equipped.

12. Install the exhaust pipe to the manifold using a new gasket where required.

13. Install the power steering pump drive belt and adjust the tension as required.

14. Refill the pump using the correct fluid and bleed the system.

3.3L and 3.8L Engines

1. Disconnect negative battery cable and isolate using appropriate insulation.

2. Remove the serpentine belt from the engine.

3. Raise and safely support the vehicle. Place a drain pan under the fluid lines on the power steering pump.

4. Remove the hose clamp and the low pressure hose at the power steering pump.

5. Remove the hose clamp and the hose to the power steering pump from the remote fluid reservoir. Drain the excess fluid from the hoses.

6. Remove the pressure line from the pump. Drain the excess fluid from the hose.

7. Remove the right front tire and wheel assembly from the vehicle.

8. Remove the 3 bolt holding the power steering pump to the alternator, power steering and belt tensioner mounting bracket.

9. Remove the strut from the engine block to the pump and lay the power steering pump on top of the power steering gear. It will be removed from the top later in the procedure.

10. Remove the serpentine belt tensioner from the mounting bracket. Lower the vehicle.

11. Remove the 2 bolts holding the power steering fluid reservoir to the alternator bracket and remove the reservoir. Remove the bolts attaching the tube/hose assembly to the power steering pump bracket and remove tube/hose assembly.

12. Remove the engine wiring harness clip from the routing bracket and relocate the harness aside.

13. Loosen but do not remove the bolt holding the engine bracket assembly to the engine support assembly.

14. Remove the upper alternator to alternator bracket mounting bolts and rotate the assembly back toward the dash panel. Remove the alternator from the mounting bracket and remove the mounting bracket from the engine. Lay the alternator on top of the intake manifold.

15. Remove the power steering pump through the top in the area of the alternator. Transfer parts as required.

To install:

16. Install the power steering pump in the vehicle, laying it on the steering gear.

17. Install the alternator back onto the lower mounting bracket and install the bracket with alternator attached, to the engine.

18. Align the bolt holes in the alternator bracket by temporarily installing the serpentine belt through the mounting bracket. Install the bracket retainer bolts and torque to 40 ft. lbs. (54 Nm). Remove the bolt from the bracket. Tighten the bolt holding the engine bracket assembly to the engine support assembly to 110 ft. lbs. (150 Nm).

19. Attach the engine wiring harness to the alternator bracket and secure.

20. Install the alternator to alternator bracket mounting bolts and tighten to 40 ft. lbs. (54 Nm).

21. Install the power steering fluid reservoir and tube/hose assembly to the power steering pump bracket.

22. Raise and safely support the vehicle. Install the strut assembly power steering/alternator bracket to the engine.

23. Install the serpentine belt tensioner onto the bracket. Torque the retainers to 40 ft. lbs. (54 Nm).

24. Install power steering pump onto mounting bracket aligning holes. Install mounting bolts and tighten to 40 ft. lbs. (54 Nm).

25. Install the bracket support strut. Install the power steering fluid pressure line with new O-ring in place and tighten the fitting to 275 inch lbs. (31 Nm).

26. Install the power steering pump low pressure line to the pump and the reservoir. Be sure all hose clamps are reinstalled.

27. Secure right front tire and wheel assembly on vehicle and lower.

28. Install the serpentine belt making sure positioning on all pulleys is correct.

29. Fill the reservoir to the correct level using the proper fluid, do not use automatic transmission fluid.

30. Start the engine and add fluid to bring the level to the correct level.

31. To purge the system of air, turn the steering wheel from side to side without contacting the stops.

32. Return the wheel to the straight-ahead position and operate the engine for 2 minutes before road testing.

BELT ADJUSTMENT

NOTE: The belt tension is automatically adjusted by a dynamic tensioner on 3.0L, 3.3L and 3.8L engines. Adjustment is not possible.

1. Loosen the bracket mounting bolts.

2. On vehicles with a square drive adjusting bracket use a 1/2 in. drive breaker bar in the square hole provided in the bracket to move the pump away from the engine. Do not pry against the fluid reservoir.

3. Adjust the pump so the belt deflects about 1/4–1/2 in. under a 10 lb. load, tighten the bolts.

SYSTEM BLEEDING

1. Fill the reservoir with power steering fluid.

2. Turn the wheels to the full left turn position and add fluid until the reservoir is full.

3. Start the engine and add fluid to bring the level to the correct level.

4. To purge the system of air, turn the steering wheel from side to side without contacting the stops.

5. Return the wheel to the straight-ahead position and operate the engine for 2 minutes before road testing.

Tie Rod Ends

REMOVAL AND INSTALLATION

1. Raise the vehicle and support safely.

2. Remove the cotter pin and nut from the tie rod end.

3. Using a puller, separate the tie rod from the steering knuckle.

4. Loosen the sleeve clamp nut and bolt, if equipped, and unscrew the tie rod end from the sleeve or inner tie rod.

5. The installation is the reverse of the removal procedure. Torque the stud nuts to 45 ft. lbs. (61 Nm) and install a new cotter pin.

6. Perform a front end alignment, as required.

BRAKES

Master Cylinder

REMOVAL AND INSTALLATION

1. Disconnect the negative battery cable.

2. Disconnect and plug the brake lines from the master cylinder.

3. Remove the nuts attaching the master cylinder to the power booster.

4. Remove the master cylinder from the mounting studs.

5. Remove the fluid reservoir from the cylinder.

To install:

6. Fill the master cylinder with clean brake fluid and bench bleed.

7. Install cylinder to the mounting studs on the booster and secure.

8. Install the brake lines to the master cylinder loosely. Have a helper slowly depress the brake pedal while the lines at the master cylinder are tightened.

9. Bleed the complete brake system.

10. Connect the negative battery cable, add brake fluid to fill reservoir to the appropriate level and check the brakes for proper operation.

Combination Valve

REMOVAL AND INSTALLATION

1. Disconnect the negative battery cable. Raise the vehicle and support safely.

2. Tag and disconnect the brake lines from the valve.

3. Disconnect the wires to the pressure switch.

4. Remove the combination valve from the frame bracket.

5. Installation is the reverse of the removal procedure.

6. Bleed the brakes in the following order:
   a. Right rear wheel cylinder or caliper
   b. Left rear wheel cylinder or caliper
   c. Right front caliper
   d. Left front caliper

Power Brake Booster

REMOVAL AND INSTALLATION

1. Disconnect the negative battery cable. Disconnect the vacuum hose(s) from the booster.
2. Remove the master cylinder from the brake booster.
3. From inside the passenger compartment, remove the clip that secures the booster pushrod to the brake pedal.
4. Remove the nuts that attach the booster to the dash panel. Remove the booster from the vehicle.
5. The installation is the reverse of the removal procedure.
6. Tighten booster mounting nuts and master cylinder mounting nuts to 21 ft. lbs. (29 Nm).
7. Connect the negative battery cable and check the brakes for proper operation.

Brake Caliper

REMOVAL AND INSTALLATION

1. Raise the vehicle and support safely.
2. Remove the tire and wheel assembly.
3. Remove the caliper mounting pins.
4. Lift the caliper off the rotor. Remove the outer pad from the caliper.
5. Remove the brake hose retaining bolt from the caliper.
To install:
6. Install the brake hose to the caliper using new copper washers.
7. Position the caliper over the rotor so the caliper engages the adaptor correctly. Install the mounting pins and tighten to 35 ft. lbs. (47 Nm).
8. Fill the master cylinder to the appropriate level and bleed the brakes.

Disc Brake Pads

REMOVAL AND INSTALLATION

All Front Brakes and Rear Brakes

1. Depressurize the hydraulic accumulator, if equipped with anti-lock brakes. Remove some of the fluid from the master cylinder.
2. Raise and safely support the vehicle. Remove the tire and wheel assemblies.
3. Unbolt and remove the caliper assembly. Remove the outer brake pad from the caliper.

4. Remove the inner brake pad from the caliper.
To install:
5. Use a large C-clamp or equivalent, to compress the disc brake piston back into the caliper bore.
6. Install the inboard shoe by inserting the retaining clip into the piston cavity.
7. Install the outboard shoe by sliding the retaining clip over the caliper fingers.
8. Position the caliper over the rotor so the caliper engages the adaptor correctly and install the retainer pin(s).
9. Install the hold-down spring, if removed.
10. Refill the master cylinder. Pump the brake pedal until a firm pedal is achieved prior to moving the vehicle. This will seat the brakes against the rotors.
11. Bleed brake system if necessary.

Brake Rotor

REMOVAL AND INSTALLATION

1. Raise the vehicle and support safely. Remove the tire and wheel assembly.
2. Remove the caliper and brake pads.
3. Remove the factory installed clips, if equipped. It is not necessary to reinstall these clips.
4. Remove the adaptor, if necessary. Remove the rotor from the hub.
5. The installation is the reverse of the removal procedure.

Brake Drum

REMOVAL AND INSTALLATION

1. Raise the vehicle and support safely.
2. Remove the wheel and tire assembly.
3. Remove the dust cap.
4. Remove the cotter pin and nut lock.
5. Remove the wheel bearing nut and washer from the spindle.
6. Remove the outer wheel bearing.
7. Remove the drum with the inner wheel bearing from the spindle. If the drum is difficult to remove, remove the plug from the rear of the backing plate and push the self adjuster lever away from the star wheel. Rotate the star wheel to re-

tract the shoes. Remove the grease seal.
To install:
8. Lubricate and install the inner wheel bearing. Install a new grease seal.
9. Install the drum to the spindle.
10. Lubricate and install the outer wheel bearing, washer and nut. When the bearing preload is properly set, install the nut lock and a new cotter pin.
11. Install the grease cap.
12. Install the wheel and tire assembly. Adjust the rear brakes as required.

Brake Shoes

REMOVAL AND INSTALLATION

1. Raise the vehicle and support safely. Remove the wheel, tires and the brake drums.
2. Remove the automatic adjuster spring and lever.
3. Rotate the automatic adjuster star wheel so both shoes move out far enough to be free of the wheel cylinder boots.
4. Disconnect the parking brake cable from the actuating lever.
5. Remove the lower shoe-to-shoe or shoe-to-anchor spring(s).
6. With the shoes held together by the upper shoe-to-shoe spring, remove them from the backing plate.
To install:
7. Thoroughly clean and dry the backing plate. To prepare the backing plate, lubricate the bosses, anchor pin and parking brake actuating lever pivot surface lightly with lithium based grease.
8. Remove, clean and dry all parts still on the old shoes. Lubricate the star wheel shaft threads with anti-seize lubricant and transfer all parts to their proper locations on the new shoes.
9. Install the lower spring(s).
10. Connect the parking brake cable to the brake shoe.
11. Install the automatic adjuster lever and spring.
12. Adjust the star wheel so a slight resistance is felt when installing the drum to the spindle.
13. Remove any grease from the linings, install the brake drum, wheel bearing washer and end nut to the spindle. Adjust the bearing pre-load and install new cotter pin.
14. Install the tire and wheel assembly.
15. Complete the brake adjustment with the wheels installed.

Wheel Cylinder

REMOVAL AND INSTALLATION

1. Raise the vehicle and support safely.

2. Remove the wheel, drum and brake shoes.

3. Remove and plug the brake line from the wheel cylinder.

4. Remove the wheel cylinder bolts and remove the cylinder from the backing plate.

To install:

5. Apply a very thin coating of silicone sealer to the cylinder mounting surface, install the cylinder to the backing plate and install the retaining bolts.

6. Connect the brake line to the wheel cylinder.

7. Install all brake parts that were removed.

8. Install the tire and wheel assembly.

9. Bleed the complete brake system.

Parking Brake Cables

ADJUSTMENT

Drum Brakes

1. Release the parking brakes fully.

2. Raise the vehicle and support safely.

3. Adjust the rear brakes.

4. Loosen the adjusting nut until there is slack in all the cables.

5. Rotate the rear wheels and tighten the cable adjusting nut until there is a slight drag at the wheels.

6. Continue to rotate the rear wheels and loosen the nut until all drag is eliminated.

7. Back off the nut an additional 2 turns.

8. Apply and release the parking brake several times. Upon the least release, verify there is no drag at the wheels.

9. To check the operation, make sure the parking brake holds on an incline.

Rear Disc Brakes

1. Fully release the parking brakes and pump the brakes several times. Raise the vehicle and support safely.

2. Tighten the cable adjusting nut until a very slight drag is felt at each rear wheel.

3. Loosen the adjusting nut 5 turns.

4. Actuate the parking brake lever on the rear calipers by manually pulling down and releasing each rear parking brake cable at the rear of the vehicle.

5. The parking brake lever should be touching the stop pin on both rear calipers. If not, loosen the adjusting nut 1 turn.

6. Repeat Steps 4 and 5 until the parking brake lever returns against the stop pin on both calipers.

7. When the adjustment is complete, the actuating levers on both calipers should return against the stop pins when the parking brakes are released and the wheels must rotate freely.

8. To confirm proper operation, make sure the parking brake holds on an incline.

REMOVAL AND INSTALLATION

Front Cable

1. Disconnect the negative battery cable.

2. Loosen the adjusting nut and disengage the front cable from the equalizer bracket.

3. Lift the carpet and floor matting and remove the floor pan seal.

4. Pull the cable end forward and disconnect from the clevis.

5. Pull the cable through the hole and remove.

6. The installation is the reverse of the removal procedure.

7. Adjust the cables, connect the negative battery cable and check the parking brakes for proper operation.

Rear Cable

DRUM BRAKES

1. Disconnect the negative battery cable. Raise the vehicle and support safely.

2. Remove the rear wheels. Back off the adjusting nut enough to provide slack in all cables and disconnect cables from the cable connectors.

3. Remove the brake drums. Disconnect the cable from the brake shoe lever.

4. Compress the retaining clips on the end of the cable housing and pull the cable from the backing plate. A small hose clamp may be used to compress retaining clip.

5. Remove the retaining clip at the support bracket and remove the cable from the trailing arm assembly.

6. The installation is the reverse of the removal procedure.

7. Adjust the cables, connect the negative battery cable and check the parking brakes for proper operation.

DISC BRAKES

1. Disconnect the negative battery cable. Raise the vehicle and support safely. Remove the rear wheels.

2. Remove the brake cable retaining clips from the hanger bracket and caliper.

3. Disconnect the cable from the parking brake lever on the caliper.

4. Remove the cable guide attaching nut and screw.

5. Pull the cable assembly out from the hanger bracket and caliper.

6. The installation is the reverse of the removal procedure.

7. Adjust the cables, connect the negative battery cable and check the parking brakes for proper operation.

Brake System Bleeding

EXCEPT ANTI-LOCK BRAKES

NOTE: If using a pressure bleeder, follow the instructions furnished with the unit and choose the correct adaptor for the application. Do not substitute an adapter that almost fits as it will not work and could be dangerous.

Master Cylinder

If the master cylinder is off the vehicle, it can be bench bled.

1. Connect 2 short pieces of brake line to the outlet fittings, bend them until the free end is below the fluid level in the master cylinder reservoirs.

2. Fill the reservoir with fresh brake fluid. Pump the piston slowly until no more air bubbles appear in the reservoirs.

3. Disconnect the 2 short lines, refill the master cylinder and securely install the cylinder caps.

4. If the master cylinder is on the vehicle, it can still be bled, using a flare nut wrench.

5. Open the brake lines slightly with the flare nut wrench while pressure is applied to the brake pedal by a helper inside the vehicle.

6. Be sure to tighten the line before the brake pedal is released.

7. Repeat the process with both lines until no air bubbles come out.

8. Bleed the complete brake system.

Calipers and Wheel Cylinders

1. Fill the master cylinder with fresh brake fluid. Check the level often during the procedure.

2. Starting with the right rear wheel, remove the protective cap from the bleeder, and place where it will not be lost. Clean the bleed screw.

CAUTION
When bleeding the brakes, keep face away from the brake area. Spewing fluid may cause facial and/or visual damage. Do not allow brake fluid to spill on the car's finish; it will remove the paint.

3. If the system is empty, the most efficient way to get fluid down to the wheel is to use a pressure bleeder. Once fluid is at the bleeder, close it before the pedal is released inside the vehicle.

NOTE: If the pedal is pumped rapidly, the fluid will churn and create small air bubbles, which are difficult to remove from the system. These air bubbles will eventually congregate and a spongy pedal will result.

4. Once fluid has been pumped to the caliper or wheel cylinder, open the bleed screw again, have the helper press the brake pedal to the floor, lock the bleeder and have the helper slowly release the pedal. Wait 15 seconds and repeat the procedure (including the 15 second wait) until no more air comes out of the bleeder upon application of the brake pedal. Remember to close the bleeder before the pedal is released inside the vehicle each time the bleeder is opened. If not, air will be induced into the system.

5. Repeat the procedure on remaining wheel cylinders in order:
   a. Left rear
   b. Right front
   c. Left front

6. Hydraulic brake systems must be totally flushed if the fluid becomes contaminated with water, dirt or other corrosive chemicals. To flush, bleed the entire system until all fluid has been replaced with new fluid.

7. Install the bleeder cap(s) on the bleeder to keep dirt out. Always road test the vehicle after brake work of any kind is done.

Anti-Lock Brakes

PRESSURE BLEEDING

The brake lines may be pressure bled, using a standard diaphragm type pressure bleeder. Only diaphragm type pressure bleeding equipment should be used to bleed the system.

1. The ignition should be turned **OFF** and remain **OFF** throughout this procedure.

2. Depressurize the hydraulic accumulator as follows:
   a. Disconnect the negative battery cable.
   b. Pump the brake pedal a minimum of 40 times.
   c. A noticeable difference in pedal pressure should be noticed. When this occurs, press the pedal an additional 10 times.

CAUTION
Failure to depressurize the hydraulic accumulator, prior to performing this operation may result in personal injury and/or damage to the painted surfaces from pressurized brake fluid.

3. Remove the electrical connector from fluid level sensor on the reservoir cap(s) and remove the reservoir cap(s).

4. Install the correct pressure bleeder adapter.

5. Attach the bleeding equipment to the bleeder adapter. Charge the pressure bleeder to approximately 20 psi (138 kPa).

6. Connect a transparent hose to the caliper bleed screw. Submerge the free end of the hose in a clear glass container, which is partially filled with clean, fresh brake fluid.

7. With the pressure turned **ON**, open the caliper bleed screw 1/2–3/4 turn and allow fluid to flow into the container. Leave the bleed screw open until clear, bubble-free fluid flows from the hose. If the reservoir has been drained or the hydraulic assembly removed from the vehicle prior to the bleeding operation, slowly pump the brake pedal 1–2 times while the bleed screw is open and fluid is flowing. This will help purge air from the hydraulic assembly. Tighten the bleeder screw to 7.5 ft. lbs. (10 Nm).

8. Repeat Step 7 at all calipers. Calipers should be bled in the following order:
   a. Left rear
   b. Right rear
   c. Left front
   d. Right front

9. After bleeding all 4 calipers, remove the pressure bleeding equipment and bleeder adapter by closing the pressure bleeder valve and slowly unscrewing the bleeder adapter from the hydraulic assembly reservoir.

CAUTION
Failure to release pressure in the reservoir will cause spillage of brake fluid and could result in injury or damage to painted surfaces.

10. Using a syringe or equivalent method, remove excess fluid from the reservoir to bring the fluid level to full level.

11. Install the reservoir cap and connect the fluid level sensor connector. Turn the ignition **ON** and allow the pump to charge the accumulator.

MANUAL BLEEDING

1. Depressurize the hydraulic accumulator as follows:
   a. Disconnect the negative battery cable.
   b. Pump the brake pedal a minimum of 40 times.
   c. A noticeable difference in pedal pressure should be noticed. When this occurs, press the pedal an additional 10 times.

CAUTION
Failure to depressurize the hydraulic accumulator, prior to performing this operation may result in personal injury and/or damage to the painted surfaces from pressurized brake fluid.

2. Connect a transparent hose to the caliper bleed screw. Submerge the free end of the hose in a clear glass container, which is partially filled with clean, fresh brake fluid.

3. Slowly pump the brake pedal several times, using full strokes of the pedal and allowing approximately 5 seconds between pedal strokes. After 2 or 3 strokes, continue to hold pressure on the pedal, keeping it at the bottom of its travel.

4. With pressure on the pedal, open the bleed screw 1/2–3/4 turn. Leave the bleed screw open until fluid no longer flows from the hose. Tighten the bleed screw and release the pedal.

5. Repeat this procedure until clear, bubble-free fluid flows from the hose.

6. Repeat all steps at each of the calipers. Calipers should be bled in the following order:
   a. Left rear
   b. Right rear
   c. Left front
   d. Right front

7. Fill the hydraulic assembly to the proper level using clean brake fluid meeting DOT 3 brake fluid.

8. Install both reservoir caps. Turn the ignition to the **ON** position

to allow the pump/motor to recharge the system.

Anti-Lock Brake System Service

PRECAUTIONS

Failure to observe the following precautions may result in system damage.
- Before performing electric arc welding on the vehicle, disconnect the Electronic Brake Control Module (EBCM) and the hydraulic modulator connectors.
- When performing painting work on the vehicle, do not expose the Electronic Brake Control Module (EBCM) to temperatures in excess of 185°F (85°C) for longer than 2 hrs. The system may be exposed to temperatures up to 200°F (95°C) for less than 15 min.
- Never disconnect or connect the Electronic Brake Control Module (EBCM) or hydraulic modulator connectors with the ignition switch ON.
- Never disassemble any component of the Anti-Lock Brake System (ABS) which is designated non-serviceable; the component must be replaced as an assembly.
- When filling the master cylinder, always use brake fluid which meets DOT-3 specifications; petroleum-based fluid will destroy the rubber parts.

DEPRESSURIZING THE HYDRAULIC ACCUMULATOR

1. With the ignition **OFF**, pump the brake pedal a minimum of 40 times, using approximately 50 lbs. (222 N) pedal force. A noticeable change in pedal feel will occur when the accumulator is discharged.
2. When a definite increase in pedal effort is felt, stroke the pedal 10 additional times. This should remove all hydraulic pressure from the system.
3. Install the return hose to the nipple on the reservoir.
4. Install the pressure hose to the hydraulic assembly; be sure the 2 washers are in there proper position. Tighten the banjo bolt to 13 ft. lbs. (18 Nm).
5. Fill the reservoir to the top of the screen.
6. Connect all electrical connectors to the hydraulic assembly.
7. Bleed the entire brake system.

8. Install the crosscar brace, if disturbed. Install the fresh air intake duct.
9. Connect the negative battery cable and check the assembly for proper operation.

Pump/Motor Assembly

REMOVAL AND INSTALLATION

1. Disconnect the negative battery cable.
2. Depressurize the hydraulic accumulator.

──────── CAUTION ────────
Failure to depressurize the hydraulic accumulator, prior to performing this operation may result in personal injury and/or damage to the painted surfaces.

3. Remove the fresh air intake ducts from the engine.
4. Remove the clip holding the high pressure line to the battery tray or body of the vehicle.
5. Disconnect the electrical connectors running across the engine compartment in the vicinity of the pump/motor high and low pressure hoses. One of these connectors is the one for the pump/motor assembly.
6. Disconnect the high and low pressure hoses from the hydraulic assembly. Cap or plug the reservoir fitting.
7. Disconnect the pump/motor electrical connector from the engine mount.
8. Remove the heat shield bolt from the front of the pump bracket. Remove the heat shield.
9. Lift the pump/motor assembly from the bracket and lift assembly out of the vehicle.
   To install:
10. Fit the pump motor assembly onto the bracket; install the heat shield and its retaining bolt.
11. Install the pump/motor electrical connector to the engine mount.
12. Connect the high and low pressure hose to the hydraulic assembly. Tighten the high pressure line to 145 inch lbs. (16 Nm). Tighten the hose clamp on the low pressure hose to 10 inch lbs. (1 Nm).
13. Connect the electrical connectors removed for access.
14. Install the high pressure line retaining clip to the battery tray if removed.
15. Install the fresh air intake ducts. Bleed the brake system.

Hydraulic Assembly

REMOVAL AND INSTALLATION

1. Disconnect the negative battery cable. Depressurize the hydraulic accumulator.

──────── CAUTION ────────
Failure to depressurize the hydraulic accumulator, prior to performing this operation may result in personal injury and/or damage to the painted surfaces.

2. Remove the fresh air intake ducts.
3. Disconnect all electrical connectors from the hydraulic unit and pump/motor.
4. Remove as much of the fluid as possible from the reservoir on the hydraulic assembly.
5. Remove the pressure hose fitting (banjo bolt) from the hydraulic assembly. Use care not to drop the 2 washers used to seal the pressure hose fitting to the hydraulic assembly inlet.
6. Disconnect the return hose from the reservoir nipple. Cap the spigot on the reservoir.
7. Disconnect all brake tubes from the hydraulic assembly. Remove the driver's side sound insulation panel.
8. Disconnect the pushrod from the brake pedal by using a small, flat tool to release the retainer clip on the brake pedal pin. The center tang on the clip must be moved back enough to allow the lock tab to clear the pin. Disconnect the pushrod from the pedal pin.
9. Remove the 4 underdash hydraulic assembly mounting nuts. Remove the hydraulic assembly.
   To install:
10. Position the hydraulic assembly on the vehicle. Install and torque the mounting nuts to 21 ft. lbs. (28 Nm).
11. Using Lubriplate™ or equivalent, coat the bearing surface of the pedal pin. Connect the pushrod to the pedal and install a new retainer clip.
12. Install the brake tubes. It the proportioning valves were removed from the hydraulic assembly, reinstall valves and tighten to 30 ft. lbs. (40 Nm).
13. Install the return hose to the nipple on the reservoir.
14. Install the pressure hose to the hydraulic assembly; be sure both washers are in there proper position. Tighten the banjo bolt to 13 ft. lbs. (18 Nm).

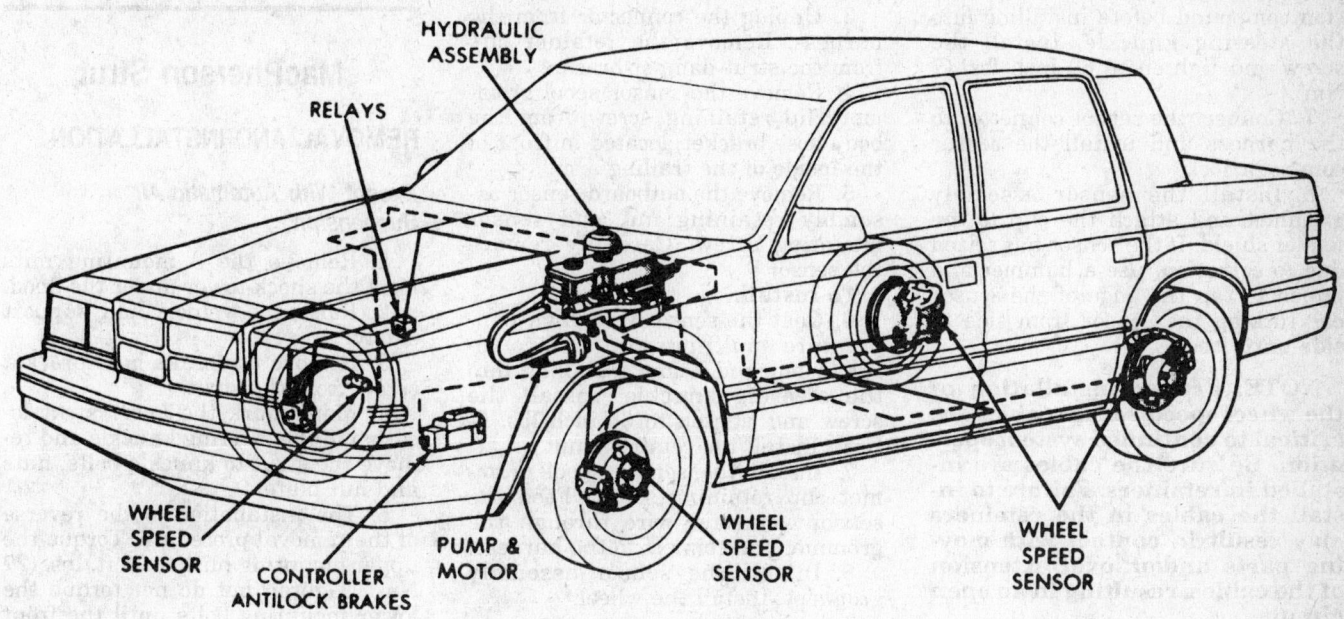

Bendix System 10 anti-lock brake system schematic

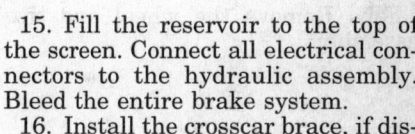

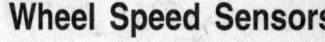

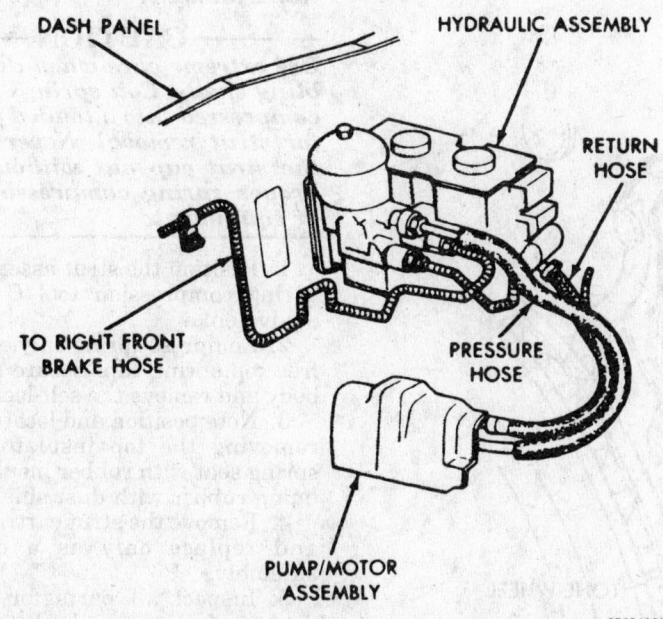

Hydraulic assembly, pump/motor assembly and related parts

15. Fill the reservoir to the top of the screen. Connect all electrical connectors to the hydraulic assembly. Bleed the entire brake system.

16. Install the crosscar brace, if disturbed. Install the fresh air intake duct.

17. Connect the negative battery cable and check the assembly for proper operation.

Wheel Speed Sensors

REMOVAL AND INSTALLATION

Front Sensor

1. Raise the vehicle and support safely. Remove the wheel and tire assembly.

2. Remove the screw from the clip that holds the sensor to the fender shield.

3. Carefully pull the sensor assembly grommet from the fender shield. Do not pull on the sensor wiring during removal.

4. Unplug the connector from the harness. Remove the retainer clip from the strut damper bracket.

5. Remove the sensor mounting screw. Carefully remove the sensor head from the steering knuckle.

To install:

6. Coat the sensor with high temperature multi-purpose anti-corrosion compound before installing into the steering knuckle. Install the screw and tighten to 60 inch lbs. (7 Nm).

7. Connect the sensor connector to the harness and install the sensor connector lock.

8. Install the sensor assembly grommet and attach the clip to the fender shield. If the sensor has seized due to corrosion, use a hammer and punch to tap the edge of the sensor ear rocking the sensor from side to side until free.

NOTE: Proper installation of the wheel speed sensor cables are critical to continued system operation. Be sure the cables are installed in retainers. Failure to install the cables in the retainers may result in contact with moving parts and/or over-extension of the cables, resulting in an open circuit.

9. Install the wheel.

Rear Sensor

1. Raise the vehicle and support safely. Remove the wheel and tire assembly.

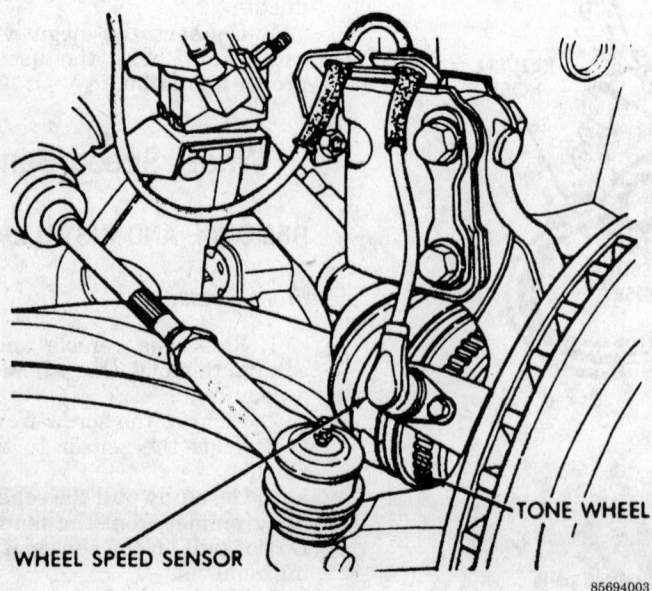

WHEEL SPEED SENSOR

TONE WHEEL

85694003

Front wheel speed sensor location

2. Carefully pull the sensor assembly grommet from the underbody and pull the harness through the hole.

3. Unplug the connector from the harness. Remove the retainer clip from the strut damper bracket.

4. Remove the sensor spool grommet clip retaining screw from the body hose bracket, located in front of the inside of the trailing arm.

5. Remove the outboard sensor assembly retaining nut and sensor mounting screw. Carefully remove the sensor.

To install:

6. Coat the sensor with high temperature multi-purpose anti-corrosion compound before installing into the steering knuckle. Install the screw and tighten to 60 inch lbs. (7 Nm). Install the retaining nut.

7. Install the sensor spool grommet clip retaining screw. Feed the sensor connector wire through the grommet and connect to the harness.

8. Install the sensor assembly grommet. Install the wheel.

FRONT SUSPENSION

MacPherson Strut

REMOVAL AND INSTALLATION

Except With Automatic Air Suspension

1. Remove the 3 mounting nuts from the shock tower under the hood.

2. Raise the vehicle and support safely.

3. Remove the brake hose bracket screw from the strut.

4. Matchmark the lower strut location to the steering knuckle and remove the strut to knuckle bolts, nuts and nut plate.

5. The installation is the reverse of the removal procedure. Torque the upper mounting nuts to 20 ft. lbs. (27 Nm). Tighten but do not torque the lower mounting bolts until the front end alignment has been completed.

6. Perform a front end alignment. Torque the strut to knuckle nuts to 75 ft. lbs. (100 Nm) plus 1/4 turn.

Strut Cartridge

REPLACEMENT

———— **CAUTION** ————

Use extreme care when disassembling struts. Coil springs must be compressed into a loaded position for strut removal. Never remove the strut cap nut without using proper spring compression tools or equipment.

1. Position the strut assembly into spring compression tool C–4838 or equivalent.

2. Compress spring only enough to free top spring cap. Secure the strut body and remove the self-locking nut.

3. Note position and location when removing the top insulator, upper spring seat with rubber insulator and bump rubber with dust shield.

4. Remove the strut cartridge body and replace only as a complete assembly.

5. Inspect all parts for wear or damage, be sure to check top spring support bearing for smooth operation. Replace any parts found to be worn or defective.

To install:

6. Position strut assembly in the vertical position and install strut cartridge body into spring assembly.

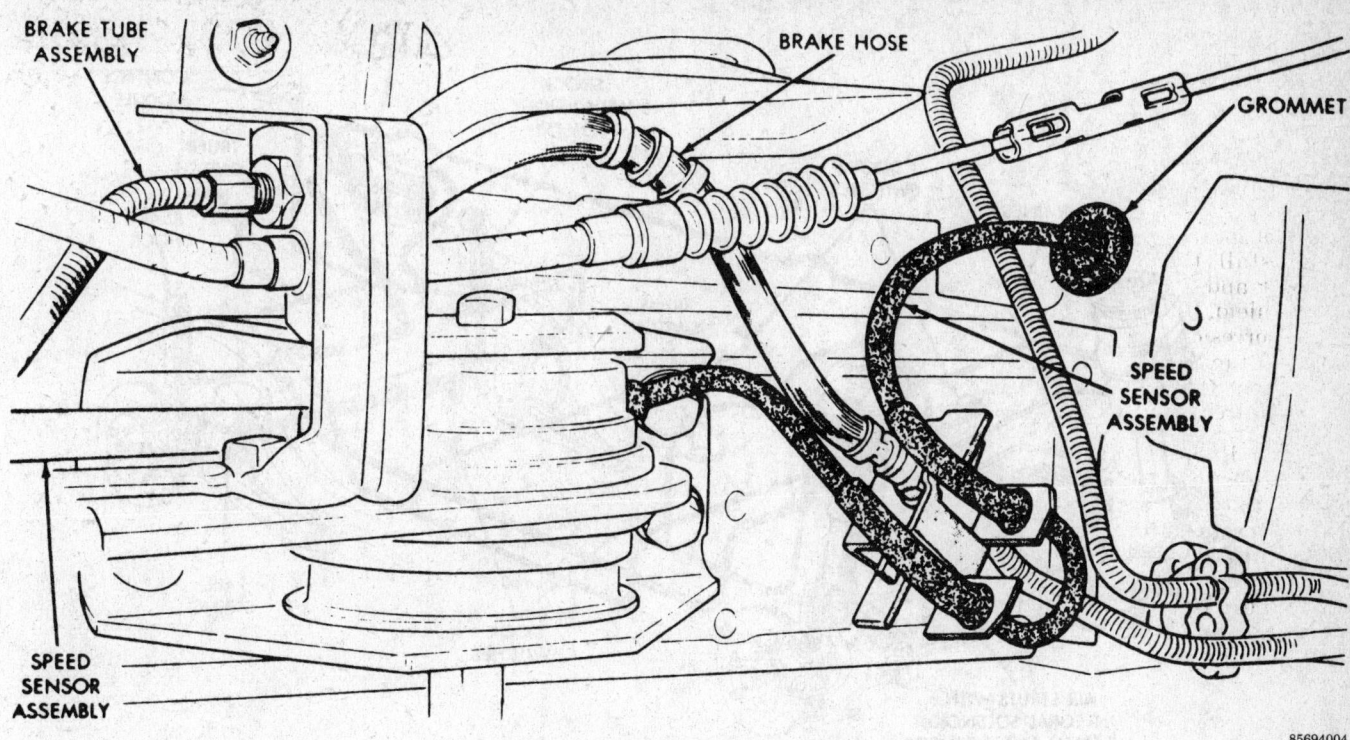

Rear speed sensor wiring routing along the body

85694004

7. Install dust boot, spring seat with rubber spring pad and top spring insulator.

8. Install the strut shaft retaining nut. Using tool L–4558 and torque the retaining nut to 55 ft. lbs. (75 Nm) plus ¼ turn.

9. Release spring compression tool while seating spring against perch.

Air Suspension Strut

REMOVAL AND INSTALLATION

1. Disconnect the negative battery cable.

2. Raise the vehicle and support safely. Remove the wheel and tire assembly.

3. To disconnect the air line, pull back on the plastic ring and pull the air line from the fitting.

4. Disconnect the electrical leads from the solenoid and the height sensor.

5. The solenoid has a molded square tang that fits into stepped notches in the air spring housing to provide for exhaust and a retaining positions. To vent the air spring:

a. Release the retaining clip.

b. Rotate the solenoid to the first step in the housing and allow the air pressure to vent.

c. Rotate the solenoid farther to the release slot and remove it from the housing.

6. Matchmark the assembly to the knuckle.

7. Remove cam bolt, knuckle bolt, and washers. Disconnect the brake hose bracket retaining bolt.

8. Hold or support the strut. Remove the upper nuts from the shock tower. Remove the strut assembly.

NOTE: Disassembly is restricted to the upper mount and bearing housing. The strut, air spring, height sensor, solenoid and wiring harness cannot be disassembled or serviced. They are replaced as a unit.

To install:

9. Install the strut assembly into the fender reinforcement, then install the retaining nuts and washers. Tighten to 20 ft. lbs. (27 Nm).

10. Position the knuckle into strut. Install washers with cam and knuckle bolts.

11. Attach brake hose retainer and tighten to 10 ft. lbs. (13 Nm).

12. Index the strut to the marks made during removal.

13. Use C-clamp to hold strut and knuckle. Tighten the clamp just enough to eliminate any looseness between the knuckle and the strut.

14. Check alignment of matchmarks. Tighten the nuts on the cam and knuckle bolts to 75 ft. lbs. (100 Nm) plus ¼ turn.

15. Remove the C-clamp.

16. Install the solenoid to the top step in the housing.

17. Connect the electrical leads to the solenoid and height sensor.

18. Connect the air line by pushing it into place; it will lock in place.

19. Connect the negative battery cable.

20. Recharge the air spring as follows:

a. To activate the left front spring solenoid, ground Pin **S31** to Pin **X20** of the controller connector.

b. To activate the right front spring solenoid, ground Pin **S30** to Pin **X20** of the controller connector.

c. To activate the right rear spring solenoid, ground Pin **S32** to Pin **X20** of the controller connector.

d. Run the compressor for 60 seconds by jumping from pin **S08** to pin **X20** of the controller connector.

21. Install the wheel and tire.

22. Check the system for proper operation.

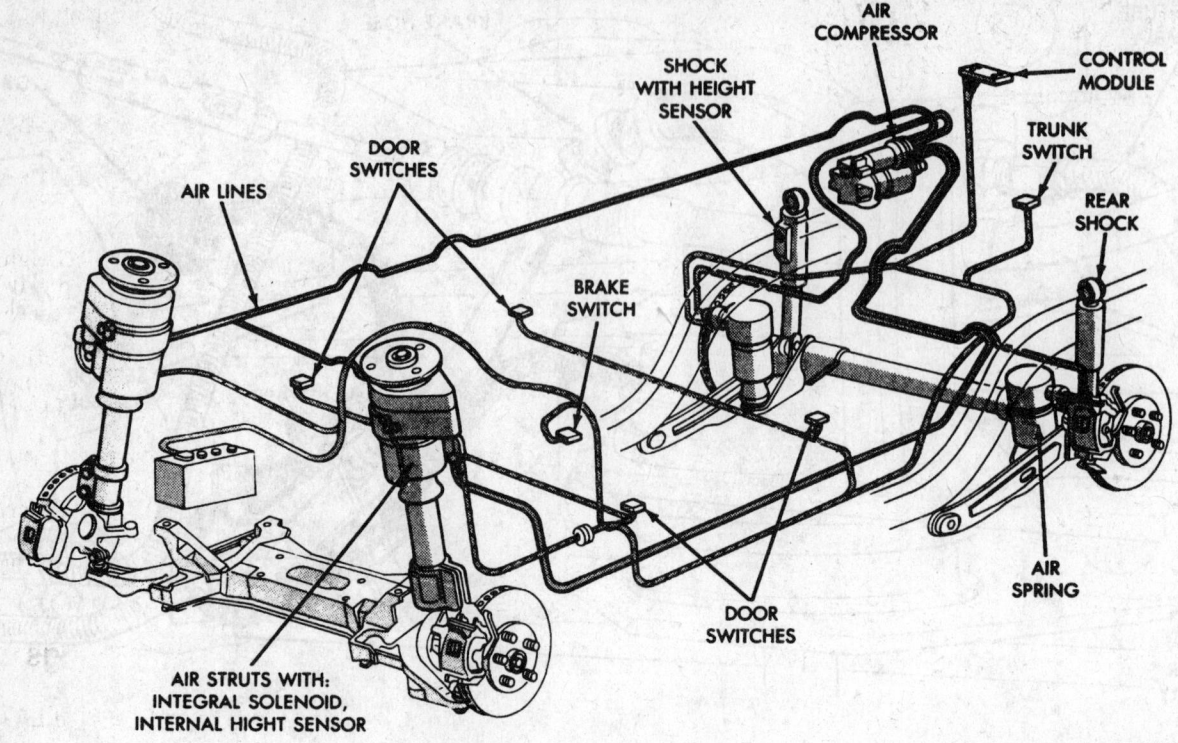

AIR
COMPRESSOR

SHOCK
WITH HEIGHT
SENSOR

CONTROL
MODULE

TRUNK
SWITCH

DOOR
SWITCHES

AIR LINES

REAR
SHOCK

BRAKE
SWITCH

DOOR
SWITCHES

AIR
SPRING

AIR STRUTS WITH:
INTEGRAL SOLENOID,
INTERNAL HIGHT SENSOR

84704059

Automatic air suspension components

Lower Ball Joints

INSPECTION

To inspect the ball joints, grasp the grease fitting by hand with the vehicle on the ground. If the grease fitting can be moved at all by hand, the ball joint should be replaced.

REMOVAL AND INSTALLATION

1. Raise the vehicle and support safely. Remove the tire and wheel assembly.
2. Remove the lower control arm from the vehicle.
3. Pry off the ball joint seal. Position the receiver cup tool C–46992 or equivalent, to support the lower control arm while receiving the ball joint assembly.
4. Press against the ball joint upper housing to remove the ball joint from the lower control arm.
   To install:
5. By hand, position the ball joint assembly into the bore in the lower control arm. Be sure the ball joint is not cocked in the bore of the control arm.
6. Position arm assembly in press with installer tool C–46992 or

equivalent, supporting the control arm.
7. Apply pressure against the ball joint assembly until the joint is fully seated against the bottom of the control arm. Do not apply excessive pressure against the control arm.
8. Position a new seal over the stud of the ball joint so it is against the ball joint housing, and using a 1½ in. socket, press the seal onto ball joint housing until it is seated against the top surface of the control arm.
9. Install the control arm on the vehicle.
10. Install the tire and wheel assembly.

Lower Control Arms

REMOVAL AND INSTALLATION

1. Raise the vehicle and support safely. Remove the tire and wheel assembly.
2. Remove the sway bar to lower control arm retainer on both sides of the vehicle. Rotate the bar down away from the control arm.
3. Remove the ball joint stud retaining bolt and nut.
4. Pry the lower control arm from the steering knuckle.

5. Remove the control arm to crossmember bolts, nuts bushings and retainers.
6. Remove the control arm from the vehicle.
   To install:
7. Transfer all reusable parts to the new control arm and lubricate.
8. Position the control arm onto the vehicle and install the attaching bolts. Loosely assemble the nuts to the attaching bolts.
9. Install the ball joint to the steering knuckle and tighten the retaining nut and bolt to 105 ft. lbs. (145 Nm).
10. Position the sway bar against the lower control arm and install the retainers and torque to 50 ft. lbs. (70 Nm). Install the tire and wheel assembly.
11. Lower the vehicle so the suspension is supporting the weight of the vehicle. Tighten the lower crossmember to control arm mounting bolts to 125 ft. lbs. (169 Nm).
12. Align the front suspension.

Sway Bar

REMOVAL AND INSTALLATION

1. Raise the vehicle and support safely.

2. Remove the front sway bar brackets and retainers.

3. Remove the sway bar support brackets and bushings from the lower control arm. Remove the sway bar from the vehicle.

4. The installation is the reverse of the removal procedure.

NOTE: Do not lubricate the sway bar bushings to eliminate a squeak. Oil based lubricants will deteriorate the rubber and only provide a temporary fix.

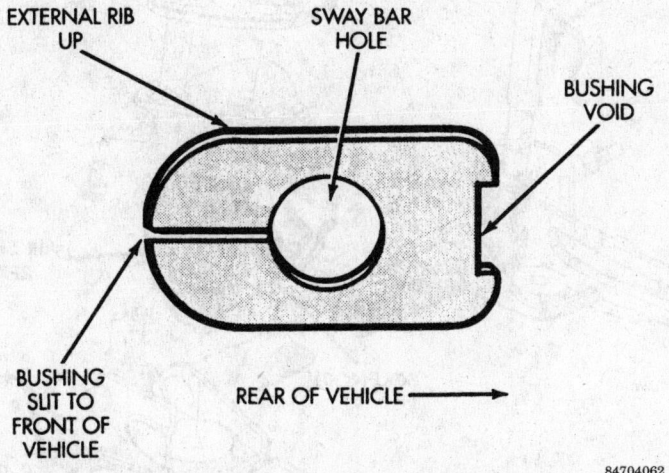

84704062

Sway to crossmember bushing positioning

REAR SUSPENSION

Shock Absorbers

REMOVAL AND INSTALLATION

1. Raise the vehicle and support safely. Disconnect the height sensor and air line, if equipped. The air line is released by pulling back on the plastic retaining ring.

2. Remove the bolts that attach the shock to the frame or bracket.

3. Remove the shock from the vehicle.

4. The installation is the reverse of the removal procedure.

5. Tighten upper shock mounting bolt to 45 ft. lbs. (61 Nm) and tighten lower mounting bolt to 40 ft. lbs. (54 Nm).

Coil Springs

REMOVAL AND INSTALLATION

1. Raise the vehicle and support safely.

2. Using the proper equipment, support the weight of the rear axle.

3. Remove the bolts that attach the shock to the lower mounting bracket.

4. Slowly lower the axle and remove the coil spring from the vehicle.

5. The installation is the reverse of the removal procedure.

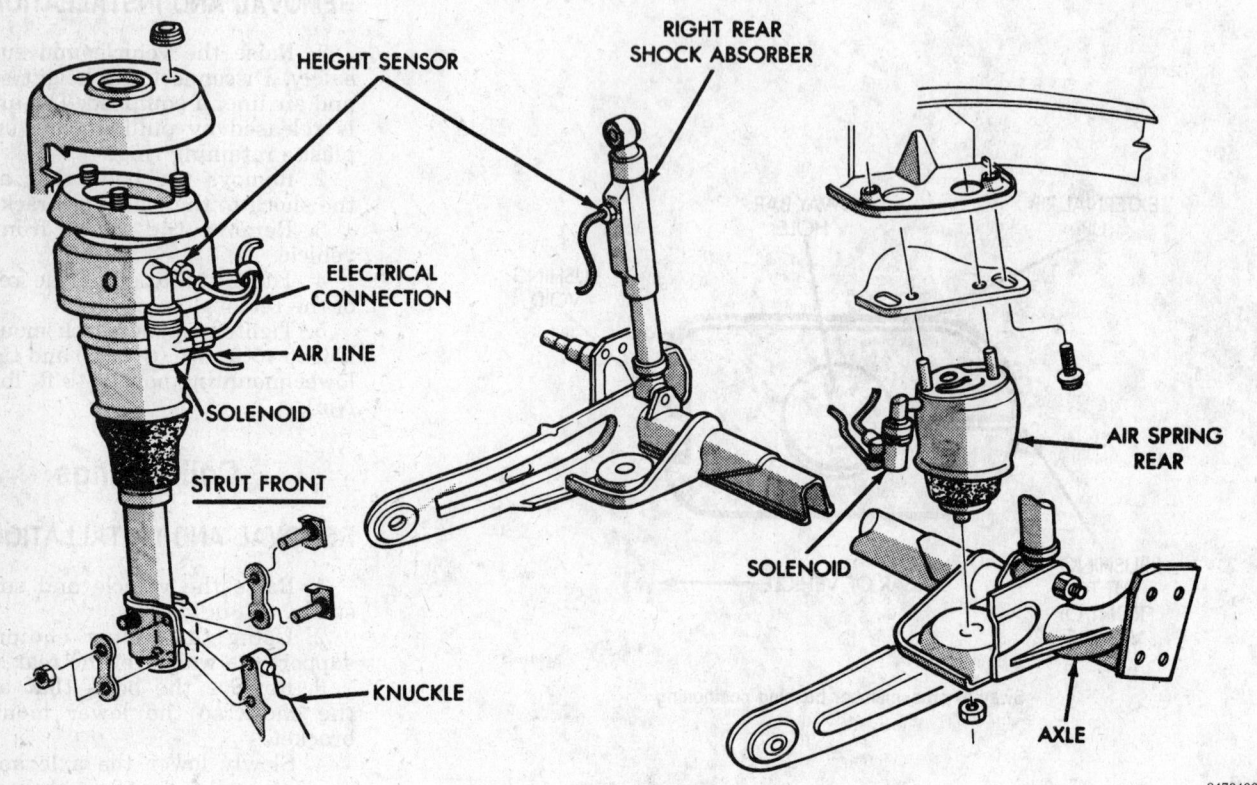

HEIGHT SENSOR

RIGHT REAR
SHOCK ABSORBER

ELECTRICAL
CONNECTION

AIR LINE

SOLENOID

STRUT FRONT

KNUCKLE

AIR SPRING
REAR

SOLENOID

AXLE

84704060

Front and rear air springs

Air Springs

REMOVAL AND INSTALLATION

1. Disconnect the negative battery cable.
2. Raise and safely support the vehicle. Remove the wheel.
3. Disconnect line to the air spring by pulling back on the plastic ring and pull the air line from the fitting.
4. Disconnect the electrical leads from the solenoid and height sensor.
5. The solenoid has a molded square tang that fits into stepped notches in the air spring housing to provide for exhaust and retaining positions. To vent the air spring:
  a. Release the retaining clips.
  b. Rotate the solenoid to the first step in the housing and allow the air to vent.
  c. Rotate the solenoid to the next step to release and remove the solenoid.
6. Release the upper spring alignment retaining clips.
7. Remove the nut that attaches the lower portion of the spring to the axle.
8. Pry the assembly down, and pull the alignment studs through the retaining clips to remove the assembly from the vehicle.

To install:

9. Position the lower stud into its seat in the axle and upper alignment pins through the frame rail adaptor. Install the retaining clips.
10. Install the lower mounting nut but do not tighten.
11. Install the solenoid to the top step in the housing.
12. Connect the electrical lead to the solenoid.
13. Connect the air line by pushing it into place; it will lock into position.
14. Connect the negative battery cable.
15. Partially charge the air spring and install the lower mounting nut.

Torque the mounting nut to 50 ft. lbs. (68 Nm).

16. Correct the air pressure as desired and install the wheel and tire assembly.

Rear Wheel Bearings

REMOVAL AND INSTALLATION

1. Disconnect the negative battery cable.

2. Raise the vehicle and support safely. Remove the wheel and tire assembly.

3. Remove and position the caliper out of the way using wire. Do not let the caliper hang from the brake hose.

4. Remove the grease cap, cotter pin, nut lock, nut, thrust washer and outer wheel bearing.

5. Carefully slide the drum or hub from the spindle making sure not to drag the inner bearing or grease seal over the threaded stub axle or damage may occur.

6. Using the appropriate puller tool, remove the grease seal and the inner bearing from the drum or hub. Discard the grease seal.

7. Thoroughly clean all old grease from all bearings, bearing races and hub or drum cavity. Clean bearings by soaking in an appropriate solvent. Dry bearing thoroughly.

--- **CAUTION** ---
Do not spin bearing with compressed air during drying or personal injury or parts damage may occur.

8. Inspect bearing cones for pitting or other damage and replace if necessary.
To install:
9. Pack both the inner and the outer bearing with grade 2 EP Grease. If bearing and cups are to be replaced, remove the old races from the drum or hub using a brass drift and install new races using the appropriate size driver.

10. Coat the hub cavity and cup with grease and install the inner bearing. Install the grease seal using the appropriate size driver.

11. Before installing the hub or drum, inspect the stub axle for burrs or rough surfaces and smooth out all rough surfaces.

12. Slide the drum or hub assembly onto the stub axle shaft. Install the outer bearing, washer and nut.

13. Tighten the wheel bearing nut to 20–25 ft. lbs. (27–34 Nm) while rotating the wheel. Back off the adjuster nut ¼ turn, then retighten finger-tight only.

14. Position the nut lock over the flats of the adjusting nut and install a new cotter pin. Install the grease cap.

15. Install the tire and wheel assembly and lower the vehicle.

ADJUSTMENT

1. Raise the vehicle and support safely.

2. Remove the tire and wheel assembly.

3. If equipped with rear disc brakes, remove the caliper and the rotor. Support the caliper aside using wire. Do not let the caliper hang from the brake hose.

4. Remove the grease cap, cotter pin and nut lock.

5. Tighten the wheel bearing nut to 20–25 ft. lbs. (27–34 Nm) while rotating the wheel. Back off the adjuster nut ¼ turn, then retighten finger-tight only.

6. Position the nut lock over the flats of the adjusting nut and install a new cotter pin. Install the grease cap.

7. Install the tire and wheel assembly and lower the vehicle.

Rear Axle Assembly

REMOVAL AND INSTALLATION

1. Raise the vehicle and support safely.

2. Separate the park brake cable at the connector. Detach the cable housing from the hanger.

3. Separate the brake tube assembly from the brake hose mounting bracket. If equipped with rear disc brakes, remove the caliper assembly and support aside.

4. Remove the lower shock absorber through bolts and the track bar to axle pivot bolt. Support the track bar end with wire.

5. Lower the axle until the spring and isolator assemblies can be removed.

6. Support the pivot bushing end of the trailing arms as well as the axle beam with jackstands. Remove the pivot bushing hanger bracket to frame screws. Lower and remove the axle from the vehicle.
To install:
7. Raise the axle in position and support the axle on jackstands.

8. Install the shock absorber and track bar through bolts loosely.

9. Install the brake assemblies and related components to the axle assembly, if removed, and adjust bearing preload.

10. Attach parking brake mechanism to the rear suspension and brake actuators.

11. Install the brake hose and fitting into the bracket and install the lock. Attach the brake tube to the hose fitting and tighten to 140 inch lbs. (16 Nm).

12. Install the tire and wheel assemblies. Lower the vehicle so the weight of the vehicle is resting on the suspension. Tighten the lower shock absorber bolts to 45 ft. lbs. (61 Nm) and the track bar bolt to 70 ft. lbs. (95 Nm).

13. Adjust the rear brakes and the parking brake cable. Bleed the brake system.

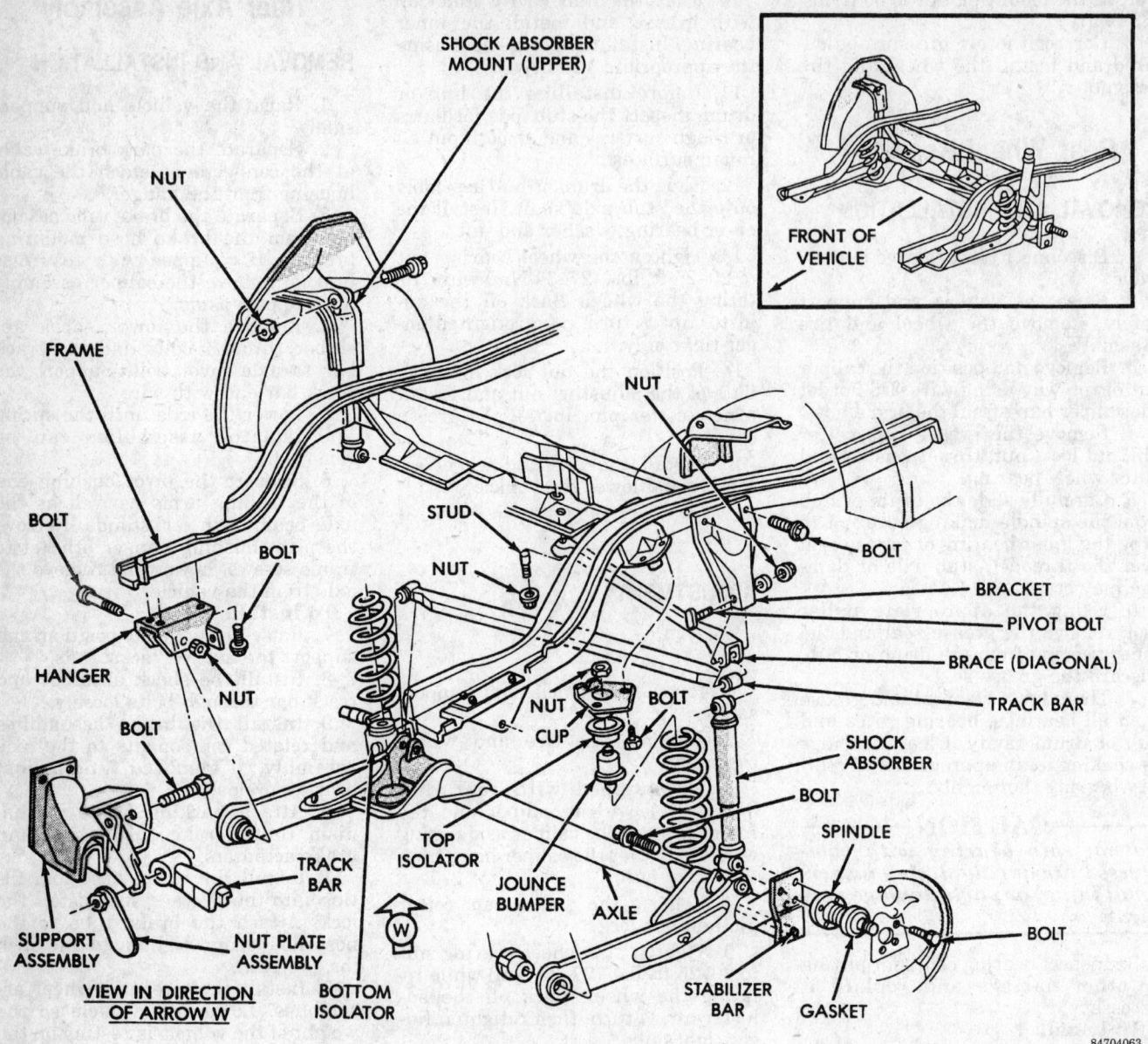

Trailing arm rear suspension

84704063

Chrysler Corporation 4

CHRYSLER—Concorde • New Yorker • LHS **DODGE**—Intrepid **EAGLE**—Vision

FIRING ORDERS

NOTE: To avoid confusion, always replace spark plug wires one at a time.

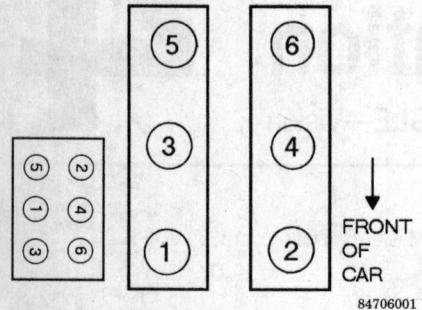

84706001

3.3L and 3.5L Engines
Engine Firing Order: 1–2–3–4–5–6
Distributorless Ignition System

ENGINE ELECTRICAL

NOTE: Disconnecting the negative battery cable on some vehicles may interfere with the functions of the on-board computer systems and may require the computers to undergo a relearning process, once the negative battery cable is reconnected.

Distributorless Ignition System

REMOVAL AND INSTALLATION

Crankshaft Position Sensor

1. Disconnect negative battery cable.
2. Disconnect the electrical connector from the crankshaft position sensor.
3. Remove the sensor mounting screw and lift the sensor from the transaxle housing.
4. Installation is the reverse of the removal procedure. Torque the crankshaft position sensor retainer screw to 105 inch lbs. (12 Nm).

Camshaft Position Sensor

1. Disconnect negative battery cable.
2. Disconnect the electrical connector from the sensor.

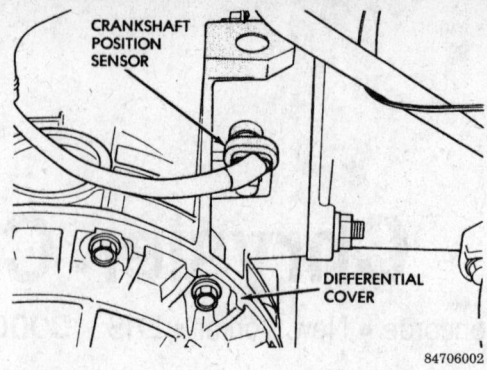

84706002

Crankshaft sensor located at the differential housing

3. Without pulling on the connector wires, pull the sensor up and out of the chain case cover.
4. If installing the original sensor, clean off the old spacer from the sensor face. A new spacer must be installed during installation. If installing a new sensor, confirm that a new paper spacer is attached to the face of the sensor and a new O-ring is positioned in the groove on the sensor body.

To install:

5. Install the sensor into the chain case cover and push the sensor downward until contact is made with the camshaft sprocket. While holding the sensor in this position, install and tighten the retainer bolt to 105 inch lbs. (12 Nm).
6. Connect the sensor wire harness connector and the negative battery cable.

Electronic Ignition Coil Pack

3.3L ENGINE

1. Disconnect negative battery cable.
2. Disconnect the electrical connector from the coil pack.
3. Remove the coil pack mounting screws. The ignition coil pack towers are numbered for cylinder identifica-

tion. Label the spark plug cables to aid in installation and remove cables from the coil pack.
4. Remove the coil pack from the engine.
5. Installation is the reverse of the removal procedure. Tighten the mounting screws to 105 inch lbs. (12 Nm).

3.5L ENGINE

1. Disconnect negative battery cable.
2. Disconnect and remove the air cleaner hose.
3. Disconnect the electrical connector from the wire harness of the ignition coil.
4. Remove the coil pack mounting screws and remove the coil. The spark plug cables and the coil pack towers are numbered for cylinder identification. Transfer spark plug cables to new coil pack.

To install:

5. Install the coil pack to the right cylinder head and secure using the retaining screws, tightened to 105 inch lbs. (12 Nm).
6. Connect the sensor wire harness connector and install the air cleaner hose.
7. Reconnect the negative battery cable.

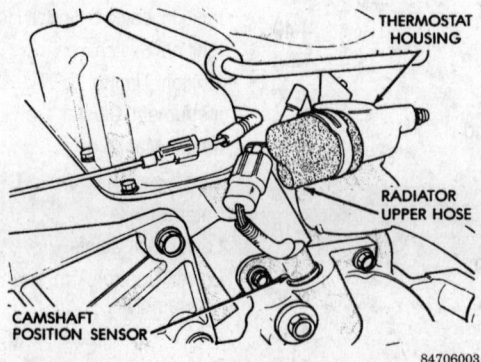

84706003

Camshaft position sensor location — 3.3L engine

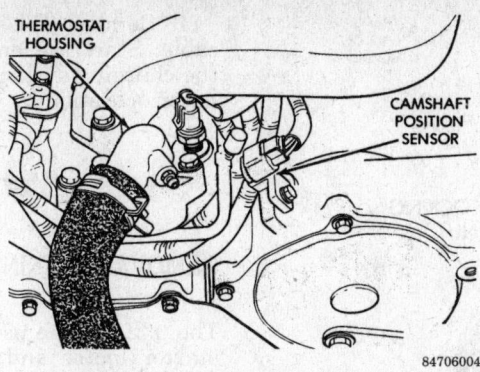

Camshaft position sensor location — 3.5L engine

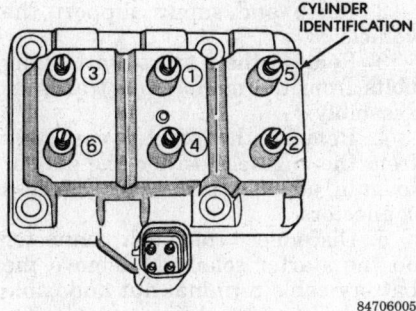

Coil pack with towers numbered for identification

Knock Sensor

3.5L ENGINE

The 3.5L engine uses 2 knock sensors that thread into the cylinder block, directly below the intake intake manifold.

1. Disconnect negative battery cable.
2. Drain the cooling system. Remove the intake manifold plenum and intake manifold.
3. Disconnect the electrical connector from the knock sensor.
4. Using a crows foot socket, remove the knock sensor from the sensor.

To install:

5. Install the knock sensor into the engine block and tighten to 7 ft. lbs. (10 Nm).

NOTE: Over tightening or under tightening of the knock sensor will effect sensor performance, possibly causing improper spark control.

6. Attach the electrical connector to the sensor.
7. Install the intake manifold and the intake manifold plenum.
8. Refill the cooling system to the proper level and connect the negative

battery cable. Start the engine and allow to reach normal operating temperature. Check for leaks and proper engine fluid levels.

Ignition Timing

ADJUSTMENT

The 3.3L and 3.5L engines use a fixed ignition system. The Power Control Module (PCM) regulates ignition timing. Basic ignition timing is not adjustable.

Alternator

PRECAUTIONS

Several precautions must be observed with alternator-equipped vehicles to avoid damage to the unit.

• If the battery is removed for any reason, make sure it is reconnected with the correct polarity. Reversing the battery connections may result in damage to the 1-way rectifiers.

• When utilizing a booster battery as a starting aid, always connect the positive to positive terminals and the negative terminal from the booster

battery to a good engine ground on the vehicle being started.

• Never use a fast charger as a booster to start vehicles.

• Disconnect the battery cables when charging the battery with a fast charger.

• Never attempt to polarize the alternator.

• Do not use test lamps of more than 12 volts when checking diode continuity.

• Do not short across or ground any of the alternator terminals.

• The polarity of the battery, alternator and regulator must be matched and considered before making any electrical connections within the system.

• Never separate the alternator on an open circuit. Make sure all connections within the circuit are clean and tight.

• Disconnect the battery ground terminal when performing any service on electrical components.

• Disconnect the battery if arc welding is to be done on the vehicle.

BELT TENSION ADJUSTMENT

1. Inspect belt tension with the use of belt tensioning tool kit C-4162 or equivalent, making sure tension reading agrees with the desired tension of 120 lbs. (54 Kg) for used belt or 140–160 lbs. (64–73 Kg) for a new belt.
2. If tension requires adjustment, loosen the alternator mounting bolts.
3. On 3.3L engine, adjust belt tension by turning the screw on the mounting bracket to maintain the proper tension.
4. On 3.5L engine, adjust belt tension by adjusting the tensioner pulley located on the timing belt cover to maintain the proper tension.
5. Tighten the alternator mounting bolts to 40 ft. lbs. (54 Nm).

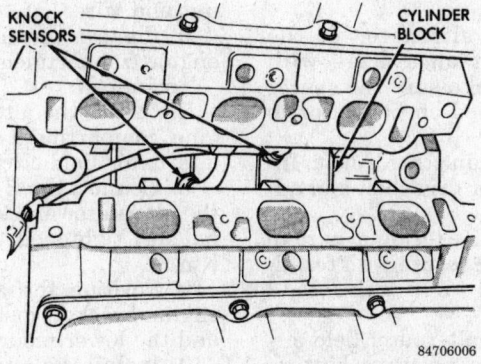

Knock sensor location — 3.5L engine

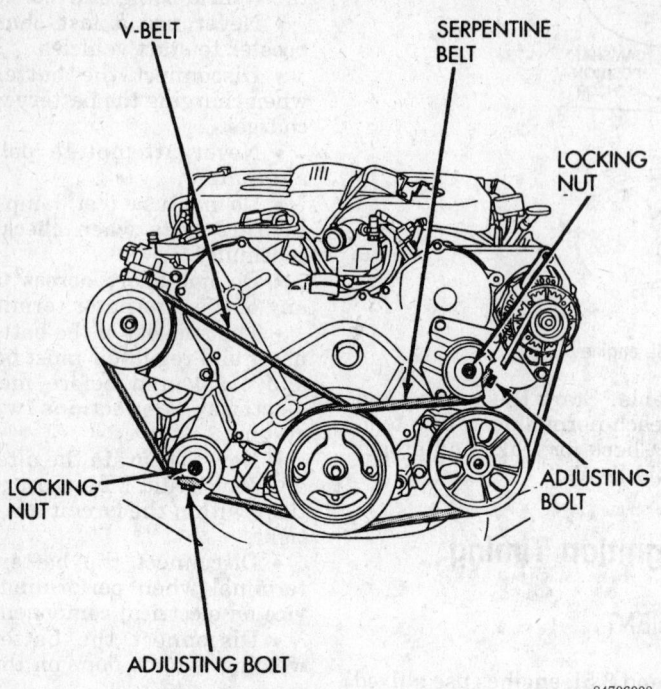

Accessory drive belt tension adjustment point — 3.5L engine

LABELS: V-BELT · SERPENTINE BELT · LOCKING NUT · LOCKING NUT · ADJUSTING BOLT · ADJUSTING BOLT · 84706008

REMOVAL AND INSTALLATION

3.3L Engine

1. Disconnect negative battery cable.

2. Disconnect the alternator field circuit plug. Remove the B+ terminal nut and wire.

3. Loosen the adjusting T-bolt and the pivot bolts. Do not remove at this time.

4. Remove the alternator drive belt.

5. Remove the adjusting T-bolt and the pivot bolt. Be careful not to loose the spacer from the pivot bolt.

6. Remove the alternator from the engine.

To install:

7. Install the alternator to the mounting bracket and secure with the pivot bolt. Make sure the spacer is properly installed on bolt prior to installation.

8. Install the adjusting T-bolt. Install the alternator drive belt and adjust tension.

9. Connect the B+ terminal wire to the alternator and secure with terminal nut tightened to 75 inch lbs. (9 Nm).

10. Connect the alternator field circuit plug and the negative battery cable.

11. Start the engine and inspect the charging system for proper alternator operation.

3.5L Engine

1. Disconnect negative battery cable.

2. Loosen the lower mounting bolt and the pivot bolt. Do not remove the bolts at this time.

3. Loosen the belt adjustment bolt and remove the drive belt.

4. Remove the bracket and the lower bolt. Remove the pivot bolt and the alternator from the mounting bracket.

5. Disconnect the alternator field circuit plug. Remove the B+ terminal nut and wire.

6. Remove the alternator from the engine compartment.

To install:

7. Install the alternator to the engine compartment and connect the alternator field circuit plug.

8. Connect the B+ terminal wire to the alternator and secure with terminal nut tightened to 75 inch lbs. (9 Nm).

9. Position the alternator on the engine bracket, install the pivot bolt and the lower mounting bolts.

10. Install the alternator drive belt and adjust the tension.

11. Connect the negative battery cable. Start the engine and inspect the charging system for proper alternator operation.

Starter

REMOVAL AND INSTALLATION

The 3.3L engine uses a Nippondenso starter motor and the 3.5L engine uses a Delco starter motor.

1. Disconnect the negative battery cable.

2. Raise and safely support the vehicle.

3. Remove the 3 starter attaching bolts from the engine and transaxle assembly.

4. Remove the starter assembly from the engine. Position the starter to gain access to the wire harness connectors.

5. Disconnect the push connector on the starter solenoid. Remove the battery cable terminal nut and cable from the starter solenoid.

6. Remove the starter from the vehicle.

To install:

7. Clean corrosion and dirt from the wore terminals and install onto the starter solenoid. Install the starter assembly in position and secure using mounting bolts. Make sure the ground wire is installed on the lower mounting bolt during installation.

8. Tighten 3 mounting bolts to 40 ft. lbs. (54 Nm).

9. Connect the negative battery terminal.

CHASSIS ELECTRICAL

Air Bag

NOTE: The air bag system is a sensitive, complex electro-mechanical unit. Before attempting to diagnose or repair the system, the system must first be disarmed. Failure to disarm the system prior to component diagnosis or repairs may result in accidental deployment and possible personal injury.

DISARMING

1. Disconnect the negative battery terminal and isolate using an appropriate insulator.
2. Allow the system capacitor to discharge for 2 minutes prior to starting repairs on any air bag system or related components.

Heater Blower Motor

REMOVAL AND INSTALLATION

1. Disconnect the negative battery cable.
2. Remove the lower right under panel silencer duct.
3. Remove the blower motor housing cover.
4. Remove the blower motor retainer screws and lower the blower motor from the housing. Disconnect the wire harness connector.
5. if replacement of the blower motor is required, the blower motor and the wheel must be replaced as an assembly.

To install:
6. Install the blower motor into the housing and secure with retainer screws.
7. Connect harness connector and install the blower motor housing cover.
8. Install the lower right under panel silencer duct and connect the negative battery terminal.

Windshield Wiper Motor

REMOVAL AND INSTALLATION

1. Disconnect the negative battery cable.
2. Remove the wiper arms and the blades. Disconnect hoses from connector at the base of each arm.
3. Remove the cowl top plastic screen and disconnect the washer hose at the inline connector. Make sure the connector is not lost.
4. Disconnect the motor connector at the back side of the housing. Remove the 4 wiper housing module mounting screws then remove the housing.
5. Remove the nut and disconnect the wiper drive link from the motor crank.
6. Remove the 3 motor mounting screws and lift the motor and mounting plate out of the housing.
7. Disconnect the motor harness grommet from the housing.

To install:
8. Connect the motor harness grommet to the housing.
9. Position the motor and mounting plate in the housing and install 3 mounting screws. Tighten the mounting screws to 106 inch lbs. (12 Nm). Connect the wiper drive link to the motor crank and install the retainer nut. Tighten the crank nut to 89–124 inch lbs. (11–14 Nm).
10. Install the wiper housing and secure using 4 mounting screws. Connect the motor connector at the back side of the housing.
11. Connect the washer hose at the inline connector and install the cowl top plastic screen.
12. Install the wiper arms and the blades. Connect hoses from connector at the base of each arm.
13. Connect the negative battery cable.

Instrument Cluster

REMOVAL AND INSTALLATION

1. Disconnect negative battery cable. Disarm the air bag system, if equipped.

NOTE: Before attempting to diagnose or repair the vehicle, the air bag system must first be disarmed. Failure to disarm the system prior to component diagnosis or repairs may result in accidental deployment and possible personal injury.

2. Remove the instrument panel left end cap and the headlight bezel.
3. Remove the 2 headlight switch screws and move switch to allow clearance for the instrument panel cluster bezel and instrument cluster removal.
4. Remove the instrument panel upper center bezel. Remove the hazard switch and the steering column shroud.
5. Tilt the steering column down. Remove the instrument panel cluster bezel. If equipped with message center, disconnect the wire connector. The message center lamps may be replaced at this point, if required.
6. Remove the instrument cluster retainer screws and disengage the upper latch.
7. Pull the instrument cluster forward slightly and disconnect the wire harness connector at the back of the unit. Remove the instrument cluster from the panel.

To install:
8. Connect the wire harness to the instrument cluster and install cluster into the instrument panel. Install the retainer screws.
9. Connect the message center wire connector. Install the instrument panel cluster bezel and secure in position.
10. Install the hazard switch and the steering column shroud.
11. Install the instrument panel upper center bezel, headlight switch and headlight bezel to the instrument panel.
12. Install the instrument panel end cap. Connect the negative battery cable and check for proper operation of the instrument cluster gauges.

Speedometer

REMOVAL AND INSTALLATION

Type A and C Gauge Option

1. Disconnect negative battery cable. Disarm the air bag system, if equipped.

NOTE: Before attempting to diagnose or repair the vehicle, the air bag system must first be disarmed. Failure to disarm the system prior to component diagnosis or repairs may result in accidental deployment and possible personal injury.

2. Remove the instrument cluster from the instrument panel.
3. Remove the 6 back cover retaining screws and the cover from the cluster.
4. Disconnect the transaxle range indicator and odometer connectors from the printed circuit board.
5. Remove the 4 lens retaining screws and remove the lens cover.
6. Remove the trip odometer reset knob by gently pulling rearward.
7. Remove the speedometer/tachometer assembly from the cluster.

NOTE: The speedometer/tachometer assembly and the transaxle range indicator is serviced as 1 component.

To install:
8. Install the speedometer/tachometer assembly into the cluster. Install the trip odometer reset knob.
9. Install the lens cover and secure using the 4 retainer screws.
10. Connect the transaxle range indicator and odometer connectors to the printed circuit board.

11. Install the cover and the 6 retaining screws to the back of the cluster.

12. Install the cluster to the instrument panel and connect the negative battery terminal. Check for proper operation of the instrument cluster gauges and speedometer.

Type B Gauge Option

1. Disconnect negative battery cable. Disarm the air bag system.

NOTE: Before attempting to diagnose or repair the vehicle, the air bag system must first be disarmed. Failure to disarm the system prior to component diagnosis or repairs may result in accidental deployment and possible personal injury.

2. Remove the instrument cluster from the instrument panel.

3. Remove the trip odometer reset knob by gently pulling rearward.

4. Remove the 5 cluster back cover retainer screws and remove the rear cover from the cluster.

5. Disconnect the transaxle range indicator and odometer connectors from the printed circuit board.

6. Remove the 4 lens retaining screws and remove the lens cover.

7. Remove the tachometer and the fuel/temperature gauge from the cluster.

8. Remove the speedometer from the cluster.

To install:

9. Install the speedometer, tachometer and the fuel/temperature gauge into the cluster.

10. Install the lens cover and secure with the 4 lens retainer screws.

11. Connect the transaxle range indicator and odometer connectors to the printed circuit board.

12. Install the cluster back cover and the 5 retaining screws.

13. Install the cluster assembly into the instrument panel.

14. Connect the negative battery cable and check for proper operation of the instrument cluster gauges and speedometer.

Headlight Switch

REMOVAL AND INSTALLATION

1. Disconnect negative battery cable.

2. Open the left front door and remove the instrument panel left end cover.

3. Remove the screw from the left end of the instrument panel and pull the bezel rearward to disengage locking clips.

4. With the bezel removed, remove the 3 screws on the headlight switch. Pull the switch out and disconnect the wiring connector. Remove the switch from the instrument panel.

5. Installation is the reverse of the removal procedure.

Combination Switch

The combination switch incorporates the hazard switch, wiper switch, the pulse wiper switch, washer switch and turn signal switch operations.

REMOVAL AND INSTALLATION

1. Disconnect negative battery cable.

2. Disarm the air bag system.

3. Remove the tilt lever.

NOTE: Before attempting to diagnose or repair the vehicle, the air bag system must first be disarmed. Failure to disarm the system prior to component diagnosis or repairs may result in accidental deployment and possible personal injury.

4. Remove both the upper and the lower steering column shrouds.

5. Remove the combination switch mounting screws and remove the switch from the column.

To install:

6. Install the switch to the column and secure using the mounting screws. Tighten the combination switch to column mounting screws to 17 inch lbs. (2 Nm).

7. Install the upper and the lower steering column shrouds tightening the retainers to 17 inch lbs. (2 Nm).

8. Install the tilt lever and connect the negative battery cable. Check all functions of the combination switch.

Ignition Switch

REMOVAL AND INSTALLATION

The ignition switch attaches to the lock cylinder housing opposite the lock cylinder.

1. Disconnect negative battery cable. Disarm the air bag system.

NOTE: Before attempting to diagnose or repair the vehicle, the air bag system must first be disarmed. Failure to disarm the system prior to component diagnosis or repairs may result in accidental deployment and possible personal injury.

2. Remove the tilt lever attaching screws and the tilt lever from the steering column.

3. Remove the upper and the lower covers from the steering column.

4. Remove the combination switch for the LHS and New Yorker.

5. Disconnect the electrical connector from the ignition switch.

6. Remove the ignition switch mounting screws and the switch.

To install:

7. Position the ignition switch so the tab on the switch is aligned to the notch in the cylinder housing. Also, a slot in the end of the end of the ignition switch fits over the shaft in the end of the lock cylinder housing. Use the ignition key to rotate the lock cylinder to align the ignition switch with the lock cylinder housing.

8. Install the ignition switch mounting screws.

9. Install the combination switch for the LHS and New Yorker.

10. Attach the electrical connector to the switch.

11. Install the tilt lever, upper and the lower steering column covers.

12. Connect the negative battery cable. Check operation of the ignition switch.

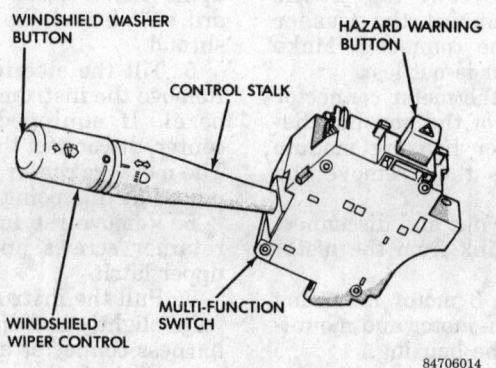

WINDSHIELD WASHER BUTTON

HAZARD WARNING BUTTON

CONTROL STALK

WINDSHIELD WIPER CONTROL

MULTI-FUNCTION SWITCH

84706014

Combination switch assembly

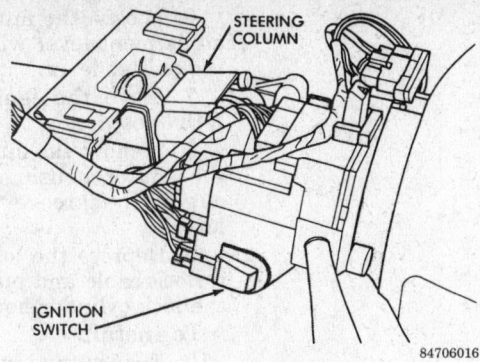

Ignition switch location

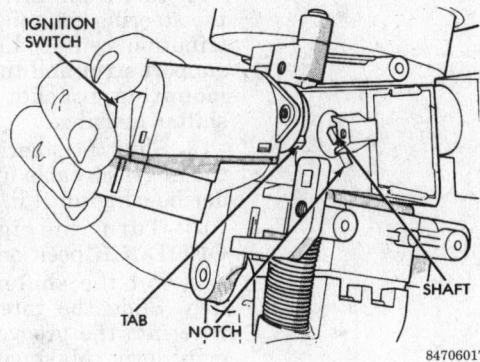

Ignition switch adjustment

Ignition Lock Cylinder Housing

REMOVAL AND INSTALLATION

1. Disconnect negative battery cable. Disarm the air bag system.

NOTE: Before attempting to diagnose or repair the vehicle, the air bag system must first be disarmed. Failure to disarm the system prior to component diagnosis or repairs may result in accidental deployment and possible personal injury.

2. Remove the tilt lever attaching screws and the tilt lever from the steering column.
3. Remove the upper and the lower covers from the steering column.
4. Turn the ignition key to **RUN** and depress the lock cylinder retainer tab using a small tipped tool.
5. With the tab depressed, pull the lock cylinder out.
   To install:
6. Install the key in the lock cylinder and turn the key to **RUN**. In this

position, the tab on the lock cylinder can be depressed.

7. The shaft at the end of the lock cylinder aligns with the socket in the housing. Align the lock cylinder with the grooves in the housing. Slide the lock cylinder into the housing until the tab sticks through the opening in the housing.

8. Turn the key **OFF** and remove the key from the ignition lock cylinder.

9. If equipped with column shift and a new lock cylinder was in-

stalled, replace and adjust the interlock cassette at this time.

NOTE: The interlock system on a column shift vehicle is only adjusted after installing a new cassette. It can only be adjusted once. If the system operation is incorrect, install and adjust a new interlock cassette.

10. If equipped with floor shift, adjust or replace the interlock cable at this time.
11. Install the tilt lever, upper and lower steering column covers.
12. Connect the negative battery cable.

Interlock Cassette/Cable

REMOVAL AND INSTALLATION

Column Shift

The interlock cassette slides into the housing behind the lock cylinder.

1. Depress the tab on top of the cassette.
2. Slide the interlock cassette out of the housing.
3. Remove the cable from the locking arm on the shifter mechanism and remove the cassette from the vehicle.
   To install:
4. Make sure the spring loaded latch rotates freely on the shifter gate. Position the shifter in **P** and remove the key from the ignition lock cylinder.
5. Install the cable over the hook on the locking arm of the shifter mechanism and slide the cassette into the housing until it locks in position.
6. To adjust, push the adjustment tab in until it stops. The adjustment tab will click as it moves into posi-

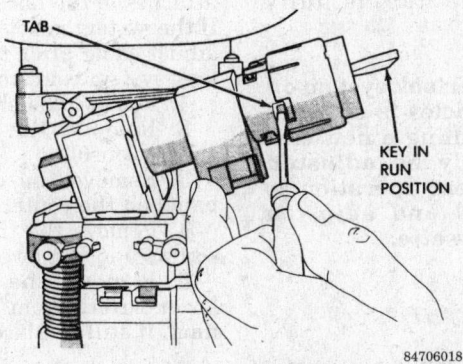

Ignition lock cylinder removal

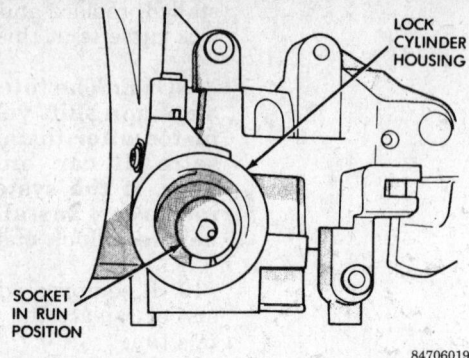

Socket positioning inside of ignition lock cylinder housing

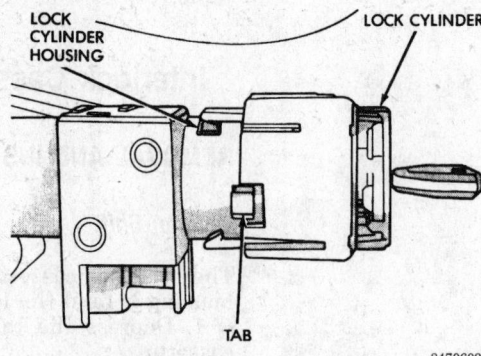

Installation of ignition lock cylinder

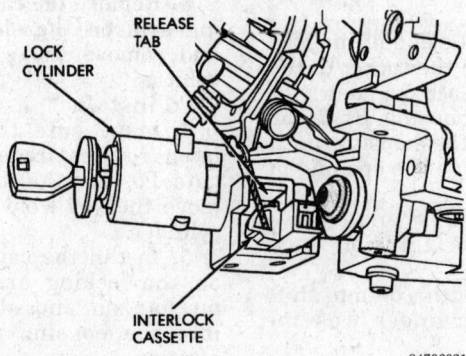

Ignition interlock cassette — if equipped with column shift

tion. Ensure the tab is fully depressed.

NOTE: The interlock system on column shift vehicles is only adjusted after installing a new cassette. It can only be adjusted once. If the system operation is incorrect, install and adjust a new interlock cassette.

Floor Shift

The interlock cable slides into the housing behind the lock cylinder and attaches to the floor mounted shifter. If the system is not working properly, adjust cable prior to replacing interlock system components.

1. Remove the shifter handle.
2. Remove the bezel from the shifter console.
3. Remove the drivers side kick panel on the center console.
4. Remove the tilt lever attaching screws and the lever.
5. Remove the upper and the lower covers from the steering column, if still in place.

6. Loosen the nut on the interlock adjustment lever which is located on the shifter lever.
7. Move the ignition key to the **RUN** position.
8. Remove the interlock cable from the shifter housing. Slide the cable out of the groove in the interlock lever.
9. Depress the lock tab on the interlock cable and pull cable out from the lock cylinder housing.
   To install:
10. Ensure the ignition switch is in the **ON** position.
11. Route the interlock cable down the steering column, past the air distribution center duct, between the support strut and the air bag module mounting bracket and down the shifter housing.
12. Slide the steering column end of the interlock cable into the lock cylinder housing until it snaps into place.
13. Turn the ignition key to **OFF/LOCK** position.
14. Put the shifter in the **P** position. Slide the interlock cable core wire into the grooves on the adjustment lever. Make sure the cable end is seated in the groove.
15. Slip the cable into the housing until it snaps into place. Ensure the shifter lever is in the **P** position and remove the key from the lock cylinder.
16. Loosen the adjuster nut on the shifter lever, which will allow the cable to set itself to in the correct position. Tighten the adjustment nut.
17. Inspect the interlock cable with the ignition in the **OFF** position and the ignition key removed. The cable core wire should not move when pulled. If the cable core moves, the cable is improperly installed or kinked. With the ignition in the **RUN** position, the cable core wire should slide freely when pulled. The cable should also return to the bottomed out position when released. If not, the cable is improperly installed or adjusted.
18. Check the interlock adjustment. With the ignition key in the **OFF** position, the shifter should be locked in **PARK**. If not, repeat the adjustment procedure.
19. Without starting the engine, place the ignition switch in the **RUN** position. Move the shifter lever to **R**. You should be unable to remove the ignition key from the cylinder. If you can remove the key, repeat the adjustment position.
20. Place the shifter in the **P** position and turn the ignition **OFF**. Remove the key from the ignition. If you

are unable to do so, repeat the adjustment procedure.

21. Install the bezel on the shifter console. Install the shifter handle.

22. Install the lower kick panel.

23. Install the tilt lever and both steering column covers.

ADJUSTMENT

Floor Shift Interlock

1. Remove the shifter handle.

2. Remove the bezel from the shifter console.

3. Loosen the adjuster nut on the shifter lever.

4. Move the key to the **RUN** position. Remove the interlock cable from the shifter housing. Slide the cable from the groove in the interlock lever.

5. Inspect the interlock cable with the ignition in the **OFF** position and the ignition key removed. The cable core wire should not move when pulled. If the cable core moves, the cable is improperly installed or kinked. With the ignition in the **RUN** position, the cable core wire should slide freely when pulled. The cable should also return to the bottomed out position when released. If not, the cable is improperly installed or adjusted.

6. Put the shifter in the **P** position. Slide the interlock cable core wire into the groove on the adjustment lever. Ensure the cable end seats in the groove.

7. Slip the cable in the housing until it snaps in place.

8. Ensure the shifter lever is in the **P** position and remove the key from the lock cylinder.

9. Loosen the adjuster nut on the shifter lever, which will allow the cable to set itself to in the correct position. Tighten the adjustment nut.

10. Check the interlock adjustment. With the ignition key in the **OFF** position, the shifter should be locked in **PARK**. If not, repeat the adjustment procedure.

11. Without starting the engine, place the ignition switch in the **RUN** position. Move the shifter lever to **R**. You should be unable to remove the ignition key from the cylinder. If you can remove the key, repeat the adjustment position.

12. Place the shifter in the **P** position and turn the ignition **OFF**. Remove the key from the ignition. If you are unable to do so, repeat the adjustment procedure.

13. Install the bezel on the shifter console. Install the shifter handle.

14. Install the lower kick panel.

15. Install the tilt lever and both steering column covers.

Brake Light Switch

ADJUSTMENT

1. Push the switch and the retaining bracket forward as far as it will go. The brake pedal will move forward slightly.

2. Gently pull back on the brake pedal as far as it will go. This will cause the switch ratchet backward to the correct position.

REMOVAL AND INSTALLATION

1. Disconnect negative battery cable. Remove the under instrument panel silencer duct.

2. Pull the switch assembly rearward off brake bracket and remove the electrical connector from the brake bracket.

3. Disconnect the wire harness connectors from the body wire harness and remove the switch.

4. Installation is the reverse of the removal procedure. Adjust the brake light switch after installation.

Manual Valve Lever Position Sensor (MVLPS)

The Manual Valve Lever Position Sensor (MVLPS) provides for Park/Neutral only starter operation. The MVLPS electrical connector extends outside the transaxle assembly, on the left side next to the fill tube.

REMOVAL AND INSTALLATION

1. Disconnect the MVLPS electrical connector.

2. Remove the valve body from the transaxle.

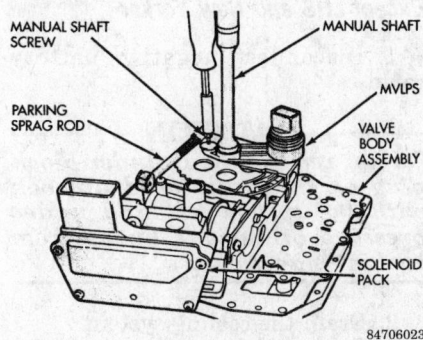

Manual Valve Lever Position Sensor (MVLPS) location on transaxle valve body

3. Remove the manual shaft retainer screw and slide the MVLPS from the shaft.

4. Installation is the reverse of the removal procedure.

Fuses, Circuit Breakers and Relays

LOCATION

Fuses

Power Distribution Center — located on the left side of the engine compartment at the firewall.

Multi-Purpose Fuse Block — inside the vehicle, on the left side behind of the driver's knee protector.

Fusible Links

Fuse Links — in the engine compartment, just behind the battery.

Relays

Hazard Flasher Relay — located on the left side of the passenger compartment, between the junction block and the brake pedal.

Anti-Lock Brake System Relays — left side of the engine compartment, mounted on the side of the power distribution center.

Horn Relay — multi-purpose fuse block inside the vehicle, on the left side behind the driver's knee protector.

Door Lock Relay — multi-purpose fuse block inside the vehicle, on the left side behind the driver's knee protector.

Cruise Control Relay — multi-purpose fuse block inside the vehicle, on the left side behind the driver's knee protector.

Engine Starter Relay — located in the power distribution center on the left side of the engine compartment at the firewall.

Fuel Pump Relay — located in the power distribution center on the left side of the engine compartment at the firewall.

Intermittent Wiper Relay — located in the power distribution center on the left side of the engine compartment at the firewall.

Radiator Fan Relay — located in the power distribution center on the left side of the engine compartment at the firewall.

Anti-Lock Brake System (ABS) Pump Relay — located in the power distribution center on the left side of the engine compartment at the firewall.

Computers

LOCATION

Engine Controller — inside the engine compartment mounted on the right front fender.

Body Control Module — right side of passenger compartment, behind the kick pane.

Daytime Running Lamp Module — inside the engine compartment, mounted on the right front area of the engine compartment.

Transmission Control Module — inside the engine compartment, mounted on the left front fender, behind the battery.

Anti-Lock Brake System (ABS) Controller — left front the engine compartment, on the right side of the battery.

Climate Control Module — under the right side of the instrument panel.

Air Bag Control Module — under the left side of the instrument panel.

Remote Keyless Entry Module — under the right side of the instrument panel.

Cruise Control

ADJUSTMENT

If the cruise control system is functioning improperly, inspect the control cable to assure both ends are securely attached. If either end is loose, the cruise control system will be inoperative.

ENGINE COOLING

Radiator

REMOVAL AND INSTALLATION

LHS and New Yorker

1. Disconnect the negative battery cable.

─────── **CAUTION** ───────
Do not remove the cylinder block plug or the radiator draincock with the system hot and under pressure or serious burns from coolant may occur.

2. Remove the sight shield from the radiator crossmember.

3. Remove the right and left headlight modules as follows:

   a. Remove the headlight module retaining screws.

   b. Separate the headlight module from the mounting adapter.

   c. Disengage the wiring harness from the headlight and fog light assembly.

   d. Remove the headlight modules from the vehicle.

4. Drain the cooling system. Discharge the air conditioning system into an approved recycling facility.

5. Disconnect and plug the automatic transaxle cooler lines and coolant hoses.

6. Disconnect the cooling fan wiring.

7. Disconnect the air conditioning lines at the condenser.

8. Remove the upper radiator mounting bolts and lift the radiator module from the vehicle.

9. Remove the cooling fan and other components if replacing the radiator.

To install:

10. Install the cooling fan and other components onto the new radiator.

11. Slide the radiator module into position. Make sure the lower insulators are in place.

12. Connect the air conditioning lines and torque the radiator mounting bolts to 105 inch lbs. (12 Nm).

13. Connect the transaxle and coolant hoses to the radiator.

14. Connect all electrical wiring to the radiator.

15. Refill the radiator with coolant. Evacuate, recharge and leak test the air conditioning system.

16. Install the headlight modules and sight shield to the radiator crossmember.

17. Connect the battery cable, start the engine and check for leaks and coolant level.

Except LHS and New Yorker

1. Disconnect negative battery cable.

─────── **CAUTION** ───────
Do not remove the cylinder block plug or the radiator draincock with the system hot and under pressure or serious burns from coolant may occur.

2. Drain the cooling system.

3. Remove the upper radiator crossmember. Remove the hose clamps and hoses from the radiator.

4. Disconnect the automatic transaxle hoses from the cooler and plug.

5. Disconnect the fan electrical harness connector from the RFI module.

6. Remove the upper radiator mounting screws. Disconnect the engine block heater wire, if equipped.

7. Remove the air conditioning condenser attaching screws located at the front of the radiator, if equipped. Lean the condenser forward against the bumper taking care not to damage condenser assembly.

8. Lift the radiator assembly from the vehicle. Take care not to damage the cooling fins or the water tubes on the radiator during removal.

To install:

9. Slide the radiator and the fan module down into position, seat the radiator assembly lower rubber isolator in the mount holes provided.

10. Attach the air conditioning condenser to the radiator, if equipped. Torque the mounting screws to 45 inch lbs. (5 Nm).

11. Install and torque the radiator mounting bolts to 123 inch lbs. (14 Nm).

12. Connect the lower radiator hose and clamp, then the automatic transaxle cooler hoses. Torque the radiator hose clamps to 22 inch lbs. (2.5 Nm).

13. Install the upper radiator hose and align so it will not interfere with the hood.

14. Connect the fan motor electrical connector and connect the negative battery cable.

15. Fill the cooling system. Start the engine and allow to run until normal operating temperature is reached.

16. Check the cooling system and automatic transaxle for leaks and correct fluid level.

Electric Cooling Fan

TESTING

1. Disconnect negative battery cable.

2. Disconnect the wire connector at the cooling fan. Remove the radiator sight shield for LHS and New Yorker.

3. Attach the fan motor terminals to the battery terminals making sure to observe fan motor polarity. If correct polarity is not followed, damage to the motor will occur.

4. If the motor fails to operate, it is assumed defective and replacement is required.

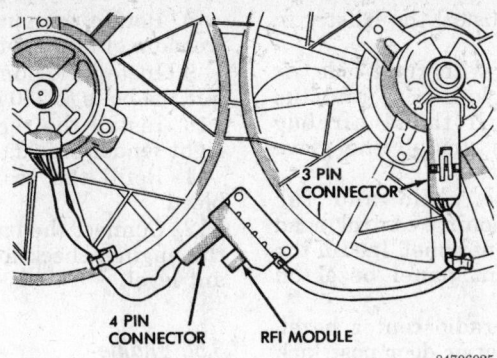

84706025

Electric fan motor RFI module

REMOVAL AND INSTALLATION

1. Disconnect negative battery cable.

2. Disconnect the electrical connector from the RFI module.

3. Remove the fans and shroud assembly from the radiator.

4. Disconnect the fan from the shroud by removing the motor fasteners from the shroud and separating.

To install:

5. Position the fan on the shroud and install the retainer nuts. Tightened the right fan mounting nuts to 25 inch lbs. (3 Nm) or 45 inch lbs. (5 Nm) for the left fan.

6. Install the fan assembly to the radiator and tighten the attaching fasteners to 45 inch lbs. (5 Nm). Install the retaining clips.

7. Connect the fan motor electrical connector and install the radiator sight shield, if equipped.

8. Connect the negative battery cable.

Heater Core

REMOVAL AND INSTALLATION

1. Disconnect the negative battery cable. Disarm the air bag system.

NOTE: Before attempting to repair the vehicle, the air bag system must first be disarmed. Failure to disarm the system prior to component repairs may result in accidental deployment and possible personal injury.

— CAUTION —

R-134A service equipment or the vehicle air conditioning system should not be pressure tested or leak tested with compressed air. Some mixtures or R-134A have been shown to be combustible at elevated pressures. These mixtures are potentially dangerous

and may result in fire or explosion causing personal injury or property damage.

2. Using an air conditioning recovery unit manufactured for servicing R-134A type refrigerant, remove all R-134A refrigerant from the air conditioning system.

— CAUTION —

Avoid breathing air conditioning refrigerant and lubricant vapor or mist. Exposure may irritate eyes, nose and throat. Use only approved service equipment meeting SAE requirements to discharge R-134A systems. If accidental system discharge occurs, ventilate the work area before resuming service.

3. Remove the air cleaner hose and the air distribution duct from the engine. Drain the cooling system.

4. Disconnect the heater hoses at the dash panel. Plug the heater core inlet and outlet tubes to prevent antifreeze from leaking inside of the vehicle.

5. Remove both air conditioning lines from the expansion valve using tool 7193 or equivalent, to disconnect the quick connectors. After removing the lines, cap the expansion valve openings to prevent system contamination.

NOTE: The lubricant used in this air conditioning system absorbs moisture readily. Do not leave any portion of the system open to the atmosphere for any extended period of time.

6. From inside the vehicle, remove the 3 retaining nuts from the mounting studs. Remove the right and the left instrument panel end caps, which are held in place by a series of clips.

7. Remove the right and left interior door post kick panel. Remove the

right side bezel from the instrument panel.

8. Remove the radio center bezel which is held in place by 6 clips, by carefully prying from the instrument panel.

9. Remove the radio and the heater/air conditioning control head from the instrument panel and set aside.

10. Remove the center instrument panel bezel by carefully prying from the panel.

11. Remove the center console from the vehicle, if equipped.

12. If equipped with passenger side air bag, lower the glove box from the panel and remove the 4 air bag mounting screws. Close the glove box.

13. Remove the lower bolster retainer screws. Lower the bolster and disconnect the trunk release and glove box light wiring. Remove the lower bolster from the vehicle.

14. Carefully pry up on 1 end of the instrument panel top cover until the retaining clips release. Repeat the procedure on the remaining side of the cover and gradually pry the rear edge of the cover along the entire width of the panel. Remove the instrument panel top cover from the vehicle.

15. Remove both windshield pillar post trim panels. Remove the 5 bolts at the base of the windshield which retain the instrument panel to the cowl.

16. Remove the DRB II scan tool connector from brace. Remove the instrument panel ground strap located under the lower left side of the console.

17. Remove the left knee blocker support bracket. This will allow for access to the 60-way connector. Disconnect all related wiring connectors.

18. Disconnect the fuse panel wiring connectors. Remove the brake light switch connector.

19. Remove the steering column covers. Remove the steering column retainer bolts and allow the column to lower to the floor. Do not completely remove the column from the vehicle.

20. Remove the air bag connectors. Remove the right side floor air duct.

21. Disconnect the 10-way connector, blower motor connector and blower module connector from the heater/air conditioning assembly.

22. Remove the body controller from the vehicle. Disconnect the right side connector and antenna connector.

23. Remove the right and left side upper instrument panel mounting screws located in the door jam. Remove the upper instrument panel from the vehicle with the aid of a helper.

24. Remove the air duct for rear heater vents, which is held in place by a bracket/push pin near the rear of the duct. Remove the air bag module and the brace from the vehicle.

25. Remove the 3 attaching bolts which holds the heater housing to the dash panel. Carefully roll the heater housing out of the vehicle.

26. Remove the drain tube from the heater housing. Pull the heater core retainer clips back and pull the heater core from the case.

To install:

27. Install the heater core into the housing and install the retainer brackets. Secure using the screws supplied with the new heater core.

28. Install the housing into the vehicle and secure using the 3 attaching bolts. Install the air bag module and brace into the vehicle.

29. Install the air duct for rear heater vents. Install the upper instrument panel into the vehicle with the aid of a helper. Install the right and left side upper instrument panel mounting screws located in the door jam.

30. Connect the right side electrical connector.

31. Install the body controller in the vehicle. Connect the 10-way connector, blower motor connector and blower module connector to the heater/air conditioning assembly.

32. Connect the air bag harness connectors. Install the right side floor air duct.

33. Raise the steering column and install the steering column retainer bolts. Install the upper and lower steering column covers.

34. Connect the fuse panel wiring connectors, brake light switch connector and remaining harness connectors disconnected during the removal procedures.

35. Install the DRB II scan tool connector to the mounting brace. Install the instrument panel ground strap under the lower left side of the center console.

36. Install both windshield pillar post trim panels and the instrument panel top cover. Connect the trunk release and glove box light wiring to

the bolster and install the bolster in vehicle.

37. If equipped with right side air bag, lower the glove box from the panel and install the 4 air bag mounting screws. Install the glove box.

38. Install the radio and the heater/air conditioning control head into the instrument panel. Install the center instrument panel bezel on panel.

39. Install the radio center bezel, right and left interior door post kick panels. Install the right side bezel to the instrument panel.

40. Install the 3 retaining nuts onto the mounting studs. Install the right and left instrument panel end caps.

41. Install both air conditioning lines to the expansion valve using new O-rings at the connections.

NOTE: The O-rings used in this system are made of a special type of rubber that is not affected by R-134A refrigerant. Do not substitute an O-ring not manufactured for R-134A refrigerant type system or leakage will occur within a short period of time.

42. Connect the heater hoses at the dash panel and refill the cooling system. Install the air cleaner hose and the air distribution duct to the engine.

43. Connect the negative battery cable. Evacuate and charge the refrigerant system. Refill and bleed the cooling system.

Water Pump

REMOVAL AND INSTALLATION

3.3L Engine

1. Disconnect the negative battery cable and drain the cooling system.
2. Remove the serpentine belt and right front fender shield.
3. Remove the water pump pulley bolts and pulley.
4. Remove the water pump mounting bolts and pump. Discard the O-ring seal.
5. Clean the gasket sealing surfaces. Do not scratch the aluminum surfaces.

To install:

6. Install a new O-ring and the water pump to the timing chain case.
7. Install the retaining bolts and torque to 105 inch lbs. (12 Nm).

8. Rotate the pump and check for freedom of movement.
9. Install the pump pulley and torque the bolts to 250 inch lbs. (30 Nm).
10. Install the serpentine belt and right fender shield.
11. Refill the cooling system and bleed.
12. Connect the battery cable, start the engine, check for leaks and coolant level.

3.5L Engine

1. Disconnect the negative battery cable and drain the cooling system.
2. Remove the timing belt.
3. Remove the water pump mounting bolts and pump. Discard the O-ring seal.
4. Clean the gasket sealing surfaces. Do not scratch the aluminum surfaces.

To install:

5. Install a new O-ring and wet with clean coolant .
6. Install the water pump and O-ring to the engine block.
7. Install the retaining bolts and torque to 105 inch lbs. (12 Nm).
8. Rotate the pump and check for freedom of movement.
9. Install the timing belt.
10. Refill the cooling system and bleed.
11. Connect the battery cable, start the engine, check for leaks and coolant level.

Thermostat

REMOVAL AND INSTALLATION

1. Disconnect negative battery cable.
2. Allow cooling system to cool completely. Drain the cooling system to a level below the thermostat.
3. Remove the thermostat bolts and housing.
4. Remove the thermostat and discard the gasket. Clean both gasket sealing surfaces.

To install:

5. Install the thermostat into the recess in the intake manifold. Place a new gasket moistened with water, on the water box mating surface.
6. Install the housing over the gasket and thermostat and tighten to 21 ft. lbs. (28 Nm).
7. Refill and bleed the cooling system.

Cooling System Bleeding

NOTE: This procedure should be followed after any cooling system component has been replaced or removed and installed. It is essential that coolant does not contact the accessory drive belt or pulleys. Chemicals deteriorate the synthetic materials in the belt. Always protect the the serpentine belt and pulleys with clean shop towels. When installing the drain hose to the air bleed valve on the thermostat housing, route the hose away from the belt, pulleys and cooling fan.

1. Attach one end of a 4 foot long ¼ in. hose to the air bleed on the thermostat housing. Route the hose away from the drive belt and pulleys. Place the other end of the hose in a clean container. The purpose of this hose is to keep coolant away from the belt and pulleys.
2. Open the bleed valve.
3. Slowly fill the coolant pressure bottle until a steady stream of coolant flows from the hose attached to the bleed valve. Close the bleed valve and continue filling to the full mark on the bottle. The full mark is the top of the post inside the bottle. Install the cap tightly on the coolant pressure bottle.
4. Remove the hose from the bleed valve.

FUEL SYSTEM

Fuel System Service Precautions

Safety is an important factor when servicing the fuel system. Failure to conduct maintenance and repairs in a safe manner may result in serious personal injury. Maintenance and testing of the vehicle's fuel system components can be accomplished safely and effectively by adhering to the following rules and guidelines.
• To avoid the possibility of fire and personal injury, always disconnect the negative battery cable unless the repair or test procedure requires that battery voltage be applied.
• Always relieve the fuel system pressure prior to disconnecting any fuel system component (injector, fuel rail, pressure regulator, etc.), fitting or fuel line connection. Exercise extreme caution whenever relieving fuel system pressure to avoid exposing skin, face and eyes to fuel spray. Please be advised that fuel under pressure may penetrate the skin or any part of the body that it contacts.
• Always place a shop towel or cloth around the fitting or connection prior to loosening to absorb any excess fuel due to spillage. Ensure that all fuel spillage is quickly removed from engine surfaces. Ensure that all fuel soaked cloths or towels are deposited into a suitable waste container.
• Always keep a dry chemical (Class B) fire extinguisher near the work area.
• Do not allow fuel spray or fuel vapors to come into contact with a spark or open flame.
• Always use a backup wrench when loosening and tightening fuel line connection fittings. This will prevent unnecessary stress and torsion to fuel line piping. Always follow the proper torque specifications.
• Always replace worn fuel fitting O-rings. Do not substitute fuel hose where fuel pipe is installed.

NOTE: Flexible Fuel Vehicles (FFV) are available in specific model production. Although many of the components are similar they cannot be interchanged. These vehicles can operate on a fuel mixture of gasoline and methanol up to 85 percent methanol. Components for Flexible Fuel Vehicles (FFV) can be identified by a green coloring or have a green label or tag attached.

RELIEVING FUEL SYSTEM PRESSURE

NOTE: Do not smoke or allow open flame near the fuel system or components during fuel system service.

1. Disconnect negative battery cable.
2. Remove the protective cap from the fuel pressure test port on the fuel rail.
3. Place the open end of fuel pressure release hose tool C-4799-1 or equivalent, into an approved gasoline container.
4. Connect the other end of the hose to the fuel pressure test port. Fuel pressure will bleed off through the hose into the gasoline container.

Fuel Tank

REMOVAL AND INSTALLATION

1. Disconnect negative battery cable. Release the fuel system pressure.
2. Drain the fuel tank using the appropriate equipment.
3. Raise and safely support the vehicle. Remove both rear tires.
4. Remove the exhaust pipe rubber insulators off the mounting studs of the rear of the vehicle and in front of the exhaust tank.
5. Using grease pencil or equivalent marking technique, place alignment marks on the fuel filler hose, filler tube, vent hose and vent tube.
6. Remove the rear splash shield from the right rear wheel well.
7. Disconnect the filler hose and the vent hose.
8. Disconnect the fuel supply tube from the inlet side of the fuel filter.

NOTE: Prior to disconnecting the fuel lines, wrap a shop rag around the connection to absorb any fuel spillage due to residual pressure in the lines.

9. Disconnect the fuel return tube and vent tube near the fuel filter.
10. Disconnect both ends of the sway bar from the stabilizer links. Mark the position of the crossmember ends on the frame rail.
11. Remove the crossmember mounting bolts and pull the crossmember down until it stops.
12. Place a jack under the tank to support it's weight.

NOTE: The sway bar bracket bolts must be replaced after loosening or removal. Only use original equipment bolts as replacement

13. Remove the sway bar mounting bracket, heatshield and fuel tank straps. To prevent the sway bar from falling down, install sway bar mounting bracket with bolts finger-tight only.
14. Lower the jack to drop the tank enough to gain access to the fuel line and the electrical connections at the top of the tank. Disconnect the electrical connections.
15. Slightly lower the front of the tank. Slide tank away from the crossmember while pushing the filler vent and fill tube over the crossmember. Lower the fuel tank.
   To install:
16. Position the tank on the jack with the shield and the tank strap in

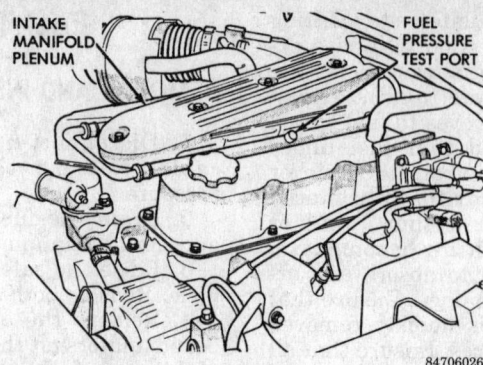

Fuel pressure test port — 3.3L engine

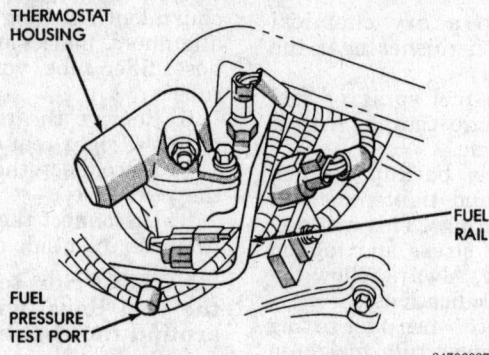

Fuel pressure test port — 3.5L engine

place. Raise the tank over the cross-member enough to connect the wiring to the fuel pump module.

17. Push the vent and the filler tube over the crossmember. Rotate the sway bar into position and install the sway bar brackets.

18. Raise the tank into place and position the sway bar mounting bracket and the tank straps in place. Tighten the bolts to 44 ft. lbs. (60 Nm).

19. Raise the crossmember into position and align with the locating marks made during removal. Install bolts and tighten to 70 ft. lbs. (95 Nm).

20. Connect the filler tube and vent tubes making sure to align marks made during removal.

21. Connect the sway bar ends to the link arms and tighten sway bar mounting nuts to 74 ft. lbs. (100 Nm).

22. Install the exhaust onto the hangers.

23. Connect the fuel supply, return and vent tubes. After installation of the quick connect fittings, check for proper connection by pulling back on the quick connect fitting. The tube should lock in place. If the connection is not complete, make sure the black plastic ring is not causing the locking

retainer to jam in the release position.

24. Lower the vehicle. Install the filler cap and reconnect the negative battery cable.

25. With the ignition in the **ON** position, access the DRB II ASD Fuel System Test to pressurize the fuel system. Check for leaks.

NOTE: When using the ASD Fuel System Test, the Auto-Shutdown (ASD) relay will remain energized for 7 minutes or until the test is stopped or until the ignition key is turned OFF.

26. Install the tires and perform a rear wheel alignment.

Fuel Filter

The fuel filter is located on the frame rail in front of the fuel tank.

REMOVAL AND INSTALLATION

1. Disconnect negative battery cable.

2. Release the fuel system pressure.

3. Disconnect the quick connect fittings at the fuel filter as follows:

    a. Remove any loose dirt from the quick connect fitting.

    b. Wrap a shop towel around hose to catch any fuel spillage.

    c. Push the quick connect fitting toward the fuel tube while depressing the built in release tool on the tube side of the fitting. Slightly twist the fitting and pull it off the fuel tube.

    d. Cover the fitting to prevent contamination of the fuel system.

4. Remove the fuel filter mounting bracket and remove the filter.

    To install:

5. The inlet and the outlet side of the filter are marked for correct installation. Install the filter with the inlet side of the filter toward the tank. Place the filter in the mounting and install to the frame rail. Tighten the mounting bolts to 105 inch lbs. (12 Nm).

6. Apply a light coating of clean 30 wt. engine oil to the fuel filter nipples. Install the fuel tubes to the filter, with new O-rings installed on the quick connect fittings. Check for proper connection by pulling back on the quick connect fitting. The tube should lock in place. If the connection is not complete, make sure the black plastic ring is not causing the locking retainer to jam in the release position.

7. Lower the vehicle. Install the filler cap and reconnect the negative battery cable.

8. With the ignition in the **ON** position, access the DRB II ASD Fuel System Test to pressurize the fuel system. Check for leaks.

NOTE: When using the ASD Fuel System Test, the ASD relay will remain energized for 7 minutes or until the test is stopped or until the ignition key is turned OFF.

Electric Fuel Pump

PRESSURE TESTING

1. Release the fuel system pressure.

2. Remove the protective cover on the fuel rail.

3. Connect a fuel pressure gauge C-4799B or exact equivalent, to the fuel rail test port.

4. Turn the ignition **ON** but do not start the engine. Using the DRB II, access the ASD Fuel System Test. This test will activate the fuel pump and pressurize the fuel system.

5. The desired fuel pressure on 3.3L engine is 55 psi (379 kPa) or 48 psi (331 kPa) for 3.5L engine with the pressure regulator vacuum line disconnected and engine not running.

6. Start the engine and allow to idle. The fuel pressure should be 46 psi (317 kPa) for 3.3L engine or 39 psi (269 kPa) for 3.5L engine with the vacuum line connected.

7. If fuel pressure is too low, check for a clogged fuel filter, a defective fuel pressure regulator or a defective fuel pump, any of which will require replacement.

8. If fuel pressure is too high, the fuel pressure regulator is defective and will have to be replaced or the fuel return is bent or clogged. If the fuel pressure reading does not change when the vacuum hose is disconnected, the hose is clogged or the valve is stuck in the fuel pressure regulator and it will have to be replaced.

9. Turn the ignition **OFF**. Release the fuel system pressure.

10. Remove the fuel pressure gauge from the fuel pressure test port and install the protective cap.

REMOVAL AND INSTALLATION

1. Remove the fuel tank filler cap. Relieve fuel system pressure.

2. Disconnect the negative battery cable.

3. Raise and safely support the vehicle.

4. The fuel pump is located in the fuel tank. Drain the fuel from the fuel tank. Lower the vehicle.

5. Remove the trunk liner and the fuel pump module access panel fasteners.

6. Remove the access panel and the gasket from the base of the trunk. Inspect the gasket and replace, if necessary.

7. Disconnect the fuel supply and return lines from the module. Disconnect the hose from the pressure relief/rollover valve.

8. Loosen the band clamp until the fuel pump module rises up from the tank.

9. To absorb possible fuel spillage, place shop towels around access opening. Without removing module, tip the tank backwards to empty the fuel reservoir of fuel.

10. The float arm of the level sensor will catch on the side of the inside of the tank while removing the module.

Tilt the module to one side and remove from the tank.

11. Remove the fuel pump module and the gasket from the tank.

To install:

12. The fuel pump module and fuel tank have alignment marks. The tank has 2 molded lines at the 10 o'clock position. The fuel pump module has a triangular alignment mark. Install the module straight into the tank with new gasket in place. Align the triangular alignment mark so it is pointing between the 2 lines on the tank.

13. Seat the module in the tank by pushing the top down. Make sure the gasket does not become dislodge or move out of position. While holding down on the module, install and tighten the clamp over the edge of the pump module and the lip of the tank. Tighten the band clamp to 31 inch lbs. (4 Nm).

14. Install the fuel tubes over the fuel return and supply nipples on the module.

15. Connect the vent line to the pressure relief/rollover valve.

16. Attach the electrical connector to the fuel pump module. Connect the negative battery cable.

17. Turn the ignition **ON** but do not start the engine. Using the DRB II, access the ASD Fuel System Test. This test will activate the fuel pump and pressurize the fuel system. Check for leaks.

18. Install the access cover and gasket. Tighten the fasteners.

19. Install the trunk liner.

Fuel Injection

IDLE SPEED ADJUSTMENT

The 3.3L and the 3.5L engines use a sequential multi-port electronic fuel injection system. In this system, the Powertrain Control Module (PCM) controls the engine idle speed, no adjustment is required.

IDLE MIXTURE ADJUSTMENT

The 3.3L and the 3.5L engines use a sequential multi-port electronic fuel injection system. In this system, the Powertrain Control Module (PCM) operates the system and control the engine idle speed, no adjustment is required.

Fuel Injector

REMOVAL AND INSTALLATION

3.3L Engine

1. Disconnect negative battery cable.

2. Release the fuel system pressure.

3. Remove the fuel rail from the intake manifold as follows:

a. Disconnect the air plenum from the air cleaner and the throttle body.

b. With the throttle held in the wide open position, disconnect the throttle linkage and the cruise control linkage from the throttle shaft. Compress the locking tabs on both cables and remove cables from mounting bracket.

c. Disconnect the electrical connector from the solenoid on the EGR valve transducer and the MAP Sensor.

d. Disconnect the vacuum hose from the PCV valve and the fuel pressure regulator. Disconnect the brake booster hose at the rear of the intake manifold.

e. Disconnect the electrical connector from the Throttle Position Sensor (TPS) and the Idle Air Control (IAC) motor.

f. Remove the EGR tube mounting screws and the intake manifold plenum. Remove the intake manifold plenum mounting bolts and the plenum from the engine.

g. Disconnect the fuel supply and the return tube at the rear of the intake manifold. Allow the fuel remaining in the rail to drain into an approved container. Remove the screws from the fuel tube clamp and separate from the fuel tubes from the bracket.

h. Tag and disconnect the electrical harness from the injectors and turn toward the center of the engine.

i. Remove the fuel rail mounting bolts and lift fuel rail straight up and off the engine.

4. Remove the fuel injector retainer clip and gently pull the injector out of the cup on the fuel rail.

To install:

5. Apply a light coating of clean engine oil to the upper O-ring.

6. Install the injector to the cup on the fuel rail and secure by installing retainer clip.

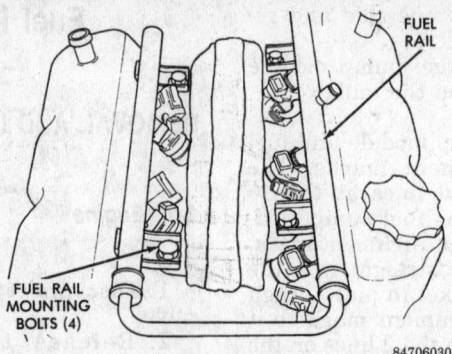

Fuel rail mounting bolt locations — 3.3L engine

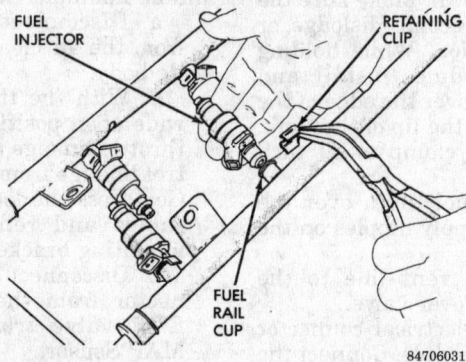

Fuel injector removal and installation — 3.3L engine

7. Install the fuel rail to the intake manifold as follows:

a. Apply a light coat of clean engine oil to the O-ring on the nozzle end of each injector.

b. Insert the fuel injector nozzles into the openings in the intake manifold. Seat the injectors in place and install the fuel rail mounting bolts, tightening to 16 ft. lbs. (22 Nm).

c. Attach the electrical connectors to each fuel injector. Rotate the injectors toward the cylinder head covers.

d. Connect the fuel supply and return tubes to the fuel rail.

e. Install the intake plenum with new gasket onto the intake manifold. Loosely install the mounting bolts.

f. Install the EGR tube to the manifold with new gasket in place. Loosely install the mounting screws.

g. Tighten the intake manifold plenum mounting bolts to 21 ft. lbs. (28 Nm) following the outlined sequence.

h. Tighten the EGR tube mounting bolts.

i. Attach the electrical connectors and the vacuum hoses re-moved during the removal procedure.

j. Install the throttle cable and speed control cable to the mounting bracket and connect to the throttle body lever while holding lever in the wide-open position.

k. Connect the purge hose to the throttle body. Connect the air plenum to the air cleaner and the throttle body.

8. Reconnect the negative battery cable.

3.5L Engine

1. Disconnect negative battery cable.

2. Release the fuel system pressure.

3. Remove the engine cover from the top of the intake manifold.

4. Remove the accelerator and the cruise control cable from the accelerator lever.

5. Disconnect the electrical connector from the idle air control motor, charge air temperature sensor and the manifold absolute pressure sensor.

6. Disconnect the vacuum hoses from the manifold tuning valve, PCV hose, idle air control motor supply hose and the purge hose from the throttle bodies.

7. Disconnect the brake booster hose and the remaining vacuum hoses from the intake manifold. If required, label for proper installation.

8. Remove the support bracket mounting bolts on each side of the plenum. Remove the intake plenum mounting bolts.

NOTE: The intake manifold plenum uses 2 different length bolts. Take note of their position and make sure they are installed in the same location during installation.

9. Remove the intake manifold plenum from the intake manifold. Discard the old gasket. Cover the intake manifold openings.

10. Disconnect the fuel supply and return tube at the fuel rail. Connect fuel gauge adapter 6631 or exact equivalent, to the fuel supply tube end of the fuel rail. Connect fuel hose 6668 or exact equivalent, to the fuel return tube end of the fuel rail.

11. Place the other end of fuel hose 6668 into an approved gasoline container.

12. Drain the gasoline from the fuel rail. To purge the fuel from the fuel rail, spray a maximum of 55 psi of compressed air into the end of adapter 6631.

NOTE: The fuel rail must be void of gasoline prior to injector removal. If the fuel rail is not drained, the gasoline in the rail will enter the engine cylinders when the injectors are removed.

13. Tag all injector harness connectors noting cylinder location for reference during assembly. Disconnect the harness connectors from each injector.

14. Remove the vacuum hose from the fuel pressure regulator.

15. Remove the fuel rail mounting bolts and the injector clamp screw. Slide the injector clamp toward the rear of the engine, then lift the clamp off the rail.

16. Install the fuel rail mounting bolts finger-tight only.

17. Using a flat tipped tool, pry the fuel injector out of the fuel rail. Ensure the upper and the lower O-rings were removed with the injector. If not, remove them from the injector well in the fuel rail.

To install:

18. Lightly lubricate the O-rings with clean engine oil. Install the injector making sure to align the notch on the injector with the alignment tab on the fuel rail.

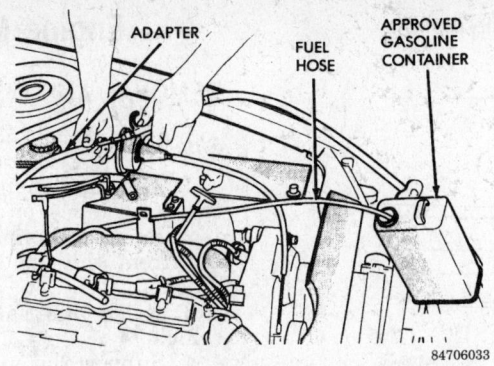

Purging the fuel from the fuel rail — 3.5L engine

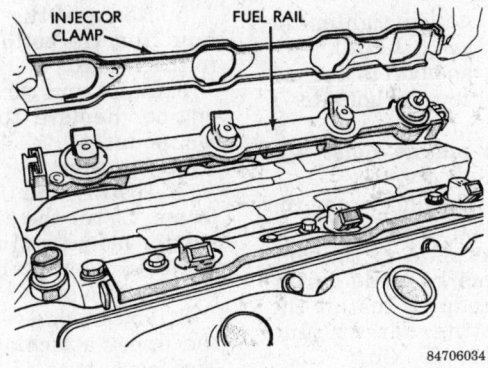

Injector clamp positioning on the fuel rail — 3.5L engine

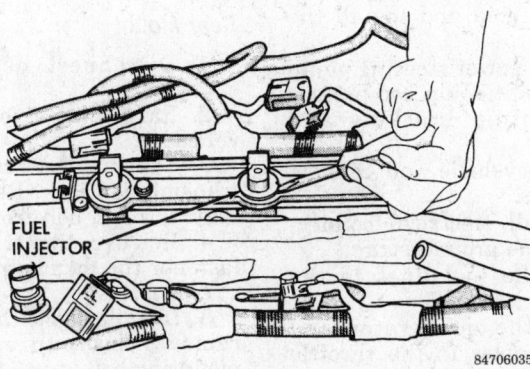

Removing fuel injector — 3.5L engine

19. Remove the fuel rail mounting bolts. Install the fuel injector clamps.
20. Install the fuel rail using new gasket, and secure with retainers tightened to 8 ft. lbs. (11 Nm).
21. Attach the electrical harness connectors to the injectors making sure of correct location.
22. Install the intake manifold plenum with a new gasket in place. Tighten mounting bolts in proper sequence to 20 ft. lbs. (28 Nm).
23. Install and tighten the support bracket bolts.

24. Attach the electrical connectors to the manifold absolute pressure sensor, throttle position sensor, idle air control motor and charge air temperature sensor.
25. Connect the vacuum hoses, and remaining electrical connectors disconnected during removal.
26. Install the EGR tube. Rotate the throttle lever to the wide-open position and connect the speed control and throttle cables.
27. Install the air cleaner plenum and connect plenum hose. Install the cover on the intake manifold plenum.

28. Connect the negative battery cable.

EMISSION CONTROLS

Emission Warning Lamp

The emission warning lamp will come **ON** each time the ignition key is turned **ON** and stays ON for a few seconds as a bulb test. If the Power Control Module (PCM) detects a malfunction with a checked system component, the check engine light on the instrument panel is illuminated to notify the operator that repairs are required.

RESETTING

Once repair of the faulty system or component has been completed, the malfunction indicator light will go out. To erase the diagnostic code, connect the DRB II scan tool to the diagnostic connector and access the ERASE TROUBLE CODE data screen. If a scan tool is not available, the PCM will erase the diagnostic code after 51 cycles of the ignition key.

ENGINE MECHANICAL

NOTE: Disconnecting the negative battery cable on some vehicles may interfere with the functions of the on-board computer systems and may require the computer to undergo a relearning process, once the negative battery cable is reconnected.

Engine Assembly

REMOVAL AND INSTALLATION

1. Disconnect negative battery cable. Release the fuel system pressure. Remove the radiator sight shield, if equipped.
2. Matchmark the hood and hinges and remove the hood assembly. Drain the cooling system.

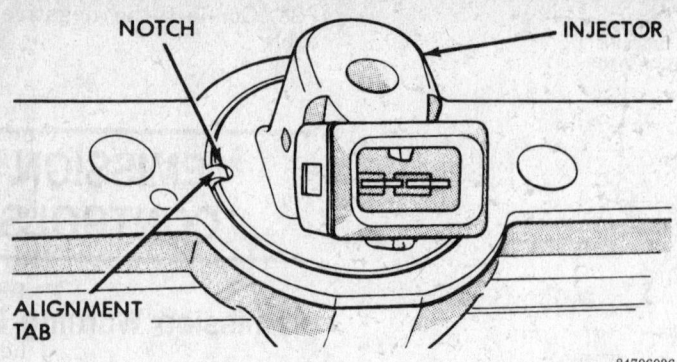

NOTCH — INJECTOR

ALIGNMENT TAB

84706036

Fuel injector alignment — 3.5L engine

3. Label and disconnect all electrical connections.

4. Remove the coolant hoses from the radiator and the engine.

5. Remove the radiator and the fan shroud.

6. Disconnect the fuel tubes and the accelerator and cruise control cables from the throttle body.

7. Remove the air cleaner assembly. Raise and safely support the vehicle.

8. Drain the engine oil. Remove the air conditioning compressor mounting bolts and position the compressor aside. It is not necessary to disconnect the refrigerant lines from the compressor.

9. Disconnect the exhaust pipe from the exhaust manifold.

10. Remove the transaxle inspection cover and mark the flexplate for reference during installation.

11. Remove the screws holding the torque converter to the flexplate. Attach a C-clamp on the converter housing to prevent the converter from falling out during removal of the engine.

12. Remove the power steering pump mounting bolts and position the pump aside.

13. Remove the 2 lower transaxle-to-block screws. Remove the starter motor from the transaxle housing.

14. Lower the vehicle and disconnect the the vacuum lines and ground strap. Support the transaxle with a floor jack.

15. Attach an engine lifting hoist to the engine and support.

16. Remove the upper transaxle mounting bolts.

17. Remove the insulator mounting nuts from the engine mounts.

18. Remove the engine from the vehicle.

To install:

19. Lower the engine into the engine compartment. Align the engine mounts and install all nuts. Once all mount bolts are installed, tighten the fasteners to 45 ft. lbs. (61 Nm).

20. Install the transaxle to the engine block and tighten the bolts to 75 ft. lbs. (102 Nm).

21. Remove the engine hoist and the transaxle holding fixture.

22. Remove the C-clamp from the converter housing, if installed.

23. Align the flexplate to the converter using the marks made during the removal procedure. Install the converter mounting screws and tighten to 55 ft. lbs. (75 Nm).

24. Install the transaxle inspection cover.

25. Connect the exhaust system to the engine manifold and install the starter.

26. Install the power steering pump and the air conditioning compressor to their mounting brackets and secure.

27. Lower the vehicle and connect all vacuum lines.

28. Connect all electrical connectors including the ground strap.

29. Connect the fuel lines to the fuel rail.

30. Connect the accelerator and cruise control cables to the throttle lever.

31. Install the radiator and the fan shroud.

32. Connect the fan motor electrical harness connector. Reinstall the radiator hoses and sight shield, if equipped.

33. Fill the crankcase with the proper amount of engine oil.

34. Install the hood onto the vehicle aligning the marks made during removal.

35. Connect the negative battery cable.

36. Start the engine and allow to idle until normal operating temperature is reached. Inspect all fluid systems for leaks and correct level.

37. Road test the vehicle. Adjust the transaxle linkage, as necessary.

Engine Mounts

REMOVAL AND INSTALLATION

Side Mounts

1. Disconnect negative battery cable.

2. Remove the insulator attaching nut from the top of the mounting bracket.

3. Raise and safely support the vehicle.

4. Support the engine using an appropriate jack and a block of wood across the full width of the oil pan.

5. Remove the lower attaching nuts from the bottom of the insulator to the frame.

6. Raise and carefully support the engine. Remove the insulator from it's mount.

To install:

7. Install the insulator to the frame. Lower the engine onto the insulator mount and install the insulator to frame nuts. Tighten nuts to 45 ft. lbs. (61 Nm).

8. Lower the vehicle and install the upper attaching nuts to mount. Tighten nuts to 45 ft. lbs. (61 Nm).

9. Connect the negative battery cable.

Rear Mount

1. Disconnect negative battery cable.

2. Raise and safely support the vehicle.

3. Support the transaxle with a transmission jack. Remove the insulator through bolt from the mount.

4. Remove the transaxle mount fastener the mount from the vehicle.

To install:

5. Installation is the reverse of the removal procedure. Tighten the mounting bolts to 45 ft. lbs. (65 Nm).

Cylinder Head

REMOVAL AND INSTALLATION

3.3L Engine

1. Disconnect negative battery cable.

2. Release the fuel system pressure.

3. Drain the cooling system.

4. Remove the intake manifold and throttle body.

5. Disconnect the coil wires, sending unit wire, heater hoses and bypass hose.

6. Remove the valve covers from the cylinder heads.

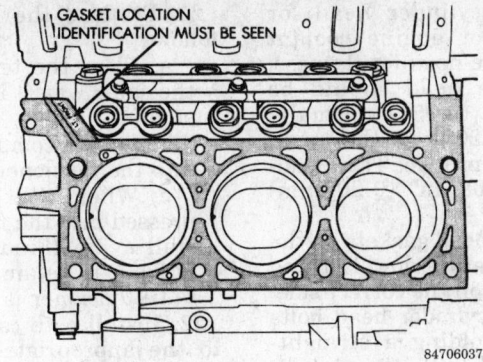

Head gasket installation — 3.3L engine

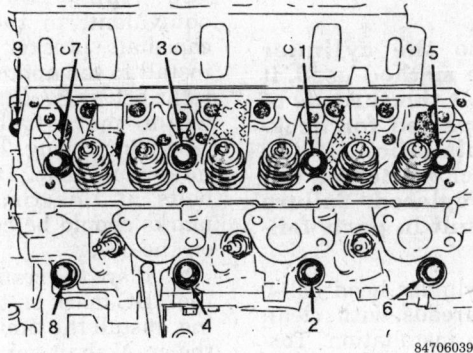

Cylinder head bolt torque sequence — 3.3L engine

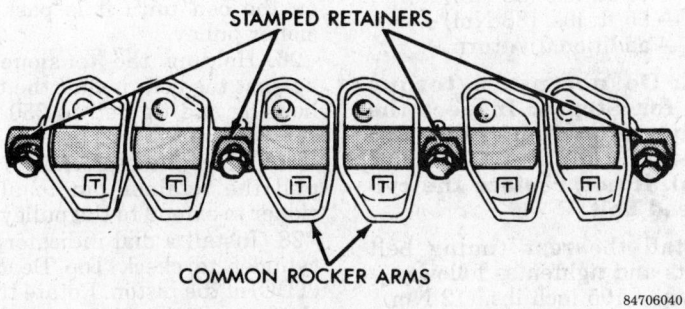

Rocker arm shaft retainer positioning — 3.3L engine

7. Remove the exhaust manifolds from the engine. Remove rocker arm and shaft assemblies. Remove pushrods and identify to assure installation in original location.

8. Remove the 9 head bolts from the cylinder head and remove head from the block.

To install:

9. Thoroughly clean and dry the mating surfaces of the head and block. Check the cylinder head for cracks, damage or engine coolant leakage. Remove scale, sealing compound and carbon. Clean oil passages

thoroughly. Check the head for flatness. End to end, the head should be within 0.002 in. (0.051mm) normally with 0.008 in. (0.203mm) the maximum allowed out of true. The total thickness allowed to be removed from the head and block is 0.008 in. (0.203mm) maximum.

10. Place a new head gasket on the cylinder block with the identification marks facing upward. Do not use sealer on the gasket.

11. Inspect the cylinder head bolts for necking by holding a straightedge against the threads of each bolt.

If all of the threads are not contacting the the scale, the bolt should be replaced.

NOTE: Due to the cylinder head bolt torque method used, it is imperative that the threads of the bolts be inspected for necking prior to installation. If the threads are necked down, the bolt should be replaced. Failure to do so may result in parts failure or damage.

12. Install the cylinder head bolts. Torque bolts Nos. 1–8 following the proper sequence as listed below:
Step 1 — 45 ft. lbs. (61 Nm)
Step 2 — 65 ft. lbs. (88 Nm)
Step 3 — 65 ft. lbs. (88 Nm)
Step 4 — additional ¼ turn

NOTE: Do not use a torque wrench for Step 4. Inspect the bolt torque after tightening. The torque should be over 90 ft. lbs. (122 Nm). If not, replace the cylinder head bolt.

13. Tighten bolt No. 9 to 25 ft. lbs. (33 Nm).

14. Inspect the pushrods and replace worn or bent rods. Install the pushrods, rocker arm and shaft assemblies with the stamped steel retainers in the forward positions. Tighten the rocker shaft retainers to 105 inch lbs. (12 Nm).

15. Install the valve covers with new gaskets in place. Tighten the retainers to 105 inch lbs. (12 Nm).

16. Using all new gaskets, install the intake manifold, throttle body, air intake plenum and exhaust manifold, following the proper torque sequences.

NOTE: The intake manifold gasket is made of very thin metal and is very sharp. Handle with care or personal injury may occur.

17. Connect the coil wires, sending unit wire, heater hoses and bypass hose.

18. Install the air intake hose.

19. Change the engine oil and oil filter.

20. Fill and bleed the cooling system.

21. Connect the negative battery cable, run the vehicle until the thermostat opens and fill the radiator completely.

22. Once the vehicle has cooled, recheck the coolant level.

3.5L Engine

1. Disconnect negative battery cable.

2. Release the fuel system pressure. Drain the cooling system.

3. Remove the air cleaner assembly and the intake manifold plenum. Cover the lower intake manifold during service.

4. Remove the upper radiator hose and the accessory drive belts.

5. Remove the engine valve covers as follows:

a. Disconnect and relocate the spark plug wires.

b. Loosen the air conditioning compressor mounting bracket and pull away from the cylinder head.

c. Remove the spark plug tube nut and O-ring.

d. Remove the rocker cover screws and the rocker cover from the cylinder head.

6. Remove the timing belt covers.

7. Mark the timing belt running direction for installation. Align the camshaft sprockets with the marks on the rear covers. Remove the timing belt and tensioner.

8. Hold the camshaft sprocket with 1⁷⁄₁₆ in. box wrench, loosen and remove the sprocket retaining bolt and washer.

NOTE: To remove the camshaft sprocket retainer bolt while the engine is in the vehicle, it may be necessary to raise that side of the engine due to the length of the retainer bolt. The right bolt is 8⅜ in. (212.6mm) long, while the left bolt is 10.0 in. (long. These bolts are not interchangeable and their original location during removal should be noted.

9. Remove the camshaft sprocket from the camshaft. The camshaft sprockets are not interchangeable from side to side.

10. Remove the intake manifold assembly.

11. Remove the rear timing belt cover to cylinder head fasteners. If the right timing belt cover is to be removed, there are O-rings located behind it for the water pump passages.

12. Remove the cylinder head mounting bolts and the cylinder head from the vehicle.

To install:

13. Thoroughly clean and dry the mating surfaces of the head and block.

NOTE: When cleaning the cylinder head and block mating surfaces, do not use a metal scraper because the surfaces could be cut or damaged. Instead, use a scraper made of wood or plastic.

14. Check the cylinder head for cracks, damage or engine coolant leakage. Check the head for flatness. End to end, the head should be within 0.002 in. (0.051) normally with 0.008 in. (0.203mm) the maximum allowed out of true. The grinding limit is 0.008 in. (0.203mm) maximum.

15. Place a new head gaskets on the cylinder block locating dowels being sure the gasket is on the correct side.

16. Inspect the cylinder head bolts for necking by holding a straightedge against the threads of each bolt. If all of the threads are not contacting the the scale, the bolt should be replaced.

NOTE: Due to the cylinder head bolt torque method used, it is imperative that the threads of the bolts be inspected for necking prior to installation. If the threads are necked down, the bolt should be replaced. Failure to do so may result in parts failure or damage.

17. Install the cylinder head bolts, lubricating the threads with clean engine oil prior to installation. Torque bolts following the proper sequence as listed below:

Step 1 — 45 ft. lbs. (61 Nm)
Step 2 — 65 ft. lbs. (88 Nm)
Step 3 — 65 ft. lbs. (88 Nm)
Step 4 — additional ¼ turn

NOTE: Do not use a torque wrench for Step 4. Inspect the bolt torque after tightening. The torque should be over 90 ft. lbs. (122 Nm). If not, replace the cylinder head bolt.

18. Install the rear timing belt cover bolts and tighten as follows:

M6 bolts — 105 inch lbs. (12 Nm)
M8 bolts — 21 ft. lbs. (28 Nm)
M10 bolts — 40 ft. lbs. (54 Nm)

19. Install the intake manifold assembly and torque bolts following the proper sequence to 21 ft. lbs. (28 Nm).

NOTE: The following procedure can only be used when the camshaft sprockets have been loosened or removed from the shafts. If the camshaft sprockets have not been removed or loosened, refer to "Timing Belt and Tensioner" for installation instructions.

20. When the camshaft sprockets are loosened or removed, the camshafts must be timed to the engine. Install the camshaft alignment tools 6642-A or exact equivalent, to the rear of the cylinder heads.

21. Pre-load the belt tensioner as follows:

a. Place the tensioner in a vise the same way it is mounted on the engine.

b. Slowly compress the plunger into the tensioner body.

c. When the plunger is compressed into the tensioner body install a pin through the body and plunger to retain plunger in place until tensioner is installed.

22. Install both camshaft sprockets to the appropriate shafts. The left camshaft sprocket has the DIS pickup as part of the sprocket.

23. Apply Loctite® 277 or equivalent, to the threads of the camshaft sprocket retainer bolts and install to the appropriate shafts. The right bolt is 8⅜ in. (213.00mm) long, while the left bolt is 10.0 in. (254.00mm) long. These bolts are not interchangeable. Do not tighten the bolts at this time. The camshaft marks should be between the marks on the cover.

24. Place the crankshaft sprocket to the TDC mark on the oil pump housing. Install the timing belt starting at the crankshaft sprocket and working in a counterclockwise direction.

25. After the belt is installed around the last sprocket keep tension on the belt until it is past the tensioner pulley.

26. Holding the tensioner pulley against the belt, install the tensioner housing and tighten to 250 inch lbs. (28 Nm)

27. When the tensioner is in place pull the retainer pin to allow tensioner to extend to the pulley bracket.

28. Install a dial indicator in No. 1 cylinder to check Top Dead Center (TDC) of the piston. Rotate the crankshaft until the piston is exactly at TDC. Hold the camshaft sprocket hex with a 1⁷⁄₁₆ in. wrench and tighten the camshaft sprocket bolt to 95 ft. lbs. (127 Nm).

29. Remove the dial indicator and install the spark plug. Tighten the spark plug to 20 ft. lbs.

30. Remove the camshaft alignment tools from the back of the cylinder heads and install the cam covers and new O-rings. Tighten the fasteners to 250 inch lbs. (28 Nm). Repeat this procedure on the other camshaft.

31. Install the timing belt covers.

32. Install the valve covers as follows:

a. Clean the cylinder head mating surfaces and install a new gasket.

b. Install valve cover and tighten bolts to 105 inch lbs. (12 Nm).

c. Install the spark plug tube nut and O-ring. Tighten the nut to 60 inch lbs. (7 Nm). Install the spark plug and tighten to 20 ft. lbs. (28 Nm).

d. Install the air conditioning compressor to the mounting bracket.

33. Install the upper radiator hose and the accessory drive belts.

34. Install the air cleaner and intake manifold plenum.

35. Change the engine oil and oil filter.

36. Fill and bleed the cooling system.

37. Connect the negative battery cable, run the vehicle until the thermostat opens and fill the radiator completely.

38. Once the vehicle has cooled, recheck the coolant level.

Valve Lifters

REMOVAL AND INSTALLATION

3.3L Engine

1. Disconnect negative battery cable. Remove the fuel filler cap. Release the fuel system pressure.

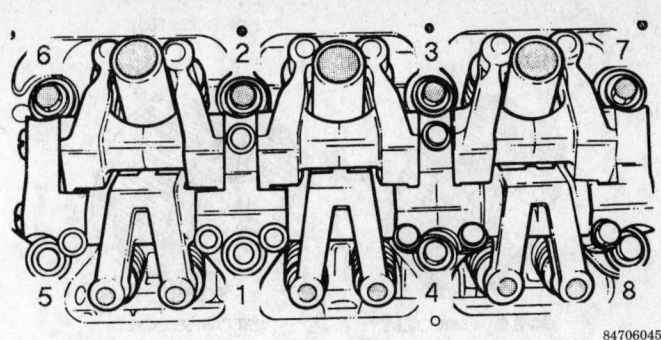

Cylinder head bolt torque sequence — 3.5L engine

2. Drain the cooling system. Disconnect the air tube from the air cleaner and the throttle body.

3. Hold the throttle lever in the wide-open position and remove the throttle cable and the speed control cable from the lever. Compress the locking tabs on the cables and remove from the mounting brackets.

4. Disconnect the electrical connector from the solenoid on the EGR valve transducer, MAP sensor, throttle position sensor and the idle air control motor.

5. Disconnect the vacuum hoses from the power brake booster at the intake manifold nipple. Disconnect

the vacuum line at the fuel pressure regulator.

6. Disconnect the purge hose from the throttle body.

7. Remove the EGR tube mounting screws at the intake manifold plenum.

8. Remove the intake manifold mounting bolts and remove the manifold from the engine. Cover the intake manifold to prevent foreign material from entering the engine.

9. Disconnect the fuel supply and return tubes at the rear of the intake manifold. Remove the screw from the fuel clamp and separate the fuel tubes from the bracket.

10. Tag and disconnect the electrical harness from the injectors and turn toward the center of the engine.

11. Remove the fuel rail mounting bolts and lift fuel rail straight up and off the engine.

12. Remove the upper radiator hose, heater hose and the rear intake manifold hose.

13. Remove the intake manifold bolts and the manifold from the engine. Remove the intake manifold seal retainers screws and remove the intake manifold gasket.

14. Remove the valve covers from the cylinder head.

15. Remove the cylinder head from the engine.

16. Remove the yoke retainer(s) and aligning yokes. Using tool C-4129 or equivalent, remove the tappets from their bores. If all tappets are to be removed, identify tappets to insure installation in their original location.

To install:

17. Lubricate tappets and install in their original location. Install the aligning yokes and retainers and tighten to 105 inch lbs. (12 Nm).

18. Install the cylinder head, fuel rail and injectors, valve covers and intake manifold.

19. Reconnect the electrical harness connectors and the vacuum

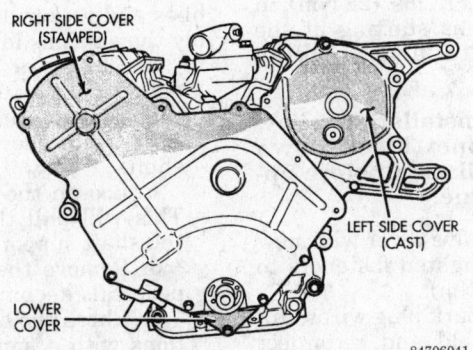

Timing belt front covers — 3.5L engine

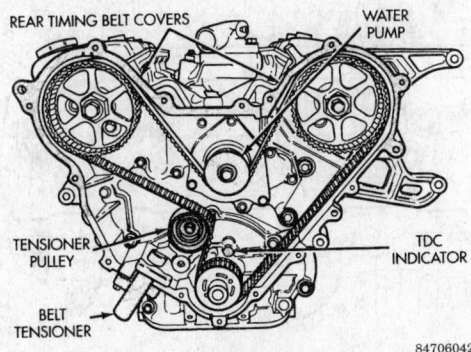

Timing belt components — 3.5L engine

 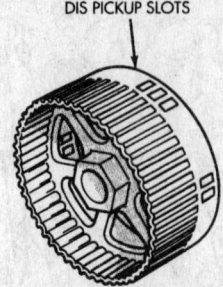

RIGHT CAM SPROCKET   LEFT CAM SPROCKET

84706046

Camshaft sprocket identification — 3.5L engine

hoses disconnected during the removal procedure.

20. Install the EGR tube to the air intake plenum.

21. Install the cruise control cable and the accelerator cable to the mounting bracket. Hold the throttle lever in the wide-open position and connect the throttle cable and the speed control cable to the lever at the throttle body.

22. Connect the air tube to the air cleaner and the throttle body.

23. Fill and bleed the cooling system.

24. Raise and safely support the vehicle. Drain and replace the engine oil and the oil filter.

25. Connect the negative battery cable, run the vehicle until the thermostat opens and fill the radiator completely.

26. Once the vehicle has cooled, recheck the coolant level.

3.5L Engine

The hydraulic lash adjusters are precision units installed in the machined openings in the valve actuating ends of the rocker arms and are serviced as an assembly.

NOTE: Do not disassemble the hydraulic lash adjusters from the rocker arm assembly or damage to the adjuster or the rocker arm may occur.

Rocker Arms/Shafts

REMOVAL AND INSTALLATION

3.3L Engine

1. Disconnect negative battery cable.

2. Remove the fuel filler cap. Release the fuel system pressure. Drain the cooling system.

3. Remove the upper intake manifold assembly.

4. Disconnect the spark plug wires from the plugs. Remove by pulling on the boot in a straight out in line with the spark plug.

5. Remove the valve cover and gasket from the engine.

6. Remove the 4 rocker shaft bolts and retainers. Remove the rocker arms and shafts from the engine.

7. Inspect rocker arm and components for wear or damage and replace as required. If the rocker shaft is disassembled for cleaning or replacement, make sure to install components in their original location.

To install:

8. Install rocker arms and shaft assemblies with the stamped steel retainers in the 4 positions. Tighten the retainer bolts to 21 ft. lbs. (28 Nm), in 3 even progressions starting at the centermost bolts and working outward.

NOTE: After installation, allow 20 minutes tappet bleed down time after installation before operating the engine.

9. Install the valve cover with new gasket in place. Tighten fasteners to 105 inch lbs. (12 Nm).

10. Install the spark plug wires, upper intake manifold and reconnect the negative battery cable.

3.5L Engine

1. Disconnect negative battery cable.

2. Remove the fuel filler cap. Release the fuel system pressure.

3. Remove the air cleaner assembly and the intake manifold plenum. Cover the lower intake manifold during service.

4. Remove the valve covers as follows:

   a. Disconnect and relocate the spark plug wires.

   b. Loosen the air conditioning compressor mounting bracket and pull away from the cylinder head.

   c. Remove the spark plug tube nut and O-ring.

   d. Remove the rocker cover screws and the rocker cover from the cylinder head.

5. Remove the rocker arm assembly mounting bolts and remove the assembly from the engine.

6. Inspect the rocker arms for wear or damage. Inspect the roller for scuffing or wear. Replace assembly as necessary.

NOTE: Do not remove the lash adjusters from the rocker arm assembly. The rocker arm and the adjuster are serviced as an assembly.

7. Identify the rocker arm assemblies and rocker arms and disassembly the shaft as follows:

   a. Thread a nut, washer and spacer onto a 4mm screw.

   b. Insert and tighten a 4mm screw into the dowel pin on the shaft.

   c. Loosen the nut on the screw. This will pull the dowel pin from the shaft support.

   d. Remove the rocker arms and pedestals keeping in order.

   e. Check the oil holes for restrictions with a small wire and clean as required.

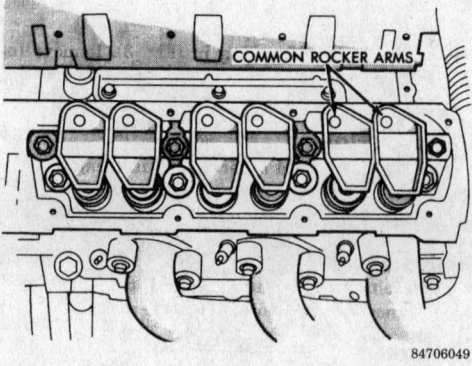

84706049

Rocker arm locations as seen on left cylinder head —
3.3L engine

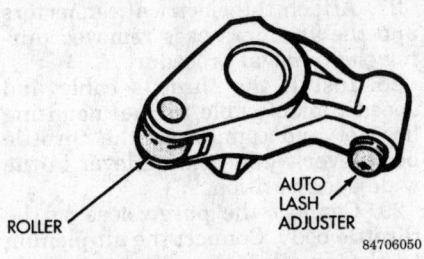

Rocker arm and lash adjuster — 3.5L engine

To install:

8. Assembly the rocker shaft as follows:

    a. Install the rocker arms and pedestals onto the shaft keeping in original order.

    b. Press the dowel pins into the pedestals until they bottom out in the pedestals.

9. Position the camshaft so there will be no load on the shaft during installation. Install the rocker shafts so the identification marks are facing toward the front of the engine.

10. Install the oil feed bolt in the correct location on the rocker shaft

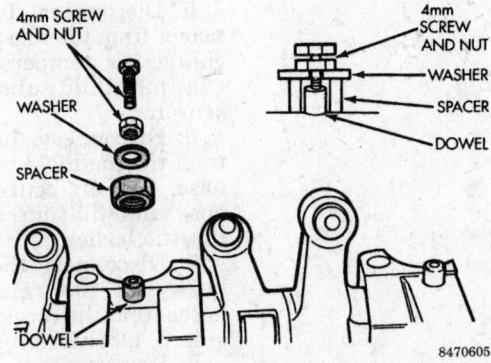

Removing dowel from rocker arm shaft — 3.5L engine

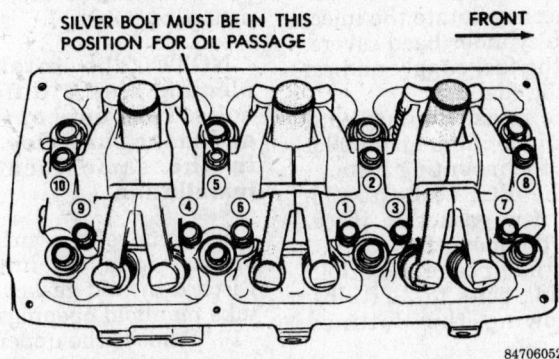

Rocker arm shaft assembly torque sequence (right side) — 3.5L engine

retainer. Tighten the bolts in proper sequence to 23 ft. lbs. (31 Nm).

11. Install the valve covers as follows:

    a. Clean the cylinder head mating surfaces and install a new gasket.

    b. Install valve cover and tighten bolts to 105 inch lbs. (12 Nm).

    c. Install the spark plug tube nut and O-ring. Tighten the nut to 60 inch lbs. (7 Nm). Install the spark plug and tighten to 20 ft. lbs. (28 Nm).

    d. Install the air conditioning compressor to the mounting bracket.

12. Install the intake manifold plenum and the air cleaner assembly.

13. Reconnect the negative battery cable.

Intake Manifold

REMOVAL AND INSTALLATION

3.3L Engine

1. Disconnect negative battery cable. Remove the fuel filler cap. Release the fuel system pressure.

2. Drain the cooling system. Disconnect the air tube from the air cleaner and the throttle body.

3. Hold the throttle lever in the wide-open position and remove the throttle cable and the speed control cable from the lever. Compress the locking tabs on the cables and remove from the mounting brackets.

4. Disconnect the electrical connector from the solenoid on the EGR valve transducer, MAP sensor, throttle position sensor and the idle air control motor.

5. Disconnect the vacuum hoses from the power brake booster at the intake manifold nipple. Disconnect the vacuum line at the fuel pressure regulator.

6. Disconnect the purge hose from the throttle body.

7. Remove the EGR tube mounting screws at the intake manifold plenum.

8. Remove the intake manifold mounting bolts and remove the manifold from the engine. Cover the intake manifold to prevent foreign material from entering the engine.

9. Disconnect the fuel supply and return tubes at the rear of the intake manifold. Remove the screw from the fuel clamp and separate the fuel tubes from the bracket.

10. Disconnect the electrical harness from the injectors and turn toward the center of the engine.

11. Remove the fuel rail mounting bolts and lift fuel rail straight up and off the engine.

12. Remove the upper radiator hose, heater hose and the rear intake manifold hose.

13. Remove the intake manifold bolts and the manifold from the engine.

14. Remove the intake manifold seal retainers screws and remove the intake manifold gasket. Clean all mating surfaces.

15. Inspect the manifold for damage, cracks or clogged passages. Repair, clean or replace the manifold as required.

    To install:

16. Place a drop of sealant onto each of the 4 corners of the intake manifold gasket. Carefully install the intake manifold gasket and tighten the seal retainers to 105 inch lbs. (12 Nm).

NOTE: The intake manifold is made of very thin metal and cause personal injury, handle with care.

17. Install the intake manifold and 8 mounting bolts tightened to 10 inch lbs. (1 Nm).

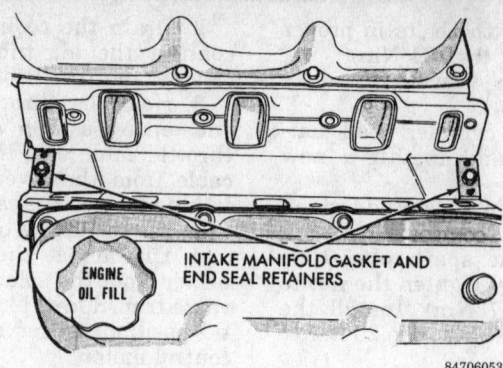

INTAKE MANIFOLD GASKET AND
END SEAL RETAINERS

ENGINE
OIL FILL

84706053

Intake manifold gasket retainers — 3.3L engine

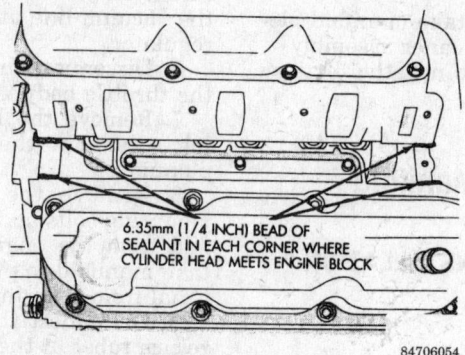

6.35mm (1/4 INCH) BEAD OF
SEALANT IN EACH CORNER WHERE
CYLINDER HEAD MEETS ENGINE BLOCK

84706054

Intake manifold gasket sealing — 3.3L engine

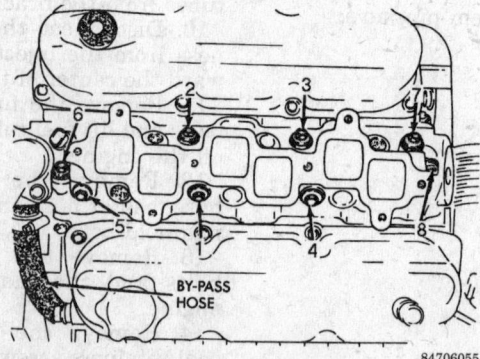

BY-PASS
HOSE

84706055

Intake manifold retainer removal and installation
sequence — 3.3L engine

18. Tighten intake manifold bolts in the proper sequence to 16 ft. lbs. (22 Nm). Once all bolts are torque, repeat the torquing sequence again tightening the bolts to 16 ft. lbs. (22 Nm). Inspect to make sure all seals are still in place.

19. Apply a light coat of clean engine oil to the O-ring on the nozzle end of each injector.

20. Insert the fuel injector nozzles into the openings in the intake manifold. Seat the injectors in place and install the fuel rail mounting bolts, tightening to 16 ft. lbs. (22 Nm).

21. Attach the electrical connectors to each fuel injector. Rotate the injectors toward the cylinder head covers.

22. Connect the fuel supply and return tubes to the fuel rail.

23. Install the intake plenum with new gasket onto the intake manifold. Loosely install the mounting bolts.

24. Install the EGR tube to the manifold with new gasket in place. Loosely install the mounting screws.

25. Tighten the intake manifold plenum mounting bolts to 21 ft. lbs. (28 Nm) following the outlined sequence.

26. Tighten the EGR tube mounting bolts.

27. Attach the electrical connectors and the vacuum hoses removed during the removal procedure.

28. Install the throttle cable and speed control cable to the mounting bracket and connect to the throttle body lever while holding lever in the wide-open position.

29. Connect the purge hose to the throttle body. Connect the air plenum to the air cleaner and the throttle body.

30. Raise and safely support the vehicle. Drain and replace the engine oil and the oil filter.

31. Connect the negative battery cable, run the vehicle until the thermostat opens and fill the radiator completely.

32. Once the vehicle has cooled, recheck the coolant level.

3.5L Engine

1. Disconnect negative battery cable. Drain the cooling system.

2. Release the fuel system pressure.

3. Remove the engine cover from the top of the intake manifold.

4. Remove the accelerator and the cruise control cable from the accelerator lever.

5. Disconnect the electrical connector from the idle air control motor, charge air temperature sensor and the manifold absolute pressure sensor.

6. Disconnect the vacuum hoses from the manifold tuning valve, PCV hose, idle air control motor supply hose and the purge hose from the throttle bodies.

7. Disconnect the brake booster hose and the remaining vacuum hoses from the intake manifold. If required, label for proper installation.

8. Remove the support bracket mounting bolts on each side of the plenum. Remove the intake plenum mounting bolts.

NOTE: The intake manifold plenum uses 2 different length bolts. Take note of their position and make sure they are installed in the same location during installation.

9. Remove the intake manifold plenum from the intake manifold. Discard the old gasket. Cover the intake manifold openings.

10. Remove the upper radiator hose from the thermostat housing and the heater hose from the rear of the intake manifold.

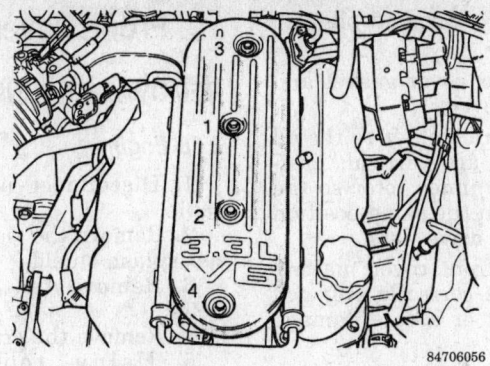

Intake manifold plenum torque sequence — 3.3L engine

84706056

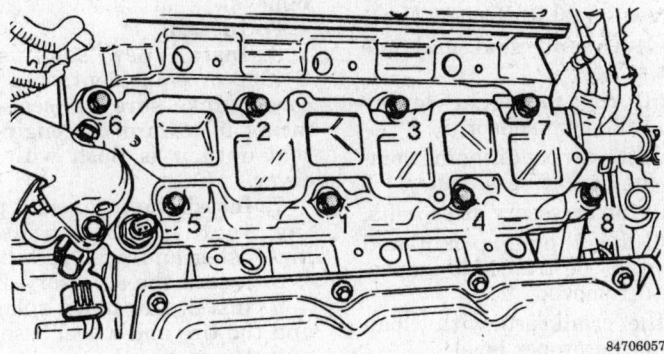

Intake manifold torque sequence — 3.5L engine

84706057

11. Remove the intake manifold retaining bolts and the manifold from the engine. Clean all gasket mating surfaces and inspect for straightness.

To install:

12. Install the manifold with new gasket in place. Tighten bolts in proper sequence to 21 ft. lbs. (28 Nm).

13. Connect the upper radiator hose to the thermostat housing and the heater hose to the rear of the intake manifold.

14. Ensure the ignition cables are routed out of the way of the intake plenum. Install the intake manifold plenum with new gasket in place and tighten in sequence to 21 ft. lbs. (28 Nm).

15. Install the intake manifold plenum with a new gasket in place. Tighten mounting bolts in proper sequence to 20 ft. lbs. (28 Nm).

16. Install and tighten the support bracket bolts.

17. Attach the electrical connectors to the manifold absolute pressure sensor, throttle position sensor, idle air control motor and charge air temperature sensor.

18. Connect the vacuum hoses, and remaining electrical connectors disconnected during removal.

19. Install the EGR tube. Rotate the throttle lever to the wide-open position and connect the speed control and throttle cables.

20. Install the air cleaner plenum and connect plenum hose. Install the cover on the intake manifold plenum.

21. Attach the ground wire the the intake manifold plenum. Connect the brake booster hose to the fitting on the intake manifold plenum.

22. Install the cover on the intake manifold plenum.

23. Connect the negative battery cable. Fill and bleed the cooling system.

24. Raise and safely support the vehicle. Change the engine oil and filter.

Exhaust Manifold

REMOVAL AND INSTALLATION

3.3L Engine

1. Disconnect the negative battery cable. Raise and safely support the vehicle.

2. Separate the EGR tube from the manifold and disconnect the heated oxygen sensor electrical connector.

3. Disconnect the exhaust pipe from the manifold.

4. Remove the screws attaching the heatshield to the manifold.

5. Remove the manifold attaching bolts and remove the manifold from the cylinder head.

6. Inspect the manifold for damage or cracks. Check for distortion against a straight-edge. Replace manifold as required.

To install:

7. Install the exhaust manifold to the cylinder head and install the retainer bolts. Tighten the retainer bolts to 17 ft. lbs. (23 Nm).

8. Install the EGR tube to the manifold.

9. Connect the exhaust pipe to the manifold and tighten nuts to 21 ft. lbs. (28 Nm).

10. Install the heatshield to the manifold and tighten the retainers to 17 ft. lbs. (23 Nm).

11. Connect the electrical connector at the oxygen sensor.

12. Lower the vehicle and reconnect the negative battery cable.

3.5L Engine

1. Disconnect the negative battery cable. Raise and safely support the vehicle.

2. Disconnect the heated oxygen sensor electrical connector.

3. Disconnect the exhaust pipes from the exhaust manifold.

4. Lower the vehicle and remove the screws attaching the heatshield to the manifold.

5. Remove the manifold attaching bolts and remove the manifold from the cylinder head.

6. Inspect the manifold for damage or cracks. Check for distortion against a straight-edge. Replace manifold as required.

To install:

7. Install the gasket and exhaust manifold to the cylinder head and install the retainer bolts. Tighten the retainer bolts to 15 ft. lbs. (20 Nm).

8. Connect the exhaust pipe to the manifold and tighten nuts to 21 ft. lbs. (28 Nm).

9. Install the heatshield to the manifold and tighten the retainers to 11 ft. lbs. (15 Nm).

10. Connect the electrical connector on the oxygen sensor.

11. Lower the vehicle and reconnect the negative battery cable.

Timing Chain Front Cover

REMOVAL AND INSTALLATION

3.3L Engine

1. Disconnect negative battery cable.
2. Drain the cooling system.
3. Raise and safely support the vehicle.
4. Remove the oil pan and the oil pump pickup. It may be necessary to remove the transaxle inspection cover.
5. Remove the accessory drive belts and tensioner pulley bracket.
6. Remove the air compressor mounting bolts and set compressor aside. Remove the compressor mounting bracket. It is not necessary to drain the R-134A from the air conditioning system.
7. Using an appropriate puller, remove the crankshaft pulley.
8. Remove the tensioner pulley bracket.
9. Remove the camshaft sensor from the chain case cover.
10. Remove the timing chain case cover mounting bolts and the cover from the front of the engine.
11. Clean the gasket material from the mating surfaces of the cover and the block.

12. Remove the crankshaft oil seal.
To install:
13. Install a new cover gasket and O-ring onto the cover.
14. Rotate the crankshaft so the oil pump drive flats are vertical. Position the oil pump inner rotor so the mating flats are in the same position as the crankshaft drive flats.
15. Install the front cover making sure the pump is correctly engaged on the crankshaft or severe damage may result.
16. Install the chain case cover screws and snug the 2 bottom screws and the top center screw. Ensure the cover is seated to the block then torque all screws to 20 ft. lbs. (27 Nm).
17. Install the oil seal and the crankshaft pulley.
18. Install the tensioner pulley bracket and the cam sensor.
19. Install the air conditioning compressor to the mounting bracket.
20. Install the accessory drive belts.
21. Install the oil pump pickup and oil pan. Install the transaxle inspection cover, if removed.
22. Fill the crankcase with clean engine oil to the proper level.
23. Fill and bleed the cooling system. Connect the negative battery cable.

Front Cover Oil Seal

REMOVAL AND INSTALLATION

3.3L Engine

1. Disconnect negative battery cable.
2. Remove the right wheel and inner splash shield.
3. Remove the accessory drive belts.
4. Remove the crankshaft pulley.
5. Using tool C-4991 or equivalent, remove the front case oil seal. Be careful not to damage the surface of the crankshaft during removal.
To install:
6. Install new seal using tool C-4992 or equivalent, into the front cover. Make sure the seal spring is facing in toward the engine. Install seal until it is flush with the case cover.
7. Install the crankshaft pulley using tool L-4524 thrust bearing/washer and a 5.9 inch bolt.
8. Install the accessory drive belt.
9. Install the inner splash shield and the tire and wheel assembly.
10. Reconnect the negative battery cable.

Timing Chain and Sprockets

REMOVAL AND INSTALLATION

3.3L Engine

1. Disconnect negative battery cable. Release the fuel system pressure.
2. Drain the cooling system.
3. Remove the timing chain front cover.
4. Remove the camshaft sprocket attaching bolts. Remove the timing chain with the camshaft sprocket.
5. Using an appropriate puller, remove the crankshaft sprocket.
To install:
6. Position a new crankshaft sprocket on the shaft and install using a properly sized driver and mallet.
7. Rotate the crankshaft so the timing arrow is at the 12 o'clock position.
8. Position the camshaft sprocket so the timing arrow is at the 6 o'clock position. Place the timing chain around the camshaft sprocket aligning the dark colored link of the chain with the dot on the camshaft sprocket.

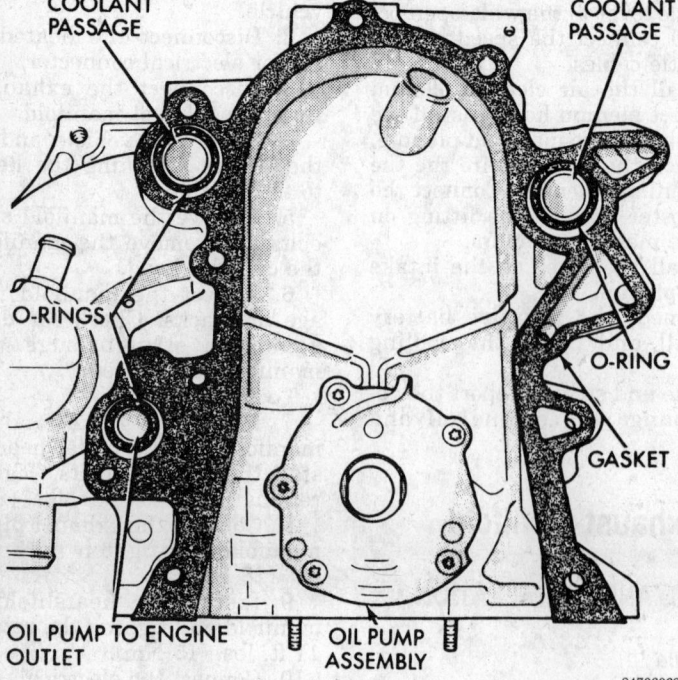

COOLANT PASSAGE
COOLANT PASSAGE
O-RINGS
O-RING
GASKET
OIL PUMP TO ENGINE OUTLET
OIL PUMP ASSEMBLY

84706062

Timing chain case cover gaskets and O-rings

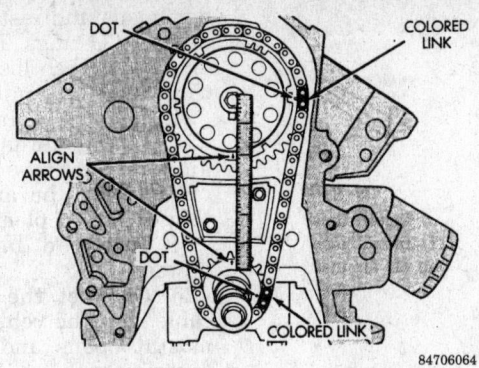

Alignment of timing marks — 3.3L engine

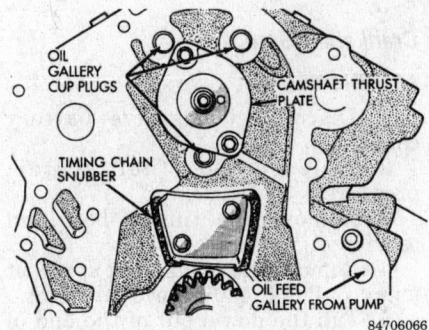

Camshaft thrust plate and snubber location — 3.3L engine

9. Place the timing chain around the crankshaft sprocket aligning the dot on the crankshaft sprocket with the dark colored link on the chain. Install the camshaft sprocket in position on the shaft.

10. Using a straight-edge, check the alignment of the timing arrows. Install the camshaft bolt and washer and tighten to 40 ft. lbs. (54 Nm).

11. Rotate the crankshaft 2 revolutions in the direction of engine rotation. Check the alignment of the timing arrows, which should align with each other. If they do not align, remove the camshaft sprocket and retime the engine. Rotate the crankshaft 2 revolutions in the direction of rotation, and confirm alignment of the timing marks.

12. Check the camshaft endplay. With new thrust plate the specification is 0.005–0.012 in. (0.0127–0.3040mm) or 0.012 in. (0.3040mm) for old thrust plate. If not within specifications, replace thrust plate.

13. Install the timing chain snubber and tighten the retaining screws to 105 inch lbs. (12 Nm).

14. Install the timing chain front cover using new seals and O-rings.

15. Install the crankshaft pulley and accessory drive belt.

16. Refill and bleed the cooling system.

17. Reconnect the negative battery cable.

Timing Belt Front Cover

REMOVAL AND INSTALLATION

3.5L Engine

1. Disconnect negative battery cable. Release the fuel system pressure.

2. Drain the cooling system.

3. Remove the radiator sight shield for LHS and New Yorker. Remove the upper radiator hose and the accessory drive belts.

4. Remove the timing belt cover mounting screws and the covers from the front of the engine.

5. Installation is the reverse of the removal procedure.

Timing Belt and Tensioner

REMOVAL AND INSTALLATION

3.5L Engine

1. Disconnect negative battery cable.

2. Release the fuel system pressure. Drain the cooling system.

3. Remove the air cleaner assembly and the intake manifold plenum. Cover the lower intake manifold during service.

4. Remove the radiator sight shield, if equipped, upper radiator hose and the accessory drive belts.

5. Remove the timing belt covers.

6. Mark the timing belt running direction for installation. Align the camshaft sprockets with the marks on the rear covers.

7. Remove the timing belt and tensioner.

To install:

NOTE: This procedure can only be used when the camshaft sprockets have not been loosened or removed from the camshafts.

8. Pre-load the belt tensioner as follows:

a. Place the tensioner in a vise the same way it is mounted on the engine.

b. Slowly compress the plunger into the tensioner body.

c. When the plunger is compressed into the tensioner body install a pin through the body and plunger to retain plunger in place until tensioner is installed.

9. Align the crankshaft sprocket with the TDC mark on the oil pump cover.

10. Align the camshaft sprockets between the marks on the covers.

11. Install the timing belt starting at the crankshaft sprocket and going in a counterclockwise direction. After the belt is installed on the right sprocket keep tension on the belt until it is past the tensioner pulley.

12. Holding the tensioner pulley against the belt, install the tensioner into the housing and tighten to 21 ft. lbs. (28 Nm).

13. When the tensioner is in place pull the retainer pin to allow tensioner to extend to the pulley bracket.

14. Rotate the crankshaft sprocket 2 revolutions and check for proper alignment of the timing marks on the camshaft and the crankshaft.

15. Install the timing belt covers and remaining components.

16. Refill and bleed the cooling system.

17. Reconnect the negative battery cable.

Timing Belt Sprockets

REMOVAL AND INSTALLATION

Camshaft Sprocket

3.5L ENGINE

NOTE: When the camshaft sprockets are loosened or removed, the camshafts must be timed to the engine. The following procedure can only be used when the camshaft sprockets have been loosened or removed from the shafts.

1. Disconnect negative battery cable.

2. Release the fuel system pressure. Drain the cooling system.

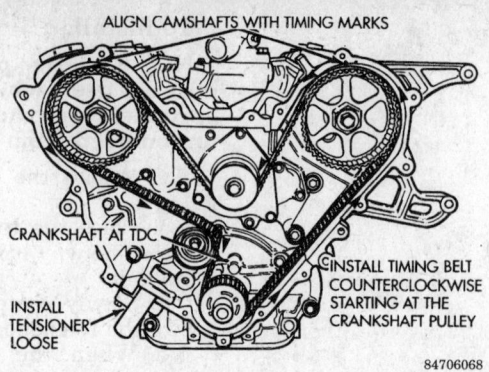

ALIGN CAMSHAFTS WITH TIMING MARKS

CRANKSHAFT AT TDC

INSTALL TENSIONER LOOSE

INSTALL TIMING BELT COUNTERCLOCKWISE STARTING AT THE CRANKSHAFT PULLEY

84706068

Timing belt mark alignment — 3.5L engine

3. Remove the air cleaner assembly and the intake manifold plenum. Cover the lower intake manifold during service.

4. Remove the upper radiator hose and the accessory drive belts.

5. Remove the timing belt covers. Do not remove the sealer on the cover, it is reusable.

6. Mark the timing belt running direction for installation. Align the camshaft sprockets with the marks on the rear covers.

7. Remove the timing belt and tensioner.

8. Hold the camshaft sprocket with 1⁷⁄₁₆ in. box wrench, loosen and remove the sprocket retaining bolt and washer.

NOTE: To remove the camshaft sprocket retainer bolt while the engine is in the vehicle, it may be necessary to raise that side of the engine due to the length of the retainer bolt. The right bolt is 8³⁄₈ in. (213.00) long, while the left bolt is 10.0 in. (254.00) long. These bolts are not interchangeable and their original location during removal should be noted.

9. Remove the camshaft sprocket from the camshaft. The camshaft sprockets are not interchangeable from side to side.

To install:

NOTE: The following procedure can only be used when the camshaft sprockets have been loosened or removed from the shafts.

10. Place the crankshaft sprocket to the TDC mark on the oil pump housing.

11. When the camshaft sprockets are loosened or removed, the camshafts must be timed to the engine. Install the camshaft alignment tools 6642-A or exact equivalent, to the rear of the cylinder heads.

12. Pre-load the belt tensioner as follows:

  a. Place the tensioner in a vise the same way it is mounted on the engine.

  b. Slowly compress the plunger into the tensioner body.

  c. When the plunger is compressed into the tensioner body install a pin through the body and plunger to retain plunger in place until tensioner is installed.

13. Install both camshaft sprockets to the appropriate shafts. The left camshaft sprocket has the DIS pickup as part of the sprocket.

14. Apply Loctite® 277 or equivalent, to the threads of the camshaft sprocket retainer bolts and install to the appropriate shafts. The right bolt is 8³⁄₈ in. (213.00mm) long, while the left bolt is 10.0 in. (254.00mm) long. These bolts are not interchangeable. Do not tighten the bolts at this time. The camshaft marks should be between the marks on the cover.

15. Install the timing belt starting at the crankshaft sprocket and working in a counterclockwise direction. Keep tension on the belt until it is past the tensioner pulley.

16. Holding the tensioner pulley against the belt, install the tensioner housing and tighten to 250 inch lbs. (28 Nm)

17. When the tensioner is in place pull the retainer pin to allow tensioner to extend to the pulley bracket.

18. Install a dial indicator in No. 1 cylinder to check Top Dead Center (TDC) of the piston. Rotate the crankshaft until the piston is exactly at TDC. Hold the camshaft sprocket hex with a 1⁷⁄₁₆ in. wrench and tighten the camshaft sprocket bolt to 95 ft. lbs. (127 Nm).

19. Remove the dial indicator. Install the spark plug and tighten to 20 ft. lbs. (28 Nm).

20. Remove the camshaft alignment tools from the back of the cylin-der heads and install the cam covers and new O-rings. Tighten the fasteners to 250 inch lbs. (28 Nm). Repeat this procedure on the other camshaft.

21. Install the timing belt covers.

22. Install the upper radiator hose and the accessory drive belts.

23. Install the air cleaner and intake manifold plenum.

24. Fill and bleed the cooling system.

25. Connect the negative battery cable, run the vehicle until the thermostat opens and fill the radiator completely.

26. Once the vehicle has cooled, recheck the coolant level.

Crankshaft Sprocket

3.5L ENGINE

1. Disconnect negative battery cable.

2. Release the fuel system pressure.

3. Remove the timing belt and tensioner.

4. Remove the crankshaft sprocket using puller L-4407A or equivalent.

5. Tap the dowel out of the end of the crankshaft.

6. Remove the crankshaft seal using tool 6341 or equivalent, taking care not to nick the shaft seal surface or seal bore during removal.

To install:

7. Inspect the crankshaft seal lip surface for varnish and polish using 400 grit paper to remove as necessary.

8. Install crankshaft seal using seal installer tool 6342 or equivalent.

9. Install the dowel into the crankshaft to 0.047 inch (1.2mm).

10. Install the crankshaft sprocket using tool C-4685C1, thrust bearing, washer and 12mm bolt.

11. Install the timing belt and tensioner and set the engine timing. Install the timing belt covers and related components.

12. Refill and bleed the cooling system.

13. Reconnect the negative battery cable.

Camshaft

REMOVAL AND INSTALLATION

3.3L Engine

1. Disconnect battery negative cable.

2. Relieve the fuel system pressure.

3. Remove the engine from the vehicle.

4. With the engine removed from the vehicle, remove the intake manifold, cylinder head covers and cylinder heads from the engine.

5. Remove the timing case cover and timing chain from the engine.

6. Remove the rocker arm and shaft assemblies.

7. Remove the pushrods and tappets; identify so each can be installed in its original location.

8. Remove the camshaft thrust plate.

9. Install a long bolt into the front of the camshaft to aid in removal. Remove the camshaft being careful not to damage the cam bearings with the cam lobes.

10. Inspect the bearing journals and the lobes on the shaft for damage and replace as required.

To install:

11. Inspect the bearing journals on the camshaft and install the shaft within 2 in. (51.00mm) of its final position in the cylinder block.

NOTE: Chrysler recommends the addition of 1 pint of Chrysler Crankcase Conditioner or equivalent, be added to the crankcase when the camshaft has been replaced. This will aid in break in. Leave the oil mixture in the engine for a minimum of 500 miles and drained at the next normal oil change.

12. Install the camshaft thrust plate with the 2 screws and tighten to 105 inch lbs. (12 Nm).

13. Rotate the crankshaft so the timing arrow is in the 12 o'clock position.

14. Position the camshaft sprocket so the timing arrow is at the 6 o'clock position. Place the timing chain around the camshaft sprocket aligning the dark colored link of the chain with the dot on the camshaft sprocket.

15. Place the timing chain around the crankshaft sprocket aligning the dot on the crankshaft sprocket with the dark colored link on the chain. Install the camshaft sprocket in position on the shaft.

16. Using a straight-edge, check the alignment of the timing arrows. Install the camshaft bolt and washer and tighten to 40 ft. lbs. (54 Nm).

17. Rotate the crankshaft 2 revolutions in the direction of engine rotation. Check the alignment of the timing arrows, which should align with each other. If they do not align, re-move the camshaft sprocket and re-time the engine. Rotate the crankshaft 2 revolutions in the direction of rotation, and confirm alignment of the timing marks.

18. Check the camshaft endplay. With new thrust plate the specification is 0.005–0.012 in. (0.0127–0.3040mm) or 0.012 in. (0.3040mm) for old thrust plate. If not within specifications, replace thrust plate.

19. Install the timing chain snubber and tighten the retaining screws to 105 inch lbs. (12 Nm).

20. Lubricate and install the tappets and the pushrods in their original position. If the camshaft was replaced, all tappets must be replaced.

21. Install the timing chain front cover using new seals and O-rings.

22. Install the intake manifold, cylinder head covers and cylinder heads onto the engine.

23. Install the engine into the vehicle.

24. Fill all fluid levels to the proper level and start the engine. Inspect for leaks and test drive the vehicle.

3.5L Engine

Camshafts are serviced from the rear of the cylinder head. The cylinder head must be removed from the vehicle.

1. Disconnect negative battery cable.

2. Release the fuel system pressure. Drain the cooling system.

3. Remove the cylinder head from the engine.

4. Mark the rocker arm assembly to note component locations prior to disassembly. Remove the rocker arm and shaft assemblies the head.

5. Remove the rear camshaft cover and O-ring from the head.

6. Remove the camshaft from the rear of the head taking care not to nick or scratch the journals when removing.

7. Inspect camshaft journals for wear or damage. If wear is present, inspect the cylinder head for damage. Inspect the head oil holes for clogging. Replace the camshaft as required.

To install:

8. Lubricate the camshaft journals and cam with clean engine oil. Install camshaft into cylinder head.

9. Install the camshaft cover and O-ring to the head and tighten to 21 ft. lbs. (28 Nm).

10. Install the rocker arm assemblies in their original location.

11. Install the cylinder head to the engine block.

12. Refill and bleed the cooling system.

13. Connect the negative battery cable.

Piston and Connecting Rod

POSITIONING

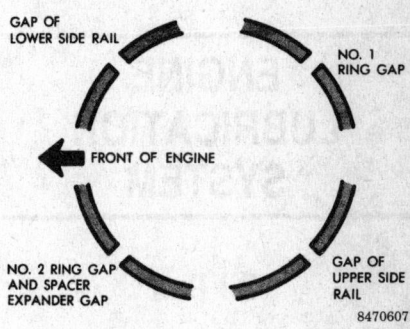

Piston ring end gap positioning — 3.3L engine

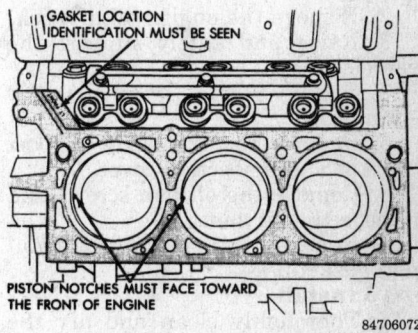

Piston positioning — 3.3L engine

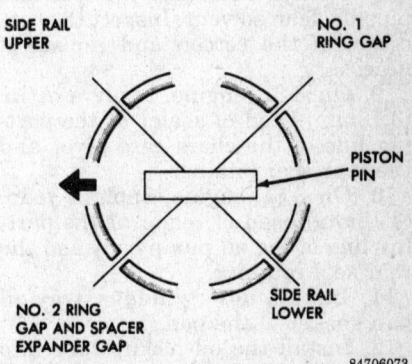

Piston ring end gap positioning — 3.5L engine

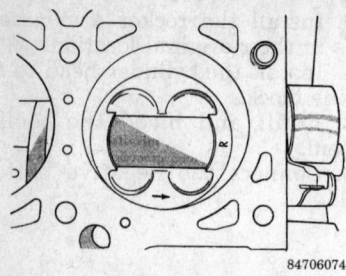

Piston positioning. Install the piston with the arrow facing the front of the engine and the R on the right (passenger) side or the L on the left (driver) side — 3.5L engine

ENGINE LUBRICATION SYSTEM

Oil Pan

REMOVAL AND INSTALLATION

1. Disconnect negative battery cable.
2. Remove the engine oil dipstick.
3. Raise and safely support the vehicle.
4. Remove the sway bar, if equipped.
5. Remove the transaxle support bracket and inspection cover.
6. Remove the oil pan screws and remove the oil pan.
7. Remove the windage tray/oil pan gaskets.

To install:

8. Thoroughly clean and dry the oil pan, cylinder block bolts and bolt holes. Inspect the oil pan flange for bends or distortion. Straighten flange if necessary. Clean the oil screen and pipe in clean solvent. Inspect the condition of the screen and replace if necessary.
9. On 3.3L engine, apply a 1/8 in. (3.18mm) bead of sealer at the parting line of the chain case cover and the rear seal retainer.
10. On 3.5L engine, apply a 1/8 in. (3.18mm) bead of sealer at the parting line of the oil pump body and the rear seal retainer.
11. Install new windage tray/oil pan gasket to the pan.
12. Install the oil pickup tube into the pump body and tighten the screws to 20 ft. lbs. (28 Nm).

13. Install the oil pan and retaining bolts. Tighten screws to 17 ft. lbs. (23 Nm).
14. Install the transaxle support bracket and sway bar, if equipped.
15. Lower the vehicle and install the oil dipstick.
16. Connect the negative battery cable.
17. Fill the crankcase with the proper amount of clean SAE 5W-30 engine oil.
18. Start the engine and check for leaks.

Oil Pump

REMOVAL AND INSTALLATION

3.3L Engine

1. Disconnect negative battery cable and drain the cooling system.
2. Raise and safely support the vehicle.
3. Remove the oil pan and the oil pump pickup. It may be necessary to remove the transaxle inspection cover.
4. Remove the accessory drive belts and tensioner pulley bracket.
5. Remove the air compressor mounting bolts and set compressor aside. Remove the compressor mounting bracket. It is not necessary to drain the R-134A from the air conditioning system.
6. Using an appropriate puller, remove the crankshaft pulley.
7. Remove the tensioner pulley bracket.
8. Remove the camshaft sensor from the chain case cover.
9. Remove the timing chain case cover mounting bolts and the cover from the front of the engine.
10. Clean the gasket material from the mating surfaces of the cover and the block.

11. Remove the oil pump cover retaining screws from the timing cover. Lift off the oil pump cover.
12. Remove the pump rotors. Wash all parts in solvent and inspect carefully for damage or wear.

To install:

13. Assemble the oil pump with new parts as required. Install the inner rotor with chamfer facing the cast iron oil pump cover.
14. Install the pump cover and tighten the fasteners to 9 ft. lbs. (12 Nm).
15. Prime the oil pump prior to installation by filling the rotor cavity with clean engine oil.
16. Remove the crankshaft oil seal from the front cover.
17. Install a new cover gasket and O-ring onto the cover.
18. Rotate the crankshaft so the oil pump drive flats are vertical. Position the oil pump inner rotor so the mating flats are in the same position as the crankshaft drive flats.
19. Install the front cover making sure the pump is correctly engaged on the crankshaft or severe damage may result.
20. Install the chain case cover screws and snug the 2 bottom screws and the top center screw. Ensure the cover is seated to the block then torque all screws to 20 ft. lbs. (27 Nm).
21. Install the oil seal and the crankshaft pulley.
22. Install the tensioner pulley bracket and the cam sensor.
23. Install the air conditioning compressor to the mounting bracket.
24. Install the accessory drive belts.
25. Install the oil pump pickup and oil pan. Install the transaxle inspection cover, if removed.
26. Fill the crankcase with clean engine oil to the proper level.
27. Fill and bleed the cooling system. Connect the negative battery cable.

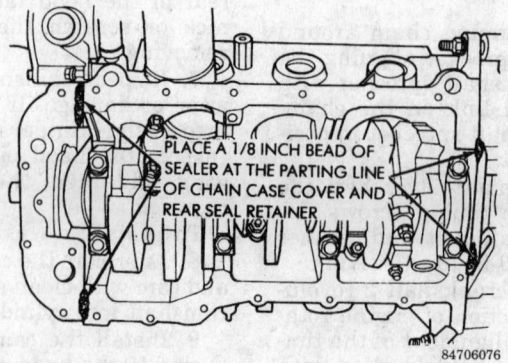

Oil pan sealing points — 3.3L engine

3.5L Engine

1. Disconnect negative battery cable. Drain the cooling system.

2. Remove the upper radiator hoses and radiator.

3. Remove the accessory drive belt.

4. Remove the timing belt and tensioner.

5. Remove the crankshaft sprocket and vibration damper using puller L-4407A or equivalent.

6. Remove the oil pump mounting screws and the pump from the crankshaft.

7. Remove the oil pump cover retaining screws and lift off the oil pump cover.

8. Remove the pump rotors. Wash all parts in solvent and inspect carefully for damage or wear.

To install:

9. Assemble the oil pump with new parts as required.

10. Install the pump cover and tighten the fasteners to 9 ft. lbs. (12 Nm).

11. Prime the oil pump prior to installation by filling the rotor cavity with clean engine oil.

12. Install the oil pump over the crankshaft carefully. Tighten the retaining screws as follows:

M8 screws — 21 ft. lbs. (28 Nm).

M10 screws — 40 ft. lbs. (55 Nm).

13. Install the crankshaft sprocket using tool C-4685C1, thrust bearing, washer and 12mm bolt.

14. Install the timing belt and tensioner and set the engine timing.

15. Install the timing belt covers and related components.

16. Refill and bleed the cooling system.

17. Connect the negative battery cable.

CHECKING

3.3L Engine

1. Clean all parts thoroughly. The mating surfaces of the chain case cover should be smooth. Replace the pump cover if scratched or grooved.

2. Place a straight-edge across the pump cover surface and inspect for warpage by inserting a feeler gauge between the cover and the straight-edge. If a 0.003 in. (0.076mm) feeler gauge can be inserted, the cover should be replaced.

3. Measure the thickness and diameter of the outer rotor. If the outer rotor thickness measures 0.0301 in. (7.64mm) or less or the diameter is 3.148 in. (79.95mm) or less, replace the outer rotor.

4. Measure the inner rotor. If the inner rotor measures 0.301 in. (7.64mm) or less replace the inner rotor.

5. Place the outer rotor into the chain case cover and push to one side with fingers. Measure the clearance between the chain case cover and the the rotor while holding the rotor in that position. If the measurement is 0.015 in. (0.39mm) or more and the outer rotor is within specifications, replace the pump body.

6. Install the inner rotor into the chain case cover. If the clearance between the inner and the outer rotor is 0.008 in. (0.203mm) or more, replace both rotors.

7. Place a straight-edge across the face of the chain case cover between the bolt holes. If a 0.004 in. (0.102mm) or more feeler gauge can be inserted between the rotors and the straight-edge and the rotors are in specification, replace the pump assembly.

8. Remove the relief valve as follows:

a. Remove the cotter pin.

b. Drill a 1/8 in. (3.175mm) hole into the relief valve retainer cap

and insert a self-threading screw into the cap.

c. Clamp screw in vise while supporting the oil pump body. Remove the cap by tapping the oil pump body with a soft hammer. Discard the retainer cap and remove the spring and relief valve.

9. Inspect the oil pressure relief valve plunger for scoring and free operation. Small marks may be removed using 400 grit wet or dry sandpaper.

10. Inspect the relief valve spring for spring pressure. Compressed to $1^{11}/_{32}$ in. (34.00mm) the spring should test to 19.5 lbs. (8.8 Kg). Replace the spring if it fails to meet specification.

11. If oil pressure is low and the pump is within specifications, inspect for worn engine bearings or other reason for oil pressure loss.

3.5L Engine

1. Clean all parts thoroughly. The mating surfaces of the oil pump housing should be smooth. Replace the pump cover if scratched or grooved.

2. Place a straight-edge across the pump cover surface and inspect for warpage by inserting a feeler gauge between the cover and the straight-edge. If a 0.003 in. (0.076mm) feeler gauge can be inserted, the cover should be replaced.

3. Measure the thickness and diameter of the outer rotor. If the outer rotor thickness measures 0.3695 in. (9.39mm) or less or the diameter is 3.141 in. (79.78mm) or less, replace the outer rotor.

4. Measure the inner rotor. If the inner rotor measures 0.3695 in. (9.39mm) or less replace the inner rotor.

5. Place the outer rotor into the pump body and push to one side with fingers. Measure the clearance between the body and the the rotor while holding the rotor in that position. If the measurement is 0.015 in. (0.39mm) or more and the outer rotor is within specifications, replace the pump body.

6. Install the inner rotor into the pump body. If the clearance between the inner and the outer rotor is 0.008 in. (0.20mm) or more, replace both rotors.

7. Place a straight-edge across the face of the pump body between the bolt holes. If a 0.004 in. (0.102mm) feeler gauge can be inserted between the rotors and the straight-edge and the rotors are in specification, replace the pump body.

PLACE A 1/8 INCH BEAD OF SEALER AT THE PARTING LINE OF CHAIN CASE COVER AND REAR SEAL RETAINER

84706078

Oil pan sealing points — 3.5L engine

8. Remove the relief valve as follows:

   a. Remove the cotter pin.

   b. Drill a ⅛ in. (3.175mm) hole into the relief valve retainer cap and insert a self-threading screw into the cap.

   c. Clamp screw in vise while supporting the oil pump body. Remove the cap by tapping the oil pump body with a soft hammer. Discard the retainer cap and remove the spring and relief valve.

9. Inspect the oil pressure relief valve plunger for scoring and free operation. Small marks may be removed using 400 grit wet or dry sandpaper.

10. Inspect the relief valve spring for spring pressure. Compressed to 1¹¹/₃₂ in. (34.00mm) the spring should test to 19.5 lbs. (8.8 Kg). Replace the spring if fails to meet specification.

11. If oil pressure is low and the pump is within specifications, inspect for worn engine bearings or other reason for oil pressure loss.

Rear Main Bearing Oil Seal

REMOVAL AND INSTALLATION

1. Disconnect the negative battery cable.

2. Remove the transaxle from the vehicle.

3. Remove the driveplate as required.

4. If the rear seal retainer is leaking remove the mounting bolts and the retainer from the engine. Remove the seal from the retainer. Clean mating surfaces of oil and gasket material.

5. If oil is leaking from the just the seal, remove the oil seal from the retainer using a prying tool. Take care not to damage the crankshaft flange seal surface or retainer bore during seal removal.

To install:

6. Install the oil seal retainer to the engine using new gasket, if removed. Tighten the retainer bolts to 105 inch lbs. (12 Nm). To assure correct positioning, install the seal retainer to the engine without the seal in place.

7. Place seal pilot tool C-4681 on crankshaft. Coat the outside diameter of the seal with Loctite® Stud N' Bearing Mount or equivalent.

8. Place the seal over the pilot tool and tap in place with a plastic hammer.

9. Install the driveplate and secure using new bolts, if removed.

Tighten the retainer bolts to 75 ft. lbs. (101 Nm).

10. Install the transaxle into the vehicle.

11. Connect the negative battery cable and check for leaks.

AUTOMATIC TRANSAXLE

Transaxle Assembly

REMOVAL AND INSTALLATION

The transaxle can be removed without removing the engine. Use Mopar Type 7176 Automatic Transmission Fluid only. Do not substitute transaxle fluid. If the differential sump requires fluid, use 80W-90 petroleum based Hypoid gear lubricant.

1. Disconnect negative battery cable.

2. Remove the engine air inlet tube.

3. The crankshaft position sensor is located on the upper right side of the transaxle bellhousing. Disconnect the crankshaft position sensor connector and remove sensor.

4. Disconnect the transaxle wiring connectors located on the right shock tower.

5. Raise and safely support the vehicle.

6. Remove the front wheels.

7. Remove the strut to steering knuckle bolts on both sides of the vehicle. Disconnect the tie-rod ends if required.

8. Remove the Anti-lock Brake System (ABS) wheel speed sensor, if equipped.

9. Remove the driveshafts from the transfer case by inserting a prybar between the driveshaft and the transaxle case and pry the shaft from the transaxle housing. Swing the shafts out of the way keeping the joints straight and suspend using wire. Be careful not to damage the driveshaft seals.

NOTE: Do not let the driveshafts or CV-joints hang unsupported. Internal joint damage may result if allowed to hang free.

10. Remove the transaxle bellhousing cover.

11. Mark the flexplate to the torque converter and remove the torque con-

verter bolts. The flexplate-to-torque converter bolts are not to be reused.

12. Unbolt and remove the starter assembly from the bellhousing and allow the starter motor to sit between the engine and the frame.

13. Disconnect the oil cooler lines from the transaxle and plug to prevent excess fluid leakage.

14. Disconnect the gear selector cable from the transaxle.

15. Disconnect the exhaust pipe from the exhaust manifold and position out of the way. If the clearance will not allow for transaxle removal, remove the exhaust system from the vehicle.

16. Support the transaxle using a transmission jack. Raise the transaxle slightly to relieve the weight of the rear transaxle mount.

17. Remove the engine to transaxle brackets and the transaxle mount through bolt.

18. Remove the rear crossmember mounting bolts. Pry the transaxle mount rearward to separate the mount from the transaxle. Remove the rear crossmember.

19. Lower the rear of the transaxle to gain access to the bellhousing bolts. Remove the bellhousing bolts.

20. Place a drain pan under the dipstick in the transaxle to catch transaxle fluid that will drain out of the case. Remove the dipstick tube from the transaxle and plug hole.

21. Remove the engine to transaxle bolts and lower the transaxle from the vehicle.

NOTE: The driveplate to torque converter bolts and the driveplate to crankshaft bolts must not be reused. Install new bolts when ever these bolts are removed.

22. Inspect the driveplate for cracks. If cracks are present, replace the driveplate.

To install:

23. Install the driveplate to the vehicle and secure using new fasteners. Tighten the fastener to 75 ft. lbs. (101 Nm).

24. Install the transaxle into the vehicle and install the engine to transaxle case mounting bolts. Tighten the bolts to 75 ft. lbs. (101 Nm).

25. Install the rear transaxle case mount and the rear crossmember in position and secure all fasteners.

26. Install the dipstick tube.

27. Connect the exhaust pipe to the engine exhaust manifold.

28. Connect the gear selector cable to the transaxle. Connect the transaxle oil cooler lines.

29. Install the starter assembly and secure with the mounting bolts tightened to 40 ft. lbs. (54 Nm).

30. Position the torque converter so matchmarks made during disassembly are in alignment. Install new torque converter to driveplate bolts and tighten to 60 ft. lbs. (81 Nm).

31. Install the transaxle bellhousing cover. Install the engine to transaxle brackets.

32. While pulling the top of the steering knuckle outward, install the inner CV-joint with new retainer clip in place, into the transaxle.

33. Install the ABS wheel sensor, if removed. Install the strut to steering knuckle bolts and securer.

34. Install the front tire and wheel assemblies.

35. Connect the transaxle wiring harness connector on the right shock tower.

36. Install and connect the crankshaft position sensor.

37. Install the air inlet tube and connect the negative battery cable.

38. Start the engine and allow to idle for 2 minutes. Apply parking brake and move selector through each gear position, ending in **N**. Recheck fluid level and add if necessary. Make sure the vehicle is level when refilling the transaxle. Use Mopar Type 7176 Automatic Transmission Fluid only. Do not substitute transaxle fluid. If the differential sump requires fluid, use 80W-90 petroleum based Hypoid gear lubricant.

39. Check the transaxle or proper operation. Make sure the reverse lamps come on when in reverse.

SHIFT LINKAGE ADJUSTMENT

Column Shift

1. Disconnect the negative battery cable.

2. Remove the upper steering column shroud.

3. Rotate the cable adjuster into the unlocked position.

4. Tilt the steering column in the full up position. Make sure the transaxle shift lever on the transaxle is in the **P** position.

5. Place the shifter in the **P** position and remove the key.

6. Adjust by rotating adjuster into lock position.

7. Install the upper steering column shroud and check shifter operation. The shifter should operate smoothly and not bind. The engine should crank in **P** or **N** only.

8. Start the engine and check the fluid level, adjust as required.

Floor Shift

1. Disconnect negative battery cable.

2. Remove the console bezel and the shifter handle.

3. Loosen the nut on the shifter cable adjuster. The nut is accessible through the access hole in the top of the floor shifter assembly.

4. Set the shifter lever in the **P** position at the transaxle. This is the most rearward position.

5. Place the shifter in **P**. Place the ignition in the LOCK position and remove the key.

6. Tighten the adjuster nut at the shifter.

7. Reinstall the console bezel and the shifter handle.

8. Check the shifter operation. The shifter should operate smoothly and not bind. The engine should crank in **P** or **N** only.

9. Start the engine and check the fluid level, adjust as required.

DRIVE AXLE

Halfshaft

REMOVAL AND INSTALLATION

NOTE: Allowing the CV-joint assemblies to dangle unsupported or pulling or pushing the ends can damage boots or CV-joints. Always support both ends of the halfshaft to prevent damage or disengaging the Tripod joint.

1. Disconnect the negative battery cable.

2. Raise and support the vehicle safely.

3. Remove the front wheel and tire assemblies.

4. Remove the front caliper assembly from the steering knuckle.

5. Remove the front brake rotor from the hub by pulling it straight off wheel mounting studs.

6. Remove the speed sensor cable routing bracket from the strut assembly.

7. Remove the hub and bearing to stub axle retainer nut.

8. Dislodge the inner Tripod joint from the stub shaft retaining snapring on the transaxle. To do this, insert a prybar between the transaxle case and the inner Tripod joint and prying on Tripod joint.

NOTE: Do not try to remove the inner Tripod joint from the transaxle stub shaft at this time. Only disengage the inner Tripod joint from the retainer snapring.

9. Remove the strut assembly to steering knuckle attaching bolts from the strut assembly.

NOTE: The strut assembly to steering knuckle bolts are serrated where they go through the strut assembly and steering knuckle. When removing the bolts, turn the nuts off the bolt. Do not turn the bolts in the steering knuckle or damage to the steering knuckle will result.

10. Separate the top of the steering knuckle from the lower end of the strut.

11. Hold the outer joint assembly with 1 hand. Grasp the steering knuckle with the other hand and rotate it out and to the rear of the vehicle, until the outer CV-joint clears the hub and bearing assembly.

12. Remove the halfshaft inner joint from the transaxle stub shaft by grasping the inner Tripod joint and the interconnecting shaft and pulling both pieces at the same time. Take care not to pull on the interconnecting shaft to remove or separation of the spider assembly will occur.

To install:

13. Replace the inner Tripod joint retaining circlip and O-ring seal on the transaxle stub shaft. These components are not reusable and must be replaced whenever the halfshaft is removed.

14. Apply an even coat of grease on the splines of the inner Tripod joint.

15. Install the halfshaft through the hole in the splash shield. Grasp the inner joint in 1 hand and interconnecting shaft in the other. Align the inner Tripod joint spline with the stub shaft spline on the transaxle. Use a rocking motion with the inner Tripod joint to get it past the circlip on the transaxle stub shaft.

16. Continue pushing Tripod joint onto transaxle stub shaft until it stops moving. The O-ring on the stub shaft should not be visible when the inner Tripod joint is fully installed. Check that the inner Tripod joint is locked in position by grasping the inner joint and pulling. If locked in position, the joint will not move on the stub shaft.

17. Hold the outer CV-joint assembly with 1 hand. Grasp the steering knuckle with the other and rotate it

out and to the rear of the vehicle. Install the outer CV-joint into the hub and bearing assembly.

18. Install the top of the steering knuckle into the strut assembly. Align the steering knuckle to strut assembly mounting holes.

19. Install the strut assembly to steering knuckle attaching bolts. Install the nuts to the attaching bolts and while holding the bolt heads, tighten nuts to 125 ft. lbs. (169 Nm).

NOTE: The strut assembly to steering knuckle bolts are serrated where they go through the strut assembly and steering knuckle. When removing the bolts, turn the nuts off the bolt. Do not turn the bolts in the steering knuckle or damage to the steering knuckle will result.

20. Install a new hub and bearing assembly to stub shaft retainer nut. Tighten but do not torque the nut at this time.

21. Install the speed sensor cable routing bracket and secure attaching screw.

22. Install the brake disc and the caliper assembly. Install the caliper to steering knuckle retainer bolts and tighten to 14 ft. lbs. (19 Nm).

23. Install the tire and wheel assembly. Lower the vehicle to the ground. Pump the brakes until a firm pedal is obtained.

24. Apply the brakes and tighten the new stub shaft to hub and bearing assembly retainer nut to 95 ft. lbs. (122 Nm).

CV-Boot

REMOVAL AND INSTALLATION

Inner Tripod Boot

1. Remove the halfshaft requiring bolt replacement.

2. Remove the large boot clamp which retains the inner Tripod joint boot to the Tripod joint housing. Remove the small clamp which retains the inner Tripod joint boot to the interconnecting shaft.

3. Remove the boot from the Tripod joint housing and slide it down the shaft.

4. Slide the interconnecting shaft and spider assembly out of the Tripod joint housing.

5. Remove the snapring which retains the spider assembly to the shaft. Slide the spider assembly off the shaft. If the spider assembly will not come off the shaft, tap on the spider body using a brass drift. Do not hit the outer Tripod bearings in an attempt to remove the spider assembly.

6. Slide the boot from the interconnecting shaft.

7. Thoroughly clean and inspect the spider assembly, Tripod joint housing and interconnecting shaft for excess wear.

NOTE: If any parts show excess wear, the halfshaft assembly will require replacement. Component parts of the driveshaft assemblies are not serviceable. The inner Tripod joint boot is made of 2 types of material depending on the application. The high temperature application is made from silicone rubber, which is soft. The standard temperature application boot is composed of Hytrel plastic which is hard. When replacement boot must be of the same composition as the original boot.

To install:

8. Slide the new boot retainer clamp onto the inner connecting shaft followed by the new boot.

9. Install the spider assembly onto the shaft and install snapring. Make sure the snapring is fully seated in the groove of the shaft.

10. Distribute ½ of the grease provided in the boot service kit into the Tripod housing. Put the remaining grease into the CV-boot.

11. Slide the spider assembly and the interconnecting shaft into the Tripod joint housing. Position the sealing boot over the retaining groove on the interconnecting shaft.

12. Install the boot retaining clamp in position over the boot and crimp closed using tool C-4975 or equivalent.

13. Position the sealing boot into the Tripod housing retainer groove. Install clamp on boot. Make sure the inner Tripod joint in at the correct position. The distance between the inner clamp and the end of the housing is 8.5 in. (216mm) for standard application joint or 7.8 in. (198mm) on high temperature applications. With the distance at the correct value, crimp the sealing boot onto the Tripod housing using tool C-4975 or equivalent.

14. Install the driveshaft into the vehicle.

Outer CV-Joint Boot

1. Remove the halfshaft requiring bolt replacement.

2. Remove the large boot clamp which retains the CV-joint boot to the CV-joint housing. Remove the small clamp which retains the CV-boot to the interconnecting shaft.

3. Remove the boot from the joint housing and slide it down the shaft.

4. Wipe any grease away to expose the outer CV-joint to shaft retaining snapring. Spread the snapring and remove the CV-joint assembly off the end of the shaft.

5. Slide the boot off the shaft. Thoroughly clean and inspect the CV-joint assembly and interconnecting shaft for damage or excess wear.

NOTE: If any parts show signs of excess wear, the halfshaft assembly will require replacement. Component parts for the halfshaft assemblies are not serviceable.

To install:

6. Slide a new seal boot to interconnecting shaft retainer clamp followed by the new boot onto the shaft. Install the outer CV-joint assembly onto the interconnecting shaft pushing on the shaft until the retaining snapring is seated in the groove on the shaft. Be sure the snapring is fully seated.

7. Distribute ½ of the grease provided in the boot service kit into the

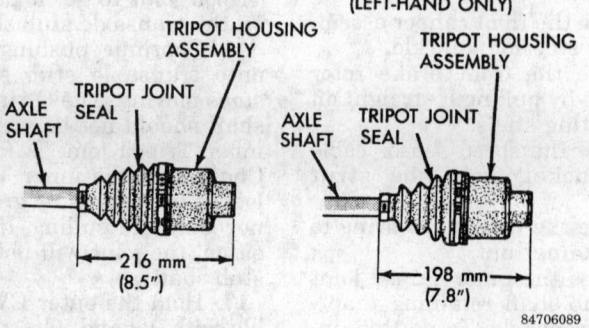

STANDARD APPLICATION

TRIPOT HOUSING ASSEMBLY

TRIPOT JOINT SEAL

AXLE SHAFT

216 mm (8.5")

HI TEMP APPLICATION (LEFT-HAND ONLY)

TRIPOT HOUSING ASSEMBLY

TRIPOT JOINT SEAL

AXLE SHAFT

198 mm (7.8")

84706089

Proper inner Tripod joint boot positioning

joint housing. Put the remaining grease into the CV-boot.

8. Position the sealing boot over the retaining groove on the interconnecting shaft. Install the boot retaining clamp in position over the boot and crimp closed using tool C-4975 or equivalent.

9. Position the sealing boot into the boot retaining groove on the CV-joint housing. Install clamp on boot and crimp using tool C-4975 or equivalent.

10. Install the driveshaft into the vehicle.

Front Wheel Hub and Bearing

REMOVAL AND INSTALLATION

1. Disconnect the negative battery cable.
2. Raise and support the vehicle safely.
3. Remove the front wheel and tire assemblies.
4. Remove the front caliper assembly from the steering knuckle.
5. Remove the front brake rotor from the hub by pulling it straight off wheel mounting stud.
6. Remove the Anti-lock Brake (ABS) system speed sensor cable routing bracket from the strut assembly. Remove the screw attaching the speed sensor to the steering knuckle. If the sensor is seized, use a hammer and a punch and tap the edge of the sensor ear, rocking sensor side to side until it is free.
7. Remove the hub and bearing to stub axle retainer nut.
8. Remove the 3 steering knuckle to hub and bearing assembly attaching bolts.

NOTE: If the metal seal on the hub and bearing assembly is seized to the steering knuckle and becomes dislodged on hub and bearing during removal, the hub and bearing must be replaced. If the flinger disc becomes damaged during the removal procedure, the hub and bearing assembly must be replaced.

9. Remove the hub and bearing assembly from the steering knuckle by sliding it straight out of the knuckle and off the ends of the stub shaft.
   To install:
10. Clean the hub and bearing mounting surfaces of dirt and make sure there are no nicks present. Install the hub and bearing to the stub

shaft and the steering knuckle. Install the 3 bearing assembly mounting bolts and tighten equally until the bearing assembly is seated squarely against the front of the steering knuckle. At this point, tighten the 3 mounting bolts to 80 ft. lbs. (110 Nm).

11. Install a new hub and bearing assembly to stub shaft retainer nut. Tighten but do not torque the nut at this time.

12. Install the speed sensor cable routing bracket and secure attaching screw. Coat the head of the speeds sensor with high temperature multi-purpose grease and install it into the steering knuckle. Tighten the retaining screw to 60 inch lbs. (7 Nm).

13. Install the brake disc and the caliper assembly. Install the caliper to steering knuckle retainer bolts and tighten to 14 ft. lbs. (19 Nm).

14. Install the tire and wheel assembly. Lower the vehicle to the ground. Pump the brakes until a firm pedal is obtained.

15. Apply the brakes and tighten the new stub shaft to hub and bearing assembly retainer nut to 95 ft. lbs. (122 Nm).

Steering Knuckle

REMOVAL AND INSTALLATION

1. Disconnect the negative battery cable.
2. Raise and support the vehicle safely.
3. Remove the front wheel and tire assemblies.
4. Remove the front caliper assembly from the steering knuckle.
5. Remove the front brake rotor from the hub by pulling it straight off wheel mounting studs.
6. Remove the Anti-lock Brake (ABS) system speed sensor cable routing bracket from the strut assembly. Remove the screw attaching the speed sensor to the steering knuckle. If the sensor is seized, use a hammer and a punch and tap the edge of the sensor ear rocking sensor side to side until it is free.
7. Remove the hub and bearing to stub axle retainer nut.
8. Remove the 3 steering knuckle to hub and bearing assembly attaching bolts.

NOTE: If the metal seal on the hub and bearing assembly is seized to the steering knuckle and becomes dislodged on hub and bearing during removal, the hub and bearing must be re-

placed. If the flinger disc becomes damaged during the removal procedure, the hub and bearing assembly must be replaced.

9. Remove the hub and bearing assembly from the steering knuckle by sliding it straight out of the knuckle and off the ends of the stub shaft.

10. Remove the ball joint stud to steering knuckle clamp nut and bolt. Do not allow the ball joint seal to hit against the steering knuckle when the lower arm is separated from the steering knuckle.

11. Carefully insert a prybar between the lower control arm and the steering knuckle. Push down on the prybar to separate the ball joint stud from the steering knuckle. Take care not to cut the ball joint seal during disassembly.

12. Remove the strut assembly to steering knuckle nuts from the bolts.

NOTE: The steering knuckle bolts are serrated where they go through the strut assembly and steering knuckle. Do not turn the bolts during removal or damage to the knuckle will result.

13. Remove the steering knuckle from the vehicle.
   To install:
14. Install the steering knuckle onto the ball joint stud and tighten bolt to 40 ft. lbs. (55 Nm).

15. Position the steering knuckle neck into the strut assembly and align the bolt holes.

16. Install the strut assembly to steering knuckle retaining bolts and while holding the bolt heads stationary with a wrench, tighten nuts to 125 ft. lbs. (169 Nm). Do not allow the bolts to turn in the steering knuckle or damage to the knuckle will result.

17. Clean the hub and bearing mounting surfaces of dirt and make sure there are no nicks present. Install the hub and bearing to the stub shaft and the steering knuckle. Install the 3 bearing assembly mounting bolts and tighten equally until the bearing assembly is seated squarely against the front of the steering knuckle. At this point, tighten the 3 mounting bolts to 80 ft. lbs. (110 Nm).

18. Install a new hub and bearing assembly to stub shaft retainer nut. Tighten but do not torque the nut at this time.

19. Install the speed sensor cable routing bracket and secure attaching screw. Coat the head of the speeds sensor with high temperature multi-

purpose grease and install it into the steering knuckle. Tighten the retaining screw to 60 inch lbs. (7 Nm).

20. Install the brake disc and the caliper assembly. Install the caliper to steering knuckle retainer bolts and tighten to 14 ft. lbs. (19 Nm)

21. Install the tire and wheel assembly. Lower the vehicle to the ground. Pump the brakes until a firm pedal is obtained.

22. Apply the brakes and tighten the new stub shaft to hub and bearing assembly retainer nut to 95 ft. lbs. (122 Nm).

Differential Carrier

REMOVAL AND INSTALLATION

The valve body and solenoid wiring connector must be removed from the transaxle in order to remove the differential from the transaxle. If any bearings in the differential require replacement, all the bearings on the differential carrier and transfer shaft must be replaced. The differential adjusters must also be replaced when differential bearings are replaced.

1. Remove the transaxle assembly from the vehicle.

2. Remove the valve body and drive chain cover.

3. Remove the chain oiler, chain snubber, output shaft sprocket snapring and wave washer.

4. Remove the transfer (pinion) shaft snapring and wave washer. Install a chain spreader tool 6550 or equivalent and remove the chain and sprockets as an assembly.

5. Remove the long stub shaft snapring and remove the long stub shaft (driver side) with a slide hammer tool 6669 or equivalent.

6. Remove the inner differential adjuster lock from inside the bellhousing.

7. Remove the outer differential adjuster lock.

8. Loosen the outer adjuster with tool 6503 or equivalent.

9. Remove the differential side cover, carrier and ring gear assembly.

10. Remove the inner adjuster by turning clockwise with socket tool 6502–B or equivalent.

11. Unstake the transfer (pinion) shaft nut to prevent thread damage. This can be done with a die grinder or a small chisel. Remove the nut.

12. Press the transfer shaft downward to remove the rear bearing cone. But, the transfer shaft can not be removed at this time.

13. Install special tool 6577 or equivalent to remove the rear transfer bearing cup. Remove the preload shim and retain if the bearings are going to be reused.

14. Remove the transfer shaft and seals from the transaxle case.

15. Remove the front transfer shaft bearing cup using special tool 6495 and handle C4171. Press the bearing assembly from the transfer shaft.

To install:

NOTE: Failure to adjust transfer (pinion) shaft depth correctly could cause gear noise and/or transaxle failure. The adjustment factor is stamped onto the transfer shaft.

16. Determine the correct shim thickness as follows:

a. Install the front transfer shaft bearing cup with tool 6494 or equivalent. Make sure the cup is completely seated in the transaxle case.

b. Install the centering block tool 6549–2 into the transaxle case. Screw the block into the inner adjuster hole of the case until it bottoms.

0.681 - 0.707	0.924 - 0.950
0.708 - 0.734	0.951 - 0.977
0.735 - 0.761	0.978 - 1.004
0.762 - 0.788	1.005 - 1.031
0.789 - 0.815	1.032 - 1.058
0.816 - 0.842	1.059 - 1.085
0.843 - 0.869	1.086 - 1.112
0.870 - 0.896	1.113 - 1.139
0.897 - 0.923	

84706094

Pinion head shim selection

3.53 - 3.55	4.13 - 4.15
3.56 - 3.58	4.16 - 4.18
3.59 - 3.61	4.19 - 4.21
3.62 - 3.64	4.22 - 4.24
3.65 - 3.67	4.25 - 4.27
3.68 - 3.70	4.28 - 4.30
3.71 - 3.73	4.31 - 4.33
3.74 - 3.76	4.34 - 4.36
3.77 - 3.79	4.37 - 4.39
3.80 - 3.82	4.40 - 4.42
3.83 - 3.85	4.43 - 4.45
3.86 - 3.88	4.46 - 4.48
3.89 - 3.91	4.49 - 4.51
3.92 - 3.94	4.52 - 4.54
3.95 - 3.97	4.55 - 4.57
3.98 - 4.00	4.58 - 4.60
4.01 - 4.03	4.61 - 4.63
4.04 - 4.06	4.64 - 4.66
4.07 - 4.09	4.67 - 4.69
4.10 - 4.12	

84706095

Transfer shaft rear shim selection

c. Install the new front bearing onto gauge disc tool 6549-3. Install the disc and bearing into case using the gauge disc rod. Install the centering disc tool 6494-2 and nut onto the gauge disc rod. Hand-tighten the nut until all play is removed.

d. Install a dial indicator into the locating block and zero the indicator.

e. Pivot the dial indicator back and forth on the centering pin to obtain the shortest distance. This will be the highest reading on the dial indicator. Record and recheck the reading. Rotate the gauge disc ⅓ turn and recheck. Rotate the gauge disc another ⅓ and average the 3 readings.

f. To determine the required shim thickness the transfer (pinion) shaft depth measurement must be adjusted, use the table provided. Convert the adjustment number to the corresponding adjustment factor. Add or subtract the adjustment factor to calculate the required shim thickness. Example: the measured pinion shaft depth is 0.789mm, the adjustment number on the transfer shaft is +2 and the adjustment factor is −0.051mm. The shim size needed is 0.789 minus 0.051mm = 0.738mm.

g. Remove the dial indicator and install the shim selected onto the transfer shaft. Press the front bearing onto the transfer shaft with the shim in place.

17. Remove the outer adjuster from the differential case with tool 6503 and remove the old stub shaft seals.

18. Install new seals into both adjusters.

19. Lubricate adjuster threads with gear oil. Screw in the inner adjuster using tool 6502B until it is under flush with the inside of the case.

20. Install the differential assembly and cover. Do not seal at this time. Tighten all bolts evenly.

21. Install a seal protector tool 6591 or equivalent, and screw in the outer adjuster finger-tight.

22. Insert special tool 6548 to check the turning torque of the differential assembly. Rotate the differential 3 times before checking the turning torque. The turning torque for new bearings should be 19–23 inch lbs. (2.13–2.58 Nm). Do not attempt this procedure for used bearings.

23. Tighten the outer adjuster with tool 6503 until the turning torque reading is obtained on the inch lbs. torque wrench 6548 or equivalent.

24. Remove the differential carrier, cover and inner adjuster

25. Install the transfer shaft as follows:

a. Install the transfer shaft into the case after installing the front shaft seal. Install the seal using tool 6567A and a press. The tool will set the seal depth.

b. Install the rear shaft seal with installation tool 6567A or equivalent. The seal spring should face the rear of the vehicle

c. Install the transfer shaft bearing cup into the case using a press and tool 6560. Install the preload shim that was removed.

d. Install a new transfer shaft nut and torque to 200 ft. lbs. (271 Nm) using socket 6497 and shaft socket 6498.

e. Check the transfer shaft turning torque with an inch lbs. torque wrench. The turning torque should be 5–12 inch lbs. (0.5–1.3 Nm). If the turning torque is too high, install a thicker preload shim and vise versa if too low.

f. Stake the locknut with tool 6589 or equivalent.

26. Install new seals and the inner adjuster into the case.

27. Install the differential assembly into the case and check ring gear-to-pinion gear backlash as follows:

a. The backlash should be 0.006–0.009 in. (0.15–0.23mm).

b. Hold the transfer shaft with one hand and rock the ring gear back and forth. Backlash should be felt between the gears. If not, use special tool 6502B to turn the inner adjuster so it raises the differential. This will increase backlash.

c. If there is too much backlash, turn the inner adjuster so it lowers the differential assembly.

28. Apply a ⅛ in. (3.18mm) of sealer to the differential cover flange and install. Torque the cover bolts to 250 inch lbs. (29 Nm).

29. Install the outer adjuster with new seals and tighten until a turning torque of 19–23 inch lbs. (2.13–2.58 Nm) is reached.

30. Recheck the ring gear-to-pinion gear backlash with a dial indicator mounted in the inspection hole in the differential case. The reading should be 0.006–0.009 in. (0.15–0.23mm). If there too much backlash, loosen the outer adjuster and turn the inner adjuster so it moves away from the ring gear. After the backlash has been adjusted, readjust the bearing preload.

31. Install the inner and outer adjuster locking brackets and new inspection plug. Refill the differential

with 32 ounces of 80W–90W Hypoid gear oil.

32. Install the transaxle assembly into the vehicle.

STEERING

Steering Wheel

NOTE: If equipped with air bags, be sure to disarm the system before starting repairs on the vehicle. Failure to do so could result in possible personal injury. The fasteners, screws and bolts originally used for the air bag components have a special coating on them specifically designed for use in this system. They must never be replaced with any substitutes. Anytime new fasteners are needed, replace with the correct fasteners.

REMOVAL AND INSTALLATION

1. Disconnect negative battery cable and isolate from the battery. Disarm the air bags as follows:

a. Disconnect the negative battery cable and isolate.

b. Wait 2 minutes for the reserve capacitor to discharge before removing a non-deployed air bag module.

2. Remove both speed control switched from the steering wheel. If not equipped with cruise control, pry off the covers on the side of the steering wheel.

3. Remove the 2 bolts attaching the air bag module to the steering wheel.

4. Lift the air bag module from the steering wheel and disconnect the electrical harness connections. Remove the module from the vehicle.

5. Remove the steering wheel retainer nut. Use a steering wheel puller C-3428B or equivalent, to remove the steering wheel from the steering shaft. Do not hammer on steering wheel to remove.

To install:

6. Align the master splines on the steering wheel and the steering shaft and install the steering wheel to the shaft. Install wheel retainer nut and tighten to 45 ft. lbs. (61 Nm).

7. Connect the electrical wires from the body harness to the air bag module and position module so it is at the center of the steering spokes. Install the 2 bolts attaching the air bag

module to the steering wheel and tighten to 8 ft. lbs. (10 Nm).

8. Connect both harness connectors to the speed control switches and install to the steering wheel, if equipped. If not equipped with cruise control, install the covers on the side of the steering wheel.

9. Reconnect the negative battery cable. Check operation of all components disturbed during this procedure.

Steering Column

REMOVAL AND INSTALLATION

1993

1. Disconnect negative battery cable and isolate from the battery. Disarm the air bags.

2. Remove the steering wheel from the steering shaft.

3. Remove the instrument panel left and right end covers. Remove fuses 7 and 19 from the junction block, which are air bag fuses.

4. Remove the instrument panel lower cover by pulling the bezel straight rearward along the radio and air conditioning control openings to disengage the clips.

5. Remove the ashtray receiver and the left under instrument panel silencer.

6. Remove the lower dash panel assembly from the vehicle.

7. Remove the under steering column air outlet duct. Tilt the steering column in the full down position.

8. Remove the tilt lever, upper and lower steering shrouds.

9. If equipped with column shifter, remove the shift cable from the steering column as follows:

   a. Install the tilt lever on the steering column.

   b. Tilt the column to the up position.

   c. Pry the shift cable off the shifter pin on the shifter mechanism. Remove the shift cable retaining clip at the shift cable support bracket, being careful not to damage the cable bracket.

NOTE: When the ignition is in the RUN position, do not rotate the steering column shaft. If steering column shaft is turned, damage to the clockspring will occur.

10. Turn the ignition to the **RUN** position to unlock the steering column. Depress the tab and remove the floor shift interlock cable from the steering column socket.

11. Remove the coupling bolt retaining pin from the lower steering column coupler bolt. Remove the coupler bolt and separate the coupler from the intermediate shaft.

12. Loosen but do not remove the 2 bolts attaching the lower steering column assembly bracket to steering column mounting bracket.

13. While supporting the weight of the steering column to prevent damage to the lower bracket and plastic adapter tabs, loosen and remove the 2 nuts and washers attaching the upper steering column assembly assembly bracket to the steering column mounting bracket.

14. Remove the steering column from its mounting bracket and lay column on the floor of the vehicle.

15. Remove the harness wire connectors from the turn signal/multifunction switch and the ignition switch.

16. Remove the wiring harness connectors from the halo light and the clockspring. Carefully remove the steering column wiring trough from it s mounting bracket by depressing tab.

17. Remove the steering column assembly out of the vehicle through the passenger compartment.

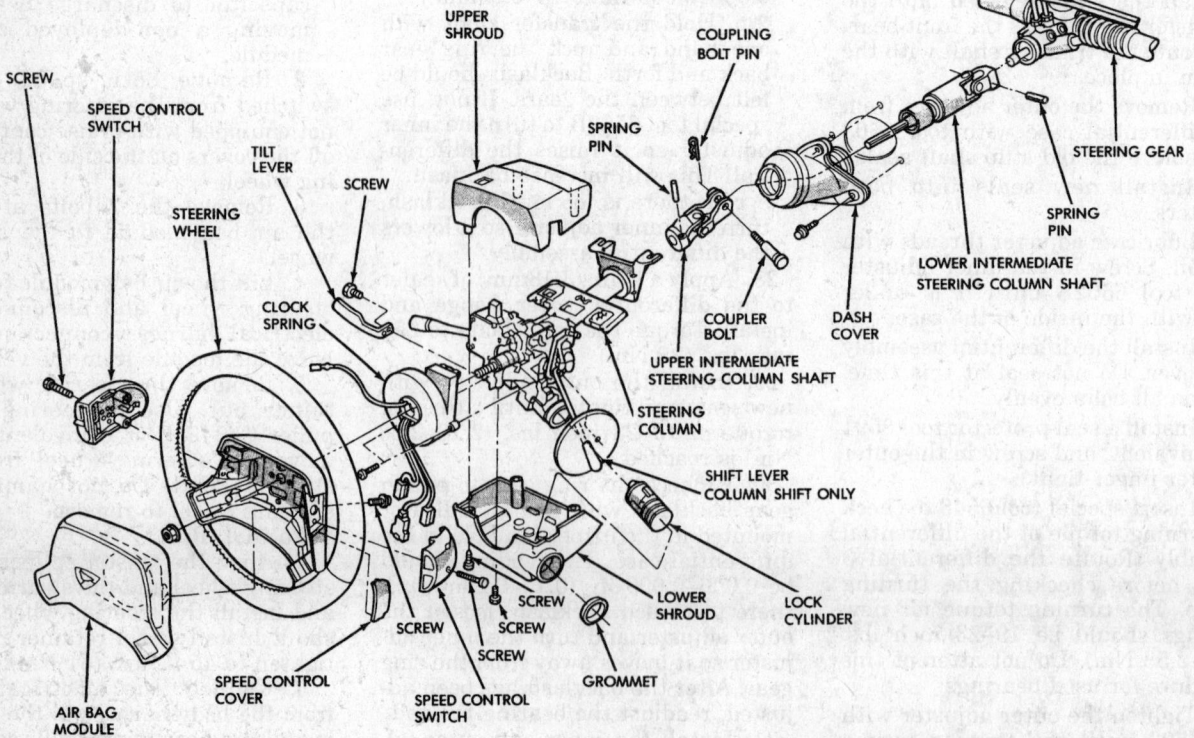

Saginaw tilt steering column and related components

84706096

To install:

18. Position the steering column on the floor of the vehicle. Reconnect all wire connectors and reposition in trough. The yellow connector mates to air bag clockspring connector. Be sure to route the wiring through the clips on the multi-function switch and the on side of clockspring. Be sure wiring is taut and free of moving parts.

19. Install the steering column back onto its bracket by first sliding the lower steering column bracket onto bolts in mounting bracket. Install but do not tighten these bolts at this time.

20. Raise the top of the steering column until the upper steering column mounting bracket is installed on studs in the steering column mounting bracket. Install but do not tighten the 2 retaining nuts at this time.

21. Position the steering column so the lower bracket rests on the lower column mounting bolts. Temporarily install the upper and the lower steering column shrouds and the center instrument panel outlet bezel. Visually center the steering column shrouds in the instrument panel opening with the steering column in the full up position. Tighten the upper and the lower fasteners. Remove the upper and the lower steering column shrouds and the center instrument panel outlet bezel.

22. Be sure both breakaway capsules are fully seated in the slots of the steering column upper support bracket. Torque the 2 upper steering column mounting nuts to 95 inch lbs. (11 Nm). Next, torque the lower steering column mounting nuts to 95 inch lbs. (11 Nm).

23. Install the upper steering column coupler onto the lower coupler shaft. Install the coupler bolt and torque to 21 ft. lbs. (28 Nm). Install the coupling retainer pin into the coupling bolt.

24. If equipped with floor shift, turn the key to **RUN** and install the shift interlock cable into the steering column socket. Be sure the locking tab on the interlock cable is fully engaged with the steering column socket.

25. If equipped with column shifter, install a new interlock cassette and adjust.

26. If equipped with column shift, correctly route shift cable to cable support bracket and install attaching clip. Make sure clip is fully seated and bracket does not get bent during installation. Verify clearance to steering column jacket by tilting steering column. Install the shift

cable onto the mechanism, check and adjust the interlock system.

27. Install the upper and the lower steering column shrouds. Install the tilt lever and the lower steering column air outlet duct.

28. Install the lower dash panel assembly and the left side under instrument panel silencer duct back into the vehicle.

29. Install the console or instrument panel lower center cover and ashtray receiver. Install the left and the right cowl area trim panels.

30. Install the 2 air bag system fuses into the junction block.

31. Install the instrument panel left and right end covers.

32. Install the steering wheel and air bag module to the steering shaft. Tighten the steering wheel retainer nut to 45 ft. lbs. (61 Nm) and the air bag module retainer bolts to 8 ft. lbs. (10 Nm).

33. Connect both harness connectors to the speed control switches and install switches to the steering wheel, if equipped. If not equipped with cruise control, install the covers on the side of the steering wheel.

34. Reconnect the negative battery cable. Check operation of all electrical components disturbed during this procedure. Operate the steering column and make sure operation is smooth. Road test the vehicle to assure proper operation of the steering column.

1994–96

1. Disconnect the negative battery cable.

2. Turn the steering wheel 180 degrees and lock in position.

3. Remove the 2 speed control switches from the steering wheel to gain access to the air bag module retaining screws. Pry out the covers on the sides of the steering wheel for access to the air bag retaining screws.

4. Remove the air bag module and steering wheel using a puller.

5. Remove the instrument panel left and right end covers.

6. Remove the 2 air bag fuses No. 7 and 19 from the fuse panel.

7. Remove the left and right lower cowl area trim panels, ashtray receiver and lower center trim bezel. The center bezel is removed by carefully prying along the edge of the bezel. Be careful not to scratch the components.

8. Remove the center upper outlet bezel from the upper instrument panel. This bezel is removed by prying on the right side of the bezel from

the instrument panel. Disconnect the traction control switch, if equipped.

9. Remove the lower knee bolster-to-upper instrument panel screw.

10. Disconnect the cigar lighter and ashtray wiring harnesses. Remove the 2 nuts located at the rear of the ashtray.

11. Remove the 6 screws inside the glove box retaining the lower knee bolster to the cowl panel. Remove the knee bolster screws and remove the bolster. Disconnect the glove box light and trunk release button. The knee bolster should be removed from the passenger side of the vehicle.

12. Remove the under steering column heater and A/C ducts.

13. Tilt the steering column to the down position and remove the lower steering column shroud.

14. Tilt the steering column to the up position and remove the tilt lever.

15. If equipped with a column shifter, proceed as follows:

   a. Remove the shift cable from the shifter assembly by prying the cable off the attaching pin of the column shifter mechanism.

   b. Remove the shaft cable retaining clip at the shaft cable support bracket. Do not bend the cable.

16. If equipped with a floor shifter, proceed as follows:

   a. Turn the ignition key to the **RUN** position to unlock the steering column.

   b. Depress the tab and remove the floor shift interlock cable from the steering column socket.

17. Remove the steering column coupler bolt pin and bolt from the coupler. Separate the coupler from the intermediate shaft.

18. Loosen but do not remove the 2 bolts that retain the column to the mounting bracket. Support the weight of the steering column and remove the 2 nut/washer assemblies.

19. Remove the column and lay on the floor. Disconnect the wiring harnesses and remove the assembly from the vehicle.

To install:

20. Install the plastic capsules into the bracket slots before installation.

21. Connect the wiring harnesses and position the column into place. Make sure the wiring harnesses are routed correctly.

22. Install but do not tighten the 2 nuts on the top mounting bracket.

23. Position the steering column so the lower mounting bracket is resting against the 2 lower mounting bolts. This will determine the fore-and-aft position of the steering column. Temporarily install the column shrouds

and visually center in the instrument panel opening.

24. Torque the upper mounting nuts and lower bracket nuts to 105 inch lbs. (12 Nm).

25. Connect the shift interlock cable to the steering column.

26. Tilt the steering column to the up position and install the tilt lever.

27. Tilt the steering column to the down position and install the lower steering column shroud.

28. Install the under steering column heater and A/C ducts.

29. Connect the glove box light and trunk release button. Install the knee bolster from the passenger side of the vehicle.

30. Connect the cigar lighter and ashtray wiring harnesses. Install the 2 nuts located at the rear of the ashtray.

31. Install the lower knee bolster-to-upper instrument panel screw.

32. Install the center upper outlet bezel to the upper instrument panel.

33. Install the left and right lower cowl area trim panels, ashtray receiver and lower center trim bezel. Be careful not to scratch the components.

34. Install the 2 air bag fuses No. 7 and 19 to the fuse panel.

35. Install the instrument panel left and right end covers.

36. Install the steering wheel and air bag module. Torque the steering wheel nut to 45 ft. lbs. (61 Nm) and the air bag screws to 8 ft. lbs. (10 Nm).

37. Install the 2 speed control switches and air bag covers.

38. Connect the negative battery cable.

39. Check all steering column operated components for correct function. Road test the vehicle for proper steering performance and speed control function.

Power Steering Rack and Pinion

The power steering gear should not be serviced or adjusted. If a malfunction or oil leak should occur, the complete gear should be replaced.

REMOVAL AND INSTALLATION

1. Disconnect negative battery cable. Disarm the air bag system.

2. Raise and safely support the vehicle.

3. Remove the gear shift cable from the shifter lever on the transaxle.

4. Loosen the bolt at the gear shift cable to transaxle mount. Remove the cable from the transaxle.

5. Lower the vehicle.

6. If equipped with 3.5L engine, disconnect the throttle cable from the throttle body and remove throttle cable bracket.

7. Remove both wiper arm assemblies from the wiper arm pivots. Remove the cowl closure panel and weatherstrip as an assembly from the cowl.

8. Disconnect the air plenum from the throttle body, PCV make up air tube and the idle air control motor. Remove the plenum from the right side of the vehicle.

9. Disconnect the wiper module harness connector from the vehicle wiring harness.

10. Remove the wiper module from the cowl panel. Disconnect the vacuum connector from the power brake booster at the intake manifold.

11. Turn the front wheels to the full left position. The turn the wheels back in the other direction until the roll pin in the lower steering coupler is accessible. Position the ignition in the LOCK position. Do not allow the rotate beyond the normal range in either direction or the clockspring will be damaged.

12. Using paint, mark the steering coupling and steering gear shaft for orientation. Using the correct size punch, remove the roll pin from the steering coupling.

13. Remove the pedal travel sensor from the brake booster as follows:

   a. Pump the brake pedal approximately 20 times. This will bleed the vacuum stored in the booster.

   b. Remove the wiring harness connector from the sensor.

   c. Using a small flat tipped tool, lift the retainer ring from the notch. Then remove the retaining ring from the grommet.

   d. Remove the pedal travel sensor from the brake booster by carefully pulling it straight out of its mounting grommet. Do not twist the sensor.

14. Loosen and remove the 2 nuts attaching the master cylinder to the brake booster. Remove the master cylinder and position aside.

15. Remove the power steering pressure hose and return hose from the power steering gear.

16. Bend back the retaining tabs on bolt attaching the tie rods to the steering gear and remove the bolts.

17. Lay the tie rods, bolts and plate as an assembly on the bellhousing of the transaxle.

18. Remove the 4 bolts attaching the steering gear assembly to the crossmember. Slide the steering gear forward in the vehicle to disengage steering coupler from the steering gear shaft. After gear is disengaged, do not rotate the steering gear shaft.

19. Remove the steering gear assembly from the vehicle through the area in the cowl that the windshield wiper module was previously removed from.

To install:

20. If a replacement rack is being installed, grasp the shaft of the steering gear and rotate until steering gear center take off is in a full left turn position. Install the steering gear into the vehicle through the wiper module opening in cowl.

21. If the original gear is being installed, align the paint mark on the steering coupler with the mark on the steering gear shaft and install the steering gear shaft into the steering gear coupler.

22. If a replacement rack is being installed, the steering gear shaft and steering coupler must be aligned. Rotate the steering gear shaft back from the full left turn position until the master spline on the steering gear shaft is aligned with the master spline on the steering coupler. At this point, install the steering gear into the coupler.

23. Align the steering gear wit the mounting holes in the crossmember and install bolts. Be sure the brake line routing clip is installed under the left steering gear mounting bracket. Tighten the mounting bolts to 50 ft. lbs. (68 Nm).

24. Install the steering coupler to steering gear shaft retaining roll pin until it is flush with the top edge of the steering coupler.

25. If equipped with 3.5L engine, correct orientation of the power steering pressure hose at the power steering pump must be maintained. Be sure the power steering hose is installed in orientation clip at the power steering pump prior to tightening tube fitting. Attach the power steering pressure and return lines onto the proper ports of the power steering gear. Torque both fittings to 23 ft. lbs. (31 Nm).

26. Align the center take off on the steering gear with the tie rod assemblies. Install the tie rod attaching bolts and washers into the steering gear assembly. Be sure the washers are installed between the tie rods and the steering gear. Torque the tie rod to steering gear attaching bolts to 55

ft. lbs. (75 Nm). Bend the retaining tabs against the heads of the bolts.

27. Install the pedal travel sensor retainer ring on the travel sensor grommet in the vacuum booster. The tab on the retaining ring should be located in top notch of the mounting grommet.

28. Sparingly lubricate pedal travel sensor O-ring with fresh brake fluid. Install the pedal travel O-ring into the pedal travel sensor mounting grommet. Coat the end of the sensor with fresh brake fluid and install by pushing straight into the mounting grommet on the brake booster until the tab on the sensor is past the retaining ring on grommet.

29. Install the wire harness connector to the pedal travel sensor.

30. Install the master cylinder and tighten nuts to 250 inch lbs. (28 Nm).

31. Install the power booster vacuum hose to the intake manifold. Install the windshield wiper module to the cowl panel. Connect the electrical harness to the module.

32. If equipped with 3.5L engine, install the air intake plenum and connect to the idle air control motor, PCV make up air tube and throttle body.

33. Install the cowl closure panel and tighten the 6 mounting screws. Install the weather strip on shock towers.

34. Install the windshield washer hoses on the wiper arms, then install arms on the windshield wiper pivots.

35. If equipped with 3.5L engine, install the throttle cable to the bracket and install to the throttle body.

36. Raise and safely support the vehicle.

37. Install the gear shift cable onto the shift lever on transaxle. Install gear shift cable on cable mounting bracket of transaxle and securely tighten bolt.

38. Lower the vehicle. Install the tire and wheel assemblies. Connect the negative battery cable.

39. Fill the pump reservoir to the correct lever with Mopar Power Steering Fluid or equivalent. Start the engine and turn the steering wheel several times from stop to stop to bleed the air from the fluid in the system. Check and adjust fluid level as required.

40. Adjust the front suspension toe setting.

Power Steering Pump

REMOVAL AND INSTALLATION

1. Disconnect negative battery cable and isolate.

2. If equipped with 3.3L engine, loosen the power steering drive belt by loosening the alternator mounting pivot bolts and turning the adjuster bolt. Remove the drive belt from the pump pulley.

3. If equipped with 3.5L engine, loosen the power steering drive belt by loosening the adjuster pulley locking nut and then loosening the adjuster bolt. Remove the drive belt from the pump pulley.

4. Raise and safely support the vehicle.

5. Position an oil drain pan under the vehicle to catch leaking power steering fluid. Remove the hose clamps from the power steering fluid inlet hose at the pump. Remove the hose at the pump.

6. Loosen and remove the power steering pressure hose from the power steering pump discharge fitting.

7. Loosen and remove the 3 bolts attaching the pump to the power steering pump mounting bracket. Access to the pump mounting bolts is through the holes in the pump pulley.

8. Remove the power steering pump and drive pulley as an assembly out the bottom of the engine compartment.

9. Remove the power steering pump pulley as follows:

    a. Mount the pump in a vise using the mounting bosses.

    b. Remove the power steering pump pulley from the shaft using special puller tool C-4333 or equivalent.

NOTE: Do not press or hammer on the shaft of the pump. This will cause internal pump damage.

10. Transfer parts to replacement pump, as required.

To install:

11. Install the power steering pump pulley as follows:

    a. Place the pulley onto the shaft and make sure it is installed squarely.

    b. Install the spacer provided with the replacement pump into the hub of the pulley.

    c. Insert the pulley installer tool C-4063 (without adapters) through the hole in the spacer. Thread the tool into the pump shaft and tighten the tool into the shaft.

    d. Hold the installer with one wrench so it does not rotate. Turn the hex down threaded rod of installer to push the pulley onto the shaft. Make sure the pulley does not become cocked during installation.

    e. Continue to push the pulley onto the shaft until the tool will not turn.

    f. Remove the installer tool and spacer. Turn the pulley and make sure it does not wobble. If it does, remove the pulley and check for a bent pump shaft, bent pulley or other malfunction.

12. Install the power steering pump back into the vehicle from below the engine compartment. Install mounting bolts and tighten to 40 ft. lbs. (54 Nm).

13. If equipped with 3.5L engine, correct orientation of the power steering pressure hose at the power steering pump must be maintained. Be sure the power steering hose is installed in orientation clip at the power steering pump prior to tightening tube fitting. Attach the power steering pressure hose on the outlet port of the pump and tighten fitting to 25 ft. lbs. (34 Nm).

14. Install the hose from the remote fluid reservoir to the low pressure hose on the power steering pump.

15. Install the accessory drive belt over the power steering pulley. Lower the vehicle.

16. Adjust the belt tension and connect the negative battery cable.

17. Fill the pump reservoir to the correct lever with Mopar Power Steering Fluid or equivalent. Start the engine and turn the steering wheel several times from stop to stop to bleed the air from the fluid in the system. Check and adjust fluid level as required.

BELT ADJUSTMENT

1. Inspect belt tension with the use of belt tensioning tool kit C-4162 or equivalent, making sure tension reading agrees with the desired tension of 120 lbs. (54 Kg) for used belt or 140-160 lbs. (64-73 Kg) for a new belt.

2. If tension requires adjustment, loosen the alternator mounting bolts.

3. On 3.3L engine, adjust belt tension by turning the screw on the mounting bracket to maintain the proper tension.

4. On 3.5L engine, adjust belt tension by adjusting the tensioner pulley located on the timing belt cover to maintain the proper tension.

5. Tighten the alternator mounting bolts to 40 ft. lbs. (54 Nm).

BLEEDING

To bleed the power steering system, start the vehicle and allow to idle. Turn the steering wheel several times from 1 stop to the other. Stop the engine and check the fluid level. If required, fill the remote reservoir to the correct level and repeat procedure.

Power Steering Pump Reservoir

REMOVAL AND INSTALLATION

1. Raise and safely support the vehicle.
2. Position a drain pan under the reservoir and disconnect the hoses.
3. Lower the vehicle.
4. Disconnect the battery cables and remove the battery.
5. Remove the battery tray, reservoir retaining bolts and reservoir.
To install:
6. Install the reservoir and torque the bolts to 60 inch lbs. (7 Nm).
7. Install the battery tray and battery.
8. Raise and safely support the vehicle.
9. Connect the power steering hoses to the reservoir.
10. Lower the vehicle, connect the battery cables and bleed the power steering system.

Tie Rod Ends

REMOVAL AND INSTALLATION

1. Raise and safely support the vehicle.
2. Remove the tire and wheel assembly.
3. Loosen the outer tie rod to adjustment sleeve jam nut.
4. Loosen but do not remove the outer tie rod to strut assembly steering arm attaching nut. Then remove the outer tie rod from the steering arm using puller MB-990635 or equivalent.
5. Remove the outer tie rod from the adjustment sleeve.
To install:
6. Install replacement outer rod into the adjustment sleeve. Make sure the jam nut is on the outer tie rod end.

7. Install the outer tie rod into the steering arm on front strut assembly. Install the tie rod to steering arm attaching nut and torque to 27 ft. lbs. (37 Nm).
8. Install the tire and wheel assembly. Check the front wheel toe setting on the vehicle and adjust as required. Make sure the maximum number of threads exposed past the outer adjusting nut does not exceed the limit of 19.
9. Install the correct size wrench on the flat of the adjustment sleeve to keep sleeve from turning. Tighten outer tie rod to adjustment sleeve jam nut to 55 ft. lbs. (75 Nm). While continuing to hold the adjustment sleeve from turning, tighten the inner tie rod to adjusting sleeve jam nut to 55 ft. lbs. (75 Nm).
10. Lower the vehicle.
11. Adjust the front suspension toe setting.

BRAKES

Master Cylinder

REMOVAL AND INSTALLATION

1. Disconnect the negative battery cable.
2. Disconnect the fluid level sensor connector.
3. Disconnect the brake tubes from the master cylinder. Install plugs at the brake tube outlets.
4. Remove the 2 nuts securing the master cylinder to the booster and remove the cylinder from the mounting studs.
5. Remove the brake reservoir as follows:
   a. Clean the master cylinder housing and brake reservoir.
   b. Remove the reservoir caps and empty the reservoir of fluid.
   c. Position the master cylinder in a vise.
   d. Remove the 2 reservoir retaining pins.
   e. Rock the reservoir from side to side and remove the reservoir from the rubber bushings.
To install:
6. Install the brake reservoir as follows:
   a. Install new bushings into the housing.
   b. Lubricate the bushings with clean brake fluid.

   c. Install the reservoir by rocking back and forth until it is fully seated.
   d. Install the reservoir retaining pins.
7. Bench bleed the master cylinder.
8. Install master cylinder to the mounting studs aligning the push rod with the master cylinder piston. Install the retainer nuts and tighten to 21 ft. lbs. (28 Nm).
9. Connect the brake tubes to the ports on the side of the master cylinder. Have a helper depress the brake pedal while the brake tubes are tighten to 145 inch lbs. (17 Nm).
10. Check brake fluid level in reservoir and correct as required.

Proportioning Valve

REMOVAL AND INSTALLATION

Except Anti-lock Brake System

1. Disconnect the negative battery cable.
2. Locate the proportioning valve located below the master cylinder mounted to the frame rail.
3. Tag and disconnect the brake lines from the valve.
4. Remove the proportioning valve from the engine compartment.
5. The installation is the reverse of the removal procedure.
6. Bleed the brake system.

Anti-lock Brake System

1. Disconnect negative battery cable.
2. Remove the Hydraulic Control Unit (HCU) assembly from the vehicle.
3. Remove the required proportioning valve from the valve block of the HCU.
To install:
4. Install the proportioning valve into the valve block of the HCU. Torque the valve to 106 inch lbs. (12 Nm).
5. Install the HCU onto the vehicle. Install the brake tube onto the proportioning valve. Tighten the tube nut to 11 ft. lbs. (15 Nm).
6. Bleed the air from the hydraulic system.

NOTE: When bleeding the brake system, visually inspect all line fittings that were previously disconnected for any signs of leakage.

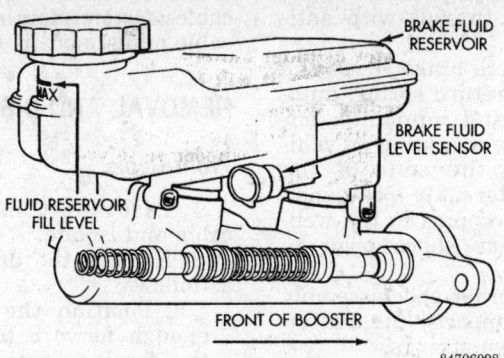

Master cylinder components

Power Brake Booster

REMOVAL AND INSTALLATION

1. Disconnect the negative battery cable.
2. Remove both wiper arm assemblies and the cowl panel to expose the wiper module.
3. Remove the 5 screws attaching the module to the dash panel. Remove the module.
4. Remove the 2 nuts attaching the master cylinder to the brake booster. Slide the master cylinder carefully off the mounting studs and allow the assembly to rest against the left shock tower.
5. Disconnect the vacuum hose from the brake booster check valve. Do not remove the check valve from the booster assembly.
6. From under the instrument panel, position a small tipped prying tool between the center tang on the power brake booster input rod to brake pedal pin retaining clip. Rotate the tool enough to allow the retainer clip center tang to pass over the end of brake pedal pin and pull the retainer clip off pin. Discard retainer clip.
7. From under the instrument panel, remove the 4 nuts attaching the power booster assembly to the dash panel.
8. Slide the booster up and to the right on the dash panel, then tilt outboard and up to remove.

NOTE: Do not attempt to disassemble the power brake unit as the booster is serviced only as a complete assembly.

To install:
9. Position the power brake unit on the dash panel and secure using the retaining screws. Tighten the screws to 21 ft. lbs. (29 Nm).

10. Position the master cylinder onto the booster mounting studs and secure with mounting nuts tightened to 21 ft. lbs. (29 Nm).
11. Connect the vacuum hose to the brake booster check valve.
12. Coat the bearing surface of the brake pedal pin with lubriplate. Connect the brake booster input rod to the brake pedal pin and install a new retainer clip. Do not use the old retainer clip during installation.
13. Check stop light operation.
14. Install the wiper module and the cowl panel onto the vehicle.
15. Install the wiper arm assemblies onto the pivots. Connect the washer hoses.

Brake Caliper

REMOVAL AND INSTALLATION

1. Disconnect the negative battery cable.
2. Raise and support the vehicle safely.
3. Remove the front wheel and tire assemblies.
4. Remove the 2 caliper guide pin bolts and remove the front caliper assembly from the steering knuckle.
5. Remove the bolt retaining the hose to the caliper. Remove the caliper from the vehicle.
To install:
6. Connect the brake hose to the caliper using new gasket.
7. Install the brake shoes into the caliper and install the caliper to the adapter.
8. Install the guide pins and tighten to 15 ft. lbs. (20 Nm) for front caliper or 17 ft. lbs. (22 Nm) for rear caliper.
9. Install the wheel and tire assembly, lower the vehicle, pump the

break pedal to seat the pads against the rotors. Bleed the brake system.

Disc Brake Pads

REMOVAL AND INSTALLATION

1. Remove some of the fluid from the master cylinder.
2. Raise the vehicle and support safely. Remove the tire and wheel assemblies.
3. Remove the 2 caliper guide pin bolts and remove the caliper assembly from the adapter.
4. Remove the outboard shoe by prying brake shoe retaining clip over raised area on the caliper. Then slide the shoe down and off the caliper.
5. Remove the inboard shoe by pulling away from piston until the retainer clip is free from the cavity in the piston.
To install:
6. Use a large C-clamp, completely retract the piston into the caliper. Lubricate both adapter to caliper mating surfaces with multi-purpose lubricant.
7. Install brake pads into the caliper assembly making sure both pads are seated securely onto the caliper.
8. Install the caliper onto the adapter and install the caliper guide pin bolts. Tighten pin bolts to 17 ft. lbs. (22 Nm).
9. Install the tire and wheel assembly. Lower the vehicle and refill the master cylinder to the appropriate level.
10. Before moving the vehicle, pump the brakes until a firm pedal is obtained. Road test the vehicle to make sure the brake operation is normal.

Brake Rotor

REMOVAL AND INSTALLATION

1. Raise the vehicle and support safely. Remove the tire and wheel assembly.
2. Remove the caliper and brake pads.
3. Remove the factory installed clips, if equipped. It is not necessary to reinstall these clips.
4. Remove the rotor from the hub assembly by pulling straight off wheel mounting studs.
5. The installation is the reverse of the removal procedure.

Brake Drum

REMOVAL AND INSTALLATION

1. Raise the vehicle and support safely.

2. Remove the wheel and tire assembly.

3. Remove the brake drum from the rear hub and bearing assembly. If the drum is difficult to remove, increase the clearance between the brake shoes and the drum as follows:

    a. Remove the rubber plug from the top of the brake support plate.

    b. Rotate the automatic shoe adjuster screw with an upward motion using a medium size flat tipped tool.

4. Installation is the reverse of the removal procedure.

Brake Shoes

REMOVAL AND INSTALLATION

1. Raise the vehicle and support safely. Remove the wheel and tire assemblies and the drums.

2. Remove the rear hub and bearing assembly dust cap. Then remove the cotter pin and the locknut from the spindle.

3. Remove the rear hub and bearing assembly retainer nut and washer. Remove the rear hub and bearing from the spindle.

4. Remove the automatic adjuster spring from the adjuster lever.

5. Rotate the automatic adjuster star wheel enough so both shoes move out far enough to be free of the wheel cylinder boots.

6. Disconnect the parking brake cable from the actuating lever. Only disconnect parking brake cable 1 side at a time.

7. Remove the lower brake shoe to anchor spring(s).

8. Remove the 2 brake shoe assembly to support plate hold-down springs from the brake shoes.

9. Remove the brake shoes, upper shoe to shoe return spring, automatic adjuster and automatic adjuster lever from the backing plate as an assembly.

To install:

10. Thoroughly clean and dry the backing plate. To prepare the backing plate, lubricate the bosses, anchor pin and parking brake actuating lever pivot surface lightly with lithium based grease.

11. Remove, clean and dry all parts still on the old shoes. Lubricate the star wheel shaft threads with anti-seize lubricant.

12. Assemble both brake shoes, the top shoe to shoe return spring, automatic adjuster and automatic adjuster lever before mounting on vehicle. Make sure the ends of the automatic adjusters are positioned above the extruded pins in the webbing of the brake shoes prior to installation.

13. Install the brake shoe assembly onto the brake support plate and install the hold-down springs.

14. Install the lower spring(s) and connect the parking brake cable.

15. Rotate the serrated adjuster nut to remove the free-play from the adjuster assembly. Install the automatic adjuster lever spring on the lead brake shoe assembly and the automatic adjuster lever.

16. Install the rear hub and bearing assembly. Install washers and retainer nuts and tighten to 124 ft. lbs. (168 Nm).

17. Install nut lock, new cotter pin and dust cover to the rear spindle.

18. Adjust brake shoes so not to interfere with brake drum installation. Install the rear brake drums.

19. Install the tire and wheel assemblies. Road the the vehicle. The automatic adjusters will continue brake adjustment during the road test of the vehicle.

Wheel Cylinder

REMOVAL AND INSTALLATION

1. Raise the vehicle and support safely. Remove the wheel, drum and brake shoes.

2. Remove the brake hose bracket from the support plate.

3. Disconnect the brake hose from the wheel cylinder.

4. Remove the rear wheel cylinder attaching bolts and pull the wheel cylinder off the brake support.

5. Installation is the reverse of the removal procedure. Tighten the cylinder mounting bolts 75 inch lbs. (8 Nm) and the tube to cylinder fitting to 145 inch lbs. (17 Nm). Bleed the brake system and refill the master cylinder to the appropriate level.

Parking Brake Cable

ADJUSTMENT

The parking brake foot lever assembly contains a self-adjuster for the cables system. Routine parking brake cable adjustment is not required.

REMOVAL AND INSTALLATION

Front Cable

1. Disconnect negative battery cable and isolate.

2. Remove the drivers front seat as follows:

    a. Position the front seat far enough forward to gain access to the from mounting bolts on the floor. Remove the bolts.

    b. Disengage the front seat wiring harness connector from the body connector.

    c. Remove the bolts holding the rear of the seat track to the floor.

    d. Separate and remove the seat from the vehicle.

3. On 6 passenger models, remove the rear seat cushion.

4. Remove the shifter knob from the floor shifter if equipped, by removing the Allen head setscrew located on the drivers side of the knob and pulling knob straight up.

5. Remove the upper center console cover, if equipped.

6. Remove the lower dash panel assembly from the vehicle.

7. Remove the drivers side door opening sill molding. Remove drivers side cowl kick molding to expose the brake pedal mechanism.

8. Remove the rear console mounting bracket from the park brake cable reaction bracket and the rear passenger compartment heat duct, if equipped.

9. Remove the throttle pedal and bracket from the dash panel and fold the carpet back to expose the front brake cable and routing clips on 5 passenger models or the front brake cable, routing clips, reaction bracket cover and equalizer on 6 passenger models. Remove the cover from the equalizer, if equipped.

NOTE: Park brake pedal mechanism self-adjuster must be reloaded and locked, to remove spring tension before attempting to remove the front parking brake cable from the park brake pedal or equalizer. Failure to do so will make assembly extremely difficult and could lead to serious injury.

10. Reload the parking brake self-adjuster assembly as follows:

    a. Insert a ¼ in. drive ratchet and extension into the hole located in the sector part of the parking brake pedal mechanism.

b. Pull on the ratchet and extension rotating the sector toward the rear of the vehicle until the ratchet extension contact the back of the brake pedal mechanism. This will unwind the sector spring.

c. Insert a pin or drill bit ⅛ in. (3.14mm) in diameter into the park brake lever mechanism to lock sector shaft in place. Make sure the pin or drill bit is long enough to go through both sides of the park brake lever mechanism.

11. Remove the front park brake cable from the park brake cable equalizer. Remove the front cable retaining clip.

12. Remove the front park brake cable from the reacting bracket. Remove the screw attaching the parking brake cable routing clip to floor pan. Remove the parking brake cable from the mounting clips at the crossmember.

13. Remove the bolt attaching the parking brake mechanism to the left front door frame. Loosen but do not remove the 2 bolt attaching the mechanism to the cowl panel. Disconnect the electrical connector from the switch on parking brake mechanism.

14. Remove the parking brake mechanism and the front cable from the vehicle as an assembly.

15. Mount parking brake assembly in vise and remove the remove the front parking brake cable to mechanism retainer clip.

16. Rotate the cable to align with the notch in cable attaching hole on the parking brake mechanism. Lift the lead of the cable out of the retaining hole in the park brake mechanism, then remove the cable from the mechanism.

To install:

17. Install the parking brake cable into the mechanism and rotate into position. Be sure cable is properly seated in the cam surface tract of foot lever assembly. Install the cable retaining clip.

18. Install the park brake mechanism to the 2 loosely installed mounting bolts on the cowl panel. Install the retainer bolt into the door frame. Torque 3 mounting bolts to 19 ft. lbs. (27 Nm).

19. Connect the brake warning light connector to the switch.

20. Route the cable along the floor of the vehicle. Install end of cable into the hole in the reaction bracket and install retainer clip. Tap the clip with a hammer until fully seated on cable.

21. Install all parking brake cable routing clips and retainers.

22. Ensure cable is correctly routed in cam surface tract of the parking brake mechanism. Using pliers, firmly grasp the lock pin previously installed in the park brake mechanism. Remove the lock pin using a firm and rapid pull. When removed, the parking brake cables will automatically adjust. Activate and release the parking brake mechanism to assure proper operation.

23. Install the equalizer cover tightening the retainers to 88 inch lbs. (10 Nm), if equipped. Fold the carpet back into position and reinstall the throttle pedal and bracket.

24. Install the rear passenger compartment heat duct, rear console mounting bracket, drivers side cowl kick molding and the door opening sill molding.

25. Install the lower dash panel assembly, upper center console cover and shifter knob, as required.

26. Install the drivers side seat assembly as follows:

a. Place the seat in the vehicle and bolt the rear of the tract to the floor.

b. Install bolts to hold front of the seat tract to the floor.

c. Connect the front seat wire connector to the body connector.

d. Check for proper seat operation.

27. Install the rear seat cushion, if removed. Connect the negative battery cable and adjust the rear brakes.

Rear Cable

REAR DRUM BRAKES

NOTE: When servicing the rear parking brake cable, remove 1 rear brake cable from rear brake shoes at a time. Failure to do so will result in high efforts required to connect park brake cables to equalizer or park brake lever.

1. Raise and safely support the vehicle.
2. Disconnect the park brake cable from the park brake lever on the rear brake assembly.
3. Position a ½ in. wrench over the retainer on the end of the parking brake cable. Compress the cable housing retainer fingers and start the housing out of the support plate.
4. Remove the retainer clips holding cable to floor pan and from of vehicle.
5. Remove the drivers front seat as follows:

a. Position the front seat far enough forward to gain access to

the from mounting bolts on the floor. Remove the bolts.

b. Disengage the front seat wiring harness connector from the body connector.

c. Remove the bolts holding the rear of the seat track to the floor.

d. Separate and remove the seat from the vehicle.

6. On 6 passenger models, remove the rear seat cushion.

7. Remove the shifter knob from the floor shifter if equipped, by removing the Ahead setscrew located on the drivers side of the knob and pulling knob straight up.

8. Remove the upper center console cover, if equipped.

9. Remove the drivers side door opening sill molding. Remove drivers side cowl kick molding to expose the brake pedal mechanism.

10. Remove the rear console mounting bracket from the park brake cable reaction bracket and the rear passenger compartment heat duct, if equipped.

11. Remove the rear parking brake cable from the equalizer and remove cable end from the brake support plate.

To install:

12. Install the brake cable into the rear support plate. Be sure the retainers are fully expanded to lock cable into position. Connect the parking brake cable to the park brake shoe lever.

13. Install parking brake cable into the mounting hole in the floor pan and install the cable retainers.

14. Connect the cable to the parking brake equalizer. The equalizer can be moved rearward to aid in cable connection.

15. Install the rear passenger compartment heat duct, rear console mounting bracket, drivers side cowl kick molding and the door opening sill molding.

16. Install the upper center console cover and shifter knob, as required.

17. Install the drivers side seat assembly as follows:

a. Place the seat in the vehicle and bolt the rear of the tract to the floor.

b. Install bolts to hold front of the seat tract to the floor.

c. Connect the front seat wire connector to the body connector.

d. Check for proper seat operation.

18. Install the rear seat cushion, if removed. Connect the negative battery cable and adjust the rear brakes.

REAR DISC BRAKES

NOTE: When servicing the rear parking brake cable, remove 1 rear brake cable from rear brake shoes at a time. Failure to do so will result in high efforts required to connect park brake cables to equalizer or park brake lever.

1. Raise and safely support the vehicle.

2. Remove the rear disc brake caliper from the adapter. Remove the brake disc from the vehicle.

3. Remove the parking brake shoes as follows:

   a. Remove the dust cap from the rear hub. Remove the cotter pin and nut lock from the spindle.

   b. Remove the hub and bearing retainer nut and washer. Pull the hub and bearing from the spindle.

   c. Remove the rear brake shoe hold-down clip. Turn the parking brake adjuster wheel to its shortest length.

   d. Remove the parking brake shoe adjuster assembly from the shoes. Remove the lower shoe to shoe spring. Pull the shoes away from the anchor and remove the shoe assembly.

   e. Remove the front parking brake shoe hold-down spring and remove shoe.

4. Disconnect the parking brake cable from the brake actuator lever.

5. Remove the parking brake cable from adapter by compressing the tangs on cable. Remove the 4 routing clips from the cable.

6. Remove the drivers front seat as follows:

   a. Position the front drivers side seat far enough forward to gain access to the front mounting bolts on the floor. Remove the bolts.

   b. Disengage the front seat wiring harness connector from the body connector.

   c. Remove the bolts holding the rear of the seat track to the floor.

   d. Separate and remove the seat from the vehicle.

7. On 6 passenger models, remove the rear seat cushion.

8. Remove the shifter knob from the floor shifter if equipped, by removing the Allen head setscrew located on the drivers side of the knob and pulling knob straight up.

9. Remove the drivers side door opening sill molding and fold the carpet forward to expose the brake pedal

equalizer cover attached to the cable reaction bracket.

10. Remove the rear console mounting bracket from the park brake cable reaction bracket and the rear passenger compartment heat duct, if equipped.

11. Remove the rear parking brake cable from the equalizer and remove cable end from the rear disc brake adapter cable mounting hole.

To install:

12. Install cable end into the rear disc brake adapter cable mounting hole. Be sure the cable retainer tabs are expanded around the hole opening and lock the cable in position.

13. Connect the parking brake cable end to the brake shoe assembly actuator lever.

14. Install the parking brake cable into the cable mounting hole in floor pan. Be sure the cable tabs are expanded in the opening and lock the cable in position. Install the 4 routing clips securing cable to floor.

15. Connect the park brake cable to the brake equalizer. The equalizer can be moved toward the rear of the vehicle to aid in cable connection.

16. Install the parking brake shoes as follows:

   a. Install the front parking brake shoe hold-down spring and remove shoe.

   b. Install the rear parking brake shoe and upper parking brake shoe to shoe spring.

   c. Install the shoe to shoe return spring. Install the adjuster assembly with the star wheel rearward.

   d. Install rear parking brake shoe hold-down clip.

   e. Adjust the parking brake shoes to a diameter of 6.75 in. (171.5mm).

17. Install the rear bearing and hub assembly. Torque the hub retainer nut to 124 ft. lbs. (168 Nm). Install the nut lock and new cotter pin.

18. Install rear disc and caliper assembly.

19. Install the tire and wheel assembly.

20. Install the equalizer cover tightening the retainers to 88 inch lbs. (10 Nm), if equipped. Fold the carpet back into position and reinstall the door opening sill molding.

21. Install the rear passenger compartment heat duct, rear console mounting bracket and drivers side cowl kick molding.

22. Install the lower dash panel assembly, upper center console cover and shifter knob, as required.

23. Install the drivers side seat assembly as follows:

   a. Place the seat in the vehicle and bolt the rear of the tract to the floor.

   b. Install bolts to hold front of the seat tract to the floor.

   c. Connect the front seat wire connector to the body connector.

   d. Check for proper seat operation.

24. Install the rear seat cushion, if removed. Connect the negative battery cable and adjust the rear brakes.

Brake System Bleeding

EXCEPT ANTI-LOCK BRAKES

NOTE: If using a pressure bleeder, follow the instructions furnished with the unit and choose the correct adaptor for the application. Do not substitute an adapter that "almost fits" as it will not work and could be dangerous.

Master Cylinder

If the master cylinder is off the vehicle, it can be bench bled.

1. Connect 2 short pieces of brake line to the outlet fittings, bend them until the free end is below the fluid level in the master cylinder reservoirs.

2. Fill the reservoir with fresh brake fluid. Pump the piston slowly until no more air bubbles appear in the reservoirs.

3. Disconnect the 2 short lines, refill the master cylinder and securely install the cylinder caps.

4. If the master cylinder is on the vehicle, it can still be bled, using a flare nut wrench.

5. Open the brake lines slightly with the flare nut wrench while pressure is applied to the brake pedal by a helper inside the vehicle.

6. Be sure to tighten the line before the brake pedal is released.

7. Repeat the process with both lines until no air bubbles come out.

Calipers and Wheel Cylinders

1. Fill the master cylinder reservoir with fresh brake fluid. Check the level often during the procedure.

2. Starting with the right rear wheel, remove the protective cap from the bleeder, if equipped, and place where it will not be lost. Clean the bleed screw.

CAUTION

When bleeding the brakes, keep face away from the brake area. Spewing fluid may cause facial and/or visual damage. Do not allow brake fluid to spill on the car's finish; it will remove the paint.

3. If the system is empty, the most efficient way to get fluid down to the wheel is to loosen the bleeder about 1/2–3/4 turn, place a finger firmly over the bleeder and have a helper pump the brakes slowly until fluid comes out the bleeder. Once fluid is at the bleeder, close it before the pedal is released inside the vehicle.

NOTE: If the pedal is pumped rapidly, the fluid will churn and create small air bubbles, which are almost impossible to remove from the system. These air bubbles will eventually congregate and a spongy pedal will result.

4. Once fluid has been pumped to the caliper or wheel cylinder, open the bleed screw again, have the helper press the brake pedal to the floor, lock the bleeder and have the helper slowly release the pedal. Wait 15 seconds and repeat the procedure (including the 15 second wait) until no more air comes out of the bleeder upon application of the brake pedal. Remember to close the bleeder before the pedal is released inside the vehicle each time the bleeder is opened. If not, air will be induced into the system.

5. If a helper is not available, connect a small hose to the bleeder, place the end in a container of brake fluid and proceed to pump the pedal from inside the vehicle until no more air comes out the bleeder. The hose will prevent air from entering the system.

6. Repeat the procedure on remaining wheel cylinder and calipers in order:
   a. Left rear
   b. Right front
   c. Left front

7. Hydraulic brake systems must be totally flushed if the fluid becomes contaminated with water, dirt or other corrosive chemicals. To flush, bleed the entire system until all fluid has been replaced with the correct type of new fluid.

8. Install the bleeder cap(s) on the bleeder to keep dirt out. Always road test the vehicle after brake work of any kind is done.

ANTI-LOCK BRAKES

The bleeding procedure is a 3 step process, 1 of which will require use of the DRB II scan tool. Bleed the system as follows:

1. Connect a pressure bleeder to the master cylinder.
2. Fully bleed the brakes hydraulic system using the conventional method in the following sequence:
   a. Right rear wheel
   b. Left rear wheel
   c. Right front wheel
   d. Left front wheel
3. Locate the diagnostic connector under the dash panel to the right of the steering column.
4. Connect the DRB II scan tool to the connector. Install cartridge for the Teves Mark IV Anti-Lock Brake system. Perform the bleeding procedure using the DRB II according to the procedure outlined in the scan tool literature.
5. Once bleeding with the scan tool is complete, repeat the bleed procedure outlined in Step 2. Remove the pressure bleeder from the master cylinder.
6. Fill the master cylinder reservoir to the proper level.
7. Road test the vehicle to check for proper brake system operation.

Anti-Lock Brake System Service

PRECAUTIONS

Failure to observe the following precautions may result in system damage.

- Before performing electric arc welding on the vehicle, disconnect the ABS controller and the hydraulic modulator connectors.
- When performing painting work on the vehicle, do not expose the ABS controller to temperatures in excess of 185°F (85°C) for longer than 2 hrs. The system may be exposed to temperatures up to 200°F (95°C) for less than 15 minutes.
- Never disconnect or connect the ABS controller or hydraulic modulator connectors with the ignition switch ON.
- Never disassemble any component of the Anti-Lock Brake System (ABS) which is designated non-serviceable; the component must be replaced as an assembly.
- When filling the master cylinder, always use brake fluid which meets DOT-3 specifications; petroleum base fluid will destroy the rubber parts.

Hydraulic Control Unit (HCU)

REMOVAL AND INSTALLATION

1. Raise and safely support the vehicle. Remove the left front tire and wheel assembly.
2. Disconnect the battery cables and remove the battery from the vehicle. Remove the 4 fasteners and remove the battery tray from the vehicle.
3. Verify that the ignition is in the **OFF** position. Disconnect the 37-way connector from the Controller Anti-Lock Brake (CAB).
4. Label all tube connections to aid in installation. Disconnect the 2 brake tube supply lines from the master cylinder at the HCU. Disconnect the 2 brake fluid output lines from the valve block on the HCU. Disconnect the brake fluid supply hose from the master cylinder reservoir and lug end of supply hose to prevent fluid from leaking.
5. Remove the HCU bracket to the left inner fender attaching bolts. Remove the 2 bracket-to-left frame rail mounting bolts.
6. Remove the HCU and the mounting bracket as an assembly.
   To install:
7. Install the HCU and the mounting bracket onto the vehicle as an assembly.
8. Install but do not tighten the mounting bracket to frame rail attaching bolts. Install the inner fender to bracket retainer bolts and tighten to 14 ft. lbs. (19 Nm). Tighten the frame rail mounting bolts to 18 inch lbs. (2 Nm).
9. Connect the 2 brake fluid supply tubes from the master cylinder to the inlet ports of the HCU. Connect the 2 HCU brake fluid outlet tubes. Torque all fitting to 14 ft. lbs. (19 Nm).
10. Connect the 2 rear brake tubes to the proportioning valve and tighten the fittings to 14 ft. lbs. (19 Nm).
11. Connect the fluid supply tube and install the clamp.
12. With the ignition in the OFF position, connect the 35-way connector to the CAB as follows:
    a. Install connector on CAB with the connector pins located in latch.
    b. Rotate the rear of the connector down into the CAB until fully seated onto connector pins.
    c. Rotate the connector latch forward and down until seated on top of the CAB connector.

13. Connect the pump motor and the fluid sensor connectors to the connections on the HCU.

14. Install the battery tray and the battery into the vehicle.

15. Bleed the air from the hydraulic system.

NOTE: When bleeding the system, visually inspect the lines that were disconnected during the replacement procedure for fluid leaks.

16. Install the left front tire and wheel assembly.

17. Lower the vehicle and install the heat shield onto the HCU.

18. Reconnect the negative battery cable.

Pump/Motor Assembly

REMOVAL AND INSTALLATION

The Pump/Motor assembly on the Teves Mark IV Anti-Lock brake system can only be serviced as part of the Hydraulic Control Unit (HCU).

Pedal Travel Sensor

REMOVAL AND INSTALLATION

1. Pump the brake pedal approximately 20 times. This will bleed the vacuum stored in the booster.

2. Remove the wiring harness connector from the sensor.

3. Using a small flat tipped tool, lift the retainer ring from the notch, then remove the retaining ring from the grommet.

4. Remove the pedal travel sensor from the brake booster by carefully pulling it straight out of its mounting grommet. Do not twist the sensor.

To install:

5. Install the pedal travel sensor retainer ring on the travel sensor grommet in the vacuum booster. The tab on the retaining ring should be located in top notch of the mounting grommet.

6. Sparingly lubricate pedal travel sensor O-ring with fresh brake fluid. Install the pedal travel O-ring into the pedal travel sensor mounting grommet.

7. Coat the end of the sensor with fresh brake fluid and install by pushing straight into the mounting grommet on the brake booster until the tab on the sensor is past the retaining ring on grommet.

8. Install the wire harness connector to the pedal travel sensor.

9. Test drive the vehicle to assure correct operation of the pedal travel sensor and the vacuum brake booster.

Wheel Speed Sensor

REMOVAL AND INSTALLATION

Front Wheel Sensor

1. Disconnect the negative battery cable. Raise and safely support the vehicle. Remove the tire and wheel from the vehicle.

2. Remove the screw from the grommet retainer clip that holds the cable grommet into the fender shield.

3. Carefully pull the sensor assembly grommet from the fender shield.

4. Unplug the sensor harness connector from the vehicle wire harness. Remove the sensor wire harness routing bracket from the strut.

5. Remove the screw attaching the sensor head to the steering knuckle. Carefully remove the sensor. It the sensor has seized, use a hammer and a punch to top on the edge of the sensor ear, rocking the sensor back and forth. Do not use pliers on the sensor head.

To install:

6. Coat the sensor with high temperature multi-purpose grease and install into the steering knuckle. Install retainer screw and tighten to 60 inch lbs. (7 Nm).

7. Install sensor electrical harness into the original retainers. Correct routing of the cable is critical for proper operation of the sensor.

8. Connect the sensor wire harness connector to the vehicle wire harness making sure the locking tab on the connector is securely latched.

9. Push the sensor grommet into the fender shield and install grommet retainer screw.

10. Install the tire and wheel assembly.

Rear Wheel Sensor

1. Disconnect the negative battery cable.

2. Remove the bottom cushion and the back cushion from the back seat of the vehicle.

3. Lift the edge of the sound insulation on the rear bulkhead. Locate the speed sensor cable to vehicle wiring harness connector and disconnect.

4. Raise and safely support the vehicle. Remove the tire and wheel from the vehicle.

5. Remove the screw from the grommet retainer clip that holds the cable grommet into the rear inner fender. Carefully pull the sensor assembly grommet from the inner fender. Remove the speed sensor cable retainers.

6. Remove the speed sensor head attaching bolt from the rear caliper adapter and remove the speed sensor from the adapter. If the sensor has seized, use a hammer and a punch to tap on the edge of the sensor ear, rocking the sensor back and forth. Do not use pliers on the sensor head.

To install:

7. Coat the sensor with high temperature multi-purpose grease and install into the steering knuckle. Install retainer screw and tighten to 60 inch lbs. (7 Nm).

8. Install sensor electrical harness into the original retainers. Correct routing of the cable is critical for proper operation of the sensor.

9. Push the sensor grommet into the fender shield and install grommet retainer screw. Install the tire and wheel assembly onto the vehicle.

10. Lower the vehicle and connect the sensor wiring harness to the vehicle harness connector. Be sure the locking tab on the connector is securely latched.

11. Install the rear seat back cushion and the seat lower cushion back into the vehicle. Reconnect the negative battery cable.

FRONT SUSPENSION

MacPherson Strut

REMOVAL AND INSTALLATION

1. Raise and safely support vehicle. Do not support vehicle by placing supports under the suspension arms.

2. Remove the wheel and tire assemblies.

3. Remove the stabilizer bar attaching link at the strut assembly. Loosen but do not remove the outer tie rod end to strut assembly steering arm attaching nut. Then remove the outer tie rod end from the steering arm using puller MB-990635 or equivalent.

4. If equipped with ABS, remove the speed sensor wire harness mounting bracket from the strut.

5. Remove the brake caliper assembly and wire aside. Remove the front braking disc.

6. The strut assembly to steering knuckle bolts are serrated where they go through the strut and steering knuckle. Do not turn the bolts during removal. Hold the bolt head with a wrench and turn the nuts off the bolts.

NOTE: The strut assembly to steering knuckle bolts are serrated where they go through the strut and steering knuckle. Do not turn the bolts during removal. If bolts are turned, damage to the steering knuckle will result.

7. Remove the 3 strut assembly upper mount to shock tower mounting nuts and washers. Remove the strut from the vehicle.

To install:

8. Install the front strut into the shock tower and install the 3 upper mount nuts and washers. Tighten mounting nuts to 25 ft. lbs. (33 Nm).

9. Position the steering knuckle neck into the strut assembly. Install the strut assembly to steering knuckle bolts. Install the nuts onto the attaching bolts and tighten to 125 ft. lbs. (169 Nm). Do not turn the bolt heads during installation.

NOTE: The strut assembly to steering knuckle bolts are serrated where they go through the strut and steering knuckle. Do not turn the bolts during removal. If bolts are turned, damage to the steering knuckle will result.

10. Install the brake disc and the caliper assembly to the adapter. Tighten the caliper mounting bolts 14 ft. lbs. (19 Nm).

11. Install the front speed sensor cable routing bracket onto the front strut, if equipped.

12. Install the outer tie rod on steering arm and tighten attaching nut to 27 ft. lbs. (37 Nm).

13. Install the stabilizer link assembly onto the strut assembly and tighten the attaching nut to 70 ft. lbs. (95 Nm).

14. Install the tire and wheel assembly onto the vehicle.

DISASSEMBLY

────── **CAUTION** ──────

Do not remove the MacPherson strut upper nut without using an approved MacPherson strut compressor C–4838 or equivalent. The coil spring is under extreme pressure and can cause severe bodily injury if the nut is removed without a spring compressor.

NOTE: There is no strut cartridge replacements available. The MacPherson strut assembly has to be replaced as an assembly. The strut assembly is available with 2 calibrations. Make sure the strut is replaced with an assembly with the same calibration as the old.

1. Raise and safely support the vehicle.

2. Remove the strut assembly from the vehicle.

3. Matchmark the strut, lower spring insulator, spring and upper strut mount for indexing during assembly.

4. Compress the spring with a suitable spring compressor C–4838 and remove the strut rod nut using a strut rod socket L–4558 or equivalent. Use a 10mm wrench to keep the strut shaft from turning and remove the strut nut. Gradually release the spring compressor.

5. Remove the upper spring seat, jounce bumper, dust shield, coil spring and lower spring seat from the strut.

To assemble:

6. Install the lower spring seat, coil spring, dust shield, jounce bumper and upper spring seat to the strut. Install the bearing seat with the notches facing down.

7. Align all matchmarks and compress the spring with the spring compressor. Install the strut rod nut. Tighten the nut to 70 ft. lbs. (94 Nm). Gradually release the spring compressor.

8. Install the strut assembly in the strut tower. Install the 4 strut attaching nuts and tighten to 25 ft. lbs. (33 Nm).

9. Lower the vehicle.

10. Align the front end.

Coil Spring

REMOVAL AND INSTALLATION

Service of the spring requires spring compressor tool C-4838. It is required that 5 coils be captured within the jaws on the compressor tool.

1. Remove the strut from the vehicle.

2. Securely mount the strut into a vise. Using paint, mark the strut unit, lower spring isolator, spring and upper strut mount for indexing of the parts at assembly.

3. Position spring compressor C-4838 or equivalent, onto the strut. Compress the coil spring until all load is off upper strut mount assembly.

4. Install strut rod socket tool L-4558 or L-4558A on the strut shaft nut. Using a 10mm socket on end of strut shaft to keep shaft from turning. Remove the strut shaft nut.

5. Remove the upper mount assembly, jounce bumper and seat bearing and dust shield as an assembly.

6. Remove the coil spring and the compressor as an assembly from the strut. Remove the lower spring isolator from the strut assembly lower spring seat.

7. Inspect all components for abnormal wear, oil leakage or failure. Replace parts as required.

To install:

8. Install the lower spring isolator on strut unit. Install the compressed coil spring onto the strut assembly aligning the paint marks made during removal.

9. Install the strut bearing into the bearing seat. Bearing must be installed into seat with notches on bearings facing down.

10. Lower the seat bearing and dust shield onto the strut and spring assembly. Align the paint marks made during removal.

11. Install jounce bumper and upper mount on the strut shaft aligning the paint marks.

12. Install the strut mount to shaft retainer nut. Inspect all alignment marks made during removal and align as required. While holding the strut shaft from turning with a 10mm socket, tighten the strut shaft nut to 70 ft. lbs. (94 Nm).

13. Equally loosen the spring compressor tool until all tension is released. Remove the spring compressor tool.

14. Install the strut assembly into the vehicle.

Tension Strut

REMOVAL AND INSTALLATION

To remove the tension strut from the vehicle, the lower control arm and the tension arm must be removed as an assembly.

1. Remove the lower control arm and the tension strut from the vehicle as an assembly.

2. Separate the tension strut from the lower control arm by removing from the tension strut bushing.

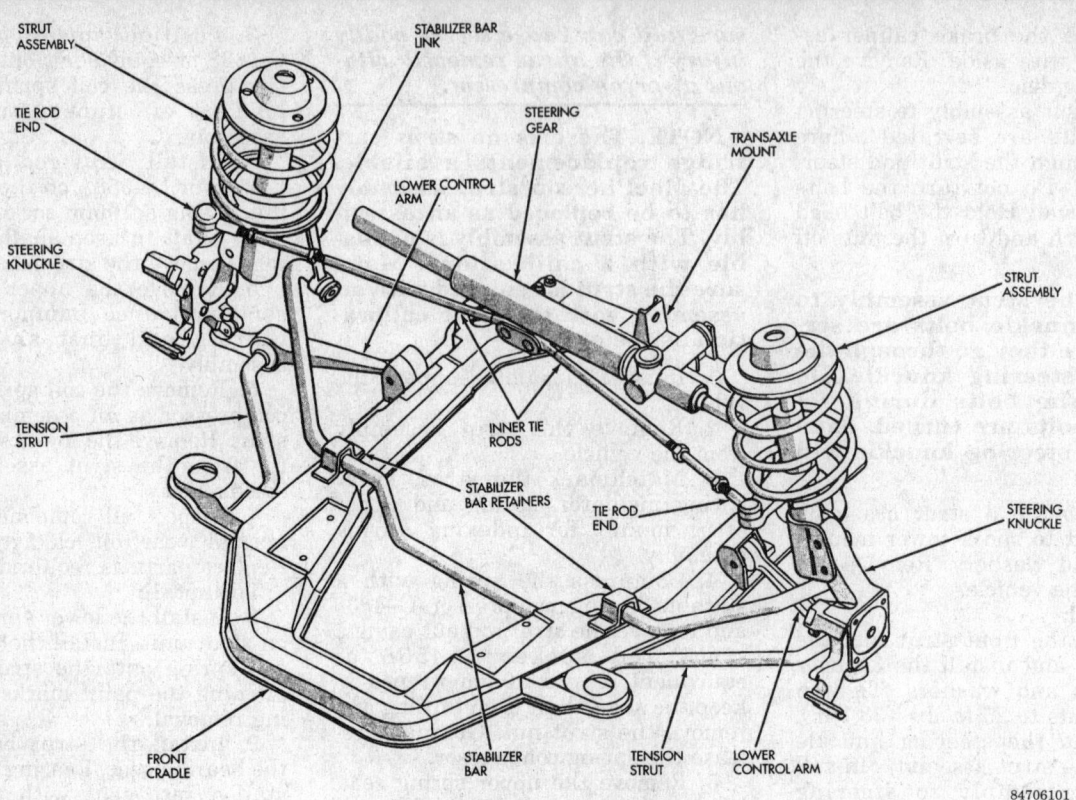

STRUT ASSEMBLY
TIE ROD END
STEERING KNUCKLE
TENSION STRUT
FRONT CRADLE
STABILIZER BAR LINK
LOWER CONTROL ARM
STEERING GEAR
INNER TIE RODS
STABILIZER BAR RETAINERS
TIE ROD END
STABILIZER BAR
TENSION STRUT
TRANSAXLE MOUNT
STRUT ASSEMBLY
STEERING KNUCKLE
LOWER CONTROL ARM

84706101

Front suspension component location

3. Installation is the reverse of the removal procedure.

Lower Ball Joints

INSPECTION

1. Safely raise the front of the vehicle using a frame contact hoist so the wheels are off the ground and the suspension is in the full rebound position.
2. Grasp tire at top and bottom and apply an in and out force on the tire. Look for movement between the lower ball joint and the lower control arm.
3. If any movement is noticed, the lower ball joint is worn and the lower control arm requires replacement.

REMOVAL AND INSTALLATION

If the lower ball joint shows signs of wear, the lower control and assembly will require replacement. The lower ball joint is not serviced as an assembly.

Lower Control Arm and Tension Strut Assembly

REMOVAL AND INSTALLATION

1. Raise and safely support the vehicle.
2. Remove the tire and wheel assembly.
3. Remove the ball joint stud to steering knuckle clamp nut and bolt.
4. Carefully insert a prybar between the lower control arm and the steering knuckle and separate ball joint from knuckle. Make sure ball joint seal does not get damaged during separation.

NOTE: Pulling the steering knuckle out from the vehicle after releasing from the ball joint can separate the inner Tripod joint. Do not separate the inner Tripod joint.

5. Remove tension strut to cradle attaching nut and washer from end of tension strut. When removing nut, keep the strut from turning by holding tension strut at flat using open end wrench. Discard the tension strut to cradle retainer nut. A new

nut should be used during installation.

NOTE: A new tension strut to cradle attaching nut must be used when installing the tension strut.

6. Loosen and remove the lower control arm pivot bushing to cradle assembly pivot bolt.
7. Separate the lower control arm and tension strut from the cradle assembly by first removing the pivot bushing from the cradle and then sliding tension strut out of isolator bushing.
To install:
8. Install the lower control arm and hold in place by installing the lower control arm to cradle bracket attaching bolt. Do not tighten the bolt at this time.
9. Install the washer and new nut on end of tension strut. Torque the tension strut to cradle bracket retainer nut to 130 ft. lbs. (175 Nm), while holding the tension strut flat with an open end wrench.
10. Install the lower ball joint stud into the steering knuckle and install the clamp bolt and nut. Tighten the bolt to 40 ft. lbs. (55 Nm).
11. Install the tire and wheel assembly and lower the vehicle so the

suspension is supporting the weight of the vehicle.

12. Torque the lower control arm pivot bushing to cradle bracket attaching bolt to 90 Ft. lbs. (123 Nm).

Stabilizer Bar

REMOVAL AND INSTALLATION

When removing the front stabilizer bar from the vehicle, it is necessary to remove the entire cradle module from the vehicle. It will be necessary to support the engine and transaxle assembly using fixture support tool 7137 or equivalent.

1. Disconnect the negative battery cable.
2. Install the engine supporting fixture safely.
3. Raise and safely support the vehicle.
4. Remove both front tire and wheel assemblies from the vehicle.
5. Remove both side ball joint stud to steering knuckle clamp nuts and bolts. Carefully insert a prybar between the lower control arm and the steering knuckle and separate ball joint from knuckle. Make sure ball joint seal does not get damaged during separation.

NOTE: Pulling the steering knuckle out from the vehicle after releasing from the ball joint can separate the inner Tripod joint. Do not separate the inner Tripod joint.

6. Remove the ground strap, located on the right side of the cradle below the halfshaft from the cradle assembly.
7. Remove the 4 nuts attaching the motor mounts to cradle assembly. Remove the 4 bolts attaching the transaxle mount to the rear of the cradle assembly.
8. Remove the bolts attaching the stabilizer bushing retainer and bushing to the cradle assembly.

── **CAUTION** ──
The jackstands are required to support the cradle assembly and transaxle assembly during cradle assembly removal from the vehicle. Do not attempt to remove the cradle from the vehicle without using jackstands to support components.

9. Position a jackstand under front of cradle and at center of transaxle to cradle assembly mount. Raise the jackstand at transaxle mount until

transaxle mount just lifts off the cradle assembly.

10. Loosen but do not fully remove the 2 rear cradle assembly to body attaching bolts.
11. Loosen and remove the 2 front cradle assembly to body attaching bolts.
12. With a helper supporting the rear of the cradle assembly and the jackstand supporting the transaxle, remove the 2 rear cradle assembly to body attaching bolts.
13. Slowly lower front jackstand until weight of engine is supported by engine support fixture and motor mounts bolts are clear the cradle assembly. With a helper at the rear of the cradle, lift front of cradle assembly off jackstand and remove from the vehicle.
14. Remove the 2 stabilizer bar to stabilizer bar link attaching nuts and remove the bar from the vehicle.

To install:
15. Install the stabilizer bar, isolator bushings and retainers back into the vehicle as an assembly. Be sure stabilizer bar is installed through the openings in the splash shields. Install the stabilizer bar link to stabilizer bar attaching nut and tighten to 70 ft. lbs. (95 Nm).
16. Tie the stabilizer bar up against the 2 transaxle to engine block bracket. This will hold bar out of the way during cradle installation.
17. With the aid of a helper, raise the cradle into vehicle resting front of cradle on jackstand. Raise the rear of the cradle far enough to by hand to start the 2 rear cradle to body attaching bolts. Install bolts far enough to securely hold the cradle in place. Do not tighten the bolts at this time.
18. Using jackstands, raise the front of the cradle up against the bottom of the motor mounts, making sure all 4 mount studs come through the holes in the cradle assembly.
19. Continue to raise the cradle and engine assembly until the 2 front cradle to body attaching bolts can be started.
20. Lower the transaxle and align the transaxle mount with the 4 transaxle mount attaching holes in the cradle. Install but do not tighten the transaxle mount to cradle assembly attaching bolts.

NOTE: The 2 long bolts go through the front cradle assembly to transaxle mount holes. Before tightening cradle assembly to body attaching bolts, check that all 4 cradle assembly to body mounting bolts are installed straight into mounting

plates in frame rails and mounting plates are not cocked inside the frame rails.

21. Using crisscross pattern, tighten all 4 cradle assembly to body attaching bolts until cradle is seated up against the body. Then repeating the crisscross pattern, torque all 4 bolts to 115 ft. lbs. (155 Nm).
22. Untie the stabilizer bar from the brackets and position it on cradle assembly. Align the bar bushing retainers with the mounting holes in the cradle assembly. Install but do not tighten the 4 bushing retainer to cradle mounting bolts. The bolts will be tightened when the vehicle is lowered to the ground.

NOTE: When the stabilizer bar is installed, position so lower part of bar is centered in the middle of the cradle assembly. Failure to do this may cause the stabilizer bar to come in contact with other suspension components.

23. Install the 4 motor mount to cradle assembly attaching nuts and tighten to 45 ft. lbs. (61 Nm).
24. Install the ground strap to the cradle assembly.
25. Install the lower ball joint stud into the steering knuckle. Install the retainer nut and tighten to 40 ft. lbs. (55 Nm).
26. Install the tire and wheel assembly.
27. Lower the vehicle to the ground. With the full weight of the vehicle supported by the suspension, tighten the 4 stabilizer bar bushing retainer to cradle assembly attaching bolts to 40 ft. lbs. (55 Nm).
28. Remove the engine support fixture. Position the vehicle on an alignment rack and check that the front suspension toe setting is correct. Adjust the toe setting as required.

REAR SUSPENSION

MacPherson Strut

REMOVAL AND INSTALLATION

1. Raise and safely support the vehicle.
2. Remove the rear wheel and tire assembly.
3. If equipped with rear disc brakes, remove the caliper assembly and disc from the hub. If equipped

with rear drum brakes, disconnect the brake flex hose from the support bracket and wheel cylinder.

4. If equipped with rear disc brakes, remove the speed sensor cable routing bracket and tube.

5. Remove the bolts attaching the lateral links to the rear spindle assembly.

6. Remove the rear strut assembly to stabilizer bar attaching link at the stabilizer bar. Hold the hex on the attaching link stud while breaking nut loose. The attaching link does not have to be removed from the strut.

7. Remove the rear spindle to strut assembly pinch bolt. Install a center punch in hole on spindle and tap punch into hole until jammed. This will spread spindle casting allowing it to be removed from strut.

8. Using a hammer, tap on the top surface of the spindle driving spindle down and off the end of the strut assembly. Let the spindle and assembled components hang from the trailing arm while the strut is being serviced.

9. Lower the vehicle. From inside the trunk of the vehicle, remove the 3 upper strut mounting bolts and remove the strut from the vehicle.

To install:

10. Position the strut in vehicle and install the 3 upper mounting nuts tightening to 20 ft. lbs. (28 Nm).

11. Install the spindle assembly onto bottom of strut. Push or tap spindle assembly onto strut until notch in spindle is tightly seated against locating tap on strut assembly. Remove the center punch from the hole in the spindle.

12. Install the strut to spindle pinch bolt and tighten to 40 ft. lbs. (55 Nm).

13. Install the lateral link to the spindle attaching bolt and tighten to 105 ft. lbs. (140 Nm).

14. Install the stabilizer bar attaching link onto the stabilizer bar and install stabilizer link to stabilizer bar attaching nut. Tighten attaching nut to 70 ft. lbs. (95 Nm), while holding the stabilizer link stud at hex with wrench.

15. If equipped with rear disc brakes, mount rear speed sensor cable routing tube and bracket in position. Install rear disc brake rotor and caliper assembly to the adapter plate. Tighten caliper mounting bolts to 16 ft. lbs. (22 Nm).

16. If equipped with rear drum brakes, install rear brake flex hose to the wheel cylinder and support plate. The brake system will require bleeding.

17. Install the tire and wheel assembly and lower the vehicle. Bleed the brake system, if equipped with rear drum brakes.

18. Check and reset the rear wheel toe to specifications.

DISASSEMBLY

———— **CAUTION** ————

Do not remove the MacPherson strut upper nut without using an approved MacPherson strut compressor C-4838 or equivalent. The coil spring is under extreme pressure and can cause severe bodily injury if the nut is removed without a spring compressor.

NOTE: There is no strut cartridge replacements available. The MacPherson strut assembly has to be replaced as an assembly. The strut assembly is available with 2 calibrations. Make sure the strut is replaced with an assembly with the same calibration as the old.

1. Raise and safely support the vehicle.

2. Remove the strut assembly from the vehicle.

3. Matchmark the strut, lower spring insulator, spring and upper strut mount for indexing during assembly.

4. Compress the spring with a suitable spring compressor C-4838 and remove the strut rod nut using a strut rod socket L-4558 or equivalent. Use a 8mm Allen wrench to keep the strut shaft from turning and remove the strut nut. Gradually release the spring compressor.

5. Remove the upper spring seat, jounce bumper, dust shield, coil spring and lower spring seat from the strut.

To assemble:

6. Install the lower spring seat, coil spring, dust shield, jounce bumper and upper spring seat to the strut.

7. Align all matchmarks and compress the spring with the spring compressor. Install the strut rod nut. Tighten the nut to 70 ft. lbs. (94 Nm). Gradually release the spring compressor.

8. Install the strut assembly in the strut tower. Install the 3 strut attaching nuts and tighten to 25 ft. lbs. (33 Nm).

9. Lower the vehicle.

10. Align all 4 wheels.

Stabilizer Bar

REMOVAL AND INSTALLATION

1. Raise and safely support the vehicle.

2. Remove both tire and wheel assemblies.

3. Position a transmission jack under the fuel tank just forward of the crossmember to help support the fuel tank when crossmember is removed.

4. Remove the 4 crossmember to frame rail attaching bolts. Remove the fuel tank.

5. Remove the stabilizer bar to link assembly attaching nuts and remove the bar and isolator bushings as an assembly from the vehicle.

To install:

6. Install the stabilizer bar and isolator bushings back into the vehicle as an assembly making sure bar is centered in vehicle so it doesn't contact other suspension components.

7. Install stabilizer bar attaching link onto stabilizer bar. Install new link to bar attaching nuts and tighten to 70 ft. lbs. (95 Nm).

NOTE: Replace the sway bar bracket bolt with new after loosening or removing them. Only use original equipment bolts as replacements.

8. Position the crossmember on frame rails and install 4 mounting bolts. Torque attaching bolts to 70 ft. lbs. (95 Nm).

9. Remove transmission jack from under the fuel tank.

10. Install the tire and wheel assembly.

11. Lower the vehicle, check and reset the rear wheel toe to specifications.

Lateral Links

REMOVAL AND INSTALLATION

Left Side

1. Raise and safely support the vehicle. Remove the left rear tire and wheel assembly.

2. Remove the nut and bolt attaching the left lateral links to the spindle.

3. Remove the nut and bolt attaching the left lateral link to the crossmember and remove the link from the vehicle.

4. Installation is the reverse of the removal procedure. Install the link attaching bolts so the bolt heads are

facing the front of the vehicle. Torque the link attaching bolts to 105 ft. lbs. (140 Nm).

5. Check and reset rear wheel toe to specifications.

Right Side

1. Raise and safely support the vehicle. Remove the left rear tire and wheel assembly.

2. Remove the nut and bolt attaching the left lateral links to the spindle.

3. Position a transmission jack under the fuel tank just forward of the crossmember to help support the fuel tank when crossmember is lowered.

4. Remove the 4 crossmember to frame rail attaching bolts and lower the crossmember far enough so right lateral link to crossmember attaching bolt will clear the fuel tank.

5. Remove the nut and bolt attaching the right lateral links to the rear crossmember. Remove the lateral link.

To install:

6. Install replacement lateral links to crossmember as follows:

a. Solid lateral link is installed on crossmember toward the front of the vehicle.

b. The adjustable lateral link is installed on crossmember toward rear of vehicle, with the adjustable link positioned toward the spindle.

7. Install the right lateral bolts at the crossmember with the heads of the bolts facing toward the front of the vehicle.

8. Position the crossmember on the frame rail and install the 4 attaching bolts. Tighten attaching bolts to 70 ft. lbs. (95 Nm). Remove the transmission jack from under fuel tank.

9. Torque the lateral link to crossmember attaching bolt to 105 ft. lbs. (140 Nm).

10. Align the lateral link with the spindle and install the lateral link to spindle attaching bolts. Tighten the bolts to 105 ft. lbs. (140 Nm).

11. Install the tire and wheel assembly.

12. Lower the vehicle and check the toe setting of the rear wheels. Adjust the toe to specifications as required.

Rear Spindle

REMOVAL AND INSTALLATION

1. Raise and safely support the vehicle.

2. Remove the rear wheel and tire assembly.

3. If equipped with rear disc brakes, remove the caliper assembly and support aside. Remove the brake disc or brake drum from the rear hub. If equipped with rear drum brakes, disconnect the brake flex hose from the support bracket and wheel cylinder.

4. Remove the rear hub and bearing assembly retainer nut and washer. Remove the hub and bearing assembly from the spindle.

5. If equipped with rear drum brakes, remove the 4 bolts attaching the rear brake support plate to the rear spindle. Remove the rear brake support plate, with the parking brake cable attached from the spindle.

6. If equipped with rear disc brakes, remove the speed sensor cable routing bracket and tube. Remove the speed sensor head from the rear disc brake adapter.

7. If equipped with rear disc brakes, remove the adapter, disc shield, park brake shoes and park brake cable from the spindle as an assembly.

8. Remove the bolts attaching the lateral links to the rear spindle assembly.

9. Remove the rear spindle to strut assembly pinch bolt. Install a center punch in hole on spindle and tap punch into hole until jammed. This will spread spindle casting allowing it to be removed from strut.

10. Using a hammer, tap on the top surface of the spindle driving spindle down and off the end of the strut assembly.

To install:

11. Install the spindle assembly onto bottom of strut. Push or tap spindle assembly onto strut until notch in spindle is tightly seated against locating tap on strut assembly. Remove the center punch from the hole in the spindle.

12. Install the strut to spindle pinch bolt and tighten to 40 ft. lbs. (55 Nm).

13. Install the lateral link to the spindle attaching bolt and tighten to 105 ft. lbs. (140 Nm).

14. Install the bolt attaching the trailing arm to the trailing arm bracket on the bottom of the spindle. Torque the trailing arm to trailing arm bracket attaching bolt to 74 ft. lbs. (100 Nm).

15. If equipped with rear disc brakes, mount rear speed sensor cable routing tube and bracket in position.

16. If equipped with rear drum brakes, install the rear brake support plate onto spindle and secure with 4 attaching bolts tightened to 85 ft. lbs. (115 Nm).

17. If equipped with rear disc brakes, install the wheel speed sensor head to the adapter and tighten the retaining bolt to 60 inch lbs. (7 Nm).

18. Install the rear hub and bearing assembly onto spindle. Install hub and bearing retainer washer and nut on spindle and tighten nut to 124 ft. lbs. (168 Nm).

19. If equipped with rear disc brakes, install the adapter, rear disc brake rotor and caliper assembly to the adapter plate. Tighten the adapter mounting bolts to 85 ft. lbs. (115 Nm) and the caliper mounting bolts to 16 ft. lbs. (22 Nm).

20. If equipped with rear drum brakes, install rear brake flex hose to the wheel cylinder and support plate. The brake system will require bleeding.

21. Install the tire and wheel assembly and lower the vehicle.

22. If equipped with rear drum brakes, bleed the brake system.

23. Check and reset the rear wheel toe to specifications.

Rear Wheel Bearings

REMOVAL AND INSTALLATION

The rear wheel bearing/hub assembly is permanently lubricated and sealed at the factory. No periodic lubrication or maintenance is required.

1. Raise the vehicle and support safely. Remove the rear wheel.

2. Remove the brake caliper and rotor if equipped with rear disc brakes. Remove the brake drum if equipped with drum brakes.

3. Remove the bearing dust cap using a suitable prybar.

4. Remove the cotter pin, nut retainer, nut and bearing/hub assembly from the spindle.

To install:

5. Install the bearing/hub assembly and nut. Torque the nut to 124 ft. lbs. (168 Nm). Install the nut retainer and new cotter pin. Bend over the cotter pin.

6. Install the dust cap.

7. Install the brake drum or rotor and caliper.

8. Install the rear wheel and torque the lug nuts, in 2 steps to 95 ft. lbs. (130 Nm). Lower the vehicle safely.

Rear Crossmember

REMOVAL AND INSTALLATION

1. Raise and safely support the vehicle. Remove both rear tire and wheel assemblies.

2. Remove the nuts and bolts attaching the lateral links to the spindle.

3. Position a transmission jack under the fuel tank just forward of the crossmember to help support the fuel tank when crossmember is removed.

4. Remove the 4 crossmember to frame rail attaching bolts and remove the crossmember and lateral links as an assembly.

To install:

5. Transfer lateral links to replacement crossmember. The adjustable lateral link is to be positioned to the rear of the vehicle on crossmember. Tighten the lateral link to crossmember attaching bolts to 105 ft. lbs. (140 Nm). Make sure the bolts are installed with the heads facing toward the front of the vehicle.

6. Position the crossmember on the frame rails and tighten cross-member mounting bolts to 70 ft. lbs. (95 Nm).

7. Align the lateral links with spindles and install the attaching bolts. Tighten the lateral link to spindle attaching bolts to 105 ft. lbs. (140 Nm).

8. Remove the transmission jack supporting the fuel tank.

9. Install the tire and wheel assemblies onto the vehicle and lower vehicle to the ground.

10. Check and reset the rear wheel toe to specifications, as required.

Ford Motor Company

FORD—Escort, Tempo **MERCURY**—Tracer, Topaz

FIRING ORDERS

NOTE: To avoid confusion, always replace spark plug wires one at a time.

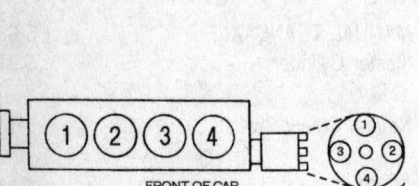

1.8L Engine
Engine Firing Order: 1–3–4–2
Distributor Rotation: Counterclockwise

84707001

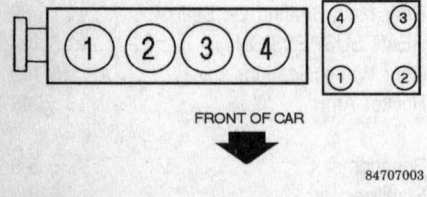

1.9L Engine
Engine Firing Order: 1–3–4–2
Distributorless Ignition System

84707003

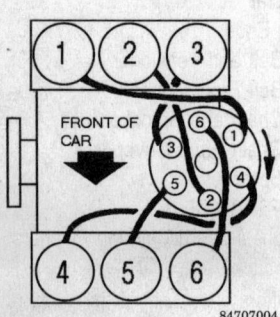

3.0L Engine
Engine Firing Order:
1–4–2–5–3–6
Distributor Rotation: Clockwise

84707004

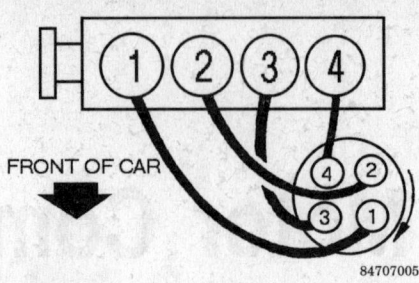

FRONT OF CAR

2.3L Engine
Engine Firing Order: 1–3–4–2
Distributor Rotation: Clockwise

84707005

ENGINE ELECTRICAL

NOTE: Disconnecting the negative battery cable on some vehicles may interfere with the functions of the on board computer systems and may require the computer to undergo a relearning process, once the negative battery cable is reconnected.

Distributor

REMOVAL

1. Turn the engine over until the piston in No. 1 cylinder is at TDC on the compression stroke.
2. Mark the position of the No. 1 cylinder spark plug wire on the distributor base.

NOTE: This is necessary for installation reference, in case the timing is disturbed while the distributor is removed from the engine.

3. Disconnect the negative battery cable.
4. Disconnect the distributor electrical connector. Disconnect the coil wire on the 1.8L engine.
5. Loosen the distributor cap retaining screws. Remove the distributor cap and position it aside with the spark plug wires attached.
6. Scribe or paint an alignment mark on the distributor body, showing the position of the rotor. Place another mark on the distributor body and cylinder head or block, showing the position of the body in relation to the head or block. These marks are used for reference when installing the distributor.

7. Remove the 2 distributor retaining bolts at the base of the distributor housing on 1.8L and 1.9L engines. Remove distributor hold-down bolt and clamp on the 2.3L and 3.0L engines.
8. Pull the distributor out of the head or block. Cover the opening in the block or head with a clean shop towel to prevent the entry of dirt or foreign material into the engine.
9. Inspect the distributor O-ring for cuts or other damage and replace, as necessary.

INSTALLATION

Timing Not Disturbed

1. Lubricate the distributor O-ring.
2. On the 1.8L and 1.9L engines, install the distributor in the cylinder head, seating the tang(s) of the drive coupling into the groove(s) at the end of the camshaft. Align the reference marks that were made in the removal procedure.
3. On the 2.3L and 3.0L engines, install the distributor in the engine block, aligning the reference marks that were made during the removal procedure.
4. Install the distributor hold-down bolt(s). Tighten the bolt(s) enough so the distributor is not loose but can still be moved by hand for ignition timing purposes.
5. Install the distributor cap and connect the distributor electrical connector. Connect the coil wire on 1.8L engine.
6. Connect the negative battery cable.
7. Check and if necessary, adjust the ignition timing.
8. After the timing has been set, tighten the distributor hold-down bolt(s) to 14–19 ft. lbs. (19–25 Nm) on 1.8L engine, 44–62 inch lbs. (5–7 Nm) on 1.9L engine or 17–25 ft. lbs. (23–34 Nm) on 2.3L and 3.0L engines.

Timing Disturbed

1. If the crankshaft was rotated while the distributor was removed, the piston in No. 1 cylinder must be brought to TDC on the compression stroke.
2. Disconnect the No. 1 cylinder spark plug wire and remove the spark plug. Place a finger over the spark plug hole and rotate the crankshaft slowly in the direction of normal rotation, until engine compression is felt.

NOTE: Turn the engine only in the direction of normal rotation.

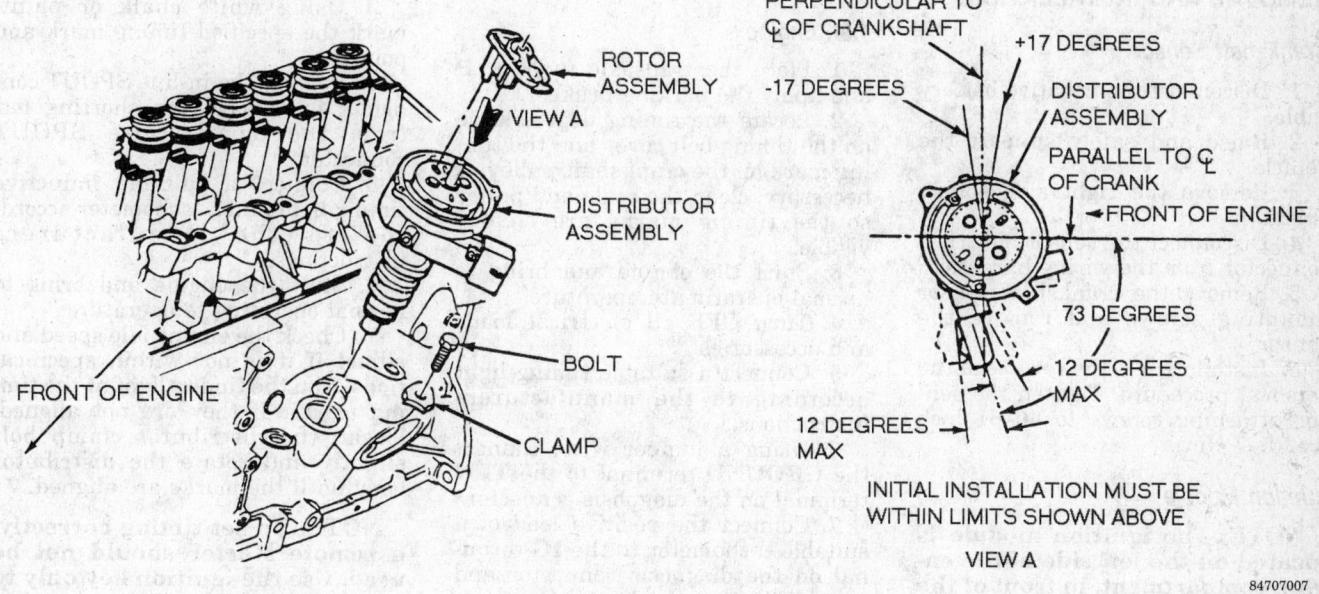

Distributor mounting — 2.3L engine

ROTOR ASSEMBLY

VIEW A

DISTRIBUTOR ASSEMBLY

BOLT

CLAMP

FRONT OF ENGINE

PERPENDICULAR TO ₵ OF CRANKSHAFT

+17 DEGREES

-17 DEGREES

DISTRIBUTOR ASSEMBLY

PARALLEL TO ₵ OF CRANK

FRONT OF ENGINE

73 DEGREES

12 DEGREES MAX

12 DEGREES MAX

INITIAL INSTALLATION MUST BE WITHIN LIMITS SHOWN ABOVE

VIEW A

84707007

3. When engine compression is felt at the spark plug hole, indicating that the piston is approaching TDC, continue to turn the crankshaft until the timing mark on the pulley is aligned with the **0** mark on the engine front cover or the timing pointer on the engine front cover is aligned with the **0** mark on the damper, as applicable.

4. Turn the distributor shaft until the ignition rotor is aligned with the mark made on the distributor base during Step 2 of the removal procedure.

5. On the 1.8L and 1.9L engines, install the distributor in the cylinder head, seating the tang(s) of the drive coupling into the groove(s) at the end of the camshaft. Align the distributor body-to-cylinder head reference marks that were made in the removal procedure.

6. On the 2.3L and 3.0L engines, install the distributor in the engine block, aligning the distributor body-to-engine block reference marks that were made during the removal procedure.

7. Install the distributor hold-down bolt(s). Tighten the bolt(s) enough so the distributor is not loose but can still be moved by hand for ignition timing purposes.

8. Install the distributor cap and connect the distributor electrical connector. Connect the coil wire on 1.8L engine.

9. Install the spark plug in the No. 1 cylinder and tighten to 11–17 ft. lbs. (14–23 Nm) on 1.8L engine, 8–15 ft. lbs. (11–20 Nm) on 1.9L engine, 6–10 ft. lbs. (7–14 Nm) on 2.3L engine or 5–11 ft. lbs. (7–15 Nm) on 3.0L engine. Connect the spark plug wire to the spark plug.

10. Connect the negative battery cable.

11. Check and adjust the ignition timing.

12. After the timing has been set, tighten the distributor hold-down bolt(s) to 14–19 ft. lbs. (19–25 Nm) on 1.8L engine, 44–62 inch lbs. (5–7 Nm) on 1.9L engine or 17–25 ft. lbs. (23–34 Nm) on 2.3L and 3.0L engines.

Distributorless Ignition

The 1.9L engine is equipped with a Distributorless Ignition System (DIS). The DIS consists of the following components: crankshaft sensor, ignition module, ignition coil pack, the spark angle portion of the PCM and the related wiring.

The crankshaft sensor is a variable reluctance-type sensor triggered by a 36-minus-1 tooth trigger wheel configuration pressed onto the rear of the crankshaft dampener. The signal generated by this sensor is called a Variable Reluctance Sensor (VRS) signal. The VRS signal provides engine position and rpm information to the ignition module.

The ignition module is a microprocessor that receives input from the crankshaft sensor in regards to engine position and engine speed and input from the PCM pertaining to spark advance. The ignition module uses this information to direct which coil to fire and to calculate the turn on and turn off times of the coils required to achieve the correct dwell and spark advance.

The ignition coil pack contains 2 separate ignition coils. Each ignition coil fires 2 cylinders simultaneously. When 1 cylinder is firing on the compression stroke, the other is firing on the exhaust stroke. During the next engine revolution, the reverse occurs. The spark plug fired on the exhaust stroke uses very little of the ignition coil's stored energy; the majority of the energy is used by the spark plug on the compression stroke. Since these 2 spark plugs are connected in series, the firing voltage of 1 plug will be negative with respect to ground, while the voltage of the other will be positive with respect to ground.

REMOVAL AND INSTALLATION

Crankshaft Sensor

1. Disconnect the negative battery cable.
2. Raise and safely support the vehicle.
3. Remove the right side splash shield.
4. Disconnect the sensor electrical connector from the wiring harness.
5. Remove the crankshaft sensor mounting screws and remove the sensor.
6. Installation is the reverse of the removal procedure. Tighten the sensor attaching screws to 40–61 inch lbs. (5–7 Nm).

Ignition Module

NOTE: The ignition module is located on the left side of the engine compartment, in front of the left strut tower.

1. Disconnect the negative battery cable.
2. Remove the 3 module sub-bracket attaching nuts.
3. Gently pull the sub-bracket and module assembly straight up and disconnect the module electrical harness.
4. Remove the 2 module attaching screws from the sub-bracket. Remove the ignition module from the sub-bracket.
5. Installation is the reverse of the removal procedure. Tighten the module attaching screws to 24–35 inch lbs. (3–4 Nm). Tighten the sub-bracket attaching nuts to 62–88 inch lbs. (7–10 Nm).

Ignition Coil Pack

1. Disconnect the negative battery cable.
2. Disconnect the electrical connector from the coil pack.
3. Remove the spark plug wires by squeezing the locking tabs to release the coil boot retainers. Tag the wires and mark their position on the coil pack prior to removal.
4. Remove the coil pack attaching bolts and remove the coil pack.

NOTE: Save the capacitor for installation with the new coil pack.

5. Installation is the reverse of the removal procedure. Tighten the attaching bolts to 40–62 inch lbs. (5–7 Nm).

Ignition Timing

ADJUSTMENT

1.8L Engine

1. Place the transaxle in **N** or **P** and apply the parking brake.
2. Locate the timing degree scale on the timing belt cover and the timing mark on the crankshaft pulley. If necessary, clean the scale and pulley so the timing marks are clearly visible.
3. Start the engine and bring to normal operating temperature.
4. Turn OFF all electrical loads and accessories.
5. Connect a suitable timing light according to the manufacturers instructions.
6. Using a jumper wire, connect the **GROUND** terminal to the **TEN** terminal on the diagnosis connector.
7. Connect the positive lead of a suitable tachometer to the **IG** terminal on the diagnosis connector and connect the negative lead to the negative battery post.
8. Aim the timing light at the timing degree scale and inspect the ignition timing. The ignition timing should be 9–11 degrees BTDC at 700–800 rpm. The yellow mark on the crankshaft pulley should be aligned with the corresponding mark on the timing belt cover.
9. If the marks are not aligned, loosen the distributor mounting bolts and turn the distributor until the ignition timing is within specification.
10. Tighten the distributor mounting bolts to 14–19 ft. lbs. (19–25 Nm), then recheck the timing to make sure it did not move when the bolts were tightened.
11. Remove the jumper wire from the diagnosis connector and remove the timing light and tachometer.

2.3L and 3.0L Engines

On the 2.3L engine, the timing marks are located on the flywheel and are visible through an access hole in the transaxle case. If equipped with manual transaxle, the timing cover plate must be removed in order to view the timing marks and adjust the timing.

On the 3.0L engine, the timing marks are located on the crankshaft damper and timing chain cover.

1. Place the transaxle in **P** or **N** and apply the parking brake. Make sure the air conditioner and heater are OFF.
2. Open the hood, locate the timing marks and clean with a stiff brush or solvent. If equipped with

2.3L engine and manual transaxle, it will be necessary to remove the cover plate which allows access to to the timing marks.

3. Using white chalk or paint, mark the specified timing mark and pointer.
4. Remove the in-line SPOUT connector or remove the shorting bar from the double wire SPOUT connector.
5. Connect a suitable inductive timing light and a tachometer according to the manufacturers instructions.
6. Start the engine and bring to normal operating temperature.
7. Check the engine idle speed and adjust if it is not within specifications. Aim the timing light at the timing marks. If they are not aligned, loosen the distributor clamp bolt slightly and rotate the distributor body until the marks are aligned.

NOTE: To set timing correctly, a remote starter should not be used. Use the ignition key only to start the vehicle. Disconnecting the start wire at the starter relay will cause the TFI module to revert to start mode timing after the vehicle is started. Reconnecting the start wire after the vehicle is running will not correct the timing.

8. Tighten the distributor clamp bolt, then recheck the ignition timing to make sure it did not change when the bolt was tightened.
9. Shut the engine **OFF** and remove all test equipment. Reconnect the in-line SPOUT connector or reinstall the shorting bar on the double wire SPOUT connector.
10. If equipped with 2.3L engine and manual transaxle, reinstall the cover plate.

Alternator

PRECAUTIONS

Several precautions must be observed with alternator equipped vehicles to avoid damage to the unit.

• If the battery is removed for any reason, make sure it is reconnected with the correct polarity. Reversing the battery connections may result in damage to the 1-way rectifiers.

• When utilizing a booster battery as a starting aid, always connect the positive to positive terminals and the negative terminal from the booster battery to a good engine ground on the vehicle being started.

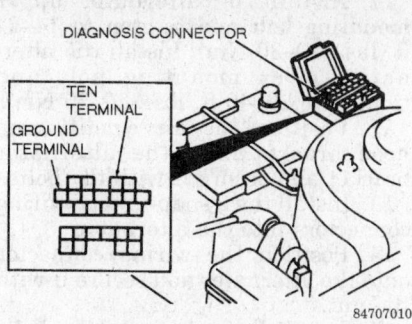

Diagnosis connector location — 1.8L engine

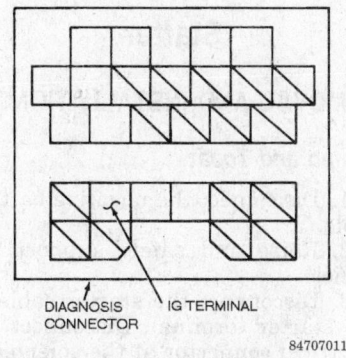

Diagnosis connector terminals — 1.8L engine

- Never use a fast charger as a booster to start vehicles.
- Disconnect the battery cables when charging the battery with a fast charger.
- Never attempt to polarize the alternator.
- Do not use test lights of more than 12 volts when checking diode continuity.
- Do not short across or ground any of the alternator terminals.
- The polarity of the battery, alternator and regulator must be matched and considered before making any electrical connections within the system.
- Never separate the alternator on an open circuit. Make sure all connections within the circuit are clean and tight.
- Disconnect the battery ground terminal when performing any service on electrical components.
- Disconnect the battery if arc welding is to be done on the vehicle.

BELT TENSION ADJUSTMENT

1.8L Engine

1. Loosen the alternator adjusting bolt.

2. Raise and safely support the vehicle.
3. Loosen the alternator mounting bolt.

NOTE: Do not pry against the stator frame. Position the prybar against a stronger point, such as the area around a case bolt.

4. Position a suitable belt tension gauge on the longest accessible span of belt and tighten the belt. Adjust the tension to 85.8–103.4 lbs. for a new belt or 68.2–85.8 lbs. for a used belt.

NOTE: A belt is considered used if it has been in use for more than 10 minutes

5. If a belt tension gauge is not available, adjust the tension to 0.31–0.35 in. (8–9mm) deflection for a new belt or 0.35–0.39 in. (9–10mm) deflection for a used belt.
6. Tighten the alternator adjusting bolt to 14–19 ft. lbs. (19–25 Nm).
7. Tighten the alternator mounting bolt to 27–38 ft. lbs. (37–52 Nm).
8. Lower the vehicle.

1.9L Engine

NOTE: An automatic tensioner maintains correct belt tension during operation on the 1.9L engine. No adjustment is necessary.

1. Loosen the alternator pivot and adjustment bolts.
2. Install a ½ inch breaker bar or equivalent, to the support bracket that is located behind the alternator.
3. Apply tension to the belt using the breaker bar. Using a belt tension gauge, adjust the tension to 140–180 lbs. for a new belt or 120–140 lbs. for a used belt. While maintaining proper belt tension, tighten the alternator adjustment bolt to 30 ft. lbs. (40 Nm).

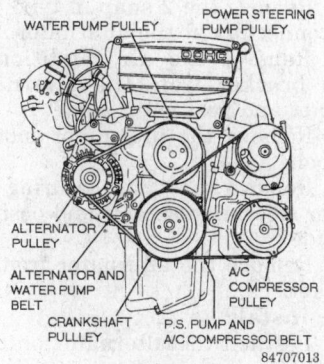

Drive belt arrangement — 1.8L engine

4. Remove the belt tension gauge and breaker bar, start the engine and let it idle for 5 minutes.
5. Stop the engine and check the belt tension. If the tension is below 120 lbs., retension the belt to 120–140 lbs. and then tighten the adjustment bolt.
6. Tighten the alternator pivot bolt to 50 ft. lbs. (68 Nm) and the support bracket bolt to 35 ft. lbs. (47 Nm).

2.3L Engine

NOTE: An automatic tensioner maintains correct belt tension during operation on the 1992–95 2.3L engine. No adjustment is necessary.

1. Loosen the alternator pivot and adjustment bolts.
2. Using adjustable pliers or equivalent, apply tension to the belt. Place the bottom jaw of the pliers under the alternator adjustment boss and the top jaw in the notch at the top of the alternator adjustment bracket.

NOTE: A suitable tensioning tool can be made by modifying a 4 inch C-clamp.

3. Squeeze the pliers together and, using a belt tension gauge, adjust the tension to 160 lbs. for a new belt or 140 lbs. for a used belt. While maintaining the proper belt tension, tighten the alternator adjustment bolt to 26 ft. lbs. (35 Nm).
4. Remove the belt tension gauge, start the engine and let it idle for 5 minutes.
5. Stop the engine and recheck the belt tension. Adjust to the proper specifications and retighten the adjustment bolt.
6. Tighten the alternator pivot bolt to 52 ft. lbs. (70 Nm).

3.0L Engine

An automatic tensioner maintains correct belt tension during operation on the 3.0L engine. No adjustment is necessary.

REMOVAL AND INSTALLATION

Tempo and Topaz

1. Disconnect the negative battery cable.
2. Disconnect the wire harness attachments to the integral alternator/regulator assembly. Pull the 2 connectors straight out.

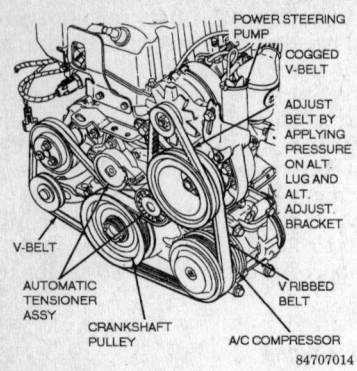

Drive belt arrangement — 2.3L engine

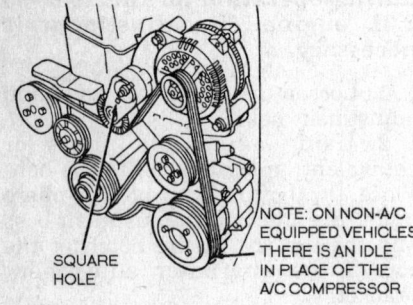

Drive belt arrangement — 3.0L engine

3. Loosen the alternator pivot bolt. Remove the adjustment arm bolt from the alternator.

4. Disengage the alternator drive belt from the alternator pulley.

5. Remove the alternator pivot bolt and alternator/regulator assembly.

6. Remove the alternator fan shield, if equipped.

To install:

7. Position the integral alternator/regulator assembly on the engine.

8. Install the alternator pivot and adjuster arm bolts. Do not tighten the bolts until the belt is tensioned.

9. Install the drive belt over the alternator pulley.

10. Adjust the belt tension.

11. Connect wiring harness to the alternator/regulator assembly. Push both connectors straight in.

12. Attach the alternator fan shield to the alternator, if equipped.

13. Connect the negative battery cable.

Escort and Tracer

1.8L ENGINE

1. Disconnect the negative battery cable.

2. Remove the nut securing the wiring connector to the alternator.

3. Remove the field terminal wiring connector.

4. Remove the upper mounting bolt securing the alternator to the alternator to the alternator bracket.

5. Loosen the lower alternator mounting bolt and pivot the alternator forward.

6. Remove the alternator belt from the pulley and position the belt aside.

7. Raise and safely support the vehicle.

8. Remove the lower splash shield located under the accessory belts.

9. Remove the alternator lower mounting bolt and remove the alternator from the vehicle.

To install:

10. Position the alternator into the vehicle and install the lower mounting bolt.

11. Install the lower splash shield.

12. Lower the vehicle.

13. Position the alternator belt onto the pulley and adjust the belt.

14. Tighten the upper mounting bolt to 14–19 ft. lbs. (19–25 Nm) and the lower mounting bolt to 27–38 ft. lbs. (37–52 Nm).

15. Install the field terminal wiring connector.

16. Position the wiring connector to the alternator and secure it with the nut.

17. Connect the negative battery cable.

1.9L ENGINE

1. Disconnect the negative battery cable.

2. Using a ⅜ in. drive ratchet or breaker bar inserted in the automatic tensioner, pull the tool toward the front of the vehicle. While releasing the belt tension, remove the drive belt from the alternator.

3. Remove the nut securing the wiring connector to the alternator.

4. Remove the 2 snap-in type wiring connectors at the alternator.

5. Remove the air conditioning hose bracket from the alternator bracket and position it aside.

6. Remove the alternator mounting bolts.

7. Remove the bolts securing the power steering reservoir and position it aside.

8. Remove the alternator from its bracket.

To install:

9. Position the alternator onto its bracket.

10. Position the power steering reservoir and secure it with the bolts.

11. Install the alternator upper mounting bolt and tighten to 14–22 ft. lbs. (20–30 Nm). Install the alternator lower mounting bolt and tighten to 29–40 ft. lbs. (40–55 Nm).

12. Position the air conditioning hose bracket onto the alternator bracket and secure it with the bolts.

13. Install the 2 snap-in type wiring connectors into the alternator.

14. Position the wiring connector onto the alternator and secure it with the nut.

15. Install the accessory drive belt.

16. Connect the negative battery cable.

Starter

REMOVAL AND INSTALLATION

Tempo and Topaz

1. Disconnect the negative battery cable.

2. Raise and safely support the vehicle.

3. Disconnect the starter cable at the starter terminal. Disconnect the electrical connector at the solenoid.

NOTE: When disconnecting the plastic hard shell connector at the solenoid S terminal, grasp the plastic connector, depress the plastic tab and pull off the lead assembly. Do not pull on the lead wire or damage may result.

4. Remove the 2 bolts attaching the starter rear support bracket, if equipped. Remove the bracket.

5. If equipped with roll restrictor brace-to-starter studs on the transaxle housing, remove the nuts and remove the brace.

6. Remove the starter retaining bolts and remove the starter.

7. For installation, reverse the removal procedure. Tighten the attaching studs or bolts to 16–20 ft. lbs. (21–27 Nm).

Escort and Tracer

1.8L ENGINE

1. Disconnect the negative battery cable.

2. Remove the air duct that connects to the throttle body and resonance chamber.

3. Remove the starter motor upper mounting bolts.

4. Raise and safely support the vehicle.

5. Remove the intake plenum support bracket mounting bolts and remove the bracket.

6. Disconnect the **S** terminal connector from the starter solenoid.

NOTE: When disconnecting the plastic hard shell connector at the solenoid S terminal, grasp the plastic connector, depress the plastic tab and pull off the lead assembly. Do not pull on the lead wire or damage may result.

7. Remove the **B** terminal attaching nut and disconnect the cable from the terminal.

8. Remove the starter motor lower mounting bolt and remove the starter motor.

To install:

9. Place the starter motor into its mounting position and install the lower mounting bolt. Tighten the bolt to 15–20 ft. lbs. (20.3–27.0 Nm).

10. Connect the cable to the starter solenoid **B** terminal and install the attaching nut to the terminal. Tighten the nut to 80–120 inch lbs. (9.0–13.5 Nm).

11. Connect the electrical connector to the starter solenoid **S** terminal.

12. Install the intake plenum support bracket and tighten the attaching bolts to 27–38 ft. lbs. (37–52 Nm) and the attaching nut to 14–19 ft. lbs. (19–25 Nm).

13. Lower the vehicle.

14. Install the starter motor upper mounting bolts and tighten to 15–20 ft. lbs. (20.3–27.0 Nm).

15. Install the air duct that connects to the throttle body and resonance chamber.

16. Connect the negative battery cable.

1.9L ENGINE

1. Disconnect the negative battery cable.

2. If equipped with an automatic transaxle, remove the kickdown cable routing bracket from the engine block.

3. Disconnect the wire from the starter solenoid **S** terminal.

NOTE: When disconnecting the plastic hard shell connector at the solenoid S terminal, grasp the plastic connector, depress the plastic tab and pull off the lead assembly. Do not pull on the lead wire or damage may result.

4. Remove the attaching nut from the starter solenoid **B** terminal and disconnect the cable from the terminal.

5. Remove the starter motor mounting bolts and remove the starter motor.

To install:

6. Place the starter motor into its mounting position and install the mounting bolts. Tighten the bolts to 15–20 ft. lbs. (20.3–27.0 Nm).

7. Connect the cable to the starter solenoid **B** terminal and install the attaching nut. Tighten the nut to 80–120 inch lbs. (9–13.5 Nm).

8. Connect the wire to the starter solenoid **S** terminal.

9. If equipped with an automatic transaxle, install the kickdown cable routing bracket to the engine block.

10. Connect the negative battery cable.

CHASSIS ELECTRICAL

Air Bag

A driver's side air bag can be installed as optional equipment on Tempo and Topaz vehicles.

DISARMING

1992–96 Vehicles

1. Disconnect the positive battery cable.

2. Wait 1 minute for the backup power supply to deplete its stored energy.

3. Remove the 4 nut and washer assemblies retaining the air bag to the steering wheel.

4. Disconnect the air bag electrical connector.

5. Attach air bag simulator tool 105–00008 or equivalent on the clockspring to simulate the air bag.

6. Connect the positive battery cable.

Heater Blower Motor

REMOVAL AND INSTALLATION

Escort and Tracer

1. Disconnect the negative battery cable.

2. Remove the trim panel below the glove compartment.

3. Remove the wiring bracket and bolt.

4. Disconnect the blower motor electrical connector.

5. Remove the 3 blower motor mounting bolts and remove the blower motor.

6. Remove the blower wheel retaining clip and remove the blower wheel from the blower motor.

7. Installation is the reverse of the removal procedures.

Tempo and Topaz

1. Disconnect the negative battery cable.

2. Remove the contents from the glove compartment and remove the glove compartment door.

3. Disconnect the blower motor wires from the blower motor resistor.

4. Loosen the instrument panel at the lower right side prior to removing the blower motor assembly through the glove compartment opening.

5. Remove the 4 screws retaining the blower motor and mounting plate to the heater case (without air conditioning) or evaporator case (with air conditioning).

6. Rotate the motor until the mounting plate flats clear the edge of the glove compartment opening. Then, remove the motor and mounting plate from the vehicle.

7. Remove the blower motor and mounting plate seal from the mounting plate and make sure the mounting surface is clean.

8. Remove the pushnut from the blower wheel shaft and remove the blower wheel from the motor shaft.

9. Installation is the reverse of the removal procedure. Be sure to use a new mounting plate seal.

Windshield Wiper Motor

REMOVAL AND INSTALLATION

Front

TEMPO AND TOPAZ

1. Disconnect the negative battery cable.

2. Lift the water shield cover from the cowl on the passenger side.

3. Disconnect the electrical connector from the motor.

4. Remove the linkage retaining clip from the operating arm on the motor by lifting locking tab up and pulling clip away from pin.

5. Remove the 3 retaining bolts from the motor and bracket assembly.

6. Remove the operating arm from the motor. Unscrew the 3 bolts and separate the motor from the mounting bracket, if necessary.

7. Installation is the reverse of the removal procedure.

ESCORT AND TRACER

1. Disconnect the negative battery cable.
2. Remove the wiper arm attaching nut covers, remove the attaching nuts and pull the wiper arms from the pivot shafts.
3. With the hood closed, remove the 7 screw covers.
4. Remove the 7 cowl grille retaining screws and remove the cowl grille.
5. Pry up the 4 baffle retaining clips and remove the baffle trim piece.

NOTE: Make sure the motor is in the PARK position before disconnecting the linkage.

6. Remove the wiper linkage retaining clip and disconnect the wiper linkage from the motor.
7. Disconnect the 2 motor electrical connectors.
8. Remove the 3 motor mounting bolts until they are loose from the sheet metal mounting surface. Remove the motor.
9. Installation is the reverse of the removal procedure. Tighten the 3 motor mounting bolts to 61–87 inch lbs. (7–9 Nm).

Rear

ESCORT AND TRACER

1. Disconnect the negative battery cable.
2. Remove the wiper arm by lifting the wiper arm attaching nut cover, removing the attaching nut and pulling the wiper arm from the pivot shaft.
3. Remove the shaft seal from the outer bushing attaching nut.
4. Remove the outer bushing attaching nut and remove the outer bushing.
5. Remove the liftgate trim panel.
6. Disconnect the wiper motor electrical connector.
7. Remove the 3 wiper motor mounting bolts and washers and remove the wiper motor.
8. Installation is the reverse of the removal procedure. Tighten the mounting bolts to 61–87 inch lbs. (7–9 Nm) and the outer bushing attaching nut to 35–52 inch lbs. (4–6 Nm).

Windshield Wiper Switch

REMOVAL AND INSTALLATION

TILT STEERING WHEEL

1. Disconnect the negative battery cable.
2. Remove the steering column shroud.
3. Peel back the side shield and disconnect the switch wiring connector.
4. Remove the screw attaching the wiring retainer to the steering column.
5. Grasp the switch handle and pull straight out to disengage the wiper switch from the turn signal switch.
6. Installation is the reverse of the removal procedure.

Escort and Tracer

Windshield wiper control is a function of the combination switch.

Tempo and Topaz

1. Disconnect the negative battery cable.
2. Insert a suitable prying tool into the small slot on top of the switch bezel. Push down on the tool to work the top of the switch bezel away from the instrument panel.
3. Insert the prying tool into the small slot on the bottom of the switch bezel. Push up on the tool to work the bottom of the switch bezel away from the instrument panel.
4. Remove the switch from the panel opening. Hold the switch and pull the wiring at the rear of the switch until the switch connector can be easily disconnected. Disconnect the connector and allow the wiring to hang from the switch mounting opening.
To install:
5. Connect the wiring connector to the new switch and route the wiring back into the mounting opening. Insert the switch into the opening so the graphics are properly aligned.
6. Push on the switch until the bezel seats against the instrument panel and the clips lock the switch into place.
7. Connect the negative battery cable.

Instrument Cluster

REMOVAL AND INSTALLATION

Escort and Tracer

1. Disconnect the negative battery cable.
2. If equipped with a tilt column, tilt the steering wheel down.
3. If equipped with a standard column, remove the 4 bolts securing the steering column to the instrument panel frame.
4. Lower the steering column.
5. Disconnect the speedometer cable from the instrument panel.
6. Remove the cap screws securing the instrument cluster bezel to the instrument panel and remove the instrument cluster bezel.
7. Remove the screws and bolts securing the instrument cluster to the instrument panel.
8. Pull the instrument cluster out slightly and disconnect the electrical connectors from the rear of the instrument cluster.
9. Remove the cluster from the instrument panel.
10. Installation is the reverse of the removal procedure. Make sure the instrument cluster is held in its forward most position while attaching the 2 upper screws.

Tempo and Topaz

1. Disconnect the negative battery cable.
2. Remove 2 retaining screws at the bottom of the steering column opening and snap the steering column cover out.
3. Remove the steering column trim shroud.
4. Remove the snap-in lower cluster finish panels.
5. Remove 4 cluster opening finish panel retaining screws and pull the panel rearward.
6. Disconnect the speedometer cable at the transaxle.
7. Remove the 4 screws retaining the instrument cluster and carefully pull rearward enough to disengage the speedometer cable. Disconnect the speedometer cable by pressing on the flat surface of the plastic connector located behind the instrument cluster.
8. Carefully pull the cluster away from the instrument panel. Disconnect the electrical connectors at the rear of the cluster.
9. Installation is the reverse of the removal procedure.

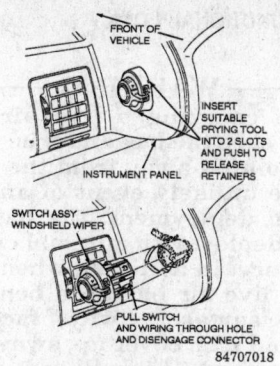

Wiper switch installation — Tempo and Topaz

CAUTION

If gauges are being removed from the cluster assembly, do not remove the gauge pointer because the magnetic gauges cannot be recalibrated.

Speedometer

REMOVAL AND INSTALLATION

Tempo and Topaz

1. Disconnect the negative battery cable.
2. Remove the instrument cluster.
3. Remove the 7 screws that retain the lens and mask to the backplate.
4. Remove the 2 nuts retaining the fuel gauge assembly to the backplate. Remove the fuel gauge assembly and then remove the speedometer assembly.

To install:

5. Apply a 3/16 in. ball of speedometer cable lubricant D7AZ–19A331–A or equivalent, in the drive hole of the speedometer head. Install speedometer head assembly into cluster.

NOTE: The speedometer is calibrated at the time of manufacture. Excessive rough handling of the speedometer may disturb the calibration.

6. Install the retaining screws to retain the lens and mask to the backplate.
7. Install the instrument cluster.
8. Connect the negative battery cable and check the operation of the speedometer.

Escort and Tracer

1. Disconnect the negative battery cable.
2. Remove the instrument cluster.
3. Remove the instrument cluster lens and shroud.

4. Remove the speedometer from the instrument cluster.
5. Installation is the reverse of the removal procedure. Be careful when handling the speedometer so as not to disturb the factory calibration.

Headlight Switch

REMOVAL AND INSTALLATION

Tempo and Topaz

1. Disconnect the negative battery cable.
2. If without air conditioning, remove the left side air vent control cable retaining screws and let the cable hang.
3. Remove the fuse panel bracket retaining screws. Move the fuse panel assembly aside to gain access to the headlight switch.
4. Pull the headlight knob out to the **ON** position. Depress the headlight knob and shaft retainer button and remove the knob and shaft assembly from the switch.
5. Remove the headlight switch retaining bezel. Disconnect the multiple connector plug and remove the switch from the instrument panel.

To install:

6. Install the headlight switch into the instrument panel. Connect the multiple connector and install the headlight switch retaining bezel.
7. Install the knob and shaft assembly by inserting the shaft into the switch and gently pushing until the shaft locks in position.
8. Move the fuse panel back into position and install the fuse panel bracket with the 2 retaining screws.
9. If without air conditioning, install the left side air vent control cable and bracket.
10. Connect the negative battery cable.

Combination Switch

On Tempo and Topaz, the combination switch assembly is a multi-function switch comprising turn signal, hazard, headlight dimmer and flash-to-pass functions. The switch lever on the left side of the upper steering column controls the turn signal, headlight dimmer and flash-to-pass functions. The hazard function is controlled by the actuating knob on the lower side of the upper steering column.

On Escort and Tracer, the combination switch assembly is a multi-function switch that controls the

headlights, parking lights and taillights, the turn signals, headlight dimmer and window wipers.

REMOVAL AND INSTALLATION

Tempo and Topaz

1. Disconnect the negative battery cable.
2. Remove the 5 column shroud screws and remove the lower column shroud.
3. Loosen the 4 steering column attaching nuts enough to allow the removal of the upper trim shroud.
4. Remove the upper shroud.
5. Remove the turn signal switch lever by pulling the lever straight out from the switch. To make removal easier, work the outer end of the lever around with a slight rotary movement before pulling it out.
6. Peel back the foam sight shield from the turn signal switch.
7. Disconnect the turn signal switch electrical connectors.
8. Remove the 2 self-tapping screws that attach the turn signal switch to the lock cylinder housing and disengage the switch from the housing.

To install:

9. Align the turn signal switch mounting holes with the corresponding holes in the lock cylinder housing and install 2 self-tapping screws until tight.
10. Apply the foam sight shield to the turn signal switch.
11. Install the turn signal switch lever into the switch by aligning the key on the lever with the keyway in the switch and pushing the lever toward the switch to full engagement.
12. Install the turn signal switch electrical connectors to full engagement.
13. Install the upper steering column trim shroud.
14. Torque the steering column attaching nuts to 15–22 ft. lbs. (20–30 Nm).
15. Attach the lower steering column shroud to the upper shroud with the 5 screws.
16. Connect the negative battery cable.
17. Check the steering column and switch for proper operation.

Escort and Tracer

1. Disconnect the negative battery cable.
2. Remove the steering wheel cover retaining screws from the back side of the steering wheel and remove the cover.

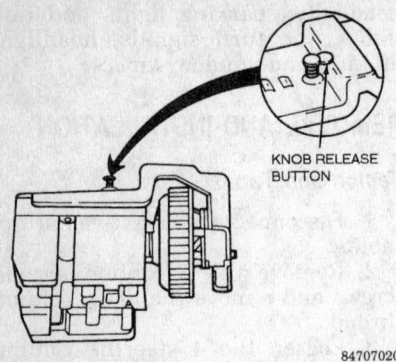

84707020

Headlight switch — Tempo and Topaz

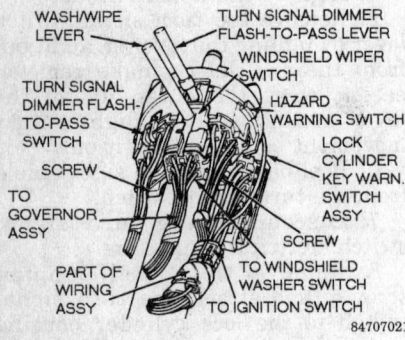

WASH/WIPE LEVER

TURN SIGNAL DIMMER FLASH-TO-PASS LEVER

WINDSHIELD WIPER SWITCH

TURN SIGNAL DIMMER FLASH-TO-PASS SWITCH

HAZARD WARNING SWITCH

LOCK CYLINDER KEY WARN. SWITCH ASSY

SCREW

TO GOVERNOR ASSY

SCREW

PART OF WIRING ASSY

TO WINDSHIELD WASHER SWITCH

TO IGNITION SWITCH

84707021

Stalk mounted switch levers and wiring harnesses — Tempo and Topaz

3. Disconnect the horn electrical connector and the speed control electrical connectors, if equipped.

4. Remove the steering wheel mounting nut or bolt.

─── CAUTION ───

Do not attempt to remove the steering wheel by hitting the column shaft with a hammer. The column may collapse.

5. Remove the steering wheel using a suitable puller.

6. Remove the 4 retaining screws from the steering column lower cover and remove the cover. Remove the upper cover.

7. Disconnect the 3 multi-function switch electrical connectors.

8. Remove the multi-function switch retaining screw, pull the electrical connectors from the retaining brackets and remove the switch.

9. Installation is the reverse of the removal procedure. Tighten the steering wheel mounting bolt to 34–46 ft. lbs. (46–63 Nm).

Ignition Lock

REMOVAL AND INSTALLATION

Tempo and Topaz

FUNCTIONAL LOCK

The following procedure is for vehicles that have functional lock cylinders. Lock cylinder keys are available for these vehicles or the lock cylinder key numbers are known and the proper key can be made.

1. Disconnect the negative battery cable.

2. If equipped with a tilt steering column, remove the upper extension shroud by unsnapping the shroud from the retaining clip at the 9 o'clock position.

3. Remove the steering column lower shroud on Escort and Tracer. On Tempo and Topaz, remove the 5 attaching screws and the 2 trim shroud halves.

4. Disconnect the key warning buzzer electrical connector. With the lock cylinder key, rotate the cylinder to the **RUN** position.

5. Take a 1/8 in. diameter pin or small wire punch and push on the cylinder retaining pin. The pin is visible through a hole in the mounting surrounding the key cylinder. Push on the pin and withdraw the lock cylinder from the housing.

To install:

6. Install the lock cylinder by turning it to the **RUN** position and depressing the retaining pin. Insert the lock cylinder into the housing. Be sure the lock cylinder is fully seated and aligned in the interlocking washer before turning the key to the **OFF** position. This action will permit the cylinder retaining pin to extend into the cylinder housing hole.

7. Rotate the lock cylinder, using the lock cylinder key, to ensure correct mechanical operation in all positions.

8. Install the electrical connector for the key warning buzzer.

9. Install the lower steering column shroud or trim shroud halves.

10. Connect the negative battery cable.

11. Check for proper start in **P** or **N**. Also, make certain the start circuit cannot be actuated in the **D** and **R** positions and that the column is locked in the **LOCK** position.

NON-FUNCTIONAL LOCK

─── WARNING ───

When carrying a live air bag, make sure the bag and trim cover are pointed away from the body. In the unlikely event of an accidental deployment, the bag will then deploy with minimal chance of injury. In addition, when placing a live air bag on a bench or other surface, always face the bag and trim cover up, away from the surface. This will reduce the motion of the module if it is accidentally deployed.

The following procedure applies to vehicles in which the ignition lock is inoperative and the lock cylinder cannot be rotated due to a lost or broken lock cylinder key, the key number is not known or the lock cylinder cap is damaged and/or broken to the extent the lock cylinder cannot be rotated.

1. Make sure the wheels are in the straight-ahead position and the column is locked. Disconnect the negative battery cable.

NOTE: If equipped with an air bag, a backup power supply is included in the system to provide air bag deployment in the event the battery or cables are damaged in an accident before the sensors can close. The power supply is a capacitor that will leak down in approximately 15 minutes after the battery is disconnected or 1 minute if the battery positive cable is grounded. If the system is equipped with a backup power supply, it must be disconnected to disarm the system.

2. If equipped with an air bag, perform the following procedure:

a. Disconnect the positive battery cable and wait 1 minute for the backup power supply to be depleted.

b. Remove the 4 nut and washer assemblies retaining the air bag assembly to the steering wheel.

c. Disconnect the air bag electrical connector from the contact assembly connectors and remove the air bag assembly.

d. Remove the steering wheel retaining bolt and remove the vibration damper, then reinstall the bolt loosely on the shaft.

e. Loosen the steering wheel on the shaft using a suitable puller.

f. Remove and discard the steering wheel retaining bolt and remove the steering wheel.

g. Remove the upper and lower shrouds.

h. Disconnect the air bag clockspring connector from the column harness.

NOTE: Before removing the air bag clockspring from the steering shaft, the clockspring must be taped to prevent the clockspring rotor from being turned accidentally and damaging the clockspring.

i. Remove the 2 screws that secure the clockspring to the retainer plate and remove the clockspring.

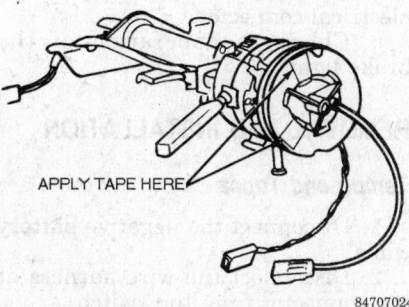

APPLY TAPE HERE

84707024

Air bag clockspring taping locations

3. If not equipped with an air bag, perform the following procedure:

a. Remove the horn pad cover by removing 2 or 4 screws from the back of the steering wheel assembly.

NOTE: The emblem assembly is removed after the horn pad cover is removed, by pushing out from the backside of the emblem.

b. Remove the energy absorbing foam from the wheel assembly, if equipped. Remember to reinstall when the steering wheel is reassembled.

c. Disconnect the horn pad wiring connector.

d. Loosen the steering wheel retaining bolt 4–6 turns. Do not remove the bolt.

e. Loosen the steering wheel on the shaft using a suitable puller.

f. Remove and discard the steering wheel retaining bolt and remove the steering wheel.

g. If equipped with a tilt column, remove the upper extension shroud by unsnapping the shroud from the retaining clip at the 9 o'clock position.

h. Remove the 2 trim shroud halves by removing the 5 retaining screws.

4. Remove the electrical connector from the key warning switch.

5. Using a 1/8 in. diameter drill bit, drill out the retaining pin, being careful not to drill deeper than 1/2 in. (12.7mm).

6. Place a suitable chisel at the base of the ignition lock cylinder cap and, using a suitable hammer, strike the chisel with sharp blows to break the cap away from the lock cylinder.

7. Using a 3/8 in. diameter drill bit, drill down the middle of the ignition lock key slot approximately 1 3/4 in. (44mm) until the lock cylinder breaks loose from the breakaway base of the lock cylinder. Remove the lock cylinder and drill shavings from the lock cylinder housing.

8. Remove the retainer, washer and steering column lock gear. Thoroughly clean all drill shavings and other foreign materials from the casting.

9. Carefully inspect the lock cylinder housing for damage. If any damage is evident, the housing must be replaced.

To install:

10. Install the ignition lock drive gear, washer and retainer.

11. Install the ignition lock cylinder and check for smooth operation.

12. Connect the electrical connector to the key warning switch.

13. If equipped with an air bag, install the clockspring, steering wheel and air bag module as follows:

a. Place the clockspring onto the steering shaft. Install the 2 retaining screws that secure the clockspring to the retainer plate. Make sure the ground wire is secured with the lower retaining screw. Remove the tape that was installed during the removal procedure.

b. Connect the clockspring wire to the column harness.

c. Install the upper and lower shrouds.

d. Install the steering wheel on the steering column, making sure the alignment marks are correct. Install the vibration damper and a new retaining bolt. Tighten the bolt to 23–33 ft. lbs. (31–45 Nm).

e. Connect the air bag module wire to the clockspring connector and place the air bag module on the steering wheel. Install the 4 retaining nuts and tighten to 35–53 inch lbs. (4–6 Nm).

f. Connect the positive battery cable.

g. Connect the negative battery cable and verify the air bag indicator.

14. If not equipped with an air bag, complete the installation as follows:

a. Install the trim shroud halves.

b. Install the steering wheel assembly on the steering column making sure the alignment marks are correct. Install a new retaining bolt and tighten to 23–33 ft. lbs. (31–45 Nm).

c. Connect the horn pad wiring connector. If equipped, install the energy absorbing foam.

d. Install the horn pad cover and 2 or 4 retaining screws. Make sure the wires are not pinched. Tighten the screws to 8–10 inch lbs. (0.9–1.1 Nm).

e. Connect the negative battery cable.

Escort and Tracer

1. Disconnect the negative battery cable.

2. Remove the steering wheel cover retaining screws from the back side of the steering wheel and remove the cover.

3. Disconnect the horn electrical connector and the cruise control electrical connectors, if equipped.

4. Remove the steering wheel mounting nut or bolt.

5. Remove the steering wheel using a suitable puller.

6. Remove the combination switch.

7. Disconnect the ignition switch electrical connector.

8. Remove the shift-lock cable mounting bracket bolt and position the bracket and cable aside.

9. Remove the 4 steering column upper mounting bracket bolts and lower the column.

10. Using a suitable hammer and chisel, make a groove in the head of each of the 2 column lock mounting bracket bolts.

11. Remove the bolts with a suitable flat bladed tool and discard the bolts.

12. Remove the steering column lock and mounting bracket.

To install:

13. Position the steering column lock and mounting bracket and install 2 new bolts, tightening them only enough to hold the column lock in position.

14. With the key in the ignition, verify the operation of the column lock. If necessary, reposition the column lock until it operates properly.

15. Tighten the mounting bracket bolts until the bolt heads break off.

16. Position the steering column and install the 4 upper mounting bracket bolts. Tighten the bolts to 80–123 inch lbs. (9–14 Nm).

17. If equipped with a tilt steering wheel, remove the upper mounting bracket retaining pin.

18. Position the shift-lock cable mounting bracket and install the bolt. Tighten to 37–55 inch lbs. (4–6 Nm).

19. Connect the ignition switch electrical connector.

20. Install the combination switch.

21. Install the steering wheel and the mounting nut or bolt. Tighten the bolt to 34–46 ft. lbs. (46–63 Nm).

22. Connect the horn electrical connector and the speed control electrical connectors, if equipped.

23. Position the steering wheel cover and install the retaining screws.

24. Connect the negative battery cable.

Ignition Switch

REMOVAL AND INSTALLATION

Tempo and Topaz

1. Disconnect the negative battery cable.

2. If equipped, remove the steering column lower cover from the instrument panel by removing the 2 screws from the bottom and disengaging the snap-in retainers at the top.

3. Remove the steering column shroud self-tapping screws.

4. Remove 2 bolts and nuts holding the steering column assembly to the steering column bracket assem-

bly and lower the steering column to the seat.

5. Remove the steering column shrouds.

6. Disconnect the electrical connector from the ignition switch.

7. Rotate ignition lock cylinder to the **RUN** position.

8. Remove 2 screws attaching the switch to the lock cylinder housing.

9. Disengage the ignition switch from the actuator pin.

To install:

10. Check to see that the actuator pin slot in the ignition switch is in the **RUN** position.

NOTE: A new switch assembly will be pre-set in the RUN position.

11. Make certain the ignition key lock cylinder is in approximately the **RUN** position to properly locate the lock actuator pin. The **RUN** position is achieved by rotating the key lock cylinder approximately 90 degrees from the **LOCK** position.

12. Install the ignition switch onto the actuator pin. It may be necessary to move the switch slightly back and fourth to align the switch mounting holes with the column lock housing threaded holes.

13. Install the new screws and tighten to 50–70 inch lbs. (5.6–7.9 Nm).

14. Connect the electrical connector to ignition switch.

15. Connect the negative battery cable.

16. Check the ignition switch for proper function including **START** and **ACC** positions. Also make certain the steering column is locked when in the **LOCK** position.

17. Position the top half of the shroud on the steering column.

18. Install the 2 bolts and nuts attaching the steering column assembly to the steering column bracket assembly. Tighten to 15–25 ft. lbs. (20–34 Nm).

19. Position lower shroud to upper shroud and install 5 self-tapping screws. Install the steering column lower cover on the instrument panel, if equipped.

Escort and Tracer

1. Disconnect the negative battery cable.

2. Remove the combination switch.

3. Disconnect the ignition switch electrical connector.

4. Remove the 3 ignition switch mounting screws and remove the ignition switch.

5. Installation is the reverse of the removal procedure. Check the switch for proper operation.

Brake Light Switch

ADJUSTMENT

Escort and Tracer

1. Measure the distance from the center of the brake pedal pad to the floor. The distance should be 7.60–7.72 in. (193–196mm). If not, proceed to Step 2.

2. Disconnect the brake light switch electrical connector.

3. Loosen the brake light locknut and turn the brake light switch until it does not contact the brake pedal.

4. Loosen the rod locknut and turn the rod until the brake pedal height is within specification.

5. Turn the brake light switch until it contacts the brake pedal, then turn it an additional ½ turn.

6. Tighten the brake light switch locknut and the rod locknut.

7. Connect the brake light switch electrical connector.

8. Check the operation of the brake lights.

REMOVAL AND INSTALLATION

Tempo and Topaz

1. Disconnect the negative battery cable.

2. Disconnect the wire harness at the connector from the switch.

NOTE: The locking tab must be lifted before the connector can be removed.

3. Remove the hairpin retainer and white nylon washer. Slide the brake light switch and the pushrod away from the pedal. Remove the switch by sliding the switch up/down.

NOTE: Since the switch side plate nearest the brake pedal is slotted, it is not necessary to remove the brake master cylinder pushrod black bushing and 1 white spacer washer nearest the pedal arm from the brake pedal pin.

To install:

4. Position the switch so the U-shaped side is nearest the pedal and directly over/under the pin. The black bushing must be in position in the pushrod eyelet with the washer face on the side closest to the retaining pin.

5. Slide the switch up/down, trapping the master cylinder pushrod and black bushing between the switch side plates. Push the switch and pushrod assembly firmly towards the brake pedal arm. Assemble the outside white plastic washer to the pin and install the hairpin retainer to trap the whole assembly.

NOTE: Do not substitute other types of pin retainers. Replace only with production hairpin retainer.

6. Connect the wire harness connector to the switch.
7. Connect negative battery cable.
8. Check the brake light switch for proper operation. Brake lights should illuminate with less than 6 lbs. applied to the brake pedal at the pad.

NOTE: The brake light switch wire harness must have sufficient length to travel with the switch during full stroke at the pedal.

Escort and Tracer

1. Disconnect the negative battery cable.
2. Disconnect the brake light switch electrical connector.
3. Remove the brake light switch retaining nuts and remove the brake light switch.
4. Installation is the reverse of the removal procedure. Adjust the switch.

Clutch Switch

ADJUSTMENT

Tempo and Topaz

1. Remove panel above clutch pedal.
2. Disengage the wiring connector by flexing the retaining tab on the

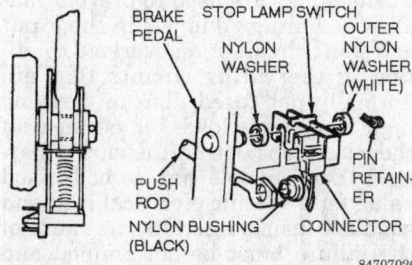

Brake light switch installation — Tempo and Topaz

switch and withdrawing the connector.
3. Using a test light, check to see that the switch is open with the clutch pedal up (engaged) and closed at approximately 1 in. (25.4mm) from the clutch pedal full down position (disengaged).
4. If the switch does not operate as outlined in Step 3, check to see if the self-adjusting clip is out of position on the rod. It should be near the end of the rod.
5. If the self-adjusting clip is out of position, remove and reposition the clip approximately 1 in. (25.4mm) from the end of the rod.
6. Reset the switch by pressing the clutch pedal to the floor. Repeat Step 3. If the switch is damaged or the clips do not remain in place, replace the switch.

Escort and Tracer

1. Disconnect the negative battery cable.
2. Disconnect the clutch engage electrical connector.
3. Using an ohmmeter, check the resistance between the connector terminals.
4. The ohmmeter should show continuity when the switch rod is pushed into the switch. The ohmmeter should show no continuity with the switch rod released.
5. Replace the switch if it does not perform as specified.

REMOVAL AND INSTALLATION

Tempo and Topaz

1. Disconnect the negative battery cable.
2. Remove panel above clutch pedal.
3. Disconnect the switch wiring connector.

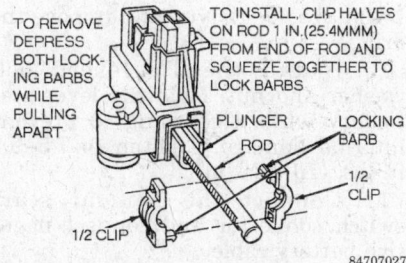

Starter/clutch interlock switch adjustment — Tempo and Topaz

4. Remove clutch interlock attaching screw and hairpin clip and remove the switch.
To install:

NOTE: Always install the switch with the self-adjusting clip about 1 in. (25.4mm) from the end of the rod. The clutch pedal must be fully up (clutch engaged). Otherwise, the switch may be misadjusted.

5. Insert the eyelet end of the rod over the clutch pedal pin and secure it with the hairpin clip.
6. Swing the switch around to align the hole in the mounting boss with the corresponding hole in the bracket. Attach with the screw.
7. Reset the clutch interlock switch by pressing the clutch pedal to the floor.
8. Connect the wiring connector.
9. Install the panel above the clutch.
10. Connect the negative battery cable.

Escort and Tracer

1. Disconnect the negative battery cable.
2. Disconnect the electrical connector.
3. Remove the 2 retaining nuts.
4. Remove the clutch engage switch.
5. Installation is the reverse of the removal procedure.

Neutral Safety Switch

ADJUSTMENT

Tempo and Topaz

The mounting location of the neutral safety switch does not provide for adjustment of the switch position when installed. If the engine will not start in **P** or **N** or if it will start in **R** or any of the **D** ranges, check the control linkage adjustment and/or replace with a known good switch.

Escort and Tracer

The neutral safety switch function is performed by the Manual Lever Position Switch (MLPS). The MLPS is an adjustable switch that informs the automatic transaxle control unit of the position of the transaxle manual shaft. The MLPS will allow the vehicle to be started with the gear selector in the **P** or **N** positions when properly adjusted. The MLPS is located externally on the transaxle

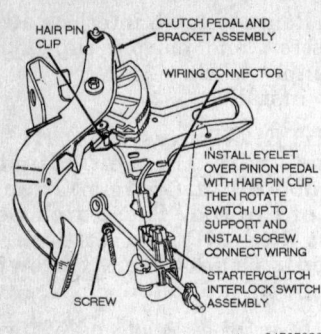

84707028

Starter/clutch interlock switch installation — Tempo and Topaz

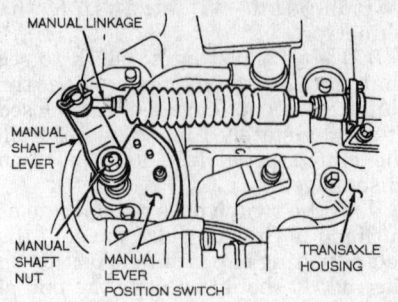

84707029

Manual lever position switch location — Escort and Tracer

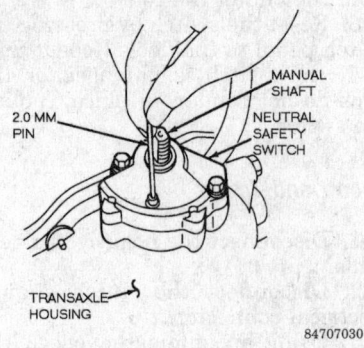

84707030

Manual lever position switch adjustment — Escort and Tracer

housing and is positioned on the manual shaft.

1. Remove the air cleaner assembly and air inlet tube.

2. Remove the nut securing the manual shaft lever to the transaxle manual shaft.

3. Remove the lever from the manual shaft.

4. Turn the manual shaft to the **N** position.

5. Loosen the MLPS mounting bolts.

6. Align the hole of the MLPS with the hole on the manual shaft lever by inserting a 0.079 in. (2.0mm) outside diameter pin.

7. Tighten the MLPS mounting bolts to 69–95 inch lbs. (8–11 Nm). Remove the pin.

8. Check the continuity of the switch as follows:

   a. Disconnect the switch connector.

   b. Using an ohmmeter, check the switch for continuity at the connector.

   c. On 1992 vehicles, there should be continuity between the **BK/BL** and **BK/R** terminals with the shift lever in the **P** or **N** position.

   d. On 1993–96 vehicles, there should be continuity between the **BK/DB** and **BK/R** terminals with the shift lever in the **P** or **N** position.

9. If there is no continuity, replace the MLPS.

10. Position the manual shaft lever to the manual shaft and install the nut. Tighten to 33–47 ft. lbs. (44–64 Nm).

11. Install the air cleaner assembly and air inlet tube.

REMOVAL AND INSTALLATION

Tempo and Topaz

1. Set the parking brake.

2. Disconnect the negative battery cable.

3. Disconnect the wire connector from the neutral safety switch.

4. Remove the nut and lock washer holding the TV lever. Hold the lever stationary while loosening to prevent internal damage.

5. Remove the 2 retaining screws from the neutral start switch and remove the switch.

To install:

6. Place the manual lever in **N**.

7. Place the switch on the manual shift shaft and loosely install the retaining bolts.

8. Use a No. 43 (0.089 in.) drill and insert it into the hole provided in the switch.

9. Tighten the retaining bolts to 7–9 ft. lbs. (9–12 Nm) and remove the drill.

10. Install the TV lever, lock washer and nut. Hold the lever stationary while tightening to prevent internal damage. Tighten to 7.5–9.5 ft. lbs. (10–13 Nm).

11. Connect the neutral start switch connector and connect negative battery cable.

12. Check the ignition switch for proper starting in **P** or **N**. Also make certain the start circuit cannot be actuated in the **D** or **R** position.

Escort and Tracer

1. Disconnect the negative battery cable.

2. Remove the air cleaner assembly and air inlet tube.

3. Remove the nut securing the manual shaft lever to the transaxle manual shaft and remove the lever.

4. Disconnect the 3 electrical connectors located on the top of the transaxle.

5. Disconnect the electrical connector located on the front side of the transaxle.

6. Remove the 2 bolts securing the MLPS and the bolts securing the electrical connector brackets to the top of the transaxle.

7. Remove the MLPS from the manual shaft.

To install:

8. Position the MLPS onto the manual shaft.

9. Install the bolts securing the electrical connectors to the transaxle housing.

10. Install the bolts securing the MLPS but do not tighten yet.

11. Connect the electrical connectors' located on the top and on the side of the transaxle.

12. Adjust the MLPS.

13. Install the air cleaner assembly and the air inlet tube.

14. Connect the negative battery cable.

Fuses, Circuit Breakers and Relays

LOCATION

Fuses

A fuse panel is located under the instrument panel to the left of the steering column. On Escort and Tracer, a fuse block is mounted in the left side of the engine compartment.

Fusible Links

Fusible links are used to prevent major wire harness damage in the event of a short circuit or an overload condition in the wiring circuits that are normally not fused, due to carrying high amperage loads of because of their locations within the wiring harness. Each fusible link is of a fixed value for a specific electrical load and should a fusible link fail, the cause of the failure must be determined and repaired prior to installing a new fusible link of the same value. Please be advised that the color coding of replacement fusible links may vary from the production color coding or replacement fusible links may vary from the production color coding that is outlined in this text.

Gray 12 Gauge Wire — On Tempo and Topaz, there is 1 link located in the charging circuit near the starter motor relay.

Dark Green 14 Gauge Wire — On Tempo and Topaz, there is 1 link for the cooling fan relay in the wiring assembly on the starter motor relay.

Black 16 Gauge Wire — On Tempo and Topaz, there is 1 link for the headlight feed located in the engine compartment on the starter relay and 1 link for the ignition feed near the starter relay.

Brown 18 Gauge Wire — On Tempo and Topaz, there is 1 link used to protect the rear window defogger and the fuel door release; there is 1 link in the charging circuit near the starter relay. On Tempo and Topaz, there is 1 link near the starter motor relay to protect the EEC module.

Dark Blue 20 Gauge Wire — On all Tempo and Topaz, there is 1 link for the air bag module located in the engine compartment near the starter relay; 1 link for the passive restraint module located in the engine compartment on the starter relay; 1 link for the heated oxygen sensor, 4WD and air conditioning fan controller located near the left shock tower and 1 link for the ignition coil, TFI module and the ECA relay located near the left shock tower. On the Tempo and Topaz, there is 1 link in the wiring assembly near the starter motor relay for the EEC power relay and fuel pump relay.

—————— **CAUTION** ——————
Always disconnect the negative battery cable before servicing the high current fuses or serious personal injury may result.
——————————————————

Fuse Link Cartridge

Fuse link cartridges are used on Escort and Tracer. Fuse link cartridges have a colored plastic housing with a clear window at the top. To check a cartridge, look at the fuse element through the clear window. The cartridges are located in the engine compartment fuse box. The following fuse link cartridges are listed according to their labels on the fuse box:

FUEL INJ — Pink 30 amp: protects the electronic engine control circuit.

HEAD — Pink 30 amp: protects the headlight circuit and the daytime running lights circuit.

MAIN — Black 80 amp for 1.8L engine or Dark Blue 100 amp for 1.9L engine: protects all circuits, except starter and starter solenoid circuits.

BTM — Yellow 60 amp for 1.8L engine or Green 40 amp for 1.9L engine: protects the courtesy lights, electronic automatic transaxle, electronic engine control, exterior lights, horn interior lights, passive restraint, power door locks, radio, shift lock and warning chime circuits.

COOLING FAN — Pink 20 amp for 1.8L engine or Green 40 amp for 1.9L engine: protects the cooling fan(s) circuit.

Circuit Breakers

Circuit breakers are used to protect the various components of the electrical system, such as headlights and windshield wipers. They are located either in the control switch or mounted on or near the fuse panel.

TEMPO AND TOPAZ

Headlight and Highbeam Indicator — a 22 amp circuit breaker incorporated in the lighting switch.

Power Windows, Power Seats, Power Door Locks and Power Lumbar — A 20 amp circuit breaker located in the fuse panel.

Windshield Wipers — a 8.25 amp circuit breaker located in the fuse panel.

ESCORT AND TRACER

Heater Blower Motor — a 30 amp circuit breaker located in the fuse panel under the dash, to the left of the steering column.

Relays

TEMPO AND TOPAZ

All Wheel Drive Relay — located behind the right side of the instrument panel.

Door Lock Control Relay — located below the left side of the instrument panel, near the fuse panel.

Cooling Fan Relay — located in the left front of the engine compartment.

Electronic Engine Control Power Relay — located behind the right side of the instrument panel.

Fuel Pump Relay — located behind the right side of the instrument panel.

Horn Relay — located behind the left side of the instrument panel, above the fuse panel.

Starter Relay — located on the left front fender apron in front of the strut tower.

Rear Window Defrost Relay — located behind the left side of the instrument panel, to the right of the steering column.

Shift Indicator Dimmer Relay — located behind the left side of the instrument panel, on the right side of the brake pedal support.

Window Safety Relay — located behind the left side of the instrument panel, above the fuse panel.

ESCORT AND TRACER

Air Conditioning Relay — located in the rear corner of the engine compartment on the firewall on.

Cooling Fan Lo and Hi Speed Relays — located on the front of the left fender apron.

Cooling Fan Relay — located on top of the left front wheel well, in the engine compartment fuse block.

Door Lock Relay — located behind the left side of the instrument panel, near the cowl.

Daytime Running Lights Relay — located behind the right side of the instrument panel, near the blower motor.

Electronic Engine Control Power Relay — located behind the center of the instrument panel.

Fuel Pump Relay — located behind the center of the instrument panel.

Headlight Relay — located behind the left side of the instrument panel, near the cowl.

Horn Relay — located behind the left side of the instrument panel, near the cowl.

Ignition Relay — located on top of the left front wheel well, in the engine compartment fuse block.

Parking Light Relay — located behind the left side of the instrument panel.

Vane Air Flow Meter Relay — located behind the center of the instrument panel.

Wide Open Throttle Cutout Relay — located in the right rear corner or the engine compartment, on the firewall.

Computers

LOCATION

The Electronic Engine Control (EEC) module is located behind the center of the instrument panel.

Turn Signal/Hazard Warning Flashers

LOCATION

Tempo and Topaz

Turn signal flasher — located on the front side of the fuse panel.
Hazard flasher — located on the rear of the fuse panel behind the turn signal flasher.

Escort and Tracer

Turn signal/Hazard flasher unit — located with the combination switch.

Cruise Control

ADJUSTMENT

Actuator Cable

1.8L AND 1.9L ENGINES

1. Remove the cable adjusting clip from the cable housing.
2. Pull tightly on the cable until all of the slack is taken out.
3. Install the cable adjusting clip.

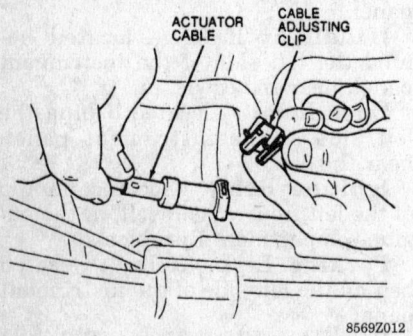

Cruise control actuator cable adjustment — 1.8L and 1.9L engines

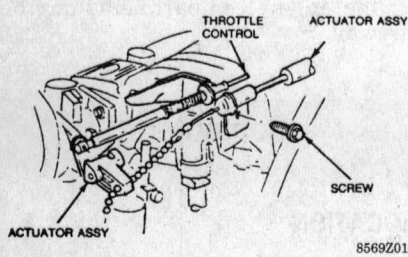

Cruise control actuator cable adjustment — 2.3L engine

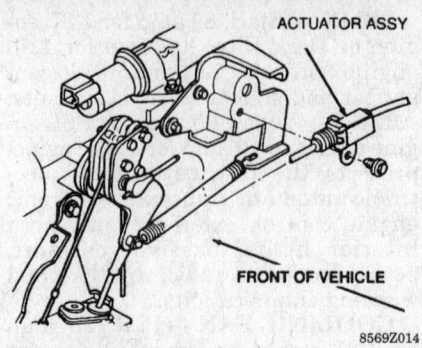

Cruise control actuator cable adjustment — 3.0L engine

2.3L ENGINE

1. With the engine **OFF**, set the throttle linkage so the throttle place is closed.
2. Remove the locking pin.
3. Pull the bead chain through the adjuster.
4. Insert the locking pin in the best hole of the adjuster to draw the bead chain tight without opening the throttle plate.

3.0L ENGINE

1. Remove the actuator cable retaining clip.
2. Pull the actuator cable through the adjuster until slight tension is felt.
3. Insert the cable retaining clip and snap into place.

Vacuum Dump Valve

1. Firmly depress the brake pedal and hold in position.
2. Push in the dump valve until the valve collar bottoms against the retaining clip.
3. Place a 0.050–0.10 in. (1.27–2.54mm) shim between the white button of the valve and the pad on the brake pedal.
4. Firmly pull the brake pedal rearward to its normal position, allowing the dump valve to ratchet backwards in the retaining clip.

Clutch Switch

ESCORT AND TRACER

1. Measure the distance from the bulkhead to the upper center of the clutch pedal pad. The distance should be 7.72–8.03 in. (196–204mm). If not, proceed to Step 2.
2. Disconnect the clutch switch electrical connector.
3. Loosen the switch locknut and turn the switch until the specified distance is achieved. Tighten the locknut to 10–13 ft. lbs. (14–18 Nm).

4. Push the clutch pedal down by hand until clutch resistance is felt.
5. Measure the distance between the upper pedal height and where resistance is felt. The free-play should be 0.20–0.51 in. (5–13mm). If not, proceed to Step 6.
6. Loosen the pushrod locknut and turn the pushrod until the specified free-play is achieved.
7. Check that disengagement height is correct when the pedal is fully depressed. Minimum disengagement height is 1.6 in. (41mm).
8. Tighten the pushrod locknut to 9–12 ft. lbs. (12–17mm) and connect the clutch switch electrical connector.

ENGINE COOLING

Radiator

REMOVAL AND INSTALLATION

Tempo and Topaz

1. Disconnect the negative battery cable. Remove the radiator cap.

— **CAUTION** —
Never remove the radiator cap while the engine is running or personal injury from scalding hot coolant or steam may result. If possible, wait until the engine has cooled to remove the radiator cap. If this is not possible, wrap a thick cloth around the radiator cap and turn it slowly to the first stop. Step back while the pressure is released from the cooling system. When it is certain all the pressure has been released, press down on the cap, still with the cloth, and turn and remove it.

2. Position a suitable container under the radiator and open the draincock to drain the radiator.
3. Remove the upper hose from the radiator.
4. Remove the 2 fasteners retaining the upper end of the fan shroud to the radiator.

NOTE: If equipped with air conditioning, remove the nut and screw retaining the upper end of the fan shroud to the radiator at the cross support and nut and screw at the inlet end of the tank. Properly discharge the air conditioning system.

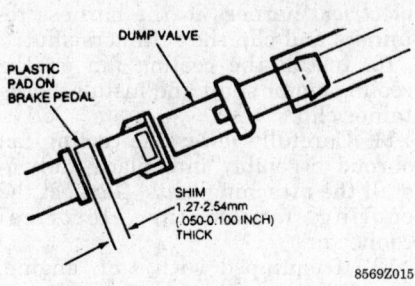

Vacuum dump valve adjustment

DUMP VALVE

PLASTIC PAD ON BRAKE PEDAL

SHIM 1.27-2.54mm (.050-0.100 INCH) THICK

8569Z015

5. Disconnect the electric cooling fan motor wires and air conditioning discharge line, if equipped, from the shroud and remove the fan shroud from the vehicle.

6. Loosen the hose clamp and disconnect the radiator lower hose from the radiator.

7. Disconnect the overflow hose from the radiator filler neck.

8. If equipped with an automatic transaxle, disconnect the oil cooler hoses at the transaxle using quick-disconnect tool T82L–9500–AH or equivalent. Cap the oil tubes and plug the oil cooler hoses.

9. Remove the 2 nuts retaining the top of the radiator to the radiator support. If the stud loosens, make sure it is tightened before the radiator is installed. Tilt the top of the radiator rearward to allow clearance with the upper mounting stud and lift the radiator from the vehicle. Make sure the mounts do not stick to the radiator lower mounting brackets.

To install:

10. Make sure the lower radiator isomounts are installed over the bolts on the radiator support.

11. Position the radiator to the radiator support making sure the radiator lower brackets are positioned properly on the lower mounts.

12. Position the top of the radiator to the mounting studs on the radiator support and install 2 retaining nuts. Tighten to 5–7 ft. lbs. (7–9.5 Nm).

13. Connect the radiator lower hose to the engine water pump inlet tube. Install the hose clamp between alignment marks on the hose.

14. Check to make sure the radiator lower hose is properly positioned on the outlet tank and install the hose clamp. The stripe on the lower hose should be indexed with the rib on the tank outlet.

15. Connect the oil cooler hoses to the automatic transaxle oil cooler lines, if equipped. Use an appropriate oil resistant sealer.

16. Position the fan shroud to the radiator lower mounting bosses. nstall 2 screws or nuts and bolts retaining the upper end of the fan shroud to the radiator. Tighten the fasteners on Tempo and Topaz to 35–41 inch lbs. (3.9–4.6 Nm).

17. Connect the electric cooling fan motor wires to the wire harness.

18. Connect the upper hose to the radiator inlet tank fitting and install the hose clamp.

19. Connect the overflow hose to the nipple just below the radiator filler neck.

20. Install the air intake tube, if necessary.

21. Connect the negative battery cable.

22. Refill the cooling system and recharge the air conditioning system, if equipped. Start the engine and allow to come to normal operating temperature. Check for leaks. Confirm the operation of the electric cooling fan.

Escort and Tracer

1. Disconnect the negative battery cable. Remove the radiator cap.

---------- **CAUTION** ----------
Never remove the radiator cap while the engine is running or personal injury from scalding hot coolant or steam may result. If possible, wait until the engine has cooled to remove the radiator cap. If this is not possible, wrap a thick cloth around the radiator cap and turn it slowly to the first stop. Step back while the pressure is released from the cooling system. When it is certain all the pressure has been released, press down on the cap, still with the cloth, and turn and remove it.

---

2. Position a suitable container under the radiator and open the draincock to drain the radiator.

3. Raise and safely support the vehicle.

4. Remove the right side and front splash shields and remove the lower radiator hose.

5. If equipped with automatic transaxle, remove the lower oil cooler line from the radiator. Remove the oil cooler line brackets from the bottom of the radiator.

6. Lower the vehicle.

7. If equipped with automatic transaxle and air conditioning, remove the seal located between the radiator and fan shroud.

8. If equipped with automatic transaxle, remove the upper oil cooler line from the radiator.

9. If equipped with 1.8L engine, remove the resonance duct from the radiator isomounts.

10. Disconnect the cooling fan motor electrical connector and the cooling fan thermoswitch electrical connector.

11. Remove the 3 fan shroud attaching bolts and remove the shroud assembly by pulling it straight up.

12. Remove the upper radiator hose and the 2 upper radiator isomounts. Remove the radiator by lifting it straight up.

To install:

13. Make sure the radiator lower isomounts are installed over the bolts on the radiator support.

14. Position the radiator to the radiator support, making sure the radiator lower brackets are positioned properly on the lower isomounts.

15. Install the radiator upper isomounts, making sure the radiator locating pegs are positioned correctly. Install the upper radiator hose.

16. Lower the cooling fan shroud assembly into place and install the 3 shroud attaching bolts.

17. Connect the cooling fan motor electrical connector and thermoswitch electrical connector.

18. If equipped with 1.8L engine, install the resonance duct on the radiator isomounts.

19. Install the upper oil cooler line on the radiator.

20. If equipped with automatic transaxle and air conditioning, install the seal between the radiator and fan shroud.

21. Raise and safely support the vehicle. If equipped with automatic transaxle, install the lower oil cooler line on the radiator.

22. Install the lower radiator hose and install the right side and front splash shields.

23. Lower the vehicle and fill the cooling system.

24. Connect the negative battery cable. Start the engine and allow to come to normal operating temperature. Check for coolant leaks. Check the coolant level and add coolant as necessary.

Electric Cooling Fan

TESTING

Tempo and Topaz

1. Check the fuse or circuit breaker for power to the cooling fan motor.
2. Remove the connector(s) at the cooling fan motor(s). Connect a jumper wire and apply battery voltage to the positive terminal of the cooling fan motor.
3. Using an ohmmeter, check for continuity in the cooling fan motor.

NOTE: Remove the cooling fan connector at the fan motor before performing continuity checks. Perform continuity check of the motor windings only. The cooling fan control circuit is connected electrically to the PCM through the cooling fan relay center. Ohmmeter battery voltage must not be applied to the PCM.

4. Ensure proper continuity of the cooling fan motor ground circuit at the chassis ground connector.

Escort and Tracer

1. Make sure the ignition key is **OFF**.
2. Apply 12 volts to the **Y** wire at the cooling fan motor on all except 1.8L engine vehicles equipped with 4EAT automatic transaxle or 1.9L engine vehicles equipped with air conditioning. Replace the motor if it does not run.
3. On 1.8L engine vehicles equipped with 4EAT automatic transaxle or 1.9L engine vehicles equipped with air conditioning, apply 12 volts to the **BL** wire on the 1.8L engine or the **LG/Y** wire on the 1.9L engine at the cooling fan motor. Replace the motor if it does not run.

REMOVAL AND INSTALLATION

Tempo and Topaz

NOTE: On 1992–95, the cooling fan motors for the 2.3L and 3.0L engines are similar in design, but cannot be interchanged. If the incorrect fan motor is installed, the vehicle may overheat or the fan motor may burnout.

1. Disconnect the negative battery cable.
2. Disconnect the wiring connector from the fan motor. Disconnect the wire loom from the clip on the shroud by pushing down on the lock fingers and pulling the connector from the motor end.
3. Remove the fasteners retaining the fan motor and shroud assembly and remove from the vehicle.
4. Remove the fan motor retaining screws.
5. Remove the retaining clip from the motor shaft and remove the fan.

NOTE: A metal burr may be present on the motor shaft after the retaining clip has been removed. If necessary, remove burr to facilitate fan removal.

6. Unbolt and withdraw the fan motor from the shroud.

To install:

7. Install the fan motor in position in the fan shroud. Install the retaining nuts and washers or screws and tighten to 44–66 inch lbs. (5.0–7.5 Nm).
8. Position the fan assembly on the motor shaft and install the retaining clip.
9. Position the fan, motor and shroud as an assembly in the vehicle. Install the retaining nuts or screws and tighten nut to 35–41 inch lbs. (3.9–4.6 Nm) and screw to 31–41 inch lbs. (3.5–4.6 Nm).
10. Install the fan motor wire loom in the clip provided on the fan shroud. Connect the wiring connector to the fan motor. Be sure the lock fingers on the connector snap firmly into place.
11. Reconnect the battery cable.
12. Check the fan for proper operation.

Escort and Tracer

1. Disconnect the negative battery cable.
2. On 1.8L engine equipped vehicles, remove the resonance duct from the radiator isomounts.
3. Disconnect the cooling fan motor electrical connector.
4. Remove the 3 shroud attaching bolts and remove the cooling fan shroud assembly by pulling it straight up.
5. Working on a bench, remove the cooling fan retainer clip. Remove the cooling fan from the motor shaft.
6. Unclip the cooling fan motor electrical harness retainers and remove the harness from the retainers.
7. Remove the cooling fan motor attaching screws and remove the cooling fan motor from the shroud assembly.

To install:

8. Position the cooling fan motor on the shroud assembly and install the attaching screws.
9. Position the cooling fan motor electrical harness in the harness retainers and clip the retainers shut.
10. Install the cooling fan on the cooling motor shaft and install the retainer clip.
11. Carefully lower the cooling fan shroud assembly into place and install the attaching bolts. Connect the cooling fan motor electrical connector.
12. If equipped with 1.8L engine, install the resonance duct on the radiator isomounts.
13. Connect the negative battery cable.

Heater Core

REMOVAL AND INSTALLATION

Tempo and Topaz

1. Disconnect the negative battery cable.
2. Drain the cooling system.
3. Disconnect the heater hoses from the heater core.
4. From inside the vehicle, remove the 2 screws retaining floor duct to plenum. Remove screw retaining floor duct to instrument panel. Remove the floor duct.
5. Remove the 4 screws attaching the heater core cover to the heater case assembly.
6. Remove the heater core and cover from the plenum.
7. Installation is the reverse of the removal procedures. Check the system for proper operation.

Escort and Tracer

1. Disconnect the negative battery cable and drain the cooling system.
2. Disconnect the heater hoses at the bulkhead.
3. Disconnect the instrument panel as follows:
    a. Remove the 4 bolts securing the steering column to the instrument panel frame. Lower the steering column.
    b. Disconnect the speedometer cable from the instrument panel.
    c. Remove the cap screws securing the instrument cluster bezel to the instrument panel and remove the instrument cluster bezel.
    d. Remove the screws and bolts securing the instrument cluster to the instrument panel. Pull the instrument cluster out slightly and disconnect the electrical connectors from the rear of the instrument cluster.

e. Remove the instrument cluster fro the instrument panel.

f. Detach the hood release cable from the left lower dash trim panel. Carefully pry out both dash side panels.

g. Remove the 4 retaining screws and the left lower dash trim panel. Disconnect all necessary electrical connectors.

h. Remove the 2 hinge-to-instrument panel retaining screws and remove the glove compartment.

i. Remove the climate control assembly and ashtray.

j. Remove the 7 accessory console retaining screws. Disconnect the radio antenna, radio wire and cigarette lighter connectors.

k. Remove the retaining screws and the right lower dash trim panel. Disconnect the 3 amplifier wire connectors.

l. Remove the 4 bolts attaching the instrument panel frame to floor pan. Remove the bolts from both of the lower instrument panel mounts.

m. Remove the 2 bolts from both of the upper instrument panel mounts. Remove the retaining screw and the defroster duct bezel.

n. Remove the 3 mounting bolts that attach the upper instrument panel to the cowl.

o. Pull the instrument panel slightly away from its mounting position and make sure all electrical connectors are disconnected.

p. Remove the instrument panel from the vehicle.

NOTE: Use care to prevent any damage to the instrument panel or the surrounding interior trim.

4. Disconnect the mode selector and temperature control cables from the cams and retaining clips.
5. Remove the necessary defroster duct screws and loosen the capscrew that secures the heater-to-blower clamp.
6. Remove the 3 heater unit mounting nuts and disconnect the antenna lead from the retaining clip. Remove the heater unit.
7. Remove the insulator and the 4 brace capscrews. Remove the brace.
8. Remove the heater core from the heater unit.
To install:
9. Install the heater core into the heater unit and install the brace.

10. Install the brace capscrews and the insulator.

NOTE: If a new heater unit is being installed, save the keys that are found on the new unit for mode selector and temperature control cable adjustment.

11. Position the heater unit and attach the defroster and floor ducting. Install the heater unit mounting nuts.
12. Tighten the heater-to-blower clamp capscrew and install the defroster duct screws. Connect the antenna lead to the retaining clip.
13. Install the instrument panel by reversing the removal procedure.
14. Connect the mode selector cable and adjust as follows:
a. Move the mode selector lever to the **DEFROST** position on the climate control assembly.
b. Insert cable locating key PN E7GH-18C408-A or equivalent, through the mode cam key slot and heater case key boss opening to secure the cam in the proper position.
c. Remove the trim panel below the glove compartment, if equipped.
d. Disconnect the cable from the retaining clip next to the mode selector cam. The mode selector cam is located on the right side of the heater unit.
e. Move the mode selector lever to the **DEFROST** position.
f. Connect the cable straight to the retaining clip. Do not exert any force on the cam during cable installation.
g. Remove the cable locating key. Install the trim panel, if equipped.
h. Make sure the mode selector lever moves its full stroke. If after performing the adjustment, air bleeds through the panel vents when in the **FLOOR, MIX** or **DEFROST** position, lengthen the adjustment rod 1–2 turns.
15. Connect the temperature control cable and adjust as follows:
a. Move the temperature control lever to the **COLD** position on the climate control assembly.
b. To secure the cam in the proper position, insert cable locating key PN E7GH-18G408-A or equivalent, through the cam key slot to the heater case key boss opening.
c. Disconnect the cable from the retaining clip next to the temperature control cam. The temperature control cam is located on the left side of the heater unit.

d. Connect the cable to the retaining clip.
e. Remove the cable locating key.
f. Make sure the temperature control lever moves its full stroke.
16. Connect the heater hoses at the bulkhead.
17. Fill the cooling system and connect the negative battery cable. Start the engine and check for leaks. Check the coolant level and fill as necessary.

Water Pump

REMOVAL AND INSTALLATION

1.8L Engine

1. Disconnect the negative battery cable.
2. Drain the cooling system.
3. Remove the timing belt.
4. Raise and safely support the vehicle.
5. Remove the engine oil dipstick tube bracket bolt from the water pump.
6. Remove the 2 bolts and the gasket from the water inlet pipe.
7. Remove all but the uppermost water pump mounting bolt.
8. Lower the vehicle.
9. Remove the remaining bolt and the water pump assembly.
10. If it is being reused, remove all gasket material from the water pump. Remove all gasket material from the engine block.
To install:
11. Install a new gasket onto the water pump.
12. Place the water pump into its mounting position, then install the uppermost bolt.
13. Raise and safely support the vehicle.
14. Install the remaining water pump mounting bolts and tighten all bolts to 14–19 ft. lbs. (19–25 Nm).
15. Install a new gasket onto the water inlet pipe.
16. Install the 2 bolts from the water inlet pipe to the water pump and tighten to 14–19 ft. lbs. (19–25 Nm).
17. Install the bolt to the engine oil dipstick tube bracket.
18. Lower the vehicle.
19. Install the timing belt.
20. Fill the cooling system.
21. Connect the negative battery cable.
22. Start the engine and allow to come to operating temperature. Check for coolant leaks. Check the coolant level and add coolant, as necessary.

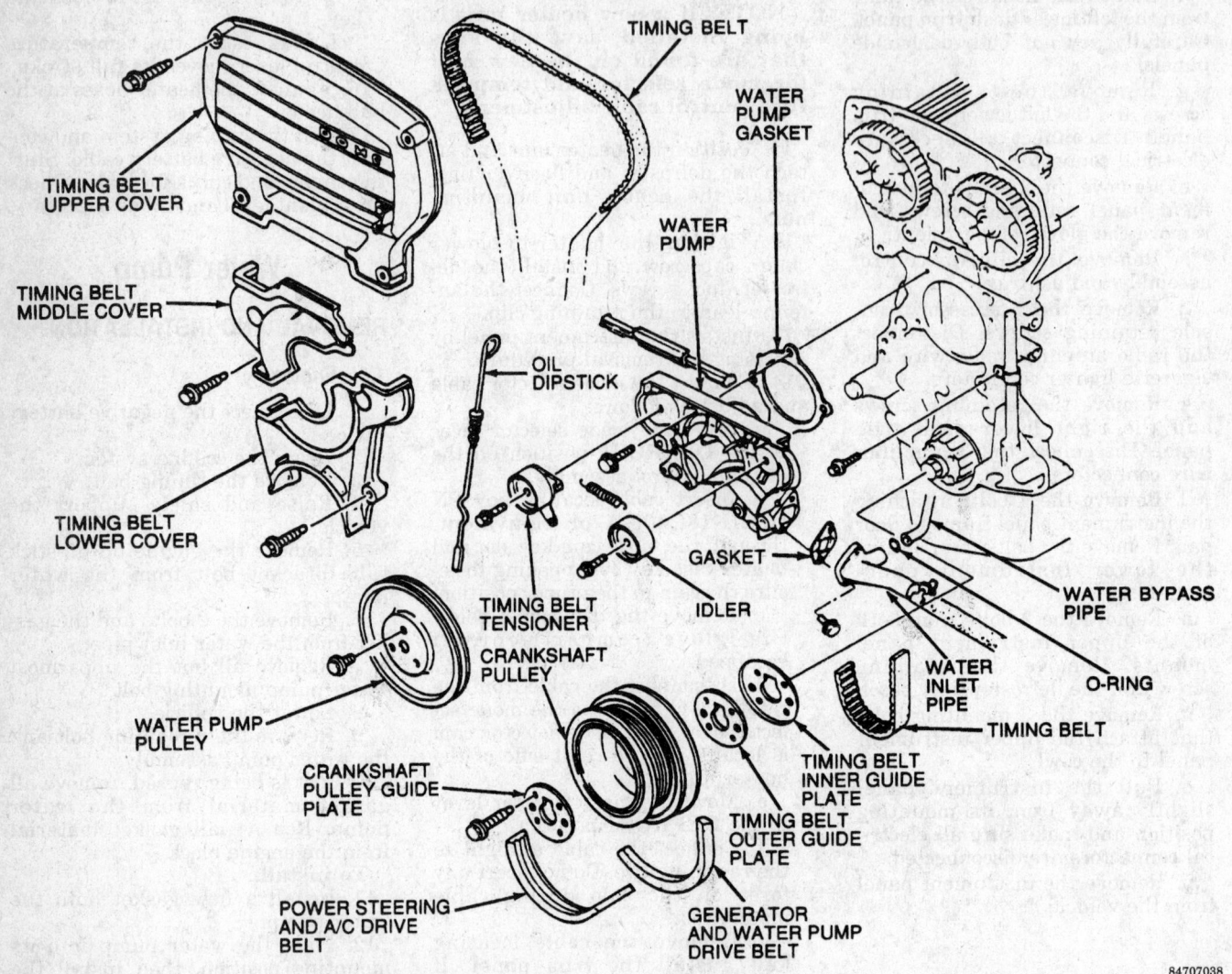

TIMING BELT

WATER PUMP GASKET

WATER PUMP

TIMING BELT UPPER COVER

TIMING BELT MIDDLE COVER

OIL DIPSTICK

TIMING BELT LOWER COVER

WATER BYPASS PIPE

GASKET

O-RING

IDLER

TIMING BELT TENSIONER

WATER INLET PIPE

TIMING BELT

WATER PUMP PULLEY

CRANKSHAFT PULLEY

CRANKSHAFT PULLEY GUIDE PLATE

TIMING BELT INNER GUIDE PLATE

TIMING BELT OUTER GUIDE PLATE

POWER STEERING AND A/C DRIVE BELT

GENERATOR AND WATER PUMP DRIVE BELT

84707038

Water pump installation — 1.8L engine

1.9L Engine

ESCORT AND TRACER

1. Disconnect the negative battery cable.
2. Drain the cooling system.
3. Remove the accessory drive belt and its automatic tensioner.
4. Remove the timing belt cover and the timing belt.
5. Raise and safely support the vehicle.
6. Remove the lower radiator hose and remove the heater hose from the water pump.
7. Lower the vehicle.
8. Support the engine with a suitable floor jack.

9. Remove the right engine mount attaching bolts and roll the engine mount aside.
10. Remove the 4 water pump attaching bolts.
11. Using the floor jack, raise the engine enough to provide clearance for removing the water pump.
12. Remove the water pump and the gasket from the engine through the top of the engine compartment.

To install:

13. Make sure the mating surfaces of the cylinder block and water pump are clean and free of gasket material.
14. If the water pump is to be replaced, transfer the timing belt ten-

sioner components to the new water pump.
15. With the engine supported and raised with a suitable floor jack, place the water pump and the gasket on the cylinder block and install the 4 attaching bolts. Tighten the bolts to 15–22 ft. lbs. (20–30 Nm).
16. Install the timing belt and cover.
17. Roll the right engine mount into position and install the mount bolts. Remove the floor jack.
18. Raise and safely support the vehicle.
19. Install the lower radiator hose and install the heater hose on the pump.

20. Install the crankshaft dampener and the splash shield.

21. Lower the vehicle.

22. Install the accessory drive belt automatic tensioner and the accessory drive belt.

23. Connect the negative battery cable.

24. Refill the cooling system.

25. Start the engine and allow to come to normal operating temperature. Check for coolant leaks. Check the coolant level and add as necessary.

2.3L Engine

1. Drain the cooling system.

2. Disconnect the negative battery cable.

3. Loosen the water pump idler pulley and remove the belt from the water pump pulley.

4. Disconnect the heater hose at the water pump inlet tube.

5. Remove A/C hose bracket from cylinder block, if equipped.

6. Disconnect the water pump inlet tube.

7. Remove the 3 water pump retaining bolts and remove the water pump from its mounting.

To install:

8. Thoroughly clean both gasket mating surfaces on the water pump and cylinder block.

9. Coat the new gasket on both sides with a water resistant sealer and position on the cylinder block.

10. Install the water pump retaining bolts and tighten to 15–22 ft. lbs. (20–30 Nm).

11. Connect the water pump inlet tube.

12. Attach A/C hose bracket to cylinder block, if equipped.

13. Connect the heater hose.

14. Install water pump belt on the pulley and adjust the tension.

15. Connect the negative battery cable.

16. Fill the cooling system. Operate the engine until normal operating temperature is reached. Check for leaks and recheck the coolant level.

3.0L Engine

1. Disconnect the negative battery cable.

2. Drain the cooling system.

3. Remove the water pump drive belt as follows:

a. Mark the direction of rotation on the accessory drive belt so it can be reinstalled in the same direction.

b. Remove the plastic belt shield from the power steering pump.

c. Using a ½ in. drive breaker bar or equivalent, inserted in the idler pulley tensioner, release the tension on the accessory drive belt and remove the belt.

d. Raise and safely support the vehicle.

e. Mark the direction of rotation on the water pump drive belt so it can be reinstalled in the same direction.

f. Use a suitable wrench to turn the water pump belt idler pulley tensioner clockwise and release the tension on the belt. Remove the water pump drive belt.

4. Lower the vehicle and remove the water pump to front cover hose.

5. Raise and safely support the vehicle.

6. Loosen and remove the retaining nut from the upper bracket and the bolt from the lower bracket. Gently grasp the tube at the water end and pull the tube out of the water pump. Remove the lower water pump tube.

7. Lower the vehicle.

8. Remove the heater hose from the rear of the water pump and remove the water pump pulley shield.

9. Remove the water pump from the bracket.

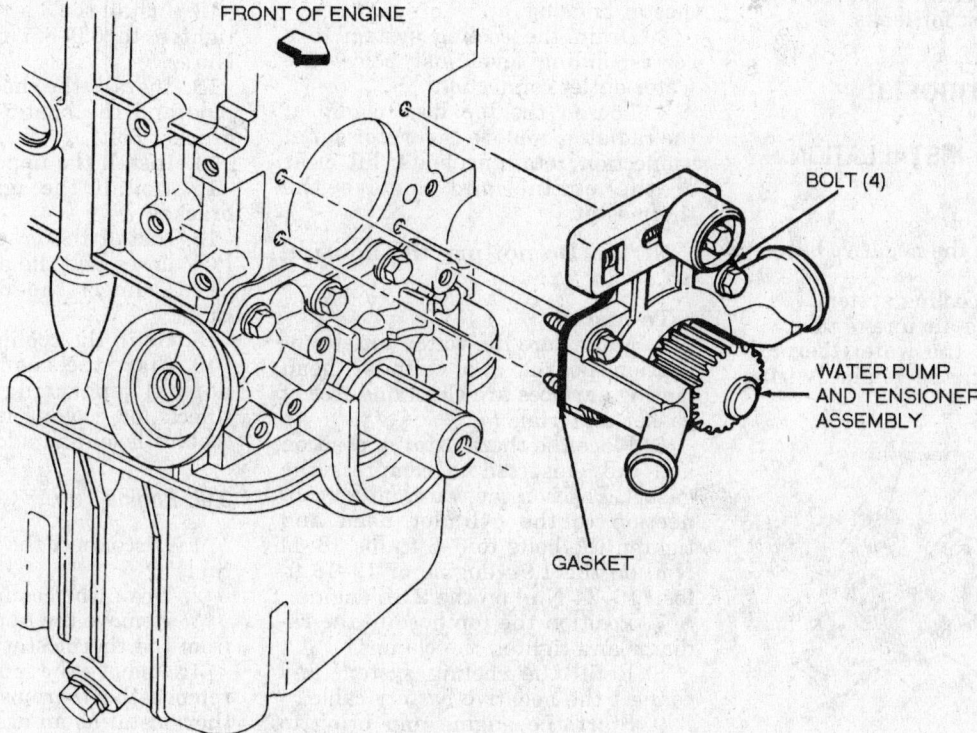

FRONT OF ENGINE

BOLT (4)

WATER PUMP AND TENSIONER ASSEMBLY

GASKET

84707152

Water pump installation — 1.9L engine, Escort and Tracer

To install:

10. If replacing the water pump, transfer the pulley to the new pump.

11. Align the water pump to the bracket and install the mounting bolts. Tighten to 15–22 ft. lbs. (20–30 Nm).

12. Raise and safely support the vehicle.

13. Install the lower water pump tube. Lubricate the water pump end of the tube with compound ESE–M99B144–A or equivalent, before inserting into the water pump.

14. Install the retaining nut to the upper bracket stud bolt and tighten to 5 ft. lbs. (7 Nm). Install the lower tube bracket retaining bolt and tighten to 71–106 inch lbs. (8–12 Nm).

15. Lower the vehicle.

16. Install the water pump pulley shield and tighten the retaining nut to 7–10 ft. lbs. (9–14 Nm).

17. Install the heater hose to the rear of the pump. Make sure the hose is clamped securely.

18. Install the water pump to front cover hose. Tighten the clamps to 19–37 inch lbs. (2.1–4.1 Nm).

19. Install the water pump and accessory drive belts.

20. Fill and bleed the cooling system.

21. Connect the negative battery cable. Start and operate the engine until normal operating temperature is reached. Check for leaks.

Thermostat

REMOVAL AND INSTALLATION

1.8L Engine

1. Disconnect the negative battery cable.
2. Drain the cooling system.
3. Remove the air intake tube.
4. Disconnect the water thermoswitch connector, the engine wiring

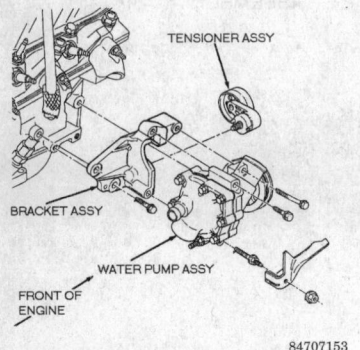

84707153

Water pump installation — 3.0L engine

harness ground strap from the connector above the housing and the exhaust gas oxygen sensor electrical connector.

5. Remove the upper radiator hose from the housing.

6. Remove the thermostat housing attaching bolt and nut and remove the housing. Remove the gasket and the thermostat.

To install:

7. Clean the thermostat housing and cylinder head gasket surfaces.

8. Position the thermostat, gasket and housing on the cylinder head.

9. Install the attaching bolt and nut and tighten to 14–19 ft. lbs. (19–26 Nm).

10. Install the upper radiator hose.

11. Connect the oxygen sensor electrical connector, the engine wiring harness ground strap and the thermoswitch electrical connector.

12. Install the air intake tube.

13. Connect the negative battery cable.

14. Start the engine and bring to normal operating temperature. Check for coolant leaks. Check the coolant level and add as necessary.

2.3L Engine

1. Disconnect the negative battery cable.
2. Disconnect the wiring connector from the thermal switch in the thermostat housing.
3. Drain the cooling system to a corresponding level just below the water outlet connection.
4. Loosen the top hose clamp at the radiator, remove the water outlet connection retaining bolts, lift clear of the engine and remove the thermostat.

NOTE: Do not pry the housing off.

To install:

5. Make sure the water outlet connection pocket and cylinder head mating surfaces are clean and free of gasket material.

6. Place the thermostat in position and fully inserted to compress the gasket. Position the water outlet connection to the cylinder head and tighten the bolts to 6–8 ft. lbs. (8–11 Nm) on the 1.9L engine or 12–18 ft. lbs. (16–24 Nm) on the 2.3L engine.

7. Position the top hose to the radiator and tighten the clamps.

8. Refill the cooling system and connect the negative battery cable.

9. Start the engine and bring to normal operating temperature. Check for coolant leaks. Check the coolant level and add as necessary.

1.9L Engine

1. Disconnect the negative battery cable.
2. Drain the cooling system.
3. Remove the air intake tube, crankcase breather and PCV hose.
4. Remove the ignition coil pack and bracket.
5. Remove the upper radiator hose.
6. Remove the heater hose inlet tube bracket bolt and remove the heater hose inlet tube from the thermostat housing.
7. Remove the 3 thermostat housing attaching bolts and remove the thermostat housing and gasket.

NOTE: Do not pry off the housing.

8. Remove the thermostat and the rubber seal from the housing.

To install:

9. Clean the thermostat housing pocket and cylinder head mating surfaces.

10. Place the thermostat into position and fully inserted to compress the rubber seal inside the housing.

NOTE: Make sure the thermostat tabs engage properly into the housing slots.

11. Position the thermostat housing and gasket on the cylinder head.

12. Install the 3 attaching bolts and tighten to 6.0–8.5 ft. lbs. (8.0–11.5 Nm).

13. Install the heater hose inlet pipe and the heater hose inlet pipe bracket bolt.

14. Install the upper radiator hose.

15. Install the ignition coil and bracket.

16. Install the crankcase breather, PCV hoses and the air intake tube.

17. Connect the negative battery cable.

18. Refill the cooling system.

19. Start the engine and bring to normal operating temperature. Check for coolant leaks. Check the coolant level and add as necessary.

3.0L Engine

1. Disconnect the negative battery cable.
2. Drain the cooling system.
3. Remove the upper radiator hose from the thermostat housing.
4. Remove the mounting bolts and remove the thermostat housing and thermostat as an assembly.
5. Clean the gasket mating surfaces, being careful not to gouge the metal.

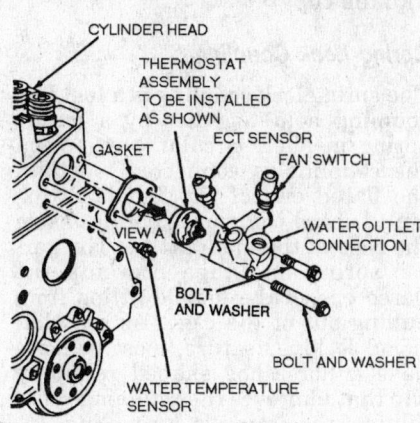

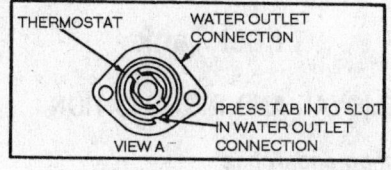

Thermostat installation — 2.3L engine

To install:
6. Install the thermostat into the housing, making sure the jiggle valve is facing up.
7. Install a new gasket onto the thermostat housing. Install the housing and tighten the bolts to 9 ft. lbs. (12 Nm).
8. Install the upper radiator hose and tighten the clamp to 20–30 inch lbs. (2.3–3.4 Nm).
9. Fill and bleed the cooling system.
10. Connect the negative battery cable. Start the engine and bring to normal operating temperature. Check for leaks.

Cooling System Bleeding

When the entire cooling system is drained, the following procedure should be used to ensure a complete fill.
1. Install the block drain plug, if removed, and close the draincock. With the engine off, add a 50/50 mixture of anti-freeze and water to the radiator until it reaches the radiator filler neck seat. Wait several minutes, as the coolant level in the radiator drops, and continue to add the

50/50 mixture until the radiator remains full.

NOTE: 1.9L engines have a float/seat de-gas system in the water outlet connection that improves coolant fill when the thermostat is closed.

2. Install the radiator cap to the first notch to keep spillage to a minimum.
3. Start the engine and let it idle until the upper radiator hose is warm. This indicates that the thermostat is open and coolant is flowing through the entire system.
4. Carefully remove the radiator cap and top off the radiator with the 50/50 mixture. Install the cap on the radiator securely.
5. Fill the coolant recovery reservoir to the FULL HOT mark with the 50/50 mixture. This will ensure that a proper mixture is in the coolant recovery bottle.
6. Check for leaks at the draincock and the block drain plug.

FUEL SYSTEM

Fuel System Service Precautions

Safety is the most important factor when performing not only fuel system maintenance but any type of maintenance. Failure to conduct maintenance and repairs in a safe manner may result in serious personal injury or death. Maintenance and testing of the vehicle's fuel system components can be accomplished safely and effectively by adhering to the following rules and guidelines.
• To avoid the possibility of fire and personal injury, always disconnect the negative battery cable unless the repair or test procedure requires that battery voltage be applied.
• Always relieve the fuel system pressure prior to disconnecting any fuel system component (injector, fuel rail, pressure regulator, etc.), fitting or fuel line connection. Exercise extreme caution whenever relieving fuel system pressure to avoid exposing skin, face and eyes to fuel spray. Please be advised that fuel under pressure may penetrate the skin or any part of the body that it contacts.
• Always place a shop towel or cloth around the fitting or connection

prior to loosening to absorb any excess fuel due to spillage. Ensure that all fuel spillage (should it occur) is quickly removed from engine surfaces. Ensure that all fuel soaked cloths or towels are deposited into a suitable waste container.
• Always keep a dry chemical (Class B) fire extinguisher near the work area.
• Do not allow fuel spray or fuel vapors to come into contact with a spark or open flame.
• Always use a backup wrench when loosing and tightening fuel line connection fittings. This will prevent unnecessary stress and torsion to fuel line piping. Always follow the proper torque specifications.
• Always replace worn fuel fitting O-rings with new. Do not substitute fuel hose or equivalent, where fuel pipe is installed.

RELIEVING FUEL SYSTEM PRESSURE

The pressure in the fuel system must be released before disconnecting any fuel lines or components.

Except Escort and Tracer
1. Disconnect the negative battery cable.
2. A special valve is incorporated in the fuel rail assembly for the purpose of relieving the pressure in the fuel system.
3. Remove the fuel tank cap and remove the cap from the pressure relief valve.
4. Attach pressure gauge tool T80L–9974–B or equivalent, to the fuel pressure valve on the fuel rail assembly and release the pressure from the system into a suitable container.

Escort and Tracer
1. Start the engine.
2. Remove the rear seat cushion and disconnect the fuel pump electrical connectors.
3. Wait for the engine to stall, then turn **OFF** the ignition switch.
4. Connect the fuel pump electrical connectors and install the rear seat cushion.

Fuel Line Couplings

REMOVAL AND INSTALLATION

There are several methods used to connect the fuel lines and fuel system components. The hairpin clip push

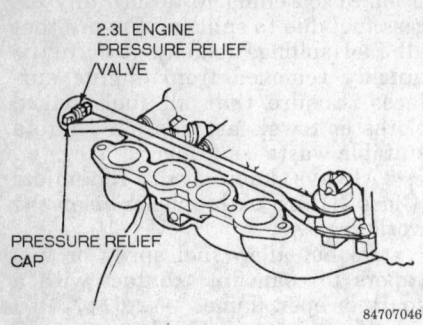

Pressure relief valve location — 2.3L engine

connect fitting, the duck bill clip push connect fitting and the spring lock coupling each require a different procedure to disconnect and connect.

Hairpin Clip Fitting

1. Inspect the internal portion of the fitting for dirt accumulation. If more than a light coating of dust is present, clean the fitting before disassembly.

2. Remove the hairpin clip from the fitting by first bending the shipping tab downward so it will clear the body. This is done, using hands only, by spreading the 2 clip legs about ⅛ in. (3.2mm) each to disengage the body and pushing the legs into the fitting. Complete removal is accomplished by lightly pulling from the triangular end of the clip and working it clear of the tube and fitting.

NOTE: Do not use any tools when disconnecting the clip.

3. Grasp the fitting and hose assembly and pull in an axial direction to remove the fitting from the steel tube. Adhesion between sealing surfaces may occur. A slight twist of the fitting may be required to break this adhesion for easier removal.

NOTE: On 90 degree elbow connectors, excessive side loading could break the connector body.

4. When the fitting is removed from the tube end, inspect the clip to make sure it has not been damaged. If damaged, replace the clip. If undamaged, immediately install the clip to prevent loss or damage. To install the clip, insert the clip into any 2 adjacent openings with the triangular portion pointing away from the fitting opening. Install the clip to fully engage the body (legs of the hairpin clip locked on the outside of the body). Piloting with an index finger is necessary.

To install:

5. Before installing the fitting on the tube, wipe the tube end with a clean cloth. Inspect the inside of the fitting to make sure it is free of dirt and/or obstructions. Apply a light coat of engine oil to the tube end for ease of assembly.

6. To install the fitting onto the tube, align the fitting and tube axial and push the fitting onto the tube end. When the fitting is engaged, a definite click will be heard. Pull on the fitting to make sure it is fully engaged.

Duck Bill Clip Fitting

1. To disengage the tube from the fitting, align the slot on the quick connect/disconnect tool T82L–9500–AH or equivalent, with either tab on the clip, 90 degrees from the slots on the side of the fitting, and insert the tool.

2. This disengages the duck bill from the tube. Holding the tool and the tube with 1 hand, pull the fitting away from the tube.

NOTE: Only moderate effort is required if the tube has been properly disengaged. Use hands only.

3. After disassembly, inspect and clean the tube sealing surface. Also inspect the inside of the fitting for damage to the retaining clip. If the retaining clip appears to be damaged, replace it.

NOTE: Some fuel tubes have a secondary bead which aligns with the outer surface of the clip. These beads can make tool insertion difficult. If there is extreme difficulty, it may be necessary to replace the fuel line.

To install:

4. Install the clip into the body by inserting 1 of the retaining clip serrated edges on the duck bill portion into 1 of the window openings. Push

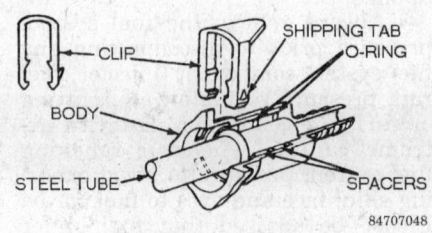

Hairpin clip push connect fitting

on the other side until the clip snaps into place. Slide the fuel line back into the clip.

Spring Lock Coupling

The spring lock coupling is a fuel line coupling held together by a garter spring inside a circular cage. When the coupling is connected together, the flared end of the female fitting slips behind the garter spring inside the cage of the male fitting. The garter spring and cage prevents the flared end of the female fitting from pulling out of the cage. As an additional locking feature, most vehicles have a horseshoe shaped retaining clip that improves the retaining reliability of the spring lock coupling.

Fuel Tank

REMOVAL AND INSTALLATION

Tempo and Topaz

1. Disconnect the negative battery cable.

2. Properly relieve the fuel system pressure.

3. Fuel should be drained from the tank as completely as possible prior to tank removal. This is accomplished by siphoning or pumping fuel out through the fuel filler neck.

NOTE: There are reservoirs inside the fuel tank to maintain fuel near the fuel pickup during vehicle cornering maneuvers and under low fuel operating conditions. These reservoirs could block siphon tubes or hoses from reaching the bottom of the fuel tank. This situation can be overcome with a few repeated attempts using different hose orientations.

4. Disconnect the fuel hoses and tubes. Disconnect the push connect fittings.

5. Disconnect the electrical hookup to the fuel tank sender unit. On some vehicles, the electrical connection is inaccessible on top of the tank and no intermediate connection point is provided. In these cases, the electrical connector must be disconnected from the fuel sender with the tank partially removed from the vehicle.

6. If equipped with all-wheel drive, perform the following procedure to gain access to the fuel tank:

   a. Remove the exhaust system.

   b. Position a suitable jack under the rear axle.

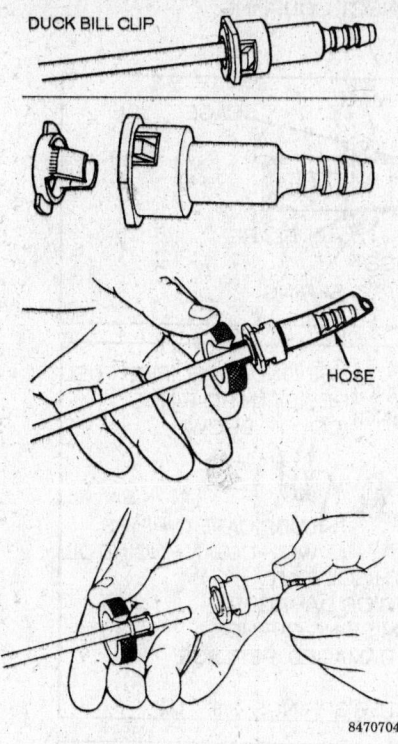

DUCK BILL CLIP

HOSE

84707047

Duck bill clip push connect fitting

c. Remove the bolts from the torque tube support bracket.

d. Remove 1 bolt each from the left and center differential support brackets.

e. Lower the differential approximately 6–8 inches (15-20 cm).

f. Remove 2 horizontal bolts retaining the axle pinion support crossmember.

7. On all vehicles, place a safety support under the fuel tank and remove the bolts or nuts from 1 end of the fuel tank straps. The straps are hinged at 1 end. Remove the bolts from the unhinged end and swing the straps aside.

8. Partially remove the tank and disconnect the fuel lines and the electrical connector from the fuel gauge sender, if required.

9. Remove the tank from the vehicle.

To install:

10. Before proceeding, check the following:

a. Leak check the sender unit. If necessary, use fuel tank sender wrench T74P–9275–A or equivalent.

b. Make sure the fuel vapor separator valve is installed completely on the tank top.

c. Make all required fuel line, fuel return line, vapor vent and electrical connections which will be inaccessible after the tank is installed.

11. Position the fuel tank in the vehicle.

12. Bring the fuel tank straps around the tank and start attaching the nut or bolt. Align the tank with the straps.

13. Check the hoses and wiring mounted on the tank top, to make sure they are correctly routed and will not be pinched between tank and body.

14. Tighten the fuel tank strap attaching bolts to 25–39 ft. lbs. (34–54 Nm).

15. Connect the fuel tank hoses and lines. Verify that the fuel supply, fuel return and vapor vent connections are made correctly.

16. Connect the electrical connections.

17. Install the fuel filler hoses that connect the fuel tank to the fuel filler pipe. Install new hose clamps and tighten.

18. With all-wheel drive, perform the following procedure:

a. Position the crossmember axle pinion support and install 2 retaining bolts.

b. Raise the differential assembly into position.

c. Install the bolts retaining the left and center differential support brackets.

d. Install the torque tube support bracket retaining bolts.

e. Remove the jack.

f. Install the exhaust system.

19. Replace the fuel that was drained from the tank.

20. Check all connections for leaks.

21. Connect the negative battery cable.

22. Turn the ignition key **ON** to run the fuel pump and pressurize the system. Check for fuel leaks.

Escort and Tracer

1. Properly relieve the fuel system pressure.

2. Disconnect the negative battery cable.

3. Completely drain the fuel tank by siphoning or pumping out the fuel through the fuel filler hose.

4. Remove the rear seat cushion and disconnect the fuel pump electrical connector.

5. Remove the ground strap retaining screw and the 3 remaining fuel pump assembly cover screws.

6. Remove the fuel pump assembly cover.

7. Remove the clips from the fuel hoses.

8. Disconnect the fuel hoses from the fuel pump assembly.

9. Raise and safely support the vehicle.

10. Loosen the filler neck clamp and disconnect the filler neck hose from the filler neck.

11. Loosen the clamp and disconnect the filler neck overflow hose from the overflow tube.

12. Disconnect the vapor hose(s) from the vapor tube(s).

13. Remove the exhaust middle pipe heatshield.

14. Support the fuel tank with a suitable jack.

15. Remove the mounting bolts from the fuel tank straps, unclip the straps and remove them.

16. Remove the 3 fuel tank heatshield attaching bolts from the fuel tank and remove the fuel tank.

To install:

17. Place the fuel tank onto the fuel tank heatshield and install the heatshield attaching bolts into the fuel tank.

18. Clip the fuel tank straps into their mounting positions.

19. Install the fuel tank strap mounting bolts and tighten to 27–38 ft. lbs. (37–52 Nm).

20. Remove the support jack from under the fuel tank.

21. Install the exhaust middle pipe heat shield.

22. Connect the vapor hose(s) to the vapor tube(s).

23. Connect the filler neck hose to the filler neck and install the attaching clamp.

24. Connect the filler neck overflow hose to the overflow tube and install the attaching clamp.

25. Lower the vehicle.

26. Connect the fuel hoses to the fuel pump assembly.

27. Install the clips onto the fuel hoses.

28. Position the fuel pump assembly cover and ground strap and install the retaining screws.

29. Connect the fuel pump assembly electrical connector.

30. Install the rear seat cushion.

31. Replace the fuel that was drained from the tank during the removal procedure. Check for leaks.

32. Connect the negative battery cable.

33. Turn the ignition switch **ON** to run the fuel pump and pressurize the system. Check for fuel leaks.

TO DISCONNECT COUPLING

CAUTION - RELIEVE FUEL PRESSURE BEFORE DISCONNECTING COUPLING

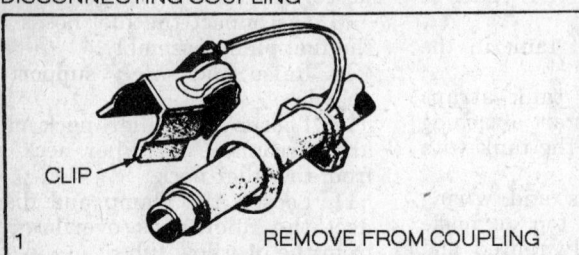

CLIP

1   REMOVE FROM COUPLING

TO CONNECT COUPLING

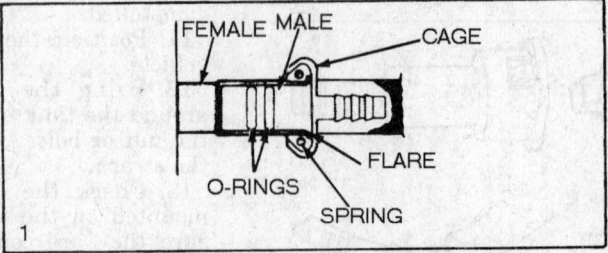

FEMALE   MALE   CAGE

O-RINGS

FLARE

SPRING

1

USE SPECIFIED TOOL OR EQUIVALENT

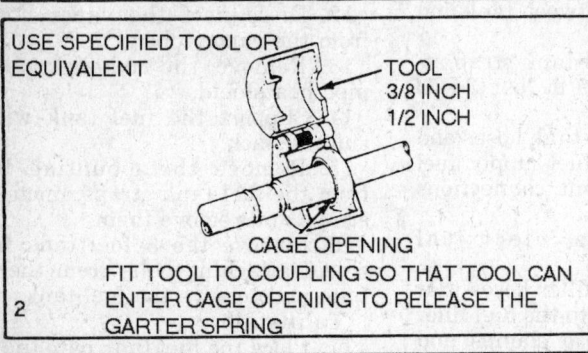

TOOL
3/8 INCH
1/2 INCH

CAGE OPENING

FIT TOOL TO COUPLING SO THAT TOOL CAN ENTER CAGE OPENING TO RELEASE THE GARTER SPRING

2

REPLACEMENT O-RINGS
(3/8 INCH DIA. 2 PER FITTING)
(1/2 INCH DIA. 2 PER FITTING)

USE ONLY SPECIFIED FUEL RESISTANT O-RINGS
(COLOR: BROWN)

CHECK FOR CORROSION

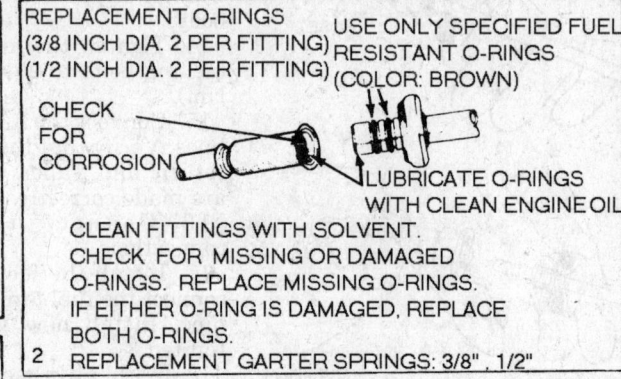

LUBRICATE O-RINGS WITH CLEAN ENGINE OIL

CLEAN FITTINGS WITH SOLVENT.
CHECK FOR MISSING OR DAMAGED
O-RINGS. REPLACE MISSING O-RINGS.
IF EITHER O-RING IS DAMAGED, REPLACE
BOTH O-RINGS.

2   REPLACEMENT GARTER SPRINGS: 3/8", 1/2"

PUSH TOOL INTO CAGE OPENING

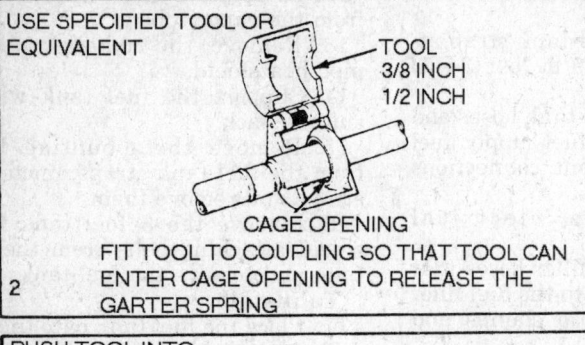

NOTE: SPECIFIED TOOL WILL FIT AROUND RUBBER COVERED FUEL LINE

PUSH THE TOOL INTO THE CAGE OPENING TO RELEASE THE FEMALE FITTING FROM THE GARTER SPRING

3

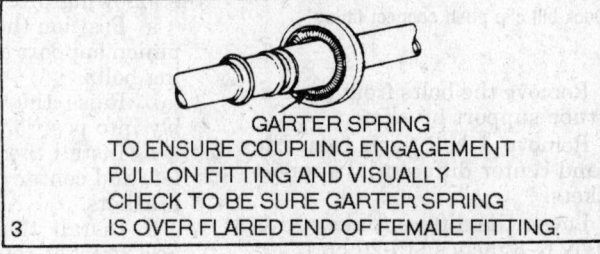

GARTER SPRING

TO ENSURE COUPLING ENGAGEMENT PULL ON FITTING AND VISUALLY CHECK TO BE SURE GARTER SPRING IS OVER FLARED END OF FEMALE FITTING.

3

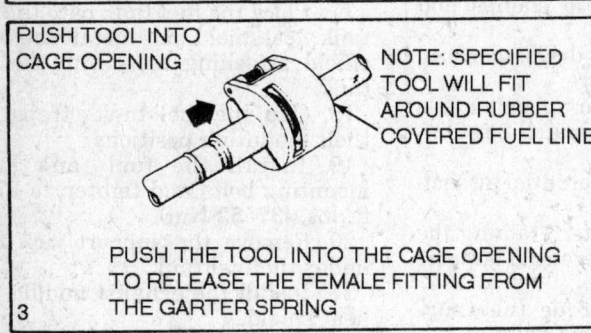

PULL THE COUPLING MALE AND FEMALE FITTINGS APART

4

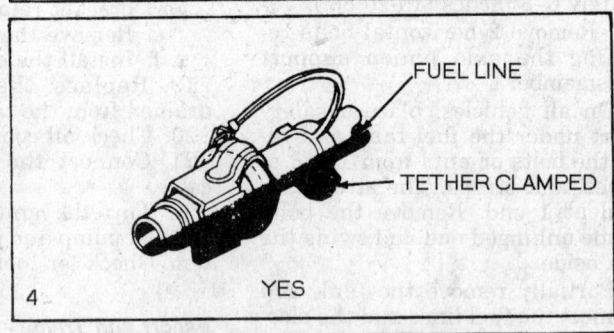

FUEL LINE

TETHER CLAMPED

YES

4

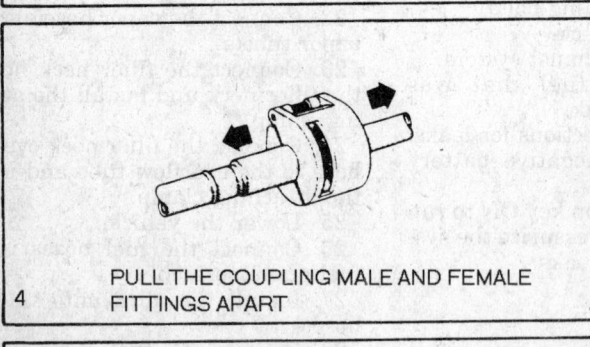

REMOVE THE TOOL FROM THE DISCONNECTED SPRING LOCK COUPLING

5

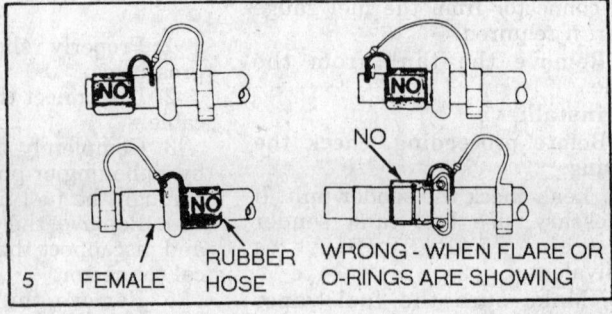

NO

NO

FEMALE   RUBBER HOSE

WRONG - WHEN FLARE OR O-RINGS ARE SHOWING

5

84707049

Spring lock coupling connect and disconnect procedure

Fuel Filter

REMOVAL AND INSTALLATION

Tempo and Topaz

1. Disconnect the negative battery cable.
2. Properly relieve the fuel system pressure.
3. Remove the push connect fittings. Install new retainer clips in each connector fitting.

NOTE: The flow arrow direction should be noted to ensure proper flow of fuel through the replacement filter.

4. Remove the filter from the bracket by loosening the filter retaining clamp enough to allow the filter to pass through.
To install:
5. Install the filter in the bracket, ensuring the proper direction of flow, as noted earlier. Tighten the clamp to 15–25 inch lbs. (1.7–2.8 Nm).
6. Install push connect fittings at both ends of the filter.
7. Connect the negative battery cable.
8. Start the engine and inspect for leaks.

Escort and Tracer

1. Properly relieve the fuel system pressure.
2. Disconnect the negative battery cable.
3. Position a suitable container below the fuel filter to collect any excess fuel that may leak from the filter and lines.
4. Remove the retaining clip from the fuel filter upper hose.
5. Disconnect the upper hose from the fuel filter and drain any excess fuel into the container. Plug the hose.
6. Loosen the fuel filter mounting clamp.
7. Raise and safely support the vehicle.
8. Remove the retaining clip from the fuel filter lower hose.
9. Disconnect the lower hose from the fuel filter and drain any excess fuel into the container. Plug the hose.
10. Lower the vehicle.
11. Remove the fuel filter.
To install:
12. Position the fuel filter and tighten the filter mounting clamp.
13. Connect the filter upper hose to the filter and install the upper hose retaining clip.
14. Raise and safely support the vehicle.

15. Connect the filter lower hose to the filter and install the lower hose retaining clip.
16. Lower the vehicle.
17. Connect the negative battery cable.
18. Start the engine and check for leaks.

Electric Fuel Pump

PRESSURE TESTING

Except 1.8L Engine

1. Make sure the ignition key is in the **OFF** position.
2. Properly relieve the fuel system pressure.
3. Disconnect the fuel pump output line and connect a suitable pressure tester.
4. Ground the fuel pump lead of the Self-Test connector through a jumper wire at the **FP** lead.
5. Turn the ignition key **ON**, to operate the fuel pump, and observe the fuel pressure.
6. The fuel pressure should be 50–60 psi on the 2.3L engine or 35–40 psi on the 1.9L EFI and 3.0L engines.
7. Turn the ignition key **OFF** and remove the jumper wire.
8. Properly relieve the fuel system pressure and remove the pressure tester.
9. Reconnect the fuel line.

1.8L Engine

1. Make sure the ignition key is in the **OFF** position.
2. Properly relieve the fuel system pressure.
3. Install a suitable fuel pressure tester in the fuel line between the fuel filter and the fuel rail.
4. Jump the fuel pump test connector terminals together, terminal **LG** and terminal **BK** at the Self-Test connector.

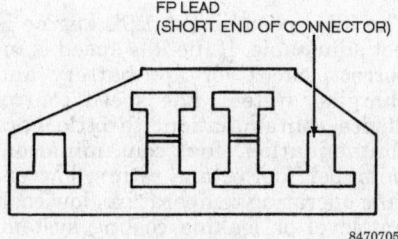

FP LEAD
(SHORT END OF CONNECTOR)

84707050

Self-Test connector — except 1.8L engine

5. Turn the ignition key to **RUN**, to operate the fuel pump, and observe the fuel pressure.
6. The fuel pressure should be 64–85 psi.
7. Turn the ignition key **OFF** and remove the jumper wire.
8. Properly relieve the fuel system pressure and remove the pressure tester.

REMOVAL AND INSTALLATION

NOTE: The fuel pump is mounted on the fuel sender assembly inside the fuel tank.

Tempo and Topaz

1. Properly relieve the fuel system pressure.
2. Disconnect the negative battery cable.
3. Remove the fuel tank.
4. Remove any dirt that has accumulated around the fuel pump retaining flange so it will not enter the fuel tank during removal and installation.
5. Turn the fuel pump locking ring counterclockwise using fuel tank sender wrench D84P–9257–A or equivalent, and remove the lock ring.
6. On all except all-wheel drive vehicles, remove the fuel pump and bracket assembly and remove the seal gasket and discard.
7. On all-wheel drive vehicles, proceed as follows:
   a. Partially lift up the sender unit and disconnect the jet pump line and the electrical connector to the resistor.
   b. Remove the fuel pump and bracket assembly and remove the seal gasket and discard.
   c. Remove the jet pump assembly attaching screw and remove the jet pump assembly.
To install:
8. Clean the fuel pump mounting flange and fuel tank mounting surface and seal ring groove.
9. Put a light coating of multi-purpose lubricant C1AZ–19590–BA or equivalent, on a new seal ring to hold it in place during assembly and install it in the fuel ring groove.
10. On all-wheel drive vehicles, install the jet pump assembly and attaching screw. Tighten the screw to 10–15 ft. lbs. (14–20 Nm).
11. Install the fuel pump and sender assembly carefully to ensure that the filter is not damaged. Make sure the locating keys are in the keyways and the seal ring remains in place.

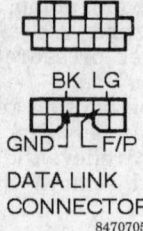

BK LG

GND ⌐ L F/P

DATA LINK
CONNECTOR
84707051

**Fuel pump test
connector
terminals — 1.8L
engine**

12. On all-wheel drive vehicles, connect the jet pump line and the electrical connector to the resistor. Make sure the locating keyways and seal ring remain in place.

13. Hold the assembly in place and install the locking ring finger-tight. Make sure all locking tabs are under the tank lock ring tabs.

14. Rotate the locking ring clockwise using fuel tank sender wrench D84P-9275-A or equivalent, until the ring stops against the stops.

15. Install the fuel tank into the vehicle.

16. Connect the negative battery cable.

Escort and Tracer

1. Properly relieve the fuel system pressure.

2. Disconnect the negative battery cable.

3. Remove the rear seat cushion. Disconnect the electrical connector at the fuel pump.

4. Remove the ground strap retaining screw and the 3 remaining fuel pump assembly cover screws.

5. Remove the fuel pump assembly cover.

6. Remove the clips from the fuel hoses.

7. Disconnect the fuel hoses from the fuel pump assembly.

8. Using a suitable removal tool, carefully remove and, if necessary, discard the fuel pump assembly spanner nut.

9. Remove the fuel pump assembly and discard the gasket.

To install:

10. Install a new gasket and position the fuel pump assembly in the tank.

11. Install the fuel pump assembly spanner nut.

12. Connect the fuel hoses to the fuel pump assembly and install the clips.

13. Position the fuel pump assembly cover and ground strap and install the retaining screws.

14. Connect the fuel pump assembly electrical connector.

15. Connect the negative battery cable.

16. Turn the ignition switch **ON** to run the fuel pump and pressurize the fuel system. Check for fuel leaks.

17. Install the rear seat cushion.

Fuel Injection

IDLE SPEED ADJUSTMENT

1.8L Engine

1. Apply the parking brake and make sure the vehicle is in **N** or **P**.

2. Start the engine and warm it to normal operating temperature.

3. Turn OFF all electrical loads and accessories.

4. Using a jumper wire, connect the **GROUND** terminal to the **TEN** terminal on the diagnosis connector.

5. Connect the positive lead of a suitable tachometer to the **IG** terminal on the diagnosis connector and the tachometer negative lead to the negative battery terminal.

6. Check the vehicle idle speed when the electric cooling fan is not operating. The idle speed should be 700–800 rpm.

NOTE: When the parking brake is not applied, the idle speed for automatic transaxle vehicles sold in Canada is approximately 800 rpm.

7. If the idle speed is not within specification, adjust the idle speed by turning the idle speed adjusting screw until the idle speed is within specification.

8. Remove the jumper wire from the diagnosis connector and remove the tachometer.

1.9L EFI Engine

The idle speed on the 1.9L engine is not adjustable. If the idle speed is incorrect, check for low battery and charging system, idle speed control device contamination, throttle bore contamination, fuel contamination, improper fuel octane rating, low engine operating temperature, low coolant level or leaking cooling system, clogged PCV system, faulty clutch or transmission, brakes not releasing, ignition system fault, exhaust system or EGR fault or vacuum leaks.

2.3L Engine

1. Connect the SUPER STAR II tester, tool number 007-00028 or other suitable scan tool to the Self-Test connector. Activate the Key On Engine Running (KOER) Self-Test.

2. After Code 1 or 111 has been displayed, unlatch and within 4 seconds, latch the STI button.

3. A single pulse code indicates the entry mode, then observe the Self-Test Output (STO) on the tester for the following:

a. A constant tone, solid light or **STO LO** readout means the base idle speed is within the correct range. To exit the test, unlatch the STI button, then wait 4 seconds for reinitialization. After 10 minutes, the tool will exit by itself.

b. A beeping tone, flashing light or **STO LO** readout at 8 Hz indicates the Throttle Position Sensor (TPS) is out of range due to over adjustment. Adjustment may be required.

c. A beeping tone, flashing light or **STO LO** readout at 4 Hz indicates the base idle speed is too fast and adjustment is required. Proceed to Step 5.

d. A beeping tone, flashing light or **STO LO** readout at 1 Hz indicates the base idle speed is too low and adjustment is required. Proceed to Step 4.

4. If the idle speed is too low, check for the presence of a throttle plate orifice plug. If there is no plug, turn the throttle screw clockwise until the conditions in Step 3a exist. If there is a plug from previous service, remove the plug and then adjust the screw in either direction, as required. The screw must be in contact with the lever pad after adjustment.

5. If the idle speed is too high, proceed as follows:

a. Turn the engine OFF.

b. Block off the orifice in the throttle plate temporarily with tape. If the orifice already has a plug, proceed to Step d.

c. Reattach the air intake hose. Restart the engine and check the idle speed using the Self-Test. If the engine stalled, crack open the plate with the throttle return screw.

d. If the idle speed continues to be fast, run the Key On Engine Off (KOEO) Self-Test and check for a TPS output code.

e. If the output code is within range, remove the tape and check for vacuum leaks, throttle linkage binding, or other causes for excessive high idle.

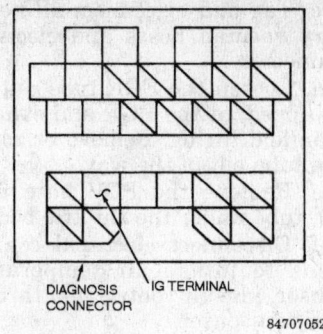

IG terminal location — Escort and Tracer with 1.8L engine

84707052

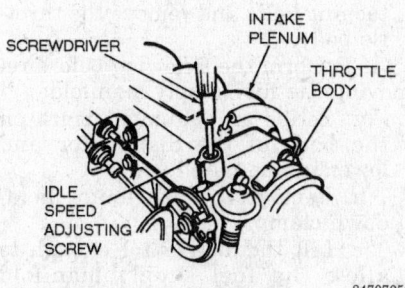

Idle speed adjusting screw location — Escort and Tracer with 1.8L engine

84707053

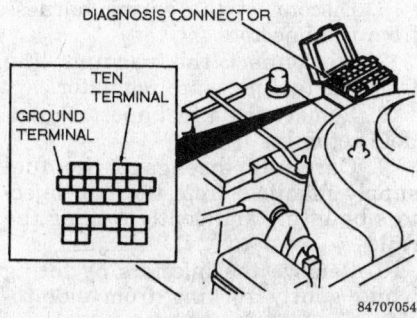

Diagnosis connector location — Escort and Tracer with 1.8L engine

84707054

f. If the output code is out of range, adjust the throttle screw to obtain the proper code. The lever pad must be in contact with the screw after adjustment.

g. If the idle speed drops to or below the desired level, as indicated by the Self-Test Output tone, turn the engine OFF, disconnect the air cleaner hose and remove the tape.

h. Install the proper plug in the throttle plate orifice.

i. Reconnect the air cleaner hose. Start the engine and turn the throttle plate stopscrew clockwise

until the conditions in Step 3a exist. Do not turn the screw counterclockwise as this may cause the throttle plate to stick at idle.

6. Run the KOEO Self-Test for proper TPS output code.

7. Make sure the throttle is not stuck in the bore and the linkage is not preventing the throttle from closing.

3.0L Engine

1. Connect the SUPER STAR II tester, tool number 007–00028 or other suitable scan tool to the Self-Test connector. Activate the Key On Engine Running (KOER) Self-Test.

2. After Code 1 or 111 has been displayed, unlatch and within 4 seconds, latch the STI button.

3. A single pulse code indicates the entry mode, then observe the Self-Test Output (STO) on the tester for the following:

a. A constant tone, solid light or **STO LO** readout means the base idle speed is within the correct range. To exit the test, unlatch the STI button, then wait 4 seconds for reinitialization. After 10 minutes, the tool will exit by itself.

b. A beeping tone, flashing light or **STO LO** readout at 8 Hz indicates the Throttle Position Sensor (TPS) is out of range due to over adjustment. Adjustment may be required.

c. A beeping tone, flashing light or **STO LO** readout at 4 Hz indicates the base idle speed is too fast and adjustment is required. Proceed to Step 5.

d. A beeping tone, flashing light or **STO LO** readout at 1 Hz indicates the base idle speed is too low and adjustment is required. Proceed to Step 4.

4. If the idle speed is too low, check for the presence of a throttle plate orifice plug. If there is no plug, turn the throttle screw clockwise until the conditions in Step 3a exist. If there is a plug from previous service, remove the plug and then adjust the screw in either direction, as required. The screw must be in contact with the lever pad after adjustment.

5. If the idle speed is too high, proceed as follows:

a. Turn the engine OFF.

b. Block off the orifice in the throttle plate temporarily with tape. If the orifice already has a plug, proceed to Step d.

c. Reattach the air intake hose. Restart the engine and check the idle speed using the Self-Test. If the engine stalled, crack open the

plate with the throttle return screw.

d. If the idle speed continues to be fast, run the Key On Engine Off (KOEO) Self-Test and check for a TPS output code.

e. If the output code is within range, remove the tape and check for vacuum leaks, throttle linkage binding or other causes for excessive high idle.

f. If the output code is out of range, adjust the throttle screw to obtain the proper code. The lever pad must be in contact with the screw after adjustment.

g. If the idle speed drops to or below the desired level, as indicated by the Self-Test Output tone, turn the engine OFF, disconnect the air cleaner hose and remove the tape.

h. Install the proper plug in the throttle plate orifice.

i. Reconnect the air cleaner hose. Start the engine and turn the throttle plate stopscrew clockwise until the conditions in Step 3a exist. Do not turn the screw counterclockwise as this may cause the throttle plate to stick at idle.

6. Run the KOEO Self-Test for proper TPS output code.

7. Make sure the throttle is not stuck in the bore and the linkage is not preventing the throttle from closing.

IDLE MIXTURE ADJUSTMENT

Idle mixture is controlled by the Powertrain Control Module and is not adjustable.

Fuel Injector

REMOVAL AND INSTALLATION

1.8L Engine

1. Properly relieve the fuel system pressure.

2. Disconnect the negative battery cable.

3. Disconnect the fuel pressure and return lines from the fuel rail.

4. Disconnect the PCV hose from the intake plenum and cylinder head cover.

5. Disconnect the fuel pressure regulator vacuum hose and the fuel injector wiring harness electrical connectors.

6. Remove the fuel rail mounting bolts and remove the fuel rail.

7. Remove the fuel injectors, grommets and insulators.

8. Installation is the reverse of the removal procedure. Lubricate new O-rings with clean engine oil and install them on the fuel injectors prior to installation.

1.9L EFI Engine

1. Properly relieve the fuel system pressure and disconnect the negative battery cable.
2. Remove vacuum line from fuel pressure regulator.
3. Remove spring-lock coupling retainer clips from fuel inlet and return fittings.
4. Disconnect fuel supply and return lines.
5. Disconnect the fuel injector wiring harness.
6. Carefully remove connectors from individual injectors(s) as required.
7. Remove the 2 bolts securing the injector manifold assembly and remove the assembly.
8. Grasping the injector's body, pull up while gently rocking the injector from side-to-side.
9. Inspect the injector O-rings (2 per injector) for signs of deterioration. Replace as required.
10. Inspect the injector "plastic hat" (covering the injector pintle) and washer for signs of deterioration. Replace as required. If hat is missing, look for it in the intake manifold.
To install:
11. Use a light grade oil to lubricate new O-rings and install 2 on each injector .
12. Install the injector(s). Use a light, twisting, pushing motion to install the injector(s).
13. Carefully seat the fuel injector manifold assembly on the injectors and secure the manifold with the attaching bolts. Tighten to 15–22 ft. lbs. (20–30 Nm).
14. Connect fuel supply and fuel return lines.
15. Reconnect spring-lock coupling retaining clips on fuel inlet and return fittings.
16. Connect the vacuum line to the fuel pressure regulator.
17. Check entire assembly for proper alignment and seating.
18. Connect the negative battery cable. With the fuel injector electrical connectors disconnected, turn the ignition switch to the **RUN** position and let the fuel pump pressurize the system. Check for fuel leaks and correct, as necessary.
19. Turn the ignition switch **OFF**.
20. Connect the fuel injector wiring harness connectors.
21. Start the engine and check for leaks.

2.3L Engine

1. Properly relieve the fuel system pressure.
2. Disconnect the engine air cleaner outlet tube from the air intake throttle body and the throttle position sensor from the wiring harness.
3. Disconnect the vacuum lines from the upper manifold and disconnect the EGR tube at the manifold connection.
4. Disconnect the air bypass valve connector, remove the accelerator and, if equipped, speed control cables and remove the manifold upper support bracket top bolt.
5. Remove the fuel supply manifold shield and the 4 upper manifold retaining bolts and 1 retaining shoulder stud.
6. Remove the upper manifold assembly and gasket and set it aside.
7. Disconnect the fuel supply and return lines and the vacuum line at the pressure regulator.
8. Disconnect the fuel injector wiring harness and disconnect the connectors from the injectors.
9. Remove the fuel supply manifold retaining bolts and remove the fuel supply manifold.
10. Grasping the injector body, pull up while gently rocking the injector from side-to-side.
11. Inspect the injector O-rings, the injector plastic hat and washer for signs of deterioration. Replace as necessary. If the hat is missing, look for it in the intake manifold.
To install:
12. Installation is the reverse of the removal procedure. Lubricate new O-rings with light engine oil and install on the injectors prior to installation. Tighten the fuel supply manifold retaining bolts and the upper intake manifold retaining bolts to 15–22 ft. lbs. (20–30 Nm).

3.0L Engine

1. Disconnect the negative battery cable.
2. Properly relieve the fuel system pressure.
3. Remove the air intake throttle body as follows:
   a. Remove the air cleaner tube from the throttle body. Remove the idle speed control solenoid shield.
   b. Disconnect the throttle cable and, if equipped, throttle valve cable.
   c. Tag and disconnect all necessary vacuum hoses and electrical connectors.
   d. Loosen the EGR tube nuts, if equipped, at the EGR and exhaust manifold fitting. Remove or rotate the tube out of the way.
   e. Remove the PCV hose from the tube under the throttle body.
   f. Disconnect electrical connections to intake air temperature sensor, idle air control and throttle position sensor.
   g. Remove the retaining nuts from the alternator brace and remove the brace.
   h. Remove the 6 throttle body attaching bolts and remove the throttle body.
4. Perform the following before removing the fuel supply manifold:
   a. Scribe an alignment mark on the base of the distributor and lower intake manifold.
   b. Remove the distributor hold-down clamp.
   c. Lift the distributor enough to allow the fuel supply manifold crossover tube to clear the distributor housing and lower intake manifold.
5. Disconnect the fuel supply and return lines.
6. Disconnect the wiring harness from the injectors.
7. Disconnect the vacuum line from the fuel pressure regulator.
8. Remove the 4 fuel injector manifold retaining bolts.
9. Carefully disengage the fuel supply manifold from the fuel injectors by lifting and gently rocking the rail.
10. Remove the injectors by lifting while gently rocking from side-to-side.
To install:
11. Lubricate new O-rings with engine oil and install 2 on each injector.
12. Make sure the injector cups are clean and undamaged.
13. Install the injectors in the fuel supply manifold using a light twisting-pushing motion.
14. Perform the following:
   a. Lift the distributor enough to allow the fuel supply manifold crossover tube to clear the distributor housing and lower intake manifold and position the fuel supply manifold.
   b. Lower the distributor into position.
   c. Install the distributor hold-down clamp and align the scribe marks. Tighten the hold-down clamp bolt to 18 ft. lbs. (24 Nm).

15. Carefully install the fuel supply manifold and injectors into the lower intake manifold, 1 side at a time. Make sure the O-rings are seated by pushing down on the fuel supply manifold.

16. While holding the fuel supply manifold in place, install the 2 retaining bolts and tighten to 7 ft. lbs. (10 Nm).

17. Connect the fuel supply and return lines.

18. Before connecting the fuel injector harness, connect the negative battery cable and turn the ignition switch to the **ON** position. This will pressurize the fuel system.

19. Using a clean paper towel, check for leaks where the injector connects to the fuel supply manifold. Correct any leaks, as necessary.

20. Turn the ignition switch **OFF** and disconnect the negative battery cable.

21. Connect the fuel injector wiring harness and connect the vacuum line to the fuel pressure regulator.

22. Install the air intake throttle body in the reverse order of removal. Use a new gasket and tighten the 6 attaching bolts to 15–22 ft. lbs. (20–30 Nm).

23. Connect the negative battery cable.

EMISSION CONTROLS

Emission Warning Lamps

RESETTING

These vehicles have a CHECK ENGINE or SERVICE ENGINE SOON light that will light when there is a fault in the engine control system. Depending upon the system or sensor involved, the light may go out if the fault is intermittent. However, the fault code will remain stored in the PCM until the system is serviced and the PCM memory cleared. When a fault is detected in certain systems or sensors, the light will remain lit until the system is serviced. When the system has been diagnosed, the problem corrected and the PCM memory cleared, the light will go out.

ENGINE MECHANICAL

NOTE: Disconnecting the negative battery cable on some vehicles may interfere with the functions of the on board computer systems and may require the computer to undergo a relearning process, once the negative battery cable is reconnected.

Engine Assembly

REMOVAL AND INSTALLATION

1.8L Engine

WITH AUTOMATIC TRANSAXLE

The 1.8L engine can be removed without removing the transaxle from the vehicle. The engine can be split from the transaxle and lifted out of the engine compartment.

1. Disconnect the negative battery cable.
2. Mark the position of the hood hinges and remove the hood.
3. If equipped with air conditioning, properly discharge the system.
4. Drain the cooling system and engine oil.
5. Remove the air duct connecting the throttle body and resonance chamber.
6. Disconnect the power brake vacuum supply hose from the power booster.
7. If equipped with cruise control, disconnect the necessary vacuum hoses from the intake plenum.

NOTE: Mark the position of the connectors prior to removal to ease reinstallation.

8. Disconnect the electrical connectors from the power steering pump, water thermoswitch, temperature sending unit, oil pressure switch, fuel injector wiring harness, exhaust gas oxygen sensor, throttle position sensor and distributor.
9. Disconnect all engine ground straps.
10. Disconnect the ignition coil high-tension lead from the distributor.
11. Disconnect the accelerator and kickdown cables from the throttle cam.
12. Remove the accelerator and kickdown cable bracket from the intake plenum and set the assembly aside.

13. Disconnect the heater core inlet and outlet hoses at the bulkhead.
14. Properly relieve the fuel system pressure.
15. Remove the necessary fuel line clips and disconnect the fuel pressure and return lines.
16. Remove the upper radiator hose.
17. Disconnect the electrical connectors from the cooling fan and the radiator thermoswitch.
18. Remove the starter motor.
19. Raise and safely support the vehicle.
20. Remove the right upper and both left and right lower splash shields.
21. Remove the radiator lower hose.
22. Disconnect the 2 transaxle cooling lines from the radiator and plug the lines.
23. If necessary, remove the air conditioner line routing bracket from the radiator and position the line aside.
24. Remove the halfshaft bearing support.
25. Remove the inspection plate from the oil pan, place a wrench on the crankshaft pulley, and rotate the crankshaft to gain access to the torque converter nuts. Remove the nuts.
26. Remove the power steering and, if equipped, air conditioner drive belt.
27. Remove the crankshaft pulley.
28. Remove the exhaust flex-pipe and mounting flange assembly from the exhaust manifold.
29. If equipped with air conditioning, remove the compressor.
30. Remove the power steering pump and bracket assembly with the hoses still connected. Suspend the pump with wire, aside of the work area.
31. Remove all accessible transaxle-to-engine bolts from the engine block.
32. Lower the vehicle.
33. Remove the radiator mounting brackets and the resonance duct.
34. Remove the radiator, fan and shroud assembly from the vehicle.
35. Remove the vacuum chamber canister located next to the intake plenum.
36. Remove the pressure regulator and bracket assembly and set it aside.
37. Remove the shutter valve actuator and bracket assembly and set it aside.
38. Remove the alternator and water pump drive belt and remove the alternator.
39. Install a suitable engine removal sling onto the engine lifting

brackets. Place a suitable engine hoist into position and support the engine.

40. Remove the oil pan-to-transaxle attaching bolts and the remaining transaxle-to-engine bolts from the engine block.

41. Remove the engine vibration dampener.

42. Remove the engine mount and the transaxle-to-engine upper right-hand bolt.

43. Carefully separate the engine from the transaxle, then remove the engine from the vehicle.

44. Install the engine onto a suitable engine stand.

To install:

45. Install a suitable engine removal sling onto the engine lifting brackets.

46. Place a suitable engine hoist into position and install the engine sling. Remove the engine from the engine stand and lower it into the engine compartment.

47. Install the transaxle-to-engine upper right bolt and tighten to 41–59 ft. lbs. (55–80 Nm).

NOTE: Make sure the torque converter studs are properly seated in the flexplate mounting holes.

48. Install the engine mount. Tighten the bolt and nuts to 49–69 ft. lbs. (67–93 Nm).

49. Install the engine vibration dampener. Tighten the bolt and nuts to 41–59 ft. lbs. (55–80 Nm).

50. Remove the engine sling from the lifting brackets and remove the engine hoist.

51. Install the remaining transaxle-to-engine bolts and tighten to 41–59 ft. lbs. (55–80 Nm).

52. Install the alternator and the alternator and water pump drive belt.

53. Install the shutter valve actuator and bracket assembly.

54. Install the pressure regulator and bracket assembly.

55. Install the vacuum chamber canister located next to the intake plenum.

56. Place the power steering pump and bracket assembly into its mounting position.

57. Place the radiator, fan and shroud assembly into its mounting position.

58. Install the radiator mounting brackets along with the resonance duct. Tighten the mounting bolts to 69–95 inch lbs. (7.8–11.0 Nm).

59. Connect the cooling fan and radiator thermoswitch electrical connectors.

60. Raise and safely support the vehicle.

61. Install the oil pan-to-transaxle attaching bolts and tighten to 27–38 ft. lbs. (37–52 Nm).

62. Install the power steering pump and bracket assembly. Tighten the bolts to 27–38 ft. lbs. (37–52 Nm).

63. Install the lower radiator hose and clamps.

64. Connect the 2 transaxle cooling lines to the radiator.

65. If equipped, install the air conditioning compressor.

66. Install the air conditioning hose routing bracket to the radiator, if equipped. Tighten the bracket attaching nuts to 56–82 inch lbs. (6.4–9.3 Nm).

67. Install the crankshaft pulley and tighten the bolts to 109–152 inch lbs. (12–17 Nm).

68. Place a wrench on the crankshaft pulley and rotate the crankshaft to gain access to the torque converter studs. Install the torque converter nuts and tighten to 25–36 ft. lbs. (34–49 Nm). Install the transaxle inspection plate.

69. Install the power steering and air conditioning drive belt.

70. Install the halfshaft bearing support and tighten the bolts to 31–46 ft. lbs. (42–62 Nm).

71. Install the starter motor.

72. Connect the heater core inlet and outlet hoses at the bulkhead.

73. Install the exhaust flex-pipe, with a new gasket, to the exhaust manifold. Tighten the pipe-to-converter attaching nuts to 23–34 ft. lbs. (31–46 Nm).

74. Install the right and left lower splash shields and the right upper splash shield. Tighten the bolts to 69–95 inch lbs. (7.8–11.0 Nm).

75. Lower the vehicle.

76. Install the upper radiator hose and clamps.

77. Unplug the fuel pressure and return lines and connect them to the fuel rail. Install the necessary fuel line clips.

78. Install the accelerator and kickdown cable bracket onto the intake plenum. Tighten the bolts to 69–95 inch lbs. (7.8–11.0 Nm). Install the accelerator and kickdown cables onto the throttle cam.

79. Connect the power brake vacuum supply hose to the vacuum booster.

80. If equipped, connect the cruise control vacuum hoses to the intake plenum.

81. Connect all engine ground straps.

82. Connect all remaining electrical connectors to their original locations, as marked during the removal procedure.

83. Connect the ignition coil high-tension lead into the distributor.

84. Install the air duct between the throttle body and resonance chamber assembly.

85. Fill the cooling system. Fill the crankcase with the proper type and quantity of engine oil.

86. If equipped, recharge the air conditioning system.

87. Install the hood, aligning the marks that were made during the removal procedure.

88. Connect the negative battery cable.

89. Start the engine and check for leaks. Stop the engine and check the fluid levels.

WITH MANUAL TRANSAXLE

The engine and transaxle must be removed as an assembly. Lift the assembly out of the engine compartment.

1. Disconnect the negative battery cable.

2. Mark the position of the hood on the hinges and remove the hood.

3. If equipped with air conditioning, properly discharge the system.

4. Drain the cooling system and the engine oil.

5. Remove the resonance duct and the air cleaner assembly.

6. Remove the battery and the battery tray.

7. Disconnect the accelerator cable from the throttle cam and remove the accelerator cable bracket from the intake plenum.

8. Remove the upper radiator hose and disconnect the radiator overflow hose from the radiator filler neck.

9. Disconnect the radiator thermoswitch and cooling fan electrical connectors.

10. Remove the attaching nuts to the radiator mounting brackets and remove the brackets.

NOTE: Mark the position of the connectors prior to removal to ease reinstallation.

11. Disconnect the alternator, oil pressure switch, throttle position sensor, idle speed control, manual lever position switch, fuel injector wiring harness, backup light switch, water thermoswitch, oxygen sensor, power steering pump and distributor electrical connectors.

12. Disconnect all engine ground straps.

13. Disconnect the ignition coil high-tension lead from the distributor.

14. Properly relieve the fuel system pressure.

15. Disconnect the fuel pressure and return lines.

NOTE: Mark the position of the hoses prior to removal to ease reinstallation.

16. Disconnect the heater core inlet and outlet, power brake vacuum supply, purge control vacuum and, if equipped, cruise control vacuum hoses.

17. Raise and safely support the vehicle.

18. Remove the right upper and lower splash shields.

19. Remove the clutch slave cylinder pipe bracket from the transaxle with the hose still connected. Position the slave cylinder aside.

NOTE: Be careful not to damage the pipe or the hose.

20. Disconnect the shift control rod and the extension bar from the transaxle.

21. Remove the battery duct.

22. Remove the radiator lower hose.

23. Remove the power steering and, if equipped, air conditioning compressor drive belt.

24. Remove the power steering pump and bracket assembly with the hoses still connected. Suspend the pump with wire aside of the work area.

25. Remove the air conditioning hose routing bracket, if equipped, from the transaxle crossmember and position the air conditioning hose aside.

26. If equipped, remove the air conditioning compressor with the hoses still connected. Suspend the compressor with wire aside of the work area.

27. Disconnect the speedometer cable from the transaxle.

28. Remove the exhaust pipe front mounting flange and support bracket from the exhaust manifold.

29. Mark the location and disconnect the wires from the starter motor.

30. Remove the stabilizer bar.

31. Remove the tie rod ends from the steering knuckles.

32. Remove the halfshafts from the transaxle.

33. Remove the transaxle front and rear mount attaching nuts from the crossmember.

34. Lower the vehicle.

35. Remove the radiator, fan and shroud assembly from the vehicle.

36. Install a suitable engine removal sling onto the engine lifting brackets.

37. Place a suitable engine hoist into position and support the engine.

38. Remove the engine vibration dampener.

39. Remove the engine mount, transaxle upper mount and the transaxle support bracket.

40. Remove the engine and transaxle assembly.

41. Remove the intake plenum support bracket.

42. Remove the starter motor.

43. Remove the transaxle front mount.

44. Remove all oil pan-to-transaxle bolts and transaxle-to-engine attaching bolts from the engine block and separate the transaxle from the engine.

45. Remove the clutch assembly from the engine.

46. Install the engine onto a suitable engine stand.

To install:

47. Install a suitable engine removal sling onto the engine lifting brackets. Place a suitable engine hoist into position and install the engine sling.

48. Remove the engine from the engine stand and lower the engine with the hoist still supporting it.

49. Install the clutch assembly.

50. Install the transaxle onto the engine.

51. Install the transaxle-to-engine bolts and tighten to 47–66 ft. lbs. (64–89 Nm).

52. Install the oil pan-to-transaxle attaching bolts and tighten to 27–38 ft. lbs. (37–52 Nm).

53. Position the transaxle front mount onto the transaxle and install the attaching bolts. Tighten the bolts to 27–38 ft. lbs. (37–52 Nm).

54. Position the starter motor into the transaxle housing and install the mounting bolts. Tighten the bolts to 27–38 ft. lbs. (37–52 Nm).

55. Install the intake plenum support bracket. Tighten the bolts to 27–38 ft. lbs. (37–52 Nm) and the nut to 14–19 ft. lbs. (19–25 Nm).

56. Using the engine hoist, position the engine and transaxle assembly into the engine compartment and align the engine mounting points with the engine mount and the mounting holes in the transaxle crossmember.

57. Install the attaching nuts to the transaxle front and rear mounts and the transaxle crossmember.

58. Position the engine mount into the vehicle.

59. Install the engine mount through-bolt and nut. Tighten them to 49–69 ft. lbs. (67–93 Nm).

60. Install the engine mount-to-engine attaching nuts. Tighten the nuts to 54–76 ft. lbs. (74–103 Nm).

61. Install the engine mount vibration dampener and attaching bolt and nut. Tighten the bolt and nut to 41–59 ft. lbs. (55–80 Nm).

62. Place the clutch slave cylinder and pipe assembly into its proper mounting position.

63. Install the transaxle support bracket and attaching bolts. Tighten the bolts to 41–59 ft. lbs. (55–80 Nm).

64. Install the transaxle upper mount and install the attaching bolts. Tighten the bolts to 32–45 ft. lbs. (43–61 Nm).

65. Install the transaxle upper mount attaching nuts. Tighten the nuts to 49–69 ft. lbs. (67–93 Nm).

66. Place the radiator, fan and shroud assembly into its mounting position.

67. Install the radiator mounting brackets and tighten the nuts to 69–95 inch lbs. (7.8–11.0 Nm).

68. Install the upper radiator hose and connect the expansion reservoir overflow tube to the radiator filler neck.

69. Connect the cooling fan and radiator thermoswitch electrical connectors.

70. Raise and safely support the vehicle.

71. Install the lower radiator hose.

72. Install the halfshafts.

73. Install the tie rod ends into the steering knuckle.

74. Install the stabilizer bar.

75. Connect the wires to the starter motor according to their positions as marked during the removal procedure.

76. Install the exhaust front mounting flange to the exhaust manifold while making sure to install a new gasket. Tighten the flange-to-manifold attaching nuts to 23–34 ft. lbs. (31–46 Nm).

77. Install the exhaust pipe support bracket. Tighten the bracket attaching bolts to 27–38 ft. lbs. (37–52 Nm).

78. Install the speedometer cable into the transaxle.

79. If equipped, install the air conditioning compressor. Tighten the mounting bolts to 15–22 ft. lbs. (20–30 Nm).

80. Install the air conditioning routing bracket, if equipped, to the transaxle crossmember. Tighten the bolt to 56–82 inch lbs. (6.4–9.3 Nm).

81. Install the power steering pump and bracket assembly. Tighten the

pump mounting bolts to 27–38 ft. lbs. (37–52 Nm).

82. Install the power steering and air conditioning drive belt.

83. Install the battery duct and tighten the attaching bolts to 69–95 inch lbs. (7.8–11.0 Nm).

84. Install the extension bar to the transaxle and tighten the attaching nut to 23–34 ft. lbs. (31–46 Nm).

85. Connect the shift control rod to the transaxle and tighten the attaching nut to 12–17 ft. lbs. (16–23 Nm).

86. Install the clutch slave cylinder attaching bolts and tighten to 12–17 ft. lbs. (16–23 Nm).

87. Position the slave cylinder pipe and install the routing bracket and attaching bolt. Tighten the bolt to 12–17 ft. lbs. (16–23 Nm).

88. Install the right upper and lower splash shields. Tighten the bolts to 69–95 inch lbs. (7.8–11.0 Nm).

89. Lower the vehicle.

90. Connect the heater core and vacuum hoses according to their original positions as marked during the removal procedure.

91. Connect the fuel pressure and return lines.

92. Connect the ignition coil high tension lead into the distributor.

93. Connect all engine ground straps.

94. Connect all remaining electrical connectors according to the locations marked during the removal procedure.

95. Install the accelerator cable bracket to the intake plenum and connect the accelerator cable to the throttle cam.

96. Install the battery tray and the battery.

97. Install the air cleaner assembly and the resonance duct.

98. Fill the cooling system. Fill the engine with the proper type and quantity of oil.

99. If equipped, recharge the air conditioning system.

100. Install the hood, aligning the marks that were made during the removal procedure.

101. Connect the negative battery cable.

102. Start the engine and check for leaks. Stop the engine and check the fluid levels.

1.9L Engine

WITH AUTOMATIC TRANSAXLE

The engine is removed without the transaxle attached. The engine is lifted from the engine compartment with the transaxle assembly remaining in the vehicle, attached to the mounts.

1. Mark the position of the hood on the hinges and remove the hood.

2. Disconnect the negative battery cable.

3. Drain the cooling system and the engine oil.

4. Remove the air intake duct.

5. Remove the crankcase ventilation hose from the valve cover and the vacuum hose from the bottom side of the throttle body.

6. Disconnect the power brake booster supply hose.

NOTE: Mark the position of the electrical connectors prior to removal to aid reinstallation.

7. Disconnect the following electrical connectors:

   a. Fuel charging harness, located at the right shock tower.

   b. Alternator harness, from the back side of the alternator.

   c. Oxygen sensor.

   d. Ignition coil.

   e. Radio suppressor, mounted on the coil bracket.

   f. Engine coolant temperature sensor, cooling fan sensor and temperature gauge sending unit, mounted on a common water tube near the thermostat housing.

   g. Radiator cooling fan.

8. Remove the idle air control valve.

9. Remove the ground strap from the stud on the left side of the cylinder head near the ignition coil.

10. Disconnect the accelerator cable and the transaxle kickdown cable from the throttle lever. Remove the cable bracket from the intake manifold and position aside.

11. Disconnect both heater hoses at the engine compartment bulkhead.

12. Properly relieve the fuel system pressure and disconnect the fuel supply and return hoses at the fuel supply manifold.

13. Remove the upper radiator hose.

14. Raise and safely support the vehicle.

15. Remove the right side and the right and left front splash shields.

16. Remove the lower radiator hose from the radiator.

17. Position a drain pan under the radiator and remove the lower transaxle oil cooler line.

18. Remove the 2 oil cooler line retaining bracket bolts from the bottom of the radiator.

19. Remove the radiator fan shroud lower mounting bolts.

20. Lower the vehicle.

21. Remove the radiator fan shroud upper mounting bolts and remove the fan and shroud assembly from the vehicle.

22. Remove the upper transaxle oil cooler line from the radiator and remove the radiator from the vehicle.

23. If equipped with air conditioning, properly discharge the system.

24. Disconnect the air conditioning suction line at the suction accumulator/drier. Plug or cap the openings to prevent the entrance of dirt and moisture.

25. Remove the accessory drive belt.

26. Remove the power steering return hose from the pump reservoir and the high-pressure hose from the power steering pump.

27. Remove the power steering and air conditioner line retainer bracket bolts from the alternator bracket. Position the hoses aside.

28. Remove the accessory drive belt automatic tensioner assembly.

29. Raise and safely support the vehicle.

30. Remove the drive belt idler pulley.

31. If equipped, remove the 4 air conditioning compressor mounting bolts. Remove the compressor assembly with the lines attached and position aside. Safety wire the compressor to the vehicle sub-frame.

32. Remove the catalytic converter inlet pipe.

33. Remove the transaxle kickdown cable support bracket from the back side of the engine block. Position the cable and the bracket aside.

34. Disconnect the oil pressure switch.

35. Disconnect the relay wire and the positive battery cable from the starter.

36. Remove the flywheel inspection shield.

37. Remove the 4 torque converter attaching nuts.

38. Remove the crankshaft dampener.

39. Remove the 5 engine-to-transaxle bolts.

40. Lower the vehicle.

41. Remove the 3 starter motor mounting bolts and remove the starter out of the top of the engine compartment.

42. Remove the 2 transaxle-to-engine mounting bolts.

43. Connect an engine removal sling to suitable engine lifting brackets. Position a suitable engine hoist and support the engine.

44. Remove the right engine mount dampener and mount assembly.

45. With the engine assembly supported by the engine hoist, carefully separate the assembly from the transaxle.

46. Lift the engine assembly out of the vehicle.

47. Install the engine onto a suitable engine stand.

To install:

48. Attach the engine removal sling to the engine lifting brackets and remove the engine from the stand with the engine hoist.

49. Carefully lower the engine into the vehicle and join the engine to the transaxle. Make sure the torque converter studs correctly engage the flywheel and the alignment dowels engage the transaxle housing.

50. Install the 2 transaxle-to-engine bolts, but do not fully tighten them at this time.

51. Install the right engine mount insulator and dampener.

52. Position the engine hoist aside and remove the sling from the engine lifting brackets.

53. Raise and safely support the vehicle.

54. Install the 5 engine-to-transaxle bolts, but do not fully tighten them at this time.

55. Install the crankshaft dampener and tighten the attaching bolt to 81–96 ft. lbs. (110–130 Nm).

56. Install the 4 torque converter attaching nuts and tighten to 25–36 ft. lbs. (34–49 Nm). Install the flywheel inspection plate.

57. Connect the oil pressure switch.

58. Install the kickdown cable support bracket.

59. If equipped, position the air conditioning compressor on the bracket and install the 4 mounting bolts. Tighten the bolts to 15–22 ft. lbs. (20–30 Nm).

60. Install the catalytic converter inlet pipe.

61. Lower the vehicle.

62. From above, position the starter motor and install the 3 mounting bolts. Connect the positive battery cable and the relay wire to the starter.

63. Tighten the 2 transaxle-to-engine bolts to 40–59 ft. lbs. (55–80 Nm).

64. Install the power steering high-pressure hose on the pump.

65. Install the accessory drive belt idler pulley and automatic tensioner.

66. Install the power steering return hose on the pump reservoir.

67. Install the power steering hose retainer bracket on the alternator bracket.

68. Install the accessory drive belt.

69. If equipped, connect the air conditioner suction line to the accumulator.

70. Install the radiator assembly.

71. Connect the upper transaxle oil cooler line at the radiator.

72. Position the cooling fan and shroud assembly and install the upper mounting bolts.

73. Raise and safely support the vehicle.

74. Install the lower shroud bolts and connect the lower transaxle oil cooler line.

75. Install the oil cooler line retaining bracket bolts.

76. Install the lower radiator hose.

77. Tighten the 5 engine-to-transaxle bolts to 27–38 ft. lbs. (37–52 Nm).

78. Install the left and right front splash shields and the right side splash shield.

79. Lower the vehicle.

80. Install the upper radiator hose.

81. Connect both heater hoses at the engine compartment bulkhead.

82. Install the accelerator cable bracket and attach the accelerator and kickdown cables to the throttle lever.

83. Install the idle air control valve.

84. Install the ground strap on the stud at the front left side of the cylinder head, near the ignition coil.

85. Connect the remaining electrical connectors according to the positions marked during the removal procedure.

86. Connect the fuel supply and return lines. Be sure to install the fuel line safety clips.

87. Connect the power brake supply hose, the vacuum hose on the bottom side of the throttle body, and the crankcase ventilation hose to the valve cover.

88. Install the air intake duct.

89. Connect the negative battery cable.

90. Fill the cooling system. Fill the crankcase with the proper type and quantity of engine oil.

91. Install the hood, aligning the marks that were made during the removal procedure.

92. Start the engine and check for leaks. Stop the engine and check the fluid levels.

93. If equipped, evacuate and recharge the air conditioning system.

WITH MANUAL TRANSAXLE

The engine is removed with the transaxle attached. The engine is lifted out of the engine compartment.

1. Mark the position of the hood on the hinges and remove the hood.

2. Disconnect the battery cables and remove the battery and the battery tray.

3. Drain the cooling system and the engine oil.

4. Remove the air cleaner.

5. Disconnect the crankcase ventilation hose from the valve cover and the vacuum hose from the bottom side of the throttle body.

6. Remove the power brake supply hose.

NOTE: Mark the position of the electrical connectors prior to removal to aid reinstallation.

7. Disconnect the following electrical connectors:
  a. Fuel charging harness, located at the right shock tower.
  b. Alternator harness, from the back side of the alternator.
  c. Oxygen sensor.
  d. Ignition coil.
  e. Radio suppressor, mounted on the coil bracket.
  f. Engine coolant temperature sensor, cooling fan sensor and temperature gauge sending unit, mounted on a common water tube near the thermostat housing.
  g. Radiator cooling fan.

8. Remove the idle air control valve.

9. Remove the ground strap from the stud on the left side of the cylinder head near the ignition coil.

10. Disconnect the accelerator cable from the throttle lever. Remove the cable bracket from the intake manifold and position aside.

11. Disconnect both heater hoses at the engine compartment bulkhead.

12. Properly relieve the fuel system pressure and disconnect the fuel supply and return hoses at the fuel supply manifold.

13. Remove the upper radiator hose.

14. If equipped, properly discharge the air conditioning system and disconnect the suction line at the accumulator.

15. Remove the accessory drive belt and the automatic tensioner and idler pulley.

16. Disconnect the power steering return hose from the pump reservoir and the high pressure hose from the pump.

17. Remove the power steering hose and air conditioning line retainer brackets from the alternator bracket.

18. Raise and safely support the vehicle.

19. Remove the right and left side and front splash shields.

20. Disconnect the lower radiator hose from the radiator and remove

the radiator fan shroud lower mounting bolts.

21. If equipped, remove the 4 air conditioning compressor mounting bolts. Remove the compressor assembly with the lines attached and position aside. Safety wire the compressor to the vehicle sub-frame.

22. Remove the catalytic converter inlet pipe.

23. Disconnect the oil pressure switch.

24. Disconnect the relay wire and the positive battery cable at the starter.

25. Remove the transaxle extension bar and shift control rod.

26. Remove the crankshaft dampener.

27. Remove the front wheel and tire assemblies.

28. Remove both halfshaft assemblies.

29. Install suitable transaxle plugs into the differential side gears.

━━ WARNING ━━
Failure to install the transaxle plugs may allow the differential side gears to move out of position. Should the gears become misaligned, the differential will have to be removed from the transaxle to align the gears.

30. Disconnect the speedometer cable and the neutral switch on the transaxle.

31. Remove the clutch slave cylinder and line as an assembly from the transaxle and set it aside.

32. Remove the transaxle front and rear mount bolts.

33. Lower the vehicle.

34. Remove the radiator fan shroud upper mounting bolts and remove the fan shroud assembly from the vehicle.

35. Connect a suitable engine removal sling to the engine lifting brackets. Connect the sling to a suitable engine hoist, position the hoist and support the engine.

36. Remove the right engine mount dampener and mount assembly.

37. Remove the transaxle upper mount.

38. Lift the engine and transaxle assembly out of the vehicle and set it down on the floor.

To install:

39. Carefully lower the engine and transaxle assembly into the vehicle with the engine hoist.

40. Position the transaxle on its mounts and install the transaxle upper mount.

41. Install the right engine mount and mount damper.

42. Remove the engine removal sling and the hoist.

43. Position the fan shroud assembly and install the upper mounting bolts.

44. Raise and safely support the vehicle.

45. Install the front and rear transaxle mount bolts.

46. Install the clutch slave cylinder and line assembly.

47. Connect the neutral switch and the speedometer cable.

48. Remove the transaxle plugs and install the halfshaft assemblies.

49. Install the crankshaft dampener and tighten the bolt to 81–96 ft. lbs. (110–130 Nm).

50. Install the transaxle extension bar and shift control rod.

51. Connect the relay wire and the positive battery cable to the starter.

52. Connect the oil pressure switch.

53. Install the catalytic converter inlet pipe.

54. If equipped, position the air conditioning compressor on its bracket and install the 4 mounting bolts.

55. Install the radiator fan shroud lower mounting bolts and install the lower radiator hose.

56. Install the left and right side and front splash shields.

57. Lower the vehicle.

58. Install the power steering hoses and install the power steering hose and air conditioner line retainer brackets.

59. Install the accessory drive belt idler pulley and automatic tensioner and install the accessory drive belt.

60. If equipped, connect the air conditioner suction line.

61. Install the upper radiator hose.

62. Connect the fuel supply and return hoses to the fuel supply manifold.

63. Connect both heater hoses.

64. Install the accelerator cable bracket on the intake manifold and connect the cable to the throttle lever.

65. Install the ground strap on the stud at the front left side of the cylinder head.

66. Install the idle air control valve.

67. Connect the remaining electrical connectors according to the positions marked during the removal procedure.

68. Connect the power brake supply hose, the crankcase ventilation hose and the vacuum line at the bottom of the throttle body.

69. Install the air cleaner assembly.

70. Install the battery tray and the battery. Connect the battery cables.

71. Fill the cooling system. Fill the crankcase with the proper type and quantity of oil.

72. Install the hood, aligning the marks that were made during the removal procedure.

73. Start the engine and check for leaks. Stop the engine and check the fluid levels.

74. If equipped, evacuate and recharge the air conditioning system.

2.3L Engine

NOTE: This procedure describes the removal and installation of the engine and transaxle as an assembly.

1. Mark the position of the hood on the hinges and remove the hood.

2. Disconnect the negative battery cable.

3. Properly relieve the fuel system pressure. Remove the air cleaner.

4. Remove lower radiator hose to drain the engine coolant.

5. Remove upper radiator hose and disconnect transaxle cooler lines at rubber hoses below radiator, if equipped with automatic transaxle.

6. Disconnect the coolant fan at the electrical connection.

7. Remove radiator shroud and cooling fan as an assembly. Remove radiator.

8. Properly discharge air conditioning system, if equipped and remove pressure and suction lines from compressor.

━━ CAUTION ━━
Use extreme care when discharging air conditioning system, as the refrigerant is under high pressure and may cause personal injury.

9. Identify, tag and disconnect all electrical and vacuum lines as necessary.

10. If equipped, disconnect the TV linkage at the automatic transaxle. If equipped, disconnect the clutch cable from the shift lever on the transaxle.

11. Disconnect accelerator linkage and fuel lines.

12. Remove coil and brackets assembly.

13. Disconnect power steering lines at pump and remove the bracket at the cylinder head, if equipped.

14. Install 2 engine lifting eyes and install engine support tool D88L–6000–A or equivalent, to engine lifting eyes.

15. Raise and safely support the vehicle.

16. Remove battery cable from starter and remove hose from catalytic converter.

17. Remove bolt attaching exhaust pipe bracket-to-oil pan and 2 exhaust pipe-to-manifold attaching nuts.

18. Remove exhaust inlet pipe-to-exhaust manifold retaining nuts, pull exhaust system out of rubber insulating grommets and set aside.

19. Remove speedometer cable from transaxle.

20. Remove 1 heater hose from water pump inlet tube and the other from the steel heater inlet tube.

21. Remove the clamp retaining bolts or nuts at the underside of the oil pan and remove the inlet tube.

22. Remove bolts attaching control arms to body. Remove stabilizer bar brackets retaining bolts and remove brackets.

23. Remove both halfshaft assemblies. After removing the halfshafts, install transaxle plugs T81P–1177–B or equivalent, in the differential side gears.

WARNING

Failure to install the plugs can result in dislocation of the differential side gears. If the gears become misaligned, the differential must be removed from the transaxle to realign the gears.

24. On manual transaxle equipped vehicles, remove roll restrictor nuts from transaxle. Pull roll restrictor from mounting bracket.

25. On manual transaxle equipped vehicles, remove shift stabilizer bar to transaxle attaching bolts. Remove shift mechanism to shift shaft attaching nut and bolt at transaxle.

26. On automatic transaxle equipped vehicles, disconnect manual shift cable clip from lever on transaxle. Remove manual shift linkage bracket bolts from transaxle and remove bracket.

27. Remove the left rear insulator mount bracket from body bracket.

28. Remove the left front insulator to transaxle mounting bolts.

29. Lower the vehicle. Install lifting equipment to the 2 lifting eyes on engine.

NOTE: Do not allow front wheels to touch floor.

30. Remove the engine support tool.

31. Remove right No. 3A insulator intermediate bracket-to-engine bracket bolts, intermediate bracket-to-insulator attaching nuts and the nut on the bottom of the double ended stud which attaches the intermediate bracket-to-engine bracket. Remove bracket.

32. Carefully lower engine and transaxle assembly to the floor.

To install:

33. Raise and safely support the vehicle.

34. Position engine and transaxle assembly directly below engine compartment.

35. Slowly lower vehicle over engine and transaxle assembly.

NOTE: Do not allow the front wheels to touch the floor.

36. Install lifting equipment to both existing engine lifting eyes on engine.

37. Raise engine and transaxle assembly up through engine compartment and position accordingly.

38. Install right side No. 3A insulator intermediate attaching nuts to intermediate bracket. Tighten to 55–75 ft. lbs. (75–100 Nm). Attach intermediate bracket-to-engine bracket bolts. Tighten to 52–70 ft. lbs. (70–95 Nm). Install nut on bottom of double-ended stud that attaches the intermediate bracket-to-engine bracket. Tighten to 60–90 ft. lbs. (80–120 Nm).

39. Install engine support tool D88L–6000–A or equivalent, to engine lifting eye.

40. Remove lifting equipment.

41. Raise and safely support the vehicle.

42. Position transaxle jack under engine. Raise engine and transaxle assembly into mounted position.

43. Install insulator-to-bracket nut and tighten to 45–65 ft. lbs. (61–68 Nm). Tighten the left rear No. 4 insulator bracket-to-body bracket nuts to 45–65 ft. lbs. (61–68 Nm).

44. If equipped with manual transaxle, position roll restrictor onto starter studs. Install nuts attaching roll restrictor to transaxle and tighten to 25–39 ft. lbs. (35–50 Nm).

45. Install starter cable to starter. Install water pump inlet tube and tighten the fastener to 71–97 inch lbs. (8–11 Nm).

46. Install lower radiator hose.

47. If equipped with manual transaxle, install shift stabilizer bar-to-transaxle attaching bolt. Tighten to 23–35 ft. lbs. (31–47 Nm).

48. If equipped with manual transaxle, install shift mechanism-to-input shift shaft (on transaxle) bolt and nut. Tighten to 7–10 ft. lbs. (9–13 Nm).

49. If equipped with automatic transaxle, install manual shift linkage bracket bolts to transaxle. Install cable clip to lever on transaxle.

50. Install lower radiator hose to radiator.

51. Install speedometer cable to transaxle.

52. Position exhaust system up and into insulating rubber grommets located at rear of vehicle.

53. Install exhaust pipe-to-exhaust manifold studs. Install exhaust pipe bracket-to-oil pan bolt.

54. Connect pulse air hose to catalytic converter.

55. Place stabilizer bar and control arm assembly into position. Install control arm-to-body attaching bolts. Install stabilizer bar brackets and tighten all fasteners.

56. Install the halfshaft assemblies.

57. Lower vehicle.

58. Remove engine support tool.

59. Connect any remaining electrical and vacuum lines.

60. Install heater hose.

61. Install air conditioning discharge and suction lines to compressor, if equipped. Do not charge at this time.

62. Connect fuel supply and return lines to engine.

63. Connect accelerator cable.

64. Install power steering pressure and return lines.

65. If equipped with automatic transaxle, connect TV linkage at transaxle.

66. If equipped with manual transaxle, connect clutch cable to shift lever on transaxle. Check clutch adjustment.

67. Install radiator shroud and coolant fan assembly. Connect the coolant fan electrical connector and install the upper radiator hose.

68. If equipped with automatic transaxle, connect transaxle cooler lines to rubber hoses below radiator.

69. Fill cooling system.

70. Install the coil and the air cleaner assembly.

71. Connect the negative battery cable.

72. Install the hood, aligning the marks made during the removal procedure.

73. Charge air conditioning system, if equipped.

74. Check all fluid levels.

75. Start the engine and check for leaks.

3.0L Engine

1. Disconnect the battery cables and remove the battery. Remove the battery tray with the air cleaner assembly attached.

2. Drain the cooling system.

3. If equipped, properly discharge the air conditioning system.

4. Mark the position of the hood on its hinges and remove the hood.

5. Properly relieve the fuel system pressure, then disconnect the fuel lines and position them aside.

6. Remove the upper radiator hose.

7. Tag and disconnect all necessary electrical connectors and vacuum lines.

8. Disconnect the lines from the power steering pump and remove the power steering reservoir.

9. Disconnect the air conditioning lines from the condenser, leaving the manifold lines attached to the compressor.

10. Disconnect the accelerator linkage, transaxle throttle valve linkage and cruise control cable, if equipped.

11. Disconnect the speedometer cable.

12. If equipped with automatic transaxle, disconnect the transaxle cooler lines from the radiator.

13. Remove the coolant overflow bottle and the lower radiator hose.

14. Remove the power steering lines at the rear of the engine above the transaxle.

15. Raise and safely support the vehicle.

16. Drain the engine oil and remove the heater hoses.

17. Remove the front wheel and tire assemblies.

18. Support the exhaust system and remove the exhaust Y-pipe.

19. Remove the bolt retaining the air conditioner line to the engine block.

20. Disconnect the tie rod ends from the spindles.

21. Disconnect the lower ball joints and pull down on the control arms to disengage them from the spindles.

22. Remove both halfshaft assemblies. After removing the halfshafts, install transaxle plugs T81P–1177–B or equivalent, in the differential side gears.

------ WARNING ------
Failure to install the plugs can result in dislocation of the differential side gears. If the gears become misaligned, the differential must be removed from the transaxle to realign the gears.
------

23. Lower the vehicle.

24. Remove the ignition coil bracket bolts and position the coil assembly aside.

25. Install suitable engine lifting eyes to the engine at the front of the right cylinder and at the rear of the left cylinder head. Attach suitable engine lifting equipment to the lifting eyes.

26. Remove the through bolts from the engine mounts.

27. Carefully lift the engine from the vehicle. The engine must be tilted to clear the master cylinder.

To install:

28. Carefully lower the engine into the engine compartment, being careful to clear the master cylinder.

29. Position the engine and install the through bolts in the engine mounts.

30. Remove the engine lifting equipment and the lifting eyes.

31. Position the ignition coil/bracket assembly and install the attaching bolts.

32. Raise and safely support the vehicle.

33. Remove the plugs and install the halfshaft assemblies.

34. Connect the lower ball joints and the tie rod ends to the spindles.

35. Install the bolt retaining the air conditioning line to the engine block.

36. Install the exhaust Y-pipe.

37. Install the front wheel and tire assemblies.

38. Connect the heater hoses.

39. Lower the vehicle.

40. Connect the power steering lines at the rear of the engine above the transaxle.

41. Install the lower radiator hose and the coolant overflow bottle.

42. If equipped with automatic transaxle, connect the transaxle cooler lines to the radiator.

43. Connect the speedometer cable.

44. Connect the accelerator linkage, transaxle throttle valve linkage and cruise control cable, if equipped.

45. Connect the air conditioning lines to the condenser.

46. Install the power steering fluid reservoir and connect the lines to the power steering pump.

47. Connect all vacuum lines and electrical connectors that were marked and disconnected during the removal procedure.

48. Install the upper radiator hose.

49. Connect the fuel lines.

50. Install the hood on the hinges, aligning the marks that were made during the removal procedure.

51. Install the battery tray and battery. Connect the battery cables.

52. Fill the cooling system.

53. Start the engine and bring to normal operating temperature. Check for leaks and check all fluid levels.

54. If equipped, properly evacuate and charge the air conditioning system.

Engine Mounts

REMOVAL AND INSTALLATION

Escort and Tracer

1. Disconnect the negative battery cable.

2. Raise and support the vehicle safely.

3. Drain the cooling system and disconnect the upper and lower radiator hoses, as necessary.

4. Position a jack with a block of wood, under the engine.

5. Remove the engine-to-mount bolts and mount-to-frame bolts.

6. Relieve the pressure from the mount by jacking the engine until the mount can be removed. Remove the mount.

7. Installation is the reverse order of the removal procedure.

8. Fill the cooling system to correct level.

9. Connect the negative battery cable.

Tempo and Topaz

RIGHT ENGINE INSULATOR (NO. 3A)

1. Disconnect the negative battery cable. Place a floor jack and a block of wood under the engine oil pan. Raise the engine approximately ½ in. or enough to take the load off the insulator.

2. Remove the insulator attaching nut from the bottom of the double-ended stud.

3. Remove the insulator lower attaching nuts through the right side front wheel opening. Remove the insulator lower retaining nuts through the engine compartment.

4. If equipped with 2.3L engine, remove the 2 bolts attaching the insulator-to-engine bracket.

5. If equipped with 3.0L engine, remove the 2 nuts and 1 bolt attaching the insulator-to-engine bracket.

6. Remove the insulator from the vehicle.

To install:

7. Position the insulator into the body opening.

8. Loosely install the retaining nuts and bolts. Tighten the nuts to 73–97 ft. lbs. (98–132 Nm) and bolts to 40–53 ft. lbs. (53–71 Nm).

9. If equipped with 2.3L engine, loosely install the retaining bolts and nut. Tighten the bolts and nut to 65–87 ft. lbs. (88–118 Nm).

10. If equipped with 3.0L engine, loosely install the retaining nuts, attaching bolt and retaining lower nut. Tighten to 51–67 ft. lbs. (68–92 Nm),

22–29 ft. lbs. (30–40 Nm) and 65–87 ft. lbs. (88–118 Nm).

11. Lower the engine and remove the jack. Connect the negative battery cable.

RIGHT ENGINE INSULATOR (NO. 2A — 3.0L ENGINE)

1. Disconnect the negative battery cable. Place a floor jack and a block of wood under the engine oil pan. Raise the engine approximately ½ in. or enough to take the load off the insulator.
2. Remove the insulator lower nut.
3. Remove the stabilizer bar bracket bolts.
4. Remove the insulator-to-A/C bracket bolt.
5. Remove the insulator from the vehicle.

To install:
6. Position the insulator onto the A/C bracket and loosely attach the bolt. Tighten the bolt to 26–36 ft. lbs. (34–46 Nm).
7. Position the insulator onto the stabilizer bar bracket and loosely attach the nut. Loosely attach the stabilizer bar bracket bolts and tighten to 40–53 ft. lbs. (53–72 Nm). Tighten the nut to 26–36 ft. lbs. (34–46 Nm).
8. Lower the engine and remove the jack. Connect the negative battery cable.

LEFT REAR ENGINE INSULATOR (NO. 4)

1. Disconnect the negative battery cable. Raise the vehicle and support safely. Place a transaxle jack and a block of wood under the transaxle.
2. Raise the transaxle approximately ½ in. or enough to take the load off the insulator.
3. Remove the insulator attaching nuts from the support bracket. Remove the 2 through bolts and remove the insulator from the transaxle.

To install:
4. Install the insulator over the left rear transaxle housing and support bracket studs.
5. Install the 2 insulator through bolts and tighten to 30–40 ft. lbs. (41–54 Nm).
6. Install 2 insulator-to-support bracket attaching nuts. Tighten to 73–97 ft. lbs. (98–132 Nm).
7. Lower vehicle and remove floor jack. Connect negative battery cable.

NOTE: To remove the left rear support bracket, remove the left rear engine insulator No. 4. Then remove the support bracket attaching bolts. When installing the support bracket, torque the attaching bolts to 51–67 ft. lbs. (68–92 Nm).

LEFT FRONT ENGINE INSULATOR (NO. 1)

1. Disconnect the negative battery cable. Raise and the vehicle and support safely. Place a transaxle jack and a block of wood under the transaxle. Raise the transaxle approximately ½ in. or enough to take the load off the insulator.
2. Remove the insulator-to-support bracket attaching nut(s). Remove the insulators and transaxle attaching bolts and remove the insulator from the vehicle.
3. Complete the installation of the insulator by reversing the removal procedure. Torque the insulator to transaxle attaching bolts to 26–36 ft. lbs. (34–46 Nm). Torque the insulator-to-support bracket nuts to 26–36 ft. lbs. (34–46 Nm).

Cylinder Head

REMOVAL AND INSTALLATION

1.8L Engine

1. Properly relieve the fuel system pressure.
2. Disconnect the negative battery cable.
3. Drain the cooling system.
4. Remove the bolts from the timing belt upper and middle covers. Remove the covers and gaskets.
5. Rotate the crankshaft by hand in the direction of normal engine rotation and align the timing marks located on the camshaft pulleys and seal plate.
6. Loosen the timing belt tensioner lock bolt and temporarily secure the tensioner spring in the fully extended position.

NOTE: Do not allow the timing belt to become contaminated by oil or grease. Mark the direction of rotation on the timing belt prior to removal so it can be reinstalled in the same direction.

7. Remove the timing belt from the camshaft pulleys and secure it aside to prevent damage during the removal and installation of the cylinder head.
8. Tag and disconnect the vacuum hoses from the cylinder head cover.
9. Tag and disconnect the spark plug wires from the spark plugs and position the wires aside.
10. Remove the cylinder head cover and gasket.
11. Remove the air duct from the resonance chamber and throttle body.
12. Disconnect the accelerator cable and, if equipped with automatic tran-

saxle, the kickdown cable from the throttle cam. Remove the cable bracket from the intake plenum.
13. Tag and disconnect all vacuum lines from the intake plenum.
14. Tag and disconnect all necessary electrical connectors from the cylinder head, exhaust manifold, intake plenum, and throttle body. Disconnect the ground straps.
15. Remove the upper radiator hose.
16. Remove the transaxle-to-engine block upper-right bolt.
17. Disconnect the fuel pressure and return lines and plug the lines.
18. Disconnect the ignition coil high-tension lead from the distributor.
19. Tag and disconnect the necessary hoses connected to the cylinder head and intake plenum.
20. Remove the 2 bolts from the transaxle vent tube routing brackets.
21. Raise and safely support the vehicle.
22. Remove the bolt from the water pump-to-cylinder head hose bracket.
23. Remove the exhaust front mounting flange and exhaust pipe support bracket from the exhaust manifold.
24. Remove the intake plenum support bracket.
25. Lower the vehicle.
26. Disconnect the heater hoses from the cylinder head.
27. Remove the cylinder head bolts in the proper sequence.

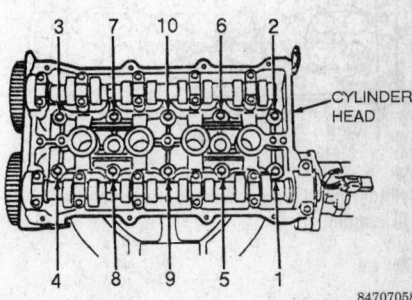

Cylinder head bolt removal sequence — 1.8L engine

28. Remove the cylinder head assembly, with the intake plenum and exhaust manifold attached, from the vehicle.
29. Remove the intake plenum and exhaust manifold.
30. Inspect the cylinder head for damage, cracks, and leakage of water and oil. Measure the cylinder head for warpage in 6 directions. The maximum distortion allowable is 0.004 in. (0.10mm).

31. If the cylinder head distortion exceeds specification, machine the cylinder head surface. The cylinder head must be replaced if the cylinder head height is not within 5.268–5.276 in. (133.8–134.0mm).

32. Inspect the manifold contact surface distortion in 4 directions. The maximum distortion allowable is 0.006 in. (0.15mm). If the distortion exceeds specification, machine the manifold contact surface or replace the cylinder head, as necessary.

To install:

33. Remove all dirt, oil and old gasket material from all gasket contact surfaces.

34. Install the intake plenum and exhaust manifold.

35. Install a new head gasket onto the top of the engine block, using the dowel pins for reference.

36. Place the cylinder head into its mounting position on top of the engine block.

37. Lubricate the cylinder head bolts with engine oil and install them finger-tight. Tighten the bolts in the proper sequence to 56–60 ft. lbs. (76–81 Nm).

38. Install the 2 bolts to the transaxle vent tube routing brackets.

39. Connect the heater hoses to the cylinder head and install the clamps.

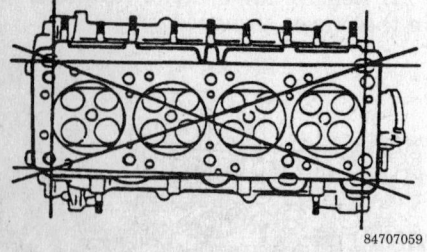

Cylinder head warpage measuring locations — 1.8L engine

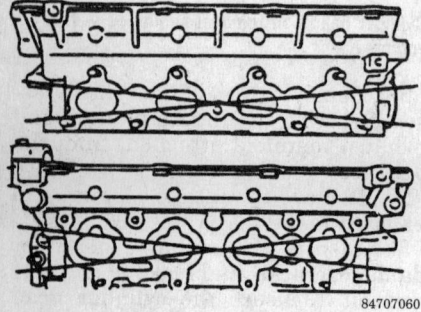

Manifold contact surface warpage measuring location — 1.8L engine

40. Connect the ignition coil high-tension lead to the distributor.

41. Connect the fuel pressure and return lines to the fuel supply manifold and install the safety clips.

42. Install the transaxle-to-engine block upper-right bolt. If equipped with manual transaxle, tighten the bolt to 47–66 ft. lbs. (64–89 Nm). If equipped with automatic transaxle, tighten the bolt to 41–59 ft. lbs. (55–80 Nm).

43. Install the upper radiator hose and clamps.

44. Connect the ground straps and connect the electrical connectors that were disconnected at the cylinder head, exhaust manifold, intake plenum, and throttle body.

45. Connect the vacuum lines to the intake plenum.

46. Install the accelerator and kickdown cable bracket onto the intake plenum and tighten the bolts to 69–95 inch lbs. (7.8–11.0 Nm). Connect the cable(s) to the throttle cam.

47. Install the cylinder head cover and gasket, then connect the hose running from the plenum to the cylinder head cover. Tighten the cover bolts to 43–78 inch lbs. (4.9–8.8 Nm).

48. Install the air duct to the resonance chamber and throttle body and tighten the clamps. Connect the hose going from the air duct to the cylinder head cover.

49. Install and connect the spark plug wires.

50. Raise and safely support the vehicle.

51. Install the intake plenum support bracket. Tighten the bolts to 27–38 ft. lbs. (37–52 Nm) and the nut to 14–19 ft. lbs. (19–25 Nm).

52. Install the bolt to the water pump-to-cylinder head hose bracket.

53. Install the exhaust front mounting flange with a new gasket to the exhaust manifold. Tighten the flange-to-manifold attaching nuts to 23–34 ft. lbs. (31–46 Nm).

54. Install the exhaust pipe support bracket. Tighten the bracket attaching bolts to 27–38 ft. lbs. (37–52 Nm).

55. Make sure the yellow ignition timing mark on the crankshaft pulley is aligned with the TDC mark on the timing belt cover.

56. Lower the vehicle.

57. Make sure the timing marks on the camshaft pulleys and seal plate are aligned. Install the timing belt, in the original direction of rotation, so there is no looseness at the idler pulley side or between the 2 camshaft pulleys.

NOTE: Do not turn the crankshaft counterclockwise.

58. Turn the crankshaft 2 turns clockwise by hand and verify that the yellow ignition timing mark on the crankshaft pulley is aligned with the timing mark on the timing belt cover. Verify that the timing marks on the camshaft pulley and seal plate are aligned.

NOTE: If the timing marks are not aligned, remove the timing belt and repeat the procedure beginning with Step 55.

59. Turn the crankshaft 1⅚ turns clockwise by hand and align the 4th tooth to the right of the **I** and **E** timing marks on the camshaft pulleys with the seal plate alignment marks.

60. Loosen the timing belt tensioner lock bolt and apply tension to the timing belt. Tighten the tensioner lock bolt to 27–38 ft. lbs. (37–52 Nm).

61. Turn the crankshaft 2⅙ turns clockwise and verify that the timing marks on the camshaft pulleys and the seal plate are aligned.

62. Install new gaskets onto the timing belt upper and middle covers and install the covers. Tighten the mounting bolts to 69–95 inch lbs. (8–11 Nm).

63. Fill the cooling system.

64. Connect the negative battery cable.

65. Start the engine and check for leaks.

1.9L Engine

1. Properly relieve the fuel system pressure.

2. Disconnect the negative battery cable.

3. Drain the cooling system.

4. Remove the air intake duct.

5. Remove the crankcase breather hose from the rocker arm cover and the vacuum hose from the bottom of the throttle body.

6. Remove the power brake supply hose.

NOTE: Tag the connectors prior to removal to aid reinstallation.

7. Disconnect the electrical connectors at the following:
   a. Fuel charging harness.
   b. Alternator harness.
   c. Crank angle sensor.
   d. Oxygen sensor.
   e. Ignition coil.
   f. Radio suppressor.
   g. Engine coolant temperature sensor, cooling fan sensor and temperature sending unit.

8. Remove the ground strap from the stud on the left side of the cylinder head.

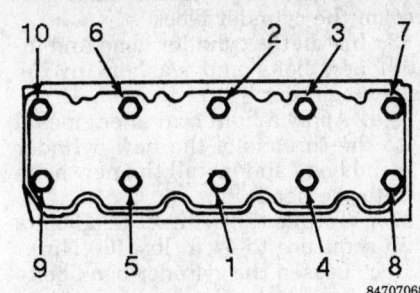

Cylinder head bolt torque sequence — 1.8L engine

Cylinder head bolt torque sequence — 2.3L engine

TIGHTENING SEQUENCE
CYLINDER HEAD ATTACHING BOLTS

9	3	1	5	7	
○	○	○	○	○	INTAKE
○	○	○	○	○	EXHAUST
8	6	2	4	10	

84707064

Cylinder head bolt torque sequence — 1.9L engine

9. Disconnect the accelerator and the transaxle kickdown cables from the throttle lever and remove the cable bracket from the intake manifold.

10. Disconnect the heater hose containing the coolant temperature switches at the bulkhead.

11. Remove the upper radiator hose.

12. Disconnect the fuel supply and return lines.

13. Remove the oil level indicator tube mounting nut from the cylinder head stud.

14. Remove the power steering hose and the air conditioner line retainer

bracket bolts from the alternator bracket.

15. Remove the accessory drive belt, alternator, and the drive belt automatic tensioner.

16. Raise and safely support the vehicle.

17. Remove the right side splash shield and remove the crankshaft dampener.

18. Remove the catalytic converter inlet pipe.

19. Remove the starter wiring harness from the retaining clip below the intake manifold.

20. Set the engine No. 1 cylinder on TDC.

21. Lower the vehicle.

22. Remove the timing belt cover.

23. Loosen the belt tensioner attaching bolt and pry the tensioner as far toward the rear of the engine as possible. Tighten the attaching bolt while in this position.

NOTE: Do not allow the timing belt to become contaminated by oil or grease. Mark the direction of rotation on the timing belt prior to removal so it can be reinstalled in the same direction.

24. Remove the timing belt.

25. Remove the heater hose support bracket retaining bolt and the alternator bracket-to-cylinder head mounting bolt.

26. Remove the rocker arm cover.

27. Remove and discard the cylinder head bolts.

28. Remove the cylinder head with the exhaust and intake manifolds attached. Discard the cylinder head gasket.

NOTE: Do not lay the cylinder head flat. Damage to the spark plugs, valves or gasket surfaces may result.

To install:

29. Clean all gasket material from the mating surfaces on the cylinder head and block and clean out the head bolt holes in the block.

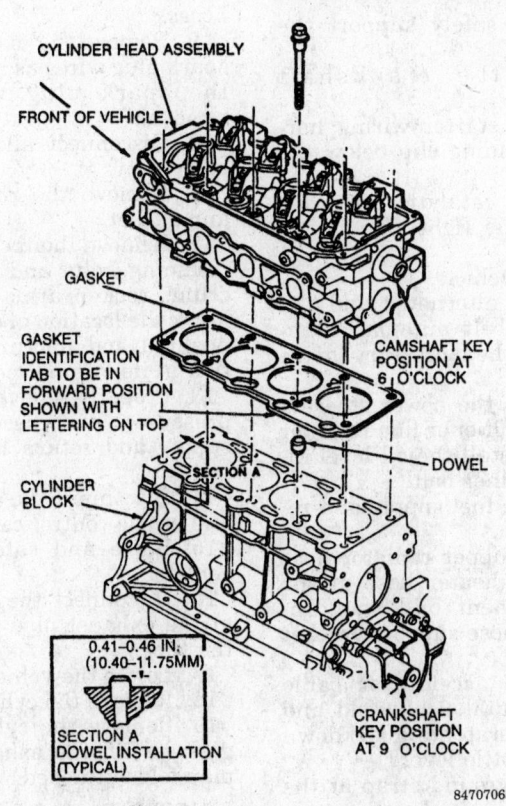

Cylinder head installation — 1.9L engine

30. Before final installation of the cylinder head to the engine, check the piston squish height as follows:

NOTE: Squish height is the clearance of the piston dome to the combustion chamber at piston TDC. No cylinder block deck machining or use of replacement crankshaft, piston or connecting rod causing the assembled squish height to be over or under tolerance specification, is permitted. If no parts other than the head gasket are replaced, the squish height should be within specification. If parts other than the head gasket are replaced, check the squish height. If the squish height is out of specification, replace the parts again and recheck the squish height.

a. Place a small amount of soft lead solder or shot of an appropriate thickness on the piston spherical areas shown.

b. Rotate the crankshaft to lower the piston in the bore and install the head gasket and cylinder head.

NOTE: A compressed (used) head gasket is preferred.

c. Install used head bolts and tighten the head bolts to 30–44 ft. lbs. (40–60 Nm) following the proper sequence.

d. Rotate the crankshaft to move the piston through its TDC position.

e. Remove the cylinder head and measure the thickness of the compressed solder to determine squish height at TDC. The solder should be 0.039–0.070 in. (1.0–1.77mm) for all engines.

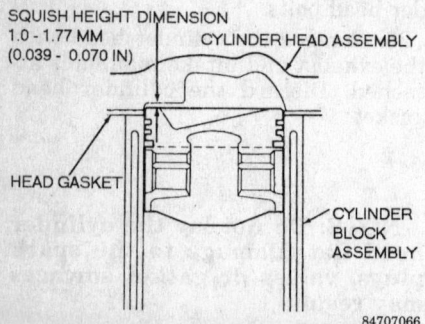

SQUISH HEIGHT DIMENSION
1.0 - 1.77 MM
(0.039 - 0.070 IN)
CYLINDER HEAD ASSEMBLY

HEAD GASKET

CYLINDER BLOCK ASSEMBLY

84707066

Piston squish height — 1.9L engine

31. Install the dowels in the cylinder block, if removed. Check the dowel height, it should be 0.41–0.46 in. (10.40–11.75mm) above the surface of the block. A dowel that is too long will not allow the cylinder head to sit properly.

32. Position the cylinder head gasket on the cylinder block.

33. Install the cylinder head and install new bolts and washers in the following order:

a. Apply a light coat of engine oil to the threads of the new cylinder head bolts and install the new bolts into the head.

b. Torque the cylinder head bolts in sequence to 44 ft. lbs. (60 Nm).

c. Loosen the cylinder head bolts approximately 2 turns and then torque again to 44 ft. lbs. (60 Nm) using the same torque sequence.

d. After setting the torque again, turn the head bolts 90 degrees in sequence and to complete the head bolt installation, turn the head bolts an additional 90 degrees in the same torque sequence.

NOTE: The cylinder head attaching bolts cannot be tightened to the specified torque more than once and must therefore be replaced when installing a cylinder head.

34. Install the rocker arm cover and the alternator bracket-to-cylinder head bolt.

35. Make sure cylinder No. 1 is at TDC.

36. Install the timing belt and the timing belt cover.

37. Raise and safely support the vehicle.

38. Install the crankshaft dampener.

39. Install the starter wiring harness on the retaining clip below the intake manifold.

40. Install the catalytic converter inlet pipe and the right side splash shield.

41. Lower the vehicle.

42. Install the alternator and the accessory drive belt automatic tensioner. Install the accessory drive belt.

43. Install both the power steering hose and air conditioner line retainer bracket bolts. Install the oil level indicator tube retainer bolt.

44. Connect the fuel supply and return lines.

45. Install the upper radiator hose and connect the heater hose at the engine compartment bulkhead. Install the heater hose support bracket retaining bolt.

46. Install the accelerator cable bracket on the intake manifold and connect the accelerator and kickdown cables to the throttle lever.

47. Install the ground strap at the left side of the cylinder head.

48. Connect all remaining electrical connectors according to their positions marked during the removal procedure.

49. Connect the power brake supply hose, crankcase breather hose and the vacuum line at the bottom of the throttle body.

50. Install the air intake duct.

51. Connect the negative battery cable.

52. Fill and bleed the cooling system.

53. Start the engine and check for leaks. Stop the engine and check the coolant level.

2.3L Engine

1. Disconnect the negative battery cable.

2. Disconnect the electric cooling fan switch at the plastic connector.

3. Drain the cooling system at the lower radiator hose.

4. On 1993–95 models, remove dipstick tube bolt.

5. Disconnect the heater hose at the heater inlet tube and disconnect the adapter hose at the water outlet connector.

6. Disconnect the upper radiator hose at the cylinder head.

7. Remove the air cleaner assembly.

8. Tag and disconnect the required electrical connectors and vacuum hoses.

9. Remove the distributor cap and spark plug wires as an assembly. Tag the spark plug wires prior to removal.

10. Disconnect all accessory drive belts.

11. Remove the rocker arm cover and gasket.

12. Remove the rocker arm fulcrum retaining bolts and remove the fulcrum, rocker arms and pushrods. Mark the location of each rocker arm, pushrod and fulcrum for reinstallation in its original position.

13. Properly relieve the fuel system pressure, then disconnect the fuel supply and return lines at the fuel rail.

14. Disconnect the accelerator cable and cruise control cable, if equipped.

15. Raise and safely support the vehicle.

16. Disconnect the exhaust system at the exhaust pipe and the hose at the tube.

17. Lower the vehicle.

18. Remove the cylinder head bolts.

19. Remove the cylinder head and gasket with the exhaust and intake manifolds attached.

NOTE: Do not lay the cylinder head flat. Damage to spark plugs or gasket surfaces may result.

To install:

20. Clean all gasket material from the mating surfaces of the cylinder head and block.

21. Position the head gasket on the cylinder block.

NOTE: Before installing the cylinder head, thread 2 cylinder head alignment studs T84P-6065-A or equivalent, into the block at opposite corners.

22. Install the cylinder head over the alignment studs onto the cylinder block. Start and run down several head bolts until snug. Remove the alignment studs and install the remaining head bolts. Tighten the bolts in sequence in 2 steps, first to 52-59 ft. lbs. (70-80 Nm) and then to 70-76 ft. lbs. (95-103 Nm).

23. Raise and safely support the vehicle.

24. Connect the exhaust system at the exhaust pipe and the hose to the metal tube.

25. Lower the vehicle.

26. Connect the accelerator cable and cruise control cable, if equipped.

27. Connect the fuel supply and return lines.

28. Install the fulcrums, rocker arms and pushrods in their original positions. Tighten the fulcrum bolts to 20-26 ft. lbs. (26-38 Nm).

29. Install the rocker arm cover gasket and cover.

30. Install the distributor cap and spark plug wires as an assembly.

31. Connect the accessory drive belts.

32. Connect the required electrical connectors and vacuum hoses.

33. Install the air cleaner assembly.

34. Connect the cooling fan switch at the plastic connector.

35. Connect the upper radiator hose and the heater hose.

36. On 1993-95 models, install dipstick tube bolt.

37. Fill the cooling system.

38. Connect the negative battery cable.

39. Start the engine and check for leaks.

40. After the engine has reached operating temperature, check and, if necessary, add coolant.

3.0L Engine

1. Rotate the crankshaft until the No. 1 cylinder piston is at TDC on the compression stroke.

2. Disconnect the negative battery cable.

3. Drain the cooling system.

4. Remove the PCV closure hose from the rocker arm cover and clean air flex tube.

5. Remove the clean air flex tube from the throttle body and mass air flow sensor.

6. Properly relieve the fuel system pressure, then disconnect the fuel lines.

7. Tag and disconnect all necessary vacuum lines.

8. Disconnect the TPS, idle air control valve, ECT, PFE, distributor, ignition coil and engine coolant temperature sending unit electrical connectors. Tag the location of each so they can be reconnected properly.

9. Disconnect the upper radiator hose from the thermostat housing.

10. Loosen the EGR tube retaining nuts and remove the tube.

11. Disconnect the throttle and TV cable from the throttle body linkage.

12. Remove the retaining nuts from the alternator brace and remove the brace.

13. Remove the 6 throttle body retaining bolts and remove the throttle body.

14. Disconnect the fuel injector harness retaining stand-offs from the inboard rocker arm cover studs. Carefully disconnect the electrical connections at each injector and remove the harness from the engine.

15. Disconnect the heater hose.

16. Tag and disconnect the ignition wires from the spark plugs, then remove the harness retaining stand-offs from the rocker arm cover studs.

17. Remove the distributor cap. Mark the position of the distributor rotor in relation to the distributor body and the position of the distributor body in relation to the engine block. Remove the distributor hold-down bolt and remove the distributor.

18. Remove the oil cooler tube assembly retaining bolt from the ignition coil bracket. Remove the ignition coil from the left cylinder head.

19. Remove the rocker arm covers.

20. Remove the rocker arms and pushrods. Keep all rocker arms, fulcrums and pushrods in order so they can be reinstalled in their original locations.

NOTE: Regardless of the cylinder head being removed, the No. 3 cylinder intake valve rocker arm and pushrod must be removed in order to remove the intake manifold.

21. Remove the intake manifold retaining bolts. Wedge a prybar between the manifold and engine block and pry upward to break the manifold-to-engine block seal, using the area between the thermostat and transaxle as a leverage point.

NOTE: The intake manifold may be removed with the fuel supply manifold and injectors in place.

22. If removing the right (rear) cylinder head, proceed as follows:

a. Remove the accessory and water pump drive belts.

b. Remove the water pump to front cover hose.

c. Raise and safely support the vehicle.

d. Remove the lower water pump tube. Loosen and remove the retaining nut from the upper bracket and the bolt from the lower bracket. Gently grasp the tube at the water pump end and pull the tube out of the water pump. Set the assembly aside.

e. Loosen and remove the exhaust inlet pipe flange retaining nuts from the exhaust manifold studs.

f. Lower the vehicle.

g. Remove the heater hose from the rear of the water pump.

h. Remove the water pump pulley shield. Remove the nut from the stud bolt.

i. Remove the water pump from the bracket.

j. Remove the exhaust manifold heatshield and the exhaust manifold.

23. If removing the left (front) cylinder head, proceed as follows:

a. Remove the accessory drive belt.

b. Remove the power steering pulley shield and the accessory belt tensioner.

c. Remove the 3 alternator bracket to cylinder head retaining bolts.

d. Remove the upper alternator retaining bolt.

e. Remove the 3 A/C brace retaining bolts and remove the brace.

f. Move the assembly away from the cylinder head slightly.

g. Remove the exhaust inlet pipe flange retaining nuts from the exhaust manifold studs.

h. Remove the 2 exhaust manifold heatshield retaining nuts and remove the shield.

i. Remove the engine oil dipstick tube or rotate it aside.

j. Remove the exhaust manifold retaining bolts and studs and remove the exhaust manifold.

24. Remove and discard the cylinder head bolts.

25. Remove the cylinder head(s). If the cylinder head is stuck to the gasket, place a prybar into the intake port and rock the cylinder head to break the seal.

NOTE: When breaking the seal, be careful not to damage machined surfaces or the intake valve.

26. Remove the cylinder head and discard the gasket.

27. If any coolant leaked into the cylinder bores from the cylinder head removal, immediately wipe the cylinder dry and apply a light coating of engine oil to the cylinder bore surface.

NOTE: Engine coolant is corrosive to engine bearing material and piston rings.

To install:

28. Lightly oil all bolt and stud threads prior to installation. Always use new cylinder heads bolts.

29. Place shop rags in the lifter valley, cylinder bores and cylinder block coolant passages to catch any dirt or gasket material. Clean the sealing surfaces of the cylinder head, intake manifold, rocker arm covers and cylinder block.

30. If the cylinder head was removed for head gasket replacement, check the cylinder head and block for flatness using a straight-edge and feeler gauge. Warpage should not exceed 0.003 inch in 6 inch span. Replace or machine the cylinder head, as necessary. If machining, do not grind off more than 0.010 in. (0.254mm).

31. Position new head gasket(s) on the cylinder block, with the V-cut toward the front of the engine. Use dowels to align and hold the gasket in place.

NOTE: Replace any dowels that are damaged or loose.

32. Install and hand-tighten the new cylinder head bolts. Tighten as follows:

   a. Tighten, in sequence, to 52–66 ft. lbs. (70–90 Nm).

   b. Back off all bolts 1 turn.

   c. Tighten, in sequence, to 33–41 ft. lbs. (45–55 Nm).

   d. Tighten, in sequence, to 63–73 ft. lbs. (85–99 Nm).

33. Apply a ¼ in. (6mm) drop of silicone sealer to the intersection of the cylinder block and cylinder head at the 4 corners of the lifter valley.

34. Position the intake gaskets on the cylinder heads and align the locking tabs to the cylinder head gaskets.

35. Install the front and rear intake manifold seals and secure with the retaining features.

36. Carefully lower the intake manifold into position, aligning the manifold bolt holes with the holes in the cylinder heads. Be careful not to disturb the sealer.

37. Install the No. 1, 2, 3 and 4 bolts and hand-tighten. Install the remaining bolts and tighten all bolts, in sequence, in 2 steps. First tighten to 15–22 ft. lbs. (20–30 Nm), then again in sequence, to 19–24 ft. lbs. (26–32 Nm).

38. Lubricate the distributor gear teeth and the distributor O-ring with engine oil. Install the distributor, aligning the marks that were made during the removal procedure. Install the hold-down bolt and snug.

39. Lubricate the pushrods and rocker arms with engine oil, then install them in their original locations. Snug the retaining bolts.

40. Rotate the crankshaft 1 turn clockwise. Tighten the rocker arm retaining bolts on the No. 1 intake valve, No. 2 exhaust valve, No. 4 intake valve and No. 5 exhaust valve to 5–11 ft. lbs. (7–15 Nm), making sure the rocker arms are seated on the pushrods and the rocker arm fulcrums are seated on the cylinder head.

41. Rotate the crankshaft 120 degrees clockwise. Tighten the remaining rocker arm retaining bolts to 5–11 ft. lbs. (7–15 Nm), making sure the rocker arms are seated on the pushrods and the rocker arm fulcrums are seated on the cylinder head.

42. Final tighten the rocker arm retaining bolts to 19–28 ft. lbs. (26–38 Nm) with the crankshaft in any position.

43. Install the rocker arm covers.

44. If the right (rear) cylinder head was removed, proceed as follows:

   a. Install the exhaust manifold and tighten the retaining bolts and studs to 15–22 ft. lbs. (20–30 Nm). Install the heatshield and tighten the retaining nuts to 12–15 ft. lbs. (16–20 Nm).

   b. Install the water pump to the bracket and tighten the retaining bolts and stud to 15–22 ft. lbs. (20–30 Nm).

   c. Install the water pump pulley shield and tighten the retaining nut to 7–10 ft. lbs. (9–14 Nm).

   d. Connect the heater hose at the fitting on the rear of the water pump and tighten the clamp.

   e. Raise and safely support the vehicle.

   f. Lubricate the water pump end of the water pump tube with soapy water and install it into the water pump. Install the retaining nut to the upper bracket stud bolt and tighten to 5 ft. lbs. (7 Nm). Install the lower tube bracket retaining bolt and tighten to 71–106 inch lbs. (8–12 Nm).

   g. Install the exhaust pipe flange nuts and tighten to 25–34 ft. lbs. (34–47 Nm).

   h. Lower the vehicle.

   i. Install the water pump to the front cover hose and tighten the clamp.

   j. Install the water pump drive belt. If the left (front) cylinder head was not removed, at this time install the accessory drive belt.

45. If the left (front) cylinder head was removed, proceed as follows:

   a. Install the exhaust manifold and tighten the retaining bolts and studs to 15–22 ft. lbs. (20–30 Nm).

   b. Rotate into position or install the engine oil dipstick tube, as required.

   c. Install the exhaust manifold heatshield and tighten the retaining nuts to 12–15 ft. lbs. (16–20 Nm).

   d. Install the exhaust pipe flange nuts and tighten to 25–34 ft. lbs. (34–47 Nm).

   e. Install the alternator bracket to the cylinder head and tighten the retaining bolts to 30–41 ft. lbs. (40–55 Nm).

   f. Install the A/C brace and the retaining bolts and upper alternator bolt. Tighten the long bolts to 30–41 ft. lbs. (40–55 Nm) and the remaining bolt to 15–22 ft. lbs. (20–30 Nm).

   g. Install the accessory belt tensioner and tighten the retaining bolt to 30–41 ft. lbs. (40–55 Nm).

   h. Install the accessory drive belt.

   i. Install the power steering pulley shield and tighten the retaining bolts to 6–8 ft. lbs. (8.5–11.0 Nm).

46. Install the fuel injector electrical harness to the injectors and secure the harness with the stand-offs to the inboard rocker arm cover studs.

47. Install the oil cooler tube assembly retaining bolt to the ignition coil bracket. Install the ignition coil and tighten the retaining bolts to 15–22 ft. lbs. (20–30 Nm).

48. Install the distributor cap and ignition wires. Install the wire harness stand-offs to the rocker arm cover studs and connect the wires to the spark plugs and ignition coil.

49. Install the throttle body, using a new gasket. Tighten the throttle body mounting bolts to 15–22 ft. lbs. (20–30 Nm).

50. Install the alternator brace to the throttle body and alternator bracket. Tighten the nuts to 12 ft. lbs. (16 Nm).

51. Connect the PCV hose to the tube under the throttle body.

52. Install the EGR tube from the exhaust manifold to the EGR valve. Tighten the retaining nuts to 26–48 ft. lbs. (36–65 Nm).

53. Connect the fuel lines to the fuel supply manifold. Install the fuel line safety clips.

54. Install the upper radiator hose and heater hose and tighten the clamps.

55. Connect all removed vacuum lines to their original locations as marked during the removal procedure.

56. Connect the electrical connectors at the TPS, idle air control, ECT, PFE, distributor, ignition coil and engine coolant temperature sending unit.

57. Connect the throttle and TV cables to the throttle body linkage.

58. Fill and bleed the cooling system.

59. Drain the crankcase and fill with the proper type and quantity of engine oil.

NOTE: Engine coolant is corrosive to all engine bearing material. Changing the oil after the replacement of a coolant carrying component prevents failure later.

60. Install the air cleaner tube between the throttle body and mass air flow sensor. Tighten the clamps to 24–35 inch lbs. (2.7–4.0 Nm).

61. Install the PCV closure hose to the rocker arm cover and clean air flex tube.

62. Connect the negative battery cable. Start the engine and check for leaks.

63. Check, and if necessary, adjust the ignition timing.

64. Install the idle air control shield.

Valve Lifters

REMOVAL AND INSTALLATION

1.8L Engine

NOTE: Hydraulic lash adjusters are used on the 1.8L engine between the valve stem and the camshaft to reduce noise and to provide maintenance-free valve clearance.

1. Disconnect the negative battery cable.

2. Remove the camshafts.

3. Mark the hydraulic lash adjusters and the cylinder head with alignment marks so the hydraulic lash adjusters can be installed in their original mounting positions.

4. Remove the hydraulic lash adjusters from the cylinder head.

To install:

5. Apply clean engine oil to the hydraulic lash adjuster friction surfaces.

6. If the hydraulic lash adjusters are being reused, install them in the positions from which they were removed.

7. Make sure the hydraulic lash adjusters move smoothly in their bores.

8. Install the camshafts.

9. Connect the negative battery cable.

1.9L Engine

1. Disconnect the negative battery cable.

2. Remove air cleaner assembly. Remove valve cover and gasket.

3. Remove rocker arms, lifter guides, lifter retainers and lifters.

NOTE: Always return lifters to the original bores unless they are being replaced.

To install:

4. Lubricate each lifter bore with engine oil.

5. Install the lifters with the plunger upward and position guide flats of lifters to be parallel with centerline of camshaft. If equipped, color orientation dots on lifters should be opposite the oil feed holes in cylinder head.

6. If equipped with roller lifters, install the lifter guide plates over the lifter guide flats with notch toward exhaust side.

7. Lubricate lifter plunger cap and valve tip with engine oil.

8. Install lifter guide plates retainers into rocker arm fulcrum slots, in both intake and exhaust side. The tab should be located on the intake seal fulcrum slot.

9. Install 4 rocker arms in lifter position No's 3, 6, 7 and 8.

10. Lubricate rocker arm surface that will contact fulcrum surface with engine oil.

11. Install 4 fulcrums. Fulcrums must be fully seated in slots of cylinder head.

12. Install 4 bolts. Tighten to 17–22 ft. lbs. (23–30 Nm).

13. Rotate the engine until the camshaft sprocket keyway is in the 6 o'clock position.

14. Repeat steps 9–12 in lifter position No's 1, 2, 4 and 5.

15. Install valve cover and gasket. Install air cleaner assembly.

16. Connect negative battery cable.

2.3L Engine

NOTE: Before replacing a lifter for noisy operation, make sure the noise is not caused by improper collapsed lifter gap, worn rocker arms, pushrods or valve tips.

1. Disconnect the negative battery cable. Remove the cylinder head and related parts.

2. Using a magnet, remove the lifters. Identify, tag and place the lifters in a rack so they can be installed in their original positions.

3. If the lifters are stuck in their bores by excessive varnish or gum, it may be necessary to use a hydraulic lifter puller tool to remove the lifters. Rotate the lifters back and forth to loosen any gum and varnish which may have formed.

To install:

4. Install the hydraulic lifters through the pushrod openings with a magnet.

5. Install the cylinder head and related parts.

6. Connect negative battery cable.

3.0L Engine

NOTE: Before replacing a lifter for noisy operation, make sure the noise is not caused by improper collapsed lifter gap, worn rocker arms, pushrods or valve tips.

1. Rotate the crankshaft until the No. 1 cylinder piston is at TDC on the compression stroke.

2. Disconnect the negative battery cable.

3. Drain the cooling system.

4. Remove the PCV closure hose from the rocker arm cover and clean air flex tube.

5. Remove the clean air flex tube from the throttle body and mass air flow sensor.

6. Properly relieve the fuel system pressure, then disconnect the fuel lines.

7. Tag and disconnect all necessary vacuum lines.

8. Disconnect the TPS, idle control, ECT, PFE, IAT, distributor, ignition coil and coolant temperature

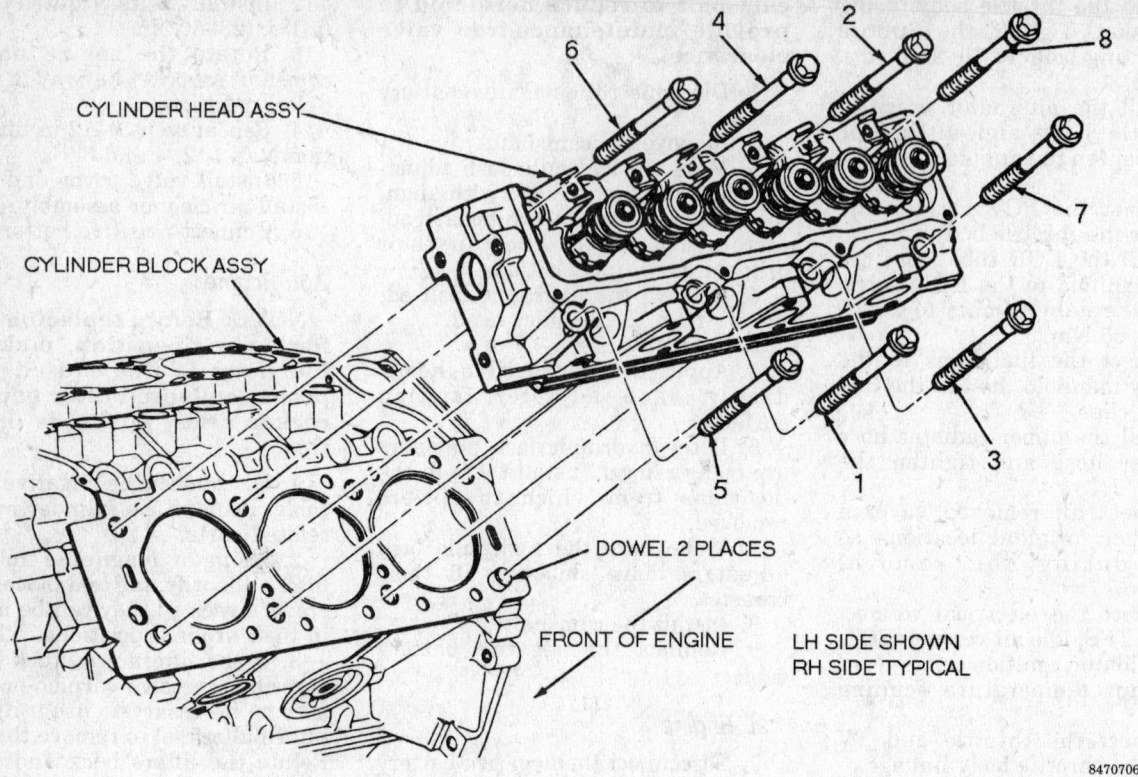

CYLINDER HEAD ASSY

CYLINDER BLOCK ASSY

DOWEL 2 PLACES

FRONT OF ENGINE

LH SIDE SHOWN
RH SIDE TYPICAL

84707069

Cylinder head bolt torque sequence — 3.0L engine

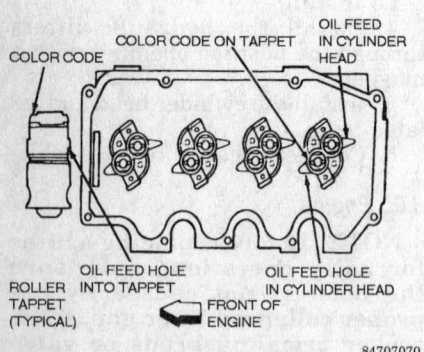

COLOR CODE

COLOR CODE ON TAPPET

OIL FEED
IN CYLINDER
HEAD

OIL FEED HOLE
INTO TAPPET

OIL FEED HOLE
IN CYLINDER HEAD

ROLLER
TAPPET
(TYPICAL)

FRONT OF
ENGINE

84707070

Roller lifter assembly installation — 1.9L engine

sending unit electrical connectors. Tag the location of each so they can be reconnected properly.

9. Disconnect the upper radiator hose from the thermostat housing.

10. Loosen the EGR tube retaining nuts and remove the tube.

11. Disconnect the throttle and TV cable from the throttle body linkage.

12. Remove the retaining nuts from the alternator brace and remove the brace.

13. Remove the 6 throttle body retaining bolts and remove the throttle body.

14. Disconnect the fuel injector harness retaining stand-offs from the inboard rocker arm cover studs. Carefully disconnect the electrical connections at each injector and remove the harness from the engine.

15. Disconnect the heater hose.

16. Disconnect the ignition wires from the spark plugs, then remove the harness retaining stand-offs from the rocker arm cover studs.

17. Remove the distributor cap. Mark the position of the distributor rotor in relation to the distributor body and the position of the distributor body in relation to the engine block. Remove the distributor hold-down bolt and remove the distributor.

18. Remove the oil cooler tube assembly retaining bolt from the ignition coil bracket. Remove the ignition coil from the left cylinder head.

19. Remove the rocker arm covers.

20. Regardless of the lifter(s) being removed, the No. 3 cylinder intake valve rocker arm and pushrod must be removed in order to remove the intake manifold.

21. Remove the intake manifold retaining bolts. Wedge a prybar between the manifold and engine block and pry upward to break the manifold-to-engine block seal, using the

area between the thermostat and transaxle as a leverage point.

NOTE: The intake manifold may be removed with the fuel supply manifold and injectors in place.

22. Remove the rocker arm, fulcrum and pushrod of the lifter(s) being replaced. Keep the rocker arms, fulcrums and pushrods in order so they can be reinstalled in their original positions.

23. Loosen the 2 roller lifter guide plate retaining bolts and remove the guide plate retainer assembly from the lifter valley.

24. Remove the lifter guide plate(s) from the lifters by lifting straight up.

25. Remove the lifter by grasping it and pulling in line with the bore. If the lifter(s) are stuck in the bore(s) due to excessive varnish or gum deposits, it may be necessary to use a claw-type tool to aid removal. Rotate the lifter back and forth to loosen it from the deposits.

To install:

26. Lightly oil all retaining bolt and stud threads prior to installation.

27. Clean the gasket mating surfaces of the intake manifold and cylinder head. Before scraping, lay a clean cloth in the lifter valley to catch any gasket material. After scraping,

remove the cloth, being careful not to let any particles fall into the drain holes or cylinder head.

28. Lubricate the lifter(s) and bore(s) with clean engine oil and install the lifter(s) into the bore(s).

29. Align the lifter flats and install the lifter guide plate. Install the plate with the word **UP** and or button visible.

30. Install the guide plate retainer assembly over the guide plates with the 2 retainer bolts. Tighten the bolts to 8–10 ft. lbs. (10–14 Nm).

31. Apply a ¼ in. (6mm) drop of silicone sealer to the intersection of the cylinder block and cylinder head at the 4 corners of the lifter valley.

32. Position the intake gaskets on the cylinder heads and align the locking tabs to the cylinder head gaskets.

33. Install the front and rear intake manifold seals and secure with the retaining features.

34. Carefully lower the intake manifold into position, aligning the manifold bolt holes with the holes in the cylinder heads. Be careful not to disturb the sealer.

35. Install the No. 1, 2, 3 and 4 bolts and hand-tighten. Install the remaining bolts and tighten all bolts, in sequence, in 2 steps. First tighten to 15–22 ft. lbs. (20–30 Nm), then again in sequence, to 19–24 ft. lbs. (26–32 Nm).

36. Lubricate the distributor gear teeth and the distributor O-ring with engine oil. Install the distributor, aligning the marks that were made during the removal procedure. Install the hold-down bolt and snug.

37. Lubricate the pushrods and rocker arms with engine oil, then install them in their original locations. Snug the retaining bolts.

38. Before tightening each retaining bolt, rotate the crankshaft until the lifter is on the base circle of the camshaft lobe. Tighten the retaining bolt to 5–11 ft. lbs. (7–15 Nm), making sure the rocker arm is fully seated on the pushrod and the fulcrum is fully seated on the cylinder head. Final tighten the retaining bolt to 19–28 ft. lbs. (26–38 Nm).

39. Install the rocker arm covers.

40. Install the fuel injector electrical harness to the injectors and secure the harness with the stand-offs to the inboard rocker arm cover studs.

41. Install the ignition coil and tighten the retaining bolts to 15–22 ft. lbs. (20–30 Nm). If equipped, install the oil cooler tube assembly bracket to the ignition coil bracket

and tighten the retaining bolt to 15–22 ft. lbs. (20–30 Nm).

42. Install the distributor cap and ignition wires. Install the wire harness stand-offs to the rocker arm cover studs and connect the wires to the spark plugs and ignition coil.

43. Install the throttle body, using a new gasket. Tighten the throttle body mounting bolts to 15–22 ft. lbs. (20–30 Nm).

44. Install the alternator brace to the throttle body and alternator bracket. Tighten the nuts to 12 ft. lbs. (16 Nm).

45. Connect the PCV hose to the tube under the throttle body.

46. Install the EGR tube from the exhaust manifold to the EGR valve. Tighten the retaining nuts to 26–48 ft. lbs. (36–65 Nm).

47. Connect the fuel lines to the fuel supply manifold. Install the fuel line safety clips.

48. Install the upper radiator hose and heater hose and tighten the clamps.

49. Connect all removed vacuum lines to their original locations as marked during the removal procedure.

50. Connect the electrical connectors at the TPS, idle air control, ECT, PFE, IAC, distributor, ignition coil and coolant temperature sending unit.

51. Connect the throttle and TV cables to the throttle body linkage.

52. Fill and bleed the cooling system.

53. Drain the crankcase and fill with the proper type and quantity of engine oil.

NOTE: Engine coolant is corrosive to all engine bearing material. Changing the oil after the replacement of a coolant carrying component prevents failure later.

54. Install the air cleaner tube between the throttle body and mass air flow sensor. Tighten the clamps to 24–35 inch lbs. (2.7–4.0 Nm).

55. Install the PCV closure hose to the rocker arm cover and clean air flex tube.

56. Connect the negative battery cable. Start the engine and check for leaks.

57. Check, and if necessary, adjust the ignition timing.

58. Install the idle air control shield.

Valve Lash

ADJUSTMENT

Collapsed Lifter Clearance

1.9L ENGINE

1. Connect an auxiliary starter switch in the starting circuit. Crank the engine with the ignition switch **OFF** until the No. 1 piston is at TDC on the compression stroke.

2. With the crankshaft in position, place hydraulic lifter compressor tool T81P–6500–A or equivalent, on the rocker arm. Slowly apply pressure to bleed down the lifter until it completely bottoms. Hold the lifter in this position and check the available clearance between the rocker arm and the valve stem tip with a feeler gauge. The feeler gauge width must not exceed ³⁄₈ in., in order to fit between the rails on the rocker arm.

3. The clearance should be 0–4.5mm, 2.2mm normal.

4. If the clearance is not within specifications, check the fulcrum, lifter, camshaft lobe and valve tip for wear.

5. With the No. 1 piston on TDC at the end of the compression stroke check the following valves: No. 1 intake, No. 1 exhaust, No. 2 intake.

6. Rotate the crankshaft 180 degrees and check the following valves: No. 3 intake, No. 3 exhaust.

7. Rotate the crankshaft another 180 degrees TDC and check the following valves: No. 4 intake, No. 4 exhaust, No. 2 exhaust.

2.3L ENGINE

NOTE: This clearance check is usually only needed when the valves, valve seats and/or cylinder head gasket surface have been machined or new parts have been installed. Clearance must be checked when the lifter is completely collapsed.

1. Disconnect the negative battery cable.

2. Remove the rocker arm cover.

3. Rotate the engine until the No. 1 cylinder is at TDC of its compression stroke. The timing marks on the camshaft and crankshaft gears will be together. Check the clearance on No. 1 intake, No. 1 exhaust, No. 2 intake and No. 3 exhaust valves.

4. To check the clearance, use lifter bleed down wrench T71P–6513–B or equivalent, to push down on the rocker arm and bleed the oil from the lifter.

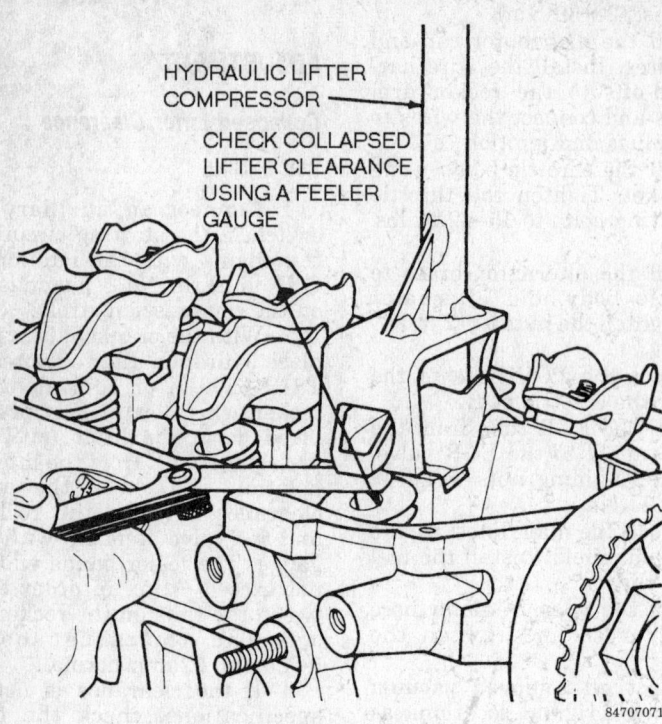

HYDRAULIC LIFTER COMPRESSOR

CHECK COLLAPSED LIFTER CLEARANCE USING A FEELER GAUGE

84707071

Checking collapsed lifter clearance — 1.9L engine

5. Insert the appropriate thickness feeler gauge between the rocker arm and valve stem to check the clearance.

6. Rotate the crankshaft 1 complete turn. Check the clearance on No. 2 exhaust, No. 3 intake, No. 4 intake and No. 4 exhaust.

7. The clearance between the rocker arm and the valve stem tip should be 0.072–0.174 in. (1.80–4.34mm) with the lifter on the base circle of the cam.

8. If the clearance is less than specified, shorter pushrods are available to correct the problem. If the clearance is greater than specified, longer pushrods are available.

3.0L ENGINE

NOTE: This clearance check is usually only needed when the valves, valve seats and/or cylinder head gasket surface have been machined or new parts have been installed. Clearance must be checked when the lifter is completely collapsed.

1. Disconnect the negative battery cable.

2. Remove the rocker arm covers.

3. Rotate the engine until the No. 1 cylinder is at TDC of its compression stroke and check the clearance between the rocker arm and the following valves: No. 1 intake and exhaust, No. 2 exhaust, No. 3 intake, No. 4 exhaust and No. 6 intake.

4. To check the clearance, use lifter bleed down wrench T71P–6513–B or equivalent, to push down on the rocker arm and bleed the oil from the lifter.

5. Insert the appropriate thickness feeler gauge between the rocker arm and valve stem to check the clearance.

6. Rotate the crankshaft 360 degrees and check the clearance between the rocker arm and the following valves: No. 2 intake, No. 3 exhaust, No. 4 intake, No. 5 intake and exhaust and No. 6 exhaust.

7. The clearance should be 0.09–0.19 in. (2.3–4.8mm).

8. If the clearance is less than specified, shorter pushrods are available to correct the problem. If the clearance is greater than specified, longer pushrods are available.

Rocker Arms

REMOVAL AND INSTALLATION

1.9L Engine

1. Disconnect the negative battery cable and remove the air cleaner assembly.

2. Remove and tag all necessary vacuum hoses from the rocker cover. Remove the spark plug wire retainers, if equipped. Remove the rocker cover from the cylinder head.

3. Remove the rocker cover and gasket from the engine.

4. Remove the rocker arm nuts, fulcrums, rocker arms and fulcrum washers. Keep all parts in order so they can be reinstalled to their original position.

To install:

5. Before installation, coat the valve tips, rocker arm and fulcrum contact areas with Lubriplate® or equivalent.

6. Rotate the engine until the lifter is on the base circle of the cam (valve closed).

NOTE: Be sure to turn the engine only in the normal rotation. Backward rotation will cause the camshaft belt to slip or lose teeth, altering the valve timing and causing serious engine damage.

7. Install the rocker arm and components and torque the rocker arm bolts to 17–22 ft. lbs. (23–30 Nm). Be sure the lifter is on the base circle of the cam for each rocker arm as it is installed.

8. Install a new gasket and the rocker arm cover. Install the 3 retaining bolts and tighten to 4–9 ft. lbs. (5–12 Nm).

NOTE: Do not use any type of sealer with the rocker arm cover silicone gasket.

9. Connect all vacuum hoses and install the spark plug wire retainers, if equipped.

10. Connect the negative battery cable.

2.3L Engine

1. Disconnect the negative battery cable.

2. Remove and tag all necessary vacuum hoses from the rocker cover. Remove the oil fill cap and set it aside. Disconnect the PCV hose and set it aside.

3. Remove the rocker arm cover bolts. Remove the rocker cover from the engine.

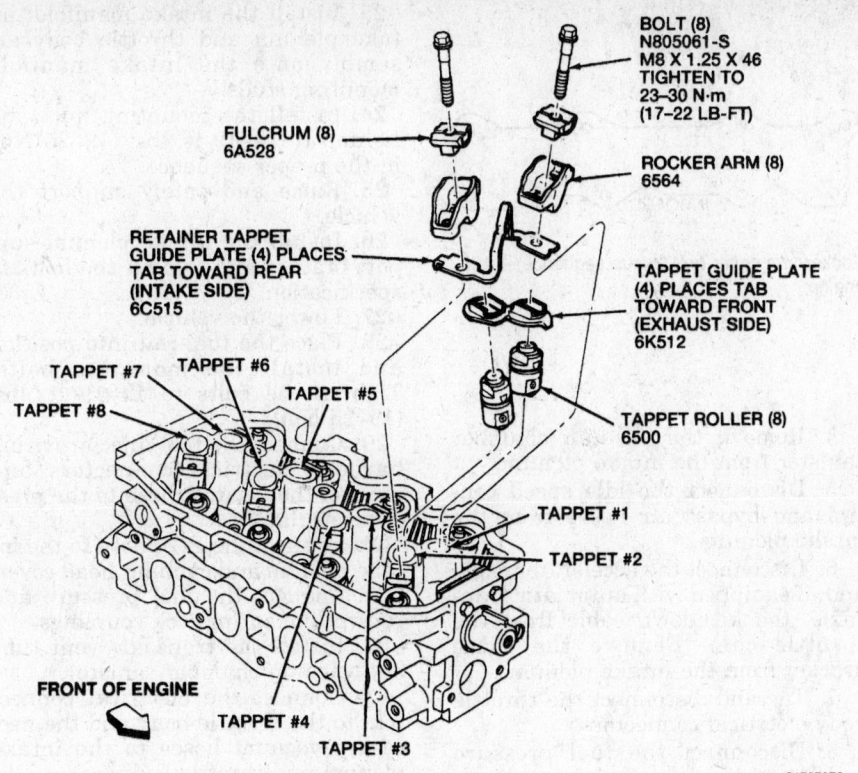

BOLT (8)
N805061-S
M8 X 1.25 X 46
TIGHTEN TO
23–30 N·m
(17–22 LB-FT)

FULCRUM (8)
6A528

ROCKER ARM (8)
6564

RETAINER TAPPET
GUIDE PLATE (4) PLACES
TAB TOWARD REAR
(INTAKE SIDE)
6C515

TAPPET GUIDE PLATE
(4) PLACES TAB
TOWARD FRONT
(EXHAUST SIDE)
6K512

TAPPET #7
TAPPET #6
TAPPET #5
TAPPET #8

TAPPET ROLLER (8)
6500

TAPPET #1
TAPPET #2

FRONT OF ENGINE

TAPPET #4
TAPPET #3

84707072

Rocker arm removal — 1.9L engine

4. Remove the rocker arm bolts, fulcrums, rocker arms and fulcrum washers. Keep all parts in order so they can be reinstalled to their original position.

To install:

5. Before installation, coat the valve tips, rocker arm and fulcrum contact areas with Lubriplate® or equivalent.

6. For each valve, rotate the engine until the lifter is on the base circle of the cam (valve closed).

7. Install the rocker arm and components and torque the rocker arm bolts in 2 steps: the first to 4.5–7.5 ft. lbs. (6–10 Nm) and the second torque to 20–26 ft. lbs. (26–38 Nm). Be sure the lifter is on the base circle of the cam for each rocker arm as it is installed. For the final tightening, the camshaft may be in any position.

8. Clean the rocker cover rail on the cylinder head.

NOTE: The rocker arm cover has a reusable "mould in place gasket". If the gasket is damaged by a cut/nick of about ⅛ in. (maximum 2 places), the damaged area may be filled in with RTV sealer. If the gasket is damaged by cuts longer than ⅛ in. or by more than 2 cuts/nicks, replace the rocker arm cover.

9. Install the rocker arm cover with the retaining bolts and tighten to 5.9–8.5 ft. lbs. (8.0–11.5 Nm). Apply suitable threadlock adhesive to the bolts if they are being reused, to prevent leaks.

10. Install oil fill cap, all necessary vacuum hoses and the PCV hose.

11. Connect negative battery cable.

3.0L Engine

1. Disconnect the negative battery cable.

2. Disconnect the ignition wires from the spark plugs. Remove the ignition wire/separator assembly from the rocker arm cover retaining studs and move aside.

3. If the left rocker arm cover is being removed, proceed as follows:

   a. Disconnect the air cleaner closure system hose.

   b. Remove the fuel injector harness stand-offs from the inboard rocker arm cover studs. Move the harness aside.

4. If the right rocker arm cover is being removed, proceed as follows:

   a. Remove the air cleaner duct hose from the throttle body.

   b. Remove the idle speed control solenoid shield.

   c. Disconnect the throttle and TV cable from the throttle body linkage.

   d. Tag and disconnect the necessary vacuum hoses from the throttle body.

   e. Loosen the EGR tube nuts, if equipped, at the EGR valve and exhaust manifold fitting. Remove or rotate the tube aside.

   f. Remove the PCV hose from the tube under the throttle body.

   g. Disconnect the electrical connectors at the air charge temperature sensor, idle speed control solenoid and throttle position sensor.

   h. Remove the retaining nuts from the alternator brace and remove the brace.

   i. Remove the throttle body mounting bolts and remove the throttle body. Discard the gasket.

   j. Remove the fuel injector harness stand-offs from the inboard rocker arm cover studs. Move the fuel injector harness aside.

5. Loosen the rocker arm cover retaining bolts and studs. Carefully slide a sharp, thin bladed knife between the cylinder head and rocker arm cover gasket at the rail step where the intake manifold mates to the cylinder head, 2 places each side. Cut only the RTV sealer and not the integral gasket, then remove the cover making sure the RTV sealer does not pull the integral gasket from the cover.

6. Remove the rocker arm retaining bolts, rocker arms and fulcrums. If the rocker arms are to be reused, keep all parts in order so they can be reinstalled in their original positions.

To install:

7. Lubricate the rocker arm and fulcrum contact surfaces and the valve stem tips with clean engine oil. Install the rocker arms and fulcrums in their original locations and snug the retaining bolts.

8. Before tightening each retaining bolt, rotate the crankshaft until the lifter is on the base circle of the camshaft lobe. Tighten the retaining bolt to 5–11 ft. lbs. (7–15 Nm), making sure the rocker arm is fully seated on the pushrod and the fulcrum is fully seated on the cylinder head. Final tighten the retaining bolt to 19–28 ft. lbs. (26–38 Nm).

9. Apply a bead of silicone sealer at the cylinder head to intake manifold rail step, 2 places per rail.

10. Position the cover on the cylinder head and hand-tighten the retaining bolts and studs. Then, tighten in sequence to 8–10 ft. lbs. (10–14 Nm).

11. If the left rocker arm cover is being installed, proceed as follows:

a. Connect the air cleaner closure system hose to the nipple.

b. Install the fuel injector harness stand-offs to the appropriate inboard rocker arm cover studs.

12. If the right rocker arm cover is being installed, proceed as follows:

a. Install the fuel injector harness stand-offs to the appropriate inboard rocker arm cover studs.

b. Clean the gasket mating surfaces of the intake manifold and throttle body.

c. Install the throttle body, using a new gasket and tighten the mounting bolts to 15–22 ft. lbs. (20–30 Nm).

d. Install the alternator brace the throttle body and alternator bracket. Tighten the nuts to 12 ft. lbs. (16 Nm).

e. Connect the PCV hose to the tube under the throttle body.

f. Install the EGR tube to the EGR valve and exhaust manifold fitting, if equipped. Tighten to 37 ft. lbs. (50 Nm).

g. Connect the vacuum hoses to the locations marked during the removal procedure.

h. Connect the electrical connectors to the air charge temperature sensor, idle speed control solenoid and throttle position sensor.

i. Connect the throttle and TV cables to the throttle body linkage.

j. Connect the air cleaner duct hose to the throttle body and air cleaner assembly. Tighten the clamp to 36 inch lbs. (4 Nm).

k. Check the TV cable adjustment.

l. Install the shield on the idle speed control solenoid.

13. Connect the ignition wires to the spark plugs. Install the ignition wire separator stand-offs to the appropriate rocker arm cover studs.

14. Connect the negative battery cable, start the engine and check for oil and vacuum leaks.

Intake Manifold

REMOVAL AND INSTALLATION

1.8L Engine

1. Properly relieve the fuel system pressure.

2. Disconnect the negative battery cable.

3. Tag and disconnect the necessary vacuum hoses from the intake manifold and plenum.

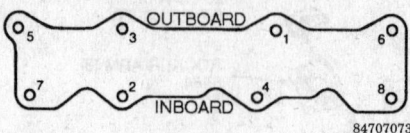

Rocker arm cover bolt torque sequence — 3.0L engine

84707073

4. Remove the vacuum chamber canister from the intake plenum.

5. Disconnect the idle speed control and bypass air hoses from the intake plenum.

6. Disconnect the accelerator cable and, if equipped with automatic transaxle, the kickdown cable from the throttle cam. Remove the cable bracket from the intake plenum.

7. Tag and disconnect the throttle body electrical connectors.

8. Disconnect the fuel pressure and return line spring lock couplings.

9. Disconnect the PCV hose from the intake plenum and cylinder head cover.

10. Disconnect the fuel pressure regulator vacuum hose and the fuel injector wiring harness electrical connectors.

11. Remove the fuel rail mounting bolts and remove the fuel rail.

12. Remove the 2 bolts from the transaxle vent tube and remove the vent tube from the intake plenum.

13. Remove the intake manifold upper mounting nuts.

14. Raise and safely support the vehicle.

15. Remove the intake plenum support bracket and the intake manifold lower mounting nuts.

16. Lower the vehicle.

17. Remove the intake manifold, intake plenum and throttle body as an assembly from the vehicle.

18. Remove the intake manifold gasket.

19. If necessary, separate the intake plenum and throttle body from the intake manifold.

20. Clean all gasket mating surfaces.

To install:

21. If necessary, install the throttle body and intake plenum onto the intake manifold.

22. Install the intake manifold gasket.

23. Install the intake manifold, intake plenum and throttle body assembly onto the intake manifold mounting studs.

24. Install the mounting nuts and tighten to 14–19 ft. lbs. (19–25 Nm) in the proper sequence.

25. Raise and safely support the vehicle.

26. Install the intake plenum support bracket and tighten the bolts to specification.

27. Lower the vehicle.

28. Place the fuel rail into position and install the mounting bolts. Tighten the bolts to 14–19 ft. lbs. (19–25 Nm).

29. Connect the fuel injector wiring harness electrical connectors and connect the vacuum hose to the pressure regulator.

30. Connect the PCV hose to the intake plenum and cylinder head cover.

31. Connect the fuel pressure and return line spring lock couplings.

32. Install the transaxle vent tube and vacuum chamber canister.

33. Connect the electrical connectors to the throttle body and the necessary vacuum hoses to the intake plenum and throttle body.

34. Connect the idle speed control and bypass air hoses to the intake plenum.

35. Install the cable bracket onto the intake plenum and connect the accelerator and, if equipped, kickdown cables to the throttle cam.

36. Install the inlet air duct that connects to the throttle body and the resonance chamber.

37. Connect the negative battery cable.

1.9L Engine

1. Properly relieve the fuel system pressure.

2. Disconnect the negative battery cable.

3. Partially drain the cooling system.

4. Remove the air intake tube.

5. Disconnect the fuel injector harness from the engine control harness at the right shock tower.

6. Disconnect the crankshaft position sensor.

7. Disconnect the fuel supply and return lines.

8. On 1993–95 models, disconnect the cylinder identification (CID) sensor.

9. Remove the accelerator cable and, if equipped with automatic transaxle, kickdown cable from the throttle lever. Remove the cable bracket from the intake manifold and position the cables aside.

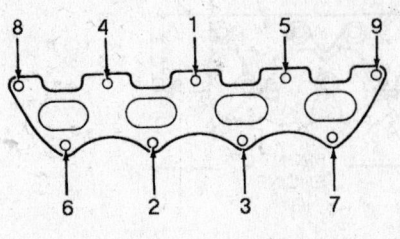

84707074

Intake manifold bolt torque sequence — 1.8L engine

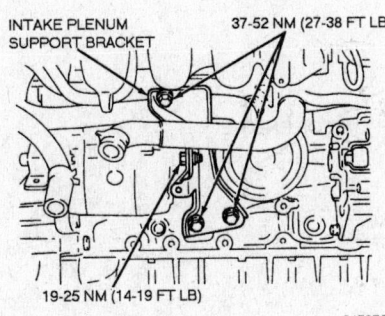

INTAKE PLENUM SUPPORT BRACKET

37-52 NM (27-38 FT LB)

19-25 NM (14-19 FT LB)

84707075

Intake plenum support bracket torque specifications — 1.8L engine

10. Remove the power brake supply hose, PCV line and the vacuum line from the bottom of the throttle body.

11. Remove the 7 attaching nuts from the intake manifold studs, slide the manifold assembly off the studs and remove it from the cylinder head. Remove and discard the intake manifold gasket.

To install:

12. Clean and inspect the mounting faces of the intake manifold and cylinder head. Both surfaces must be clean and flat.

13. Clean and oil the manifold studs and position a new gasket over them.

14. Install the intake manifold and the attaching nuts. Tighten the nuts to 12–15 ft. lbs. (16–20 Nm).

15. Install the vacuum line on the bottom of the throttle body, the power brake supply hose and the PCV line.

16. Install the accelerator cable bracket and connect the accelerator cable and, if equipped, kickdown cable on the throttle lever.

17. Connect the crankshaft position sensor electrical connector.

18. Connect the fuel supply and return lines. Install the fuel line retaining clips.

19. On 1993–95 models, connect the cylinder identification (CID) sensor.

20. Connect the 2 fuel injector harness connectors to the engine control harness at the right shock tower.

21. Install the air intake tube.

22. Refill the cooling system.

23. Connect the negative battery cable.

24. Start the engine and bring to normal operating temperature. Check for leaks. Stop the engine and check the coolant level.

2.3L Engine

1. Disconnect the negative battery cable.

2. Properly relieve the fuel system pressure.

3. Remove the air duct from between the throttle body and air cleaner.

4. Disconnect the accelerator and, if equipped, cruise control cables from the mounting bracket and throttle lever.

5. Tag and disconnect the rear vacuum line to the dash panel vacuum tree, the vacuum line at the intake manifold, MAP sensor vacuum line and fuel pressure regulator vacuum line.

6. Disconnect the hoses from the PCV valve at the intake manifold.

7. Disconnect the EGR vacuum line at the EGR valve and EGR tube. Disconnect the EGR tube from the upper intake manifold by supporting the connector while loosening the compression nut.

8. Disconnect the upper support manifold bracket by removing the top bolt only. Leave the bottom bolts attached.

9. Tag and disconnect the electrical connectors at the main engine harness, near the No. 4 runner.

10. Disconnect the fuel supply and return lines.

11. Remove the 8 manifold mounting fasteners.

12. Disconnect the lower support manifold bracket by removing the top bolt only. Leave the bottom bolts attached.

13. Remove the manifold with the wiring harness. Discard the gasket.

To install:

14. Clean and inspect the mounting faces of the manifold and cylinder head. Both surfaces must be clean and flat.

15. Install a new gasket and the manifold assembly. Install and finger-tighten the fasteners.

16. Connect the fuel return line to the fitting in the fuel supply manifold.

17. Tighten all manifold fasteners, in sequence, to 15–22 ft. lbs. (20–30 Nm).

18. Connect the upper and lower manifold support brackets and tighten to 15–22 ft. lbs. (20–30 Nm).

19. Install the EGR tube with the oil-coated compression nut and tighten to 30–40 ft. lbs. (40–55 Nm).

20. Connect the large PCV vacuum line to the upper manifold fitting.

21. Connect the rear manifold vacuum connections at the dash panel vacuum tree and connect the vacuum line(s) to the upper manifold.

22. Connect the accelerator and, if equipped, the cruise control cables.

23. Connect the wiring harness at the electronic engine control harness.

24. Connect the fuel supply hose from the filter to the fuel supply manifold.

25. Connect the negative battery cable. Start the engine and check for fuel and/or vacuum leaks.

3.0L Engine

1. Disconnect the negative battery cable.

2. Drain the cooling system.

3. Remove the PCV closure hose from the rocker arm cover and clean air flex tube.

4. Remove the clean air flex tube from the throttle body and mass air flow sensor.

5. Properly relieve the fuel system pressure, then disconnect the fuel lines.

6. Tag and disconnect all necessary vacuum lines.

7. Disconnect the TPS, idle air control, IAT, ECT, PFE, distributor, ignition coil and coolant temperature sending unit electrical connectors. Tag the location of each so they can be reconnected properly.

8. Disconnect the upper radiator hose from the thermostat housing.

9. Loosen the EGR tube retaining nuts and remove the tube.

10. Disconnect the throttle and TV cable from the throttle body linkage.

11. Remove the retaining nuts from the alternator brace and remove the brace.

12. Remove the 6 throttle body retaining bolts and remove the throttle body.

13. Disconnect the fuel injector harness retaining stand-offs from the inboard rocker arm cover studs. Carefully disconnect the electrical connections at each injector and remove the harness from the engine.

14. Disconnect the heater hose.

15. Disconnect the ignition wires from the spark plugs, then remove

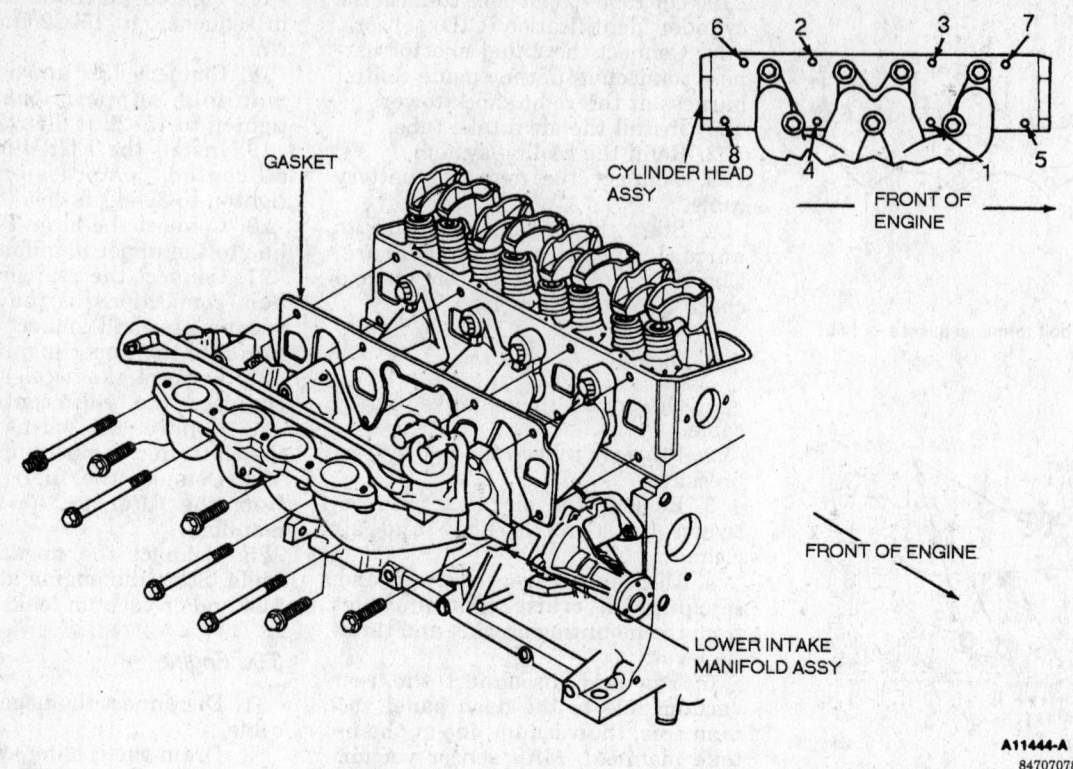

Intake manifold bolt torque sequence — 2.3L engine

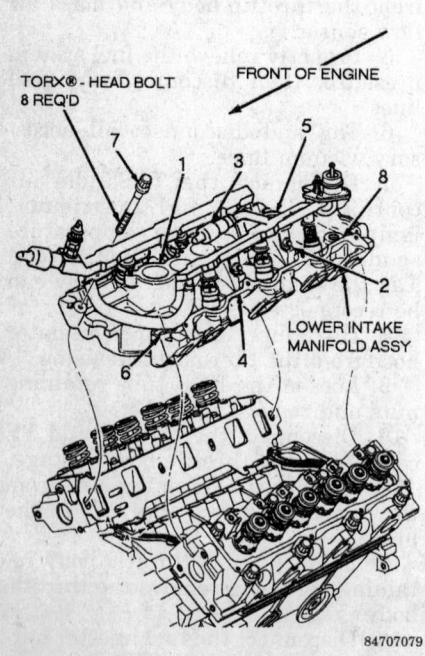

Intake manifold bolt torque sequence — 3.0L engine

the harness retaining stand-offs from the rocker arm cover studs.

16. Remove the distributor cap. Mark the position of the distributor rotor in relation to the distributor body and the position of the distributor body in relation to the engine block. Remove the distributor hold-down bolt and remove the distributor.

17. Remove the oil cooler tube assembly retaining bolt from the ignition coil bracket. Remove the ignition coil from the left cylinder head.

18. Remove the rocker arm covers.

19. Remove the No. 3 cylinder intake valve rocker arm and pushrod.

20. Remove the intake manifold retaining bolts. Wedge a prybar between the manifold and engine block and pry upward to break the manifold-to-engine block seal, using the area between the thermostat and transaxle as a leverage point.

NOTE: The intake manifold may be removed with the fuel supply manifold and injectors in place.

To install:

21. Lightly oil all retaining bolt and stud threads prior to installation.

22. Clean the gasket mating surfaces of the intake manifold and cylinder head. Before scraping, lay a clean cloth in the lifter valley to catch any gasket material. After scraping, remove the cloth, being careful not to let any particles fall into the drain holes or cylinder head.

23. If installing a new intake manifold, transfer the ECT sensor, thermostat gasket and housing, heater hose elbow and coolant temperature sending unit to the new manifold.

24. If removed, install the fuel supply manifold. Apply light grade oil to the fuel injector O-rings prior to installation. Install the injectors into the fuel supply manifold and carefully align the assembly to the intake manifold injector holes. Push 1 side into place at a time until the manifold "clicks" into place. Install the fuel supply manifold retaining bolts and tighten to 71–106 inch lbs. (8–12 Nm).

25. Apply a 1/4 in. (6mm) drop of silicone sealer to the intersection of the cylinder block and cylinder head at the 4 corners of the lifter valley.

26. Position the intake gaskets on the cylinder heads and align the locking tabs to the cylinder head gaskets.

27. Install the front and rear intake manifold seals and secure with the retaining features.

28. Carefully lower the intake manifold into position, aligning the manifold bolt holes with the holes in the

cylinder heads. Be careful not to disturb the sealer.

29. Install the No. 1, 2, 3 and 4 bolts and hand-tighten. Install the remaining bolts and tighten all bolts, in sequence, in 2 steps. First tighten to 15–22 ft. lbs. (20–30 Nm), then again in sequence, to 19–24 ft. lbs. (26–32 Nm).

30. Lubricate the distributor gear teeth and the distributor O-ring with engine oil. Install the distributor, aligning the marks that were made during the removal procedure. Install the hold-down bolt and snug.

31. Lubricate the No. 3 cylinder intake valve pushrod and rocker arm with engine oil, then install. Snug the retaining bolt.

32. Before tightening the retaining bolt, rotate the crankshaft until the lifter is on the base circle of the camshaft lobe. Tighten the retaining bolt to 5–11 ft. lbs. (7–15 Nm), making sure the rocker arm is fully seated on the pushrod and the fulcrum is fully seated on the cylinder head. Final tighten the retaining bolt to 19–28 ft. lbs. (26–38 Nm).

33. Install the rocker arm covers.

34. Install the fuel injector electrical harness to the injectors and secure the harness with the stand-offs to the inboard rocker arm cover studs.

35. Install the ignition coil and tighten the retaining bolts to 15–22 ft. lbs. (20–30 Nm). If equipped, install the oil cooler tube assembly bracket to the ignition coil bracket and tighten the retaining bolt to 15–22 ft. lbs. (20–30 Nm).

36. Install the distributor cap and ignition wires. Install the wire harness stand-offs to the rocker arm cover studs and connect the wires to the spark plugs and ignition coil.

37. Install the throttle body, using a new gasket. Tighten the throttle body mounting bolts to 15–22 ft. lbs. (20–30 Nm).

38. Install the alternator brace to the throttle body and alternator bracket. Tighten the nuts to 12 ft. lbs. (16 Nm).

39. Connect the PCV hose to the tube under the throttle body.

40. Install the EGR tube from the exhaust manifold to the EGR valve. Tighten the retaining nuts to 26–48 ft. lbs. (36–65 Nm).

41. Connect the fuel lines to the fuel supply manifold. Install the fuel line safety clips.

42. Install the upper radiator hose and heater hose and tighten the clamps.

43. Connect all removed vacuum lines to their original locations as marked during the removal procedure.

44. Connect the electrical connectors at the TPS, idle air control, ECT, PFE, distributor, ignition coil and coolant temperature sending unit.

45. Connect the throttle and TV cables to the throttle body linkage.

46. Fill and bleed the cooling system.

47. Drain the crankcase and fill with the proper type and quantity of engine oil.

NOTE: Engine coolant is corrosive to all engine bearing material. Changing the oil after the replacement of a coolant carrying component prevents failure later.

48. Install the air cleaner tube between the throttle body and mass air flow sensor. Tighten the clamps to 24–35 inch lbs. (2.7–4.0 Nm).

49. Install the PCV closure hose to the rocker arm cover and clean air flex tube.

50. Connect the negative battery cable. Start the engine and check for leaks.

51. Check, and if necessary, adjust the ignition timing.

52. Install the idle air control shield.

Exhaust Manifold

REMOVAL AND INSTALLATION

1.8L Engine

1. Disconnect the negative battery cable.
2. Remove the resonance duct.
3. Partially drain the cooling system and disconnect the upper radiator hose.
4. Remove the cooling fan.
5. Raise and safely support the vehicle.
6. Remove the exhaust pipe from the exhaust manifold and remove the gasket.
7. Remove the 2 bolts from the exhaust pipe support bracket.
8. Remove the left lower splash shield.
9. Lower the vehicle.
10. Disconnect the oxygen sensor electrical connector.
11. Remove the exhaust manifold heatshield mounting bolts and remove the shield.
12. Remove the exhaust manifold mounting nuts and remove the assembly.

13. Remove all gasket material from the cylinder head and exhaust manifold.

To install:

14. Install a new gasket onto the exhaust manifold mounting studs.
15. Place the exhaust manifold onto the mounting studs and install the manifold mounting nuts. Tighten the nuts to 28–34 ft. lbs. (38–46 Nm).
16. Place the heatshield into its mounting position and install the shield mounting bolts. Tighten the bolts to 69–95 inch lbs. (7.8–11.0 Nm).
17. Connect the oxygen sensor electrical connector.
18. Install the cooling fan.
19. Connect the upper radiator hose.
20. Install the resonance duct.
21. Raise and safely support the vehicle.
22. Install the exhaust pipe support bracket.
23. Install a new gasket and install the exhaust pipe to the exhaust manifold. Tighten the attaching nuts to 23–34 ft. lbs. (31–46 Nm).
24. Install the left lower splash shield and tighten the bolts to 69–95 inch lbs. (7.8–11.0 Nm).
25. Lower the vehicle.
26. Refill the cooling system.
27. Connect the negative battery cable.

1.9L Engine

1. Disconnect the negative battery cable.
2. Remove the accessory drive belt.
3. Remove the alternator.
4. Remove the radiator cooling fan and the shroud assembly.
5. Remove the exhaust manifold heat shield.
6. Raise and safely support the vehicle.
7. Remove the 2 catalytic converter inlet pipe-to-exhaust manifold attaching nuts.
8. Lower the vehicle.
9. Remove the 8 exhaust manifold attaching nuts and remove the exhaust manifold and gasket.

To install:

10. Clean the cylinder head and exhaust manifold gasket surfaces.
11. Position the new gasket onto the manifold mounting studs.
12. Position the exhaust manifold on the cylinder head and install the attaching nuts. Tighten the nuts to 16–19 ft. lbs. (21–26 Nm).
13. Raise and safely support the vehicle.

14. Install the catalytic converter inlet pipe-to-exhaust manifold attaching nuts.

15. Lower the vehicle.

16. Install the exhaust manifold heat shield.

17. Install the radiator cooling fan and shroud assembly.

18. Install the alternator and the accessory drive belt.

19. Connect the negative battery cable.

2.3L Engine

1. Disconnect the negative battery cable.

2. Properly relieve the fuel system pressure.

3. Drain the cooling system.

4. Remove the accelerator cable and position to the side.

5. Remove air cleaner assembly and heat stove tube at heat shield.

6. Identify, tag and disconnect all necessary vacuum lines.

7. Disconnect the exhaust pipe-to-exhaust manifold retaining nuts.

8. Disconnect the oxygen sensor wire at the connector.

9. Disconnect the throttle linkage.

10. Disconnect the cruise control cable, if equipped.

11. Disconnect the fuel supply and return lines at the rubber connector.

12. Disconnect EGR tube from the EGR valve.

13. Remove the intake manifold.

14. Remove the exhaust manifold retaining nuts. Remove the exhaust manifold from the vehicle.

To install:

15. Position exhaust manifold to the cylinder head using guide bolts in holes 2 and 3.

16. Install the attaching bolts in the remaining holes.

17. Tighten the attaching bolts until snug, then remove guide bolts and install the remaining attaching bolts.

18. Tighten all exhaust manifold bolts to specification using the following tightening procedure: torque retaining bolts in sequence to 5–7 ft. lbs. (7–10 Nm) then retorque, in sequence, to 20–30 ft. lbs. (27–41 Nm).

19. Install the intake manifold gasket and bolts. Torque the intake manifold retaining bolts, in the proper sequence to 15–22 ft. lbs. (20–30 Nm).

20. Connect the oxygen sensor wire at the connector.

21. Connect the EGR tube to EGR valve.

22. Install exhaust manifold studs.

23. Connect exhaust pipe to exhaust manifold.

24. Connect the fuel supply and return lines.

25. Install vacuum lines.

26. Install air cleaner assembly.

27. Install accelerator cable and cruise control cable, if equipped.

28. Connect the negative battery cable.

29. Fill the cooling system.

30. Start engine and check for leaks.

3.0L Engine

LEFT SIDE

1. Disconnect the negative battery cable.

2. Remove the 2 retaining nuts and remove the heat shield.

3. Remove the engine oil dipstick tube or rotate it out of the way.

4. Remove the exhaust pipe retaining nuts from the exhaust manifold studs.

5. Remove the exhaust manifold retaining bolts and stud.

6. Remove the manifold from the cylinder head, being careful not to damage the spark plugs.

To install:

7. Lightly oil all bolt and stud threads.

8. Clean the mating surfaces of the cylinder head, manifold and exhaust pipe.

9. Align the exhaust manifold studs with the exhaust pipe flange and install the exhaust manifold to the cylinder head. Install the retaining bolts and stud and tighten to 15–22 ft. lbs. (20–30 Nm).

10. Install the exhaust pipe retaining nuts and tighten to 25–34 ft. lbs. (34–47 Nm).

11. Rotate or install the dipstick tube bracket to the manifold retaining stud and tighten the nut to 11–14 ft. lbs. (15–20 Nm).

12. Install the heatshield and tighten the retaining nuts to 12–14 ft. lbs. (16–20 Nm).

13. Connect the negative battery cable. Start the engine and check for exhaust and oil leaks.

RIGHT SIDE

1. Disconnect the negative battery cable.

2. Drain the cooling system.

3. Disconnect the Pressure Feedback EGR (PFE) sensor hose connection to the EGR tube.

4. Loosen the EGR supply tube nuts at the manifold and EGR valve and remove the tube.

5. Remove the water pump.

6. Remove the exhaust pipe retaining nuts from the exhaust manifold studs.

7. Remove the heatshield retaining nuts and remove the shield.

8. Remove the exhaust manifold retaining bolts and studs. Remove the manifold from the cylinder head, being careful not to damage the spark plugs.

To install:

9. Lightly oil all bolt and stud threads.

10. Clean the mating surfaces of the cylinder head, manifold, exhaust pipe and EGR tube.

11. If installing a new manifold, install the EGR tube adapter/orifice, noting the small hole end (orifice) goes to the manifold.

12. Align the exhaust manifold studs with the exhaust pipe flange and install the exhaust manifold to the cylinder head. Install the retaining bolts and stud and tighten to 15–22 ft. lbs. (20–30 Nm).

13. Install the exhaust pipe retaining nuts and tighten to 25–34 ft. lbs. (34–47 Nm).

14. Install the heatshield and tighten the retaining nuts to 12–15 ft. lbs. (16–20 Nm).

15. Install the water pump.

16. Install the EGR tube and tighten the nuts to 26–48 ft. lbs. (35–65 Nm).

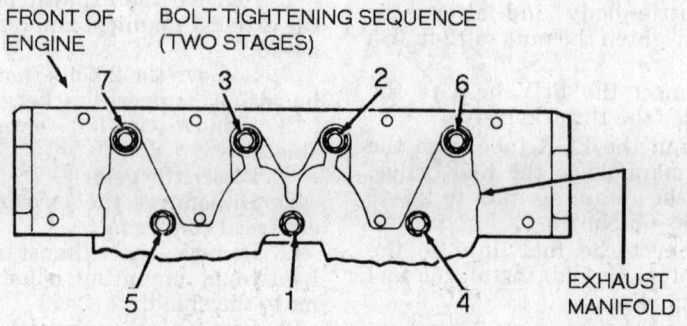

Exhaust manifold bolt torque sequence — 2.3L engine

17. Connect the PFE hose to the EGR tube.

18. Fill and bleed the cooling system.

19. Connect the negative battery cable. Start the engine and check for coolant and exhaust leaks.

Timing Chain Front Cover

REMOVAL AND INSTALLATION

2.3L Engine

1. Remove the engine and transaxle from the vehicle as an assembly and position in a suitable holding fixture. Remove the dipstick.

2. Remove accessory drive pulley, if equipped. Remove the crankshaft pulley attaching bolt and washer and remove pulley.

3. Remove front cover attaching bolts from front cover. Pry the top of the front cover away from the block.

4. Clean any gasket material from the surfaces.

5. Check timing chain and sprockets for excessive wear. If the timing chain and sprockets are worn, replace with new.

6. Check timing chain tensioner blade for wear depth. If the wear depth exceeds 0.060 in. (1.5mm), replace tensioner.

7. Remove the oil pan.

NOTE: Oil pan removal is recommended to ensure proper sealing to front cover.

To install:
8. Clean and inspect all parts before installation. Clean the oil pan, cylinder block and front cover of gasket material and dirt.

9. Apply oil resistant sealer to a new front cover gasket and position gasket into front cover.

10. Remove the front cover oil seal and position the front cover on the engine.

11. Position front cover alignment tool T84P–6019–C or equivalent, onto the end of the crankshaft, ensuring the crank key is aligned with the keyway in the tool. Bolt the front cover to the engine and torque bolts to 6–9 ft. lbs. (8–12 Nm). Remove the front cover alignment tool.

12. Replace the front cover seal with new. Lubricate the hub of the crankshaft pulley with multi-purpose grease to prevent damage to the seal during installation and initial engine start. Install crankshaft pulley.

13. Install the oil pan.

14. Install the accessory drive pulley, if equipped.

15. Install crankshaft pulley attaching bolt and washer. Tighten to 140–170 ft. lbs. (190–230 Nm).

16. Remove engine from work stand and install in vehicle.

3.0L Engine

1. Remove the engine assembly and install on a suitable workstand.

2. Remove the accessory drive belts.

3. Remove the oil pan.

4. Remove the water pump-to-front cover hose.

5. Remove both belt tensioner assemblies.

6. Remove the vibration damper using a suitable puller.

7. Remove the front cover retaining bolts and remove the front cover. If replacing the front cover, transfer the engine mount to the cover mounting pad.

To install:
8. Lightly oil all bolt and stud threads except those specifying special sealant.

9. Carefully clean all gasket material and sealant from the timing cover, cylinder block and oil pan.

10. Pry out the crankshaft seal from the timing cover. Lubricate and install a new seal, using a seal installer.

11. Install a new timing cover gasket over the cylinder block dowels.

12. Install the timing cover, being careful not to damage the crankshaft seal.

13. Hand start the timing cover retaining bolts. Apply pipe sealant to bolt No. 1, 2 and 3 prior to installation.

14. Tighten the retaining bolts, in sequence, to 15–22 ft. lbs. (20–30 Nm).

15. Clean the oil pan and install, using new gaskets. Tighten the bolts to 9 ft. lbs. (12 Nm).

16. Install the crankshaft damper and pulley. Lubricate the seal mating surface prior to installation. Tighten the damper bolt to 107 ft. lbs. (145 Nm) and the 4 pulley bolts to 26 ft. lbs. (35 Nm).

17. Install the automatic belt tensioners. Tighten the retaining nuts and bolt to 35 ft. lbs. (48 Nm).

18. Install the accessory drive belts.

19. Install the water pump to the front cover hose.

20. Install the engine assembly.

21. Start the engine and check for coolant, exhaust and oil leaks.

Front Cover Oil Seal

REPLACEMENT

NOTE: The removal and installation of the front cover oil seal on the 2.3L and 3.0L engines can only be accomplished with the engine removed from the vehicle.

2.3L Engine

1. Remove the engine from the vehicle and position in a suitable holding fixture.

2. Remove bolt and washer at crankshaft pulley.

3. Remove the crankshaft pulley using a suitable puller.

4. Using a suitable tool, remove the front cover oil seal.

To install:
5. Coat a new seal with grease. Using a suitable installation tool, install the seal into the cover. Drive the seal in until it is fully seated. Check the seal after installation to be sure the spring is properly positioned in the seal.

6. Install crankshaft pulley, attaching bolt and washer. Torque the crankshaft pulley bolt to 140–170 ft. lbs. (190–230 Nm).

7. Install the engine in the vehicle.

3.0L Engine

1. Remove the engine assembly and install on a suitable workstand.

2. Remove the accessory drive belts.

3. Remove the crankshaft damper retaining bolt and washer.

4. Remove the damper from the crankshaft using a suitable puller.

5. Using a small prybar, pry the seal from the front cover. Be careful not to damage the crankshaft or front cover.

To install:
6. Inspect the front cover and shaft seal surface of the crankshaft damper for damage, nicks, burrs or other roughness which may cause the seal to fail. Service as necessary.

7. Clean the crankshaft and front cover of all dirt and old sealer.

8. Lubricate the seal lip with clean engine oil and install the seal using a suitable seal installer.

9. Coat the crankshaft damper sealing surface with clean engine oil. Apply silicone sealer to the damper keyway prior to installation. Install the damper using installation tool T82L–6316–A or equivalent.

10. Install the damper retaining bolt and washer. Tighten to 93–121 ft. lbs. (125–165 Nm).

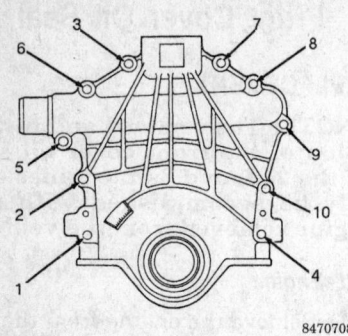

84707082

Timing chain front cover bolt torque sequence — 3.0L engine

11. Install the accessory drive belts.
12. Install the engine in the vehicle. Start the engine and check for leaks.

Timing Chain and Sprockets

REMOVAL AND INSTALLATION

2.3L Engine

1. Disconnect negative battery cable.
2. Remove engine and transaxle from vehicle as an assembly and position in a suitable holding fixture. Remove the dipstick.
3. Remove the front cover from the engine.
4. Check timing chain deflection as follows:
   a. Rotate crankshaft counterclockwise, as viewed from the front of the engine, to take up slack on the left side of chain.
   b. Make a reference mark on the block at approximately mid-point of chain. Measure from this point to chain.
   c. Rotate crankshaft in opposite direction to take up slack on the right side of the chain. Force left side of chain out with fingers and measure distance between reference point and chain. The deflection is the difference between the 2 measurements.
   d. If deflection measurement exceeds 0.5 in. (12.7mm), replace timing chain and sprockets. If wear on tensioner face exceeds 0.06 in. (1.5mm), replace tensioner.
5. Turn engine over until the timing marks are aligned. Remove camshaft sprocket attaching bolt and washer. Slide both sprockets and timing chain forward and remove as an assembly.
6. If equipped, check timing chain vibration damper for excessive wear

and replace if necessary. The damper is located inside the front cover.
7. Remove the oil pan.

NOTE: Oil pan removal is recommended to ensure proper sealing to front cover upon installation.

To install:
8. Clean and inspect all parts before installation. Clean the oil pan, cylinder block and front cover of gasket material and dirt.
9. Slide both sprockets and timing chain onto the camshaft and crankshaft with timing marks aligned. Install camshaft bolt and washer and tighten 41–56 ft. lbs. (55–75 Nm). Oil timing chain, sprockets and tensioner after installation with clean engine oil.
10. Install the front cover.
11. Install the oil pan.
12. Install the accessory drive pulley, if equipped.
13. Install crankshaft pulley attaching bolt and washer. Tighten to 140–170 ft. lbs. (190–230 Nm).
14. Remove engine from work stand and install in vehicle.
15. Connect negative battery cable.

3.0L Engine

1. Remove the engine assembly and install on a suitable workstand.
2. Remove the front cover.
3. Check the timing chain deflection as follows:
   a. Remove the left rocker arm cover.
   b. Loosen the No. 5 exhaust rocker arm and rotate to 1 side.
   c. Install a dial indicator on the end of the pushrod.
   d. Turn the crankshaft clockwise until the No. 1 piston is at TDC. The damper timing mark should point to TDC on the timing degree indicator. This will take up slack on the right side of the chain.
   e. Zero the dial indicator.
   f. Slowly turn the crankshaft counterclockwise until the slightest movement is seen on the dial indicator. Stop, and observe the damper timing mark for the number of degrees of travel from TDC.
   g. If the reading on the timing degree indicator exceeds 6 degrees, replace the timing chain and sprockets.
4. Check the camshaft endplay as follows:
   a. Remove the rocker arm covers.
   b. Back off all rocker arm retaining bolts to relieve the valve train load on the camshaft.

   c. Attach a suitable dial indicator to the front of the engine. Position the indicator foot on the camshaft retaining bolt.
   d. Push the camshaft toward the rear of the engine, then zero the dial indicator.
   e. Pull the camshaft forward and release it. Observe the reading on the dial indicator.
   f. If endplay exceeds 0.005 in (0.127mm) the thrust plate, then recheck the endplay.
   g. If endplay is still excessive, check the camshaft for excessive wear.
5. Turn the crankshaft until the marks on the camshaft and crankshaft gears are aligned.
6. Remove the camshaft sprocket retaining bolt and washer.
7. Remove the timing chain and sprockets.
To install:
8. Lubricate the timing chain and sprockets with clean engine oil and install as an assembly. Make sure the marks are aligned.
9. Inspect the camshaft sprocket retaining bolt for blockage of the drilled oil passages and clean, as necessary. Install the bolt and washer and tighten to 37–51 ft. lbs. (50–70 Nm).

─────── WARNING ───────
Do not replace the camshaft sprocket retaining bolt with a standard bolt or severe engine damage will result. This bolt is an oil carrying, precision component.
─────────────────────────

10. Install the front cover and install the engine in the vehicle.
11. Fill and bleed the cooling system. Fill the crankcase with the proper type and quantity of engine oil.
12. Start the engine and check for oil, coolant and exhaust leaks.

Timing Belt Front Cover

REMOVAL AND INSTALLATION

1.8L Engine

1. Disconnect the negative battery cable.
2. Remove the timing belt upper cover and gasket.
3. Loosen the water pump pulley bolts.
4. Remove the alternator and water pump accessory drive belt.
5. Remove the water pump pulley bolts and remove the pulley.

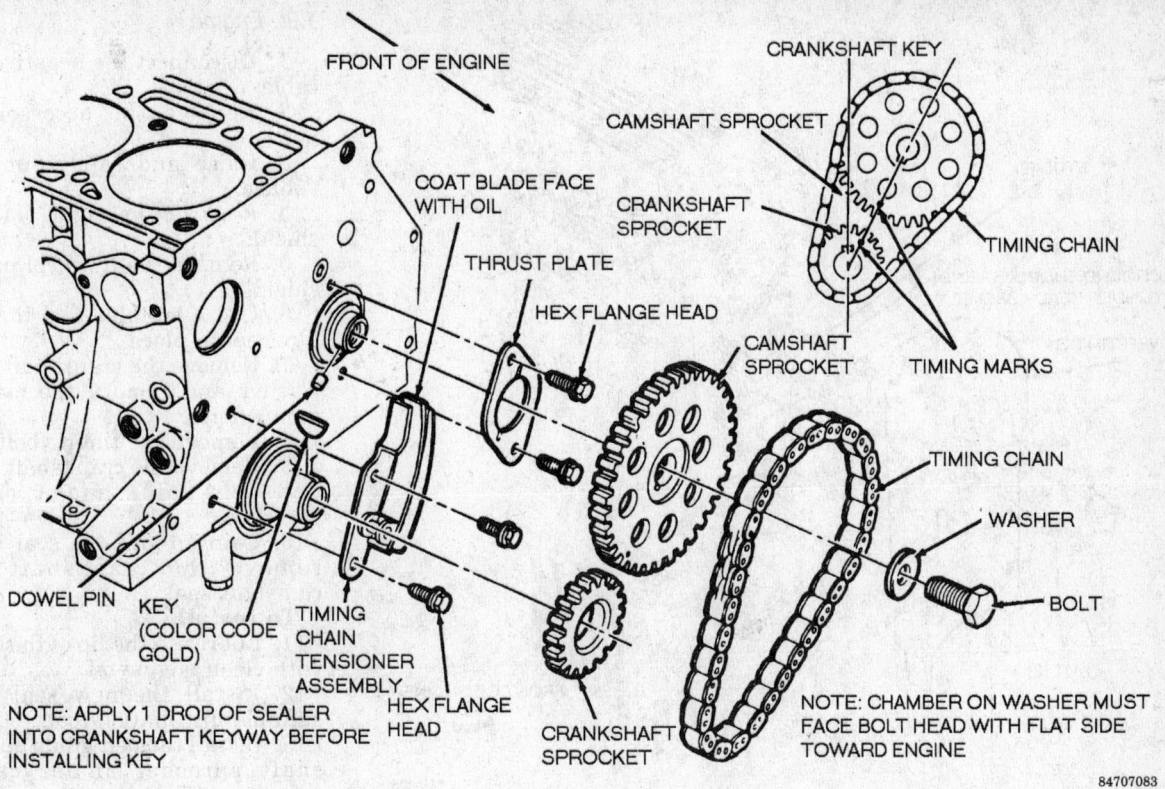

FRONT OF ENGINE

CRANKSHAFT KEY

CAMSHAFT SPROCKET

COAT BLADE FACE WITH OIL

CRANKSHAFT SPROCKET

TIMING CHAIN

THRUST PLATE

HEX FLANGE HEAD

CAMSHAFT SPROCKET

TIMING MARKS

TIMING CHAIN

WASHER

BOLT

DOWEL PIN KEY (COLOR CODE GOLD) TIMING CHAIN TENSIONER ASSEMBLY HEX FLANGE HEAD CRANKSHAFT SPROCKET

NOTE: APPLY 1 DROP OF SEALER INTO CRANKSHAFT KEYWAY BEFORE INSTALLING KEY

NOTE: CHAMBER ON WASHER MUST FACE BOLT HEAD WITH FLAT SIDE TOWARD ENGINE

84707083

Timing chain tensioner, sprockets and timing chain installation — 2.3L engine

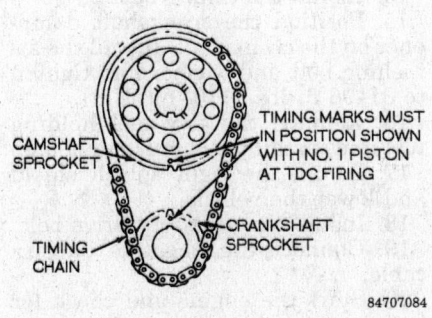

CAMSHAFT SPROCKET

TIMING MARKS MUST IN POSITION SHOWN WITH NO. 1 PISTON AT TDC FIRING

CRANKSHAFT SPROCKET

TIMING CHAIN

84707084

Timing sprockets alignment — 3.0L engine

6. Raise and safely support the vehicle.

7. Remove the right wheel and tire assembly.

8. Remove the right upper and lower splash shields.

9. Remove the air conditioning, if equipped, and power steering accessory drive belt.

10. Remove the crankshaft pulley, crankshaft pulley guide plate and timing belt outer and inner guide plates.

11. Remove the timing belt middle and lower covers along with the gaskets.

To install:

12. Install the timing belt middle and lower covers along with the gaskets.

13. Install the timing belt inner and outer guide plates, the crankshaft pulley and the crankshaft pulley guide plate. Tighten the bolts to 109–152 inch lbs. (12–17 Nm).

14. Install the air conditioning, if equipped, and power steering accessory drive belt.

15. Install the splash shields and tighten the bolts to 69–95 inch lbs. (7.8–11.0 Nm).

16. Install the water pump pulley and tighten the bolts to 69–95 inch lbs. (7.8–11.0 Nm).

17. Install the alternator and water pump accessory drive belt.

18. Install the right wheel and tire assembly and lower the vehicle.

19. Install the timing belt upper cover and gasket. Tighten the bolts to 69–95 inch lbs. (7.8–11.0 Nm).

20. Connect the negative battery cable.

1.9L Engine

1. Disconnect the negative battery cable.

2. Remove the accessory drive belt.

3. Remove the drive belt automatic tensioner, if equipped.

4. On 1993–95 models, Support the engine with a suitable floor jack.

   a. Remove the right engine mount damper.

   b. Remove the right engine mount bolts and loosen the engine mount through bolt.

   c. Roll the engine mount out of the way.

5. Remove the timing cover retaining nuts.

6. Installation is the reverse of the removal procedure. Tighten the retaining nuts to 3–5 ft. lbs. (5–7 Nm).

OIL SEAL REPLACEMENT

1.8L Engine

1. Disconnect the negative battery cable.

2. Remove the timing belt.

3. Remove the crankshaft oil seal as follows:

   a. Remove the crankshaft sprocket locking bolt and remove the crankshaft sprocket. If necessary, use a suitable puller.

   b. Remove the Woodruff® key.

   c. If necessary, cut the lip of the crankshaft oil seal to ease removal.

   d. Use a suitable prying tool to remove the crankshaft oil seal.

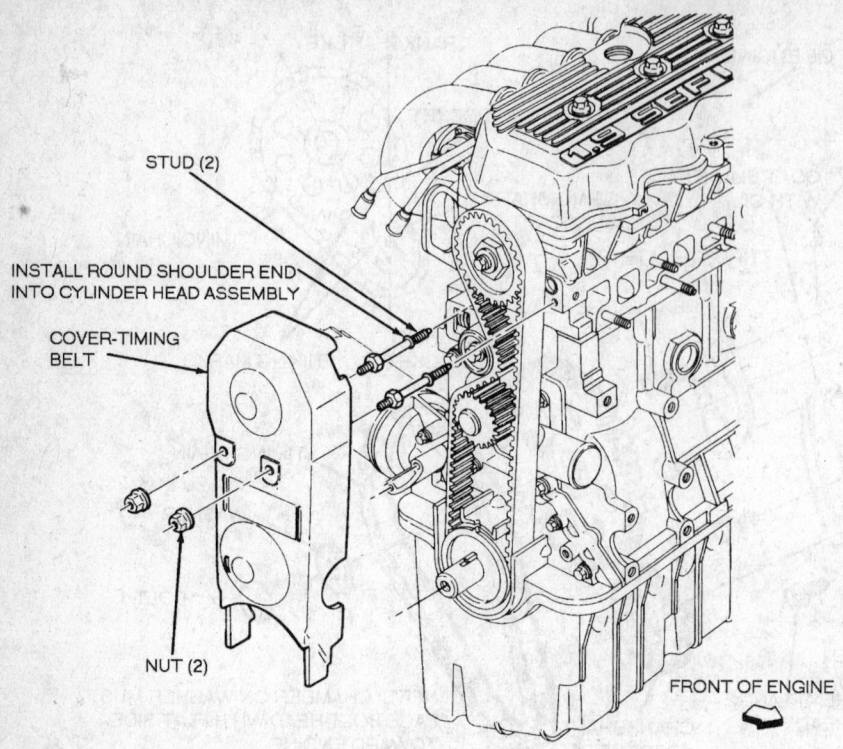

STUD (2)

INSTALL ROUND SHOULDER END
INTO CYLINDER HEAD ASSEMBLY

COVER-TIMING
BELT

NUT (2)

FRONT OF ENGINE

84707085

Timing belt cover removal and installation — 1.9L engine

4. Remove the camshaft oil seal(s) as follows:

a. Tag and disconnect the vacuum hoses at the cylinder head cover.

b. Disconnect the ignition wires from the spark plugs and position aside.

c. Remove the cylinder head cover mounting bolts and remove the cover.

d. Hold the camshaft with a wrench and remove the camshaft sprocket lock bolt. Remove the camshaft sprocket.

e. Remove the seal plate mounting bolts and remove the seal plate.

f. Remove the camshaft seal using a suitable tool.

To install:

5. Install the new crankshaft oil seal as follows:

a. Lubricate the lip of the new crankshaft oil seal with clean engine oil.

b. Using a suitable installation tool, install the seal evenly until it is flush with the edge of the oil pump body.

c. Install the crankshaft sprocket onto the shaft, making sure to match the alignment grooves.

d. Install the Woodruff® key with the tapered end facing the oil pump.

e. Install the crankshaft sprocket locking bolt. Tighten the locking bolt to 80–87 ft. lbs. (108–118 Nm).

6. Install the new camshaft oil seal(s) as follows:

a. Apply a small amount of clean engine oil to the lip of a new camshaft oil seal.

b. Install the seal, using a suitable seal installer.

c. Install the seal plate and tighten the mounting bolts to 69–95 inch lbs. (7.8–11.0 Nm).

d. Install the camshaft sprocket with the timing mark aligned with the timing mark on the seal plate.

e. Hold the camshaft with a wrench and install the lock bolt. Tighten to 36–45 ft. lbs. (49–61 Nm).

f. Install the cylinder head cover with a new gasket. Tighten the cylinder head cover bolts to 43–78 inch lbs. (4.9–8.8 Nm).

g. Connect the ignition wires and the vacuum hoses.

7. Install the timing belt.

8. Connect the negative battery cable.

1.9L Engine

1. Disconnect the negative battery cable.

2. Remove the accessory drive belt.

3. Raise and safely support the vehicle.

4. Remove the right side splash shield.

5. Remove the flywheel inspection shield.

6. Use a suitable tool to hold the flywheel in place.

7. Remove the crankshaft bolt and washer and remove the crankshaft dampener.

8. Remove the timing belt.

9. Remove the crankshaft sprocket and belt guide and/or camshaft sprocket.

10. Using a suitable seal remover, remove the crankshaft and/or camshaft seal.

To install:

11. Lubricate the lip of the new seal with clean engine oil.

12. Install the new seal using a suitable installation tool.

13. Install the belt guide and crankshaft sprocket and/or camshaft sprocket. Tighten the camshaft sprocket bolt to 71–84 ft. lbs. (95–115 Nm).

14. Install the timing belt.

15. Position the crankshaft dampener on the crankshaft. Install the attaching bolt and washer and tighten to 81–96 ft. lbs. (110–130 Nm).

16. Remove the flywheel holding tool and install the inspection shield.

17. Install the right splash shield and lower the vehicle.

18. Install the accessory drive belt.

19. Connect the negative battery cable.

20. Start the engine and check for leaks.

Timing Belt and Tensioner

ADJUSTMENT

1.8L Engine

1. Disconnect the negative battery cable.

2. Remove the timing belt upper and middle covers and gaskets.

3. Place a wrench onto the crankshaft sprocket and rotate the crankshaft clockwise so the timing marks located on the camshaft sprocket and the seal plate are aligned.

4. Rotate the crankshaft clockwise 2 complete revolutions and align the timing marks on the camshaft sprockets and seal plate.

5. Make sure the yellow ignition timing mark on the crankshaft sprocket is aligned with the TDC mark on the timing belt cover.

6. Measure the timing belt deflection by applying 22 lbs. of pressure on the belt, at a point between the camshaft sprockets. The timing belt deflection should be 0.35–0.45 in. (9.0–11.5mm).

7. If the deflection is not within specification, loosen the tensioner lock bolt. Using a suitable prying tool to move the tensioner, tighten or loosen the belt, as required, so the deflection will meet specification. Tighten the tensioner lock bolt to 27–38 ft. lbs. (37–52 Nm) and recheck the timing belt deflection beginning with Step 3.

8. If the timing belt will not meet specification, it must be replaced.

9. Install new gaskets onto the timing belt covers and install. Tighten the bolts to 69–95 inch lbs. (7.8–11.0 Nm).

1.9L Engine

The timing belt tensioner is spring-loaded on the 1.9L engine. The spring automatically maintains the proper tension and periodic belt tension adjustments are not necessary.

REMOVAL AND INSTALLATION

1.8L Engine

1. Disconnect the negative battery cable.

2. Remove the upper, middle, and lower timing belt covers.

3. Rotate the crankshaft and align the timing marks located on the camshaft sprockets and the seal plate.

4. If the timing belt is to be re-used, mark an arrow on the belt to indicate its rotational direction for installation reference.

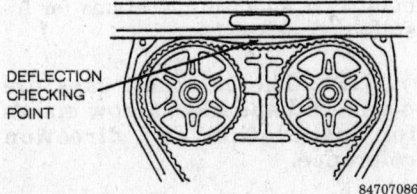

DEFLECTION CHECKING POINT

84707086

Timing belt deflection checking point — 1.8L engine

5. Loosen the timing belt tensioner lock bolt and remove the timing belt.

To install:

6. Temporarily secure the timing belt tensioner in the far left position with the spring fully extended, then tighten the lock bolt.

7. Make sure the timing marks on the timing belt sprocket and the engine block are aligned.

8. Make sure the timing marks on the camshaft sprockets and the seal plate are aligned.

9. Install the timing belt.

10. Loosen the tensioner lock bolt. Using a prybar, position the timing belt tensioner so the timing belt is taut, then tighten the tensioner lock bolt.

11. Turn the crankshaft 2 turns clockwise and align the timing belt sprocket mark with the mark on the engine block.

12. Make sure the camshaft sprocket marks are aligned with the seal plate marks.

NOTE: If the timing marks are not aligned, remove the belt and repeat the procedure.

13. Turn the crankshaft $1\frac{5}{6}$ turns clockwise and align the timing belt sprocket mark with the tension set mark, at approximately the 10 o'clock position.

14. Apply tension to the timing belt tensioner and install the tensioner lock bolt. Tighten the bolt to 27–38 ft. lbs. (37–52 Nm).

15. Turn the crankshaft $2\frac{1}{6}$ turns clockwise and make sure the timing marks are aligned.

16. Measure the timing belt deflection by applying 22 lbs. of pressure on the belt between the camshaft sprockets. The timing belt deflection should be 0.35–0.45 in. (9.0–11.5mm). If necessary, adjust the timing belt deflection.

17. Turn the crankshaft 2 turns clockwise and make sure the timing marks are aligned.

NOTE: If the timing marks are not aligned, repeat the procedure beginning at Step 9.

18. Install the timing belt covers and the remaining components.

19. Connect the negative battery cable.

1.9L Engine

1. Disconnect the negative battery cable.

2. Remove the accessory drive belt automatic tensioner and the accessory drive belt.

3. Remove the timing belt cover.

4. Align the timing mark on the camshaft sprocket with the timing mark on the cylinder head.

5. Confirm that the timing mark on the crankshaft sprocket is aligned with the timing mark on the oil pump housing.

6. Loosen the belt tensioner attaching bolt, pry the tensioner away from the timing belt and retighten the bolt.

7. Remove the spark plugs. Remove the right engine mount on 1993–95 models.

8. Raise and safely support the vehicle.

9. Remove the right side splash shield.

10. Remove the flywheel inspection shield.

11. Use a suitable tool to hold the flywheel in place.

12. Remove the crankshaft damper bolt and washer and remove the damper.

13. Remove the timing belt.

NOTE: With the timing belt removed and the No. 1 piston at TDC, do not rotate the camshaft. If the camshaft must be rotated, align the crankshaft damper 90 degrees BTDC.

To install:

14. Install the timing belt over the sprockets in a counterclockwise direction starting at the crankshaft. Keep the belt span from the crankshaft to the camshaft tight while installing over the remaining sprocket.

15. Loosen the belt tensioner attaching bolt, allowing the tensioner to snap against the belt.

16. Rotate the crankshaft clockwise 2 complete revolutions, stopping at TDC. This will allow the tensioner spring to load the timing belt.

NOTE: Do not turn the engine counterclockwise to align the timing marks. Do not rotate the crankshaft with the spark plugs installed.

17. Recheck the camshaft and crankshaft timing marks for alignment, to make sure the timing belt has not skipped a tooth during rotation. Repeat the procedure if the timing marks are not aligned.

18. Tighten the tensioner attaching bolt to 17–22 ft. lbs. (23–30 Nm).

19. Install the crankshaft damper and the bolt and washer. Tighten the bolt to 81–96 ft. lbs. (110–130 Nm).

20. Install the flywheel inspection shield.

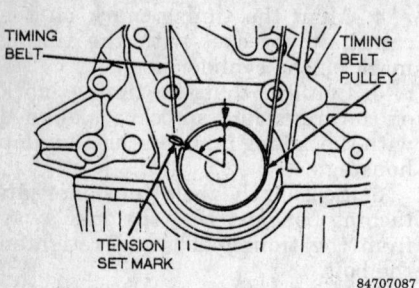

Timing belt tension set position — 1.8L engine

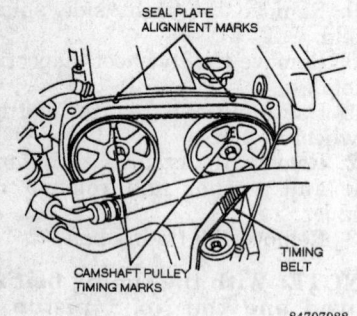

Camshaft sprocket alignment marks — 1.8L engine

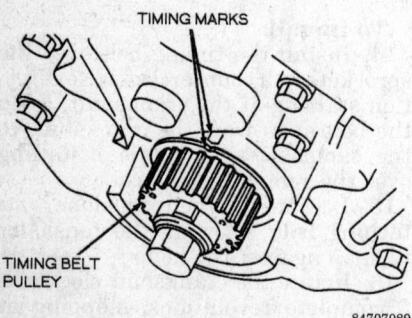

Crankshaft sprocket alignment marks — 1.8L engine

21. Install the splash shield and lower the vehicle.
22. Install the right engine mount on 1993–95 models. Install the spark plugs.
23. Install the timing belt cover.
24. Install the accessory drive belt automatic tensioner and the accessory drive belt.
25. Connect the negative battery cable.

Timing Sprockets

REMOVAL AND INSTALLATION

1.8L Engine

1. Disconnect the negative battery cable.
2. Remove the timing belt.
3. Disconnect the vacuum hoses from the cylinder head cover.
4. Tag and disconnect the spark plug wires from the spark plugs and position the wires aside.
5. Remove the cylinder head cover mounting bolts and remove the cover and gasket.
6. While holding the camshaft with a wrench, remove the camshaft sprocket lock bolt. Remove the camshaft sprocket.
7. Remove the timing belt crankshaft sprocket locking bolt.
8. Remove the timing belt sprocket. If necessary, use a suitable puller.
9. Remove the Woodruff® key from the crankshaft.
To install:
10. Install the timing belt sprocket onto the crankshaft while making sure to match the alignment grooves.
11. Install the Woodruff® key with the tapered end facing the oil pump.
12. Install the timing belt sprocket locking bolt and tighten to 80–87 ft. lbs. (108–118 Nm).
13. Install the camshaft sprocket with the timing mark aligned with the timing mark on the seal plate.
14. While holding the camshaft with a wrench, install the camshaft sprocket lock bolt. Tighten the bolt to 36–45 ft. lbs. (49–61 Nm).
15. Install a new cylinder head cover gasket onto the cylinder head.
16. Place the cylinder head cover into its mounting position and install the mounting bolts. Tighten the cylinder head cover bolts to 43–78 inch lbs. (4.9–8.8 Nm).
17. Connect the spark plug wires to the spark plugs and connect the vacuum hoses to the cylinder head cover.
18. Install the timing belt and timing belt covers.

1.9L Engine

1. Disconnect the negative battery cable.
2. Remove the timing belt cover and timing belt.

NOTE: With the timing belt removed and pistons at TDC, do not rotate the engine. If the camshaft

must be rotated, align the crankshaft sprocket to 90 degrees BTDC.

3. Remove the camshaft sprocket attaching bolt and washer and camshaft sprocket.
4. Remove the crankshaft sprocket.
To install:
5. Install the camshaft sprocket and attaching bolt and washer. Tighten to 71–84 ft. lbs. (95–115 Nm).
6. Install the crankshaft sprocket.
7. Install the timing belt and cover.
8. Connect the negative battery cable.

Camshaft

REMOVAL AND INSTALLATION

1.8L Engine

1. Disconnect the negative battery cable.
2. Remove the distributor assembly.
3. Remove the camshaft sprockets.
4. Remove the seal plate mounting bolts and remove the seal plate.
5. Loosen the camshaft cap bolts in the correct sequence.

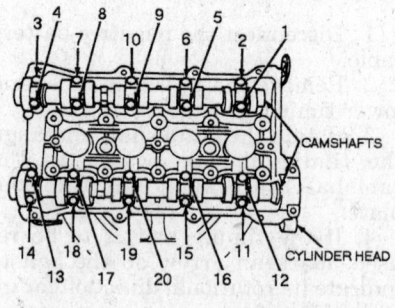

Camshaft cap bolt loosening sequence — 1.8L engine

6. Remove the camshaft caps and note their mounting locations for installation reference.

NOTE: The camshaft caps are numbered and have arrow marks for installation and direction reference.

7. Remove the camshaft and camshaft oil seal.
To install:
8. Apply clean engine oil to the camshaft journals and bearings.

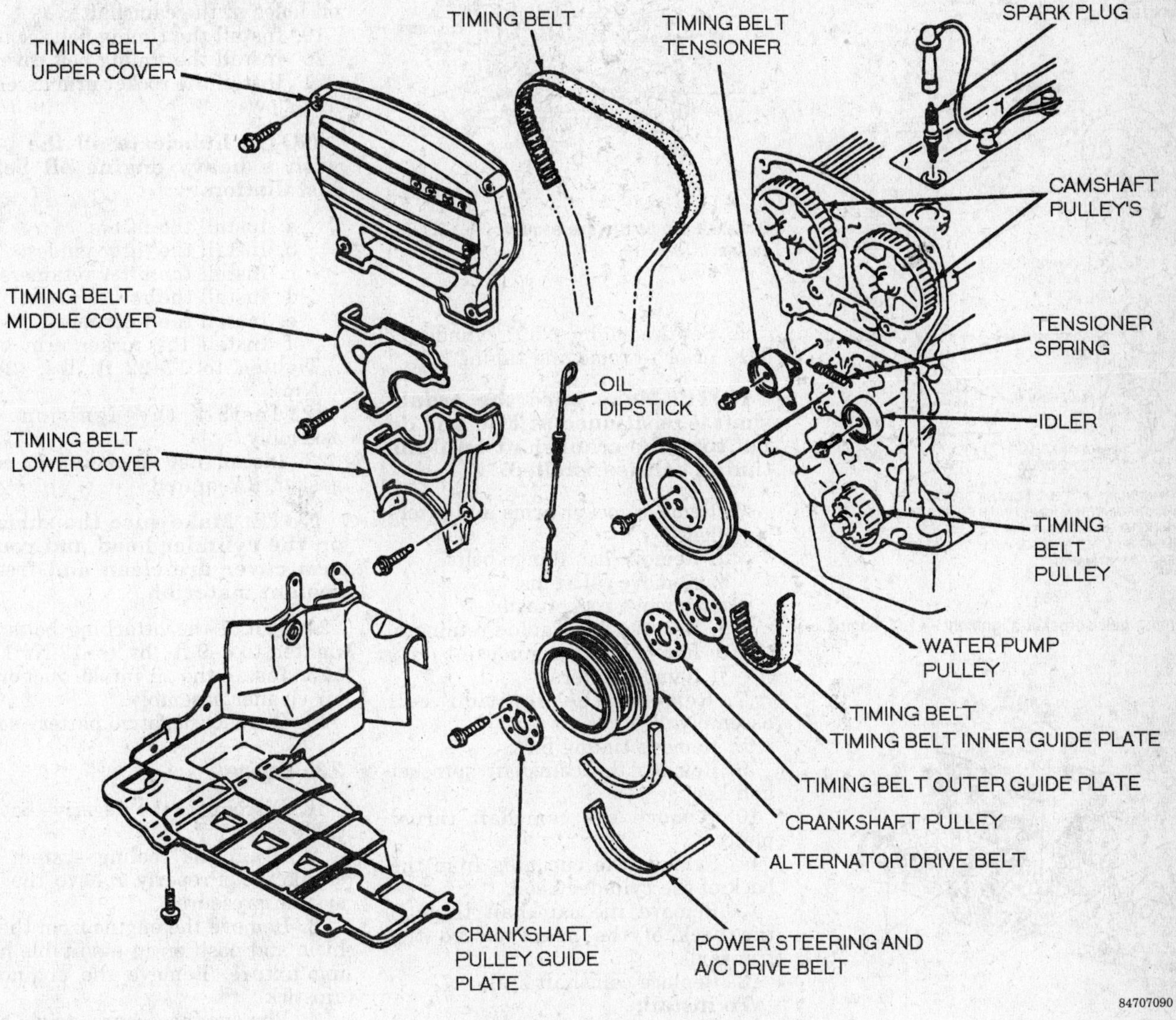

TIMING BELT UPPER COVER

TIMING BELT

TIMING BELT TENSIONER

SPARK PLUG

CAMSHAFT PULLEY'S

TIMING BELT MIDDLE COVER

OIL DIPSTICK

TENSIONER SPRING

IDLER

TIMING BELT LOWER COVER

TIMING BELT PULLEY

WATER PUMP PULLEY

TIMING BELT

TIMING BELT INNER GUIDE PLATE

TIMING BELT OUTER GUIDE PLATE

CRANKSHAFT PULLEY

ALTERNATOR DRIVE BELT

CRANKSHAFT PULLEY GUIDE PLATE

POWER STEERING AND A/C DRIVE BELT

84707090

Timing belt removal and installation — 1.8L engine

9. Place the camshaft into its mounting position.

NOTE: The exhaust camshaft has a groove which must be installed into the distributor drive gear.

10. Apply silicone sealant to the required areas.

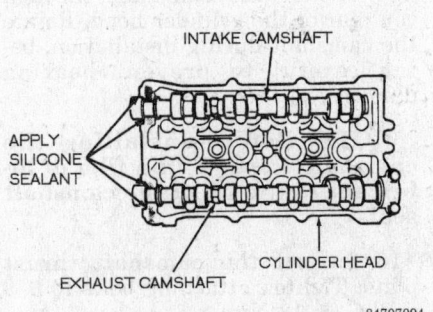

INTAKE CAMSHAFT

APPLY SILICONE SEALANT

EXHAUST CAMSHAFT

CYLINDER HEAD

84707094

Silicone sealer application points — 1.8L engine

11. Install the camshaft caps according to the cap numbers and arrow marks.

12. Install the camshaft cap bolts and tighten them in the proper sequence to 100–126 inch lbs. (11.3–14.2 Nm).

13. Apply a small amount of clean engine oil to the lip of a new camshaft oil seal. Using a suitable installation tool, install the new seal.

14. Place the seal plate into its mounting position and install the mounting bolts. Tighten the bolts to 69–95 inch lbs. (7.8–11.0 Nm).

15. Install the camshaft sprockets and the distributor assembly.

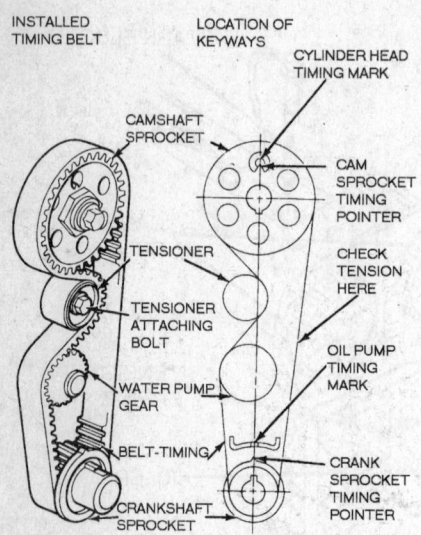

CRANKSHAFT AT T.D.C. (CRANK SPROCKET)
TIMING POINTER ALIGNED WITH OIL PUMP
TIMING MARK AND CAMSHAFT SPROCKET
TIMING POINTER ALIGNED WITH CYLINDER
HEAD TIMING MARK)

84707091

Timing belt sprocket alignment — 1.9L engine

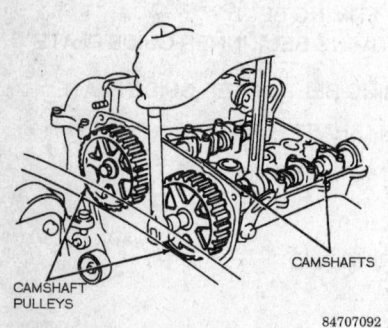

84707092

Hold the camshaft with a wrench when removing or installing the camshaft sprocket lock bolt — 1.8L engine

16. Connect the negative battery cable.

1.9L Engine

1. Disconnect the negative battery cable.
2. Remove the air cleaner or air intake duct.
3. Remove the accessory drive belts and crankshaft damper.
4. Remove the timing belt cover and rocker arm cover.

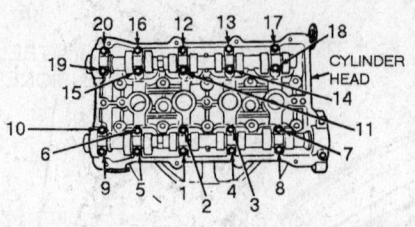

84707095

Camshaft cap bolt torque sequence — 1.8L engine

5. Set the engine No. 1 cylinder at TDC prior to removing timing belt.

NOTE: Make sure the crankshaft is positioned at TDC and do not turn the crankshaft until the timing belt is installed.

6. Remove rocker arms and lifters as follows:
   a. Remove hex flange bolts.
   b. Remove fulcrums.
   c. Remove rocker arms.
   d. Remove lifter guide retainers.
   e. Remove lifters guides.
   f. Remove lifters.
7. Remove the ignition coil assembly.
8. Remove timing belt.
9. Remove the camshaft sprocket and key.
10. Remove the camshaft thrust plate.
11. Remove the cup plug from the back of the cylinder head.
12. Remove the camshaft through the back of the head toward the transaxle.
13. Replace camshaft seal.
   To install:
14. Thoroughly coat the camshaft bearing journals, cam lobe surfaces and thrust plate groove with a suitable lubricant.
15. Install the camshaft through the rear of the cylinder head. Rotate the camshaft during installation, being careful to prevent bearing damage.

NOTE: Before installing the camshaft, apply a thin film of lubricant to the lip of the camshaft seal.

16. Install the camshaft thrust plate. Tighten attaching bolts to 6–9 ft. lbs. (8–13 Nm).
17. Align and install the cam sprocket over the cam key. Install attaching washer and bolt. While holding camshaft stationary, tighten the bolt to 71–84 ft. lbs. (95–115 Nm).

18. Install the cup plug using a suitable sealer. Use the sealer sparingly, as excess sealer may clog the oil holes in the camshaft.
19. Install the timing belt.
20. Install the timing belt cover.
21. Install the rocker arm assembly as follows:

NOTE: Lubricate all the parts with a heavy engine oil before installation.

   a. Install the lifters.
   b. Install the lifter guides.
   c. Install the lifter retainers.
   d. Install the rocker arms.
   e. Install the fulcrums.
   f. Install the rocker arm bolts. Tighten to 17–22 ft. lbs. (23–30 Nm).
22. Install the ignition coil assembly.
23. Install new rocker arm cover gasket, if required.

NOTE: Make sure the surfaces on the cylinder head and rocker arm cover are clean and free of sealant material.

24. Install the attaching bolts and tighten to 4–9 ft. lbs. (5–12 Nm).
25. Install the air intake duct or the air cleaner assembly.
26. Connect negative battery cable.

2.3L Engine

1. Disconnect the negative battery cable.
2. Drain the cooling system and crankcase. Properly relieve the fuel system pressure.
3. Remove the engine from the vehicle and position in a suitable holding fixture. Remove the engine oil dipstick.
4. Remove necessary drive belts and pulleys.
5. Remove the cylinder head.
6. Remove the distributor.
7. Using a magnet, remove the hydraulic lifters and label them so they can be installed in their original positions. If the lifters are stuck in the bores by excessive varnish, etc., use a suitable puller to remove them.
8. Remove the crankshaft pulley.
9. Remove the oil pan.
10. Remove the cylinder front cover and gasket.
11. Check the camshaft endplay as follows:
   a. Push the camshaft toward the rear of the engine and install a dial indicator tool, so the indicator foot is positioned on the camshaft sprocket attaching bolt.
   b. Zero the dial indicator. Position a small prybar or equivalent,

between the camshaft sprocket or gear and block.

c. Pull the camshaft forward and release it. Compare the dial indicator reading with the camshaft endplay specification of 0.009 in.

d. If the camshaft endplay is over the amount specified, replace the thrust plate.

12. Remove the timing chain, sprockets and timing chain tensioner. On 1992–95 models, remove the VRS sensor (located near base of distributor on the block).

13. Remove camshaft thrust plate. Carefully remove the camshaft by pulling it toward the front of the engine. Use caution to avoid damaging bearings, journals and lobes.

To install:

14. Clean and inspect all parts before installation.

15. Lubricate camshaft lobes and journals with heavy engine oil. Carefully slide the camshaft through the bearings in the cylinder block.

16. Install the thrust plate. Tighten attaching bolts to 6–9 ft. lbs (8–12 Nm).

17. Install the timing chain, sprockets and timing chain tensioner. On 1992–95 models, install the VRS sensor (located near base of distributor on the block).

18. Install the cylinder front cover and crankshaft pulley.

19. Clean the oil pump inlet tube screen, oil pan and cylinder block gasket surfaces. Prime oil pump by filling the inlet opening with oil and rotate the pump shaft until oil emerges from the outlet tube. Install oil pump, oil pump inlet tube screen and oil pan.

20. Install the accessory drive belts and pulleys.

21. Lubricate the lifters and lifter bores with heavy engine oil. Install lifters into their original bores.

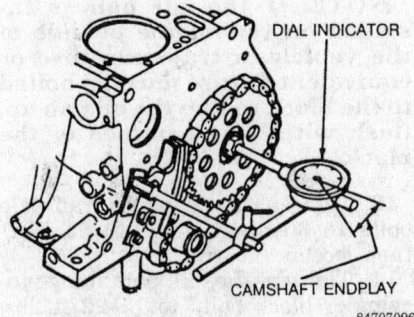

DIAL INDICATOR

CAMSHAFT ENDPLAY

84707096

Checking camshaft endplay — 2.3L engine

22. Install cylinder head.

23. Position No. 1 piston at TDC after the compression stroke. Position distributor in the block with the rotor at the No. 1 firing position. Install distributor retaining clamp.

24. Install engine in vehicle.

25. Connect engine temperature sending unit wire. Connect coil primary wire. Install distributor cap. Connect spark plug wires and the coil high tension lead.

26. Fill the cooling system and crankcase to the proper levels.

27. Connect negative battery cable.

28. Start the engine. Check and adjust ignition timing. Check for leaks.

3.0L Engine

1. Remove the engine from the vehicle and position on a suitable workstand.

2. Rotate the crankshaft until the piston in No. 1 cylinder is at TDC on the compression stroke.

3. Remove the intake manifold.

4. Remove the lifters.

5. Remove the oil pan.

6. Remove the timing chain cover.

7. Check the camshaft endplay as follows:

a. Attach a suitable dial indicator to the front of the engine. Position the indicator foot on the camshaft retaining bolt.

b. Push the camshaft toward the rear of the engine, then zero the dial indicator.

c. Pull the camshaft forward and release it. Observe the reading on the dial indicator.

d. If endplay exceeds 0.005 in., replace the thrust plate, then recheck the endplay.

e. If endplay is still excessive, check the camshaft for excessive wear.

8. Remove the timing chain and sprockets.

9. Remove the 2 camshaft thrust plate retaining bolts and the thrust plate.

10. Remove the camshaft by pulling it slowly toward the front of the engine, being careful not to damage the camshaft bearings, journals or lobes.

To install:

11. Clean all gasket mating surfaces. Clean and inspect all components and replace, as necessary.

12. Lubricate the camshaft lobes, journals and distributor drive gear with clean engine oil. Carefully slide the camshaft through the bearings into the cylinder block.

13. Lubricate the camshaft thrust plate with clean engine oil and install with the 2 retaining bolts. Tighten the bolts to 7 ft. lbs. (10 Nm).

14. Install the timing chain and sprockets.

15. Install the timing chain cover.

16. Install the oil pan.

17. Install the lifters.

18. Install the intake manifold, pushrods, rocker arms, rocker arm covers and distributor.

19. Install the engine assembly in the vehicle.

20. Fill the crankcase with the proper type and quantity of engine oil. Fill and bleed the cooling system.

21. Start the engine and check for coolant, oil, exhaust, vacuum and fuel leaks. Check and, if necessary, adjust the timing.

Piston and Connecting Rod

POSITIONING

NOTE: On 1.8L engine, the piston and rod assembly must be positioned in the engine block with the F mark facing the front of the engine.

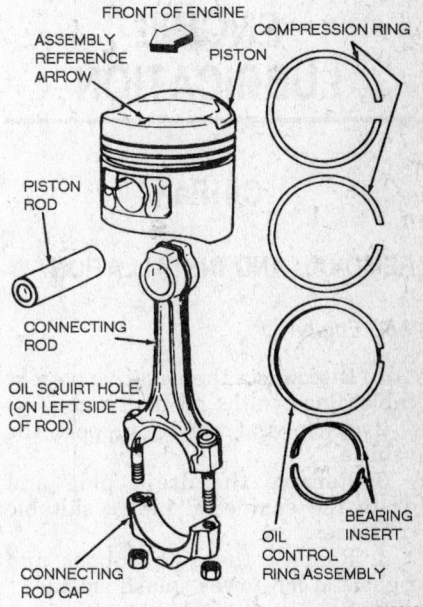

FRONT OF ENGINE

COMPRESSION RING

ASSEMBLY REFERENCE ARROW

PISTON

PISTON ROD

CONNECTING ROD

OIL SQUIRT HOLE (ON LEFT SIDE OF ROD)

BEARING INSERT

OIL CONTROL RING ASSEMBLY

CONNECTING ROD CAP

84707098

Piston and rod assembly — 1.9L engine

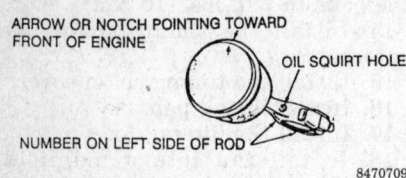

ARROW OR NOTCH POINTING TOWARD
FRONT OF ENGINE

OIL SQUIRT HOLE

NUMBER ON LEFT SIDE OF ROD

84707097

Piston and rod assembly — 2.3L engine

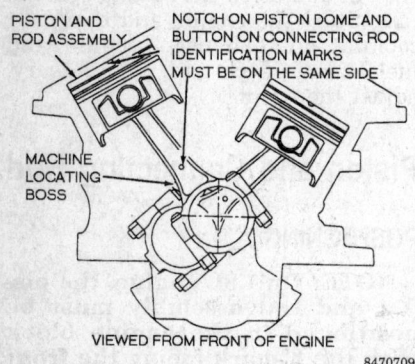

PISTON AND
ROD ASSEMBLY

NOTCH ON PISTON DOME AND
BUTTON ON CONNECTING ROD
IDENTIFICATION MARKS
MUST BE ON THE SAME SIDE

MACHINE
LOCATING
BOSS

VIEWED FROM FRONT OF ENGINE

84707099

Piston and rod assembly — 3.0L engine

ENGINE LUBRICATION

Oil Pan

REMOVAL AND INSTALLATION

1.8L Engine

1. Disconnect the negative battery cable. Remove the oil filler cap.
2. Raise and safely support the vehicle.
3. Remove the drain plug and drain the engine oil into a suitable container.
4. Remove the right upper and right and left lower splash shields.
5. Remove the exhaust pipe front mounting flange and exhaust pipe support bracket from the exhaust manifold.
6. Remove the oil pan-to-transaxle attaching bolts.
7. Support the oil pan with a suitable jackstand.

8. Remove the oil pan-to-engine block attaching bolts.

NOTE: Do not force a prying tool between the engine block and the oil pan contact surface when trying to remove the oil pan. This may damage the oil pan contact surface and cause oil leakage.

9. Only at the most rearward points of the oil pan, next to the transaxle, use a suitable tool to carefully pry the oil pan away from the engine block and remove the oil pan.
10. Use a suitable tool to pry the crankcase stiffeners away from the engine block and/or oil pan.
11. Remove the front and rear oil pan gaskets and end seals. Remove all sealant material from the engine block and oil pan.

NOTE: When removing the crankcase stiffeners and sealant material from the oil pan and engine block, be careful not to damage the oil pan and engine block contact surfaces.

To install:
12. Apply a bead of silicone sealant to the crankcase stiffeners along the inside of the bolt holes.
13. Install the crankcase stiffeners onto the oil pan.
14. Apply sealant to the proper areas of the end seals. Be sure to install the end seals with the projections in the notches.
15. Install the front and rear end seals onto the oil pan.
16. Apply a continuous bead of silicone sealant to the oil pan along the inside of the bolt holes. Overlap the sealant ends.
17. Place the oil pan into its mounting position and install the oil pan-to-engine block attaching bolts. Tighten the bolts to 69–95 inch lbs. (7.8–11.0 Nm).

NOTE: If the oil pan attaching bolts are to be reused, the old sealant must be removed from the bolt threads. Tightening the old attaching bolts with old sealant still on them may cause cracking inside the bolt holes.

18. Install the oil pan-to-transaxle attaching bolts and tighten to 27–38 ft. lbs. (37–52 Nm).
19. Install the oil drain plug and tighten to 22–30 ft. lbs. (29–41 Nm).
20. Install the exhaust front mounting flange to the exhaust manifold using a new gasket. Tighten the mounting flange-to-exhaust manifold attaching nuts to 23–34 ft. lbs. (31–46 Nm).

21. Install the exhaust pipe support bracket and tighten the bolts to 27–38 ft. lbs. (37–52 Nm).
22. Install the splash shields. Tighten the bolts to 69–95 inch lbs. (7.8–11.0 Nm).
23. Lower the vehicle.
24. Fill the crankcase with the proper type and quantity of engine oil. Install the filler cap.
25. Connect the negative battery cable.

1.9L Engine

1. Disconnect negative battery cable.
2. Raise the vehicle and support safely.
3. Drain the crankcase.
4. Remove the 2 oil pan-to-transaxle bolts.
5. Disconnect the exhaust inlet pipe at the manifold and converter. Remove pipe.
6. Remove oil pan retaining bolts and oil pan.
7. Remove oil pan gasket and discard.

To install:
8. Clean the oil pan gasket surface and the mating surface on the cylinder block. Wipe the oil pan rail with a solvent-soaked cloth to remove oil traces.
9. Remove and clean the oil pump pick up tube and screen assembly. Install tube and screen assembly using a new gasket.
10. Apply a bead of silicone rubber sealer at the corner of the block and at the seating point of the oil pump and the rear seal retainer joint.
11. Install the gasket in oil pan ensuring press fit tabs are fully engaged in oil pan gasket channel.
12. Install the oil pan and the attaching bolts. Tighten the bolts lightly until the 2 oil pan-to-transmission bolts can be installed.

NOTE: If the oil pan is installed on the engine outside of the vehicle, a transaxle case or equivalent fixture must be bolted to the block to line the oil pan up, flush with the rear face of the block.

13. Tighten the 2 pan-to-transaxle bolts to 30–40 ft. lbs. (40–54 Nm), then loosen ½ turn.
14. Tighten the oil pan flange-to-cylinder block bolts to 15–22 ft. lbs. (20–30 Nm) in the proper sequence. Retighten the 2 oil pan-to-transaxle bolts to 30–40 ft. lbs. (40–55 Nm).
15. Install the transaxle inspection plate.

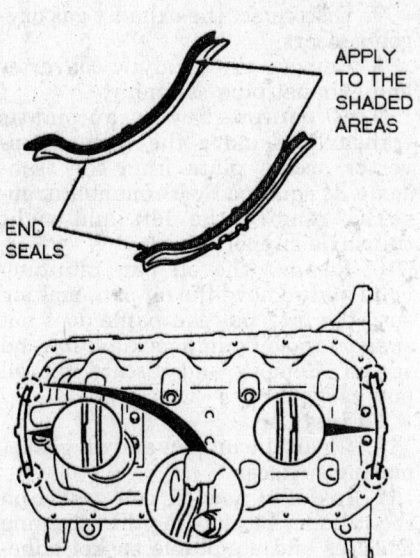

Sealant application areas and oil pan end seal installation — 1.8L engine

16. Install the exhaust inlet pipe. Lower the vehicle and fill the crankcase with the proper type and quantity of engine oil.

17. Connect negative battery cable.

18. Start the engine and check for oil leaks.

2.3L Engine

1992

1. Disconnect the negative battery cable. Raise the vehicle and support safely.

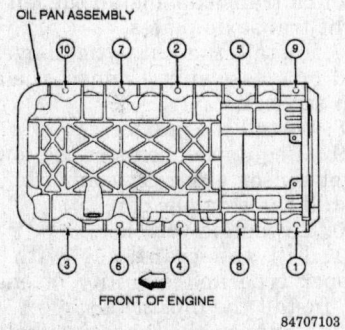

Oil pan attaching bolt torque sequence — 1.9L engine

2. Drain the crankcase and drain the cooling system by removing the lower radiator hose.

3. Remove the roll restrictor on manual transaxle equipped vehicles.

4. Disconnect the starter cable.

5. Remove the starter.

6. Disconnect the exhaust pipe from oil pan.

7. Remove the engine coolant tube from the lower radiator hose, water pump and at the tabs on the oil pan. Position air conditioner line off to the side. Remove the retaining bolts and remove the oil pan.

To install:

8. Clean both mating surfaces of oil pan and cylinder block making certain all traces of RTV sealant are removed. Ensure that the block rails, front cover and rear cover retainer are also clean.

9. Remove and clean oil pump pickup tube and screen assembly. After cleaning, install tube and screen assembly.

10. Apply RTV E8AZ–19562–A Sealer or equivalent, in oil pan groove. Completely fill oil pan groove with sealer. Sealer bead should be 0.200 in. (5mm) wide and 0.080–0.150 in. (2.0–3.8mm) high, above oil pan surface, in all areas except the half-rounds. The half-rounds should have a bead 0.200 in. (5mm) wide and 0.150–0.200 in. (3.8–5.1mm) high, above the oil pan surface.

NOTE: Applying RTV in excess of the specified amount will not improve the sealing of the oil pan, and could cause the oil pickup screen to become clogged with sealer. Use adequate ventilation when applying sealer.

11. Install oil pan to cylinder block within 5 minutes to prevent skinning over. RTV needs to cure completely before coming in contact with any engine oil, about 1 hour at ambient temperature between 65–75°F.

12. Install oil pan bolts lightly until the 2 oil pan-to-transmission bolts can be installed.

NOTE: If oil pan is installed on engine out of vehicle, a transaxle case or equivalent fixture must be bolted to the block to line the oil pan up, flush with the rear face of block.

13. Install 2 oil pan-to-transaxle bolts. Tighten to 30–39 ft. lbs. (40–54 Nm) to align oil pan with transaxle. Loosen bolts ½ turn.

14. Tighten all oil pan flange bolts to 15–22 ft. lbs. (20–30 Nm).

15. Tighten 2 oil pan-to-transmission bolts to 30–39 ft. lbs. (40–54 Nm).

16. If required, rework exhaust bracket to fit to oil pan.

17. Replace water inlet tube O-ring and install tube.

18. Install the starter.

19. Connect the starter cable.

20. Install roll restrictor, if equipped.

21. Lower vehicle.

22. Fill the crankcase with the proper type and quantity of engine oil. Fill and bleed the cooling system.

23. Connect negative battery cable.

24. Start engine and check for coolant and oil leaks.

1993–94

1. Disconnect the negative battery cable. Raise the vehicle and support safely.

2. Drain the crankcase and drain the cooling system.

3. Remove the rear oil pan-to-transaxle bolts.

4. Remove the secondary air injection tubes and disconnect the rubber hose at the check valve on manual transaxle equipped vehicles.

5. Disconnect the starter cable and remove the starter.

6. Remove the heater supply tube from the water pump inlet tube assembly. Remove bolt bracket at the block and water pump inlet tube assembly.

7. Remove bracket from the air conditioning compressor line above the oil pan and remove the 2 bolts.

8. Remove the retaining bolts and remove the oil pan.

To install:

9. Clean both mating surfaces of oil pan and cylinder block making certain all traces of RTV sealant are removed. Ensure that the block rails, front cover and rear cover retainer are also clean.

10. Remove and clean oil pump pickup tube and screen assembly. After cleaning, install tube and screen assembly.

11. Apply RTV E8AZ–19562–A Sealer or equivalent, in oil pan groove. Completely fill oil pan groove with sealer. Sealer bead should be 0.200 in. (5mm) wide and 0.15 in. (4mm) high, above oil pan surface, in all areas except the half-rounds. The half-rounds should have a bead 0.200 in. (5mm) wide and 0.25 in. (6mm) high, above the oil pan surface.

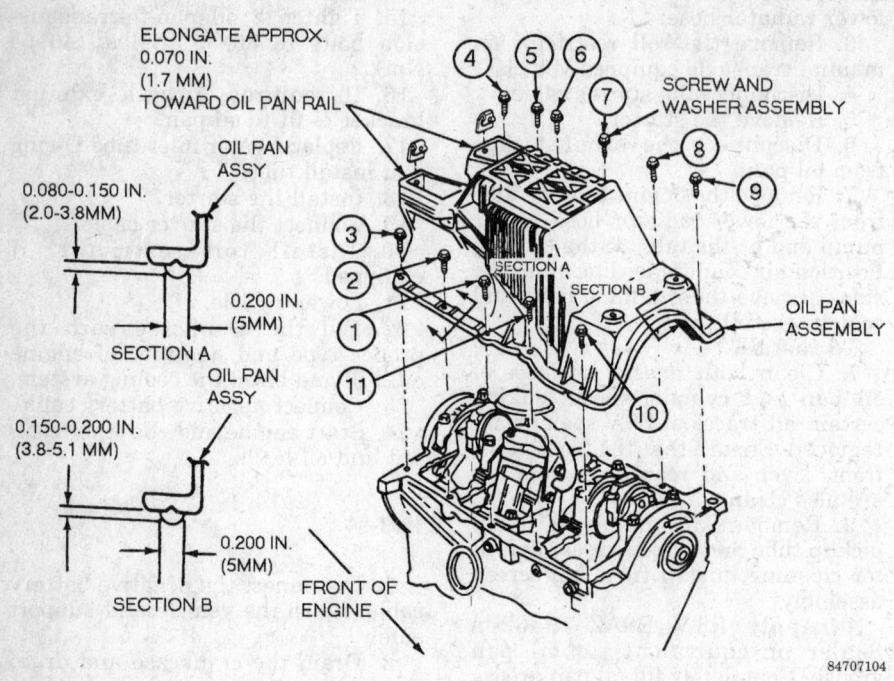

ELONGATE APPROX.
0.070 IN.
(1.7 MM)
TOWARD OIL PAN RAIL

OIL PAN
ASSY

0.080-0.150 IN.
(2.0-3.8MM)

0.200 IN.
(5MM)

SECTION A

OIL PAN
ASSY

0.150-0.200 IN.
(3.8-5.1 MM)

0.200 IN.
(5MM)

SECTION B

SECTION A

SECTION B

FRONT OF
ENGINE

SCREW AND
WASHER ASSEMBLY

OIL PAN
ASSEMBLY

84707104

Oil pan installation — 2.3L engine

WARNING

Applying RTV in excess of the specified amount will not improve the sealing of the oil pan, and could cause the oil pickup screen to become clogged with sealer. Use adequate ventilation when applying sealer.

---

12. Install oil pan to cylinder block within 5 minutes to prevent skinning over. RTV needs to cure completely before coming in contact with any engine oil, about 1 hour at ambient temperature between 65–75°F.

13. Install oil pan bolts lightly until the 2 oil pan-to-transmission bolts can be installed.

NOTE: If oil pan is installed on engine outside of vehicle, a transaxle case or equivalent fixture must be bolted to the block to line the oil pan up, flush with the rear face of block.

14. Install 2 oil pan-to-transaxle bolts. Tighten to 30–39 ft. lbs. (40–54 Nm) to align oil pan with transaxle. Loosen bolts ½ turn.

15. Tighten all oil pan flange bolts to 15–22 ft. lbs. (20–30 Nm).

16. Tighten 2 oil pan-to-transmission bolts to 30–39 ft. lbs. (40–54 Nm).

17. Install bracket from the air conditioning compressor line above the oil pan.

18. Install bracket at the block and water pump inlet tube assembly.

19. Install the starter.

20. Connect the starter cable.

21. Connect the secondary air injection tubes and connect the rubber hose at the check valve on manual transaxle equipped vehicles.

22. Lower vehicle.

23. Fill the crankcase with the proper type and quantity of engine oil. Fill and bleed the cooling system.

24. Connect negative battery cable.

25. Start engine and check for coolant and oil leaks.

3.0L Engine

1. Disconnect the negative battery cable.

2. Remove the engine oil dipstick.

3. Raise and safely support the vehicle.

4. If equipped, remove the low oil level sensor retainer clip and disconnect the electrical connector at the sensor.

5. Drain the engine oil from the crankcase into a suitable container.

6. Remove the starter.

7. Disconnect the exhaust gas oxygen sensors.

8. Remove the catalytic converter and exhaust pipe assembly.

9. If equipped with automatic transaxle, remove the torque converter access plate from the transaxle. If equipped with manual transaxle, remove the left and right transaxle support plates.

10. Remove the oil pan retaining bolts and remove the oil pan, making sure the internal pan baffle does not snag on the oil pump pickup tube and screen. Remove and discard the oil pan gasket.

To install:

11. Clean the oil pan and all gasket mating surfaces.

12. Install a new oil pan gasket on the cylinder block using the retaining features and a suitable gasket adhesive. Snug retaining bolts at the 4 corners and 2 middle places on the cylinder block to support the gasket until the adhesive cures.

13. Apply a 3/16 in. (4.75mm) bead of silicone sealer to the junction of the rear main bearing cap and cylinder block and the junction of the front cover and cylinder block.

NOTE: Do not let the sealer cure longer than 4 minutes prior to oil pan installation or 7 total minutes before bolts are tightened to specification.

14. Position the oil pan and install the retaining bolts, hand tight.

15. Tighten the 4 corner bolts to 7–10 ft. lbs. (10–14 Nm), then tighten the remaining bolts to the same specification.

16. If equipped with automatic transaxle, install the torque converter access plate. If equipped with manual transaxle, install the left and right transaxle plates.

17. Install the catalytic converter and pipe assembly. Connect the oxygen sensors.

18. Install the starter.

19. If equipped, connect the low oil level sensor electrical connector and install the retainer clip.

20. Lower the vehicle.

21. Fill the crankcase with the proper type and quantity of engine oil. Install the dipstick.

22. Connect the negative battery cable, start the engine and check for oil and exhaust leaks.

Oil Pump

REMOVAL AND INSTALLATION

1.8L Engine

1. Disconnect the negative battery cable.
2. Remove the timing belt and crankshaft sprocket.
3. Remove the oil pan.
4. Remove the oil strainer mounting bolts and remove the oil strainer and gasket.
5. If equipped, remove the air conditioning compressor mounting bolts and position the compressor so it is free from the work area.
6. Remove the air conditioning compressor mounting bracket.
7. Remove the mounting bolt from the engine oil dipstick tube bracket and remove the alternator lower mounting bolt.
8. Remove all oil pump mounting bolts and remove the oil pump. Remove all gasket material from the oil pump.
To install:
9. Install a new gasket onto the oil pump.
10. Place the oil pump into its mounting position and install the pump mounting bolts. Tighten the bolts to 14–19 ft. lbs. (19–25 Nm).
11. Place the dipstick tube bracket bolt into its mounting position and install the mounting bolt.
12. Install the alternator lower mounting bolt and tighten to 27–38 ft. lbs. (37–52 Nm).
13. Install a new gasket onto the oil strainer, place the strainer into its mounting position and install the mounting bolts. Tighten to 69–95 inch lbs. (7.8–11.0 Nm).
14. Install the oil pan.
15. If equipped, place the air conditioning compressor bracket into its mounting position and install the mounting bolts. Tighten the bolts to 30–40 ft. lbs. (40–55 Nm).
16. If equipped, install the air conditioning compressor into its mounting position and install the mounting bolts. Tighten to 15–22 ft. lbs. (20–30 Nm).
17. Install the crankshaft sprocket and timing belt.
18. Connect the negative battery cable.

1.9L Engine

1. Disconnect the negative battery cable.
2. Remove the accessory drive belt and the automatic tensioner.

3. Support the engine with a suitable floor jack.
4. Remove the right engine mount dampener and remove the right engine mount bolts from the mount bracket.
5. Loosen the mount through bolt and roll the mount aside.
6. Remove the timing belt cover.
7. Make sure the No. 1 cylinder is at TDC.
8. Roll the engine mount back into place and install the 2 mount bolts. Remove the floor jack.
9. Loosen the belt tensioner attaching bolt and pry the tensioner to the rear of the engine. Tighten the attaching bolt.
10. Raise and safely support the vehicle.
11. Remove the right side splash shield.
12. Remove the catalytic converter inlet pipe.
13. Drain and remove the oil pan. Remove the oil filter.
14. Remove the crankshaft damper and the timing belt.
15. Remove the crankshaft sprocket and the timing belt guide from the crankshaft.
16. Disconnect the crank angle sensor.
17. Remove the 6 oil pump-to-engine bolts and remove the oil pump assembly from the engine. Remove and discard the gasket.
18. Remove the crankshaft seal from the pump and discard.
To install:
19. Make sure the pump mating surfaces on the cylinder block and oil pump are clean and free of gasket material.
20. Remove the oil pickup tube and screen assembly from the pump for cleaning.
21. Lubricate the outside diameter of the crankshaft seal with engine oil and install the seal with a suitable installation tool. Lubricate the seal lip with engine oil.
22. Position the oil pump gasket on the cylinder block.
23. Prime the oil pump with engine oil and position the pump over the crankshaft. Using a suitable tool, position the pump drive gear to allow the pump to pilot over the crankshaft and seat firmly on the cylinder block.

NOTE: The pump drive gear can be accessed through the oil pickup hole in the body of the pump. Do not install the oil pump pickup tube and screen until the pump has been correctly installed on the cylinder block.

24. Install the 6 oil pump bolts and tighten to 8–12 ft. lbs. (11–16 Nm).

NOTE: When the oil pump bolts are tightened, the gasket must not be below the cylinder block sealing surface.

25. Install the pickup tube and screen assembly on the oil pump using a new gasket. Tighten the attaching screws to 7–9 ft. lbs. (10–13 Nm).
26. Install the timing belt guide over the end of the crankshaft and install the crankshaft sprocket.
27. Make sure the No. 1 cylinder is at TDC.
28. Position the timing belt over the sprockets.
29. Connect the crank angle sensor.
30. Install the oil pan and the crankshaft damper.
31. Install the catalytic converter inlet pipe.
32. Install the splash shield and lower the vehicle.
33. Install the timing belt. Tighten the tensioner attaching bolt to 17–22 ft. lbs. (23–30 Nm).
34. Support the engine with a suitable floor jack.
35. Remove the right engine mount bolts and roll the mount back.
36. Install the timing belt cover.
37. Roll the engine mount back into place and install the attaching bolts. Tighten the mount through bolt and install the mount damper.
38. Remove the floor jack.
39. Install the accessory drive belt automatic tensioner and the accessory drive belt.
40. Fill the crankcase with the proper type and quantity of engine oil.
41. Connect the negative battery cable, start the engine and check for leaks.

2.3L Engine

1. Disconnect the negative battery cable.
2. Raise and safely support the vehicle.
3. Remove oil pan.
4. Remove oil pump attaching bolts and remove oil pump and intermediate driveshaft.
To install:
5. Prime oil pump by filling inlet port with engine oil. Rotate pump shaft until oil flows from outlet port.
6. If screen and cover assembly have been removed, replace gasket. Clean screen and reinstall screen and cover assembly. Tighten attaching bolts and nut.
7. Position intermediate driveshaft into distributor socket.

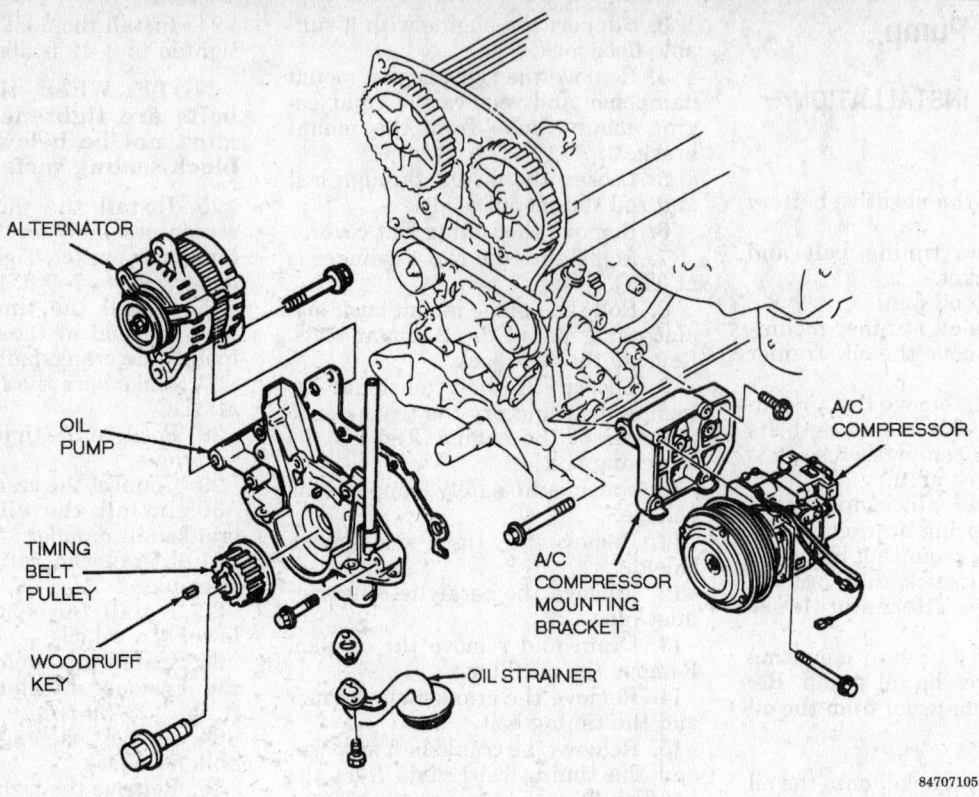

ALTERNATOR

OIL
PUMP

TIMING
BELT
PULLEY

WOODRUFF
KEY

A/C
COMPRESSOR

A/C
COMPRESSOR
MOUNTING
BRACKET

OIL STRAINER

84707105

Oil pump installation — 1.8L engine

8. Insert intermediate driveshaft into oil pump. Install pump and shaft as an assembly.

──────── **CAUTION** ────────
Do not attempt to force the pump into position if it will not seat. The shaft hex may be misaligned with the distributor shaft. To align, remove the oil pump and rotate the intermediate driveshaft into a new position.

9. Tighten the oil pump attaching bolts to 15–22 ft. lbs. (20–30 Nm).
10. Install oil pan with new gasket.
11. Connect negative battery cable.
12. Fill the crankcase with the proper type and quantity of engine oil. Start engine and check for leaks.

3.0L Engine

1. Disconnect the negative battery cable.
2. Remove the oil pan.
3. Remove the oil pump retaining bolt and remove the pump from the main bearing cap. The intermediate shaft will remain in the oil pump. If the pump is to be replaced, remove the intermediate shaft by pulling it from the pump. Check the retaining clip for damage and replace, as necessary.

To install:
4. Insert the intermediate shaft into the hex drive hole in the oil pump until the retainer "clicks" into place.
5. Prime the oil pump by filling the inlet port with engine oil. Rotate the intermediate shaft until oil flows from the outlet port.
6. Install the oil pump with the intermediate shaft through the intermediate shaft hole in the rear main bearing cap. Position the pump over the locating pins.
7. Install the retaining bolt and tighten to 30–40 ft. lbs. (40–55 Nm).
8. Install the oil pan.
9. Fill the crankcase with the proper type and quantity of engine oil.
10. Connect the negative battery cable. Start the engine and check for leaks.

CHECKING

1.8L Engine

1. Remove the oil pump from the vehicle.
2. Disassemble the pump, clean all parts with a suitable solvent and allow to dry.
3. Use a suitable feeler gauge to check the outer rotor tooth tip clear-ance. The maximum allowable clear-ance is 0.0079 in. (0.20mm).
4. Use a suitable feeler gauge to inspect the outer rotor-to-pump body clearance. The maximum allowable clearance is 0.0087 in. (0.22mm).
5. Use a straightedge and a feeler gauge to inspect the oil pump side clearance. The maximum allowable side clearance is 0.0055 in. (0.14mm).
6. Inspect the pressure spring for breakage or weak retraction. Inspect the pressure spring free length; it should be 1.791 in. (45.5mm).
7. If the pump is damaged or toler-ances are not within specification, re-place the oil pump.

1.9L Engine

1. Remove the oil pump from the vehicle.
2. Disassemble the pump, clean all parts with a suitable solvent and allow to dry.
3. Use a suitable feeler gauge to check the inner-to-outer gear tip clearance. The maximum allowable clearance is 0.007 in. (0.18mm).
4. Use a suitable feeler gauge to inspect the outer gear-to-housing clearance. The maximum allowable clearance is 0.0063 in. (0.161mm).
5. Use a straightedge and a feeler gauge to inspect the inner and outer

gear-to-cover clearance (endplay). The maximum allowable clearance is 0.0035 in. (0.089mm).

6. Inspect the relief valve spring for breakage or weak retraction. The spring tension should be 9.3–10.3 lbs. (41.4–45.8 N) at 1.11 in. (28.1mm).

7. If the pump is damaged or tolerances are not within specification, replace the oil pump.

2.3L and 3.0L Engines

1. Remove the oil pump from the vehicle.

2. Disassemble the pump and clean all parts in solvent. Allow to dry.

3. Inspect the inside of the pump housing for damage or excessive wear.

4. Check the mating surface for wear. Minor scuff marks are normal, but if the cover, gears or housing are excessively worn, scored or grooved, replace the pump.

5. Inspect the rotor for nicks, burrs or score marks. Remove minor imperfections with an oil stone.

6. Measure the inner-to-outer rotor tip clearance. The clearance must not exceed 0.012 in. (0.30mm) with a feeler gauge inserted ½ in. (12.7mm) minimum with the rotors removed from the pump housing.

7. With the rotor assembly installed in the housing, place a straightedge across the rotor assembly and housing. Measure the rotor endplay or clearance, between the straightedge and both the inner rotor and outer race. Maximum clearance must not exceed 0.005 in. (0.13mm).

8. Check the relief valve spring tension. On the 2.3L engine, the tension should be 14.2–16.2 lbs. (63.5–72.1 N) at 1.2 in. (30.4mm). On the 3.0L engine, the tension should be 9.1–10.1 lbs. (40.5–44.9 N) at 1.11 in. (28.2mm). If the spring is worn or damaged, replace the pump. Check the relief valve piston for freedom of movement in the bore.

9. If the pump is damaged or tolerances are not within specification, replace the oil pump.

Rear Main Bearing Oil Seal

REMOVAL AND INSTALLATION

1.8L Engine

1. Disconnect the negative battery cable.

2. Remove the transaxle assembly.

3. If equipped with manual transaxle, remove the clutch disc and pressure plate assembly. Remove the flywheel or flexplate.

4. If necessary, remove the rear cover mounting bolts and remove the rear cover.

5. Using a suitable prybar, remove the crankshaft rear oil seal. Be careful not to damage the crankshaft seal surface or seal housing.

To install:

6. If removed, install the rear cover and attaching bolts. Tighten the bolts to 69–95 inch lbs. (7.8–11.0 Nm).

7. Lubricate the lip of a new seal and install, using a suitable installation tool.

8. Install the flywheel or flexplate. Tighten the flywheel or flexplate bolts to 71–76 ft. lbs. (96–103 Nm).

9. Install the transaxle.

10. Connect the negative battery cable.

1.9L Engine

1. Disconnect the negative battery cable.

2. Raise the vehicle and support it safely. Remove the transaxle.

3. Remove flywheel and the engine cover plate.

4. With a suitable tool, remove the oil seal.

NOTE: Use caution to avoid damaging the oil seal surface.

To install:

5. Inspect the crankshaft seal area for any damage which may cause the seal to leak. If damage is evident, service or replace the crankshaft, as necessary.

6. Coat the crankshaft seal area and the seal lip with engine oil.

7. Using a suitable seal installer tool, install the seal.

8. Install the engine cover plate and the flywheel. Tighten the flywheel attaching bolts to 54–64 ft. lbs. (73–87 Nm).

9. Install the transaxle assembly.

10. Connect the negative battery cable, start the engine and check for leaks.

2.3L Engine

1. Disconnect the negative battery cable.

2. Remove transaxle.

3. Remove flywheel.

4. Remove rear cover plate.

5. Insert a suitable tool into seal cavity and pry out old seal.

NOTE: Use caution to avoid damaging the oil seal surface.

To install:

6. Inspect the crankshaft seal area for any damage which may cause the seal to leak. If damage is evident, service or replace the crankshaft, as necessary.

7. Coat the crankshaft seal area and the seal lip with engine oil.

8. Using a suitable seal installer tool, install the seal.

9. Install rear cover plate and 2 dowels.

10. Install the flywheel. Tighten attaching bolts to 54–64 ft. lbs. (73–87 Nm).

11. Install the transaxle assembly.

12. Connect the negative battery cable, start the engine and check for leaks.

3.0L Engine

1. Remove the engine and position on a suitable workstand.

2. Using a sharp awl, punch a hole into the seal metal surface between the lip and the block. Thread a screw into the hole and remove the seal, using a slide hammer.

NOTE: Use care to prevent scratching or damaging the oil seal surface.

To install:

3. Apply clean engine oil to the outer lips and inner edge of a new seal.

4. Install the seal, using suitable seal installer.

5. Install the engine.

MANUAL TRANSAXLE

Transaxle Assembly

REMOVAL AND INSTALLATION

Tempo and Topaz With 2.3L Engine

1. Disconnect the negative battery cable. Wedge a 7 in. wooden block under the clutch pedal to hold the pedal up slightly beyond its normal position. Grasp the clutch cable, pull it forward and disconnect it from the clutch release shaft assembly. Remove the clutch casing from the rib on the top surface of the transaxle case.

2. Remove the upper 2 transaxle-to-engine bolts. Remove the air cleaner on Tempo and Topaz or the

air management valve bracket-to-transaxle upper bolt on Escort and Tracer.

3. Raise and safely support the vehicle.

4. On Tempo and Topaz, remove the front stabilizer bar-to-control arm nut and washer, on the driver's side and discard the nut. Remove both front stabilizer bar mounting brackets and discard the bolts.

5. Remove the lower control arm ball joint-to-steering knuckle nut/bolt and discard the nut/bolt; repeat this procedure on the opposite side.

6. Using a large prybar, pry the lower control arm from the steering knuckle; repeat this procedure on the opposite side.

NOTE: Be careful not to damage or cut the ball joint boot and do not contact the lower arm.

7. Using a large prybar, pry the left-side inboard CV-joint assembly from the transaxle.

NOTE: Plug the seal opening (both sides), with transaxle plugs T81P–1177–B or equivalent, to prevent lubricant leakage.

8. Grasp the left-hand steering knuckle and swing it and the half-shaft outward from the transaxle; this will disconnect the inboard CV-joint from the transaxle.

NOTE: If the CV-joint assembly cannot be pried from the transaxle, insert a differential rotator tool through the left-side and tap the joint out; the tool can be used from either side of transaxle.

9. Using mechanics wire, support the halfshaft in a near level position to prevent damage to the assembly during the remaining operations; repeat this procedure on the opposite side.

10. Disengage the locking tabs and remove the backup light switch connector from the transaxle backup light switch.

11. On 1992 Tempo and Topaz, remove the starter studs-to-engine roll restrictor bracket nuts and the engine roll restrictor. Remove the starter stud bolts.

12. On 1993–94 Tempo and Topaz, remove the three nuts from the starter mounting studs. Remove the ground strap. Remove the starter stud bolts.

13. On Escort and Tracer, remove the starter bolts.

14. Remove the shift mechanism-to-shift shaft nut/bolt, the control selector indicator switch arm and the shift shaft.

15. Remove the shift mechanism stabilizer bar-to-transaxle bolt, control selector indicator switch and bracket assembly.

16. Using a crowfoot wrench, remove the speedometer cable from the transaxle.

17. On Tempo and Topaz, remove both oil pan-to-clutch housing bolts. On Escort and Tracer, remove 2 stiffener brace retaining bolts.

18. Using a floor jack and a transaxle support, position it under the transaxle and secure the transaxle to it.

19. On Tempo and Topaz, remove the both left-hand rear No. 4 insulator-to-body bracket nuts and the left-hand front No. 1 insulator-to-body bracket bolts.

20. On Escort and Tracer, remove both rear mount-to-floorpan bolts, loosen the nut at the bottom of the front mount and remove the front mount-to-transaxle bolts.

21. Lower the floor jack, until the transaxle clears the rear insulator. Support the engine by placing wood under the oil pan.

22. Remove the engine-to-transaxle bolts and lower the transaxle from the vehicle.

NOTE: On Tempo and Topaz, 1 of the engine-to-transaxle bolts attaches the ground strap and wiring loom stand off bracket.

To install:

23. Raise the transaxle into position and engage the input shaft with the clutch plate. Install the lower engine-to-transaxle bolts and torque to 28–31 ft. lbs. (38–42 Nm).

——— WARNING ———
Never attempt to start the engine prior to installing the CV-joints or differential side gear for dislocation and/or damage may occur.

24. On Escort and Tracer, install the front mount-to-transaxle bolts and torque to 25–35 ft. lbs. (34–47 Nm); also, tighten the nut on the bottom of the front transaxle mount.

25. On Tempo, tighten the left front No. 1 insulator bolts to 25–35 ft. lbs. (34–47 Nm) and the left rear No. 4 insulator bolts to 35–50 ft. lbs. (47–68 Nm).

26. On Escort and Tracer install the air management valve-to-transaxle upper bolt, finger-tight and the bottom bracket bolt to 28–31 ft. lbs. (38–42 Nm).

27. On Escort and Tracer, install both rear mount-to-floorpan brace bolts to 40–51 ft. lbs. (55–70 Nm).

28. Remove the floor jack and adapter.

29. Using a crowfoot wrench, install the speedometer cable; be careful not to cross-thread the cable nut.

30. On Tempo and Topaz, install the oil pan-to-transaxle bolts and tighten to 28–38 ft. lbs. (38–51 Nm). On Escort and Tracer, install the 2 stiffener brace bolts and tighten to 15–21 ft. lbs. (21–28 Nm).

31. Install the shifter stabilizer bar/control selector indicator switch-to-transaxle bolt and torque to 23–35 ft. lbs. (31–47 Nm).

32. Install the shift mechanism-to-shift shaft, the switch actuator bracket clamp and torque the bolt to 7–10 ft. lbs. (9–13 Nm); be sure to shift the transaxle into **4th** for 4-speed or **5th** for 5-speed and align the actuator.

33. On Escort and Tracer, install the starter bolts and tighten to 30–40 ft. lbs. (41–54 Nm). On Tempo and Topaz, install the starter stud bolts and tighten to 30–40 ft. lbs. (41–54 Nm) and install the engine roll restrictor on 1992 models, and the attaching nuts. Tighten the attaching nuts to 14–20 ft. lbs. (19–27 Nm).

34. Install the backup light switch connector to the transaxle switch.

35. Install the new circlip onto both inner joints of the halfshafts, insert the inner CV-joints into the transaxle and fully seat them; lightly, pry outward to confirm that the retaining rings are seated.

NOTE: When installing the halfshafts, be careful not to tear the oil seals.

36. Connect the lower ball joint to the steering knuckle, insert a new pinch bolt and torque the new nut to 37–44 ft. lbs. (50–60 Nm); be careful not to damage the boot.

37. Refill the transaxle and lower the vehicle.

38. On Escort and Tracer, install the upper air management valve bracket-to-transaxle bolt and torque to 28–31 ft. lbs. (38–42 Nm). On Tempo and Topaz, install the air cleaner.

39. Install the both upper transaxle-to-engine bolts and torque to 28–31 ft. lbs. (38–42 Nm).

40. Connect the clutch cable to the clutch release shaft assembly and remove the wooden block from under

the clutch pedal. Connect the negative battery cable.

NOTE: Prior to starting the engine, set the hand brake and pump the clutch pedal several times to ensure proper clutch adjustment.

Escort and Tracer

1. Disconnect the battery cables and remove the battery and the battery tray.
2. Remove the air hose and the resonance chamber.
3. Disconnect the speedometer cable at the transaxle.
4. Remove the retaining clip, then disconnect the slave cylinder line from the slave cylinder hose and plug the hose.
5. Disconnect the ground strap from the transaxle.
6. Remove the tie wrap and disconnect the 3 electrical connectors located above the transaxle. Remove the electrical connector support bracket.
7. Mount engine support bar D88L–6000–A or equivalent, and attach it to the engine hangers.
8. Remove the 3 nuts from the upper transaxle mount. Loosen the mount pivot nut and rotate the mount out of position. Remove the 3 bolts and the upper transaxle mount bracket.
9. Remove the 2 upper transaxle-to-engine bolts.
10. Raise and safely support the vehicle.
11. Remove the front wheel and tire assemblies.
12. Remove the inner fender splash shields.
13. Drain the transaxle fluid and install the drain plug.
14. Remove the halfshafts. Install 2 transaxle plugs T88C–7025–AH or equivalent, between the differential side gears.

─── **WARNING** ───
Failure to install the transaxle plugs may cause the differential side gears to become improperly positioned. If the gears become misaligned, the differential will have to be removed from the transaxle to align them.

15. Remove the plenum support bracket and remove the starter.
16. Remove the nut and the extension bar.
17. Remove the bolt and nut and remove the shift control rod from the transaxle.

18. Remove both lower splash shields.
19. Remove the 2 transaxle mount-to-crossmember nuts and remove the lower crossmember.
20. Remove the front transaxle mount and tubing bracket.
21. Position and secure a suitable jack under the transaxle.
22. Remove the 5 lower engine-to-transaxle bolts and lower the transaxle out of the vehicle.

To install:

23. Apply a thin coating of suitable grease to the spline of the input shaft.
24. Place the transaxle onto a suitable jack. Make sure the transaxle is secure.
25. Raise the transaxle into position on the engine.
26. Install the 5 lower engine-to-transaxle bolts and tighten to 27–38 ft. lbs. (37–52 Nm).
27. Install the front transaxle mount and tubing bracket. Tighten the bolts to 12–17 ft. lbs. (16–23 Nm).
28. Install the lower crossmember. Tighten the nuts and bolts to 47–66 ft. lbs. (64–89 Nm).
29. Install the 2 transaxle mount-to-crossmember nuts and tighten to 27–38 ft. lbs. (37–52 Nm).
30. Install both lower splash shields.
31. Install the shift control rod bolt and nut and tighten to 23–34 ft. lbs. (31–46 Nm).
32. Install the extension bar nut and tighten to 12–17 ft. lbs. (16–23 Nm).
33. Install the starter and the plenum support bracket.
34. Remove the transaxle plugs and install the halfshafts.
35. Install the inner fender splash shields.
36. Install the wheel and tire assemblies. Tighten the lug nuts to 65–87 ft. lbs. (88–118 Nm).
37. Lower the vehicle.
38. Install the 2 upper engine-to-transaxle bolts and tighten to 47–66 ft. lbs. (64–89 Nm).
39. Install the upper transaxle mount bracket and tighten the 3 bolts to 47–66 ft. lbs. (64–89 Nm). Rotate the mount into position and tighten the pivot nut. Install and tighten the 3 upper mount nuts to 47–66 ft. lbs. (64–89 Nm).
40. Remove the engine support bar.
41. Install the electrical connector support bracket. Connect the 3 electrical connectors and secure with the tie wrap.
42. Connect the ground strap to the transaxle.

43. Connect the slave cylinder line to the slave cylinder hose and install the retaining clip.
44. Add the proper type and amount of fluid to the transaxle.
45. Connect the speedometer cable.
46. Install the air hose and the resonance chamber.
47. Install the battery tray and the battery. Connect the battery cables.
48. Check for fluid leaks and proper operation.

Tempo and Topaz with 3.0L Engine

1. Prop the clutch pedal to keep it from moving toward the floor when the clutch cable is disconnected.
2. Disconnect the negative battery cable.
3. Disconnect the mass air flow sensor and air charge temperature sensor connectors at the air cleaner.
4. Remove the air cleaner retaining bolt, loosen the outlet tube at the throttle body and remove the air cleaner assembly.
5. Remove the retaining bolts and remove the coil bracket assembly from the left cylinder head. Position the assembly aside.
6. Install engine lifting bracket tools T70P–6000 or equivalent, on the rear of the left cylinder head.
7. Disconnect and remove the backup light switch.
8. Disconnect the clutch cable from the clutch release lever.
9. Remove the nut attaching the starter cable bracket to the left front transaxle support.
10. Remove the 2 top left-hand front transaxle mount-to-engine bolts.
11. Remove the nuts attaching the power steering line bracket to the engine.
12. Remove the top 4 transaxle-to-engine bolts.
13. Disconnect the vehicle speed sensor connector from the speed sensor.
14. Remove the speedometer cable from the speed sensor. Do not remove the clip retaining the cable to the speed sensor.
15. Install 3 bar engine support tool D88L–6000–A or equivalent, and connect the J-hook to the engine lifting bracket.
16. Loosen, but do not remove, the 2 Torx® head bolts attaching the right engine mounts to the right frame rail.
17. Raise and safely support the vehicle.
18. Remove the front wheel and tire assemblies.

19. Remove and discard both lower steering knuckle ball joint pinch bolts. Using a small prybar, slightly spread the knuckle pinch joint and separate each ball joint from the steering knuckle. A drift punch may be used to remove the bolt. Be careful not to damage the ball joint boot seal.

NOTE: Make sure the steering column is in the unlocked position. Do not use a hammer to separate the ball joint from the knuckle.

20. Remove the cotter pins and the nuts from the tie-rod ends. Use a suitable tool to disconnect the tie-rod ends from the steering knuckles.

21. Use a suitable prybar to disengage the CV-joints from the transaxle. Install transaxle plugs T81P–1177–B or equivalent, to prevent transaxle fluid from leaking from the transaxle.

22. Remove the nuts attaching the halfshafts to the hubs and remove the halfshafts.

23. Remove the bolt attaching the shift lever linkage to the transaxle shift rod and position the linkage aside.

24. Remove the bolt attaching the stabilizer rod to the transaxle and position the stabilizer rod aside.

25. Disconnect the neutral sensing switch connector.

26. Remove the starter support bracket and the starter.

27. Loosen the a front retaining bolt from each side on the engine-to-transaxle support bracket.

28. Remove the 2 rear retaining bolts on the engine-to-transaxle bracket and remove the 2 bracket-to-transaxle bolts.

29. On 1993–95 models, remove the accessory drive belt tensioner and install damper tool T93P6316-A or equivalent.

30. From the right wheel well, loosen, but do not remove, 2 right engine mount retaining nuts.

31. Remove the lower retaining bolt from the left front transaxle mount. Loosen the through bolt and pivot the mount up away from the transaxle.

32. Remove the 2 retaining nuts from the rear transaxle mount.

33. Carefully lower the engine/transaxle assembly using the engine support fixture until the crankshaft damper just contacts the right frame rail.

NOTE: Do not let the weight of the engine rest on the crankshaft damper or the damper and crankshaft thrust bearings may be damaged.

34. Position a transaxle jack under the transaxle and install safety chains. Lower the transaxle.

35. Remove the 2 remaining transaxle-to-engine bolts.

36. Remove the transaxle from the vehicle. After clearing the clutch assembly, rotate the transaxle clutch housing toward the front of the vehicle to clear the suspension stabilizer bar.

NOTE: Do not move the vehicle with the wheels on the ground with the transaxle removed.

To install:

37. Position the transaxle on the transaxle jack with safety chains.

38. Raise the transaxle into position. Rotate the transaxle clutch housing to the front of the engine compartment to allow the rear of the transaxle to clear the suspension stabilizer bar.

39. Align the transaxle input shaft with the clutch splines and locating pin on the engine and seat the transaxle against the engine.

40. Install 2 transaxle-to-engine bolts.

41. Using the engine support fixture, raise the engine/transaxle assembly into position.

42. Position the engine-to-transaxle support bracket to the transaxle and install but do not tighten the 2 bolts, 1 on each side.

43. Install 2 rear engine support bracket-to-engine bolts, 1 on each side.

44. Tighten the support bracket-to-engine bolts.

45. From the right wheel well, tighten the 2 right engine mount nuts to 73–97 ft. lbs. (98–132 Nm).

46. Install the lower left front engine mount-to-engine bolt and tighten to 26–33 ft. lbs. (34–46 Nm). Tighten the transaxle mount through bolt.

47. Install 2 left rear engine mount-to-body bracket nuts and tighten to 73–97 ft. lbs. (98–132 Nm).

48. Remove the transaxle jack.

49. On 1993–95 models, remove damper tool T93P6316-A or equivalent and install the accessory drive belt tensioner.

50. Install the starter and the starter bracket.

51. Connect the neutral sensing switch connector.

52. Install the transaxle stabilizer bar and tighten the bolt.

53. Position the shift linkage on the shift rod and install the bolt, washer and nut.

54. Position the halfshafts in the vehicle and insert the outer CV-joints through the hub assemblies. Install the retaining nuts and tighten to 180–200 ft. lbs. (244–271 Nm).

55. Remove the plugs from the transaxle that were installed during the removal procedure.

56. Install new clips on the inner CV-joint stub axles. Install the halfshafts into the transaxle. Pull on the CV-joints to make sure they are fully seated in the transaxle.

57. Install the ball joints into the steering knuckles using new bolts. Tighten the bolts to 38–45 ft. lbs. (52–60 Nm).

58. Check the transaxle fluid level and add fluid, if necessary.

59. Lower the vehicle. Remove the engine support and lifting eye.

60. Position the coil bracket and install the retaining bolts.

61. Install the speedometer cable into the speed sensor. Pull on the cable to make sure it is fully seated in the sensor. Connect the electrical connector to the speed sensor.

62. Connect the clutch cable to the clutch release lever.

63. Coat the threads of the backup light switch with pipe sealant and install the switch. Tighten to 12–15 ft. lbs. (16–20 Nm).

64. Install the 4 upper transaxle-to-engine bolts and tighten to 25–34 ft. lbs. (34–47 Nm).

65. Position the power steering line bracket to the upper transaxle-to-engine stud bolts and install the 2 nuts.

66. Install the 2 bolts in the left front transaxle mount.

67. Position the starter cable bracket and install the attaching nut.

68. Install the air cleaner and outlet tube.

69. Connect the mass air flow sensor and air charge temperature sensor connectors at the air cleaner.

70. Tighten the top 2 right mount-to-body Torx® bolts to 40–52 ft. lbs. (54–71 Nm).

71. Connect the negative battery cable.

72. Remove the prop from the clutch pedal. Road test the vehicle.

CLUTCH

Clutch Assembly

REMOVAL AND INSTALLATION

1. Disconnect the negative battery cable. Raise and safely support the vehicle. Remove the transaxle.

2. If the clutch assembly is to be reused, matchmark the pressure plate and the flywheel so they can be assembled in the same position.

3. Loosen the pressure plate-to-flywheel bolts 1 turn at a time, in sequence, until spring tension is relieved to prevent pressure plate cover distortion.

4. Support the pressure plate and remove the bolts. Remove the pressure plate and clutch disc from the flywheel.

5. Inspect the flywheel, clutch disc, pressure plate, release bearing, pilot bearing and the clutch fork for wear; replace parts, as required.

NOTE: If the flywheel shows any signs of overheating (blue discoloration) or if it is badly grooved or scored, it should be refaced or replaced.

To install:
6. If removed, install a new pilot bearing using a suitable installation tool.

7. If removed, install the flywheel. Make sure the flywheel and crankshaft flange mating surfaces are clean. Tighten the flywheel bolts to 71–76 ft. lbs. (96–103 Nm) on 1.8L engine, 54–67 ft. lbs. (73–91 Nm) on 1.9L engine, 54–64 ft. lbs. (73–86 Nm) on 2.3L engine or 59 ft. lbs. (80 Nm) on 3.0L engine.

8. Clean the pressure plate and flywheel surfaces thoroughly. Position the clutch disc and pressure plate into the installed position and support them with a dummy shaft or clutch aligning tool. If the clutch assembly is being reused, align the matchmarks that were made during the removal procedure.

9. Install the pressure plate-to-flywheel bolts. Tighten them gradually in a criss-cross pattern to 12–24 ft. lbs. (17–32 Nm) on all except Escort and Tracer, where the torque should be 13–20 ft. lbs. (18–26 Nm). Remove the alignment tool.

10. If the release bearing was removed, lubricate the release fork where it contacts the bearing and install the bearing in the fork.

11. Install the transaxle assembly. Lower the vehicle and connect the negative battery cable.

PEDAL HEIGHT/FREE-PLAY ADJUSTMENT

Tempo and Topaz

The pedal height and free-play are controlled by a self-adjusting feature.

Escort and Tracer

PEDAL HEIGHT

To determine if the pedal height requires adjustment, measure the distance from the bulkhead to the upper center of the pedal pad. The distance should be 7.72–8.03 in. (196–204mm). If adjustment is necessary, proceed as follows:

1. Disconnect the clutch switch electrical connector.

2. Loosen the clutch switch locknut.

3. Turn the clutch switch until the correct height is achieved.

4. Tighten the locknut to 10–13 ft. lbs. (14–18 Nm).

5. Measure the pedal free-play.

6. Connect the electrical connector.

PEDAL FREE-PLAY

To determine if the pedal free-play requires adjustment, depress the clutch pedal by hand until clutch resistance is felt. Measure the distance between the upper pedal height and where the resistance is felt. Free-play should be 0.20–0.51 in. (5–13mm). If an adjustment is necessary, proceed as follows:

1. Loosen the pushrod locknut.

2. Turn the pushrod until the pedal free-play is within specification.

3. Check that the disengagement height is correct when the pedal is fully depressed. Minimum disengagement height is 1.6 in. (41mm).

4. Tighten the pushrod locknut to 9–12 ft. lbs. (12–17 Nm).

Clutch Cable

ADJUSTMENT

Tempo and Topaz

The clutch control system is self-adjusting. After proper installation of the cable, adjustment is completed by pulling the clutch pedal to its upmost position.

REMOVAL AND INSTALLATION

Tempo and Topaz

NOTE: Whenever the clutch cable is disconnected for any reason, such as transaxle or clutch removal, clutch pedal components or clutch cable replacement, it is imperative that the proper method for installing the clutch cable be followed.

1. Disconnect the negative battery cable.

2. On the Tempo or Topaz, remove the panel from above the clutch pedal pad.

3. Prop up the clutch pedal to lift the pawl free of the quadrant which is part of the self-adjuster mechanism.

4. Remove the air cleaner to gain access to the clutch cable.

5. Using a pair of pliers, grasp the extended tip of the clutch cable, pull it forward and disconnect it from the clutch bearing lever.

NOTE: Do not grasp the wire strand portion of the inner cable since it may cut the wires and cause cable failure.

6. Remove the clutch casing from the insulator which is located on the rib on the top of the transaxle case.

7. Remove the rear screw and move the clutch shield away from the brake pedal support bracket. Loosen the front retaining screw, located near the toe board, rotate the shield aside and snug the screw to retain the shield.

8. With the clutch pedal raised to release the pawl, rotate the gear quadrant forward, unhook the clutch cable and allow the quadrant to swing rearward; do not allow the quadrant to snap back.

9. Pull the cable through the recess between the clutch pedal and the gear quadrant and from the insulator on the pedal assembly.

10. Remove the cable from the engine compartment.

To install:
11. Lift the clutch pedal to disengage the adjusting mechanism. This must be done during cable installation as failure to do so will result in damage to the self-adjuster mechanism.

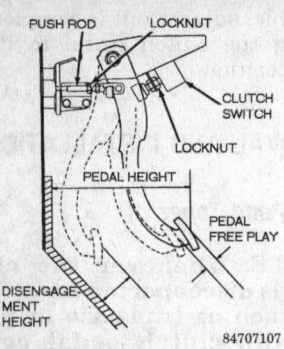

Pedal height/pedal free-play adjustment — Escort and Tracer

12. Insert the clutch cable through the dash panel and the dash panel grommet.

NOTE: Be sure the clutch cable is routed under the brake lines and not trapped at the spring tower by the brake lines. If equipped with power steering, route the cable inboard of the power steering hose.

13. Push the clutch cable through the insulator on the stop bracket and through the recess between the pedal and the gear quadrant.
14. Lift the clutch pedal to release the pawl, rotate the gear quadrant forward and hook the cable into the gear quadrant.
15. Install the clutch shield on the brake pedal support bracket.
16. On the Tempo or Topaz, install the panel above the clutch pedal.
17. Using a piece of wire, cord or tape, secure the pedal in the upmost position.
18. Insert the clutch cable through the insulator and connect the cable to the clutch release lever in the engine compartment.
19. Remove the device used to temporarily secure the pedal against its stop.
20. Adjust the clutch by depressing the clutch pedal several times. Install the air cleaner and connect the negative battery cable.

Clutch Master Cylinder

REMOVAL AND INSTALLATION

Escort and Tracer

1. Disconnect the battery cables and remove the battery and battery tray.
2. Disconnect the clutch pipe from the master cylinder using a suitable line wrench.

3. Disengage the clamp and remove the master cylinder hose from the clutch master cylinder. Prevent excess fluid loss by plugging the hose.
4. Remove the external mounting nut.
5. Remove the internal mounting nut and remove the master cylinder.

To install:

6. Align the pushrod and install the clutch master cylinder.
7. Install the external and internal mounting nuts and tighten to 14–19 ft. lbs. (19–25 Nm).
8. Connect the clutch pipe and tighten the nut to 10–16 ft. lbs. (13–22 Nm).
9. Install the hose and the clamp to the master cylinder.
10. Install the battery and battery tray.
11. Bleed the air from the system.
12. Test the system and make sure there is no leakage.
13. Connect the negative battery cable.

Clutch Slave Cylinder

ADJUSTMENT

Escort and Tracer

The clutch slave cylinder is not adjustable. The only adjustments necessary on the clutch control system are pedal height and pedal free-play.

REMOVAL AND INSTALLATION

Escort and Tracer

1. Disconnect the pressure line. Plug the line to prevent leaking.
2. Remove the attaching bolts and remove the slave cylinder.

To install:

3. Install the slave cylinder.
4. Install the attaching bolts and tighten to 12–17 ft. lbs. (16–23 Nm).
5. Connect the pressure line and tighten the nut to 10–16 ft. lbs. (13–22 Nm).
6. Bleed the air from the system.
7. Press on the clutch pedal and make sure there is no leakage.

Hydraulic Clutch System Bleeding

NOTE: The fluid level in the reservoir must be maintained at the ¾ level or higher during air bleeding.

1. Remove the bleeder cap from the slave cylinder and attach a vinyl hose to the bleeder screw.

2. Place the other end of the hose in a container.
3. Slowly pump the clutch pedal several times.
4. With the clutch pedal depressed, loosen the bleeder screw to release the fluid and air.
5. Tighten the bleeder screw.
6. Repeat the last 3 steps until no air bubbles appear in the fluid.

AUTOMATIC TRANSAXLE

Transaxle Assembly

REMOVAL AND INSTALLATION

Tempo and Topaz

1. Disconnect the negative battery cable.

NOTE: Due to automatic transaxle case configuration, on all except the 3.0L engine, the right-side halfshaft assembly must be removed first. The differential rotator tool T81P-4026-A or equivalent, is then inserted into the transaxle to drive the left-side inboard CV-joint assembly from the transaxle.

2. Remove the air cleaner assembly.
3. Disconnect the electrical harness connector from the neutral safety switch.
4. Disconnect the throttle valve linkage, throttle cable if equipped with 3.0L engine, and the manual lever cable from their levers.

NOTE: Failure to disconnect the linkage or cable and allowing the transaxle to hang, will fracture the throttle valve cam shaft joint, which is located under the transaxle cover.

5. To prevent contamination, cover the timing window in the converter housing. If equipped, remove the bolts retaining the thermactor hoses and position out of the way.
6. If equipped, remove the ground strap, located above the upper engine mount, and the coil and bracket assembly.

NOTE: If equipped with 3.0L engine, be careful not to damage the TV cable while accessing the upper retaining bolts.

7. Remove both transaxle-to-engine upper bolts; the bolts are located below and on both sides of the distributor. Install 3 bar engine support D88L–6000–A or equivalent.

8. Raise and safely support the vehicle. Remove the front wheel and tire assemblies.

9. Remove the nut from the control arm-to-steering knuckle attaching bolt, at the ball joint. Using a hammer and a punch, drive the bolt from the steering knuckle; repeat this step on the other side. Discard the nut and bolt.

NOTE: Be careful not to damage or cut ball joint boot. The prybar must not contact lower arm.

10. Using a prybar, disengage the control arm from the steering knuckle; repeat this step on the other side.

NOTE: Do not hammer on the knuckle to remove the ball joints. The plastic shield installed behind the rotor contains a molded pocket into which the lower control arm ball joint fits. When disengaging the control arm from the knuckle, clearance for the ball joint can be provided by bending the shield back toward the rotor. Failure to provide clearance for the ball joint can result in damage to the shield.

11. Remove the stabilizer bar bracket-to-frame rail bolts and discard the bolts; repeat this step on the other side.

12. Remove the stabilizer bar-to-control arm nut/washer and discard the nut; repeat this step on the other side.

13. Pull the stabilizer bar from of the control arms.

14. Remove the brake hose routing clip-to-suspension strut bracket bolt; repeat this step on the other side.

15. Remove the steering gear tie rod-to-steering knuckle nut and disengage the tie rod from the steering knuckle; repeat this step on the other side.

16. Using a halfshaft removal tool, pry the halfshaft from the right side of the transaxle and support the end of the shaft with mechanics wire.

NOTE: It is normal for some fluid to leak from the transaxle when the halfshaft is removed. Be careful not to damage the transaxle case or the bottom of the oil pan flange when prying the halfshaft out.

17. Using differential rotator tool T81P–4026–A or equivalent, drive the left-side halfshaft from the differential side gear.

18. Pull the halfshaft from the transaxle and support the end of the shaft with mechanics wire.

NOTE: Do not allow the shaft to hang unsupported, as damage to the outboard CV-joint may result.

19. Install transaxle plugs T81P–1177–B or equivalent, into the differential seals.

20. Remove the starter support bracket, if equipped. Disconnect the starter cable. Remove the starter bolts and the starter. If equipped, remove the hose and bracket bolts on the starter and a bolt at the converter and disconnect the hoses.

21. If equipped, remove the transaxle support bracket. Remove the dust cover from the torque converter housing.

22. Remove the torque converter-to-flywheel nuts by turning the crankshaft pulley bolt to bring the nuts into position.

23. Position a suitable transmission jack under the transaxle and remove the rear support bracket nuts.

24. Remove the left front insulator-to-body bracket nuts, the bracket-to-body bolts and the bracket.

25. Disconnect the transaxle cooler lines.

26. Remove the manual lever bracket-to-transaxle case bolts.

27. Support the engine. Make sure the transaxle is supported and remove the remaining transaxle-to-engine bolts.

28. Make sure the torque converter studs will be clear the flywheel. Insert a prybar between the flywheel and the converter, then, pry the transaxle and converter away from the engine. When the converter studs are clear of the flywheel, lower the transaxle about 2–3 in. (51–76mm).

29. Disconnect the speedometer cable and lower the transaxle.

NOTE: When moving the transaxle away from the engine, watch the No. 1 insulator. If it contacts the body before the converter studs clear the flywheel, remove the insulator.

To install:

30. Raise the transaxle and align it with the engine and flywheel. Install the No. 1 insulator, if removed. Torque the transaxle-to-engine bolts to 25–33 ft. lbs. (34–45 Nm) on the 1.9L and 2.3L engines or 34–47 ft. lbs. (46–63 Nm) on the 3.0L engine.

Tighten the torque converter-to-flywheel bolts to 23–39 ft. lbs. (31–53 Nm).

31. Install the manual lever bracket-to-transaxle case bolts and connect the transaxle cooler lines.

32. Install the left front insulator-to-body bracket nuts and torque the nuts to 40–50 ft. lbs. (55–70 Nm). Install the bracket-to-body and torque the bolts to 55–70 ft. lbs. (75–90 Nm).

33. Install the transaxle support bracket and the dust cover to the torque converter housing.

34. If equipped, install the hose and bracket bolts on the starter and a bolt to the converter and connect the hoses. Install the starter and the support bracket; torque the starter-to-engine bolts to 30–40 ft. lbs. (41–54 Nm). Connect the starter cable.

35. Remove the seal plugs from the differential seals and install the halfshaft by performing the following procedures:

   a. Prior to installing the halfshaft in the transaxle, install a new circlip onto the CV-joint stub.

   b. Install the halfshaft in the transaxle by carefully aligning the CV-joint splines with the differential side gears. Be sure to push the CV-joint into the differential until the circlip is felt to seat in the differential side gear. Use care to prevent damage to the differential oil seal.

   c. Attach the lower ball joint to the steering knuckle, taking care not to damage or cut the ball joint boot. Insert a new pinch bolt and a new nut. While holding the bolt with a 2nd wrench, torque the nut to 40–54 ft. lbs. (54–74 Nm).

36. Engage the tie rod with the steering knuckle and torque the nut to 23–35 ft. lbs. (31–47 Nm).

37. Install the brake hose routing clip-to-suspension strut bracket and torque the bolt to 8 ft. lbs. (11 Nm).

38. Install the stabilizer bar to control arm and using a new nut, torque it to 98–125 ft. lbs. (133–169 Nm).

39. Install the stabilizer bar bracket-to-frame rail bolts and using new bolts, torque them to 60–70 ft. lbs. (81–95 Nm).

40. Install the wheel and tire assemblies and lower the vehicle. Install the upper transaxle-to-engine bolts and torque to 25–33 ft. lbs. (34–45 Nm) on 1.9L and 2.3L engines or 34–47 ft. lbs. (46–63 Nm) on 3.0L engine.

41. If equipped, install the ground strap, located above the upper engine mount, and the coil and bracket assembly.

42. If equipped, install the bolts retaining the thermactor hoses. Uncover the timing window in the converter housing.

43. Connect the throttle valve linkage or cable and the manual lever cable to their levers.

44. Connect the electrical harness connector from the neutral safety switch.

45. Install the air cleaner assembly.

46. Connect the negative battery cable and road test the vehicle.

Escort and Tracer

1. Disconnect the battery cables and remove the battery and battery tray.

2. Disconnect the wiring harness retaining clip from the battery tray.

3. Remove the air cleaner assembly.

4. Disconnect the shift control cable from the manual lever.

5. Disconnect the speedometer cable from the transaxle by unsnapping the cable at the speedometer driven gear.

6. Disconnect the transaxle electronic control electrical connectors and separate the harness from the transaxle clips.

7. Remove the manual lever position switch wiring brackets and disconnect the ground cables from the top of the transaxle.

8. Remove the starter.

9. Disconnect the manual lever position switch wiring connectors.

10. Install engine support D88L–6000–A or equivalent, to support the engine.

11. Disconnect the kickdown cable at the throttle cam.

12. Place a suitable drain pan under the transaxle and disconnect the transaxle cooler lines at the transaxle.

13. Remove the upper transaxle mount bolts, the mount and the upper transaxle housing bolts.

14. Disconnect the oxygen sensor electrical connector, the transaxle vent hose, and the electrical connector at the vehicle speed sensor.

15. Raise and safely support the vehicle.

16. Remove the front wheel and tire assemblies.

17. Using a suitable hammer and a flat punch, straighten the detent in the halfshaft nut.

18. Remove the nuts securing the halfshafts to the steering knuckles and remove the nuts and bolts securing the lower ball joints to the steering knuckles. Separate the lower ball joints from the steering knuckles. Remove the nuts securing the tie rods to the steering knuckles.

19. Disconnect the halfshaft mid-bearing bracket from the back of the engine.

20. Remove the halfshafts from both steering knuckles.

21. Remove the 3 engine/transaxle lower splash shields and the torque converter inspection plate. Remove the nuts securing the torque converter to the flexplate.

22. Remove the bolts securing the lower transaxle to the engine oil pan. Disconnect the lower crossmember from the chassis and the transaxle mounts.

23. Remove the driver's side and then the passenger's side halfshafts. Install 2 transaxle plugs T88C–7025–AH or equivalent into the differential side gears.

——— WARNING ———
Failure to install the transaxle plugs may cause the differential side gears to become improperly positioned. If the gears become misaligned, the differential will have to be removed from the transaxle to align them.

24. Position a drain pan and remove the drainplug from the transaxle. Drain the fluid from the differential cavity. Remove the transaxle pan and drain the transaxle fluid, then install the pan and drainplug.

25. Position a suitable transmission jack under the transaxle. Secure the transaxle to the jack.

26. Remove the lower bolts securing the transaxle to the engine and carefully lower the transaxle out of the vehicle.

To install:

NOTE: A pin is used for securing the throttle cam in a fixed position on new and rebuilt transaxles. This pin must be removed to allow proper transaxle operation. If the pin is not removed, the throttle lever will remain in a fixed position. After removing the pin, apply sealant to the bolt from the previous transaxle. Install the bolt and tighten to 69–95 inch lbs. (8–11 Nm).

27. Secure the transaxle on the transmission jack.

28. Raise the transaxle into position and install the lower transaxle-to-engine bolts. Tighten the bolts to 41–59 ft. lbs. (55–80 Nm).

29. Position the torque converter to the flexplate and install the nuts.

Tighten the nuts to 25–36 ft. lbs. (34–49 Nm). Install the torque converter inspection plate.

30. Remove the 2 transaxle plugs and install the halfshafts.

31. Connect the crossmember to the transaxle mounts and the chassis. Tighten the crossmember-to-transaxle mount nuts to 27–38 ft. lbs. (37–52 Nm). Tighten the crossmember-to-chassis nuts and bolts to 47–66 ft. lbs. (64–89 Nm).

32. Install the lower transaxle-to-engine oil pan bolts and tighten to 27–38 ft. lbs. (37–52 Nm). Install the engine/transaxle splash shields and the starter.

33. Position the lower ball joints into the steering knuckles and secure with the nuts and bolts. Tighten the nuts and bolts to 32–43 ft. lbs. (43–59 Nm).

34. Position the tie rod ends into the steering knuckles and install the nuts. Tighten to 31–42 ft. lbs. (42–57 Nm).

35. Install the wheel and tire assemblies. Tighten the lug nuts to 65–88 ft. lbs. (88–118 Nm).

36. Lower the vehicle.

37. Install the transaxle-to-engine bolts and tighten to 41–59 ft. lbs. (55–80 Nm).

38. Install the upper transaxle mount and tighten the nuts to 49–69 ft. lbs. (67–93 Nm).

39. Connect the transaxle vent hose, the electrical connector at the speed sensor, the speedometer cable and the oxygen sensor connector.

40. Connect the transaxle cooler lines and connect the kickdown cable at the throttle body.

41. Remove the engine support.

42. Connect the ground wires to the transaxle and connect the manual lever position switch bracket and wiring connectors.

43. Connect the shift control cable to the cable bracket and to the selector lever. Tighten the selector lever attaching locknut to 33–47 ft. lbs. (44–64 Nm).

NOTE: Do not use any type of power wrench to tighten the locknut. Damage to the transaxle may result.

44. Install the battery tray and battery. Connect the wiring harness retaining clip to the battery tray.

45. Install the air cleaner assembly.

46. Connect the battery cables.

47. Add the proper type and quantity of transaxle fluid.

48. Check the transaxle for leaks and for proper operation.

SHIFT LINKAGE ADJUSTMENT

Tempo and Topaz

1. Place the gear shift selector into **D**. The shift lever must be in the **D** position during linkage adjustment.
2. Working at the transaxle, loosen the transaxle manual lever-to-control cable nut.
3. Make sure the transaxle lever is in the **D** position, 2nd detent from the most rearward position.
4. Torque the retaining nut to 10–15 ft. lbs. (14–20 Nm).
5. Make sure all gears engage correctly and the vehicle will only start in **P** or **N**.

Escort and Tracer

1. Move the gear selector lever to **P**.
2. Disconnect the negative battery cable. This will deactivate the shift-lock system.
3. Remove the screw securing the gear selector knob to the gear selector lever. Remove the knob.
4. Remove the shift console as follows:
   a. Remove the rear seat ash tray and position both front seats to the rear-most position.
   b. Remove the 2 front retaining screws from the parking brake console and recline both front seats.
   c. Remove the 2 rear retaining screws from the parking brake console.
   d. With the parking brake engaged, remove the parking brake console.
   e. Remove the 2 front retaining screws from the shift console and remove the console.
5. Remove the position indicator mounting screws and disconnect the illumination bulb from the position indicator.
6. Disconnect the shift-lock servo and park range switch electrical connectors.
7. Remove the position indicator.

NOTE: Make sure the detent spring roller is in the P detent.

8. Loosen the shift control cable bracket mounting bolts.
9. Push the gear selector lever against the **P** range and hold it.
10. Tighten the shift control cable bracket mounting bolts to 69–95 inch lbs. (8–11 Nm).
11. Lightly press the gear selector pushrod and make sure the guide plate and guide pin clearances are within specifications.
12. Check that the guide plate and guide pin clearances are within the

appropriate specifications when the selector lever is shifted to **N** and **OD**. If the clearances are not as specified, readjust the shift control cable.

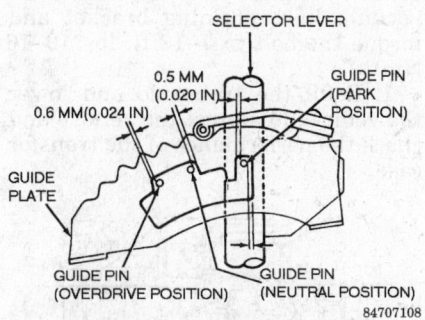

Shift control cable adjustment clearances — Escort and Tracer

13. Make sure the gear selector operates properly.
14. Connect the illumination bulb to the position indicator.
15. Connect the shift-lock servo and park range switch electrical connectors.
16. Install the position indicator and secure it with the mounting screws.
17. Install the shift console by reversing the removal procedure.
18. Position the gear selector knob onto the gear selector lever and secure the knob with the screw.
19. Connect the negative battery cable.

THROTTLE LINKAGE ADJUSTMENT

2.3L Engine

1. Disconnect the negative battery cable.
2. Remove the splash shield from the cable retainer bracket.
3. Loosen the trunnion bolt on the throttle valve rod.
4. Install plastic clip using TV linkage adjustment tool T91P–7000–A or equivalent, to bottom of throttle valve rod; be sure the clip keeps the rod from telescoping.
5. Be sure the return spring is connected between the throttle valve rod and the retaining bracket to hold the transaxle throttle valve lever at it's idle position.
6. Make sure the throttle lever is resting on the throttle return control screw.
7. Tighten the throttle valve rod trunnion bolt and remove the plastic clip.

8. Install the splash shield. Connect the negative battery cable and check the vehicle's operation.

3.0L Engine

1. Remove the splash shield from the cable retainer bracket.
2. Unsnap the white adjuster locking clip at the cable retainer bracket.
3. Hold the transaxle lever in the idle position against the idle stop.
4. Make sure the throttle lever adjusting screw is resting against the idle stop.
5. Snap the white adjuster locking clip into the lock position.
6. Install the splash shield.
7. Check the linkage for proper operation.

TRANSFER CASE

Transfer Case Assembly

REMOVAL AND INSTALLATION

1. Disconnect the negative battery cable.
2. Raise and safely support the vehicle.
3. Loosen the 2 rear engine mount bolts far enough to gain access to the transfer cup plug. Using a light hammer and a dull chisel, remove the cup plug from the transfer case and drain the oil.
4. Remove the vacuum line retaining bracket bolt.
5. Remove the driveshaft front retaining bolts and caps; disengage the front of the driveshaft from the drive yoke.
6. If the transfer case is to be disassembled, check the backlash through the cup plug opening before removal in order to reset to existing backlash at installation. The backlash should be as follows:
• Vehicles except transaxle models PMA-BX through PMA-BX10 — 0.012–0.047 in. (0.30–1.20mm).
• Vehicles with transaxle models PMA-BX through PMA-BX10 — 0.031–0.066 in. (0.78–1.68mm).
7. Remove the vacuum motor shield bolts and the shield.
8. Remove the vacuum lines from the vacuum servo.
9. Remove the transfer case-to-transaxle bolts; note and record the length and locations of the bolts.
10. Remove the the transfer case from the vehicle.

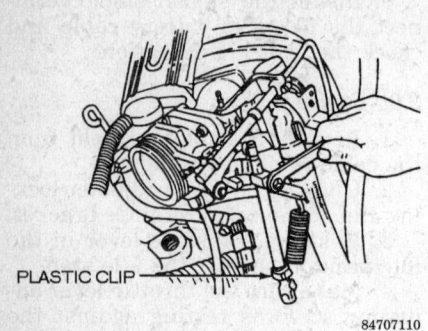

PLASTIC CLIP

84707110

Throttle valve linkage adjustment — 2.3L engine

To install:

11. Position new maximum thickness gasket 7A191–H onto the transfer case. For transaxle models PMA–BX through PMA–BX 10, install a 7A191–J gasket.

12. Position the transfer case to the transaxle.

13. Install the transfer case bolts in the proper positions and torque the bolts, in sequence, to 12–15 ft. lbs. (16–20 Nm).

14. Install backlash measuring gauge T87P–4020–B or equivalent, through the cup plug opening into the input gear. Tighten the wing nut on the end of the backlash tool.

15. Make sure the transaxle is in **P**. Remove 1 bolt from the transfer case. Install a rod on the transaxle panrail and secure a suitable dial indicator to the rod. Rotate both front wheels together until the park gear is wedged tight against the park pawl. Maintain the load on the park gear, park pawl and wheels while reading the backlash. Position the indicator foot on the end of the backlash measuring gauge. Push the backlash measuring gauge upward and zero the dial indicator.

16. Pushing down on the backlash measuring gauge, measure the backlash. The backlash should be within the range specified in Step 6.

17. If the backlash measurement is within specification, proceed to Step 18. If the measurement is not within specification, select the proper gasket from the gasket selection charts. Remove the transfer case, install the gasket and recheck the backlash. If the backlash is correct, proceed to Step 18.

18. Remove the measuring tools and reinstall the cup plug. Tighten the 2 rear engine mount bolts.

19. Install the vacuum motor supply hose connector, vacuum motor

shield and torque the bolts to 7–12 ft. lbs. (9–16 Nm).

20. Install the driveshaft to the drive yoke, lubricate the bolts with Loctite® and torque the bolts to 15–17 ft. lbs. (21–23 Nm). Install the vacuum line retaining bracket and torque the bolt to 7–12 ft. lbs. (9–16 Nm).

21. Refill the transaxle and lower the vehicle. Road test the vehicle and check the performance of the transfer case.

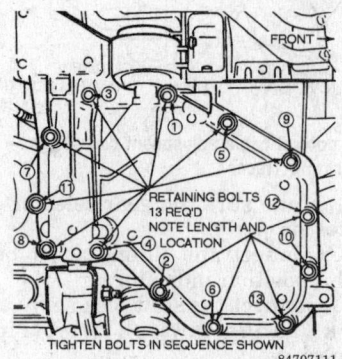

FRONT

RETAINING BOLTS 13 REQ'D NOTE LENGTH AND LOCATION

TIGHTEN BOLTS IN SEQUENCE SHOWN

84707111

Transfer case bolt torque sequence

SELECT GASKET CHART TRANSAXLE MODEL PMA-BX THROUGH PMA-BX10

Measurement Obtained	Select Gasket Required
0.78-1.68mm (.031-.066 inch)	7A191-J
1.68mm (.066 inch) or greater	7A191-I
0.78mm (.031 inch) or less	7A191-K

84707114

Transfer case gasket selection chart — transaxle model PMA-BX through PMA-BX 10

DRIVE AXLE

Halfshaft

REMOVAL AND INSTALLATION

Tempo and Topaz and All Wheel Drive Rear Halfshaft

NOTE: Halfshaft assembly removal and installation procedures are the same for automatic and manual transaxles, except on the automatic transaxle, the

right side halfshaft must be removed first. Differential rotator tool T81P–4026–A or equivalent, is then inserted into the transaxle to drive the left side inboard CV-joint assembly from the transaxle. If only the left side halfshaft assembly is to be removed for service, remove the right side halfshaft assembly from the transaxle only. After removal, support it with a length of wire, then drive the left side halfshaft assembly from the transaxle.

1. Remove the cap from the hub and loosen the hub nut. Set the parking brake. The nut must be loosened without unstaking; the use of a chisel or similar tool may damage the spindle thread.

2. Raise and safely support the vehicle. Remove the wheel and tire assembly. Remove the hub nut/washer and discard the nut.

3. Remove the brake hose routing clip-to-strut bolt.

4. Remove the nut from the ball joint-to-steering knuckle bolt. Using a hammer and a punch, drive the bolt from the steering knuckle and discard the bolt/nut.

5. Using a prybar, separate the ball joint from the steering knuckle. Position the end of the prybar outside of the bushing pocket to avoid damage to the bushing; be careful not to damage the ball joint or CV-joint boot.

NOTE: The lower control arm ball joint fits into a pocket formed in the plastic disc brake rotor shield; bend the shield away from the ball joint while prying the ball joint from the steering knuckle.

6. Using a prybar, pry the halfshaft from the differential housing. Position the prybar between the differential housing and the CV-joint assembly. Be careful not to damage the differential oil seal, case, CV-joint boot or the transaxle.

—————— **WARNING** ——————
Shipping plugs T81P–1177–B or equivalent, must be installed in the differential housing after halfshaft removal. Failure to do so can result in dislocation of the differential side gears. Should the gears become misaligned, the differential will have to be removed from the transaxle to realign the gears.

7. Using a piece of wire, support the end of the shaft from a convenient underbody component.

NOTE: Do not allow the shaft to hang unsupported, as damage to the outboard CV-joint may result.

8. Using a front hub removal tool, press the halfshaft's outboard CV-joint from the hub.

NOTE: Never use a hammer to separate the outboard CV-joint stub shaft from the hub. Damage to the CV-joint internal components may result.

To install:

9. Install a new circlip onto the inboard CV-joint stub shaft; the outboard CV-joint stub shaft does not have a circlip. To install the circlip properly, start one end in the groove and work the circlip over the stub shaft end and into the groove; this will avoid over expanding the circlip.

NOTE: Do not reuse the old circlip. A new circlip must be installed each time the inboard CV-joint is installed into the differential.

10. Carefully, align the splines of the inboard CV-joint stub shaft with the splines in the differential. Push the CV-joint into the differential until the circlip is seated in the differential side gear. Use care to prevent damage to the differential oil seal.

NOTE: A non-metallic mallet may be used to aid in seating the circlip into the differential side gear groove; if a mallet is necessary, tap only on the outboard CV-joint stub shaft.

11. Carefully, align the outboard CV-joint stub shaft splines with the hub splines and push the shaft into the hub, as far as possible.

12. Temporarily fasten the rotor to the hub with 2 lug nuts. Insert a steel rod or equivalent, into the rotor and rotate clockwise to contact the knuckle and keep the rotor from turning.

13. Manually thread a new retainer nut onto the CV-joint shaft as far as possible.

14. Connect the control arm-to-steering knuckle and torque the new nut/bolt to 40–54 ft. lbs. (54–74 Nm). A new bolt and nut must be used.

15. Position the brake hose routing clip on the suspension strut and torque the bolt to 8 ft. lbs. (11 Nm).

16. Tighten the hub retainer nut to 170–236 ft. lbs. (230–320 Nm) on 1992–94 vehicles.

NOTE: Do not use power or impact tools to tighten the hub nut.

17. Install the wheel/tire assembly and torque the lug nuts to 80–105 ft. lbs. (108–144 Nm). Lower the vehicle.

18. Refill the transaxle and road test.

All Wheel Drive Rear Halfshaft

1. Raise and safely support the vehicle. Remove the rear suspension control arm bolt.

2. Remove the outboard U-joint retaining bolts and straps. Remove the inboard U-joint retaining bolts and straps.

3. Slide the shafts together; do not allow the splined shafts to contact with excessive force. Remove the halfshafts; do not drop the halfshafts as the impact may cause damage to the U-joint bearing cups.

4. Retain the bearing cups. Inspect the U-joint assemblies for wear or damage, replace the U-joint if necessary. **To install:**

5. Install the halfshaft at the inboard U-joint; the inboard shaft has a larger diameter than the outboard shaft. Install the U-joint retaining caps and bolts and torque them to 15–17 ft. lbs. (21–23 Nm).

NOTE: Be sure to apply Loctite® to the U-joint bolts.

6. Install the halfshaft at the outboard U-joint. Install the U-joint retaining caps and bolts and torque them to 15–17 ft. lbs. (21–23 Nm).

7. Install the rear suspension control arm and torque the bolt to 60–86 ft. lbs. (82–116 Nm).

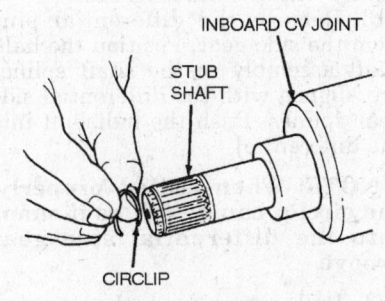

INBOARD CV JOINT

STUB SHAFT

CIRCLIP

84707118

Stub shaft circlip installation

Escort and Tracer

LEFT SIDE — 1.8L AND 1.9L ENGINES, RIGHT SIDE — 1.9L ENGINE

1. Raise and safely support the vehicle.

2. Remove the wheel and tire assembly.

3. Remove the splash shield.

4. Carefully raise the staked portion of the halfshaft retaining nut using a suitable small chisel. Remove and discard the retaining nut.

5. Remove the cotter pin and nut from the tie rod end and remove the tie rod end from the steering knuckle using a suitable removal tool.

6. Remove the lower ball joint clamp bolt. Carefully pry down on the lower control arm to separate the ball joint from the steering knuckle.

7. Pull outward on the steering knuckle/brake assembly. Carefully pull the halfshaft from the steering knuckle and position it aside.

8. Removal of the left side halfshaft requires removal of the crossmember to allow access with a prybar. If the left side halfshaft is being removed, proceed as follows:

    a. Support the transaxle with a suitable transmission jack.

    b. Remove the 4 transaxle mount-to-crossmember attaching nuts.

    c. Remove the 2 crossmember attaching nuts at the rear of the crossmember.

    d. While supporting the rear of the crossmember, remove the 2 front mounting bolts. Remove the crossmember.

9. Position a drain pan under the transaxle.

10. Insert a prybar between the halfshaft and the transaxle case. Gently pry outward to release the halfshaft from the differential side gears. Be careful no to damage the transaxle case, oil seal, CV-joint or CV-joint boot.

11. Remove the halfshaft.

WARNING
Install suitable plugs after removing the halfshafts to prevent the differential side gears from becoming mispositioned. Should the gears become misaligned, the differential will have to be removed from the transaxle to align the gears.

To install:

12. Position a new circlip on the inner CV-joint spline so the circlip gap is at the top. Lubricate the splines lightly with suitable grease.

13. Remove the plugs that were installed in the differential side gears.

14. Position the halfshaft so the CV-joint splines are aligned with the differential side gear splines. Push the halfshaft into the differential.

NOTE: When seated properly, the circlip can be felt as it snaps into the differential side gear groove.

15. Pull outward on the steering knuckle/brake assembly and insert the halfshaft into the steering knuckle.

16. Pry downward on the control arm and position the lower ball joint in the steering knuckle.

17. For left side halfshaft installation, proceed as follows:

a. Position the crossmember in place.

b. Install the 2 mounting bolts and the 2 attaching nuts. Tighten the nuts and bolts to 47–66 ft. lbs. (64–89 Nm).

c. Install the 4 transaxle mount-to-crossmember attaching nuts. Tighten the nuts to 27–38 ft. lbs. (37–52 Nm).

d. Remove the transmission jack.

18. Install the lower ball joint clamp bolt and tighten to 32–43 ft. lbs. (43–59 Nm).

19. Install the tie rod end in the steering knuckle. Install the nut to the tie rod end and tighten to 31–42 ft. lbs. (42–57 Nm). Install a new cotter pin.

20. Install a new halfshaft retaining nut and tighten to 174–235 ft. lbs. (235–319 Nm). Stake the halfshaft retaining nut using a suitable chisel with a rounded cutting edge.

NOTE: If the nut splits or cracks after staking, replace it with a new nut.

21. Install the splash shield.

22. Install the wheel and tire assembly and lower the vehicle.

23. Check and refill the transaxle with the proper type and quantity of fluid.

RIGHT SIDE — 1.8L ENGINE

NOTE: The right side halfshaft assembly is a 2 piece shaft with a bearing support bracket positioned between the 2 halves. The bearing support bracket is mounted on the cylinder block and must be unbolted if the entire halfshaft assembly is to be removed. If only the CV-joints/boots are to be serviced, the outboard shaft assembly may

be removed, leaving the bearing support bracket mounted on the engine cylinder block.

1. Raise and safely support the vehicle.

2. Remove the right front wheel and tire assembly.

3. Remove the splash shield.

4. Carefully raise the staked portion of the halfshaft retaining nut using a suitable small chisel. Remove and discard the retaining nut.

5. Remove the cotter pin and nut from the tie rod end and remove the tie rod end from the steering knuckle using a suitable removal tool.

6. Remove the lower ball joint clamp bolt. Carefully pry down on the lower control arm to separate the ball joint from the steering knuckle.

7. Pull outward on the steering knuckle/brake assembly. Carefully pull the halfshaft from the steering knuckle and position it aside.

8. Position a drain pan under the transaxle.

9. Remove the 3 bearing support bracket mounting bolts.

10. Insert a prybar between the bearing support bracket and the starter bracket. Gently pry outward on the damper until the halfshaft disengages from the differential side gear.

11. Remove the halfshaft assembly. Install an appropriate differential plug in the differential side gear.

——— WARNING ———
If both halfshafts are removed, plugs must be installed to keep the differential side gears from becoming mispositioned. If the gears become misaligned, the differential will have to be removed from the transaxle to align the gears.

To install:

12. Position a new circlip on the inner CV-joint spline so the circlip gap is at the top. Lubricate the splines lightly with a suitable grease.

13. Remove the differential plug from the side gear. Position the halfshaft assembly so the shaft splines are aligned with the differential side gear splines. Push the halfshaft into the differential.

NOTE: When seated properly, the circlip can be felt as it snaps into the differential side gear groove.

14. Pull outward on the steering knuckle/brake assembly and insert the halfshaft into the steering knuckle.

15. Pry downward on the control arm and position the lower ball joint in the steering knuckle. Install the lower ball joint clamp bolt and tighten to 32–43 ft. lbs. (43–59 Nm).

16. Install the tie rod end in the steering knuckle. Install the nut to the tie rod end and tighten to 31–42 ft. lbs. (42–57 Nm). Install a new cotter pin.

17. Position the bearing support bracket and install the 3 mounting bolts. Tighten the bolts in the proper sequence to 31–46 ft. lbs. (42–62 Nm).

18. Install a new halfshaft retaining nut and tighten to 174–235 ft. lbs. (235–319 Nm). Stake the retaining nut using a suitable chisel with the cutting edge rounded off.

NOTE: If the nut splits or cracks after staking, it must be replaced with a new nut.

19. Install the splash shield.

20. Install the right front wheel and tire assembly and lower the vehicle.

21. Check and refill the transaxle with the proper type and quantity of fluid.

CV-Boot

REPLACEMENT

NOTE: When replacing a CV-boot, be aware of the transaxle type, transaxle ratio, engine size, CV-joint type, right or left side and inboard or outboard end.

Tempo and Topaz

NOTE: There are several different types of CV-joints used, each requiring different removal procedures.

DOUBLE OFFSET JOINT INBOARD CV-JOINT BOOT

1. Disconnect the negative battery cable.

2. Remove halfshaft assembly from vehicle. Place halfshaft in vise. Do not allow vice jaws to contact the boot or its clamp. The vise should be equipped with jaw caps to prevent damage to any machined surfaces.

3. Cut the large boot clamp using side cutters and peel away from the boot. After removing the clamp, roll boot back over shaft.

4. Remove wire ring ball retainer.

5. Remove outer race.

6. Pull inner race assembly out until it rests on the circlip. Using snapring pliers, spread stopring and move it back on shaft.

7. Slide inner race assembly down the shaft to allow access to the circlip. Remove circlip.

8. Remove inner race assembly. Remove boot.

NOTE: Circlips must not be reused. Replace with new circlips before assembly.

9. When replacing damaged CV-boots, the grease should be checked for contamination. If the CV-joints were operating satisfactorily and the grease does not appear to be contaminated, add grease and replace the boot. If the lubricant appears contaminated, proceed with a complete CV-joint disassembly and inspection.

10. Remove balls by prying from cage.

NOTE: Exercise care to prevent scratching or other damage to the inner race or cage.

11. Rotate inner race to align lands with cage windows. Lift inner race out through the wider end of the cage.

To install:

12. Clean all parts (except boots) in a suitable solvent.

13. Inspect all CV-joint parts for excessive wear, looseness, pitting, rust and cracks.

NOTE: CV-joint components are matched during assembly. If inspection reveals damage or wear the entire joint must be replaced as an assembly. Do not replace a joint merely because the parts appear polished. Shiny areas in ball races and on the cage spheres are normal.

14. Install a new circlip, supplied with the service kit, in groove nearest end of shaft. Do not over-expand or twist circlip during installation.

15. Install inner race in the cage. The race is installed through the large end of the cage with the circlip counterbore facing the large end of the cage.

16. With the cage and inner race properly aligned, install the balls by pressing through the cage windows with the heel of the hand.

17. Assemble inner race and cage assembly in outer race.

18. Push the inner race and cage assembly by hand, into the outer race. Install with inner race chamfer facing out.

19. Install ball retainer into groove inside of outer race.

20. Install new CV-boot.

21. Tighten clamp securely but not to the point where the clamp bridge is cut or the boot is damaged.

22. Position stopring and new circlip into grooves on shaft.

23. Fill CV-joint outer race with 3.2 oz. (90 grams) of grease, then spread 1.4 oz. (40 grams) of grease evenly inside boot for a total combined fill of 4.6 oz. (130 grams).

24. With boot peeled back, install CV-joint using soft tipped hammer. Ensure splines are aligned prior to installing CV-joint onto shaft.

25. Remove all excess grease from the CV-joint external surfaces.

26. Position boot over CV-joint. Before installing boot clamp, move CV-joint in or out, as necessary, to adjust to the proper length.

NOTE: Insert a suitable tool between the boot and outer bearing race and allow the trapped air to escape from the boot. The air should be released from the boot only after adjusting to the proper dimensions.

27. Ensure boot is seated in its groove and clamp in position.

28. Tighten clamp securely but not to the point where the clamp bridge is cut or the boot is damaged.

29. Install halfshaft assembly in vehicle.

30. Connect negative battery cable.

TRIPOD INBOARD CV-JOINT BOOT

1. Disconnect the negative battery cable.

2. Remove halfshaft assembly from vehicle. Place halfshaft in vice. Do not allow vise jaws to contact the boot or its clamp. The vise should be equipped with jaw caps to prevent damage to any machined surfaces.

3. Cut the large boot clamp using side cutters and peel away from the boot. After removing the clamp, roll boot back over shaft.

4. Bend retaining tabs back slightly to allow for tripod removal.

5. Separate outer race from tripod.

6. On all except 1992–95 vehicles with 2.3L engine, move stopring back on shaft using snapring pliers. On 1992–95 vehicles with 2.3L engine, remove the tripod snapring.

7. On all except 1992–95 vehicles with 2.3L engine, move tripod assembly back on shaft to allow access to circlip. Remove the circlip and stopring from the shaft.

8. Remove tripod assembly from shaft.

9. Remove the boot.

10. When replacing damaged CV-boots, the grease should be checked for contamination. If the CV-joints were operating satisfactorily and the grease does not appear to be contaminated, add grease and replace the

boot. If the lubricant appears contaminated, proceed with a complete CV-joint disassembly and inspection.

To install:

11. Clean all parts (except boots) in a suitable solvent.

12. Inspect all CV-joint parts for excessive wear, looseness, pitting, rust and cracks.

NOTE: CV-joint components are matched during assembly. If inspection reveals damage or wear the entire joint must be replaced as an assembly. Do not replace a joint merely because the parts appear polished. Shiny areas in ball races and on the cage spheres are normal.

13. Install new CV-boot.

14. Tighten clamp securely but not to the point where the clamp bridge is cut or the boot is damaged.

15. If equipped, install the stop ring. Install tripod assembly on shaft with chamfered side inboard.

16. Install new circlip or snapring, as required.

NOTE: To install the circlip, start 1 end in the groove and work the circlip over the stub shaft end and into the groove. This will avoid overexpanding the circlip. A new circlip must be used.

17. If equipped, compress circlip and slide tripod assembly forward over circlip to expose stopring groove. Move stopring into groove using snapring pliers, making sure it is fully seated in groove.

18. Fill CV-joint outer race with 3.5 oz. (100 grams) of grease and fill CV-boot with 2.1 oz. (60 grams) of grease.

19. Install outer race over tripod assembly and bend 6 retaining tabs back into their original position.

20. Remove all excess grease from CV-joint external surfaces. Position boot over CV-joint. Move CV-joint in and out as necessary, to adjust to proper length.

NOTE: Insert a suitable tool between the boot and outer bearing race and allow the trapped air to escape from the boot. The air should be released from the boot only after adjusting to the proper dimensions.

21. Ensure boot is seated in its groove and clamp in position.

22. Tighten clamp securely but not to the point where the clamp bridge is cut or the boot is damaged.

23. Install a new circlip, supplied with service kit, in groove nearest end of shaft by starting one end in

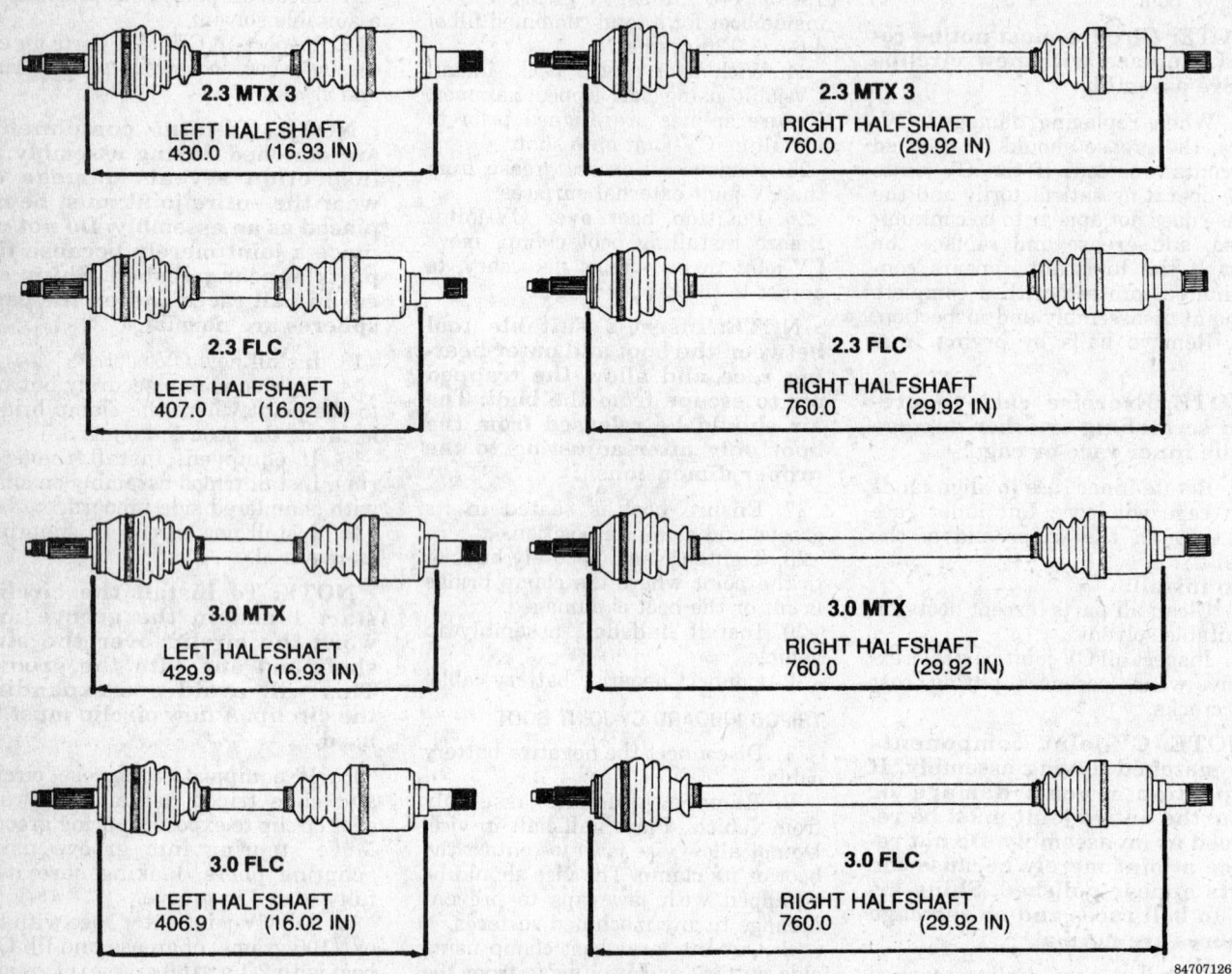

2.3 MTX 3
LEFT HALFSHAFT
430.0   (16.93 IN)

2.3 MTX 3
RIGHT HALFSHAFT
760.0   (29.92 IN)

2.3 FLC
LEFT HALFSHAFT
407.0   (16.02 IN)

2.3 FLC
RIGHT HALFSHAFT
760.0   (29.92 IN)

3.0 MTX
LEFT HALFSHAFT
429.9   (16.93 IN)

3.0 MTX
RIGHT HALFSHAFT
760.0   (29.92 IN)

3.0 FLC
LEFT HALFSHAFT
406.9   (16.02 IN)

3.0 FLC
RIGHT HALFSHAFT
760.0   (29.92 IN)

84707126

Halfshaft assembled lengths — Tempo and Topaz

the groove and working clip over stub shaft end and into groove.

24. Install halfshaft assembly in vehicle.

25. Connect negative battery cable.

OUTBOARD CV-JOINT BOOT

The outboard CV-joint cannot be removed from the shaft on these vehicles. If it is necessary to replace the outboard CV-joint boot, the inboard CV-joint and boot must be removed.

Escort and Tracer

1. Raise and safely support the vehicle.

2. Remove the halfshaft assembly from the vehicle.

3. Secure the halfshaft in a vise with protective jaw covers.

4. Using a suitable tool, pry up the locking tabs of the inner CV-boot bands. Remove the bands with pliers.

5. Slide the boot back to expose the tripod CV-joint. Mark the shaft and the CV-joint housing to ensure correct assembly.

6. Remove the retainer ring from the CV-joint housing and remove the CV-joint housing from the halfshaft.

7. Mark the tripod bearing and the shaft to ensure correct assembly. Using snaring pliers, remove the tripod snaring.

8. Using a soft-faced mallet, gently tap the tripod bearing from the shaft.

9. Wrap the shaft splines with tape to protect the CV-boot if the boot is to be reused.

10. Slide the inner CV-joint boot off the shaft. If the outer CV-joint boot is to be replaced, continue with the procedure.

11. On 1.9L right side halfshafts, pry up the rubber damper retaining band locking clip using a suitable tool. Remove the retaining band using pliers and remove the rubber damper from the shaft.

12. Using a suitable tool, pry up the outer CV-boot band locking tabs. Remove the bands with pliers.

13. Slide the outer CV-boot off the shaft.

NOTE: When replacing a damaged boot, check the grease for contamination by rubbing it between 2 fingers. Any gritty feeling indicates a contaminated CV-joint. A contaminated inner CV-joint must be completely disassembled, cleaned and inspected. The outer CV-joint is not serviceable and should be replaced as an assembly, if necessary. If the grease is not contaminated and the CV-joint has been operating satisfactorily, replace only the boot and add the required lubricant.

To install:

14. Cover the halfshaft splines with tape and install the outer CV-joint boot.

NOTE: The outer and inner CV-joint boots are different. Failure to correctly install the boot on the proper end of the halfshaft could lead to premature boot and/or CV-joint wear.

CV Boot Specifications

	1.9L Engine		1.8L Engine	
	Right Side	Left Side	Right Side	Left Side
Ⓐ	84.0 mm (3.31 in)	90.0 mm (3.54 in)	89.9 mm (3.54 in)	
Ⓑ	89.0 mm (3.50 in)		85.2 mm (3.35 in)	

84707129

CV-boot specifications — Escort and Tracer

15. Fill the outer CV-joint housing with the proper type and amount of lubricant.

16. Position the CV-boot. Make sure the boot is fully seated in the shaft grooves and the CV-joint housing.

17. Insert a suitable tool between the boot and the CV-joint housing to allow trapped air to escape.

18. Position new bands on the outer CV-joint boot.

NOTE: Always use new bands. The bands should be mounted in the direction opposite the forward revolving direction of the halfshaft.

19. Wrap the bands around the boot in a clockwise direction, pull them tight with pliers and bend the locking tabs to secure the bands in position.

20. Work the CV-joint through it's full range of travel at various angles. The CV-joint should flex, extend and compress smoothly.

21. On 1.9L right side halfshafts, position the rubber damper on the halfshaft. Position a new band on the damper. Pull the band tight with pliers and fold it back. Lock the end of the band by bending the locking clip.

22. Position the inner CV-joint boot on the halfshaft.

23. Align the marks on the tripod bearing and the halfshaft. Install the tripod bearing on the halfshaft. If necessary, using a soft-faced mallet, tap the bearing into place.

24. Install the snapring.

25. Fill the inner CV-joint housing with the proper type and amount of lubricant. Coat the tripod bearing with the same lubricant.

26. Position the inner CV-joint housing over the tripod bearing, making sure to align the alignment marks. Install the retainer ring in the CV-joint housing.

27. Slide the inner CV-boot in place. Make sure the boot is fully seated in the shaft grooves and in the housing.

28. Insert a small prybar between the boot and the CV-joint housing to allow trapped air to escape.

29. Position new bands on the inner CV-joint boot.

NOTE: Always use new bands. The bands should be mounted in the direction opposite the forward revolving direction of the halfshaft.

30. Wrap the bands around the boot in a clockwise direction, pull them tight with pliers and bend the locking tabs to secure the bands in position.

31. Work the CV-joint through it's full range of travel at various angles. The CV-joint should flex, extend and compress smoothly.

32. Measure the length of the assembled halfshaft. If the length is not as specified, check the CV-joints for freedom of movement to ensure that it was assembled correctly. Repair or replace any components as necessary.

Driveshaft and U-Joints

REMOVAL AND INSTALLATION

Tempo and Topaz with All Wheel Drive

1. Raise the vehicle and support safely.

2. To maintain the driveshaft balance, mark the U-joints so they may be installed in their original position.

3. Remove the front U-joint retaining bolts and straps.

4. Support the driveshaft near the center bearing. Remove the driveshaft center bearing retaining bolts.

5. Slide the driveshaft toward the rear of the vehicle to disengage from the transfer case.

6. Remove the rear U-joint bolts and straps retaining the driveshaft, from the torque tube yoke flange.

7. Slide the driveshaft toward the front of the vehicle to disengage. Do not allow the splined shafts to contact with excessive force.

8. Remove the center bearing retaining bolts. Remove the driveshaft and retain the bearing cups with tape, if necessary.

9. Inspect the U-joint assemblies for wear and or damage, and replace if necessary.

To install:

10. Install the driveshaft at the rear torque yoke flange. Ensure that the U-joint is in its original position.

11. Install the U-joint retaining bolts and caps. Torque them to 15–17 ft. lbs. (21–23 Nm). Position the front U-joint. Install the U-joint retaining caps and bolts. Torque them to 15–17 ft. lbs. (21–23 Nm).

12. Install the center bearing and retaining bolts. Torque to 23–30 ft. lbs. (31–41 Nm). Do not drop the assembled driveshafts as the impact may cause damage to the U-joint bearing cups.

Front Wheel Hub, Knuckle and Bearings

REMOVAL AND INSTALLATION

Tempo and Topaz

1. Remove wheel cover/hub cover from wheel and tire assembly and loosen wheel nuts.

2. Remove hub nut retainer and washer by applying sufficient torque to overcome the prevailing torque of the nut. The hub nut must be discarded after removal.

FLUID SPECIFICATIONS

Halfshaft Assemblies	1.9L Engine		1.8L Engine	
	Right Side	Left Side	Right Side	Left Side
Differential Side	220 g (7.77 oz.) Lt. Yellow	140 g (4.94 oz.) Yellow	145 g (5.12 oz.) Yellow	145 g (5.12 oz.) Yellow
Wheel Side	140 g (4.94 oz.) Black	140 g (4.94 oz.) Black	90 g (3.18 oz.) Black	90 g (3.18 oz.) Black

CV-boot lubricant specifications — Escort and Tracer

3. Raise and safely support the vehicle. Remove wheel and tire assembly.

4. Remove brake caliper by loosening caliper locating pins and rotating caliper off rotor starting from lower end of caliper and lifting upward. Do not remove caliper pins from caliper assembly. Lift caliper off rotor and hang it free of rotor. Do not allow caliper assembly to hang from brake hose. Support caliper assembly with a length of wire.

5. Remove rotor from hub by pulling it off hub bolts. If rotor is difficult to remove from hub, strike rotor sharply between studs with a rubber or plastic hammer. If rotor will not pull off, apply rust penetrator to inboard and outboard rotor hub mating surfaces. Install a 3 jaw puller and remove rotor by pulling on rotor outside diameter and pushing on hub center.

6. If excessive force is required for removal, check rotor for lateral runout. Lateral runout must be checked with wheel nuts clamping hat section of rotor.

7. Remove rotor splash shield.

8. Disconnect lower control arm and tie rod from knuckle (leave strut attached).

9. Loosen the 2 strut top mount-to-apron nuts.

10. Install a suitable hub removal tool and remove hub/bearing/knuckle assembly by pushing out CV-joint outer shaft until it is free of assembly.

11. Support knuckle with a length of wire, remove strut bolt and slide hub/knuckle assembly off strut.

12. Carefully remove support wire and transfer hub/bearing/knuckle assembly to bench.

13. Install front hub puller D80L–1002–L and shaft protector D80L–625–1 or equivalents, with jaws of puller on the knuckle bosses and remove hub.

NOTE: Ensure the shaft protector is centered, clears the bearing inside diameter and rests on the end face of the hub journal.

14. Remove snapring which retains bearing knuckle assembly and discard.

15. Using a hydraulic press, place a suitable front bearing spacer step side up on press plate and position knuckle on spacer with outboard side up. Install bearing removal tool on bearing inner race and press bearing out of knuckle.

16. Discard bearing.

17. Remove halfshaft.

18. Place halfshaft in vise. Remove bearing dust seal by uniformly tapping on outer edge with a light-duty hammer and a small prybar. Discard dust seal.

To install:

19. Place halfshaft in vise. Install a new dust seal using a suitable seal installer. Seal flange must face outboard.

20. Install halfshaft.

21. On bench, remove all foreign material from knuckle bearing bore

Item	Model	1.8L Engine	1.9L Engine
Halfshaft			
Length of joint (between center of joint)	Right side	631.2 mm (24.85 in)	918.7 mm (36.16 in)
	Left side	621.7 mm (24.48 in)	640.7 mm (25.22 in)
Shaft diameter	Right side	23.0 mm (0.91 in)	
	Left side	23.0 mm (0.91 in)	

Halfshaft length specifications — Escort and Tracer

and hub bearing journal to ensure correct seating of new bearing.

NOTE: If hub bearing journal is scored or damaged, replace hub. Do not attempt to service. The front wheel bearings are of a cartridge design and are pregreased, sealed and require no scheduled maintenance. The bearings are preset and cannot be adjusted. If a bearing is disassembled for any reason, it must be replaced as a unit. No individual service seals, rollers or races are available.

22. Place suitable bearing spacer step side down on hydraulic press plate and position knuckle on spacer with outboard side down. Position a new bearing in inboard side of knuckle. Install a suitable front bearing installer on bearing outer race face with undercut side facing bearing and press bearing into knuckle. Ensure that bearing seats completely against shoulder of knuckle bore.

NOTE: Ensure proper positioning of bearing installer during installation to prevent bearing damage.

23. Install a new snapring in knuckle groove using snapring pliers.
24. Place suitable front bearing spacer on arbor press plate and position hub on tool with lugs facing downward. Position knuckle assembly on hub barrel with outboard side down. Place a suitable front bearing installer on inner race of bearing and press down on tool until bearing is fully seated onto hub. Make sure hub rotates freely in knuckle after installation.
25. Suspend hub/knuckle/bearing assembly on vehicle with wire and attach strut loosely to knuckle. Lubricate CV-joint stub shaft splines with SAE 30 weight motor oil and insert shaft into hub splines as far as possible using hand pressure only. Check that spline are properly engaged.
26. Install suitable front hub installer and wheel bolt adapter to hub and stub shaft. Tighten hub installer tool to 120 ft. lbs. (162 Nm) to ensure that hub is fully seated. Remove tool and install washer and new hub nut retainer. Tighten hub nut retainer finger-tight.
27. Install washer and new hub nut. Rotate nut clockwise to seat CV-joint. Tighten hub nut to 188–236 ft. lbs. (255–320 Nm). Do not tighten with impact gun and do not move vehicle before retainer is tightened.
28. Complete installation of front suspension components.

29. Install disc brake rotor to hub assembly.
30. Install disc brake caliper over rotor.
31. Ensure outer brake shoe spring end is seated under upper arm of knuckle.
32. Install wheel and tire assembly, tightening wheel nuts finger-tight.
33. Lower vehicle and block wheels to prevent vehicle from rolling.
34. Tighten wheel nuts to 85–105 ft. lbs. (115–142 Nm).
35. Install wheel cover or hub cover and lower vehicle completely to ground.
36. Remove wheel blocks.

Escort and Tracer

1. Raise and safely support the vehicle.
2. Remove the front wheel and tire assembly, brake caliper and rotor.
3. Remove the nut securing the halfshaft to the hub.
4. Remove the outer tie rod end at the steering knuckle.
5. Remove the nuts and bolts and separate the shock/strut assembly from the steering knuckle.
6. Remove the nut and bolt and separate the lower ball joint from steering knuckle.
7. Remove the front hub/steering knuckle assembly from the halfshaft.
8. Remove the oil seal from the rear of the hub/steering knuckle assembly.
9. Position the hub/steering knuckle assembly on a hydraulic press and press the front hub out of the steering knuckle using a suitable removal tool.

NOTE: If the bearing inner race remains on the hub, use a grinder to grind a section of the bearing inner race until only 0.020 in. (0.5mm) remains. Remove the inner race with a suitable chisel.

10. Remove the E-clip from the steering knuckle.
11. Position the steering knuckle onto a hydraulic press and, using an appropriate bearing remover, press the bearing out of the steering knuckle.

NOTE: If the dust cover is removed, it must be replaced.

12. Scribe a mark in the dust cover and steering knuckle. Using a suitable chisel, remove the dust cover.
   To install:
13. Scribe a mark on the new dust cover in the same position as on the previous mark. Align the marks on

the steering knuckle to the mark on the dust cover and, using a suitable tool, press the dust cover onto the steering knuckle.
14. Position the steering knuckle onto a press and press the bearing into the steering knuckle, using a suitable bearing installer. Apply threadlocking compound to the wheel bearing outer race, prior to installation.
15. Install the E-clip.
16. Position the hub onto the knuckle and press the hub into the bearing and the steering knuckle, using a suitable installation tool.
17. Using an appropriate seal installer, install a new oil seal onto the inboard side of the steering knuckle. Make sure the oil seal mounts flush with the steering knuckle.
18. Install the hub/steering knuckle assembly onto the ball joint and install the nut and bolt. Tighten to 32–43 ft. lbs. (43–59 Nm). Apply Loctite® to the nut and bolt threads prior to installation.
19. Install the outer tie rod.
20. Install the steering knuckle to the shock/strut assembly. Tighten the nuts and bolts to 69–93 ft. lbs. (93–127 Nm).
21. Install a new locknut securing the halfshaft to the front hub. Tighten the locknut to 174–235 ft. lbs. (235–319 Nm). Stake the locknut to prevent it from loosening.
22. Install the brake rotor, caliper and wheel and tire assembly.
23. Lower the vehicle.

Axle Housing

REMOVAL AND INSTALLATION

Tempo and Topaz with All Wheel Drive

1. Disconnect the negative battery cable.
2. Raise and safely support the vehicle.

NOTE: Anytime a U-joint retaining bolt is removed, Loctite® or equivalent, must be applied to the retaining bolts prior to installation.

3. Position a hoist or jack under rear axle housing.
4. Remove muffler and exhaust system from catalytic converter back.
5. Remove rear U-joint retaining bolts and straps retaining driveshaft from torque tube yoke flange. Remove driveshaft center bearing bolts. Disengage driveshaft from axle yoke and position driveshaft off to 1 side.

6. Remove 4 retaining bolts from torque tube support bracket. Remove damper.

7. Disconnect axle vent hose clip form body.

8. Remove axle retaining bolt from left side differential support bracket.

9. Remove axle retaining bolt from center differential support bracket.

10. Lower axle assembly and remove inboard U-joint retaining bolts and straps from each halfshaft. Remove and wire halfshaft assemblies aside.

11. Remove rear axle assembly.

To install:

12. Position rear axle assembly under vehicle. Raise axle far enough for U-joint and halfshaft assemblies to be installed.

13. Position each inboard U-joint to rear axle. Install U-joint straps and retaining bolts. Using a T-30 Torx® bit, tighten bolts to 15–17 ft. lbs. (21–23 Nm).

14. Raise into position being careful not to trap or pinch axle vent hose. Install bolts attaching differential housing to left side and center differential support bracket. Tighten to 70–80 ft. lbs. (95–108 Nm).

15. Attach axle vent hose clip to body.

16. Position torque tube and mounting bracket and damper to crossmember. Install 4 attaching bolts. Tighten to 28–35 ft. lbs. (38–47 Nm). Install driveshaft and retaining bolts to torque tube yoke flange. Using a T-30 Torx® bit, tighten to 15–17 ft. lbs. (21–23 Nm).

17. Install exhaust from catalytic converter back.

18. Check lubricant level in axle.

19. Lower vehicle.

STEERING

Steering Wheel

CAUTION

If equipped with an air bag, the negative battery cable and backup power supply must be disconnected, before working on the system. Failure to do so may result in deployment of the air bag and possible personal injury.

REMOVAL AND INSTALLATION

Tempo and Topaz

1. Make sure the wheels are in the straight-ahead position and the column is locked. Disconnect the negative battery cable.

NOTE: If equipped with an air bag, a backup power supply is included in the system to provide air bag deployment in the event the battery or cables are damaged in an accident before the sensors can close. The power supply is a capacitor that will leak down in approximately 15 minutes after the battery is disconnected or 1 minute if the battery positive cable is grounded. If the system is equipped with a backup power supply, it must be disconnected to disarm the system.

CAUTION

When carrying a live air bag, make sure the bag and trim cover are pointed away from the body. In the unlikely event of an accidental deployment, the bag will then deploy with minimal chance of injury. In addition, when placing a live air bag on a bench or other surface, always face the bag and trim cover up, away from the surface. This will reduce the motion of the module if it is accidentally deployed.

---

2. On vehicles equipped with an air bag, perform the following procedure:

a. Disconnect the positive battery cable and wait 1 minute for the backup power supply to be depleted.

b. Remove the 4 nut and washer assemblies retaining the air bag assembly to the steering wheel.

c. Disconnect the air bag electrical connector from the contact assembly connectors and remove the air bag assembly.

3. If not equipped with an air bag, remove the horn pad cover by removing the retaining screws from the steering wheel assembly.

NOTE: The emblem assembly is removed after the horn pad cover is removed, by pushing it out from the backside of the emblem.

4. Remove the energy absorbing foam from the wheel assembly, if equipped. Remember the energy absorbing foam must be installed when the steering wheel is assembled. Disconnect the horn pad wiring connector, if not equipped with an air bag.

5. Loosen the steering wheel retaining bolt 4–6 turns but do not remove. On air bag equipped vehicles, remove the bolt completely to remove the vibration damper, then reinstall the bolt loosely on the shaft.

6. Remove the steering wheel with a suitable puller. Do not use a knock-off type puller, because it will cause damage to the collapsible steering column. Remove the retaining bolt, grasp the rim of the steering wheel and pull the steering wheel from the upper shaft.

To install:

7. Install the steering wheel assembly on the steering column, making sure the alignment marks are correct.

8. Install a new retaining bolt. Torque the bolt to 23–33 ft. lbs. (31–45 Nm). On air bag equipped vehicles, install the vibration damper before installing the bolt.

9. If equipped with air bag, connect the air bag module wire to clockspring connector and place the module on the steering wheel with the 4 attaching nuts, torque the nuts to 35–53 inch lbs. (4–6 Nm).

10. If without air bag, connect the horn pad wiring connector and, if equipped, install the energy absorbing foam. Install the horn pad cover and torque the retaining screws to 8–10 inch lbs. (0.9–1.1 Nm).

11. Reconnect the negative battery cable and check the steering wheel and horn for proper operation.

Escort and Tracer

1. Disconnect the negative battery cable.

2. Remove the steering wheel cover retaining screws from the back side of the steering wheel and remove the cover.

NOTE: On 2-spoke steering wheels there are 2 retaining screws, and on 4-spoke steering wheels there are 4 retaining screws.

3. Disconnect the horn electrical connector and the cruise control electrical connector, if equipped.

4. Remove the steering wheel mounting nut or bolt and remove the steering wheel with a suitable puller.

WARNING

Do not attempt to remove the steering wheel by hitting the column shaft with a hammer; the column may collapse.

To install:

5. Position the steering wheel and install the mounting nut or bolt. Tighten the nut to 29–36 ft. lbs. (39–49 Nm) or the bolt to 34–46 ft. lbs. (46–63 Nm).

6. Connect the horn electrical connector and the cruise control electrical connector, if equipped.

7. Position the steering wheel cover and install the retaining screws.

8. Connect the negative battery cable.

Steering Column

REMOVAL AND INSTALLATION

Tempo and Topaz

NOTE: On air bag equipped vehicles, whenever the steering column is separated from the steering gear for any reason, the steering column must be locked to prevent the steering wheel from being rotated, which in turn will prevent damage to the air bag clockspring.

1. Disconnect the negative battery cable.

NOTE: Before disconnecting cable on air bag equipped vehicles, ensure wheels are in straight-ahead position. Turn ignition switch to LOCK position and rotate steering wheel about 16 degrees counterclockwise until locked into position.

2. Remove steering column cover on lower portion of instrument panel (2 screws).

3. Remove cruise control module, if equipped (2 screws).

4. Remove lower steering column shroud (5 screws).

5. Loosen, but do not remove, 2 nuts and 2 bolts retaining steering column to support bracket and remove upper shroud.

6. Disconnect all steering column electrical connections: ignition, washer/wiper, turn signal, key warning buzzer, cruise control. On console shift automatic transaxle, remove interlock cable retaining screw and disconnect cable from steering column.

7. Loosen steering column to intermediate shaft clamp connection and remove bolt or nut.

8. Remove 2 nuts and 2 bolts retaining steering column to support bracket.

9. Pry open steering column shaft in area of clamp on each side of bolt

groove with steering column locked. Open enough to disengage shafts with minimal effort. Do not use excessive force.

10. Inspect 2 steering column bracket clips for damage. If clips have been bent or excessively distorted, they must be replaced.

To install:

11. Engage lower steering shaft to intermediate shaft and hand start clamp bolt and nut.

12. Align 2 bolts on steering column support bracket assembly with outer tube mounting holes and hand start 2 nuts. Check for presence of 2 clips on outer bracket. The clips must be present to ensure adequate performance of vital parts and systems. Hand start 2 bolts through outer tube upper bracket and clip and into support bracket nuts. On console shift automatic transaxles, install interlock cable and retaining screw. Tighten to 30–38 inch lbs. (3.3–4.3 Nm).

13. Connect all quick-connect electrical connections: turn signal, wash/wipe, key warning buzzer, ignition, cruise control and air bag clockspring connector, if equipped.

14. Install upper shroud.

15. Tighten steering column mounting nuts and bolts to 15–25 ft. lbs. (20–34 Nm).

16. On air bag equipped vehicles, unlock steering column and cycle steering wheel 1 turn left and 1 turn right to align intermediate shaft into column shaft. Power steering vehicles must have engine running.

17. Tighten steering shaft clamp nut to 20–30 ft. lbs. (27–40 Nm).

18. Install lower trim shroud with 5 screws.

19. Install cruise control module, if equipped, with 2 screws.

20. Install steering column cover on instrument panel with 2 screws.

21. Connect battery ground cable.

22. Check steering column for proper operation.

Escort and Tracer

1. Disconnect the negative battery cable.

2. Remove the steering wheel.

3. Remove the combination switch and disconnect the ignition switch electrical connector.

4. Remove the shift-lock cable mounting bracket bolt and place the bracket and cable aside.

5. Remove the 4 steering column upper mounting bracket bolts and lower the column.

6. Remove the 5 set plate mounting nuts and remove the set plate.

7. Remove the intermediate shaft-to-pinion shaft bolt.

8. Remove the 2 steering column lower mounting bracket nuts and remove the column.

To install:

9. Position the steering column and install the 2 lower mounting bracket nuts.

10. Install the intermediate shaft-to-pinion shaft bolt and tighten to 30–36 ft. lbs. (40–50 Nm).

11. Position the set plate and install the 5 mounting nuts.

12. Install the 4 steering column upper mounting bracket bolts and tighten to 80–123 inch lbs. (9–14 Nm).

13. Position the shift-lock cable mounting bracket and install the bolt. Tighten the bolt to 37–55 inch lbs. (4–6 Nm).

14. Connect the ignition switch electrical connector and install the combination switch.

15. Install the steering wheel.

16. Connect the negative battery cable and inspect the shift-lock system.

Manual Rack and Pinion

REMOVAL AND INSTALLATION

Escort and Tracer

1. Working inside the vehicle, remove the nuts securing the set plate and remove the set plate.

2. Remove the intermediate shaft-to-pinion shaft bolt from inside the vehicle.

3. Raise and safely support the vehicle.

4. Remove the front wheel and tire assemblies.

5. Remove the cotter pins and nuts securing the tie rod ends to the steering knuckles. Separate the tie rod ends from the steering knuckles using a suitable tool.

6. If equipped with manual transaxle, disconnect the extension bar.

7. Remove the nuts securing the steering gear brackets to the bulkhead. Remove the brackets.

8. Remove the steering gear from the vehicle.

To install:

9. Position the steering gear into its mounting position and install the brackets and nuts. Tighten the nuts to 27–38 ft. lbs. (37–52 Nm).

10. If equipped with a manual transaxle, connect the extension bar. Tighten the nut to 23–34 ft. lbs. (31–46 Nm).

11. Attach the tie rod ends to the steering knuckles. Install the nuts and tighten to 31–42 ft. lbs. (42–57 Nm). Install new cotter pins.

12. Install the front wheel and tire assemblies.

13. Lower the vehicle.

14. Install the intermediate shaft-to-pinion shaft bolt and tighten to 13–20 ft. lbs. (18–27 Nm).

15. Position the set plate and secure it with the nuts.

ADJUSTMENT

Escort and Tracer

RACK PRELOAD/SUPPORT YOKE ADJUSTMENT

1. Remove the rack and pinion assembly from the vehicle and mount it in a suitable vice.

2. Loosen the locknut.

3. Tighten the adjusting bolt using yoke adjustment adapter T90P–3504–JH in the yoke plug to 8.7 inch lbs. (1 Nm), then loosen the adjusting bolt 10–40 degrees from that position.

4. Measure the pinion turning torque using pinion shaft adapting tool T86P–3504–K. The correct torque at the neutral position ± 90 degrees should be 9–12 inch lbs. (1.0–1.3 Nm). At any other position the torque should be 14.7 inch lbs. (1.6 Nm) or less.

5. If the pinion torque is not within specification, re-adjust the adjusting bolt to achieve the correct pinion torque. Tighten the adjusting bolt locknut.

Power Rack and Pinion

REMOVAL AND INSTALLATION

Tempo and Topaz

1. Disconnect the negative battery cable.

2. Turn the ignition key to the **RUN** position.

3. Remove access panel from dash below the steering column.

4. Remove screws from steering column boot at the dash panel and slide boot up intermediate shaft.

5. Remove intermediate shaft bolt at gear input shaft and loosen the bolt at the steering column shaft joint.

6. With a suitable tool, spread the slots enough to loosen intermediates shaft at both ends. The intermediate shaft and gear input shaft cannot be separated at this time.

7. Separate pressure and return lines at steering gear and drain fluid.

8. Remove the pressure switch.

9. Disconnect the exhaust secondary air tube at check valve. Raise the vehicle and support it safely. Disconnect exhaust system at intermediate connection and remove exhaust system.

10. Separate tie rod ends from steering knuckles.

11. Remove left tie rod end from tie rod on manual transaxle vehicles. This will allow tie rod to clear the shift linkage.

NOTE: Mark location of rod end prior to removal.

12. Disconnect speedometer cable at transaxle, if equipped with automatic transaxle. Remove the vehicle speed sensor.

13. Remove transaxle shift cable assembly at transaxle on vehicles equipped with automatic transaxle.

14. Turn steering wheel to full left turn stop for easier gear removal.

15. On Escort and Tracer, remove screws holding the heater water tube to shake brace below the oil pan.

16. On Escort and Tracer, remove nut from the lower of 2 bolts holding engine mount support bracket to transaxle housing. Tap bolt out as far as it will go.

17. Remove the gear mounting brackets and insulators.

18. Drape cloth towel over both apron opening edges to protect bellows during gear removal.

19. Separate gear from intermediate shaft by either pushing up on shaft with a bar from underneath the vehicle while pulling the gear down or with an assistant removing the shaft from inside the vehicle.

20. Rotate gear forward and down to clear the input shaft through the dash panel opening.

21. Make sure input shaft is in full left turn position. Move gear through the right (passenger) side apron opening until left tie rod clears left apron opening and other parts so it may be lowered. Guide the power steering hoses around the nearby components as the gear is being removed.

22. Lower the left side of the gear and remove the gear out of the vehicle. Use care not to tear the bellows.

To install:

23. Rotate the input shaft to a full left turn stop. Position the right road wheel to a full left turn.

24. Start the right side of the gear through the opening in the right apron. Move the gear in until the left

tie rod clears all parts so it may be raised to the left apron opening.

25. Raise the gear and insert the left side through the apron opening. Move the power steering hoses into their proper position at the same time. Rotate the gear so the joint shaft enters the dash panel opening.

26. With an assistant guiding the intermediate shaft from the inside of the vehicle, insert the input shaft into the intermediate shaft coupling. Insert the intermediate shaft clamp bolts finger-tight. Do not tighten at this time.

27. Install the gear mounting insulators and brackets in their proper places. Ensure the flat in the left mounting area is parallel to the dash panel. Tighten the bracket bolts to 40–55 ft. lbs. (54–75 Nm) in the sequence as described below:

　a. Tighten the left (driver's side) upper bolt halfway.

　b. Tighten the left side lower bolt.

　c. Tighten the left side upper bolt.

　d. Tighten the right side bolts.

　e. Do not forget that the right and left side insulators and brackets are not interchangeable side to side.

28. Attach the tie rod ends to the steering knuckles. Tighten the castellated nuts to 27–32 ft. lbs. (36–43 Nm), then tighten the nuts until the slot aligns with the cotter pin hole. Insert a new cotter pin.

29. Install the exhaust system. Install the speedometer cable, if removed. Install the vehicle speed sensor and the transaxle shift cable.

30. Connect the secondary air tube at the check valve. Connect the pressure and return lines at the intermediate connections or steering gear.

31. Install the pressure switch.

32. Tighten the gear input shaft to intermediate shaft coupling clamp bolt first. Then, tighten the upper intermediate shaft clamp bolt. Tighten to 20–30 ft. lbs. (27–40 Nm).

33. Install the steering weather boot to dash panel and the access panel below the steering column. Turn the ignition key to the **OFF** position.

34. Fill the system. Check and adjust the toe. Tighten the tie rod end jam nuts to 40–50 ft. lbs. (54–68 Nm), check for twisted bellows.

35. Connect negative battery cable.

Escort and Tracer

1. From inside the passenger compartment, remove the 5 set plate nuts and remove the set plate.

2. Remove the intermediate shaft-to-pinion shaft bolt.

3. Raise and safely support the vehicle.

4. Remove the front wheel and tire assemblies.

5. Remove the cotter pins and attaching nuts from the tie rod ends. Using a suitable tool, separate the tie rod ends from the steering knuckles.

6. On 1992 models equipped with the 1.8L engine, remove the 2 screws from the power steering line retaining bracket and remove the bracket from the steering gear housing. On all 1993–96 models and 1992 models equipped with the 1.9L engine, remove the strap that holds the power steering lines to the steering gear housing and discard the strap.

7. Disconnect the high-pressure and return lines from the steering gear and plug the lines.

8. If equipped with manual transaxle, disconnect the extension bar and shift control rod from the transaxle.

9. Remove the nuts from the 2 steering gear mounting brackets.

10. Remove the splash shield from the left wheel well.

11. Remove the steering gear from the left side of the vehicle.

To install:

12. Position the steering gear in its mounting location and install the splash shield in the left wheel well.

13. Position the 2 steering gear mounting brackets and install the 2 nuts to each bracket. Tighten the nuts to 27–38 ft. lbs. (37–52 Nm).

14. If equipped with a manual transaxle, connect the extension bar and shift control rod. Tighten the extension bar nut to 23–34 ft. lbs. (31–46 Nm) and the shift control rod nut to 12–17 ft. lbs. (16–23 Nm).

15. Remove the plugs and connect the pressure and return lines to the steering gear. Tighten the flare nuts to 22–28 ft. lbs. (29–39 Nm).

16. On 1992 models equipped with 1.8L engine, position the power steering line retaining bracket and install the 2 screws. On all 1993–96 models and 1992 models equipped with 1.9L engine, install a new strap to hold the power steering lines to the steering gear housing.

17. Position the tie rod ends in the steering knuckles and install the attaching nuts. Tighten the nuts to 31–42 ft. lbs. (42–57 Nm). Install new cotter pins.

18. Install the wheel and tire assemblies and lower the vehicle.

19. From inside the vehicle, install the intermediate shaft-to-pinion shaft bolt. Tighten the bolt to 13–20 ft. lbs. (18–27 Nm).

20. Position the set plate and install the 5 set plate nuts.

21. Fill the system with steering fluid and check for leaks.

ADJUSTMENT

Tempo and Topaz

The power rack and pinion steering gear provides for only rack yoke plug preload adjustment. This adjustment can be performed only with the gear out of the vehicle. To check rack yoke plug preload, proceed as follows:

1. Disconnect the negative battery cable.

2. Raise and safely support the vehicle.

3. Remove power rack and pinion assembly from vehicle.

4. Clean exterior of steering gear thoroughly.

5. Mount steering gear in a suitable rack housing holding fixture.

NOTE: Do not mount gear in vise.

6. Do not remove external pressure lines, unless they are leaking or damaged. If these lines are removed, they must be replaced with new lines.

7. Drain power steering fluid by rotating input shaft lock-to-lock twice using input shaft torque adapter T81P–3504–R or equivalent. Position adapter and wrench on input shaft.

8. Loosen yoke plug locknut with yoke locknut wrench T81P–3504–G or equivalent.

9. Loosen yoke plug using yoke plug adapter T87P–3504–G or equivalent.

10. With rack at center of travel, tighten yoke plug to 44–50 inch lbs. (5.0–5.7 Nm). Clean threads of yoke plug prior to tightening to prevent a false reading.

11. Install yoke plug adapter T87P–3504–G or equivalent. Mark location of 0 degree mark on housing. Back off adjuster so 48 degree mark lines up with 0 degree mark.

12. Place yoke locknut wrench T81P–3504–G or equivalent, on yoke plug locknut. While holding yoke plug, tighten locknut to 40–50 ft. lbs. (54–68 Nm). Do not allow yoke plug to move while tightening or preload will be affected. Check input shaft torque after tightening locknut.

13. If external pressure lines were removed, the Teflon® seal rings must be replaced. Clean out Teflon® seal shreds from housing ports prior to installation of new lines.

14. Install power rack assembly in vehicle.

15. Lower vehicle.

16. Connect negative battery cable.

Power Steering Pump

REMOVAL AND INSTALLATION

Escort and Tracer

1.8L ENGINE

1. Disconnect the negative battery cable.

2. Loosen the power steering fluid reservoir-to-pump hose clamp and pull the hose from the reservoir. Plug the hose.

3. Remove the 2 reservoir mounting bolts and lift the reservoir from its mounting position.

4. Loosen the return hose clamp and pull the return hose from the reservoir. Plug the hose and remove the reservoir.

5. Disconnect the electrical connector from the power steering pressure switch.

6. Loosen the high-pressure line flarenut and disconnect the line from the pump. Plug the line.

7. Raise and safely support the vehicle.

8. Remove the 5 right front undercover bolts and remove the undercover.

9. Remove the belt tensioner adjustment bolt and remove the accessory drive belt from the pulley.

10. Lower the vehicle.

11. Remove the 3 pump mounting bracket bolts and remove the pump and the bracket.

12. Remove the bolt that attaches the pump to the mounting bracket.

13. Remove the nut and bolt that attaches the tensioner to the pump mounting bracket and remove the nut and bolt that attaches the tensioner to the pump.

To install:

14. Position the tensioner to the pump and install the bolt and nut. Tighten the nut to 14–19 ft. lbs. (19–25 Nm).

15. Position the tensioner to the pump mounting bracket and install the bolt and nut. Tighten the nut to 23–34 ft. lbs. (31–46 Nm).

16. Install the bolt that attaches the pump to the mounting bracket and tighten to 27–40 ft. lbs. (36–54 Nm).

17. Position the pump and bracket and install the 3 pump mounting bracket bolts. Tighten the bolts to 27–38 ft. lbs. (37–54 Nm).

18. Raise and safely support the vehicle.

19. Position the accessory drive belt on the pulley and install the belt tensioner adjustment bolt.

20. Position the right front undercover and install the 5 bolts.

21. Lower the vehicle.

22. Unplug the high-pressure line and connect the line to the pump. Tighten the flarenut to 12–17 ft. lbs. (16–24 Nm).

23. Connect the power steering pressure switch electrical connector.

24. Unplug the return hose and connect the hose to the reservoir. Tighten the clamp.

25. Position the reservoir and install the 2 mounting bolts.

26. Unplug the reservoir-to-pump hose and connect the hose to the reservoir. Tighten the clamp.

27. Fill the system with power steering fluid and adjust the accessory drive belt tension.

1.9L ENGINE

1. Disconnect the negative battery cable and drain the cooling system.

2. Loosen the belt tensioner and remove the drive belt from the pulley. Remove the belt tensioner bolt and remove the tensioner.

3. Support the engine with a suitable floor jack.

4. Remove the engine vibration damper nut and bolt and remove the damper.

5. Remove the 2 front engine mount nuts. Loosen the engine mount pivot bolt and nut and position the engine mount aside.

6. Raise the engine to gain access to the power steering pump pulley.

7. Hold the pulley in position with a suitable tool and remove the 3 pulley mounting bolts. Remove the pulley and lower the engine.

8. Position the engine mount and install the 2 nuts.

9. Raise and safely support the vehicle.

10. Loosen the clamp and disconnect the return line from the pump. Loosen the flarenut from the high-pressure line and disconnect the line from the pump.

11. Remove the 2 passenger side splash shields.

12. If equipped, remove the 4 compressor mounting bolts and position the air conditioning compressor aside.

13. Remove the lower radiator hose.

14. Remove the 3 power steering pump mounting bolts and remove the pump.

To install:

15. Position the power steering pump and install the 3 mounting bolts. Tighten the bolts to 30–45 ft. lbs. (40–62 Nm).

16. Install the lower radiator hose.

17. If equipped, position the air conditioning compressor and install the 4 mounting bolts. Tighten the bolts to 30–40 ft. lbs. (40–55 Nm).

18. Install the 2 passenger side splash shields and lower the vehicle.

19. Connect the high-pressure line to the power steering pump and tighten the nut. Connect the return line to the pump and position the clamp. Lower the vehicle.

20. Support the engine with a suitable floor jack.

21. Remove the 2 front engine mount nuts and raise the engine to gain access to the pulley.

22. Position the pulley and, holding the pulley in place with a suitable tool, install the 3 pulley mounting bolts. Tighten the bolts to 15–22 ft. lbs. (20–30 Nm).

23. Lower the engine.

24. Position the engine mount and install the 2 nuts. Tighten the engine mount pivot bolt and nut.

25. Position the engine vibration dampener and install the bolt and nut.

26. Position the belt tensioner and install the bolt loosely. Position the accessory drive belt on the pulley and tighten the tensioner mounting bolt to 30–41 ft. lbs. (40–55 Nm).

27. Fill the cooling system.

28. Add the proper type and quantity of power steering fluid.

29. Connect the negative battery cable. Check that the pump operates properly and that there are no leaks.

Tempo and Topaz

2.3L ENGINE

1. Disconnect the negative battery cable.

2. Disconnect the fluid return line at the remote reservoir and drain the power steering fluid into a suitable container.

3. Disconnect the pressure hose from the pump outlet and drain the fluid into a suitable container.

4. Loosen the tensioner and remove the drive belt from the pump pulley.

5. Remove the 4 bolts from the pump pulley and remove the pulley.

6. Remove the 3 pump retaining bolts and remove the pump.

To install:

7. Position the pump on its bracket and install the retaining bolts.

8. Install the pulley and secure with the 4 bolts.

9. Connect the pressure line to the pump but do not overtighten the fitting. Swivel and/or endplay of the fitting is normal and does not indicate a loose fitting.

10. Connect the inlet hose to the pump and secure with the hose clamp.

11. Fill the reservoir with the proper type of fluid.

12. Connect the negative battery cable and bleed the system. Check for leaks.

3.0L ENGINE

1. Disconnect the negative battery cable.

2. Disconnect the fluid return hose from the pump inlet and drain the fluid into a suitable container.

3. Remove the pressure line from the pump outlet and drain the fluid into a suitable container.

4. Remove the plastic pulley guard.

5. Loosen the tensioner and remove the drive belt from the pulley.

6. Remove the pulley-to-pump shaft bolt or nut and remove the pulley from the pump shaft.

7. Remove the pump-to-bracket bolts and remove the pump.

To install:

8. Install the pump onto the pump bracket and install the retaining screws. Tighten to 47–63 inch lbs. (5.2–7.2 Nm).

9. Install the pulley on the pump shaft and secure with the bolt or nut.

10. Install the drive belt on the pulley.

11. Install the plastic pulley guard.

12. Connect the pressure line to the pump but do not overtighten the fitting. Swivel and/or endplay of the fitting is normal and does not indicate a loose fitting.

13. Connect the inlet hose to the pump and secure with the hose clamp.

14. Fill the reservoir with the proper type of fluid.

15. Connect the negative battery cable and bleed the system. Check for leaks.

BELT ADJUSTMENT

1.8L Engine

1. Raise and safely support the vehicle.

2. Loosen the power steering pump mounting bolt and nuts.

3. Adjust the belt tension by turning the pump adjusting bolt.

4. Tighten the power steering pump mounting nut near the pump adjusting bolt.

5. Check the belt tension using either a belt tension gauge or using the deflection method.

6. If using a belt tension gauge, position the gauge on the longest accessible span of belt. The tension for a new belt should be 110–132 lbs. The tension for a used belt (more than 10 minutes running time) should be 95–110 lbs.

7. If using the deflection method, apply approximately 22 lbs. pressure midway between the pulleys. The deflection on a new belt should be 0.31–0.35 in. (8–9mm). The deflection on a used belt (more than 10 minutes running time) should be 0.35–0.39 in. (9–10mm).

8. Tighten the power steering pump mounting nut, located near the adjusting bolt, to 27–38 ft. lbs. (37–52 Nm).

9. Tighten the pump mounting bolt behind the pulley to 27–40 ft. lbs. (36–54 Nm) and the remaining pump mounting nut to 23–34 ft. lbs. (31–46 Nm).

10. Lower the vehicle.

2.3L, 3.0L and 1.9L Engines

Belt tension is maintained by an automatic belt tensioner and does not require adjustment.

SYSTEM BLEEDING

If air bubbles are present in the power steering fluid, bleed the system by performing the following:

1. Fill the reservoir to the proper level.

2. Operate the engine until the fluid reaches normal operating temperature of 165–175°F (73.8–79.4°C).

3. Turn the steering wheel all the way to the left then all the way to the right several times. Do not hold the steering wheel in the far left or far right position stops.

4. Check the fluid level and recheck the fluid for the presence of trapped air. If apparent that air is still in the system, fabricate or obtain a vacuum tester and purge the system as follows:

   a. Remove the pump dipstick cap assembly.

   b. Check and fill the pump reservoir with fluid to the **COLD FULL** mark on the dipstick.

   c. Disconnect the ignition coil wire or the coil pack electrical connector if equipped with distributorless ignition, and raise the

front of the vehicle and support safely.

   d. Crank the engine with the starter and check the fluid level. Do not turn the steering wheel at this time.

   e. Fill the pump reservoir to the **COLD FULL** mark on the dipstick. Crank the engine with the starter while cycling the steering wheel lock-to-lock. Check the fluid level.

   f. Tightly insert a suitable size rubber stopper and air evacuator pump into the reservoir fill neck. Connect the ignition coil wire or coil pack electrical connector.

   g. With the engine idling, apply a 15 in. of Hg vacuum to the reservoir for 3 minutes. As air is purged from the system, the vacuum will drop off. Maintain the vacuum on the system as required throughout the 3 minutes.

   h. Remove the vacuum source. Fill the reservoir to the **COLD FULL** mark on the dipstick.

   i. With the engine idling, re-apply 15 in. of Hg vacuum source to the reservoir. Slowly cycle the steering wheel to lock-to-lock stops for approximately 5 minutes. Do not hold the steering wheel on the stops during cycling. Maintain the vacuum as required.

   j. Release the vacuum and disconnect the vacuum source. Add fluid, as required.

   k. Start the engine and cycle the wheel slowly and check for leaks at all connections.

   l. Lower the front wheels.

5. In cases of severe aeration, repeat the bleeding procedure.

Tie Rod Ends

REMOVAL AND INSTALLATION

1. Raise and safely support the vehicle. Remove the wheel and tire assembly.

2. Remove and discard cotter pin and nut from worn tie rod end ball stud.

3. Disconnect tie rod end from spindle, using tie rod end remover tool 3290-D and adapter T81P-3504–W or equivalent.

4. Holding tie rod end with a wrench, loosen tie rod jam nut.

5. Note depth to which tie rod was located, using jam nut as a marker. Grip tie rod hex flats with a pair of suitable locking pliers, and remove tie rod end assembly from tie rod.

To install:

6. Clean tie rod threads. Apply a light coating of disc brake caliper slide grease D7AZ-19590–A or equivalent, to tie rod threads. Thread new tie rod end on tie rod to same depth as the removed tie rod end. Tighten jam nut.

7. Place tie rod end stud into steering spindle.

8. Install a new nut on tie rod end stud. Tighten nut to 27–32 ft. lbs. (36–43 Nm) on all except Escort and Tracer where the torque is 31–42 ft. lbs. (42–57 Nm), and continue tightening nut to align next castellation with cotter pin hole in stud. Install a new cotter pin.

9. Set toe to specification and tighten jam nuts to 42–50 ft. lbs. (57–68 Nm) on all except Escort and Tracer where the torque is 25–29 ft. lbs. (34–49 Nm). Do not twist bellows.

BRAKES

Master Cylinder

REMOVAL AND INSTALLATION

Tempo and Topaz

1. Disconnect the negative battery cable.

2. Disconnect and plug the brake lines from the primary and secondary outlet ports of the master cylinder and pressure control valves.

3. Remove the nuts attaching the master cylinder to the brake booster assembly. Disconnect the brake warning light wire.

4. Slide the master cylinder forward and upward from the vehicle.

To install:

5. Before installation, bench bleed the new master cylinder as follows:

   a. Mount the new master cylinder in a suitable holding fixture. Be careful not to damage the housing.

   b. Fill the master cylinder reservoir with brake fluid.

   c. Using a suitable tool inserted into the booster pushrod cavity, push the master cylinder piston in slowly. Place a suitable container under the master cylinder to catch the fluid being expelled from the outlet ports.

   d. Place a finger tightly over each outlet port and allow the master cylinder piston to return.

e. Repeat the procedure until clear fluid only is expelled from the master cylinder. Plug the outlet ports and remove the master cylinder from the holding fixture.

6. Position the master cylinder over the booster pushrod and booster mounting studs. Install the nuts and tighten to 13–25 ft. lbs. (18–33 Nm) on 1992 models and 16–21 ft. lbs. (21–29 Nm) on 1993–94 vehicles.

7. Remove the plugs and connect the brake lines. Tighten the fittings.

8. Make sure the master cylinder reservoir is full. Have an assistant push down on the brake pedal. When the pedal is all the way down, crack open the brake line fittings, 1 at a time, to expel any remaining air in the master cylinder and brake lines. Tighten the fittings, then have the assistant allow the brake pedal to return.

9. Repeat Step 8 until all air is expelled from the master cylinder and brake lines. Final tighten the brake line fittings to 10–18 ft. lbs. (14–24 Nm).

10. Connect the brake warning indicator connector.

11. Make sure the master cylinder reservoir is full.

12. If necessary, bleed the brake system.

13. Connect the negative battery cable. Check for fluid leaks and check for proper operation.

Escort and Tracer

WITHOUT ABS

1. Disconnect the battery cables and remove the battery.

2. Disconnect the low fluid level sensor electrical connector.

3. Loosen the brake line fittings and disconnect the brake lines from the master cylinder.

4. If equipped with manual transaxle, remove the clamp and pull the clutch hose from the brake/clutch fluid reservoir.

5. Cap the lines and the master cylinder ports.

6. Remove the 2 mounting nuts and remove the master cylinder assembly.

To install:

7. Adjust the piston to pushrod clearance as follows:

a. Place the master cylinder in a soft-jawed vise.

b. Using the Master Cylinder Gauge tool T87C-2500-A, loosen the set screw and retract the gauge rod. Position the gauge on the brake master cylinder.

c. Push lightly on the end of the gauge rod, until the gauge rod bottoms on the brake master cylinder primary piston.

d. Tighten the set screw, securing the gauge rod in place.

e. Apply 19.7 in. Hg of vacuum to the power brake booster with a vacuum pump.

f. Invert the gauge and place it over the power brake booster pushrod. Check to make sure there is no space between the end of the adjustment gauge and the power brake booster pushrod. If there is space between the end of the gauge and the pushrod, loosen the pushrod locknut and adjust the pushrod until there is no space.

g. The brake master cylinder piston-to-power brake booster pushrod clearance is 0.016–0.024 in. (0.4–0.6mm) for no vacuum or 0.004–0.012 in. (0.1–0.4mm) for 500mm Hg of vacuum.

8. Before installation, bench bleed the new master cylinder as follows:

a. Mount the new master cylinder in a suitable holding fixture. Be careful not to damage the housing.

b. Fill the master cylinder reservoir with brake fluid.

c. Using a suitable tool inserted into the booster pushrod cavity, push the master cylinder piston in slowly. Place a suitable container under the master cylinder to catch the fluid being expelled from the outlet ports.

d. Place a finger tightly over each outlet port and allow the master cylinder piston to return.

e. Repeat the procedure until clear fluid only is expelled from the master cylinder. Plug the outlet ports and remove the master cylinder from the holding fixture.

9. Position the master cylinder over the booster pushrod and booster mounting studs. Install the nuts and tighten to 8–12 ft. lbs. (10–16 Nm).

10. If equipped with manual transaxle, connect the clutch hose onto the brake/clutch fluid reservoir and install the clamp.

11. Remove the caps and connect the brake lines. Tighten the fittings.

12. Make sure the master cylinder reservoir is full. Have an assistant push down on the brake pedal. When the pedal is all the way down, crack open the brake line fittings, 1 at a time, to expel any remaining air in the master cylinder and brake lines. Tighten the fittings, then have the assistant allow the brake pedal to return.

13. Repeat Step 12 until all air is expelled from the master cylinder and brake lines. Tighten the brake line fittings to 10–16 ft. lbs. (13–22 Nm).

14. Connect the low fluid level sensor electrical connector.

15. Install the battery and connect the negative battery cable.

16. Make sure the master cylinder reservoir is full. Bleed the brakes, if necessary.

17. Check for brake fluid leaks and for proper brake operation.

WITH ABS

ABS was introduced on the 1994 Escort and Tracer.

1. Disconnect the negative battery cable. Use a syringe to remove the brake fluid from the master cylinder reservoir.

2. If equipped, remove the speed control wire from its bracket.

3. If equipped, disconnect the clutch master cylinder.

4. Disconnect the brake master cylinder sensor electrical connector.

5. Disconnect the brake tubes from the master cylinder. Cap the tubes and ports.

6. Remove the master cylinder-to-power brake booster nuts and the master cylinder.

To install:

7. To adjust master cylinder pushrod length, perform the following procedure:

a. Place the master cylinder in a soft-jawed vise.

b. Using the Master Cylinder Gauge tool T92C-2500-A, loosen the brass holding screw and retract the gauge rod. Attach the gauge to the power brake booster and tighten the gauge nuts to 8–12 ft. lbs. (10–16 Nm).

c. Start the engine and allow it to idle for approx. 15 seconds.

d. Push lightly on the end of the gauge rod, until the gauge rod just contacts the power brake booster pushrod.

e. Tighten the brass holding screw, securing the gauge rod in place.

NOTE: Be careful when removing the gauge from the power brake booster. If the gauge rod setting is changed during removal, a faulty measurement will be recorded and may lead to unnecessary adjustment of the pushrod.

f. Remove the gauge from the power brake booster and turn the engine **OFF**.

g. Using a depth gauge, measure and record the height of the master cylinder gauge rod.

h. Loosen the master cylinder gauge brass holding screw and set opposite end of the gauge on the brake master cylinder.

i. Push lightly on the end of the gauge rod, until the it bottoms in the brake master cylinder piston; then, tighten the brass holding screw.

j. Remove the master cylinder gauge from the brake master cylinder.

k. Using a depth gauge, measure and record the height of the master cylinder gauge rod.

l. Determine the difference between the 2 measurements. If the 2nd measurement is larger than the 1st, subtract the 1st from the 2nd. If the 1st measurement is larger than the 2nd, subtract the 2nd from the 1st. Adjust the power booster pushrod nut to lengthen or shorten the power brake booster pushrod the amount equal to the difference between the 1st and 2nd. If the measurement of 1st is larger than 2nd, the pushrod must be lengthened. If the measurement of 2nd is larger than 1st, the pushrod must be shortened.

m. Recheck the pushrod measurement.

8. Install the master cylinder and torque the nuts to 8–12 ft. lbs. (10–16 Nm).

9. Connect the short lengths of brake tubes to the master cylinder and route the tubes back to the master cylinder reservoir.

10. Fill the master cylinder reservoir and pump the brake pedal until clear fluid comes out of the tubes.

11. Place a clean shop towel over the top of the reservoir and remove the temporary brake tubes.

12. Connect the brake tubes to the master cylinder and tighten the fittings to 10–16 ft. lbs. (13–22 Nm).

13. If equipped, install the speed control wire in its bracket. If equipped, connect the clutch master cylinder hose.

14. Fill the master cylinder reservoir and bleed the brakes.

Proportioning/Combination Valve

REMOVAL AND INSTALLATION

Except 1992 Escort and Tracer

There are 2 pressure control valves housed in the master cylinder assembly. The valves reduce rear brake system hydraulic pressure when the pressure exceeds a preset value. The rear brake hydraulic pressure is limited in order to minimize rear wheel skidding during hard braking. Remove and install the pressure control valves as follows:

1. Disconnect the primary or secondary brake line, as necessary.

2. Loosen and remove the pressure control valve from the master cylinder housing. On 1993–96 Escort and Tracers, remove and discard the O-rings.

To install:

3. On 1993–96 Escort and Tracers, install new O-rings.

4. Install the pressure control valve in the master cylinder housing port and tighten to 10–18 ft. lbs. (14–24 Nm) or 33–40 ft. lbs. (44–54 Nm) on 1993–96 Escort and Tracers.

5. Connect the brake line and tighten the fitting to 10–18 ft. lbs. (14–24 Nm).

6. Fill and bleed the brake system.

1992 Escort and Tracer

1. Loosen the brake line fittings and disconnect the brake lines from the proportioning valve.

2. Remove the 2 mounting bolts and remove the valve.

To install:

3. Position the valve and install the mounting bolts. Tighten to 14–17 ft. lbs. (19–23 Nm).

4. Connect the brake lines and tighten the fittings to 10–16 ft. lbs. (13–22 Nm).

5. Properly bleed the brake system.

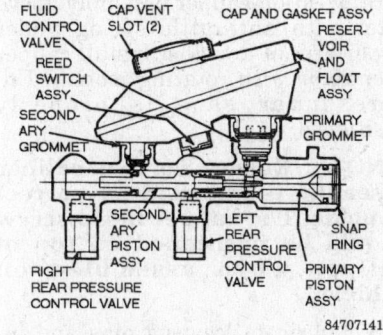

Master cylinder and pressure control valve assembly — except 1992 Escort and Tracer

Power Brake Booster

REMOVAL AND INSTALLATION

Tempo and Topaz

1. Disconnect the battery ground cable and remove the brake lines from the master cylinder.

2. Remove the retaining nuts and remove the master cylinder.

3. From under the instrument panel, remove the brake light switch wiring connector from the switch. Remove the pushrod retainer and outer nylon washer from the brake pin, slide the brake light switch along the brake pedal pin, far enough for the outer hole to clear the pin.

4. Remove the switch by sliding it upward. Remove the booster to dash panel retaining nuts. Slide the booster pushrod and pushrod bushing off the brake pedal pin.

5. Disconnect the manifold vacuum hose from the booster check valve and move the booster forward until the booster studs clear the dash panel and remove the booster.

To install:

6. Align the pedal support and support spacer inside the vehicle and place the booster in position on the dash panel. Hand-start the retaining nuts.

7. Working inside the vehicle, install the pushrod and pushrod bushing on the brake pedal pin. Tighten the booster-to-dash panel retaining nuts to 13–25 ft. lbs. (18–33 Nm) on 1992 or 16–21 ft. lbs. (21–29 Nm) on 1993–94.

8. Position the brake light switch so it straddles the booster pushrod with the brake light switch slot toward the pedal blade and the hole just clearing the pin. Slide the brake light switch down onto the pin. Slide the assembly toward the pedal arm, being careful not to bend or deform the switch. Install the nylon washer on the pin and secure all parts to the pin with the hairpin retainer. Make sure the retainer is fully installed and locked over the pedal pin. Install the brake light switch connector on the brake light switch.

9. Connect the manifold vacuum hose to the booster check valve using a hose clamp.

10. Install the master cylinder.

11. Bleed the brake system.

12. Connect the negative battery cable and start the engine. Check the power brake function.

13. If equipped with cruise control, adjust the dump valve as follows:

a. Firmly depress and hold the brake pedal.

b. Push in the dump valve until the valve collar bottoms against the retaining clip.

c. Place a 0.050–0.10 in. (1.27–2.54mm) shim between the white button of the valve and the pad on the brake pedal.

d. Firmly pull the brake pedal rearward to its normal position, allowing the dump valve to ratchet backward in the retaining clip.

Escort and Tracer

1. Disconnect the negative battery cable.

2. Remove the master cylinder assembly.

3. Loosen the vacuum hose clamp and remove the hose from the power brake booster.

4. From inside the vehicle, remove the pin and discard.

5. Remove the clevis pin.

6. Remove the 4 booster mounting nuts and remove the booster. Remove and discard the gasket.

To install:

7. Install a new gasket over the studs and position the power brake booster.

8. From inside the vehicle, install the 4 mounting nuts and tighten to 14–19 ft. lbs. (19–25 Nm).

9. Lubricate the clevis pin with white lithium grease and install. Install a new pin.

10. Position the vacuum hose to the booster and install the clamp.

11. Install the master cylinder, making sure to check the master cylinder pushrod clearance.

12. Adjust the brake pedal as follows:

a. Press the brake pedal several times to eliminate the vacuum in the booster.

b. Carefully press the pedal and measure the amount of free-play until resistance is felt. If the free-play is 0.039–0.079 in. (1–2mm), the pedal free-play is within specification. If the free-play is not within specification, proceed to Step c.

c. Loosen the rod locknut and rotate the rod either in or out to obtain the specified free-play.

d. While holding the rod in position, tighten the rod locknut.

e. Measure the distance from the center of the brake pedal to the floor. If the distance measures 7.60–7.72 in. (193–196mm), the pedal height is within specification.

If the pedal height is not within specification, proceed to Step f.

f. Disconnect the brake light switch electrical connector, loosen the switch locknut and turn the switch until it does not contact the brake pedal.

g. Loosen the rod locknut and turn the rod until the brake pedal height is within specification.

h. Turn the brake light switch until it contacts the brake pedal, then turn it an additional ½ turn. Tighten the brake light locknut and the rod locknut.

i. Connect the brake light switch electrical connector and check the operation of the brake lights and brake system.

Brake Caliper

REMOVAL AND INSTALLATION

Tempo and Topaz

1. Disconnect the negative battery cable.

2. Raise and safely support the vehicle.

3. Remove wheel and tire assembly from rotor mounting face.

4. Disconnect flexible brake hose from caliper. Remove hollow retaining bolt that connects hose fitting to caliper. Remove hose assembly from caliper and plug hose.

5. Remove caliper locating pins using Torx® drive bit D79P–2100–T40 or equivalent.

6. Lift caliper off rotor and integral knuckle and anchor plate using rotating motion.

--- **WARNING** ---

Do not pry directly against plastic piston or damage to piston will occur.

To install:

7. Retract piston fully in piston bore. Position caliper assembly above rotor with anti-rattle spring under upper arm of knuckle. Install caliper over rotor with rotating motion. Ensure inner shoe is properly positioned.

NOTE: Ensure correct caliper assembly is installed on correct knuckle. The caliper bleed screw should be positioned on top of caliper when assembled on vehicle.

8. Lubricate locating pins and inside of insulators with silicone grease. Install locating pins through caliper insulators and into knuckle

attaching holes. The caliper locating pins must be inserted and threads started by hand.

9. Using Torx® drive bit D79P–2100–T40 or equivalent, tighten caliper locating pins to 18–25 ft. lbs. (24–34 Nm).

10. Remove plug and install brake hose on caliper with new gasket on each side of fitting outlet. Insert attaching bolt through washers and fittings. Tighten bolt to 30–40 ft. lbs. (40–54 Nm).

11. Bleed brake system. Always replace rubber bleed screw cap after bleeding.

12. Fill master cylinder as required.

13. Install wheel and tire assembly. Tighten wheel lug nuts to 85–105 ft. lbs. (115–142 Nm).

14. Connect negative battery cable.

15. Pump brake pedal prior to moving vehicle to position brake linings.

16. Road test vehicle.

Escort and Tracer

FRONT CALIPER

1. Disconnect the negative battery cable.

2. Raise and safely support the vehicle. Remove the wheel and tire assembly.

3. Remove the brake pads.

4. Clamp the brake hose and remove the brake hose attaching bolt.

5. Disconnect the brake hose from the caliper and discard the 2 copper washers.

6. Remove the 2 caliper mounting bolts and remove the caliper.

To install:

7. Position the caliper and install the 2 caliper mounting bolts. Tighten the bolts to 29–36 ft. lbs. (39–49 Nm).

8. Install 2 new copper washers to the brake hose. Position the brake hose onto the caliper and install the attaching bolt. Tighten the bolt to 16–22 ft. lbs. (22–29 Nm).

9. Remove the clamp from the brake hose.

10. Install the brake pads.

11. Bleed the brake system.

12. Install the wheel and tire assembly and lower the vehicle.

13. Connect negative battery cable.

REAR CALIPER

1. Disconnect the negative battery cable.

2. Raise and safely support the vehicle. Remove the wheel and tire assembly.

3. Remove the brake pads.

4. Remove the parking brake cable bracket bolt and position the bracket aside.

5. Remove the parking brake cable from the operating lever.

6. Clamp the brake hose, remove the brake line attaching bolt and remove the 2 washers. Discard the washers.

7. Disconnect the brake line and slide the caliper off the mounting bracket.

To install:

8. Position the caliper on the mounting bracket.

9. Install 2 new washers to the brake line. Position the brake line to the caliper and install the attaching bolt. Tighten the bolt to 16–22 ft. lbs. (22–29 Nm).

10. Remove the clamp from the brake hose.

11. Attach the parking brake cable to the operating lever. Position the bracket and install the bracket bolt.

12. Install the brake pads.

13. Bleed the brake system.

14. Install the wheel and tire assembly and lower the vehicle.

15. Connect negative battery cable.

Disc Brake Pads

REMOVAL AND INSTALLATION

Tempo and Topaz

1. Disconnect the negative battery cable.

2. Remove master cylinder cap and check fluid level in reservoir. Remove brake fluid until reservoir is ½ full. Discard removed fluid.

3. Raise and safely support the vehicle.

4. Remove wheel and tire assembly.

5. Remove caliper locating pins.

6. Lift caliper assembly from integral knuckle and anchor plate and rotor using rotating motion. Do not pry directly against plastic piston or damage will occur.

7. Remove outer shoe and lining assembly.

8. Remove inner shoe and lining assembly.

9. Inspect both rotor braking surfaces. Minor scoring or buildup of lining material does not require machining or replacement of rotor. Hand-sand glaze from both rotor braking surfaces using garnet paper 100-A (medium grit) or aluminum oxide 150-J (medium).

10. Suspend caliper inside fender housing with wire. Use care not to damage caliper or stretch brake hose.

To install:

11. Use a 4 in. C-clamp and wood block 2¾ in. x 1 in. (70mm x 25mm)

and approximately ¾ in. (19mm) thick to seat caliper hydraulic piston in its bore.

CAUTION

Extra care must be taken during this procedure to prevent damage to the plastic piston. Metal or sharp objects cannot come into direct contact with the piston surface or damage will result.

---

12. Remove all rust buildup from inside of caliper legs where the outer shoe makes contact.

13. Install inner shoe and lining assembly in caliper piston(s). Do not bend shoe clips during installation in piston.

14. Install correct outer shoe and lining assembly. Ensure clips are properly seated.

15. Install caliper over rotor.

16. Install wheel and tire assembly. Tighten wheel nuts to 85–105 ft. lbs. (115–142 Nm).

17. Pump brake pedal prior to moving vehicle to position brake linings. Check the fluid level in the master cylinder.

18. Connect negative battery cable.

19. Road test vehicle.

Escort and Tracer

FRONT DISC BRAKE PADS

1. Remove master cylinder cap and check fluid level in reservoir. Remove brake fluid until reservoir is ½ full. Discard removed fluid.

2. Raise and safely support the vehicle.

3. Remove wheel and tire assembly.

4. Remove the 2 brake pad pins and remove the M-spring and the W-spring.

5. Remove the brake pads and shims from the caliper.

To install:

6. Use a suitable tool to push the piston into the caliper bore.

7. Apply suitable grease between the shims and the brake pad guide plates and position the brake pads and shims into the caliper.

8. Install the W-spring and the M-spring. Install the 2 brake pad pins.

9. Install the wheel and tire assembly and lower the vehicle.

10. Pump brake pedal prior to moving vehicle to position brake linings. Check the fluid level in the master cylinder.

11. Road test vehicle.

REAR DISC BRAKE PADS

1. Disconnect the negative battery cable.

2. Remove master cylinder cap and check fluid level in reservoir. Remove brake fluid until reservoir is ½ full. Discard removed fluid.

3. Raise and safely support the vehicle.

4. Remove wheel and tire assembly.

5. If necessary, remove the screw plug and turn the adjustment gear counterclockwise with an Allen wrench to pull the piston fully inward.

6. Remove the lower caliper lock bolt.

7. Using a suitable tool, pivot the caliper on its mounting bracket to access the brake pads. If the upper lock bolt requires lubrication or service, remove it and suspend the caliper with mechanics wire.

8. Remove the brake pads, shims, spring and guides.

To install:

9. Apply an appropriate brake pad grease between the shims and the brake pads.

10. Using a suitable tool, pivot the caliper on its mounting bracket and position the brake pads, shims, spring and guides to the rotor.

11. Lubricate and install the lower lock bolt. Tighten the bolt to 33–43 ft. lbs. (45–59 Nm).

12. If necessary, turn the adjustment gear clockwise with an Allen wrench until the brake pads just touch the rotor, then loosen the gear ⅓ of a turn. Install the screw plug and tighten to 9–12 ft. lbs. (12–16 Nm).

13. Install the wheel and tire assembly and lower the vehicle.

14. Pump brake pedal prior to moving vehicle to position brake linings. Check the fluid level in the master cylinder.

15. Connect negative battery cable.

16. Road test vehicle.

Brake Rotor

REMOVAL AND INSTALLATION

Tempo and Topaz

1. Disconnect the negative battery cable.

2. Raise and safely support the vehicle.

3. Remove wheel and tire assembly.

4. Remove caliper locating pins.

5. Lift caliper assembly from integral knuckle and anchor plate and rotor using rotating motion. Do not pry directly against plastic piston or damage will occur.

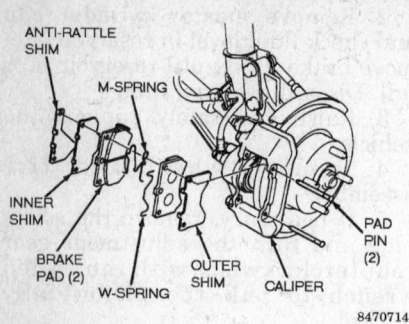

Front disc brake pad assembly — Escort and Tracer

6. Position caliper aside and support it with a length of wire to avoid damaging caliper.

7. Remove rotor from hub assembly by pulling it off the hub studs. Inspect the rotor and refinish or replace, as necessary. If refinishing, check the minimum thickness specification.

To install:

8. If rotor is being replaced, remove protective coating from new rotor with carburetor degreaser. If original rotor is being installed, make sure rotor braking and mounting surfaces are clean.

9. Install rotor on hub assembly.

10. Install caliper assembly on rotor.

11. Install wheel and tire assembly. Tighten wheel nuts to 85–105 ft. lbs. (115–142 Nm).

12. Pump brake pedal prior to moving vehicle to position brake linings.

13. Connect negative battery cable.

14. Road test vehicle.

Escort and Tracer

FRONT BRAKE ROTOR

1. Disconnect the negative battery cable.

2. Raise and safely support the vehicle.

3. Remove the wheel and tire assembly.

4. Remove the 2 caliper mounting bolts.

5. Secure the caliper aside with mechanics wire.

6. Pull the rotor from the hub. Inspect the rotor and refinish or replace, as necessary. If refinishing, check the minimum thickness specification.

To install:

7. If rotor is being replaced, remove protective coating from new rotor with carburetor degreaser. If original rotor is being installed, make sure rotor braking and mounting surfaces are clean.

8. Position the rotor onto the hub.

9. Remove the mechanics wire and position the caliper.

10. Install the 2 caliper mounting bolts and tighten to 29–36 ft. lbs. (39–49 Nm).

11. Install the wheel and tire assembly and lower the vehicle.

12. Connect negative battery cable.

REAR BRAKE ROTOR

1. Disconnect the negative battery cable.

2. Raise and safely support the vehicle.

3. Remove the wheel and tire assembly.

4. Remove the brake pads.

5. Remove the 2 rotor mounting screws.

6. Using a suitable tool, pivot the caliper on its mounting bracket and remove the rotor. Inspect the rotor and refinish or replace, as necessary. If refinishing, check the minimum thickness specification.

To install:

7. Using a suitable tool, pivot the caliper on its mounting bracket and position the rotor.

8. Install the 2 mounting screws.

9. Install the brake pads.

10. Install the wheel and tire assembly and lower the vehicle.

11. Connect negative battery cable.

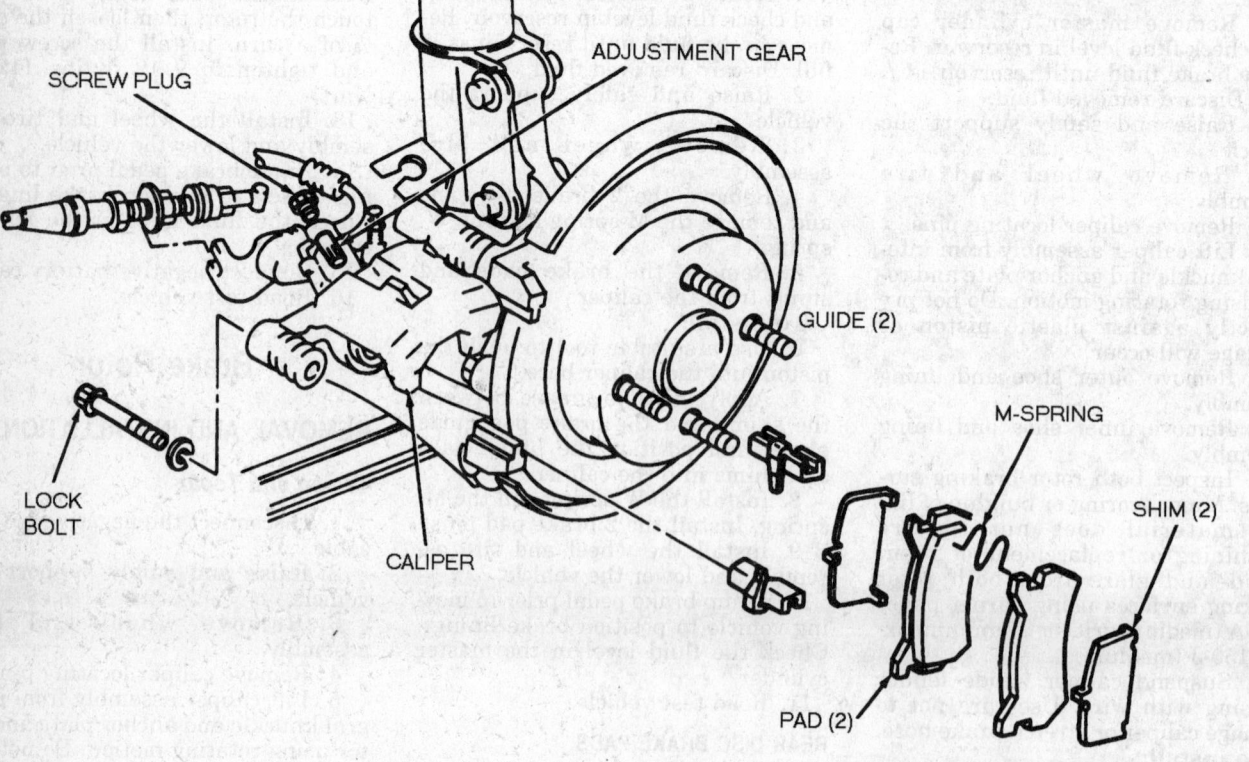

Rear disc brake pad assembly — Escort and Tracer

Brake Drums

REMOVAL AND INSTALLATION

Except Escort and Tracer and Tempo/Topaz with All Wheel Drive

1. Raise and safely support the vehicle.
2. Remove wheel and tire assembly.
3. Remove grease cap from hub. Remove cotter pin, nut lock, adjusting nut and keyed flat washer from spindle. Remove outer bearing.
4. Remove hub and drum assembly as a unit.

NOTE: **If the hub/drum assembly will not come off, pry the rubber plug from the backing plate inspection hole. If with 7 inch brakes, insert a suitable tool in the hole until it contacts the adjuster assembly pivot. Apply side pressure on this pivot point to allow the adjuster quadrant to ratchet and release the brake adjustment. If with 8 inch brakes, remove the brake line-to-axle retention bracket. This will allow sufficient room for insertion of suitable tools to disengage the adjusting lever and back-off the adjusting screw.**

5. Inspect the brake drum and refinish or replace, as necessary. If refinishing, check the maximum inside diameter specification.

   To install:
6. Inspect and lubricate bearings, as necessary. Replace grease seal if any damage is visible.
7. Clean spindle stem and apply a thin coat of wheel bearing grease.
8. Install hub and drum assembly on spindle.
9. Install outer bearing into hub on spindle.
10. Install keyed flat washer and adjusting nut. Tighten nut finger-tight.
11. Adjust wheel bearing. Install nut retainer and a new cotter pin.
12. Install grease cap.
13. Install wheel and tire assembly. Tighten wheel nuts to 85–105 ft. lbs. (115–142 Nm).
14. Pump brake pedal prior to moving vehicle to position brake linings.
15. Connect negative battery cable.
16. Road test vehicle.

Escort and Tracer and Tempo/Topaz With All Wheel Drive

1. Raise and safely support the vehicle.

2. Remove wheel and tire assembly.
3. Remove the spring nut or attaching screws, if necessary.
4. Pull the brake drum from the hub. Inspect the drum and refinish or replace, as necessary. If refinishing, check the maximum inside diameter specification.

   To install:
5. Position the brake drum on the hub.
6. Install the 2 drum attaching screws, if applicable.
7. Install the wheel and tire assembly and lower the vehicle.

Brake Shoes

REMOVAL AND INSTALLATION

Tempo and Topaz

1. Raise and safely support the vehicle.
2. Remove the wheel, tire, and hub and drum assembly.
3. Remove 2 shoe hold-down springs and pins.
4. Lift the brake shoes, springs and adjuster assembly off backing plate and wheel cylinder assembly. Be careful not to bend adjusting lever during assembly removal.

5. Remove the parking brake cable from the parking brake lever.
6. Remove the retracting springs from the lower brake shoe attachments and upper shoe-to-adjusting lever attachment points. This will separate the brake shoes and disengage the adjuster mechanism.
7. Remove the horseshoe retaining clip and spring washer and slide the lever off the parking brake lever pin on the trailing shoe.

   To install:
8. Apply a light coating of high temperature grease at the points where the brake shoes contact the backing plate.
9. Apply a light coating of lubricant to the adjuster screw threads and the socket end of the adjusting screw. Install the stainless steel washer over the socket end of the adjusting screw and install the socket. Turn the adjusting screw into the adjusting pivot nut to the limit of the threads and then back-off ½ turn.
10. Assemble the parking brake lever to the trailing shoe by installing the spring washer and a new horseshoe retaining clip. Crimp the clip until it retains the lever to the shoe securely.
11. Attach the parking brake cable to the parking brake lever.

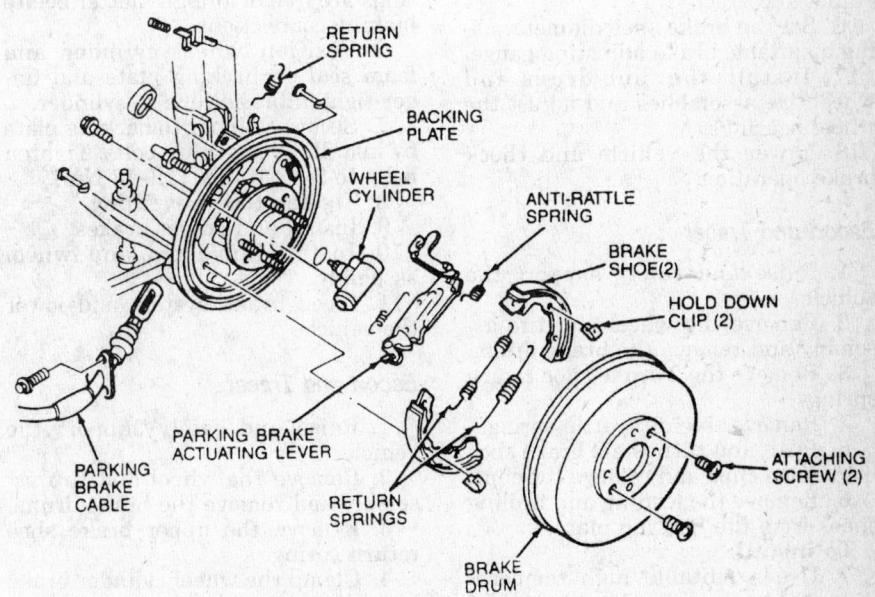

8470c089

Brake drum assembly exploded view — Escort and Tracer

12. Attach the lower shoe retracting spring to the leading and trailing shoe assemblies and install to backing plate. It will be necessary to stretch the retracting spring as the shoes are installed downward over the anchor plate to inside of shoe retaining plate.

13. Install the adjuster screw assembly between the leading shoe slot and the slot in the trailing shoe and parking brake lever. The adjuster socket end slot must fit into the trailing shoe and parking brake lever.

NOTE: The adjuster socket blade is marked R or L for the right or left brake assemblies. The R or L adjuster blade must be installed with the letter R or L in the upright position, facing the wheel cylinder, on the correct side to ensure that the deeper of the 2 slots in the adjuster sockets fits into the parking brake lever.

14. Assemble the adjuster lever in the groove located in the parking brake lever pin and into the slot of the adjuster socket that fits into the trailing shoe web.

15. Attach the upper retracting spring to the leading shoe slot. Using a suitable spring tool, stretch the other end of the spring into the notch on the adjuster lever. If the adjuster lever does not contact the star wheel after installing the spring, it is possible that the adjuster socket is installed incorrectly.

16. Set the brake shoe diameter using a suitable brake adjusting gauge.

17. Install the hub/drum and wheel/tire assemblies and adjust the wheel bearings.

18. Lower the vehicle and check brake operation.

Escort and Tracer

1. Raise and safely support the vehicle.

2. Remove the wheel and tire assembly and remove the brake drum.

3. Remove the 2 brake shoe return springs.

4. Remove the anti-rattle spring.

5. Push and turn the 2 brake shoe hold-down clips and remove the clips.

6. Remove the leading and trailing shoes from the backing plate.

To install:

7. Use a suitable high temperature grease to lubricate the brake shoe contact points on the backing plate.

8. Position the trailing brake shoe on the backing plate and install 1 of the brake shoe hold-down clips.

9. Position the leading brake shoe on the backing plate and install the other brake shoe hold-down clip.

10. Install the anti-rattle spring.

11. Install the 2 brake shoe return springs.

12. Press the brake pedal to verify operation of the automatic brake adjuster.

13. Install the brake drum and the wheel and tire assembly. Lower the vehicle.

14. Firmly apply the brakes 2 or 3 times to adjust the rear brakes.

Wheel Cylinder

REMOVAL AND INSTALLATION

Tempo and Topaz

1. Raise and safely support the vehicle. Remove wheel/tire and hub/drum assemblies.

2. Remove brake shoe assembly.

3. Disconnect brake tube from wheel cylinder.

4. Remove wheel cylinder attaching bolts and remove wheel cylinder.

NOTE: Use caution to prevent brake fluid from contacting brake linings and drum braking surface. Contaminated linings must be replaced.

To install:

5. Ensure ends of hydraulic fittings are free of foreign matter before making connections.

6. Position wheel cylinder and foam seal on backing plate and finger-tighten brake tube to cylinder.

7. Secure cylinder to backing plate by installing attaching bolts. Tighten bolts to 9–13 ft. lbs. (12–18 Nm).

8. Tighten tube nut fitting.

9. Install and adjust brakes.

10. Install hub/drum and wheel assembly.

11. Bleed brake system and lower the vehicle.

Escort and Tracer

1. Raise and safely support the vehicle.

2. Remove the wheel and tire assembly and remove the brake drum.

3. Remove the upper brake shoe return spring.

4. Clamp the wheel cylinder brake hose.

5. Using a suitable flarenut wrench, loosen the wheel cylinder-to-brake line flare nut.

6. Pull the clip from the brake hose retaining bracket and remove

the brake hose from the retaining bracket.

7. Remove the brake line from the wheel cylinder.

8. Remove the 2 wheel cylinder mounting bolts and remove the wheel cylinder from the backing plate.

9. Remove and discard the wheel cylinder gasket.

To install:

10. Install a new wheel cylinder gasket onto the backing plate.

11. Position the wheel cylinder onto the backing plate and install the 2 mounting bolts. Tighten the bolts to 89–115 inch lbs. (10–13 Nm).

12. Position the brake line into the wheel cylinder fitting and tighten the wheel cylinder-to-brake line flarenut to 12–16 ft. lbs. (16–22 Nm).

13. Position the brake hose into the retaining bracket and install the clip. Remove the clamp from the wheel cylinder brake hose.

14. Install the brake shoe return spring.

15. Press the brake pedal to verify the operation of the automatic brake adjuster.

16. Install the brake drum and the wheel and tire assembly.

17. Bleed the brake system and lower the vehicle.

Parking Brake Cable

ADJUSTMENT

Tempo and Topaz

NOTE: The rear brake shoes should be properly adjusted before adjusting the parking brake.

1. With the engine running, apply approximately 100 lbs. pedal effort to the hydraulic service brake 3 times before adjusting the parking brake.

2. Block the front wheels and place the transaxle in N. Raise and safely support the rear of the vehicle just enough to rotate the wheels.

3. Place the parking brake control assembly in the 12th notch position, 2 notches from full application. Tighten the adjusting nut until approximately 1 in. (25mm) of threaded rod is exposed beyond the nut. Release the parking brake control and rotate the rear wheels by hand. There should be no brake drag.

4. If the brakes drag when the control assembly is fully released, or the handle travels too far on full apply, repeat the procedure and adjust the nut accordingly.

Escort and Tracer

1. Start the engine and place the transaxle in **R**.

2. With the vehicle moving in reverse, depress the brake pedal several times.

3. Stop the vehicle and place the transaxle in **P**. Turn the engine OFF.

4. Remove the parking brake console as follows:

   a. Remove the rear seat ash tray.

   b. Position both front seats to the rear-most position.

   c. Remove the 2 front retaining screws from the parking brake console.

   d. Recline both front seats.

   e. Remove the 2 rear retaining screws and with the parking brake engaged, remove the parking brake console.

   f. Release the parking brake lever.

5. Turn the adjusting nut until the parking brake lever stroke is 5–7 notches when pulled with a force of 22 lbs.

6. Install the parking brake console by reversing the removal procedure.

REMOVAL AND INSTALLATION

Tempo and Topaz

1. Place control assembly in seventh notch position and loosen adjusting nut. Completely release control assembly.

2. Raise and safely support the vehicle. Remove rear parking brake cable from equalizer.

3. Remove hairpin clip holding cable to floor pan tunnel bracket.

4. Remove wire retainer holding cable to fuel tank mounting bracket. Remove cable from wire retainer. Remove cable and clip from the fuel pump bracket.

5. Remove screw holding cable retaining clip to rear sidemember. Remove cable from clip.

6. Remove the wheel and tire assembly and rear brake drum.

7. Disengage cable end from brake assembly parking brake lever. Depress cable prongs holding cable to backing plate. Remove cable through hole in backing plate.

To install:

8. Insert cable through hole in backing plate. Attach cable end to rear brake assembly parking brake lever.

9. Insert conduit end fitting into backing plate. Ensure retention prongs are locked into place.

10. Insert cable into rear attaching clip and attach clip to rear sidemember with screw.

11. Route cable through bracket in floorpan tunnel and install hairpin retaining clip.

12. Install cable end into equalizer.

13. Insert cable into wire retainer and snap retainer into hole in fuel tank mounting bracket. Insert cable and install clip into suspension torque box bracket.

14. Install rear drum, wheel and tire assembly and wheel cover.

15. Lower vehicle.

16. Adjust parking brake.

Escort and Tracer

1. Remove the parking brake console as follows:

   a. Remove the rear seat ash tray.

   b. Position both front seats to the rear-most position.

   c. Remove the 2 front retaining screws from the parking brake console.

   d. Recline both front seats.

   e. Remove the 2 rear retaining screws and with the parking brake engaged, remove the parking brake console.

   f. Release the parking brake lever.

2. Remove the cable adjusting nut.

3. Raise and safely support the vehicle.

4. Remove the rear exhaust pipe and resonator heat shields.

5. Disconnect the equalizer return spring and remove the cables from the equalizer.

6. Remove the clip that attaches the cable to the retaining bracket located near the equalizer. Remove the cable from the bracket.

7. Remove the cable routing bracket bolt from the floorpan and remove the bracket.

8. Remove the 2 cable routing bracket nuts from the trailing link and remove the bracket.

9. Remove the 2 cable retaining bracket bolts from the backing plate and remove the bracket.

10. Remove the cable from the parking brake actuating lever.

To install:

11. Position the cable onto the parking brake actuating lever.

12. Position the parking brake cable bracket onto the backing plate and install the 2 bolts. Tighten the bolts to 14–19 ft. lbs. (19–25 Nm).

13. Position the cable routing bracket onto the trailing link and install the 2 nuts. Tighten the nuts to 12–17 ft. lbs. (16–23 Nm).

14. Position the cable routing bracket to the floor pan and install the mounting bolt. Tighten the bolt to 14–19 ft. lbs. (19–25 Nm).

15. Position the cable into the retaining bracket near the equalizer and install the clip.

16. Install the cables into the equalizer and install the cable return spring.

17. Install the rear exhaust pipe and resonator heat shields.

18. Lower the vehicle.

19. Install the adjusting nut.

20. Adjust the parking brake cable and install the parking brake console in the reverse order of removal.

Brake System Bleeding

1. Clean all the dirt from around the master cylinder filler cap.

2. Fill the reservoir with brake fluid. The reservoir must be at least $\frac{3}{4}$ full throughout the bleeding procedure.

3. If the master cylinder is known or suspected to have air in the bore, it must be bled before any wheel cylinders or calipers.

4. To bleed the master cylinder, loosen 1 outlet fitting approximately $\frac{3}{4}$ turn. Have an assistant push the brake pedal down slowly through full travel. Close the outlet fitting, then return the pedal slowly to the full released position. Wait 5 seconds, then repeat the operation until the air bubbles cease to appear.

5. Loosen the other outlet fitting approximately $\frac{3}{4}$ turn and repeat Step 4.

6. To continue to bleed the system, remove the rubber cap dust cap from the wheel cylinder bleeder fitting or caliper fitting. Check to make sure the bleeder fitting is positioned at the upper half on the front of the caliper, if not the caliper is located on the wrong side.

7. Attach a suitable length of rubber hose to the fitting. Submerge the free end of the hose in a container partially filled with clean brake fluid and loosen the bleeder fitting approximately $\frac{3}{4}$ of a turn.

8. Have the assistant push brake pedal down slowly through full travel. Close the bleeder fitting, then return the pedal to the full release position. Wait 5 seconds, then repeat this operation until the air bubbles cease to appear at the submerged end of the bleeder hose.

9. When the fluid is completely free of air bubbles, properly tighten the bleeder fitting and reinstall the rubber dust cap. Repeat this process

on the opposite diagonal system. Refill the master cylinder reservoir after each wheel cylinder or caliper is bled and reinstall the master cylinder cap.

NOTE: If all wheels are to be bled, proceed as follows: right rear, left front, left rear and right front.

10. When the bleeding operation is completed, the fluid level should be filled to the maximum fill level indicated on the reservoir. Always ensure the disc brake pistons are returned to their normal positions by depressing the brake pedal several times until the normal pedal travel is established. Check the pedal feel. If the pedal feels spongy, repeat the bleeding procedure.

Anti-Lock Brake System Service

PRECAUTIONS

• Certain components within the ABS system are not intended to be serviced or repaired individually. Only those components with removal and installation procedures should be serviced.

• Do not use rubber hoses or other parts not specifically specified for and ABS system. When using repair kits, replace all parts included in the kit. Partial or incorrect repair may lead to functional problems and require the replacement of components.

• Lubricate rubber parts with clean, fresh brake fluid to ease assembly. Do not use lubricated shop air to clean parts; damage to rubber components may result.

• Use only DOT 3 brake fluid from an unopened container.

• If any hydraulic component or line is removed or replaced, it may be necessary to bleed the entire system.

• A clean repair area is essential. Always clean the reservoir and cap thoroughly before removing the cap. The slightest amount of dirt in the fluid may plug an orifice and impair the system function. Perform repairs after components have been thoroughly cleaned; use only denatured alcohol to clean components. Do not allow ABS components to come into contact with any substance containing mineral oil; this includes used shop rags.

• The Anti-Lock control unit is a microprocessor similar to other computer units in the vehicle. Ensure that the ignition switch is **OFF** before removing or installing controller harnesses. Avoid static electricity discharge at or near the controller.

• If any arc welding is to be done on the vehicle, the ALCU connectors should be disconnected before welding operations begin.

Hydraulic Actuator Assembly

REMOVAL AND INSTALLATION

1. Disconnect the battery terminals. Remove the battery and the battery tray. Remove the acid shield.
2. Label and disconnect the electrical connectors from the hydraulic actuator.
3. Label and disconnect the brake fluid tubes from the hydraulic actuator.
4. Loosen the front nut and the 2 rear nuts; then, remove the hydraulic actuator.

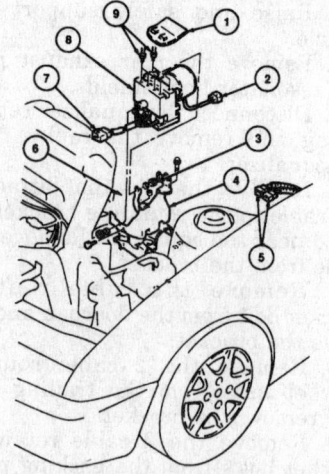

Item	Part Number	Description
1	—	Acid Shield
2	—	Electrical Connector
3	—	Nut
4	—	Hydraulic Anti-Lock Actuator Assembly Bracket
5	—	Electrical Connector
6	—	Nut
7	—	Electrical Connector
8	2C257	Hydraulic Anti-Lock Actuator Assembly
9	—	Brake Tube

85697001

Exploded view the hydraulic anti-lock actuator assembly — 1994–95 Escort and Tracer

To install:
5. Position the hydraulic actuator in the vehicle and make sure the electrical connectors are properly routed.
6. Install the brake fluid tubes to the hydraulic actuator and torque the fittings to 10–16 inch lbs. (13–22 Nm).
7. Connect both electrical connectors.
8. Install the acid shield, the battery tray and the battery. Connect the battery terminals.
9. Bleed the brake system.

Anti-Lock Brake Pressure Control Valve

REMOVAL AND INSTALLATION

The brake pressure control valve regulates the hydraulic pressure to the rear brake circuit. It is located on the cowl and reduces the hydraulic brake pressure to the rear brake circuit.
1. Disconnect the negative battery cable.
2. Using a tubing wrench, loosen the 4 brake tubes at the brake pressure control valve and the 2 brake tubes at the brake master cylinder.
3. Remove the brake tubes between the brake pressure control valve and the brake master cylinder.
4. Disconnect all brake tubes from the brake pressure control valve.
5. Remove the brake pressure control valve-to-cowl bolts and the valve.
To install:
6. Position the brake pressure control valve on the cowl and loosely install a bolt.

NOTE: The brake pressure control valve is equipped with R marks which should be facing the driver's side.

7. Loosely install the brake tubes to the brake pressure control valve and the master cylinder.
8. Install the other bolt to the brake pressure control valve and torque the bolts to 14–17 ft. lbs. (19–23 Nm).
9. Torque the brake tube fittings to 10–16 ft. lbs. (13–22 Nm).
10. Connect the negative battery cable. Bleed the brake system.

NOTE: If the system is being manually bled, bleed the brake tubes at the brake pressure control valve 1st and then at the wheels.

Anti-Lock Brake Control Module

REMOVAL AND INSTALLATION

The brake control module is located under the passenger's seat.

——— **CAUTION** ———
The electronic module is sensitive to static electrical charges. If exposed to these charges, damage may result.

1. Disconnect the negative battery cable. Remove the passenger's seat.
2. Disconnect the electrical connectors from the anti-lock brake control module.
3. Remove the 3 anti-lock brake control module-to-vehicle bolts and the module.

To install:

4. Install the anti-lock brake control module and torque the bolts to 61–86 inch lbs. (7–10 Nm).
5. Connect the electrical connectors to the anti-lock brake control module.
6. Install the passenger's seat and connect the negative battery cable.

Anti-Lock Brake Relay

REMOVAL AND INSTALLATION

The brake relay is located on the front left side of the engine compartment, next to the radiator coolant recovery reservoir.

1. Disconnect the negative battery cable.
2. Remove the air cleaner. Remove the air cleaner intake tube bolt and the intake tube.
3. Remove the anti-lock relay bracket bolts.

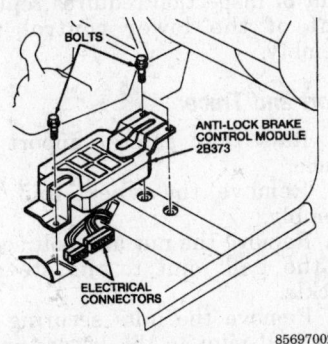

Exploded view the anti-lock brake control module — 1994–95 Escort and Tracer

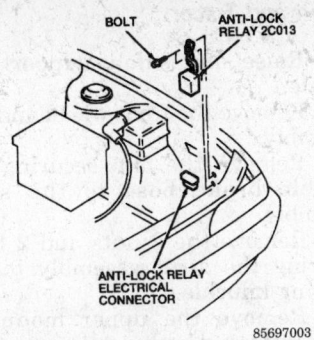

Exploded view the anti-lock relay — 1994–95 Escort and Tracer

4. Disconnect the anti-lock relay electrical connector and remove the relay.
5. To install, reverse the removal procedures and torque the relay bracket bolts to 61–86 inch lbs. (7–10 Nm).

Anti-Lock Brake Sensor

REMOVAL AND INSTALLATION

Front Sensor

1. Disconnect the negative battery cable. For left front sensor, it may be necessary to remove the battery.
2. From inside the engine compartment, near the strut tower, disconnect the sensor's electrical connector. Pinch grommet's sides and push the grommet through the hole in the shock tower.
3. Raise and safely support the front of the vehicle. Remove the wheel and tire assembly.
4. Remove the sensor's wiring clip from the bracket on the wheel well. Remove the upper wiring harness bracket from the bracket on the wheel well.
5. Remove the wiring harness clip from the bracket on the front shock absorber. Remove the lower wiring harness bracket from the bracket on the front shock absorber.
6. Remove sensor-to-steering knuckle bolts and the sensor.

To install:

7. Install the sensor-to-steering knuckle and torque the bolts to 12–17 ft. lbs. (16–23 Nm).
8. Install the wiring harness into lower and upper brackets and secure with the clips.
9. Install the wheel and tire assembly; torque the wheel hub nuts to 65–87 ft. lbs. (88–118 Nm).
10. Connect the wiring harness electrical connector. Connect the negative battery cable.

Rear Sensor

1. Disconnect the negative battery cable. Remove the rear quarter trim panel.
2. Disconnect the rear sensor's electrical connector. Pinch grommet's sides and push the grommet through the hole in the chassis.
3. Raise and safely support the rear of the vehicle. Remove the wheel and tire assembly.
4. Remove the sensor's wiring clip from the upper and lower brackets.
5. Remove sensor-to-rear knuckle bolts and the sensor.

To install:

6. Install the sensor-to-rear knuckle and torque the bolts to 12–17 ft. lbs. (16–23 Nm).
7. Install the wiring harness into lower and upper brackets and secure with the clips.
8. Install the wheel and tire assembly; torque the wheel hub nuts to 65–87 ft. lbs. (88–118 Nm).
9. Connect the wiring harness electrical connector. Connect the negative battery cable.

FRONT SUSPENSION

MacPherson Strut

REMOVAL AND INSTALLATION

Tempo and Topaz

NOTE: All vehicles are equipped with gas pressurized shock absorbers which will extend unassisted. Do not apply heat or flame to the shock strut tube during removal.

1. Loosen but do not remove the 2 top mount-to-shock tower nuts.
2. Raise and safely support the vehicle. Raise vehicle to a point where it is possible to reach the 2 top mount-to-shock tower nuts and the strut-to-knuckle pinch bolt.
3. Remove wheel and tire assembly.
4. Remove brake flex line-to-strut bolt.
5. Remove strut-to-knuckle pinch bolt.
6. Using a suitable tool, spread knuckle-to-strut pinch joint slightly.
7. Using a suitable bar, place top of bar under fender apron and pry down on knuckle until strut sepa-

rates from knuckle. Be careful not to pinch brake hose.

NOTE: Do not pry against caliper or brake hose bracket.

8. Remove 2 top mount-to-shock tower nuts and remove strut from vehicle.

———— **WARNING** ————
Attempting to remove the spring from the strut without first compressing the spring with a tool designed for that purpose could cause bodily injury.

9. Install spring compressor in bench mount, install strut in compressor and compress spring.

10. Place deep 18mm socket on strut shaft nut. Insert an 8mm deep socket with ¼ inch drive wrench. Remove top shaft mounting nut from shaft while holding ¼ inch drive socket with a suitable extension.

NOTE: Do not attempt to remove shaft nut by turning shaft and holding nut. The nut must be turned and the shaft held to avoid possible damage to the shaft.

11. Loosen spring compressor tool and remove top mount bracket assembly, bearing, insulator and spring.
To install:
12. Install replacement strut in spring compressor.

NOTE: During reassembly of strut/spring assembly, be certain to follow correct sequence and proper positioning of bearing plate and seal assembly. If bearing and seal assembly are out of position, damage to the bearing will result.

13. Install spring, insulator, bearing and top mount bracket assembly.

14. Install top shaft mounting nut while holding shaft with ¼ drive 8mm deep socket and extension. Tighten nut to 35–50 ft. lbs. (48–68 Nm).

15. Install strut assembly in vehicle. Install 2 top mount-to-shock tower nuts. Tighten to 25–30 ft. lbs. (37–41 Nm).

16. Slide strut mounting flange onto knuckle.

17. Install strut-to-knuckle pinch bolt. Tighten to 68–80 ft. lbs. (92–110 Nm).

18. Install brake flex line-to-strut bolt.

19. Install wheel and tire assembly.

20. Lower vehicle.

21. Check alignment.

Escort and Tracer

1. Raise and safely support the vehicle.

2. Remove the front wheel and tire assembly.

3. Remove the clip securing the flexible brake hose to the strut assembly.

4. Remove the 2 nuts and 2 bolts securing the strut assembly to the steering knuckle.

5. Remove the upper mounting block nuts and remove the strut assembly from the vehicle.

6. Remove the cap from the top of the strut assembly.

7. Secure the strut assembly mounting block in a vise. Turn the piston rod nut 1 revolution to loosen.

———— **CAUTION** ————
Attempting to remove the spring from the strut without first compressing the spring with a tool designed for that purpose could cause bodily injury.

8. Install an appropriate spring compressor onto the strut spring and compress the spring.

9. Remove the nut, mounting block, thrust bearing, upper spring seat, rubber spring seat, coil spring and bound stopper.
To install:
10. Position the bound stopper onto the strut piston rod.

11. With the coil spring compressed, position the spring onto the strut assembly.

12. Install the rubber spring seat, upper spring seat, thrust bearing, mounting block and piston rod nut. Tighten the piston rod nut to 58–81 ft. lbs. (79–110 Nm).

13. With the nut tightened to specification, carefully remove the spring compressor from the spring while making sure the spring is properly seated in the upper and lower spring seats.

14. Install the cap.

15. Position the strut assembly into the wheel housing. Make sure the direction indicator on the mounting block faces inboard.

16. Secure the upper mounting block to the strut tower with the 4 nuts. Tighten the nuts to 22–30 ft. lbs. (29–40 Nm).

17. Attach the strut assembly to the steering knuckle and install the bolts and nuts. Tighten to 69–93 ft. lbs. (93–127 Nm).

18. Position the flexible brake hose to the strut assembly and secure it with the brake hose clip.

19. Install the front wheel and tire assembly. Tighten the lug nuts to 65–87 ft. lbs. (88–118 Nm).

20. Lower the vehicle and check the front wheel alignment.

Lower Ball Joints

INSPECTION

Tempo and Topaz

1. Raise and safely support the vehicle so wheels are in the full-down position.

2. Have an assistant grasp lower edge of the tire and move wheel and tire assembly in and out.

3. As wheel is being moved in and out, observe lower end of knuckle and lower control arm. Any movement indicates abnormal ball joint wear.

4. If any movement is observed, install new lower control arm assembly.

Escort and Tracer

1. Remove the lower ball joint.

2. Secure the ball joint bracket in a vise.

3. Thread the ball joint attaching nut onto the ball joint stud until the nut bottoms out on the stud.

4. Install a torque wrench onto the nut and measure the torque required to keep the stud in motion. The correct turning torque is 14–25 ft. lbs. (20–34 Nm).

5. If the turning torque is not within specification, replace the ball joint.

REMOVAL AND INSTALLATION

Tempo and Topaz

The lower ball joint is integral to the lower control assembly and cannot be serviced individually. Any movement of the lower ball joint detected as a result of inspection requires replacement of the lower control arm assembly.

Escort and Tracer

1. Raise and safely support the vehicle.

2. Remove the wheel and tire assembly.

3. Remove the nut and bolt securing the ball joint to the steering knuckle.

4. Remove the nuts securing the lower ball joint to the lower control arm. Remove the lower ball joint.

5. Mount the lower ball joint in a vise.

6. Place a suitable chisel between the ball joint and the dust boot. Lightly tap on the chisel to separate the dust boot from the ball joint.

To install:

7. Position the dust boot over the ball joint and, using a suitable tool, press down on the tool to secure the dust boot to the ball joint.

8. Install the ball joint into the lower control arm and install the mounting nuts. Tighten the nuts to 69–86 ft. lbs. (93–117 Nm).

9. Install the lower ball joint into the steering knuckle and secure it with the nut and bolt. Tighten the nut to 32–43 ft. lbs. (43–59 Nm). Apply Loctite® to the nut and bolt threads prior to installation.

10. Install the wheel and tire assembly and lower the vehicle.

Lower Control Arms

REMOVAL AND INSTALLATION

Tempo and Topaz

1. Raise and safely support the vehicle.
2. Remove nut from stabilizer bar end. Pull off large dished washer.
3. Remove lower control arm inner pivot nut and bolt.
4. Remove lower control arm ball joint pinch bolt. Using a suitable tool, slightly spread knuckle pinch joint and separate control arm from steering knuckle. A drift punch may be used to remove bolt.

— **CAUTION** —
Do not allow the steering knuckle/halfshaft to move outward. Over extension of the tripod CV-joint could result in separation of internal parts, causing failure of the joint.

5. Remove stabilizer bar spacer from the arm bushing.

NOTE: Make sure steering column is in unlocked position. Do not use a hammer to separate ball joint from knuckle.

To install:

6. Assemble lower control arm ball joint stud to the steering knuckle, ensuring that the ball stud groove is properly positioned.
7. Insert a new pinch bolt and nut. Tighten to 38–40 ft. lbs. (52–55 Nm).
8. Insert stabilizer bar spacer into arm bushing with flange facing forward.

9. Clean stabilizer bar threads to remove dirt and contamination.
10. Position lower control arm onto stabilizer bar and position lower control arm to the inner underbody mounting. Install a new nut and bolt. Tighten to 48–55 ft. lbs. (65–74 Nm).
11. Assemble stabilizer bar, dished washer and a new nut to stabilizer. Tighten nut to 98–115 ft. lbs. (132–156 Nm).
12. Lower vehicle.

Escort and Tracer

1. Raise and safely support the vehicle.
2. Remove the front wheel and tire assembly.
3. Remove the front stabilizer nuts, washers, bushings, bolts and sleeves.
4. Remove the lower control arm front bushing bolt and washer.
5. Remove the bolts securing the lower control arm rear bushing retaining strap.
6. Remove the nut and bolt securing the lower ball joint to the steering knuckle. Separate the steering knuckle from the lower ball joint.
7. Remove the lower control arm.
8. Remove the nut and washers from the lower control arm rear pivot bolt.
9. Remove the lower control arm rear bushing.

To install:

10. Position the lower control arm rear bushing onto the rear pivot bolt.
11. Install the washers and nut onto the lower control arm pivot bolt. Tighten the nut to 69–86 ft. lbs. (93–117 Nm).
12. Install the ball joint into the steering knuckle. Install the ball joint retaining nut and bolt and tighten the nut to 32–43 ft. lbs. (43–59 Nm). Apply Loctite® to the nut and bolt threads prior to installation.
13. Install the lower control arm rear bushing retaining strap to the lower frame. Install the bolts and tighten to 69–86 ft. lbs. (93–117 Nm).
14. Install the lower control arm front pivot bolt and washer. Tighten the nut to 69–93 ft. lbs. (93–127 Nm).
15. Install the stabilizer bolts, washers, bushings, sleeves and nuts. Tighten the stabilizer nuts so 0.67–0.75 in. (17–19mm) of thread is exposed at the end of the bolt.
16. Install the wheel and tire assembly. Tighten the lug nuts to 65–87 ft. lbs. (88–118 Nm).
17. Lower the vehicle.

Stabilizer Bar

REMOVAL AND INSTALLATION

Tempo and Topaz

1. Raise and safely support the vehicle.
2. Remove nut from stabilizer bar at each lower control arm and pull off large dished washer. Discard nuts.
3. Remove stabilizer bar insulator U-bracket bolts and U-brackets and remove stabilizer bar assembly. Discard bolts.

NOTE: Stabilizer bar U-bracket insulators can be serviced without removing the stabilizer bar assembly.

To install:

4. Slide new insulators onto the stabilizer bar and position them in the approximate location.
5. Clean stabilizer bar threads to remove dirt and contamination.
6. Install spacers into the control arm bushings from forward side of control arm so washer end of spacer will seat against stabilizer bar machined shoulder and push mounting brackets over insulators.
7. Insert end of stabilizer bar into the lower control arms. Using new bolts, attach the stabilizer bar and the insulator U-brackets to the bracket assemblies. Hand start all 4 U-bracket bolts. Tighten all bolts halfway, then tighten bolts to 82–88 ft. lbs. (110–120 Nm).
8. Using new nuts and the original dished washers (dished side away from bushing), attach the stabilizer bar to the lower control arm. Tighten nuts to 99–112 ft. lbs. (133–153 Nm).
9. Lower vehicle.

Escort and Tracer

1. Support the engine with engine support D88L–6000–A or equivalent.
2. Raise and safely support the vehicle.
3. Remove the front wheel and tire assemblies.
4. Remove the nuts securing the steering gear mounting brackets and position the steering gear slightly forward.
5. Remove the stabilizer bar nuts, washers, bushings, sleeves and bolts from the lower control arm.
6. Remove the rear crossmember nuts from the rear transaxle mount and the vehicle frame.
7. Loosen the front crossmember bolts and nuts from the front transaxle mount and the vehicle frame.

Lower the rear end of the crossmember.

8. Remove the nuts and bolts securing the chassis frame to the vehicle frame. Lower the chassis frame.

NOTE: The engine and transaxle mounts will support the chassis frame when unbolting the chassis frame from the vehicle frame.

9. Unbolt the stabilizer bar from the chassis frame and remove the stabilizer bar from the vehicle.

To install:
10. Position the stabilizer bar into the vehicle.
11. Secure the stabilizer bar to the chassis frame with the bolts. Tighten the bolts to 32–43 ft. lbs. (43–59 Nm).
12. Install the chassis frame to the vehicle frame with the bolts and nuts. Tighten the bolts and nuts to 69–93 ft. lbs. (93–127 Nm).
13. Position the crossmember to the vehicle frame and the transaxle mounts. Tighten the bolts and nuts to the specified torque.
14. Install the stabilizer bar bolts, sleeves, bushings, washers and nuts. Tighten the stabilizer bolts so 0.67–0.75 in. (17–19mm) of thread is exposed at the end of the bolt.
15. Position the steering gear and secure it with the brackets and nuts. Tighten the nuts to 28–38 ft. lbs. (37–52 Nm).
16. Install the wheel and tire assemblies. Tighten the lug nuts to 65–87 ft. lbs. (88–118 Nm).
17. Lower the vehicle and remove the engine support.

REAR SUSPENSION

MacPherson Strut

REMOVAL AND INSTALLATION

Escort and Tracer

1. Raise and safely support the vehicle.
2. Remove the wheel and tire assembly.
3. Remove the clip securing the flexible brake hose to the rear strut assembly.
4. Remove the nuts and bolts securing the rear strut assembly to the rear wheel spindle assembly.

5. On hatchback and wagon, remove the quarter lower trim panel.
6. Remove the mounting block nuts and remove the rear strut assembly from the vehicle.
7. Position the strut assembly into a vise and secure the assembly at the mounting block.
8. Remove the cap and loosen the piston rod nut 1 turn. Do not remove the piston rod nut at this time.

— **CAUTION** —
Attempting to remove the spring from the strut without first compressing the spring with a tool designed for that purpose could cause bodily injury.

9. Install an appropriate coil spring compressor onto the coil spring and compress the coil spring.
10. Remove the piston rod nut, washer, retainer and mounting block.
11. Remove the coil spring.
12. Remove the bound stopper seat and stopper from the strut piston.

To install:
13. Position the strut assembly into a vise and secure.
14. Install the bound stopper seat and stopper onto the strut piston rod.
15. Install the coil spring onto the strut assembly.
16. Install the mounting block, then align the mounting block studs and the lower bracket of the strut assembly.
17. Install the retainer, washer and piston rod nut. Tighten the nut to 41–50 ft. lbs. (55–68 Nm).
18. Make sure the spring is properly aligned and carefully release the spring into the seats of the strut.
19. Remove the spring compressor from the coil spring and install the cap.
20. Position the strut assembly into the vehicle wheel housing.
21. Install the mounting block nuts and tighten to 22–27 ft. lbs. (29–40 Nm).
22. On hatchback and wagon, install the quarter lower trim panel.
23. Install the nuts and bolts securing the strut assembly to the rear spindle assembly. Tighten the lower strut bolts to 69–93 ft. lbs. (93–127 Nm).
24. Install the clip securing the flexible brake hose to the rear strut assembly.
25. Install the wheel and tire assembly. Tighten the lug nuts to 65–87 ft. lbs. (88–118 Nm).
26. Check the rear alignment and lower the vehicle.

Tempo and Topaz

NOTE: All Tempo and Topaz vehicles are equipped with gas-pressurized shock absorbers which will extend unassisted. Do not apply heat or flame to the shock strut during removal.

1. Open luggage compartment and loosen but do not remove, 2 nuts retaining the upper strut mount to body.
2. Raise and safely support the vehicle. Remove the wheel and tire assembly.
3. Place a jackstand under the control arms to support the suspension.

NOTE: Care should be taken when removing the strut that the rear brake flex hose is not stretched or the steel brake tube is not bent.

4. Remove bolt attaching brake hose bracket to strut and move it aside.
5. Remove 2 bolts attaching shock strut to spindle.
6. Remove 2 upper mount-to-body nuts.
7. Remove strut from vehicle.
8. Place strut, spring and upper mount assembly in spring compressor.

— **CAUTION** —
Attempting to remove the spring from the strut without first compressing the spring with a tool designed for that purpose could cause bodily injury.

NOTE: Do not attempt to remove shaft nut by turning shaft and holding nut. Nut must be turned and shaft held to avoid possible fracture of shaft at base of hex.

9. With the spring compressed, remove strut shaft-to-mount nut and then remove spring, strut and mount from compressor tool.
To install:
10. With spring compressed, install spring, spring insulator, top mount and upper washer on strut shaft.
11. Ensure spring is properly located in upper and lower spring seats. The spring end must be within 0.39 in. (10mm) of the step in the spring seat.
12. Tighten shaft nut to 35–46 ft. lbs. (47–63 Nm). Use 18mm deep socket to turn the nut and ¼ inch drive 8mm deep socket to hold shaft so it will not turn while tightening nut.

13. Insert 2 upper mount studs into strut tower and hand start 2 new nuts. Do not tighten at this time.

14. Position spindle into lower strut mount and install 2 new bolts. Tighten to 85–96 ft. lbs. (115–130 Nm).

15. Install brake flex-hose bracket on the strut.

16. Install wheel and tire assembly.

17. Remove jackstand and lower vehicle to the ground.

18. Tighten 2 top mount-to-body nuts to 23–29 ft. lbs. (30–40 Nm).

Rear Control Arms

REMOVAL AND INSTALLATION

Escort and Tracer

1. Raise and safely support the vehicle.

2. Remove the wheel and tire assembly.

3. Remove the stabilizer nuts, washers, bushings, sleeves and bolts.

4. Remove the bolts securing the stabilizer bar brackets and grommets to the rear suspension crossmember.

5. Remove the stabilizer bar.

6. Remove the cap covering the front and rear lateral link pivot bolts.

7. Position a floor jackstand under the rear suspension crossmember.

8. Remove the bolts securing the rear suspension crossmember to the vehicle frame.

9. Lower the floor jackstand to allow the rear suspension crossmember to be lowered from the vehicle frame.

10. Remove the front and rear lateral link pivot nut, washer and bolt from the rear suspension crossmember.

11. Remove the front and rear lateral links from the rear suspension crossmember.

12. Remove the bolt, washers and nut securing the front and rear lateral links to the rear wheel spindle and remove the lateral links.

13. Remove the nuts securing the parking brake cable and cable bracket to the trailing link.

14. Remove the rear trailing link bolts and washers from the vehicle frame and rear wheel spindle. Remove the rear trailing link.
To install:

15. Position the rear trailing link and install the bolts and washers. Tighten the trailing link front bolt to 46–69 ft. lbs. (63–93 Nm) and the rear bolt to 69–93 ft. lbs. (93–127 Nm).

16. Position the parking brake cable and bracket to the trailing link and secure it with the nuts.

17. Position the front and rear lateral links to the rear wheel spindle and install the washers, bolt and nut. Tighten the front and rear lateral link nut at the rear wheel spindle to 63–86 ft. lbs. (85–117 Nm).

18. Position the front and rear lateral links to the rear suspension crossmember. Tighten the front and rear lateral link nut at the rear suspension crossmember to 50–70 ft. lbs. (68–95 Nm).

19. Install the cap.

20. Raise the floor jackstand to position the rear suspension crossmember to the vehicle frame. Install and tighten the bolts. Remove the floor jackstand from under the vehicle.

21. Position the grommets onto the stabilizer bar and align the grommets to the positions painted on the bar.

22. Position the stabilizer bar to the rear suspension crossmember and secure it in place with the straps and bolts. Tighten the bolts to 32–43 ft. lbs. (43–59 Nm).

23. Install the stabilizer bolts, washers, grommets, sleeves and nuts. Tighten the stabilizer nuts so 0.64–0.72 in. (16.2–17.0mm) of thread is exposed at the end of the bolt.

24. Install the wheel and tire assembly. Tighten the lug nuts to 65–87 ft. lbs. (88–118 Nm).

25. Check the wheel alignment and lower the vehicle.

Tempo and Topaz

1. Raise and safely support the vehicle.

2. Remove and discard arm-to-spindle bolt and nut.

3. Remove and discard center retaining bolt and nut.

4. Remove arm from vehicle.
To install:

NOTE: When installing new control arms, the bushing with the 0.39 in. (10mm) hole is installed to the center of the vehicle and the bushing with the 0.48 in. (12mm) hole is installed to the spindle. The offset on the arm must face up on the right side of the vehicle and down on the left side of the vehicle. The flange edge of the arm stamping must also face the rear of the vehicle.

5. Position arm at center of vehicle and insert new bolt and nut. Do not tighten at this time.

6. Move arm end up to spindle and insert new bolt, washer and nut. Ensure bolt engages both arms and spindle.

7. Tighten arm-to-body bolt to 41–46 ft. lbs. (55–63 Nm).

8. Tighten arm-to-spindle nut to 60–80 ft. lbs. (81–109 Nm).

9. Lower vehicle.

Rear Wheel Bearings

REMOVAL AND INSTALLATION

Except Tempo and Topaz with AWD and Escort and Tracer

1. Raise and safely support the vehicle.

2. Remove wheel and tire assembly. Remove grease cap from hub.

3. Remove cotter pin, nut retainer, adjusting nut and flat washer from spindle. Discard cotter pin.

4. Pull hub and drum assembly off spindle being careful not to drop outer bearing assembly.

5. Remove outer bearing assembly.

6. Using seal remover, remove and discard grease seal. Remove inner bearing assembly from hub.

7. Wipe all lubricant from spindle and inside of hub. Cover spindle with a clean cloth and vacuum all loose dust and dirt from brake assembly. Carefully remove cloth to prevent dirt from falling on spindle.

8. Clean both bearing assemblies and, cups using solvent. inspect bearing assemblies and cups for excessive wear, scratches, pits or other damage. Replace all worn or damaged parts as required.

NOTE: Allow solvent to dry before repacking bearings. Do not spin-dry bearings with air pressure.

9. If cups are replaced, remove them with wheel hub cup remover D80L–927–A and bearing cup puller T77F–1102–A or equivalent.
To install:

10. If inner or outer bearing cups were removed, install replacement cups using driver handle T80T–4000–W and bearing cup replacers T77F–1202–A and T73T–1217–A or equivalent. Support drum hub on wood block to prevent

damage. Insure cups are properly seated in hub.

NOTE: Do not use cone and roller assembly to install cup as this will cause damage to bearing cup and cone and roller assembly.

11. Ensure all spindle and bearing surfaces are clean.

12. Using a bearing packer, pack bearing assemblies with a suitable wheel bearing grease. If a packer is not available, work in as much grease as possible between the rollers and the cages. Grease the cup surfaces.

13. Place inner bearing cone and roller assembly in inner cup. Apply light film of grease to lips of a new grease seal and install seal with rear hub seal replacer T81P–1249–A or equivalent. Ensure retainer flange is seated all around.

14. Apply light film of grease on spindle shaft bearing surfaces.

15. Install hub and drum assembly on spindle. Keep hub centered on spindle to prevent damage to grease seal and spindle threads.

16. Install outer bearing assembly and keyed flat washer on spindle. Install adjusting nut finger-tight. Adjust wheel bearings. Install a new cotter pin and install grease cap.

17. Install wheel and tire on drum.

18. Lower vehicle.

Tempo and Topaz with AWD

1. Raise and support the vehicle safely. Remove the tire and wheel assembly.

2. Remove the brake drum. Remove the parking brake cable from the brake backing plate.

3. Remove the brake line from the wheel cylinder. Remove the outboard U-joint retaining bolts. Remove the outboard end of the halfshaft from the wheel stub shaft yoke and wire it to the control arm.

4. Remove and discard the control arm to spindle bolt, washer and nut. Remove the tie rod nut, bushing and washer and discard the nut.

5. Remove and discard the 2 bolts retaining the spindle to the strut. Remove the spindle from the vehicle. Mount the spindle and backing plate assembly in a suitable vise.

6. Remove the cotter pin and nut attaching the stub shaft yoke to the stub shaft. Discard the cotter pin.

7. Remove the spindle and backing plate assembly from the vise. Remove the stub shaft yoke using a 2 jaw puller and shaft protector. After removing end yoke from spindle as-

sembly, inspect the nylon bushing and replace, as necessary.

8. Position the spindle and backing plate assembly into a vise and remove the wheel stub shaft.

9. Remove the snapring retaining the bearing. Remove the bolts retaining the spindle to the backing plate and remove the backing plate.

10. Remove the spindle from the vise and mount it into a suitable press. With the spindle side facing upward, carefully press out the bearing from the spindle, using a driver handle and bearing cup driver. Discard the bearing after removal.

To install:

11. Mount the spindle in a press, spindle side facing down. Position a new bearing in the outboard side of the spindle and carefully press in the new bearing using a driver handle and bearing installer.

12. Remove the spindle from the press and mount it in a vise. Install the snapring retaining the bearing. Position the backing plate to the spindle and install the retaining bolts.

13. Install the wheel stub shaft. Install the stub shaft yoke and attaching nut. Torque the nut to 120–150 ft. lbs. (163–204 Nm) install a new cotter pin.

14. Remove the spindle and backing plate assembly from the vise. Position the spindle onto the tie rod and then into the strut lower bracket. Insert 2 new strut-to-spindle bolts. Do not tighten at this time.

15. Install the tie rod bushing washer and new nut. Install the new control arm to spindle bolt, washers and nut. Do not tighten them at this time.

16. Install a jackstand to support the suspension at the normal curb height before tightening the fasteners.

17. Torque the spindle to strut bolts to 70–96 ft. lbs. (95–130 Nm). Torque the tie rod nut to 52–74 ft. lbs. (71–101 Nm). Torque the control arm to spindle nut to 60–86 ft. lbs. (82–117 Nm).

18. Position the outboard end of the halfshaft to the wheel stub shaft yoke. Install the retaining caps and bolts and torque them to 15–17 ft. lbs.

19. Install the brake line to wheel cylinder. Install the parking brake cable and brake drum. Install the wheel assembly, torque the lugs nuts to 80–105 ft. lbs. (109–140 Nm).

20. Lower the vehicle and bleed the brake system. Check and adjust the toe, if necessary.

Escort and Tracer

1. Raise and safely support the vehicle.

2. Remove the wheel and tire assembly.

3. Remove the brake drum or brake caliper and rotor, as necessary.

4. Remove the nut securing the rear wheel hub to the spindle and remove the hub and bearing assembly.

To install:

5. Install the rear wheel hub and bearing assembly onto the spindle.

6. Install the hub nut onto the spindle and tighten to 130–174 ft. lbs. (177–235 Nm).

7. Stake the hub nut and install the cap.

8. Install the brake drum or the brake caliper and rotor, as necessary.

9. Install the wheel and tire assembly. Tighten the lug nuts to 65–87 ft. lbs. (88–118 Nm).

10. Lower the vehicle.

ADJUSTMENT

Except Tempo and Topaz with AWD and Escort and Tracer

1. Raise and safely support the vehicle.

2. Remove wheel cover or ornament and nut covers. Remove grease cap from hub.

3. Remove cotter pin and nut retainer. Discard cotter pin.

4. Back-off adjusting nut 1 full turn. Ensure nut turns freely on spindle threads. Correct any binding condition.

5. Tighten adjusting nut to 17–25 ft. lbs. (23–34 Nm) while rotating hub and drum assembly to seat bearings. Loosen adjusting nut ½ turn and tighten adjusting nut to 24–28 inch lbs. (2.7–3.2 Nm) using inch lb. torque wrench.

6. Position adjusting nut retainer over adjusting nut so slots in nut retainer flange are in line with cotter pin hole in spline.

7. Install a new cotter pin and bend ends around retainer flange.

8. Check hub rotation. If hub rotates freely, install grease cap. If not, check bearings for damage and replace as necessary.

9. Install wheel and tire assembly, wheel cover or ornaments, and nut covers as required.

10. Lower vehicle.

Tempo and Topaz with AWD

Bearings on 4WD vehicles are not adjustable.

Ford Motor Company

6

FORD—Festiva

FIRING ORDERS

NOTE: To avoid confusion, always replace spark plug wires one at a time.

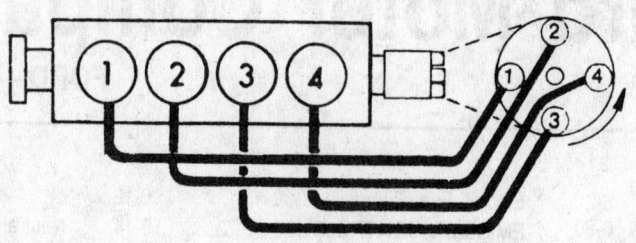

84708001

1.3L Engine
Engine Firing Order 1–3–4–2
Distributor Rotation: Counterclockwise

ENGINE ELECTRICAL

NOTE: Disconnecting the negative battery cable on some vehicles may interfere with the functions of the on-board computer systems and may require the computer to undergo a relearning process, once the negative battery cable is reconnected.

Distributor

REMOVAL

1. Disconnect the negative battery cable.
2. Disconnect the coil wire from the distributor.
3. Remove the distributor cap attaching screws, pull off the distributor cap and position it aside.

NOTE: If replacing the distributor cap, mark the distributor cap towers with the cylinder numbers before removing the spark plug wires, to aid reinstallation.

4. Disconnect the distributor electrical connector.
5. Scribe a timing reference mark across the distributor mounting flange and cylinder head surface to ensure that the distributor will be installed without altering the timing. Note the position of the rotor.

6. Remove the base flange mounting bolts and remove the distributor assembly from its mounting bore.
7. Remove the flange base O-ring and inspect for damage. Replace the O-ring as required. Coat the O-ring with clean engine oil and install into the flange base.

INSTALLATION

Timing Not Disturbed

1. Insert the distributor assembly into the cylinder head mounting bore. Rotate the distributor until the offset drive tang aligns and engages with the camshaft slot. The rotor position should be the same as when removed.
2. After the distributor is engaged with the camshaft, align the timing reference marks scribed across the flange base and cylinder head. When the timing marks are aligned, install and tighten the mounting bolts to 14–18 ft. lbs. (19–25 Nm).
3. Connect the distributor electrical connector.
4. Install the distributor cap and connect the coil wire. If the spark plug wires were removed, connect them to the proper distributor cap towers, as marked during the removal procedure.
5. Connect the negative battery cable.

Timing Disturbed

1. If the crankshaft was rotated while the distributor was removed, the piston in No. 1 cylinder must be

brought to TDC on the compression stroke.
2. Remove the No. 1 spark plug. Place a finger over the hole and rotate the crankshaft slowly in the direction of normal rotation, until engine compression is felt.

NOTE: Turn the engine only in the direction of normal rotation. Backward rotation may cause the cam belt to slip or lose teeth, altering engine timing.

3. When engine compression is felt at the spark plug hole, indicating that the piston is approaching TDC, continue to turn the crankshaft until the TDC timing mark on the pulley is aligned with the TDC mark on the engine front cover.
4. Insert the distributor assembly into the cylinder head mounting bore. Rotate the distributor until the offset drive tang aligns and engages with the camshaft slot. Install the mounting bolts, leaving them loose enough that the distributor can be moved by hand.
5. Connect the distributor electrical connector.
6. Install the distributor cap and connect the coil wire. If the spark plug wires were removed, connect them to the proper distributor cap towers, as marked during the removal procedure.
7. Connect the negative battery cable. Start the engine and check and adjust the ignition timing. When the timing is set, tighten the distributor mounting bolts to 14–18 ft. lbs. (19–25 Nm).

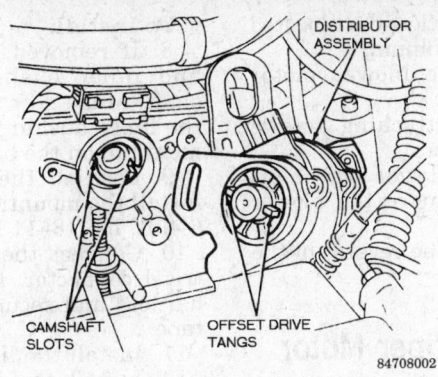

Distributor offset drive tangs and camshaft slots

Ignition Timing

ADJUSTMENT

1. Place the transaxle in **P** or **N**, then make sure the air conditioner and heater fan is **OFF**.

2. Connect an inductive timing light to the No. 1 spark plug wire. Connect a tachometer to the 1-pin white test connector. The connector has a yellow/green wire and is located near the brake master cylinder.

3. Start the engine and allow it to warm up to normal operating temperature.

4. Ground the black 1-pin STI self-test connector (yellow/black wire) located near the brake master cylinder.

5. Check and adjust the idle speed, if necessary.

6. Check the base ignition timing. The white ignition timing mark on the crankshaft pulley should align with the white pointer on the timing belt cover.

7. If the white timing mark and the white pointer do not line up, loosen the distributor mounting bolts and rotate the distributor until the timing marks are properly aligned.

8. Tighten the distributor mounting bolts to 14–18 ft. lbs. (19–25 Nm).

9. Remove the jumper wire connecting the STI connector to ground.

10. Increase the engine rpm and check the timing marks to be sure the ignition timing changes.

11. Remove the timing light and tachometer.

Alternator

PRECAUTIONS

Several precautions must be observed to avoid damage to the alternator.

• If the battery is removed for any reason, make sure it is reconnected with the correct polarity. Reversing the battery connections may result in damage to the one-way rectifiers.

• When utilizing a booster battery as a starting aid, always connect the positive to positive terminals and the negative terminal from the booster battery to a good engine ground on the vehicle being started.

• Never use a fast charger as a booster to start vehicle. Disconnect the battery cables when charging the battery with a fast charger.

• Never attempt to polarize the alternator.

• Do not use test lamps of more than 12 volts when checking diode continuity.

• Do not short across or ground any of the alternator terminals.

• The polarity of the battery, alternator and regulator must be matched and considered before making any electrical connections within the system.

• Never separate the alternator on an open circuit. Make sure all connections within the circuit are clean and tight.

• Disconnect the battery ground terminal when performing any service on electrical components.

• Disconnect the battery if arc welding is to be done on the vehicle.

BELT TENSION ADJUSTMENT

1. Inspect the condition of the drive belt prior to adjustment. If the inspection reveals a severely glazed, frayed, oil contaminated or cracked belt, the belt must be replaced.

2. Loosen the alternator adjustment bolt.

3. Raise the vehicle and support it safely.

4. Loosen the lower alternator mounting/pivot bolt.

5. Lower the vehicle.

6. Position a suitable prybar between the engine and the alternator. Position the bar against the alternator in an area around a case bolt. Do not pry on the stator frame.

7. Adjust the belt tension by prying on the bar. Measure the belt tension using a belt tension gauge or by using the deflection method.

8. If using a belt tension gauge, position the gauge on the longest accessible belt span. The belt tension should be 110–132 lbs. (50–60 Kg) for a new belt or 95–110 lbs. (43–50 Kg) for a used belt (more than 10 minutes running time).

9. If using the deflection method, apply approximately 22 lbs. (10 Kg) of pressure to the middle of the longest accessible belt span. The deflection should be 0.31–0.35 in. (8–9mm) for a new belt or 0.35–0.39 in. (9–10mm) for a used belt (more than 10 minutes running time).

10. When the belt tension is as specified, tighten the adjustment bolt to 14–19 ft. lbs. (19–25 Nm).

11. Raise and safely support the vehicle.

12. Tighten the alternator mounting/pivot bolt to 27–46 ft. lbs. (37–52 Nm).

13. Lower the vehicle.

REMOVAL AND INSTALLATION

1. Disconnect the negative battery cable.

2. If equipped, pull the rubber boot away from the **B** terminal to expose the terminal nut. Remove the nut and electrical lead from the terminal post.

3. Remove the alternator adjusting bracket bolt.

4. Disconnect the remaining electrical connector(s) from the alternator housing.

5. Raise and safely support the vehicle. Remove the alternator mounting/pivot bolt.

6. Disconnect the drive belt from the alternator.

7. Remove the alternator. If necessary, bend the catalytic converter shield brace to allow enough clearance.

8. Installation is the reverse of the removal procedure. Adjust the belt tension and tighten the adjustment bolt to 14–19 ft. lbs. (19–25 Nm) and

the mounting/pivot bolt to 27–46 ft. lbs. (37–52 Nm).

Starter

REMOVAL AND INSTALLATION

Automatic Transaxle

1. Disconnect the negative battery cable.
2. Remove the 2 upper starter mounting bolts.
3. Raise and safely support the vehicle.
4. Remove the 2 bolts that secure the manifold-to-cylinder block bracket, then remove the bracket.
5. Remove the bolt that secures the mounting bracket to the support bracket and remove the support bracket.
6. Remove the 2 nuts and washers that secure the mounting bracket to the starter and remove the mounting bracket.
7. Disconnect the **B** and **S** terminal connectors at the starter solenoid.
8. Remove the lower starter mounting bolt and remove the starter.
9. Installation is the reverse of removal procedure. Tighten the starter mounting bolts to 23–34 ft. lbs. (31–46 Nm).

Manual Transaxle

1. Disconnect the negative battery cable.
2. Disconnect the **B** and **S** terminal connectors at the starter solenoid.
3. Remove the 2 bolts that secure the starter support bracket to the transaxle.
4. Remove the starter mounting bolts and remove the starter.
5. Installation is the reverse of removal procedure. Tighten the starter mounting bolts to 23–34 ft. lbs. (31–46 Nm).

CHASSIS ELECTRICAL

Heater Blower Motor

REMOVAL AND INSTALLATION

1. Disconnect the negative battery cable.

2. Remove the airflow duct located below the steering column.
3. Disconnect the blower motor wiring.
4. Remove the attaching screws and the blower motor.
5. Remove the blower wheel attaching nut and remove the blower wheel and washer.
6. Installation if the reverse of the removal procedure.

Windshield Wiper Motor

REMOVAL AND INSTALLATION

Front

1. Disconnect the negative battery cable. Disconnect the wiring at the wiper motor.
2. Remove the wiper motor attaching bolts.
3. Remove the access plate attaching screws and pull the plate away from the dash panel.
4. Using a suitable tool, pry the linkage pivot off the output arm. Remove the wiper motor from the vehicle.
   To install:
5. Position the motor on the access plate and connect the output arm to the linkage pivot.
6. Position the mounting plate and install the attaching screws.
7. Install the wiper motor attaching bolts and tighten to 61–87 inch lbs. (7–10 Nm). Make sure the ground wire is installed with the top left attaching bolt.
8. Connect the wiper motor wiring connector and the negative battery cable. Check the wiper motor for proper operation and linkage movement.

Rear

1. Disconnect the negative battery cable.
2. Lift the attaching nut cover and remove the wiper arm attaching nut.
3. Carefully pry on the arm to disengage it from the tapered splines on the motor shaft; remove the wiper arm.
4. Remove the boot from the outer bushing attaching nut and remove the nut and bushing.
5. Remove the liftgate trim panel.
6. Peel back the wiring harness routing tape and separate the wiper motor electrical connector.
7. Remove the mounting bolts and the wiper motor. If necessary, remove the inner bushing and O-ring from the motor shaft.

To install:
8. If removed, install the O-ring and inner bushing on the motor shaft. Make sure the locating tab on the inner bushing engages the alignment tab on the brush lead cover tab.
9. Position the wiper motor and install the mounting bolts. Tighten to 6–8 ft. lbs. (8–11 Nm).
10. Connect the wiper motor electrical connector. Position the wiring harness and secure with the routing tape.
11. Install the liftgate trim panel.
12. Install the outer bushing and the attaching nut. Tighten to 2–4 ft. lbs. (3–5 Nm).
13. Install the boot onto the outer bushing attaching nut.
14. Adjust the wiper arm on the motor shaft so that the tip of the wiper blade is 3.14 in. (80.0mm) from the edge of the liftgate window seal. Install the wiper arm, torque the nut to 7 ft. lbs. (10 Nm) and install the cover.
15. Connect the negative battery cable and turn the ignition switch **ON**.
16. Turn the rear wiper motor ON, allow it to cycle several times, then turn it OFF. This will locate the wiper arm shaft in the park position.
17. Turn the ignition switch **OFF**.
18. Install the wiper arm on the motor shaft so the tip of the wiper blade is 3.14 in. (80mm) from the edge of the liftgate window seal.
19. Install the wiper arm attaching nut and tighten to 4–7 ft. lbs. (5.0–9.5 Nm). Push the nut cover downward into position.

Windshield Wiper Switch

REMOVAL AND INSTALLATION

Front

Control of the front wipers is a function of the combination switch.

Rear

1. Disconnect the negative battery cable.
2. Remove the steering column covers.
3. Remove the screws securing the instrument cluster bezel to the instrument panel and pull the bezel away from the instrument panel. Disconnect the electrical connector from the wiper switch.
4. Compress the switch lock tabs and remove it from the bezel.
5. Installation is the reverse of the removal procedure.

Instrument Cluster

REMOVAL AND INSTALLATION

1. Disconnect the battery negative cable.
2. Remove the steering column covers.
3. Remove the screws securing the instrument cluster bezel to the instrument panel.
4. Pull the instrument cluster bezel away from the instrument panel.
5. If equipped with rear window defroster, disconnect the wiring from the switch.
6. If equipped with rear window wiper, disconnect the wiring from the switch.
7. Remove the screws securing the instrument cluster in the instrument panel.
8. Pull the cluster away from the instrument panel.
9. Reach behind the cluster, press the lock tab and disconnect the speedometer cable.
10. Lift the lock tab and disconnect the 2 electrical connectors from the back of the instrument cluster.
11. Remove the instrument cluster from the vehicle.
   To install:
12. Position the instrument cluster in the instrument panel opening.
13. Connect the electrical connectors to the back of the instrument cluster.
14. Connect the speedometer cable.
15. Slide the instrument cluster into the instrument panel.
16. Install and tighten the instrument cluster attaching screws.
17. Position the instrument cluster bezel in the instrument panel opening. If necessary, connect the rear defogger and rear wiper switch wiring.
18. Install and tighten the instrument cluster bezel attaching screws.
19. Install the steering column covers.
20. Connect the negative battery cable.
21. Check the operation of all instruments, gauges and indicator lights.

Speedometer

REMOVAL AND INSTALLATION

1. Disconnect the negative battery cable. Remove the instrument cluster from the vehicle.

2. Remove the odometer reset button, if necessary.
3. Remove the cluster illumination bar attaching screws, remove the screws attaching the illumination bar wiring to the cluster circuit board and remove the bar.
4. Press down on the lock tabs and remove the cluster lens.
5. Remove the circuit board attaching screws and remove the circuit board and gauges from the cluster housing.
6. Remove the speedometer.
7. Installation is the reverse of the removal procedure. Check the speedometer for proper operation.

Combination Switch

The combination switch controls the windshield wiper, turn signal and headlight operation. The headlight and turn signal stalk can be serviced separately.

REMOVAL AND INSTALLATION

1. Disconnect the negative battery cable.
2. Remove the steering wheel.
3. Remove the attaching screws from the upper half of the lower steering column cover, then remove the cover half.
4. Remove the upper steering column cover.
5. Remove the 5 clips from the lower half of the lower steering column cover.
6. Release the wiring harness clip and unplug the 4 wiring harness connectors from the rear of the combination switch. From below the steering column, loosen the band clamp securing the switch hub to the steering column jacket.
7. Pull the switch assembly off the steering column.
   To install:
8. Slide the combination switch assembly onto the steering column seating the switch against the column jacket. Make certain that the switch is level, then, tighten the band clamp on the switch hub to hold the switch assembly in place.
9. Plug the 4 wiring harness connectors into the rear of the switch and clip the harness in place.
10. Position the lower half of the lower steering column cover and install the clips.
11. Install the upper steering column cover.

12. Position the upper half of the lower steering column cover and install the attaching screws.
13. Install the steering wheel. Connect the negative battery cable.

Headlight and Turn Signal Stalk

REMOVAL AND INSTALLATION

1. Disconnect the negative battery cable.
2. Remove the combination switch from the steering column.
3. Remove the 3 switch retaining screws.
4. Rotate the stalk to the parking light position and remove the 2 detent plate retaining screws and plate.
5. Pivot the stalk out of the switch base. Use care to prevent the loss of the detent balls and springs.
   To install:
6. Position the stalk in the combination switch base. Install the detent balls and springs. Push the detent balls inward against the springs and pivot the switch stalk into position.
7. Install the detent plate and screws.
8. Turn the switch to the OFF position.
9. Position the headlight and turn signal switch onto the switch base and install the retaining screws.
10. Install the combination switch, connect the battery cable and check for proper operation.

Ignition Lock

REMOVAL AND INSTALLATION

1. Disconnect the negative battery cable. Remove the steering wheel, combination switch and ignition switch.
2. If necessary, remove the shift-lock cable attaching bolt and disconnect the cable from the lock housing.
3. Using slim-nose locking pliers, grip and remove the round head mounting screws securing the steering lock housing and cap to the steering column jacket. Remove the lock housing and discard the screws.
   To install:
4. Position the steering lock housing onto the steering column jacket and install the mounting cap with new mounting screws. Tighten the screws enough to hold the lock in position.
5. Using the ignition key, verify that the mechanism locks and un-

locks positively and without binding. If necessary, reposition the lock housing until proper operation is obtained, then tighten the mounting screws until the heads break off.

6. If necessary, install the shift-lock cable and attaching bolt. Tighten the bolt to 37–54 inch lbs. (4–6 Nm).

7. Install the ignition switch, combination switch and steering wheel. Connect the negative battery cable.

Ignition Switch

REMOVAL AND INSTALLATION

1. Disconnect the negative battery cable.

2. Remove the 4 screws from the upper half of the lower steering column cover, then remove the cover half.

3. Remove the upper steering column cover.

4. Remove the 5 clips from the lower half of the lower steering column cover, then remove the cover half.

5. Remove the 4 shield nuts and the steering column shield.

6. Remove the 2 shield bracket bolts and the shield bracket.

7. Remove the air discharge duct located below the steering column.

8. Remove the steering column attaching nuts and lower the steering column mounting bracket.

9. Remove the tie strap securing the key warning buzzer switch wires to the lock cylinder housing.

10. Remove the ignition switch attaching screw and remove the switch harness from the routing clip.

11. Separate the ignition switch wiring connectors and remove the switch.

To install:

12. Position the ignition switch in the lock cylinder housing and install the attaching screw.

13. Connect the switch wiring connectors. Position the switch wiring in the routing clip and close the clip.

14. Position the key warning buzzer switch wires and secure them to the lock cylinder housing with the tie strap.

15. Raise the steering column into position and install the attaching bolts. Tighten the bolts to 23–34 ft. lbs. (31–46 Nm).

16. Install the air discharge duct.

17. Install the shield bracket and the shield with the attaching bolts and nuts.

18. Install the steering column covers.

19. Connect the negative battery cable.

Brake Light Switch

ADJUSTMENT

1. Disconnect the switch wiring connector.

2. Loosen the upper and lower attaching nuts enough to allow for rotation of the switch.

3. Connect an ohmmeter across the switch terminals.

4. Rotate the switch until the ohmmeter indicates continuity.

5. Slowly rotate the switch toward the brake pedal until the ohmmeter indicates that the switch is open (infinite resistance).

6. Rotate the switch toward the brake pedal ½ additional turn and tighten the attaching nuts to retain the adjustment.

7. Connect the switch wiring connector and check the switch for proper operation.

REMOVAL AND INSTALLATION

1. Disconnect the negative battery cable. Disconnect the brake light switch wiring connector.

2. Remove the upper attaching nut and lower the switch from the bracket.

3. Remove the lower attaching nut from the switch.

4. Installation is the reverse of the removal procedure. Adjust the switch after installation.

Clutch Switch

ADJUSTMENT

1992

1. To eliminate the possibility that the clutch cable is affecting the pedal height, loosen the cable adjusting nut and disengage the cable pin from the transaxle release lever.

2. Move the floor carpet and insulation out of the way of the dash panel to gain sufficient room for an accurate measurement.

3. Measure the distance from the upper center of the pedal to the cowl panel. The pedal height should be 8.2–8.4 in. (208.2–213.2mm).

4. If the pedal height is within this range, no adjustment is necessary. If the pedal height is not within specification, proceed to Step 5.

5. Remove the air duct from under the instrument panel.

6. Locate the clutch switch and loosen the attaching nuts. Turn the switch in or out until the pedal height is within specification. Tighten the attaching nuts.

7. Connect the clutch cable to the transaxle release lever and adjust the pedal free-play.

8. Measure the clutch pedal height. If the pedal height has changed after connecting the clutch cable, check for binding along the cable route.

9. Install the air duct. Place the insulation and floor carpet in their original positions.

1993

If the vehicle does not start with the clutch pedal engaged, adjustment of the Starter Clutch Pedal Position (SCPP) switch may be necessary.

1. Loosen the switch screws slightly.

2. Depress the clutch and attempt to start the engine.

3. The switch is properly adjusted when the switch will close the starter motor circuit and allow the vehicle to start.

4. Tighten the switch retaining screws.

REMOVAL AND INSTALLATION

1. Disconnect the negative battery cable. Move the floor carpet aside.

2. Remove the air duct located under the steering column.

3. Disconnect the clutch switch wiring connector.

4. For 1992 vehicles, loosen the switch upper attaching nut and lower the switch from the mounting bracket. Remove the lower attaching nut.

5. For 1993 vehicles, remove the 2 clutch switch retaining screws and switch.

6. Installation is the reverse of the removal procedure. Adjust the clutch pedal height after installation.

Neutral Safety Switch

The neutral safety switch is located in the lower right side of the automatic transaxle. The switch is not adjustable.

REMOVAL AND INSTALLATION

1. Disconnect the negative battery cable. Raise and support the vehicle safely.

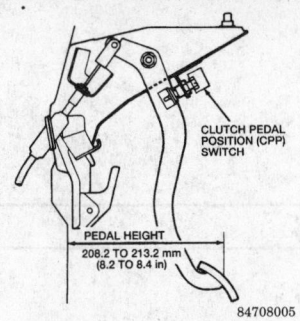

Clutch switch and pedal height adjustment — 1992 clutch switch and pedal height adjustment, 1993 pedal height adjustment

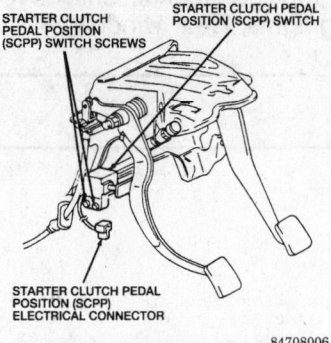

Clutch switch adjustment — 1993

2. Disconnect the neutral safety switch electrical wires.

3. Place a drain pan under the transaxle, to catch any excess transaxle fluid.

4. Remove the neutral safety switch from its mounting.

5. Installation is the reverse of the removal procedure. Be sure to replace any lost fluid.

Fuses, Fusible Links and Relays

LOCATION

Fuses

The fuse panel is located in the passenger compartment, to the left of the steering column. It is concealed behind an access panel that clips into position on the instrument panel. The fuses are the cartridge type that must be removed for inspection. When making replacements, install only cartridge type fuses with the same amperage rating as the fuse that was removed.

Fusible Links

The main fuse links are located in the engine compartment on the front of the left strut tower. The main fuse link panel contains 3 fusible links — **EGI**, **MAIN** and **HEAD**. The ends of the fusible links are connected to the main fuse panel through standard push-on connectors. To remove a link, grasp the insulator and pull until the connector separates from the panel. Install the new link by reversing the removal procedure.

Relays

Air Conditioning Relays — located in the left front corner of the engine compartment, left of the cooling fan. There are 3 air conditioning relays, the main relay, the wide open throttle cut-off relay and the condenser fan relay.

Cooling Fan Relay — located on the fender apron, behind the left headlight.

Daytime Running Light Relay — located on the fender apron, behind the left headlight on Canadian vehicles only.

Fuel Pump Relay — located on the left side of the instrument panel, to the left of the electronic control unit.

Headlight Relay — located on the fender apron, behind the left headlight.

Horn Relay — located behind left corner of instrument panel.

Main Relay — located in the left front corner of the engine compartment, attached to the fender apron.

Parking Light Relay — located in the right front corner of the engine compartment, on the fender apron.

Computers

LOCATION

The electronic control unit is located behind the instrument panel on the driver's side of the vehicle.

Flashers

LOCATION

the turn signal and hazard flashers are controlled by a single flasher unit. The flasher unit is located under the instrument panel, behind the electronic control unit.

FUSE CHART—1992–93 VEHICLES

Fuse	Item for Circuit Affected	Fuse	Item for Circuit Affected
TAIL (15A)	License lamp, Parking / side marker lamps, Front parking lamps, Illumination lamps and tail lamps	F. WIPER (15A)	Front wiper and washer
STOP (15A)	Horn, Stoplamps and Hi-mount Stoplamp	ENG. (10A)	Charging system and Emission control system
HAZARD (15A)	Seat belt warning, Interior light, Luggage compartment lamp, Turn and hazard flasher lamps, Ignition key reminder buzzer and Radio system	METER (10A)	Seat belt warning, Turn and hazard flasher lamps, Cooling fan system, Backup lamp and cluster and warning lamps
CIGAR (15A)	Radio system, Cigar lighter and remote control mirror	R. DEF. (15A)	Rear window defroster
R. WIPER (15A)	Rear wiper and washer	R. DEF. (15A)	Rear window defroster
HEATER (15A)	Heater and Air conditioner	BELT (30A)	Passive Restraint System
FAN (15A)	Heater and Air conditioner and Cooling fan system	BELT (30A)	Passive Restraint System

85569Z017

Fuse chart

MAIN FUSE LINK CHART

Main Fuse	Item for Circuit Affected
PTC or EGI Fusible Link (Brown, 15A)	EFE Heater (carbureted engine) or EFI (EFI engine)
Main Fusible Link (Red, 25A)	Parking/side marker lamps, Illumination lamps, Tail lamps, Horn & stop-lamps, Interior lamp, Luggage compartment lamp, Turn & hazard flasher lamps, Radio, Charging system, Cigar lighter, Rear wiper & washer, Air conditioning & heater, Cooling fan system, Front wiper & washer, Emission control system, Backup lamps, Cluster & warning lights, Rear window defroster, Ignition system, Starting system
Head Fusible Link (Brown, 15A)	Headlamp

8569Z018

Main fuse link chart

ENGINE COOLING

Radiator

REMOVAL AND INSTALLATION

1. Disconnect the negative battery cable.
2. Remove the radiator pressure cap from the filler neck.

—— **CAUTION** ——
Never remove the radiator cap while the engine is running or personal injury from scalding hot coolant or steam may result. If possible, wait until the engine has cooled to remove the radiator cap. If this is not possible, wrap a thick cloth around the radiator cap and turn it slowly to the first stop. Step back while the pressure is released from the cooling system. When it is certain all the pressure has been released, press down on the cap, still with the cloth, and turn and remove it.

3. Position a suitable container under the radiator and open the draincock to drain the radiator.

4. Disconnect the coolant recovery hose from the filler neck.
5. Loosen the retaining clamp and disconnect the upper radiator hose from the radiator.
6. Disconnect the cooling fan wiring harness connector. Disengage the wiring harness from the routing clamps on the cooling fan shroud.
7. Loosen the retaining clamp and disconnect the lower radiator hose.
8. Remove the 4 bolts attaching the radiator upper tank brackets to the vehicle body and remove the radiator/cooling fan assembly. Separate the fan and shroud assembly from the radiator, if necessary.

To install:
9. If removed, install the fan and shroud assembly on the radiator.
10. Lower the radiator/cooling fan assembly into the engine compartment, making sure the mounting insulators engage with their supports. Attach the radiator to the mounting brackets with the 4 bolts.
11. Connect the cooling fan wiring and position the wiring harness in the routing clips on the fan shroud.
12. Connect the coolant recovery hose and the upper and lower radiator hoses.
13. Close the radiator draincock. Connect the negative battery cable.

14. Fill and bleed the cooling system. Check for leaks.

Electric Cooling Fan

TESTING

1. Check for voltage at the cooling fan motor as follows:
   a. Turn the ignition key **ON**, but do not start the engine.
   b. Use a voltmeter to measure the voltage at the cooling fan motor **Y** terminal.
   c. If the voltage is greater than 10 volts, proceed to Step 2.
   d. If the voltage is less than 10 volts, service the **Y** wire from the 20 amp cooling fan fuse to the cooling fan motor.
2. Check for operation of the cooling fan motor as follows:
   a. Turn the ignition key **ON**, but do not start the engine.
   b. Ground the **Y/R** terminal at the cooling fan motor with a jumper wire.
   c. If the cooling fan operates, proceed to Step 3.
   d. If the cooling fan does not operate, service the motor side of the cooling fan harness. If the harness is okay, replace the cooling fan motor.

3. Check for power at the cooling fan relay as follows:

a. Turn the ignition key **ON**, but do not start the engine.

b. Disconnect the cooling fan relay.

c. Using a voltmeter, measure the voltage at the cooling fan relay **Y/R** wire.

d. If the voltage is greater than 10 volts, proceed to Step 4.

e. If the voltage is not greater than 10 volts, service the **Y/R** wire from the cooling fan motor to the cooling fan relay, air conditioning relay and Powertrain Control Module.

4. Check the voltage supply at the cooling fan relay as follows:

a. Turn the ignition key **ON**, but do not start the engine.

b. Disconnect the cooling fan relay.

c. Using a voltmeter, measure the voltage at the cooling fan relay **BK/Y** terminal.

d. If the voltage is greater than 10 volts, proceed to Step 5.

e. If the voltage is not greater than 10 volts, service the **BK/Y** wire from the cooling fan relay to the 10 amp METER fuse.

5. Check the cooling fan relay as follows:

a. Make sure the ignition key is **OFF**.

b. Remove the cooling fan relay.

c. Apply battery power to the relay **A** terminal.

d. Using an ohmmeter, measure the resistance between relay **B** and **C** terminals.

e. Ground the relay **D** terminal with a jumper wire.

f. If the resistance is greater than 10,000 ohms with the **D** terminal grounded and less than 5 ohms with the **D** terminal ungrounded, proceed to Step 6.

g. If the resistance is not as specified in Step 5f, replace the cooling fan relay.

6. Check the coolant temperature switch voltage as follows:

a. Turn the ignition key **ON**, but do not start the engine.

b. Disconnect the coolant temperature switch.

c. Using a voltmeter, measure the voltage at the coolant temperature switch **GN/Y** terminal.

d. If the voltage is greater than 10 volts, proceed to Step 7.

e. If the voltage is not greater than 10 volts, service the **GN/Y** wire, that runs from the cooling fan relay to the coolant temperature switch.

7. Check the coolant temperature switch operation as follows:

a. Let the engine cool completely.

b. Remove the radiator cap.

c. Place a suitable thermometer/pyrometer probe in the radiator, under the coolant surface.

d. Using an ohmmeter, measure the resistance between the coolant temperature switch terminal and ground.

e. Start the engine. Run the engine until the coolant temperature exceeds 207°F (97°C), then shut the engine **OFF**.

f. If the switch opens at 207°F (97°C) and then closes when the coolant temperature falls below 194°F (90°C), service the cooling fan relay ground **BK** wire.

g. If the switch does not perform as specified in Step 7f, replace the cooling fan switch.

REMOVAL AND INSTALLATION

1. Disconnect the negative battery cable. Partially drain the radiator to a level just below the upper radiator hose.

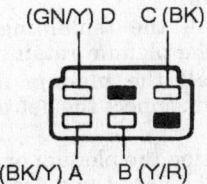

84708009

Cooling fan relay terminals

2. Loosen the retaining clamp and disconnect the upper radiator hose at the radiator.

3. Disconnect the cooling fan wiring harness connector and disengage the wiring harnesses from the routing clamps on the cooling fan shroud.

4. Remove the bolts attaching the top of the fan shroud to the radiator.

5. Support the fan/shroud assembly and remove the bolts attaching the bottom of the fan shroud to the radiator. Remove the fan/shroud assembly from the vehicle.

6. Remove the nut and washer and remove the fan from the motor shaft.

7. Remove the wiring harness routing strap.

8. Remove the attaching screws and remove the cooling fan motor from the fan shroud.

To install:

9. Install the cooling fan motor attaching screws.

10. Install the wiring harness routing strap.

11. Install the fan to the motor, nut and washer. Torque the nut to 10 ft. lbs. (13 Nm).

12. Install the fan/shroud assembly to the vehicle.

13. Install the bolts attaching the top of the fan shroud to the radiator.

14. Connect the cooling fan wiring harness connector and engage the wiring harnesses to the routing clamps on the cooling fan shroud.

15. Connect the upper radiator hose and tighten the retaining clamp.

16. Refill the cooling system to the proper level and connect the battery cable.

Heater Core

REMOVAL AND INSTALLATION

1. Disconnect the negative battery cable.

SWITCH OPERATION		
Coolant	Temperature	Resistance
At opening temp.	97°C (207°F) (rising)	Greater than 10,000 ohms
Above	97°C (207°F)	Greater than 10,000 ohms
Below closing temp.	90°C (194°F) (falling)	Less than 5 ohms

● **Does the switch operate correctly?**

84708010

Coolant temperature switch operation

2. Remove the instrument panel as follows:

a. Remove the steering wheel, steering column covers and the combination switch.

b. Remove the screws securing the instrument cluster bezel and move the bezel toward the rear of the vehicle.

c. Disconnect the electrical connectors from the switches on the instrument cluster bezel and remove the bezel.

d. Remove the left and right heater ducts.

e. Disconnect the speedometer cable at the transaxle.

f. Remove the 4 screws securing the instrument cluster and move the cluster toward the rear of the vehicle.

g. Disconnect the instrument cluster electrical connectors and the speedometer cable from the instrument cluster. Remove the instrument cluster.

h. Remove the 4 shield nuts and the shield and remove the 2 shield bracket bolts and the shield bracket.

i. Remove the screws securing the glove box hinges to the glove box and remove the glove box.

j. Open the fuse panel cover, remove the fuse panel attaching screws and push the fuse panel forward. Do not remove the fuse panel.

k. If equipped with a shift lever console, remove the shift lever knob and the console attaching screws. Remove the console.

l. If equipped, remove the support bracket bolts and nut and remove the support bracket.

m. Remove the radio and disconnect the cigarette lighter connector.

n. Disconnect the cables from the mode selector, temperature control lever and recirc/fresh air lever.

o. Remove the screws securing the heater/air conditioner control assembly to the instrument panel. Pull the control assembly away from the instrument panel, disconnect the blower motor switch, air conditioning switch and illumination light wiring connectors and remove the control assembly.

p. Remove the snap-in trim inserts concealing the instrument panel attaching bolts and remove the 7 instrument panel attaching bolts.

q. Remove the 2 instrument panel attaching stud nuts, tag and

disconnect the remaining electrical connectors and remove the instrument panel.

3. Drain the cooling system.

4. In the engine compartment, disconnect the heater hoses.

5. Disconnect the wiring at the blower motor and the blower resistor.

6. Disengage the wiring harness and antenna lead from the routing bracket on the front of the air distribution housing.

7. Loosen the clamp screw securing the connector duct to the air inlet housing.

8. Remove the attaching nuts at the top and bottom of the plenum, disengage the plenum from the defroster ducts and remove the plenum.

9. Disconnect the link connecting the 2 defroster doors.

10. Remove the attaching screw located just above and to the right of the blower resistor.

11. Turn the plenum around and remove the attaching screw located just to the left of the blower motor opening.

12. Remove the clips securing the 2 halves of the plenum and separate the plenum halves.

13. Remove the heater core and remove the tube insert from the heater core.

To install:

14. Install the heater core tube insert and position the heater core in the plenum.

15. Install the remaining plenum half and the plenum retaining clips.

16. Install the plenum attaching screws and connect the defroster door link.

17. Position the plenum on the dash panel. Make sure the defroster ducts and connector duct are properly seated on the plenum.

18. Install the plenum attaching nuts and tighten the connector duct clamp screw.

19. Connect the blower motor and blower resistor wiring.

20. Route the wiring harness and antenna lead through the routing bracket on the front of the plenum.

21. Install the instrument panel in the reverse order of removal.

22. Connect the heater hoses.

23. Fill the cooling system to the proper level.

24. Start the engine and allow to come operating temperature. Check the operation of the heating system. Check for coolant leaks.

25. Stop the engine and check the coolant level.

Water Pump

REMOVAL AND INSTALLATION

1. Disconnect the negative battery cable.

2. Remove the timing belt.

3. Drain the cooling system.

4. Remove the radiator lower hose and heater return hose from the water pump inlet tube.

5. Remove the bolts attaching the inlet tube to the water pump housing. Remove the inlet tube and gasket.

6. Remove the water pump-to-cylinder block attaching bolts. Remove the water pump and gasket from the cylinder block surface.

7. Remove all existing gasket material from the cylinder block and inlet tube gasket surfaces.

To install:

8. Coat both sides of the new water pump and inlet tube gaskets with a suitable water resistant sealer. Apply the gaskets to the engine and inlet tube surfaces. Make certain the gasket holes are aligned with the bolt holes.

9. Position the water pump against the gasket. Make sure the holes in the water pump are aligned with the gasket holes and that the pump does not shift the position of the gasket.

10. Install the water pump-to-cylinder block attaching bolts and torque to 14–19 ft. lbs. (19–26 Nm). Position the inlet tube and gasket against the water pump housing and install the attaching bolts. Torque the bolts to 14–22 ft. lbs. (19–30 Nm). Tighten the inlet tube bracket nut to 27–38 ft. lbs. (37–52 Nm).

11. Connect the inlet tube hoses and install the timing belt.

12. Fill the cooling system to the proper level. Connect the negative battery cable.

13. Start the engine and allow to reach normal operating temperature. Check for coolant leaks.

Thermostat

REMOVAL AND INSTALLATION

1. Disconnect the negative battery cable.

2. Disconnect the cooling fan temperature switch wire.

3. Remove the radiator cap and drain the cooling system to a level below the radiator upper hose. Disconnect the radiator upper hose from the thermostat housing.

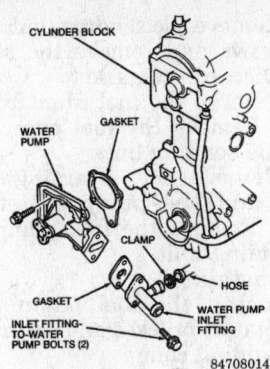

CYLINDER BLOCK
WATER PUMP
GASKET
CLAMP
GASKET
HOSE
INLET FITTING-TO-WATER PUMP BOLTS (2)
WATER PUMP INLET FITTING

84708014

Water pump removal and installation

4. Remove the thermostat housing-to-cylinder head attaching bolts. Remove the thermostat housing and housing gasket. Withdraw the thermostat from the cylinder head.

5. Remove all gasket material from the thermostat housing and cylinder block surfaces.

To install:

6. Install the thermostat in the cylinder head, with the valve end first and the sub valve at the top.

7. Coat a new gasket with a suitable water resistant sealer. Apply the gasket to the cylinder block surface making sure the gasket and cylinder block holes are aligned.

8. Position the thermostat housing onto the cylinder head making sure the bolt holes are aligned and the gasket does not shift. Install the housing attaching bolts. Before tightening the bolts, ensure that the thermostat flange is properly seated against the recess of the housing. Torque the bolts to 14–19 ft. lbs. (19–26 Nm).

9. Connect the radiator upper hose to the thermostat housing. Fill the cooling system to the proper level and install the radiator cap. Connect the cooling fan temperature switch wire and the negative battery cable.

10. Start the engine and allow to reach normal operating temperature. Inspect for leaks.

Cooling System Bleeding

When the entire cooling system is drained, the following procedure should be used to ensure a complete fill.

1. Install the block drain plug, if removed and close the draincock. With the engine off, add anti-freeze to the radiator to a level of 50 percent of the total cooling system capacity. Then add water until it reaches the radiator filler neck seat.

2. Install the radiator cap to the first notch to keep spillage to a minimum.

3. Start the engine and let it idle until the upper radiator hose is warm. This indicates that the thermostat is open and coolant is flowing through the entire system.

4. Carefully remove the radiator cap and top off the radiator with water. Install the cap on the radiator securely.

5. Fill the coolant recovery reservoir to the **FULL COLD** mark with anti-freeze, then add water to the **FULL HOT** mark. This will ensure that a proper mixture is in the coolant recovery bottle.

6. Check for leaks at the draincock and block plug.

FUEL SYSTEM

Fuel System Service Precautions

Safety is the most important factor when performing not only fuel system maintenance but any type of maintenance. Failure to conduct maintenance and repairs in a safe manner may result in serious personal injury. Maintenance and testing of the vehicle's fuel system components can be accomplished safely and effectively by adhering to the following rules and guidelines.

• To avoid the possibility of fire and personal injury, always disconnect the negative battery cable unless the repair or test procedure requires that battery voltage be applied.

• Always relieve the fuel system pressure prior to disconnecting any fuel system component (injector, fuel rail, pressure regulator, etc.), fitting or fuel line connection. Exercise extreme caution whenever relieving fuel system pressure to avoid exposing skin, face and eyes to fuel spray. Please be advised that fuel under pressure may penetrate the skin or any part of the body that it contacts.

• Always place a shop towel or cloth around the fitting or connection prior to loosening to absorb any excess fuel. Ensure that all fuel spillage (should it occur) is quickly removed from engine surfaces. Ensure that all fuel soaked cloths or towels are de-posited into a suitable waste container.

• Always keep a dry chemical (Class B) fire extinguisher near the work area.

• Do not allow fuel spray or fuel vapors to come into contact with a spark or open flame.

• Always use a backup wrench when loosening and tightening fuel line connection fittings. Always follow the proper torque specifications.

• Always replace worn fuel fitting O-rings with new. Do not substitute fuel hose or equivalent where fuel pipe is installed.

RELIEVING FUEL SYSTEM PRESSURE

1. Remove the rear seat cushion.

2. Disconnect the electrical connector from the fuel pump/sending unit.

3. Start the engine and let it run until it stalls. Turn the ignition key **OFF**.

4. Reconnect the electrical lead.

Fuel Tank

REMOVAL AND INSTALLATION

1. Remove the rear seat as follows:
   a. Remove the right and left front attaching bolts.
   b. Fold the rear seat forward.
   c. Remove the right and left anchor nuts on the rear side of the seat and remove the seat.

2. Remove the screw and retainers and remove the left rear quarter trim panel.

3. Start the engine and disconnect the fuel pump/sending unit connector. After the engine stalls, turn the ignition key **OFF**.

4. Disconnect the negative battery cable.

5. Drain the fuel from the tank as completely as possible. This is accomplished by siphoning or pumping the fuel out through the fuel filler neck.

6. Remove the rear carpet hold-down pins using a suitable tool. Fold the carpet forward until the sending unit access plate is uncovered.

7. Remove the sending unit access plate attaching screws, lift the access plate and disconnect the sending unit wiring.

8. Disconnect the fuel supply line at the sending unit and the fuel return line from the top of the fuel tank.

9. Remove the fuel tank cover plate.

10. Disconnect the filler neck hose, overflow hose and the 2 vapor separator hoses from the fuel tank.

11. Raise and safely support the vehicle.

12. Disconnect the vapor hose from the vapor line.

13. Position a suitable jack under the fuel tank and remove the 4 attaching bolts.

14. Move the fuel tank toward the left and lower it from the vehicle.

To install:

15. Raise the fuel tank and slide it into position from the left side of the vehicle. Install the attaching bolts.

16. Connect the vapor hose to the vapor line and lower the vehicle.

17. Connect the vapor separator hoses, overflow hose and fuel filler hose to the fuel tank.

18. Connect the fuel return hose to the fitting on the top of the fuel tank and the fuel supply hose to the fitting on the fuel sending unit.

19. Add fuel to the tank and check for leaks.

20. Connect the negative battery cable and the fuel sending unit wiring. Start the engine and check for leaks. Stop the engine.

21. Install the fuel line cover plate and the fuel sender access plate.

22. Position the rear carpet and secure it in position with the retainers.

23. Install the left rear quarter panel and the rear seat.

Fuel Filter

REMOVAL AND INSTALLATION

The fuel filter is located in the rear left corner of the engine compartment next to the carbon canister.

1. Properly relieve the fuel system pressure.

2. Disconnect the negative battery cable.

3. Remove the clamp and line at the inlet of the fuel filter. Plug the end to prevent spillage.

4. Remove the attaching bolts from the outlet of the fuel filter.

5. Remove the fuel filter from it's brace.

To install:

6. Install the fuel filter into it's brace.

7. Install the line onto the filter outlet with the attaching bolts. Tighten the bolts to 18–25 ft. lbs. (25–34 Nm).

8. Unplug and install the supply line onto the fuel filter inlet and secure with the clamp.

9. Connect the fuel pump connector and install the rear seat cushion. Connect the negative battery cable.

10. Run the engine and check for leaks.

Electric Fuel Pump

PRESSURE TESTING

1. Properly relieve the fuel system pressure.

2. Disconnect the negative battery cable.

3. Connect a suitable fuel pressure gauge between the fuel filter outlet and the fuel rail.

4. Connect the negative battery cable.

5. Connect the **BK** and **GN/R** terminals together on the fuel pump test connector.

6. Turn the ignition key **ON** but do not start the engine.

7. The fuel pressure reading should be 64–85 psi.

8. Turn the ignition key **OFF** and remove the jumper wire from the **BK** and **GN/R** terminals.

9. Properly relieve the fuel system pressure.

10. Disconnect the negative battery cable.

11. Remove the fuel pressure tester and reconnect the fuel line and fuel rail.

12. Connect the negative battery cable. Start the engine and check for fuel leaks.

REMOVAL AND INSTALLATION

The fuel pump is located in the fuel tank as part of the sending unit assembly.

1. Properly relieve the fuel system pressure.

2. Disconnect the negative battery cable.

3. Remove the rear seat as follows:
   a. Remove the right and left front attaching bolts.
   b. Fold the rear seat forward.
   c. Remove the right and left anchor nuts on the rear side of the seat and remove the seat.

4. Remove the rear carpet hold-down pins and fold the carpet forward until the sending unit access plate is uncovered.

5. Remove the access plate attaching screws, lift the access plate and disconnect the sending unit wiring.

6. Disconnect and plug the fuel line at the sending unit.

7. Remove the sending unit retaining screws and remove the sending unit. Discard the gasket.

8. Remove the fuel filter from the pump. Remove the fuel pump wires from the sending unit.

9. Remove the retaining clamp screw and the pump outlet hose clamp. Remove the fuel pump from the sending unit.

To install:

10. Install the fuel pump to the sending unit bracket and secure with the retaining clamp.

11. Install the pump outlet hose and secure with the clamp.

12. Connect the fuel pump wires to the sending unit and install the fuel pump filter.

13. Position a new gasket on the fuel tank and install the sending unit with the attaching screws.

14. Connect the fuel line and the sending unit wiring.

15. Connect the negative battery cable. Start the engine and check for leaks at the fuel line connections. Stop the engine.

16. Install the access cover with the attaching screws.

17. Position the carpet and install the retaining pins.

18. Install the rear seat.

Fuel Injection

IDLE SPEED ADJUSTMENT

1. Disconnect the cooling fan electrical connector. Check the ignition timing and adjust if necessary.

2. Apply the parking brake. Make certain the air conditioning system is **OFF**. Be sure all lights and electrical accessories are **OFF**.

3. Connect a tachometer to the check connector (clear, pin No. 1 for 1992 vehicles) or to the 1 pin white tachometer test connector for 1993 vehicles. Connect a jumper wire between the black test connector (1 pin, Y/BL wire) and ground.

4. Check the idle speed on the tachometer. The idle speed should be 680–720 rpm on manual transaxle vehicles in **N** or 830–870 on automatic transaxle vehicles in **P**.

5. If necessary, turn the idle air adjust screw to obtain the correct idle speed.

6. After adjustment, remove the jumper wire and the tachometer.

IDLE MIXTURE ADJUSTMENT

The idle mixture is preset at the factory and controlled by the Powertrain

1. Rollover Vent Valve
2. Vapor Separator
3. Return Line
4. Supply Line
5. Fuel Filter
6. Fuel Injectors (4)
7. Fuel Rail
8. Fuel Pressure Regulator
9. Fuel Pump

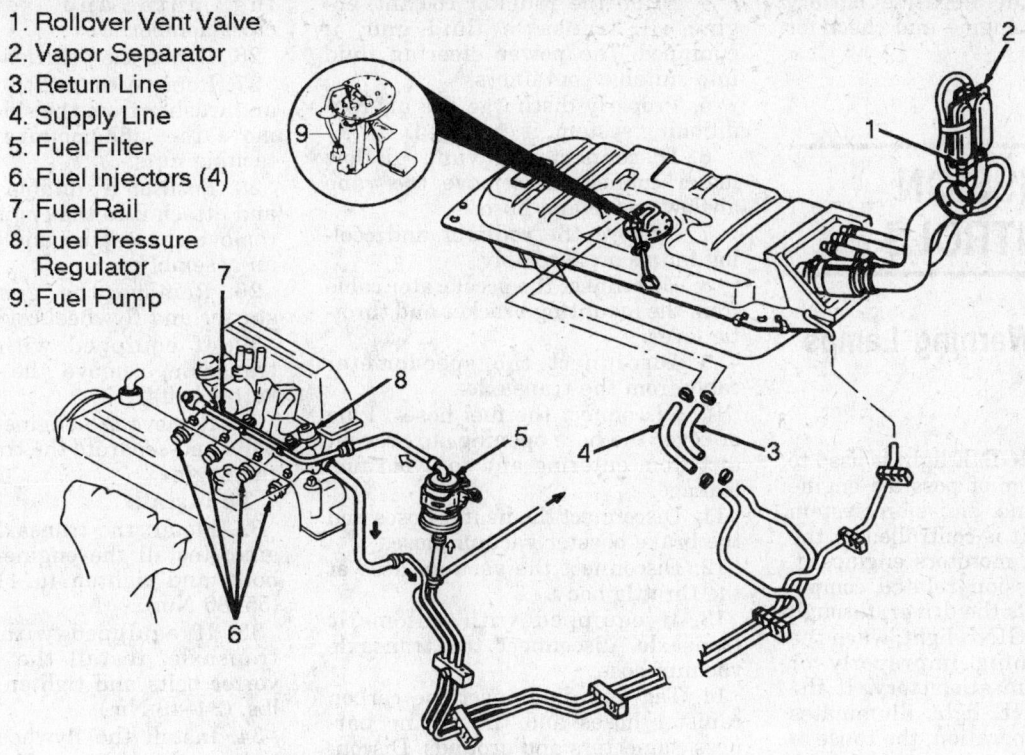

84708015

Engine fuel supply system

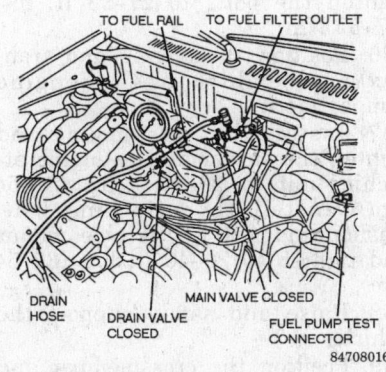

84708016

Electric fuel pump pressure testing

Control Module (PCM). Idle mixture cannot be adjusted.

Fuel Injector

REMOVAL AND INSTALLATION

1. Properly relieve the fuel system pressure.
2. Disconnect the negative battery cable.
3. Remove the intake plenum as follows:
   a. Drain the cooling system.

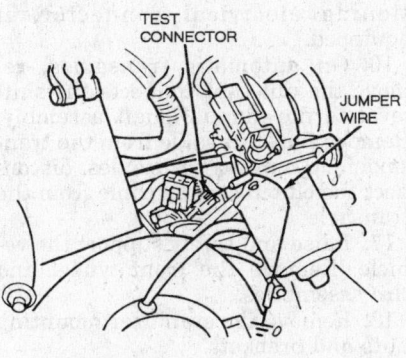

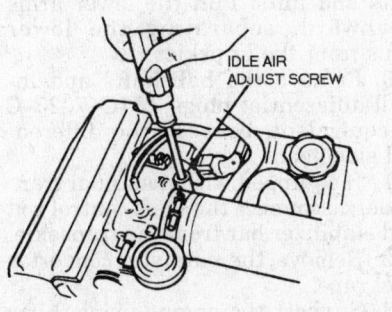

84708017

Engine test connector and idle air control adjusting screw locations

   b. Disconnect the throttle cable and the air duct from the throttle body.
   c. Mark all vacuum and coolant hoses for ease of reassembly and remove the hoses from the throttle body.
   d. Disconnect the electrical connector at the throttle position sensor.
   e. Remove the intake plenum retaining bolts and/or nuts and remove the intake plenum and gasket.
4. Remove the fuel inlet and return lines from the fuel rail.
5. Remove the electrical connectors at the injectors.
6. Remove the pressure regulator.
7. Remove the attaching bolts and the fuel rail. Remove the injectors.
   To install:
8. Install new O-rings onto the injectors and lubricate with clean gasoline.
9. Position the injectors into the cylinder head and fuel rail into the injectors. Install the fuel rail bolts.
10. Install the fuel pressure regulator and connect the electrical connectors.
11. Connect the fuel inlet, return and vacuum line.
12. Install the intake plenum and connect the fuel rail connectors.

13. Connect the negative battery cable, start the engine and check for fuel leaks.

EMISSION CONTROLS

Emission Warning Lamps

RESETTING

The CHECK ENGINE light is used to inform the driver of possible engine malfunctions and emission system failure. The light is controlled by the PCM. The PCM monitors engine, ignition and emission related components and signals the driver, through the CHECK ENGINE light, when the engine is running improperly or emissions are unsatisfactory. If the CHECK ENGINE light illuminates during vehicle operation, the cause of the fault or malfunction must be determined and corrected. After the problem area is repaired, the CHECK ENGINE light can be turned OFF by disconnecting the negative battery cable for at least 10 seconds.

ENGINE MECHANICAL

NOTE: Disconnecting the negative battery cable on some vehicles may interfere with the functions of the on-board computer systems and may require the computer to undergo a relearning process, once the negative battery cable is reconnected.

Engine Assembly

REMOVAL AND INSTALLATION

NOTE: The engine and transaxle are removed as an assembly.

1. Properly relieve the fuel system pressure.
2. Disconnect the battery cables. Remove the battery and battery tray.
3. Mark the hinge location and remove the hood.

4. Drain the radiator coolant, engine oil, transaxle fluid and, if equipped, the power steering fluid into suitable containers.
5. Properly discharge the air conditioning system, if equipped.
6. Disconnect the vane airflow meter connector. Remove the vane airflow meter and hose.
7. Remove the radiator and cooling fan as an assembly.
8. Disconnect the accelerator cable from the mounting bracket and throttle lever.
9. Disconnect the speedometer cable from the transaxle.
10. Disconnect the fuel hoses. Plug or cover the hose openings to prevent dirt from entering and to avoid fuel leakage.
11. Disconnect the heater hoses and the brake booster vacuum hose.
12. Disconnect the vacuum hose at the throttle body.
13. If equipped with automatic transaxle, disconnect the transaxle vacuum hose.
14. Tag and disconnect the carbon canister hoses and the engine harness connectors and grounds. Disconnect the distributor wiring at the coil.
15. Disconnect the power steering lines, if equipped. Disconnect the air conditioning lines and the air conditioning electrical connector, if equipped.
16. On automatic transaxles, remove the nut that connects the shift lever to the manual shaft assembly. Remove the shift cable from the transaxle. On manual transaxles, disconnect the clutch control cable from the transaxle.
17. Raise and safely support the vehicle. Remove the front wheel and tire assemblies.
18. Remove the stabilizer mounting nuts and brackets.
19. Remove the lower arm clamp bolts and nuts. Pull the lower arms downward, separating the lower arms from the knuckles.
20. Remove the halfshafts and install differential plugs T87C–7025–C or equivalent, between the differential side gears.
21. If equipped with a manual transaxle, disconnect the shift control rod and stabilizer bar from the transaxle.
22. Remove the catalytic converter inlet pipe.
23. Support the engine using 3-bar engine support D88L–6000–A or equivalent.
24. Remove the crossmember attaching bolts.
25. Remove the front and rear engine mount-to-crossmember attach-

ing nuts and remove the crossmember.
26. Lower the vehicle.
27. Remove the attaching bolt, nut and washer from the side mount. Remove the side mount-to-engine attaching nuts.
28. Position a suitable jack or hoist and attach it to the engine. Carefully remove the engine and transaxle as an assembly.
29. Remove the gusset plates, starter and flywheel cover.
30. If equipped with automatic transaxle, remove the torque converter bolts.
31. Remove the engine-to-transaxle bolts and separate the transaxle from the engine.

To install:

32. Mount the transaxle to the engine. Install the engine-to-transaxle bolts and tighten to 41–59 ft. lbs. (55–80 Nm).
33. If equipped with automatic transaxle, install the torque converter bolts and tighten to 26–36 ft. lbs. (34–49 Nm).
34. Install the flywheel cover and tighten the bolts to 61–87 inch lbs. (7–10 Nm). Install the starter.
35. Install the gusset plates and tighten the bolts to 27–38 ft. lbs. (37–52 Nm).
36. Position the engine and transaxle assembly in the engine compartment.
37. Install the side mount and tighten the side mount-to-engine attaching nuts to 29–40 ft. lbs. (39–54 Nm). Install the attaching bolt, washer and nut to the side mount and tighten to 29–40 ft. lbs. (39–54 Nm).
38. Raise and safely support the vehicle.
39. Position the crossmember and install the attaching bolts. Tighten the bolts to 47–66 ft. lbs. (64–89 Nm).
40. Install the front and rear engine mount-to-crossmember attaching nuts. Tighten the front nuts to 32–38 ft. lbs. (43–52 Nm) and the rear nut to 21–34 ft. lbs. (28–46 Nm).
41. Install the catalytic converter inlet pipe and tighten the nuts to 23–34 ft. lbs. (31–46 Nm).
42. If equipped with manual transaxle, install the shift control rod and stabilizer bar.
43. Remove the differential plugs and install the halfshafts. Install the lower arm ball joint to the knuckle and tighten the clamp nut and bolt to 32–40 ft. lbs. (43–54 Nm).
44. Install the stabilizer bracket and mounting nuts. Tighten the

mounting nuts to 40–50 ft. lbs. (54–68 Nm).

45. Install the front wheel and tire assemblies and lower the vehicle.

46. If equipped with manual transaxle, connect the clutch cable. If equipped with automatic transaxle, install the shift lever on the manual shaft assembly and tighten the nut to 34–47 ft. lbs. (44–64 Nm). Attach the shift cable to the transaxle.

47. Connect the distributor wiring to the coil and connect all engine harness connectors and grounds.

48. If equipped with air conditioning, connect the lines and the electrical connector.

49. If equipped with automatic transaxle, connect the transaxle vacuum hose.

50. Connect the vacuum hose at the throttle body.

51. Connect the brake booster vacuum hose, the carbon canister hoses, the heater hoses and the fuel lines.

52. Connect the speedometer cable and connect the accelerator cable to the throttle lever and mounting bracket.

53. If equipped, connect the power steering lines.

54. Install the radiator and cooling fan.

55. Install the vane airflow meter and hose. Connect the vane airflow meter connector.

56. Install the hood, aligning the marks that were made during the removal procedure.

57. Install the battery carrier and the battery. Connect the battery cables.

58. Add the proper types and quantities of engine oil, transaxle fluid and coolant.

59. If equipped, add power steering fluid to the reservoir.

60. If equipped, evacuate, recharge and leak test the air conditioning system.

61. Start the engine. Check for leaks and proper fluid levels. Road test.

Engine Mounts

REMOVAL AND INSTALLATION

Front Mount

1. Disconnect the negative battery cable. Remove the front mount through bolt attaching nut.

2. Properly support the engine.

3. Raise and support the vehicle safely.

4. Remove the front mount to crossmember attaching nuts.

5. Raise the vehicle, as required, to gain sufficient clearance to remove the front mount. Remove the front mount from the crossmember. Note and record the position of the mount to ensure proper installation.

To install:

6. Install the engine mount onto the crossmember in the original installation position.

7. Secure the mount to the crossmember with the attaching nuts. Torque the attaching nuts to 32–38 ft. lbs. (43–52 Nm).

8. Lower the vehicle.

9. Move the engine as necessary until the holes in the mount align with the holes in the engine bracket. Install the through bolt and attaching nut. Torque the nut to 29–40 ft. lbs. (39–54 Nm).

10. Remove the engine support.

Rear Mount

1. Disconnect the negative battery cable. Raise the vehicle and support safely.

2. Properly support the engine.

3. Remove the mount-to-crossmember attaching nut.

4. Remove the mount-to-engine attaching bolts.

5. If necessary, raise the engine to gain access to the rear mount. Remove the mount from the crossmember.

To install:

6. Position the mount onto the rear engine bracket.

7. Install the mount to engine bracket bolts. Torque the bolts to 29–40 ft. lbs. (39–54 Nm).

8. Lower the engine and mount onto the crossmember.

9. Install the attaching nut and torque to 21–34 ft. lbs. (28–46 Nm).

10. Remove the engine support.

Side Mount

1. Disconnect the negative battery cable. Properly support the engine.

2. Remove the through bolt, nut and washer.

3. Remove the bracket-to-engine attaching nuts.

4. Remove the side mount and bracket as an assembly.

To install:

5. Position the engine mount and bracket onto the engine.

6. Install the engine-to-bracket attaching nuts. Torque the nuts to 29–40 ft. lbs. (39–54 Nm).

7. Position the washer against the mount. Install the through bolt and nut. Torque the nut and bolt to 29–40 ft. lbs. (39–54 Nm).

8. Remove the engine support.

Cylinder Head

REMOVAL AND INSTALLATION

1. Disconnect the negative battery cable. Drain the cooling system.

2. Position the engine at TDC on the compression stroke.

3. Remove the valve cover. Remove the timing belt cover and timing belt.

4. Remove the exhaust manifold. Remove the intake manifold.

5. Remove the spark plug wires and spark plugs. Remove the distributor.

6. Remove the front and rear engine lift hangers. Remove the engine ground wire.

7. Remove the wiring harness connector. Remove the upper radiator hose. Remove the bypass hose and bracket.

8. Remove the cylinder head retaining bolts. Remove the cylinder head from the engine. Discard the gasket.

9. Clean all mating surfaces of dirt and old gasket material.

To install:

10. Position the cylinder head gasket on the engine block. Install the cylinder head and tighten the bolts, in sequence, in 2 equal steps. The final torque should be 56–60 ft. lbs. (75–81 Nm).

11. Connect the radiator hose, bypass hose, wiring harness connectors, engine lift hangers and engine ground wire.

12. Install the distributor, spark plugs and wires.

13. Install the intake and exhaust manifolds. Install the timing belt and cover.

14. Install the valve cover.

15. Fill the cooling system.

16. Connect the negative battery cable. Start the engine and check for leaks.

Valve Lifters

REMOVAL AND INSTALLATION

All engines are equipped with hydraulic lash adjusters that automatically maintain valve lash.

1. Disconnect the negative battery cable.

2. Remove the valve cover and the rocker arm shaft assemblies.

3. Remove the hydraulic lash adjuster from the rocker arm.

To install:

4. Pour engine oil into the oil reservoir in the rocker arm. Apply en-

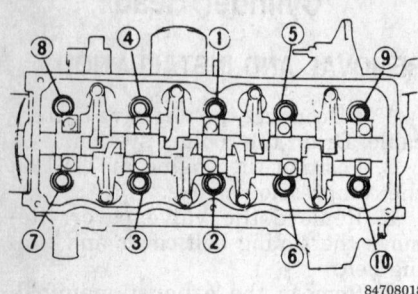

84708018

Cylinder head bolt torque sequence and rocker arm positioning

gine oil to the new hydraulic lash adjuster.

5. Install the hydraulic lash adjuster into the rocker arm.

NOTE: Be careful not to damage the O-ring when installing the hydraulic lash adjuster.

6. Install the rocker arm shaft assemblies and install the valve cover.

7. Connect the negative battery cable.

Valve Lash

ADJUSTMENT

Inspect hydraulic lash adjuster operation by pushing down each rocker arm by hand. If a rocker arm moves down, replace the hydraulic lash adjuster. No valve lash adjustment is required or possible.

Rocker Arms/Shafts

REMOVAL AND INSTALLATION

1. Disconnect the negative battery cable.

2. Remove the air hose and the resonance chamber.

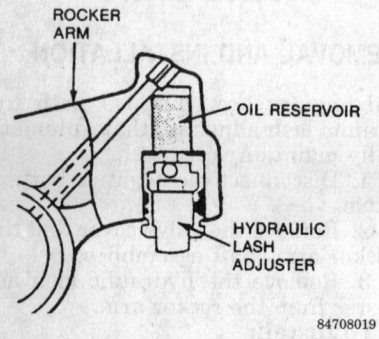

84708019

Rocker arm and hydraulic lash adjuster assembly

3. Disconnect the accelerator cable from the throttle lever and routing bracket. Remove the PCV valve.

4. Remove the spark plug wires from the routing clips. Remove the upper timing belt cover.

5. Remove the valve cover retaining bolts. Remove the valve cover. Discard the gasket.

6. Remove the rocker arm shaft retaining bolts and remove the rocker arms/shafts assemblies from the engine. If the shafts are to be disassembled, keep all parts in order so they can be assembled in their correct positions.

To install:

7. Clean all gasket mating surfaces.

8. If disassembled, coat the rocker arms and shafts with clean engine oil and reassemble.

9. Install the rocker arms/shafts assemblies with the shaft retaining bolts. Tighten the bolts, in sequence, to 16–21 ft. lbs. (22–28 Nm).

10. Install the valve cover with a new gasket. Tighten the valve cover retaining bolts to 44–79 inch lbs. (5–9 Nm).

11. Install the remaining components in the reverse order of removal.

Intake Manifold

REMOVAL AND INSTALLATION

1. Relieve the fuel system pressure. Disconnect the negative battery cable and drain the cooling system.

2. Remove the intake manifold bracket.

3. Disconnect the accelerator cable.

4. Identify, tag and disconnect the necessary vacuum hoses and electrical connectors.

5. Disconnect the fuel line(s).

6. Support the intake manifold by hand and remove the retaining bolts.

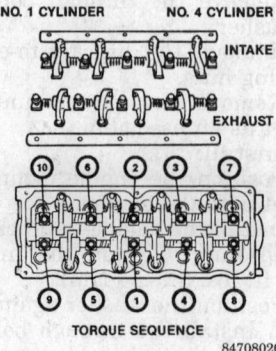

84708020

Rocker arm shaft bolt torque sequence

Remove the intake manifold from the cylinder head.

7. Remove the old gasket material and thoroughly clean the intake manifold and cylinder head surfaces.

To install:

8. Apply a new gasket to the cylinder head surface and hold in place.

9. Position the intake manifold onto the new gasket and install the retaining bolts. Torque the retaining bolts to 14–20 ft. lbs. (19–26 Nm) in a crisscross pattern, from the inside out.

10. Connect the vacuum hoses and electrical wiring to their respective connections. Install the accelerator cable.

11. Connect the fuel line(s).

12. Install the intake manifold bracket and tighten to 22–34 ft. lbs. (31–46 Nm).

13. Refill the cooling system to the proper level. Connect the negative battery cable.

14. Start the engine and check for leaks.

Exhaust Manifold

REMOVAL AND INSTALLATION

1. Disconnect the negative battery cable.

2. Raise and safely support the vehicle.

3. Disconnect the catalytic converter inlet pipe from the exhaust manifold.

4. If equipped, remove the pulse air tube-to-catalytic converter inlet pipe attaching nuts.

5. Unbolt the catalytic converter support bracket.

6. Lower the vehicle.

7. Remove the throttle body-to-air cleaner hose.

8. Remove the exhaust manifold heat shroud.

9. Separate the oxygen sensor wiring connector from the routing bracket and disconnect the electrical connector.

10. If equipped, unbolt the pulse air routing bracket clamp. Remove the pulse air tube and gaskets. Discard the gaskets.

11. Support the exhaust manifold by hand and remove the attaching nuts and bolts. Separate the exhaust manifold from the cylinder head and inlet pipe. Remove the inlet pipe and exhaust manifold gaskets and discard.

12. If necessary, remove the oxygen sensor. Inspect the sensor gasket for damage and replace if necessary.

To install:

13. Remove all existing gasket material from the exhaust manifold, cylinder head inlet pipe and, if equipped, the pulse air tube flange surfaces. Clean all threaded surfaces.

14. If removed, position the gasket onto the oxygen sensor and install into the exhaust manifold.

15. Apply a new gasket onto the cylinder head studs and position the exhaust manifold onto the gasket. Install the attaching nuts and bolts and torque to 12–17 ft. lbs. (16–23 Nm).

16. Install the heat shroud.

17. If equipped, install the pulse air tube and mounting bracket clamp. Install the air hose.

18. Connect the oxygen sensor electrical connector and secure the connector in the routing bracket.

19. Raise the vehicle and support it safely.

20. Position a new gasket over the exhaust manifold studs and, if equipped, 2 new gaskets onto the pulse air tube studs.

21. Raise the catalytic converter inlet pipe into position on the exhaust manifold and pulse air tube studs and support by hand. Install the attaching nuts and torque to 23–34 ft. lbs. (31–46 Nm).

22. Install the catalytic converter inlet pipe support bracket.

23. Lower the vehicle and connect the negative battery cable.

24. Start the engine and inspect for exhaust gas leaks.

Timing Belt Front Cover

REMOVAL AND INSTALLATION

1. Disconnect the negative battery cable. Remove the drive belts.

2. Remove the 3 water pump pulley attaching bolts and remove the water pump pulley.

3. Raise and safely support the vehicle.

4. Remove the right front wheel and tire assembly and the right inner fender panel.

5. Remove the 4 attaching bolts and the screws from the crankshaft pulley. Remove the spacer and outer pulley, if equipped. Remove the inner spacer, inner pulley and the baffle or guide plates, as required.

6. Remove the attaching bolts and the upper and lower covers.

To install:

7. Install the upper and lower covers. Install the attaching bolts and tighten to 69–95 inch lbs. (8–11 Nm).

8. Install the crankshaft pulley baffle with the curved lip facing outward or install the large guide plate and then the small guide plate, as required.

9. Install the inner pulley with the deep recess facing outward. Install the spacer and then the outer pulley, spacer and screws. Install the pulley bolts and tighten to 109–152 inch lbs. (12–17 Nm).

10. Install the inner fender panel and the wheel and tire assembly. Lower the vehicle.

11. Install the water pump pulley and tighten the bolts to 36–45 ft. lbs. (49–61 Nm).

12. Install the drive belts. Connect the negative battery cable.

OIL SEAL REPLACEMENT

1. Disconnect the negative battery cable.

2. Remove the timing belt covers and timing belt.

3. If replacing the crankshaft oil seal, proceed as follows:

   a. If equipped with manual transaxle, place the shift lever in 4th gear and apply the parking brake.

   b. If equipped with automatic transaxle, install flywheel holding tool T84P–6375–A or equivalent, to lock the flywheel.

   c. Remove the crankshaft sprocket attaching bolt, sprocket and key.

   d. Use a suitable tool to pry the crankshaft seal from the oil pump housing.

4. If replacing the camshaft oil seal, proceed as follows:

   a. Remove the valve cover.

   b. Use a large open-end wrench to hold the camshaft and remove the camshaft sprocket attaching bolt.

   c. Remove the sprocket.

   d. Drive the old seal through the cylinder head. Cut the seal with side cutters and remove the seal.

To install:

5. If replacing the camshaft oil seal, proceed as follows:

   a. Clean the camshaft and cylinder head seal surface.

   b. Lubricate the seal lip and camshaft seal surface with clean engine oil.

   c. Install the seal using a seal installer.

   d. Install the camshaft sprocket and bolt.

   e. Hold the camshaft with a large open-end wrench and tighten the sprocket bolt to 36–45 ft. lbs. (49–61 Nm).

   f. Install the valve cover and tighten the bolts to 44–80 inch lbs. (5–9 Nm).

6. If replacing the crankshaft oil seal, proceed as follows:

   a. Lubricate the lip of the new seal and the crankshaft seal surface with clean engine oil.

   b. Use a suitable tool to install the seal into the oil pump housing.

   c. Install the crankshaft sprocket and key.

   d. Coat the threads of the crankshaft sprocket bolt with a non-hardening sealer. Install the bolt and tighten to 80–85 ft. lbs. (108–118 Nm).

   e. Remove the flywheel holding tool.

7. Install the timing belt and timing belt covers.

8. Connect the negative battery cable.

Timing Belt and Tensioner

REMOVAL AND INSTALLATION

1. Disconnect the negative battery cable.

2. Remove the timing belt covers. Mark the direction of rotation of the timing belt, if the belt is to be reused.

3. Remove the timing belt tensioner spring and retaining bolt. Remove the timing belt.

To install:

4. Align the camshaft and crankshaft timing marks with the marks located on the cylinder head and oil pump housing.

5. If reusing the original timing belt, install the timing belt with the mark made indicating the direction of rotation.

6. Install the timing belt tensioner spring and cover on the pulley. Position the tensioner and spring assembly on the engine and install the attaching bolt. Do not tighten the bolt at this time.

7. Reconnect the free end of the spring to the spring anchor. Torque the tensioner bolt to 14–19 ft. lbs. (19–26 Nm).

8. Install the timing belt covers and connect the negative battery cable.

Timing Sprockets

REMOVAL AND INSTALLATION

Camshaft Sprocket

1. Disconnect the negative battery cable.

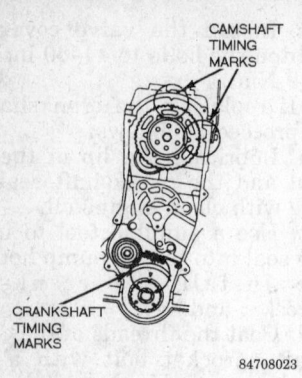

Camshaft and crankshaft timing mark locations

taining bolt to 36–45 ft. lbs. (49–61 Nm).

8. Install the timing belt and tensioner.

9. Install the valve cover and tighten the bolts to 44–80 inch lbs. (5–9 Nm).

10. Connect the negative battery cable.

Crankshaft Sprocket

1. Disconnect the negative battery cable.

2. Remove the timing belt and timing belt tensioner.

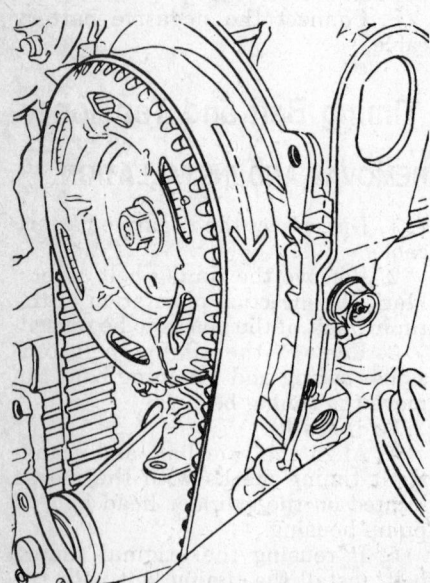

Direction of timing belt rotation

2. Remove the timing belt and timing belt tensioner.

3. Remove the valve cover.

4. With a large open-end wrench, hold the camshaft stationary and remove the camshaft sprocket retaining bolt.

5. Pull the camshaft sprocket with dowel pin from the camshaft. Take care not to lose the dowel pin.

To install:

6. Install the camshaft sprocket, dowel pin and retaining bolt.

7. Hold the camshaft stationary with the wrench and torque the re-

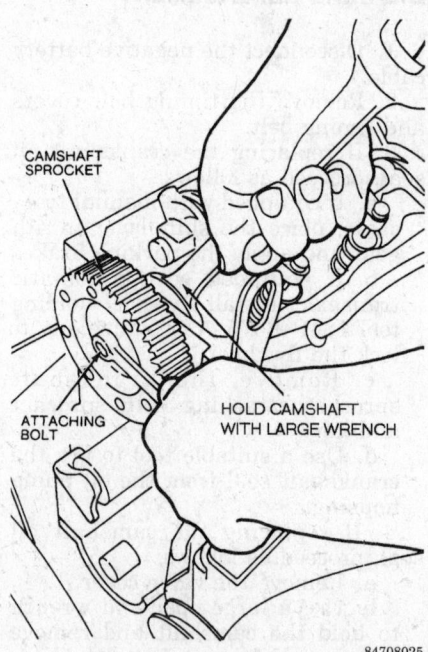

Camshaft sprocket removal

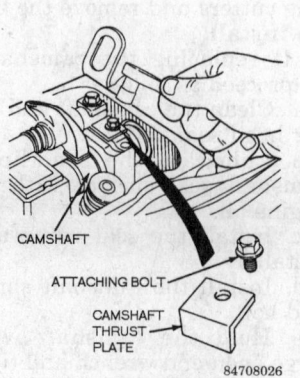

Camshaft thrust plate and bolt

3. If equipped with manual transaxle, place the shift lever in 4th gear and apply the parking brake. If equipped with automatic transaxle vehicle, install flywheel holding tool T84P–6375–A or equivalent.

4. Remove the crankshaft sprocket retaining bolt.

5. Pull the crankshaft sprocket and key from the crankshaft. Make certain not to lose the key when removing the crankshaft sprocket. Replace the key if worn or damaged.

To install:

6. Position the crankshaft sprocket onto the crankshaft and align the keyways. Install the key.

7. Coat the threads of the retaining bolt with non-hardening sealer. Install the retaining bolt and torque to 80–85 ft. lbs. (108–118 Nm).

8. Remove the flywheel holding tool.

9. Install the timing belt.

10. Connect the negative battery cable.

Camshaft

REMOVAL AND INSTALLATION

1. Disconnect the negative battery cable. Drain the cooling system.

2. Remove the cylinder head from the engine.

3. Position the cylinder head in a suitable holding fixture. Remove the camshaft sprocket. Remove the rocker arm/shaft assemblies.

4. Remove the camshaft thrust plate and the camshaft from the cylinder head.

5. Remove the camshaft seal.

To install:

6. Lubricate the camshaft journals, lobes and bearings with clean engine oil.

7. Carefully slide the camshaft into the cylinder head, being careful not to damage the journals, lobes or bearings. Install the camshaft thrust plate.

8. Lubricate the lip of the new camshaft seal with engine oil and install, using a seal installer.

9. Install the rocker arm/shaft assemblies and tighten the mounting bolts, in sequence, to 16–21 ft. lbs. (22–28 Nm).

10. Install the camshaft sprocket. Hold the camshaft with an open-end wrench and tighten the sprocket bolt to 36–45 ft. lbs. (49–61 Nm).

11. Install the cylinder head.

12. Fill the cooling system and connect the negative battery cable.

13. Start the engine and bring to normal operating temperature. Check for leaks.

Piston and Connecting Rod

POSITIONING

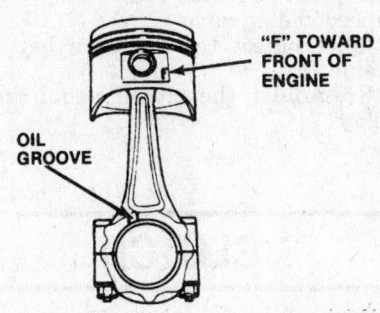

Piston and connecting rod positioning

ENGINE LUBRICATION

Oil Pan

REMOVAL AND INSTALLATION

1. Disconnect the negative battery cable. Raise and support the vehicle safely. Drain the engine oil.

2. Remove the flywheel dust cover retaining bolts and remove the cover.

NOTE: Depending on the position of the crankshaft, the oil pan may encounter interference during removal from the crankshaft counterweights or connecting rods. If necessary, rotate the crankshaft retaining bolt until the oil pan can be removed without crankshaft interference.

3. Support the oil pan and remove the oil pan to cylinder block bolts, nuts and stiffeners. Lower the oil pan. Discard the oil pan gasket.

4. As required, remove the baffle plate from the oil pan.

To install:

5. Clean the oil pan and cylinder block sealing surfaces to remove all traces of existing gasket material. From beneath the engine, apply a suitable oil resistant sealant to the joint line formed at the cylinder block and front and rear engine covers.

6. If equipped, install the baffle plate.

7. Apply the new rubber gasket to the oil pan.

8. Raise the oil pan and gasket against the cylinder block. Install the stiffeners, bolts and nuts. Torque the oil pan bolts in an alternate pattern to 69–78 inch lbs. (8–9 Nm).

9. Install the flywheel dust cover and attaching bolts. Torque the bolts to 61–87 inch lbs. (7–10 Nm).

10. Install the oil pan drain plug and lower the vehicle. Fill the crankcase to the proper level. Connect the negative battery cable.

11. Start the engine and allow the oil to reach normal operating temperature. Check for oil leaks and correct as required.

Oil Pump

REMOVAL AND INSTALLATION

1. Disconnect the negative battery cable. Raise and support the vehicle safely. Remove the crankshaft sprocket.

2. Drain the engine oil. Remove the oil pan.

3. Remove the oil pump assembly retaining bolts. Remove the oil pump assembly and gasket from the engine. Discard the gasket.

4. Remove the pickup tube and screen.

5. Remove the screws from the oil pump cover. Remove the cover. Remove the oil pump gears.

6. Remove the front seal from the pump assembly. Remove the cotter pin, spring and relief valve from the oil pump body.

To install:

7. Clean the oil pump housing and components with a suitable solvent and allow to dry.

8. Lubricate the oil pump relief valve and install into the bore. Install the spring, retainer and cotter pin.

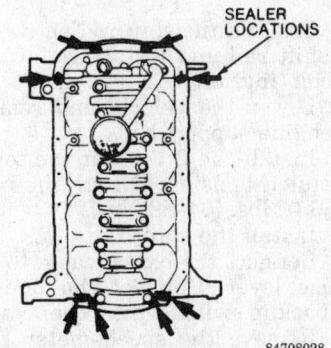

Oil pan sealant application points

9. Lubricate the lip of the new crankshaft seal and install the seal into the pump, using a suitable installation tool.

10. Lubricate and install the gears in the pump body and install the pump body cover. Coat the screws with a suitable locking compound and tighten.

11. Clean the cylinder block contact surface to remove the old gasket material and sealant. Thoroughly coat both sides of the new oil pump gasket with a suitable sealant compound. Apply the gasket to the oil pump and remove any excess sealant.

NOTE: Do not allow the sealant compound to enter the oil pump discharge opening once the gasket is in place. This opening must be free and clear before the oil pump is installed onto the cylinder block.

12. Position the oil pump against the cylinder block surface and install the retaining bolts. Torque the bolts to 14–19 ft. lbs. (19–25 Nm).

13. Install a new gasket onto the oil pump inlet and bolt the pickup tube to the oil pump. Torque the bolts to 69–95 inch lbs. (8–11 Nm).

14. Install the oil pan and the crankshaft sprocket.

15. Lower the vehicle. Fill the crankcase to the proper level with engine oil. Connect the negative battery cable.

16. Start the engine and allow the oil to reach normal operating temperature. Check for leaks and correct as required.

CHECKING

1. Remove the oil pump assembly from the vehicle and disassemble. Clean all parts in solvent and allow to dry.

2. Measure the inner gear tip-to-outer gear clearance at the minimum clearance point. The clearance should be 0.0078 in. (0.198mm) maximum.

3. Inspect the oil pump body for scoring in the outer gear bore. A slight amount of scoring is acceptable.

4. Measure the housing-to-outer gear clearance with a feeler gauge. The clearance should be no more than 0.0087 in. (0.22mm).

5. Measure the gear endplay. Gear endplay should not exceed 0.0055 in. (0.140mm). If the pump clearances are not within specification, replace the gears or the body. Clean the relief valve internals and inspect for nicks,

burrs or binding operation. Clean the pickup tube and screen.

6. Assemble the oil pump relief valve into the bore. Install the spring, retainer and cotter pin.

7. Press or drive a new oil seal into the oil pump body bore.

8. Coat the cover attaching screws with a suitable thread locking compound and install the cover.

9. Install the oil pump assembly in the vehicle.

Rear Main Bearing Oil Seal

REMOVAL AND INSTALLATION

1. Disconnect the negative battery cable.

2. Remove the transaxle from the vehicle.

3. Remove the flywheel. If necessary, remove the cover plate.

4. Remove the seal retainer. Remove the crankshaft seal.

To install:

5. Clean the sealing surface on the cover plate.

6. Apply engine oil to the inside and outside of a new seal. Install the seal into the cover plate using a seal installer, with the hollow part of the seal facing the engine.

7. Install the seal retainer and tighten to 69–95 inch lbs. (8–11 Nm).

8. Trim the excess gasket material off the seal retainer gasket after installation.

9. Install the cover plate and tighten the attaching bolts to 69–95 inch lbs. (8–11 Nm).

10. Install the flywheel and tighten the bolts to 71–76 ft. lbs. (96–103 Nm).

11. Install the transaxle. Connect the negative battery cable.

MANUAL TRANSAXLE

Transaxle Assembly

REMOVAL AND INSTALLATION

1. Disconnect the negative battery cable.

2. Disconnect the backup light switch wiring connector.

3. Disconnect the neutral switch wiring connector.

4. Loosen the clutch cable adjusting nut and disengage the cable from the release lever.

5. Remove the starter.

6. Disconnect the speedometer cable.

7. Remove the 2 bolts from the top of the clutch housing.

8. Install 3 bar engine support tool D88L–6000–A, or equivalent. Raise and support the vehicle safely.

9. Remove the nut and bolt attaching the shift rod to the input shift rail.

10. Remove the nuts and bolts attaching the lower control arms to the steering knuckles.

11. Disengage the halfshafts from the differential side gears.

12. Install differential side gear plug tool T87C–7025–C or equivalent, to prevent the side gears from moving.

13. Remove the mounting bracket attaching bolts and the mounting brackets.

14. Remove the crossmember.

15. Position a suitable transmission jack under the transaxle and secure it with a safety chain.

16. Remove the remaining lower transaxle attaching bolts. Pull the transaxle away from the engine and lower it from the vehicle.

To install:

17. Raise the transaxle into position and seat it against the rear of the engine.

18. Install the lower transaxle attaching bolts. Torque the bolts to 47–66 ft. lbs. (64–89 Nm).

19. Install the mounting brackets and remove the transmission jack.

20. Install the crossmember and remove the differential plugs.

21. Remove and discard the old halfshaft circlips. Install new circlips and engage the halfshafts with the differential side gears.

22. Connect the lower control arms to the steering knuckles. Install the lower control arm attaching bolts and nuts.

23. Position the shift rod on the input shift rail and install the attaching bolt and nut.

24. Lower the vehicle and remove the engine support bar.

25. Install the 2 bolts at the top of the clutch housing. Torque the bolts 47–66 ft. lbs. (64–89 Nm).

26. Install the starter.

27. Connect the clutch cable to the release lever. Connect the neutral and backup switch wiring connectors.

28. Remove the speedometer gear and sleeve assembly from the transaxle case bore. With a clean rag,

wipe the assembly and reinsert the sleeve into the transaxle. Remove the sleeve and check the oil level. The oil level should be between the **F** and **L** marks on the gear sleeve. If the level is not within the normal operating range, add oil through the speedometer bore as required.

29. Install the speedometer sleeve and gear assembly and connect the speedometer cable.

30. Connect the negative battery cable.

31. Adjust the clutch pedal free-play.

CLUTCH

Clutch Assembly

REMOVAL AND INSTALLATION

1. Disconnect the negative battery cable.

2. Remove the transaxle assembly.

NOTE: During the removal procedure, do not allow oil or grease to come in contact with the clutch disc facing if the disc is to be reused. Handle the disc with clean rags wrapped around the edges and do not touch the disc facing. Even a small amount of dirt or grease may cause the clutch to grab or slip.

3. If the pressure plate is to be reused, paint or scribe alignment marks on the pressure plate and flywheel for assembly reference.

4. Install an appropriate locking tool to prevent the flywheel from turning.

5. Loosen the pressure plate attaching bolts in an alternate pattern 1 turn at a time. This will relieve the pressure plate spring tension evenly and prevent distortion of the pressure plate. Remove the pressure plate and clutch disc after the bolts are removed. Replace all clutch components as required.

6. Inspect the flywheel for scoring, cracks and heat checks. Resurface or replace the flywheel, as necessary.

7. Inspect the pilot bearing for damage. Make sure the bearing turns easily. If replacement is necessary, remove the flywheel and remove the pilot bearing.

To install:

8. If necessary, install a new pilot bearing using a suitable installation

tool. Use only a driver tool that contacts the bearing outer race. A driver tool that contacts the inner race or the bearing area is unsuitable.

9. If the flywheel was removed, clean the sealant from the flywheel attaching bolts. Coat the bolt threads with a suitable sealer compound.

10. Make sure the crankshaft flange and the back of the flywheel are clean. Position the flywheel on the crankshaft and install the attaching bolts. Tighten the bolts to 71–76 ft. lbs. (96–103 Nm).

11. Position the clutch disc on the flywheel and install a clutch alignment tool to hold the disc in place.

NOTE: When installing the clutch disc, make sure the disc dampener springs are facing away from the flywheel. A new disc will be stamped FLYWHEEL to indicate the correct installation position.

12. Align the reference marks, if present, and position the pressure plate on the flywheel and install the attaching bolts. Torque the bolts evenly, in an alternate pattern, to 13–20 ft. lbs. (18–26 Nm). The bolts must be tightened in this manner to prevent distortion of the pressure plate.

13. Remove the clutch alignment tool.

14. Clean the clutch disc splines on the input shaft with a dry rag and coat the spline surfaces with a light film of clutch grease.

15. Install the transaxle.

16. Connect the negative battery cable.

17. Adjust the clutch pedal free-play.

PEDAL HEIGHT ADJUSTMENT

1. To eliminate the possibility that the clutch cable is affecting the pedal height, disconnect it at the transaxle release lever. Move the floor carpet and insulation out of the way of the dash panel to ensure an accurate measurement.

2. Measure the distance from the upper center of the pedal to the cowl panel. The pedal height should be from 8.2–8.4 in. (208.2–213.2mm). If the pedal height is within this range, no adjustment is necessary. If the pedal height is not within specification, inspect the clutch pedal mounting for damaged, worn or missing parts. If the mounting appears to be satisfactory, proceed as follows:

   a. Remove the air duct located under the steering column.

b. Locate the clutch switch and loosen the attaching nuts. Thread the switch in or out until the pedal height is within specification. Tighten the attaching nuts when the correct height is obtained.

c. Connect the clutch cable to the transaxle release lever and adjust the pedal free-play.

d. If the pedal height changes after connecting the clutch cable, check for binding along the cable route.

e. Install the air duct. Place the insulation and floor carpet in their original positions.

FREE-PLAY ADJUSTMENT

1. Carefully move the clutch pedal back and forth and measure the amount of travel. If the clutch pedal free-play is 0.35–0.59 in. (9–15mm), no adjustment is necessary. If the free-play is not within specification, proceed to Step 2.

2. Pull back the transaxle release lever and measure the clearance between the lever and the cable pin. Thread the adjuster in or out until the clearance between the pin and the lever is 0.06–0.10 in. (1.5–2.5mm).

3. Check the free-play at the clutch. If it is not within specifica-

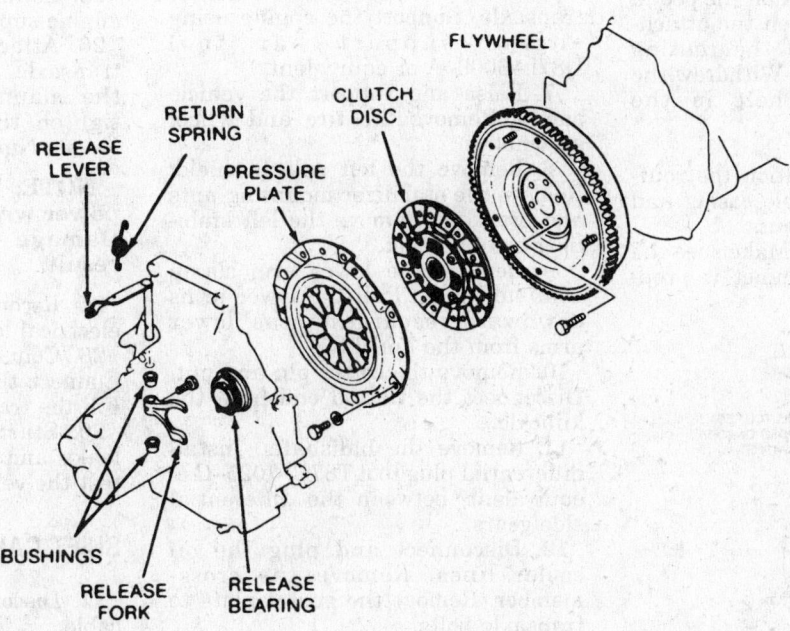

RELEASE LEVER

RETURN SPRING

PRESSURE PLATE

CLUTCH DISC

FLYWHEEL

BUSHINGS

RELEASE FORK

RELEASE BEARING

84708031

Exploded view of the clutch assembly

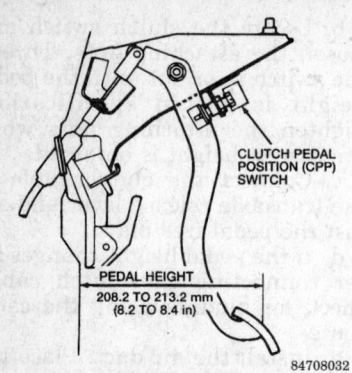

CLUTCH PEDAL
POSITION (CPP)
SWITCH

PEDAL HEIGHT
208.2 TO 213.2 mm
(8.2 TO 8.4 in)

84708032

Clutch pedal height adjustment

tion, inspect the clutch release components for a problem.

Clutch Cable

REMOVAL AND INSTALLATION

1. Loosen the clutch cable adjuster nut at the transaxle release lever until the cable can be disengaged from the lever.
2. Unbolt the cable routing bracket from the transaxle housing.
3. Remove the air duct located under the steering column.
4. Remove the clip securing the cable casing to the pedal support bracket.
5. Pull upward on the cable to disengage it from the hook on the pedal.
6. If necessary, loosen the attaching nut and remove the routing bracket from the cable. Withdraw the cable through the hole in the bulkhead.
   To install:
7. If necessary, position the routing bracket on the cable casing and tighten the attaching nuts.
8. Install the cable. Make sure the instrument panel grommet is properly seated.

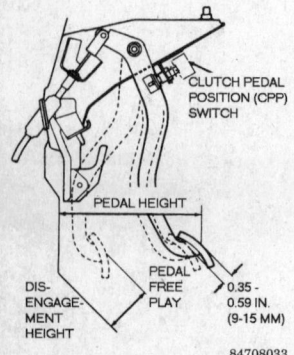

CLUTCH PEDAL
POSITION (CPP)
SWITCH

PEDAL HEIGHT

DIS-
ENGAGE-
MENT
HEIGHT

PEDAL
FREE
PLAY

0.35 -
0.59 IN.
(9-15 MM)

84708033

Clutch cable free-play adjustment

9. Pull upward on the cable and hook it over the top of the clutch pedal.
10. Install the cable casing retaining clip.
11. Install the air duct.
12. Connect the cable to the release lever. Check the clutch pedal freeplay and adjust if necessary.

AUTOMATIC TRANSAXLE

Transaxle Assembly

REMOVAL AND INSTALLATION

1. Disconnect the negative battery cable. Loosen the front wheel bolts.
2. Drain the transaxle fluid. Disconnect the speedometer cable from the transaxle.
3. Disconnect the transaxle electrical connectors, which are located next to the governor.
4. Disconnect the transaxle ground wire. Disconnect the transaxle vacuum hose.
5. Remove the nut which connects the shift linkage to the manual shaft assembly.
6. Remove the shift cable from the transaxle. Support the engine using engine support bar tool D87L–6000–A or equivalent.
7. Raise and support the vehicle safely. Remove the tire and wheel assemblies.
8. Remove the left splash shield. Remove the stabilizer mounting nuts and brackets. Remove the left stabilizer body bracket.
9. Remove the lower arm clamp bolts and nuts. Pull the lower arms downward, separating the lower arms from the knuckles.
10. Remove the cotter pin and nut. Disconnect the tie rod end from the knuckle.
11. Remove the halfshafts. Install differential plug tool T87C–7025–C or equivalent, between the differential side gears.
12. Disconnect and plug the oil cooler lines. Remove the crossmember. Remove the gusset plate to transaxle bolts.
13. Remove the flywheel cover. Remove the torque converter retaining bolts. Remove the starter.
14. Properly support the transaxle assembly.

15. Remove the engine-to-transaxle retaining bolts. Carefully remove the transaxle from the vehicle.
    To install:
16. Position the transaxle in the vehicle. Install the engine-to-transaxle bolts. Tighten to 41–59 ft. lbs. (55–80 Nm).
17. Install the starter. Install the torque converter bolts and tighten to 26–36 ft. lbs. (34–49 Nm).
18. Install the flywheel cover and tighten the bolts to 61–87 inch lbs. (7–10 Nm).
19. Install the crossmember and tighten the bolts to 47–66 ft. lbs. (64–89 Nm). Install the front engine mount-to-crossmember attaching nuts and tighten to 32–38 ft. lbs. (43–52 Nm). Install the rear engine mount-to-crossmember attaching nut and tighten to 21–34 ft. lbs. (28–46 Nm).
20. Install the halfshafts. Connect the oil cooler lines.
21. Connect the tie rod ends to the steering knuckles and tighten the attaching nuts to 26–30 ft. lbs. (35–40 Nm). Install new cotter pins.
22. Attach the lower arm ball joints to the knuckles. Tighten the lower arm clamp nuts and bolts to 32–40 ft. lbs. (43–54 Nm).
23. Install the stabilizer body bracket and mounting nuts. Tighten the nuts to 40–45 ft. lbs. (54–61 Nm).
24. Install the splash shield and the front wheel and tire assemblies.
25. Lower the vehicle. Remove the engine support tool.
26. Attach the shift cable to the transaxle. Install the shift linkage on the manual shaft assembly and tighten the nut to 34–47 ft. lbs. (44–64 Nm).

NOTE: Do not use any type of power wrench to tighten the nut. Damage to the transaxle may result.

27. Reconnect the vacuum hose and electrical leads.
28. Connect the speedometer cable. Connect the negative battery cable. Fill the transaxle to the proper level.
29. Start the engine. Check for leaks and proper fluid level. Road test the vehicle.

SHIFT CABLE ADJUSTMENT

1. Disconnect the negative battery cable.
2. Remove the shift lever knob and the shift console attaching screws. Remove the shift console.
3. Shift the selector lever to the **P** position.

4. Remove the 4 shift quadrant attaching screws and the shift quadrant.

NOTE: Make sure the detent spring roller is in the P detent.

5. Loosen adjustment nuts "A" and "B" until they reach the ends of the cable thread.
6. Move the shift lever on the transaxle to the **P** position.
7. Tighten adjustment nut "A" by hand until it lightly contacts the T-joint, then tighten adjustment nut "B" to 80–97 inch lbs. (9–11 Nm).
8. Lightly press the selector pushrod and make sure the guide plate and guide pin clearances are within specification.
9. Check that the plate and pin clearances are within the same specifications when the selector lever is shifted to **N** and **D**. If the clearances are not as specified, readjust the shift cable.
10. Make sure the selector lever operates properly.
11. Install the shift quadrant, shift console and selector lever knob.
12. Connect the negative battery cable.

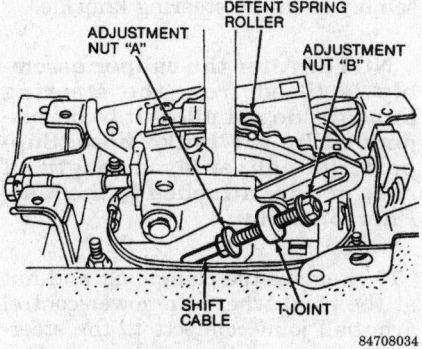

Shift cable adjustment points

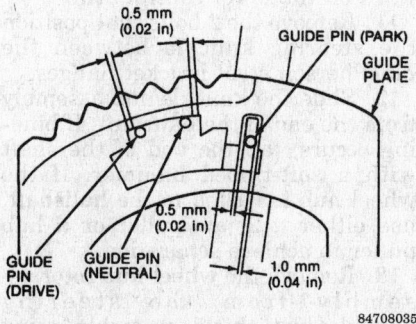

Guide plate and guide pin clearances

SHIFT QUADRANT ADJUSTMENT

1. Remove the shift console.
2. Shift the selector into the **P** position.
3. Remove the selector lever knob and locknut.
4. Remove the shift quadrant attaching screws and quadrant. Make sure the detent is in the **P** position.
5. Align the holes in the slider and the shift quadrant, then install an alignment pin to hold the slider in this position.
6. Position the shift quadrant and tighten the attaching screws. Remove the alignment pin.
7. Verify that the clearance between the lock lever and the emergency override lever is within 0.02–0.20 in. (0.5–3.0mm).
8. Install the locknut and selector lever knob. Torque the locknut to 15 ft. lbs. (20 Nm).
9. Install the shift console and check for proper operation.

DRIVE AXLE

Halfshaft

REMOVAL AND INSTALLATION

1. Disconnect the negative battery cable.
2. Raise the vehicle and support it safely.
3. Drain the transaxle fluid.
4. Remove the front wheel and tire assembly. Remove the splash shields.
5. Bend back the lockwing tab on the halfshaft nut. Have an assistant apply the brakes, then loosen but do not remove, the halfshaft locknut.
6. Remove the stabilizer mounting nuts and brackets.
7. Remove the clamp bolt and nut from the lower suspension control arm. With a suitable prybar, pry the lower suspension control arm downward to disconnect the ball joint. Be careful not to tear or puncture the dust boot when disconnecting the ball joint.
8. Using a small prybar, separate the halfshaft from the transaxle.

NOTE: The halfshaft must be separated from the transaxle gradually. If the halfshaft is pulled or jerked suddenly, the oil seal may be damaged.

9. Remove and discard the halfshaft locking nut.
10. Withdraw the halfshaft from the wheel hub. Be careful not to damage the oil seal. If the halfshaft is stuck in the hub, use a suitable puller to push out the halfshaft.
11. Install differential plug tool T87C–7025–C or equivalent, to prevent the differential side gear from moving.

To install:
12. Inspect the differential and wheel hub oil seals for damage and replace, as required.
13. Remove the circlip from the inboard halfshaft spline end and replace with new. Coat the inboard and outboard halfshaft spline ends with grease.
14. Remove the differential gear holding plug.
15. Position and install the inboard end of the halfshaft into the differential side gear. Take care not to damage the differential oil seal.
16. Position and install the outboard end of the halfshaft into the wheel hub. Take care not to damage the wheel hub oil seal.
17. Install the halfshaft locknut onto the halfshaft and tighten by hand.
18. Raise the lower suspension control arm and connect the arm to the ball joint. Take care not to damage the ball joint dust boot.
19. Install the lower suspension arm clamp nut and bolt. Hold the bolt stationary and torque the nut to 32–40 ft. lbs. (43–54 Nm).
20. Have an assistant apply the brakes, then torque the outboard halfshaft locknut to 116–174 ft. lbs. (157–235 Nm). Stake the nut using a suitable tool.

NOTE: Do not stake the locking tab with a pointed tool. Make sure the locking tab is depressed at least 0.16 in. (4mm) into the locknut slot to ensure proper locking capability. After the lockwasher is locked into place, grasp the wheel hub and pull to ensure that the halfshaft is installed properly. Rotate the wheel hub by hand to ensure that the wheel hub turns smoothly.

21. Install the stabilizer brackets and mounting bracket nuts. Tighten the nuts to 40–50 ft. lbs. (54–68 Nm).
22. Install the splash shields and the wheel and tire assemblies. Install and tighten the transaxle drain plug.
23. Fill the transaxle with the proper grade and type fluid to specification. Lower the vehicle.

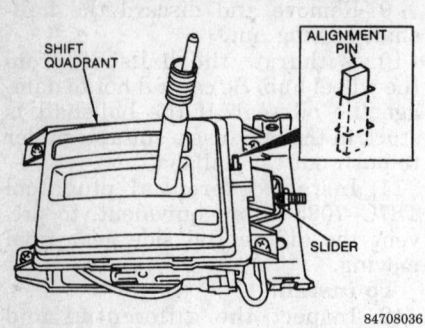

SHIFT QUADRANT

ALIGNMENT PIN

SLIDER

84708036

Shift quadrant adjustment and alignment pin location

CV-Boot

REMOVAL AND INSTALLATION

There are 2 different types of CV–joints used. All vehicles are equipped with Tripot type inboard CV–joints and Birfield outboard CV–joints. The Tripot CV–joints can be disassembled and serviced, however the Birfield CV–joint is serviced only as an assembly with the shaft. Consequently, if outboard CV–joint boot replacement is necessary, the inboard CV–joint must first be disassembled.

1. Raise and support the vehicle safely.

2. Remove the halfshaft from the vehicle. Support the assembly in a vise with protective jaws.

3. Use side cutters to cut and remove the large boot clamp from the inboard CV–joint. Roll the boot back over the shaft.

4. Check the grease for contamination by rubbing it between 2 fingers. Any gritty feeling indicates a contaminated CV–joint. A contaminated joint must be completely disassembled, cleaned and inspected. If the grease is not contaminated and the CV–joint has been operating properly, continue with boot replacement and add the required grease.

5. Remove the wire ring bearing retainer. Paint alignment marks on the outer race and Tripot bearing for installation reference, then remove the outer race.

6. Paint alignment marks on the Tripot bearing and shaft for assembly reference, then remove the Tripot bearing snapring. Using a brass drift and hammer, remove the Tripot bearing from the shaft.

7. Remove the small clamp and the CV–joint boot from the halfshaft. If the boot is to be reused, cover the

splines with tape before removing the boot.

8. If replacing the right outboard CV–joint boot, remove the dynamic damper.

9. If replacing the outboard CV–joint boot, remove the clamps and slide the boot off the shaft from the inboard side.

To install:

10. Cover the halfshaft splines with tape.

11. If replacing the outboard CV–joint boot, slide the boot onto the halfshaft and onto the outboard CV–joint. Insert a small prybar between the boot and joint to allow trapped air to escape from the boot.

12. Wrap new clamps around the boots in a clockwise direction, pull tight with pliers and bend the locking tabs to secure in position.

13. If removed, install the dynamic damper onto the halfshaft at a distance of 18.99–19.27 in. (482.5–489.5mm) from the outboard end of the halfshaft with the outboard halfshaft fully pushed onto the halfshaft.

14. Install the inboard CV–joint boot onto the halfshaft, then remove the tape.

15. Install the Tripot assembly on the halfshaft using a brass drift and hammer, making sure the marks made during the removal procedure are aligned.

16. Install the Tripot assembly retaining ring.

17. Fill the CV–joint outer race with 3.5 oz. of high temperature CV–joint grease. Install the outer race over the Tripot joint and install the wire ring bearing retainer. Align the marks that were made during the removal procedure.

18. Position the CV–joint boot. Make sure the boot is fully seated in the grooves in the shaft and outer race. Extend or compress the joint, as necessary, until the distance between the CV–joint boot clamp grooves measures 3.5 in. (90mm).

19. Insert a small prybar between the boot and the outer bearing race to allow trapped air to escape from the boot. Install the boot clamps, wrapping them around the boots in a clockwise direction. Pull the clamps tight with a suitable tool and bend the locking tabs to secure in position.

20. Work the CV–joint through its full range of travel at various angles. The joint should flex, extend and compress smoothly.

21. Install the halfshaft in the vehicle.

Front Wheel Hub, Knuckle and Bearings

REMOVAL AND INSTALLATION

1. Disconnect the negative battery cable.

2. Raise the vehicle and support it safely.

3. Unbolt and remove front wheel from the hub assembly.

4. With a small chisel, straighten the staked edge of the halfshaft attaching nut. Take care not to damage the halfshaft threads.

5. Remove and discard the halfshaft attaching nut.

6. Remove the retaining clip securing the caliper hose to the strut bracket.

7. Remove the cotter pin and tie rod end attaching nut. Discard the cotter pin and set the nut aside. Inspect the nut for damage and replace as required.

8. Using a tie rod end separator tool, release the tie rod end from the steering knuckle arm. If the tie rod appears to be seized, strike the knuckle sharply with a soft-tipped hammer to achieve separation.

9. Remove the brake caliper attaching bolts and lift the caliper assembly from the steering knuckle.

NOTE: After the caliper assembly is lifted from the steering knuckle, do not allow it to be suspended by the brake hose. Support the caliper by a length of rope or wire attached to the MacPherson strut.

10. Remove the clamp bolt and nut at the point where the lower control arm ball joint connects to the steering knuckle. With a medium prybar, release the lower ball joint from the steering knuckle by prying downward on the lower control arm.

11. Remove the 2 bolts that position the steering knuckle between the MacPherson strut bracket flanges.

12. Slide the knuckle/hub assembly from the end of the halfshaft. If binding occurs, tap the end of the shaft with a soft-tipped hammer. If the wheel hub is rusted to the halfshaft, use either a 2 jaw puller or a hub puller to achieve separation.

13. Remove the wheel hub/rotor assembly from the steering knuckle/dust shield assembly using knuckle puller tool T87C–1104–A or equivalent.

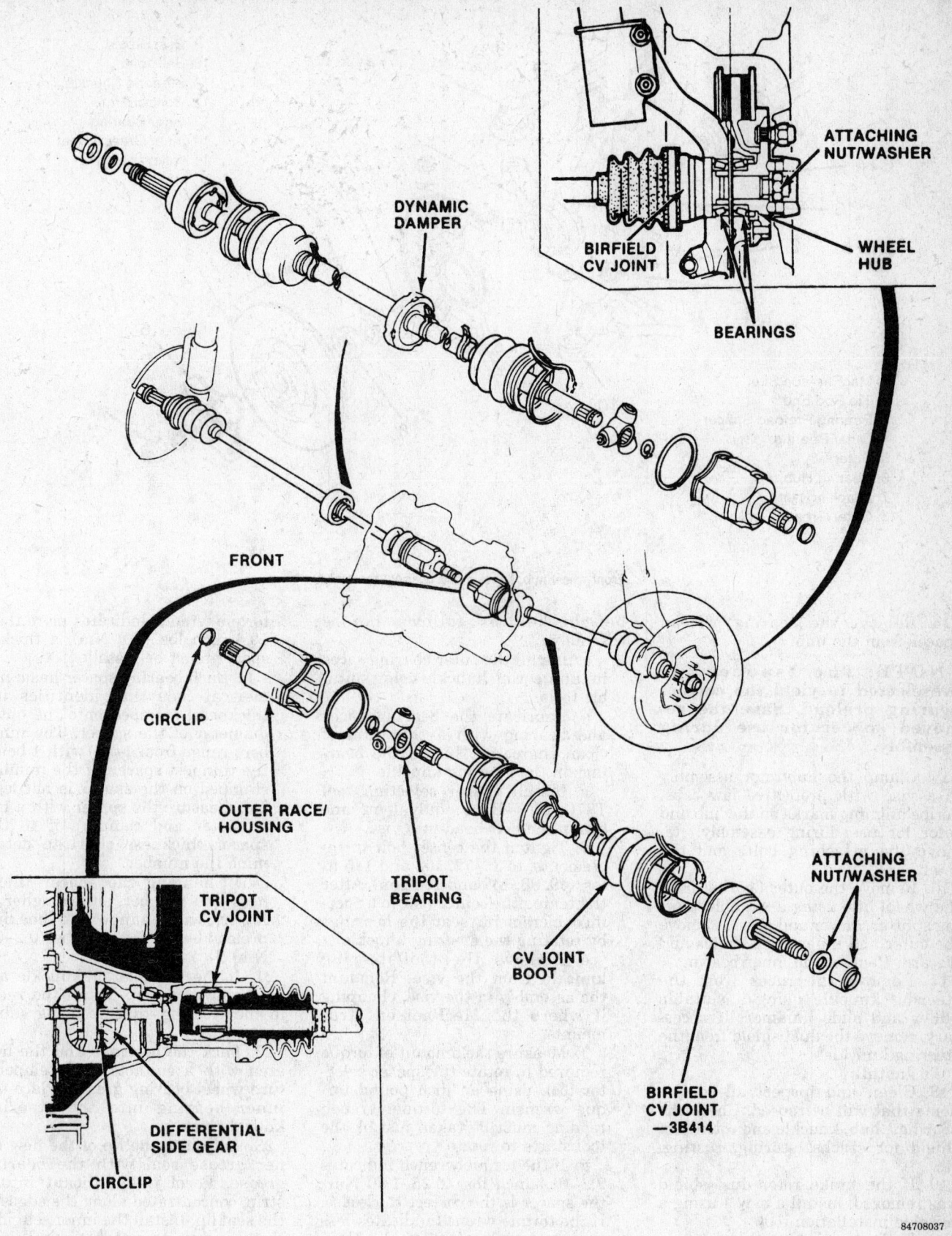

ATTACHING
NUT/WASHER

BIRFIELD
CV JOINT

WHEEL
HUB

BEARINGS

DYNAMIC
DAMPER

FRONT

CIRCLIP

OUTER RACE/
HOUSING

TRIPOT
BEARING

TRIPOT
CV JOINT

DIFFERENTIAL
SIDE GEAR

CIRCLIP

CV JOINT
BOOT

ATTACHING
NUT/WASHER

BIRFIELD
CV JOINT
—3B414

84708037

Halfshaft assembly

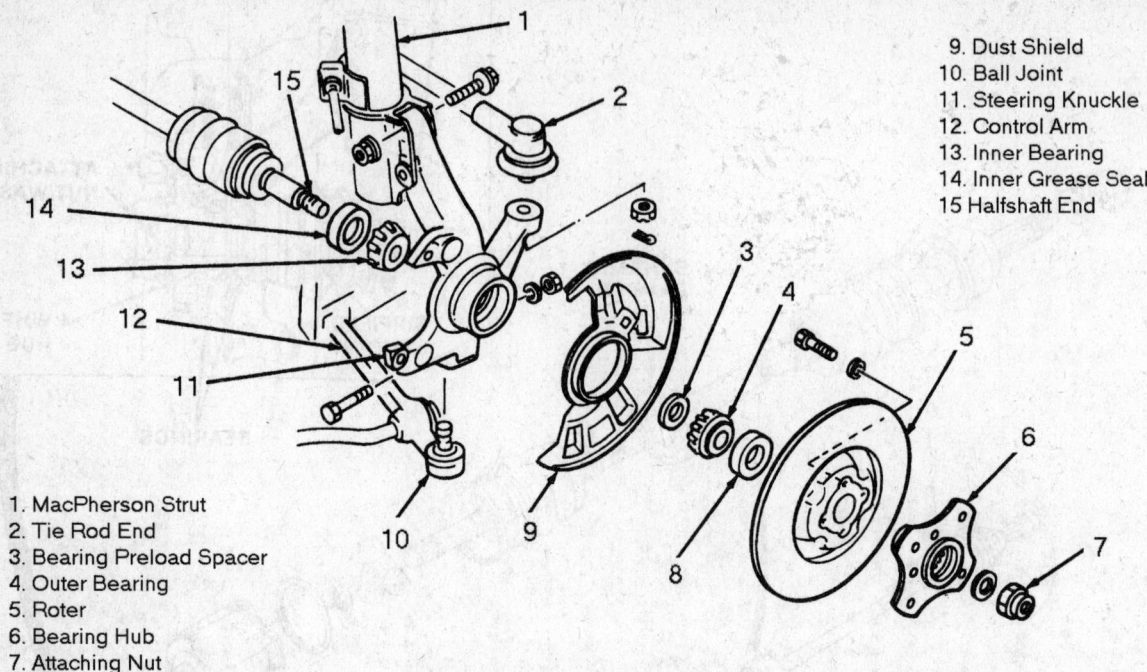

9. Dust Shield
10. Ball Joint
11. Steering Knuckle
12. Control Arm
13. Inner Bearing
14. Inner Grease Seal
15 Halfshaft End

1. MacPherson Strut
2. Tie Rod End
3. Bearing Preload Spacer
4. Outer Bearing
5. Roter
6. Bearing Hub
7. Attaching Nut
8. Outer Grease Seal

84708038

Front wheel hub, knuckle and bearing assembly

14. Remove the bearing preload spacer from the hub.

NOTE: The spacer is preselected to yield the correct bearing preload. Save the removed spacer for use during assembly.

15. Clamp the hub/rotor assembly in a vise with protective jaw caps. Scribe aligning marks on the hub and rotor for use during assembly. Remove the attaching bolts and the rotor.

16. Remove the outer bearing from the wheel hub using a suitable bearing splitter, driver and press. Remove the outer and inner grease seals and discard. Remove the inner bearing.

17. Remove the races from the steering knuckle using a suitable puller and slide hammer. If necessary, remove the dust shield from the steering knuckle.

To install:

18. Clean and inspect all components that will be reused. Check the bearings, hub, knuckle and rotor dust shield for cracks, scoring, rusting, etc.

19. If the brake rotor dust shield was removed, install a new 1 using a suitable installation tool.

20. If the bearings or knuckle are being replaced, bearing preload must be checked as follows before assembly.

a. Install the outer bearing races in the steering knuckle using suitable tools.

b. Lubricate the bearing races and bearing with a thin film of clean engine oil. Install the bearings in the steering knuckle.

c. Install spacer selection tool T87C–1104–B or equivalent, and clamp the bolt head in a vise.

d. Tighten the center bolt in increments, to 36, 72, 108 and 145 ft. lbs. (49, 98, 147 and 196 Nm). After tightening the center bolt to a specified increment, seat the bearings by rotating the steering knuckle.

e. Remove the tool/steering knuckle from the vise. Remount the assembly in the vise, clamping it where the MacPherson strut mounts.

f. Measure the amount of torque required to rotate the spacer selector tool, using an inch pound torque wrench. The torque wrench reading must be taken just as the tool starts to rotate.

g. If the torque wrench indicates 2.2–10.4 inch lbs. (0.25–1.80 Nm), the spacer is the correct thickness. If the torque wrench indicates less than 2.2 inch lbs. (0.25 Nm), a thinner spacer must be installed. If the torque wrench indicates more than 10.4 inch lbs. (1.8 Nm), a thicker spacer must be installed.

h. Each bearing spacer has a numerical code that identifies it's thickness, stamped onto the outer diameter of the spacer. The numbers range from 1–21, with 1 being the thinnest spacer. If the number stamped on the spacer is not legible, measure the spacer with a micrometer and compare it to the spacer thickness chart to determine the number.

i. Changing the spacer thickness by 1 number, either higher or lower, will change the bearing preload by 1.7–3.5 inch lbs. (0.2–0.4 Nm).

21. If the bearings or knuckle are not being replaced, install the races in the steering knuckle using suitable tools.

22. Pack the bearings and the hub area with a suitable high temperature wheel bearing grease. Place the inner bearing into the steering knuckle bore.

23. Lubricate the lip of the new inner grease seal with the bearing grease. Form the lubricant into a strip, concentrated along the edges of the seal lip. Install the inner seal into the bore, using a suitable installation tool.

24. Place the original bearing preload spacer or the spacer selected from the bearing preload check procedure, in the steering knuckle bore. Position the bearing removed from the wheel hub in the steering knuckle bore.

25. Lubricate the lip of the new outer grease seal with the bearing grease. Form the lubricant into a strip, concentrated along the edges of the seal lip. Install the outer seal into the bore, using a suitable installation tool.

26. Position the rotor on the hub, observing the original aligning marks, and install the attaching bolts. Tighten the attaching bolts to 33–40 ft. lbs. (44–54 Nm).

27. Position the hub/rotor assembly in the steering knuckle bore and press it into position using a suitable driver.

28. Clean the halfshaft spline end and lubricate with a coating of wheel bearing grease. Apply a thin film of clean SAE 30 weight oil to the steering knuckle/rotor hub assembly up to the point where the uppermost arm of the steering knuckle seats into the MacPherson strut bracket. Guide the steering knuckle/rotor/hub assembly onto the halfshaft and the MacPherson strut.

29. Install the strut-to-steering knuckle bolts and attaching nuts. Tighten the nuts to 69–86 ft. lbs. (93–117 Nm).

30. Position the lower control arm ball joint in the steering knuckle. Install the lower control arm pinch bolt and attaching nut. Tighten the nut to 32–40 ft. lbs. (43–54 Nm).

31. Position the caliper on the steering knuckle and install the attaching bolts. Tighten the bolts to 29–36 ft. lbs. (39–49 Nm). Position the caliper hose in the strut routing bracket and install the retaining clip.

32. Install a new halfshaft attaching nut and tighten to 116–174 ft. lbs. (157–235 Nm). After installation, the wheel hub assembly must rotate freely by hand. Stake the halfshaft attaching nut into the shaft groove.

NOTE: Do not use a pointed tool to stake the nut. If the nut cracks even slightly during staking, replace it with another new one.

33. Connect the tie rod end to the steering knuckle and install the attaching nut. Tighten the attaching nut to 22–33 ft. lbs. (29–44 Nm). Install a new cotter pin through the nut and ball stud. If the openings in the nut and the hole in the ball stud are not aligned, tighten the nut slightly, just to the point of alignment. Never loosen the nut.

34. Install the wheel and tire assembly. Tighten the attaching bolts to 65–87 ft. lbs. (88–118 Nm). Lower the vehicle.

STEERING

Steering Wheel

REMOVAL AND INSTALLATION

1. Disconnect the negative battery cable.

2. Remove the 2 screws from the back of the steering wheel. Disconnect the horn wire and remove the steering wheel cover.

3. Remove the steering wheel nut.

4. Remove the attaching screws and washers located to the left and right of the steering column stud, if equipped. Remove the 2 screws from the back of the steering wheel spokes. Disconnect the horn wire and remove the cover assembly.

5. Matchmark the steering wheel and steering column shaft for assembly reference. Using a steering wheel puller tool, remove the steering wheel.

Stamped mark	Thickness
1	6.285 mm (0.2474 in)
2	6.325 mm (0.2490 in)
3	6.365 mm (0.2506 in)
4	6.405 mm (0.2522 in)
5	6.445 mm (0.2538 in)
6	6.485 mm (0.2554 in)
7	6.525 mm (0.2570 in)
8	6.565 mm (0.2586 in)
9	6.605 mm (0.2602 in)
10	6.645 mm (0.2618 in)
11	6.685 mm (0.2634 in)
12	6.725 mm (0.2650 in)
13	6.765 mm (0.2666 in)
14	6.805 mm (0.2682 in)
15	6.845 mm (0.2698 in)
16	6.885 mm (0.2714 in)
17	6.925 mm (0.2730 in)
18	6.965 mm (0.2746 in)
19	7.005 mm (0.2762 in)
20	7.045 mm (0.2778 in)
21	7.085 mm (0.2794 in)

84708040

Front wheel bearing preload spacer thickness

6. Installation is the reverse of the removal procedure. Position the steering wheel onto the steering column shaft and align the matchmarks. Tighten the nut to 29–36 ft. lbs. (39–49 Nm).

NOTE: When installing the steering wheel, make certain the cutouts in the rear cover engage the turn signal canceling cam.

Steering Column

REMOVAL AND INSTALLATION

1. Disconnect the negative battery cable.

2. Remove the steering wheel, combination switch and ignition switch.

3. Remove the steering column shield and the air duct from below the steering column.

4. Remove the 2 nuts securing the steering column upper mounting bracket to the instrument panel crossmember. When free, the upper end of the column may be lowered as needed for access to the intermediate shaft universal joint at the lower end.

5. With paint or marking pen, make an index mark at the juncture of the steering column shaft and the intermediate shaft upper universal joint to assure correct alignment during assembly. Remove the universal joint clamp screw.

6. Loosen the 2 nuts securing the steering column hinge bracket to the clutch/brake pedal support. Remove the steering column assembly by pulling to the rear, disengaging it from the universal joint. Remove the shim clips from the upper mounting bracket.

To install:

7. Install the joint clamp bolt but do not tighten it at this time. The bolt may need to be shifted up or down on the shaft to line up with the steering column without binding.

8. Install the steering column, aligning the index marks on the column shaft and universal joint and engaging the column hinge bracket with the pedal support studs. Do not tighten the universal joint clamp bolt yet.

9. Tighten the hinge bracket nuts and raise the upper end of the column to seat under the instrument panel. Position the shim clips on the column upper bracket flanges.

10. Install the 2 steering column upper retaining nuts.

11. Turn the steering wheel lock-to-lock several times to align the universal joints, then tighten both universal joint clamp bolts.

12. Install the instrument panel brace or steering column shield, as necessary. Install the air duct.

13. Install the ignition switch, combination switch and the steering wheel.

Manual Steering Rack and Pinion

ADJUSTMENT

Only the rack preload is adjustable and only to a limited degree, since it is primarily determined by the yoke spring. Since adjustment requires removal of the steering gear, it should only be undertaken after a thorough inspection of front suspension and steering column components fails to reveal damage or binding elsewhere.

If necessary, adjust the rack yoke preload as follows:

1. Remove the steering rack from the vehicle.

2. Center the steering rack in a protected jaw vise, make sure there is equal left and right tie rod extension.

3. Remove the locknut and the yoke plug and clean the yoke plug threads. Apply sealant to the yoke plug threads and install the yoke plug. Tighten to 78–95 inch lbs. (9–11 Nm).

4. Slowly cycle the rack back and forth through 90 percent of it's full stroke. Then center the rack so the tie rods are equally extended.

1. Steering Column - Upper Half
2. Steering Wheel
3. Cover
4. Attaching Nut
5. Combination Switch
6. Steering Column Cover - Lower Half
7. Lower Steering Column Cover
8. Universal Joint/Boot
9. Steering Column

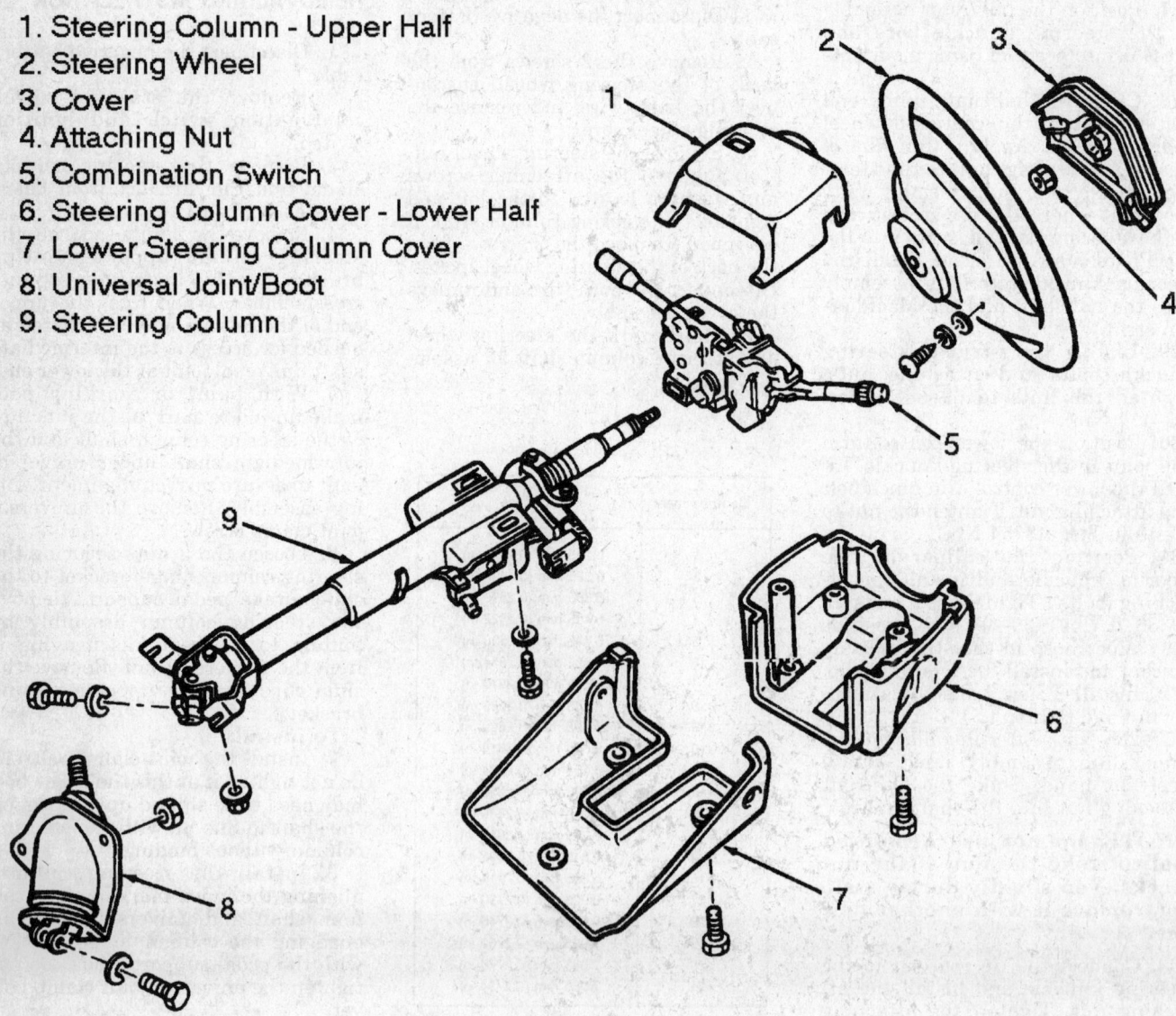

84708041

Steering column assembly and related components

5. Loosen the yoke plug, then tighten it to 22–30 inch lbs. (2.5–3.4 Nm).

6. Use a spring scale to measure the force needed to turn the pinion 180 degrees from the rack center position.

7. Adjust the pinion to the position where the most force was needed to turn it.

8. Tighten the yoke plug to 48 inch lbs. (5.4 Nm), then back it off 5–10 degrees. Install the locknut and tighten to 29–36 ft. lbs. (39–49 Nm).

REMOVAL AND INSTALLATION

1. Disconnect the negative and positive battery cables and remove the battery from the vehicle.

2. Matchmark the steering column lower universal joint and steering rack pinion for assembly reference. Remove the steering column and intermediate shaft assembly from the vehicle.

3. Cut the plastic tie wrap securing the steering column boot to the steering rack.

4. Raise the vehicle and support safely. Remove the front tire and wheel assemblies.

5. Using the proper tool, separate both tie rod ends from the steering knuckles.

6. Remove the catalytic converter.

7. Remove the plastic tie rod splash shield from the right inner fender.

8. Remove the steering rack mounting bolts and lower the steering rack until it is free of the steering column boot. Slide the rack to the right, through the inner fender tie rod opening, until the left tie rod is clear of the left inner fender, then lower the left end until the steering rack assembly can be withdrawn from the left side of the vehicle.

NOTE: While maneuvering the tie rod boots in and out of the inner fender openings, guide the steering rack assembly carefully to avoid cutting or nicking the boots.

To install:

9. From under the vehicle, insert the right side tie rod through the right inner fender tie rod opening, far enough to allow raising the left end of the assembly to enter the left inner fender opening. Shift the assembly to the left taking care not to catch the boots.

10. Align the steering rack pinion shaft housing with the steering column boot. Raise the steering rack into the boot.

11. Install the steering rack mounting bolts from left to right. Torque the bolts to 23–34 ft. lbs. (31–46 Nm).

12. Connect the tie rod ends to the steering knuckles. If the tie rod ends are not properly aligned with the knuckle ends during installation, release the small end boot clips before rotating the tie rods. This is done to avoid twisting the boots.

13. Attach the right side tie rod splash shield on the right inner fender panel.

14. Install the catalytic converter.

15. Install the tire and wheel assemblies and lower the vehicle.

16. Secure the steering column boot to the steering rack housing with a new tie wrap.

17. Align the matchmarks made on the steering column lower universal joint and the steering rack pinion shaft. Install the steering column when the proper alignment is achieved.

18. Install the battery and connect the battery cables.

Power Steering Rack and Pinion

REMOVAL AND INSTALLATION

1. Disconnect the negative battery cable.

2. Remove the intermediate shaft.

3. Disconnect and plug the high pressure and return lines.

4. Raise the vehicle and support safely. Remove the front tire and wheel assemblies.

5. Remove the tie rod end cotter pins and attaching nuts. Using the proper tool, separate both tie rod ends from the steering knuckles.

6. Remove the tie rod end splash shields and the right fender splash shield.

7. Remove the front catalytic converter nuts and separate the converter from the inlet pipe.

8. Place alignment marks on the right tie rod end to ease installation. Loosen the jam nut and remove the right tie rod end.

9. Remove the steering rack mounting bolts and lower the steering rack until it is free of the steering column boot. Slide the rack to the left and pull the right tie rod through the fender opening. Remove the steering gear by sliding it to the right.

To install:

10. Position the steering rack in it's mounting location.

11. Attach the intermediate shaft to the steering gear pinion and tighten the clamp bolt to 13–20 ft. lbs. (18–26 Nm). Guide the intermediate shaft into the steering column hole.

12. Lower the vehicle.

13. With an assistant lifting the steering gear, align the intermediate shaft with the universal joint and install the clamp bolt.

14. Raise and safely support the vehicle.

15. Install the steering rack mounting bolts and tighten to 23–34 ft. lbs. (31–46 Nm).

16. Install the right tie rod end and attach the tie rod ends to the steering knuckles. Install the tie rod end nuts and tighten to 23–34 ft. lbs. (39–44 Nm). Install new tie rod end cotter pins.

17. Attach the catalytic converter to the inlet pipe and install the attaching nuts. Tighten the nuts to 23–34 ft. lbs. (31–46 Nm).

18. Install the tie rod end splash shields and the right fender splash shield.

19. Install the front wheel and tire assemblies and lower the vehicle.

20. Connect the high pressure and return lines.

21. Connect the negative battery cable.

22. Add power steering fluid and bleed the air from the system. Check for leaks.

Power Steering Pump

REMOVAL AND INSTALLATION

1. Disconnect the negative battery cable.

2. Remove the air duct and air cleaner unit.

3. Disconnect the electrical connector from the fluid pressure switch.

4. Disconnect and plug the fluid lines.

5. Remove the adjustment bolt and the locknut, washer and bracket bolt.

6. Loosen the mounting bolt and disconnect the drive belt. Remove the mounting bolt and remove the power steering pump.

7. Installation is the reverse of the removal procedure. Tighten the high pressure line nuts to 29–36 ft. lbs. (39–49 Nm). Adjust the drive belt tension.

BELT TENSION ADJUSTMENT

1. Remove the air duct and air cleaner.

2. Loosen the pump mounting bolt. Loosen the adjusting locknut.

3. Using a belt tension gauge or the deflection method, adjust the tension at the adjusting bolt.

4. If using a belt tension gauge, position the gauge in the middle of the longest accessible belt span and set new belt tension to 110–132 lbs. (50–60 Kg) or used belt (more than 10 minutes of run time) tension to 95–110 lbs. (43–50 Kg).

5. If using the deflection method, apply approximately 22 lbs. (10 Kg) of pressure to the middle of the longest accessible belt span. Adjust the tension to 0.31–0.35 in. (8–9mm) for a new belt or 0.35–0.39 in. (9–10mm) for a used belt (more than 10 minutes of run time).

6. Tighten the pump mounting bolt to 27–40 ft. lbs. (36–54 Nm) and the adjustment locknut to 27–38 ft. lbs. (37–52 Nm).

7. Install the air cleaner and air duct.

SYSTEM BLEEDING

1. Add power steering fluid to the **L** mark on the reservoir cap dipstick.

2. Run the engine until it reaches normal operating temperature.

3. Turn the steering wheel lock to lock approximately 10 times.

4. Shut the engine OFF with the wheels in the straight-ahead position.

5. Check the fluid level, the level should be between the **L** and **H** marks on the reservoir cap dipstick. Repeat the procedure if needed.

Tie Rod Ends

REMOVAL AND INSTALLATION

1. Raise the vehicle and support it safely.

2. Remove the wheel and tire assembly.

3. Remove the cotter pin and nut from the tie rod end stud. Discard the cotter pin. Examine the nut for damage and replace as required.

4. Separate the tie rod end from the steering knuckle using tie rod end remover tool T85M-3395-A or equivalent.

5. With paint or a suitable marker, mark the tie rod end, jam nut and tie rod to ease assembly without changing the toe-in setting.

6. Loosen the jam nut and unscrew the tie rod end counting the number of turns required for re-

moval. Replace the tie rod end as required.

NOTE: If new tie rod ends are being installed, place the old and new ends side-by-side and place alignment marks in the new end that match as closely as possible to the marks on the old end. Please be advised that the existing jam nut may not seat in exactly the same position on the new end and the toe-in setting may have to be checked and/or readjusted as a precaution.

To install:

7. When replacing a tie rod end, install a new dust boot over the stud with a suitable adapter. A ¾ in. socket will accomplish the task simply and effectively.

8. Thread the jam nut and tie rod end onto the tie rod and align the index marks made during the removal procedure.

9. Install the tie rod end into the steering knuckle. If the tie rod is correctly aligned, the taper should seat without twisting the tie rod or boot. Torque the stud nut to 26–30 ft. lbs. (35–40 Nm) and install a new cotter pin. If the cotter pin does not align with stud bore, tighten (do not loosen) the nut until the castellations align with the pin bore.

10. Install the wheel and tire assembly. Lower the vehicle and connect the negative battery cable. Check the toe-in setting, if necessary.

BRAKES

Master Cylinder

REMOVAL AND INSTALLATION

1. Disconnect the negative battery cable. Disconnect the low fluid level sensor connector.

2. Disconnect the brake lines from the master cylinder connections. Plug or cover the line openings and master cylinder ports.

3. Remove the attaching nuts and washers and separate the master cylinder from the power booster mounting studs. Clean the master cylinder and power booster contact surfaces with a clean shop towel.

To install:

4. If a new master cylinder is being installed, check the pushrod length adjustment as follows:

   a. Position master cylinder gauge T87C-2500-A or equivalent, on the end of the master cylinder, loosen the set screw and push the gauge plunger against the bottom of the primary piston.

   b. While holding the gauge in position, tighten the set screw.

   c. Invert the master cylinder gauge and place it over the brake booster pushrod.

   d. If the clearance is not zero, loosen the pushrod locknut and adjust the pushrod.

NOTE: Proper pushrod length adjustment is critical. If the pushrod is adjusted too long, the brakes will drag. If the pushrod is adjusted too short, the brake pedal will be low.

5. Before installation, bench bleed a new master cylinder as follows:

   a. Mount the new master cylinder in a suitable holding fixture. Be careful not to damage the housing.

   b. Fill the master cylinder reservoir with brake fluid.

   c. Using a suitable tool inserted into the booster pushrod cavity, push the master cylinder piston in slowly. Place a suitable container under the master cylinder to catch the fluid being expelled from the outlet ports.

   d. Place a finger tightly over each outlet port and allow the master cylinder piston to return.

   e. Repeat the procedure until clear fluid only is expelled from the master cylinder. Plug the outlet ports and remove the master cylinder from the holding fixture.

6. Position the master cylinder onto the power booster mounting studs.

7. Install the attaching washers and nuts. Torque the nuts to 7–12 ft. lbs. (10–16 Nm).

8. Connect the brake lines to master cylinder connections.

9. Make sure the master cylinder reservoir is full. Have an assistant slowly push down on the brake pedal. When the pedal is all the way down, crack open the brake line fittings, 1 at a time, to expel any remaining air in the master cylinder and brake lines. Tighten the fittings, then have the assistant allow the brake pedal to return.

10. Repeat Step 9 until all air is expelled from the master cylinder and brake lines. Tighten the brake line fittings.

11. Connect the low fluid level sensor.

12. Make sure the master cylinder reservoir is full. If necessary, bleed the entire brake system.

13. Connect the negative battery cable.

Proportioning Valve

The proportioning valve is located in the engine compartment. It is mounted to the dash panel below and to the right of the brake booster. The valve is not repairable and must be replaced if determined to be faulty.

REMOVAL AND INSTALLATION

1. Disconnect the negative battery cable. Loosen the connector nuts and disconnect the brake lines from the proportioning valve. Plug or cover the line openings to prevent the entry of dirt and grease.

2. Loosen the valve attaching bolts and remove the valve from the dash panel.

3. Installation is the reverse of the removal procedure.

4. Bleed the brake system.

5. Inspect for proper brake operation and inspect for leaks around the valve connections.

Power Brake Booster

REMOVAL AND INSTALLATION

1. Disconnect the negative battery cable. Remove the master cylinder.

NOTE: It may be possible to remove the master cylinder from the booster assembly without disconnecting the brake lines from the cylinder. If possible, position the master cylinder to the side.

2. Disconnect the vacuum hose from the brake booster unit.

3. From inside the vehicle, remove and discard the cotter pin securing the clevis pin. Remove the clevis pin from the clevis.

4. Have an assistant support the power booster unit in the engine compartment.

5. From inside the vehicle, remove the 4 nuts securing the unit to the bulkhead. Remove the unit from the engine compartment.

6. Remove the gasket between the power booster unit and the bulkhead. Replace the gasket, as required.

To install:

7. Position the gasket onto the power brake booster studs and have an assistant position the unit against the bulkhead.

8. From inside the vehicle, secure the power booster to the bulkhead with the 4 retaining nuts. Torque the retaining nuts to 12–17 ft. lbs. (16–23 Nm).

9. Lubricate the clevis with a coating of white lithium grease or equivalent. From inside the vehicle, attach the clevis to the brake pedal with the clevis pin. Secure the clevis pin with a new cotter pin.

10. Connect the vacuum to the power brake booster.

11. Install the master cylinder.

12. Bleed the brake system.

Brake Caliper

REMOVAL AND INSTALLATION

1. Raise and safely support the vehicle.

2. Remove the wheel and tire assembly.

3. Remove the brake pads. Remove the brake hose attaching bolt and plug the hose end. Discard the seal washers.

4. Remove the caliper attaching bolts and the anti-squeak caps.

5. Remove the caliper from the vehicle.

6. Installation is the reverse of the removal procedure.

7. Tighten the caliper mounting bolts to 29–36 ft. lbs. (39–49 Nm). Use new seal washers on the brake hose and tighten the brake hose attaching bolt to 16–22 ft. lbs. (22–29 Nm). Bleed the brake system.

Disc Brake Pads

REMOVAL AND INSTALLATION

1. Remove approximately 1/3 of the brake fluid from the master cylinder. Raise and support the vehicle safely.

2. Remove the tire and wheel assembly.

3. Place a C-clamp on the caliper and tighten the clamp to move the caliper piston in the cylinder bore approximately 1/8 in. (3mm). Remove the clamp.

NOTE: Do not pry the piston away from the rotor.

4. Remove the brake pad pin retainer. Disengage the anti-rattle spring from the brake pads.

5. Remove the brake pad pins and the anti-rattle spring.

6. Remove the brake pads and shims. Do not discard the shims found behind the brake pads.

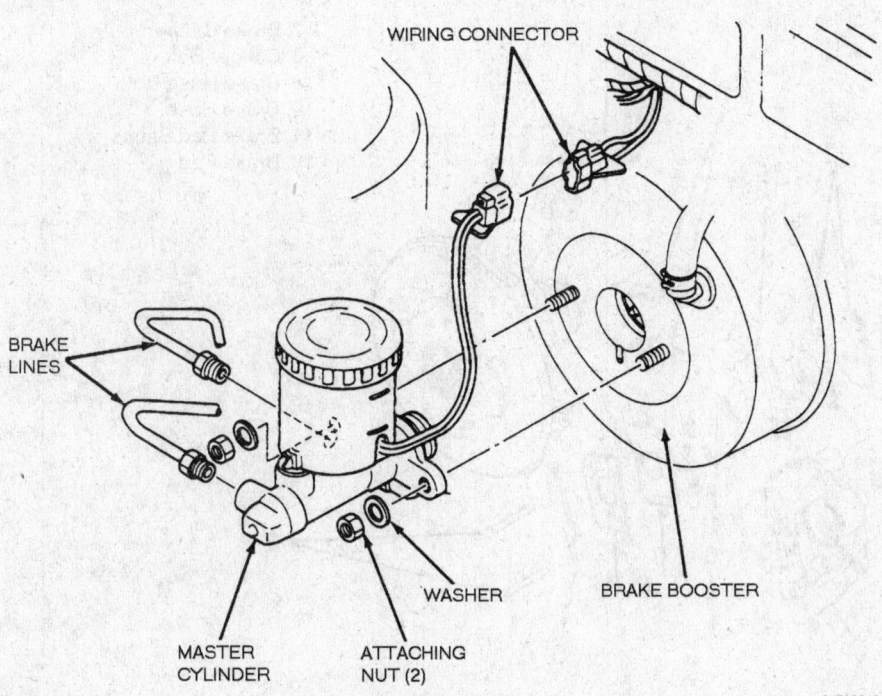

WIRING CONNECTOR

BRAKE LINES

MASTER CYLINDER

ATTACHING NUT (2)

WASHER

BRAKE BOOSTER

84708043

Master cylinder assembly

To install:

7. Push the piston back into the caliper bore.

8. Apply the grease supplied with the brake pad set to both surfaces of the inner shim and to the back of the brake pad.

9. Install the brake pads, making sure the shims are installed.

10. Install the brake pad pins, anti-rattle spring and brake pad pin retainer.

11. Install the wheel and tire assembly and lower the vehicle.

12. Apply the brake several times to seat the pads. Check the brake fluid level in the master cylinder. Add fluid as necessary.

Brake Rotor

REMOVAL AND INSTALLATION

1. Disconnect the negative battery cable.

2. Raise the vehicle and support it safely.

3. Unbolt and remove front wheel from the hub assembly.

4. With a suitable tool, straighten the staked edge of the halfshaft attaching nut. Take care not to damage the halfshaft threads.

5. Remove and discard the half-shaft attaching nut.

6. Remove the retaining clip securing the caliper hose to the strut bracket.

7. Remove the cotter pin and tie rod end attaching nut. Discard the cotter pin and set the nut aside. Inspect the nut for damage and replace as required.

8. Using a tie rod end separator tool, release the tie rod end from the steering knuckle arm. If the tie rod appears to be seized, strike the knuckle sharply with a soft-tipped hammer to achieve separation.

9. Remove the brake caliper attaching bolts. Lift the caliper assembly from the steering knuckle.

NOTE: After the caliper assembly is lifted from the steering knuckle, do not allow it to be suspended by the brake hose. Support the caliper by a length of rope or wire attached to the Mac-Pherson strut.

10. Remove the clamp bolt and nut at the point where the lower control arm ball joint connects to the steering knuckle. With a medium prybar, release the lower ball joint from the steering knuckle by prying downward on the lower control arm.

11. Remove the 2 bolts that position the steering knuckle between the MacPherson strut bracket flanges.

12. Slide the knuckle/hub assembly from the end of the halfshaft. If binding occurs, tap the end of the shaft with a soft-tipped hammer. If the wheel hub is rusted to the halfshaft, use either a 2 jaw puller or a hub puller to achieve separation.

13. Remove the wheel hub/rotor assembly from the steering knuckle/dust shield assembly using puller tool T87C–1104–A or equivalent.

14. Remove the bearing preload spacer from the hub.

NOTE: The spacer is preselected to yield the correct bearing preload. Save the removed spacer for use during assembly.

15. Clamp the hub/rotor assembly in a vise with protective jaw caps. If the rotor is to be reused, scribe aligning marks on the hub and rotor for use during assembly. Remove the attaching bolts and the rotor.

To install:

16. Place the bearing preload spacer in the steering knuckle bore.

17. Position the rotor on the hub, observing the original aligning marks if the rotor is being reused and install

1. Anti-Squeak Caps
2. Brake Pad Pins
3. Pin Retainer
4. Brake Pad Shim
5. Brake Pad
6. Anti-Rattle Spring

7. Brake Caliper
8. Caliper Bolt
9. Brake Hose Bolt
10. Brake Hose
11. Brake Pad Shims
12. Brake Pad

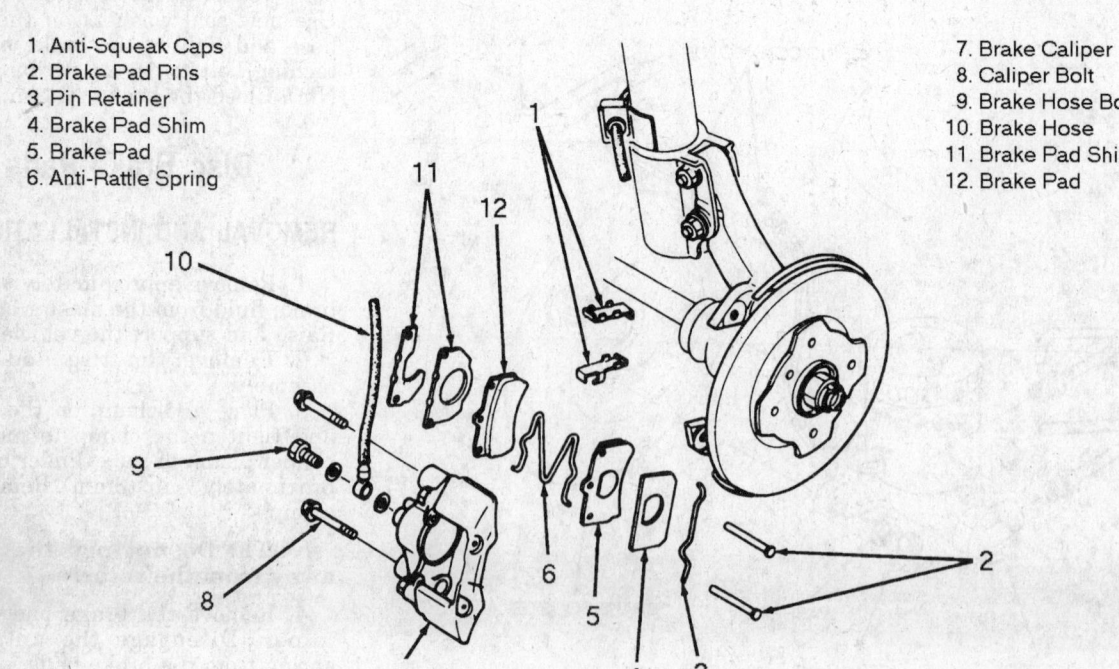

Front disc brake assembly

84708044

the attaching bolts. Tighten the attaching bolts to 33–40 ft. lbs. (44–54 Nm).

18. Position the hub/rotor assembly in the steering knuckle bore and press it into position using a suitable driver.

19. Clean the halfshaft spline end and lubricate with a coating of wheel bearing grease. Apply a thin film of clean SAE 30 weight oil to the steering knuckle/rotor hub assembly up to the point where the uppermost arm of the steering knuckle seats into the MacPherson strut bracket. Guide the steering knuckle/rotor/hub assembly onto the halfshaft and the MacPherson strut.

20. Install the strut-to-steering knuckle bolts and attaching nuts. Tighten the nuts to 69–86 ft. lbs. (93–117 Nm).

21. Position the lower control arm ball joint in the steering knuckle. Install the lower control arm pinch bolt and attaching nut. Tighten the nut to 32–40 ft. lbs. (43–54 Nm).

22. Position the caliper on the steering knuckle and install the attaching bolts. Tighten the bolts to 29–36 ft. lbs. (39–49 Nm). Position the caliper hose in the strut routing bracket and install the retaining clip.

23. Install a new halfshaft attaching nut and tighten to 116–174 ft. lbs. (157–235 Nm). After installation, the wheel hub assembly must rotate freely by hand. Stake the halfshaft attaching nut into the shaft groove.

NOTE: Do not use a pointed tool to stake the nut. If the nut cracks even slightly during staking, replace it with another new one.

24. Connect the tie rod end to the steering knuckle and install the attaching nut. Tighten the attaching nut to 22–33 ft. lbs. (29–44 Nm). Install a new cotter pin through the nut and ball stud. If the openings in the nut and the hole in the ball stud are not aligned, tighten the nut slightly, just to the point of alignment. Never loosen the nut.

25. Install the wheel and tire assembly. Tighten the attaching bolts to 65–87 ft. lbs. (88–118 Nm). Lower the vehicle.

Brake Drums

REMOVAL AND INSTALLATION

1. Raise and safely support the vehicle.

2. Remove the tire and wheel assembly.

3. On Type 1 nuts, carefully raise the staked portion of the attaching nut using a small cape chisel. On Type 2 nuts, remove the cotter pin and nut retaining cap.

4. Remove the locknut. Discard Type 1 locknuts or the Type 2 cotter pin.

NOTE: Some locknuts are right and left hand thread. The left hand threaded locknut is located on the right side of the vehicle. Turn this locknut clockwise to loosen. The right hand threaded locknut is located on the left side of the vehicle and is turned counterclockwise to loosen.

5. Remove the brake drum and bearings as an assembly. Be careful not to let the outer bearing fall out of the hub during removal.

To install:

6. Make sure the bearings and the hub contain adequate lubricant.

7. Position the brake drum, bearings and hub assembly on the spindle. Keep the drum centered on the spindle to prevent damage to the grease seal and spindle threads.

8. Install the outer bearing, washer and locknut.

9. Properly adjust the wheel bearing preload.

Brake Shoes

REMOVAL AND INSTALLATION

1. Raise and support the vehicle safely.

2. Remove the tire and wheel assembly. Remove the brake drum.

3. Remove the brake shoe hold-down springs and pins.

4. Remove the brake shoe return springs. Pull the brake shoes away from the backing plate and remove.

To install:

5. Lubricate the backing plate shoe pads with a suitable high temperature grease.

6. Install the brake shoe upper return spring on the primary brake shoe. Position the primary brake shoe on the backing plate and install the hold-down pin and spring.

7. Connect the upper return spring to the secondary brake shoe and position the shoe against the backing plate. Install the secondary brake shoe hold-down pin and spring.

8. Install the parking brake return spring and the lower brake shoe return spring.

9. Set the self adjuster to the fully released position. Place a suitable tool against the adjuster cam and push it to the released position.

10. Install the brake drum, wheel and tire assembly and lower the vehicle.

11. Push the brake pedal several times to set the self adjuster.

Wheel Cylinder

REMOVAL AND INSTALLATION

1. Raise and support the vehicle safely.

2. Remove the rear brake shoes.

3. Disconnect the brake line from the wheel cylinder. Plug or cover the brake line opening to prevent the entry of dirt or grease.

4. Remove the 2 wheel cylinder attaching bolts and remove the wheel cylinder from the backing plate.

To install:

5. Position the wheel cylinder onto the backing plate and install the retaining bolts. Torque the retaining bolts to 7–9 ft. lbs. (10–13 Nm).

6. Connect the brake line to the wheel cylinder.

7. Install the rear brake shoes.

8. Bleed the brake system.

Parking Brake Cable

ADJUSTMENT

1. Make sure the parking brake is fully released.

2. Remove the parking brake console access cover.

3. Remove the locking clip from the cable adjuster nut.

4. Raise and support the vehicle safely. Make sure the rear wheels are free to turn.

5. Tighten the cable adjuster nut until there is a slight brake drag when the rear wheels are rotated.

6. Back off on the adjuster nut until the brake drag disappears.

7. Check the operation of the parking brake. The rear brakes should be fully applied when the brake lever is pulled upward 11–16 notches.

8. Install the locking clip onto the cable adjuster nut.

9. Install the parking brake console access cover.

REMOVAL AND INSTALLATION

1. Remove the parking brake console and parking brake lever as follows:

   a. Slide both front seats all the way forward.

   b. Remove the bolts that attach the lap belt buckles to their mounting brackets.

   c. Remove the 2 console attaching screws.

   d. Remove the retainer located at the front of the console.

   e. Remove the access cover and remove the parking brake console.

   f. Remove the locking clip from the cable adjuster nut and remove the cable adjuster nut.

   g. Disconnect the wiring connector from the parking brake light switch.

   h. Remove the attaching bolts and the parking brake lever.

2. Remove the attaching screws and parking brake console mounting bracket.

3. Remove the bolts attaching the lower half of the rear seat hinge to the floor pan.

4. Fold the rear seat forward and remove the bolts attaching the upper half of the rear seat hinge to the floor pan.

5. Remove the rear seat.

6. Remove the rear carpet push retainers and carefully pull the carpeting forward to expose the parking brake cable guide.

7. Disconnect the parking brake cable guide by removing the attaching screws.

8. Raise and support the vehicle safely.

9. Remove the rear wheel and tire assemblies.

10. Remove the cotter pin and clevis pin attaching the parking brake cable ends to the rear brake levers.

11. Remove the routing bracket retaining clips.

12. Disengage the parking brake routing sleeves from the torsion beam routing brackets.

13. Remove the nut and bolt attaching the parking brake routing bracket to the fuel tank.

14. Remove the parking brake cable equalizer attaching bolts.

15. Withdraw the lever end of the cable through the body opening and remove from the vehicle.

To install:

16. Position the lever end of the cable through the body opening.

17. Position the cable routing bracket on the fuel tank and install the attaching bolt and nut.

18. Make sure the cable seal is properly positioned in the floor pan.

19. Position the cable equalizer and install the attaching bolts. Make sure the equalizer spacers are in position before tightening the attaching bolts.

20. Route the cable ends through the body brackets and install the retaining clips.

21. Seat the cable sleeves in the torsion beam routing brackets.

22. Attach the cable ends to the brake levers using the clevis pins and new cotter pins.

23. Install the rear wheel and tire assemblies and lower the vehicle.

24. Route the end of the cable through the park brake lever.

25. Position the cable guide and secure with the attaching screws.

26. Position the carpet and install the push retainers. Install the rear seat and torque the retaining bolts to 28–38 ft. lbs. (38–51 Nm).

27. Position the console mounting bracket and install the attaching screws.

28. Install the parking brake lever and console as follows:

   a. Position the parking brake lever and install the attaching bolts. Tighten the bolts to 12–17 ft. lbs. (16–23 Nm).

   b. Connect the wiring connector to the parking brake light switch.

   c. Install the adjuster nut and adjust the parking brake cable.

   d. Install the locking clip.

   e. Position the console over the parking brake lever.

   f. Install the access cover and the console retainer.

   g. Install the console attaching screws.

   h. Position the lap belt buckles and install the buckle-to-bracket bolts.

   i. Slide the seats to their original position.

Brake System Bleeding

When any part of the hydraulic system has been disconnected for service, air may enter the system and cause spongy pedal action. The bleeding procedure is used to remove air from the hydraulic circuits.

The brake hydraulic circuits form a split diagonal hydraulic system. The left front and right rear form 1 circuit while the right front and left rear form the other circuit. When bleeding 1 of these circuits, bleed the rear wheel first and then the front wheel at the opposite corner.

Never reuse brake fluid that has been drained from the hydraulic system or that has been allowed to stand in an open container for an extended period of time.

Bleed the brake system as follows:

1. Clean all dirt from the master cylinder filler cap. Fill the master cylinder with DOT 3 brake fluid.

NOTE: Do not allow the master cylinder to run dry during the bleeding procedure.

2. If the master cylinder is known or suspected to contain air, it must be bled before the wheel cylinders or caliper. Bleed the master cylinder as follows:

   a. Loosen the front line fitting and have an assistant push the brake pedal slowly through it's full travel.

   b. While the assistant holds the pedal down, tighten the brake line fitting. After the line fitting is tightened, the assistant may release the brake pedal.

   c. Repeat the procedure on the rear brake line.

   d. Repeat the entire process several times to make sure all air has been removed from the master cylinder.

3. Remove the bleeder screw cap from the appropriate rear wheel cylinder. Position a box end wrench on the bleeder fitting.

4. Attach a rubber hose to the bleeder fitting. The hose must fit snugly around the bleeder fitting.

5. Submerge the other end of the hose in a container partially filled with brake fluid.

6. Loosen the bleeder fitting approximately 3/4 turn. Have an assistant push the brake pedal slowly through it's full travel and hold it there.

7. Close the bleeder fitting, then have the assistant release the brake pedal.

8. Repeat Steps 6 and 7 until air bubbles no longer appear at the submerged end of the bleeder hose.

9. When the fluid entering the bottle is completely free of bubbles, tighten the bleeder screw, remove the hose and install the bleeder screw cap.

10. Repeat Steps 3–9 at the front caliper located diagonally to the wheel cylinder just completed.

11. If necessary, bleed the other diagonal circuit in the same manner.

12. Check the master cylinder fluid level and add, if necessary.

13. Check the pedal feel. If the pedal is still spongy, repeat the bleeding procedure.

FRONT SUSPENSION

MacPherson Strut

REMOVAL AND INSTALLATION

1. Raise the vehicle and support it safely.
2. Remove the wheel and tire assembly.
3. Remove the brake line clip from the strut lower mounting bracket and disengage the brake line.
4. Remove the 2 nuts and bolts securing the strut lower bracket to the steering knuckle.
5. In the engine compartment, remove the 2 nuts securing the strut mounting block in the strut tower.
6. Disengage the strut lower bracket from the steering knuckle and lower the strut clear of the wheel well.
7. Attach spring compressor tool T81P–5310–A or equivalent, and compress the coil spring.
8. Pry out the mounting block cap and remove the strut upper nut and lockwasher.
9. Remove the strut mounting block and spacer plate. Remove the washer, bearing seal and bearing from the strut rod.
10. Remove the upper spring seat, seat insulator and spring. Slide the jounce bumper/shield off the strut.

NOTE: If replacing the spring, release the spring compressor progressively to prevent spring arching. Open the compressor jaws wide enough to grip the new spring in the same position and tighten the compressor screws progressively, compressing the spring until the strut can be assembled without interference.

To install:
11. Check the condition of the jounce bumper and spring seat insulator and replace, as necessary. Make sure the bearing operates smoothly. Check the spring for uniform coil spacing, for nicks or burrs and compare the spring length with a new spring to check for excessive spring set; replace as necessary.

12. Slide the jounce bumper/shield onto the strut rod and over the body. Install the compressed spring, upper spring seat insulator and upper seat, positioning the spring ends against the steps in the seats.
13. Install the bearing, seal and plain washer on the strut rod. Install the strut mounting block with the white alignment spot on the same side of the strut as the steering knuckle mounting bracket.
14. Install the spacer plate. Install the lockwasher and nut and tighten to 40–50 ft. lbs. (54–67 Nm). Release and remove the spring compressor.
15. Place the strut assembly with spacer plate in the strut tower with the white alignment mark facing outward.
16. Install the upper mounting block stud nuts and torque to 22–27 ft. lbs. (29–36 Nm).
17. Engage the steering knuckle in the strut tower lower bracket and install the mounting bolts and nuts. Torque to 69–86 ft. lbs. (93–117 Nm).
18. Position the brake line into the strut lower mounting bracket cutout and install the retaining clip.
19. Install the wheel and tire assembly and lower the vehicle.

Strut Cartridge

REPLACEMENT

——————— **CAUTION** ———————
Do not remove the MacPherson strut upper nut without using an approved MacPherson strut compressor, T81P–5310–A or equivalent. The coil spring is under extreme pressure and can cause severe bodily injury if the nut is removed without a spring compressor.
——————————————————————

1. Raise the vehicle and support safely.
2. Remove the front wheel assembly.
3. Remove the MacPherson strut assembly from the vehicle.
4. Install a MacPherson strut spring compressor T81P–5310–A or equivalent.
5. Compress the coil spring and remove the mounting block cap, strut shaft nut and washer. Gradually release the spring compressor. Be careful not to strip the threads on the strut shaft as the spring extends.
6. Remove the mounting block spacer plate, washer, bearing seal and bearing.

7. Slide the jounce bumper/shield off the strut and remove the spring.
To install:
8. Install the coil spring and jounce bumper.
9. Install the upper seat insulator, upper seat and position the ends of the spring ends against the steps in the seat. Make sure the spring ends are positioned correctly in the spring seats. If not, suspension height may be affected.
10. Install the bearing, seal, and plain washer to the strut.
11. Install the strut mounting block with the alignment slot on the same side of the steering knuckle mounting bracket.
12. Install the washer and strut shaft nut. Torque the nut to 50 ft. lbs. (67 Nm).
13. Gradually release the spring compressor and install the strut assembly into the vehicle.
14. Torque the mounting nuts to 46 ft. lbs. (63 Nm).
15. Install the front wheels and lower the vehicle safely.

Lower Ball Joints

NOTE: The ball joint is an integral part of the control arm. If inspection proves the ball joint to be bad, the entire lower control arm must be replaced.

INSPECTION

Control Arm Installed

Check for ball joint wear by raising and safely supporting the vehicle until the wheel and tire assembly is clear of the floor. Support the lower control arm so there is no load on the suspension strut. Try to rock the wheel top-to-bottom; if any wobble is felt, look for movement between the control arm and steering knuckle. If the ball joint appears tight, check and adjust the wheel bearing preload, then repeat the wobble check. Any movement still present is a sign of ball joint wear. Replace the lower control arm.

Control Arm Removed

Make sure the ball joint stud swivels freely but is not loose. Grip the ball joint stud with a suitable adapter and check the stud rotating torque with a low-reading torque wrench. It should be in the range of 16–27 inch lbs. (1.8–3.1 Nm).

Lower Control Arms

REMOVAL AND INSTALLATION

1. Raise and support the vehicle safely. Remove the lower control arm pivot bolt at the frame bracket.
2. Remove the ball joint clamp bolt and and nut from the steering knuckle assembly.
3. Remove the stabilizer bar bushing retaining nut from the rear of the control arm and remove the rear bushing washer and bushing.
4. Lower the control arm, prying the ball joint stud out of the steering knuckle, if necessary. Disengage and remove the control arm from the stabilizer end.
5. Inspect the control arm for deformation or cracks and check the pivot bushing for deterioration. Verify that the ball joint swivels freely but is not loose. If the control arm pivot bushing is to be replaced, remove the old bushing with C-frame tool T74P-3044-A1, bushing tool T81P-5493-B2 and receiver cup tool T88C-5493E or equivalents. Center the new bushing in the center of the control arm eye and install using the removal tools. Replace the lower control arm/ball joint assembly as required.
6. If the ball joint boot is damaged or deteriorated, pry the boot off with a small cold chisel. Install the new boot onto the ball joint using a suitable adapter such as a ¾ in. socket to properly seat the boot.

To install:
7. Position the front bushing washer and bushing onto the stabilizer end. Engage the control arm with the stabilizer.
8. Raise the control arm inner end into the pivot bracket on the frame and start the pivot bolt to hold the control arm in place. Do not completely tighten the bolt at this time.
9. Engage the control arm ball joint stud with the clamp bore in the steering knuckle and install the clamp bolt and nut.
10. Install the stabilizer rear bushing and washer onto the stabilizer end with the retaining nut. Torque the retaining nut to 47–57 ft. lbs. (64–77 Nm). Install the cotter pin.
11. Torque the pivot bolt at the control arm frame bracket to 32–40 ft. lbs. (43–54 Nm).
12. Hold the steering clamp bolt stationary and torque the clamp nut to 32–40 ft. lbs. (43–54 Nm).
13. Lower the vehicle.

Stabilizer Bar

REMOVAL AND INSTALLATION

1. Raise and safely support the vehicle.
2. Remove the stabilizer mounting bracket nuts and mounting brackets.
3. Remove the split bushings from the stabilizer bar. Replace deteriorated or worn bushings as required.
4. Remove the stabilizer bushing nuts at the lower control arms and remove the rear washers and bushings.
5. Pull the stabilizer bar forward to disengage it from both lower control arms. Remove the bushings and washers. Replace deteriorated or worn bushings as required.

To install:
6. Install the control arm bushing washers on the ends of the stabilizer bar and install the control arm front bushings.
7. Support the stabilizer bar by hand and insert the ends of the bar into the lower control arms. Install the control arm bushings and washers with the retaining nuts. Make the retaining nuts finger-tight.
8. Install the split bushings on the the stabilizer bar cross bar with the split side forward and position them next to the white alignment marks on the bar.
9. Install the stabilizer bar mounting brackets. Torque the bracket retaining nuts to 40–50 ft. lbs. (54–68 Nm).
10. Torque the control arm bushing retaining nuts to 47–57 ft. lbs. (64–77 Nm). Install cotter pins.
11. Lower the vehicle.

REAR SUSPENSION

MacPherson Strut

REMOVAL AND INSTALLATION

1. Raise the vehicle and support it safely.
2. Remove the rear wheel and tire assembly.
3. Install spring compressor tool T81P-5310-A or equivalent, and compress the spring.
4. From the cargo compartment, remove the rear quarter trim panel.
5. Remove the jam nut and flanged nut from the strut rod and remove the bushing washer and upper bushing.
6. Remove the strut lower end mounting bolt from the torsion beam.
7. Withdraw the strut assembly downward and separate it from the spring and seat insulator. Remove the spring compressor.
8. Remove the lower grommet and jounce bumper seat from the strut rod. Slide the jounce bumper off the strut.
9. Inspect the material condition of the jounce bumper, spring seat insulator and strut rod bushings. Inspect the strut for leakage, endplay or erratic action. Inspect the strut lower end bushing for damage or deterioration. Replace any damaged or deteriorated components, as required.

To install:
10. Slide the jounce bumper onto the strut rod. Install the bumper seat and lower bushing on the strut rod.
11. If the upper spring seat insulator is replaced, install the new insulator on the spring upper end, seating the end of the coil against the step in the insulator. Position the spring on the strut, making sure the end of the coil seats against the step in the strut spring seat. When the spring is properly seated, reinstall the spring compressor.
12. Guide the strut tower into the strut mounting hole through the wheel well.
13. Align the strut lower end with the mounting hole in the torsion beam. Start the mounting bolt in by hand to hold the strut in position.
14. From the cargo compartment, install the rod upper end bushing, bushing washer and flanged nut. Torque the flanged nut to 12–18 ft. lbs. (16–24 Nm). Hold the flanged nut stationary and tighten the locknut.
15. Torque the lower strut mounting bolt to 40–50 ft. lbs. (54–68 Nm).
16. Back off on the spring compressor slowly to release the spring tension. Remove the spring compressor.
17. Install the rear quarter trim panel.
18. Install the wheel and tire assembly. Lower the vehicle.

Rear Wheel Bearings

REMOVAL AND INSTALLATION

1. Raise the vehicle and support it safely. Make sure the parking brake is fully released.
2. Remove the wheel and tire assembly.

3. Remove the grease/dust cap.

4. On Type 1 nuts, carefully raise the staked portion of the locknut using a small cape chisel. On Type 2 nuts, remove the cotter pin and nut retaining cap.

NOTE: Some locknuts may have left hand thread. The left hand threaded locknut is located on the right side of the vehicle. Turn this locknut clockwise to loosen. The right hand threaded locknut is located on the left side of the vehicle and is turned counterclockwise to loosen.

5. Remove the locknut. Discard the Type 1 locknut or Type 2 cotter pin.

6. Pull the brake drum bearings and hub assembly away from the spindle shaft. Take care not to damage the spindle shaft threads.

7. With a small roll head prybar or equivalent, remove the bearing grease seal from the bearing hub. Discard the seal regardless of condition.

8. Remove the inner and outer bearings from the bearing hub. If the bearings are to be reused, identify and tag each bearing for installation reference. Replace worn or damaged bearings as required.

9. If the bearings are being replaced, remove the bearing races using a suitable tool.

To install:

10. If the bearings are being replaced, install the new bearing races in the hub using suitable installation tools.

11. Pack the bearings and the hub with high temperature wheel bearing grease.

12. Position the inner bearing in the hub. Install and seat a new grease seal with a suitable driving tool. Lubricate the lip of the seal with the wheel bearing grease.

13. Position the brake drum and hub assembly on the spindle. Keep the hub centered during positioning to prevent damage to the new grease seal and spindle threads.

14. Install the outer bearing, washer and locknut.

15. Adjust the bearing preload.

16. Install the grease cap, wheel and tire assembly.

17. Lower the vehicle and connect the negative battery cable.

ADJUSTMENT

1. Make sure the parking brake is fully released.

2. Raise the vehicle and support it safely. Remove the wheel and tire assembly.

3. Remove the grease cap. Rotate the brake drum to make sure there is no brake drag.

4. On Type 1 nuts, carefully raise the staked portion of the locknut using a small cape chisel. On Type 2 nuts, remove the cotter pin and nut retaining cap.

NOTE: Some locknuts may have left hand thread. The left hand threaded locknut is located on the right side of the vehicle. Turn this locknut clockwise to loosen. The right hand threaded locknut is located on the left side of the vehicle and is turned counterclockwise to loosen.

5. Remove the locknut. Discard the Type 1 locknut or Type 2 cotter pin.

6. To seat the bearings, torque the locknut to 18–22 ft. lbs. (25–29 Nm). Rotate the brake drum by hand while tightening the locknut.

7. Loosen the locknut until it can be turned by hand.

8. Before the bearing preload can be set, the amount of seal drag must be measured and added to the the required preload.

9. To measure the seal drag on Type 1 nuts, proceed as follows:

   a. Install a lug bolt and rotate the brake drum until the stud is in the 12 o'clock position.

   b. Place an inch pound torque wrench onto the bolt to measure the amount of force required to rotate the break drum.

   c. Pull the torque wrench and note and record the torque reading when rotation begins.

10. To measure the seal drag on Type 2 nuts, use a pull scale. Measure the oil seal drag by pulling on the scale until the wheel begins to turn. Record the value.

11. To determine the specified preload on Type 1 nuts, add the amount of seal drag to the required preload, which is 1.3–4.3 inch lbs. (0.15–0.49 Nm). To calculate the preload, add the seal drag value to the minimum and maximum preload specifications. For example, if the seal drag was 2.2 inch lbs. (0.25 Nm), then the minimum preload specification would be 1.3 inch lbs. (0.15 Nm)

+ 2.2 inch lbs. (0.25 Nm) = 3.5 inch lbs. (0.40 Nm) and the maximum preload specification would be 4.3 inch lbs. (0.49 Nm) + 2.2 inch lbs. (0.25 Nm) = 6.5 inch lbs. (0.74 Nm). Therefore, for a seal drag of 2.2 inch lbs. (0.25 Nm), the bearing preload should be within the range of 3.5–6.5 inch lbs. (0.40–0.74 Nm).

12. On Type 2 nuts, add the oil seal drag value obtained in Step 10 to the specified value of 0.6–1.9 lbs. (2.6–8.5 N). This is the standard bearing preload.

13. On Type 1 locknuts, tighten the locknut slightly. Rotate the brake drum until the nut and wheel are returned to the 12 o'clock position. Position the inch lb. torque wrench onto the nut and measure the amount of pull required to rotate the brake drum. Tighten the locknut until the torque shown on the torque wrench is within the range calculated in Step 11.

14. On Type 2 locknuts, turn the locknut slowly to adjust to the standard bearing preload, while checking with the pull scale.

15. On Type 1 locknuts, stake the locknut in place using a cold chisel with the cutting edge rounded.

NOTE: If the nut splits or cracks after staking, it must be replaced with a new nut.

16. On Type 2 nuts, install the nut retaining cap and a new cotter pin.

17. Install the grease cap.

18. Install the wheel and tire assembly. Lower the vehicle.

Torsion (Axle) Beam

REMOVAL AND INSTALLATION

1. Raise and safely support the vehicle.

2. Remove the wheel and tire assemblies.

3. Remove the rear struts and disconnect the brake lines.

4. Disconnect the parking brake cable clevises at the brake backing plates.

5. Remove the parking brake equalizer and cables from the torsion beam.

6. Remove the 4 nuts from the back of each brake assembly to release the backing plates and wheel spindle supports.

7. Remove the torsion beam pivot bolts from the body brackets and

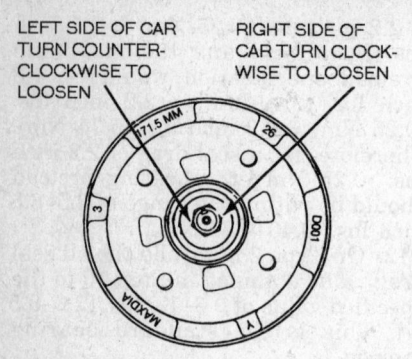

LEFT SIDE OF CAR TURN COUNTER-CLOCKWISE TO LOOSEN

RIGHT SIDE OF CAR TURN CLOCKWISE TO LOOSEN

84708049

Rear wheel bearing nut turning direction

carefully lower the torsion beam from the vehicle.

NOTE: If the torsion beam body brackets are not to be replaced, it may be desirable to leave them in place on the body. The bracket mounting holes are slotted to permit side-to-side adjustment of the torsion beam for true tracking of the rear suspension. If removed, they require alignment when the torsion beam is installed. However, if the torsion beam is repaired or replaced, the alignment must be checked at assembly.

To install:

8. If removed, install the torsion beam pivot brackets on the body with flatwashers, lockwashers and 3 bolts on each side. Do not tighten the mounting bolts at this time.

9. If installing a new torsion beam, install the pivot bushings in the beam arms.

10. Install the bushing flange washers and position the beam arms in the body brackets. Align the pivot bolt holes and install the bolts but do not tighten the nuts yet.

11. Install the brake backing plates and wheel spindle support assemblies with 4 nuts each, tightening to 32–45 ft. lbs. (43–61 Nm).

12. Install the parking brake equalizer assembly on the torsion beam and connect the cable clevises to the brake levers with the clevis pins and cotter pins.

13. Connect the right and left brake lines at the routing brackets and clip in place.

14. Install the rear suspension struts.

15. Install the wheel and tire assemblies. Use a suitable jack to raise the torsion beam into normal ride height position.

16. With the torsion beam in position, tighten the torsion beam pivot bolts at the body brackets to 69–87 ft. lbs. (93–118 Nm).

17. Check the rear suspension alignment by locating and marking the center of the underbody, at a point equidistant from the right and left body bracket inboard mounting bolts. From this point, measure the distance to the centers of the strut lower mounting bolts, right and left. If these measurements are not within 0.2 in. (5mm), shift the torsion beam body brackets side-to-side to center the suspension.

18. When centered, tighten the body bracket mounting bolts, the upper bolts to 40–50 ft. lbs. (54–68 Nm) and the lower bolt to 69–87 ft. lbs. (93–118 Nm).

19. Bleed the rear brakes and lower the vehicle.

FIRING ORDERS

NOTE: To avoid confusion, always replace spark plug wires one at a time.

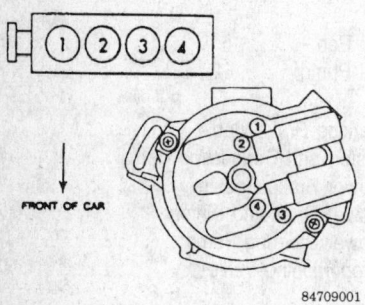

84709001

2.0L Engine
Engine Firing Order: 1–3–4–2
Distributor rotation: Clockwise

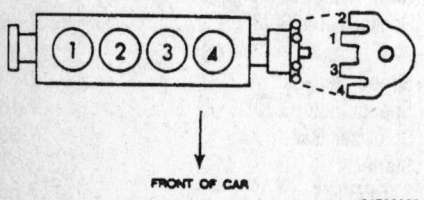

84709002

2.2L Engine
Engine Firing Order: 1–3–4–2
Distributor Rotation: Counterclockwise

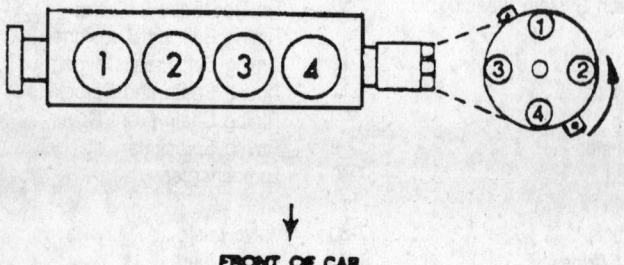

84709003

2.2L Turbocharged Engine
Engine Firing Order: 1–3–4–2
Distributor Rotation: Counterclockwise

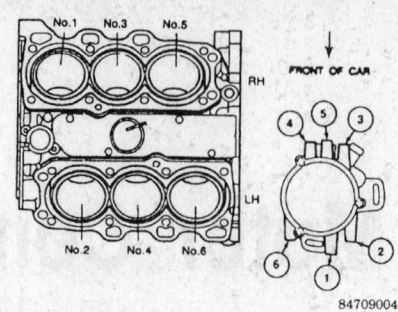

84709004

2.5L Engine
Engine Firing Order: 1–2–3–4–5–6
Distributor Rotation: Counterclockwise

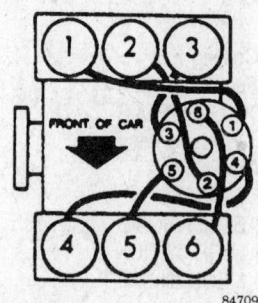

84709005

3.0L Engine
Engine Firing Order: 1–4–2–5–3–6
Distributor Rotation: Clockwise

ENGINE ELECTRICAL

NOTE: Disconnecting the negative battery cable on some vehicles may interfere with the functions of the on board computer systems and may require the computer to undergo a relearning process, once the negative battery cable is reconnected.

Distributor

REMOVAL

Except 2.5L Engine

1. Disconnect the negative battery cable.
2. Remove the distributor cap and position aside, leaving the spark plug wires connected. Before removing the distributor, mark the position of the No. 1 spark plug wire tower on the distributor cap.
3. On 2.0L engine, disconnect the distributor electrical connector. If equipped with automatic transaxle, disconnect the coil connector.
4. On 2.2L non-turbocharged engine, disconnect the vacuum hoses from the distributor diaphragm and the wiring harness at the coil. Tag the hoses and wires prior to removal so they can be reinstalled in their original locations.
5. On 2.2L turbocharged engine, disconnect the distributor wiring harness connector located near the distributor.
6. On 3.0L engine, disconnect the primary wiring connector from the distributor and disconnect the TFI-IV wiring harness connector at the ignition module.
7. Using a wrench on the crankshaft pulley, rotate the crankshaft to position the No. 1 piston at TDC on the compression stroke. The crankshaft pulley notch should align with the timing plate indicator and the distributor rotor should be pointing to the No. 1 spark plug tower position on the distributor cap.
8. Using chalk or paint, mark the position of the distributor housing on the cylinder head on 2.0L and 2.2L engines, or the position of the distributor housing on the cylinder block on 3.0L engine.
9. Remove the distributor hold-down bolt(s) and remove the distributor.
10. Inspect the O-ring on the distributor housing and replace it, if it is damaged or worn.

2.5L Engine

1. Disconnect the negative battery cable.
2. Remove the 2 fresh air duct nuts and 3 bolts. Loosen the spring clamp at the front of the air cleaner assembly and slide it forward. Remove the fresh air duct.
3. Loosen the clamp on the front of the air flow meter and disconnect the air duct. Disconnect the air flow

meter electrical connector at the left side of the air cleaner.

4. Disconnect the evaporative canister hose from the routing clip on the front of the air cleaner. Remove the fuel pressure regulator control solenoid from the air cleaner and position aside.

5. Remove the nuts and bolt and remove the air cleaner assembly.

6. Tag and disconnect the spark plug wires from the distributor cap. Disconnect the electrical connectors from the top of the distributor.

7. Using chalk or paint, mark the position of the distributor housing on the cylinder head. Remove the distributor hold-down bolts and remove the distributor.

INSTALLATION

Timing Not Disturbed

EXCEPT 2.5L ENGINE

1. Using clean engine oil, lubricate the distributor O-ring.

2. Install the distributor. Make sure the distributor rotor aligns with the No. 1 spark plug tower position on the distributor cap and the distributor housing mark aligns with the cylinder head or cylinder block mark.

NOTE: On 2.0L engine, there are existing marks on the distributor shaft and housing, which when aligned, indicate the No. 1 spark plug wire tower position. On 2.2L engine, make sure the distributor drive gear engages with the slot in the camshaft.

3. Install and loosely tighten the distributor hold-down bolt(s).

4. Connect the electrical connectors and, if equipped, vacuum hoses to their original locations. Install the distributor cap.

5. Connect the negative battery cable. Start the engine and check or adjust the ignition timing.

2.5L ENGINE

1. Align the distributor shaft with the camshaft end and install the distributor.

NOTE: The tangs on the distributor shaft are different sizes, allowing the distributor to be installed in only 1 position.

2. Install the distributor hold-down bolts. Align the mark that was made on the distributor housing with the mark that was made on the cylinder head and loosely tighten the bolts.

3. Connect the electrical connectors to the distributor and the spark plug wires to the distributor cap.

4. Install the air cleaner assembly and tighten the nuts and bolt to 18 ft. lbs. (25 Nm).

5. Install the fuel pressure regulator solenoid and connect the evaporative canister hose into the routing clip.

6. Connect the air flow meter electrical connector. Connect the air duct and tighten the clamp.

7. Align the fresh air duct and install the hose to the air cleaner assembly. Loosen the spring clamp and slide it into position. Install the fresh air duct nuts and bolts and tighten to 71–88 inch lbs. (8–10 Nm).

8. Connect the negative battery cable. Start the engine and check or adjust the ignition timing.

Timing Disturbed

EXCEPT 2.5L ENGINE

1. Using clean engine oil, lubricate the distributor O-ring.

2. Disconnect the spark plug wire from the No. 1 cylinder spark plug. Remove the spark plug from the No. 1 cylinder and press a thumb over the spark plug hole.

3. Using a wrench on the crankshaft pulley, rotate the crankshaft until pressure is felt at the spark plug hole, indicating the piston is approaching TDC on the compression stroke. Continue rotating the crankshaft until the crankshaft pulley mark aligns with the timing cover indicator.

4. Position the distributor rotor so it aligns with the No. 1 spark plug wire tower on the distributor cap.

5. Install the distributor. Be sure to engage the drive gear with the camshaft slot on 2.2L engines. Align the mark that was made on the distributor housing with the mark that was made on the cylinder head or cylinder block. Loosely tighten the distributor hold-down bolts.

6. Connect the electrical connectors and, if equipped, vacuum hoses to their original locations. Install the distributor cap.

7. Install the spark plug in the No. 1 cylinder and connect the spark plug wire.

8. Connect the negative battery cable. Start the engine and check or adjust the ignition timing.

2.5L ENGINE

1. Align the distributor shaft with the camshaft end and install the distributor.

NOTE: The tangs on the distributor shaft are different sizes, allowing the distributor to be installed in only 1 position.

2. Install the distributor hold-down bolts. Align the mark that was made on the distributor housing with the mark that was made on the cylinder head and loosely tighten the bolts.

3. Connect the electrical connectors to the distributor and the spark plug wires to the distributor cap.

4. Install the air cleaner assembly and tighten the nuts and bolt to 18 ft. lbs. (25 Nm).

5. Install the fuel pressure regulator solenoid and connect the evaporative canister hose into the routing clip.

6. Connect the air flow meter electrical connector. Connect the air duct and tighten the clamp.

7. Align the fresh air duct and install the hose to the air cleaner assembly. Loosen the spring clamp and slide it into position. Install the fresh air duct nuts and bolts and tighten to 71–88 inch lbs. (8–10 Nm).

8. Connect the negative battery cable. Start the engine and check or adjust the ignition timing.

Ignition Timing

ADJUSTMENT

2.0L Engine

1. Apply the parking brake. If equipped with manual transaxle, place the shift lever in neutral. If equipped with automatic transaxle, place the shift lever in **P**.

2. Locate the timing marks on the crankshaft pulley and the timing indicator scale on the engine front cover. If the marks are hard to see, clean them with degreaser and a wire brush.

3. Start the engine and bring to normal operating temperature. Make sure all accessories are **OFF**.

4. Connect a tachometer and timing light to the engine according to the manufacturer's instructions.

5. If equipped with manual transaxle, remove the shorting bar from the double wire SPOUT connector. If equipped with automatic transaxle, connect a jumper wire between the STI (TEN) terminal and the GND terminal on the data link connector.

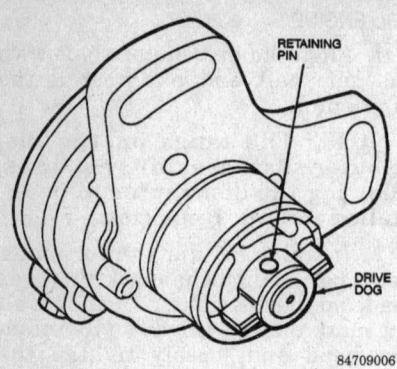

Distributor drive gear — 2.2L engine

84709006

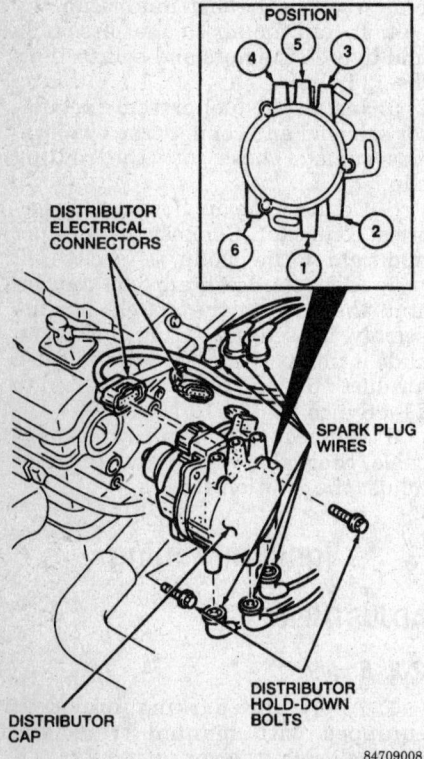

POSITION

DISTRIBUTOR ELECTRICAL CONNECTORS

SPARK PLUG WIRES

DISTRIBUTOR HOLD-DOWN BOLTS

DISTRIBUTOR CAP

84709008

Distributor installation — 2.5L engine

6. Check the idle speed and adjust, if necessary; it should be 700 ± 50 rpm.

7. Aim the timing light at the timing marks; the timing should be 10 ± 1 degrees if equipped with manual transaxle or 12 ± 1 degrees if equipped with automatic transaxle.

8. If the timing marks are not aligned, loosen the distributor hold-down bolt and turn the distributor housing to adjust. When the marks align, tighten the hold-down bolt to 19 ft. lbs. (25 Nm). Recheck the timing after the bolt has been tightened.

9. If equipped with manual transaxle, install the shorting bar to the

double wire SPOUT connector. If equipped with automatic transaxle, remove the jumper wire from the data link connector.

10. Remove all test equipment.

2.2L Engine

NON-TURBOCHARGED ENGINE

1. Apply the parking brake. If equipped with manual transaxle, place the shift lever in neutral. If equipped with automatic transaxle, place the shift lever in **P**.

2. Locate the timing marks on the crankshaft pulley and timing belt cover. If the marks are hard to see, clean them off with some degreasing cleaner and a wire brush.

3. Start the engine and bring to normal operating temperature. Make sure all accessories are **OFF**.

4. Connect a tachometer and inductive timing light according to the manufacturer's instructions.

NOTE: The tachometer can be connected without removing the coil connector. Insert an alligator clip into the back of the connector onto the dark green/yellow dotted wire, then connect the tachometer lead to the alligator

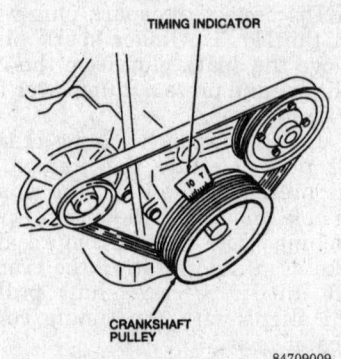

TIMING INDICATOR

CRANKSHAFT PULLEY

84709009

Timing mark location — 2.0L engine

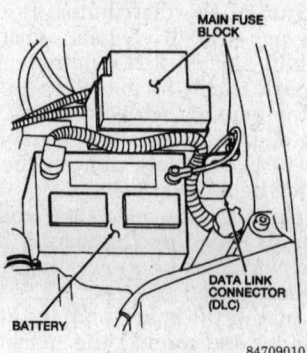

MAIN FUSE BLOCK

DATA LINK CONNECTOR (DLC)

BATTERY

84709010

Data link connector location — 1993–96 Probe

clip. Do not allow the clip to accidently ground to a metal surface, as it may permanently damage the coil.

5. Check the idle speed and adjust, if necessary; it should be 750 ± 25 rpm.

6. Shut OFF the engine. Disconnect and plug the vacuum hoses at the distributor vacuum diaphragm. On 1992 vehicles, connect a jumper wire between the black 1-pin STI test connector, located near the left strut tower, and ground.

7. Start the engine and allow the idle to stabilize.

8. Aim the timing light at the timing marks. The timing should be 6 ± 1 degrees.

9. If the marks are not aligned, loosen the distributor lock bolt just enough to turn the distributor housing. While aiming the timing light at the timing marks, turn the distributor until the marks are aligned. Tighten the distributor lock bolt to 14–19 ft. lbs. (19–25 Nm) and recheck the timing.

10. Reconnect the vacuum hoses and remove the jumper wire. Remove all test equipment.

TURBOCHARGED ENGINE

1. Apply the parking brake. If equipped with manual transaxle, place the shift lever in neutral. If equipped with automatic transaxle, place the shift lever in **P**.

2. Locate the timing marks on the crankshaft pulley and timing belt cover. If the marks are hard to see, clean them off with some degreasing cleaner and a wire brush.

3. Start the engine and allow it to come to normal operating temperature. Make sure all accessories are **OFF**.

4. Connect a tachometer and inductive timing light according to the manufacturer's instructions.

NOTE: The tachometer can be connected without removing the coil connector. Insert an alligator clip into the back of the connector onto the dark green/yellow dotted wire, then connect the tachometer lead to the alligator clip. Do not allow the clip to accidently ground to a metal surface, as it may permanently damage the coil.

5. Check the idle speed and adjust, if necessary; it should be 750 ± 25 rpm.

6. Shut OFF the engine. Connect a jumper wire between the black 1-pin

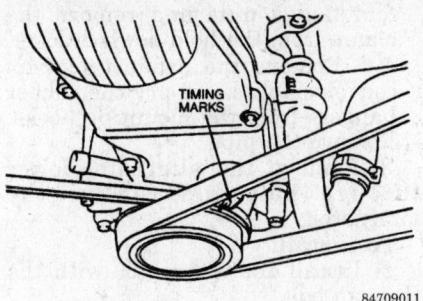

Timing mark location — 2.2L engine

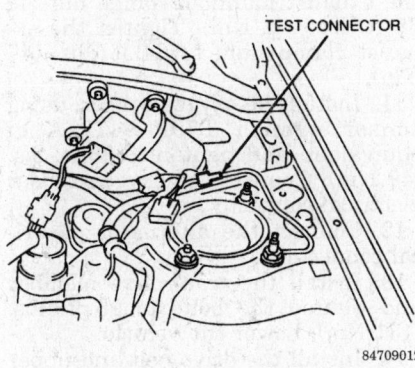

STI test connector location — 2.2L engine

STI test connector, located near the left strut tower, and ground.

7. Start the engine and allow the idle to stabilize.

8. Aim the timing light at the timing marks. The timing should be 9 ± 1 degrees.

9. If the marks are not aligned, loosen the distributor lock bolt just enough to turn the distributor housing. While aiming the timing light at the timing marks, turn the distributor until the marks are aligned. Tighten the distributor lock bolt to 14–19 ft. lbs. (19–25 Nm) and recheck the timing.

10. Shut OFF the engine. Remove the jumper wire and test equipment.

2.5L Engine

1. Apply the parking brake. If equipped with manual transaxle, place the shift lever in neutral. If equipped with automatic transaxle, place the shift lever in **P**.

2. Locate the timing marks on the crankshaft pulley and timing belt cover. If the marks are hard to see, clean them off with some degreasing cleaner and a wire brush.

3. Start the engine and allow it to come to normal operating tempera-

ture. Make sure all accessories are **OFF**.

4. Connect a tachometer and inductive timing light according to the manufacturer's instructions.

5. Connect terminals STI (TEN) and GND on the data link connector with a jumper wire.

6. Check the idle speed and adjust, if necessary; it should be 650 ± 50 rpm.

7. Aim the timing light at the timing marks. The timing should be 9–11 degrees.

8. If the marks are not aligned, loosen the distributor hold-down bolts just enough to turn the distributor housing. While aiming the timing light at the timing marks, turn the distributor until the marks are aligned. Tighten the distributor hold-down bolts to 14–19 ft. lbs. (19–25 Nm) and recheck the timing.

9. Shut OFF the engine. Remove the jumper wire and test equipment.

3.0L Engine

1. Apply the parking brake. If equipped with manual transaxle, place the shift lever in neutral. If equipped with automatic transaxle, place the shift lever in **P**.

2. Locate the timing marks on the crankshaft pulley and timing belt cover. If the marks are hard to see, clean them off with some degreasing cleaner and a wire brush.

3. Connect a suitable inductive timing light according to the manufacturer's instructions.

4. Disconnect the single wire inline SPOUT connector, located near the distributor, by pulling the plug from the connector housing.

5. Start the engine and allow it to warm to operating temperature. Make sure the idle speed is correct.

NOTE: To set timing correctly, a remote starter should not be used. Use the ignition key only to

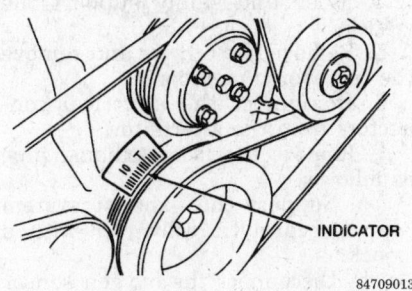

Timing mark locations — 2.2L engine

start the vehicle. Disconnecting the start wire at the starter relay will cause the TFI module to revert to start mode timing after the vehicle is started. Reconnecting the start wire after the vehicle is running will not correct the timing.

6. Aim the timing light at the timing marks. The timing should be 10 degrees BTDC. If the timing is correct, proceed to Step 8. If the timing is incorrect, proceed to Step 7.

7. Loosen the distributor hold-down bolt just enough to turn the distributor housing. While aiming the timing light at the timing marks, turn the distributor until the marks are aligned. Tighten the distributor hold-down bolt to 17–25 ft. lbs. (23–34 Nm) and recheck the timing.

8. Reconnect the single wire inline SPOUT connector. Check the timing advance to verify the distributor is advancing beyond the initial setting.

9. Remove the inductive timing light.

Alternator

PRECAUTIONS

Several precautions must be observed with alternator equipped vehicles to avoid damage to the unit.

• If the battery is removed for any reason, make sure it is reconnected with the correct polarity. Reversing the battery connections may result in damage to the one-way rectifiers.

• When utilizing a booster battery as a starting aid, always connect the positive to positive terminals and the negative terminal from the booster battery to a good engine ground on the vehicle being started.

• Never use a fast charger as a booster to start vehicles.

• Disconnect the battery cables when charging the battery with a fast charger.

• Never attempt to polarize the alternator.

• Do not use test lights of more than 12 volts when checking diode continuity.

• Do not short across or ground any of the alternator terminals.

• The polarity of the battery, alternator and regulator must be matched and considered before making any electrical connections within the system.

• Never separate the alternator on an open circuit. Make sure all connections within the circuit are clean and tight.

• Disconnect the battery ground terminal when performing any service on electrical components.

• Disconnect the battery if arc welding is to be done on the vehicle.

BELT TENSION ADJUSTMENT

2.0L Engine

1. Apply approximately 22 lbs. pressure to the drive belt at a point midway between the alternator and water pump pulleys. The belt should deflect 0.26–0.27 in. (6.5–7.0mm) for new or 0.28–0.35 in. (7–9mm) for used.

NOTE: Always check the belt tension when the engine is cold or has been stopped for at least ½ hour. The alternator belt can be considered new if it has been in used on a running engine less than 5 minutes.

2. If the belt deflection is not as specified, loosen the alternator adjusting bolt and upper mounting bolt.
3. Raise and safely support the vehicle. Remove the right splash shield and loosen the alternator through bolt.
4. Lower the vehicle.
5. Turn the alternator adjusting bolt until the belt deflection is as specified in Step 1.
6. Tighten the alternator upper mounting bolt to 18 ft. lbs. (25 Nm).
7. Raise and safely support the vehicle. Tighten the alternator lower through bolt to 38 ft. lbs. (51 Nm).
8. Install the right splash shield and lower the vehicle.

2.2L Engine

1. Apply approximately 22 lbs. pressure to the alternator belt at a point midway between the crankshaft and alternator pulleys. The belt should deflect 0.24–0.31 in. (6–8mm) for new or 0.27–0.35 in. (7–9mm) for used.

NOTE: Always check the belt tension when the engine is cold or has been stopped for at least ½ hour. The alternator belt can be considered new if it has been in used on a running engine less than 5 minutes.

2. If the belt deflection is not as specified, loosen the alternator adjustment bolt and through bolt.
3. Turn the alternator adjustment bolt to adjust the belt tension.
4. After adjustment, tighten the through bolt to 38 ft. lbs. (52 Nm) and

the adjusting bolt to 18 ft. lbs. (25 Nm).

2.5L Engine

1. If not equipped with A/C, apply approximately 22 lbs. pressure to the alternator drive belt at a point midway between the alternator and crankshaft pulleys. The alternator belt should deflect 0.24–0.27 in. (6–7mm) for new or 0.28–0.31 in. (7–8mm) for used.
2. If equipped with A/C, apply approximately 22 lbs. pressure to the alternator belt at a point midway between the A/C compressor and crankshaft pulleys. The belt should deflect 0.22–0.25 in. (5.5–6.5mm) if the belt is new or 0.26–0.29 in. (6.5–7.5mm) for used.

NOTE: Always check the belt tension when the engine is cold or has been stopped for at least ½ hour. The alternator belt can be considered new if it has been in used on a running engine less than 5 minutes.

3. If the belt deflection is not as specified, loosen the tensioner pulley locknut and turn the tensioner adjusting bolt until the belt tension is correct.
4. After adjustment, tighten the tensioner pulley locknut to 34 ft. lbs. (46 Nm).

3.0L Engine

The 3.0L engine uses an automatic tensioner to maintain proper belt tension. No adjustment is necessary.

REMOVAL AND INSTALLATION

2.0L Engine

1. Disconnect the negative battery cable.
2. Remove the alternator upper mounting bolt.
3. Loosen the alternator adjusting bolt and remove the drive belt from the alternator pulley.
4. Raise and safely support the vehicle.
5. Remove the 6 bolts and remove the transverse member.
6. Disconnect the electrical connectors from the alternator.
7. Remove the front exhaust pipe as follows:
   a. Support the exhaust system at the catalytic converter with a jack.
   b. Disconnect the oxygen sensor electrical connector and remove the sensor using sensor wrench T79P–9472–A or equivalent.

c. Remove the 3 exhaust manifold flange nuts and remove the clamp from the hold-down bracket.
   d. Remove the exhaust pipe-to-converter nuts and pry the rubber hangers from the mounting hooks. Remove the pipe.
8. Remove the alternator lower through bolt and remove the alternator.

To install:
9. Install the alternator with the through bolt.
10. Install the exhaust pipe, using new gaskets. Tighten the pipe-to-converter nuts to 66 ft. lbs. (89 Nm) and the exhaust manifold flange nuts to 38 ft. lbs. (52 Nm). Tighten the exhaust clamp nuts to 34 ft. lbs. (47 Nm).
11. Install the oxygen sensor, using sensor wrench T79P–9472–A or equivalent, and tighten to 36 ft. lbs. (49 Nm). Connect the oxygen sensor electrical connector.
12. Connect the alternator electrical connectors.
13. Install the transverse member and tighten the bolts to 96 ft. lbs. (131 Nm). Lower the vehicle.
14. Install the drive belt and upper mounting bolt. Adjust the belt tension. Tighten the lower through bolt to 38 ft. lbs. (52 Nm) and the upper mounting bolt to 10 ft. lbs. (15 Nm).
15. Connect the negative battery cable.

2.2L Engine

1. Disconnect the negative battery cable.
2. Raise and safely support the vehicle.
3. Remove the right halfshaft.
4. From the rear of the alternator, depress the lock tabs on the wiring terminals and pull the terminals straight off. Mark the location of the wires prior to removal so they can be reinstalled in their original positions.
5. Loosen the alternator adjustment and through bolts enough to allow the alternator to pivot. Remove the alternator drive belt.
6. Remove the alternator adjustment bracket, lock bolt and through bolt.
7. Hold the alternator to prevent it from falling and remove it through the space left by removing the halfshaft.

To install:
8. Position the alternator and loosely install the mounting and adjustment bolts.
9. Install the drive belt and adjust the tension. Tighten the through bolt

to 38 ft. lbs. (52 Nm) and the adjusting bolt to 19 ft. lbs. (25 Nm).

10. Connect the wiring terminals at the rear of the alternator.

11. Install the right halfshaft.

12. Lower the vehicle. Connect the negative battery cable.

2.5L Engine

1. Disconnect the negative battery cable.

2. Disconnect the electrical connectors from the alternator.

3. Loosen the belt tensioner locknut and tension adjusting bolt. Remove the alternator upper mounting bolt.

4. Raise and safely support the vehicle.

5. Remove the right splash shield.

6. Remove the drive belt from the alternator pulley.

7. Remove the A/C compressor mounting bolts and and support the compressor aside, leaving the refrigerant lines connected.

8. Remove the alternator through bolt and the alternator.

9. Installation is the reverse of the removal procedure. Adjust the drive belt tension and tighten the alternator through bolt to 38 ft. lbs. (51 Nm) and the upper mounting bolt to 18 ft. lbs. (25 Nm). Tighten the A/C compressor mounting bolts to 26 ft. lbs. (35 Nm).

3.0L Engine

1. Disconnect the negative battery cable.

2. Remove the accessory drive belt.

3. Remove and set aside the windshield washer reservoir.

4. Remove the power steering pump reservoir return hose from the pump assembly.

5. Remove the power steering pump high pressure hose from the pump assembly.

6. Remove the upper and middle accessory support bracket mounting bolts.

7. Pull back on the idler tensioner, using a 1/2 in. drive breaker bar and remove the lower accessory support bracket mounting bolt.

8. Remove the mounting bolt from the side of the accessory bracket at the air conditioning compressor brace.

9. Raise the alternator/accessory support bracket to clear the engine and set aside carefully to remove the electrical connectors.

10. Disconnect the electrical connectors from the alternator. Place the

alternator/accessory support bracket on a bench for alternator removal.

11. Remove the alternator pivot bolt and remove the mounting bolt from the back side of the alternator. Remove the alternator from the accessory support bracket.

To install:

12. Position the alternator on the accessory support bracket and install the alternator pivot bolt.

13. Install the alternator mounting bolt at the rear of the alternator.

14. Position the alternator/accessory support bracket in the engine compartment and connect the electrical connectors on the back side of the alternator.

15. Position the alternator/accessory support bracket on the engine. Install the mounting bolt through the air conditioning compressor brace into the support bracket.

16. Install the middle accessory support bracket mounting bolt.

17. Pull back on the idler tensioner, using the 1/2 in. drive breaker bar and install the lower accessory support bracket mounting bolt.

18. Install the upper accessory support bracket mounting bolt.

19. Connect the power steering pressure and return hoses to the pump.

20. Install the accessory drive belt.

21. Replace the windshield washer reservoir and connect the negative battery cable.

22. Fill and bleed the power steering system.

Starter

REMOVAL AND INSTALLATION

2.0L Engine

1. Disconnect the negative battery cable.

2. Remove the air duct and air cleaner assembly.

3. Remove the upper starter mounting bolts.

4. Raise and safely support the vehicle.

5. Remove the intake manifold support bracket bolts and the bracket.

6. Disconnect the electrical connectors from the starter solenoid.

7. Remove the lower starter mounting bolt and remove the starter.

8. Installation is the reverse of the removal procedure. Tighten the starter mounting bolts to 34 ft. lbs.

(46 Nm). The upper mounting bolts must be tightened first.

2.2L Engine

1. Disconnect the negative battery cable. Raise and support the vehicle, safely.

2. If equipped with a manual transaxle, remove the exhaust pipe bracket.

3. Remove the transaxle-to-engine bracket and intake manifold-to-engine bracket.

4. Disconnect the electrical connectors from the starter.

5. Remove the starter mounting bolts and the starter.

To install:

6. Install the starter and torque the bolts to 34 ft. lbs. (46 Nm).

7. Connect the electrical connectors to the starter.

8. Install the intake manifold-to-engine bracket and tighten the bolts to 22 ft. lbs. (30 Nm).

9. If equipped with an automatic transaxle, install the transaxle-to-engine bracket and torque the bellhousing bolt to 86 ft. lbs. (117 Nm) and the 3 other mounting bolts to 38 ft. lbs. (52 Nm).

10. If equipped with a manual transaxle, install the transaxle-to-engine bracket and connect the exhaust pipe bracket. Tighten the bracket bolts to 45 ft. lbs. (61 Nm).

11. Lower the vehicle.

12. Connect the negative battery cable and check the starter for proper operation.

2.5L Engine

1. Disconnect the negative battery cable.

2. Remove the fresh air duct and the air cleaner assembly.

3. If equipped with automatic transaxle, proceed as follows:

a. Use a small prybar to pry the shift cable from the shift lever.

b. Squeeze the lock tabs on the shift cable and remove the cable from the cable bracket.

c. Label and disconnect the electrical connectors from the knock sensor, throttle position sensor, fuel rail, distributor, neutral safety switch, automatic transaxle and wiring harness.

d. Position the wiring harness aside.

e. Remove the 2 selector cable bracket mounting bolts and the bracket.

f. Remove the 2 nuts and bolt from the starter bracket and remove the bracket.

4. Disconnect the electrical connectors from the starter solenoid.

5. Remove the 3 starter mounting bolts and remove the starter.

6. Installation is the reverse of the removal procedure. Tighten the starter mounting bolts to 33 ft. lbs. (46 Nm).

3.0L Engine

1. Disconnect the negative battery cable.

2. Raise and safely support the vehicle.

3. If equipped with automatic transaxle, remove the kickdown cable routing bracket from the engine block.

4. Disconnect the wire from the starter solenoid S-terminal.

NOTE: When disconnecting the plastic hard shell connector at the solenoid S-terminal, grasp the plastic connector, depress the plastic tab, and pull off the lead assembly. Do not pull on the lead wire or damage may result.

5. Remove the attaching nut from the starter solenoid B-terminal and disconnect the cable from the terminal.

6. Remove the starter mounting bolts and remove the starter.

To install:

7. Position the starter and install the mounting bolts. Tighten the bolts to 20 ft. lbs. (27 Nm).

8. Connect the cable to the starter solenoid B-terminal and install the attaching nut. Tighten the nut to 120 inch lbs. (13.5 Nm).

9. Connect the wire to the starter solenoid S-terminal.

10. If necessary, install the kickdown cable routing bracket to the engine block.

11. Lower the vehicle. Connect the negative battery cable and check the starter for proper operation.

CHASSIS ELECTRICAL

Air Bag

DISARMING

1. Disconnect the negative battery cable.

2. Wait 1 minute for the backup power supply in the diagnostic monitor to deplete its stored energy.

3. Remove the 4 bolts retaining the air bag to the steering wheel.

4. Disconnect the air bag/horn electrical connector. Disconnect the cruise control switch electrical connector, if equipped.

5. Remove the air bag module from the steering wheel.

CAUTION

When carrying a live air bag, make sure the bag and trim cover are pointed away from the body. In the unlikely event of an accidental deployment, the bag will then deploy with minimal chance of injury. When placing a live air bag on a bench or other surface, always face the bag and trim cover up, away from the surface. This will reduce the motion of the module if it is accidentally deployed.

Heater Blower Motor

REMOVAL AND INSTALLATION

1992

1. Disconnect the negative battery cable.

2. Remove the sound deadening panel from the passenger side.

3. Remove the glove box assembly and the brace.

4. Remove the cooling hose from the blower motor assembly.

5. Disconnect the electrical connector from the blower motor.

6. Remove the 3 blower motor-to-blower motor housing screws and blower motor.

7. If necessary, remove the blower wheel-to-blower motor clip and the wheel.

8. To install, reverse the removal procedure and check the blower motor operation.

1993–96

1. Disconnect the negative battery cable.

2. Remove the 2 hush panel screws and disconnect the courtesy light electrical connector. Remove the hush panel.

3. Disconnect the blower motor electrical connector and remove the 3 blower motor retaining screws. Remove the blower motor.

4. If necessary, remove the clip from the motor shaft and remove the blower wheel from the motor.

5. Installation is the reverse of the removal procedure.

Windshield Wiper Motor

REMOVAL AND INSTALLATION

Front

1992

1. Disconnect the negative battery cable.

2. Unscrew the retaining nut and remove the wiper arm and blade assemblies.

3. Disconnect the hose from the washer jet nozzle.

4. Remove the lower cowl moulding and wiper linkage cover.

5. Pull the wiper linkage off the wiper motor output arm.

6. Disconnect the electrical connectors from the wiper motor.

7. Remove the wiper motor mounting bolts and remove the motor from the vehicle.

8. Installation is the reverse of the removal procedure. Install the wiper arm and blade assemblies so the tip of the wiper blade is 0.79–1.18 in. (20–30mm) from the bottom of the windshield. Tighten the wiper arm retaining nut to 10 ft. lbs. (14 Nm).

1993–96

1. Disconnect the negative battery cable.

2. Remove the wiper arm cover cap and attaching nut and remove the wiper arm and blade assemblies.

3. Remove the lower windshield moulding.

4. Use a small prybar to pry the wiper linkage from the wiper motor output arm.

5. Remove the wiring harness bracket from the wiper motor mounting bracket.

6. Remove the 4 wiper motor mounting bracket bolts.

7. Disconnect the wiper motor ground and electrical connector and remove the wiper motor.

8. Installation is the reverse of the removal procedure. Tighten the wiper motor bolts to 87 inch lbs. (9 Nm). Install the wiper arm and blade assemblies so the tips of the blades are 1.12–1.28 in. (28–32mm) from the top of the cowl grille. Tighten the wiper arm nuts to 121 inch lbs. (15 Nm).

Rear

1992

1. Disconnect the negative battery cable.

2. Lift the cover and remove the wiper arm and blade assembly retaining nut. Remove the wiper arm and blade assembly.

3. Remove the boot, nut and mount from the wiper motor pivot.

4. Remove the liftgate interior trim panel.

5. Disconnect the electrical connector from the wiper motor.

6. Remove the wiper motor mounting bolts and remove the wiper motor.

7. Installation is the reverse of the removal procedure. Install the wiper arm and blade assembly so the tip of the wiper blade is 0.79–1.18 in. (20–30mm) from the bottom of the rear window.

1993–96

1. Disconnect the negative battery cable.

2. Lift the wiper arm nut cover and remove the nut. Remove the wiper arm and blade assembly.

3. Remove the cover and remove the wiper motor shaft support nut.

4. Remove the liftgate lower trim.

5. Disconnect the wiper motor electrical connector.

6. Remove the 3 wiper motor mounting bolts and disconnect the ground wire. Remove the wiper motor.

7. Installation is the reverse of the removal procedure. Tighten the wiper motor mounting bolts to 87 inch lbs. (9 Nm) and the shaft support nut to 52 inch lbs. (5 Nm). Install the wiper arm and blade assembly so the tip of the wiper blade is 1.0–1.6 in. (25–40mm) from the shaded glass area. Tighten the wiper arm nut to 87 inch lbs. (9 Nm).

Windshield Wiper Switch

REMOVAL AND INSTALLATION

Front

1992

1. Disconnect the negative battery cable.

2. Remove the instrument cluster module as follows:

  a. Remove the steering wheel.

  b. Remove the 2 column cover screws and remove the cover.

  c. Remove the 9 cluster module mounting screws.

  d. Carefully pull the cluster module outward and disconnect the 7 electrical connectors from the cover.

  e. Remove the ignition switch illumination bulb and remove the cluster module.

3. Gently pull the washer/interval rate control switch knob and wiper control switch knob from the windshield wiper switch.

4. From the rear of the instrument cluster module cover, remove the windshield wiper switch housing screws and the switch.

5. Installation is the reverse of the removal procedure. Check windshield wiper switch operation.

1993–96

Windshield wiper control is a function of the combination switch.

Rear

1992

1. Disconnect the negative battery cable.

2. Remove the instrument cluster module as follows:

  a. Remove the steering wheel.

  b. Remove the 2 column cover screws and remove the cover.

  c. Remove the 9 cluster module mounting screws.

  d. Carefully pull the cluster module outward and disconnect the 7 electrical connectors from the cover.

  e. Remove the ignition switch illumination bulb and remove the cluster module.

3. Gently pull the front washer/interval rate control switch knob and the front wiper control switch knob from the windshield wiper switch.

4. From the rear of the instrument cluster module cover, remove the windshield wiper switch housing screws and the switch.

5. Remove the rear wiper/washer switch-to-instrument cluster module cover screws.

6. Remove the control switch button by releasing the tangs. Remove the rear wiper/washer switch.

7. Installation is the reverse of the removal procedure. Check the windshield wiper/washer switch and the rear wiper/washer switch operation.

1993–96

1. Disconnect the negative battery cable.

2. Remove the floor console as follows:

  a. Remove the armrest.

  b. If equipped with manual transaxle, unscrew the shifter knob. If equipped with automatic transaxle, remove the emergency override key switch cover.

  c. Apply the parking brake.

  d. Gently pull up on the upper half of the floor console to separate it from the lower half.

  e. Disconnect the cigar lighter electrical connectors.

  f. Remove the ashtray light bulb from the upper half of the console.

3. Remove the 2 control console bezel screws and move the bezel away from the instrument panel to gain access to the wiper switch electrical connector.

4. Disconnect the wiper switch electrical connector. Squeeze the switch tabs and remove the switch from the control console bezel.

5. Installation is the reverse of the removal procedure.

Instrument Cluster

REMOVAL AND INSTALLATION

1992

1. Disconnect the negative battery cable.

2. Remove the instrument cluster module as follows:

  a. Remove the steering wheel.

  b. Remove the 2 column cover screws and remove the cover.

  c. Remove the 9 cluster module mounting screws.

  d. Carefully pull the cluster module outward and disconnect the 7 electrical connectors from the cover.

  e. Remove the ignition switch illumination bulb and remove the cluster module.

3. Loosen the 2 cover hinge screws and remove the 6 upper cluster cover screws. Remove the cover.

NOTE: During removal, be careful not to rip the rubber seal that joins the upper and lower portions of the cluster cover panels.

4. Remove the lower cluster cover panel and remove the 4 cluster mounting screws.

5. Disconnect the electrical connectors from the back of the cluster. If equipped with analog instrument cluster, disconnect the speedometer cable.

6. Remove the cluster from the vehicle.

7. Installation is the reverse of the removal procedure.

1993–96

1. Disconnect the negative battery cable.

2. Loosen the hood release handle mounting nut and remove the lower instrument panel cover screw.

3. Turn the courtesy light bulb ¼ turn counterclockwise and pull it straight out from the lower instrument panel cover. Remove the lower instrument panel cover.

4. Remove the 5 instrument cluster bezel screws and disconnect the resistor panel light dimmer switch electrical connector. Remove the instrument cluster bezel.

5. Remove the 2 upper steering column mounting bolts and lower the steering column.

6. Remove the 4 instrument cluster screws and pull the cluster out to gain access to the electrical connectors at the rear of the cluster.

7. Disconnect the 2 electrical connectors and remove the instrument cluster.

8. Installation is the reverse of the removal procedure.

Speedometer

REMOVAL AND INSTALLATION

1992

ELECTRONIC INSTRUMENT CLUSTER

The electronic speedometer is not serviceable. If the speedometer malfunctions, the entire instrument cluster must be replaced.

ANALOG INSTRUMENT CLUSTER

1. Disconnect the negative battery cable.

2. Remove the instrument cluster.

3. Remove the cluster lens.

4. Remove the speedometer attaching screws and the speedometer from the cluster.

5. Installation is the reverse of the removal procedure.

1993–96

1. Disconnect the negative battery cable.

2. Remove the instrument cluster.

3. Remove the printed circuit board from the instrument cluster as follows:

   a. Push in the lock tabs and remove the lens from the lens bezel. Push in the lock tabs and remove the lens bezel from the cluster housing.

   b. Remove the 2 fuel indicator module plastic cover attaching screws.

   c. Flip up the lower right corner of the plastic cover and disconnect the fuel indicator module electrical connector. Remove the fuel indicator module.

   d. Turn each of the 18 bulbs in the cluster housing a ¼ turn counterclockwise and pull straight out.

   e. Remove the 21 circuit board attaching screws and remove the printed circuit board.

4. Carefully pry out the oil pressure and battery gauge cluster and fuel and temperature gauge cluster from the cluster housing.

5. Remove the speedometer and tachometer gauge cluster from the cluster housing.

6. Press in the 2 tabs and remove the speedometer printed circuit board.

7. Installation is the reverse of the removal procedure.

Concealed Headlights

MANUAL OPERATION

A manual control knob is located on each headlight retractor motor. If the power headlight door system becomes inoperative, turn the manual control knob to raise the headlights. On 1992 vehicles, the knob is covered by a rubber boot and is accessed under the front fascia. On 1993–96 vehicles, the manual control knob can be operated through the engine compartment.

Headlight Switch

REMOVAL AND INSTALLATION

1992

1. Disconnect the negative battery cable. Remove the turn signal switch.

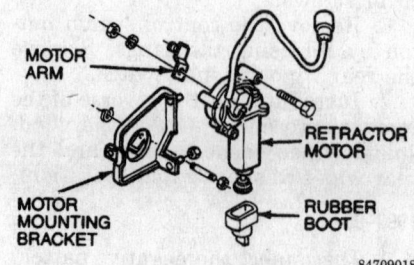

Headlight retractor motor assembly — 1992 Probe

2. Gently pull the rotary knob from the headlight switch.

3. From the rear of the instrument cluster module cover, remove the rotary switch housing screws and the switch.

4. Installation is the reverse of the removal procedure. Check headlight switch operation.

1993–96

Headlight operation control is a function of the combination switch.

Combination Switch

On 1992 vehicles, the combination switch is located on the instrument cluster module and incorporates the turn signal and dimmer switch functions. On 1993–96 vehicles, the combination switch is located on the steering column and controls the function of the headlights, turn signals and window wipers/washers.

REMOVAL AND INSTALLATION

1992

1. Disconnect the negative battery cable. Remove the steering wheel.

2. Remove the center cover mounting screws and the cover.

3. Remove cluster module mounting screws, pull the cluster module away from the dash and disconnect the electrical connectors. Remove the cluster module.

4. Remove the switch lever-to-switch screw and the lever.

5. From the rear of the instrument cluster module, remove the switch screws and the switch.

6. Installation is the reverse of the removal procedure. Check turn signal and headlight dimmer operation.

1993–96

1. Center the wheels to the straight-ahead position.

2. Disconnect the negative battery cable. Wait 1 minute for the backup power supply in the diagnostic monitor to deplete its stored energy.

3. Remove the 4 bolts retaining the air bag to the steering wheel.

4. Disconnect the air bag/horn electrical connector. Disconnect the cruise control switch electrical connector, if equipped.

5. Remove the air bag module from the steering wheel.

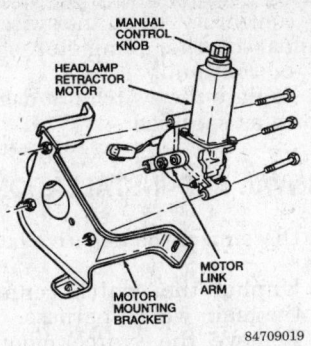

MANUAL CONTROL KNOB

HEADLAMP RETRACTOR MOTOR

MOTOR LINK ARM

MOTOR MOUNTING BRACKET

84709019

Headlight retractor motor assembly — 1993–96 Probe

────── CAUTION ──────

When carrying a live air bag, make sure the bag and trim cover are pointed away from the body. In the unlikely event of an accidental deployment, the bag will then deploy with minimal chance of injury. When placing a live air bag on a bench or other surface, always face the bag and trim cover up, away from the surface. This will reduce the motion of the module if it is accidently deployed.

6. Make alignment marks on the steering wheel and column shaft so they can be reassembled in the same position.

7. Remove the steering wheel nut and remove the steering wheel with a suitable puller. Route the wiring harness through the steering wheel as the wheel is lifted off the shaft.

NOTE: Do not try to remove the steering wheel by hitting the column shaft with a hammer, as the column shaft will collapse.

8. Remove the 4 lower steering column panel screws and separate the upper and lower steering column panels.

9. Remove the lock cylinder illumination bulb from the lower steering column panel and remove the upper and lower steering column panels.

10. Apply 2 strips of tape across the clockspring and housing to prevent accidental rotation.

11. Remove the 3 clockspring assembly screws and pull the clockspring assembly off the steering column shaft.

12. Disconnect the ground wire and electrical connector and remove the clockspring assembly.

13. Remove the cancel cam and spring. Remove the 3 combination switch screws.

14. Disconnect the electrical connectors and remove the combination switch.

To install:

15. Slide the combination switch over the column shaft and connect the electrical connectors.

16. Secure the switch with the screws and install the cancel cam and spring.

17. Make sure the front wheels are in the straight-ahead position.

NOTE: If the clockspring has been accidently rotated, turn the clockspring clockwise until it stops, then rotate counterclockwise 2.75 turns. Align the marks on the clockspring with the marks on the outer housing.

18. Install the clockspring ground wire screw and position the clockspring assembly on the column shaft. Connect the clockspring electrical connector.

19. Install the clockspring screws and tighten to 26 inch lbs. (3 Nm). Remove the tape strips from the clockspring and housing.

20. Install the upper and lower steering column panels. Install the lock cylinder illumination bulb and the 4 lower steering column panel screws.

21. Route the wiring harness through the steering wheel opening and position the steering wheel on the column shaft. Align the marks that were made during removal.

22. Install the steering wheel nut and tighten to 36 ft. lbs. (49 Nm).

23. Connect the air bag module and, if equipped, cruise control electrical connectors. Install the air bag module with the 4 bolts. Tighten the bolts to 54 inch lbs. (6 Nm).

24. Connect the negative battery cable.

Ignition Switch

REMOVAL AND INSTALLATION

1992

1. Disconnect the negative battery cable.

2. Remove the lower instrument cluster cover as follows:

   a. Remove the steering wheel.

   b. Remove the 2 column cover screws and the cover.

   c. Remove the 9 cluster module mounting screws.

   d. Carefully pull the cluster module outward and disconnect the electrical connectors.

   e. Remove the ignition switch illumination bulb and remove the cluster module.

   f. Loosen the 2 cover hinge screws and the 6 upper cluster cover screws. Remove the cover.

   g. Remove the lower cluster cover panel.

3. If equipped with automatic transaxle, remove the shift-lock cable attaching bolt and disconnect the cable from the lock cylinder housing.

4. Remove the steering column lower panel and lower plate.

5. Remove the side register duct.

6. If equipped, remove the tilt lever through-bolt, tilt lever and attaching nuts. Remove the tilt lever housing attaching bolts and spring.

7. Disconnect the ignition switch electrical connectors and remove the ignition switch retaining screw.

8. Remove the retainers from the lock cylinder electrical connector and disconnect the connector from the lock cylinder housing.

9. Remove the ignition switch from the lock cylinder housing.

To install:

10. Install the electrical connector into the lock cylinder housing.

11. Install the electrical connector retainers onto the lock cylinder housing and connector.

12. Install the ignition switch into the lock cylinder housing and install the retaining screw.

13. Connect all other ignition switch electrical connectors.

14. If necessary, install the tilt lever housing attaching bolts and spring, and the tilt lever, through bolt, and attaching nuts.

15. Install the side register duct. Install the steering column lower plate and lower panel.

16. If equipped with automatic transaxle, connect the shift-lock cable to the lock cylinder housing and install the bracket attaching bolt.

17. Install the lower cluster cover panel and the cluster cover.

18. Install the ignition switch illumination bulb. Connect the electrical connectors and install the cluster module with the attaching screws.

19. Install the column cover and the steering wheel.

20. Connect the negative battery cable and check ignition switch operation.

1993–96

1. Disconnect the negative battery cable.

2. Remove the 4 lower steering column panel screws and separate

the upper and lower steering column panels.

3. Remove the lock cylinder illumination bulb from the lower steering column panel and remove the upper and lower steering column panels.

4. Disconnect the electrical connector, remove the retaining screw and remove the switch.

5. Installation is the reverse of the removal procedure.

Ignition Lock

REMOVAL AND INSTALLATION

1992

1. Disconnect the negative battery cable.

2. Remove the ignition switch.

3. Remove the 2 lock cylinder assembly mounting screws and remove the lock cylinder assembly.

4. Installation is the reverse of the removal procedure.

1993–96

1. Disconnect the negative battery cable.

2. Remove the combination switch.

3. If equipped with automatic transaxle, remove the shift-lock cable screw.

4. Disconnect the shift-lock cable from the ignition switch/lock cylinder assembly.

5. Use a chisel to remove the 2 ignition switch/lock cylinder bolts and remove the ignition switch/lock cylinder assembly from the steering column shaft.

6. Disconnect the ignition key reminder switch electrical connector.

7. Drill out the 4 pins holding the lock cylinder to the housing. Remove the 3 shift-lock cable mechanism screws.

8. Remove the shift lock cable mechanism and the lock cylinder. If necessary, remove the ignition key reminder switch.

9. Installation is the reverse of the removal procedure. Use new ignition switch/lock cylinder bolts and tighten them until the heads break.

Brake Light Switch

ADJUSTMENT

1992

1. Check the distance between the center of the brake pedal pad to the

floor. The distance should be 8.74–8.94 in. (222–227mm).

2. If adjustment is necessary, disconnect the brake light switch electrical connector and loosen the switch locknut.

3. Rotate the switch until the pedal height is within specification.

4. Tighten the locknut and connect the electrical connector.

REMOVAL AND INSTALLATION

1992

1. Disconnect the negative battery cable.

2. Disconnect the electrical connector from the brake light switch.

3. Remove the brake light switch locknut and the switch.

4. Installation is the reverse of removal procedure. Adjust the switch.

1993–96

1. Disconnect the negative battery cable.

2. Remove the lower steering column trim.

3. Disconnect the switch electrical connector.

4. Remove the switch by pulling it straight out from the brake pedal.

5. Installation is the reverse of the removal procedure. To make sure it is properly adjusted, push in the switch until it bottoms out against the brake pedal.

Clutch Switch

ADJUSTMENT

1. Unplug the switch connector from the main wiring harness.

2. Using an ohmmeter, check the resistance between the 2 connector terminals. When the switch rod is pushed in, the ohmmeter should

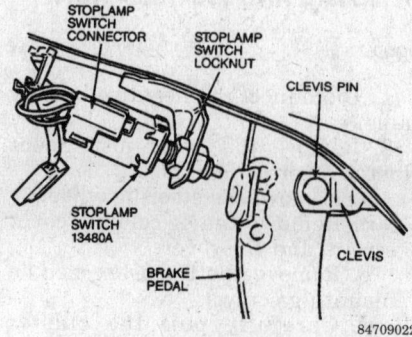

Brake light switch location — 1992

show continuity; when the switch rod is released, the ohmmeter should show no continuity.

3. Replace the switch if it does not perform as specified.

REMOVAL AND INSTALLATION

1. Disconnect the negative battery cable.

2. Unplug the switch connector from the main wiring harness.

3. Remove the switch mounting bolts and remove the switch.

4. Installation is the reverse of the removal procedure.

Neutral Safety Switch

The neutral safety switch is located on the top of the transaxle, toward the front of the vehicle.

ADJUSTMENT

1992

1. Unplug the 3-pronged neutral safety switch connector, located under the battery tray. Connect an ohmmeter between terminals **A** and **B**.

2. With the transaxle selector lever in **P** or **N**, there should be continuity between the terminals.

3. If continuity does not exist, adjust the switch as follows:

   a. Raise and safely support the vehicle.

   b. On turbocharged vehicles, remove the intercooler inlet and outlet hoses.

   c. Turn the manual shaft to the **N** position and loosen the switch mounting bolts.

   d. Remove the screw from the switch and insert a 0.079 in. (2.0mm) pin.

   e. Move the neutral safety switch until the pin engages the switch alignment hole.

   f. Tighten the switch mounting bolts to 69–96 inch lbs. (8–11 Nm), remove the pin and install the screw.

   g. On turbocharged vehicles, install the intercooler inlet and outlet hoses.

4. Retest continuity with the transaxle selector lever in **P** or **N**. If continuity does not exist, replace the neutral safety switch.

1993–96

1. Disconnect the negative battery cable.

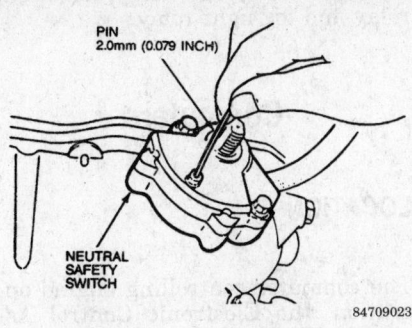

Neutral safety switch adjustment — 1992

2. Remove the air cleaner assembly.

3. Pry the shift cable from the neutral safety switch arm, using a small prybar.

4. Disconnect the neutral safety switch connector. Rotate the switch shaft to the neutral mark and loosen the switch mounting bolts.

5. Connect a suitable volt/ohmmeter to the switch and check the switch continuity.

6. Tighten the switch mounting bolts to 88 inch lbs. (10 Nm) and connect the switch connector.

7. Make sure the switch shaft is still aligned with the neutral mark.

8. Install the shift cable onto the switch arm.

9. Install the air cleaner assembly and connect the negative battery cable.

REMOVAL AND INSTALLATION

1992

1. Disconnect the negative battery cable.

2. On turbocharged vehicles, remove the intercooler inlet and outlet hoses.

3. Remove the shift cable and the shift cable bracket retaining nut.

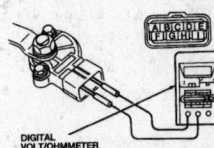

Neutral safety switch adjustment — 1993–96

4. Remove the 2 bolts retaining the switch to the case.

5. Disconnect the neutral safety switch electrical connector and then remove the switch from the vehicle.

To install:

6. Turn the manual shaft to the **N** position.

7. Install the neutral safety switch and loosely tighten the bolts. Connect the electrical connector.

8. Remove the screw from the switch and insert a 0.079 in. (2.0mm) pin. Move the neutral safety switch until the pin engages the switch alignment hole.

9. Tighten the switch mounting bolts to 95 inch lbs. (11 Nm), remove the pin and install the screw.

10. Install the shift cable bracket nut and connect the shift cable.

11. On turbocharged vehicles, install the intercooler inlet and outlet hoses.

12. Connect the negative battery cable.

1993–96

1. Disconnect the negative battery cable.

2. Remove the air cleaner assembly.

3. Pry the shift cable from the neutral safety switch arm, using a small prybar.

4. Disconnect the neutral safety switch connector.

5. Remove the switch mounting bolts and remove the switch.

To install:

6. Install the switch and loosely tighten the mounting bolts. Adjust the switch.

7. After the switch has been adjusted, tighten the mounting bolts to 88 inch lbs. (10 Nm). Connect the switch electrical connector.

8. Install the shift cable onto the switch arm.

9. Install the air cleaner assembly and connect the negative battery cable.

Fuses, Circuit Breakers and Relays

LOCATION

Fuses

The main fuse block is located in the left side of the engine compartment near the battery. The interior fuse block is located behind the left side kick panel.

Circuit Breakers

A bi-metal circuit breaker, used to protect the rear window defroster circuit, is located in the joint box, which is just above the interior fuse panel on 1992 vehicles.

Relays

1992

The main relay box is located in the engine compartment on the upper left side of the firewall (bulkhead). There is also a relay box located inside the vehicle under the left side of the instrument panel.

EFI Main Relays (2) — located the main relay box.

Horn Relay — located in the main relay box.

Cooling Fan Relay No. 1 — located in the main relay box.

Cooling Fan Relay No. 2 — located in the main relay box.

Turn Signal/Hazard Flasher Relay — located in the relay box.

Fuel Pump Relay — located in the relay box.

Rear Window Defroster Relay — located in the relay box.

Intermittent Wiper Relay — located in the relay box.

Stoplight/Taillight Checker Relay — located in the relay box.

Fog Light Relay — located in the relay box.

ABS Relay — located in the engine compartment, near the master cylinder.

Air Conditioning Relay — on Probe LX only, located behind the right side of the instrument panel, to the left of the blower motor.

Blower Motor Relay — located in the engine compartment, forward of the battery.

Condenser Fan Relay — on Probe GL and GT only, located in the engine compartment, on the right front of the condenser.

Dimmer Relay — located in the engine compartment, forward of the washer reservoir.

Power Door Lock Relay — located behind the left interior rear quarter trim panel.

NOTE: Cooling fan relay No. 1 is used only on vehicles equipped with an electronically controlled 4EAT automatic transaxle.

1993–96

Several main relays are located within the main fuse block. There include the starter relay, main relay, fuel pump relay, parking light/turn signal relay, horn relay, daytime running light relay, A/C relay, headlight relay and fog light relay.

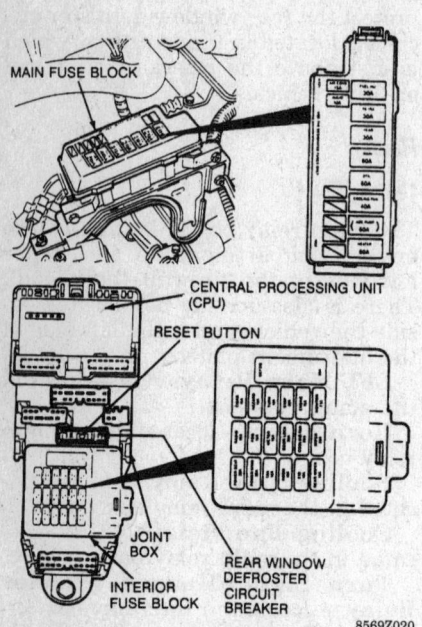

Main and interior fuse blocks — 1992

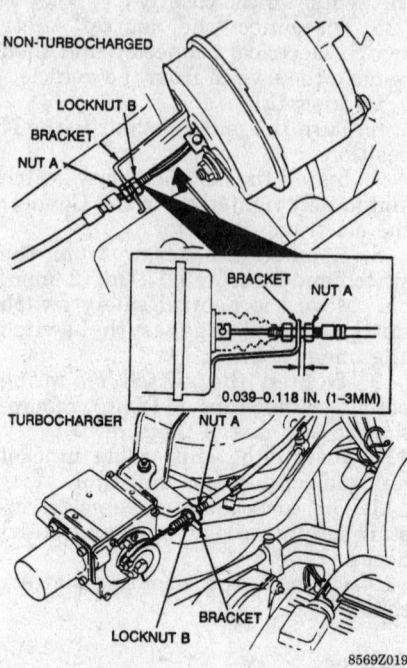

Cruise control actuator cable adjustment — 2.2L engines

Computers

LOCATION

The computer controlling engine operation, the Electronic Control Assembly (ECA), is located behind the instrument panel forward of the center console.

On 1992 vehicles, the control units for the anti-lock brake system and the variable assist power steering are both located under the driver's seat. On 1993–96 vehicles, the control unit for the anti-lock brake system is located behind the left side kick panel and air bag diagnostic monitor is located under the left side of the instrument panel.

A central processing unit is located directly above the interior fuse block. This microprocessor controls the warning chime systems and the theft warning and the illuminated entry systems, if equipped.

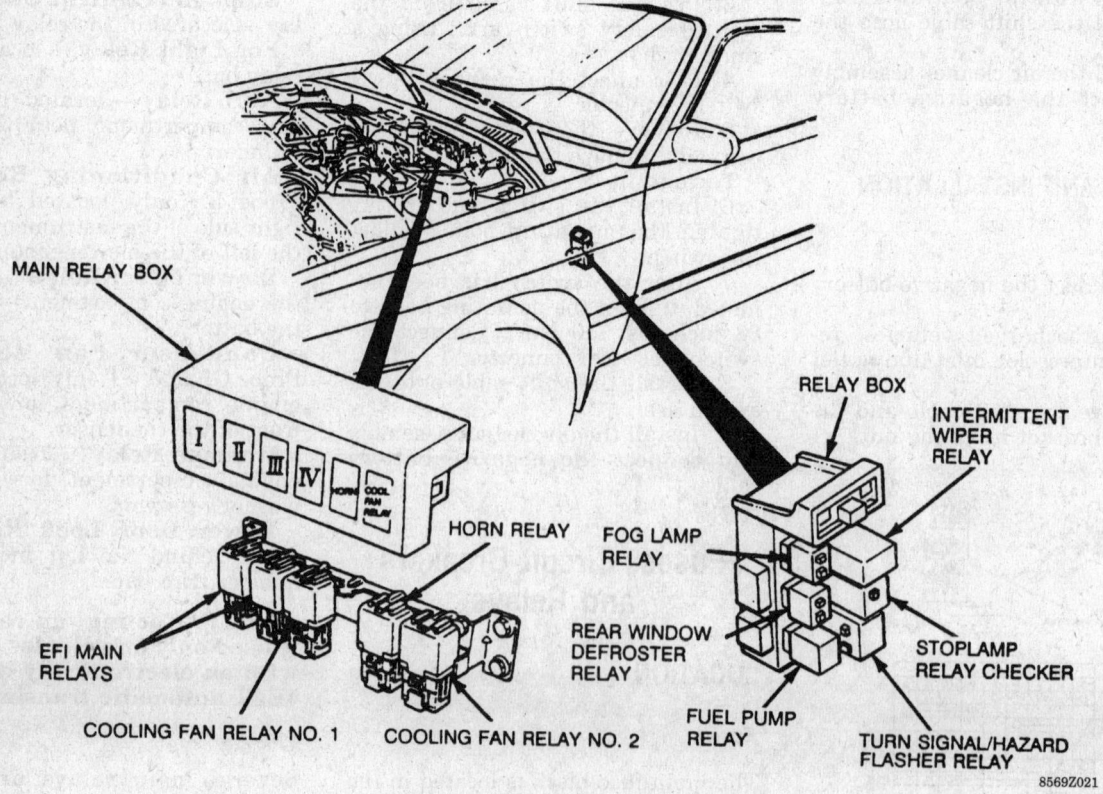

Main relay box and relay box contents and locations — 1992

Flashers

LOCATION

The turn signal/flasher relay is located in the relay box under the instrument panel on 1992 vehicles and in the main fuse block on 1993–96 vehicles.

Cruise Control

ADJUSTMENT

2.2L Engine

NON-TURBOCHARGED ENGINE

1. Loosen the locknut and adjusting nuts.
2. Pull on the cable housing without moving the actuator rod.
3. Position adjusting nut A until there is 0.039–0.118 in. (1–3mm) clearance between nut A and the bracket.
4. Tighten the locknut B securely.

TURBOCHARGED ENGINE

1. Remove the plastic cover.
2. Loosen the locknut and adjusting nuts.
3. Pull on the cable housing without the actuator spool.
4. Position adjusting nut A until there is 0.039–0.118 in. (1–3mm) clearance between nut A and the bracket.
5. Tighten the locknut B securely.
6. Install the plastic cover.

2.0L and 2.5L Engines

ACTUATOR CABLE

1. Remove the cable adjusting clip from the cable housing.
2. Pull lightly on the cable until all of the slack is taken out.
3. Install the cable adjusting clip.

VACUUM DUMP VALVE

1. Remove the dump valve-to-actuator vacuum hose at the actuator.
2. Connect a suitable vacuum tester to the end of the hose at the actuator.
3. Pump up the vacuum to approximately 10–15 in. Hg.

NOTE: If vacuum cannot be obtained, check the hose and vacuum dump valve for leaks.

4. Depress the brake pedal and vacuum should release.

5. If the vacuum does not release, adjust the vacuum dump valve as follows:

a. When the brake pedal is released and in the upright position, the vacuum dump valve plunger should protrude 4–5mm from the body.

b. If the plunger protrudes more than 5mm, move the vacuum dump valve position in the adjusting clip until the plunger is within specification.

6. Repeat Steps 2–4. If the vacuum does not release, replace the vacuum dump valve.

3.0L Engine

1. Remove the cruise control actuator cable retaining clip.
2. Push the actuator cable through the adjuster until slight tension is felt.
3. Insert the cable retaining clip and snap into place.

ENGINE COOLING

Radiator

REMOVAL AND INSTALLATION

1. Disconnect the negative battery cable and the cooling fan wiring harness connectors.
2. On 1993–96 vehicles, remove the fresh air duct.
3. Remove the radiator pressure cap from the filler neck.

—— **CAUTION** ——
Never remove the radiator pressure cap while the engine is running or personal injury from

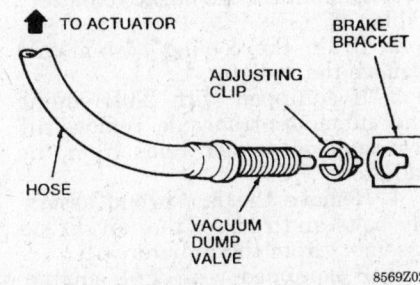

Vacuum dump valve — 2.0L and 2.5L engines

scalding hot coolant or steam may result. If possible, wait until the engine has cooled to remove the radiator pressure cap. If this is not possible, wrap a thick cloth around the cap and turn it slowly to the first stop. Step back while the pressure is released from the cooling system. When it is certain all the pressure has been released, press down on the cap, still with the cloth, and turn and remove it.

4. Position a drain pan under the radiator drain valve and drain the cooling system.
5. On all except 2.5L engine, disconnect the overflow hose from the filler neck. If equipped with 2.5L engine, disconnect the overflow hose from the expansion tank.
6. If equipped with 2.5L engine, disconnect the hoses and remove the expansion tank.
7. Disconnect the upper and lower radiator hoses.
8. Disconnect and plug the oil cooler lines, if equipped with automatic transaxle.
9. Disconnect the coolant temperature sensor wires, if equipped.
10. Remove the radiator upper mounting brackets.
11. Remove the radiator and cooling fan(s) as an assembly.
12. If necessary, remove the fan and shroud assembly from the radiator.

To install:
13. If removed, install the fan and shroud assembly. Tighten the mounting bolts to 88 inch lbs. (10 Nm).
14. Install the radiator, making sure the bottom of the radiator engages the insulators.
15. Install the upper brackets and tighten the retaining bolts to 95 inch lbs. (11 Nm) on 1992 vehicles or 18 ft. lbs. (25 Nm) on 1993–96 vehicles.
16. Unplug and connect the oil cooler lines, if required.
17. Install the upper and lower radiator hoses to the radiator.
18. Connect the overflow hose and connect the cooling fan wiring connector.
19. If equipped with 2.5L engine, install the expansion tank.
20. Close the radiator drain valve and fill the system with coolant.
21. Connect the negative battery cable, warm the engine to pressurize the system and check for leaks.
22. Recheck the coolant level and refill if necessary.

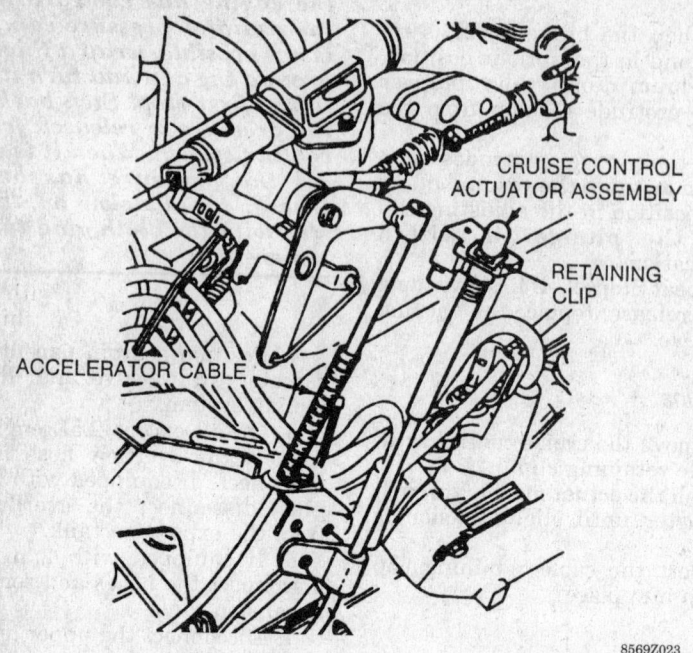

CRUISE CONTROL
ACTUATOR ASSEMBLY

RETAINING
CLIP

ACCELERATOR CABLE

8569Z023

Cruise control actuator cable adjustment — 3.0L engines

Electric Cooling Fan

TESTING

1. Disconnect the cooling fan electrical connector.

2. Connect a jumper wire from the **BK** (black) terminal of the cooling fan connector to ground.

3. Connect a jumper wire from the other terminal of the cooling fan connector to the positive battery terminal. The cooling fan should operate.

NOTE: If the cooling fan connector has 3 terminals, connect the positive terminal lead to either of the terminals other than ground.

4. If the cooling fan motor does not operate, it must be replaced.

5. If the cooling fan motor operates during this procedure, but does not operate during normal engine operation, check the fan motor fuse, cooling fan relay(s) and temperature switches.

REMOVAL AND INSTALLATION

1992

1. Disconnect the negative battery cable.

2. Disconnect the cooling fan electrical connectors.

3. Remove the fan shroud-to-radiator screws and the fan/shroud assembly.

4. If removing the fan motor from the shroud, remove the fan blade-to-motor nut and washer, the fan motor-to-shroud bolts and the motor.

5. Installation is the reverse of the removal procedure. Tighten the cooling fan blade attaching nut to 69–95 inch lbs. (8–11 Nm), the motor-to-shroud screws to 23–46 inch lbs. (2.6–5.2 Nm) and the shroud-to-radiator screws to 61–87 inch lbs. (7–10 Nm).

1993–96

1. Disconnect the negative battery cable.

2. Drain the cooling system and remove the radiator.

3. If equipped with 2.0L engine and automatic transaxle, remove the transaxle oil cooler lines from the radiator.

4. Remove the fan/shroud assembly bolts and remove the fan/shroud assembly from the radiator.

5. If equipped with 2.0L engine, remove the shroud insert.

6. Remove the cooling fan clip and remove the cooling fan.

7. Remove the cooling fan motor mounting bolts and remove the cooling fan.

8. Installation is the reverse of the removal procedure. Tighten the motor mounting bolts to 19 inch lbs. (2.1 Nm) and the shroud attaching bolts to 88 inch lbs. (10 Nm).

Heater core

REMOVAL AND INSTALLATION

1992

1. Disconnect the negative battery cable. Drain the cooling system into a suitable container. If equipped with air conditioning, properly discharge the refrigerant.

2. Remove the instrument panel assembly as follows:

a. Remove the steering wheel and the instrument cluster.

b. Remove the lower dash trim and the driver's side sound deadening panel.

c. Remove the instrument panel shake brace and the lower dash ducts.

d. Remove the instrument cluster carrier.

e. Remove the lower steering column bracket retaining screws and lower column.

f. Remove the shift indicator and shift indicator bezel.

g. Remove the ashtray and the shift handle.

h. Remove the floor console.

i. Remove the radio and, if equipped, the compact disc player.

j. If equipped, remove the trip computer display by removing the display cover bezel, then remove the 2 display housing attaching screws and pull the housing straight out of the dash. It may be necessary to gently pry the display free from the instrument panel. Disconnect the electrical connector and remove the display.

k. If not equipped with a trip computer, remove the center mounting nut access cover.

l. Remove the passenger side lower instrument panel and remove the glove box.

m. Remove the left and right console kick panels.

n. Remove the heater control bezel. Disconnect the remove the heater control.

o. Slide the accessory console back far enough to access the mounting bolts at the floor. Remove the bolts.

p. Remove the left and right dash side covers and the bolts from the left and right sides of the dash.

NOTE: On 1992, there are 3 bolts on each side of the dash.

q. Remove the instrument panel center mounting nut.

r. Remove the hood release cable handle.

s. Remove the left and right A to B pillar trim.

NOTE: The remaining removal Steps require the help of an assistant.

t. Lift the instrument panel and tilt it toward the rear of the vehicle.

u. Disconnect all remaining electrical connectors, including the dash harness, the wire connector at the left hand main harness, and the shift lock wiring connector.

v. Remove the instrument panel from the vehicle.

3. Disconnect the heater hoses from the heater core extension tubes and cap the extension tubes to prevent spilling coolant into the passenger compartment.

4. On non-air conditioned vehicles, remove the main air duct from the vehicle.

5. If equipped with air conditioning, remove the evaporator casing from the vehicle as follows:

a. Remove the carbon canister.

b. Disconnect the air conditioning lines from the evaporator. Plug the lines to prevent dirt and moisture from entering the system.

c. Disconnect the electrical connectors from the air conditioning relays at the top of the evaporator case.

d. Remove the air duct bands and remove the drain hose.

e. Remove the evaporator case attaching nuts and carefully remove the case from the vehicle.

NOTE: Disconnecting and connecting the refrigerant lines requires spring lock coupling tools T81P-19623-G2 and T83P-19623-C or equivalents.

6. Remove the 3 heater case mounting nuts.

7. If equipped with automatic temperature control, disconnect the electrical connectors from the function control and temperature blend actuator motors.

8. Remove the heater case by pulling it straight out, being careful not to damage the extension tubes.

9. Remove the 2 screws attaching the heater core tube braces to the heater case and remove the tube braces. Remove the heater core by pulling it straight out.

To install:
10. Install the heater core in the heater case. Install the heater core tube braces and secure them with the screws.

11. Position the heater case onto its mounting studs being careful not to damage the heater core extension tubes. Install the 3 mounting nuts.

12. If equipped with automatic temperature control, connect the electrical connectors to the actuator motors.

13. On non-air conditioned vehicles, install the main air duct. If equipped with air conditioning, install the evaporator case as follows:

a. Carefully position the evaporator case into the vehicle and install the attaching nuts.

b. Install the drain hose to the evaporator case.

c. Install and secure the air duct bands and connect the electrical connectors.

d. Unplug the liquid line and install it into the evaporator inlet.

e. Unplug the suction line and install it into the evaporator outlet.

f. Install the carbon canister.

14. Make sure the rubber grommets for the extension tubes are still in place in the engine side of the bulkhead.

15. Uncap the extension tubes and connect the heater hoses. Secure them with the clamps.

16. Install the instrument panel in the reverse order of removal.

17. Fill the cooling system and connect the negative battery cable. Check the operation of the heater system and check for leaks.

18. If equipped with air conditioning, evacuate and charge the system.

1993–96

1. Disconnect the negative battery cable. Drain the cooling system.

2. Disconnect the heater hoses at the firewall.

3. Remove the instrument panel as follows:

a. Loosen the hood release cable nut and remove the hood release cable from the lower instrument panel cover.

b. Remove the lower instrument panel cover screw and remove the courtesy light bulb from the lower instrument panel cover. Remove the lower instrument panel cover.

c. Remove the 4 lower steering column panel screws and separate the upper and lower steering column panels. Remove the ignition switch illumination bulb from the lower panel and remove the upper and lower panels.

d. Remove the 2 upper steering column bolts and lower the steering column.

e. Remove the instrument cluster and the glove compartment.

f. Remove the 2 hush panel screws and the courtesy light bulb from the hush panel. Remove the hush panel.

g. Remove the armrest, if equipped. If equipped with manual transaxle, unscrew the shift knob. If equipped with an automatic transaxle, remove the emergency override key switch cover.

h. Apply the parking brake and gently pull up on the upper half of the floor console. Disconnect the cigar lighter electrical connectors and remove the ashtray illumination bulb.

i. Remove the control console bezel and the floor heater duct covers. Remove the lower half of the floor console.

j. Remove the control panel assembly screws and pull the panel carefully from the dash. Disconnect the electrical connectors, vacuum hoses and control cables. Remove the control panel.

k. Remove the 2 side instrument panel covers and the 2 side instrument panel bolts.

l. Remove the upper instrument panel bolt and the 4 lower instrument panel bolts.

m. Remove the A-pillar trim.

n. Tip the instrument panel forward and disconnect the necessary electrical connectors.

o. Carefully remove the instrument panel.

4. Loosen the upper left evaporator/blower unit nut to allow for the removal or the heater unit.

5. Remove the wire harness screw and the 3 heater unit screws. Remove the heater unit.

6. Remove the 4 brace screws and the brace from the heater unit.

7. Remove the heater core from the heater unit.

To install:
8. Install the heater core into the heater unit.

9. Install the brace core tubes and install the brace retaining screws.

10. Position the heater unit in the vehicle and install the 3 screws.

11. Install the wire harness screw and tighten the upper left evaporator/blower unit nut.

12. Install the instrument panel in the reverse order of removal.

13. Connect the heater hoses at the firewall.

14. Connect the negative battery cable. Fill and bleed the cooling system.

15. Run the engine and check for leaks. Check for proper heater operation.

Water Pump

REMOVAL AND INSTALLATION

2.0L Engine

1. Disconnect the negative battery cable. Drain the cooling system.
2. Remove the accessory drive belts.
3. Loosen the cylinder head cover bolts in 2–3 steps in the reverse of the torque sequence. Remove the cylinder head cover.
4. Raise and safely support the vehicle.
5. Remove the water pump pulley using pulley tool T92C–6312–AH or equivalent, to hold the pulley while the bolts are removed.
6. Remove the splash shields and the timing belt.
7. Remove the 5 water pump mounting bolts and remove the water pump.

To install:

8. Clean all gasket mating surfaces.
9. Install a new gasket on the water pump and install the water pump on the engine. Install the mounting bolts and tighten to 19 ft. lbs. (25 Nm).
10. Install the water pump pulley and bolts. Hold the pulley with the tool and tighten the bolts to 88 inch lbs. (10 Nm).
11. Install the timing belt.
12. Install the splash shields and tighten the bolts to 88 inch lbs. (10 Nm).
13. Lower the vehicle and install the cylinder head cover. Tighten the bolts in 2–3 steps to 69 inch lbs. (7 Nm) in the proper sequence.
14. Install the accessory drive belts and adjust the tension.
15. Connect the negative battery cable. Fill and bleed the cooling system.
16. Start the engine and bring to normal operating temperature. Check for leaks.

2.2L Engine

1. Disconnect the negative battery cable.
2. Drain the cooling system.

3. Remove the timing belt.
4. Remove the water pump-to-engine bolts, the water pump and the O-ring. Discard the O-ring.

To install:

5. Clean the mating surfaces of the water pump and the engine block.
6. Install a new O-ring onto the water pump.
7. Install the water pump and torque the bolts 14–19 ft. lbs. (19–25 Nm).
8. Install the timing belt.
9. Fill the cooling system.
10. Connect the negative battery cable, start the engine and check for leaks. Check the coolant level and add coolant, as necessary.

2.5L Engine

1. Disconnect the negative battery cable. Drain the cooling system.
2. Remove the timing belt covers and the timing belt.
3. Use pulley removal tool T92C–6312–AH or equivalent, to hold the water pump pulley and remove the bolts. Remove the water pump pulley.
4. Position a drain pan under the water pump.
5. Remove the 5 water pump mounting bolts and remove the water pump.

To install:

6. Clean the mating surfaces of the water pump and the engine block.
7. Install a new O-ring onto the water pump.
8. Install the water pump and torque the bolts 18 ft. lbs. (25 Nm).
9. Install the water pump pulley with the bolts. Hold the pulley with the tool and tighten the bolts to 88 inch lbs. (10 Nm).
10. Install the timing belt and timing covers.
11. Connect the negative battery cable. Fill and bleed the cooling system.
12. Start the engine and bring to normal operating temperature. Check for leaks.

3.0L Engine

1. Disconnect the negative battery cable. Raise and safely support the vehicle.
2. Drain the cooling system and remove the water pump belt.

NOTE: The accessory drive belt may be left installed and the pump belt pulled aside. The accessory drive belt must be removed however, if the water pump belt is to be replaced.

3. Remove the upper water pump and heater hoses from the water pump.
4. Remove the lower radiator hose from the water pump steel tube.
5. Remove the steel tube brace bolt from the water pump mounting bracket.
6. Remove the water pump mounting bolts and remove the water pump.

To install:

7. Install the the water pump onto the mounting bracket and tighten the mounting bolts to 15–22 ft. lbs. (20–30 Nm).
8. Install the steel tube brace bolt. Install the lower radiator hose on the steel tube.
9. Install the heater and upper water pump hoses.
10. Install the water pump belt and lower the vehicle.
11. Connect the negative battery cable and fill the cooling system. Start the engine and check for leaks. Check the coolant level and add coolant, as necessary.

Thermostat

REMOVAL AND INSTALLATION

2.0L Engine

1. Disconnect the negative battery cable. Drain the cooling system.
2. Remove the lower radiator hose from the thermostat housing.
3. Remove the thermostat housing mounting bolts and remove the thermostat housing.
4. Remove the thermostat.

To install:

5. Clean the thermostat housing and engine block thermostat housing mating surfaces.
6. Install the thermostat, aligning the tab on the thermostat with the tab on the engine block thermostat housing.
7. Install the thermostat housing and tighten the bolts to 18 ft. lbs. (25 Nm).
8. Connect the lower radiator hose.
9. Connect the negative battery cable. Fill and bleed the cooling system.
10. Start the engine and bring to normal operating temperature. Check for leaks.

2.2L Engine

1. Disconnect the negative battery cable. Drain the radiator to below the level of the thermostat.

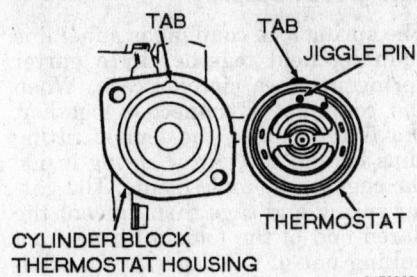

TAB   TAB
JIGGLE PIN

CYLINDER BLOCK
THERMOSTAT HOUSING

THERMOSTAT

84709034

Thermostat–to–engine block thermostat housing alignment — 2.0L and 2.5L engines

2. Disconnect the coolant temperature switch at the thermostat housing.

3. Remove the upper radiator hose.

4. Remove the mounting nuts, thermostat housing, thermostat and gasket.

NOTE: Do not pry the housing off.

To install:

5. Clean the thermostat housing and the cylinder head mating surfaces.

6. Insert the thermostat into the rear cylinder head housing with the jiggle pin at the top. The spring side of the thermostat should face the housing.

7. Install a new gasket onto the studs with the seal print side facing the rear cylinder housing.

8. Install the thermostat housing and 2 nuts. Tighten the nuts to 14–22 ft. lbs. (19–30 Nm).

9. Connect the coolant temperature switch and install the upper radiator hose.

10. Fill the cooling system. Connect the negative battery cable, start the engine and check for leaks. Check the coolant level and add coolant, as necessary.

2.5L Engine

1. Disconnect the negative battery cable. Drain the cooling system.

2. Remove the fresh air duct and air cleaner assembly.

3. Remove the lower radiator hose from the coolant inlet pipe.

4. Remove the coolant inlet pipe mounting bolt and pull the coolant inlet pipe away from the thermostat housing.

5. Remove the thermostat housing bolts and remove the thermostat housing. Discard the O-ring.

6. Remove the thermostat.

To install:

7. Clean the thermostat housing and engine block thermostat housing mating surfaces.

8. Install the thermostat, aligning the tab on the thermostat with the tab on the engine block thermostat housing.

9. Install the thermostat housing and tighten the bolts to 18 ft. lbs. (25 Nm).

10. Install a new thermostat housing O-ring and connect the coolant inlet pipe to the thermostat housing.

11. Install the coolant inlet pipe mounting bolt and tighten to 18 ft. lbs. (25 Nm).

12. Connect the lower radiator hose to the coolant inlet pipe.

13. Connect the negative battery cable. Fill and bleed the cooling system.

14. Start the engine and bring to normal operating temperature. Check for leaks.

3.0L Engine

1. Disconnect the negative battery cable. Drain the cooling system.

2. Remove the radiator hose from the thermostat housing.

3. Disconnect the wiring harness bracket and remove the ground wire.

4. Remove the thermostat housing mounting bolts, the thermostat housing and the thermostat.

5. Remove the gasket and discard.

To install:

6. Clean the thermostat housing and cylinder head gasket surfaces.

7. Position the thermostat in the thermostat housing, rotating in a clockwise direction to secure in place. Align the jiggle pin with the recess located near the top of the thermostat housing.

8. Position a new gasket and install the thermostat housing. Tighten the bolts to 8–10 ft. lbs. (10–14 Nm).

9. Position the harness bracket and ground wire, then install the nut.

10. Fill the cooling system. Connect the negative battery cable, start the engine and check for leaks. Check the coolant level and add coolant, as necessary.

Cooling System Bleeding

When the entire cooling system is drained, the following procedure should be used to ensure a complete fill.

1. Close the drain valve. With the engine OFF, add a 50/50 mixture of water and anti-freeze to the cooling system. On 1992 vehicles, fill to the

FULL mark on the reservoir. On 1993–96 vehicles with 2.0L engine, fill to the bottom of the radiator filler neck seat. On 1993–96 vehicles with 2.5L engine, fill to the top of the coolant elbow.

2. Install the radiator pressure cap to the first notch to keep spillage to a minimum.

3. Start the engine and let it idle until the upper radiator hose is warm. This indicates that the thermostat is open and coolant is flowing through the entire system.

4. Carefully remove the radiator pressure cap. On all except 2.5L engine, top off the radiator with the water/anti-freeze mixture. On 2.5L engine, add the coolant mixture until it reaches the top of the coolant elbow, then stop the engine and check the coolant level in the filler port. Add coolant, if required to restore the level.

5. Install the radiator pressure cap securely.

6. Fill the coolant reservoir with the water/anti-freeze mixture to the FULL mark on the reservoir on 1992 vehicles. On 1993–96 vehicles, fill to the **F** mark on the coolant level dipstick.

FUEL SYSTEM

Fuel System Service Precautions

Safety is the most important factor when performing not only fuel system maintenance but any type of maintenance. Failure to conduct maintenance and repairs in a safe manner may result in serious personal injury or death. Maintenance and testing of the vehicle's fuel system components can be accomplished safely and effectively by adhering to the following rules and guidelines.

• To avoid the possibility of fire and personal injury, always disconnect the negative battery cable unless the repair or test procedure requires that battery voltage be applied.

• Always relieve the fuel system pressure prior to disconnecting any fuel system component (injector, fuel rail, pressure regulator, etc.), fitting or fuel line connection. Exercise extreme caution whenever relieving fuel system pressure to avoid exposing skin, face and eyes to fuel spray.

Please be advised that fuel under pressure may penetrate the skin or any part of the body that it contacts.

• Always place a shop towel or cloth around the fitting or connection prior to loosening to absorb any excess fuel due to spillage. Ensure that all fuel spillage, should it occur, is quickly removed from engine surfaces. Ensure that all fuel soaked cloths or towels are deposited into a suitable waste container.

• Always keep a dry chemical (Class B) fire extinguisher near the work area.

• Do not allow fuel spray or fuel vapors to come into contact with a spark or open flame.

• Always use a backup wrench when loosening and tightening fuel line connection fittings. This will prevent unnecessary stress and torsion to fuel line piping. Always follow the proper torque specifications.

• Always replace worn fuel fitting O-rings with new. Do not substitute fuel hose or equivalent where fuel pipe is installed.

RELIEVING FUEL SYSTEM PRESSURE

1. Start the engine.
2. On 1992 vehicles, remove the fuel pump relay from the relay box, located under the left side of the instrument panel. On 1993–96 vehicles, remove the fuel pump relay from the main fuse box, located in the engine compartment next to the battery.
3. After the engine stalls, turn the ignition switch **OFF** and reinstall the fuel pump relay.

Fuel Lines

REMOVAL AND INSTALLATION

Vehicles equipped with the 3.0L engine use several methods to connect the fuel lines and fuel system components. Two of these methods, the hairpin clip push connect fitting and the spring lock coupling, require certain procedures to disconnect and connect.

Hairpin Clip Push Connect Fitting

1. Inspect the visible internal portion of the fitting for dirt accumulation. If more than a light coating of dust is present, clean the fitting before disassembly.
2. Some adhesion between the seals in the fitting and the tubing will occur with time. To separate, twist the fitting on the tube, then push and pull the fitting until it moves freely on the tube.
3. Remove the hairpin clip from the fitting by first bending and breaking the shipping tab. Next, spread the 2 clip legs by hand about ⅛ in. each to disengage the body and push the legs into the fitting. Lightly pull the triangular end of the clip and work it clear of the tube and fitting.

NOTE: Do not use hand tools to complete this operation.

4. Grasp the fitting and pull in an axial direction to remove the fitting from the tube. Be careful on 90 degree elbow connectors, as excessive side loading could break the connector body.
5. After disassembly, inspect and clean the tube end sealing surfaces. The tube end should be free of scratches and corrosion that could provide leak paths. Inspect the inside of the fitting for any internal parts such as O-rings and spacers that may have been dislodged from the fitting. Replace any damaged connector.

To connect:

6. Install a new connector if damage was found. Insert a new clip into any 2 adjacent openings with the triangular portion pointing away from the fitting opening. Install the clip until the legs of the clip are locked on the outside of the body. Piloting with an index finger is necessary.
7. Before installing the fitting on the tube, wipe the tube end with a clean cloth. Inspect the inside of the fitting to make sure it is free of dirt and/or obstructions.
8. Apply a light coating of engine oil to the tube end. Align the fitting and tube axially and push the fitting onto the tube end. When the fitting is engaged, a definite click will be heard. Pull on the fitting to make sure it is fully engaged.

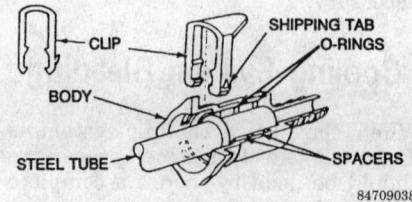

84709038

Hairpin clip push connect fitting — 3.0L engine

Spring Lock Coupling

The spring lock coupling is a fuel line coupling held together by a garter spring inside a circular cage. When the coupling is connected together, the flared end of the female fitting slips behind the garter spring inside the cage of the male fitting. The garter spring and cage then prevent the flared end of the female fitting from pulling out of the cage. As an additional locking feature, most vehicles have a horseshoe shaped retaining clip that improves the retaining reliability of the spring lock coupling.

Fuel Tank

REMOVAL AND INSTALLATION

1992

1. Relieve the fuel system pressure.
2. Disconnect the negative battery cable.
3. Depress the clips on each end of the rear seat cushion and remove the cushion.
4. Disconnect the sending unit electrical connector, remove the 4 attaching screws and the sending unit access cover.
5. Disconnect the fuel supply and return lines from the sending unit.
6. Raise and safely support the vehicle.
7. Position a suitable container under the fuel tank drain plug. Remove the plug and drain the fuel tank.
8. Disconnect the vapor hoses and fuel filler neck hose at the fuel filler neck assembly.
9. Remove the 2 parking brake cable retaining brackets from the chassis to gain access to the fuel tank.
10. Remove the fuel tank mounting strap.
11. Support the fuel tank, remove the 3 attaching bolts and brackets and remove the fuel tank.

To install:

12. Position the fuel tank and install the 3 attaching bolts and brackets. Tighten the bolts to 16–22 ft. lbs. (22–30 Nm).
13. Install the fuel tank mounting strap. Tighten the mounting bolt to 32–45 ft. lbs. (43–61 Nm).
14. Install the 2 parking brake cable retaining brackets to the chassis.
15. Connect the fuel tank filler neck hose and the 3 vapor hoses to the fuel tank filler neck assembly.

16. Install the fuel tank drain plug and tighten to 9–13 ft. lbs. (12–18 Nm).

17. Lower the vehicle and connect the fuel supply and return hoses to the sending unit.

18. Install the sending unit access cover with the 4 attaching screws. Reconnect the sending unit electrical connector.

19. Position the rear seat cushion over the floor, making sure to align the retaining pins with the clips. Push down firmly until the 2 retaining pins are locked into the rear seat retaining clips.

20. Fill the fuel tank with fuel and check for leaks.

21. Connect the negative battery cable.

1993–96

1. Relieve the fuel system pressure. Disconnect the negative battery cable.

2. Remove the fuel tank filler cap. Siphon or pump the fuel from the tank out through the filler neck into a suitable container.

3. Raise and safely support the vehicle.

4. Disconnect the filler neck, overflow and vapor line hoses.

5. Disconnect the fuel supply and return line hoses.

6. Disconnect the fuel pump/sending unit electrical connector.

7. Remove the 4 nuts and the exhaust heatshield.

8. Remove the 1 nut from the fuel tank shield.

9. Support the tank with a jack and remove the center and right-hand fuel tank straps.

10. Remove the fuel tank heatshield.

11. Remove the left side fuel tank strap and remove the fuel tank.

To install:

12. Raise the fuel tank into position and install the left side tank strap. Tighten the bolts to 45 ft. lbs. (69 Nm).

13. Install the fuel tank shield.

14. Install the right-hand and center fuel tank straps. Tighten the bolts to 45 ft. lbs. (69 Nm).

15. Install the fuel tank shield nut and tighten to 97 inch lbs. (11 Nm).

16. Install the exhaust heatshield and tighten the nuts to 97 inch lbs. (11 Nm).

17. Connect the fuel pump/sending unit electrical connector and the fuel supply and return lines.

18. Connect the vapor line, overflow and filler neck hoses and tighten the clamps.

19. Lower the vehicle.

20. Fill the tank with fuel and check for leaks. Start the engine and check for leaks.

Fuel Filter

REMOVAL AND INSTALLATION

1. Relieve the fuel system pressure.

2. Disconnect the fuel lines from both ends of the fuel filter. Plug the lines to prevent leakage.

3. On 1992 vehicles, loosen the bolt and nut and remove the in-line fuel filter from its mounting bracket. On 1993–96 vehicles, remove the mounting nuts and remove the filter from the mounting bracket.

4. Installation is the reverse of the removal procedure. Check for any fuel leaks.

Electric Fuel Pump

PRESSURE TESTING

1. Relieve the pressure in the fuel system, then disconnect the negative battery cable.

2. Install a suitable fuel pressure gauge between the fuel filter and the fuel rail.

3. On 2.0L and 2.5L engines, connect a jumper wire between the **F/P** and **GND** terminals on the data link connector, located next to the battery. On 2.2L engines, connect a jumper wire between the **BK** and **LG** terminals of the fuel pump test connector. On the 3.0L engine, ground the fuel pump lead of the self-test connector through a jumper wire at the **FP** lead.

4. Connect the negative battery cable, turn the ignition key **ON** and check the fuel pump pressure. The pressure should be 64–92 psi. on the 2.0L engine, 64–85 psi. on the 2.2L engines, 72–92 psi. on the 2.5L engine or 35–40 psi. on the 3.0L engine.

5. If there is no fuel pressure, remove the fuel tank cap and try to hear if the fuel pump is operating. If the pump sounds like it's running, check for a restriction in the fuel line. If the pump is not running, check for power to the pump and check the pump motor ground. If there is no power to the pump, check all electri-cal connections and check the fuel pump relay.

6. If fuel pressure is low, check for a restriction in the fuel line or clogged fuel filters.

7. Remove the jumper wire, relieve the fuel system pressure and disconnect the negative battery cable.

8. Remove the fuel pressure gauge and reconnect the fuel line.

9. Connect the negative battery cable.

REMOVAL AND INSTALLATION

The fuel pump is mounted on the fuel sending unit assembly in the fuel tank.

1992

1. Relieve the fuel pressure and disconnect the negative battery cable.

2. Depress the clips on each end of the rear seat cushion and remove the cushion.

3. Disconnect the electrical connector from the fuel pump/sending unit.

4. Remove the attaching screws from the fuel pump/sending unit access cover and remove the cover.

5. Disconnect the fuel supply and return hoses from the fuel pump/sending unit.

6. Remove the attaching screws and the fuel pump/sending unit from the fuel tank.

7. Disconnect the sending unit electrical connector, remove the sending unit attaching nuts and remove the sending unit from the fuel pump assembly.

To install:

8. Attach the sending unit to the fuel pump assembly and install the nuts. Connect the sending unit electrical connector.

9. Install the fuel pump/sending unit into the fuel tank and install the mounting screws.

10. Connect the fuel supply and return lines.

11. Install the access cover and the mounting screws.

12. Connect the sending unit electrical connector.

13. Position the rear seat cushion over the floor, making sure to align the retaining pins with the clips. Push down firmly until the 2 retaining pins are locked into the rear seat retaining clips.

14. Connect the negative battery cable, start the engine and check for proper system operation and for fuel leaks.

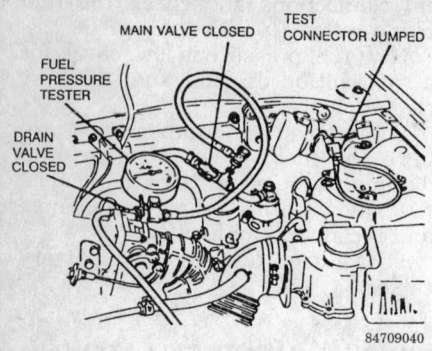

Fuel pump pressure testing — 2.2L engine

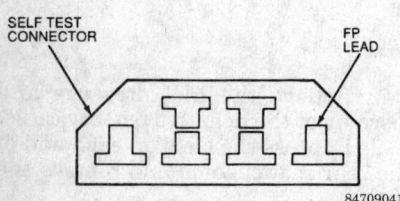

Self-test connector terminal location — 3.0L engine

1993–96

1. Disconnect the negative battery cable.

2. Remove the fuel tank and place it on a bench.

3. Remove any dirt that has accumulated around the fuel pump retaining flange so it will not enter the tank during pump removal and installation.

4. Turn the fuel pump locking ring counterclockwise and remove the locking ring.

5. Remove the fuel pump and bracket assembly. Remove and discard the seal ring.

To install:

6. Clean the fuel pump mounting flange, fuel tank mounting surface and seal ring groove.

7. Apply a light coating of grease on a new seal ring to hold it in place during assembly and install in the seal ring groove.

8. Install the fuel pump and bracket assembly carefully to ensure the filter is not damaged. Make sure the locating keys are in the keyways and the seal ring remains in the groove.

9. Hold the pump assembly in place and install the locking ring fin-

ger-tight. Make sure all the locking tabs are under the tank lock ring tabs.

10. Rotate the locking ring clockwise until the ring is against the stops.

11. Install the fuel tank in the vehicle. Add a minimum of 10 gallons of fuel to the tank and check for leaks.

12. Connect the negative battery cable, start the engine and check for proper system operation and for fuel leaks.

Fuel Injection

IDLE SPEED ADJUSTMENT

2.0L Engine

AUTOMATIC TRANSAXLE

1. Place the gearshift lever in **N** or **P** and apply the parking brake.

2. Start the engine and bring to normal operating temperature.

3. Turn OFF all electrical loads and accessories.

4. Using a jumper wire, connect the **GND** terminal to the **STI (TEN)** terminal on the data link connector, located next to the battery.

5. Connect a suitable tachometer according to the manufacturer's instructions.

6. Observe the idle speed; it should be 650–750 rpm. Do not check the idle speed while the cooling fan is running.

7. If the idle speed is not as specified, adjust it by turning the idle speed adjusting screw.

8. Remove the jumper wire and the tachometer.

MANUAL TRANSAXLE

1. Start the engine and bring to normal operating temperature.

2. Turn the engine **OFF**.

3. Turn OFF all accessories.

4. Connect a suitable tachometer according to the manufacturer's instructions.

5. Disconnect the Idle Air Control Bypass Air (IAC BPA) valve connector.

6. Start and run the engine at 2500 rpm for 30 seconds.

7. Let the engine idle and make a note of the idle speed.

8. Turn the idle speed adjusting screw until the idle speed is 650–750 rpm.

9. Turn the engine **OFF** and rerun the test to make sure the idle speed is correct.

10. Connect the IAC BPA valve connector and remove the tachometer.

2.2L Engine

1. Check the ignition timing and adjust to specification, if necessary.

2. Turn OFF all lights and other unnecessary electrical loads. Idle speed adjustment must be done while the radiator cooling fan is not operating.

3. Set the parking brake and place the transaxle selector lever in neutral on manual transaxle vehicles or **P** on automatic transaxle vehicles. Warm the engine and run it for 3 minutes at 2500–3000 rpm.

4. Ground the black 1-pin test connector located near the driver's side strut tower.

5. Attach a suitable tachometer according to the manufacturer's instructions.

6. Check the idle speed. It should be 750 rpm ± 25 rpm.

7. If the idle speed is not correct, remove the blind cap from the throttle body and adjust the idle speed by turning the idle air adjust screw.

8. After adjusting the idle speed, install the blind cap, disconnect the jumper wire from the test connector and remove the tachometer from the engine.

NOTE: Do not tamper with the adjustment screw located just to the left of the idle air adjust screw. Doing so may result in damage to the throttle body.

2.5L Engine

1. Apply the parking brake. If equipped with manual transaxle, place the gearshift lever in neutral. If equipped with automatic transaxle, place the gearshift lever in **P**.

2. Start the engine and bring to normal operating temperature.

3. Make sure all electrical loads are turned OFF.

4. Connect a suitable tachometer according to the manufacturer's instructions.

5. Connect a jumper wire between the **GND** and **STI (TEN)** terminals of the data link connector, located next to the battery.

6. Observe the idle speed; it should be 650 ± 50 rpm. Do not check the idle speed while the cooling fan is operating.

7. If the idle speed is not as specified, proceed to Step 8.

8. Connect a suitable timing light according to the manufacturer's instructions.

9. Aim the timing light at the marks on the crankshaft pulley and timing belt cover and make sure the

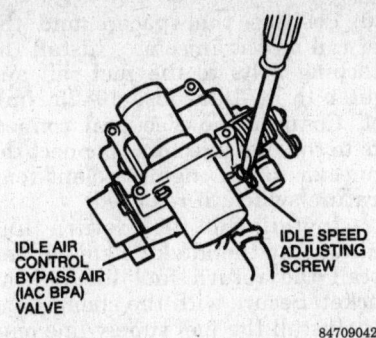

IDLE AIR CONTROL BYPASS AIR (IAC BPA) VALVE — IDLE SPEED ADJUSTING SCREW

84709042

Idle speed adjusting screw location — 2.0L engine

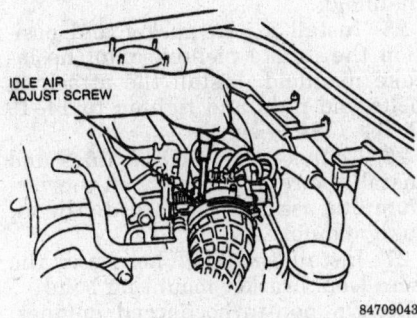

IDLE AIR ADJUST SCREW

84709043

Idle speed adjustment location — 2.2L engine

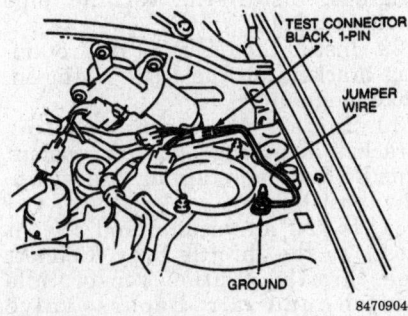

TEST CONNECTOR BLACK, 1-PIN — JUMPER WIRE — GROUND

84709044

Idle speed adjustment test connector location — 2.2L engine

timing is 10 degrees BTDC ± 1 degree.

10. If the timing is not within specification, loosen the distributor bolts and turn the distributor until the timing is correct. Tighten the bolts to 18 ft. lbs. (25 Nm) and verify the timing.

11. Remove the jumper wire from between the **GND** and **STI (TEN)** terminals.

12. Verify that the ignition timing is 6–18 degrees BTDC.

13. Reconnect the jumper wire between the **GND** and **STI (TEN)** terminals.

14. Turn the idle speed adjusting screw to set the idle speed to specification.

15. Turn the engine **OFF**. Remove the jumper wire, tachometer and timing light.

3.0L Engine

The curb idle and fast idle speeds are controlled by the ECA and the idle rpm control device and cannot be adjusted. This procedure should only be attempted if there is a change in idle speed and the following possible causes have been eliminated:

• Contamination within the throttle bore.
• Contamination within the idle speed control device.
• Contaminated or defective oxygen sensor.
• Throttle sticking or binding.
• Engine not reaching operating temperature.
• Ignition timing out of specification.
• Vacuum leaks at the intake manifold, vacuum hoses, vacuum reservoirs, power brake booster, etc.

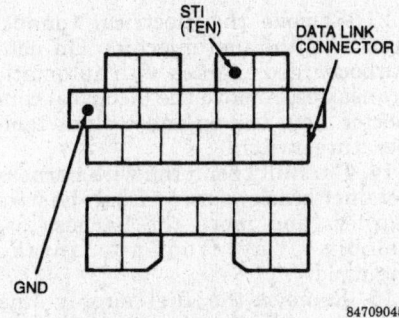

STI (TEN) — DATA LINK CONNECTOR — GND

84709045

Data link connector terminal location — 2.0L and 2.5L engines

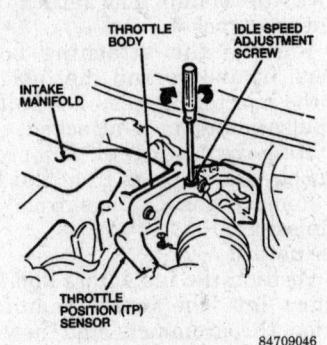

THROTTLE BODY — IDLE SPEED ADJUSTMENT SCREW — INTAKE MANIFOLD — THROTTLE POSITION (TP) SENSOR

84709046

Idle speed adjustment screw location — 2.5L engine

This procedure requires the use of the Ford SUPER STAR II tester, or equivalent.

1. Apply the parking brake. Place the transaxle selector lever in neutral on manual transaxle vehicles or **P** on automatic transaxle vehicles.

2. Start the engine and bring to normal operating temperature. Make sure the heater and all accessories are **OFF**.

3. Make sure the throttle lever is resting on the throttle plate stop screw and the ignition timing is set to specification.

4. Make sure all engine malfunctions have been resolved.

5. Activate the Engine Running Self-Test.

6. After Code 1, 11 or 111 has been displayed, quickly (within 4 seconds) unlatch and latch the STI button.

7. A single pulse code indicates the entry mode, then observe the Self-Test Output (STO) of the tester for the following:

a. A constant tone, solid light, or "STO LO" readout means the base idle rpm is within range. To exit the test, unlatch the STI button, then wait 4 seconds for reinitialization. (After 10 seconds it will exit by itself.)

b. A beeping tone, flashing light, or "STO LO" readout at 8 Hz indicates the Throttle Position (TP) sensor is out of range due to over adjustment. Adjustment may be required.

c. A beeping tone, flashing light, or "STO LO" readout at 4 Hz indicates the base idle rpm is too fast and adjustment is required.

d. A beeping tone, flashing light, or "STO LO" readout at 1 Hz indicates the base idle rpm is too slow, adjustment is required.

8. If the idle rpm is too slow, turn the throttle plate stop screw clockwise until the beeping tone, flashing light, or "STO LO" readout is constant.

9. If the idle rpm is too high, turn the throttle plate stop screw counterclockwise until the beeping tone, flashing light, or "STO LO" readout is constant.

10. Run the Key On Engine Off Self-Test and check for a TP sensor output code.

11. Make sure the throttle is not stuck in the bore and the linkage is not preventing the throttle from closing.

IDLE MIXTURE ADJUSTMENT

The air/fuel mixture is controlled by the ECA and is not adjustable.

Fuel Injector

REMOVAL AND INSTALLATION

2.0L Engine

1. Relieve the fuel system pressure and disconnect the negative battery cable.
2. Label and disconnect the fuel injector wiring harness.
3. Disconnect and plug the fuel lines at the fuel rail.
4. Disconnect the vacuum hose from the fuel pressure regulator.
5. Remove the fuel line mounting bracket bolt.
6. Remove the fuel rail mounting bolts, spacers, insulators and the fuel rail, with the injectors attached.
7. Remove the fuel injectors, grommets and O-rings from the fuel rail. Remove the O-rings from the fuel injectors.
   To install:
8. Apply a small amount of clean engine oil to new O-rings and install them and the grommets on the fuel injectors.
9. Install the insulators and injectors on the intake manifold.
10. Install the grommets and the fuel rail onto the injectors.
11. Install the fuel rail attaching bolts and tighten to 18 ft. lbs. (25 Nm).
12. Connect the vacuum hose to the fuel pressure regulator and the fuel lines to the fuel rail.
13. Install the fuel line mounting bracket and tighten the bolt to 97 inch lbs. (11 Nm).
14. Connect the fuel injector wiring harness.
15. Connect the negative battery cable and turn the ignition switch **ON** to pressurize the fuel system. Check for leaks and correct as necessary, before starting the engine.

2.2L Engine

1. Relieve the fuel system pressure.
2. Disconnect the negative battery cable and drain the cooling system.
3. Remove the accelerator cables and the air duct from the throttle body.
4. Mark all vacuum and coolant hoses for ease of reassembly and remove the hoses from the throttle body.

5. Disconnect the throttle position sensor, idle switch and air bypass valve connectors.
6. Remove the engine lifting bracket mounting bolt and coolant line/EGR hose retaining bracket from the throttle body.
7. Remove the throttle cable retaining brackets and wire loom bracket from the right side of the intake plenum.
8. On the turbocharged 2.2L engine, disconnect the vacuum pipe mounting bolts from the right side of the intake plenum. On non-turbocharged 2.2L engines, remove the EGR back-pressure variable transducer bracket from the right side of the intake plenum.
9. Remove the PCV hose from the intake plenum.
10. Remove the retaining nuts and bolts from the vacuum line assembly bracket at the rear of the intake plenum.
11. Mark all vacuum lines for ease of reassembly and remove the lines from the intake plenum.
12. Remove the intake plenum retaining bolts and nuts and remove the intake plenum and gasket.

NOTE: After removing the intake plenum, cover the intake manifold ports with a clean cloth to prevent dust and dirt from entering.

13. Remove the electrical connectors from the fuel injectors. On non-turbocharged engines with automatic transaxles, remove the electrical connector from the engine coolant temperature switch.
14. Carefully bend the wire harness retainer brackets away from the wire harness and move the harness assembly away from the intake manifold.
15. Remove the fuel supply line from the pulsation damper.
16. Remove the fuel return line bracket from the intake manifold and remove the clamp and return fuel line at the bracket.
17. Remove the attaching bolts, spacers, insulators and the fuel rail with the injectors, pressure regulator and pulsation damper attached.
18. Remove the fuel injectors, grommets and O-rings from the fuel rail. Remove the O-rings from the fuel injectors.
   To install:
19. Position the insulators and fuel injectors into the intake manifold. Position the grommets and new O-rings onto the fuel injectors. Apply a small amount of engine oil to the O-rings during installation.

20. Position the spacers and the fuel rail on the injectors. Install the attaching bolts to the fuel rail and tighten to 14–19 ft. lbs. (19–25 Nm).
21. Connect the electrical connectors to the fuel injectors. Connect the connector to the engine coolant temperature switch, if removed.
22. Install the fuel return line bracket onto the intake manifold and install the return fuel line at the bracket. Secure with the clamp.
23. Install the fuel supply line onto the pulsation damper and secure with the clamp.
24. Remove all old gasket material from the intake plenum and intake manifold.
25. Install a new gasket and position the intake plenum onto the intake manifold. Install the attaching bolts and nuts and tighten to 14–19 ft. lbs. (19–25 Nm).
26. Connect the vacuum lines and install the retaining bolts on the vacuum line assembly bracket to the intake manifold.
27. Install the PCV hose and the wire loom bracket mounting bolts.
28. On non-turbocharged engines, install the EGR back-pressure variable transducer bracket to the right side of the intake. On turbocharged engines, install the vacuum pipe mounting bolts.
29. Install the throttle cable retaining brackets on the front of the intake plenum.
30. Install the engine lifting bracket mounting bolt and coolant line/EGR hose retaining bracket to the throttle body.
31. Install all vacuum and coolant hoses to the throttle body. Connect the throttle position sensor, idle switch and air bypass valve connectors.
32. Install the air duct and the accelerator cables to the throttle body. Check the adjustment of the accelerator cable.
33. Install the wire harness into the retainer brackets and carefully bend the brackets toward the wire harness.
34. Connect the negative battery cable and properly fill and bleed the cooling system.
35. Turn the ignition switch **ON** to pressurize the fuel system. Check for fuel leaks and correct as necessary before starting the engine.

2.5L Engine

1. Relieve the fuel system pressure and disconnect the negative battery cable.

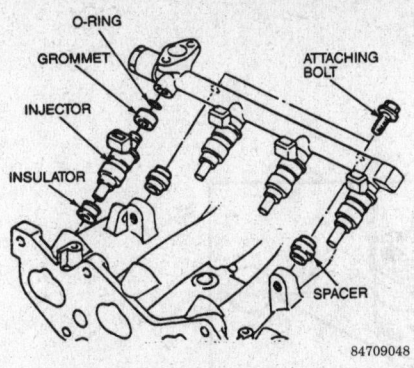

Fuel rail and injector assembly — 2.2L engine

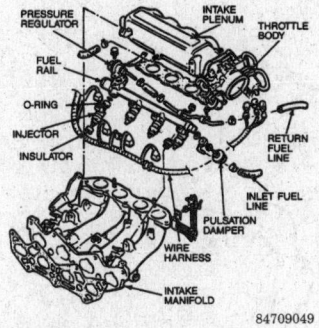

Air intake plenum and manifold assembly — 2.2L engine

2. Remove the air cleaner housing and air ducts.

3. Label and disconnect the fuel injector electrical connectors.

4. Disconnect and plug the fuel supply and return lines. Discard the copper crush washers.

5. Remove the fuel pressure regulator mounting bolts and the fuel pressure regulator.

6. Remove the fuel rail mounting bolts and the fuel rails.

7. Remove the 6 insulators.

8. Remove the 7 distribution harness attaching screws and remove the distribution harness from the fuel rails.

9. Remove and discard the spacer from the top of each fuel injector. Remove the fuel injectors from the fuel rails by rotating back and forth.

To install:

10. Apply clean engine oil to new O-rings and install them on the injectors. Install the injectors into the fuel rails.

11. Install new spacers on the injectors, then install the distribution harness with the screws. Tighten the screws to 31 inch lbs. (3 Nm).

12. Install the 6 insulators and the fuel rails. Install the fuel rail mount-

ing bolts and tighten to 18 ft. lbs. (25 Nm).

13. Install the fuel pressure regulator and tighten the bolts to 86 inch lbs. (9 Nm).

14. Using new copper crush washers, connect the fuel supply and return lines.

15. Connect the fuel injector electrical connectors.

16. Install the air ducts and air cleaner housing.

17. Connect the negative battery cable. Turn the ignition switch **ON** to pressurize the fuel system. Check for fuel leaks and correct as necessary before starting the engine.

3.0L Engine

1. Relieve the fuel system pressure.

2. Disconnect the negative battery cable.

3. Remove the air cleaner tube and plastic shield from the throttle body.

4. Remove the EGR supply tube and disconnect all the vacuum hoses from the air intake throttle body. Tag the hoses prior to removal for ease of installation.

5. Disconnect the air charge temperature sensor, idle speed control solenoid and throttle position sensor.

6. Remove the manifold absolute pressure sensor from the throttle body.

7. Disconnect the throttle cable and the throttle valve control cable, if equipped with an automatic transaxle, from the throttle lever.

8. Remove the fuel rail bracket bolt from the throttle body.

9. Remove the 6 air intake throttle body mounting bolts and lift off the throttle body.

10. Disconnect the fuel supply and return lines.

11. Disconnect the fuel injector wiring harness.

12. Disconnect the vacuum line from the fuel pressure regulator.

13. Remove the 4 fuel injector manifold mounting bolts.

14. Disengage the fuel rail assembly by lifting and gently rocking the rail.

15. Remove the injectors by lifting while gently rocking side to side.

NOTE: Handle the injectors and rail assembly with extreme care to prevent damage to the sealing areas and metering orifices.

To install:

16. Inspect the injector O-rings for wear or damage. Install new O-rings, if required.

17. Lubricate new O-rings with a light grade oil and install 2 on each injector.

18. Make sure the injector cups are free of contamination or damage.

19. Install the injectors in the fuel rail using a light twisting-pushing motion.

20. Install the rail assembly and the injectors carefully into the lower intake manifold, one side at a time.

21. Push down on the fuel rail to make sure the O-rings are seated.

22. Install the retaining bolts and tighten to 7 ft. lbs. (10 Nm) while holding the fuel rail in place.

23. Connect the fuel supply and return lines.

24. Before connecting the fuel injector harness, connect the negative battery cable and turn the key to the **ON** position. This will pressurize the fuel system.

25. Check for leaks where the injector is installed into the intake manifold and fuel rail; correct as necessary.

26. Turn the ignition key **OFF** and disconnect the negative battery cable.

27. Connect the fuel injector wiring harness.

28. Position the air intake throttle body and gasket on the lower intake manifold.

NOTE: Lightly oil all bolt threads before installation.

29. Install the mounting bolts and tighten to 15–22 ft. lbs. (20–30 Nm).

30. Install the fuel rail bracket on the throttle body and tighten securely.

31. Install the throttle cable and, if equipped, the throttle valve control cable on the throttle lever.

32. Install the manifold absolute pressure sensor on the throttle body.

33. Connect the throttle position sensor, idle speed control solenoid and the air charge temperature sensor.

34. Connect all vacuum hoses to the air intake throttle body.

35. Install the EGR supply tube. Install the plastic shield on the throttle body.

36. Install the air cleaner tube onto the throttle body and connect the negative battery cable.

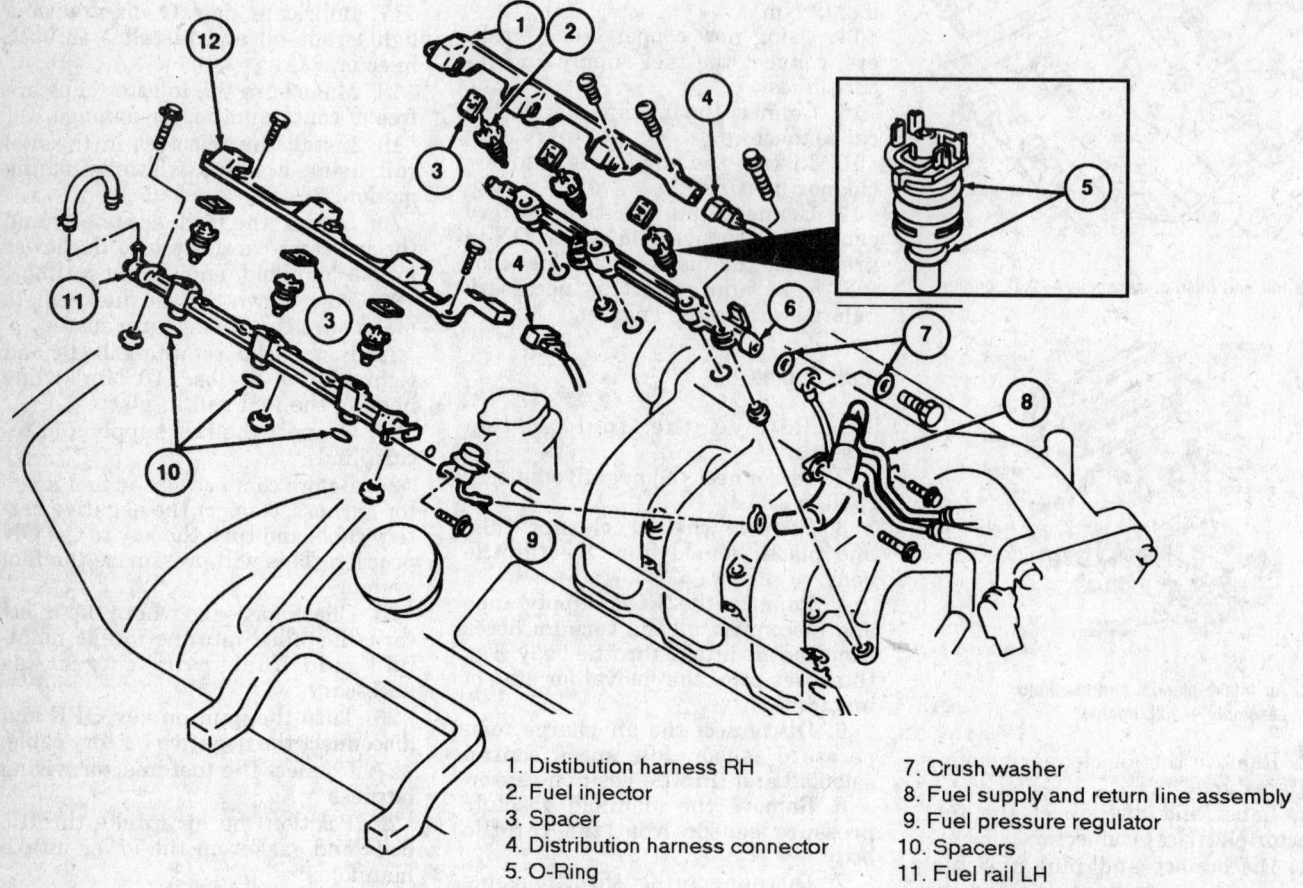

1. Distibution harness RH
2. Fuel injector
3. Spacer
4. Distribution harness connector
5. O-Ring
6. Fuel rail
7. Crush washer
8. Fuel supply and return line assembly
9. Fuel pressure regulator
10. Spacers
11. Fuel rail LH
12. Distibution harness LH

84709050

Fuel rail and injectors — 2.5L engine

EMISSION CONTROLS

Emission Warning Lamps

All vehicles are equipped with a **CHECK ENGINE** light. This light should come ON briefly when the ignition key is turned **ON** but should turn OFF when the engine is started. If the light stays ON after the engine is started or if it comes ON at any time during engine operation, a problem in the electronic engine control system is indicated.

On 1992 vehicles, there are also 2 different service interval reminder systems, the Vehicle Maintenance Monitor or System Scanner. The Vehicle Maintenance Monitor is available only on vehicles with an analog instrument cluster. It will indicate a service interval check on a module located on the front center portion of the headliner, just above the rear view mirror. The System Scanner is found on vehicles with electronic instrument clusters. It will indicate a service interval check on a display, located in the lower left corner of the instrument cluster.

RESETTING

To reset the service interval light on vehicles equipped with the Vehicle Maintenance Monitor, insert a small pointed instrument into the service interval cancel switch. Depress the switch once.

To cancel the service check message on the System Scanner, press the **SERV** button on the keyboard, located to the right of the instrument cluster, and hold until 3 tones are sounded.

the back right-hand side of the intake manifold.

12. Disconnect the vacuum line connecting the evaporative canister and the metal EGR vacuum line. If equipped, disconnect the EGR temperature sensor connector.

13. Disconnect the accelerator cable. Disconnect the power booster vacuum line from the back left-hand side of the intake manifold.

14. Disconnect the heater hoses and remove the upper starter mounting bolts. Raise and safely support the vehicle.

15. Remove the splash shields. Remove the starter and the intake manifold support bracket.

16. Remove the halfshaft support bearing mounting bolts and disconnect the oil pressure sensor connector.

17. Remove the torque converter-to-flexplate nuts. Remove the 3 engine-to-transaxle bolts and the transaxle-to-engine mounting bolts.

18. Disconnect the oxygen sensor connector. Remove and discard the exhaust pipe-to-catalytic converter nuts.

19. Remove the exhaust support bolts. Remove and discard the exhaust pipe-to-exhaust manifold nuts and remove the exhaust pipe. Support the remaining exhaust system with mechanics wire.

20. Label and disconnect the remaining alternator wiring. Remove the wiring harness bracket from the back of the alternator, remove the through bolt and remove the alternator.

21. Use a suitable holding tool to hold the crankshaft pulley and remove the pulley bolt. Remove the crankshaft pulley. Lower the vehicle.

22. Raise the engine slightly with a jack and remove the right-hand engine mount. Attach suitable engine lifting equipment to the lifting eyes on the engine.

23. Remove the remaining transaxle-to-engine mounting bolts and carefully remove the engine from the vehicle.

24. Remove the flexplate from the crankshaft and mount the engine on a workstand.

To install:

25. Remove the engine from the workstand. Remove the old sealant from the flexplate mounting bolts and bolt holes.

26. If reusing the flexplate bolts, apply silicone sealant to the bolt

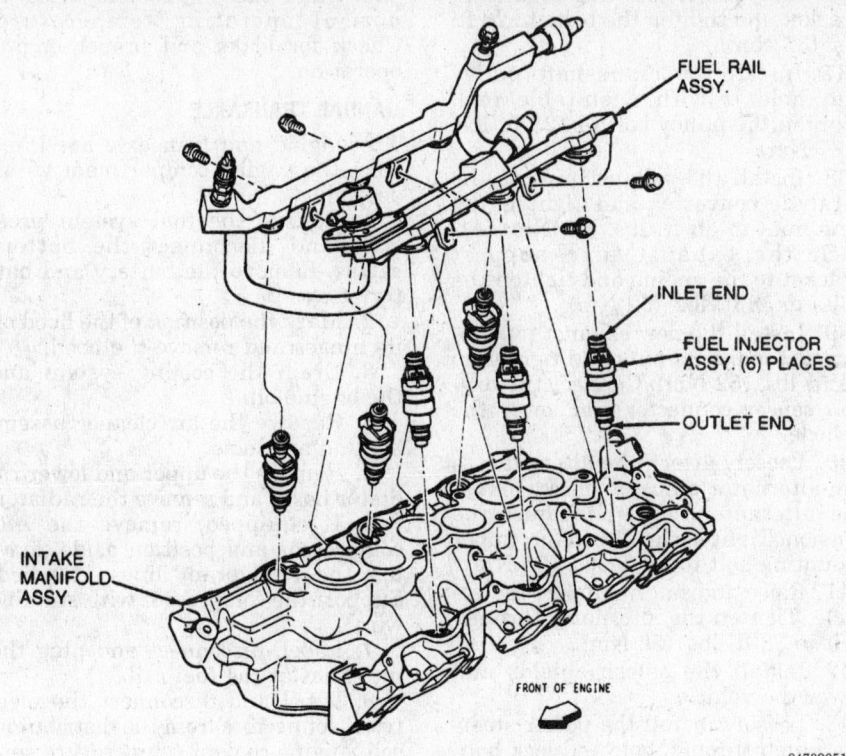

Fuel rail and injector assembly — 3.0L engine

FUEL RAIL ASSY.

INLET END

FUEL INJECTOR ASSY. (6) PLACES

OUTLET END

INTAKE MANIFOLD ASSY.

FRONT OF ENGINE

84709051

ENGINE MECHANICAL

NOTE: Disconnecting the negative battery cable on some vehicles may interfere with the functions of the on board computer systems and may require the computer to undergo a relearning process, once the negative battery cable is reconnected.

Engine Assembly

REMOVAL AND INSTALLATION

2.0L Engine

AUTOMATIC TRANSAXLE

The engine is lifted from the engine compartment, leaving the transaxle in the vehicle.

1. Relieve the fuel system pressure and disconnect the battery cables. Remove the battery and battery tray.

2. Mark the position of the hood on its hinges and remove the hood.

3. Drain the cooling system and the engine oil.

4. Remove the air cleaner assembly and air ducts.

5. If equipped, remove the A/C compressor and position aside, leaving the refrigerant lines attached. Support the compressor with suitable wire.

6. Label, disconnect and plug the fuel lines at the fuel rail.

7. Label and disconnect the electrical connectors from the distributor, engine coolant temperature sensor, cooling fan temperature sensor, coolant temperature gauge sensor, throttle position sensor, air bypass valve, idle switch, fuel injectors, EGR solenoids and alternator.

8. Remove the power steering belt shield and the power steering belt. Remove the power steering hose brackets from the cylinder head cover.

9. Remove the power steering belt adjuster and disconnect the power steering pressure switch connector. Remove the power steering pump and position aside, leaving the hoses connected.

10. Loosen the alternator adjusting bolt, remove the upper mounting bolt and remove the alternator belt.

11. Remove the upper and lower radiator hoses. If equipped, disconnect the cruise control vacuum hose from

threads. Install the flexplate and loosely install the bolts.

NOTE: New flexplate mounting bolts come with sealant already on them.

27. Tighten the flexplate bolts in 2–3 steps to 75 ft. lbs. (103 Nm) in a crisscross pattern.

28. Carefully lower the engine into the vehicle and install it to the transaxle. Install the transaxle-to-engine bolts and tighten mounting bolts **A** to 73 ft. lbs. (99 Nm).

29. Raise the engine slightly with the jack and install the right-hand engine mount. Tighten the mount through bolt to 86 ft. lbs. (117 Nm) and mount nuts to 75 ft. lbs. (103 Nm). Remove the engine lifting equipment.

30. Raise and safely support the vehicle. Install the torque converter to the flexplate and tighten the nuts to 45 ft. lbs. (60 Nm). Rotate the flexplate, as necessary, to gain access to all of the nuts.

31. Install the remaining transaxle-to-engine mounting bolts. Tighten mounting bolt **B** to 73 ft. lbs. (99 Nm) and mounting bolt **C** to 38 ft. lbs. (51 Nm).

32. Install the engine-to-transaxle mounting bolts. Tighten mounting bolt **D** to 18 ft. lbs. (25 Nm), **E** to 38 ft. lbs. (51 Nm) and **F** to 73 ft. lbs. (99 Nm).

33. Install the alternator and loosely install the through bolt. Connect the alternator wiring and install the harness bracket to the back of the alternator.

34. Install the starter and tighten the bolts to 34 ft. lbs. (46 Nm). Install the intake manifold support bracket and tighten the bolts to 38 ft. lbs. (52 Nm).

35. Install the halfshaft support bearing bolts and tighten, in sequence, to 45 ft. lbs. (61 Nm).

36. Connect the oil pressure sensor connector. If equipped, install the

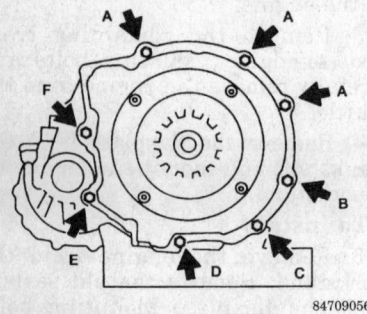

Engine and transaxle mounting bolt identification — 2.0L engine with automatic transaxle

A/C compressor on the mounting bracket and tighten the bolts to 26 ft. lbs. (35 Nm).

37. Install the crankshaft pulley and hold it with a suitable tool. Tighten the pulley bolt to 123 ft. lbs. (167 Nm).

38. Install the exhaust pipe to the catalytic converter and tighten the new nuts to 38 ft. lbs. (52 Nm). Attach the exhaust pipe support bracket to the engine and tighten the bolts to 38 ft. lbs. (52 Nm).

39. Install the new exhaust pipe-to-exhaust manifold nuts and tighten to 38 ft. lbs. (52 Nm). Connect the oxygen sensor connector and lower the vehicle.

40. Loosely attach the alternator to the alternator adjuster block. Install the alternator belt and adjust the tension. Tighten the alternator upper mounting bolt to 18 ft. lbs. (25 Nm).

41. Raise and safely support the vehicle. Tighten the alternator through bolt to 38 ft. lbs. (52 Nm).

42. Install the splash shields and lower the vehicle.

43. Loosely install the power steering pump through bolt and lock bolt. Connect the power steering switch connector and install the power steering belt.

44. Adjust the power steering belt tension, then tighten the through bolt to 45 ft. lbs. (61 Nm) and the lock bolt to 34 ft. lbs. (46 Nm).

45. Install the power steering pump belt shield and tighten the bolts to 86 inch lbs. (9 Nm). Install the power steering hose brackets to the cylinder head cover and tighten the bolts to 88 inch lbs. (10 Nm).

46. Connect the heater hoses. If equipped, connect the cruise control vacuum line to the back right-hand side of the intake manifold.

47. Connect the vacuum line connecting the evaporative canister to the metal EGR vacuum line. Connect the power brake booster vacuum line to the back left-hand side of the intake manifold.

48. Connect the fuel lines to the fuel rail and all remaining electrical connectors.

49. Install the accelerator cable and the radiator hoses. Install the air cleaner and air ducts.

50. Install the battery tray and battery. Connect the battery cables.

51. Install the hood, aligning the marks that were made during removal.

52. Fill the engine with the proper type and quantity of oil. Fill and bleed the cooling system.

53. Start the engine and bring to normal operating temperature. Check for leaks and proper engine operation.

MANUAL TRANSAXLE

The engine and transaxle are lifted from the engine compartment as an assembly.

1. Relieve the fuel system pressure and disconnect the battery cables. Remove the battery and battery tray.

2. Mark the position of the hood on its hinges and remove the hood.

3. Drain the cooling system and the engine oil.

4. Remove the air cleaner assembly and air ducts.

5. Remove the upper and lower radiator hoses and remove the radiator.

6. If equipped, remove the A/C compressor and position aside, leaving the refrigerant lines attached. Support the compressor with suitable wire.

7. Label, disconnect and plug the fuel lines at the fuel rail.

8. Label and disconnect the electrical connectors from the distributor, coil, engine coolant temperature sensor, coolant temperature gauge sensor, throttle position sensor, air bypass valve, fuel injectors, EGR solenoids and alternator.

9. Remove the power steering belt shield and the power steering belt. Remove the power steering hose brackets from the cylinder head cover.

10. Remove the power steering belt adjuster and disconnect the power steering pressure switch connector. Remove the power steering pump and position aside, leaving the hoses connected.

11. Loosen the alternator adjusting bolt, remove the upper mounting bolt and remove the alternator belt.

12. If equipped, disconnect the cruise control vacuum hose from the back right-hand side of the intake manifold.

13. Disconnect the vacuum line connecting the evaporative canister and the metal EGR vacuum line. If equipped, disconnect the EGR temperature sensor connector.

14. Disconnect the accelerator cable. Disconnect the power booster vacuum line from the back left-hand side of the intake manifold.

15. Disconnect the heater hoses and remove the upper starter mounting bolts. If equipped, disconnect the cruise control actuator electrical connector, remove the actuator mounting nuts and position the actuator aside.

16. Remove the ignition coil. Remove the fuel filter bracket bolts and position the filter and bracket aside.

17. Remove the ignition control module. Remove the ground wire bracket from between the transaxle and rear transaxle mount.

18. Remove the rear transaxle mount through bolt and remove the transaxle ground from the top rear of the transaxle.

19. Label and disconnect the brake on/off switch and vehicle speed sensor connectors from the rear of the transaxle.

20. Disconnect and plug the slave cylinder hydraulic line at the slave cylinder. Pull the spring clips from the slave cylinder line mounting brackets, then remove the rubber line from the metal line.

21. Label and disconnect the park/neutral position switch from the front of the transaxle. Raise and safely support the vehicle.

22. Remove the splash shields and the front wheel and tire assemblies.

23. Remove the 6 transverse member bolts and the transverse member. Remove the 6 transaxle cradle nuts and 2 bolts and remove the transaxle cradle.

24. Remove the 2 transaxle lower mount bolts and the transaxle lower mount.

25. Remove the halfshafts. Install transaxle plug tools T88C–7025–AH or equivalent, into the differential side gears.

NOTE: If the plugs are not installed, the differential side gears may become mispositioned. If the gears are mispositioned, the differential may have to be removed to reposition them.

26. Remove the intake manifold support bracket. Remove the 3 rear transaxle mount bolts and remove the rear transaxle mount.

27. Remove the starter. Label and disconnect the oil pressure sensor and oxygen sensor electrical connectors.

28. Remove and discard the exhaust pipe-to-catalytic converter nuts. Remove the exhaust support bolts. Remove and discard the exhaust pipe-to-exhaust manifold nuts and remove the exhaust pipe.

29. Remove the extension bar nut and washer, then disengage the bar from the transaxle. Remove the transaxle shift linkage through bolt and nut, then disengage the linkage from the transaxle.

30. Remove the wiring harness bracket from the rear of the alternator and remove the alternator

through bolt. Label and disconnect the remaining alternator wiring and remove the alternator.

31. Hold the crankshaft pulley with a suitable tool and remove the pulley bolt. Remove the crankshaft pulley.

32. Lower the vehicle. Raise the engine slightly with a jack and remove the right-hand engine mount.

33. Attach suitable engine lifting equipment to the lifting eyes on the engine. Remove the left-hand transaxle mount nuts, bolt and through bolt and remove the mount.

34. Carefully remove the engine/transaxle assembly from the vehicle.

35. Remove the transaxle-to-engine bolts and the engine-to-transaxle bolts. Separate the transaxle from the engine.

36. Remove the clutch assembly, flywheel and crankshaft rear cover plate. Mount the engine on a workstand.

To install:

37. Remove the engine from the workstand. Install the crankshaft rear cover plate and tighten the bolt to 88 inch lbs. (10 Nm). Install the flywheel and clutch assembly.

38. Install the transaxle on the engine. Install the transaxle-to-engine bolts. Tighten bolts **A** to 86 ft. lbs. (116 Nm), **B** to 38 ft. lbs. (51 Nm) and **C** to 18 ft. lbs. (25 Nm).

39. Install the engine-to-transaxle bolts. Tighten bolt **D** to 38 ft. lbs. (51 Nm) and bolt **E** to 86 ft. lbs. (116 Nm).

40. Lower the engine/transaxle assembly into the engine compartment.

41. Install the left-hand transaxle mount and tighten the nuts and bolt to 68 ft. lbs. (93 Nm). Tighten the mount through bolt to 86 ft. lbs. (116 Nm).

42. Raise the engine slightly with a jack and install the right-hand engine mount. Tighten the mount through bolt to 86 ft. lbs. (116 Nm) and the mount attaching nuts to 75

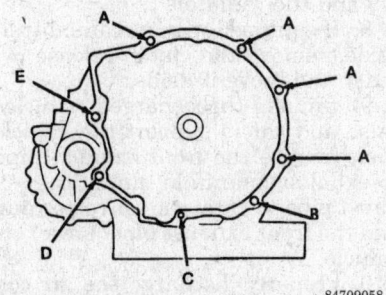

Engine and transaxle mounting bolt identification — 2.0L engine with manual transaxle

ft. lbs. (103 Nm). Remove the engine lifting equipment.

43. Raise and safely support the vehicle. Install the alternator and loosely install the alternator through bolt. Connect the alternator wiring and install the wiring harness bracket to the rear of the alternator.

44. Connect the extension bar to the transaxle with the washer and nut. Tighten the nut to 38 ft. lbs. (51 Nm).

45. Connect the shift linkage to the transaxle with the through bolt and nut. Tighten the through bolt to 18 ft. lbs. (25 Nm).

46. Install the exhaust pipe to the catalytic converter and tighten the new nuts to 38 ft. lbs. (52 Nm). Attach the exhaust pipe support bracket to the engine and tighten the bolts to 38 ft. lbs. (52 Nm).

47. Install the new exhaust pipe-to-exhaust manifold nuts and tighten to 38 ft. lbs. (52 Nm). Connect the oxygen sensor and oil pressure sensor connectors.

48. Install the starter and tighten the bolts to 34 ft. lbs. (46 Nm). Install the rear transaxle mount and tighten the 3 bolts to 68 ft. lbs. (93 Nm).

49. Install the intake manifold support bracket and tighten the bolts to 38 ft. lbs. (52 Nm).

50. Remove the plugs from the differential side gears and install the halfshafts.

51. Install the transaxle lower mount and tighten the bolts to 68 ft. lbs. (93 Nm).

52. Install the transaxle cradle. Tighten bolts and nuts **B** to 68 ft. lbs. (93 Nm), nuts **A** to 77 ft. lbs. (104 Nm) and nuts **C** to 44 ft. lbs. (60 Nm).

53. Install the transverse member and tighten the 4 bolts to 96 ft. lbs. (131 Nm).

54. Install the crankshaft pulley and hold it with a suitable tool. Install the pulley bolt and tighten to 123 ft. lbs. (167 Nm). Lower the vehicle.

55. Loosely attach the alternator to the alternator adjuster block. Install the alternator belt and adjust the tension. Tighten the alternator upper mounting bolt to 18 ft. lbs. (25 Nm).

56. Raise and safely support the vehicle. Tighten the alternator through bolt to 38 ft. lbs. (52 Nm).

57. Install the splash shields and the wheel and tire assemblies. Lower the vehicle and connect the park/neutral position switch.

58. Remove the plug and install the rubber line to the clutch hydraulic metal line. Install the spring clips to the hydraulic line mounting brackets.

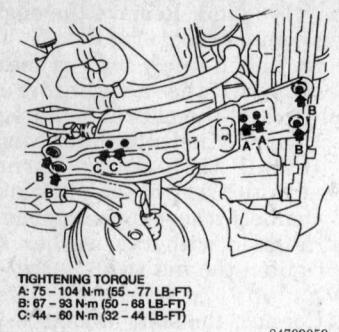

TIGHTENING TORQUE
A: 75 – 104 N·m (55 – 77 LB-FT)
B: 67 – 93 N·m (50 – 68 LB-FT)
C: 44 – 60 N·m (32 – 44 LB-FT)

84709059

Transaxle cradle bolt/nut identification — 2.0L and 2.5L engines

Install the hydraulic line fitting on the slave cylinder.

59. Connect the vehicle speed sensor and brake on/off switch electrical connectors at the rear of the transaxle.

60. Install the ground wire bracket between the transaxle and the rear transaxle mount. Install the rear transaxle mount through bolt and tighten to 68 ft. lbs. (93 Nm). Install the transaxle ground at the top rear of the transaxle.

61. Install the ignition control module. Install the fuel filter and bracket on the upper transaxle mount and tighten the bolts to 97 inch lbs. (11 Nm). Install the ignition coil.

62. If equipped, install the cruise control actuator and tighten the nuts. Connect the cruise control actuator electrical connector.

63. Install the starter mounting bolts and tighten to 34 ft. lbs. (46 Nm). Connect the heater hoses and connect the power brake booster vacuum line to the back left-hand side of the intake manifold.

64. Connect the accelerator cable. Connect the EGR temperature sensor, if equipped.

65. Connect the vacuum line between the evaporative canister and the metal EGR vacuum line. If equipped, connect the cruise control vacuum line to the back right-hand side of the intake manifold.

66. Loosely install the power steering pump through bolt and lock bolt. Connect the power steering switch connector and install the power steering belt.

67. Adjust the power steering belt tension, then tighten the through bolt to 45 ft. lbs. (61 Nm) and the lock bolt to 34 ft. lbs. (46 Nm).

68. Install the power steering pump belt shield and tighten the bolts to 86 inch lbs. (9 Nm). Install the power steering hose brackets to the cylinder

head cover and tighten the bolts to 88 inch lbs. (10 Nm).

69. Connect all remaining electrical connectors.

70. Unplug and connect the fuel lines. If equipped, install the A/C compressor and tighten the mounting bolts to 26 ft. lbs. (35 Nm).

71. Install the radiator and the radiator hoses.

72. Install the air cleaner and air ducts. Install the battery tray and battery. Connect the battery cables.

73. Install the hood, aligning the marks that were made during removal.

74. Fill the engine with the proper type and quantity of oil. Fill and bleed the cooling system. Bleed the clutch hydraulic system.

75. Start the engine and bring to normal operating temperature. Check for leaks and proper engine operation.

2.2L Engine

1. Properly relieve the fuel system pressure and disconnect the negative battery cable.

2. Mark the hood hinge-to-hood locations and remove the hood.

3. Drain the cooling system, the engine oil, power steering fluid and, if equipped, automatic transaxle fluid into suitable containers.

4. Remove the battery, the battery carrier and the fuse holder.

5. Remove the air filter assembly and ducts. Disconnect the accelerator cable, throttle valve, and the cruise control cable, if equipped.

6. Label and disconnect the electrical connectors from the electronic fuel injection system, the ignition coil, the thermostat housing sensors, the oxygen sensor, the radiator and the cooling fan assembly.

7. If equipped with an automatic transaxle, disconnect and plug the cooler lines from the radiator. Remove the radiator cooling fan assembly and the radiator.

8. If equipped with a manual transaxle, remove the clutch release cylinder and move it aside.

9. On non-turbocharged vehicles, raise and safely support the vehicle, then remove the front exhaust pipe-to-exhaust manifold nuts, the exhaust pipe-to-catalytic converter nuts and the front exhaust pipe. Lower the vehicle.

10. Properly discharge the air conditioning system and remove the air conditioning lines from the compressor. Immediately plug the lines and the compressor openings to prevent

the entrance of moisture. Disconnect the electrical connector from the compressor clutch.

11. Disconnect and plug the power steering lines from the power steering pump.

12. Disconnect the ground strap from the engine.

13. Disconnect and plug the heater hoses and the fuel lines.

14. Label and disconnect the vacuum lines from the brake booster chamber, the carbon canister, the bulkhead mounted solenoids and the distributor.

15. If equipped with an automatic transaxle, label and disconnect the electrical connectors from the transaxle.

16. Disconnect the speedometer cable from the transaxle.

17. If equipped with a turbocharger, disconnect the hoses and pipe. Cover the turbocharger with a clean rag.

18. Raise and safely support the vehicle. Remove the halfshafts from the transaxle.

19. Disconnect the shift control cable, if equipped with an automatic transaxle, or disconnect the rod, if equipped with a manual transaxle, from the transaxle. Lower the vehicle.

20. Using a suitable engine lifting device, attach it to the engine and support its weight.

21. Disconnect the engine mount bolts and remove the engine/transaxle assembly from the vehicle.

22. If necessary, remove the transaxle-to-engine bolts and support the engine on an engine stand.

To install:

23. If the transaxle was removed from the engine, install it and torque the bolts to 66–86 ft. lbs. (89–117 Nm).

24. Lower the engine/transaxle assembly into the vehicle and secure the engine mount bolts.

25. Install the halfshafts.

NOTE: When installing the halfshafts, hold the shafts to prevent damage to the seals, boots and joints caused by moving the joints through angles greater than 20 degrees.

26. Depending on which transaxle the vehicle is equipped with, connect the shift control cable or rod. If equipped with a manual transaxle, install the clutch release cylinder. If equipped with an automatic transaxle, connect the electrical connectors to the transaxle.

27. Connect the speedometer cable to the transaxle and the power steering lines to the power steering pump.

28. If equipped with air conditioning, use new O-rings and connect the pressure and suction lines to the compressor. Reconnect the electrical connector to the compressor clutch.

29. Connect the engine ground strap. On non-turbocharged vehicles, install the front exhaust pipe. If equipped with a turbocharger, connect the oil pipe and hoses to the turbocharger.

30. Install the radiator and the cooling fan assembly and reconnect the electrical connectors. If equipped with an automatic transaxle, reconnect the oil cooler lines to the radiator.

31. Connect the vacuum lines to the carbon canister, the bulkhead mounted solenoids, distributor and the brake booster.

32. Connect the heater hoses to the engine and the fuel lines to the fuel system. Connect the electrical connectors to the oxygen sensor, thermostat housing sensors, the coil and the electronic fuel injection assembly.

33. Install the accelerator cable, throttle valve cable and the cruise control cable, if equipped. Install the air filter and ducts.

34. Install the battery carrier, battery and the fuse holder. Connect the battery cables.

35. Refill the cooling system. Fill the crankcase with the proper type and quantity of engine oil. If equipped, fill the automatic transaxle with the proper type and quantity of fluid. Refill the power steering reservoir and bleed the system.

36. Start the engine, allow it to reach normal operating temperatures and check for leaks. Charge the air conditioning system.

37. Install the hood, aligning the marks that were made during the removal procedure.

2.5L Engine

AUTOMATIC TRANSAXLE

The engine and transaxle are lifted from the engine compartment as an assembly.

1. Relieve the fuel system pressure. Disconnect the battery cables and remove the battery and battery tray. Mark the position of the hood on its hinges and remove the hood.

2. Remove the air cleaner assembly and fresh air duct. Loosen the alternator belt tensioner locknut and adjuster bolt and remove the belt.

3. Raise and safely support the vehicle. Remove the front wheel and

tire assemblies and the splash shields.

4. Remove the 6 transverse member bolts and remove the transverse member.

5. Disconnect the front and rear oxygen sensor connectors. Remove the exhaust pipe-to-exhaust manifold nuts.

6. Disconnect the oil pressure switch electrical connector, located at the oil filter. Remove the halfshafts.

7. Loosen the power steering belt tensioner locknut and adjuster bolt and remove the belt.

8. Remove the 3 power steering pump mounting bolts through the holes in the pump pulley. Remove the power steering hose bracket-to-power steering pump bolt and the pump rear bracket bolt. Secure the pump aside with mechanics wire, leaving the hoses connected.

9. If equipped, remove the 4 A/C compressor mounting bolts and secure the compressor aside with mechanics wire, leaving the refrigerant lines attached. Do not let the compressor hang by the refrigerant lines.

10. Lower the vehicle and drain the cooling system.

11. Remove the radiator hoses and overflow hose. Disconnect the cooling fan electrical connectors. Disconnect and plug the transaxle cooler lines. Remove the radiator/cooling fan assembly.

12. Label and disconnect the wiring from the alternator. Remove the 2 A/C and alternator wiring harness retaining bolts, then disconnect the harness from the engine block.

13. Label and disconnect the electrical connectors from the fuel rail, vehicle speed sensor, starter, throttle position sensor, knock sensor, EGR air bypass valve, EGR valve position sensor, neutral safety switch, engine coolant temperature sensor, cooling fan engine coolant temperature sensor, temperature gauge sending unit and crank position sensor.

14. Label and disconnect the vacuum hoses from the cruise control actuator, EGR, throttle body, power brake booster, A/C control head and fuel pressure regulator.

15. Remove the 2 heater hoses from the thermostat housing. Remove the wiring harness grounds.

16. If equipped, disconnect the cruise control actuator electrical connector. Remove the 2 nuts from the actuator bracket and position the actuator and bracket aside.

17. Disconnect the fuel supply and return lines and discard the copper

crush washer. Remove the 2 fuel line retaining bolts from the fuel line bracket.

18. Disconnect the throttle cable from the throttle body. Remove the 2 nuts from the fuel filter bracket and position the filter aside, without disconnecting the fuel lines.

19. Remove the spring clip from the shift cable bracket and pull the cable from the switch. Remove the 2 bolts from the cooling fan relay bracket and position the bracket aside.

20. Raise and safely support the vehicle. Remove the front and rear transaxle mount through bolts.

21. Lower the vehicle. Attach suitable lifting equipment to the engine lifting eyes and remove any slack.

22. Remove the left-hand transaxle mount through bolt and the right-hand transaxle mount through bolt and 2 nuts. Remove the right-hand engine mount from the vehicle.

23. Carefully lift the engine/transaxle assembly from the vehicle. Separate the transaxle from the engine, if necessary.

To install:

24. If necessary, connect the engine and transaxle. Tighten the engine-to-transaxle bolts and the transaxle-to-engine bolts to 73 ft. lbs. (99 Nm).

25. Carefully lower the engine/transaxle assembly into position in the engine compartment. Install the right-hand engine mount. Tighten the through bolt to 68 ft. lbs. (93 Nm) and the nuts to 76 ft. lbs. (103 Nm).

26. Install the left-hand transaxle mount through bolt and tighten to 86 ft. lbs. (116 Nm). Remove the engine lifting equipment.

27. Raise and safely support the vehicle. Install the front and rear transaxle mount through bolts and tighten to 86 ft. lbs. (116 Nm).

28. Lower the vehicle. Align the cooling fan relay bracket and install the 2 bolts. Tighten to 88 inch lbs. (10 Nm).

29. Install the shift cable and retain with the spring clip. Align the fuel filter and install the nuts. Tighten to 88 inch lbs. (10 Nm).

30. If equipped, connect the vacuum line to the A/C control head. Connect the vacuum line to the power brake booster.

31. Connect the throttle cable and vacuum lines to the throttle body. Connect the vacuum line to the fuel pressure regulator.

32. Align the fuel line bracket and install the bolts. Tighten to 88 inch lbs. (10 Nm). Connect the fuel supply and return lines, using a new copper

crush washer. Tighten the supply line to 25 ft. lbs. (34 Nm).

33. If equipped, align the cruise control actuator and install the nuts. Connect the actuator electrical connector.

34. Install the wiring harness grounds and connect the heater hoses to the thermostat housing.

35. Connect the electrical connectors for the crank position sensor, engine coolant temperature sensor, cooling fan engine coolant temperature sensor, temperature gauge sending unit, neutral safety switch, EGR valve position sensor, air bypass valve solenoid, EGR, knock sensor, throttle position sensor, starter, vehicle speed sensor and fuel rail.

36. Connect the vacuum hose to the EGR and, if equipped, cruise control actuator.

37. Align the A/C and alternator wiring harness and install the 2 bolts. Connect the 2 electrical connectors to the top of the distributor.

38. Install the radiator/cooling fan assembly and connect the cooling fan electrical connectors. Unplug and connect the transaxle oil cooler lines and install the radiator hoses.

39. Raise and safely support the vehicle. If equipped, install the A/C compressor and tighten the bolts to 38 ft. lbs. (51 Nm).

40. Align the power steering pump and install the rear bracket bolt. Tighten to 34 ft. lbs. (46 Nm). Install the power steering hose bracket bolt and tighten to 34 ft. lbs. (46 Nm).

41. Install the 3 power steering pump bolts through the pulley and tighten to 34 ft. lbs. (46 Nm). Install the power steering belt and adjust the tension.

42. Install the halfshafts. Connect the oil pressure switch electrical connector.

43. Install the exhaust pipe to the manifolds and tighten the nuts to 41 ft. lbs. (55 Nm). Connect the front and rear oxygen sensor connectors.

44. Align the transverse member and install the 6 bolts. Tighten to 93 ft. lbs. (126 Nm).

45. Install the splash shields and the wheel and tire assemblies. Lower the vehicle.

46. Install the alternator belt and adjust the tension. Make sure all electrical connectors and vacuum hose are connected.

47. Install the air cleaner assembly and fresh air duct. Install the hood, aligning the marks that were made during removal.

48. Install the battery tray and battery. Connect the battery cables.

49. Fill the cooling system. If necessary, fill the engine and transaxle with the proper types and quantities of oil.

50. Start the engine and bring to normal operating temperature. Check for leaks and proper operation. Stop the engine and check all fluid levels.

MANUAL TRANSAXLE

The engine and transaxle are lifted from the engine compartment as an assembly.

1. Relieve the fuel system pressure. Disconnect the battery cables and remove the battery and battery tray.

2. Mark the position of the hood on its hinges and remove the hood. Remove the air cleaner assembly and fresh air duct.

3. Raise and safely support the vehicle. Remove the front wheel and tire assemblies and the splash shields.

4. Remove the 6 transverse member bolts and remove the transverse member.

5. Remove the 2 bolts and 6 nuts from the transaxle cradle and remove the cradle.

6. Disconnect the front and rear oxygen sensor connectors and remove the exhaust pipe-to-exhaust manifold nuts.

7. Remove the extension bar, nut and washer, then remove the extension bar from the transaxle. Remove the transaxle shift linkage through bolt and nut, then disengage the linkage from the transaxle.

8. Disconnect the A/C and oil pressure switch electrical connectors. Disconnect and plug the hydraulic line at the slave cylinder, then remove the 2 spring clips from the line.

9. Remove the halfshafts. Remove the 3 bolts from the rear transaxle mount and remove the mount.

10. Loosen the locknut and adjuster bolt on the power steering belt tensioner and remove the belt. Remove the 3 power steering pump mounting bolts working through the pulley holes.

11. Remove the rear bracket bolt from the power steering pump and secure the pump aside with mechanics wire.

12. If equipped, remove the 4 A/C compressor mounting bolts and secure the compressor aside with mechanics wire, leaving the refrigerant lines attached. Do not let the compressor hang by the refrigerant lines.

13. Remove the power steering hose bracket from the pump. Loosen the

alternator belt tensioner locknut and adjuster bolt and remove the belt.

14. Remove the radiator hoses and overflow hose. Disconnect the cooling fan electrical connectors. Remove the radiator/cooling fan assembly.

15. Label and disconnect the electrical connectors at the alternator. Remove the 2 A/C and alternator wiring harness bolts, then disconnect the harness from the engine block.

16. Label and disconnect the electrical connectors from the distributor, fuel rail, vehicle speed sensor, starter, throttle position sensor, engine coolant temperature sensor, cooling fan engine coolant temperature sensor, temperature gauge sending unit, knock sensor, crank position sensor, EGR valve, park/neutral position switch, air bypass valve solenoid, EGR valve position sensor and, if equipped, cruise control actuator.

17. Label and disconnect the vacuum hoses from the cruise control actuator, if equipped, EGR valve and fuel pressure regulator.

18. Remove the ground-to-engine bracket bolt located near the starter. If equipped, remove the 2 nuts from the cruise control actuator and position aside.

19. Remove the transaxle ground and backup light switch from the rear of the transaxle. Remove the starter-to-chassis ground.

20. Disconnect the heater hoses from the engine. Disconnect the fuel supply and return lines. Remove the 2 fuel line retaining bolts and bracket.

21. Label and disconnect the vacuum lines and the accelerator cable from the throttle body. Label and disconnect the vacuum line from the intake manifold to the A/C control head and the power brake booster vacuum hose.

22. Remove the 2 fuel filter mounting nuts and position the filter aside, leaving the fuel lines connected.

23. Attach suitable engine lifting equipment to the engine lifting eyes and take up any slack.

24. Remove both of the left-hand transaxle mount nuts and through bolt. Remove both front transaxle mount nuts and remove the 2 nuts and the through bolt from the right-hand engine mount.

25. Carefully lift the engine/transaxle assembly from the vehicle. Separate the engine and transaxle, if necessary.

To install:

26. If necessary, assemble the engine and transaxle. Tighten the engine-to-transaxle and transaxle-to-

engine bolts to the proper specification.

27. Carefully lower the engine/transaxle assembly into position in the engine compartment.

28. Install the rear transaxle mount. Tighten the nuts to 68 ft. lbs. (93 Nm) and the through bolt to 86 ft. lbs. (116 Nm).

29. Install the front transaxle mount. Tighten the nuts to 75 ft. lbs. (102 Nm) and the through bolt to 86 ft. lbs. (116 Nm).

30. Install the left-hand transaxle mount. Tighten the nuts to 77 ft. lbs. (104 Nm) and the through bolt to 86 ft. lbs. (116 Nm).

31. Install the right-hand transaxle mount. Tighten the nuts to 77 ft. lbs. (104 Nm) and the through bolt to 68 ft. lbs. (93 Nm). Remove the engine lifting equipment.

32. Raise and safely support the vehicle. Install the power steering pump and tighten the bolts to 34 ft. lbs. (46 Nm).

33. Tighten the power steering pump rear bracket bolt to 34 ft. lbs. (46 Nm). Install the power steering belt and adjust the tension.

34. Install the A/C compressor and tighten the bolts to 38 ft. lbs. (51 Nm). Install the alternator and A/C belt and adjust the tension.

35. Align the extension bar and tighten the nut to 33 ft. lbs. (46 Nm). Install the shift linkage and tighten the bolt to 16 ft. lbs. (22 Nm).

36. Install the halfshafts. Install the transaxle cradle. Tighten the cradle mounting bolts and nuts **B** to 68 ft. lbs. (93 Nm), nuts **A** to 77 ft. lbs. (104 Nm) and nuts **C** to 44 ft. lbs. (60 Nm).

37. Install the exhaust pipe to the exhaust manifolds and tighten the nuts to 41 ft. lbs. (55 Nm). Connect the oxygen sensor connectors.

38. Install the transverse member and tighten the bolts to 93 ft. lbs. (126 Nm). Install the splash shields

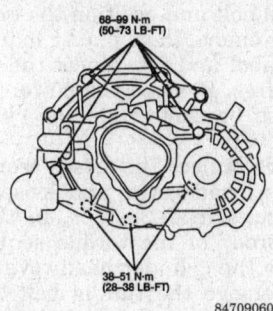

68—99 N·m
(50—73 LB-FT)

38—51 N·m
(28—38 LB-FT)

84709060

Engine and transaxle mounting bolt identification — 2.5L engine with manual transaxle

and wheel and tire assemblies and lower the vehicle.

39. Install the power steering hose bracket bolt to the pump.

40. Connect the electrical connectors to the knock sensor, engine coolant temperature sensor, cooling fan engine coolant temperature sensor, temperature gauge sending unit, crank position sensor, EGR solenoids, EGR valve position sensor, vehicle speed sensor, starter, backup light switch, fuel injectors, throttle position sensor, distributor and park/neutral position switch.

41. Connect the vacuum hoses to the A/C control head, located in the right-hand rear of the engine compartment, EGR valve, fuel pressure regulator and, if equipped, cruise control actuator.

42. Install the starter-to-chassis grounds, the transaxle ground and the ground-to-engine bracket bolt.

43. Connect the heater hoses. Connect the fuel supply and return lines. Tighten the fuel line bracket bolts to 88 inch lbs. (10 Nm) and the fuel supply line to 25 ft. lbs. (34 Nm).

44. Install the fuel filter to the bracket and install the 2 nuts. Install the cruise control actuator with the nuts and connect the electrical connector.

45. Connect the vacuum lines to the throttle body and connect the accelerator cable. Connect the power brake booster vacuum hose.

46. Connect the air bypass valve, oil pressure switch, A/C compressor and alternator electrical connectors. Connect the A/C and alternator harness bracket to the engine.

47. Install the battery tray. Connect the hydraulic line to the slave cylinder and install the line bracket spring clips.

48. Install the radiator/cooling fan assembly and connect the cooling fan electrical connectors. Install the radiator hoses.

49. Install the air cleaner housing and ducts. Connect all vacuum and electrical connectors.

50. Install the battery and connect the cables. Install the hood, aligning the marks that were made during removal.

51. Fill the cooling system. If necessary, fill the engine and transaxle with the proper types and quantities of oil.

52. Bleed the air from the clutch hydraulic system.

53. Start the engine and bring to normal operating temperature. Check for leaks and proper operation.

Stop the engine and check all fluid levels.

3.0L Engine

1. Properly relieve the fuel system pressure and disconnect the battery cables. Mark the position of the hood on its hinges and remove the hood assembly.

2. Drain the cooling system and the engine oil into suitable containers. Properly discharge the air conditioning system.

3. Remove the air cleaner assembly from the engine compartment and the vacuum valve assembly from the right side shock tower.

4. Disconnect and plug the fuel lines.

5. Remove the upper radiator hose.

6. Tag and disconnect the alternator, air conditioning compressor clutch, ignition coil and the engine coolant temperature sensor connectors.

7. Tag and disconnect the TFI module connector, injector wiring harness, air charge temperature sensor and the throttle position sensor.

8. Disconnect the oil pressure sending switch, ground straps at the intake manifold on both sides of the engine and the block heater, if equipped.

9. Disconnect the EGR sensor and the oil level sensor, located on the back side of the oil pan.

10. Tag and disconnect all vacuum lines, heater hoses and crankcase ventilation hoses.

11. Disconnect and plug the high pressure and return lines at the power steering pump.

12. Disconnect the air conditioning lines from the condenser and chassis, leaving the manifold lines attached to the compressor.

13. Disconnect the accelerator linkage, transaxle throttle valve linkage and the cruise control cable, if equipped.

14. Remove the battery, battery tray and the fuse box assembly.

15. Disconnect and set aside the cruise control servo assembly and the transaxle shift cable, if equipped with an automatic transaxle.

16. Disconnect all automatic transaxle wiring connectors and the speedometer cable on conventional (analog) cluster vehicles.

17. Disconnect the Vehicle Speed Sensor (VSS) connector on electronic cluster vehicles.

18. Disconnect and plug the cooler lines at the transaxle, if equipped with automatic transaxle.

19. Remove the clutch slave cylinder, leaving the pressure line attached, if equipped with a manual transaxle, and set it aside.

20. Remove the radiator, cooling fan and shroud.

21. Raise and safely support the vehicle. Remove the front wheel and tire assemblies.

22. Remove the lower radiator hose, the front exhaust pipe and the starter motor.

NOTE: On vehicles with an automatic transaxle, it is advised that the torque converter nuts be removed at this time to facilitate the removal of the transaxle assembly from the engine after the engine/transaxle assembly is removed from the vehicle.

23. Remove the shift control rod and the extension bar on manual transaxle vehicles.

24. Remove the stabilizer links and tie rod ends and disconnect the lower ball joints. Pull down on the control arms to disengage them from the spindle.

25. Remove the dynamic damper mounting bolts on the right halfshaft assembly.

26. Disengage both halfshafts by pulling outward on both side brake and spindle assemblies. In this procedure, the halfshaft assemblies are left in the chassis.

27. Install two T88C–7025–AH transaxle plugs or equivalent, into the differential side gears.

NOTE: Failure to install the transaxle plugs may allow the differential side gears to become misaligned, making halfshaft installation difficult or impossible, without disassembling the differential.

28. Disconnect the lower transaxle mount and safely, lower the vehicle.

29. Install and position suitable engine lifting devices. Disconnect the lower front engine mount.

30. Disconnect the right side upper engine mount at the timing cover and the left side upper engine mount at the transaxle case.

31. Carefully, lift the engine and the transaxle assembly out of the vehicle.

To install:

32. Lower the engine and the transaxle assembly into the vehicle.

33. Connect and tighten the upper and lower engine mounts. Remove the engine lifting devices.

34. Remove both transaxle plugs and install the halfshafts on both sides.

35. Install the dynamic damper mounting bolts on the right side halfshaft.

36. Engage the control arms and install the lower ball joints, tie rod ends and the stabilizer links.

37. Install the shift control rod and extension bar, if equipped with a manual transaxle.

38. Replace the torque converter nuts, if equipped with an automatic transaxle.

39. Install the starter, front exhaust pipe and the lower radiator hose.

40. Replace the front tires and wheels. Safely, lower the vehicle.

41. Install the cooling fan, shroud and the radiator.

42. Install the clutch release cable with the hose attached, if equipped.

43. Reconnect the cooler lines at the transaxle, if equipped.

44. Connect the Vehicle Speed Sensor (VSS) on electronic cluster vehicles.

45. Connect all automatic transaxle wiring connectors and the speedometer cable on conventional (analog) cluster vehicles.

46. Install the cruise control servo assembly and the transaxle shift cable, if equipped.

47. Replace the battery, battery tray and the fuse box assembly.

48. Connect the accelerator linkage, transaxle throttle valve linkage and the cruise control cable, if equipped.

49. Connect the air conditioning lines from the condenser and chassis.

50. Install the high pressure and return lines to the power steering pump.

51. Reconnect all vacuum lines, heater hoses and crankcase ventilation hoses.

52. Reconnect the EGR sensor and the oil level sensor on the back side of the oil pan.

53. Connect the oil pressure sending switch connector, the ground straps on both sides of the engine and the block heater, if equipped.

54. Reconnect the TFI module connector, injector wiring harness, air charge temperature sensor and the throttle position sensor.

55. Install the alternator, air conditioning compressor clutch, ignition coil and the engine coolant temperature sensor.

56. Connect the fuel lines and replace the upper radiator hose.

57. Install the air cleaner assembly in the engine compartment and the vacuum valve assembly on the right side shock tower.

58. Refill the cooling system. Fill the crankcase with the proper type and quantity of engine oil. If equipped, fill the automatic transaxle with the proper type and quantity of fluid.

59. Reconnect the battery cables and install the hood assembly, aligning the marks that were made during the removal procedure.

60. Start the engine and bring to normal operating temperature. Check for any leaks.

61. Recharge the air conditioning system.

Engine Mounts

REMOVAL AND INSTALLATION

1. Disconnect the negative battery cable.

2. If necessary, raise and support the vehicle safely.

3. Using an engine lifting device, attach it to the engine and support it's weight.

4. Remove the engine mount-to-engine bolts/nuts, through bolt and, if necessary, the engine mount-to-chassis bolts/nuts. Remove the mount.

5. To install, reverse the removal procedure. Remove the engine lift.

Cylinder Head

REMOVAL AND INSTALLATION

2.0L Engine

1. Relieve the fuel system pressure and disconnect the negative battery cable. Drain the cooling system.

2. Remove the intake manifold.

3. Remove the accessory drive belts. Remove the power steering pump bolts and secure the pump aside with mechanics wire, leaving the hoses attached.

4. Remove the alternator bracket nut and bolt and position the bracket aside. Remove the exhaust manifold.

5. Label and disconnect the spark plug wires. Remove the power steering hose brackets from the cylinder head cover.

6. Disconnect the hoses from the cylinder head cover and loosen the cover bolts in 2–3 steps, in the reverse order of the torque sequence. Remove the cylinder head cover.

7. Remove the timing belt. Label and disconnect the distributor/coil connectors, engine coolant temperature sensor connector, cooling fan coolant temperature sensor connector

and temperature gauge sensor connector.

8. Remove the coolant temperature sensor housing from the cylinder head. Remove the distributor.

9. Remove the camshafts.

10. Loosen the cylinder head bolts, in 2–3 steps, in the reverse order of the torque sequence. Remove the bolts and the cylinder head.

11. Clean all gasket mating surfaces. Inspect the cylinder head for damage, cracks, and water and oil leakage. Check the head gasket surface for distortion using a straightedge and feeler gauge. Maximum allowable distortion is 0.004 in. (0.10mm).

To install:

12. Position a new cylinder head gasket on the cylinder block and install the cylinder head.

13. Install new cylinder head bolts and tighten in 2 steps, in sequence, to 16 ft. lbs. (22 Nm).

14. Paint a mark on the edge of each cylinder head bolt to use as a reference. Turn each bolt, in sequence, 90 degrees. Again, turn each bolt, in sequence, an additional 90 degrees.

15. Install the camshafts. Install the distributor and connect the distributor/coil connectors.

16. Install the timing belt.

17. Install a new cylinder head cover gasket on the cylinder head cover. Apply sealant to the cylinder head surface in the area adjacent to the front camshaft caps, then install the cover. Tighten the bolts in 2 steps, in sequence, to 69 inch lbs. (7 Nm).

18. Connect the hoses to the cylinder head cover. Connect the spark plug wires.

19. Install the exhaust manifold and the alternator bracket. Tighten the bracket nut and bolt to 19 ft. lbs. (25 Nm).

20. Install the alternator belt and adjust the tension.

21. Loosely install the power steering pump through and lock bolts. Connect the pump pressure switch connector.

22. Install the power steering pump belt and adjust the tension. Tighten the pump through bolt to 45 ft. lbs. (61 Nm) and the lock bolt to 34 ft. lbs. (46 Nm).

23. Install the power steering pump belt shield and tighten the bolts to 86 inch lbs. (9 Nm). Install the power steering hose brackets to the cylinder head cover and tighten the bolts to 88 inch lbs. (10 Nm).

24. Install the coolant temperature sensor housing with a new gasket. Tighten the bolts to 19 ft. lbs. (25 Nm). Connect the electrical connectors at the housing.

25. Install the intake manifold.

26. Connect the negative battery cable. Fill and bleed the cooling system. Run the engine and check for proper operation.

2.2L Engine

1. Disconnect the negative battery cable. Remove the drive belts.

2. Remove the crankshaft pulley as follows:

   a. Raise and safely support the vehicle.

   b. Remove the right front wheel and tire assembly.

   c. Remove the right inner fender panel.

   d. Remove the 6 bolts, pulley and baffle plate.

   e. Lower the vehicle.

3. Remove the timing belt covers and timing belt.

4. Remove the exhaust manifold, intake manifold and the distributor.

5. Remove rocker arm cover.

6. Drain the cooling system.

7. Remove the spark plug wires and the spark plugs.

8. Tag and disconnect the electrical connectors from the thermostat housing sensors. Remove the upper radiator hose and the water bypass hose.

9. Remove the front and rear engine lifting eyes and the engine ground wire. Remove the front and rear housings and gaskets.

10. Remove the cylinder head bolts, a little at a time, in the reverse order of installation. Remove the cylinder head and discard the gasket.

11. Clean the gasket mounting surfaces.

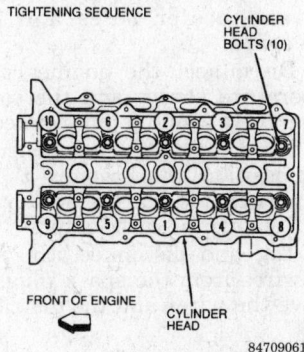

Cylinder head torque sequence — 2.0L engine

To install:

12. Position a new cylinder head gasket on the cylinder block. Install the cylinder head and torque the bolts, in sequence, to 29–32 ft. lbs. (40–42 Nm) and then again, in sequence, to 59–64 ft. lbs. (80–86 Nm).

13. Install the front and rear housings, using new gaskets, and tighten the bolts/nuts to 14–19 ft. lbs. (19–25 Nm).

14. Install the distributor and the front and rear engine lifting eyes.

15. Install the spark plugs and spark plug wires.

16. Install the intake and exhaust manifolds.

17. Install the rocker arm cover.

18. Install the timing belt and timing covers.

19. Install the crankshaft pulley and the drive belts.

20. Fill the cooling system and connect the negative battery cable.

21. Run the engine and check for any leaks. Check the ignition timing.

2.5L Engine

1. Relieve the fuel system pressure and disconnect the negative battery cable. Drain the cooling system.

2. Remove the timing belt covers and the timing belt. Remove the intake manifold.

3. Disconnect the ventilation pipe from the left cylinder head cover, remove the bolts and remove the cylinder head covers.

4. Remove the camshafts. Remove the 3 bolts and the seal plate from the front of the engine.

5. Remove the 4 coolant elbow bolts and the coolant elbow. Raise and safely support the vehicle.

6. Disconnect the oxygen sensor connectors. Remove the exhaust pipe-to-exhaust manifold nuts and lower the exhaust pipes. Lower the vehicle.

7. Remove the hydraulic lifters. Identify each lifter as it is removed so it can be reinstalled in the same position. If the lifters are to be reused, store them upside down in a sealed container.

8. Loosen the cylinder head bolts, in 2–3 steps, in the reverse order of the torque sequence. Remove the bolts and remove the cylinder heads.

9. Clean all gasket mating surfaces. Inspect the cylinder head for damage, cracks, and water and oil leakage. Check the head gasket surface for distortion using a straightedge and feeler gauge. Maximum allowable distortion is 0.004 in. (0.10mm).

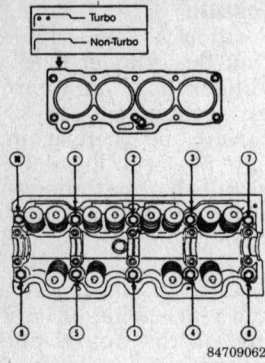

Cylinder head torque
sequence — 2.2L engine

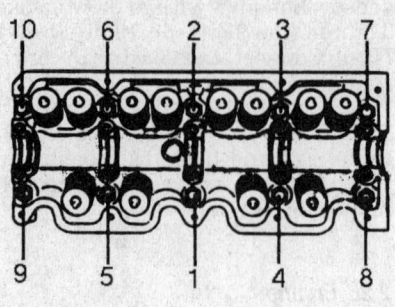

Cylinder head torque sequence — 2.5L engine

3.0L Engine

To install:

10. If removed, install the exhaust manifolds using new gaskets. Tighten the exhaust manifold nuts and bolts to 18 ft. lbs. (25 Nm). Tighten the manifold heatshield bolts to 88 inch lbs. (10 Nm).

11. Position new head gaskets on the cylinder block. The gaskets cannot be interchanged between sides and are marked **R** and **L** for right and left side.

12. Install the cylinder heads. Apply clean engine oil to the threads of new cylinder head bolts and install. Tighten the cylinder head bolts in 2–3 steps, in sequence, to 19 ft. lbs. (26 Nm).

13. Paint a mark on the edge of each cylinder head bolt to use as a reference. Turn each bolt, in sequence, 90 degrees. Again, turn each bolt, in sequence, an additional 90 degrees.

14. Apply clean engine oil to the hydraulic lifters and install them in their original positions. Make sure they move freely in the bores.

15. Install the camshafts. Raise and safely support the vehicle.

16. Connect the exhaust pipes to the manifolds and tighten the nuts to 41 ft. lbs. (55 Nm). Connect the oxygen sensor connectors.

17. Apply sealant to the cylinder head surface in the area of the front and rear camshaft caps. Install new gaskets and install the cylinder head covers. Tighten the bolts in 2 steps, in sequence, to 78 inch lbs. (8 Nm).

18. Install the intake manifold. Install the timing belt and timing belt covers.

19. Connect the negative battery cable. Fill and bleed the cooling system. Run the engine and check for proper operation.

1. Properly relieve the fuel system pressure and disconnect the negative battery cable.

2. Drain the cooling system.

3. Remove the air cleaner hoses from the throttle body and rocker arm cover.

4. Disconnect the fuel lines from the fuel supply manifold.

5. Tag and disconnect the vacuum lines from the throttle body.

6. Tag and disconnect the air charge temperature sensor, throttle position sensor and air bypass solenoid electrical connectors.

7. Remove the EGR supply tube and the MAP sensor from the throttle body.

8. Disconnect the throttle cable and, if equipped with automatic transaxle, the throttle valve control cable from the throttle lever.

9. Remove the fuel rail bracket bolt from the throttle body, remove the 6 throttle body attaching bolts and remove the throttle body.

10. Disconnect the fuel injector harness stand-offs from the inboard rocker arm cover studs and each injector and remove from the engine.

11. Disconnect the upper radiator hose and heater hoses and move them aside.

12. Disconnect the engine coolant temperature sensor and the coolant temperature sending unit connectors.

13. Mark the distributor housing to block position, then remove the distributor cap and mark the rotor position. Remove the distributor.

14. Tag and disconnect the spark plug wires from the spark plugs and remove the wires and the distributor cap.

15. Remove the ignition coil and bracket assembly from the left cylinder head and set aside.

16. If the left cylinder head is being removed, perform the following:

  a. Remove the power steering protective shroud.

  b. Using a ½ in. drive breaker bar, rotate the automatic belt tensioner clockwise and remove the accessory drive belt.

  c. Remove the automatic belt tensioner.

  d. Remove the nut and remove the power steering pulley.

  e. Remove the air conditioning brace to the power steering support retaining bolts.

  f. Remove the 3 power steering support retaining bolts.

  g. Remove the engine oil dipstick tube attaching nut from the exhaust manifold stud. Rotate or remove the tube from the manifold.

NOTE: The power steering support bracket may be pulled away from the engine with the alternator and power steering pump intact.

17. Remove the spark plugs.

18. Remove the exhaust manifold(s), heatshield(s) and inlet pipe(s).

19. Remove the rocker arm covers.

20. Loosen the rocker arm fulcrum retaining bolts and remove the rocker arms, fulcrums and retaining bolts.

NOTE: The No. 3 intake valve pushrod must be removed to allow removal of the intake manifold, regardless of which cylinder head is being removed.

21. Remove the pushrods. Note the position of each so they may be reinstalled in their original positions.

22. Remove the intake manifold.

23. Remove the cylinder head retaining bolts and remove the cylinder head(s). Remove and discard the cylinder head gasket(s).

24. Clean all gasket mating surfaces.

To install:

25. Position new head gasket(s) on the cylinder block, using the dowel pins for alignment. Carefully position the cylinder head(s) on the block.

26. Lightly oil the threads and install the cylinder head bolts, finger-tight. On 1992 vehicles, tighten the bolts, in sequence, to 59 ft. lbs. (80 Nm), then back off all bolts a minimum of 1 full turn. Retighten the bolts, in sequence, in 2 steps; first to 37 ft. lbs. (50 Nm), and then to 68 ft. lbs. (92 Nm).

27. Install the intake manifold.

28. Install the distributor, aligning the marks that were made during removal.

29. Dip each pushrod in heavy engine oil, then install in their original positions.

30. For each rocker arm, rotate the crankshaft until the lifter rests on the base circle of the camshaft lobe, before tightening the fulcrum mounting bolts. Position the rocker arms over the pushrods and tighten the fulcrum mounting bolts to 24 ft. lbs. (32 Nm). Make sure the fulcrums and pushrods are fully seated before tightening.

NOTE: If the original valve train components are being installed, a valve clearance check is not required. If a component has been replaced, perform a valve clearance check.

31. Install the exhaust manifold(s) and tighten the retaining bolts to 18 ft. lbs. (25 Nm). Install the inlet pipe retaining nuts and tighten to 20 ft. lbs. (27 Nm).

32. Install the dipstick tube into the cylinder block. Tighten the retaining nut to 13 ft. lbs. (18 Nm).

33. Install the spark plugs and tighten to 7–15 ft. lbs. (9–20 Nm).

34. Install the rocker arm covers.

35. Install the fuel injector electrical harness to the injectors and inboard rocker arm cover studs. Connect the engine harness to the main harness and secure with the retainers.

36. Install the distributor cap and connect the spark plug wires to the spark plugs.

37. Position a new gasket and the throttle body on the lower intake manifold. Install the attaching bolts and tighten to 15–22 ft. lbs. (20–30 Nm).

38. Install the fuel rail bracket bolt on the throttle body. Connect the throttle cable and, if equipped with automatic transaxle, the throttle valve control cable to the throttle lever.

39. Install the MAP sensor and the EGR supply tube to the throttle body.

40. Connect the electrical connectors for the air charge temperature sensor, throttle position sensor and air bypass solenoid.

41. Install the ignition coil and bracket. Tighten the bolts to 35 ft. lbs. (48 Nm).

42. If the left cylinder head was removed, perform the following:
 a. Install the power steering support bracket. Tighten the 3 retaining bolts to 35 ft. lbs. (48 Nm).
 b. Install the air conditioning brace to the power steering support bracket retaining bolt. Tighten the bolt to 18 ft. lbs. (25 Nm).
 c. Install the power steering pump pulley. Tighten the retaining nut to 47 ft. lbs. (64 Nm).
 d. Install the automatic belt tensioner. Tighten the retaining bolt to 35 ft. lbs. (48 Nm). Install the accessory drive belt.
 e. Install the power steering protective shroud. Tighten the 2 retaining bolts to 7 ft. lbs. (10 Nm).

43. Connect the fuel lines to the fuel supply rail.

44. Connect the upper radiator and heater hoses. Connect the vacuum lines to their original locations.

45. Change the engine oil and filter. This is necessary because engine coolant is corrosive to all engine bearing material. Replacing the engine oil after removal of a coolant carrying component guards against later failure.

46. Install the air cleaner fresh air hose to the throttle body and air cleaner. Install the closure hose to the rocker arm cover.

47. Fill the cooling system.

48. Connect the negative battery cable.

49. Start the engine and check for leaks. Check the ignition timing.

Valve Lifters

REMOVAL AND INSTALLATION

2.0L and 2.5L Engines

1. Disconnect the negative battery cable.
2. Remove the cylinder head cover(s).
3. Remove the accessory drive belts, timing belt covers and timing belt.
4. Remove the camshafts.
5. Remove the hydraulic lifters. Identify each lifter as it is removed so it can be reinstalled in the same position. If the lifters are to be reused, store them upside down in a sealed container.
To install:
6. Apply clean engine oil to the lifters, then install them in their original positions.
7. Install the camshafts.
8. Install the timing belt and timing belt covers.
9. Install the accessory drive belts and adjust the tension.
10. Install the cylinder head cover(s) and connect the negative battery cable.

2.2L Engine

NOTE: The 2.2L engine is equipped with Hydraulic Lash Adjusters (HLA) located in the rocker arms and directly contacting the valve stem tips.

1. Disconnect the negative battery cable.
2. Remove the rocker arm and shaft assemblies.
3. Pull the HLA out of the rocker arm by hand. If removal is difficult, pliers may be used. Do not remove the HLA unless it is absolutely necessary; it may leak oil if the O-ring is damaged.
To install:
4. Pour clean engine oil into the rocker arm reservoir. Apply clean engine oil to the HLA.
5. Carefully install the HLA into the rocker arm, being careful not to damage the O-ring.
6. Install the rocker arm/shaft assemblies and remaining components in the reverse order of removal.

3.0L Engine

NOTE: Before replacing a lifter for noisy operation, make sure the noise is not caused by improper valve-to-rocker arm clearance, worn rocker arms or pushrods.

1. Disconnect the negative battery cable.
2. Drain the cooling system.
3. Remove the rocker arm covers, and the throttle body and intake manifold assembly.
4. Loosen each rocker arm fulcrum mounting bolt to allow the rocker arm to be lifted off the pushrod and rotated to one side.
5. Remove the pushrods, marking the location of each pushrod to ensure the proper replacement in the original position.
6. Remove the lifter(s), using a magnet. Mark the location of each lifter to ensure the proper replacement in the original position.

NOTE: If the lifters are stuck in the bores due to excessive varnish or gum deposits, it may be necessary to use a hydraulic lifter puller or a claw-type tool to aid in removal. Rotate the lifter back and forth to loosen it from the gum or varnish that may have formed on the lifter.

To install:
7. Lubricate each lifter and bore with heavy engine oil and install the lifters into the bore. Install each lifter in the bore from which it was re-

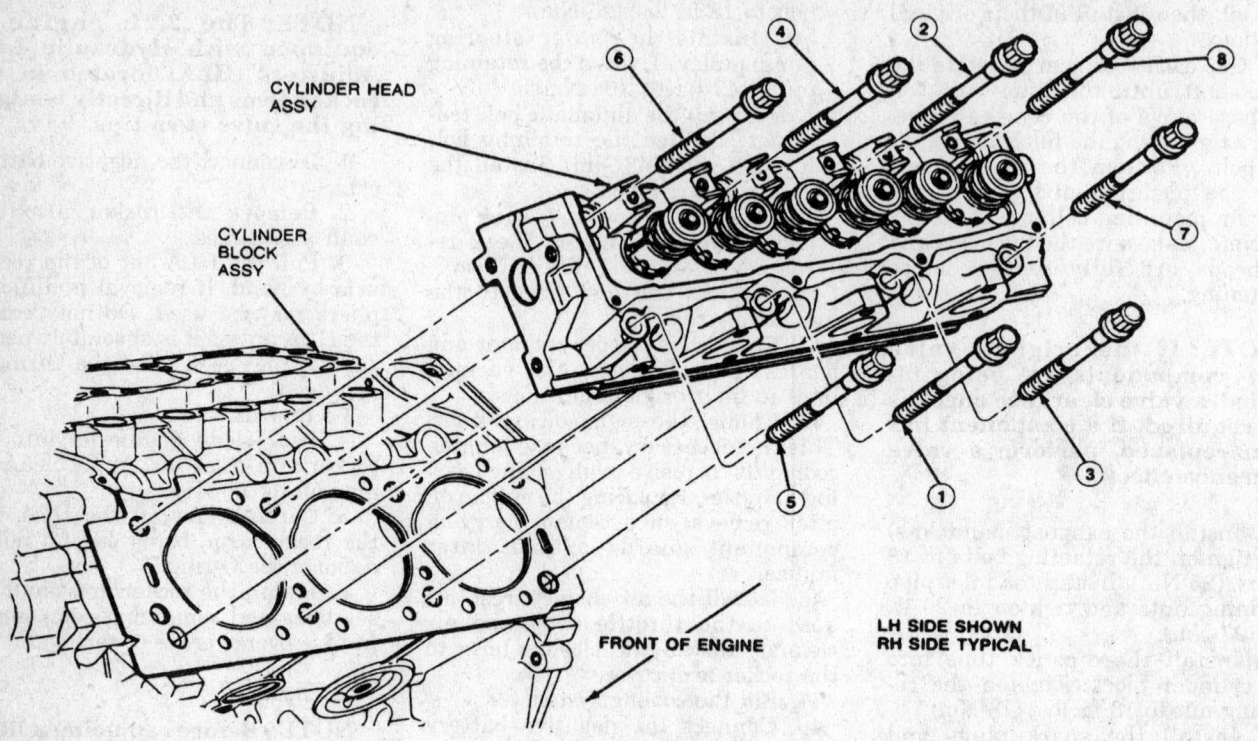

CYLINDER HEAD ASSY

CYLINDER BLOCK ASSY

FRONT OF ENGINE

LH SIDE SHOWN
RH SIDE TYPICAL

84709064

Cylinder head torque sequence — 3.0L engine

moved. If new lifters are being installed, check each one for free fit in the bore in which it is to be installed.

8. Lubricate each pushrod with the heavy engine oil and insert in their original position.

9. Place the rocker arms over the pushrods. For each rocker arm, rotate the crankshaft until the lifter rests on the base circle of the camshaft lobe, then position the fulcrums and tighten the mounting bolts to 24 ft. lbs. (32 Nm).

10. Lubricate all the rocker arm assemblies.

NOTE: Fulcrums must be fully seated in the cylinder head and the pushrods must be seated in the rocker arm sockets prior to tightening.

11. Install the throttle body and intake manifold and the rocker arm covers.

12. Connect the negative battery cable.

13. Refill the cooling system and check for leaks.

Valve Lash

CHECKING

2.0L and 2.5L Engines

The hydraulic lifters are not adjustable. When the lifters are removed from the engine, check the friction surfaces for wear or damage. Hold the lifter and try to press the plunger by hand. If the lifter is worn or damaged, or the plunger can be moved by hand, replace the lifter.

2.2L Engine

1. Warm the engine to normal operating temperature.

2. Check the condition of the engine oil and check the oil pressure. The oil pressure should be 21–36 psi at 1000 rpm.

3. Stop the engine and remove the rocker arm cover.

4. Push down on the hydraulic lash adjuster side of the rocker arm to make sure the hydraulic lash adjuster cannot be compressed.

5. If the hydraulic lash adjuster can be compressed, it must be replaced.

3.0L Engine

This clearance check is usually only needed when the valves, valve seats and/or cylinder head gasket surface have been machined or new parts have been installed. Clearance must be checked when the lifter is completely collapsed.

1. Disconnect the negative battery cable.

2. Remove the rocker arm covers.

3. Rotate the engine until the No. 1 cylinder is at TDC of its compression stroke and check the clearance between the rocker arm and the following valves: No. 1 intake and exhaust, No. 2 exhaust, No. 3 intake, No. 4 exhaust and No. 6 intake.

4. To check the clearance, use lifter bleed down wrench T71P–6513–B or equivalent, to push down on the rocker arm and bleed the oil from the lifter.

5. Insert the appropriate thickness feeler gauge between the rocker arm and valve stem to check the clearance.

6. Rotate the crankshaft 360 degrees and check the clearance between the rocker arm and the following valves: No. 2 intake, No. 3 exhaust, No. 4 intake, No. 5 intake and exhaust and No. 6 exhaust.

7. The clearance should be 0.09–0.19 in. (2.3–4.8mm).

8. If the clearance is less than specified, shorter pushrods are available to correct the problem. If the clearance is greater than specified, longer pushrods are available.

Rocker Arms/Shafts

REMOVAL AND INSTALLATION

2.2L Engine

1. Remove the rocker arm cover.
2. Remove the rocker arm and shaft assembly mounting bolts. Start at the ends and work toward the center of the shafts, when removing the bolts.
3. If necessary, separate the rocker arms and springs from the shafts; be sure to keep the parts in order for reinstallation purposes.
4. Clean and inspect the shafts and rocker arms for wear. Measure the difference between the rocker arm shaft outside diameter and the rocker arm inside diameter; this is the oil clearance. If the oil clearance exceeds 0.004 in. (0.10mm), replace the shaft and/or the rocker arm(s).

To install:

5. If they were disassembled, coat the rocker arm shafts and rocker arms with engine oil and assemble them with the springs. When assembling and installing on the cylinder head, note the notches at the ends of the shafts; they are different on the intake and exhaust side and cannot be interchanged.
6. Install the rocker arm/shaft assemblies onto the cylinder head and torque the rocker arm shaft-to-cylinder head bolts, in sequence, to 13–20 ft. lbs. (18–26 Nm), in 2 steps.
7. Install the rocker arm cover.

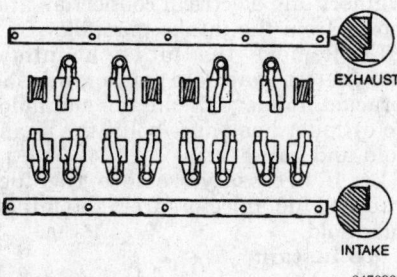

Exploded view of the rocker arm/shaft assemblies — 2.2L engine

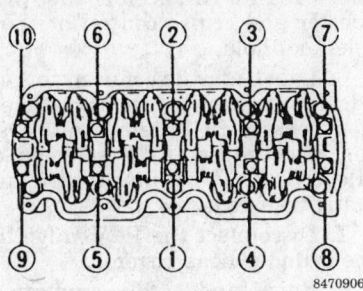

Rocker arm shaft bolt torque sequence — 2.2L engine

3.0L Engine

NOTE: The rocker arm covers on 1992 3.0L engines are equipped with integral (built-in) gaskets that should last the life of the vehicle. Be sure to adhere to the instructions given in the following procedure that pertain to 1992 vehicles. If the integral gaskets become damaged and cannot be reused, replacement gaskets are available.

1. Disconnect the negative battery cable.
2. Tag and disconnect the spark plug wires from the spark plugs. Remove the spark plug wire separator stand-offs from the rocker arm cover studs.
3. If the left side (front) rocker arm cover is being removed, proceed as follows:
   a. Remove the wiring harness from the rocker arm cover studs and position the harness aside.
   b. Disconnect the crankcase hose from the rocker arm cover.
4. If the right side (rear) rocker arm cover is being removed, proceed as follows:
   a. Remove the air intake throttle body assembly.
   b. Remove the PCV valve.
   c. Remove the wiring harness from the rocker arm cover studs and position the harness aside.
5. On 1992 vehicles, proceed as follows:
   a. Loosen the rocker arm cover retaining bolts enough to disengage them from the cylinder head. Do not remove the retaining bolts from the rocker arm cover as they are captive to the built in gasket.
   b. Using caution, slide a sharp, thin bladed knife between the cylinder head gasket surface and the rocker arm cover gasket at the 4 RTV junctions. Cut only the RTV sealer and avoid cutting the gasket.

   c. Carefully lift the cover from the cylinder head, making sure RTV sealer is not pulling the gasket from the cover.
6. Remove the rocker arm mounting bolts, fulcrums and rocker arms. Identify the position of the rocker arms and fulcrums so they may be reinstalled in their original positions.
7. Inspect the rocker arms, fulcrums and pushrods for wear and/or damage and replace as necessary.

To install:

8. If removed, dip each pushrod in heavy engine oil and install in it's original position. If not removed, lubricate the pushrod ends with heavy engine oil.
9. Dip each rocker arm and fulcrum in heavy engine oil and install in its original position. For each rocker arm, rotate the crankshaft until the lifter rests on the base circle of the camshaft lobe, before tightening the fulcrum mounting bolts to 24 ft. lbs. (32 Nm). Make sure the fulcrum is fully seated in the cylinder head and the pushrod is fully seated in the rocker arm socket before tightening.

NOTE: If the original valve train components are being installed, a valve clearance check is not required. If a component has been replaced, perform a valve clearance check.

10. Lightly oil all bolt and stud threads before installation. Using solvent, clean the cylinder head and rocker arm cover sealing surfaces. On 1992 vehicles, remove all silicone sealer and dirt; do not allow solvent to come in contact with the integral rocker arm gasket.
11. If the integral gasket is no longer usable on 1992 vehicles, it can be replaced as follows:
    a. Remove the gasket by pulling it from the rocker arm gasket channel. Note the bolt and stud locations before removing.
    b. Clean the gasket channel with a soft cloth to remove all dirt.
    c. Using a suitable solvent, clean off any remaining RTV sealer.
    d. Aligning the fastener holes, lay the new gasket onto the channel and install it with your finger.
    e. Install a gasket to each fastener by securing the fastener head with a nut driver or socket. Seat the fastener against the cover and, at the same time, roll the gasket around the fastener collar. If installed correctly, all fasteners will be secured by the gasket and will not fall out.
    f. Check the gasket for correct installation. A new gasket will lay

flat to the rocker arm cover in both the channel and the fastener areas. If the gasket is installed incorrectly, there will be oil leaks.

12. On 1992 vehicles, apply a bead of silicone sealer at the cylinder head-to-intake manifold rail step (2 places per rail). Carefully position the cover on the cylinder head and install the bolts and studs. Tighten to 9 ft. lbs. (12 Nm).

NOTE: When positioning the cover to the cylinder head, use a straight down approach to align the bolt holes. Once the cover contacts the RTV sealer, any adjustment for bolt alignment can roll the gasket from the channel, causing oil leaks.

13. If the left side (front) rocker arm cover is being installed, proceed as follows:

    a. Connect the wiring harness to the rocker arm cover studs.

    b. Connect the crankcase hose to the rocker arm cover.

14. If the right side (rear) rocker arm cover is being installed, proceed as follows:

    a. Connect the wiring harness to the rocker arm cover studs.

    b. Install the PCV valve and connect the hoses.

    c. Install the air intake throttle body assembly.

15. Connect the spark plug wires to the spark plugs. Install the spark plug wire separator stand-offs to the rocker arm cover studs.

16. Connect the negative battery cable. Start the engine and bring to normal operating temperature. Check for leaks.

Intake Manifold

REMOVAL AND INSTALLATION

2.0L Engine

1. Relieve the fuel system pressure and disconnect the negative battery cable. Drain the cooling system.

2. Disconnect the mass air flow sensor electrical connector. Remove the air ducts and air cleaner assembly.

3. Remove the fuel line mounting bracket and disconnect the throttle cable. Disconnect and plug the fuel lines.

4. Disconnect the coolant lines from the air bypass valve and throttle body.

5. Label and disconnect the vacuum lines at the throttle body, and the vacuum lines for the brake booster and cruise control at the intake manifold.

6. Label and disconnect the electrical connectors for the throttle position sensor, EGR temperature sensor, if equipped, EGR solenoid and idle switch, if equipped with automatic transaxle.

7. Disconnect the PCV valve from the cylinder head cover.

8. Raise and safely support the vehicle.

9. Remove the intake manifold support bracket and remove the EGR pipe from the intake manifold.

10. Lower the vehicle. Remove the 5 bolts and 2 nuts and remove the intake manifold.

To install:

11. Clean all gasket mating surfaces.

12. Install the intake manifold, using a new gasket. Tighten the nuts and bolts, in sequence, to 19 ft. lbs. (25 Nm).

13. Raise and safely support the vehicle.

14. Attach the EGR pipe to the manifold and install the intake manifold support bracket. Tighten the support bracket bolts to 38 ft. lbs. (51 Nm).

15. Lower the vehicle.

16. Connect the PCV valve to the cylinder head cover. Connect the electrical connectors, vacuum lines and coolant lines.

17. Connect the throttle cable and the fuel lines. Install the fuel line mounting bracket and tighten the bolt to 97 inch lbs. (11 Nm).

18. Install the air cleaner assembly and ducts. Connect the mass air flow sensor connector.

19. Connect the negative battery cable. Fill and bleed the cooling system. Run the engine and check for leaks.

TIGHTENING SEQUENCE

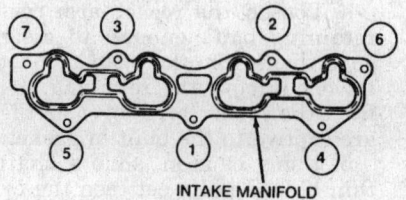

INTAKE MANIFOLD

84709069

Intake manifold bolt torque sequence — 2.0L engine

2.2L Engine

1. Properly relieve the fuel system pressure and disconnect the negative battery cable.

2. Drain the cooling system.

3. From the bottom of the intake manifold, remove the water hose.

4. Disconnect the accelerator cables from the throttle body.

5. Remove the air duct from the throttle body.

6. Label and disconnect the vacuum lines and coolant hoses from the throttle body.

7. Tag and disconnect the electrical connectors from the throttle position sensor, the idle switch and the bypass air control valve.

8. Remove the engine lifting bracket mounting bolts from the throttle body and the engine block.

9. Disconnect the coolant line/EGR hose bracket from the throttle body and the throttle cable brackets from the intake plenum.

10. Remove the wire loom bracket. On non-turbocharged engines, remove the EGR back-pressure variable transducer bracket from the right-hand side of the intake plenum. On turbocharged engines, remove the vacuum pipe mounting bolts from the right-hand side of the intake plenum.

11. Remove the PCV hose from the intake plenum. Remove the nuts and bolts retaining the vacuum line assembly bracket at the rear of the intake plenum.

12. Label and disconnect the vacuum lines from the intake plenum.

13. Remove the plenum-to-intake manifold nuts and bolts, the plenum and the gasket.

14. Disconnect the electrical connectors from the fuel injectors. Carefully, bend the wire harness retainer brackets away from the wire harness and move the harness assembly away from the intake manifold.

15. Disconnect the fuel pressure and return lines at the fuel rail.

16. Disconnect the EGR pipe from the intake manifold. Label and disconnect any electrical connectors and hoses from the intake manifold.

17. Remove the intake manifold bracket-to-manifold nuts and the bracket. Remove the intake manifold-to-cylinder head nuts/bolts, the manifold and gasket.

18. If necessary, remove the fuel rail and fuel injectors from the intake manifold.

To install:

19. Clean all gasket mating surfaces.

20. Using a new gasket, position the intake manifold on the cylinder

head studs and torque the nuts/bolts to 14–22 ft. lbs. (19–30 Nm).

21. Install the intake manifold bracket-to-manifold nuts and tighten to 14–22 ft. lbs. (19–30 Nm).

22. Connect the fuel lines to the fuel rail. Connect the electrical connectors to the fuel injectors.

23. Using a new gasket, install the intake plenum onto the intake manifold and torque the nuts/bolts to 14–19 ft. lbs. (19–25 Nm).

24. Connect the vacuum lines to the intake manifold. Install the retaining bolts and nuts on the vacuum line assembly bracket to the intake plenum.

25. Install the PCV hose to the intake plenum.

26. Install the wire loom bracket and the EGR variable transducer bracket or vacuum pipe bracket to the right side of the plenum.

27. Install the throttle cable bracket, engine lifting bracket mounting bolt and coolant line/EGR hose bracket to the intake plenum and throttle body.

28. Install the vacuum and coolant hoses to the throttle body.

29. Connect the throttle position sensor, idle switch and bypass air control valve connectors.

30. Install the air duct and the throttle cables to the throttle body.

31. Connect the EGR pipe and connect the water hose to the bottom of the intake manifold.

32. Connect the negative battery cable and fill the cooling system. Start the engine and check for leaks.

2.5L Engine

1. Relieve the fuel system pressure and disconnect the negative battery cable. Drain the cooling system.

2. Disconnect the vacuum hoses and electrical connectors from the air cleaner housing. Remove the air cleaner assembly.

3. Disconnect the knock sensor connector and remove the knock sensor bracket from the intake manifold. Remove the crankshaft position sensor bracket from the right side of the intake manifold.

4. Remove the right bank (rear) spark plug wires from the spark plugs and the routing clips. Remove the Variable Resource Induction System (VRIS) solenoid connector bracket from the rear of the intake manifold.

5. Label and disconnect the necessary vacuum hoses from the rear of the intake manifold and EGR valve. Disconnect the PCV valve hose from the intake manifold, near the throttle body.

6. Label and disconnect the throttle position sensor and fuel rail electrical connectors. Disconnect the throttle cable from the throttle body and the vacuum hose from the evaporative canister.

7. Disconnect and plug the fuel supply line at the fuel rails and discard the copper crush washers. Disconnect the fuel and vacuum lines from the fuel pressure regulator.

8. Disconnect the EGR breather tube. Remove the intake manifold mounting nuts and bolts in 2–3 steps, then remove the intake manifold.

To install:

9. Clean all gasket mating surfaces.

10. Position new gaskets and install the intake manifold. Tighten the nuts and bolts in 2–3 steps to 18 ft. lbs. (25 Nm).

11. Connect the EGR breather tube and connect the fuel and vacuum lines to the fuel pressure regulator.

12. Connect the fuel supply line to the fuel rail, using new copper crush washers.

13. Connect the vacuum hoses to the evaporative canister, intake manifold, throttle body and EGR valve.

14. Connect the throttle position sensor electrical connector. Install the VRIS solenoid connector bracket.

15. Connect the spark plug wires to the spark plugs and routing clips. Install the crankshaft position sensor bracket.

16. Install the knock sensor bracket and connect the knock sensor electrical connector.

17. Install the air cleaner assembly and connect the vacuum hoses and electrical connectors to the air cleaner housing.

18. Connect the negative battery cable. Fill and bleed the cooling system. Run the engine and check for leaks.

3.0L Engine

1. Properly relieve the fuel system pressure and disconnect the negative battery cable.

2. Drain the cooling system.

3. Remove the air cleaner hoses from the throttle body and rocker cover.

4. Disconnect the fuel lines from the fuel supply manifold. Cover the fuel line ends with clean shop rags to prevent dirt from entering.

5. Tag and disconnect the vacuum lines and electrical connectors from the throttle body.

6. Remove the plastic shield and the EGR supply tube from the throttle body.

7. Disconnect the throttle cable and, if equipped with automatic transaxle, the throttle valve control cable from the throttle lever.

8. Remove the fuel rail bracket bolt and the 6 throttle body mounting bolts. Remove the throttle body.

9. Disconnect the fuel injector harness stand-offs from the injector inboard rocker cover studs and each injector and remove from the engine.

10. Remove the brace from the fuel supply manifold and throttle body. Remove the fuel supply manifold and fuel injectors.

NOTE: The intake manifold assembly can be removed with the fuel supply manifold and fuel injectors in place.

11. Disconnect the upper radiator hose from the thermostat housing and disconnect the heater hoses.

12. Disconnect the engine coolant temperature sensor and coolant temperature sending unit connectors.

13. Tag and disconnect the spark plug wires from the spark plugs.

14. Remove the distributor cap. Mark the position of the rotor and the distributor in the engine and remove the distributor.

15. Remove the ignition coil and bracket assembly from the left side (front) cylinder head and set aside.

16. Remove the rocker arm covers.

17. Loosen the retaining bolt from the No. 3 intake valve and rotate the rocker arm fulcrum away from the valve retainer. Remove the pushrod.

18. Remove the intake manifold retaining bolts. Before attempting to remove the manifold, break the seal between the manifold and cylinder block. Place a suitable prybar between the manifold, near the thermostat, and the transaxle. Carefully pry upward to loosen the manifold.

19. Lift the intake manifold away from the engine. Place shop rags in the lifter valley to catch any dirt or gasket material. Clean all gasket mating surfaces. Be careful when scraping aluminum to prevent gouging, which may cause leak paths.

To install:

20. Lightly oil all attaching bolt and stud threads. Apply silicone sealer to the intersection of the cylinder block and cylinder head assembly at the 4 corners of the lifter valley.

21. Install the front and rear intake manifold seals. Install the intake manifold gaskets onto the cylinder

heads and insert the locking tabs on the cylinder head gaskets.

NOTE: Make sure the side of the gasket marked TO INTAKE MANIFOLD is facing away from the cylinder head.

22. Carefully lower the intake manifold into position to prevent disturbing the silicone sealer. Install bolts No. 1, 2, 3 and 4 and snug. Install the remaining bolts and tighten, in sequence, to 11 ft. lbs. (15 Nm). Then tighten, in sequence, to 21 ft. lbs. (28 Nm).

23. Install the thermostat and housing, if removed, using a new gasket. Tighten the mounting bolts to 9 ft. lbs. (12 Nm).

24. If removed, lubricate and install new O-rings on the fuel injectors and install the fuel injectors in the fuel rail, using a light twisting-pushing motion. Install the fuel rail and injectors into the intake manifold, pushing down to seat the O-rings. While holding the fuel rail assembly in place, install the 4 retaining bolts and tighten to 7 ft. lbs. (10 Nm).

25. Install the distributor assembly, aligning the housing and rotor with the marks that were made during the removal procedure.

26. Install the No. 3 cylinder intake valve pushrod. Apply oil to the pushrod and fulcrum prior to installation. Rotate the crankshaft to place the lifter on the base circle of the camshaft and tighten the rocker arm bolt to 24 ft. lbs. (32 Nm).

27. Install the rocker arm covers and connect the fuel injector electrical harness.

28. Position a new gasket and the throttle body on the intake manifold. Install the mounting bolts and tighten to 15–22 ft. lbs. (20–30 Nm).

29. Install the fuel rail bracket bolt on the throttle body and connect the throttle cable and, if equipped, the throttle valve control cable to the throttle lever.

30. Install the MAP sensor and the EGR tube to the throttle body.

31. Connect the vacuum hoses and the electrical connectors in their original positions on the throttle body. Install the plastic shield on the throttle body.

32. Install the fuel supply manifold brace. Tighten the retaining bolts to 7 ft. lbs. (10 Nm).

33. Connect the PCV hose at the PCV valve. Connect all remaining vacuum hoses.

34. Install the EGR tube and nut, if equipped. Tighten the nuts on both ends to 37 ft. lbs. (50 Nm).

35. Connect the fuel lines to the fuel rail.

36. Install the distributor cap and connect the spark plug wires to the spark plugs. Install the wiring stand-offs to the rocker arm cover studs.

37. Install the ignition coil and bracket assembly. Tighten the mounting bolts to 35 ft. lbs. (48 Nm).

38. Connect the engine coolant temperature sensor and coolant temperature sending unit connectors.

39. Install the upper radiator and heater hoses. Fill the cooling system.

40. Change the engine oil and filter. This is necessary because engine coolant is corrosive to all engine bearing material. Replacing the engine oil after removal of a coolant carrying component guards against later failure.

41. Install the air cleaner hoses to the throttle body and rocker cover.

42. Connect the negative battery cable. Start the engine and check for coolant, oil, fuel and vacuum leaks. Check the ignition timing.

Exhaust Manifold

REMOVAL AND INSTALLATION

2.0L Engine

1. Disconnect the negative battery cable.

2. Remove the 7 exhaust manifold heatshield bolts and the heatshield.

3. Disconnect the oxygen sensor electrical connector.

4. Raise and safely support the vehicle.

5. Remove and discard the exhaust pipe-to-exhaust manifold nuts. Suspend the exhaust system with wire.

6. Disconnect the EGR pipe from the exhaust manifold and lower the vehicle.

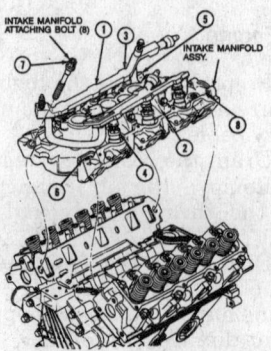

84709070

Intake manifold torque
sequence — 3.0L engine

7. Remove the 2 nuts and 8 bolts and remove the exhaust manifold. Discard the nuts.

To install:

8. Clean all gasket mating surfaces.

9. Position a new exhaust manifold gasket over the studs and install the exhaust manifold. Tighten the 8 mounting bolts to 17 ft. lbs. (23 Nm).

10. Install 2 new manifold mount nuts and tighten to 21 ft. lbs. (28 Nm). Raise and safely support the vehicle.

11. Connect the exhaust pipe to the manifold. Install new nuts and tighten to 38 ft. lbs. (52 Nm). Connect the oxygen sensor connector.

12. Connect the EGR pipe to the back of the exhaust manifold and tighten to 34 ft. lbs. (47 Nm). Lower the vehicle.

13. Install the heatshield and tighten the bolts to 88 inch lbs. (10 Nm). Connect the negative battery cable.

2.2L Engine

1. Disconnect the negative battery cable and the oxygen sensor connector.

2. Remove the turbocharger assembly, if equipped.

3. Remove the oxygen sensor from the exhaust manifold on non-turbocharged vehicles.

4. Disconnect the exhaust pipe from the exhaust manifold and remove the outer heatshield.

5. Remove the exhaust manifold-to-cylinder head bolts and the exhaust manifold, inner heatshield and gaskets.

6. Clean the mating surfaces on the exhaust manifold and the cylinder head.

To install:

7. Position the inner heatshield on the studs.

8. Install the exhaust manifold gaskets with the raised edge of the gasket facing the exhaust manifold.

9. Install the exhaust manifold and tighten the bolts to 16–21 ft. lbs. (22–28 Nm).

10. Install the outer heatshield and tighten the bolts to 14–22 ft. lbs. (19–30 Nm).

11. Install the exhaust gas oxygen sensor on non-turbocharged vehicles.

12. Install the turbocharger assembly, if equipped.

13. Connect the exhaust pipe to the exhaust manifold, using a new gasket. Tighten the bolts to 26–36 ft. lbs. (34–49 Nm).

14. Connect the exhaust gas oxygen sensor wire and connect the negative battery cable.

2.5L Engine

1. Disconnect the negative battery cable. Raise and safely support the vehicle.

2. Disconnect the oxygen sensor connectors.

3. Remove the nuts from the front and rear exhaust pipes and lower the exhaust system. Both pipes must be disconnected, even if only one manifold is to be removed.

4. If removing the rear (right side) manifold, disconnect the EGR pipe.

5. Remove the 3 heatshield bolts and remove the heatshield.

6. Remove the 2 nuts and 5 bolts and remove the exhaust manifold.

To install:

7. Clean all gasket mating surfaces.

8. Install the exhaust manifold, using a new gasket, and tighten the nuts and bolts to 18 ft. lbs. (25 Nm).

9. Install the heatshield and tighten the bolts to 88 inch lbs. (10 Nm).

10. If installing the rear (right side) manifold, connect the EGR pipe.

11. Connect the exhaust pipes to the manifolds, using new gaskets and nuts, and tighten the nuts to 38 ft. lbs. (52 Nm).

12. Connect the oxygen sensor connectors and the negative battery cable.

3.0L Engine

LEFT SIDE (FRONT) MANIFOLD

1. Remove the oil dipstick tube, support bracket and heatshield retaining nuts. Carefully rotate the tube away from the manifold stud.

2. Raise and safely support the vehicle.

3. Remove the exhaust manifold-to-front exhaust pipe attaching nuts.

4. Lower the vehicle and remove the exhaust manifold attaching bolts and the manifold.

To install:

5. Clean all gasket mating surfaces. Lightly oil the bolt and stud threads.

6. Install the exhaust manifold on the cylinder head with the attaching bolts. Tighten the bolts to 18 ft. lbs. (25 Nm).

7. Raise and safely support the vehicle.

8. Connect the exhaust pipe to the manifold and tighten the attaching nuts to 20 ft. lbs. (27 Nm). Lower the vehicle.

9. Rotate the oil dipstick tube and bracket into position over the manifold stud. Install the heatshield and retaining nuts. Tighten the nuts to 13 ft. lbs. (18 Nm).

RIGHT SIDE (REAR) MANIFOLD

1. Raise and safely support the vehicle.

2. Remove the EGR supply tube from the exhaust manifold, if equipped. Use a backup wrench on the lower fitting adapter.

3. Remove the heatshield retaining nuts and the manifold-to-exhaust pipe retaining nuts.

4. Remove the exhaust manifold retaining bolts and the manifold.

To install:

5. Clean all gasket mating surfaces. Lightly oil the bolt and stud threads.

6. Install the exhaust manifold on the cylinder head with the attaching bolts. Tighten the bolts to 15–22 ft. lbs. (20–30 Nm).

7. Connect the exhaust pipe to the manifold. Tighten the attaching nuts to 20 ft. lbs. (27 Nm).

8. Install the spark plug heatshield and retaining nuts. Tighten the nuts to 12–15 ft. lbs. (16–20 Nm).

9. Connect the EGR supply tube to the exhaust manifold. Tighten to 37 ft. lbs. (50 Nm). Lower the vehicle.

Turbocharger

REMOVAL AND INSTALLATION

Before starting the following procedure, clean the area around the turbocharger assembly with a non-caustic solution. After the turbocharger is removed, cover the openings to prevent the entry of foreign material while it is off the engine.

During removal, be careful not to bend, nick, or in any way damage the compressor wheel blades. Damage may result in rotating assembly imbalance, and bearing and oil seal failure. Any time a turbocharger assembly has been removed, gently spin the turbine wheel before reassembly to ensure the rotating assembly does not bind.

Any time an engine bearing (main bearing, connecting rod bearing, camshaft bearing) has been damaged in a turbocharged engine, the oil and filter should be changed and the turbocharger flushed with clean engine oil to reduce the possibility of contamination.

1. Disconnect the negative battery cable.

2. Drain the cooling system.

3. Remove the air inlet and outlet hoses from the turbocharger assembly.

4. Remove the heatshields from the exhaust manifold and turbocharger.

5. Disconnect the oxygen sensor electrical connector and place the wire over the front of the vehicle, away from the heatshield.

6. From the top of the turbocharger, remove the oil feed line. From the lower portion of the turbocharger, remove oil return line and gasket.

7. Disconnect the coolant inlet and outlet hoses from the turbocharger.

8. Remove the EGR tube from the exhaust manifold. Disconnect the turbo boost control solenoid valve electrical connector.

9. Remove the air tube from the turbo boost control solenoid valve at the turbocharger outlet air hose.

10. From under the turbocharger, remove the retaining bracket-to-turbocharger bolt.

11. Properly discharge the air conditioning system and remove the refrigerant line from the head of the compressor.

12. Remove the oxygen sensor from the turbocharger.

13. Disconnect the converter inlet pipe from the turbocharger joint pipe. Remove the exhaust manifold-to-cylinder head bolts, the exhaust manifold/turbocharger assembly and the gasket from the vehicle.

14. Remove the exhaust manifold-to-turbocharger nuts, the manifold and the gasket from the turbocharger. Remove the joint pipe-to-turbocharger nuts, the pipe, heatshield and the gasket from the turbocharger.

15. Clean the gasket mounting surfaces.

To install:

16. Using a new gasket, install the joint pipe and heatshield assembly on the turbocharger and torque the nuts to 27–46 ft. lbs (37–63 Nm).

17. Using a new gasket, install the exhaust manifold on the turbocharger and torque the nuts to 20–29 ft. lbs. (27–39 Nm).

18. Using a new gasket, position the exhaust manifold/turbocharger assembly onto the cylinder head and torque the nuts to 16–21 ft. lbs. (22–28 Nm).

19. Using a new gasket, install the converter inlet pipe to the joint pipe and torque the nuts to 26–36 ft. lbs. (34–49 Nm).

20. Install the mounting bolt to the retaining bracket under the turbocharger assembly.

21. Install the oil return line and coolant outlet hose to the turbocharger assembly.

22. Install the air tube to the turbocharger outlet air hose.

23. Connect the turbo boost control solenoid valve electrical connector.

24. Install the oxygen sensor. To ease the remaining installation procedure, leave the wiring assembly aside of the heatshield assembly.

25. Install the EGR tube onto the exhaust manifold and install the coolant inlet hose onto the turbocharger assembly.

26. Pour 0.85 oz. (25ml) of engine oil in the oil inlet fitting, then install the oil feed line onto the turbocharger assembly.

27. Install the heatshields onto the exhaust manifold and turbocharger assembly.

28. Install the inlet and outlet hoses on the turbocharger compressor housing.

29. Connect the oxygen sensor electrical connector and install the wiring assembly.

30. Connect the refrigerant line to the compressor.

31. Fill the cooling system and connect the negative battery cable.

32. After replacing the turbocharger, perform the following:

 a. Disconnect the electrical connector from the ignition coil.

 b. Crank the engine for approximately 20 seconds.

 c. Reconnect the electrical connector to the ignition coil.

 d. Start the engine and operate it at idle for approximately 30 seconds.

 e. Stop the engine, disconnect the negative battery cable and depress the brake pedal for at least 5 seconds to cancel the malfunction code.

 f. Reconnect the negative battery cable.

33. Start the engine, allow it to reach normal operating temperatures and check for leaks and engine operation. Recharge the air conditioning system.

Timing Chain Front Cover

REMOVAL AND INSTALLATION

3.0L Engine

1. Disconnect the negative battery cable.

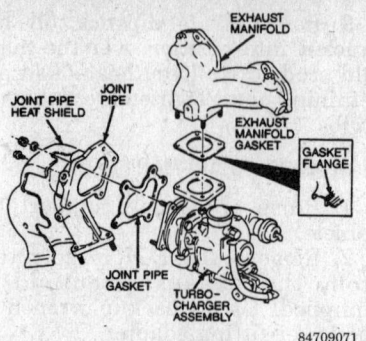

84709071

Turbocharger/exhaust manifold assembly — 2.2L engine

2. Drain the cooling system.

3. Remove the 2 retaining bolts and remove the power steering protective shroud.

4. Using a suitable tool on the idler pulley tensioner, release the tension on the accessory drive belt and remove the belt. Remove the belt tensioner.

5. Raise and safely support the vehicle.

6. Remove the right front wheel and tire assembly and the plastic inner fender shield. Using a suitable tool, turn the water pump idler pulley tensioner clockwise to release the tension on the water pump belt. Remove the belt.

7. Lower the vehicle and support the engine with a floor jack.

8. If equipped with manual transaxle, remove the right engine mount from the water pump bracket.

9. Remove the 3 nuts that attach the right upper engine mount to the timing cover. Lower the floor jack carefully, allowing the engine to rest on the remaining mounts.

10. Raise and safely support the vehicle.

11. Remove the crankshaft damper bolt and flat washer. Using a suitable puller, remove the damper from the crankshaft.

12. Remove the 3 nuts and 1 bolt that attach the right side of the subframe to the body. Pull the subframe down slightly to remove the damper from the vehicle.

13. Disconnect the water pump-to-front cover hose from the water pump connection.

NOTE: The timing cover may be removed with the water pump hose attached.

14. Drain the engine oil and remove the oil pan. Discard the oil pan gasket.

15. Remove the 4 lowest timing cover retaining bolts and lower the vehicle.

16. Support the bottom of the engine using care to prevent damage to the crankshaft and oil pump assembly. Remove the 3 nuts and 1 bolt attaching the upper engine mount to the top of the front cover.

17. Remove the 6 remaining timing cover mounting bolts. Pry the timing cover away from the cylinder block. Carefully pull the cover over the end of the crankshaft and lower it through the bottom of the engine compartment.

To install:

18. Clean all gasket material and old silicone sealer from all gasket mating surfaces. Pry the old crankshaft seal from the timing cover.

19. Lubricate the lip of a new crankshaft seal and install in the timing cover, using a seal installation tool.

20. Install a new timing cover gasket over the cylinder block dowels and install the timing cover. Install the 6 upper mounting bolts, fingertight. Apply pipe sealant to bolt No. 5 prior to installation.

21. Raise and safely support the vehicle.

22. Install the 4 lower mounting bolts, finger-tight. Apply pipe sealant to bolt No. 2 prior to installation.

23. Tighten the timing cover bolts, in sequence, to 18 ft. lbs. (25 Nm).

24. Lower the vehicle and install the upper engine mount.

25. Raise and safely support the vehicle.

26. Install the oil pan with a new gasket. Tighten the mounting bolts to 9 ft. lbs. (12 Nm).

27. Coat the crankshaft damper sealing surface with clean engine oil. Install the damper, using a suitable tool. Install the damper bolt and flat washer and tighten to 92–122 ft. lbs. (125–165 Nm).

28. Lower the vehicle. Using a suitable floor jack, raise the engine and install the right engine mount nuts. Tighten the nuts to 55–76 ft. lbs. (74–103 Nm).

29. Install the subframe nuts and bolt. Tighten the bolt to 27–40 ft. lbs. (36–54 Nm) and the nuts to 69–97 ft. lbs. (93–132 Nm).

30. Lower the engine and remove the floor jack. If equipped with manual transaxle, install the mount to the water pump bracket.

31. Raise and safely support the vehicle. Install the water pump belt, plastic shield and the right front wheel and tire assembly.

32. Connect the hose from the timing cover to the water pump.

33. Lower the vehicle.

34. Install the accessory drive belt.

35. Install the power steering protective shroud. Tighten the retaining bolts to 7 ft. lbs. (10 Nm).

36. Fill the crankcase with the proper type and quantity of engine oil. Fill the cooling system.

37. Connect the negative battery cable, start the engine and check for leaks.

Front Cover Oil Seal

REPLACEMENT

3.0L Engine

1. Remove the plastic belt shield from the power steering pump. Using a ½ inch drive breaker bar on the idler pulley tensioner, release the tension on the accessory drive belt and remove the belt.

2. Raise and safely support the vehicle.

3. Remove the right front wheel and tire assembly and the plastic inner fender shield.

4. Using a wrench, turn the water pump idler pulley tensioner clockwise to release tension on the water pump belt. Remove the belt.

5. Lower the vehicle and support the engine with a floor jack.

6. If equipped with manual transaxle, remove the right engine mount from the water pump bracket.

7. Remove the 3 nuts that attach the right upper engine mount to the timing cover. Lower the floor jack carefully, allowing the engine to rest on the remaining mounts.

8. Raise and safely support the vehicle.

9. Remove the crankshaft damper bolt and flat washer. Using a suitable puller, remove the damper from the crankshaft.

10. Remove the 3 nuts and 1 bolt that attach the right side of the subframe to the body. Pull the subframe

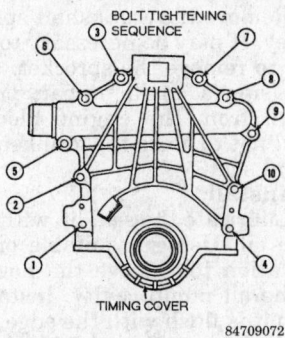

BOLT TIGHTENING SEQUENCE

TIMING COVER

84709072

Timing chain front cover bolt torque sequence — 3.0L engine

down slightly to remove the damper from the vehicle.

11. Remove the front cover oil seal using a small prybar.

To install:

12. Inspect the timing cover and shaft seal surface of the crankshaft damper for damage, nicks, burrs or other roughness which may cause the new seal to fail. Service or replace components, as necessary.

13. Lubricate the seal lip with clean engine oil and install the seal in the timing cover, using a suitable installation tool.

14. Coat the crankshaft damper sealing surface with clean engine oil. Install the damper, using a suitable tool. Install the damper bolt and flat washer and tighten to 92–122 ft. lbs. (125–165 Nm).

15. Lower the vehicle. Using a suitable floor jack, raise the engine and install the right engine mount nuts. Tighten the nuts to 55–76 ft. lbs. (74–103 Nm).

16. Install the subframe nuts and bolt. Tighten the bolt to 27–40 ft. lbs. (36–54 Nm) and the nuts to 69–97 ft. lbs. (93–132 Nm).

17. Lower the engine and remove the floor jack. If equipped with manual transaxle, install the mount to the water pump bracket.

18. Raise and safely support the vehicle. Install the water pump belt, plastic shield and the right front wheel and tire assembly.

19. Lower the vehicle.

20. Install the accessory drive belt and the power steering pulley shield.

Timing Chain and Sprockets

REMOVAL AND INSTALLATION

3.0L Engine

1. Disconnect the negative battery cable. Drain the cooling system and crankcase.

2. Remove the crankshaft pulley and damper. Remove the timing cover.

3. Rotate the crankshaft until the No.1 piston is at Top Dead Center (TDC) and the timing marks are aligned.

4. Remove the camshaft sprocket retaining bolt and washer.

5. Slide the sprockets and the chain forward and remove as an assembly.

6. Clean and inspect all the parts prior to installation.

To install:

7. Slide the sprockets and the chain on as an assembly with the timing marks aligned.

8. Install the camshaft retaining bolt and washer. Tighten the retaining bolt to 41–51 ft. lbs. (55–70 Nm) and lubricate the chain and sprockets with engine oil.

NOTE: The camshaft retaining bolt has a drilled passage for timing chain lubrication. If damaged, do not replace with a standard bolt. Clean the oil passage with solvent prior to installation.

9. Position the timing cover gasket onto the cylinder block alignment dowels.

10. Install the timing cover onto the cylinder block, being careful not to damage the seal.

11. Install the oil pan using a new gasket.

12. Install the crankshaft damper and pulley.

13. Refill the crankcase and the cooling system. Connect the negative battery cable.

14. Start the engine and check for any leaks. Recheck the timing.

Timing Belt Front Cover

REMOVAL AND INSTALLATION

2.0L Engine

1. Disconnect the negative battery cable.

2. Remove the power steering hose brackets from the cylinder head cover. Label and disconnect the spark plug wires and wire clips.

3. Disconnect the breather tube and PCV valve from the cylinder head cover. Remove the bolts, in 2 steps, in the reverse order of the torque sequence. Remove the cylinder head cover.

4. Remove the power steering belt shield. Loosen the power steering adjusting bolt, lock bolt and through bolt and remove the power steering belt.

5. Loosen the alternator adjusting bolt and upper mounting bolt. Remove the alternator belt.

6. Support the engine with engine support tool 014–00750 or equivalent. Raise the engine slightly with a jack and remove the right side engine mount.

7. Remove the timing belt upper cover. Raise and safely support the vehicle.

8. Remove the splash shields. Using holder tool T92C–6316–AH or

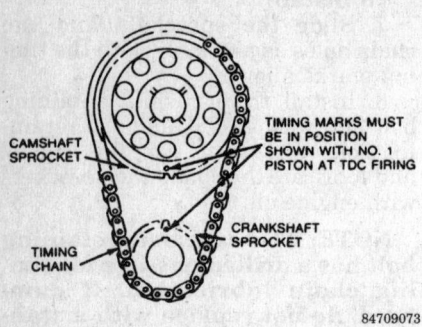

CAMSHAFT SPROCKET

TIMING MARKS MUST BE IN POSITION SHOWN WITH NO. 1 PISTON AT TDC FIRING

CRANKSHAFT SPROCKET

TIMING CHAIN

84709073

Timing mark alignment — 3.0L engine

equivalent, hold the crankshaft pulley and remove the pulley bolt. Use a suitable puller to remove the pulley, then remove the guide plate.

9. Remove the timing belt lower cover.

To install:

10. Install the timing belt lower cover and tighten the bolts to 88 inch lbs. (10 Nm).

11. Install the guide plate, crankshaft pulley and pulley bolt. Hold the pulley with the holder tool and tighten the bolt to 123 ft. lbs. (167 Nm).

12. Install the splash shields and lower the vehicle.

13. Raise the engine slightly with the jack and install the right side engine mount. Tighten the mount through bolt to 86 ft. lbs. (116 Nm) and the mount attaching nuts to 75 ft. lbs. (103 Nm). Remove the engine support tool.

14. Install the upper timing belt cover and tighten the bolts to 88 inch lbs. (10 Nm).

15. Apply silicone sealant to the cylinder surface in the area adjacent to the front camshaft bearing caps. Apply sealant to a new gasket and install it on the cylinder head cover.

16. Install the cylinder head cover and tighten the bolts in 2 steps, in sequence, to 69 inch lbs. (7 Nm).

17. Install the power steering hose brackets and tighten the bolts to 88 inch lbs. (10 Nm). Connect the spark plug wires and wire clips. Connect the breather tube and PCV valve.

18. Install the alternator belt and adjust the tension. Tighten the upper mounting bolt to 18 ft. lbs. (25 Nm) and the lower through bolt to 38 ft. lbs. (52 Nm).

19. Install the power steering belt and adjust the tension. Tighten the through bolt to 45 ft. lbs. (61 Nm) and the lock bolt to 34 ft. lbs. (46 Nm). Install the power steering belt shield and tighten the bolts to 86 inch lbs. (9 Nm).

20. Connect the negative battery cable.

2.2L Engine

1. Disconnect the negative battery cable.

2. Loosen the air conditioning compressor and alternator adjusting and pivot bolts, rotate the compressor and alternator toward the engine and remove the drive belts.

3. Raise and safely support the vehicle.

4. Remove the right front wheel and tire assembly and the right inner fender panel. Remove the 6 bolts, the crankshaft pulley and baffle plate.

5. Lower the vehicle.

6. Support the engine with a floor jack. Remove the 2 nuts and dowels from the right engine mount and remove the mount.

7. Remove the 7 bolts that retain the timing belt covers and remove the covers.

To install:

8. Install the lower cover gasket and the lower cover. Tighten the bolts to 61–87 inch lbs. (7–10 Nm).

9. Install the upper cover gasket and the upper cover. Tighten the bolts to 61–87 inch lbs. (7–10 Nm).

10. Position the engine mount on the engine and install the 2 nuts and dowels. Remove the floor jack.

11. Install the crankshaft sprocket baffle with the curved outer lip facing outward. Install the crankshaft pulley with the deep recess facing out and install the 6 bolts. Tighten the bolts to 109–152 inch lbs. (12–17 Nm).

12. Install the drive belts. Adjust the belt tension and tighten the adjusting and pivot bolts.

13. Install the right inner fender panel and wheel and tire assembly. Connect the negative battery cable.

2.5L Engine

1. Disconnect the negative battery cable.

2. Label and disconnect the electrical connectors from the coolant elbow. Label and disconnect the electrical connectors from the knock sensor and crankshaft position sensor.

3. Loosen the drive belt tensioner locknuts and adjusting bolts. Remove the accessory drive belts.

4. Raise and safely support the vehicle. Remove the lower bolt from the A/C and alternator tensioner bracket.

5. Hold the crankshaft damper with holder tool T92C–6316–AH or equivalent, and remove the damper bolt. Remove the crankshaft damper.

6. Remove the timing belt cover lower bolts. Lower the vehicle.

7. Remove the A/C and alternator belt tensioner. Remove the engine oil dipstick tube.

8. Hold the water pump pulley with holder tool T92C–6312–AH or equivalent, remove the 4 bolts and the water pump pulley.

9. Remove the upper timing cover bolts and remove the timing covers.

To install:

10. Install the timing covers with the upper bolts. Tighten to 88 inch lbs. (10 Nm).

11. Install the water pump pulley and bolts. Hold the pulley with the holder tool and tighten the bolts to 88 inch lbs. (10 Nm).

12. Install the dipstick tube and the A/C and alternator belt tensioner. Raise and safely support the vehicle.

13. Install the timing belt cover lower bolts and tighten to 88 inch lbs. (10 Nm).

14. Install the crankshaft damper with the bolt. Hold the damper with the holder tool and tighten to 122 ft. lbs. (166 Nm).

15. Install the lower bolt into the A/C and alternator tensioner bracket and lower the vehicle.

16. Install the accessory drive belts and adjust the tension. Connect the electrical connectors and the negative battery cable.

OIL SEAL REPLACEMENT

1. Disconnect the negative battery cable. Remove the timing belt.

2. On 2.2L engine, proceed as follows:

   a. If equipped with manual transaxle, place the shift lever in **4TH** gear and apply the parking brake.

   b. If equipped with automatic transaxle, remove the lower flywheel cover and lock the flywheel with a suitable tool.

   c. Remove the crankshaft sprocket-to-crankshaft bolt.

3. Remove the crankshaft sprocket and key. It may be necessary to use a puller to remove the sprocket.

4. Using a small prybar, pry the oil seal from the engine block; be careful not to score the crankshaft or the seal seat.

To install:

5. Lubricate the seal lip with clean engine oil. Using a suitable oil seal installation tool, drive the new seal into the oil pump cavity. Install the seal so it is flush with the edge of the pump body on 2.0L and 2.2L engines. On 2.5L engine, install the seal so it protrudes 0.03 in. (0.7mm).

6. Install the crankshaft key and sprocket.

7. On 2.2L engine, torque the crankshaft sprocket-to-crankshaft bolt to 108–116 ft. lbs. (147–157 Nm). If necessary, remove the flywheel locking tool.

8. Install the timing belt and connect the negative battery cable.

Timing Belt and Tensioner

REMOVAL AND INSTALLATION

2.0L Engine

1. Remove the timing belt covers. Temporarily reinstall the crankshaft pulley bolt.

2. Turn the crankshaft until the timing mark on the crankshaft sprocket aligns with the timing mark on the oil pump and the camshaft sprocket timing marks, **E** and **I**, line up on the camshaft sprockets.

3. Lower the vehicle. Insert camshaft sprocket holding tool T92C–6256–AH or equivalent, between the camshaft sprockets.

4. Turn the timing belt tensioner with an Allen wrench and remove the tensioner spring from the hook pin.

5. If the timing belt is to be reused, mark the direction of rotation on the timing belt. Remove the timing belt.

To install:

6. Make sure the timing marks on the camshaft and crankshaft sprockets are still aligned.

7. Install the timing belt. If reusing the original timing belt, make sure it is installed in the same direction of rotation.

8. Turn the tensioner clockwise with an Allen wrench and install the tensioner spring. Remove the holding tool from between the camshaft sprockets.

9. Rotate the crankshaft 2 turns in the normal direction of rotation and align the timing marks. Make sure all marks are still correctly aligned.

10. Raise and safely support the vehicle. Remove the crankshaft pulley bolt and install the timing belt covers.

2.2L Engine

1. Bring the No. 1 cylinder piston to Top Dead Center (TDC) on the compression stroke. The notch on the crankshaft damper should align with the TDC mark on the front cover.

2. Disconnect the negative battery cable.

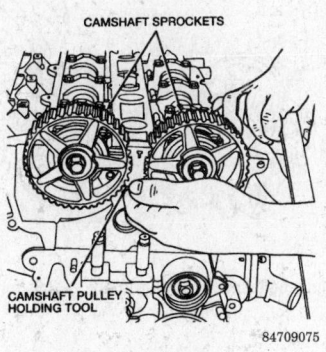

Timing belt sprocket alignment — 2.0L engine

84709074

Installing the camshaft sprocket holding tool — 2.0L engine

84709075

3. Remove the drive belts, crankshaft pulley and the timing belt covers.

4. Remove the timing belt tensioner spring and retaining bolt. Remove the idler pulley retaining bolt.

5. If the timing belt is to be reused, mark the direction of rotation so it can be reinstalled in the same direction.

6. Remove the timing belt.

To install:

7. Align the camshaft and crankshaft sprockets with the marks on the cylinder head front housing and the oil pump housing.

8. Install the timing belt. If reusing the old belt, observe the direction of rotation mark made during the removal procedure.

9. Place the timing belt tensioner and spring in position. Temporarily secure the tensioner with the spring fully extended. Make sure the timing belt is installed so there is no looseness at the water pump pulley at the idler side.

10. Loosen the idler bolt. Turn the crankshaft twice in the direction of rotation; align the timing marks.

NOTE: Always turn the crankshaft in the correct direction of rotation only. If the crankshaft is turned in the opposite direction, the timing belt may lose tension and correct belt timing may be lost.

11. Check to see that the timing marks are correctly aligned. If they are not aligned, remove the timing belt and align the timing marks, then repeat Steps 8–11.

12. Tighten the tensioner bolt to 27–38 ft. lbs. (37–52 Nm).

13. Measure the belt deflection between the crankshaft and camshaft pulleys. The correct deflection should be 0.30–0.33 (7.5–8.5mm) at 22 ft. lbs. (98 Nm) of pressure. If the deflection is not correct, loosen the tensioner bolt and repeat Steps 10 and 11.

14. Install the timing belt covers, crankshaft pulley and drive belts.

15. Connect the negative battery cable.

2.5L Engine

1. Remove the timing belt covers. Temporarily reinstall the crankshaft pulley bolt.

2. Remove the nuts and through bolt from the right side engine mount and remove the mount.

3. Turn the crankshaft until the timing mark on the crankshaft sprocket aligns with the timing mark on the oil pump and the camshaft sprocket timing marks align with the marks on the cylinder head.

4. Remove the 2 bolts from the automatic tensioner, removing the lower one first.

5. If the timing belt is to be reused, mark the direction of rotation on the timing belt. Remove the timing belt.

To install:

6. Position the automatic tensioner in a suitable press. Set a flat washer under the tensioner body to prevent damage to the body plug.

7. Compress the tensioner until the hole in the piston is aligned with the 2nd hole in the tensioner case. Insert a 0.060 in. (1.6mm) diameter wire or pin through the 2nd hole to keep the piston compressed.

8. Make sure the camshaft sprocket timing marks are still aligned. Turn the crankshaft counterclockwise until the timing sprocket is offset from TDC by 1 tooth.

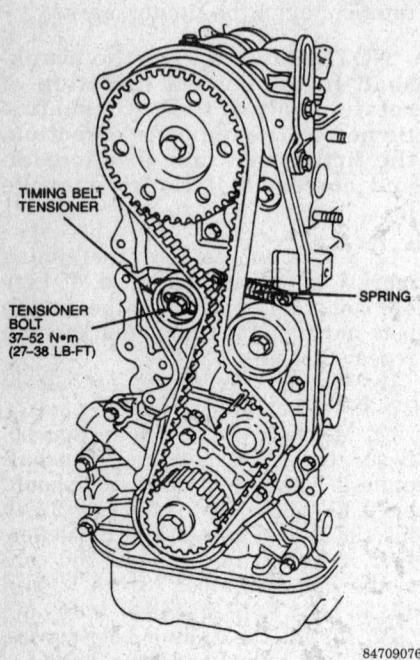

Timing belt installation — 2.2L engine

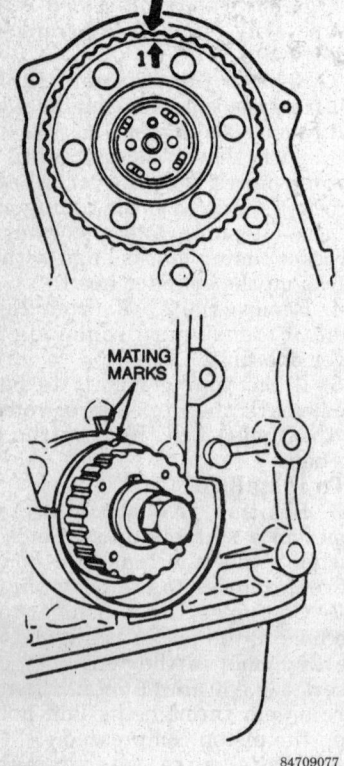

Timing mark locations — 2.2L engine

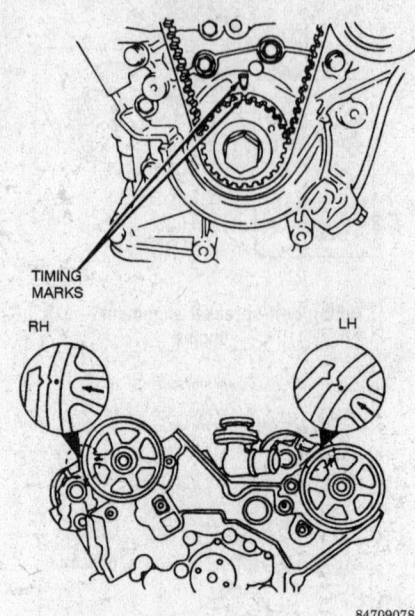

Timing belt sprocket alignment — 2.5L engine

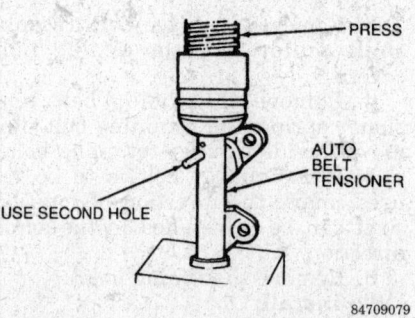

Compressing the automatic tensioner piston — 2.5L engine

9. Install the timing belt. If the original belt is being reused, make sure it is installed in the same direction of rotation.

10. Turn the crankshaft clockwise, until the crankshaft sprocket timing mark is again at TDC. This should place all of the belt slack in the automatic tensioner portion of the belt.

11. Install the automatic belt tensioner and tighten the bolts to 18 ft. lbs. (25 Nm). Remove the wire or pin from the tensioner.

12. Rotate the crankshaft 2 turns in the normal direction of rotation and align the timing marks. Make sure all marks are still correctly aligned.

13. Install the right side engine mount. Tighten the nuts to 76 ft. lbs. (103 Nm) and the through bolt to 68 ft. lbs. (93 Nm).

14. Remove the crankshaft damper bolt and install the timing belt covers.

Timing Sprockets

REMOVAL AND INSTALLATION

2.0L and 2.5L Engines

1. Disconnect the negative battery cable.

2. Remove the timing belt and the cylinder head covers.

3. There is a hexagon cast into the camshaft. Hold the camshaft with a wrench on the hexagon and remove the camshaft sprocket bolts. Remove the sprockets.

4. Use a suitable puller to remove the crankshaft sprocket.

To install:

5. Install the crankshaft sprocket on the crankshaft.

6. Install the camshaft sprockets and bolts. On 2.0L engine, install the camshaft sprockets so the **E** and **I** marks are aligned with the top of the cylinder head.

7. Hold the camshaft with the wrench on the hexagon and tighten the bolts to 45 ft. lbs. (61 Nm) on 2.0L engine or 103 ft. lbs. (140 Nm) on 2.5L engine.

8. Install the timing belt and the cylinder head covers. Connect the negative battery cable.

2.2L Engine

1. Disconnect the negative battery cable. Remove the timing belt.

2. Insert a proper tool through one of the camshaft sprocket holes to keep it from turning.

3. Remove the sprocket bolt and the sprocket from the camshaft.

4. If equipped with a manual transaxle, place the shift lever in **4th** gear and apply the parking brake. If equipped with an automatic transaxle, remove the flywheel dust cover and install a flywheel locking tool to hold the flywheel.

5. Remove the crankshaft sprocket bolt, sprocket and key.

To install:

6. Install the camshaft sprocket, aligning the dowel with the number **1** mark.

7. Install the camshaft sprocket bolt. Hold the sprocket with a suitable tool and tighten the bolt to 35–48 ft. lbs. (47–65 Nm).

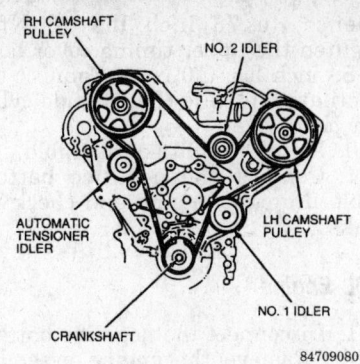

Timing belt and sprockets — 2.5L engine

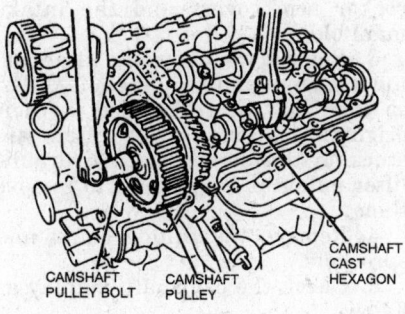

Removing the camshaft sprocket — 2.0L and 2.5L engines

8. Install the crankshaft sprocket and key. Align the keyway with the timing mark on the oil pump housing.

9. Install the crankshaft sprocket bolt. Install the flywheel locking tool, if equipped with automatic transaxle, or place the shift lever in **4th** gear and apply the parking brake, if equipped with manual transaxle. Tighten the bolt to 108–116 ft. lbs. (147–157 Nm).

10. Install the timing belt and connect the negative battery cable.

Camshaft

REMOVAL AND INSTALLATION

2.0L Engine

1. Disconnect the negative battery cable.

2. Remove the power steering hose brackets from the cylinder head cover.

3. Label and disconnect the spark plug wires and spark plug wire clips.

4. Disconnect the breather tube and PCV valve from the cylinder head cover. Loosen the cylinder head

cover in 2–3 steps, in the reverse order of the torque sequence. Remove the cylinder head cover.

5. Remove the accessory drive belts, timing belt covers and timing belt. Remove the camshaft sprockets.

6. Note the location of the numbers on top of the camshaft caps, so the caps can be reinstalled in their original positions.

7. Loosen the camshaft cap bolts in 2–3 steps, in the reverse order of the torque sequence. Remove the camshaft caps and the oil seals.

8. Remove the camshafts.

To install:

9. Lubricate the camshaft lobes and journals with clean engine oil and install the camshafts on the cylinder head. Make sure none of the lobes are located directly on the hydraulic lifters.

10. Apply silicone sealant to the cylinder head on the front camshaft caps mating surface. Do not get sealant on the camshaft journals.

11. Install the camshaft bearing caps in their original locations. Install the bolts and tighten, in sequence, in 3 steps:
   Step 1: 35 inch lbs. (4 Nm)
   Step 2: 71 inch lbs. (8 Nm)
   Step 3: 126 inch lbs. (14 Nm)

12. Apply clean engine oil to the lips of new camshafts seals. Install the seals using a suitable seal installer.

13. Install the camshaft sprockets, timing belt and timing belt covers. Install the accessory drive belts and adjust the tension.

14. Apply silicone sealant to a new cylinder head cover gasket and install the gasket on the cylinder head cover.

15. Apply silicone sealant to the cylinder head in the area adjacent to the front camshaft caps.

16. Install the cylinder head cover. Tighten the bolts in 2 steps, in sequence, to 69 inch lbs. (7 Nm). Torque the cover starting at the camshaft pulley and move around the cover.

17. Install the power steering hose brackets and tighten the bolts to 88 inch lbs. (10 Nm). Connect the spark plug wires and clips.

18. Connect the breather hose and PCV valve.

19. Connect the negative battery cable, run the engine and check for leaks.

2.2L Engine

1. Disconnect the negative battery cable. Drain the cooling system to a level below the thermostat housing.

2. Remove the timing belt covers, the timing belt and the camshaft sprocket.

3. Disconnect the upper radiator hose and the electrical connectors from the thermostat housing.

4. Mark the position of the distributor housing and the rotor and remove the distributor.

5. Remove the rocker arm cover and the front and rear housings. If necessary, pry out the camshaft seal from the front housing.

6. Remove the rocker arm/shaft assemblies.

7. Remove the camshaft bearing caps and the camshaft.

To install:

8. Clean all gasket mating surfaces.

9. Apply a liberal amount of clean engine oil to the camshaft journals and bearings. Install the camshaft on the cylinder head with the dowel pin facing straight up.

10. Apply silicone sealant to the cylinder head area under the front and rear camshaft bearing caps. Do not let sealer come in contact with the camshaft bearings or journals.

11. Install the camshaft bearing caps with the arrows facing the front of the engine. Install the rocker arm/shaft assemblies, making sure the notches on the end of the shafts are in the correct position. Tighten the bolts, in sequence, to 13–20 ft. lbs. (18–26 Nm) in 2 equal steps.

12. Install a new gasket and the rear housing. Tighten the bolts to 14–19 ft. lbs. (19–25 Nm).

13. If the camshaft seal was removed, lubricate the lip of a new seal and install in the front housing, using a suitable installation tool. Install a new gasket and the front housing. Tighten the bolts to 14–19 ft. lbs. (19–25 Nm).

14. Install the rocker arm cover, tightening the retaining bolts to 52–69 inch lbs. (6–8 Nm).

15. Install the distributor, aligning the marks that were made during the removal procedure.

16. Connect the electrical connectors and the upper radiator hose.

17. Install the camshaft sprocket, the timing belt and the timing belt covers.

18. Fill the cooling system, connect the negative battery cable and start the engine. Check the ignition timing and check for leaks.

2.5L Engine

1. Disconnect the negative battery cable.

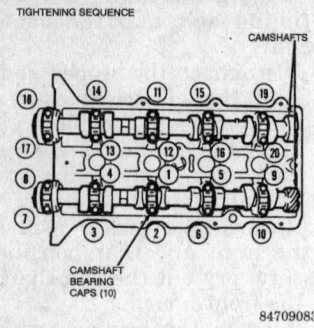

Camshaft cap bolt torque sequence — 2.0L engine

2. Remove the intake manifold. Label and disconnect the spark plug wires from the spark plugs.

3. Remove the upper timing belt cover bolts. If removing the left cylinder head cover, disconnect the ventilation pipe from the front of the left side (front) cylinder head cover.

4. Remove the bolts and the cylinder head cover.

5. Remove the timing belt and the camshaft sprockets.

6. Turn the camshafts so the knock pins are aligned with the marks on the camshaft caps. This will reduce the pressure on the hydraulic lifters.

7. Note the markings on the camshaft caps prior to removal, so they can be reinstalled in the same positions. The right hand (rear) caps are marked with numbers and the left hand (front) caps are marked with letters.

8. Loosen the front camshaft cap bolts in sequence, in 5–6 steps. Remove the front camshaft caps.

9. Remove the remaining camshaft cap bolts in the proper sequence. Remove the caps, being sure to remove the thrust caps last. Do not damage the cylinder head thrust bearing support.

10. Remove the camshafts and oil seals.

To install:

11. Install new oil seals on the camshafts. Apply clean engine oil to the camshaft lobes, journals and supports.

12. Install the camshafts so the gear marks align.

13. Apply silicone sealant to the cylinder head surface in the area forward of the camshaft gear cavity and to the left cylinder head on the rear exhaust camshaft cap mating surface.

14. Install the thrust caps. Tighten the thrust cap bolts until the caps are fully seated on the cylinder head.

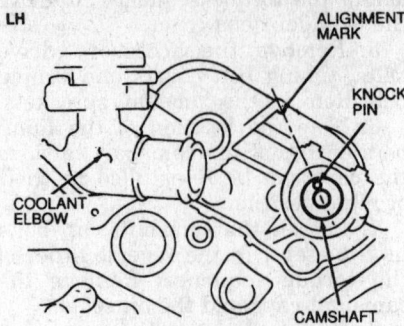

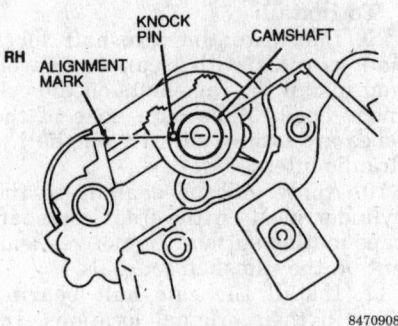

Place the camshafts in this position for removal, to reduce the pressure on the lifters — 2.5L engine

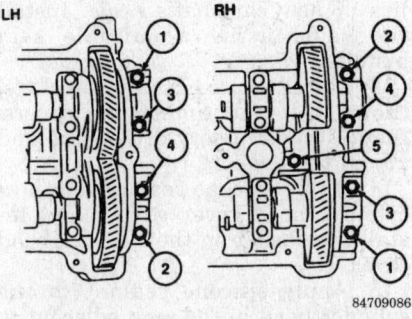

Front camshaft cap bolt loosening sequence — 2.5L engine

15. Install the remaining camshaft caps in their original positions. Tighten the caps, in sequence, in 5 equal steps, with the final step being 10 ft. lbs. (14 Nm).

16. Install the camshaft sprockets and the timing belt.

17. Remove any sealant and gasket material from the cylinder head cover contact surfaces.

18. Apply silicone sealant to the cylinder head in the area adjacent to the front and rear camshaft caps. Install a new gasket on the cylinder head.

19. Install the cylinder head cover. Tighten the bolts in 2 steps, in sequence, to 78 inch lbs. (8 Nm). Tighten the upper timing cover bolts to 88 inch lbs. (10 Nm). Connect the ventilation pipe to the left side cylinder head cover.

20. Install the intake manifold.

21. Connect the negative battery cable. Run the engine and check for leaks.

3.0L Engine

1. Disconnect the negative battery cable. Remove the engine assembly from the vehicle and place it on a suitable workstand.

2. Remove the timing covers, rocker arm covers and the intake manifold.

3. Remove the hydraulic lifters using a magnet and keep them in order, so they may be reinstalled in their original positions. If the lifters are stuck in the bores, use a hydraulic lifter puller or equivalent, to remove them.

4. Remove the timing chain and sprockets.

5. Check the camshaft endplay as follows:

   a. Mount a dial indicator on the front of the cylinder block and rest the indicator foot on the end of the camshaft.

   b. Move the camshaft back and forth in the cylinder block and observe the dial indicator. If necessary, use a prybar to move the camshaft, but be careful not to damage the camshaft lobes or journals.

   c. If the endplay exceeds 0.005 in. (0.127mm), replace the thrust plate.

6. Remove the camshaft thrust plate. Remove the camshaft by pulling it toward the front of the engine.

NOTE: Use caution to avoid damaging the bearings, journals and lobes.

7. Clean and inspect all parts prior to installation.

To install:

8. Lubricate the camshaft lobes and the journals with engine assembly lube. Carefully slide the camshaft through the bearings in the cylinder block.

9. Install the thrust plate and tighten the bolts to 6–8 ft. lbs. (8–12 Nm).

10. Install the timing chain and sprockets. Check the camshaft sprocket bolt for blockage of the drilled oil passages.

11. Install the timing cover and the crankshaft damper.

15. Fill the cooling system and the crankcase. Run the engine and check for leaks.

Piston and Connecting Rod

POSITIONING

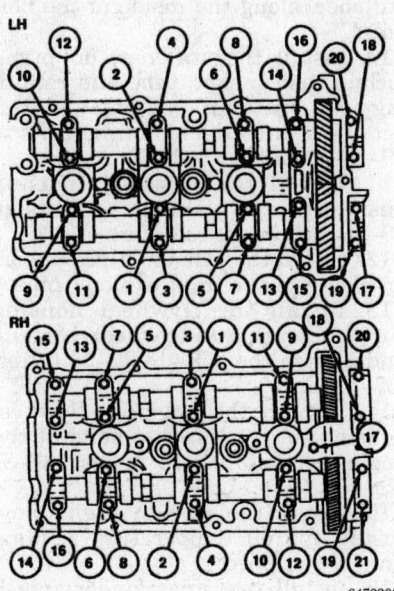

Camshaft cap bolt loosening sequence — 2.5L engine

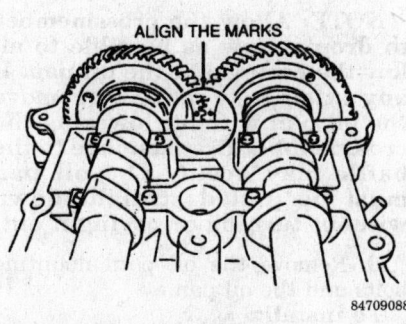

Align the gears when installing the camshafts — 2.5L engine

12. Lubricate the lifters and lifter bores with heavy engine oil and install the lifters into their original bores.

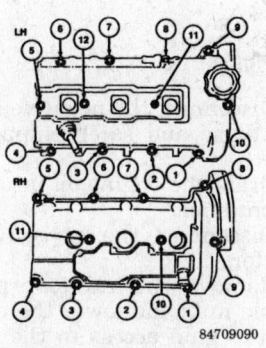

Camshaft cap bolt torque sequence — 2.5L engine

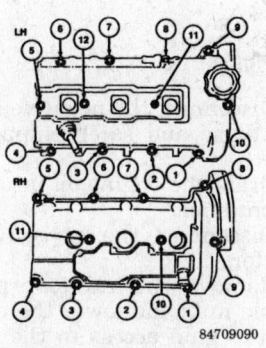

Cylinder head cover bolt torque sequence — 2.5L engine

13. Install the pushrods, rocker arms, rocker covers and intake manifold.
14. Install the engine assembly and connect the negative battery cable.

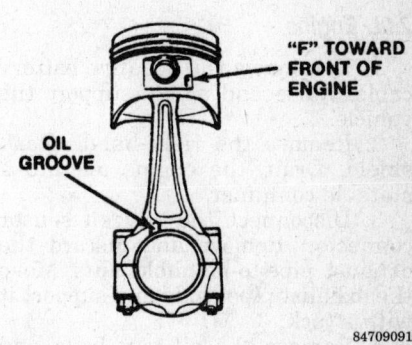

Piston and connecting rod — 2.0L and 2.2L engine

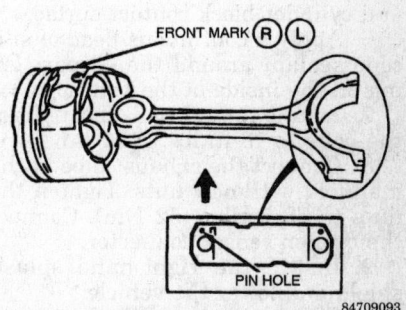

The L mark should face front of the left bank, R mark should face front on the right bank — 2.5L engine

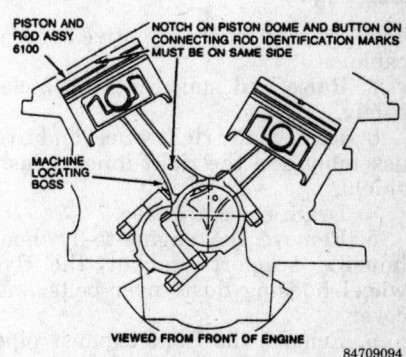

Piston and connecting rod — 3.0L engine

ENGINE LUBRICATION

Oil Pan

REMOVAL AND INSTALLATION

2.0L Engine

1. Disconnect the negative battery cable. Raise and safely support the vehicle.

2. Remove the right-hand splash shield. Drain the engine oil into a suitable container.

3. Disconnect the oxygen sensor connector. Remove and discard the exhaust pipe-to-manifold nuts. Move the exhaust pipe aside and support it with a jack.

4. Remove the oil pan bolts and the oil pan.
   To install:

5. Clean the oil pan. Clean all dirt, oil and old sealant from the oil pan and cylinder block contact surfaces.

6. Apply a continuous bead of silicone sealant around the oil pan, going on the inside of the bolt holes.

7. Install the oil pan and tighten the bolts to 19 ft. lbs. (25 Nm).

8. Connect the exhaust pipe to the manifold with new nuts. Tighten the nuts to 38 ft. lbs. (52 Nm). Connect the oxygen sensor connector.

9. Install the right-hand splash shield and lower the vehicle.

10. Fill the engine with the proper type and quantity of engine oil. Connect the negative battery, run the engine and check for leaks.

2.2L Engine

1. Disconnect the negative battery cable.

2. Raise and support the vehicle, safely.

3. Remove the right wheel and tire assembly and the right inner splash shield.

4. Drain the crankcase.

5. Remove the engine-to-flywheel housing support bracket, the flywheel housing dust cover bolts and cover.

6. Remove the front exhaust pipe and the exhaust pipe support bracket.

7. Remove the oil pan-to-engine bolts, the oil pan, the oil pickup tube and the stiffener.

8. Clean the gasket mounting surfaces.

To install:

9. Using silicone sealant, apply a continuous bead on both sides of the stiffener, along the inside of the bolt holes.

10. Install the stiffener, oil pump pickup tube gasket, tube and retaining bolts. Install the oil pan and gasket and tighten the mounting bolts to 69–104 inch lbs. (8–12 Nm).

11. Install the flywheel housing dust cover and tighten the bolts to 49–96 inch lbs. (8–11 Nm).

12. Install the exhaust pipe support bracket and the front exhaust pipe.

13. Install the flywheel housing support bracket-to-flywheel housing and tighten the bolts to 27–38 ft. lbs. (37–52 Nm).

14. Tighten the engine-to-flywheel housing support bracket bolts at the engine block to 27–38 ft. lbs. (37–52 Nm).

15. Install the oil pan drain plug. Install the oil temperature sending unit, if equipped.

16. Install the inner fender splash shield and the wheel and tire assembly. Lower the vehicle.

17. Add engine oil to the proper level.

18. Connect the negative battery cable, start the engine and check for leaks.

2.5L Engine

1. Disconnect the negative battery cable. Raise and safely support the vehicle.

2. Drain the engine oil into a suitable container.

3. Disconnect the oxygen sensor connectors.

4. Remove the exhaust pipe-to-manifold nuts and lower the exhaust system to gain access to the oil pan bolts.

5. Remove the oil pan bolts and the oil pan.

To install:

6. Clean the oil pan. Clean all dirt, oil and old sealant from the oil pan and cylinder block contact surfaces. Remove the old sealant from the threads of the oil pan bolts and the bolt holes in the block.

NOTE: Failure to remove the old sealant from the bolts and bolt holes may cause the block to crack.

7. Apply a continuous bead of silicone sealant along the inside of the bolt holes, overlapping the ends.

8. Install the oil pan. Tighten oil pan bolts **A** to 18 ft. lbs. (25 Nm) and bolts **B** to 88 inch lbs. (10 Nm).

9. Connect the exhaust pipes to the manifolds with new gaskets and tighten the nuts to 41 ft. lbs. (55 Nm). Connect the oxygen sensors.

10. Lower the vehicle. Fill the engine with the proper type and quantity of engine oil. Run the engine and check for leaks.

3.0L Engine

1. Disconnect the negative battery cable. Raise and safely support the vehicle.

2. Drain the engine oil and remove the starter motor.

3. Remove the front and rear transaxle-to-engine braces.

4. Disconnect the low oil level sensor connector from the dash panel side of the oil pan.

5. Remove the exhaust inlet pipe from the manifolds and position it aside.

6. Drain the cooling system and remove the water pump.

7. Remove the water pump bracket and idler pulley tensioner.

8. Remove the mounting bolts and nut from the front end of the right crossmember.

9. Loosen, but do not remove the bolts and nut from the rear end of the right crossmember.

NOTE: Allow the crossmember to drop as low as possible to allow the removal of the oil pan. If any attempt is made to remove the oil pan without lowering the crossmember first, damage to the baffle may occur. The oil pan must be pulled straight down without turning or prying it out.

10. Remove the oil pan mounting bolts and the oil pan.
   To install:

11. Clean the oil pan and all gasket contact surfaces.

12. Apply a ⅕ in. (4–5mm) bead of silicone sealer to the junction of the rear main bearing cap and the cylinder block and the junction of the front cover assembly and the cylinder block.

13. Position the oil pan gasket on the engine block and secure with gasket adhesive.

14. Place the oil pan on the cylinder block and tighten the mounting bolts to 9 ft. lbs. (12 Nm).

15. Lift the right crossmember into place and tighten all the nuts and bolts.

16. Install the water pump mounting bracket and the idler pulley tensioner.

17. Install the water pump and the exhaust inlet pipe.

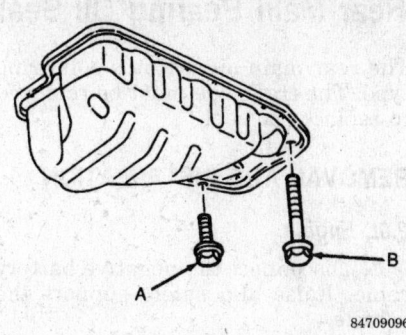

Oil pan bolt identification — 2.5L engine

18. Connect the oil level sensor and install the transaxle-to-engine braces.

19. Install the starter motor.

20. Lower the vehicle. Refill the crankcase and the cooling system.

21. Connect the negative battery cable. Run the engine and check for leaks.

Oil Pump

REMOVAL AND INSTALLATION

2.0L Engine

1. Disconnect the negative battery cable.

2. Remove the timing belt and the crankshaft sprocket.

3. Remove the A/C compressor and secure it aside, leaving the refrigerant lines attached. Remove the compressor mounting bracket.

4. Remove the oil pan.

5. Remove the oil pickup tube and discard the gasket.

6. Remove the rear main seal housing-to-stiffener nuts and remove the stiffener.

7. Remove the oil pump attaching bolts and remove the oil pump.

To install:

8. Clean the oil, dirt and old sealant from all contact surfaces.

9. Apply a bead of silicone to the oil pump-to-cylinder block contact surface, going inside the bolt holes.

10. Install the oil pump and tighten the bolts to 19 ft. lbs. (25 Nm).

11. Apply a bead of silicone sealant to the perimeter of the stiffener, going inside the bolt holes.

12. Install the stiffener and the mounting bolts. Tighten the bolts in 2 steps, in sequence, to 19 ft. lbs. (25 Nm). Tighten the rear main seal housing-to-stiffener nuts to 88 inch lbs. (10 Nm).

13. Install a new gasket and the oil pump pickup tube. Tighten the

mounting bolts to 88 inch lbs. (10 Nm).

14. Install the oil pan.

15. Install the A/C compressor bracket and tighten the bolts to 38 ft. lbs. (52 Nm). Install the A/C compressor and tighten the bolts to 26 ft. lbs. (35 Nm).

16. Install the remaining components in the reverse order of removal. Fill the engine with the proper type and quantity of oil. Run the engine and check for leaks.

2.2L Engine

1. Disconnect the negative battery cable. Raise and safely support the vehicle.

2. Remove the crankshaft sprocket. Drain the engine oil and remove the oil pan.

3. Remove the oil pump pickup tube-to-oil pump bolts, the tube and gasket.

4. Remove the oil pump-to-cylinder block bolts, the pump and gasket.

5. If necessary, pry the oil seal from the pump and clean the seal bore.

6. Clean the gasket mounting surfaces. Inspect the pump and gears for wear.

To install:

7. If necessary, press a new seal into the oil pump until it is flush with the edge of the pump housing and lubricate the seal lip with engine oil. Install a new O-ring into the oil pump body.

8. Apply a continuous bead of silicone sealer to the oil pump gasket surface.

NOTE: When using sealant, do not allow the sealant to squeeze into the pump's outlet hole in the pump or cylinder block.

9. Install the oil pump to the cylinder block; be careful not to cut the oil seal lip. Tighten the 8mm oil pump-

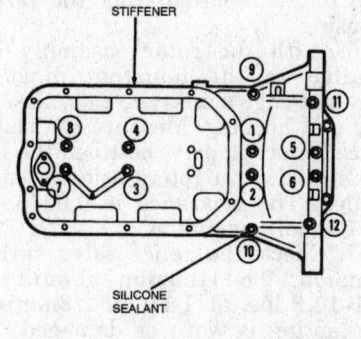

Stiffener bolt torque sequence — 2.0L engine

to-cylinder block bolts to 14–19 ft. lbs. (19–25 Nm) and the 10mm oil pump-to-cylinder block bolts to 27–38 ft. lbs. (37–52 Nm).

10. Install the oil pump pickup tube using a new gasket.

11. Install the oil pan and the crankshaft sprocket.

12. Connect the negative battery cable and refill the crankcase. Start the engine and check for leaks.

2.5L Engine

1. Remove the timing belt and the oil pan.

2. Properly discharge the refrigerant from the A/C system.

3. Remove the A/C compressor and the compressor bracket.

4. Remove the power steering pump and tensioner bolts from the engine block. Remove the pump and tensioner and position aside.

5. Remove the crankshaft sprocket.

6. Remove the 9 oil pump mounting bolts and the 2 oil strainer-to-oil pump bolts. Remove the oil pump.

7. Remove the pump O-ring. If necessary, press the oil seal from the housing.

To install:

8. Clean the oil, dirt and old sealant from all contact surfaces.

9. If removed, press a new oil seal into the pump housing.

10. Install a new O-ring onto the oil pump. Apply a continuous bead of silicone sealant to the oil pump mating surface and install the pump.

11. Install the oil pump mounting bolts. Tighten bolts **A** and **B** to 18 ft. lbs. (25 Nm).

12. Install the crankshaft sprocket and key.

13. Install the power steering pump and tensioner. Tighten the 2 power steering belt tensioner upper bolts and the power steering pump rear bracket bolt to 33 ft. lbs. (46 Nm). Tighten the tensioner lower bolt to 18 ft. lbs. (25 Nm).

14. Install the A/C compressor bracket and tighten the bolts to 38 ft. lbs. (51 Nm). Install the A/C compressor and tighten the bolts to 38 ft. lbs. (51 Nm).

15. Install the 2 oil strainer-to-oil pump bolts and tighten to 88 inch lbs. (10 Nm).

16. Install the remaining components in the reverse order of removal. Fill the engine with the proper type and quantity of oil. Run the engine and check for leaks.

17. Evacuate and charge the A/C system.

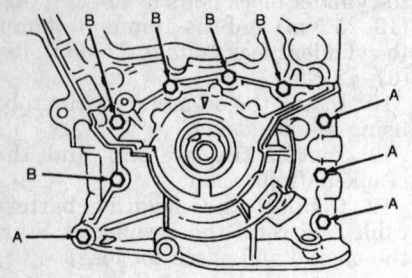

BOLT A : 40mm (1.57 IN.)
BOLT B : 25mm (0.98 IN.)

84709100

Oil pump bolt identification — 2.5L engine

3.0L Engine

1. Disconnect the negative battery cable. Raise and support the vehicle, safely. Drain the engine oil.
2. Remove the oil pan and the oil pump mounting bolt.
3. Remove the oil pump and the intermediate shaft from the rear main bearing cap.
4. Pull the intermediate shaft out of the oil pump.
To install:
5. Insert the pump intermediate shaft into the drive hole in the pump assembly until it clicks into place.
6. Pour a small amount of clean oil into the outlet hole in the body of the oil pump.
7. Lift the oil pump assembly into place guiding the intermediate shaft through the hole in the rear main bearing cap. Seat the pump securely on the locating dowels.
8. Install the pump mounting bolt and tighten to 35 ft. lbs. (48 Nm).
9. Install the oil pan.
10. Lower the vehicle and refill the crankcase. Connect the negative battery cable, run the engine and check for leaks.

CHECKING

Except 3.0L Engine

1. Remove the pump cover screws and remove the pump cover. Remove the inner and outer rotor.
2. Using snapring pliers, remove the internal snapring and remove the pressure relief valve assembly.
3. Using a small prybar, remove the oil seal from he pump body. Discard the seal.
4. Clean all parts in solvent and allow to dry. Check for obvious signs of wear: scoring, galling or distortion of the pump body or cover, worn or damaged pressure relief valve plunger, or a weak or broken spring plunger.

5. Measure the side clearance using a straight-edge and feeler gauge. The clearance must not exceed 0.0047 in. (0.12mm) on 2.0L engine, 0.004 in. (0.10mm) on 2.2L engine or 0.0051 in. (0.13mm) on 2.5L engine.
6. Measure the tooth tip clearance using a feeler gauge. The clearance must not exceed 0.007 in. (0.18mm) on 2.2L engine or 0.0079 in. (0.20mm) on 2.0L and 2.5L engines.
7. Measure the outer rotor-to-pump body clearance using a feeler gauge. The clearance must not exceed 0.0083 in. (0.21mm) on 2.0L engine, 0.008 in. (0.20mm) on 2.2L engine or 0.0087 in. (0.22mm) on 2.5L engine.
8. Replace parts or the entire assembly, as necessary.
9. When reassembling the pump, install the inner and outer rotors with the dimples aligned and facing the pump cover.

3.0L Engine

1. Disassemble the pump and wash all parts in solvent. Use a brush to clean the inside of the pump housing and the pressure relief valve chamber, making sure all dirt and metal particles are removed. Allow the parts to dry.
2. Inspect the inside of the pump housing for damage or excessive wear.
3. Check the mating surface for wear. Minor scuff marks are normal but if the cover, gears or housing are excessively worn, scored or grooved, replace the pump.
4. Inspect the rotor for nicks, burrs, or score marks. Remove minor imperfections with an oil stone.
5. Measure the inner-to-outer rotor tip clearance using a feeler gauge. The clearance must not exceed 0.010 in. (0.254mm) with a feeler gauge inserted ½ in. (12.7mm) minimum with the rotors removed from the pump housing.
6. With the rotor assembly installed in the housing, place a straight-edge across the rotor assembly and housing. Measure the clearance (rotor endplay) between the the inner and outer rotors using a feeler gauge. The clearance is 0.0055 in. (0.140mm) maximum.
7. Check the relief valve spring tension. The tension should be 9.1–10.1 lbs. at 1.11 in. (28mm). If the spring is worn or damaged, replace the pump. Check the relief valve piston for freedom of movement in the bore.

Rear Main Bearing Oil Seal

The rear main oil seal is a solid ring type. The transaxle must be removed to replace the seal.

REMOVAL AND INSTALLATION

2.0L Engine

1. Disconnect the negative battery cable. Raise and safely support the vehicle.
2. Remove the transaxle. If equipped with manual transaxle, remove the clutch assembly.
3. Remove the flywheel or flexplate.
4. Remove the rear main seal housing-to-stiffener nuts. Remove the 6 rear main seal housing-to-block bolts and remove the housing.
5. Pry the seal from the housing.
To install:
6. Apply a small amount of clean engine oil to the lip of the new seal. Use a suitable installation tool to install the seal until it is flush with the edge of the housing.
7. Apply a bead of silicone sealant to the housing, going inside the bolt holes.
8. Install the seal housing and tighten the bolts to 88 inch lbs. (10 Nm). Tighten the seal housing-to-stiffener nuts to 88 inch lbs. (10 Nm).
9. Install the flywheel or flexplate. Remove the old sealant from the flywheel bolts and apply new sealant. Install the bolts and tighten in 2–3 steps, in a crisscross pattern to 75 ft. lbs. (103 Nm).
10. If equipped with manual transaxle, install the clutch assembly.
11. Install the transaxle and lower the vehicle.
12. Connect the negative battery cable. Run the engine and check for leaks.

2.2L Engine

1. Disconnect the negative battery cable.
2. Raise and safely support the vehicle.
3. Remove the transaxle assembly.
4. If equipped with a manual transaxle, remove the clutch and flywheel assembly.
5. If equipped with an automatic transaxle, remove the flexplate-to-crankshaft bolts, the flexplate and shim plates.
6. If necessary, remove the rear engine plate.
7. Remove the rear oil seal housing mounting bolts, the housing and the gasket.

8. Using a small prybar, pry the oil seal from the oil seal housing. Clean the gasket mounting surfaces.

To install:

9. Clean the oil seal housing. Coat the oil seal and the housing with clean engine oil.

10. Press the seal into the seal housing using a suitable installer. Make sure the hollow side of the seal is facing toward the engine.

11. Using a new gasket, install the rear oil seal housing and torque the seal housing-to-engine bolts to 69–104 inch lbs. (8–12 Nm). Trim the excess gasket material off the housing after installation.

12. Install the rear engine plate, if removed. Tighten the bolts to 14–22 ft. lbs. (19–30 Nm).

13. Install the clutch and flywheel assembly or the flexplate, as applicable. Tighten the flywheel or flexplate bolts to 71–76 ft. lbs. (96–103 Nm).

14. Install the transaxle, lower the vehicle and connect the negative battery cable.

2.5L and 3.0L Engines

1. Disconnect the negative battery cable.

2. Raise and safely support the vehicle.

3. Remove the transaxle assembly.

4. Remove the clutch/flywheel assembly if equipped with manual transaxle or the flexplate if equipped with automatic transaxle.

5. Using a sharp awl, punch a hole into the seal metal surface between the lip and the block. Use a screw and a slide hammer to pull the seal out.

To install:

6. Apply engine oil to the outer lips and inner seal edge. Using a seal installation tool, install the new rear main oil seal. Make sure the seal is seated properly.

7. Install the clutch/flywheel assembly or flexplate, as applicable.

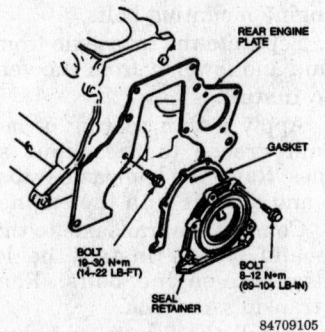

Rear main bearing oil seal assembly — 2.2L engine

Tighten the flywheel or flexplate bolts, in 2–3 steps to 45–49 ft. lbs. (61–67 Nm) on 2.5L engine or 54–64 ft. lbs. (73–87 Nm). Tighten the bolts in a crisscross pattern.

8. Install the transaxle assembly and lower the vehicle. Connect the negative battery cable.

MANUAL TRANSAXLE

Transaxle Assembly

REMOVAL AND INSTALLATION

1992

1. Disconnect the battery cables, negative cable first. Remove the battery and the battery tray.

2. Disconnect the main fuse block and disconnect the coil wire from the distributor. Disconnect and mark the wiring assembly, as necessary.

3. Disconnect the electrical connector from the air flow meter and remove the air cleaner assembly.

4. On 2.2L non-turbocharged engine, remove the resonance chamber and bracket. On 2.2L turbocharged engine, remove the throttle body-to-intercooler air hose and the air cleaner-to-turbocharger air hose.

5. Disconnect the speedometer cable (analog cluster) or cluster harness (electronic cluster).

6. If equipped with the 3.0L engine, drain the engine coolant and close the drain valve. Remove the upper radiator hose.

7. Disconnect both ground wires from the transaxle. Raise and safely support the vehicle.

8. Remove the front wheel and tire assemblies and the splash shields. Drain the transaxle.

9. Remove the slave cylinder and move it aside.

10. Remove the tie rod ends-to-steering knuckle cotter pins and nuts. Disconnect the tie rod ends from the steering knuckle.

11. Remove the stabilizer link assemblies from the lower control arm.

12. Remove the lower control ball joint-to-steering knuckle nut/bolt. Using a prybar, pry the lower control arm downward to separate the ball joint from the steering knuckle.

13. Remove the right-hand joint shaft bracket.

14. Position a prybar between the halfshaft and transaxle case; pry the halfshafts from the transaxle and suspend them on a wire.

15. Install 2 transaxle plugs, T88C–7025–AH or equivalent, between the differential side gears to keep the gears from becoming mispositioned.

16. Remove the gusset plate-to-transaxle bolts on 2.2L engine. Disconnect the extension bar and shift control rod.

17. Remove the front exhaust pipe on the 3.0L engine.

18. Remove the flywheel inspection plate on the 2.2L engine.

19. Remove the starter motor and the access brackets.

20. Attach engine support bar D87L–6000–A or equivalent to the engine and support its weight.

21. Remove the center transaxle mount and bracket, the left transaxle mount and the right transaxle mount-to-frame nut and bolt.

22. Remove the crossmember and the left-hand side lower arm as an assembly.

23. Attach and secure a suitable jack to the transaxle.

24. Remove the transaxle-to-engine bolts, lower the transaxle and remove it from the vehicle.

To install:

25. Apply a small amount of grease to the input shaft splines.

26. Raise and position the transaxle. Install the transaxle-to-engine bolts and torque to 66–86 ft. lbs. (89–117 Nm).

27. Install the center transaxle mount and bracket and torque the bolts to 27–40 ft. lbs. (36–54 Nm) and the nuts to 47–66 ft. lbs. (64–89 Nm).

NOTE: Do not install the nut that braces the throttle air inlet hose bracket.

28. Install the left transaxle mount and torque the left transaxle-to-mount bolts on the 2.2L non-turbocharged engine to 27–38 ft. lbs. (37–52 Nm) or on the 2.2L turbocharged engine and 3.0L engine to 49–69 ft. lbs. (67–93 Nm). Torque the mount-to-bracket nut and bolt to 49–69 ft. lbs. (67–93 Nm).

29. Install the crossmember and the left side lower arm as an assembly. Tighten the bolts to 27–40 ft. lbs. (36–54 Nm) and the nuts to 55–69 ft. lbs. (75–93 Nm).

30. Install the right transaxle mount bolt and nut and tighten to 63–86 ft. lbs. (85–117 Nm).

31. Install the starter motor and access brackets.

32. Install the flywheel inspection cover on 2.2L engine. Tighten the bolts to 69–96 inch lbs. (8–11 Nm).

33. Connect the extension rod and control rod. Install the front exhaust pipe on 3.0L engine.

34. Install the slave cylinder and tighten the bolts to 14–19 ft. lbs. (19–26 Nm).

35. Install the gusset plate-to-transaxle bolts on the 2.2L engine and tighten to 27–38 ft. lbs. (37–52 Nm).

36. On the end of each halfshaft, install a new circlip. This must be done whenever halfshafts are serviced.

37. Remove the transaxle plugs and install the halfshaft until the clips snap into place. Attach the lower arm ball joints to the knuckles.

38. Install and torque the tie rod end-to-steering knuckle nut to 22–33 ft. lbs. (29–44 Nm) and install a new cotter pin. Tighten the lower control arm ball joint-to-steering knuckle nut and bolt to 32–40 ft. lbs. (43–54 Nm).

39. Install the stabilizer link assembly-to-lower control arm. Turn the upper nuts (on each assembly) until 0.79 in. (20mm) of bolt thread can be measured above the nuts.

40. Install the splash shields and the front wheel and tire assemblies; torque the lug nuts to 65–87 ft. lbs. (88–118 Nm). Lower the vehicle.

41. Connect the ground wires to the transaxle case and tighten to 69–96 inch lbs. (8–11 Nm).

42. On the 2.2L non-turbocharged engine, install the resonance chamber and bracket; torque to 69–96 inch lbs. (8–11 Nm). On turbocharged engines, install the throttle body-to-intercooler air hose and torque the bracket-to-mount nut to 47–66 ft. lbs. (64–89 Nm).

43. On 3.0L engine, install the upper radiator hose and fill the cooling system.

44. Install the air cleaner assembly and tighten to 69–96 inch lbs. (8–11 Nm).

45. Connect the electrical connector to the air flow meter. Connect the previously marked wiring assembly, if disconnected.

46. Reconnect the main fuse block and connect the coil wire to the distributor.

47. Remove the engine support bracket.

48. Connect the speedometer cable or harness, as applicable.

49. Install the battery tray, battery and connect the battery cables.

50. Refill the transaxle assembly. Connect the negative battery cable, start the engine and check for leaks.

1993–96

1. Remove the fresh air duct and air cleaner assembly. Disconnect the battery cables and remove the battery and battery tray.

2. Remove the transaxle ground straps. Label and disconnect the vehicle speed sensor connector at the top right-hand rear corner of the transaxle.

3. Label and disconnect the park/neutral position switch electrical connector from the lower front of the transaxle. Label and disconnect the backup light switch electrical connector from the rear of the transaxle.

4. Disconnect the 2 spring clips from the clutch slave cylinder hydraulic line and remove the slave cylinder mounting bolts. Position the slave cylinder aside, without disconnecting the hydraulic line.

5. Support the engine with engine support tool 014–00750 or equivalent.

6. Remove the upper transaxle-to-engine mounting bolts and the upper starter bolts. Remove the fuel filter mounting nuts and position the filter aside, without disconnecting the fuel lines.

7. Remove the 2 nuts and the through bolt from the left side transaxle mount. Raise and safely support the vehicle.

8. If equipped with 2.0L engine, remove the intake manifold support bracket.

9. Disconnect the wiring from the starter, remove the lower starter bolt and remove the starter.

10. Remove the drain plug and drain the transaxle fluid into a suitable container. Discard the drain plug washer.

11. Remove the front wheel and tire assemblies. Unstake the halfshaft attaching nuts. Have an assistant apply the brakes to keep the hubs from turning, then remove the nuts and discard them.

12. Remove the lower splash shields. Remove the 6 transverse member bolts and the transverse member.

13. Remove the lower ball joint pinch bolt and nut from the left side knuckle. Pry the lower ball control arm down to separate the ball joint from the knuckle. Be careful not to damage the ball joint dust boot.

14. Pull the hub/knuckle assembly outward to separate it from the halfshaft. If the halfshaft is stuck in the hub, push it out using a suitable puller.

15. Position a prybar between the transaxle case and inner CV-joint.

Pry the left halfshaft from the transaxle case. Install transaxle plug tool T88C–7025–AH or equivalent, to keep the differential side gear from becoming mispositioned.

16. If equipped with anti-lock brakes, remove the clips from the wheel speed sensor and the wheel speed sensor mounting nuts from the sensor harness mount on the left side of the vehicle.

17. If equipped with 2.5L engine, disconnect the oxygen sensor connectors. Remove and discard the exhaust pipe-to-manifold nuts. Lower the exhaust system enough to gain access to the right side halfshaft support bearing.

18. Remove the 3 right halfshaft support bearing bolts. If equipped with anti-lock brakes, remove the clips from the wheel speed sensor and the wheel speed sensor mounting nuts from the sensor harness mount on the right side of the vehicle.

19. Remove the lower ball joint pinch bolt and nut from the right side knuckle. Pry the lower ball control arm down to separate the ball joint from the knuckle. Be careful not to damage the ball joint dust boot.

20. Pull the hub/knuckle assembly outward to separate it from the halfshaft. If the halfshaft is stuck in the hub, push it out using a suitable puller.

21. Pull the right halfshaft from the transaxle case. Install transaxle plug tool T88C–7025–AH or equivalent, to keep the differential side gear from becoming mispositioned.

22. Remove the 6 nuts and 2 bolts from the transaxle cradle and remove the cradle.

23. Disconnect the shift linkage and extension bar from the transaxle.

24. Remove the 3 rear transaxle mount-to-transaxle bolts. Support the transaxle with a jack.

25. Remove the 3 rear transaxle mount bolts and the rear transaxle mount. Remove the lower transaxle-to-engine mounting bolts.

26. Separate the transaxle from the engine and lower it from the vehicle.

To install:

27. Apply a thin coating of molybdenum grease to the input shaft splines. Raise the transaxle into position and align it with the engine.

28. Connect the transaxle to the engine and loosely install the lower transaxle-to-engine bolts. Remove the transmission jack.

29. Install the 2 nuts and through bolt into the left transaxle mount. Tighten the nuts to 44 ft. lbs. (60 Nm)

and the through bolt to 86 ft. lbs. (116 Nm).

30. Install the rear transaxle mount with the 3 bolts. Tighten the bolts to 68 ft. lbs. (93 Nm).

31. Connect the extension bar and shift linkage to the transaxle. Tighten the extension bar nut to 38 ft. lbs. (51 Nm) and the shift linkage nut to 18 ft. lbs. (25 Nm).

32. Install the transaxle cradle and tighten the bolts and nuts to specification.

33. Remove the transaxle plug from the right side and install the right halfshaft. Pull out on the right hub/knuckle assembly and install the halfshaft into the hub.

34. Pry the lower control arm down and insert the lower ball joint stud into the knuckle. Install the pinch bolt and nut and tighten to 41 ft. lbs. (56 Nm).

35. If equipped with anti-lock brakes, install the wheel speed sensor harness mounting nuts and tighten to 88 inch lbs. (10 Nm). Install the sensor harness clips.

36. Install the 3 halfshaft support bearing bracket bolts. Tighten the bolts, in sequence, to 45 ft. lbs. (61 Nm).

37. Remove the transaxle plug from the left side and install the left halfshaft. Pull out on the left hub/knuckle assembly and install the halfshaft into the hub.

38. Pry the lower control arm down and insert the lower ball joint stud into the knuckle. Install the pinch bolt and nut and tighten to 41 ft. lbs. (56 Nm).

39. If equipped with anti-lock brakes, install the wheel speed sensor harness mounting nuts and tighten to 88 inch lbs. (10 Nm). Install the sensor harness clips.

40. If equipped with 2.5L engine, connect the exhaust pipes to the manifolds and tighten the new nuts to 41 ft. lbs. (55 Nm). Connect the oxygen sensor connectors.

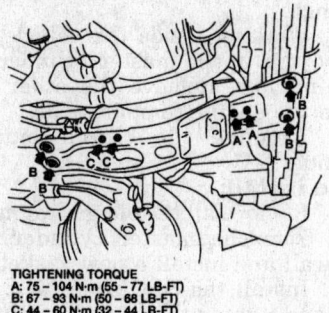

TIGHTENING TORQUE
A: 75 – 104 N·m (55 – 77 LB-FT)
B: 67 – 93 N·m (50 – 68 LB-FT)
C: 44 – 60 N·m (32 – 44 LB-FT)

84709107

Transaxle cradle torque sequence — 1993–96 vehicles

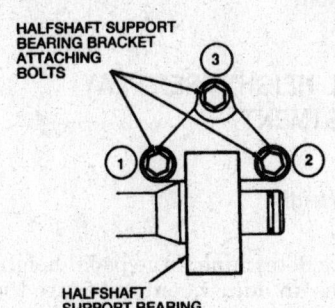

2.0L

HALFSHAFT SUPPORT BEARING BRACKET ATTACHING BOLTS

HALFSHAFT SUPPORT BEARING BRACKET

2.5L

HALFSHAFT SUPPORT BEARING ATTACHING BOLTS

HALFSHAFT SUPPORT BEARING

84709108

Halfshaft support bearing bracket bolt torque sequence — 1993–96 vehicles

41. Install the transverse member and tighten the bolts to 96 ft. lbs. (131 Nm).

42. Install new halfshaft locknuts. Have an assistant apply the brakes to lock the hubs, then tighten the nuts to 235 ft. lbs. (319 Nm). Stake the nuts in place.

43. Install the wheel and tire assemblies. Install a new washer on the transaxle drain plug and tighten it to 43 ft. lbs. (58 Nm).

44. Install the starter and tighten the lower bolt to 38 ft. lbs. (52 Nm). Connect the starter wiring.

45. If equipped with 2.0L engine, install the intake manifold support bracket and tighten the bolts to 38 ft. lbs. (52 Nm).

46. Install the lower splash shields.

47. If equipped with 2.0L engine, install the transaxle-to-engine and engine-to-transaxle bolts **B, C, D** and **E.** Tighten bolts **B** and **D** to 38 ft. lbs. (51 Nm), bolt **C** to 18 ft. lbs. (25 Nm) and bolt **E** to 86 ft. lbs. (116 Nm).

48. If equipped with 2.5L engine, tighten the lower transaxle-to-engine bolts to 38 ft. lbs. (51 Nm).

49. Install the 3 rear transaxle mount-to-transaxle bolts and tighten to 68 ft. lbs. (93 Nm).

50. Fill the transaxle with the proper type of fluid to a level even with the lower edge of the oil level plug port, with the vehicle level. Install the plug, using a new washer, and tighten to 43 ft. lbs. (58 Nm). Lower the vehicle.

51. Install the fuel filter and tighten the nuts to 88 inch lbs. (10 Nm).

52. If equipped with 2.0L engine, install transaxle-to-engine mounting bolts **A** and tighten to 86 ft. lbs. (116 Nm). If equipped with 2.5L engine, install the upper transaxle-to-engine bolts and tighten to 73 ft. lbs. (99 Nm).

53. Install the upper starter bolts and tighten to 38 ft. lbs. (51 Nm). Remove the engine support tool.

54. Install the clutch slave cylinder and tighten the bolts to 16 ft. lbs. (22 Nm).

55. Connect the electrical connectors and ground straps. Install the battery and battery tray.

56. Install the air cleaner assembly and air duct.

57. Connect the battery cables. Run the engine and check for leaks. Check transaxle operation.

CLUTCH

Clutch Assembly

REMOVAL AND INSTALLATION

1. Disconnect the negative battery cable. Raise and safely support the vehicle.

2. Remove the transaxle assembly.

3. Position a suitable clutch alignment tool through the pressure plate, clutch disc and into the pilot bearing; this will keep the assembly from dropping when the bolts are removed.

4. Install flywheel holding tool T74P–6375–A or equivalent, to keep the flywheel from turning. Remove the pressure plate-to-flywheel bolts, a little at a time, evenly, to relieve the spring pressure.

5. Remove the pressure plate, clutch disc and alignment tool.

6. Inspect the pressure plate and clutch disc for wear and/or damage and replace, as necessary.

7. Inspect the pilot bearing for excessive wear or scoring. Remove it, using a suitable puller, only if replacement is necessary.

8. Inspect the flywheel for scoring, cracks, worn or broken teeth, or other damage. Remove the flywheel if machining or replacement is neces-

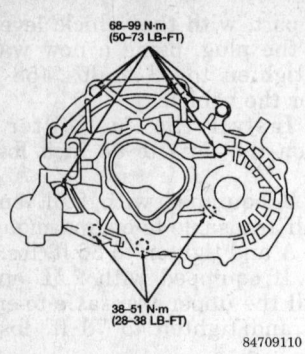

Transaxle mounting bolt torque sequence — 2.5L engine

sary. Use care when removing the last bolt to prevent dropping the flywheel.

9. Remove the release bearing and fork. Inspect them for wear or damage and replace, as necessary

To install:

10. Apply molybdenum grease to the release bearing where it contacts the release fork. Apply molybdenum grease to the release fork at the pivot point and to the area where it contacts the release bearing.

11. Install the release fork and bearing.

12. If removed, install the flywheel. Make sure the crankshaft flange and flywheel mating surfaces are clean. On 1993–96 vehicles, remove the old sealant from the flywheel bolts and apply stud and bearing mount sealant to them. If the old sealant cannot be removed, replace the bolts.

13. Install the flywheel holding tool. Tighten the flywheel bolts, in sequence, to 75 ft. lbs. (102 Nm) on 2.0L and 2.2L engines, 49 ft. lbs. (67 Nm) on 2.5L engines or 54–64 ft. lbs. (73–87 Nm) on the 3.0L engine.

14. If removed, install a new pilot bearing using a suitable installation tool. When installed, the pilot bearing should be 0.150–0.165 in. (3.8–4.2mm) below the surface of the crankshaft flange on 1992 vehicles or 0–0.016 in. (0–0.4mm) below the surface of the crankshaft flange on 1993–96 vehicles.

15. Apply a small amount of molybdenum grease to the clutch disc and input shaft splines. Do not let grease get on the clutch face.

16. Install the clutch disc and alignment tool with the clutch spring plate side of the disc toward the transaxle.

17. Install the pressure plate to the flywheel. Install the pressure plate-to-flywheel bolts and torque, evenly, a little at a time, to 18 ft. lbs. (26 Nm) in the proper sequence.

18. Install the transaxle assembly and lower the vehicle.

19. Connect the negative battery cable. Check for proper clutch operation.

PEDAL HEIGHT/FREE-PLAY ADJUSTMENT

Pedal Height

1. To determine if the pedal height requires an adjustment, measure the distance from the bulkhead to the upper center of the pedal pad. The distance should be 8.524–8.720 in. (216.5–221.5mm) on 1992 vehicles or

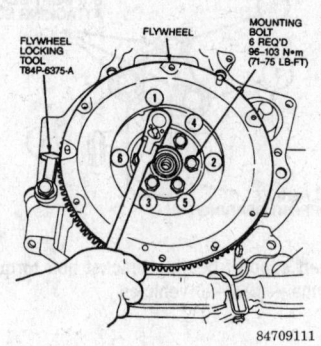

Flywheel bolt torque sequence — 2.2L and 3.0L engines

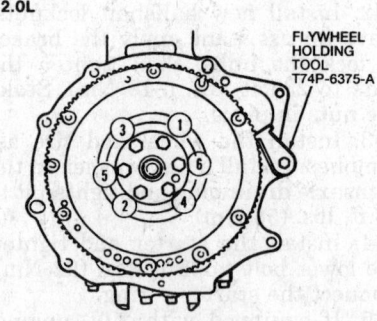

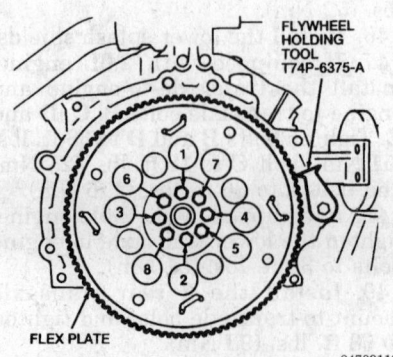

Flywheel bolt torque sequence — 2.0L and 2.5L engines

7.32–8.31 in. (186–211mm) on 1993–96 vehicles.

2. If adjustment is required, proceed as follows:

a. On 1992 vehicles, remove the lower dash panel and the air ducts.

b. Loosen the locknut and turn the stopper bolt until the desired pedal height is reached.

c. Tighten the locknut.

d. Install the ducts and the lower dash panel, if required.

Pedal Free-Play

1. Measure the pedal height.

2. Depress the clutch pedal by hand and measure the height of the pedal when resistance is felt.

3. The free-play should be 0.20–0.51 in. (5–13mm) on 1992 vehicles or 0.04–0.12 in. (1–3mm) on 1993–96 vehicles.

4. If adjustment is necessary, proceed as follows:

a. On 1992 vehicles, remove the lower dash panel and the air ducts.

b. Loosen the locknut and turn the clutch master cylinder pushrod until the pedal play is within specifications.

c. Measure the distance from the floor to the center of the pedal pad when the pedal is fully depressed. The distance should be 2.7 in. (68mm) or more.

d. Tighten the locknut and replace the lower dash panel and the air ducts, if required.

Clutch Master Cylinder

REMOVAL AND INSTALLATION

1. Disconnect the negative battery cable. On 1992 vehicles, remove the ABS relay box, if equipped.

2. On 1993–96 vehicles, disconnect and plug the hose from the brake fluid reservoir.

3. Disconnect the hydraulic line at the master cylinder, using a tubing wrench.

4. Working inside the vehicle, remove the upper master cylinder retaining nut. Remove the other nut from the engine compartment.

5. Remove the clutch master cylinder.

To install:

6. Remove all the old gasket material from the master cylinder and firewall and install a new gasket.

7. Install the clutch master cylinder and tighten the mounting nuts to 14–19 ft. lbs. (19–26 Nm).

8. Connect the hydraulic line and tighten the nut securely.

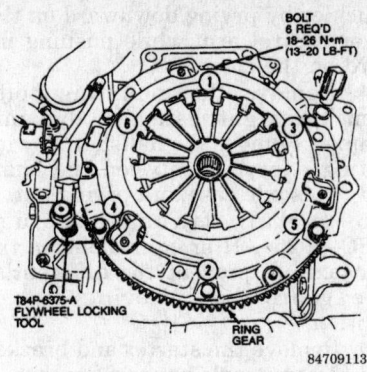

BOLT
6 REQ'D
18–26 N•m
(13–20 LB-FT)

T84P-6375-A
FLYWHEEL LOCKING
TOOL

RING
GEAR

84709113

Pressure plate bolt torque sequence

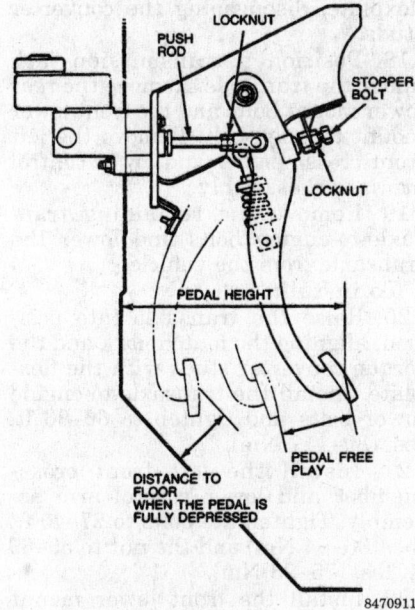

LOCKNUT

PUSH
ROD

STOPPER
BOLT

LOCKNUT

PEDAL HEIGHT

PEDAL FREE
PLAY

DISTANCE TO
FLOOR
WHEN THE PEDAL IS
FULLY DEPRESSED

84709114

Clutch pedal adjustment

9. On 1993–96 vehicles, unplug and connect the hose to the brake fluid reservoir.

10. Install the ABS relay box, if equipped.

11. Bleed the air from the clutch hydraulic system, connect the negative battery cable and road test the vehicle.

Clutch Slave Cylinder

REMOVAL AND INSTALLATION

1. Disconnect the negative battery cable.

2. Disconnect the hydraulic line at the slave cylinder using a tubing wrench. Plug the line to prevent leakage.

3. Remove the slave cylinder mounting bolts and remove the slave cylinder.

To install:

4. Install the slave cylinder and tighten the mounting bolts to 12–16 ft. lbs. (16–22 Nm).

5. Connect the hydraulic line and tighten the nut to 10–15 ft. lbs. (13–21 Nm).

6. Connect the negative battery cable.

7. Bleed the air from the clutch hydraulic system and road test the vehicle.

Hydraulic Clutch System Bleeding

NOTE: The fluid reservoir must be maintained at the ¾ level or higher during air bleeding.

1. Remove the bleeder cap from the slave cylinder and attach a vinyl hose to the bleeder screw.

2. Place the other end of the hose in a clear container partially filled with brake fluid.

3. Have an assistant slowly pump the clutch pedal several times.

4. With the clutch pedal depressed, loosen the bleeder screw to release the fluid and air.

5. Tighten the bleeder screw. Repeat this procedure until there are no air bubbles in the fluid in the container.

AUTOMATIC TRANSAXLE

Transaxle Assembly

REMOVAL AND INSTALLATION

1992

2.2L ENGINE

1. Disconnect the battery cables (negative cable first). Remove the battery and the battery tray.

2. Disconnect the main fuse block and disconnect the coil wire from the distributor.

3. Disconnect the electrical connector from the air flow meter and remove the air cleaner assembly.

4. Remove the resonance chamber and bracket.

5. Disconnect the speedometer cable (analog cluster) or harness (electronic cluster).

6. Disconnect the transaxle electrical connectors and separate the harness from the transaxle clips.

7. Disconnect both ground wires, the range selector cable and the kickdown cable from the transaxle. Raise and safely support the vehicle.

8. Remove the front wheel and tire assemblies and the splash shields. Drain the transaxle fluid.

9. Disconnect and plug the oil cooler hoses from the transaxle. Insert plugs to prevent fluid leakage.

10. Remove the tie rod ends-to-steering knuckle cotter pins and nuts. Disconnect the tie rod ends from the steering knuckle.

11. Remove the stabilizer link assemblies from the lower control arm.

12. Remove the lower control ball joint-to-steering knuckle nut/bolt. Using a prybar, pry the lower control arm downward to separate the ball joint from the steering knuckle.

13. Remove the right-hand half-shaft bracket.

14. Position a prybar between the halfshaft and transaxle case; pry the halfshafts from the transaxle.

15. Install 2 transaxle plugs T88C–7025–AH or equivalent, into the halfshaft openings of the transaxle case; this will keep the differential side gears from becoming mispositioned.

16. Remove the gusset plate-to-transaxle bolts.

17. Remove the torque converter-to-transaxle cover, the starter and the access brackets.

18. Using paint or chalk, match-mark the torque converter-to-flexplate position and remove the mounting nuts.

19. Mount engine support bar D87L–6000–A or equivalent, to the engine and support its weight.

20. Remove the center transaxle mount and bracket, the left transaxle mount and the nut and bolt attaching the right-hand transaxle mount to the frame.

21. Remove the crossmember and the left lower arm as an assembly.

22. Position a suitable jack under the transaxle and secure the transaxle to the jack.

23. Position a prybar between the torque converter and flexplate; pry the torque converter studs off the flexplate.

24. Remove the transaxle-to-engine bolts, lower the transaxle and remove it from the vehicle.

To install:

25. Raise and position the transaxle, align the torque converter-to-flexplate matchmark and studs. Install the transaxle-to-engine bolts and torque to 66–86 ft. lbs. (89–117 Nm).

26. Install the center transaxle mount and bracket and torque the bolts to 27–40 ft. lbs. (36–54 Nm) and the nuts to 47–66 ft. lbs. (64–89 Nm).

27. Install the left transaxle mount. Tighten the transaxle-to-mount nut to 63–86 ft. lbs. (85–117 Nm). Tighten the mount-to-bracket bolt and nut to 49–69 ft. lbs. (67–93 Nm).

28. Install the crossmember and left lower arm as an assembly. Tighten the bolts to 27–40 ft. lbs. (36–54 Nm) and the nuts to 55–69 ft. lbs. (75–93 Nm).

29. Install the right transaxle mount bolt and nut. Tighten to 63–86 ft. lbs. (85–117 Nm).

30. Install the starter motor and access brackets.

31. Install the torque converter nuts and tighten to 32–45 ft. lbs. (43–61 Nm).

32. Install the torque converter cover and tighten the bolts to 69–96 inch lbs. (8–11 Nm).

33. Install the gusset plate-to-transaxle bolts and tighten to 27–38 ft. lbs. (37–52 Nm).

34. On the end of each halfshaft, install a new circlip.

35. Remove the transaxle plugs and install the halfshaft until the circlips snap into place.

36. Attach the lower ball joints to the steering knuckle.

37. Install the tie rods and tighten to 22–33 ft. lbs. (29–44 Nm). Install new cotter pins.

38. Install the bolts and nuts to the lower arm ball joints and tighten to 32–40 ft. lbs. (43–54 Nm).

39. Install the stabilizer link assembly-to-lower control arm. Turn the upper nuts (on each assembly) until 0.79 inch (20mm) of bolt thread can be measured above the nuts.

40. Install the oil cooler hoses to the transaxle.

41. Install the splash shields and the front wheel and tire assemblies; torque the lug nuts to 65–87 ft. lbs. (88–118 Nm).

42. Connect and adjust the kickdown cable. Connect the range selector cable and torque the bolt to 33–47 ft. lbs. (44–64 Nm).

43. Install the resonance chamber and bracket; torque to 69–96 inch lbs. (8–11 Nm).

44. Connect the electrical connectors and attach the harness to the transaxle clips. Connect the ground wires.

45. Connect the speedometer cable or harness, as necessary.

46. Install the air filter assembly and connect the air flow meter connector.

47. Connect the center distributor terminal lead and main fuse block.

48. Install the battery carrier and the battery. Connect the battery cables.

49. Remove the engine support bracket.

50. Refill the transaxle and check for leaks and proper operation.

3.0L ENGINE

1. Disconnect the battery cables and remove the battery and battery tray.

2. Disconnect the main fuse block.

3. Disconnect the air cleaner hose from the air cleaner, remove the bolt/nut/washer assemblies and remove the air cleaner.

4. Remove the cruise control actuator mounting bolts and nut and move the assembly aside.

5. Disconnect the speed sensor or speedometer cable from the transaxle.

6. Move the pinch clamps on the transaxle cooler lines aside, then disconnect and plug the lines at the radiator.

7. Disconnect the transaxle electrical connectors, then disconnect the harness from the routing brackets.

8. Disconnect the shift cable from the transaxle and routing bracket. Remove the transaxle wiring harness bracket and disconnect the 2 ground straps from the transaxle.

9. Disconnect the kickdown cable from the cable bracket and the throttle cam.

10. Install engine support bar D88L–6000–A or equivalent to support the engine and transaxle. Remove all accessible transaxle-to-engine bolts from the top of the engine compartment and remove the transaxle upper mount nuts.

11. Raise and safely support the vehicle.

12. Remove the front wheel and tire assemblies and the inner fender splash shields. Drain the transaxle fluid.

13. Disconnect the stabilizer links from the lower control arms and the bolts/nuts from the ball joints. Separate the ball joints from the steering knuckles by prying downward on the lower control arm while pushing inward on the rotor.

14. Remove the mounting bolts from the right halfshaft dynamic damper. Remove the halfshafts by inserting a prybar between the shaft and transaxle case and prying out.

15. Install transaxle plugs T88C–7025–AH or equivalent, in the transaxle to prevent the differential side gears from moving out of position.

16. Remove the starter and bracket and the transaxle support bracket.

17. Remove the torque converter inspection plate. Matchmark the converter and the flexplate and remove the attaching nuts. Use a prybar to move the converter away from the flexplate, disengaging the converter studs.

18. Position a transmission jack under the transaxle. Remove the rear lower mount bolts and the front lower mount through-bolt. Remove the left front crossmember and lower control arm as an assembly.

19. Remove the remaining transaxle-to-engine bolts and lower the transaxle from the vehicle.

To install:

20. Raise the transaxle into position, aligning the matchmark and the torque converter studs with the flexplate. Install the transaxle-to-engine lower bolts and tighten to 66–86 ft. lbs. (89–117 Nm).

21. Install the left front crossmember and lower control arm assembly. Tighten the bolts to 27–40 ft. lbs. (36–54 Nm) and the nut to 55–69 ft. lbs. (75–93 Nm).

22. Install the front lower mount through bolt and tighten to 66–86 ft. lbs. (85–117 Nm). Install the rear lower mount bolts and tighten to 49–69 ft. lbs. (67–93 Nm).

23. Install the torque converter attaching nuts and tighten to 32–45 ft. lbs. (43–61 Nm). Install the inspection plate and mounting bolt.

24. Install the transaxle support bracket and the starter motor and bracket.

25. Install a new circlip on the end of each halfshaft. Remove the transaxle plugs and install the halfshaft, making sure the clips lock in place.

26. Install the mounting bolts to the right halfshaft dynamic damper. Tighten to 31–46 ft. lbs. (42–62 Nm).

27. Attach the ball joints to the steering knuckles. Install the bolts and nuts and tighten to 27–40 ft. lbs. (36–54 Nm).

28. Install the stabilizer link assemblies. Turn the nuts until 0.79 in.

(20mm) of bolt thread can be measured from the upper nut.

29. Install the splash guards and the wheel and tire assemblies. Tighten the lug nuts to 65–87 ft. lbs. (88–118 Nm). Lower the vehicle.

30. Install the upper mount nuts and tighten to 47–66 ft. lbs. (64–89 Nm). Install the remaining transaxle-to-engine bolts and tighten to 66–86 ft. lbs. (89–117 Nm).

31. Remove the engine support bar.

32. Connect the kickdown cable to the throttle cam and the cable bracket. Tighten the adjusting nuts.

33. Connect the ground straps and install the wiring harness bracket.

34. Connect the shift cable to the routing bracket and the transaxle. Install the attaching nut and tighten to 33–47 ft. lbs. (44–64 Nm).

35. Connect the transaxle electrical connectors, then connect the harness routing brackets to the transaxle.

36. Unplug the transaxle cooler lines and connect them to the radiator. Install the pinch clamps.

37. Connect the speed sensor or speedometer cable to the transaxle.

38. Position the cruise control actuator and install the mounting bolts and nut.

39. Position the air cleaner assembly and install the bolt/nut/washer assemblies. Connect the air cleaner hose and install the clamp.

40. Connect the main fuse block.

41. Install the battery tray and battery. Connect the battery cables.

42. Refill the transaxle and check for leaks and proper operation. Adjust the kickdown cable.

1993–96

1. Disconnect the battery cables and remove the battery and battery tray.

2. Remove the air cleaner assembly.

3. Pry the shift cable from the transaxle manual lever. Remove the cable bracket lock tab retainer, press in on the lock tabs and pull the cable through the bracket.

4. Disconnect the neutral safety switch connector. Disconnect the oxygen sensor connector(s) and disconnect the transaxle electrical connector.

5. Remove the wiring harness bracket from the cable bracket. If equipped with 2.5L engine, remove the starter.

6. Disconnect the vehicle speed sensor connector. Remove the ground wire bracket and the ground wire.

7. Remove the harness support bracket to the engine block, located at the rear transaxle mount.

8. Disconnect and plug the oil cooler lines. Remove the 4 transaxle-to-engine mounting bolts.

9. Support the engine with engine support tool 014–00750 or equivalent. Remove the 2 left side transaxle mount nuts and bolt and the mount through bolt.

10. Remove the 2 fuel filter bracket nuts from the left transaxle mount. Position the filter and bracket, aside, without disconnecting the fuel lines.

11. Remove the left side transaxle mount. Disconnect the pulse signal generator connector.

12. Raise and safely support the vehicle. Remove the front wheel and tire assemblies and the splash shields.

13. Remove the 6 transverse member bolts and the transverse member. Remove the 6 transaxle cradle nuts and 2 bolts and remove the transaxle cradle.

14. Remove the 2 transaxle lower mount bolts and remove the lower mount.

15. Remove the halfshafts.

16. If equipped with 2.0L engine, remove the intake manifold support bracket and the starter.

17. Disconnect the transaxle vent hose and the dipstick tube.

18. If equipped with 2.0L engine, remove the seal rubber located next the starter opening. Use a small prybar to hold the flexplate and reach through the opening to remove the torque converter nuts.

19. If equipped with 2.5L engine, remove the 3 inspection cover bolts. Use a small prybar to hold the flexplate and remove the torque converter nuts.

20. Support the transaxle with a jack. Secure the transaxle to the jack to keep it from falling.

21. Remove the engine-to-transaxle and transaxle-to-engine bolts. Remove the 3 rear transaxle mount bolts.

22. Use a small prybar to separate the transaxle from the engine. Slightly tilt the transaxle and engine to ease removal.

23. Remove the transaxle from the engine and lower the transaxle from the vehicle.

To install:

24. Raise the transaxle into position. Align the torque converter studs with the flexplate.

25. If equipped with 2.0L engine, install the transaxle-to-engine and engine-to-transaxle bolts. Tighten bolt **B** to 73 ft. lbs. (99 Nm), bolt **C** to 38 ft. lbs. (51 Nm), bolt **D** to 18 ft. lbs.

(25 Nm), bolt **E** to 38 ft. lbs. (51 Nm) and bolt **F** to 73 ft. lbs. (99 Nm).

26. If equipped with 2.5L engine, install the engine-to-transaxle bolts and tighten to 73 ft. lbs. (99 Nm).

27. Install the 3 rear transaxle mount bolts and tighten to 68 ft. lbs. (93 Nm). Install the torque converter-to-flexplate nuts and tighten to 45 ft. lbs. (60 Nm).

28. On 2.0L engine, install the seal rubber. On 2.5L engine, install the inspection cover.

29. If equipped with 2.0L engine, install the intake manifold support bracket. Tighten the bolts to 38 ft. lbs. (52 Nm). Install the starter.

30. Connect the transaxle vent hose and install the dipstick tube. Tighten the dipstick tube mounting bolts to 88 inch lbs. (10 Nm).

31. Install the halfshafts.

32. Install the transaxle lower mount and tighten the bolts to 68 ft. lbs. (93 Nm). Remove the transmission jack.

33. Install the transaxle cradle. Tighten the cradle-to-body bolts and nuts to 68 ft. lbs. (93 Nm). Tighten the cradle-to-front mount nuts to 77 ft. lbs. (104 Nm) and the cradle-to-rear mount nuts to 44 ft. lbs. (60 Nm).

34. Install the transverse member and tighten the bolts to 96 ft. lbs. (131 Nm).

35. Install the splash shields and the wheel and tire assemblies. Lower the vehicle.

36. If equipped with 2.0L engine, install transaxle-to-engine bolts **A** and tighten to 73 ft. lbs. (99 Nm). If equipped with 2.5L engine, install the upper transaxle-to-engine bolts and tighten to 73 ft. lbs. (99 Nm).

37. Connect the vehicle speed sensor and pulse signal generator connectors. Install the ground wire bracket and the ground wire.

38. Install the harness support bracket to the engine block located at the rear transaxle mount.

39. Install the left side transaxle mount. Tighten the 2 nuts and bolt to 68 ft. lbs. (93 Nm) and the through bolt to 86 ft. lbs. (116 Nm). Remove the engine support tool.

40. Install the fuel filter bracket and tighten the nuts to 88 inch lbs. (10 Nm). Connect the oil cooler lines.

41. If equipped with 2.5L engine, install the starter.

42. Connect the transaxle electrical connector and the oxygen sensor connector(s).

43. Insert the shift cable through the cable bracket and pull the cable until the lock tabs engage. Install the

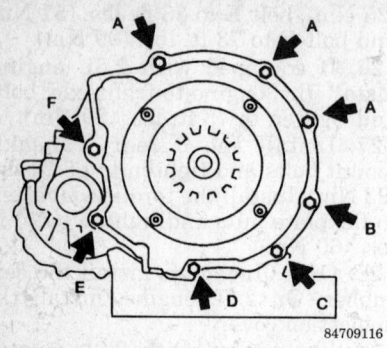

Transaxle mounting bolt identification — 2.0L engine with automatic transaxle

lock tab retainer. Connect the shift cable to the manual lever arm.

44. Connect the neutral safety switch connector. Snap the wiring harness bracket on the cable bracket.

45. Install the air cleaner assembly. Install the battery tray and battery. Connect the battery cables.

46. Fill the transaxle with the proper type and quantity of fluid. Run the engine and check for leaks. Road test and check for proper transaxle operation.

SHIFT CABLE ADJUSTMENT

1992

1. Disconnect the negative battery cable. Shift the gear selector to the **P** detent.

2. Remove the selector knob mounting screws and remove the selector knob.

3. Remove the selector trim piece and the 4 position indicator mounting screws. Disconnect the illumination bulb.

4. Disconnect the shift control switch and programmed ride control switch wiring harnesses.

5. Remove the position indicator.

NOTE: Make sure the detent spring roller is in the P detent.

6. Loosen nuts **A** and **B**. The loosen the shift control cable attaching trunnion bolt.

7. Turn the transaxle-mounted shift lever clockwise to put the transaxle in the **P** position.

8. Tighten nut **A** by hand until it contacts the spacer, then an additional ½ turn.

9. Tighten the trunnion bolt to 67–96 inch lbs. (8–11 Nm). Tighten nut **B** to 67–96 inch lbs. (8–11 Nm).

10. Lightly, press the selector pushrod and make sure the guide plate and guide pin clearances are within the specifications.

11. Check that the guide plate and guide pin clearances are within the specifications when the selector lever is shifted to **N** and **D**.

12. Connect the illumination bulb.

13. Connect the shift control switch and the programmed ride control switch wiring harnesses.

14. Install the position indicator and tighten the mounting screws.

15. Install the selector trim piece and position the selector knob. Tighten the knob screws.

16. Connect the negative battery cable.

1993–96

1. Disconnect the negative battery cable. Remove the floor console.

2. Move the gearshift lever to **P**.

3. Remove the position indicator mounting screws and lift the position indicator out of the way.

4. Slide the lock cover back and disconnect the set button.

5. Move the gearshift lever to adjust the **P** position.

6. Connect the set button and slide the lock cover to lock the set button in place.

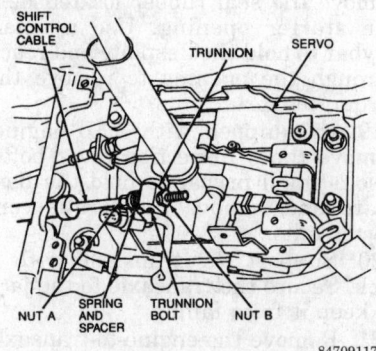

Shift cable adjustment — 1992 vehicles

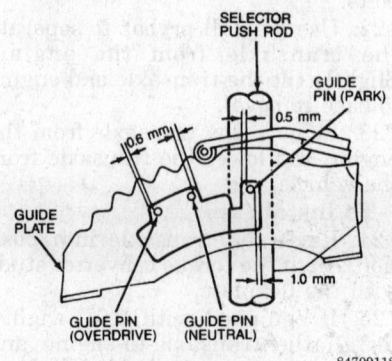

Guide plate and pin clearances — 1992 vehicles

7. Install the position indicator and tighten the mounting screws to 26 inch lbs. (2.9 Nm).

8. Install the floor console and connect the negative battery cable.

KICKDOWN CABLE ADJUSTMENT

1992

1. From the left front wheel well, remove the splash shield.

2. At the transaxle, remove the square head plug, marked **L**, and install an adapter and a suitable pressure gauge in the hole.

3. Rotate the kickdown cable locknuts to the furthest point from the throttle cam to loosen the cable all the way.

4. Place the transaxle into the **P** position and warm the engine; the idle speed should be 750 ± 25 rpm.

5. Rotate the locknuts toward the throttle cam until the line pressure exceeds 63–66 psi, rotate the locknuts away from the throttle cam until the line pressure is 63–66 psi and tighten the locknuts.

6. Turn the engine **OFF**, install the square head plug and torque to 43–87 inch lbs. (5–10 Nm).

7. When installing a new kickdown cable, fully open the throttle valve, crimp the pin with the protector installed. Remove the protector.

DRIVE AXLE

Halfshaft

REMOVAL AND INSTALLATION

1. Disconnect the negative battery cable. Raise and safely support the vehicle.

2. Remove the front wheel and tire assembly and the necessary inner fender splash guards.

3. Remove the stabilizer link assembly from the lower control arm.

4. Using a cape chisel and a hammer, raise the staked portion of the hub nut.

5. Using an assistant to depress the brake pedal, loosen but do not remove, the hub nut.

6. Remove the lower control arm ball joint clamp bolt. Using a prybar, pry the lower control arm downward

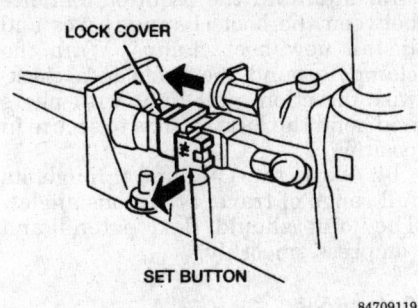

84709119

Shift cable adjustment — 1993–96 vehicles

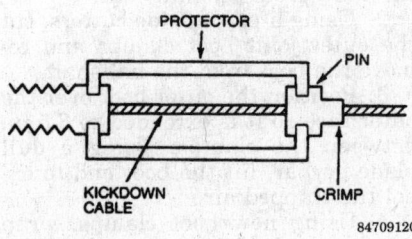

84709120

Crimping the pin on a new kickdown cable — 1992 vehicles

to separate the ball joint from the steering knuckle.

NOTE: If removing the right halfshaft, remove the support bearing bracket from the cylinder block.

7. Separate the halfshaft from the transaxle by positioning a prybar between the halfshaft and transaxle case. Pry out the halfshaft while pulling out on the steering knuckle. Be careful not to damage the transaxle case, transaxle oil seal, CV-joint or CV-joint boot.
8. Remove and discard the hub nut. Pull the halfshaft out of the wheel hub.

NOTE: If the halfshaft binds in the hub splines, use a plastic hammer to tap it out or a wheel puller to press it out. Never use a metal hammer.

9. Install transaxle plugs T88C-7025–AH or equivalent, into the halfshaft openings of the transaxle case and into the differential side gears; this will keep the differential side gears from becoming mispositioned.
To install:
10. On the end of each halfshaft, install a new circlip. Start 1 end of the

clip in the groove and work the clip over the stub shaft end and into the groove. This will prevent over-expanding the clip. Make sure the end gap is positioned at the top of the splines.
11. Remove the transaxle plugs and inspect the transaxle oil seals. Replace, if necessary.
12. Lubricate the halfshaft splines with a suitable grease, align the splines with the differential side gears and push the halfshaft into the differential. Make sure the retaining clip is seated in the differential side gear groove.
13. Position the halfshaft through the wheel hub and install a new attaching nut. Do not tighten the nut at this time.

NOTE: If installing the right halfshaft, install the halfshaft support bearing and tighten the mounting bolts to 31–46 ft. lbs. (42–62 Nm). On 2.0L and 2.5L engines, the bolts must be torqued in the proper sequence.

14. Position the ball joint in the steering knuckle and install the clamp bolt/nut. Tighten the nut to 32–40 ft. lbs. (43–54 Nm).
15. Install the stabilizer link assemblies. On 1992 vehicles, turn the nuts until 1.0 in. (25.4mm) of bolt thread can be measured from the upper nut. When the length is reached, secure the upper nut and back off the lower nut until a torque of 12–17 ft. lbs. (16–23 Nm) is reached. On 1993–96 vehicles, tighten the nut to 40 ft. lbs. (54 Nm).
16. Install the splash shields.
17. Have an assistant apply the brakes and tighten the halfshaft attaching nut to 116–174 ft. lbs. (157–235 Nm) on 1992 vehicles or 174–235 ft. lbs. (235–319 Nm) on 1993–96 vehicles. Stake the nut using a suitable chisel with a rounded cutting edge.

NOTE: If the nut splits or cracks after staking, it must be replaced with a new nut.

18. Install the wheel and tire assembly.

CV-Boot

REMOVAL AND INSTALLATION

Inner Boot

MANUAL TRANSAXLE

1. Clamp the halfshaft in a soft jawed vise. Do not allow the vise to contact the boot or boot clamps.

2. Remove the large boot clamp. After removing the clamp, roll the boot back over the shaft.

NOTE: The grease should be checked at this time for contamination. Rub some grease between your fingers, if grit can be felt the grease is contaminated. A contaminated joint should be disassembled, cleaned and inspected. If the grease is not contaminated and the CV-joint has been operating satisfactorily, replace only the boot and add the required lubricant.

3. Remove the wire ring bearing retainer. Before removing the bearing retainer, paint alignment marks on the outer race and shaft for assembly reference.
4. Remove the outer race.
5. Remove the inner race snapring from the end of the halfshaft. Before removing the snapring, paint alignment marks on the inner race and shaft.
6. Remove the inner race, cage and ball bearings from the shaft as an assembly.
7. Carefully pry the ball bearing out of the bearing cage using a small prybar. Be careful not to damage the bearing or cage surfaces. Matchmark the inner race and bearing cage for proper assembly.
8. Rotate the inner race to align the bearing lands with the windows in the bearing cage. Remove the inner race through the larger end of the cage.
9. Remove the small clamp and the boot from the halfshaft. If the boot is to be reused, wrap the halfshaft splines with tape before removing.
To install:
10. Clean and inspect all parts for wear and/or damage. Replace as necessary.
11. Cover the halfshaft splines with tape to prevent cutting the CV-joint boot. Install the boot.
12. Lubricate the inner race, bearing cage and ball bearings with high temperature CV-joint grease E43Z–19590–A or equivalent.
13. Position the inner race in the bearing cage and align the match marks. Install the race with the chamfered splines facing the large end of the cage.
14. Install the ball bearings in the bearing cage. The balls can be pressed into the cage windows with the heel of the hand.
15. Install the inner race, cage and balls onto the halfshaft as an assembly. Make sure the chamfer on the

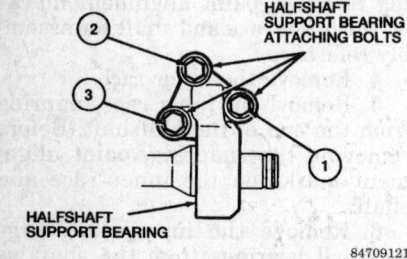

2.0L

HALFSHAFT SUPPORT
BEARING BRACKET
ATTACHING
BOLTS

HALFSHAFT
SUPPORT BEARING
BRACKET

2.5L

HALFSHAFT
SUPPORT BEARING
ATTACHING BOLTS

HALFSHAFT
SUPPORT BEARING

84709121

Halfshaft support bearing bracket bolt torque sequence — 1993–96 vehicles

bearing cage faces the snapring and that the paint marks made during removal are aligned. Install the inner race snapring.

16. Lubricate the outer race with 2 oz. of high temperature CV-joint grease E43Z–19590–A or equivalent. Install the outer race and add an additional ounce of the same grease. Install the wire ring bearing retainer.

17. Position the boot, making sure it is fully seated in the grooves in the shaft and outer race. Extend or compress the CV-joint as necessary until the distance between the boot clamp grooves is 3.5 in. (90mm). Do not allow this dimension to change until the boot clamps are installed.

18. Insert a small prybar with a dulled edge between the boot and the outer bearing race to allow any trapped air to escape.

19. Install the new boot clamps. Wrap the clamps around the boots in a clockwise direction, pull tight with pliers and bend the locking tabs to secure in position.

20. Work the CV-joint through its full range of travel at various angles. The joint should flex, extend and compress smoothly.

AUTOMATIC TRANSAXLE

1. Clamp the halfshaft in a soft jawed vise. Do not allow the vise to contact the boot or boot clamps.

2. Remove the large boot clamp. After removing the clamp, roll the boot back over the shaft.

NOTE: The grease should be checked at this time for contamination. Rub some grease between your fingers, if grit can be felt the grease is contaminated. A contaminated joint should be disassembled, cleaned and inspected. If the grease is not contaminated and the CV-joint has been operating satisfactorily, replace only the boot and add the required lubricant.

3. Remove the wire ring bearing retainer. Remove the outer race, after painting or scribing matchmarks on the outer race and tripot bearing for assembly reference.

4. Remove the tripot bearing snapring, after painting matchmarks on the tripot bearing and shaft for assembly reference.

5. Using a brass drift and hammer, remove the tripot bearing assembly from the shaft. Remove the small clamp and the CV-joint boot. If the boot is to be reused, wrap the halfshaft splines with tape before removing.

To install:

6. Clean and inspect all parts for wear and/or damage. Replace as necessary.

7. Lubricate all components with high temperature CV-joint grease E43Z–19590–A or equivalent.

8. Cover the halfshaft splines with tape to prevent cutting the CV-joint boot. Install the boot.

9. Install the tripot bearing on the shaft with the matchmarks aligned. Use a brass drift and hammer, if necessary, to tap the assembly into place. Install the snapring.

10. Fill the CV-joint outer race with 3.5 oz. of high temperature CV-joint grease, E43Z–19590–A or equivalent. Install the outer race over the tripot joint, with matchmarks aligned, and install the wire ring bearing retainer.

11. Position the CV-joint boot into the grooves in the shaft and outer race. Make sure the boot is fully seated.

12. Extend or compress the joint, as necessary, until the distance between the CV-joint boot clamp grooves is 3.5 in. (90mm). Insert a small prybar with a dulled edge between the boot and outer race to allow any trapped air to escape.

13. Maintain the required distance between the boot clamp grooves and install new boot clamps. Wrap the clamps around the boots in a clockwise direction, pull tight with pliers and bend the locking tabs to secure in position.

14. Work the CV-joint through its full range of travel at various angles. The joint should flex, extend and compress smoothly.

Outer Boot

The outer CV-joint is not serviceable and must be replaced with the shaft as an assembly.

1. Remove the inner joint and boot assembly from the halfshaft.

2. Using a pair of side cutters, cut the outer joint boot clamps and remove the boot from the halfshaft.

3. Position the outer boot over the outer race so it is extended to 3.5 in. between the clamps. Using a dull blade prybar, lift the boot end to expel the trapped air.

4. Using new boot clamps, wrap them around the boots in a clockwise direction, pull them tight using a pair of pliers and bend the locking tabs to secure them in place.

5. To complete the installation, reverse the removal procedures. Install the halfshaft into the vehicle.

Front Wheel Hub, Knuckle/Spindle and Bearings

REMOVAL AND INSTALLATION

1. Raise and safely support the vehicle. Remove the front wheel and tire assembly.

2. Using a small cape chisel and a hammer, raise the staked portion of the hub nut.

3. Have an assistant apply the brakes and remove the hub nut. Discard the nut after removal; it must not be reused.

4. On 1992 vehicles, remove the stabilizer bar-to-control arm, bolt, nut, washers and bushings. On 1993–96 vehicles, remove the stabilizer bar link nut.

5. At the tie rod end, remove the cotter pin and nut. Using a tie rod end separator tool or equivalent, separate the tie rod end from the steering knuckle.

6. If equipped with anti-lock brakes, remove the wheel speed sensor and the sensor harness routing bracket.

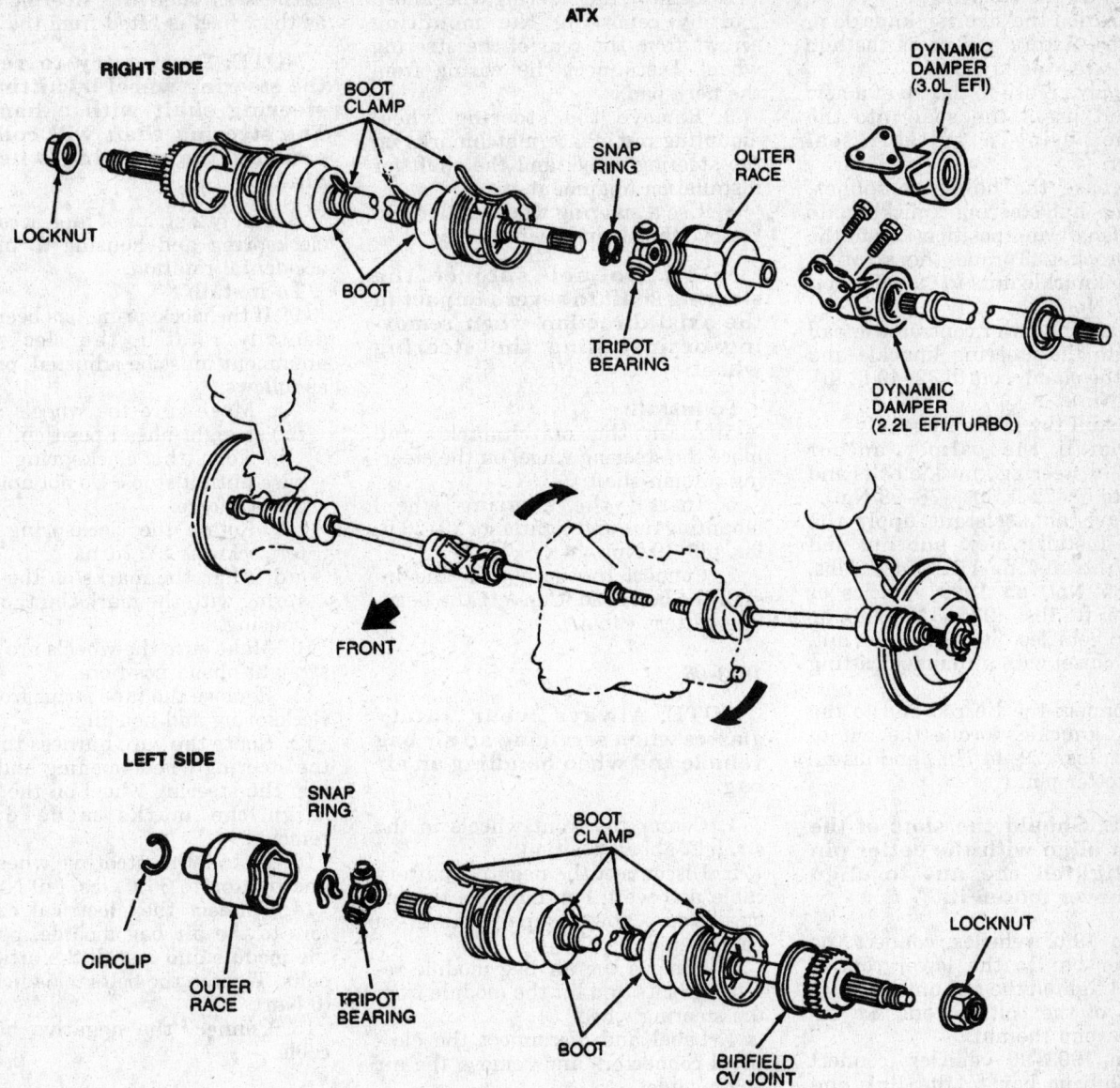

Exploded view of the automatic transaxle halfshafts

7. Remove the caliper and anchor bracket and suspend the caliper assembly from the coil spring with mechanics wire.

8. Remove the brake disc rotor.

9. Remove the lower control arm ball joint clamp nut/bolt. Using a prybar, pry the lower control arm downward and separate the ball joint from the steering knuckle.

10. Remove the steering knuckle-to-strut attaching bolts and slide the steering knuckle assembly from the strut bracket.

11. Slide the steering knuckle assembly from the halfshaft and support the halfshaft with mechanics wire; be careful not to damage the seals. Should the wheel hub bind on the halfshaft, use a plastic hammer to jar it free.

NOTE: If the halfshaft splines bind in the hub, it may be necessary to use a 2-jawed wheel puller to separate them.

12. Using a prybar, pry the grease seal from the knuckle.

13. Position the steering knuckle in a suitable fixture and press the hub from the knuckle.

NOTE: If the inner race remains on the hub, grind a section of the inner race to approximately 0.020 in. (0.5mm) and use a chisel to remove it.

14. Remove the snapring from the steering knuckle.

15. Position the steering knuckle in a suitable fixture and press the bearing from the knuckle.

NOTE: Unless the disc brake dust shield is damaged, it should be left on the steering knuckle; it is pressed on and is difficult to remove without damaging it.

To install:

16. Inspect the steering knuckle and hub for cracks, wear and scoring. Replace parts as necessary.

17. Position the steering knuckle in a suitable fixture and press in the wheel bearing.

18. Install the snapring.

19. Position the steering knuckle in a suitable fixture and press the hub into the steering knuckle.

20. Apply grease to the lip of a new seal and press the seal into the knuckle, using a suitable seal installer.

21. Grease the halfshaft splines. Slide the hub/steering knuckle onto the halfshaft and position it into the strut bracket. Torque the strut-to-steering knuckle nuts to 69–86 ft. lbs. (93–117 Nm).

22. Push the lower control arm ball joint into the steering knuckle and torque the clamp bolt to 32–40 ft. lbs. (43–54 Nm).

23. Install the brake rotor.

24. Install the caliper anchor bracket-to-steering knuckle bolts and torque to 58–72 ft. lbs. (78–98 Nm).

25. Have an assistant apply the brakes. Install a new hub nut and torque the nut to 116–174 ft. lbs. (157–235 Nm) on 1992 vehicles or 174–235 ft. lbs. (235–319 Nm) on 1993–96 vehicles. Stake the hub nut, using a chisel with a rounded cutting edge.

26. Connect the tie rod end to the steering knuckle, torque the nut to 22–33 ft. lbs. (29–44 Nm) and install a new cotter pin.

NOTE: Should the slots of the nut not align with the cotter pin hole, tighten the nut to align them; never loosen it.

27. On 1992 vehicles, connect the stabilizer bar to the lower control arm and tighten the nut until 0.79 in. (20mm) of the bolt threads are exposed beyond the nut.

28. On 1993–96 vehicles, connect the stabilizer bar to the link and tighten the nut to 40 ft. lbs. (54 Nm).

29. Install the wheel and tire assembly and torque the lug nuts to 65–87 ft. lbs. (88–118 Nm).

STEERING

Steering Wheel

REMOVAL AND INSTALLATION

1992

1. Disconnect the negative battery cable.

2. Remove the steering wheel horn pad by removing the mounting screws from the rear of the steering wheel. Disconnect the wiring from the horn pad.

3. Remove the steering wheel mounting nut. Place matchmarks on the steering wheel and the shaft for installation alignment.

4. Use a steering wheel puller and remove the steering wheel.

NOTE: Do not subject the steering shaft to severe impact in the axial direction when removing or installing the steering wheel.

To install:

5. Align the matchmarks and place the steering wheel on the steering column shaft.

6. Install the steering wheel mounting nut and tighten to 29–36 ft. lbs. (39–49 Nm).

7. Connect the horn wire and install the horn pad. Connect the negative battery cable.

1993–96

NOTE: Always wear safety glasses when servicing an air bag vehicle and when handling an air bag.

1. Center the front wheels in the straight-ahead position.

2. Disconnect the negative battery cable and wait 1 minute for the air bag backup power supply energy to be depleted.

3. Remove the air bag module retaining bolts and lift the module from the steering wheel.

4. Label and disconnect the electrical connectors and remove the air bag module.

--- **CAUTION** ---

When carrying a live air bag, make sure the bag and trim cover are pointed away from the body. In the unlikely event of an accidental deployment, the bag will then deploy with minimal chance of personal injury. When placing a live air bag on a bench or other surface, always face the bag and trim cover up, away from the surface. This will reduce the motion of the module if it is accidentally deployed.

5. Make an alignment mark on the steering wheel and steering shaft for assembly reference.

6. Remove the steering wheel nut.

7. Remove the steering wheel using a suitable puller. Route the wire harness through the steering wheel as the wheel is lifted from the shaft.

NOTE: Do not try to remove the steering wheel by hitting the steering shaft with a hammer. The steering shaft will collapse, causing the steering wheel to bind.

8. Apply 2 strips of tape across the clockspring and housing to prevent accidental rotation.

To install:

9. If the clockspring has been accidentally rotated, the clockspring alignment must be adjusted, proceed as follows:

a. Make sure the wheels are in the straight-ahead position.

b. Turn the clockspring clockwise until it stops. Do not apply excessive force.

c. Rotate the clockspring counterclockwise $2\frac{3}{4}$ turns.

d. Align the marks on the clockspring with the marks on the outer housing.

10. Make sure the wheels are in the straight-ahead position.

11. Remove the tape strips from the clockspring and housing.

12. Route the wire harness through the steering wheel opening and position the steering wheel on the shaft. Align the marks made during removal.

13. Install the steering wheel nut and tighten to 36 ft. lbs. (49 Nm).

14. Connect the electrical connectors to the air bag module, position the module and install the attaching bolts. Tighten the bolts to 54 inch lbs. (6 Nm).

15. Connect the negative battery cable.

Steering Column

REMOVAL AND INSTALLATION

1992

1. Disconnect the negative battery cable.

2. Remove the steering wheel.

3. Remove the column cover screws and the cover.

4. Remove the 9 attaching screws from the instrument cover. Carefully, pull the cover outward and disconnect the electrical connectors from the cover. Remove the ignition illumination bulb and the instrument cover.

5. Loosen the 2 instrument cluster cover-to-hinge screws, remove the 6 instrument cluster cover-to-dash

screws and the instrument cluster cover.

6. Remove the lower panel, the lap duct and the defrost duct.

7. Disconnect the electrical connectors from the ignition switch and turn signal cancel switch.

8. Remove the upper U-joint cinch bolt from the lower end of the steering shaft.

9. Remove the mounting nuts from the hinge bracket.

10. Remove the 4 cluster support nuts and the 2 nuts and 4 bolts from the upper steering column brackets. Remove the steering shaft assembly.

11. At the steering rack, lift the boot from the intermediate shaft U-joint and remove the lower U-joint cinch bolt.

12. Remove the 4 intermediate shaft dust cover assembly nuts, the intermediate shaft and the dust cover assembly.

To install:

13. Using an assistant to support the intermediate shaft and dust cover assembly, guide the lower U-joint onto the steering rack pinion.

14. Install the lower intermediate shaft U-joint cinch bolt and torque it to 13–20 ft. lbs. (18–26 Nm). Install the dust cover nuts.

15. Using an assistant to support the steering column, guide the column into the upper intermediate U-joint. Do not install the cinch bolt at this time.

16. Install the hinge bracket nuts, but do not tighten at this time.

17. Install the upper cinch bolt into the intermediate U-joint and tighten to 13–20 ft. lbs. (18–26 Nm).

18. Install the upper column bracket bolts. Tighten the hinge bracket nuts to 12–17 ft. lbs. (16–23 Nm) and the upper bracket bolts to 6.5–10 ft. lbs. (8.8–14 Nm).

19. Install the cluster support nuts and tighten to 6.5–10 ft. lbs. (8.8–14 Nm).

20. Connect the electrical connectors at the ignition switch and turn signal cancel switch.

21. Install the lap duct and the defrost duct. Install the lower panel.

22. Position the instrument cluster cover and install the attaching screws. Tighten the 2 cover hinge screws.

23. Connect the electrical connectors and install the ignition illumination bulb into the instrument cover and install the cover.

24. Install the column cover and the steering wheel. Connect the negative battery cable.

1993–96

1. Center the front wheels in the straight-ahead position.

2. Disconnect the negative battery cable and wait 1 minute for the air bag backup power supply energy to be depleted.

3. Remove the steering wheel.

4. Remove the clockspring assembly as follows:

a. Apply 2 strips of tape across the clockspring and housing to prevent accidental rotation.

b. Remove the 3 clockspring screws and pull the clockspring assembly off the steering column shaft.

c. Remove the clockspring ground wire screw and disconnect the clockspring electrical connector.

d. Remove the clockspring assembly.

5. Remove the combination switch.

6. Loosen the hood release cable nut and remove the hood release cable from the lower instrument panel cover.

7. Remove the lower instrument panel screw. Disconnect the courtesy light electrical connector and remove the lower instrument panel.

8. Label and disconnect the necessary electrical connectors. If equipped with automatic transaxle, disconnect the shift-lock cable.

9. Remove the intermediate shaft bolt. Remove the 2 lower column bracket nuts and the 2 upper column bracket bolts.

10. Remove the steering column.

To install:

11. Position the steering column in the vehicle. Install the column bracket nuts and bolts and tighten to 17 ft. lbs. (23 Nm).

12. Install the intermediate shaft bolt and tighten to 20 ft. lbs. (26 Nm).

13. Connect the electrical connectors. If equipped with automatic transaxle, connect the shift-lock cable.

14. Connect the courtesy light electrical connector and install the lower instrument panel. Install the panel screw.

15. Connect the hood release cable to the lower instrument panel cover and tighten the nut.

16. Install the combination switch.

17. Install the clockspring as follows:

a. Make sure the wheels are in the straight-ahead position.

b. If the clockspring has been accidentally rotated, the clockspring alignment must be adjusted: Turn

the clockspring clockwise until it stops; do not use excessive force. Rotate the clockspring counterclockwise 2¾ turns and align the clockspring and outer housing marks.

NOTE: If a new clockspring is being installed, the alignment is already set.

c. Install the clockspring ground wire screw and position the clockspring assembly on the steering column shaft.

d. Connect the clockspring electrical connector.

e. Install the 3 clockspring screws and tighten to 26 inch lbs. (3 Nm).

f. Remove the tape strips from the clockspring and housing.

18. Install the steering wheel and connect the negative battery cable.

Power Rack and Pinion

ADJUSTMENT

1992

STANDARD POWER STEERING

1. Disconnect the negative battery cable. Remove the steering gear from the vehicle and place it in a holding fixture.

2. Using pinion torque adapter tool T88C-3504–BH or equivalent, and an inch pound torque wrench, check the pinion turning torque; it should be 89–124 inch lbs. (10–14 Nm).

3. If the torque is not to specifications, loosen the locknut.

4. Using yoke torque gauge tool T88C-3504–AH or equivalent, torque the adjusting cover to 7.2 ft. lbs. (9.8 Nm), loosen the cover, retorque to 3.6 ft. lbs. (4.9 Nm) and loosen the cover 45 degrees.

5. Using yoke locknut wrench tool T88C-3504–KH or equivalent, torque the locknut to 36–43 ft. lbs. (49–59 Nm).

6. Install the steering gear. Refill the power steering reservoir. Start the engine and bleed the system. Test drive and check the steering operation.

ELECTRONIC POWER STEERING

1. Disconnect the negative battery cable. Remove the steering gear from the vehicle and place it in a holding fixture.

2. Using pinion torque adapter tool T88C-3504–BH or equivalent, and an inch pound torque wrench, check the pinion turning torque; it

should be 89–124 inch lbs. (10–14 Nm).

3. If the torque is not to specifications, loosen the locknut.

4. Using yoke torque gauge tool T88C–3504–AH or equivalent, torque the adjusting cover to 39–48 inch lbs. (4.5–5.5 Nm), then loosen it 35 degrees.

5. Using yoke locknut wrench tool T88C–3504–KH or equivalent, torque the locknut to 29–36 ft. lbs. (40–50 Nm).

6. Install the steering gear. Refill the power steering reservoir. Connect the negative battery cable.

7. Start the engine and bleed the system. Test drive and check the steering operation.

1993–96

1. Remove the steering gear from the vehicle and secure it in a soft jawed vise.

2. Measure the pinion preload using pinion torque adapter T92C–3504–AH or equivalent. The correct torque at the neutral position ± 90 degrees, should be 9–12 inch lbs. (1.0–1.4 Nm). At any other position, the torque should be 15 inch lbs. (1.6 Nm).

3. If the pinion preload is not within specification, loosen the adjusting cover locknut.

NOTE: Apply thread locking compound to the exposed threads of the adjusting cover.

4. Use yoke plug adapter T81P–3504–U or equivalent, to tighten the adjusting cover to 87 inch lbs. (9 Nm), then loosen it. Tighten the adjusting cover again to 48 inch lbs. (5 Nm), then loosen it 45 degrees.

NOTE: Do not allow the adjusting cover to turn.

5. Install the adjusting cover locknut. Use yoke locknut wrench T88C–3504–KH or equivalent, to tighten the adjusting cover locknut while holding the adjusting cover to 43 ft. lbs. (59 Nm).

REMOVAL AND INSTALLATION

1992

STANDARD POWER STEERING

1. Disconnect the negative battery cable.

2. Raise and safely support the vehicle. Remove the front wheel and tire assemblies.

3. Remove the cotter pins and nuts from the tie rod end studs. Sepa-

rate the tie rod ends from the steering knuckles using separator tool T85M–3395–A or equivalent.

NOTE: If the tie rod end does not separate easily, give the steering knuckle a sharp blow with a brass hammer or drift to shock the taper.

4. From both sides of the vehicle, remove the lower inner fender plastic splash shield.

5. At the steering assembly, pull back the steering column dust boot, turn the steering shaft until the clamp bolt is accessible and lock the steering column. Using paint, matchmark the steering column pinion shaft-to-intermediate shaft lower universal joint location.

6. Remove the clamp bolt from the intermediate shaft lower universal joint.

7. Disconnect and plug both hydraulic lines at the steering gear. Position the lines aside.

8. Remove the 6 steering gear-to-chassis bolts and lower the steering gear until it rests on the crossmember. Slide the steering gear toward the right side until the left tie rod clears the left lower control arm, then carefully slide the steering gear to the left and remove from the vehicle.

To install:

9. Move the steering gear into position through the right side lower inner fender well opening, until the pinion shaft is just below the intermediate shaft universal joint.

10. Raise the steering gear into position, align the pinion shaft-to-intermediate universal joint matchmark and install the steering gear-to-chassis bolts. Torque the bolts to 27–40 ft. lbs. (36–54 Nm).

11. Install the pinion shaft-to-intermediate universal joint clamp bolt and torque to 13–20 ft. lbs. (18–26 Nm).

12. Connect the hydraulic lines to the steering gear. Tighten the large hydraulic line to 25–33 ft. lbs. (34–44 Nm) and the small hydraulic line to 18–22 ft. lbs. (25–29 Nm).

13. Connect the tie rod ends to the steering knuckles. Install the attaching nuts and tighten to 22–33 ft. lbs. (29–44 Nm), then install new cotter pins.

14. Install the splash shields.

15. Install the wheel and tire assemblies.

16. Lower the vehicle. Refill the power steering reservoir. Start the engine, bleed the power steering system and check for leaks.

ELECTRONIC POWER STEERING

1. Disconnect the negative battery cable.

2. Raise and safely support the vehicle. Remove the front wheel and tire assemblies.

3. Remove the cotter pins and nuts from the tie rod end studs. Separate the tie rod ends from the steering knuckles using separator tool T85M–3395–A or equivalent.

NOTE: If the tie rod end does not separate easily, give the steering knuckle a sharp blow with a brass hammer or drift to shock the taper.

4. From both sides of the vehicle, remove the lower inner fender plastic dust shields.

5. At the steering assembly, pull back the steering column dust boot, turn the steering shaft until the clamp bolt is accessible and lock the steering column. Using paint, matchmark the steering column pinion shaft-to-intermediate shaft lower universal joint location.

6. Remove the clamp bolt from the intermediate shaft lower universal joint.

7. Disconnect the electrical connector from the solenoid valve and the power steering pressure switch.

8. Disconnect and plug the hydraulic lines at the steering gear; discard both copper washers from each fitting and position the lines aside.

9. Remove the steering gear-to-chassis bolts and lower the steering gear until it clears the bulkhead. Slide the steering gear toward the right side until the left tie rod clears the left lower control arm, then carefully slide it to the left and remove from the vehicle.

To install:

10. Slide the steering gear into position through the right side lower inner fender well opening, until the pinion shaft is just below the intermediate shaft universal joint.

11. Raise the steering gear into position, align the pinion shaft-to-intermediate universal joint matchmark and install the steering gear-to-chassis bolts. Torque the bolts to 27–40 ft. lbs. (36–54 Nm).

12. Install the pinion shaft-to-intermediate universal joint clamp bolt and torque to 13–20 ft. lbs. (18–26 Nm).

13. Using new copper washers, connect the hydraulic lines to the steering gear. Connect the electrical connectors to the solenoid valve and the power steering pressure switch.

14. Connect the tie rod ends to the steering knuckles. Install the attaching nuts and tighten to 22–33 ft. lbs. (29–44 Nm), then install new cotter pins.

15. Install the front wheel and tire assemblies. Lower the vehicle.

16. Refill the power steering reservoir. Start the engine, bleed the power steering system and check for leaks.

1993–96

1. Disconnect the negative battery cable.

2. Support the engine with engine support tool D88L–6000–A or equivalent.

3. Raise and safely support the vehicle. Remove the wheel and tire assemblies.

4. Remove the cotter pins and nuts from the tie rod ends. Use tool 3290–D or equivalent to separate the tie rod ends from the steering knuckles.

5. Remove the splash shields. Remove the 6 transverse member bolts and remove the transverse member.

6. Remove the 2 bolts and 6 nuts from the transaxle cradle and remove the cradle.

7. If equipped with 2.5L engine, disconnect the oxygen sensor connectors. Remove the exhaust pipe-to-manifold nuts and separate the pipes from the manifolds. Move the front exhaust pipe aside.

8. Disconnect and plug the power steering pressure and return hoses.

9. Remove the ground wire bracket from the rear engine mount. Remove the 3 rear engine mount-to-transaxle bolts, the mount through bolt and remove the mount.

10. Remove the 4 bolts from the 2 steering gear mounting brackets and remove the brackets. Remove the intermediate shaft-to-pinion shaft bolt.

11. If equipped with manual transaxle, remove the extension bar nut and position the extension bar aside.

12. Position a jack under the front crossmember. Remove the 6 front crossmember bolts and 2 nuts.

13. Remove the vent tube attached to the drivers side of the front crossmember. Remove the stabilizer bar-to-stabilizer control link nuts.

14. Lower the front crossmember to allow removal of the steering gear. Remove the steering gear from the drivers side of the vehicle.
  To install:
15. Position the steering gear in the vehicle. Install the intermediate shaft-to-pinion shaft bolt and tighten to 20 ft. lbs. (26 Nm).

16. Raise the front crossmember into position. Install the crossmember mounting bolts and nuts and tighten to 97 ft. lbs. (131 Nm). Remove the jack supporting the front crossmember.

17. Install the stabilizer bar-to-stabilizer control link nuts and tighten to 40 ft. lbs. (54 Nm). Install the vent tube.

18. Position the steering gear mounting brackets and install the mounting bolts. Tighten to 40 ft. lbs. (54 Nm).

19. Position the rear engine mount and install the through bolt. Tighten the through bolt to 86 ft. lbs. (117 Nm).

20. Install the 3 rear engine mount-to-transaxle bolts and tighten to 68 ft. lbs. (93 Nm). Install the ground wire bracket to the rear engine mount.

21. Remove the plugs and connect the power steering lines. If equipped with manual transaxle, install the extension bar bolt and tighten to 38 ft. lbs. (51 Nm).

22. If equipped with 2.5L engine, connect the exhaust pipes to the manifolds and tighten the nuts to 38 ft. lbs. (51 Nm). Connect the oxygen sensor connectors.

23. Position the transverse member and install the bolts. Tighten the bolts to 97 ft. lbs. (131 Nm).

24. Position the transaxle cradle and install the bolts and nuts. Tighten the cradle-to-chassis bolts and nuts to 68 ft. lbs. (93 Nm), the cradle-to-front mount nuts to 77 ft. lbs. (104 Nm) and the cradle-to-rear mount nuts to 44 ft. lbs. (60 Nm).

25. Connect the tie rod ends to the steering knuckles and tighten the nuts to 33 ft. lbs. (44 Nm). Install new cotter pins.

26. Install the splash shields and the wheel and tire assemblies. Lower the vehicle.

27. Remove the engine support tool.

28. Fill the power steering system with the proper type of fluid. Connect the negative battery cable and bleed the air from the system.

Power Steering Pump

REMOVAL AND INSTALLATION

2.0L Engine

1. Disconnect the negative battery cable.

2. Remove the 2 power steering pump belt shield bolts.

3. Remove the lock and adjusting bolts. Remove the power steering belt.

4. Insert a small prybar through a hole in the power steering pump pulley to hold it in place. Loosen the pulley nut and remove the pulley.

5. Remove the 2 supply line manifold bolts and remove the high pressure line banjo bolt.

6. Disconnect the pump pressure switch and remove the pump through bolt. Remove the power steering pump.
  To install:
7. Position the power steering pump and loosely install the through bolt.

8. Install the high pressure line banjo bolt, using new washers, and tighten to 33 ft. lbs. (44 Nm).

9. Connect the supply line manifold and tighten the bolts to 13 ft. lbs. (18 Nm).

10. Install the power steering pump pulley and the retaining nut. Insert a small prybar through a hole in the pulley to hold it in place and torque the nut to 43 ft. lbs. (59 Nm).

11. Install the power steering belt and the lock and adjusting bolts. Adjust the belt tension.

12. Install the 2 power steering pump belt shield bolts and connect the negative battery cable. Fill the power steering system with the proper fluid and bleed the air from the system.

2.2L Engine

1. Disconnect the negative battery cable.

2. At the right fender, remove the inner fender splash shield.

3. Loosen the power steering pump and remove the drive belt.

4. Disconnect and plug the pressure and return hoses from the pump.

5. Remove the pump-to-bracket bolts and the pump; if necessary, remove the drive pulley from the pump.
  To install:
6. Position the pump on the bracket and torque the bolts to 27–34 ft. lbs. (31–46 Nm).

7. Connect the pressure and return hoses to the pump.

8. Install the drive belt. Refill the power steering reservoir. Connect the negative battery cable, start the engine and bleed the system.

2.5L Engine

1. Disconnect the negative battery cable.

2. Remove the high pressure line hold-down bracket bolt and the high pressure line banjo bolt.

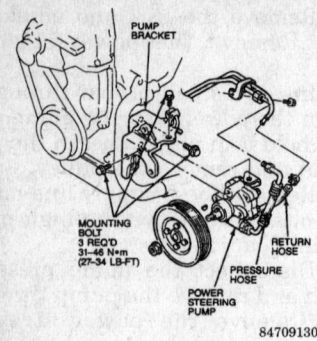

Power steering pump removal and installation — 2.2L engine

84709130

3. Raise and safely support the vehicle. Remove the passenger side front tire and wheel assembly and the splash shield.

4. Loosen the adjusting bolt and remove the power steering pump belt.

5. Insert a small prybar through a hole in the power steering pump pulley to hold it in place. Loosen the pulley nut and remove the pulley.

6. Remove the 2 supply line manifold bolts and remove the high pressure line hold-down bracket nut.

7. Disconnect the power steering pump pressure switch.

8. Remove the 4 power steering pump bracket-to-engine bolts and the power steering pump.

To install:

9. Position the power steering pump and install the pump bracket-to-engine bolts. Tighten to 34 ft. lbs. (46 Nm). Connect the pressure switch connector.

10. Install the high pressure line bracket nut and tighten to 86 inch lbs. (9 Nm). Install the supply line manifold bolts and tighten to 13 ft. lbs. (18 Nm).

11. Install the power steering pump pulley and the retaining nut. Insert a small prybar through a hole in the pulley to hold it in place and torque the nut to 43 ft. lbs. (59 Nm).

12. Install the power steering pump belt and adjust the tension.

13. Install the splash shield and the front wheel and tire assembly. Lower the vehicle.

14. Install the high pressure line banjo bolt, using new washers, and tighten to 33 ft. lbs. (44 Nm).

15. Install the high pressure line hold-down bracket bolt and tighten to 86 ft. lbs. (9 Nm).

16. Connect the negative battery cable. Fill the power steering system with the proper fluid and bleed the air from the system.

3.0L Engine

1. Disconnect the negative battery cable.

2. Remove the washer reservoir and place aside.

3. Remove the plastic shield and the accessory drive belt.

4. Remove the drive pulley from the pump.

5. Disconnect and plug both power steering hoses at the pump.

6. Remove the pump mounting bolts and lift the pump from the accessory support bracket.

To install:

7. Position the pump on the accessory support bracket.

8. Install the pump mounting bolts and tighten to 15–22 ft. lbs. (20–30 Nm).

9. Install the drive pulley and replace both power steering hoses.

10. Install the drive belt and the plastic shield. Install the washer reservoir and connect the negative battery cable.

11. Fill the pump reservoir and bleed the system.

BELT ADJUSTMENT

2.0L Engine

1. Apply approximately 22 lbs pressure to the drive belt at a point midway between the power steering pump pulley and the crankshaft pulley.

NOTE: Always check belt deflection when the engine is cold, or has been stopped for at least 30 minutes. A drive belt is considered new if it has been used on a running engine for less than 5 minutes.

2. The belt should deflect 0.30–0.35 in. (7.5–9.0mm) for new or 0.32–0.37 in. (8.0–9.5mm) for used.

3. If the belt tension is not as specified, loosen the adjusting bolt, lock bolt and through bolt.

4. Turn the adjusting bolt until the belt tension is correct. Tighten the lock bolt to 34 ft. lbs. (46 Nm) and the through bolt to 44 ft. lbs. (60 Nm).

2.2L Engine

1. Apply approximately 22 lbs pressure to the drive belt at a point midway between the A/C compressor pulley and the crankshaft pulley.

NOTE: Always check belt deflection when the engine is cold, or has been stopped for at least 30 minutes. A drive belt is consid-

ered new if it has been used on a running engine for less than 5 minutes.

2. The belt should deflect 0.27–0.35 in. (7–9mm) for new or 0.31–0.39 in. (8–10mm) for used.

3. If the belt tension is not as specified, loosen the air conditioning compressor pivot and adjustment lock bolts.

4. Turn the tension adjusting bolt until the belt tension is as specified.

5. After adjustment, tighten the lock and pivot bolts to 38 ft. lbs. (51 Nm).

2.5L Engine

1. Apply approximately 22 lbs. pressure to the drive belt at a point midway between the power steering pump and water pump pulleys.

NOTE: Always check belt deflection when the engine is cold, or has been stopped for at least 30 minutes. A drive belt is considered new if it has been used on a running engine for less than 5 minutes.

2. The belt should deflect 0.24–0.28 in. (6–7mm) for new or 0.28–0.31 in. (7–8mm) for used.

3. If the belt tension is not as specified, loosen the tensioner locknut. Turn the adjusting bolt until the tension is correct.

4. After adjustment, tighten the tensioner locknut to 34 ft. lbs. (46 Nm).

3.0L Engine

Power steering belt tension is maintained by an automatic tensioner. No adjustment is necessary.

SYSTEM BLEEDING

1. Raise and support the vehicle, safely.

2. Disconnect the coil wire. Refill the power steering pump reservoir to the specified level.

3. Crank the engine. Check and refill the reservoir.

4. Crank the engine and rotate the steering wheel from lock-to-lock.

NOTE: The front wheels must be off the ground during lock-to-lock rotation of the steering wheel.

5. Check and refill the power steering pump reservoir.

6. Connect the coil wire, start the engine and allow it to run for several minutes.

7. Rotate the steering wheel from lock-to-lock several times, until the air bubbles are eliminated from the fluid.

8. Turn the engine **OFF**. Check and/or refill the reservoir.

9. Disconnect the negative battery cable, depress the brake pedal for at least 5 seconds and reconnect the negative battery cable.

Tie Rod Ends

REMOVAL AND INSTALLATION

1. Raise and safely support the vehicle. Remove the wheel and tire assembly.

2. Remove the cotter pin and the nut from the tie rod end stud.

3. Separate the tie rod end from the steering knuckle using separator tool T85M–3395–A or equivalent. If the tie rod end does not separate easily, give the steering knuckle a sharp blow with a brass hammer or drift to shock the taper.

4. Paint or mark an alignment stripe on the tie rod end, jam nut, and tie rod.

5. Loosen the jam nut and remove the tie rod end.

To install:

6. Thread the jam nut and tie rod end onto the tie rod.

7. Align the marks made during removal and tighten the jam nut to 51–72 ft. lbs. (69–98 Nm).

8. Install the tie rod end in the steering knuckle. Install the nut and tighten to 22–33 ft. lbs. (29–44 Nm).

9. Install a new cotter pin. If the slots in the nut do not align with the hole in the tie rod end stud, tighten the nut for proper alignment; never loosen the nut.

10. Install the wheel and tire assembly and lower the vehicle. Check the front end alignment.

BRAKES

Master Cylinder

REMOVAL AND INSTALLATION

1. Disconnect the negative battery cable. On 1993–96 vehicles, remove the cruise control actuator from its bracket.

2. Disconnect the electrical connector from the fluid level sensor.

3. Disconnect the brake lines from the master cylinder. On 1993–96 vehicles, with manual transaxle, disconnect and plug the reservoir hose for the clutch master cylinder.

4. Cap the brake lines and the master cylinder ports.

5. Remove the mounting nuts and remove the master cylinder.

To adjust:

6. On all except 1992–93 vehicles with anti-lock brakes and 1993–96 vehicles with automatic transaxle, adjust the master cylinder pushrod as follows:

a. Install adjustment gauge T87C–2500–A or equivalent on the end of the master cylinder.

b. Loosen the setscrew and push the gauge plunger against the bottom of the primary piston. While holding the gauge in position, tighten the setscrew.

c. Apply 19.7 in. Hg of vacuum to the booster using a hand vacuum pump.

d. Invert gauge T87C–2500–A or equivalent onto the booster.

e. Check the clearance between the end of the gauge and the master cylinder pushrod. There should be no clearance between the gauge and the pushrod.

f. If adjustment is necessary, loosen the pushrod locknut and adjust the clearance.

7. On 1992–93 vehicles with anti-lock brakes and 1993–96 vehicles with automatic transaxle, adjust the master cylinder pushrod as follows:

a. Loosen the brass holding screw on master cylinder gauge T92C–2500–A or equivalent and retract the gauge rod. Attach the gauge to the booster and tighten the retaining nuts to 87–140 inch lbs. (10–16 Nm).

b. Start the engine and let it idle for approximately 15 seconds.

c. Push lightly on the end of the gauge rod until it just contacts the power brake pushrod. Tighten the brass holding screw to secure the gauge rod in place.

d. Remove the master cylinder gauge from the booster and turn the engine **OFF**.

NOTE: Be very careful not to disturb the gauge rod setting when removing the gauge from the booster. If the setting is changed during removal, a faulty measurement will be recorded and may cause unnecessary pushrod adjustment.

e. Using a depth gauge, measure and record the height of the master cylinder gauge rod. This measurement will be called "D1".

f. Loosen the master cylinder gauge brass holding screw and place the gauge on the master cylinder.

g. Push lightly on the end of the gauge rod, until it just bottoms in the master cylinder piston. Tighten the brass screw.

h. Remove the master cylinder gauge from the master cylinder.

NOTE: Be very careful not to disturb the gauge rod setting when removing the gauge from the master cylinder. If the setting is changed during removal, a faulty measurement will be recorded and may cause unnecessary pushrod adjustment.

i. Using a depth gauge, measure and record the height of the gauge rod. This measurement will be called "D2".

j. Subtract D1 from D2. Adjust the power brake pushrod nut to lengthen or shorten the booster pushrod the amount equal to the difference between D1 and D2. If measurement D1 is larger than D2, the pushrod must be lengthened. If measurement D2 is larger than D1, the pushrod must be shortened.

To install:

8. Position the master cylinder on the power brake booster studs.

9. Install the master cylinder mounting nuts and tighten to 8–12 ft. lbs. (10–16 Nm).

10. Connect short lengths of brake line to the master cylinder that point back into the reservoir. Position the ends of the lines so they will be submerged in brake fluid.

11. Fill the master cylinder reservoir with DOT-3 brake fluid and cover the reservoir with a shop towel. Slowly pump the brake pedal until clear fluid comes out of both temporary brake lines.

12. Remove the temporary brake lines and connect the brake lines to the master cylinder. Tighten the brake line nuts to 10–16 ft. lbs. (13–22 Nm). If the lines are connected with banjo bolts, use new washers and tighten the banjo bolts to 16–22 ft. lbs. (22–29 Nm).

13. Connect the clutch master cylinder supply hose, if equipped.

14. Connect the fluid level sensor electrical connector.

15. Fill the master cylinder reservoir to the proper level and bleed the brake system.

Proportioning Valve

REMOVAL AND INSTALLATION

1. On 1992 vehicles, remove the 2 bolts from the fuel filter bracket and position the fuel filter aside.

2. If necessary, remove the master cylinder and hydraulic actuation assembly on 1992 vehicles with anti-lock brakes, to gain access to the proportioning valve.

3. Using a tubing wrench, loosen all of the brake lines connected to the proportioning valve and the brake lines at the master cylinder.

4. Remove the brake lines between the proportioning valve and the master cylinder.

5. Disconnect all the brake lines connected to the proportioning valve and remove the valve.

To install:

6. Position the valve on the bulkhead and loosely install one of the attaching bolts. On 1993–96 vehicles, install the valve with the **R** marks facing the drivers side.

7. Loosely install the brake lines between the master cylinder and the proportioning valve and loosely install the 6 brake lines into the valve.

8. Install the other attaching bolt into the valve and tighten both bolts to 14–17 ft. lbs. (19–23 Nm).

9. Tighten all the brake lines to 10–16 ft. lbs. (13–22 Nm).

10. If removed, install the hydraulic actuation assembly and the master cylinder.

11. Bleed the brakes. Bleed the lines at the proportioning valve first and then at the wheels.

Power Brake Booster

REMOVAL AND INSTALLATION

1. Remove the master cylinder.

2. Disconnect the hose connecting the intake manifold to the power brake booster.

3. Working under the instrument panel, remove the spring clip in the brake pedal clevis pin. Remove the clevis pin and brake pedal pushrod from the brake pedal.

4. Remove the 4 attaching nuts that hold the booster to the bulkhead and remove the power brake booster.

To install:

5. Have an assistant position the power brake booster on the bulkhead so the 4 retaining studs protrude through the bulkhead into the passenger compartment.

6. Working under the instrument panel, install the 4 booster retaining nuts and tighten to 19 ft. lbs. (25 Nm).

7. Apply lithium grease to the clevis pin and install it through the brake pedal pushrod and the brake pedal.

8. Install the clevis pin spring clip in the clevis pin.

9. Connect the hose connecting the power brake booster to the intake manifold. Because there is a check valve located in the center of the hose, make sure the arrow on the hose points toward the engine.

10. On all except 1992–93 vehicles with anti-lock brakes and 1993–96 vehicles with automatic transaxle, adjust the master cylinder pushrod as follows:

a. Install adjustment gauge T87C–2500–A or equivalent on the end of the master cylinder.

b. Loosen the setscrew and push the gauge plunger against the bottom of the primary piston. While holding the gauge in position, tighten the setscrew.

c. Apply 19.7 in. Hg of vacuum to the booster using a hand vacuum pump.

d. Invert gauge T87C–2500–A or equivalent onto the booster.

e. Check the clearance between the end of the gauge and the master cylinder pushrod. There should be no clearance between the gauge and the pushrod.

f. If adjustment is necessary, loosen the pushrod locknut and adjust the clearance.

11. On 1992–93 vehicles with anti-lock brakes and 1993–96 vehicles with automatic transaxle, adjust the master cylinder pushrod as follows:

a. Loosen the brass holding screw on master cylinder gauge T92C–2500–A or equivalent and retract the gauge rod. Attach the gauge to the booster and tighten the retaining nuts to 87–140 inch lbs. (10–16 Nm).

b. Start the engine and let it idle for approximately 15 seconds.

c. Push lightly on the end of the gauge rod until it just contacts the power brake pushrod. Tighten the brass holding screw to secure the gauge rod in place.

d. Remove the master cylinder gauge from the booster and turn the engine **OFF**.

NOTE: Be very careful not to disturb the gauge rod setting when removing the gauge from the booster. If the setting is changed during removal, a faulty measurement will be recorded and may cause unnecessary pushrod adjustment.

e. Using a depth gauge, measure and record the height of the master cylinder gauge rod. This measurement will be called "D1".

f. Loosen the master cylinder gauge brass holding screw and place the gauge on the master cylinder.

g. Push lightly on the end of the gauge rod, until it just bottoms in the master cylinder piston. Tighten the brass screw.

h. Remove the master cylinder gauge from the master cylinder.

NOTE: Be very careful not to disturb the gauge rod setting when removing the gauge from the master cylinder. If the setting is changed during removal, a faulty measurement will be recorded and may cause unnecessary pushrod adjustment.

i. Using a depth gauge, measure and record the height of the gauge rod. This measurement will be called "D2".

j. Subtract D1 from D2. Adjust the power brake pushrod nut to lengthen or shorten the booster pushrod the amount equal to the difference between D1 and D2. If measurement D1 is larger than D2, the pushrod must be lengthened. If measurement D2 is larger than D1, the pushrod must be shortened.

12. Install the master cylinder.

Brake Caliper

REMOVAL AND INSTALLATION

Front

1. Raise and safely support the vehicle.

2. Remove the wheel and tire assembly.

3. Remove the banjo bolt attaching the brake hose to the caliper, and discard the 2 sealing washers. Plug the hose to prevent fluid leakage.

4. Remove the caliper mounting bolt and pivot the caliper upward and off the brake pads.

5. Slide the caliper from the guide pin and remove from the vehicle.

To install:

6. Remove the guide pin bushing dust boots and push out the caliper guide pin bushing.

7. Lubricate the guide pin bushings with high temperature grease and install them in the caliper. In-

stall the guide pin bushing dust boots.

8. Slide the caliper onto the guide pin and pivot the caliper down onto the brake pads. To provide the necessary clearance, it may be necessary to pull slightly outward on the caliper.

9. Install the caliper mounting bolt and tighten to 23–30 ft. lbs. (31–41 Nm) on 1992 vehicles or 33–36 ft. lbs. (44–49 Nm) on 1993–96 vehicles.

10. Install 2 new copper washers and the banjo bolt on the brake hose banjo fitting.

11. Position the brake hose on the caliper and install the banjo bolt. Tighten the bolt to 16–22 ft. lbs. (22–29 Nm).

12. Bleed the brakes.

13. Install the wheel and tire assembly and tighten the lug nuts to 65–87 ft. lbs. (80–118 Nm). Lower the vehicle.

Rear

1. Raise and safely support the vehicle. Remove the wheel and tire assembly.

2. On 1993–96 vehicles, remove the parking brake cable retaining clip.

3. Loosen the parking brake cable housing adjustment nut. Remove the cable housing from the bracket and the parking brake lever.

4. Remove the banjo bolt mounting the brake hose to the caliper.

5. Remove and discard the copper washers from the banjo fitting.

6. Remove the caliper mounting bolt.

7. Pivot the caliper off the brake pads and slide the caliper off the guide pin.

To install:

8. Lubricate the guide pin bushings with high temperature grease. Install the caliper onto the guide pin and pivot the caliper over the brake pads. Tighten the mounting bolt to 12–17 ft. lbs. (16–24 Nm) On 1992 vehicles or 25–29 ft. lbs. (34–39 Nm) on 1993–96 vehicles.

9. Install new copper washers and the banjo bolt mounting the brake hose to the caliper. Tighten the banjo bolt to 16–20 ft. lbs. (22–26 Nm).

10. Position the parking brake cable into the parking brake lever and bracket. Install the retaining clip, if equipped.

11. Adjust the parking brake cable so there is no clearance between the cable end and the parking brake lever. Tighten the parking brake cable locknut.

12. Bleed the brakes.

13. Install the wheel and tire assembly and lower the vehicle.

Disc Brake Pads

REMOVAL AND INSTALLATION

Front

1. Remove approximately ⅔ of the brake fluid from the master cylinder reservoir.

2. Raise and safely support the vehicle.

3. Remove the wheel and tire assembly.

4. If necessary, clean the brake assembly with brake cleaner and allow to dry.

5. Remove the caliper mounting bolt. Pivot the caliper upward on the fixed guide pin and secure it out of the way.

— WARNING —
Do not allow the caliper to hang by the brake hose.

6. On 1993–96 vehicles, remove the 2 anti-rattle springs.

7. Remove the shims. Tag the shims so they can be reinstalled in their original position.

8. Remove the brake pads and retaining clips from the caliper anchor.

9. Inspect the disc brake rotor and machine or replace, as necessary.

To install:

10. Install the retaining clips.

11. Install the brake pads into the caliper anchor. The pad with the wear indicator is the inboard pad.

12. Install the shims in their original position.

13. Compress the caliper piston into its bore using pliers or another suitable tool.

14. Pivot the caliper down over the brake pads. On 1993–96 vehicles, install the anti-rattle springs. Install the caliper mounting bolt and tighten the bolt to 23–30 ft. lbs. (31–34 Nm) on 1992 vehicles or 33–36 ft. lbs. (44–49 Nm) on 1993–96 vehicles.

15. Install the wheel and tire assembly. Tighten the lug nuts to 65–87 ft. lbs. (80–118 Nm).

16. Lower the vehicle. Pump the brake pedal several times to position the caliper piston.

17. Check the fluid level in the master cylinder reservoir.

Rear

1. Remove approximately ⅔ of the brake fluid from the master cylinder reservoir.

2. Raise and support the vehicle, safely.

3. Remove the wheel and tire assembly. On 1993–96 vehicles, remove the parking brake cable retaining clip.

4. Loosen the parking brake cable housing adjusting nut. Remove the cable housing from the bracket and the parking brake lever.

5. On 1993–96 vehicles, insert an Allen wrench into the back of the caliper and turn the manual adjustment gear counterclockwise, to pull the caliper piston inward. Turn the gear until it stops.

6. Remove the caliper mounting bolt and pivot the caliper to clear the brake pads. Remove the caliper and suspend it with mechanics wire from the rear strut.

7. Remove the anti-rattle spring from the disc brake pads. Remove the disc brake pads, the shims and retaining clips.

NOTE: If the brake pads and shims are to be reused, they must be installed in their original positions.

To install:

8. Install the retaining clips. Position the shims on the disc brake pads and install the pads into the caliper anchor bracket.

9. Install the V-spring onto the disc brake pads.

10. On 1992 vehicles, use brake piston turning tool T75P–2588–B or equivalent, to rotate the caliper piston clockwise and screw the piston fully into the bore.

11. Lubricate the guide pin bushings with high temperature grease and install the caliper onto the guide pin. Pivot the caliper over the disc brake pads.

12. Install the caliper mounting bolt and tighten to 12–17 ft. lbs. (16–24 Nm) on 1992 vehicles or 25–29 ft. lbs. (34–39 Nm) on 1993–96 vehicles.

13. Install the parking brake cable into the parking brake lever and bracket. On 1993–96 vehicles, install the parking brake cable retaining clip.

14. Adjust the cable so there is no clearance between the cable end and the parking brake lever. Tighten the parking brake cable locknut.

15. On 1993–96 vehicles, turn the caliper manual adjustment gear clockwise with an Allen wrench until the brake pads just touch the rotor, then back off ⅓ turn.

16. Install the wheel and tire assembly and lower the vehicle.

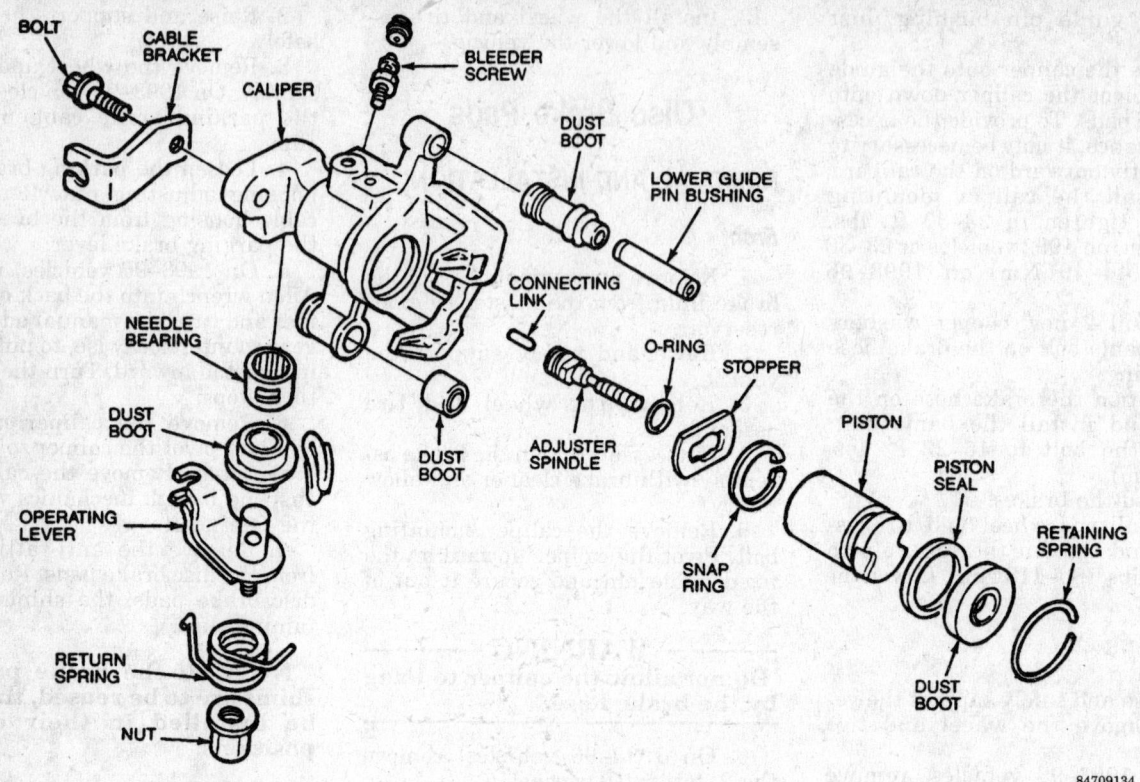

BOLT CABLE BRACKET CALIPER BLEEDER SCREW DUST BOOT LOWER GUIDE PIN BUSHING NEEDLE BEARING DUST BOOT CONNECTING LINK O-RING STOPPER PISTON PISTON SEAL RETAINING SPRING DUST BOOT ADJUSTER SPINDLE SNAP RING OPERATING LEVER DUST BOOT RETURN SPRING NUT

84709134

Rear disc brake caliper assembly

17. Pump the brake pedal several times to position the caliper piston. Check the fluid level in the master cylinder reservoir and add clean brake fluid, if necessary.

Brake Rotor

REMOVAL AND INSTALLATION

Front

1. Raise and safely support the vehicle.
2. Remove the wheel and tire assembly.
3. Remove the caliper anchor bracket bolts and remove the anchor bracket and caliper as an assembly. Support the caliper assembly from the coil spring with mechanics wire or string; do not disconnect the brake hose.

NOTE: Do not let the caliper assembly hang by the brake hose.

4. Remove the disc brake rotor. Handle the rotor with care, to prevent nicking or scratching the rotor surface.
To install:
5. Attach the disc brake rotor to the hub.

6. Install the caliper anchor bracket and tighten the bolts to 58–72 ft. lbs. (78–98 Nm).
7. Install the wheel and tire assembly. Tighten the lug nuts to 65–87 ft. lbs. (80–118 Nm).
8. Lower the vehicle. Apply the brake pedal several times to make sure the caliper piston is positioned.

Rear

1992

1. Raise and safely support the vehicle.
2. Remove the wheel and tire assembly.
3. Remove the 2 anchor bracket bolts and remove the caliper and anchor bracket assembly. Do not disconnect the brake hose from the caliper. Support the caliper with mechanics wire from the coil spring.

NOTE: Do not let the caliper hang by the brake hose.

4. Remove the grease cap. Unstake the wheel bearing nut, using a cape chisel. Remove the nut and washer and discard the nut.
5. Remove the disc brake rotor.
To install:
6. Install the rotor/hub assembly on the spindle.

7. Install the washer and a new nut. Tighten the nut to 73–131 ft. lbs. (98–178 Nm).
8. Stake the nut using a chisel with a rounded cutting edge. If the nut splits or cracks after staking, it must be replaced with a new nut.
9. Install the grease cap.
10. Install the caliper and anchor bracket assembly. Tighten the anchor bracket bolts to 33–49 ft. lbs. (45–67 Nm).
11. Install the wheel and tire assembly. Tighten the lug nuts to 65–87 ft. lbs. (80–118 Nm). Lower the vehicle.

1993–96

1. Raise and safely support the vehicle. Remove the wheel and tire assembly.
2. Remove the 2 anchor bracket bolts and remove the caliper and anchor bracket assembly. Do not disconnect the brake hose from the caliper. Support the caliper with mechanics wire from the coil spring.

NOTE: Do not let the caliper hang by the brake hose.

3. Remove the disc brake rotor from the hub.
4. Installation is the reverse of the removal procedure. Tighten the cali-

per anchor bracket bolts to 33–49 ft. lbs. (45–67 Nm).

Brake Drums

REMOVAL AND INSTALLATION

1992

1. Raise and safely support the vehicle.
2. Remove the wheel and tire assembly and remove the grease cap.
3. Carefully raise the staked portion of the attaching nut using a suitable chisel.
4. Remove and discard the hub nut. Remove the brake drum/bearing assembly.
   To install:
5. Position the brake drum/bearing assembly on the spindle and install a new locknut. Tighten the locknut to 73–131 ft. lbs. (98–178 Nm).
6. Stake the attaching nut using a suitable chisel with a rounded cutting edge.

   NOTE: If the nut splits or cracks after staking, it must be replaced with a new nut.

7. Install the grease cap and the wheel and tire assembly. Tighten the lug nuts to 65–87 ft. lbs. (88–118 Nm).
8. Lower the vehicle.

1993–96

1. Raise and safely support the vehicle.
2. Remove the wheel and tire assembly.
3. Remove the grease cap.
4. Remove the 2 brake drum screws and remove the brake drum.
5. Installation is the reverse of the removal procedure. Tighten the brake drum screws to 123 inch lbs. (14 Nm).

Brake Shoes

REMOVAL AND INSTALLATION

1992

1. Raise and safely support the vehicle.
2. Remove the wheel and tire assembly and the brake drum. Clean the brake assembly using brake cleaner.
3. Remove the brake shoe return springs and anti-rattle spring.

4. Remove the brake shoe hold-down springs. Push the hold-down spring inward using a small prybar, and twist the hold-down pin using needle-nose pliers until the head of the pin aligns with the slot in the spring. Release the spring and pin.
5. Remove the front and rear brake shoes from the parking brake strut.

NOTE: Unless they are broken or worn, leave the parking brake strut, adjuster mechanism and the adjuster spring in place.

To install:

6. Inspect the anti-rattle and return springs for separated or twisted coils, twisted, bent or damaged shanks or discoloration. Discoloration indicates brake overheating; overheated springs lose some of their tension and should be replaced.
7. Using high temperature grease, lubricate the 6 shoe contact pads and the adjuster mechanism.

NOTE: If new shoes are being installed, the brake drums should always be resurfaced. This removes glazing, ensures an equal friction surface from side-to-side, and corrects out of round and bell mouth conditions.

8. Position the rear brake shoe in the parking brake strut and install the rear hold-down pin and spring.
9. Position the front brake shoe against the parking brake strut and backing plate and install the hold-down pin and spring.
10. Install the brake shoe return springs.
11. Insert a small prybar between the knurled quadrant and the parking brake strut; twist the prybar until the quadrant just touches the backing plate.
12. Install the brake drum, and wheel and tire assembly. Lower the vehicle.
13. Firmly apply the brakes 2–3 times to adjust the rear brakes.

1993–96

1. Raise and safely support the vehicle.
2. Unstake the hub locknut. Have an assistant apply the brakes to lock the hub, then remove the locknut.
3. Remove the brake drum and the hub.
4. Remove the brake shoe hold-down springs. Push the hold-down spring inward using a small prybar, and twist the hold-down pin using needle-nose pliers until the head of

the pin aligns with the slot in the spring. Release the spring and pin.
5. Remove the parking brake cable from the parking brake anchor plate.
6. Remove the brake shoe return springs and remove the brake shoes.
   To install:
7. Using high temperature grease, lubricate the 6 shoe contact pads and the anchor plate.

NOTE: If new shoes are being installed, the brake drums should always be resurfaced. This removes glazing, ensures an equal friction surface from side-to-side, and corrects out of round and bell mouth conditions.

8. Position the rear brake shoe in the parking brake strut and install the rear hold-down pin and spring.
9. Position the front brake shoe against the parking brake strut and backing plate and install the hold-down pin and spring.
10. Install the brake shoe return springs. Connect the parking brake cable.
11. Measure the drum inside diameter using gauge tool D81L–1103–A or equivalent. Insert a small prybar into the knurled quadrant of the parking brake strut and adjust the brake shoes to the same measurement as the brake drum.
12. Install the hub and the brake drum. Install a new locknut and tighten to 130–174 ft. lbs. (177–235 Nm). Stake the locknut using a dull bladed chisel.
13. The brake shoes should just touch the brake drum when properly adjusted.
14. Install the wheel and tire assembly and lower the vehicle.

Wheel Cylinder

REMOVAL AND INSTALLATION

1. Raise and safely support the vehicle. Remove the wheel and tire assembly.
2. Remove the brake drum and hub and the brake shoes.
3. Using a tubing wrench, disconnect the brake line from the wheel cylinder.
4. Remove the wheel cylinder-to-backing plate bolts and the wheel cylinder.
   To install:
5. Install the wheel cylinder and loosely install the mounting bolts.
6. Connect the brake line to the wheel cylinder and tighten the fitting, using a tubing wrench.

7. Tighten the wheel cylinder mounting bolts to 7–9 ft. lbs. (10–13 Nm).

8. Install the brake shoes and the hub and brake drum.

9. Bleed the brakes.

10. Install the wheel and tire assembly and lower the vehicle.

Parking Brake Cable

ADJUSTMENT

1. Start the engine and depress the brake pedal several times while the vehicle is moving in reverse.

2. Stop the engine.

3. Remove the center console. On 1993–96 vehicles, remove the parking brake lever cover.

4. Adjust the parking brake adjusting nut so the brakes are fully applied when the parking brake lever can be lifted 7–10 notches on 1992 vehicles or 5–7 notches on 1993–96 vehicles.

5. Make sure the brakes do not drag.

6. Reinstall the lever cover, if necessary, and the center console.

REMOVAL AND INSTALLATION

1992

1. Raise and safely support the vehicle.

2. Using a pair of needle-nose pliers, remove the parking brake return spring from each backing plate; be careful not to overextend the spring.

3. If equipped with drum brakes, remove the attaching bolts from the parking brake cable housing and pull it away from the backing plate. Disconnect the cables from the backing plate parking brake levers.

4. If equipped with disc brakes, loosen the locknut and remove the parking brake cable from the lever.

5. Unbolt the cable housing clamps from the trailing arms and the body.

6. Disconnect the parking brake return spring from the parking brake equalizer.

7. Disconnect the parking brake cable from the equalizer and remove the cable from the vehicle.

8. Inspect the parking brake cable for free movement in the cable housing. If the cable does not move freely, lubricate or replace the cable assembly, as necessary.

To install:

9. Install the 2 cable ends in the parking brake equalizer. Apply multi-purpose grease to the cable clamps and the brake cable.

10. Install the cable housing clamps on the body and the trailing arms.

11. Connect the cables to the backing plate parking brake levers.

NOTE: On rear disc brakes, there must be no clearance between the cable end and the lever.

12. If equipped with drum brakes, position the parking brake cable against the backing plate and install the attaching bolts.

13. If equipped with disc brakes, tighten the locknut to 12–17 ft. lbs. (16–22 Nm).

14. Lower the vehicle and adjust the parking brake.

1993–96

1. Raise and safely support the vehicle. Remove the wheel and tire assemblies.

2. If equipped with drum brakes, proceed as follows:

   a. Remove the brake drum and hub.

   b. Remove the parking brake cable from the parking brake anchor plate.

   c. Remove the cable from the hole in the backing plate.

   d. Disconnect the parking brake return spring from the parking brake strut.

3. If equipped with disc brakes, loosen the parking brake cable adjusting nut and remove the cable from the parking brake lever.

4. Remove the 4 cable housing clamp nuts from the rear suspension trailing arms.

5. Remove the exhaust heatshield.

6. Remove the 2 cable housing clamp nuts from the body and remove the cables from the equalizer and housing bracket.

To install:

7. Install the cable ends into the parking brake equalizer and housing brackets.

8. Apply suitable grease to the cable clamps and the cable, then install the cable housing support clamps on the body.

9. Install the cable housing brackets on each rear suspension trailing arm and tighten the nuts to 19 ft. lbs. (25 Nm).

10. Install the exhaust heatshield.

11. If equipped with drum brakes, proceed as follows:

   a. Route the parking brake cable through the hole in the backing plate and connect it to the parking brake anchor plate.

   b. Connect the parking brake return spring to the parking brake strut.

   c. Install the hub and the brake drum.

12. If equipped with disc brakes, proceed as follows:

   a. Connect the parking brake cable to the parking brake lever.

   b. Install the parking brake cable retaining clip.

   c. Tighten the parking brake cable adjusting nut.

NOTE: On rear disc brakes, there must be no clearance between the cable end and the lever.

13. Install the wheel and tire assembly.

14. Lower the vehicle and adjust the parking brake.

Brake System Bleeding

SYSTEM PRIMING

When a new master cylinder has been installed, or the brake system emptied or partially emptied, fluid may not flow from the bleeder screws during normal bleeding. It may be necessary to prime the system using the following procedure:

1. Disconnect the brake lines from the master cylinder.

2. Install short brake lines in the master cylinder ports and position them that they point back into the reservoir and the ends of the lines are submerged in brake fluid.

3. Fill the reservoir with clean DOT-3 brake fluid and cover the reservoir with a shop towel.

4. Slowly pump the brake pedal until clear, bubble-free fluid comes out of both temporary brake lines.

NOTE: Do not allow brake fluid to spill on the vehicle's finish; it will remove the paint. In case of a spill, flush the area with water.

5. Remove the short brake lines and reconnect the vehicle brake lines to the master cylinder.

6. Bleed each brake line at the master cylinder as follows:

   a. Have an assistant slowly pump the brake pedal 10 times and then hold firm pressure on the pedal.

   b. Position a shop towel under the rear most brake line fitting. Open the fitting with a tubing wrench until a stream of brake fluid comes out. Have the assistant maintain pressure on the brake pedal until the brake line fitting is tightened.

c. Repeat Steps a and b until clear, bubble-free fluid comes out from around the tubing fitting.

d. Repeat the operation on the front brake line fitting.

7. If any of the brake lines, calipers, or wheel cylinders have been removed, it may be helpful to prime the system by gravity bleeding. This should be done after the master cylinder is primed and bled. To prime the system:

a. Fill the master cylinder with clean DOT-3 brake fluid.

b. Loosen both wheel cylinder bleeder screws, if equipped, and leave them open until clear brake fluid flows out. Frequently check the master cylinder reservoir to make sure it does not run dry.

c. Tighten the wheel cylinder bleeder screws.

d. One at a time, loosen the caliper bleeder screws and leave them open until clear fluid flows out. Frequently check the master cylinder reservoir to make sure it does not run dry.

e. Tighten the bleeder screws.

8. After the master cylinder has been primed, the lines bled at the master cylinder, and the brake system primed, proceed with normal brake system bleeding.

MANUAL BLEEDING

1. Clean all dirt from the master cylinder filler cap.

2. If the master cylinder is known or suspected of having air in the bore, it must be bled before any of the wheel cylinders and/or calipers are bled. Use the System Priming procedure.

3. Bleed the wheel cylinders and/or calipers as follows:

a. Begin at the rear bleeder screw.

NOTE: The brake system is diagonally split. If bleeding is begun at the right rear wheel, bleed the left front caliper next, followed by the left rear and right front. If bleeding is begun at the left rear wheel, bleed the right front caliper next, followed by the right rear and left front.

b. Attach a drain hose to the bleeder screw. The end of the hose should fit snugly around the end of the bleeder screw.

c. Place the other end of the hose in a container partially filled with clean brake fluid.

d. Have an assistant slowly pump the brake pedal 5–10 times and maintain pressure on the pedal after the last stroke.

e. Loosen the bleeder screw approximately ¾ turn. Make sure your assistant keeps constant pressure on the pedal until the pedal drops all the way down and the bleeder screw is closed again. If the pedal pressure is released, air will be drawn back into the system.

f. Tighten the bleeder screw.

g. Repeat this operation until the fluid is clear and air bubbles no longer appear in the container.

h. Repeat these steps at the other wheel cylinder and calipers.

NOTE: Never reuse the brake fluid expelled from the bleeder screws during the bleeding operation.

4. After the bleeding procedure is completed, make sure the fluid level is correct in the master cylinder reservoir.

Anti-Lock Brake System Service

PRECAUTION

Failure to observe the following precautions may result in system damage or personal injury.

• Before servicing any high pressure component, be sure to discharge the hydraulic pressure from the system.

• Do not allow the brake fluid to contact any of the electrical connectors.

• Use care when opening the bleeder screws due to the high system pressure from the accumulator.

RELIEVING ANTI-LOCK BRAKE SYSTEM PRESSURE

1. Turn the ignition key **OFF**.

2. Pump the brake pedal a minimum of 20 times until an increase in pedal force is clearly felt.

Hydraulic Actuation Unit

REMOVAL AND INSTALLATION

1992

1. Disconnect the negative battery cable.

2. Remove the air cleaner assembly.

3. Disconnect the electrical connectors at the ignition coil.

4. Remove the 2 mounting nuts at the coil and module bracket and remove the coil and module bracket.

5. Remove the 4 mounting nuts at the fuel filter bracket and move the filter and bracket aside.

6. Disconnect the 2 electrical connectors leading to the hydraulic actuation unit.

7. Disconnect the brake lines from the hydraulic actuation unit. Remove the brake lines necessary for actuation unit removal.

8. Remove the mounting nuts and the hydraulic actuation unit.

To install:

9. Install the hydraulic actuation unit and tighten the nuts to 14–19 ft. lbs. (19–25 Nm).

10. Connect the brake lines and tighten to 10–16 ft. lbs. (13–22 Nm).

11. Connect the electrical connectors leading to the actuation unit.

12. Position the fuel filter and bracket and tighten the mounting nuts.

13. Install the ignition coil and module bracket. Tighten the mounting nuts.

14. Connect the electrical connectors at the ignition coil.

15. Install the air cleaner assembly.

16. Fill and bleed the brake system. Connect the negative battery cable.

1993–96

1. Disconnect the negative battery cable.

2. Slide the evaporative canister out of its bracket and position it aside.

3. Remove the cruise control vacuum actuator from its bracket, if equipped.

4. Disconnect the 2 electrical connectors at the hydraulic actuation assembly.

5. Loosen the 3 hydraulic assembly mounting nuts and remove the front-left brake line bolt.

NOTE: Note the routing of the brake lines to ensure proper installation.

6. Remove the brake line fittings from the actuation assembly using a tubing wrench.

7. Remove the 3 mounting nuts and washers and remove the hydraulic actuation assembly.

8. Installation is the reverse of the removal procedures. Tighten the brake lines to 10–16 ft. lbs. (13–22 Nm). Bleed the brake system.

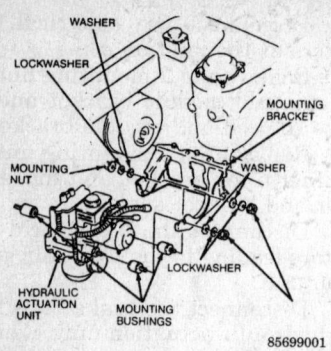

Hydraulic actuation unit removal and installation

Wheel Sensor Rotor

REMOVAL AND INSTALLATION

Front

1. Raise and safely support the vehicle. Remove the wheel and tire assembly.
2. Remove the halfshaft assembly.
3. On 1992, use a soft-faced drift to tap the sensor rotor from the outboard CV-joint. On 1993–96, use a suitable bearing puller to remove the sensor rotor.

To install:

4. Position the sensor rotor on the CV-joint with the chamfered edge facing the halfshaft.
5. On 1992, use a soft-faced drift to tap the sensor rotor onto the outboard CV-joint. On 1993–96, use installation tools T88P-20202-A and T92C-20202-AH or equivalent, to press the sensor rotor into place.
6. Install the halfshaft.
7. Install the wheel and tire assembly and lower the vehicle.

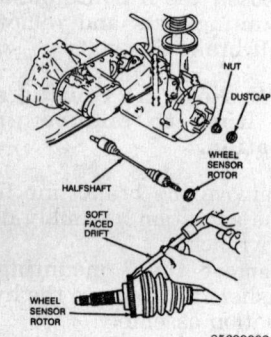

Front wheel sensor rotor removal — 1992 — 1993–96 similar

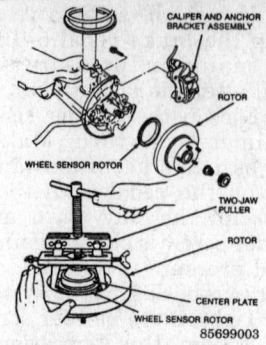

Rear wheel sensor rotor removal — 1992 — 1993–96 similar

Rear

1. Raise and safely support the vehicle. Remove the wheel and tire assembly.
2. Remove the caliper and anchor bracket, without disconnecting the brake hose. Support the caliper from the coil spring with mechanics wire or string.

NOTE: Do not let the caliper hang by the brake hose.

3. Remove the disc brake rotor and hub.
4. Remove the sensor rotor from the disc brake rotor or hub, using a 2-jaw puller and center plate.

To install:

5. Position the rotor or hub in a press with the wheel studs facing down.
6. Using sensor ring installer tool T88C-20202-AH or equivalent, press the sensor onto the disc brake rotor or hub.
7. Install the rotor, caliper and anchor bracket.
8. Install the wheel and tire assembly and lower the vehicle.

Speed Sensor

REMOVAL AND INSTALLATION

Front

1. Disconnect the negative battery cable. Raise and safely support the vehicle.
2. Remove the front wheel and tire assembly.
3. Remove the retaining bolts and the speed sensor from the steering knuckle.
4. Remove the routing bracket from the strut assembly.
5. Remove the routing bracket from the inner fender well and disconnect the wiring harness.

6. Remove the speed sensor.

NOTE: The left and right speed sensors are not interchangeable. L or R is indicated on the bracket.

To install:

7. Route the sensor wiring harness in the vehicle and connect the wiring harness.
8. Install the routing bracket onto the inner fender well.
9. Install the routing bracket onto the strut assembly. Tighten the bolt to 13–17 ft. lbs. (18–23 Nm).
10. Install the speed sensor into the knuckle and tighten the bolts to 12–17 ft. lbs. (16–23 Nm).
11. Make sure the wiring harness will clear all suspension components.
12. Install the wheel and tire assembly and lower the vehicle. Connect the negative battery cable.

Rear

1. Disconnect the negative battery cable. Raise and safely support the vehicle.
2. Remove the front wheel and tire assembly.
3. Remove the retaining bolt and the speed sensor from the knuckle.
4. Remove the routing bracket from the strut assembly.
5. Remove the routing bracket from the inner fender well.
6. Remove the interior panels as necessary to gain access to the wiring harness.
7. Disconnect the wiring harness and remove the speed sensor.

NOTE: The left and right speed sensors are not interchangeable. L or R is indicated on the bracket.

To install:

8. Route the sensor wiring harness in the vehicle and connect the wiring harness.
9. Install the routing bracket onto the inner fender well.
10. Install the routing bracket onto the strut assembly. Tighten the bolt to 13–17 ft. lbs. (18–23 Nm).
11. Install the speed sensor into the knuckle and tighten the bolt to 12–17 ft. lbs. (16–23 Nm).
12. Make sure the wiring harness will clear all suspension components.
13. Install any interior panels that were removed.
14. Install the wheel and tire assembly and lower the vehicle. Connect the negative battery cable.

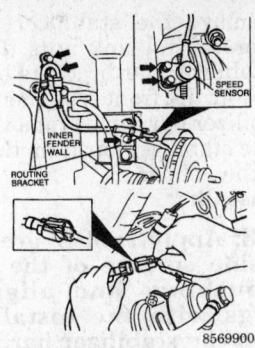

Front speed sensor
location — 1992 — 1993–96
similar

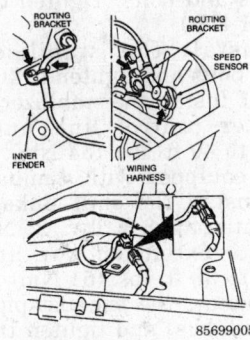

Rear speed sensor
location — 1992 — 1993–96
similar

FRONT SUSPENSION

MacPherson Strut

REMOVAL AND INSTALLATION

1. Raise and support the vehicle safely.
2. Remove the wheel and tire assembly.
3. On 1992 vehicles, remove the rubber cap from the strut mounting block. If equipped, disconnect the programmed ride control module connector.
4. At the inside of the strut mounting block and chassis strut tower, place an alignment mark.
5. On 1992 vehicles, if equipped, remove the programmed ride control actuator.
6. If equipped with anti-lock brakes, disconnect the electrical harness and remove the bracket.
7. Remove the brake caliper-to-steering knuckle bolts and suspend

the caliper with mechanics wire; do not disconnect the pressure hose.
8. Remove the U-clip from the brake line hose and slide it out of the strut bracket.
9. Remove the strut-to-steering knuckle bolts.
10. On 1992 vehicles, remove the vane airflow meter assembly and the ignition coil bracket.
11. Remove the strut-to-chassis nuts and remove the strut from the vehicle.
12. Place the strut assembly in a suitable holding fixture. Loosen, but do not remove the shock nut. Compress the spring with a suitable compressor tool, then remove the shock nut. Gradually release the spring compressor.
13. Remove the programmed ride control module bracket, if equipped, strut mounting block, spring seat, dust boot, bump stopper and the coil spring from the strut assembly.

To install:

14. Install the coil spring, bump stopper, dust boot and the upper spring seat on the strut assembly.
15. Install the strut mounting block and the programmed ride control module bracket, if equipped, making sure the notch on the mounting block is 180 degrees from the knuckle mounting bracket on the strut.
16. Compress the spring with the compressor tool and install the shock nut. Tighten the nut to 47–69 ft. lbs. (64–84 Nm) on 1992 vehicles or 66–86 ft. lbs. (89–117 Nm) on 1993–96 vehicles. Gradually release the compressor tool and remove from the strut assembly.
17. Install the strut in the shock tower. Align the strut-to-chassis matchmark and torque the strut-to-chassis nuts to 34–46 ft. lbs. (46–63 Nm).
18. On 1992 vehicles, install the vane airflow meter assembly and the ignition coil bracket.
19. On 1992 vehicles, if equipped, install the programmed ride control module and the connector.
20. On 1992 vehicles, install the rubber cap on the strut tower.
21. Align the strut to the steering knuckle and torque the nuts/bolts to 69–86 ft. lbs. (93–117 Nm).
22. Install the brake caliper and the brake hose in its bracket. If equipped with anti-lock brakes, install the bracket and harness.
23. Install the wheel and tire assembly. Tighten the lug nuts to 65–87 ft. lbs. (88–118 Nm). Lower the vehicle.

Strut Cartridge

REPLACEMENT

—————— **CAUTION** ——————
Do not remove the MacPherson strut upper nut without using an approved MacPherson strut compressor D85P-7178-A or equivalent. The coil spring is under extreme pressure and can cause severe bodily injury if the nut is removed without a spring compressor.

1. Raise the vehicle and support safely.
2. Remove the front wheel assembly.
3. Remove the MacPherson strut assembly from the vehicle.
4. Place the strut assembly in a suitable vise.
5. Loosen, but do not remove the upper strut shaft nut. Remove the strut assembly from the vise and install a MacPherson strut spring compressor D85P-7178-A or equivalent.
6. Compress the coil spring and remove the strut shaft nut. Gradually release the spring compressor. Be careful not to strip the threads on the strut shaft as the spring extends.
7. Remove the programmed ride control bracket, if equipped, mounting block, strut bearing, upper spring seat, rubber spring seat, dust boot, bump stopper and coil spring.

To install:

8. Install the coil spring, bump stopper, dust boot, and upper rubber seat onto the strut assembly.
9. Install the strut mounting block and programmed ride control bracket, if equipped. Make sure the notch on the mounting block is 180 degrees from the knuckle mounting bracket on the strut. Make sure the spring ends are positioned correctly in the spring seats. If not, suspension height may be affected.
10. Compress the spring using the spring compressor D85P-7178-A or equivalent.
11. Compress the spring and install the upper strut nut and torque to 47–70 ft. lbs. (64–84 Nm).
12. Gradually release the spring compressor and install the strut assembly into the vehicle. Make sure the alignment mark on the strut mounting block faces the mark on the chassis strut tower.
13. Torque the mounting nuts to 46 ft. lbs. (63 Nm).
14. Install the front wheels and lower the vehicle safely.

Lower Ball Joints

INSPECTION

Raise and safely support the vehicle until the front wheel is clear of the floor. Try to rock the wheel up and down. If any play is felt, have an assistant rock the wheel while observing the lower ball joint. If any movement is seen between the steering knuckle and control arm, the ball joint is bad. If not, any wheel play indicates wheel bearing wear.

REMOVAL AND INSTALLATION

The lower ball joint is an integral part of the lower control arm and cannot be serviced separately. If the lower ball joint is defective, the entire lower control arm must be replaced.

Lower Control Arms

REMOVAL AND INSTALLATION

1. Raise and safely support the vehicle. Remove the wheel and tire assembly.
2. Remove the brake caliper and support it with mechanics wire from the coil spring.
3. On 1992 vehicles, remove the stabilizer link assembly from the lower control arm. On 1993–96 vehicles, remove the stabilizer control link-to-control arm nut.
4. Remove the ball-joint clamp bolt from the steering knuckle. Using a prybar, pry downward to separate the ball joint from the steering knuckle.
5. On 1992 vehicles, if equipped, remove the harmonic damper from the chassis sub-frame; the damper is located on the left side of the vehicle.
6. Remove the lower control arm-to-chassis mounting bolts and nuts and remove the lower control arm.
To install:
7. Install the control arm and tighten the mounting bolts to 69–93 ft. lbs. (93–127 Nm) on 1992 vehicles. On 1993–96 vehicles, install the lower control arm rear bushing bolts and tighten to 69–96 ft. lbs. (93–131 Nm), then install the lower control arm front bushing bolt and tighten to 58–78 ft. lbs. (78–106 Nm).
8. On 1992 vehicles, install the harmonic damper, if equipped.
9. Install the ball joint stud into the steering knuckle and tighten the clamp bolt to 32–40 ft. lbs. (43–54 Nm).

10. On 1992 vehicles, install the stabilizer bar link assembly. Tighten the nut until 0.79 in. (20mm) of thread remains above the nut.
11. On 1993–96 vehicles, install the stabilizer control link-to-lower control arm nut and tighten to 40 ft. lbs. (54 Nm).
12. Install the brake caliper.
13. Install the wheel and tire assembly. Tighten the lug nuts to 65–87 ft. lbs. (88–118 Nm). Lower the vehicle.

Stabilizer Bar

REMOVAL AND INSTALLATION

1992

1. Raise and safely support the vehicle.
2. Remove the wheel and tire assemblies.
3. Remove the stabilizer bar link assembly mounting bolts from the lower control arm.
4. Remove the mounting bolt from the stabilizer bar bushing. Remove the stabilizer bar.
To install:
5. Install the stabilizer bar link assembly mounting bolts at the control arm. Hand-tighten only.
6. Install the stabilizer bar bushing. Tighten the bushing bolt to 27–40 ft. lbs. (36–54 Nm).
7. Tighten the link nut until 0.79 in. (20mm) of thread remains above the nut.
8. Install the wheel and tire assemblies. Tighten the lug nuts to 65–87 ft. lbs. (88–118 Nm). Lower the vehicle.

1993–96

1. Disconnect the negative battery cable. Raise and safely support the vehicle.
2. Remove the front wheel and tire assemblies.
3. Remove the 6 transverse member bolts and remove the transverse member.
4. Remove the 2 bolts and 6 nuts and remove the transaxle cradle.
5. Disconnect the oxygen sensor connector(s). Disconnect the exhaust pipe(s) from the manifold(s) and position aside.
6. If equipped with manual transaxle, remove the extension bar nut and shift linkage bolt.
7. Position a jack under the front crossmember. Remove the 4 bolts and 2 nuts attaching the front crossmember to the body.

8. Remove the stabilizer bar-to-stabilizer control link nuts. Remove the 4 stabilizer bar brackets bolts.
9. Lower the front crossmember so the stabilizer bar can be removed. Remove the stabilizer bar from the right side of the vehicle.
To install:

NOTE: Apply rubber grease to the inside surface of the stabilizer bushings and align the bushings with the installation mark on the stabilizer bar.

10. Install the stabilizer bar from the right side of the vehicle. Raise the crossmember into position and install the nuts and bolts. Tighten to 96 ft. lbs. (131 Nm).
11. Install the stabilizer bar bracket bolts and tighten to 40 ft. lbs. (54 Nm). Install the stabilizer bar-to-stabilizer control link nuts and tighten to 40 ft. lbs. (54 Nm).
12. If equipped with manual transaxle, install the shift linkage bolt and tighten to 18 ft. lbs. (25 Nm). Install the extension bar nut and tighten to 38 ft. lbs. (51 Nm).
13. Connect the exhaust pipe(s) to the manifold(s) and tighten the nuts to 38 ft. lbs. (51 Nm). Connect the oxygen sensor connector(s).
14. Install the transaxle cradle with the nuts and bolts. Tighten the cradle-to-chassis nuts and bolts to 68 ft. lbs. (93 Nm), the cradle-to-front mount nuts to 77 ft. lbs. (104 Nm) and the cradle-to-rear mount nuts to 44 ft. lbs. (60 Nm).
15. Install the transverse member and tighten the bolts to 96 ft. lbs. (131 Nm).
16. Install the wheel and tire assemblies and lower the vehicle. Connect the negative battery cable.

REAR SUSPENSION

MacPherson Strut

REMOVAL AND INSTALLATION

1992

1. Raise and support the vehicle, safely. Remove the wheel and tire assembly.
2. Remove the upper trunk side garnish and lower trunk side trim to gain access to the strut assembly.
3. If equipped with programmed ride control, disconnect the program-

med ride control module connector and removed the module.

4. If equipped with anti-lock brakes, remove the anti-lock brake harness and remove the bracket.

5. If equipped with drum brakes, remove the drum and backing plate assembly. If equipped with rear disc brakes, remove the rear disc brake caliper and rotor assembly.

6. Remove the brake line U-clip from the strut housing.

7. Loosen, but do not completely remove, the trailing arm bolt. Remove the spindle-to-strut bolts.

8. From inside the vehicle, remove the strut-to-chassis nuts. Remove the strut assembly.

9. Mount the strut assembly in a suitable vise and loosen, but do not completely remove the shock absorber nut.

10. Remove the strut assembly from the vise and compress the spring, using spring compressor 086–00029 or equivalent.

11. Remove the shock absorber nut.

12. Gradually release the spring compressor. Be careful not to strip the threads on the shock absorber as the spring expands.

13. Remove the strut mounting block, upper rubber spring seat, dust boot, bump stopper and the coil spring from the shock absorber.

To install:

14. Install the coil spring, bump stopper, dust boot and the upper spring seat on the shock absorber.

15. Install the strut mounting block. The mounting block will not seat on the shock absorber unless the notches on the block line up with those on the shock absorber.

16. Compress the spring with the compressor tool and install the shock absorber nut. Tighten the nut to 47–69 ft. lbs. (64–84 Nm).

17. Gradually release the compressor tool and remove from the strut assembly.

18. Position the strut into the strut tower and torque the strut-to-chassis nuts to 34–46 ft. lbs. (46–63 Nm).

19. If equipped with programmed ride control, install the module and reconnect the connector.

20. Install the lower trunk side trim and the upper trunk side garnish.

21. Install the spindle-to-strut mounting bolts and tighten to 69–86 ft. lbs. (93–117 Nm). Tighten the trailing arm mounting bolt to 64–86 ft. lbs. (86–117 Nm).

22. Install the brake drum and backing plate or the caliper and rotor

assembly, as applicable. Install the brake line U-clip onto the strut.

23. If equipped, install the ABS brake harness and bracket.

24. Install the wheel and tire assembly and tighten the lug nuts to 65–87 ft. lbs. (88–118 Nm). Lower the vehicle.

1993–96

1. Raise and safely support the vehicle. Remove the rear wheel and tire assembly.

2. If equipped with anti-lock brakes, remove the speed sensor routing bracket.

3. Remove the brake line U-clip from the strut housing.

4. Remove the 2 spindle-to-strut mounting bolts.

5. Remove the trunk side panel to gain access to the strut assembly.

6. Remove the 3 upper strut attaching nuts and remove the strut.

7. Use spring compressor tool D85P–7178–A or equivalent, to compress the coil spring.

8. Remove the nut from the strut and remove the shock absorber.

To install:

9. Position the shock absorber in the compressed coil spring.

10. Install the nut and tighten to 87 ft. lbs. (117 Nm). Release the compressor and remove the strut.

11. Position the strut in the vehicle and install the 3 upper strut nuts. Tighten to 46 ft. lbs. (63 Nm).

12. Install the trunk side panel.

13. Install the 2 spindle-to-strut bolts and tighten to 87 ft. lbs. (117 Nm).

14. Install the brake line U-clip. Install the wheel speed sensor bracket, if equipped.

15. Install the wheel and tire assembly and lower the vehicle.

Strut Cartridge

REPLACEMENT

——— CAUTION ———

Do not remove the MacPherson strut upper nut without using an approved MacPherson strut compressor, D85P-7178-A or equivalent. The coil spring is under extreme pressure and can cause severe bodily injury if the nut is removed without a spring compressor.

1. Raise the vehicle and support safely.

2. Remove the rear wheel assembly.

3. Remove the MacPherson strut assembly from the vehicle. Remove the programmed ride control actuator, if equipped.

4. Install a MacPherson strut spring compressor D85P-7178-A or equivalent.

5. Compress the coil spring and remove the strut shaft nut. Gradually release the spring compressor. Be careful not to strip the threads on the strut shaft as the spring extends.

6. Remove the mounting block, upper spring seat, rubber spring seat, dust boot, bump stopper and coil spring.

To install:

7. Install the coil spring, bump stopper, dust boot, and upper rubber seat onto the strut assembly.

8. Install the strut mounting block. Make sure the spring ends are positioned correctly in the spring seats. If not, suspension height may be affected.

9. Compress the spring using the spring compressor D85P-7178-A or equivalent.

10. Install the upper strut nut and torque to 66–87 ft. lbs. (89–117 Nm).

11. Gradually release the spring compressor and install the strut assembly into the vehicle.

12. Torque the mounting nuts to 46 ft. lbs. (63 Nm).

13. Install the rear wheels and lower the vehicle safely.

Rear Control Arms

REMOVAL AND INSTALLATION

1992

1. Raise and support the vehicle, safely.

2. Remove the tire and wheel assembly.

3. Remove the brake drum and the backing plate assembly or the rear brake caliper and rotor assembly, if equipped.

4. Loosen, but do not completely remove, the spindle to strut assembly mounting bolts.

5. Remove the common lateral link arm bolt and nut from the spindle.

6. Remove the trailing arm mounting bolt at the spindle and the spindle to strut assembly mounting bolts.

7. Remove the spindle from the strut assembly.

8. Remove the rear stabilize bar.

9. Remove the nut from the common lateral link mounting bolt at the

rear crossmember and remove the rear lateral link.

NOTE: Because of lack of clearance between the fuel tank and the common lateral link mounting bolt, the bolt and the front lateral link cannot be removed at this time.

10. Remove the parking brake mounting bolts from the trailing arm assembly.

11. Remove the trailing arm mounting bolt and the trailing arm.

12. Remove the exhaust mounting bolts and the brake line retaining bracket from the rear crossmember. Remove the mounting bolts from the end of the crossmember.

13. Remove the rear crossmember and front lateral link as an assembly. Remove the common lateral link mounting bolt from the rear crossmember and remove the front lateral link from the crossmember.

To install:

14. Position the front lateral link on the crossmember and install the common lateral link mounting bolt.

15. Install the crossmember into the vehicle and install the mounting bolts, exhaust mounting bolts and the brake line retaining bracket bolt to the crossmember.

16. Tighten the crossmember mounting bolts to 27–40 ft. lbs. (36–54 Nm) and the brake line retaining bracket bolt to 13–20 ft. lbs. (18–26 Nm).

17. Position the trailing arm into the body mounting bracket and tighten the mounting bolt to 49–69 ft. lbs. (63–93 Nm).

18. Install the parking brake cable mounting bolts to the trailing arm.

19. Position the rear lateral link onto the common lateral link mounting bolt at the rear crossmember and install the nut to the bolt. Tighten the mounting bolt and nut at the rear crossmember to 64–86 ft. lbs. (86–117 Nm).

20. Install the rear stabilizer bar assembly.

21. Place the spindle onto the strut assembly mounting bracket and tighten the mounting bolts to 69–86 ft. lbs. (93–117 Nm).

22. Install the common lateral link arm bolt and nut through the spindle and tighten to 64–86 ft. lbs. (86–117 Nm).

23. Install the trailing arm mounting bolt and tighten to 64–86 ft. lbs. (86–117 Nm).

24. Install the brake drum and backing plate assembly or the brake

caliper and rotor assembly, as applicable.

25. Install the wheel and tire assembly and tighten the lug nuts to 65–87 ft. lbs. (88–118 Nm). Lower the vehicle.

1993–96

TRAILING ARM

1. Raise and safely support the vehicle.

2. Remove the parking brake cable bracket from the trailing arm.

3. Remove the trailing arm-to-spindle and trailing arm-to-frame bolts and remove the trailing arm.

4. Installation is the reverse of the removal procedure. Tighten the trailing arm mounting bolts to 86 ft. lbs. (117 Nm).

FRONT LATERAL LINK

1. Raise and safely support the vehicle.

2. Remove the spindle through bolt.

3. Position a jack under the rear crossmember.

4. Remove the 4 rear crossmember-to-frame bolts and lower the crossmember enough to gain access to the front lateral link to crossmember bolt.

5. Remove the access hole cap.

6. Remove the front lateral link-to-rear crossmember bolt and remove the front lateral link.

7. Installation is the reverse of the removal procedure. Tighten the spindle through bolt and front lateral link-to-rear crossmember bolt to 86 ft. lbs. (117 Nm). Tighten the rear crossmember-to-frame bolts to 40 ft. lbs. (54 Nm).

REAR LATERAL LINK

1. Raise and safely support the vehicle.

2. Remove the spindle through bolt.

3. Remove the stabilizer control link.

4. Paint an alignment mark on the cam plate and crossmember for assembly reference. Remove the adjusting cam bolt and remove the rear lateral link.

5. Installation is the reverse of the removal procedure. Tighten the spindle through bolt to 86 ft. lbs. (117 Nm). Align the marks made during removal and tighten the adjusting cam bolt to 86 ft. lbs. (117 Nm). Tighten the stabilizer link nuts to 40 ft. lbs. (54 Nm).

REAR CROSSMEMBER

1. Raise and safely support the vehicle.

2. Remove the spindle through bolt.

3. Remove the stabilizer bar.

4. Remove the rear lateral link.

5. Remove the 4 rear crossmember-to-frame bolts and remove the rear crossmember.

6. Remove the front lateral link.

7. Installation is the reverse of the removal procedure. Tighten the rear crossmember-to-frame bolts to 40 ft. lbs. (54 Nm) and the spindle through bolt to 86 ft. lbs. (117 Nm). Tighten the stabilizer control link and stabilizer bracket nuts and bolts to 40 ft. lbs. (54 Nm).

Rear Wheel Bearings

REMOVAL AND INSTALLATION

1992

1. Raise and support the vehicle, safely.

2. Remove the wheel and tire assembly and the grease cap.

3. Using a cape chisel and a hammer, raise the staked portion of the hub nut.

4. Remove and discard the hub nut.

5. Remove the brake drum or disc brake rotor assembly from the spindle.

6. Using a small prybar, pry the grease seal from the brake drum or rotor and discard it.

7. Remove the snapring. Using a shop press, press the wheel bearing from the brake drum or rotor.

To install:

8. Using a shop press, press the new wheel bearing into the brake drum or rotor until it seats and install the snapring.

9. Lubricate the new seal lip with grease and install the seal, using a suitable installation tool.

10. Position the brake drum or rotor onto the wheel spindle.

11. Install a new locknut and tighten to 73–131 ft. lbs. (98–178 Nm).

12. Using a dull cold chisel, stake the locknut.

NOTE: If the nut splits or cracks after staking, it must be replaced with a new nut.

13. Install the grease cap and the wheel and tire assembly. Tighten the lug nuts to 65–87 ft. lbs. (88–118 Nm). Lower the vehicle.

1993–96

NOTE: On 1993–96 vehicles, the bearing cannot be disassembled from the hub.

1. Raise and safely support the vehicle. Remove the wheel and tire assembly.

2. Unstake the locknut. Have an assistant apply the brakes to lock the hub, then remove the locknut. Discard the nut; it must not be reused.

3. Remove the brake drum or, if equipped, rear disc brake caliper and rotor.

4. Remove the hub/bearing assembly.

5. Installation is the reverse of the removal procedure. Tighten a new locknut to 174 ft. lbs. (235 Nm), then stake the nut in place using a dull bladed chisel.

ADJUSTMENT

1. Raise and safely support the vehicle. Make sure the parking brake is fully released.

2. Remove the wheel and tire assembly.

3. On 1993–96 vehicles, install the lug nuts to hold the drum or rotor in place.

4. Rotate the drum or rotor to make sure there is no brake drag.

5. Position a suitable dial indicator with the indicator foot resting on the dust cap.

6. Check the wheel bearing endplay. Endplay should not exceed 0.008 in. (0.2mm) on 1992 vehicles or 0.002 in. (0.05mm) on 1993–96 vehicles.

7. If the endplay exceeds specification, replace the wheel bearing or hub/bearing assembly, as required.

Rear Axle/Spindle Assembly

REMOVAL AND INSTALLATION

1992

1. Raise and support the vehicle safely.

2. Remove the wheel and tire assembly.

3. Remove the brake drum and backing plate if equipped with drum brakes. Remove the brake caliper and rotor if equipped with disc brakes.

4. Loosen, but do not remove the spindle-to-shock absorber mounting nuts.

5. Remove the common lateral link arm bolt and nut from the spindle.

6. Remove the trailing arm mounting bolt at the spindle

7. Remove the spindle-to-shock absorber mounting nuts.

8. Remove the spindle from the shock absorber.

To install:

9. Position the spindle onto the shock absorber mounting bracket and install the spindle-to-shock absorber mounting bolts. Torque the bolts to 75 ft. lbs. (100 Nm).

10. Install the common lateral link arm and nut through the spindle and torque the bolt to 75 ft. lbs. (100 Nm).

11. Install the trailing arm mounting bolt and torque to 75 ft. lbs. (100 Nm).

12. Install the brake drum and backing plate if equipped with drum brakes. Install the brake caliper and rotor if equipped with disc brakes.

13. Install the wheel and tire assembly.

14. Lower the vehicle safely and have the rear suspension.

1993–96

1. Raise and support the vehicle safely.

2. Remove the wheel and tire assembly.

3. Remove the brake drum and backing plate if equipped with drum brakes. Remove the brake caliper and rotor if equipped with disc brakes.

4. Remove the hub and wheel bearing assembly.

5. Remove the ABS speed sensor retaining bolt and speed sensor, if equipped.

6. Remove the spindle-to-strut mounting nuts.

7. Remove the trailing arm mounting bolt at the spindle

8. Remove the spindle through bolt.

9. Remove the spindle.

To install:

10. Position the spindle into position and install the spindle through bolt. Torque the bolts to 75 ft. lbs. (100 Nm).

11. Install the trailing arm and spindle-to-strut mounting bolts. Torque the bolts to 75 ft. lbs. (100 Nm).

12. Install the speed sensor and retaining bolt, if equipped. Torque the bolt to 50 inch lbs. (5.0 Nm).

13. Install the hub and bearing assembly.

14. Install the brake drum and backing plate if equipped with drum brakes. Install the brake caliper and rotor if equipped with disc brakes.

15. Install the wheel and tire assembly.

16. Lower the vehicle safely and have the rear suspension.

Ford Motor Company 8

FORD—Taurus **LINCOLN**—Continental **MERCURY**—Sable

FIRING ORDERS

NOTE: To avoid confusion, always replace spark plug wires one at a time.

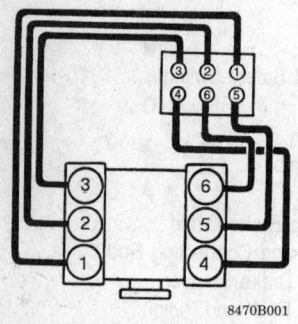

3.0L and 3.2L SHO Engines
Engine Firing Order:
1–4–2–5–3–6
Distributorless Ignition System

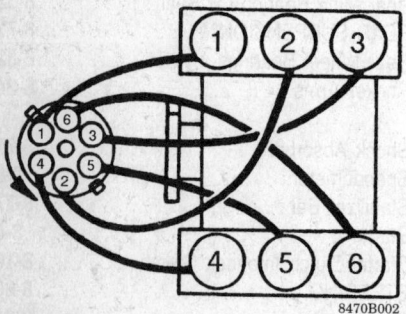

3.8L Engine
Engine Firing Order: 1–4–2–5–3–6
Distributor Rotation: Counterclockwise

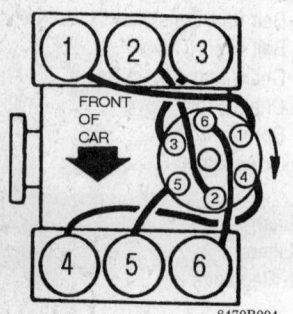

3.0L Engine
Engine Firing Order:
1–4–2–5–3–6
Distributor Rotation: Clockwise

ENGINE ELECTRICAL

NOTE: Disconnecting the negative battery cable on some vehicles may interfere with the functions of the on-board computer systems and may require the computer to undergo a relearning process once the negative battery cable is reconnected.

Distributor

REMOVAL

1. Disconnect the negative battery cable.
2. Disconnect the wiring connector from the distributor.
3. Mark the position of the No. 1 cylinder wire tower on the distributor base.
4. Remove distributor cap and position it and the attached wires aside.
5. Mark the position of the rotor in relation to the distributor housing and mark the position of the distributor housing on the engine.
6. Remove the distributor hold-down bolt and clamp and remove the distributor.
7. Use a clean shop towel to cover the distributor opening in the engine to prevent the entry of dirt or foreign material.

INSTALLATION

NOTE: Before installation, inspect the distributor O-ring and drive gear for wear and/or damage. Rotate the distributor shaft to make sure it moves freely, without binding.

Timing Not Disturbed

1. Install the distributor, aligning the distributor housing and rotor with the marks that were made during the removal procedure.
2. Install the distributor hold-down bolt and clamp. Only snug the bolt at this time.
3. Connect the distributor to the wiring harness.
4. Install the distributor cap. Make sure the ignition wires are securely connected to the distributor cap and spark plugs. Tighten the distributor cap screws to 18–23 inch lbs. (2.0–2.6 Nm).
5. Check the ignition timing and adjust, if necessary.

6. Tighten the distributor hold-down bolt to 14–21 ft. lbs. (19–28 Nm) on the 3.0L engine or 20–29 ft. lbs. (27–40 Nm) on the 3.8L engine.
7. Recheck the ignition timing after tightening the hold-down bolt.

Timing Disturbed

1. Disconnect the spark plug wire from the No. 1 cylinder spark plug and remove the spark plug.
2. Place a finger over the spark plug hole. Rotate the engine clockwise until compression is felt at the spark plug hole.
3. Align the timing pointer with the TDC mark on the crankshaft damper.
4. Rotate the distributor shaft so the rotor tip is pointing to the distributor cap No. 1 spark plug tower position.
5. Install the distributor, aligning the marks that were made on the distributor housing and engine.
6. Install the distributor hold-down bolt and clamp. Only snug the bolt at this time.
7. Connect the distributor to the wiring harness and install the distributor cap. Tighten the distributor cap hold-down screws to 18–23 inch lbs. (2.0–2.6 Nm).
8. Install the No. 1 cylinder spark plug and connect the spark plug wire.
9. Check and adjust the ignition timing.
10. Tighten the distributor hold-down bolt to 14–21 ft. lbs. (19–28 Nm) on the 3.0L engine or 20–29 ft. lbs. (27–40 Nm) on the 3.8L engine.
11. Recheck the ignition timing and adjust if necessary.

Distributorless Ignition System

The 3.0L and 3.2L SHO engines are equipped with a Distributorless Ignition System (DIS) which consists of the following components:
Crankshaft timing sensor
Camshaft sensor
DIS ignition module
Ignition coil pack
The spark angle portion of the EEC–IV module

REMOVAL AND INSTALLATION

Crankshaft Timing Sensor

1. Disconnect the negative battery cable.
2. Loosen the tensioner pulleys for the air conditioning compressor and

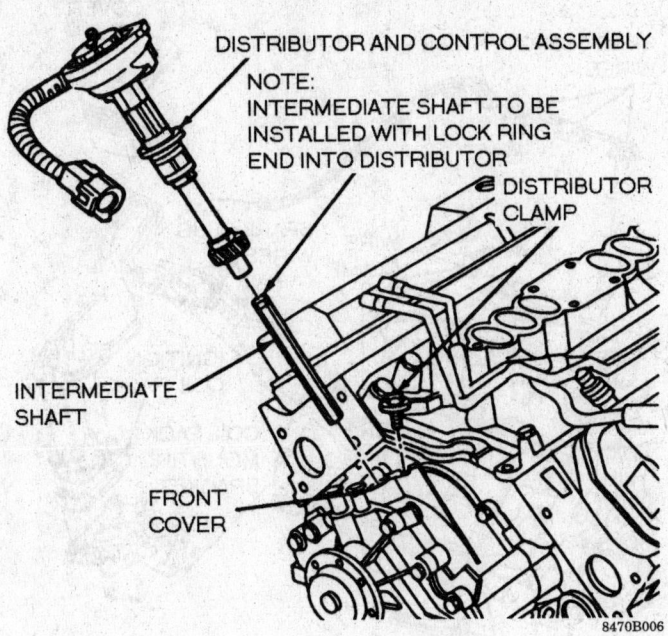

DISTRIBUTOR AND CONTROL ASSEMBLY

NOTE:
INTERMEDIATE SHAFT TO BE INSTALLED WITH LOCK RING END INTO DISTRIBUTOR

DISTRIBUTOR CLAMP

INTERMEDIATE SHAFT

FRONT COVER

8470B006

Distributor Installation — 3.8L engine

power steering pump belts. Remove the belts from the crankshaft pulley.

3. Disconnect the DIS module and remove the intake manifold crossover tube.

4. Remove the upper timing belt cover.

5. Disconnect the sensor wiring harness at the connector and route the wiring harness through the belt cover.

6. Raise the vehicle and support it safely.

7. Remove the right front wheel and tire assembly.

8. Remove the crankshaft pulley using universal puller T67L–3600–A or equivalent.

9. Remove the center and lower timing belt covers.

10. Rotate the crankshaft by hand, to position the metal vane of the shutter outside of the sensor air gap.

11. Remove the crankshaft sensor mounting screws and remove the sensor.

To install:

12. Route the sensor wiring harness through the belt cover. Install the sensor assembly on the mounting pad and install but do not tighten, the retaining screws.

13. Use a 0.03 in. (0.8mm) feeler gauge to set the clearance between the crankshaft sensor assembly and 1

vane on the crankshaft timing pulley and vane assembly. Tighten the screws to 22–31 inch lbs. (2.5–3.5 Nm).

— **WARNING** —
This is a critical torque. Over-tightening can cause damage to the timing sensor.

14. Install the lower timing belt cover. Install the crankshaft pulley using a suitable tool. Tighten the pulley bolt to 112–127 ft. lbs. (152–172 Nm).

15. Install the center timing belt cover.

16. Install the right front wheel and tire assembly. Lower the vehicle.

17. Route and connect the sensor wiring harness.

18. Install the upper timing belt cover.

19. Install the intake manifold crossover tube and connect the DIS module.

20. Install the air conditioning and power steering belts and adjust them to the proper tension.

21. Connect the negative battery cable.

Camshaft Sensor Assembly

1. Disconnect the negative battery cable.

2. Remove the engine torque strut.

3. Remove the power steering belt and the pump pulley.

4. Disconnect the camshaft sensor wiring connector.

5. Remove the mounting bolts and remove the sensor.

6. To install, reverse the removal procedure. Tighten the mounting bolts to 22–31 inch lbs. (2.5–3.5 Nm).

DIS Ignition Module

1. Disconnect the negative battery cable.

2. Disconnect the wiring connectors at the module.

3. Remove the module mounting bolts and remove the module from the upper intake manifold.

4. To install, reverse the removal procedure. Apply a uniform coating of silicone dielectric compound to the mounting surface of the DIS module before it is installed. Tighten the mounting bolts to 22–31 inch lbs. (2.5–3.5 Nm).

Ignition Coil Pack

1. Disconnect the negative battery cable.

2. Remove the cover from the coil pack and disconnect the electrical connector.

3. Remove the spark plug wires by squeezing the locking tabs to release the coil boot retainers.

4. Remove the coil pack mounting screws and remove the coil pack.

5. To install, reverse the removal procedure. Tighten the mounting screws to 40–62 inch lbs. (4.5–7 Nm).

Ignition Timing

ADJUSTMENT

Except 3.0L and 3.2L SHO Engines

The 3.0L and 3.8L engines have the timing marks on the crankshaft pulley and a timing pointer near the pulley.

1. Place the transaxle in the **P** or **N** position. Firmly apply the parking brake and block the wheels. The air conditioner and heater must be in the **OFF** position.

2. Locate the timing marks and clean with a stiff brush or solvent.

3. Using white chalk or paint, mark the specified timing mark and pointer.

4. Remove the in-line SPOUT connector or remove the shorting bar from the double wire SPOUT connector.

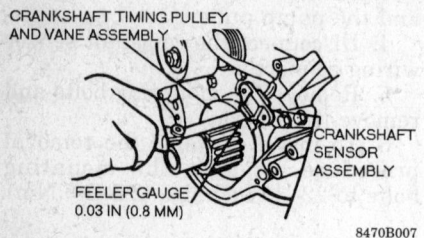

Adjusting crankshaft sensor-to-vane clearance — 3.0L and 3.2L engines

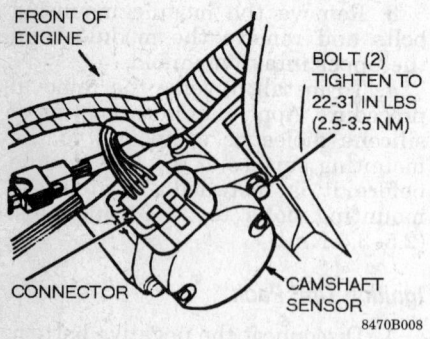

DIS camshaft sensor assembly location — 3.0L and 3.2L engines

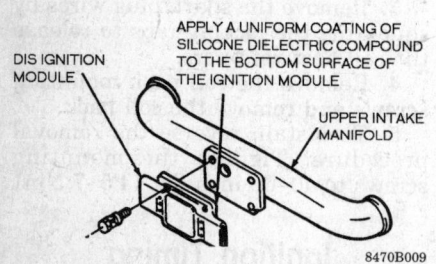

DIS ignition module removal and installation — 3.0L and 3.2L engines

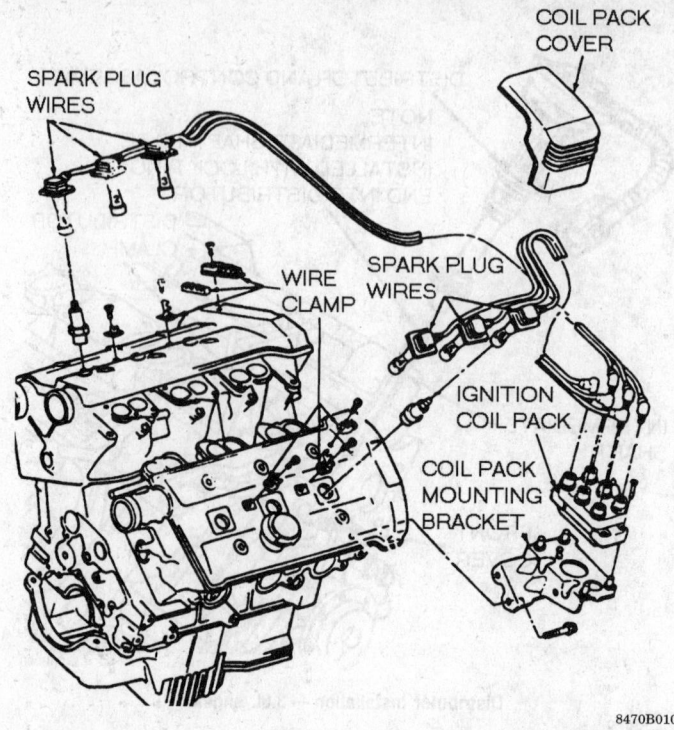

DIS ignition coil pack removal and installation — 3.0L and 3.2L engines

5. Connect a suitable inductive type timing light to the No. 1 spark plug wire. Do not, puncture and ignition wire with any type of probing device.

NOTE: The high ignition coil charging currents generated in the EEC–IV ignition system may falsely trigger timing lights with capacitive or direct connect pickups. It is necessary that an inductive type timing light be used in this procedure.

6. Connect a suitable tachometer to the engine. The ignition coil connector allows a test lead with an alligator clip to be connected without removing the coil connector. Insert the alligator clip into the back of the connector, onto the dark green/yellow dotted wire.

— **WARNING** —
Do not allow the alligator clip to accidently ground to a metal surface. It may permanently damage the coil.

7. Start the engine and let it run until it reaches normal operating temperature.

NOTE: Only use the ignition key to start the vehicle. Do not use a remote starter, as disconnecting the start wire at the starter relay will cause the TFI module to revert to start mode timing, after the vehicle is started. Reconnecting the start wire after the vehicle is running will not correct the timing.

8. Check the engine idle speed and adjust as necessary. When the idle speed is correct, aim the timing light at the timing marks. If the marks are not aligned, loosen the distributor clamp bolt slightly. Rotate the dis-

tributor body until the marks are aligned.
9. Tighten the distributor clamp bolt and recheck the ignition timing. Readjust the idle speed. Shut the engine OFF, remove all test equipment, reconnect the in-line SPOUT connector.

3.0L and 3.2L SHO Engines

The base ignition timing is set at 10 degrees BTDC and is not adjustable.

Alternator

PRECAUTIONS

Several precautions must be observed with alternator equipped vehicles to avoid damage to the unit.
• If the battery is removed for any reason, make sure it is reconnected with the correct polarity. Reversing the battery connections may result in damage to the one-way rectifiers.
• When utilizing a booster battery as a starting aid, always connect the positive to positive terminals and the negative terminal from the booster battery to a good engine ground on the vehicle being started.
• Never use a fast charger as a booster to start vehicles.

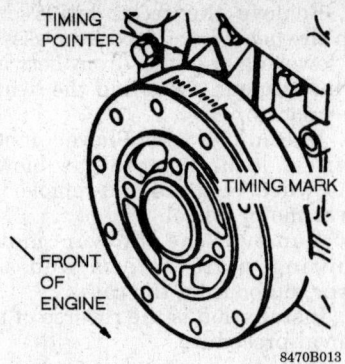

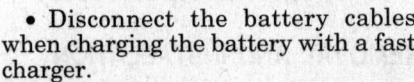

8470B013

Timing marks location — 3.0L engine

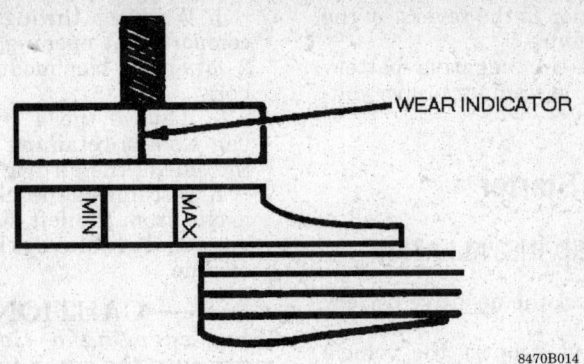

8470B014

Automatic tensioner drive belt wear indicator

• Disconnect the battery cables when charging the battery with a fast charger.

• Never attempt to polarize the alternator.

• Do not use test lights of more than 12 volts when checking diode continuity.

• Do not short across or ground any of the alternator terminals.

• The polarity of the battery, alternator and regulator must be matched and considered before making any electrical connections within the system.

• Never separate the alternator on an open circuit. Make sure all connections within the circuit are clean and tight.

• Disconnect the battery ground terminal when performing any service on electrical components.

• Disconnect the battery if arc welding is to be done on the vehicle.

BELT TENSION ADJUSTMENT

3.0L (1993–96), 3.2L SHO and 3.8L Engines

The V-ribbed belts used on these engines, utilize an automatic belt tensioner which maintains the proper belt tension for the life of the belt. The automatic belt tensioner has a belt wear indicator mark and **MIN** and **MAX** marks. If the indicator mark is not between the **MIN** and **MAX** marks, the belt is worn or an incorrect belt is installed.

3.0L Engine — 1992 Vehicles

1. Disconnect the negative battery cable.

2. Loosen the alternator adjustment and pivot bolts.

3. Apply tension to the belt using the adjusting screw.

4. Using a belt tension gauge, set the belt to the proper tension. The

tension should be 200 lbs. for a new belt or 150 lbs. for a used belt.

5. When the belt is properly tensioned, tighten the alternator adjustment bolt to 27 ft. lbs. (37 Nm).

6. Remove the tension gauge and run the engine for 5 minutes.

7. With the engine **OFF** and the belt tension gauge in place, check that the adjusting screw is in contact with the bracket before loosening the alternator adjustment bolt. Rotate the adjustment screw until the belt is tensioned to 150 lbs.

8. Tighten the alternator adjustment bolt to 27 ft. lbs. (37 Nm) and the pivot bolt to 43 ft. lbs. (58 Nm).

3.0L SHO Engine

1. Disconnect the negative battery cable.

2. Loosen the idler pulley nut.

3. Turn the adjusting bolt until the belt is adjusted to specification.

4. Position a belt tension gauge midway between the pulleys on the longest accessible belt span. The belt tension should be 220–265 lbs. for a new belt or 148–192 lbs. for a used belt.

NOTE: Turning the wrench to the right tightens the belt adjustment and turning the wrench to the left loosens the belt tension.

5. Tighten the idler pulley nut to 25–37 ft. lbs. (34–50 Nm) and check the belt tension.

REMOVAL AND INSTALLATION

Except 3.0L SHO Engine

1. Disconnect the negative battery cable.

2. If equipped with an automatic belt tensioner, rotate the tensioner counterclockwise and remove the drive belt from the pulley.

3. If not equipped with an automatic tensioner, loosen the alternator

pivot bolt and remove the adjustment arm bolt from the alternator.

  a. Remove the alternator belt from the pulley.

  b. Tag and disconnect the wire harness from the alternator.

  c. Remove the alternator mounting bolts or the pivot bolt, as required, and remove the alternator.

4. Installation is the reverse of the removal procedure. Adjust the belt tension, if not equipped with an automatic belt tensioner.

3.0L SHO Engine

1. Disconnect the battery cables and remove the battery and battery tray.

2. Tag and disconnect the wire harness from the alternator.

3. Loosen the belt tensioner and remove the alternator belt from the pulley.

4. Remove the mounting bolts and the alternator.

5. Installation is the reverse of the removal procedure. Tighten the front mounting bolt to 36–53 ft. lbs. (48–72 Nm) and the rear mounting bolts to 25–37 ft. lbs. (34–50 Nm). Adjust the belt tension.

Voltage Regulator

ADJUSTMENT

The electronic voltage regulator is calibrated and preset by the manufacturer. No adjustment is required or possible.

REMOVAL AND INSTALLATION

1. Disconnect the negative battery cable.

2. Disconnect the electrical connectors from the wiring harness.

3. Remove the regulator mounting screws and the regulator.

4. Installation is the reverse of the removal procedure.

5. Connect the negative battery cable. Test the system for proper voltage regulation.

Starter

REMOVAL AND INSTALLATION

1. Disconnect the negative battery cable.

2. Raise and support the vehicle safely.

3. Disconnect the wiring connection(s) at the starter.

4. Remove the cable support and ground cable connection from the upper starter stud bolt, if necessary.

5. If equipped, remove the starter brace from the cylinder block and the starter.

6. Remove the starter-to-bell housing bolts and remove the starter.

7. Installation is the reverse of the removal procedure.

CHASSIS ELECTRICAL

Air Bag

DISARMING

1. Disconnect the positive battery cable.

2. Wait 1 minute for the backup power supply in the diagnostic monitor to deplete its stored energy.

3. Remove the 4 nuts attaching the air bag module to the steering wheel. Disconnect the air bag connector and connect air bag simulator tool 105–00008 or equivalent, to the vehicle harness connector.

NOTE: If equipped with optional passenger side air bag, both driver and passenger air bag modules must be disconnected.

4. On Taurus/Sable, if equipped with a passenger air bag, proceed as follows:

a. Remove the right-hand and left-hand finish panels.

b. Remove the instrument panel finish panel retaining spear clips.

c. Open the glove compartment, press the side inward and lower the glove compartment to the floor.

d. Working through the glove compartment opening, remove the 2 lower air bag module retaining bolts.

e. Remove the 4 remaining air bag module retaining screws from the side of the air bag cover.

f. Disconnect the electrical connector from the left side of the air bag and remove the air bag module.

— CAUTION —

When carrying a live air bag, make sure the bag and trim cover are pointed away from the body. In the unlikely event of an accidental deployment, the bag will then deploy with minimal chance of injury. In addition, when placing a live air bag on a bench or other surface, always face the bag and trim cover up, away from the surface. This will reduce the motion of the unit if it is accidentally deployed.

g. Connect air bag simulator tool 105–00008 or equivalent, to the vehicle harness connector.

5. On Continental, if equipped with passenger side air bag, proceed as follows:

a. Open the glove compartment and rotate all the way down, past the stops.

b. Disconnect the air bag connector and connect air bag simulator tool 105–00008 or equivalent, to the vehicle harness connector.

6. Connect the positive battery cable.

Heater Blower Motor

REMOVAL AND INSTALLATION

1. Disconnect the negative battery cable.

2. Open the glove compartment door, release the door retainers and lower the door.

3. Remove the screw attaching the recirculation duct support bracket to the instrument panel cowl.

4. If equipped with automatic temperature control, remove the nut holding the electrical connector bracket to the recirculation duct. Release the 3 connectors from the bracket and remove the bracket.

5. Remove the vacuum connection of the recirculation door vacuum motor. If equipped, disconnect the 2 aspirator hoses from the muffler.

6. Remove the screws attaching the recirculation duct to the heater or evaporator assembly.

7. Remove the recirculation duct from the heater or evaporator assembly, lowering the duct from between the instrument panel and the heater or evaporator case.

8. Disconnect the blower motor electrical lead. Remove the blower motor wheel pushnut and remove the blower motor wheel.

9. Remove the blower motor mounting plate screws and the blower motor from the case.

10. Installation is the reverse of the removal procedure.

Windshield Wiper Motor

REMOVAL AND INSTALLATION

Front

1. Disconnect the negative battery cable.

2. Disconnect the power lead from the motor.

3. Remove the left wiper arm by first applying downward pressure on the wiper arm head, while holding the wiper arm. Lift the arm to the highest position and using finger pressure only, grasp the slide latch tab and slide the latch out from under the arm head. Remove the arm and blade assembly.

4. On Continental and Taurus and Sable, lift the water shield cover from the cowl on the passenger side.

5. Remove the linkage retaining clip from the operating arm on the motor by lifting the locking tab up and pulling the clip away from the pin.

6. Remove the attaching screws from the motor and bracket assembly and remove.

7. Installation is the reverse of the removal procedure.

Rear — Station Wagon

1. Disconnect the negative battery cable.

2. Raise the wiper arm and blade assembly away from the glass and insert a 0.062 in. (1.6mm) pin in the holes in the retainer arm. Let the arm move toward the glass to relieve the arm spring tension and lift the arm off the pivot shaft.

3. Remove the pivot shaft retaining nut and spacers.

4. Disconnect the electrical connector to the wiper motor.

5. Remove the nut retaining the motor to the handle and remove the motor.

6. Installation is the reverse of the removal procedure.

Windshield Wiper Switch

REMOVAL AND INSTALLATION

Front

The front wiper switch is a function of the combination switch.

Rear — Station Wagon

1. Disconnect the negative battery cable.
2. Remove the cluster opening finish panel as follows:
   a. Engage the parking brake.
   b. Remove the ignition lock cylinder.
   c. If equipped with a tilt column, tilt the column to the full down position and remove the tilt lever.
   d. Remove the 4 bolts and the opening cover from under the steering column.
   e. Remove the steering column trim shrouds. Disconnect all electrical connections from the combination switch.
   f. Remove the 2 screws retaining the combination switch and remove the switch.
   g. Pull the gear shift lever to the full down position.
   h. Remove the cluster opening finish panel retaining screws and, if necessary, the light switch knob and retaining nut.
   i. Remove the finish panel by pulling it toward the driver to unsnap the snap-in retainers and disconnect the wiring from the switches, clock and warning lights.
3. Remove the wiper switch from the cluster opening finish panel.

To install:

4. Push the rear wiper switch into the cluster finish panel until it snaps into place.
5. Install the cluster opening finish panel in the reverse order of removal.
6. Connect the negative battery cable.

Instrument Cluster

REMOVAL AND INSTALLATION

Conventional

1. Disconnect the negative battery cable.
2. Remove the ignition lock cylinder to allow removal of the steering column shrouds.
3. Remove the steering column trim shrouds.

4. Remove the lower left and radio finish panel screws and snap the panels out.
5. On Taurus, remove the clock assembly (or clock cover) to gain access to the finish panel screw behind the clock.
6. Remove the cluster opening finish panel retaining screws and jam nut behind the headlight switch. Remove the finish panel by rocking the upper edge toward the driver.
7. On column shift vehicles, disconnect the transaxle selector indicator from the column by removing the retaining screw and cable loop.
8. Disconnect the upper speedometer cable from the lower speedometer cable in the engine compartment.
9. Remove the 4 cluster-to-instrument panel retaining screws and pull the cluster assembly forward.
10. Disconnect the cluster electrical connector and speedometer cable. Press the cable latch to disengage the cable from the speedometer head while pulling the cable away from the cluster. Remove the cluster.

To install:

11. Position the cluster in front of the cluster opening.
12. Connect the speedometer cable and electrical connectors.
13. Install the cluster and the 4 cluster-to-instrument panel retaining screws.
14. Connect the upper speedometer cable to the lower speedometer cable in the engine compartment.
15. On column shift vehicles, connect the transaxle selector indicator.
16. Install the cluster opening finish panel.
17. On Taurus vehicles, install the clock assembly or clock cover.
18. Install the lower left and radio finish panels.
19. Install the steering column trim shrouds.
20. Install the ignition lock cylinder and connect the negative battery cable.

Electronic

TAURUS AND SABLE

1. Disconnect the negative battery cable.
2. Remove the lower trim covers.
3. Remove the steering column cover and disconnect the shift indicator cable from the cluster by removing the retaining screws.
4. Disconnect the switch module and remove the cluster trim panel.
5. Remove the cluster mounting screws and pull the bottom of the cluster toward the steering wheel.

6. Reach behind and under the cluster, disconnect the 3 electrical connectors.
7. Swing the bottom of the cluster out to clear the top of the cluster from the crash pad and remove.

To install:

8. Insert the top of the cluster under the crash pad, leaving the bottom out.
9. Connect the 3 connectors.
10. Properly seat the cluster and install the retaining screws.
11. Connect the battery ground cable and check the cluster for proper operation.
12. Connect the shift indicator assembly to the cluster and secure with the retaining screw. Install the steering column cover.
13. Connect the switch module to the cluster and install the cluster trim panel.
14. Install the lower trim covers.

CONTINENTAL

1. Position the vehicle on a flat surface to prevent movement when the gear shift selector is out of position. Apply the parking brake and block the wheels.
2. Disconnect the negative battery cable.
3. Rotate the ignition switch to unlock the the shift lever and move the lever from the front of the cluster. Tilt the steering wheel as far as possible.
4. Remove the right and left finish mouldings by pulling upwards to unsnap the 2 clips. Disconnect the electrical connectors and set the mouldings aside.
5. Remove the 5 Torx® screws that secure the applique below the instrument cluster. Unsnap the applique along the top and pull away from the panel.
6. Disconnect the switch assembly connector from the instrument cluster and set the applique aside.
7. Remove the screws from the bottom of the steering column shroud.
8. Raise the top section of the shroud to release a clip located on the left side near the steering wheel. Separate the upper section of the shroud from the side section near the ignition switch. Slide the upper section off the shift lever.
9. Remove the 4 Torx® screws attaching the instrument cluster to the instrument panel.
10. Place a clean, soft cloth on the steering column to prevent scratching the surface of the steering column as the instrument cluster is removed.

11. Tilt the top of the instrument cluster slightly toward the rear of the vehicle. Disconnect the shift indicator assembly from the cluster by undoing the 2 snaps located under the cluster.

12. Reach around the back of the instrument cluster to disconnect the connectors. The connectors have locking tabs that must be pressed in to release.

13. Loosen the 2 clips retaining the shift indicator assembly to the cluster. Pull the shift indicator down and to the right to position it aside.

14. Push the bottom of the instrument cluster into the instrument panel cavity. Tilt the top of the instrument cluster toward the rear of the vehicle. Push the cluster up and out of the cavity.

To install:

15. Position the instrument cluster in front of the instrument panel cavity.

16. Connect the electrical connectors.

17. Install the cluster into the instrument panel cavity.

18. Connect the shift indicator assembly to the instrument cluster.

19. Install the 4 Torx® screws.

20. Install the upper section of the steering column shroud and install the screws in the bottom section.

21. Connect the switch assembly connector and install the applique. Install the 5 Torx® screws that secure the applique.

22. Connect the electrical connectors and install the right and left finish mouldings.

23. Move the shift lever to the **P** position and the ignition switch to the **LOCK** position.

24. Connect the negative battery cable.

Speedometer

REMOVAL AND INSTALLATION

Taurus and Sable

ANALOG

1. Disconnect the negative battery cable.
2. Remove the instrument cluster.
3. Remove the 8 mask and lens mounting screws. Remove the mask and lens.
4. Remove the 2 screws attaching the transaxle selector indicator or the filler bezel to the speedometer and remove the indicator or filler bezel from the cluster.
5. Lift the speedometer from the instrument cluster.

6. Installation is the reverse of the removal procedure.

ELECTRONIC

The speedometer is part of a single electronic instrument cluster module and cannot be removed separately.

Continental

The speedometer is part of a single electronic instrument cluster module and cannot be removed separately.

Headlight Switch

REMOVAL AND INSTALLATION

Taurus and Sable

1. Disconnect the negative battery cable.
2. Pull off the headlight switch knob and remove the retaining nut.
3. Remove the instrument cluster finish panel as follows:
   a. Apply the parking brake.
   b. Remove the ignition lock cylinder.
   c. If equipped with a tilt column, tilt the column to the most downward position and remove the tilt lever.
   d. Remove the 4 bolts and opening cover from under the steering column.
   e. Remove the steering column trim shrouds. Disconnect all electrical connections from the steering column combination switch.
   f. Remove the 2 screws retaining the combination switch and remove the switch.
   g. Pull the gear shift lever to the full down position.
   h. Remove the cluster opening finish panel retaining screws. Remove the finish panel by pulling it toward the driver to unsnap the snap-in retainers and disconnect the wiring from the switches, clock and warning lights.
4. Remove the 2 screws retaining the headlight switch, pull the switch out of the instrument panel and disconnect the electrical connector.
5. Installation is the reverse of the removal procedure.

Continental

1. Disconnect the negative battery cable.
2. Gently pull off the headlight switch knob.
3. Snap out the right and left mouldings, remove the 5 cluster opening finish panel retaining screws and the panel.

4. Remove the 2 screws retaining the headlight switch to the finish panel, disconnect the electrical connector and remove the switch.
5. Installation is the reverse of the removal procedure.

Combination Switch

The combination switch incorporates the turn signal, headlight dimmer, headlight flash-to-pass, hazard warning, cornering lights and windshield washer/wiper functions.

REMOVAL AND INSTALLATION

1. Disconnect the negative battery cable. If equipped with a tilt steering column, set the tilt column to its lowest position and remove the tilt lever.
2. Remove the ignition lock cylinder. Remove the steering column shroud screws and remove the upper and lower shrouds.
3. Remove the self tapping screws attaching the switch to the steering column and disengage the switch from the steering column casting.
4. Remove the wiring harness retainer, if equipped and disconnect the electrical connectors.

To install:

5. Connect the electrical connectors. Install the wiring harness retainer, if equipped.
6. Align the turn signal switch mounting holes with the corresponding holes in the steering column and install self-tapping screws. Torque the screws to 17–26 inch lbs. (2–3 Nm).
7. Install the upper and lower steering column shroud and shroud retaining screws, torque the screws to 6–10 inch lbs. (0.7–1.1 Nm).
8. Install the ignition lock cylinder. Attach the tilt lever, if removed.
9. Connect the negative battery cable. Check the switch and the steering column for proper operation.

Ignition Lock Cylinder

REMOVAL AND INSTALLATION

Functional Lock

The following procedure applies to vehicles that have functional lock cylinders. Lock cylinder keys are available for these vehicles or the lock cylinder key numbers are known and the proper key can be made.

1. Disconnect the negative battery cable.

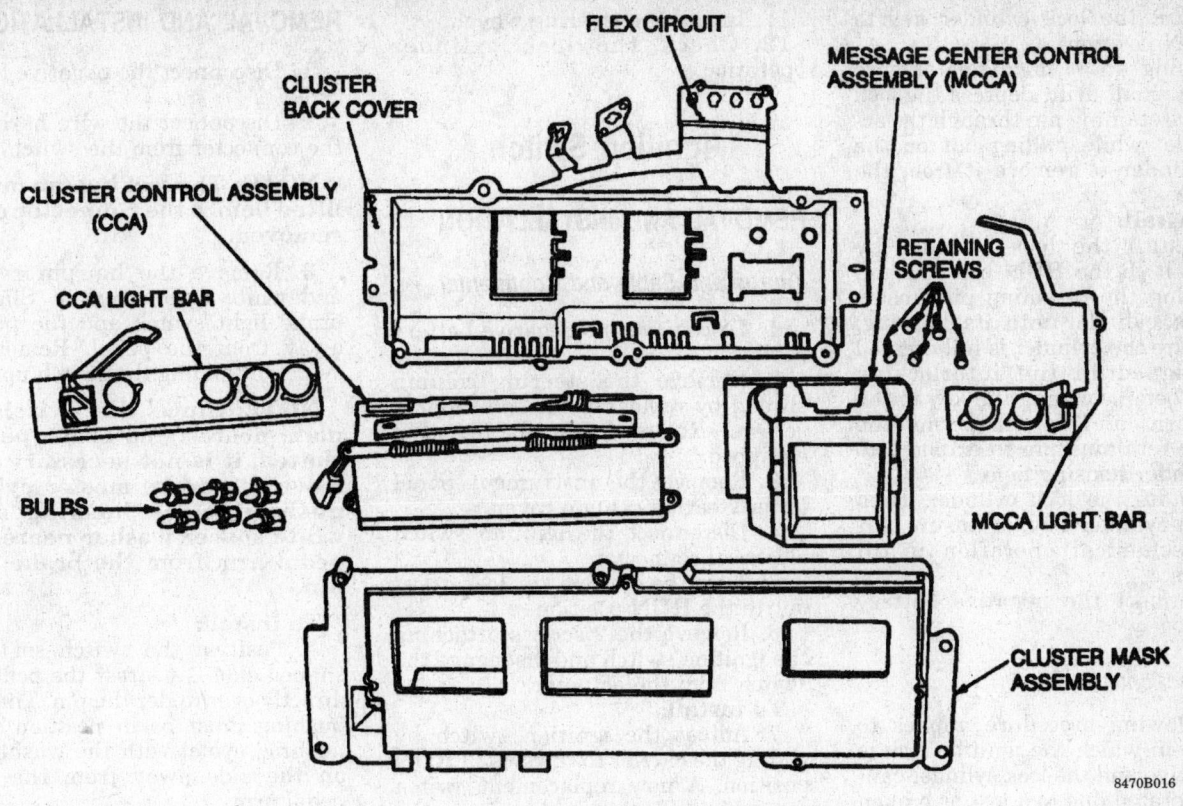

Electronic instrument cluster assembly — Continental

8470B016

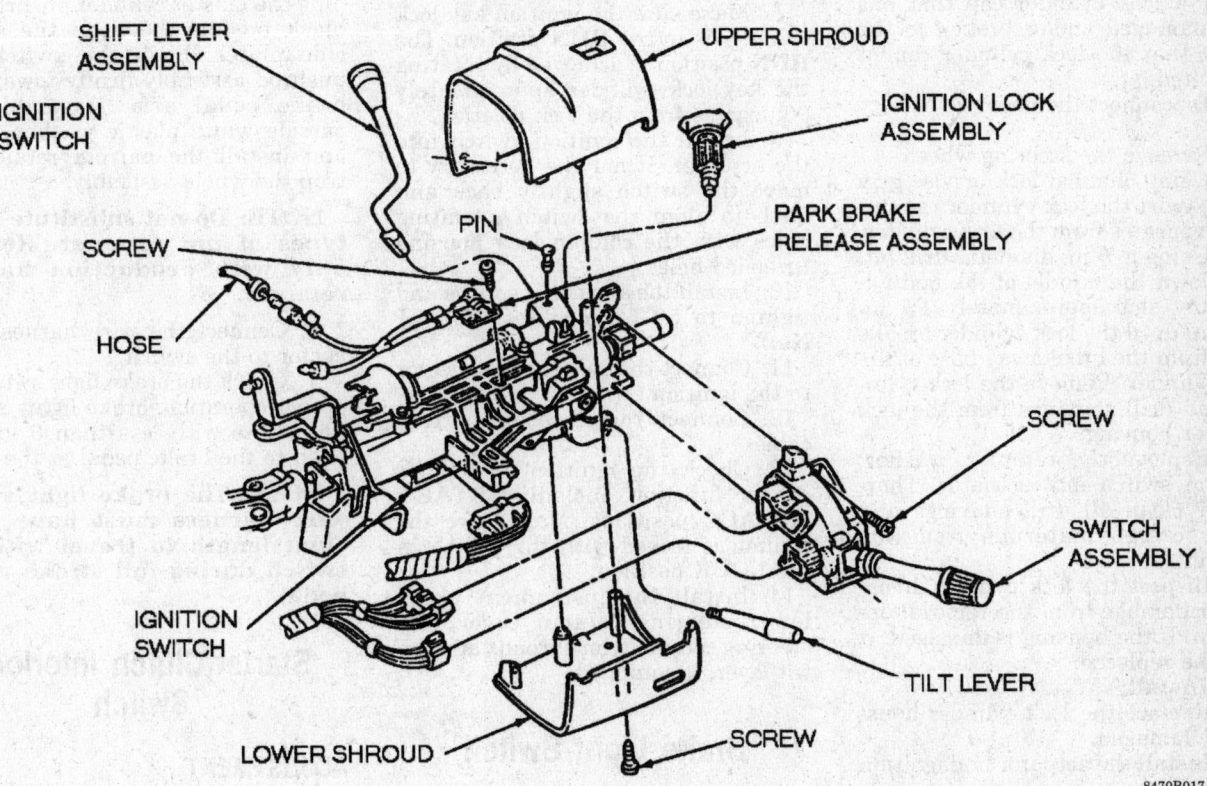

Combination switch removal and installation — Taurus, Sable and Continental

8470B017

2. Turn the lock cylinder key to the **RUN** position.

3. Using an ⅛ in. diameter wire pin or a small drift, depress the lock cylinder retaining pin through the access hole, while pulling out on the lock cylinder to remove it from the column.

To install:

4. Install the lock cylinder by turning it to the **RUN** position and depressing the retaining pin. Insert the lock cylinder into its housing. Make sure the cylinder is fully seated and aligned in the interlocking washer before turning the key to the **OFF** position. This will permit the cylinder retaining pin to extend into the cylinder housing hole.

5. Rotate the lock cylinder using the lock cylinder key, to ensure correct mechanical operation in all positions.

6. Connect the negative battery cable.

Non-Functional Lock

The following procedure applies to vehicles in which the ignition lock is inoperative and the lock cylinder cannot be rotated due to a lost or broken lock cylinder key, unknown key number or a lock cylinder cap that has been damaged and/or broken to the extent that the lock cylinder cannot be rotated.

1. Disconnect the negative battery cable.

2. Remove the steering wheel.

3. Using channel lock or vise grip pliers, twist the lock cylinder cap until it separates from the lock cylinder.

4. Using a ⅜ in. diameter drill bit, drill down the middle of the ignition lock key slot approximately 1¾ in. (44mm) until the lock cylinder breaks loose from the breakaway base of the lock cylinder. Remove the lock cylinder and drill shavings from the lock cylinder housing.

5. Remove the retainer, washer, ignition switch and actuator. Thoroughly clean all drill shavings and other foreign materials from the casting.

6. Inspect the lock cylinder housing for damage from the removal operation. If the housing is damaged, it must be replaced.

To install:

7. Replace the lock cylinder housing, if damaged.

8. Install the actuator and ignition switch.

9. Install the trim and electrical parts.

10. Install the ignition lock cylinder.

11. Install the steering wheel.

12. Check the lock cylinder operation.

Ignition Switch

REMOVAL AND INSTALLATION

Taurus and Sable and Continental

1. Disconnect the negative battery cable.

2. Remove the steering column shroud by removing the self-tapping screws. Remove the tilt lever, if equipped.

3. Remove the instrument panel lower steering column cover.

4. Disconnect the ignition switch electrical connector.

5. Turn the ignition key lock cylinder to the **RUN** position.

6. Remove the 2 screws attaching the ignition switch and disengage the switch from the actuator.

To install:

7. Adjust the ignition switch by sliding the carrier to the switch **RUN** position. A new replacement switch assembly will already be set in the **RUN** position.

8. Make sure the ignition key lock cylinder is in the **RUN** position. The **RUN** position is achieved by rotating the key lock cylinder approximately 90 degrees from the lock position.

9. Install the ignition switch into the actuator. It may be necessary to move the switch slightly back and forth to align the switch mounting holes with the column lock housing threaded holes.

10. Install the attaching screws and tighten to 50–69 inch lbs. (5.6–7.9 Nm).

11. Connect the electrical connector to the ignition switch.

12. Connect the negative battery cable.

13. Check the ignition switch for proper function, including **START** and **ACC** positions. Make sure the column is locked with the switch in the **LOCK** position.

14. Install the instrument panel lower steering column cover, the steering column trim shrouds and the tilt lever, if equipped.

Brake Light Switch

The mechanical brake light switch assembly is installed on the pin of the brake pedal arm, so it straddles the master cylinder pushrod.

REMOVAL AND INSTALLATION

1. Disconnect the negative battery cable.

2. Disconnect the wire harness at the connector from the switch.

NOTE: The locking tab must be lifted before the connector can be removed.

3. Remove the hairpin retainer and white nylon washer. Slide the brake light switch and the pushrod away from the pedal. Remove the switch by sliding the switch up/down.

NOTE: Since the switch side plate nearest the brake pedal is slotted, it is not necessary to remove the brake master cylinder pushrod black bushing and 1 white spacer washer nearest the pedal arm from the brake pedal pin.

To install:

4. Position the switch so the U-shaped side is nearest the pedal and directly over/under the pin. The black bushing must be in position in the pushrod eyelet with the washer face on the side away from the brake pedal arm.

5. Slide the switch up/down, trapping the master cylinder pushrod and black bushing between the switch side plates. Push the switch and pushrod assembly firmly toward the brake pedal arm. Assemble the outside white plastic washer to pin and install the hairpin retainer to trap the whole assembly.

NOTE: Do not substitute other types of pin retainer. Replace only with production hairpin retainer.

6. Connect the wire harness connector to the switch.

7. Check the brake light switch for proper operation. brake lights should illuminate with less than 6 lbs. applied to the brake pedal at the pad.

NOTE: The brake light switch wire harness must have sufficient length to travel with the switch during full stroke at the pedal.

Starter/Clutch Interlock Switch

ADJUSTMENT

1. Remove the panel above clutch pedal.

2. Disengage the wiring connector by flexing the retaining tab on the

switch and withdrawing the connector.

3. Using a test light, check that the switch is open with the clutch pedal up (clutch engaged) and closed at approximately 1 in. (25.4mm) from the clutch pedal full down position (clutch disengaged).

4. If the switch does not operate as outlined in Step 3, check if the self-adjusting clip is out of position on the rod. It should be near the end of the rod.

5. If the self-adjusting clip is out of position, remove and reposition the clip approximately 1 in. (25.4mm) from the end of the rod.

6. Reset the switch by pressing the clutch pedal to the floor. Repeat Step 3. If the switch is damaged or the clips do not remain in place, replace the switch.

REMOVAL AND INSTALLATION

1. Disconnect the negative battery cable.

2. Remove the panel above the clutch pedal.

3. Disconnect the switch wiring connector.

4. Remove clutch interlock attaching screw and hairpin clip and then remove the switch.

To install:

NOTE: Always install the switch with the self-adjusting clip about 1 in. (25.4mm) from the end of the rod. The clutch pedal must be fully up (clutch engaged). Otherwise, the switch may be misadjusted.

5. Insert the eyelet end of the rod over the clutch pedal pin and secure with the hairpin clip.

6. Align the mounting boss with the corresponding hole in the bracket and attach with a screw.

7. Reset clutch interlock switch by pressing the clutch pedal to the floor.

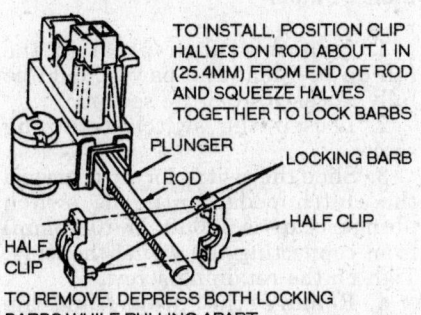

TO INSTALL, POSITION CLIP HALVES ON ROD ABOUT 1 IN (25.4MM) FROM END OF ROD AND SQUEEZE HALVES TOGETHER TO LOCK BARBS

PLUNGER
ROD
LOCKING BARB
HALF CLIP
HALF CLIP

TO REMOVE, DEPRESS BOTH LOCKING BARBS WHILE PULLING APART

8470B018

Starter/clutch interlock switch

8. Connect the wiring connector.

9. Install the panel above the clutch.

Neutral Safety Switch

REMOVAL AND INSTALLATION

ATX/FLC Transaxle

1. Disconnect the negative battery cable and set the parking brake.

2. Disconnect the wire connector from the neutral safety switch.

3. Remove the nut and washer holding the Throttle Valve (TV) lever. Hold the lever stationary while loosening to prevent internal damage. Remove the lever from the TV shaft.

4. Remove the 2 neutral safety switch attaching bolts and remove the neutral safety switch.

To install:

5. Place the manual lever in **N**.

6. Install the neutral safety switch on the manual shaft.

7. Loosely install the 2 neutral safety switch attaching bolts, lock washers and flat washers.

8. Insert a No. 43 (0.089 in.) drill bit through the hole provided in the switch. Tighten the attaching bolts to 7–9 ft. lbs. (9–12 Nm) and remove the drill bit.

9. Connect the neutral safety switch connector.

10. Install the TV lever, lock washer and nut. Hold the lever stationary while tightening to prevent internal damage. Tighten to 7.5–9.5 ft. lbs. (10–13 Nm).

11. Connect the negative battery cable.

12. Check the ignition switch for proper starting in **P** or **N**. Also make certain the start circuit cannot be actuated in the **D** or **R** position and that the column is locked in the **LOCK** position.

Fuses, Circuit Breakers and Relays

LOCATION

Fuses

All vehicles have a fuse panel located under the left side of the instrument panel. In addition, Continental and 1992–94 Taurus/Sable are equipped with a high-current fuse panel located in the engine compartment on the left fender apron.

Circuit Breakers

Circuit breakers protect electrical circuits by interrupting the current flow. A circuit breakers conducts current through an arm make of 2 types of metal bonded together. If the arm starts to carry too much current, it heats up. As 1 metal expands faster than the other, the arm bends, opening the contacts and interrupting the current flow.

TAURUS AND SABLE

Station Wagon Rear Window/Washer — a 4.5 amp circuit breaker located on the instrument panel brace.

Windshield Wipers and Washer Pump — a 8.25 amp circuit breaker located on the fuse panel.

Cigar Lighter, Horn Relay and Horns — a 20 amp circuit breaker located on the fuse panel.

Power Windows, Power Locks and Power Seats — a 20 amp circuit breaker located on the fuse panel.

Headlights — a 22 amp circuit breaker incorporated in the headlight switch.

CONTINENTAL

Windshield Wipers and Washer Pump — a 8.25 amp circuit breaker located on the fuse panel.

Relays

TAURUS AND SABLE

Anti-lock Motor Relay — located in the lower left front of engine compartment, if equipped with anti-lock brakes.

Anti-lock Power Relay — located in the right rear of engine compartment on firewall on early 1992 vehicles or on the front of left front fender apron on late 1992–96 vehicles, if equipped with anti-lock brakes.

Autolight Dual Coil Relay — located behind the center of the instrument panel on the instrument panel brace, if equipped with automatic headlights.

Fog Light Relay — located behind the center of the instrument panel on the instrument panel brace.

Horn Relay — located behind the center of the instrument panel on the instrument panel brace.

LCD Dimming Relay — located behind the center of the instrument panel on the instrument panel brace, is equipped with automatic headlights.

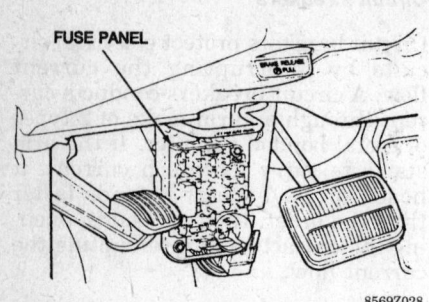
FUSE PANEL

8569Z028

Fuse panel location — Continental

Liftgate Release Relay — located in the right rear corner of the cargo area.

Low Oil Level Relay — located behind the center of the instrument panel on the instrument panel brace.

Moonroof Relay — located behind the right side of the instrument panel.

Police Accessory Relay — located behind the center of the instrument panel.

CONTINENTAL

Alternator Output Control Relay — if equipped with heated windshield, is located in front right fender.

Anti-lock Motor Relay — if equipped with anti-lock brakes, is located on the lower left front of the engine compartment, on the bracket behind the radiator.

Anti-lock Power Relay — If equipped with anti-lock brakes, is located on the left side of the engine compartment, on the front of the power distribution box.

Autolight Relay — located behind the center of the instrument panel.

Compressor Relay — located on the engine cowl or on the front of the power distribution box.

Hard Shock Relay — located below the left side of the rear package tray.

Hi-Lo Beam Relay — locate behind the center of the instrument panel.

Horn Relay — located behind the lower center of the instrument panel, near the left side of the warning chime module.

LCD Dimming Relay — located behind the center of the instrument panel.

Soft Shock Relay — located below the left side of the rear package tray.

Starter Relay — located on the left fender apron.

Window Safety Relay — located behind the center of the instrument panel.

Computers

LOCATION

Taurus and Sable

Electronic Engine Control Module — located on the passenger side of the firewall.

Anti-lock Brake Control Module — located at the front of the engine compartment next to the passenger side fender, except on Taurus SHO where it is located at the front of the engine compartment on the driver's side.

Automatic Temperature Control Module — located behind the center of the instrument panel.

Heated Windshield Control Module — located behind the left side of the instrument panel, to the right of the steering column.

Integrated Control Module — located at the front of the engine compartment, on the upper radiator support.

Air Bag Diagnostic Module — located behind the right side of the instrument panel, Above the glove box.

Continental

Electronic Engine Control Module — located on the passenger side of the firewall.

Anti-lock Brake Control Module — located in the trunk on the passenger side under the package tray.

Air Bag Diagnostic Module — located behind the left side of the instrument panel above the fuse panel.

Automatic Temperature Control Module — located behind the center of the instrument panel.

Heated Windshield Control Module — located behind the left side of the instrument panel.

Integrated Control Module — located at the front of the engine compartment, on the upper radiator support.

Air Suspension Control Module — located in the left side of the trunk.

Flashers

LOCATION

An electronic combination turn signal and emergency warning flasher is attached to the lower left instrument panel reinforcement above the fuse panel.

Cruise Control

ADJUSTMENT

Actuator Cable

3.0L AND 3.8L ENGINES

1. Remove the retaining clip.
2. Push the actuator cable through the adjuster until slight tension is felt.
3. Insert cable retaining clip and snap into place.

Vacuum Dump Valve

The vacuum dump valve is adjustable in its mounting bracket. It should be adjusted so it is closed (no vacuum leak) when the brake pedal is in the normal release position (not depressed) and open when the pedal is depressed. Use a hand vacuum pump or equivalent to make the adjustment.

Clutch Switch

1. Prop the clutch pedal in the full-up position. The pawl should be fully released from the sector.
2. Loosen the switch retaining screw.
3. Slide the switch forward toward the clutch pedal until the switch plunger cap is 0.030 in (0.76mm) from connecting the switch housing. Tighten the retaining screw.
4. Remove the prop from the clutch pedal and test drive for clutch switch cancellation of cruise control.

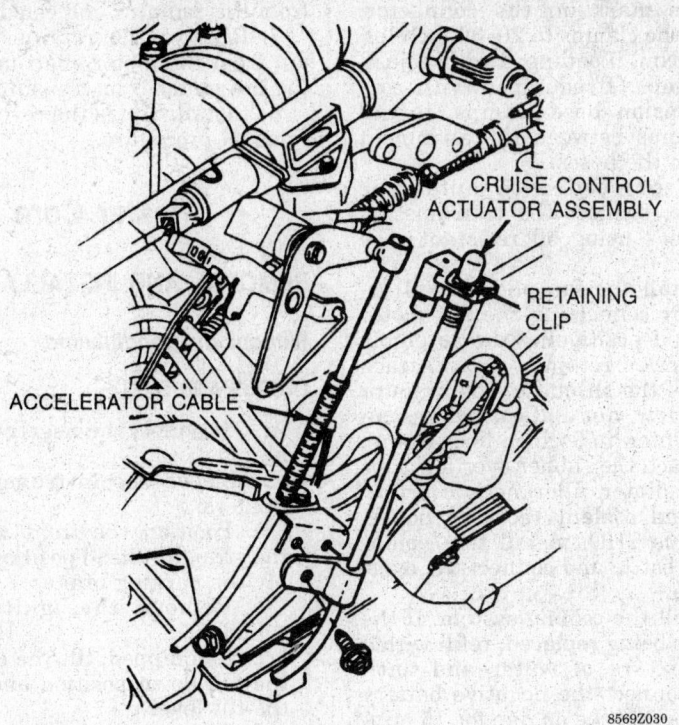

CRUISE CONTROL
ACTUATOR ASSEMBLY

RETAINING
CLIP

ACCELERATOR CABLE

8569Z030

Cruise control actuator cable assembly — 3.0L engine

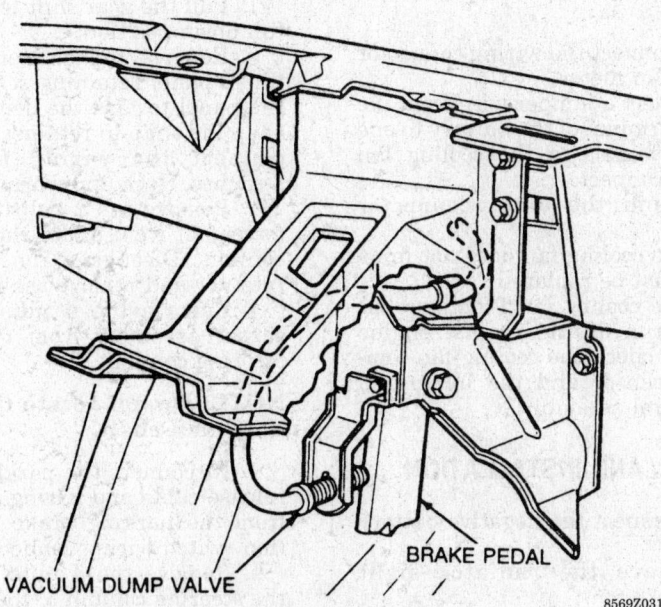

VACUUM DUMP VALVE

BRAKE PEDAL

8569Z031

Vacuum dump valve location

ENGINE COOLING

Radiator

REMOVAL AND INSTALLATION

—————— CAUTION ——————
Never remove the radiator cap while the engine is running or personal injury from scalding hot coolant or steam may result. If possible, wait until the engine has cooled to remove the radiator cap. If this is not possible, wrap a thick cloth around the radiator cap and turn it slowly to the first stop. Step back while the pressure is released from the cooling system. When it is certain all the pressure has been released, press down on the cap, still with the cloth, and turn and remove it.

1. Disconnect the negative battery cable.
2. Drain the cooling system by removing the radiator cap and opening the draincock located at the lower rear corner of the radiator inlet tank.
3. Remove the rubber overflow tube from the coolant recovery bottle and detach it from the radiator. On Taurus SHO, disconnect the tube from the radiator and remove the recovery bottle.
4. Remove 2 upper shroud retaining screws and lift the shroud out of the lower retaining clips.
5. Disconnect the electric cooling fan motor wires and remove the fan and shroud assembly.
6. Loosen the upper and lower hose clamps at the radiator and remove the hoses from the radiator connectors.
7. If equipped with an automatic transaxle, disconnect the transmission oil cooling lines from the radiator fittings using disconnect tool T82L–9500–AH or equivalent.
8. If equipped with 3.0L or 3.0L SHO engine — 1992, remove 2 radiator upper retaining screws. If equipped with the 3.8L engine or 3.0L and 3.2L SHO engines — 1993–96, remove 2 hex nuts from from the right radiator support bracket and 2 screws from the left radiator support bracket and remove the brackets.
9. Tilt the radiator rearward approximately 1 in. and lift it directly upward, clear of the radiator support.

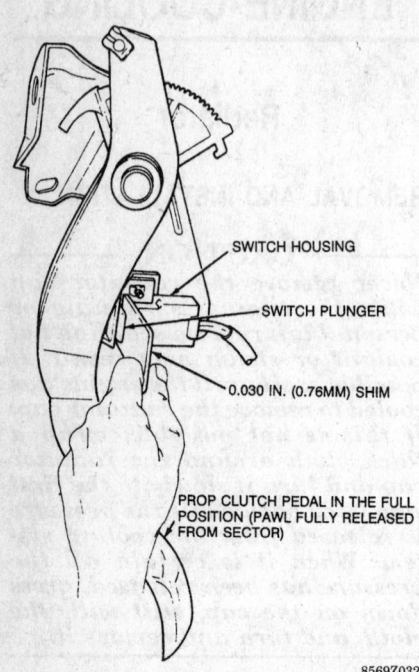

SWITCH HOUSING

SWITCH PLUNGER

0.030 IN. (0.76MM) SHIM

PROP CLUTCH PEDAL IN THE FULL
POSITION (PAWL FULLY RELEASED
FROM SECTOR)

8569Z032

Cruise control clutch switch adjustment

10. Remove the radiator lower support rubber pads, if pad replacement is necessary.

To install:

11. Position the radiator lower support rubber pads to the lower support, if removed.

12. Position the radiator into the engine compartment and to the radiator support. Insert the moulded pins at the bottom of each tank through the slotted holes in the lower support rubber pads.

13. Make sure the plastic pads on the bottom of the radiator tanks are resting on the rubber pads. Install 2 upper retaining bolts to attach the radiator to the radiator support. Tighten the bolts to 46–60 inch lbs. (5–7 Nm). If equipped with the 3.8L engine or 3.0L and 3.2L SHO engines — 1993–96, tighten the bolts to 13–20 ft. lbs. (17–27 Nm).

14. If equipped with the 3.8L engine or 3.0L and 3.2L SHO engines — 1993–96, fasten the left radiator support bracket to the radiator support with 2 screws. Tighten the screws to 9–17 ft. lbs. (12–24 Nm). Attach the right support bracket to the radiator support with 2 hex nuts. Tighten the nuts to 9–17 ft. lbs. (12–24 Nm).

15. Attach the radiator upper and lower hoses to the radiator. Position the hose on the radiator connector so the index arrow on the hose is in line with the mark on the connector. Tighten the clamps to 20–30 inch lbs. (2.3–3.4 Nm) if equipped with adjustable clamps. If equipped with constant tension hose clamps, install hose clamps between the alignment marks on the hoses.

16. If equipped with automatic transaxle, connect the transmission cooler lines using oil resistant pipe sealer.

17. Install the fan and shroud assembly by connecting the fan motor wiring and positioning the assembly on the lower retainer clips. Attach the top of the shroud to the radiator with 2 screw, nut and washer assemblies. Tighten to 35 inch lbs. (4 Nm).

18. Attach the rubber overflow tube to the radiator filler neck overflow nipple and coolant recovery bottle. On Taurus SHO, install the coolant recovery bottle and connect the overflow hose.

19. Refill the cooling system. If the coolant is being replaced, refill with a 50/50 mixture of water and antifreeze. Connect the negative battery cable. Operate the engine for 15 minutes and check for leaks. Check the coolant level and add, as required.

Electric Cooling Fan

TESTING

1. Disconnect the wiring connector from the fan motor.

2. Connect a jumper wire from the positive terminal of the battery to one of the terminals in the cooling fan electrical connector.

3. Ground the other connector terminal.

4. If the cooling fan does not function, it must be replaced.

5. If the cooling fan functions but does not run during normal engine operation, check the cooling fan temperature sensor and the integrated relay control assembly.

REMOVAL AND INSTALLATION

1. Disconnect the negative battery cable.

2. Remove the radiator sight shield.

3. Disconnect the electrical connector and remove the integrated relay control assembly located on the radiator support.

4. Disconnect the fan electrical connector.

5. If necessary, remove the air bag crash sensor.

6. Unbolt the fan/shroud assembly from the radiator and remove.

7. Remove the retainer and the fan from the motor shaft and unbolt the fan motor from the shroud.

8. Installation is the reverse of the removal procedure.

Heater Core

REMOVAL AND INSTALLATION

Without Air Conditioning

TAURUS AND SABLE

1. Disconnect the negative battery cable.

2. Remove the instrument panel as follows:

a. Position the front wheels in the straight-ahead position and apply the parking brake.

b. Remove the ignition lock cylinder.

c. If equipped, tilt the column to the full down position and remove the tilt lever.

d. Remove the 4 bolts and opening cover from under the steering column. Remove the steering column trim shrouds.

e. Disconnect the electrical connectors from the combination switch and remove the switch.

f. Pull the gear shift lever to the full down position.

g. Remove the cluster opening finish panel retaining screws. Pull the panel toward the driver to unsnap the snap-in retainers and disconnect the wiring from the switches, clock and warning lights.

h. Remove the 2 bolts and reinforcement from under the steering column. Disengage the insulator retainer and remove the insulator.

i. Remove the 4 nuts and absorber assembly from under the steering column.

NOTE: Do not rotate the steering column shaft.

j. Disconnect the parking brake release cable and wiring connector from the parking brake and ignition switch wiring connector.

k. Remove the 4 nuts retaining the steering column to the support, disconnect the shift position indicator cable if equipped with column shift and lower the column on the front seat. Cover the front seat to protect from damage.

l. Install the lock cylinder to make sure the steering column shaft does not turn.

m. Remove the 4 retaining screws from the cluster, disconnect the wiring and remove.

n. Remove the 1 bolt at the steering column opening attaching the instrument panel to the brace. Remove the 1 instrument panel brace retaining bolt from under the radio area.

o. Remove the sound insulator under the glove compartment by removing the 2 pushnuts that secure the insulator to the studs on the climate control case.

p. Remove the 3 screws attaching the glove compartment assembly to the instrument panel and remove the door assembly.

q. Remove the air cleaner, battery and battery tray. Disconnect the main wire loom in the engine compartment. Disengage the rubber grommet from the dash panel, then feed the wiring through the hole in the dash panel into the passenger compartment.

r. Remove the right and left cowl side trim panels. Disconnect the wires from the instrument panel at the right and left cowl sides.

s. Support the panel and remove the 3 screws attaching the top of the panel to the cowl top and disconnect any remaining wires. Remove the instrument panel and lay it on the front seat.

3. Drain the coolant from the radiator.

4. Disconnect and plug the heater hoses at the heater core. Plug the heater core tubes.

5. Disconnect the vacuum supply hose from the in-line vacuum check valve in the engine compartment. Remove the screw holding the instrument panel shake brace to the heater case and remove the shake brace.

6. Remove the floor register and rear floor ducts from the bottom of the heater case. Remove the 3 nuts attaching the heater case to the dash panel in the engine compartment.

7. Remove the 2 screws attaching the brackets to the cowl top panel. Pull the heater case assembly away from the dash panel and remove from the vehicle.

8. Remove the vacuum source line from the heater core tube seal and remove the seal from the heater core tubes.

9. Remove the 4 heater core access cover attaching screws and remove the access cover from the heater case. Lift the heater core and seals from the heater case.

To install:

10. Transfer the 3 foam core seals to the new heater core. Install the heater core and seals into the heater case.

11. Position the heater case access cover on the case and install the 4 screws.

12. Install the seal on the heater core tubes and install the vacuum source line through the seal.

13. Position the heater case assembly to the dash panel and cowl top panel at the air inlet opening. Install the 2 screws to attach the support brackets to the cowl top panel.

14. Install the 3 nuts in the engine compartment to attach the heater case to the dash panel. Install the floor register and rear floor ducts on the bottom of the heater case.

15. Install the instrument panel shake brace and screw to the heater case. Install the instrument panel by reversing the removal procedure.

16. Connect the heater hoses to the heater core. Connect the black vacuum supply hose to the vacuum check valve in the engine compartment.

17. Fill the radiator and bleed the cooling system.

18. Connect the negative battery cable and check the system for proper operation.

With Air Conditioning

NOTE: It is necessary to remove the evaporator case in order to remove the heater core. Whenever an evaporator case is removed, it will be necessary to replace the suction accumulator/drier.

TAURUS AND SABLE

1. Disconnect the negative battery cable.

2. Remove the instrument panel as follows:

a. Position the front wheels in the straight-ahead position and apply the parking brake.

b. Remove the ignition lock cylinder.

c. If equipped, tilt the column to the full down position and remove the tilt lever.

d. Remove the 4 bolts and opening cover from under the steering column. Remove the steering column trim shrouds.

e. Disconnect the electrical connectors from the combination switch and remove the switch.

f. Pull the gear shift lever to the full down position.

g. Remove the cluster opening finish panel retaining screws. Pull the panel toward the driver to unsnap the snapin retainers and disconnect the wiring from the switches, clock and warning lights.

h. Remove the 2 bolts and reinforcement from under the steering column. Disengage the insulator retainer and remove the insulator.

i. Remove the 4 nuts and absorber assembly from under the steering column.

NOTE: Do not rotate the steering column shaft.

j. Disconnect the parking brake release cable and wiring connector from the parking brake and ignition switch wiring connector.

k. Remove the 4 nuts retaining the steering column to the support, disconnect the shift position indicator cable if equipped with column shift and lower the column on the front seat. Cover the front seat to protect from damage.

l. Install the lock cylinder to make sure the steering column shaft does not turn.

m. Remove the 4 retaining screws from the cluster, disconnect the wiring and remove.

n. Remove the 1 bolt at the steering column opening attaching the instrument panel to the brace. Remove the 1 instrument panel brace retaining bolt from under the radio area.

o. Remove the sound insulator under the glove compartment by removing the 2 pushnuts that secure the insulator to the studs on the climate control case.

p. Remove the 3 screws attaching the glove compartment assembly to the instrument panel and remove the door assembly.

q. Remove the air cleaner, battery and battery tray. Disconnect the main wire loom in the engine compartment. Disengage the rubber grommet from the dash panel, then feed the wiring through the hole in the dash panel into the passenger compartment.

r. Remove the right and left cowl side trim panels. Disconnect the wires from the instrument panel at the right and left cowl sides.

s. Support the panel and remove the 3 screws attaching the top of the panel to the cowl top and disconnect any remaining wires. Remove the instrument panel and lay it on the front seat.

3. Drain the coolant from the radiator. Properly discharge the air conditioning system.

4. Disconnect and plug the heater hoses at the heater core. Plug the heater core tubes.

5. Disconnect the vacuum supply hose from the in-line vacuum check valve in the engine compartment.

6. Disconnect the air conditioning lines from the evaporator core at the dash panel. Cap the lines and the core to prevent entrance of dirt and moisture.

7. Remove the screw holding the instrument panel shake brace to the evaporator case and remove the shake brace.

8. Remove the 2 screws attaching the floor register and rear seat duct to the bottom of the evaporator case. Remove the 3 nuts attaching the evaporator case to the dash panel in the engine compartment.

9. Remove the 2 screws attaching the support brackets to the cowl top panel. Carefully pull the evaporator assembly away from the dash panel and remove the evaporator case from the vehicle.

10. Remove the vacuum source line from the heater core tube seal and remove the seal from the heater core tubes.

11. If equipped with automatic temperature control, remove the 3 screws attaching the blend door actuator to the evaporator case and remove the actuator.

12. Remove the 4 heater core access cover attaching screws and remove the access cover and seal from the evaporator case. Lift the heater core and seals from the evaporator case.

To install:
13. Transfer the seal to the new heater core. Install the heater core into the evaporator case.

14. Position the heater core access cover on the evaporator case and install the 4 attaching screws. If equipped with automatic temperature control, position the blend door actuator to the blend door shaft and install the 3 attaching screws.

15. Install the seal on the heater core tubes and install the vacuum source line through the seal.

16. Position the evaporator case assembly to the dash panel and cowl top panel at the air inlet opening. Install the 2 screws attaching the support brackets to the cowl top panel.

17. Install the 3 nuts in the engine compartment attaching the evaporator case to the dash panel. Install the floor register and rear seat duct to the evaporator case and tighten the 2 attaching screws.

18. Install the instrument panel shake brace and screw to the evapo-

rator case. Install the instrument panel in the reverse order of removal.

19. Connect the air conditioning lines to the evaporator core and the heater hoses to the heater core.

20. Connect the black vacuum supply hose to the vacuum check valve in the engine compartment.

21. Fill and bleed the cooling system. Connect the negative battery cable.

22. Leak test, evacuate and charge the air conditioning system. Observe all safely precautions.

23. Check the system for operation.

CONTINENTAL

1. Disconnect both battery cables. Wait 1 minute for the backup power supply in the air bag diagnostic monitor to deplete its stored energy.

2. Remove the instrument panel as follows:

a. Open the glove compartment door and depress the sides inward. Lower the glove compartment assembly toward the floor.

b. Remove the 4 nut and washer assemblies retaining the driver air bag module to the steering wheel. Disconnect the driver air bag module connector and attach a jumper wire to the air bag terminals on the clockspring. Remove the air bag from the vehicle.

c. Disconnect the passenger air bag connector. Attach air bag simulator tool 105-00008 or equivalent, to the vehicle harness connector. Remove the 4 bolts/screws attaching the passenger air bag module to the instrument panel and remove the air bag from the vehicle.

———— CAUTION ————

When carrying a line air bag module, make sure the bag and trim cover are pointed away from the body. In the unlikely event of an accidental deployment, the bag will then deploy with minimal chance of injury. In addition, when placing a live air bag module on a bench or other surface, always face the bag and trim cover up, away from the surface. This will reduce the motion of the module if it is accidentally deployed.

d. Remove the right finish moulding by pulling upward to unsnap the 5 clips. Disconnect the wiring. Remove the left finish moulding by pulling upward to unsnap the 2 clips.

e. Remove the right and left lower insulators. Remove the screws retaining the lower instru-

ment panel steering column cover and remove the cover. Remove the 4 screws retaining the lower instrument panel steering column reinforcement and remove the reinforcement.

f. If equipped, remove the 4 retaining nuts and the absorber assembly. Remove the 3 screws retaining the upper steering column shroud and remove. Remove the tilt wheel lever.

g. Remove the lock cylinder by pushing a small Allen wrench into the groove located under the lock cylinder. Place the key into the ignition and gently wiggle to work the cylinder free.

h. Remove the lower steering column shroud by pulling out. Remove the bolt retaining the shift indicator cable to the steering column. Remove the steering wheel. Disconnect all electrical connectors.

i. Disconnect the hood and brake release cables. Remove the 4 nuts retaining the steering column and lower the column. Remove the screw(s) at the steering column opening retaining the instrument panel to the brake pedal support.

j. Remove the 2 screws under the ashtray that hold the instrument panel to the air conditioning plenum case. Remove the headlight switch knob.

k. Remove the 5 screws from the cluster opening finish panel and remove the panel. Remove the 4 screws retaining the air conditioning control. Disconnect the electrical connectors and 1 vacuum connector.

l. Remove the 4 screws retaining the cluster and disconnect the electrical connectors. Remove the 3 screws to remove the glove compartment assembly.

m. Remove the 2 screws from the instrument panel to cowl top brace and 1 screw from the passenger air bag support bracket. Remove both speaker grilles by snapping out to release. Remove the 2 screws seated in the plastic push clips and remove the center defrost grille.

n. Working under the hood, disconnect all electrical connectors of the main wire loom. Disengage the rubber grommet from the dash panel and feed the wiring and connectors through the hole into the instrument panel area.

o. Remove the 3 screws (2 located on the sill Plate) at both right and left cowl trim panels and remove the panels. Disconnect the wiring at the right and left cowl side panels.

p. Remove the lower 2 screws from the instrument panel, 1 at each end. Remove the 3 upper instrument panel retaining screws and carefully lower the instrument panel.

q. Disconnect the remaining electrical and vacuum connectors and remove the instrument panel.

3. Drain the coolant from the radiator and properly discharge the refrigerant from the air conditioning system.

4. Disconnect and plug the heater hoses at the heater core. Plug the heater core tubes. Disconnect the vacuum supply hose from the in-line vacuum check valve in the engine compartment.

5. Disconnect the air conditioner lines from the evaporator core at the dash panel. Cap the lines and the core to prevent the entrance of dirt and moisture.

6. Remove the screw holding the instrument panel shake brace to the evaporator case. Remove the shake brace. Remove the 2 screws attaching the floor register to the evaporator case.

7. Disconnect the vacuum line, electrical connections and aspirator hose from the evaporator case.

8. Remove the 3 nuts retaining the evaporator case to the dash panel in the engine compartment. Remove the 2 screws retaining the support bracket to the cowl top panel.

9. Carefully pull the evaporator case assembly away from the dash panel and remove from the vehicle.

10. Remove the vacuum source line from the heater core tube seal. Remove the seal from the heater core tube seal. Remove the seal from the heater core tubes.

11. Remove the 3 screws attaching the blend door actuator to the evaporator case and remove the actuator.

12. Remove the 4 heater core access cover retaining screws and remove the access cover and seal from the evaporator case. Lift the heater core and seals from the evaporator case.

To install:

13. Transfer 3 foam core seals to the new heater core. Install the heater core in the evaporator case.

14. Position the heater core access cover on the evaporator case and install the 4 retaining screws.

15. Position the blend door actuator to the blend door shaft. Install the 3 retaining screws.

16. Install the seal on the heater core tubes. Install the vacuum source line through the seal.

17. Position the evaporator case assembly against the dash panel and cowl top panel at the air inlet opening. Install the 2 screws retaining the support brackets to the cowl top panel.

18. Install the 3 nuts in the engine compartment retaining the evaporator case to the dash panel. Install the floor register to the evaporator case and tighten the 2 retaining screws.

19. Connect the vacuum line, electrical connections and aspirator hose at the evaporator case. Install the instrument panel shake brace.

20. Install the instrument panel in the reverse order of removal

21. Connect the air conditioner lines at the evaporator core and the heater hoses at the heater core. Connect the black vacuum supply hose to the vacuum check valve in the engine compartment.

22. Fill and bleed the cooling system. Connect the negative battery cable.

23. Leak test, evacuate and charge the air conditioning system. Observe all safety precautions.

24. Check the system for proper operation.

Water Pump

REMOVAL AND INSTALLATION

3.0L Engine Except SHO

1. Disconnect the negative battery cable and place a drain pan under the radiator drain cock.

2. Remove the radiator cap, open the drain cock on the radiator and drain the cooling system.

3. Loosen the 4 water pump pulley retaining bolts while the accessory drive belts are still tight.

4. Loosen the alternator belt adjuster jack screw to provide enough clearance for removal of the alternator belt.

5. Using a ½ in. breaker bar, rotate the automatic tensioner down and to the left. Remove the power steering/air conditioner belt.

6. Remove the 2 nuts and 1 bolt retaining the automatic tensioner to the engine.

7. Disconnect and remove the lower radiator and heater hose from the water pump.

8. Remove the water pump to engine retaining bolts and lift the water pump and pulley up and out of the vehicle.

To install:

9. Clean the gasket surfaces on the water pump and front cover.

10. Install the water pump with the pulley loosely positioned on the hub, using a new gasket.

11. Install and tighten the retaining bolts. Tighten bolts 3–9 to 15–22 ft. lbs. (20–30 Nm) and bolts 11–15 to 71–106 inch lbs. (8–12 Nm). Apply pipe sealant to bolt No. 3 prior to installation.

12. Hand tighten the water pump pulley retaining bolts.

13. Install the automatic belt tensioner assembly. Tighten the 2 retaining nuts and bolt to 35 ft. lbs. (48 Nm).

14. Install the alternator and power steering belts. Final tighten the water pump pulley retaining bolts to 16 ft. lbs. (21 Nm).

15. Install the lower radiator and heater hoses. Fill and bleed the cooling system with the appropriate quantity and coolant type.

16. Connect the negative battery cable. Start the engine and check for leaks.

3.0L and 3.2L SHO Engines

1. Disconnect the battery cables and remove the battery and the battery tray.

2. Drain the cooling system and remove the accessory drive belts.

3. Remove the bolts retaining the air conditioning and alternator idler pulley and bracket assembly.

4. Disconnect the electrical connector from the ignition module and ground strap.

5. Loosen the clamps on the upper intake connector tube, remove the retaining bolts and remove the connector tube.

6. Raise and safely support the vehicle. Remove the right wheel and tire assembly.

7. Remove the splash shield.

8. Remove the upper timing belt cover, crankshaft pulley and lower timing belt cover.

9. Remove the bolts from the center timing belt cover and position it aside.

10. Remove the water pump attaching bolts and remove the water pump.

11. To install, reverse the removal procedure. Tighten the water pump bolts to 12–16 ft. lbs. (15–23 Nm). Tighten the crankshaft pulley bolt to 113–126 ft. lbs. (152–172 Nm).

3.8L Engine

1. Disconnect the negative battery cable. Drain the cooling system.

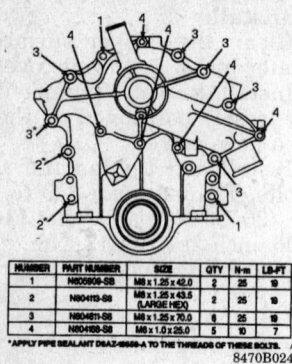

NUMBER	PART NUMBER	SIZE	QTY	N·m	LB-FT
1	N805909-S8	M8 x 1.25 x 42.0	2	25	19
2	N604113-S8	M8 x 1.25 x 43.5 (LARGE HEX)	2	25	19
3	N604611-S8	M8 x 1.25 x 70.0	6	25	19
4	N604108-S8	M6 x 1.0 x 25.0	5	10	7

*APPLY PIPE SEALANT D8AZ-19559-A TO THE THREADS OF THESE BOLTS.

8470B024

Water pump bolt identification — 3.0L engine

2. Support the engine using engine support bar D88L–6000–A or equivalent. Remove the lower nut on both right engine mounts. Raise the engine.

3. Loosen the accessory drive belt idler. Remove the drive belt and water pump pulley.

4. Remove the air suspension pump.

5. Remove the power steering pump mounting bracket attaching bolts. Leaving hoses connected, place pump/bracket assembly aside in a position to prevent fluid from leaking out.

6. If equipped with air conditioning, remove the compressor front support bracket. Leave the compressor in place.

7. Disconnect coolant bypass and heater hoses at the water pump.

8. Remove the water pump-to-engine block attaching bolts and remove the pump from the vehicle. Discard the gasket and replace with new.

To install:

9. Lightly oil all bolt and stud threads before installation except those that require sealant. Thoroughly clean the water pump and front cover gasket contact surfaces.

10. Apply a coating of contact adhesive to both surfaces of the new gasket. Position a new gasket on water pump sealing surface.

11. Position water pump on the front cover and install attaching bolts.

12. Tighten the attaching bolts to 15–22 ft. lbs. (20–30 Nm).

13. Connect the cooling bypass hose, heater hose and radiator lower hose to water pump and tighten the clamps.

14. If equipped with air conditioning, install compressor front support bracket.

15. Position the power steering pump and mounting bracket and install the retaining bolts.

16. Position the accessory drive belt over the pulleys.

17. Lower the engine.

18. Install and tighten the lower right engine mount nuts. Remove the engine support bar.

19. Fill cooling system to the proper level.

20. Start engine and check for coolant leaks.

Thermostat

REMOVAL AND INSTALLATION

3.0L Engine

1. Disconnect the negative battery cable.

2. Place a suitable drain pan under the radiator.

3. Remove the radiator cap and open the draincock. Drain the cooling system.

4. Remove the upper radiator hose from the thermostat housing.

5. Remove the 3 retaining bolts from the thermostat housing.

6. Remove the housing and the thermostat as an assembly.

To install:

7. Make sure all sealing surfaces are free of old gasket material.

8. Install the thermostat into the housing and rotate clockwise to lock in. Make sure the jiggle valve is in the up position.

9. Position a new gasket onto the housing using the bolts as a holding device. Install the thermostat assembly and tighten the bolts to 9 ft. lbs. (12 Nm).

10. Install the upper radiator hose and tighten the clamp.

11. Fill and bleed the cooling system. Connect the negative battery cable, start the engine and check for

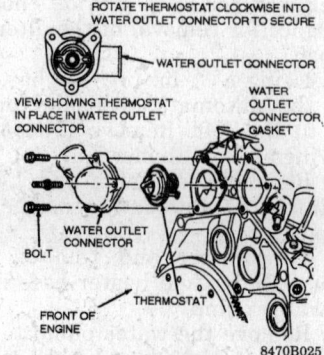

ROTATE THERMOSTAT CLOCKWISE INTO WATER OUTLET CONNECTOR TO SECURE

WATER OUTLET CONNECTOR

VIEW SHOWING THERMOSTAT IN PLACE IN WATER OUTLET CONNECTOR

WATER OUTLET CONNECTOR GASKET

WATER OUTLET CONNECTOR

BOLT

THERMOSTAT

FRONT OF ENGINE

8470B025

Thermostat installation — 3.0L engine

coolant leaks. Check the coolant level and add as required.

3.0L and 3.2L SHO Engines

1. Disconnect the negative battery cable.

2. Place a suitable drain pan below the radiator. Remove the radiator cap and open the draincock. Partially drain the cooling system and then close the draincock.

3. Remove the air cleaner tube.

4. Disconnect the hose from the water outlet tube.

5. Remove the 2 retaining nuts and remove the water outlet tube.

6. Remove the thermostat and seal from the water outlet housing.

To install:

7. Install the seal around the outer rim of the thermostat and install the thermostat into the water outlet housing. Align the jiggle valve of the thermostat with the upper bolt on the water outlet housing.

8. Install the water outlet tube. Tighten the 2 retaining nuts to 5–8 ft. lbs. (7–11 Nm).

9. Install the air cleaner tube.

10. Refill the cooling system. Connect the negative battery cable. Start the engine and check for leaks. Check the coolant level and add as necessary.

3.8L Engine

1. Disconnect the negative battery cable.

2. Place a suitable drain pan below the radiator.

3. Remove the radiator cap and open the draincock. Drain the radiator to a level below the water outlet connection and then close the draincock.

4. Loosen the top hose clamp at the radiator, remove the water outlet connection retaining bolts and lift the water outlet clear of the engine. Remove the thermostat by rotating it counterclockwise in the water outlet connection until the thermostat becomes free to remove.

NOTE: Do not pry the housing off.

To install:

5. Make sure the water outlet connection pocket and all mating surfaces are clean.

6. Install the thermostat into the water outlet connection by rotating it clockwise until the engaging ramps on the thermostat are secure. Install the water outlet connection on the intake manifold with a new gasket and tighten the mounting bolts to 15–22 ft. lbs. (20–30 Nm). Position the top

hose to the radiator and tighten the clamps.

7. Refill the cooling system. Connect the negative battery cable. Start the engine and check for leaks. Check the coolant level and add as required.

Cooling System Bleeding

When the entire cooling system is drained, the following procedure should be used to ensure a complete fill.

1. Install the block drain plug, if removed and close the draincock. With the engine **OFF**, add a 50/50 mixture of coolant and water to the radiator to a level just below the filler neck seat.

2. Place the heater temperature selector in the **MAX HEAT** position.

3. Install the radiator cap to the first notch to keep spillage to a minimum.

4. Start the engine and let it idle until the upper radiator hose is warm. This indicates that the thermostat is open and coolant is flowing through the entire system.

5. Carefully remove the radiator cap and top off the radiator with water. Install the cap on the radiator securely.

6. Fill the coolant recovery reservoir to the **FULL HOT** mark with the 50/50 mixture of coolant and water.

7. Check for leaks at the draincock AND block plug .

FUEL SYSTEM

Fuel System Service Precautions

Safety is the most important factor when performing not only fuel system maintenance but any type of maintenance. Failure to conduct maintenance and repairs in a safe manner may result in serious personal injury or death. Maintenance and testing of the vehicle's fuel system components can be accomplished safely and effectively by adhering to the following rules and guidelines.

• To avoid the possibility of fire and personal injury, always disconnect the negative battery cable unless the repair or test procedure requires that battery voltage be applied.

• Always relieve the fuel system pressure prior to disconnecting any fuel system component (injector, fuel rail, pressure regulator, etc.), fitting or fuel line connection. Exercise extreme caution whenever relieving fuel system pressure to avoid exposing skin, face and eyes to fuel spray. Please be advised that fuel under pressure may penetrate the skin or any part of the body that it contacts.

• Always place a shop towel or cloth around the fitting or connection prior to loosening to absorb any excess fuel due to spillage. Ensure that all fuel spillage (should it occur) is quickly removed from engine surfaces. Ensure that all fuel soaked cloths or towels are deposited into a suitable waste container.

• Always keep a dry chemical (Class B) fire extinguisher near the work area.

• Do not allow fuel spray or fuel vapors to come into contact with a spark or open flame.

• Always use a backup wrench when loosening and tightening fuel line connection fittings. This will prevent unnecessary stress and torsion to fuel line piping. Always follow the proper torque specifications.

• Always replace worn fuel fitting O-rings with new. Do not substitute fuel hose or equivalent where fuel pipe is installed.

RELIEVING FUEL SYSTEM PRESSURE

The pressure in the fuel system must be released before attempting to disconnect any fuel lines. A special valve is incorporated in the fuel rail assembly for the purpose of relieving the pressure in the fuel system.

1. Remove the fuel tank cap.

2. Remove the cap from the pressure relief Schrader valve on the fuel rail.

3. Attach pressure gauge tool T80L–9974–A or equivalent, to the fuel pressure relief valve.

4. Release the pressure from the system into a suitable container.

5. Remove the pressure gauge and install the cap on the pressure relief valve. Install the fuel tank cap.

Fuel Line Couplings

REMOVAL AND INSTALLATION

There are several methods used to connect the fuel lines and fuel system components. The hairpin clip push connect fitting and the spring lock coupling each require a different procedure to disconnect and connect.

Hairpin Clip Push Connect Fitting

1. Inspect the internal portion of the fitting for dirt accumulation. If more than a light coating of dust is present, clean the fitting before disassembly.

2. Remove the hairpin clip from the fitting by first bending the shipping tab downward so it will clear the body. This is done, using hands only, by spreading the 2 clip legs about 1/8 in. (3.2mm) each to disengage the body and pushing the legs into the fitting. Complete removal is accomplished by lightly pulling from the triangular end of the clip and working it clear of the tube and fitting.

NOTE: Do not use any tools when disconnecting the clip.

3. Grasp the fitting and hose assembly and pull in an axial direction to remove the fitting from the steel tube. Adhesion between sealing surfaces may occur. A slight twist of the fitting may be required to break this adhesion for easier removal.

NOTE: On 90 degree elbow connectors, excessive side loading could break the connector body.

4. When the fitting is removed from the tube end, inspect the clip to make sure it has not been damaged. If damaged, replace the clip. If undamaged, immediately install the clip to prevent loss or damage. To install the clip, insert the clip into any 2 adjacent openings with the triangular portion pointing away from the fitting opening. Install the clip to fully engage the body — legs of the hairpin clip locked on the outside of the body. Piloting with an index finger is necessary.

To install:

5. Before installing the fitting on the tube, wipe the tube end with a clean cloth. Inspect the inside of the fitting to make sure it is free of dirt and/or obstructions. Apply a light coat of engine oil to the tube end for ease of assembly.

6. To install the fitting onto the tube, align the fitting and tube axial and push the fitting onto the tube end. When the fitting is engaged, a definite click will be heard. Pull on the fitting to make sure it is fully engaged.

Spring Lock Coupling

The spring lock coupling is a fuel line coupling held together by a garter

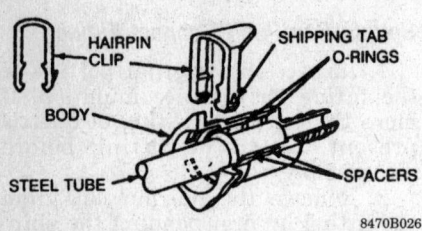

Hairpin clip push connect fitting

8470B026

spring inside a circular cage. When the coupling is connected together, the flared end of the female fitting slips behind the garter spring inside the cage of the male fitting. The garter spring and cage then prevent the flared end of the female fitting from pulling out of the cage. As an additional locking feature, most vehicles have a horseshoe shaped retaining clip that improves the retaining reliability of the spring lock coupling.

Fuel Tank

REMOVAL AND INSTALLATION

1. Disconnect the negative battery cable.
2. Relieve the fuel system pressure.
3. Siphon or pump the fuel from the fuel tank, through the filler neck, into a suitable container.

NOTE: There are reservoirs inside the fuel tank to maintain fuel near the fuel pickup during cornering and under low fuel operating conditions. These reservoirs could block siphon tubes or hoses from reaching the bottom of the tank. A few repeated attempts using different hose orientations can overcome this situation.

4. Raise and safely support the vehicle.
5. Loosen the filler pipe and vent hose clamps at the tank and remove the hoses from the tank.
6. Place a safety support under the fuel tank and remove the bolts from the rear of the fuel tank straps. The straps are hinged at the front and will swing aside.
7. Partially remove the tank. Remove the hairpin clips from the push connect fitting and disconnect the

fuel lines. Disconnect the electrical connector from the fuel sender/pump assembly.
8. Remove the fuel tank.
    To install:
9. Raise the fuel tank into position. Connect the fuel lines and the electrical connector.
10. Bring the fuel tank straps around the tank and start the retaining bolt. Align the tank as far forward in the vehicle as possible while securing the retaining bolts.

NOTE: If equipped with a heat shield, make sure it is installed with the straps and positioned correctly on the tank.

11. Check the hoses and wiring mounted on the tank top, to make sure they are correctly routed and will not be pinched between the tank and the body.
12. Tighten the fuel tank strap retaining bolts to 22–30 ft. lbs. (29–41 Nm).
13. Install the fuel filler hoses and tighten the clamps. Refill the fuel tank.
14. Check all connections for leaks. Connect the negative battery cable.

Fuel Filter

REMOVAL AND INSTALLATION

1. Disconnect the negative battery cable. Relieve the fuel system pressure.
2. Remove the push connect fittings at both ends of the fuel filter.
3. Remove the filter from the mounting bracket by loosening the worm gear mounting clamp enough to allow the filter to pass through.
    To install:
4. Install the filter in the mounting bracket, ensuring that the flow direction arrow is pointing forward. Locate the fuel filter against the tab at the lower end of the bracket.
5. Install the push connect fittings at both ends of the fuel filter.
6. Tighten the worm gear mounting clamp to 15–25 inch lbs. (1.7–2.8 Nm).
7. Start the engine and check for leaks.

Electric Fuel Pump

PRESSURE TESTING

1. Properly relieve the fuel system pressure.

2. Ground the fuel pump lead of the self-test connector through a jumper wire at the **FP** lead.
3. Connect a suitable fuel pressure tester to the fuel pump outlet.
4. Turn the ignition key **ON** to operate the fuel pump. Do not start the engine.
5. The fuel pressure should be 30–45 psi on 3.0L and 3.2L SHO engines or 35–40 psi on 3.0L and 3.8L engines.

REMOVAL AND INSTALLATION

1. Disconnect the negative battery cable.
2. Relieve the fuel system pressure.
3. Remove the fuel tank from the vehicle and place it on a work bench. Remove any dirt from around the fuel pump attaching flange.
4. Turn the fuel pump locking ring counterclockwise and remove the lock ring.
5. Remove the fuel pump from the fuel tank and discard the flange gasket.
    To install:
6. Clean the fuel pump mounting flange and fuel tank mounting surface and seal ring groove.
7. Put a light coating of grease on the new seal gasket to hold it in place during assembly and install it in the fuel ring groove.
8. Install the fuel pump and sender assembly. Make sure the locating keys are in the keyways and the seal gasket remains in place.
9. Hold the assembly in place and install the lock ring making sure all locking tabs are under the tank lock ring tabs. Tighten the lock ring by turning it clockwise until it is up against the stops.
10. Install the fuel tank.
11. Fill the tank with a minimum of 10 gallons of fuel and check for leaks.
12. Turn the ignition switch to the **ON** position 5–10 times, leaving it ON for 3 seconds at a time, until the system is pressurized. Check for leaks at the fittings.
13. Start the engine and recheck for leaks.

Fuel Injection

IDLE SPEED ADJUSTMENT

3.0L Engine

1. Place the transaxle in **P** and apply the parking brake.

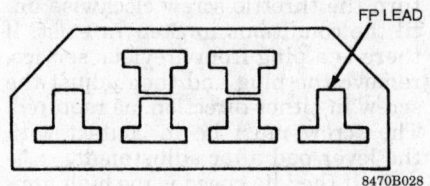

Self test connector

2. Start the engine and bring to normal operating temperature. Make sure the heater, air conditioning and all other accessories are **OFF**.

3. Check and if necessary, adjust the ignition timing.

4. Make sure the fuel pressure is correct. Any indicated vehicle malfunction service codes should be resolved before proceeding further.

5. Connect the SUPER STAR II tester, tool number 007–00028 or other suitable scan tool to the Self-Test connector. Activate the Key On Engine Running (KOER) Self-Test.

6. After Code **1** or **111** has been displayed, unlatch and within 4 seconds, latch the **STI** button.

7. A single pulse code indicates the entry mode, then observe the Self-Test Output (STO) on the tester for the following:

a. A constant tone, solid light or **STO LO** readout means the base idle speed is within the correct range. To exit the test, unlatch the **STI** button, then wait 4 seconds for reinitialization. After 10 minutes, the tool will exit by itself.

b. A beeping tone, flashing light or **STO LO** readout at 8 Hz indicates the Throttle Position Sensor (TPS) is out of range due to over adjustment. Adjustment may be required.

c. A beeping tone, flashing light or **STO LO** readout at 4 Hz indicates the base idle speed is too fast and adjustment is required. Proceed to Step 9.

d. A beeping tone, flashing light or **STO LO** readout at 1 Hz indicates the base idle speed is too low and adjustment is required. Proceed to Step 8.

8. If the idle speed is too low, check for the presence of a throttle plate orifice plug. If there is no plug, turn the throttle screw clockwise until the conditions in Step 7a exist. If there is a plug from previous service, remove the plug and then adjust the screw in either direction, as required.

The screw must be in contact with the lever pad after adjustment.

9. If the idle speed is too high, proceed as follows:

a. Turn the engine **OFF**.

b. Block the orifice in the throttle plate temporarily with tape. If the orifice already has a plug, proceed to Step d.

c. Reattach the air intake hose. Restart the engine and check the idle speed using the Self-Test. If the engine stalled, crack open the plate with the throttle return screw.

d. If the idle speed continues to be fast, run the Key On Engine Off (KOEO) Self-Test and check for a TPS output code.

e. If the output code is within range, remove the tape and check for vacuum leaks, throttle linkage binding, or other causes for excessive high idle.

f. If the output code is out of range, adjust the throttle screw to obtain the proper code. The lever pad must be in contact with the screw after adjustment.

g. If the idle speed drops to or below the desired level, as indicated by the Self-Test Output tone, turn the engine **OFF**, disconnect the air cleaner hose and remove the tape.

h. Install the proper plug in the throttle plate orifice.

i. Reconnect the air cleaner hose. Start the engine and turn the throttle plate stop screw clockwise until the conditions in Step 7a exist. Do not turn the screw counterclockwise as this may cause the throttle plate to stick at idle.

10. Run the KOEO Self-Test for proper TPS output code.

11. Make sure the throttle is not stuck in the bore and the linkage is not preventing the throttle from closing.

12. Check the Throttle Valve (TV) pressure adjustment.

3.0L SHO Engine

1. Apply the parking brake, turn the air conditioning control selector **OFF** and block the wheels.

2. Connect a tachometer and an inductive timing light to the engine. Start the engine and allow it to reach normal operating temperatures.

3. Stop the engine and disconnect the negative battery cable for 5 minutes, then reconnect it.

4. Start the engine and let it stabilize for 2 minutes, then rev the engine and let it return to idle. Lightly depress and release the accelerator

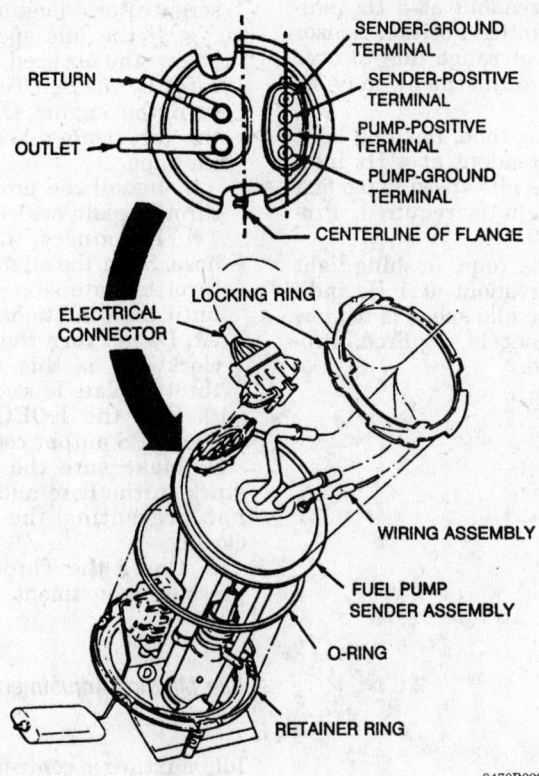

Electric fuel pump assembly

and let the engine idle. Check that the engine idles properly.

NOTE: If the cooling fan comes ON, wait until it turns OFF.

5. If the engine does not idle properly, proceed to Step 6.

6. Unplug the SPOUT line at the distributor, then check and/or adjust the ignition timing to the specification listed on the underhood emission calibration decal.

7. Stop the engine and disconnect and plug the PCV hose at the intake manifold. Remove the CANP hose from the intake manifold and connect tool T89P–9600–AH or equivalent, between the PCV and CANP ports.

8. Disconnect the idle speed control/air bypass solenoid.

9. Start the engine and let it idle. Place the transaxle selector lever in **N**.

10. Check and/or adjust the idle speed to 800 ± 30 rpm by turning the throttle plate stop screw.

11. Shut the engine **OFF** and disconnect the battery for 10 minutes minimum.

12. Stop the engine and remove all test equipment. Reconnect the SPOUT line. Remove tool T89P–9600–AH or equivalent, and unplug the PCV hose. Connect the PCV and CANP hoses. Reconnect the idle speed control/air bypass solenoid.

13. Make sure the throttle is not stuck in the bore and the linkage is not preventing the throttle from closing.

3.2L SHO Engine

The throttle body is not adjustable on this vehicle. If the idle speed is not within the specified limits, 750 ± 30 rpm, look for other possible causes or replace the throttle body unit.

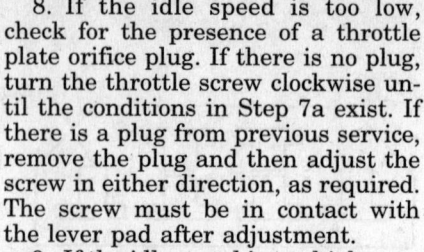

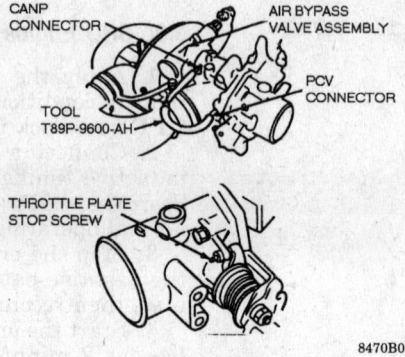

8470B032

Throttle plate stop screw location — 3.0L SHO engine

3.8L Engine

1. Place the transaxle in **P** and apply the parking brake.

2. Start the engine and bring to normal operating temperature. Make sure the heater, air conditioning and all other accessories are **OFF**.

3. Check and if necessary, adjust the ignition timing.

4. Make sure the fuel pressure is correct. Any indicated vehicle malfunction service codes should be resolved before proceeding further.

5. Connect the SUPER STAR II tester, tool number 007–00028 or other suitable scan tool to the Self-Test connector. Activate the Key On Engine Running (KOER) Self-Test.

6. After Code **1** or **111** has been displayed, unlatch and within 4 seconds, latch the **STI** button.

7. A single pulse code indicates the entry mode, then observe the Self-Test Output (STO) on the tester for the following:

a. A constant tone, solid light or **STO LO** readout means the base idle speed is within the correct range. To exit the test, unlatch the **STI** button, then wait 4 seconds for reinitialization. After 10 minutes, the tool will exit by itself.

b. A beeping tone, flashing light or **STO LO** readout at 8 Hz indicates the Throttle Position Sensor (TPS) is out of range due to over adjustment. Adjustment may be required.

c. A beeping tone, flashing light or **STO LO** readout at 4 Hz indicates the base idle speed is too fast and adjustment is required. Proceed to Step 9.

d. A beeping tone, flashing light or **STO LO** readout at 1 Hz indicates the base idle speed is too low and adjustment is required. Proceed to Step 8.

8. If the idle speed is too low, check for the presence of a throttle plate orifice plug. If there is no plug, turn the throttle screw clockwise until the conditions in Step 7a exist. If there is a plug from previous service, remove the plug and then adjust the screw in either direction, as required. The screw must be in contact with the lever pad after adjustment.

9. If the idle speed is too high, proceed as follows:

a. Turn the engine **OFF**.

b. Block the orifice in the throttle plate temporarily with tape. If the orifice already has a plug, proceed to Step d.

c. Reattach the air intake hose. Restart the engine and check the idle speed using the Self-Test. If the engine stalled, crack open the plate with the throttle return screw.

d. If the idle speed continues to be fast, run the Key On Engine Off (KOEO) Self-Test and check for a TPS output code.

e. If the output code is within range, remove the tape and check for vacuum leaks, throttle linkage binding, or other causes for excessive high idle.

f. If the output code is out of range, adjust the throttle screw to obtain the proper code. The lever pad must be in contact with the screw after adjustment.

g. If the idle speed drops to or below the desired level, as indicated by the Self-Test Output tone, turn the engine **OFF**, disconnect the air cleaner hose and remove the tape.

h. Install the proper plug in the throttle plate orifice.

i. Reconnect the air cleaner hose. Start the engine and turn the throttle plate stop screw clockwise until the conditions in Step 7a exist. Do not turn the screw counterclockwise as this may cause the throttle plate to stick at idle.

10. Run the KOEO Self-Test for proper TPS output code.

11. Make sure the throttle is not stuck in the bore and the linkage is not preventing the throttle from closing.

12. Check the Throttle Valve (TV) pressure adjustment.

Idle Mixture Adjustment

Idle mixture is controlled by the electronic control unit. No adjustment is possible.

Fuel Injector

REMOVAL AND INSTALLATION

3.0L Engine

1. Disconnect the negative battery cable.
2. Relieve the fuel system pressure.
3. Remove the air intake throttle body as follows:

   a. Tag and disconnect the vacuum hoses at the vacuum tree.

   b. Loosen the EGR tube nuts, if equipped, at the EGR valve and exhaust manifold fitting. Remove or rotate the tube aside.

   c. Remove the PCV hose from the tube under the throttle body.

   d. Remove the air cleaner duct hose and the idle speed control solenoid shield.

   e. Disconnect the throttle and TV cables from the throttle body linkage.

   f. Tag and disconnect the electrical connectors from the air charge temperature sensor, idle speed control solenoid and throttle position sensor.

   g. Remove the alternator brace.

   h. Remove the throttle body retaining bolts and remove the throttle body. Note the location of the bolts so they can reinstalled in their original positions.
4. Scribe an alignment mark on the base of the distributor and lower intake manifold. Remove the distributor hold-down clamp and lift the distributor enough to allow the fuel rail crossover tube to clear the distributor housing and lower intake manifold.
5. Disconnect the fuel supply and fuel return lines.
6. Disconnect the wiring harness from the injectors.
7. Disconnect the vacuum line from the fuel pressure regulator valve.
8. Remove the 4 fuel injector manifold retaining bolts.
9. Carefully disengage the fuel rail assembly from the fuel injectors by lifting and gently rocking the rail.
10. Remove the injectors by lifting while gently rocking from side to side.

To install:

11. Lubricate new O-rings with engine oil and install 2 on each injector.
12. Make sure the injector cups are clean and undamaged.
13. Install the injectors in the fuel rail using a light twisting-pushing motion.

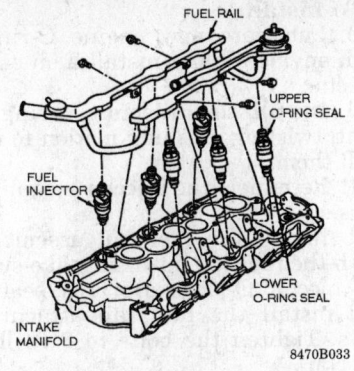

Injector removal and installation — 3.0L engine

14. Carefully install the rail assembly and injectors into the lower intake manifold, 1 side at a time. Make sure the O-rings are seated by pushing down on the fuel rail.
15. While holding the fuel rail assembly in place, install the 2 retaining bolts and tighten to 7 ft. lbs. (10 Nm).
16. Connect the fuel supply and fuel return lines.
17. Before connecting the fuel injector harness, connect the negative battery cable and turn the ignition switch to the **ON** position. This will pressurize the fuel system.
18. Using a clean paper towel, check for leaks where the injector connects to the fuel rail.
19. Install the air intake throttle body in the reverse order of removal. Tighten the throttle body retaining bolts to 15–22 ft. lbs. (20–30 Nm).
20. Connect the vacuum line to the fuel pressure regulator. Connect the fuel injector harness, start the engine and let it idle for 2 minutes.
21. Using a clean paper towel, check for leaks where the injector is installed into the intake manifold.

3.0L and 3.2L SHO Engines

1. Disconnect the negative battery cable.
2. Relieve the fuel system pressure.
3. Remove the intake manifold as follows:

   a. Drain the cooling system.

   b. Remove the intake air tube from the throttle body and mass air flow sensor. Disconnect the throttle cables.

   c. Disconnect the electrical connectors at the throttle position sensor, air bypass valve, vacuum switching valve and DIS module.

   d. Disconnect the coolant bypass hoses and vacuum lines.

   e. Disconnect the EGR pipe from the EGR valve.

   f. Remove the 8 bolts at the intake manifold support brackets and remove the brackets.

   g. Remove the bolt retaining the coolant hose bracket and disconnect the PCV hoses.

   h. Remove the 12 manifold retaining bolts and remove the intake manifold and throttle body assembly.
4. Disconnect the electrical connectors at the fuel injectors.
5. Remove the fuel rail retaining bolts.
6. Raise and slightly rotate the fuel rail assembly and remove the injectors.

To install:

7. Lubricate new O-rings with engine oil and install them on the fuel injectors.
8. Install the injectors in the fuel rail by lightly twisting and pushing the injectors into position.
9. Install the fuel rail, making sure the injectors seat properly in the cylinder head.
10. Install the fuel rail retaining bolts and tighten to 12–16 ft. lbs. (16–23 Nm) for 1992 models or 11–17 ft. lbs. (15–23 Nm) for 1993–96 models.
11. Connect the electrical connectors at the injectors. Install the intake manifold by reversing the removal procedure.
12. Run the engine and check for leaks.

3.8L Engine

1. Disconnect the negative battery cable.
2. Remove the fuel cap at the tank and release the pressure.
3. Relieve the pressure from the fuel system.
4. Remove the upper intake manifold and the fuel supply manifold as follows:

   a. Disconnect the electrical connectors at the air bypass valve, throttle position sensor and EGR position sensor.

   b. Disconnect the throttle linkage at the throttle ball and the transmission linkage from the throttle body. Remove the 2 bolts securing the bracket to the intake manifold and position the bracket with the cables aside.

   c. Disconnect the vacuum lines to the vacuum tree or chassis vacuum tube, EGR valve and pressure regulator. On Continental, disconnect and remove the chassis vacuum tube.

d. Disconnect the PCV hose and remove the nut retaining the EGR transducer to the upper intake manifold. Disconnect the wire from the EGR transducer.

e. Loosen the EGR tube at the exhaust manifold and disconnect at the EGR valve.

f. Remove 2 bolts retaining the EGR valve to the upper intake manifold and remove the EGR valve and EGR transducer as an assembly.

g. Remove the 2 canister purge lines from the fittings on the throttle body and remove the 6 upper intake manifold retaining bolts.

h. Remove 2 retaining bolts on the front and rear edges of the upper intake manifold where the manifold support brackets are located.

i. Remove the nut retaining the alternator bracket to the upper intake manifold and the 2 bolts retaining the alternator bracket to the water pump and alternator.

j. Remove the upper intake manifold and throttle body as an assembly.

k. Disconnect the fuel supply and return lines from the fuel rail assembly.

l. Remove the fuel rail assembly retaining bolts, carefully disengage the fuel rail from the fuel injectors and remove the fuel rail.

5. Remove the injector retaining clips.

6. Remove the electrical connectors from the fuel injectors.

7. To remove the injector, pull it up while gently rocking it from side-to-side.

8. Inspect the injector pintle protection cap (plastic hat) and washer for deterioration and replace, as required. If the plastic hat is missing, look for it in the intake manifold.

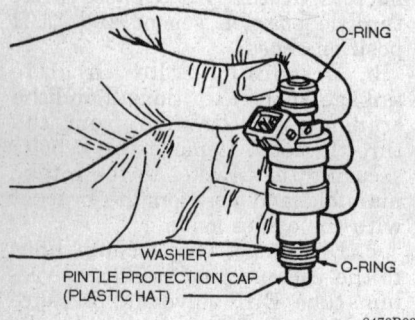

Fuel injector — 3.8L engine

8470B034

To install:

9. Lubricate new engine O-rings with engine oil and install 2 on each injector.

10. Install the injectors, using a light, twisting, pushing motion to install them.

11. Reconnect the injector retaining clips.

12. Install the fuel rail assembly. Push the fuel rail down to make sure all injector O-rings are fully seated and install the fuel rail attaching bolts. Tighten the bolts to 8 ft. lbs. (10 Nm).

13. Connect the electrical harness connectors to the injectors.

14. Install the upper intake manifold by reversing the removal procedure. Tighten the center 4 bolts to 8 ft. lbs. (10 Nm), then each end bolt/stud to 8 ft. lbs. (10 Nm). Repeat the tightening procedure in 2 steps, first to 15 ft. lbs. (20 Nm) and finally to 24 ft. lbs. (32 Nm).

15. Install the fuel cap at the tank.

16. Connect the negative battery cable.

17. Turn the ignition switch from **ON** to **OFF** position several times without starting the engine to pressurize the system. Check for fuel leaks.

EMISSION CONTROLS

Emission Warning Lamps

These vehicles have a Check Engine light that will light when there is a fault in the engine control system. This light cannot be reset without diagnosing the fault in the system. When the system has been diagnosed and the problem corrected, the light will go out.

ENGINE MECHANICAL

NOTE: Disconnecting the negative battery cable on some vehicles may interfere with the functions of the on board computer systems and may require the computer to undergo a relearning process, once the negative battery cable is reconnected.

Engine Assembly

REMOVAL AND INSTALLATION

3.0L Engine

1. Disconnect the battery cables and drain the cooling system. Mark the position of the hood on the hinges and remove the hood.

2. Evacuate the air conditioning system safely and properly. Relieve the fuel system pressure. Remove the air cleaner assembly. Remove the battery and the battery tray.

3. Remove the integrated relay controller, cooling fan and radiator with fan shroud. Remove the engine bounce damper bracket on the shock tower.

4. Remove the evaporative emission line, upper radiator hose, starter brace and lower radiator hose.

5. Remove the exhaust pipes from both exhaust manifolds. Remove and plug the power steering pump lines.

6. Remove the fuel lines and remove and tag all necessary vacuum lines.

7. Disconnect the ground strap, heater lines, accelerator cable linkage, throttle valve linkage and cruise control cable.

8. Disconnect and label the following wiring connectors; alternator, air conditioning clutch, oxygen sensor, ignition coil, radio frequency suppressor, cooling fan voltage resistor, engine coolant temperature sensor, coolant temperature sending switch, Thick film ignition module, injector wiring harness, ISC motor wire, throttle position sensor, oil pressure sending switch, ground wire, block heater, if equipped, knock sensor, EGR sensor and oil level sensor.

9. Raise the vehicle and support it safely. Remove the engine mount bolts and engine mounts. Remove the transaxle to engine mounting bolts and transaxle brace assembly.

10. Lower the vehicle. Install a suitable engine lifting plate onto the engine and use a suitable engine hoist to remove the engine from the vehicle. Remove the main wiring harness from the engine.

To install:

11. Install the main wiring harness on the engine. Position the engine in the vehicle and remove the engine lifting plate.

12. Raise the vehicle and support it safely. Install the engine mounts and

bolts and tighten to 40–55 ft. lbs. (54–75 Nm). Install the transaxle brace assembly and tighten the bolts to 40–55 ft. lbs. (54–75 Nm).

13. Connect all wiring connectors according to their labels.

14. Connect the ground strap, heater lines, accelerator cable linkage, throttle valve linkage and speed control cables.

15. Connect the power steering pump lines.

16. Connect the exhaust pipes to the exhaust manifolds.

17. Connect the fuel lines and vacuum lines.

18. Install the evaporative emission line, upper radiator hose, starter brace and lower radiator hose.

19. Install the integrated relay controller, cooling fan and radiator with fan shroud. Install the engine bounce damper bracket on the shock tower.

20. Install the battery tray and the battery.

21. Install the air cleaner assembly and charge the air conditioning system.

22. Fill the cooling system with the proper type and quantity of coolant. Fill the crankcase with the correct type of motor oil to the required level.

23. Install the hood.

24. Connect the negative battery cable. Start the engine and check for leaks.

3.0L and 3.2L SHO Engines

1. Disconnect the battery cables and remove the battery and battery tray.

2. Drain the cooling system and relieve the fuel system pressure.

3. Disconnect the wiring connector retaining the under hood light, if equipped. Mark the position of the hood hinges and remove the hood.

4. Remove the oil level indicator.

5. Disconnect the alternator and voltage regulator wiring assembly.

6. Remove the radiator upper sight shield.

7. Discharge the air conditioning system.

8. Remove the radiator coolant recovery reservoir assembly.

9. Remove the integrated relay controller, air cleaner hose assembly, upper radiator hose, electric fan and shroud assembly.

10. Remove the lower radiator hose and the radiator.

11. Disconnect the fuel inlet and return hose.

12. Remove the Barometric Air Pressure (BAP) sensor.

13. Remove the engine vibration damper and bracket assembly from the right side of the engine.

14. Remove the engine to damper bracket.

15. Remove the retaining bolt from the power steering reservoir and place the reservoir aside. Disconnect the hose to the power steering cooler at the pump.

16. Disconnect the throttle linkage and disconnect and tag the vacuum hoses.

17. Disconnect the heater hoses at the heater core.

18. Disconnect the electrical connectors from the harness on the rear of the engine.

19. For 3.0L engine, loosen the belt tensioner pulleys and remove the air conditioning compressor/alternator belt and the steering pump belt. Remove the lower tensioner pulley.

20. For 3.2L engine, loosen belt tensioner pulley and remove single accessory drive belt.

21. Disconnect the cycling switch on the top of the suction accumulator/drier.

22. Disconnect the air conditioning line at the dash panel and remove the accumulator and bracket assembly.

23. Remove the alternator assembly.

24. Disconnect the air conditioning discharge hose and remove the air conditioning compressor and bracket assembly.

25. Raise the vehicle and support it safely.

26. Place a drain pan under the oil pan. Drain the motor oil and remove the filter element.

27. Remove the wheel and tire assemblies. Disconnect the oil level sensor switch.

28. Disconnect the right lower ball joint, tie rod end and stabilizer bar.

29. Disconnect the center support bearing bracket and right-hand CV-joint from the transaxle.

30. Disconnect the oxygen sensor assembly and the 4 exhaust catalyst to engine retaining bolts.

31. Remove the starter motor assembly.

32. Remove the lower transaxle to engine retaining bolts.

33. Remove the engine mount to sub-frame nuts.

34. Remove the crankshaft pulley assembly.

35. Lower the vehicle and remove the upper transaxle to engine retaining bolts.

36. Install engine lifting bracket D89L–6001–A or equivalent.

37. Position a floor jack under the transaxle.

38. Position suitable engine lifting equipment, raise the transaxle assembly slightly and remove the engine from the vehicle.

To install:

39. Position the engine assembly in the vehicle.

40. Install the upper transaxle to engine bolts and remove the floor jack and engine lifting equipment. Remove the engine lifting eyes.

41. Raise the vehicle and support it safely.

42. Install the crankshaft pulley assembly. Tighten the retaining bolt to 113–126 ft. lbs. (152–172 Nm).

43. Install the engine mount to sub-frame nuts and the lower transaxle to engine retaining bolts. Tighten the bolts to 25–35 ft. lbs. (34–47 Nm).

44. Install the starter motor assembly.

45. Install the 4 exhaust catalyst to engine retaining nuts and tighten them to 19–34 ft. lbs. (27–47 Nm). Apply anti-seize compound to the threads, then install the oxygen sensor assembly. Tighten to 27–33 ft. lbs. (37–45 Nm).

46. Connect the center support bearing bracket and install the right-hand CV-joint.

47. Connect the right lower ball joint, tie rod end and stabilizer bar.

48. Connect the oil level sensor and install the wheel and tire assemblies.

49. Install the oil filter. Install the oil drain plug and tighten to 15–24 ft. lbs. (20–33 Nm).

50. Lower the vehicle.

51. Install the air conditioning compressor and bracket assembly, tighten to 27–40 ft. lbs. (36–55 Nm) and connect the air conditioning discharge hose.

52. Install the alternator assembly and tighten to 36–53 ft. lbs. (48–72 Nm).

53. Install the accumulator and bracket assembly and connect the cycling switch to the top of the accumulator.

54. For 3.0L engine, install the lower belt tensioner. Install the power steering and air conditioning compressor-alternator belts and tighten the tensioner pulleys.

55. For 3.2L engine, install single accessory drive belt and release tensioner.

56. Connect the electrical connectors from the harness on the rear of the engine.

57. Connect the heater hoses, vacuum hoses and throttle linkage.

58. Connect the hose from the power steering cooler at the pump and install the power steering reservoir.

59. Install the damper bracket to the engine and install the engine vibration damper and bracket assembly to the right side of the engine.

60. Install the BAP sensor.

61. Connect the fuel inlet and return hoses.

62. Install the radiator assembly and the lower radiator hose.

63. Install the electric fan and shroud assembly, upper radiator hose, air cleaner hose, integrated relay controller, radiator coolant recovery reservoir and radiator upper sight shield.

64. Connect the alternator and voltage regulator wiring.

65. Install the oil level indicator tube.

66. Install the hood and connect the under hood light wiring, if equipped.

67. Install the battery tray and the battery.

68. Connect the battery cables.

69. Fill the cooling system with the proper type and quantity of coolant and fill the crankcase with the proper type of motor oil to the required level.

70. Drain, evacuate, pressure test and recharge the air conditioning system.

71. Start the engine and check for leaks.

3.8L Engine

TAURUS AND SABLE

1. Drain the cooling system and disconnect the negative battery cable. Properly relieve the fuel system pressure.

2. Disconnect the underhood light wiring connector. Mark position of hood hinges and remove hood.

3. Remove the oil level indicator tube.

4. Disconnect alternator to voltage regulator wiring assembly.

5. Remove the radiator upper sight shield. Remove the engine cooling fan motor relay retaining bolts and position cooling fan motor relay aside.

6. Remove the air cleaner assembly.

7. Disconnect the radiator electric fan and motor assembly. Remove fan shroud.

8. Remove upper radiator hose.

9. Disconnect the transaxle oil cooler inlet and outlet tubes and cover the openings to prevent the entry of dirt and grease. Disconnect the heater hoses.

10. Disconnect the power steering pressure hose assembly.

11. Disconnect the air conditioner compressor clutch wire assembly. Discharge the air conditioning system and disconnect the compressor-to-condenser line.

12. Remove the radiator coolant recovery reservoir assembly. Remove the wiring shield.

13. Remove accelerator cable mounting bracket.

14. Disconnect fuel inlet and return lines.

15. Disconnect power steering pump pressure and return tube brackets.

16. Disconnect the engine control sensor wiring assembly.

17. Identify, tag and disconnect all necessary vacuum hoses.

18. Disconnect the ground wire assembly. Remove the duct assembly.

19. Disconnect one end of the throttle control valve cable. Disconnect the bulkhead electrical connector and transaxle pressure switches.

20. Remove transaxle support assembly retaining bolts and remove transaxle and support assembly from vehicle.

21. Raise the vehicle and support safely. Remove the wheel and tire assemblies. Drain the engine oil and remove the filter.

22. Disconnect the oxygen sensor assembly.

23. Loosen and remove drive belt assembly. Remove the crankshaft pulley and drive belt tensioner assemblies.

24. Remove the starter motor assembly. Remove the catalytic converter housing assembly and remove the converter and inlet pipe assembly.

25. Remove the left and right front engine mount retaining nuts.

26. Remove the converter-to-flywheel nuts.

27. Disconnect the oil level indicator sensor. Remove crankshaft pulley assembly.

28. Disconnect the lower radiator hose.

29. Remove the engine-to-transaxle bolts and partially lower engine. Remove the wheel and tire assemblies.

30. Remove the water pump pulley retaining bolts and the water pump pulley.

31. Remove the distributor cap and position aside. Remove distributor rotor.

32. Remove the exhaust manifold bolt lock retaining bolts. Remove the thermactor air pump retaining bolts and the thermactor air pump, if equipped.

33. Disconnect the oil pressure engine unit gauge assembly.

34. Install engine lifting eyes D81L–60001–D or equivalent, and connect suitable lifting equipment to the lifting eyes.

35. Position a suitable jack under the transaxle and raise the transaxle a small amount.

36. Remove the engine from the vehicle and position in a suitable holding fixture.

To install:

NOTE: Lightly oil all bolt and stud threads before installation except those specifying special sealant.

37. Remove the engine assembly from the work stand and position it in the vehicle.

38. Install the engine to transaxle bolts and remove the jack from under the transaxle and the engine lifting equipment. Remove the engine lifting eyes.

39. Tighten the engine to transaxle bolts to 41–50 ft. lbs. (55–68 Nm).

40. Connect the oil pressure engine unit gauge assembly.

41. Install the air conditioning compressor and tighten the retaining bolts to 30–45 ft. lbs. (41–61 Nm). Connect the compressor to condenser discharge line and the compressor clutch wire assembly.

42. Connect the heater hoses, vacuum hoses and the fuel inlet hose and return line hose.

43. Connect the engine control module wiring assembly.

44. Connect the transaxle oil cooler inlet and outlet tubes.

45. Install the radiator assembly.

46. Partially raise the vehicle and support it safely.

47. Install the converter to flywheel bolts and tighten to 20–34 ft. lbs. (27–46 Nm).

48. Install the left and right transaxle and engine mount retaining nuts and install the converter housing cover.

49. Install the starter motor.

50. Connect the lower radiator hose.

51. Install the drive belt tensioner assembly and the crankshaft pulley assembly. Tighten the crankshaft pulley retaining bolts to 20–28 ft. lbs. (26–38 Nm).

52. Install the catalytic converter assembly and connect the heated exhaust gas oxygen sensor.

53. Install the oil filter and connect the oil level indicator sensor.

54. Lower the vehicle.

55. Position the thermactor air supply pump, if equipped, and install the retaining bolts.

56. Connect the vacuum pump and install the exhaust air supply pump pulley assembly.

57. Install the wiring shield.

58. Install the distributor cap and rotor.

59. Install the radiator coolant recovery reservoir assembly, upper radiator hose and water pump pulley.

60. Connect the alternator-to-voltage regulator wiring assembly and the engine control module wiring assembly.

61. Connect the wiring assembly ground.

62. Install the accelerator cable mounting bracket.

63. Connect the power steering pressure hose assembly and the power steering line.

64. Install the fan shroud.

65. Connect the radiator electric motor assembly and install the engine cooling fan motor relay assembly.

66. Install the drive belts.

67. Position and install the transaxle support assembly.

68. Install the radiator upper sight shield.

69. Raise the vehicle and support it safely. Install the wheel and tire assemblies.

70. Install the hood and connect the negative battery cable.

71. Fill the cooling system with the proper type and quantity of coolant and fill the crankcase with the proper type of motor oil to the required level.

72. Drain, evacuate, pressure test and recharge the air conditioning system.

73. Start the engine and check for leaks.

CONTINENTAL

1. Disconnect the negative battery cable.

2. Relieve the fuel system pressure, drain the cooling system and properly discharge the air conditioning system.

3. Tag and disconnect the alternator-to-voltage regulator, electric cooling fan, transaxle pressure switch, air conditioning compressor clutch, electronic engine control and ground wiring.

4. Disconnect the heater hoses, power steering hoses and brackets, air conditioning discharge hose, transaxle oil cooler tubes and fuel lines.

5. Tag and disconnect the vacuum lines. Disconnect the throttle cable at the throttle valve.

6. Remove the electric cooling fan and motor assembly. Remove the fan shroud.

7. Remove the engine oil dipstick and the radiator sight shield. Remove the integrated controller relay and position aside.

8. Remove the air cleaner assembly.

9. Disconnect the upper radiator hose and remove the coolant recovery reservoir. Remove the wiring shield.

10. Remove the air suspension compressor and position aside. Remove the accelerator cable mounting bracket.

11. Remove the transaxle support assembly. Remove the air conditioning compressor.

12. Raise and safely support the vehicle.

13. Drain the engine oil and remove the oil filter. Disconnect the oxygen sensor.

14. Release the tension at the drive belts. Remove the crankshaft pulley and drive belt tensioner.

15. Remove the starter. Remove the catalytic converter housing cover and remove the converter and inlet pipe assembly from the engine.

16. Remove the nuts at the transaxle and engine mounts. Remove the torque converter-to-flywheel nuts.

17. Disconnect the oil level indicator sensor and the lower radiator hose.

18. Loosen the engine-to-transaxle bolts, leaving them loosely installed.

19. Partially lower the vehicle and remove the front wheel and tire assemblies.

20. Remove the drive belts and the water pump pulley. Remove the radiator assembly.

21. Remove the distributor cap and position aside. Remove the distributor rotor.

22. Remove the exhaust manifold lock bolts and the thermactor air pump, if equipped. Disconnect the oil pressure sending unit.

23. Install suitable engine lifting equipment and position a transmission jack. Completely remove the engine-to-transaxle bolts.

24. Raise the transaxle assembly using the jack and lift the engine from the vehicle.

To install:

25. Position the engine assembly in the vehicle and align the engine-to-transaxle bolt bores. Install the engine-to-transaxle bolts that are accessible but do not tighten at this time.

26. Remove the transmission jack and the engine lifting equipment.

27. Install the oil pressure sending unit. Install the air conditioning compressor and tighten the retaining bolts to 30–45 ft. lbs. (41–61 Nm).

28. Connect the air conditioning compressor discharge hose and the clutch wiring to the compressor.

29. Connect the heater hoses and the fuel lines. Connect the vacuum hoses and routing clips.

30. Connect the transaxle oil cooler lines and the transaxle pressure switch wiring.

31. Install the radiator assembly. Raise and safely support the vehicle.

32. Install the remaining transaxle-to-engine bolts. Tighten all the bolts to 40–50 ft. lbs. (55–68 Nm).

33. Install the torque converter-to-flywheel bolts and tighten to 20–34 ft. lbs. (27–46 Nm). Install the converter housing cover.

34. Install the transaxle mount retaining nuts and tighten to 50–70 ft. lbs. (68–95 Nm).

35. Install the starter and the lower radiator hose.

36. Install the drive belt tensioner assembly and the crankshaft pulley assembly. Tighten the crankshaft pulley retaining bolts to 20–28 ft. lbs. (26–38 Nm).

37. Install the catalytic converter and inlet pipe assembly. Connect the oxygen sensor.

38. Install the oil filter and the oil drain plug. Connect the low oil level sensor.

39. Partially lower the vehicle.

40. Install the thermactor air pump, if equipped, and tighten the mounting bolts to 30–40 ft. lbs. (40–55 Nm). Install the vacuum hose at the pump and the air pump pulley.

41. Install the wiring shield. Install the distributor rotor and cap and connect the distributor wiring.

42. Install the coolant recovery reservoir and connect the top radiator hose.

43. Install the air suspension compressor and connect the wiring. Install the water pump pulley.

44. Connect the alternator to voltage regulator wiring, the electronic engine control wiring and the ground wires.

45. Connect the power steering hoses and the throttle cable at the throttle valve. Install the accelerator cable mounting bracket.

46. Install the fan shroud and connect the fan wiring. Install the cooling fan relay and position the drive belts.

47. Install the transaxle support assembly and the upper radiator sight shield. Partially raise the vehicle.

48. Install the exhaust air supply pump valve and hose assembly. Install the drive belts. Partially lower the vehicle.

49. Install the integrated controller relay and the engine oil dipstick. Install the front wheel and tire assemblies and tighten the lug nuts to 85–105 ft. lbs. (115–142 Nm).

50. Lower the vehicle. Install the hood, aligning the marks that were made during the removal procedure.

51. Install the air cleaner assembly and connect the negative battery cable.

52. Fill the engine with the proper type and quantity of engine oil and coolant. Leak test, evacuate and charge the air conditioning system. Observe all safety precautions.

53. Start the engine and check for leaks.

Engine Mounts

REMOVAL AND INSTALLATION

3.0L Engines

RIGHT REAR ENGINE INSULATOR (NO. 3)

1. Disconnect the negative battery cable. Raise and support the vehicle safely.

2. Place a suitable jack and a block of wood under the engine block.

3. Remove the nut attaching the right front and rear insulators to the frame.

4. Raise the engine with the jack until enough of a load is taken off the insulator.

5. Remove the insulator retaining bolts and remove the insulator from the engine support bracket.

6. Installation is the reverse of the removal procedure. Tighten the insulator to engine support bracket to 40–55 ft. lbs. (54–75 Nm). Tighten the nut attaching the right, front and rear insulators to frame to 55–75 ft. lbs. (75–102 Nm).

LEFT ENGINE INSULATOR AND SUPPORT ASSEMBLY

1. Disconnect the negative battery cable. Raise and support the vehicle safely. Remove the wheel and tire assembly.

2. Place a suitable jack and a block of wood under the transaxle and support the transaxle.

3. Remove the nuts attaching the insulator to the support assembly. Remove the through bolts attaching the insulator to the frame.

4. Raise the transaxle with the jack enough to relieve the weight on the insulator.

5. Remove the bolts attaching the support assembly to the transaxle. Remove the insulator and/or transaxle support assembly.

6. Installation is the reverse of the removal procedure. Tighten the support assembly retaining bolts to 40–55 ft. lbs. (54–75 Nm). Tighten the insulator-to-frame bolts to 60–86 ft. lbs. (81–116 Nm). Tighten the insulator to support assembly nuts to 55–75 ft. lbs. (74–102 Nm).

RIGHT FRONT ENGINE INSULATOR (NO. 2)

1. Disconnect the negative battery cable. Remove the lower damper nut or bolt from the right side of the engine. Raise and support the vehicle safely.

2. Place a jack and a block of wood under the engine block.

3. Remove the nuts attaching the right front and rear insulators to the frame.

4. Raise the engine with the jack until enough load is taken off the insulator.

5. Remove the bolt(s) and the insulator from the engine bracket.

6. Installation is the reverse of the removal procedure. Tighten the insulator-to-engine bracket bolt(s) to 71–95 ft. lbs. (90–130 Nm) on 3.0L engine. Tighten the nut attaching the right front and right rear insulators to frame to 55–75 ft. lbs. (75–102 Nm).

3.0L and 3.2L SHO Engines

RIGHT FRONT (NO. 2) AND RIGHT REAR (NO. 3)

1. Remove the lower damper bolt from the right side of the engine.

2. Raise the vehicle and support it safely.

3. Place a jack and a wood block in a suitable place under the engine.

4. Remove the roll damper to engine retaining nuts and remove the roll damper.

5. Raise the engine enough to unload the insulator.

6. Remove the 2 through bolts and remove the insulators from the engine bracket.

7. Installation is the reverse of the removal procedure. Tighten the insulator-to-engine bracket bolts to 40–55 ft. lbs. (54–75 Nm). Tighten the insulator to frame nuts to 50–70 ft. lbs. (68–95 Nm). Tighten the roll damper retaining nuts to 40–55 ft. lbs. (54–75

Nm). Tighten the engine damper to engine bolt to 40–55 ft. lbs. (54–75 Nm).

LEFT ENGINE INSULATOR AND SUPPORT ASSEMBLY

1. Remove the bolt retaining the roll damper to the lower damper bracket and place the damper shaft aside.

2. Remove speed control servo and bracket.

3. Raise the vehicle and support it with jackstands under the vehicle body, allowing the sub-frame to hang.

4. Remove the left tire and wheel assembly.

5. Place a jack and wood block under the transaxle.

6. Remove the nuts retaining the lower damper bracket to engine mount and the bolts retaining the insulator to the transaxle and sub-frame.

7. Raise the transaxle with the jack enough to unload the insulator.

8. Remove the insulator and lower damper bracket.

9. Installation is the reverse of the removal procedure. Tighten the damper bracket to insulator nuts to 40–55 ft. lbs. (54–75 Nm). Tighten the insulator to transaxle bolts to 70–95 ft. lbs. (95–130 Nm). Tighten the insulator to frame bolts to 60–85 ft. lbs. (81–116 Nm). Tighten the damper to damper bracket bolt to 40–55 ft. lbs. (54–75 Nm).

3.8L Engine

RIGHT FRONT ENGINE INSULATOR

1. Remove the mount upper retaining nut through the engine compartment using a long extension and an 18mm swivel socket.

2. Install 3 bar engine support D88L–6000–A or equivalent.

3. Raise and safely support the vehicle.

4. Loosen the right rear and right front lower mount retaining nuts.

5. Lower the vehicle.

6. Raise the engine approximately 1 in. using the engine support tool.

7. Raise and safely support the vehicle. Remove the engine mount.

8. Installation is the reverse of the removal procedure. Tighten the lower mount retaining nuts to 51–70 ft. lbs. (68–95 Nm). Tighten the upper mount retaining nut to 40–55 ft. lbs. (54–75 Nm).

RIGHT REAR ENGINE INSULATOR (NO. 3)

1. Disconnect the negative battery cable and raise and support the vehicle safely.

2. Remove the nuts retaining the right front and right rear engine mounts to the frame.

3. Lower the vehicle.

4. Use 3 bar engine support tool D88L–6000–A or equivalent to support the engine. Raise the engine about 1 in.

5. Loosen the retaining nut on the right rear (No. 3) mount and heat shield assembly.

6. Raise and support the vehicle safely.

7. Remove the insulator retaining nut and the insulator and heat shield assembly.

8. Installation is the reverse of the removal procedure. Tighten the top retaining nut on the insulator to 40–55 ft. lbs. (54–75 Nm). Tighten the retaining nuts on the right front and right rear engine mounts to 51–70 ft. lbs. (68–95 Nm).

LEFT ENGINE MOUNT AND SUPPORT ASSEMBLY

1. Raise the vehicle and support it safely.

2. Remove the tire and wheel assembly.

3. Place a jack and wood block under the transaxle and support the transaxle.

4. Remove the 2 bolts retaining the vertical restrictor assembly, if equipped.

5. Remove the nut retaining the transaxle mount to the support assembly.

6. Remove the 2 through bolts retaining the transaxle mount to the frame.

7. Raise the transaxle with the jack enough to unload the mount.

8. Remove the bolts retaining the support assembly to the transaxle and remove the mount and/or transaxle support assembly.

9. Installation is the reverse of the removal procedure. Tighten the support assembly to transaxle bolts to 40–55 ft. lbs. (54–75 Nm).

10. Tighten the mount to frame bolts to 60–86 ft. lbs. (81–116 Nm).

11. Tighten the transaxle mount to support nut to 55–75 ft. lbs. (74–102 Nm). If equipped, tighten the 2 bolts retaining the vertical restrictor assembly to 40–55 ft. lbs. (54–75 Nm).

Cylinder Head

REMOVAL AND INSTALLATION

3.0L Except SHO Engine

1. Disconnect the negative battery cable. Properly relieve the fuel system pressure. Drain the cooling system. Remove the air cleaner assembly.

2. Loosen the accessory drive belt idler pulley, remove the drive belt.

3. If the left cylinder head is being removed, perform the following:

   a. Disconnect the alternator electrical connectors.

   b. Rotate the tensioner clockwise and remove the accessory drive belt.

   c. Remove the automatic belt tensioner assembly.

   d. Remove the alternator.

   e. Remove the power steering mounting bracket retaining bolts. Leave the hoses connected and place the pump aside in a position to prevent fluid from leaking out.

   f. Remove the engine oil dipstick tube from the exhaust manifold.

4. If the right head is being removed, perform the following:

   a. Remove the alternator belt tensioner bracket.

   b. Remove the heater supply tube retaining brackets from the exhaust manifold.

   c. Remove the vehicle speed sensor cable retaining bolt and the EGR vacuum regulator sensor and bracket.

5. Remove the exhaust manifolds from both heads. Remove the PCV and the rocker arm covers. Loosen the rocker arm fulcrum attaching bolts enough to allow the rocker arm to be lifted off the pushrod and rotated to one side.

NOTE: Regardless of the cylinder head being removed, the No. 3 cylinder intake valve pushrod must be removed to allow removal of the intake manifold.

6. Remove the pushrods. Be sure to identify and label the position of each pushrod. The pushrods should be installed in their original position during reassembly.

7. Remove the intake manifold.

8. Remove the cylinder head attaching bolts and remove the cylinder heads from the engine. Remove and discard the old cylinder head gaskets.

To install:

9. Lightly oil all bolt and stud bolt threads before installation. Clean the cylinder head, intake manifold,

rocker arm cover and cylinder head gasket contact surfaces. If the cylinder head was removed for a cylinder head gasket replacement, check the flatness of the cylinder head and block gasket surfaces.

NOTE: If the flat surface of the cylinder head is warped, do not plane or grind off more than 0.010 in. If the head is machined past its resurface limit, the head will have to be replaced with a new one.

10. Position new head gaskets on the cylinder block using the dowels in the engine block for alignment. If the dowels are damaged, they must be replaced.

11. Position the cylinder head on the cylinder block. Tighten the cylinder head attaching bolts in 2 steps following the proper torque sequence. The first step is 37 ft. lbs. (50 Nm) and the second step is 68 ft. lbs. (92 Nm).

NOTE: When cylinder head bolts have been tightened, it is not necessary to retighten the bolts after extended engine operation. The bolts can be rechecked for tightness if desired.

12. Install the intake manifold. Connect the coolant temperature sending unit connectors.

13. Dip each pushrod end in oil conditioner or heavy engine oil. Install the pushrods in their original position.

14. Before installation, coat the valve tips, rocker arm and fulcrum contact areas with Lubriplate® or equivalent.

15. Rotate the engine until the lifter is on the base circle of the cam (valve closed).

16. Install the rocker arm and components and torque the rocker arm fulcrum bolts to 24 ft. lbs. (32 Nm). Be sure the lifter is on the base circle of the cam for each rocker arm as it is installed.

NOTE: The fulcrums must be fully seated in the cylinder head and the pushrods must be seated in the rocker arm sockets prior to the final tightening.

17. Install the exhaust manifolds and oil dipstick tube. Install the remaining components by reversing the removal procedure.

18. Start the engine and check for leaks.

19. Check and if necessary, adjust the transaxle throttle linkage and cruise control. Install the air cleaner outlet tube duct.

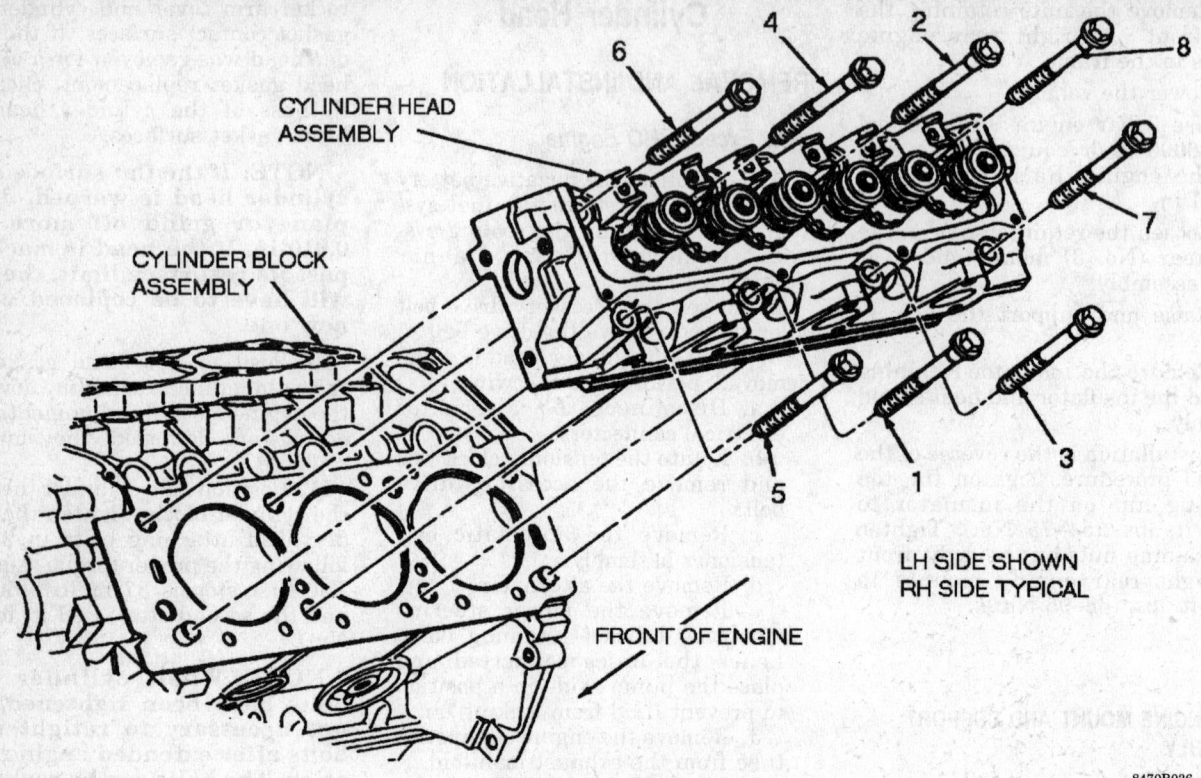

CYLINDER HEAD
ASSEMBLY

CYLINDER BLOCK
ASSEMBLY

FRONT OF ENGINE

LH SIDE SHOWN
RH SIDE TYPICAL

8470B036

Cylinder head bolt torque sequence — 3.0L engine

3.0L and 3.2L SHO Engines

1. Disconnect the negative battery cable.

2. Drain the cooling system. Properly relieve the fuel system pressure.

3. Remove the air cleaner outlet tube.

4. Remove the intake manifold.

5. Loosen the accessory drive belt idlers and remove the drive belts.

6. Remove the upper timing belt cover.

7. Remove the left idler pulley and bracket assembly.

8. Raise the vehicle and support it safely.

9. Remove the right wheel and inner fender splash shield.

10. Remove the crankshaft damper pulley.

11. Remove the lower timing belt cover.

12. Align both camshaft pulley timing marks with the index marks on the upper belt cover.

13. Release the tension on the belt by loosening the tensioner nut and rotating the tensioner with a hex head wrench. When tension is released, tighten the nut. This will hold the tensioner in place. Lower the vehicle until the wheels touch but keep the vehicle supported.

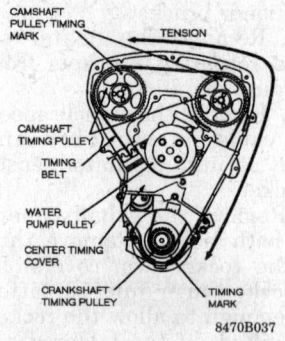

CAMSHAFT
PULLEY TIMING
MARK

TENSION

CAMSHAFT
TIMING PULLEY

TIMING
BELT

WATER
PUMP PULLEY

CENTER TIMING
COVER

CRANKSHAFT
TIMING PULLEY

TIMING
MARK

8470B037

Timing mark alignment — 3.0L and 3.2L SHO engines

14. Disconnect the crankshaft sensor wiring assembly.

15. Remove the center cover assembly.

16. Remove the timing belt noting the location of the **KOA** for 3.0L engine or **KOB** for 3.2L engine, on the belt. The belt must be installed in the same direction.

17. Remove the cylinder head covers.

18. Remove the camshaft timing sprockets.

19. Remove the upper rear and the center rear timing belt covers.

20. If the left cylinder head is being removed, remove the DIS coil bracket and the oil dipstick tube. If the right cylinder head is being removed, remove the coolant outlet hose.

21. Remove the exhaust manifold on the left cylinder head. On the right cylinder head the exhaust manifold must be removed with the head.

22. Remove the cylinder head to block retaining bolts.

23. Remove the cylinder head.

   To install:

   NOTE: Lightly oil all bolt and stud bolt threads before installation except those specifying special sealant.

24. Clean the cylinder head and engine block mating surfaces of all gasket material.

25. Position the cylinder head and gasket on the engine block and align with the dowel pins.

26. Install the cylinder head bolts and tighten, in sequence, in 2 steps; the first to 37–50 ft. lbs. (49–69 Nm) and finally to 62–68 ft. lbs. (83–93 Nm).

27. If installing the left cylinder head, install the exhaust manifold, DIS coil bracket and oil dipstick tube. If installing the right cylinder head, install the coolant outlet hose and connect the exhaust catalyst.

28. Install the upper rear and center rear timing belt covers.

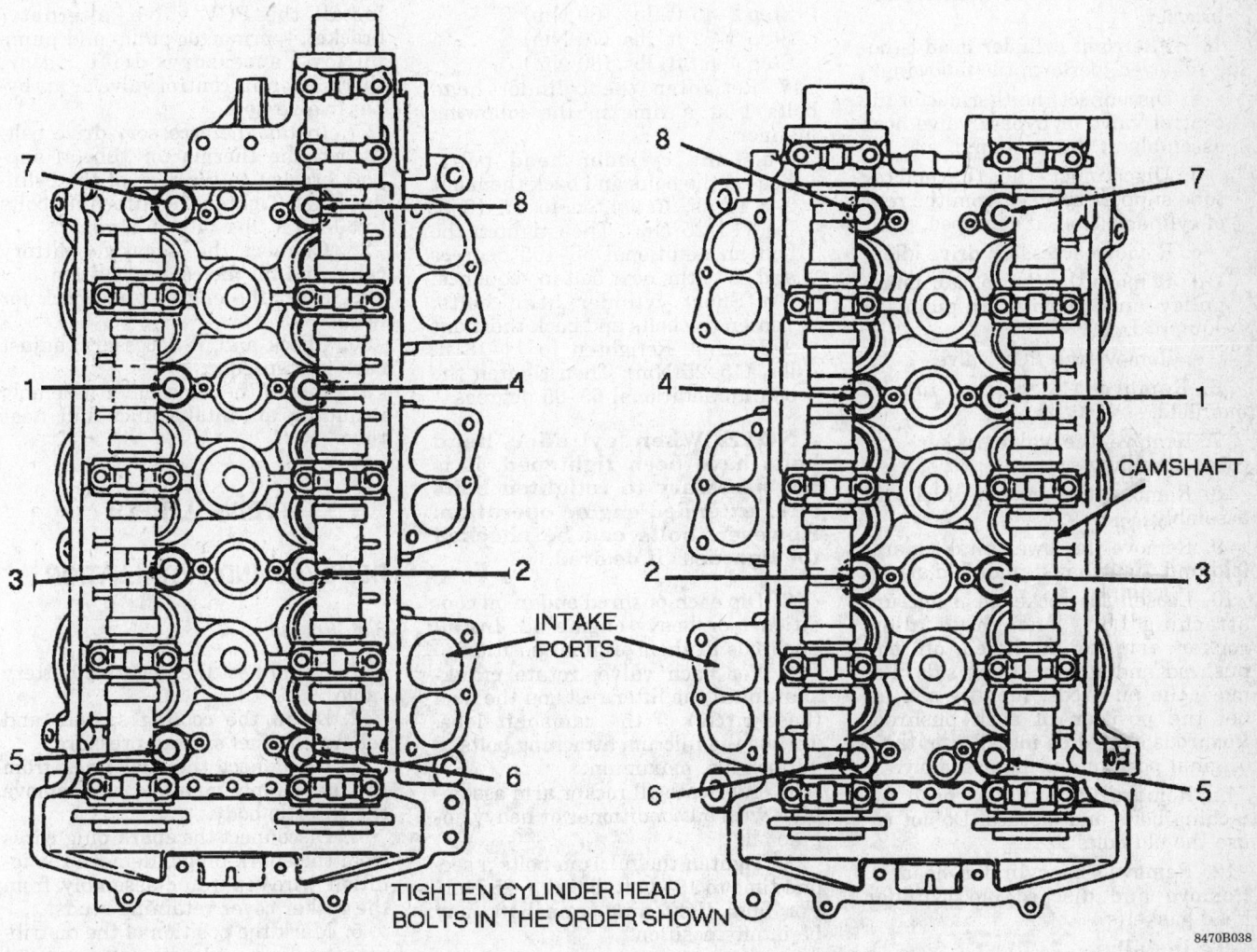

TIGHTEN CYLINDER HEAD
BOLTS IN THE ORDER SHOWN

INTAKE
PORTS

CAMSHAFT

8470B038

Cylinder head bolt torque sequence — 3.0L and 3.2L SHO engines

29. Install the camshaft sprockets in the timed position.

30. Install the cylinder head covers.

31. Install and adjust the timing belt.

32. Install the center timing belt cover.

33. Connect the crankshaft sensor wiring assembly and install the lower timing belt cover.

34. Raise the vehicle and support it safely.

35. Install the inner fender splash shield and the right wheel and tire assembly.

36. Install the left idler pulley and bracket.

37. Install the upper timing belt cover.

38. Install the accessory drive belts.

39. Install the intake manifold.

40. Install the air cleaner outlet tube.

41. Connect the negative battery cable.

42. Fill the engine cooling system with the proper type and quantity of coolant.

43. Start the engine and check for coolant, fuel or oil leaks.

3.8L Engine

1. Drain the cooling system and disconnect the negative battery cable.

2. Properly relieve the fuel system pressure. Remove the air cleaner assembly including air intake duct and heat tube.

3. Loosen the accessory drive belt idler and remove the drive belt.

4. If the right head is being removed, proceed to Step 5. If the left cylinder head is being removed, perform the following:

   a. Remove the oil fill cap.

   b. Remove the power steering pump. Leave the hoses connected and place the pump/bracket assembly aside in a position to prevent fluid from leaking out.

   c. If equipped with air conditioning, remove mounting bracket attaching bolts. Leaving the hoses connected, position the compressor aside.

d. Remove the alternator and bracket.

5. If the right cylinder head is being removed, perform the following:

a. Disconnect the thermactor air control valve or bypass valve hose assembly at the air pump.

b. Disconnect the thermactor tube support bracket from the rear of cylinder head, if equipped.

c. Remove accessory drive idler.

d. Remove the thermactor pump pulley and thermactor pump, if equipped.

e. Remove the PCV valve.

6. Remove the upper intake manifold.

7. Remove the valve rocker arm cover attaching screws.

8. Remove the injector fuel rail assembly.

9. Remove the lower intake manifold and the exhaust manifold(s).

10. Loosen the rocker arm fulcrum attaching bolts enough to allow rocker arm to be lifted off the pushrod and rotate to one side. Remove the pushrods. Identify and label the position of each pushrod. Pushrods should be installed in their original position during assembly.

11. Remove the cylinder head attaching bolts and discard. Do not reuse the old bolts.

12. Remove the cylinder head(s). Remove and discard old cylinder head gasket(s).

To install:

13. Lightly oil all bolt threads before installation.

14. Clean cylinder head, intake manifold, valve rocker arm cover and cylinder head gasket contact surfaces. If cylinder head was removed for a cylinder head gasket replacement, check flatness of cylinder head and block gasket surfaces.

15. Position the new head gasket(s) onto cylinder block using dowels for alignment. Position cylinder head(s) onto block.

NOTE: Always use new cylinder head bolts to ensure a leaktight assembly. Torque retention with used bolts can vary, which may result in coolant or compression leakage at the cylinder head mating surface area.

16. Tighten the cylinder head attaching bolts, in sequence, to the following specifications:

Step 1–37 ft. lbs. (50 Nm)
Step 2–45 ft. lbs. (60 Nm)
Step 3–52 ft. lbs. (70 Nm)
Step 4–59 ft. lbs. (80 Nm)

17. Retighten the cylinder head bolts 1 at a time in the following manner:

a. Long cylinder head bolts: Loosen the bolts and back them out 2–3 turns. Retighten to 11–18 ft. lbs. (15–25 Nm). Then tighten the bolt an additional 85–105 degrees and go to the next bolt in sequence.

b. Short cylinder head bolts: Loosen the bolts and back them out 2–3 turns. Retighten to 11–18 ft. lbs. (15–25 Nm). Then tighten the bolt an additional 65–85 degrees.

NOTE: When cylinder head bolts have been tightened, it is not necessary to retighten bolts after extended engine operation. However, bolts can be checked for tightness if desired.

18. Dip each pushrod end in oil conditioner or heavy engine oil. Install pushrods in their original position.

19. For each valve, rotate crankshaft until the lifter rests on the heel (base circle) of the camshaft lobe. Torque the fulcrum attaching bolts to 43 inch lbs. maximum.

20. Lubricate all rocker arm assemblies with oil conditioner or heavy engine oil.

21. Tighten the fulcrum bolts a second time to 19–25 ft. lbs. (25–35 Nm). For final tightening, camshaft may be in any position.

NOTE: If original valve train components are being installed, a valve clearance check is not required. If a component has been replaced, perform a valve clearance check.

22. Install the exhaust manifold(s), lower intake manifold and injector fuel rail assembly.

23. Position the cover(s) and new gasket on cylinder head and install attaching bolts. Note location of spark plug wire routing clip stud bolts. Tighten attaching bolts to 80–106 inch lbs. (9–12 Nm).

24. Install the upper intake manifold and connect the secondary wires to the spark plugs.

25. If the left cylinder head is being installed, perform the following: install oil fill cap, compressor mounting and support brackets, power steering pump mounting and support brack-

ets and the alternator/support bracket.

26. If the right cylinder head is being installed, perform the following: install the PCV valve, alternator bracket, thermactor pump and pump pulley, accessory drive idler, thermactor air control valve or air bypass valve hose.

27. Install the accessory drive belt. Attach the thermactor tube(s) support bracket to the rear of the cylinder head. Tighten the attaching bolts to 30–40 ft. lbs. (40–55 Nm).

28. Connect the negative battery cable and fill the cooling system.

29. Start the engine and check for leaks.

30. Check and, if necessary, adjust curb idle speed.

31. Install the air cleaner assembly including air intake duct and heat tube.

Valve Lifters

REMOVAL AND INSTALLATION

3.0L Engine

1. Disconnect the negative battery cable.

2. Drain the cooling system and relieve the fuel system pressure.

3. Disconnect the fuel lines from the fuel supply manifold and remove the throttle body.

4. Disconnect the spark plug wires from the spark plugs. Remove the ignition wire/separator assembly from the rocker cover retaining studs.

5. Mark the position of the distributor housing and rotor and remove the distributor.

6. Remove the rocker arm covers. Loosen the No. 3 intake valve rocker arm retaining bolt to allow the rocker arm to be rotated to 1 side. Remove the pushrod.

7. Remove the intake manifold assembly.

8. Loosen the rocker arm fulcrum retaining bolt enough to allow the rocker arm to be lifted off the pushrod and rotated to 1 side.

9. Remove the pushrod(s). If more than 1 is removed, identify each pushrod's location. The pushrods should be installed in their original position during reassembly.

10. If equipped with roller lifters, loosen the 2 roller lifter guide plate retaining bolts and remove the guide plate retainer assembly from the lifter valley. Remove the lifter guide plate(s) from the lifters by lifting straight up.

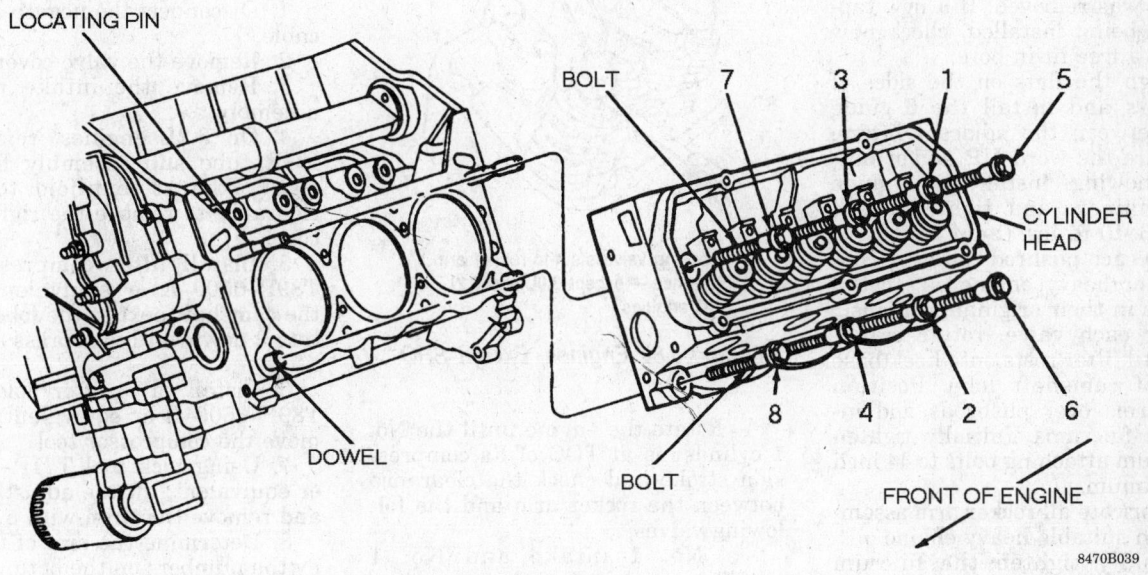

Cylinder head bolt torque sequence — 3.8L engine

11. Remove the lifter(s) using a magnet, or grasp the lifter and pull in line with the bore.

NOTE: If the lifter(s) are stuck in the bore(s) due to excessive varnish or gum deposits, it may be necessary to use a claw-type tool to aid removal. Rotate the lifter back and forth to loosen it from the gum or varnish that may have formed on the lifter.

To install:

12. Clean all gasket mating surfaces. Place a rag in the lifter valley to catch any stray gasket material.

13. Lubricate each lifter and bore with heavy engine oil. Install the lifter in the bore, checking for free fit.

14. If equipped with roller lifters, align the lifter flats and install the lifter guide plate. Install the plate with the word **UP** and/or button visible. Install the guide plate retainer assembly over the guide plates. Retainer orientation is not important. Loosely install the retaining bolts, then tighten to 8–10 ft. lbs. (10–14 Nm).

15. Install the intake manifold and the distributor.

16. Dip each pushrod end in oil conditioner and install in it's original position.

17. For each valve, rotate the crankshaft until the lifter rests on the base circle of the camshaft lobe. Position the rocker arms over the pushrod and valve. Tighten the retaining bolt to 8 ft. lbs. (11 Nm) to initially seat the fulcrum into the cylinder head and onto the pushrod. Final tighten the bolt to 24 ft. lbs. (32 Nm).

18. Install the rocker arm covers.

19. Install the throttle body and connect the fuel lines to the fuel supply manifold. Install the safety clips.

20. Install the coolant hoses. Fill and bleed the cooling system. Drain and change the crankcase oil.

21. Connect the air cleaner hoses to the throttle body and rocker cover.

22. Connect the negative battery cable, start the engine and check for leaks. Check the ignition timing.

3.8L Engine

1. Disconnect the negative battery cable. Disconnect the secondary ignition wires at the spark plugs.

2. Remove the plug wire routing clips from mounting studs on the rocker arm cover attaching bolts. Lay plug wires with routing clips toward the front of engine.

3. Remove the upper intake manifold, rocker arm covers and lower intake manifold.

4. Sufficiently loosen each rocker arm fulcrum attaching bolt to allow the rocker arm to be lifted off the pushrod and rotated to one side.

5. Remove the pushrods. The location of each pushrod should be identified and labeled. When engine is assembled, each pushrod should be installed in its original position.

6. Remove the 2 lifter guide plate retainers and 6 guide plates.

7. Remove the lifters using a magnet. The location of each lifter should be identified and labeled. When engine is assembled, each lifter should be installed in its original position.

NOTE: If lifters are stuck in bores due to excessive varnish or gum deposits, it may be necessary to use a hydraulic lifter puller tool to aid removal. When using a remover tool, rotate lifter back and forth to loosen it from gum or varnish that may have formed on the lifter.

To install:

8. Lightly oil all bolt and stud threads before installation. Using solvent, clean the cylinder head and valve rocker arm cover sealing surfaces.

9. Lubricate each lifter and bore with oil conditioner or heavy engine oil.

10. Install each lifter in bore from which it was removed. If a new tappet(s) is being installed, check new lifter for a free fit in bore.

11. Align the flats on the sides of the lifters and install the 6 guide plates between the adjacent lifters. Make sure the word **UP** and/or button is showing. Install the 3 guide plate retainers and tighten the 4 bolts to 6–10 ft. lbs. (8–14 Nm).

12. Dip each pushrod end in oil conditioner or heavy engine oil. Install pushrods in their original positions.

13. For each valve, rotate crankshaft until lifter rests onto heel (base circle) of camshaft lobe. Position rocker arms over pushrods and install the fulcrums. Initially tighten the fulcrum attaching bolts to 44 inch lbs. maximum.

14. Lubricate all rocker arm assemblies with suitable heavy engine oil.

15. Finally tighten the fulcrum bolts to 19–25 ft. lbs. (25–35 Nm). For the final tightening, the camshaft may be in any position.

NOTE: Fulcrums must be fully seated in the cylinder head and pushrods must be seated in rocker arm sockets prior to the final tightening.

16. Complete the installation of the lower intake manifold, valve rocker arm covers and the upper intake manifold by reversing the removal procedure.

17. Install the plug wire routing clips and connect wires to the spark plugs.

18. Start the engine and check for oil or coolant leaks.

Valve Lash

CHECKING

The valve stem-to-rocker arm clearance for all engines except the 3.0L and 3.2L SHO engines should be within specification with the valve lifter completely collapsed. With the crankshaft in the designated positions, install lifter bleed down wrench T71P–6513–B or equivalent, on the rocker arm. Slowly apply pressure to the lifter until the plunger is completely collapsed, then use a feeler gauge to determine the rocker arm to valve lifter clearance.

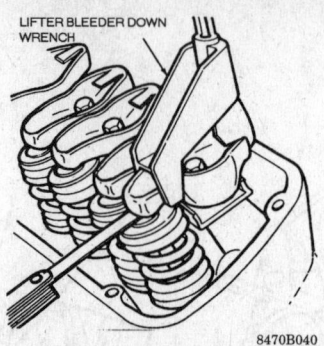

Checking valve stem-to-rocker arm clearance — except 3.0L and 3.2L SHO engines

3.0L and 3.8L Engines, Except SHO

1. Rotate the engine until the No. 1 cylinder is at TDC of its compression stroke and check the clearance between the rocker arm and the following valves.
   a. No. 1 intake and No. 1 exhaust
   b. No. 3 intake and No. 2 exhaust
   c. No. 6 intake and No. 4 exhaust
2. Rotate the crankshaft 360 degrees and check the clearance between the rocker arm and the following valves.
   a. No. 2 intake and No. 3 exhaust
   b. No. 4 intake and No. 5 exhaust
   c. No. 5 intake and No. 6 exhaust
3. The clearance should be 0.09–0.19 in. (2.25–4.79mm).

3.0L and 3.2L SHO Engines

1. Remove the valve cover.
2. Remove the intake manifold assembly.
3. On 3.2L engines, remove the EGR tube sub assembly from the right exhaust manifold to obtain clearance to remove the right rocker cover.
4. Insert a feeler gauge under the cam lobe at a 90 degree angle to the camshaft. Clearance for the intake valves should be (cold) 0.006–0.010 in. (0.15–0.25mm). Clearance for the exhaust valves should be (cold) 0.010–0.014 in. (0.25–0.35mm).

NOTE: The cam lobes must be directed 90 degrees or more away from the valve lifters.

ADJUSTMENT

3.0L and 3.2L SHO Engines

1. Disconnect the negative battery cable.
2. Remove the valve cover.
3. Remove the intake manifold assembly.
4. On 3.2L engines, remove the EGR tube sub assembly from the right exhaust manifold to obtain clearance to remove the right rocker cover.
5. Install lifter compressor tool T89P–6500–A or equivalent, under the camshaft next to the lobe and rotate it downward to depress the valve lifter.
6. Install valve lifter holding tool T89P–6500–B or equivalent, and remove the compressor tool.
7. Using pick tool T71P–19703–C or equivalent, lift the adjusting shim and remove the shim with a magnet.
8. Determine the size of the shim by the numbers on the bottom face of the shim or by measuring with a micrometer. Install the replacement that will permit the specified clearance.
9. Install the replacement shim with the numbers down. Make sure the shim is properly seated.
10. Release the lifter holder tool by installing the compressor tool.
11. Repeat the procedure for each valve by rotating the crankshaft as necessary.

Rocker Arms

REMOVAL AND INSTALLATION

3.0L Engine

1. Disconnect the negative battery cable. Disconnect and tag the spark plug wires.
2. Remove the ignition wire/separator assembly from the rocker arm attaching bolt studs. If the left rocker arm cover is being removed, remove the oil fill cap, disconnect the air cleaner closure system hose and remove the fuel injector harness from the inboard rocker arm cover studs.
3. If the right rocker arm cover is being removed, remove the throttle body as follows:
   a. Tag and disconnect the vacuum hoses at the vacuum tree.
   b. Loosen the EGR tube nuts, if equipped, at the EGR valve and exhaust manifold fitting. Remove or rotate the tube aside.

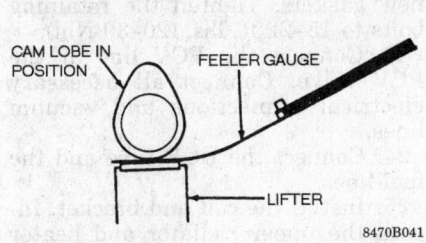

Checking valve clearance — 3.0L and 3.2L SHO engines

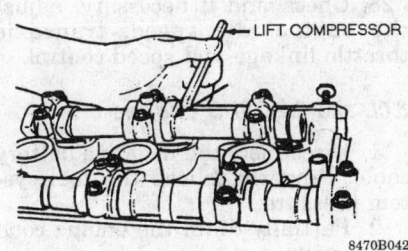

Valve lifter compression tool — 3.0L and 3.2L SHO engines

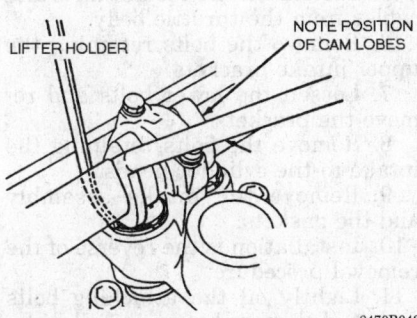

Valve lifter holding tool — 3.0L and 3.2L SHO engines

c. Remove the PCV hose from the tube under the throttle body.

d. Remove the air cleaner duct hose and the idle speed control solenoid shield.

e. Disconnect the throttle and TV cables from the throttle body linkage.

f. Tag and disconnect the electrical connectors from the air charge temperature sensor, idle speed control solenoid and throttle position sensor.

g. Remove the alternator brace.

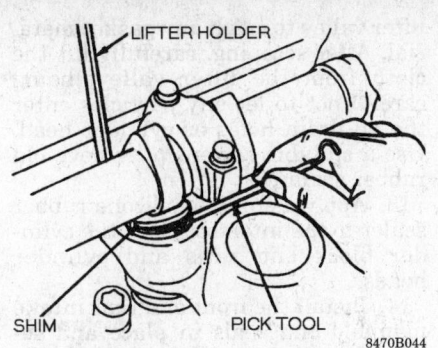

Removing the shim from the valve lifter — 3.0L and 3.2L SHO engines

h. Remove the throttle body retaining bolts and remove the throttle body. Note the location of the bolts so they can reinstalled in their original positions.

4. If removing the right rocker arm cover, remove the PCV valve, loosen the lower EGR tube, if equipped, retaining nut and rotate the tube aside, and move the fuel injection harness aside.

5. Remove the rocker arm cover attaching screws and the covers and gaskets from the vehicle.

6. Remove the rocker arm bolts, fulcrums, rocker arms and fulcrum washers. Keep all parts in order so they can be reinstalled to their original position.

To install:

7. Coat the valve tips, rocker arm and fulcrum contact areas with Lubriplate® or equivalent. Lightly oil all the bolt and stud threads before installation.

8. Rotate the engine until the lifter is on the base circle of the cam (valve closed).

9. Install the rocker arm and components and torque the rocker arm fulcrum bolts in 2 steps: the first to 8 ft. lbs. (11 Nm) and the final to 24 ft. lbs. (32 Nm). Be sure the lifter is on the base circle of the cam for each rocker arm as it is installed.

10. Clean the cylinder head and rocker arm cover sealing surfaces of all dirt and old sealer. If not equipped with integral gaskets, make sure all old gasket material is removed.

11. Apply a bead of silicone sealant at the cylinder head to intake manifold rail step. If not equipped with integral gaskets, install a new rocker arm cover gasket.

12. Install the rocker arm cover and the bolts and studs. Tighten to 9 ft. lbs. (12 Nm). Tighten the cover in the proper sequence.

13. Install the remaining components in the reverse order of their removal.

3.8L Engine

1. Disconnect the negative battery cable.

2. Tag and disconnect the spark plug wires from the spark plugs.

3. If the left cover is being removed, remove the oil fill cap.

4. If the right cover is being removed, position the air cleaner assembly aside and remove the PCV valve.

5. Remove the rocker arm cover mounting bolts and remove the rocker arm cover.

6. Remove the rocker arm bolt, fulcrum and rocker arm. Keep all parts in order so they can be reinstalled in their original positions.

To install:

7. Coat the valve tips, rocker arm and fulcrum contact areas with Lubriplate® or equivalent. Install the rocker arm, fulcrum and rocker arm bolt.

8. Rotate the crankshaft until the lifter rests on the base circle of the camshaft lobe, then tighten the rocker arm bolt. Tighten in 2 steps, first to 44 inch lbs. (5 Nm) and finally to 19–25 ft. lbs. (25–35 Nm).

9. Clean the rocker arm cover and cylinder head mating surfaces of old gasket material and dirt.

10. Position a new gasket onto the cylinder head. Install the rocker arm cover and the mounting bolts. Note the location of the spark plug wire routing clip stud bolts. Tighten the bolts to 80–106 inch lbs. (9–12 Nm).

11. Install the remaining components in the reverse order of their removal.

Intake Manifold

REMOVAL AND INSTALLATION

3.0L Except SHO Engine

1. Disconnect the negative battery cable and drain the engine cooling system. Relieve the fuel system pressure.

2. Loosen the hose clamp attaching the flex hose to the throttle body. Remove the air cleaner flex hose.

3. Identify, tag and disconnect and all vacuum connections to the throttle body.

4. Loosen the lower EGR tube nut and rotate the tube away from the valve. Disconnect the throttle and TV cable from the throttle linkage.

5. Disconnect the throttle position sensor, air charge temperature sensor and idle speed control electrical connectors.

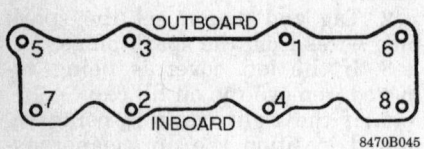

Rocker arm cover bolt torque sequence — 3.0L engine

6. Disconnect the PCV hose and disconnect the alternator support brace. Remove the throttle body retaining bolts and the throttle body.

7. Disconnect the fuel lines. Remove the fuel injection wiring harness from the engine.

8. Disconnect and tag the spark plug wires and remove the rocker arm covers.

9. Disconnect the upper radiator hose and heater hoses. Mark the position of the distributor housing and rotor and remove the distributor assembly.

10. Disconnect the engine coolant temperature sensor and temperature sending unit connector. Loosen the intake valve rocker arm retaining bolt from cylinder No. 3 and rotate the rocker arm from the pushrod and away from the valve stem. Remove the pushrod.

11. Remove the intake manifold attaching bolts. Use a suitable prybar to loosen the intake manifold. Pry upward using the area between the thermostat and transaxle as a leverage point. Remove the manifold and old gaskets and seals.

NOTE: The manifold assembly can be removed with the fuel supply manifold and injectors in place.

To install:

NOTE: Lightly oil all the attaching bolts and stud threads before installation. When using a silicone rubber sealer, assembly must occur within 15 minutes after the sealer has been applied. After this time, the sealer may start to set-up and its sealing quality may be reduced. In high temperature/humidity conditions, the sealant will start to set up in approximately 5 minutes.

12. Clean the gasket mating surfaces of the intake manifold and cylinder head. Lay a shop rag in the lifter valley to catch any gasket material. After scraping, carefully lift the cloth from the lifter valley, being careful not to let any particles enter the oil drain holes or cylinder head. Use a suitable solvent to remove old rubber sealant.

13. Apply a suitable silicone rubber sealer to the intersection of the cylinder block end rails and cylinder heads.

14. Install the front and rear intake manifold end seals in place and secure. Install the intake manifold gaskets, aligning the locking tabs to the provisions on the cylinder head gaskets.

15. Carefully lower the intake manifold into position on the cylinder block and cylinder heads to prevent smearing the silicone sealer and causing gasket voids.

16. Install the retaining bolts and tighten the bolts, in sequence, to 11 ft. lbs. (15 Nm), then retorque to 21 ft. lbs. (28 Nm).

17. Install the fuel supply manifold and injectors, if removed. Apply lubricant to the injector holes in the intake manifold and fuel supply manifold prior to injector installation. Install the fuel supply manifold retaining bolts and tighten to 7 ft. lbs. (10 Nm).

18. Install the thermostat housing and a new gasket, if removed. Tighten the retaining bolts to 9 ft. lbs. (12 Nm).

19. Install the distributor assembly, aligning the marks that were made during the removal procedure.

20. Install the No. 3 cylinder intake valve pushrod. Apply Lubriplate® or equivalent, to the pushrod and valve stem prior to installation. Position the lifter on the base circle of the camshaft and tighten the rocker arm bolt in 2 steps, first to 8 ft. lbs. (11 Nm) and then to 24 ft. lbs. (32 Nm).

21. Install the rocker arm covers. Install the fuel injector harness and attach to the injectors.

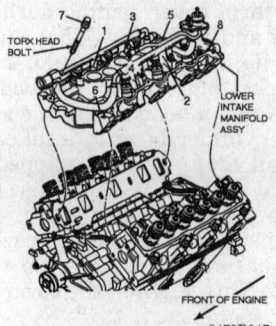

Intake manifold bolt torque sequence — 3.0L engine

22. Install the throttle body with new gaskets. Tighten the retaining bolts to 15–22 ft. lbs. (20–30 Nm).

23. Connect the PCV line at the PCV valve. Connect all necessary electrical connections and vacuum lines.

24. Connect the EGR tube and the fuel lines.

25. Install the coil and bracket. Install the upper radiator and heater hose.

26. Install and connect the air cleaner assembly and outlet tube. Fill the cooling system.

27. Reconnect the negative battery cable, start the engine and check for coolant, fuel and oil leaks.

28. Check and if necessary, adjust the engine idle speed, transaxle throttle linkage and speed control.

3.0L and 3.2L SHO Engines

1. Disconnect the negative battery cable. Properly relieve the fuel system pressure.

2. Partially drain the engine cooling system.

3. Tag and disconnect all electrical connectors and vacuum lines from the intake assembly.

4. Remove the air cleaner tube.

5. Disconnect the coolant lines and cables from the throttle body.

6. Remove the bolts retaining the upper intake brackets.

7. Loosen the lower bolts and remove the brackets.

8. Remove the bolts retaining the intake to the cylinder heads.

9. Remove the intake assembly and the gaskets.

10. Installation is the reverse of the removal procedure.

11. Lightly oil the attaching bolts and stud threads before installation.

NOTE: The intake gasket is reusable.

12. Install the retaining bolts and tighten to 11–17 ft. lbs. (15–23 Nm).

3.8L Engine

1. Disconnect the negative battery cable. Drain the cooling system.

2. Properly relieve the fuel system pressure. Remove the air cleaner assembly including air intake duct and heat tube.

3. Disconnect the accelerator cable at throttle body assembly. Disconnect cruise control cable, if equipped.

4. Disconnect the transaxle linkage at the upper intake manifold.

5. Remove the attaching bolts from accelerator cable mounting bracket and position cables aside.

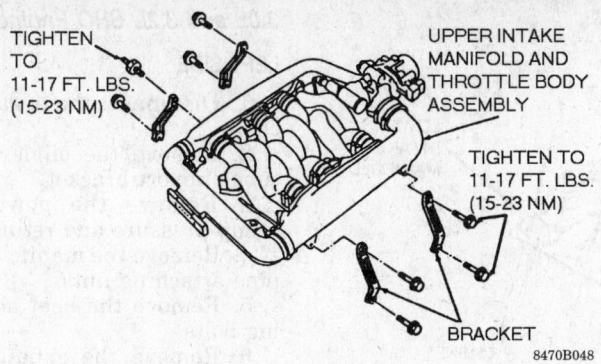

TIGHTEN TO 11-17 FT. LBS. (15-23 NM)

UPPER INTAKE MANIFOLD AND THROTTLE BODY ASSEMBLY

TIGHTEN TO 11-17 FT. LBS. (15-23 NM)

BRACKET

8470B048

Intake manifold cover bolt torque sequence — 3.0L and 3.2L SHO engines

6. Disconnect the thermactor air supply hose at the check valve, if equipped.

7. Disconnect the flexible fuel lines from steel lines over rocker arm cover.

8. Disconnect the fuel lines at injector fuel rail assembly.

9. Disconnect the radiator hose at thermostat housing connection.

10. Disconnect the coolant bypass hose at manifold connection.

11. Disconnect the heater tube at the intake manifold. Remove the heater tube support bracket attaching nut. Remove the heater hose at rear of heater tube. Loosen hose clamp at heater elbow and remove heater tube with hose attached. Remove heater tube with fuel lines attached and set the assembly aside.

12. Disconnect vacuum lines at fuel rail assembly and intake manifold.

13. Identify, tag and disconnect all necessary electrical connectors.

14. If equipped with air conditioning, remove the compressor support bracket.

15. Disconnect the PCV lines. One is located on upper intake manifold. The second is located at the left rocker cover and the lower intake stud.

16. Remove the throttle body assembly and remove the EGR valve assembly from the upper manifold.

17. Remove the attaching nut and remove wiring retainer bracket located at the left front of the intake manifold and set aside with the spark plug wires.

18. Remove the upper intake manifold attaching bolts/studs. Remove the upper intake manifold.

19. Remove the injectors with fuel rail assembly.

20. Remove the heater water outlet hose.

21. Remove the lower intake manifold attaching bolts/stud and remove

the lower intake manifold. Remove the manifold side gaskets and end seals. Discard and replace with new.

NOTE: The manifold is sealed at each end with RTV-type sealer. To break the seal, it may be necessary to pry on the front of the manifold with a small or medium prybar. If it is necessary to pry on the manifold, use care to prevent damage to the machined surfaces.

To install:

22. Lightly oil all attaching bolt and stud threads before installation.

NOTE: When using silicone rubber sealer, assembly must occur within 15 minutes after sealer application. After this time, the sealer may start to set-up and its sealing effectiveness may be reduced. The lower intake manifold, cylinder head and cylinder block mating surfaces should be clean and free of old gasket material. Use a suitable solvent to clean these surfaces.

23. Apply a bead of contact adhesive to each cylinder head mating surface. Press the new intake manifold gaskets into place, using locating pins as necessary to aid in assembly alignment.

24. Apply a ⅛ in. bead of silicone sealer at each corner where the cylinder head joins the cylinder block.

25. Install the front and rear intake manifold end seals.

26. Carefully lower the intake manifold into position on cylinder block and cylinder heads. Use locating pins as necessary to guide the manifold.

27. Install the retaining bolts and stud bolts in their original locations. Torque the retaining bolts, in sequence, in 2 steps:

Step 1: Tighten to 8 ft. lbs. (11 Nm)
Step 2: Tighten to 11 ft. lbs. (15 Nm)

28. Connect the rear PCV line to upper intake tube. Install the front PCV tube so the mounting bracket sits over the lower intake stud.

29. Install the injectors and fuel rail assembly. Tighten the screws to 6–8 ft. lbs. (8–11 Nm).

30. Position the upper intake gasket and manifold on top of the lower intake. Use locating pins to secure position of gasket between manifolds.

31. Install bolts and studs in their original locations. Tighten the 4 center bolts, then tighten the end bolts, to 8 ft. lbs. (11 Nm). Repeat the tightening procedure 2 more times in the same manner, increasing the torque first to 15 ft. lbs. (20 Nm) and finally to 24 ft. lbs. (32 Nm).

32. Install the EGR valve assembly on the manifold. Tighten the attaching nuts to 15–22 ft. lbs. (20–30 Nm).

33. Install the throttle body. Crosstighten the retaining nuts to 15–22 ft. lbs. (20–30 Nm).

34. Connect the rear PCV line at PCV valve and upper intake manifold connections. If equipped with air conditioning, install the compressor support bracket. Tighten attaching fasteners to 15–22 ft. lbs. (20–30 Nm).

35. Connect all electrical connectors and vacuum hoses.

36. Connect the heater tube hose to the heater elbow. Position the heater tube support bracket and tighten attaching nut to 15–22 ft. lbs. (20–30 Nm). Connect the heater hose to the rear of the heater tube and tighten hose clamp.

37. Connect coolant bypass and upper radiator hoses and secure with hose clamps.

38. Connect the fuel line(s) at injector fuel rail assembly and connect the flexible fuel lines to steel lines.

39. Position the accelerator cable mounting bracket and install and tighten attaching bolts to 15–22 ft. lbs. (20–30 Nm).

40. Connect the cruise control cable, if equipped. Connect the transaxle linkage at upper intake manifold.

41. Fill the cooling system to the proper level.

42. Start the engine and check for coolant or fuel leaks.

43. Check and, if necessary, adjust engine idle speed, transaxle throttle linkage and cruise control.

44. Install the air cleaner assembly and air intake duct.

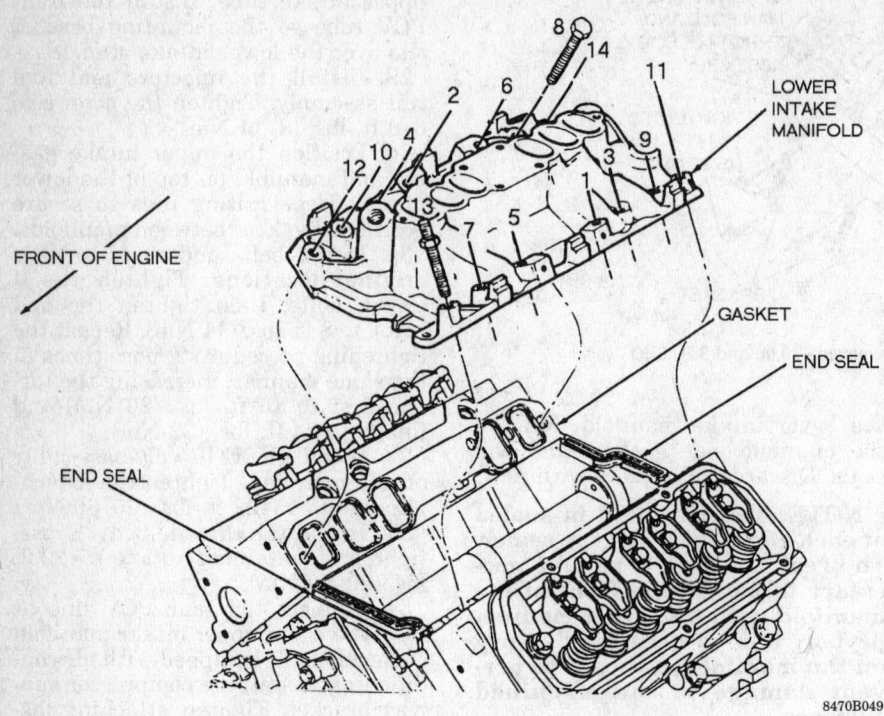

Intake manifold bolt torque sequence — 3.8L engine

Exhaust Manifold

REMOVAL AND INSTALLATION

3.0L Engine

LEFT SIDE

1. Disconnect the negative battery cable. Remove the oil level indicator support bracket retaining nut.
2. Remove the electrical harness connected to the dipstick support bracket, if necessary. Remove the dipstick and tube.
3. Raise and safely support the vehicle. Remove the manifold-to-exhaust pipe retaining nuts.
4. Lower the vehicle. Remove the exhaust manifold attaching bolts and the manifold.
5. Installation is the reverse of the removal procedure. Clean all mating surfaces and lightly oil all bolt and stud threads prior to installation. Tighten the exhaust manifold retaining bolts to 19 ft. lbs. (25 Nm) and tighten the exhaust pipe attaching nuts to 30 ft. lbs. (41 Nm).

RIGHT SIDE

1. Disconnect the negative battery cable.
2. Remove the heater hose support bracket and disconnect and plug the heater hoses, if necessary.
3. Disconnect the pressure feedback hose from the EGR tube. Remove the EGR tube from the exhaust manifold. Use a backup wrench on the lower adapter.
4. Remove the coolant bypass tube, if necessary.
5. Raise the vehicle and support it safely. Remove the manifold-to-exhaust pipe attaching nuts and remove the pipe from the manifold.
6. Lower the vehicle. Remove the exhaust manifold attaching bolts and remove the exhaust manifold from the vehicle.
7. Installation is the reverse of the removal procedure. Clean all mating surfaces and lightly oil all bolt and stud threads prior to installation. Tighten to the following:
Exhaust manifold retaining bolts — 19 ft. lbs. (25 Nm)
Exhaust pipe attaching nuts — 30 ft. lbs. (41 Nm)
EGR tube to exhaust manifold — 31 ft. lbs. (42 Nm).

3.0L and 3.2L SHO Engines

LEFT SIDE

1. Disconnect the negative battery cable.
2. Remove the oil level indicator tube support bracket.
3. Remove the power steering pump pressure and return hoses.
4. Remove the manifold to exhaust pipe attaching nuts.
5. Remove the heat shield retaining bolts.
6. Remove the exhaust manifold retaining nuts and manifold.
7. Installation is the reverse of the removal procedure. Clean all mating surfaces and lightly oil all bolt and stud threads before installation. Tighten the manifold retaining nuts to 26–38 ft. lbs. (35–52 Nm), the heat shield retaining bolts to 11–17 ft. lbs. (15–23 Nm) and the exhaust pipe to manifold nuts to 16–24 ft. lbs. (21–32 Nm).

RIGHT SIDE

1. Disconnect the negative battery cable.
2. Remove the right cylinder head.
3. Remove the heat shield retaining bolts.
4. Remove the exhaust manifold retaining nuts and manifold.
5. Installation is the reverse of the removal procedure. Clean all mating surfaces and lightly oil all bolt and stud threads prior to installation. Tighten the manifold retaining nuts to 26–38 ft. lbs. (35–52 Nm). Tighten the heat shield retaining bolts to 11–17 ft. lbs. (15–23 Nm).

3.8L Engine

LEFT SIDE

1. Disconnect the negative battery cable. Remove the oil level dipstick tube support bracket.
2. Tag and disconnect the spark plug wires.
3. Raise the vehicle and support safely.
4. Remove the manifold-to-exhaust pipe attaching nuts.
5. Lower the vehicle.
6. Remove the exhaust manifold retaining bolts and remove the manifold from vehicle.
   To install:
7. Lightly oil all bolt and stud threads before installation. Clean the mating surfaces on the exhaust manifold, cylinder head and exhaust pipe.
8. Position the exhaust manifold on the cylinder head. Install the lower front bolt hole on No. 5 cylinder as a pilot bolt.

9. Install the remaining manifold retaining bolts. Tighten the bolts 15–22 ft. lbs. (20–30 Nm).

NOTE: A slight warpage in the exhaust manifold may cause a misalignment between the bolt holes in the head and the manifold. Elongate the holes in the exhaust manifold as necessary to correct the misalignment, if apparent. Do not elongate the pilot hole, the lower front bolt on No. 5 cylinder.

10. Raise the vehicle and support safely.
11. Connect the exhaust pipe to the manifold. Tighten the attaching nuts to 16–24 ft. lbs. (21–32 Nm).
12. Lower the vehicle.
13. Connect the spark plug wires. Install dipstick tube support bracket attaching nut. Tighten to 15–22 ft. lbs. (20–30 Nm).
14. Start the engine and check for exhaust leaks.

RIGHT SIDE

1. Disconnect the negative battery cable. Remove the air cleaner assembly and tube. If equipped, disconnect the thermactor hose from the downstream air tube check valve.
2. Tag and disconnect the coil secondary wire from coil and the wires from spark plugs. Remove the spark plugs.
3. Disconnect the EGR tube.
4. Raise the vehicle and support safely.
5. Remove the transaxle dipstick tube. If necessary, remove the thermactor air tube by cutting the tube clamp at the underbody catalyst fitting with a suitable cutting tool.
6. Remove the manifold-to-exhaust pipe attaching nuts.
7. Lower the vehicle.
8. Remove the exhaust manifold retaining bolts and the exhaust manifold.
To install:
9. Lightly oil all bolt and stud threads before installation. Clean the mating surfaces on exhaust manifold cylinder head and exhaust pipe.
10. Position the inner half of the heat shroud, if equipped, gasket and exhaust manifold on cylinder head. Start 2 attaching bolts to align the manifold with the cylinder head. Install the remaining retaining bolts and tighten to 15–22 ft. lbs. (20–30 Nm).

NOTE: A slight warpage in the exhaust manifold may cause a misalignment between the bolt holes in the head and the mani-
fold. Elongate the holes in the exhaust manifold as necessary to correct the misalignment, if apparent. Do not elongate the pilot hole, the lower rear bolt on No. 2 cylinder.

11. Raise the vehicle and support safely.
12. Connect the exhaust pipe to manifold. Tighten the attaching nuts to 16–24 ft. lbs. (21–32 Nm). If necessary, position the thermactor hose to the downstream air tube and clamp tube to the underbody catalyst fitting.
13. Install the transaxle dipstick tube and lower vehicle.
14. Install the outer heat shroud, if equipped, and tighten the retaining screws to 50–70 inch lbs. (5–8 Nm).
15. Install the spark plugs. Connect the wires to their respective spark plugs and connect coil secondary wire to coil.
16. Connect the EGR tube. If equipped, connect the thermactor hose to the downstream air tube and secure with clamp. Install the air cleaner outlet tube assembly.
17. Start the engine and check for exhaust leaks.

Timing Chain Front Cover

REMOVAL AND INSTALLATION

3.0L Engine

1. Disconnect the negative battery cable.
2. Loosen the 4 water pump pulley bolts while the water pump drive belt is in place.
3. Loosen the alternator belt-adjuster jackscrew to provide enough slack in the alternator drive belt for removal.
4. Using a ½ in. drive breaker bar, rotate the automatic belt tensioner to remove the water pump drive belt. Remove the automatic belt tensioner bolt and nuts.
5. Drain the cooling system.
6. Remove the lower radiator hose and the heater hose from the water pump.
7. Remove the crankshaft pulley and damper.
8. Drain and remove the oil pan.
9. Remove the retaining bolts from the timing cover to the block and remove the timing cover.

NOTE: The timing cover and water pump may be removed as an assembly by not removing bolts 11 through 15.

To install:
10. Lightly oil all bolt and stud threads except those specifying special sealant.
11. Clean all old gasket material and sealer from the timing cover, oil pan and cylinder block.
12. Inspect the timing cover seal for wear or damage and replace if necessary.
13. Align a new timing cover gasket over the cylinder block dowels.
14. Install the timing cover/water pump assembly onto the cylinder block with the water pump pulley loosely attached to the water pump hub.
15. Apply pipe sealant to bolt numbers 1, 2 and 3 and hand start them along with the rest of the cover retaining bolts. Tighten bolts 1–10 to 19 ft. lbs. (25 Nm) and 11–15 to 7 ft. lbs. (10 Nm).
16. Install the oil pan and tighten the retaining bolts to 9 ft. lbs. (12 Nm).
17. Hand tighten the water pump pulley retaining bolts.
18. Install the crankshaft damper and pulley. Torque the damper bolt to 107 ft. lbs. (145 Nm) and the 4 pulley bolts to 37 ft. lbs. (50 Nm).
19. Install the automatic belt tensioner. Tighten the 2 retaining nuts and bolt to 35 ft. lbs. (48 Nm).
20. Install the water pump and accessory drive belts. Torque the water pump pulley retaining bolts to 16 ft. lbs. (21 Nm).
21. Install the lower radiator hose and the heater hose and tighten the clamps.
22. Fill the crankcase with the correct amount and type of engine oil. Connect the negative battery cable. Fill and bleed the cooling system.
23. Start the engine and check for coolant and oil leaks.

3.8L Engine

1. Disconnect the negative battery cable. Drain the cooling system and crankcase.
2. Remove the air cleaner assembly and air intake duct.
3. Loosen the accessory drive belt idler. Remove the drive belt and water pump pulley.
4. Remove the power steering pump mounting bracket attaching bolts. Leaving the hoses connected, place the pump/bracket assembly in a position that will prevent the loss of power steering fluid.
5. If equipped with air conditioning, remove the compressor front support bracket. Leave the compressor in place.

6. Disconnect coolant bypass and heater hoses at the water pump. Disconnect radiator upper hose at thermostat housing.

7. Disconnect the coil wire from distributor cap and remove cap with the spark plug wires attached. Remove the distributor retaining clamp and lift distributor out of the front cover.

8. Raise the vehicle and support safely.

9. Remove the crankshaft damper and pulley.

NOTE: If the crankshaft pulley and vibration damper have to be separated, mark the damper and pulley so they may be reassembled in the same relative position. This is important as the damper and pulley are initially balanced as a unit. If the crankshaft damper is being replaced, check if the original damper has balance pins installed. If so, new balance pins E0SZ-6A328-A or equivalent, must be installed on the new damper in the same position as the original damper. The crankshaft pulley must also be installed in the original installation position.

10. Remove the oil filter, disconnect the radiator lower hose at the water pump and remove the oil pan.

NOTE: The front cover cannot be removed without lowering the oil pan.

11. Lower the vehicle.
12. Remove the front cover attaching bolts.

────── WARNING ──────
Do not overlook the cover attaching bolt located behind the oil filter adapter. The front cover will break if pried upon if all attaching bolts are not removed.

13. Remove the ignition timing indicator.

14. Remove the front cover and water pump as an assembly. Remove the cover gasket and discard.

NOTE: The front cover houses the oil pump. If a new front cover is to be installed, remove the water pump and oil pump from the old front cover.

To install:
15. Lightly oil all bolt and stud threads before installation. Clean all gasket surfaces on the front cover, cylinder block and fuel pump. If reusing the front cover, replace crankshaft front oil seal.

16. If a new front cover is to be installed, complete the following:

   a. Install the oil pump gears.

   b. Clean the water pump gasket surface. Position a new water pump gasket on the front cover and install the water pump. Install the pump attaching bolts and tighten to 15–22 ft. lbs.

17. Install the distributor drive gear.

18. Lubricate the crankshaft front oil seal with clean engine oil.

19. Position a new cover gasket on the cylinder block and install the front cover/water pump assembly using dowels for proper alignment. A suitable contact adhesive is recommended to hold the gasket in position while the front cover is installed.

20. Position the ignition timing indicator.

21. Install the front cover attaching bolts. Apply Loctite® or equivalent, to the threads of the bolt installed below the oil filter housing prior to installation. This bolt is to be installed and tightened last. Tighten all bolts to 15–22 ft. lbs. (20–30 Nm).

22. Raise the vehicle and support safely.

23. Install the oil pan. Connect the radiator lower hose. Install a new oil filter.

24. Coat the crankshaft damper sealing surface with clean engine oil. Apply a small amount of silicone sealant to the crankshaft keyway.

25. Position the crankshaft pulley key in the crankshaft keyway.

26. Install the damper with damper washer and attaching bolt. Tighten the bolt to 104–132 ft. lbs. (140–180 Nm).

27. Install the crankshaft pulley and tighten the attaching bolts 19–28 ft. lbs. (26–28 Nm).

28. Lower the vehicle.

29. Connect the coolant bypass hose.

30. Rotate the crankshaft, as necessary, to position piston No. 1 at TDC on the compression stroke. Install the distributor with rotor pointing at No. 1 distributor cap tower. Install the distributor cap and coil wire.

31. Connect the radiator upper hose at thermostat housing.

32. Connect the heater hose.

33. If equipped with air conditioning, install compressor and mounting brackets.

34. Install the power steering pump and mounting brackets.

35. Position the accessory drive belt over the pulleys.

36. Install the water pump pulley. Position the accessory drive belt over

water pump pulley and tighten the belt.

37. Connect the negative battery cable. Fill the crankcase and cooling system to the proper level.

38. Start the engine and check for leaks.

39. Check the ignition timing and curb idle speed; adjust as required.

40. Install the air cleaner assembly and air intake duct.

Front Cover Oil Seal

REPLACEMENT

3.0L Engine

1. Disconnect the negative battery cable and remove the accessory drive belts.

2. Raise the vehicle and support safely. Remove the right front wheel and tire assembly.

3. Remove the pulley-to-damper attaching bolts and remove the crankshaft pulley.

4. Remove the crankshaft damper retaining bolt and washer. Remove the damper from the crankshaft using a damper removal tool.

5. Pry the seal from the timing cover with a suitable tool, being careful not to damage the front cover and crankshaft.

To install:

NOTE: Before installation, inspect the front cover and shaft seal surface of the crankshaft damper for damage, nicks, burrs or other roughness which may cause the new seal to fail. Service or replace components as necessary.

6. Lubricate the seal lip with clean engine oil and install the seal using a seal installer tool.

7. Coat the crankshaft damper sealing surface with clean engine oil. Apply RTV to the keyway of the damper prior to installation. Install the damper using a damper installation tool. Install the damper retaining bolt and washer. Tighten to 107 ft. lbs. (145 Nm).

8. Position the crankshaft pulley and install the attaching bolts. Tighten the attaching bolts to 37 ft. lbs. (50 Nm).

9. Install the right front wheel and tire assembly and lower the vehicle.

10. Position the drive belt over the crankshaft pulley. Check the drive belt for proper routing and engagement in the pulleys.

11. Reconnect the negative battery cable, start the engine and check for oil leaks.

3.8L Engine

1. Disconnect the negative battery cable.
2. Loosen the accessory drive belt idler.
3. Raise the vehicle and support safely.
4. Disengage the accessory drive belt and remove crankshaft pulley.
5. Remove the crankshaft damper using a suitable puller.
6. Remove the seal from the front cover with a suitable prying tool. Use care to prevent damage to front cover and crankshaft.

To install:

NOTE: Inspect the front cover and crankshaft damper for damage, nicks, burrs or other roughness which may cause the seal to fail. Service or replace components as necessary.

7. Lubricate the seal lip with clean engine oil and install the seal using a suitable seal installer.
8. Lubricate the seal surface on the damper with clean engine oil. Install the damper using a suitable installation tool. Install the damper attaching bolt and tighten to 103–132 ft. lbs. (140–180 Nm).
9. Position the crankshaft pulley and install the retaining bolts. Tighten to 19–28 ft. lbs. (26–38 Nm).
10. Position accessory drive belt over crankshaft pulley.
11. Lower the vehicle.
12. Check accessory drive belt for proper routing and engagement in the pulleys. Adjust the drive belt tension.
13. Connect the negative battery cable. Start the engine and check for leaks.

Timing Chain and Sprockets

REMOVAL AND INSTALLATION

3.0L Engine

1. Check timing chain deflection as follows:
   a. Remove the left rocker arm cover.
   b. Loosen the No. 5 exhaust rocker arm and rotate to 1 side. Install a dial indicator on the end of the pushrod.
   c. Turn the crankshaft clockwise until the No. 1 piston is at TDC on the compression stroke. The damper timing mark should point to TDC on the timing degree indicator. The slack should now be taken up on the right side of the chain. Zero the dial indicator.
   d. Slowly turn the crankshaft counterclockwise until the slightest movement is seen on the dial indicator. Stop and observe the damper timing mark for number of degrees of travel from TDC.
   e. If the reading on the timing degree indicator exceeds 6 degrees, replace the timing chain and sprockets.
2. Disconnect the negative battery cable. Drain the cooling system and crankcase. Remove the crankshaft pulley and front cover assemblies.
3. Rotate the crankshaft until the No. 1 piston is at the TDC on its compression stroke and the timing marks are aligned.
4. Remove the camshaft sprocket attaching bolt and washer. Slide both sprockets and timing chain forward and remove as an assembly.

To install:

NOTE: Before installation, clean and inspect all parts. Clean the gasket material and dirt from the oil pan, cylinder block and front cover.

5. Slide both sprockets and timing chain onto the camshaft and crankshaft with the timing marks aligned. Install the camshaft bolt and washer and torque to 46 ft. lbs. (63 Nm). Apply clean engine oil to the timing chain and sprockets after installation.

NOTE: The camshaft bolt has a drilled oil passage in it for timing chain lubrication. If the bolt is damaged, do not replace it with a standard bolt. Clean the oil passage with solvent prior to installation.

6. Install the timing cover and the crankshaft pulley and damper. Tighten the crankshaft damper bolt to 107 ft. lbs. (145 Nm) and the pulley bolts to 37 ft. lbs. (50 Nm).
7. Fill the crankcase with the proper type and quantity of oil and the cooling system with coolant. Connect the negative battery cable.

3.8L Engine

1. Disconnect the negative battery cable. Drain the cooling system and crankcase.
2. Remove the air cleaner assembly and air intake duct.
3. Loosen the accessory drive belt idler. Remove the drive belt and water pump pulley.
4. Remove the power steering pump mounting bracket attaching bolts. Leaving the hoses connected, place the pump/bracket assembly in a position that will prevent the loss of power steering fluid.
5. If equipped with air conditioning, remove the compressor front support bracket. Leave the compressor in place.
6. Disconnect coolant bypass and heater hoses at the water pump. Disconnect radiator upper hose at thermostat housing.
7. Disconnect the coil wire from distributor cap and remove cap with the spark plug wires attached. Remove the distributor retaining clamp and lift distributor out of the front cover.
8. Raise the vehicle and support safely.
9. Remove the crankshaft damper and pulley.

NOTE: If the crankshaft pulley and vibration damper have to be separated, mark the damper and pulley so they may be reassembled in the same relative position. This is important as the damper and pulley are initially balanced as a unit. If the crankshaft damper is being replaced, check if the original damper has balance pins installed. If so, new balance pins E0SZ-6A328-A or equivalent, must be installed on the new damper in the same position as the original damper. The crankshaft pulley must also be installed in original installation position.

10. Remove the oil filter, disconnect the radiator lower hose at the water pump and remove the oil pan.

NOTE: The front cover cannot be removed without lowering the oil pan.

11. Lower the vehicle.
12. Remove the front cover attaching bolts.

— WARNING —
Do not overlook the cover attaching bolt located behind the oil filter adapter. The front cover will break if pried upon if all attaching bolts are not removed.

13. Remove the ignition timing indicator.
14. Remove the front cover and water pump as an assembly. Remove the cover gasket and discard.

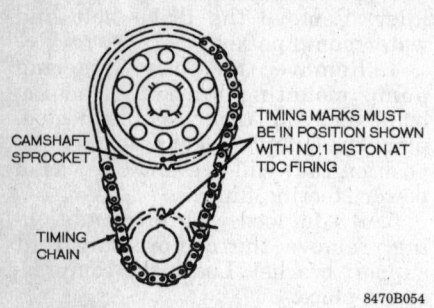

CAMSHAFT
SPROCKET

TIMING MARKS MUST
BE IN POSITION SHOWN
WITH NO.1 PISTON AT
TDC FIRING

TIMING
CHAIN

8470B054

Timing sprocket alignment — 3.0L engine

15. Remove the camshaft bolt and washer from end of the camshaft. Remove the distributor drive gear.

16. Remove the camshaft sprocket, crankshaft sprocket and timing chain. If the crankshaft sprocket is difficult to remove, pry it off using a pair of small prybars positioned on both sides of the sprocket.

17. Pull back on the chain tensioner ratcheting mechanism and install a pin through the hole in the bracket to relieve tension. Remove the 3 bolts and the chain tensioner assembly.

NOTE: The front cover houses the oil pump. If a new front cover is to be installed, remove the water pump and oil pump from the old front cover.

To install:

18. Lightly oil all bolt and stud threads before installation. Clean all gasket surfaces on the front cover, cylinder block and fuel pump. If reusing the front cover, replace crankshaft front oil seal.

19. If a new front cover is to be installed, complete the following:

   a. Install the oil pump gears.

   b. Clean the water pump gasket surface. Position a new water pump gasket on the front cover and install water pump. Install the pump attaching bolts and tighten to 15–22 ft. lbs.

20. Rotate the crankshaft as necessary to position piston No. 1 at TDC and the crankshaft keyway at the 12 o'clock position.

21. Install the tensioner assembly. Make sure the ratcheting mechanism is in the retracted position with the pin pointing outward from the hole in the bracket assembly. Tighten the retaining bolts to 6–10 ft. lbs. (8–14 Nm).

22. Lubricate timing chain with clean engine oil. Install the camshaft sprocket, crankshaft sprocket and timing chain.

23. Remove the pin from the tensioner assembly to load the tensioner arm against the chain. Make certain the timing marks are positioned across from each other.

24. Install the distributor drive gear.

25. Install the washer and bolt at end of camshaft and tighten to 30–37 ft. lbs. (40–50 Nm).

26. Lubricate the crankshaft front oil seal with clean engine oil.

27. Position a new cover gasket on the cylinder block and install the front cover/water pump assembly using dowels for proper alignment. A suitable contact adhesive is recommended to hold the gasket in position while the front cover is installed.

28. Position the ignition timing indicator.

29. Install the front cover attaching bolts. Apply Loctite® or equivalent, to the threads of the bolt installed below the oil filter housing prior to installation. This bolt is to be installed and tightened last. Tighten all bolts to 15–22 ft. lbs. (20–30 Nm).

30. Raise the vehicle and support safely.

31. Install the oil pan. Connect the radiator lower hose. Install a new oil filter.

32. Coat the crankshaft damper sealing surface with clean engine oil. Apply a small amount of silicone sealant to the crankshaft keyway.

33. Position the crankshaft pulley key in the crankshaft keyway.

34. Install the damper with damper washer and attaching bolt. Tighten the bolt to 104–132 ft. lbs. (140–180 Nm).

35. Install the crankshaft pulley and tighten the attaching bolts 19–28 ft. lbs. (26–28 Nm).

36. Lower the vehicle.

37. Connect the coolant bypass hose.

38. Install the distributor with rotor pointing at No. 1 distributor cap tower. Install the distributor cap and coil wire.

39. Connect the radiator upper hose at thermostat housing.

40. Connect the heater hose.

41. If equipped with air conditioning, install compressor and mounting brackets.

42. Install the power steering pump and mounting brackets.

43. Position the accessory drive belt over the pulleys.

44. Install the water pump pulley. Position the accessory drive belt over water pump pulley and tighten the belt.

45. Connect battery ground cable. Fill the crankcase and cooling system to the proper level.

46. Start the engine and check for leaks.

47. Check the ignition timing and curb idle speed; adjust as required.

48. Install the air cleaner assembly and air intake duct.

Timing Belt Front Cover

REMOVAL AND INSTALLATION

3.0L SHO Engine

NOTE: The front cover on the 3.0L SHO engine is made up of 3 sections.

1. Disconnect the battery cables and remove the battery. Remove the right-hand engine roll damper.

2. Disconnect the wiring to the ignition module. Remove the intake manifold crossover tube bolts, loosen the crossover tube clamps and remove the crossover tube.

3. Loosen the alternator/air conditioner belt tensioner pulley and relieve the tension on the belt by backing out the adjustment screw. Remove the belt.

4. Loosen the water pump/power steering belt tensioner pulley and relieve the tension on the belt by backing out the adjustment screw. Remove the belt.

5. Remove the alternator/air conditioner belt tensioner pulley and bracket assembly. Remove the water pump/power steering belt tensioner pulley only.

6. Remove the upper timing belt cover.

7. Disconnect the crankshaft sensor connectors.

8. Raise and safely support the vehicle. Remove the right front wheel and tire assembly.

9. Loosen the fender splash shield and move aside. Remove the crankshaft damper using a suitable puller.

10. Remove the center and lower timing belt covers.

11. Installation is the reverse of the removal procedure. Tighten the timing belt cover retaining bolts to 60–90 inch lbs. (7–11 Nm) and the crankshaft damper bolt to 113–126 ft. lbs. (152–172 Nm).

3.2L SHO Engine

NOTE: The front cover on the 3.2L SHO engine is made up of 3 sections.

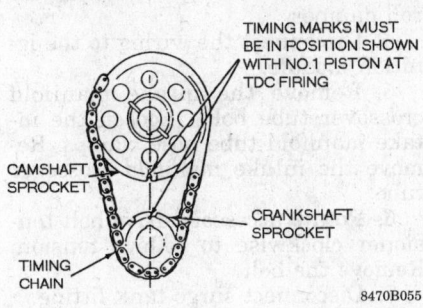

TIMING MARKS MUST BE IN POSITION SHOWN WITH NO.1 PISTON AT TDC FIRING

CAMSHAFT SPROCKET

CRANKSHAFT SPROCKET

TIMING CHAIN

8470B055

Timing sprocket alignment — 3.8L engine

1. Disconnect the battery cables and remove the battery. Remove the right-hand engine roll damper.

2. Disconnect the wiring to the ignition module. Remove the intake manifold crossover tube bolts, loosen the crossover tube clamps and remove the crossover tube.

3. Rotate accessory drive belt tensioner clockwise to relieve tension. Remove the belt.

4. Disconnect surge tank fittings.

5. Remove bolts retaining upper and lower idler pulleys to engine and remove pulleys.

6. Using strap wrench D85L-6000-A or equivalent, to hold power steering pump pulley, remove nut, washer and remove power steering pulley.

7. Remove retaining bolt from belt tensioner and remove tensioner.

8. Remove the upper and center timing belt cover.

9. Disconnect the crankshaft sensor connectors.

10. Raise and safely support the vehicle. Remove the right front wheel and tire assembly.

11. Loosen the fender splash shield and move aside. Remove the crankshaft damper using a suitable puller.

12. Remove the lower timing belt cover.

13. Installation is the reverse of the removal procedure. Tighten the timing belt cover retaining bolts to 12–17 ft. lbs. (16–23 Nm) and the crankshaft damper bolt to 112–127 ft. lbs. (152–172 Nm).

OIL SEAL REPLACEMENT

3.0L and 3.2L SHO Engines

CRANKSHAFT SEAL

1. Loosen the accessory drive belts.

2. Raise the vehicle and support it safely.

3. Remove the right front wheel.

4. Remove the damper attaching bolt and the accessory drive belts from the crankshaft damper.

5. Using a suitable puller, remove the crankshaft damper from the crankshaft.

6. Remove the timing belt.

7. Remove the crankshaft timing gear using a suitable puller.

NOTE: Be careful not to damage the crankshaft sensor or shutter.

8. Remove the crankshaft front oil seal using a suitable puller.

To install:

9. Inspect the front cover and shaft seal surface of the crankshaft damper for damage, nicks, burrs or other roughness which may cause the new seal to fail. Repair or replace as necessary.

10. Using suitable tools, install a new crankshaft front oil seal and the crankshaft timing gear.

11. Install the timing belt.

12. Install the crankshaft damper using a suitable tool. Tighten the damper attaching bolt to 113–126 ft. lbs. (152–172 Nm).

13. Install the accessory drive belts.

14. Lower the vehicle.

15. Start the engine and check for oil leaks.

CAMSHAFT SEAL

1. Remove the timing belt covers and timing belt.

2. Remove the camshaft sprocket(s). Note the location of the dowel pin(s).

3. Remove the camshaft seal using a suitable puller.

To install:

4. Clean and inspect the seal surface area.

5. Apply silicone rubber or equivalent, to the seal outer diameter and seal seating surface.

6. Install the camshaft seal using a suitable seal installer.

7. Install the camshaft sprocket(s). Tighten the retaining bolt to 15–18 ft. lbs. (21–25 Nm).

8. Install the timing belt and timing belt covers.

Timing Belt and Tensioner

REMOVAL AND INSTALLATION

3.0L SHO Engine

1. Disconnect the battery cables.

2. Remove the battery.

3. Remove the right-hand engine roll damper.

4. Disconnect the wiring to the ignition module.

5. Remove the intake manifold crossover tube bolts. Loosen the intake manifold tube hose clamps. Remove the intake manifold crossover tube.

6. Loosen the alternator/air conditioning belt tensioner pulley and relieve the tension on the belt by backing out the adjustment screw. Remove the alternator/air conditioning belt.

7. Loosen the water pump/power steering belt tensioner pulley and relieve the tension on the belt by backing out the adjustment screw. Remove the water pump/power steering belt.

8. Remove the alternator/air conditioning belt tensioner pulley and bracket assembly.

9. Remove the water pump/power steering belt tensioner pulley only.

10. Remove the upper timing belt cover.

11. Disconnect the crankshaft sensor connectors.

12. Place the gear selector in **N**.

13. Rotate the crankshaft until the No. 1 cylinder piston is at TDC on the compression stroke. Make sure the white mark on the crankshaft damper aligns with the **0** degree index mark on the lower timing belt cover and the marks on the intake camshaft sprockets align with the index marks on the metal timing belt cover.

14. Raise the vehicle and support safely.

15. Remove the right front wheel and tire assembly.

16. Loosen the fender splash shield and place it aside.

17. Using a suitable puller, remove the crankshaft damper.

18. Remove the lower timing belt cover.

19. Remove the center timing belt cover and disconnect the crankshaft sensor wire and grommet from the slot in the cover and the stud on the water pump.

20. Loosen the timing belt tensioner, rotate the pulley 180 degrees clockwise and tighten the tensioner nut to hold the pulley in the unload position.

21. Lower the vehicle and remove the timing belt.

WHITE MARK

8470B057

Crankshaft damper to lower timing cover index mark alignment — 3.0L SHO engine

To install:

NOTE: Before installing the timing belt, inspect it for cracks, wear or other damage and replace, if necessary. Do not allow the timing belt to come into contact with gasoline, oil, water, coolant or steam. Do not twist or turn the belt inside out.

22. Make sure the engine is at TDC on the No. 1 cylinder. Check that the camshaft sprocket marks line up with the index marks on the upper steel belt cover and that the crankshaft sprocket aligns with the index mark on the oil pump housing.

NOTE: The timing belt has 3 yellow lines. Each line aligns with the index marks.

23. Install the timing belt over the crankshaft and camshaft sprockets. The lettering on the belt **KOA** should be readable from the rear of the engine; top of the lettering to the front of the engine. Make sure the yellow lines are aligned with the index marks on the sprockets.
24. Release the tensioner locknut and leave the nut loose.
25. Raise the vehicle and support safely.

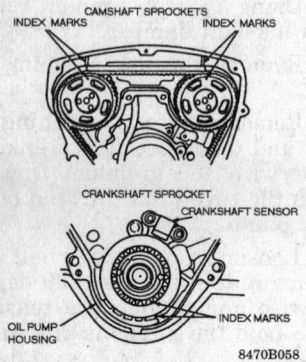

CAMSHAFT SPROCKETS
INDEX MARKS   INDEX MARKS

CRANKSHAFT SPROCKET
CRANKSHAFT SENSOR

OIL PUMP HOUSING   INDEX MARKS

8470B058

Timing belt index marks — 3.0L SHO engine

26. Install the center timing belt cover. Make sure the crankshaft sensor wiring and grommet are installed and routed properly. Tighten the mounting bolts to 60–90 inch lbs. (7–11 Nm).
27. Install the lower timing belt cover. Tighten the bolts to 60–90 inch lbs. (7–11 Nm).
28. Using a suitable tool, install the crankshaft damper. Tighten the damper attaching bolt to 113–126 ft. lbs. (152–172 Nm).
29. Rotate the crankshaft 2 revolutions in the clockwise direction until the yellow mark on the damper aligns with the **0** degree mark on the lower timing belt cover.
30. Remove the plastic door in the lower timing belt cover. Tighten the tensioner locknut to 25–37 ft. lbs. (33–51 Nm) and install the plastic door.
31. Rotate the crankshaft 60 degrees more in the clockwise direction until the white mark on the damper aligns with the **0** degree mark on the lower timing belt cover.
32. Lower the vehicle.
33. Make sure the index marks on the camshaft sprockets align with the marks on the rear metal timing belt cover.
34. Route the crankshaft sensor wiring and connect with the engine wiring harness.
35. Install the upper timing belt cover. Tighten the bolts to 60–90 inch lbs. (7–11 Nm).
36. Install the water pump/power steering tensioner pulley. Tighten the nut to 11–17 ft. lbs. (15–23 Nm).
37. Install the alternator/air conditioning tensioner pulley and bracket assembly. Tighten the bolts to 11–17 ft. lbs. (15–23 Nm).
38. Install the water pump/power steering and alternator/air conditioning belts and set the tension. Tighten the idler pulley nut to 25–36 ft. lbs. (34–50 Nm).
39. Install the intake manifold crossover tube. Tighten the bolts to 11–17 ft. lbs. (15–23 Nm).
40. Install the engine roll damper and the battery.
41. Connect the wiring to the ignition module.
42. Connect the battery cables.
43. Raise the vehicle and support safely.
44. Install the splash shield and the right front wheel and tire assembly.
45. Lower the vehicle.

3.2L SHO Engine

1. Disconnect the battery cables.
2. Remove the battery.

3. Remove the right-hand engine roll damper.
4. Disconnect the wiring to the ignition module.
5. Remove the intake manifold crossover tube bolts. Loosen the intake manifold tube hose clamps. Remove the intake manifold crossover tube.
6. Rotate accessory drive belt tensioner clockwise to relieve tension. Remove the belt.
7. Disconnect surge tank fitting.
8. Remove bolts retaining upper and lower idler pulleys to engine and remove pulleys.
9. Using strap wrench D85L-6000-A or equivalent, to hold power steering pump pulley, remove nut, washer and remove power steering pulley.
10. Remove retaining bolt from belt tensioner and remove tensioner.
11. Remove the upper and center timing belt cover.
12. Disconnect the crankshaft sensor connectors.
13. Place the transaxle selector in **N**.
14. Rotate the crankshaft until the No. 1 cylinder piston is at TDC on the compression stroke. Make sure the white mark on the crankshaft damper aligns with the **0** degree index mark on the lower timing belt cover and the marks on the intake camshaft sprockets align with the index marks on the metal timing belt cover.
15. Raise the vehicle and support safely.
16. Remove the right front wheel and tire assembly.
17. Loosen the fender splash shield and place it aside.
18. Using a suitable puller, remove the crankshaft damper.
19. Remove the lower timing belt cover and belt guide.
20. Remove the upper timing belt tensioner bolt.
21. Slowly loosen the lower timing belt tension bolt and remove the tensioner.
22. Lower the vehicle and remove the timing belt.
To install:

NOTE: Before installing the timing belt, inspect it for cracks, wear or other damage and replace, if necessary. Do not allow the timing belt to come into contact with gasoline, oil, water, coolant or steam. Do not twist or turn the belt inside out.

23. Slowly compress timing belt tensioner in a soft jawed vice until

hole in tensioner housing aligns with hole in tensioner rod.

— CAUTION —

Use caution when compressing timing belt tensioner in vice to insure that tensioner does not slip from vice.

24. Insert a ¹/₂₀ inch (1.5mm) hex wrench through holes.
25. Release tension from vice.
26. If a new belt is being installed, loosen timing belt idler bolt.
27. Make sure the engine is at TDC on the No. 1 cylinder. Check that the camshaft sprocket marks line up with the index marks on the upper steel belt cover and that the crankshaft sprocket aligns with the index mark on the oil pump housing.

NOTE: The timing belt has 3 yellow lines. Each line aligns with the index marks.

28. Install the timing belt over the crankshaft and camshaft sprockets. The lettering on the belt **KOB** should be readable from the rear of the engine; top of the lettering to the front of the engine. Make sure the yellow lines are aligned with the index marks on the sprockets.

— WARNING —

Do not install timing belt tensioner with rod extended.

29. Install timing belt tensioner on the cylinder block while pushing timing belt idler toward belt. Tighten tensioner bolts to 12–17 ft. lbs. (16–23 Nm).
30. Install grommets between timing belt tensioner and oil pump.
31. Remove ¹/₂₀ inch (1.5mm) hex wrench from timing belt tensioner.
32. If a new belt is being installed, perform the following steps:

    a. Position timing belt tensioner tool T93P-6254-B or equivalent, using power steering pump bracket holes.

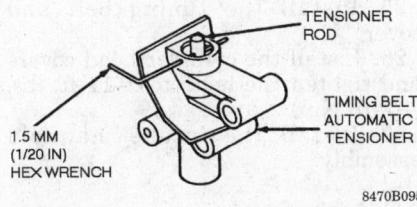

Timing belt automatic tensioner — 3.2L SHO engine

    b. Hand-tighten timing belt idler bolt.

    c. Using torque wrench with attachment T93P-6254-A, rotate clockwise to 4.3 inch lbs. (0.5 Nm).

    d. Tighten timing belt tensioner bolts to 27–37 ft. lbs. (36–50 Nm), then remove timing belt tensioning tool.

33. Raise the vehicle and support safely.
34. Install the belt guide and lower timing belt cover. Tighten the retaining bolts to 12–17 ft. lbs. (16–23 Nm).
35. Using a suitable tool, install the crankshaft damper. Tighten the damper attaching bolt to 113–126 ft. lbs. (152–172 Nm).
36. Rotate the crankshaft 2 revolutions in the clockwise direction until the yellow mark on the damper aligns with the **0** degree mark on the lower timing belt cover.
37. Lower the vehicle.
38. Make sure the index marks on the camshaft sprockets align with the marks on the rear metal timing belt cover.
39. Route the crankshaft sensor wiring and connect with the engine wiring harness.
40. Install the center and upper timing belt covers. Tighten the bolts to 12–17 ft. lbs. (16–23 Nm).

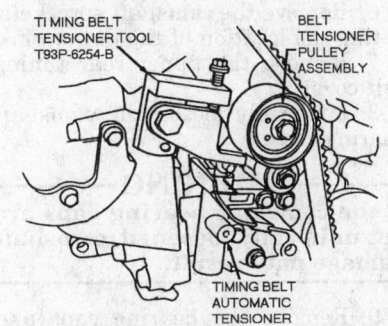

Timing belt tensioner pulley adjustment — 3.2L SHO engine

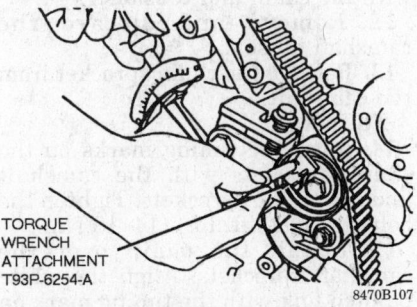

Timing belt tensioner pulley torque adjustment — 3.2L SHO engine

41. Install the water pump pulley. Tighten the nut to 12–17 ft. lbs. (16–23 Nm).
42. Install the single accessory drive belt while rotating accessory drive belt tensioner clockwise.
43. Install surge tank fitting.
44. Install the intake manifold crossover tube. Tighten the bolts to 11–17 ft. lbs. (15–23 Nm).
45. Install the engine roll damper and the battery.
46. Connect the wiring to the ignition module.
47. Connect the battery cables.
48. Raise the vehicle and support safely.
49. Install the splash shield and the right front wheel and tire assembly.
50. Lower the vehicle.

Timing Sprockets

REMOVAL AND INSTALLATION

3.0L SHO Engine

1. Disconnect the negative battery cable.
2. Remove the timing belt.
3. Remove the camshaft and crankshaft timing belt sprockets. Note the location of the dowel pins when removing the camshaft sprockets.
4. Install in the reverse order of removal. Tighten the camshaft timing belt sprocket bolts to 15–18 ft. lbs. (21–25 Nm) and the crankshaft sprocket bolt to 113–126 ft. lbs. (152–172 Nm).

Camshaft

REMOVAL AND INSTALLATION

3.0L Except SHO Engine

1. Drain the cooling system and crankcase. Relieve the fuel system pressure.
2. Remove the engine from the vehicle and position in a suitable holding fixture.
3. Remove the accessory drive components from the front of the engine.
4. Remove the throttle body and the fuel injector harness. Remove the distributor assembly.
5. Remove and tag the spark plug wires and rocker arm covers. Loosen the rocker arm fulcrum nuts and position the rocker arms to the side. Remove the pushrods and label them so they may be installed in their original positions.

6. Remove the intake manifold.

7. Remove the lifter guide plates. Using a suitable magnet or lifter removal tool, remove the hydraulic lifters and keep them in order so they can be installed in their original positions. If the lifters are stuck in the bores by excessive varnish use a hydraulic lifter puller to remove the lifters.

8. Remove the crankshaft pulley and damper using a suitable removal tool. Remove the oil pan assembly.

9. Remove the front cover assembly. Align the timing marks on the camshaft and crankshaft gears. Check the camshaft endplay as follows:

  a. Push the camshaft toward the rear of the engine and install a dial indicator tool, so the indicator point is on the camshaft sprocket attaching screw.

  b. Zero the dial indicator. Position a small prybar or equivalent, between the camshaft sprocket or gear and block.

  c. Pull the camshaft forward and release it. Compare the dial indicator reading with the camshaft endplay service limit specification of 0.005 in.

  d. If the camshaft endplay is over the amount specified, replace the thrust plate.

10. Remove the timing chain and sprockets.

11. Remove the camshaft thrust plate. Carefully remove the camshaft by pulling it toward the front of the engine. Remove it slowly to avoid damaging the bearings, journals and lobes.

To install:

12. Clean and inspect all parts before installation.

13. Lubricate camshaft lobes and journals with heavy engine oil. Carefully insert the camshaft through the bearings in the cylinder block.

14. Install the thrust plate. Tighten the retaining bolts to 7 ft. lbs. (10 Nm).

15. Install the timing chain and sprockets. Check the camshaft sprocket bolt for blockage of drilled oil passages prior to installation and clean, if necessary.

16. Install the front timing cover and crankshaft damper and pulley.

17. Lubricate the lifters and lifter bores with a heavy engine oil. Install the lifters into their original bores. Install the lifter guide plates, making sure the word **UP** and/or button is visible. Tighten the guide plate retainer bolts to 9 ft. lbs. (12 Nm).

18. Install the intake manifold assembly and the distributor.

19. Lubricate the pushrods and rocker arms with heavy engine oil. Install the pushrods and rocker arms into their original positions. Rotate the crankshaft to set each lifter on its base circle, then tighten the rocker arm bolt. Tighten the rocker arm bolts to 24 ft. lbs. (32 Nm).

20. Install the oil pan and the rocker covers.

21. Install the fuel injector harness and the throttle body. Connect the spark plug wires to the spark plugs.

22. Install the accessory drive components and install the engine assembly.

23. Connect the negative battery cable. Start the engine and check for leaks. Check and adjust the ignition timing.

3.0L and 3.2L SHO Engines

1. Disconnect the negative battery cable. Properly relieve the fuel system pressure.

2. Set the engine on TDC on No. 1 cylinder.

3. Remove the intake manifold assembly.

4. Remove the timing cover and belt.

5. Remove the cylinder head covers.

6. Remove the camshaft sprockets, noting the location of the dowel pins.

7. Remove the upper rear timing belt cover.

8. Uniformly loosen the camshaft bearing caps.

——— **WARNING** ———
If the camshaft bearing caps are not uniformly loosened, camshaft damage may result.

9. Remove the bearing caps and note their positions for installation.

10. Remove the camshaft chain tensioner mounting bolts.

11. Remove the camshafts together with the chain and tensioner.

12. Remove and discard the camshaft oil seal.

13. Remove the chain sprocket from the camshaft.

  To install:

14. Align the timing marks on the chain sprockets with the camshaft and install the sprockets. Tighten the bolts to 10–13 ft. lbs. (14–18 Nm).

15. Install the chain over the camshaft sprockets. Align the white painted link with the timing mark on the sprocket.

16. Rotate the camshafts approximately 60 degrees counterclockwise.

Set the chain tensioner between the sprockets and install the camshafts on the cylinder head.

NOTE: The left and right chain tensioners are NOT interchangeable.

17. Apply a thin coat of engine oil to the camshaft journals and install bearing caps No. 2 through No. 5 and loosely install the bolts. Install the bearing caps in their original location.

NOTE: The arrows on the bearing caps point to the front of the engine when installed.

18. Apply silicone sealer to outer diameter of the new camshaft seal and the seal seating area on the cylinder head. Install the camshaft seal.

19. Apply silicone sealer to the No. 1 bearing cap and install the bearing cap.

20. Tighten the bearing caps, in sequence, in 2 steps. First tighten to 71–106 inch lbs. (8–12 Nm) and then to 12–16 ft. lbs. (16–22 Nm).

NOTE: For left camshaft installation, apply pressure to the chain tensioner to avoid damage to the bearing caps.

21. Install the chain tensioner and tighten the bolts to 11–14 ft. lbs. (15–19 Nm). Rotate the camshafts 60 degrees clockwise and check for proper alignment of the timing marks. Marks on the camshaft sprockets should align with the cylinder head cover mating surface.

22. Install the camshaft positioning tool T89P–6256–C or equivalent, on the camshafts to check for correct positioning. The flats on the tool should align with the flats on the camshaft. If the tool does not fit and/or timing marks will not line up, repeat the procedure from Step 14.

23. Install the timing belt rear cover and tighten the bolts to 70 inch lbs. (8.8 Nm).

24. Install the camshaft sprockets and tighten the bolts to 15–18 ft. lbs. (21–25 Nm).

25. Install the timing belt and cover.

26. Install the cylinder head covers and tighten the bolts to 8–11 ft. lbs. (10–16 Nm).

27. Install the intake manifold assembly.

3.8L Engine

1. Disconnect the negative battery cable.

2. Properly relieve the fuel system pressure.

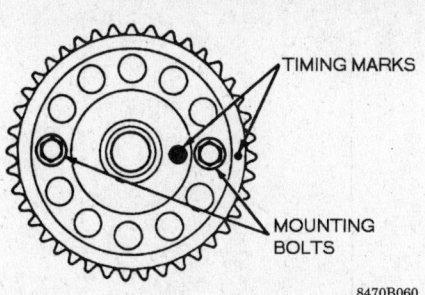

Timing chain sprocket and camshaft alignment — 3.0L and 3.2L SHO engines

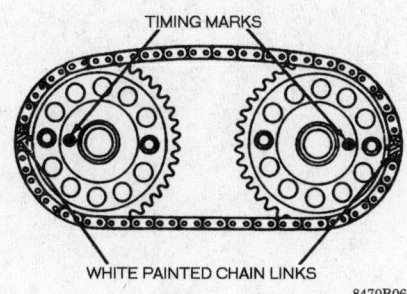

Aligning the timing chain with the timing marks — 3.0L and 3.2L SHO engines

3. Drain the cooling system and crankcase.

4. Remove the engine from the vehicle and position in a suitable holding fixture.

5. Remove the intake manifold.

6. Remove the rocker arm covers, rocker arms, pushrods and lifters.

7. Remove the oil pan.

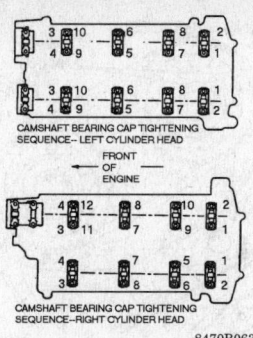

Camshaft bearing cap tightening sequence — 3.0L and 3.2L SHO engines

8. Remove the front cover and timing chain.

9. Remove the thrust plate. Remove the camshaft through the front of the engine, being careful not to damage bearing surfaces.

To install:

10. Lightly oil all attaching bolts and stud threads before installation. Lubricate the cam lobes, thrust plate and bearing surfaces with a suitable heavy engine oil.

11. Install the camshaft being careful not to damage bearing surfaces while sliding into position. Install the thrust plate and tighten the bolts to 6–10 ft. lbs. (8–14 Nm).

12. Install the front cover and timing chain.

13. Install the oil pan.

14. Install the lifters.

15. Install the upper and lower intake manifolds.

16. Install the engine assembly.

17. Fill the cooling system and crankcase to the proper level and connect the negative battery cable.

18. Start the engine. Check and adjust the ignition timing and engine idle speed as necessary. Check for leaks.

Balance Shaft

REMOVAL AND INSTALLATION

3.8L Engine

1. Remove the engine from the vehicle.

2. Remove the intake manifolds.

3. Remove the oil pan.

4. Remove the front cover and timing chain and camshaft sprocket.

5. Remove the balance shaft drive gear and spacer.

6. Remove the balance shaft gear, thrust plate and shaft assembly.

To install:

7. Thoroughly coat the balance shaft bearings in the block with engine oil.

8. Install the balance shaft gear.

9. Install the balance shaft, thrust plate and gear and tighten the retaining bolts to 6–10 ft. lbs. (8–14 Nm).

10. Install the timing chain and camshaft sprocket.

11. Install the oil pan.

12. Install the timing cover.

13. Install the intake manifolds.

14. Install the engine in the vehicle.

Piston and Connecting Rod

POSITIONING

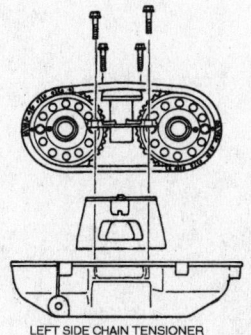

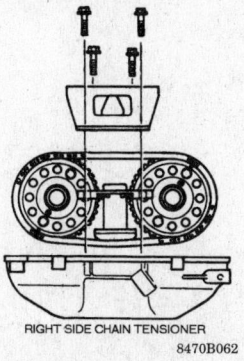

Chain tensioner installation — 3.0L and 3.2L SHO engines

Piston and connecting rod assembly — 3.8L engine

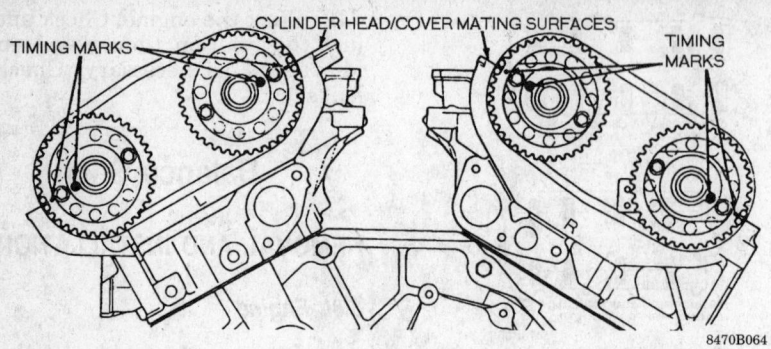

8470B064

Camshaft sprocket timing mark to cylinder head cover mating surface alignment — 3.0L and 3.2L SHO engines

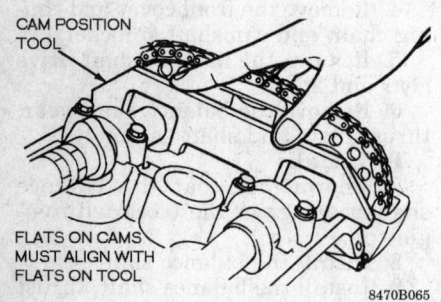

8470B065

Camshaft positioning tool — 3.0L and 3.2L SHO engines

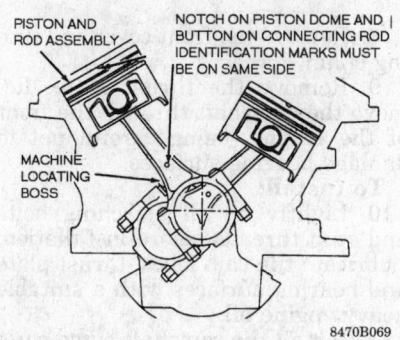

8470B069

Piston and connecting rod assembly — 3.0L engine

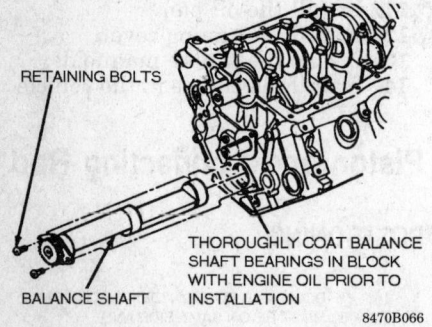

8470B066

Balancer shaft — 3.8L engine

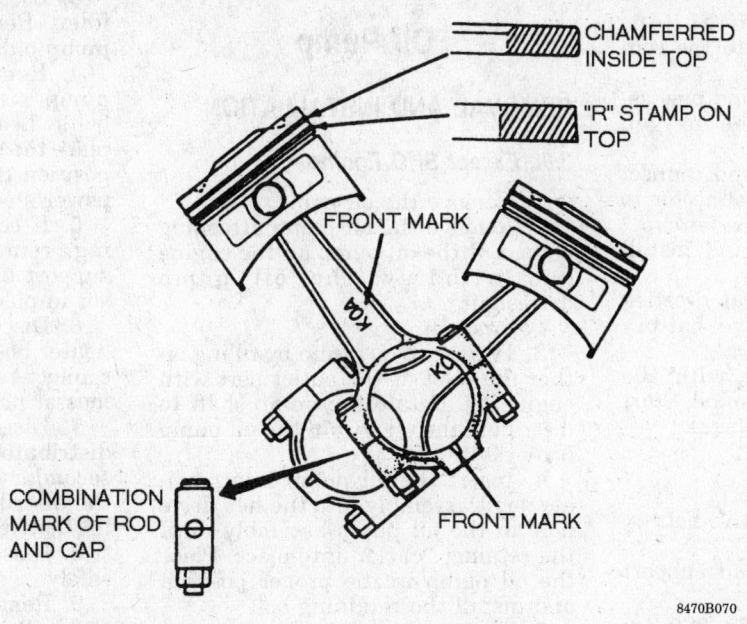

Piston and connecting rod assembly — 3.0L SHO engine shown — 3.2L engine front mark reads KOB

ENGINE LUBRICATION

Oil Pan

REMOVAL AND INSTALLATION

3.0L Except SHO Engine

1. Disconnect the negative battery cable and remove the oil level dipstick.
2. Raise the vehicle and support safely. If equipped with a low level sensor, remove the retainer clip at the sensor. Remove the electrical connector from the sensor.
3. Drain the crankcase. Remove the starter motor and disconnect the electrical connector from the oxygen sensor.
4. Remove the catalyst and pipe assembly. Remove the lower engine/flywheel dust cover from the torque converter housing.
5. Remove the oil pan attaching bolts and slowly remove the oil pan from the engine block. Remove the oil pan gasket.

To install:

6. Clean the gasket surfaces on the cylinder block and oil pan. Apply a ¼ in. bead of silicone sealer to the junction of the rear main bearing cap and cylinder block junction of the front cover assembly and cylinder block.

NOTE: When using a silicone sealer, the assembly process should occur within 15 minutes after the sealer has been applied. After this time, the sealer may start to set-up and its sealing effectiveness may be affected.

7. Position the oil pan gasket over the oil pan and secure the gasket with a suitable sealer contact adhesive.
8. Position the oil pan on the engine block. Install the oil pan attaching bolts and tighten the bolts to 8–10 ft. lbs. (10–14 Nm). Back off all bolts and retighten.
9. Install the lower engine/flywheel dust cover to the torque converter housing. Install the catalyst and pipe assembly. Connect the oxygen sensor connector.
10. Install the starter motor. Install the low oil level sensor connector to the sensor and install the retainer clip. Lower the vehicle and replace the oil level dipstick.

11. Connect the negative battery cable. Fill the crankcase. Start the engine and check for oil and exhaust leaks.

3.0L and 3.2L SHO Engines

1. Disconnect the negative battery cable.
2. Remove the oil level dipstick.
3. Remove the accessory drive belts.
4. Remove the timing belt.
5. Raise the vehicle and support it safely.
6. If equipped with a low oil level sensor, remove the retainer clip and the electrical connector from the sensor.
7. Drain the engine oil.
8. Remove the starter motor.
9. Disconnect the oxygen sensors.
10. Remove the catalyst and pipe assembly.
11. Remove the lower flywheel dust cover from the converter housing.
12. Remove the oil pan attaching bolts and the oil pan.

To install:

13. Clean the gasket surfaces of the cylinder block and the oil pan.
14. Position the oil pan gasket on the oil pan and secure with silicone sealer.

15. Position the oil pan and tighten the retaining bolts to 11–16 ft. lbs. (15–23 Nm).

16. Install the lower engine/flywheel dust cover to the converter housing.

17. Install the catalyst and pipe assembly and connect the oxygen sensors.

18. Install the starter and connect the low oil level sensor connector to the sensor. Install the retainer clip.

19. Lower the vehicle and install the accessory drive belts.

20. Replace the oil level dipstick and connect the negative battery cable.

21. Fill the crankcase with the proper type and quantity of oil. Start the vehicle and check for leaks.

3.8L Engine

1. Disconnect the negative battery cable.

2. Raise the vehicle and support safely.

3. Drain the crankcase and remove the oil filter element.

4. Remove the catalytic converter assembly, starter motor and converter housing cover.

5. Remove the retaining bolts and remove the oil pan.

To install:

6. Clean the gasket surfaces on cylinder block, oil pan and oil pickup tube.

7. Trial fit oil pan to cylinder block. Ensure enough clearance has been provided to allow oil pan to be installed without sealant being scraped off when pan is positioned under engine.

8. Apply a bead of silicone sealer to the oil pan flange. Also apply a bead of sealer to the front cover/cylinder block joint and fill the grooves on both sides of the rear main seal cap.

NOTE: When using silicone rubber sealer, assembly must occur within 15 minutes after sealer application. After this time, the sealer may start to harden and its sealing effectiveness may be reduced.

9. Install the oil pan and secure to the block with the attaching screws. Tighten the screws to 7–9 ft. lbs. (9–12 Nm).

10. Install a new oil filter element. Install the torque converter housing cover and starter motor.

11. Install the catalytic converter assembly and lower the vehicle.

12. Fill the crankcase and connect the negative battery cable.

13. Start the engine and check for leaks.

Oil Pump

REMOVAL AND INSTALLATION

3.0L Except SHO Engine

1. Remove the oil pan.

2. Remove the oil pump attaching bolts. Lift the oil pump off the engine and withdraw the oil pump driveshaft.

To install:

3. Prime the oil pump by filling either the inlet or the outlet port with engine oil. Rotate the pump shaft to distribute the oil within the oil pump body cavity.

4. Insert the oil pump intermediate shaft assembly into the hex drive hole in the oil pump assembly until the retainer "clicks" into place. Place the oil pump in the proper position and install the retaining bolt.

5. Torque the oil pump retaining bolt to 35 ft. lbs. (48 Nm).

6. Install the oil pan with new gasket.

7. Fill the crankcase. Start engine and check for leaks.

3.0L and 3.2L SHO Engines

1. Remove the oil pan.

2. Remove the crankshaft timing belt sprocket.

3. Remove the sump to oil pump bolts.

4. Remove the oil pump to block bolts and remove the pump.

To install:

5. Align the oil pump on the crankshaft and install the oil pump retaining bolts. Tighten the bolts to 11–17 ft. lbs. (15–23 Nm).

6. Install the oil sump to oil pump retaining bolts and tighten to 6–8 ft. lbs. (7–11 Nm).

7. Install the crankshaft timing belt sprocket.

8. Install the oil pan with a new gasket.

9. Fill the crankcase with the proper type and quantity of oil.

10. Start the engine and check for leaks.

3.8L Engine

NOTE: The oil pump, oil pressure relief valve and pump drive intermediate shaft are contained in the front cover assembly.

1. Disconnect the negative battery cable. Drain the cooling system and crankcase.

2. Remove the air cleaner assembly and air intake duct.

3. Loosen the accessory drive belt idler. Remove the belt and water pump pulley.

4. Remove the power steering pump mounting bracket attaching bolts. Leaving the hoses connected, place the pump/bracket assembly in a position that will prevent the loss of power steering fluid.

5. If equipped with air conditioning, remove the compressor front support bracket. Leave the compressor in place.

6. Disconnect coolant bypass and heater hoses at the water pump. Disconnect radiator upper hose at thermostat housing.

7. Disconnect the coil wire from distributor cap and remove cap with secondary wires attached. Remove the distributor hold-down clamp and lift distributor out of the front cover.

8. Raise the vehicle and support safely.

9. Remove the crankshaft damper and pulley.

NOTE: If the crankshaft pulley and vibration damper have to be separated, mark the damper and pulley so they may be reassembled in the same relative position. This is important as the damper and pulley are initially balanced as a unit. If the crankshaft damper is being replaced, check if the original damper has balance pins installed. If so, new balance pins E0SZ–6A328–A or equivalent, must be installed on the new damper in the same position as the original damper. The crankshaft pulley must also be installed in original installation position.

10. Remove the oil filter, disconnect the radiator lower hose at the water pump and remove the oil pan.

11. Lower the vehicle.

12. Remove the front cover.

─────── **WARNING** ───────
Do not overlook the cover attaching bolt located behind the oil filter adapter. The front cover will break if pried upon if all attaching bolts are not removed.

13. Remove the oil pump cover attaching bolts and remove the cover. Lift the pump gears off the front cover pocket. Remove the cover gasket and replace with new.

To install:

14. Clean the front cover oil pump gasket contact surface. Place a straight-edge across the oil pump

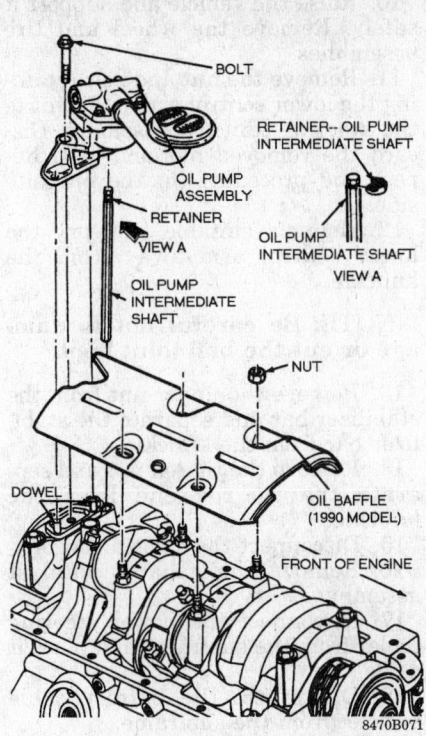

BOLT

RETAINER-- OIL PUMP INTERMEDIATE SHAFT

OIL PUMP ASSEMBLY

RETAINER

VIEW A

OIL PUMP INTERMEDIATE SHAFT

OIL PUMP INTERMEDIATE SHAFT

VIEW A

NUT

DOWEL

OIL BAFFLE (1990 MODEL)

FRONT OF ENGINE

8470B071

Oil pump installation — 3.0L engine

cover mounting surface and check for wear or warpage using a feeler gauge. If the surface is out of flat by more than 0.0016 in. (0.04mm), replace the cover.

15. Lightly pack the gear pocket with petroleum jelly or coat all pump gear surfaces with oil conditioner.

16. Install the gears in the pocket. Make certain the petroleum jelly fills the gap between the gears and the pocket.

────── **WARNING** ──────
Failure to properly coat the oil pump gears may result in failure of the pump to prime when the engine is started.
────────────────────

17. Position the oil pump cover gasket and install the oil pump cover. Tighten the oil pump cover retaining bolts to 18–22 ft. lbs. (25–30 Nm).

18. Clean the gasket surfaces of the front cover and cylinder block.

19. Position a new gasket and the front cover on the cylinder block.

20. Install the front cover attaching bolts. Apply Loctite® or equivalent, to the threads of the bolt installed below the oil filter housing prior to installation. This bolt is to be installed and tightened last. Tighten all bolts to 15–22 ft. lbs. (20–30 Nm).

21. Raise the vehicle and support safely.

22. Install the oil pan. Connect the radiator lower hose. Install a new oil filter.

23. Coat the crankshaft damper sealing surface with clean engine oil.

24. Position the crankshaft pulley key in the crankshaft keyway.

25. Install the damper with damper washer and attaching bolt. Tighten the bolt to 104–132 ft. lbs. (140–180 Nm).

26. Install the crankshaft pulley and tighten the attaching bolts 19–28 ft. lbs. (26–28 Nm).

27. Lower the vehicle.

28. Connect the coolant bypass hose.

29. Rotate the crankshaft, as necessary, to bring the piston in No. 1 cylinder to TDC on the compression stroke. Install the distributor with rotor pointing at No. 1 distributor cap tower. Install the distributor cap and coil wire.

30. Connect the radiator upper hose at thermostat housing.

31. Connect the heater hose.

32. If equipped with air conditioning, install compressor and mounting brackets.

33. Install the power steering pump and mounting brackets.

34. Position the accessory drive belt over the pulleys.

35. Install the water pump pulley. Position the accessory drive belt over water pump pulley and tighten the belt.

36. Connect battery ground cable. Fill the crankcase and cooling system to the proper level.

37. Start the engine and check for leaks.

38. Check the ignition timing and curb idle speed, adjust as required.

39. Install the air cleaner assembly and air intake duct.

CHECKING

3.0L Engine

1. Remove the oil pump from the vehicle. Disassemble the pump, clean the parts in a suitable solvent and allow to dry.

2. Inspect the inside of the pump housing for damage or excessive wear.

3. Check the mating surface for wear. Minor scuff marks are normal but if the cover, gears or housing are excessively worn, scored or grooved, replace the pump.

4. Inspect the rotor for nicks, burrs, or score marks. Remove minor imperfections with an oil stone.

5. Measure the inner-to-outer rotor tip clearance. The clearance must not exceed 0.012 in. (0.30mm) with a feeler gauge inserted ½ in. minimum with the rotors removed from the pump housing.

6. With the rotor assembly installed in the housing, place a straight-edge across the rotor assembly and housing. Measure the clearance (rotor endplay) between the the inner and outer rotors. The clearance is 0.005 in. (0.13mm) maximum.

7. Check the relief valve spring tension. It should be 9.1–10.1 lbs. at 1.11 in. If the spring is worn or damaged, replace the pump. Check the relief valve piston for freedom of movement in the bore.

3.0L and 3.2L SHO Engines

1. Remove the oil pump from the vehicle. Disassemble the pump, clean the parts in a suitable solvent and allow to dry.

2. Inspect the inside of the pump housing for damage or excessive wear.

3. Check the mating surface for wear. Minor scuff marks are normal but if the cover, gears or housing are excessively worn, scored or grooved, replace the pump.

4. Check the inner rotor tip-to-outer rotor tip clearance using a feeler gauge. The clearance must not exceed 0.0024–0.0071 in. (0.06–0.18mm) with the feeler gauge inserted ½ in. (12.7mm) minimum and the rotors removed from the pump housing.

5. With the rotor assembly installed in the pump housing, place a straight-edge over the rotor assembly and the housing. Measure the clearance (rotor endplay) between the straight-edge and the rotor and outer race. The clearance should be 0.0012–0.0035 in. (0.03–0.09mm).

6. Check the relief valve spring tension. It should be 34.5 lbs. per inch. If the spring is worn or damaged, replace the pump. Check the relief valve piston for freedom of movement in the bore.

3.8L Engine

PUMP GEAR END CLEARANCE

1. Inspect the pump cover mating surface on the front cover and pump body. Visually inspect the O-ring for any cuts and/or nicks and replace, if necessary. Remove any burrs or nicks.

2. Measure the thickness of the gear using a micrometer. The gear

should measure 1.19–1.20 in. (30.455–30.480mm) thick.

3. If the gear is less than the specified minimum thickness, replace the gear. If the gear thickness is within specification, it may be necessary to replace the pump body. If the gear thickness is within the specified limits, proceed to Step 4.

4. Measure the depth of the gear pocket in the oil pump body. The depth should be 1.200–1.202 in. (30.49–30.54mm).

5. If the depth is more than 1.202 in. (30.54mm), replace the oil pump body.

PUMP GEAR SIDE CLEARANCE

1. Measure the side clearance by inserting a feeler gauge between the gear tooth and the side wall of the gear pocket.

2. The clearance should be a maximum of 0.005 in. (0.13mm) and the gears should be free to turn. If the clearance is greater than 0.005 in. (0.13mm), proceed to Step 3.

3. Measure the diameter of the gear using a micrometer. The gear should be 1.505–1.509 in. (38.252–38.332mm) wide.

4. If the gear is less than 1.505 in. (38.252mm) in diameter, replace the gear and measure the clearance as in Step 1. If the diameter of the gear is within the specified limits, go to Step 5.

5. Measure the diameter of the gear pocket in the front cover. The diameter should be 1.504–1.507 in. (38.22–38.30mm). If the diameter is less than 1.504 in. (38.22mm), replace the front cover and measure the clearance as in Step 1.

Rear Main Bearing Oil Seal

REMOVAL AND INSTALLATION

1. Disconnect the negative battery cable.

2. Raise the vehicle and support it safely. Remove the transaxle.

3. Remove flywheel. Remove the cover plate, if necessary.

4. With a suitable tool, remove the oil seal.

NOTE: Use caution to avoid damaging the oil seal surface.

To install:

5. Inspect the crankshaft seal area for any damage which may cause the seal to leak. If damage is evident, service or replace the crankshaft as necessary.

6. Coat the crankshaft seal area and the seal lip with engine oil.

7. Using a seal installer tool, install the seal. Tighten the 2 bolts of the seal installer tool evenly so the seal is straight and seats without mis-alignment.

8. Install the flywheel. Tighten attaching bolts to 54–64 ft. lbs. (73–87 Nm) on all except the 3.0L and 3.2L SHO engines. On the 3.0L and 3.2L SHO engines, tighten the bolts in 2 steps, first to 29–43 ft. lbs. (39–50 Nm) and then to 51–58 ft. lbs. (69–78 Nm).

9. Install rear cover plate, if necessary.

10. Install the transaxle and connect the negative battery cable.

MANUAL TRANSAXLE

Transaxle Assembly

REMOVAL AND INSTALLATION

1. Disconnect the negative battery cable.

2. Wedge a 7 in. block of wood under the clutch pedal to hold the pedal up beyond it's normal position.

3. Remove the air cleaner hose.

4. Grasp the clutch cable and pull it forward, disconnecting it from the clutch release shaft assembly.

5. Disconnect the clutch cable casing from the rib on top of the transaxle case.

6. Install engine lifting eyes.

7. Tie up the wiring harness and power steering cooler hoses.

8. Disconnect the speedometer cable and speed sensor wire.

9. Support the engine using engine support bar 014–00750 or equivalent.

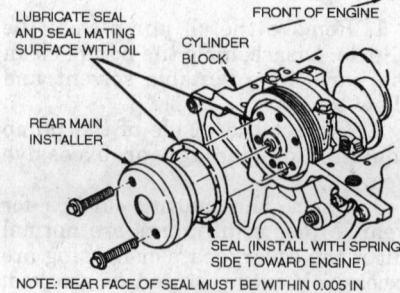

NOTE: REAR FACE OF SEAL MUST BE WITHIN 0.005 IN (0.127 MM) OF THE REAR FACE OF THE BLOCK

8470B072

Rear main oil seal installation — 3.8L engine shown

10. Raise the vehicle and support it safely. Remove the wheel and tire assemblies.

11. Remove the nut and bolt retaining the lower control arm ball joint to the steering knuckle assembly. Discard the removed nut and bolt. Repeat the procedure on the opposite side.

12. Using a suitable tool, pry the lower control arm away from the knuckle.

NOTE: Be careful not to damage or cut the ball joint boot.

13. Remove the upper nut from the stabilizer bar and separate the stabilizer bar from the knuckle.

14. Remove the tie rod nut and separate the tie rod end from the knuckle.

15. Disconnect the oxygen sensor.

16. Remove the exhaust catalyst assembly.

17. Disconnect the power steering cooler from the subframe and place it aside.

18. Disconnect the battery cable bracket from the subframe.

19. Using a large prybar, pry the left inboard CV-joint assembly from the transaxle. Install transaxle plug T81P–1177–B or equivalent, into the seal to prevent fluid leakage. Remove the CV-joint from the transaxle by grasping the left steering knuckle and swinging the knuckle and half-shaft outward from the transaxle. Repeat the procedure on the right side.

NOTE: If the CV-joint assembly cannot be pried from the transaxle, insert differential rotator tool T81P–4026–A or equivalent, through the left side and tap the joint out. The tool can be used from either side of the transaxle.

20. Support the halfshaft assembly with wire in a near level position to prevent damage to the assembly during the remaining operations. Repeat the procedure on the opposite side.

21. Remove the retaining bolts from the center support bearing and remove the right halfshaft from the transaxle.

22. Remove the 2 steering gear retaining nuts from the sub-frame. Support the steering gear by wiring up the tie rod ends to the coil springs.

23. Remove the transaxle to engine retaining bolts.

24. Remove the shift mechanism stabilizer bar-to-transaxle retaining bolt, shift rod-to-shift shaft retaining nut and bolt and remove the rods from the transaxle.

25. Remove the engine mount bolts.

26. Position jacks under the body mount positions and remove the 4 bolts, lower the sub-frame and position it aside.

27. Remove the starter motor assembly.

28. Remove the left engine vibration dampener lower bracket.

29. Remove the backup light switch connector from the transaxle backup light switch, located on top of the transaxle and remove the backup light switch.

30. Position a suitable support jack under the transaxle.

31. Lower the transaxle, remove it from the engine and lower it from the vehicle.

To install:

32. Raise the transaxle into position. Engage the input shaft spline into the clutch disc and work the transaxle onto the dowel sleeves. Make sure the transaxle assembly is flush with the rear face of the engine before installation of the retaining bolts.

33. Install the engine to transaxle retaining bolts. Tighten to 28–31 ft. lbs. (38–42 Nm).

34. Install the backup light switch and tighten to 12–15 ft. lbs. (16–20 Nm). Connect the electrical connector.

35. Install the starter motor. Tighten the retaining bolts to 30–40 ft. lbs. (41–54 Nm).

36. Using jacks, position the subframe and raise it into position. Install the 4 bolts and tighten to 65–85 ft. lbs. (90–115 Nm).

37. Install the left vibration dampener lower bracket.

38. Install the engine mount bolts and tighten to 40–55 ft. lbs. (54–75 Nm).

39. Connect the stabilizer and shift rod to the transaxle. Tighten the stabilizer bolt to 35–46 ft. lbs. (47–63 Nm). Tighten the shift rod clamp bolt and nut to 80–106 inch lbs. (9–12 Nm).

40. Install the engine to transaxle bolts and tighten to 28–31 ft. lbs. (38–42 Nm).

41. Install the steering gear retaining nuts and tighten to 85–100 ft. lbs. (115–135 Nm).

42. Install the center support bearing retaining bolts and tighten to 85–100 ft. lbs. (115–135 Nm).

43. Install the right halfshaft into the transaxle.

44. Install the left inboard CV-joint assembly into the transaxle.

45. Connect the battery cable bracket to the sub-frame.

46. Connect the power steering cooler to the subframe.

47. Install the exhaust catalyst retaining bolts and tighten to 25–34 ft. lbs. (34–47 Nm).

48. Connect the oxygen sensor.

49. Install the tie rod in the knuckle and the tie rod retaining nut. Tighten to 35–47 ft. lbs. (47–64 Nm).

50. Position the stabilizer bar to the knuckle and install the nut.

51. Install the lower control arm ball joint to steering knuckle assembly. Install and tighten a new retaining nut and bolt to 37–44 ft. lbs. (50–60 Nm).

52. Install the wheel and tire assemblies.

53. Check the transaxle fluid level.

54. Lower the vehicle.

55. Remove the engine support tool.

56. Install the speedometer cable. Connect the speedometer cable and speed sensor wire.

57. Remove the engine lifting eyes.

58. Connect the clutch cable to the transaxle.

59. Install the air cleaner hose and remove the wood block from the clutch pedal.

60. Connect the negative battery cable and check the transaxle for fluid leaks.

CLUTCH

Clutch Assembly

REMOVAL AND INSTALLATION

1. Disconnect the negative battery cable. Raise the vehicle and support it safely. Remove the transaxle.

2. If the pressure plate is to be reused, mark the pressure plate and the flywheel so they can be assembled in the same position.

3. Loosen the attaching bolts 1 turn at a time, in sequence, until spring tension is relieved to prevent pressure plate cover distortion.

4. Support the pressure plate and remove the bolts. Remove the pressure plate and clutch disc from the flywheel.

5. Inspect the flywheel, clutch disc, pressure plate, release bearing and the release fork for wear. Replace parts as required. If the flywheel shows any signs of overheating (blue discoloration) or if it is badly grooved

or scored, it should be refaced or replaced.

To install:

6. Install the flywheel, if removed. Tighten attaching bolts in 2 steps, first to 29–43 ft. lbs. (39–50 Nm) and then to 51–58 ft. lbs. (69–78 Nm).

7. Clean the pressure plate and flywheel surfaces thoroughly. Place the clutch disc and pressure plate into the installed position. The clutch disc must be installed so the flatter side is toward the flywheel. Align the marks made during the removal procedure if components are being reused. Support the clutch disc and pressure plate with a suitable dummy shaft or clutch aligning tool.

8. Install the pressure plate-to-flywheel bolts. Tighten them gradually in a criss-cross pattern to 12–24 ft. lbs. (17–32 Nm). Remove the alignment tool.

9. If the release bearing was removed, apply a light film of grease to the outer surface of the transaxle bearing retainer and the tips of the release lever where they contact the bearing. Fill the bearing groove with grease. Slide the bearing onto the bearing retainer and attach to the release lever with the retaining pin.

10. Install the transaxle and connect the negative battery cable.

PEDAL HEIGHT/FREE-PLAY ADJUSTMENT

The clutch control system is self-adjusting during normal operation. There is no provision for pedal height/free-play adjustment.

Clutch Cable

REMOVAL AND INSTALLATION

NOTE: Whenever the clutch cable is disconnected for any reason, such as transaxle removal or clutch, clutch pedal components or clutch cable replacement, the proper method for installing the clutch cable must be followed.

1. Disconnect the negative battery cable.

2. Prop up the clutch pedal to lift the pawl free of the quadrant which is part of the self-adjuster mechanism.

3. Remove the air cleaner assembly to gain access to the clutch cable.

4. Grasp the extended tip of the clutch cable with a pair of pliers and unhook the clutch cable from the clutch bearing release lever.

WARNING

Do not grasp the wire strand portion of the inner cable since this might cut the wires and result in cable failure.

---

5. Disconnect the cable from the insulator that is located on the rib of the transaxle.

6. Position the clutch shield away from the mounting plate bracket by removing the rear retaining screw. Loosen the front retaining screw located near the toe board and rotate the shield aside. Secure by snugging up the front screw. The rear retaining screw is nearest the instrument panel.

7. With the clutch pedal lifted up to release the pawl, rotate the gear quadrant forward. Unhook the clutch cable from the gear quadrant. Let the quadrant swing rearward but do not let it snap back.

8. Pull the cable out through the recess between the clutch pedal and gear quadrant, and from the insulator on the pedal assembly. Remove the cable by withdrawing it through the engine compartment.

To install:

NOTE: The clutch pedal must be lifted to disengage the adjusting mechanism during cable installation. Failure to do so will result in damage to the self adjuster mechanism. A prying instrument must never be used to install the cable into the quadrant.

9. Insert the clutch cable assembly from the engine or passenger compartment through the dash panel and dash panel grommet. Make sure the cable is routed inboard of the brake lines and not trapped at the spring tower by the brake lines.

10. Push the clutch cable through the insulator on the stop bracket and through the recess between the pedal and the gear quadrant.

11. With the clutch pedal lifted up to release the pawl, rotate the gear quadrant forward. Hook the cable into the gear quadrant.

12. Secure the clutch shield on the clutch mounting plate.

13. Using a piece of wire, cord or tape, secure the pedal in the upper most position.

14. Install the clutch cable in the insulator on the rib of the transaxle.

15. Hook the cable into the clutch release lever in the engine compartment.

16. Remove the device that was used to temporarily secure the pedal against its stop.

17. Adjust the clutch by depressing the clutch pedal several times.

18. Install the air cleaner and connect the negative battery cable.

AUTOMATIC TRANSAXLE

Transaxle Assembly

REMOVAL AND INSTALLATION

1. Disconnect the battery cables and remove the battery and battery tray.

2. Remove the air cleaner assembly, hoses and tubes.

3. Disconnect the electrical connectors from the engine and remove the bolt retaining the main wiring harness bracket.

4. Remove the shift lever. Remove the EGR bracket and throttle body bracket retaining bolts and install engine lifting eyes.

5. Secure the wiring harness aside and remove the radiator sight shield. Position engine support tool D88L–6000–D or equivalent.

6. If equipped with air suspension, turn the air suspension switch located in the luggage compartment to the **OFF** position.

7. Remove the dipstick and disconnect the power steering line bracket. Remove the 4 torque converter housing bolts from the top of the transaxle.

8. Raise and safely support the vehicle. Remove the front wheel and tire assemblies.

9. Disconnect the left-hand outer tie rod end. Remove the suspension height sensor, if equipped. Disconnect the brake line support brackets.

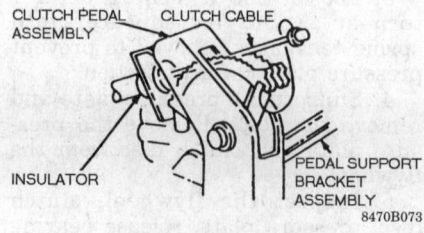

CLUTCH PEDAL ASSEMBLY   CLUTCH CABLE

INSULATOR   PEDAL SUPPORT BRACKET ASSEMBLY

8470B073

Clutch cable installation

---

10. Remove the retaining bolts from the front stabilizer bar assembly. Remove the ball joint pinch bolts and disconnect the right and left lower arm assemblies from the knuckles.

11. Remove the steering gear retaining nuts from the sub-frame. Disconnect the oxygen sensors and remove the exhaust pipe, catalytic converter assembly and mounting bracket.

12. Remove 2 bolts from the transaxle mount and the 4 bolts from the left engine support. Remove the support.

13. Support the sub-frame with suitable jacks. Remove the steering gear from the sub-frame and secure to the rear of the engine compartment. Remove the sub-frame-to-body bolts and lower the sub-frame.

14. Remove the starter and the dust cover.

15. Rotate the engine at the crankshaft pulley to align the torque converter bolts with the starter drive hole. Remove the 4 torque converter-to-flywheel retaining nuts.

16. Disconnect the transaxle cooler lines. Remove the engine-to-transaxle retaining bolts.

17. Remove the speedometer sensor heat shield. Remove the vehicle speed sensor from the transaxle.

NOTE: Vehicles with electronic instrument clusters do not use a speedometer cable.

18. Position a suitable transaxle jack. Remove the halfshafts.

19. Remove the last 2 torque converter housing bolts, carefully separate the transaxle from the engine and lower out of the vehicle.

20. Installation is the reverse of the removal procedure. During installation be sure to observe the following:

a. Clean the transaxle oil cooler lines.

b. Install new circlips on the inboard CV-joint stub shafts.

c. Carefully install the halfshafts in the transaxle by aligning the splines of the CV-joint with the splines of the differential.

d. Attach the lower ball joint to the steering knuckle with a new nut and bolt. Tighten the nut to 40–53 ft. lbs. (53–72 Nm).

e. When installing the transaxle to the engine, verify that the converter-to-transaxle engagement is maintained. Prevent the converter from moving forward and disengaging during installation.

f. Adjust the TV and manual linkages. Check the transaxle fluid level.

g. Tighten the following bolts to the torque specifications listed:

Transaxle-to-engine bolts: 41–50 ft. lbs. (55–68 Nm)

Control arm-to-knuckle bolts: 40–53 ft. lbs. (53–72 Nm)

Stabilizer U-clamp-to-bracket bolts

1992 models: 60–70 ft. lbs. (81–95 Nm)

1993–96 models: 23–29 ft. lbs. (30–40 Nm)

Tie rod-to-knuckle nut: 23–35 ft. lbs. (31–47 Nm)

Starter-to-transaxle bolts: 30–40 ft. lbs. (41–54 Nm)

Converter-to-flywheel bolts: 23–39 ft. lbs. (31–53 Nm)

Insulator-to-bracket bolts: 55–70 ft. lbs. (75–90 Nm)

SHIFT CABLE ADJUSTMENT

1. Position the selector lever in the **OD** position. If equipped with floor shift, the shift lever must be held in the rearward position using a constant force of 3 lbs. (1.4 Kg) while the linkage is being adjusted. If equipped with column shift, a 3 lb. (1.4 Kg) weight should be hung on the shift lever to make sure the lever is firmly located in the overdrive detent.
2. Loosen the manual lever-to-control cable retaining nut.
3. Move the transaxle manual lever to the **OD** position, second detent from the most rearward position.
4. Tighten the retaining nut to 12–19 ft. lbs. (16–27 Nm).
5. Check the operation of the transaxle in each selector lever position. Make sure the park and neutral start switch are functioning properly.

DRIVE AXLE

Halfshaft

——— WARNING ———

When removing both the left and right halfshafts on vehicles equipped with manual transaxle or 3-speed automatic transaxle, install transaxle plug tools T81P–1177–B or equivalent, to prevent dislocation of the differ-

ential side gears. Should the gears become misaligned, the differential will have to be removed from the transaxle to re-align the side gears.

NOTE: Due to the 3-speed automatic transaxle case configuration, the right halfshaft assembly must be removed first. Differential rotator tool T81P–4026–A or equivalent, is then inserted into the transaxle to drive the left inboard CV-joint assembly from the transaxle. If only the left halfshaft assembly is to be removed for service, remove the right halfshaft assembly from the transaxle first. After removal, support it with a length of wire, then drive the left halfshaft assembly from the transaxle.

REMOVAL AND INSTALLATION

1. Disconnect the negative battery cable. Remove the wheel cover/hub cover from the wheel and tire assembly and loosen the wheel nuts.
2. Raise the vehicle and support safely. Remove the wheel and tire assembly. Remove the hub nut and washer and discard the hub nut.
3. Remove the nut from the ball joint to steering knuckle attaching bolts. Drive the bolt out of the steering knuckle using a punch and hammer. Discard the bolt and nut after removal.
4. If equipped with anti-lock brakes, remove the anti-lock brake sensor and position aside. If equipped with air suspension, remove the height sensor bracket retaining bolt and wire sensor bracket to inner fender. Position the sensor link aside.
5. Separate the ball joint from the steering knuckle using a suitable prybar. Position the end of the prybar outside of the bushing pocket to avoid damage to the bushing. Use care to prevent damage to the ball joint boot. Remove the stabilizer bar link at the stabilizer bar.

NOTE: The remaining removal procedures differ according to transaxle application: manual transaxle, 4-speed automatic overdrive (AXOD or AXODE) transaxle or 3-speed automatic (ATX/FLC) transaxle.

6. If equipped with AXOD or AXODE transaxle and removing the right or left halfshaft, or if equipped with manual transaxle and removing the left halfshaft, proceed as follows:

a. Install the CV-joint puller tool T86P–3514–A1 or equivalent, between CV-joint and transaxle case. Turn the steering hub and/or wire strut assembly aside.

b. Screw extension tool T86P–3514–A2 or equivalent, into the CV-joint puller and hand tighten. Screw an impact slide hammer onto the extension and remove the CV-joint from the transaxle.

c. Support the end of the shaft by suspending it from a convenient underbody component with a piece of wire. Do not allow the shaft to hang unsupported; damage to the outboard CV-joint may occur.

d. Separate the outboard CV-joint from the hub using front hub remover tool T81P–1104–C or equivalent, metric adapter tools T83–P–1104–BH, T86P–1104–Al and front hub installer T81P–1104–A or equivalent.

e. Remove the halfshaft assembly from the vehicle.

7. If equipped with ATX/FLC or manual transaxle and removing the right halfshaft, proceed as follows:

a. Remove the bolts attaching the bearing support to the bracket. Slide the link shaft out of the transaxle. Support the end of the shaft by suspending it from a convenient underbody component with a piece of wire. Do not allow the shaft to hang unsupported, damage to the outboard CV-joint may occur.

b. Separate the outboard CV-joint from the hub using front hub remover tool T81P–1104–C or equivalent, metric adapter tools T83–P–1104–BH, T86P–1104–Al and front hub installer T81P–1104–A or equivalent.

——— WARNING ———

Never use a hammer to separate the outboard CV-joint stub shaft from the hub. Damage to the CV-joint threads and internal components may result. The right side link shaft and halfshaft assembly is removed as a complete unit.

8. If equipped with ATX/FLC transaxle and removing the left halfshaft, proceed as follows:

NOTE: Due to the automatic transaxle case configuration, the right halfshaft assembly must be removed first. Differential rotator tool T81P–4026–A or equivalent, is then inserted into the transaxle to drive the left inboard CV-joint assembly from the transaxle. If only the left halfshaft assembly is to be removed for service, remove the right halfshaft assembly from the transaxle first. After removal, support it with a length of wire, then drive the left halfshaft assembly from the transaxle.

a. Support the end of the shaft by suspending it from a convenient underbody component with a piece of wire. Do not allow the shaft to hang unsupported as damage to the outboard CV-joint may occur.

b. Separate the outboard CV-joint from the hub front hub remover tool T81P–1104–C or equivalent, metric adapter tools T83–P–1104–BH, T86P–1104–Al and front hub installer T81P–1104–A or equivalent.

c. Remove the halfshaft assembly from the vehicle.

To install:

9. Install a new circlip on the inboard CV-joint stub shaft and/or link shaft. The outboard CV-joint does not have a circlip. When installing the circlip, start one end in the groove and work the circlip over the stub shaft end into the groove. This will avoid over expanding the circlip.

NOTE: The circlip must not be re-used. A new circlip must be installed each time the inboard CV-joint is installed into the transaxle differential.

10. Carefully align the splines of the inboard CV-joint stub shaft with the splines in the differential. Exerting some force, push the CV-joint into the differential until the circlip is felt to seat in the differential side gear. Use care to prevent damage to the differential oil seal. If equipped, torque the link shaft bearing retaining bolts to 16–23 ft. lbs. (21–32 Nm).

NOTE: A non-metallic mallet may be used to aid in seating the circlip into the differential side gear groove. If a mallet is necessary, tap only on the outboard CV-joint stub shaft.

11. Carefully align the splines of the outboard CV-joint stub shaft with the splines in the hub and push the shaft into the hub as far as possible.

12. Temporarily fasten the rotor to the hub with washers and 2 wheel lug nuts. Insert a steel rod into the rotor and rotate clockwise to contact the knuckle to prevent the rotor from turning during the CV-joint installation.

13. Install the hub nut washer and a new hub nut. Manually thread the retainer onto the CV-joint as far as possible.

14. Connect the control arm to the steering knuckle and install a new nut and bolt. Tighten the nut to 40–55 ft. lbs. (54–74 Nm).

15. Install the anti-lock brake sensor and/or the ride height sensor bracket, if equipped.

16. Connect the stabilizer link to the stabilizer bar. Tighten to 35–48 ft. lbs. (47–65 Nm).

17. Tighten the hub retainer nut to 180–200 ft. lbs. (245–270 Nm). Remove the steel rod.

18. Install the wheel and tire assembly and lower the vehicle. Tighten the wheel nuts to 80–105 ft. lbs. (108–144 Nm). Fill the transaxle to the proper level with the specified fluid.

CV-Boot

REMOVAL AND INSTALLATION

Outboard CV-Joint Boot

1. Disconnect the negative battery cable. Raise and safely support the vehicle.

2. Remove the halfshaft assembly from the vehicle.

3. Clamp the halfshaft in a vise that is equipped with soft jaw covers. Do not allow the vise jaws to contact the boot or boot clamp.

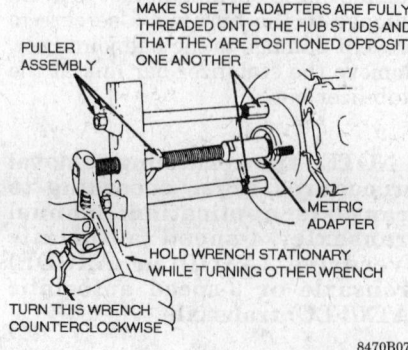

MAKE SURE THE ADAPTERS ARE FULLY THREADED ONTO THE HUB STUDS AND THAT THEY ARE POSITIONED OPPOSITE ONE ANOTHER

PULLER ASSEMBLY

METRIC ADAPTER

HOLD WRENCH STATIONARY WHILE TURNING OTHER WRENCH

TURN THIS WRENCH COUNTERCLOCKWISE

8470B075

Removing stub shaft from hub assembly

4. Cut the large boot clamp with a pair of side cutters and peel the clamp away from the boot. Roll the boot back over the shaft after the clamp has been removed.

5. Clamp the interconnecting shaft in a soft jawed vise and angle the CV-joint so the inner bearing race is exposed.

6. Using a brass drift and hammer, give a sharp tap to the inner bearing race to dislodge the internal snapring and separate the CV-joint from the interconnecting shaft. Take care to secure the CV-joint so it does not drop after separation. Remove the clamp and boot from the shaft.

7. Remove and discard the circlip at the end of the interconnecting shaft. Remove the stopring, located just below the circlip. The stopring should be replaced only if damaged or worn.

8. Inspect the CV-joint grease for contamination. If the CV-joint is operating satisfactorily and the grease does not appear to be contaminated, proceed to Step 19. If the lubricant appears contaminated, proceed to Step 9 and continue with disassembly.

9. Clamp the CV-joint stub shaft in a soft jawed vise with the outer face facing up. Be careful not to damage the dust seal.

10. Press down on the inner race until it tilts enough to remove the ball. A tight assembly can be tilted by tapping the inner race with a wooden dowel and hammer. Do not hit the cage.

11. With the cage sufficiently tilted, remove the ball from the cage. Continue until all balls are removed. If the balls are tight in the cage, use a small prybar with blunt edges to pry the balls from the cage.

NOTE: Use care to prevent damaging the inner race or cage spheres.

12. Pivot the cage and inner race assembly until it is straight up and down in the outer race. Align the cage windows with the outer race lands while pivoting the bearing cage. With the cage pivoted and aligned, lift the assembly from the outer race.

13. Pivot the inner race until it is straight up and down in the cage. Align 1 of the inner race lands with 1 of the cage windows and position the race through the window. Rotate the inner race up and out of the cage.

14. Clean all CV-joint parts (except boots) in solvent. Inspect the boots for cuts or other damage. Inspect the

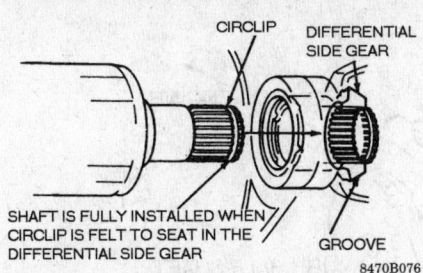

Seating circlip in transaxle differential side gear

CV-joint parts for excessive wear, looseness, pitting, rust and cracks.

NOTE: CV-joint parts are matched during assembly. Individual components are not available. If a part is found to be unserviceable, the entire CV-joint must be replaced.

To install:

15. Apply a light coating of suitable CV-joint grease on the inner and outer races. Install the inner race in the bearing cage.

16. Install the inner race and cage assembly in the outer race. Install the assembly vertically and pivot 90 degrees into position.

17. Align the bearing cage and inner race with the outer race. Tilt the inner race and cage and install a ball. Repeat until all 6 balls are installed.

18. The left and right interconnecting shafts are different, depending on year and vehicle application. The outboard end of the shaft is shorter from the end of the shaft to the end of the boot groove than the inboard end. Take a measurement to insure correct installation.

19. Install the new boot. Make sure the boot is seated in the mounting groove and secure it in position with a new clamp. Tighten the clamp securely using suitable boot clamp pliers, but not to the point where the clamp bridge is cut or the boot is damaged.

20. Clean the interconnecting shaft splines and install a new circlip and stop ring. To install the circlip correctly, start one end in the groove and work the circlip over the shaft end and into the groove.

21. Pack the CV-joint with at least 3½ oz. (100 g) of CV-joint grease.

22. With the boot peeled back, position the CV-joint on the shaft and tap into position using a plastic tipped hammer. The CV-joint is fully seated when the circlip locks into the groove cut into the CV-joint inner bearing race. Check for seating by attempting to pull the joint away from the shaft.

23. Remove all excess grease form the CV-joint external surface and position the boot over the joint.

24. Before installing the boot clamp, make sure all air pressure that may have built up in the boot is removed. Pry up on the boot lip to allow the air to escape.

25. The large end clamp should be installed after making sure the boot is seated in its groove. Tighten the clamp securely, but not to the point where the clamp bridge is cut or the boot is damaged.

26. Install the halfshaft assembly and lower the vehicle. Connect the negative battery cable.

Inboard CV-Joint Boot

1. Disconnect the negative battery cable. Raise and safely support the vehicle.

2. Remove the halfshaft assembly from the vehicle.

3. Clamp the halfshaft in a vise that is equipped with soft jaw covers. Do not allow the vise jaws to contact the boot or boot clamp.

4. Cut and remove both boot clamps and slide the boot back on the shaft. Remove the clamp by engaging the pincer jaws of boot clamp pliers

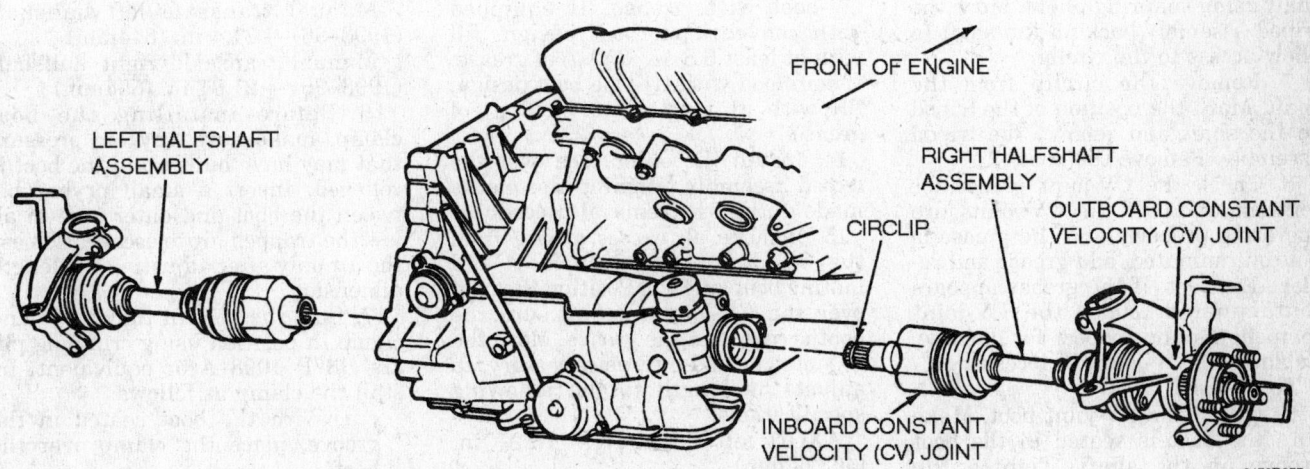

Halfshaft assembly removal and installation — AXOD and AXODE transaxle

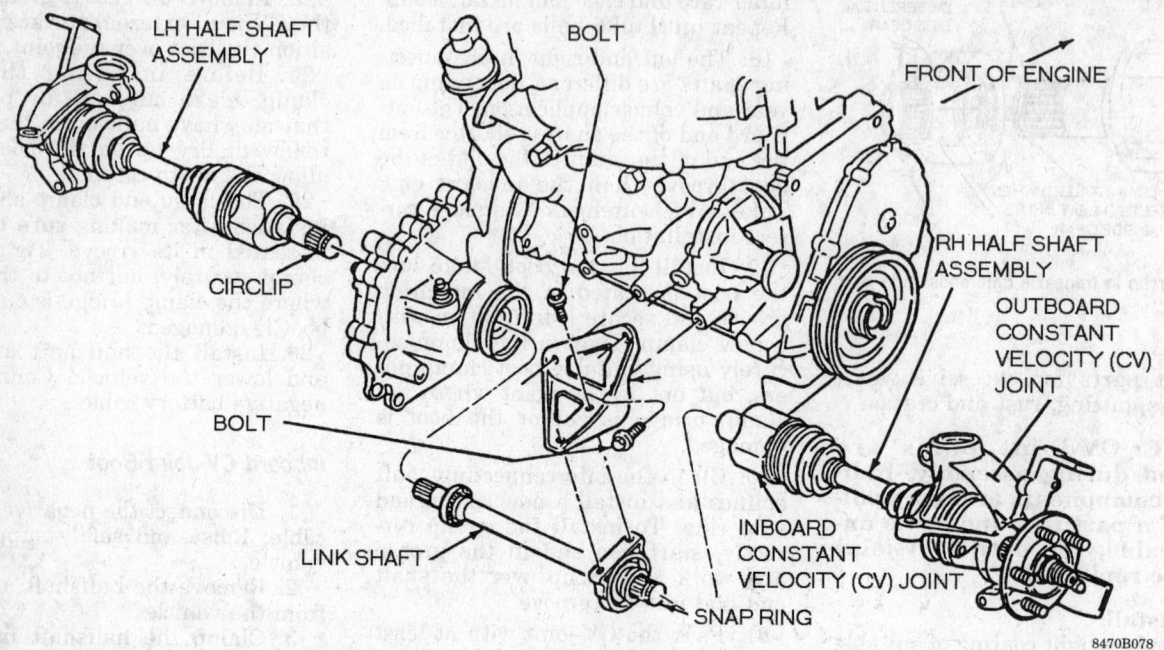

LH HALF SHAFT ASSEMBLY

BOLT

FRONT OF ENGINE

CIRCLIP

RH HALF SHAFT ASSEMBLY

OUTBOARD CONSTANT VELOCITY (CV) JOINT

BOLT

LINK SHAFT

INBOARD CONSTANT VELOCITY (CV) JOINT

SNAP RING

8470B078

Halfshaft assembly removal and installation — manual transaxle

D87P–1090–A or equivalent, in the closing hooks on the clamp and draw together. Disengage the windows and locking hooks and remove the clamp.

5. Mark the position of the outer race in relation to the shaft and remove the outer race.

6. Move the stoping back on the shaft using snapring pliers. Move the tripod assembly back on the shaft to allow access to the circlip.

7. Remove the circlip from the shaft. Mark the position of the tripod on the shaft and remove the tripod assembly. Remove the boot.

8. Check the CV-joint grease for contamination. If the CV-joints are operating properly and the grease is not contaminated, add grease and replace the boot. If the grease appears contaminated, clean the CV-joint components and inspect for damage. Replace the CV-joint, if necessary.

To install:

9. Install the CV-joint boot. Make sure the boot is seated in the boot groove on the shaft. Tighten the clamp using crimping pliers, but do not tighten to the point where the clamp bridge is cut or the boot is damaged.

10. Install the tripod assembly with chamfered side toward the stopring. Be sure to align the marks that were made during the removal procedure.

11. Install a new circlip. Compress the circlip and slide tripod assembly forward over the circlip to expose stopring groove.

12. Move the stopring into the groove using snapring pliers, making sure it is fully seated in the groove.

13. Fill the CV-joint outer race and CV-boot with grease. If equipped with conventional boot design, fill with at least 8.8 oz. (250 g) of grease. If equipped with tri-lobe boot design, fill with at least 6 oz. (170 g) of grease.

14. Install the outer race over the tripod assembly, aligning the marks made during the removal procedure.

15. Remove all excess grease from the CV-joint external surfaces and mating boot surface. Position the boot over the CV-joint making sure the boot is seated in the groove. Move the CV-joint in and out, as necessary, to adjust the length to the following specifications:

AXOD left halfshaft — 18.27 in. (463.65mm)

AXOD right halfshaft — 23.58 in. (598.55mm)

AXODE (1993–96 3.2L SHO engine) left halfshaft — 18.27 in. (463.65mm)

AXODE (1993–96 3.2L SHO engine) right halfshaft — 23.85 in. (606mm)

ATX/FLC left halfshaft — 22.80 in. (578.75mm)

ATX/FLC right halfshaft — 20.09 in. (510.05mm)

Manual transaxle left halfshaft (1992) — 21.24 in. (539.05mm)

Manual transaxle right halfshaft (1992) — 21.63 in. (549.05mm)

Manual transaxle left halfshaft (1993–96) — 21.4 in. (544mm)

Manual transaxle right halfshaft (1993–96) — 21.81 in. (554mm)

16. Before installing the boot clamp, make sure any air pressure that may have built up in the boot is relieved. Insert a small prybar between the boot and outer race to allow the trapped air to escape. Release the air only after adjusting the length dimension.

17. Seat the boot in the groove and clamp in position using crimping pliers D87P–1098–A or equivalent. Install the clamp as follows:

a. With the boot seated in the groove, place the clamp over the boot.

b. Engage hook C in the window.

c. Place the pincer jaws of the crimping pliers in closing hooks A and B.

d. Secure the clamp by drawing the closing hooks together. When windows 1 and 2 are above locking hooks D and E, the spring tab will

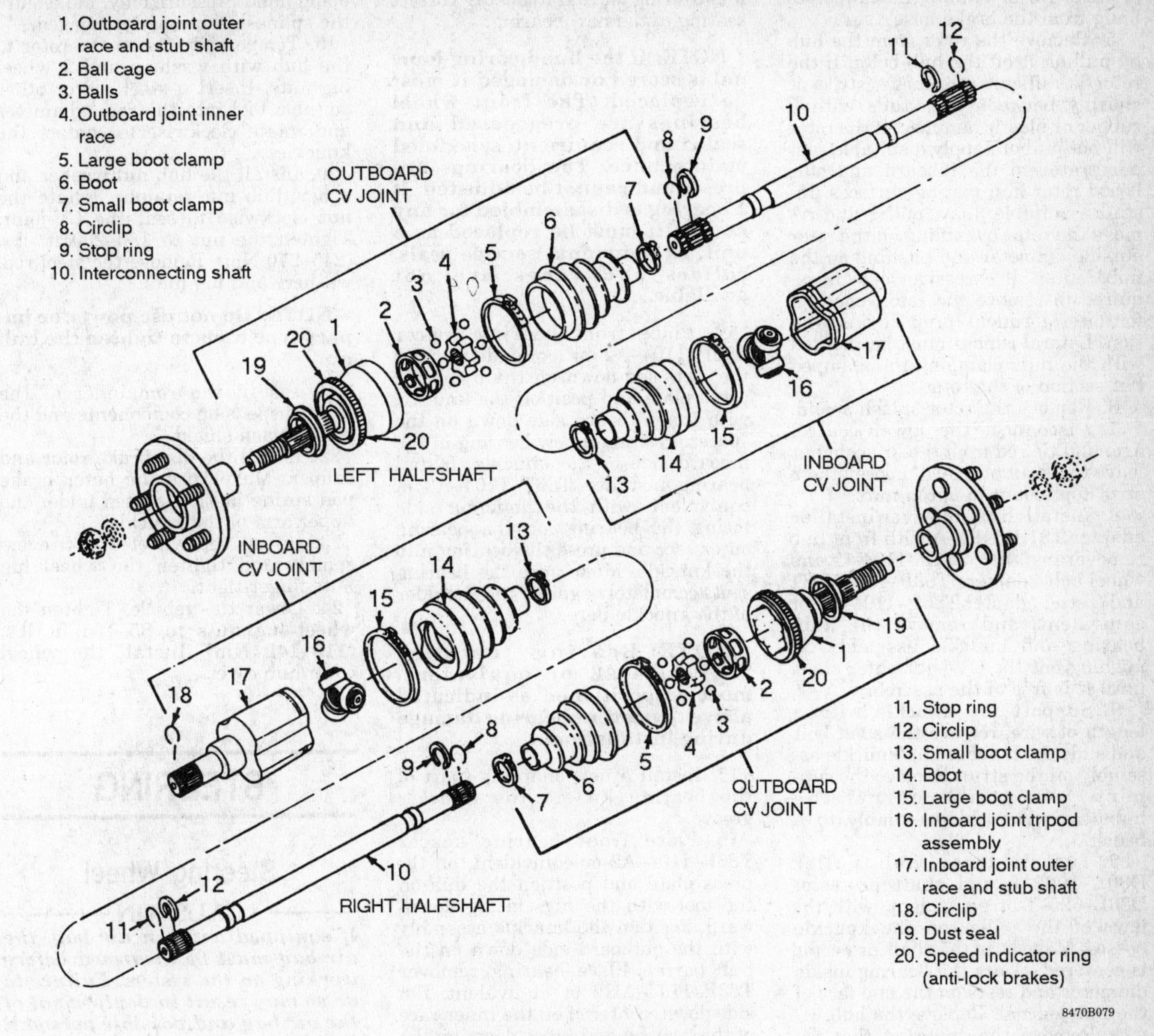

1. Outboard joint outer race and stub shaft
2. Ball cage
3. Balls
4. Outboard joint inner race
5. Large boot clamp
6. Boot
7. Small boot clamp
8. Circlip
9. Stop ring
10. Interconnecting shaft

OUTBOARD CV JOINT

LEFT HALFSHAFT

INBOARD CV JOINT

INBOARD CV JOINT

RIGHT HALFSHAFT

OUTBOARD CV JOINT

11. Stop ring
12. Circlip
13. Small boot clamp
14. Boot
15. Large boot clamp
16. Inboard joint tripod assembly
17. Inboard joint outer race and stub shaft
18. Circlip
19. Dust seal
20. Speed indicator ring (anti-lock brakes)

8470B079

Halfshaft and CV-joint disassembly view

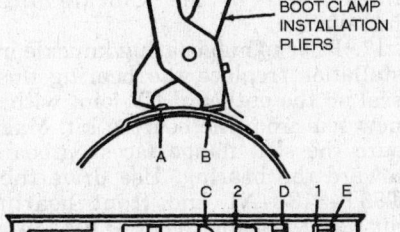

LOW PROFILE BOOT CLAMP INSTALLATION PLIERS

A B

C 2 D 1 E

A CLOSED B

8470B080

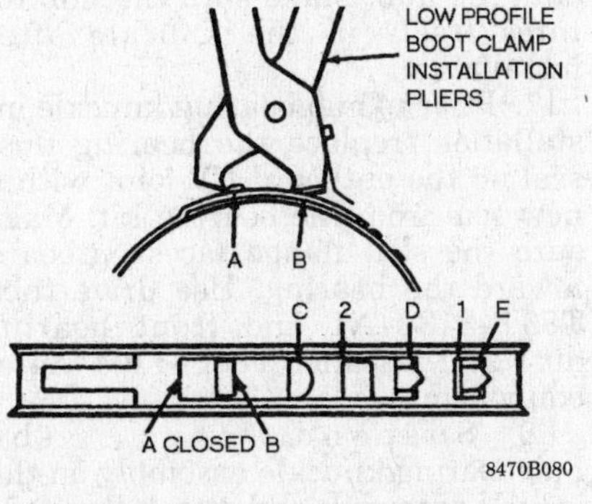

Inboard CV-joint boot clamp tightening procedure

press the windows over the locking hooks and engage the clamp.

18. Install the halfshaft and lower the vehicle. Connect the negative battery cable.

Front Wheel Hub, Knuckle and Bearings

REMOVAL AND INSTALLATION

1. Remove the wheel cover/hub cover and loosen the wheel nuts.

2. Remove the hub nut retainer and washer by applying sufficient torque to the nut to overcome the pre-

vailing torque feature of the crimp in the nut collar. Do not use an impact-type tool to remove the hub nut retainer. The hub nut retainer is not reusable and must be discarded after removal.

3. Raise the vehicle and support it safely. Remove the wheel and tire assembly.

4. Remove the brake caliper by loosening the caliper locating pins and rotating the caliper off the rotor, starting from the lower end of the caliper and lifting upwards. Do not remove the caliper pins from the caliper assembly. Once the caliper is free of the rotor, support it with a length

of wire. Do not allow the caliper to hang from the brake hose.

5. Remove the rotor from the hub by pulling it off the hub bolts. If the rotor is difficult to remove, strike it sharply between the studs with a rubber or plastic hammer. If the rotor will not pull off, apply a suitable rust penetrator to the inboard and outboard rotor hub mating surfaces. Install a suitable 3-jaw puller and remove the rotor by pulling on the rotor outside diameter and pushing on the hub center. If excessive force is required to remove the rotor, check it for lateral runout prior to installation. Lateral runout must be checked with the nuts clamping the stamped hat section of the rotor.

6. Remove the rotor splash shield.

7. Disconnect the lower control arm and tie rod from the knuckle but leave the strut attached. Loosen the 2 strut top mount-to-apron nuts.

8. Install hub remover/installer adapter T81P–1104–A with front hub remover/installer T81P–1104–C and wheel bolt adapters T83P–1104–BH1 and 2 stud adapter T86P–1104–A1 or equivalent, and remove the hub, bearing and knuckle assembly by pushing out the CV-joint outer shaft until it is free of the assembly.

9. Support the knuckle with a length of wire, remove the strut bolt and slide the hub/bearing/knuckle assembly off the strut. Remove the support wire and carry the hub/bearing/knuckle assembly to a bench.

10. Install front hub puller D80L–1002–L and shaft protector D80L–625–1 or equivalent, with the jaws of the puller on the knuckle bosses. Make sure the shaft protector is centered, clears the bearing inside diameter and rests on the end face of the hub journal. Remove the hub.

11. Remove the snapring that retains the bearing in the knuckle assembly and discard.

12. Using a suitable hydraulic press, place front bearing spacer T86P–1104–A2 or equivalent, on the press plate with the step side facing up and position the knuckle with the outboard side up on the spacer. Install front bearing remover T83P–1104–AH2 or equivalent, centered on the bearing inner race and press the bearing out of the knuckle. Discard the bearing.

To install:

13. Remove all foreign material from the knuckle bearing bore and

hub bearing journal to ensure correct seating of the new bearing.

NOTE: If the hub bearing journal is scored or damaged it must be replaced. The front wheel bearings are pregreased and sealed and require no scheduled maintenance. The bearings are preset and cannot be adjusted. If a bearing is disassembled for any reason, it must be replaced as a unit, as individual service seals, rollers and races are not available.

14. Place front bearing spacer T86P–1104–A2 or equivalent, with the step side down on the hydraulic press plate and position the knuckle with the outboard side down on the spacer. Position a new bearing in the inboard side of the knuckle. Install bearing installer T86P–1104–A3 or equivalent, with the undercut side facing the bearing, on the bearing outer race and press the bearing into the knuckle. Make sure the bearing seats completely against the shoulder of the knuckle bore.

NOTE: Bearing installer T86P–1104–A3 or equivalent, must be positioned as indicated above to prevent bearing damage during installation.

15. Install a new snapring (part of the bearing kit) in the knuckle groove.

16. Place front bearing spacer T86P–1104–A2 or equivalent, on the press plate and position the hub on the tool with the lugs facing downward. Position the knuckle assembly with the outboard side down on the hub barrel. Place bearing remover T83P–1104–AH2 or equivalent, flat side down, centered on the inner race of the bearing and press down on the tool until the bearing is fully seated onto the hub. Make sure the hub rotates freely in the knuckle after installation.

17. Prior to hub/bearing/knuckle installation, replace the bearing dust seal on the outboard CV-joint with a new seal from the bearing kit. Make sure the seal flange faces outboard toward the bearing. Use drive tube T83T–3132–A1 and front bearing dust seal installer T86P–1104–A4 or equivalent.

18. Suspend the hub/bearing/knuckle assembly on the vehicle with wire and attach the strut loosely to the knuckle. Lubricate the CV-joint stub shaft with SAE 30 weight motor oil and insert the shaft into the hub splines as far as possible

using hand pressure only. Make sure the splines are properly engaged.

19. Temporarily fasten the rotor to the hub with washers and 2 wheel lug nuts. Insert a steel rod or other suitable tool into the rotor diameter and rotate clockwise to contact the knuckle.

20. Install the hub nut washer and a new hub nut retainer. Rotate the nut clockwise to seat the CV-joint. Tighten the nut to 180–200 ft. lbs. (245–270 Nm). Remove the steel rod, washers and lug nuts.

NOTE: Do not use power or impact-type tools to tighten the hub nut.

21. Install the remainder of the front suspension components and the rotor splash shield.

22. Install the disc brake rotor and caliper. Make sure the outer brake pad spring hook is seated under the upper arm of the knuckle.

23. Install the wheel and tire assembly and tighten the wheel lug nuts finger-tight.

24. Lower the vehicle. Tighten the wheel lug nuts to 85–105 ft. lbs. (115–142 Nm). Install the wheel cover/hub cover.

STEERING

Steering Wheel

—— CAUTION ——
If equipped with an air bag, the air bag must be disarmed before working on the system. Failure to do so may result in deployment of the air bag and possible personal injury. Always wear safety glasses when servicing an air bag vehicle and when handling an air bag.

REMOVAL AND INSTALLATION

Taurus, Sable and Continental

1. Center the front wheels in the straight-ahead position. Disconnect the negative battery cable.

2. Disconnect the positive battery cable and wait 1 minute for the backup power supply in the diagnostic monitor to deplete its stored energy.

3. Remove the 4 air bag module retaining nuts and lift the module from the wheel. Disconnect the air bag wire harness from the air bag module

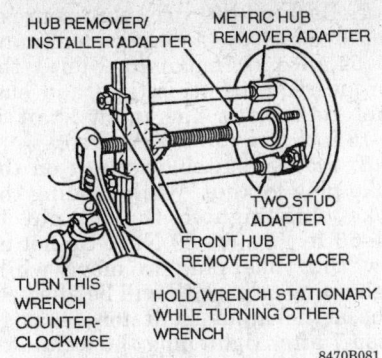

Separating the hub from the outer CV-joint

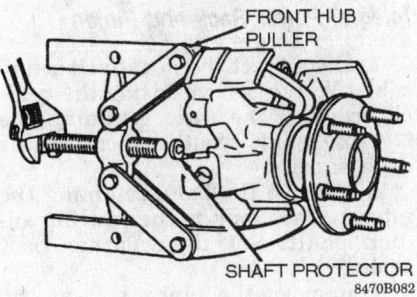

Removing the hub from the knuckle

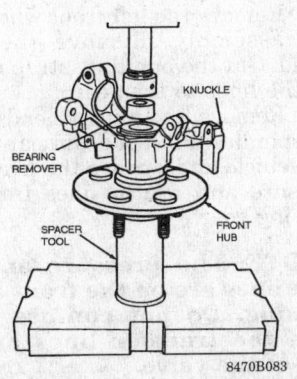

Front wheel bearing installation

and remove the module from the wheel. On 1993–96 Taurus SHO, remove steering wheel back cover plugs and 2 air bag module retaining nuts.

―――――― **CAUTION** ――――――
When carrying a live air bag, make sure the bag and trim cover are pointed away from the body. In the unlikely event of an accidental deployment, the bag will then deploy with minimal chance of injury. In addition, when placing a live air bag on a bench or other surface, always face the bag and trim cover up, away from the surface. This will reduce the motion of the module if it is accidentally deployed.

4. Disconnect the cruise control wire harness from the steering wheel. Remove and discard the steering wheel retaining bolt.
5. Install a suitable steering wheel puller and remove the steering wheel. Route the contact assembly wire harness through the steering wheel as the wheel is lifted off the shaft.

To install:
6. Make sure the vehicle's front wheels are in the straight-ahead position.
7. Route the contact assembly wire harness through the steering wheel opening at the 3 o'clock position and install the steering wheel on the shaft. The steering wheel and shaft alignment marks should be aligned. Make sure the air bag contact wire is not pinched.
8. Install a new steering wheel retaining bolt and tighten to 23–33 ft. lbs. (31–45 Nm).
9. Connect the cruise control wire harness to the wheel and snap the connector assembly into the steering wheel clip. Make sure the wiring does not get trapped between the steering wheel and contact assembly.
10. Connect the air bag wire harness to the air bag module and install the module to the steering wheel. Tighten the module retaining nuts to 36–47 inch lbs. (4.0–5.4 Nm). On 1993–96 Taurus SHO, tighten the module retaining nuts to 7.5–10 ft. lbs. (10.2–13.8 Nm) and install back cover plugs.
11. Connect the air bag backup power supply and the battery cable(s). Verify the air bag warning indicator.

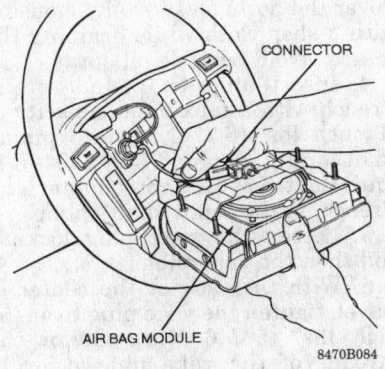

Air bag module removal

Steering Column

REMOVAL AND INSTALLATION

Taurus, Sable and Continental

1. Disconnect the negative battery cable. Disconnect the positive battery cable and wait 1 minute for the backup power supply in the diagnostic monitor to deplete its stored energy.
2. Remove the steering wheel.
3. Remove the left and right lower mouldings from the instrument panel by pulling up and snapping out of the retainers.
4. Remove the instrument panel lower trim cover and the lower steering column shroud.
5. Disconnect the air bag clockspring contact assembly wire harness. Apply 2 strips of tape across the contact assembly stator and rotor to prevent accidental rotation. Remove the 3 contact assembly retaining screws and pull the contact assembly off the steering column shaft.
6. Remove the tilt lever by unscrewing it from the column.
7. Rotate the ignition lock cylinder to the **RUN** position. Using an ⅛ in. drift, depress the lock cylinder retaining pin through the access hole and remove the lock cylinder.
8. Remove the 4 retaining screws from the lower shroud and remove the steering column shrouds.
9. Remove the 2 instrument panel reinforcement brace retaining bolts and remove the reinforcement.
10. If equipped with column shift, disconnect the shift position indicator cable from the actuator housing by removing 1 screw and disconnect the cable loop from the shift tube hook. If equipped with console shift, remove the interlock cable retaining screws and remove the cable.
11. Remove the 2 combination switch retaining screws and set the switch aside.
12. Remove the pinch bolt from the steering shaft flex coupling.
13. Disconnect the shift cable from the selector lever pivot. Remove the shift cable and bracket from the lower column mounting. Remove the column skid plate.
14. While supporting the column assembly, remove the 4 column assembly retaining nuts. Lower the column and disconnect the vacuum hoses at the parking brake release switch or remove the vacuum release assembly.
15. Remove the column from the vehicle.

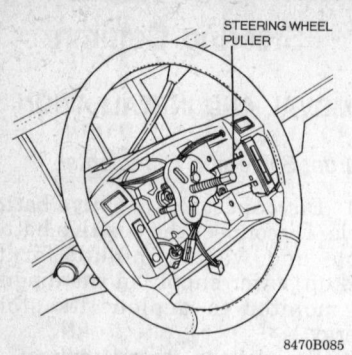

STEERING WHEEL PULLER

8470B085

Steering wheel removal — Taurus, Sable and Continental

To install:

16. Align the column lower universal joint to the lower shaft. Install 1 bolt and tighten to 31–41 ft. lbs. (41–56 Nm). Connect the parking brake release vacuum hoses.

17. Support the column assembly to the column support bracket. Install the 4 retaining nuts and tighten to 10–14 ft. lbs. (13–19 Nm).

18. Position the shift cable bracket, with the shift cable attached, to the lower 2 screws of the column. Tighten to 5–8 ft. lbs. (7–11 Nm). Snap the shift cable onto the shift selector pivot ball.

19. If equipped with automatic console shift, position the interlock cable and install the retaining screws.

20. Position the combination switch and install the 2 retaining screws. Tighten to 18–26 inch lbs. (2–3 Nm). Connect all electrical connectors.

21. If equipped with column shift, attach the shift position indicator cable loop on the shift selector hook and install the cable bracket to the actuator housing. Install the retaining screw and tighten to 5–8 ft. lbs. (7–11 Nm).

22. Install the steering column skid plate and tighten the retaining nuts to 15–25 ft. lbs. (20–34 Nm).

23. Install the upper and lower column shrouds and the instrument panel reinforcement brace.

24. Install the lower instrument panel cover. Snap the right and left lower instrument panel mouldings into place.

25. Install the lock cylinder assembly and the tilt lever.

26. Install the air bag clockspring contact assembly screws and tighten to 18–26 inch lbs. (2–3 Nm). Route

the contact assembly down the column and connect to the wire harness.

NOTE: If a new contact assembly is being installed, remove the plastic lock mechanism after the contact assembly is secured to the column.

27. Install the steering wheel with a new bolt. Tighten to 23–33 ft. lbs. (31–48 Nm). Position the air bag module to the steering wheel. Install the 4 retaining nuts and tighten to 36–47 inch lbs. (4.0–5.4 Nm).

28. Connect the battery cable(s).

Power Rack and Pinion

The Integral Power Rack and Pinion system is standard equipment on most Taurus and Sable vehicles. The Variable Assist Power Steering (VAPS) system is optional on the Taurus GL and standard on most Sables and all Continentals. The VAPS system can be identified by the actuator valve on the power steering gear assembly.

ADJUSTMENT

Integral Power Rack and Pinion

RACK YOKE PLUG CLEARANCE

NOTE: The rack yoke clearance adjustment is not a normal service adjustment. It is only required when the input shaft and valve assembly is removed.

1. Remove the steering gear from the vehicle. Clean the exterior of the steering gear thoroughly.

2. Install the steering gear in a suitable holding fixture. Do not remove the external transfer tubes unless they are leaking or damaged. If these lines are removed, they must be replaced with new ones.

3. Drain the power steering fluid by rotating the input shaft lock-to-lock twice, using a suitable tool. Cover the ports on the valve housing with a shop cloth while draining the gear to avoid possible oil spray.

4. Insert an inch pound torque wrench with a maximum capacity of 60 inch lbs. (6.77 Nm) into pinion shaft torque adapter T74P–3504–R or equivalent. Position the adapter and wrench on the input shaft splines.

5. Loosen the yoke plug locknut and then the yoke plug.

6. With the rack at the center of travel, tighten the yoke plug to 45–50 inch lbs. (5–5.6 Nm). Clean the threads of the yoke plug prior to tightening to prevent a false reading.

7. Back off the yoke plug approximately ⅛ turn, 44 degrees minimum to 54 degrees maximum, until the torque required to initiate and sustain rotation of the input shaft is 7–18 inch lbs. (0.78–2.03 Nm).

8. Place a suitable wrench on the yoke plug locknut. While holding the yoke plug, tighten the locknut to 44–66 ft. lbs. (60–89 Nm). Do not allow the yoke plug to move while tightening or preload will be affected. Check the input shaft torque as in Step 7 after tightening the locknut.

9. Install the steering gear.

REMOVAL AND INSTALLATION

Integral Power Rack and Pinion

1. Disconnect the negative battery cable. Working from inside the vehicle, remove the nuts retaining the steering shaft weather boot to the dash panel.

2. Remove the bolts retaining the intermediate shaft to the steering column shaft. Set the weather boot aside.

3. Remove the pinch bolt at the steering gear input shaft and remove the intermediate shaft. Raise the vehicle and support safely.

4. Remove the left front wheel and tire assembly. Remove the heat shield. Cut the bundling strap retaining the lines to the gear.

5. Remove the tie rod ends from the spindles. Place a drain pan under the vehicle and remove the hydraulic pressure and return lines from the steering gear.

NOTE: The pressure and return lines are on the front of the housing. Do not confuse them with the transfer lines on the side of the valve.

6. Remove the nuts from the gear mounting bolts. The bolts are pressed into the gear housing and should not be removed during gear removal.

7. Push the weather boot end into the vehicle and lift the gear out of the mounting holes. Rotate the gear so the input shaft will pass between the brake booster and the floor pan. Carefully start working the steering gear out through the left fender apron opening.

8. Rotate the input shaft so it clears the left fender apron opening and complete the removal of the steering gear. If the steering gear seems to be stuck, check the right tie rod to ensure the stud is not caught on anything.

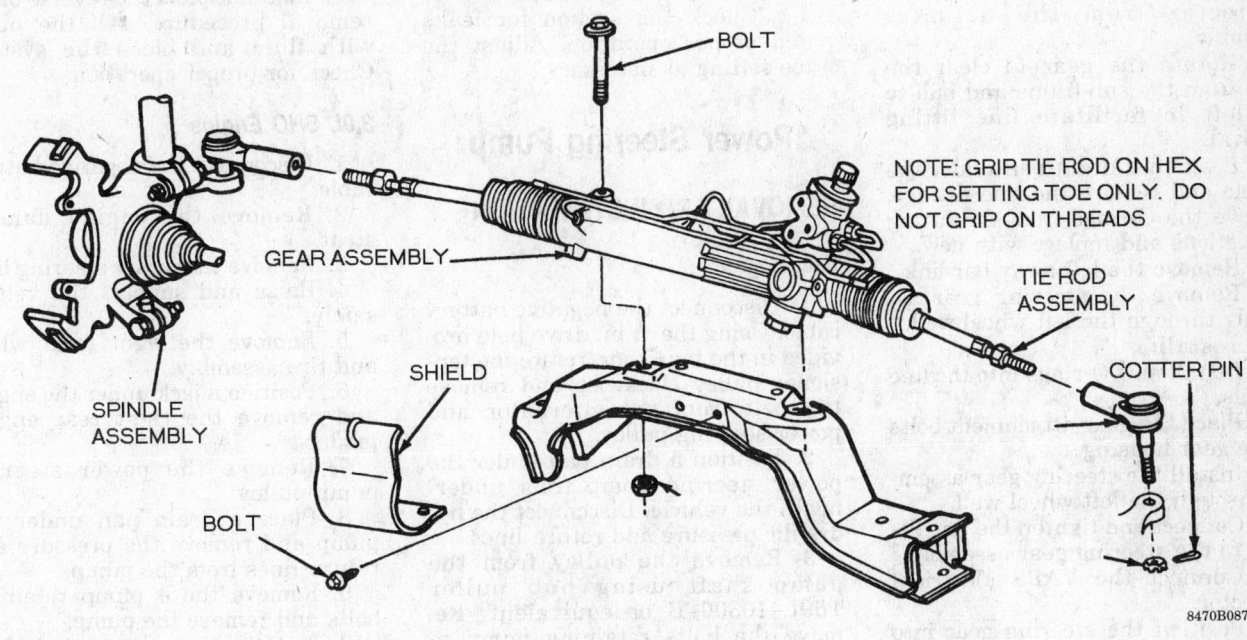

BOLT

NOTE: GRIP TIE ROD ON HEX FOR SETTING TOE ONLY. DO NOT GRIP ON THREADS

GEAR ASSEMBLY

TIE ROD ASSEMBLY

SHIELD

COTTER PIN

SPINDLE ASSEMBLY

BOLT

8470B087

Integral power rack and pinion

To install:

9. Install new plastic seals on the hydraulic line fittings.

10. Insert the steering gear through the left fender apron. Rotate the input shaft forward to completely clear the fender apron opening.

11. To allow the gear to pass between the brake booster and the floorpan, rotate the input shaft rearward. Align the steering gear bolts to the bolt holes. Install the mounting nuts and torque them to 85–100 ft. lbs. (115–135 Nm). Lower the vehicle.

12. From inside the engine compartment, install the hydraulic pressure and return lines. Tighten the pressure line to 15–20 ft. lbs. (20–28 Nm) and the return line to 15–20 ft. lbs. (20–28 Nm). Swivel movement of the lines is normal when the fittings are properly tightened.

13. Raise the vehicle and support safely. Secure the pressure and return lines to the transfer tube with a bundle strap. Install the heat shield.

14. Install the tie rod ends to spindles. Torque the castle nuts to 35 ft. lbs. (48 Nm). If necessary, torque the nuts a little bit more to align the slot in the nut for the cotter pin. Install the cotter pin.

15. Install the left front wheel and tire assembly and lower the vehicle.

Working from inside the vehicle, pull the weather boot end out of the vehicle and install it over the valve housing. Install the intermediate shaft to the steering gear input shaft. Install the the inner weather boot to the floor pan.

16. Install the intermediate shaft to the steering column shaft. Fill the power steering system.

17. Check the system for leaks and proper operation. Adjust the toe setting as necessary.

Variable Assist Power Steering (VAPS) System

The Variable Assist Power Steering (VAPS) system used on these vehicles consists of a micro-processor based module, a power rack and pinion steering gear, an actuator valve assembly, hose assemblies and a high efficiency power steering pump.

1. Disconnect the negative battery cable.

2. On the Taurus and Sable:

a. Working from inside the vehicle, remove the nuts retaining the steering shaft weather boot to the dash panel.

b. Remove the 2 bolts retaining the intermediate shaft to the steering column shaft. Set the weather boot aside.

c. Remove the pinch bolt at the steering gear input shaft and remove the intermediate shaft. Raise the vehicle and support safely.

3. On the Continental:

a. Remove primary steering column boot attachments.

b. Remove the bolts retaining the intermediate shaft and remove the intermediate shaft.

c. Remove the secondary column boot from inside of passenger compartment. Raise the vehicle and support safely.

4. Remove the front wheel and tire assemblies. Support the vehicle under the rear edge of the sub-frame.

5. Remove the tie rod cotter pins and nuts. Remove the tie rod ends from the spindle.

6. Remove the tie rod ends from the shaft. Mark the position of the jam nut to maintain the alignment.

7. Remove the nuts from the gear-to-sub-frame attaching bolts.

8. Remove both height sensor attachments on Continental.

9. Remove the rear sub-frame-to-body attaching bolts.

10. Remove the exhaust pipe-to-catalytic converter attachment.

11. Lower the vehicle carefully until the subframe separates from the body; approximately 4 in.

12. Remove the heat shield band and fold the shield down.

13. Disconnect the VAPS electrical connector from the actuator assembly.

14. Rotate the gear to clear the bolts from the sub-frame and pull to the left to facilitate line fitting removal.

15. Position a drain pan under the vehicle and remove the line fittings. Remove the O-rings from the fitting connections and replace with new.

16. Remove the left sway bar link.

17. Remove the steering gear assembly through the left wheel well.

To install:

18. Install new O-rings into the line fittings.

19. Place the gear attachment bolts in the gear housing.

20. Install the steering gear assembly through the left wheel well.

21. Connect and tighten the line fittings to the steering gear assembly.

22. Connect the VAPS electrical connector.

23. Position the steering gear into the sub-frame.

24. Install the tie rod ends onto the shaft.

25. Install the heat shield band.

26. Attach the tie rod ends onto the spindle. Install the nuts and secure with new cotter pins.

27. Attach the sway bar link.

28. Raise the vehicle until the sub-frame contacts the body. Install the sub-frame attaching bolts.

29. Install the gear-to-sub-frame nuts and torque to 85–100 ft. lbs. (115–135 Nm).

30. Attach the exhaust pipe to the catalytic converter.

31. Attach the height sensors on Continental, install the wheel and tire assemblies and lower the vehicle.

32. Fill the power steering system.

33. On the Continental:

  a. Install the secondary steering column boot and attach the intermediate shaft to the steering gear. Tighten the bolt to 30–38 ft. lbs. (41–51 Nm).

  b. Install the primary steering column boot and attach the intermediate shaft to the steering column.

  c. Bleed the system and align the front end.

34. On the Taurus and Sable:

  a. Working from inside the vehicle, pull the weather boot end out of the vehicle and install it over the valve housing. Install the intermediate shaft to the steering gear input shaft. Install the the inner weather boot to the floor pan.

  b. Install the intermediate shaft to the steering column shaft. Fill the power steering system.

  c. Check the system for leaks and proper operation. Adjust the toe setting as necessary.

Power Steering Pump

REMOVAL AND INSTALLATION

3.8L Engine

1. Disconnect the negative battery cable. Using the ½ in. drive hole provided in the tensioner, rotate the tensioner pulley clockwise and remove the belt from the alternator and power steering pulley.

2. Position a drain pan under the power steering pump from underneath the vehicle. Disconnect the hydraulic pressure and return lines.

3. Remove the pulley from the pump shaft using hub puller T69L–10300–B or equivalent. Remove the bolts retaining pump to bracket and remove the power steering pump.

4. Installation is the reverse of the removal procedure. Fill the pump with fluid and bleed the system. Check the system for proper operation.

NOTE: To install the power steering pump pulley, use steering pump pulley replacer T65P–3A733–C or equivalent. When using this tool, the small diameter threads must be fully engaged in the pump shaft before pressing on the pulley. Hold the head screw and turn the nut to install the pulley. Install the pulley face flush with the pump shaft within ± 0.100 in. (0.25mm).

3.0L Engine, Except SHO

1. Disconnect the negative battery cable. Loosen the idler pulley and remove the power steering belt.

2. Remove the radiator overflow bottle in order to gain access to the 3 screws attaching the pulleys to the pulley hub.

3. Matchmark both pulley to hub positions to maintain balance.

4. Remove the pulleys from the pulley hub.

5. Remove the return line from the pump. Be prepared to catch any spilled fluid in a suitable container.

6. Back off the pressure line attaching nut completely. The line will separate from the pump connection when the pump is removed.

7. Remove the pump mounting bolts and remove the pump.

8. Installation is the reverse of the removal procedure. Fill the pump with fluid and bleed the system. Check for proper operation.

3.0L SHO Engine

1. Disconnect the negative battery cable.

2. Remove the engine damper strut.

3. Remove the power steering belt.

4. Raise and support the vehicle safely.

5. Remove the right front wheel and tire assembly.

6. Position a jack under the engine and remove the right rear engine mount.

7. Remove the power steering pump pulley.

8. Place a drain pan under the pump and remove the pressure and return lines from the pump.

9. Remove the 4 pump retaining bolts and remove the pump.

10. Installation is the reverse of the removal procedure. Tighten the pump retaining bolts to 15–24 ft. lbs. (20–33 Nm). Fill the pump with fluid and bleed the system. Check for proper operation.

BELT ADJUSTMENT

Except 3.0L SHO Engine

Belt tension is maintained by an automatic tensioner and does not require adjustment.

3.0L SHO Engine

1. Loosen the idler pulley nut and turn the adjusting screw until the belt is adjusted.

2. Measure the belt tension at a point mid-way between the pulleys, using a suitable offset belt tension gauge. New belts should measure 154–198 lbs. or used belts 112–157 lbs. The allowable minimum belt tension is 80 lbs.

3. Tighten the idler pulley nut to 25–37 ft. lbs. (34–50 Nm).

SYSTEM BLEEDING

1. Disconnect the ignition coil wire.

2. Fill the reservoir with power steering fluid.

3. Raise and safely support the vehicle so the front wheels are off the ground.

4. Crank the engine with the starter and add fluid to the reservoir

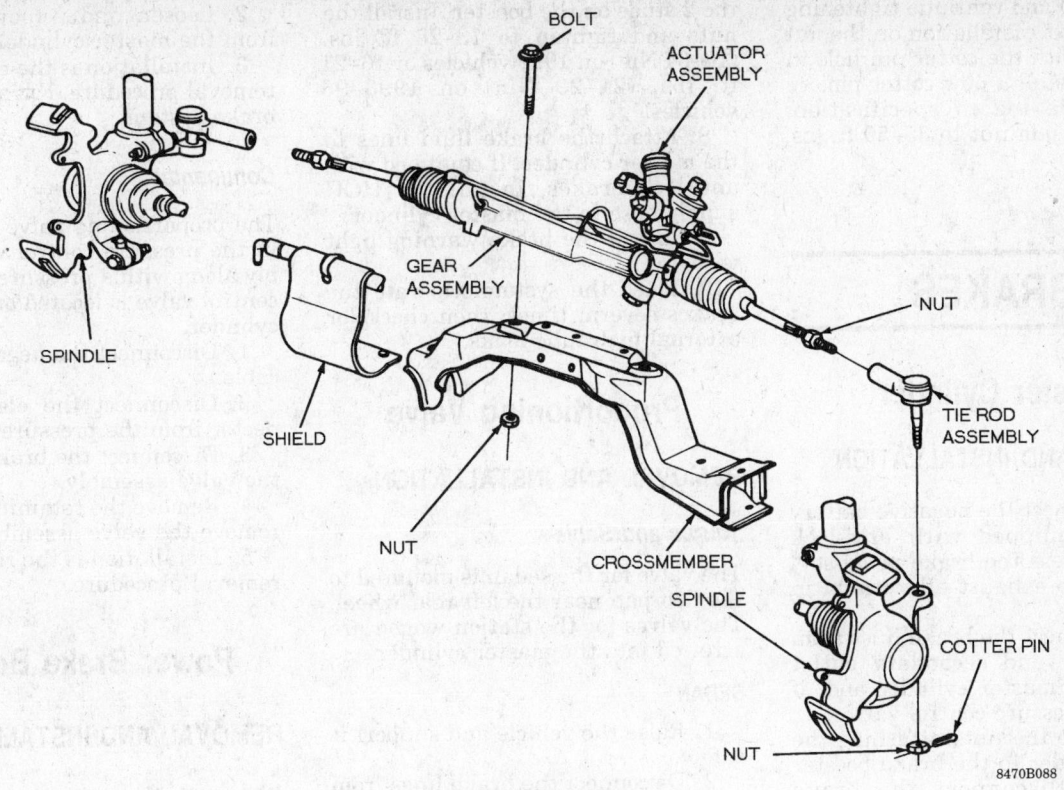

VAPS power rack and pinion

until the level remains constant. Rotate the steering wheel from lock-to-lock while cranking the engine.

NOTE: The front wheels must be off the floor during lock-to-lock rotation of the steering wheel.

5. Check the fluid level and add, as necessary.
6. Connect the ignition coil wire and lower the front wheels.
7. Start the engine and let it run for several minutes. Rotate the steering wheel from lock-to-lock.
8. Turn the engine **OFF** and check the fluid level. Add fluid, if necessary.
9. Check the fluid for the presence of trapped air. If apparent that air is still in the system, fabricate or obtain a vacuum tester and purge the system as follows:
    a. Remove the pump dipstick cap assembly.
    b. Check and fill the pump reservoir with fluid to the **COLD FULL** mark on the dipstick.
    c. Disconnect the ignition coil wire. Raise the front of the vehicle and support safely.
    d. Crank the engine with the starter and check the fluid level. Do not turn the steering wheel at this time.

    e. Fill the pump reservoir to the **COLD FULL** mark on the dipstick. Crank the engine with the starter while cycling the steering wheel lock-to-lock. Check the fluid level.
    f. Tightly insert a suitable size rubber stopper and air evacuator pump into the reservoir fill neck. Connect the ignition coil wire.
    g. With the engine idling, apply a 15 in. Hg vacuum to the reservoir for 3 minutes. As air is purged from the system, the vacuum will drop off. Maintain the vacuum on the system as required throughout the 3 minutes.
    h. Remove the vacuum source. Fill the reservoir to the **COLD FULL** mark on the dipstick.
    i. With the engine idling, re-apply 15 in. Hg vacuum source to the reservoir. Slowly cycle the steering wheel from lock-to-lock every 30 seconds for approximately 5 minutes. Do not hold the steering wheel on the stops during cycling. Maintain the vacuum as air purges.
    j. Release the vacuum and disconnect the vacuum source. Add fluid as required.
    k. Start the engine and cycle the wheel slowly. Check for leaks at all connections.

    l. Lower the front wheels.
10. In cases of severe aeration, repeat the procedure.

Tie Rod Ends

REMOVAL AND INSTALLATION

1. Remove and discard the cotter pin and nut from the worn tie rod end ball stud.
2. Disconnect the tie rod end from the steering spindle, using tie rod remover tool 3290–D or equivalent.
3. Hold the tie rod end with a wrench and loosen the tie rod jam nut.
4. Note the depth to which the tie rod was located using the jam nut as a marker, then grip the tie rod with a pair of suitable pliers and remove the tie rod end assembly from the tie rod.
    To install:
5. Clean the tie rod threads. Thread the new tie rod end into the tie rod to the same depth as the removed tie rod end.
6. Place the tie rod end stud into the steering spindle. Make sure the front wheels are pointed straight-ahead before connecting the stud to the spindle.
7. Install a new nut on the tie rod end stud. Tighten the nut to 35 ft.

lbs. (48 Nm) and continue tightening until the next castellation on the nut is aligned with the cotter pin hole in the stud. Install a new cotter pin.

8. Set the toe to specification. Tighten the jam nut to 35–50 ft. lbs. (47–68 Nm).

BRAKES

Master Cylinder

REMOVAL AND INSTALLATION

1. Disconnect the negative battery cable. If equipped with anti-lock brakes, depress the brake pedal several times to exhaust all vacuum in the system.

2. Disconnect the brake lines from the primary and secondary outlet ports of the master cylinder and, if equipped, pressure control valves.

3. Remove the nuts attaching the master cylinder to the brake booster assembly. Disconnect the brake warning light wire. If equipped with anti-lock brakes, disconnect the Hydraulic Control Unit (HCU) supply hose at the master cylinder and secure in a position to prevent loss of brake fluid.

4. Slide the master cylinder forward and upward from the vehicle.

To install:

5. Before installation, bench bleed the new master cylinder as follows:

a. Mount the new master cylinder in a holding fixture. Be careful not to damage the housing.

b. Fill the master cylinder reservoir with brake fluid.

c. Using a suitable tool inserted into the booster pushrod cavity, push the master cylinder piston in slowly. Place a suitable container under the master cylinder to catch the fluid being expelled from the outlet ports.

d. Place a finger tightly over each outlet port and allow the master cylinder piston to return.

e. Repeat the procedure until clear fluid only is expelled from the master cylinder. Plug the outlet ports and remove the master cylinder from the holding fixture.

6. Install a new seal in the groove in the master cylinder mounting face on vehicles equipped with anti-lock brakes.

7. Position the master cylinder over the booster pushrod and onto the 2 studs on the booster. Install the nuts and tighten to 13–25 ft. lbs. (18–34 Nm) on 1992 vehicles or 16–21 ft. lbs. (21–29 Nm) on 1993–96 vehicles.

8. Attach the brake fluid lines to the master cylinder. If equipped with anti-lock brakes, install the HCU supply hose to the master cylinder.

9. Install the brake warning light wire.

10. Bleed the system. Operate the brakes several times, then check for external hydraulic leaks.

Proportioning Valve

REMOVAL AND INSTALLATION

Taurus and Sable

The valve for the sedan is mounted to the floorpan near the left rear wheel. The valves for the station wagon are screwed into the master cylinder.

SEDAN

1. Raise the vehicle and support it safely.

2. Disconnect the brake lines from the valve assembly and note their position.

3. Remove the screw retaining the valve bracket to the lower suspension arm. Remove the 2 screws retaining the valve bracket to the underbody and remove the assembly.

NOTE: The service replacement valve will have a red plastic gauge clip on the valve and must not be removed until it is installed on the vehicle.

To install:

4. Make sure the rear suspension is in the full rebound position.

5. Make sure the red plastic gauge clip is in position on the valve and that the operating rod lower adjustment screw is loose.

6. Position the valve lower mounting bracket to the lower suspension arm. Install 1 retaining screw and tighten to 4–6 ft. lbs. (6–8 Nm). Make sure the valve adjuster is resting on the lower bracket and install the setscrew.

7. Connect the brake lines in the same position as removed. Bleed the rear brakes.

8. Remove the red plastic gauge clip and lower the vehicle.

WAGON

1. Disconnect the primary or secondary brake line from the master cylinder, as necessary.

2. Loosen and remove the valve from the master cylinder housing.

3. Installation is the reverse of the removal procedure. Fill and bleed the brake system.

Continental

The proportioning valve is contained in the pressure control valve assembly along with a pressure switch. The control valve is located on the master cylinder.

1. Disconnect the negative battery cable.

2. Disconnect the electrical connector from the pressure switch.

3. Disconnect the brake lines from the valve assembly.

4. Remove the retaining screw and remove the valve assembly.

5. Installation is the reverse of the removal procedure.

Power Brake Booster

REMOVAL AND INSTALLATION

Without Anti-lock Brakes

1. Disconnect the battery ground cable and remove the brake lines from the master cylinder.

2. Disconnect the manifold vacuum hose and the warning indicator. Remove the retaining nuts and the master cylinder.

3. From under the instrument panel, remove the brake light switch wiring connector from the switch. Remove the pushrod retainer and outer nylon washer from the brake pin. Slide the brake light switch along the brake pedal pin, far enough for the outer hole to clear the pin.

4. Remove the switch by sliding it upward. Remove the booster to dash panel retaining nuts. Slide the booster pushrod and pushrod bushing off the brake pedal pin.

5. Remove the screws and position the vacuum fitting at the dash panel aside. Position the wire harness aside. Remove the transaxle shift cable and bracket.

6. Move the booster forward until the booster studs clear the dash panel and remove the booster.

7. Installation is the reverse of the removal procedure. Bleed the brake system.

NOTE: If equipped with cruise control, the vacuum dump valve must be adjusted if the brake booster has been removed.

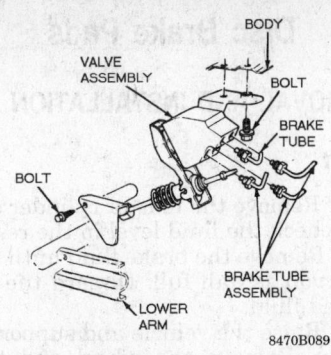

**Brake pressure control valve —
Taurus and Sable sedan**

With Anti-lock Brake

1. Disconnect the negative battery cable. Pump the brake pedal until all vacuum is removed from the booster. This will prevent the O-ring from being sucked into the booster during disassembly.

2. Disconnect the manifold vacuum hose from the booster check valve and the electrical connector from the master cylinder reservoir cap.

3. Remove the brake lines from the primary and secondary outlet ports of the master cylinder and remove the Hydraulic Control Unit (HCU) supply hose. Plug the ports and reservoir feed to prevent brake fluid from leaking onto paint and wiring.

4. Working under the instrument panel, remove the brake light switch wiring connector from the switch. Disengage the pedal position switch from the stud. Remove the hairpin retainer and outer nylon washer from the pedal pin. Slide the brake light switch off the brake pedal just far enough for the outer arm to clear the pin. Remove the switch.

5. Remove the booster to dash panel attaching nuts. Slide the bushing and booster pushrod off the brake pedal pin.

6. Move the booster forward until the booster studs clear the dash panel. Remove the booster and master cylinder assembly.

7. Place the booster and master cylinder assembly on a bench. Remove the 2 nuts attaching the master cylinder to the booster and remove the master cylinder.

To install:

8. Slide the master cylinder onto the booster studs. Make sure the O-ring is in place in the groove on the master cylinder and install the 2 attaching nuts. Tighten the nuts to 13–25 ft. lbs. (18–34 Nm) on 1992 ve-

hicles or 16–21 ft. lbs. (21–29 Nm) on 1993–96 vehicles.

9. Position the booster/master cylinder assembly on the dash panel.

10. Working under the instrument panel, install the booster pushrod and bushing on the brake pedal pin. Fasten the booster to the dash panel with self-locking nuts. Tighten the nuts to 12–22 ft. lbs. (16–30 Nm) on 1992 vehicles or 16–21 ft. lbs. (21–29 Nm) on 1993–96 vehicles.

11. Position the brake light switch so it straddles the booster pushrod with the switch slot towards the pedal blade and hole just clearing the pin. Slide the switch completely onto the pin.

12. Install the outer nylon washer on the pin and secure all parts to the pin with the hairpin retainer. Make sure the retainer is fully installed and locked over the pedal pin. Install the brake light switch wiring connector.

13. Install the pedal travel switch. To adjust the switch, push the switch plunger fully into the switch housing. This zeros out the switch adjustment so it can be automatically reset to the correct dimension during the following steps:

   a. Slowly pull the arm back out of the switch housing past the detent point. At this point it should be impossible to reattach the arm to the pin unless the brake pedal is forced down.

   b. Depress the brake pedal until the switch hook can be snapped onto the pin. Snap the hook onto the pin and pull the brake pedal back up to its normal at rest position. This automatically sets the switch to the proper adjustment.

14. Connect the brake lines to the master cylinder and tighten to 10–18 ft. lbs. (14–24 Nm). Connect the HCU supply hose to the reservoir.

15. Connect the manifold vacuum hose to the booster check valve and the electrical connector to the master cylinder reservoir cap.

16. Connect the negative battery cable and bleed the brake system.

Brake Caliper

REMOVAL AND INSTALLATION

Front

1. Raise and support the vehicle safely.

2. Remove the wheel and tire assembly. Mark the caliper to ensure that it is reinstalled on the correct knuckle.

3. Disconnect the flexible brake hose from the caliper. Remove the hollow retaining bolt that connects the hose fitting to the caliper. Remove the hose assembly from the caliper and plug the hose.

4. Remove the caliper locating pins.

5. Lift the caliper off of the rotor, integral knuckle and anchor plate using a rotating motion.

———— **WARNING** ————
Do not pry directly against the plastic piston or damage to the piston will result.

To install:

6. Retract the piston fully in the piston bore. Position the caliper assembly above the rotor with the anti-rattle spring under the upper arm of the knuckle. Install the caliper over the rotor with a rotating motion. Make sure the inner and outer shoes are properly positioned and the outer anti-rattle spring is properly positioned. Make sure the correct caliper assembly, as marked during removal, is installed on the correct knuckle. The caliper bleed screw should be positioned on top of the caliper when assembled on the vehicle.

7. Lubricate the locating pins and the inside of the insulators with silicone grease. Install the locating pins through the caliper insulators and hand start the threads into the knuckle attaching holes. Tighten the locating pins to 18–25 ft. lbs. (24–34 Nm).

8. Remove the plug and install the brake hose on the caliper with a new copper washer on each side of the fitting outlet. Insert the attaching bolt through the washers and fittings and tighten to 30–45 ft. lbs. (40–60 Nm).

9. Bleed the brake system, filling the master cylinder as required.

10. Install the wheel and lower the vehicle. Pump the brake pedal prior to moving the vehicle to position the brake linings.

Rear

1. Raise and support the vehicle safely.

2. Remove the wheel and tire assembly.

3. Remove the brake flex hose from the caliper assembly.

4. Remove the retaining clip from the parking brake at the caliper. Disengage the parking brake cable end from the lever arm.

5. Hold the slider pin hex-heads with an open-end wrench and remove the pinch bolts. Lift the caliper as-

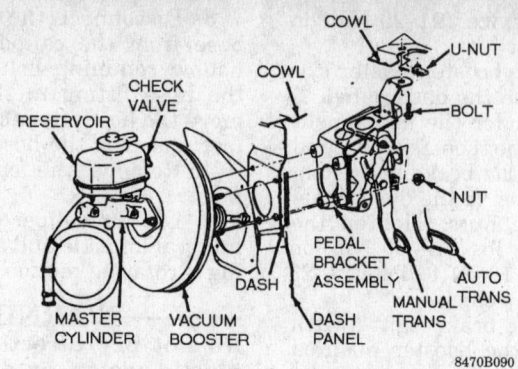

CONSTANT VELOCITY
JOINT

Brake booster assembly with anti-lock brakes

Disc Brake Pads

REMOVAL AND INSTALLATION

Front

1. Remove the master cylinder cap and check the fluid level in the reservoir. Remove the brake fluid until the reservoir is half full. Discard the removed fluid.

2. Raise the vehicle and support it safely. Remove the wheel and tire assembly.

3. Remove the caliper locating pins. Lift the caliper assembly from the integral knuckle and anchor plate and rotor using a rotating motion. Suspend the caliper inside the fender housing with wire. Do not allow the caliper to hang from the brake hose.

— **WARNING** —
Do not pry directly against the plastic piston or damage will result.

4. Remove the inner and outer brake pads. Inspect the rotor braking surfaces for scoring and machine as necessary. Refer to the minimum rotor thickness specification when machining. If machining is not necessary, hand sand the glaze from the

sembly away from the anchor plate. Remove the slider pins and boots from the anchor plate.
To install:
6. Apply silicone dielectric compound to the inside of the slider pin boots and to the slider pins.
7. Position the slider pins and boots in the anchor plate. Position the caliper assembly on the anchor plate. Make sure the brake pads are installed correctly.
8. Remove the residue from the pinch bolt threads and apply 1 drop of threadlock and sealer. Install the pinch bolts and tighten to 23–26 ft.

lbs. (31–35 Nm) while holding the slider pins with an open-end wrench.
9. Attach the cable end to the parking brake lever. Install the cable retaining clip on the caliper assembly.
10. Using new washers, connect the brake flex hose to the caliper. Tighten the retaining bolt to 8–11 ft. lbs. (11–16 Nm).
11. Bleed the brake system, filling the master cylinder as required.
12. Install the wheel and lower the vehicle. Pump the brake pedal prior to moving the vehicle to position the brake pads.

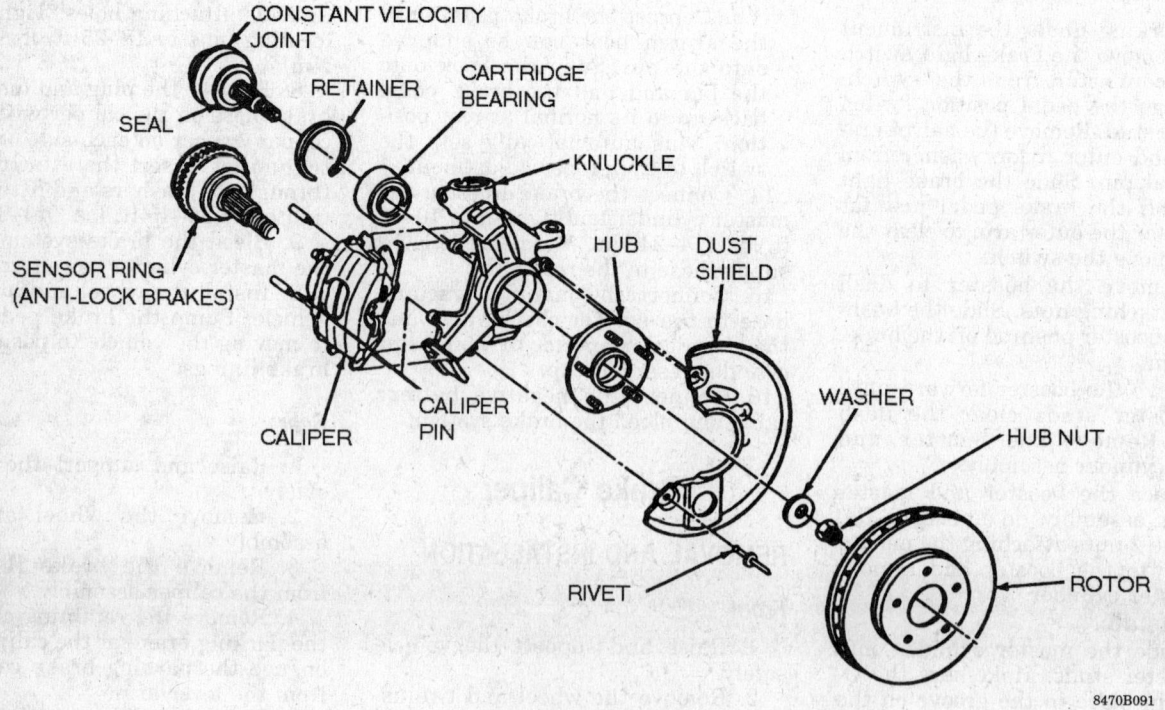

Front disc brake assembly

braking surfaces with medium grit sand paper.

To install:

5. Use a 4 in. C-clamp and a wood block 2¾ in. x 1 in. x ¾ in. thick to seat the caliper piston in its bore. This must be done to provide clearance for the caliper assembly with the new brake pads to fit over the rotor during installation. Care must be taken during this procedure to prevent damage to the plastic piston. Do not allow metal or sharp objects to come into direct contact with the piston surface or damage will result.

6. Remove all rust buildup from the inside of the caliper legs. Install the inner pad in the caliper piston. Do not bend the pad clips during installation in the piston or distortion and rattles can occur. Install the outer pad. Make sure the clips are properly seated.

7. Install the caliper over the rotor and install the wheel. Lower the vehicle.

8. Pump the brake pedal prior to moving the vehicle to position the brake linings. Refill the master cylinder.

Rear

1. Remove the master cylinder cap and check the fluid level in the reservoir. Remove the brake fluid until the reservoir is half full. Discard the removed fluid.

2. Raise the vehicle and support it safely.

3. Remove the wheel and tire assembly.

4. Remove the screw retaining the brake hose bracket to the shock absorber bracket. Remove the retaining clip from the parking brake cable at the caliper. Remove the cable end from the parking brake lever.

5. Hold the slider pin hex-heads with an open-end wrench. Remove the upper pinch bolt. Rotate the caliper away from the rotor.

6. Remove the brake pads.

To install:

7. Using caliper piston turning tool T87P–2588–A or equivalent, rotate the piston clockwise until it is fully seated. Make sure 1 of the 2 slots in the piston face is positioned so it will engage the nib on the brake pad.

8. Install the brake pads in the anchor plate. Rotate the caliper assembly over the rotor into position on the anchor plate. Make sure the brake pads are installed correctly.

9. Remove the residue from the pinch bolt threads and apply 1 drop

of threadlock and sealer. Install and tighten the pinch bolts to 23–26 ft. lbs. (31–35 Nm) while holding the slider pins with an open-end wrench.

10. Attach the cable end to the parking brake lever. Install the cable retaining clip on the caliper assembly. Position the brake flex hose and bracket assembly to the shock absorber bracket and install the retaining screw. Tighten the screw to 8–11 ft. lbs. (11–16 Nm).

11. Install the wheel and tire assembly and lower the vehicle. Pump the brake pedal prior to moving the vehicle to position the brake linings. Refill the master cylinder.

Brake Rotor

REMOVAL AND INSTALLATION

Front

1. Raise the vehicle and support it safely.

2. Remove the wheel and tire assembly.

3. Remove the caliper assembly from the rotor. Position the caliper aside and support it with a length of wire. Do not allow the caliper to hang by the brake hose.

4. Remove the rotor from the hub assembly by pulling it off the hub studs. If additional force is required to remove the rotor, apply rust penetrator on the front and rear rotor/hub mating surfaces and then strike the rotor between the studs with a plastic hammer. If this does not work, attach a 3-jaw puller and remove the rotor.

NOTE: If excessive force must be used to remove the rotor, it should be checked for lateral runout before installation.

5. Check the rotor for scoring and/or other wear. Machine or replace, as necessary. If machining, observe the minimum thickness specification.

6. Install the rotor in the reverse order of removal.

Rear

1. Raise the vehicle and support it safely.

2. Remove the wheel and tire assembly.

3. Remove the caliper assembly from the rotor and support it with a length of wire. Do not let the caliper hang from the brake line.

4. Remove the 2 rotor retaining nuts and remove the rotor from the hub.

5. Check the rotor for scoring and/or other wear. Machine or replace, as necessary. If machining, observe the minimum thickness specification.

6. Install the rotor in the reverse order of removal.

Brake Drums

REMOVAL AND INSTALLATION

1. Raise the vehicle and support it safely.

2. Remove the wheel cover and nut covers, as required.

3. Remove the lug nuts and the wheel and tire assembly.

4. Remove the 2 drum retaining nuts and the drum.

NOTE: If the drum will not come off, pry the rubber plug from the backing plate inspection hole. Remove the brake line-to-axle retention bracket. This will allow sufficient room to insert suitable brake tools through the inspection hole to disengage the adjusting lever and back off the adjusting screw.

5. Inspect the drum for scoring and/or other wear. Machine or replace, as necessary. If machining, observe the maximum permissible drum diameter specification.

6. Installation is the reverse of the removal procedure.

Brake Shoes

REMOVAL AND INSTALLATION

1. Raise the vehicle and support it safely.

2. Remove the wheel and tire assembly and the brake drum.

3. Remove the 2 shoe hold-down springs and pins.

4. Lift the brake shoes, springs and adjuster assembly off the backing plate and wheel cylinder assembly. When removing the assembly, be careful not to bend the adjusting lever.

5. Remove the parking brake cable from the parking brake lever.

6. Remove the retracting springs from the lower brake attachments and upper shoe-to-adjusting lever attachment points. This will separate the brake shoes and disengage the adjuster mechanism.

7. Remove the horse shoe retaining clip and spring washer and slide

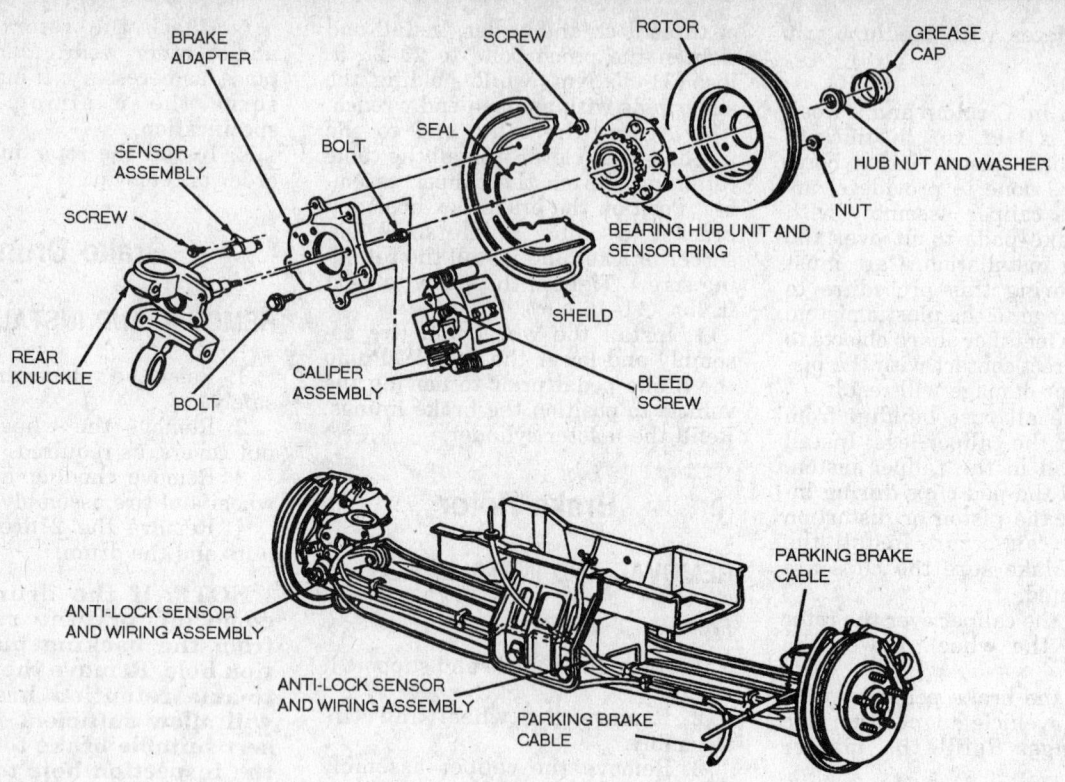

Rear disc brake assembly

the lever off the parking brake lever pin on the trailing shoe.

To install:

8. Apply a light coating of disc brake caliper slide grease at the points where the brake shoes contact the backing plate.

9. Apply a thin coat of lubricant to the adjuster screw threads and socket end of the adjusting screw. Install the stainless steel washer over the socket end of the adjusting screw and install the socket. Turn the adjusting screw into the adjusting pivot nut to the limit of the threads and then back off ½ turn.

10. Assemble the parking brake lever to the trailing shoe by installing

the spring washer and a new horse shoe retaining clip. Crimp the clip until it retains the lever to the shoe securely.

11. Attach the parking brake cable to the parking brake lever.

12. Attach the lower shoe retracting spring to the leading and trailing shoe and install to the backing plate. It will be necessary to stretch the retracting spring as the shoes are installed downward over the anchor plate to the inside of the shoe retaining plate.

13. Install the adjuster screw assembly between the leading shoe slot and the slot in the trailing shoe and parking brake lever. The adjuster

socket end slot must fit into the trailing shoe and parking brake lever.

14. Assemble the adjuster lever in the groove located in the parking brake lever pin and into the slot of the adjuster socket that fits into the trailing shoe web.

15. Attach the upper retracting spring to the leading shoe slot. Using a suitable spring tool, stretch the other end of the spring into the notch on the adjuster lever. If the adjuster lever does not contact the star wheel after installing the spring, it is possible that the adjuster socket is installed incorrectly.

NOTE: The adjuster socket blade is marked R for the right-hand or L for the left-hand brake assemblies. The R or L adjuster blade must be installed with the letter R or L in the upright position, facing the wheel cylinder, on the correct side to ensure that the deeper of the 2 slots in the adjuster sockets fits into the parking brake lever.

16. Adjust the brake shoes.

17. Install the brake drum and wheel and tire assembly. Lower the vehicle.

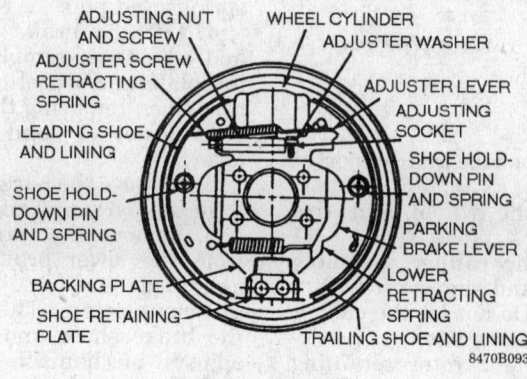

Brake shoe assembly

Wheel Cylinder

REMOVAL AND INSTALLATION

1. Raise and support the vehicle safely.
2. Remove the wheel and tire assembly.
3. Remove the brake drum.
4. Remove the brake shoes, retainers and springs from the backing plate.
5. Disconnect and plug the brake line at the rear-side of the wheel cylinder.
6. Remove the wheel cylinder-to-backing plate bolts and remove the wheel cylinder.
7. To install, reverse the order of removal. Tighten the wheel cylinder-to-backing plate bolts to 8–10 ft. lbs. (10–14 Nm). Bleed the rear brake system.

Parking Brake Cable

ADJUSTMENT

Drum Brakes

1. Make sure the parking brake is fully released. Place the transaxle in the N position.
2. Raise the vehicle and support it safely. Working in front of the left rear wheel, tighten the adjusting nut against the cable equalizer causing a rear wheel brake drag. Then loosen the adjusting nut until the rear brakes are fully released. There should be no brake drag.
3. If the brake cables were replaced, stroke the parking brake several times, then release control and repeat Step 2.
4. Check for operation of the parking brake with the vehicle supported and the parking brake fully released. If there is any slack in the cables or if the rear brakes drag when the wheels are turned, adjust as required.
5. Lower the vehicle.

Disc Brakes

1. Make sure the parking brake is fully released.
2. Raise and safely support the vehicle.
3. Tighten the adjusting nut against the cable adjuster bracket until there is a slight, less than 1/16 in. (1.59mm), movement of either rear parking brake lever at the caliper.
4. If the brake cables were replaced, stroke the parking brake several times, then release the control and repeat Step 3.

5. Lower the vehicle.

REMOVAL AND INSTALLATION

Front Cable

1992

1. Raise the front of the vehicle and support safely.
2. Loosen the adjuster nut at the cable adjuster bracket.
3. Lower the vehicle.
4. Disconnect the cable from the control assembly at the clevis.
5. Raise the vehicle and support safely.
6. At the cable connector, disconnect the front cable from the rear cable.
7. Remove the cable and push-in prong retainer from the cable bracket, using a 13mm box end wrench to depress the retaining prongs. Allow the cable to hang.
8. Push the grommet up through the floor pan and lower the vehicle.
9. Remove the left cowl side panel. Pull the carpet away from the cowl panel.
10. From inside the vehicle, remove the cable end from the clevis and remove the conduit retainer from the control assembly.
11. Pull the cable assembly through the floorpan hole.
12. Installation is the reverse of the removal procedure. Adjust the parking brake and check the brake for proper operation.

1993–96

1. Raise the front of the vehicle and support safely.
2. Loosen the adjuster nut at the cable adjuster bracket.
3. Lower the vehicle.
4. Disconnect the cable from the control assembly at the clevis using a 13mm box end wrench to depress the retaining prongs and remove cable end pronged fitting from brake control.
5. Remove the left cowl side panel. Pull the carpet away from the cowl panel to expose the cable.
6. Raise the vehicle and support safely.
7. At the cable connector, disconnect the front cable from the rear cable.
8. Remove the cable and push-in prong retainer from the cable bracket, using a 13mm box end wrench to depress the retaining prongs.
9. Pull the grommet down from the floorpan.

10. Installation is the reverse of the removal procedure. Adjust the parking brake and check the brake for proper operation.

Rear Cable

LEFT SIDE

1. Raise the vehicle and support safely.
2. Remove the parking brake cable adjusting nut.
3. Remove the rear cable end fitting from the front cable connector.
4. Remove the wheel and drum assembly if equipped with drum brakes.
5. Disconnect the brake cable from the parking brake actuating lever. On drum brake vehicles, use a 13mm box end wrench to depress the conduit retaining prongs and remove the cable end pronged fitting from the backing plate. On disc brake vehicles, remove the E-clip from the conduit end of the fitting at the caliper.
6. Push the plastic snap-in grommet rearward to disconnect it from the side rail bracket.
7. Remove the pronged connector from the parking park adjuster bracket. Remove the cable assembly.
8. Installation is the reverse of the removal procedure. Make sure all pronged connectors are locked in place. Adjust the parking brake.

RIGHT SIDE

1. Raise the vehicle and support it safely.
2. Remove the parking brake cable adjuster nut.
3. Use a 13mm box wrench to remove the conduit retainer prongs and remove the cable from the frame side rail bracket.
4. Remove the rear wheel and drum assembly if equipped with drum brakes.
5. Disconnect the brake cable from the parking brake actuating lever. On drum brake vehicles, use a 13mm box end wrench to depress the conduit retaining prongs and remove the cable end pronged fitting from the backing plate. On disc brake vehicles, remove the E-clip from the conduit end of the fitting at the caliper.
6. On Taurus/Sable sedan vehicles, perform the following:
  a. Remove the brake pressure control valve bracket at the control arm.
  b. Remove the cable retaining screw and clip from the lower suspension arm.
  c. Remove one screw from the cable bracket at the crossmember.

d. Remove the entire right cable assembly.

7. On station wagon vehicles, perform the following:

a. Remove the cable retaining clip and screw from each lower suspension arm.

b. Remove the cable clip retaining screw from lower suspension arm inner mounting bracket.

8. Installation is the reverse of the removal procedure. Make sure the pronged fitting is securely locked in place. Adjust the parking brake.

Brake System Bleeding

WITHOUT ANTI-LOCK BRAKES

1. Clean all dirt from the master cylinder filler cap.

2. If the master cylinder is known or suspected to have air in the bore, it must be bled before any of the wheel cylinders or calipers. To bleed the master cylinder, loosen the upper secondary left front outlet fitting approximately ¾ turn. Have an assistant depress the brake pedal slowly through it's full travel. Close the outlet fitting and let the pedal return slowly to the fully released position. Wait 5 seconds and then repeat the operation until all air bubbles disappear.

3. Repeat Step 2 with the right-hand front outlet fitting.

4. Continue to bleed the brake system by removing the rubber dust cap from the wheel cylinder bleeder fitting or caliper fitting at the right rear of the vehicle. Place a suitable box wrench on the bleeder fitting and attach a rubber drain tube to the fitting. The end of the tube should fit snugly around the bleeder fitting. Submerge the other end of the tube in a container partially filled with clean brake fluid and loosen the fitting ¾ turn.

5. Have an assistant push the brake pedal down slowly through its full travel. Close the bleeder fitting and allow the pedal to slowly return to its full release position. Wait 5 seconds and repeat the procedure until no bubbles appear at the submerged end of the bleeder tube. Secure the bleeder fitting and remove the bleeder tube. Install the rubber dust cap on the bleeder fitting.

6. Repeat the procedure in Steps 4 and 5 in the following sequence: left front, left rear and right front. Refill the master cylinder reservoir after each wheel cylinder or caliper has been bled and install the master cylinder cover and gasket. When brake bleeding is completed, the fluid level should be filled to the maximum level indicated on the reservoir.

7. Always make sure the disc brake pistons are returned to their normal positions by depressing the brake pedal several times until normal pedal travel is established. If the pedal feels spongy, repeat the bleeding procedure.

WITH ANTI-LOCK BRAKES

The anti-lock brake system must be bled in 2 steps.

1. The master cylinder and hydraulic control unit must be bled using the Rotunda Anti-Lock Brake Breakout Box/Bleeding Adapter tool T90P–50–ALA or equivalent. If this procedure is not followed, air will be trapped in the hydraulic control unit which will eventually lead to a spongy brake pedal. To bleed the master cylinder and the hydraulic control unit, disconnect the 55-pin plug from the electronic control unit and install the Anti-Lock Brake Breakout Box/Bleeding Adapter to the wire harness 55-pin plug.

a. Place the Bleed/Harness switch in the BLEED position.

b. Turn the ignition to the ON position. At this point the red off light should come ON.

c. Push the motor button on the adapter down to start the pump motor. The red OFF light will turn OFF and the green ON light will turn ON. The pump motor will run for 60 seconds after the motor button is pushed. If the pump motor is to be turned off for any reason before the 60 seconds has elapsed, push the ABORT button to turn the pump motor OFF.

d. After 20 seconds of pump motor operation, push and hold the valve button down. Hold the valve button down for 20 seconds and then release it.

e. The pump motor will continue to run for an additional 20 seconds after the valve button is released.

2. The brake lines can now be bled in the normal fashion. Bleed the brake system by removing the rubber dust cap from the caliper fitting at the right rear of the vehicle. Place a suitable box wrench on the bleeder fitting and attach a rubber drain tube to the fitting. The end of the tube should fit snugly around the bleeder fitting. Submerge the other end of the tube in a container partially filled with clean brake fluid and loosen the fitting ¾ turn.

3. Have an assistant push the brake pedal down slowly through it's full travel. Close the bleeder fitting and allow the pedal to slowly return to it's full release position. Wait 5 seconds and repeat the procedure until no bubbles appear at the submerged end of the bleeder tube. Secure the bleeder fitting and remove the bleeder tube. Install the rubber dust cap on the bleeder fitting.

4. Repeat the bleeding procedure at the left front, left rear and right front in that order. Refill the master cylinder reservoir after each caliper has been bled and install the master cylinder and gasket. When brake bleeding is completed, the fluid level should be filled to the maximum level indicated on the reservoir.

5. Always make sure the disc brake pistons are returned to their normal positions by depressing the brake pedal several times until normal pedal travel is established. If the pedal feels spongy, repeat the bleeding procedure.

Anti-Lock Brake System Service

PRECAUTION

Failure to observe the following precautions may result in system damage.

• Before servicing any high pressure component, be sure to discharge the hydraulic pressure from the system.

• Do not allow the brake fluid to contact any of the electrical connectors.

• Use care when opening the bleeder screws due to the high pressures available from the accumulator.

RELIEVING ANTI-LOCK BRAKE SYSTEM PRESSURE

Before servicing any components which contain high pressure, it is mandatory that the hydraulic pressure in the system be discharged. To discharge the system, turn the ignition OFF and pump the brake pedal a minimum of 20 times until an increase in pedal force is clearly felt.

Hydraulic Control Unit (HCU)

REMOVAL AND INSTALLATION

1. On all vehicles, except Taurus SHO, disconnect the battery cables and remove the battery from the vehicle. Remove the battery tray. Remove the 3 plastic push pins holding the acid shield to the HCU mounting bracket and remove the acid shield. On Taurus SHO, it is only necessary to disconnect the negative battery cable and remove the electronic control unit and it's mounting bracket from the top of the HCU mounting bracket.

2. Disconnect the 19-pin connector from the HCU to the wiring harness and disconnect the 4-pin connector from the HCU to the pump motor relay.

3. Remove the 2 lines from the inlet ports and the 4 lines from the outlet ports of the HCU. Plug each port to prevent brake fluid from spilling onto the paint and wiring.

4. Remove the 3 nuts retaining the HCU assembly to the mounting bracket and remove the assembly from the vehicle. The nut on the front of the HCU also retains the relay mounting bracket.

5. Install in the reverse order of removal. Tighten the 3 retaining nuts to 12–18 ft. lbs. (16–24 Nm) and the brake lines to 10–18 ft. lbs. (14–24 Nm). Bleed the brake system and check for fluid leaks.

Wheel Sensors

REMOVAL AND INSTALLATION

Front

1. Disconnect the sensor connector located in the engine compartment.

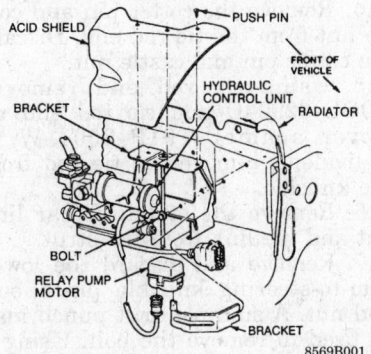

Anti-lock brake hydraulic control unit

2. For the right front sensor, remove the 2 plastic push studs to loosen the front section of the splash shield in the wheel well. For the left front sensor, remove the 2 plastic push studs to loosen the rear section of the splash shield.

3. Thread the sensor wires through the holes in the fender apron. For the right front sensor, remove the 2 retaining clips behind the splash shield.

4. Raise and support the vehicle safely. Remove the wheel and tire assembly.

5. Disengage the sensor wire grommets at the height sensor bracket and from the retainer clip on the shock strut just above the spindle.

6. Loosen the sensor retaining screw and remove the sensor assembly from the front knuckle.

7. Install in the reverse order of removal. Tighten the sensor retaining screws to 40–60 inch lbs. (4.5–6.8 Nm).

Rear

TAURUS/SABLE SEDAN

1. Remove the rear seat and seat back insulation.

2. Disconnect the sensor from the harness and tie the sensor connector to the rear seat sheetmetal bracket with wire or string.

3. Push the sensor wire grommet and connector through the floorpan drawing the string or wire from the sensor from underneath the vehicle.

4. Disconnect the string or wire from the sensor from underneath the vehicle.

5. Disconnect the routing clips from the suspension arms and remove the sensor retaining bolts from the rear brake adapters.

6. Install in the reverse order of removal. Use string or wire to pull the new sensor connector through the hole in the floorpan. Tighten the sensor retaining bolt to 40–60 inch lbs. (4.5–6.8 Nm).

TAURUS/SABLE WAGON

1. Raise and safely support the vehicle.

2. Remove the sensor wire with the attached grommet from the hole in the floorpan.

3. Disconnect the sensor from the harness.

4. Remove the routing clips, then remove the sensor attaching bolt and sensor.

5. Installation is the reverse of the removal procedure. Tighten the sen-

sor attaching bolt to 40–60 inch lbs. (4.5–6.8 Nm).

CONTINENTAL

1. Turn the air suspension switch in the luggage compartment to the **OFF** position. Disconnect the sensor connector in the luggage compartment.

2. Push the rubber grommet through the sheetmetal floorpan.

3. Raise and safely support the vehicle. Remove the retainer clips for the sensor wire and remove the wire from it's routing position.

4. Loosen the sensor retaining screw at the caliper anchor plate and remove the sensor.

5. Installation is the reverse of the removal procedure. Tighten the sensor retaining screw to 40–60 inch lbs. (4.5–6.8 Nm).

Electronic Control Unit (ECU)

REMOVAL AND INSTALLATION

Taurus and Sable

The ECU is located on the front right side of the engine compartment next to the washer bottle, except on Taurus SHO. On Taurus SHO, it is mounted on the left side on top of the HCU mounting bracket.

1. Disconnect the negative battery cable.

2. Disconnect the 55-pin connector from the ECU. Unlock the connector by completely pulling up the lever. Move the top of the connector away from the ECU until all terminals are clear, then pull the connector up out of the slots in the ECU.

3. Remove the screws attaching the ECU and remove the ECU.

4. Install in the reverse order of removal. Connect the 55-pin connector by installing the bottom part of the connector into the slits in the ECU and pushing the top portion of the connector into the ECU. Then pull the locking lever completely down to ensure proper installation. Tighten the retaining screws to 15–20 inch lbs. (1.7–2.3 Nm).

Continental

1. Disconnect the negative battery cable.

2. Remove the trim panel in the luggage compartment (behind the back seat) to gain access to the ECU.

3. Disconnect the connector from the ECU.

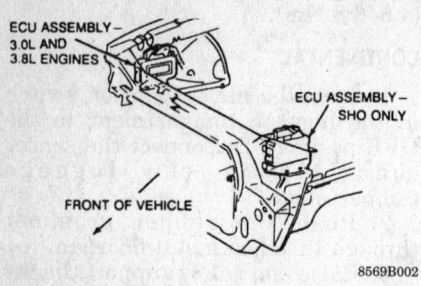

Anti-lock brake system electronic control unit location — Taurus and Sable

4. Remove the screws attaching the ECU to the panel and remove the ECU.

5. Installation is the reverse of the removal procedure. Tighten the retaining screws to 15–20 inch lbs. (1.7–2.3 Nm).

FRONT SUSPENSION

MacPherson Strut

REMOVAL AND INSTALLATION

Taurus and Sable

1. Place the ignition switch in the **OFF** position and the steering column in the **UNLOCKED** position.

2. Remove the hub nut. Loosen the 3 top mount-to-shock tower nuts; do not remove the nuts at this time.

3. Raise and support the vehicle safely.

——— CAUTION ———
When raising the vehicle, do not lift by the lower control arms.

4. Remove the tire and wheel assembly. Remove the brake caliper, supporting it on a wire. Remove the rotor.

5. At the tie rod end, remove the cotter pin and the castle nut. Discard the cotter pin and nut and replace with new.

6. Using tie rod end remover tool 3290–D and the tie rod remover adapter tool T81P–3504–W or equivalents, separate the tie rod from the steering knuckle.

7. Remove the stabilizer bar link nut and the link from the strut.

8. Remove the lower arm-to-steering knuckle pinch bolt and nut; it may be necessary to use a drift punch

to remove the bolt. Using a suitable tool, spread the knuckle-to-lower arm pinch joint and remove the lower arm from the steering knuckle. Discard the pinch nut/bolt and replace with new.

9. Remove the halfshaft from the hub and support it on a wire.

——— WARNING ———
When removing the halfshaft, do not allow it to move outward as the internal parts of the tripod CV-joint could separate, causing failure of the joint.

10. Remove the strut-to-steering knuckle pinch bolt. Using a small prybar, spread the pinch bolt joint and separate the strut from the steering knuckle. Remove the steering knuckle/hub assembly from the strut.

11. Remove the 3 top mount-to-shock tower nuts and the strut assembly from the vehicle.

12. Compress the coil spring using a suitable spring compressor. Use a 10mm box end wrench to hold the top of the strut shaft while removing the nut with a 21mm 6-point crow foot wrench and ratchet.

13. Loosen the spring compressor, then remove the top mount bracket assembly, bearing plate assembly and spring.

To install:

14. Install the spring compressor. Install the spring, bearing plate assembly, lower washer and top mount bracket assembly.

15. Compress the spring. Install the upper washer and nut on the shock strut shaft. Tighten the nut with the 21mm 6-point crow foot wrench and ratchet while holding the shaft with the 10mm box end wrench.

16. Install the strut assembly and the 3 top mount-to-shock tower nuts.

17. Install the steering knuckle and hub assembly to the strut.

18. Install a new strut-to-steering knuckle pinch bolt. Tighten the bolt to 73–97 ft. lbs. (98–132 Nm).

19. Install the halfshaft into the hub.

20. Install the lower arm to the steering knuckle and install a new pinch bolt and nut. Tighten to 40–53 ft. lbs. (54–72 Nm).

21. Install the stabilizer link to the strut and install a new stabilizer bar link nut. Tighten to 57–75 ft. lbs. (77–101 Nm).

22. Install the tie rod end onto the knuckle using a new castle nut. Tighten the castle nut to 23–35 ft. lbs. (31–47 Nm). Retain the castle nut with a new cotter pin.

23. Install the disc brake rotor, caliper and tire and wheel assembly.

24. Tighten the 3 top mount-to-shock tower nuts to 23–29 ft. lbs. (30–40 Nm).

25. Lower the vehicle and tighten the hub nut to 170–202 ft. lbs. (230–275 Nm).

26. Depress the brake pedal several times before moving the vehicle. Check the front end alignment.

Continental

1. Turn OFF the air suspension switch, located in the left side of the luggage compartment.

2. Place the ignition switch in the **OFF** position and the steering column in the **UNLOCKED** position.

3. Remove the plastic cover from the shock tower to gain access to the upper mounting nuts and dual damping actuator.

4. Remove the actuator retaining screws. Remove the actuator and place it aside.

5. Remove the hub nut.

6. Loosen the 3 top mount-to-shock tower nuts but do not remove them at this time.

7. Raise the vehicle and support it safely.

——— CAUTION ———
Do not raise the vehicle by the lower control arms.

8. Remove the tire and wheel assembly.

9. Remove the brake line bracket from the strut assembly.

10. Disconnect the height sensor link from the ball stud pin at the lower control arm.

11. Disconnect the air line from the solenoid valve.

12. Disconnect the electrical connector at the solenoid valve.

13. Remove the brake caliper and the disc brake rotor. Support the caliper with wire; do not let the caliper hang by the brake hose.

14. Remove the cotter pin and castle nut from the tie rod end. Discard the cotter pin and castle nut.

15. Using tie rod end remover TOOL–3290–D and tie rod end remover adapter T81P–3504–W or equivalent, remove the tie rod from the knuckle.

16. Remove the stabilizer bar link nut and the link from the strut.

17. Remove and discard the lower arm-to-steering knuckle pinch bolt and nut. A suitable drift punch may be used to remove the bolt. Using a small prybar, slightly spread the knuckle-to-lower arm pinch joint and

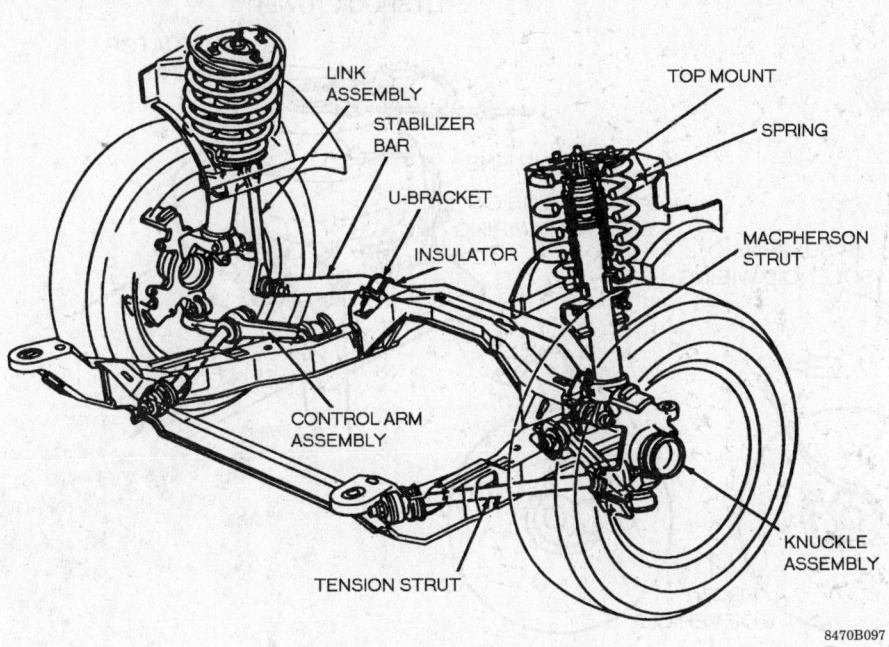

Front suspension — Taurus and Sable

LINK ASSEMBLY
STABILIZER BAR
U-BRACKET
INSULATOR
CONTROL ARM ASSEMBLY
TENSION STRUT
TOP MOUNT
SPRING
MACPHERSON STRUT
KNUCKLE ASSEMBLY

8470B097

remove the lower arm from the steering knuckle.

18. Remove the halfshaft from the hub.

------ **CAUTION** ------

When removing the halfshaft, do not allow the halfshaft to move outward. This could result in separation of the internal parts of the tripod CV-joint, causing failure of the joint.

19. Remove the strut-to-steering knuckle pinch bolt. Using a small prybar, slightly spread the knuckle-to-strut pinch joint to remove the strut from the steering knuckle.

20. Remove the 3 top mount-to-shock tower nuts and remove the strut from the vehicle.

To install:

21. Install the strut with the 3 top mount-to-shock tower nuts and leave the nuts loose.

22. Install the steering knuckle and hub assembly to the strut. Install a new strut-to-steering knuckle pinch bolt. Tighten the bolt to 73–97 ft. lbs. (98–132 Nm).

23. Install the halfshaft into the hub.

24. Install the lower arm to the steering knuckle and install a new pinch bolt and nut. Tighten to 40–53 ft. lbs. (54–72 Nm).

25. Install the stabilizer bar link to the strut and install a new stabilizer bar link nut. Tighten to 57–75 ft. lbs. (77–101 Nm).

26. Install the tie rod end onto the knuckle using a new castle nut. Before tightening the nut, make sure the steering wheel and wheels are in the straight-ahead position. Tighten the castle nut to 23–35 ft. lbs. (31–47 Nm). Install a new cotter pin in the castle nut.

27. Install the brake caliper and rotor.

28. Connect the electrical connector and the air line to the solenoid valve and position them properly.

29. Install the height sensor link on the ball stud pin on the control arm.

30. Install the brake line bracket to the strut assembly.

31. Install the wheel and tire assembly.

32. Tighten the 3 top mount-to-shock tower nuts to 20–30 ft. lbs. (27–40 Nm).

33. Install the dual damping actuator and the plastic shock tower cover.

Correctly position the actuator wiring.

34. Refill the air spring prior to fully lowering the vehicle. The refill procedure is as follows:

a. Place the air suspension service switch in the **ON** position.

b. Turn the ignition switch **OFF**.

c. Connect a battery charger to reduce battery drain.

d. Open the access door in the left-hand luggage compartment trim panel to plug the SUPER STAR II tester or equivalent, into the air suspension diagnostics wiring harness connector.

e. The tester button should be in the **HOLD** (up) position.

f. With the brake pedal depressed hard, turn the ignition switch to the **RUN** position.

g. Move the tester button to the **TEST** (down) position.

h. The air suspension control module will now start sending out the spring fill selection codes to be displayed on the tester. These codes will be displayed in a scrolling manner.

i. Select the desired spring fill operation by releasing the tester button when the desired code is displayed. Select either Code **24** or Code **25** to inflate either the right front or left front air spring. As long as the tester button is released the inflation will continue. To stop inflation, move the tester button back down to the **TEST** position. The spring fill codes will again be displayed.

NOTE: Do not apply a load to the suspension until after the air spring has been inflated at least 60 seconds.

j. To exit the spring fill mode, turn the ignition switch to the **OFF** position and unplug the tester.

35. Lower the vehicle and tighten the hub nut to 170–202 lbs. (230–275 Nm).

36. Turn ON the air suspension.

37. Depress the brake pedal several times before moving the vehicle. Check the front end alignment.

MacPherson Strut Cartridge

REPLACEMENT

The strut assembly is not serviceable and must be replaced as an assembly.

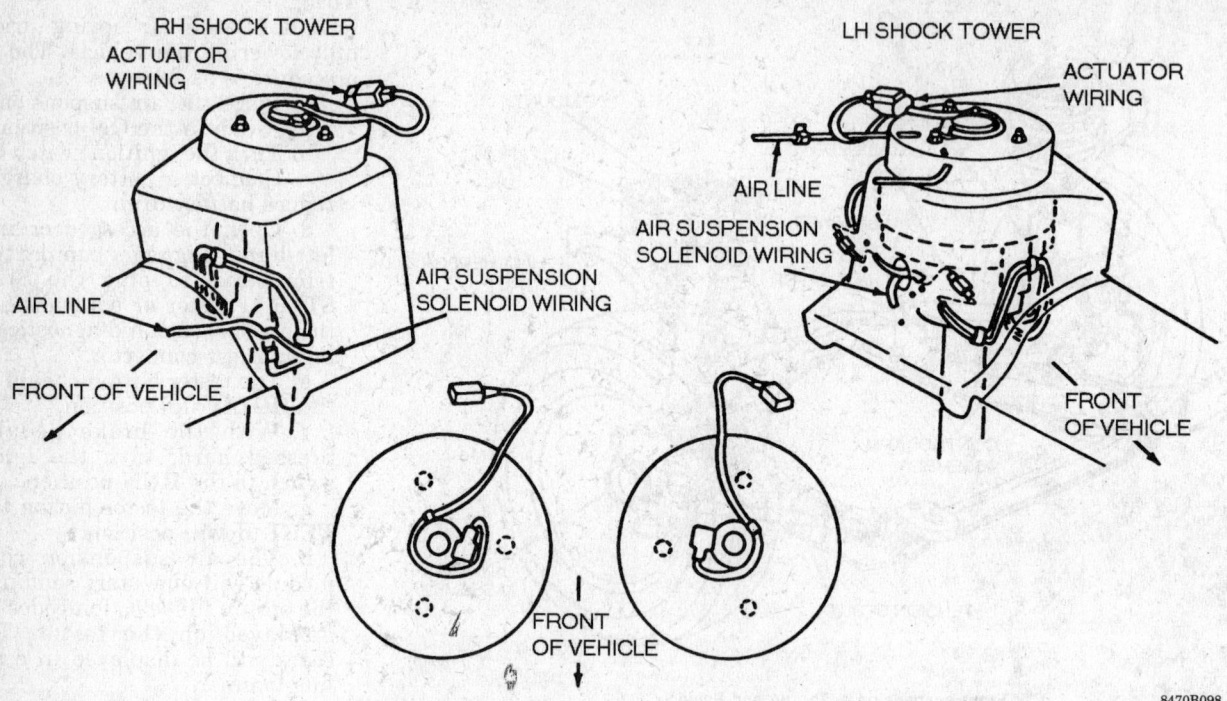

Air line and actuator wiring positioning — Continental

Code	Description
21	Vent R.F.
22	Vent L.F.
23	Vent R.R.
24	Inflate R.F.
25	Inflate L.F.
26	Inflate R.R.
27	Vent L.R.
28	Inflate L.R.

8470B099

Air suspension spring fill codes — Continental

Lower Ball Joints

INSPECTION

1. On Continental, turn **OFF** the air suspension switch, located in the left side of the luggage compartment.

2. Raise the vehicle and safely support it so the wheels fall to the full-down position.

3. Have an assistant grasp the lower edge of the tire and move the wheel and tire assembly in and out.

4. Observe the lower end of the knuckle and the lower control arm as the wheel is being moved in and out.

Any movement indicates abnormal ball joint wear.

5. If there is any movement, install a new lower control arm assembly.

6. Lower the vehicle. On Continental, turn **ON** the air suspension.

REMOVAL AND INSTALLATION

Ball joints are integral parts of the lower control arms. If an inspection reveals an unsatisfactory ball joint, the entire lower control arm assembly must be replaced.

Lower Control Arms

REMOVAL AND INSTALLATION

1. On Continental, turn **OFF** the air suspension switch, located in the left side of the luggage compartment.

2. Raise and support the front of the vehicle safely. Remove the wheel and tire assembly. Position the steering column in the unlocked position.

3. Disconnect the height sensor link from the ball stud pin on Continental.

4. Remove the tension strut-to-control arm nut and the dished washer. Discard the nut.

5. Remove and discard the lower control ball joint pinch bolt. Using a small prybar, spread the pinch joint and separate the control arm from the steering knuckle. A drift punch may be used to remove the bolt.

NOTE: When separating the control arm from the steering knuckle, do not use a hammer. Be careful not to damage the ball joint boot seal.

6. Remove and discard the control arm-to-frame nut/bolt, then the control arm from the frame and the tension strut.

——— **WARNING** ———
Do not allow the halfshaft to move outward or the tripod CV-joint internal parts could separate, causing failure of the joint.

7. To install, use a new tension strut nut, ball joint pinch nut/bolt and lower control arm inner pivot bolt nut and reverse the removal procedures. Tighten the bolts to the following torque specifications:
Control arm-to-frame 73–97 ft. lbs. (98–132 Nm)
Control arm-to-steering knuckle 40–53 ft. lbs. (54–72 Nm)

Tension strut-to-control arm 73–97 ft. lbs. (98–132 Nm)

Wheel lug nuts 80–105 ft. lbs. (109–142 Nm)

8. Check the front end alignment.

Stabilizer Bar

REMOVAL AND INSTALLATION

1. Raise and support the front of the vehicle on jackstands behind the subframe.

NOTE: Do not raise or support the vehicle on the front control arms.

2. Remove and discard the stabilizer bar link-to-stabilizer bar nut, the stabilizer bar link-to-strut nut and the link from the vehicle.

3. Remove the steering gear-to-subframe nuts and move the gear from the sub-frame.

4. Position another set of jackstands under the subframe and remove the rear subframe retaining bolts. Lower the rear of the subframe to gain access to the stabilizer bar brackets.

5. Remove the stabilizer bar U-bracket bolts and the stabilizer bar from the vehicle.

NOTE: When removing the stabilizer bar, replace the insulators and the U-bracket bolts with new ones.

To install:

6. To install, reverse the removal procedure. Tighten the bolts to the following torque specifications:

U-bracket-to-subframe 23–29 ft. lbs. (30–40 Nm)

Subframe-to-steering gear 85–100 ft. lbs. (115–135 Nm)

Stabilizer bar-to-stabilizer bar link 35–46 ft. lbs. (47–63 Nm)

Stabilizer bar-to-strut 57–75 ft. lbs. (77–101 Nm)

7. Prior to assembly, coat the inside diameter of the new insulators with Rubber Suspension Insulator Lube E25Y–19553–A or equivalent lubricant. Do not use any mineral or petroleum base lubricants as they will cause deterioration of the rubber insulators.

REAR SUSPENSION

Shock Absorbers

REMOVAL AND INSTALLATION

Taurus/Sable Wagon

1. Raise and support the vehicle safely.

2. Remove the wheel and tire assembly.

3. Position a jack stand under the lower suspension arm. Remove the 2 nuts retaining the shock absorber to the lower suspension arm.

4. From inside the vehicle, remove the rear compartment access panels.

5. Remove and discard the top shock absorber attaching nut using a crow's foot wrench and ratchet while holding the shock absorber shaft stationary with an open end wrench.

—————— **WARNING** ——————
If the shock absorber is to be reused, do not grip the shaft with pliers or vise grips. Gripping the shaft in this manner will damage the shaft surface finish and will result in severe oil leakage.

6. Remove the rubber insulator from the shock and the shock from the vehicle.

NOTE: The shocks are gas filled. It will require an effort to collapse the shock in order to remove it from the lower arm.

To install:

7. Install a new washer and insulator on the upper shock absorber rod.

8. Maneuver the upper part of the shock absorber into the shock tower opening in the body. Push slowly on the lower part of the shock absorber until the mounting studs are aligned with the mounting holes in the lower suspension arm.

9. Install new lower attaching nuts but do not tighten at this time.

10. Install a new insulator, washer and nut on top of the shock absorber. Torque the nut to 19–25 ft. lbs. (26–34 Nm.).

11. Install the rear compartment access panel.

12. Torque the 2 lower attaching nuts to 15–19 ft. lbs. (19–26 Nm).

13. Install the wheel and tire assembly. Remove the safety stand supporting the lower suspension arm and lower the vehicle.

MacPherson Strut

REMOVAL AND INSTALLATION

Taurus/Sable Sedan

1. Raise and support the rear of the vehicle safely. Remove the wheel and tire.

—————— **CAUTION** ——————
Do not raise or support the vehicle using the tension struts.

2. Raise the luggage compartment lid and loosen but do not remove the upper strut-to-body nuts.

3. Remove the brake differential control valve-to-control arm bolt. Using a wire, secure the control arm to the body to ensure proper support leaving at least 6 in. clearance to aid in the strut removal.

4. Remove the brake hose-to-strut bracket clip and move the hose aside.

5. If equipped, remove the stabilizer bar U-bracket from the vehicle.

6. If equipped, remove the stabilizer bar-to-stabilizer link nut, washer and insulator, then separate the stabilizer bar from the link.

NOTE: When removing the strut, be sure the rear brake flex hose is not stretched or the steel brake tube is not bent.

7. Remove the tension strut-to-spindle nut, washer and insulator. Move the spindle rearward to separate it from the tension strut.

8. Remove the shock strut-to-spindle pinch bolt. If necessary, use a medium prybar, spread the strut-to-spindle pinch joint to remove the strut. Discard the bolt and replace it.

9. Lower the jackstand and separate the shock strut from the spindle.

10. Support the shock strut, then loosen the top strut-to-body nuts completely and remove the strut from the vehicle.

11. Remove the nut, washer and insulator attaching link to strut and remove link. Mark the location of the insulator to top mount, then compress the spring, using a suitable spring compressor.

12. Use a 10mm box end wrench to hold the top of the strut shaft while removing the nut with a 21mm 6-point crow foot wrench and ratchet. Loosen the spring compressor, then remove the top mount bracket assembly, spring insulator and spring.

To install:

13. Using the spring compressor, install the spring, spring insulator, bottom washer, if equipped, top mount, upper washer and nut on the

strut shaft. Make sure the spring is properly located in the upper and lower spring seats and the mount washers are positioned correctly.

14. Tighten the rod nut to 35–50 ft. lbs. (48–68 Nm). Use a 21mm crow foot wrench to turn the nut and a 10mm box end wrench to hold the shaft. Do not use pliers or vise grips on the strut rod.

15. Position the stabilizer bar link in the strut bracket. Install the insulator, washer and nut and tighten to 5–7 ft. lbs. (7–9.5 Nm).

16. Insert the 3 upper mount studs into the strut tower in the apron and hand start 3 new nuts. Do not tighten the nuts at this time.

17. Partially raise the vehicle.

18. Install the strut into the spindle pinch joint. Install a new pinch bolt into the spindle and through the strut bracket. Tighten the bolt to 50–70 ft. lbs. (68–95 Nm).

19. Move the spindle rearward and install the tension strut into the spindle. Install the insulator, washer and nut on the tension strut. Tighten the nut to 35–50 ft. lbs. (48–68 Nm).

20. Position the link into the stabilizer bar. Install the insulator, washer and nut on the link. Tighten to 5–7 ft. lbs. (7–9.5 Nm).

21. Position the stabilizer bar U-bracket on the body. Install the bolt and tighten to 25–37 ft. lbs. (34–50 Nm).

22. Install the brake hose to the strut bracket.

23. Install the brake control differential valve on the control arm and remove the retaining wire.

24. Install the top mount-to-body nuts and tighten to 19–26 ft. lbs. (26–35 Nm).

25. Install the wheel and tire assembly and lower the vehicle.

Continental

1. Turn **OFF** the air suspension switch located in the luggage compartment.

2. From inside the luggage compartment, disconnect the electrical connector from the dual dampening actuator.

3. Loosen but do not remove the 3 nuts retaining the strut to the upper body.

4. Raise and support the vehicle safely. Remove the wheel and tire assembly.

—————— CAUTION ——————
Do not raise the vehicle by the tension strut.

5. Disconnect the air line and electrical connector from the solenoid valve.

6. Remove the brake hose retainer at the strut bracket.

7. Disconnect the parking brake cable from the brake caliper. Remove all the wire retainers and parking brake cable retainers from the lower suspension arm.

8. Disconnect the height sensor link from the ball stud pin on the lower arm.

9. Remove the caliper assembly from the spindle and position it off to the side with a piece of wire. Do not kink or place a load on the brake hose.

10. Bleed the air spring by performing the following:
   a. Remove the solenoid clip.
   b. Rotate the solenoid counterclockwise to the first stop.
   c. Slowly pull the solenoid straight out to the second stop and bleed the air from the system.

—————— CAUTION ——————
Do not fully release the solenoid until the air is fully bled from the spring or personal injury may result.

   d. After the air is fully bled from the system, rotate the solenoid to the third stop and remove the solenoid from the housing.

11. Mark the position of the notch on the toe adjustment cam.

12. Remove the torsion spring clamp from the spindle-to-strut bolt.

13. Remove the nut from the inboard bushing on the suspension arm.

14. Install torsion spring remover tool T88P-5310-A or equivalent, on the suspension arm. Pry up on the tool and arm using a ¾ in. drive ratchet to relieve the pressure on the pivot bolt. An assistant may be required to pull outboard on the spindle simultaneously to fully relieve the tension on the bolt. Remove the bolt and lower arm. Repeat this procedure for the opposite arm.

15. Remove the torsion spring from the arms.

16. Remove the stabilizer U-bracket from the body.

17. Remove the nut, washer and insulator attaching the stabilizer bar to the link. Separate the stabilizer bar from the link.

18. Remove the nut, washer and insulator retaining the tension strut to the spindle. Move the spindle rearward enough to separate it from the tension strut.

19. Remove and discard the strut-to-spindle pinch bolt. With a suitable prybar, spread the strut-to-spindle pinch joint as required to assist in removing the bolt.

20. Separate the spindle from the strut. Remove the spindle as an assembly with the arms attached.

21. From inside the luggage compartment area, support the shock strut by hand and remove and discard the 3 upper mount-to-body nuts. Care should be taken not to drop the strut when removing the upper nuts. Guide the electric actuator wire through the opening to prevent snagging and damage while removing the strut assembly.

To install:

22. Install the solenoid valve on the air spring.

23. Guide the electric actuator wire through the opening and install the strut assembly. Install 3 new upper mount nuts.

24. Install the spindle and arms to the strut. Install a new strut-to-spindle pinch bolt. Do not tighten the bolt until the control arms are attached to the body and the cams are centered.

25. Position the tension strut to the spindle. Install the insulator, washer and nut retaining the tension strut to the spindle. Tighten the nut to 35–50 ft. lbs. (48–68 Nm).

26. Install the stabilizer bar to the link. Install the insulator, washer and retaining nut. Tighten the nut to 5–7 ft. lbs. (7–9.5 Nm).

27. Install the stabilizer U-bracket to the body. Tighten the bolt to 25–37 ft. lbs. (34–50 Nm).

28. Install the torsion spring to the arms.

29. Position the inboard bushing using torsion spring remover T88P-5310-A or equivalent, and install the bolt. An assistant may be required to pull outboard on the spindle to align the bushing so the bolt can be inserted. Repeat the procedure for the opposite lower arm.

30. Install the nut to the inboard bushing on the suspension arm but do not tighten at this time.

31. Tighten the spindle-to-strut bolt to 51–70 ft. lbs. (68–95 Nm).

32. Set the toe adjustment cam to the alignment mark.

33. Remove the wire from the caliper and install the caliper to the spindle.

34. Connect the height sensor link to the ball stud pin on the lower arm.

35. Install the torsion spring clamp and secure.

36. Install all wire retainers and parking brake cable retainers to the lower suspension arm.

37. Connect the parking brake cable to the brake caliper and install the brake hose retainer at the strut bracket.

38. Connect the air line and the electrical connector to the solenoid valve.

39. Install the wheel and tire assembly and partially lower the vehicle.

40. Tighten the 3 nuts retaining the strut to the upper body to 19–26 ft. lbs. (26–35 Nm).

41. From inside the luggage compartment, connect the electrical connector for the dual dampening actuator.

42. Turn ON the air suspension switch and fill the air spring as follows:

a. Place the air suspension service switch in the **ON** position.

b. Turn the ignition switch **OFF**.

c. Connect a battery charger to reduce battery drain.

d. Open the access door in the left-hand luggage compartment trim panel to plug the SUPER STAR II tester or equivalent, into the air suspension diagnostics wiring harness connector.

e. The tester button should be in the **HOLD** (up) position.

f. With the brake pedal depressed hard, turn the ignition switch to the **RUN** position.

g. Move the tester button to the **TEST** (down) position.

h. The air suspension control module will now start sending out the spring fill selection codes to be displayed on the tester. These codes will be displayed in a scrolling manner.

i. Select the desired spring fill operation by releasing the tester button when the desired code is displayed. Select either Code **26** or Code **28** to inflate either the right rear or left rear air spring. As long as the tester button is released the inflation will continue. To stop inflation, move the tester button back down to the **TEST** position. The spring fill codes will again be displayed.

NOTE: Do not apply a load to the suspension until after the air spring has been inflated at least 60 seconds.

j. To exit the spring fill mode, turn the ignition switch to the **OFF** position and unplug the tester.

43. Lower the vehicle all of the way. Check the toe setting and adjust if necessary.

44. Tighten the inboard bushing nut to 45–65 ft. lbs. (61–88 Nm).

MacPherson Strut Cartridge

REPLACEMENT

The strut assembly is not serviceable and must be replaced as an assembly.

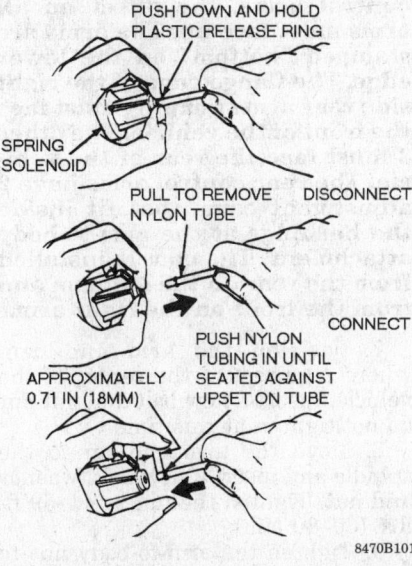

Air suspension air line connect and disconnect procedure — Continental

Code	Description
21	Vent R.F.
22	Vent L.F.
23	Vent R.R.
24	Inflate R.F.
25	Inflate L.F.
26	Inflate R.R.
27	Vent L.R.
28	Inflate L.R.

8470B102

Air suspension spring fill codes — Continental

Coil Springs

REMOVAL AND INSTALLATION

Taurus/Sable Wagon

1. Raise the rear of the vehicle and support safely on the pads of the underbody forward of the tension strut bracket. Position a floor jack under the lower suspension arm and raise the lower arm to normal curb height.

2. Remove the wheel and tire assembly.

3. Locate the bracket retaining the flexible hose to the body. Remove the bracket retaining bolt and bracket from the body.

4. Remove the stabilizer bar U-bracket from the lower suspension arm.

5. Remove and discard the nuts attaching the shock absorber to the lower suspension arm.

6. Disconnect and remove the parking brake cable and clip from the lower suspension arm.

7. If equipped with rear disc brakes, remove the ABS cable from the clips on the lower suspension arm.

8. Remove and discard the bolt and nut attaching the tension strut to the lower suspension arm.

9. Suspend the spindle and upper suspension arms from the body with a piece of wire to prevent them from dropping.

10. Remove the nut, bolt, washer and adjusting cam that retain the lower suspension arm to the spindle. Discard the nut, bolt and washer and replace with new. Set the cam aside.

11. With the floor jack, slowly lower the suspension arm until the spring, lower and upper insulators can be removed. Replace the spring and insulators as required.

To install:

12. Position the lower insulator on the lower suspension arm and press the insulator downward into place. Make sure the insulator is properly seated.

13. Position the upper insulator on top of the spring. Install the spring on the lower suspension arm. Make sure the spring is properly seated.

14. With the floor jack, slowly raise the suspension arm. Guide the upper spring insulator onto the upper spring underbody seat.

15. Position the spindle in the lower suspension arm with a new bolt, nut washer, and the existing cam. Install the bolt with the head of the bolt toward the front of the vehicle. Do not tighten the bolt at this time.

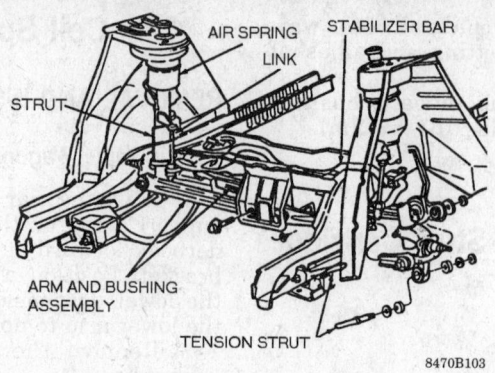

Rear suspension — Continental

8470B103

16. Remove the wire supporting the spindle and suspension arms.

17. Install the tension strut in the lower suspension arm using a new nut and bolt; do not tighten at this time.

18. Attach the parking brake cable and clip to the lower suspension arm.

19. If equipped with rear disc brakes, install the ABS cable into the clips on the lower suspension arm.

20. Position the shock absorber on the lower suspension arm and install 2 new nuts. Torque the nuts to 15–19 ft. lbs. (19–26 Nm).

21. Attach the stabilizer bar and U-bracket to the lower suspension arm using a new bolt. Torque the bolt to 23–30 ft. lbs. (30–40 Nm).

22. Attach the flexible brake hose to the body and tighten the bolt to 8–12 ft. lbs. (11–16 Nm).

23. With the floor jack, raise the lower suspension to normal curb height. Torque the lower suspension arm-to-spindle nut to 40–52 ft. lbs. (54–71 Nm). Torque the bolt that attaches the tension strut to the body bracket to 40–52 ft. lbs. (54–71 Nm).

24. Install the wheel and tire assembly. Remove the floor jack and lower the vehicle.

25. Check the rear wheel alignment and adjust if necessary.

Rear Control Arms

REMOVAL AND INSTALLATION

Taurus/Sable Sedan

1. Raise the vehicle and support it safely. Do not raise the vehicle by the tension strut.

2. Disconnect the brake proportioning valve from the left side front arm.

3. Disconnect the parking brake cable from the front arms.

4. Remove and discard the arm-to-spindle bolt, washer and nut.

5. Remove and discard the arm-to-body bolt and nut.

6. Remove the arm from the vehicle.

To install:

NOTE: When installing new control arms, the offset on all arms must face up. The arms are stamped "bottom" on the lower edge. The flange edge of the right side rear arm stamping must face the front of the vehicle. The other 3 must face the rear of the vehicle. The rear control arms have 2 adjustment cams that fit inside the bushings at the arm-to-body attachment. The cam is installed from the rear on the left arm and from the front on the right arm.

7. Position the arm and cam where required, at the center of the vehicle. Insert a new bolt and nut but do not tighten at this time.

8. Move the arm end up to the spindle and insert a new bolt, washer and nut. Tighten the nut to 44–59 ft. lbs. (60–80 Nm).

9. Tighten the arm-to-body nut to 50–67 ft. lbs. (68–92 Nm).

10. Attach the parking brake cable to the front arms and the brake proportioning valve to the left side front arm.

11. Lower the vehicle and check the alignment.

Continental

1. Turn **OFF** the air suspension switch located in the luggage compartment.

2. Raise and support the vehicle safely.

3. Remove all wire retainers and parking brake cable retainers from the lower suspension arm.

4. Disconnect the height sensor link from the ball stud pin on the lower arm.

5. Mark the position of the notch on the toe adjustment cam.

6. Remove the torsion spring retaining clamp at the spindle.

7. Remove the nut from the inboard bushing on the suspension arm.

8. Install torsion spring remover T88P–5310–A or equivalent, on the arm. Using a ¾ in. ratchet, pry up on the tool and arm to relieve the pressure on the pivot bolt. An assistant may also be required to pull outward on the spindle at the same time to fully relieve the tension on the bolt. Remove the bolt and lower the arm.

9. Remove the nut retaining the torsion spring to the arm and separate the spring from the arm.

10. Remove the outboard attaching bolt at the spindle.

11. Repeat the removal procedure for the other arm.

To install:

NOTE: When installing new control arms, the offset must face up. The arms are stamped bottom on the lower edge. The rear control arms have adjustment cams that fit inside the bushings at the arm-to-body attachment. The cams are installed from the front of both arms.

12. Loosely attach the arm(s) at the spindle. Attach the torsion spring(s) to the arm(s).

13. Position the inboard bushing using torsion spring remover T88P–5310–A or equivalent, and install the bolt. It may be required to have an assistant pull outward on the spindle to align the bushing so the bolt can be inserted. Repeat this step for the opposite side.

14. Set the toe adjustment cam to the alignment mark for rear arm only.

15. Connect the height sensor link to the ball stud pin on the lower arm for right front only.

16. Install all wire retainers and parking brake cable retainers to the lower suspension arm.

17. Lower the vehicle and then turn **ON** the air suspension switch.

18. With the vehicle suspension at curb height, tighten the control arm-to-spindle bolt to 44–59 ft. lbs. (60–80 Nm) and the control arm-to-body bolt to 50–68 ft. lbs. (68–92 Nm).

19. Check the rear toe setting.

Taurus/Sable Wagon

UPPER ARMS

1. Raise the vehicle and support it with wood blocks on jackstands so the suspension is at normal curb height.

2. Remove the wheel and tire assembly.

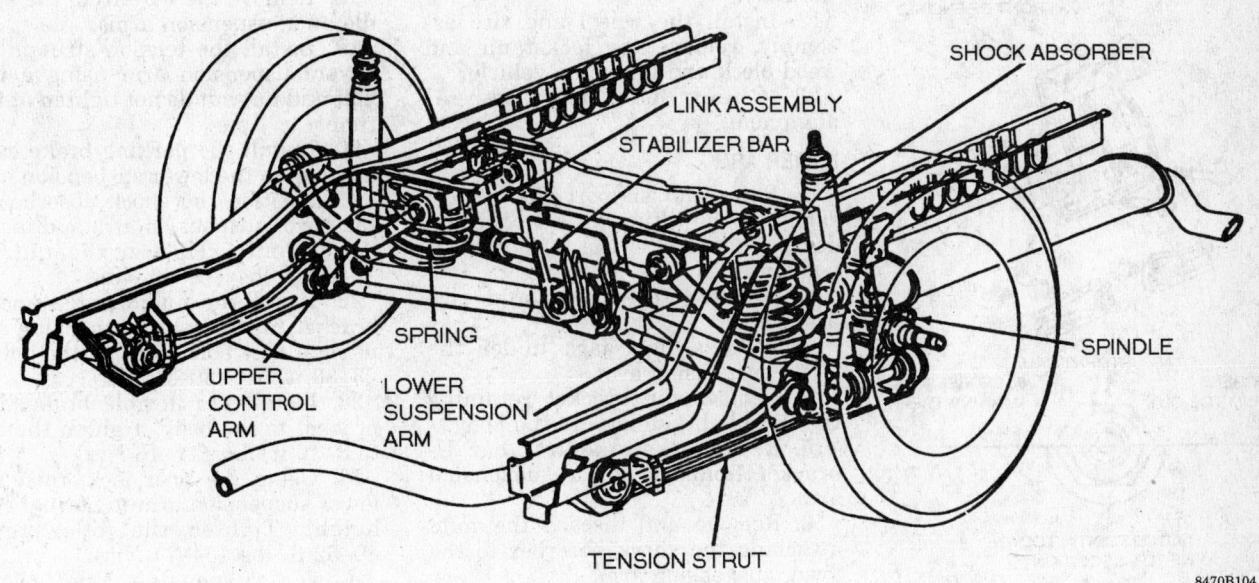

SHOCK ABSORBER

LINK ASSEMBLY

STABILIZER BAR

SPRING

SPINDLE

UPPER CONTROL ARM

LOWER SUSPENSION ARM

TENSION STRUT

8470B104

Rear suspension — Taurus and Sable wagon

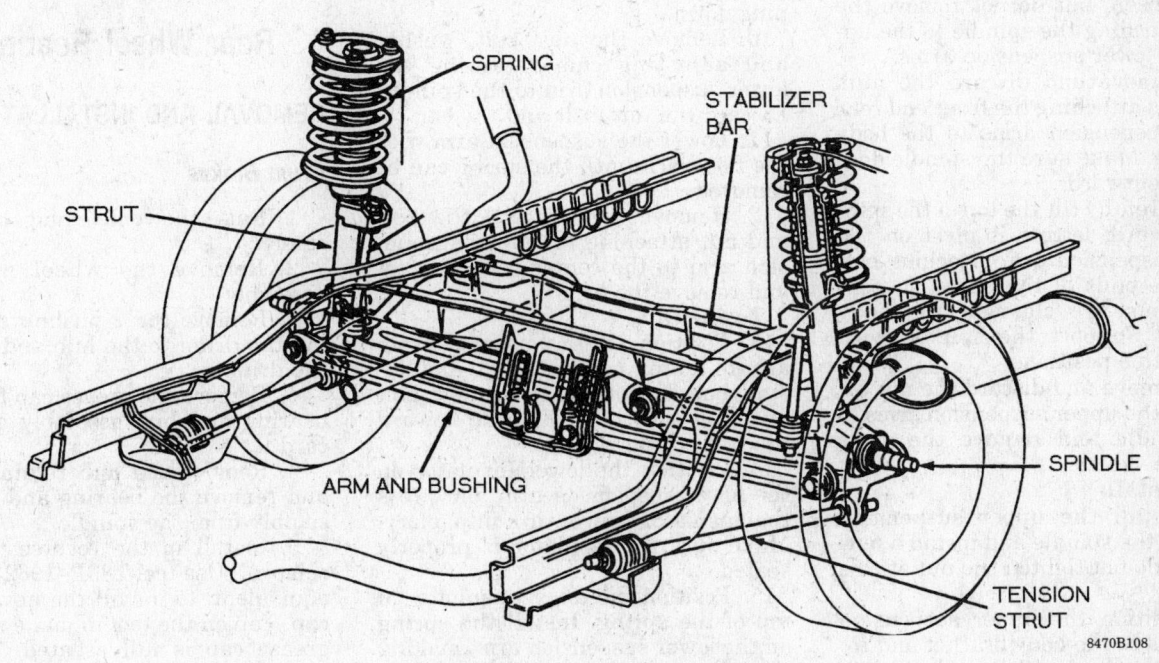

SPRING

STABILIZER BAR

STRUT

SPINDLE

ARM AND BUSHING

TENSION STRUT

8470B108

Rear suspension — Taurus and Sable sedan

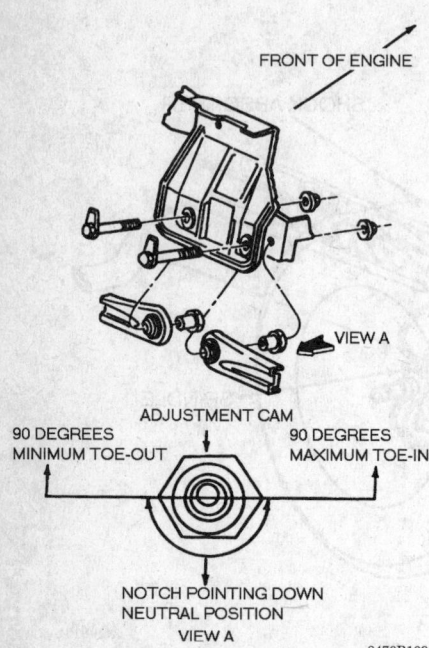

FRONT OF ENGINE

VIEW A

ADJUSTMENT CAM

90 DEGREES
MINIMUM TOE-OUT

90 DEGREES
MAXIMUM TOE-IN

NOTCH POINTING DOWN
NEUTRAL POSITION
VIEW A

8470B109

Rear control arm adjustment — Taurus and Sable sedan and Continental

3. Remove the brake line flexible hose bracket from the body.

4. Loosen, but do not remove the nuts attaching the spindle to the upper and lower suspension arms.

5. Remove and discard the nuts and bolts attaching the front and rear upper suspension arms to the body brackets. Make sure the spindle does not fall outward.

6. Carefully tilt the top of the spindle outward, letting it pivot on the lower suspension arm attaching bolt until the ends of the upper suspension arms are clear of the body bracket. Support the spindle with wire in this position.

7. Remove and discard the nut attaching the upper suspension arms to the spindle and remove the arms from the vehicle.

To install:

8. Install the upper suspension arms on the spindle and install a new nut but do not tighten the nut at this time.

9. Position the upper suspension arm ends to the body bracket and install new nuts and bolts. Tighten to 73–97 ft. lbs. (95–129 Nm). Remove the wire from the spindle.

10. Tighten the nut attaching the upper suspension arms to the spindle to 150–190 ft. lbs. (204–257 Nm). Tighten the nut attaching the lower

suspension arm to the spindle to 40–52 ft. lbs. (54–71 Nm).

11. Install the brake line bracket to the body.

12. Install the wheel and tire assembly, remove the jackstand and wood block and lower the vehicle.

13. Check the rear wheel alignment.

LOWER ARM

1. Raise and support the vehicle safely on the lifting pads on the underbody forward of the tension strut body bracket.

2. Remove the wheel and tire assembly.

3. Place a floor jack under the lower suspension arm.

4. Remove the bracket retaining the flexible brake hose to the body.

5. Remove the stabilizer bar U-bracket from the lower suspension arm.

6. Remove and discard the nuts attaching the shock absorber to the lower suspension arm.

7. Remove the parking brake cable and clip from the lower suspension arm.

8. Remove and discard the bolt and nut attaching the tension strut to the lower suspension arm.

9. Support the spindle and upper suspension arms by wiring them to the body, to prevent them from dropping down.

10. Remove the nut, bolt, washer and adjusting cam retaining the lower suspension arm to the spindle. Discard the nut, bolt and washer.

11. Lower the suspension arm with the floor jack until the spring can be removed.

12. Remove and discard the bolt and nut attaching the lower suspension arm to the center body bracket and remove the arm.

To install:

13. Position the lower suspension arm-to-center body bracket and install but do not tighten a new bolt and nut with the bolt head toward the front of the vehicle.

14. Position the lower insulator on the lower suspension arm and press the insulator downward into place. Make sure the insulator is properly seated.

15. Position the upper insulator on top of the spring. Install the spring on the lower suspension arm, making sure the spring is properly seated.

16. Raise the suspension arm with the floor jack and guide the upper spring insulator onto the upper spring seat on the underbody.

17. Position the spindle in the lower suspension arm and install, but do

not tighten, a new bolt, nut, washer and the existing cam, with the bolt head toward the front of the vehicle.

18. Remove the wire from the spindle and suspension arms.

19. Install the tension strut in the lower suspension arm using a new bolt and nut but do not tighten at this time.

20. Install the parking brake cable and clip to the lower suspension arm.

21. Position the shock absorber on the lower suspension arm and install 2 new nuts. Tighten the nuts to 15–19 ft. lbs. (19–26 Nm).

22. Install the stabilizer bar and U-bracket to the lower suspension arm using a new bolt. Tighten the bolt to 23–30 ft. lbs. (30–40 Nm).

23. Install the flexible brake hose bracket to the body. Tighten the bolt to 8–12 ft. lbs. (11–16 Nm).

24. Using the floor jack, raise the lower suspension arm to normal curb height. Tighten the following to 40–52 ft. lbs. (54–71 Nm):

Lower suspension arm-to-body bracket nut

Lower suspension arm-to-spindle nut

Tension strut-to-body bracket bolt

25. Install the wheel and tire assembly and lower the vehicle.

26. Check the rear wheel alignment.

Rear Wheel Bearings

REMOVAL AND INSTALLATION

Drum Brakes

1. Raise the vehicle and support it safely.

2. Remove the wheel and tire assembly.

3. Remove the 2 pushnuts retaining the drum to the hub and remove the drum.

4. Remove the grease cap from the bearing and hub assembly and discard it.

5. Remove the hub retaining nut and remove the bearing and hub assembly from the spindle.

6. Install in the reverse order of removal. Use tool T89P–19623–FH or equivalent, to install the new grease cap. Tap on the tool to make sure the grease cap is fully seated. Tighten the hub retaining nut to 188–254 ft. lbs. (255–345 Nm).

Disc Brakes

1. Raise the vehicle and support it safely.

2. Remove the wheel and tire assembly.

3. Remove the caliper assembly from the brake adapter. Support the caliper assembly with a length of wire; do not let it hang by the brake hose.

4. Remove the push on nuts that retain the rotor to the hub and remove the rotor.

5. Remove the grease cap from the bearing and hub assembly and discard the grease cap.

6. Remove the bearing and hub assembly retaining nut and remove the bearing and hub assembly from the spindle.

7. Install in the reverse order of removal. Install a new grease cap using tool T89P–19623–FH or equivalent. Tap on the tool until the grease cap is fully seated. Tighten the hub retaining nut to 188–254 ft. lbs. (255–345 Nm).

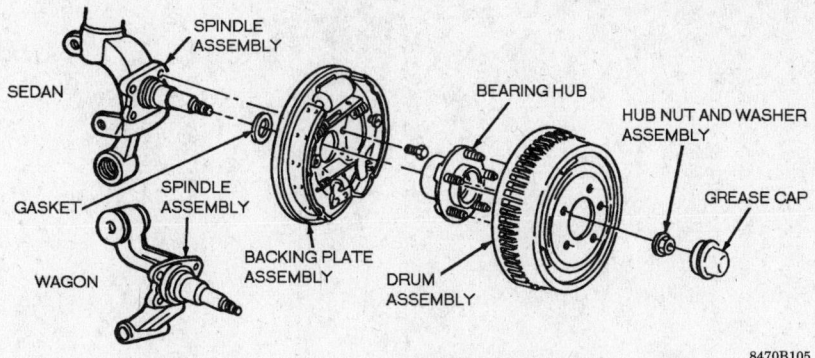

8470B105

Rear wheel hub and bearing assembly — vehicles with drum brakes

Ford/Lincoln/Mercury

LINCOLN—MARK VII, MARK VIII **MERCURY**—Cougar **FORD**—Mustang, Thunderbird

FIRING ORDERS

NOTE: To avoid confusion, always replace spark plug wires one at a time.

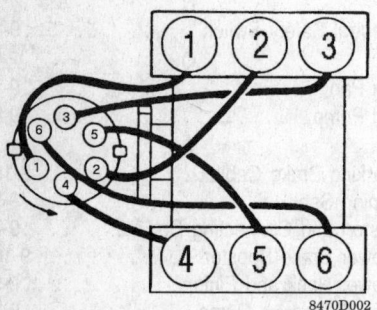

3.8L Engine (except SC)
Engine Firing Order: 1–4–2–5–3–6
Distributor Rotation: Counterclockwise

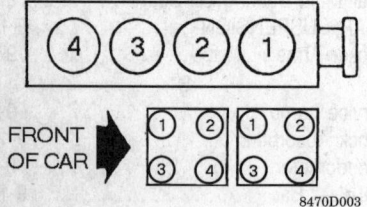

2.3L Engine
Engine Firing Order: 1–3–4–2
Distributorless Ignition System

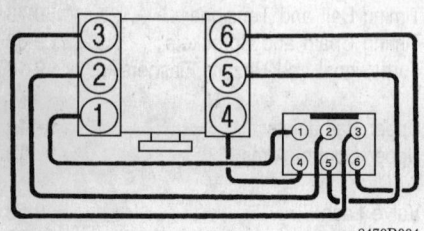

3.8L SC Engine
Engine Firing Order: 1–4–2–5–3–6
Distributorless Ignition System

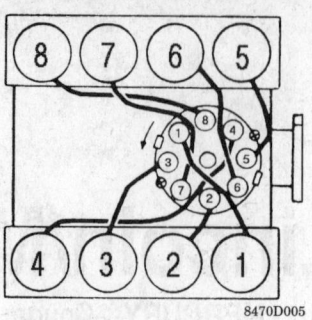

5.0L Engine
Engine Firing Order:
1–3–7–2–6–5–4–8
Distributor Rotation:
Counterclockwise

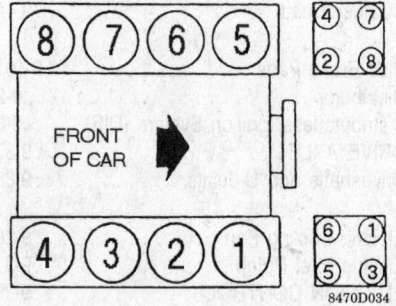

4.6L Engine
Engine Firing Order: 1–3–7–2–6–5–4–8
Distributorless Ignition System

ENGINE ELECTRICAL

NOTE: Disconnecting the negative battery cable on some vehicles may interfere with the functions of the on board computer systems and may require the computer to undergo a relearning process, once the negative battery cable is reconnected.

Distributor

REMOVAL

1. Disconnect the negative battery cable.
2. Mark the position of the No. 1 cylinder wire tower on the distributor base.

NOTE: This reference is necessary in case the engine is disturbed while the distributor is removed.

3. Remove the distributor cap and position the cap and ignition wires to the side. Disconnect the wiring harness plug from the distributor connector.
4. Scribe a mark on the distributor body to indicate the position of the rotor tip. Scribe a mark on the distributor housing and engine block or timing cover to indicate the position of the distributor in the engine.
5. Remove the hold-down bolt and clamp located at the base of the distributor. Remove the distributor from the engine. Note the direction the rotor tip points if it moves from the No. 1 position when the drive gear disengages. For reinstallation purposes, the rotor should be at this point to insure proper gear mesh and timing.
6. Cover the distributor opening in the engine to prevent the entry of dirt or foreign material.
7. Avoid turning the crankshaft, if possible, while the distributor is removed. If the engine is disturbed, the No. 1 cylinder piston will have to be brought to TDC on the compression stroke before the distributor is installed.

INSTALLATION

NOTE: Before installing, visually inspect the distributor. The drive gear should be free of nicks, cracks and excessive wear. The distributor driveshaft should move freely, without binding. The O-ring should fit tightly and be free of cuts.

Timing Not Disturbed

1. Position the distributor in the engine, aligning the rotor and distributor housing with the marks that were made during removal. If the distributor does not fully seat in the engine block or timing cover, it may be because the distributor is not engaging properly with the oil pump intermediate shaft. Remove the distributor and, using a suitable tool, turn the intermediate shaft until the distributor will seat properly.
2. Install the hold-down clamp and bolt. Snug the mounting bolt so the distributor can be turned for ignition timing purposes.
3. Install the distributor cap and connect the distributor to the wiring harness.
4. Connect the negative battery cable. Check and, if necessary, adjust the ignition timing.

5. After the timing has been set, tighten the distributor hold-down clamp bolt to:

1992 3.8L engine 20–29 ft. lbs. (27–40 Nm)

1993–96 3.8L engine 15–22 ft. lbs. (20–30 Nm)

5.0L engine 18–26 ft. lbs. (24–35 Nm)

6. Recheck the ignition timing after tightening the bolt.

Timing Disturbed

1. Disconnect the No. 1 cylinder spark plug wire and remove the No. 1 cylinder spark plug.

2. Place a finger over the spark plug hole and crank the engine slowly until compression is felt.

3. Align the TDC mark on the crankshaft pulley with the pointer on the timing cover. This places the piston in No. 1 cylinder at TDC on the compression stroke.

4. Turn the distributor shaft until the rotor points to the distributor cap No. 1 spark plug tower, as marked during the removal procedure.

5. Install the distributor in the engine, aligning the rotor and distributor housing with the marks that were made during removal. If the distributor does not fully seat in the engine block or timing cover, it may be because the distributor is not engaging properly with the oil pump intermediate shaft. Remove the distributor and, using a suitable tool, turn the intermediate shaft until the distributor will seat properly.

6. Install the hold-down clamp and bolt. Snug the mounting bolt so the distributor can be turned for ignition timing purposes.

7. Install the No. 1 cylinder spark plug and connect the spark plug wire. Install the distributor cap and connect the distributor to the wiring harness.

8. Connect the negative battery cable and set the ignition timing.

9. After the timing has been set, tighten the distributor hold-down clamp bolt to:

1992 3.8L engine 20–29 ft. lbs. (27–40 Nm)

1993–96 3.8L engine 15–22 ft. lbs. (20–30 Nm)

5.0L engine 18–26 ft. lbs. (24–35 Nm)

10. Recheck the ignition timing after tightening the bolt.

Distributorless Ignition System (DIS)

The 3.8L SC, 2.3L and 4.6L engines are equipped with Distributorless Ignition Systems. The DIS consists of the following components: crankshaft sensor, ignition module, ignition coil pack, the spark angle portion of the ECU and the related wiring. The system used on the 3.8L SC engine includes a camshaft sensor.

The DIS eliminates the need for a distributor by using multiple ignition coils. Each coil fires 2 spark plugs at the same time. The plugs are paired so as 1 fires during the compression cycle, the other fires during the exhaust stroke. The next time the coil is fired, the plug that was on exhaust will be on compression and the 1 that was on compression will be on exhaust. The spark in the exhaust cylinder is wasted but little of the coil energy is lost. The ignition coils are mounted together in coil packs. There are 2 coil packs used on the 2.3L and 4.6L engines, each containing 2 ignition coils. The 3.8L SC engine uses 1 coil pack containing 3 separate ignition coils.

The crankshaft sensor is a Hall effect magnetic switch, activated by vanes on the crankshaft damper and pulley assembly. The signal generated by this sensor is called the Profile Ignition Pickup (PIP). The PIP signal provides base timing and rpm information to the ECU. In addition, the crankshaft sensor on the 2.3L engine provides a Cylinder Identification (CID) signal. The CID signal is used to synchronize the ignition coils.

The camshaft sensor used on the 3.8L SC engine is a Hall effect magnetic switch, activated by a single vane which is driven by the camshaft. This sensor provides CID information for the ignition coil and for fuel system synchronization.

The ignition module is a microprocessor that receives input from the crankshaft and camshaft sensors in regards to engine position, base timing and engine speed and input from the ECU pertaining to spark advance. The ignition module uses this information to direct which coil to fire and to calculate the turn on and turn off times of the coils required to achieve the correct dwell and spark advance.

REMOVAL AND INSTALLATION

Crankshaft Sensor

2.3L ENGINE

1. Disconnect the negative battery cable.

2. Disconnect the sensor electrical connectors from the engine harness.

3. Remove the large electrical connector from the crankshaft position sensor assembly.

4. Remove the accessory drive belt. Remove the 4 screws retaining the crankshaft pulley hub assembly and remove the pulley.

5. Remove the timing belt outer cover. Rotate the crankshaft by hand till the keyway is at the 10 o'clock position.

6. Remove the 2 sensor retaining bolts and the plastic wire harness retainer that secures the sensor harness to it's mounting bracket. Remove the sensor, sliding the electrical wires out from behind the inner timing belt cover.

To install:

7. Remove the large electrical connector from the new crankshaft timing sensor.

8. Slide the electrical wires behind the inner timing belt cover and position the sensor. Hold the sensor loosely in place with the retaining bolts, but do not tighten at this time.

9. Install the large electrical connector onto the sensor.

NOTE: Make sure the 4 wires to the large electrical connector are installed in the proper locations as indicated. The sensor will not function properly if the wires are installed in the wrong locations.

10. Reconnect both sensor electrical connectors to the engine harness.

11. Rotate the crankshaft so the outer vane on the crankshaft pulley hub assembly engages both sides of the crankshaft Hall effect sensor positioner T89P–6316–A or equivalent, and tighten the sensor retaining bolts.

12. Rotate the crankshaft so the vane on the crankshaft pulley hub is no longer engaged in the positioning tool. Remove the tool.

13. Install the new plastic wire harness retainer to secure the sensor harness to it's mounting bracket. Trim off the excess.

14. Install the timing belt outer cover.

15. Install the crankshaft pulley and tighten the 4 attaching bolts to 15–22 ft. lbs. (20–30 Nm). Install the accessory drive belts.

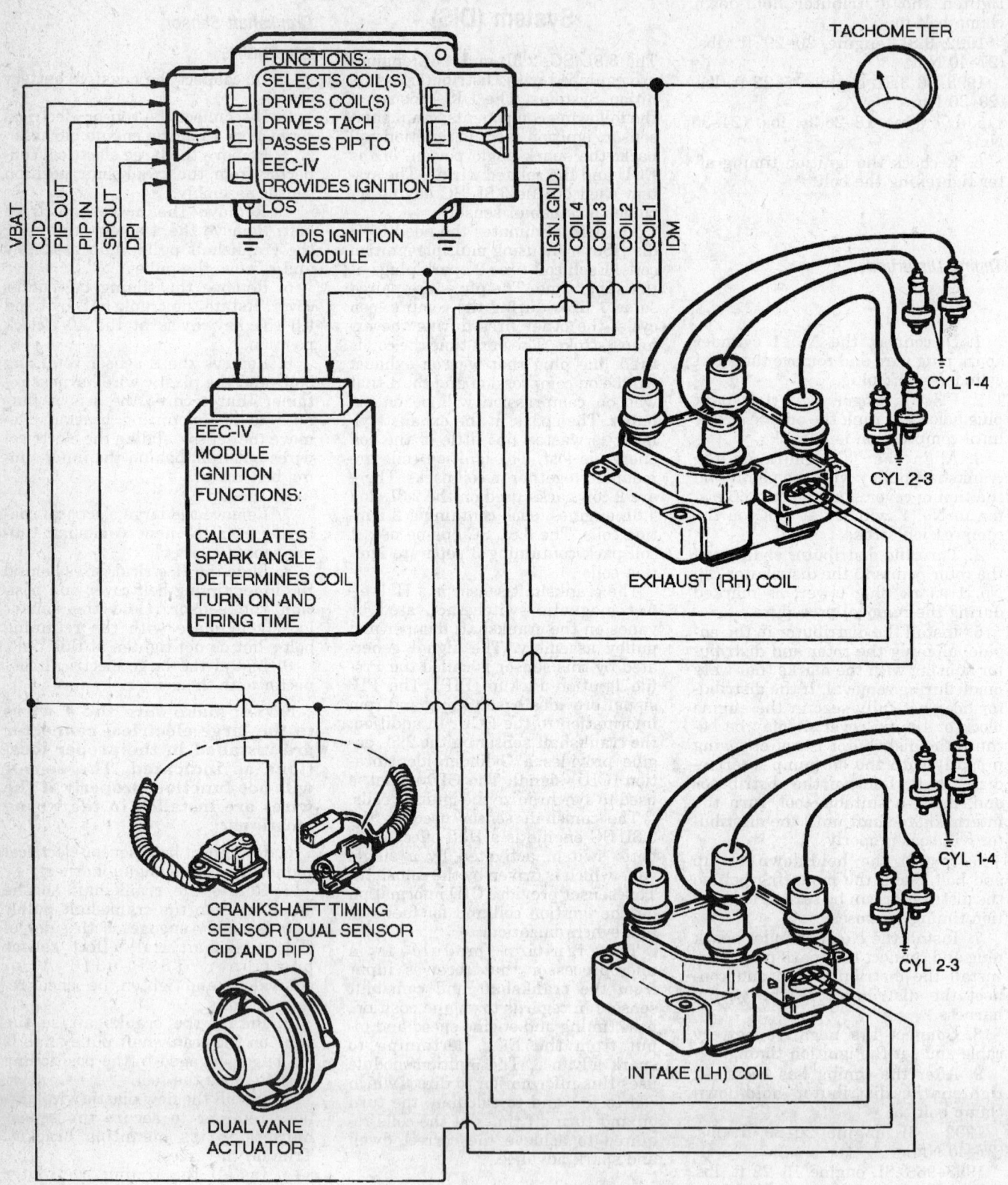

Distributorless ignition system — 2.3L engine

8470D006

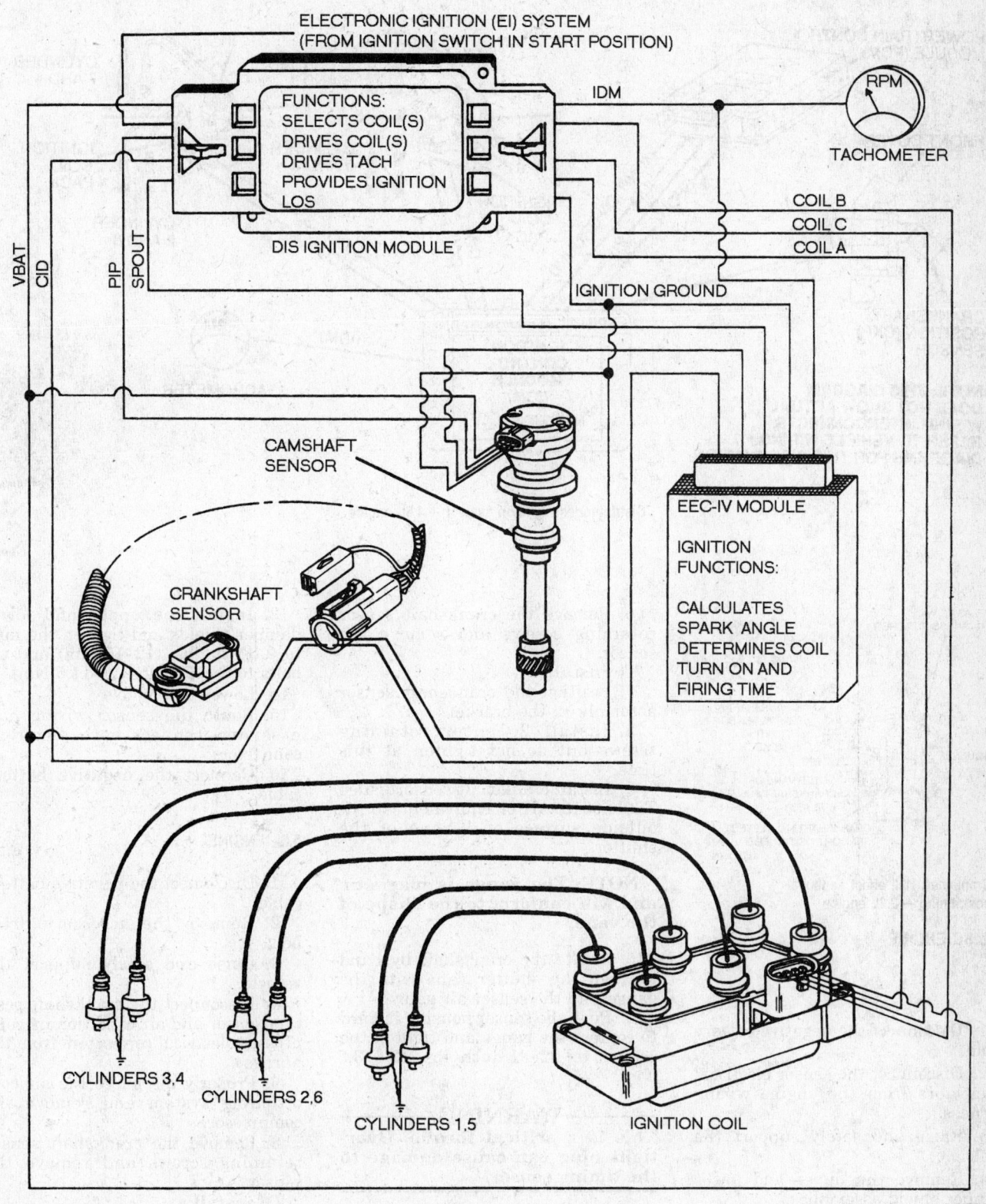

Distributorless ignition system — 3.8L SC engine

8470D007

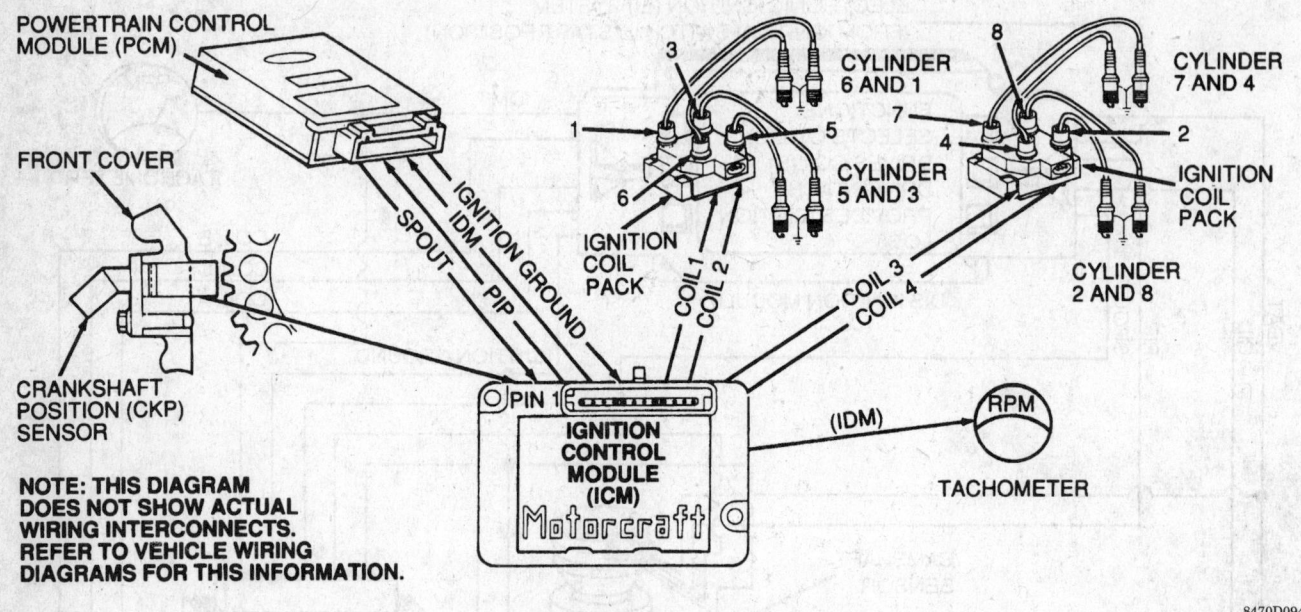

Distributorless ignition system — 4.6L engine

8470D094

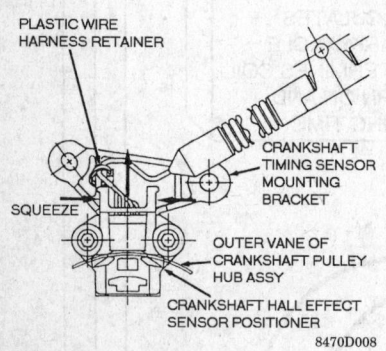

Crankshaft Hall effect sensor positioning — 2.3L engine

8470D008

3.8L SC ENGINE

1. Disconnect the negative battery cable.

2. Disconnect the sensor electrical connectors from the engine wiring harness.

3. Raise and safely support the vehicle.

4. Remove the upper and lower damper shield assemblies.

5. Rotate the crankshaft by hand to position the metal vane of the shutter, attached to the rear of the damper, outside of the sensor air gap.

6. Remove the crankshaft sensor retaining screws and remove the sensor.

To install:

7. Position the crankshaft sensor assembly on the bracket.

8. Install 2 sensor retaining screws but do not tighten at this time.

9. Install crankshaft sensor gauge T89P–6316–AH or equivalent, to the outside surface of 1 vane of the shutter.

NOTE: The gauge is magnetic and will conform to the shape of the vane.

10. Rotate the crankshaft by hand to align the shutter vane with the gauge into the sensor air gap.

11. Push the sensor housing inward to contact the gauge and tighten the screws to 22–31 inch lbs. (2.5–3.5 Nm).

— WARNING —
This is a critical torque. Over-tightening can cause damage to the timing sensor.

12. Rotate the crankshaft by hand to position the shutter vane with the gauge outside of the air gap. Remove the magnetic gauge.

13. Install the upper and lower damper shields and tighten the nuts to 9–11 ft. lbs. (12–15 Nm) and the bolts to 6–8.5 ft. lbs. (8–11.5 Nm).

14. Lower the vehicle.

15. Route the sensor wiring harness and connect both electrical connectors.

16. Connect the negative battery cable.

4.6L ENGINE

1. Disconnect the negative battery cable.

2. Remove the accessory drive belt.

3. Raise and safely support the vehicle.

4. Disconnect the crankshaft position sensor and air conditioning compressor electrical connectors from the harness.

5. Properly discharge the air conditioning system and remove the compressor.

6. Remove the crankshaft sensor retaining screws and remove the sensor.

To install:

7. Make sure the sensor mounting surface is clean and O-ring is in the proper location. Position the crankshaft sensor assembly on the bracket.

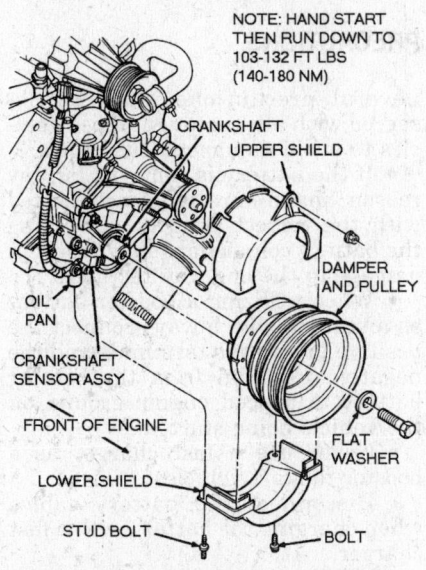

NOTE: HAND START THEN RUN DOWN TO 103-132 FT LBS (140-180 NM)

CRANKSHAFT

UPPER SHIELD

DAMPER AND PULLEY

OIL PAN

CRANKSHAFT SENSOR ASSY

FRONT OF ENGINE

FLAT WASHER

LOWER SHIELD

STUD BOLT

BOLT

NOTE: LUBRICATE SEAL SURFACE (O.D.) AND I.D. OF DAMPER HUB WITH ESE-M2C39-F OIL OR ESE-M1C104-A GREASE PRIOR TO ASSEMBLY. SEAL SURFACE MUST BE FREE OF DIRT OR GRIT.

8470D009

Crankshaft position sensor removal and installation — 3.8L engine

8. Install 2 sensor retaining screws and tighten to 71–106 inch lbs. (8–12 Nm).

——— WARNING ———
This is a critical torque. Overtightening can cause damage to the timing sensor.

9. Install the A/C compressor. Evacuate and recharge the A/C system.
10. Connect the crankshaft position sensor and air conditioning compressor electrical connectors to the harness.
11. Lower the vehicle.
12. Install the accessory drive belt.
13. Connect the negative battery cable.

Camshaft Sensor

3.8L SC ENGINE

1. Disconnect the negative battery cable.
2. Disconnect the camshaft sensor electrical connector.
3. Remove the camshaft sensor retaining screws and remove the sensor.
4. Installation is the reverse of the removal procedure. Tighten the retaining screws to 22–31 inch lbs. (2.5–3.5 Nm).

Synchronizer Assembly

3.8L SC ENGINE

The synchronizer assembly mounts in place of the distributor. It provides the mechanical link between the camshaft sensor and the camshaft.

NOTE: Before starting this procedure, set the No. 1 cylinder to 26 degrees after TDC on the compression stroke. Then note the position of the camshaft sensor electrical connector. The installation procedure requires that the connector be located in the same position.

1. Disconnect the negative battery cable.
2. Remove the camshaft sensor assembly.
3. Remove the synchronizer clamp, bolt and washer.
4. Remove the synchronizer from the front engine cover, by pulling it out. The oil pump intermediate shaft will come out with the assembly.

To install:

——— WARNING ———
If the replacement synchronizer does not contain a plastic locator cover tool, a special service tool such as synchro positioner tool T89P-12200-A or equivalent, must be used to install the synchronizer. Failure to use this special tool will cause the synchronizer timing to be out of adjustment, and could lead to engine damage.

5. If the plastic locator cover tool is not attached to the replacement synchronizer, attach synchro positioner tool T89P-12200-A or equivalent, as follows:
   a. Engage the synchronizer vane into the tool's radial slot.
   b. Rotate the tool on the synchronizer base until the tool boss engages the base notch. The cover tool should be square and in contact with the entire top surface of the synchronizer base.
6. Install the intermediate oil pump shaft onto the replacement synchronizer.
7. Position the synchronizer so gear engagement occurs when the arrow on the locator tool is pointed 30 degrees counterclockwise from the front face of the engine block. This will locate the camshaft sensor electrical connector to the position it was in before removal.
8. Install the synchronizer base clamp and tighten the mounting bolt to 15–22 ft. lbs. (20–30 Nm).

9. Remove the positioner tool and install the camshaft sensor. Connect the sensor electrical lead and connect the negative battery cable.

——— WARNING ———
If the camshaft sensor electrical connector is not positioned properly — contacting the A/C bracket or forward of the supercharger drive belt, do not reposition the connector by rotating the synchronizer base. This will result in the ignition and fuel systems being out of time with the engine, possibly causing engine damage. If the sensor electrical connector is not properly positioned, remove the synchronizer and repeat the installation procedure.

Ignition Module

1. Disconnect the negative battery cable.
2. Disconnect the electrical connectors at the module.
3. Remove the module retaining screws and remove the module.

To install:
4. Apply an even coating of silicone dielectric compound WA–IO, D7AZ–19A331–A or equivalent to the mounting surface of the module.
5. Install the module and the retaining screws. Tighten the screws to 22–31 inch lbs. (2.5–3.5 Nm).
6. Connect the electrical connectors to the module and connect the negative battery cable.

Ignition Coil Pack

2.3L ENGINE

1. Disconnect the negative battery cable.
2. Squeeze the locking tabs of the coil wire retainer by hand and remove the spark plug wires with a twisting and pulling motion. Do not pull on the wire.
3. Disconnect the engine harness electrical connector from the ignition coil assembly.
4. Remove the 4 retaining screws and remove the ignition coil.
5. Installation is the reverse of removal procedure.

3.8L SC AND 4.6L ENGINES

1. Disconnect the negative battery cable.
2. Disconnect the electrical harness connector from the coil pack. On 4.6L engine, disconnect the capacitor.
3. Remove the spark plug wires by squeezing the locking tabs to release the coil boot retainers.

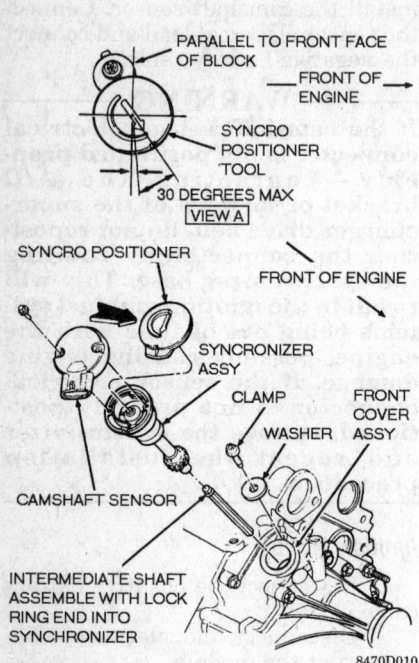

PARALLEL TO FRONT FACE OF BLOCK

FRONT OF ENGINE

SYNCRO POSITIONER TOOL

30 DEGREES MAX
VIEW A

SYNCRO POSITIONER

FRONT OF ENGINE

SYNCHRONIZER ASSY

CLAMP

WASHER

FRONT COVER ASSY

CAMSHAFT SENSOR

INTERMEDIATE SHAFT ASSEMBLE WITH LOCK RING END INTO SYNCHRONIZER

8470D010

Synchronizer assembly installation — 3.8L SC engine

4. Remove the coil pack retaining screws and remove the coil pack. On 4.6L engines, save the capacitor for installation with the new coil pack.

5. Installation is the reverse of the removal procedure. Tighten the screws to 40–62 inch lbs. (4.5–7.0 Nm).

Ignition Timing

ADJUSTMENT

NOTE: Always refer to the Vehicle Emission Information Label to verify the timing adjustment procedure.

Distributorless Ignition Systems

Base timing for distributorless engines is set from the factory at 10 degrees BTDC and is not adjustable.

Distributor Ignition System

1. Locate the timing marks and pointer on the crankshaft pulley and the timing cover. Clean the marks so they will be visible with a timing light. Apply chalk or bright-colored paint, if necessary.

2. Place the transaxle in **P** or **N**. The air conditioning and heater controls should be in the **OFF** position.

3. Connect a suitable tachometer and inductive timing light according to the manufacturer's instructions.

NOTE: The tachometer can be connected to the ignition coil without removing the coil connector. Insert an alligator clip into the back of the connector, onto the dark green/yellow dotted wire. Do not let the clip accidently ground to a metal surface as it may permanently damage the coil.

4. Disconnect the single wire inline SPOUT connector or remove the shorting bar from the double wire SPOUT connector.

5. Start the engine and allow it to warm up to operating temperature.

NOTE: To set timing correctly, a remote starter should not be used. Use the ignition key only to start the vehicle. Disconnecting the start wire at the starter relay will cause the TFI module to revert to start mode timing after the vehicle is started. Reconnecting the start wire after the vehicle is running will not correct the timing.

6. With the engine at the timing rpm specified, check the initial timing by aiming the timing light at the timing marks and pointer. Refer to the underhood Vehicle Emission Information Label for specifications.

7. If the marks align, shut OFF the engine and proceed to Step 8. If the marks do not align, shut OFF the engine and loosen the distributor hold-down clamp bolt. Start the engine, aim the timing light and turn the distributor until the timing marks align. Shut OFF the engine and tighten the distributor hold-down clamp bolt. Recheck the timing after the bolt has been tightened.

8. Reconnect the single wire inline SPOUT connector or reinstall the shorting bar on the double wire SPOUT connector. Check the timing advance to verify the distributor is advancing beyond the initial setting.

9. Remove the inductive timing light and tachometer.

Alternator

PRECAUTIONS

Several precautions must be observed with alternator equipped vehicles to avoid damage to the unit.

• If the battery is removed for any reason, make sure it is reconnected with the correct polarity. Reversing the battery connections may result in damage to the one-way rectifiers.

• When utilizing a booster battery as a starting aid, always connect the positive to positive terminals and the negative terminal from the booster battery to a good engine ground on the vehicle being started.

• Never use a fast charger as a booster to start vehicles.

• Disconnect the battery cables when charging the battery with a fast charger.

• Never attempt to polarize the alternator.

• Do not use test lamps of more than 12V when checking diode continuity.

• Do not short across or ground any of the alternator terminals.

• The polarity of the battery, alternator and regulator must be matched and considered before making any electrical connections within the system.

• Never separate the alternator on an open circuit. Make sure all connections within the circuit are clean and tight.

• Disconnect the battery ground terminal when performing any service on electrical components.

• Disconnect the battery if arc welding is to be done on the vehicle.

BELT TENSION ADJUSTMENT

All vehicles are equipped with an automatic belt tensioner. No adjustment is necessary or possible. The belt tensioner is equipped with a belt wear indicator; when 1 percent belt stretch is indicated, the drive belt must be replaced. If the wear indicator is difficult to see on the 3.8L or 5.0L engines, locate the tab on the tensioner face plate. The tab should be approximately between the stops.

REMOVAL AND INSTALLATION

1. Disconnect the negative battery cable.

2. Tag and disconnect the wiring connectors from the rear of the alternator.

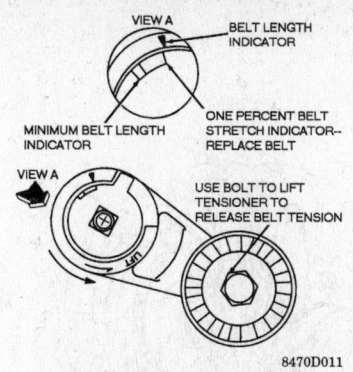

Belt tensioner — 3.8L and 5.0L engines

3. Loosen the alternator pivot bolt and remove the adjusting bolt. Disengage the drive belt from the alternator pulley.

4. Remove the alternator pivot bolt and the alternator.

5. Installation is the reverse of the removal procedure.

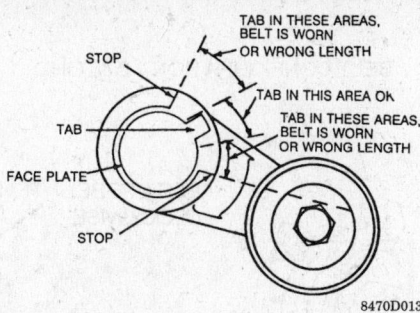

Belt replacement checking — 3.8L 4.6L and 5.0L engines

Voltage Regulator

REMOVAL AND INSTALLATION

1. Disconnect the negative battery cable.

2. Disconnect the wire connectors, remove the regulator mounting screws and remove the regulator.

NOTE: Always disconnect the connector plug from the regulator before removing the mounting screws.

3. Installation is the reverse of the removal procedure.

Starter

REMOVAL AND INSTALLATION

1. Disconnect the negative battery cable.

2. Raise the vehicle and support it safely.

3. Disconnect the starter cable from the starter. If equipped with starter mounted solenoid, disconnect the push-on connector from the solenoid.

NOTE: To disconnect the hard-shell connector from the solenoid S terminal, grasp the plastic shell and pull off; do not pull on the wire. Pull straight off to prevent damage to the connector and S terminal.

4. Remove the starter bolts and the starter.

5. Position the starter to the engine and tighten the mounting bolts to 15–20 ft. lbs. (20–27 Nm).

6. Reconnect the starter cable and, if equipped, solenoid wire. Connect the negative battery cable.

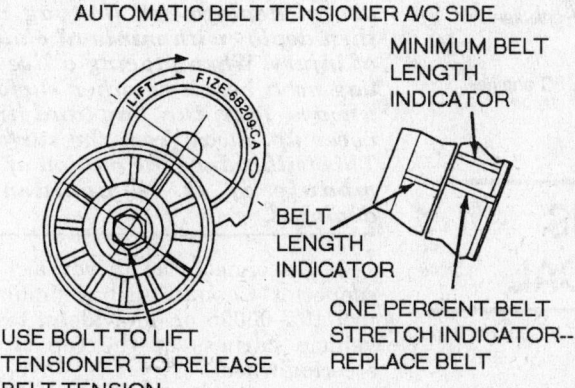

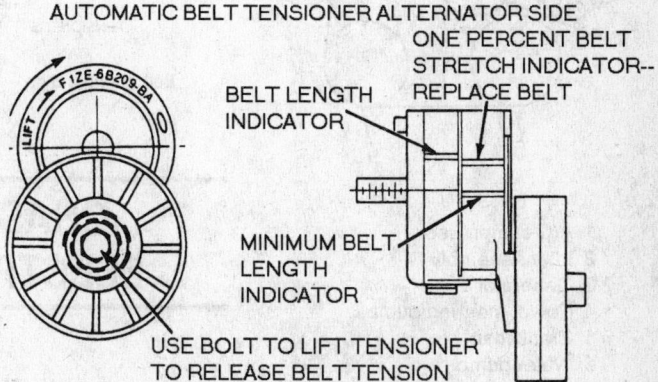

Belt wear indicator marks — 2.3L engine

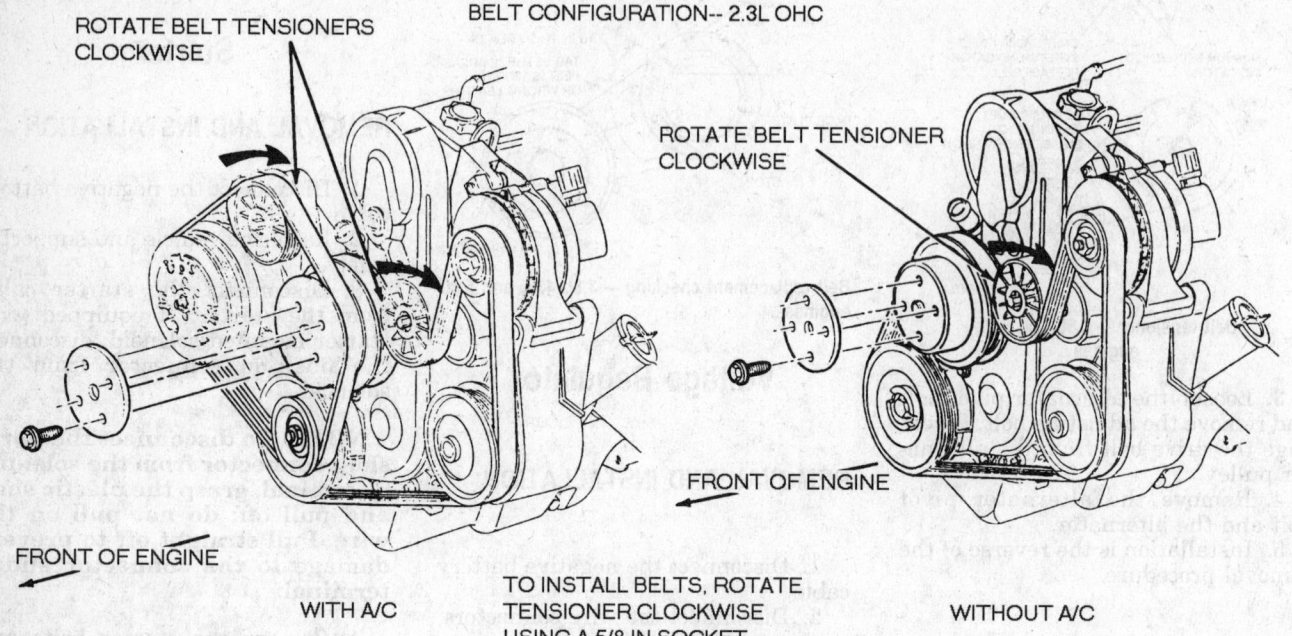

ROTATE BELT TENSIONERS CLOCKWISE

BELT CONFIGURATION-- 2.3L OHC

ROTATE BELT TENSIONER CLOCKWISE

FRONT OF ENGINE

FRONT OF ENGINE

WITH A/C

TO INSTALL BELTS, ROTATE TENSIONER CLOCKWISE USING A 5/8 IN SOCKET.

WITHOUT A/C

8470D014

Belt configuration — 2.3L engine

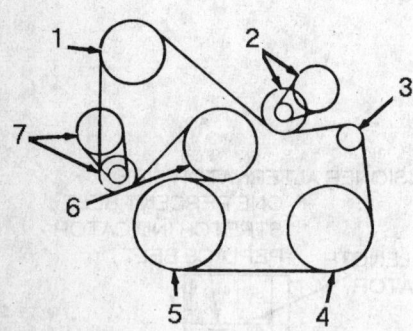
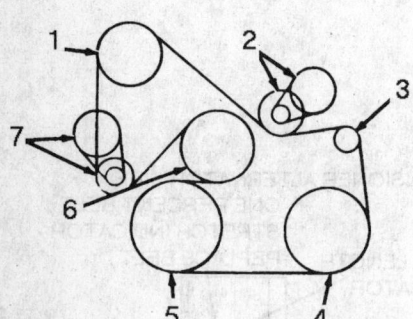

1. A/C compressor
2. Idler Assembly
3. Generator
4. Power steering pump
5. Crankshaft
6. Water pump
7. Tensioner assembly

8470D095

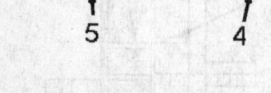

Belt configuration — 3.8L engine

AUTO TENSIONERS
SUPER-CHARGER
AUTO TENSIONERS
A/C COMPRESSOR
GENERATOR
POWER STEERING PUMP
IDLER PULLEY
WATER PUMP PULLEY
AUTO TENSIONERS
CRANKSHAFT

8470D096

Belt configuration — 3.8L SC engine

CHASSIS ELECTRICAL

Air Bag

DISARMING

1. Disconnect the positive battery cable. Wait 1 minute for the backup power supply in the diagnostic monitor to deplete its stored energy.

2. Remove the 4 nut and washer assemblies (2 screws on Mark VIII) retaining the driver air bag module to the steering wheel.

---CAUTION---
When carrying a live air bag, make sure the bag and trim cover are pointed away from the body. In the unlikely event of an accidental deployment, the bag will then deploy with minimal chance of injury. When placing a live air bag on a bench or other surface, always face the bag and trim cover up, away from the surface. This will reduce the motion of the module if it is accidently deployed.

---

3. Disconnect the driver air bag connector. Connect air bag simulator tool 105–00008 or equivalent, to the vehicle harness at the top of the steering wheel.

Heater Blower Motor

REMOVAL AND INSTALLATION

Mustang

1. Disconnect the negative battery cable.

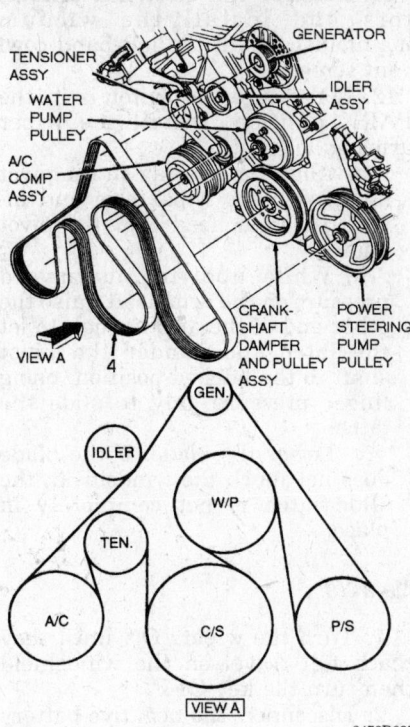

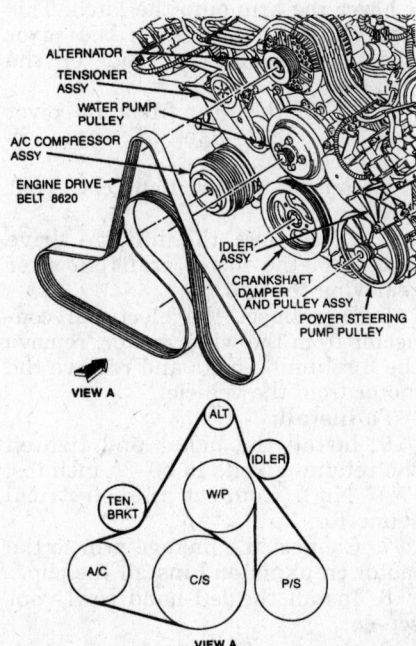

Belt configuration — 4.6L (DOHC) engine

8470D097

Belt configuration — 4.6L (SOHC) engine

8470E005

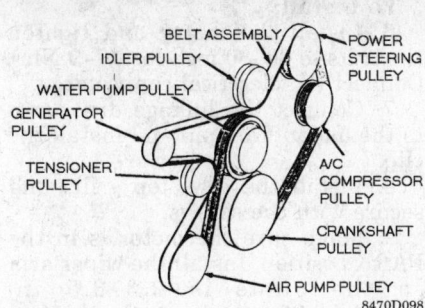

Belt configuration — Thunderbird and Cougar with 5.0L engine

8470D098

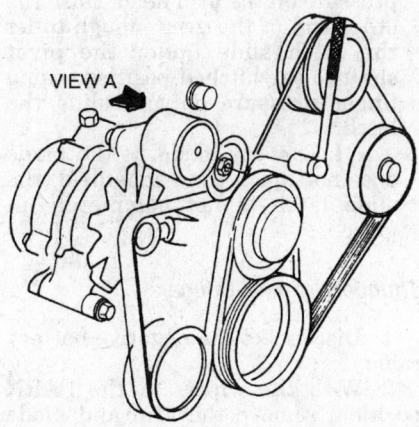

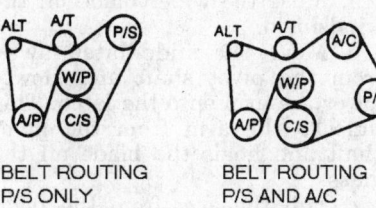

BELT ROUTING P/S ONLY

BELT ROUTING P/S AND A/C

8470D099

Belt configuration — Mustang with 5.0L engine

2. Squeeze the sides of the glove compartment together to disengage the retaining tabs. Let the glove compartment hang down in front of the instrument panel.

3. Disconnect the blower motor electrical connector and the vacuum hose from the outside-recirc door vacuum motor.

4. Remove the housing assembly-to-bracket case retaining nut. Close the glove compartment door and remove the lower screws from the blower motor housing.

5. Lift the blower motor housing and air inlet duct/recirc door assemblies away from the heater case. Re-

moving the lower right trim panel will allow for easier removal.

6. Disconnect the cooling tube from the blower motor.

7. Remove the retaining screws and pull the blower motor and wheel from the housing.

8. Remove the pushnut from the blower motor shaft and remove the wheel.

To install:

9. Install gasket material, jumper wire harness, wheel and pushnut onto a new blower motor.

10. Install the blower motor into the housing and secure with the screws.

11. Connect the blower motor cooling tube.

12. Tape the blower motor power lead to the air inlet duct to keep the wire away from the blower outlet during installation.

13. Install the air inlet duct and blower housing to the evaporator case, inserting the flange at the top of the blower outlet into the opening in the evaporator case.

14. Install 2 lower blower motor housing-to-heater case retaining screws.

15. Use a suitable vacuum pump to hold the outside-recirc door open and rotate the blower wheel to make sure it rotates freely. If there is interference, remove the blower motor and wheel and correct the problem.

16. Connect the blower motor power lead to the harness connector and connect the vacuum hose to the outside-recirc door vacuum motor.

17. Make sure the blower motor functions properly and make sure there are no air leaks between the blower motor housing and heater case.

18. Install the blower housing-to-bracket retaining nut. Install the lower right trim panel, if removed.

Thunderbird and Cougar

1. Disconnect the negative battery cable.

2. Remove the glove compartment liner to gain access to the blower motor mounting screws.

3. Remove the 4 retaining screws and remove the blower motor and wheel assembly from the blower housing.

4. Remove the pushnut from the blower motor shaft and remove the blower wheel from the shaft.

5. Installation is the reverse of removal. Connect the negative battery cable.

Mark VII

1. Disconnect the negative battery cable.

2. Remove the recirc duct assembly and disconnect the blower electrical connector.

3. Remove the 4 retaining screws and remove the blower motor and wheel assembly from the blower housing.

4. Remove the pushnut from the blower motor shaft and remove the blower wheel from the shaft.

5. Installation is the reverse of the removal. Connect the negative battery cable.

Mark VIII

1. Disconnect the negative battery cable.

2. Lower the glove compartment door to gain access to the rear of the A/C evaporator housing.

3. Remove the 2 retaining screws and remove the muffler and automatic temperature control sensor hose and elbow.

4. Remove the screw and pull the A/C blower motor out of the housing. Pull the blower motor wheel retainer off of the shaft.

5. Installation is the reverse of the removal. Connect the negative battery cable.

Windshield Wiper Motor

REMOVAL AND INSTALLATION

Mustang

1. Disconnect the negative battery cable.

2. Remove the right hand wiper arm assembly as follows:

   a. Raise the wiper blade off the windshield.

   b. Move the slide latch away from the pivot shaft and slowly lower the arm onto the latch. This unlocks the arm from the pivot shaft and holds the blade off the glass.

   c. Pull the arm from the pivot shaft. The use of tools is unnecessary.

3. Remove the cowl top grille retaining screws and grille.

4. Disconnect the linkage drive arm from the motor crankpin after removing the clip.

5. Disconnect the electrical connector from the wiper motor, remove the 3 retaining bolts and remove the motor from the vehicle.

To install:

6. Install the motor and tighten the bolts to 60–80 inch lbs. (7–9 Nm). Connect the electrical connector.

7. Connect the linkage drive arm to the motor crankpin and install the clip.

8. Install the cowl top grille and secure with the screws.

9. Make sure the motor is in the PARK position. Install the wiper arm so the blade is 2.3–3.5 in. (58.42–88.90mm) from the bottom windshield moulding. Install the arm as follows:

   a. Install the arm head over the pivot shaft.

   b. While applying downward pressure on the arm head, raise the other end of the arm enough to let the latch slide under the pivot shaft to the latched position, using finger pressure only to slide the latch.

   c. Lower the blade. If the blade does not touch the windshield, the slide latch is not completely in place.

Thunderbird and Cougar

1. Disconnect the negative battery cable.

2. With the wipers in the PARK position, remove the arm and blade assemblies as follows:

   a. Raise the wiper blade off the windshield.

   b. Move the slide latch away from the pivot shaft and slowly lower the arm onto the latch. This unlocks the arm from the pivot shaft and holds the blade off the glass.

   c. Pull the arm from the pivot shaft. The use of tools is unnecessary.

3. Remove the left-hand cowl vent screen.

4. Remove the vacuum manifolds from the wiper module and disconnect the electrical connectors.

5. Remove the 5 screws and 1 nut from the wiper module and remove the wiper module.

6. Disconnect the linkage drive arm from the motor crankpin after removing the clip.

7. Remove the 3 wiper motor retaining screws and pull the motor from the opening.

To install:

8. Install the motor and secure with the retaining screws.

9. Connect the linkage arm to the motor crankpin and install the clip.

10. Install the wiper module and secure with the screws and nut.

11. Connect the electrical connectors and install the vacuum manifolds. Install the left-hand cowl vent screen.

12. Make sure the motor is in the PARK position. Install the wiper arms as follows:

   a. Align the keyway on the pivot shaft with the wiper arm and install the arm head over the pivot shaft.

   b. While applying downward pressure on the arm head, raise the other end of the arm enough to let the latch slide under the pivot shaft to the latched position, using finger pressure only to slide the latch.

   c. Lower the blade. If the blade does not touch the windshield, the slide latch is not completely in place.

Mark VII

1. Turn the wipers ON until they reach full travel on the windshield then turn the key **OFF**.

2. Disconnect the negative battery cable and remove the arm and blade assemblies as follows:

   a. Raise the wiper blade off the windshield.

   b. Move the slide latch away from the pivot shaft and slowly lower the arm onto the latch. This unlocks the arm from the pivot shaft and holds the blade off the glass.

   c. Pull the arm from the pivot shaft. The use of tools is unnecessary.

3. Remove the left hand cowl vent screen.

4. Disconnect the linkage drive arm from the motor crankpin after removing the clip.

5. Disconnect the electrical connector from the wiper motor, remove the 3 retaining bolts and remove the motor from the vehicle.

To install:

6. Install the motor and tighten the retaining bolts to 60–80 inch lbs. (7–9 Nm). Connect the electrical connector.

7. Connect the linkage arm to the motor crankpin and install the clip.

8. Install the left-hand cowl vent screen.

9. Connect the negative battery cable and turn the wiper switch **ON**. Let the motor move the pivot shafts 3–4 cycles, then turn the wiper switch **OFF**. The pivot shafts will now be in the PARK position.

10. Install the arms so the wiper blades are 0–0.83 in. (0–21mm) from

the bottom windshield moulding. Install the wiper arms as follows:

a. Install the arm head over the pivot shaft.

b. While applying downward pressure on the arm head, raise the other end of the arm enough to let the latch slide under the pivot shaft to the latched position, using finger pressure only to slide the latch.

c. Lower the blade. If the blade does not touch the windshield, the slide latch is not completely in place.

Mark VIII

1. Turn the wipers ON until they reach midway (straight up) on the windshield then turn the key **OFF**.

2. Disconnect the negative battery cable and remove the right and left wiper arms

3. Remove the cowl top to hood seal and the right and left cowl vent screens.

4. Remove the 4 screws and the cowl top extension.

5. Disconnect the electrical connector from the wiper motor, remove the 5 retaining bolts and 1 nut.

6. Lift the module to disengage the support bracket from the mounting stud, move the module about 2 inches toward the passenger side and remove the module.

7. Disconnect the linkage drive arm from the motor crankpin after removing the clip. Check the location of the support bracket on the module.

8. Remove the 3 screws and separate the motor from the module.

To install:

9. Connect the motor to the module assembly and tighten the retaining bolts to 7.5–10 ft. lbs. (10–14 Nm).

10. Connect the linkage arm to the motor crankpin and install the clip.

11. Install the 5 retaining bolts and 1 nut and connect the electrical connector. Install the cowl top extension.

12. Install the left and right cowl vent screens and cowl top to hood seal.

NOTE: Before installing the wiper arms to the pivot shafts, cycle the motor to make sure the linkage is in the park position.

13. Connect the wiper arms and the negative battery cable.

Instrument Cluster

REMOVAL AND INSTALLATION

Standard Cluster

MUSTANG

1. Disconnect the negative battery cable.

2. Remove the switch assembly on the right and left sides of the cluster assembly.

3. Remove the 2 upper and 3 lower retaining screws from the instrument cluster trim cover and remove the trim cover.

4. Remove the 4 retaining screws from the instrument cluster to panel.

5. Pull the cluster away from the instrument panel. Reach behind the instrument cluster to disconnect the speedometer cable. Disconnect the cable by pressing on the flat surface of the plastic connector (quick disconnect).

6. Pull the cluster further away from the instrument panel and disconnect the cluster printed circuit connectors from their receptacles in the cluster backplate.

7. Remove the cluster.

8. Installation is the reverse of the removal procedure. Apply a $^3/_{16}$ in. (4.6mm) diameter ball of silicone damping grease in the drive hole of the speedometer head prior to installation.

THUNDERBIRD AND COUGAR

1. Disconnect the negative battery cable.

2. Remove the 2 retaining screws and remove the cluster trim panel.

3. Remove the 4 cluster mounting screws.

4. Pull the bottom of the cluster toward the steering wheel.

5. Reach behind and under the cluster and unplug the 2 connectors. On Thunderbird SC, disconnect the vacuum line for the boost gauge.

6. Remove the cluster by swinging the bottom of the cluster out to clear the top of the steering column shroud.

7. Installation is the reverse of removal.

MARK VII LSC

1. Disconnect the negative battery cable.

2. Remove the instrument cluster finish panel, disconnecting the warning indicator module connectors.

3. Remove the instrument panel binnacle moulding.

4. Remove the 5 mask to backplate retaining screws. Do not remove the

3 top screws securing the lens to the mask. Remove the mask and lens assembly.

5. Lift the main dial assembly from the backplate. Some effort may be required to pull the quick connect terminals from the clips.

6. Installation is the reverse of the removal procedure.

MARK VIII

1. Disconnect the negative battery cable.

2. Remove the instrument cluster finish panel.

3. Remove the 4 cluster to panel retaining screws. Do not remove screws securing lens and mask to backplate.

4. Rotate the cluster face down and disconnect the instrument cluster connector.

5. Slide the cluster to the right of the instrument panel opening and unhook the harness from the back of the instrument panel. Remove the cluster assembly from the panel.

6. Installation is the reverse of the removal procedure.

Electronic Cluster

THUNDERBIRD AND COUGAR

1. Disconnect the negative battery cable.

2. Remove the headlight switch knob.

3. Remove the cluster finish panel by removing 2 screws on the upper inside surface. Carefully pull away the finish panel while detaching the spring clips surrounding the finish panel.

4. Unplug the connector on the rear of the switch assembly. If equipped, disconnect the autolamp module.

5. Place a clean, soft cloth over the steering column shroud to prevent scratching or damage. Remove the 4 cluster retaining screws.

6. Pull the bottom of the cluster toward the steering wheel. Place a clean, soft cloth over the lens to prevent potential scratches.

7. Reach behind and under the cluster to unplug the 2 connectors. Swing the bottom of the cluster out to clear the crash pad and remove the cluster.

8. Installation is the reverse of the removal procedure.

MARK VII

1. Disconnect the negative battery cable.

2. Remove the instrument cluster trim bezel. Remove the headlight switch knob.

3. Remove the screws retaining the instrument panel pad and rotate the pad toward the steering wheel and remove. Remove the headlight switch trim panel.

4. Remove the 4 screws retaining the instrument cluster to the instrument panel and remove the cluster.

5. Disconnect the electrical connector at the lower left rear corner of the cluster.

6. Installation is the reverse of the removal procedure.

Speedometer

REMOVAL AND INSTALLATION

Except Electronic Cluster

MUSTANG, THUNDERBIRD AND COUGAR

1. Disconnect the negative battery cable.

2. Remove the instrument cluster assembly.

3. Remove the 7 screws retaining the mask and lens assembly.

4. Remove the speedometer head assembly retaining screws and remove the speedometer.

5. Installation is the reverse of the removal procedure.

MARK VII LSC

1. Disconnect the negative battery cable.

2. Remove the instrument cluster finish panel, disconnecting the warning indicator module connectors.

3. Remove the instrument panel binnacle moulding.

4. Remove the 5 mask to backplate retaining screws. Do not remove the 3 top screws securing the lens to the mask. Remove the mask and lens assembly.

5. Lift the main dial assembly from the backplate. Some effort may be required to pull the quick connect terminals from the clips.

6. Remove the screws retaining the fuel gauge, temperature gauge and tachometer. The speedometer is integral with the main dial.

7. Installation is the reverse of the removal procedure.

MARK VIII

1. Disconnect the negative battery cable.

2. Remove the instrument cluster assembly.

3. Remove the 7 screws retaining the mask and lens assembly.

4. Remove the mask assembly and lens. Grasp the speedometer at top and bottom using fingers only. Gently

pull forward until speedometer comes out.

5. Installation is the reverse of the removal procedure.

Electronic Cluster

The speedometer is an integral part of the electronic cluster and cannot be removed separately.

Headlight Switch

REMOVAL AND INSTALLATION

Mustang

1. Disconnect the negative battery cable.

2. Disengage the 2 locking tabs on the left side of the switch, under the paddles, by pushing the tabs in with a small prybar and pulling on the paddles.

3. Using a small prybar, pry the right side of the switch out of the instrument panel.

4. Pull the switch out of the opening and disconnect the 2 connectors.

5. To install, assemble the connectors, insert the switch into the panel opening and push until the locking tabs on both sides of the switch snap into place.

Thunderbird and Cougar

1. Disconnect the negative battery cable.

2. Remove the 2 cluster finish panel retaining screws.

3. Pull the headlight switch knob off.

4. Unsnap the cluster finish panel.

5. Disconnect the electrical connector to the headlight dimmer sensor assembly.

6. Through the opening in the instrument panel, depress the shaft release button on the switch and remove the shaft. The switch must be

in the full **ON** position to release the shaft.

7. Remove the headlight switch retaining nut and pull the switch through the opening to disconnect the wiring connector.

8. Installation is the reverse of removal.

Mark VII

1. Disconnect the negative battery cable.

2. Remove the center moulding and the headlight switch knob.

3. Remove the 5 screws retaining the cluster finish panel and snap out the headlight switch lens.

4. Remove the 2 screws retaining the headlight switch. Remove the switch from the instrument panel and disconnect the electrical connector.

5. Installation is the reverse of the removal procedure.

Mark VIII

1. Disconnect the negative battery cable.

2. Pull off the headlight switch knob.

3. Remove the lamp switch knob applique by pulling at the left end to unsnap it from the finish panel and twist out the bulb socket.

4. Remove the 2 screws retaining the left end of the finish panel to the instrument panel.

5. Pull up on the forward edge to unsnap the 4 snap in tabs from the upper steering column cover.

6. Pull back on the left finish panel far enough to disconnect the 2 electrical connectors.

7. Remove the 2 screws retaining the switch to the center finish panel.

8. Installation is the reverse of the removal procedure.

Combination Switch

The combination switch incorporates the turn signal, dimmer and wiper switch functions.

REMOVAL AND INSTALLATION

Mustang, Thunderbird and Cougar

1. Disconnect the negative battery cable.

2. Remove the shroud retaining screws and remove the upper and lower shrouds.

3. Remove the switch retaining screws and lift the switch assembly.

4. With the wiring connectors exposed, carefully lift the connector re-

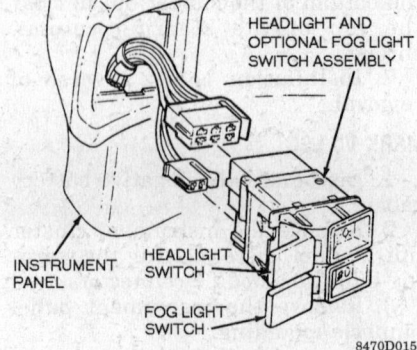

Headlight switch installation — Mustang

8470D015

tainer tabs and disconnect the connectors.

5. Installation is the reverse of the removal procedure.

Mark VII and Mark VIII

1. Disconnect the negative battery cable.

2. If equipped with tilt column, move to the lowest position and remove the tilt lever.

3. Remove the ignition lock cylinder.

4. Remove the shroud screws and remove the upper and lower shrouds.

5. Remove the 2 self-tapping screws attaching the combination switch to the steering column casting and remove the switch.

6. Disconnect the 2 electrical connectors.

7. Installation is the reverse of the removal procedure.

Ignition Lock

REMOVAL AND INSTALLATION

Functional Lock

The following procedure is for vehicles with functioning lock cylinders. Ignition keys are available for these vehicles, or the ignition key numbers are known and the proper key can be made.

1. Disconnect the negative battery cable. If equipped, properly disarm the air bag system.

2. On Thunderbird, Cougar and Mustang equipped with tilt column, remove the upper extension shroud by unsnapping the shroud retaining clip at the 9 o'clock position.

3. On all except Mark VII and Mark VIII, remove the trim shroud halves by removing the attaching screws. Remove the electrical connector from the key warning switch.

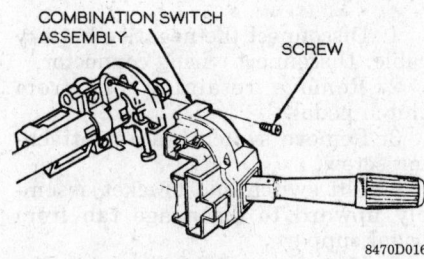

COMBINATION SWITCH ASSEMBLY

SCREW

8470D016

Combination switch — Mustang

4. Place the gear shift lever in **P**, for column shift only, and turn the ignition to the **RUN** position.

5. Place a ⅛ in. diameter wire pin or small drift punch in the hole in the casting surrounding the lock cylinder and depress the retaining pin while pulling out on the lock cylinder to remove it from the column housing.

To install:

6. To install the lock cylinder, turn it to the **RUN** position and depress the retaining pin. Insert the lock cylinder into its housing in the lock cylinder casting.

7. Make sure the cylinder is fully seated and aligned in the interlocking washer before turning the key to the **OFF** position. This action will permit the cylinder retaining pin to extend into the hole in the lock cylinder housing.

8. Using the ignition key, rotate the cylinder to ensure the correct mechanical operation in all positions.

9. Check for proper start in **P** or **N**. Also make sure the start circuit cannot be actuated in **D** or **R** positions and that the column is locked in the **LOCK** position.

10. Connect the key warning buzzer electrical connector and install the trim shrouds, if required.

Non-Functional Lock

The following procedure is for vehicles with non-functioning locks. On these vehicles, the lock cylinder cannot be rotated due to a lost or broken key, the key number is not known, or the lock cylinder cap is damaged and/or broken, preventing the lock cylinder from rotating.

1. Disconnect the negative battery cable. If equipped, properly disarm the air bag system.

2. Remove the steering wheel.

3. On Thunderbird, Cougar and and Mustang equipped with tilt column, remove the upper extension shroud by unsnapping the shroud retaining clip at the 9 o'clock position.

4. On all except Mark VII and VIII:

   a. Remove the trim shroud halves by removing the attaching screws. Remove the electrical connector from the key warning switch.

   b. Drill out the retaining pin using a ⅛ in. diameter drill, being careful not to drill deeper than ½ in.

   c. Position a chisel at the base of the ignition lock cylinder. Strike the chisel with sharp blows, using a hammer, to break the cap away from the lock cylinder.

5. On Mark VII and Mark VIII, use suitable pliers to to twist lock cylinder clip until it separates from lock cylinder.

6. Drill approximately 1¾ in. down the middle of the ignition key slot, using a ⅜ in. diameter drill bit, until the lock cylinder breaks loose from the breakaway base of the lock cylinder. Remove the lock cylinder and drill shavings from the lock cylinder housing.

7. Remove the snapring or retainer, washer and steering column lock gear. Thoroughly clean all drill shavings and other foreign materials from the casting.

8. Inspect the lock cylinder housing for damage and replace, as necessary.

To install:

9. Install the ignition lock drive gear, washer and retainer.

10. Install the ignition lock cylinder and check for smooth operation.

11. Connect the electrical connector to the key warning switch.

12. Install the trim shrouds, if necessary.

13. Install the new lock cylinder housing assembly.

14. Install the steering wheel and connect the negative battery cable.

Ignition Switch

REMOVAL AND INSTALLATION

1. Disconnect the negative battery cable.

2. Remove the steering column shroud. On Mark VII and Mark VIII, remove the steering column opening trim cover and remove the cover.

3. Disconnect the switch electrical connector.

4. Turn the ignition lock cylinder to **RUN**.

5. Remove the screws attaching the switch and disengage the switch from the actuator.

To install:

6. Adjust the new ignition switch by sliding the carrier to the **RUN** position.

7. Make sure the ignition key lock cylinder is in the **RUN** position. The **RUN** position is achieved by rotating the key lock cylinder approximately 90 degrees from the **LOCK** position.

8. Install the ignition switch onto the actuator pin or install the switch pin in the column hole, as required.

9. Align the switch mounting holes and install the attaching screws. Tighten the screws to 50–69 inch lbs. (5.6–7.9 Nm).

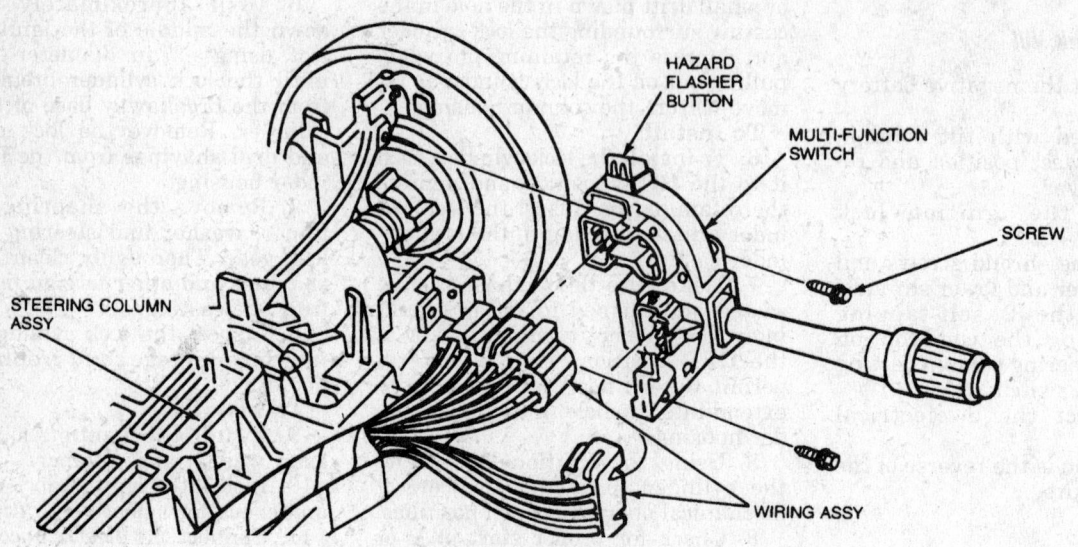

HAZARD FLASHER BUTTON

MULTI-FUNCTION SWITCH

SCREW

STEERING COLUMN ASSY

WIRING ASSY

8470D100

Combination switch — Mark VII and Mark VIII

10. Connect the electrical connector to the ignition switch.

11. Connect the negative battery cable. Check the ignition switch for proper function in **START** and **ACC** positions. Make sure the column is locked in the **LOCK** position.

12. Install the remaining components in the reverse order of removal.

Brake Light Switch

REMOVAL AND INSTALLATION

1. Disconnect the negative battery cable.

2. Disconnect the wire harness at the connector from the switch. The locking tab on the connector must be lifted before the connector can be removed.

3. Remove the hairpin retainer. Slide the brake light switch, the pushrod and the nylon washers and bushings away from the pedal and remove the switch.

NOTE: Since the switch side plate nearest the brake pedal is slotted, it is not necessary to remove the brake master cylinder pushrod and 1 washer from the brake pedal pin.

To install:

4. Position the switch so the U-shaped side is nearest the pedal and directly over/under the pin. Then slide the switch down/up trapping the master cylinder pushrod and black bushing between the switch side plates. Push the switch and pushrod assembly firmly toward the brake pedal arm. Assemble the outside white plastic washer to the pin and install the hairpin retainer to trap the whole assembly.

5. Assemble the wire harness connector to the switch. Check the switch for proper operation.

NOTE: The brake light switch wire harness must be long enough to travel with the switch during full pedal stroke. If wire length is insufficient, reroute the harness or service, as required.

Clutch Switch

ADJUSTMENT

1. If necessary, remove the panel above the clutch pedal.

2. Disconnect the electrical connector at the switch.

3. Using test light, make sure the switch is open with the clutch pedal

up (clutch engaged) and closed at approximately 1 in. from the clutch pedal full-down position (clutch disengaged).

4. If the switch does not operate as specified, check if the self-adjusting clip is out of position on the rod; it should be near the end of the rod.

5. If the clip is out of position, remove it and reposition about 1 in. from the end of the rod. Reset the switch by pushing the clutch pedal to the floor.

6. Repeat Step 3. If the switch is damaged or the clips do not stay in place, replace the switch.

REMOVAL AND INSTALLATION

Mustang

1. Disconnect the negative battery cable. Disconnect wiring connector.

2. Remove retaining pin from clutch pedal.

3. Remove switch bracket attaching screw.

4. Lift switch and bracket assembly upward to disengage tab from pedal support.

5. Move the switch outward to disengage actuating rod eyelet from clutch pedal pin and remove switch from vehicle.

To install:

NOTE: Always install the switch with the self-adjusting clip about 1.0 in. (25.4mm) from the end of the rod. The clutch pedal must be fully up (clutch engaged). Otherwise, the switch may be misadjusted.

6. Place eyelet end of rod onto pivot pin.
7. Swing switch assembly around to line up hole in mounting boss with hole in bracket.
8. Install attaching screw.
9. Replace retaining pin on clutch pedal.
10. Connect wiring connector.

Thunderbird and Cougar

1. Disconnect the negative battery cable.
2. Disconnect wiring connector from the switch.
3. Remove the C-clip from the clutch pedal switch pin and slide the pushrod off the pin.
4. Remove the C-clip from the end of the clutch pedal switch rod.
5. Remove the switch pushrod from the switch.
6. Disconnect the switch from the plastic bracket.
7. Installation is the reverse of removal. Check switch operation.

Neutral Safety Switch

REMOVAL AND INSTALLATION

Mustang with 2.3L Engine

1. Disconnect the negative battery cable.
2. Disconnect the switch wiring harness connector.

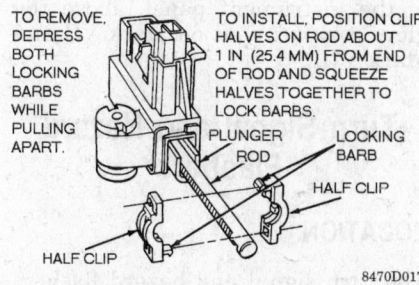

TO REMOVE, DEPRESS BOTH LOCKING BARBS WHILE PULLING APART. TO INSTALL, POSITION CLIP HALVES ON ROD ABOUT 1 IN (25.4 MM) FROM END OF ROD AND SQUEEZE HALVES TOGETHER TO LOCK BARBS. PLUNGER ROD LOCKING BARB HALF CLIP HALF CLIP

8470D017

Clutch switch clip installation — Mustang

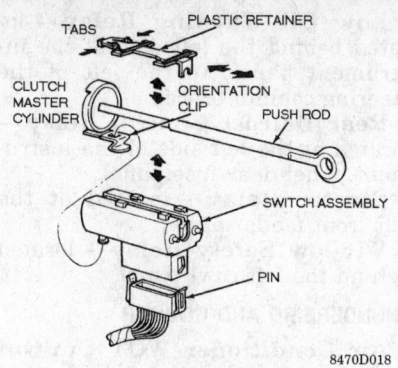

TABS PLASTIC RETAINER CLUTCH MASTER CYLINDER ORIENTATION CLIP PUSH ROD SWITCH ASSEMBLY PIN

8470D018

Clutch switch installation — Thunderbird

3. Remove the neutral safety switch and O-ring using socket tool T74P–77247–A or equivalent.

NOTE: Use of different tools could crush or puncture the walls of the switch.

To install:
4. Install the neutral safety switch and new O-ring using socket tool T74P–77247–A or equivalent.
5. Tighten the switch to 7–10 ft. lbs. (10–14 Nm).
6. Connect the neutral safety switch to the wiring harness.
7. Connect the negative battery cable.
8. Check that the vehicle starts only in the **N** or **P** position.

Mustang with 5.0L Engine, Thunderbird, Cougar and Mark VII

1. Place the selector lever in the manual **L** position.
2. Disconnect the negative battery cable.
3. Raise and support the vehicle safely.
4. Disconnect the neutral safety switch electrical harness from the switch by pushing the harness straight up off the switch using a small long-bladed prybar under the rubber plug section of the harness.
5. Install socket tool T74P–77247–A or equivalent, and rachet on the neutral safety switch. Once the ratchet and socket tool are over the switch, reach from the rear of the transmission over the extension housing area and remove the neutral safety switch and O-ring.

NOTE: Use of different tools could crush or puncture the walls of the switch.

To install:
6. Install the neutral safety switch and new O-ring using socket tool T74P–77247–A or equivalent.

7. Tighten the switch to 8–11 ft. lbs. (11–15 Nm).
8. Connect the neutral safety switch to the wiring harness.
9. Lower the vehicle and connect the negative battery cable.
10. Check that the vehicle starts only in the **N** or **P** position.

Fuses, Circuit Breakers and Relays

LOCATION

Fuses

All vehicles are equipped with a fuse panel located on the left side of the lower instrument panel. In addition, Thunderbird and Cougar are equipped with a high-current fuse box located in the engine compartment on the left fender apron.

Fusible Links

Fusible links are used to protect the main wiring harness and selected branches from complete burn-out, should a short circuit or electrical overload occur. A fusible link is a short length of insulated wire, integral with the engine compartment wiring harness. It is several wire gauges smaller than the circuit it protects and generally located in-line directly from the positive terminal of the battery.

Circuit Breakers

Circuit breakers are used on certain electrical components requiring high amperage. The advantage of the circuit breaker is ability to open and close the electrical circuit as the load demands, rather than the necessity of a part replacement.

MUSTANG

Windshield Wiper Circuit — a 8.25 amp circuit breaker located on the fuse panel.
Power Windows — a 20 amp circuit breaker located on the fuse panel.
Power Windows, Power Seats, Power Door Locks — a 20 amp circuit breaker located at the starter relay.
Headlight and High Beam — a 22 amp circuit breaker incorporated in the lighting switch.
Convertible Top — a 25 amp circuit breaker located at the lower instrument panel-reinforcement.

THUNDERBIRD AND COUGAR

Windshield Wiper Circuit — a 8.25 amp circuit breaker located on the fuse panel.

Power Windows and Moon Roof Motor — a 20 amp circuit breaker located on the fuse panel.

Power Seats, Door Locks and Fuel Door Release Solenoid — a 20 amp circuit breaker located on the fuse panel.

Cigar Lighter and High Beam — a 20 amp circuit breaker located on the fuse panel.

MARK VII

Windshield Wiper circuit — a 6 amp circuit breaker located on the fuse panel.

Cigar Lighters/Horns — a 20 amp circuit breaker located on the fuse panel.

Power Windows and Sun Roof — a 20 amp circuit breaker located at the starter relay.

Power Windows, Seats and Door Locks — a 20 amp circuit breaker located at the starter relay.

Headlight and High Beam — a 22 amp circuit breaker incorporated in the lighting switch.

MARK VIII

Power Roof, Power Windows, One Touch Down Module — a 20 amp circuit breaker located on the fuse panel.

Power Seats, Fuel Fill Door, Luggage Compartment Release and Shock Damping Control — a 20 amp (yellow) circuit breaker located on the fuse panel.

Horn, Cigar Lighter — a 30 amp circuit breaker located on the fuse panel.

Relays

MUSTANG

Air Conditioner WOT CUT-OUT Relay — located on the right fender apron.

Convertible Top Lower and Raise Relays — located in luggage compartment, behind rear seat.

EEC Power Relay — located behind the right cowl panel, above the the EEC control module.

Fuel Pump Relay — located on the right side of the engine compartment, on the lower front of the wheel-well on 1992–96.

Horn Relay — located behind the center of the instrument panel, above the warning chime module.

LCD Illumination Relay — located behind the center of the instrument panel.

Low Oil Warning Relay — located behind the left side of the instrument panel, to the left of the steering column brace.

Rear Defrost Control Relay — located at the left side of the instrument panel near fuse panel.

Starter Relay — located at the left front fender apron.

Window Safety Relay — located behind the left cowl panel.

THUNDERBIRD AND COUGAR

Air Conditioner WOT Cut-Out Relay — located at the right front of the firewall, on the relay bracket.

Anti-Lock Hydraulic Pump Motor Relay — located at the right front of the firewall, on the relay bracket.

Anti-Lock Power Relay — located at the right front of the firewall, on the relay bracket.

Autolamp Dual Coil Relay — located at the left side of the instrument panel to the right of the steering column.

EEC Power Relay — located at the left fender apron inside the power distribution box.

Fuel Pump Relay — located in the left side of the trunk, behind the wheel well.

Hard Ride Relay — located under the rear package tray.

Horn Relay — located in the left side of the engine compartment, inside the power distribution box.

LCD Illumination Relay — located behind the left side of the instrument pane., near the steering column.

Soft Ride Relay — located under the rear package tray.

Starter Relay — located on the left fender apron.

MARK VII

Air Conditioning WOT Cut-Out Relay — located on the left fender apron, near the shock tower.

Air Suspension Compressor Relay — located on the left fender apron, near the shock tower.

Anti-Lock Brake Hydraulic Pump Motor Relay — located in front of the firewall, behind the brake master cylinder.

Anti-Lock Power Relay — located in front of the firewall, behind the brake master cylinder.

ATC Feedback Isolation Relay — located behind the left side of the instrument panel, to the right of the steering column.

Autolamp Relay — located behind the left side of the instrument panel, to the right of the steering column.

EEC Power Relay — located in the right rear of the engine compartment.

Fuel Pump Relay — located at the outside of the left deck lid hinge support.

Hi-Lo Beam Relay — located to the right of the steering column, behind the instrument panel.

Horn Relay — located in the right rear corner of the engine compartment on the firewall.

Low Oil Level Relay — located behind the left side of the instrument panel.

Moonroof Relay — located at the center rear of the roof above the headliner.

Starter Relay — located on the left fender apron.

MARK VIII

Anti-Lock Brake Control Module — located in the power distribution box, left inner fender (black).

Parking Lamp — located in the power distribution box, left inner fender (black).

Fuel Pump Relay — located in the power distribution box, left inner fender (black).

Hi-Lo Auto-Lamp — located in the power distribution box, left inner fender (black).

Horn Relay — located in the power distribution box, left inner fender (black).

Computers

LOCATION

The engine electronic control module is located behind the right cowl panel. The anti-lock brake control module is located under the center of the rear package tray. The automatic temperature control module is located behind the center of the instrument panel. The air bag diagnostic module is located behind the lower center of the instrument panel on Mustang or behind the top right side of the instrument panel, above the glove compartment on Mark VII and Mark VIII.

Turn Signal and Hazard Flashers

LOCATION

The turn signal and hazard flashers are attached to the fuse panel or the instrument panel reinforcement over the fuse panel on Mustang and Mark

VII. On Thunderbird and Cougar, an electronic flasher is located behind the left side of the instrument panel, to the right of the steering column.

Cruise Control

ADJUSTMENT

Actuator Cable

1. Remove the cable retaining clip.
2. Push the cable through the adjuster until a slight tension is felt.
3. Insert the cable retaining clip and snap into place.

Vacuum Dump Valve

The vacuum dump valve is movable in its mounting bracket. It should be adjusted so it is closed (no vacuum leaks) when the brake pedal is in its normal release position (not depressed) and open when the pedal is depressed. Use a hand vacuum pump to make this adjustment.

Clutch Switch

MUSTANG

1. Prop the clutch pedal in the full-up position, pawl fully released from the sector.
2. Loosen the switch retaining screw.
3. Slide the switch forward toward the clutch pedal until the switch plunger cap is 0.030 in. (0.76mm) from contacting the switch housing. Then, tighten the retaining screw.
4. Remove the prop from the clutch pedal and test drive for clutch switch cancellation of cruise control.

THUNDERBIRD

1. disconnect the wiring harness from the switch.
2. Using a volt-ohmmeter, probe the switch terminals with the switch installed and the clutch pedal at the up or engaged position.

3. The EFI switch, terminals 5 and 6, should be normally open and close within approximately 2 in. (50mm) of clutch pedal travel.
4. The cruise control release switch, terminals 3 and 4, should be normally closed and open within approximately 2 in. (50mm) of clutch travel.
5. The clutch interlock switch, terminals 1 and 2, should be normally open and close when the clutch pedal has been moved to approximately 1 in (25mm) from full travel.
6. Replace the clutch switch if any of the conditions in Steps 3, 4 and 5 are not as specified.

ENGINE COOLING

Radiator

REMOVAL AND INSTALLATION

Except 3.8L SC Engine

1. Disconnect the negative battery cable.

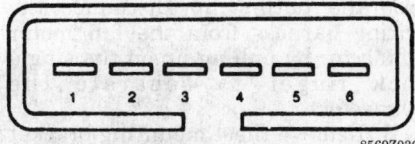

8569Z036

Clutch switch terminal locations — Thunderbird

2. Remove the radiator cap. Place a drain pan under the radiator, open the draincock and drain the coolant.

CAUTION

Never remove the radiator cap while the engine is running or personal injury from scalding hot coolant or steam may result. If possible, wait until the engine has cooled to remove the radiator cap. If this is not possible, wrap a thick cloth around the radiator cap and turn it slowly to the first stop. Step back while the pressure is released from the cooling system. When it is certain all the pressure has been released, press down on the cap, still with the cloth, and turn and remove it.

3. Disconnect the upper, lower and overflow hoses at the radiator.
4. If equipped with an automatic transmission, disconnect the fluid cooler lines at the radiator.
5. On Mustang with 2.3L engine and Mark VIII, remove the electric cooling fan/shroud assembly. On all other vehicles, remove the 2 upper fan shroud retaining bolts at the radiator support, lift the fan shroud sufficiently to disengage the lower retaining clips and lay the shroud back over the fan.
6. Remove the radiator upper support retaining bolts and remove the supports. Lift the radiator from the vehicle.

To install:

7. If a new radiator is to be installed, transfer the petcock from the old radiator to the new one. If equipped with automatic transmission, transfer the fluid cooler line fittings from the old radiator.
8. Position the radiator assembly into the vehicle. Install the upper supports and the retaining bolts. If equipped with automatic transmission, connect the fluid cooler lines.
9. On Mustang with the 2.3L engine and Mark VIII, install the electric cooling fan/shroud assembly. On all other vehicles, place the fan shroud into the clips on the lower radiator support and install the 2 upper shroud retaining bolts. Position the shroud to maintain approximately 0.38 in. (9.7mm) radial clearance between the fan blades and the shroud.
10. Connect the radiator hoses. Close the radiator petcock. Fill and bleed the cooling system.
11. Start the engine and bring to operating temperature. Check for coolant and transmission fluid leaks.
12. Check the coolant and transmission fluid levels.

CORRECTLY ADJUSTED DUMP VALVE
DUMP VALVE
PAD ON BRAKE PEDAL
0.050 INCH
DUMP VALVE BLACK HOUSING MUST CLEAR WHITE PLASTIC PAD ON BRAKE PEDAL WITH BRAKE PEDAL PULLED TO REARMOST POSITION
8569Z035

Cruise control dump valve adjustment

3.8L SC Engine

1. Disconnect the negative battery cable.

2. Remove the charge air cooler.

3. Remove the radiator cap. Place a drain pan under the radiator, open the draincock and drain the coolant.

--------- CAUTION ---------

Never remove the radiator cap while the engine is running or personal injury from scalding hot coolant or steam may result. If possible, wait until the engine has cooled to remove the radiator cap. If this is not possible, wrap a thick cloth around the radiator cap and turn it slowly to the first stop. Step back while the pressure is released from the cooling system. When it is certain all the pressure has been released, press down on the cap, still with the cloth, and turn and remove it.

4. Disconnect the upper and lower radiator hoses and the overflow hose at the radiator.

5. If equipped with an automatic transmission, disconnect the fluid cooler lines at the radiator.

6. Remove the overflow hose from the clip on the fan shroud. Remove the 2 shroud upper retaining bolts at the radiator support and remove the wiring harness retaining clip from the fan shroud. Lift the electric cooling fan/shroud assembly from the radiator, disengaging the shroud from the lower retaining clips.

7. Remove the 2 bolts retaining the top of the air duct to the charge air cooler and remove the upper 2 radiator retaining bolts. Tilt the radiator and support assembly toward the engine and lift the radiator from the vehicle.

To install:

8. If a new radiator is to be installed and the vehicle is equipped with automatic transmission, transfer the fluid cooler line fittings from the old radiator.

9. Position the radiator and support assembly in the vehicle and install the 2 upper retaining bolts.

10. Cut the retaining strap from the air duct. The duct should spring out from the support assembly. Lift the top of the duct and insert the tabs on the bottom of the duct into the clips at the bottom of the charge air cooler. Install the 2 bolts that retain the top of the duct to the charge air cooler.

11. Connect the fluid cooler lines to the radiator. Position the engine cooling fan and stud assembly into the radiator lower clips. Attach the top of the radiator to the top of the support with the 2 bolts.

12. Connect the radiator and overflow hoses to the radiator. Route the overflow hose through the retaining clip. Make sure the draincock is closed and fill the cooling system.

13. Install the charge air cooler. Connect the cooling fan electrical connector and install the harness clip to the fan shroud.

14. Start the engine and bring to operating temperature. Check for coolant and transmission fluid leaks.

15. Check the coolant and transmission fluid levels.

Electric Cooling Fan

TESTING

1. Disconnect the electrical connector at the cooling fan motor.

2. Connect a jumper wire between the negative motor lead and ground.

3. Connect another jumper wire between the positive motor lead and the positive terminal of the battery.

4. If the cooling fan motor does not run, it must be replaced.

REMOVAL AND INSTALLATION

Mustang with 2.3L Engine

1. Disconnect the negative battery cable.

2. Remove the fan wiring harness from the routing clip. Disconnect the wiring harness from the fan motor connector by pulling up on the single lock finger to separate the connectors.

3. Remove the 4 mounting bracket attaching screws and remove the fan assembly from the vehicle.

4. Remove the retaining clip from the end of the motor shaft and remove the fan.

NOTE: A metal burr may be present on the motor after the retaining clip is removed. Deburring of the shaft may be required to remove the fan.

5. Remove the nuts attaching the fan motor to the mounting bracket.

6. Installation is the reverse of the removal procedure.

Thunderbird and Cougar with 3.8L SC Engine

1. Disconnect the negative battery cable.

2. Disconnect the fan motor wiring connector at the side of the fan shroud. Remove the male terminal connector retaining clip from the shroud mounting tab.

3. Remove the overflow hose from the fan shroud retaining clip and remove the 2 shroud upper retaining bolts at the radiator support.

4. Lift the cooling fan module past the radiator, disengaging the shroud from the 2 lower retaining clips.

5. Installation is the reverse of the removal procedure. Tighten the shroud retaining bolts to 36 inch lbs. (4 Nm).

Thunderbird, Cougar and Mark VIII with 4.6L engine

1. Disconnect the negative battery cable.

2. Remove the fan shroud bolts and fan shroud from the mounts. Remove the lower radiator hose from the fan shroud.

3. Lift the radiator electric fan/shroud assembly from the vehicle.

4. Disconnect the radiator electric motor wiring harness at the electric motor.

5. Installation is the reverse of the removal procedure.

Heater Core

REMOVAL AND INSTALLATION

Without Air Conditioning

MUSTANG

1. Disconnect the negative battery cable.

2. Remove the floor console and instrument panel as follows:

a. Remove the 2 access covers at the rear of the console by snapping them out. Remove the 4 armrest-to-floor bracket retaining bolts and remove the armrest assembly by snapping it out of the console.

b. Remove the gear shift lever opening finish panel by snapping out. If equipped with a manual transmission, the shift boot is attached to the bottom of the finish panel. Remove the shift knob and slide the boot and finish panel up the shift lever to remove.

c. Pull up the emergency brake lever. Remove the 4 retaining screws and lift up the top finish panel. Disconnect the necessary wire connectors.

d. Remove the 2 console-to-rear floor bracket retaining screws. Insert a small prybar into the 2 notches at the bottom of the front upper finish panel and snap it out.

e. Remove the radio assembly. Open the glove compartment door and drop the glove compartment assembly down. Remove the 2 console-to-instrument panel retaining screws.

f. Remove the 4 console-to-bracket retaining screws and remove the console.

g. Disconnect all underhood wiring connectors from the main wiring harness. Disengage the rubber grommet seal from the dash panel and push the wiring harness and connector into the passenger compartment.

h. Remove the 3 bolts attaching the steering column opening cover and reinforcement panel. Remove the cover.

i. Remove the steering column opening reinforcement by removing the 2 bolts, remove the 2 bolts retaining the lower steering column opening reinforcement and remove the reinforcement.

j. Remove the 6 steering column retaining nuts. Two are retaining the hood release mechanism and 4 retain the column to the lower brake pedal support. Lower the steering column to the floor.

k. Remove the steering column upper and lower shrouds and disconnect the wiring from the combination switch.

l. Remove the brake pedal support nut and snap out the defroster grille.

m. Remove the screws from the speaker covers. Snap out the speaker covers. Remove the front screws retaining the right and left scuff plates at the cowl trim panel. Remove the right and left side cowl trim panels.

n. Disconnect the wiring at the right and left cowl sides. Remove the cowl side retaining bolts, 1 on each side.

o. Open the glove compartment door and flex the glove compartment bin tabs inward. Drop down the glove compartment door assembly.

p. Remove the 5 cowl top screw attachments. Gently pull the instrument panel away from the cowl. Disconnect the speedometer cable and wire connectors.

3. Drain the coolant from the cooling system and remove the hoses from the heater core. Plug the hoses and core.

4. Remove the screw attaching the air inlet duct and blower housing assembly support bracket to the cowl top panel.

5. Disconnect the black vacuum supply hose from the in-line vacuum check valve in the engine compartment.

6. Disconnect the blower motor wire harness from the resistor and motor head.

7. Working under the hood, remove the 2 nuts retaining the heater assembly to the dash panel.

8. In the passenger compartment, remove the screw attaching the heater assembly support bracket to the cowl top panel. Remove the 1 screw retaining the bracket below the heater assembly to the dash panel.

9. Carefully pull the heater assembly away from the dash panel and remove from the vehicle.

10. Remove the 4 heater core access cover attaching screws and remove the access cover from the case.

11. Lift the heater core and seal from the case. Remove the seal from the heater core tubes.

To install:

12. Install the heater core tube seal on the heater core tubes. Inspect the heater core sealer in the heater case and replace, it necessary.

13. Install the heater core in the case with the seals on the outside of the case. Position the heater core access cover on the case and install the 4 attaching screws.

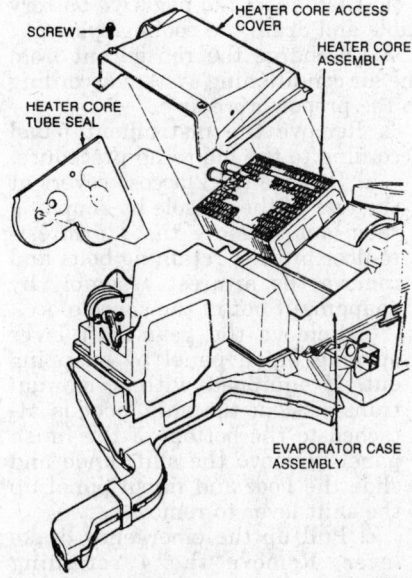

Heater core installation — Mustang

14. Position the heater assembly in the vehicle. Install the screw attaching the heater assembly support bracket to the cowl top panel.

15. Check the heater assembly drain tube to make sure it is through the dash panel and is not pinched or kinked.

16. Working under the hood, install the 2 nuts retaining the heater assembly to the dash panel. Install the air inlet duct and blower housing support bracket attaching screw. Install 1 screw to the retainer bracket below the heater assembly to the dash panel.

17. Connect the blower motor ground wire to ground and the harness to the resistor and blower motor lead.

18. Connect the black vacuum supply hose to the vacuum check valve in the engine compartment.

19. Install the instrument panel and floor console by reversing the removal procedure.

20. Connect the heater hoses to the heater core and fill the cooling system. Check the system for proper operation.

THUNDERBIRD AND COUGAR

1. Disconnect the negative battery cable.

2. Remove the instrument panel as follows:

a. Disconnect the underhood wiring at the left side of the dash panel.

b. Disengage the wiring connector from the dash panel and push the wiring harness into the passenger compartment.

c. Remove the steering column lower trim cover by removing the 3 screws at the bottom, 1 screw on the left side and pulling to disengage the 5 snap-in retainers across the top.

d. Remove the steering column lower opening reinforcement; 6 screws retain the reinforcement to the instrument panel.

e. Remove the steering column upper and lower shrouds and disconnect the wiring from the steering column.

f. Remove the shift interlock switch and disconnect the steering column universal joint.

g. Support the steering column and remove the 4 nuts retaining the column to the support. Remove the column from the vehicle.

h. Remove the 1 screw retaining the left side of the instrument panel to the parking brake bracket.

i. Install the steering column lower opening reinforcement using the 4 screws, 1 at each corner. This will prevent the instrument panel from twisting when being removed.

j. Remove the right and left cowl side trim panels.

k. Remove the console assembly and remove the 2 nuts retaining the center of the instrument panel to the floor.

l. Open the glove compartment, squeeze the sides of the bin and lower to the full open position. From under the instrument panel and through the glove compartment opening, disconnect the wiring, vacuum lines and control cables.

m. Remove 2 screws from the right side and 2 screws from the left side retaining the instrument panel to the cowl side.

n. Remove the right and left upper finish panels by pulling up to disengage the snap-in retainers. There are 3 on the right side, 4 on the left side.

o. Remove the 4 screws retaining the instrument panel to the cowl top. Remove the right and left roof rail trim panel. Remove the door frame weatherstrip.

p. Carefully pull the instrument panel away from the cowl and disconnect any remaining wiring or controls.

3. Remove the right instrument panel brace located above the heater case and attached to the cowl.

4. Drain the coolant from the cooling system and remove the hoses from the heater core. Plug the hoses and the core.

5. Disconnect the black vacuum supply hose from the in-line vacuum check valve in the engine compartment.

6. Disconnect the blower motor wire harness from the resistor and motor lead.

7. Working under the hood, remove the 3 nuts retaining the heater assembly to the dash panel.

8. In the passenger compartment, remove the screw attaching the heater assembly support bracket to the cowl top panel.

9. Remove the 1 screw retaining the bracket below the heater assembly to the dash panel.

10. Carefully pull the heater assembly away from the dash panel and remove the heater assembly from the vehicle.

11. Remove the 4 heater core access cover attaching screws and remove the access cover.

12. Remove the seal from the heater core tubes and pull the heater core from the case.

To install:

13. Inspect the heater core sealer in the case and replace, if necessary.

14. Install the heater core in the case with the seals on the outside of the case. Install the heater corer tube seal on the heater core tubes.

15. Position the heater core access cover and seal on the case and install the 4 attaching screws.

16. Position the heater assembly in the vehicle. Install the screw attaching the heater assembly support bracket to the cowl top panel.

17. Working under the hood, install the 3 nuts retaining the heater assembly to the dash panel.

18. Install 1 screw to retain the bracket below the heater assembly to the dash panel.

19. Connect the blower motor and the harness to the resistor and blower motor lead.

20. Connect the black vacuum supply hose to the vacuum check valve in the engine compartment.

21. Install the right instrument panel brace and install the instrument panel by reversing the removal procedure.

22. Connect the heater hoses to the heater core and fill the cooling system. Check heater operation.

With Air Conditioning

MUSTANG

1. Disconnect the negative battery cable and drain the cooling system.

2. Discharge the refrigerant from the air conditioning system according to the proper procedure.

3. Remove the instrument panel according to the following procedure:

a. Remove the 2 access covers at the rear of the console by snapping them out. Remove the 4 armrest-to-floor bracket retaining bolts and remove the armrest assembly by snapping it out of the console.

b. Remove the gear shift lever opening finish panel by snapping out. If equipped with a manual transmission, the shift boot is attached to the bottom of the finish panel. Remove the shift knob and slide the boot and finish panel up the shift lever to remove.

c. Pull up the emergency brake lever. Remove the 4 retaining screws and lift up the top finish panel. Disconnect the necessary wire connectors.

d. Remove the 2 console-to-rear floor bracket retaining screws. Insert a small prybar into the 2

notches at the bottom of the front upper finish panel and snap it out.

e. Remove the radio assembly. Open the glove compartment door and drop the glove compartment assembly down. Remove the 2 console-to-instrument panel retaining screws.

f. Remove the 4 console-to-bracket retaining screws and remove the console.

g. Disconnect all underhood wiring connectors from the main wiring harness. Disengage the rubber grommet seal from the dash panel and push the wiring harness and connector into the passenger compartment.

h. Remove the 3 bolts attaching the steering column opening cover and reinforcement panel. Remove the cover.

i. Remove the steering column opening reinforcement by removing the 2 bolts, remove the 2 bolts retaining the lower steering column opening reinforcement and remove the reinforcement.

j. Remove the 6 steering column retaining nuts. Two are retaining the hood release mechanism and 4 retain the column to the lower brake pedal support. Lower the steering column to the floor.

k. Remove the steering column upper and lower shrouds and disconnect the wiring from the combination switch.

l. Remove the brake pedal support nut and snap out the defroster grille.

m. Remove the screws from the speaker covers. Snap out the speaker covers. Remove the front screws retaining the right and left scuff plates at the cowl trim panel. Remove the right and left side cowl trim panels.

n. Disconnect the wiring at the right and left cowl sides. Remove the cowl side retaining bolts, 1 on each side.

o. Open the glove compartment door and flex the glove compartment bin tabs inward. Drop down the glove compartment door assembly.

p. Remove the 5 cowl top screw attachments. Gently pull the instrument panel away from the cowl. Disconnect the speedometer cable and wire connectors.

4. Disconnect the liquid line and the accumulator/drier inlet tube from the evaporator core at the dash panel. Cap the refrigerant lines and evaporator core tube to prevent the entrance of dirt and moisture.

5. Disconnect the heater hoses and tubes.

6. Remove the screw attaching the air inlet duct and blower housing assembly support brace to the cowl top panel.

7. Disconnect the black vacuum supply hose from the in-line vacuum check valve in the engine compartment. Disconnect the blower motor wires from the wire harness and disconnect the wire harness from the blower motor resistor.

8. Working under the hood, remove the 2 nuts retaining the evaporator case to the dash panel. Inside the passenger compartment, remove the 2 screws attaching the evaporator case support brackets to the cowl top panel.

9. Remove the 1 screw retaining the bracket below the evaporator case to the dash panel. Carefully pull the evaporator case away from the dash panel and remove the evaporator case assembly from the vehicle.

NOTE: Whenever an evaporator case is replaced, it will be necessary to replace the suction accumulator/drier.

10. Remove the 4 heater core access cover attaching screws and remove the cover from the case.

11. Lift the heater core and seal from the case. Remove the seal from the heater core tubes.

To install:

12. Install the heater core tube seal on the heater core tubes.

13. Inspect the heater core sealer in the evaporator case. Replace with suitable caulking cord, if necessary.

14. Install the heater core in the case with the seals on the outside of the case. Position the heater core access cover on the case and install the 4 attaching screws.

15. Position the evaporator case assembly in the vehicle. Install the screws attaching the evaporator case support brackets to the cowl top panel. Check the evaporator case drain tube to make sure it is through the dash panel and is not pinched or kinked.

16. Install 1 screw retaining the bracket below the evaporator case to the dash panel. Working under the hood, install the 2 nuts retaining the evaporator case to the dash panel. Tighten the 4 nuts and 2 screw in the engine compartment. Tighten the 2 screws in the passenger compartment and the 2 support bracket attaching screws.

17. Connect the blower motor wire harness to the resistor and blower motor. Connect the black vacuum

supply hose to the vacuum check valve in the engine compartment.

18. Using new O-rings lubricated with clean refrigerant oil, connect the liquid line and suction accumulator inlet to the evaporator core tubes. Tighten each connection using a backup wrench to prevent component damage.

19. Install the instrument panel by reversing the removal procedure.

20. Connect the heater hoses to the heater core and fill the cooling system.

21. Connect the negative battery cable. Leak test, evacuate and charge the refrigerant system according to the proper procedures. Observe all safely precautions.

22. Check the system for proper operation.

THUNDERBIRD AND COUGAR

1. Disconnect the negative battery cable and drain the cooling system.

2. Discharge the refrigerant from the air conditioning system according to the proper procedure.

3. Remove the instrument panel according to the following procedure:

a. Disconnect the underhood wiring at the left side of the dash panel.

b. Disengage the wiring connector from the dash panel and push the wiring harness into the passenger compartment.

c. Remove the steering column lower trim cover by removing the 3 screws at the bottom, 1 screw on the left side and pulling to disengage the 5 snap-in retainers across the top.

d. Remove the steering column lower opening reinforcement; 6 screws retain the reinforcement to the instrument panel.

e. Remove the steering column upper and lower shrouds and disconnect the wiring from the steering column.

f. Remove the shift interlock switch and disconnect the steering column lower universal joint.

g. Support the steering column and remove the 4 nuts retaining the column to the support. Remove the column from the vehicle.

h. Remove the 1 screw retaining the left side of the instrument panel to the parking brake bracket.

i. Install the steering column lower opening reinforcement using the 4 screws, 1 at each corner. This will prevent the instrument panel from twisting when being removed.

j. Remove the right and left cowl side trim panels.

k. Remove the console assembly and remove the 2 nuts retaining the center of the instrument panel to the floor.

l. Open the glove compartment, squeeze the sides of the bin and lower to the full open position. From under the instrument panel and through the glove compartment opening, disconnect the wiring, vacuum lines and control cables.

m. Remove 2 screws from the right side and 2 screws from the left side retaining the instrument panel to the cowl side.

n. Remove the right and left upper finish panels by pulling up to disengage the snap-in retainers. There are 3 on the right side, 4 on the left side.

o. Remove the 4 screws retaining the instrument panel to the cowl top. Remove the right and left roof rail trim panel. Remove the door frame weatherstrip.

p. Carefully pull the instrument panel away from the cowl and disconnect any remaining wiring or controls.

4. Disconnect the liquid line and accumulator/drier inlet tube from the evaporator core at the dash panel. Cap the refrigerant lines and evaporator core to prevent the entrance of dirt and moisture.

5. Disconnect the refrigerant lines and wiring connector from the suction accumulator/drier. Remove the suction accumulator/drier and bracket.

6. If necessary, remove the throttle cable bracket and position aside.

7. Disconnect the heater hoses from the heater core. Plug the hoses and heater core tubes.

8. Disconnect the black vacuum supply hose from the in-line vacuum check valve in the engine compartment. Disconnect the blower motor wiring.

9. Working under the hood, remove the nuts retaining the evaporator case to the dash panel. In the passenger compartment, remove the screw attaching the evaporator case support bracket to the cowl top panel.

10. Remove 1 nut retaining the bracket below the evaporator case to the dash panel. Carefully pull the evaporator case away from the dash panel and remove the evaporator case assembly from the vehicle.

NOTE: Whenever an evaporator case is replaced, it will be necessary to replace the suction accumulator/drier.

11. Remove the 4 heater core access cover attaching screws and remove the access cover from the evaporator case.

12. Remove the tube seal from the heater core tubes. Slide the heater core and seals from the evaporator case.

To install:

13. Install the heater core in the evaporator case with the tube seal on the outside of the case.

14. Position the heater core access cover on the evaporator case and install the 4 attaching screws.

15. Position the evaporator case assembly in the vehicle and install the screw attaching the evaporator case support bracket to the cowl top panel. Check the evaporator case drain tube to make sure it is through the dash panel and is not pinched or kinked.

16. Install 1 nut retaining the mounting bracket at the left end of the evaporator case to the dash panel and another nut to retain the bracket below the evaporator case to the dash panel.

17. Working under the hood, install the nuts retaining the evaporator case to the dash panel. Tighten the 4 nuts, 2 in the engine compartment and 2 in the passenger compartment and the 1 support bracket attaching screw.

18. Connect the black vacuum supply hose to the vacuum check valve in the engine compartment.

19. Install the suction accumulator/drier and bracket. Using new O-rings lubricated with clean refrigerant oil, connect the refrigerant lines to the suction accumulator/drier. Connect the wire harness to the pressure switch.

20. Install the throttle cable bracket, if removed.

21. Using new O-rings lubricated with clean refrigerant oil, connect the liquid line and suction accumulator inlet tube to the evaporator core.

22. Install the instrument panel by reversing the removal procedure.

23. Connect the heater hoses to the heater core and fill the cooling system.

24. Leak test, evacuate and charge the system according to the proper procedure. Observe all safety precautions.

25. Check the system for proper operation.

MARK VII

1. Disconnect the negative battery cable and drain the cooling system. Remove the air intake duct.

2. Discharge the refrigerant from the air conditioning system according to the proper procedure.

3. Remove the instrument panel as follows:

   a. Disconnect all underhood electrical connectors of the main wiring harness. Disengage the rubber grommet from the dash panel.

   b. Remove the right and left sound insulator assemblies from under the instrument panel. Remove the bulb and socket assemblies, if necessary.

   c. Remove the steering column opening trim cover and the lower steel reinforcement.

   d. Remove the left and right cowl trim panels. Remove the screws attaching the hood release to the cowl panel before removing the left trim panel.

   e. Remove the steering column trim shroud screws and remove the shrouds.

   f. Disconnect all electrical connector quick couplers from the steering column switches.

   g. Remove the 4 nuts attaching the steering column to the support. Lower the column to rest on the seat cushion.

   h. Snap out the defroster opening grille panel and remove the screws attaching the floor console to the instrument panel and floor. Move the console rearward.

   i. Remove the screw(s) attaching the instrument panel to the floor. Remove the screws attaching the instrument panel to the cowls. Remove the bolt or nut attaching the instrument panel to the support bracket.

   j. Disconnect the main wiring harness behind the instrument panel, on the right side of the steering column support, at the blower motor and at the left and right cowl panels.

   k. Disconnect the radio antenna lead from the radio. Disconnect any vacuum hoses attached to the instrument panel.

   l. Remove the right and left A-pillar garnish mouldings.

   m. Remove the 3 screws attaching the instrument panel to the dash panel and pull/push the wiring harness and connectors into the passenger compartment. Remove the instrument panel.

4. Disconnect the heater hoses from the heater core. Plug the hoses and the core. Disconnect the wire harness connector from the clutch cycling pressure switch, located on top of the suction accumulator/drier.

5. Disconnect the liquid line and the accumulator/drier inlet tube from the evaporator core tubes. Use a backup wrench to prevent component damage. Cap all fittings to prevent the entrance of dirt and moisture.

6. Working under the hood, remove the 2 nuts retaining the accumulator/drier bracket to the dash panel. Position the accumulator/drier and liquid line aside and remove the 2 evaporator assembly retaining nuts.

7. Disconnect the wiring harness connectors, as necessary. Disconnect the harness connectors from the blower motor wires and blower motor speed controller.

8. Disconnect the automatic temperature control sensor hose and elbow from the evaporator case. Disconnect the automatic temperature control harness at the control assembly.

9. Disconnect the rear seat duct adapter from the floor duct. Remove the 3 evaporator attaching screws and remove the evaporator assembly from the vehicle.

NOTE: Whenever an evaporator case is replaced, it will be necessary to replace the suction accumulator/drier.

10. Remove the 5 heater core access cover attaching screws and remove the access cover from the evaporator case.

11. Lift the heater core and seal from the evaporator case. Remove the seal from the heater core tubes.

To install:

12. Install the heater core in the evaporator case.

13. Position the heater core access cover on the evaporator case and install the 5 attaching screws. Install the heater core seal.

14. Position the evaporator assembly to the dash panel. Install the 3 attaching screws located in the passenger compartment, but do not tighten at this time. Check the evaporator drain tube to be certain it is through the opening.

15. Working in the engine compartment, install 2 nuts to retain the evaporator assembly to the dash panel; then, tighten the retaining nuts and attaching screws.

16. Position the instrument panel near the dash panel and connect the radio antenna, automatic temperature control harness to control assembly, harness to blower motor speed controller and blower motor wires. Also attach any additional wire harness connectors disconnected during removal.

17. Move the instrument panel into position and install attaching screws. Connect the automatic temperature control sensor hose and elbow assembly.

NOTE: Make sure the air conditioning plenum (attached to the instrument panel) is correctly aligned and sealed at the evaporator outlet opening. Air leakage to the floor area will result if the plenum is not sealed at the evaporator case outlet.

18. Install the nut retaining the instrument panel to the brake pedal and steering column support and install the retainer nuts.

19. Install the steering column opening reinforcement and shroud. Install the screws to attach the lower center of the instrument panel to the floor brace.

20. Install the defroster opening grille and the right and left side cowl trim panels. Install the right and left instrument panel sound insulators.

21. Install the rear seat duct adapter and the console assembly. Install the instrument panel right hand finish panel and the steering column opening cover.

22. Position the accumulator/drier mounting bracket over the studs on the dash panel and loosely install the 2 nuts.

23. Connect the accumulator/drier inlet tube to the evaporator core outlet tube using a new O-ring lubricated with clean refrigerant oil. Do not tighten the connection.

24. Connect the liquid line to the evaporator core inlet tube using a new O-ring lubricated with clean refrigerant oil. Do not tighten the connection.

25. Tighten the 2 nuts retaining the accumulator/drier to the dash panel. Tighten the 2 refrigerant line connections at the evaporator core. Use a backup wrench to prevent component damage.

26. Connect the harness connector to the clutch cycling pressure switch. Connect the heater hoses to the heater core and fill the cooling system.

27. Connect the negative battery cable. Leak test, evacuate and charge the refrigerant system according to the proper procedure. Observe all safety precautions.

28. Check the automatic temperature control system and all instrument panel functions for proper operation.

MARK VIII

1. Disconnect the negative battery cable. Wait one minute for the air bag diagnostic monitor to deplete the air bag backup power supply.

2. Remove the instrument panel as follows:

   a. Loosen the main wiring connector bolt in the engine compartment at the left side of the instrument panel.

   b. Remove the radio antenna stanchion and disconnect the radio antenna lead in cable from the radio.

   c. Remove the right and left windshield garnish mouldings. Remove the right and left front door scuff plates and weatherstrips.

   d. Remove the cowl side trim panels.

   e. Remove the instrument panel steering column cover. Unsnap the 3 clips across the top of the instrument panel steering column cover.

   f. Remove the ignition switch lock cylinder.

   g. Remove the steering column shrouds and install the ignition switch lock cylinder to prevent the steering wheel from turning.

   h. Disconnect the wiring connectors to the turn signal and wiper switch. Remove the 1 screw for the evaporator register duct from under the steering column.

   i. Disconnect the wiring from the bottom of the steering column tube.

   j. Remove the pinch bolt at the lower end of the steering column yoke and slightly spread the joint with a suitable tool.

   k. While supporting the tube, remove the 4 steering column retaining nuts. Remove the interlock cable and shift actuator cable fitting. Carefully remove the steering column from the vehicle.

   l. Loosen the main wiring connector at the left side of the steering column opening.

   m. Disconnect the stoplight switch. Pull the floor carpet as required to disconnect the window regulator safety relay switch wiring and the Powertrain Control Module (PCM) from the main wiring.

   n. Open the glove compartment to the stop and unsnap the hydraulic lift from the right side of the glove compartment.

   o. Remove the glove compartment from the vehicle. Reach through the opening and disconnect the wiring and vacuum hoses that connect to the evaporator housing.

   p. Disconnect the wiring connector from the speed control amplifier.

   q. Remove the floor console assembly.

   r. Install a protective cover over the instrument panel to protect from damage.

   s. Using a putty knife or similar tool, insert under the left and right corner of the instrument panel upper finish panel and pry up on the instrument panel upper finish panel to release one snap clip. Unsnap the remaining 4 clips pulling up by hand, working toward the opposite side of the vehicle.

   t. Remove the 2 nuts retaining the left side of the instrument panel-to-cowl side. Remove the console bracket bolts from instrument panel.

   u. With the help of an assistant, remove the 6 retaining bolts at the top of the instrument panel.

   v. Carefully pull the instrument panel away from the windshield glass while checking for any remaining wiring connectors. Disengage the antenna wire grommet from the sheet metal and pull the radio antenna lead in cable through.

   w. Transfer all components if the panel is being replaced.

3. Partially drain the cooling system and remove the A/C evaporator housing.

4. Remove the heater core access cover from the housing.

5. Remove the tube gasket from the heater core tubes and remove the heater core. Try not to damage the seals.

To install:

6. Install the heater core with the tube gasket on the outside of the case.

7. Install the core cover and A/C evaporator housing into the vehicle.

8. Install the instrument panel as follows:

   a. Loosen the main wiring connector bolt in the engine compartment at the left side of the instrument panel.

   b. Transfer all components if the panel is being replaced.

   c. With the help of an assistant, carefully push the instrument panel toward the windshield glass while checking obstructions. Connect the radio antenna lead in cable.

   d. Install the 6 retaining bolts at the top of the instrument panel.

e. Install the 2 nuts retaining the left side of the instrument panel-to-cowl side. Install the console bracket bolts to instrument panel.

f. Make sure the panel is snapped into place.

g. Install the floor console assembly.

h. Connect the wiring connector to the speed control amplifier.

i. Connect the wiring and vacuum hoses. Install the glove compartment to the vehicle.

j. Install the glove compartment door.

k. Connect the stoplight switch, window regulator safety relay switch wiring and the Powertrain Control Module (PCM) to the main wiring.

l. Install the main wiring connector at the left side of the steering column opening.

m. Connect the interlock and shift cables. Install the steering column and 4 steering column retaining nuts.

n. Install the pinch bolt at the lower end of the steering column yoke.

o. Connect the wiring to the bottom of the steering column tube.

p. Connect the wiring connectors to the turn signal and wiper switch.

q. Install the steering column shrouds and ignition switch lock cylinder.

r. Install the instrument panel steering column cover.

s. Install the cowl side trim panels.

t. Install the right and left windshield garnish mouldings. Install the right and left front door scuff plates and weatherstrips.

u. Install the radio antenna stanchion and connect the radio antenna lead in cable to the radio.

9. Refill the cooling system, connect the battery cable, start the engine and check for leaks.

Water Pump

REMOVAL AND INSTALLATION

2.3L Engine

1. Disconnect the negative battery cable and drain the cooling system.
2. Remove the 4 bolts retaining the pulley to the water pump shaft. Remove the fan and shroud.
3. Remove the air conditioning and power steering belts. Remove the water pump pulley.

4. Remove the heater hose to the water pump and the lower radiator hose.
5. Remove the timing belt outer cover bolt, release the interlocking tabs and remove the cover.
6. Remove the water pump retaining bolts and remove the water pump.
7. Installation is the reverse of the removal procedure. Clean all gasket mating surfaces prior to installation. Apply pipe sealant to the water pump bolts and tighten to 14–21 ft. lbs. (20–30 Nm). Tighten the pulley retaining bolts to 15–22 ft. lbs. (20–30 Nm).
8. Fill and bleed the cooling system. Operate the engine until normal operating temperatures have been reached and check for leaks.

3.8L Engine

1. Disconnect the negative battery cable and drain the cooling system.
2. On all except supercharged engine, remove the fan/clutch assembly and shroud.
3. Rotate the main accessory drive belt tensioner. Remove the main drive belt and water pump pulley.
4. Remove the power steering pump pulley and remove the water pump to power steering pump brace.

NOTE: On supercharged engines, it may be necessary to remove the charge air cooler to gain access to the power steering pump pulley.

5. On all except supercharged engine, disconnect the coolant bypass hose(s) and the heater hose at the water pump. On supercharged engine, disconnect the oil cooler tube and bypass hose and remove the upper crankshaft sensor cover.
6. Disconnect the lower radiator hose. Remove the water pump retaining bolts and the pump. If a prybar is used to assist removal, be careful not to damage the mating surfaces.
7. Installation is the reverse of the removal procedure. Clean all gasket mating surfaces prior to installation. Tighten the water pump retaining bolts to 15–22 ft. lbs. (20–30 Nm). Fill and bleed the cooling system. Operate the engine until normal operating temperatures have been reached and check for leaks.

NOTE: The threads of the No. 1 water pump retaining bolt must be coated with pipe sealant before installing.

4.6L (DOHC) Engine

1. Disconnect the negative battery cable and drain the cooling system.
2. Remove the 4 bolts retaining the pulley to the water pump shaft.
3. Release belt tensioner and remove the drive belts. Remove 4 bolts retaining water pump pulley and remove the pulley.
4. Remove the 4 water pump retaining bolts and remove the water pump.
5. Installation is the reverse of the removal procedure. Clean all gasket mating surfaces prior to installation. Tighten the water pump bolts and pulley retaining bolts to 15–22 ft. lbs. (20–30 Nm).
6. Fill and bleed the cooling system. Operate the engine until normal operating temperatures have been reached and check for leaks.

4.6L (SOHC) Engine

1. Disconnect the negative battery cable and drain the cooling system.
2. Release the drive belt tensioner and remove the belt.
3. Remove the water pump pulley bolts and pulley.
4. Remove the pump-to-block bolts and pump.
5. Installation is the reverse of the removal procedure. Clean all gasket mating surfaces prior to installation. Tighten the water pump bolts and pulley retaining bolts to 15–22 ft. lbs. (20–30 Nm).
6. Fill and bleed the cooling system. Operate the engine until normal operating temperatures have been reached and check for leaks.

5.0L Engine

1. Disconnect the negative battery cable.
2. Drain the cooling system. Remove the air inlet tube, if equipped.
3. On Thunderbird and Cougar, disconnect the upper radiator hose at the engine.
4. On all except Thunderbird and Cougar, remove the fan shroud attaching bolts and position the shroud over the fan. Remove the fan and clutch assembly from the water pump shaft and remove the shroud.
5. On Thunderbird and Cougar, remove the fan and clutch assembly from the water pump shaft using fan clutch holding tool T84T–6312–C or equivalent, and fan clutch nut wrench T84T–6312–D or equivalent, and position the fan and clutch assembly in the fan shroud. The nut is turned counterclockwise. Remove the

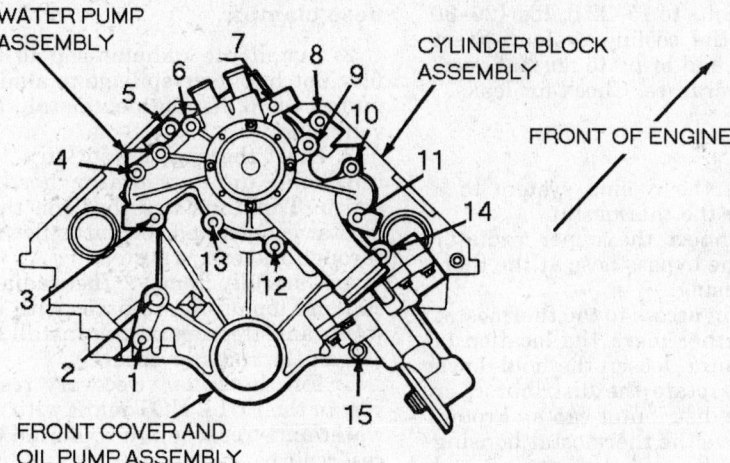

FASTENER AND HOLE NO.	HOLE NO.		FASTENERS	
	WATER PUMP	FRONT COVER	PART NO.	PART NAME
1.		4	N805112	STUD
2.		2	N805112	STUD
3.	2	9	N804853	STUD
4.	1	8	N804853	STUD
5.		10	N605787	BOLT
6.	9	15	N605908	BOLT
7.	8	16	N605908	BOLT
8.		11	N605787	BOLT
9.	7	17	N804756	STUD BOLT
10.	6	1	N804852	STUD BOLT
11.	5	7	N804853	STUD
12.*	4	13	N605908	BOLT
13.	3	14	N605908	BOLT
14.		6	N804839	BOLT
15.		5	N804841	CAP SCREW
3, 4, 10, 11	2, 1, 5	9, 8, 7	N804578	NUT

*EFI ENGINE IS A BOLT, SUPERCHARGED ENGINE IS A STUD.

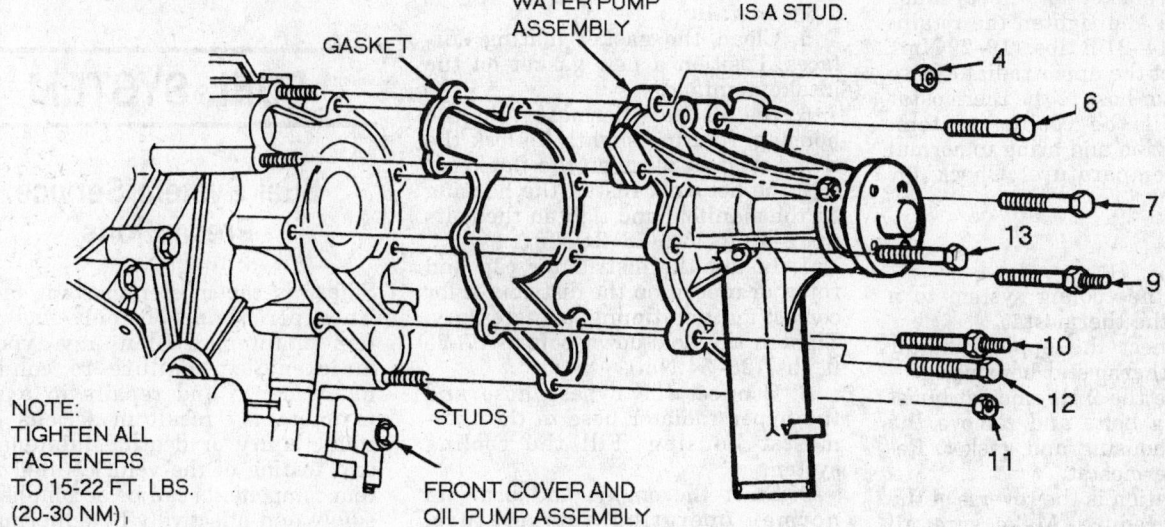

Water pump fastener and hole location — 3.8L engine

8470D024

fan shroud and fan/clutch as an assembly.

6. Loosen the water pump pulley bolts. Rotate the tensioner away from the accessory drive belt and remove the belt. Remove the water pump pulley.

7. Remove all accessory brackets that attach to the water pump.

8. Disconnect the lower radiator hose, heater hose and water pump bypass hose at the water pump.

9. Remove the water pump attaching bolts and remove the water pump. Discard the gasket.

10. Installation is the reverse of the removal procedure. Clean all gasket mating surfaces prior to installation.

Tighten the water pump attaching bolts to 12–18 ft. lbs. (16–24 Nm).

11. Fill and bleed the cooling system. Operate the engine until normal operating temperatures have been reached and check for leaks.

Thermostat

REMOVAL AND INSTALLATION

2.3L Engine

1. Drain the cooling system to a level below the thermostat.

2. Remove the upper radiator hose and disconnect the heater hose at the

thermostat housing located on the left front lower side of the engine.

3. Remove the thermostat housing retaining bolts and remove the housing. Remove the thermostat by rotating counterclockwise in the housing until the thermostat becomes free to remove. Do not pry out the thermostat.

4. Remove and discard the gasket.
To install:

5. Clean all gasket mating surfaces and position a new gasket on the cylinder head opening. The gasket must be positioned on the cylinder head, before the thermostat is installed.

6. Install the thermostat into the housing with the bridge section in the housing. Turn the thermostat clockwise to lock it into position on the flats cast into the housing.

NOTE: It is important that the rubber thermostat gasket be pressed and the correct thermostat installation alignment be made to provide coolant flow to the heater. Insert and rotate the thermostat to the left or right until it stops in the thermostat housing. Visually check for full width of heater outlet tube opening to be visible within the thermostat port in assembly. This port alignment at assembly is required to provide maximum coolant flow to the heater.

7. Position the thermostat housing against the gasket on the cylinder head. Install and tighten the retaining bolts to 14–21 ft. lbs. (19–29 Nm).
8. Connect the upper radiator hose and the heater hose to the thermostat housing. Fill the cooling system. Start the engine and bring to normal operating temperature. Check for leaks.

3.8L Engine

1. Drain the cooling system to a level below the thermostat.
2. Disconnect the upper radiator hose at the thermostat housing.
3. Remove the 2 thermostat housing retaining bolts and remove the thermostat housing and gasket. Remove the thermostat.
4. Installation is the reverse of the removal procedure. Make sure all mating surfaces are clean prior to installation. Install the thermostat into the housing and turn clockwise to lock into position on the flats cast into the housing.
5. Tighten the thermostat housing retaining bolts to 15–22 ft. lbs. (20–30 Nm). Fill the cooling system. Start the engine and bring to normal operating temperature. Check for leaks.

4.6L Engine

1. Drain the cooling system to a level below the thermostat.
2. Disconnect the lower radiator hose (upper hose for Thunderbird/Cougar), engine return hose and bypass from the thermostat housing.
3. Remove the 2 thermostat housing retaining bolts and remove the thermostat housing and O-ring. Remove the thermostat.
4. Installation is the reverse of the removal procedure. Make sure all

mating surfaces are clean prior to installation.
5. Tighten the thermostat housing retaining bolts to 15–22 ft. lbs. (20–30 Nm). Fill the cooling system. Start the engine and bring to normal operating temperature. Check for leaks.

5.0L Engine

1. Drain the cooling system to a level below the thermostat.
2. Disconnect the upper radiator hose and the bypass hose at the thermostat housing.
3. To gain access to the thermostat housing, either mark the location of the distributor, loosen the hold-down clamp and rotate the distributor, or remove the distributor cap and rotor.
4. Remove the thermostat housing retaining bolts and the housing and gasket. Remove the thermostat.
To install:
5. Clean the gasket mating surfaces. Position a new gasket on the intake manifold.
6. Install the thermostat in the housing, rotating slightly to lock the thermostat in place on the flats cast into the housing. Install the housing on the manifold and tighten the bolts to 12–18 ft. lbs. (16–24 Nm).
7. Install the distributor cap and rotor, or reposition the distributor for correct ignition timing, as necessary. Tighten the hold-down bolt to 17–25 ft. lbs. (23–34 Nm).
8. Connect the bypass hose and the upper radiator hose to the thermostat housing. Fill the cooling system.
9. Start the engine and bring to normal operating temperature. Check for leaks.

Cooling System Bleeding

When the entire cooling system is drained, the following procedure should be used to ensure a complete fill.

1. Install the block drain plug, if removed and close the draincock. On 3.8L engine, remove the vent plug on the intake manifold behind the thermostat housing. With the engine OFF, add a 50/50 mixture of water and anti-freeze to the radiator until it reaches the radiator filler neck seat.

NOTE: On Mustang equipped with the 2.3L engine, disconnect the heater hose at the connection on the thermostat housing. Fill the radiator until coolant is visible at the connection in the thermostat housing or the coolant

level in the radiator reaches the radiator filler neck seat. Install the heater hose and tighten the hose clamps.

2. Install the radiator cap to the first notch to keep spillage to a minimum. On 3.8L engine, install the vent plug.
3. Start the engine and let it idle until the upper radiator hose is warm. This indicates that the thermostat is open and coolant is flowing through the entire system.
4. Carefully remove the radiator cap and top off the radiator with the water/anti-freeze mixture. Install the cap on the radiator securely.
5. Fill the coolant recovery reservoir to the FULL HOT mark with the water/anti-freeze mixture. Install the reservoir cap.

FUEL SYSTEM

Fuel System Service Precautions

Safety is the most important factor when performing not only fuel system maintenance but any type of maintenance. Failure to conduct maintenance and repairs in a safe manner may result in serious personal injury or death. Maintenance and testing of the vehicle's fuel system components can be accomplished safely and effectively by adhering to the following rules and guidelines.

• To avoid the possibility of fire and personal injury, always disconnect the negative battery cable unless the repair or test procedure requires that battery voltage be applied.
• Always relieve the fuel system pressure prior to disconnecting any fuel system component (injector, fuel rail, pressure regulator, etc.), fitting or fuel line connection. Exercise extreme caution whenever relieving fuel system pressure to avoid exposing skin, face and eyes to fuel spray. Please be advised that fuel under pressure may penetrate the skin or any part of the body that it contacts.
• Always place a shop towel or cloth around the fitting or connection prior to loosening to absorb any excess fuel due to spillage. Ensure that all fuel spillage (should it occur) is quickly removed from engine surfaces. Ensure that all fuel soaked

cloths or towels are deposited into a suitable waste container.

• Always keep a dry chemical (Class B) fire extinguisher near the work area.

• Do not allow fuel spray or fuel vapors to come into contact with a spark or open flame.

• Always use a backup wrench when loosening and tightening fuel line connection fittings. This will prevent unnecessary stress and torsion to fuel line piping. Always follow the proper torque specifications.

• Always replace worn fuel fitting O-rings with new. Do not substitute fuel hose or equivalent where fuel pipe is installed.

RELIEVING FUEL SYSTEM PRESSURE

Fuel supply lines on all fuel injected engines will remain pressurized for some period of time after the engine is shut OFF. This pressure must be relieved before servicing the fuel system. Pressure is relieved through the fuel pressure relief valve. To relieve the fuel system pressure, first remove the fuel tank cap to relieve pressure in the tank, then remove the cap on the fuel pressure relief valve, located on the fuel rail. Attach fuel pressure gauge T80L–9974–A or equivalent, and drain the system through the drain tube into a suitable container. Remove the fuel pressure gauge and replace the cap on the relief valve.

Fuel Line Couplings

REMOVAL AND INSTALLATION

There are 3 methods used to connect the fuel lines and fuel system components: the hairpin clip push connect fitting, the duck bill clip push connect fitting and the spring lock coupling. Each requires a different procedure to disconnect and connect.

Hairpin Clip Push Connect Fitting

1. Inspect the visible internal portion of the fitting for dirt accumulation. If more than a light coating of dust is present, clean the fitting before disassembly.

2. Some adhesion between the seals in the fitting and the tubing will occur with time. To separate, twist the fitting on the tube, then push and pull the fitting until it moves freely on the tube.

NOTE: Use care when separating 90 degree elbow connectors, as excessive side loading could break the connector body.

3. Remove the hairpin clip from the fitting by first bending and breaking the shipping tab. Next, spread the 2 clip legs by hand about 1/8 in. each to disengage the body and push the legs into the fitting. Lightly pull the triangular end of the clip and work it clear of the tube and fitting.

NOTE: Do not use hand tools to complete this operation.

4. Grasp the fitting and pull in an axial direction to remove the fitting from the tube.

5. After disassembly, inspect and clean the tube end sealing surfaces. The tube end should be free of scratches and corrosion that could provide leak paths. Inspect the inside of the fitting for any internal parts such as O-rings and spacers that may have been dislodged from the fitting. Replace any damaged connector.

To connect:

6. Install a new connector if damage was found. Insert a new clip into any 2 adjacent openings with the triangular portion pointing away from the fitting opening. Install the clip until the legs of the clip are locked on the outside of the body. Piloting with an index finger is necessary.

7. Before installing the fitting on the tube, wipe the tube end with a clean cloth. Inspect the inside of the fitting to make sure it is free of dirt and/or obstructions.

8. Apply a light coating of engine oil to the tube end. Align the fitting and tube axially and push the fitting onto the tube end. When the fitting is engaged, a definite click will be heard. Pull on the fitting to make sure it is fully engaged.

Duck Bill Clip Push Connect Fitting

1. Inspect the visible internal portion of the fitting for dirt accumulation. If more than a light coating of dust is present, clean the fitting before disassembly.

2. Some adhesion between the seals in the fitting and the tubing will occur with time. To separate, twist the fitting on the tube, then push and pull the fitting until it moves freely on the tube.

3. Align the slot on push connect disassembly tool T82L–9600–AH or equivalent, with either tab on the clip, 90 degrees from the slots on the side of the fitting and insert the tool. This disengages the duck bill retainer from the tube.

4. Holding the tool and the tube with 1 hand, pull the fitting away from the tube.

NOTE: Use hands only. Only moderate effort is required if the tube has been properly disengaged.

5. After disassembly, inspect and clean the tube end sealing surfaces. The tube end should be free of scratches and corrosion that could provide leak paths. Inspect the inside of the fitting for any internal parts such as O-rings and spacers that may have been dislodged from the fitting. Replace any damaged connector.

6. Some fuel tubes have a secondary bead which aligns with the outer surface of the clip. These beads can make tool insertion difficult. If there is extreme difficulty, use the following disassembly method:

a. Using pliers with a jaw width of 0.2 in. (5mm) or less, align the jaws with the openings in the side of the fitting case and compress the portion of the retaining clip that engages the fitting case. This disengages the retaining clip from the case. Often 1 side of the clip will disengage before the other. The clip must be disengaged from both openings.

b. Pull the fitting off the tube by hand only. Only moderate effort is required if the retaining clip has been properly disengaged.

c. After disassembly, inspect and clean the tube end sealing surfaces. The tube end should be free of scratches and corrosion that could provide leak paths. Inspect the inside of the fitting for any internal parts such as O-rings and spacers that may have been dislodged from the fitting. Replace any damaged connector.

d. The retaining clip will remain on the tube. Disengage the clip from the tube bead and remove.

To connect:

7. Install a new connector if damage was found. Install the new replacement clip into the body by inserting 1 of the retaining clip serrated edges on the duck bill portion into 1 side of the window openings. Push on the other side until the clip snaps into place.

8. Before installing the fitting on the tube, wipe the tube end with a clean cloth. Inspect the inside of the fitting to make sure it is free of dirt and/or obstructions.

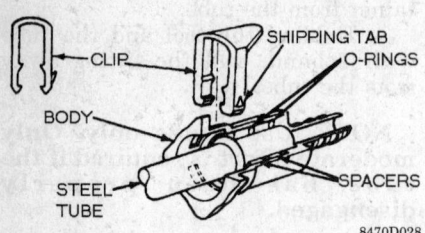

Hairpin clip push connect fitting

9. Apply a light coating of engine oil to the tube end. Align the fitting and tube axially and push the fitting onto the tube end. When the fitting is engaged, a definite click will be heard. Pull on the fitting to make sure it is fully engaged.

Spring Lock Coupling

The spring lock coupling is a fuel line coupling held together by a garter spring inside a circular cage. When the coupling is connected together, the flared end of the female fitting slips behind the garter spring inside the cage of the male fitting. The gar-

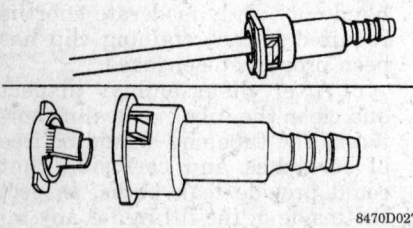

Duck bill clip push connect fitting

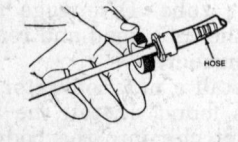

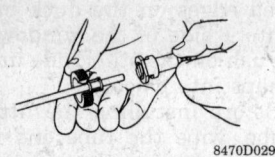

Duck bill clip push connect fitting disconnect tool

ter spring and cage then prevent the flared end of the female fitting from pulling out of the cage. As an additional locking feature, most vehicles have a horseshoe shaped retaining clip that improves the retaining reliability of the spring lock coupling.

Fuel Tank

REMOVAL AND INSTALLATION

1. Disconnect the negative battery cable and relieve the fuel system pressure.
2. Siphon or pump as much fuel as possible out through the fuel filler pipe.

NOTE: All vehicles have reservoirs inside the fuel tank to maintain fuel near the fuel pickup during cornering and under low fuel operating conditions. These reservoirs could block siphon tubes or hoses from reaching the bottom of the fuel tank. Repeated attempts using different hose orientations can overcome this obstacle.

3. Raise and safely support the vehicle.
4. On Mark VIII, Thunderbird and Cougar, remove the exhaust pipe and exhaust shield, if equipped. Disconnect the fuel fill and vent hoses connecting the filler pipe to the tank. Disconnect 1 end of the vapor crossover hose at the rear over the driveshaft.
5. If equipped with a metal retainer that fastens the filler pipe to the fuel tank, remove the screw attaching the retainer to the fuel tank flange.
6. Disconnect the fuel lines and the electrical connector to the fuel tank sending unit. On some vehicles, these are inaccessible on top of the tank. In these cases they must be disconnected with the tank partially removed.
7. Place a safety support under the fuel tank and remove the bolts from the fuel tank straps. Allow the straps to swing out of the way. Be careful not to deform the fuel tank.
8. Partially remove the tank and disconnect the fuel lines and electrical connector from the sending unit, if required.
9. Remove the tank from the vehicle.
To install:
10. Raise the fuel tank into position in the vehicle. Connect the fuel lines and sending unit electrical connector

if it is necessary to connect them before the tank is in the final installed position.
11. Lubricate the fuel filler pipe with water base tire mounting lubricant and install the tank onto the filler pipe, then bring the tank into final position. Be careful not to deform the tank.
12. Bring the fuel tank straps around the tank and start the retaining nut or bolt. Align the tank with the straps. If equipped, make sure the fuel tank shields are installed with the straps and are positioned correctly on the tank. On Mark VIII, Thunderbird and Cougar, align the tank with the driveshaft.
13. Check the hoses and wiring mounted on the tank top to make sure they are correctly routed and will not be pinched between the tank and body. On Mark VIII, Thunderbird and Cougar, make sure the fuel vent hose is positioned above the vent retainer and not contacting the driveshaft.
14. Tighten the fuel tank strap retaining nuts or bolts to 22–30 ft. lbs. (29–41 Nm).
15. If not already connected, connect the fuel hoses and lines which were disconnected. Make sure the fuel supply, fuel return, if present, and vapor vent connections are made correctly. If not already connected, connect the sending unit electrical connector.
16. On Mark VIII, Thunderbird and Cougar, install the exhaust pipe shield, if equipped, and exhaust pipe.
17. Lower the vehicle. Replace the fuel that was drained from the tank. Check all connections for leaks.

Fuel Filter

REMOVAL AND INSTALLATION

1. Disconnect the negative battery cable and relieve the fuel system pressure.
2. Raise and safely support the vehicle. On Mark VIII, remove the right front fender liner.
3. Remove the push connect fittings at both ends of the filter. Install new retainer clips in each push connect fitting.
4. Remove the fuel filter from the bracket by loosening the worm gear clamp on all vehicles except the Mark VIII. Note the direction of the flow arrow as installed in the bracket to ensure proper direction of fuel flow through the replacement filter.

5. On Mark VIII, remove the screw from the apron and remove retainer tab from sheetmetal.

To install:

6. Install the fuel filter into the bracket, ensuring the proper direction of flow. Tighten the worm gear clamp to 15–25 inch lbs. (1.7–2.8 Nm) on all vehicles except the Mark VIII.

7. On Mark VIII, insert tab into sheetmetal and install screw.

8. Install the push connect fittings onto the filter ends. Start the engine and check for leaks. On Mark VIII, install the fender liner.

9. Lower the vehicle.

Electric Fuel Pump

PRESSURE TESTING

1. Relieve the fuel system pressure and connect a fuel pressure gauge to the valve on the fuel rail.

2. Ground the fuel pump lead of the self-test connector through a jumper wire at the **FP** lead.

3. Turn the ignition key to the **RUN** position to operate the fuel pump.

4. Observe the fuel pressure gauge. The indicated pressure should be 35–40 psi.

5. Remove the fuel pressure gauge and the jumper wire.

REMOVAL AND INSTALLATION

1. Disconnect the negative battery cable and properly relieve the fuel system pressure.

2. Remove the fuel tank and place it on a bench.

3. Remove any dirt that has accumulated around the fuel pump retaining flange so it will not enter the tank during pump removal and installation.

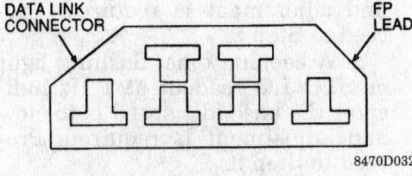

DATA LINK CONNECTOR   FP LEAD

8470D032

Self-test connector terminal location

4. Turn the fuel pump locking ring counterclockwise and remove the locking ring.

5. Remove the fuel pump and bracket assembly. Remove and discard the seal ring.

To install:

6. Clean the fuel pump mounting flange, fuel tank mounting surface and seal ring groove.

7. Apply a light coating of grease on a new seal ring to hold it in place during assembly and install in the seal ring groove.

8. Install the fuel pump and bracket assembly carefully to ensure the filter is not damaged. Make sure the locating keys are in the keyways and the seal ring remains in the groove.

9. Hold the pump assembly in place and install the locking ring finger-tight. Make sure all the locking tabs are under the tank lock ring tabs.

10. Rotate the locking ring clockwise until the ring is against the stops.

11. Install the fuel tank in the vehicle. Add a minimum of 10 gallons of fuel to the tank and check for leaks.

12. Install a suitable fuel pressure gauge to the valve on the fuel rail.

13. Turn the ignition switch from **OFF** to **ON** for 3 seconds. Repeat this procedure 5–10 times until the pressure gauge shows at least 35 psi. Check for fuel leaks.

14. Remove the pressure gauge, start the engine and check for leaks.

Fuel Injection

IDLE SPEED ADJUSTMENT

2.3L Engine

1. Connect the SUPER STAR II tester, tool number 007–00028 or other suitable scan tool to the Self-

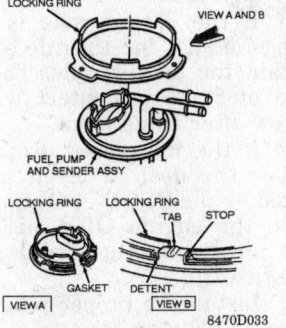

LOCKING RING   VIEW A AND B

FUEL PUMP AND SENDER ASSY

LOCKING RING   LOCKING RING TAB   STOP

GASKET   DETENT

VIEW A   VIEW B

8470D033

Electric fuel pump installation — Except Mark VIII

Test connector. Activate the Key On Engine Running (KOER) Self-Test.

2. After Code 1 or 111 has been displayed, unlatch and within 4 seconds, latch the STI button.

3. A single pulse code indicates the entry mode, then observe the Self-Test Output (STO) on the tester for the following:

a. A constant tone, solid light or **STO LO** readout means the base idle speed is within the correct range. To exit the test, unlatch the STI button, then wait 4 seconds for reinitialization. After 10 minutes, the tool will exit by itself.

b. A beeping tone, flashing light or **STO LO** readout at 8 Hz indicates the Throttle Position Sensor (TPS) is out of range due to over adjustment. Adjustment may be required.

c. A beeping tone, flashing light or **STO LO** readout at 4 Hz indicates the base idle speed is too fast and adjustment is required. Proceed to Step 5.

d. A beeping tone, flashing light or **STO LO** readout at 1 Hz indicates the base idle speed is too low and adjustment is required. Proceed to Step 4.

4. If the idle speed is too low, check for the presence of a throttle plate orifice plug. If there is no plug, turn the throttle screw clockwise until the conditions in Step 3a exist. If there is a plug from previous service, remove the plug and then adjust the screw in either direction, as required. The screw must be in contact with the lever pad after adjustment.

5. If the idle speed is too high, proceed as follows:

a. Turn the engine **OFF**.

b. Block off the orifice in the throttle plate temporarily with tape. If the orifice already has a plug, proceed to Step d.

c. Reattach the air intake hose. Restart the engine and check the idle speed using the Self-Test. If the engine stalled, crack open the plate with the throttle return screw.

d. If the idle speed continues to be fast, run the Key On Engine Off (KOEO) Self-Test and check for a TPS output code.

e. If the output code is within range, remove the tape and check for vacuum leaks, throttle linkage binding, or other causes for excessive high idle.

f. If the output code is out of range, adjust the throttle screw to obtain the proper code. The lever

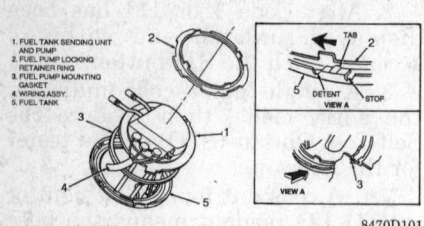

1. FUEL TANK SENDING UNIT
   AND PUMP
2. FUEL PUMP LOCKING
   RETAINER RING
3. FUEL PUMP MOUNTING
   GASKET
4. WIRING ASSY.
5. FUEL TANK

8470D101

Electric fuel pump installation — Mark VIII

pad must be in contact with the screw after adjustment.

g. If the idle speed drops to or below the desired level, as indicated by the Self-Test Output tone, turn the engine **OFF**, disconnect the air cleaner hose and remove the tape.

h. Install the proper plug in the throttle plate orifice.

i. Reconnect the air cleaner hose. Start the engine and turn the throttle plate stop screw clockwise until the conditions in Step 3a exist. Do not turn the screw counterclockwise as this may cause the throttle plate to stick at idle.

6. Run the KOEO Self-Test for proper TPS output code.

7. Make sure the throttle is not stuck in the bore and the linkage is not preventing the throttle from closing.

3.8L Engine, Except SC

1. Place the transaxle in **P** and apply the parking brake.

2. Start the engine and bring to normal operating temperature. Make sure the heater, air conditioning and all other accessories are OFF.

3. Check and if necessary, adjust the ignition timing.

4. Make sure the fuel pressure is correct. Any indicated vehicle malfunction service codes should be resolved before proceeding further.

5. Connect the SUPER STAR II tester, tool number 007–00028 or other suitable scan tool to the Self-Test connector. Activate the Key On Engine Running (KOER) Self-Test.

6. After Code 1 or 111 has been displayed, unlatch and within 4 seconds, latch the STI button.

7. A single pulse code indicates the entry mode, then observe the Self-Test Output (STO) on the tester for the following:

a. A constant tone, solid light or **STO LO** readout means the base

idle speed is within the correct range. To exit the test, unlatch the STI button, then wait 4 seconds for reinitialization. After 10 minutes, the tool will exit by itself.

b. A beeping tone, flashing light or **STO LO** readout at 8 Hz indicates the Throttle Position Sensor (TPS) is out of range due to over adjustment. Adjustment may be required.

c. A beeping tone, flashing light or **STO LO** readout at 4 Hz indicates the base idle speed is too fast and adjustment is required. Proceed to Step 9.

d. A beeping tone, flashing light or **STO LO** readout at 1 Hz indicates the base idle speed is too low and adjustment is required. Proceed to Step 8.

8. If the idle speed is too low, check for the presence of a throttle plate orifice plug. If there is no plug, turn the throttle screw clockwise until the conditions in Step 7a exist. If there is a plug from previous service, remove the plug and then adjust the screw in either direction, as required. The screw must be in contact with the lever pad after adjustment.

9. If the idle speed is too high, proceed as follows:

a. Turn the engine **OFF**.

b. Block off the orifice in the throttle plate temporarily with tape. If the orifice already has a plug, proceed to Step d.

c. Reattach the air intake hose. Restart the engine and check the idle speed using the Self-Test. If the engine stalled, crack open the plate with the throttle return screw.

d. If the idle speed continues to be fast, run the Key On Engine Off (KOEO) Self-Test and check for a TPS output code.

e. If the output code is within range, remove the tape and check for vacuum leaks, throttle linkage binding, or other causes for excessive high idle.

f. If the output code is out of range, adjust the throttle screw to obtain the proper code. The lever pad must be in contact with the screw after adjustment.

g. If the idle speed drops to or below the desired level, as indicated by the Self-Test Output tone, turn the engine **OFF**, disconnect the air cleaner hose and remove the tape.

h. Install the proper plug in the throttle plate orifice.

i. Reconnect the air cleaner hose. Start the engine and turn the

throttle plate stop screw clockwise until the conditions in Step 7a exist. Do not turn the screw counterclockwise as this may cause the throttle plate to stick at idle.

10. Run the KOEO Self-Test for proper TPS output code.

11. Make sure the throttle is not stuck in the bore and the linkage is not preventing the throttle from closing.

12. Check the Throttle Valve (TV) pressure adjustment.

3.8L SC Engine

1. Place the transaxle in **P** and apply the parking brake.

2. Start the engine and bring to normal operating temperature. Make sure the heater, air conditioning and all other accessories are OFF.

3. Check and if necessary, adjust the ignition timing.

4. Make sure the fuel pressure is correct. Any indicated vehicle malfunction service codes should be resolved before proceeding further.

5. Connect the SUPER STAR II tester, tool number 007–00028 or other suitable scan tool to the Self-Test connector. Activate the Key On Engine Running (KOER) Self-Test.

6. After Code 1 or 111 has been displayed, unlatch and within 4 seconds, latch the STI button.

7. A single pulse code indicates the entry mode, then observe the Self-Test Output (STO) on the tester for the following:

a. A constant tone, solid light or **STO LO** readout means the base idle speed is within the correct range. To exit the test, unlatch the STI button, then wait 4 seconds for reinitialization. After 10 minutes, the tool will exit by itself.

b. A beeping tone, flashing light or **STO LO** readout at 8 Hz indicates the Throttle Position Sensor (TPS) is out of range due to over adjustment. Adjustment may be required.

c. A beeping tone, flashing light or **STO LO** readout at 4 Hz indicates the base idle speed is too fast and adjustment is required. Proceed to Step 9.

d. A beeping tone, flashing light or **STO LO** readout at 1 Hz indicates the base idle speed is too low and adjustment is required. Proceed to Step 8.

8. If the idle speed is too low, do not clean the throttle body. Turn the air trim screw counterclockwise until the conditions in Step 7a are satisfied.

9. If the idle speed is too high, do not clean the throttle body. Turn the air trim screw clockwise until the conditions in Step 7a are satisfied.

4.6L Engine

The idle speed is not adjustable on the 4.6L engine

5.0L Engine

1992–93 THUNDERBIRD AND COUGAR

1. Place the transaxle in **P** and apply the parking brake.
2. Start the engine and bring to normal operating temperature. Make sure the heater, air conditioning and all other accessories are OFF.
3. Check and if necessary, adjust the ignition timing.
4. Make sure the fuel pressure is correct. Any indicated vehicle malfunction service codes should be resolved before proceeding further.
5. Connect the SUPER STAR II tester tool 007–00028 or other suitable scan tool, to the Self-Test connector. Activate the Key On Engine Running (KOER) Self-Test.
6. After Code 1 or 111 has been displayed, unlatch and within 4 seconds, latch the STI button.
7. A single pulse code indicates the entry mode, then observe the Self-Test Output (STO) on the tester for the following:
    a. A constant tone, solid light or **STO LO** readout means the base idle speed is within the correct range. To exit the test, unlatch the STI button, then wait 4 seconds for reinitialization. After 10 minutes, the tool will exit by itself.
    b. A beeping tone, flashing light or **STO LO** readout at 8 Hz indicates the Throttle Position Sensor (TPS) is out of range due to over adjustment. Adjustment may be required.
    c. A beeping tone, flashing light or turn the air trim screw counterclockwise until the conditions in Step 7a are satisfied.
8. If the idle speed is too high, do not clean the throttle body. Turn the air trim screw clockwise until the conditions in Step 7a are satisfied.

1992–93 MUSTANG AND MARK VII

1. Place the transaxle in **P** and apply the parking brake.
2. Start the engine and bring to normal operating temperature. Make sure the heater, air conditioning and all other accessories are OFF.
3. Check and if necessary, adjust the ignition timing.

4. Make sure the fuel pressure is correct. Any indicated vehicle malfunction service codes should be resolved before proceeding further.
5. Disconnect the negative battery terminal for 5 minutes, then reconnect. Start the engine and stabilize for 2 minutes, then goose the engine and let it return to idle. Lightly depress and release the accelerator and let the engine idle. Check the engine idle.
6. If the engine does not idle properly, shut the engine OFF and place a 0.025 in. feeler gauge between the throttle plate stop screw and throttle lever.
7. Start the engine and let it idle. Check the idle speed; it should be 675 ± 50 rpm.
8. If the idle speed is too low, proceed as follows:
    a. Shut the engine OFF. Do not clean the throttle body, but check the throttle plate for an orifice plug.
    b. If there is no plug, start the engine and let it idle for 2 minutes, then adjust the idle to the desired speed, ± 25 rpm.
    c. If there is a plug, remove it, then start the engine and let it idle for 2 minutes. Adjust the idle to the desired speed, ± 25 rpm.
    d. The screw must be in contact with the lever pad after adjustment.
9. If the idle speed is too high, proceed as follows:
    a. Shut the engine OFF and disconnect the air cleaner hose.
    b. Block off the orifice in the throttle plate temporarily with tape. If the orifice already has a plug, proceed to Step d.
    c. Reattach the air intake hose. Restart the engine and check the idle speed. If the engine stalled, crack open the plate with the throttle return screw.
    d. If the idle speed continues to be fast, connect a suitable scan tool and run the Key On Engine Off (KOEO) Self-Test and check for a TPS output code.
    e. If the output code is within range, remove the tape and check for vacuum leaks, throttle linkage binding, or other causes for excessive high idle.
    f. If the output code is out of range, adjust the throttle screw to obtain the proper code. The lever pad must be in contact with the screw after adjustment.
    g. If the idle speed drops to or below the desired level, turn the

engine **OFF**, disconnect the air cleaner hose and remove the tape.
    h. Install the proper plug in the throttle plate orifice.
    i. Reconnect the air cleaner hose. Start the engine and turn the throttle plate stop screw clockwise to the nominal idle speed, ± 25 rpm. Do not turn the screw counterclockwise as this may cause the throttle plate to stick at idle.
10. Remove the feeler gauge from between the throttle plate stop screw and throttle lever.
11. Shut the engine OFF and disconnect the battery for 10 minutes minimum.
12. Run the KOEO Self-Test for proper TPS output code.
13. Start the engine and let the idle stabilize for 2 minutes. Rev the engine and let it return to idle. Lightly depress and release the accelerator; let the engine idle.
14. If equipped with automatic overdrive transmission, check the throttle valve pressure adjustment.

IDLE MIXTURE ADJUSTMENT

The idle mixture is controlled by the electronic control unit and cannot be adjusted.

Fuel Injector

REMOVAL AND INSTALLATION

2.3L Engine

1. Disconnect the negative battery cable.
2. Remove the fuel tank cap and relieve the fuel system pressure.
3. Disconnect the air intake, electrical connectors, throttle linkage, vacuum lines and EGR tube from the upper intake manifold and throttle body. Tag the electrical connectors and vacuum lines prior to removal for installation reference.
4. Remove the upper intake manifold retaining bolts and remove the upper intake manifold and throttle body assembly.
5. Disconnect the electrical connectors from the injectors.
6. Disconnect the fuel lines from the fuel supply manifold.
7. Remove the fuel supply manifold retaining bolts, carefully disengage the manifold and fuel injectors from the engine and remove the manifold and injectors.
8. Remove the fuel injectors from the manifold.

To install:

9. Lubricate new O-rings with clean light grade oil and install 2 on each injector.

NOTE: Never use silicone grease as it will clog the injectors.

10. Install the fuel supply manifold and injectors into the intake manifold. Push the fuel rail down to make sure all the fuel injector O-rings are fully seated in the fuel rail cups and intake manifold.

11. Install the fuel manifold assembly retaining bolts and tighten to 15–22 ft. lbs. (20–30 Nm) while holding the assembly down.

12. Connect the fuel lines to the manifold assembly.

13. After the fuel rail assembly has been installed and before the fuel injector wire connectors have been connected, connect the negative battery cable and turn the key to the **ON** position. This will cause the fuel pump to run for 2–3 seconds and pressurize the system.

14. Check for fuel leaks, especially where the fuel injector is installed into the fuel rail.

15. Disconnect the negative battery cable.

16. Install the upper intake manifold in the reverse order of removal. Tighten the retaining bolts, in sequence, to 15–22 ft. lbs. (20–30 Nm).

17. Connect the fuel injector wire connectors.

18. Connect the negative battery cable. Start the engine and let it idle.

19. Turn the engine **OFF** and check for fuel leaks.

3.8L Engine

EXCEPT SUPERCHARGED ENGINE

1. Disconnect the negative battery cable.

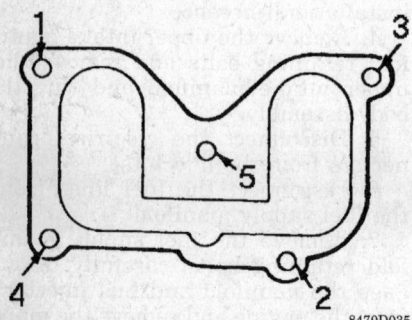

Upper intake manifold bolt torque — 2.3L engine

8470D035

2. Remove the fuel tank cap and relieve the fuel system pressure.

3. Disconnect the electrical connectors at the idle air bypass valve, TP sensor and EGR position sensor.

4. Disconnect the throttle linkage at the throttle ball and the transmission linkage from the throttle body.

5. Remove the 2 bolts securing the bracket to the intake manifold and position the bracket with the cables aside.

6. Disconnect all the vacuum lines and PCV from the upper intake manifold and throttle assembly. Tag all lines prior to removal for ease of reinstallation.

7. Remove the upper intake manifold retaining bolts and remove the upper intake manifold and throttle body assembly.

8. Disconnect the fuel lines from the fuel rail assembly.

9. Remove the fuel pressure regulator.

10. Disconnect the electrical connectors from the fuel injectors. Remove the injector retaining clips, as required.

11. Remove the fuel rail retaining bolts. Carefully disengage the fuel rail from the fuel injectors and remove the fuel rail.

NOTE: It may be easier to remove the injectors with the fuel rail as an assembly.

12. Grasping the injector body, pull while gently rocking the injector from side-to-side to remove the injector from the fuel rail or the intake manifold.

13. Inspect the pintle protection cap (plastic hat) and washer for signs of deterioration. Replace the complete injector, as required. If the cap is missing, look for it in the intake manifold.

NOTE: The pintle protection cap is not available as a separate part.

To install:

14. Lubricate new O-rings with light grade oil and install 2 on each injector.

NOTE: Never use silicone grease as it will clog the injectors.

15. Install the injectors in the intake manifold using a light, twisting pushing motion.

16. Install the fuel rail, pushing it down to ensure all injector O-rings are fully seated in the fuel rail cups and intake manifold.

17. Install the retaining bolts while holding the fuel rail down and tighten to 87 inch lbs. (10 Nm). Reinstall the injector retaining clips, as required.

18. Install the fuel pressure regulator retaining bolt and tighten to 15–22 ft. lbs. (20–30 Nm).

19. Connect the fuel lines to the fuel rail.

20. With the injector wiring disconnected, connect the negative battery cable and turn the ignition to the **RUN** position to allow the fuel pump to pressurize the system. Check for fuel leaks.

21. Disconnect the negative battery cable.

22. Connect the fuel injector wiring harness.

23. Install the upper intake manifold and throttle body assembly by reversing the removal procedure. Tighten the upper intake manifold retaining bolts to 24 ft. lbs. (32 Nm).

24. Connect the negative battery cable, start the engine and check for fuel leaks.

SUPERCHARGED ENGINE

1. Disconnect the negative battery cable.

2. Remove the fuel tank cap and relieve the fuel system pressure.

3. Remove the supercharger assembly.

4. Disconnect the fuel lines from the fuel rail assembly.

5. Remove the 4 fuel rail assembly retaining bolts and remove the fuel pressure regulator bracket retaining bolt.

6. Disconnect the electrical connectors from the injectors.

7. Carefully disengage the fuel rail from the fuel injectors and remove the fuel rail.

NOTE: It may be easier to remove the injectors with the fuel rail as an assembly.

8. Grasping the injector body, remove the injector from the fuel rail or intake manifold by pulling while gently rocking the injector from side-to-side.

9. Inspect the pintle protection cap (plastic hat) and washer for signs of deterioration. Replace the complete injector, as required. If the cap is missing, look for it in the intake manifold.

NOTE: The pintle protection cap is not available as a separate part.

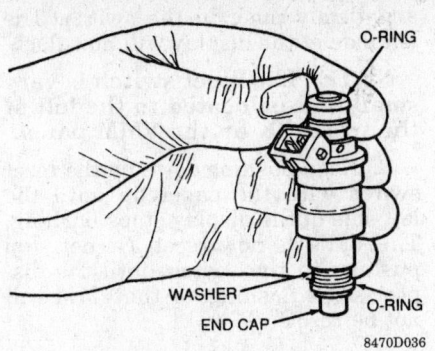

Fuel injector — typical

8470D036

To install:

10. Lubricate new O-rings with light grade oil and install 2 on each injector.

NOTE: Never use silicone grease as it will clog the injectors.

11. Install the injectors, using a light, twisting, pushing motion.

12. Place the fuel rail assembly over each of the injectors and seat the injectors into the fuel rail.

NOTE: It may be easier to seat the injectors in the fuel rail and then seat the entire assembly in the lower intake manifold.

13. Install the fuel rail assembly retaining bolts and tighten to 70–97 inch lbs. (8–11 Nm). Install the fuel pressure regulator bracket retaining bolt and tighten to 15–22 ft. lbs. (20–30 Nm).

14. Install the supercharger assembly.

15. Connect the negative battery cable. Turn the ignition from **OFF** to **ON** several times without starting the engine to check for fuel leaks. Check all connections at the fuel rail and injectors.

16. Start the engine and warm to operating temperature. Check for fuel or coolant leaks.

4.6L (SOHC) Engine

1. Disconnect the negative battery cable.

2. Remove the fuel tank cap and relieve the fuel system pressure.

3. Disconnect the vacuum line at the pressure regulator.

4. Disconnect the fuel lines from the fuel rail.

5. Disconnect the electrical connectors from the injectors.

6. Remove the fuel rail assembly retaining bolts.

7. Carefully disengage the fuel rail from the fuel injectors and remove the fuel rail.

NOTE: It may be easier to remove the injectors with the fuel rail as an assembly.

8. Grasping the injector body, pull while gently rocking the injector from side-to-side to remove the injector from the fuel rail or intake manifold.

9. Inspect the pintle protection cap and washer for signs of deterioration. Replace the complete injector, as required. If the cap is missing, look for it in the intake manifold.

NOTE: The pintle protection cap is not available as a separate part.

To install:

10. Lubricate new O-rings with light grade oil and install 2 on each injector.

NOTE: Never use silicone grease as it will clog the injectors.

11. Install the injectors using a light, twisting, pushing motion.

12. Install the fuel rail, pushing it down to ensure all injector O-rings are fully seated in the fuel rail cups and intake manifold.

13. Install the retaining bolts while holding the fuel rail down and tighten to 71–106 inch lbs. (8–12 Nm).

14. Connect the fuel lines to the fuel rail and the vacuum line to the pressure regulator.

15. With the injector wiring disconnected, connect the negative battery cable and turn the ignition switch to the **RUN** position to allow the fuel pump to pressurize the system.

16. Check for fuel leaks.

17. Disconnect the negative battery cable.

18. Connect the electrical connectors to the fuel injectors.

19. Connect the negative battery cable and start the engine. Let it idle for 2 minutes.

20. Turn the engine **OFF** and check for leaks.

4.6L (DOHC) Engine

1. Disconnect the negative battery cable.

2. Remove the fuel tank cap and relieve the fuel system pressure.

3. Remove engine cover and air inlet tube.

4. Disconnect the vacuum line at the fuel pressure regulator and brake booster.

5. Disconnect the fuel lines from the fuel rail assembly.

6. Remove the 10 fuel injection supply manifold assembly bolts.

NOTE: It may be easier to remove the injectors with the fuel rail as an assembly.

7. Disconnect the electrical connectors from the fuel injectors.

8. Carefully disengage the fuel rail from the fuel injectors and remove the fuel rail.

9. Grasping the injector body, pull while gently rocking the injector from side-to-side to remove the injector from the fuel rail or the intake manifold.

To install:

10. Lubricate new O-rings with light grade oil and install 2 on each injector.

NOTE: Never use silicone grease as it will clog the injectors.

11. Install the injectors in the intake manifold using a light, twisting pushing motion.

12. Install the fuel rail, pushing it down to ensure all injector O-rings are fully seated in the fuel rail cups and intake manifold.

13. Install the retaining bolts while holding the fuel rail down and tighten to 71–106 inch lbs. (8–12 Nm).

14. Connect the fuel lines to the fuel rail.

15. Connect the vacuum line to the fuel pressure regulator and brake booster.

16. With the injector wiring disconnected, connect the negative battery cable and turn the ignition to the **RUN** position to allow the fuel pump to pressurize the system. Check for fuel leaks.

17. Disconnect the negative battery cable.

18. Connect the fuel injector wiring harness. Install air inlet tube.

19. Connect the negative battery cable, start the engine and check for fuel leaks. Turn engine **OFF** and install the engine cover.

5.0L Engine

1. Disconnect the negative battery cable.

2. Remove the fuel tank cap and relieve the fuel system pressure.

3. Partially drain the cooling system into a suitable container.

4. Disconnect the electrical connectors at the idle air bypass valve, TP sensor and EGR sensor.

5. Disconnect the throttle linkage at the throttle ball and transmission linkage from the throttle body. Remove the 2 bolts securing the bracket the bracket to the intake manifold and position the bracket with the cables aside.

6. Disconnect the upper intake manifold vacuum fitting connections by disconnecting all vacuum lines to the vacuum tree, vacuum lines to the EGR valve, vacuum line to the fuel pressure regulator and canister purge line.

7. Disconnect the PCV system by disconnecting the hose from the fitting on the rear of the upper manifold and disconnect the PCV vent closure tube at the throttle body.

8. Remove the 2 EGR coolant lines from the fittings on the EGR spacer.

9. Remove the 6 upper intake manifold retaining bolts.

10. Remove the upper intake and throttle body as an assembly from the lower intake manifold.

11. Disconnect the fuel lines from the fuel rail.

12. Remove the 4 fuel rail assembly retaining bolts.

13. Disconnect the electrical connectors from the injectors.

14. Carefully disengage the fuel rail from the fuel injectors.

NOTE: It may be easier to remove the injectors with the fuel rail as an assembly.

15. Grasping the injector body, pull up while gently rocking the injector from side-to-side to remove the injector from the fuel rail or intake manifold.

16. Inspect the pintle protection cap (plastic hat) and washer for signs of deterioration. Replace the complete injector, as required. If the cap is missing, look for it in the intake manifold.

NOTE: The pintle protection cap is not available as a separate part.

To install:

17. Lubricate new O-rings with light grade oil and install 2 on each injector.

NOTE: Never use silicone grease as it will clog the injectors.

18. Install the injectors using a light, twisting, pushing motion.

19. Install the fuel rail, pushing it down to ensure all the injector O-rings are fully seated in the fuel rail cups and intake manifold.

20. Install the retaining bolts while holding the fuel rail down and tighten to 70–105 inch lbs. (8–12 Nm).

21. Connect the fuel lines to the fuel rail.

22. With the injector wiring disconnected, connect the negative battery cable and turn the ignition switch to the **RUN** position to allow the fuel pump to pressurize the system.

23. Check for fuel leaks.

24. Disconnect the negative battery cable.

25. Connect the electrical connectors to the injectors.

26. Install the upper intake manifold and throttle body assembly by reversing the removal procedure. Tighten the retaining bolts to 12–17 ft. lbs. (16–24 Nm).

27. Refill the cooling system and connect the negative battery cable.

28. Start the engine and let it idle for 2 minutes. Turn the engine **OFF** and check for leaks.

EMISSION CONTROLS

Emission Warning Lamps

RESETTING

These vehicles have a CHECK ENGINE lamp that will light when there is a fault in the engine control system. This light cannot be reset without diagnosing the fault in the system. When the system has been diagnosed and the problem corrected, the light will go out.

Service Lamp

THUNDERBIRD AND COUGAR

The optional Vehicle Maintenance Monitor (VMM) alerts the vehicle operator to when engine oil needs to be changed and when fuel, oil, coolant and washer fluids are low. To reset the VMM after an oil change, proceed as follows:

1. Turn the ignition key **OFF**, then turn it **ON**, but do not start the engine.

2. Within 16 seconds of turning the key to **ON**, stick a straightened paperclip into the reset switch hole and firmly push in the switch. The left side of the display will now flash.

NOTE: The reset switch is very small and is located to the left of the word OK on the VMM panel.

3. Keep pushing down on the reset switch with the paperclip until the left side of the display stops flashing. The VMM is now reset. Do not stop pushing in the switch until the display stops flashing, or the VMM will not be reset.

ENGINE MECHANICAL

NOTE: Disconnecting the negative battery cable on some vehicles may interfere with the functions of the on board computer systems and may require the computer to undergo a relearning process, once the negative battery cable is reconnected.

Engine Assembly

REMOVAL AND INSTALLATION

2.3L Engine

1. Disconnect the negative battery cable and relieve the fuel system pressure.

2. Drain the cooling system and the crankcase.

3. Mark the position of the hood on the hinges and remove the hood.

4. Remove the air cleaner outlet hose.

5. Remove the radiator upper and lower hoses. Disconnect the electrical connector to the cooling fan and remove the fan and shroud. If equipped with automatic transmission, disconnect the oil cooler lines from the radiator. Remove the radiator.

6. Disconnect the heater hose from the heater core. Tag and disconnect the wires from the alternator and starter. Disconnect the accelerator cable from the throttle body.

7. If equipped with air conditioning, remove the compressor from the mounting bracket and position it aside, leaving the refrigerant lines attached.

8. If equipped with power steering, remove the pump and position aside, leaving the hoses attached.

9. Disconnect the flexible fuel line at the fuel rail and plug the fuel line.

10. Disconnect the coil primary wire, the water temperature sending unit connector and the injector wiring harness connectors from the main wiring harness.

11. Remove the starter and remove the engine mount bolts.

12. Raise and safely support the vehicle. Remove the flywheel or converter housing upper retaining bolts.

13. Disconnect the muffler inlet pipe at the exhaust manifold. Disconnect the engine right and left mounts at the No. 2 crossmember pedestals. Remove the flywheel or converter housing cover.

14. If equipped with a manual transmission, remove the flywheel housing lower retaining bolts. If equipped with an automatic transmission, disconnect the converter from the flywheel and disconnect the transmission oil cooler lines, if attached to the engine at the pan rail. Remove the converter housing lower retaining bolts.

15. Lower the vehicle. Support the transmission and flywheel or converter housing with a jack.

16. Attach suitable engine lifting equipment to the engine lifting brackets. Carefully lift the engine out of the engine compartment and install on a workstand.

To install:

17. Install the clutch, if removed.

18. Carefully lower the engine into the engine compartment. Make sure the studs on the exhaust manifold are aligned with the holes in the muffler inlet pipe.

19. If equipped with an automatic transmission, start the converter pilot into the crankshaft. If equipped with a manual transmission, start the transmission input shaft into the clutch disc. It may be necessary to adjust the position of the transmission in relation to the engine if the input shaft will not enter the clutch disc.

NOTE: If the engine hangs up after the shaft enters, turn the crankshaft slowly in a clockwise direction, with the transmission in gear, until the shaft splines mesh with the clutch disc splines.

20. Install the flywheel or converter housing upper retaining bolts. Remove the engine lifting equipment.

21. Remove the jack from the transmission. Raise and safely support the vehicle.

22. Install the flywheel or converter housing lower retaining bolts. If equipped with an automatic transmission, attach the converter to the flywheel and tighten the retaining nuts to 20–34 ft. lbs. (27–46 Nm).

23. Install the flywheel or converter housing dust cover. Install the left and right engine mounts to the No. 2 crossmember pedestal. Tighten the nuts and bolts to 80–106 ft. lbs. (108–144 Nm).

24. Connect the muffler inlet pipe to the manifold. Connect the fuel line to the fuel rail.

25. Install the starter and connect the starter cable.

26. Lower the vehicle. Connect the oil pressure and water temperature sending unit connectors. Connect the coil and alternator wires. Connect the accelerator cable and the heater hoses.

27. If equipped with air conditioning, install the compressor in the mounting bracket. If equipped with power steering, install the pump. Install the drive belt.

28. Install the radiator, cooling fan and shroud. Connect the fan electrical connector. If equipped with automatic transmission, connect the oil cooler lines to the radiator. Install the upper and lower radiator hoses.

29. Install the air cleaner outlet hose.

30. Fill the crankcase with the proper type and quantity of oil. Fill and bleed the cooling system.

31. Connect the negative battery cable, start the engine and bring to normal operating temperature. Check for leaks. Check all fluid levels.

32. Align the hood on the hinges with the marks that were made during removal. Secure with the mounting bolts.

3.8L Engine

1. Disconnect the negative battery cable. Drain the crankcase and the cooling system.

2. Relieve the fuel system pressure and discharge the air conditioning system.

3. Disconnect the electrical connector to the underhood lamp. Mark the position of the hood on the hinges and remove the hood.

4. Remove the left cowl vent screen and wiper module. On non-supercharged engines, disconnect the alternator to voltage regulator wiring assembly.

5. On supercharged engines, remove the upper charge air cooler tube at the supercharger and cooler assemblies. Remove the bolt retaining the cooler tube to the alternator bracket and remove the tube.

6. Remove the radiator upper sight shield. Release the belt tension and remove the drive and accessory/supercharger belts. Remove the air cleaner-to-throttle body tube.

7. On supercharged engines, disconnect the cooling fan electrical connector and remove the cooling fan/shroud assembly. On non-supercharged engines, remove the fan and shroud.

8. Remove the upper radiator hose and disconnect the heater hoses. If equipped with an automatic transmission, disconnect the oil cooler lines from the radiator.

9. Disconnect the lower radiator hose at the water pump. Remove the radiator. On supercharged engines it will also be necessary to remove the 2 push pins retaining the charge air cooler to the radiator assembly.

10. Disconnect the power steering pressure hose assembly. On non-supercharged engines, remove the power steering pump and bracket assembly and position aside.

11. Disconnect the air conditioner compressor clutch wire. Disconnect and plug the refrigerant lines. Remove the compressor.

12. Remove the coolant recovery reservoir and remove the wiring shield. Remove the accelerator cable mounting bracket and position aside.

13. Disconnect the fuel lines from the fuel rail. Tag and disconnect the engine control module (PCM) wiring, engine feed harnesses and vacuum hoses.

14. On non-supercharged engines, disconnect the ground and coil wires. On supercharged engines, disconnect the DIS module wiring, remove the coil pack retaining bolts and position the coil pack aside.

15. On supercharged engines, remove the nuts retaining the lower charge air cooler tube to the supercharger elbow and lower charge air cooler tube bracket and remove the charge air cooler tube retaining bolt and nut at the alternator bracket.

16. On supercharged engines, remove the alternator bracket bolts, disconnect the alternator wiring and remove the alternator. Remove the power steering pump bracket assembly and position aside.

17. Disconnect the canister purge line and disconnect 1 end of the throttle control valve cable.

18. Raise and safely support the vehicle. Remove the oil filter element.

19. On supercharged engines, remove the 2 nuts retaining the lower charge air cooler tube to the charge

air cooler and remove the charge air cooler and charge air cooler tube.

20. Remove the exhaust pipe-to-manifold nuts and remove the left exhaust shield. Disconnect the oxygen sensors.

21. If equipped with an automatic transmission, remove the inspection plug and remove the torque converter bolts.

22. Remove the engine-to-transmission bolts and remove the engine mount through bolts. On supercharged engines, remove the left mount retaining strap bolt.

23. Remove the crankshaft pulley assembly.

NOTE: If the crankshaft pulley and vibration damper have to be separated, mark the damper and pulley so they may be reassembled in the same relative position. This is important as the damper and pulley are initially balanced as a unit. If the crankshaft damper is being replaced, check if the original damper has balance pins installed. If so, new balance pins must be installed on the new damper in the same position as the original damper.

24. Remove the starter. Remove the ground cable and remove the left and right starter harness retainers.

25. Disconnect the oil level indicator sensor and partially lower the vehicle. Disconnect the oil pressure sending unit gauge assembly.

26. Position a floor jack under the transmission and position suitable engine lifting equipment.

27. Remove the engine from the vehicle and position on a workstand.

To install:

28. Remove the engine assembly from the workstand and install engine lifting equipment.

29. Position the engine in the vehicle and install 2 engine-to-transmission bolts. Lower the engine onto the mounting seats, left side first, and remove the lifting equipment. Remove the jacks.

30. Tighten the 2 engine-to-transmission bolts to 40–50 ft. lbs. (55–68 Nm) and connect the oil pressure sending unit gauge assembly. Raise and safely support the vehicle.

31. Install the remaining engine-to-transmission bolts and tighten to 40–50 ft. lbs. (55–68 Nm).

32. Install the torque converter bolts and tighten to 20–34 ft. lbs. (27–46 Nm). Install the inspection plug.

33. Install and tighten the engine mount through bolts to 35–50 ft. lbs. (47–68 Nm). On supercharged en-

gines, install the left mount retaining strap bolt and tighten to 33–45 ft. lbs. (45–61 Nm).

34. Install the starter. Install the starter harness retainer, ground cable and transmission oil cooler line bracket. Install the exhaust pipe-to-manifold nuts.

35. Install the crankshaft pulley assembly and tighten the bolts to 20–28 ft. lbs. (26–30 Nm).

36. Connect the oxygen sensors and the oil level indicator sensor. Install a new oil filter and lower the vehicle.

37. Connect the throttle control valve cable and the canister purge line.

38. On supercharged engines, perform the following:

a. Install the lower charge air cooler tube, charge air cooler and power steering pump bracket assembly.

b. Install the alternator, connect the wiring and install the alternator bracket bolts.

c. Install the charge air cooler tube bolts at the power steering bracket and install the nuts retaining the lower charge air cooler tube to the lower charge air cooler tube bracket and supercharger elbow.

d. Install the coil pack and retaining bolts.

39. Install the coolant recovery reservoir.

40. Connect the alternator-to-voltage regulator wiring, the engine control module (PCM) wiring assembly and engine feed harnesses. Connect the vacuum hoses.

41. On non-supercharged engines, connect the wiring assembly ground and coil wire. On supercharged engines, connect the DIS module wiring.

42. Connect the fuel lines to the fuel rail. Install the accelerator cable mounting bracket and the wiring shield.

43. Install the air conditioning compressor and retaining bolts. Tighten the bolts to 30–45 ft. lbs. (41–61 Nm).

44. Remove the plugs from the air conditioner compressor lines and connect the lines to the compressor. Connect the compressor clutch wire.

45. On non-supercharged engines, install the power steering pump bracket assembly. Connect the power steering hoses.

46. Install the radiator. On supercharged engines, install the charge air cooler to the radiator and install the retaining push pins.

47. Connect the lower radiator hose to the water pump and install the heater hoses. If equipped with an au-

tomatic transmission, install the oil cooler lines to the radiator.

48. Install the upper radiator hose and the fan and fan shroud. On supercharged engines, connect the cooling fan electrical connector.

49. Position the drive belts and the accessory/supercharger belts. Install the radiator sight shield.

50. On supercharged engines, install the charge air cooler tube and bolts retaining the tube to the power steering bracket. Install the upper charge air cooler tube to the supercharger and cooler assemblies.

51. Install the cowl vent screen and wiper module. Install the hood, aligning the marks that were made during removal. Connect the underhood lamp wiring.

52. Fill the crankcase with the proper type and quantity of engine oil. Fill and bleed the cooling system.

53. Connect the negative battery cable, start the engine and bring to normal operating temperature. Check for leaks. Check all fluid levels.

54. Leak test, evacuate and charge the air conditioning system. Observe all safety precautions.

4.6L (SOHC) Engine

1. Disconnect the negative battery cable, drain the cooling system and discharge/recycle the A/C refrigerant.

2. Remove the ciar cleaner outlet tube and air cleaner assembly.

3. Remove the fan blade and shroud.

4. Relieve the fuel system pressure.

5. Disconnect the 42-pin and 8-pin connectors and position out of the way.

6. Label all components for reassembly. Disconnect the accelerator cable, speed control actuator, throttle valve control cable, canister purge electrical connector and vacuum lines.

7. Disconnect the power supply from the power distribution box and starter relay.

8. Disconnect the transmission oil cooler tubes from the transmission, upper radiator hose and heater hoses.

9. Disconnect the engine-to-frame ground straps. Partially raise the vehicle and support safely. Remove the front wheels.

10. Disconnect the right and left front anti-lock sensor and brackets.

11. Remove the right and left disc brake caliper bolts. Remove the calipers and support with wire to a frame member.

12. Disconnect the right and left front suspension upper arms from the spindles.

13. Disconnect the front springs and shocks from the lower arms.

14. Raise the vehicle and support safely.

15. Drain the engine oil.

16. Disconnect the dual converter Y-pipe from the manifolds. Disconnect the transmission shift cable and bracket.

17. Index the driveshaft centering socket yoke to the rear axle universal joint flange.

18. Remove the 4 bolts connecting the driveshaft centering socket yoke to the rear axle universal joint flange. Support the rear axle assembly with a jackstand.

19. Remove the rear axle assembly to rear sub-frame bolts. Loosen the rear differential bracket-to-body bolts and lower.

20. Slide the driveshaft rearward until it is free of the extension housing.

21. Remove the lower radiator hose, power steering lines and steering oil cooler.

22. Disconnect the wiring connector at the bulkhead. Support the front sub-frame using Rotunda Powertrain Lift 014-00765 and Adapter 014-00341 or equivalent.

23. Remove the rear engine support insulator bolts and disconnect the steering coupling at the pinch bolt joint.

24. Remove the 8 sub-frame bolts and lower the engine/transmission assembly.

25. Label and remove all needed components. Separate the engine from the transmission and place the engine on a suitable workstand.

To install:

26. Install engine lifting brackets 014-00334. Install the transmission to the engine. Make sure the torque converter studs align with the holes in the flywheel. Torque the bellhousing retaining bolts to 30–44 ft. lbs. (40–60 Nm). Torque the torque converter bolts to 25 ft. lbs. (35 Nm).

27. Install the transmission housing cover, starter motor and transmission-to-engine block brackets.

28. Position the transmission oil cooler tube bracket to the transmission case.

29. Raise the engine/transmission assembly and carefully lower onto the front sub-frame.

30. Install the right and left front engine support insulator through bolts. Torque the bolts to 22 ft. lbs. (30 Nm).

31. Install the power steering lines and remove the engine lift brackets from the cylinder heads.

32. Raise the engine/transmission/sub-frame assembly using the Powertrain Lift 014-00765 and Adapter 014-00341 into the vehicle.

33. Align the sub-frame-to-body and install the bolts. Torque bolts to 100 ft. lbs. (130 Nm).

34. Connect the steering pinch joint and driveshaft. Raise the rear axle assembly into the vehicle and torque the rear sub-frame bolts to 89 ft. lbs. (120 Nm). Torque the 2 rear axle differential insulator nuts to 94 ft. lbs. (127 Nm).

35. Align the driveshaft centering socket yoke to the rear axle universal joint flange and install the 4 retaining bolts and torque to 162 ft. lbs. (220 Nm).

36. Connect the transmission shift linkage, front suspension arms and lower radiator hose.

37. Connect the power steering hoses to steering cooler, ground straps and dual converter Y-pipe.

38. Connect the front suspension upper arms to the spindles and torque to 98 ft. lbs. (92 Nm).

39. Connect the anti-lock sensor and install the calipers. Install the front wheels.

40. Lower the vehicle and connect the A/C lines, transmission cooler lines and radiator hoses.

41. Connect all remaining hoses, lines, electrical connectors and cables.

42. Install the fan/ shroud and air cleaner.

43. Refill the cooling system. Evacuate, recharge and leak test the A/C system.

44. Connect the negative battery cable, fill the engine with oil, start the engine and check for leaks.

4.6L (DOHC) Engine

1. Disconnect the negative battery cable. Drain the crankcase and the cooling system.

2. Properly relieve the fuel system pressure and discharge the air conditioning system.

3. Disconnect IAT sensor connector and crankcase vent tube from air cleaner outlet tube. Loosen air cleaner outlet to throttle body bolt and disconnect the tube.

4. Remove remaining bolt from support bracket clamp on right valve cover and remove air cleaner outlet tube assembly and resonator assembly.

5. Remove the hush panel to expose the windshield wiper module, remove screw, lower module and bracket assembly and disconnect electrical connector. Remove the wiper module.

6. Remove the cooling fan and shroud.

7. Disconnect fuel lines. Remove 42 pin connector from retaining bracket on left fender well. Disconnect connector and position aside.

8. Remove power distribution box and disconnect alternator **B+** connector from inside of box.

9. Disconnect engine harness connector from canister purge solenoid assembly. Disconnect accelerator and speed control cables from throttle body and from accelerator cable bracket.

10. Disconnect canister purge vacuum line at throttle body and chassis vacuum supply hose at connection on cowl support.

11. Disconnect heater supply and return hose at rear of right cylinder head and upper radiator hose at coolant crossover tube.

12. Remove power steering return and supply hoses from reservoir and drain fluid into appropriate container. Remove reservoir retaining bolt and stud from left coil bracket and remove reservoir.

13. Remove upper transmission cooler line from radiator.

14. Install suitable engine lifting eyes. Disconnect and plug air conditioning compressor lines and disconnect retaining clips from pump.

15. Raise and safely support the vehicle. Remove b wheel and tire assemblies.

16. Disconnect right and left ride height sensor electrical connectors.

17. Remove right and left caliper bolts and remove calipers from rotors. Support calipers with mechanics wire.

18. Disconnect right and left upper control arms from spindles.

19. Remove Y-pipe from both exhaust manifolds and resonator. Disconnect ground strap from right fender apron.

20. Disconnect power steering pressure line from steering rack at power steering pump connection.

21. Remove lower radiator hose. Remove right and left lower strut to control arm bolts and nuts.

22. Disconnect transmission wiring harness and shift linkage. Disconnect lower transmission cooler line from radiator.

23. Index driveshaft to rear axle companion flange.

24. Remove 4 bolts connecting driveshaft to rear axle companion flange. Support rear axle housing with jackstand.

25. Remove 2 nut and bolt assemblies retaining the front of the differential to the undercarriage. Loosen rear differential bracket to body bolts and lower.

26. Slide driveshaft rearward until it is free of transmission extension housing.

27. Remove 2 nuts from bottom front cover studs and remove starter cable.

28. Disconnect low oil level sensor connector and wiring harness from oil pan. Remove starter.

29. Support subframe with Rotunda Powertrain Lift 014-00765 and adapter 014-00341, or equivalent. Remove rear transmission mount bolts.

30. Disconnect steering shaft coupler at rag joint. Remove 8 subframe bolts.

31. Lower engine and transmission assembly from vehicle.

32. Remove motor mount through bolts.

33. Install suitable engine lifting equipment on the engine lifting eyes and lift engine and transmission from subframe.

34. Lower engine and transmission. Support the transmission on a level, stationary surface for transmission storage.

35. Remove transmission to cylinder block mounting bolts and separate engine from transmission/torque converter assembly. Place engine on suitable workstand. Remove engine lifting equipment.

36. Remove right and left motor mounts from block. Remove right and left water jacket pipe plugs in cylinder block and drain coolant. Reinstall plugs.

37. Disconnect EGR to exhaust manifold tube from left exhaust manifold connector, differential pressure feedback EGR hose connections and loosen EGR tube connector at EGR control valve. Remove EGR valve to exhaust manifold tube.

38. Remove exhaust manifolds and discard gaskets.

To install:

39. Install exhaust manifolds with new gaskets. Tighten nuts in sequence to 15–22 ft. lbs. (20–30 Nm).

40. Install EGR to exhaust manifold tube to EGR control valve, left exhaust manifold and differential pressure feedback EGR hose.

41. Install left and right motor mounts to block. Install engine lifting bracket.

42. Remove engine from stand using suitable lifting equipment.

43. Connect transmission to cylinder block. Tighten bolts to 30–44 ft. lbs. (40–60 Nm).

44. Position engine and transmission on subframe assembly. Install mount through bolts and tighten to 15–22 ft. lbs. (20–30 Nm).

45. Raise engine, transmission and subframe assembly into position.

46. Align subframe to body and install bolts. Tighten to 73–100 ft. lbs. (95–130 Nm).

47. Connect steering shaft coupler at rag joint. Install rear transmission mount bolt and tighten to 15–22 ft. lbs. (20–30 Nm). Remove lifting equipment.

48. Install starter, low oil level sensor and lower engine wiring harness.

49. Install starter cable and 2 retaining nuts to lower front cover studs.

50. Install driveshaft to transmission. Lift rear differential into position. Install 2 nut and bolt assemblies retaining the front of the differential to the rear subframe and tighten to 72–89 ft. lbs. (98–120 Nm).

51. Tighten 2 differential mounts to 75–89 ft. lbs. (102–127 Nm). Align driveshaft to companion flange and install 4 bolts. Tighten to 70–96 ft. lbs. (95–130 Nm).

52. Connect lower transmission cooler line to the radiator. Connect the transmission wiring harness and shift linkage.

53. Position lower control arms to strut and install bolt. Tighten to 118–162 ft. lbs. (160–220 Nm).

54. Install lower radiator hose and power steering pressure line. Connect ground strap to right fender apron.

55. Install exhaust Y-pipe.

56. Connect upper control arms to spindles. Tighten to 50–68 ft. lbs. (68–92 Nm). Connect right and left ride height sensor electrical connectors.

57. Install brake calipers. Install front tire and wheel assemblies. Lower the vehicle.

58. Unplug and connect the air conditioning lines. Remove the engine lifting brackets and eyelets.

59. Connect upper transmission cooler line.

60. Install power steering reservoir, power steering return line and power steering supply hose.

61. Install coolant supply hose to reservoir. Connect upper radiator hose at crossover pipe and connect heater supply and return hoses.

62. Connect chassis vacuum supply and canister purge vacuum hoses.

63. Connect accelerator and speed control cables. Connect engine wiring harness to canister purge solenoid assembly.

64. Connect alternator **B+** connector and install power distribution box. Connect 42 pin connector and attach to retaining bracket.

65. Connect the fuel lines. Install cooling fan and shroud.

66. Install windshield wiper module. Install engine air cleaner outlet tube assembly and resonator assembly.

67. Connect IAT sensor and crankcase vent tube.

68. Fill the engine with the proper type and quantity of engine oil. Fill and bleed the cooling system.

69. Fill the power steering system with the proper type and quantity of fluid. Connect the negative battery cable.

70. Start the engine and bring to normal operating temperature. Check for leaks. Check all fluid levels.

71. Leak test, evacuate and charge the air conditioning system. Observe all safety precautions.

5.0L Engine

MUSTANG AND MARK VII

1. Disconnect the negative battery cable. Drain the crankcase and the cooling system.

2. Properly relieve the fuel system pressure and discharge the air conditioning system.

3. Mark the position of the hood on the hinges and remove the hood. Disconnect the battery ground cables from the cylinder block.

4. Remove the air intake duct.

5. Disconnect the upper radiator hose from the thermostat housing and the lower hose from the water pump. If equipped with an automatic transmission, disconnect the oil cooler lines from the radiator.

6. Remove the bolts attaching the radiator fan shroud to the radiator. Remove the radiator. Remove the fan, belt, pulley and shroud.

7. Remove the alternator bolts and position the alternator aside.

8. Disconnect the oil pressure sending unit wire from the sending unit and, if equipped, the low oil level sensor wire from the left side of the oil pan. Disconnect the flexible fuel line at the fuel tank line. Plug the fuel tank line.

9. Disconnect the accelerator cable from the throttle body. Disconnect the TV rod if equipped with an auto-

matic transmission. Disconnect the cruise control cable, if equipped.

10. Disconnect the transmission filler tube bracket from the cylinder block.

11. If equipped with air conditioning, disconnect the lines and electrical connectors at the compressor and remove the compressor. Plug the lines and the compressor fittings to prevent the entrance of dirt and moisture.

12. Disconnect the power steering pump bracket from the cylinder head. Position the power steering pump aside in a position that will prevent the fluid from leaking.

13. Disconnect the power brake vacuum line from the intake manifold.

14. Disconnect the heater hoses from the heater tubes. Disconnect the electrical connector from the coolant temperature sending unit.

15. Remove the flywheel or converter housing-to-engine upper bolts.

16. Disconnect the wiring harness at the two 10-pin connectors.

17. Raise and safely support the vehicle. Disconnect the starter cable from the starter and remove the starter.

18. Disconnect the muffler inlet pipes from the exhaust manifolds. Disconnect the engine mounts from the chassis. Disconnect the downstream thermactor tubing and check valve from the right exhaust manifold stud, if equipped.

19. If equipped with automatic transmission, disconnect the transmission cooler lines from the retainer and remove the converter housing inspection cover. Disconnect the flywheel from the converter and secure the converter assembly in the housing.

20. Remove the remaining converter or flywheel housing-to-engine bolts.

21. Lower the vehicle and then support the transmission. Attach engine lifting equipment and hoist the engine.

22. Raise the engine slightly and carefully pull it from the transmission. Carefully lift the engine out of the engine compartment. Avoid bending or damaging the rear cover plate or other components. Install the engine on a workstand.

To install:

23. Attach the engine lifting equipment and remove the engine from the workstand.

24. Lower the engine carefully into the engine compartment. Make sure the exhaust manifolds are properly aligned with the muffler inlet pipes.

25. Start the converter pilot, or manual transmission input shaft, into the crankshaft. Align the paint mark on the flywheel to the paint mark on the torque converter.

26. Install the flywheel or converter housing upper bolts, making sure the dowels in the cylinder block engage the housing.

27. Install the engine mount-to-chassis attaching fasteners and remove the engine lifting equipment.

28. Raise and safely support the vehicle. Connect both muffler inlet pipes to the exhaust manifolds. Install the starter and connect the starter cable.

29. If equipped with automatic transmission, remove the retainer holding the converter in the housing. Attach the converter to the flywheel. Install the converter housing inspection cover.

30. Install the remaining flywheel or converter housing attaching bolts. Remove the support from the transmission and lower the vehicle.

31. Connect the wiring harness at the two 10-pin connectors.

32. Connect the coolant temperature sending unit wire and connect the heater hoses. Connect the wiring to the sensors.

33. Connect the transmission filler tube bracket, if equipped with automatic transmission.

34. Connect the accelerator cable and TV cable. Connect the cruise control cable, if equipped.

35. Remove the plug from the fuel tank line and connect the fuel line and the oil pressure sending unit wire.

36. Install the pulley, water pump belt and fan/clutch assembly.

37. Position the alternator bracket and install the alternator bolts. Connect the alternator and ground cables.

38. Install the air conditioning compressor. Unplug and connect the refrigerant lines and connect the electrical connector to the compressor.

39. Install the power steering pump bracket and the accessory drive belt. Connect the power brake vacuum line.

40. Place the shroud over the fan and install the radiator. Connect the radiator hoses and the transmission oil cooler lines. Position the shroud and install the bolts.

41. Connect the heater hoses to the heater tubes. Fill and bleed the cooling system. Fill the crankcase with the proper type and quantity of en-

gine oil. Adjust the transmission throttle linkage, if equipped with automatic transmission.

42. Connect the negative battery cable. Start the engine and bring to normal operating temperature. Check for leaks. Check all fluid levels.

43. Install the air intake duct assembly. Install the hood, aligning the marks that were made during removal.

44. Leak test, evacuate and charge the air conditioning system. Observe all safety precautions.

THUNDERBIRD AND COUGAR

1. Disconnect the negative battery cable. Drain the crankcase and the cooling system.

2. Properly relieve the fuel system pressure and discharge the air conditioning system.

3. Disconnect the electrical connector for the underhood lamp. Mark the position of the hood on the hinges and remove the hood.

4. Remove the oil dipstick. Disconnect and plug the refrigerant lines at the air conditioning compressor.

5. Disconnect the compressor clutch and power steering pressure switch electrical connectors. Disconnect the alternator wiring harness from the alternator and position the harness aside.

6. Remove the fan shroud and the fan. Remove the upper radiator hose.

7. Remove the air cleaner-to-throttle body tube. Disconnect and plug the transmission oil cooler lines at the radiator.

8. Disconnect the throttle and kickdown cables from the throttle body and remove the cable bracket retaining bolts. Position the cable and bracket assembly aside.

9. Tag and disconnect the vacuum lines at the upper intake manifold vacuum tree, air conditioning control panel vacuum supply hose, thermactor valve and EGR valve. Disconnect the electrical connector at the EGR valve.

10. Remove the upper intake manifold as follows:

a. Disconnect the electrical connectors at the idle air bypass valve, throttle position sensor and EGR position sensor.

b. Disconnect the vacuum line from the fuel pressure regulator and the PCV hose from the fitting on the rear of the upper manifold.

c. Remove the upper intake manifold retaining bolts and remove the manifold.

11. Disconnect the main engine wiring harness connectors at the

right side of the dash panel. Position the engine wiring harness so it can be removed with the engine.

12. Disconnect the heater hoses at the engine. Disconnect the wiring harness from the coil and distributor and position the harness aside.

13. Disconnect and plug the fuel lines at the fuel supply manifold.

14. Disconnect the lower radiator hose from the water pump. Remove the radiator retaining bolts and remove the radiator.

15. Raise and safely support the vehicle. Remove the oil filter.

16. Remove the starter. Disconnect the oxygen sensors for the right and left catalytic converters. Disconnect the negative battery cable from the left side of the engine.

17. On the right side of the engine, disconnect the brackets for the transmission cooler lines, engine-to-body ground straps and the starter wiring harness.

18. Remove the torque converter inspection cover and mark 1 of the converter studs to the flywheel for alignment during reassembly. Remove the torque converter attaching nuts.

19. Remove the exhaust manifold heat shield at the left manifold flange and disconnect the exhaust pipe from the flange. Disconnect the right exhaust manifold flange.

20. Loosen the transmission mount retaining nut. Remove the converter housing to engine bolts and the motor mount through bolts.

21. Lower the vehicle and disconnect the power steering lines. Cap the lines to prevent contamination.

22. Support the transmission with a floor jack. Install suitable engine lifting equipment on the engine lifting eyes.

23. Lift the engine assembly clear of the engine mounts and remove the engine from the vehicle. Place the engine on a workstand.

To install:

24. Install suitable engine lifting equipment on the engine lifting eyes and lift the engine from the workstand.

25. Carefully lower the engine into the engine compartment. Make sure the exhaust manifolds are properly aligned with the muffler inlet pipes.

26. Start the converter pilot into the crankshaft. Align the mark on the flywheel to the mark on the torque converter.

27. Position the retaining clip for the left oxygen sensor wiring near the left upper transmission-to-engine bolt. Install the converter housing upper bolts. Make sure the dowels in

the cylinder block engage the converter housing.

28. Raise and safely support the vehicle. Install the remaining converter housing bolts and install the motor mount through bolts. Tighten the transmission mount retaining nut to 65–85 ft. lbs. (88–115 Nm).

29. Connect the right exhaust manifold flange. Connect the exhaust pipe to the left exhaust manifold flange and install the heat shield.

30. Install the torque converter retaining nuts and the inspection cover.

31. On the right side of the engine, install the brackets for the transmission cooler lines, engine-to-body ground strap and the starter wiring harness.

32. Connect the negative battery cable to the left side of the engine. Connect the oxygen sensors for the catalytic converters.

33. Install the starter. Install a new oil filter and the oil pan drain plug. Lower the vehicle and connect the power steering lines.

34. Install the radiator. Connect the coolant overflow hose and the lower radiator hose.

35. Connect the fuel lines to the fuel supply manifold.

36. Position and connect the wiring harness for the coil and distributor. Connect the heater hoses at the engine. Connect the main engine wiring harness connectors at the right side of the dash panel.

37. Install the upper intake manifold in the reverse order of removal. Be sure to use a new gasket.

38. Connect the vacuum lines at the upper intake manifold vacuum tee, air conditioning control panel vacuum supply hose, thermactor valve and EGR valve. Connect the electrical connector to the EGR valve.

39. Connect the throttle and kickdown cables to the throttle body and install the cable bracket retaining bolts.

40. Connect the transmission oil cooler lines and the upper radiator hose. Install the fan shroud and the fan. Install the air cleaner-to-throttle body tube assembly.

41. Position and connect the wiring harness for the alternator. Connect the compressor clutch electrical connector and connect the refrigerant lines to the compressor.

42. Install the hood, aligning the marks that were made during removal. Connect the wiring connector for the underhood lamp.

43. Fill the engine with the proper type and quantity of engine oil. Fill

and bleed the cooling system. Install the dipstick.

44. Fill the power steering system with the proper type and quantity of fluid. Connect the negative battery cable.

45. Start the engine and bring to normal operating temperature. Check for leaks. Check all fluid levels.

46. Leak test, evacuate and charge the air conditioning system. Observe all safety precautions.

Engine Mounts

REMOVAL AND INSTALLATION

2.3L Engine

FRONT

1. Disconnect the negative battery cable. Raise and safely support the vehicle. Support the engine using a wood block and jack placed under the engine.

2. Remove the through bolts attaching both mounts to the No. 2 crossmember pedestal bracket. On convertible, remove the nuts.

3. Disconnect shift linkage.

4. Raise the engine sufficiently to disengage the mount from the crossmember pedestal bracket.

5. Remove the bolts attaching the mount to the engine and remove the mount.

To install:

6. Position the mount on the engine and install the attaching bolts. Tighten to 35–46 ft. lbs. (47–63 Nm).

7. Lower the engine into position making sure the mounts are seated flat on the No. 2 crossmember. Hand start the bolts, lower the engine completely, then tighten the through bolts to 35–46 ft. lbs. (47–63 Nm) for 1992 vehicles or 72–98 ft. lbs. (97–133 Nm) for 1993–96 vehicles.

8. On convertible, tighten the flange nut to 73–106 ft. lbs. (98–144 Nm).

9. Install shift linkage. Lower the vehicle and connect the negative battery cable.

REAR

1. Disconnect the negative battery cable. Raise and safely support the vehicle.

2. Support the transmission with a jack and a wood block. Remove the nut(s) retaining the rear mount to the crossmember.

3. Remove the 2 bolts and nuts retaining the crossmember to the body brackets. Remove the crossmember

by raising the transmission slightly with the jack.

4. Remove the 2 bolts retaining the rear mount to the transmission and remove the mount and retainer. If equipped with automatic transmission, remove the 2 bolts retaining the rear mount to the intermediate bracket.

To install:

5. Position the rear mount and retainer on the transmission. Install the 2 retaining bolts and tighten to 51–70 ft. lbs. (68–96 Nm). On 1992 vehicles equipped with automatic transmission, tighten the 2 bolts to 35–50 ft. lbs. (47–68 Nm).

6. Install the crossmember to the body brackets. Tighten the retaining nuts and bolts to 35–50 ft. lbs. (47–68 Nm).

7. Lower the transmission and install the mount to crossmember retaining nuts. Tighten to 26–35 ft. lbs. (34–48 Nm). If equipped with automatic transmission, tighten the nut to 65–87 ft. lbs. (88–119 Nm).

8. Lower the vehicle. Connect the negative battery cable.

3.8L Engine

FRONT

1. Disconnect the negative battery cable.

2. Remove fan shroud retaining screws. Remove the air tube to the remote air cleaner.

3. Raise and safely support the vehicle. Support engine using a jack and wood block placed under the engine.

4. Remove the engine mount through bolt. On supercharged engines, remove the retaining strap bolt from the left side.

5. Remove shift linkage.

6. Raise engine high enough to clear clevis brackets.

NOTE: Raise the engine carefully so as not to damage the lines and hoses at the rear of the engine.

7. Remove any accessory and oil cooler line retaining clips from the engine support brackets.

8. Remove bolts retaining the engine mount and bracket assembly to engine. Remove the mount and bracket assembly.

NOTE: The left hand front engine mount removal on the supercharged engine may require lowering the front sub frame.

To install:

9. Position the engine mount and bracket assembly to the engine, install the retaining bolts and tighten to 26–34 ft. lbs. (34–47 Nm).

10. Install the accessories to the lower front engine mount support bracket stud. Tighten to 26–34 ft. lbs. (34–47 Nm).

11. Lower the engine into position and make sure the engine mounts are seated flat on the front sub frame; the left mount must seat first. Install the through-bolt and tighten to 35–50 ft. lbs. (47–68 Nm). On supercharged engines, install the retaining strap bolt and tighten to 34–44 ft. lbs. (45–61 Nm).

12. Lower the vehicle and install the air tube and the fan shroud retaining screws. Connect the negative battery cable.

REAR

1. Disconnect the negative battery cable. Raise and safely support the vehicle.

2. Support the transmission with a jack and a wood block. Remove the rear nut attaching the mount-to-crossmember. Keep transmission weight on the mount during nut removal.

3. Remove the 2 bolts retaining the crossmember-to-body brackets. Remove the crossmember by raising the transmission slightly with the jack.

4. Remove the bolts retaining the rear engine mount to the transmission. Remove the mount.

To install:

5. Position the engine mount and retainer on the transmission. Install the 2 retaining bolts and tighten to 35–50 ft. lbs. (47–68 Nm).

6. Install the crossmember-to-body brackets. Tighten the retaining bolts or nuts to 34–47 ft. lbs. (45–65 Nm).

7. Lower the transmission. Install the mount-to-crossmember nut. Tighten to 65–84 ft. lbs. (88–115 Nm).

8. Lower the vehicle and connect the negative battery cable.

4.6L Engine

FRONT

1. Disconnect the negative battery cable.

2. Remove the engine cover. Remove the air tube to the remote air cleaner.

3. Install engine lifting bracket. Install Three Bar Engine Support D88L-6000-A or equivalent, to engine lifting bracket and support engine.

4. Raise and safely support the vehicle.

5. Remove the engine mount through bolt. Remove any accessory and oil cooler clips from front subframe assembly.

6. Remove front anti-lock brake wire harness from body and front subframe assembly retainers.

7. Remove steering column pinch bolt and separate steering column from intermediate steering shaft.

8. Support front lower control arms and remove front strut through bolts. Separate studs from control arms.

9. Slowly lower control arms until they hang freely.

10. Support the front subframe with jackstands. Remove 8 front subframe retaining bolts.

11. Slowly lower the front subframe to gain access to the engine mounts. Remove engine mount and bracket assembly bolts.

12. Remove bolts retaining the engine mount and bracket assembly to engine. Remove the mount and bracket assembly.

To install:

13. Installation is the reverse of the removal procedure.

Engine mounts and bracket assembly to engine bolts and studs to 40–53 ft. lbs. (53–71 Nm).

Subframe assembly bolts to 72–97 ft. lbs. (97–132 Nm).

Front strut to control arm bolts to 90–118 ft. lbs. (120–160 Nm).

Steering coupling pinch bolt to 20–29 ft. lbs. (28–40 Nm).

Engine mount through bolt to 35–50 ft. lbs. (47–68 Nm).

REAR

1. Disconnect the negative battery cable. Raise and safely support the vehicle.

2. Support the transmission with a jack and a wood block. Remove the rear nuts attaching the mount-to-crossmember.

3. Remove the 2 bolts retaining the crossmember-to-body brackets. Remove the crossmember.

4. Remove the 2 nuts retaining the rear engine mount to the transmission bracket. Remove the mount.

To install:

5. Position the engine mount and retainer on the transmission. Install the 2 retaining bolts and tighten to 50–72 ft. lbs. (68–96 Nm).

6. Install the crossmember-to-body brackets. Tighten the retaining bolts or nuts to 35–50 ft. lbs. (47–68 Nm).

7. Lower the transmission. Install the mount-to-crossmember nuts. Tighten to 25–35 ft. lbs. (34–48 Nm).

8. Lower the vehicle and connect the negative battery cable.

5.0L Engine

FRONT

1. Disconnect the negative battery cable. Remove fan shroud attaching screws.

2. Raise and safely support the vehicle. Support the engine using a jack and wood block placed under the engine.

3. Remove the nuts or bolts attaching the mounts to the No. 2 crossmember. On Thunderbird and Cougar, remove the through bolts.

4. Disconnect shift linkage on all except Thunderbird and Cougar.

5. Raise the engine sufficiently with the jack to disengage the mount from the crossmember. If equipped, remove the transmission brace attached at the left or right engine mount bracket.

6. Remove the engine mount and bracket assembly to the cylinder block attaching bolts. Remove the engine mount.

To install:

7. Position the mount on the engine and install the attaching bolts. Tighten the bolts to 45–59 ft. lbs. (61–81 Nm).

8. Attach the transmission brace to the right or left engine mount, if equipped. Tighten the nut to 45–59 ft. lbs. (60–81 Nm).

9. Lower the engine into position making sure the mounts are seated flat on the No. 2 crossmember and the insulator studs are at the bottom of the slots.

NOTE: On Thunderbird and Cougar, the left mount, with the locating pin, must seat before the right mount.

10. Install and tighten the mount nuts to 73–106 ft. lbs. (98–144 Nm). On Thunderbird and Cougar, install the through bolts and tighten to 35–45 ft. lbs. (45–61 Nm).

11. Lower the vehicle and install the fan shroud attaching screws. Connect the negative battery cable.

REAR — MUSTANG

1. Disconnect the negative battery cable. Raise and safely support the vehicle.

2. Support the transmission with a jack and wood block. Remove the 2 nuts attaching the mount to the crossmember.

3. Remove the 2 bolts and nuts attaching the crossmember to the body brackets and remove the crossmember by raising the transmission slightly with the jack.

4. Remove the 2 bolts attaching the rear mount to the transmission and remove the mount and retainer.

To install:

5. Position the rear mount and retainer on the transmission. Install the 2 attaching bolts and tighten to 51–70 ft. lbs. (68–96 Nm).

6. Install the crossmember to the body brackets. Tighten the attaching nuts to 35–50 ft. lbs. (47–68 Nm).

7. Lower the transmission and install the mount-to-crossmember attaching nuts. Tighten to 26–35 ft. lbs. (34–48 Nm).

8. Lower the vehicle and connect the negative battery cable.

REAR — THUNDERBIRD AND COUGAR

1. Disconnect the negative battery cable. Raise and safely support the vehicle.

2. Remove the nut attaching the rear mount-to-crossmember.

NOTE: This must be done while the transmission weight is still on the mount.

3. Support the transmission with a jack and a wood block. Remove the bolts that attach the crossmember to the body brackets and remove the crossmember.

4. Remove the bolts attaching the mount to the transmission bracket and remove the mount.

To install:

5. Position the mount on the transmission bracket. Install bolts and tighten to 35–50 ft. lbs. (47–68 Nm).

6. Install the crossmember to the body brackets and tighten the bolts to 34–47 ft. lbs. (45–65 Nm).

7. Lower the transmission and install the nut. Tighten the nut to 65–85 ft. lbs. (88–115 Nm).

8. Lower the vehicle and connect the negative battery cable.

REAR — MARK VII

1. Disconnect the negative battery cable. Raise and safely support the vehicle.

2. Support the transmission with a jack and wood block. Remove the bolts that attach the rear mounts and crossmember to the transmission.

3. Remove the lower rebound mount.

4. Raise the transmission slightly with the jack. Remove the upper mounts.

To install:

5. Position the upper mounts between the crossmember and the transmission.

6. Position the lower mounts and hand start the attaching bolts. Lower the transmission and tighten the crossmember-to-body bolts to 45–70 ft. lbs. (60–96 Nm) and the crossmember-to-transmission bolts to 35–50 ft. lbs. (47–68 Nm).

7. Lower the vehicle and connect the negative battery cable.

Cylinder Head

REMOVAL AND INSTALLATION

2.3L Engine

1. Disconnect the negative battery cable. Drain the cooling system and relieve the fuel system pressure.

2. Remove the air cleaner assembly.

3. Remove the engine and alternator wiring harnesses. Remove the heater hose retaining screw from the rocker arm cover, if equipped.

4. Tag and disconnect the spark plug wires from the spark plugs. Remove the spark plug wires and, if equipped, the distributor cap. Remove the spark plugs.

5. Tag and disconnect the required vacuum hoses. Remove the dipstick and disconnect the dipstick tube from the bracket.

6. Remove the upper intake manifold and throttle body as follows:

   a. Tag and disconnect the electrical connectors and vacuum hoses.

   b. Disconnect the throttle linkage, cruise control and kickdown cable. Unbolt the accelerator cable from the bracket and position the cable aside.

   c. Disconnect the crankcase vent hose. Disconnect the PCV hose from the fitting on the underside of the upper intake manifold.

   d. Disconnect the EGR tube from the EGR valve. Remove the upper intake manifold mounting bolts and the manifold.

7. Remove the rocker cover retaining bolts and remove the cover. Remove the intake manifold retaining bolts.

8. Remove the accessory drive belt, loosen the retaining bolt and swing the alternator aside.

9. Remove the upper radiator hose. Remove the timing belt cover retaining bolts and remove the cover.

10. Loosen the timing belt idler retaining bolts. Position the idler in the unloaded position and tighten the retaining bolts.

11. Remove the timing belt from the camshaft sprocket and the auxiliary sprocket.

12. Remove the exhaust manifold retaining bolts. Remove the timing belt idler and 2 bracket bolts. Remove the timing belt idler spring stop from the cylinder head.

13. Disconnect the oil sending unit wire, if necessary.

14. Remove the cylinder head bolts and the cylinder head. Clean all gasket mating surfaces and blow the oil out of the cylinder head bolt block holes.

15. Check the cylinder head for flatness using a straight-edge and a feeler gauge. If the head gasket surface is warped greater than 0.006 in., it must be resurfaced. Do not grind more than 0.010 in. from the cylinder head.

To install:

16. Position the head gasket on the block. Position the camshaft with the pin approximately 30 degrees to the right of the 6 o' clock position when facing the front of the cylinder head. The camshaft must be positioned this way to protect protruding valves.

17. Position the cylinder head on the block and install new cylinder head bolts. Tighten the bolts, in sequence, in 2 steps, 1st to 50–60 ft. lbs. (60–81 Nm) and then to 80–90 ft. lbs. (108–122 Nm).

18. Connect the oil sending unit wire, if necessary. Install the timing belt tensioner spring stop to the cylinder head.

19. Position the timing belt tensioner and tensioner spring to the cylinder head and install the retaining bolts. Rotate the tensioner against the spring with belt tensioner tool T74P-6254-A or equivalent, and temporarily tighten.

20. Install the exhaust manifold retaining bolts. Tighten the bolts, in sequence, in 2 steps, 1st to 178–204 inch lbs. (20–23 Nm) and then to 20–30 ft. lbs. (27–40 Nm).

21. If equipped with a distributor, align the distributor rotor with the No. 1 plug location on the distributor cap. Align the camshaft sprocket with the pointer and align the crankshaft pulley with the pointer on the timing belt cover.

22. Install the timing belt over the sprockets. Loosen the tensioner retaining bolts, rotate the engine by hand 1 complete revolution and check the timing alignment.

23. Tighten the 10mm tensioner bolt to 28–40 ft. lbs. (38–54 Nm) and the 8mm bolt to 14–21 ft. lbs. (19–29 Nm).

24. Install the timing belt cover and tighten the retaining bolts to 6–9 ft. lbs. (8–12 Nm).

25. Install the rocker arm cover and tighten the retaining bolts to 62–97 inch lbs. (7–11 Nm).

26. Install the intake manifold. Tighten the bolts, in sequence, to 19–28 ft. lbs. (26–38 Nm).

27. Install the upper intake manifold and throttle body in the reverse order of removal. Tighten the upper intake-to-lower intake bolts, in sequence, to 15–22 ft. lbs. (20–30 Nm).

28. Position the alternator and install the drive belt. Install the upper radiator hose.

29. Install the dipstick and connect the necessary vacuum hoses. Install the spark plugs, spark plug wires and distributor cap, if equipped.

30. Position and connect the engine and alternator wiring harnesses. Install the hose from the air cleaner to the throttle body. If equipped, install the retaining heater hose screw to the rocker cover.

31. Fill and bleed the cooling system. Connect the negative battery cable, start the engine and bring to normal operating temperature. Check for leaks. If equipped with distributor ignition, check the ignition timing.

3.8L Engine

1. Disconnect the negative battery cable.

2. Relieve the fuel system pressure. Drain the cooling system.

3. Remove air cleaner assembly including the air intake duct and heat tube.

4. Loosen accessory drive belt idler. Remove drive belt.

5. If the left cylinder head is being removed, perform the following:

   a. On supercharged engines, remove the charge air cooler and charge air cooler tubes.

   b. Remove oil fill cap.

   c. Remove the power steering pump front mounting bracket attaching bolts.

   d. Remove the alternator assembly and accessory drive belt main idler.

   e. Remove the power steering/pump alternator bracket retaining bolts.

   f. Leaving the hoses connected, place the power steering pump/alternator bracket assembly aside in a position to prevent the fluid from leaking out.

6. If the right cylinder head is being removed, perform the following:

   a. If equipped, disconnect the thermactor tube support bracket from the rear of the cylinder head.

Remove the thermactor pump pulley and remove the pump.

   b. If equipped, remove the air conditioner compressor belt and main drive belt.

   c. If equipped, remove the compressor mounting bracket retaining bolts. Leave the hoses connected and position the compressor aside.

   d. Remove the PCV valve.

7. On supercharged engines, remove the supercharger. On non-supercharged engines, remove the upper intake manifold as follows:

   a. Disconnect the electrical connectors at the idle air bypass valve, throttle position sensor and EGR position sensor.

   b. Disconnect the throttle and transmission linkage from the throttle body. Remove the cable bracket from the manifold and position the bracket and cables aside.

   c. Tag and disconnect the vacuum lines at the upper manifold vacuum tree, EGR valve and fuel pressure regulator.

   d. Disconnect the PCV hose from the fitting at the rear of the upper manifold.

   e. Remove the retaining bolts and remove the upper intake manifold.

8. Remove valve rocker arm cover attaching screws. Remove the fuel rail and the lower intake manifold.

9. Remove the exhaust manifold(s).

10. Loosen rocker arm fulcrum attaching bolts enough to allow the rocker arm to be lifted off the pushrod and rotated to 1 side.

11. Remove the pushrods. Identify the position of each rod. The rods should be installed in their original position during assembly.

12. Remove the cylinder head attaching bolts and discard.

13. Remove the cylinder head(s). Clean all gasket mating surfaces.

14. Check the flatness of the cylinder head gasket surface using a straight-edge and a feeler gauge. The allowable warpage is 0.003 in. for every 6.0 inches. Do not machine more than 0.010 in.

To install:

NOTE: Lightly oil all bolt and stud bolt threads before installation except those specifying special sealant.

15. Position new head gasket(s) on the cylinder block using the dowels for alignment.

16. Position the cylinder head(s) on the block.

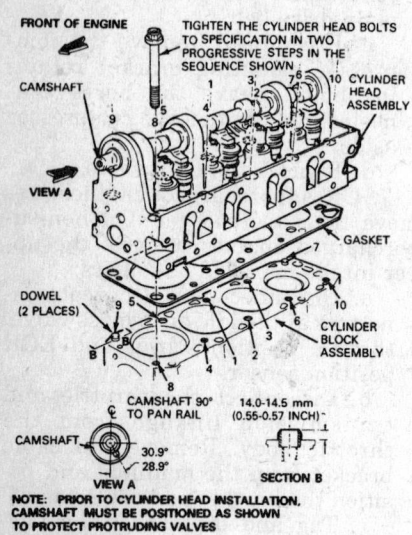

Cylinder head bolt torque sequence — 2.3L engine

8470D037

17. Install new cylinder head bolts.

NOTE: Always use new cylinder head bolts to assure a leaktight assembly. Torque retention with used bolts can vary, which may result in coolant or compression leakage at the cylinder head mating surface area.

18. Tighten the new cylinder head attaching bolts in numerical sequence as follows:

   a. 37 ft. lbs. (50 Nm)
   b. 45 ft. lbs. (60 Nm)
   c. 52 ft. lbs. (70 Nm)
   d. 59 ft. lbs. (80 Nm)
   e. Back-off the attaching bolts 2–3 turns.
   f. On supercharged engines, tighten each long and short bolt to 48–55 ft. lbs. (65–75 Nm), rotate an additional 90–110 degrees, then go to the next bolt in sequence.
   g. On non-supercharged engines, tighten each long bolt to 11–18 ft. lbs. (15–25 Nm), rotate an additional 85–105 degrees on 1992 vehicles or 85–96 degrees on 1993–96 vehicles, then go to the next bolt in sequence. Do the same for each short bolt except only rotate the short bolts 65–85 degrees on 1992

vehicles or 85–96 degrees on 1993–96 vehicles.

NOTE: When cylinder head attaching bolts have been tightened using multi-step torque procedure, it is not necessary to retighten the bolts after extended engine operation.

19. Lubricate each pushrod with heavy engine oil and install, in their original positions.
20. For each valve, rotate the crankshaft until the lifter rests on the base circle of the camshaft lobe, before tightening the fulcrum attaching bolts to 43 inch lbs. (5 Nm).
21. Lubricate the rocker arm assemblies with heavy engine oil and final tighten the fulcrum bolts to 19–25 ft. lbs. (25–35 Nm). Fulcrums must be fully seated in cylinder head and pushrods must be seated in rocker arm sockets prior to final tightening. Final tightening can be done with the camshaft in any position.

NOTE: If the original valve train components are being installed, a valve clearance check is not required. If a component has been replaced, perform a valve clearance check.

22. Install the exhaust manifold(s).
23. Install the lower intake manifold and the fuel rail.
24. Position cover and new gasket on the cylinder head and install attaching bolts. Note the location of spark plug wire routing clip stud bolts. Tighten attaching bolts to 80–106 inch lbs. (9–12 Nm).
25. Install the upper intake manifold. On supercharged engines, install the supercharger.
26. Install the spark plugs, if removed.
27. Connect the spark plug wires to the spark plugs.
28. If the left cylinder head is being installed, perform the following:
   a. Install the oil filler cap.
   b. Install the alternator/power steering pump mounting bracket.
   c. Install the alternator assembly.
   d. Install the main accessory drive belt tensioner assembly.
   e. Install the power steering pump assembly.
   f. Install the power steering pump support bracket.
   g. On supercharged engines, install the charge air cooler tubes.
29. If the right cylinder head is being installed, perform the following:
   a. Install PCV valve.

   b. If equipped with air conditioning, install the compressor mounting and support brackets and install the compressor.
   c. If equipped, install the thermactor pump and pump pulley.
   d. If equipped, install the accessory drive belt idler pulley.
   e. If equipped, install the thermactor air control valve or idle air bypass valve hose. Tighten the clamps securely to the air pump assembly.
30. Install the accessory drive belt. If equipped, attach the thermactor tube(s) support bracket to the rear of the cylinder head. Tighten attaching bolts to 30–40 ft. lbs. (40–55 Nm).
31. Connect the negative battery cable.
32. Fill and bleed the cooling system.
33. Start engine and check for coolant, fuel and oil leaks.
34. Check and, if necessary, adjust the curb idle speed.
35. Install the air cleaner assembly including the air intake duct and heat tube.

4.6L (SOHC) Engine

1. Disconnect the negative battery cable.
2. Drain the cooling system and remove the cooling fan and shroud.
3. Relieve the fuel system pressure and disconnect the fuel lines.
4. Remove the air inlet tube and the wiper module. Release the belt tensioner and remove the accessory drive belt.
5. Tag and disconnect the ignition wires from the spark plugs. Disconnect the ignition wire brackets from the camshaft cover studs and remove the 2 bolts retaining the ignition wire tray to the coil brackets.
6. Remove the bolt retaining the air conditioner high pressure line to the right coil bracket. Disconnect both ignition coils and CID sensor.
7. Remove the nuts retaining the coil brackets to the front cover. Slide the ignition coil brackets and ignition wire assembly off the mounting studs and remove from the vehicle.
8. Remove the water pump pulley. Disconnect the generator wiring harness from the junction block, fender apron and generator. Disconnect the bolts retaining the generator to the intake manifold and engine block and remove the generator.
9. Disconnect the positive battery cable at the power distribution box. Remove the retaining bolt from the positive battery cable bracket located on the side of the right cylinder head.

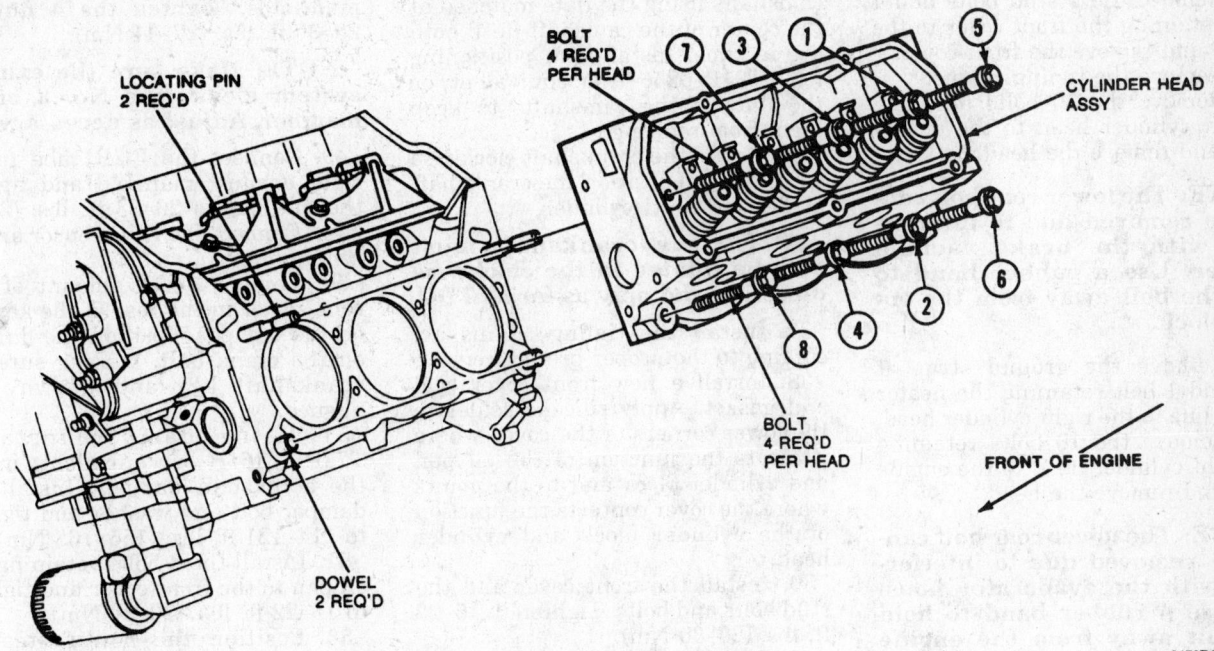

LOCATING PIN 2 REQ'D

BOLT 4 REQ'D PER HEAD

CYLINDER HEAD ASSY

FRONT OF ENGINE

DOWEL 2 REQ'D

BOLT 4 REQ'D PER HEAD

8470D038

Cylinder head bolt torque sequence — 3.8L engine

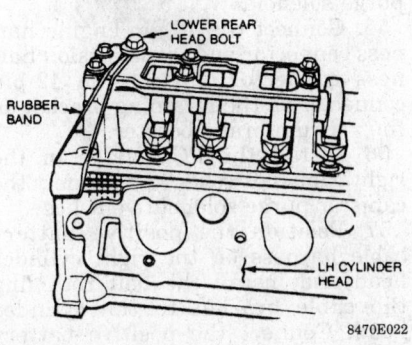

LOWER REAR HEAD BOLT

RUBBER BAND

LH CYLINDER HEAD

8470E022

Supporting left lower head bolt with rubberband — 4.6L SOHC engine

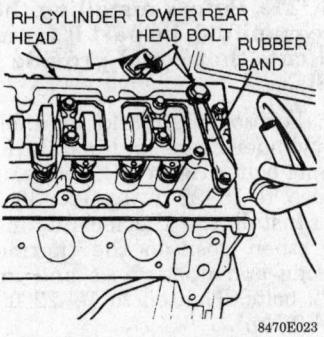

RH CYLINDER HEAD

LOWER REAR HEAD BOLT

RUBBER BAND

8470E023

Supporting right lower head bolt with rubberband — 4.6L SOHC engine

10. Disconnect the vent hose from the canister purge solenoid and position the positive battery cable out of the way. Disconnect the canister purge solenoid vent hose from the PCV valve and remove the PCV valve from the camshaft cover.

11. Remove the 42-pin engine harness connector from the retaining bracket on the brake vacuum booster, disconnect and position out of the way.

12. Disconnect the HDR sensor, air conditioning compressor clutch and canister purge solenoid connectors.

13. Raise and safely support the vehicle.

14. Remove the bolts retaining the power steering pump to the engine block and front cover. The front lower bolt on the power steering pump will not come all the way out. Wire the power steering pump out of the way.

15. Remove the 4 bolts retaining the oil pan to the front cover. Remove the crankshaft damper retaining bolt and remove the damper, using a suitable puller.

16. Disconnect the EVO sensor and oil sending unit. Position the EVO sensor and oil pressure sending unit harness out of the way.

17. Disconnect the EGR tube from the right exhaust manifold. Disconnect the exhaust pipes from the exhaust manifolds. Lower the exhaust pipes and hang with wire from the crossmember.

18. Remove the bolt retaining the starter wiring harness to the rear of the right cylinder head. Lower the vehicle.

19. Remove the bolts and stud bolts retaining the camshaft covers to the cylinder heads and remove the covers.

20. Disconnect the accelerator, cruise control and throttle valve cables. Remove the accelerator cable bracket from the intake manifold and position out of the way.

21. Disconnect the vacuum hose from the throttle body elbow vacuum port, both oxygen sensors and the heater supply hose.

22. Remove the 2 bolts retaining the thermostat housing to the intake manifold and position the upper hose and thermostat housing out of the way.

NOTE: Two thermostat housing bolts also retain the intake manifold.

23. Remove the 9 bolts retaining the intake manifold to the cylinder

heads and remove the intake manifold and gaskets.

24. Remove the 7 stud bolts and 4 bolts retaining the front cover to the engine and remove the front cover.

25. Remove the timing chains.

26. Remove the 10 bolts retaining the left cylinder head to the engine block and remove the head.

NOTE: The lower rear bolt cannot be removed due to interference with the brake vacuum booster. Use a rubber band to hold the bolt away from the engine block.

27. Remove the ground strap, 1 stud and 1 bolt retaining the heater return line to the right cylinder head.

28. Remove the 10 bolts retaining the right cylinder head to the engine block and remove the head.

NOTE: The lower rear bolt cannot be removed due to interference with the evaporator housing. Use a rubber band to hold the bolt away from the engine block.

29. Clean all gasket mating surfaces. Check the cylinder head and engine block for flatness. Check the cylinder head for scratches near the coolant passage and combustion chamber that could provide leak paths. Machine as necessary.

To install:

30. Rotate the crankshaft counterclockwise 45 degrees. The crankshaft keyway should be at the 9 o'clock position viewed from the front of the engine. This ensures that all pistons are below the top of the engine block deck face.

31. Rotate the camshaft to a stable position where the valves do not extend below the head face.

32. Position new head gaskets on the engine block. Install the lower rear bolts on both cylinder heads and retain with rubber bands as explained during the removal procedure.

33. Position the cylinder heads on the engine block dowels, being careful not to score the surface of the head face. Apply clean oil to the head bolts, remove the rubber band from the lower rear bolt and install all bolts hand-tight.

34. Tighten the head bolts as follows:
   a. Tighten the bolts, in sequence, to 15–22 ft. lbs. (20–30 Nm).
   b. Rotate each bolt, in sequence, 85–96 degrees.
   c. Rotate each bolt, in sequence, an additional 85–96 degrees.

35. Position the heater return hose and install the 2 bolts. Rotate the camshafts using the flats matched at the center of the camshaft until both are in time. Install cam positioning tools T91P-6256-A or equivalent, on the flats of the camshafts to keep them from rotating.

36. Rotate the crankshaft clockwise 45 degrees to position the crankshaft at TDC on No. 1 cylinder.

NOTE: The crankshaft must only be rotated in the clockwise direction and only as far as TDC.

37. Install the timing chains according to the proper procedure.

38. Install a new front cover seal and gasket. Apply silicone sealer to the lower corners of the cover where it meets the junction of the oil pan and cylinder block and to the points where the cover contacts the junction of the cylinder block and cylinder head.

39. Install the front cover and the stud bolts and bolts. Tighten to 15–22 ft. lbs. (20–30 Nm).

40. Position new intake manifold gaskets on the cylinder heads. Make sure the alignment tabs on the gaskets are aligned with the holes in the cylinder heads.

NOTE: Before installing the intake manifold, inspect it for nicks and cuts that could provide leak paths.

41. Position the intake manifold on the cylinder heads and install the retaining bolts. Tighten the bolts, in sequence, to 15–22 ft. lbs. (20–30 Nm).

42. Install the thermostat and O-ring, then position the thermostat housing and upper hose and install the 2 bolts. Tighten to 15–22 ft. lbs. (20–30 Nm).

43. Connect the heater supply hose and both oxygen sensors. Connect the vacuum hose to the throttle body adapter vacuum port.

44. Connect and, if necessary, adjust the throttle valve cable. Install the accelerator cable bracket on the intake manifold and connect the accelerator and cruise control cables to the throttle body.

45. Apply silicone sealer to both places where the front cover meets the cylinder head. Install new gaskets on the camshaft covers.

46. Install the camshaft covers on the cylinder heads. Install the bolts and stud bolts and tighten to 6.0–8.8 ft. lbs. (8–12 Nm).

47. Raise and safely support the vehicle. Position the starter wiring harness to the right cylinder head and install the retaining bolt.

48. Cut the wire and position the exhaust pipes to the exhaust manifolds. Tighten the 4 nuts to 20–30 ft. lbs. (27–41 Nm).

NOTE: Make sure the exhaust system clears the No. 3 crossmember. Adjust as necessary.

49. Connect the EGR tube to the right exhaust manifold and tighten the line nut to 26–33 ft. lbs. (35–45 Nm). Connect the EVO sensor and oil sending unit.

50. Apply a small amount of silicone sealer in the rear of the keyway on the damper. Position the damper on the crankshaft, making sure the crankshaft key and keyway are aligned.

51. Using damper installer T74P-6316-B or equivalent, install the crankshaft damper. Install the damper bolt and washer and tighten to 114–121 ft. lbs. (155–165 Nm).

52. Install the 4 bolts retaining the oil pan to the front cover and tighten to 15–22 ft. lbs. (20–30 Nm).

53. Position the power steering pump on the engine and install the 4 retaining bolts. Tighten to 15–22 ft. lbs. (20–30 Nm). Lower the vehicle.

54. Connect the air conditioning compressor, HDR sensor and canister purge solenoid.

55. Connect the 42-pin engine harness connector and transmission harness connector. Install the 42-pin connector on the retaining bracket on the vacuum brake booster.

56. Install the PCV valve in the right camshaft cover and connect the canister purge solenoid vent hose.

57. Position the positive battery cable harness on the right cylinder head and install the bolt retaining the cable bracket to the cylinder head. Connect the positive battery cable at the power distribution box and battery.

58. Position the generator and install the 2 retaining bolts. Tighten to 15–22 ft. lbs. (20–30 Nm). Install the 2 bolts retaining the generator brace to the intake manifold and tighten to 6–8 ft. lbs. (8–12 Nm).

59. Install the water pump pulley and tighten the bolts to 15–22 ft. lbs. (20–30 Nm).

60. Position the ignition coil brackets and ignition wire assembly onto the mounting studs. Install the 7 nuts retaining the coil brackets to the front cover and tighten to 15–22 ft. lbs. (20–30 Nm).

61. Install the 2 bolts retaining the ignition wire tray to the coil bracket and tighten to 6.0–8.8 ft. lbs. (8–12 Nm). Connect both ignition coils and CID sensor.

MUSTANG, THUNDERBIRD FORD/LINCOLN/MERCURY 9

62. Position the air conditioner high pressure line on the right coil bracket and install the bolt. Connect the ignition wires to the spark plugs and install the bracket onto the camshaft cover studs.

63. Install the accessory drive belt and the wiper module. Connect the fuel lines and install the cooling fan and shroud. Fill and bleed the cooling system.

64. Install the air inlet tube and connect the negative battery cable. Start the engine and bring to normal operating temperature. Check for leaks. Check all fluid levels.

4.6L (DOHC) Engine

1. Disconnect the negative battery cable.

2. Relieve the fuel system pressure. Drain the cooling system.

3. Remove the engine front cover and valve covers.

4. Raise and safely support the vehicle. Disconnect the exhaust Y-pipe and support aside with mechanics wire. Lower the vehicle.

5. Disconnect the EGR tube from left catalyst.

6. Remove the intake manifold assembly.

7. Remove the crankshaft position sensor tooth wheel and rotate the engine by hand to No. 1 cylinder TDC.

8. Install camshaft positioning tool T93P-6256-A, or equivalent, in rear D-slots of camshafts.

9. Remove 2 right tensioner bolts and remove tensioner. Remove 2 left tensioner bolts and remove tensioner.

10. Remove right and left primary timing chains.

11. Install crankshaft holding tool T93P-6303-A, or equivalent. Remove the the roller followers from intake and exhaust valves on cylinder head being removed.

12. Loosen the ten cylinder head bolts using the reverse order of the tightening sequence. Discard the bolts.

NOTE: The lower rear bolt cannot be removed because of interference with the brake vacuum booster. Use a rubber band or suitable device to hold the away from the block.

13. Remove the cylinder head and discard the gasket.

14. Clean all gasket mating surfaces. Check the flatness of the cylinder head using a straight-edge and a feeler gauge. If there is any warpage, machine cylinder as necessary.

To install:

15. Rotate the crankshaft 90 degrees to ensure all pistons are below top of engine block deck face.

16. Install new exhaust manifold gaskets and install exhaust manifolds.

17. Position new cylinder gasket on engine block. Install lower rear bolt on right and left heads and hold in place with rubber band or suitable device.

18. Position left head on dowels. Oil all cylinder head bolts with clean engine oil prior to installation.

19. Remove rubber band and install the remaining head bolts and hand-tighten.

20. Tighten cylinder head bolts in 3 steps:
   Tighten bolts in sequence to 27–32 ft. lbs. (37–43 Nm).
   Rotate bolts, in sequence 85–96 degrees.
   Rotate bolts, in sequence an additional 85–96 degrees.

21. Position right head on dowels. Oil all cylinder head bolts with clean engine oil prior to installation.

22. Remove rubber band and install the remaining head bolts and hand-tighten.

23. Tighten cylinder head bolts in 3 steps:
   Tighten bolts in sequence to 27–32 ft. lbs. (37–43 Nm).
   Rotate bolts, in sequence 85–96 degrees.
   Rotate bolts, in sequence an additional 85–96 degrees.

24. Install heater return hose. Install primary timing chains and set valve timing. Make sure the copper link on the timing chain aligns the timing on the camshaft sprocket.

25. Install the rocker followers. Install the crankshaft position sensor tooth wheel.

26. Install the intake manifold.

27. Install front engine cover. Connect the EGR tube to the left catalyst.

28. Raise and safely support the vehicle. Connect the exhaust Y-pipe. Lower the vehicle.

29. Install valve covers and connect the negative battery cable.

30. Fill and bleed the cooling system.

31. Start engine and check for coolant, fuel and oil leaks.

5.0L Engine

1. Disconnect the negative battery cable.

2. Drain the cooling system and relieve the fuel system pressure.

3. Remove the upper and lower intake manifold and throttle body assembly.

4. If the left cylinder head is to be removed and the vehicle is equipped with air conditioning, proceed as follows:
   a. Discharge the air conditioning system.
   b. Disconnect and plug the refrigerant lines at the compressor. Cap the openings on the compressor.
   c. Disconnect the electrical connector to the compressor.
   d. Remove the compressor and the necessary mounting brackets.

5. If the left cylinder head is to be removed, disconnect the power steering pump bracket from the cylinder head. Position the pump aside in a position that will prevent the oil from draining out.

6. Disconnect the oil level indicator tube bracket from the exhaust manifold stud.

7. If the right cylinder head is to be removed, remove the alternator mounting bracket from the cylinder head.

8. Remove the thermactor crossover tube from the rear of the cylinder heads. Remove the fuel line from the clip at the front of the right cylinder head.

9. Raise and safely support the vehicle. Disconnect the exhaust manifolds from the muffler inlet pipes. Lower the vehicle.

10. Loosen the rocker arm fulcrum bolts so the rocker arms can be rotated to the side. Remove the pushrods in sequence so they may be installed in their original positions.

11. Remove the cylinder head attaching bolts and the cylinder heads. If necessary, remove the exhaust manifolds to gain access to the lower bolts. Remove and discard the head gaskets.

12. Clean all gasket mating surfaces. Check the flatness of the cylinder head using a straight-edge and a feeler gauge. The cylinder head must not be warped any more than 0.003 in. in any 6.0 in.; 0.006 in. overall. Machine as necessary.

To install:

13. Position the new cylinder head gasket over the dowels on the block. Position the cylinder heads on the block and install the attaching bolts.

14. On 1992 models, tighten the bolts, in sequence, in 2 steps, 1st to 55–65 ft. lbs. (75–88 Nm), then to 65–72 ft. lbs. (88–97 Nm).

15. On 1993–96 models, there are 2 types of bolts, flanged hex head and

9-49

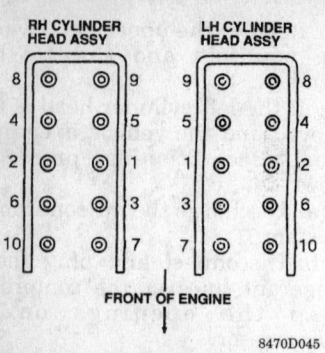

RH CYLINDER HEAD ASSY   LH CYLINDER HEAD ASSY

FRONT OF ENGINE

8470D045

Cylinder head bolt torque sequence — 4.6L engine

non-flanged hex head. If equipped with non-flanged hex head bolts, tighten the bolts, in sequence, in 2 steps, 1st to 55–65 ft. lbs. (75–88 Nm), then to 65–72 ft. lbs. (88–97 Nm). If equipped with flanged hex head bolts, tighten the bolts, in sequence, in 3 steps, 1st to 25–35 ft. lbs. (34–47 Nm), then to 45–55 ft. lbs. (61–75 Nm), then tighten an additional ¼ turn (85–96 degrees).

NOTE: When the cylinder head bolts have been tightened following this procedure, it is not necessary to retighten the bolts after extended operation.

16. If removed, install the exhaust manifolds. Tighten the retaining bolts to 18–24 ft. lbs. (24–32 Nm).

17. Clean the pushrods, making sure the oil passages are clean. Check the ends of the pushrods for wear. Visually check the pushrods for straightness or check for runout using a dial indicator. Replace pushrods, as necessary.

18. Apply a suitable grease to the ends of the pushrods and install them in their original positions. Position the rocker arms over the pushrods and the valves.

19. Before tightening each fulcrum bolt, bring the lifter for the fulcrum bolt to be tightened onto the base circle of the camshaft by rotating the engine. When the lifter is on the base circle of the camshaft, tighten the fulcrum bolt to 18–25 ft. lbs. (24–34 Nm).

NOTE: If all the original valve train parts are reinstalled, a valve clearance check is not necessary. If any valve train components are replaced, a valve clearance check must be performed.

20. Install new rocker arm cover gaskets on the rocker arm covers and install the covers on the cylinder heads. Tighten the retaining bolts to 10–13 ft. lbs. (14–18 Nm), wait 2 min-

utes, then retighten to the same specification.

21. Raise and safely support the vehicle. Connect the exhaust manifolds to the muffler inlet pipes. Lower the vehicle.

22. If necessary, install the air conditioning compressor and brackets. Connect the refrigerant lines and electrical connector to the compressor.

23. If necessary, install the alternator bracket.

24. If the left cylinder head was removed, install the power steering pump.

25. Install the drive belt. Install the thermactor tube at the rear of the cylinder heads.

26. Install the intake manifold. Fill and bleed the cooling system.

27. Connect the negative battery cable, start the engine and bring to normal operating temperature. Check for leaks. Check all fluid levels.

28. If necessary, leak test, evacuate and charge the air conditioning system. Observe all safety precautions.

Valve Lifters

REMOVAL AND INSTALLATION

2.3L Engine

The 2.3L engine is equipped with hydraulic lash adjusters which, while not being exactly the same as a conventional hydraulic lifter, perform the same function — maintain proper valve train clearance.

1. Disconnect the negative battery cable.

2. If equipped with distributor ignition, tag and disconnect the spark plug wires from the spark plugs. Move the wires aside.

3. Remove the hose and the retaining bolts from the rocker arm cover and remove the cover.

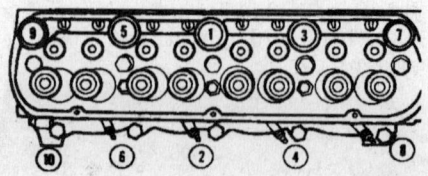

8470D039

Cylinder head bolt torque sequence — 5.0L engine

4. Rotate the camshaft so the base circle of the cam is facing the cam follower to be removed.

5. Using valve spring compressor tool T88T–6565–BH or equivalent, compress the lash adjuster as required and/or depress the valve spring if necessary and slide the cam follower over the lash adjuster and out.

6. Lift out the hydraulic lash adjuster.

To install:

7. Rotate the camshaft so the base circle of the camshaft is facing the lash adjuster and cam follower to be installed. Lubricate the hydraulic lash adjuster with clean engine oil and position it in the bore.

8. Using valve spring compressor tool T88T–6565–BH or equivalent, compress the lash adjuster, as necessary, to position the cam follower over the lash adjuster and the valve stem.

9. Before rotating the camshaft to the next position, make sure the lash adjuster just installed is fully compressed and released.

10. Clean the gasket mating surface of the rocker arm cover and cylinder head. Install a new gasket and the rocker arm cover. Install the mounting screws and tighten to 62–97 inch lbs. (7–11 Nm).

11. Install the remaining components in the reverse order of removal. Start the engine and check for oil leaks.

3.8L Engine

NOTE: Before replacing a lifter for noisy operation, be sure the noise is not caused by improper valve to rocker arm clearance or by worn rocker arms or pushrods.

1. Disconnect the negative battery cable. Tag and disconnect the spark plug wires at the spark plugs.

2. Remove plug wire routing clips from the studs on the rocker arm cover attaching bolts. Lay the plug wires, with the routing clips toward the front of the engine.

3. Remove the upper intake manifold. On supercharged engine, remove the supercharger.

4. Remove the rocker arm covers. Remove the lower intake manifold.

5. Sufficiently loosen each rocker arm fulcrum attaching bolt to allow the rocker arm to be lifted off the pushrod and rotated to 1 side.

6. Remove the pushrods. The location of each pushrod should be identified. When the engine is assembled

each rod should be installed in its original position.

7. Remove the 4 bolts holding the 2 guide plate retainers in place; the bolts are held captive in the retainers. Remove the 6 guide plates from the adjacent lifters.

8. Remove the lifters using a magnet. The location of each lifter should be identified. When the engine is assembled, each lifter should be installed in its original position.

NOTE: If the lifters are stuck in the bores due to excessive varnish or gum deposits, it may be necessary to use a claw-type tool to aid removal. When using a remover tool, rotate the lifter back and forth to loosen it from gum or varnish that may have formed on the lifter.

To install:

9. Clean the rocker arm cover and cylinder head mating surfaces.

10. Install each lifter in the bore from which it was removed. If new lifters are being installed, check the new lifters for free fit in the bores.

11. Align the flats on the side of the lifters and install the 6 guide plates between the adjacent lifters. Make sure the word **UP** is showing. Install the 2 guide plate retainers and tighten the 4 captive bolts to 7–10 ft. lbs. (9–14 Nm).

12. Dip each pushrod in heavy engine oil and install in its original position.

13. For each valve, rotate the crankshaft until the lifter rests on the base circle of the camshaft lobe. Position the rocker arms over the pushrods. Install the fulcrums and tighten the bolts to 5–11 ft. lbs. (7–15 Nm).

14. Lubricate all rocker arm assemblies with heavy engine oil. Final tighten the fulcrum bolts to 19–25 ft. lbs. (25–35 Nm). For final tightening the camshaft may be in any position.

NOTE: The fulcrums must be fully seated in the cylinder head and the pushrods must be seated in the rocker arm sockets prior to final tightening.

15. Install the lower intake manifold and the rocker arm covers. On non-supercharged engines, install the upper intake manifold. On supercharged engines, install the supercharger.

16. Install the spark plug wire routing clips and connect the wires to the spark plugs. Connect the negative battery cable, start the engine and check for oil and coolant leaks.

4.6L (SOHC) Engine

The 4.6L engine is equipped with hydraulic lash adjusters which, while not being exactly the same as a conventional hydraulic lifter, perform the same function — maintain proper valve train clearance.

1. Disconnect the negative battery cable.

2. Remove the right camshaft cover as follows:

a. Disconnect the positive battery cable at the battery and at the power distribution box. Remove the retaining bolt from the positive battery cable bracket located on the side of the right cylinder head.

b. Disconnect the High Data Rate (HDR) sensor, air conditioning compressor clutch and canister purge solenoid connectors. Position the harness out of the way.

c. Disconnect the vent hose from the purge solenoid and position the positive battery cable out of the way.

d. Disconnect the ignition wires from the spark plugs. Remove the ignition wire brackets from the camshaft cover studs and position the wires out of the way.

e. Remove the PCV valve from the camshaft cover grommet and position out of the way.

f. Remove the bolts and stud bolts and remove the camshaft cover.

3. Remove the left camshaft cover as follows:

a. Remove the air inlet tube. Relieve the fuel system pressure and disconnect the fuel lines.

b. Raise and safely support the vehicle.

c. Disconnect the EVO sensor and oil pressure sending unit and position the harness out of the way. Lower the vehicle.

d. Remove the 42-pin engine harness connector from the retaining bracket on the brake vacuum booster. Disconnect and position out of the way.

e. Remove the windshield wiper module.

f. Disconnect the ignition wires from the spark plugs. Remove the ignition wire brackets from the studs and position the wires out of the way.

g. Remove the bolts and stud bolts and remove the camshaft cover.

4. Position the piston of the cylinder being serviced at the bottom of its stroke and position the camshaft lobe on the base circle.

5. Install valve spring spacer tool T91P–6565–AH or equivalent, between the spring coils to prevent valve seal damage.

NOTE: If the valve spring spacer tool is not used, the retainer will hit the valve stem seal and damage the seal.

6. Install valve spring compressor tool T91P–6565–A or equivalent, under the camshaft and on top of the valve spring retainer.

7. Compress the valve spring and remove the roller follower. Remove the valve spring compressor and spacer.

8. Remove the hydraulic lash adjuster.

To install:

9. Check the hydraulic lash adjusters. They must have no more than 1.5mm of plunger travel prior to installation.

10. Apply engine oil to the valve stem and tip, roller follower contact surfaces and lash adjuster bore. Install the lash adjusters.

11. Install valve spring spacer tool T91P–6565–AH or equivalent, between the spring coils. Compress the valve spring using valve spring compressor tool T91P–6565–A or equivalent, and install the roller follower.

NOTE: The piston must be at the bottom of its stroke and the camshaft at the base circle.

12. Remove the valve spring compressor and spacer.

13. Clean the sealing surfaces of the camshaft covers and cylinder heads. Apply silicone sealer to the places where the front cover meets the cylinder head.

14. Position new gaskets onto the camshaft covers and install the covers. Install the bolts and stud bolts and tighten to 6.0–8.8 ft. lbs. (8–12 Nm).

15. When installing the right camshaft cover, proceed as follows:

a. Install the PCV valve into the camshaft cover grommet.

b. Install the ignition wire brackets on the studs and connect the wires to the spark plugs.

c. Position the harness and connect the canister purge solenoid, air conditioning compressor clutch and HDR sensor.

d. Position the positive battery cable harness on the right cylinder head. Install the bolt retaining the cable bracket to the cylinder head.

e. Connect the positive battery cable at the power distribution box and the battery.

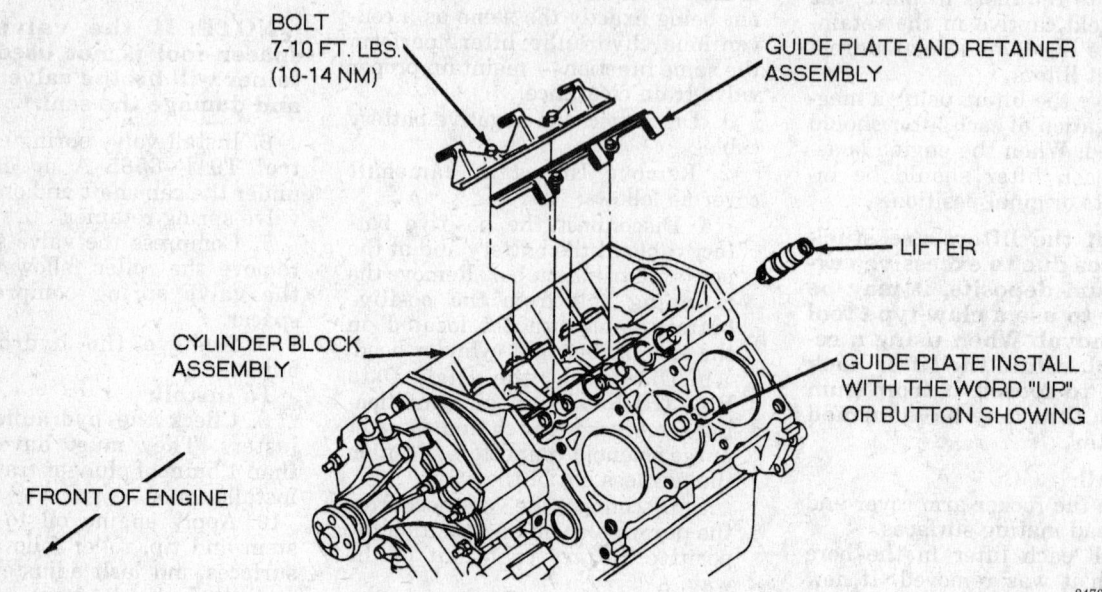

BOLT
7-10 FT. LBS.
(10-14 NM)

GUIDE PLATE AND RETAINER
ASSEMBLY

LIFTER

CYLINDER BLOCK
ASSEMBLY

GUIDE PLATE INSTALL
WITH THE WORD "UP"
OR BUTTON SHOWING

FRONT OF ENGINE

8470D040

Valve lifter installation — 3.8L engine

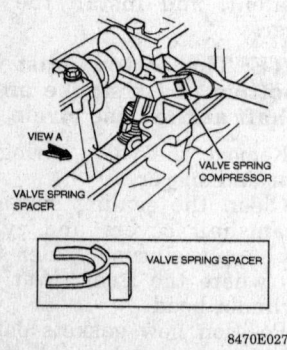

VIEW A

VALVE SPRING
COMPRESSOR

VALVE SPRING
SPACER

VALVE SPRING SPACER

8470E027

Valve spring compressor and
spacer 4.6L SOHC engine

16. When installing the left
camshaft cover, proceed as follows:

a. Install the ignition wire
brackets on the studs and connect
the wires to the spark plugs.

b. Install the windshield wiper
module.

c. Connect the 42-pin connector
and transmission harness connector. Install the connector on the retaining bracket.

d. Raise and safely support the
vehicle. Position and connect the
EVO sensor and oil pressure sending unit harness.

e. Lower the vehicle. Connect
the fuel lines.

17. Connect the negative battery
cable. Start the engine and check for
leaks.

4.6L (DOHC) Engine

1. Disconnect the negative battery
cable.

2. Disconnect the necessary hoses
from the valve covers and remove the
covers.

3. Rotate the camshaft so the base
circle of the cam is facing the cam
follower to be removed.

4. Using valve spring compressor
tool T93P–6565–A or equivalent,
compress the lash adjuster as required and remove the roller
follower.

5. Remove the hydraulic lash
adjuster.

6. Repeat steps 3 through 5 for adjusters being removed.

To install:

7. Rotate the camshaft so the base
circle of the cam is facing the cam
follower to be installed.

8. Lubricate the lash adjuster,
valve stem and tip, roller follower
contact surfaces and lash adjuster
bore. Install the lash adjusters in
their original bores. Lash adjusters
must have no more than 1.5 mm of
plunger travel prior to installation.

9. Compress exhaust valve spring
and install roller follower.

10. Compress primary intake valve
spring and install roller follower.
Compress secondary intake valve
spring and install roller follower.

11. Remove valve spring compressor. Repeat steps 7 through 11 until
all lash adjusters are installed.

12. Install the rocker arm covers
and necessary hoses. Connect the
negative battery cable, start the engine and check for leaks.

5.0L Engine

1. Disconnect the negative battery
cable. Remove the intake manifold
and related parts.

2. Disconnect the necessary hoses
from the rocker arm covers. Tag and
disconnect the spark plug wires, then
remove the wires and brackets from
the rocker arm cover attaching studs.
Remove the upper intake manifold.

3. Remove the rocker arm covers.
Loosen the rocker arm fulcrum bolts
and rotate the rocker arms to the
side.

4. Remove the valve pushrods and
identify them so they can be installed
in their original position.

5. Remove the lifter guide retainer
bolts. Remove the retainer and lifter
guide plates. Identify the guide

plates so they may be reinstalled in their original positions.

6. Using a magnet, remove the lifters and place them in a rack so they can be installed in their original bores.

NOTE: If the lifters are stuck in the bores due to excessive varnish or gum deposits, it may be necessary to use a claw-type tool to aid removal. When using a remover tool, rotate the lifter back and forth to loosen it from gum or varnish that may have formed on the lifter.

To install:

7. Lubricate the lifters and install them in their original bores. If new lifters are being installed, check them for free fit in their respective bores.

8. Install the lifter guide plates in their original positions, then install the guide plate retainer.

9. Install the pushrods in their original positions. Apply grease to the ends prior to installation.

10. Lubricate the rocker arms and fulcrum seats with heavy engine oil. Position the rocker arms over the pushrods and install the fulcrum bolts.

11. Before tightening each fulcrum bolt, rotate the crankshaft until the lifter is on the base circle of the cam. Tighten the fulcrum bolt to 18–25 ft. lbs. (24–34 Nm). Check the valve clearance.

12. Install the rocker arm covers and the intake manifold. Connect the negative battery cable, start the engine and check for leaks.

Valve Lash

ADJUSTMENT

2.3L Engine

1. Disconnect the negative battery cable.
2. Remove the valve cover assembly.
3. Position the camshaft so the base circle of the lobe is facing the cam follower of the valve to be checked.
4. Using valve spring compressor tool T88T–6565–BH or equivalent, slowly apply pressure to the cam follower until the the lash adjuster is completely collapsed.
5. With follower collapsed, insert a feeler gauge between the base circle of the camshaft and follower. The clearance should not be more than 0.035–0.055 in.

6. If the clearance is excessive, remove the cam follower and inspect for damage.

7. If the cam follower appears to be intact and not excessively worn, measure the valve spring assembled height to make sure the valve is not sticking.

8. If the valve spring assembled height is correct, check the camshaft for wear. If the camshaft dimensions are correct, replace the lash adjuster.

9. Install the valve cover and all remaining components.

3.8L Engine

The valve lash is not adjustable. If the collapsed lifter clearance is found to be incorrect, there are replacement pushrods available to compensate for excessive or insufficient clearance.

1. Disconnect the negative battery cable.
2. Remove the valve cover assembly on the side to be checked.
3. Turn the engine until the No. 1 piston is at TDC on the compression stroke.
4. The following valves can be checked with the engine in this position:
   a. No. 1 intake — No. 1 exhaust
   b. No. 3 intake — No. 2 exhaust
   c. No. 6 intake — No. 4 exhaust
5. Rotate the engine 360 degrees and check the following valves:
   a. No. 2 intake — No. 3 exhaust
   b. No. 4 intake — No. 5 exhaust
   c. No. 5 intake — No. 6 exhaust
6. Check each of the lifters by placing hydraulic lifter compressor tool T71P–6513–B or equivalent, on the rocker arm and slowly applying pressure to the lifter, until the lifter is collapsed.
7. Hold the lifter in this position and check the clearance between the rocker arm and the valve stem tip. The clearance should be 0.09–0.19 in. (2.25–4.79mm).

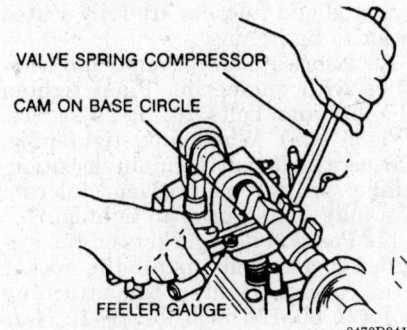

VALVE SPRING COMPRESSOR

CAM ON BASE CIRCLE

FEELER GAUGE

8470D041

Checking collapsed lifter valve clearance — 2.3L engine

8. Repeat this operation for each valve to be checked.

9. If the clearance is greater than specification, replace the pushrod with a longer one. If the clearance is less than specified, replace the pushrod with a shorter one.

5.0L Engine

The valve lash is not adjustable. If the collapsed lifter clearance is found to be incorrect, there are replacement pushrods available to compensate for excessive or insufficient clearance.

1. Install an auxiliary starter switch. Crank the engine with the ignition switch OFF until the No. 1 piston is at TDC on the compression stroke.

2. With the crankshaft in the positions designated in Steps 4, 5 and 6, position lifter bleed down wrench tool T71P–6513–B or equivalent, on the rocker arm. Slowly apply pressure to bleed down the lifter until the plunger is completely bottomed. Hold the lifter in this position and check the available clearance between the rocker arm and the valve stem tip with a feeler gauge.

3. The clearance should be 0.123–0.146 in. If the clearance is less than specification, install a shorter pushrod. If the clearance is greater than specification, install a longer pushrod.

4. The following valves can be checked with the engine in position 1, No. 1 piston at TDC on the compression stroke.
   a. No. 1 intake — No. 1 exhaust
   b. No. 4 intake — No. 3 exhaust
   c. No. 8 intake — No. 7 exhaust
5. Rotate the engine 360 degrees (1 revolution) from the 1st position and check the following valves:
   a. No. 3 intake — No. 2 exhaust
   b. No. 7 intake — No. 6 exhaust
6. Rotate the engine 90 degrees (¼ revolution) from the 2nd position and check the following valves:
   a. No. 2 intake — No. 4 exhaust
   b. No. 5 intake — No. 5 exhaust
   c. No. 6 intake — No. 8 exhaust

Rocker Arms

REMOVAL AND INSTALLATION

2.3L Engine

1. Disconnect the negative battery cable.
2. If equipped with distributor ignition, tag and disconnect the spark plug wires from the spark plugs. Move the wires aside.

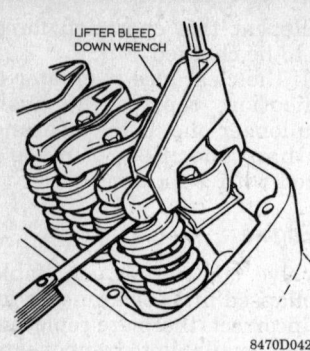

Checking collapsed lifter valve clearance — 3.8L and 5.0L engine

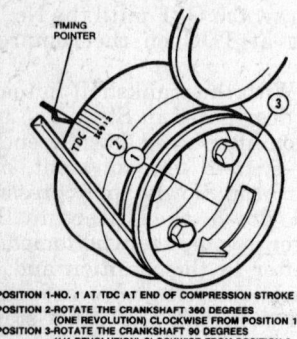

POSITION 1-NO. 1 AT TDC AT END OF COMPRESSION STROKE
POSITION 2-ROTATE THE CRANKSHAFT 360 DEGREES (ONE REVOLUTION) CLOCKWISE FROM POSITION 1
POSITION 3-ROTATE THE CRANKSHAFT 90 DEGREES (1/4 REVOLUTION) CLOCKWISE FROM POSITION 2

8470D043

Engine valve adjusting positions — 5.0L engine

3. Remove the hose and the retaining bolts from the rocker arm cover and remove the cover.

4. Rotate the camshaft so the base circle of the cam is facing the cam follower to be removed.

5. Using valve spring compressor tool T88T-6565-BH or equivalent, compress the lash adjuster as required and/or depress the valve spring if necessary and slide the cam follower over the lash adjuster and out.

To install:

6. Using valve spring compressor tool T88T-6565-BH or equivalent, compress the lash adjuster, as necessary, to position the cam follower over the lash adjuster and the valve stem.

7. Before rotating the camshaft to the next position, make sure the lash adjuster just installed is fully compressed and released.

8. Clean the gasket mating surface of the rocker arm cover and cylinder head. Install a new gasket and the rocker arm cover. Install the mounting screws and tighten to 62–97 inch lbs. (7–11 Nm).

9. Install the remaining components in the reverse order of removal.

Start the engine and check for oil leaks.

3.8L Engine

1. Disconnect the negative battery cable.

2. Disconnect the spark plug wires from the spark plugs. Remove the spark plug wire routing clips from the rocker arm cover attaching bolt studs.

3. To remove the left rocker arm cover, proceed as follows:

a. Remove the oil fill cap.

b. Remove the crankcase vent tube.

c. On supercharged engines, remove the charge air cooler tubes and the oil cooler inlet tube.

4. To remove the right rocker arm cover, proceed as follows:

a. Remove the PCV valve.

b. Position the air cleaner assembly aside, if necessary.

c. On supercharged engines, remove the air inlet tube and remove the throttle body assembly.

5. Remove the rocker arm cover attaching screws and remove the rocker arm covers.

6. Remove the rocker arm, fulcrum and bolt assemblies. Keep each assembly together and identify the assemblies so they may be reinstalled in their original positions.

To install:

7. Clean all gasket mating surfaces on the rocker arm covers and cylinder heads. Clean the rocker arms and fulcrums and inspect for wear or damage. Replace as necessary.

8. Apply grease to the pushrod tips and valve stem tips. Lubricate the fulcrums and rocker arms with heavy engine oil and install them over the pushrods and valve stems.

9. For each valve, rotate the crankshaft until the lifter is on the base circle of the camshaft. Install the fulcrum bolt and tighten to 5–11 ft. lbs. (7–15 Nm). Make sure the pushrod and fulcrum are fully seated prior to tightening.

10. Lubricate all rocker arm assemblies with engine oil. Final tighten the fulcrum bolts to 19–25 ft. lbs. (25–35 Nm). When final tightening, the camshaft may be in any position. Make sure the pushrod and fulcrum are fully seated prior to tightening.

11. Position new gaskets on the cylinder heads and install the rocker arm covers. Tighten the attaching bolts to 80–106 inch lbs. (9–12 Nm). Note the location of the spark plug wire routing clip stud bolts prior to installation.

12. After installing the left rocker arm cover, proceed as follows:

a. Install the oil fill cap.

b. Install the crankcase vent tube.

c. On supercharged engines, install the charge air cooler tubes and the oil cooler inlet tube.

13. After installing the right valve cover, proceed as follows:

a. Install the PCV valve.

b. Install the air cleaner assembly, if necessary.

c. On supercharged engines, install the air inlet tube and the throttle body assembly.

14. Install the spark plug wire routing clips and connect the wires to the spark plugs.

15. Connect the negative battery cable, start the engine and check for leaks.

4.6L Engine

1. Disconnect the negative battery cable.

2. Disconnect the necessary hoses from the valve covers and remove the covers.

3. Rotate the camshaft so the base circle of the cam is facing the cam follower to be removed.

4. Using valve spring compressor tool T93P-6565-A or equivalent, compress the lash adjuster as required and remove the roller follower.

5. Repeat steps 3 and 4 for followers being removed.

To install:

6. Rotate the camshaft so the base circle of the cam is facing the cam follower to be installed.

7. Compress exhaust valve spring and install roller follower.

8. Compress primary intake valve spring and install roller follower. Compress secondary intake valve spring and install roller follower.

9. Remove valve spring compressor. Repeat steps 6 through 10 until all followers are installed.

10. Install the rocker arm covers and necessary hoses. Connect the negative battery cable, start the engine and check for leaks.

5.0L Engine

1. Disconnect the negative battery cable.

2. Before removing the right rocker arm cover, disconnect the PCV closure tube from the oil fill stand pipe at the rocker cover.

3. Remove the thermactor bypass valve and air supply hoses as necessary to provide clearance.

4. Tag and disconnect the spark plug wires from the spark plugs. Remove the wires and bracket assembly from the rocker arm cover attaching stud and position the wires aside.

5. Remove the upper intake manifold as follows:

a. Disconnect the electrical connectors at the idle air bypass valve, throttle position sensor and EGR position sensor.

b. Disconnect the throttle and transmission linkage from the throttle body. Remove the cable bracket from the manifold and position the cables and bracket aside.

c. Tag and disconnect the vacuum lines at the upper intake manifold vacuum tree, EGR valve, fuel pressure regulator and evaporative canister.

d. Disconnect the PCV hose from the fitting on the rear of the upper manifold and disconnect the PCV vent closure tube at the throttle body.

e. Partially drain the cooling system and remove the 2 EGR coolant lines from the fittings on the EGR spacer.

f. Remove the retaining bolts and remove the upper intake manifold and throttle body assembly.

6. Remove the attaching bolts and remove the covers.

7. Remove the rocker arm fulcrum bolt, fulcrum seat and rocker arm. Keep all rocker arm assemblies together. Identify each assembly so it may be reinstalled in its original position.

To install:

8. Clean all gasket mating surfaces of the rocker arm covers and cylinder heads. Clean and inspect the rocker arm assemblies for wear and/or damage. Replace as necessary.

9. Apply grease to the pushrod and valve stem tips and the underside of the fulcrum seats.

10. Rotate the crankshaft until the lifter is on the camshaft base circle and install the rocker, fulcrum seat and fulcrum bolt. Tighten the bolts to 18–25 ft. lbs. (24–34 Nm). Make sure the pushrod and fulcrum are fully seated prior to tightening.

11. Position new rocker arm cover gaskets and install the rocker arm covers. Tighten the bolts to 10–13 ft. lbs. (14–18 Nm), wait 2 minutes and tighten again to the same specification.

12. Install the crankcase ventilation tube in the right cover. Install the upper intake manifold in the reverse order of removal. Tighten the

retaining bolts to 12–17 ft. lbs. (16–24 Nm).

13. Install the spark plug wires and bracket assembly on the rocker cover attaching stud. Connect the spark plug wires.

14. Install the air cleaner intake duct assembly. Install the thermactor bypass valve and air supply hoses, if required.

15. Connect the negative battery cable, start the engine and check for leaks.

Intake Manifold

REMOVAL AND INSTALLATION

2.3L Engine

1. Disconnect the negative battery cable.

2. Relieve the fuel system pressure and drain the cooling system.

3. Disconnect and label the electrical connectors at the following:

a. Idle air control valve

b. Throttle positioning sensor

c. Injector wiring harness

d. Air charge temperature sensor

e. Engine coolant temperature sensor

f. EGR valve, if necessary

g. Fan switch, if necessary

h. Ignition control assembly, if equipped

4. Tag and disconnect the necessary vacuum lines.

5. Remove the throttle linkage shield. Disconnect the throttle linkage and if equipped, the cruise control and kickdown cables. Unbolt the accelerator cable from the bracket and position the cable aside.

6. Disconnect the air intake hose and crankcase vent hose.

7. Disconnect the PCV system hose from the fitting on the underside of the upper intake manifold.

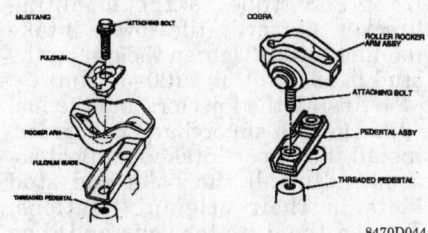

8470D044

Rocker arm assembly — 5.0L engine

8. Disconnect the water bypass hose at the lower intake manifold.

9. Loosen the EGR flange nut and disconnect the EGR tube.

10. Remove the engine oil dipstick bracket retaining bolt.

11. Remove the upper intake manifold retaining bolts and/or studs and remove the upper intake manifold assembly.

12. Disconnect the fuel lines from the fuel supply manifold.

13. Disconnect the electrical connectors from the fuel injectors and move the harness aside.

14. Remove the fuel supply manifold retaining bolts and remove the manifold carefully. Injectors can be removed at this time by exerting a slight twisting/pulling motion.

15. Remove the lower intake manifold retaining bolts and remove the lower intake manifold. The front 2 bolts also secure an engine lifting bracket.

To install:

16. Clean all gasket mating surfaces. Clean and oil the manifold bolt threads. Install a new intake manifold gasket.

17. Position the lower intake manifold to the head with the engine lift bracket. Install the manifold retaining bolts finger-tight.

18. Tighten the manifold retaining bolts, in sequence, to 15–22 ft. lbs. (20–30 Nm).

19. Install the fuel supply manifold and injectors. Connect the electrical connectors to the injectors.

20. Install a new gasket and the upper intake manifold. Tighten the bolts to 15–22 ft. lbs. (20–30 Nm) in the proper sequence. Connect the fuel lines to the fuel supply manifold.

21. Install the engine oil dipstick and retaining bolt. Connect the EGR tube, water bypass line and PCV hose.

22. Connect the electrical connectors and vacuum lines to their original locations. Connect the throttle linkage.

23. Fill and bleed the cooling system. Connect the negative battery cable, start the engine and check for leaks.

3.8L Engine

1. Disconnect the negative battery cable.

2. Drain the cooling system and relieve the fuel system pressure.

3. Remove the air cleaner assembly or air inlet tube.

4. Disconnect the accelerator cable at the throttle body. Disconnect the cruise control cable, if equipped.

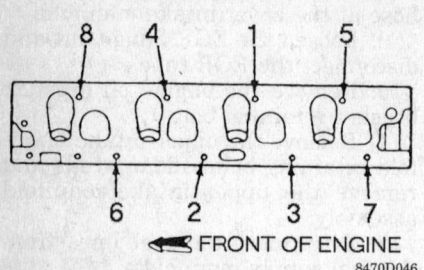

Intake manifold to cylinder head torque sequence — 2.3L engine

8470D046

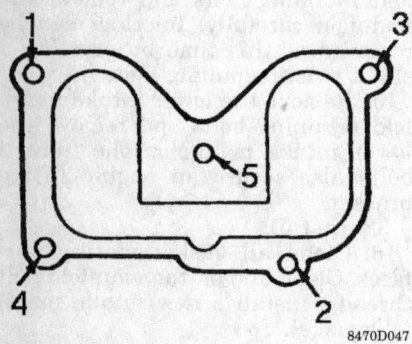

Upper intake manifold bolt torque sequence — 2.3L engine

8470D047

5. If equipped with an automatic transmission, disconnect the transmission linkage at the upper intake manifold. Remove the retaining bolts from the accelerator cable mounting bracket and position the cables aside.

6. If equipped, disconnect the thermactor air supply hose at the check valve. The valve is located in the Y-pipe assembly.

7. Disconnect the fuel lines. If equipped, remove the supercharger.

8. Disconnect the radiator hose at the thermostat housing and the coolant bypass hose at the manifold.

9. Disconnect the heater tube at the intake manifold and remove the tube support bracket retaining nut. Remove the heater hose at the rear of the heater tube. Loosen the hose clamp at the heater elbow and remove the heater tube with the hose attached. Remove the heater tube with the lines attached and set the assembly aside.

10. Tag and disconnect the vacuum lines at the fuel rail assembly and intake manifold. Tag and disconnect the necessary electrical connectors.

11. If equipped with air conditioning, remove the compressor support bracket. Disconnect the 1 PCV line at the upper intake manifold and at the

valve. Remove the 2nd PCV line from the left rocker arm cover.

12. Remove the throttle body assembly. Remove the EGR valve assembly from the upper manifold.

13. Remove the retaining nut and remove the wiring retainer bracket located at the left front of the intake manifold and set aside with the spark plug wires.

14. Remove the upper intake manifold retaining bolts/studs and remove the upper intake manifold.

15. Remove the injectors and fuel rail assembly. Remove the heater water outlet hose.

16. Remove the lower intake manifold retaining bolts/studs and remove the lower intake manifold.

NOTE: The manifold is sealed at each end with RTV-type sealer. To break the seal, it may be necessary to pry on the front of the manifold with a small prybar. If it is necessary to pry on the manifold, use care to prevent damage to the machined surfaces.

To install:

17. Clean all gasket mating surfaces. Lightly oil all retaining bolt and stud threads.

18. Apply a dab of gasket adhesive to each cylinder head mating surface. Press new intake manifold gaskets in place, using location pins as necessary to aid in installation.

19. Apply a $1/8$ in. bead of silicone sealer at each corner where the cylinder head joins the cylinder block. Install the front and rear intake manifold end seals.

20. Carefully lower the intake manifold into place on the cylinder heads and cylinder block. Use locating pins as necessary to guide the manifold.

21. Install the bolts and stud bolts in their original locations.

22. On all supercharged engines and 1992–93 non-supercharged engines, tighten the bolts, in sequence, in 2 steps, 1st to 8 ft. lbs. (11 Nm) and then to 11 ft. lbs. (15 Nm).

23. Connect the rear PCV line to the upper intake tube. Install the front PCV tube so the mounting bracket sits over the lower intake manifold stud. Tighten the nut on the stud to 15–22 ft. lbs. (20–30 Nm).

24. Install the injectors and the fuel rail. On non-supercharged engines, install the upper intake manifold assembly. Install the bolts and stud bolts in their original locations. Tighten the 4 center bolts and then the end bolts in 3 steps, 1st to 8 ft. lbs. (10 Nm), then to 15 ft. lbs. (20 Nm), and finally to 24 ft. lbs. (32 Nm).

25. On supercharged engines, install the supercharger.

26. Install the EGR valve. Install the throttle body and cross-tighten the retaining nuts to 15–22 ft. lbs. (20–30 Nm).

27. Connect the rear PCV line at the PCV valve on the upper intake manifold. If equipped with air conditioning, install the compressor support bracket.

28. Connect the necessary electrical connectors and vacuum hoses. Connect the heater tube hose to the heater elbow and position the heater tube support bracket. Tighten the retaining nut to 15–22 ft. lbs. (20–30 Nm).

29. Connect the heater hose to the heater tube and connect the coolant bypass hose and radiator upper hose.

30. Connect the fuel lines. Position the accelerator cable mounting bracket and tighten the mounting bolts to 15–22 ft. lbs. (20–30 Nm).

31. Connect the transmission linkage at the upper intake manifold. If equipped, connect the cruise control cable.

32. Fill and bleed the cooling system. Connect the negative battery cable, start the engine and check for leaks.

33. Check and if necessary, adjust the engine idle speed, transmission throttle linkage and cruise control.

4.6L (SOHC) Engine

1. Disconnect the negative battery cable.

2. Drain the cooling system. Relieve the fuel system pressure and disconnect the fuel lines.

3. Remove the wiper module and the air inlet tube. Release the belt tensioner and remove the accessory drive belt.

4. Tag and disconnect the ignition wires from the spark plugs. Disconnect the ignition wire brackets from the camshaft cover studs.

5. Disconnect both ignition coils and CID sensor. Tag and disconnect all ignition wires from both ignition coils. Remove the 2 bolts retaining the ignition wire tray to the coil brackets and remove the ignition wire assembly.

6. Disconnect the generator wiring harness from the junction block at the fender apron and generator. Remove the bolts retaining the generator brace to the intake manifold and the generator to the engine block and remove the generator.

7. Raise and safely support the vehicle. Disconnect the oil sending unit

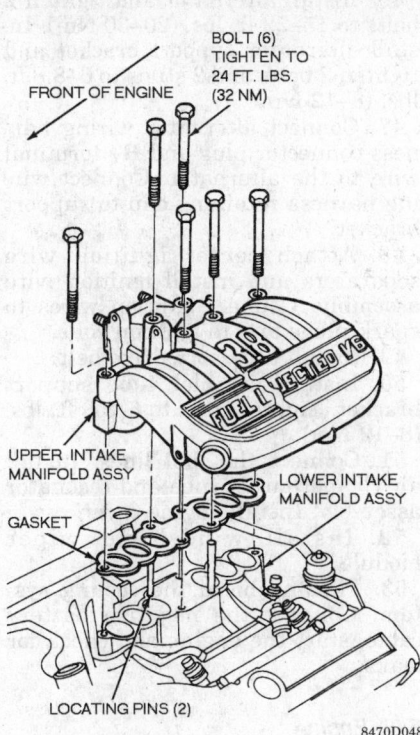

Upper intake manifold installation — 3.8L engine

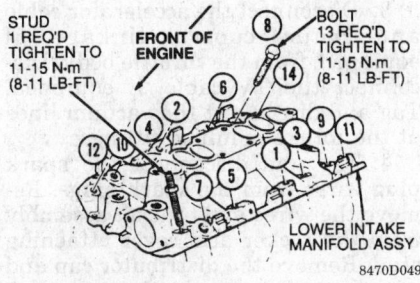

Lower intake manifold bolt torque sequence — 3.8L engine

and EVO harness sensor and position the wiring harness out of the way.

8. Disconnect the EGR tube from the right exhaust manifold and lower the vehicle.

9. Remove the 42-pin engine harness connector from the retaining bracket on the vacuum brake booster and disconnect the connector.

10. Disconnect the air conditioning compressor, HDR sensor and canister purge solenoid.

11. Remove the PCV valve from the camshaft cover and disconnect the canister purge vent hose from the PCV valve.

12. Disconnect the accelerator and cruise control cables from the throttle body. Remove the accelerator cable bracket from the intake manifold and position out of the way.

13. Disconnect the throttle valve cable from the throttle body and the vacuum hose from the throttle body adapter port.

14. Disconnect both oxygen sensors and the heater supply hose.

15. Remove the 2 bolts retaining the thermostat housing to the intake manifold and position the upper hose and thermostat housing out of the way.

NOTE: The 2 thermostat housing bolts also retain the intake manifold.

16. Remove the bolts retaining the intake manifold to the cylinder heads and remove the intake manifold. Remove and discard the gaskets.

To install:

17. Clean all gasket mating surfaces. Position new intake manifold gaskets on the cylinder heads. Make sure the alignment tabs on the gaskets are aligned with the holes in the cylinder heads.

18. Install the intake manifold and the retaining bolts. Tighten the bolts, in sequence, to 15–22 ft. lbs. (20–30 Nm).

19. Inspect and if necessary, replace the O-ring seal on the thermostat housing. Position the housing and upper hose and install the 2 bolts. Tighten to 15–22 ft. lbs. (20–30 Nm).

20. Connect the heater supply hose and connect both oxygen sensors.

21. Connect the vacuum hose to the throttle body adapter vacuum port. Connect and, if necessary, adjust the throttle valve cable.

22. Install the accelerator cable bracket on the intake manifold and connect the accelerator and cruise control cables to the throttle body.

23. Install the PCV valve in the camshaft cover and connect the canister purge solenoid vent hose. Connect the air conditioning compressor, HDR sensor and canister purge solenoid.

24. Connect the 42-pin engine harness connector. Install the connector on the retaining bracket on the vacuum brake booster.

25. Raise and safely support the vehicle. Connect the EGR tube to the right exhaust manifold and tighten the line nut to 26–33 ft. lbs. (35–45 Nm).

26. Connect the EVO sensor and oil sending unit. Lower the vehicle.

27. Position the generator and install the retaining bolts. Tighten to 15–22 ft. lbs. (20–30 Nm). Install the 2 bolts retaining the generator brace to the intake manifold and tighten to 6.0–8.8 ft. lbs. (8–12 Nm).

28. Connect the generator wiring harness to the generator, right-hand fender apron and junction block.

29. Position the ignition wire assembly on the engine and install the 2 bolts retaining the ignition wire tray to the coil brackets. Tighten the bolts to 6.0–8.8 ft. lbs. (8–12 Nm).

30. Connect the ignition wires to the ignition coils in their proper positions. Connect the ignition wires to the spark plugs.

31. Connect the ignition wire brackets on the camshaft cover studs. Connect both ignition coils and CID sensor.

32. Install the accessory drive belt and the air inlet tube. Install the wiper module and connect the fuel lines.

33. Fill and bleed the cooling system. Connect the negative battery cable, start the engine and check for leaks.

4.6L (DOHC) Engine

1. Disconnect the negative battery cable.

2. Drain the cooling system and relieve the fuel system pressure.

3. Remove engine cover. Remove air cleaner outlet tube and resonator assembly.

4. Disconnect fuel lines.

5. Remove the hush panel to expose the windshield wiper module, remove screw, lower module and bracket assembly and disconnect electrical connector. Remove the wiper module.

6. Remove accessory drive belt.

7. Remove air inlet tube support bracket. Remove left and right ignition wire covers.

8. Label and disconnect ignition wires from spark plugs and from ignition coils. Detach center ignition wire separators and remove ignition wire assembly.

9. Disconnect alternator wiring harness at **B+** terminal and stator connector plug. Disconnect wiring harness retaining clip from alternator support bracket.

10. Remove 2 bolts and 2 studs retaining support bracket to alternator and intake manifold.

11. Disconnect upper radiator hose and coolant bypass hose at coolant crossover tube.

12. Remove coolant crossover tube. Remove the alternator.

13. Disconnect the accelerator and speed control cables from the throttle body and from cable mounting bracket. Set aside.

14. Disconnect chassis vacuum supply hose from intake manifold and position aside.

15. Tag and disconnect the following vacuum lines:
Fuel pressure regulator
Right and left IMRC vacuum controls
EGR control valve
EGR vacuum regulator control
IMRC vacuum control solenoids
Intake manifold connections.

16. Disconnect PCV hose connector from throttle body. Remove PCV valve from left valve cover and position PCV tube assembly aside.

17. Disconnect 4 engine harness retaining clips from intake manifold studs and 1 clip from fuel regulator bracket.

18. Disconnect fuel injector electrical connectors.

19. Remove upper bolt retaining accelerator cable bracket to left cylinder head. Loosen lower bolt and position bracket against left valve cover.

20. Remove 2 bolts retaining EGR control valve to intake manifold. Remove EGR control valve.

21. Remove 20 bolts and studs retaining intake manifold using a reverse torque pattern.

22. Lift engine harness upward for intake manifold removal clearance.

23. Lift front of intake manifold and IMRC assembly and move assembly forward to obtain access to the rear of the intake manifold and disconnect connector at idle air control, throttle position switch and harness clip at idle air control retaining stud.

24. Remove intake manifold assembly. Remove fuel injector supply manifold from fuel injectors.

25. Remove right and left IMRC units. Remove gaskets and load limiting spacers. Discard the gaskets.

26. Remove and discard EGR and lower intake gaskets.

To install:

27. Clean and inspect all sealing surfaces. Remove paper from adhesive backing on new upper intake manifold gasket. Install onto top of right IMRC unit. Use tapered pins at end bolt hole locations for proper alignment. Repeat for left IMRC.

28. Assemble IMRC units onto intake manifold and hand-tighten 4 bolts.

29. Install fuel injection supply manifold onto fuel injectors and tighten 4 retaining screws to 26–45 inch lbs. (3–5 Nm). Install 2 fuel pressure regulator retaining bracket screws and tighten to 6–8.8 ft. lbs. (8–12 Nm).

30. Position new IMRC gaskets onto cylinder heads. Use gaskets integral location pins to align gasket.

31. Place intake manifold under engine harness and connect wiring harness plugs to idle air control valve, throttle position sensor and connect wiring clip to idle air control valve retaining clip.

32. Move intake manifold into position and install new EGR valve gasket. Hand-tighten 2 retaining bolts.

33. Install 10 long bolts and studs in outer holes of intake manifold. Do not tighten.

34. Install 10 short bolts and studs in inner holes of intake manifold. Hand-tighten all 20 fasteners.

35. Tighten bolts and studs in sequence as follows:
Numbers 5, 7, 9 and 11 to 8.8–11 ft. lbs. (12–15 Nm)
All others to 13–16 ft. lbs. (18–22 Nm)
Rotate, in sequence, 85–96 degrees.

36. Tighten 4 IMRC retaining bolts to 6–7.5 ft. lbs. (8–10 Nm). Rotate, in sequence, 85–96 degrees.

37. Tighten 2 EGR retaining bolts to 15–22 ft. lbs. (20–30 Nm).

38. Install upper retaining bolt into accelerator cable bracket and tighten both upper and lower bolts to 15–22 ft. lbs. (20–30 Nm).

39. Connect engine harness to fuel injectors.

40. Connect engine harness clips to intake manifold studs and connect harness clip to fuel pressure regulator bracket. Connect PCV system.

41. Connect vacuum harness to fuel pressure regulator, right and left IMRC vacuum controls, EGR vacuum regulator control, IMRC vacuum control solenoids and intake manifold vacuum at rear connection.

42. Connect chassis vacuum supply hose and spring clamp to intake manifold vacuum at forward connection.

43. Connect the accelerator and speed control cables to the throttle body and to the cable mounting bracket.

44. Replace O-rings on coolant crossover tubes if necessary. Insert crossover tube support tube support braces over intake manifold inner studs and press crossover tube into place. Install nuts and tighten to 6–8.8 ft. lbs. (8–12 Nm).

45. Connect ECT and temperature gauge sensor connections. Connect upper radiator hose and coolant bypass hose at coolant crossover tube.

46. Install alternator and tighten 2 bolts to 15–22 ft. lbs. (20–30 Nm). Install alternator support bracket and tighten 2 bolts and 2 studs to 6–8.8 ft. lbs. (8–12 Nm).

47. Connect alternator wiring harness connector plug and **B+** terminal wire to the alternator. Connect wiring harness retaining clip to support bracket.

48. Attach center ignition wire separators and install ignition wire assembly. Connect ignition wires to spark plugs and to ignition coils.

49. Install accessory drive belt.

50. Install air inlet tube support bracket. Tighten nuts to 6–8.8 ft. lbs. (8–12 Nm).

51. Connect the fuel lines. Install air cleaner outlet tube and resonator assembly. Install engine cover.

52. Install windshield wiper module.

53. Fill and bleed the cooling system. Connect the negative battery cable, start the engine and check for leaks.

5.0L Engine

1. Disconnect the negative battery cable.

2. Drain the cooling system and relieve the fuel system pressure.

3. Disconnect the accelerator cable and cruise control linkage, if equipped, from the throttle body. Disconnect the TV cable, if equipped. Tag and disconnect the vacuum lines at the intake manifold fitting.

4. Tag and disconnect the spark plug wires from the spark plugs. Remove the wires and bracket assembly from the rocker arm cover attaching stud. Remove the distributor cap and wires assembly.

5. Disconnect the fuel lines and the distributor wiring connector. Mark the position of the rotor on the distributor housing and the distributor housing in the block. Remove the hold-down bolt and remove the distributor.

6. Disconnect the upper radiator hose at the thermostat housing and the water temperature sending unit wire at the sending unit. Disconnect the heater hose from the intake manifold and disconnect the 2 throttle body cooler hoses, except on Cobra.

7. Disconnect the water pump bypass hose from the thermostat housing. Tag and disconnect the connectors from the engine coolant temperature, air charge temperature, throttle position and EGR sensors and the idle speed control solenoid. Disconnect the injector wire connec-

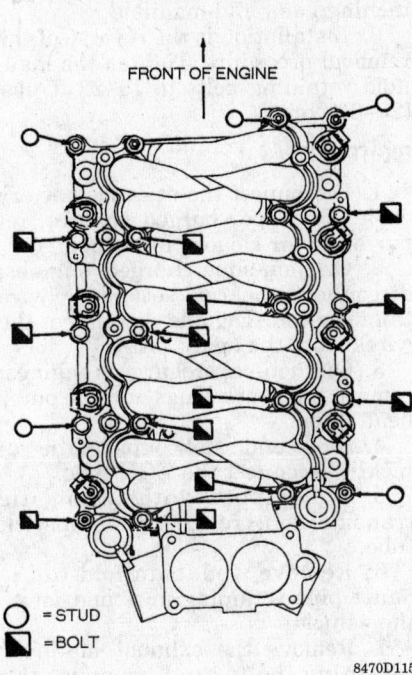

Intake manifold bolt and stud locations — 4.6L (DOHC) engine

⭕ = STUD
◼ = BOLT

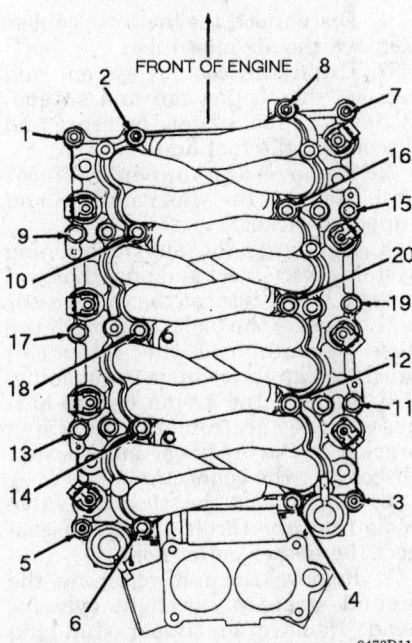

Intake manifold bolt torque sequence — 4.6L (DOHC) engine

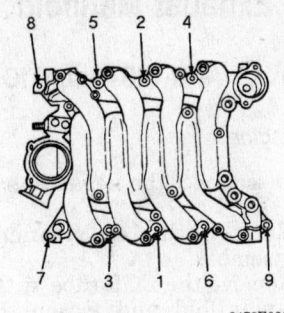

Intake manifold torque sequence — 4.6L (SOHC) engine

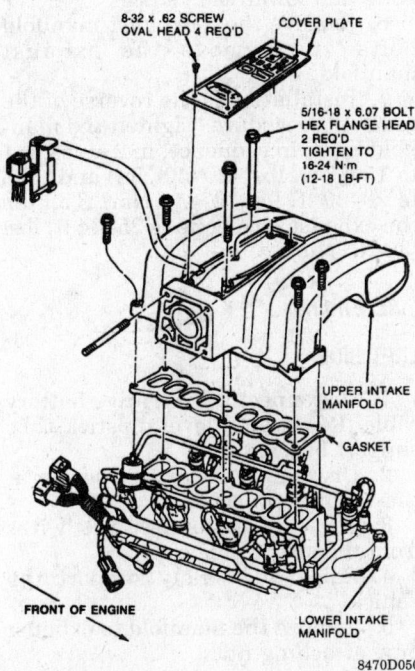

Upper intake manifold installation — 5.0L engine

tions and the fuel charging assembly wiring.

8. Remove the PCV valve from the grommet at the rear of the lower intake manifold. Disconnect the fuel evaporative purge hose from the plastic connector at the front of the upper intake manifold.

9. Remove the upper intake manifold cover plate, except on Cobra, and upper intake bolts. Remove the upper intake manifold.

10. Remove the heater tube assembly from the lower intake manifold.

11. Remove the lower intake manifold retaining bolts and remove the lower intake manifold.

NOTE: If it is necessary to pry the intake manifold away from the cylinder heads, be careful to avoid damaging the gasket sealing surfaces.

To install:

12. Clean all gasket mating surfaces. Apply a 1/8 in. bead of silicone sealer to the points where the cylinder block rails meet the cylinder heads.

13. Position new seals on the cylinder block and new gaskets on the cylinder heads with the gaskets interlocked with the seal tabs. Make sure the holes in the gaskets are aligned with the holes in the cylinder heads.

14. Apply a 1/16 in. bead of sealer to the outer end of each intake manifold seal for the full width of the seal.

15. sing guide pins to ease installation, carefully lower the intake manifold into position on the cylinder block and cylinder heads.

NOTE: After the intake manifold is in place, run a finger around the seal area to make sure the seals are in place. If the seals are not in place, remove the intake manifold and position the seals.

16. Make sure the holes in the manifold gaskets and the manifold are in alignment. Remove the guide pins. Install the intake manifold attaching bolts and tighten, in sequence, to:
1992 vehicles 15–20 ft. lbs. (20–27 Nm)
1993–96 vehicles, in sequence, to 8 ft. lbs. (11 Nm), then to 16 ft. lbs. (22 Nm), finally to 24 ft. lbs. (32 Nm).

17. Install the heater tube assembly to the lower intake manifold.

18. Install the water pump bypass hose on the thermostat housing. Install the hoses to the heater tubes.

19. Connect the upper radiator hose and connect the heater hose at the intake manifold. Connect the fuel lines.

20. Install the distributor, aligning the housing and rotor with the marks that were made during removal. Install the distributor cap. Position the spark plug wires in the harness brackets on the rocker arm cover attaching stud and connect the wires to the spark plugs.

21. Install a new gasket and the upper intake manifold. Tighten the bolts to 12–18 ft. lbs. (16–24 Nm). Install the cover plate and connect the crankcase vent tube.

22. Connect the TV cable and cruise control cable, if equipped, to the throttle body. Connect the electrical connectors and vacuum lines.

23. Connect the coolant hoses to the EGR spacer. Fill and bleed the cooling system.

24. Connect the negative battery cable, start the engine and check for leaks. Check the ignition timing.

25. Operate the engine at fast idle. When engine temperatures have stabilized, tighten the intake manifold bolts to 23–25 ft. lbs. (31–34 Nm).

26. Connect the air intake duct and the crankcase vent hose.

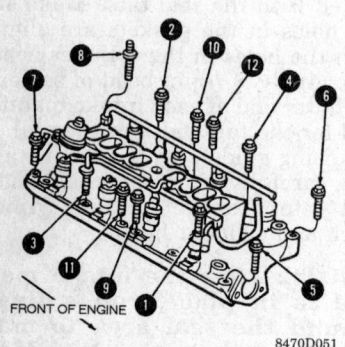

Lower intake manifold bolt torque sequence — 5.0L engine

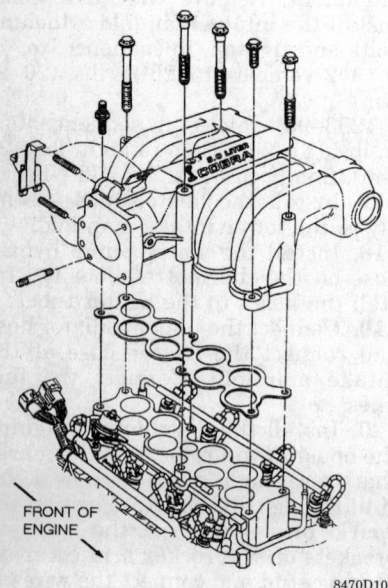

Upper intake manifold installation — 5.0L Cobra engine

Exhaust Manifold

REMOVAL AND INSTALLATION

2.3L Engine

1. Disconnect the negative battery cable.

2. Remove the air cleaner and duct assembly.

3. Remove the EGR tube at the exhaust manifold and loosen at the EGR valve.

4. Disconnect and, if necessary, remove the oxygen sensor from the exhaust manifold.

5. Raise and safely support the vehicle. Remove the 2 exhaust pipe bolts and lower the vehicle.

6. Remove the 8 exhaust manifold bolts and remove the exhaust manifold.

7. Installation is the reverse of the removal procedure. Tighten the manifold bolts, in sequence, in 2 steps, 1st to 15–17 ft. lbs. (20–30 Nm) and then to 20–30 ft. lbs. (27–41 Nm). Tighten the exhaust pipe bolts to 25–34 ft. lbs. (36–46 Nm).

3.8L Engine

LEFT SIDE

1. Disconnect the negative battery cable. Remove oil level dipstick tube support bracket.

2. Disconnect the oxygen sensor at the wiring connector.

3. Tag and disconnect the wires from the spark plugs.

4. Raise and safely support the vehicle.

5. Remove the manifold to exhaust pipe attaching nuts.

6. Lower the vehicle.

7. On supercharged engines, remove the charge air cooler tubes and remove the oil cooler tube and dipstick tube support brackets from the studs.

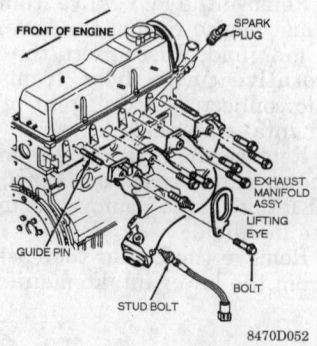

Exhaust manifold installation and torque sequence — 2.3L engine

8. Remove exhaust manifold attaching bolts and manifold.

9. Installation is the reverse of the removal procedure. Tighten the manifold retaining bolts to 15–22 ft. lbs. (20–30 Nm).

RIGHT SIDE

1. Disconnect the negative battery cable. On supercharged engines, remove the air cleaner inlet tube.

2. On non-supercharged engines, disconnect the coil secondary wire from the coil. Tag and disconnect the wires from the spark plugs.

3. On non-supercharged engines, remove the spark plugs and the outer heat shield.

4. Raise and safely support the vehicle. Disconnect the EGR tube.

5. If equipped with automatic transmission, remove the dipstick tube.

6. Remove the manifold-to-exhaust pipe retaining nuts and lower the vehicle.

7. Remove the exhaust manifold retaining bolts and remove the manifold.

8. Installation is the reverse of the removal procedure. Tighten the exhaust manifold retaining bolts to 15–22 ft. lbs. (20–30 Nm).

4.6L (SOHC) Engine

1. Disconnect the battery cables. Remove the air inlet tube.

2. Drain the cooling system and remove the cooling fan and shroud. Relieve the fuel system pressure and disconnect the fuel lines.

3. Remove the upper radiator hose. Remove the wiper module and support bracket.

4. Discharge the air conditioning system. Disconnect and plug the compressor outlet hose at the compressor and remove the bolt retaining the hose assembly to the right coil bracket. Cap the compressor opening.

5. Remove the 42-pin engine harness connector from the retaining bracket on the brake vacuum booster. Disconnect the connector.

6. Disconnect the throttle valve cable from the throttle body. Disconnect the heater outlet hose.

7. Remove the nut retaining the ground strap to the right cylinder head. Remove the upper stud and lower bolt retaining the heater outlet hose to the right cylinder head and position out of the way.

8. Remove the blower motor resistor and remove the bolt retaining the right engine insulator to the lower engine bracket. Disconnect both oxygen sensors.

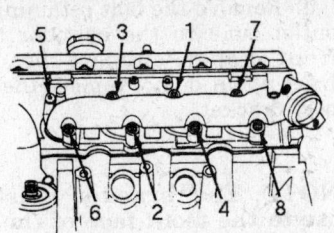

NOTE: ENGINE SHOWN REMOVED FOR CLARITY
NOTE: LH EXHAUST MANIFOLD SHOWN RH EXHAUST MANIFOLD TYPICAL

8470E033

Exhaust manifold torque sequence — 4.6L (SOHC) engine

9. Raise and safely support the vehicle. Remove the engine mount through bolts.

10. Remove the EGR tube line nut from the right exhaust manifold.

11. Disconnect the exhaust pipes from the manifolds. Lower the exhaust system and hang it from the crossmember with wire.

12. To remove the left exhaust manifold, remove the engine mount from the engine block and remove the 8 bolts retaining the exhaust manifold.

13. Position a jack and a block of wood under the oil pan, rearward of the oil drain hole. Raise the engine approximately 4 in. (100mm).

14. Remove the 8 bolts retaining the right exhaust manifold and remove the manifold.

To install:

15. If the exhaust manifolds are being replaced, transfer the oxygen sensors and tighten to 27–33 ft. lbs. (37–45 Nm). On the right manifold, transfer the EGR tube connector and tighten to 33–48 ft. lbs. (45–65 Nm).

16. Clean the mating surfaces of the exhaust manifolds and cylinder heads.

17. Position the exhaust manifolds to the cylinder heads and install the retaining bolts. Tighten, in sequence, to 15–22 ft. lbs. (20–30 Nm).

18. Position and connect the EGR valve and tube assembly to the exhaust manifold. Tighten the line nut to 26–33 ft. lbs. (35–45 Nm).

19. Install the left engine mount and tighten the bolts to 15–22 ft. lbs. (20–30 Nm). Lower the engine onto the mounts and remove the jack. Install the engine mount through bolts and tighten to 15–22 ft. lbs. (20–30 Nm).

20. Cut the wire and position the exhaust system. Tighten the nuts to 20–30 ft. lbs. (27–41 Nm).

NOTE: Make sure the exhaust system clears the No. 3 crossmember. Adjust as necessary.

21. Lower the vehicle. Connect both oxygen sensors and install the bolt retaining the right engine mount to the frame. Tighten to 15–22 ft. lbs. (20–30 Nm).

22. Install the blower motor resistor. Position the heater outlet hoses. Install the upper stud and lower bolt and tighten to 15–22 ft. lbs. (20–30 Nm). Install the ground strap onto the stud and tighten the nut to 15–22 ft. lbs. (20–30 Nm).

23. Connect the heater outlet hose. Connect and if necessary, adjust the throttle valve cable.

24. Connect the 42-pin connector and transmission harness connector. Install the connector to the retaining bracket on the brake vacuum booster.

25. Connect the air conditioning compressor outlet hose to the compressor and install the bolt retaining the hose assembly to the right coil bracket.

26. Install the upper radiator hose and connect the fuel lines. Install the wiper module and retaining bracket.

27. Install the cooling fan and shroud. Install the air inlet tube. Connect the battery cables, start the engine and check for leaks.

28. Leak test, evacuate and charge the air conditioning system according to the proper procedure. Observe all safety precautions.

4.6L (DOHC) Engine

RIGHT SIDE

1. Disconnect the negative battery cable.

2. Remove engine appearance cover. Disconnect intake air temperature sensor connector and crankcase vent tube from air cleaner outlet tube.

3. Completely loosen air cleaner outlet to throttle body bolt. Disconnect air cleaner outlet tube.

4. Remove remaining bolt from support bracket clamp on right valve cover to air cleaner outlet tube assembly and remove assembly and resonator.

5. Disconnect the oxygen sensor connector.

6. Remove 4 manifold to cylinder head bolts from upper side of exhaust manifold.

7. Disconnect exhaust pipe from catalyst and remove catalyst. Remove 4 lower exhaust manifold retaining

bolts and remove manifold. Remove exhaust manifold gasket and discard.

8. Installation is the reverse of the removal procedure. Tighten the manifold retaining bolts in sequence to 15–22 ft. lbs. (20–30 Nm).

LEFT SIDE

1. Turn **OFF** air suspension switch located in luggage compartment.

2. Disconnect the negative and positive battery cables.

3. Disconnect the oxygen sensor. Install engine support tripod onto engine compartment and attach to engine.

4. Raise and safely support the vehicle.

5. Remove the front wheel and tire assemblies.

6. Disconnect EGR tube at left catalyst. Disconnect the left exhaust pipe at the catalyst and right catalyst at the exhaust manifold.

7. Disconnect left and right ride height sensor wiring connectors and remove right and left brake caliper bolts. Remove brake calipers and support with mechanics wire.

8. Disconnect left and right upper control arms from spindles. Disconnect steering shaft coupler at rag joint.

9. Remove power steering line clamp from subframe.

10. Support subframe with engine jack.

11. Remove 2 motor mount through bolts. Remove left and right lower strut control arm nuts and bolts.

12. Remove 8 subframe bolts. Lower the subframe.

13. Remove the 8 manifold attaching nuts and remove left exhaust manifold. Remove and discard gaskets.

14. Installation is the reverse of the removal procedure. Tighten the manifold retaining bolts in sequence to 15–22 ft. lbs. (20–30 Nm).

5.0L Engine

THUNDERBIRD AND COUGAR

1. Disconnect the negative battery cable.

2. If removing the left manifold, remove the oil dipstick tube nut and pull the bracket from the manifold stud.

3. Raise and safely support the vehicle.

4. Carefully tap upward on the dipstick tube and remove it from the vehicle.

5. If removing the left manifold, disconnect the oxygen sensor connector.

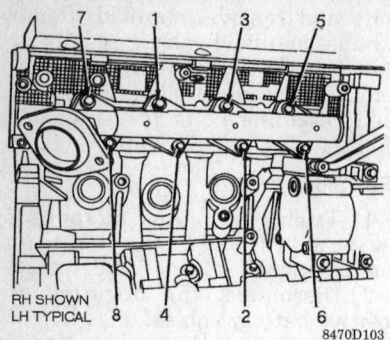

RH SHOWN
LH TYPICAL

8470D103

**Exhaust manifold bolt torque sequence —
4.6L (DOHC) engine**

6. Disconnect the exhaust manifold(s) from the exhaust pipe(s). Lower the vehicle.

7. If removing the right exhaust manifold, disconnect the electrical connector from the mass air flow sensor, located on the air cleaner assembly. Remove the air cleaner and inlet duct assembly.

8. Tag and disconnect the spark plug wires.

9. If removing the right exhaust manifold, remove the alternator rear brace and the thermactor hose assembly and EGR tube.

10. Remove the retaining bolts and remove the exhaust manifold(s) through the top of the engine compartment.

11. Installation is the reverse of the removal procedure. Clean the manifold and cylinder head mating surfaces prior to installation. Working from the center to the ends, tighten the exhaust manifold-to-cylinder head bolts to 18–24 ft. lbs. (24–32 Nm).

MUSTANG AND MARK VII

1. Disconnect the negative battery cable.

2. If removing the right exhaust manifold, remove the thermactor hardware.

3. Tag and disconnect the spark plug wires. Remove the spark plugs.

4. Raise and safely support the vehicle.

5. Disconnect the exhaust pipe(s) from the manifold(s). Lower the vehicle.

6. Remove the retaining bolts and remove the exhaust manifold(s).

7. Installation is the reverse of the removal procedure. Clean the manifold and cylinder head mating surfaces prior to installation. Working from the center to the ends, tighten the exhaust manifold attaching bolts to 18–24 ft. lbs. (24–32 Nm) on 1992 vehicles or 26–32 ft. lbs. (32–43 Nm) on 1993–96 vehicles.

Supercharger

REMOVAL AND INSTALLATION

3.8L SC Engine

NOTE: Before beginning any supercharger service, clean the area around the supercharger assembly. Cover the engine and supercharger openings while the supercharger is removed, to prevent damage by foreign material.

1. Disconnect the negative battery cable and partially drain the cooling system.

2. Remove the throttle body air inlet tube and the cowl vent screens.

3. Tag and disconnect the right side spark plug wires at the coil and position aside. Tag and disconnect the electrical connections at the idle air bypass valve, throttle position sensor and air charge temperature sensors.

4. Tag and disconnect the vacuum lines from the inlet/plenum assembly. If equipped, remove the EGR transducer from the bracket and disconnect the vacuum line. Disconnect the PCV tube.

5. Disconnect the throttle linkage at the throttle housing. Remove the linkage bracket retaining bolts and position the bracket aside. Disconnect the cruise control, if equipped.

6. Remove the 2 EGR valve attaching bolts and move the EGR valve away from the intake assembly, if equipped. Disconnect the coolant hoses from the throttle body, if equipped.

7. Remove the supercharger drive belt. Remove the charge air cooler inlet and outlet tubes as follows:

a. Disconnect the inlet tube from the supercharger outlet adapter using spanner nut wrench tool T89P–6634–A or equivalent. Remove the 4 nuts retaining the inlet and outlet tubes to the charge air cooler.

b. Remove the nut and push-on nut retaining the inlet tube to the alternator-power steering pump bracket. Remove the stud from the alternator-power steering pump bracket. Remove the inlet tube.

NOTE: Use extreme care during removal and installation of the charge air cooler tubes so as not to scratch, nick or contaminate the sealing surfaces.

c. Remove the 2 nuts retaining the outlet tube to the intake elbow assembly. Raise and safely support the vehicle.

d. Remove the bolt retaining the outlet tube to the cylinder block front upper support bracket. Loosen, but do not remove the support bracket.

NOTE: The bracket must be close to the front face of the cylinder block to allow the bracket to pivot during outlet tube reinstallation.

e. Remove the nut and push-on nut retaining the outlet tube to the alternator-power steering pump bracket. Remove the power steering pump drive belt.

f. Tag and disconnect the spark plug wires from the coil. Remove the power steering pump bracket brace to water pump retaining stud nuts. Remove 2 power steering pump bracket to cylinder head retaining bolts and 1 stud nut.

g. Install a 10 x 1.5mm x 170mm bolt, 6½ in. long into the top hole in the power steering pump bracket. Thread the bolt into the cylinder head approximately 5 turns. This will aid in holding the power steering pump bracket in position.

h. Remove the power steering pump filler cap. Slide the power steering pump bracket assembly forward on the stud and bolt that was installed in the previous step.

i. Remove the outlet tube by pulling underneath the power steering pump bracket assembly and up through the engine compartment. It may be necessary to pivot the outlet tube clamping connector to gain clearance during removal.

8. Remove the 3 intake elbow retaining bolts and the 3 supercharger retaining bolts. Lift the supercharger and intake elbow assembly from the vehicle as a unit.

To install:

9. Clean and inspect all gasket surfaces. Position a new gasket on the intake manifold using guide pins, if available.

10. Install the supercharger, throttle body and intake elbow as an assembly. Tighten the two 8mm bolts to 15–22 ft. lbs. (20–30 Nm). Tighten the 12mm bolt to 52–70 ft. lbs. (70–96 Nm).

11. Install the 3 intake elbow retaining bolts and tighten to 20–28 ft. lbs. (26–38 Nm). Install the charge air cooler tubes as follows:

a. Clean and inspect the sealing surfaces of the supercharger outlet adapter intake elbow, charge air cooler and tubes.

NOTE: Make sure there are no foreign particles on the sealing surfaces of the tubes. It is important that the charge air cooler tubes seal completely. Any air leak will cause poor operation and performance.

b. Install gasket sealant tape ESE–M4G168–B or equivalent, to the spherical seat surfaces of the charge air cooler tubes. Install the tape approximately ⅛ in. (3mm) from the inner diameter of the tubes. Overlap the tape ends approximately ¼ in. (6mm). Do not stretch the tape during installation or the seal may leak. During proper installation, a slight wrinkling will occur on the tape edge at the inner diameter.

NOTE: The system must be torqued in sequence and to the specification for that step. This is required for proper alignment of the system to ensure sealing of the charge air cooler tubes.

c. Guide the outlet tube down through the engine compartment and underneath the power steering pump bracket assembly. It may be necessary to rotate the lower outlet tube clamping connector to gain clearance.

NOTE: Use extreme care during installation of the charge air cooler tubes so as not to scratch, nick or contaminate the sealing surfaces.

d. Slide the power steering pump bracket assembly into position. Install the power steering pump bracket retaining stud nut and tighten to 30–40 ft. lbs. (40–55 Nm).

e. Remove the bolt installed in Step 7g of the removal procedure. Install the power steering pump bracket to cylinder head bolts and tighten to 30–40 ft. lbs. (40–55 Nm).

f. Install the power steering pump bracket brace to water pump retaining stud nuts and tighten to 15–22 ft. lbs. (20–30 Nm). Install the outlet tube over the lower stud on the alternator-power steering pump bracket.

g. Install the push-on nut onto the stud, tight enough to retain the tube against the alternator-power steering pump bracket surface but free enough to allow tube movement to ensure seating of the spherical seat on the outlet tube to intake elbow assembly.

h. Install the outlet tube clamping connector over the studs on the intake elbow assembly and secure with the 2 nuts. Tighten both nuts to 15–22 ft. lbs. (20–30 Nm). The clamping connector should be installed so it is visually parallel to the stud mounting face of the intake elbow assembly.

i. Install the nut to the stud on the alternator-power steering pump bracket and tighten to 30–40 ft. lbs. (40–55 Nm). Install the bolt to secure the outlet tube to the cylinder block support bracket and tighten to 30–40 ft. lbs. (40–55 Nm). Tighten the support bracket to front of cylinder block retaining nut to 15–22 ft. lbs. (20–30 Nm) and bolt to 52–70 ft. lbs. (70–96 Nm).

j. Apply anti-seize compound to the inner backside spherical seat surface and threads of the supercharger outlet adapter collar. Position the inlet tube, then install the upper stud into the alternator-power steering pump bracket.

k. Install the push-on nut onto the stud, tight enough to retain the tube against the alternator-power steering pump bracket surface but free enough to allow tube movement to ensure seating of the spherical seat on the inlet tube to supercharger outlet adapter.

l. Fully hand-tighten the supercharger outlet adapter collar onto the threaded tube end of the inlet tube assembly. Install the charge air cooler assembly to the inlet and outlet tubes. Install the nuts to the studs tight enough to retain the charge air cooler and tubes together but free enough to allow movement on the spherical seats. Do not tighten at this time.

m. Tighten the supercharger outlet adapter collar to inlet tube to 148 ft. lbs. (200 Nm).

n. Wait 10 minutes minimum and retighten the supercharger outlet collar to 148 ft. lbs. (200 Nm).

NOTE: When 1st compressed, the sealant tape flows and forms to the sealing surface. If the collar is not retightened, the torque of the collar will drop causing a leak at this joint.

o. Tighten the inlet and outlet tube to charge air cooler nuts to 15–22 ft. lbs. (20–30 Nm). The clamping connectors should be installed so they are visually parallel to the stud mounting face of the charge air cooler assembly.

p. Install the nut retaining the inlet tube to the alternator-power steering pump support bracket and tighten to 30–40 ft. lbs. (40–55 Nm).

12. Install the supercharger drive belt. Connect the coolant hoses to the throttle body, if equipped.

13. Connect the EGR valve with a new gasket to the intake manifold, if equipped. Tighten the retaining bolts to 14–22 ft. lbs. (20–30 Nm).

14. Install the throttle linkage bracket and connect the throttle linkage. Tighten to 10–15 ft. lbs. (14–20 Nm).

15. Connect the vacuum lines to the inlet assembly and connect the PCV tube. If equipped, connect the vacuum line to the EGR transducer and install the transducer in the bracket.

16. Install the right side spark plug wires. Connect the electrical connectors at the idle air bypass valve, throttle position sensor and air charge temperature sensor.

17. Install the cowl covers and the throttle body air inlet tube.

18. Fill and bleed the cooling system. Connect the negative battery cable. Start the engine and check for leaks and proper operation.

Timing Chain Front Cover

REMOVAL AND INSTALLATION

3.8L Engine

1. Disconnect the negative battery cable and drain the cooling system.

2. Remove the air cleaner assembly and air intake duct.

3. On non-supercharged engines, remove the fan/clutch assembly and shroud. On supercharged engines, remove the electric cooling fan assembly.

4. Remove the accessory drive belt idlers, drive belts and the water pump pulley.

5. Remove the power steering pump bracket retaining bolts. Leaving the hoses connected, place the pump/bracket assembly aside in a position to prevent fluid from leaking out.

6. If equipped with air conditioning, remove the compressor front support bracket but leave the compressor in place.

7. Disconnect the coolant bypass hose and heater hose at the water pump. Disconnect the upper radiator hose at the thermostat housing.

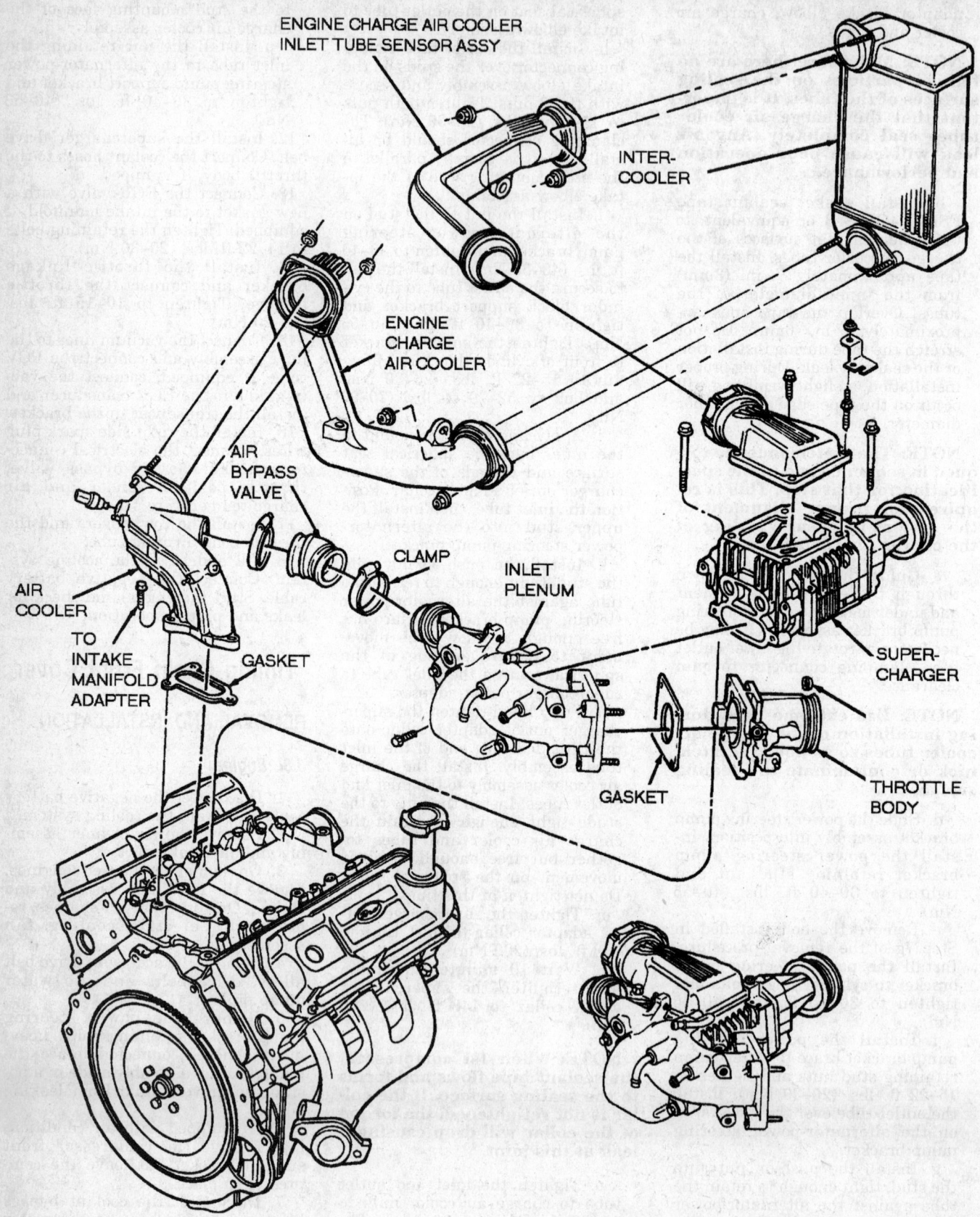

ENGINE CHARGE AIR COOLER
INLET TUBE SENSOR ASSY

INTER-
COOLER

ENGINE
CHARGE
AIR COOLER

AIR
BYPASS
VALVE

CLAMP

INLET
PLENUM

SUPER-
CHARGER

AIR
COOLER

TO
INTAKE
MANIFOLD
ADAPTER

GASKET

GASKET

THROTTLE
BODY

8470D054

Supercharger system components — 3.8L SC engine

8. On non-supercharged engines, disconnect the coil wire from the distributor cap and remove the cap with the secondary wires attached.

9. On non-supercharged engines, mark the position of the rotor in relation to the distributor housing and mark the position of the distributor housing on the front cover. Remove the distributor hold-down clamp and lift the distributor out of the front cover.

10. On supercharged engines, remove the hold-down clamp and lift the camshaft synchronizer from the front cover.

11. Raise and safely support the vehicle. Remove the crankshaft damper and pulley using a puller.

NOTE: If the crankshaft pulley and vibration damper have to be separated, mark the damper and pulley so they may be reassembled in the same relative position. This is important as the damper and pulley are initially balanced as a unit. If the crankshaft damper is being replaced, check if the original damper has balance pins installed. If so, new balance pins must be installed on the new damper in the same position as the original damper. The crankshaft pulley, new or original, must also be installed in the same relative position as originally installed.

12. Remove the oil filter. On supercharged engines, remove the oil cooler.

13. Disconnect the lower radiator hose at the water pump. Remove the oil pan.

NOTE: The front cover cannot be removed without lowering the oil pan.

14. Lower the vehicle. Remove the front cover retaining bolts. It is not necessary to remove the water pump.

NOTE: Do not overlook the cover retaining bolt located behind the oil filter adapter. The front cover will break if pried on and all retaining bolts are not removed.

15. Remove the front cover and water pump as an assembly. Remove and discard the cover gasket.

NOTE: The front cover contains the oil pump and water pump. If a new front cover is to be installed, remove the water pump and oil pump from the old front cover.

To install:

16. Clean all gasket mating surfaces. If reusing the front cover, replace the front cover oil seal.

17. Position a new gasket on the cylinder block and install the front cover using dowels for proper alignment. Install the front cover retaining bolts and tighten to 15–22 ft. lbs. (20–30 Nm).

18. Raise and safely support the vehicle. Install the oil pan. Connect the lower radiator hose and install the oil filter.

19. Coat the crankshaft damper sealing surface with clean engine oil. Apply a small amount of silicone sealer to the crankshaft keyway.

20. Position the crankshaft pulley key in the crankshaft keyway and install the damper, using a suitable installation tool.

21. Install the damper washer and retaining bolt and tighten to 103–132 ft. lbs. (140–180 Nm). Install the crankshaft pulley and tighten the retaining bolts to 20–28 ft. lbs. (26–38 Nm).

22. Lower the vehicle. Connect the coolant bypass hose.

23. On non-supercharged engines, install the distributor, aligning the marks that were made during the removal procedure. Install the distributor cap and coil wire. On supercharged engines, install the camshaft synchronizer.

24. Connect the upper radiator hose at the thermostat housing. Connect the heater hose.

25. If equipped with air conditioning, install the compressor and mounting brackets. Tighten retaining bolts to 30–45 ft. lbs. (41–61 Nm).

26. Install the power steering pump and mounting bracket. Tighten the retaining bolts to 30–45 ft. lbs. (41–61 Nm).

27. Install the water pump pulley. Position the accessory drive belts over the pulleys.

28. On non-supercharged engines, install the fan/clutch assembly and fan shroud. Cross-tighten the fan/clutch assembly retaining bolts to 12–18 ft. lbs. (16–24 Nm).

29. On supercharged engines, install the electric cooling fan assembly and connect the harness connector to the fan motor.

30. Fill the crankcase with the proper type and quantity of engine oil. Fill and bleed the cooling system. Connect the negative battery cable.

31. Start the engine and check for leaks. Check the ignition timing and curb idle speed and adjust, as necessary.

4.6L (SOHC) Engine

1. Disconnect the negative battery cable.

2. Remove the cooling fan and shroud. Loosen the water pump pulley bolts, remove the accessory drive belt and remove the water pump pulley.

3. Raise and safely support the vehicle.

4. Remove the bolts retaining the power steering pump to the engine block and cylinder front cover. The lower front bolt on the power steering pump will not come all the way out. Wire the power steering pump out of the way.

5. Remove the 4 bolts retaining the oil pan to the front cover. Remove the crankshaft damper retaining bolt and washer. Remove the damper using a puller.

6. Lower the vehicle. Remove the bolt retaining the air conditioner high pressure line to the right coil bracket.

7. Remove the front bolts and loosen the remaining bolts on the camshaft covers. Using plastic wedges or similar tools, prop up both camshaft covers. Disconnect both ignition coils and CID sensor.

8. Remove the 3 nuts retaining the right coil bracket to the front cover. Position the power steering hose out of the way.

9. Remove the 4 nuts retaining the left coil bracket to the front cover. Slide both coil brackets and ignition wires off the mounting studs and lay the assembly on top of the engine.

10. Disconnect the High Data Rate (HDR) sensor. Remove the 7 stud bolts and 4 bolts retaining the front cover to the engine and remove the front cover.

To install:

11. Inspect and replace the front cover seal as necessary and clean the sealing surfaces of the cylinder block. Apply silicone sealer to the oil pan where it meets the cylinder block and to the points where the cylinder head meets the cylinder block.

12. Install the front cover and the attaching studs and bolts. Tighten to 15–22 ft. lbs. (20–30 Nm). Connect the HDR sensor.

13. Position the coil brackets and ignition wires as an assembly onto the mounting studs. Position the power steering hose and install the 7 nuts retaining the coil brackets to the front cover. Tighten the nuts to 15–22 ft. lbs. (20–30 Nm). Connect both ignition coils and CID sensor.

14. Remove the plastic wedges holding up the camshaft covers. Ap-

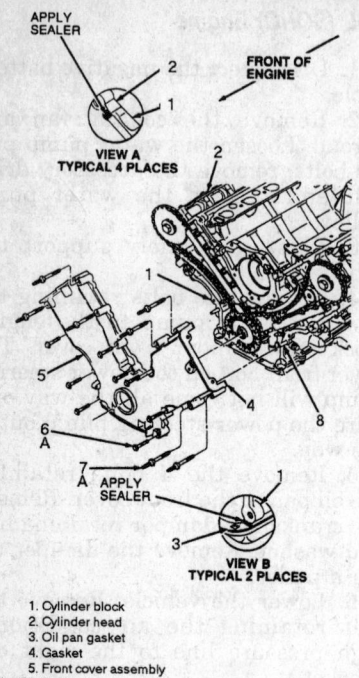

1. Cylinder block
2. Cylinder head
3. Oil pan gasket
4. Gasket
5. Front cover assembly
6A. Bolts
7A. Studs
8. Dowel

8470E034

Timing chain front cover installation — 4.6L (SOHC) engine

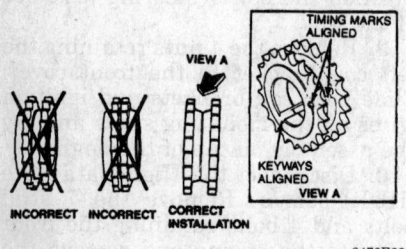

8470E035

Crankshaft sprocket positioning — 4.6L (SOHC) engine

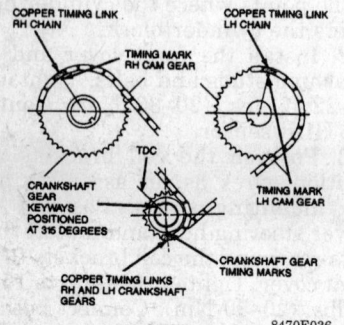

8470E036

Timing chain and sprocket alignment — 4.6L (SOHC) engine

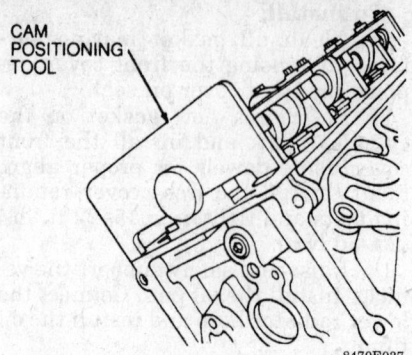

8470E037

Cam positioning tool — 4.6L (SOHC) engine

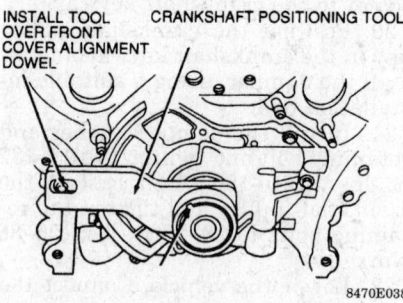

8470E038

Crankshaft positioning tool — 4.6L (SOHC) engine

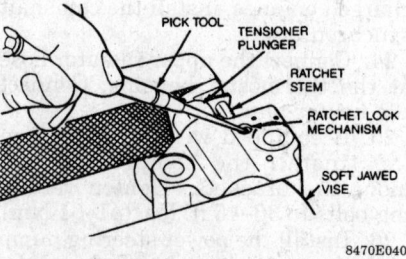

8470E040

Timing chain tensioner bleeding procedure — 4.6L (SOHC) engine

ply silicone sealer where the front cover meets the cylinder head and make sure the camshaft cover gaskets are properly positioned. Install the front retaining bolts into the camshaft cover and tighten the bolts to 6.0–8.8 ft. lbs. (8–12 Nm).

15. Position the air conditioner high pressure line on the right coil bracket and install the bolt. Raise and safely support the vehicle.

16. Apply a small amount of silicone sealer in the rear of the keyway in the damper. Position the damper on the crankshaft and install, using a

suitable installation tool. Install the damper bolt and washer and tighten to 114–121 ft. lbs. (155–165 Nm).

17. Install the 4 bolts retaining the oil pan to the front cover. Tighten to 15–22 ft. lbs. (20–30 Nm).

18. Position the power steering pump on the engine and install the 4 retaining bolts. Tighten to 15–22 ft. lbs. (20–30 Nm). Lower the vehicle.

19. Install the water pump pulley with the 4 bolts. Tighten to 15–22 ft. lbs. (20–30 Nm). Install the accessory drive belt and the cooling fan and shroud.

20. Connect the negative battery cable, start the engine and check for leaks.

4.6L (DOHC) Engine

1. Disconnect the negative battery cable and drain the cooling system.

2. Remove the windshield wiper module assembly.

3. Remove the engine appearance cover.

4. Remove coolant bypass and upper radiator hoses at coolant crossover tube. Loosen water pump pulley bolts.

5. Remove accessory drive belt. Remove water pump pulley and lower water pump to cylinder block bolt for front cover removal clearance.

6. Remove 2 bolts retaining power steering pump reservoir to left coil bracket.

7. Raise and safely support the vehicle. Using a suitable puller, remove the power steering pump pulley.

8. Remove power steering pump to engine block and cylinder front cover bolts. The front lower bolt on the power steering pump will not come all the way out. Position pump and reservoir aside.

9. Remove 4 bolts retaining oil pan to front cover. Remove the crankshaft damper bolt and washer. Using a suitable puller, remove the damper.

10. Lower the vehicle.

11. Remove front bolts and loosen valve cover bolts. Prop up valve covers with plastic wedges or equivalent devices.

12. Disconnect both ignition coils and camshaft position sensor.

13. Remove 3 right coil bracket to front cover bolts. Remove 3 nuts and 1 bolt retaining left coil bracket to front cover. Slide both coil brackets and ignition wires off mounting studs and position aside.

14. Remove accessory drive belt idler pulley. Disconnect crankshaft position sensor.

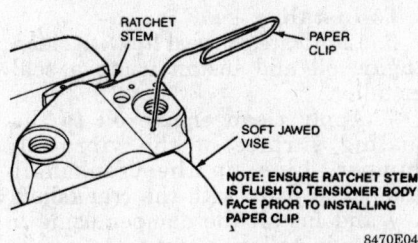

**Timing chain tensioner locking procedure —
4.6L (SOHC) engine**

15. Remove 7 studs and 8 bolts retaining front cover to engine block and remove the front cover.

To install:

16. Clean all mating surfaces. Replace front cover gasket and front cover oil seal.

17. Apply silicone sealer to six locations. Place bottom of front cover on oil pan and roll cover into place. Do not slide cover into place.

18. Attach front cover to engine. Install 7 studs and 8 bolts attaching front cover to engine block. Tighten in sequence to 15–22 ft. lbs. (20–30 Nm).

19. Connect crankshaft position sensor.

20. Install right and left coil brackets. Tighten to 15–22 ft. lbs. (20–30 Nm). Connect ignition coils and camshaft position sensor.

21. Apply silicone sealer to point where cylinder head meets front cover. Make sure camshaft cover gaskets are in proper position.

22. Remove plastic wedges and install valve covers. Tighten to 6–8.8 ft. lbs. (8–12 Nm).

23. Raise and safely support the vehicle.

24. Apply silicone sealer in keyway of damper. Install crankshaft damper and tighten bolt to 114–121 ft. lbs. (155–165 Nm).

25. Install 4 oil pan to front cover bolts. Tighten to 15–22 ft. lbs. (20–30 Nm).

26. Install power steering pump and tighten retaining bolts to 15–22 ft. lbs. (20–30 Nm). Install power steering pump pulley and lower the vehicle.

27. Install water pump lower bolt. Tighten to 15–22 ft. lbs. (20–30 Nm). Install water pump pulley and accessory drive belt.

28. Install air cleaner outlet tube and resonator. Install engine appearance cover.

29. Fill the crankcase with the proper type and quantity of engine oil. Fill and bleed the cooling system. Connect the negative battery cable.

30. Start the engine and check for leaks.

5.0L Engine

1. Disconnect the negative battery cable.

2. Drain the cooling system. Remove the air inlet tube, if equipped.

3. On Thunderbird and Cougar, disconnect the upper radiator hose at the engine.

4. On all except Thunderbird and Cougar, remove the fan shroud attaching bolts and position the shroud over the fan. Remove the fan and clutch assembly from the water pump shaft and remove the shroud.

5. On Thunderbird and Cougar, remove the fan and clutch assembly from the water pump shaft using fan clutch holding tool T84T–6312–C or equivalent, and fan clutch nut wrench T84T–6312–D or equivalent, and position the fan and clutch assembly in the fan shroud. The nut is turned counterclockwise. Remove the fan shroud and fan/clutch as an assembly.

6. Loosen the water pump pulley bolts. Rotate the tensioner away from the accessory drive belt and remove

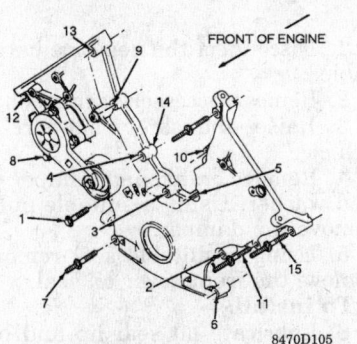

**Front cover bolt torque sequence —
4.6L (DOHC) engine**

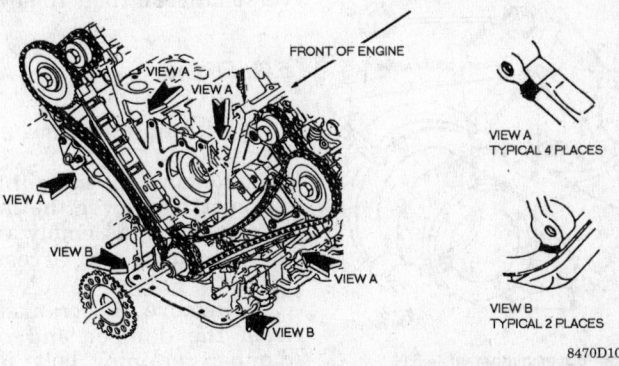

Front cover sealer points — 4.6L (DOHC) engine

the belt. Remove the water pump pulley.

7. Remove all accessory brackets that attach to the water pump.

8. Disconnect the lower radiator hose, heater hose and water pump bypass hose at the water pump.

9. Remove the crankshaft pulley from the crankshaft vibration damper. Remove the damper attaching bolt and washer and remove the damper using a puller.

10. Remove the oil pan-to-front cover attaching bolts. Use a thin blade knife to cut the oil pan gasket flush with the cylinder block face prior to separating the cover from the cylinder block.

11. Remove the cylinder front cover and water pump as an assembly.

NOTE: Cover the front oil pan opening while the cover assembly is off to prevent foreign material from entering the pan.

To install:

12. If a new front cover is to be installed, remove the water pump from the old front cover and install it on the new front cover.

13. Clean all gasket mating surfaces. Pry the old oil seal from the front cover and install a new 1, using a seal installer.

14. Coat the gasket surface of the oil pan with sealer, cut and position the required sections of a new gasket on the oil pan and apply silicone sealer at the corners. Apply sealer to a new front cover gasket and install on the block.

15. Position the front cover on the cylinder block. Use care to avoid seal damage or gasket mislocation. It may be necessary to force the cover downward to slightly compress the pan gasket. Use front cover aligner tool T61P–6019–B or equivalent to assist the operation.

16. Coat the threads of the front cover attaching screws with pipe sealant and install. While pushing in

on the alignment tool, tighten the oil pan to cover attaching screws to 9–12 ft. lbs. (12–16 Nm).

17. Tighten the front cover to cylinder block attaching bolts to 12–18 ft. lbs. (16–24 Nm). Remove the alignment tool.

18. Apply multi-purpose grease to the sealing surface of the vibration damper. Apply silicone sealer to the keyway of the vibration damper.

19. Line up the vibration damper keyway with the crankshaft key and install the damper using a suitable installation tool. Tighten the retaining bolt to 70–90 ft. lbs. (95–122 Nm). Install the crankshaft pulley.

20. Install the remaining components in the reverse order of their removal.

21. Fill the crankcase with the proper type and quantity of engine oil. Fill and bleed the cooling system.

22. Connect the negative battery cable, start the engine and check for leaks.

Front Cover Oil Seal

REPLACEMENT

3.8L Engine

1. Disconnect the negative battery cable.

2. On non-supercharged engines, remove the fan shroud and position it back over the fan. Remove the fan/clutch assembly and shroud.

3. On supercharged engines, disconnect the electric cooling fan connector and remove the fan assembly.

4. Loosen the accessory drive belt idlers. Raise and safely support the vehicle.

5. Disengage the drive belts and remove the crankshaft pulley. On su-

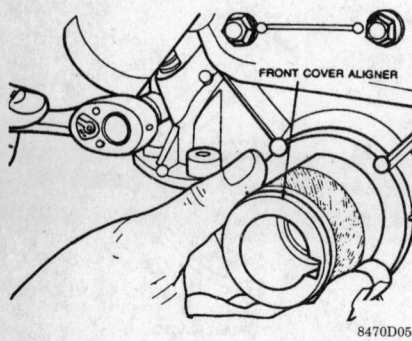

8470D055

Timing chain front cover alignment — 5.0L engine

percharged engines, remove the upper and lower crankshaft shields.

6. Remove the crankshaft damper retaining bolt and remove the damper using a puller.

7. Using a small prybar, remove the seal from the front cover. Use care to prevent damage to the cover and crankshaft.

To install:

8. Inspect the front cover and crankshaft damper for damage, nicks, burrs or other roughness which may cause the seal to fail. Service or replace components as necessary.

9. Lubricate the seal lip using clean engine oil. Install the seal using a suitable seal installer.

10. Lubricate the seal surface on the damper with clean engine oil. Install the damper using a suitable installation tool.

11. Install the damper retaining bolt and tighten to 103–132 ft. lbs. (140–180 Nm). Install the crankshaft pulley and tighten the retaining bolts to 20–28 ft. lbs. (26–38 Nm).

12. Install the remaining components in the reverse order of their removal. Connect the negative battery cable, start the engine and check for leaks.

4.6L Engine

1. Disconnect the negative battery cable.

2. Remove accessory drive belt.

3. Raise and safely support the vehicle.

4. Remove crankshaft damper bolt and washer. Using a suitable puller, remove the damper.

5. Using a suitable seal remover, remove the front cover oil seal.

To install:

6. Lubricate oil seal lip and bore with clean engine oil. Install seal with a suitable seal installer. Install the remaining components in the reverse order of their removal.

5.0L Engine

1. Disconnect the negative battery cable.

2. Remove the fan shroud and position it back over the fan. Remove the fan/clutch assembly and shroud.

3. Remove the accessory drive belts.

4. Remove the crankshaft pulley from the damper and remove the damper retaining bolt. Remove the damper using a puller.

5. Remove the seal using a seal removal tool.

To install:

6. Lubricate the seal lip with clean engine oil and install using a seal installer.

7. Apply clean engine oil to the sealing surface of the vibration damper. Line up the crankshaft damper keyway with the crankshaft key and install the damper using a damper installation tool.

8. Install the damper retaining bolt and tighten to 70–90 ft. lbs. (95–122 Nm).

9. Install the remaining components in the reverse order of their removal.

Timing Chain and Sprockets

REMOVAL AND INSTALLATION

3.8L Engine

1. Disconnect the negative battery cable and drain the cooling system.

2. Remove the air cleaner assembly and air intake duct.

3. On non-supercharged engines, remove the fan/clutch assembly and shroud. On supercharged engines, remove the electric cooling fan assembly.

4. Remove the accessory drive belt idlers, drive belts and the water pump pulley.

5. Remove the power steering pump bracket retaining bolts. Leaving the hoses connected, place the pump/bracket assembly aside in a position to prevent fluid from leaking out.

6. If equipped with air conditioning, remove the compressor front support bracket but leave the compressor in place.

7. Disconnect the coolant bypass hose and heater hose at the water pump. Disconnect the upper radiator hose at the thermostat housing.

8. On non-supercharged engines, disconnect the coil wire from the distributor cap and remove the cap with the secondary wires attached.

9. On non-supercharged engines, remove the distributor hold-down clamp and lift the distributor out of the front cover.

10. On supercharged engines, remove the hold-down clamp and lift the camshaft synchronizer from the front cover.

11. Raise and safely support the vehicle. Remove the crankshaft damper and pulley using a puller.

NOTE: If the crankshaft pulley and vibration damper have to be separated, mark the damper and pulley so they may be reassembled in the same relative position. This is important as the damper and pulley are initially balanced as a unit. If the crankshaft damper is being replaced, check if the original damper has balance pins installed. If so, new balance pins must be installed on the new damper in the same position as the original damper. The crankshaft pulley, new or original, must also be installed in the same relative position as originally installed.

12. Remove the oil filter. On supercharged engines, remove the oil cooler.

13. Disconnect the lower radiator hose at the water pump. Remove the oil pan.

NOTE: The front cover cannot be removed without lowering the oil pan.

14. Lower the vehicle. Remove the front cover retaining bolts. It is not necessary to remove the water pump.

NOTE: Do not overlook the cover retaining bolt located behind the oil filter adapter. The front cover will break if pried on and all retaining bolts are not removed.

15. Remove the front cover and water pump as an assembly. Remove and discard the cover gasket.

NOTE: The front cover contains the oil pump and water pump. If a new front cover is to be installed, remove the water pump and oil pump from the old front cover.

16. Remove the camshaft bolt and washer from the end of the camshaft.

17. Remove the distributor drive gear, camshaft sprocket, crankshaft sprocket and timing chain.

NOTE: If the crankshaft sprocket is difficult to remove, pry the sprocket off the shaft using a pair of large prybars positioned on both sides of the sprocket.

To install:

18. Clean all gasket mating surfaces. If reusing the front cover, replace the front cover oil seal.

19. Rotate the crankshaft to position the No. 1 piston at TDC and the crankshaft keyway at the 12 o'clock position.

20. Lubricate the timing chain with engine oil.

21. Install the camshaft sprocket, crankshaft sprocket and timing chain. Make sure the timing marks align.

22. Install the distributor drive gear. Install the bolt and washer assembly on the end of the camshaft and tighten to 30–37 ft. lbs. (40–50 Nm).

23. Position a new gasket on the cylinder block and install the front cover using dowels for proper alignment. Install the front cover retaining bolts and tighten to 15–22 ft. lbs. (20–30 Nm).

24. Raise and safely support the vehicle. Install the oil pan. Connect the lower radiator hose and install the oil filter.

25. Coat the crankshaft damper sealing surface with clean engine oil. Apply a small amount of silicone sealer to the crankshaft keyway.

26. Position the crankshaft pulley key in the crankshaft keyway and install the damper, using a suitable installation tool.

27. Install the damper washer and retaining bolt and tighten to 103–132 ft. lbs. (140–180 Nm). Install the crankshaft pulley and tighten the retaining bolts to 20–28 ft. lbs. (26–38 Nm).

28. Lower the vehicle. Connect the coolant bypass hose.

29. On non-supercharged engines, install the distributor with the rotor pointing at the No. 1 distributor cap tower. Install the distributor cap and coil wire. On supercharged engines, install the camshaft synchronizer.

30. Connect the upper radiator hose at the thermostat housing. Connect the heater hose.

31. If equipped with air conditioning, install the compressor and mounting brackets. Tighten retaining bolts to 30–45 ft. lbs. (41–61 Nm).

32. Install the power steering pump and mounting bracket. Tighten the retaining bolts to 30–45 ft. lbs. (41–61 Nm).

33. Install the water pump pulley. Position the accessory drive belts over the pulleys.

34. On non-supercharged engines, install the fan/clutch assembly and fan shroud. Cross-tighten the fan/clutch assembly retaining bolts to 12–18 ft. lbs. (16–24 Nm).

35. On supercharged engines, install the electric cooling fan assembly

and connect the harness connector to the fan motor.

36. Fill the crankcase with the proper type and quantity of engine oil. Fill and bleed the cooling system. Connect the negative battery cable.

37. Start the engine and check for leaks. Check the ignition timing and curb idle speed and adjust, as necessary.

4.6L (SOHC) Engine

NOTE: This is not a free wheeling engine. If it has "jumped time" there will be damage to the valves and/or pistons and will require the removal of the cylinder heads.

1. Disconnect the negative battery cable.

2. Remove the camshaft covers and the timing chain front cover.

3. Remove the High Data Rate (HDR) wheel.

4. Rotate the engine to set the No. 1 piston at TDC on the compression stroke.

5. Install cam positioning tools T91P–6256–A or equivalent, on the flats of the camshaft. This will prevent accidental rotation of the camshafts.

6. Remove the 2 bolts retaining the right tensioner to the cylinder head and remove the tensioner. Remove the right tensioner arm.

7. Remove the 2 bolts retaining the right chain guide to the cylinder head and remove the chain guide. Remove the right chain and right crankshaft sprocket. Remove the right camshaft sprocket retaining bolt, washer, sprocket and spacer.

NOTE: Cam positioning tools T91P–6256–A or equivalent, must be installed on the camshaft to prevent the camshaft from rotating.

8. Remove the 2 bolts retaining the left tensioner to the cylinder head and remove the tensioner. Remove the left tensioner arm.

9. Remove the 2 bolts retaining the left chain guide to the cylinder head and remove the chain guide. Remove the left chain and left crankshaft sprocket. Remove the left camshaft sprocket retaining bolt, washer, sprocket and spacer.

NOTE: Cam positioning tools T91P–6256–A or equivalent, must be installed on the camshaft to prevent the camshaft from rotating.

10. Inspect the friction material on the tensioner arms and chain guides.

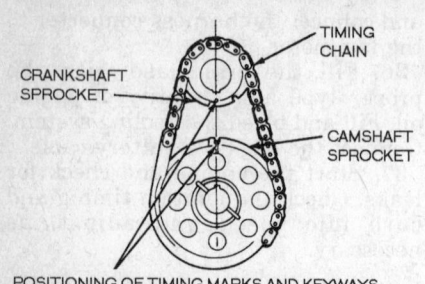

POSITIONING OF TIMING MARKS AND KEYWAYS IN CAMSHAFT AND CRANKSHAFT SPROCKETS MUST BE IN LINE AS SHOWN WITH NO. 1 PISTON AT TOP DEAD CENTER FIRING.

8470D056

Timing chain sprocket alignment — 3.8L engine

If worn or damaged, remove and clean the oil pan and replace the oil pickup tube.

NOTE: At no time, when the timing chains are removed and the cylinder heads are installed, may the crankshaft and/or camshafts be rotated. Failure to follow these directions will result in valve and/or piston damage.

To install:

11. Make sure cam positioning tools T91P–6256–A or equivalent, are installed on the camshafts to prevent them from rotating.

12. Position the camshaft spacers and sprockets on the camshafts and install the washers and retaining bolts. Tighten the retaining bolts to 81–96 ft. lbs. (110–130 Nm).

13. Install the left crankshaft sprocket with the tapered part of the sprocket facing away from the engine block.

NOTE: The crankshaft sprockets are identical. They may only be installed one way, with the tapered part of the sprocket facing each other.

14. Install the left timing chain on the camshaft and crankshaft sprockets. Make sure the copper links of the chain line up with the timing marks of the sprockets.

NOTE: If the copper links of the timing chain are not visible, pull the chain taught until the opposite sides of the chain contact one another and lay it on a flat surface. Mark the links at each end of the chain and use them in place of the copper links.

15. Install the right crankshaft sprocket with the tapered part of the sprocket facing the left crankshaft sprocket.

16. Install the right timing chain on the camshaft and crankshaft sprockets. Make sure the copper links of the chain line up with the timing marks of the sprockets.

17. It is necessary to bleed the timing chain tensioners before installation. Proceed as follows:

a. Position the timing chain tensioner in a soft-jawed vice.

b. Using a small pick or similar tool, hold the ratchet lock mechanism away from the ratchet stem and slowly compress the tensioner plunger by rotating the vise handle.

NOTE: The tensioner must be compressed slowly or damage to the internal seals will result.

c. Once the tensioner plunger bottoms in the tensioner bore, continue to hold the ratchet lock mechanism and push down on the ratchet stem until flush with the tensioner face.

d. While holding the ratchet stem flush to the tensioner face, release the ratchet lock mechanism and install a paper clip or similar tool in the tensioner body to lock the tensioner in the collapsed position.

e. The paper clip must not be removed until the timing chain, tensioner, tensioner arm and timing chain guide are completely installed on the engine.

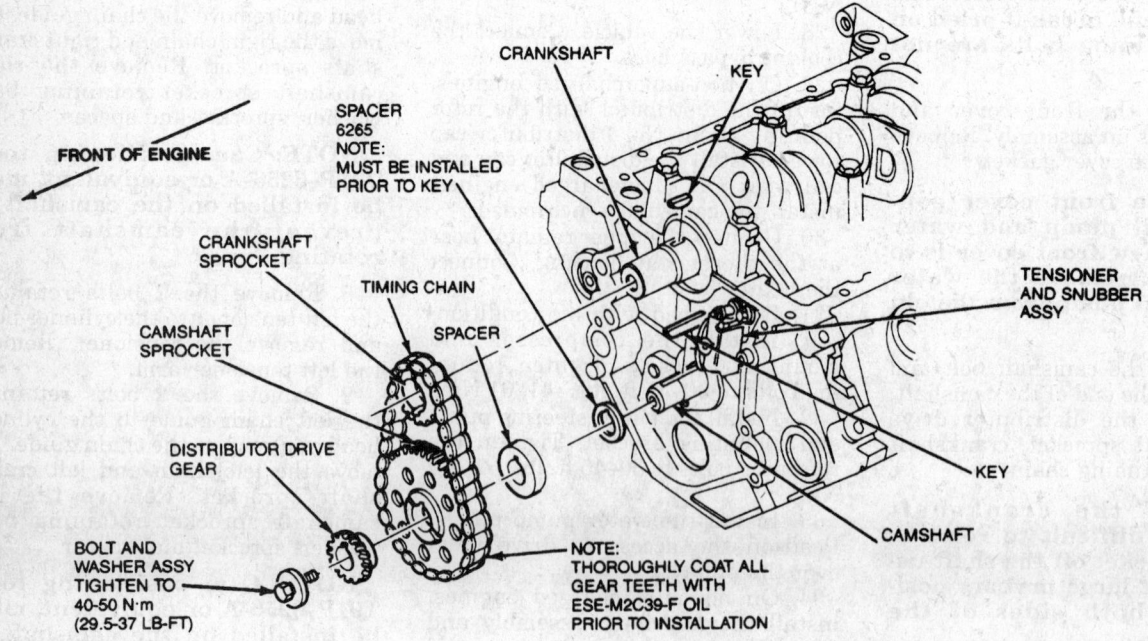

FRONT OF ENGINE

CRANKSHAFT

KEY

SPACER 6265 NOTE: MUST BE INSTALLED PRIOR TO KEY

CRANKSHAFT SPROCKET

TIMING CHAIN

SPACER

TENSIONER AND SNUBBER ASSY

CAMSHAFT SPROCKET

DISTRIBUTOR DRIVE GEAR

KEY

CAMSHAFT

BOLT AND WASHER ASSY TIGHTEN TO 40-50 N·m (29.5-37 LB-FT)

NOTE: THOROUGHLY COAT ALL GEAR TEETH WITH ESE-M2C39-F OIL PRIOR TO INSTALLATION

8470D058

Timing chain and sprockets installation — 3.8L engine

18. Lubricate the tensioner arm contact surfaces with engine oil and install the right and left tensioner arms on their dowels.

19. Install the right and left timing chain tensioners and secure with 2 bolts on each. Tighten the bolts to 15–22 ft. lbs. (20–30 Nm).

20. Install the right and left timing chain guides and secure with 2 bolts on each. Tighten the bolts to 6.0–8.8 ft. lbs. (8–12 Nm).

21. Remove the paper clips from the timing chain tensioners and make sure all timing marks are aligned.

22. Remove the camshaft positioning tools.

23. Installation of the remaining components is the reverse of removal.

24. Connect the negative battery cable, start the engine and check for leaks and proper operation.

4.6L (DOHC) Engine

NOTE: Because the 4.6L engine is not free wheeling, damage to the valves and pistons may occur if the timing chain is out of alignment.

1. Disconnect the negative battery cable and drain the cooling system.

2. Remove the timing chain front cover.

3. Remove the crankshaft position sensor tooth wheel. Rotate the engine to No. 1 TDC.

4. Install camshaft positioning tool T93P-6256-A, or equivalent, in rear D-slots of camshafts. Remove 2 bolts retaining right tensioner to cylinder head and remove tensioner.

5. Remove bolt retaining right tensioner arm and remove right tensioner arm.

6. Remove bolt retaining right chain guide and remove right chain guide. Note the location of the longer bolts which retain the chain guide to the cylinder head.

7. Remove right chain from camshaft and crankshaft gears. Install camshaft torquing tool at center area of camshafts.

NOTE: Camshaft positioning tool must be installed to prevent the camshafts from rotating.

8. Remove cam sprocket retaining bolts. Compress secondary chain tensioners and remove secondary timing chain and sprockets.

——— WARNING ———
Secondary chain tensioner plunger is spring loaded. Care must be taken to prevent plunger from dropping out of the tensioner during disassembly.

9. Remove 2 bolts retaining left tensioner to cylinder head and remove tensioner.

10. Remove bolt retaining left tensioner arm and remove left tensioner arm.

11. Remove bolt retaining left chain guide and remove left chain guide.

12. Remove left chain from camshaft and crankshaft gears. Install camshaft torquing tool at center area of camshafts.

NOTE: Camshaft positioning tool must be installed to prevent the camshafts from rotating.

13. Remove cam sprocket retaining bolts. Compress secondary chain tensioners and remove secondary timing chain and sprockets.

——— WARNING ———
Secondary chain tensioner plunger is spring loaded. Care must be taken to prevent plunger from dropping out of the tensioner during disassembly.

14. Inspect friction material on tensioner arms and chain guides. If worn or damaged, remove and clean oil pan and oil pickup tube.

To install:

15. Install left secondary tensioner. Tighten bolts to 6–9 ft. lbs. (8–12 Nm). Install secondary sprockets and chain as an assembly. Note direction of hubs.

16. Install left primary camshaft sprocket and spacer on left camshaft.

17. Install washers and camshaft sprocket retaining bolts. Hand-tighten bolts.

NOTE: Secondary sprockets must be free to turn.

18. Install secondary chain tensioning tool on left secondary tensioner.

19. If removed, install camshaft positioning tool T93P-6256-A, or equivalent, into D-slots. Install camshaft torquing tool at center area of camshafts. Tighten camshaft sprocket bolts to 81–96 ft. lbs. (110–130 Nm). Do not remove camshaft positioning tool.

20. Repeat steps 14 through 18 for the right side.

21. Install left crankshaft sprocket. Make sure tapered part of sprocket faces away from engine block.

22. Install primary timing chain on left primary camshaft sprocket. Make sure copper link of chain aligns with the timing mark on the camshaft sprocket.

23. Install primary timing chain on crankshaft sprocket. Make sure copper link of chain aligns with the timing mark on the crankshaft sprocket. Make sure tapered part of sprocket faces toward engine block.

24. Repeat steps 20 through 22 for right primary timing chain.

25. Install right and left chain guides. Tighten bolts to 15–22 ft. lbs. (20–30 Nm).

26. Lubricate tensioner arm contact surfaces with clean engine oil and install right and left tensioner arms and tighten bolts to 7–11 ft. lbs. (10–15 Nm). Do not remove tensioner locking pins until timing chain guides are installed.

27. Install right and left timing chain tensioners. Tighten 2 bolts on each tensioner to 15–22 ft. lbs. (20–30 Nm).

28. Remove locking pins from timing chain tensioners and make sure all timing marks are aligned. Remove camshaft positioning tool.

29. Install the remaining parts and fill the crankcase with the proper type and quantity of engine oil. Fill and bleed the cooling system. Connect the negative battery cable.

30. Start the engine and check for leaks. Check the ignition timing and curb idle speed and adjust, as necessary.

5.0L Engine

1. Disconnect the negative battery cable and drain the cooling system.

2. Remove the timing chain front cover.

3. Rotate the crankshaft until the timing marks on the sprockets are aligned.

4. Remove the camshaft retaining bolt, washer and eccentric, if equipped. Slide both sprockets and the timing chain forward and remove them as an assembly.

To install:

5. Position the sprockets and timing chain on the camshaft and crankshaft simultaneously. Make sure the timing marks on the sprockets are aligned.

6. Install the washer, eccentric if equipped, and camshaft sprocket retaining bolt. Tighten the bolt to 40–45 ft. lbs. (54–61 Nm).

7. Install the timing chain front cover and remaining components.

8. Fill and bleed the cooling system. Connect the negative battery cable, start the engine and check for leaks.

9. Check and adjust the ignition timing and idle speed, as necessary.

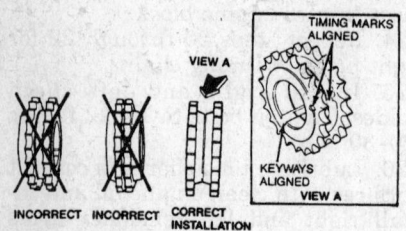

Crankshaft sprocket alignment — 4.6L engine

Timing Belt Front Cover

REMOVAL AND INSTALLATION

2.3L Engine

1. Disconnect the negative battery cable and drain the cooling system. Remove the 4 water pump pulley bolts.

2. Remove the automatic belt tensioner and accessory drive belt. Remove the upper radiator hose.

3. Remove the crankshaft pulley bolt and pulley. Remove the thermostat housing and gasket.

4. Remove the timing belt outer cover retaining bolt(s). Release the cover interlocking tabs, if equipped, and remove the cover.

To install:

5. Position the timing belt front cover. Snap the interlocking tabs into place, if necessary. Install the timing belt outer cover retaining bolt(s) and tighten to 71–106 inch lbs. (8–12 Nm).

6. Install the thermostat housing and a new gasket. Install the upper radiator hose.

7. Install the crankshaft pulley and retaining bolt. Tighten to 114–151 ft. lbs. (155–205 Nm) on 1992–93 vehicles.

8. Install the water pump pulley and the automatic belt tensioner. Install the accessory drive belt.

9. Connect the negative battery cable, start the engine and check for leaks.

OIL SEAL REPLACEMENT

2.3L Engine

1. Disconnect the negative battery cable.

2. Remove the timing belt front cover and timing belt.

3. Use a suitable puller to remove the crankshaft, camshaft and auxiliary shaft sprockets, as necessary.

4. Use seal remover tool T74P-6700-B or equivalent, to remove the crankshaft, camshaft and auxiliary shaft seals, as necessary. Position the tool so the jaws are gripping the thin edge of the seal. Operate the jackscrew on the tool to remove the seal.

To install:

5. Lubricate the lips of the new seal(s) with clean engine oil.

6. Use seal replacer tool T74P-6150-A or equivalent, to install the seal(s).

7. Install the crankshaft, camshaft and auxiliary shaft sprockets, as necessary. Tighten the camshaft sprocket retaining bolt to 52–70 ft. lbs. (70–96 Nm) and the auxiliary sprocket retaining bolt to 30–41 ft. lbs. (40–55 Nm).

8. Install the timing belt and timing belt front cover.

9. Connect the negative battery cable, start the engine and check for leaks.

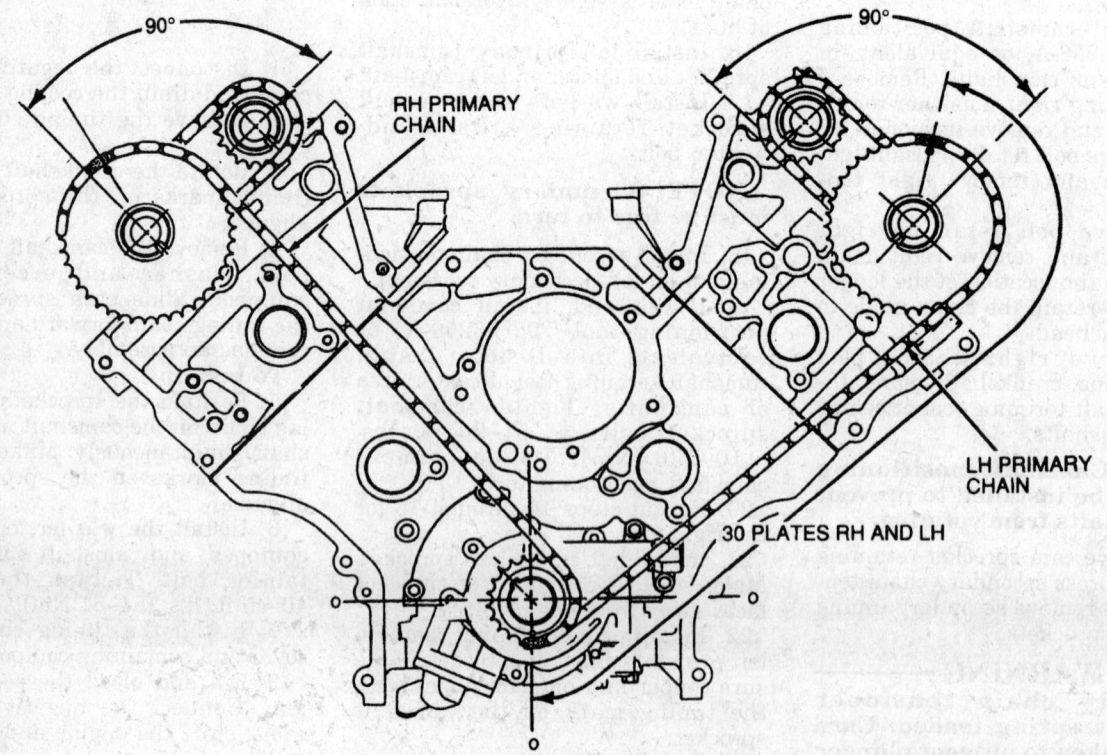

Timing chain alignment to TDC — 4.6L (DOHC) engine

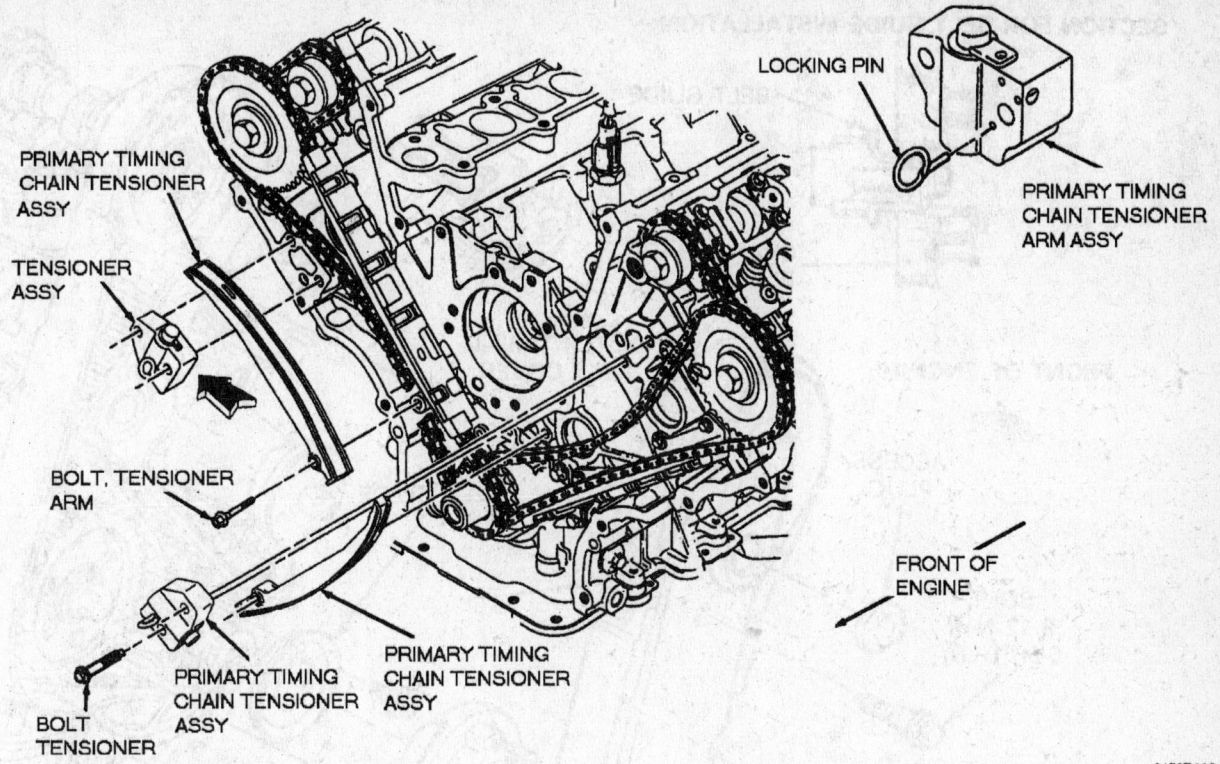

Timing chain tensioner installation — 4.6L (DOHC) engine

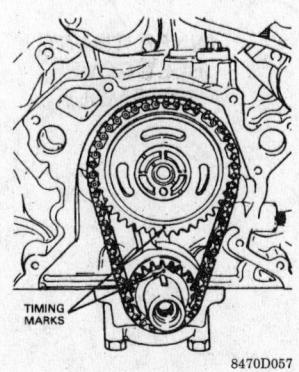

Timing chain sprocket
alignment — 5.0L engine

Timing Belt and Tensioner

REMOVAL AND INSTALLATION

2.3L Engine

1. Disconnect the negative battery cable.
2. Remove the timing belt front cover.
3. Loosen the belt tensioner adjustment screw, position belt tensioner tool T74P-6254-A or equivalent, on the tension spring roll pin and release the belt tensioner.

Tighten the adjustment screw to hold the tensioner in the released position.

4. On 1992–93 vehicles, remove the bolts holding the timing sensor in place and pull the sensor assembly free of the dowel pin.

5. Remove the crankshaft pulley, hub and belt guide. Remove the timing belt. If the belt is to be reused, mark the direction of rotation so it may be reinstalled in the same direction.

To install:

6. Position the crankshaft sprocket to align with the TDC mark and the camshaft sprocket to align with the camshaft timing pointer.

7. Install the timing belt over the crankshaft sprocket and then counterclockwise over the auxiliary and camshaft sprockets. Align the belt fore-and-aft on the sprockets.

8. Loosen the tensioner adjustment bolt to allow the tensioner to move against the belt. If the spring does not have enough tension to move the roller against the belt, it may be necessary to manually push the roller against the belt and tighten the bolt.

9. To make sure the belt does not jump time during rotation in Step 10, remove a spark plug from each cylinder.

10. Rotate the crankshaft 2 complete turns in the direction of normal rotation to remove the slack from the belt. Tighten the tensioner adjustment to 29–40 ft. lbs. (40–55 Nm) and pivot bolts to 14–22 ft. lbs. (20–30 Nm). Check the alignment of the timing marks.

11. Install the crankshaft belt guide.

12. On 1992–93 vehicles, proceed as follows:

a. Install the timing sensor onto the dowel pin and tighten the 2 longer bolts to 14–22 ft. lbs. (20–30 Nm).

b. Rotate the crankshaft 45 degrees counterclockwise and install the crankshaft pulley and hub assembly. Tighten the bolt to 114–151 ft. lbs. (155–205 Nm).

c. Rotate the crankshaft 90 degrees clockwise so the vane of the crankshaft pulley engages with timing sensor positioner tool T89P-6316-A or equivalent. Tighten the 2 shorter sensor bolts to 14–22 ft. lbs. (20–30 Nm).

d. Rotate the crankshaft 90 degrees counterclockwise and remove the sensor positioner tool.

e. Rotate the crankshaft 90 degrees clockwise and measure the outer vane to sensor air gap. The air gap must be 0.018–0.039 in. (0.458–0.996mm).

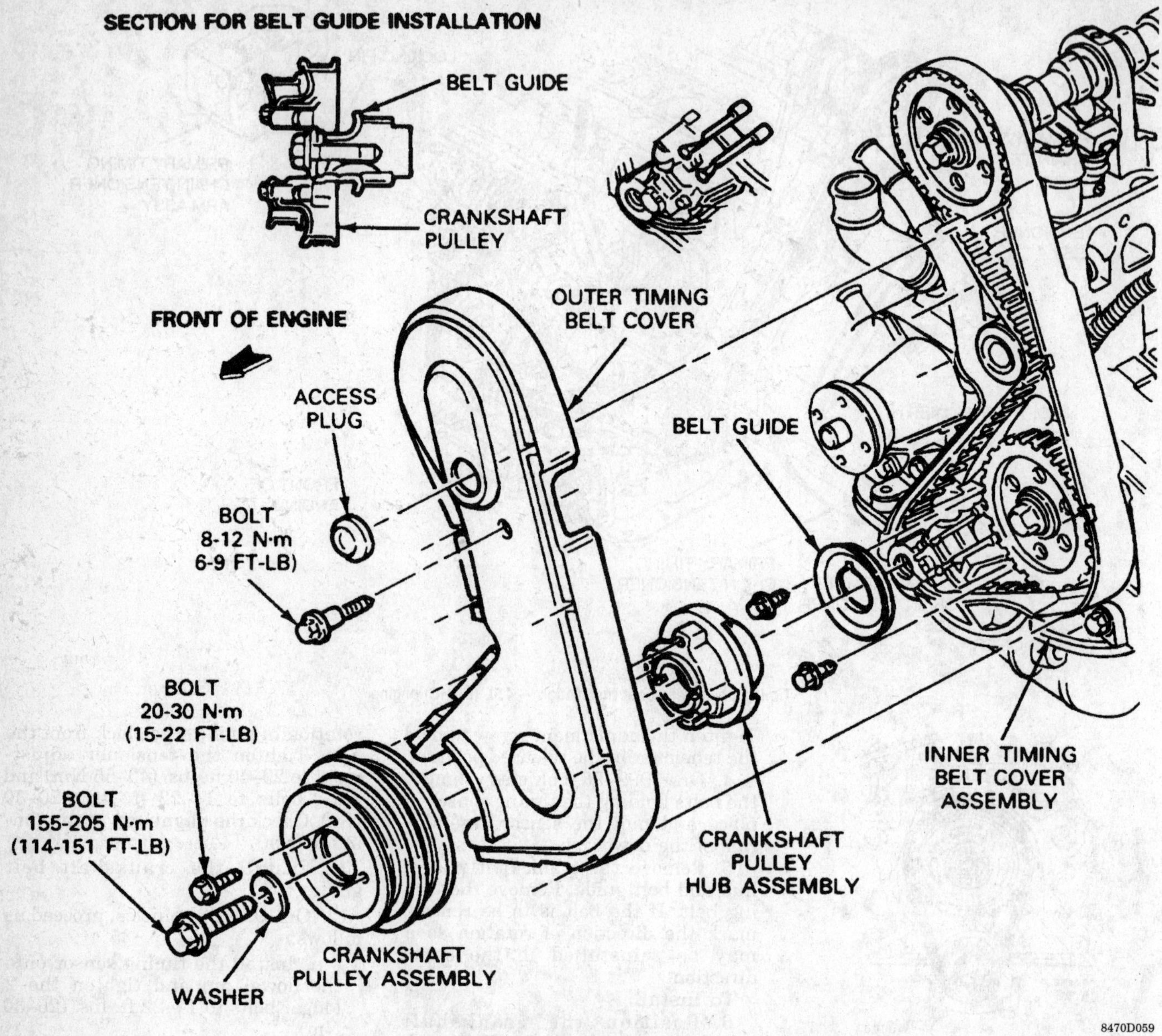

SECTION FOR BELT GUIDE INSTALLATION

BELT GUIDE

CRANKSHAFT PULLEY

FRONT OF ENGINE

ACCESS PLUG

BOLT
8-12 N·m
6-9 FT-LB)

BOLT
20-30 N·m
(15-22 FT-LB)

BOLT
155-205 N·m
(114-151 FT-LB)

WASHER

CRANKSHAFT
PULLEY ASSEMBLY

OUTER TIMING
BELT COVER

BELT GUIDE

CRANKSHAFT
PULLEY
HUB ASSEMBLY

INNER TIMING
BELT COVER
ASSEMBLY

8470D059

Timing belt front cover installation — 2.3L engine

13. Install the timing belt front cover, spark plugs and remaining components.

14. Connect the negative battery cable, start the engine and check the ignition timing.

Timing Sprockets

REMOVAL AND INSTALLATION

2.3L Engine

1. Disconnect the negative battery cable.

2. Remove the timing belt front cover and the timing belt.

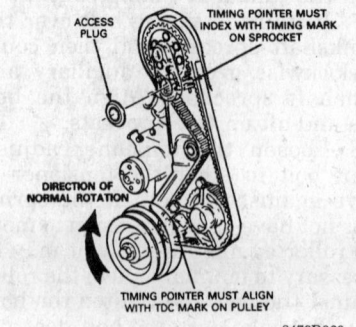

ACCESS PLUG

TIMING POINTER MUST INDEX WITH TIMING MARK ON SPROCKET

DIRECTION OF NORMAL ROTATION

TIMING POINTER MUST ALIGN WITH TDC MARK ON PULLEY

8470D060

Timing belt and sprockets positioning — 2.3L engine

3. Remove the camshaft and auxiliary shaft sprocket retaining bolts. Remove the crankshaft, camshaft and auxiliary shaft sprockets using suitable pullers.

To install:

4. Install the crankshaft, camshaft and auxiliary shaft sprockets. Tighten the camshaft sprocket retaining bolt to 52–70 ft. lbs. (70–96 Nm) and the auxiliary sprocket retaining bolt to 30–41 ft. lbs. (40–55 Nm).

5. Install the timing belt and timing belt front cover.

6. Connect the negative battery cable.

Camshaft

REMOVAL AND INSTALLATION

2.3L Engine

1. Disconnect the negative battery cable and drain the cooling system.
2. Remove the air intake and the throttle body.
3. Disconnect the radiator hoses. Remove the cooling fan, shroud and radiator assembly.
4. Tag and disconnect the spark plug wires and position aside.
5. Tag and disconnect the necessary electrical connectors and vacuum lines and position aside.
6. Remove the rocker cover retaining bolts and the rocker cover.
7. Remove the timing belt front cover and the timing belt.
8. Compress the valve springs using valve spring compressor lever T88T–6565–BH or equivalent and remove the cam followers.
9. Remove the camshaft sprocket retaining bolt. Remove the camshaft sprocket using a suitable puller. Remove the camshaft seal using a seal removal tool.
10. Remove the 2 screws and the camshaft rear retainer.
11. Raise and safely support the vehicle. Remove the right and left engine support bolts and nuts.
12. Position a block of wood and a jack under the engine. Raise the engine as high as it will go. Place blocks of wood between the engine mounts and chassis brackets and remove the jack.
13. Lower the vehicle and remove the camshaft.

To install:

14. Make sure the threaded plug is in the rear of the camshaft. If not, remove the plug from the old camshaft and install.
15. Coat the camshaft lobes with multi-purpose grease and lubricate the journals with heavy engine oil before installation. Carefully slide the camshaft through the bearings.
16. Install the camshaft rear retainer and tighten the 2 screws to 6–9 ft. lbs. (8–12 Nm). Install a new camshaft seal using a suitable seal installer.
17. Install the camshaft sprocket and tighten the retaining bolt to 52–70 ft. lbs. (70–96 Nm).
18. Install the timing belt and timing belt front cover.

19. Raise and safely support the vehicle. Position a block of wood and a jack and raise the engine. Remove the blocks of wood, lower the engine and remove the jack.
20. Install the engine support bolts and nuts and lower the vehicle.
21. Install the remaining components in the reverse order of removal.
22. Connect the negative battery cable, start the engine and check for leaks. Check the ignition timing, if necessary.

3.8L and 5.0L Engines

1. Disconnect the negative battery cable and drain the cooling system.
2. Relieve the fuel system pressure and discharge the air conditioning system.
3. Remove the radiator. If equipped with air conditioning, remove the condenser.
4. Remove the grille.
5. Remove the intake manifolds and the lifters. On the 3.8L engine, remove the oil pan.
6. Remove the timing chain front cover, the timing chain and spacer.
7. Remove the thrust plate. Remove the camshaft, being careful not to damage the bearing surfaces.

To install:

8. Lubricate the cam lobes and journals with heavy engine oil. Install the camshaft, being careful not to damage the bearing surfaces while sliding into position.
9. Install the thrust plate. Tighten the bolts to 6–10 ft. lbs. (8–14 Nm) on the 3.8L engine or 9–12 ft. lbs. (12–16 Nm) on the 5.0L engine.
10. Install the timing chain and sprockets. Install the engine front cover.
11. Install the lifters and the intake manifolds. On 3.8L engine, install the oil pan.
12. Install the grille. If equipped with air conditioning, install the condenser.
13. Install the radiator. Fill and bleed the cooling system.
14. Connect the negative battery cable. Start the engine and check for leaks.

4.6L (SOHC) Engine

1. Disconnect the negative battery cable and drain the cooling system. Relieve the fuel system pressure.
2. Remove the right and left camshaft covers.
3. Remove the timing chain front cover. Remove the timing chains.

4. Rotate the crankshaft counterclockwise 45 degrees from TDC to make sure all pistons are below the top of the engine block deck face.

NOTE: The crankshaft must be in this position prior to rotating the camshafts or damage to the pistons and/or valve train will result.

5. Install valve spring compressor tool T91P–6565–A or equivalent, under the camshaft and on top of the valve spring retainer.

NOTE: Valve spring spacer tool T91P–6565–AH or equivalent, must be installed between the spring coils and the camshaft must be at the base circle before compressing the valve spring.

6. Compress the valve spring far enough to remove the roller follower. Repeat Steps 5 and 6 until all roller followers are removed.
7. Remove the bolts retaining the camshaft cap cluster assemblies to the cylinder heads. Tap upward on the camshaft caps at points near the upper bearing halves and gradually lift the camshaft clusters from the cylinder heads.
8. Remove the camshafts straight upward to avoid bearing damage.

To install:

9. Apply heavy engine oil to the camshaft journals and lobes. Position the camshafts on the cylinder heads.
10. Install and seat the camshaft cap cluster assemblies. Hand start the bolts.
11. Tighten the camshaft cluster retaining bolts in sequence to 6.0–8.8 ft. lbs. (8–12 Nm).

NOTE: Each camshaft cap cluster assembly is tightened individually.

12. Loosen the camshaft cap cluster retaining bolts approximately 2 turns or until the heads of the bolts are free. Retighten all bolts, in sequence, to 6.0–8.8 ft. lbs. (8–12 Nm).

NOTE: The camshafts should turn freely with a slight drag.

13. Install cam positioning tools T91P–6256–A or equivalent, on the flats of the camshafts and install the spacers and camshaft sprockets. Install the bolts and washers and tighten to 81–96 ft. lbs. (110–130 Nm).
14. Install valve spring compressor T91P–6565–A or equivalent, under

the camshaft and on top of the valve spring retainer.

NOTE: Valve spring spacer tool T91P–6565–AH or equivalent, must be installed between the spring coils and the camshaft must be at the base circle before compressing the valve spring.

15. Compress the valve spring far enough to install the roller followers.

16. Repeat Steps 14 and 15 until all roller followers are installed.

17. Rotate the crankshaft clockwise 45 degrees to position the crankshaft at TDC.

NOTE: The crankshaft must only be rotated in the clockwise direction and only as far as TDC.

18. Install the timing chains and install the timing chain front cover. Install the camshaft covers.

19. Install the remaining components in the reverse order of removal.

20. Connect the negative battery cable. Start the engine and check for leaks.

4.6L (DOHC) Engine

1. Disconnect the negative battery cable and drain the cooling system.

2. Remove the windshield wiper module.

3. Remove the valve covers.

4. Remove the the front cover.

5. Remove the timing chains.

6. Rotate the crankshaft counter clockwise 45 degrees to ensure all pistons are below the top of the cylinder block deck face.

7. Install valve spring compressor T91P-6565-A, or equivalent, under the exhaust camshaft and on top of the exhaust valve spring retainer.

8. Install valve spring compressor T91P-6565-A, or equivalent, under the intake camshaft and on top of the primary intake valve spring retainer.

9. Install valve spring compressor T91P-6565-A, or equivalent, under the intake camshaft and on top of the secondary valve spring retainer.

10. Compress valve spring far enough to remove roller follower. Repeat steps 7 through 10 until all followers are removed.

11. Remove 13 bolts retaining exhaust camshaft cap cluster assemblies to cylinder head to remove exhaust camshaft.

12. Remove 12 bolts retaining intake camshaft cap cluster assemblies to cylinder head to remove intake camshaft.

13. Lightly tap upward on camshaft cap with rubber or plastic hammer and gradually lift camshaft cap cluster from cylinder head.

14. Remove camshaft straight up to avoid bearing damage. Repeat steps 7 through 14 to remove the other camshafts.

To install:

15. Clean and inspect valve cover, front cover and cylinder head mating surfaces.

16. Apply clean engine oil to all journals and lobes of the camshaft. Position camshaft on cylinder head.

17. Install and seat camshaft cap cluster assemblies. Hand-tighten all 25 cap cluster retaining bolts. Tighten in sequence the cap cluster retaining bolts to 6–8.8 ft. lbs. (8–12 Nm). Tighten each camshaft cluster cap assembly individually.

18. Loosen all 25 cap cluster retaining bolts 2 turns or until head of bolt is free. Retighten in sequence the cap cluster retaining bolts to 6–8.8 ft. lbs. (8–12 Nm). The camshaft should turn freely with a slight drag.

19. Check the camshaft endplay. The play should be between 0.001–0.009 inches.

20. Install timing chains and set valve timing.

21. Install valve spring compressor T91P-6565-A, or equivalent, under the exhaust camshaft and on top of the exhaust valve spring retainer.

22. Install valve spring compressor T91P-6565-A, or equivalent, under the intake camshaft and on top of the primary intake valve spring retainer.

23. Install valve spring compressor T91P-6565-A, or equivalent, under the intake camshaft and on top of the secondary valve spring retainer.

24. Compress valve spring far enough to install the roller follower. Repeat steps 21 through 24 until all followers are installed.

25. Inspect and replace if necessary front cover seal. Replace front cover gasket.

26. Install front cover. Install valve covers.

27. Install windshield wiper module.

28. Fill and bleed the cooling system. Connect the negative battery cable, start the engine and check for leaks.

Auxiliary Shaft

REMOVAL AND INSTALLATION

2.3L Engine

1. Disconnect the negative battery cable. Remove the front timing belt cover.

2. Remove the timing belt. Remove the auxiliary shaft sprocket retaining bolt. Remove the sprocket using a puller.

3. Remove the auxiliary shaft cover and thrust plate.

4. Withdraw the auxiliary shaft from the block being careful not to damage the bearings.

To install:

5. Dip the auxiliary shaft in engine oil before installing. Slide the auxiliary shaft into the cylinder block, being careful not to damage the bearings.

6. Install the thrust plate. Tighten the thrust plate screws to 6–9 ft. lbs. (8–12 Nm).

7. Install a new gasket and auxiliary shaft cover. Tighten the cover screws to 6–9 ft. lbs. (8–12 Nm).

NOTE: The auxiliary shaft cover and cylinder front cover share a common gasket. Cut off the old gasket around the cylinder cover and use half of the new gasket on the auxiliary shaft cover.

8. Insert the distributor, aligning the housing-to-engine block marks, and install the auxiliary shaft sprocket.

9. Align the timing marks and install the timing belt.

10. Install the timing belt cover.

11. Check the ignition timing.

Piston and Connecting Rod

POSITIONING

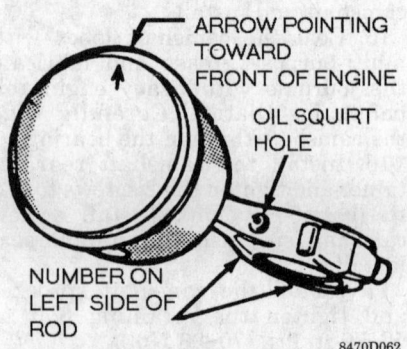

ARROW POINTING TOWARD FRONT OF ENGINE

OIL SQUIRT HOLE

NUMBER ON LEFT SIDE OF ROD

8470D062

Piston and rod assembly — 2.3L engine

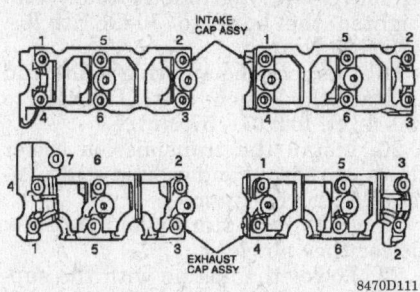

Bolt torque sequence for camshaft cap cluster assemblies — 4.6L (DOHC) engine

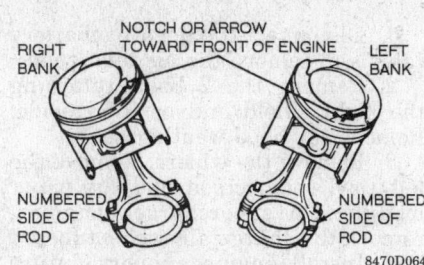

Piston and rod assembly — 4.6L and 5.0L engines

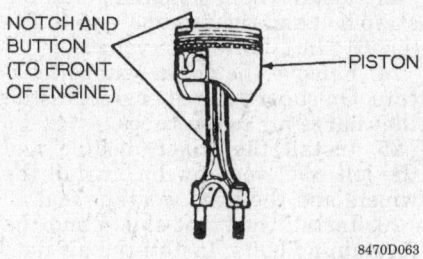

Piston and rod assembly — 3.8L engine

ENGINE LUBRICATION

Oil Pan

REMOVAL AND INSTALLATION

2.3L Engine

1. Disconnect the negative battery cable. Remove the air cleaner outlet tube at the throttle body.

2. Remove the engine oil dipstick.

3. Install engine support fixture D88L–6000–A or equivalent.

4. Raise and safely support the vehicle.

5. Remove the engine mount through bolts.

6. Drain the engine oil.

7. Disconnect the cable from the starter and remove the starter.

8. Disconnect the exhaust manifold tube to the inlet pipe bracket and disconnect the catalytic converter at the inlet pipe.

9. Remove the transmission. If equipped with manual transmission, remove the clutch pressure plate and disc.

10. Remove the flywheel retaining bolts and remove the flywheel.

11. If equipped with automatic transmission, remove the oil cooler lines from the retainer at the block.

12. Lower the vehicle. Raise the engine using the engine support fixture, then raise and safely support the vehicle.

13. Remove the oil pan attaching bolts and lower the oil pan to the chassis. Remove the oil pump and pickup tube and lay the assembly in the oil pan.

14. Remove the pan and pump from the vehicle.

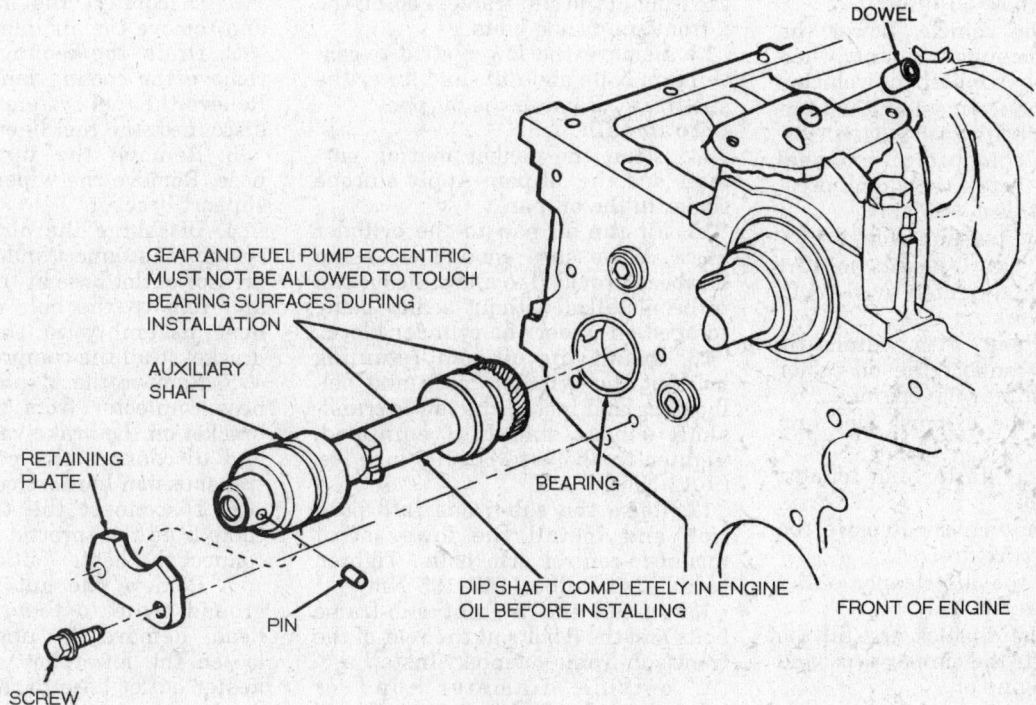

Auxiliary shaft installation — 2.3L engine

15. Clean the oil pan and all gasket mating surfaces. Clean the oil pump exterior and pickup tube screen.

To install:

16. Install the oil pan gasket in the groove in the oil pan.

17. Lay the oil pump and pickup tube assembly in the oil pan and position the pan on the crossmember.

18. Install the oil pump and pickup tube assembly. Tighten the oil pump mounting bolts to 14–21 ft. lbs. (19–29 Nm) and the oil pump strap nut to 30–41 ft. lbs. (40–55 NM).

19. Apply silicone sealer to the points where the rear main bearing cap meets the cylinder block, to the corners of the engine front cover and to where the front cover meets the cylinder block.

20. Install the oil pan assembly. Install the oil pan flange bolts tight enough to compress the oil pan gasket to the point that the 2 transmission holes are aligned with the 2 tapped holes in the oil pan, but loose enough to allow movement of the pan, relative to the block.

21. Install the 2 oil pan/transmission bolts and tighten to 30–36 ft. lbs. (40–50 Nm) to align the oil pan with the transmission, then loosen the bolts ½ turn.

22. Tighten all oil pan flange bolts to 90–120 inch lbs. (10–13 Nm). Tighten the 2 oil pan/transmission bolts to 30–39 ft. lbs. (40–54 Nm).

23. Install a new oil filter.

24. Lower the vehicle. Lower the engine onto the engine mounts, then raise and safely support the vehicle.

25. Install the flywheel and tighten the attaching bolts to 54–64 ft. lbs. (73–87 Nm). If equipped with manual transmission, install the clutch pressure plate and disc assembly.

26. Install the transmission.

27. Install the engine mount through bolts and tighten to 65–85 ft. lbs. (88–115 Nm).

28. If equipped with automatic transmission, connect the oil cooler line retainer clip to the engine.

29. Connect the exhaust pipe and the inlet pipe.

30. Install the starter and connect the starter cable.

31. Lower the vehicle. Remove the engine support fixture.

32. Connect the air cleaner outlet tube to the throttle body.

33. Install the dipstick and fill the crankcase with the proper type and quantity of engine oil.

34. Connect the negative battery cable, start the engine and check for leaks.

3.8L Engine

1. Disconnect the negative battery cable and remove the air inlet tube.

2. Remove the 2 bolts retaining the sight shield and position aside. Remove the hood weather seal.

3. Remove the wipers. Remove the left cowl vent screen and the wiper module. On supercharged engines, remove the charge air cooler tubes.

4. Install engine support fixture tool D88L–6000–A or equivalent. Raise and safely support the vehicle.

5. Remove the engine mount through bolts. On supercharged engine, remove the left mount retaining strap bolt.

6. Partially lower the vehicle and raise the engine with the support fixture.

7. Raise and safely support the vehicle. Remove the starter.

8. Drain the crankcase and remove the oil filter.

9. Remove the wire loom, ground strap and automatic transmission oil cooler lines, if equipped.

10. Remove the oil pan-to-bellhousing bolts and the bolts at the crankshaft position sensor shield, if equipped. Remove the remaining oil pan retaining bolts.

11. Remove the steering shaft pinch bolts and separate the steering shaft. Position a jack under the front of the sub-frame.

12. Remove the 6 rearward bolts on the front of the sub-frame. Loosen the 2 front sub-frame bolts.

13. Remove the lower strut-to-control arm bolts and nuts and lower the sub-frame. Remove the oil pan.

To install:

14. Clean the gasket mating surfaces and the oil pan. Apply silicone sealer to the oil pan.

15. Fit the oil pan to the cylinder block. Make sure enough clearance has been provided to allow the oil pan to be installed without sealer being scraped off under the cylinder block.

16. Install the oil pan retaining bolts at the cylinder block and bellhousing and install the lower crankshaft sensor shield, if equipped. Tighten the bolts to 80–106 inch lbs. (9–12 Nm).

17. Raise the sub-frame into position and install the lower strut mount-to-control arm bolts. Tighten to 103–144 ft. lbs. (140–195 Nm).

18. Install the 2 front sub-frame bolts and the 6 bolts at the rear of the front sub-frame member. Install a ¾ in. outside diameter pipe or equivalent, into both front left and right sub-frame and body alignment holes. Tighten 1 bolt at each corner.

Remove the alignment tools and tighten the bolts to 70–96 ft. lbs. (95–130 Nm).

19. Connect the steering shaft and install the pinch bolt. Tighten to 30–42 ft. lbs. (41–57 Nm).

20. Install the transmission cooler lines, wire loom and ground strap. Install a new oil filter.

21. Install the starter and partially lower the vehicle.

22. Lower the engine with the support fixture. Seat the left side locating pin before the right. Partially raise the vehicle and support safely.

23. Install the engine mount through bolts and tighten to 35–50 ft. lbs. (47–68 Nm). On supercharged engine, install the left mount retaining strap bolt and tighten to 33–45 ft. lbs. (45–61 Nm). Lower the vehicle.

24. Remove the engine support fixture. On supercharged engine, install the charge air cooler tubes.

25. Install the wiper module and the left cowl vent screen. Install the wipers and the hood weather seal.

26. Install the sight shield and the 2 retaining bolts. Install the air duct assembly. Fill the crankcase with the proper type and quantity of engine oil.

27. Connect the negative battery cable, start the engine and check for leaks.

4.6L (SOHC) Engine

1. Disconnect the battery cables and remove the air inlet tube.

2. Drain the cooling system and remove the cooling fan and shroud. Relieve the fuel system pressure and disconnect the fuel lines.

3. Remove the upper radiator hose. Remove the wiper module and support bracket.

4. Discharge the air conditioning system. Disconnect and plug the compressor outlet hose at the compressor and remove the bolt retaining the hose assembly to the right coil bracket. Cap the compressor outlet.

5. Remove the 42-pin engine harness connector from the retaining bracket on the brake vacuum booster and disconnect the connector and transmission harness connector.

6. Disconnect the throttle valve cable from the throttle body and disconnect the heater outlet hose.

7. Remove the nut retaining the ground strap to the right cylinder head. Remove the upper stud and loosen the lower bolt retaining the heater outlet hose to the right cylinder head and position out of the way.

8. Remove the blower motor resistor. Remove the bolt retaining the

right engine mount to the lower engine bracket.

9. Disconnect the vacuum hoses from the EGR valve and tube. Remove the 2 bolts retaining the EGR valve to the intake manifold.

10. Raise and safely support the vehicle. Drain the crankcase and remove the engine mount through bolts.

11. Remove the EGR tube line nut from the right exhaust manifold and remove the EGR valve and tube assembly.

12. Disconnect the exhaust from the exhaust manifolds. Lower the exhaust system and support it with wire from the crossmember.

13. Position a jack and a block of wood under the oil pan, rearward of the oil drain hole. Raise the engine approximately 4 in. and insert 2 wood blocks approximately 2½ in. thick under each engine mount. Lower the engine onto the wood blocks and remove the jack.

14. Remove the 16 bolts retaining the oil pan to the engine block and remove the oil pan.

NOTE: It may be necessary to loosen, but not remove, the 2 nuts on the rear transmission mount and with a jack, raise the transmission extension housing slightly to remove the pan.

To install:
15. Clean the oil pan and the gasket mating surfaces.

16. Position a new gasket on the oil pan. Apply silicone sealer to where the front cover meets the cylinder block and rear seal retainer meets the cylinder block. Position the oil pan on the engine and install the bolts. Tighten the bolts, in sequence, to 15–22 ft. lbs. (20–30 Nm).

17. Position the jack and wood block under the oil pan, rearward of the oil drain hole and raise the engine enough to remove the wood blocks. Lower the engine and remove the jack.

18. Install the engine mount through bolts and tighten to 15–22 ft. lbs. (20–30 Nm).

19. Position the EGR valve and tube assembly in the vehicle and connect to the exhaust manifold. Tighten the line nut to 26–33 ft. lbs. (35–45 Nm).

NOTE: Loosen the line nut at the EGR valve prior to installing the assembly into the vehicle. This will allow enough movement to align the EGR valve retaining bolts.

20. Cut the wire and position the exhaust system to the manifolds. Install the 4 nuts and tighten to 20–30 ft. lbs. (27–41 Nm). Make sure the exhaust system clears the crossmember. Adjust as necessary.

21. Install a new oil filter and lower the vehicle.

22. Install the bolt retaining the right engine mount to the lower engine bracket. Tighten to 15–22 ft. lbs. (20–30 Nm).

23. Install a new gasket on the EGR valve and position on the intake manifold. Install the 2 bolts retaining the EGR valve to the intake manifold and tighten to 15–22 ft. lbs. (20–30 Nm). Tighten the EGR tube line nut at the EGR valve to 26–33 ft. lbs. (35–45 Nm). Connect the vacuum hoses to the EGR valve and tube.

24. Install the blower motor resistor. Position the heater outlet hose, install the upper stud and tighten the upper and lower bolts to 15–22 ft. lbs. (20–30 Nm). Install the ground strap on the stud and tighten to 15–22 ft. lbs. (20–30 Nm).

25. Connect the heater outlet hose and the throttle valve cable. If necessary, adjust the throttle valve cable.

26. Connect the 42-pin connector and transmission harness connector. Install the harness connector on the brake vacuum booster.

27. Connect the air conditioning compressor outlet hose to the compressor and install the bolt retaining the hose to the right coil bracket.

28. Install the upper radiator hose and connect the fuel lines. Install the wiper module and retaining bracket.

29. Install the cooling fan and shroud and fill the cooling system. Fill the crankcase with the proper type and quantity of engine oil.

30. Connect the negative battery cable and install the air inlet tube. Start the engine and check for leaks.

31. Evacuate and recharge the air conditioning system.

4.6L (DOHC) Engine

1. Turn **OFF** air suspension switch located in luggage compartment, if equipped.

2. Disconnect the negative and positive battery cables.

3. Remove oil dipstick. Install engine support tripod onto engine compartment and attach to engine.

4. Raise and safely support the vehicle.

5. Remove the front wheel and tire assemblies.

6. Drain the engine oil.

7. Disconnect left and right ride height sensor wiring connectors and

remove right and left brake caliper bolts. Remove brake calipers and support with mechanics wire.

8. Disconnect left and right upper control arms from spindles. Disconnect steering shaft coupler at rag joint.

9. Remove power steering line clamp from subframe.

10. Support subframe with engine jack.

11. Remove 2 motor mount through bolts. Remove left and right lower strut control arm nuts and bolts.

12. Remove 8 subframe bolts. Lower the subframe.

13. Disconnect low oil level sensor connector and sensor wiring clips from oil pan rail in 2 places.

14. Remove 16 oil pan bolts. and remove the pan. Clean the oil pan and mating surfaces and inspect for damage.

To install:
15. Position new gasket on oil pan. Apply silicone sealer where front cover meets cylinder block and rear seal retainer meets cylinder block. Position oil pan on cylinder block and install 16 oil pan bolts. Tighten the bolts to 15–22 ft. lbs. (20–30 Nm).

16. Connect low oil level sensor connector and sensor wiring clips to oil pan rail.

17. Raise the subframe into position. Install lower strut to control arm bolts.

18. Install the motor mount through bolts. Install the 8 subframe bolts. Install power steering line clamps.

19. Connect steering shaft at rag joint. Partially lower the vehicle.

20. Install the left and right ride height sensor wiring connectors. Install right and left brake calipers and caliper retaining bolts.

21. Connect left and right upper control arms to spindles. Install wheel and tire assemblies. Lower the vehicle.

22. Remove engine support. Install dipstick.

23. Fill the crankcase with the proper type and quantity of engine oil.

24. Connect the negative battery cable, start the engine and check for leaks.

25. Turn **ON** air suspension switch located in luggage compartment.

5.0L Engine

MUSTANG AND MARK VII

1. Disconnect the negative battery cable and remove the air cleaner tube.

2. Remove the oil level indicator from the left side of the cylinder block. Remove the fan shroud and position the shroud over the fan.

3. Raise and safely support the vehicle. Drain the crankcase and remove the oil level sensor wiring from the oil pan.

4. Disconnect the electrical connectors from the starter and remove the starter. Remove the catalytic converter and muffler inlet pipes.

5. Remove the engine mount-to-No. 2 crossmember attaching bolts or nuts. Support the transmission and remove the No. 3 crossmember and rear mount support assemblies.

6. Remove the steering gear attaching bolts and position the steering gear forward aside.

7. Position a jack and wood block under the oil pan. Raise the engine and install wood blocks between the engine mounts and frame. Lower the engine onto the wood blocks and remove the jack.

8. Remove the oil pan attaching bolts and lower the pan to the crossmember. Remove the oil pump and pickup tube assembly and allow to drop into the pan. Remove the pan.

To install:

9. Clean the oil pan and the gasket mating surfaces. Clean the oil pump exterior and pickup tube screen. Apply gasket sealer to the gasket mating surfaces and install new oil pan gaskets.

10. With the oil pump and pickup tube assembly positioned in the oil pan, raise the pan onto the crossmember. Install the oil pump and then the pan. Tighten the oil pan bolts to 9 ft. lbs. (12 Nm).

11. Position the oil pan and the wood block under the oil pan. Raise the engine and remove the wood blocks. Lower the engine and remove the jack. Install the engine mount-to-No. 2 crossmember attaching nuts or bolts. Tighten to 80–106 ft. lbs. (108–144 Nm).

12. Position the steering gear and install the retaining bolts. Install the starter and connect the electrical connectors. Connect the oil level sensor wire to the oil pan.

13. Install the rear mount and the No. 3 crossmember. Tighten the attaching bolts to 80–106 ft. lbs. (108–144 Nm). Install the catalytic converter and muffler inlet pipes. Lower the vehicle.

14. Install the fan shroud and install the oil level indicator to the side of the cylinder block. Install the air cleaner assembly.

15. Fill the crankcase with the proper type and quantity of engine oil. Connect the negative battery cable, start the engine and check for leaks.

THUNDERBIRD AND COUGAR

1. Disconnect the negative battery cable and remove the oil level dipstick. Disconnect the air cleaner cover retaining clips to allow free movement when the engine is raised.

2. Remove the 2 bolts retaining the radiator shroud to the radiator and pull the shroud loose from the lower retaining clips.

3. Install engine support fixture tool D88L-6000-A or equivalent. Raise and safely support the vehicle.

4. Drain the crankcase and remove the engine mount through bolts. Loosen the transmission mount nut to allow the mount to move when the engine is raised. Partially lower the vehicle.

5. Raise the engine approximately 2 in. using the support fixture. Raise and safely support the vehicle.

6. Remove the power steering cooler line retaining clips. Remove the bolt securing the transmission lines to the right side of the engine block.

7. Disconnect the electrical connector from the low oil level sensor located in the oil pan, if equipped. Remove the oil pan retaining bolts.

8. Remove the steering shaft pinch bolt and separate the steering shaft from the power steering rack assembly.

9. Position 2 jackstands under the engine support sub-frame. Remove the lower strut-to-control arm bolts and nuts from both sides.

10. While supporting the engine support sub-frame on jackstands, remove the 6 rearward bolts on the subframe. Loosen the 2 froward bolts on the sub-frame. Lower the sub-frame.

11. Remove the oil pump/pickup tube assembly and place it in the oil pan. Remove the pan.

To install:

12. Clean the oil pan and the gasket mating surfaces. Clean the oil pump exterior and the pickup tube screen.

13. Apply a thin coat of silicone sealer to the engine block and to the engine block side of a new oil pan gasket. Allow the adhesive to set-up for approximately 5 minutes, before positioning the gasket to the engine.

14. Place the oil pump and pickup tube assembly in the oil pan and position the pan on the sub-frame. Install the oil pump/pickup tube and oil

pump drive to the engine. Tighten the oil pump retaining bolts to 22–32 ft. lbs. (30–43 Nm).

15. Position the oil pan to the engine and install all the pan bolts hand tight, then tighten the bolts evenly to 9 ft. lbs. (12 Nm). Connect the electrical connector to the low oil level sensor, if equipped.

16. Raise the sub-frame into position while supporting the sub-frame on the jackstands. Install a ¾ in. outside diameter pipe or equivalent, into both front left and right subframe and body alignment holes. Tighten 1 bolt at each corner. Remove the alignment tools and tighten the bolts to 70–96 ft. lbs. (95–130 Nm).

17. Install the lower strut-to-control arm bolts and nuts and tighten to 103–144 ft. lbs. (140–195 Nm). Remove the 2 jackstands used for installing the sub-frame.

18. Connect the steering shaft and install the steering shaft pinch bolt. Tighten the pinch bolt to 30–42 ft. lbs. (41–57 Nm). Install the bolt securing the transmission lines to the right side of the engine block.

19. Secure the power steering cooler line retaining clips and partially lower the vehicle. Lower the engine onto the engine mounts and remove the engine support fixture.

20. Raise and safely support the vehicle. Tighten the transmission mount nut to 65–85 ft. lbs. (88–115 Nm). Install the engine mount through bolts.

21. Install a new oil filter and lower the vehicle. Position the fan shroud into the lower retaining clips and install the 2 bolts. Connect the air filter cover retaining clips.

22. Fill the crankcase with the proper type and quantity of engine oil. Install the dipstick and connect the negative battery cable. Start the engine and check for leaks.

Oil Pump

REMOVAL AND INSTALLATION

Except 3.8L and 4.6L Engines

1. Disconnect the negative battery cable. Remove the oil pan.

2. Remove the oil pump inlet tube and screen assembly.

3. Remove the oil pump attaching bolts and gasket. Remove the oil pump intermediate shaft.

To install:

4. Prime the oil pump by filling either the inlet or outlet ports with engine oil and rotating the pump shaft

to distribute the oil within the pump body.

5. Position the intermediate driveshaft into the distributor socket. With the shaft firmly seated in the distributor socket, the stop on the shaft should touch the roof of the crankcase. Remove the shaft and position the stop, as necessary.

6. Position a new gasket on the pump body, insert the intermediate shaft into the oil pump and install the pump and shaft as an assembly.

NOTE: Do not attempt to force the pump into position if it will not seat readily. The driveshaft hex may be misaligned with the distributor shaft. To align, rotate the intermediate shaft into a new position.

7. Tighten the oil pump attaching screws to 14–21 ft. lbs. (19–29 Nm) on the 2.3L engine or 22–32 ft. lbs. (30–43 Nm) on the 5.0L engine.

8. Clean and install the oil pump inlet tube and screen assembly.

9. Install the oil pan and the remaining components.

3.8L Engine

NOTE: The timing chain front cover houses the oil pump on the 3.8L engine. If the oil pump housing is scored, worn or grooved, the entire front cover will have to be replaced.

1. Disconnect the negative battery cable. Raise and safely support the vehicle.

2. Remove the oil filter.

3. Remove the cover/filter mount assembly. On supercharged engines, remove the oil cooler assembly.

4. Lift the pump gears from their mounting pocket in the front cover.

5. Clean all gasket mounting surfaces.

6. Inspect the mounting pocket for wear. If excessive wear is present, complete timing cover assembly replacement is necessary.

7. Inspect the cover/filter mount gasket to timing cover surface for flatness. Place a straight-edge across the flat and check clearance with a feeler gauge. If the measured clearance exceeds 0.0016 in. (0.04mm), replace the cover/filter mount.

8. Replace the pump gears if wear is excessive.

9. Remove the plug from the end of the pressure relief valve passage using a small drill and slide hammer. Use caution when drilling.

10. Remove the spring and valve from the bore. Clean all dirt and metal chips from the bore and valve. Inspect all parts for wear. Replace as necessary.

To install:

11. Install the valve and spring after lubricating them with engine oil. The end with the smaller diameter goes in first.

12. Install a new plug. The plug can be tapped into the bore using a plastic tipped hammer. Make sure the plug is 0–0.010 in. (0–0.25mm) below the machined surface.

13. Lightly pack the gear pocket with petroleum jelly. Install the gears in the cover pocket, making sure petroleum jelly fills all the voids between the gears and pockets.

NOTE: Failure to properly coat the oil pump gears may result in failure of the pump to prime when the engine is started.

14. Position the pump body O-ring seal and install the pump body to the front cover using alignment dowels on the front cover.

15. Tighten the pump body retaining bolts to 18–22 ft. lbs. (25–30 Nm) for M8 bolts and 30–40 ft. lbs. (40–55 Nm) for M10 bolts.

16. Install the oil cooler on supercharged engine. Install a new oil filter. Fill the crankcase with the proper type and quantity of engine oil.

17. Connect the negative battery cable, start the engine and check for leaks and proper oil pressure.

4.6L Engine

1. Disconnect the negative battery cable. Remove the front cover.

2. Remove the oil pan and pickup tube.

3. Remove primary timing chains. Remove crankshaft timing sprockets.

4. Remove 4 bolts retaining the oil pump to cylinder block. Remove the oil pump. Clean mating surfaces and inspect for damage.

To install:

5. Rotate the inner rotor of oil pump to align with flats on crankshaft and install oil pump flush with cylinder block.

6. Install 4 retaining bolts and tighten to 6–8.8 ft. lbs. (8–12 Nm).

7. Replace oil filter. Install timing chains.

8. Install pickup tube and oil pan.

9. Install front cover. Fill the crankcase with the proper type and quantity of engine oil.

10. Connect the negative battery cable, start the engine and check for leaks and proper oil pressure.

CHECKING

1. Check the inside of the pump housing and the inner and outer gears for damage or excessive wear.

2. Check the mating surface of the pump cover for wear. Minor scuff marks are normal, but if the cover, gears or housing surfaces are excessively worn, scored or grooved, replace the pump. Inspect the rotor for nicks, burrs or score marks. Remove minor imperfections with an oil stone.

3. Measure the inner to outer rotor tip clearance. With the rotor assembly removed from the pump and resting on a flat surface, the inner and outer rotor tip clearance must not exceed 0.012 in. (0.30mm) with the feeler gauge inserted 0.5 in. (13mm) minimum.

4. With the rotor assembly installed in the housing, place a straight-edge over the rotor assembly and the housing. Measure the rotor endplay between the straight-edge and both the inner and outer race. The maximum clearance must not exceed 0.005 in. (0.13mm).

5. Inspect the relief valve spring to see if it is collapsed or worn. Check the relief valve spring tension. Specifications are as follows:

2.3L engine — 12.6–14.5 lbs. at 1.20 in.

3.8L engine — 15.2–17.1 lbs. at 1.20 in.

5.0L engine — 10.6–12.2 lbs. at 1.704 in.

6. If the spring tension is not within specification and/or the spring is worn or damaged, replace the pump. Check the relief valve piston for free operation in the bore.

NOTE: Except on the 3.8L engine, internal oil pump components are not serviced. If any component is out of specification, the entire pump must be replaced.

Rear Main Bearing Oil Seal

REMOVAL AND INSTALLATION

1. Disconnect the negative battery cable. Remove the transmission. If equipped with manual transmission, remove the clutch and flywheel.

2. Punch 2 holes in the crankshaft rear oil seal on opposite sides of the crankshaft, just above the bearing cap to cylinder block split line. Install a sheetmetal screw in each of the holes or use a small slide hammer

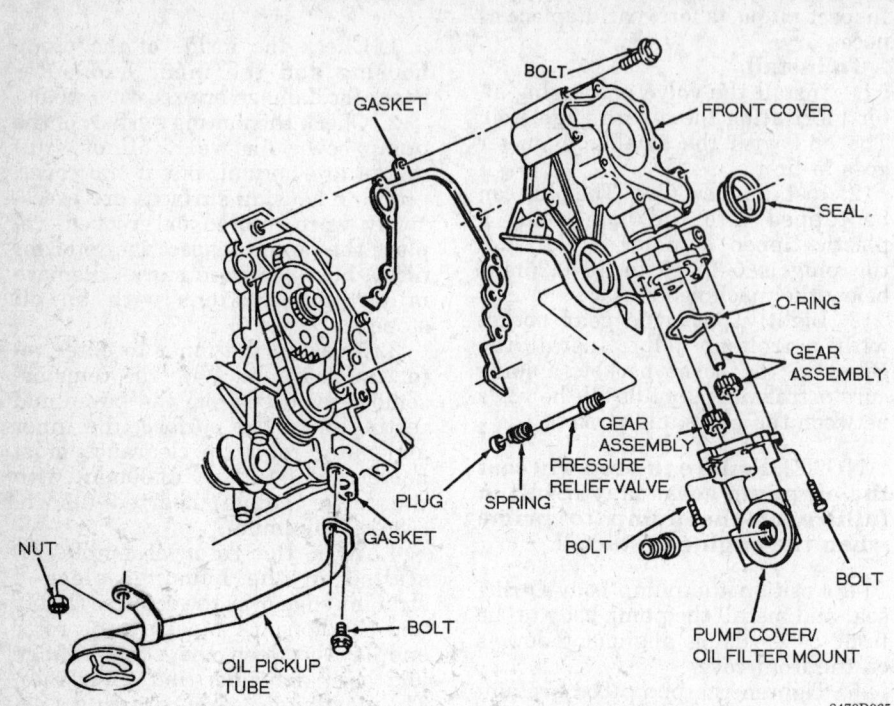

Oil pump and timing chain front cover exploded view — 3.8L engine

8470D065

and pry the crankshaft rear main oil seal from the block.

NOTE: Use extreme caution not to scratch the crankshaft oil seal surface.

3. Clean the oil seal recess in the cylinder block and main bearing cap.

4. Coat the seal and all of the seal mounting surfaces with oil. Position the seal on rear main seal installer T82L–6701–A or equivalent, and position the tool and seal to the rear of the engine.

5. Alternate bolt tightening to seat the seal properly. The rear face of the seal must be within 0.005 in. (0.127mm) of the rear face of the block.

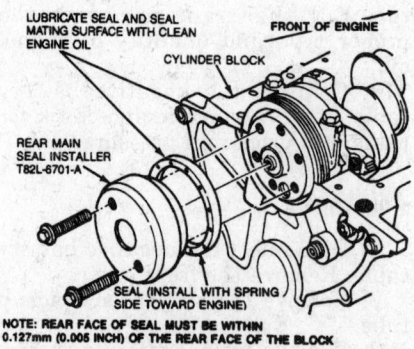

8470D066

Rear main bearing oil seal installation

MANUAL TRANSMISSION

Transmission Assembly

REMOVAL AND INSTALLATION

Mustang

1. Disconnect the negative battery cable.

2. Raise and support the vehicle safely.

3. Mark the position of the driveshaft on the axle flange so it can be reinstalled in the same position. Disconnect the driveshaft from the flange. Slide the driveshaft off the transmission output shaft and install a suitable plug to prevent lubricant from leaking.

4. Remove the catalytic converter.

5. Remove the 2 nuts attaching the rear transmission support to the crossmember. Remove the bolts.

6. Support the engine and transmission with a suitable jack.

7. Remove the 2 nuts from the crossmember bolts. Remove the bolts, raise the jack slightly and remove the crossmember.

8. Lower the transmission to expose the 2 bolts securing the shift handle to the shift tower. Remove the 2 nuts and bolts and remove the shift handle.

9. Disconnect the wiring harness from the backup lamp switch. On the 5.0L engine, disconnect the neutral sensing switch.

10. Remove the bolt from the speedometer cable retainer and remove the speedometer driven gear from the transmission.

11. Remove the 4 bolts that secure the transmission to the flywheel housing.

12. Move the transmission and jack rearward until the transmission input shaft clears the flywheel housing. If necessary lower the engine enough to obtain clearance for removing the transmission.

NOTE: Do not depress the clutch while the transmission is removed.

To install:

13. Make sure the mounting surface of the transmission and flywheel housing are clean and free of dirt, paint and burrs.

14. Install 2 guide pins in the flywheel housing lower mounting bolt holes. Raise the transmission and move forward on the guide pins until the input shaft splines enter the clutch hub splines and the case is positioned against the flywheel housing.

15. Install the 2 upper transmission-to-flywheel housing mounting bolts snug and remove the 2 guide pins. Install the 2 lower mounting bolts and tighten all the bolts to 45–65 ft. lbs. (61–88 Nm).

16. Raise the transmission with a jack until the shift handle can be secured to the shift tower. Install and

tighten the attaching bolts and washers to 23–32 ft. lbs. (31–43 Nm).

17. Connect the speedometer cable to the extension housing and tighten the attaching screw to 54–115 inch lbs. (6–13 Nm).

18. Raise the rear of the transmission with the jack and install the transmission support. Install and tighten the attaching bolts to 36–50 ft. lbs. (48–68 Nm).

19. With the transmission extension housing resting on the engine rear support, install the attaching bolts and tighten to 35 ft. lbs. (48 Nm).

20. Connect the backup lamp switch wiring harness. On 5.0L engine, connect the neutral sensing switch to the wiring harness.

21. Install the catalytic converter. Tighten the attaching bolts to 20–30 ft. lbs. (27–41 Nm).

22. Remove the extension housing installation tool and slide the forward end of the driveshaft over the transmission output shaft. Connect the driveshaft to the axle flange. Make sure the marks align that were made during removal. Tighten the U-bolt nuts to 42–57 ft. lbs. (56–77 Nm).

23. Fill the transmission with the proper type and quantity of fluid.

24. Lower the vehicle. Check the shift and crossover motion for full shift engagement and smooth crossover operation.

Thunderbird and Cougar

1. Disconnect the negative battery cable.

2. Shift the transmission into the N position.

3. Remove the shift knob and the console top cover.

4. Remove the 2 shifter retaining bolts and remove the shifter.

5. Raise and support the vehicle safely.

6. Remove the drain plug and drain the oil from the transmission.

7. Remove the body reinforcement in front of the axle.

8. Disconnect the rear exhaust assembly from the resonator.

9. Remove the 4 bolts retaining the driveshaft to the companion flange. If the rear driveshaft yoke and companion flange are not marked, mark the position for reassembly.

10. Position an axle stand under the front axle housing and remove the forward retaining nuts and bushings. Loosen the rear retaining nuts to allow the axle to tilt for driveshaft removal.

11. Pull the vent tube from the hole in the sub-frame.

12. Lower the front of the axle housing with the axle stand and slide the driveshaft out of the transmission above the axle housing. Let the driveshaft rest on the front driveshaft support and axle assembly.

13. Remove the catalytic converter.

14. Disconnect the hydraulic clutch line.

15. Disconnect the electrical connectors and remove the starter.

16. Position a transmission jack under the transmission. Remove the crossmember and the bellhousing to engine bolts.

17. Move the transmission to the rear until the input shaft clears the flywheel and lower the transmission from the vehicle.

To install:

18. Install guide studs in the engine block and raise the transmission until the input shaft splines are aligned with the clutch disc splines.

19. Slide the transmission forward on the guide studs until it is against the bellhousing. Install the bellhousing-to-engine retaining bolts and tighten to 28–38 ft. lbs. (38–51 Nm).

20. Install the crossmember and tighten the bolts to 35–50 ft. lbs. (47–68 Nm). Remove the transmission jack.

21. Install the starter and connect the electrical connectors. Connect the hydraulic clutch line.

22. Install the catalytic converter assembly.

23. Lubricate the splines with grease and slide the driveshaft into the transmission.

24. Raise the axle housing with the axle stand and install the bushings and retaining nuts. Tighten the retaining nuts to 68–100 ft. lbs. (92–136 Nm) and remove the axle stand.

25. Position the vent tube in the hole of the sub-frame.

26. Align the driveshaft yoke and companion flange and install the retaining bolts. Tighten to 71–96 ft. lbs. (95–129 Nm).

27. Connect the exhaust pipe muffler assembly to the resonator. Lower the vehicle.

28. Position the shifter and install the retaining bolts. Tighten to 18–24 ft. lbs. (24–33 Nm). Install the console top cover and the shifter knob.

29. Connect the negative battery cable. Check transmission operation.

CLUTCH

Clutch Assembly

REMOVAL AND INSTALLATION

Mustang

1. Disconnect the negative battery cable. Lift the clutch pedal to its uppermost position to disengage the pawl and quadrant. Push quadrant forward, unhook cable from quadrant and allow quadrant to slowly swing rearward.

2. Raise and safely support the vehicle. Remove the dust shield, if equipped.

3. Disconnect cable from the release lever. Remove the retaining clip and remove the clutch cable from the flywheel housing.

4. Remove the starter. If equipped with 5.0L engine, remove the bolts that secure engine rear plate to front lower part of flywheel housing. If equipped with 2.3L engine, remove the flywheel housing-to-oil pan bolts.

5. Remove the transmission, then the flywheel housing.

6. Remove the clutch release lever boot. Remove clutch release lever from housing by pulling it through the window in housing until retainer spring is disengaged from pivot. Remove release bearing from release lever.

7. Loosen the pressure plate cover attaching bolts evenly to release spring tension gradually and avoid distorting cover. If same pressure plate and cover are to be installed, mark cover and flywheel so pressure plate can be installed in its original position.

8. Inspect the flywheel for scoring, cracks or other damage and machine or replace, as necessary. Inspect the pilot bearing for damage and free movement. Replace, as necessary.

To install:

9. If removed, install the flywheel. Make sure the mating surfaces of the flywheel and the crankshaft flange are clean prior to installation. Tighten the flywheel bolts to 56–64 ft. lbs. (73–87 Nm) on 2.3L engines or 75–85 ft. lbs. (102–115 Nm) on 5.0L engine.

10. Position the clutch disc and pressure plate assembly on the flywheel. The 3 dowel pins on the flywheel must be properly aligned with the pressure plate. Bent, damaged or missing dowels must be replaced.

Start the pressure plate bolts but do not tighten them.

11. Align the clutch disc using a suitable alignment tool inserted in the pilot bearing. Alternately tighten the bolts a few turns at a time, until they are all tight. Final torque the bolts to 12–24 ft. lbs. (17–32 Nm). Remove the alignment tool.

12. Apply a light coating of multi-purpose long-life grease to the release bearing contact surface of the transmission bearing retainer, the pressure plate fingers contact surface of the release bearing, the release lever pivot pocket, release lever fork and flywheel housing pivot ball. Fill the grease groove of the release bearing hub with the same grease. Clean all excess grease from the inside bore of the bearing hub.

13. Install the release bearing on the release lever and install the lever in the flywheel housing. Install the boot.

14. Install the flywheel housing. Tighten the bolts to 29–38 ft. lbs. (38–52 Nm) on the 2.3L engine or 38–55 ft. lbs. (52–74 Nm) on the 5.0L engine.

15. Install the remaining components in the reverse order of removal.

Thunderbird and Cougar

1. Disconnect the negative battery cable.

2. Disconnect the clutch hydraulic system master cylinder from the clutch pedal.

3. Raise and support the vehicle safely.

4. Remove the starter.

5. Disconnect the hydraulic coupling at the transmission with tool T88T–70522–A or equivalent, by sliding the white plastic sleeve toward the slave cylinder and applying a slight tug on the tube.

6. Remove the transmission.

7. Matchmark the assembled position of the pressure plate to the flywheel.

8. Loosen the pressure plate attaching bolts evenly until the pressure plate springs are expanded, and remove the bolts. Be sure to support the pressure plate before removing the last bolt.

9. Remove the pressure plate and clutch disc from the flywheel.

10. Inspect the flywheel for scoring, cracks or other damage and machine or replace, as necessary. Inspect the pilot bearing for damage and free movement. Replace, as necessary.

To install:

11. If removed, install the flywheel. Make sure the mating surfaces of the flywheel and the crankshaft flange are clean prior to installation. Tighten the flywheel bolts to 54–64 ft. lbs. (73–87 Nm).

12. Position the clutch disc on the flywheel so a suitable alignment tool can enter the clutch pilot bearing and align the disc.

13. If reinstalling the original pressure plate, align the matchmarks. Position the pressure plate on the flywheel and install the retaining bolts hand tight. Tighten the bolts, in sequence, to 20–28 ft. lbs. (27–39 Nm). Remove the alignment tool.

14. Install the remaining components in the reverse order of removal. Tighten the flywheel housing-to-engine bolts to 40–49 ft. lbs. (54–67 Nm).

NOTE: Reuse the aluminum washers under the attaching bolts to prevent galvanic corrosion.

Clutch Cable

REMOVAL AND INSTALLATION

Mustang

NOTE: Whenever the clutch cable is disconnected, it is mandatory that the proper method for installing the clutch cable be followed.

1. Lift the clutch pedal to its upward most position to disengage the pawl and quadrant. Push the quadrant forward, unhook the cable from the quadrant and allow it to slowly swing rearward.

2. Remove the screw that holds the cable insulator to the dash panel and pull the cable through the dash panel and into the engine compartment.

3. Remove the cable bracket screw from the fender apron.

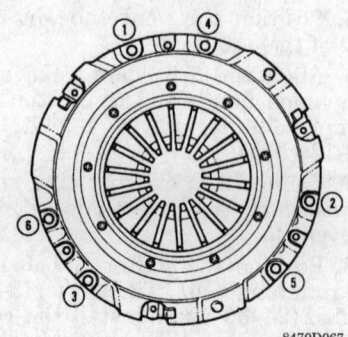

8470D067

Pressure plate bolt torque sequence — Thunderbird and Cougar

4. Raise and support the vehicle safely.

5. On 5.0L engine, remove the dust cover from the bellhousing.

6. Remove the clip retainer holding the cable to the bellhousing.

7. On the 5.0L engine, slide the ball on the end of the cable through the hole in the clutch release lever and remove the cable.

8. On the 2.3L engine, remove the hairpin clip, clevis pin and clevis from the end of the cable.

To install:

NOTE: The clutch pedal must be lifted to disengage the adjusting mechanism during cable installation. Failure to do so will cause damage the self-adjuster mechanism. A prying instrument should never be used to install the cable into the quadrant.

9. Slide the cable through the hole in the bellhousing and through the hole in the the release lever. On the 5.0L engine, slide the ball on the end of the cable assembly into the cable ball pocket on the clutch release lever. On the 2.3L engine, place the cable ball into the clevis. Install the clevis and clevis pin onto the clutch release lever and into the clevis pin.

10. Install the clutch cable retaining clip on the bellhousing.

11. On the 5.0L engine, install the dust shield on the bellhousing.

12. Push the cable assembly into the engine compartment and lower the vehicle. Install the cable bracket screw in the fender apron.

13. Push the cable into the hole in the dash panel and secure the insulator with a screw.

14. Install the cable assembly by lifting the clutch pedal to disengage the pawl and quadrant. Then, pushing the quadrant forward, hook the end of the cable over the rear of the quadrant.

15. Depress the clutch pedal several times to adjust the cable.

Clutch Master Cylinder

REMOVAL AND INSTALLATION

Thunderbird and Cougar

1. Disconnect the negative battery cable.

2. Disconnect the clutch pedal from the pushrod.

3. Disconnect the hydraulic line from the slave cylinder by depressing the white retainer bushing with tool T88T–70522–A or equivalent, while pulling slightly on the line.

4. Remove the 2 push pins retaining the clutch master cylinder reservoir to the left shock tower.

5. Rotate the master cylinder 45 degrees counterclockwise, then carefully pull the master cylinder through the dash panel, noting the routing of the hydraulic line to the slave cylinder.

6. If the master cylinder is to be replaced, position the master cylinder in a vise and drive out the roll pin using a drift. Remove the O-ring from the tube connection of the master cylinder.

To install:

7. Install a new O-ring onto the clutch tube and install the tube into the master cylinder. Install the roll pin.

8. Position the clutch master cylinder in the engine compartment and route the hydraulic line to the slave cylinder.

9. Install the master cylinder to the dash panel and install the clutch master cylinder fluid reservoir.

10. Push the hydraulic line male connector onto the slave cylinder female connector. Connect the pushrod to the clutch pedal.

11. Fill the reservoir and bleed the system.

Clutch Slave Cylinder

REMOVAL AND INSTALLATION

Thunderbird and Cougar

1. Disconnect the negative battery cable.
2. Disconnect the master cylinder pushrod from the clutch pedal.
3. Raise and support the vehicle safely.
4. Disconnect the hydraulic line from the slave cylinder by depressing

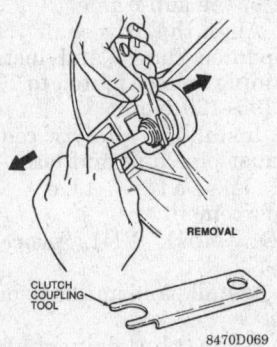

REMOVAL

CLUTCH COUPLING TOOL

8470D069

Disconnecting the clutch hydraulic line from the slave cylinder — Thunderbird and Cougar

the white retainer bushing with tool T88T–70522–A or equivalent, while pulling slightly on the line.

5. Remove the transmission.
6. Remove the clutch release bearing by rotating the assembly against the spring tension until the spring pushes the bearing off the slave cylinder.
7. Remove the clutch slave cylinder retaining bolts and remove the slave cylinder.

To install:

8. Position the slave cylinder over the input shaft aligning the bleeder screw and line coupling with holes in the transmission housing.

9. Install the slave cylinder retaining bolts and tighten to 15–19 ft. lbs. (20–27 Nm).

10. Install the release bearing and transmission.

11. Push the hydraulic line male connector onto the slave cylinder female connector.

12. Connect the master cylinder pushrod to the clutch pedal. Bleed the system.

Hydraulic Clutch System

BLEEDING

Thunderbird and Cougar

NOTE: Be sure to pump the clutch at least 30 times to make sure air is in the system. If the slave cylinder is pushed off the clutch plate, a similar pedal feel may occur. Pumping the clutch pushes fluid from the clutch reservoir into the slave cylinder, pushing it out to meet the clutch plate.

1. Clean all dirt and grease from the cap to make sure no foreign substances enter the system.
2. Remove the cap and diaphragm and fill the reservoir to the top with the proper fluid.
3. Raise and support the vehicle safely.
4. Attach a hose to the bleeder valve at the slave cylinder.

NOTE: Keep the clutch fluid reservoir full at all times to prevent air from being pulled into the system.

5. While the clutch pedal is being depressed, slightly open the bleeder valve and observe air bubbles in the clutch fluid at the end of the hose.
6. Close the bleeder valve before releasing the clutch pedal.

7. Repeat Steps 5 and 6, as necessary, until no air bubbles are observed.
8. Lower the vehicle and fill the reservoir. Road test the vehicle.

AUTOMATIC TRANSMISSION

Transmission Assembly

REMOVAL AND INSTALLATION

1. Disconnect the negative battery cable. Raise the vehicle and support safely.
2. Drain the fluid from the transmission by removing all oil pan bolts except the 2 at the front. Loosen the 2 at the front and drop the oil pan at the rear to allow the fluid to drain into a container. When drained, reinstall a few of the bolts to hold the pan in place.
3. Remove the access cover and remove the converter drain plug, if equipped, to allow the converter to drain. After the converter has drained, reinstall the drain plug and tighten. Remove the converter to flywheel nuts by turning the converter to expose the bolts.

NOTE: Crank the engine over with a wrench on the crankshaft pulley attaching bolt. On belt driven OHC engines, never rotate the pulley in a counterclockwise direction as viewed from the front.

4. On Mustang and Mark VII, mark the position of the driveshaft on the axle flange so it can be reinstalled in the same position. Disconnect the driveshaft from the flange and slide the driveshaft from the transmission. Install a suitable plug in the extension housing to prevent fluid leakage.

5. On Thunderbird and Cougar, proceed as follows:
   a. Remove the catalytic converter.
   b. Remove the body reinforcement.
   c. Remove the exhaust pipe and muffler assembly.
   d. Mark the position of the driveshaft on the axle flange so it can be reinstalled in the same position. Disconnect the driveshaft from the flange.

e. Loosen the differential housing assembly rear mounting nuts approximately ¼ in.

f. Position an axle stand under the front of the differential housing and remove the forward mounting nuts and bushings. Pull the vent tube from the hole in the subframe.

g. Lower the front of the differential housing with the axle stand and slide the driveshaft out of the transmission above the axle housing. Let the driveshaft rest on the front driveshaft support and axle assembly.

6. On Mark VIII, proceed as follows:

a. Mark the position of the driveshaft to rear axle so it can be reinstalled in the same position. Disconnect the driveshaft from the rear axle.

b. Remove the catalytic converter inlet pipe.

c. Lower the exhaust pipe and muffler assembly.

d. Loosen the rear axle housing bolts.

e. Lower the housing enough for driveshaft clearance. Slide the driveshaft out of the transmission and position over rear axle housing.

f. Remove transmission oil inlet tube.

7. Remove the speedometer cable or sensor from the extension housing.

8. Disconnect the manual control shift rod or cable and the downshift rod or cable from the transmission control levers.

9. Remove the starter cable and remove the starter.

10. Remove the electrical wires and vacuum lines, as required from the transmission assembly. Remove the bellcrank bracket, if equipped, from the converter housing.

11. Place a support under the transmission and slightly raise it. It may be necessary to raise the engine hood and loosen the fan shroud.

12. Remove the rear crossmember and engine rear support. Disconnect and remove any interfering exhaust components.

13. Lower the transmission to expose the oil cooler line fittings. Disconnect the lines from the transmission.

14. On Mark VIII, loosen EGR retaining nut on left converter and position aside.

15. Support the engine and remove the dipstick tube and all the bellhousing retaining bolts except for the top 2.

16. Chain the transmission to the jack or support unit for safety.

17. Remove the 2 top bolts from the converter housing and move the transmission rearward and down from under the vehicle. Hold the converter in place to avoid having it drop from the transmission.

18. On Mark VIII, remove the transmission pad from the left side of the converter housing using a hacksaw. Wear proper eye protection.

To install:

19. Tighten the converter drain plug to 8–28 ft. lbs. (11–38 Nm) or to 21–23 ft. lbs. (28–30 Nm) on Mark VIII.

20. Position the converter to the transmission and rotate into position to make sure the drive flats are fully engaged in the pump gear.

NOTE: Lubricate the pilot with chassis grease.

21. Raise the converter and transmission assembly into position. Rotate the converter until the studs and drain plug are in alignment with the holes in the flywheel. Align the orange balancing marks on the converter stud and flywheel bolt hole if balancing marks are present.

NOTE: The converter face must rest squarely against the flywheel. This indicates that the converter pilot is not binding in the engine crankshaft. To ensure the converter is properly seated, grasp a converter stud. It should move freely back and forth in the flywheel hole. If the converter will not move, the transmission must be removed and the converter repositioned so the impeller hub is properly engaged in the pump gear.

22. Install the transmission-to-engine attaching bolts. Tighten the bolts to 40–50 ft. lbs. (55–68 Nm) on all except 2.3L engine. On 2.3L engine, tighten the bolts to 28–38 ft. lbs. (38–51 Nm).

23. Remove the safety chain from around the transmission.

24. Install a new O-ring on the lower end of the transmission filler tube, if equipped. Install the tube to the transmission case and secure with the retaining bolt.

25. Connect the speedometer cable to the transmission case, if equipped.

26. Connect the oil cooler lines to the right side of the transmission case.

27. Position the crossmember on the side supports. Position the rear mount on the crossmember and install the attaching bolts and/or nuts.

28. Secure the engine rear support to the extension housing.

29. Install any exhaust system components, if removed.

30. Lower the transmission and remove the jack.

31. Secure the crossmember to the side supports with the attaching bolts.

32. Connect the TV linkage rod or cable and the manual linkage rod.

33. Install the converter to flywheel attaching nuts and tighten to 20–34 ft. lbs. (27–46 Nm). Install the converter housing cover.

34. Secure the starter motor in place and connect all electrical connections.

35. Install the driveshaft, making sure the index marks are aligned. On Thunderbird and Cougar, proceed as follows:

a. Raise the differential housing with the axle stand and install the bushings and retaining nuts. Tighten to 68–100 ft. lbs. (92–136 Nm). Remove the axle stand.

b. Tighten the differential rear retaining nuts to 122–156 ft. lbs. (165–211 Nm).

c. Position the vent tube in the hole of the sub-frame.

d. Align the driveshaft yoke and companion flange and install the retaining bolts. Tighten to 70–96 ft. lbs. (95–129 Nm).

e. Install the catalytic converter, exhaust pipe and muffler.

f. Install the body reinforcement.

36. On Mark VIII, proceed as follows:

a. Install transmission oil inlet tube.

b. Slide the driveshaft into position.

c. Align marks made during removal and connect the driveshaft to the rear axle.

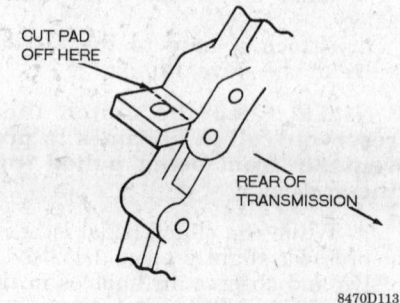

CUT PAD OFF HERE

REAR OF TRANSMISSION

8470D113

Transmission pad removal — Mark VIII

d. Tighten the rear axle housing bolts.

e. Install exhaust system.

37. Lower the vehicle. Fill the transmission with the proper type and quantity of fluid, start the engine and check the transmission for leakage. Adjust the linkage as required.

MANUAL LINKAGE ADJUSTMENT

1. Position the transmission selector lever in the **OVERDRIVE** position.

NOTE: The shift lever should be held against the rearward OVERDRIVE stop when the linkage is adjusted.

2. Raise and safely support the vehicle. Loosen the manual lever shift cable or rod retaining nut. Move the transmission manual lever to the **OVERDRIVE** position.

3. With the transmission selector lever and manual lever in the **OVERDRIVE** position, tighten the retaining nut to 10–18 ft. lbs. (13–25 Nm).

4. Check the operation of the transmission in each selector lever position.

THROTTLE VALVE CABLE ADJUSTMENT

Automatic Overdrive Transmission

1. Set the parking brake and place the shift selector in **N**.

2. Remove the air cleaner cover and inlet tube from the throttle body inlet to access the throttle lever and cable.

3. Using a small prybar, pry the grooved pin on the cable assembly out of the grommet on the throttle body. Then push out the white locking tab.

4. Check the plastic block with pin and tab; it should slide freely on the notched rod. If not, the white tab may not be pushed out far enough.

5. While holding the throttle lever firmly against the idle stop, push the grooved pin into the grommet on the throttle lever as far as it will go.

6. Make sure the throttle lever does not move while pushing the pin into the grommet.

7. Install the air cleaner cover and inlet tube.

DRIVE AXLE

Rear Halfshaft

REMOVAL AND INSTALLATION

Mark VIII, Thunderbird and Cougar

NOTE: Before removing the rear halfshafts, new inboard CV-joint stub shaft circlips, new differential oil seals and new hub retainer nuts must be available for assembly.

1. Remove the wheelcover/hub cover and remove the hub retainer nut. Loosen the wheel nuts.

2. Raise and support the vehicle safely by the frame only. Remove the wheel nuts and remove the wheel and tire assembly.

3. If equipped with drum brakes, remove the brake drum.

4. If equipped with disc brakes, perform the following:

a. Remove the anti-lock brake sensors, if equipped.

b. Use needle-nose pliers to slide the parking brake cable adjusting clip downward until the cable is free.

c. Remove the parking brake cable from the brake caliper.

d. Remove the upper and lower caliper retaining bolts and remove the caliper. Support the caliper aside with a wire, do not allow it to hang from the brake hose.

e. Remove the brake rotor, except Mark VIII.

5. Remove the upper control arm nuts and bolt. Wire the upper control arm to the top of the shock absorber.

6. Using a paint marker, mark the position of the lower control arm in relation to the knuckle with the lower bushings in the relaxed position.

NOTE: Failure to mark this relationship will result in bushing wind-up on assembly and incorrect ride height, causing misalignment and premature tire wear.

7. Use a suitable puller to free the halfshaft from the hub.

8. On Thunderbird and Cougar, proceed as follows:

a. Remove the lower control arm to knuckle attaching bolts. Remove the knuckle assembly while supporting the outboard CV-joint and boot. Carefully rest the halfshaft on the lower control arm.

b. If equipped with drum brakes, wire the knuckle assembly to the top of the shock. Do not allow the knuckle assembly to hang from the brake hose.

c. Remove the halfshaft from the differential using CV-joint remover tool T89P–3514–A or equivalent. Push the tool outward until the CV-joint is freed from the differential side gear.

NOTE: Be careful not to damage the differential oil seal, differential housing and/or CV-joint boot.

d. Remove the halfshaft from the vehicle. Insert plugs into the differential housing to prevent fluid loss.

9. On Mark VIII, proceed as follows:

a. Remove the lower control arm to knuckle attaching nuts. Push the halfshaft through the hub while positioning CV-joint and knuckle to allow the front lower bolt to clear the CV-joint and remove the bolt. Remove and save the washers.

b. Remove rear bolt, washer, and knuckle assembly.

NOTE: Be careful not to damage the differential oil seal, differential housing and/or CV-joint boot.

c. Remove the halfshaft from the vehicle. Insert plugs into the differential housing to prevent fluid loss.

To install:

10. Remove the differential plugs and install new differential oil seals.

11. Install a new circlip on the halfshaft. Start the ends in the groove and push the circlip into the groove, to prevent over expanding the circlip.

12. Lightly lubricate the stub shaft splines and carefully align the splines on the shaft with the splines in the differential.

13. Push the halfshaft inward to seat the circlip in the differential side gear groove. Use care not to damage the seal.

14. Engage the hub splines with the outboard CV-joint splines.

15. Install the lower control arm bolts and nuts. Align the paint marks and tighten the bolts to 119–147 ft. lbs. (160–200 Nm) or to 94–131 ft. lbs. (128–178 Nm) on Mark VIII.

16. Install a new hub retaining nut and pull the CV-joint into the hub as far as possible by hand.

17. Install the upper arm retaining bolt and nut and tighten to 119–147 ft. lbs. (160–200 Nm) or to 117–142 ft. lbs. (158–193 Nm) or Mark VIII.

18. If equipped with drum brakes, install the brake drum. If equipped with disc brakes, proceed as follows:

a. Install the brake rotor, except Mark VIII.

b. Install the brake caliper assembly to the rotor with the outer brake shoe against the rotor's braking surface. This prevents pinching the piston boot between the inner brake shoe and the piston.

c. Install the upper and lower caliper retaining bolts and tighten to 80–99 ft. lbs. (108–135 Nm) or to 64–88 ft. lbs. (87–119 Nm) on Mark VIII.

d. Install the parking brake cable to the brake caliper. Install the cable adjustment clip.

e. Install the anti-lock brake sensor, if equipped. Tighten the retaining bolts to 15–19 ft. lbs. (19–27 Nm).

19. Check inboard CV-joint circlip engagement by attempting to pull the inboard CV-joint from the axle. If the CV-joint circlip is not seated, push the CV-joint in until the circlip is fully engaged in the side gear.

20. Check the axle lube level and fill, as necessary.

21. Install the wheel and tire assembly and tighten the wheel nuts to 80–106 ft. lbs. (108–144 Nm). Lower the vehicle.

22. Tighten the hub nut to 250 ft. lbs. (340 Nm). Install the wheelcover/hub cover.

CV-Boot

REMOVAL AND INSTALLATION

Mark VIII, Thunderbird and Cougar

1. Remove the halfshaft from the vehicle and clamp in a vise. Do not allow the vise jaws to contact the boot or its clamp.

NOTE: The vise should be equipped with jaw caps to prevent damage to any machined surfaces.

2. Cut and remove both boot clamps and slide the boot back on the shaft.

3. Slide the outer race off the tripod.

NOTE: When replacing damaged CV-joint boots, the grease should be checked for contamination or gritty feeling. If the CV-joints are operating satisfactory and the grease does not feel contaminated, add grease and re-place the boot. If the grease appears contaminated, the CV-joint should be disassembled and inspected.

4. Remove trilobe insert from outer race.

5. Move the stopring back on the shaft using snapring pliers.

6. Move the tripod back on the shaft to allow access to the circlip.

7. Remove the circlip and the tripod from the shaft.

8. Remove the stopring and remove the inboard CV-joint boot.

9. Reposition the halfshaft in the vise and remove the outboard CV-joint boot.

NOTE: The outboard CV-joint is permanently retained to the inter-connecting shaft and cannot be disassembled. Outboard CV-joints are serviced as an assembly, including the inter-connecting shaft, boot, clamps grease and circlips.

To install:

10. Slide the outboard boot on the shaft. Before positioning the boot over the CV-joint, pack the CV-joint and boot with grease.

1992 vehicles, the total amount of grease required is 7.05 ounces (200 grams) with 3.8L engine

1992 vehicles, the total amount of grease required is 8.82 ounces (250 grams) with 3.8L SC or 5.0L engine.

1993–96 vehicles, the total amount of grease required is 5.28 ounces (150 grams) with 3.8L engine

1993–96 vehicles, the total amount of grease required is 7.92 ounces (225 grams) with 3.8L SC, 4.6L or 5.0L engine.

11. Position the boot on the CV-joint and install the boot clamps.

12. Slide the inboard CV-joint boot on the shaft.

13. With the stopring installed past the splines, install the tripod assembly with the chamfered side toward the stopring.

14. Start 1 end of a new circlip in the groove of the halfshaft and work the circlip over the stub shaft end and into the groove. This will avoid over-expanding the circlip.

15. Compress the circlip and slide the tripod assembly forward over the circlip to expose the stopring groove.

16. Move the stopring into the groove using snapring pliers and make sure it is fully seated in the groove.

17. Fill the CV-joint outer race and boot with grease.

1992 vehicles, the total amount of grease required is 9 ounces (250 grams) without anti-lock brakes

1992 vehicles, the total amount of grease required is 10.58 ounces (300 grams) with anti-lock brakes.

1993–96 vehicles, the total amount of grease required is 5 ounces (140 grams) with 3.8L engine

1993–96 vehicles, the total amount of grease required is 8.8 ounces (250 grams) with 3.8L SC, 4.6L or 5.0L engine.

18. Install the outer race on the tripod assembly.

19. Position the boot over the CV-joint. Move the CV-joint in and out, as necessary, to adjust to the proper length.

20. Release any air pressure by inserting a small prybar with a dulled blade between the boot and the outer bearing race.

21. Seat the boot in the groove and clamp in position without cutting the boot.

Driveshafts and U-Joints

REMOVAL AND INSTALLATION

Except Mark VIII, Thunderbird and Cougar

1. Raise and safely support the vehicle. Matchmark the rear driveshaft yoke and the companion flange so they can be reassembled in the same position to maintain balance.

NOTE: Mark VII vehicles may have a balance weight attached to 1 of the flange bolts. This bolt should be reinstalled in it's original position.

2. Remove the flange bolts and disconnect the driveshaft from the axle companion flange.

3. Allow the rear of the driveshaft to drop down slightly. Pull the driveshaft and slip yoke out of the transmission extension housing.

4. Plug the transmission to prevent fluid leakage.

To install:

5. Lubricate the yoke splines and install the yoke into the transmission extension housing, aligning the splines. Be careful not to bottom the slip yoke hard against the transmission seal.

6. Rotate the pinion flange, as necessary, to align the matchmarks made during removal. Install the driveshaft yoke to the pinion flange.

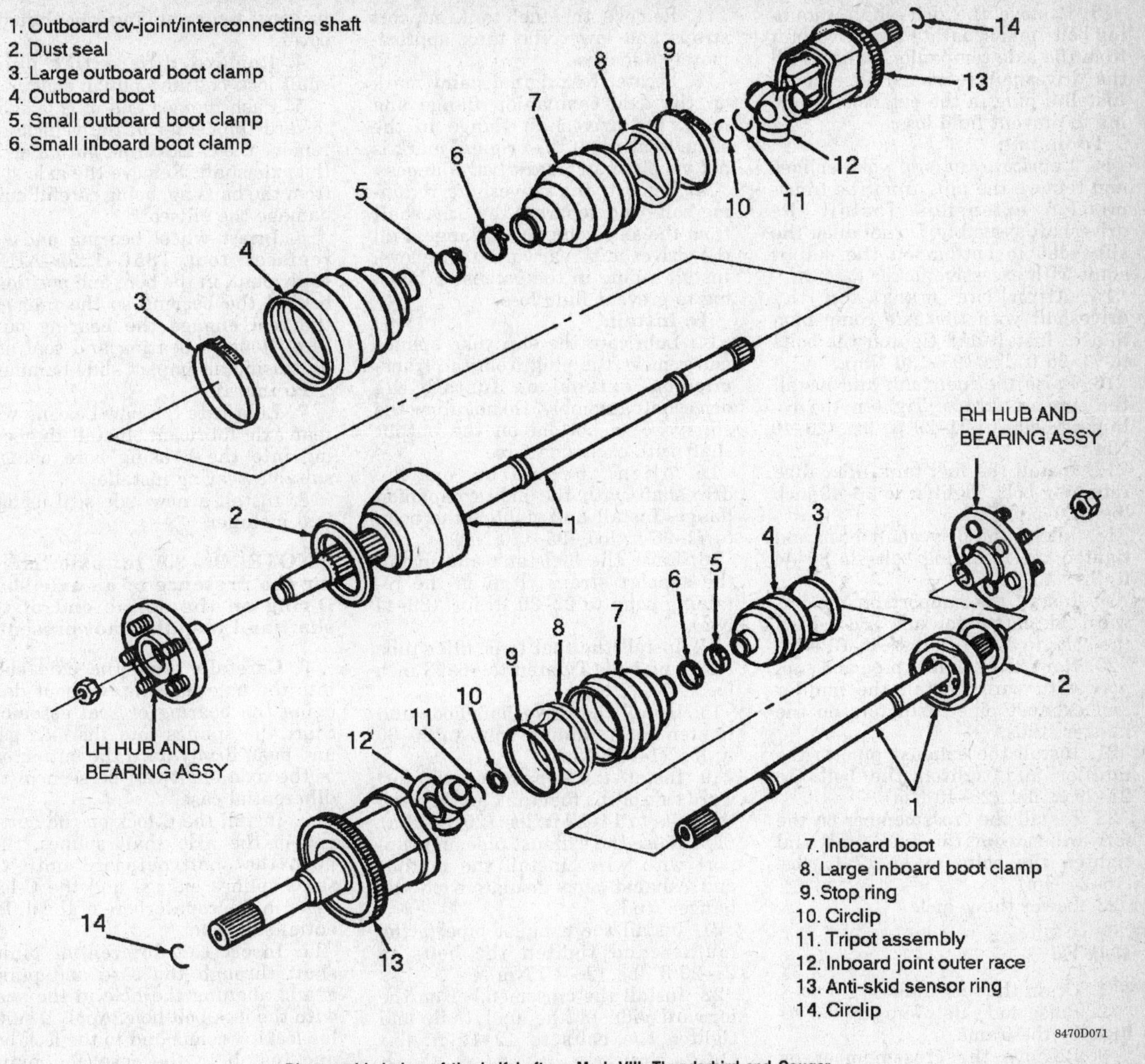

1. Outboard cv-joint/interconnecting shaft
2. Dust seal
3. Large outboard boot clamp
4. Outboard boot
5. Small outboard boot clamp
6. Small inboard boot clamp

RH HUB AND BEARING ASSY

LH HUB AND BEARING ASSY

7. Inboard boot
8. Large inboard boot clamp
9. Stop ring
10. Circlip
11. Tripot assembly
12. Inboard joint outer race
13. Anti-skid sensor ring
14. Circlip

8470D071

Disassembled view of the halfshafts — Mark VIII, Thunderbird and Cougar

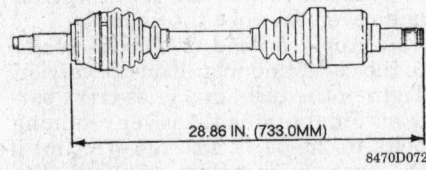

28.86 IN. (733.0MM)

8470D072

Halfshaft assembled length — Mark VIII, Thunderbird and Cougar

Install the bolts and tighten to 71–96 ft. lbs. (95–130 Nm).

Thunderbird and Cougar

1. Drain the fuel tank.
2. Raise and safely support the vehicle by the frame.
3. Remove the crossmember on the forward side of the fuel tank.
4. Remove the exhaust pipe at the muffler. Lower the pipe and support with a wire.
5. Remove the exhaust pipe rear insulator from the exhaust pipe hanger stud.
6. Remove the muffler insulator from the hanger stud. Remove the exhaust system from the vehicle.

7. Remove the driveshaft hoop on the rear side of the tank.
8. Remove the fuel tank filler tube retaining bolt from the right frame rail.
9. Carefully place a transmission jack under the fuel tank and remove the front heat shield.
10. Remove the support on the forward side of the fuel tank.
11. Remove the fuel tank support straps and lower the tank approximately 6 in.
12. Locate the original paint mark on the axle companion flange and mark the driveshaft flange in the same location. If the original mark is not visible matchmark both flanges.

13. Remove the driveshaft retaining bolts and separate the driveshaft from the axle companion flange. Pull the driveshaft rearward to remove. Install a plug in the extension housing to prevent fluid loss.

To install:

14. Lubricate the slip yoke splines and remove the plug from the transmission extension. Install the driveshaft assembly. Do not allow the slip yoke to bottom on the output shaft with excessive force.

15. Align the marks on the driveshaft with the axle companion flange. Install and tighten the bolts to 71–96 ft. lbs. (95–130 Nm).

16. Raise the fuel tank and install the support straps. Tighten the retaining bolts to 21–29 ft. lbs. (28–40 Nm).

17. Install the fuel tank filler tube retaining bolt. Tighten to 36–48 inch lbs. (4.0–5.5 Nm).

18. Install the driveshaft hoop and tighten the retaining bolts to 30–44 ft. lbs. (40–61 Nm).

19. Install the support on the forward side of the fuel tank and tighten the bolts to 30–44 ft. lbs. (40–61 Nm).

20. Raise the exhaust pipe and support with wire. Install the muffler and exhaust pipe insulators on the hanger studs.

21. Install the exhaust pipe to the muffler and tighten the bolts to 21–29 ft. lbs. (28–40 Nm).

22. Install the crossmember on the forward side of the fuel tank and tighten the bolts to 12–17 ft. lbs. (16–24 Nm).

23. Lower the vehicle.

Mark VIII

1. Drain the fuel tank.
2. Raise and safely support the vehicle by the frame.
3. Remove the crossmember on the forward side of the fuel tank.
4. Remove the exhaust pipe at the muffler. Lower the pipe and support with a wire.
5. Remove the exhaust pipe rear insulator from the exhaust pipe hanger stud.
6. Support mufflers and remove muffler rear hangers from rear frame rails. Remove the exhaust system from the vehicle.
7. Remove the fuel tank filler tube retaining bolt from the right frame rail.
8. Carefully place a transmission jack under the fuel tank.
9. Remove the support on the forward side of the fuel tank.
10. Remove the driveshaft hoop on the rear side of the tank.

11. Remove the fuel tank support straps and lower the tank approximately 6 inches.
12. Locate the original paint mark on the axle companion flange and mark the driveshaft flange in the same location. If the original mark is not visible matchmark both flanges.
13. Remove the driveshaft retaining bolts and separate the driveshaft from the axle companion flange. Pull the driveshaft rearward to remove. Install a plug in the extension housing to prevent fluid loss.

To install:

14. Lubricate the slip yoke splines and remove the plug from the transmission extension. Install the driveshaft assembly. Do not allow the slip yoke to bottom on the output shaft with excessive force.

15. Align the marks on the driveshaft with the axle companion flange. Install and tighten the bolts to 71–96 ft. lbs. (95–130 Nm).

16. Raise the fuel tank and install the support straps. Tighten the retaining bolts to 22–30 ft. lbs. (29–41 Nm).

17. Install the fuel tank filler tube retaining bolt. Tighten to 16–23 inch lbs. (2.7–3.7 Nm).

18. Install the driveshaft hoop and tighten the retaining bolts to 20–30 ft. lbs. (14–22 Nm).

19. Install the support on the forward side of the fuel tank and tighten the bolts to 14–22 ft. lbs. (20–30 Nm).

20. Raise the exhaust pipe and support with wire. Install the muffler and exhaust pipe insulators on the hanger studs.

21. Install the exhaust pipe to the muffler and tighten the bolts to 21–29 ft. lbs. (28–40 Nm).

22. Install the crossmember on the forward side of the fuel tank and tighten the bolts to 12–17 ft. lbs. (16–24 Nm).

23. Lower the vehicle.

Rear Axle Shaft, Bearing and Seal

REMOVAL AND INSTALLATION

Except Mark VIII, Thunderbird and Cougar

1. Raise and safely support the vehicle. Remove wheel and tire assembly and remove brake drum or brake rotor.
2. If equipped, remove the anti-lock brake speed sensor.
3. Clean all dirt from the area of the carrier cover. Drain the axle lu-

bricant by removing the housing cover.

4. Remove differential pinion shaft lock bolt and pinion shaft.

5. Push flanged end of axle shafts toward the center of the vehicle and remove the C-lock from button end of the axle shaft. Remove the axle shaft from the housing, being careful not to damage the oil seal.

6. Insert wheel bearing and seal replacer tool T85L–1225–AH or equivalent, in the bore and position it behind the bearing so the tangs on the tool engage the bearing outer race. Remove bearing and seal as a unit using an impact slide hammer.

To install:

7. Lubricate the new bearing with rear axle lubricant. Install the bearing into the housing bore using a suitable bearing installer.

8. Install a new axle seal using a seal installer.

NOTE: On 8.8 in. axle, check for the presence of an axle shaft O-ring on the spline end of the shaft and install, if not present.

9. Carefully slide the axle shaft into the axle housing, without damaging the bearing or seal assembly. Start the splines into the side gear and push firmly until the button end of the axle shaft can be seen in the differential case.

10. Install the C-lock on the button end of the axle shaft splines, then push the shaft outboard until the shaft splines engage and the C-lock seats in the counterbore of the differential side gear.

11. Insert the differential pinion shaft through the case and pinion gears, aligning the hole in the shaft with the lock bolt hole. Apply a suitable locking compound to the lock bolt and install in the case and pinion shaft. Tighten to 15–30 ft. lbs. (20–41 Nm).

12. Cover the inside of the differential case with a shop rag and clean the machined surface of the carrier and cover. Remove the shop rag.

13. Apply a bead of silicone sealer to the cover and install on the carrier. Tighten the bolts in a criss-cross pattern. Final torque the cover retaining bolts to 25–34 ft. lbs. (34–47 Nm) if the cover is metal or 15–19 ft. lbs. (20–27 Nm) if the cover is plastic.

14. Add rear axle lubricant to the carrier to a level $1/4$–$9/16$ in. below the bottom of the fill hole. Install the filler plug and tighten to 15–30 ft. lbs. (20–41 Nm).

15. Install the anti-lock speed sensor, if equipped. Tighten the retain-

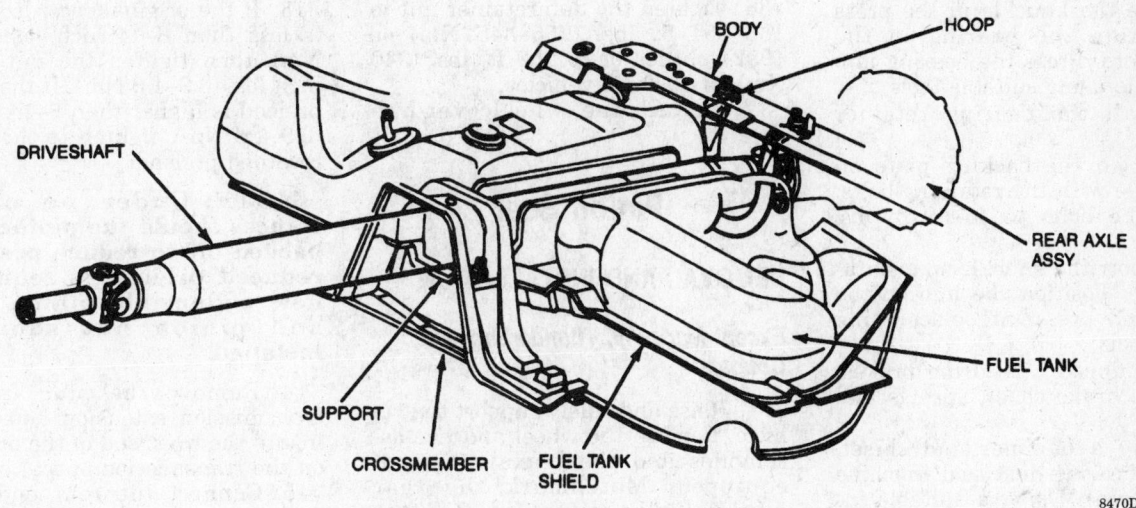

Driveshaft installation — Mark VIII, Thunderbird and Cougar

ing bolt to 40–60 inch lbs. (4.5–6.8 Nm).

16. Install the brake calipers and rotors or the brake drums, as required. Install the wheel and tire assembly and lower the vehicle.

Mark VIII, Thunderbird and Cougar

NOTE: A new hub retainer nut must be used in this procedure.

1. Remove the wheelcover/hub cover from the wheel and tire assembly and loosen the lug nuts.
2. Remove and discard the hub nut and washer.

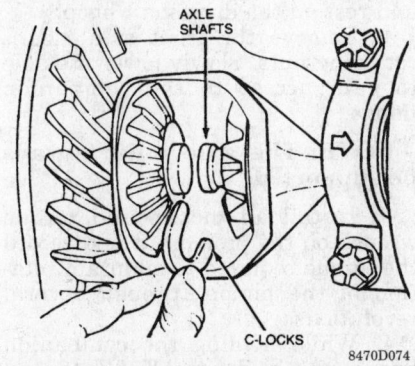

Removing the axle shaft C-locks

3. Raise and safely support the vehicle. Remove the wheel and tire assembly.
4. Use needle-nose pliers to slide the parking brake cable adjusting clip downward, until the cable is free.
5. If equipped with disc brakes, remove the parking brake cable from the caliper.
6. Remove the caliper from the disc brake rotor, leaving the brake hose connected. Wire the caliper to the brake line junction bracket; do not let it hang by the brake hose.
7. Remove the brake rotor or brake drum except on Mark VIII.
8. If equipped with disc brakes, remove the splash shield.
9. If equipped with drum brakes, disconnect the parking brake cable and disconnect the brake line from the wheel cylinder.
10. Remove the upper control arm nut and bolt. Wire the upper control arm to the body to prevent damage to the CV-joint boots when the knuckle and hub assembly is removed.
11. Attach hub removal tool T81P–1104–C or other equivalent puller tool, to the hub studs and turn the tool shaft until the halfshaft is free in the hub.
12. Mark the position of the control arm in relation to the knuckle with

the bushings in the relaxed position. When the upper control arm bolt is removed from the knuckle, the lower arm bushings will return to the relaxed position.

NOTE: Failure to mark the position will cause bushing wind up at assembly resulting in improper ride height. This can cause incorrect alignment and tire wear.

13. If the knuckle is being replaced, note the approximate angle of the knuckle in the relaxed position by measuring the distance from the upper bushing to a point on the vehicle body.
14. Remove the lower control arm-to-knuckle retaining bolts and nuts and remove the knuckle assembly from the halfshaft.
15. Position the knuckle and hub assembly in a vise.
16. If equipped with drum brakes, remove the brake shoes, springs and adjuster from the backing plate. Remove the screws retaining the backing plate to the knuckle.
17. Position a suitable 3-jaw puller on the knuckle and press the hub out of the knuckle.
18. Remove the backing plate and remove the bearing retainer snapring.

19. Position the knuckle and bearing assembly on a press and, using suitable tools, press the bearing from the knuckle.

To install:

20. Place the knuckle in the press and position the bearing in the knuckle bore. Press the bearing into the knuckle using suitable tools.

21. Install the bearing retainer snapring.

22. Position the backing plate on the knuckle with the retaining bolts. Tighten the bolts to 45–59 ft. lbs. (61–81 Nm).

23. Support the knuckle on a suitable fixture. Position the hub on the bearing and press into place using suitable tools.

24. If equipped with drum brakes, install the brake shoes, springs and adjuster.

25. Using a hammer and chisel, drive the bearing dust seal from the outer CV-joint. Using a suitable installation tool, install a new seal on the CV-joint, making sure the seal flange faces out toward the bearing.

26. Place the knuckle and hub assembly on the halfshaft splines and install the lower control arm-to-knuckle bolts and nuts. Position the knuckle so the marks made during the removal procedure align with the marks on the control arm. If a new knuckle is being installed, set the knuckle at the approximate angle noted during removal before tightening the bolts.

27. Push the knuckle and hub assembly firmly onto the halfshaft splines. Install the upper control arm bolt and nut and tighten the nut to 118–148 ft. lbs. (160–200 Nm).

28. Install a new hub nut and washer and tighten by hand.

29. If equipped with disc brakes, install the splash shield to the knuckle and tighten the retaining bolts to 45–59 ft. lbs. (61–81 Nm).

30. If equipped with drum brakes, connect the brake line to the wheel cylinder and connect the parking brake cable.

31. Install the brake rotor or drum.

32. If equipped with disc brakes, install the caliper over the rotor and the outer brake pad against the rotor, to prevent pinching the piston boot between the inner pad and piston. Install the caliper-to-knuckle bolts and tighten to 44–60 ft. lbs. (59–81 Nm) or to 64–88 ft. lbs. (87–119 Nm) on Mark VIII.

33. If equipped with disc brakes, connect the parking brake cable to the caliper and install the adjustment clip.

34. Bleed the brake system, if equipped with drum brakes.

35. Install the wheel and tire assembly, lower the vehicle and apply the parking brake.

36. Tighten the hub retainer nut to 188–254 ft. lbs. (255–345 Nm) on 1992 vehicles or to 250 ft. lbs. (340 Nm) on 1993–96 vehicles.

37. Install the wheelcover/hub cover.

Pinion Seal

REMOVAL AND INSTALLATION

Except Mark VIII, Thunderbird and Cougar

1. Raise and safely support the vehicle. Remove the wheel and tire assemblies and the brake drums, if equipped. Matchmark the rear driveshaft yoke and the axle flange so they may be reassembled in the same position to maintain balance.

2. Disconnect the driveshaft from the rear axle companion flange, remove the driveshaft and remove the driveshaft from the extension housing. Plug the extension housing to prevent leakage.

3. Install an inch pound torque wrench on the pinion nut and record the torque required to maintain rotation of the pinion through several revolutions.

4. While holding the companion flange with holder tool T78P–4851–A or equivalent, remove the pinion nut.

5. Clean the area around the oil seal and place a pan under the seal.

6. Mark the companion flange in relation to the pinion shaft so the flange can be installed in the same position.

7. Remove the rear axle companion flange using tool T65L–4851–B or equivalent. Do not use a hammer.

8. Pry the seal out of the housing using a prybar.

To install:

9. Clean the oil seal seat surface and install the seal in the carrier using seal replacer tool T79P–4676–A or equivalent. Apply lubricant to the lips of the seal.

10. Apply a small amount of lubricant to the companion flange splines, align the marks on the flange and and the pinion shaft and install the flange.

11. Install a new nut on the pinion shaft and apply lubricant on the washer side of the nut.

12. Hold the flange with the holder tool while tightening the nut. Rotate the pinion to ensure proper seating and take frequent pinion bearing torque preload readings until the original recorded preload reading is obtained.

13. If the original recorded preload is less than 8–14 inch lbs. (0.9–1.6 Nm), then tighten the nut to 8–14 inch lbs. (0.9–1.6 Nm). If the original preload is higher than 8–14 inch lbs. (0.9–1.6 Nm), tighten to the original recorded preload.

NOTE: Under no circumstances should the pinion nut be backed off to reduce preload. If reduced preload is required, a new collapsible pinion spacer and pinion nut should be installed.

14. Remove the plug from the transmission extension housing and install the front end of the driveshaft on the transmission output shaft.

15. Connect the rear end of the driveshaft to the axle companion flange, aligning the scribe marks and tighten the 4 bolts to 71–96 ft. lbs. (95–130 Nm).

16. Add lubricant to the axle until it is 1/4–9/16 in. below the bottom of the fill hole with the axle in operating position.

17. Make sure the axle vent is not plugged with debris. Install the brake drums and tire and wheel assemblies.

Mark VIII, Thunderbird and Cougar

1. Raise and safely support the vehicle on the frame.

2. Place a screw type jackstand under the rear axle pinion nose and remove the rear axle mount to axle cover retaining bolts and nuts.

3. Install the rear axle mount bolt in the lower bolt hole to allow the axle to pivot forward.

4. Mark the driveshaft in relation to the companion flange and remove the driveshaft retaining bolts.

5. Slide the driveshaft forward and rest on the driveshaft hoop.

6. Remove the front axle mount retaining nuts. Slowly lower the axle to gain access to the companion flange.

NOTE: The axle must always be supported.

7. Install an inch pound torque wrench on the pinion nut and record the torque required to maintain rotation of the pinion through several revolutions.

8. While holding the companion flange with holder tool T78P–4851–A or equivalent, remove the pinion nut.

9. Mark the companion flange in relation to the pinion shaft so the flange can be installed in the same position.

10. Place a pan under the companion flange.

11. Remove the rear axle companion flange using tool T65L–4851–B or equivalent.

12. Pry the seal out of the housing using a prybar.

To install:

13. Clean the pinion seal seat surface and install the seal in the carrier using seal replacer tool T79P–4676–A or equivalent. Apply lubricant to the lips of the seal.

14. Apply a small amount of lubricant to the companion flange splines, align the marks on the flange and and the pinion shaft and install the flange.

15. Install a new nut on the pinion shaft and apply lubricant on the washer side of the nut.

16. Hold the flange with the holder tool while tightening the nut. Rotate the pinion to ensure proper seating and take frequent pinion bearing torque preload readings until the original recorded preload reading is obtained.

17. If the original recorded preload is less than 8–14 inch lbs. (0.9–1.6 Nm), then tighten the nut to 8–14 inch lbs. (0.9–1.6 Nm). If the original preload is higher than 8–14 inch lbs. (0.9–1.6 Nm), tighten to the original recorded preload.

NOTE: Under no circumstances should the pinion nut be backed off to reduce preload. If reduced preload is required, a new collapsible pinion spacer and pinion nut should be installed.

18. Using a jackstand, raise and locate the axle on the front mounting bolts.

19. Install the front mounting nuts and tighten to 68–100 ft. lbs. (92–136 Nm).

20. Remove the rear mount bolt from the pivot position.

21. Install the rear mount bolts in the axle cover mount and tighten to 80–100 ft. lbs. (108–136 Nm).

22. Align the marks on the driveshaft and the companion flange, install the retaining bolts and tighten to 70–96 ft. lbs. (95–129 Nm).

23. Fill the rear axle with lubricant to level with the bottom of the filler hole. Install the filler plug and tighten to 20–30 ft. lbs. (28–40 Nm).

24. Lower the vehicle.

Axle Housing

REMOVAL AND INSTALLATION

Except Mark VIII, Thunderbird and Cougar

1. Raise and safely support the vehicle. Position safety stands under the rear frame crossmember.

2. Remove the cover and drain the axle lubricant.

3. Remove the wheel and tire assemblies. Remove the brake drums or brake rotors.

4. Remove the lock bolt from the pinion shaft and remove the shaft.

5. Remove the anti-lock brake sensor before removing the axle shafts, if equipped.

6. Push the axle shafts inward to remove the C-locks and remove the axle shafts.

7. If necessary, remove the bolt attaching the brake junction block to rear cover.

8. Remove the 4 retaining nuts from each backing plate and wire the backing plate to the underbody.

9. Matchmark the driveshaft yoke and companion flange. Disconnect the driveshaft at the companion flange and wire it to the underbody.

10. Support the axle housing with jackstands. Disengage the brake line from the clips that retain the line to the axle housing.

11. Disconnect the vent from the rear axle housing.

NOTE: Some axle vents may be secured to the housing assembly through the brake junction block. At assembly, a thread lock/sealer must be applied to ensure retension.

12. If equipped with air springs, proceed as follows:

  a. Disconnect the negative battery cable. Turn **OFF** the air suspension switch located in the trunk.

  b. Disconnect the electrical connector and the air line from the air spring solenoid, located on the air spring.

  c. Remove the solenoid clip and rotate the solenoid counterclockwise to the 1st stop.

  d. Pull the solenoid straight out slowly to the 2nd stop to bleed the air from the system.

--- **CAUTION** ---
Do not fully release the solenoid until the air is completely bled from the air spring, or personal injury may result.

  e. After the air is fully bled from the system, rotate the solenoid counterclockwise to the 3rd stop and remove the solenoid from the solenoid housing.

  f. Remove the bolts retaining the springs to the lower arms.

13. Disconnect the lower shock absorber studs from the mounting brackets on the axle housing. If equipped, disconnect the quad shock from the quad shock bracket.

14. Disconnect the upper arms from the mountings on the axle housing ear brackets.

15. Lower the axle housing assembly until the coil springs are released and lift out the coil springs.

16. Disconnect the suspension lower arms at the axle housing.

17. Lower the axle housing and remove it from the vehicle.

To install:

18. Position the axle housing under the vehicle and raise the axle with a hoist or jack. Connect the lower suspension arms to their mounting brackets on the axle housing. Do not tighten the bolts and nuts at this time.

19. Reposition the rear coil springs or air springs, as required.

20. Raise the housing into position.

21. Connect the upper arms to the mounting ears on the housing. Tighten the nuts and bolts to 100 ft. lbs. (135 Nm). Tighten the lower arm bolts and nuts to 100 ft. lbs. (35 Nm).

22. Connect the air springs to the axle housing.

23. Install the axle vent and the the brake line to the clips that retain the line to the axle housing. If equipped with air springs, proceed as follows:

  a. Check the solenoid O-rings for damage and replace, as required. Lightly grease the O-ring area of the solenoid and the larger solenoid housing O-ring with silicone dielectric compound.

  b. Insert the solenoid into the air spring end cap and rotate clockwise to the 3rd stop, push in to the 2nd stop, then rotate clockwise to the 1st stop.

  c. Install the solenoid clip. Connect the air line and the electrical connector.

24. Install the brake backing plates on the axle housing flanges.

25. Connect the lower shock absorber studs to the mounting bracket on the axle housing. If equipped, connect the quad shock to the quad shock bracket.

26. Connect the driveshaft to the companion flange and tighten the

bolts and nuts to 70–96 ft. lbs. (95–130 Nm).

27. Slide the rear axle shafts into the housing until the splines enter the side gear. Push the axle shafts inward and install the C-lock at the end of each shaft spline. Pull the shafts outboard until the C-lock enters the recess in the side gears.

28. Install the pinion shaft. Apply Loctite® to the pinion shaft lock bolt and tighten to 15–30 ft. lbs. (20–41 Nm).

29. Install the anti-lock sensor, if equipped.

30. Install the rear brake drums or disc brake rotors and calipers.

31. Install the rear carrier cover using new silicone sealer. Tighten the retaining bolts on metal covers to 25–34 ft. lbs. (34–47 Nm) or 15–19 ft. lbs. (20–27 Nm) on plastic covers.

32. Install the brake junction block on the carrier cover and tighten to 11–17 ft. lbs. (14–24 Nm).

33. Fill the axle with lubricant to the bottom of the filler hole. Install the filler plug and tighten to 15–30 ft. lbs. (20–41 Nm).

34. If equipped with air springs, proceed as follows:

a. Connect the negative battery cable and turn ON the air suspension switch. Leave the diagnostic pigtail ungrounded.

b. Connect a suitable battery charger to the battery.

c. Open the drivers door, but leave all other doors shut. Turn the ignition switch to the RUN position for 5 seconds minimum, then turn the switch OFF.

d. Connect a jumper wire between the diagnostic pigtail and ground. The pigtail must remain grounded for the remainder of the spring fill procedure.

e. Leaving the driver s door open, apply the brakes and turn the ignition switch to RUN, but do not start the engine. The warning indicator will blink continuously once every 2 seconds, to indicate the spring pump sequence has been entered.

f. Close and open the drivers door once. After a 6 second delay, the rear spring will be filled for 60 seconds.

g. After completing the spring fill, turn the air suspension switch OFF to prevent deflation of the air springs while the vehicle is raised. Inspect the air springs for proper inflation: no folds or creases.

35. Lower the vehicle. If equipped with air suspension, turn the air suspension switch ON.

NOTE: If equipped with air suspension, any further leveling will be done during normal vehicle operation on the ground.

Mark VIII, Thunderbird and Cougar

NOTE: Before removing the rear halfshafts, new inboard CV-joint stub shaft circlips, new differential oil seals and new hub retainer nuts must be available for assembly.

1. Disconnect the negative battery cable. On Mark VIII, turn OFF the air suspension switch located in the trunk.

2. Remove the right wheel-cover/hub cover and remove the hub retainer nut. Loosen the wheel nuts.

3. Raise and support the vehicle safely by the frame only. Remove the wheel nuts and remove the right wheel and tire assembly.

4. If equipped with drum brakes, remove the right brake drum.

5. If equipped with disc brakes, perform the following:

a. Remove the anti-lock brake sensor, if equipped.

b. Use needle-nose pliers to slide the parking brake cable adjusting clip downward until the cable is released.

c. Remove the parking brake cable from the brake caliper.

d. Remove the retaining bolts and remove the right caliper. Support the caliper from the brake junction bracket with a wire; do not allow it to hang from the brake hose.

e. Remove the right brake rotor, except on Mark VIII.

6. Remove the right upper control arm nut and bolt. Wire the upper control arm to the top of the shock absorber.

7. Using a paint marker, mark the position of the right lower control arm in relation to the knuckle with the lower bushings in the relaxed position.

NOTE: Failure to mark this relationship will result in bushing wind-up on assembly and incorrect ride height, causing misalignment and premature tire wear.

8. If equipped with drum brakes, proceed as follows:

a. Use hub remover tool T81P-1104-C or other suitable puller to free the right halfshaft from the hub.

b. Remove the lower control arm-to-knuckle attaching bolts.

c. Remove the right knuckle assembly from the halfshaft.

d. Carefully rest the halfshaft on the lower arm and wire the knuckle assembly to the top of the shock. Do not allow the knuckle assembly to hang from the brake hose.

e. Remove the right halfshaft from the differential using CV-joint remover tool T89P-3514-A or equivalent. Push the tool inward until the CV-joint is freed from the differential side gear.

NOTE: Be careful not to damage the differential oil seal, differential housing and/or CV-joint boot.

f. Remove the halfshaft from the vehicle. Insert a plug into the differential housing to prevent fluid loss.

9. If equipped with disc brakes, proceed as follows:

a. Remove the lower control arm-to-knuckle attaching bolts.

b. Remove the right halfshaft from the differential using CV-joint remover tool T89P-3514-A or equivalent. Push the tool inward until the CV-joint is freed from the differential side gear.

NOTE: Be careful not to damage the differential oil seal, differential housing and/or CV-joint boot.

c. Remove the halfshaft and knuckle assembly from the vehicle.

d. Insert a plug into the differential housing to prevent fluid loss.

10. Mark the driveshaft in relation to the companion flange. Remove the driveshaft retaining bolts, slide the driveshaft forward and let it rest on the driveshaft hoop.

11. With a jack supporting the rear axle, remove the rear axle mount to crossmember retaining nuts. Remove the rear mount from the axle cover.

12. Remove the axle front retaining bolts, nuts, bushings and washers.

13. Remove the inboard CV-joint of the left halfshaft from the differential housing using CV-joint remover tool T89P-3514-A or equivalent, by pushing the tool inward, toward the carrier.

14. Partially lower the axle assembly. While lowering the axle, move it to the right and disengage the axle from the left stub shaft. Be careful not to damage the CV-joint boot.

15. Install a plug into the left side of the differential and lower the axle from the vehicle.

To install:

16. Replace the differential oil seals. Install a new circlip on the left inboard stub shaft.

17. Position the axle on the jack and partially raise to align the left CV-joint stub shaft into the differential side gear. Lightly lubricate the stub shaft splines prior to installation.

NOTE: Be careful not to damage the differential pilot bearing or oil seal during halfshaft installation and spline alignment.

18. Locate the axle on the front mounting bolts and push in the CV-joint until the circlip seats in the differential side gear.

19. Install the bushings, washers and nuts on the front differential mount. Tighten the retaining nuts to 68–100 ft. lbs. (92–136 Nm). The bushings must be installed properly.

20. Install the rear mount to the differential cover. Tighten to 80–100 ft. lbs. (108–136 Nm).

21. Install the rear mount-to-crossmember retaining bolts and nuts. Tighten to 122–156 ft. lbs. (165–211 Nm).

22. Align the marks on the driveshaft and companion flange. Install the retaining bolts and tighten to 70–96 ft. lbs. (95–129 Nm).

23. Install a new circlip on the right inboard stub shaft, by sliding it into the groove on the splined end of the shaft.

24. Lightly lubricate the stub shaft splines and carefully align the splines on the shaft with the splines in the differential.

25. Push the halfshaft inward to seat the circlip in the differential side gear groove. Use care not to damage the seal.

26. If equipped with drum brakes, proceed as follows:

　a. Engage the hub splines with the outboard CV-joint splines.

　b. Install the lower control arm bolts and nuts. Align the paint marks and tighten the bolts to 119–147 ft. lbs. (160–200mm).

　c. Install a new hub retaining nut and pull the CV-joint into the hub as far as possible by hand.

　d. Install the upper arm retaining bolt and nut and tighten to 119–147 ft. lbs. (160–200 Nm).

　e. Install the brake drum.

27. If equipped with disc brakes, proceed as follows:

　a. Install the lower control arm bolts and nuts. Align the paint marks and tighten the bolts to 119–147 ft. lbs. (160–200mm).

　b. Install the upper arm retaining bolt and nut and tighten to 119–147 ft. lbs. (160–200 Nm).

　c. Install the brake rotor, except on Mark VIII.

　d. Install the brake caliper assembly to the rotor with the outer brake shoe against the rotor's braking surface. This prevents pinching the piston boot between the inner brake shoe and the piston.

　e. Install the caliper retaining bolts and tighten to 45–88 ft. lbs. (60–90 Nm) or to 64–88 ft. lbs. (87–119 Nm) on Mark VIII.

　f. Install the parking brake cable to the brake caliper. Install the cable adjustment clip.

　g. Install the anti-lock brake sensor, if equipped. Tighten the retaining bolts to 14–20 ft. lbs. (19–27 Nm).

28. Fill the axle with the proper type and quantity of lubricant. Install the differential fill plug and tighten to 20–30 ft. lbs. (28–40 Nm).

29. Install the wheel and tire assembly and tighten the wheel nuts to 80–106 ft. lbs. (108–144 Nm). Lower the vehicle.

30. If equipped with drum brakes, tighten the hub nut to 250 ft. lbs. (340 Nm). Install the wheelcover/hub cover.

STEERING

Steering Wheel

REMOVAL AND INSTALLATION

Mustang, Mark VII and Mark VIII with Air Bag

1. Center the front wheels in the straight-ahead position.

2. Disarm the air bag system as follows:

　a. Disconnect the positive battery cable. Wait 1 minute for the backup power supply in the diagnostic monitor to deplete its stored energy.

　b. Remove the 4 nut and washer assemblies retaining the driver air bag module to the steering wheel and remove the air bag module.

—————— CAUTION ——————
When carrying a live air bag, make sure the bag and trim cover are pointed away from the body.

In the unlikely event of an accidental deployment, the bag will then deploy with minimal chance of injury. When placing a live air bag on a bench or other surface, always face the bag and trim cover up, away from the surface. This will reduce the motion of the module if it is accidentally deployed.

　c. Disconnect the driver air bag connector. Connect air bag simulator tool 105–00008 or equivalent, to the vehicle harness at the top of the steering wheel.

3. Disconnect the cruise control wire harness from the steering wheel, if equipped.

4. Remove and discard the steering wheel bolt. Remove the steering wheel using a suitable puller. Route the contact assembly wire harness through the steering wheel as the wheel is lifted off the shaft.

NOTE: Do not use a knock-off type steering wheel puller or strike the retaining bolt with a hammer. This could cause damage to the steering shaft bearing.

To install:

5. Make sure the front wheels are in the straight-ahead position.

6. Route the contact assembly wire harness through the steering wheel opening at the 3 o'clock position and install the steering wheel on the steering shaft. The steering wheel and shaft alignment marks should be aligned. Make sure the air bag contact wire is not pinched.

7. Install a new steering wheel retaining bolt and tighten to 23–33 ft. lbs. (31–48 Nm).

8. If equipped, connect the cruise control wire harness to the wheel and snap the connector assembly into the steering wheel clip. Make sure the wiring does not get trapped between the steering wheel and contact assembly.

9. Connect the air bag wire harness to the air bag module and install the module to the steering wheel. Tighten the module retaining nuts to 3–4 ft. lbs. (4–6 Nm) on Mustang and Mark VII or tighten the screws to 8–10 ft. lbs. (10–14 Nm) on Mark VIII.

10. Connect the air bag backup power supply and battery cable. Verify the air bag warning indicator.

Except Mustang and Mark VII with Air Bag

1. Disconnect the negative battery cable.

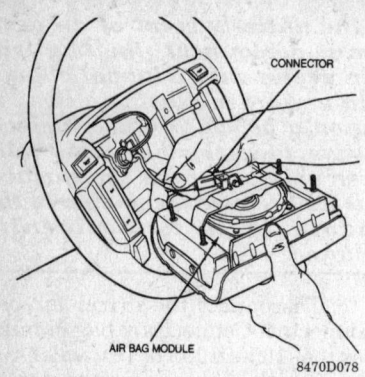

CONNECTOR

AIR BAG MODULE

8470D078

Air bag module removal — Mustang shown

2. Remove the horn pad and cover assembly. Disconnect the horn electrical connector.

3. Disconnect the cruise control switch electrical connector, if equipped.

4. Remove and discard the steering wheel bolt. Remove the steering wheel using a suitable puller.

NOTE: Do not use a knock-off type steering wheel puller or strike the retaining bolt with a hammer. This could cause damage to the steering shaft bearing.

To install:

5. Align the index marks on the steering wheel and shaft and install the steering wheel.

6. Install a new steering wheel retaining bolt and tighten to 23–33 ft. lbs. (31–45 Nm).

7. Connect the cruise control electrical connector, if equipped.

8. Connect the horn electrical connector and install the horn pad and cover.

9. Connect the negative battery cable.

Steering Column

REMOVAL AND INSTALLATION

Mustang

1. Disconnect the negative battery cable. On 1992–96 Mustang equipped with an air bag, disconnect the positive battery cable and wait 1 minute for the backup power supply in the diagnostic monitor to deplete its stored energy.

NOTE: If equipped with an air bag, do not remove the steering column wheel and air bag module as an assembly unless the column is locked or the steering

shaft is secured to keep it from turning. This will avoid damage to the clockspring assembly.

2. Remove the 2 nuts that attach the flexible coupling to the flange on the steering input shaft. Disengage the safety strap and bolt assembly from the flexible coupling.

3. Remove the steering column trim shrouds.

4. Remove the steering column cover and hood release mechanism directly under the column.

5. Disconnect the electrical connectors to the steering column switches.

6. Remove the 4 screws that attach the dust boot to the dash panel.

7. Remove the 4 attaching nuts holding the column to the brake pedal support. Lower the column to clear the 4 mounting bolts. On 1992–96 vehicles with automatic transmission, remove the interlock cable. Pull the column out, so the U-joint assembly will pass through the clearance hole in the dash panel.

To install:

8. Install the steering column by inserting the U-joint assembly through the opening in the dash panel. Be careful not to damage the column during installation. On 1992–96 vehicles with automatic transmission, install the interlock cable

9. Align the 4 bolts on the brake pedal support with the mounting holes on the column collar and bracket. Attach the nuts and tighten to 20–37 ft. lbs. (27–50 Nm).

10. Connect the electrical connectors to the steering column switches.

11. Engage the safety strap and bolt assembly to the flange on the steering gear input shaft. Install the 2 nuts that attach the steering column lower shaft and U-joint assembly to the flange on the steering gear input shaft. Tighten the nuts to 20–37 ft. lbs. (27–50 Nm).

NOTE: The safety strap must be properly positioned to prevent metal-to-metal contact after tightening the nuts. The flexible coupling must not be distorted when the nuts are tightened. Pry the steering shaft up or down with a suitable prybar to achieve ± ⅛ in. (3mm) coupling insulator flatness.

12. Engage the dust boot at the base of the steering column to the dash panel opening. Install the 4 screws that attach the dust boot to the dash panel.

13. Install the steering wheel and the trim shrouds.

14. Install the hood release mechanism and steering column cover beneath the steering column.

15. Connect the battery cable(s). Check the steering column for proper operation.

Mark VII and Mark VIII

1. Make sure the front wheels are in the straight-ahead position. Disconnect the negative battery cable. Disconnect the positive battery cable and wait 1 minute for the backup power supply in the diagnostic monitor to deplete its stored energy.

2. Remove the steering wheel.

3. Remove the right and left lower mouldings from the instrument panel by pulling up and snapping out of the retainers.

4. Remove the instrument panel lower trim cover.

5. Remove the air bag clockspring contact assembly as follows:

   a. Disconnect the contact assembly wire harness.

   b. Apply 2 strips of tape across the contact assembly stator and rotor to prevent accidental rotation.

   c. Remove the 3 contact assembly retaining screws and pull the contact assembly off the column shaft.

6. Unscrew the tilt lever from the column.

7. Place the ignition lock cylinder in the **RUN** position. Using an ⅛ in. drift, depress the lock cylinder retaining pin through the access hole and remove the lock cylinder.

8. Remove the 4 retaining screws and remove the column shrouds.

9. Remove the instrument panel reinforcement.

10. Remove the 2 interlock cable retaining screws and remove the cable.

11. Remove the 2 combination switch retaining screws and set the combination switch aside.

12. Remove the parking brake vacuum release assembly or disconnect the hoses at the switch.

13. Remove the pinch bolt from the steering shaft flex coupling.

14. Remove the interlock cable retaining screws and cable end assembly.

15. While supporting the column assembly, remove the 4 column assembly retaining nuts. Remove the column from the vehicle.

To install:

16. Align the column lower universal joint to the lower shaft. Install 1 bolt and tighten to 29–41 ft. lbs. (40–56 Nm).

17. Install the interlock cable retaining screws and cable end assembly.

18. Position the steering column assembly to the column support bracket. Install the 4 retaining nuts and tighten to 10–14 ft. lbs. (13–19 Nm).

19. Install the combination switch with the 2 retaining screws. Tighten to 18–26 inch lbs. (2–3 Nm). Connect all electrical connectors.

20. Install the instrument panel reinforcement brace and tighten the bolts to 25–38 ft. lbs. (34–52 Nm).

21. Install the lock cylinder and the tilt lever.

22. Install the air bag clockspring contact assembly as follows:

  a. Make sure the front wheels are in the straight-ahead position and the steering column shaft alignment mark is at the 12 o'clock position.

  b. Align the contact assembly to the column shaft and mounting bosses and slide the contact assembly onto the shaft.

  c. Install the 3 retaining screws and tighten to 18–26 inch lbs. (2–3 Nm). Remove the tape strips.

  d. Route the contact assembly down the column assembly and connect to the wire harness.

NOTE: If a new contact assembly is being installed, remove the plastic lock mechanism after the contact assembly is secured to the column.

23. Install the shroud assembly and the lower instrument panel cover and snap the right and left lower instrument panel mouldings into place.

24. Install the steering wheel. Install a new bolt and tighten to 23–33 ft. lbs. (31–48 Nm).

25. Position the air bag module to the wheel and install the 4 retaining nuts and tighten to 3–4 ft. lbs. (4–6 Nm) on Mark VII or tighten the screws to 8–10 ft. lbs. (10–14 Nm) on Mark VIII. Install screw cover plugs.

26. Connect the battery cable(s) and the air bag backup power supply. Verify the air bag warning indicator.

Thunderbird and Cougar

1. Disconnect the negative battery cable.

2. Remove lower left finish panel retaining bolts.

3. Carefully pull the lower left finish panel to disengage the retaining clips.

4. Remove the lower left reinforcement panel retaining bolts and remove the reinforcement panel.

5. Remove the steering column upper and lower shroud retaining screws and remove the shroud.

6. Disconnect the electrical connectors for the ignition key courtesy lamp, cruise control, ignition switch, combination switch and steering shock absorber sensor.

7. Remove the steering universal shaft pinch bolt.

8. Remove the steering column retaining nuts.

9. Disconnect the hazard warning wire connector.

10. Remove the brake shift interlock switch retaining screw and remove the switch.

11. Remove the steering column from the vehicle.

  To install:

12. Position the steering column and loosely install 1 retaining nut.

13. Install the brake shift interlock switch and connect the hazard warning wire connector.

14. Install the steering column upper shroud.

15. Align the steering column universal.

16. Install the steering column retaining nuts.

17. Install the universal pinch bolt and tighten to 30–42 ft. lbs. (41–57 Nm).

18. Connect the wire connectors to the steering shock absorber sensor, combination switch, ignition switch, cruise control and ignition key courtesy lamp.

19. Position the steering column harness wiring and secure in place.

20. Install the lower steering column shroud and retaining screws.

21. Position the lower left reinforcement panel and install the retaining bolts.

22. Position the lower left finish panel and install the retaining bolts.

23. Connect the negative battery cable and check column operation.

Power Rack and Pinion

ADJUSTMENT

Rack Yoke Plug Clearance

The rack yoke plug clearance adjustment is not a normal service adjustment. It is only required when the input shaft and valve assembly is removed.

1. Clean the exterior of the steering rack thoroughly.

2. Install 2 long bolts and washers through the bushings and attach the rack to bench mounted holding fixture T57L–500–B or equivalent.

3. Do not remove the external pressure lines, unless they are leaking or damaged. If the lines are removed, install new seals. If the lines are damaged, they must be replaced.

4. Drain the power steering fluid by rotating the input shaft lock-to-lock twice using pinion shaft torque adapter tool T74P–3504–R or equivalent. Cover the ports on the valve housing with a shop cloth while draining the gear to avoid possible oil spray.

5. Insert an inch pound torque wrench with a maximum capacity of 30–60 inch lbs. (3.39–6.77 Nm) into the pinion shaft torque adapter tool. Position the adapter and wrench on the input shaft splines.

6. Loosen the yoke plug locknut with pinion housing locknut wrench T78P–3504–H or equivalent. Loosen the yoke plug with a ³/₄ in. socket wrench.

7. With the rack at the center of travel, tighten the yoke plug to 45–50 inch lbs. (5.0–5.6 Nm). Clean the threads of the yoke plug prior to tightening to prevent a false reading.

8. Back off the yoke plug approximately ⅛ turn, 44 degrees minimum to 54 degrees maximum, until the torque required to initiate and sustain rotation of the input shaft is 7–18 inch lbs. (0.79–2.03 Nm) for base power steering or 7–24 inch lbs. (0.79–2.71 Nm) for handling package on 1992 models or 4–24 inch lbs. (0.45–2.71 Nm) on 1993–96 Mark VIII, Thunderbird and Cougar.

9. Place pinion housing yoke locknut wrench T78P–3504–H or equivalent, on the yoke plug locknut. While holding the yoke plug, tighten the locknut to 44–66 ft. lbs. (60–89 Nm).

NOTE: Do not allow the yoke plug to move while tightening or the preload will be affected.

10. Install the steering rack in the vehicle.

REMOVAL AND INSTALLATION

Except Thunderbird and Cougar

1. Disconnect the negative battery cable. Turn the ignition switch to the **RUN** position.

2. On Mark VII, turn **OFF** the air suspension switch, located in the luggage compartment.

3. Raise and safely support the vehicle. Position a drain pan to catch the fluid from the power steering lines.

4. Remove the 1 bolt retaining the flexible coupling to the input shaft.

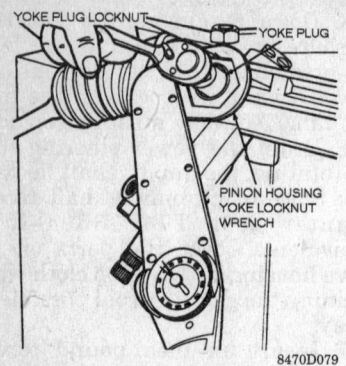

YOKE PLUG LOCKNUT
YOKE PLUG
PINION HOUSING YOKE LOCKNUT WRENCH

8470D079

Rack yoke plug clearance adjustment

5. Remove the cotter pins and nuts from the tie rod ends and separate the tie rod studs from the spindles.

6. Remove the 2 nuts, insulator washers and bolts retaining the steering gear to the crossmember. Remove the front rubber insulators.

7. Position the gear to allow access to the hydraulic lines and disconnect the lines.

8. Remove the steering gear.

To install:

9. Install new plastic seals on the hydraulic line fittings.

10. Install the gear on the mounting spikes and install the hydraulic lines. Tighten the fittings to 20–25 ft. lbs. (27–33 Nm).

NOTE: The hoses are designed to swivel when properly tightened. Do not attempt to eliminate looseness by over-tightening the fittings.

11. Install the front rubber insulators. Make sure all rubber insulators are pushed completely inside the gear housing before installing the mounting bolts.

12. Insert the input shaft into the flexible coupling. Install the mounting bolts, insulator washers and nuts. Tighten the nuts to 30–40 ft. lbs. (41–54 Nm) while holding the bolts. Install and tighten the flexible coupling bolt to 20–30 ft. lbs. (28–40 Nm).

13. Connect the tie rod ends to the spindle arms and install the retaining nuts. Tighten to 35–47 ft. lbs. (48–63 Nm). After tightening, tighten the nuts to their nearest cotter pin castellation and install 2 new cotter pins.

14. Lower the vehicle. Turn the ignition switch to **OFF** and connect the negative battery cable. On Mark VII, turn the air suspension switch **ON**.

15. Fill the power steering system with the proper type and quantity of fluid. Bleed the air from the system. If the tie rod ends were loosened,

check and adjust the front end alignment.

Mark VIII, Thunderbird and Cougar

1. Disconnect the negative battery cable. Raise and safely support the vehicle.

2. Remove the front wheel and tire assemblies.

3. Remove the cotter pins and nuts from the tie rod ends. Separate the tie rods from the spindles using a suitable tool.

4. Place a drain pan under the vehicle. Disconnect and plug the power steering return line hose. Disconnect the power steering pressure line at the intermediate fitting and position aside.

5. Remove the steering shaft retaining bolt. Remove the rack-to-subframe bolts and nuts. The nuts are accessed through the hole in the front crossmember.

6. Lower the rack as necessary to remove the pressure line inlet tube. Remove and discard the plastic seal on the inlet tube. Cut the tie strap securing the pressure line to each tube.

7. Remove the steering rack from the vehicle.

To install:

8. Install a new seal on the pressure line inlet tube.

9. Install the insulators from the rear side of the rack housing making sure they are fully seated. Use a suitable rubber lubricant to aid in installation.

10. Install and position the rack to the front crossmember. Install the pressure line inlet tube to the rack.

11. Align the steering shaft to allow the rack to completely seat on the crossmember. Install the steering rack retaining bolts and nuts. Tighten the bolts to 100–144 ft. lbs. (135–195 Nm).

12. Install the steering shaft retaining bolt and tighten to 20–30 ft. lbs. (28–40 Nm).

13. Secure the pressure line to the rack tube with a new tie strap. Connect the power steering pressure line.

14. Connect the power steering return line and tighten the clamp to 12–18 inch lbs. (1.4–2.0 Nm).

15. Install the outer tie rod ends to the spindles. Install the nuts and tighten to 39 ft. lbs. (53 Nm). Continue to tighten the nuts until the castellations line up with the stud bores, then install new cotter pins.

16. Install the front wheel and tire assemblies and lower the vehicle.

17. Fill the power steering system with the proper type and quantity of

fluid. Bleed the air from the system. If the tie rods were loosened, check and adjust the front end alignment.

Power Steering Pump

REMOVAL AND INSTALLATION

NOTE: On the 3.8L SC engine, the charge air cooler and charge air cooler tubes must be removed to gain access to the power steering pump.

1. Disconnect the negative battery cable.

2. Disconnect the fluid return hose at the reservoir and drain the fluid into a container.

3. Remove the pressure hose from the pump fitting, but do remove the fitting from the pump.

4. Remove the pump mounting bracket. Disconnect the belt from the pulley and remove the pump.

5. On engines with the fixed pump system, remove the pulley before removing the pump.

To install:

6. On non-fixed pump systems, install the pulley on the pump, if removed.

7. Place the pump on the mounting bracket and install the bolts at the front of the pump. Tighten to 30–45 ft. lbs. (40–62 Nm) or to 15–22 ft. lbs. (20–30 Nm) on Mark VIII.

8. On fixed pump systems, install the pulley.

9. Place the belt on the pump pulley and adjust the tension, if necessary.

10. Install the pressure hose to the pump fitting. Tighten the tube nut with a tube nut wrench rather than with an open-end wrench. Tighten to 20–25 ft. lbs. (27–34 Nm) or to 34–45 ft. lbs. (47–60 Nm) on Mark VIII.

NOTE: Do not overtighten this fitting. Swivel and/or end-play of the fitting is normal and does not indicate a loose fitting. Overtightening the tube nut can collapse the tube nut wall, resulting in a leak and requiring replacement of the entire pressure hose assembly. Use of an open-end wrench to tighten the nut can deform the tube nut hex which may result in improper torque and may make further servicing of the system difficult.

11. Connect the return hose to the pump and tighten the clamp. Fill the reservoir with the proper type and quantity of fluid. Bleed the air from the system.

BELT ADJUSTMENT

All vehicles are equipped with an automatic belt tensioner. No adjustment is necessary or possible. The belt tensioner is equipped with a belt wear indicator; when 1 percent belt stretch is indicated, the drive belt must be replaced. If the wear indicator is difficult to see on the 3.8L or 5.0L HO engines, locate the tab on the tensioner face plate. The tab should be approximately between the stops.

SYSTEM BLEEDING

1. Disconnect the ignition coil(s).
2. Raise and safely support the vehicle so the front wheels are off the floor.
3. Fill the power steering fluid reservoir.
4. Crank the engine with the starter and add fluid until the level remains constant.
5. While cranking the engine, rotate the steering wheel from lock-to-lock.

NOTE: The front wheels must be off the floor during lock-to-lock rotation of the steering wheel.

6. Check the fluid level and add fluid, if necessary.
7. Connect the ignition coil wire. Start the engine and allow it to run for several minutes.
8. Rotate the steering wheel from lock-to-lock.
9. Shut off the engine and check the fluid level. Add fluid, if necessary.
10. If air is still present in the system, purge the system of air using power steering pump air evacuator tool 021–00014 or equivalent, as follows:

   a. Make sure the power steering pump reservoir is full to the COLD FULL mark on the dipstick.
   b. Tightly insert the rubber stopper of the air evacuator assembly into the pump reservoir fill neck.
   c. Apply 15 in. Hg maximum vacuum on the pump reservoir for a minimum of 3 minutes with the engine idling. As air purges from the system, vacuum will fall off. Maintain adequate vacuum with the vacuum source.
   d. Release the vacuum and remove the vacuum source. Fill the reservoir to the COLD FULL mark.
   e. With the engine idling, apply 15 in. Hg vacuum to the pump reservoir. Slowly cycle the steering wheel from lock-to-lock every 30 seconds for approximately 5 minutes. Do not hold the steering wheel on the stops while cycling. Maintain adequate vacuum with the vacuum source as the air purges.
   f. Release the vacuum and remove the vacuum source. Fill the reservoir to the COLD FULL mark.
   g. Start the engine and cycle the steering wheel. Check for oil leaks at all connections. In severe cases of aeration, it may be necessary to repeat Steps 10b–10f.

Tie Rod Ends

REMOVAL AND INSTALLATION

1. Raise and safely support the vehicle.
2. Remove the cotter pin and nut from the tie rod end ball stud. Disconnect the tie rod end from the spindle using ball stud remover tool 3290–D or equivalent.
3. Holding the tie rod end with a wrench, loosen the tie rod jam nut. Grip the tie rod end with pliers and remove the assembly from the tie rod, but 1st note the depth to which the tie rod was located by using the jam nut as a marker.
To install:
4. Clean the tie rod threads.
5. Thread the new tie rod end onto the tie rod to the same depth as the removed tie rod end.
6. Place the tie rod end ball stud into the spindle and install the nut. Make sure the front wheels are in the straight-ahead position.
7. Tighten the nut to 35 ft. lbs. (48 Nm) and continue tightening the nut to align the next castellation of the nut with the cotter pin hole in the stud. Install a new cotter pin.
8. Set the toe to specification. Tighten the jam nut to 35–50 ft. lbs. (48–68 Nm).

BRAKES

Master Cylinder

REMOVAL AND INSTALLATION

Except Mark VII, Thunderbird and Cougar with Anti-Lock Brakes

NOTE: The master cylinder on Mark VII, Thunderbird and Cougar with anti-lock brakes is part of the hydraulic actuation assembly and cannot be removed separately.

1. Disconnect the negative battery cable.
2. Remove the brake lines from the primary and secondary outlet ports of the master cylinder, except on Mark VIII.
3. On Mark VIII, depress brake pedal several times to exhaust vacuum in the system. Disconnect the hydraulic control unit supply hose at the master cylinder and plug the hose.
4. Disconnect the brake warning indicator connector.
5. Remove the nuts attaching master cylinder to the brake booster assembly.
6. Slide the master cylinder forward and upward from the vehicle.
To install:
7. Position the master cylinder over the booster pushrod and onto the 2 studs on the booster. Install the retaining nuts and tighten to 14–25 ft. lbs. (18–34 Nm) or to 16–21 ft. lbs. (21–29 Nm) on Mark VIII.
8. Install short brake lines in the master cylinder outlet ports and position them so they point back into the reservoir and the ends of the lines are submerged in brake fluid, except Mark VIII.
9. Fill the reservoir with brake fluid and cover the reservoir with a shop towel.
10. Pump the brakes until clear, bubble-free fluid comes out of both brake lines. If any brake fluid spills on the paint, wash it off immediately with water.
11. Remove the short brake lines and connect the vehicle brake lines to the master cylinder. Bleed each brake line at the master cylinder using the following procedure, except on Mark VIII:

   a. Have an assistant pump the brake pedal 10 times and then hold firm pressure on the pedal.

b. Crack the rear most brake line fitting with a tubing wrench until a stream of brake fluid comes out. Have the assistant maintain pressure on the brake pedal until the brake line fitting is tightened again.

c. Repeat this operation until clear, bubble free fluid comes out from around the brake line fitting.

d. Repeat this bleeding operation at the front brake line fitting.

12. On Mark VIII, unplug the hose and connect the hydraulic control unit supply hose to the master cylinder.

13. Connect the brake warning indicator switch connector.

14. Bleed the system. Operate the brakes several times, then check for external hydraulic leaks.

Brake Control Valves

There are several types of valves in use. Not all valves perform the same function nor are they located in the same place on every vehicle.

Mustang — a brake control valve which contains a proportioning valve and shuttle valve located on the fender apron.

Thunderbird and Cougar — Vehicles without anti-lock brakes have 2 pressure control valves housed in the master cylinder. Vehicles with anti-lock brakes have a control valve which is located on a bracket below the hydraulic actuation unit.

Mark VII — a proportioning valve is located in the rear outlet port of the hydraulic actuator.

Mark VIII — a brake control valve which contains a proportioning valve located on the fender apron.

REMOVAL AND INSTALLATION

1. Disconnect the negative battery cable.

2. Disconnect the brake line(s) from the valve. Disconnect the electrical connector, if equipped.

3. Unscrew the valve from the master cylinder or remove the mounting screw from the frame or fender apron, as required.

4. Installation is the reverse of the removal procedure. Bleed the brake system.

Power Brake Booster

REMOVAL AND INSTALLATION

1. Disconnect the negative battery cable. Remove the air cleaner.

2. On Mustang equipped with the 2.3L engine, perform the following:

a. Relieve the fuel system pressure.

b. Disconnect the accelerator cable from the throttle body. Remove the screw that secures the accelerator cable to the accelerator shaft bracket and remove the cable from the bracket.

c. Remove the screws that secure the accelerator shaft bracket to the manifold and rotate the bracket toward the engine. Remove the horn.

d. Disconnect the 2 manifold injector connectors located near the oil dipstick retaining bracket. Disconnect the 2 fuel hoses to the fuel supply manifold.

e. Remove the 3 bolts holding the oil dipstick bracket to the upper intake manifold. Remove the dipstick and bracket.

f. Remove the windshield wiper motor and remove the vacuum hoses directly over the brake booster at the dash panel vacuum tee.

g. Remove the bolt holding the clutch cable stand, move the bracket to the side rail at the fender inner panel.

h. If equipped with cruise control, move the cruise control cable aside to clear the booster.

3. Disconnect the manifold vacuum hose from the booster check valve.

4. Disconnect the brake lines from the master cylinder, remove the master cylinder-to-booster retaining nuts and remove the master cylinder.

5. On Mark VIII, 1993–96 Thunderbird and Cougar, remove the windshield wiper module.

6. Working inside the vehicle below the instrument panel, remove the brake light switch connector. Remove the switch retaining pin and slide the switch off the brake pedal pin just far enough for the outer arm to clear the pin, then remove the switch. Be careful not to damage the switch.

7. On Mark VIII, remove the brake pedal support to cowl bolt.

8. Remove the booster-to-dash panel attaching nuts.

9. On Mustang, Thunderbird and Cougar equipped with cruise control, remove and set aside the control am-

plifier which is mounted to the lower outboard booster stud.

10. Slide the booster pushrod, washers and bushing off the brake pedal pin. Remove the booster.

11. Installation is the reverse of the removal procedure. Tighten the booster-to-dash panel attaching nuts and the master cylinder attaching nuts to 14–25 ft. lbs. (18–34 Nm). Bleed the brake system.

Brake Caliper

REMOVAL AND INSTALLATION

Front

1. Raise and safely support the vehicle. Remove the front wheel and tire assembly.

2. On all except Mustang with 2.3L engine, remove the hollow brake hose retaining bolt and plug the brake hose.

3. On Mustang with 2.3L engine, loosen the brake line fitting that connects the brake hose to the brake line at the frame bracket. Remove the retaining clip from the hose and bracket and disengage the hose from the bracket. Unscrew the hose from the caliper.

4. Remove the caliper locating pins and remove the caliper. If removing both calipers, mark the right and left sides so they may be reinstalled correctly.

To install:

5. Install the caliper over the rotor with the outer brake shoe against the rotor's braking surface. On Thunderbird and Cougar, make sure the antrattle spring is under the arm of the knuckle.

6. Lubricate the inside of the locating pin insulators with silicone dielectric grease. Install the caliper locating pins and start the threads by hand. Tighten to 45–65 ft. lbs. (61–88 Nm) on Mustang and Mark VII. On Thunderbird and Cougar, tighten the locating pins to 19–25 ft. lbs. (25–34 Nm). On Mark VIII, tighten caliper side pin to 16–24 ft. lbs. (22–32 Nm)

NOTE: On Mustang with 2.3L engine, new caliper locating pins must be used.

7. On all except Mustang with 2.3L engine, install new copper washers on each side of the brake hose fitting outlet and install the bolt, through the hose fitting and into the caliper. Tighten the bolt to 30–40 ft. lbs. (40–55 Nm) on Mark VIII, Thunderbird and Cougar. On Mustang and

Mark VII, tighten the bolt to 17–25 ft. lbs. (23–34 Nm).

8. On Mustang with 2.3L engine, thread the brake hose into the caliper and tighten to 20–30 ft. lbs. (28–41 Nm).

NOTE: This is a special self-sealing fitting that does not require a gasket. When the hose is correctly tightened, there should be 1 or 2 threads of the fitting still showing at the caliper. It is not necessary for the hose fitting to be flush with the caliper for sealing, so do not over-tighten.

9. On Mustang with 2.3L engine, position the brake hose in its bracket and install the retaining clip. Connect the brake line to the hose and tighten the line fitting nut.

10. Bleed the brake system, install the wheel and tire assembly and lower the vehicle.

11. To position the brake pads, apply the brake pedal several times before moving the vehicle.

Rear

MARK VIII, THUNDERBIRD, COUGAR AND 1992 MARK VII

1. Raise and safely support the vehicle. Remove the rear wheel and tire assembly.

2. Remove the brake hose from the caliper.

3. Release the parking brake cable tension, if necessary. Remove the cable retaining clip and disconnect the cable end from the lever.

4. Hold the slider pin hex heads with an open end wrench and remove the pinch bolts.

5. Lift the caliper assembly away from the anchor plate. Remove the slider pins and boots from the anchor plate.

To install:

6. Apply silicone dielectric compound to the inside of the slider pin boots and to the slider pins.

7. Position the slider pins and boots in the anchor plate. Position the caliper assembly on the anchor plate. Make sure the brake shoes and anti-rattle springs are installed correctly.

8. Remove the residue from the pinch bolt threads and apply locking compound. Install the pinch bolts and tighten to 23–26 ft. lbs. (31–35 Nm) while holding the slider pins with an open end wrench.

9. Attach the cable end to the parking brake lever and install the cable retaining clip. Adjust the parking brake.

10. Using new washers, connect the brake flex hose to the caliper. Tighten the retaining bolt to 30–45 ft. lbs. (40–60 Nm).

11. Bleed the brake system, install the wheel and tire assembly and lower the vehicle.

12. Pump the brake pedal prior to moving the vehicle to position the linings.

Disc Brake Pads

REMOVAL AND INSTALLATION

Front

1. Remove and discard half the brake fluid from the master cylinder reservoir.

2. Raise and safely support vehicle. Remove the front wheel and tire assemblies.

3. Remove the caliper locating pins and remove the caliper from the anchor plate and rotor, but do not disconnect the brake hose.

4. Lift the caliper assembly from the knuckle or spindle.

5. Remove the outer brake pad from the caliper assembly and remove the inner brake pad from the caliper piston.

6. Inspect the disc brake rotor for scoring and wear. Replace or machine, as necessary. If machining, observe the minimum thickness specification.

7. Suspend the caliper inside the fender housing with a length of wire. Do not let the caliper hang by the brake hose.

To install:

8. Use a large C-clamp and wood block to push the caliper piston back into its bore.

9. Install the inner brake pad, then the outer brake pad, making sure the clips are properly seated.

10. Install the caliper and the wheel and tire assembly. Lower the vehicle.

11. Pump the brake pedal prior to moving the vehicle to seat the brake pads. Refill the master cylinder.

Rear

MARK VIII, THUNDERBIRD, COUGAR AND 1992 MARK VII

1. Remove and discard half the brake fluid from the master cylinder.

2. Raise and safely support vehicle. Remove the rear wheel and tire assembly.

3. Remove the caliper from the anchor plate and rotor, but do not

disconnect the brake hose. Suspend the caliper inside the fender housing with a length of wire. Do not let the caliper hang by the brake hose.

4. Remove the brake pads from the anchor plate.

5. Inspect the disc brake rotor for scoring and wear. Replace or machine, as necessary. If machining, observe the minimum thickness specification.

To install:

6. Using brake piston turning tool T87P–2588–A or equivalent, rotate the caliper piston clockwise until it is fully seated. Make sure 1 of the 2 slots in the piston face is positioned so it will engage the nib on the brake pad.

7. Install the brake pads on the anchor plate. Install the caliper and wheel and tire assembly and lower the vehicle.

8. Pump the brake pedal prior to moving the vehicle to seat the brake pads. Refill the master cylinder.

Brake Rotor

REMOVAL AND INSTALLATION

Front

MUSTANG AND MARK VII

1. Raise and safely support the vehicle. Remove the wheel and tire assembly.

2. Remove the caliper, but do not disconnect the brake hose. Suspend the caliper inside the fender housing with a length of wire. Do not let the caliper hang by the brake hose.

3. Remove the grease cap from the hub and remove the cotter pin, nut lock, adjusting nut and flat washer.

4. Remove the outer roller bearing assembly and remove the hub and rotor assembly.

5. Inspect the rotor for scoring and wear. Replace or machine as necessary. If machining, observe the minimum thickness specification.

6. Installation is the reverse of removal. Make sure the grease in the rotor is clean and adequate. Adjust the wheel bearings.

MARK VIII, THUNDERBIRD AND COUGAR

1. Raise and safely support the vehicle. Remove the wheel and tire assembly.

2. Remove the caliper, but do not disconnect the brake hose. Suspend the caliper inside the fender housing with a length of wire. Do not let the caliper hang by the brake hose.

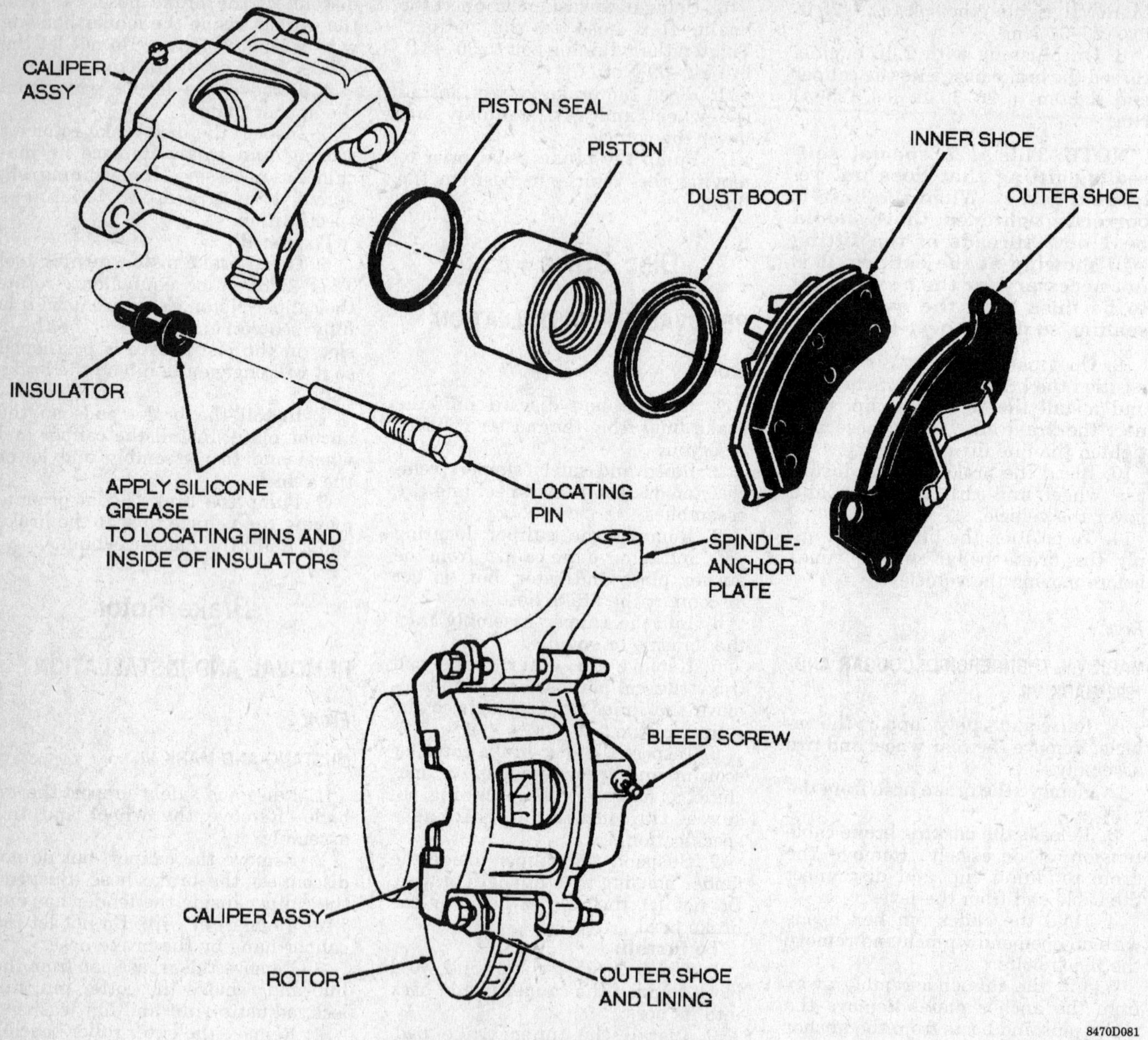

CALIPER ASSY

PISTON SEAL

PISTON

DUST BOOT

INNER SHOE

OUTER SHOE

INSULATOR

APPLY SILICONE GREASE TO LOCATING PINS AND INSIDE OF INSULATORS

LOCATING PIN

SPINDLE-ANCHOR PLATE

BLEED SCREW

CALIPER ASSY

ROTOR

OUTER SHOE AND LINING

8470D081

Front disc brake assembly — Mark VII

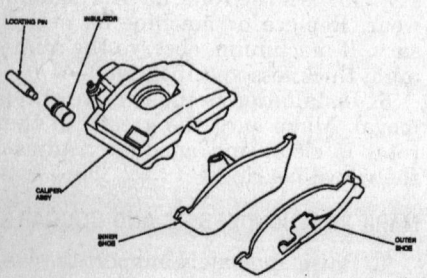

LOCATING PIN   INSULATOR

CALIPER ASSY

INNER SHOE   OUTER SHOE

8470D083

Front disc brake assembly — Thunderbird and Cougar

3. Remove the rotor retaining push nuts, if equipped, and remove the rotor from the hub.

4. Inspect the rotor for scoring and wear. Replace or machine as necessary. If machining, observe the minimum thickness specification.

5. Installation is the reverse of the removal procedure.

Rear

1. Raise and safely support the vehicle. Remove the wheel and tire assembly.

2. Remove the caliper, but do not disconnect the brake hose. Suspend the caliper inside the fender housing with a length of wire. Do not let the caliper hang by the brake hose.

3. Remove the caliper anchor plate.

4. Remove the rotor retaining push nuts, if equipped, and remove the rotor from the hub.

5. Inspect the rotor for scoring and wear. Replace or machine as necessary. If machining, observe the minimum thickness specification.

6. Installation is the reverse of the removal procedure. Tighten the anchor plate retaining bolts to 45–65 ft. lbs. (60–90 Nm) on Thunderbird and Cougar, 64–88 ft. lbs. (87–119 Nm) on Mark VIII or 80–110 ft. lbs. (108–149 Nm) on Mark VII.

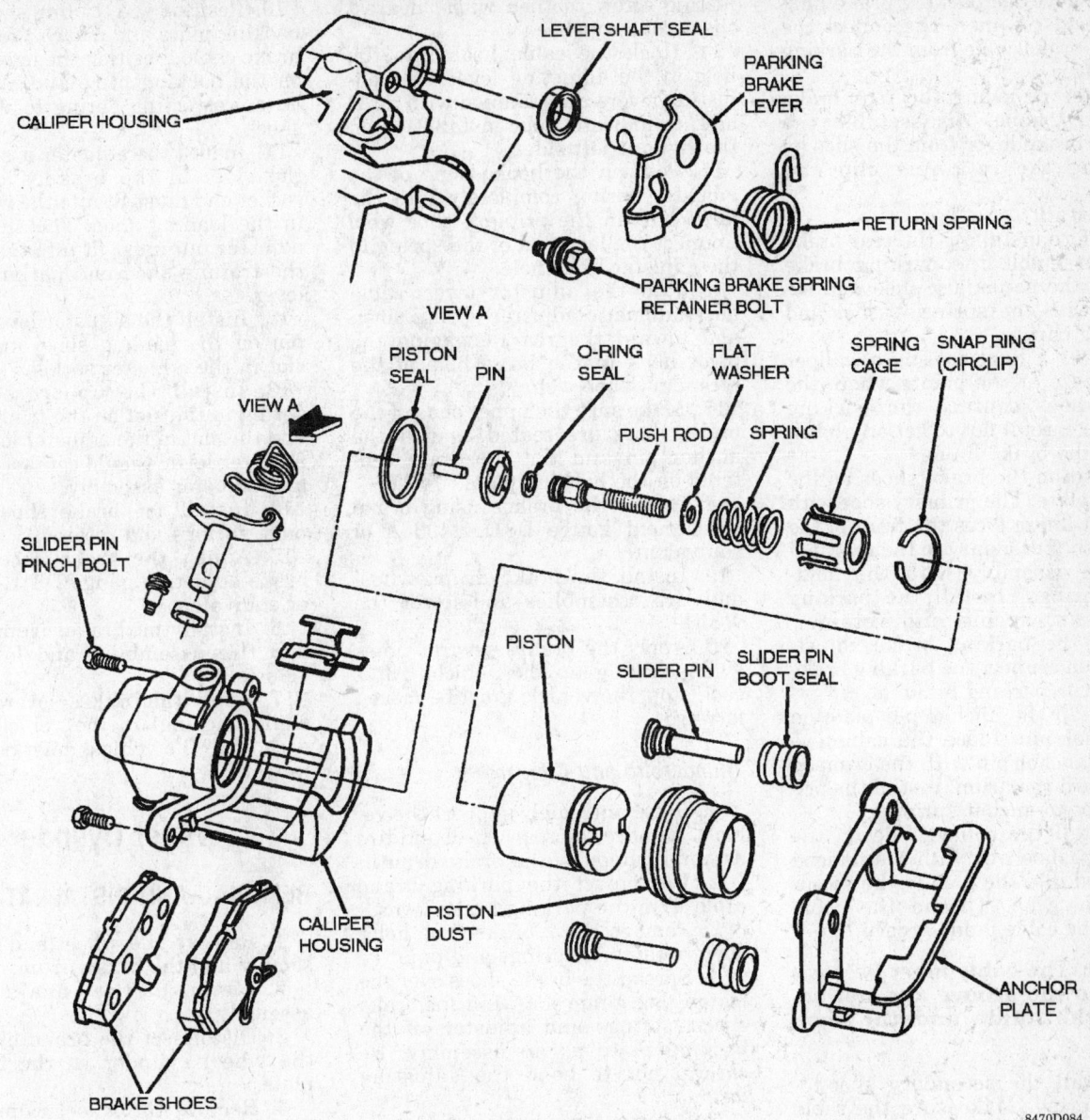

Exploded view of the rear disc brakes — Mark VIII, Thunderbird, Cougar and 1992 Mark VII

Brake Drum

REMOVAL AND INSTALLATION

1. Raise and safely support the vehicle.
2. Remove the wheel and tire assembly.
3. Remove the drum retaining nuts and remove the brake drum.

NOTE: If the drum will not come off, pry the rubber plug from the backing plate. Insert a narrow rod through the hole in the backing plate and disengage the adjusting lever from the ad-justing screw. While holding the adjustment lever away from the screw, back off the adjusting screw with a brake adjusting tool.

4. Inspect the brake drum for scoring and wear. Replace or machine as necessary. If machining, observe the maximum diameter specification.
5. Installation is the reverse of removal.

Brake Shoes

REMOVAL AND INSTALLATION

Mustang

1. Raise and safely support the vehicle. Remove the rear wheel and tire assembly. Remove the brake drum.
2. Remove the shoe-to-anchor springs and unhook the cable eye from the anchor pin. Remove the anchor pin plate.
3. Remove the shoe hold-down springs, shoes, adjusting screw, pivot nut, socket and automatic adjustment parts.

4. Remove the parking brake link, spring and retainer. Disconnect the parking brake cable from the parking brake lever.

5. After removing the rear brake secondary shoe, disassemble the parking brake lever from the shoe by removing the retaining clip and spring washer.

To install:

6. Before installing the rear brake shoes, assemble the parking brake lever to the secondary shoe and secure it with the spring washer and retaining clip.

7. Apply a light coating of caliper slide grease at the points where the brake shoes contact the backing plate. Be careful not to get any lubricant on the brake linings.

8. Position the brake shoes on the backing plate. The primary shoe with the short lining faces the front of the vehicle, the secondary to the rear. Secure the assembly with the hold-down springs. Install the parking brake link, spring and retainer. Back-off the parking brake adjustment, then connect the parking brake cable to the parking brake lever.

9. Install the anchor pin plate on the anchor pin. Place the cable eye over the anchor pin with the crimped side toward the drum. Install the primary shoe-to-anchor spring.

10. Install the cable guide on the secondary shoe web with the flanged hole fitted into the hole in the secondary shoe web. Thread the cable around the cable guide groove.

NOTE: The cable must be positioned in the groove and not between the guide and the shoe web.

11. Install the secondary shoe-to-anchor spring. Make sure the cable eye is not cocked or binding on the anchor pin when installed. All parts should be flat on the anchor pin.

12. Apply a thin coat of lubricant to the threads and the socket end of the adjusting screw. Turn the adjusting screw into the adjusting pivot nut to the limit of the threads, then back-off ½ turn.

NOTE: Make sure the socket end of the adjusting screw is stamped with an R or L, indicating the right or left side of the vehicle. The adjusting screw assemblies must be installed on the correct side for proper brake shoe adjustment.

13. Place the adjusting socket on the screw and install the assembly between the shoe ends with the ad-justing screw toothed wheel nearest the secondary shoe.

14. Hook the cable hook into the hole in the adjusting lever. The adjusting levers are stamped with an **R** or **L** to indicate their installation on the right or left side.

15. Position the hooked end of the adjuster spring completely into the large hole in the primary shoe web. Connect the loop end of the spring to the adjuster lever hole.

16. Pull the adjuster lever, cable and automatic adjuster spring down and toward the rear, engaging the pivot hook in the large hole of the secondary shoe web.

17. Make sure the upper ends of the brake shoes are seated against the anchor pin and the shoes are centered on the backing plate.

18. Adjust the brakes using brake adjustment gauge D81L–1103–A or equivalent.

19. Install the brake drum, wheel and tire assemblies and lower the vehicle.

20. Apply the brakes several times while backing up the vehicle. After each stop, the vehicle must be moved forward.

Thunderbird and Cougar

1. Raise and safely support the vehicle. Remove the rear wheel and tire assembly. Remove the brake drum.

2. Disconnect the parking brake cable from the parking brake lever.

3. Remove the 2 brake shoe hold-down retainers, springs and pins.

4. Spread the brake shoes over the piston shoe guide slots. Lift the brake shoes, springs and adjuster off the backing plate as an assembly. Be careful not to bend the adjusting lever.

5. Remove the adjuster spring. To separate the shoes, remove the retracting springs.

6. Remove the parking brake lever retaining clip and spring washer. Remove the lever from the pin.

To install:

7. Apply a light coating of caliper slide grease to the backing plate brake shoe contact areas.

8. Apply a light coat of lubricant to the threaded areas of the adjuster screw and socket. Assemble the brake adjuster with the stainless steel washer. Turn the socket all the way down on the screw, then back off ½ turn.

9. Install the parking brake lever to the trailing shoe with the spring washer and new retaining clip. Crimp the clip to securely retain the lever.

10. Position the trailing shoe on the backing plate and attach the parking brake cable. Position the leading shoe on the backing plate and attach the lower retracting spring to the brake shoes.

11. Install the adjuster assembly to the slots in the brake shoes. The socket end must fit into the wider slot in the leading shoe. The slot in the adjuster nut must fit into the slots in the trailing shoe and parking brake lever.

12. Install the adjuster lever on the pin on the leading shoe and to the slot in the adjuster socket.

13. Install the upper retracting spring in the slot on the trailing shoe and the slot in the adjuster lever. The adjuster lever should contact the star and adjuster assembly.

14. Install the brake shoe anchor pins, springs and retainers.

15. Adjust the brake shoes using brake adjusting gauge D81L–1103–A or equivalent.

16. Install the brake drum, wheel and tire assemblies and lower the vehicle.

17. Apply the brakes several times while backing up the vehicle. After each stop, the vehicle must be moved forward.

Wheel Cylinder

REMOVAL AND INSTALLATION

1. Remove the wheel and tire assembly and the brake drum.

2. Remove the brake shoe assembly.

3. Disconnect the brake line from the wheel cylinder at the backing plate.

4. Remove the wheel cylinder attaching bolts and remove the wheel cylinder.

5. Installation is the reverse of the removal procedure. Tighten the wheel cylinder attaching bolts to 10–20 ft. lbs. (14–28 Nm) on Mustang. On Thunderbird and Cougar, tighten the attaching bolts to 106–160 inch lbs. (12–18 Nm).

6. Bleed the brake system.

Parking Brake Cable

ADJUSTMENT

Mustang and 1992 Mark VII

1. Make sure the parking brake is fully released.

2. Place the transmission in **N**. Raise and safely support the vehicle.

3. Tighten the adjusting nut against the cable equalizer, causing a rear wheel brake drag. Loosen the adjusting nut until the rear brakes are fully released. There should be no brake drag.

4. Lower the vehicle and check the operation of the parking brake.

Mark VIII, Thunderbird and Cougar

1. Apply the parking brake control fully on. Release the parking brake control. Repeat the application and release.

2. Place the transmission in **N**. Raise and safely support the vehicle by the axles.

3. On 1992–93 vehicles, proceed as follows:

a. With the parking brake control in the **OFF** position, grasp the tensioner around the housing, then using a hook tool, hook the end into the rounded end of the clip between the clip and the housing.

b. Unlock the clip by pulling downward with the tool and support tensioner; the tensioner spring will take up cable slack and preload the cables.

c. While holding the tensioner, lock the clip by pushing up on the bottom of the clip. If the clip does not slide up, move the assembly slightly to align the closest groove on the adjuster rod to the clip.

4. Examine the tensioner for remaining cable take up capability. If none is present, check all cables, parking brake control and brackets for possible damage or deflection.

REMOVAL AND INSTALLATION

Front Cable

MARK VIII, THUNDERBIRD AND COUGAR, EXCEPT SUPER COUPE

1. Make sure the parking brake is fully released. Raise and safely support the vehicle on the axles.

2. Remove the cable tension as follows:

a. Unlock the tensioner by pulling downward on the clip.

b. While the clip is disengaged, have an assistant apply the parking brake control fully to the last notch position. The tensioner spring will compress allowing cable slack to return.

c. Lock the tensioner by pushing up on the clip.

d. Make sure the locking lever is secure by rotating it toward the threaded rod. Wrap tape or wire around the locking lever and threaded rod to prevent any accidental release.

3. Disconnect the front cable from the intermediate cable at the connector.

4. Remove the cable snap-in retainer from the cable bracket and allow the cable to hang. Lower the vehicle.

5. Remove the left cowl trim panel.

6. Disconnect the cable from the control assembly at the clevis. Remove the cable snap-in retainer and pull the cable and grommet up through the floor pan.

7. Installation is the reverse of the removal procedure. Adjust the parking brake.

THUNDERBIRD SUPER COUPE

1. Make sure the parking brake is fully released. Raise and safely support the vehicle on the axles.

2. Remove the cable tension as follows:

a. Unlock the tensioner by pulling downward on the clip.

b. While the clip is disengaged, have an assistant apply the parking brake control fully to the last notch position. The tensioner spring will compress allowing cable slack to return.

c. Lock the tensioner by pushing up on the clip.

d. Make sure the locking lever is secure by rotating it toward the threaded rod. Wrap tape or wire around the locking lever and threaded rod to prevent any accidental release.

3. Disconnect the front cable from the right rear cable at the connector.

4. Remove the cable snap-in retainer from the tensioner housing. Remove the cable routing clip from the body rear crossmember by squeezing the clip together between the cable and crossmember. Allow the cable to hang.

5. Lower the vehicle. Remove the rear seat and the console.

6. Disconnect the cable from the control at the clevis hook. Remove the cable snap-in retainer from the hand control assembly.

7. Pull the cable and grommet up through the rear floor. Pull the cable out from under the carpet.

8. Installation is the reverse of the removal procedure. Adjust the parking brake.

MARK VII

1. Raise and safely support the vehicle. Loosen the adjusting nut at the adjuster.

2. Disconnect the front cable from the equalizer lever assembly and remove the cable from the body bracket. Lower the vehicle.

3. Inside the passenger compartment, remove the retainer holding the cable conduit to the parking brake control and remove the cable.

4. Installation is the reverse of the removal procedure. Adjust the parking brake.

Intermediate Cable

MARK VIII, THUNDERBIRD AND COUGAR, EXCEPT SUPER COUPE

1. Make sure the parking brake is fully released. Raise and safely support the vehicle on the axles.

2. Remove the cable tension as follows:

a. Unlock the tensioner by pulling downward on the clip.

b. While the clip is disengaged, have an assistant apply the parking brake control fully to the last notch position. The tensioner spring will compress allowing cable slack to return.

c. Lock the tensioner by pushing up on the clip.

d. Make sure the locking lever is secure by rotating it toward the threaded rod. Wrap tape or wire around the locking lever and threaded rod to prevent any accidental release.

3. Disconnect the intermediate cable from the right rear cable and front cable at the connector.

4. Remove the cable snap-in retainer from the tensioner housing and body bracket.

5. Remove the cable routing clips for body side rails and rear crossmember by squeezing the clip together between the cable and the crossmembers. Remove the cable.

6. Installation is the reverse of the removal procedure. Adjust the parking brake.

MARK VII

1. Raise and safely support the vehicle. Remove the cable adjusting nut.

2. Disconnect the intermediate cable ends from the left rear and the transverse cable.

3. Remove the cotter pin, washer and spring from the pin protruding through the equalizer lever assembly and remove the lever.

NOTE: The intermediate cable cannot be separated from the lever assembly.

4. Installation is the reverse of the removal procedure. Adjust the parking brake.

Transverse Cable

MARK VII

1. Raise and safely support the vehicle. Loosen the adjusting nut on the adjusting rod until it is off the rod.
2. Remove the cable ends from the right rear and intermediate cables.
3. Remove hairpin clips or conduit bracket, as required, to remove the transverse cable from the vehicle.
4. Installation is the reverse of the removal procedure. Adjust the parking brake.

Rear Cables

MUSTANG, EXCEPT COBRA

1. Place the parking brake control in the released position. Release the cable tension as follows:
   a. Remove the floor console.
   b. With an assistant inside the vehicle, raise and safely support the vehicle.
   c. Have another assistant pull the equalizer rearward approximately 1–2½ in. to rotate the self-adjuster reel backward.
   d. Insert a steel lockpin through the holes in the lever and control assembly. This locks the ratchet wheel in the cable released position.

NOTE: Do not remove the steel lockpin until the cables are connected to the equalizer. Pin removal releases the tension in the ratchet wheel causing the spring to unwind and release tension. If the pin is removed without the cables attached, the entire assembly must be removed to reset the spring tension.

2. Raise and safely support the vehicle. Remove the rear cables from the equalizer.
3. Remove the cable snap fitting from the body. Remove the retaining clip that attaches the cable to the underbody.
4. Remove the wheel and tire assemblies and the brake drums.
5. Remove the self adjuster springs and remove the cable retainers from the backing plates.
6. Disconnect the cable ends from the parking brake levers, compress the cable retainer prongs and pull the cable ends from the backing plates.
7. Installation is the reverse of removal procedure. Adjust the parking brake.

MUSTANG COBRA

1. Place the parking brake control in the released position. Release the cable tension as follows:
   a. Remove the floor console.
   b. With an assistant inside the vehicle, raise and safely support the vehicle.
   c. Have another assistant pull the equalizer rearward approximately 1–2½ in. to rotate the self-adjuster reel backward.
   d. Insert a steel lockpin through the holes in the lever and control assembly. This locks the ratchet wheel in the cable released position.

NOTE: Do not remove the steel lockpin until the cables are connected to the equalizer. Pin removal releases the tension in the ratchet wheel causing the spring to unwind and release tension. If the pin is removed without the cables attached, the entire assembly must be removed to reset the spring tension.

2. Raise and safely support the vehicle. Remove the rear cables from the rear calipers.
3. Remove trailing arm brackets. Remove the rear cables from the equalizer.
4. Remove cables from tunnel brackets and remove cables.
5. Installation is the reverse of the removal procedure. Adjust the parking brake.

THUNDERBIRD AND COUGAR WITH DRUM BRAKES

1. Make sure the parking brake is fully released. Raise and safely support the vehicle on the axles.
2. Remove the cable tension as follows:
   a. Unlock the tensioner by pulling downward on the clip.
   b. While the clip is disengaged, have an assistant apply the parking brake control fully to the last notch position. The tensioner spring will compress allowing cable slack to return.
   c. Lock the tensioner by pushing up on the clip.
   d. Make sure the locking lever is secure by rotating it toward the threaded rod. Wrap tape or wire around the locking lever and threaded rod to prevent any accidental release.
3. Remove the wheel and tire assemblies and the brake drums.
4. Disconnect the parking brake cable end from the parking brake ac-

tuating lever. Depress the conduit retaining prongs and remove the cable and pronged fitting from the backing plate.
5. Remove the cable snap-in retainer from the frame bracket.
6. Disconnect the cable end from the tensioner or intermediate cable at the connector. Remove the rear cable by sliding the cable through the clip on the lower control arm.
7. Installation is the reverse of removal procedure. Adjust the parking brake.

MARK VIII, THUNDERBIRD AND COUGAR WITH DISC BRAKES

1. Make sure the parking brake is fully released. Raise and safely support the vehicle on the axles.
2. Remove the cable tension as follows:
   a. Unlock the tensioner by pulling downward on the clip.
   b. While the clip is disengaged, have an assistant apply the parking brake control fully to the last notch position. The tensioner spring will compress allowing cable slack to return.
   c. Lock the tensioner by pushing up on the clip.
   d. Make sure the locking lever is secure by rotating it toward the threaded rod. Wrap tape or wire around the locking lever and threaded rod to prevent any accidental release.
3. Disconnect the rear cable end from the tensioner or intermediate/front cable at the connector.
4. Remove the cable snap-in retainer from the frame bracket. Disconnect the rear cable end from the caliper housing and remove the cable from the parking brake lever arm on the caliper.
5. Remove the cable retainer from the rear stabilizer bar.
6. Installation is the reverse of the removal procedure. Adjust the parking brake.

MARK VII

1. Raise and safely support the vehicle. Loosen the adjusting nut at the adjuster assembly.
2. With the cables slackened, disconnect the rear cables from the right and left rear cable connectors. The left cable connects to the end of the intermediate cable, The right cable connects to the transverse cable.
3. Disconnect the rear cables from the body brackets or caliper brackets.
4. Slide the cable out of the brake lever arm and remove from the vehicle.

5. Installation is the reverse of the removal procedure. Adjust the parking brake.

Brake System Bleeding

WITHOUT ANTI-LOCK BRAKES

1. Clean all dirt from the master cylinder filler cap.

2. If the master cylinder is known or suspected to have air in the bore, it must be bled before any of the wheel cylinders or calipers. To bleed the master cylinder, loosen the upper secondary left front outlet fitting approximately ¾ turn. Have an assistant depress the brake pedal slowly through it's full travel. Close the outlet fitting and let the pedal return slowly to the fully released position. Wait 5 seconds and then repeat the operation until all air bubbles disappear.

3. Repeat Step 2 with the right-hand front outlet fitting.

4. Continue to bleed the brake system by removing the rubber dust cap from the wheel cylinder bleeder fitting or caliper fitting at the right-hand rear of the vehicle. Place a suitable box wrench on the bleeder fitting and attach a rubber drain tube to the fitting. The end of the tube should fit snugly around the bleeder fitting. Submerge the other end of the tube in a container partially filled with clean brake fluid and loosen the fitting ¾ turn.

5. Have an assistant push the brake pedal down slowly through it's full travel. Close the bleeder fitting and allow the pedal to slowly return to it's full release position. Wait 5 seconds and repeat the procedure until no bubbles appear at the submerged end of the bleeder tube. Secure the bleeder fitting and remove the bleeder tube. Install the rubber dust cap on the bleeder fitting.

6. Repeat the procedure in Steps 4 and 5 in the following sequence: left front, left rear and right front. Refill the master cylinder reservoir after each wheel cylinder or caliper has been bled and install the master cylinder cover and gasket. When brake bleeding is completed, the fluid level should be filled to the maximum level indicated on the reservoir.

7. Always make sure the disc brake pistons are returned to their normal positions by depressing the brake pedal several times until normal pedal travel is established. If the pedal feels spongy, repeat the bleeding procedure.

WITH ANTI-LOCK BRAKES

The front brakes can be bled in the same manner as a vehicle without anti-lock brakes or they can be bled with a pressure bleeder. The rear brakes must be bled with a pressure bleeder or with a fully charged accumulator.

Pressure Bleeding

1. Clean all dirt from the reservoir filler cap area. Attach a suitable pressure bleeder to the reservoir cap opening.

2. Maintain 35 psi pressure on the system through the pressure bleeder.

3. Remove the dust cap from the right front caliper bleeder fitting. Attach a rubber drain tube to the fitting, making sure the tube fits snugly.

4. With the ignition switch in the **OFF** position and the brake pedal in the fully released position, open the bleeder fitting for 10 seconds at a time until an air-free stream of brake fluid flow is observed.

5. Repeat the procedure at the left front, right rear and left rear calipers, in that order.

6. Place the ignition switch in the **RUN** position and pump the brake pedal several times to complete the bleeding procedure and to fully charge the accumulator.

7. Turn the ignition switch to the **OFF** position and remove the pressure bleeder. Siphon off the excess fluid in the reservoir to adjust the level to the **MAX** mark with a fully charged accumulator.

Rear Brake Bleeding With a Fully Charged Accumulator

1. Remove the dust cap from the right rear caliper bleeder fitting. Attach a rubber drain tube to the fitting, making sure the tube fits snugly.

2. Turn the ignition switch to the **RUN** position. This will turn on the electric pump to charge the accumulator, as required.

3. Have an assistant hold the brake pedal in the applied position. Open the bleeder fitting for 10 seconds at a time until an air-free stream of brake fluid flow is observed.

CAUTION

To prevent possible injury, care must be used when opening the bleeder screws due to the high pressures available from a fully charged accumulator.

4. Repeat the procedure at the left rear caliper.

5. Pump the brake pedal several times to complete the bleeding procedure.

6. Adjust the fluid level in the reservoir to the MAX mark with a fully charged accumulator.

NOTE: If the pump motor is allowed to run continuously for approximately 20 minutes, a thermal safety switch inside the motor may shut the motor off to prevent it from overheating. If that happens, a 2–10 minute cool down period is typically required before normal operation can resume.

Anti-Lock Brake System Service

PRECAUTIONS

- Before servicing any high pressure component, discharge the hydraulic pressure from the system.
- Do not allow brake fluid to contact any electrical connections.
- Use care when opening the bleeder screws due to the high system pressure from the accumulator.

RELIEVING ANTI-LOCK BRAKE SYSTEM PRESSURE

CAUTION

Before servicing any component which contains high pressure, it is mandatory that the hydraulic pressure in the system be discharged or personal injury could result.

To discharge the system, turn the ignition **OFF** and pump the brake pedal a minimum of 20 times until an increase in pedal force is clearly felt.

Hydraulic Control Unit (HCU)

REMOVAL AND INSTALLATION

The hydraulic actuation assembly contains all the anti-lock brake hydraulic components: master cylinder and fluid reservoir, hydraulic pump motor and accumulator and solenoid valve block assembly.

1. Discharge the hydraulic pressure in the system.

2. Disconnect the negative battery cable.

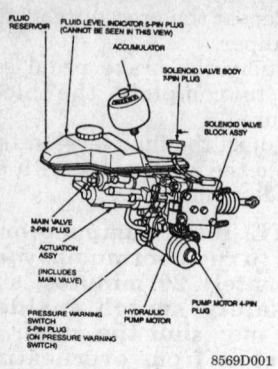

8569D001

**Anti-Lock Brake Hydraulic
Control Unit (HCU)**

3. On Thunderbird and Cougar, remove the air cleaner housing and duct assembly.

4. Label and disconnect the electrical connectors from the fluid level indicator, main valve, solenoid valve block, pressure warning switch, hydraulic pump motor and ground connector from the master cylinder portion of the assembly.

5. Disconnect the brake line fittings. Immediately plug each port to prevent fluid loss and contamination.

NOTE: Do not allow brake fluid to come in contact with any electrical connectors.

6. On Mark VII, remove the accumulator. On Thunderbird and Cougar, remove the trim panel under the steering column.

7. Disconnect the actuation assembly pushrod from the brake pedal by removing the hairpin connector next to the stoplight switch. Slide the switch, pushrod and plastic bushings off the pedal pin.

8. Remove the 4 retaining nuts that hold the actuation assembly to the brake pedal support bracket.

9. Remove the actuation assembly.

To install:

10. Mount the actuation assembly with the rubber boot and foam gasket to the engine side of the dash panel with the 4 mounting studs and pushrod inserted in the proper holes.

11. Working in the passenger compartment, loosely start 4 retaining locknuts attaching the actuation assembly to the pedal support bracket.

12. Connect the pushrod to the brake pedal pin by sliding the flanged plastic bushing, pushrod and washer onto the brake pedal pin. Position the stoplight switch so the slot on the switch bracket straddles the pushrod on the brake pedal pin, with the hole on the opposite leg of the switch bracket just clearing the pin. Slide

the switch onto the pedal pin until it bottoms. Install the outer nylon bushing and secure the assembly with the hairpin retainer.

13. Tighten the locknuts to 13–25 ft. lbs. (18–34 Nm).

14. From the engine compartment, connect the brake tubes and tighten the nuts 10–15 ft. lbs. (13–20 Nm). Connect the electrical connectors.

15. On Mark VII, screw in the accumulator, making sure the O-ring is in place. Tighten to 30–34 ft. lbs. (40–46 Nm). On Thunderbird and Cougar, install the air cleaner and duct assembly.

16. Connect the negative battery cable and bleed the brake system.

Front Wheel Speed Sensor

REMOVAL AND INSTALLATION

Thunderbird and Cougar

1. Disconnect the negative battery cable. Raise and safely support the vehicle.

2. From under the vehicle, near the front radiator support, disconnect the sensor electrical connector for right or left front sensor.

3. Remove routing clips along wiring harness.

4. Remove Torx® head screws securing sensor to front spindle.

NOTE: If the toothed speed indicator ring is damaged, replace it.

To install:

5. Install sensor into hole in spindle. No adjustment is necessary. Install Torx® head screw and tighten to 40–60 inch lbs. (4.5–6.8 Nm).

6. Route wiring using clips previously removed. Ensure wiring is routed properly.

7. Connect sensor wiring connector to harness connector.

Mark VII

1. Disconnect the negative battery cable.

2. From inside the engine compartment, disconnect sensor electrical connector for right or left front sensor.

3. Raise and safely support the vehicle. Disengage wire grommet at right or left shock tower and pull sensor cable connector through hole. Use care not to damage connector.

4. Remove sensor wire from bracket on shock strut and side rail.

5. Remove wheel and tire assembly.

6. Loosen 5mm setscrew holding sensor to sensor bracket post. Remove sensor through hole in disc brake splash shield.

7. To remove sensor bracket or sensor bracket post in case of damage, the caliper and hub and rotor assembly must be removed. After removing the hub and rotor assembly, remove 2 brake splash shield attaching bolts that attach sensor bracket.

NOTE: Replace the toothed sensor ring, if damaged.

To install:

8. Install sensor bracket with sensor bracket post, if removed. Tighten sensor retaining bolt to 40–53 inch lbs. (4.5–6.0 Nm) and splash shield attaching bolts to 10–15 ft. lbs. (13–20 Nm). Install hub and rotor assembly and caliper.

9. If a sensor is to be reused or adjusted, pole face must be clean of all foreign material. Carefully scrape pole face with a dull knife or similar tool, to ensure that sensor slides freely on the post. Glue a new front paper spacer on pole face, front paper spacer is marked with an **F** and is 0.051 in. (1.3mm) thick. Also, the steel sleeve around post bolt must be rotated to provide a new surface for setscrew to indent and lock into.

10. Install sensor through brake shield onto sensor bracket post. Ensure paper spacer on sensor is intact and does not come off during installation.

11. Push sensor toward toothed sensor ring until new paper sensor contacts the ring. Hold sensor against sensor ring and tighten the 5mm setscrew to 21–26 inch lbs. (2.4–3.0 Nm).

12. Insert sensor cable into bracket on shock strut, rail bracket; then through inner fender apron to engine compartment and seat grommet. Install wheel and tire assembly.

13. Lower vehicle and from inside engine compartment, connect sensor electrical connection. Connect the negative battery cable.

Rear Wheel Speed Sensor

REMOVAL AND INSTALLATION

Thunderbird and Cougar

1. Disconnect the negative battery cable.

2. From inside luggage compartment, disconnect wheel sensor electrical connector located rearward of wheel well, behind carpeting on sides of luggage compartment.

3. Lift luggage compartment carpet and push sensor wire grommet through hole in luggage compartment floor.

4. Raise and safely support the vehicle.

5. Remove the plastic clip holding sensor wire to axle carrier housing. Do not bend the clip open more than the amount necessary to remove the clip from the axle housing.

6. Remove wheel sensor retaining bolt using a ½ in. socket.

To install:

7. Align sensor locating tab and bolt hole with axle housing and push into position.

8. Install sensor retaining bolt and tighten to 14–20 ft. lbs. (19–27 Nm).

9. Install plastic clip retaining sensor wire to axle carrier housing and push electrical connector through hole in floor into luggage compartment. Ensure that rubber grommet is properly seated in hole in floor.

10. Lower the vehicle. Connect sensor electrical connector to connector on harness.

Mark VII

1. Disconnect the negative battery cable.

2. From inside the luggage compartment, disconnect the wheel sensor electrical connector located behind the forward luggage compartment trim panel.

3. Lift the luggage compartment carpet and push the sensor wire grommet through the hole in the luggage compartment floor.

4. Raise the vehicle and remove the appropriate wheel and tire assembly.

5. Carefully remove the wheel sensor wiring from the axle shaft housing. The wiring harness has 3 different types of retainers:

   a. The inboard retainer is a clip located on top of the differential housing. Bent the clip out of the way enough to remove the wiring harness.

   b. The second retainer is a C-clip located in the center of the axle shaft housing. Pull rearward on the clip to disengage the clip from the axle housing.

NOTE: Do not bend the clip open beyond the amount necessary to remove the clip from the axle housing.

   c. The third clip is at the connection between the rear wheel brake tube and the flexible hose. Remove

the hold-down bolt and open the clip to remove the wiring harness.

6. Remove the sensor retaining bolts and remove the sensor.

NOTE: Replace the toothed sensor ring, if damaged.

To install:

7. Install the sensor in the rear brake adapter and tighten the retaining screws to 11–15 ft. lbs. (15–20 Nm).

8. Install the sensor wire in the retainers along the axle housing. Push the connector through the hole in the luggage compartment and seat the grommet in the luggage compartment floorpan.

9. Install the wheel and tire assembly and lower the vehicle.

10. From inside the luggage compartment, connect the cable electrical connector. Install the carpet, as necessary.

11. Check the sensor function by driving the vehicle and observing the CHECK ANTI-LOCK BRAKES indicator.

FRONT SUSPENSION

NOTE: If equipped with the level ride air suspension, power to the air system must be shut OFF before servicing the suspension. The switch is located in the luggage compartment, on the drivers side rear fender well.

MacPherson Strut

REMOVAL AND INSTALLATION

Mustang

1. Disconnect the negative battery cable.

2. Place the ignition switch in the **UNLOCKED** position to permit free movement of the front wheels.

3. Raise the vehicle by the lower control arms until the wheels are just off the ground. From the engine compartment, remove and discard the 3 upper mount retaining nuts. Do not remove the pop-rivet holding the camber plate position.

4. Continue to raise the front of the vehicle by the lower control arms and position safety stands under the frame jacking pads, rearward of the wheels.

5. Remove the wheel and tire assembly and remove the brake caliper.

Support the caliper with a length of wire; do not let the caliper hang by the brake hose.

6. Remove the 2 lower nuts that attach the strut to the spindle, leaving the bolts in place. Carefully remove both spindle-to-strut bolts, push the bracket free of the spindle and remove the strut.

7. Compress the strut to clear the upper mount of the body mounting pad. Remove the upper mount and jounce bumper, if necessary.

To install:

8. Install the upper mount and jounce bumper, if removed.

9. Position the 3 upper mount studs into the body mounting pad and camber plate and start 3 new nuts.

10. Compress the strut and position into the spindle. Install 2 new lower retaining bolts and hand start the nuts. Remove the suspension load from the control arms by lowering the vehicle. Tighten the lower retaining nuts to 140–200 ft. lbs. (190–271 Nm).

11. Raise the suspension control arms and tighten the 3 new upper mount retaining nuts to 45–59 ft. lbs. (60–81 Nm).

12. Install the brake caliper and the wheel and tire assembly.

13. Lower the vehicle to the ground and check the front end alignment.

Thunderbird and Cougar

1. Remove the plastic cover at the upper strut mount, if equipped. If equipped with automatic ride control, remove the actuator assembly as follows:

   a. Make sure the vehicle is level. Turn the ignition switch **OFF**.

   b. Disconnect the actuator connector from the wiring harness connector. Remove the actuator cover by snapping off.

   c. Slide the actuator connector off the cover by inserting a small prybar tip between the connector and track to separate the 2 parts prior to sliding the connector off.

   d. Squeeze the 2 actuator retaining tabs firmly inward with 1 hand and lift the actuator off the mounting bracket with the other hand.

   e. Grasp the piston rod end at the 9mm hex with a socket wrench.

   f. Loosen the nut retaining the actuator mounting bracket to the strut with a 19mm box wrench while holding the socket wrench.

   g. Remove the nut and mounting bracket.

2. Remove the 3 upper strut retaining nuts and collar plate from the

mounting studs in the engine compartment.

3. Raise and safely support the vehicle. Remove the wheel and tire assembly.

4. Remove the lower strut mounting bolt and nut and remove the nut at the stabilizer link upper mounting stud. Separate the link from the spindle using a suitable joint separator tool.

5. Support the lower control arm with a jack. Raise the control arm and spindle with the jack until the stabilizer link can be completely separated from the spindle. Position the link aside.

6. Remove and discard the spindle to upper control arm retaining nut and bolt. Lower the jack to separate the spindle from the upper control arm. Support the spindle with a length of wire; do not let it hang free.

7. Lower the support for the lower control arm and remove the strut assembly from the vehicle.

To install:

8. Position the strut over the lower arm. Insert the lower strut bolt into the control arm.

9. Using a jack, raise the control arm and strut into position. Align the upper strut mounting studs with the holes.

10. Remove the wire supporting the spindle and position the spindle to the upper control arm. Raise the lower control arm using the jack and attach the spindle to the upper control arm.

11. Install a new spindle retaining bolt from the front of the vehicle and install the nut. Tighten to 59–66 ft. lbs. (80–90 Nm).

12. Position the stabilizer bar link and lower the spindle assembly until the link can be installed. Install the nut on the link stud and tighten to 48–55 ft. lbs. (65–75 Nm) on 1992 vehicles or to 39–53 ft. lbs. (53–77 Nm) on 1993–96 vehicles.

13. Remove the jack from the lower arm. Install the lower strut nut, but do not tighten at this time.

14. Install the wheel and tire assembly and lower the vehicle. Make sure the upper strut mounting studs are aligned with the holes.

15. Install the collar plate and 3 nuts to the upper mounting studs. Tighten to 17–22 ft. lbs. (22–31 Nm).

16. Install the washer, nut and automatic ride actuator, if equipped. Install the plastic cover, if equipped.

17. Neutralize the front suspension bushings by pushing down and releasing on the front of the vehicle.

Then tighten the lower strut nut to 140–162 ft. lbs. (190–220 Nm).

NOTE: The lower strut nut must be tightened with the vehicle weight on the wheels.

Mark VII

1. Turn the air suspension switch **OFF**.

2. Turn the ignition switch to the **UNLOCKED** position to allow free movement of the front wheels.

3. From inside the engine compartment, loosen but do not remove, the 1 strut-to-upper mount retaining nut. A small prybar positioned in the slot will hold the rod stationary while loosening the nut.

4. Raise the vehicle and position safety stands under the lower control arms as far outboard as possible, verifying the lower sensor mounting bracket is clear. Lower the vehicle until vehicle weight is supported by the lower arms.

5. Remove the wheel and tire assembly. Remove the brake caliper and support with a length of wire. Do not let the caliper hang by the brake hose.

6. Remove and discard the strut-to-upper mount retaining nut and then the 2 lower nuts and bolts attaching the strut to the spindle.

NOTE: The strut should be held firmly during removal of the last bolt since the gas pressure will cause the strut to fully extend when removed.

7. Lift the strut up from the spindle to compress the rod and then remove the strut. Remove the jounce bumper.

To install:

8. Prime the new strut by extending and compressing the strut 5 times. Install the jounce bumper.

9. Place the strut rod through the upper mount and hand start a new nut. Tighten the nut to 55–92 ft. lbs. (75–125 Nm).

10. Compress the strut and position onto the spindle. Install 2 new lower retaining bolts and hand start the nuts.

11. Raise the vehicle to remove the vehicle load from the lower control arms. Tighten the lower retaining nuts to 140–200 ft. lbs. (190–271 Nm).

12. Install the brake caliper and the wheel and tire assembly. Remove the safety stand and lower the vehicle to the ground.

13. Turn the air suspension switch **ON**. Check the front end alignment.

Coil Springs

REMOVAL AND INSTALLATION

Mustang

1. Raise and safely support the vehicle, allowing the control arms to hang free.

2. Remove the wheel and tire assembly and the brake caliper. Suspend the caliper with a length of wire; do not let the caliper hang by the brake hose.

3. Disconnect the tie rod end from the steering spindle and disconnect the stabilizer link from the lower arm.

4. Remove the steering gear bolts, if necessary and position the gear so the suspension arm bolt can be removed.

5. If equipped with 2.3L engine, use spring compressor tool T82P-5310-A or equivalent to place the upper plate in position into the spring pocket cavity on the crossmember. The hooks on the plate should be facing the center of the vehicle.

6. If equipped with 5.0L engine, use spring compressor tool D78P-5310-A or equivalent, to install a plate between the coils near the toe of the spring. Mark the location of the upper plate on the coils for installation.

7. Install the compression rod into the lower arm spring pocket hole, through the coil spring and into the upper plate.

8. Install the lower plate, lower ball nut, thrust washer and bearing and forcing nut onto the compression rod. Tighten the forcing nut until a drag on the nut is felt.

9. Remove the suspension arm-to-crossmember nuts and bolts. The compressor tool forcing nut may have to be tightened or loosened for easy bolt removal.

10. Loosen the compression rod forcing nut until spring tension is relieved and remove the forcing nut. Remove the compression rod and coil spring.

To install:

11. Place the insulator on top of the spring. Position the spring into the lower arm pocket. Make sure the spring pigtail is positioned between the 2 holes in the lower arm spring pocket.

12. Position the spring into the upper spring seat in the crossmember.

13. If equipped with 2.3L engine, insert the compression rod through the control arm and spring, then

hook it to the upper plate. The upper plate is installed with the hooks facing the center of the vehicle.

14. If equipped with 5.0L engine, install the upper plate between the coils in the location marked during removal.

15. Install the lower plate, ball nut, thrust washer and bearing and forcing nut onto the compression rod.

16. Tighten the forcing nut, position the lower arm into the crossmember and install new lower arm-to-crossmember bolts and nuts. Do not tighten at this time.

17. Remove the spring compressor tool from the vehicle. Raise the suspension arm to a normal attitude position with a jack. Tighten the lower arm-to-crossmember attaching nuts to 110–150 ft. lbs. (149–203 Nm). Remove the jack.

18. Install the steering gear-to-crossmember bolts and nuts, if removed. Hold the bolts and tighten the nuts to 90–100 ft. lbs. (122–135 Nm).

19. Connect the stabilizer bar link to the lower suspension arm. Tighten the attaching nut to 6–17 ft. lbs. (8–24 Nm).

20. Position the tie rod into the steering spindle and install the retaining nut. Tighten the nut to 35 ft. lbs. (47 Nm) and continue tightening the nut to align the next castellation with the hole in the stud. Install a new cotter pin.

21. Install the brake caliper and the wheel and tire assembly. Lower the vehicle.

Thunderbird and Cougar

1. Remove the strut assembly from the vehicle.

NOTE: The upper strut mount cannot be rotated when the strut and spring are assembled. Mark the position of the upper mount to the coil spring with chalk or paint, prior to disassembly. If the upper mount is not properly positioned during assembly, it will not install in the vehicle.

2. Position the strut assembly in spring compressor tool 086–00029 or equivalent.

3. Compress the spring. Remove the strut nut and washer and remove the upper mount.

4. Release the spring compressor to remove the coil spring.

To install:

5. If installing a new spring or upper mount, transfer the reference marks from the removed part to the new part.

6. Position the strut and the spring in the spring compressor tool and compress the spring to install the upper mount.

7. Install the upper mount, aligning the reference marks. Install the washer and nut and tighten to 37–52 ft. lbs. (50–71 Nm).

8. Release the spring compressor, making sure the spring is properly seated at top and bottom.

9. Install the strut assembly in the vehicle.

Air Springs

REMOVAL AND INSTALLATION

Mark VII

1. Turn the air suspension switch **OFF**.

2. Raise and safely support the vehicle on the frame. The suspension must be at full rebound.

3. Remove the wheel and tire assembly. Remove the air spring solenoid as follows:

  a. Disconnect the electrical connector and then disconnect the air line.

  b. Remove the solenoid clip.

  c. Rotate the solenoid counterclockwise to the 1st stop.

  d. Pull the solenoid straight out slowly to the 2nd stop to bleed air from the system.

NOTE: Do not fully release the solenoid until the air is completely bled from the air spring.

  e. After the air is fully bled from the system, rotate counterclockwise to the 3rd stop and remove the solenoid from the solenoid housing. Remove the large O-ring from the solenoid housing.

4. Remove the clip retaining the spring to the lower arm. Push down on the spring clip on the collar of the air spring and rotate the collar counterclockwise to release the spring from the body spring seat.

5. Remove the air spring.

To install:

6. Install the air spring solenoid as follows:

  a. Check the solenoid O-rings for cuts or abrasion. Replace the O-rings as required. Lightly grease the O-ring area of the solenoid and the larger solenoid housing O-ring with silicone dielectric compound.

  b. Insert the solenoid into the air spring end cap and rotate clockwise to the 3rd stop, push in to the 2nd stop, then rotate clockwise to the 1st stop.

  c. Install the solenoid clip. Inspect the wire harness connector and ensure the rubber gasket is in place at the bottom of the connector cavity.

7. For left side installations, position the notch on the collar to be in-line with the centerline of the solenoid. For right side installations, the flat on the collar is to be in-line with the centerline of the solenoid.

8. Install the air spring into the body spring seat, taking care to keep the solenoid air and electrical connections clean and free of damage. Rotate the air spring collar until the spring clip snaps into place. Make sure the air spring collar is retained by the 3 rolled tabs on the body spring seat.

9. Connect the air line and electrical connector to the solenoid.

10. Align and secure the lower arm-to-spring attachment with the suspension at full rebound and supported by the shock absorbers.

NOTE: The air springs may be damaged if the suspension is allowed to compress before the spring is inflated.

11. Refill the air spring as follows:

  a. Turn the air suspension switch **ON**. Leave the diagnostic pigtail ungrounded.

  b. Connect a battery charger to reduce battery drain.

  c. Turn the ignition switch from the **OFF** to the **RUN** position, hold in the **RUN** position for a minimum of 5 seconds, then return to the **OFF** position. The drivers door must be open but all other doors must be shut.

  d. Ground the diagnostic pigtail by connecting a jumper wire from the pigtail to vehicle ground. The pigtail must remain grounded during the spring fill sequence.

  e. While applying the brakes, turn the ignition switch to the **RUN** position. The door must be open but do not start the vehicle. The warning indicator will blink continuously once every 2 seconds to indicate the spring pump sequence has been entered.

  f. To fill the front spring(s), close and open the door twice. After a 6 second delay, the front spring will be filled for 60 seconds.

  g. Immediately after completion of the air spring fill, turn the air suspension switch **OFF** to prevent deflation of the air springs while the vehicle is raised. Inspect all springs for proper inflation; no folds or creases.

12. Install the wheel and tire assembly and lower the vehicle. Turn the air suspension switch **ON**.

NOTE: Any further vehicle leveling will be done when the vehicle is in normal operation on the ground.

Mark VIII

1. Turn the air suspension switch **OFF**.
2. Raise and safely support the vehicle. Make sure the suspension is in full rebound. Remove the wheel and tire assembly.

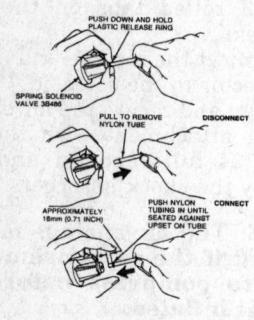

8470D088

Air line disconnect/connect procedure — Mark VII and Mark VIII

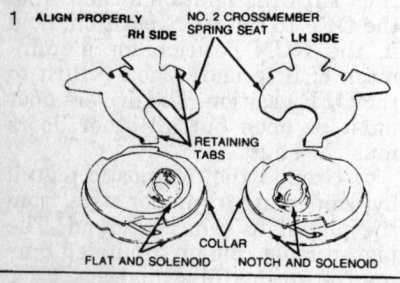

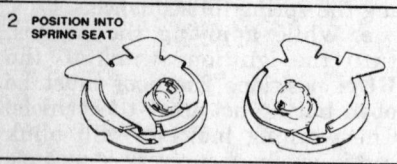

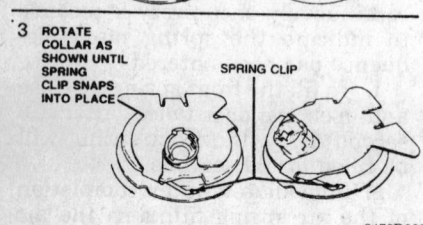

8470D089

Air spring-to-body spring seat installation — Mark VII

3. Remove the forward section of the front wheel splash shield far enough to disconnect the connector. Pull out the height sensor clips. Remove the sensor.
4. Disconnect the air spring solenoid connector and air line. Remove the solenoid clip.
5. Rotate the solenoid counterclockwise to the 1st stop. Pull the solenoid straight out slowly to the 2nd stop to bleed air from the system. When air is fully bled from the system, rotate the solenoid to the 3rd stop and remove the solenoid.
6. From inside the engine compartment, remove the appearance cover from over the air spring attachments.
7. Remove the 3 nuts and and the collar retaining the 3 air spring studs to the shock tower. Remove the lower nut and bolt to detach shock from the lower suspension arm. Remove the shock.

NOTE: Do not remove the front shock's large center nut. It may cause a permanent air leak.

To install:
8. Insert the solenoid into the air spring end cap and rotate clockwise to the 3rd stop, push into the 2nd stop, then rotate clockwise to the 1st stop.
9. Install the solenoid clip. Position and fasten the 3 upper air spring studs through the shock tower and hand-tighten the 3 nuts and the collar. The solenoid socket for the left or right spring should be oriented forward of the spring.
10. Place the lower end of the shock over the lower suspension arm and hand-tighten the nut and bolt.
11. Tighten the 3 upper attachment bolts to 17–23 ft. lbs. (23–32 Nm). Attach the appearance cover over the top of the shock tower.
12. Connect the air line and electrical connector to the solenoid. Install the height sensor and connect the connector.
13. Refill the air spring as follows:
   a. Make sure the air suspension switch is turned **OFF**.
   b. Connect SUPER STAR II diagnostic tool, or equivalent, to the data link connector located on the front side of the right shock tower.
   c. Connect a battery charger to reduce battery drain.
   d. Enter function test to pump appropriate air springs. Left front spring=212. Right front spring=214. Any further leveling will be done when the vehicle is in normal operation.

14. Install the tire and wheel assembly. Lower the vehicle.
15. Neutralize the front suspension bushings by pushing down then releasing the front end.
16. Tighten the lower shock nut to 199–243 ft. lbs. (170–230 Nm).
17. Turn the air suspension switch **ON**. Check the front end alignment.

Upper Ball Joints

INSPECTION

Mark VIII, Thunderbird and Cougar

1. Raise the vehicle and place jacks under the sub-frame. This will minimize the load on the ball joints.
2. Attach a dial indicator in such a way as to measure the lateral movement between the spindle and the arm.
3. Grasp the tire at the top and bottom and slowly move the tire in and out. Note the reading on the dial indicator. If the reading exceeds 0.015 in. (0.4mm), replace the ball joint.

REMOVAL AND INSTALLATION

Mark VIII, Thunderbird and Cougar

The ball joint is an integral part of the upper control arm. If the ball joint is defective, the entire upper control arm must be replaced.

Lower Ball Joints

INSPECTION

Mustang and Mark VII

1. Support the vehicle in normal driving position with ball joints loaded.
2. Wipe the wear indicator and ball joint cover checking surface clean.
3. The checking surface should project outside the cover. If the checking surface is inside the cover, replace the lower arm assembly.

Mark VIII, Thunderbird and Cougar

1. Raise the vehicle and place jacks under the sub-frame. This will minimize the load on the ball joints.
2. Attach a dial indicator in such a way as to measure the lateral movement between the spindle and the arm.
3. Grasp the tire at the top and bottom and slowly move the tire in and out. Note the reading on the dial

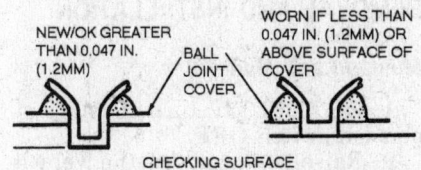

Lower ball joint cover checking surface — Mustang and Mark VII

indicator. If the reading exceeds 0.015 in. (0.4mm), replace the ball joint.

REMOVAL AND INSTALLATION

Mustang and Mark VII

The ball joint is an integral part of the lower control arm. If the ball joint is defective, the entire lower control arm must be replaced.

Mark VIII, Thunderbird and Cougar

1. Remove the lower control arm.
2. Remove and discard the joint boot seal.
3. Press out the ball joint using ball joint remover tool D89P–3010–A and cup tool D84P–3395–A4 or equivalent, and a suitable press.

To install:

4. When installing a new ball joint, leave the protective cover in place during installation to protect the ball joint seal. It may be necessary to cut off the end of the cover to allow it to pass through the receiving cup.
5. Install the ball joint with ball joint replacer tool D89P–3010–B, cup tool D84P–3395–A4 or equivalent, and a suitable press.
6. Make sure the ball joint is fully seated in the control arm and the ball joint seal is free of cuts or tears.
7. Install the lower control arm. Check the front end alignment.

Upper Control Arms

REMOVAL AND INSTALLATION

Mark VIII, Thunderbird and Cougar

1. Raise and safely support the vehicle. Remove the wheel and tire assembly.
2. On Mark VIII, disconnect the height sensor.

3. Remove and discard the upper spindle-to-ball joint bolt and nut. Slightly spread the spindle at the slot and remove the ball joint.
4. Lower the vehicle. Break off the flags on the upper control arm pivot bolt heads.
5. Remove the upper control arm bolts and the control arm.

To install:

6. Position the upper control arm and install new bolts without the flags and nuts.
7. Hold the upper control arm at a horizontal position and tighten the nuts to 72–88 ft. lbs. (98–120 Nm).

NOTE: If it is necessary to tighten the bolts, due to nut access, tighten the bolts to 82–88 ft. lbs. (110–120 Nm).

8. Raise the vehicle. Attach the spindle to the upper control arm. Install a new bolt and nut from the front of the vehicle and tighten to 59–66 ft. lbs. (80–90 Nm).
9. On Mark VIII, connect the height sensor.
10. Install the wheel and tire assembly and lower the vehicle. Check the front end alignment.

Lower Control Arms

REMOVAL AND INSTALLATION

Mustang and Mark VII

1. On Mark VII, turn the air suspension switch **OFF**.
2. Raise and safely support the vehicle. Allow the control arms to hang free. Remove the wheel and tire assembly.
3. If necessary, remove the brake caliper and suspend with a length of wire; do not let the caliper hang by the brake hose. Remove the brake rotor and dust shield.

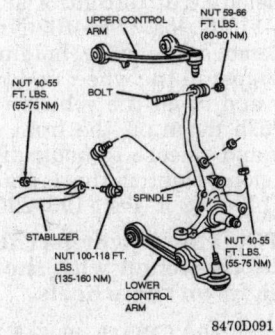

Front suspension assembly — Mark VIII, Thunderbird and Cougar

4. Disconnect the tie rod end from the steering spindle. Disconnect the stabilizer bar link from the lower arm.
5. Remove the steering gear bolts and lower the gear aside to provide clearance, if necessary, for suspension arm bolt removal.
6. On Mark VII, disconnect the lower end of the height sensor from the lower control arm sensor mounting stud. Remove the sensor mounting stud and screw from the lower arm, noting the position of the stud on the lower arm bracket.
7. Remove the cotter pin and loosen the lower ball joint stud nut 1–2 turns. Do not remove the nut at this time. Tap the spindle boss sharply to relieve the stud pressure.
8. On Mustang, install a suitable spring compressor and compress the spring so it is free in the seat. On Mark VII, proceed as follows:

   a. Disconnect the electrical connector and then disconnect the air line.

   b. Remove the solenoid clip.

   c. Rotate the solenoid counterclockwise to the 1st stop.

   d. Pull the solenoid straight out slowly to the 2nd stop to bleed the air from the system.

   e. Push in, then rotate clockwise to the 1st stop.

   f. Install the solenoid clip. Inspect the wire harness connector and ensure the rubber gasket is in place at the bottom of the connector cavity.

   g. Remove and discard the air spring-to-lower arm fastener clip.

9. Remove and discard the ball joint nut and raise the entire strut and spindle assembly. Wire aside to obtain working room.
10. Remove and discard the control arm-to-crossmember nuts and bolts. Remove the lower control arm and, on Mustang, remove the coil spring.

To install:

11. On Mustang, position the coil spring into the lower arm pocket. Make sure the spring pigtail is positioned between the 2 holes in the pocket.
12. Position the lower arm to the crossmember and install new arm-to-crossmember bolts and nuts. Do not tighten at this time.
13. Remove the wire from the strut and spindle assembly and attach the spindle to the ball joint stud. Install a new ball joint stud nut, but do not tighten at this time.
14. On Mustang, raise the control arm with a jack to a normal attitude

position and remove the spring compressor.

15. On Mark VII, position the air spring in the arm and install the new fastener. Install the sensor mounting stud and screw to the lower arm in the same position as on the replaced arm. Connect the lower end of the sensor to the lower arm mounting stud. Raise the control arm to curb height with a jack.

16. With the jack in place, tighten the lower arm-to-crossmember attaching nuts to 110–150 ft. lbs. (149–203 Nm).

17. Tighten the ball joint stud nut to 100–120 ft. lbs. (136–163 Nm) and install a new cotter pin. Remove the jack.

18. Install the dust shield, rotor and brake caliper, if removed. Install the steering gear-to-crossmember bolts and nuts, if removed. Hold the bolts and tighten the nuts to 90–100 ft. lbs. (122–136 Nm).

19. Position the tie rod into the steering spindle and install the retaining nut. Tighten the nut to 35 ft. lbs. (47 Nm) and continue tightening the nut to align the next castellation with the hole in the stud. Install a new cotter pin.

20. Connect the stabilizer bar link to the lower control arm. Tighten the retaining nut to 6–17 ft. lbs. (8–24 Nm).

21. On Mustang, install the wheel and tire assembly and lower the vehicle. Check the front end alignment.

22. On Mark VII, proceed as follows:

a. Connect the air line and then the electrical connector to the air spring solenoid.

b. Turn the air suspension switch **ON**. Leave the diagnostic pigtail ungrounded.

c. Connect a battery charger to reduce battery drain.

d. Turn the ignition switch from the **OFF** to the **RUN** position, hold in the **RUN** position for a minimum of 5 seconds, then return to the **OFF** position. The drivers door should be open, with all other doors shut.

e. Ground the diagnostic pigtail by connecting a jumper wire from the pigtail to vehicle ground. The pigtail must remain grounded during the spring fill sequence.

f. While applying the brakes, turn the ignition switch to the **RUN** position. The door must be open; do not start the vehicle. The warning indicator will blink continuously once every 2 seconds to indi-cate the spring pump sequence has been entered.

g. To fill the front spring(s), close and open the door twice. After a 6 second delay, the front spring will be filled for 60 seconds.

h. Immediately after completion of the air spring fill, turn the air suspension switch **OFF** to prevent deflation of the air springs while the vehicle is raised. Inspect all springs for proper inflation; no folds or creases.

i. Install the wheel and tire assembly and lower the vehicle. Turn the air suspension switch **ON**. Check the front end alignment.

NOTE: Any further vehicle leveling will be done when the vehicle is in normal operation on the ground.

Mark VIII, Thunderbird and Cougar

1. Raise and safely support the vehicle. Remove the wheel and tire assembly.

2. Loosen the ball joint nut 3–4 turns. Rap the spindle to separate the ball joint. Leave the nut attached.

3. Support the spindle with a wire. Mark the position of the camber adjusting cam. Remove and discard the nut attaching the tension strut to the control arm.

4. Remove the lower strut bolt and remove the pivot bolt.

5. Remove the ball joint nut and remove the control arm.

To install:

6. Position the control arm in the vehicle and loosely install the pivot bolt and new nut.

7. Install the tension strut washer and insulators and loosely install the strut to control arm attaching nut.

8. Loosely install a new ball joint nut. Install a new lower strut bolt and nut, but do not tighten at this time.

9. Tighten the ball joint nut to 82–118 ft. lbs. (110–160 Nm). Tighten the tension strut to control arm nut to 103–118 ft. lbs. (140–160 Nm).

10. Remove the wire holding the spindle. Install the wheel and tire assembly and lower the vehicle.

11. Push down on the front of the vehicle and release to neutralize the suspension. Tighten the lower strut nut to 140–162 ft. lbs. (190–220 Nm).

NOTE: The lower strut nut must be tightened with the vehicle weight on the wheels.

12. Align the camber marks at the pivot bolt and tighten the nut to 98–114 ft. lbs. (135–155 Nm).

13. Check the front end alignment.

Stabilizer Bar

REMOVAL AND INSTALLATION

Mustang and Mark VII

1. On Mark VII, turn the air suspension switch **OFF**.

2. Raise the front of the vehicle and place jackstands under the lower control arms.

3. Disconnect the stabilizer bar from the links and the insulator mounting clamps. Remove the stabilizer bar.

4. Cut the worn insulators from the stabilizer bar.

5. Installation is the reverse of the removal procedure. Coat the necessary parts of the stabilizer bar with rubber lubricant prior to installation.

Mark VIII, Thunderbird and Cougar

1. Disconnect the negative battery cable.

2. Remove the air inlet tube. Remove the stabilizer bar retaining bracket bolts and brackets.

3. Remove the serpentine drive belt. Raise and safely support the vehicle.

4. Remove the wheel and tire assemblies. Remove the crankshaft vibration damper.

5. Remove the cotter pins and nuts from the tie rod ends. Separate the tie rod ends from the spindles.

6. Remove the transmission oil cooler line bracket. Remove the stabilizer bar to lower link retaining nuts.

7. Remove the stabilizer bar link from the stabilizer bar using joint separator tool D88L-3006-A or equivalent. Be careful not to damage the ball joint seal.

8. Remove the stabilizer bar through the right wheel opening. Remove the bushings from the stabilizer bar.

To install:

9. Install the bushings onto the stabilizer bar and position the bar in the vehicle.

10. Attach the stabilizer links to the bar and tighten the retaining nuts to 48–55 ft. lbs. (65–75 Nm).

11. Install the stabilizer bar bracket and retaining bolts. Tighten to 48–55 ft. lbs. (65–75 Nm).

12. Install the transmission oil cooler lines. Install the tie rod ends to the spindles. Tighten the nuts to 39–54 ft. lbs. (53–73 Nm) and install new cotter pins.

13. Install the crankshaft damper. Install the wheel and tire assemblies and lower the vehicle.

14. Install the serpentine drive belt and the air inlet tube. Connect the negative battery cable.

Front Wheel Bearings

ADJUSTMENT

Mustang and Mark VII

1. On Mark VII, turn the air suspension switch **OFF**.
2. Raise and safely support the front of the vehicle.
3. Remove the wheel cover and grease cap.
4. Remove the cotter pin and nut retainer.
5. Loosen the adjusting nut 3 turns and rock the wheel back and forth a few times to release the brake pads from the rotor.
6. While rotating the wheel and hub assembly in a counterclockwise direction, tighten the adjusting nut to 17–25 ft. lbs. (23–34 Nm).
7. Back off the adjusting nut ½ turn, then retighten to 10–28 inch lbs. (1.1–3.2 Nm).
8. Install the nut retainer and a new cotter pin. Check the wheel rotation. If it is noisy or rough, the bearings either need to be cleaned and repacked or replaced. After adjustment is completed, replace the grease cap.
9. Lower the vehicle. Before driving the vehicle, pump the brake pedal several times to restore normal brake pedal travel. On Mark VII, turn the air suspension switch **ON**.

Mark VIII, Thunderbird and Cougar

The front wheel bearings are of a hub unit design and are pregreased, sealed and require no maintenance. The bearings are preset and cannot be adjusted.

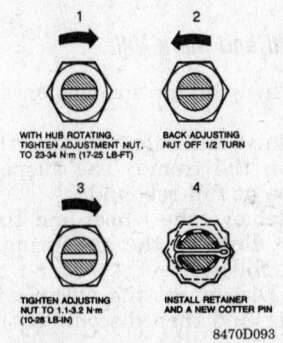

Wheel bearing adjustment procedure — Mustang and Mark VII

REMOVAL AND INSTALLATION

Mustang and Mark VII

1. On Mark VII, turn the air suspension switch **OFF**.
2. Raise and support the vehicle safely. Remove the wheel and tire assembly and the caliper. Suspend the caliper with a length of wire; do not let it hang from the brake hose.
3. Pry off the dust cap. Remove the cotter pin, nut retainer, adjusting nut and flat washer. Remove the outer roller bearing assembly.
4. Pull off the brake disc and wheel hub assembly.
5. Remove the inner grease seal using a prybar. Remove the inner roller bearing assembly.
6. Clean the bearings with solvent and inspect them for pits, scratches and excessive wear. Wipe all the old grease from the hub and inspect the bearing races. If either bearings or races are damaged, the bearing races must be removed and the bearings and races replaced as an assembly.
7. If the bearings are to be replaced, drive out the races from the hub using a brass drift.
8. Make sure the spindle, hub and bearing assemblies are clean prior to installation.
To install:
9. If the bearing races were removed, install new ones using a suitable bearing race installer. Pack the bearings with a bearing packer. If a packer is not available, work as much grease as possible between the rollers and cages.
10. Coat the inner surface of the hub and bearing races with grease.
11. Install the inner bearing in the hub. Lubricate the lips of a new seal with grease and install the seal in the hub, using a seal installer.
12. Install the hub/disc assembly on the spindle, being careful not to damage the oil seal.
13. Install the outer bearing, washer and spindle nut. Install the caliper and the wheel and tire assembly and adjust the bearings.

Mark VIII, Thunderbird and Cougar

1. Raise and safely support the vehicle. Remove the wheel and tire assembly.
2. Remove and discard the grease cap from the hub.
3. Remove the brake caliper. Suspend the caliper with a length of wire; do not let it hang from the brake hose.
4. Remove the rotor. Remove and discard the wheel hub nut.

5. Remove the hub and bearing assembly.
To install:
6. Install the hub and bearing assembly. Install a new wheel hub nut and tighten to 238 ft. lbs. (322 Nm).
7. Install the rotor and a new grease cap. Install the brake caliper.
8. Install the wheel and tire assembly and lower the vehicle.

REAR SUSPENSION

Shock Absorbers

REMOVAL AND INSTALLATION

1. On Mark VII, turn the air suspension switch **OFF**. On Mark VIII, Thunderbird and Cougar, proceed as follows to remove the actuation assembly, if equipped with automatic ride control:
   a. Make sure the vehicle is on a flat surface and the ignition is in the **OFF** position.
   b. Remove the luggage compartment side trim panel and disconnect the actuator wiring connector.
   c. Squeeze the 2 actuator retaining tabs firmly inward with 1 hand and lift the actuator off the mounting bracket with the other hand.
   d. Grasp the actuator mounting bracket with water pump pliers and hold firmly. While holding the bracket, loosen the bracket retaining nut. Remove the bracket.
2. Raise the vehicle and support it by the rear axle housing. Open the luggage compartment. On Mustang 3-door, open the hatch back door.
3. Remove the trim panels, as necessary, to gain access to the shock absorber. Remove the shock absorber retaining nut washer and insulator.
4. Remove the shock absorber bolt washer and nut at the lower arm and remove the shock absorber.

NOTE: Vehicles are equipped with gas pressurized shock absorbers which will extend unassisted.

To install:
5. Prime the new shock absorber as follows:
   a. With the shock absorber right side up, extend it fully.
   b. Turn the shock upside down and fully compress it.

c. Repeat the previous 2 steps at least 3 times to make sure any trapped air has been expelled.

6. Place the inner washer and insulator on the upper retaining stud and position the stud through the shock tower mounting hole.

7. Attach the lower end of the shock absorber with the retaining bolt and nut. Tighten the bolt to 45–60 ft. lbs. (61–81 Nm) on Mark VII and Mustang with handling package or 57–70 ft. lbs. (76–96 Nm) on Mustang without handling package. Tighten the nut to 72–97 ft. lbs. (97–132 Nm) on Thunderbird and Cougar or to 82–113 ft. lbs. (113–153 Nm) on Mark VIII.

8. Install the upper insulator, washer and retaining nut and tighten to 20–25 ft. lbs. (26–35 Nm) on Mustang and Mark VII or 27–35 ft. lbs. (37–47 Nm) on Thunderbird and Cougar or to 17–23 ft. lbs. (23–31 Nm) on

9. On Mark VIII, Thunderbird and Cougar, install the shock actuator, if necessary.

10. Lower the vehicle. On Mark VII, turn the air suspension switch **ON**.

Coil Springs

REMOVAL AND INSTALLATION

Mustang

1. Raise and safely support the vehicle. Support the body at the rear body crossmember.

2. Remove the stabilizer bar, if equipped.

3. Support the axle with a suitable jack or jackstands.

4. Place another jack under the lower arm axle pivot bolt. Remove and discard the bolt and nut. Lower the jack slowly until the coil spring load is relieved.

5. Remove the coil spring and insulator from the vehicle.

To install:

6. Place the upper spring insulator on top of the spring. Place the lower spring insulator on the lower arm.

7. Position the coil spring on the lower arm spring seat, so the pigtail on the lower arm is at the rear of the vehicle and pointing toward the left side of the vehicle.

8. Slowly raise the jack until the arm is in position. Insert a new rear pivot bolt and nut with the nut facing outward. Do not tighten at this time.

9. Raise the axle to curb height. Tighten the lower arm-to-axle pivot bolt to 70–100 ft. lbs. (95–135 Nm).

10. Install the stabilizer bar, if equipped. Remove the crossmember supports and lower the vehicle.

Thunderbird and Cougar

1. Raise and safely support the vehicle. Remove the rear wheel and tire assembly.

2. Remove the rear stabilizer bar link nuts at both ends of the bar. Rotate the bar up and out of the way.

3. Disconnect the parking brake cable at the brake caliper.

4. Install 3 spring cage tools 086–00031 or equivalent to the rear spring as follows:

   a. Install 1 spring cage without an adjuster link to the inboard side, the innermost "bend" of the spring.

   b. Install 2 more spring cages, with adjusters, at 120 degree angles to the previously installed cage.

5. Place a jack under the lower rear control arm as far outboard as possible.

6. Support the rear knuckle and caliper assembly by wiring the upper control arm to the body.

7. Remove the lower shock absorber mounting bolt and nut. Mark the toe adjustment cam-to-subframe position and loosen both inboard pivot bolts on the lower control arm.

NOTE: The control arm must not be lowered until the pivot bolts are loose. Do not attempt to remove the plastic cap on the front pivot nut.

8. Remove the 2 bolts and nuts attaching the lower control arm to the knuckle. Lower the control arm by lowering the jack. Make sure the spring cages properly seat on the spring as the control arm is dropped.

9. Remove the jack, pull the control arm down fully by hand and remove the rear spring with the cages in place. Remove the spring insulators, if necessary.

10. If the springs are to be replaced, use a suitable coil spring compressor to compress the spring and remove the spring cages.

To install:

11. If a new spring is to be installed, it 1st must be compressed and caged. Compress the spring to the length of the original spring. If replacing a broken spring, compress

the spring to approximately 10½ in. (267mm).

12. Install the spring insulators, if removed. Install the spring, with the cages in place, onto the upper and lower control arm seats.

NOTE: The short cage, without the adjuster, must be inboard. the spring pigtails may be in any position.

13. Position 2 jackstands under the front bumper reinforcement to prevent the rear of the vehicle lifting off the hoist.

14. Position a jack under the lower control arm and raise the lower control arm up to the knuckle bores. Make sure the spring seats properly. Install the bolts and nuts attaching the lower control arm to the knuckle and tighten the bolts to 118–148 ft. lbs. (160–200 Nm).

15. Remove the wire supporting the knuckle, caliper and upper control arm. Install the lower shock absorber mount bolt and nut and tighten the nut to 110–120 ft. lbs. (150–162 Nm).

16. Remove the jack and the jackstands. Remove the spring cages.

17. Connect the parking brake cable to the caliper. Install the rear stabilizer bar links and retaining nuts.

18. Install the wheel and tire assembly and lower the vehicle.

19. Set the toe adjustment cam to the mark made at the time of removal. Tighten the front lower control arm-to-sub-frame nut to 185–228 ft. lbs. (250–310 Nm). Tighten the rear lower control arm-to-sub-frame nut to 126–169 ft. lbs. (170–230 Nm).

20. Check the rear wheel toe setting and adjust as necessary.

Air Springs

REMOVAL AND INSTALLATION

Mark VII and Mark VIII

1. Turn the air suspension switch **OFF**.

2. Raise and safely support the vehicle on the frame. The suspension must be at full rebound.

3. Remove the wheel and tire assembly. Remove the air spring solenoid as follows:

   a. Disconnect the electrical connector and then disconnect the air line.

   b. Remove the solenoid clip.

   c. Rotate the solenoid counterclockwise to the 1st stop.

d. Pull the solenoid straight out slowly to the 2nd stop to bleed air from the system.

NOTE: Do not fully release the solenoid until the air is completely bled from the air spring.

e. After the air is fully bled from the system, rotate counterclockwise to the 3rd stop and remove the solenoid from the solenoid housing. Remove the large O-ring from the solenoid housing.

4. On Mark VII, remove the bolts retaining the spring to the lower arm. Push down on the spring clip on the collar of the air spring and rotate the collar counterclockwise to release the spring from the body spring seat.

5. On Mark VIII, press the 4 plastic locking fingers in the bottom of the air spring's piston and remove the piston from the lower suspension arm.

6. Remove the air spring.

To install:

7. Install the air spring solenoid as follows:

a. Check the solenoid O-rings for cuts or abrasion. Replace the O-rings as required. Lightly grease the O-ring area of the solenoid and the larger solenoid housing O-ring with silicone dielectric compound.

b. Insert the solenoid into the air spring end cap and rotate clockwise to the 3rd stop, push in to the 2nd stop, then rotate clockwise to the 1st stop.

c. Install the solenoid clip. Inspect the wire harness connector and ensure the rubber gasket is in place at the bottom of the connector cavity.

8. For left side installations, position the notch on the collar to be in-line with the centerline of the solenoid. For right side installations, the flat on the collar is to be in-line with the centerline of the solenoid.

9. On Mark VII, install the air spring into the body spring seat, taking care to keep the solenoid air and electrical connections clean and free of damage. Rotate the air spring collar until the spring clip snaps into place. Make sure the air spring collar is retained by the 3 rolled tabs on the body spring seat.

10. On Mark VIII, Insert the air spring piston's 4 plastic locking fingers into the lower suspension arm until they lock in place. Make sure all 4 fingers are locked in place.

11. Connect the air line and electrical connector to the solenoid.

12. Align and secure the lower arm-to-spring attachment with the suspension at full rebound and supported by the shock absorbers.

NOTE: The air springs may be damaged if the suspension is allowed to compress before the spring is inflated.

13. On Mark VII, refill the air spring as follows:

a. Turn the air suspension switch **ON**. Leave the diagnostic pigtail ungrounded.

b. Connect a battery charger to reduce battery drain.

c. Turn the ignition switch from the **OFF** to the **RUN** position, hold in the **RUN** position for a minimum of 5 seconds, then return to the **OFF** position. The drivers door should be open with all other doors shut.

d. Ground the diagnostic pigtail by connecting a jumper wire from the pigtail to vehicle ground. The pigtail must remain grounded during the spring fill sequence.

e. While applying the brakes, turn the ignition switch to the **RUN** position. The door must be open; do not start the vehicle. The warning indicator will blink continuously once every 2 seconds to indicate the spring pump sequence has been entered.

f. To fill the rear spring(s), close and open the door once. After a 6 second delay, the rear spring will be filled for 60 seconds.

g. Immediately after completion of the air spring fill, turn the air suspension switch **OFF** to prevent deflation of the air springs while the vehicle is raised. Inspect all springs for proper inflation; no folds or creases.

14. On Mark VIII, refill the air spring as follows:

a. Make sure the air suspension switch is turned **OFF**.

b. Connect SUPER STAR II diagnostic tool, or equivalent, to the data link connector located on the front side of the right shock tower.

c. Connect a battery charger to reduce battery drain.

d. Enter function test to pump appropriate air springs. Left rear spring=216. Right rear spring=218. Any further leveling will be done when the vehicle is in normal operation.

15. Install the wheel and tire assembly and lower the vehicle. Turn the air suspension switch **ON**.

NOTE: Any further vehicle leveling will be done when the vehicle is in normal operation on the ground.

Rear Control Arms

REMOVAL AND INSTALLATION

Mustang

UPPER ARM

NOTE: If 1 arm needs to be replaced, replace the other arm also.

1. Raise and safely support the vehicle at the rear crossmember.

2. Remove and discard the upper arm pivot bolts and nuts and remove the control arm.

To install:

3. Place the upper arm into the bracket of the body side rail. Install a new pivot bolt and nut with the nut facing outboard. Do not tighten at this time.

4. Using a jack, raise the suspension until the upper arm-to-axle pivot hole is in position with the hole in the axle bushing. Install a new pivot bolt and nut with the nut facing inboard. Do not tighten at this time.

5. Raise the suspension to curb height. Tighten the front upper arm bolt to 77–105 ft. lbs. (104–142 Nm) and the rear upper arm bolt to 70–100 ft. lbs. (95–135 Nm).

6. Remove the supports and lower the vehicle.

LOWER ARM

NOTE: If 1 arm needs to be replaced, replace the other arm also.

1. Raise and safely support the vehicle at the rear crossmember.

2. Remove the stabilizer bar, if equipped.

3. Place a jack under the lower arm-to-axle pivot bolt. Remove and discard the bolt and nut. Lower the jack slowly until the coil spring can be removed.

4. Remove and discard the lower arm-to-frame pivot bolt and nut. Remove the lower arm.

To install:

5. Position the lower arm assembly into the front arm bracket. Install a new pivot bolt and nut with the nut facing outwards. Do not tighten at this time.

6. Position the coil spring on the lower arm spring seat, so the pigtail on the lower arm is at the rear of the vehicle and pointing toward the left side of the vehicle.

7. Slowly raise the jack until the arm is in position. Insert a new rear pivot bolt and nut with the nut facing outward. Do not tighten at this time.

8. Raise the axle to curb height. Tighten the lower arm front bolt to 77–105 ft. lbs. (104–142 Nm) and the rear bolt to 70–100 ft. lbs. (95–135 Nm).

9. Install the stabilizer bar, if equipped. Remove the crossmember supports and lower the vehicle.

Thunderbird and Cougar

UPPER ARM

1. Raise and safely support the vehicle. Remove the rear wheel and tire assembly.

2. Support the knuckle and hub assembly so it cannot swing outward.

3. Remove the inner and outer pivot bolts and nuts at the upper control arm and remove the arm.

To install:

4. Install the upper arm. Loosely install the bolts and nuts.

NOTE: The inner pivot bolt used for camber adjustment has a specially shaped washer under the bolt head. Make sure fasteners are used in the correct locations.

5. Install the wheel and tire assembly and lower the vehicle.

6. Tighten the outboard nut to 118–148 ft. lbs. (160–200 Nm).

7. Set the camber and tighten the inner pivot nut to 81–98 ft. lbs. (110–133 Nm) on 1992 vehicles or to 50–68 ft. lbs. (68–92 Nm) on 1993–96 vehicles.

LOWER ARM

1. Remove the coil spring.

2. Remove the inner control arm pivot bolts and nuts and remove the arm.

NOTE: Do not attempt to remove the plastic cap on the front pivot nut.

3. Remove the toe compensating link from the control arm.

To install:

4. Inspect the large nut used at the inner front arm attachment for condition of plastic cap. Use a new nut if the cap is cracked, loose or missing.

5. Install the toe compensating link on the arm.

6. Install the lower control arm to the sub-frame and loosely install the pivot bolts and nuts.

7. Tighten the toe compensating link nut to 118–148 ft. lbs. (160–200 Nm).

8. Install the spring and reattach the control arm at the knuckle.

9. Check and adjust the rear toe.

Mark VII

UPPER ARM

NOTE: If 1 arm needs to be replaced, replace the other arm also.

1. Turn the air suspension switch **OFF**.

2. Raise and safely support the vehicle. Allow the suspension to be at full rebound.

3. On the right side, disconnect the rear height sensor from the side arm. Note position of the sensor adjustment bracket on the upper arm.

4. Remove and discard the upper arm pivot bolts and nuts and remove the upper arm.

To install:

5. Place the upper arm into position and install new pivot bolts and nuts. At the body bracket, the nut must face outboard. At the axle, the nut must face inboard. Do not tighten at this time.

6. Connect the rear height sensor to the arm. Set the adjustment bracket to the same position as on the replaced arm and tighten the nut to 7–10 ft. lbs. (8–14 Nm).

7. Using a suitable jack, raise the axle to curb height. Tighten the front upper arm bolt to 80–105 ft. lbs. (108–142 Nm) and the rear upper arm bolt to 70–100 ft. lbs. (95–135 Nm).

8. Remove the supports and lower the vehicle. Turn the air suspension switch **ON**.

LOWER ARM

NOTE: If 1 arm needs to be replaced, replace the other arm also.

1. Turn the air suspension switch **OFF**.

2. Raise and safely support the vehicle. Allow the suspension to be at full rebound.

3. Remove the wheel and tire assembly.

4. Vent the air springs to atmospheric pressure as follows:

   a. Disconnect the electrical connector and then disconnect the air line.

   b. Remove the solenoid clip.

   c. Rotate the solenoid counterclockwise to the 1st stop.

   d. Pull the solenoid straight out slowly to the 2nd stop to bleed the air from the system.

   e. Push in, then rotate clockwise to the 1st stop.

   f. Install the solenoid clip. Inspect the wire harness connector and ensure the rubber gasket is in place at the bottom of the connector cavity.

   g. Reconnect the air line and electrical connector.

5. Remove and discard the 2 air spring-to-lower control arm bolts and remove the air spring from the lower arm.

6. Remove and discard the bolts and remove the arm from the vehicle.

To install:

7. Position the control arm and install new pivot bolts and nuts with the nuts facing outward. Do not tighten at this time.

8. Install 2 new air spring-to-arm bolts, but do not tighten at this time.

9. Using a jack, raise the axle to curb height. Tighten the lower arm front bolt to 80–105 ft. lbs. (108–142 Nm) and the rear bolt to 70–100 ft. lbs. (95–135 Nm).

10. Tighten the air spring-to-arm bolt to 25–35 ft. lbs. (34–48 Nm). Make sure the air spring piston is flat on the lower arm. Remove the jack.

11. Refill the air spring as follows:

   a. Turn the air suspension switch **ON**. Leave the diagnostic pigtail ungrounded.

   b. Connect a battery charger to reduce battery drain.

   c. Turn the ignition switch from the **OFF** to the **RUN** position, hold in the **RUN** position for a minimum of 5 seconds, then return to the **OFF** position. The drivers door should be open with all other doors shut.

   d. Ground the diagnostic pigtail by connecting a jumper wire from the pigtail to vehicle ground. The pigtail must remain grounded during the spring fill sequence.

   e. While applying the brakes, turn the ignition switch to the **RUN** position. The door must be open; do not start the vehicle. The warning indicator will blink continuously once every 2 seconds to indicate the spring pump sequence has been entered.

   f. To fill the rear spring(s), close and open the door once. After a 6 second delay, the rear spring will be filled for 60 seconds.

   g. Immediately after completion of the air spring fill, turn the air suspension switch **OFF** to prevent deflation of the air springs while the vehicle is raised. Inspect all springs for proper inflation; no folds or creases.

12. Install the wheel and tire assembly and lower the vehicle. Turn the air suspension switch **ON**.

NOTE: Any further vehicle leveling will be done when the vehicle is in normal operation on the ground.

Mark VIII

UPPER ARM

1. Raise and safely support the vehicle. Remove the rear wheel and tire assembly.
2. Support the knuckle and hub assembly so it cannot swing outward.
3. Remove the inner and outer pivot bolts and nuts at the upper control arm and remove the arm.
   To install:
4. Install the upper arm. Loosely install the bolts and nuts.

NOTE: The inner pivot bolt used for camber adjustment has a specially shaped washer under the bolt head. Make sure fasteners are used in the correct locations.

5. Install the wheel and tire assembly and lower the vehicle.
6. Tighten the outboard nut to 116–142 ft. lbs. (157–192 Nm).
7. Set the camber and tighten the inner pivot nut to 50–68 ft. lbs. (68–92 Nm).

LOWER ARM

1. Remove the rear knuckle/hub assembly.
2. Deflate the rear air springs. On left side only, disengage the height sensor from the lower arm ballstud attachment. Make sure the integral lower air spring clip is disengaged from lower arm.
3. Disengage the rear stabilizer bar straps from the emergency brake cables and remove the stabilizer bar link nuts at the lower arm attachment ends. Remove the link bushings, push the link ends up and out of the lower arm and rotate the bar aside.
4. Remove the inner control arm pivot bolts and nuts and remove the arm.

NOTE: Do not attempt to remove the plastic cap on the front pivot nut.

5. Mark the toe adjustment cam-to-subframe position. Loosen the inboard pivot nuts at the lower arm to subframe position. Do not remove the bolt.
6. Remove the shock to lower arm bolt, nut and washer. Note the location of the washers.
7. Remove the inner pivot bolts and nuts. Remove the control arm from the vehicle.
   To install:
8. Inspect the large nut used at the inner front arm attachment for

condition of plastic cap. Use a new nut if the cap is cracked, loose or missing.
9. Install the toe compensating link on the arm.
10. On left side only, install height sensor bracket assembly to lower control arm.
11. Install the lower control arm to the sub-frame and loosely install the pivot bolts and nuts.
12. Attach the shock and tighten to 83–113 ft. lbs. (113–153 Nm).
13. Install air spring assembly into the lower arm spring pocket opening and make sure the base of the air spring is fully seated and the air spring is not kinked.
14. Position the control arm to curb/design position and tighten lower arm to subframe to 166–203 ft. lbs. (225–275 Nm). Align the inner pivot cam bolt to the marks made during removal. Tighten to 141–191 ft. lbs. (191–258 Nm).
15. Tighten the toe compensating link nut to 83–113 ft. lbs. (113–153 Nm).
16. Install the stabilizer bar. tighten nuts to 7.5–10.2 ft. lbs. (10.2–13.8 Nm).
17. On left side only, install height sensor to lower arm bracket.
18. Install the knuckle/hub assembly. Make sure inflated air spring is properly seated and centered in the lower arm pocket. Inflate the air springs.
19. Check and adjust the rear toe.

Ford Motor Company 10

FORD—Crown Victoria **LINCOLN**—Town Car
MERCURY—Grand Marquis

FIRING ORDERS

NOTE: To avoid confusion, always replace spark plug wires one at a time.

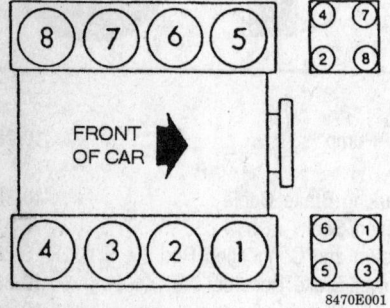

4.6L Engine
Engine Firing Order: 1–3–7–2–6–5–4–8
Distributorless Ignition System

ENGINE ELECTRICAL

NOTE: Disconnecting the negative battery cable on some vehicles may interfere with the functions of the on board computer systems and may require the computer to undergo a relearning process, once the negative battery cable is reconnected.

Distributorless Ignition System (DIS)

The 4.6L engine is equipped with a distributorless ignition system. The DIS consists of the following components: crankshaft sensor, ignition module, ignition coil packs, the spark angle portion of the ECU and the related wiring.

The DIS eliminates the need for a distributor by using multiple ignition coils. Each coil fires 2 spark plugs at the same time. The plugs are paired so as 1 fires during the compression cycle, the other fires during the exhaust stroke. The next time the coil is fired, the plug that was on exhaust will be on compression and the 1 that was on compression will be on ex-

haust. The spark in the exhaust cylinder is wasted but little of the coil energy is lost. The ignition coils are mounted together in coil packs. There are 2 coil packs used, each containing 2 ignition coils.

The crankshaft sensor is a variable reluctance-type sensor triggered by a 36-minus-1 tooth trigger wheel located inside the front cover. The signal generated by this sensor is called a Variable Reluctance Sensor (VRS) signal. The VRS signal provides engine position and rpm information to the ignition module.

The ignition module is a microprocessor that receives input from the crankshaft sensor in regards to engine position, base timing and engine speed and input from the ECU pertaining to spark advance. The ignition module uses this information to direct which coil to fire and to calculate the turn on and turn off times of the coils required to achieve the correct dwell and spark advance.

Base ignition timing is referenced to the position of the crankshaft sensor, and is set at 10 ± 2 degrees BTDC and is not adjustable.

REMOVAL AND INSTALLATION

Crankshaft Sensor

1. Disconnect the negative battery cable.
2. Remove the serpentine belt.
3. Raise and safely support the vehicle.
4. Disconnect the crankshaft sensor and air conditioning compressor electrical connectors from the engine wiring harness.
5. Properly discharge the air conditioning system and remove the air conditioning compressor.
6. Remove the crankshaft position sensor retaining screw and remove the sensor.
To install:
7. Make sure the sensor mounting surface is clean and the sensor O-ring is in the proper location on the sensor assembly.
8. Position the sensor assembly and install the retaining screw. Tighten to 71–106 inch lbs. (8–12 Nm).

NOTE: Do not overtighten the screw.

9. Install the air conditioning compressor. Evacuate and recharge the system according to the proper procedure.

10. Properly route the engine wiring harness and connect the electrical connectors to the air conditioning compressor and crankshaft sensor.
11. Lower the vehicle.
12. Install the serpentine belt and connect the negative battery cable.

Ignition Module

1. Disconnect the negative battery cable.
2. Disconnect the electrical connectors at the module by pushing in on the connector finger ends while grasping the connector body and pulling away from the module.
3. Remove 2 module retaining screws and remove the module.
To install:
4. Position the module to the inner fender and install retaining screws. Tighten the screws to 24–35 inch lbs. (3–4 Nm).
5. Connect the electrical connectors to the module by pushing until the connector fingers are locked over the locking wedge feature on the module.

NOTE: Locking the connector is important to ensure sealing of the connector/module interface.

6. Connect the negative battery cable.

Ignition Coil Pack

1. Disconnect the negative battery cable.
2. Disconnect the electrical connectors from the coil pack and capacitor.
3. Disconnect the spark plug wires by squeezing the locking tabs and twisting while pulling upward.
4. Remove the 4 coil pack retaining bolts and remove the coil pack and capacitor. Save the capacitor for installation with the new coil pack.

NOTE: Apply silicone dielectric compound D7AZ–19A331–A or equivalent, to all spark plug wire boots prior to installation.

5. Installation is the reverse of the removal procedure. Tighten the retaining bolts to 40–61 inch lbs. (5–7 Nm).

Ignition Timing

ADJUSTMENT

NOTE: Always refer to the Vehicle Emission Information Label to verify the timing adjustment procedure.

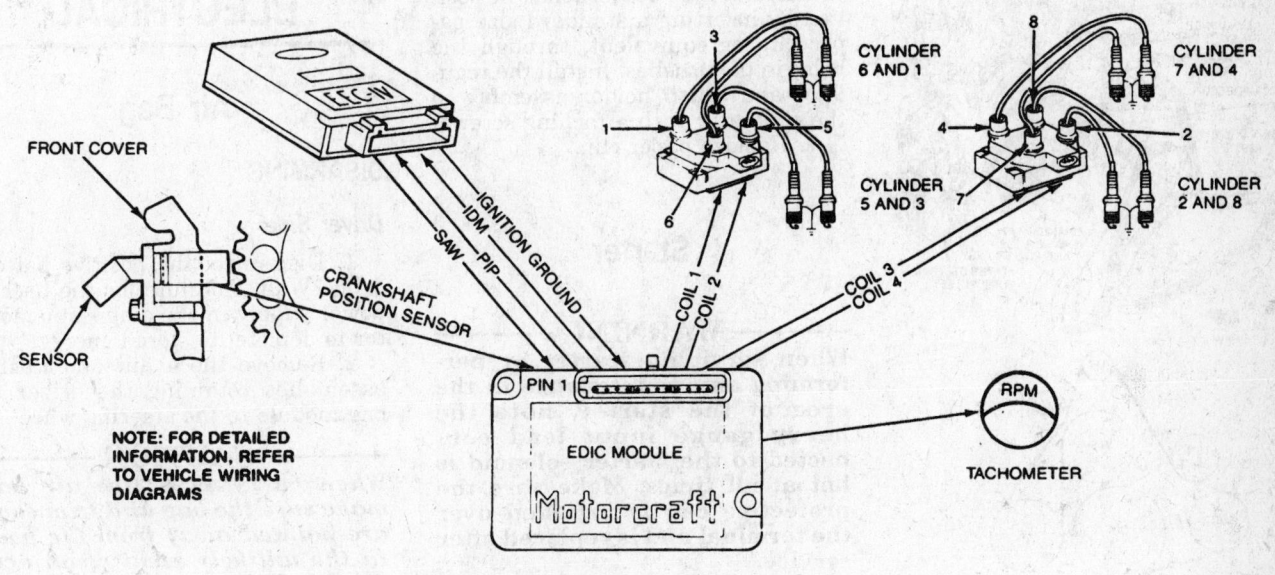

Distributorless ignition system — 4.6L engine

8470E002

4.6L Engine

Base timing for the distributorless engine is set by the factory at 10 ± 2 degrees BTDC and is not adjustable.

Generator

NOTE: To conform with J1930 standardized terminology, Ford Motor Co. will refer to an alternator as a generator.

PRECAUTIONS

Several precautions must be observed with generator equipped vehicles to avoid damage to the unit.

• If the battery is removed for any reason, make sure it is reconnected with the correct polarity. Reversing the battery connections may result in damage to the one-way rectifiers.
• When utilizing a booster battery as a starting aid, always connect the positive to positive terminals and the negative terminal from the booster battery to a good engine ground on the vehicle being started.
• Never use a fast charger as a booster to start vehicles.
• Disconnect the battery cables when charging the battery with a fast charger.

• Never attempt to polarize the generator.
• Do not use test lamps of more than 12V when checking diode continuity.
• Do not short across or ground any of the generator terminals.
• The polarity of the battery, generator and regulator must be matched and considered before making any electrical connections within the system.
• Never separate the generator on an open circuit. Make sure all connections within the circuit are clean and tight.
• Disconnect the battery ground terminal when performing any service on electrical components.
• Disconnect the battery if arc welding is to be done on the vehicle.

BELT TENSION ADJUSTMENT

4.6L Engine

Vehicles with the 4.6L engine are equipped with an automatic belt tensioner. To remove the drive belt, rotate the tensioner away from the belt using a ½ in. breaker bar and remove old belt. To install, position new belt over pulleys, ensure that all V-grooves make proper contact and relax pressure on the tensioner. No adjustment is necessary or possible.

REMOVAL AND INSTALLATION

4.6L Engine

1. Disconnect negative battery cable.
2. Disconnect the wiring harness attachments to the integral generator/regulator assembly.
3. Disengage the generator drive belt from the generator pulley.
4. Remove generator brace and mounting bolts and lift out generator.
5. Installation is reverse of the removal procedure.

Voltage Regulator

REMOVAL AND INSTALLATION

Electronic Regulator

1. Disconnect the negative battery cable.
2. Remove the regulator mounting screws, unlock the wire connectors and remove the regulator.
3. Installation is the reverse of the removal procedure.

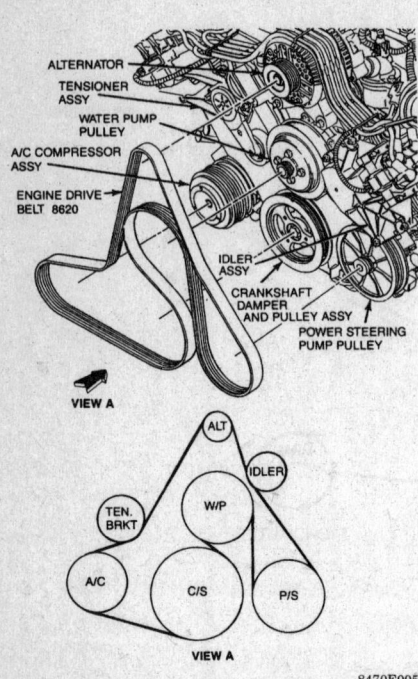

Drive belt replacement — 4.6L engine

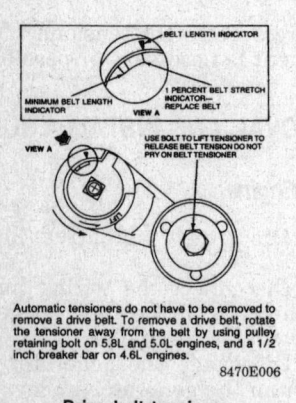

Automatic tensioners do not have to be removed to remove a drive belt. To remove a drive belt, rotate the tensioner away from the belt by using pulley retaining bolt on 5.8L and 5.0L engines, and a 1/2 inch breaker bar on 4.6L engines.

8470E006

Drive belt tensioner

Rear Mount Regulator

1. Remove the four T20 TORX® screws attaching the regulator to the generator rear housing. Remove the regulator, with the brush holder attached, from the generator.

2. Hold the regulator in one hand and pry off the cap covering the **A** screw head with a prybar.

3. Remove the two T20 TORX ® screws attaching the regulator to the brush holder. Separate the regulator from brush holder.

To install:

4. Replace brush holder to regulator and install attaching screws.

5. Replace cap on the head of the **A** terminal screw.

6. Depress the brushes into the holder and hold the brushes in position by inserting a standard size paper clip or equivalent, through the holes in the brushes. Install the regulator and brush holder assembly to the generator with attaching screws.

7. Remove paper clip.

Starter

WARNING

When servicing starter or performing any maintenance in the area of the starter, note the heavy gauge input lead connected to the starter solenoid is hot at all times. Make sure the protective cap is installed over the terminal and is replaced after service.

REMOVAL AND INSTALLATION

1. Disconnect the negative battery cable.

2. Raise the vehicle and support it safely.

3. Disconnect the starter cable from the starter. If equipped with starter mounted solenoid, disconnect the push-on connector from the solenoid.

NOTE: To disconnect the hard-shell connector from the solenoid S terminal, grasp the plastic shell and pull off; do not pull on the wire. Pull straight off to prevent damage to the connector and S terminal.

4. Remove the upper and lower starter bolts and remove starter.

To install:

5. Position the starter to the engine and tighten the mounting bolts to 15–20 ft. lbs. (20–27 Nm).

6. Reconnect the electrical leads. Be careful to push straight on and make sure connector locks in position with a notable click or detent. Install starter cable nut to starter terminal, tighten to 80–124 inch lb. (9–14 Nm).

7. Replace red solenoid safety cap. Lower vehicle to the floor.

8. Connect the negative battery cable.

CHASSIS ELECTRICAL

Air Bag

DISARMING

Driver Side

1. Disconnect the positive battery cable. Wait 1 minute for the backup power supply in the diagnostic monitor to deplete its stored energy.

2. Remove the 4 nut and washer assemblies retaining the driver air bag module to the steering wheel.

CAUTION

When carrying a live air bag, make sure the bag and trim cover are pointed away from the body. In the unlikely event of an accidental deployment, the bag will then deploy with minimal chance of injury. When placing a live air bag on a bench or other surface, always face the bag and trim cover up, away from the surface. This will reduce the motion of the module if it is accidently deployed.

3. Disconnect the driver air bag connector.

Passenger Side

1. Remove the right-hand instrument panel lower moulding.

2. Remove the cluster finish panel retaining screws and remove the panel.

3. Open the glove compartment, press the sides inward and lower the glove compartment to the floor.

4. Remove the air bag module retaining bolts. Disconnect the electrical connector and remove the module.

Heater Blower Motor

REMOVAL AND INSTALLATION

1. Disconnect the negative battery cable.

2. Disconnect the blower motor lead connector from the wiring harness connector.

3. Remove the blower motor cooling tube from the blower motor.

4. Remove the 4 retaining screws.

5. Turn the motor and wheel assembly slightly to the right so the bottom edge of the mounting plate

follows the contour of the wheel well splash panel. Lift up on the blower and remove it from the blower housing.

6. Installation is the reverse of the removal. Connect the negative battery cable.

Windshield Wiper Motor

REMOVAL AND INSTALLATION

Town Car, Crown Victoria and Grand Marquis

1. Disconnect the negative battery cable.

2. Remove the rear hood seal. Remove the wiper arm assemblies by raising the wiper blade off the windshield. Move the slide latch away from the pivot shaft and slowly lower the arm onto the latch. This unlocks the arm from the pivot shaft and holds the blade off the glass. Pull the arm from the pivot shaft.

3. Remove the cowl vent screws and disconnect the washer hoses from the washer jets.

4. Disconnect the electrical connectors from the wiper motor.

5. Remove the wiper assembly attaching screws, lift the assembly out and disconnect the washer hose.

6. Unsnap and remove the linkage cover.

7. Remove the linkage retaining clip from the motor operating arm by lifting the locking tab and pulling the clip away from the pin.

8. Remove the motor retaining screws and remove the motor from the vehicle.

To install:

9. Installation is the reverse of removal. Install the wiper arms by aligning the wiper arm key with the pivot shaft keyway.

10. Install the arm head over the pivot shaft. While applying downward pressure on the arm head, raise the other end of the arm enough to let the latch slide under the pivot shaft to the latched position, using finger pressure only to slide the latch.

11. Lower the blade. If the blade does not touch the windshield, the slide latch is not completely in place.

Wiper Switch

REMOVAL AND INSTALLATION

1. Disconnect negative battery ground cable.

2. Remove the split steering column cover retaining screws and separate both halves.

3. Remove the 2 wiper switch retaining screws. Disconnect the multiple connector at the rear of the switch.

To install:

4. Reverse removal procedure. Test system operation.

Instrument Cluster

REMOVAL AND INSTALLATION

Conventional Cluster

1. Disconnect the negative battery cable.

2. Remove the instrument cluster trim cover attaching screws and remove the trim cover.

3. Remove the lower steering column cover retaining screws and remove the lower cover.

4. On Town Car and Grand Marquis, remove the knee bolster retaining screws and remove the knee bolster.

5. Remove the screw holding the transmission indicator column bracket to the steering column. Detach the cable loop from the pin and cane shift lever. Remove the column bracket from the column.

6. Remove the 4 cluster retaining screws holding in the cluster.

7. Disconnect the cluster feed plugs from the receptacle canister assembly.

8. Remove 8 screws on Crown Victoria or 6 on Town Car and Grand Marquis from the lens and mask assembly for access to the shift indicator, gauges or speedometer. Remove shift indicator from the speedometer by releasing snaps on Crown Victoria or 2 retaining screws on Town Car and Grand Marquis.

Electronic Cluster

1. Disconnect the negative battery cable and set the parking brake.

2. Unsnap the center moulding on the left and right sides of the instrument panel. Remove the steering column cover and column shroud.

3. Remove the knobs from the auto dim and auto lamp switches, if equipped. Remove the 13 screws retaining the instrument panel and pull the panel out.

4. Move the shift lever to the **1** position, if required, for easier access.

5. Disconnect the electrical connectors from the warning lamp mod-

ule, switch module and center panel switches, if equipped.

6. Remove the instrument cluster carefully so as not to scratch the cluster lens. Disconnect the electrical connector from the front of the cluster.

7. Disconnect the transmission indicator assembly from the cluster by carefully bending the bottom tab down and pulling the indicator assembly forward.

8. Pull the cluster out and disconnect the electrical connectors on the rear of the cluster. Remove the instrument cluster.

9. Installation is the reverse of the removal procedure.

Speedometer

REMOVAL AND INSTALLATION

Conventional Cluster

CROWN VICTORIA AND GRAND MARQUIS

1. Disconnect the negative battery cable.

2. Remove the instrument cluster assembly.

3. Keeping the cluster face up, remove the lens and mask retaining screws.

4. Remove the lens and mask assembly. Use caution handling the mask to prevent scratches.

5. Remove the transmission indicator assembly. Lift the temperature gauge and fuel gauge from the cluster. Set the face up to avoid damage.

6. Lift the speedometer assembly out of the cluster.

7. Installation is the reverse of the removal procedure.

Electronic Cluster

The speedometer is an integral part of the electronic cluster and cannot be removed separately.

Headlight Switch

REMOVAL AND INSTALLATION

Town Car

1. Disconnect the negative battery cable.

2. Remove the headlight switch knob and auto dimmer knob, if equipped.

3. Remove the right and left mouldings from the instrument panel by pulling away from the instrument panel and snapping out of the retainers.

4. Remove 12 screws retaining the finish panel and remove the panel.

5. Remove the 2 headlight switch bracket retaining screws and pull the bracket and switch from the instrument panel.

6. Remove the nut retaining the switch to the bracket, disconnect the connector and remove the switch.

7. Installation is the reverse of the removal procedure.

Crown Victoria and Grand Marquis

1. Disconnect the negative battery cable.

2. Remove the right and left mouldings from the instrument panel by pulling up and snapping out of the retainers.

3. Remove the screws retaining the finish panel to the instrument panel.

4. Remove the headlight switch knob from the shaft by depressing the spring, in the knob slot, with a hooked tool. Remove the finish panel.

5. Remove the 2 headlight bracket retaining screws and pull the bracket and switch from from the instrument panel.

6. Remove the nut retaining the switch to the bracket.

7. Disconnect the electrical connector and remove the switch.

8. Installation is the reverse of removal.

Combination Switch

The combination switch incorporates the turn signal, dimmer and wiper switch functions on the turn signal lever.

REMOVAL AND INSTALLATION

1. Disconnect the negative battery cable.

2. If equipped with tilt column, move to the lowest position and remove the tilt lever.

3. Remove the ignition lock cylinder.

4. Remove the shroud screws and remove the upper and lower shrouds.

5. Remove the 2 self-tapping screws attaching the combination switch to the steering column casting and remove the switch.

6. Remove the wiring harness retainer and disconnect the 2 electrical connectors.

7. Installation is the reverse of the removal procedure.

Ignition Lock

REMOVAL AND INSTALLATION

Functional Lock

The following procedure is for vehicles with functioning lock cylinders. Ignition keys are available for these vehicles or the ignition key numbers are known and the proper key can be made.

1. Disconnect the negative battery cable. If equipped, properly disarm the air bag system.

2. Remove the steering column shroud by removing the 4 or 5 self tapping screws. Remove tilt lever if equipped.

3. Turn the ignition to the **RUN** position.

4. Place a ⅛ in. diameter wire pin or small drift punch in the hole in the casting surrounding the lock cylinder and depress the retaining pin while pulling out on the lock cylinder to remove it from the column housing.

To install:

5. To install the lock cylinder, turn it to the **RUN** position and depress the retaining pin. Insert the lock cylinder into its housing in the lock cylinder casting.

6. Make sure the cylinder is fully seated and aligned in the interlock-

1. Headlamp switch knob assembly
2. Headlamp switch bezel
3. Bulb
4. Headlamp switch bracket
5. Instrument panel assembly
6. Wiring assembly
7. Headlamp switch assembly
8. Screw
9. Cluster finish panel

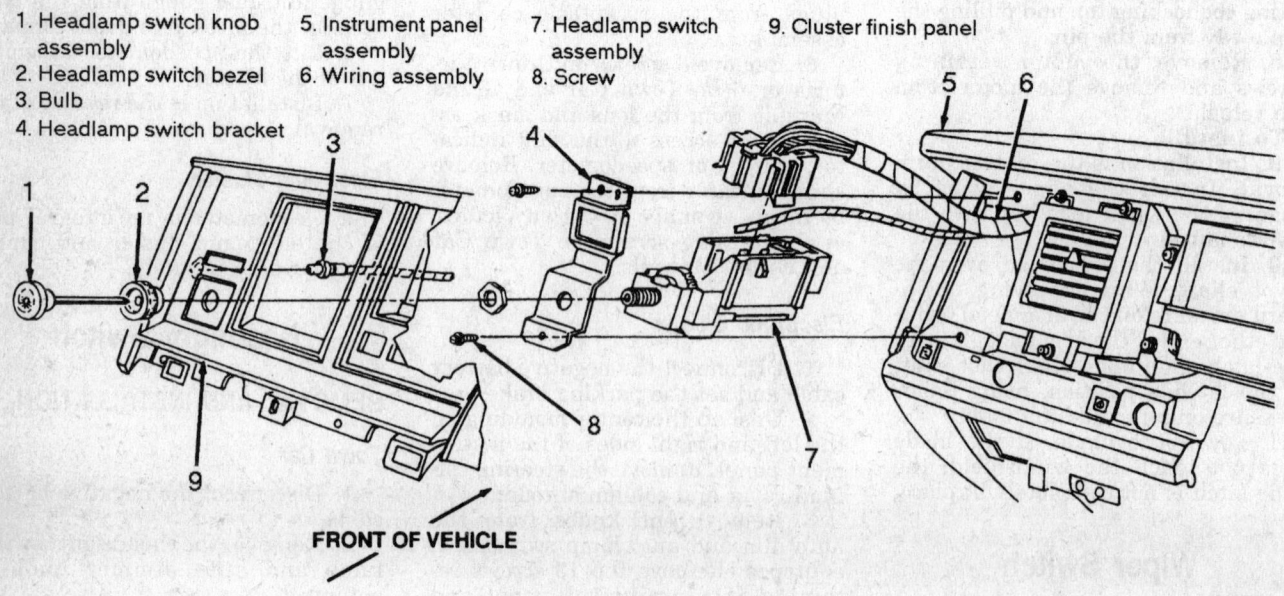

FRONT OF VEHICLE

Headlight switch installation — Town Car

8470E009

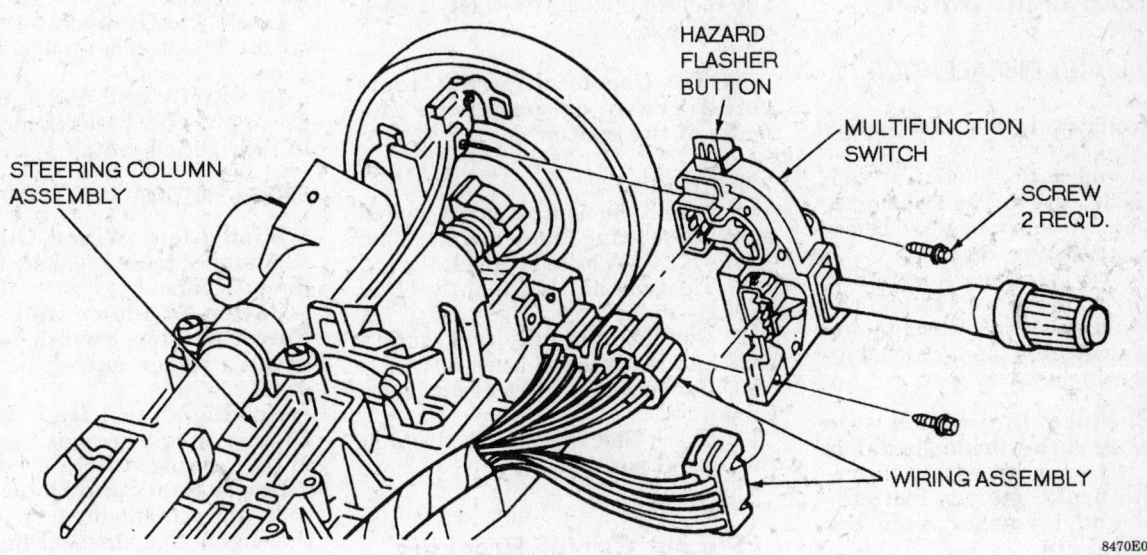

Combination switch installation

8470E010

STEERING COLUMN ASSEMBLY

HAZARD FLASHER BUTTON

MULTIFUNCTION SWITCH

SCREW 2 REQ'D.

WIRING ASSEMBLY

ing washer before turning the key to the **OFF** position. This action will permit the cylinder retaining pin to extend into the hole in the lock cylinder housing.

7. Using the ignition key, rotate the cylinder to ensure the correct mechanical operation in all positions.

8. Check for proper start in **P** or **N**. Also make sure the start circuit cannot be actuated in **D** or **R** positions and that the column is locked in the **LOCK** position.

9. Connect the key warning buzzer electrical connector and install the trim shrouds, if required.

Non-functional Lock

The following procedure is for vehicles with non-functioning locks. On these vehicles, the lock cylinder cannot be rotated due to a lost or broken key, the key number is not known, or the lock cylinder cap is damaged and/or broken, preventing the lock cylinder from rotating.

1. Disconnect the negative battery cable. If equipped, properly disarm the air bag system.

2. Remove the steering wheel.

3. Use channel lock or vise grip type pliers to twist the lock cylinder cap until it separates from the lock cylinder.

4. Drill approximately 1³/₄ in. down the middle of the ignition key slot, using a ³/₈ in. diameter drill bit, until the lock cylinder breaks loose from the breakaway base of the lock cylinder. Remove the lock cylinder and drill shavings from the lock cylinder housing.

5. Remove the snapring or retainer, washer and steering column lock gear. Thoroughly clean all drill shavings and other foreign materials from the casting.

6. Inspect the lock cylinder housing for damage and replace, as necessary.

To install:

7. Install the ignition lock cylinder and check for smooth operation.

8. Connect the electrical connector to the key warning switch and install the trim shrouds, if necessary.

9. Install the steering wheel and connect the negative battery cable.

Ignition Switch

REMOVAL AND INSTALLATION

1. Disconnect the negative battery cable.

2. Remove the steering column shroud.

3. Remove the instrument panel lower steering column cover.

4. Disconnect the electrical connector from the ignition switch.

5. Rotate the ignition key lock cylinder to the **RUN** position.

6. Remove the 2 screws attaching the ignition switch.

7. Disengage the ignition switch from the actuator pin and remove the switch.

To install:

8. Adjust the new ignition switch by sliding the carrier to the **RUN** position.

9. Check to ensure that the ignition key lock cylinder is in the **RUN** position. The **RUN** position is achieved by rotating the key lock cylinder approximately 90 degrees from the **LOCK** position.

10. Install the ignition switch onto the actuator pin.

11. Align the switch mounting holes and install the attaching screws. Tighten the screws to 50–69 inch lbs. (5.6–7.9 Nm).

12. Connect the electrical connector to the ignition switch.

13. Connect the negative battery cable. Check the ignition switch for proper function in **START** and **ACC** positions. Make sure the column is locked in the **LOCK** position.

14. Install the remaining components in the reverse order of removal.

Brake Light Switch

REMOVAL AND INSTALLATION

1. Disconnect the negative battery cable.

2. Disconnect the electrical connector at the switch. The locking tab on the connector must be lifted before the connector can be removed.

3. Remove the hairpin retainer, slide the brake light switch, the pushrod and the nylon washers and bushings away from the pedal and remove the switch.

NOTE: Since the switch side plate nearest the brake pedal is slotted, it is not necessary to remove the brake master cylinder pushrod and 1 washer from the brake pedal pin.

To install:

4. Position the switch so the U-shaped side is nearest the pedal and directly over/under the pin. Then slide the switch down/up trapping the master cylinder pushrod and black bushing between the switch side plates. Push the switch and pushrod assembly firmly toward the brake pedal arm. Assemble the outside white plastic washer to the pin and install the hairpin retainer to trap the whole assembly.

5. Assemble the wire harness connector to the switch. Check the switch for proper operation.

NOTE: The brake light switch wire harness must be long enough to travel with the switch during full pedal stroke. If wire length is insufficient, reroute the harness or service, as required.

Neutral Safety Switch

REMOVAL AND INSTALLATION

1. Set the parking brake.
2. Place the selector lever in the manual **L** position.
3. Remove the air cleaner assembly.
4. Disconnect the negative battery cable.
5. Disconnect the neutral safety switch electrical harness from the switch by lifting the harness straight up off the switch without side-to-side motion.

6. Reach in the area of the left hand dash panel, using a 24 inch extension, universal adapter and socket tool T74P–77247–A or equivalent, and remove the neutral safety switch and O-ring.

NOTE: Use of different tools could crush or puncture the walls of the switch.

To install:

7. Install the neutral safety switch and new O-ring using socket tool T74P–77247–A or equivalent.
8. Tighten the switch to 8–11 ft. lbs. (11–15 Nm).
9. Connect the neutral safety switch to the wiring harness.
10. Connect the negative battery cable.
11. Check that the vehicle starts in the **N** or **P** position.

Fuses, Circuit Breakers and Relays

LOCATION

Fuses

All vehicles are equipped with a fuse panel located on the left side of the lower instrument panel. In addition, Town Car and 1992–95 Crown Victoria and Grand Marquis are equipped with a fuse box located in the right front of the engine compartment.

Fuse Links

Fuse links are used to protect the main wiring harness and selected branches from complete burn-out, should a short circuit or electrical overload occur. A fuse link is a short length of insulated wire, integral with the engine compartment wiring harness. It is several wire gauges smaller than the circuit it protects and generally located in-line directly from the positive terminal of the battery.

Circuit Breakers

Circuit breakers are used on certain electrical components requiring high amperage. The advantage of the circuit breaker is it's ability to open and close the electrical circuit as the load demands rather than the necessity of a part replacement.

TOWN CAR

Windshield Wiper Circuit — a 8.25 amp circuit breaker located on the fuse panel.

Deck Lid Release — a 20 amp circuit breaker located on the fuse panel.

Headlight and High Beam — a 22 amp circuit breaker incorporated in the lighting switch.

CROWN VICTORIA AND GRAND MARQUIS

Windshield Wiper Circuit — a 8.25 amp circuit breaker located on the fuse panel.

Power Windows and Tailgate Power Window Switch — a 20 amp circuit breaker located on the fuse panel.

Headlight and High Beam — a 22 amp circuit breaker incorporated in the lighting switch.

Power Seats and Door Locks — a 30 amp circuit breaker located in the engine compartment fuse box.

Relays

TOWN CAR

Air Conditioner WOT Cut-Out Relay — located the the left fender apron.

Alternator Output Control Relay — located on the right side of the engine compartment.

Anti-Lock Brake Motor Relay — located in the left front of the engine compartment.

Anti-Lock Brakes Relay — located in the right front of the engine compartment, in the engine compartment fuse box.

Compressor Relay — located on the right side of the engine compartment, in the engine compartment fuse box.

Delayed Exit Relay — located behind the left side of the instrument panel.

EEC Power Relay — located at the left fender apron.

Fuel Pump Relay — located at the left fender apron.

Hi-Lo Beam Relay — located behind the left side of the instrument panel.

Moonroof Relay — located in the center of the headliner, behind the moonroof.

Starter Relay — located on the right front fender apron.

Trailer Battery Charging Relay — located in the trunk, on the left wheel well.

Trailer Exterior Lamps Relay — located in the trunk, on the left wheel well.

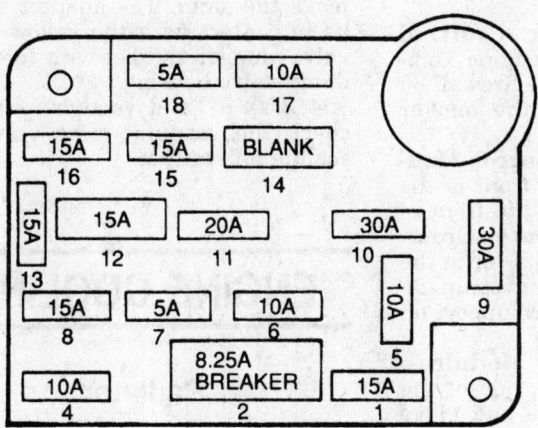

Cavity Number	Fuse Rating	Circuit Protected
1	15 Amp	Automatic Leveling Control, Electronic Cluster, CD Changer, Clock Memory, Luggage Compartment Lid Pull-Down, Cellular Telephone Connector, Power Antenna, Memory Seats, Radio Memory
2	8.25 Amp Circuit Breaker	Interval Wiper / Washer
4	10 Amp	Air Bag, Automatic Leveling Control, Electronic Cluster, Warning Chime, Warning Lamps, Speed Control
5	10 Amp	Heated Mirrors
6	10 Amp	Dome / Reading Lamps, Power Windows, Moon Roof, Radio, Warning Chime, Brake Shift Interlock, Power Antenna, Clock, Speed Control
7	5 Amp	Instrument Panel Illumination
8	15 Amp	ATC, Back Up Lamps, Auto Lamps, Daytime Running Lamps, Day / Night Mirror, Manual Lever Position Sensor, Keyless Entry, Air Suspension / EVO Steering, Anti-Theft
9	30 Amp	ATC Blower
10	30 Amp	Cigar Lighters
11	20 Amp	Anti-Theft, Exterior Lamps, Keyless Entry, Courtesy Lamps, Autolamps
12	15 Amp	Stop / Hazard Lamps, Brake Shift Interlock, Speed Control
13	15 Amp	Electronic Engine Control, Ignition Coils
14	—	Not Used
15	15 Amp	Anti-Theft, Rear Window Defroster, Trailer Tow, Flash-to-Pass, ATC Clutch, Turn Signals
16	15 Amp	Electronic Engine Control
17	10 Amp	Anti-Theft, ATC, Courtesy Lamps, Keyless Entry, Power Mirrors, Power Door Locks, Memory Seats, Warning Lamps
18	5 Amp	Anti-Lock Brakes

8470E012

View of the fuse, relay and circuit breaker panel — Town Car

Trailer Left Hand Turn Lamp Relay — located in the trunk, on the left wheel well.

Trailer Right Hand Turn Lamp Relay — located in the trunk, on the left wheel well.

Unlock Relay — located behind the right cowl panel.

Window Safety Relay — located behind the right side of the instrument panel.

CROWN VICTORIA AND GRAND MARQUIS

Alternator Output Control Relay — located in the right front of the engine compartment.

Anti-Lock Brake Motor Relay — located on the lower left front of engine compartment, on bracket near front of ABS hydraulic control unit.

Anti-Lock Brake Relay — located in right front of engine compartment, in engine compartment fuse box.

Autolamp Relay — located behind the center of the instrument panel.

Compressor Relay — located in the right front of the engine compartment, in the engine compartment fuse box.

EEC Power Relay — located in the left side of the engine compartment in the relay center.

Fuel Pump Relay — located on the left side of the engine compartment.

Horn Relay — located in the right front of the engine compartment, in the engine compartment fuse box.

LCD Dimming Relay — located behind the center of the instrument panel.

Starter Relay — located on the right fender apron.

Trailer Battery Charging Relay — located near the left side of the trunk on Sedan or above the left rear wheel well on Wagon.

Trailer Exterior Lamps Relay — located near the left side of the trunk on Sedan or above the left rear wheel well on Wagon.

Trailer Left Turn Lamp Relay — located near the left side of the trunk on Sedan or above the left rear wheel well on Wagon.

Trailer Right Turn Relay — located near the left side of the trunk on Sedan or above the left rear wheel well on Wagon.

WOT Cutout Relay — located in the left side of the engine compartment in the relay center.

Computers

LOCATION

Engine Electronic Control Unit — located in the engine compartment, attached to the firewall on the driver's side, near the master cylinder.

Anti-Lock Brake Control Module — located in the left front of the engine compartment, on the front of the upper radiator support on Crown Victoria and Grand Marquis or in the right front of the engine compartment, under the radiator support on Town Car.

Air Bag Diagnostic Module — located behind the right side of the instrument panel, above the glove compartment on Crown Victoria and Grand Marquis or behind the left side of the instrument panel on Town Car.

Automatic Temperature Control Module — located behind the center of the instrument panel.

Turn Signal and Hazard Flashers

LOCATION

The turn signal and hazard flashers are attached to the fuse panel.

Cruise Control

ADJUSTMENT

Actuator Cable

1. Remove the cable retaining clip.
2. Make sure the throttle is in the closed position.
3. Pull on the actuator cable end tube to take up any slack. Maintain a light tension on the cable.
4. Insert the cable retaining clip and snap into place.
5. Check that the throttle linkage operates freely and smoothly.

Vacuum Dump Valve

The vacuum dump valve is movable in its mounting bracket. It should be adjusted so it is closed, no vacuum leaks, when the brake pedal is in its normal release position. Adjust the dump valve as follows:

1. Hold the brake pedal down and push the dump valve forward through its adjustment collar.

2. Install a 0.05 in. (1.27mm) shim on the surface of the adapter and pull the brake pedal fully rearward.
3. Release the brake pedal and remove the shim. The adapter should be in contact with the yellow dump valve plunger and not with the black dump valve housing.
4. Use a hand vacuum pump to check the vacuum dump valve for sealing off vacuum.

ENGINE COOLING

Radiator

REMOVAL AND INSTALLATION

1. Disconnect the negative battery cable.
2. Remove the radiator cap. Place a drain pan under the radiator, open the draincock and drain the coolant.

―――― CAUTION ――――
Never remove the radiator cap while the engine is running or personal injury from scalding hot coolant or steam may result. If possible, wait until the engine has cooled to remove the radiator cap. If this is not possible, wrap a thick cloth around the radiator cap and turn it slowly to the first stop. Step back while the pressure is released from the cooling system. When it is certain all the pressure has been released, press down on the cap, still with the cloth, and turn and remove it.

3. Disconnect the upper, lower and coolant reservoir hoses at the radiator.
4. Disconnect the fluid cooler lines at the radiator.
5. Remove the 2 upper fan shroud retaining bolts at the radiator support, lift the fan shroud sufficiently to disengage the lower retaining clips and lay the shroud back over the fan.
6. Remove the radiator upper support retaining bolts and remove the supports. Lift the radiator from the vehicle.
To install:
7. If a new radiator is to be installed, transfer the petcock from the old radiator to the new one. Transfer the fluid cooler line fittings from the old radiator.
8. Position the radiator assembly into the vehicle. Install the upper

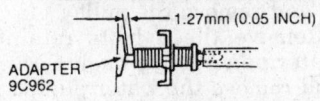

POSITION OF DUMP VALVE
WHEN BRAKE IS NOT DEPRESSED

NOTE: BLACK THREADED HOUSING
OF DUMP VALVE MUST CLEAR
ADAPTER 9C962 ON BRAKE PEDAL

1.27mm (0.05 INCH)

ADAPTER
9C962

POSITION OF DUMP VALVE
WHEN BRAKE IS DEPRESSED

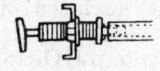

8569Z037

Cruise control vacuum dump valve adjustment

supports and the retaining bolts. Connect the fluid cooler lines.

9. Place the fan shroud into the clips on the lower radiator support and install the 2 upper shroud retaining bolts. Position the shroud to maintain approximately 1 in. (25mm) clearance between the fan blades and the shroud.

10. Connect the radiator hoses. Close the radiator petcock. Fill and bleed the cooling system.

11. Start the engine and bring to operating temperature. Check for coolant and transmission fluid leaks.

12. Check the coolant and transmission fluid levels.

Heater Core

REMOVAL AND INSTALLATION

With Automatic Temperature Control

1. Disconnect the negative battery cable.

2. Drain the cooling system and disconnect the heater hoses from the heater core tubes. Plug the hoses and the heater core tubes.

3. Remove the 3 nuts located below the windshield wiper motor attaching the left end of the plenum to the dash panel. Remove the 1 nut retaining the upper left corner of the evaporator case to the dash panel.

4. Disconnect the vacuum supply hose(s) from the vacuum source and disconnect the vacuum harness from the thermal blower lockout switch. Push the grommet and vacuum supply hoses into the passenger compartment.

5. Remove the right and left lower instrument panel insulators.

6. Remove all instrument panel mounting screws and pull the instrument panel back as far as it will go without disconnecting the wiring harness. Make sure the nuts attaching the instrument panel braces to the dash panel are removed.

7. Loosen the right door sill plate and remove the right side cowl trim panel.

8. Remove the cross body brace and disconnect the wiring harness from the temperature blend door actuator. Disconnect the ATC sensor tube from the evaporator case connector.

9. Disconnect the vacuum jumper harness at the multiple vacuum connector near the floor air distribution duct. Disconnect the white vacuum hose from the outside-recirc door vacuum motor. Remove the 2 hush panels.

10. Remove the 2 screws attaching the passenger (rear) side of the floor air distribution duct to the plenum. It may be necessary to remove the 2 screws attaching the partial (lower) panel door vacuum motor to the mounting bracket to gain access to the right screw.

11. Remove the 1 plastic push fastener retaining the floor air distribution duct to the left end of the plenum and 2 screws on the rear face of the plenum and remove the floor air distribution duct.

12. Remove 2 nuts from the 2 studs along the lower flange of the plenum. Carefully move the plenum rearward to allow the heater core tubes and the stud at the top of the plenum to clear the holes in the dash panel. Remove the plenum from the vehicle by rotating the top of the plenum forward, down and out from under the instrument panel. Carefully pull the lower edge of the instrument panel rearward, as necessary, while rolling the plenum from behind the instrument panel.

13. Remove the 4 retaining screws from the heater core cover and remove the cover from the plenum assembly. Pull the heater core and seal assembly from the plenum assembly.

To install:

14. Carefully install the heater core and seal assembly into the plenum assembly. Visually check to ensure the core seal is properly positioned. Position the heater core cover and install the 4 retaining screws.

15. Position the plenum on the rear of the dash panel with the heater core tubes and the stud at the top of the plenum through the holes in the dash panel. Install the 2 nuts removed from the lower flange of the plenum.

16. Install the plastic push fastener retaining the left end of the floor air distribution duct to the left end of the plenum.

17. Install the screws that attach the rear of the floor air distribution duct to the plenum. If necessary, tighten the screws attaching the partial (lower) panel door vacuum motor to the mounting bracket.

18. Connect the white vacuum hose from the outside-recirc door vacuum motor. Connect the vacuum jumper harness at the multiple vacuum connector near the floor air distribution duct.

19. Connect the ATC sensor tube to the evaporator case connector. Install the cross body brace and connect the wiring harness to the blend door actuator.

20. Replace the right side cowl trim panel and tighten the screws in the right door sill plate.

21. Push the instrument panel back into position and install all instrument panel mounting screws. Install the right and left lower instrument panel insulators.

22. Push the vacuum supply hose(s) into the engine compartment and seat the grommet in the dash panel. Connect the vacuum supply hoses(s) to the vacuum source and connect the vacuum harness to the thermal blower lockout switch.

23. Install the 1 nut retaining the upper left corner of the evaporator case to the dash panel. Install the 3 nuts located below the windshield wiper motor, that attach the left end of the plenum to the dash panel. Install the hush panels.

24. Unplug the heater core hoses and tubes and connect the heater hoses to the heater core tubes. Fill the cooling system.

25. Connect the negative battery cable and check the system for proper operation.

With Manual Air Conditioning

1. Disconnect the negative battery cable.

2. Drain the cooling system and disconnect the heater hoses from the heater core tubes. Plug the hoses and the heater core tubes.

3. Remove the 3 nuts located below the windshield wiper motor attaching the left end of the plenum to the dash panel. Remove the 1 nut retaining the upper left corner of the evaporator case to the dash panel.

4. Disconnect the vacuum supply hose(s) from the vacuum source. Push the grommet and vacuum supply hoses into the passenger compartment.

5. Remove the right and left lower instrument panel insulators.

6. Remove all instrument panel mounting screws and pull the instrument panel back as far as it will go without disconnecting the wiring harness. Make sure the nuts attaching the instrument panel braces to the dash panel are removed.

7. Loosen the right door sill plate and remove the right side cowl trim panel. Remove the bolt attaching the lower right end of the instrument panel to the side cowl.

8. Disengage the temperature control cable housing from the bracket on top of the plenum. Disconnect the cable from the temperature blend door crank arm.

9. Disconnect the vacuum jumper harness at the multiple vacuum connector near the floor air distribution duct. Disconnect the white vacuum hose from the outside-recirculating door vacuum motor.

10. Remove the 2 hush panels.

11. Remove 1 plastic push fastener retaining the floor air distribution duct to the left end of the plenum. Remove the left screw and loosen the right screw on the rear face of the plenum and remove the floor air distribution duct.

12. Remove the 2 nuts from the 2 studs along the lower flange of the plenum.

13. Carefully move the plenum rearward to allow the heater core tubes and the stud at the top of the plenum to clear the holes in the dash panel. Remove the plenum from the vehicle by rotating the top of the plenum forward, down and out from under the instrument panel. Carefully pull the lower edge of the instrument panel rearward, as necessary, while rolling the plenum from behind the instrument panel.

14. Remove the 4 retaining screws from the heater core cover and remove the cover from the plenum assembly. Pull the heater core and seal assembly from the plenum assembly.

To install:

15. Carefully install the heater core and seal assembly into the plenum assembly. Visually check to ensure that the core seal is properly positioned. Position the heater core cover and install the 4 retaining screws.

16. Route the vacuum supply hose through the dash panel and seat the grommet in the opening.

17. Position the plenum under the instrument panel with the register duct opening up and the heater core tubes down. Rotate the plenum up behind the instrument panel and position the plenum to the dash panel. Insert the heater core tubes and

mounting studs through their respective holes in the dash panel and the evaporator case.

18. Install the 2 nuts on the studs along the lower flange of the plenum. Install the 1 bolt or 3 nuts below the windshield wiper motor to attach the left end of the plenum to the dash panel. Install 1 nut to retain the upper left corner of the evaporator case to the dash panel.

19. Position the floor air distribution duct on the plenum. Install the 2 screws and plastic push fastener. If removed, position the panel door vacuum motor to the mounting bracket and install the 2 attaching screws.

20. Connect the white vacuum hose to the outside-recirculating door vacuum motor. Connect the vacuum jumper harness to the plenum harness at the multiple vacuum connector near the floor air distribution duct. Install the floor duct.

21. Connect the temperature control cable housing to the bracket on top of the plenum and connect the temperature control cable to the temperature blend door crank arm. Adjust the temperature cable.

22. Install the bolt to attach the lower right end of the instrument panel to the side cowl. Install the right side cowl trim panel and tighten the right door sill plate attaching screws.

23. Push the instrument panel back into position and install all instrument panel mounting screws. Install the right and left lower instrument panel insulators.

24. Push the vacuum supply hoses into the engine compartment and seat the grommet in the dash panel. Connect the vacuum supply hose(s) to the vacuum source.

25. Install the right and left lower instrument panel insulators and install the 2 hush panels.

26. Unplug the heater core tubes and the heater hoses and connect the heater hoses to the heater core tubes. Fill the cooling system.

27. Connect the negative battery cable and check the system for proper operation.

Water Pump

REMOVAL AND INSTALLATION

4.6L Engine

1. Disconnect the negative battery cable.

2. Drain the cooling system, remove the cooling fan and the shroud.

3. Release the belt tensioner and remove the accessory drive belt.

4. Remove the 4 bolts retaining the water pump pulley to the water pump and remove the pulley.

5. Remove the 4 bolts retaining the water pump to the engine assembly and remove the water pump.

To install:

6. Installation is the reverse of the removal procedure. Be sure to clean the sealing surfaces of the water pump and block and use a new O-ring. Lubricate the O-ring with clean anti-freeze prior to installation.

7. Tighten the water pump-to-engine bolts and the pulley-to-water pump bolts to 15–22 ft. lbs. (20–30 Nm). Fill and bleed the cooling system. Operate the engine until normal operating temperatures have been reached and check for leaks.

Thermostat

REMOVAL AND INSTALLATION

4.6L Engine

1. Drain the cooling system to a level below the thermostat.

2. Disconnect the upper radiator hose at the thermostat housing.

3. Remove the 2 thermostat housing retaining bolts and remove the thermostat housing.

4. Remove the thermostat and O-ring seal.

To install:

5. Installation is the reverse of the removal procedure. Make sure all mating surfaces are clean prior to installation. Use a new O-ring seal.

6. Tighten the thermostat housing retaining bolts to 15–22 ft. lbs. (20–30 Nm). Fill the cooling system. Start the engine and bring to normal operating temperature. Check for leaks.

Cooling System Bleeding

When the entire cooling system is drained, the following procedure should be used to ensure a complete fill.

1. Install the block drain plug, if removed and close the draincock. With the engine OFF, add a 50/50 mixture of water and anti-freeze to the reservoir filler neck seat on 4.6L engine.

2. Install the radiator cap to the first notch to keep spillage to a minimum.

3. Place the heater temperature selector in the maximum heat position.

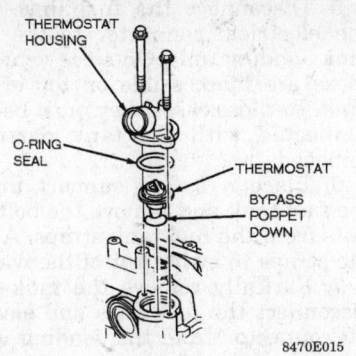

THERMOSTAT HOUSING

O-RING SEAL

THERMOSTAT

BYPASS POPPET DOWN

8470E015

Thermostat installation — 4.6L engine

4. Start the engine and let it idle until the upper radiator hose is warm. This indicates that the thermostat is open and coolant is flowing through the entire system.

5. Stop the engine and carefully remove the radiator cap. On 4.6L engine, fill the reservoir to the minimum level with the coolant mixture. Install the pressure cap securely.

FUEL SYSTEM

Fuel System Service Precautions

Safety is the most important factor when performing not only fuel system maintenance but any type of maintenance. Failure to conduct maintenance and repairs in a safe manner may result in serious personal injury or death. Maintenance and testing of the vehicle's fuel system components can be accomplished safely and effectively by adhering to the following rules and guidelines.

• To avoid the possibility of fire and personal injury, always disconnect the negative battery cable unless the repair or test procedure requires that battery voltage be applied.

• Always relieve the fuel system pressure prior to disconnecting any fuel system component (injector, fuel rail, pressure regulator, etc.), fitting or fuel line connection. Exercise extreme caution whenever relieving fuel system pressure to avoid exposing skin, face and eyes to fuel spray. Please be advised that fuel under pressure may penetrate the skin or any part of the body that it contacts.

• Always place a shop towel or cloth around the fitting or connection prior to loosening to absorb any excess fuel due to spillage. Ensure that all fuel spillage (should it occur) is quickly removed from engine surfaces. Ensure that all fuel soaked cloths or towels are deposited into a suitable waste container.

• Always keep a dry chemical (Class B) fire extinguisher near the work area.

• Do not allow fuel spray or fuel vapors to come into contact with a spark or open flame.

• Always use a backup wrench when loosening and tightening fuel line connection fittings. This will prevent unnecessary stress and torsion to fuel line piping. Always follow the proper torque specifications.

• Always replace worn fuel fitting O-rings with new. Do not substitute fuel hose or equivalent where fuel pipe is installed.

RELIEVING FUEL SYSTEM PRESSURE

Fuel supply lines on all fuel injected engines will remain pressurized for some period of time after the engine is shut OFF. This pressure must be relieved before servicing the fuel system. Pressure is relieved through the fuel pressure relief valve, located on the fuel rail.

To relieve the fuel system pressure, first remove the fuel tank cap to relieve pressure in the tank, then remove the cap on the fuel pressure relief valve. Attach fuel pressure gauge T80L–9974–A or equivalent, and drain the system through the drain tube into a suitable container. Remove the fuel pressure gauge and replace the cap on the relief valve.

Fuel Line Couplings

REMOVAL AND INSTALLATION

There are 3 methods in use to connect the fuel lines and fuel system components, the hairpin clip push connect fitting, the duck bill clip push connect fitting and the spring lock coupling. Each requires a different procedure to disconnect and connect.

Hairpin Clip Push Connect Fitting

1. Inspect the visible internal portion of the fitting for dirt accumulation. If more than a light coating of dust is present, clean the fitting before disassembly.

2. Some adhesion between the seals in the fitting and the tubing will occur with time. To separate, twist the fitting on the tube, then push and pull the fitting until it moves freely on the tube.

3. Remove the hairpin clip from the fitting by first bending and breaking the shipping tab. Next, spread the 2 clip legs by hand about 1/8 in. each to disengage the body and push the legs into the fitting. Lightly pull the triangular end of the clip and work it clear of the tube and fitting.

NOTE: Do not use hand tools to complete this operation.

4. Grasp the fitting and pull in an axial direction to remove the fitting from the tube. Be careful on 90 degree elbow connectors, as excessive side loading could break the connector body.

5. After disassembly, inspect and clean the tube end sealing surfaces. The tube end should be free of scratches and corrosion that could provide leak paths. Inspect the inside of the fitting for any internal parts such as O-rings and spacers that may have been dislodged from the fitting. Replace any damaged connector.

To connect:

6. Install a new connector if damage was found. Insert a new clip into any 2 adjacent openings with the triangular portion pointing away from the fitting opening. Install the clip until the legs of the clip are locked on the outside of the body. Piloting with an index finger is necessary.

7. Before installing the fitting on the tube, wipe the tube end with a clean cloth. Inspect the inside of the fitting to make sure it is free of dirt and/or obstructions.

8. Apply a light coating of engine oil to the tube end. Align the fitting and tube axially and push the fitting onto the tube end. When the fitting is engaged, a definite click will be heard. Pull on the fitting to make sure it is fully engaged.

Duck Bill Clip Push Connect Fitting

1. Inspect the visible internal portion of the fitting for dirt accumulation. If more than a light coating of dust is present, clean the fitting before disassembly.

2. Some adhesion between the seals in the fitting and the tubing will occur with time. To separate, twist the fitting on the tube, then push and pull the fitting until it moves freely on the tube.

3. Align the slot on push connect disassembly tool T90T–9550–B or T90T–9550–C or equivalent, with either tab on the clip, 90 degrees from

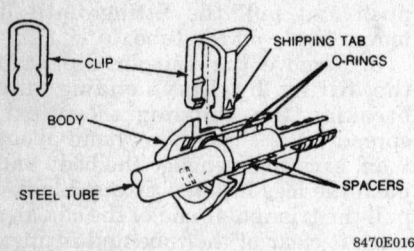

Hairpin clip push connect fitting

the slots on the side of the fitting and insert the tool. This disengages the duck bill retainer from the tube.

4. Holding the tool and the tube with 1 hand, pull the fitting away from the tube.

NOTE: Use hands only. Only moderate effort is required if the tube has been properly disengaged.

5. After disassembly, inspect and clean the tube end sealing surfaces. The tube end should be free of scratches and corrosion that could provide leak paths. Inspect the inside of the fitting for any internal parts such as O-rings and spacers that may have been dislodged from the fitting. Replace any damaged connector.

6. Some fuel tubes have a secondary bead which aligns with the outer surface of the clip. These beads can make tool insertion difficult. If there is extreme difficulty, use the following disassembly method:

• Using pliers with a jaw width of 0.2 in. (5mm) or less, align the jaws with the openings in the side of the fitting case and compress the portion of the retaining clip that engages the fitting case. This disengages the retaining clip from the case. Often 1 side of the clip will disengage before the other. The clip must be disengaged from both openings.

• Pull the fitting off the tube by hand only. Only moderate effort is required if the retaining clip has been properly disengaged.

• After disassembly, inspect and clean the tube end sealing surfaces. The tube end should be free of scratches and corrosion that could provide leak paths. Inspect the inside of the fitting for any internal parts such as O-rings and spacers that may have been dislodged from the fitting. Replace any damaged connector.

• The retaining clip will remain on the tube. Disengage the clip from the tube bead and remove.

To connect:

7. Install a new connector if damage was found. Install the new replacement clip into the body by inserting 1 of the retaining clip serrated edges on the duck bill portion into 1 side of the window openings. Push on the other side until the clip snaps into place.

8. Before installing the fitting on the tube, wipe the tube end with a clean cloth. Inspect the inside of the fitting to make sure it is free of dirt and/or obstructions.

9. Apply a light coating of engine oil to the tube end. Align the fitting and tube axially and push the fitting onto the tube end. When the fitting is engaged, a definite click will be heard. Pull on the fitting to make sure it is fully engaged.

Spring Lock Coupling

The spring lock coupling is a fuel line coupling held together by a garter spring inside a circular cage. When the coupling is connected together, the flared end of the female fitting slips behind the garter spring inside the cage of the male fitting. The garter spring and cage then prevent the flared end of the female fitting from pulling out of the cage. As an additional locking feature, most vehicles have a horseshoe shaped retaining clip that improves the retaining reliability of the spring lock coupling.

Fuel Tank

REMOVAL AND INSTALLATION

1. Disconnect the negative battery cable and relieve the fuel system pressure.
2. Siphon or pump as much fuel as possible out through the fuel filler pipe.

NOTE: Fuel injected vehicles have reservoirs inside the fuel tank to maintain fuel near the fuel pickup during cornering and under low fuel operating conditions. These reservoirs could block siphon tubes or hoses from reaching the bottom of the fuel tank. Repeated attempts using different hose orientations can overcome this obstacle.

3. Raise and safely support the vehicle.
4. If equipped with a metal retainer that fastens the filler pipe to the fuel tank, remove the screw attaching the retainer to the fuel tank flange.

5. Disconnect the fuel lines and the electrical connector to the fuel tank sending unit. On some vehicles, these are inaccessible on top of the tank. In these cases they must be disconnected with the tank partially removed.

6. Place a safety support under the fuel tank and remove the bolts or nuts from the fuel tank straps. Allow the straps to swing out of the way.

7. Partially remove the tank and disconnect the fuel lines and electrical connector from the sending unit, if required.

8. Remove the tank from the vehicle.

To install:

9. Raise the fuel tank into position in the vehicle. Connect the fuel lines and sending unit electrical connector if it is necessary to connect them before the tank is in the final installed position.

10. Lubricate the fuel filler pipe with water base tire mounting lubricant and install the tank onto the filler pipe, then bring the tank into final position. Be careful not to deform the tank.

11. Bring the fuel tank straps around the tank and start the retaining nut or bolt. Align the tank with the straps. If equipped, make sure the fuel tank shields are installed with the straps and are positioned correctly on the tank.

12. Check the hoses and wiring mounted on the tank top to make sure they are correctly routed and will not be pinched between the tank and body.

13. Tighten the fuel tank strap retaining nuts or bolts to 20–30 ft. lbs. (28–40 Nm).

14. If not already connected, connect the fuel hoses and lines which were disconnected. Make sure the fuel supply, fuel return, if present, and vapor vent connections are made correctly. If not already connected, connect the sending unit electrical connector.

15. Lower the vehicle. Replace the fuel that was drained from the tank. Check all connections for leaks.

Fuel Filter

REMOVAL AND INSTALLATION

In-line Fuel Filter

1. Disconnect the negative battery cable and relieve the fuel system pressure.
2. Raise and safely support the vehicle.

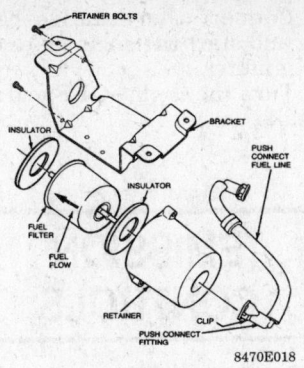

8470E018

Inline fuel filter

3. Remove the push connect fittings at both ends of the filter. Install new retainer clips in each push connect fitting.

4. Remove the fuel filter and retainer from the metal bracket. Remove the filter from the retainer. Note that the direction of the flow arrow points to the open end of the retainer. Remove the rubber insulator rings.

To install:

5. Install the rubber insulator rings, place the filter into the retainer with the flow arrow pointing out of the retainer open end, and install the retainer on the metal bracket. Tighten the retaining bolts to 27–44 inch lbs. (3–5 Nm).

6. Install the push connect fittings onto the filter ends. Start the engine and check for leaks.

7. Lower the vehicle.

Electric Fuel Pump

PRESSURE TESTING

1. Relieve the fuel system pressure and connect a fuel pressure gauge to the valve on the fuel rail.

2. Ground the fuel pump lead of the self-test connector through a jumper wire at the **FP** lead.

3. Turn the ignition key to the **RUN** position to operate the fuel pump.

4. Observe the fuel pressure gauge. the indicated pressure should be 35–40 psi.

5. Remove the fuel pressure gauge and the jumper wire.

REMOVAL AND INSTALLATION

1. Disconnect the negative battery cable and relieve the fuel system pressure.

2. Remove the fuel tank and place it on a bench.

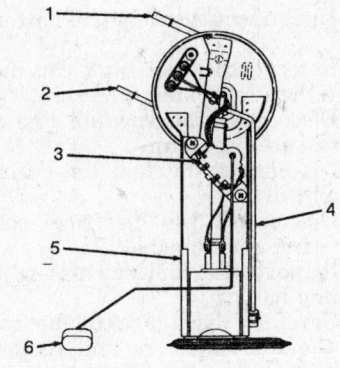

1. Fuel supply
2. Fuel return
3. Fuel gauge sender
4. Fuel return
5. Electric fuel pump
6. Sender float

8470E019

Fuel gauge and pump assembly

3. Remove any dirt that has accumulated around the fuel pump retaining flange so it will not enter the tank during pump removal and installation.

4. Turn the fuel pump locking ring counterclockwise and remove the locking ring.

5. Remove the fuel pump and bracket assembly. Remove and discard the seal ring.

To install:

6. Clean the fuel pump mounting flange, fuel tank mounting surface and seal ring groove.

7. Apply a light coating of grease on a new seal ring to hold it in place

during assembly and install in the seal ring groove.

8. Install the fuel pump and bracket assembly carefully to ensure the filter is not damaged. Make sure the locating keys are in the keyways and the seal ring remains in the groove.

9. Hold the pump assembly in place and install the locking ring finger-tight. Make sure all the locking tabs are under the tank lock ring tabs.

10. Rotate the locking ring clockwise until the ring is against the stops.

11. Install the fuel tank in the vehicle. Add a minimum of 10 gallons of fuel to the tank and check for leaks.

12. Install a suitable fuel pressure gauge to the valve on the fuel rail.

13. Turn the ignition switch from **OFF** to **ON** for 3 seconds. Repeat this procedure 5–10 times until the pressure gauge shows at least 35 psi. Check for fuel leaks.

14. Remove the pressure gauge, start the engine and check for leaks.

Fuel Injection

IDLE SPEED ADJUSTMENT

4.6L Engine

1. Place the transmission in **P** and apply the parking brake.

2. Start the engine and bring to normal operating temperature. Make sure the heater, air conditioning and all other accessories are OFF.

3. Check and if necessary, adjust the ignition timing.

4. Make sure the fuel pressure is correct. Any indicated vehicle malfunction service codes should be resolved before proceeding further.

5. Connect the SUPER STAR II tester, tool number 007–00028 or other suitable scan tool to the Self-

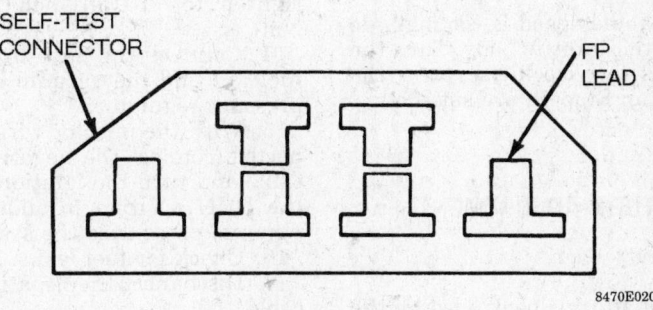

8470E020

Self-test connector terminal

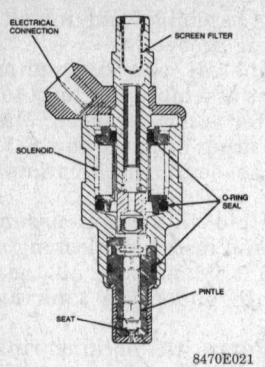

MFI fuel injector

Test connector. Activate the Key On Engine Running (KOER) Self-Test.

6. After Code **1** or **111** has been displayed, unlatch and within 4 seconds, latch the **STI** button.

7. A single pulse code indicates the entry mode, then observe the Self-Test Output (STO) on the tester for the following:

a. A constant tone, solid light or **STO LO** readout means the base idle speed is within the correct range. To exit the test, unlatch the **STI** button, then wait 4 seconds for reinitialization. After 10 minutes, the tool will exit by itself.

b. A beeping tone, flashing light or **STO LO** readout at 8 Hz indicates the Throttle Position Sensor (TPS) is out of range due to over adjustment. Adjustment may be required.

c. A beeping tone, flashing light or **STO LO** readout at 4 Hz indicates the base idle speed is too fast and adjustment is required. Proceed to Step 9.

d. A beeping tone, flashing light or **STO LO** readout at 1 Hz indicates the base idle speed is too low and adjustment is required. Proceed to Step 8.

8. If the idle speed is too low, do not clean the throttle body. Turn the air trim screw counterclockwise until the conditions in Step 7a are satisfied.

9. If the idle speed is too high, do not clean the throttle body. Turn the air trim screw clockwise until the conditions in Step 7a are satisfied.

IDLE MIXTURE ADJUSTMENT

The idle mixture is controlled by the electronic control unit and cannot be adjusted.

Fuel Injector

REMOVAL AND INSTALLATION

4.6L Engine

1. Disconnect the negative battery cable.

2. Remove the fuel tank cap and relieve the fuel system pressure.

3. Disconnect the vacuum line at the pressure regulator.

4. Disconnect the fuel lines from the fuel rail.

5. Disconnect the electrical connectors from the injectors.

6. Remove the fuel rail assembly retaining bolts.

7. Carefully disengage the fuel rail from the fuel injectors and remove the fuel rail.

NOTE: It may be easier to remove the injectors with the fuel rail as an assembly.

8. Grasping the injector body, pull while gently rocking the injector from side-to-side to remove the injector from the fuel rail or intake manifold.

9. Inspect the pintle protection cap and washer for signs of deterioration. Replace the complete injector, as required. If the cap is missing, look for it in the intake manifold.

NOTE: The pintle protection cap is not available as a separate part.

To install:

10. Lubricate new O-rings with light grade oil and install 2 on each injector.

NOTE: Never use silicone grease as it will clog the injectors.

11. Install the injectors using a light, twisting, pushing motion.

12. Install the fuel rail, pushing it down to ensure all injector O-rings are fully seated in the fuel rail cups and intake manifold.

13. Install the retaining bolts while holding the fuel rail down and tighten to 71–106 inch lbs. (8–12 Nm).

14. Connect the fuel lines to the fuel rail and the vacuum line to the pressure regulator.

15. With the injector wiring disconnected, connect the negative battery cable and turn the ignition switch to the **RUN** position to allow the fuel pump to pressurize the system.

16. Check for fuel leaks.

17. Disconnect the negative battery cable.

18. Connect the electrical connectors to the fuel injectors.

19. Connect the negative battery cable and start the engine. Let it idle for 2 minutes.

20. Turn the engine **OFF** and check for leaks.

EMISSION CONTROLS

Emission Warning Lamps

RESETTING

These vehicles have an CHECK ENGINE lamp that will light when there is a fault in the engine control system. This light cannot be reset without diagnosing the fault in the system. When the system has been diagnosed and the problem corrected, the light will go out.

ENGINE MECHANICAL

NOTE: Disconnecting the negative battery cable on some vehicles may interfere with the functions of the on board computer systems and may require the computer to undergo a relearning process, once the negative battery cable is reconnected.

Engine Assembly

REMOVAL AND INSTALLATION

4.6L Engine

1. Disconnect the battery cables. Drain the crankcase and the cooling system.

2. Relieve the fuel system pressure and discharge the air conditioning system.

3. Mark the position of the hood on the hinges and remove the hood.

4. Remove the cooling fan, shroud and radiator.

5. Remove the wiper module and support bracket. Remove the air inlet tube.

6. Remove the 42-pin connector from the retaining bracket on the brake vacuum booster. Disconnect

the 42-pin connector and transmission harness connector and position aside.

7. Disconnect the accelerator and cruise control cables. Disconnect the throttle valve cable.

8. Disconnect the electrical connector and vacuum hose from the purge solenoid. Disconnect the power supply from the power distribution box and starter relay.

9. Disconnect the vacuum supply hose from the throttle body adapter vacuum port. Disconnect the heater hoses.

10. Disconnect the generator harness from the fender apron and junction block. Disconnect the air conditioning hoses from the compressor.

11. Disconnect the EVO sensor connector from the power steering pump and disconnect the body ground strap from the dash panel.

12. Raise and safely support the vehicle.

13. Disconnect the exhaust system from the exhaust manifolds and support with wire hung from the crossmember.

14. Remove the retaining nut from the transmission line bracket and remove the 3 bolts and stud retaining the engine to the transmission knee braces.

15. Remove the starter. Remove the 4 bolts retaining the power steering pump to the engine block and position aside.

16. Remove the plug from the engine block to access the torque converter retaining nuts. Rotate the crankshaft until each of the 4 nuts is accessible and remove the nuts.

17. Remove the 6 transmission-to-engine retaining bolts. Remove the engine mount through bolts, 2 on the left mount and 1 on the right mount.

18. Lower the vehicle. Support the transmission with a floor jack and remove the bolt retaining the right engine mount to the lower engine bracket.

19. Install an engine lifting bracket to the left cylinder head on the front and the right cylinder head on the rear. Connect engine lifting equipment to the lifting brackets.

20. Raise the engine slightly and carefully separate the engine from the transmission.

21. Carefully lift the engine out of the engine compartment and position on a workstand. Remove the engine lifting equipment.

To install:

22. Install engine lifting brackets as in Step 19. Connect engine lifting

equipment to the brackets and remove the engine from the workstand.

23. Carefully lower the engine into the engine compartment. Start the converter pilot into the flexplate and align the paint marks on the flexplate and torque converter. Make sure the studs on the torque converter align with the holes in the flexplate.

24. Fully engage the engine to the transmission and lower onto the mounts. Remove the engine lifting equipment and brackets. Install the bolt retaining the right engine mount to the frame.

25. Raise and safely support the vehicle. Install the 6 engine-to-transmission bolts and tighten to 30–44 ft. lbs. (40–60 Nm).

26. Install the engine mount through bolts and tighten to 15–22 ft. lbs. (20–30 Nm). Install the 4 torque converter retaining nuts and tighten to 22–25 ft. lbs. (20–30 Nm). Install the plug into the access hole in the engine block.

27. Position the power steering pump on the engine block and install the 4 retaining nuts. Tighten to 15–22 ft. lbs. (20–30 Nm). Install the starter.

28. Position the engine to transmission braces and install the 3 bolts and 1 stud. Tighten the bolts and stud to 18–31 ft. lbs. (25–43 Nm).

29. Position the transmission line bracket to the knee brace stud and install the retaining nut. Tighten to 15–22 ft. lbs. (20–30 Nm).

30. Cut the wire and position the exhaust system to the manifolds. Install the 4 nuts and tighten to 20–30 ft. lbs. (27–41 Nm).

NOTE: Make sure the exhaust system clears the No. 3 crossmember. Adjust as necessary.

31. Lower the vehicle and connect the EVO sensor.

32. Connect the air conditioner lines to the compressor and connect the generator harness from the fender apron and junction block.

33. Connect the heater hoses and connect the vacuum supply hose to the throttle body adapter vacuum port.

34. Connect the power supply to the power distribution box and starter relay. Connect the electrical connector and vacuum hose to the purge solenoid.

35. Connect and if necessary, adjust the throttle valve cable. Connect the accelerator and cruise control cables.

36. Connect the 42-pin engine harness connector and transmission har-

ness connector. Install the 42-pin connector to the retaining bracket on the brake vacuum booster.

37. Install the wiper module and support bracket. Connect the fuel lines.

38. Install the radiator, cooling fan and shroud. Install the air inlet tube.

39. Fill the crankcase with the proper type and quantity of engine oil. Fill and bleed the cooling system.

40. Install the hood, aligning the marks that were made during removal. Connect the battery cables.

41. Start the engine and bring to operating temperature. Check for leaks. Check all fluid levels. Leak test, evacuate and charge the air conditioning system according to the proper procedure. Observe all safety precautions.

Engine Mounts

REMOVAL AND INSTALLATION

4.6L Engine

FRONT

1. Disconnect the battery cables. Drain the cooling system, relieve the fuel system pressure and discharge the air conditioning system.

2. Remove the air inlet tube and the cooling fan and shroud. Remove the upper radiator hose.

3. Disconnect the fuel lines from the fuel rail. Remove the wiper module and support bracket.

4. Disconnect the air conditioning compressor outlet hose at the compressor and remove the bolt retaining the hose assembly to the right coil bracket.

5. Remove the 42-pin engine harness connector from the retaining bracket on the brake vacuum booster. Disconnect the 42-pin connector and transmission harness connector.

6. Disconnect the throttle valve cable from the throttle body. Disconnect the heater outlet hose.

7. Remove the upper stud and loosen the lower bolt retaining the heater outlet hose to the right cylinder head and position aside.

8. Remove the blower motor resistor. Remove the bolt retaining the right engine mount to the lower engine bracket.

9. Disconnect the vacuum hoses from the EGR valve and EGR tube. Remove the 2 bolts retaining the EGR valve to the intake manifold. Disconnect both oxygen sensors.

10. Raise and safely support the vehicle. Remove the engine mount

through bolts, 2 from the left side and 1 from the right.

11. Remove the EGR tube line nut from the right exhaust manifold and remove the EGR valve and tube assembly.

12. Disconnect the exhaust pipes from the manifolds. Lower the exhaust and hang the pipes with wire from the crossmember.

13. Position a jack and a block of wood under the oil pan, rearward of the oil drain hole. Raise the engine approximately 4 in. (100mm).

14. Install a block of wood under the oil pan and lower the engine onto the wood block. Remove 3 retaining bolts each from the right and left engine mounts and remove the mounts.

To install:

15. Position the mounts on the engine block, install 3 retaining bolts and tighten to 45–60 (60–81 Nm). Raise the engine and remove the wood block.

16. Lower the engine onto the mounts. Position and connect the EGR valve and tube assembly to the exhaust manifold. Tighten the line nut to 26–33 ft. lbs.

NOTE: Loosen the line nut at the EGR valve prior to installing the assembly onto the vehicle. This will allow enough movement to align the EGR valve retaining bolts.

17. Install the engine mount through bolts and tighten to 15–22 ft. lbs. (20–30 Nm).

18. Cut the wire and position the exhaust manifolds. Install the 4 nuts and tighten to 20–30 ft. lbs. (27–41 Nm). Make sure the exhaust system clears the No. 3 crossmember; adjust as necessary.

19. Lower the vehicle and connect the oxygen sensors. Install the bolt retaining the right engine mount to the frame. Tighten to 45–60 ft. lbs. (60–81 Nm).

20. Install a new gasket on the EGR valve and position to the intake manifold. Install the 2 EGR valve retaining bolts and tighten to 15–22 ft. lbs. (20–30 Nm).

21. Tighten the EGR tube line nut at the EGR valve to 26–33 ft. lbs. (35–45 Nm). Connect the vacuum hoses to the EGR valve and tube.

22. Install the blower motor resistor. Position the heater outlet hose. Install the upper stud and tighten the upper stud and lower bolt to 15–22 ft. lbs. (20–30 Nm). Install the ground strap onto the stud and tighten the nut to 15–22 ft. lbs. (20–30 Nm). Connect the heater outlet hose.

23. Connect and if necessary, adjust the throttle valve cable. Connect the 42-pin connector and transmission harness connector. Install the 42-pin engine harness connector to the retaining bracket on the brake vacuum booster.

24. Connect the air conditioning compressor outlet hose to the compressor and install the bolt retaining the hose assembly to the right coil bracket.

25. Install the upper radiator hose and connect the fuel lines. Install the wiper module and retaining bracket.

26. Install the cooling fan and shroud. Install the air inlet tube.

27. Fill and bleed the cooling system. Connect the battery cables, start the engine and check for leaks. Leak test, evacuate and charge the air conditioning system according to the proper procedure. Observe all safety precautions.

REAR

1. Disconnect the negative battery cable. Raise and safely support the vehicle.

2. Support the transmission with a jack and wood block. Remove the 2 nuts attaching the rear mount to the crossmember.

3. Remove the 2 bolts attaching the mount to the transmission.

4. Raise the transmission with the jack and remove the mount.

To install:

5. Position the mount on the transmission. Install the 2 retaining bolts and tighten to 50–70 ft. lbs. (68–95 Nm).

6. Lower the transmission. Install the rear mount-to-crossmember retaining nuts and tighten to 35–50 ft. lbs. (48–68 Nm).

7. Lower the vehicle and connect the negative battery cable.

Cylinder Head

REMOVAL AND INSTALLATION

4.6L Engine

1. Disconnect the negative battery cable.

2. Drain the cooling system and remove the cooling fan and shroud.

3. Relieve the fuel system pressure and disconnect the fuel lines.

4. Remove the air inlet tube and the wiper module. Release the belt tensioner and remove the accessory drive belt.

5. Tag and disconnect the ignition wires from the spark plugs. Disconnect the ignition wire brackets from

the camshaft cover studs and remove the 2 bolts retaining the ignition wire tray to the coil brackets.

6. Remove the bolt retaining the air conditioner high pressure line to the right coil bracket. Disconnect both ignition coils and CID sensor.

7. Remove the nuts retaining the coil brackets to the front cover. Slide the ignition coil brackets and ignition wire assembly off the mounting studs and remove from the vehicle.

8. Remove the water pump pulley. Disconnect the generator wiring harness from the junction block, fender apron and generator. Disconnect the bolts retaining the generator to the intake manifold and engine block and remove the generator.

9. Disconnect the positive battery cable at the power distribution box. Remove the retaining bolt from the positive battery cable bracket located on the side of the right cylinder head.

10. Disconnect the vent hose from the canister purge solenoid and position the positive battery cable out of the way. Disconnect the canister purge solenoid vent hose from the PCV valve and remove the PCV valve from the camshaft cover.

11. Remove the 42-pin engine harness connector from the retaining bracket on the brake vacuum booster, disconnect and position out of the way.

12. Disconnect the HDR sensor, air conditioning compressor clutch and canister purge solenoid connectors.

13. Raise and safely support the vehicle.

14. Remove the bolts retaining the power steering pump to the engine block and front cover. The front lower bolt on the power steering pump will not come all the way out. Wire the power steering pump out of the way.

15. Remove the 4 bolts retaining the oil pan to the front cover. Remove the crankshaft damper retaining bolt and remove the damper, using a suitable puller.

16. Disconnect the EVO sensor and oil sending unit. Position the EVO sensor and oil pressure sending unit harness out of the way.

17. Disconnect the EGR tube from the right exhaust manifold. Disconnect the exhaust pipes from the exhaust manifolds. Lower the exhaust pipes and hang with wire from the crossmember.

18. Remove the bolt retaining the starter wiring harness to the rear of the right cylinder head. Lower the vehicle.

19. Remove the bolts and stud bolts retaining the camshaft covers to the

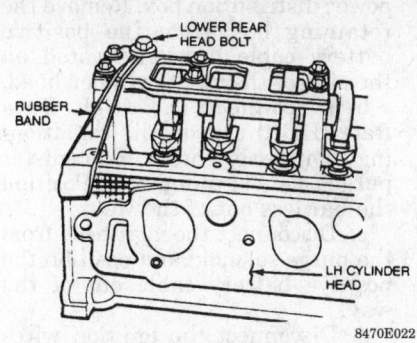

Supporting left lower head bolt with rubberband

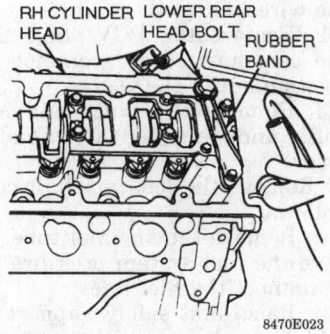

Supporting right lower head bolt with rubberband

cylinder heads and remove the covers.

20. Disconnect the accelerator, cruise control and throttle valve cables. Remove the accelerator cable bracket from the intake manifold and position out of the way.

21. Disconnect the vacuum hose from the throttle body elbow vacuum port, both oxygen sensors and the heater supply hose.

22. Remove the 2 bolts retaining the thermostat housing to the intake manifold and position the upper hose and thermostat housing out of the way.

NOTE: Two thermostat housing bolts also retain the intake manifold.

23. Remove the 9 bolts retaining the intake manifold to the cylinder heads and remove the intake manifold and gaskets.

24. Remove the 7 stud bolts and 4 bolts retaining the front cover to the engine and remove the front cover.

25. Remove the timing chains.

26. Remove the 10 bolts retaining the left cylinder head to the engine block and remove the head.

NOTE: The lower rear bolt cannot be removed due to interference with the brake vacuum booster. Use a rubber band to hold the bolt away from the engine block.

27. Remove the ground strap, 1 stud and 1 bolt retaining the heater return line to the right cylinder head.

28. Remove the 10 bolts retaining the right cylinder head to the engine block and remove the head.

NOTE: The lower rear bolt cannot be removed due to interference with the evaporator housing. Use a rubber band to hold the bolt away from the engine block.

29. Clean all gasket mating surfaces. Check the cylinder head and engine block for flatness. Check the cylinder head for scratches near the coolant passage and combustion chamber that could provide leak paths. Machine as necessary.

To install:

30. Rotate the crankshaft counterclockwise 45 degrees. The crankshaft keyway should be at the 9 o'clock position viewed from the front of the engine. This ensures that all pistons are below the top of the engine block deck face.

31. Rotate the camshaft to a stable position where the valves do not extend below the head face.

32. Position new head gaskets on the engine block. Install the lower rear bolts on both cylinder heads and retain with rubber bands as explained during the removal procedure.

33. Position the cylinder heads on the engine block dowels, being careful not to score the surface of the head face. Apply clean oil to the head bolts, remove the rubber band from the lower rear bolt and install all bolts hand-tight.

34. Tighten the head bolts as follows:

    a. Tighten the bolts, in sequence, to 15–22 ft. lbs. (20–30 Nm).

    b. Rotate each bolt, in sequence, 85–95 degrees.

    c. Rotate each bolt, in sequence, an additional 85–95 degrees.

35. Position the heater return hose and install the 2 bolts. Rotate the camshafts using the flats matched at the center of the camshaft until both are in time. Install cam positioning

tools T91P–6256–A or equivalent, on the flats of the camshafts to keep them from rotating.

36. Rotate the crankshaft clockwise 45 degrees to position the crankshaft at TDC on No. 1 cylinder.

NOTE: The crankshaft must only be rotated in the clockwise direction and only as far as TDC.

37. Install the timing chains according to the proper procedure.

38. Install a new front cover seal and gasket. Apply silicone sealer to the lower corners of the cover where it meets the junction of the oil pan and cylinder block and to the points where the cover contacts the junction of the cylinder block and cylinder head.

39. Install the front cover and the stud bolts and bolts. Tighten to 15–22 ft. lbs. (20–30 Nm).

40. Position new intake manifold gaskets on the cylinder heads. Make sure the alignment tabs on the gaskets are aligned with the holes in the cylinder heads.

NOTE: Before installing the intake manifold, inspect it for nicks and cuts that could provide leak paths.

41. Position the intake manifold on the cylinder heads and install the retaining bolts. Tighten the bolts, in sequence, to 15–22 ft. lbs. (20–30 Nm).

42. Install the thermostat and O-ring, then position the thermostat housing and upper hose and install the 2 bolts. Tighten to 15–22 ft. lbs. (20–30 Nm).

43. Connect the heater supply hose and both oxygen sensors. Connect the vacuum hose to the throttle body adapter vacuum port.

44. Connect and, if necessary, adjust the throttle valve cable. Install the accelerator cable bracket on the intake manifold and connect the accelerator and cruise control cables to the throttle body.

45. Apply silicone sealer to both places where the front cover meets the cylinder head. Install new gaskets on the camshaft covers.

46. Install the camshaft covers on the cylinder heads. Install the bolts and stud bolts and tighten to 6.0–8.8 ft. lbs. (8–12 Nm).

47. Raise and safely support the vehicle. Position the starter wiring harness to the right cylinder head and install the retaining bolt.

48. Cut the wire and position the exhaust pipes to the exhaust

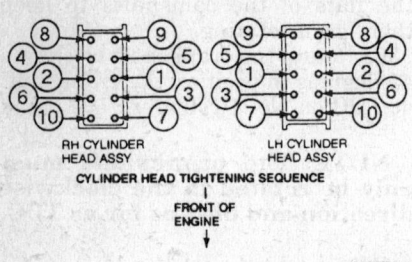

8470E024

Cylinder head torque sequence — 4.6L engine

manifolds. Tighten the 4 nuts to 20–30 ft. lbs. (27–41 Nm).

NOTE: Make sure the exhaust system clears the No. 3 crossmember. Adjust as necessary.

49. Connect the EGR tube to the right exhaust manifold and tighten the line nut to 26–33 ft. lbs. (35–45 Nm). Connect the EVO sensor and oil sending unit.

50. Apply a small amount of silicone sealer in the rear of the keyway on the damper. Position the damper on the crankshaft, making sure the crankshaft key and keyway are aligned.

51. Using damper installer T74P-6316-B or equivalent, install the crankshaft damper. Install the damper bolt and washer and tighten to 114–121 ft. lbs. (155–165 Nm).

52. Install the 4 bolts retaining the oil pan to the front cover and tighten to 15–22 ft. lbs. (20–30 Nm).

53. Position the power steering pump on the engine and install the 4 retaining bolts. Tighten to 15–22 ft. lbs. (20–30 Nm). Lower the vehicle.

54. Connect the air conditioning compressor, HDR sensor and canister purge solenoid.

55. Connect the 42-pin engine harness connector and transmission harness connector. Install the 42-pin connector on the retaining bracket on the vacuum brake booster.

56. Install the PCV valve in the right camshaft cover and connect the canister purge solenoid vent hose.

57. Position the positive battery cable harness on the right cylinder head and install the bolt retaining the cable bracket to the cylinder head. Connect the positive battery cable at the power distribution box and battery.

58. Position the generator and install the 2 retaining bolts. Tighten to 15–22 ft. lbs. (20–30 Nm). Install the 2 bolts retaining the generator brace

to the intake manifold and tighten to 6–8 ft. lbs. (8–12 Nm).

59. Install the water pump pulley and tighten the bolts to 15–22 ft. lbs. (20–30 Nm).

60. Position the ignition coil brackets and ignition wire assembly onto the mounting studs. Install the 7 nuts retaining the coil brackets to the front cover and tighten to 15–22 ft. lbs. (20–30 Nm).

61. Install the 2 bolts retaining the ignition wire tray to the coil bracket and tighten to 6.0–8.8 ft. lbs. (8–12 Nm). Connect both ignition coils and CID sensor.

62. Position the air conditioner high pressure line on the right coil bracket and install the bolt. Connect the ignition wires to the spark plugs and install the bracket onto the camshaft cover studs.

63. Install the accessory drive belt and the wiper module. Connect the fuel lines and install the cooling fan and shroud. Fill and bleed the cooling system.

64. Install the air inlet tube and connect the negative battery cable. Start the engine and bring to normal operating temperature. Check for leaks. Check all fluid levels.

Valve Lifters

REMOVAL AND INSTALLATION

4.6L Engine

The 4.6L engine is equipped with hydraulic lash adjusters which, while not being exactly the same as a conventional hydraulic lifter, perform the same function — maintain proper valve train clearance.

1. Disconnect the negative battery cable.

2. Remove the right camshaft cover as follows:

a. Disconnect the positive battery cable at the battery and at the

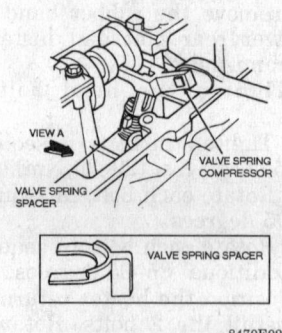

8470E027

Valve spring compressor and spacer 4.6L engine

power distribution box. Remove the retaining bolt from the positive battery cable bracket located on the side of the right cylinder head.

b. Disconnect the High Data Rate (HDR) sensor, air conditioning compressor clutch and canister purge solenoid connectors. Position the harness out of the way.

c. Disconnect the vent hose from the purge solenoid and position the positive battery cable out of the way.

d. Disconnect the ignition wires from the spark plugs. Remove the ignition wire brackets from the camshaft cover studs and position the wires out of the way.

e. Remove the PCV valve from the camshaft cover grommet and position out of the way.

f. Remove the bolts and stud bolts and remove the camshaft cover.

3. Remove the left camshaft cover as follows:

a. Remove the air inlet tube. Relieve the fuel system pressure and disconnect the fuel lines.

b. Raise and safely support the vehicle.

c. Disconnect the EVO sensor and oil pressure sending unit and position the harness out of the way. Lower the vehicle.

d. Remove the 42-pin engine harness connector from the retaining bracket on the brake vacuum booster. Disconnect and position out of the way.

e. Remove the windshield wiper module.

f. Disconnect the ignition wires from the spark plugs. Remove the ignition wire brackets from the studs and position the wires out of the way.

g. Remove the bolts and stud bolts and remove the camshaft cover.

4. Position the piston of the cylinder being serviced at the bottom of its stroke and position the camshaft lobe on the base circle.

5. Install valve spring spacer tool T91P-6565-AH or equivalent, between the spring coils to prevent valve seal damage.

NOTE: If the valve spring spacer tool is not used, the retainer will hit the valve stem seal and damage the seal.

6. Install valve spring compressor tool T91P-6565-A or equivalent, under the camshaft and on top of the valve spring retainer.

7. Compress the valve spring and remove the roller follower. Remove

the valve spring compressor and spacer.

8. Remove the hydraulic lash adjuster.

To install:

9. Check the hydraulic lash adjusters. They must have no more than 1.5mm of plunger travel prior to installation.

10. Apply engine oil to the valve stem and tip, roller follower contact surfaces and lash adjuster bore. Install the lash adjusters.

11. Install valve spring spacer tool T91P–6565–AH or equivalent, between the spring coils. Compress the valve spring using valve spring compressor tool T91P–6565–A or equivalent, and install the roller follower.

NOTE: The piston must be at the bottom of its stroke and the camshaft at the base circle.

12. Remove the valve spring compressor and spacer.

13. Clean the sealing surfaces of the camshaft covers and cylinder heads. Apply silicone sealer to the places where the front cover meets the cylinder head.

14. Position new gaskets onto the camshaft covers and install the covers. Install the bolts and stud bolts and tighten to 6.0–8.8 ft. lbs. (8–12 Nm).

15. When installing the right camshaft cover, proceed as follows:

a. Install the PCV valve into the camshaft cover grommet.

b. Install the ignition wire brackets on the studs and connect the wires to the spark plugs.

c. Position the harness and connect the canister purge solenoid, air conditioning compressor clutch and HDR sensor.

d. Position the positive battery cable harness on the right cylinder head. Install the bolt retaining the cable bracket to the cylinder head.

e. Connect the positive battery cable at the power distribution box and the battery.

16. When installing the left camshaft cover, proceed as follows:

a. Install the ignition wire brackets on the studs and connect the wires to the spark plugs.

b. Install the windshield wiper module.

c. Connect the 42-pin connector and transmission harness connector. Install the connector on the retaining bracket.

d. Raise and safely support the vehicle. Position and connect the EVO sensor and oil pressure sending unit harness.

e. Lower the vehicle. Connect the fuel lines.

17. Connect the negative battery cable. Start the engine and check for leaks.

Valve Lash

ADJUSTMENT

4.6L Engine

The valve lash is not adjustable. If the collapsed lash adjuster clearance is incorrect, check the camshaft, roller follower and valve for wear or damage.

1. Disconnect the negative battery cable.

2. Remove the camshaft covers.

3. Rotate the crankshaft until the camshaft base circle is contacting the roller follower.

4. Use a suitable tool to bleed down the lash adjuster. Slowly compress the lash adjuster until the plunger is bottomed.

5. Use a feeler gauge to check the clearance between the camshaft and the roller follower. The clearance should be 0.018–0.033 in. (0.45–0.85mm).

Rocker Arms

REMOVAL AND INSTALLATION

4.6L Engine

1. Disconnect the negative battery cable.

2. Remove the right camshaft cover as follows:

a. Disconnect the positive battery cable at the battery and at the power distribution box. Remove the retaining bolt from the positive battery cable bracket located on the side of the right cylinder head.

b. Disconnect the High Data Rate (HDR) sensor, air conditioning compressor clutch and canister purge solenoid connectors. Position the harness out of the way.

c. Disconnect the vent hose from the purge solenoid and position the positive battery cable out of the way.

d. Disconnect the ignition wires from the spark plugs. Remove the ignition wire brackets from the camshaft cover studs and position the wires out of the way.

e. Remove the PCV valve from the camshaft cover grommet and position out of the way.

f. Remove the bolts and stud bolts and remove the camshaft cover.

3. Remove the left camshaft cover as follows:

a. Remove the air inlet tube. Relieve the fuel system pressure and disconnect the fuel lines.

b. Raise and safely support the vehicle.

c. Disconnect the EVO sensor and oil pressure sending unit and position the harness out of the way. Lower the vehicle.

d. Remove the 42-pin engine harness connector from the retaining bracket on the brake vacuum booster. Disconnect and position out of the way.

e. Remove the windshield wiper module.

f. Disconnect the ignition wires from the spark plugs. Remove the ignition wire brackets from the studs and position the wires out of the way.

g. Remove the bolts and stud bolts and remove the camshaft cover.

4. Position the piston of the cylinder being serviced at the bottom of its stroke and position the camshaft lobe on the base circle.

5. Install valve spring spacer tool T91P–6565–AH or equivalent, between the spring coils to prevent valve seal damage.

NOTE: If the valve spring spacer tool is not used, the retainer will hit the valve stem seal and damage the seal.

6. Install valve spring compressor tool T91P–6565–A or equivalent, under the camshaft and on top of the valve spring retainer.

7. Compress the valve spring and remove the roller follower. Remove the valve spring compressor and spacer.

To install:

8. Apply engine oil to the valve stem and tip and roller follower contact surfaces.

9. Install valve spring spacer tool T91P–6565–AH or equivalent, between the spring coils. Compress the valve spring using valve spring compressor tool T91P–6565–A or equivalent, and install the roller follower.

NOTE: The piston must be at the bottom of its stroke and the camshaft at the base circle.

10. Remove the valve spring compressor and spacer.

11. Clean the sealing surfaces of the camshaft covers and cylinder

heads. Apply silicone sealer to the places where the front cover meets the cylinder head.

12. Position new gaskets onto the camshaft covers and install the covers. Install the bolts and stud bolts and tighten to 6.0–8.8 ft. lbs. (8–12 Nm).

13. When installing the right camshaft cover, proceed as follows:

a. Install the PCV into the camshaft cover grommet.

b. Install the ignition wire brackets on the studs and connect the wires to the spark plugs.

c. Position the harness and connect the canister purge solenoid, air conditioning compressor clutch and HDR sensor.

d. Position the positive battery cable harness on the right cylinder head. Install the bolt retaining the cable bracket to the cylinder head.

e. Connect the positive battery cable at the power distribution box and the battery.

14. When installing the left camshaft cover, proceed as follows:

a. Install the ignition wire brackets on the studs and connect the wires to the spark plugs.

b. Install the windshield wiper module.

c. Connect the 42-pin connector and transmission harness connector. Install the connector on the retaining bracket.

d. Raise and safely support the vehicle. Position and connect the EVO sensor and oil pressure sending unit harness.

e. Lower the vehicle. Connect the fuel lines.

15. Connect the negative battery cable. Start the engine and check for leaks.

Intake Manifold

REMOVAL AND INSTALLATION

4.6L Engine

1. Disconnect the negative battery cable.

2. Drain the cooling system. Relieve the fuel system pressure and disconnect the fuel lines.

3. Remove the wiper module and the air inlet tube. Release the belt tensioner and remove the accessory drive belt.

4. Tag and disconnect the ignition wires from the spark plugs. Disconnect the ignition wire brackets from the camshaft cover studs.

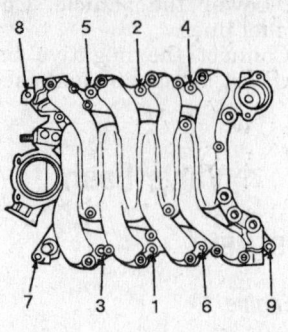

8470E030

Intake manifold torque sequence — 4.6L engine

5. Disconnect both ignition coils and CID sensor. Tag and disconnect all ignition wires from both ignition coils. Remove the 2 bolts retaining the ignition wire tray to the coil brackets and remove the ignition wire assembly.

6. Disconnect the generator wiring harness from the junction block at the fender apron and generator. Remove the bolts retaining the generator brace to the intake manifold and the generator to the engine block and remove the generator.

7. Raise and safely support the vehicle. Disconnect the oil sending unit and EVO harness sensor and position the wiring harness out of the way.

8. Disconnect the EGR tube from the right exhaust manifold and lower the vehicle.

9. Remove the 42-pin engine harness connector from the retaining bracket on the vacuum brake booster and disconnect the connector.

10. Disconnect the air conditioning compressor, HDR sensor and canister purge solenoid.

11. Remove the PCV valve from the camshaft cover and disconnect the canister purge vent hose from the PCV valve.

12. Disconnect the accelerator and cruise control cables from the throttle body. Remove the accelerator cable bracket from the intake manifold and position out of the way.

13. Disconnect the throttle valve cable from the throttle body and the vacuum hose from the throttle body adapter port.

14. Disconnect both oxygen sensors and the heater supply hose.

15. Remove the 2 bolts retaining the thermostat housing to the intake manifold and position the upper hose

and thermostat housing out of the way.

NOTE: The 2 thermostat housing bolts also retain the intake manifold.

16. Remove the bolts retaining the intake manifold to the cylinder heads and remove the intake manifold. Remove and discard the gaskets.

To install:

17. Clean all gasket mating surfaces. Position new intake manifold gaskets on the cylinder heads. Make sure the alignment tabs on the gaskets are aligned with the holes in the cylinder heads.

18. Install the intake manifold and the retaining bolts. Tighten the bolts, in sequence, to 15–22 ft. lbs. (20–30 Nm).

19. Inspect and if necessary, replace the O-ring seal on the thermostat housing. Position the housing and upper hose and install the 2 bolts. Tighten to 15–22 ft. lbs. (20–30 Nm).

20. Connect the heater supply hose and connect both oxygen sensors.

21. Connect the vacuum hose to the throttle body adapter vacuum port. Connect and, if necessary, adjust the throttle valve cable.

22. Install the accelerator cable bracket on the intake manifold and connect the accelerator and cruise control cables to the throttle body.

23. Install the PCV valve in the camshaft cover and connect the canister purge solenoid vent hose. Connect the air conditioning compressor, HDR sensor and canister purge solenoid.

24. Connect the 42-pin engine harness connector. Install the connector on the retaining bracket on the vacuum brake booster.

25. Raise and safely support the vehicle. Connect the EGR tube to the right exhaust manifold and tighten the line nut to 26–33 ft. lbs. (35–45 Nm).

26. Connect the EVO sensor and oil sending unit. Lower the vehicle.

27. Position the generator and install the retaining bolts. Tighten to 15–22 ft. lbs. (20–30 Nm). Install the 2 bolts retaining the generator brace to the intake manifold and tighten to 6.0–8.8 ft. lbs. (8–12 Nm).

28. Connect the generator wiring harness to the generator, right-hand fender apron and junction block.

29. Position the ignition wire assembly on the engine and install the 2 bolts retaining the ignition wire tray to the coil brackets. Tighten the bolts to 6.0–8.8 ft. lbs. (8–12 Nm).

30. Connect the ignition wires to the ignition coils in their proper positions. Connect the ignition wires to the spark plugs.

31. Connect the ignition wire brackets on the camshaft cover studs. Connect both ignition coils and CID sensor.

32. Install the accessory drive belt and the air inlet tube. Install the wiper module and connect the fuel lines.

33. Fill and bleed the cooling system. Connect the negative battery cable, start the engine and check for leaks.

Exhaust Manifold

REMOVAL AND INSTALLATION

4.6L Engine

1. Disconnect the battery cables. Remove the air inlet tube.

2. Drain the cooling system and remove the cooling fan and shroud. Relieve the fuel system pressure and disconnect the fuel lines.

3. Remove the upper radiator hose. Remove the wiper module and support bracket.

4. Discharge the air conditioning system. Disconnect and plug the compressor outlet hose at the compressor and remove the bolt retaining the hose assembly to the right coil bracket. Cap the compressor opening.

5. Remove the 42-pin engine harness connector from the retaining bracket on the brake vacuum booster. Disconnect the connector.

6. Disconnect the throttle valve cable from the throttle body. Disconnect the heater outlet hose.

7. Remove the nut retaining the ground strap to the right cylinder head. Remove the upper stud and lower bolt retaining the heater outlet hose to the right cylinder head and position out of the way.

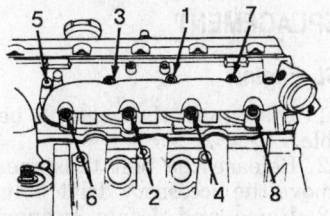

NOTE: ENGINE SHOWN REMOVED FOR CLARITY
NOTE: LH EXHAUST MANIFOLD SHOWN RH EXHAUST MANIFOLD TYPICAL

8470E033

Exhaust manifold torque sequence — 4.6L engine

8. Remove the blower motor resistor and remove the bolt retaining the right engine insulator to the lower engine bracket. Disconnect both oxygen sensors.

9. Raise and safely support the vehicle. Remove the engine mount through bolts.

10. Remove the EGR tube line nut from the right exhaust manifold.

11. Disconnect the exhaust pipes from the manifolds. Lower the exhaust system and hang it from the crossmember with wire.

12. To remove the left exhaust manifold, remove the engine mount from the engine block and remove the 8 bolts retaining the exhaust manifold.

13. Position a jack and a block of wood under the oil pan, rearward of the oil drain hole. Raise the engine approximately 4 in. (100mm).

14. Remove the 8 bolts retaining the right exhaust manifold and remove the manifold.

To install:

15. If the exhaust manifolds are being replaced, transfer the oxygen sensors and tighten to 27–33 ft. lbs. (37–45 Nm). On the right manifold, transfer the EGR tube connector and tighten to 33–48 ft. lbs. (45–65 Nm).

16. Clean the mating surfaces of the exhaust manifolds and cylinder heads.

17. Position the exhaust manifolds to the cylinder heads and install the retaining bolts. Tighten, in sequence, to 15–22 ft. lbs. (20–30 Nm).

18. Position and connect the EGR valve and tube assembly to the exhaust manifold. Tighten the line nut to 26–33 ft. lbs. (35–45 Nm).

19. Install the left engine mount and tighten the bolts to 15–22 ft. lbs. (20–30 Nm). Lower the engine onto the mounts and remove the jack. Install the engine mount through bolts and tighten to 15–22 ft. lbs. (20–30 Nm).

20. Cut the wire and position the exhaust system. Tighten the nuts to 20–30 ft. lbs. (27–41 Nm).

NOTE: Make sure the exhaust system clears the No. 3 crossmember. Adjust as necessary.

21. Lower the vehicle. Connect both oxygen sensors and install the bolt retaining the right engine mount to the frame. Tighten to 15–22 ft. lbs. (20–30 Nm).

22. Install the blower motor resistor. Position the heater outlet hoses. Install the upper stud and lower bolt and tighten to 15–22 ft. lbs. (20–30 Nm). Install the ground strap onto the stud and tighten the nut to 15–22 ft. lbs. (20–30 Nm).

23. Connect the heater outlet hose. Connect and if necessary, adjust the throttle valve cable.

24. Connect the 42-pin connector and transmission harness connector. Install the connector to the retaining bracket on the brake vacuum booster.

25. Connect the air conditioning compressor outlet hose to the compressor and install the bolt retaining the hose assembly to the right coil bracket.

26. Install the upper radiator hose and connect the fuel lines. Install the wiper module and retaining bracket.

27. Install the cooling fan and shroud. Install the air inlet tube. Connect the battery cables, start the engine and check for leaks.

28. Leak test, evacuate and charge the air conditioning system according to the proper procedure. Observe all safety precautions.

Timing Chain Front Cover

REMOVAL AND INSTALLATION

4.6L Engine

1. Disconnect the negative battery cable.

2. Remove the cooling fan and shroud. Loosen the water pump pulley bolts, remove the accessory drive belt and remove the water pump pulley.

3. Raise and safely support the vehicle.

4. Remove the bolts retaining the power steering pump to the engine block and cylinder front cover. The lower front bolt on the power steering pump will not come all the way out. Wire the power steering pump out of the way.

5. Remove the 4 bolts retaining the oil pan to the front cover. Remove the crankshaft damper retaining bolt and washer. Remove the damper using a puller.

6. Lower the vehicle. Remove the bolt retaining the air conditioner high pressure line to the right coil bracket.

7. Remove the front bolts and loosen the remaining bolts on the camshaft covers. Using plastic wedges or similar tools, prop up both camshaft covers. Disconnect both ignition coils and CID sensor.

8. Remove the 3 nuts retaining the right coil bracket to the front cover. Position the power steering hose out of the way.

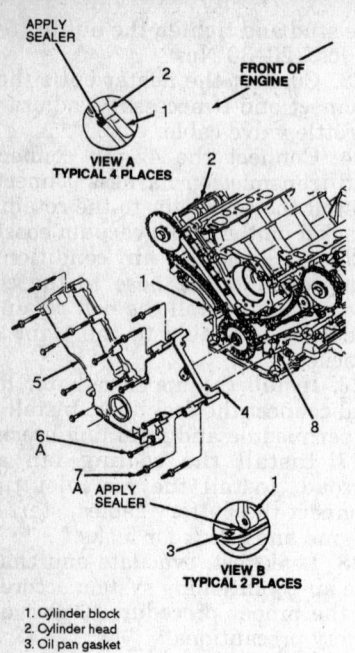

Timing chain front cover installation — 4.6L engine

1. Cylinder block
2. Cylinder head
3. Oil pan gasket
4. Gasket
5. Front cover assembly
6A. Bolts
7A. Studs
8. Dowel

8470E034

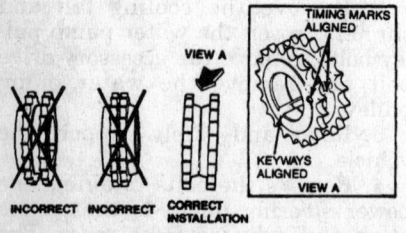

Crankshaft sprocket positioning — 4.6L engine

8470E035

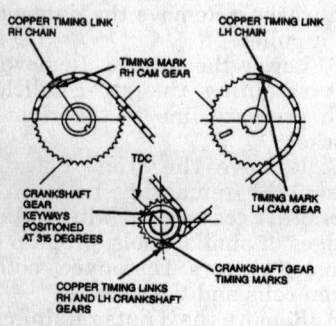

Timing chain and sprocket alignment — 4.6L engine

8470E036

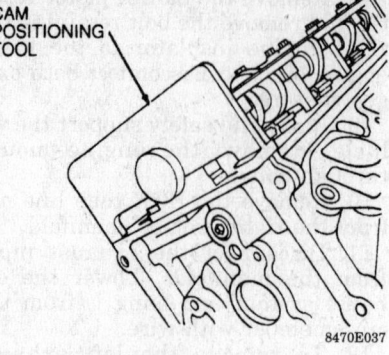

Cam positioning tool — 4.6L engine

8470E037

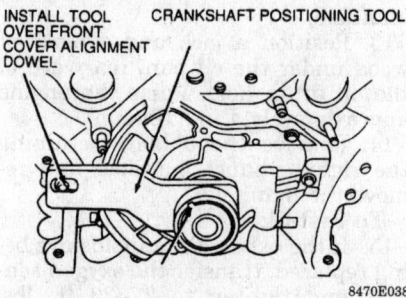

Crankshaft positioning tool — 4.6L engine

8470E038

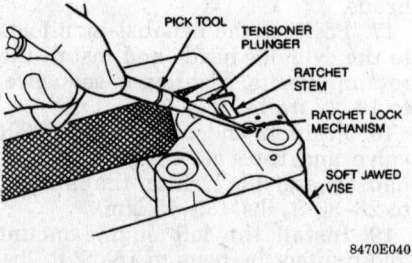

Timing chain tensioner bleeding procedure — 4.6L engine

8470E040

9. Remove the 4 nuts retaining the left coil bracket to the front cover. Slide both coil brackets and ignition wires off the mounting studs and lay the assembly on top of the engine.

10. Disconnect the High Data Rate (HDR) sensor. Remove the 7 stud bolts and 4 bolts retaining the front cover to the engine and remove the front cover.

To install:

11. Inspect and replace the front cover seal as necessary and clean the sealing surfaces of the cylinder block. Apply silicone sealer to the oil pan where it meets the cylinder block and to the points where the cylinder head meets the cylinder block.

12. Install the front cover and the attaching studs and bolts. Tighten to 15–22 ft. lbs. (20–30 Nm). Connect the HDR sensor.

13. Position the coil brackets and ignition wires as an assembly onto the mounting studs. Position the power steering hose and install the 7 nuts retaining the coil brackets to the front cover. Tighten the nuts to 15–22 ft. lbs. (20–30 Nm). Connect both ignition coils and CID sensor.

14. Remove the plastic wedges holding up the camshaft covers. Apply silicone sealer where the front cover meets the cylinder head and make sure the camshaft cover gaskets are properly positioned. Install the front retaining bolts into the camshaft cover and tighten the bolts to 6.0–8.8 ft. lbs. (8–12 Nm).

15. Position the air conditioner high pressure line on the right coil bracket and install the bolt. Raise and safely support the vehicle.

16. Apply a small amount of silicone sealer in the rear of the keyway in the damper. Position the damper on the crankshaft and install, using a suitable installation tool. Install the damper bolt and washer and tighten to 114–121 ft. lbs. (155–165 Nm).

17. Install the 4 bolts retaining the oil pan to the front cover. Tighten to 15–22 ft. lbs. (20–30 Nm).

18. Position the power steering pump on the engine and install the 4 retaining bolts. Tighten to 15–22 ft. lbs. (20–30 Nm). Lower the vehicle.

19. Install the water pump pulley with the 4 bolts. Tighten to 15–22 ft. lbs. (20–30 Nm). Install the accessory drive belt and the cooling fan and shroud.

20. Connect the negative battery cable, start the engine and check for leaks.

Front Cover Oil Seal

REPLACEMENT

4.6L Engine

1. Disconnect the negative battery cable.

2. Release the belt tensioner and remove the accessory drive belt.

3. Raise and safely support the vehicle.

4. Remove the crankshaft damper retaining bolt and washer. Remove the damper using a puller.

5. Using a small prybar, remove the front cover seal.

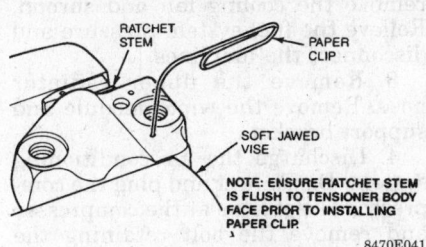

Timing chain tensioner locking procedure — 4.6L engine

To install:

6. Lubricate the seal bore in the front cover and seal lip with clean engine oil. Install the seal, using a seal installer.

7. Apply a small amount of silicone sealer to the rear of the damper keyway. Using a damper installer, install the crankshaft damper. Be sure the key on the crankshaft aligns with the keyway in the damper.

8. Install the crankshaft damper retaining bolt and washer and tighten to 114–121 ft. lbs. (155–165 Nm).

9. Lower the vehicle and install the accessory drive belt.

10. Connect the negative battery cable, start the engine and check for leaks.

Timing Chain and Sprockets

REMOVAL AND INSTALLATION

4.6L Engine

NOTE: This is not a free wheeling engine. If it has "jumped time" there will be damage to the valves and/or pistons and will require the removal of the cylinder heads.

1. Disconnect the negative battery cable.

2. Remove the camshaft covers and the timing chain front cover.

3. Remove the High Data Rate (HDR) wheel.

4. Rotate the engine to set the No. 1 piston at TDC on the compression stroke.

5. Install cam positioning tools T91P–6256–A or equivalent, on the flats of the camshaft. This will prevent accidental rotation of the camshafts.

6. Remove the 2 bolts retaining the right tensioner to the cylinder head and remove the tensioner. Remove the right tensioner arm.

7. Remove the 2 bolts retaining the right chain guide to the cylinder head and remove the chain guide. Remove the right chain and right crankshaft sprocket. Remove the right camshaft sprocket retaining bolt, washer, sprocket and spacer.

NOTE: Cam positioning tools T91P–6256–A or equivalent, must be installed on the camshaft to prevent the camshaft from rotating.

8. Remove the 2 bolts retaining the left tensioner to the cylinder head and remove the tensioner. Remove the left tensioner arm.

9. Remove the 2 bolts retaining the left chain guide to the cylinder head and remove the chain guide. Remove the left chain and left crankshaft sprocket. Remove the left camshaft sprocket retaining bolt, washer, sprocket and spacer.

NOTE: Cam positioning tools T91P–6256–A or equivalent, must be installed on the camshaft to prevent the camshaft from rotating.

10. Inspect the friction material on the tensioner arms and chain guides. If worn or damaged, remove and clean the oil pan and replace the oil pickup tube.

NOTE: At no time, when the timing chains are removed and the cylinder heads are installed, may the crankshaft and/or camshafts be rotated. Failure to follow these directions will result in valve and/or piston damage.

To install:

11. Make sure cam positioning tools T91P–6256–A or equivalent, are installed on the camshafts to prevent them from rotating.

12. Position the camshaft spacers and sprockets on the camshafts and install the washers and retaining bolts. Tighten the retaining bolts to 81–95 ft. lbs. (110–130 Nm).

13. Install the left crankshaft sprocket with the tapered part of the sprocket facing away from the engine block.

NOTE: The crankshaft sprockets are identical. They may only be installed one way, with the tapered part of the sprocket facing each other.

14. Install the left timing chain on the camshaft and crankshaft sprockets. Make sure the copper links of the chain line up with the timing marks of the sprockets.

NOTE: If the copper links of the timing chain are not visible, pull the chain taught until the opposite sides of the chain contact one another and lay it on a flat surface. Mark the links at each end of the chain and use them in place of the copper links.

15. Install the right crankshaft sprocket with the tapered part of the sprocket facing the left crankshaft sprocket.

16. Install the right timing chain on the camshaft and crankshaft sprockets. Make sure the copper links of the chain line up with the timing marks of the sprockets.

17. It is necessary to bleed the timing chain tensioners before installation. Proceed as follows:

   a. Position the timing chain tensioner in a soft-jawed vice.

   b. Using a small pick or similar tool, hold the ratchet lock mechanism away from the ratchet stem and slowly compress the tensioner plunger by rotating the vise handle.

NOTE: The tensioner must be compressed slowly or damage to the internal seals will result.

   c. Once the tensioner plunger bottoms in the tensioner bore, continue to hold the ratchet lock mechanism and push down on the ratchet stem until flush with the tensioner face.

   d. While holding the ratchet stem flush to the tensioner face, release the ratchet lock mechanism and install a paper clip or similar tool in the tensioner body to lock the tensioner in the collapsed position.

   e. The paper clip must not be removed until the timing chain, tensioner, tensioner arm and timing chain guide are completely installed on the engine.

18. Lubricate the tensioner arm contact surfaces with engine oil and install the right and left tensioner arms on their dowels.

19. Install the right and left timing chain tensioners and secure with 2 bolts on each. Tighten the bolts to 15–22 ft. lbs. (20–30 Nm).

20. Install the right and left timing chain guides and secure with 2 bolts on each. Tighten the bolts to 6.0–8.8 ft. lbs. (8–12 Nm).

21. Remove the paper clips from the timing chain tensioners and make sure all timing marks are aligned.

22. Remove the camshaft positioning tools.

23. Installation of the remaining components is the reverse of removal.

24. Connect the negative battery cable, start the engine and check for leaks and proper operation.

Camshaft

REMOVAL AND INSTALLATION

4.6L Engine

1. Disconnect the negative battery cable and drain the cooling system. Relieve the fuel system pressure.

2. Remove the right and left camshaft covers.

3. Remove the timing chain front cover. Remove the timing chains.

4. Rotate the crankshaft counterclockwise 45 degrees from TDC to make sure all pistons are below the top of the engine block deck face.

NOTE: The crankshaft must be in this position prior to rotating the camshafts or damage to the pistons and/or valve train will result.

5. Install valve spring compressor tool T91P–6565–A or equivalent, under the camshaft and on top of the valve spring retainer.

NOTE: Valve spring spacer tool T91P–6565–AH or equivalent, must be installed between the spring coils and the camshaft must be at the base circle before compressing the valve spring.

6. Compress the valve spring far enough to remove the roller follower. Repeat Steps 5 and 6 until all roller followers are removed.

7. Remove the bolts retaining the camshaft cap cluster assemblies to the cylinder heads. Tap upward on the camshaft caps at points near the upper bearing halves and gradually lift the camshaft clusters from the cylinder heads.

8. Remove the camshafts straight upward to avoid bearing damage.

To install:

9. Apply heavy engine oil to the camshaft journals and lobes. Position the camshafts on the cylinder heads.

10. Install and seat the camshaft cap cluster assemblies. Hand start the bolts.

11. Tighten the camshaft cluster retaining bolts in sequence to 6.0–8.8 ft. lbs. (8–12 Nm).

NOTE: Each camshaft cap cluster assembly is tightened individually.

12. Loosen the camshaft cap cluster retaining bolts approximately 2 turns or until the heads of the bolts are free. Retighten all bolts, in sequence, to 6.0–8.8 ft. lbs. (8–12 Nm).

NOTE: The camshafts should turn freely with a slight drag.

13. Install cam positioning tools T91P–6256–A or equivalent, on the flats of the camshafts and install the spacers and camshaft sprockets. Install the bolts and washers and tighten to 81–95 ft. lbs. (110–130 Nm).

14. Install valve spring compressor T91P–6565–A or equivalent, under the camshaft and on top of the valve spring retainer.

NOTE: Valve spring spacer tool T91P–6565–AH or equivalent, must be installed between the spring coils and the camshaft must be at the base circle before compressing the valve spring.

15. Compress the valve spring far enough to install the roller followers.

16. Repeat Steps 14 and 15 until all roller followers are installed.

17. Rotate the crankshaft clockwise 45 degrees to position the crankshaft at TDC.

NOTE: The crankshaft must only be rotated in the clockwise direction and only as far as TDC.

18. Install the timing chains and install the timing chain front cover. Install the camshaft covers.

19. Install the remaining components in the reverse order of removal.

20. Connect the negative battery cable. Start the engine and check for leaks.

Piston and Connecting Rod

POSITIONING

ENGINE LUBRICATION

Oil Pan

REMOVAL AND INSTALLATION

4.6L Engine

1. Disconnect the battery cables and remove the air inlet tube.

2. Drain the cooling system and remove the cooling fan and shroud. Relieve the fuel system pressure and disconnect the fuel lines.

3. Remove the upper radiator hose. Remove the wiper module and support bracket.

4. Discharge the air conditioning system. Disconnect and plug the compressor outlet hose at the compressor and remove the bolt retaining the hose assembly to the right coil bracket. Cap the compressor outlet.

5. Remove the 42-pin engine harness connector from the retaining bracket on the brake vacuum booster and disconnect the connector and transmission harness connector.

6. Disconnect the throttle valve cable from the throttle body and disconnect the heater outlet hose.

7. Remove the nut retaining the ground strap to the right cylinder head. Remove the upper stud and loosen the lower bolt retaining the heater outlet hose to the right cylinder head and position out of the way.

8. Remove the blower motor resistor. Remove the bolt retaining the right engine mount to the lower engine bracket.

9. Disconnect the vacuum hoses from the EGR valve and tube. Remove the 2 bolts retaining the EGR valve to the intake manifold.

10. Raise and safely support the vehicle. Drain the crankcase and remove the engine mount through bolts.

11. Remove the EGR tube line nut from the right exhaust manifold and remove the EGR valve and tube assembly.

12. Disconnect the exhaust from the exhaust manifolds. Lower the exhaust system and support it with wire from the crossmember.

13. Position a jack and a block of wood under the oil pan, rearward of the oil drain hole. Raise the engine approximately 4 in. and insert 2 wood blocks approximately 2½ in. thick under each engine mount. Lower the engine onto the wood blocks and remove the jack.

14. Remove the 16 bolts retaining the oil pan to the engine block and remove the oil pan.

NOTE: It may be necessary to loosen, but not remove, the 2 nuts on the rear transmission mount and with a jack, raise the transmission extension housing slightly to remove the pan.

To install:

15. Clean the oil pan and the gasket mating surfaces.

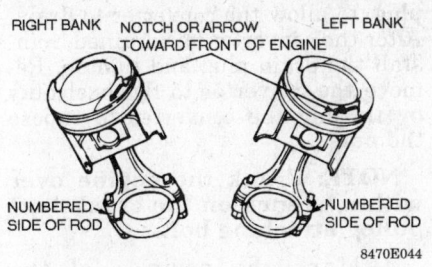

Piston position — 8 cylinder engine.

RIGHT BANK   NOTCH OR ARROW TOWARD FRONT OF ENGINE   LEFT BANK

NUMBERED SIDE OF ROD

NUMBERED SIDE OF ROD

8470E044

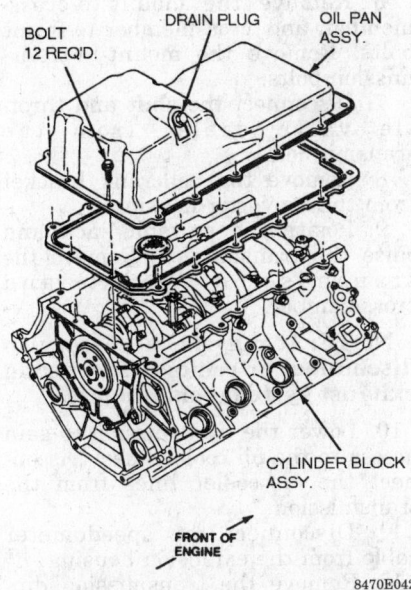

BOLT 12 REQ'D.   DRAIN PLUG   OIL PAN ASSY.

CYLINDER BLOCK ASSY.

FRONT OF ENGINE

Oil pan replacement — 4.6L engine

8470E042

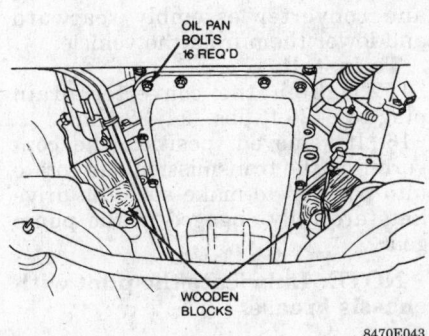

OIL PAN BOLTS 16 REQ'D

WOODEN BLOCKS

8470E043

Supporting engine on blocks for pan removal

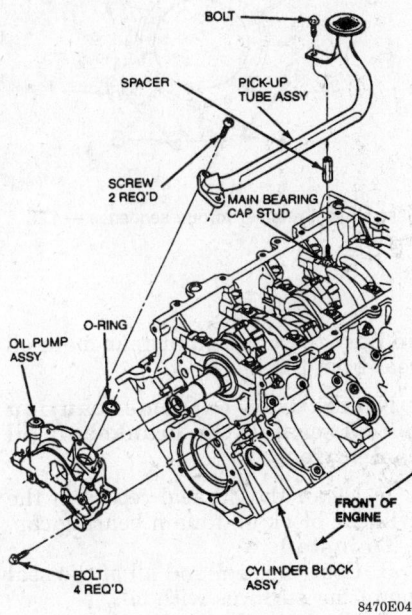

BOLT

SPACER   PICK-UP TUBE ASSY

SCREW 2 REQ'D   MAIN BEARING CAP STUD

O-RING

OIL PUMP ASSY

FRONT OF ENGINE

BOLT 4 REQ'D   CYLINDER BLOCK ASSY

8470E045

Oil pump — 4.6L engine

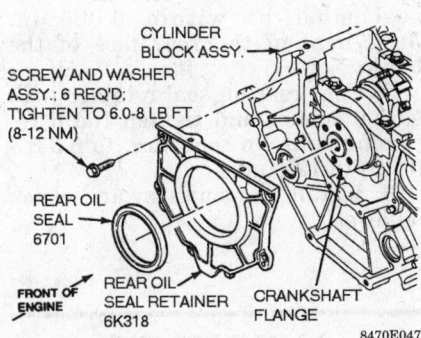

CYLINDER BLOCK ASSY.

SCREW AND WASHER ASSY.; 6 REQ'D; TIGHTEN TO 6.0-8 LB FT (8-12 NM)

REAR OIL SEAL 6701

FRONT OF ENGINE   REAR OIL SEAL RETAINER 6K318   CRANKSHAFT FLANGE

8470E047

Rear oil seal replacement — 4.6L engine

16. Position a new gasket on the oil pan. Apply silicone sealer to where the front cover meets the cylinder block and rear seal retainer meets the cylinder block. Position the oil pan on the engine and install the bolts. Tighten the bolts, in sequence, to 15–22 ft. lbs. (20–30 Nm).

17. Position the jack and wood block under the oil pan, rearward of the oil drain hole and raise the engine enough to remove the wood blocks. Lower the engine and remove the jack.

18. Install the engine mount through bolts and tighten to 15–22 ft. lbs. (20–30 Nm).

19. Position the EGR valve and tube assembly in the vehicle and connect to the exhaust manifold. Tighten the line nut to 26–33 ft. lbs. (35–45 Nm).

NOTE: Loosen the line nut at the EGR valve prior to installing the assembly into the vehicle. This will allow enough movement to align the EGR valve retaining bolts.

20. Cut the wire and position the exhaust system to the manifolds. Install the 4 nuts and tighten to 20–30 ft. lbs. (27–41 Nm). Make sure the exhaust system clears the crossmember. Adjust as necessary.

21. Install a new oil filter and lower the vehicle.

22. Install the bolt retaining the right engine mount to the lower engine bracket. Tighten to 15–22 ft. lbs. (20–30 Nm).

23. Install a new gasket on the EGR valve and position on the intake manifold. Install the 2 bolts retaining the EGR valve to the intake manifold and tighten to 15–22 ft. lbs. (20–30 Nm). Tighten the EGR tube line nut at the EGR valve to 26–33 ft. lbs. (35–45 Nm). Connect the vacuum hoses to the EGR valve and tube.

24. Install the blower motor resistor. Position the heater outlet hose, install the upper stud and tighten the upper and lower bolts to 15–22 ft. lbs. (20–30 Nm). Install the ground strap on the stud and tighten to 15–22 ft. lbs. (20–30 Nm).

25. Connect the heater outlet hose and the throttle valve cable. If necessary, adjust the throttle valve cable.

26. Connect the 42-pin connector and transmission harness connector. Install the harness connector on the brake vacuum booster.

27. Connect the air conditioning compressor outlet hose to the compressor and install the bolt retaining the hose to the right coil bracket.

28. Install the upper radiator hose and connect the fuel lines. Install the wiper module and retaining bracket.

29. Install the cooling fan and shroud and fill the cooling system. Fill the crankcase with the proper type and quantity of engine oil.

30. Connect the negative battery cable and install the air inlet tube. Start the engine and check for leaks.

31. Evacuate and recharge the air conditioning system.

Oil Pump

REMOVAL AND INSTALLATION

4.6L Engine

1. Disconnect the negative battery cable.
2. Remove the camshaft covers, front cover, and oil pan.
3. Remove the timing chains.
4. Remove the 4 bolts retaining the oil pump to the cylinder block and remove the pump.
5. Remove the 2 bolts retaining the oil pickup tube to the oil pump and remove the bolt retaining the oil pickup tube to the main bearing stud spacer. Remove the pickup tube.

To install:

6. Clean the oil pickup tube and replace the O-ring.
7. Position the tube on the oil pump and hand-start the 2 bolts. Install the bolt retaining the pickup tube to the main bearing stud spacer hand-tight.
8. Tighten the pickup tube-to-oil pump bolts to 6.0–8.8 ft. lbs. (8–12 Nm). Tighten the pickup tube to main bearing stud spacer bolt to 15–22 ft. lbs. (20–30 Nm).
9. Rotate the inner rotor of the oil pump to align with the flats on the crankshaft and install the oil pump flush with the cylinder block. Install the 4 retaining bolts and tighten to 6.0–8.8 ft. lbs. (8–12 Nm).
10. Install a new oil filter. Install the timing chains.
11. Install the oil pan, front cover and camshaft covers.
12. Fill the crankcase with the proper type and quantity of engine oil. Connect the negative battery cable, start the engine and check for leaks.

Rear Main Bearing Oil Seal

REMOVAL AND INSTALLATION

1. Disconnect the negative battery cable.
2. Remove the transmission and flywheel.
3. Remove the rear oil seal retainer from the block.
4. Punch 2 holes in the crankshaft rear oil seal on opposite sides of the crankshaft, just above the bearing cap to cylinder block split line. Install a sheetmetal screw in each of the holes or use a small slide hammer

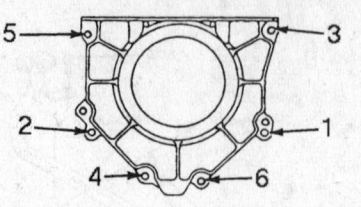

8470E048

Rear oil seal retainer torque sequence — 4.6L engine

and pry the crankshaft rear main oil seal from the block.

NOTE: Use extreme caution not to scratch the crankshaft oil seal surface.

5. Clean the oil seal recess in the cylinder block and main bearing cap.

To install:

6. Coat the seal and all of the seal mounting surfaces with oil.
7. Position the seal on rear main seal installer T82L–6701–A or equivalent, and position the tool and seal to the rear of the engine.
8. Alternate bolt tightening to seat the seal properly. The rear face of the seal must be within 0.005 in. (0.127mm) of the rear face of the block.
9. Coat rear oil seal retainer with gasket maker and tighten the 6 retaining bolts, in sequence, to 6.0–8.8 ft. lbs (8–12 Nm).
10. Install transmission and check oil level.

AUTOMATIC TRANSMISSION

Transmission Assembly

REMOVAL AND INSTALLATION

1. Disconnect the negative battery cable. Raise the vehicle and support safely.
2. Drain the fluid from the transmission by removing all oil pan bolts except the 2 at the front. Loosen the 2 at the front and drop the oil pan at the rear to allow the fluid to drain into a container. When drained, reinstall a few of the bolts to hold the pan in place.

3. Remove the converter bottom cover and remove the converter drain plug, to allow the converter to drain. After the converter has drained, reinstall the drain plug and tighten. Remove the converter to flywheel nuts by turning the converter to expose the nuts.

NOTE: Crank the engine over with a wrench on the crankshaft pulley attaching bolt.

4. Mark the position of the driveshaft on the rear axle flange and remove the driveshaft. Install a suitable plug in the transmission extension housing to prevent fluid leakage.
5. Disconnect the starter cable and remove the starter. Disconnect the wiring from the neutral safety switch.
6. Remove the mount-to-crossmember and crossmember-to-frame bolts. Remove the mount-to-transmission bolts.
7. Disconnect the shift and throttle valve cables from the transmission.
8. Remove the bellcrank bracket from the converter housing.
9. Position a suitable jack and raise the transmission. Remove the transmission mount and crossmember.

NOTE: It may be necessary to disconnect or remove interfering exhaust system components.

10. Lower the transmission to gain access to the oil cooler lines. Disconnect the oil cooler lines from the transmission.
11. Disconnect the speedometer cable from the extension housing.
12. Remove the transmission dipstick tube-to-engine block retaining bolt and remove the tube and dipstick from the transmission.
13. Secure the transmission to the jack with a chain and remove the transmission-to-engine bolts.
14. Carefully pull the transmission and converter assembly rearward and lower them from the vehicle.

To install:

15. Tighten the converter drain plug to 8–28 ft. lbs. (11–38 Nm).
16. If removed, position the converter on the transmission and rotate into position to make sure the drive flats are fully engaged in the pump gear.

NOTE: Lubricate the pilot with chassis grease.

17. Raise the converter and transmission assembly into position. Rotate the converter until the studs and drain plug are in alignment with the

holes in the flywheel. Align the orange balancing marks on the converter stud and flywheel bolt hole if balancing marks are present.

NOTE: The converter face must rest squarely against the flywheel. This indicates that the converter pilot is not binding in the engine crankshaft. To ensure the converter is properly seated, grasp a converter stud. It should move freely back and forth in the flywheel hole. If the converter will not move, the transmission must be removed and the converter repositioned so the impeller hub is properly engaged in the pump gear.

18. Install the transmission-to-engine attaching bolts. Tighten the bolts to 40–50 ft. lbs. (55–68 Nm).
19. Remove the safety chain from around the transmission.
20. Install a new O-ring on the lower end of the transmission dipstick tube and install the tube to the transmission case.
21. Connect the speedometer cable to the transmission case.
22. Connect the oil cooler lines to the right side of the transmission case.
23. Position the crossmember on the side supports. Position the rear mount on the crossmember and install the attaching bolt/nut.
24. Secure the engine rear support to the transmission extension housing.
25. Install any exhaust system components, if removed.
26. Lower the transmission and remove the jack.
27. Secure the crossmember to the side supports with the attaching bolts.
28. Connect the TV linkage and the manual linkage rod. Connect the shift cable.
29. Install the converter to flywheel attaching nuts and tighten to 20–34 ft. lbs. (27–46 Nm). Install the converter housing cover.
30. Secure the starter motor in place and connect all electrical connections.
31. Install the driveshaft, aligning the marks that were made during removal.
32. Lower the vehicle. Fill the transmission with the proper type and quantity of fluid, start the engine and check the transmission for leakage. Adjust the linkage as required.

MANUAL LINKAGE ADJUSTMENT

1. From the passenger compartment, place the steering column selector lever in **OVERDRIVE** and hold the selector lever in position by placing a 3 lb. weight on the lever.
2. Place a prybar in the slot of the slide adjuster to open the adjuster.
3. Move transmission manual shift lever to **OVERDRIVE** position, 2nd. detent from most rearward position.
4. Push slide adjuster closed.
5. Check the shift lever for proper operation. Ensure that park/neutral start switch are functioning properly.

THROTTLE VALVE CABLE ADJUSTMENT

Automatic Overdrive Transmission

1. Set the parking brake and place the shift selector in **N**.
2. Remove the air cleaner cover and inlet tube from the throttle body inlet to access the throttle lever and cable.
3. Using a small prybar, pry the grooved pin on the cable assembly out of the grommet on the throttle body lever. Push out the white locking tab.
4. Check the plastic block with pin and tab; it should slide freely on the notched rod. If not, the white tab may not be pushed out far enough.
5. While holding the throttle lever firmly against the idle stop, push the grooved pin into the grommet on the throttle lever as far as it will go.
6. Make sure the throttle lever does not move while pushing the pin into the grommet.
7. Install the air cleaner cover and inlet tube.

DRIVE AXLE

Driveshafts and U-Joints

REMOVAL AND INSTALLATION

1. Raise and safely support the vehicle. Mark the position of the driveshaft yoke on the axle companion flange so they can be reassembled in the same way to maintain balance.
2. Remove the flange bolts and disconnect the driveshaft from the axle companion flange.

3. Allow the rear of the driveshaft to drop slightly. Pull the driveshaft and slip yoke out of the transmission extension housing.
4. Plug the transmission to prevent fluid leakage.
5. Place driveshaft on a suitable workbench with a vise.
6. Prior to disassembly, mark the positions of the driveshaft components relative to the driveshaft tube. All components must be reassembled in the same relationship to maintain proper balance.
7. Using a U-joint C–clamp mounted in the vise, press out one side bearing cup. Rotate the driveshaft 180 degrees and press out bearing cap.
8. Remove slip yoke from the U-joint. Remove remaining bearing cups in the same manner.
9. Clean all foreign matter from the yoke areas of the driveshaft.
   To install:
10. Start a new bearing cup into the yoke of the driveshaft
11. Position the new U-joint in the driveshaft yoke and press the bearing cup ¼ in. (6.3mm) below the yoke surface with the C– clamp and install a new snapring.
12. Start a new bearing cup into the opposite side of the yoke. Check needles for proper position.
13. Position driveshaft in C–clamp and press the cup until the opposite cup contacts the snapring. Install snapring. Tap yoke with plastic hammer to seat the snaprings.
14. Lubricate the yoke splines and install the yoke into the transmission extension housing, aligning the splines. Be careful not to bottom the slip yoke hard against the transmission seal.
15. Rotate the axle flange, as necessary, to align the marks made during removal. Install the driveshaft yoke to the axle flange. Install the bolts and tighten to 71–95 ft. lbs. (95–130 Nm).

Rear Axle Shaft, Bearing and Seal

REMOVAL AND INSTALLATION

1. Raise and safely support the vehicle. Remove wheel and tire assembly and remove brake drum or brake rotor.
2. If equipped, remove the anti-lock brake speed sensor.
3. Clean all dirt from the area of the carrier cover. Drain the axle lu-

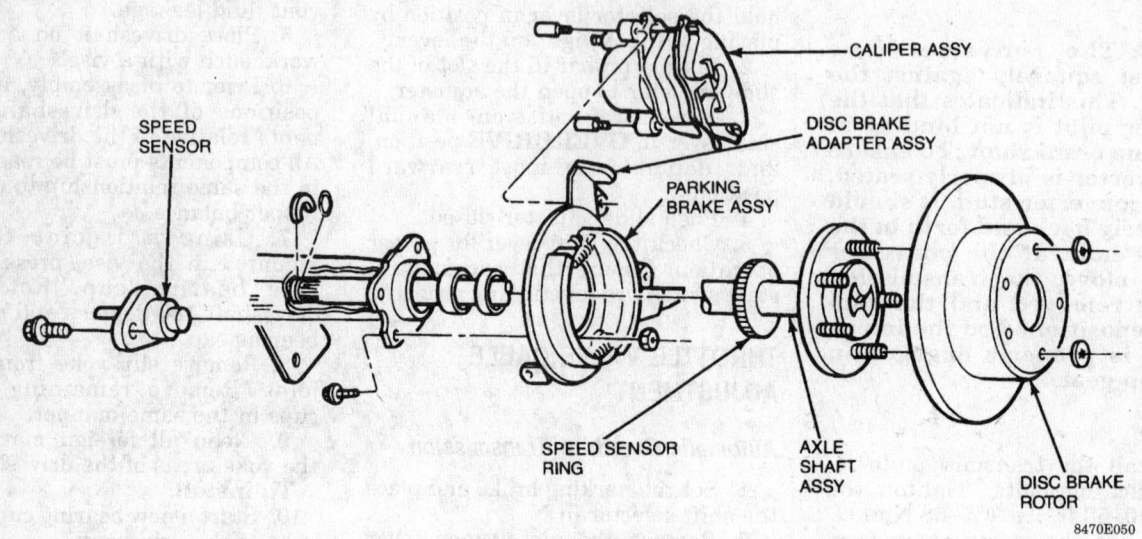

SPEED SENSOR

CALIPER ASSY

DISC BRAKE ADAPTER ASSY

PARKING BRAKE ASSY

SPEED SENSOR RING

AXLE SHAFT ASSY

DISC BRAKE ROTOR

8470E050

Axle shaft exploded view

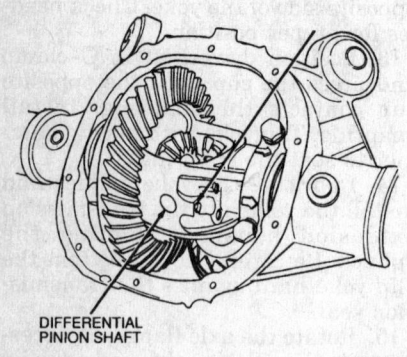

DIFFERENTIAL PINION SHAFT

8470E051

Removal of differential pinion shaft

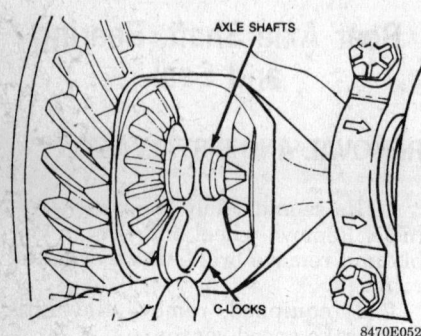

AXLE SHAFTS

C-LOCKS

8470E052

Removing axle shaft C-lock clips

bricant by removing the housing cover.

4. Remove differential pinion shaft lock bolt and pinion shaft.

5. Push flanged end of axle shafts toward the center of the vehicle and remove the C-lock from button end of the axle shaft. Remove the axle shaft from the housing, being careful not to damage the oil seal.

6. Insert wheel bearing and seal replacer tool T85L–1225–AH or equivalent, in the bore and position it behind the bearing so the tangs on the tool engage the bearing outer race. Remove bearing and seal as a unit using an impact slide hammer.

To install:

7. Lubricate the new bearing with rear axle lubricant. Install the bearing into the housing bore using a suitable bearing installer.

8. Install a new axle seal using a seal installer.

NOTE: Check for the presence of an axle shaft O-ring on the spline end of the shaft and install, if not present.

9. Carefully slide the axle shaft into the axle housing, without damaging the bearing or seal assembly. Start the splines into the side gear and push firmly until the button end

of the axle shaft can be seen in the differential case.

10. Install the C-lock on the button end of the axle shaft splines, then push the shaft outboard until the shaft splines engage and the C-lock seats in the counterbore of the differential side gear.

11. Insert the differential pinion shaft through the case and pinion gears, aligning the hole in the shaft with the lock bolt hole. Apply locking compound to the lock bolt and install in the case and pinion shaft. Tighten to 15–30 ft. lbs. (20–41 Nm).

12. Cover the inside of the differential case with a shop rag and clean the machined surface of the carrier and cover. Remove the shop rag.

13. Apply a bead of silicone sealer to the cover and install on the carrier. Tighten the bolts in a criss-cross pattern. Final torque the cover retaining bolts to 25–35 ft. lbs. (34–47 Nm).

14. Add rear axle lubricant to the carrier to a level 1/4–9/16 in. below the bottom of the fill hole. If equipped with limited slip, add friction modifier C8AZ–19B564–A or equivalent. Install the filler plug and tighten to 15–30 ft. lbs. (20–41 Nm).

15. Install the anti-lock speed sensor, if equipped. Tighten the retaining bolt to 40–60 inch lbs. (4.5–6.8 Nm).

16. Install the brake calipers and rotors or the brake drums, as required. Install the wheel and tire assembly and lower the vehicle.

Pinion Seal

REMOVAL AND INSTALLATION

1. Raise and safely support the vehicle. Mark the position of the driveshaft yoke on the axle companion flange so they may be reassembled in the same way to maintain balance.
2. Disconnect the driveshaft from the rear axle companion flange, remove the driveshaft and remove the driveshaft from the extension housing. Plug the extension housing to prevent leakage.
3. Install an inch pound torque wrench on the pinion nut and record the torque required to maintain rotation of the pinion through several revolutions.
4. While holding the companion flange with holder tool T78P–4851–A or equivalent, remove the pinion nut.
5. Clean the area around the oil seal and place a pan under the seal.
6. Mark the companion flange in relation to the pinion shaft so the flange can be installed in the same position.
7. Remove the rear axle companion flange using tool T65L–4851–B or equivalent.
8. Pry the seal out of the housing using a prybar.
To install:
9. Clean the oil seal seat surface and install the seal in the carrier using seal replacer tool T79P–4676–A or equivalent. Apply lubricant to the lips of the seal.
10. Apply a small amount of lubricant to the companion flange splines, align the marks on the flange and and the pinion shaft and install the flange.
11. Install a new nut on the pinion shaft and apply lubricant on the washer side of the nut.
12. Hold the flange with the holder tool while tightening the nut. Rotate the pinion to ensure proper seating and take frequent pinion bearing torque preload readings until the original recorded preload reading is obtained.
13. If the original recorded preload is less than 8–14 inch lbs. (0.9–1.6 Nm), then tighten the nut to 8–14 inch lbs. (0.9–1.6 Nm). If the original preload is higher than 8–14 inch lbs.

(0.9–1.6 Nm), tighten to the original recorded preload.

NOTE: Under no circumstances should the pinion nut be backed off to reduce preload. If reduced preload is required, a new collapsible pinion spacer and pinion nut should be installed.

14. Remove the plug from the transmission extension housing and install the front end of the driveshaft on the transmission output shaft.
15. Connect the rear end of the driveshaft to the axle companion flange, aligning the scribe marks. Tighten the 4 bolts to 71–95 ft. lbs. (95–130 Nm).
16. Add lubricant to the axle until it is 1/4–9/16 in. below the bottom of the fill hole with the axle in operating position. If equipped with limited slip, add friction modifier C8AZ–19B564–A or equivalent.
17. Make sure the axle vent is not plugged with debris.

Axle Housing

REMOVAL AND INSTALLATION

1. Raise and safely support the vehicle. If equipped, turn the air suspension switch **OFF**. Position safety stands under the rear frame crossmember.
2. Remove the cover and drain the axle lubricant.
3. Remove the wheel and tire assemblies. Remove the brake drums or brake rotors.
4. Remove the lock bolt from the pinion shaft and remove the shaft.
5. Remove the anti-lock brake sensor before removing the axle shafts, if equipped.
6. Push the axle shafts inward to remove the C-locks and remove the axle shafts.
7. If equipped with drum brakes, remove the 4 retaining nuts from each backing plate and wire the backing plate to the underbody.
8. If equipped with disc brakes, remove the disc brake adapter bracket, bolts and J-nuts. Remove the 4 retaining nuts from each adapter and wire the adapters to the underbody.
9. Mark the position of the driveshaft yoke on the axle companion flange. Disconnect the driveshaft at the companion flange and wire it to the underbody.
10. Support the axle housing with jackstands. Disengage the brake line

from the clips that retain the line to the axle housing.
11. Disconnect the vent from the rear axle housing.
12. If equipped with air springs, proceed as follows:
   a. Disconnect the negative battery cable. Make sure the air suspension switch, located in the trunk, is **OFF**.
   b. Remove the heat shield and spring retainer clip from the top of the air spring.
   c. Disconnect the electrical connector and the air line from the air spring solenoid, located on the air spring.
   d. Remove the solenoid clip and rotate the solenoid counterclockwise to the first stop.
   e. Pull the solenoid straight out slowly to the 2nd stop to bleed the air from the system.

—— CAUTION ——
Do not fully release the solenoid until the air is completely bled from the air spring or personal injury may result.

   f. After the air is fully bled from the system, rotate the solenoid counterclockwise to the 3rd stop and remove the solenoid from the solenoid housing.
   g. Insert air spring removal tool T90P–5310–A or equivalent, between the axle tube and spring seat on the forward side of the axle.
   h. Position the tool so its flat end rests on the piston knob. Push downward, forcing the piston and retainer clip off the axle spring seat.
   i. Remove the air spring.
13. Disconnect the lower shock absorber studs from the mounting brackets on the axle housing.
14. Disconnect the upper arms from the mountings on the axle housing ear brackets.
15. Lower the axle housing assembly until the springs are released and lift out the springs.
16. Disconnect the suspension lower arms at the axle housing.
17. Lower the axle housing and remove it from the vehicle.
To install:
18. Position the axle housing under the vehicle and raise the axle with a hoist or jack. Connect the lower suspension arms to their mounting brackets on the axle housing. Do not tighten the bolts and nuts at this time.
19. Reposition the rear springs.
20. Raise the housing into position.

21. Connect the upper arms to the mounting ears on the housing. Tighten the nuts and bolts to 103–133 ft. lbs. (140–180 Nm). Tighten the lower arm bolts and nuts to 103–133 ft. lbs. (140–180 Nm).

22. Install the axle vent and install the brake line to the clips that retain the line to the axle housing. If equipped with air springs, proceed as follows:

a. Check the solenoid O-rings for damage and replace, as required. Lightly grease the O-ring area of the solenoid and the larger solenoid housing O-ring with silicone dielectric compound.

b. Insert the solenoid into the air spring end cap and rotate clockwise to the 3rd stop, push in to the 2nd stop, then rotate clockwise to the 1st stop.

c. Install the solenoid clip. Connect the air line and the electrical connector.

d. Install the air spring into the frame spring seat. Connect the spring retainer clip to the knob of the spring cap from the top side of the frame spring seat.

e. Align the air spring piston with the axle seats. Squeeze to increase pressure and push downward on the piston, snapping the piston to the axle seat.

23. If equipped with drum brakes, install the brake backing plates on the axle housing flanges. If equipped with disc brakes, install the disc brake adapters and tighten the nuts to 20–29 ft. lbs. (27–40 Nm). Install the disc brake adapter brackets, bolts and J-nuts. Tighten to 20–39 ft. lbs. (27–54 Nm).

24. Connect the lower shock absorber studs to the mounting bracket on the axle housing.

25. Connect the driveshaft to the companion flange and tighten the bolts and nuts to 70–95 ft. lbs. (95–130 Nm).

26. Slide the rear axle shafts into the housing until the splines enter the side gear. Push the axle shafts inward and install the C-lock at the end of each shaft spline. Pull the shafts outboard until the C-lock enters the recess in the side gears.

27. Install the pinion shaft. Apply locking compound to the pinion shaft lock bolt. Install and tighten to 15–30 ft. lbs. (20–41 Nm).

28. Install the anti-lock sensor, if equipped.

29. Install the rear brake drums or disc brake rotors and calipers.

30. Install the rear carrier cover using new silicone sealer. Tighten to 25–35 ft. lbs. (34–47 Nm).

31. Add rear axle lubricant to the carrier to a level ¼–⁹⁄₁₆ in. below the bottom of the fill hole. If equipped with limited slip, add friction modifier C8AZ–19B564–A or equivalent. Install the filler plug and tighten to 15–30 ft. lbs. (20–41 Nm).

32. If equipped, fill the air springs as follows before lowering the vehicle:

a. Turn the air suspension switch ON. The ignition switch must be ON and the engine running or a battery charger must be connected to the battery to reduce battery drain.

b. Remove the right luggage compartment trim panel and connect Super Star II tester 007–0041–A or equivalent to the air suspension diagnostic connector.

c. Set the tester to EEC-IV/MCU mode. Also set the tester to FAST mode. Release the tester button to the HOLD (up) position and turn the tester ON.

d. Depress the tester button to TEST (down) position. A Code 10 will be displayed. Within 2 minutes a Code 13 will be displayed. After Code 13 is displayed, release the tester button to HOLD (up) position, wait 5 seconds and depress the tester button to TEST (down) position. Ignore any codes displayed.

e. Release the tester button to the HOLD (up) position. Wait at least 20 seconds, then depress the tester button to TEST (down) position. Within 10 seconds, the following codes will be displayed in the order shown.

f. Within 4 seconds after Code 26 is displayed, release the tester button to the HOLD (up) position. Waiting longer than 4 seconds may result in Functional Test 31 being entered. The compressor will fill the air springs with air as long as the tester button is in the HOLD (up) position. To stop filling the air springs, depress the tester button to the TEST (down) position.

NOTE: It is possible to overheat the compressor during this operation. If the compressor overheats, the self-resetting circuit breaker in the compressor will open and remain open for about 15 minutes. This allows the compressor to cool down.

g. To exit Functional Test 26, disconnect the tester and turn the ignition switch OFF.

33. Lower the vehicle.

STEERING

Steering Wheel

— CAUTION —

If equipped with an air bag, the air bag system must be disarmed, before working on the system. Failure to do so may result in deployment of the air bag and possible personal injury.

REMOVAL AND INSTALLATION

With Air Bag

1. Center the front wheels in the straight-ahead position.

2. Disarm the air bag system as follows:

a. Disconnect the positive battery cable. Wait 1 minute for the backup power supply in the diagnostic monitor to deplete its stored energy.

b. Remove the 4 nut and washer assemblies retaining the driver air bag module to the steering wheel and remove the air bag module.

— CAUTION —

When carrying a live air bag, make sure the bag and trim cover are pointed away from the body. In the unlikely event of an accidental deployment, the bag will then deploy with minimal chance of injury. When placing a live air bag on a bench or other surface, always face the bag and trim cover up, away from the surface. This will reduce the motion of the module if it is accidently deployed.

c. Disconnect the driver air bag connector. Connect air bag simulator tool 105–00008 or equivalent, to the vehicle harness at the top of the steering wheel.

3. Disconnect the cruise control wire harness from the steering wheel, if equipped.

4. Remove and discard the steering wheel bolt. Remove the steering wheel using a suitable puller. Route the contact assembly wire harness

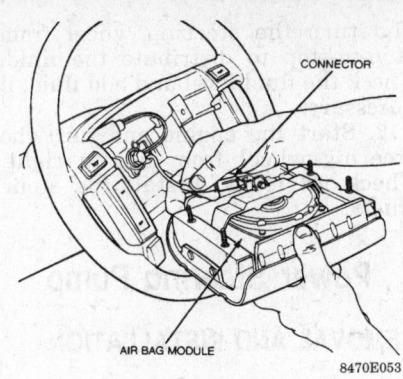

Air bag module removal

through the steering wheel as the wheel is lifted off the shaft.

NOTE: Do not use a knock-off type steering wheel puller or strike the retaining bolt with a hammer. This could cause damage to the steering shaft bearing.

To install:

5. Make sure the front wheels are in the straight-ahead position.

6. Route the contact assembly wire harness through the steering wheel opening at the 3 o'clock position and install the steering wheel on the steering shaft. The steering wheel and shaft alignment marks should be aligned. Make sure the air bag contact wire is not pinched.

7. Install a new steering wheel retaining bolt and tighten to 23–33 ft. lbs. (31–48 Nm).

8. If equipped, connect the cruise control wire harness to the wheel and snap the connector assembly into the steering wheel clip. Make sure the wiring does not get trapped between the steering wheel and contact assembly.

9. Connect the air bag wire harness to the air bag module and install the module to the steering wheel. Tighten the module retaining nuts to 3–4 ft. lbs. (4–6 Nm).

10. Connect the air bag backup power supply and negative battery cable. Verify the air bag warning indicator.

Without Air Bag

1. Disconnect the negative battery cable.

2. Remove the horn pad and cover assembly. Disconnect the horn electrical connector.

3. Disconnect the cruise control switch electrical connector, if equipped.

4. Remove and discard the steering wheel bolt. Remove the steering wheel using a suitable puller.

NOTE: Do not use a knock-off type steering wheel puller or strike the retaining bolt with a hammer. This could cause damage to the steering shaft bearing.

To install:

5. Align the index marks on the steering wheel and shaft and install the steering wheel.

6. Install a new steering wheel retaining bolt and tighten to 30 ft. lbs. (41 Nm).

7. Connect the cruise control electrical connector, if equipped.

8. Connect the horn electrical connector and install the horn pad and cover.

9. Connect the negative battery cable.

Steering Column

REMOVAL AND INSTALLATION

1. Make sure the front wheels are in the straight-ahead position. Properly disarm the air bag system.

2. Remove the steering wheel.

3. Remove the right and left lower mouldings from the instrument panel by pulling up and snapping out.

4. Remove the instrument panel lower trim panel and lower steering column shroud.

5. Remove the air bag clockspring contact assembly as follows:

  a. Disconnect the contact assembly wire harness.

  b. Apply 2 strips of tape across the contact assembly stator and rotor to prevent accidental rotation.

  c. Remove the 3 contact assembly retaining screws and pull the contact assembly off the steering column shaft.

6. Unscrew the tilt lever from the column.

7. Place the ignition lock cylinder in the **RUN** position. Using an 1/8 in. drift, depress the lock cylinder retaining pin through the access hole and remove the lock cylinder.

8. Remove the 4 retaining screws from the lower column shroud and remove the column shrouds.

9. Remove the 2 instrument panel reinforcement brace bolts and remove the reinforcement.

10. Remove the steering column to parking brake control shake brace. Disconnect the shift indicator cable from the actuator housing by removing 1 screw.

11. Remove the 2 combination switch retaining screws and set the combination switch aside.

12. Remove the pinch bolt from the steering column to extension shaft. Compress the extension shaft toward the engine and separate it from the column U-joint.

13. Disconnect the shift cable from the selector lever pivot. Remove the shift cable and bracket from the lower column mounting.

14. While supporting the column assembly, remove the 4 column assembly retaining nuts. Lower the column and disconnect the vacuum hoses at the parking brake release switch or remove the vacuum release assembly.

15. Remove the column from the vehicle.

To install:

16. Align the column lower universal joint to the lower shaft. Install 1 bolt and tighten to 31–41 ft. lbs. (40–56 Nm).

17. Connect the parking brake release vacuum hoses.

18. Position the steering column assembly to the column support bracket. Install the 4 retaining nuts and tighten to 9–14 ft. lbs. (13–19 Nm).

19. Position the shift cable bracket, with the shift cable attached, to the lower 2 screws of the column. Tighten to 5–8 ft. lbs. (7–11 Nm). Snap the shift cable onto the shift selector pivot ball.

20. Install the combination switch with the 2 retaining screws. Tighten to 18–26 inch lbs. (2–3 Nm). Connect all electrical connectors.

21. Attach the shift indicator cable loop on the shift selector hook and install the shift indicator cable bracket to the actuator housing. Install the steering column to parking brake control shake brace.

22. Install the instrument panel reinforcement brace and tighten the bolts.

23. Install the lock cylinder and the tilt lever.

24. Install the air bag clockspring contact assembly as follows:

  a. Make sure the front wheels are in the straight-ahead position and the steering column shaft alignment mark is at the 12 o'clock position.

  b. Align the contact assembly to the column shaft and mounting bosses and slide the contact assembly onto the shaft.

  c. Install the 3 retaining screws and tighten to 18–26 inch lbs. (2–3 Nm). Remove the tape strips.

d. Route the contact assembly down the column assembly and connect to the wire harness.

NOTE: If a new contact assembly is being installed, remove the plastic lock mechanism after the contact assembly is secured to the column.

25. Install the lower instrument panel cover and snap the right and left lower instrument panel mouldings into place. Install the upper and lower column shrouds.
26. Install the steering wheel. Install a new bolt and tighten to 23–33 ft. lbs. (31–48 Nm).
27. Position the air bag module to the wheel and install the 4 retaining nuts. Tighten to 3–4 ft. lbs. (4–6 Nm).
28. Connect the negative battery cable. If equipped, connect the air bag backup power supply. Verify the air bag warning indicator.

Power Steering Gear

ADJUSTMENT

Adjust the total-over-center position load to eliminate excessive lash between the sector and rack teeth as follows:
1. Disconnect the pitman arm from the sector shaft.
2. Disconnect the fluid return line at the reservoir. Cap the reservoir return line pipe.
3. Place the end of the return line in a clean container and turn the steering wheel from left stop to right stop several times to discharge the fluid from the gear.
4. Turn the steering wheel to 45 degrees from the left stop.
5. Using a ft. lb. torque wrench on the steering wheel nut, determine the torque required to rotate the shaft slowly approximately ¼ turn from the 45 degree position. If equipped with tilt column, place the steering wheel in the center tilt position.
6. Turn the steering wheel back to center and determine the torque required to rotate the shaft back and forth across the center position. If the reading is not to specification, loosen the nut and turn the adjuster screw until the reading is to specification. Tighten the wheel nut while holding the screw in place.
7. Check the readings and replace the pitman arm and steering wheel hub cover.
8. Connect the fluid return line to the reservoir and fill the reservoir.

Check the belt tension and adjust, if necessary.

REMOVAL AND INSTALLATION

1. Disconnect the negative battery cable.
2. Remove the stone shield.
3. Tag the pressure and return lines so they may be reassembled in their original positions.
4. Disconnect the pressure and return lines from the steering gear. Plug the lines and ports in the gear to prevent the entry of dirt.
5. Remove the clamp bolts retaining the flexible coupling to the steering gear.
6. Raise and safely support the vehicle. Remove the nut from the sector shaft.
7. Remove the pitman arm from the sector shaft with pitman arm remover tool T64P-3590-F or equivalent. Remove the tool from the pitman arm.

NOTE: Do not damage the seals and/or gear housing. Do not use a non-approved tool such as a pickle fork.

8. Support the steering gear and remove the steering gear retaining bolts.
9. Work the gear free of the flex coupling and remove the gear.
10. If the flex coupling did not come off with the gear, lift it off the shaft.
To install:
11. Turn the steering wheel to the straight-ahead position.
12. Center the steering gear input shaft with the indexing flat facing downward on 1991 Crown Victoria and Grand Marquis. On Town Car and 1992–95 Crown Victoria and Grand Marquis, center the steering gear input shaft with the centerline of the 2 indexing flats at 4 o'clock.
13. Slide the steering gear input shaft into the flex coupling and into place on the frame side rail. Install the retaining bolts and tighten to 50–65 ft. lbs. (68–88 Nm).
14. Make sure the wheels are in the straight-ahead position. Install the pitman arm on the sector shaft and install the lockwasher and nut. Tighten the nut to 200–250 ft. lbs. (271–339 Nm). Install and tighten the sector shaft and retaining bolts.
15. Move the flex coupling into place on the steering gear input shaft. Install the retaining bolt and tighten to 20–30 ft. lbs. (27–41 Nm).
16. Connect the pressure and return lines to the steering gear and tighten the lines. Fill the reservoir

and turn the steering wheel from stop-to-stop to distribute the fluid. Check the fluid level and add fluid, if necessary.
17. Start the engine and turn the steering wheel from left to right. Check for leaks. Install the stone shield.

Power Steering Pump

REMOVAL AND INSTALLATION

1. Disconnect the negative battery cable.
2. Disconnect the fluid return hose at the pump and drain the fluid into a container.
3. Remove the pressure hose from the pump and, if necessary, drain the fluid into a container. Do not remove the fitting from the pump.
4. Disconnect the belt from the pulley.
5. Remove the mounting bolts and remove the pump.
To install:
6. On 4.6L engine, place the pump on the mounting bosses of the engine block and install the bolts at the side of the pump. Tighten to 15–22 ft. lbs. (20–30 Nm).
7. Place the belt on the pump pulley and adjust the tension, if necessary.
8. Install the pressure hose to the pump fitting. Tighten the tube nut with a tube nut wrench rather than with an open-end wrench. Tighten to 20–25 ft. lbs. (27–34 Nm).

NOTE: Do not overtighten this fitting. Swivel and/or endplay of the fitting is normal and does not indicate a loose fitting. Overtightening the tube nut can collapse the tube nut wall, resulting in a leak and requiring replacement of the entire pressure hose assembly. Use of an open-end wrench to tighten the nut can deform the tube nut hex which may result in improper torque and may make further servicing of the system difficult.

9. Connect the return hose to the pump and tighten the clamp. Fill the reservoir with the proper type and quantity of fluid. Bleed the air from the system.

BELT ADJUSTMENT

4.6L Engine

The 4.6L engine is equipped with an automatic belt tensioner. No adjustment is necessary or possible. The belt tensioner is equipped with a belt wear indicator; when 1 percent belt stretch is indicated, the drive belt must be replaced.

SYSTEM BLEEDING

1. Disconnect the ignition coil. Raise and safely support the vehicle so the front wheels are off the floor.
2. Fill the power steering fluid reservoir.
3. Crank the engine with the starter and add fluid until the level remains constant.
4. While cranking the engine, rotate the steering wheel from lock-to-lock.

NOTE: The front wheels must be off the floor during lock-to-lock rotation of the steering wheel.

5. Check the fluid level and add fluid, if necessary.
6. Connect the ignition coil wire. Start the engine and allow it to run for several minutes.
7. Rotate the steering wheel from lock-to-lock.
8. Shut **OFF** the engine and check the fluid level. Add fluid, if necessary.
9. If air is still present in the system, purge the system of air using power steering pump air evacuator tool 021–00014 or equivalent, as follows:

a. Make sure the power steering pump reservoir is full to the COLD FULL mark on the dipstick or to just above the minimum indication on the reservoir.

b. Tightly insert the rubber stopper of the air evacuator assembly into the pump reservoir fill neck.

c. Apply 15 in. Hg maximum vacuum on the pump reservoir for a minimum of 3 minutes with the engine idling. As air purges from the system, vacuum will fall off. Maintain adequate vacuum with the vacuum source.

d. Release the vacuum and remove the vacuum source. Fill the reservoir to the COLD FULL mark or to just above the minimum indication on the reservoir.

e. With the engine idling, apply 15 in. Hg vacuum to the pump reservoir. Slowly cycle the steering wheel from lock-to-lock every 30 seconds for approximately 5 minutes. Do not hold the steering wheel on the stops while cycling. Maintain adequate vacuum with the vacuum source as the air purges.

f. Release the vacuum and remove the vacuum source. Add fluid, if necessary.

g. Start the engine and cycle the steering wheel. Check for oil leaks at all connections. In severe cases of aeration, it may be necessary to repeat Steps 9b–9f.

Tie Rod Ends

REMOVAL AND INSTALLATION

1. Raise and support the vehicle safely.
2. Remove the cotter pin and nut from the tie rod end ball stud.
3. Loosen the tie rod adjusting sleeve clamp bolts and remove the rod end from the spindle arm or center link, using ball stud remover tool 3290–D or equivalent.
4. Remove the tie rod end from the sleeve, counting the exact number of turns required to do so.

To install:

5. Install the new tie rod end into the sleeve, using the exact number of turns it took to remove the old one. Install the tie rod end ball studs into the spindle arm or center link.
6. Install the stud and stud nut. Tighten to 43–47 ft. lbs. (59–63 Nm), then continue tightening the nut to align its next castellation with the cotter pin hole in the stud. Install a new cotter pin.

NOTE: Never loosen the nut to align the nut castellation and cotter pin hole.

7. Check the toe and adjust if necessary. Loosen the clamps from the sleeve and oil the sleeve, clamps, bolts and nuts. Position the adjusting sleeve clamps so the bolts are horizontal, with the threaded end pointing toward the front of the vehicle, and tighten the clamp nuts to 20–22 ft. lbs. (27–29 Nm).

BRAKES

Master Cylinder

REMOVAL AND INSTALLATION

1. Disconnect the negative battery cable.
2. If equipped with anti-lock brakes, depress the brake pedal several times to exhaust all vacuum in the system.
3. Remove the brake lines from the primary and secondary outlet ports of the master cylinder.
4. Disconnect the brake warning indicator connector.
5. If equipped with anti-lock brakes, disconnect the Hydraulic Control Unit (HCU) supply hose at the master cylinder and secure in a position to prevent loss of brake fluid.
6. Remove the nuts attaching master cylinder to the brake booster assembly.
7. Slide the master cylinder forward and upward from the vehicle.

To install:

8. If equipped with anti-lock brakes, install a new seal in the groove in the master cylinder mounting face.
9. Install the master cylinder on the booster studs and install the mounting nuts. Tighten the nuts to 13–25 ft. lbs. (18–34 Nm) on all except vehicles with anti-lock brakes. If equipped with anti-lock brakes, tighten the nuts to 16–21 ft. lbs. (21–29 Nm).
10. Install short brake lines in the master cylinder outlet ports and position them so they point back into the reservoir and the ends of the lines are submerged in brake fluid.
11. Fill the reservoir with brake fluid and cover the reservoir with a shop towel.
12. Pump the brakes until clear, bubble-free fluid comes out of both brake lines. If any brake fluid spills on the paint, wash it off immediately with water.
13. Remove the short brake lines and connect the vehicle brake lines to the master cylinder. Bleed each brake line at the master cylinder using the following procedure:

a. Have an assistant pump the brake pedal 10 times and then hold firm pressure on the pedal.

b. Crack the rear most brake line fitting with a tubing wrench until a stream of brake fluid comes out. Have the assistant maintain pressure on the brake pedal until the brake line fitting is tightened again.

c. Repeat this operation until clear, bubble free fluid comes out from around the brake line fitting.

d. Repeat this bleeding operation at the front brake line fitting.

14. Attach the HCU supply hose to the master cylinder.
15. Connect the brake warning indicator switch connector.

16. Bleed the system. Operate the brakes several times, then check for external hydraulic leaks.

Brake Control Valves

There are several types of valves in use. Not all valves perform the same function nor are they located in the same place on every vehicle.

Town Car — Uses a brake pressure control valve that contains twin brake proportioning valves located on the frame.

Crown Victoria and Grand Marquis — a pressure control valve is screwed into the master cylinder. In addition, some vehicles have a metering valve located on the frame. Vehicles with anti-lock brakes have a proportioning valve located on the frame.

REMOVAL AND INSTALLATION

1. Disconnect the negative battery cable.
2. Disconnect the brake line(s) from the valve. Disconnect the electrical connector, if equipped.
3. Unscrew the valve from the master cylinder or remove the mounting screw from the frame or fender apron, as required.
4. Installation is the reverse of the removal procedure. Bleed the brake system.

Power Brake Booster

REMOVAL AND INSTALLATION

1. Disconnect the negative battery cable.
2. If equipped with anti-lock brakes, pump the brake pedal several times until all vacuum is removed from the booster.
3. Remove the master cylinder from the booster and move it aside without disconnecting the brake lines. Be careful not to kink the brake lines.
4. Disconnect the manifold vacuum hose from the booster check valve.
5. Working inside the vehicle below the instrument panel, remove the brake light switch connector. Remove the switch retaining pin and slide the switch off the brake pedal pin just far enough for the outer arm to clear the pin, then remove the switch. Be careful not to damage the switch.
6. Remove the booster-to-dash panel attaching nuts.

7. Slide the booster pushrod, washers and bushing off the brake pedal pin. Remove the booster.
8. Installation is the reverse of the removal procedure. Tighten the booster-to-dash panel attaching nuts and the master cylinder attaching nuts to 13–25 ft. lbs. (18–34 Nm).

Brake Caliper

REMOVAL AND INSTALLATION

Front

1. Raise and safely support the vehicle. Remove the front wheel and tire assembly.
2. Loosen the brake line fitting that connects the brake hose to the brake line at the frame bracket. Remove the retaining clip from the hose and bracket and disengage the hose from the bracket. Remove the hose from the caliper.
3. Remove the caliper locating pins and remove the caliper. If removing both calipers, mark the right and left sides so they may be reinstalled correctly.

To install:
4. Install the caliper over the rotor with the outer brake shoe against the rotor's braking surface.
5. Lubricate the inside of the locating pin insulators with silicone dielectric grease. Install the caliper locating pins and tighten to 45–60 ft. lbs. (61–81 Nm).
6. Install new sealing washers on each side of the brake hose fitting outlet and install the bolt, through the hose fitting and into the caliper. Tighten the bolt to 30 ft. lbs. (41 Nm).
7. Position the other end of the brake hose in the bracket and install the retaining clip. Make sure the hose is not twisted.
8. Connect the brake line to the brake hose and tighten the fitting nut.
9. Bleed the brake system, install the wheel and tire assembly and lower the vehicle.
10. Apply the brake pedal several times before moving the vehicle, to position the brake pads.

Rear

1. Raise and safely support the vehicle. Remove the rear wheel and tire assembly.
2. Remove the brake fitting retaining bolt from the caliper and disconnect the flexible brake hose from the caliper. Plug the hose and the caliper fitting.

3. Remove the caliper locating pins. Lift the caliper off the rotor and anchor plate using a rotating motion.

NOTE: Do not pry directly against the plastic piston or damage to the piston will occur.

To install:
4. Position the caliper assembly above the rotor with the anti-rattle spring located on the lower adapter support arm. Install the caliper over the rotor with a rotating motion. Make sure the inner pad is properly positioned.
5. Install the caliper locating pins and start them in the threads by hand. Tighten them to 19–25 ft. lbs. (26–34 Nm).
6. Install the brake hose on the caliper with a new gasket on each side of the fitting outlet. Insert the retaining bolt and tighten to 30–40 ft. lbs. (40–54 Nm).
7. Bleed the brake system, install the wheel and tire assembly and lower the vehicle.
8. Pump the brake pedal prior to moving the vehicle to position the linings.

Disc Brake Pads

REMOVAL AND INSTALLATION

Front

1. Remove and discard half the brake fluid from the master cylinder.
2. Raise and safely support vehicle. Remove the front wheel and tire assemblies.
3. Remove the caliper locating pins and remove the caliper from the anchor plate and rotor, but do not disconnect the brake hose.
4. Remove the outer brake pad from the caliper assembly and remove the inner brake pad from the caliper piston.
5. Inspect the disc brake rotor for scoring and wear. Replace or machine, as necessary.
6. Suspend the caliper inside the fender housing with a length of wire. Do not let the caliper hang by the brake hose.

To install:
7. Use a large C-clamp and wood block to push the caliper piston back into its bore.
8. Install the inner brake pad, then the outer brake pad, making sure the clips are properly seated.
9. Install the caliper and the wheel and tire assembly. Lower the vehicle.

10. Pump the brake pedal prior to moving the vehicle to seat the brake pads. Refill the master cylinder.

Rear

1. Remove and discard half the brake fluid from the master cylinder.
2. Raise and safely support vehicle. Remove the rear wheel and tire assemblies.
3. Remove the caliper locating pins and remove the caliper from the anchor plate and rotor, but do not disconnect the brake hose.
4. Remove the inner and outer brake pads.
5. Inspect the disc brake rotor for scoring and wear. Replace or machine, as necessary.
6. Suspend the caliper inside the fender housing with a length of wire. Do not let the caliper hang by the brake hose.
   To install:
7. Use a large C-clamp and wood block to push the caliper piston back into its bore.
8. Install the inner brake pad, then the outer brake pad, making sure the clips are properly seated.
9. Install the caliper and the wheel and tire assembly. Lower the vehicle.
10. Pump the brake pedal prior to moving the vehicle to seat the brake pads. Refill the master cylinder.

Brake Rotor

REMOVAL AND INSTALLATION

Front

1. Raise and safely support the vehicle. Remove the wheel and tire assembly.
2. Remove the caliper, but do not disconnect the brake hose. Suspend the caliper inside the fender housing with a length of wire. Do not let the caliper hang by the brake hose.
3. Remove the rotor retaining push nuts, if equipped, and remove the rotor from the hub.
4. Inspect the rotor for scoring and wear. Replace or machine as necessary. If machining, observe the minimum thickness specification.
5. Installation is the reverse of removal procedure.

Rear

1. Raise and safely support the vehicle. Remove the wheel and tire assembly.
2. Remove the caliper, but do not disconnect the brake hose. Suspend

the caliper inside the fender housing with a length of wire. Do not let the caliper hang by the brake hose.
3. Remove the rotor retaining push nuts and remove the rotor from the hub.
4. Inspect the rotor for scoring and wear. Replace or machine as necessary. If machining, observe the minimum thickness specification.
5. Installation is the reverse of the removal procedure.

Rear Brake Drum

REMOVAL AND INSTALLATION

1. Raise and safely support the vehicle.
2. Remove the wheel and tire assembly.
3. Remove the drum retaining clips and discard. Remove the brake drum.

NOTE: If the drum will not come off, pry the rubber plug from the backing plate. Insert a narrow rod through the hole in the backing plate and disengage the adjusting lever from the adjusting screw. While holding the adjustment lever away from the screw, back off the adjusting screw with a brake adjusting tool.

4. Inspect the brake drum for scoring and wear. Replace or machine as necessary. If machining, observe the maximum diameter specification.
5. Installation is the reverse of removal.

Rear Brake Shoes

REMOVAL AND INSTALLATION

1. Raise and safely support the vehicle. Remove the rear wheel and tire assemblies. Remove the brake drum.
2. Remove the shoe-to-anchor springs and unhook the cable eye from the anchor pin. Remove the anchor pin plate.
3. Remove the shoe hold-down springs, shoes, adjusting screw, pivot nut, socket and automatic adjustment parts.
4. Remove the parking brake link, spring and retainer. Disconnect the parking brake cable from the parking brake lever.
5. After removing the rear brake secondary shoe, disassemble the parking brake lever from the shoe by

removing the retaining clip and spring washer.
   To install:
6. Before installing the rear brake shoes, assemble the parking brake lever to the secondary shoe and secure it with the spring washer and retaining clip.
7. Apply a light coating of caliper slide grease at the points where the brake shoes contact the backing plate. Be careful not to get any lubricant on the brake linings.
8. Position the brake shoes on the backing plate. The primary shoe with the short lining faces the front of the vehicle, the secondary shoe with the long lining, to the rear. Secure the assembly with the hold-down springs. Install the parking brake link, spring and retainer. Back-off the parking brake adjustment, then connect the parking brake cable to the parking brake lever.
9. Install the anchor pin plate on the anchor pin. Place the cable eye over the anchor pin with the crimped side toward the drum. Install the primary shoe to the anchor pin.
10. Install the cable guide on the secondary shoe web with the flanged hole fitted into the hole in the secondary shoe web. Thread the cable around the cable guide groove.

NOTE: The cable must be positioned in the groove and not between the guide and the shoe web.

11. Install the secondary shoe-to-anchor spring. Make sure the cable eye is not cocked or binding on the anchor pin when installed. All parts should be flat on the anchor pin.
12. Apply a thin coat of lubricant to the threads and the socket end of the adjusting screw. Turn the adjusting screw into the adjusting pivot nut to the limit of the threads, then back-off ½ turn.

NOTE: Make sure the socket end of the adjusting screw is stamped with an R or L, indicating the right or left side of the vehicle. The adjusting screw assemblies must be installed on the correct side for proper brake shoe adjustment.

13. Place the adjusting socket on the screw and install the assembly between the shoe ends with the adjusting screw toothed wheel nearest the secondary shoe.
14. Hook the cable hook into the hole in the adjusting lever. The adjusting levers are stamped with an **R** or **L** to indicate their installation on the right or left side.

15. Position the hooked end of the adjuster spring completely into the large hole in the primary shoe web. Connect the loop end of the spring to the adjuster lever hole.

16. Pull the adjuster lever, cable and automatic adjuster spring down and toward the rear, engaging the pivot hook in the large hole of the secondary shoe web.

17. Make sure the upper ends of the brake shoes are seated against the anchor pin and the shoes are centered on the backing plate.

18. Adjust the brakes using brake adjustment gauge D81L–1103–A or equivalent.

19. Install the brake drum, wheel and tire assemblies and lower the vehicle.

20. Apply the brakes several times while backing up the vehicle. After each stop, the vehicle must be moved forward.

Wheel Cylinder

REMOVAL AND INSTALLATION

1. Remove the wheel and tire assembly and the brake drum.

2. Remove the brake shoe assembly.

3. Disconnect the brake line from the wheel cylinder at the backing plate.

4. Remove the wheel cylinder attaching bolts and remove the wheel cylinder.

5. Installation is the reverse of the removal procedure. Tighten the wheel cylinder attaching bolts to 10–20 ft. lbs. (14–28 Nm).

6. Bleed the brake system.

Parking Brake Cable

ADJUSTMENT

NOTE: The following procedure is to be used only if a new parking brake control assembly is installed. All components of the parking brake system must be installed prior to the adjustment procedure. The parking brake control with automatic tensioning is preset by means of a shipping clip. The following procedure must be followed in sequence and must be done with the vehicle weight on the axle.

1. Verify removal of the shipping clip. The take up reel will apply tension to the system.

2. Depress the parking brake control to the 8th notch.

3. Push the parking brake control pedal to release.

4. Check function as follows:

a. Apply the parking brake with a full stroke, to the 9th or 10th notch.

b. Release the parking brake by shifting the vehicle into a forward gear with the engine running. The control must release.

c. Apply the parking brake with a full stroke, to the 9th or 10th notch.

d. Manually release the parking brake with the push to release feature.

NOTE: With the control in the OFF position, the rear brakes must not drag. Check for movement of the rear cables from their conduits when the intermediate cable is deflected with a force of 10–15 lbs.

REMOVAL AND INSTALLATION

Front Cable

1. Raise and safely support the vehicle.

2. Disconnect the cable from the rear of the cable connector located along the left frame side rail.

3. Use a 13mm box end wrench to depress the retaining tabs and remove the conduit retainer from the frame. Remove screw holding the plastic inner fender apron to the frame, at the rear of the fender panel.

4. Pull back the fender apron. If equipped, remove the spring clip retainer that holds the parking brake cable to the frame.

5. Pull the cable through the frame and let it hang in the wheel housing. Lower the vehicle.

6. Inside the passenger compartment, remove the sound deadener cover from the cable at the dash panel.

7. Pull the cable until the parking brake control take up spring tang is at full clockwise position. Use a fabricated tool to retain the reel spring and disconnect the cable from the take up reel.

8. Using a 13mm box end wrench, depress the retaining tabs and remove the conduit from the cable assembly. Push the cable down through the dash panel and remove cable from inside the wheel housing.

9. Installation is the reverse of the removal procedure. Check the parking brake adjustment.

Rear Cables

WITH DRUM BRAKES

1. Raise and safely support the vehicle.

2. Remove the wheel and tire assemblies and the brake drums.

3. Working on the wheel side of the rear brake, remove the brake automatic adjuster spring. Compress the prongs on the parking brake cable so they can pass through the hole in the backing plate. Pull the cable retainer through the hole.

4. With the tension off the cable spring at the parking brake lever, lift the cable end out of the slot in the lever. Remove the cable through the backing plate hole.

5. Installation is the reverse of the removal procedure. Adjust the parking brake, if necessary.

WITH DISC BRAKES

1. Raise and safely support the vehicle. Disconnect the control cable from the rear cable at the connector.

2. Disconnect the parking brake cable retainer spring at the frame, if equipped with dual exhaust.

3. Disconnect the left cable from the right cable at the adjuster bracket. Release the right cable tabbed conduit retainer from the frame, using a 13mm box end wrench.

4. Remove the cable retainer from the left shock bracket, the wire retainer on the left axle bracket and disconnect the cable from the retainer on the right axle tube by removing the bolt and retainer.

5. Remove the cable retaining E-clip and cable eyelet from the brake lever. Pull the cable out of the disc brake adapter boss. Remove the cables.

6. Installation is the reverse of the removal procedure. Check parking brake operation.

Brake System Bleeding

Without Anti-Lock Brakes

1. Clean all dirt from the master cylinder filler cap.

2. If the master cylinder is known or suspected to have air in the bore, it must be bled before any of the wheel cylinders or calipers. To bleed the master cylinder, loosen the upper secondary left front outlet fitting approximately ¾ turn. Have an assistant depress the brake pedal slowly through it's full travel. Close the outlet fitting and let the pedal return slowly to the fully released position.

Wait 5 seconds and then repeat the operation until all air bubbles disappear.

3. Repeat Step 2 with the right-hand front outlet fitting.

4. Continue to bleed the brake system by removing the rubber dust cap from the wheel cylinder bleeder fitting or caliper fitting at the right-hand rear of the vehicle. Place a suitable box wrench on the bleeder fitting and attach a rubber drain tube to the fitting. The end of the tube should fit snugly around the bleeder fitting. Submerge the other end of the tube in a container partially filled with clean brake fluid and loosen the fitting ¾ turn.

5. Have an assistant push the brake pedal down slowly through it's full travel. Close the bleeder fitting and allow the pedal to slowly return to it's full release position. Wait 5 seconds and repeat the procedure until no bubbles appear at the submerged end of the bleeder tube. Secure the bleeder fitting and remove the bleeder tube. Install the rubber dust cap on the bleeder fitting.

6. Repeat the procedure in Steps 4 and 5 in the following sequence: left rear, right front, left front. Refill the master cylinder reservoir after each wheel cylinder or caliper has been bled and install the master cylinder cover and gasket. When brake bleeding is completed, the fluid level should be filled to the maximum level indicated on the reservoir.

7. Always make sure the disc brake pistons are returned to their normal positions by depressing the brake pedal several times until normal pedal travel is established. If the pedal feels spongy, repeat the bleeding procedure.

With Anti-Lock Brakes

NOTE: The anti-lock brake system must be bled in 2 steps.

The master cylinder and hydraulic control unit must be bled using the Rotunda Anti-Lock Brake Breakout Box/Bleeding Adapter tool T90P-50-ALA or equivalent. If this procedure is not followed, air will be trapped in the hydraulic control unit which will eventually lead to a spongy brake pedal. To bleed the master cylinder and the hydraulic control unit, disconnect the 55-pin plug from the electronic control unit and install the Anti-Lock Brake Breakout Box/Bleeding Adapter to the wire harness 55-pin plug.

1. Place the Bleed/Harness switch in the **BLEED** position.

2. Turn the ignition to the ON position. At this point the red off light should come ON.

3. Push the motor button on the adapter down to start the pump motor. The red light will turn OFF and the green light will turn ON. The pump motor will run for 60 seconds after the motor button is pushed. If the pump motor is to be turned off for any reason before the 60 seconds has elapsed, push the ABORT button to turn the pump motor OFF.

a. After 20 seconds of pump motor operation, push and hold the VALVE button down. Hold the VALVE button down for 20 seconds and then release it.

b. The pump motor will continue to run for an additional 20 seconds after the valve button is released.

4. The brake lines can now be bled in the normal fashion. Bleed the brake system by removing the rubber dust cap from the caliper fitting at the right-hand rear of the vehicle. Place a suitable box wrench on the bleeder fitting and attach a rubber drain tube to the fitting. The end of the tube should fit snugly around the bleeder fitting. Submerge the other end of the tube in a container partially filled with clean brake fluid and loosen the fitting ¾ turn.

5. Have an assistant push the brake pedal down slowly through it's full travel. Close the bleeder fitting and allow the pedal to slowly return to it's full release position. Wait 5 seconds and repeat the procedure until no bubbles appear at the submerged end of the bleeder tube. Secure the bleeder fitting and remove the bleeder tube. Install the rubber dust cap on the bleeder fitting.

6. Repeat the bleeding procedure at the left front, left rear and right front in that order. Refill the master cylinder reservoir after each caliper has been bled and install the master cylinder and gasket. When brake bleeding is completed, the fluid level should be filled to the maximum level indicated on the reservoir.

7. Always make sure the disc brake pistons are returned to their normal positions by depressing the brake pedal several times until normal pedal travel is established. If the pedal feels spongy, repeat the bleeding procedure.

Anti-Lock Brake System Service

PRECAUTIONS

- Before servicing any high pressure component, discharge the hydraulic pressure from the system.
- Do not allow brake fluid to contact any electrical connections.
- Use care when opening the bleeder screws due to the high system pressure.

RELIEVING ANTI-LOCK BRAKE SYSTEM PRESSURE

—— **CAUTION** ——
Before servicing any component which contains high pressure, it is mandatory that the hydraulic pressure in the system be discharged or personal injury could result.

To discharge the system, turn the ignition **OFF** and pump the brake pedal a minimum of 20 times until an increase in pedal force is clearly felt.

Hydraulic Control Unit (HCU)

REMOVAL AND INSTALLATION

1. Disconnect the negative battery cable.

2. Remove the air cleaner and air outlet tube.

3. Disconnect the 19-pin connector from the HCU to the wiring harness and disconnect the 4-pin connector from the HCU to the pump motor relay.

4. Remove the 2 lines from the inlet ports and the 4 lines from the outlet ports of the HCU. Plug each port to prevent brake fluid from spilling onto the paint and wiring.

5. Remove the 3 nuts retaining the HCU assembly to the mounting bracket and remove the assembly from the vehicle. The nut on the front of the HCU also retains the relay mounting bracket.

6. Install in the reverse order of removal. Tighten the 3 retaining nuts to 12-18 ft. lbs. (16-24 Nm) and the brake lines to 10-18 ft. lbs. (14-24 Nm). Bleed the brake system and check for fluid leaks.

Anti-Lock Brake Hydraulic Control Unit (HCU)

Front Wheel Speed Sensor

REMOVAL AND INSTALLATION

1. Disconnect the negative battery cable.

2. From inside engine compartment, disconnect sensor assembly 2-pin connector from the wiring harness.

3. Remove the steel routing clip attaching the sensor wire to the tube bundle on the left sensor or remove the plastic routing clip attaching the sensor wire to the frame on the right sensor.

4. Remove the rubber coated spring steel clip holding the sensor wire to the frame.

5. Remove the sensor wire from the steel routing clip on the frame and from the dust shield.

6. Remove the sensor attaching bolt from the front spindle and slide the sensor out of the mounting hole.

To install:

7. Install the sensor into the mounting hole in the front spindle and attach with the mounting bolt. Tighten to 40–60 inch lbs. (4.5–6.8 Nm).

8. Insert the sensor routing grommets into the dust shield and steel bracket on the frame. Route the wire into the engine compartment.

9. Install the rubber coated steel clip that holds the sensor wire to the frame into the hole in the frame.

10. Install the steel clip that holds sensor wire to tube bundle on left side or plastic clip that holds sensor to frame on right side.

11. Connect the 2-pin connector to wire harness. Connect the negative battery cable.

Rear Wheel Speed Sensor

REMOVAL AND INSTALLATION

1. Disconnect the negative battery cable.

2. From inside luggage compartment, disconnect 2-pin sensor connector from wiring harness and push sensor wire through hole in floor.

3. From below vehicle, remove sensor wire from routing bracket located on top of rear axle carrier housing and remove steel clip holding sensor wire and brake tube against axle housing.

4. Remove screw from clip holding sensor wire and brake tube to bracket on axle.

5. Remove sensor to rear adapter retaining bolt and remove sensor.

To install:

6. Insert sensor adapter and install retaining bolt. Tighten to 40–60 inch lbs. (4.5–6.8 Nm).

7. Attach clip holding sensor and brake tube to bracket on axle housing and secure with screw. Tighten to 40–60 inch lbs. (4.5–6.8 Nm).

8. Install steel clip around axle tube that holds sensor wire and brake tube against axle tube and push spool-shaped grommet into clip located on top of axle carrier housing.

9. Push sensor wire connector up through hole in floor and seat large round grommet into hole.

10. Push sensor wire connector up through hole in floor and seat large round grommet into hole.

11. Connect sensor 2-pin connector to wiring harness inside luggage compartment.

FRONT SUSPENSION

NOTE: If equipped with the level ride air suspension, power to the air system must be shut OFF before servicing the suspension. The switch is located in the luggage compartment, on the drivers side rear fender well.

Shock Absorbers

REMOVAL AND INSTALLATION

NOTE: Purge a new shock of air by repeatedly extending it in its normal position and compressing it while inverted.

1. Remove the nut, washer and bushing from the upper end of the shock absorber.

2. Raise and safely support the vehicle by the frame rails allowing the front wheels to hang.

3. Remove the 2 bolts securing the shock absorber to the lower control arm and remove the shock absorber.

To install:

4. Install a new bushing and washer on the top of the shock absorber and position the unit inside the front spring. Install the 2 lower attaching bolts and torque them to 12–18 ft. lbs. (16–24 Nm).

5. Lower the vehicle.

6. Place a new bushing and washer on the shock absorber top stud and install a new attaching nut. Tighten to 22–26 ft. lbs. (30–41 Nm).

Coil Springs

REMOVAL AND INSTALLATION

1. Raise and safely support the vehicle. Remove the wheel and tire assembly.

2. Remove the shock absorber. Remove the steering link from the pitman arm.

3. Using spring compressor tool D78P–5310–A or equivalent, install 1 plate with the pivot ball seat facing downward into the coils of the spring. Rotate the plate, so it is flush with the upper surface of the lower arm.

4. Install the other plate with the pivot ball seat facing upward into the coils of the spring. Insert the upper ball nut through the coils of the spring, so the nut rests in the upper plate.

5. Insert the compression rod into the opening in the lower arm, through the upper and lower plate and upper ball nut. Insert the securing pin through the upper ball nut and compression rod.

NOTE: This pin can only be inserted 1 way into the upper ball nut because of a stepped hole design.

6. With the upper ball nut secured, turn the upper plate so it walks up the coil until it contacts the upper spring seat. Then back off ½ turn.

7. Install the lower ball nut and thrust washer on the compression rod and screw on the forcing nut. Tighten the forcing nut until the spring is compressed enough so it is free in its seat.

8. Remove the 2 lower arm pivot bolts, disengage the lower arm from the frame crossmember and remove the spring.

9. If a new spring is to be installed, perform the following:

a. Mark the position of the upper and lower plates on the spring with chalk.

b. With an assistant, compress a new spring for installation and measure the compressed length and the amount of curvature of the old spring.

10. Loosen the forcing nut to relieve the spring tension and remove the tools from the spring.

To install:

11. Assemble the spring compressor and locate in the same position as indicated in Step 10a.

12. Before compressing the coil spring, make sure the upper ball nut securing the pin is inserted properly.

13. Compress the coil spring until the spring height reaches the dimension obtained in Step 10b.

14. Position the coil spring assembly into the lower arm and reverse the removal procedure.

Upper Ball Joints

INSPECTION

1. Raise the vehicle and place floor jacks beneath the lower control arms.

2. Make sure the front wheel bearings are properly adjusted.

3. Have an assistant grasp the bottom of the tire and move the wheel in and out.

4. As the wheel is being moved, observe the upper control arm where the spindle attaches to it. Any movement between the upper part of the spindle and the upper control arm indicates a bad ball joint which must be replaced.

REMOVAL AND INSTALLATION

1991 Crown Victoria and Grand Marquis

NOTE: Ford Motor Company recommends replacement of the control arm and ball joint as an assembly. However, aftermarket replacement parts are available, which can be installed using the following procedure.

1. Raise the vehicle and support on frame points so the front wheels fall to their full down position. Remove the wheel and tire assembly.

2. Drill a 1/8 in. hole completely through each ball joint attaching rivet.

3. Using a large chisel, cut off the head of each rivet and drive them from the arm.

4. Place a jack under the lower arm and raise to compress the coil spring.

5. Remove the cotter pin and attaching nut from the ball joint stud.

6. Using a ball joint removal tool, loosen the ball joint stud from the spindle and remove the ball joint from the arm.

To install:

7. Clean all metal burrs from the arm and install the new ball joint, using the service part nuts and bolts to attach the ball joint. Do not attempt to rivet the ball joint once it has been removed.

8. Install the ball joint stud into the spindle. Tighten the ball joint-to-upper spindle nut to 60–90 ft. lbs. (81–122 Nm). Continue to tighten until the slot for the cotter pin is aligned. Install a new cotter pin.

9. Install the wheel and tire assembly and lower the vehicle. Check front end alignment.

Town Car, 1992–95 Crown Victoria and Grand Marquis

1. Raise and safely support the vehicle with safety stands under the frame behind the lower arm. Remove the wheel and tire assembly.

2. Position a floor jack under the lower arm at the lower ball joint area. The floor jack will support the spring load on the lower arm.

3. Remove the retaining nut and pinch bolt from the upper ball joint stud.

4. Mark the position of the alignment cams. When replacing the ball joint this will approximate the current alignment.

5. Remove the 2 nuts retaining the ball joint to the upper arm. Remove the ball joint and spread the slot with a suitable prybar to separate the ball joint stud from the spindle.

To install:

NOTE: The upper ball joints differ from side to side. Be sure to use the proper ball joint on each side.

6. Position the ball joint on the upper arm and insert the ball stud into the spindle.

7. Install the pinch bolt and retaining nut. Tighten to 51–67 ft. lbs. (68–92 Nm).

8. Install the alignment cams to the approximate position at removal.

If not marked, install in neutral position.

9. Install the 2 nuts attaching the ball joint to the arm. Hold the cams and tighten the nuts to 90–109 ft. lbs. (122–149 Nm).

10. Remove the floor jack from the lower arm and install the wheel and tire assembly. Remove the safety stands and lower the vehicle.

11. Check and adjust the front end alignment.

Lower Ball Joints

INSPECTION

1. Support the vehicle in normal driving position with ball joints loaded.

2. Wipe the wear indicator and ball joint cover checking surface clean.

3. The checking surface should project outside the cover. If the checking surface is inside the cover, replace the lower arm assembly.

REMOVAL AND INSTALLATION

The ball joint is an integral part of the lower control arm. If the ball joint is defective, the entire lower control arm must be replaced.

Upper Control Arms

REMOVAL AND INSTALLATION

1. Raise and safely support the vehicle on safety stands positioned on the frame just behind the lower arm.

2. Remove the wheel and tire assembly and position a floor jack under the lower arm.

3. Remove the retaining nut from the upper ball joint stud to spindle pinch bolt. Tap the pinch bolt to remove from the spindle.

4. Using a suitable prybar, spread the slot to allow the ball joint stud to release out of the spindle.

5. Remove the upper arm retaining bolts and the upper arm.

To install:

6. Transfer the rebound bumper from the old arm to the new arm, or replace the bumper if worn or damaged.

7. Use reference marks from the camber and caster cams as initial settings.

8. Position the upper arm shaft to the frame bracket. Install the 2 retaining bolts and washers. Position the arm in the center of the slot ad-

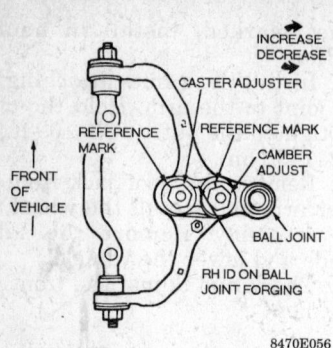

Upper control arm — Town Car, Crown Victoria and Grand Marquis

justment range and tighten to 100 ft. lbs. (136 Nm).

9. Connect the upper ball joint stud to the spindle and install the retaining pinch bolt and nut. Tighten the nut to 52–66 ft. lbs. (70–90 Nm).

10. Install the wheel and tire assembly and lower the vehicle. Check the front end alignment.

Lower Control Arms

REMOVAL AND INSTALLATION

1. Raise the front of the vehicle and position safety stands on the frame behind the lower control arms. Remove the wheel and tire assembly.

2. Remove the brake caliper and suspend with a length of wire; do not let the caliper hang by the brake hose. Remove the brake rotor and dust shield. Remove the anti-lock brake sensor, if equipped.

3. Remove the jounce bumper; inspect and save for installation if in good condition. Remove the shock absorber.

4. Disconnect the steering center link from the pitman arm.

BALL JOINT COVER

NEW OK

WORN IF BELOW SURFACE OF COVER

CHECKING SURFACE

8470E057

Lower ball joint checking cover surface

5. Remove the cotter pin and loosen the lower ball joint stud nut 1–2 turns.

NOTE: Do not remove the nut at this time.

6. Install a suitable ball joint press tool to place the ball joint stud under compression. With the stud under compression, tap the spindle sharply with a hammer to loosen the stud in the spindle. Remove the ball joint press tool.

7. Place a floor jack under the lower arm and install a suitable spring compression tool.

8. Remove the coil spring, the ball joint nut and remove the lower control arm.

To install:

9. Position the arm assembly ball joint stud into the spindle and install the nut. Tighten to 80–120 ft. lbs. (108–163 Nm). Continue to tighten until the slot for the cotter pin is aligned. Install a new cotter pin.

10. Position the coil spring into the upper spring pocket and raise the lower arm, aligning the holes in the arm with the holes in the crossmember. Install the bolts and nuts with the washer installed on the front bushing. Do not tighten at this time.

NOTE: Make sure the pigtail of the lower coil of the spring is in the proper location of the seat on the lower arm, between the 2 holes.

11. Remove the spring compressor tool.

12. Connect the steering center link at the pitman arm and install the nut. Tighten to 43–47 ft. lbs. (59–63 Nm). Continue to tighten until the slot for the cotter pin is aligned. Install a new cotter pin.

13. Install the shock absorber and the jounce bumper.

14. Install the dust shield, rotor and caliper. Install the anti-lock brake sensor, if equipped.

15. Install the wheel and tire assembly and lower the vehicle. With the vehicle supported on the wheels and tires at normal curb height, tighten the lower control arm-to-crossmember bolts to 100–140 ft. lbs. (136–190 Nm).

16. Check the front end alignment.

Stabilizer Bar

REMOVAL AND INSTALLATION

1. Raise the front of the vehicle and place jackstands under the lower control arms.

2. Remove the retaining nuts from the pinch bolts at the spindles. Spread the slots in the spindles with a prybar to free the ball studs.

3. Remove the stabilizer bar brackets from the frame and remove the stabilizer bar. If worn, cut the insulators from the stabilizer bar.

4. On Town Car, Crown Victoria and Grand Marquis, remove the retaining nuts from the ball joint studs at the end of the bar. Use removal tool 3290–D or equivalent to separate the links from the ends of the stabilizer bar.

To install:

5. Coat the necessary parts of the stabilizer bar with rubber lubricant. Slide new insulators onto the stabilizer bar.

6. On Town Car, Crown Victoria and Grand Marquis, install the ball joint links into the ends of the bar with the retaining nuts. Tighten to 30–40 ft. lbs. (40–55 Nm).

7. On Town Car, Crown Victoria and Grand Marquis, position the bar under the vehicle and engage the upper ball joint links to the spindles. Install the insulator brackets with the retaining nuts. Tighten the pinch bolts and nuts at the spindles to 30–40 ft. lbs. (40–55 Nm) Tighten the bracket-to-frame nuts to 44–59 ft. lbs. (59–81 Nm).

Front Wheel Bearings

ADJUSTMENT

The front wheel bearings are of a hub unit design and are pregreased, sealed and require no maintenance. The bearings are preset and cannot be adjusted.

REMOVAL AND INSTALLATION

1. Raise and safely support the vehicle. Remove the wheel and tire assembly.

2. Remove and discard the grease cap from the hub.

3. Remove the brake caliper. Suspend the caliper with a length of wire; do not let it hang from the brake hose.

4. Remove the rotor. Remove and discard the wheel hub nut.

5. Remove the hub and bearing assembly.

To install:

6. Install the hub and bearing assembly. Install a new wheel hub nut and tighten to 238 ft. lbs. (322 Nm).

7. Install the rotor and a new grease cap. Install the brake caliper.

8. Install the wheel and tire assembly and lower the vehicle.

REAR SUSPENSION

Shock Absorbers

REMOVAL AND INSTALLATION

Without Automatic Leveling

1. If equipped with air suspension, turn the air suspension switch **OFF**.

2. Raise and safely support the vehicle. Make sure the rear axle is supported.

3. Remove the shock absorber retaining nut, washer and insulator from the stud on the upper side of the frame. Discard the nut. Compress the shock to clear the hole in the frame and remove the inner insulator and washer from the upper retaining stud.

NOTE: All vehicles, except police applications, are equipped with gas pressurized shock absorbers which will extend unassisted.

4. Remove the self-locking retaining nut and disconnect the shock absorber lower stud from the mounting bracket on the rear axle.

To install:

5. Prime the new shock absorber as follows:

a. With the shock absorber right side up, extend it fully.

b. Turn the shock upside down and fully compress it.

c. Repeat the previous 2 steps at least 3 times to make sure any trapped air has been expelled.

6. Place the inner washer and insulator on the upper retaining stud and position the shock absorber with the stud through the hole in the frame.

7. While holding the shock absorber in position, install the outer insulator, washer and a new stud nut on the upper side of the frame. Tighten the nut to 21 ft. lbs. (29 Nm).

8. Extend the shock absorber and place the lower stud in the mounting

bracket hole on the rear axle housing. Install a new self-locking nut and tighten to 52–85 ft. lbs. (70–115 Nm).

9. Lower the vehicle and, if equipped, turn the air suspension switch **ON**.

With Automatic Leveling

NOTE: Disconnect the height sensor connector link before allowing the rear axle to hang free. Then, raise the vehicle on a hoist so the suspension arms hang free with the ignition switch in the OFF position. The rear shock absorbers will vent air through the compressor and a hissing noise will be heard. When the noise stops, the air lines can be disconnected. A residual pressure of 8–24 psi will remain in the air lines.

1. Disconnect the air line by pushing in on the retainer ring and pulling the line out.

2. Remove the top retaining nut, washer and bushing.

3. Remove the bottom retaining nut and washer. Remove the shock absorber.

To install:

4. Position the shock absorber and install the bottom retaining washer and nut. Tighten to 52–85 ft. lbs. (70–115 Nm).

5. Install the top bushing, washer and retaining nut. Tighten to 14–26 ft. lbs. (19–35 Nm).

NOTE: Check the rubber sleeve on the shock absorber to be sure it is not wrapped up. To assist in identifying wrap-up during installation, a white stripe is on the rubber sleeve and on the shock absorber body. The stripes should align. To correct a wrap-up condition, loosen the upper shock retaining nut and turn the shock to align the stripes. Retighten the retaining nut.

6. Connect the air line to the shock absorber by pushing in on the retainer ring and installing the air line.

7. Connect the height sensor connecting link and lower the vehicle.

Coil Springs

REMOVAL AND INSTALLATION

1. Raise the vehicle and support the rear axle housing. Place jackstands under the frame side rails.

2. Remove the rear stabilizer bar, if equipped.

3. Disconnect the lower studs of both rear shock absorbers from the mounting brackets on the axle tube.

4. Unsnap the right parking brake cable from the right upper arm retainer before lowering the axle.

5. Lower the axle housing until the coil springs are released. Remove the springs and insulators.

To install:

6. Position the spring in the upper and lower seats with an insulator between the upper end of the spring and frame seat.

7. Raise the axle and connect the shock absorbers to the mounting brackets. Install new retaining nuts and tighten to 52–85 ft. lbs. (70–115 Nm).

8. Snap the right parking cable into the upper arm retainer. Install the stabilizer bar, if equipped.

9. Remove the jackstands and lower the vehicle.

Air Springs

REMOVAL AND INSTALLATION

1. Turn the air suspension switch **OFF**.

2. Raise and safely support the vehicle on the frame. The suspension must be at full rebound.

3. Remove the heat shield, as required. Remove the spring retainer clip. Remove the air spring solenoid as follows:

a. Disconnect the electrical connector and then disconnect the air line.

b. Remove the solenoid clip.

c. Rotate the solenoid counterclockwise to the first stop.

d. Pull the solenoid straight out slowly to the 2nd stop to bleed air from the system.

CAUTION

Do not fully release the solenoid until the air is completely bled from the air spring or personal injury may result.

---

e. After the air is fully bled from the system, rotate counterclockwise to the 3rd stop and remove the solenoid from the solenoid housing. Remove the large O-ring from the solenoid housing.

4. Remove the spring piston-to-axle spring seat as follows:

a. Insert air spring removal tool T90P–5310–A or equivalent, between the axle tube and the spring seat on the forward side of the axle.

b. Position the tool so its flat end rests on the piston knob. Push downward, forcing the piston and retainer clip off the axle spring seat.

5. Remove the air spring.

To install:

6. Install the air spring solenoid as follows:

a. Check the solenoid O-rings for cuts or abrasion. Replace the O-rings as required. Lightly grease the O-ring area of the solenoid and the larger solenoid housing O-ring with silicone dielectric compound.

b. Insert the solenoid into the air spring end cap and rotate clockwise to the 3rd stop, push into the 2nd stop, then rotate clockwise to the 1st stop.

c. Install the solenoid clip. Inspect the wire harness connector and ensure the rubber gasket is in place at the bottom of the connector cavity.

7. Install the air spring into the frame spring seat, taking care to keep the solenoid air and electrical connections clean and free of damage.

8. Connect the push on spring retainer clip to the knob of the spring cap from the top side of the frame spring seat.

9. Connect the air line and electrical connector to the solenoid. Install the heat shield to frame spring seat, if required.

10. Align the air spring piston to axle seats. Squeeze to increase pressure and push downward on the piston, snapping the piston to axle seat at rebound and supported by the shock absorber.

NOTE: The air springs may be damaged if the suspension is allowed to compress before the spring is inflated.

11. Refill the air spring as follows:

a. Turn the air suspension switch **ON**. The ignition switch must be **ON** and the engine running or a battery charger must be connected to the battery to reduce battery drain.

b. Remove the right luggage compartment trim panel and connect Super Star II tester 007–0041–A or equivalent to the air suspension diagnostic connector.

c. Set the tester to EEC-IV/MCU mode. Also set the tester to FAST mode. Release the tester button to the HOLD (up) position and turn the tester **ON**.

d. Depress the tester button to TEST (down) position. A Code **10** will be displayed. Within 2 minutes a Code **13** will be displayed. After Code **13** is displayed, release the tester button to HOLD (up) position, wait 5 seconds and depress the tester button to TEST (down) position. Ignore any codes displayed.

e. Release the tester button to the HOLD (up) position. Wait at least 20 seconds, then depress the tester button to TEST (down) position. Within 10 seconds, the following codes will be displayed in the order shown.

f. Within 4 seconds after Code **26** is displayed, release the tester button to the HOLD (up) position. Waiting longer than 4 seconds may result in Functional Test **31** being entered. The compressor will fill the air springs with air as long as the tester button is in the HOLD (up) position. To stop filling the air springs, depress the tester button to the TEST (down) position.

NOTE: It is possible to overheat the compressor during this operation. If the compressor overheats, the self-resetting circuit breaker in the compressor will open and remain open for about 15 minutes. This allows the compressor to cool down.

g. To exit Functional Test **26**, disconnect the tester and turn the ignition switch **OFF**.

Rear Control Arms

REMOVAL AND INSTALLATION

Upper Arm

NOTE: If both arms are to be replaced, remove and install 1 at a time to prevent the axle from rolling or slipping sideways.

1. If equipped, turn the air suspension switch **OFF**.
2. Raise the vehicle and support the frame side rails with jackstands.
3. Support the rear axle under the differential pinion nose as well as under the axle.
4. Unsnap the parking brake cable from the upper arm retainer. If equipped, disconnect the height sensor from the ball stud on the left upper control arm.

5. Remove and discard the nut and bolt retaining the upper arm to the axle housing. Disconnect the arm from the housing.

6. Remove and discard the nut and bolt retaining the upper arm to the frame bracket and remove the arm.

To install:

7. Hold the upper arm in place on the front arm bracket and install a new retaining bolt and self-locking nut. Do not tighten at this time.

8. Secure the upper arm to the axle housing with new retaining bolts and nuts. The bolts must be pointed toward the front of the vehicle.

9. Raise the suspension with a jack until the upper arm rear pivot hole is in position with the hole in the axle bushing. Install a new pivot bolt and nut with the nut facing inboard.

10. Tighten the upper arm-to-axle pivot bolts to 103–133 ft. lbs. (140–180 Nm) and upper arm-to-frame pivot bolts to 120–150 ft. lbs. (162–203 Nm).

11. Snap the parking brake cable into the upper arm retainer. Connect the height sensor to the ball stud on the left upper arm, if equipped.

12. Remove the supports from the frame and axle and lower the vehicle. If equipped, turn the air suspension switch **ON**.

Lower Arm

1. If equipped, turn the air suspension switch **OFF**.
2. Raise the vehicle and support the frame side rails with jackstands.
3. Remove the stabilizer bar, if equipped.
4. Support the axle with jackstands under the differential pinion nose as well as under the axle.
5. Remove and discard the lower arm pivot bolts and nuts and remove the lower arm.

To install:

6. Position the lower arm to the frame bracket and axle. Install new bolts and nuts.

7. Raise the axle. Tighten the lower arm-to-axle pivot bolt to 103–133 ft. lbs. (140–180 Nm) and lower arm-to-frame pivot bolt to 120–150 ft. lbs. (162–203 Nm).

8. Install the stabilizer bar, if equipped.

9. Remove the jackstands and lower the vehicle. If equipped, turn the air suspension switch **ON**.

GM "A" Body
Front Wheel Drive

OLDSMOBILE—Cutlass Ciera, Cutlass Cruiser **BUICK**—Century

11

FIRING ORDERS

NOTE: To avoid confusion, always replace spark plug wires one at a time.

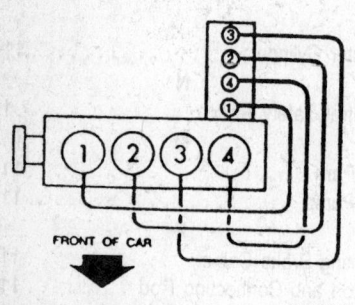

8470F001

2.2L and 2.5L Engines
Engine Firing Order: 1–3–4–2
Distributorless Ignition System

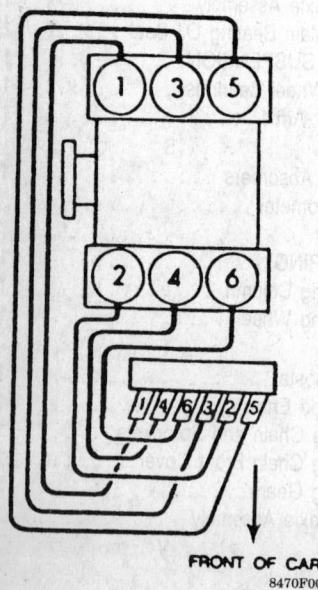

8470F003

3.1L and 3.3L Engines
3.3L Engine Firing Order: 1–6–5–4–3–2
3.1L Engine Firing Order: 1–2–3–4–5–6
Distributorless Ignition System

ENGINE ELECTRICAL

NOTE: Disconnecting the negative battery cable on some vehicles may interfere with the functions of the on–board computer systems and may require the computer to undergo a relearning process, once the negative battery cable is reconnected.

Direct Ignition System (DIS)

REMOVAL AND INSTALLATION

DIS Assembly

2.5L ENGINE

1. Disconnect the negative battery cable.
2. Disconnect the DIS electrical connectors.
3. Tag and disconnect the spark plug wires.
4. Remove the DIS assembly attaching bolts.
5. Remove the DIS assembly from the engine.
   To install:
6. Install the DIS assembly and attaching bolts.
7. Connect the spark plug wires.
8. Connect the DIS electrical connectors.
9. Connect the negative battery cable.

Ignition Coil(s)

2.5L ENGINE

1. Disconnect the negative battery cable.
2. Disconnect and tag spark plug wires.

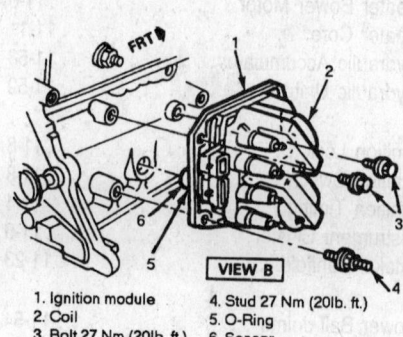

1. Ignition module
2. Coil
3. Bolt 27 Nm (20lb. ft.)
4. Stud 27 Nm (20lb. ft.)
5. O-Ring
6. Sensor

8470F004

DIS Coil System — 2.5L Engine

3. Remove ignition coil(s) attaching bolts, then the ignition coil from the module.
   To install:
4. Install the coil(s) and attaching bolts.
5. Connect the spark plug wires.
6. Connect the negative battery cable.

Ignition Module

2.5L ENGINE

1. Disconnect the negative battery cable.
2. Remove the DIS assembly from the engine.
3. Remove the coils from the assembly.
4. Remove DIS module from the assembly plate.
   To install:
5. Install the DIS module to the assembly plate.
6. Install the coils to the assembly.
7. Install the DIS assembly to the engine.
8. Connect the negative battery cable.

Crankshaft Sensor

2.5L ENGINE

1. Disconnect the negative battery cable.
2. Remove the DIS assembly.
3. Remove the sensor screws and remove the sensor from the DIS assembly.
   To install:
4. Inspect the sensor O-ring for wear, cracks or leakage. Replace as necessary. Lubricate the new O-ring with engine oil prior to installation.
5. Install the sensor to the DIS assembly and install the screws.
6. Install the DIS assembly to the vehicle.
7. Connect the negative battery cable.

Computer Controlled Coil Ignition (C³I) System

REMOVAL AND INSTALLATION

C³I Module

3.1L AND 3.3L ENGINES

1. Disconnect the negative battery cable.
2. Disconnect the 14-way connector at the ignition module.
3. Tag and disconnect the spark plug wires at the coil assembly.

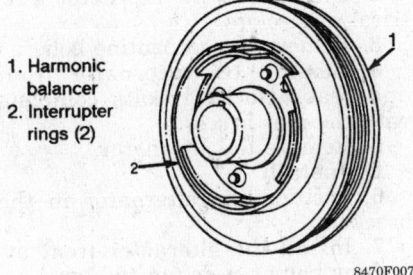

8470F006

C³I Ignition Coils and Control Module

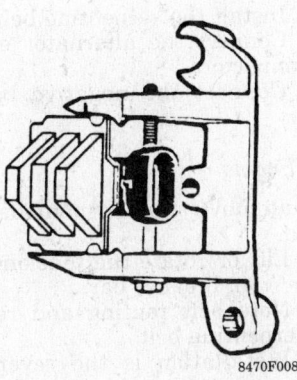

1. Harmonic balancer
2. Interrupter rings (2)

8470F007

C³I System Harmonic Balancer

C³I System Crankshaft Position Sensor

8470F008

4. Remove the nuts and washers securing the C³I module assembly to the bracket.

5. Remove the 6 nuts attaching the coil assemblies to the ignition module.

To install:

6. Install the coil assemblies to the ignition module and install the 6 attaching nuts.

7. Install the nuts and washers attaching the assembly to the bracket.

8. Connect the spark plug wires.

9. Connect the 14-way connector to the module.

---

10. Connect the negative battery cable.

Ignition Coil(s)

3.1L AND 3.3L ENGINES

1. Disconnect the negative battery cable.

2. Tag and disconnect spark plug wires.

3. Remove ignition coil(s) attaching nuts and the ignition coil from the module.

To install:

4. Install the coil(s) and attaching nuts.

5. Connect the spark plug wires.

6. Connect the negative battery cable.

Dual (24X) Crankshaft Sensor

3.1L AND 3.3L ENGINES

NOTE: The 3.1L engine is equipped with 2 separate crankshaft sensors. The 3X crankshaft sensor is mounted to the side of the engine block, above the oil pan flange and the 24X crankshaft sensor is mounted to the front timing cover, under the harmonic balancer. For the 3.1L engine with manual transaxle, the 3X crankshaft sensor is easily accessed from beneath the vehicle. For the 3.1L engine with automatic transaxle, the rack and pinion heatshield and catalytic converter intermediate exhaust assembly must be removed.

1. Disconnect battery negative cable.

2. Disconnect serpentine belt from crankshaft pulley.

3. Raise and safely support the vehicle.

4. Remove right front tire and wheel assembly, then the inner fender access cover.

5. Remove crankshaft harmonic balancer retaining bolt and crankshaft harmonic balancer.

6. Disconnect electrical connector from sensor, remove the foreign object deflector and remove the crankshaft sensor from the vehicle.

To install:

7. Loosely install the crankshaft sensor on the pedestal.

8. Position the sensor with the pedestal attached on special tool J–37089.

9. Position the tool on the crankshaft.

10. Install the bolts to hold the pedestal to the block face. Tighten to 18–26 ft. lbs. (25–35 Nm).

---

11. Tighten the pedestal pinch bolt to 26–44 inch lbs. (3–5 Nm).

12. Remove special tool J–37089 and install the foreign object deflector.

13. Place special tool J–37089 on the harmonic balancer and turn. If any vane of the harmonic balancer touches the tool, replace the balancer assembly.

14. Install the balancer on the crankshaft and install the crankshaft balancer bolt. Tighten to 104 ft. lbs. + 56 degrees (140 Nm + 56 degrees).

15. Install the inner fender shield.

16. Install the tire and wheel assembly. Tighten to 100 ft. lbs. (140 Nm).

17. Lower the vehicle.

18. Install the serpentine belt.

19. Connect the negative battery cable.

3X Crankshaft Sensor

3.1L ENGINE

NOTE: The 3X crankshaft sensor is mounted to the side of the engine block, above the oil pan flange. For the manual transaxle, the 3X crankshaft sensor is easily accessed from beneath the vehicle. For the automatic transaxle, the rack and pinion heatshield and catalytic converter intermediate exhaust assembly must be removed.

1. Disconnect the negative battery terminal.

2. Disconnect the sensor electrical connector.

3. Remove the sensor bolt and sensor from the engine.

4. Install a new O-ring and lubricate with engine oil. Install the bolt and torque to 88 inch lbs. (10 Nm).

5. Connect the negative battery terminal and check for proper operation.

Electronic Ignition (EI) System

REMOVAL AND INSTALLATION

Ignition Coil Assembly

2.2L ENGINE

1. Disconnect the negative battery cable.

2. Disconnect the electrical connectors and the spark plug wires, noting the original location of the spark plug wires.

3. Remove the ignition coil mounting bolts and remove the ignition coils.

To install:

4. Install the ignition coils to the engine and tighten the mounting bolts to 15–22 ft. lbs. (20–30 Nm).

5. Connect the spark plug wires to the respective coils and connect the coil electrical connectors.

6. Connect the negative battery cable.

Crankshaft Position Sensor

2.2L ENGINE

1. Disconnect the sensor harness connector at the module.

2. Remove the sensor–to–engine block bolt and remove the sensor.

To install:

3. Install the sensor into the hole in the block.

4. Install the sensor block bolt and connect the harness connector.

Electronic Ignition Control Module (ICM)

2.2L ENGINE

1. Disconnect the negative battery cable.

2. Remove the ignition coil from the engine.

3. Remove the coils from the coil assembly plate.

4. Remove the module from the assembly plate.

To install:

5. Install the module and the coils to the assembly plate.

6. Install the ignition coils to the engine.

7. Connect the negative battery cable.

Ignition Timing

All vehicles are equipped with either the Direct Ignition System (DIS) or the Computer Controlled Coil Ignition (C_3I) system. The systems consist of a coil pack, ignition module, crankshaft interrupter ring(s), magnetic sensor and an Electronic Control Module (ECM). Timing advance and retard are accomplished through the ECM with the Electronic Spark Timing (EST) and Electronic Spark Control (ESC) circuitry. No ignition timing adjustment is required or possible.

Alternator

PRECAUTIONS

Several precautions must be observed with alternator equipped vehicles to avoid damage to the unit.

• If the battery is removed for any reason, make sure it is reconnected with the correct polarity. Reversing the battery connections may result in damage to the one-way rectifiers.

• When utilizing a booster battery as a starting aid, always connect the positive to positive terminals and the negative terminal from the booster battery to a good engine ground on the vehicle being started.

• Never use a fast charger as a booster to start vehicles.

• Disconnect the battery cables when charging the battery with a fast charger.

• Never attempt to polarize the alternator.

• Do not use test lamps of more than 12 volts when checking diode continuity.

• Do not short across or ground any of the alternator terminals.

• The polarity of the battery, alternator and regulator must be matched and considered before making any electrical connections within the system.

• Never separate the alternator on an open circuit. Make sure all connections within the circuit are clean and tight.

• Disconnect the battery ground terminal when performing any service on electrical components.

• Disconnect the battery if arc welding is to be done on the vehicle.

BELT TENSION ADJUSTMENT

Serpentine Belt

A single serpentine belt is used to drive all engine accessories. The belt tension is maintained by a spring loaded tensioner. The belt tensioner has the ability to control the belt tension over a broad range of belt lengths. However, there are limits to which the tensioner can compensate for varying lengths. If the belt tension is below the minimum specifications, replace the belt tensioner.

Check the serpentine belt tension with tool J–23600B or equivalent, belt tension gauge in the following manner:

1. Start the engine and run until operating temperature is reached.

2. Shut the engine OFF and place the tension gauge midway between

the pulleys. Install the gauge on the longest belt span possible. If the belt is notched on the inner surface, place the middle finger of the tensioner gauge into 1 of the notches. Correct belt tension readings should be approximately:

40 lbs. (178 Nm) — 2.5L engine
50–70 lbs. (225–315 Nm) — 3.1L engine
67 lbs. (298 Nm) — 3.3L engine

REMOVAL AND INSTALLATION

Except 3.1L Engine

1. Disconnect the negative battery cable.

2. Disconnect the alternator electrical connectors.

3. Remove the serpentine belt.

4. Remove the alternator front and rear attaching bolts complete with the rear brace.

5. Remove the alternator.

To install:

6. Position the alternator in the bracket.

7. Install the alternator front attaching bolts but do not tighten.

8. Install the rear attaching bolts and brace. Tighten bolts to the proper torque specs.

9. Install the serpentine belt.

10. Connect the alternator electrical connectors.

11. Connect the negative battery cable.

3.1L Engine

1. Remove the serpentine belt shield.

2. Lift or rotate the tensioner using a 3/8 in. breaker bar.

3. Note belt routing and remove the serpentine belt.

4. Installation is the reverse of removal.

Starter

REMOVAL AND INSTALLATION

2.2L and 2.5L Engines

1. Disconnect the negative battery cable.

2. Raise and safely support the vehicle.

3. Remove the engine torque strut bracket pencil brace, from the 2.2L engine vehicle.

4. Remove the bolts from the flywheel inspection cover and remove the cover.

5. Remove the bolts from the bracket and remove the starter bolts.

6. Disconnect the starter wiring.
7. Remove the starter and any shims.

To install:

NOTE: If replacing the starter, transfer the starter bracket to the new starter.

8. Install the starter and any shims.
9. Install the 2 starter attaching bolts.
10. On the 2.5L engine, install the bolt attaching the starter bracket to the engine.
11. Install the flywheel inspection cover and install the bolts.
12. Connect the starter wires.
13. Lower the vehicle.
14. Connect the negative battery cable.

3.1L Engine

1. Disconnect the negative battery cable.
2. Raise the vehicle and safely support.
3. Disconnect the engine wiring harness from the front of the frame.
4. Remove the inspection cover and electrical connections from the starter.

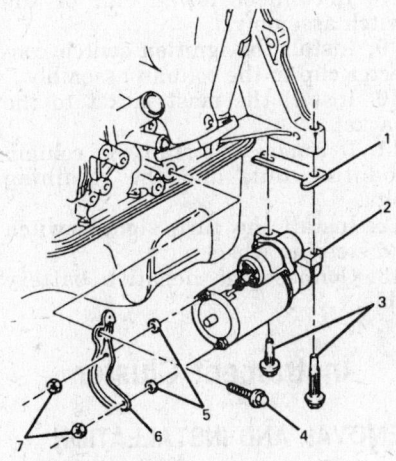

1. Starter motor shim
2. Starter motor assembly
3. Starter motor bolt/screw
4. Starter motor bracket bolt/screw
5. Starter motor washer
6. Starter motor bracket
7. Starter motor nut

8470F013

Exploded view of the starter — 2.2L engine

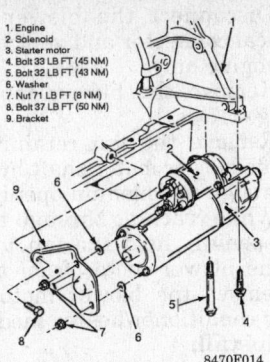

1. Engine
2. Solenoid
3. Starter motor
4. Bolt 33 LB FT (45 NM)
5. Bolt 32 LB FT (43 NM)
6. Washer
7. Nut 71 LB FT (8 NM)
8. Bolt 37 LB FT (50 NM)
9. Bracket

8470F014

Exploded view of the starter — 2.5L engine

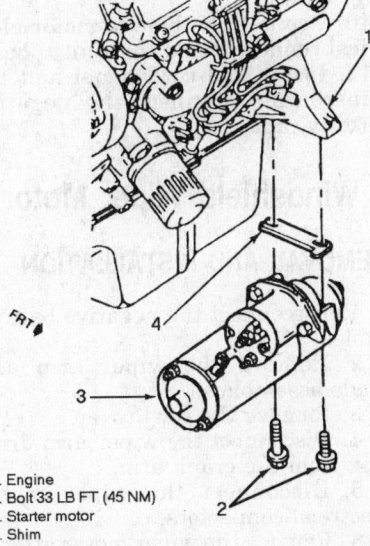

1. Engine
2. Bolt 33 LB FT (45 NM)
3. Starter motor
4. Shim

8470F015

Exploded view of the starter — 3.1L engine

5. Remove the starter bolt and starter. Save any shims that are removed.

To install:

6. Connect the solenoid battery and S terminals. Torque the battery nut to 12 ft. lbs. (16 Nm) and the S terminal nut to 27 inch lbs. (3 Nm).
7. Install the starter bolts and torque to 32 ft. lbs. (43 Nm). Install the remaining components.

3.3L Engine

1. Disconnect the negative battery cable.

2. Properly discharge the air conditioning system.
3. On 3.3L engine, remove the cooling fan assembly.
4. Remove the front exhaust manifold.
5. Raise and support the vehicle safely.
6. Remove the bolts from the flywheel inspection cover and remove the cover.
7. Disconnect the air conditioner condenser hose from the compressor and position aside.
8. Disconnect the starter motor electrical connectors.
9. Remove the 2 bolts attaching the starter.
10. Remove the starter and any shims.

To install:

11. Install the starter motor and any shims.
12. Install the 2 bolts attaching the starter. Tighten to 30 ft. lbs. (40 Nm).
13. Connect the starter motor electrical connectors.
14. Replace the condenser O-ring. Lubricate with refrigerant oil. Connect the air conditioner condenser hose to the compressor.
15. Install the flywheel inspection cover and attaching bolts.
16. Lower the vehicle.
17. Install the front exhaust manifold.
18. Install the cooling fan assembly.
19. Evacuate, recharge and leak test the air conditioning system.
20. Connect the negative battery cable.

CHASSIS ELECTRICAL

Air Bag

DISARMING

1. Align the steering wheel so the wheels are pointing in the straight-ahead position.
2. Turn the ignition switch to the **LOCK** position.
3. Remove the SIR or AIR BAG fuse from the fuse block.
4. Remove the Connector Position Assurance (CPA) device, then disengage the yellow 2-way SIR wire harness connector at the base of the steering column.

1. Bolts
2. Motor assembly

8470F016

Exploded view of the starter — 3.3L engine

To enable system:

5. Turn the ignition switch to the **LOCK** position.

6. Engage the yellow 2-way connector at the base of the steering column, then install the CPA device.

7. Reinstall the SIR or AIR BAG fuse.

8. Turn the ignition switch to the **RUN** position.

9. Verify the SIR indicator light flashes 7–9 times, if not, inspect system for malfunction.

Heater Bower Motor

REMOVAL AND INSTALLATION

Without Air Conditioning

1. Disconnect the negative battery cable.

2. Tag and disconnect the blower motor electrical leads.

3. Remove the motor retaining bolts and remove the blower motor.

4. If the blower motor is to be replaced, separate the fan from the blower motor by removing the retaining nut and sliding the fan from the shaft.

To install:

5. If the blower motor is to be replaced, install the fan to the new blower motor and install the retaining nut.

6. Install the fan in the heater module and install the retaining bolts.

7. Connect the electrical connector.

8. Connect the negative battery cable.

With Air Conditioning

1. Disconnect the negative battery cable.

2. Remove the wiper arms and the cowl panel.

3. Disconnect the blower motor electrical connector and vent tube for 3.3L engine only.

4. Remove the blower motor retaining screws.

5. Remove the fan retaining nut from the blower motor shaft by reaching through the plenum opening.

6. While reaching through the plenum opening, hold the fan to separate the blower motor from the fan and remove the blower motor from the air conditioner/heater module.

To install:

7. Install the blower motor to the air conditioner/heater module by reaching through the plenum opening to hold the fan and insert the blower motor shaft into the fan.

8. Install the fan retaining nut to the blower motor shaft.

9. Install the blower motor retaining screws.

10. Connect the blower motor electrical connector and the vent tube.

11. Install the cowl panel and the wiper arms. Connect the negative battery cable.

Windshield Wiper Motor

REMOVAL AND INSTALLATION

1. Disconnect the negative battery cable.

2. Remove the wiper arm and blade assemblies.

3. Remove the cowl cover.

4. Disconnect the wiper arm drive link from the crank arm.

5. Disconnect the wiper motor electrical connectors.

6. Remove the wiper motor attaching bolts.

7. Remove the wiper motor, guiding the crank arm through the hole.

To install:

8. Insert the wiper motor, guiding the crank arm through the hole.

9. Install the wiper motor attaching bolts.

10. Connect the electrical connectors.

11. Connect the wiper arm drive link to the crank arm.

12. Install the cowl cover.

13. Install the wiper arms.

14. Connect the negative battery cable.

Windshield Wiper Switch

REMOVAL AND INSTALLATION

1. Disconnect the negative battery cable.

2. Remove the steering wheel and turn signal switch. It may be necessary to first remove the column mounting nuts and remove the 4 bracket-to-mast jacket screws, then separate the bracket from the mast jacket to allow the connector clip on the ignition switch to be pulled from the column assembly.

3. Tag and disconnect the washer/wiper switch lower connector.

4. Remove the screws attaching the column housing to the mast jacket. Be sure to note the position of the dimmer switch actuator rod for reassembly in the same position. Remove the column housing and switch as an assembly.

NOTE: Certain tilt and travel columns are equipped with a removable plastic cover on the column housing. This provides access to the wiper switch without removing the entire column housing.

5. Turn upside down and use a drift to remove the pivot pin from the washer/wiper switch. Remove the switch.

To install:

6. Place the switch into position in the housing. Install the pivot pin.

7. Position the housing onto the mast jacket and attach by installing the screws. Install the dimmer switch actuator rod in the same position as noted when removed. Check switch operation.

8. Reconnect lower end of the switch assembly.

9. Install the ignition switch connector clip to the column assembly.

10. Install the mast jacket to the bracket.

11. If removed, install the column mounting nuts and the retaining bolts.

12. Install the turn signal switch and steering wheel.

13. Connect the negative battery cable.

Instrument Cluster

REMOVAL AND INSTALLATION

Century

1. Disconnect the negative battery cable.

2. Remove the left instrument panel trim plate.

3. Disconnect the shift indicator clip from the steering column shift bowl.

4. Remove the 4 screws cluster screws.

5. If equipped with column shift, shift the transaxle to **1**.

6. Pull the cluster outward to remove from the vehicle.

To install:

7. Install the cluster to the vehicle.

8. Install the 4 screws.

9. If equipped with column shift, shift the transaxle to **P**.

10. Install the shift indicator clip and make sure the indicator lines up properly.

11. Install the left instrument panel trim plate.

Cutlass Ciera and Cutlass Cruiser

1. Disconnect the negative battery cable. Remove upper console, if equipped.

2. Remove the accessory trim plate assembly.

3. Remove the cluster trim plate assembly.

4. Remove the steering column trim trim collar and trim cover.

5. Disconnect shift indicator clip from steering column shift bowl.

6. Remove the 4 bolts securing the cluster assembly.

7. Pull cluster rearward to remove and remove unit from the vehicle.

To install:

8. Install the cluster assembly.

9. Install the 4 bolts.

10. Connect the shift indicator clip to the shift bowl.

11. Shift the indicator to make sure needle alignment is correct.

12. Install the steering column trim cover.

13. Install the cluster trim plate.

14. Install the accessory trim plate and upper console, if equipped.

15. Connect the negative battery cable.

Speedometer

REMOVAL AND INSTALLATION

Century

1. Disconnect the negative battery cable.

2. Remove the left side trim plate.

3. Remove the 4 speedometer lens screws and remove the speedometer lens.

4. Remove the 4 screws holding the speedometer to the instrument and remove the speedometer assembly.

To install:

5. Install the speedometer assembly and the screws holding the speed-

ometer assembly to the instrument panel.

6. Install the speedometer lens and retaining screws.

7. Install the left side trim plate.

8. Connect the negative battery cable.

Cutlass Ciera and Cutlass Cruiser

1. Disconnect the negative battery cable.

2. Remove the instrument cluster assembly.

3. Remove the vehicle speed sensor bolt from the rear of the speedometer. Remove the vehicle speed sensor.

4. Remove the speedometer lens screws and remove the speedometer lens. Remove the bezel.

5. Remove the screw that holds the speedometer at the rear of the cluster.

6. Remove the front cluster screws. Remove the speedometer by gently pulling forward.

To install:

7. Install the speedometer head and install the front 2 screws.

8. Install the rear screw that holds the speedometer to the instrument cluster.

9. Install the speedometer lens and attaching screws. Install the bezel.

10. Install the vehicle speed sensor and the attaching bolt at the rear of the speedometer.

11. Install the instrument cluster assembly.

12. Connect the negative battery cable.

Headlight Switch

NOTE: Follow the steps below if equipped with dash mounted headlight switch. Refer to combination switch section if equipped with column mounted multi-function switch.

REMOVAL AND INSTALLATION

Century

1. Disconnect the negative battery cable.

2. Remove the instrument panel trim plate.

3. Remove the left side instrument panel switch trim panel by removing the 3 screws and gently rocking the panel out.

4. Remove the 3 screws and pull the switch straight out.

To install:

5. Install the switch and the 3 attaching screws.

6. Install the left side instrument panel switch trim panel and 3 attaching screws.

7. Install the instrument panel trim plate.

8. Connect the negative battery cable.

Cutlass Ciera and Cutlass Cruiser

1. Disconnect the negative battery cable.

2. Remove the left side instrument panel trim pad.

3. Unbolt the switch from the instrument panel.

4. Pull the switch rearward and remove it.

To install:

5. Install the switch and connect the electrical connectors.

6. Install the bolts attaching the switch to the instrument panel.

7. Install the left side instrument panel trim pad.

8. Connect the negative battery cable.

Dimmer Switch

NOTE: Some vehicles have the dimmer switch incorporated into the combination switch. If equipped as such, refer to the combination switch section.

REMOVAL AND INSTALLATION

1. Disconnect the negative battery cable.

2. Remove the steering wheel. Remove the trim cover.

3. Remove the turn signal switch assembly.

4. Remove the ignition switch stud and screw. Remove the ignition switch.

5. Remove the dimmer switch actuator rod by sliding it from the switch assembly.

6. Remove the dimmer switch bolts and remove the dimmer switch.

To install:

7. Install the dimmer switch and attaching bolts.

8. Install the dimmer switch actuator rod by sliding it into the switch assembly.

9. Adjust the dimmer switch by depressing the switch slightly and inserting a $3/32$ in. drill bit into the adjusting hole. Push the switch up to remove any play and tighten the dimmer switch adjusting screw.

10. Install the ignition switch, stud and screw.

11. Install the turn signal switch assembly.

12. Install the trim cover. Install the steering wheel.

13. Connect the battery negative cable.

Combination Switch

NOTE: If equipped with a dash mounted headlight switch, refer to headlight switch section.

REMOVAL AND INSTALLATION

1. Disconnect the negative battery cable. Remove the steering wheel and trim cover.

2. Loosen the cover screws. Pry the cover upward and remove it from the shaft.

3. Position U-shaped lock plate compressing tool J–23653–C on the end of the steering shaft and compress the lockplate by turning the shaft nut clockwise. Pry the wire snapring from the shaft groove.

4. Remove the tool and lift the lock plate off the shaft.

5. Slip the cancelling cam, upper bearing preload spring and thrust washer off the shaft.

6. Remove the turn signal lever. Push the flasher knob in and unscrew it. Remove the button retaining screw and remove the button, spring and knob.

7. Pull the switch connector out the mast jacket and tape the upper part to facilitate switch removal. Attach a long piece of wire to the turn signal switch connector. When installing the turn signal switch, feed this wire through the column first, and then use this wire to pull the switch connector into position. If equipped with tilt-wheel, place the turn signal and shifter housing in the lowest position and remove the harness cover.

8. Remove the 3 switch mounting screws. Remove the switch by pulling it straight up while guiding the wiring harness cover through the column.

To install:

9. Install the replacement switch by working the connector and cover down through the housing and under the bracket. If equipped with tilt-wheel, work the connector down through the housing, under the bracket and install the harness cover.

10. Install the switch mounting screws and the connector on the mast

jacket bracket. Install the column-to-dash trim plate.

11. Install the flasher knob and the turn signal lever.

12. With the turn signal lever in the middle position and the flasher knob out, slide the thrust washer, upper bearing preload spring and cancelling cam onto the shaft.

13. Position the lock plate on the shaft and press it down until a new snapring can be inserted in the shaft groove. Always use a new snapring when assembling.

14. Install the cover and the steering wheel. Connect the battery negative cable.

Ignition Lock

REMOVAL AND INSTALLATION

1. Disconnect the negative battery cable. Place the lock in the **RUN** position. Remove the steering wheel.

2. Remove the lock plate, turn signal switch and buzzer switch.

3. Remove the screw and lock cylinder.

NOTE: Be careful not to drop the screw which could fall into the column assembly requiring complete disassembly of the column to retrieve the screw.

To install:

4. Rotate the cylinder clockwise to align cylinder key with the keyway in the housing.

5. Push the lock all the way in.

6. Install the screw. Tighten the screw to 14 inch lbs. for adjustable columns or 25 inch lbs. (3 Nm) for standard columns. Connect battery negative cable.

Ignition Switch

REMOVAL AND INSTALLATION

The switch is connected to the jacket assembly of the steering column housing. The switch is actuated by a rod and rack assembly. A gear on the end of the lock cylinder engages the toothed upper end of the rod.

1. Disconnect the negative battery cable.

2. Put the ignition switch in the **OFF-LOCKED** position. Remove the steering wheel.

3. Using tool J–23653–C, depress the shaft lock and remove the shaft lock retaining ring and the shaft lock.

4. Remove the turn signal cancelling cam.

5. Remove the upper bearing spring and thrust washer.

6. Set the turn signal to the RIGHT turn setting and remove the combination switch lever.

7. Remove the screws from the actuator switch and remove the switch assembly.

8. Remove the hazard knob assembly.

9. Disconnect the turn signal switch and allow it to hang freely.

10. Remove the key from the lock cylinder set and remove the alarm assembly and clip.

11. Insert key into lock cylinder and set to **LOCK** position.

12. If equipped with cruise control, remove the housing cover end cap, unplug the connector and carefully pull through the shroud. Remove the combination switch assembly.

13. Remove the ignition switch screws and remove the switch assembly.

To install:

14. Before installing, place the new switch in **OFF-UNLOCKED** position and make sure the lock cylinder and actuating rod are in **OFF-UNLOCKED**, third detent from the top.

15. Install the activating rod into the switch and assemble the switch on the column. Tighten the mounting screws. Use only the specified screws since over-length screws could impair the collapsibility of the column.

16. Reinstall the steering column assembly. Connect battery negative cable.

Brake Light Switch

ADJUSTMENT

1. The switch is mounted on the brake pedal bracket.

2. To adjust, depress the pedal and push the switch through the circular retaining clip until it contacts the brake pedal, then pull the pedal up against the internal pedal stop. This places the switch in the correct position within the clip.

REMOVAL AND INSTALLATION

1. Disconnect the negative battery cable. Disconnect the electrical connector to the switch.

2. Remove the switch from the brake pedal bracket.

To install:

3. Install the new switch into the bracket.

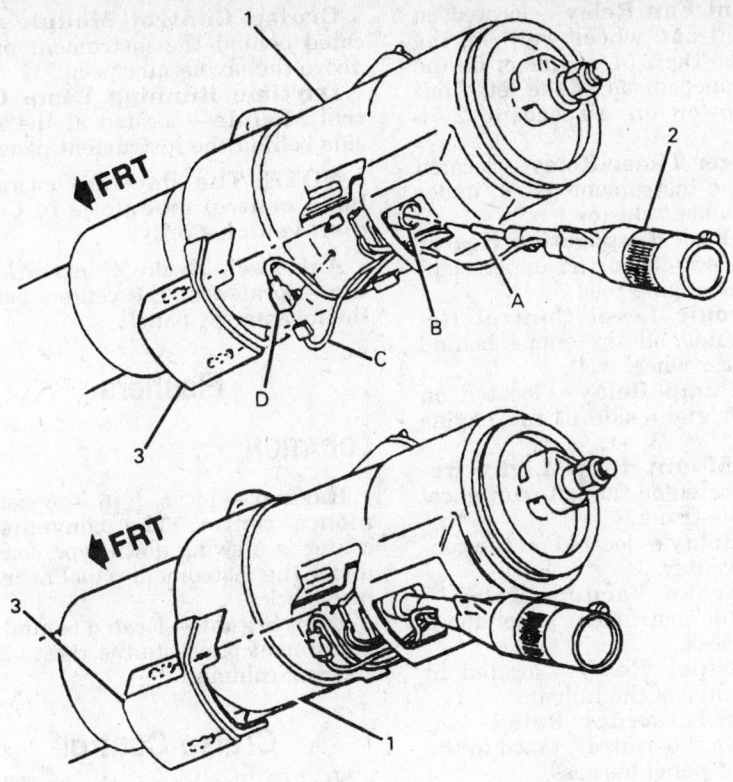

A. Tang
B. Notch
C. Lever assembly connector
D. Steering column connector
1. Steering column assembly
2. Lever assembly - turn signal, headlamp dimmer switch, cruise control actuator, windshield wiper and windshield washer
3. Steering column housing cap

8470F024

Combination switch assembly

1. Switch actuator rack
2. Dimmer and ignition switch mounting stud
3. Dimmer switch assembly
4. Ignition and dimmer switch assembly
5. Hex nut (#10-24)
6. Washer HD screw (#10-24X.25)
7. Dimmer switch actuator rod

8470F025

Removal of ignition and dimmer switches

4. Connect the electrical connector.
5. Adjust the switch. Connect battery negative cable.

Neutral Safety Switch

ADJUSTMENT

1. After the switch is installed, move the housing towards the **L** gear position.
2. Shift the gear selector into the **P** position.

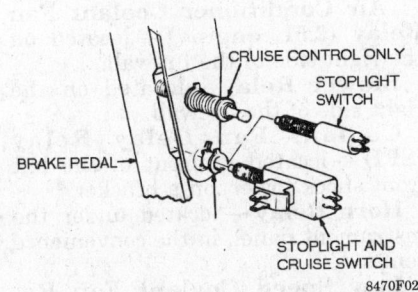

CRUISE CONTROL ONLY
STOPLIGHT SWITCH
BRAKE PEDAL
STOPLIGHT AND CRUISE SWITCH

8470F026

Brake light switch assembly

3. The main housing and the housing back should ratchet. This will provide proper switch adjustment.
4. Repeat if necessary.

REMOVAL AND INSTALLATION

Vehicles With Console Shift

1. New switches include a small plastic alignment pin. Leave this pin in place. Position the shifter assembly in **N**.
2. Disconnect the negative battery cable. Remove console to access old switch. Remove the old switch and install the replacement, align the pin

on the shifter with the slot in the switch and fasten with the 2 screws.
3. Move the shifter from the **N** position. This shears the plastic alignment pin and frees the switch.
4. If the switch is to be adjusted, insert a 3/32 in. drill bit or similar size pin and align the hole switch. Position switch, adjust as necessary. Remove the pin before shifting from **N**. Connect battery negative cable.

Vehicles with Column Shift

1. Disconnect the negative battery cable. Disconnect the electrical connectors from the combination backup and neutral safety switch.
2. Remove the 2 screws attaching the switch to the steering column.
3. Remove the switch.
To install:
4. Install the new switch and 2 attaching screws.
5. Adjust the switch by performing the following:
   a. Position the shift lever in **N**.
   b. Loosen the attaching screws. Install a 0.090mm. gauge pin into the outer hole in the switch cover.
   c. Rotate the switch until the pin goes into the alignment hole in the inner plastic slide.
   d. Tighten the switch-to-column attaching screws and remove the

gauge pin. Torque the screws to 20 inch lbs. (1 Nm) maximum.

6. Connect battery negative cable.

7. Make sure the engine starts only in the **P** and **N** positions.

Fuses, Circuit Breakers and Relays

LOCATION

Fusible Links

There are several locations where fusible links can be found. They are located ahead of the left side front shock tower, near the positive battery connection or at the starter solenoid near the front of the engine.

Circuit Breakers

Circuit breakers are used along with the fusible links to protect various components of the electrical system, such as headlights, the windshield wipers and electric windows. The circuit breakers are located either in the switch or mounted on or near the lower lip of the instrument panel, to the right or left of the steering column.

Fuse Panel

The fuse panel is located on the left side of the vehicle. It is under the instrument panel, it may be necessary to first remove the under dash padding.

Relays

EXCEPT CENTURY

Air Conditioner Compressor Relay — located on the upper right corner of the engine cowl.

Air Conditioner Delay Relay — located in the upper right corner of the engine cowl.

Air Conditioner/Heater Blower Relay — located on the plenum, on the right side of the firewall.

Altitude Advance Relay — located on the left inner fender, in front of the shock tower.

Charging System Relay — located behind the instrument panel, near the fuse block.

Constant Run Relay — located on the left inner fender wheel well.

Coolant Fan Low-Speed Relay — located on the left inner fender wheel well, on a bracket on the 2.5L engine or on the fender panel in front of the left front shock tower on all except 2.5L engine.

Coolant Fan Relay — located on the left front wheel well on the bracket on the 2.5L engine or on the fender panel ahead of the left front shock tower on all except 2.5L engine.

Defogger Timer Relay — located behind the instrument panel, under the instrument cluster.

Early Fuel Evaporation Heater Relay — located on the upper right side of the engine cowl.

Electronic Level Control Relay — located on the frame behind the left rear wheel well.

Fuel Pump Relay — located on the upper right side of the engine cowl.

High Mount Stop Light Relays — located on the left rear wheel well, in the trunk.

Horn Relay — located on the convenience center.

Low Brake Vacuum Relay — taped to the instrument panel above the fuse block.

Rear Wiper Relay — located in the top center of the tailgate.

Starter Interrupt Relay — located above the ashtray, taped to the instrument panel harness.

CENTURY

Air Conditioner Coolant Fan Relay (2.5L engine) — located on the right side of the firewall.

Blower Relay — located on the right side of the firewall.

Coolant Fan Delay Relay (SFI) — located in front of the left front shock tower, on a bracket.

Horn Relay — located under the instrument panel, in the convenience center.

Low Speed Coolant Fan Relay — located near the battery, on the left side of the radiator shroud.

Rear Wiper Relay — located in the top center of the tailgate.

Starter Interrupt Relay — taped to the instrument panel harness, above the right side ashtray.

Computers

LOCATION

Electronic Control Module — located on the right side of the vehicle. It is positioned under the instrument panel. In order to gain access to the electronic control module, it will be necessary to first remove the trim panel.

Cruise Control Module — located behind the instrument panel, above the accelerator pedal.

Daytime Running Lamp Control Module — located at the right side behind the instrument panel.

NOTE: The daytime running lamp control module is in Canadian vehicles only.

Anti-Lock Brake Control Module — located in the center, behind the instrument panel.

Flashers

LOCATION

Hazard — located in the convenience center. The convenience center is a swing down type, located under the instrument panel near the fuse block.

Turn Signal — located behind the instrument panel, to the right of the steering column.

Cruise Control

NOTE: To keep the vehicle under control and to prevent possible vehicle damage, it is not advisable to use the cruise control on slippery roads. Disengage the cruise control in conditions such as varying or heavy traffic or when traveling down a steep graded hill.

ADJUSTMENTS

1. Adjust the throttle lever to the idle position with the engine **OFF**. If equipped with an idle control solenoid, the solenoid must be de-energized.

2. Pull the servo assembly end of the cable towards the servo blade.

3. Align the holes in the servo blade with the cable pin. Install the cable pin.

ENGINE COOLING

Radiator

REMOVAL AND INSTALLATION

1. Disconnect the negative battery cable and drain the cooling system.

2. Remove the air cleaner assembly and air cleaner duct.

3. Remove the engine strut brace bolts from the upper mounting panel. Loosen the bolt to prevent damage to the bushing, then swing the strut rearward.

4. On the 2.5L engine, remove the air intake resonator mounting nut and remove the resonator.

5. Disconnect the electrical connector from the fan and remove the cooling fan attaching bolts, and then the cooling fan.

6. Disconnect the coolant hoses from the radiator and the coolant recovery tank hose. Disconnect the transaxle oil cooler lines.

7. Remove the radiator attaching bolts, then the radiator. If equipped with air conditioning, it may be necessary to raise the left side of the radiator so the radiator neck will clear the compressor.

To install:

8. Install the radiator and attaching bolts.

9. Connect the coolant hoses to the radiator. Connect the oil cooler lines.

10. Install the cooling fan and attaching bolts.

11. Install the air intake resonator to the 2.5L engine. Connect the electrical connector to the fan.

12. Install the engine forward strut bracket to the radiator and install the air cleaner assembly.

13. Connect the negative battery cable.

14. Fill cooling system and check for leaks. Start the engine and allow to come to normal operating temperature. Recheck for leaks. Top-off coolant level.

Electric Cooling Fan

TESTING

Coolant Fan Not Working

1. Turn the ignition switch to the **RUN** position. Ground the diagnostic terminal **C1/21** for 2.5L engine or **C3/E8** for 3.3L engine with a fused jumper wire.

2. If the coolant fan runs, replace the ECM. If the coolant fan does not run, go to the next step.

3. Remove the connector from the coolant fan relay which is located on the left front fender. Measure the voltage from the brown wire to the ground. Turn the ignition switch to the **RUN** position.

4. If there is no voltage present, inspect the brown and white wire for an open. Repair as necessary.

5. If there is voltage, move the voltmeter to between the brown wire

and the green wire for the 2.2L and 2.5L engine or green/white wire for 3.3L engine.

6. If there is no voltage present, inspect the green or green/white wire for an open or short. Repair as necessary.

7. If there is voltage present, measure the voltage between the **A** (red) terminal and the coolant fan relay ground at the connector.

8. If there is no voltage present, inspect the red wire for an open or short. Repair as necessary.

9. If there is voltage present, connect a fused jumper between terminals **A** and **E** of the coolant fan relay connector.

10. If the coolant fan runs, replace the coolant fan relay. If the coolant fan does not run, go to the next step.

11. With the fused jumper still in place, remove the coolant fan connector and connect a test lamp to terminal **B** of the connector and ground.

12. If the lamp does not light, inspect the wiring for an open and repair as necessary. If the lamp lights, go to the next step.

13. Move the test lamp ground lead to terminal **A** of the coolant fan connector. If the test lamp does not light, check wire for an open and repair as necessary.

Coolant Fan Runs Continuously

IGNITION SWITCH IN RUN POSITION

1. Check for diagnostic Code 14 or 15. If either of these codes are present, replace the coolant sensor. If no code is present, go to the next step.

2. Inspect the dark green and white wire for an open and repair, as necessary. If the wire shows continuity on the 2.5L engine, replace the coolant fan relay. On all other engines, go to the next step.

3. Remove the connector from the fan temperature backup switch and turn the ignition switch to **RUN**.

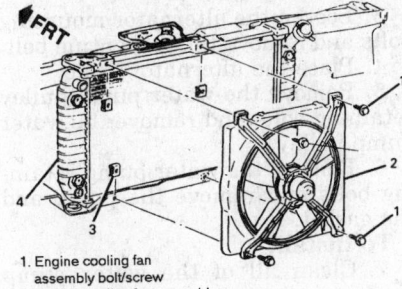

1. Engine cooling fan assembly bolt/screw
2. Engine cooling fan assembly
3. Radiator bracket nut
4. Radiator assembly

8470F028

Cooling fan assembly

4. If the coolant fan runs, replace the coolant fan relay. If the coolant fan does not run, replace the fan temperature backup switch located between the coolant fan relay and the ECM.

IGNITION SWITCH IN OFF POSITION

1. Remove the connector from the coolant fan relay.

2. If the coolant fan runs, check for a short to battery voltage. Repair as necessary.

3. If the coolant fan stops running, replace the coolant fan relay.

REMOVAL AND INSTALLATION

Engine Cooling Fan

1. Disconnect the negative battery cable.

2. Tag and disconnect the electrical connector from the fan motor and fan frame.

3. Remove the fan frame-to-radiator support bolts.

4. Remove the fan and frame assembly from the vehicle.

To install:

5. Install the fan and frame assembly to the vehicle.

6. Install the fan frame-to-radiator support bolts.

7. Connect the electrical connector to the fan motor.

8. Connect the negative battery cable.

Auxiliary Engine Cooling Fan

3.1L ENGINE

1. Remove the grille and disconnect the fan electrical connectors.

2. Remove the front end support upper bolts and bolts from the top of the fan.

3. Raise the vehicle and support safely.

4. Remove the front end lower support bolts and bolts from the bottom of the fan.

5. Remove the fan assembly.

6. Installation is the reverse of removal. Torque the fan bolts to 80 inch lbs. (9 Nm).

Heater Core

REMOVAL AND INSTALLATION

Without Air Conditioning

1. Disconnect the negative battery cable Drain the cooling system.

2. Remove the heater inlet and outlet hoses.

3. Remove the radio noise suppression strap and blow residual coolant from heater core using compressed air.

4. Remove the heater core cover retaining screws. Remove the cover.

5. Remove the heater core.

To install:

6. Install the heater core.

7. Install the heater core cover and retaining screws.

8. Install the radio noise suppression strap.

9. Install the heater inlet and outlet hoses.

10. Fill cooling system and check for leaks. Start the engine and allow to come to normal operating temperature. Check for leaks. Top off coolant level.

11. Connect the negative battery cable.

With Air Conditioning

1. Disconnect the negative battery cable. Drain the cooling system.

2. Disconnect the heater hoses at the heater core.

3. Remove the heater duct and the lower side covers.

4. Remove the lower heater outlet.

5. Remove the housing cover-to-air valve housing clips.

6. Remove the housing cover bolts. Remove the housing cover.

7. Remove the heater core retaining straps. Remove the heater core tubing retainers. Lift out the heater core.

To install:

8. Install the heater core, tubing retainers and retaining straps.

9. Install the housing cover and retaining bolts.

10. Install the housing cover-to-air valve housing clips.

11. Install the lower heater outlet.

12. Install the heater duct and the lower side covers.

13. Connect the heater hoses to the heater core.

14. Fill cooling system and check for leaks. Start the engine and allow to come to normal operation temperature. Check for leaks. Top off coolant level.

15. Connect the negative battery cable.

Water Pump

REMOVAL AND INSTALLATION

2.2L Engine

1. Disconnect the negative battery cable.

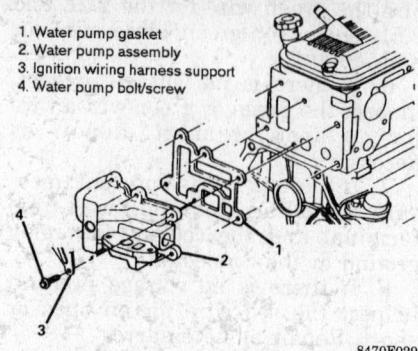

1. Water pump gasket
2. Water pump assembly
3. Ignition wiring harness support
4. Water pump bolt/screw

8470F029

Water pump assembly — 2.2L engine

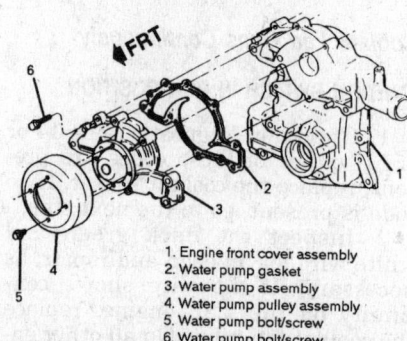

1. Coolant pump
2. Bolt/screw
3. Coolant pump inlet gasket
4. Coolant pump inlet
5. Bolt/screw
6. Coolant pump gasket

[3] GASKET, COOLANT PUMP INLET
[4] INLET, COOLANT PUMP

8470F030

Water pump assembly — 2.5L engine

2. Drain the cooling system into a suitable container.

3. Loosen the alternator mounting bolts and remove the serpentine belt.

4. Place the alternator aside.

5. Remove the water pump pulley retaining bolts and remove the water pump pulley.

6. Remove the water pump retaining bolts and remove the pump and the gasket.

To install:

7. Clean all of the water pump mating surfaces.

8. Install the gasket and install the water pump assembly. Tighten the mounting bolts to 18 ft. lbs. (25 Nm).

9. Install the water pump pulley and tighten the bolts to 22 ft. lbs. (30 Nm).

10. Install the alternator and install the serpentine belt.

11. Refill the cooling system to the proper level and connect the negative battery cable.

2.5L Engine

1. Disconnect the negative battery cable.

2. Remove the alternator and disconnect the radiator and heater hoses from the inlet.

3. Drain the cooling system.

4. Remove water pump attaching bolts and remove pump.

To install:

5. If installing a new water pump, transfer pulley from old unit. With sealing surfaces cleaned, place a 1/8 in. (3mm) bead of RTV sealant or equivalent, on the water pump sealing surface. While sealer is still wet, install pump and torque bolts to 6 ft. lbs. (7 Nm).

6. Install the radiator inlet hoses and install the alternator.

7. Connect the negative battery cable.

8. Fill cooling system and check for leaks. Start the engine and allow to come to normal operating temperature. Check for leaks. Refill coolant to proper level.

3.1L Engine

1. Disconnect the negative battery cable.

2. Drain cooling system.

3. Remove the serpentine drive belt.

4. Remove the pulley bolts and pulley.

5. Remove the water pump retaining bolts and water pump.

6. Installation is the reverse of removal. Clean the gasket mating surfaces, torque the pump retaining bolts to 18 ft. lbs. (25 Nm) and pulley bolts to 22 ft. lbs. (30 Nm).

3.3L Engine

1. Disconnect the negative battery cable.

2. Drain cooling system.

3. Remove the serpentine drive belt.

4. Remove the coolant hose at the water pump.

5. Remove the water pump pulley bolts. The long bolt should be re-

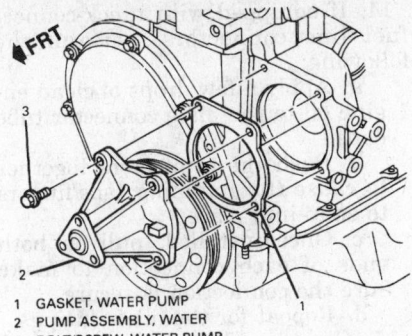

1 GASKET, WATER PUMP
2 PUMP ASSEMBLY, WATER
3 BOLT/SCREW, WATER PUMP

8569y001

Water pump assembly — 3.1L engine

moved through the access hole provided in the body side rail. Remove the pulley.

6. Remove the water pump attaching bolts and remove the water pump.

To install:

7. Install the water pump attaching bolts and install the water pump.

8. Install the pulley. Install the water pump pulley bolts. The long bolt should be installed through the access hole provided in the body side rail.

9. Install the coolant hose at the water pump.

10. Install the serpentine drive belt.

11. Connect the negative battery cable.

12. Fill cooling system and check for leaks. Start the engine and allow to come to normal operating temperature. Check for leaks. Refill coolant to the proper level.

Thermostat

REMOVAL AND INSTALLATION

Except 3.1L Engine

1. Disconnect the negative battery cable. Drain the cooling system.

2. If equipped with cruise control and vacuum modulator is connected to the thermostat housing, remove the vacuum modulator from the thermostat housing.

3. On all vehicles, unbolt the water outlet from the intake manifold. Remove the outlet and lift the thermostat from the the intake manifold.

To install:

4. Clean mating surfaces thoroughly. Apply a ⅛ inch (3mm) bead of suitable RTV sealant in the groove of the water outlet.

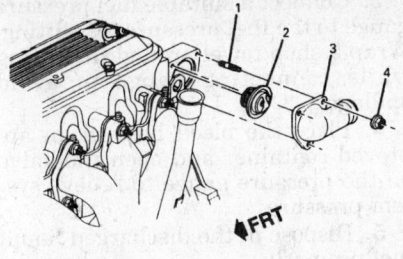

1. Water outlet stud
2. Engine coolant thermostat assembly
3. Water outlet
4. Water outlet nut

8470F033

Thermostat assembly — 2.2L engine

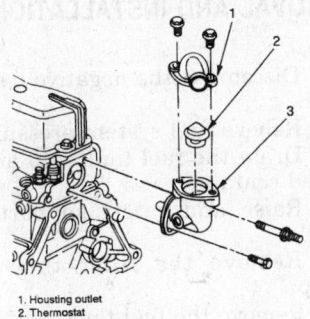

1. Housing outlet
2. Thermostat
3. Thermostat housing

8470F034

Thermostat assembly — 2.5L engine

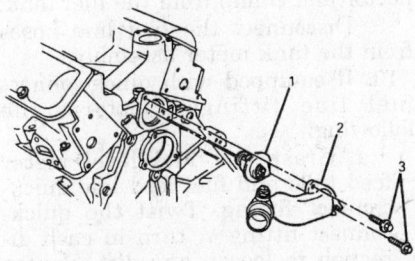

1 THERMOSTAT ASSEMBLY, ENGINE COOLANT
2 OUTLET ASSEMBLY, WATER
3 BOLT/SCREW, WATER OUTLET

8569y002

Thermostat assembly — 3.1L engine

5. Install the thermostat with the spring toward the engine. Install the water outlet. Torque bolts to 21 ft. lbs. (29 Nm).

6. If equipped with cruise control, install the vacuum modulator to the thermostat housing.

7. Connect the negative battery cable.

8. Fill cooling system and check for leaks. Start the engine and allow it to come to normal operating temperature. Check for leaks. Fill coolant to proper level.

3.1L Engine

1. Disconnect the negative battery cable. Drain the cooling system.

2. Remove the radiator hose from the water outlet.

3. Remove the outlet nuts, outlet and thermostat.

To install:

4. Clean mating surfaces thoroughly. Apply a ⅛ inch (3mm) bead of suitable RTV sealant in the groove of the water outlet.

5. Install the thermostat with the spring toward the engine. Install the water outlet. Torque bolts to 89 inch lbs. (10 Nm).

6. Connect the negative battery cable.

7. Fill cooling system and check for leaks. Start the engine and allow it to come to normal operating temperature. Check for leaks. Fill coolant to proper level.

FUEL SYSTEM

Fuel System Service Precautions

Safety is the most important factor when performing not only fuel system maintenance but any type of maintenance. Failure to conduct maintenance and repairs in a safe manner may result in serious personal injury or death. Maintenance and testing of the vehicle's fuel system components can be accomplished safely and effectively by adhering to the following rules and guidelines.

• To avoid the possibility of fire and personal injury, always disconnect the negative battery cable unless the repair or test procedure requires that battery voltage be applied.

• Always relieve the fuel system pressure prior to disconnecting any fuel system component (injector, fuel rail, pressure regulator, etc.), fitting or fuel line connection. Exercise extreme caution whenever relieving fuel system pressure to avoid exposing skin, face and eyes to fuel spray. Please be advised that fuel under pressure may penetrate the skin or any part of the body that it contacts.

• Always place a shop towel or cloth around the fitting or connection prior to loosening to absorb any excess fuel due to spillage. Ensure that all fuel spillage (should it occur) is

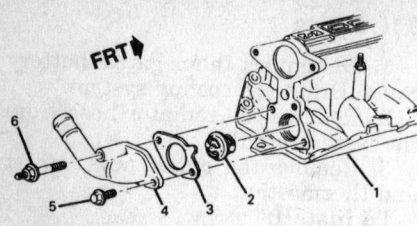

1. Intake manifold assembly
2. Engine coolant thermostat assembly
3. Engine coolant thermostat gasket
4. Water outlet
5. Water outlet bolt/screw
6. Water outlet stud

8470F036

Thermostat assembly — 3.3L engine

quickly removed from engine surfaces. Ensure that all fuel soaked cloths or towels are deposited into a suitable waste container.

• Always keep a dry chemical (Class B) fire extinguisher near the work area.

• Do not allow fuel spray or fuel vapors to come into contact with a spark or open flame.

• Always use a backup wrench when loosening and tightening fuel line connection fittings. This will prevent unnecessary stress and torsion to fuel line piping. Always follow the proper torque specifications.

• Always replace worn fuel fitting O-rings with new. Do not substitute fuel hose or equivalent where fuel pipe is installed.

RELIEVING FUEL SYSTEM PRESSURE

Throttle Body Injection (TBI)

1. On a cold engine, remove the fuse marked "Fuel Pump" from the fuse block in the passenger compartment.

2. Loosen the fuel filler cap to relive the tank pressure.

3. Start the engine and run until the fuel supply remaining in the fuel lines is exhausted. When the engine stops, engage the starter again for 3.0 seconds to assure dissipation of any remaining pressure.

4. With the ignition **OFF**, replace the fuel pump fuse.

5. Disconnect the negative battery cable.

Port Fuel Injection (PFI)

1. Disconnect the negative battery cable to avoid possible fuel discharge if an accidental attempt is made to start the engine.

2. Loosen the fuel filler cap to relieve the tank pressure.

3. Connect a suitable fuel pressure gauge to the fuel pressure test fitting. Wrap a shop towel around the fitting while connecting gauge to avoid spillage.

4. Place the bleed hose in an approved container and open the valve on the pressure gauge to relieve system pressure.

5. Dispose of the discharged liquid fuel promptly.

Fuel Tank

REMOVAL AND INSTALLATION

1. Disconnect the negative battery cable.

2. Relieve fuel system pressure.

3. Drain the fuel tank into an approved container.

4. Raise and safely support the vehicle.

5. Remove the filler tube and clamp.

6. Remove the fuel tank vent tube and clamp at the fuel tank.

7. Disconnect the electrical connectors.

8. Disconnect the vapor hose connector and clamp from the fuel tank.

9. Disconnect the fuel line hoses from the tank meter assembly.

10. If equipped with quick-connect fuel line fittings, perform the following:

a. Grasp the fuel level meter feed tube and fuel feed line quick-connect fitting. Twist the quick-connect fitting 1/4 turn in each direction to loosen any dirt. Repeat for the fuel return line quick-connect fitting.

b. Squeeze the plastic tabs of the male end of the connector and pull the connection apart. Repeat for the other fitting.

11. With the aid of an assistant, support the fuel tank and remove the 2 front fuel tank retaining strap attaching bolts, 2 rear fuel tank strap attaching nuts and bolts, bolt fuel tank retaining straps and remove the tank.

To install:

12. With the aid of an assistant, position and support the fuel tank. Install the 2 fuel tank retaining straps, front attaching bolts and rear attaching bolts and nuts. Torque front retaining bolts 9 ft. lbs. (12 Nm) and rear bolts 25 ft. lbs. (34 Nm).

13. Connect the fuel lines to the tank meter assembly.

14. If equipped with quick-connect fuel line connectors, perform the following:

a. Apply a few drops of clean engine oil to the male connector tube ends.

b. Push the connectors together to cause the retaining tabs/fingers to snap into place.

c. Once installed, pull on both ends of each connection to make sure the connection is secure.

d. Repeat for the other fittings.

15. Connect the vapor hose and clamp.

16. Connect the fuel level meter electrical connector.

17. Connect the fuel tank vent tube and clamp.

18. Connect the filler tube and clamp.

19. Lower the vehicle.

20. Add fuel to the tank and install the fuel filler cap.

21. Connect the negative battery cable.

22. Turn the ignition switch to the **ON** position for 2 seconds, then turn to the **OFF** position for 10 seconds. Turn the ignition switch back to the **ON** position and check for fuel leaks.

Fuel Filter

REMOVAL AND INSTALLATION

Threaded Fitting

The filter is an in-line unit located just ahead of the TBI unit or to the left of the fuel tank.

1. Ensure the engine is cold. Relieve fuel pressure, then unclamp and remove the fuel hose.

2. Unscrew the filter from the fuel line.

To install:

3. Place the new filter into position and connect the fuel lines.

4. Tighten the retaining clamp.

5. Start the engine and check for fuel leaks.

Quick–Connect Fitting

1. Disconnect the negative battery cable.

2. Relieve the fuel system pressure.

3. Raise and safely support the vehicle.

4. Remove the filter bracket attaching screw and filter bracket.

5. Grasp the filter and 1 fuel line fitting. Twist the quick-connect fitting 1/4 turn in each direction to loosen any dirt within the fitting. Repeat for the other fuel line fitting.

6. Use compressed air, blow out dirt from the quick-connect fittings at both ends of the fuel filter.

7. To disconnect the fuel line fittings, squeeze the plastic tabs of the male end of the connector and pull the connector apart. Repeat for the other fitting.

8. Remove the fuel filter.

To install:

9. Remove the protective caps from the new filter.

10. Install new plastic connector retainers on the filter inlet and outlet tubes. Observe the positions on the old filter and duplicate with new filter.

11. Connect the quick-connect fittings by performing the following:

   a. Apply a few drops of clean engine oil to the male tube ends of the fuel filter and fuel level meter assembly.

   b. Push the connectors together until the retaining tabs/fingers snap into place.

   c. Once installed, pull on both ends of each connector to ensure a tight connection.

12. Align the fuel filter bracket on the frame with the brake line mounting bracket and install the filter bracket attaching screw.

13. Lower the vehicle.

14. Tighten the fuel filler cap.

15. Connect the negative battery cable.

Electric Fuel Pump

PRESSURE TESTING

1. Disconnect the fuel line from the EFI unit.

2. Install a suitable pressure gauge to the fuel line.

3. Connect a jumper wire from the positive terminal on the battery to the **G** terminal of the ALDL.

4. Fuel pressure gauge should be 9–13 psi if equipped with TBI or 34–46 psi if equipped with PFI or SFI.

NOTE: If fuel pressure does not meet specifications, check the fuel line for restrictions or the fuel pump for malfunctions.

REMOVAL AND INSTALLATION

The fuel pump is attached to the fuel sending unit located inside the fuel tank.

1. Relieve the fuel system pressure, then disconnect the negative battery cable.

2. Raise and support the vehicle safely. Drain the fuel tank.

3. Disconnect wiring from the tank, then remove the ground wire retaining screw from under the body.

4. Disconnect all hoses from the tank.

5. Support the tank on a jack and remove the retaining strap nuts.

6. Lower the tank and remove it from the vehicle.

7. Remove the fuel gauge/pump retaining ring using a suitable spanner wrench.

8. Remove the gauge unit and the pump.

To install:

9. Install the gauge unit and the pump.

10. Install the fuel gauge/pump retaining ring using a suitable spanner.

11. Raise the tank and and install it to the vehicle.

12. Support the tank on a jack stand and install the retaining strap nuts.

13. Connect the hoses to the tank.

14. Connect the electrical connectors and the ground wire, if equipped.

15. Lower the vehicle.

16. Fill the fuel tank.

17. Turn the ignition switch to the **ON** position for 2 seconds, then turn to the **OFF** position for 10 seconds. Turn the ignition switch back to the **ON** position and check for fuel leaks.

Fuel Injection

IDLE SPEED MIXTURE ADJUSTMENT

Throttle Body Injection (TBI)

NOTE: This procedure should be performed only after throttle body parts have been replaced.

1. Block the drive wheels and apply the parking brake.

2. Connect a Scan tool to the ALDL connector.

3. Turn the ignition switch to the ON position.

4. Select the "Field Service Mode" on the Scan tool. This will cause the IAC valve pintle to seat in the throttle body. Wait at least 45 seconds, disconnect the IAC valve connector and exit the "Field Service Mode."

5. Place the transaxle in **P**, if equipped with an automatic transaxle or **N**, if equipped with a manual transaxle. Start the engine and allow to come to normal operating temperature.

6. Confirm the following prior to checking idle speed:

   a. Engine at normal operating temperature and in closed loop.

   b. All accessories and cooling fan OFF.

   c. Ensure that throttle and cruise control cables do not hold the throttle open.

7. Select "Engine rpm" on the Scan tool. Observe the engine speed and adjust as necessary to 600 ± 50 rpm.

8. Turn the ignition switch to the **OFF** position.

9. Connect the IAC valve electrical connector.

10. Reset the IAC valve pintle position by performing the following:

   a. Select "Engine rpm" on the Scan tool.

   b. Start the engine and hold speed above 2000 rpm. Select "Field Service Mode" for 10 seconds.

   c. Exit "Field Service Mode" and allow the engine to return to idle.

   d. Turn the ignition switch to the **OFF** position. Restart the engine and check for proper idle operation.

11. Disconnect the Scan tool.

12. Remove the block from the drive wheels.

Port Fuel Injection (PFI) and Sequential Fuel Injection (SFI)

1. Using an suitable tool, pierce the idle stop screw plug, located on the side of the throttle body, and remove it by prying it from the housing.

2. Using a jumper wire, ground the diagnostic lead of the IAC motor.

3. Turn the ignition **ON**. Do not start the engine. After 30 seconds, disconnect the IAC electrical connector. Remove the diagnostic lead ground lead and start the engine. Allow the system to go to closed loop.

4. Adjust the idle set screw to 550 rpm on automatic transaxle in **D** or 650 rpm on manual transaxle.

5. Turn the ignition **OFF** and reconnect the IAC motor lead.

6. Using a voltmeter, adjust the TPS to 0.55 ± 0.1 volt and secure the TPS.

7. Recheck the setting, then start the engine and check for proper idle operation.

8. Seal the idle stop screw with silicone sealer.

Fuel Injector

All fuel injectors are serviced as a complete assembly only. Since it is an electrical component, it should not be immersed in any type of cleaner.

REMOVAL AND INSTALLATION

Throttle Body Injection

1. Relieve fuel system pressure. Disconnect the negative battery cable.

2. Remove the air cleaner assembly.

3. Squeeze the 2 tabs on the injector electrical connector together and pull straight upward.

4. Remove the fuel meter cover retaining screws. The 2 front retaining screws are shorter than the 3 rear retaining screws. Remove the fuel meter cover.

5. With the fuel meter cover gasket in place, use a prying tool and carefully lift the injector until it is free from the fuel meter body.

6. Remove the small O-ring from the injector nozzle end. Carefully rotate the injector fuel filter back and forth and remove the filter from the base of the injector.

7. Remove and discard the fuel meter cover gasket. Remove the large O-ring and steel backup washer from

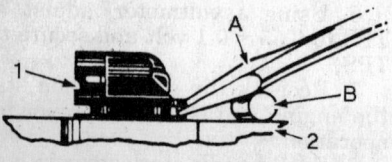

1. Injector retainer screw
2. Injector retainer
3. Fuel meter assembly
4. Fuel injector O-ring (lower)
5. Fuel injector O-ring (upper)
6. Fuel injector assembly

8470F037

TBI fuel injector assembly

1. Fuel injector assembly
2. Fuel meter body
A. Screwdriver blade
B. Fulcrum

8470F038

TBI fuel injector assembly removal

the top counterbore of the fuel meter body injector cavity.

To install:

8. Install the fuel injector nozzle filter on the nozzle end of the fuel injector, with the larger end of the filter facing the injector, so the filter covers raised rib at the base of the injector.

9. Lubricate the new small O-ring with automatic transmission fluid and push the O-ring on the nozzle end of the injector until it presses against the injector fuel filter.

10. Install the steel backup washer in the top counterbore of the fuel meter body injector cavity.

11. Lubricate the new large O-ring with automatic transmission fluid and install it directly over the backup washer. Be sure the O-ring is seated properly in the cavity and is flush with the top of the fuel meter body casting surface.

12. Install the injector into the cavity, aligning the raised lug on the injector base with cast-in notch in the fuel meter body cavity. Push down on the injector until it is fully seated in the cavity. The electrical terminals of the injector will be approximately parallel to the throttle shaft.

13. Install a new dust seal into the recess on the fuel meter body.

14. Install a new fuel outlet passage gasket on the fuel meter cover and a new cover gasket on the fuel meter body.

15. Install the fuel meter cover, making sure the pressure regulator dust seal and cover gaskets are in place; then, apply a thread locking compound to the threads on the fuel meter cover attaching screws. Install the fuel meter cover attaching screws and lock washers and torque to 28 inch lbs. (3 Nm). The 2 short screws go to the front of the injector. Connect battery negative cable.

Port Fuel Injection (PFI) and Sequential Fuel Injection (SFI)

NOTE: Always support the fuel rail to avoid damaging other components while removing the injectors.

1. Relieve fuel system pressure. Disconnect the negative battery cable.

2. Remove the intake manifold plenum.

3. Remove the fuel rail.

4. Remove the injector retaining clips and remove the injectors.

5. Remove the injector O-ring seals from both ends of the injector and discard.

To install:

6. Lubricate the new injector seals with clean engine oil and install on the injectors.

7. Install new injector retaining clips on the injectors. Position the open end of the clip facing the injector electrical connector.

8. Install the injectors into the fuel rail assembly. Push in far enough to engage the retainer clip with the machined slots on the injector socket.

9. Install the fuel rail assembly and intake manifold plenum.

10. Complete installation by reversing the removal procedure. Connect battery negative cable.

EMISSION CONTROLS

Emission Warning Lamps

RESETTING

Cutlass Ciera and Cutlass Cruiser

Vehicles equipped with an engine oil life index display as a part of the Driver Information System (DIS), have a display that will show when to change the engine oil.

The oil change interval is determined by the driver information system and will usually fall at or between the 2 recommended alternative intervals of 3000 miles and 7500 miles but it could be shorter than 3000 miles under some severe driving conditions. The driver information system will also signal the need for an oil change at 7500 miles or one year passed since the last oil change. If the drive information system does not indicate the need for an oil change after 7500 miles or one year if the engine oil life index display fails to appear, the oil should be changed and the driver information system serviced.

When the engine oil life index reaches 10 percent or less, the change oil light display will function as a reserve trip odometer, indicating the distance to an oil change. Until the engine oil lift index reset is performed, the driver information system will display the distance to the oil change and sound a beep when the ignition switch is turned to the

ACCESSORY or **RUN** position the first time each day.

When the distance to the next oil change reaches zero, the driver information system will display the change oil now light. Until an engine oil life index reset is performed the the driver information system will display the Change Oil Now Light and sound a beep when the ignition switch is turned to the **ACCESSORY** or **RUN** position the first time each day.

The driver information system will not detect dusty conditions or engine malfunctions which may affect the engine oil. If driving in severe conditions exists, change the engine oil every 3000 miles or 3 months which ever comes first, unless instructed otherwise by the driver information system. The driver information center does not measure the engine oil level, it remains the owner's responsibility to check the engine oil level. After the oil has been changed, the engine oil life index light must be reset. Reset the can be accomplished as follows:

1. The engine oil life index can be reset by pressing the RESET and OIL buttons simultaneously for at least 5 seconds while on the engine oil life index display. The driver information system will reset the engine oil life index to 100 percent and display an engine oil life index of 100 percent.

2. Oil life index 100 message appears.

NOTE: The Engine Oil Life Index is stored on a non-volatile memory chip and will not reset by disconnecting the battery and or fuse.

ENGINE MECHANICAL

NOTE: Disconnecting the negative battery cable on some vehicles may interfere with the functions of the on board computer systems and may require the computer to undergo a relearning process, once the negative battery cable is reconnected.

Engine Assembly

REMOVAL AND INSTALLATION

2.2L Engine

1. Relieve the fuel system pressure. Disconnect the negative battery cable.
2. Scribe reference marks at the hood supports and remove the hood. Install covers on both fenders.
3. Drain the cooling system. Remove the air cleaner assembly and ducts.
4. Remove the throttle control cable bracket at the intake and rocker cover.
5. Disconnect the fuel line.
6. Disconnect the vacuum, radiator and heater hose connections.
7. Remove the engine mount strut from the engine and remove the engine mount strut bracket pencil brace.
8. Disconnect the engine harness connector.
9. Rotate the engine forward.
10. Remove the power steering pump, leaving the hoses connected.
11. Disconnect the electrical connectors at the rear of the engine.
12. Remove the transaxle oil level indicator tube nut.
13. Remove all of the transaxle to engine bolts, except the upper 2 bolts.
14. Rotate the engine rearward.
15. Raise and safely support the vehicle.
16. Remove the right front tire/wheel assembly and remove the right side engine splash shield.
17. Remove the exhaust pipe and the flywheel cover.
18. Remove the starter assembly.
19. Remove the engine mount to frame nuts.
20. Remove the converter to the flywheel bolts.
21. If equipped with air conditioning, remove the air conditioning compressor from mounting brackets and set aside. Do not discharge the air conditioning system.
22. Remove the front exhaust pipe support bracket from the transaxle.
23. Remove the transaxle support bracket to transaxle bolt.
24. Lower the vehicle and rotate the engine forward.
25. Remove the rear transaxle to engine bolt and rotate the engine rearward.
26. Remove the front transaxle to engine bolt and attach an engine lifting device.
27. Lift the engine from the vehicle.

To install:
28. Lower the engine to the vehicle.
29. Remove the engine lifting device.
30. Install the front transaxle to engine bolt and rotate the engine forward.
31. Install the rear transaxle to engine bolt and rotate the engine rearward.
32. Raise and safely support the vehicle and install the transaxle support bracket to the transaxle bolt.
33. Install the front exhaust pipe support bracket to the transaxle.
34. Install the air conditioning compressor.
35. Install the convertor-to-flywheel bolts.
36. Install the engine mount-to-frame nuts and install the starter motor.
37. Install the flywheel cover and install the exhaust pipe.
38. Install the right side splash shield and install the right front tire/wheel.
39. Lower the vehicle and rotate the engine forward.
40. Install the transaxle to engine bolts.
41. Install the transaxle oil level indicator tube nut and connect the electrical connectors at the rear of the engine.
42. Install the power steering pump and rotate the engine rearward.
43. Connect the engine harness connector and install the engine mount strut bracket pencil brace and the engine mount strut.
44. Connect the heater, radiator and vacuum hoses.
45. Connect the fuel line.
46. Install the throttle control cable bracket at the intake and rocker cover.
47. Install the air cleaner and duct assembly.
48. Install the hood assembly.
49. Refill the coolant to the proper level and connect the negative battery cable. Check all fluid levels.

2.5L Engine

1. Relieve the fuel system pressure. Disconnect the negative battery cable.
2. Scribe reference marks at the hood supports and remove the hood. Install covers on both fenders.
3. Drain the cooling system. Remove the air cleaner assembly and ducts.
4. Disconnect engine harness connector.
5. Disconnect the vacuum, radiator and heater hose connections.

6. If equipped with air conditioning, remove the air conditioning compressor from mounting brackets and set aside. Do not discharge the air conditioning system.

7. Remove the alternator and the alternator bracket.

8. Remove the front engine strut assembly.

9. Disconnect the throttle and transaxle linkage.

10. Raise the vehicle and support it safely. Remove transaxle-to-engine bolts leaving the upper 2 bolts in place.

11. Remove front mount-to-cradle nuts.

12. Remove forward exhaust pipe.

13. Remove flywheel inspection cover and remove starter motor.

14. Remove torque converter-to-flywheel bolts.

15. Remove power steering pump and bracket with hoses attached and set aside.

16. Disconnect the fuel line.

17. Remove the 2 rear support bracket bolts.

18. Using a floor jack and a block of wood placed under the transaxle, raise engine and transaxle until engine front mount studs clear cradle.

19. Connect engine lift equipment and put tension on engine.

20. Remove the 2 remaining transaxle bolts.

21. Slide engine forward and remove from the vehicle.

To install:

22. Position the engine in the engine compartment, aligning the engine with the transaxle bellhousing.

23. With the engine supported by the lifting tool, install the 2 upper bellhousing bolts. Do not lower the engine while the jack is supporting the transaxle.

24. Remove the transaxle support jack and lower the engine onto the engine mounts. Remove the engine lift tool.

25. Install the bellhousing bolts.

26. Raise and safely support the vehicle. Install the front mount-to-cradle nuts.

27. Connect the fuel supply line at fuel filter.

28. Install the 2 rear transaxle support bracket bolts.

29. Install power steering pump and bracket.

30. Install torque converter-to-flywheel bolts.

31. Install starter motor and flywheel inspection cover.

32. Install forward exhaust pipe.

33. Lower the vehicle.

34. Install front engine strut assembly.

35. Install the alternator and the bracket.

36. If equipped with air conditioning, install the air conditioning mounting brackets and compressor.

37. Connect the heater, radiator and vacuum hoses.

38. Connect throttle and transaxle linkage.

39. Connect engine harness connector.

40. Install the air cleaner assembly and preheat tube.

41. Install the hood.

42. Connect the negative battery cable.

43. Fill cooling system and check for leaks. Start the engine and allow to come to normal operating temperature. Check for leaks.

3.1L Engine

1. Disconnect the battery cables and remove the air cleaner assembly.

2. Scribe the bolt locations and remove the hood with the help of an assistant.

3. Remove the heater and radiator hoses from the engine. Remove the engine torque strut at the radiator support.

4. Remove the serpentine belt from the engine.

5. Relieve the fuel system pressure. Disconnect the throttle body bracket, cables and fuel and coolant hoses.

6. Label and disconnect the electrical connections from the engine.

7. Label and disconnect the vacuum lines from the engine.

8. Disconnect the power steering lines and remove the power steering brace.

9. Remove the coolant reservoir and 2 upper A/C compressor upper bolts.

10. Disconnect the electrical connectors from the transaxle.

11. Remove the 4 upper transaxle-to-engine mounting bolts.

12. Raise the vehicle and safely support.

13. Disconnect the exhaust pipe from the manifold.

14. Remove the oil drip shield, flywheel cover and starter motor.

15. Disconnect all electrical connections from the engine.

16. Remove the flywheel-to-converter bolts.

17. Remove the A/C compressor and position aside. Do not disconnect the refrigerant lines.

18. Install a transaxle support bracket and remove the remaining transaxle bolts.

19. Remove the engine mounts and 2 remaining transaxle bolts.

20. Lower the vehicle install an approved engine lifting device.

21. Remove the engine assembly slowly and check that all components are disconnected and free from obstruction. Place the engine on a work stand.

To install:

22. Lower the engine into the vehicle and start 2 transaxle-to-engine bolts.

23. Remove the transaxle support tool.

24. Install the remaining transaxle bolts.

25. Install the engine mounts, transaxle support bracket and bolts.

26. Position the A/C compressor and tighten the bolts.

27. Install the flywheel-to-converter bolts and torque to 53 ft. lbs. (71 Nm).

28. Connect the engine grounds to the transaxle mounting bolts. Connect all accessible electrical connectors to the engine.

29. Install the starter motor, flywheel cover and oil drip shield.

30. Install the exhaust pipe-to-manifold and torque to 18 ft. lbs. (25 Nm).

31. Install the upper A/C compressor bolts, coolant reservoir and power steering brace and lines.

32. Connect all vacuum and electrical connections to the engine.

33. Connect the fuel lines and install the throttle body bracket and cable.

34. Connect the heater and radiator hoses.

35. Install the serpentine belt.

36. With the help of an assistant, install the hood to its original position.

37. Connect the battery cables, refill all engine fluids to the proper level and install the air cleaner.

38. Start the engine and check for leaks.

3.3L Engine

1992-94

1. Disconnect the negative battery cable.

2. Remove the air cleaner and duct assembly.

3. Drain the coolant and disconnect the heater and radiator hoses.

4. Remove the exhaust crossover pipe.

5. Relieve the fuel pressure and disconnect the fuel lines at the quick disconnect fittings.

6. Remove the engine torque strut.

7. Remove the serpentine drive belt.

8. Disconnect the power steering pump lines from the pump.

9. Disconnect the brake vacuum booster hose from the brake booster.

10. Disconnect the TV control cables from the throttle body and bracket.

11. Remove the alternator from the vehicle.

12. Disconnect the engine electrical harness and place harness aside.

13. Mark and disconnect the engine vacuum hoses.

14. Disconnect the engine ground wires from the transaxle mounting bolts.

15. Remove the wiring harness retaining clips from the right side of the engine compartment.

16. Raise and safely support the vehicle.

17. Drain the engine oil. Remove both front wheels.

18. Remove the exhaust pipe from the rear manifold.

19. Remove the right engine splash shield.

20. Remove the air conditioning compressor from the brackets and set aside.

21. Remove the flywheel inspection cover and remove the starter.

22. Use a scribe and mark the relationship of the torque converter to the flywheel for reassembly.

23. Remove the flywheel to converter bolts and remove the engine mount nuts from the frame.

24. Disconnect the oil pressure sensor, knock sensor and ground connectors near the power steering pump bracket.

25. Remove the transaxle support bolts from the transaxle and remove the lower rear engine to transaxle bolt (located between transaxle case and engine block and positioned in the opposite direction).

26. Lower the vehicle and remove the transaxle to engine bolts.

27. Install an engine lifting tool and remove the engine from the vehicle.

To install:

28. Install the engine in the engine compartment. Install the upper engine-to-transaxle bolts. Remove the engine lift tool.

29. Raise and safely support the vehicle.

30. Install the lower engine-to-transaxle bolts; the bolt is located behind the transaxle case and engine block.

31. Install the transaxle support bracket bolts to the transaxle.

32. Connect the ground connectors and install the engine mount to frame nuts.

33. Line up the torque converter with the flywheel and install the bolts. Tighten the bolts to 46 ft. lbs. (62 Nm).

34. Install the starter and the flywheel inspection cover with bolts.

35. Install the A/C compressor to the bracket and connect the lower radiator hose.

36. Install the right engine shield and connect the exhaust pipe to the exhaust manifold.

37. Install the front wheels, fill the engine to the proper level with oil and lower the vehicle.

38. Install the right side engine wiring harness retaining clips and connect the engine ground wires to the transaxle mounting bolts.

39. Connect the engine vacuum hoses and the engine electrical harness and connectors.

40. Install the alternator and connect the TV control cables to the throttle body and the bracket.

41. Install the brake vacuum booster hose to the brake booster. Connect the power steering lines to the power steering pump.

42. Install the serpentine drive belt and the engine torque strut.

43. Connect the fuel lines and install the exhaust crossover pipe.

44. Connect the upper and lower radiator hoses and the heater hoses.

45. Install the air cleaner and duct assembly and connect the negative battery cable.

46. Fill cooling system and check for leaks. Start the engine and allow to come to normal operating temperature. Recheck for leaks. Top-off engine coolant.

Engine Mounts

REMOVAL AND INSTALLATION

1. Disconnect the negative battery cable.

2. Raise and support the vehicle safely.

3. Using a suitable tool, support the engine and remove the engine mounting bracket nuts.

4. Raise the engine slightly until the engine mount is free from the vehicle chassis.

5. Remove the nuts holding the engine mount to the frame.

6. Remove the engine mounts and discard.

To install:

7. Install the engine mounts.

8. Install the nuts holding the engine mount to the frame.

9. Lower the engine onto the mount and install the engine mounting bracket nuts.

10. Remove the engine lift tool.

11. Connect the negative battery cable.

Cylinder Head

REMOVAL AND INSTALLATION

2.2L Engine

1. Disconnect the negative battery cable.

2. Drain the cooling system.

3. Remove the air cleaner and the duct assembly.

4. Remove the air inlet resonator at the upper tie bar and remove the lower air inlet duct.

5. Loosen the alternator mounting bolts and remove the serpentine belt. Place the alternator aside.

6. Remove the power steering mounting bolts. Do not disconnect the hoses. Place the power steering pump aside.

7. Disconnect the spark plug wires and note the original wire location.

8. Remove the throttle control cable bracket at the throttle body and the rocker cover. Disconnect the cables at the throttle body.

9. Remove the rocker arm assemblies.

10. Disconnect the intake manifold, throttle body, cylinder head and oxygen sensor electrical connectors.

11. Remove the power steering pump bracket from the intake manifold brace, located under the intake manifold.

12. Disconnect the engine strut bracket from the engine and remove the strut assembly.

13. Remove the alternator rear bracket from the engine and mark and disconnect any necessary vacuum hoses.

14. Disconnect the upper radiator and heater hose from the engine.

15. Raise and safely support the vehicle and disconnect the exhaust pipe from the exhaust manifold.

16. Lower the vehicle and properly relieve the fuel pressure.

17. Disconnect the fuel lines.

18. Remove the transaxle fluid level indicator tube from the intake manifold.

19. Remove the cylinder head bolts and remove the cylinder head.

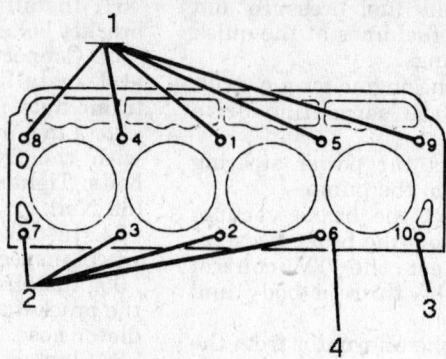

1. Long bolts
2. Short bolts
3. Stud
4. Numbers on gasket indicate torque sequence

CYLINDER HEAD BOLT TORQUE PROCEDURE

1. Tighten bolts in sequence (No. 4) to:
   Long bolts: 46 LB FT (63 NM)
   Short bolts: 43 LB FT (58 NM)
2. Tighten all bolts an additional angle of 90° in sequence (No. 4) using J 36660 of equivalent

8470F039

Cylinder head torque sequence — 2.2L engine

1. Cylinder head
2. Gasket
3. Cylinder block

NOTE: Tighten all bolts in proper sequence to 18 LB FT (25 NM) "A" through "J".
Tighten bolts "A" through "J" again (except "I") to 28 LB FT (35 NM).
Tighten bolt "I" to 18 LB FT (25 NM) following the proper sequence.
Tighten all bolts 90° with J 36660.

8470F040

Cylinder head torque sequence — 2.5L engine

To install:

20. Clean the cylinder head and block from any foreign matter, nicks or heavy scratches. Clean the cylinder head bolt threads and threads in the cylinder block.

21. Position the new cylinder head gasket over the dowel pins.

22. Carefully guide the cylinder head into place. Coat the cylinder head bolts with sealing compound and install finger-tight.

23. Torque the cylinder head bolts as follows:

   a. Torque the short bolts to 43 ft. lbs. (58 Nm) and the long bolts to 46 ft. lbs. (63 Nm) in the proper sequence.

   b. Repeat sequence. Turn all bolts 100 degrees (2 flats).

24. Install the transaxle fluid level indicator tube nut to the intake manifold.

25. Connect the fuel lines.

26. Raise and safely support the vehicle and connect the exhaust pipe to the exhaust manifold.

27. Lower the vehicle and connect the upper radiator and heater hose to the engine.

28. Connect the vacuum lines to the intake manifold.

29. Install the engine strut assembly.

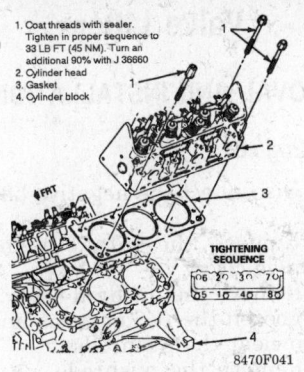

1. Coat threads with sealer. Tighten in proper sequence to 33 LB FT (45 NM). Turn an additional 90% with J 36660
2. Cylinder head
3. Gasket
4. Cylinder block

FRT

TIGHTENING SEQUENCE

8470F041

Cylinder head torque sequence — 3.1L engine

8470F042

Cylinder head torque sequence — 3.3L engine

30. Install the alternator rear bracket to the engine.

31. Connect the engine strut bracket to the engine.

32. Connect the power steering pump bracket to the intake manifold brace, located under the intake manifold.

33. Connect the electrical connectors to the oxygen sensor, cylinder head, the throttle body and the intake manifold.

34. Install the rocker arm assemblies and covers.

35. Install the throttle control cable bracket to the throttle body and rocker cover. Connect the cables at the throttle body.

36. Connect the spark plug wires.

37. Install the power steering pump and the alternator.

38. Install the drive belt.

39. Install the lower air inlet duct, the air inlet resonator and the air cleaner/duct assembly.

40. Refill the cooling system and connect the negative battery cable.

41. Start the engine and check the system for leaks.

2.5L Engine

1. Relieve the pressure in the fuel system before disconnecting any fuel line connections.

2. Disconnect the negative battery cable.

3. Raise and safely support the vehicle.

4. Disconnect the exhaust pipe and the oxygen sensor connector.

5. Lower the vehicle and disconnect the auxiliary ground cable.

6. Remove the oil level indicator tube and remove the air cleaner assembly.

7. Disconnect the wiring, throttle linkage and fuel lines from the TBI assembly.

8. Disconnect the heater hoses from the intake manifold and disconnect the vacuum hoses.

9. Disconnect the electrical connectors from the cylinder head and from the intake manifold.

10. Remove the engine torque strut bolt from the upper support.

11. Remove the serpentine belt.

12. Remove the air conditioning brackets and swing the compressor aside.

13. Remove the alternator brackets and place the alternator aside.

14. Remove the upper power steering pump bracket and remove the radiator hoses.

15. Remove the valve cover and remove the rocker arms.

16. Remove the cylinder head bolts and remove the cylinder head from the engine.

To install:

17. Clean the cylinder head and block from any foreign matter, nicks or heavy scratches. Clean the cylinder head bolt threads and threads in the cylinder block.

18. Position the new cylinder head gasket over the dowel pins.

19. Carefully guide the cylinder head into place. Coat the cylinder head bolts with sealing compound and install finger-tight.

20. Torque the cylinder head bolts as follows:

  a. Torque the cylinder head bolts gradually to 25 ft. lbs. in the proper sequence.

  b. Torque all bolts except No. 9 in sequence again to 22 ft. lbs. (28 Nm). Torque stud in sequence No. 9 to 29 ft. lbs. (40 Nm).

  c. Repeat sequence. Turn all bolts, except No. 9, 120 degrees (2 flats). Turn No. 9 a ¼ turn (90 degrees).

21. Install the rocker arms and rocker arm cover.

22. Install the power steering pump bracket and pump.

23. Connect the radiator hoses and engine strut rod bolt to the upper support.

24. Connect all vacuum and electrical connections to the cylinder head.

25. If equipped with air conditioning, install the compressor bracket bolts and install the compressor.

26. Install the serpentine belt.

27. If removed, install the alternator bracket-to-cylinder head bolts.

28. Connect the exhaust pipe and the oxygen sensor connector. Install the intake and exhaust manifolds.

29. Connect the throttle linkage and fuel lines.

30. Install the air cleaner and the oil level indicator tube.

31. Connect the negative battery cable.

32. Fill cooling system and check for leaks. Start the engine and allow to come to normal operating temperature. Check for leaks. Refill coolant to proper level.

3.1L Engine

LEFT SIDE (FRONT)

1. Drain and recover the A/C refrigerant. Disconnect the battery cables.

2. Remove the intake manifold assembly.

3. Remove the exhaust crossover pipe. Label and disconnect the spark plug wires.

4. Remove the rocker arm covers, rocker arms and pushrods. Label these components for correct installation.

5. Remove the air level indicator and tube.

6. Remove the A/C compressor bolts from the top.

7. Raise the vehicle and support safely.

8. Disconnect the A/C compressor hoses. Remove the bolts, electrical connectors and compressor.

9. Remove the A/C compressor lower brackets.

10. Lower the vehicle and remove the A/C compressor upper brackets.

11. Remove the cylinder head bolts, cylinder head and gasket.

12. Clean all mating surfaces and check for warpage.

To install:

13. Place the gasket on the block with the "This Side Up" showing. Install the cylinder head and bolts.

14. Torque the head bolts in sequence to 33 ft. lbs. (45 Nm) and then another 90 degrees torquing angle.

15. Install the compressor bracket and upper bolts.

16. Raise the vehicle and support safely.

17. Install the A/C compressor lower brackets.

18. Install the compressor. Connect the A/C compressor hoses and electrical connectors.

19. Install the air level indicator and tube.

20. Install the rocker arm covers, rocker arms and pushrods.

21. Install the exhaust crossover pipe. Connect the spark plug wires.

22. Install the intake manifold assembly.

23. Refill and recharge the A/C refrigerant. Connect the battery cables.

RIGHT SIDE (REAR)

1. Remove the lower intake manifold, ignition coil connection and alternator.

2. Remove the crossover pipe and oxygen sensor.

3. Raise the vehicle and support safely.

4. Remove the exhaust pipe from the manifold.

5. Lower the vehicle and remove the rocker cover, rocker arms and pushrods. Label these components for proper installation.

6. Remove the cylinder head bolts, cylinder head and gasket.

7. Clean all mating surfaces and check for warpage.

To install:

8. Place the gasket on the block with the "This Side Up" showing. Install the cylinder head and bolts.

9. Torque the head bolts in sequence to 33 ft. lbs. (45 Nm) and then another 90 degrees torquing angle.

10. Install the pushrods, rocker arms and rocker arm cover.

11. Raise the vehicle and support safely.

12. Install the exhaust pipe and lower the vehicle.

13. Install the oxygen sensor and crossover pipe.

14. Install the alternator, ignition coil connections and lower intake manifold.

15. Refill all fluids, connect the battery cable, start the engine and check for leaks.

3.3L Engine

1. Relieve the pressure in the fuel system before disconnecting any fuel line connections.

2. Disconnect the negative battery cable. Raise the vehicle and support it safely.

3. Drain the cooling system and lower the vehicle.

4. Remove the exhaust crossover and remove the intake manifold and exhaust manifold.

5. Remove the valve cover.

6. Remove the ignition module and coils as a unit.

7. Disconnect and tag all electrical wiring and vacuum hoses, as necessary.

8. If equipped with air conditioning, remove the air conditioning compressor and position to the side.

9. Remove the alternator and power steering pump and position to the side. Remove the belt tensioner assembly.

10. Remove the rocker arm assembly, guide plate and pushrods.

11. Remove the cylinder head bolts and remove the cylinder head.

To install:

12. Clean the cylinder head and block of any foreign matter, nicks or heavy scratches. Clean the cylinder head bolt threads and threads in the cylinder block.

13. Position the new cylinder head gasket on the block.

14. Carefully guide the cylinder head into place.

15. Coat the cylinder head bolts with sealing compound and install into the head. Tighten the cylinder head bolts according to the following procedure:

    a. Tighten in sequence to 35 ft. lbs. (47 Nm).

    b. Using an appropriate torque angle gauge, rotate each bolt in sequence an additional 130 degrees.

    c. Rotate the center 4 bolts an additional 30 degrees in sequence.

16. Install the pushrods, guide plate and rocker arm assembly. Tighten the rocker arm pivot bolts to 28 ft. lbs. (38 Nm).

17. Install the intake manifold and exhaust manifold.

18. Install the valve cover.

19. Remove the ignition module and coils as a unit, as required.

20. Connect all electrical wiring and vacuum hoses.

21. If equipped with air conditioning, install the air conditioning compressor.

22. Install the alternator and power steering pump. Remove the belt tensioner assembly.

23. Connect the negative battery cable.

24. Fill cooling system and check for leaks. Start the engine and allow to come to normal operating temperature. Check for leaks. Refill coolant to proper level.

Valve Lifters

REMOVAL AND INSTALLATION

2.5L Engine

1. Disconnect the negative battery cable.

2. Remove the intake manifold and valve cover.

3. Remove the pushrod cover.

4. Loosen the rocker arms and rotate to clear the pushrods.

5. Remove the pushrods, retainer and guide.

6. Remove the lifters. Keep all components separated so they may be reinstalled in the same location.

To install:

7. Lubricate the lifters with engine oil and install the lifters in their bore.

8. Install the guides, retainers and pushrods.

9. With the lifter on the base circle of the camshaft, tighten the rocker arm bolts to 24 ft. lbs. (32 Nm).

10. Install the pushrod cover and the intake manifold and valve cover.

11. Connect battery negative cable.

Except 2.5L Engine

1. Disconnect the negative battery cable.

2. Drain the cooling system.

3. Remove the valve cover and the intake manifold.

4. If the engine is equipped with individual rocker arms, loosen the rocker arm adjusting nut and rotate the arm so as to clear the pushrod.

5. If the engine is equipped with a rocker shaft assembly, remove the rocker shaft retaining bolts/nuts and remove the shaft assembly.

NOTE: Be sure to keep all valve train parts in order so they may be reinstalled in their original locations and with the same mating surfaces as when removed.

6. Remove the pushrods and valve lifters using tool J–3049 or equivalent.

To install:

7. Lubricate the bearing surfaces with Molykote® or equivalent.

8. Install the lifters in their original locations.

9. With the lifter on the base circle of the camshaft, tighten the rocker arm bolts to 14–20 ft. lbs. (20–27 Nm).

10. Connect the negative battery cable.

11. Adjust the valves, as required.

Valve Lash

ADJUSTMENT

All engines are originally equipped with hydraulic valve lifters. No adjustment is necessary. The 3.1L engine replacement rocker arm stud is adjustable and the adjustment can be performed as listed below.

3.1L Engine

NOTE: The following adjustment procedure should be used when reconditioning a valve seat and a new adjustable type rocker arm is used.

1. Install the rocker arms, balls and nuts. Tighten the rocker arm nuts until all of the lash (free-play) is eliminated.
2. Adjust the valves when the lifter is on the base circle of a camshaft lobe as follows:
   a. Place the engine in the No. 1 firing position. This can be determined by placing a finger on the No. 1 rocker arm as the engine alignment mark on the front face of the of the torsional damper pulley aligns with the arrow on the front cover. If the valves don't move freely, the engine is in the No. 1 firing position. If the valves move freely, the engine is in the No. 4 firing position and the engine should be rotated one full rotation to reach the No. 1 position.
   b. With the engine TDC on the No. 1 cylinder, adjust the following valves:
   • Exhaust — 1, 2, 3
   • Intake — 1, 5, 6
   c. Loosen the adjusting nut several turns backwards and then tighten until all lash (free-play) is removed. After all of the valve lash is removed turn the nut an additional 1½ turns; this will center the lifter plunger.
   d. Turn the engine 1 complete revolution until the timing tab and the alignment mark are again aligned; this will place the engine in the No. 4 firing position.
   e. With the engine TDC on the No. 4 cylinder, adjust the following valves:
   • Exhaust — 4, 5, 6
   • Intake — 2, 3, 4

Rocker Arms

REMOVAL AND INSTALLATION

2.2L and 2.5L Engines

1. Relieve pressure in the fuel system before disconnecting any fuel lines.
2. Disconnect the negative battery cable.
3. Remove the valve cover.
4. If only the pushrod is being removed, loosen the rocker arm bolt and swing the rocker arm aside.
5. Remove the rocker arm nut and ball.
6. Lift the rocker arm off the stud, keeping rocker arms in order for installation.
To install:
7. If the pushrod was removed, install through the cylinder head and into the lifter seat.
8. Install the guide, rocker arm, ball and bolt. Tighten to 24 ft. lbs. (32 Nm).
9. Install the valve cover.
10. Connect the negative battery cable.

3.1L Engine

1. Remove the rocker cover.
2. Label all components for correct installation.

NOTE: The intake and exhaust pushrods are of different lengths. The exhaust pushrods are longer than the intake rod. Intake rods are marked orange and are 6 inches long. The exhaust rods are blue and are 6 ³⁄₈ inches long.

3. Remove the rocker arm pivot balls, rocker arms, studs and pushrods.
4. Install the pushrods to there proper location.
5. Install the studs, rocker arms, rocker arm pivot balls and nuts.
6. Adjust the valve lash if any components were replaced. Torque the rocker arm nuts to 18 ft. lbs. (24 Nm) if no components were replaced. Install the rocker arm cover.
7. Refill the fluids, start the engine and check for valve train noise. Any noise should go away after the engine is warm and driven a few miles at various engine speeds.

3.3L Engine

1. Relieve pressure in the fuel system before disconnecting any fuel lines. Disconnect the negative battery cable.
2. Remove the valve covers.

3. Remove the rocker arm bolts, pivots, and rocker arms assembly. Keep all components separated so they may be reinstalled in the same location.
To install:
4. Install the rocker arms, pivots and bolts. Tighten bolts to 37 ft. lbs. (51 Nm).
5. Install the valve covers.
6. Connect the negative battery cable.

Intake Manifold

REMOVAL AND INSTALLATION

2.2L Engine

UPPER

1. Remove the throttle body from the air cleaner air inlet duct.
2. Remove the control cable bracket from the manifold and rocker cover.
3. Disconnect the brake vacuum booster hose from the manifold.
4. Remove the MAP sensor.
5. Disconnect the vacuum harness connector at the throttle body.
6. Disconnect the electrical connectors at the the throttle body and the intake manifold.
7. Remove the intake manifold bolts and remove the intake manifold and gasket.
To install:
8. Install the upper intake manifold assembly with a new gasket in place and tighten the bolts/screws to 22 ft. lbs. (30 Nm).
9. Connect the electrical connectors to the throttle body and to the intake manifold.
10. Connect the vacuum harness connector to the throttle body and install the MAP sensor.
11. Connect the brake vacuum booster hose to the manifold.
12. Install the control cable bracket to the manifold and to the rocker cover.
13. Install the throttle body to air cleaner air inlet duct assembly.

LOWER

1. Disconnect the negative battery cable and drain the cooling system.
2. Remove the air cleaner and duct assembly.
3. Rotate the engine forward.
4. Remove the throttle control cable bracket and disconnect the cables at the throttle body.
5. Disconnect the electrical connectors from the throttle body, fuel

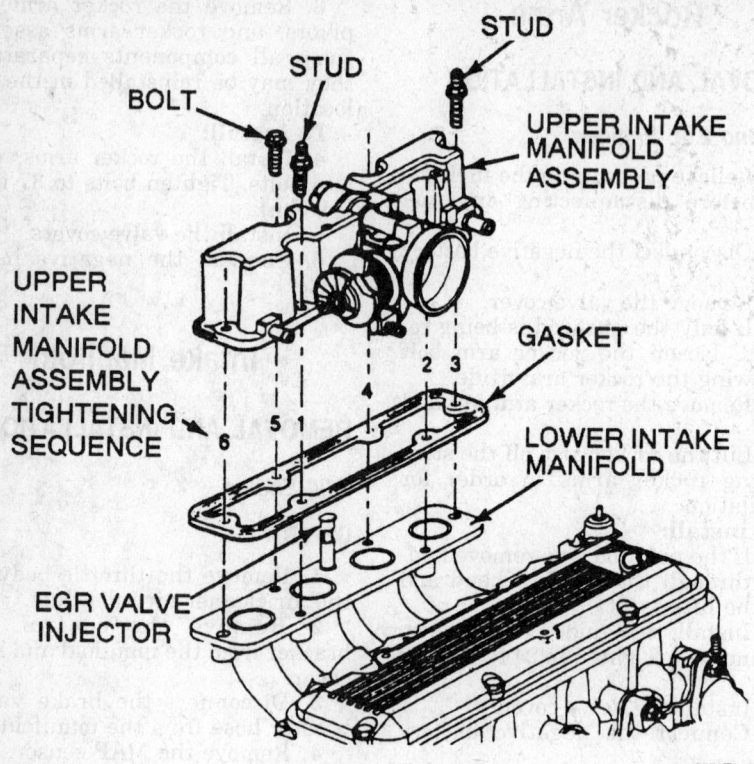

UPPER INTAKE MANIFOLD ASSEMBLY TIGHTENING SEQUENCE

BOLT

STUD

STUD

UPPER INTAKE MANIFOLD ASSEMBLY

GASKET

LOWER INTAKE MANIFOLD

EGR VALVE INJECTOR

8470F043

Intake manifold — 2.2L engine

injector connector and the wiring harness clip from under the manifold.

6. Mark and disconnect the vacuum hoses from the intake manifold, plenum and the EGR valve.

7. Remove the power steering pump bracket from the intake manifold brace.

8. Mark and disconnect the spark plug wires.

9. Properly relieve the fuel system pressure and disconnect the fuel lines. Move the fuel lines to the side.

10. Remove the transaxle fluid level indicator tube nut and position it to the side.

11. Remove the retaining nuts and remove the intake manifold with the plenum attached.

To install:

12. Clean all old gasket material from the manifold mating surfaces.

13. Install a new gasket and install the manifold assembly with the plenum attached.

14. Install the manifold retaining nuts and tighten in proper sequence to 24 ft. lbs. (33 Nm)

15. Install the transaxle fluid level indicator tube nut.

16. Connect the fuel lines and install the power steering pump bracket.

17. Connect the vacuum hoses and the electrical connectors.

1. Intake manifold gasket
2. Intake manifold
3. Bolt to 34 Nm (25ft. lb.)
4. Engine lift bracket
5. Ignition cable harness bracket

TIGHTENING SEQUENCE

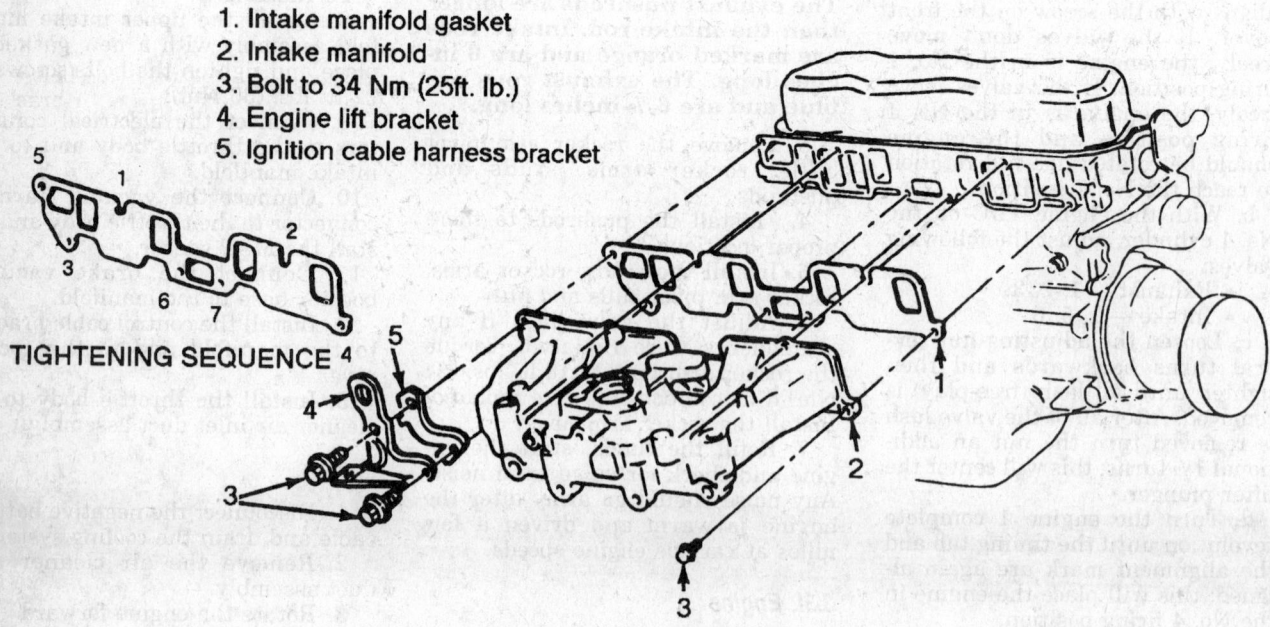

8470F044

Intake manifold — 2.5L engine

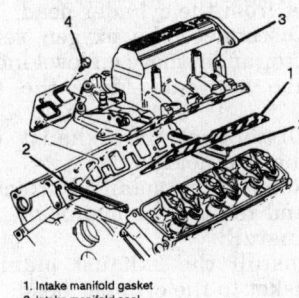

1. Cylinder head assembly
2. Lower intake manifold gasket
3. Lower intake manifold
4. Lower intake manifold bolt/screw
5. Lower intake manifold bolt/screw

8569y003

Intake manifold — 3.1L engine

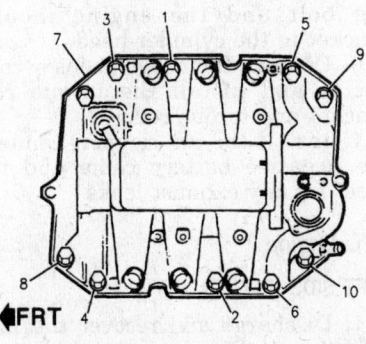

1. Intake manifold gasket
2. Intake manifold seal
3. Intake manifold
4. Bolt

8470F046

Intake manifold — 3.3L engine

8470F047

Intake manifold torque sequence — 3.3L engine

18. Install the throttle control cable bracket and connect the cables to the throttle body.

19. Rotate the engine to the proper position and install the air cleaner/duct assembly.

20. Refill the engine coolant and connect the negative battery cable. Start the engine and check for leaks.

2.5L Engine

1. Relieve the pressure in the fuel system before disconnecting any fuel line connections.

2. Disconnect the negative battery cable.

3. Drain the coolant and disconnect the PCV hose at the TBI and at the valve cover.

4. Disconnect the fuel lines and position to the side.

5. Disconnect the vacuum hoses including the power brake booster hoses.

6. Disconnect the wiring and throttle linkage from the TBI unit.

7. Disconnect the transaxle downshift linkage bracket and if equipped with cruise control, disconnect the servo cable.

8. Disconnect the throttle and TV cable and position to the side for clearance.

9. Remove the heater hose and remove the intake manifold retaining bolts.

10. Remove the intake manifold from the vehicle.

To install:

11. Clean the cylinder head and intake manifold surfaces from any foreign matter, nicks or heavy scratches.

12. Install the intake manifold with a new gasket and tighten the retaining bolts in sequence to the specified torque.

13. Connect the heater hose, throttle and TV cable.

14. If equipped with cruise control, connect the servo cable.

15. Install the transaxle downshift linkage bracket.

16. Connect the wiring and throttle linkage to the TBI assembly.

17. Connect the vacuum hoses and fuel lines. Connect the PCV hose at the TBI and at the valve cover.

18. Install the air cleaner and connect the negative battery cable.

19. Fill coolant to proper level and check for leaks. Start the engine and allow to come to normal operating temperature. Recheck for leaks. Check coolant level.

3.1L Engine

UPPER MANIFOLD

1. Disconnect the negative battery cable, drain the cooling system and remove the air cleaner.

2. Remove the throttle control cables, fuel lines and brackets from the manifold and throttle body.

3. Disconnect the vacuum lines from the upper intake manifold.

4. Remove the EGR valve and position the heater inlet hose out of the way.

5. Remove the ignition coil nuts and bolts.

6. Remove the power steering line clip from the alternator brace.

7. Remove the alternator brackets and disconnect the electrical connections from the throttle body.

8. Remove the upper intake manifold bolts and manifold from the throttle body.

9. Clean all gasket mating surfaces and sealing surfaces.

To install:

10. Apply a 2–3mm bead of Ultra Black RTV sealer on each ridge where the front and rear of the intake manifold contact the cylinder head.

11. Install a new gasket, upper manifold and bolts. Torque the bolts to 18 ft. lbs. (25 Nm).

12. Connect all vacuum and electrical connections.

13. Install the alternator brackets, power steering line clip and ignition coil fasteners.

14. Properly position heater inlet pipe hose clamps.

15. Install the EGR valve, control cable bracket, fuel lines, throttle cables and air cleaner.

16. Refill the cooling system, connect the battery cable, start the engine and check for leaks.

LOWER MANIFOLD

1. Disconnect the negative battery cable, drain the cooling system and remove the air cleaner.

2. Relieve the fuel pressure and remove the upper intake manifold.

3. Disconnect the fuel lines and remove the fuel rail.

4. Disconnect the coolant hoses and remove the serpentine belt.

5. Remove the alternator brackets and power steering pump.

6. Disconnect the upper radiator hose and heater hose from the thermostat housing.

7. Remove the ignition coil and engine torque strut.

8. Remove the rocker cover, lower manifold bolts and manifold.

To install:

9. Clean the gasket mating surfaces.

10. Apply a 2–3mm bead of Ultra Black RTV sealer on each ridge where the manifold contacts the engine block.

11. Install a new gasket, lower manifold and bolts. Torque the bolts to 116 inch lbs. (13 Nm).

12. Connect all vacuum and electrical connections.

13. Install the rocker covers, engine torque strut and ignition coils

14. Install the heater hose, radiator hose, power steering pump, alternator brackets and serpentine belt.

15. Install the fuel rail and connect the coolant hose and fuel lines.

16. Install the upper intake manifold.

17. Refill the cooling system, connect the battery cable, start the engine and check for leaks.

3.3L Engine

1. Relieve the pressure in the fuel system before disconnecting any fuel line connections.

2. Disconnect the negative battery cable and remove the air cleaner assembly.

3. Drain the cooling system.

4. Remove the serpentine belt, alternator and braces and power steering pump braces.

5. Disconnect and label the rear spark plug wires and place to the side.

6. Remove the coolant bypass hose, heater pipe and upper radiator hose.

7. Remove the air inlet duct, throttle cable bracket and cables.

8. Disconnect and tag all vacuum hoses and electrical connectors, as necessary.

9. Remove the fuel rail, vapor canister purge line and heater hose from the throttle body.

10. Remove the intake manifold retaining bolts and intake manifold.

To install:

11. Clean the cylinder head and intake manifold surfaces from any foreign matter, nicks or heavy scratches.

12. Apply sealer 12345336 or equivalent, to the ends of the manifold seals. Clean the intake manifold bolts and bolt holes. Apply thread lock compound 1052624 or equivalent, to the intake manifold bolt threads before assembly.

13. Install the new gasket and intake manifold. Tighten the intake manifold bolts twice to 88 inch lbs. (10 Nm) in the proper sequence.

14. Install the fuel rail, vapor canister purge line and heater hose from the throttle body.

15. Connect all vacuum hoses and electrical connectors including the spark plug wires.

16. Install the air inlet duct, throttle cable bracket and cables.

17. Install the coolant bypass hose, heater pipe and upper radiator hose.

18. Install the serpentine belt, alternator and braces and power steering pump braces.

19. Connect the negative battery cable.

20. Fill cooling system and check for leaks. Start the engine and allow to come to normal operating temperature. Recheck for leaks. top-off the engine coolant.

Exhaust Manifold

REMOVAL AND INSTALLATION

2.2L Engine

1. Remove the air cleaner and duct assembly.

2. Remove the air inlet resonator at the upper tie bar and remove the lower air inlet duct.

3. Loosen the alternator mounting bolts, remove the drive belt and remove the alternator. Set the alternator aside.

4. Remove the engine strut from the engine and remove the engine strut bracket assembly.

5. Remove the alternator rear support bracket.

6. Raise and safely support the vehicle. Remove the exhaust pipe from the exhaust manifold.

7. Lower the vehicle and remove the oil level indicator.

8. Disconnect the oxygen sensor connector.

9. Remove the exhaust manifold mounting nuts and remove the exhaust manifold and gaskets.

To install:

10. Clean all old gasket material from the exhaust manifold and the block.

11. Install the exhaust manifold with a new gasket and tighten the mounting bolts to 116 inch lbs. (13 Nm).

12. Connect the oxygen sensor connector.

13. Install the oil level indicator tube.

14. Raise and safely support the vehicle. Connect the exhaust pipe to the exhaust manifold and tighten the bolt to 18 ft. lbs. (25 Nm).

8470F048

Exhaust manifold — 2.2L engine

1. Stud
2. Gasket
3. Exhaust manifold
4. Nut

15. Lower the vehicle and install the alternator rear support bracket.

16. Install the engine support bracket and the engine support.

17. Install the alternator and the drive belt.

18. Install the lower air inlet duct, the air inlet resonator at the upper tie rod and air cleaner/duct assembly.

2.5L Engine

1. Disconnect the negative battery cable. Remove the air cleaner.

2. Remove the engine torque strut bolts at the cylinder head.

3. Remove the engine torque strut bracket from the cylinder head.

4. Disconnect the oxygen sensor connector and remove oil level indicator tube and nut. Move the tube aside.

5. Disconnect the exhaust pipe from the manifold.

6. Remove the manifold attaching bolts and remove the manifold.

To install:

7. Install the exhaust manifold and gasket to the cylinder head. Torque all bolts in sequence to the specified torque value.

8. Connect the exhaust pipe to the manifold.

9. Install the dipstick tube attaching bolt and the engine mount bracket to the cylinder head.

10. Connect the oxygen sensor connector and install the torque rod bracket and torque rod.

11. Install the air cleaner, connect the negative battery cable and inspect for any exhaust leaks

3.1L Engine

LEFT SIDE (FRONT)

1. Discharge and recover the A/C refrigerant. Disconnect the battery cables and drain the cooling system.

2. Disconnect the electrical connectors and heater hoses from the throttle body.

3. Relieve the fuel pressure and remove the throttle body.

4. Disconnect the fuel lines and coolant hoses.

5. Remove the crossover heatshield, crossover pipe and engine strut.

6. Remove the 2 top A/C compressor and bracket bolts.

7. Raise the vehicle and support safely.

8. Disconnect the A/C hoses and electrical connectors from the compressor.

9. Remove the lower A/C compressor bolts and compressor. Remove the lower bracket bolts and bracket.

1. Gasket
2. Manifold assembly
3. Bolt to 28 FT LB (38 NM)
4. Stud to 28 FT LB (38 NM)
5. Bolt to 37 FT LB (50 NM)
6. Stud to 37 FT LB (50 NM)

BOLT TIGHTENING SEQUENCE
TIGHTEN BOLT POSITION NUMBER IN
SEQUENCE AS FOLLOWS: 3-5-6-2-1-7-4

VIEW A

8470F049

Exhaust manifold — 2.5L engine

1. Studs
2. Exhaust manifold
3. Heat shield
4. Nuts

8470F051

Left exhaust manifold — 3.3L engine

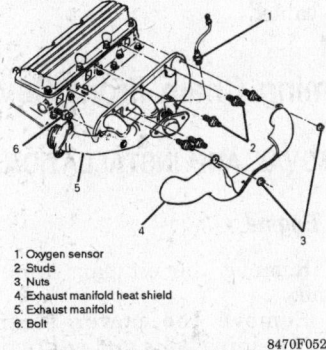

1. Oxygen sensor
2. Studs
3. Nuts
4. Exhaust manifold heat shield
5. Exhaust manifold
6. Bolt

8470F052

Right exhaust manifold — 3.3L engine

10. Lower the vehicle
11. Remove the exhaust manifold heatshield, manifold nuts and manifold.

To install:
12. Clean the gasket mating surfaces.
13. Install the gasket, manifold and nuts. Torque the nuts to 18 ft. lbs. (25 Nm). Install the heatshield.
14. Raise the vehicle and support safely.
15. Install the A/C bracket and compressor. Connect the A/C hoses and electrical connectors to the compressor. Use new sealing washers.

16. Lower the vehicle and install the upper A/C bracket and compressor bolts.
17. Install the engine torque strut, crossover pipe, heatshield and coolant hoses.
18. Connect the fuel lines and install the throttle body.
19. Refill the cooling system, evacuate the A/C system, start the engine and check for leaks.

RIGHT SIDE (REAR)

1. Drain the cooling system and disconnect the negative battery terminal.

2. Remove the throttle body.
3. Disconnect the radiator hose from the thermostat housing.
4. Remove the EGR tube.
5. Relieve the fuel pressure and disconnect the fuel lines.
6. Remove the crossover heatshield, crossover and oxygen sensor.
7. Remove the heatshield bolt from the top of the exhaust manifold.
8. Raise the vehicle and support safely.
9. Remove the exhaust pipe at the converter.
10. Remove the transaxle oil fill tube.
11. Remove the heatshield, manifold nuts and manifold.

To install:
12. Clean the gasket mating surfaces.
13. Install the gasket, manifold and nuts. Torque the nuts to 12 ft. lbs. (16 Nm). Install the heatshield.
14. Install the transaxle fill tube, exhaust pipe and lower the vehicle.
15. Install the heatshield top bolts, oxygen sensor, crossover pipe and heatshield.
16. Connect the fuel lines, EGR tube and radiator hose.
17. Install the throttle body.
18. Refill the cooling system and connect the battery cable. Start the engine and check for leaks.

3.3L Engine

LEFT SIDE

1. Remove the air cleaner assembly. Disconnect the negative battery cable.
2. Remove the alternator from the vehicle.
3. Remove the engine torque strut and mount brackets.
4. Mark and disconnect the spark plug wires and remove the spark plugs.
5. Remove the exhaust crossover pipe and remove the oil level indicator tube assembly.
6. Remove the engine cooling fan assembly.
7. Remove the exhaust heatshield and the manifold support bracket.
8. Remove the manifold studs and bolts and remove the manifold.

To install:

9. Install the manifold and torque bolts and studs to 18 ft. lbs. (25 Nm).
10. Install the manifold support bracket. Install the exhaust heatshield.
11. Install the cooling fan assembly. Install the oil indicator tube assembly.
12. Install the exhaust crossover pipe. Install the spark plugs and wires.
13. Install the engine torque strut and mount bracket
14. Install the alternator and install the air cleaner assembly.
15. Connect the negative battery cable.

RIGHT SIDE

1. Disconnect the negative battery cable. Remove the air cleaner and duct assembly.
2. Remove the serpentine belt and drain the coolant.
3. Remove the power steering pump brace and bolts and move pump forward.
4. Mark and remove spark plug wires.
5. Disconnect the oxygen sensor connector and remove the engine lift bracket nuts from the exhaust manifold.
6. Remove the coolant tube, engine lift bracket and fuel line clamp screw from the coolant tube assembly and set to the side.
7. Remove the right bank of spark plugs and remove the exhaust crossover tube.
8. Remove the transaxle fill tube retaining bolt and remove tube for access.
9. Raise and safely support the vehicle.

10. Disconnect the exhaust pipe from the manifold and lower the vehicle.
11. Remove the exhaust heatshield retaining nuts and pull shield aside.
12. Remove the manifold studs and remove the manifold. Remove the heatshield.

To install:

13. Install the manifold bolts, studs and heatshield assembly. Torque to 18 ft. lbs. (25 Nm)
14. Raise and safely support the vehicle, connect the exhaust pipe to the manifold. Lower the vehicle.
15. Install the transaxle fill tube retaining bolt and install the exhaust crossover pipe.
16. Install the right bank of spark plugs.
17. Install the coolant tube, engine lift bracket and fuel line clamp screw.
18. Install the engine lift bracket nuts to the exhaust manifold.
19. Connect the oxygen sensor connector and connect the spark plug wires.
20. Install the power steering pump brace and pump bolts to the mounting bracket.
21. Refill the coolant to the proper level and install the serpentine belt.
22. Install the air cleaner and duct assembly. Connect the negative battery cable.

Timing Chain Front Cover

REMOVAL AND INSTALLATION

2.2L Engine

1. Remove the oil pan from the engine.
2. Remove the power steering pump retaining bolts and position the pump aside.
3. Remove the alternator assembly and place it aside.
4. Remove the belt tensioner.

1. Bolt
2. Crankcase front cover

8470F053

Timing chain front cover — 2.2L Engine

5. Raise and safely support the vehicle.
6. Remove the crankshaft balancer hub assembly.
7. Remove the front/timing chain cover bolts and remove the cover.

To install:

8. Install the front cover over the dowel pins and install the mounting bolts. Tighten the bolts to 98 inch lbs. (11 Nm).
9. Install the crankshaft balancer hub. Tighten the bolt to 77 ft. lbs. (105 Nm).
10. Lower the vehicle and install the drive belt tensioner.
11. Install the alternator and the power steering pump.
12. Install the oil pan.

2.5L Engine

1. Disconnect the negative battery cable.
2. Remove the drive belt tensioner.
3. Remove the upper front cover to engine bolts.
4. Raise and safely support the vehicle. Remove the right front wheel.
5. Remove the right side engine splash shield. Remove the crankshaft pulley.
6. Remove the lower front cover bolts and remove the front cover.
7. Clean the gasket surfaces thoroughly.

To install:

8. Apply a 1/8 in. (3mm) bead of silicone sealer to the oil pan, engine block and front cover.
9. Align the front cover seal with a centering tool and install the front cover. Tighten the screws and bolts.
10. Install the pulley and right engine splash shield.
11. Install the right wheel and lower the vehicle.
12. Install the upper cover bolts and the drive belt tensioner.
13. Connect the battery negative cable.

3.1L Engine

1. Disconnect the negative battery terminal.
2. Drain the engine oil and remove the oil pan.
3. Drain the cooling system and remove the serpentine belt.
4. Remove the alternator brackets, power steering pump and belt tensioner.
5. Remove the coolant bypass adapter and coolant hose from the water pump.
6. Remove the crankshaft balancer and knock sensor.

TIGHTEN IN PROPER SEQUENCE "A" THROUGH "G"

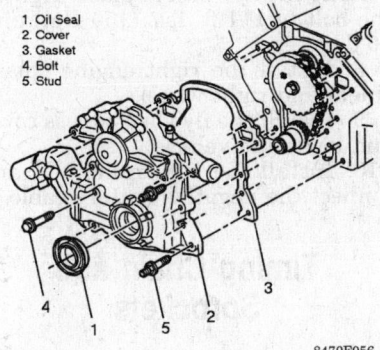

1. Bolt 89 LB IN (10 NM)
2. Front cover

8470F054

Timing chain front cover — 2.5L Engine

1. Oil Seal
2. Cover
3. Gasket
4. Bolt
5. Stud

8470F056

Timing chain front cover — 3.3L Engine

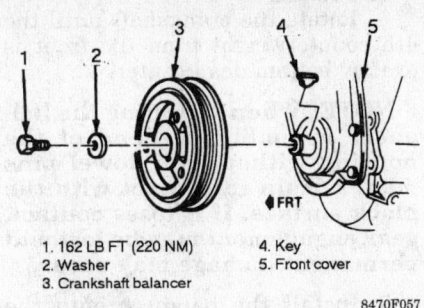

1. 162 LB FT (220 NM)
2. Washer
3. Crankshaft balancer
4. Key
5. Front cover

8470F057

Crankshaft balancer — 2.5L engine

7. Remove the front cover bolts, front cover and gasket.

To install:

8. Clean the gasket mating surfaces and apply a ⅛ in. (3mm) bead of silicone sealer to the oil pan, engine block and front cover.

9. Install the front cover bolts, front cover and gasket. Torque the small bolts to 15 ft. lbs. (21 Nm) and the large bolts to 41 ft. lbs. (55 Nm).

10. Install the crankshaft balancer and knock sensor.

11. Install the coolant bypass adapter and coolant hose to the water pump.

12. Install the alternator brackets, power steering pump and belt tensioner.

13. Refill the cooling system and install the serpentine belt.

14. Install the oil pan and refill the engine oil.

15. Connect the negative battery terminal, start the engine and check for leaks.

3.3L Engine

1. Relieve the pressure in the fuel system before disconnecting any fuel line connections. Disconnect the negative battery cable.

2. Drain the cooling system and drain the engine oil.

3. Remove the serpentine belt.

4. Remove the heater pipes. Remove the coolant bypass hose and lower radiator hose from cover.

5. Raise and support the vehicle safely.

6. Remove the inner splash shield.

7. Remove the crankshaft balancer.

8. Disconnect all electrical connectors at the camshaft sensor, crankshaft sensor and oil pressure sender.

9. Remove the oil pan-to-front cover retaining bolts, front cover retaining bolts and remove the front cover.

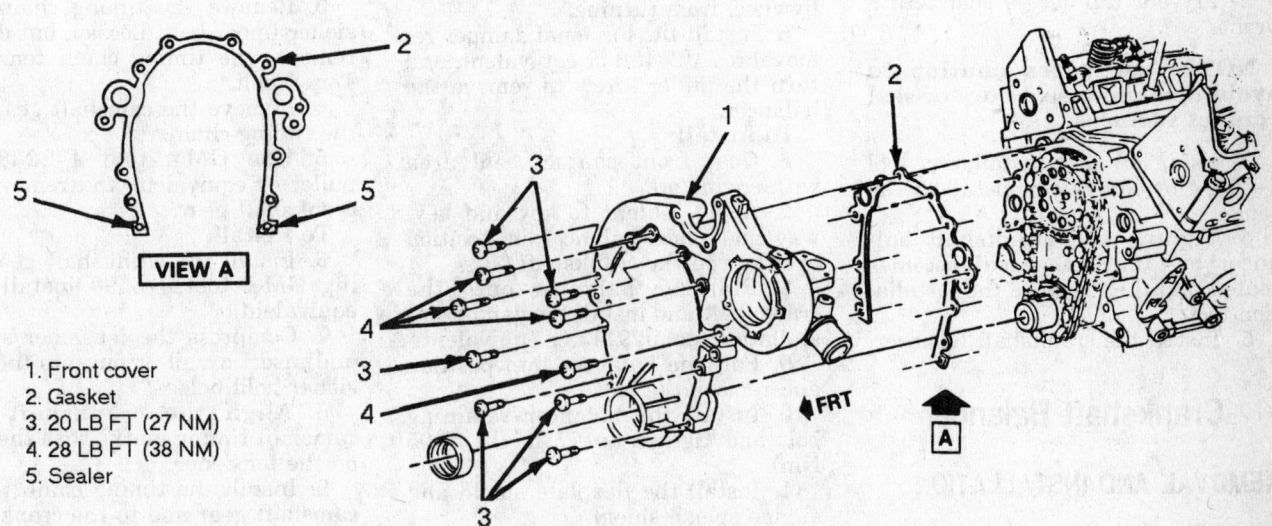

VIEW A

1. Front cover
2. Gasket
3. 20 LB FT (27 NM)
4. 28 LB FT (38 NM)
5. Sealer

8470F055

Timing chain front cover/water pump assembly — 3.1L Engine

To install:

10. Clean the mating surfaces of the front cover and cylinder block.

11. Install a new gasket on the cylinder block. Install the front cover. Apply sealer to the threads of the cover retaining bolts and secure the cover. Tighten the bolts to 22 ft. lbs. (30 Nm).

12. Install the oil pan-to-front cover bolts. Tighten the bolts to 88 inch lbs. (10 Nm).

13. Reconnect the camshaft sensor, crankshaft sensor and oil pressure sender electrical connectors. Adjust the crankshaft sensor using tool J–37087 or equivalent.

14. Install the crankshaft balancer.

15. Install the inner splash shield.

16. Lower the vehicle.

17. Install the heater pipes. Install the coolant bypass hose and lower radiator hose from cover.

18. Install the serpentine belt.

19. Connect the negative battery cable.

20. Fill cooling system and check for leaks. Start the engine and allow to come to normal operating temperature. Check for leaks. Refill coolant to proper level.

Front Cover Oil Seal

REPLACEMENT

1. Remove the harmonic crankshaft balancer.

2. Pry out the old oil seal with a prybar.

NOTE: Use extra caution to avoid damaging seal bore or seal contact surfaces.

3. Using oil seal installation tool J–35354 or equivalent install the oil seal.

4. Tighten the crankshaft balancer bolt until the seal becomes seated and then remove the installation tool.

5. Install the crankshaft balancer.

Crankshaft Balancer

REMOVAL AND INSTALLATION

2.5L Engine

1. Disconnect the negative battery cable and drain the engine oil.

2. Remove the oil pan.

3. Remove the crankshaft balancer retaining bolts and remove the balancer.

To install:

4. Rotate the crankshaft until the 4th counterweight from the front is exactly bottom dead center.

NOTE: When installing the balancer assembly, the end of the housing without the dowel pins must remain in contact with the block surface. If it loses contact, gear engagement may be lost and permanent damage may occur.

5. Install the balancer onto the block and install the balancer bolts.

6. Tighten the bolts to 107 inch lbs. (12 Nm) in the order of 3-1-2-4. Following the same sequence, tighten the short bolts to 11 ft. lbs. (15 Nm) plus 72 degrees. Tighten the long bolts to 11 ft. lbs. (15 Nm) plus 86 degrees.

7. Rotate the crankshaft several times and check clearance between the 4th counterweight and the balancer weights.

8. Install the oil pan and connect the negative battery cable. Refill the engine with oil and inspect for leaks.

2.2L and 3.1L Engines

1. Disconnect the negative battery cable.

2. Remove the serpentine belt, raise and safely support the vehicle.

3. Remove the right side inner fender splash shield and remove the flexplate shield.

4. Remove the balancer retaining bolt and have an assistant hold the flywheel from turning.

5. Install the torsional damper removal tool J2440B or equivalent, and turn the puller screw to remove the balancer.

To install:

6. Coat front contact seal area with engine oil.

7. Apply sealant to key and keyway and place balancer in position over key on the crankshaft.

8. Pull the balancer onto the crankshaft and install the damper installation tool J29113 or equivalent.

9. Pull the balancer into position and remove the tool.

10. Install the balancer retaining bolt and tighten to 77 ft. lbs. (105 Nm).

11. Install the flexplate shield and engine splash shield.

12. Install the serpentine belt and connect the negative battery cable.

3.3L Engine

1. Disconnect the negative battery cable.

2. Remove the serpentine belt.

3. Raise and safely support the vehicle. Remove the right front wheel.

4. Remove the right engine splash shield and remove the flywheel access cover.

5. Using a flywheel holding tool J37096 or equivalent, hold the flywheel and using the crankshaft balancer removal tool J38197 or equivalent, remove the crankshaft balancer.

To install:

6. Lubricate the seal surface with oil and install the crankshaft balancer.

7. Tighten the balancer bolt while holding the flywheel in place. Tighten the bolt to 111 ft. lbs. (150 Nm) plus 76 degrees.

8. Install the right engine splash shield and right wheel.

9. Install the flywheel access cover and lower the vehicle.

10. Install the serpentine belt and connect the negative battery cable.

Timing Chain and Sprockets

REMOVAL AND INSTALLATION

2.2L Engine

1. Remove the front cover assembly.

2. Align the marks on the crankshaft gear with the marks on the camshaft gear.

3. Remove the timing chain tensioner upper bolt. Loosen, but do not remove, the timing chain tensioner Torx® bolt.

4. Remove the camshaft gear and the timing chain.

5. Use GM® tool J–22888–20 puller or equivalent and remove the crankshaft gear.

To install:

6. Install the crankshaft gear using GM® tool J–5590 installer or equivalent.

7. Compress the tensioner spring and insert a nail or pin into the tensioner hold hole.

8. Align the crankshaft and camshaft timing marks with the taps on the tensioner.

9. Install the timing chain to the camshaft gear and to the crankshaft gear.

10. Align the dowel in the camshaft with the dowel hole in the camshaft gear and then install the gear to the camshaft.

11. Install the camshaft gear and tighten the mounting bolt to 77 ft. lbs. (105 Nm).

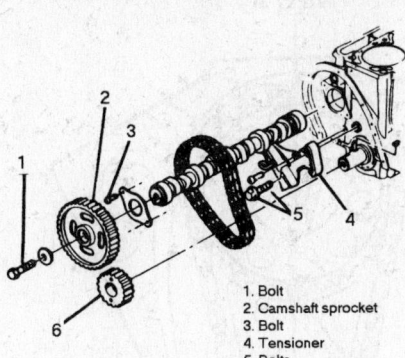

1. Bolt
2. Camshaft sprocket
3. Bolt
4. Tensioner
5. Bolts
6. Crankshaft sprocket

A - ALIGN TABS ON TENSIONER WITH MARKS ON CAMSHAFT & CRANKSHAFT SPROCKETS

8470F058

Timing chain assembly — 2.2L engine

12. Install the timing chain tensioner upper bolt and tighten to 18 ft. lbs. (24 Nm).

13. Remove the timing chain tensioner pin or nail to release the tensioner.

14. Install the front cover assembly.

Timing Gears

REMOVAL AND INSTALLATION

2.5L Engine

1. Disconnect the negative battery cable.

2. Remove the front cover.

3. Loosen the camshaft bolt. Align the cam and crankshaft timing marks and remove the camshaft bolt.

4. Remove the timing chain and sprocket.

To install:

5. Install the timing chain and sprocket. Align the cam and crankshaft (with engine at TDC).

6. Install the camshaft bolt and tighten to 43 ft. lbs. (58 Nm).

7. Install the front cover.

3.1L Engine

1. Relieve the pressure in the fuel system before disconnecting any fuel line connections. Disconnect the negative battery cable.

2. Remove the crankcase front cover.

3. Place the No. 1 piston at TDC with the marks on the camshaft and crankshaft sprockets aligned.

4. Remove the camshaft sprocket and chain.

NOTE: If the sprocket does not come off easily, a light blow with a plastic mallet on the lower edge of the sprocket should dislodge the sprocket.

5. Remove the crankshaft sprocket.

To install:

6. Install the crankshaft sprocket. Apply Molykote® or equivalent, to the sprocket thrust surface.

7. Hold the sprocket with the chain hanging down and align the marks on the camshaft and crankshaft sprockets.

8. Align the dowel in the camshaft with the dowel hole in the camshaft sprocket.

9. Draw the camshaft sprocket onto the camshaft using the mounting bolts. Tighten the camshaft sprocket mounting bolts to 18 ft. lbs. (25 Nm).

10. Lubricate the timing chain with engine oil. Install the crankcase front

1. Camshaft
2. Key
3. Tensioner
4. Bolt 43 FT LB (25 NM)
5. Bolt 43 FT LB (25 NM)
6. Washer
7. Sprocket and chain assembly
8. Bolt 89 IN LB (10 NM)
9. Bearing
10. Timing marks to be aligned as shown when engine is rotated to T.D.C.

8470F059

Timing chain assembly — 2.5L engine

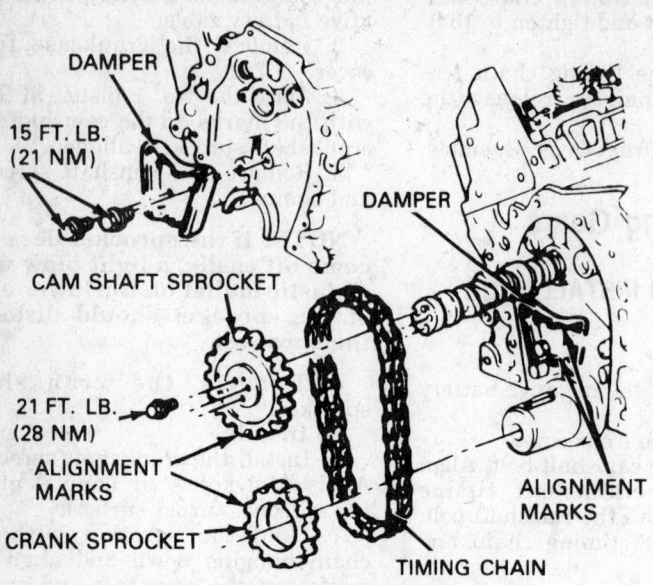

DAMPER

15 FT. LB. (21 NM)

CAM SHAFT SPROCKET

DAMPER

21 FT. LB. (28 NM)

ALIGNMENT MARKS

CRANK SPROCKET

ALIGNMENT MARKS

TIMING CHAIN

NOTE—ALIGN TIMING MARKS ON CAM & CRANK SPROCKETS USING ALIGNMENT MARKS ON DAMPER STAMPING OR CAST ALIGNMENT MARKS ON CYL & CASE

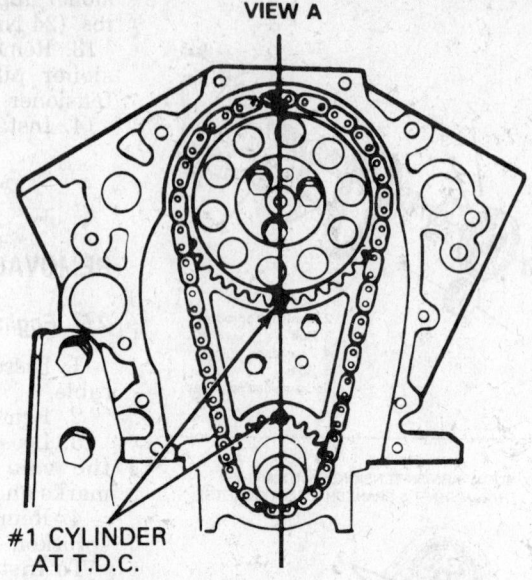

VIEW A

#1 CYLINDER AT T.D.C.

NOTE—CAMSHAFT SPROCKET MARK AT 6 O'CLOCK CRANKSHAFT SPROCKET MARK AT 12 O'CLOCK

8470M084

Timing chain and sprockets — 3.1L engine

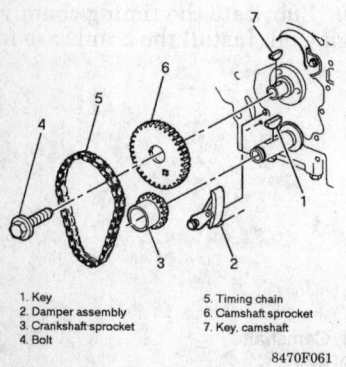

1. Key
2. Damper assembly
3. Crankshaft sprocket
4. Bolt
5. Timing chain
6. Camshaft sprocket
7. Key, camshaft

8470F061

Timing chain assembly — 3.3L engine

cover. Connect battery negative cable.

3.3L Engine

1. Relieve the pressure in the fuel system before disconnecting any fuel line connections. Disconnect the negative battery cable.
2. Remove the crankcase front cover.
3. Turn the crankshaft so the timing marks are aligned.
4. Remove the timing chain damper and camshaft sprocket bolts.

5. Remove the camshaft sprocket and chain. Remove the crankshaft sprocket.
To install:
6. Make sure the crankshaft is positioned so No. 1 piston is at TDC on compression stroke.
7. Rotate the camshaft with the sprocket temporarily installed, so the timing mark is straight down.
8. Assembly the timing chain on the sprockets with the timing marks aligned. Install the timing chain and sprocket.
9. Install the camshaft sprocket bolts. Torque the bolts to 74 ft. lbs. (100 Nm) +105 degrees using tool J–36660 or equivalent.
10. Install the timing chain damper and engine front cover. Connect battery negative cable.

Camshaft

REMOVAL AND INSTALLATION

2.2L Engine

1. Remove the engine from the vehicle as previously listed. Install the engine to a suitable engine stand.
2. Remove the drive belt tensioner and the alternator assembly. Place the alternator to the side.

3. Remove the strut bracket and the rear alternator bracket.
4. Remove the front engine mount bracket.
5. Remove the oil level indicator tube and the oil pan.
6. Remove the crankshaft balancer hub and the front cover assembly.
7. Remove the timing chain and the gears.
8. Mark and disconnect the spark plug wires.
9. Remove the rocker arm cover and gaskets.
10. Remove the rocker arms and the pushrods.
11. Remove the power steering pump bracket pencil brace.
12. Remove the cylinder head with the intake manifold and exhaust manifold intact.
13. Remove the valve lifters and the camshaft thrust plate.
14. Remove the oil pump drive assembly and remove the camshaft.
To install:
15. Lubricate the camshaft journals with GM®EOS lubricant 1052367 or equivalent.
16. Install the camshaft and the oil pump drive assembly.
17. Install the camshaft thrust plate and bolts/screws. Tighten the bolts/screws to 107 inch lbs. (12 Nm).

18. Install the valve lifters and the cylinder head with the intake and exhaust manifold attached.

19. Install the power steering pump bracket pencil brace.

20. Install the rocker arms and pushrods. Tighten the rocker arm nuts to 22 ft. lbs. (30 Nm).

21. Install the rocker arm gasket and the cover.

22. Install the spark plug wires.

23. Install the timing chain and the gears and install the front cover assembly.

24. Install the crankshaft balancer hub and the oil pan.

25. Install the oil level indicator tube and the front engine mount bracket.

26. Install the strut bracket and rear alternator bracket.

27. Install the alternator and the drive belt tensioner.

28. Install the engine to the vehicle.

2.5L Engine

1. Relieve the pressure in the fuel system before disconnecting any fuel line connections.

2. Disconnect the negative battery cable.

3. Remove the engine from the vehicle and support on a suitable engine stand.

4. Remove the rocker cover, rocker arms and pushrods.

5. Remove the spark plugs and fuel pump.

6. Remove the pushrod cover and gasket. Remove the lifters.

7. Remove the alternator, the alternator lower bracket and the front engine mount bracket assembly.

8. Remove the oil pump driveshaft and gear assembly.

9. Remove the crankshaft hub and timing gear cover.

10. Remove the 2 camshaft thrust plate screws by working through the holes in the gear.

11. Remove the camshaft and gear assembly by pulling it through the front of the block. Take care not to damage the bearings.

12. If replacement of the camshaft gear is necessary, use the following procedure:

a. Remove the camshaft gear using an arbor press and adapter.

b. Position the thrust plate to avoid damage by interference with the Woodruff® key as the gear is removed.

c. When assembling the gear onto the camshaft, support the camshaft at the back of the front journal in the arbor press using press plate adapters.

d. Press the gear on the shaft until it bottoms against the spacer ring.

e. Measure the end clearance of the thrust plate. End clearance should be 0.0015–0.0050 in. (0.0381–0.127mm).

f. If clearance is less than 0.0015 in.(0.0381mm), replace the spacer ring.

g. If clearance is more than 0.0050 in.(0.127mm), replace the thrust plate.

To install:

13. Lubricate the camshaft journals with a high quality engine oil supplement and carefully install the camshaft and gear into the cylinder block.

14. Rotate the camshaft and crankshaft so the timing marks on the gear teeth align. The engine is now in No. 4 cylinder firing position.

15. Install the camshaft thrust plate-to-block screw. Torque the screw to 90 inch lbs. (10 Nm).

16. Install the crankshaft hub and timing gear cover.

17. Install the oil pump driveshaft and gear assembly.

18. Install the lower alternator bracket, alternator and the front engine mount bracket assembly.

19. Install the spark plugs and fuel pump.

20. Install the lifters. Install the pushrod cover and gasket.

21. Install the pushrods, rocker arms and rocker cover.

22. Install the engine in the vehicle.

23. Connect the negative battery cable.

3.1L and 3.3L Engines

1. Relieve the pressure in the fuel system before disconnecting any fuel line connections.

2. Disconnect the negative battery cable.

3. Remove the engine from the vehicle and support on a suitable engine stand.

4. Label all components for correct installation. Remove the intake manifold, valve cover, rocker arms, pushrods and valve lifters.

5. Remove the crankshaft balancer and front cover.

6. Remove the timing chain and sprockets.

7. Carefully remove the camshaft. Avoid marring the camshaft bearing surfaces.

To install:

8. Coat the camshaft with lubricant 1052365 or equivalent, and install the camshaft.

9. Install the timing chain and sprocket.

10. Install the camshaft thrust button and front cover.

11. Install the crankshaft balancer.

12. Install the intake manifold, valve cover, rocker arms, pushrods and valve lifters.

13. Install the engine in the vehicle.

14. Connect the negative battery cable.

15. Adjust the valves, as required.

Piston and Connecting Rod

POSITIONING

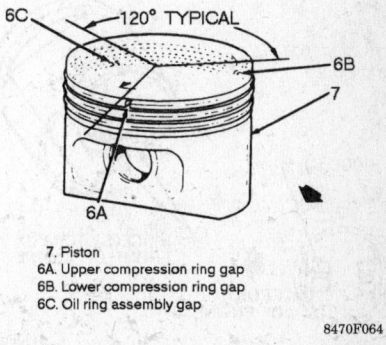

7. Piston
6A. Upper compression ring gap
6B. Lower compression ring gap
6C. Oil ring assembly gap

8470F064

Piston assembly ring gap location — 2.2L engine

1. Oil ring spacer gap (tang in hole or slot with ARC)
2. Oil ring rail gaps
3. 2nd compression ring gap
4. Top compression ring gap

8470F067

Piston ring gap locations — 2.5L, 3.1L and 3.3L engines

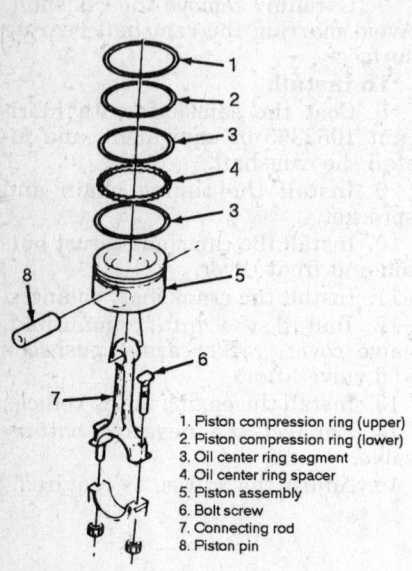

1. Piston compression ring (upper)
2. Piston compression ring (lower)
3. Oil center ring segment
4. Oil center ring spacer
3. Oil center ring segment
5. Piston assembly
6. Bolt screw
7. Connecting rod
8. Piston pin

8470F068

Piston and rod assembly — 2.5L and 3.1L engine

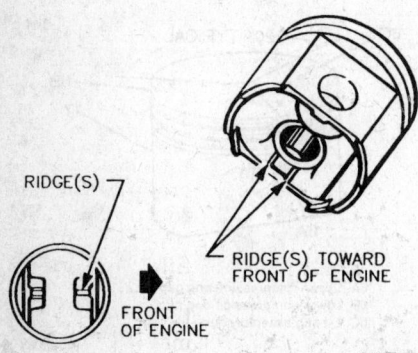

8470F070

Piston installation direction — 3.3L engine

8470F071

Oil pan assembly — 2.2L engine

8470F072

3 OIL PAN
4 OIL PAN DRAIN PLUG
1 10 N·m (89 LB. IN.)
2 OIL FILTER ACCESS PLUG

Oil pan assembly — 2.5L engine

ENGINE LUBRICATION

Oil Pan

REMOVAL AND INSTALLATION

2.2L and 2.5L Engines

1. Disconnect the negative battery cable. Remove the air cleaner and duct assembly.

2. Remove the serpentine belt. Remove the engine torque strut from the engine bracket.

3. Remove the 2 upper front air conditioning compressor bolts to the mounting bracket.

4. Raise and support the vehicle safely. Drain the oil.

5. Remove cradle-to-front engine mount nuts.

6. Disconnect exhaust pipe at manifold and at rear transaxle mount.

7. Disconnect starter and remove flywheel housing inspection cover.

8. Remove upper alternator bracket. Remove the splash shield, if equipped, in order to gain working clearance.

9. Install suitable engine support equipment and raise engine.

10. Remove lower alternator bracket and engine support bracket.

11. Remove oil pan retaining bolts and remove oil pan.

To install:

12. Thoroughly clean all gasket sealing surfaces.

13. Install rear oil pan gasket in rear main bearing cap and apply a small quantity of sealer in depressions where pan gasket engages into block.

14. Install front oil pan gasket on timing gear cover pressing tips into holes provided in cover.

15. Install side gaskets on oil pan using grease as a retainer.

16. Apply a 1/8 inch by 1/4 inch long bead of sealer at split lines of front and side gaskets.

17. Install oil pan. Bolts into timing gear cover should be installed last. They are installed at an angle and holes align after rest of pan bolts are snugged up.

18. Install lower alternator bracket and engine support bracket.

19. Lower the engine and remove engine support equipment.

20. Install upper alternator bracket. If removed, install the splash shield.

21. Install flywheel housing inspection cover. Connect starter.

22. Connect exhaust pipe at manifold and at rear transaxle mount.

23. Install cradle-to-front engine mount nuts.

24. Lower the vehicle.

25. Fill the crankcase with oil.

26. Connect the negative battery cable.

27. Start the engine and check for leaks.

3.1L Engine

NOTE: Special GM tools, engine support fixture J–28467A, engine support adapter leg J–36462 and torque wrench adapter J–39505 are needed to perform the oil pan removal and installation.

1. Disconnect the negative battery cable and drain the engine oil.

2. Remove the torque strut bolt. Raise the vehicle and support safely.

3. Remove the oil drip shield and engine mounts. Support the engine using a suitable jack.

**APPLY RTV SEALANT
AS SPECIFIED**

1. 5/16" wide x 1/8" thick
2. 9/64" wide x 3/32" thick
3. 5/64" bead in areas shown

BLOCK

FWD

PAN

8470F073

Oil pan sealer application — 2.5L engine

4. Remove the transaxle mount nuts and exhaust pipe from the manifold.
5. Raise the engine using tools J–28467–A and J–36462.
6. Lower the vehicle. Place jackstands under the frame at the front and rear center crossmembers.
7. Loosen but do not remove the rear frame bolts.
8. Remove the front frame bolts and lower front of frame.
9. Remove the front engine mount bracket bolts, bracket and mount.
10. Remove the starter motor and electrical brackets at the oil pan.
11. Remove the oil pan bolts and oil pan. The side bolts need to be removed with tool J–39505, or equivalent
To install:
12. Clean the gasket mating surfaces. Apply a bead of Ultra Black RTV sealer on the oil pan gasket tabs that insert into the gasket groove of the outer surface on the rear main bearing cap.
13. Install a new gasket, oil pan and bolts. Torque the side bolts to 37 ft. lbs. (50 Nm) with special tool J–39505. Torque the bottom bolts to 18 ft. lbs. (25 Nm).

14. Install the electrical brackets, starter motor and engine mount/bracket.
15. Raise the frame to proper position using new frame bolts. Remove the jackstands.
16. Raise the vehicle and support safely. Lower the engine to the correct position using engine support tools.
17. Install the exhaust pipe, transaxle mount, engine mount and oil drip shield.
18. Lower the vehicle and fill the engine with the proper amount of oil.
19. Install the torque strut bolt and remove the engine support fixture tools. Recheck the engine oil level, start the engine and check for leaks.

3.3L Engine

1. Disconnect the negative battery cable.
2. Raise and support the vehicle safely.
3. Drain the engine oil.
4. Remove the flywheel inspection cover and remove the right front wheel.
5. Remove the engine splash shield.
6. Remove the oil filter, oil pan retaining bolts and oil pan assembly.

To install:
7. Clean the oil pan and cylinder block mating surfaces.
8. Install a new oil pan gasket to the oil pan flange.
9. Install the oil pan and torque the oil pan to cylinder block bolts to 12 ft. lbs. (16 Nm). Torque the oil pan to front cover bolts to 10 ft. lbs. (14 Nm).
10. Install the oil filter and install the engine splash shield.
11. Install the right front wheel and install the flywheel inspection cover.
12. Lower the vehicle and fill the crankcase with oil.
13. Connect the negative battery cable.

Oil Pump

REMOVAL AND INSTALLATION

2.2L Engine

1. Disconnect the negative battery cable.
2. Remove the oil pan .
3. Remove the oil pump to rear main bearing cap bolt and remove the oil pump and extension shaft.
4. Remove the extension shaft and retainer, being careful not to crack the retainer.

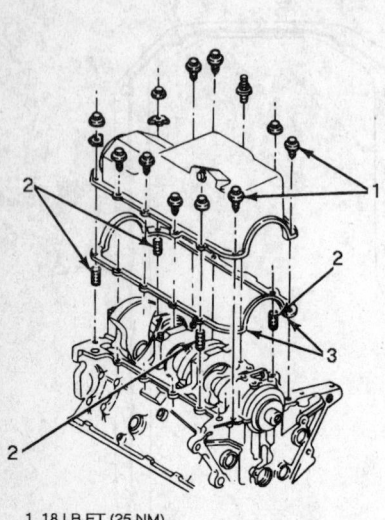

1. 18 LB FT (25 NM)
2. 13 LB FT (17 NM)
   ALL OTHERS 89 LB IN (10 NM)
3. Sealer

8470F074

Oil pan assembly — 3.1L engine

1. Gasket
2. Oil pump screen assembly
3. Bolt
4. Gasket
5. Oil pan
6. Bolt

8470F075

Oil pan assembly — 3.3L engine

1. Pickup tube and screen
2. Pump cover
3. Drive gear and shaft
4. Idler gear
5. Pump body
6. Retainer
7. Shaft
8. Bolts
9. Retaining pin
10. Pressure regulator spring
11. Pressure regulator valve
12. Gasket

8470F076

Oil pump assembly — 2.2L engine

To install:

5. Heat the retainer in hot water before assembling the the extension shaft.

6. Install the extension shaft to the oil pump, being careful not to crack the retainer.

7. Install the oil pump to the rear bearing cap and bolt.

8. Tighten the oil pump bolt to 32 ft. lbs. (44 Nm).

9. Install the oil pan and torque bolts to 89 in. lbs. (10 Nm). Connect the negative battery cable.

2.5L Engine

1. Disconnect the negative battery cable.

2. Raise and support the vehicle safely.

3. Drain the engine oil and remove the oil filter and the oil pan.

4. Remove the oil pump cover.

5. Remove the pump and screen as an assembly.

To install:

6. Remove the 4 cover attaching screws and cover from the oil pump assembly.

7. Pack the space around the oil pump gears completely full of petroleum jelly. There must be no air space left inside the pump. If the pump is not packed, it may not begin to pump oil as soon as the engine is started and engine damage may result.

8. Align the oil pump shaft to match with the oil pump drive shaft tang, then install the oil pump to the block positioning the flange over the oil pump driveshaft lower bushing. Do not use any gasket. Torque the bolts to 20 ft. lbs. (30 Nm).

9. Install the oil pan using a new gasket and seals.

10. Install the 2 flange mounting bolts and nut to the main bearing cap bolt.

11. Lower the vehicle.

12. Fill the crankcase with oil.

13. Connect the negative battery cable.

3.1L Engine

1. Disconnect the negative battery cable.

2. Raise and support the vehicle safely.

3. Drain the engine oil and remove the oil pan.

4. Remove the pump-to-rear main bearing cap bolt and remove the pump and extension shaft.

To install:

5. Remove the 4 cover attaching screws and cover from the oil pump assembly.

6. Pack the space around the oil pump gears completely full of petroleum jelly. There must be no air space left inside the pump. If the pump is not packed, it may not begin to pump oil as soon as the engine is started and engine damage may result.

7. Assemble the pump and extension shaft with retainer to rear main bearing cap, aligning the top end of the extension shaft with the lower end of the drive gear.

8. Install the pump-to-the rear bearing cap bolt. Tighten to 30 ft. lbs. (40 Nm).

9. Install the oil pan. Torque the rear pan bolts to 18 ft. lbs. (25 Nm), except for 3.1L engine or 18 ft. lbs. (25 Nm) for 3.1L engine.

10. Lower the vehicle.

11. Fill the crankcase with oil.

12. Connect the negative battery cable.

3.3L Engine

1. Disconnect the negative battery cable.

2. Remove the front engine cover. Drain the engine oil.

3. Remove the oil filter adapter, pressure regulator valve and spring.

4. Remove the oil pump cover attaching screws and cover.

5. Remove the gears.

To install:

6. Lubricate the gears with petroleum jelly.

7. Assemble the gears in the housing.

8. Pack the gear cavity with petroleum jelly.

9. Install the oil pump cover and screws. Tighten to 97 inch lbs. (11 Nm).

10. Install the pressure regulator and spring valve.

11. Install the oil filter adapter with a new gasket. Tighten the oil filter adapter bolts to 24 ft. lbs. (33 Nm).

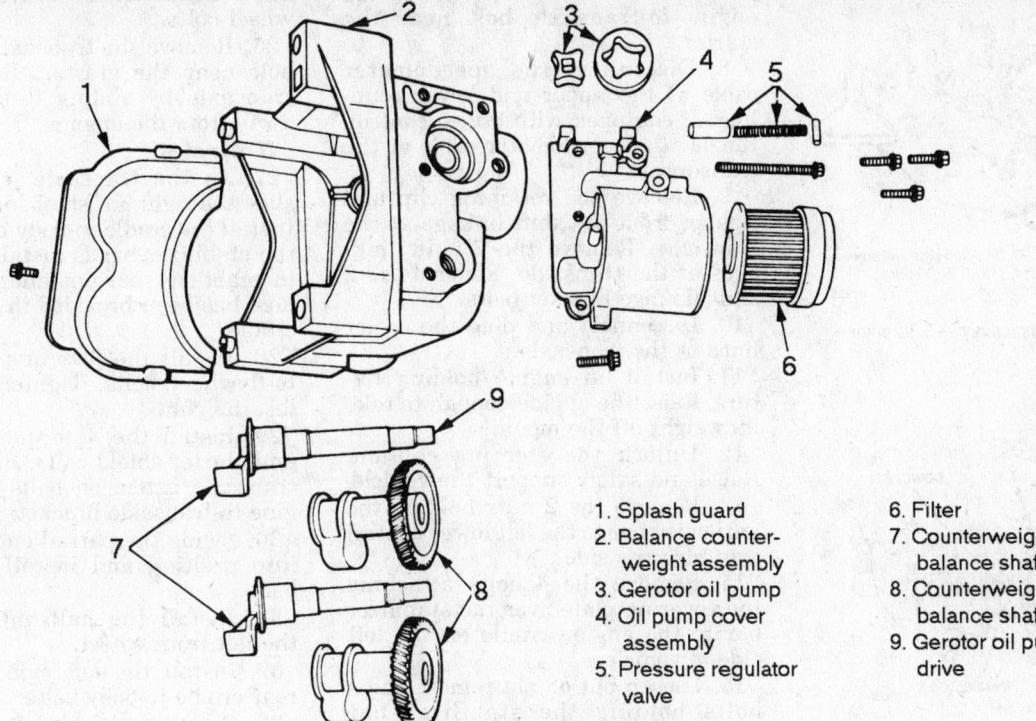

1. Splash guard
2. Balance counter-
   weight assembly
3. Gerotor oil pump
4. Oil pump cover
   assembly
5. Pressure regulator
   valve

6. Filter
7. Counterweighted
   balance shaft
8. Counterweighted
   balance shaft gear
9. Gerotor oil pump
   drive

8470F077

Oil pump/force balancer assembly — 2.5L engine

25 LB FT
(34 NM)

OIL PUMP DRIVE

OIL PUMP

30 LB FT
(41 NM)

8470F078

Oil pump assembly — 3.1L engine

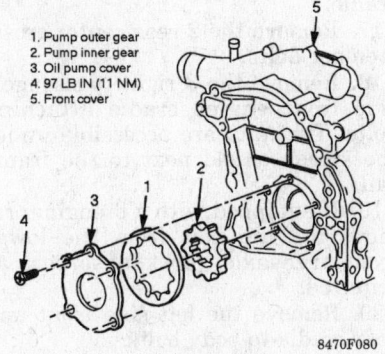

1. Pump outer gear
2. Pump inner gear
3. Oil pump cover
4. 97 LB IN (11 NM)
5. Front cover

8470F080

Oil pump and housing assembly — 3.3L
engine

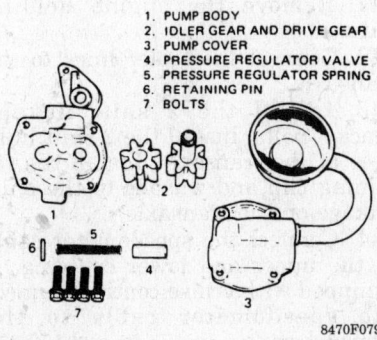

1. PUMP BODY
2. IDLER GEAR AND DRIVE GEAR
3. PUMP COVER
4. PRESSURE REGULATOR VALVE
5. PRESSURE REGULATOR SPRING
6. RETAINING PIN
7. BOLTS

8470F079

**Exploded view of the oil pump assembly —
3.1L engine**

12. Install the front cover on the engine.
13. Fill the crankcase with oil.
14. Connect the negative battery cable.

Rear Main Bearing Oil Seal

REMOVAL AND INSTALLATION

2.2L, 2.5L and 3.3L Engines

1. Disconnect the negative battery cable.

2. Support the engine. Remove the transaxle and flywheel.
3. Being careful not to scratch the crankshaft, pry out the old seal with an suitable pry tool.
   To install:
4. Coat the new seal with clean engine oil and install it by hand or use seal installer tool J–34924 onto the crankshaft. The seal backing must be flush with the block opening.
5. Install the flywheel.
6. Install the transaxle.
7. Connect the negative battery cable.

3.1L Engine

1. Disconnect the negative battery cable.
2. Support the engine with tool J–28467–A or equivalent.
3. Remove the transaxle and flywheel.
4. Carefully remove the old seal by inserting a prying tool through the dust lip at an angle. Pry out the old seal with an suitable pry tool.
   To install:
5. Coat the new seal with clean engine oil, and install it using seal installer tool J–34686 or equivalent.
6. Install the flywheel.
7. Install the transaxle.
8. Remove the engine support tool.

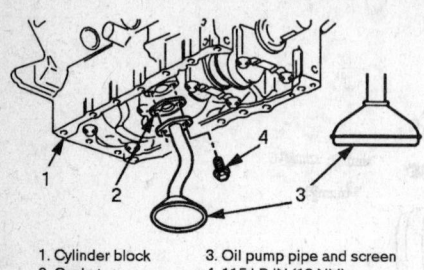

1. Cylinder block
2. Gasket
3. Oil pump pipe and screen
4. 115 LB IN (13 NM)

8470F081

Oil pump pickup assembly — 3.3L engine

ALIGNMENT HOLE

DUST LIP

DOWEL PIN

J 34686

SEAL

ATTACHING SCREWS

MANDRIL

COLLAR

8470F082

Rear main seal installation — 3.1L engine shown

9. Connect the negative battery cable.

AUTOMATIC TRANSAXLE

Transaxle Assembly

REMOVAL AND INSTALLATION

Turbo Hydro–Matic 3T40

1. Disconnect the negative battery cable.

2. Remove the air cleaner and duct assembly.

3. Remove the bolt that secures the TV cable to the transaxle.

4. Disconnect the shift cable.

5. Disconnect the electrical connector at the neutral switch.

6. Remove all the engine-to-transaxle bolts except the one near the starter. The one nearest the firewall is installed from the engine side of the vehicle.

7. Loosen but do not remove the engine-to-transaxle bolt near the starter.

8. Disconnect the speedometer cable at the upper and lower coupling. If equipped with cruise control, remove the speedometer cable at the transducer.

9. Remove the retaining clip and washer from the shift linkage at the transaxle. Remove the 2 shift linkages at the transaxle. Remove the 2 shift linkage bracket bolts.

10. Disconnect and plug the cooler lines at the transaxle.

11. Install an engine holding fixture. Raise the engine enough to take its weight off the mounts.

12. Unlock the steering column. Raise and safely support the vehicle.

13. Remove the 2 nuts holding the anti-sway bar to the left lower control arm (driver's side).

14. Remove the 4 bolts attaching the covering plate over the stabilizer bar to the engine cradle on the left side of vehicle.

15. Loosen but do not remove the 4 bolts holding the stabilizer bar bracket to the right side of the engine cradle. Pull the bar downward.

16. Disconnect the front and rear transaxle mounts at the engine cradle.

17. Remove the 2 rear center crossmember bolts.

18. Remove the 3 right (passenger) side front engine cradle attaching bolts. The nuts are accessible under the splash shield next to the frame rail.

19. If equipped with V6 engine, remove the top bolt from the lower front transaxle shock absorber, as required.

20. Remove the left side front and rear cradle-to-body bolts.

21. Remove the left front wheel. Attach an halfshaft removing tool J–28468 or equivalent, to a slide hammer. Place the tool behind the halfshaft cones and pull the cones out away from the transaxle. Remove the right shaft in the same manner. Set the shafts aside. Plug the openings in the transaxle to prevent fluid leakage and the entry of dirt.

22. Swing the partial engine cradle to the left (driver) side and wire it aside outboard of the fender well.

23. Remove the 4 torque converter and starter shield bolts. Remove the 2 transaxle extension bolts from the engine-to-transaxle bracket.

24. Attach a transaxle jack to the case.

25. Use a felt pen to matchmark the torque converter and flywheel. Re-

move the 3 torque converter-to-flywheel bolts.

26. Remove the transaxle-to-engine bolt near the starter. Remove the transaxle by sliding it to the left, away from the engine.

To install:

27. As the transaxle is installed, slide the right halfshaft into the case. Install the cradle-to-body bolts before the stabilizer bar is installed. To aid in stabilizer bar installation, a pry hole has been provided in the engine cradle.

28. Install the 3 torque converter-to-flywheel bolts. Tighten to 46 ft. lbs. (62 Nm).

29. Install the 4 torque converter and starter shield bolts. Install the 2 transaxle extension bolts to the engine-to-transaxle bracket.

30. Swing the partial engine cradle into position and install attaching bolts.

31. Install the halfshafts. Install the left front wheel.

32. Install the left side front and rear cradle-to-body bolts.

33. If equipped with V6 engine, install the top bolt to the lower front transaxle shock absorber, as required.

34. Install the 3 right (passenger) side front engine cradle attaching bolts.

35. Install the 2 rear center crossmember bolts.

36. Disconnect the front and rear transaxle mounts at the engine cradle.

37. Tighten the 4 bolts holding the stabilizer bar bracket to the right side of the engine cradle.

38. Install the 4 bolts attaching the covering plate over the stabilizer bar to the engine cradle on the left side of vehicle.

39. Install the 2 nuts holding the anti-sway bar to the left lower control arm (driver's side).

40. Lower the vehicle.

41. Remove the engine holding fixture.

42. Connect the cooler lines to the transaxle.

43. Install the 2 shift linkage bracket bolts. Install the 2 shift linkages at the transaxle. Install the retaining clip and washer to the shift linkage on the transaxle.

44. Connect the speedometer cable at the upper and lower coupling. If equipped with cruise control, connect the speedometer cable to the transducer.

45. Tighten the engine-to-transaxle bolt near the starter.

46. Install all the engine-to-transaxle bolts except the one near the starter. The one nearest the firewall is installed from the engine side of the vehicle.

47. Install the 2 transaxle strut bracket bolts at the transaxle, if equipped.

48. Connect the detent cable.

49. Install the air cleaner.

50. Connect the negative battery cable.

Turbo Hydro–Matic 4T60

1. Disconnect the negative battery cable.

2. Remove the air cleaner and disconnect the TV cable at the throttle body.

3. Disconnect the shift linkage at the transaxle.

4. Remove the engine support fixture tool J–28467 or equivalent.

5. Disconnect all electrical connectors.

6. Remove the 3 bolts from the transaxle to the engine.

7. Disconnect the vacuum line at the modulator.

8. Raise and safely support the vehicle.

9. Remove the left front wheel and tire assembly.

10. Remove the left side ball joint from the steering knuckle.

11. Disconnect the brake line bracket at the strut.

NOTE: A halfshaft seal protector tool J–34754 or equivalent should be modified and installed on any halfshaft prior to service procedures on or near the halfshaft. Failure to do so could result in seal damage or joint failure.

12. Remove the halfshafts from the transaxle.

13. Disconnect the pinch bolt at the intermediate steering shaft. Failure to do so could cause damage to the steering gear.

14. Remove the frame to stabilizer bolts.

15. Remove the stabilizer bolts at the control arm.

16. Remove the left front frame assembly.

17. Disconnect the speedometer cable or wire connector from the transaxle.

18. Remove the extension housing to engine block support bracket.

19. Disconnect the cooler pipes.

20. Remove the converter cover and converter-to-flywheel bolts.

21. Remove all of the remaining transaxle-to-engine bolts except one.

22. Position a jack under the transaxle.

23. Remove the remaining transaxle-to-engine bolt and remove the transaxle.

To install:

24. Install the transaxle in the vehicle. Install the engine-to-transaxle bolt accessible from under the vehicle. Tighten to 55 ft. lbs. (75 Nm).

25. Install all of the remaining transaxle-to-engine bolts. Tighten to 55 ft. lbs. (75 Nm).

26. Remove the jack.

27. Install the converter-to-flywheel bolts and the converter cover.

28. Connect the cooler pipes.

29. Install the extension housing-to-engine block support bracket.

30. Connect the speedometer cable or wire connector to the transaxle.

31. Install the left front frame assembly.

32. Install the stabilizer bolts at the control arm.

33. Install the frame-to-stabilizer bolts.

34. Connect the pinch bolt at the intermediate steering shaft.

35. Install the halfshafts to the transaxle.

36. Connect the brake line bracket at the strut.

37. Install the left side ball joint to the steering knuckle.

38. Install the left front wheel and tire assembly.

39. Lower the vehicle.

40. Connect the vacuum line at the modulator.

41. Install the 3 bolts from the transaxle to the engine.

42. Connect all electrical connectors.

43. Remove the engine support tool.

44. Connect the shift linkage to the transaxle.

45. Connect the TV cable at the throttle body and adjust as necessary. Install the air cleaner.

46. Connect the negative battery cable.

Turbo Hydro–Matic 4T60–E

NOTE: Special tools needed for this procedure: engine support fixture J–28467A, oil cooler and line flusher J–35944A, oil cooler and line flusher adapter J–36462 and axle seal protector J–37292B.

1. Disconnect the negative battery cable and remove the air cleaner.

2. Remove the engine torque strut from the engine.

3. Disconnect the shift control cable and remove the bracket from the transaxle case lever.

4. Disconnect the TCC switch connector and vacuum hose.

5. Remove the upper transaxle mounting bolts and install engine support fixture tool J–28467A.

6. Raise the vehicle and support safely. Remove the front tire assemblies and engine splash shields.

7. Remove the pinch bolts from the controls arms and steering shaft.

8. Remove the stabilizer shaft nuts and brackets from the frame. Separate the stabilizer from the control arm.

9. Use a $7/16$ inch drill bit to drill through the 2 spot welds located between the front and rear holes of the left front stabilizer shaft mounting.

10. Remove the front and rear transaxle mounting nuts. Disconnect the power steering cooler line bolts.

11. Disconnect the engine wiring harness from the frame.

12. Remove the right frame-to-left frame retaining bolt. Position jackstands under the frame for support.

13. Loosen the 2 right frame mounts and discard bolts. Remove the 2 left frame bolts from the frame.

14. Remove the left frame with the help of an assistant.

15. Disconnect the right lower ball joint from the steering knuckle.

16. Remove the transaxle support bracket bolts from the transaxle.

17. Disconnect the power steering cooler line support and remove the torque converter cover.

18. Remove the starter motor and torque converter bolts.

19. Remove the transaxle mount bolts and mount from the case.

20. Disconnect all electrical connectors from the transaxle.

21. Remove both halfshafts from the transaxle and install the protective covers J–37292B, or equivalent.

22. Install a suitable transaxle jack.

23. Disconnect the oil cooler lines and plug openings.

24. Remove the remaining transaxle bolts and transaxle. Remove slowly to check for components not disconnected or hanging up.

To install:

25. Place the transaxle on the jack and move into position. Install the front bolt and torque to 55 ft. lbs. (75 Nm).

26. Connect the cooler lines and remove the transaxle jack.

27. Connect all electrical, vacuum and cable connections to the lower portion of the transaxle.

28. Install the halfshafts into the transaxle and make sure they are seated properly.

29. Install the transaxle mount and torque to 41 ft. lbs. (55 Nm).

30. Install the torque converter bolts and torque to 47 ft. lbs. (63 Nm). Retorque again using same pattern.

31. Install the starter motor, converter cover, power steering cooler line and transaxle support bracket.

32. Install the pinch bolts to the control arms. Install the right and left frame assembly and torque the bolts to 40 ft. lbs. (54 Nm).

33. Install the jackstands and the remainder of the right and left frame bolts.

34. Install the transaxle rear nuts and torque to 24 ft. lbs. (33 Nm).

35. Install the stabilizer bar bolts and torque to 30 ft. lbs. (44 Nm).

36. Install the steering shaft pinch bolt.

37. Install the engine splash shields, front wheels and remove the engine support fixture.

38. Install the upper transaxle bolts and ground wires. Torque bolts to 55 ft. lbs. (75 Nm).

39. Install the engine torque strut and air cleaner.

40. Connect the battery cable, refill the transaxle fluid, start the engine and check for leaks.

SHIFT CONTROL CABLE ADJUSTMENT

1. Lift up on the locking tab at the transaxle side of the shaft cable.

2. Place the shift lever in **N**. To determine the **N** position, rotate the selector shaft clockwise from **P** through **R** to **N**.

3. Place the shift control assembly in **N**.

4. Push the tab on the cable adjuster to adjust the cable in cable mounting bracket.

PARK/LOCK CONTROL CABLE ADJUSTMENT

The shifter lever must not be able to move to any other positions with the shift lever in **P** and the key in the **LOCK** position. Also, with the key in the **RUN** position and the shift lever in **N**, ensure that the key cannot be turned to the **LOCK** position. If these conditions cannot be met, adjustment is necessary.

1. If the key cannot be removed in the **P** position, snap the connector lock button to the **UP** position.

2. Move the cable connector nose rearward until the key can be removed from the ignition.

3. Push the snap lock button down.

TV DETENT CABLE ADJUSTMENT

Except 2.2L Engine

1. With the engine **OFF**, depress and hold-down the readjust tab at the TV cable adjuster.

2. Move the cable conduit until it stops against the fitting. Release the readjustment tab.

3. Rotate the throttle lever by hand to its full throttle position. The slider must ratchet toward the lever when the lever is rotated to its full travel.

NOTE: Check that the cable moves freely. The cable may appear to function properly with the engine OFF and COLD. Recheck after the engine is HOT.

2.2L Engine

1. The cable should be in the non-adjustment position.

2. Without twisting or kinking the cable, insert cable slug into the idler pulley (cam) slot.

3. Install the accelerator cable if not done so.

4. Rotate the idler pulley in a counterclockwise direction to 65 inch lbs. (7.3 Nm).

5. The cable must move freely and function properly when the engine is stopped and cold. Road test the vehicle.

DRIVE AXLE

Halfshaft

REMOVAL AND INSTALLATION

1. Raise and safely support the vehicle. Remove the wheel and tire assembly.

2. Remove the shaft nut, using tool J–4826 or equivalent and discard. A new shaft nut must be used for reassembly.

3. Disconnect the brake hose clip from the MacPherson strut but do not disconnect the hose from the caliper. Remove the brake caliper from the spindle and support the caliper with a length of wire. Do not allow the cal-

iper to hang by the brake hose unsupported.

4. Remove the brake rotor and remove the lower ball joint and pinch bolt.

5. Install drive axle seal protector tool J–34754 or equivalent onto drive axle.

6. Remove the ball joint from the steering knuckle.

7. Remove the halfshaft from the transaxle.

8. Using spindle remover tool J–28733 or equivalent, remove the halfshaft from the hub and bearing assembly. Do not allow the halfshaft to hang unsupported. If necessary, support using a length of wire in order to prevent component damage.

To install:

9. If a new halfshaft is to be installed, a new knuckle seal should be installed first along with a boot seal protector when necessary.

10. Loosely install the halfshaft into the transaxle and steering knuckle.

11. Loosely attach the steering knuckle to the suspension strut.

12. The halfshaft is an interference fit in the steering knuckle. Press the axle into place, then install the hub nut. When the shaft begins to turn with the hub, insert a drift through the caliper into one of the cooling slots in the rotor to keep it from turning.

NOTE: On some vehicles, the hub flange has a notch in it which can be used to prevent the hub and the shaft from turning, when one of the hub bearing retainer bolts is removed, by placing a longer bolt put in its place through the notch.

13. Tighten the hub nut to 70 ft. lbs. (95 Nm) to completely seat the shaft.

14. Install the brake caliper. Tighten the caliper mounting bolts to 30 ft. lbs. (41 Nm).

15. Load the hub assembly by lowering it onto a jackstand. Align the camber cam bolt marks made during removal, install the bolt and tighten to 140 ft. lbs. (190 Nm). Tighten the upper nut to the same value.

16. Install the halfshaft all the way into the transaxle using a suitable tool inserted into the groove provided on the inner retainer. Tap the tool until the shaft seats in the transaxle. Remove the boot seal protector.

17. Connect the brake hose clip the the strut. Install the tire and wheel, lower the vehicle and tighten the hub nut to 192 ft. lbs. (261 Nm).

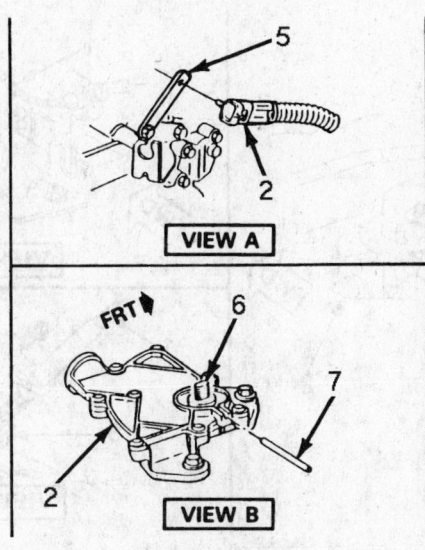

1. Bolts
   21 LB FT (28 NM)
2. Switch assembly
3. Transmission
4. Bracket (125C)
5. Bracket (440-T4)
6. Trans. shaft
7. 3/32" drill bit or
   2.34 dia. gage pin

8470F083

Park/lock control cable

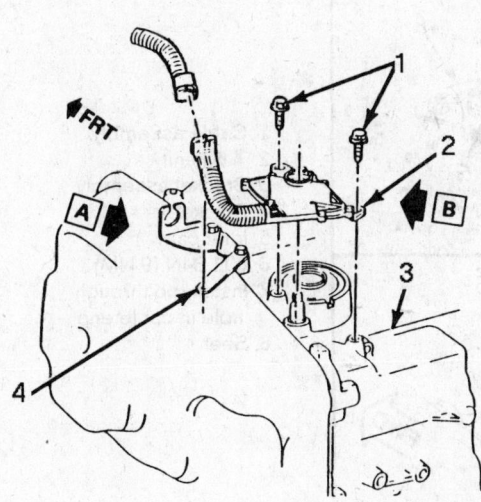

1 READJUSTMENT TAB/BUTTON
2 CABLE ASSEMBLY, TRANSAXLE THROTTLE CONTROL VALVE
3 SLIDER

8569y004

TV cable assembly — 2.2L engine

CV-Boot

REMOVAL AND INSTALLATION

Outer Boot

1. Raise and support the vehicle safely.
2. Remove the front tire and wheel assembly.
3. Remove the caliper bolts. Remove the caliper and support using a length of wire.
4. Remove the hub nut, washer and wheel bearing.

5. Using a brass drift, lightly tap around the seal retainer to loosen it. Remove the seal retainer.
6. Remove the seal retaining clamp or ring and discard.
7. Using snapring pliers, remove the race retaining ring from the halfshaft.
8. Pull the outer joint assembly and the outboard seal away from the halfshaft.
9. Flush the grease from the joint and repack with half of the grease provided. Put the remainder of the grease in the seal.

To install:
10. Assemble the inner seal retainer, outboard seal and outer seal retainer to the halfshaft. Push the joint assembly onto the shaft until the retaining ring is seated in the groove.
11. Slide the outboard seal onto the joint assembly and secure using the outer seal retainer. Using seal clamp tool J–35910 or equivalent, torque the outer clamp to 130 ft. lbs. (176 Nm) and the inner clamp to 100 ft. lbs. (136 Nm).
12. Install the wheel bearing, washer and hub nut. Tighten the hub nut to 192 ft. lbs. (260 Nm).
13. Install the caliper and caliper attaching bolts.

14. Install the front tire and wheel assembly.
15. Lower the vehicle.

Inner Boot

1. Raise and safely support the vehicle.
2. Remove the front tire and wheel assembly.
3. Remove the caliper bolts. Remove the caliper and support using a length of wire.
4. Remove the hub nut, washer and wheel bearing.
5. Remove the halfshaft. Place in a suitable holding fixture being careful not place undue pressure on the halfshaft.
6. Remove the joint assembly retaining ring. Remove the joint assembly.
7. Remove the race retaining ring and remove the seal retainer.
8. Remove the inner seal retaining clamp. Remove the inner joint seal.
9. Flush the grease from the joint and repack with half of the grease provided. Put the remainder of the grease in the seal.

To install:
10. Assemble the inner seal retainer, outboard seal and outer seal retainer to the halfshaft. Push the joint assembly onto the shaft until

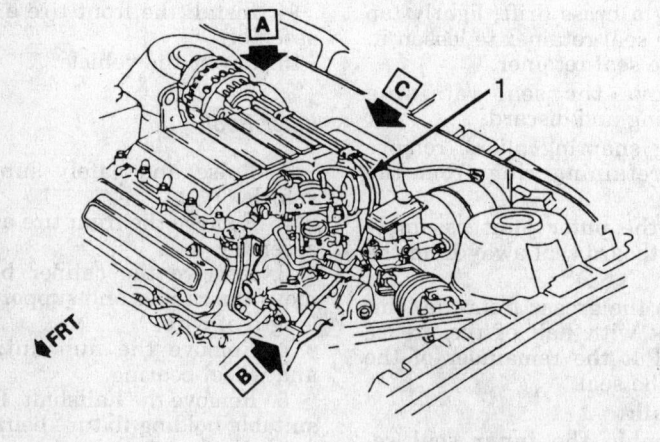

1. Cable assembly
2. T.B.I unit
3. Bracket assembly
4. Bracket
5. Idler cam
6. 80 LB IN (9 NM)
7. Install rod through hole in cable end
8. Seal

VIEW A

VIEW B

8470F084

TV cable assembly — 2.5L engine

1. Cable
2. 80 LB IN (9 NM
3. Rod
4. Install Seal 5 into transmission before installation of Cable 1
5. Seal
6. Bracket (engine)
7. Locking tangs must be expanded and locked in bracket attaching hole
8. Lever (engine)

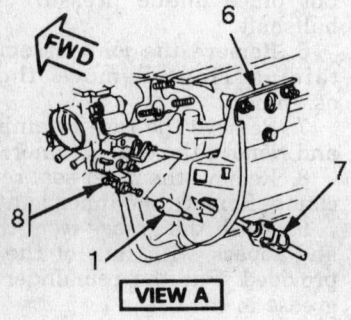

VIEW A

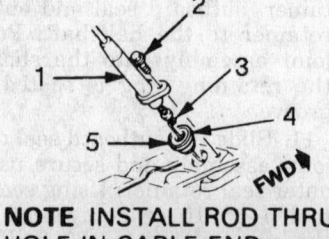

NOTE INSTALL ROD THRU HOLE IN CABLE END.

VIEW B

VIEW C

8470F085

TV cable assembly — 3.1L engine

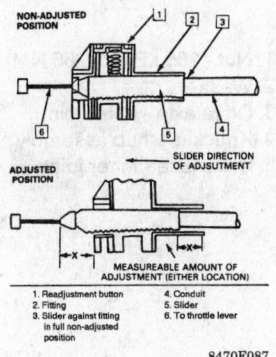

TV cable adjustment — 2.5L engine

8470F086

TV cable adjustment — 3.1L engine

1. Readjustment button
2. Fitting
3. Slider against fitting in full non-adjusted position
4. Conduit
5. Slider
6. To throttle lever

8470F087

the retaining ring is seated in the groove.

11. Slide the outboard seal onto the joint assembly and secure using the outer seal retainer. Using seal clamp tool J–35910 or equivalent, torque the outer clamp to 130 ft. lbs. (176 Nm) and the inner clamp to 100 ft. lbs. (136 Nm).

12. Install the halfshaft assembly.

13. Install the wheel bearing, washer and hub nut. Tighten the hub nut to 192 ft. lbs. (260 Nm).

14. Install the caliper and caliper attaching bolts.

15. Install the front tire and wheel assembly.

16. Lower the vehicle.

Front Wheel Hub, Knuckle and Bearings

REMOVAL AND INSTALLATION

1. Disconnect the negative battery cable.

2. Remove the wheel cover, loosen the lug nuts. Raise and safely support the vehicle.

3. Remove the tire and wheel assembly.

4. Install boot cover tool J–28712, for a double off-set joint or tool J–33162 for a tri-pot joint.

5. Remove and discard the hub nut. A new hub nut must be used during assembly.

6. Remove the brake caliper and rotor.

7. Remove the 3 hub and bearing attaching bolts. Remove the hub.

NOTE: If the old bearing is to be reused, make matchmarks on the bolts and holes for installation purposes.

8. Attach bearing puller J–28733 or equivalent, then remove the bearing.
To install:

9. Clean the mating surfaces of all dirt and corrosion. Check the knuckle bore and seal for damage. If a new bearing is to be installed, remove the old knuckle seal and install a new one. Grease the lips of new seal.

10. Push the bearing onto the half-shaft. Install a new washer and hub nut.

11. Tighten the hub nut on the half-shaft until the new bearing is seated. If the rotor and hub start to rotate as the hub nut is tightened, insert a drift through the caliper and into the rotor cooling fins to prevent rotation.

NOTE: Do not apply full torque to the hub nut at this time.

12. Install the brake shield, if removed, and the bearing retaining bolts. Torque bolts to 63 ft. lbs. (85 Nm).

13. Install the caliper and rotor. Ensure the caliper hose is not twisted. Install caliper bolts.

14. Install the wheel assembly. Torque the lug nuts to the proper torque.

15. Connect battery negative cable.

STEERING

── CAUTION ──
When performing service on or around SIR components or wiring, follow the procedures to disable the SIR system. Failure to follow procedures could result in possible air bag deployment, personal injury, or unneeded SIR system repairs.

Steering Wheel

REMOVAL AND INSTALLATION

NOTE: When installing the steering wheel, always make sure the turn signal lever is in the neutral position.

1. Disconnect the negative battery cable. Remove the trim retaining screws from behind the wheel. On steering wheels with a center cap, pull off the cap.

2. Lift the trim off and pull the horn wires from the turn signal cancelling cam.

3. Remove the retainer and the steering wheel nut.

4. Mark the wheel-to-shaft relationship and then remove the wheel with a puller.
To install:

5. Install the wheel on the shaft, aligning the previously made marks. Tighten the nut to 30 ft. lbs. (41 Nm).

6. Insert the horn wires into the cancelling cam.

7. Install the center trim and reconnect the battery cable.

Steering Column

NOTE: Once the steering column is removed from the vehicle, the column is extremely susceptible to damage. Dropping the column assembly on its end could collapse the steering shaft or loosen the plastic injections which maintain column rigidity. Leaning on the column assembly could cause the jacket to bend or deform. Any of the above damage could impair the column's collapsible design. If it is necessary to remove the steering wheel, use a standard wheel puller. Under no condition should the end of the shaft be hammered upon, as hammering could loosen the plastic injection which maintains column rigidity.

REMOVAL AND INSTALLATION

1. Disconnect the negative battery cable. Remove the left instrument panel sound insulator and trim panel.

2. If column repairs are to be made, remove the steering wheel.

3. Remove the nuts and bolts attaching the flexible coupling to the bottom of the steering column. Remove the safety strap and bolt, if equipped.

1. Nut - 185 LB FT (260 NM)
2. Washer
3. Drive axle - outer joint
4. Knuckle & hub assembly
5. Drive axle - inner joint

J 2619-01

J 33008

J 29794

8470F089

Halfshaft removal

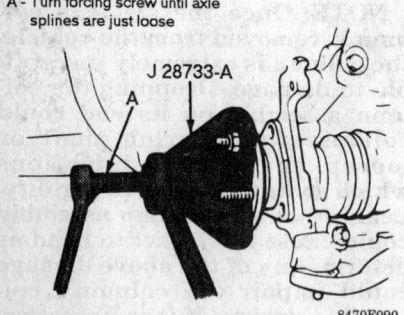

A - Turn forcing screw until axle
splines are just loose

J 28733-A

A

8470F090

**Drive axle removal from hub and bearing
assembly**

4. Remove the steering column trim shrouds and column covers. Disconnect the shift indicator cable.

5. Disconnect all wiring harness connectors. Remove the dust boot mounting screws and column mounting bracket bolts.

6. Lower the column to clear the mounting bracket and carefully remove from the vehicle.

To install:

7. Install the column in the vehicle.

8. Install the column mounting bracket bolts. Install the dust boot

mounting screws. Connect all wiring harness connectors.

9. Install the steering column trim shrouds and column covers. Connect the shift indicator cable.

10. Install the safety strap and bolt if equipped. Install the nuts and bolts attaching the flexible coupling to the bottom of the steering column.

11. If removed, install the steering wheel. Install the instrument panel sound insulator.

12. Connect the negative battery cable.

Power Steering Rack

BEARING PRELOAD ADJUSTMENT

1. Raise and safely support vehicle.

2. When adjusting, ensure front wheels are raised and the steering wheel centered.

3. Loosen the adjuster plug locknut, turn adjuster plug clockwise until it bottoms in the housing, then back adjuster plug approximately 50–70 degrees (approximately 1 flat).

4. After adjustment, check the returnability of the steering wheel.

REMOVAL AND INSTALLATION

1. Disconnect the negative battery cable. Raise and safely support vehicle. Allow the front suspension to hang freely. Disconnect the power steering hoses from the gear, where equipped.

2. Move the intermediate shaft seal upward and remove the intermediate shaft-to-stub shaft pinch bolt.

3. Remove both front wheels.

4. Remove the cotter pins and nut from both tie rod ends. Disconnect the tie rod ends from the steering knuckles.

5. Remove the AIR management system pipe bracket bolt from the crossmember.

6. Support the engine cradle with a floor jack. Remove the 2 rear cradle mount bolts and, using a jack, lower the rear of the engine cradle about 4–5 in. (24–28mm).

NOTE: Do not lower the engine cradle too far or damage to surrounding components will result.

7. Remove the rack and pinion heatshield, then the 2 rack and pinion mount bolts.

8. Remove the rack and pinion assembly through the left wheel opening.

1. Hexagon locking nut (M14 x 1.5)
3. Retaining ring
4. Shaft lock
5. Turn signal cancelling cam assembly
6. Upper bearing spring
7. Binding HD cross recess screw
8. RD wash HD screw (M4.2 x 1.41)
9. Signal switch arm
10. Turn signal switch assembly
11. Hex washer HD tapping screw
12. Thrust washer
13. Buzzer switch assembly
14. Buzzer switch retaining clip

15. Lock retaining screw
16. Lock housing cover assembly
17. Switch acuator sector
18. Steering column lock cylinder set
19. Shift lever gate
20. Rack preload spring
21. Ignition switch actuator assembly
22. Spring thrust washer
23. Upper bearing retainer
24. Bearing retaining bushing
25. Bearing assembly
26. Spring and bolt assembly

27. Horn circuit contact
28. Flat head cross recess screw
29. Switch actuator pivot pin
30. Pivot & (pulse) switch assembly
31. Col. housing cover end cap
32. Binding head cross recess screw
33. Wiring protector
34. Retaining ring

35. Steering column shaft assembly
36. Upper shift lever spring
37. Gearshift lever bowl

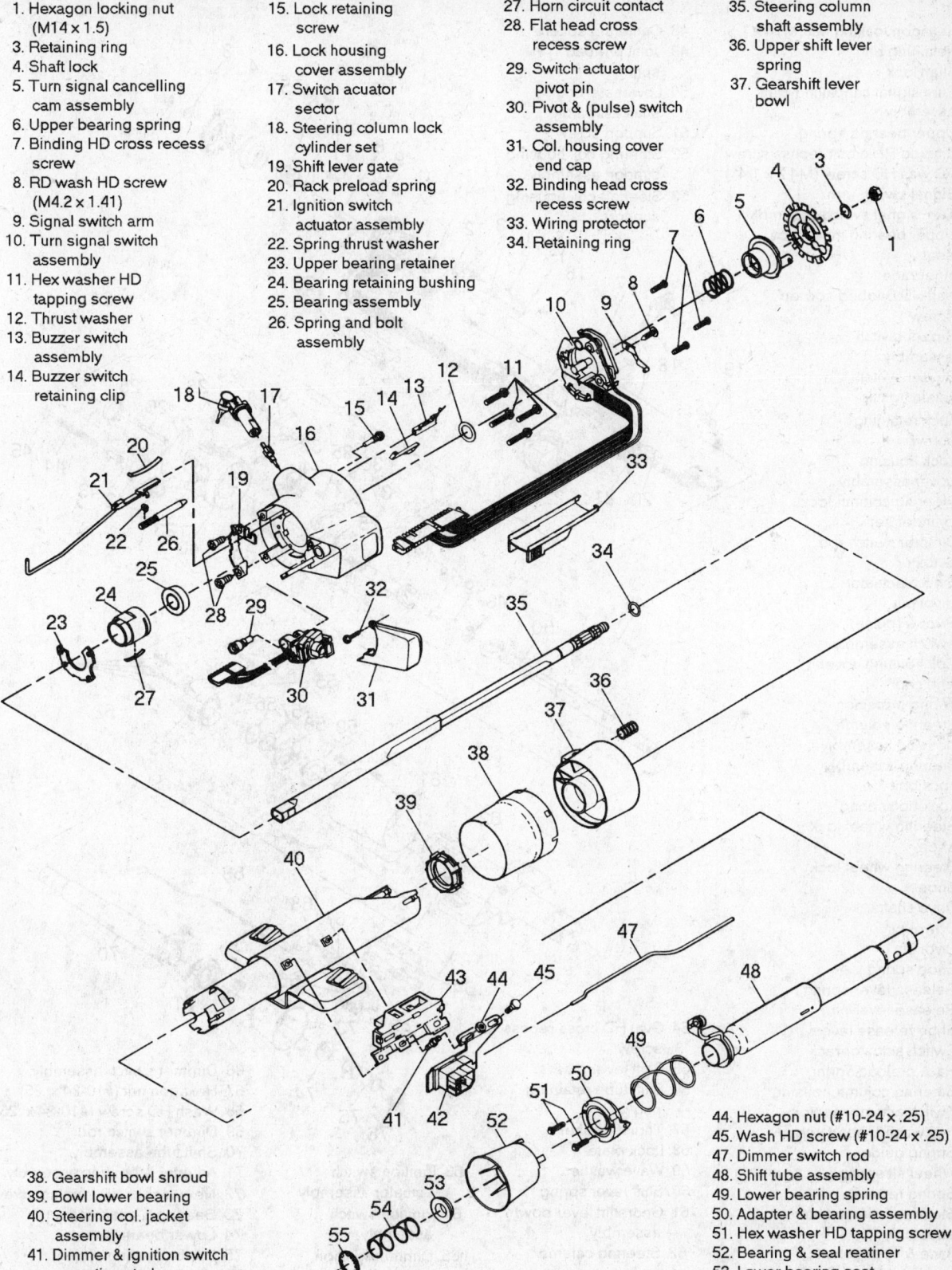

38. Gearshift bowl shroud
39. Bowl lower bearing
40. Steering col. jacket assembly
41. Dimmer & ignition switch mounting stud
42. Dimmer switch assembly
43. Ignition switch assembly

44. Hexagon nut (#10-24 x .25)
45. Wash HD screw (#10-24 x .25)
47. Dimmer switch rod
48. Shift tube assembly
49. Lower bearing spring
50. Adapter & bearing assembly
51. Hex washer HD tapping screw
52. Bearing & seal reatiner
53. Lower bearing seat
54. Shift tube return spring
55. Lower spring retainer

8470F091

Standard steering column assembly

1. Hexagon locking nut (M14 x 1.5)
3. Retaining ring
4. Shaft lock
5. Turn signal cancalling cam assembly
6. Upper bearing spring
7. Binding HD cross recess screw
8. RD was HD screw (M4.2 x 1.41)
9. Signal switch arm
10. Turn signal switch assembly
11. Upper bearing inner race seat
12. Inner race
13. Pan HD 6-lobed soc tap screw
14. Buzzer switch assembly
15. Buzzer switch retaining clip
16. Lock retaining screw
17. Lock housing cover assembly
18. Steering column lock cylinder set
19. Dimmer switch rod actuator
20. Switch actuator pivot pin
21. Pivot & (pulse) switch assembly
22. Col. housing cover end cap
23. Wiring protector
24. Steering column housing assembly
25. Bearing assembly
26. Lock bolt
27. Lock bolt spring
28. Steering wheel lock shoe
29. Steering wheel lock shoe
31. Drive shaft
32. Dowel pin
33. Pivot pin
34. Shoe spring
35. Release lever spring
36. Release lever pin
37. Shoe release lever
38. Switch actuator rack
39. Rack preload spring
40. Steering column housing
41. Switch actuator sector
42. Hex washer head screw
43. Spring guide
44. Wheel tilt spring
45. Spring retainer
46. Steering column shaft assembly
47. Race & upper shaft assembly

48. Centering sphere
49. Joint preload spring
50. Lower sterring shaft assembly
51. Support screw
52. Steering col. housing support assembly
53. Steering col. housing support

54. Oval HD cross recess screw
55. Shift lever gate
56. Shift tube retaining ring
57. Thrust washer
58. Lock plate
59. Wave washer
60. Shift lever spring
61. Gearshift lever bowl assembly
62. Steering column jacket assembly
63. Ignition switch actuator assembly
64. Ignition switch assembly
65. Dimmer/ignition switch mounting stud

66. Dimmer switch assembly
67. Hexagon nut (#10-24 x .25)
68. Wash HD screw (#10-24 x .25)
69. Dimmer switch rod
70. Shift tube assembly
71. Adapter & bearing assembly
72. Hex washer HD tapping screw
73. Bearing & seal reatiner
74. Lower bearing seat
75. Lower bearing spring
76. Lower spring retainer

Tilt steering column assembly

8470F093

To install:

9. Install the rack and pinion assembly through the left wheel opening.

10. Install the rack and pinion heatshield, then the 2 rack and pinion mount bolts. Torque the mount bolts to 66 ft. lbs. (90 Nm).

11. Raise the engine cradle into position and install the 2 rear cradle mount bolts.

12. Install the AIR management system pipe bracket bolt to the crossmember.

13. Connect the tie rod ends to the steering knuckles. Install the cotter pin and nut to both tie rod ends. Tighten the tie rod end nuts to 30 ft. lbs. (41 Nm).

14. Install both front wheels.

15. Install the intermediate shaft-to-stub shaft pinch bolt. Tighten the pinch bolt to 45 ft. lbs. (61 Nm).

16. If equipped, connect the power steering hoses to the steering gear. Refill the system.

17. Lower the vehicle. Connect the negative battery cable.

Power Steering Pump

REMOVAL AND INSTALLATION

2.2L Engine

1. Remove the serpentine drive belt.

2. Disconnect the lines/hoses from the power steering pump.

3. Remove the 4 pump retaining bolts.

4. Remove the power steering pump assembly.

   To install:

5. Install the pump and the 4 retaining bolts. Tighten the front bolts to 25 ft. lbs. (34 Nm) and the rear bolt to 23 ft. lbs. (31 Nm).

6. Connect the lines/hose to the power steering pump.

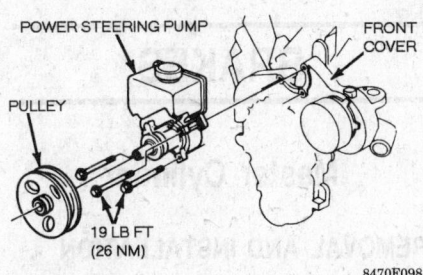

1. Steering gear
2. Busing
3. Bolt
4. Nut
5. Nut
6. Cotter pin
7. Sleeve

8470F095

Power steering rack assembly

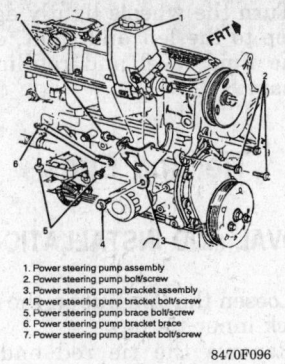

1. Power steering pump assembly
2. Power steering pump bolt/screw
3. Power steering pump bracket assembly
4. Power steering pump bracket bolt/screw
5. Power steering pump brace bolt/screw
6. Power steering pump bracket brace
7. Power steering pump bracket bolt/screw

8470F096

Power steering pump assembly — 2.2L engine

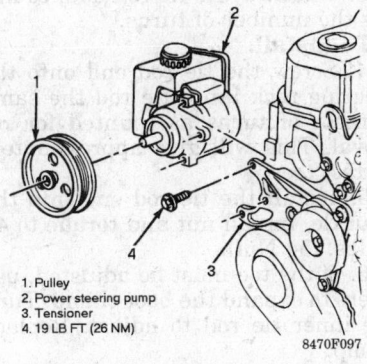

1. Pulley
2. Power steering pump
3. Tensioner
4. 19 LB FT (26 NM)

8470F097

Power steering pump assembly — 2.5L engine

POWER STEERING PUMP

FRONT COVER

PULLEY

19 LB FT (26 NM)

8470F098

Power steering pump assembly — 3.1L engine

7. Install the serpentine drive belt.

8. Fill the power steering pump with fluid and bleed any air from the system.

2.5L Engine

1. Disconnect the negative battery cable. Raise and safely support the vehicle.

2. Remove the right front wheel and right side engine splash shield.

3. Remove the serpentine belt and siphon the fluid from the pump reservoir.

4. Disconnect the hydraulic lines/hoses from the pump.

5. Remove the radiator hose clamp bolt.

6. Remove the upper and lower bolts and nuts from the front pump bracket.

7. Remove the pump from the engine.

   To install:

8. Install the pump to the engine.

9. Install the upper and lower bolts and nuts to the front pump bracket.

10. Install the radiator hose clamp bolt.

11. Connect the hydraulic lines/hoses to the pump.

12. Install serpentine belt. Refill the system.

13. Install the right side engine splash shield and right front wheel.

14. Lower the vehicle.

15. Connect the negative battery cable.

16. Bleed the system.

3.1L Engine

1. Disconnect the negative battery cable at the battery. Remove air cleaner, if necessary.

2. Disconnect the blower motor wiring and remove the blower motor.

3. Remove the coolant hose from the water pump.

4. Siphon the fluid from the pump reservoir, then disconnect the lines from the pump.

5. Remove the serpentine drive belt.

6. Remove the 1 nut which attaches the rear pump bracket to the engine bracket.

7. Remove the 2 front pump bracket-to-engine bolts, then remove the pump and bracket assembly.

   To install:

8. Install the pump and bracket assembly. Install the 2 front pump bracket-to-engine bolts.

9. Install the 1 nut which attaches the rear pump bracket to the engine bracket.

10. Install the serpentine belt.

11. Connect the lines to the pump. Refill the system.

12. Install the coolant hose to the water pump.

13. Install the blower motor. Connect the blower motor wiring.

14. If removed, install the air cleaner.

15. Connect the negative battery cable.

16. Bleed the system.

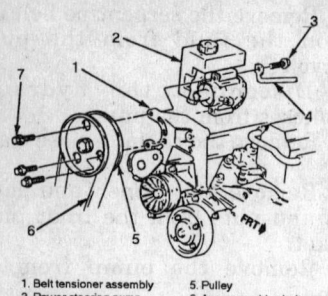

1. Belt tensioner assembly
2. Power steering pump
3. Bolt/screw
4. Belt tensioner brace
5. Pulley
6. Accessory drive belt
7. Bolt

8470F099

Power steering pump assembly — 3.3L engine

3.3L Engine

1. Disconnect the negative battery cable.
2. Remove the serpentine belt.
3. Remove the rear power steering pump bracket.
4. Disconnect the power steering lines at the pump.
5. Remove the power steering mounting bolts and remove the pump from the vehicle.
To install:
6. Install the pump and secure with the pump mounting bolts.
7. Torque mounting nuts to 21 ft. lbs. (29 Nm).
8. Connect the power steering lines to the power steering pump.
9. Install the rear power steering pump bracket.
10. Install the serpentine belt.
11. Connect the negative battery cable.
12. Bleed the system.

BELT ADJUSTMENT

The accessories are driven by a single serpentine belt. Belt tension is controlled automatically by the spring-loaded tensioner. No adjustment is necessary.

SYSTEM BLEEDING

1. Fill the fluid reservoir.
2. Let fluid stand undisturbed for 2 minutes, then crank engine for about 2 seconds. Refill reservoir if necessary.
3. Repeat Steps 1 and 2 until fluid level remains constant after cranking the engine.
4. Raise the front of the vehicle until both wheels are off the ground, then start the engine. Increase engine speed to 1500 rpm.

5. Turn the wheels lightly against the stop to the left and right, checking the fluid level and refilling, as necessary.

Tie Rod Ends

REMOVAL AND INSTALLATION

1. Loosen the jam nut on the steering rack inner tie rod.
2. Remove the tie rod end nut. Separate the tie rod end from the steering knuckle using a suitable puller.
3. Unscrew the tie rod end, counting the number of turns.
To install:
4. Screw the tie rod end onto the steering rack inner tie rod the same number of turns as counted for removal. This will give approximately correct toe.
5. Install the tie rod end into the knuckle. Install nut and torque to 40 ft. lbs. (54 Nm).
6. If the toe must be adjusted, use pliers to expand the boot clamp. Turn the inner tie rod to adjust. Replace clamp.
7. Tighten the jam nut to 59 ft. lbs. (80 Nm).

BRAKES

Master Cylinder

REMOVAL AND INSTALLATION

1. Disconnect the negative battery cable. Disconnect the electrical connector from the fluid level sensor, if equipped.
2. Disconnect and plug the hydraulic lines at master cylinder.
3. Remove the master cylinder retaining nuts and lock washers.
4. Remove the master cylinder from the vehicle.
To install:
5. Install the cylinder on the booster. Install nuts and lock washers. Tighten the attaching nuts to 20 ft. lbs. (27 Nm).
6. Install hydraulic lines. Tighten to 24 ft. lbs. (32 Nm).
7. Connect the fluid level sensor electrical connector.
8. Bleed the brakes system.

Proportioning Valve

REMOVAL AND INSTALLATION

1. Disconnect the negative battery cable.

NOTE: It may be necessary to remove the master cylinder reservoir to remove the proportioner valves.

2. Remove the proportioner valve caps (2).
3. Remove the proportioner O-rings and springs.
4. Carefully remove the valve pistons using needle nose pliers.
To install:
5. Lubricate the O-rings, proportioner valve seals and stems of valve pistons with silicone grease (supplied in repair kit).
6. Install the seals onto the proportioner pistons with the seal lips facing up toward the cap assembly.
7. Install the proportioner valve pistons and seals into the master cylinder body.
8. Install the springs into the master cylinder body.
9. Install new O-rings onto the proportioner valve caps and install to the master cylinder body. Torque the caps to 20 ft. lbs. (27 Nm).
10. Connect the negative battery cable.

Power Brake Booster

REMOVAL AND INSTALLATION

1. Disconnect the negative battery cable.
2. Remove the master cylinder attaching nuts and remove the master cylinder from the booster.
3. Disconnect the booster vacuum hose from the vacuum check valve. Remove the nuts and lock washers that secure the booster to firewall.
4. Disconnect the booster pushrod from the brake pedal. Tilt the booster slightly and work the booster pushrod off of the pedal clevis pin without putting excessive pressure on the side pin. Remove the booster from the engine compartment.
5. Remove the booster from the vehicle.
To install:
6. Install the booster to the engine compartment.
7. Working inside the vehicle, install the nuts and lock washers that secure the booster to the firewall. Tighten the mounting nuts to 20 ft.

lbs. (28 Nm). Connect the pushrod at the brake pedal.

8. Position the master cylinder on the booster and install the attaching nuts.

9. Connect vacuum hose to the vacuum check valve.

10. Connect the negative battery cable. Check operation of stop lights. Allow engine vacuum to build before applying brakes.

Brake Caliper

REMOVAL AND INSTALLATION

1. Disconnect the negative battery cable.

2. Raise and safely support the vehicle. Remove the tire and wheel assembly.

3. Remove 2/3 of the brake fluid from the master cylinder.

4. Position a 12 inch adjustable pliers over the inboard brake shoe tab and the inboard caliper housing. Squeeze the pliers to compress the piston back into the caliper bore and to provide clearance between the lining and rotor.

5. If equipped with rear disc brakes, disconnect the parking brake

cable and return spring from the parking brake lever, then the parking brake cable from the bracket.

6. On all models, remove the caliper mounting bolts, then lift caliper from bracket and remove the inner and outer pads with the anti-rattle springs.

7. Disconnect the hydraulic hose. Remove the caliper from the vehicle.

To install:

8. Connect the hydraulic hose.

9. On all models, install the caliper on the mounting brackets and install the mounting bolts. Install the inner and outer pads with the anti-rattle springs.

10. If equipped with rear disc brakes, connect the parking brake cable to the bracket and the cable and return spring to the parking brake lever.

11. Install the tire and wheel assembly.

12. Lower the vehicle.

13. Fill the master cylinder reservoir.

14. Connect the negative battery cable.

15. Bleed the brake system.

Disc Brake Pads

REMOVAL AND INSTALLATION

1. Disconnect the negative battery cable.

2. Raise and safely support the vehicle. Remove the tire and wheel assembly.

3. Remove 2/3 of the brake fluid from the master cylinder.

4. Position a 12 inch adjustable pliers over the inboard brake shoe tab and the inboard caliper housing. Squeeze the pliers to compress the piston back into the caliper bore and to provide clearance between the lining and rotor.

5. If equipped with rear disc brakes, disconnect the parking brake cable and return spring from the parking brake lever, then the parking brake cable from the bracket.

6. On all models, remove the caliper mounting bolts, then lift caliper from bracket and remove the inner and outer pads complete with the anti-rattle springs.

To install:

7. Install the inner and outer pads complete with the anti-rattle springs. Install the caliper and mounting bolts.

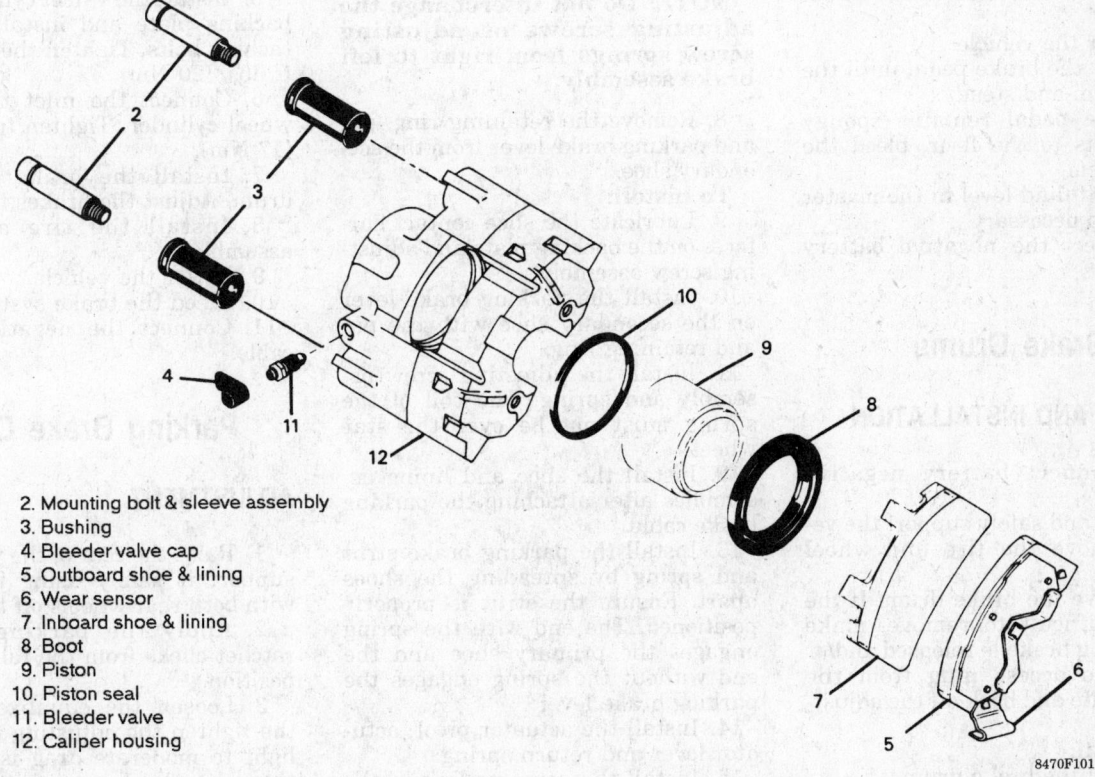

2. Mounting bolt & sleeve assembly
3. Bushing
4. Bleeder valve cap
5. Outboard shoe & lining
6. Wear sensor
7. Inboard shoe & lining
8. Boot
9. Piston
10. Piston seal
11. Bleeder valve
12. Caliper housing

8470F101

Brake caliper assembly

8. If equipped with rear disc brakes, connect the parking brake cable to the bracket and the cable and return spring to the parking brake lever.

9. Install the tire and wheel assembly.

10. Lower the vehicle.

11. Fill the master cylinder reservoir with fresh brake fluid.

12. Apply the brake pedal until the pedal is firm and steady.

13. If the pedal remains spongy and/or sinks to the floor, bleed the brake system.

14. Top-off fluid level in the master cylinder, as necessary.

Brake Rotor

REMOVAL AND INSTALLATION

1. Disconnect the negative battery cable.

2. Raise and safely support the vehicle.

3. Remove the tire and wheel assembly.

4. Remove the caliper. Support the caliper using a length of wire.

5. Remove the rotor.

To install:

6. Install the rotor.

7. Install the caliper.

8. Install the tire and wheel assembly.

9. Lower the vehicle.

10. Apply the brake pedal until the pedal is firm and steady.

11. If the pedal remains spongy and/or sinks to the floor, bleed the brake system.

12. Top-off fluid level in the master cylinder, as necessary.

13. Connect the negative battery cable.

Brake Drums

REMOVAL AND INSTALLATION

1. Disconnect battery negative cable.

2. Raise and safely support the vehicle. Remove the tire and wheel assembly.

3. Remove the brake drum. If the drum is difficult to remove, make sure parking brake is released and/or remove the access plug from the backing plate and back off the adjusting screw.

To install:

4. Install the brake drum.

5. Adjust the brakes.

6. Install the tire and wheel assembly.

7. Lower the vehicle.

8. Connect the negative battery cable.

Brake Shoes

REMOVAL AND INSTALLATION

1. Disconnect the negative battery cable.

2. Raise and safely support vehicle. Remove the tire and wheel assembly.

3. Remove the brake drum. If the drum is difficult to remove, remove the access plug from the backing plate and back off the adjusting screw.

4. Remove the return springs from the anchor using appropriate brake spring pliers.

5. Remove the hold-down springs and retaining pins. Remove the lever pivot, actuator link, actuator lever, actuator pivot and lever return spring, parking brake strut and strut spring.

6. Remove the brake shoes, then disconnect the parking brake cable.

7. Remove the adjusting screw assembly and spring. Note position of adjusting spring.

NOTE: Do not interchange the adjusting screws or adjusting screw springs from right to left brake assembly.

8. Remove the retaining ring, pin and parking brake lever from the secondary shoe.

To install:

9. Lubricate the shoe contact surfaces on the backing plate and adjusting screw assembly.

10. Install the parking brake lever on the secondary shoe with the pin and retaining ring.

11. Install the adjusting screw assembly and spring. The coil of the spring must not be over the star wheel.

12. Install the shoe and lining assemblies after attaching the parking brake cable.

13. Install the parking brake strut and spring by spreading the shoes apart. Ensure the strut is properly positioned. The end with the spring engages the primary shoe and the end without the spring engages the parking brake lever.

14. Install the actuator pivot, actuator lever and return spring.

15. Install the actuator link in the shoe retainer.

16. Install the link into the lever while holding up on the lever.

17. Install the hold-down pins, lever pivot and hold-down springs.

18. Install the shoe return springs.

19. Install the brake drum, wheel and tire assembly, then lower vehicle. Apply the brake pedal several times to seat the brake shoes. Check and adjust the parking brake, as required.

20. Check the master cylinder reservoir. Connect the negative battery cable.

Wheel Cylinder

REMOVAL AND INSTALLATION

1. Disconnect the negative battery cable.

2. Loosen the wheel lug nuts, raise and safely support the vehicle. Remove the tire and wheel assembly. Remove the drum and brake shoes. Leave the hub and wheel bearing assembly in place.

3. Remove any dirt from around the brake line fitting, then disconnect the brake line.

4. Remove the wheel cylinder attaching bolts and remove the wheel cylinder from the backing plate.

To install:

5. Install the wheel cylinder to the backing plate and install the 2 attaching bolts. Tighten the bolts to 15 ft. lbs. (20 Nm).

6. Connect the inlet tube to the wheel cylinder. Tighten to 12 ft. lbs. (17 Nm).

7. Install the brake shoes and drum. Adjust the brakes.

8. Install the tire and wheel assembly.

9. Lower the vehicle.

10. Bleed the brake system.

11. Connect the negative battery cable.

Parking Brake Cable

ADJUSTMENT

1. Raise the rear of the vehicle and support it safely using jackstands, with both rear wheels off the ground.

2. Apply the parking brake 3 ratchet clicks from the fully released position.

3. Loosen the equalizer locknut, the tighten the adjusting nut until a light to moderate drag is felt when the rear wheels are rotate. Tighten the locknut.

1. Actuator spring
2. Adjuster actuator
3. Adjuster socket
4. Adjuster screw
5. Pivot nut
6. Adjuster shoe & lining
7. Park brake lever
8. Park brake shoe & lining
9. Retractor spring
10. Bleeder valve
11. Bolt
12. Wheel cylinder assembly
13. Backing plate assembly
14. Access hole plug

8470F102

Drum brake assembly

4. Fully release parking brake and rotate rear wheels; no drag should be felt.

REMOVAL AND INSTALLATION

Front Cable

1. Raise and safely support the vehicle.
2. Loosen the equalizer nut.
3. Disconnect the front cable from the connector and equalizer.
4. Remove the clip at the frame.
5. Remove the cable from the hanger.
6. Lower the vehicle.
7. Remove the 3 screws and 1 nut and lower the driver's side sound insulator panel.
8. Remove the carpet finish molding. Lift the carpet.
9. Remove the cable retaining clip at the lever assembly.
10. Depress the retaining tangs and remove the cable and casing from the lever assembly.
11. Remove the cable from the retaining clips.
12. Remove the grommet retainer from the floor pan.
13. Unseat the grommet and pull the cable through the floor pan.

To install:
14. Insert the cable through the floor pan and grommet.
15. Seat the grommet. Install the grommet retainer to the floor pan.
16. Fasten the cable in the retaining clips.
17. Connect the cable and casing to the lever assembly. Seat the retaining tangs.
18. Install the cable retaining clip at the lever assembly.
19. Place the carpet into position. Install the carpet finish molding.
20. Install the driver's side sound insulator panel and attaching screws and nuts.
21. Raise and safely support the vehicle.
22. Fasten the cable to the hanger.
23. Install the clip to the frame.
24. Connect the front cable to the equalizer and connector.
25. Adjust the parking brake cable.
26. Lower the vehicle.

Rear Cables

1. Raise and safely support the vehicle.
2. Loosen the equalizer nut.
3. Disconnect the cable at the equalizer and connector.
4. Remove the tire, wheel and brake drum.

5. Disconnect the cable from the parking brake lever.
6. Depress the retaining tangs on the cable. Remove the cable and casing from the backing plate.

To install:
7. Install the cable through the rear of the backing plate. Seat the retaining tangs in the backing plate.
8. Connect the cable to the parking brake lever.
9. Install the brake drum, tire and wheel.
10. Connect the cable at the equalizer and connector.
11. Adjust the parking brake cable.
12. Lower the vehicle.

Brake System Bleeding

COMPONENT BLEEDING

Master Cylinder

1. Remove the vacuum reserve by applying the brakes several times, with the engine **OFF**.
2. Fill the master cylinder reservoir with brake fluid and keep it at least ½ full of fluid at all times during the bleeding operation.
3. If the master cylinder is known or suspected to have air in the bore,

bleed the unit before wheel cylinders or calipers, in the following manner:

a. Disconnect the forward brake line connection at the master cylinder.

b. Allow brake fluid to fill the master cylinder bore until it begins to flow from the forward brake line port at the master cylinder.

c. Connect the forward brake line to the master cylinder and tighten.

d. Have an assistant depress the brake pedal slowly 1 time and hold. Loosen the forward brake line connection at the master cylinder to purge air from the bore. Tighten the connection and have the assistant release the pedal slowly. Wait 15 seconds and repeat the sequence, including the 15 second pause, until all air is removed from the bore. Ensure brake fluid does not contact any painted surface.

e. Repeat the procedure at the rear master cylinder brake line connection.

f. If it is known that the calipers and wheel cylinders do not contain any air, it will not be necessary to bleed them.

Calipers and Wheel Cylinders

If it is necessary to bleed all of the wheel cylinders and calipers, follow the proper sequence: Right rear, left rear, right front, left front. Bleed individual wheel cylinders or calipers, only after all air is removed from the master cylinder.

1. Place a suitable bleeder wrench over the bleeder valve.

2. Attach a clear tube over the bleeder valve and allow the tube to hang, submerged in a clear container partially filled with brake fluid.

3. Have an assistant depress the brake pedal slowly 1 time and hold. Loosen the bleeder valve to purge the air from the cylinder. Tighten the bleeder screw and have the assistant slowly release the pedal. Wait 15 seconds and repeat the sequence, including the 15 second pause, until all air is removed.

4. If necessary, repeat the sequence to remove all of the air.

NOTE: Rapid pumping of the brake pedal pushes the master cylinder secondary piston down the bore in a way that makes it difficult to bleed the rear side of the system.

5. Check for a spongy brake pedal and the red brake warning light for

an indication of unbalanced pressure. Repeat the bleeding procedure to correct either of these conditions.

Anti-Lock Brake System Service

PRECAUTIONS

Failure to observe the following precautions may result in system damage.

• Before performing electric arc welding on the vehicle, disconnect the Electronic Brake Control Module (EBCM) and the hydraulic modulator connectors.

• When performing painting work on the vehicle, do not expose the Electronic Brake Control Module (EBCM) to temperatures in excess of 185°F (85°C) for longer than 2 hours. The system may be exposed to temperatures up to 200°F (95°C) for less than 15 minutes.

• Never disconnect or connect the Electronic Brake Control Module (EBCM) or hydraulic modulator connectors with the ignition switch **ON**.

• Never disassemble any component of the Anti-Lock Brake System (ABS) which is designated non-serviceable; the component must be replaced as an assembly.

• When filling the master cylinder, always use Delco Supreme 11 brake fluid or equivalent, which meets DOT-3 specifications; petroleum base fluid will destroy the rubber parts.

RELIEVING ANTI-LOCK BRAKE SYSTEM PRESSURE

──── **CAUTION** ────
Failure to fully depressurize the accumulator before performing any repairs could result in injury, and/or damage to the system.

With the ignition switch in the **OFF** position, apply and release the brake pedal a minimum of 20 times using approximately 50 lbs. (222 N) of force on the pedal. A change in the pedal feel will occur when the accumulator is completely discharged.

Hydraulic Unit

REMOVAL AND INSTALLATION

1. Depressurize the system, then disconnect the negative battery cable.

2. Disconnect the electrical connectors from the unit, then remove the fluid from the reservoir.

3. Remove the wire clip from the return hose fitting, then the return hose from the pump.

4. Remove the pressure hose attaching bolt, then the pressure hose and O-ring from the pump.

5. Remove the pump mounting bolt, then the energy unit from the hydraulic unit.

6. Disconnect the 4 brake lines from the valve block and hydraulic unit.

7. Disconnect the pushrod from the brake pedal, then push the dust boot forward of the rear half of the pushrod and unthread the 2 halfs of the pushrod.

8. Remove the hydraulic unit attaching bolts from the pushrod bracket, then the hydraulic unit from the vehicle.

To install:

9. Install the hydraulic unit to the pushrod bracket. Torque bolts to 37 ft. lbs. (50 Nm).

10. Thread the 2 halfs of pushrod together, reposition the dust boot, then install pushrod to the brake pedal. Torque bolts to 27 ft. lbs. (37 Nm).

11. Connect the 4 brake lines to the valve block and hydraulic unit. Torque the brake lines to 11 ft. lbs. (15 Nm).

12. Install energy unit to hydraulic unit, then the pump mounting bolt.

13. Install the pressure hose and O-ring to the pump, then the pressure hose bolt. Torque bolt to 15 ft. lbs. (20 Nm).

14. Install return hose to pump, then the wire clip to the return hose fitting.

15. Connect electrical connectors to hydraulic unit, then the battery negative cable.

Valve Block

REMOVAL AND INSTALLATION

1. Depressurize the system.
2. Remove the hydraulic unit.
3. Remove the valve block attaching nuts and bolts, then the valve block and O-rings from the vehicle.

To install:

4. Replace the O-ring. Install the valve block and attaching nuts and bolts. Tighten the valve block bolts to 18 ft. lbs. (25 Nm).

5. Install the hydraulic unit.
6. Bleed the brake system.

Pump Motor

REMOVAL AND INSTALLATION

1. Depressurize system, then disconnect the battery negative cable.

2. Remove the brake fluid from the reservoir, then disconnect the electrical connectors from the pressure switch and the pump motor.

3. Remove the hydraulic accumulator and O-ring.

4. Remove the pressure hose attaching bolt, then the pressure hose and O-ring from the pump.

5. Remove the wire clip and return hose fitting, then the return hose from the pump.

6. Remove the pump attaching bolts and grommets, then the pump from the hydraulic unit.

To install:

7. Install the pump to the hydraulic unit. Install the attaching bolts and grommets. Tighten the pump mounting bolts to 71 inch lbs. (8 Nm).

8. Connect the return hose to the pump. Install the wire clip.

9. Replace the pressure hose O-ring and install the pressure hose attaching bolt. Tighten the pressure hose bolt to 15 ft. lbs. (20 Nm).

10. Replace the hydraulic accumulator. Tighten the accumulator bolts to 17 ft. lbs. (23 Nm).

11. Connect the pump motor and pressure switch electrical connectors.

12. Fill the reservoir with brake fluid. Bleed the brake system.

13. Connect the negative battery cable.

Pressure Switch

REMOVAL AND INSTALLATION

1. Depressurize the system, then disconnect the negative battery cable.

2. Disconnect the electrical connector from the pressure switch.

3. Using tool J-35804-A or equivalent, remove the pressure switch and O-ring.

To install:

4. Replace the pressure switch O-ring. Install the pressure switch and tighten to 17 ft. lbs. (23 Nm).

5. Connect the pressure switch electrical connector. Bleed the brake system.

6. Connect the negative battery cable.

Hydraulic Accumulator

REMOVAL AND INSTALLATION

1. Depressurize the system, then disconnect the negative battery cable.

2. Remove the hydraulic accumulator bolts, the hydraulic accumulator and O-ring from the vehicle.

To install:

3. Replace the accumulator O-ring.

4. Install the accumulator and attaching bolts. Tighten the accumulator bolts to 17 ft. lbs. (23 Nm).

5. Bleed the brake system.

6. Connect the negative battery cable.

Wheel Speed Sensor

REMOVAL AND INSTALLATION

1. Raise and safely support the vehicle. Remove the wheel and tire assembly.

2. Disconnect the speed sensor electrical connector.

3. Remove the speed sensor attaching bolt, disconnect the sensor and cable from brackets, then the sensor and cable from the vehicle.

To install:

4. Install the sensor and cable into the bracket. Install the attaching bolt. Tighten to 53 inch lbs. (6 Nm).

5. Connect the speed sensor electrical connector.

6. Install the wheel and tire assembly.

7. Lower the vehicle.

FRONT SUSPENSION

MacPherson Strut

REMOVAL AND INSTALLATION

1. Loosen the wheel nuts, raise and support vehicle, then remove the wheel and tire assembly.

2. Remove the brake hose clip-to-strut bolt, if equipped. Do not disconnect the hose from the caliper. Install a halfshaft cover to protect the axle boot.

3. Mark the camber cam eccentric adjuster for assembly.

4. Remove the 2 lower strut-to-steering knuckle bolts and the 3 upper strut-to-body nuts. Remove the strut assembly.

To install:

5. Install the strut assembly. Install the 2 lower strut-to-steering knuckle bolts and 3 upper strut-to-body nuts. Realign the camber marks made upon removal.

6. Install the brake hose clip-to-strut bolt.

7. Remove the axle boot protector.

8. Install the tire and wheel assembly.

9. Lower the vehicle.

Strut Cartridge

REMOVAL AND INSTALLATION

———— **WARNING** ————
Do not remove upper bearing plate center bolt without securing the strut assembly and compressing the spring with a suitable spring compressor. Failure to take these steps could cause severe injury, or property damage.

1. Remove the three nuts under the hood attaching the bearing plate to the body.

2. Raise the vehicle and support the weight of the vehicle on jackstands under the frame.

3. Remove tire and wheel assembly.

4. Disconnect brake line bracket from the strut housing.

5. Scribe the strut and knuckle for easier alignment during assembly.

6. Remove the strut to knuckle bolts and pull the knuckle away from the strut housing.

7. Remove strut assembly from vehicle.

8. Install the strut assembly to a strut compressor.

9. Turn the compressor so that the spring becomes compressed.

10. Hold the strut shaft from turning and remove the 24mm strut nut.

11. Install special rod J-34013-38 or equivalent to the strut shaft and guide the strut out of the assembly while loosening the spring compressor.

12. Remove the strut cartridge from the assembly.

To install:

13. Install the replacement strut to the strut compressor/spring assembly.

14. Start turning the compressor screw clockwise to compress the spring while guiding the shaft through the mounting hole in the upper plate..

15. Tighten the mounting nut to 55 ft. lbs. (75 Nm) while holding the strut shaft.

16. Install strut assembly into place, aligning the upper bearing plate studs with the holes and tighten nuts to 18 ft. lbs. (25 Nm).

17. Align the scribe marks on the steering knuckle and tighten bolts 140 ft. lbs. (190 Nm).

18. Connect brake hose bracket to strut housing and tighten to 13 ft. lbs. (17 Nm).

19. Install tire and raise vehicle to remove jackstand.

20. Align vehicle.

Lower Ball Joints

INSPECTION

1. Raise and support vehicle safely.

2. Grasp the wheel at the top and bottom and shake the wheel in and out.

3. If any movement is seen of the steering knuckle relative to the control arm, the ball joints are defective and must be replaced. Note that movement elsewhere may be due to loose wheel bearings or other problems; watch the knuckle-to-control arm connection.

4. If the ball stud is disconnected from the steering knuckle and any looseness is noted, often the ball joint stud can be twisted in its socket by hand. If so, replace the ball joint.

REMOVAL AND INSTALLATION

1. Loosen the wheel nuts, raise and support vehicle safely, then remove the tire and wheel assemblies.

2. Using an ⅛ inch drill bit, drill a hole approximately ¼ inch deep in the center of each of the 3 ball joint rivets.

3. Using a ½ inch drill bit, drill off the rivet heads. Drill only enough to remove the rivet head.

4. Using a hammer and punch, remove the rivets, driving them out from the bottom.

5. Loosen the ball joint pinch bolt in the steering knuckle, then remove the ball joint.

To install:

6. Install a new ball joint in the control arm. Torque new bolts to 13 ft. lbs.

7. Install the ball stud into the steering knuckle pinch bolt fitting. It should go in easily; if not, check the stud alignment. Install the pinch bolt

from the rear to the front. Torque to 45 ft. lbs.

8. Install the wheel and lower the vehicle.

Lower Control Arms

REMOVAL AND INSTALLATION

1. Loosen the wheel nuts, raise and support vehicle safely, then remove the tire and wheel assembly.

2. Remove the stabilizer bar from the control arm.

3. Remove the ball joint from the steering knuckle.

4. Remove the control arm mounting bolts, then the control arm from the vehicle.

To install:

5. Install the control arm into the fittings. Install the pivot bolts from the rear to the front. Torque bolts to 50 ft. lbs. (68 Nm).

6. Install the ball stud into the pinch bolt fitting. It should go in easily; if not, check the ball joint stud alignment.

7. Install the pinch bolt from the rear to the front. Torque bolts 33 ft. lbs. (45 Nm).

8. Install the stabilizer bar attachment. Torque bolts to 35 ft. lbs. (47 Nm).

9. Install the tire and wheel assembly and lower the vehicle.

Stabilizer Shaft

REMOVAL AND INSTALLATION

1. Disconnect battery negative cable.

2. Raise and safely support the vehicle.

3. Remove the stabilizer shaft insulator clamp and insulator at the control arms. Do not remove the studs from the control arm.

4. Remove the plate from the frame at each side, then the stabilizer shaft and insulator bushings from the vehicle.

To install:

5. Install the stabilizer insulator bushings, stabilizer shaft and plate to the frame at each side. Tighten plate–to–frame bolts to 40 ft. lbs. (55 Nm)

6. Install the insulators at the control arms. Install the stabilizer shaft insulator clamp. Tighten insulator clamp nuts to 33 ft. lbs. (45 Nm).

7. Lower the vehicle.

8. Connect the negative battery cable.

REAR SUSPENSION

Shock Absorbers

REMOVAL AND INSTALLATION

1. Disconnect the negative battery cable.

2. Open the deck or trunk lid, then remove the trim cover and the upper shock nut. Remove and replace 1 shock at a time when replacing both shocks.

3. Raise and support the vehicle safely.

4. Remove the shock lower attaching bolt, then remove the shock. If equipped with air shocks, disconnect the air lines.

To install:

NOTE: Purge new shocks of air by repeatedly compressing them while inverted and extending them in their normal installed position.

5. Install the shock absorber and attaching bolts. Tighten to 43 ft. lbs. (58 Nm).

6. Lower the vehicle.

7. Install the upper shock absorber nut. Tighten the upper nut to 13 ft. lbs. (18 Nm).

8. Install the trim cover.

9. Connect the negative battery cable.

Coil Springs

REMOVAL AND INSTALLATION

1. Disconnect the battery negative cable.

2. Raise and safely support the vehicle using jacks that can be raised and lowered.

3. Remove the brake hose attaching brackets (right and left), allowing the hoses to hang freely. Do not disconnect the hoses.

4. Remove the track bar attaching bolts from the rear axle.

5. Lower the axle, then remove the coil spring and insulator.

NOTE: Do not suspend the rear axle by the brake hose.

To install:

6. Position the spring and insulator on the axle. The leg on the upper coil of the spring must be parallel to the axle, facing the left side of the vehicle.

7. Install the shock absorber bolts. Torque bolts to 43 ft. lbs. (57 Nm). Install track bar, if equipped, and torque to 33 ft. lbs. (45 Nm). Install the brake line brackets and torque to 8 ft. lbs. (11 Nm).

Rear Wheel Bearings

REMOVAL AND INSTALLATION

1. Disconnect battery negative cable, then raise and support vehicle.
2. Remove the wheel and brake drum. Do not hammer on the brake drum as damage to the bearing may result.
3. If equipped with anti-lock brakes, remove caliper, rotor and pads.
4. On all vehicles, remove the hub and bearing assembly attaching bolts and remove assembly from the rear axle.

NOTE: The bolts attaching the hub and bearing assembly also support the brake assembly. When removing these bolts, support the brake assembly with a length of wire. Do not let the brake assembly hang by the brake line unsupported.

To install:
5. On all vehicles, install the hub and bearing assembly attaching bolts and torque to 44 ft. lbs. (60 Nm).

6. If equipped with anti-lock brakes, install the rotor, caliper and pads.
7. Install the brake drum. Install the tire and wheel assembly.
8. Lower the vehicle.
9. Connect the negative battery cable.

Rear Axle Assembly

REMOVAL AND INSTALLATION

1. Raise and safely support the vehicle. Disconnect the negative battery cable.

NOTE: If removing the rear axle on a twin post lift, the axle assembly must be supported securely to prevent the possibility of the axle assembly slipping from the lift when certain fasteners are removed.

2. Remove the rear wheels. Remove the rear brake drums. Disconnect the parking brake from the rear axle.
3. If equipped with anti-lock brakes, remove the caliper, rotor and pads.
4. On all models, remove the brake brackets from the vehicle frame.
5. Remove the rear shock absorbers. Remove the track bar.

6. Disconnect the rear brake hoses.
7. Lower the axle assembly and remove the coil springs and insulators.
8. Remove the hub attaching bolts. Remove the hub and bearing assembly.
9. Remove the control arm bracket attaching bolts. Remove the control arms. Lower the axle from the vehicle.

To install:
10. Raise the axle assembly into position. Install the control arms and control arm bracket attaching bolts.
11. Install the hub and bearing assembly. Install the hub attaching bolts.
12. Install the coil springs and insulators. Raise the axle assembly.
13. Install the shock absorbers. Install the track bar.
14. Connect the brake hoses.
15. Install the brake brackets to the vehicle frame.
16. If equipped with anti-lock brakes, install the rotor, caliper and pads.
17. Connect the parking brake to the rear axle. Install the rear brake drums. Install the rear tire and wheel assemblies.
18. Bleed the brake system and adjust the parking brake, as required.
19. Lower the vehicle. Connect the negative battery cable.

GM "C AND H" BODY

Front Wheel Drive

BUICK—LeSabre, Park Avenue   **CADILLAC**—DeVille, Fleetwood
PONTIAC—Bonneville   **OLDSMOBILE**—Ninety Eight, 88 Royale

12

FIRING ORDERS

NOTE: To avoid confusion, always replace spark plug wires one at a time.

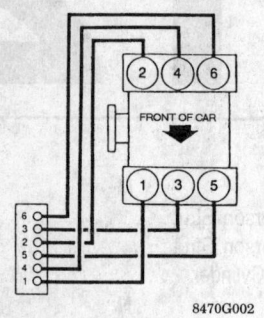

8470G002

3.8L (VIN L and 1) Engine
Engine Firing Order:
1–6–5–4–3–2
Distributorless Ignition System

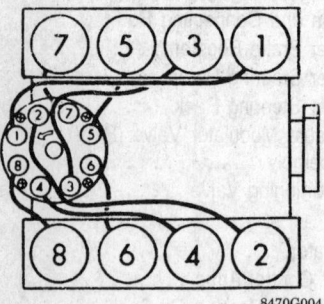

8470G004

4.9L Engine
Engine Firing Order:
1–8–4–3–6–5–7–2
Distributor Rotation:
Counterclockwise

ENGINE ELECTRICAL

NOTE: Disconnecting the negative battery cable on some vehicles may interfere with the functions of the on board computer systems and may require the computer to undergo a relearning process, once the negative battery cable is reconnected.

Distributor

The 4.9L engine is equipped with the High Energy Ignition (HEI) system, utilizing Electronic Spark Timing (EST). The EST distributor uses no mechanical or vacuum advance and is easily identified by the absence of a vacuum advance.

All other engines are equipped with Computer Controlled Coil Ignition (C_3I) system, which eliminates the distributor. The ECM provides sequential injection by processing signals received from the crankshaft and camshaft sensors.

The C_3I system consists of the coil pack, ignition module, various hall effect sensors, interrupter rings and the Electronic Control Module (ECM). Since the ECM controls the ignition timing, no timing adjustments are necessary. These systems utilize the EST signal from the ECM to control spark timing.

REMOVAL

1. Disconnect the negative battery cable.
2. Label and disconnect all wires leading from the distributor cap.
3. Remove the distributor cap by turning the 4 latches counterclockwise. Lift off the distributor cap and carefully move it aside.
4. Disconnect the electrical connector harness from the distributor, if not already done.
5. Remove the distributor holddown nut and clamp, using the proper tool.
6. Using a piece of chalk or paint, mark the rotor-to-distributor body and the distributor body-to-engine positions. Pull the distributor upward until the rotor just stops turning (counterclockwise); note the position of the rotor once again. Remove the distributor.

NOTE: Do not crank the engine with the distributor removed. On certain engines, a thrust washer is used between the distributor drive gear and the crankcase. This washer may stick to the bottom of the distributor when it is removed. Always make sure the washer is at the bottom of the distributor bore before installation.

INSTALLATION

Timing Not Disturbed

1. Rotate the distributor shaft until the rotor aligns with the second

'COIL IN CAP' DISTRIBUTOR

COIL AND CAP ASSEMBLY

TERMINALS
C–   B+

CAP SCREWS (4)

6-TERMINAL 5-WIRE CONNECTOR

CONNECTOR (DISCONNECTED FROM CAP)

8470G005

Distributor assembly — 4.9L engine

mark, when the shaft stopped moving.

2. Lubricate the drive gear with clean engine oil and install the distributor into the engine.

3. As the distributor is installed, the rotor should rotate to the first alignment mark; this will ensure proper timing.

4. If the marks do not align properly, remove the distributor and re-set; be sure to install the thrust washer, if equipped.

5. Install the clamp and hold-down nut. Tighten the nut until the distributor can just be moved with a little effort.

6. Connect all wires and hoses. Install the distributor cap.

7. Check and/or adjust the ignition timing. After ignition timing is set, tighten distributor hold-down

Timing Disturbed

1. Remove the No. 1 spark plug.
2. Rotate the crankshaft until No. 1 piston is at the TDC of its compression stroke.

NOTE: The compression stroke can be determined by placing a thumb over the hole while slowly cranking the engine. Crank until compression is felt at the hole and continue cranking slowly until the timing mark on the crankshaft pulley aligns with the 0 degrees timing mark located on the timing chain cover.

3. Position the distributor in the block but do not, at this time, allow it to engage with the drive gear.

4. Rotate the distributor shaft until the rotor points between No. 1 and No. 8 spark plug towers and lower the distributor to engage the camshaft. Be sure that distributor rotor alignment is correct after camshaft gear engagement.

NOTE: It may be necessary to turn the rotor a small amount in either direction in order to achieve this engagement. The rotor will rotate slightly as the distributor gear engages. If installed correctly, the rotor should point toward the No. 1 spark plug terminal in the distributor cap.

5. Press down firmly on the distributor housing. This will ensure that the distributor shaft engages the oil pump shaft, thereby allowing the distributor to fully contact the engine block.

6. Install the hold-down clamp and tighten the nut until it is snug, do not tighten.

7. Install the distributor cap, making sure the rotor points to No. 1 terminal in the cap.

8. Attach all wires and hoses.

9. Start the engine. Check and/or adjust the ignition timing. Torque the distributor hold-down nut to 20 ft. lbs.

NOTE: Malfunction trouble codes must be cleared after removal or adjustment of the distributor. The ECM power feed must be disconnected for at least 30 seconds to clear the codes.

Ignition Module

REMOVAL AND INSTALLATION

4.9L Engine

1. Disconnect the negative battery cable.

2. Disconnect the wires from the distributor cap and remove the distributor cap.

3. Remove the rotor.

4. Remove the module attaching screws and lift the shield and module up.

5. Disconnect the electrical leads from the module. Note the connections for installation purposes.

To install:

6. Connect the electrical leads to the module and install it along with the shield. Make sure the connections are correct.

7. Install the rotor and distributor cap and connect the spark plug and coil wires.

8. Connect the negative battery cable.

Distributorless Ignition System

REMOVAL AND INSTALLATION

Crankshaft Sensor

3.8L ENGINE

1. Disconnect the negative battery cable.

2. Remove the serpentine drive belt.

3. Raise the vehicle and support it safely.

4. Remove the right front tire and wheel assembly.

5. Remove the inner fender access panel.

6. Using the proper socket, remove the crankshaft balancer bolt and balancer.

7. Disconnect the sensor electrical connector.

8. Remove the sensor and pedestal from the block face.

9. Remove the sensor from the pedestal.

To install:

10. Loosely install the crankshaft sensor on the pedestal.

11. Position the sensor with the pedestal attached on the proper tool.

12. Position the tool No. J38197 or equivalent, on the crankshaft.

13. Install the bolts to hold the pedestal to the block face and torque to 14–28 ft. lbs.

14. Torque the pedestal pinch bolt to 36–40 ft. lbs.

15. Remove the tool.

16. Place special tool on the harmonic balancer and turn. If any vane of the harmonic balancer touches the tool, replace the balancer assembly.

17. Install the balancer on the crankshaft.

18. Torque the crankshaft bolt to 110 ft. lbs. plus 76 degrees.

19. Install the inner fender access panel.

20. Install the wheel and torque the lug nuts to 100 ft. lbs.

21. Lower the vehicle and install the serpentine belt.

22. Connect the battery cable.

Ignition Coil

1. Disconnect the negative battery cable.

2. Remove the spark plug wires and the Torx screws attaching the coil to the ignition module.

3. Position the coil assembly aside and disconnect the coil to module connector.

4. Remove the coil assembly.

To install:

5. Install the coil assembly and attaching screws.

6. Connect the electrical connectors.

7. Connect the spark plug wires.

8. Connect the negative battery cable.

Ignition Module

3.8L ENGINE

1. Disconnect the negative battery cable.

2. Remove the spark plug wires at the coil assembly.

3. Remove the ignition module bracket mounting nuts.

4. Remove the Torx screws mounting the coil to the ignition module. Mark the position of the lead wires.

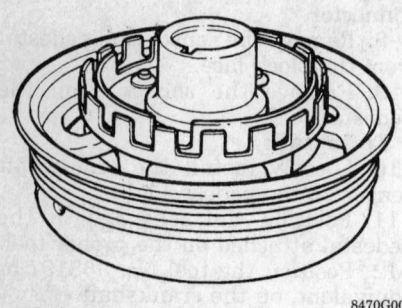

Crankshaft balancer with interrupter rings — 3.8L engines

8470G006

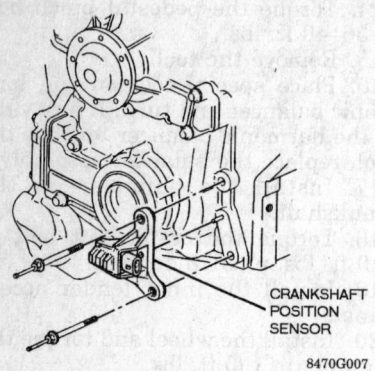

Crankshaft position sensor — 3.8L engines

CRANKSHAFT POSITION SENSOR

8470G007

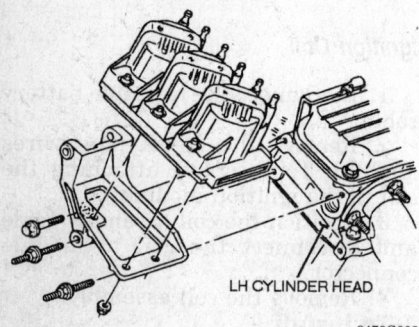

Ignition control module and coil assembly — 3.8L (VIN L) engine

LH CYLINDER HEAD

8470G008

5. Disconnect the connectors between the coil and the ignition module.

6. Remove the ignition module.

To install:

7. Install the ignition module.

8. Connect the ignition module to coil electrical connectors.

9. Install the Torx screws mounting the coil to the ignition module.

10. Install the ignition module bracket mounting nuts.

11. Install the spark plug wires at the coil assembly.

12. Connect the negative battery cable.

Ignition Timing

ADJUSTMENT

4.9L Engine

NOTE: The 4.9L engine incorporates a magnetic timing probe hole for use with special electronic timing equipment. Consult the manufacturer's instructions before using this system. The following procedure is for use with the HEI-EST distributor.

1. Connect a timing light to the No. 1 spark plug wire according to the light manufacturer's instructions; do not pierce the spark plug wire to connect the timing light.

2. Follow the instructions on the Vehicle Emission Control Information label located in the engine compartment.

3. If equipped with an Electronic Spark Timing (EST) distributor, disconnect the 4-wire terminal plug from the distributor. Some models may require grounding the diagnostic connector located under the left side of the dash.

4. Start the engine and allow it to run at idle speed.

5. Aim the timing light at the degree scale just over the harmonic balancer.

6. Adjust the timing by loosening the hold-down clamp and rotate the distributor until the desired ignition advance is achieved. When the correct timing marks are aligned, tighten the clamp.

7. Adjust the timing, replace and tighten the hold-down clamp. To advance the timing, rotate the distributor opposite the normal direction of rotor rotation. Retard the timing by rotating the distributor in the normal direction of rotor rotation.

NOTE: If equipped with Throttle Body Injection (TBI), the malfunction trouble codes must be cleared after removal or adjustment of the distributor. This is accomplished by removing battery voltage to terminal R of the distributor for 10 seconds.

3.8L Engine

The 3.8L engine uses a Computer Controlled Coil Ignition (C_3I) system. The C_3I system components replace the conventional distributor and consists of a coil pack, ignition module, crankshaft sensor and camshaft sen-

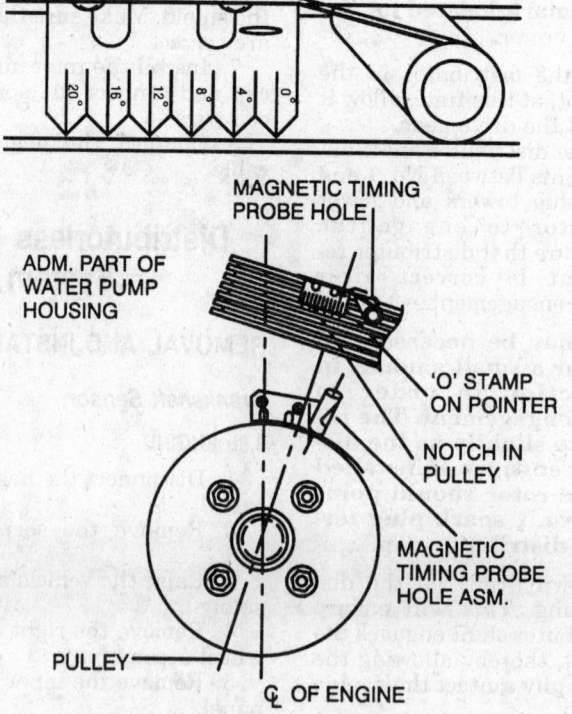

MAGNETIC TIMING PROBE HOLE

ADM. PART OF WATER PUMP HOUSING

'O' STAMP ON POINTER

NOTCH IN PULLEY

MAGNETIC TIMING PROBE HOLE ASM.

PULLEY

℄ OF ENGINE

20° 16° 12° 8° 4° 0°

8470G009

Magnetic timing probe hole — 4.9L engine

sor. No ignition timing adjustment is necessary or possible on the C₃I system.

Alternator

PRECAUTIONS

Several precautions must be observed with alternator equipped vehicles to avoid damage to the unit.

• If the battery is removed for any reason, make sure it is reconnected with the correct polarity. Reversing the battery connections may result in damage to the one-way rectifiers.

• When utilizing a booster battery as a starting aid, always connect the positive to positive terminals and the negative terminal from the booster battery to a good engine ground on the vehicle being started.

• Never use a fast charger as a booster to start vehicles.

• Disconnect the battery cables when charging the battery with a fast charger.

• Never attempt to polarize the alternator.

• Do not use test lights of more than 12 volts when checking diode continuity.

• Do not short across or ground any of the alternator terminals.

• The polarity of the battery, alternator and regulator must be matched and considered before making any electrical connections within the system.

• Never separate the alternator on an open circuit. Make sure all connections within the circuit are clean and tight.

• Disconnect the battery ground terminal when performing any service on electrical components.

• Disconnect the battery if arc welding is to be done on the vehicle.

BELT TENSION ADJUSTMENT

A single serpentine belt is used to drive all engine mounted accessories. Drive belt tension is maintained by a spring loaded tensioner. A belt squeak when the engine is started or stopped is normal and has no effect on belt durability. The drive belt tensioner can control belt tension over a broad range of belt lengths; however, there are limits to the tensioner's ability to compensate.

1. Inspect tensioner markings to see if the belt is within operating lengths. Replace belt if the belt is excessively worn or is outside of the tensioner's operating range.

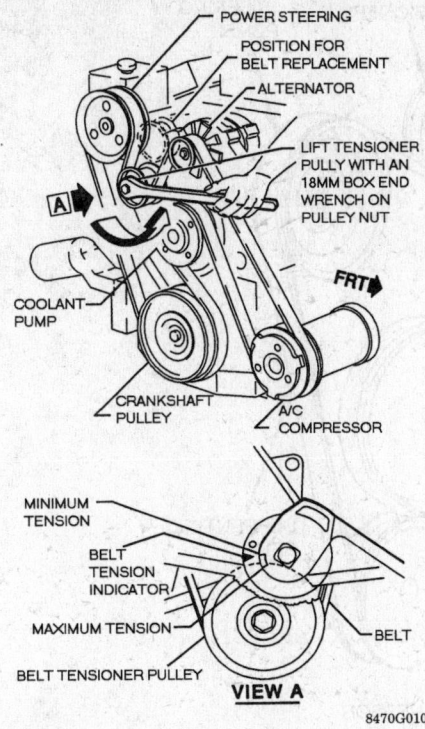

Drive belt service — 3.8L Non–supercharged engine

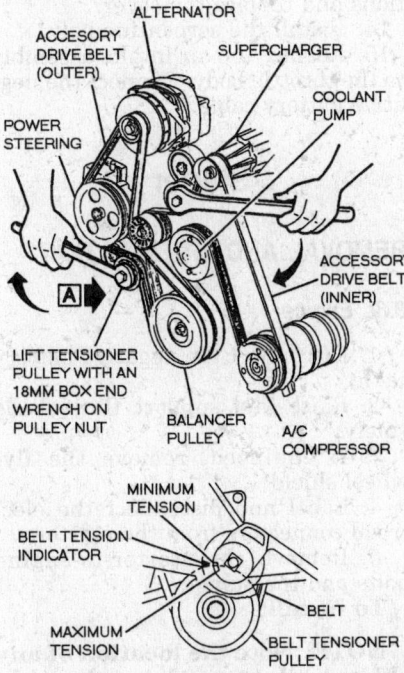

Drive belt service — 3.8L Supercharged engine

2. Run engine with the accessories OFF until the engine is warm. Turn the engine **OFF** and read belt tension with a proper belt tension gauge or equivalent placed halfway between the alternator and the air conditioning compressor. For non-air conditioning applications read tension between the power steering pump and crankshaft pulley. Remove tool.

3. Start the engine, with accessories OFF, and allow the system to stabilize for 15 seconds. Turn the engine **OFF**. Using the proper tool, apply clockwise force (tighten) to the tensioner pulley bolt. Release the force and immediately take a tension reading without disturbing belt tensioner position.

4. Apply a counterclockwise force to the tensioner pulley bolt and raise the pulley to the fully raised position. Slowly lower the pulley to engage the belt and take a tension reading without disturbing the belt tensioner position.

5. Average the 3 readings. If the average of the 3 readings is lower than the tension specified and the belt is within the tensioner's operating range, replace the belt tensioner. The drive belt tension should be 120 lbs. for 4.9L engines or never below 67 lbs. for 3.8L engine. If the belt tensioner is adjusted beyond it's movable limit, replace the serpentine drive belt.

REMOVAL AND INSTALLATION

3.8L Engine

1. Disconnect the negative battery cable.

2. Label and disconnect the electrical connectors from the back of the alternator.

3. If equipped, remove the brace at the back of the alternator and the fuel rail cover.

4. Rotate the tensioner counterclockwise to remove the serpentine drive belt.

5. While supporting the alternator, remove the mounting bolts and the alternator.

To install:

6. Support the alternator in position and install the alternator.

7. Install the serpentine drive belt and rotate the tensioner into position.

8. If equipped, install the brace at the back of the alternator and the fuel rail cover.

9. Connect the electrical connectors at the back of the alternator.

10. Connect the negative battery cable.

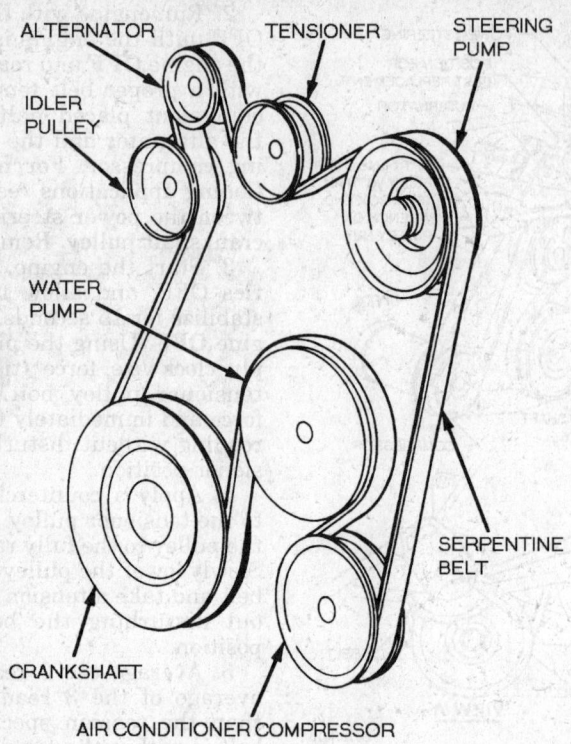

Drive belt routing — 4.9L engine

Labels on diagram:
- ALTERNATOR
- TENSIONER
- STEERING PUMP
- IDLER PULLEY
- WATER PUMP
- SERPENTINE BELT
- CRANKSHAFT
- AIR CONDITIONER COMPRESSOR

8470G012

4.9L Engine

1. Disconnect the negative battery cable.

2. Remove the air intake assembly at the throttle body.

3. Remove the serpentine belt from the tensioner pulley.

4. Remove the cover from the rear of the alternator and disconnect the electrical connections.

5. Disconnect the alternator mounting stud and the brace from the power steering pump.

6. Remove the rear alternator bolt and move the alternator upward and remove the connector.

7. Disconnect the heated windshield power module connection, if equipped.

8. Disconnect the front alternator bolt and remove the alternator.

To install:

9. Install the alternator and replace the front alternator bolt, tighten to 32 ft. lbs.

10. Connect the heated windshield power leads, if so equipped.

11. Install the alternator connector and the rear mounting bolt. Tighten the bolt to 20 ft. lbs.

12. Install the power steering brace and replace the alternator mounting stud.

13. Connect the electrical connections and replace the cover.

14. Install the serpentine belt.

15. Replace the air intake assembly to the throttle body. Connect the negative battery cable.

Starter

REMOVAL AND INSTALLATION

3.8L Engine

1. Disconnect the negative battery cable.

2. Raise and support the vehicle safely.

3. If equipped, remove the flywheel shield.

4. Label and disconnect the electrical connectors from the starter.

5. Remove the starter-to-engine bolts and the starter.

To install:

NOTE: Note the location of any shims so they may be replaced in the same positions upon installation.

6. Install the starter and starter-to-engine bolts.

7. Connect the electrical connectors to the starter.

8. If removed, install the flywheel shield.

9. Lower the vehicle.

10. Connect the negative battery cable.

4.9L Engine

1. Disconnect the negative battery cable.

2. Raise and safely support the vehicle.

3. Remove the starter motor shield and remove the exhaust front and rear pipe assembly.

4. Remove the flexplate inspection cover.

5. Disconnect the starter electrical connections.

6. Remove the starter motor mounting bolts and remove the starter from the vehicle.

To install:

7. Install the starter to the vehicle and install the mounting bolts. Tighten the bolts to 32 ft. lbs.

8. Connect the starter electrical connectors.

9. Install the flexplate inspection cover and front and rear exhaust pipe assembly.

10. Install the starter motor shield and lower the vehicle.

11. Connect the negative battery cable.

CHASSIS ELECTRICAL

Air Bag

— CAUTION —
Some vehicles are equipped with the Supplemental Inflatable Restraint (SIR) or air bag system. The SIR system must be disabled before performing service on or around SIR system components, steering column, instrument panel components, wiring and sensors. Failure to follow safety and disabling procedures could result in accidental air bag deployment, possible personal injury and unnecessary SIR system repairs.

PRECAUTIONS

Several precautions must be observed when handling the inflator module to avoid accidental deployment and possible personal injury.

• Never carry the inflator module by the wires or connector on the underside of the module.

• When carrying a live inflator module, hold securely with both hands, and ensure that the bag and trim cover are pointed away.

• Place the inflator module on a bench or other surface with the bag and trim cover facing up.

• With the inflator module on the bench, never place anything on or close to the module which may be thrown in the event of an accidental deployment.

DISABLING SIR SYSTEM

1. Disconnect the negative battery cable.

2. Remove the SIR fuse from the fuse panel.

3. Remove the left side sound insulator.

4. Remove the Connector Positive Assurance (CPA) from the yellow 2-way SIR harness connector at the base of the steering column and separate the connector.

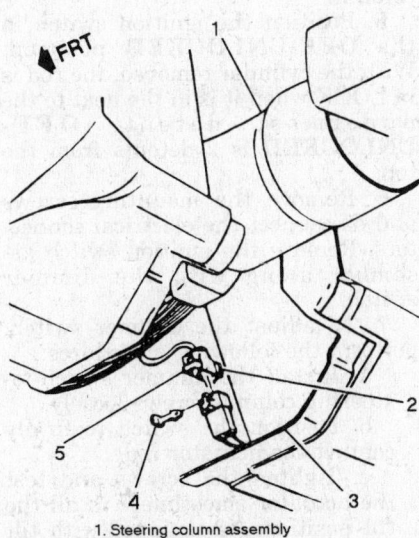

1. Steering column assembly
2. Edge metal clip
3. IP Lower tie bar assembly
4. Connector position assurance (CPA)
5. SIR harness connector

8470G018

Yellow two-way SIR harness connector — Air bag equipped vehicles

ENABLING SIR SYSTEM

1. Connect the yellow 2-way SIR connector at the base of the steering column and insert the Connector Positive Assurance (CPA).

2. Install the left side sound insulator.

3. Install the SIR fuse in the fuse panel.

4. Connect the negative battery cable.

Heater Blower Motor

REMOVAL AND INSTALLATION

1. Disconnect the negative battery cable.

2. Disconnect the electrical connections from the blower motor.

3. Disconnect the cooling hose from the blower motor.

4. Remove the mounting screws and the motor.

5. If necessary, remove the coil and spark plug wires.

To install:

6. Use a silicone sealer on the blower motor sealing surfaces.

7. If removed, connect the coil and spark plug wires.

8. Remove the motor and mounting screws.

9. Connect the cooling hose to the blower motor.

10. Connect the electrical connections to the blower motor.

11. Connect the negative battery cable.

Windshield Wiper Motor

REMOVAL AND INSTALLATION

1. Disconnect the negative battery cable. Disconnect the washer hoses.

2. Remove the wiper arms and the air inlet screen assembly.

3. Disconnect the wiper arm drive link from the crank arm.

4. Disconnect the electrical connectors and remove the wiper motor mounting bolts.

5. Guide the crank arm through the hole in the dash and remove the motor.

To install:

6. Guide the crank arm through the hole in the dash and place the motor into position.

7. Install the wiper motor mounting bolts and connect the electrical connectors.

8. Connect the wiper arm drive link to the crank arm. Install the

wiper arms and the air inlet screen assembly.

9. Connect the washer hoses and connect the negative battery cable.

Windshield Wiper Switch

REMOVAL AND INSTALLATION

1. Disconnect the negative battery cable.

2. Remove the steering wheel, the cover and the lock plate assembly.

3. Remove the turn signal actuator arm, the lever and the hazard flasher button.

4. Remove the turn signal switch screws, the lower steering column trim panel and the steering column bracket bolts.

5. Disconnect the the turn signal switch and the wiper switch connectors.

6. Pull the turn signal switch rearward 6–8 inches, remove the key buzzer switch and cylinder lock assembly.

7. Remove and pull the steering column housing rearward. Remove the housing cover screw.

8. Remove the wiper switch pivot and the switch assembly.

To install:

9. Install the pivot and switch assembly.

10. Reposition and reinstall the steering column. Replace the housing cover screw.

11. Install the cylinder lock and key buzzer assembly. Reposition the turn signal switch.

12. Connect the turn signal switch and wiper switch connectors.

13. Install the steering column bracket bolts and the column trim panel.

14. Replace the turn signal switch screws.

15. Install the hazard flasher button, turn signal actuator arm and lever.

16. Install the lock plate assembly, cover and the steering wheel.

17. Connect the negative battery cable.

Instrument Cluster

REMOVAL AND INSTALLATION

Except Cadillac

1. Disconnect the negative battery cable. Disable the SIR system.

2. Remove the steering column filler panel.

3. Lower the steering column and cover the top of the column to prevent scratching and, if necessary, disconnect the PRNDL cable.

4. Remove the instrument panel trim plate by removing the screws and/or gently prying outward.

5. Remove the cluster to instrument panel screws and pull right end of cluster rearward.

6. Disconnect the cluster connector by reaching around cluster and depressing the locking tab on the connector.

7. Pull the bottom of the cluster rearward and rotate the assembly so it is facing up.

8. Remove the cluster assembly by sliding toward the center of the vehicle.

To install:

9. Install the cluster to the vehicle and rotate into the proper position.

10. Connect the cluster connector, being careful not to damage the connector.

11. Install the cluster to instrument panel screws and install the instrument panel cluster trim plate.

12. Remove the protective cover from the steering column, connect the PRNDL cable and raise the steering column to the proper position.

13. Enable the SIR system and connect the negative battery cable.

Cadillac

1. Disable the SIR system, if equipped, and disconnect the negative battery cable.

2. Remove the upper trim pad and remove the trim plate screws and the trim plate.

3. Remove the cluster mounting screws.

4. Disconnect the electrical connector

5. Remove the shift indicator cable clip and disconnect the cable.

6. Remove the instrument cluster.

NOTE: On a digital cluster, remove the memory chip for the season odometer before sending the unit to an authorized repair center. The printed circuit must be lifted to gain access to the memory chip.

7. Remove the lens mounting screws and the speedometer retaining screws.

8. Disconnect the speedometer cable or electrical connection, if equipped.

9. Remove the speedometer assembly.

To install:

10. Install the speedometer assembly. Connect the speedometer cable or electrical connection, if so equipped.

11. Install the instrument cluster and connect the electrical connectors.

12. Install and adjust the shift indicator clip. Replace the cluster mounting screws.

13. Install the trim panel.

14. Enable the SIR system, if equipped, and connect the negative battery cable.

Headlight Switch

REMOVAL AND INSTALLATION

Except Park Avenue

1. Disconnect the negative battery cable. Remove the steering column lower cover or the instrument panel trim plate covering the headlight switch, if equipped with a rocker-type headlight switch.

2. Disconnect the electrical harness retainer below headlight switch assembly. The switch connector is integral to the instrument panel. Pull the switch outward to disconnect it, except on Cadillac.

3. On Cadillac, depress spring loaded release button on top of headlight switch and remove switch, knob and rod assembly with the switch in the **ON** position.

4. Remove screw with ground wire at bottom of switch housing and all other mounting screws.

5. Pull assembly down and rearward, disconnect wiring harness connectors, bulb(s) and remove assembly.

To install:

6. Connect wiring harness connectors, bulb(s) and install the assembly.

7. Install the screw with ground wire at the bottom of switch housing and all other mounting screws.

8. Connect the electrical harness retainer below headlight switch assembly. Push the switch inward to connect it, except on Cadillac.

9. On Cadillac, install the switch, knob and rod assembly with the switch in the **ON** position.

10. Install the steering column lower cover or the instrument panel trim plate covering the headlight switch, if equipped with a rocker-type headlight switch.

11. Connect the negative battery cable.

Park Avenue

1. Disconnect the negative battery cable.

2. Remove the driver's side door trim panel.

3. Remove the 2 head light switch to door panel attaching bolts and disconnect the electrical connector.

4. Remove the switch assembly.

To install:

5. Install the switch to the door panel and connect the electrical connector.

6. Remove the 2 bolts securing the switch to the door panel.

7. Install the driver's side door panel and connect the negative battery cable.

Dimmer Switch

The dimmer switch is attached to the lower portion of the steering column and is controlled by an actuator rod connected to the turn signal lever.

REMOVAL AND INSTALLATION

1. Disconnect the negative battery cable.

2. Remove the left side sound insulator.

3. Lower the steering column trim plate.

4. Remove the steering column-to-dash screws and lower the steering column.

5. Position the ignition switch in the **OFF-UNLOCKED** position. With the cylinder removed, the rod is in LOCK when it is in the next to the uppermost detent; **OFF-UNLOCKED** is 2 detents from the top.

6. Remove the mounting screws and disconnect the electrical connectors. Remove the ignition switch assembly along with the dimmer switch.

7. To adjust the dimmer switch, perform the following procedures:

   a. Install the dimmer switch-to-steering column screws loosely.

   b. Position the switch to firmly contact the actuator rod.

   c. Tighten the screws and test the actuator smoothness in all the tilt positions, if equipped with tilt wheel.

To install:

8. Install the dimmer switch and attach the mounting screws. Put the ignition switch in **OFF-UNLOCKED** position; make sure the lock cylinder and actuating rod are in **OFF-UNLOCKED** (third detent from the top) position.

9. Install the activating rod into the switch and assemble the switch on the column. Tighten the mounting screws.

10. Connect the electrical connections to the dimmer switch.

11. Position the steering column in place and install the column mounting screws.

12. Install the column trim plate and replace the sound insulator.

13. Connect the negative battery cable.

Turn Signal Switch

REMOVAL AND INSTALLATION

1. Disconnect the negative battery cable and remove the steering wheel and the shroud.

2. Remove the inflation restraint (air bag module) coil assembly-to-steering shaft lock screw (home boss) and retaining ring. Remove the coil assembly from the shaft and allow it to hang freely.

3. Using the lock plate compression tool or equivalent, position it on the end of the steering shaft and compress the lock plate by turning the shaft nut clockwise. Pry the wire snapring out of the shaft groove.

4. Remove the tool and lift the lock plate from the shaft.

5. Remove the cancelling cam, upper bearing preload spring, bearing seat and inner race from the shaft.

6. Position the turn signal switch in the right turn position. Remove the turn signal lever screw and the lever.

7. Remove the turn signal switch by performing the following:

   a. Remove the switch-to-steering column screws, pull the switch out and allow it to hang freely.

   b. From under the dash, remove the retainer spring and wiring protector.

c. Remove the hazard knob.

   d. Disconnect the electrical connector from the lower steering column and gently pull the wiring connector through the gear shift lever bowl, the column housing and the lock housing cover. Remove the switch.

To install:

8. Install the turn signal switch harness through the steering column housing and connect the switch.

9. Install the switch actuator arm and screw.

10. Install the inner race, bearing seat and the bearing preload spring. Replace the turn signal cancelling cam.

11. Install the lock plate, using a lock plate compression tool, compress the lock plate and install the shaft lock retaining ring.

12. Install the steering wheel and the shroud.

13. To install the inflation restraint coil, perform the following procedures:

   a. Install the home boss-to-steering column lock screw, allowing the hub to rotate.

   b. While holding the coil assembly (in one hand) with the steering wheel connector facing upwards, rotate the coil hub counterclockwise until it stops; the coil ribbon is now wound snug.

   c. Rotate the coil hub 2½ turns clockwise until the center lock hole is even with the notch in the coil housing.

   d. While holding the hub in position, install the lock screw into the center lock hole.

   e. Install the coil assembly using the horn tower on the inner ring cancelling cam and outer ring projections for alignment purposes.

14. Connect the negative battery cable.

1. Binding HD cross recess screw
2. RD wash HD screw (m4.2x1.41)
3. Signal switch arm ASM
4. Turn signal switch assy
5. Multi-function lever
6. Hazard knob assembly

8470G022

Turn signal switch assembly

Combination Switch

The combination switch is attached to the upper portion of the steering column and is part of the turn signal lever.

REMOVAL AND INSTALLATION

1. Disconnect the negative terminal from the battery and disable the SIR system.

2. Remove the left side sound insulator.

3. Lower the steering column trim plate.

4. Remove the steering column-to-dash screws and lower the steering column.

5. Remove the inflation restraint (air bag module) and the combination switch assembly.

6. Position the ignition switch in the **OFF-UNLOCKED** position. With the cylinder removed, the rod is in LOCK when it is in the next to the uppermost detent; **OFF-UNLOCKED** is 2 detents from the top.

7. Remove the mounting screws and disconnect the electrical connectors. Remove the ignition switch assembly along with the dimmer switch.

To install:

8. Adjust the dimmer switch as necessary.

9. Install the dimmer switch and attach the mounting screws. Put the ignition switch in **OFF-UNLOCKED** position; make sure the lock cylinder and actuating rod are in **OFF-UNLOCKED** (third detent from the top) position.

10. Install the activating rod into the switch and assemble the switch on the column. Tighten the mounting screws.

11. Connect the electrical connections at the dimmer switch.

12. Install the combination switch and replace the air bag module.

13. Position the steering column in place and install the column mounting screws.

14. Install the column trim plate and replace the sound insulator.

15. Connect the negative battery cable and enable the SIR system.

Ignition Switch

REMOVAL AND INSTALLATION

1. Disconnect the negative battery cable and lower the steering column; be sure to properly support it.

2. Position the switch in the **OFF-UNLOCKED** position. With the lock cylinder removed, the rod is in LOCK when it is in the next to the upper-most detent; **OFF-UNLOCKED** is 2 detents from the top.

3. Remove both switch screws and the switch assembly.

To install:

4. Place the new switch in the **OFF-UNLOCKED** position. Ensure the lock cylinder and actuating rod are in **OFF-UNLOCKED** position (3rd detent from the top).

5. Install the actuating rod into the switch and assemble the switch on the column. Tighten the mounting screws.

NOTE: Use only the specified screws since over-length screws could impair the collapsibility of the column.

6. Install the steering column.

7. Connect the negative battery cable.

Ignition Lock

REMOVAL AND INSTALLATION

1. Disconnect the negative battery cable and remove the turn signal switch assembly.

2. Remove the key from the lock cylinder. Remove the buzzer switch and clip.

3. Reinsert the key into the lock cylinder and turn it to the **LOCK** position.

4. Remove the cylinder lock-to-steering column screw and the lock set.

To install:

5. Install the cylinder lock and tighten the lock-to-steering column screw to 22 inch lbs.

6. Position the key in the **RUN** position and reverse the removal procedures. Tighten the turn signal switch-to-steering column screws to 30 inch lbs. and the turn signal lever screw to 20 inch lbs.

7. Connect the negative battery cable.

Brake Light Switch

ADJUSTMENT

1. Install the switch into the tubular clip until the switch assembly seats itself on the tubular clip.

2. Pull the brake pedal rearward against the pedal stop.

3. The switch will be moved in the tubular clip which will adjust itself properly.

4. The proper switch adjustment is achieved when no clicks are heard when the pedal is pulled upward and the brake lights stay OFF when the brake pedal is released.

REMOVAL AND INSTALLATION

1. Disconnect the negative terminal from the battery. Remove the left side sound insulator if necessary.

2. Bend in the retaining tabs to remove the switch assembly.

3. Disconnect the electrical connector from the rear of the switch assembly.

4. If so equipped, disconnect the cruise control vacuum hose from the switch.

5. Remove the brake light switch from the vehicle.

To install:

6. Install the brake light switch into the vehicle.

7. Connect the electrical connector to the rear of the switch assembly and connect the vacuum hose.

8. Install the left side sound insulator. Connect the negative battery cable.

Neutral Safety Switch

ADJUSTMENT

1. Disconnect the negative battery cable.

2. Place the transaxle shifter lever in the **N** position.

3. Loosen the switch mounting screws.

4. Rotate the switch on the shifter assembly to align the service adjustment holes.

5. Insert a gauge pin or equivalent, into the service slots. Tighten the mounting bolts.

6. Remove the gauge pin. Connect the negative battery cable.

REMOVAL AND INSTALLATION

1. Disconnect the negative battery cable.

2. Set the parking brake and shift the indicator to **N**.

3. Remove the shifter/linkage cable nut and remove the bracket from the shaft.

4. Remove the 2 neutral safety switch bolts and disconnect the electrical connector.

5. Remove the nut on the starter that connects the cable to the neutral safety switch.

6. Remove the neutral safety switch from the vehicle.

To install:

7. Install the neutral safety switch to the vehicle.

8. Connect the electrical connectors and connect the cable to the starter.

9. Insert a gauge pin into the service slot to properly align switch.

10. Install the 2 bolts and tighten to 20 ft. lbs.

11. Remove the gauge pin and install the linkage cable bracket to the switch complete with the nut.

12. Connect the negative battery cable.

Fuses, Circuit Breakers and Relays

LOCATION

Fuses

The fuse panel is located on the left side of the vehicle. It is under the instrument panel assembly. In order to gain access to the fuse panel, it may be necessary to first remove the under dash padding.

Underhood Fuse Panel

On some vehicles there is also a fuse panel under the hood on the right side of the engine. It is located along the vehicle firewall.

Circuit Breakers

The convenience center is located on the underside of the instrument panel near the fuse panel. It provides a central location for various relays, hazard flasher units and warning buzzers/chimes. All units are replaced with plug-in modules.

Relays

The relay center is located on the right side of the instrument panel. The relay center is mounted behind the glove box.

Computers

LOCATION

ECM — The Electronic Control Module is located on the right side of the vehicle. It is positioned under the instrument panel. In order to gain ac-

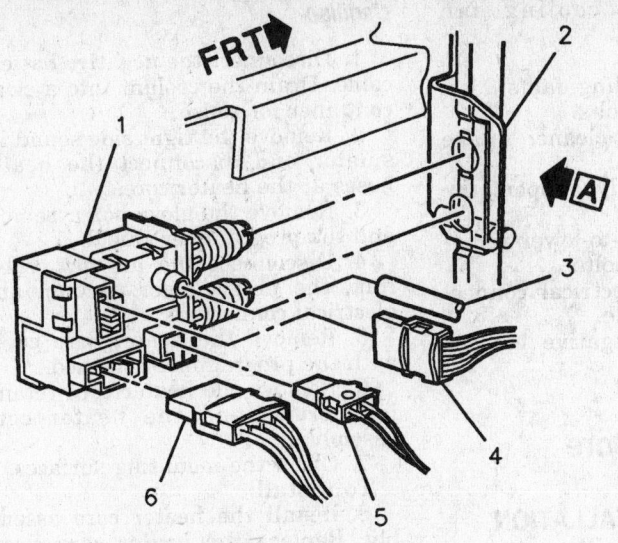

A. Retaining tabs
B. Switch barrels
1. Switch
2. Mounting bracket
3. Cruise vacuum line
4. Connector, TCC/ABS (black)
5. Connector, Stoplamp SW (gray)
6. Connector, shift-interlock/cruise (blue)

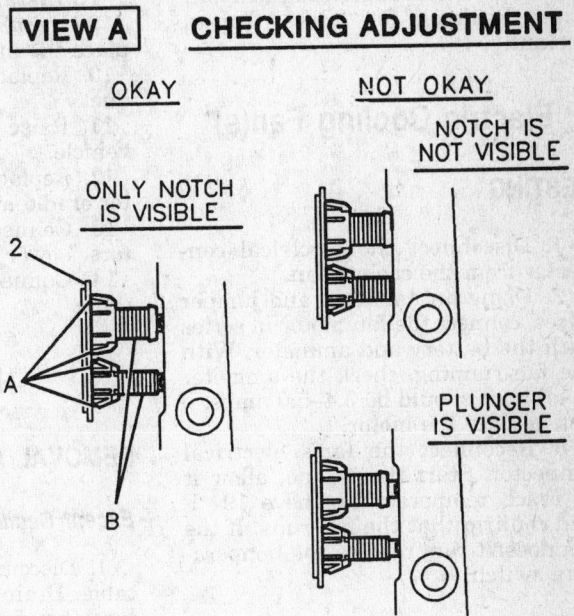

8470G024

Brake light switch assembly and adjustment

cess to the module, it will be necessary to first remove the trim panel.

BCM — The Body Control Module is located on the right side of the vehicle and positioned under the instrument panel. In order to gain access to the module, it will be necessary to first remove the trim panel.

EBCM — The Electronic Brake Control Module is located on the right side of the vehicle and positioned under the right sound insulator panel. In order to gain access to the module, it will be necessary to first remove the trim panel.

OLM — The Oil Lift Module is located on the right side of the vehicle, under the glove compartment. In order to gain access to the oil life module, the lower dash trim panel must first be removed.

HVAC Programmer — The Heating and Air Conditioner Controller is located in the center of the vehicle below the dashboard. Access to the unit can be obtained from beneath the dashboard.

Flashers

LOCATION

Turn Signal Flasher Unit — located behind the instrument panel near the steering column, along with the hazard flasher. It si secured with a plastic retainer. In order to gain access to components, it may first be necessary to remove certain under dash padding.

Hazard Flasher — located on the fuse block. It is positioned on the lower right side corner of the fuse block assembly.

Cruise Control

ADJUSTMENT

1. Turn the ignition switch **OFF**.
2. Fully retract the idle speed control motor plunger.

NOTE: The throttle lever must not touch the idle speed control plunger.

3. Connect the cruise control cable to the hole in the servo blade that leaves the minimum slack.
4. Install the retainer at the servo.

ENGINE COOLING

Radiator

REMOVAL AND INSTALLATION

1. Disconnect the negative battery cable.
2. Drain the radiator coolant. Remove the upper radiator panel.
3. Disconnect and remove the cooling fans, as required.
4. Disconnect the coolant reservoir hoses and the radiator hoses.
5. Disconnect the engine coolant lines from the radiator.
6. Disconnect the transaxle cooler lines. Remove the radiator.
To install:
7. Install the radiator. Connect the transaxle cooler lines.
8. If removed, connect the engine coolant lines to the radiator.
9. Connect the coolant reservoir hoses and the radiator hoses.
10. If removed, install the cooling fans.
11. Install the upper radiator panel.
12. Connect the negative battery cable.

13. Fill cooling system and check for leaks. Start the engine and allow to come to normal operating temperature. Recheck for leaks. Top-up coolant.

Electric Cooling Fan(s)

TESTING

1. Disconnect the electrical connector from the cooling fan.
2. Using an ammeter and jumper wires, connect the fan motor in series with the battery and ammeter. With the fan running, check the ammeter reading, it should be 3.4–5.0 amps; if not, replace the motor.
3. Reconnect the fan's electrical connector. Start the engine, allow it to reach temperatures above 194°F and confirm that the fan runs. If the fan doesn't run, replace the temperature switch.

REMOVAL AND INSTALLATION

Except Cadillac

1. Disconnect the negative battery cable.
2. Disconnect the wiring harness and remove the fan frame.
3. Remove the fan guard and the hose support, as required.
4. Remove the fan assembly from the radiator support.
To install:
5. Install the fan assembly to the radiator support.
6. If removed, install the fan guard and the hose support.
7. Install the fan frame and connect the wiring harness.
8. Connect the negative battery cable.

Cadillac

1. Disconnect the negative battery cable.
2. Raise and safely support the vehicle.
3. Disconnect the electrical connectors from the rear of the fan assemblies.
4. Remove the fan-to-lower radiator cradle bolts.
5. Lower the vehicle.
6. For right fan removal, remove the air conditioning accumulator to gain working clearance. Remove the air cleaner intake duct.
7. Remove the upper fan-to-radiator panel bolts and the upper radiator panel.

8. Remove the cooling fan assemblies.
To install:
9. Install the cooling fan(s). Replace the mounting bolts.
10. Replace the air cleaner intake duct.
11. Raise and safely support the vehicle.
12. Replace the fan-to-lower radiator cradle mounting bolts.
13. Connect the electrical connectors. Lower the vehicle.
14. Connect the negative battery cable.

Heater Core

REMOVAL AND INSTALLATION

Except Cadillac

1. Disconnect the negative battery cable. Drain the coolant into a clean container for reuse.
2. Remove the right side sound insulator and disconnect the heater hoses at the heater core.
3. Remove the center and lower instrument panel trim plates.
4. If equipped with electronic climate control, perform the following procedures:
   a. Disconnect the wires and the hose from the programmer.
   b. Remove the programmer linkage cover and linkage.
   c. Remove the programmer mounting bolts and the programmer.
5. Remove the heater core cover and heater core assembly.
To install:
6. Install the heater core assembly and heater core cover.
7. If equipped with electronic climate control, perform the following:
   a. Install the programmer mounting bolts and the programmer.
   b. Install the programmer linkage and linkage cover.
   c. Connect the wires and the hose to the programmer.
8. Install the center and lower instrument panel trim plates.
9. Install the right side sound insulator and disconnect the heater hoses at the heater core.
10. Connect the negative battery cable.
11. Fill the cooling system and check for leaks. Start the engine and allow to come to normal operating temperature. Recheck for leaks. Top-up coolant.

Cadillac

1. Disconnect the negative battery cable. Drain the coolant into a clean container for reuse.
2. Remove the right side sound insulator and disconnect the heater hoses at the heater core.
3. Remove the glove box assembly and the programmer shield.
4. Disconnect the air mix valve link, the programmer vacuum and electrical connectors.
5. Remove the heater core cover with the programmer attached.
6. Remove the heater core retaining screws and the heater core assembly.
7. Clean the mounting surfaces.
To install:
8. Install the heater core assembly. Replace the heater core cover with the programmer attached.
9. Connect the vacuum and electrical connections.
10. Connect the air mix valve link and adjust the air mix.
11. Install the glove box assembly and connect programmer shield.
12. Install the right side sound insulator and connect the heater hoses at the heater core.
13. Connect the negative battery cable.
14. Fill the cooling system and check for leaks. Start the engine and allow to come to normal operating temperature. Recheck for leaks. Top-up coolant.

Water Pump

REMOVAL AND INSTALLATION

3.8L Engine

1. Disconnect the negative battery cable. Drain the coolant into a clean container for reuse.
2. Remove the serpentine drive belt and the coolant hoses from the water pump.
3. Remove the water pump pulley bolts and the pulley; the long bolt can be removed through the access hole in the body side rail.
4. Remove the water pump-to-engine bolts and the pump.
To install:
5. Clean the gasket mounting surfaces. Install a new gasket and pump assembly.
6. Install the water pump-to-engine mounting bolts and tighten to 29 ft. lbs. (26 Nm) for the long bolts and 97 inch lbs. (11 Nm) for the short bolts.

7. Connect the coolant hoses to the water pump and install the serpentine drive belt.

8. Connect the negative battery cable.

9. Fill cooling system and check for leaks. Start the engine and allow to come to normal operating temperature. Recheck for leaks. Top-up coolant.

4.9L Engine

1. Disconnect the negative battery cable.

2. Drain the coolant into a clean container for reuse.

3. Remove the air conditioning accumulator from its bracket, move the bracket and accumulator aside without discharging the air conditioning system.

4. Remove the right cross brace and the serpentine drive belt.

5. Remove the water pump pulley-to-water pump bolts and the pulley.

6. Remove the water pump-to-engine bolts and the water pump.

7. Clean the gasket mounting surfaces.

To install:

8. Install a new gasket and pump the water pump pulley, do not fully tighten the screws.

9. Install the right cross brace.

10. Install the air conditioning accumulator bracket and accumulator.

11. Install the serpentine drive belt.

12. Tighten the water pump pulley bolts fully.

13. Connect the negative battery cable.

14. Fill cooling system and check for leaks. Start the engine and allow to come to normal operating temperature. Recheck for leaks. Top-up coolant.

Thermostat

REMOVAL AND INSTALLATION

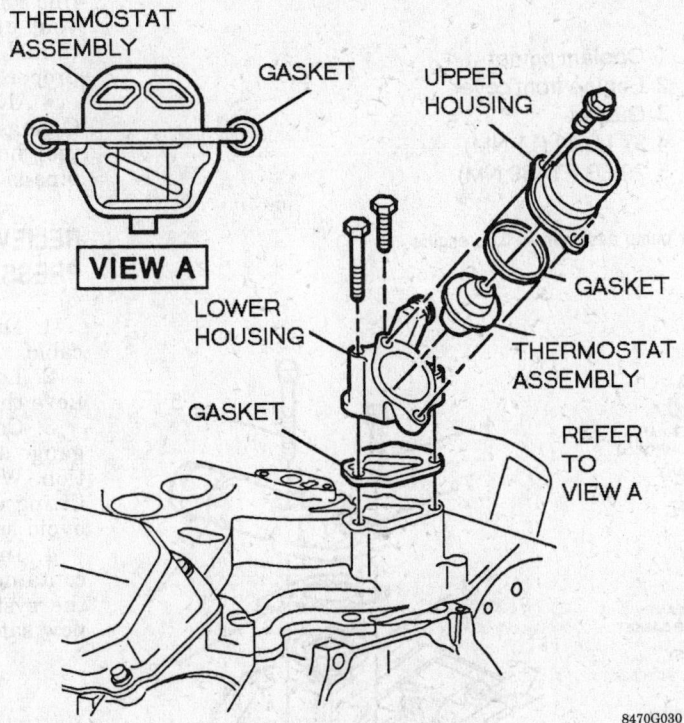

Thermostat location — 4.9L engine

8470G030

1. Disconnect the negative battery cable. Drain the coolant to below the thermostat housing.

2. Remove the thermostat housing mounting screws/bolts.

3. Remove the thermostat housing and lift out the thermostat.

To install:

4. Clean the mounting surfaces and install new gasket(s) or O-ring.

5. Install the thermostat and mounting screws/bolts.

6. Connect the negative battery cable.

7. Fill cooling system and check for leaks. Start the engine and allow to come to normal operating temperature. Recheck for leaks. Top-up coolant.

Cooling System Bleeding

To bleed air from the cooling system, remove the plug or sensor on the top of the thermostat housing. Fill the radiator with coolant until the coolant comes out the hole. Install the plug and continue to fill the radiator. This will vent all trapped air from the engine.

FUEL SYSTEM

Fuel System Service Precautions

Safety is the most important factor when performing fuel system maintenance. Failure to conduct maintenance and repairs in a safe manner may result in serious personal injury or death. Maintenance and testing of the vehicle's fuel system components

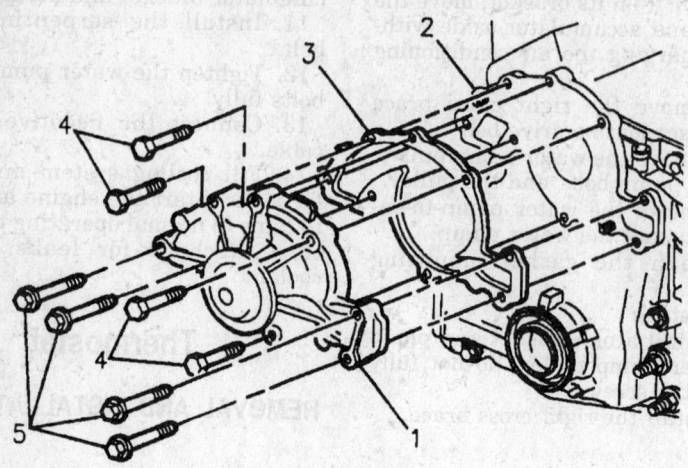

1. Coolant pump
2. Engine front cover
3. Gasket
4. 97 LB IN (11 NM)
5. 29 LB FT (39 NM)

8470G027

Water pump assembly — 3.8L engine

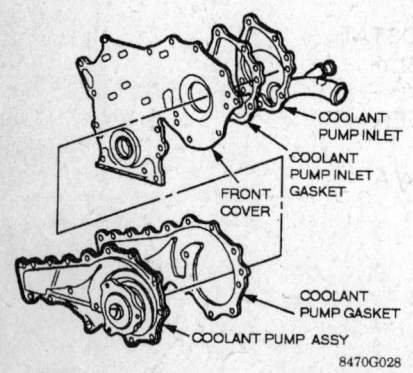

COOLANT PUMP INLET
COOLANT PUMP INLET GASKET
FRONT COVER
COOLANT PUMP GASKET
COOLANT PUMP ASSY

8470G028

Water pump assembly — 4.9L engine

can be accomplished safely and effectively by adhering to the following rules and guidelines.

• To avoid the possibility of fire and personal injury, always disconnect the negative battery cable unless the repair or test procedure requires that battery voltage be applied.

• Always relieve the fuel system pressure prior to disconnecting any fuel system component (injector, fuel rail, pressure regulator, etc.), fitting or fuel line connection. Exercise extreme caution whenever relieving fuel system pressure to avoid exposing skin, face and eyes to fuel spray.

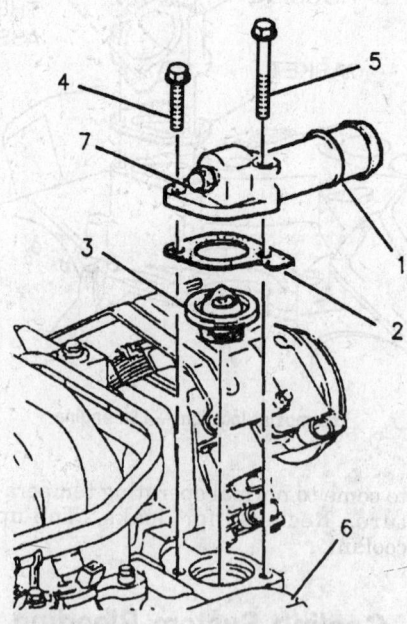

1. Outlet
2. Gasket
3. Thermostat
4. Bolt/screw
5. Bolt/screw
6. Intake manifold
7. Bleeder valve

8470G029

Thermostat location — 3.8L engine

Please be advised that fuel under pressure may penetrate the skin or any part of the body that it contacts.

• Always place a shop towel or cloth around the fitting or connection prior to loosening to absorb any excess fuel due to spillage. Ensure that all fuel spillage (should it occur) is quickly removed from engine surfaces. Ensure that all fuel soaked cloths or towels are deposited in a suitable waste container.

• Always keep a dry chemical (Class B) fire extinguisher near the work area.

• Do not allow fuel spray or fuel vapors to come into contact with a spark or open flame.

• Always use a backup wrench when loosening and tightening fuel line connection fittings. This will prevent unnecessary stress and torsion to fuel line piping. Always follow the proper torque specifications.

• Always replace worn fuel fitting O-rings with new. Do not substitute fuel hose or equivalent where fuel pipe is installed.

RELIEVING FUEL SYSTEM PRESSURE

1. Disconnect the negative battery cable.
2. Loosen the fuel filler cap to relieve the tank vapor pressure.
3. Connect a suitable fuel pressure gauge to the fuel pressure connection. Wrap a shop towel around the fitting while connecting the gauge to avoid spillage.
4. Install a bleed hose into a container and open the valve to bleed the system pressure. The system is now safe for servicing.

Fuel Tank

REMOVAL AND INSTALLATION

1. Disconnect the negative battery cable. Relieve the fuel system pressure.
2. Drain all fuel from the tank into a proper container.
3. Disconnect the sender assembly wires, tank filler and the vent hoses.
4. Disconnect the fuel pipe quick connectors.
5. Have an assistant support the fuel tank and disconnect the 2 tank retaining straps.
6. Disconnect the exhaust at the rear hanger and remove the tank from the vehicle.

To install:

7. Install the fuel tank to the vehicle and install the 2 retaining straps.

8. Raise the exhaust and connect the rear hangers.

9. Connect the fuel pipe quick connectors.

10. Connect the sender wires, the tank filler and vent hoses.

11. Refill the tank with fuel and connect the negative battery cable.

12. Inspect for any fuel leakage.

Fuel Filter

REMOVAL AND INSTALLATION

1. Disconnect the negative battery cable.

2. Raise and safely support the vehicle.

3. Disconnect the fuel lines from the filter at the fuel tank.

4. Remove the filter from the vehicle.

To install:

5. Install the filter and connect the fuel lines to the filter.

6. Secure the filter and lower the vehicle.

7. Connect the negative battery cable. Start the engine and check for leaks.

Electric Fuel Pump

PRESSURE TESTING

1. Disconnect the negative battery cable.

2. Raise and safely support the vehicle.

3. Connect a suitable fuel pressure gauge to the fuel line fitting connection at the fuel tank.

4. Lower the vehicle and connect the negative battery cable. Measure the fuel pressure while cranking the engine.

5. Raise and safely support the vehicle. Remove the fuel pressure gauge.

6. Lower the vehicle, run engine and check connections for leaks.

REMOVAL AND INSTALLATION

The electric fuel pump is located in the fuel tank.

1. Relieve the fuel system pressure. Disconnect the negative battery cable.

2. Drain the fuel from the tank. Raise and safely support the vehicle.

3. Support the tank and disconnect the tank retaining straps.

4. Lower the exhaust at the rear hanger.

5. Lower the tank enough to disconnect the wires, hoses and ground strap, if equipped. Remove the fuel tank.

6. Using a brass drift and a hammer, drive (turn) the cam lock ring-to-fuel tank counterclockwise and lift the assembly from the fuel tank.

7. Pull the fuel pump up into the attaching hose while pulling outward away from the bottom support. Take care to prevent damage to the rubber sound insulator and strainer during removal. Once the pump assembly is clear of the bottom support, pull it out of the rubber connector.

To install:

8. Install the pump into the fuel tank. Connect the fuel lines, wires and the ground strap, if equipped.

9. When installing the fuel tank, make sure all rubber sound isolators or anti-squeak spacers are replaced in their original locations.

10. Support the tank and install the tank retaining straps.

11. Lower the vehicle. Refill the fuel tank.

12. Connect the negative battery cable. Start the engine and check for fuel leaks.

Fuel Injection

ADJUSTMENTS

Idle speed and idle mixture are controlled automatically by the Electronic Control Module (ECM) and are not adjustable.

Fuel Injector

REMOVAL AND INSTALLATION

3.8L Engine

1. Properly relieve the fuel system pressure. Remove the air cleaner assembly. Disconnect the negative battery cable.

2. Label and disconnect the fuel injector electrical connectors.

3. Remove the fuel rail retaining bolts. Disconnect the fuel injector electrical connectors and the fuel supply lines.

4. Remove the fuel rail.

5. Separate the injector(s) from the fuel rail.

To install:

6. Replace the fuel injector O-rings.

7. Install the injector(s) into the fuel rail.

8. Install the fuel rail.

9. Install the fuel rail retaining bolts. Connect the the fuel injector electrical connectors and the fuel supply line.

10. Install the air cleaner assembly.

11. Connect the negative battery cable.

4.9L Engine

1. Disconnect the negative battery cable.

2. Position the power steering pump aside.

3. Relieve the fuel system pressure.

4. Disconnect the vacuum lines from the pressure regulator and the base assembly.

5. Disconnect the fuel feed line from the rear of the rail assembly. Discard the O-ring.

6. Remove the fuel return line. Discard the O-ring.

7. Disconnect the electrical connectors at the front and the rear of the rail assembly.

8. Remove the rail support bracket mounting bolts and remove the rail assembly from the intake manifold.

9. Disconnect the electrical connector from the fuel injector by pushing in the clip while pulling the connector body away from the injector.

10. Disconnect the injector retaining clip. Discard the clip.

11. Remove the fuel injector assembly, by twisting back and forth while removing. Remove and discard the O-rings from the injectors.

To install:

12. Lubricate new O-rings and install on the injector assembly.

13. Install a new injector clip on the injector.

14. Install the fuel injector into the fuel rail socket. Push in to engage the retainer clip with the fuel rail cup.

NOTE: The electrical connectors should be facing the engine front for injectors 1–4. The connectors should be facing the rear of the engine for injectors 5–8.

15. Install the electrical connector to the injector assembly.

16. Install the fuel rail assembly and connect the support bracket mounting bolts.

17. Connect the electrical connectors at the front and rear of the rail assembly.

18. Install the fuel return line, using a new O-ring.

19. Connect the fuel feed line at the rear of the rail assembly, using a new O-ring.

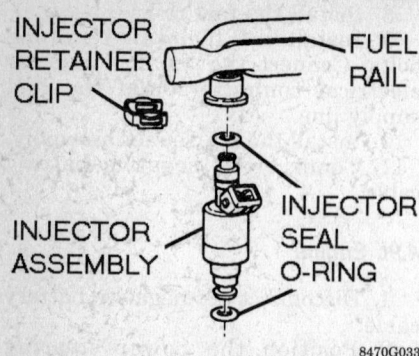

Fuel injector assembly — 4.9L engine

8470G033

20. Connect the vacuum lines to the base assembly and the pressure regulator.

21. Reposition the power steering pump and connect the negative battery cable.

22. Start the engine and check for leaks.

EMISSION CONTROLS

Emission Warning Lamps

The dash mounted "Service Soon" and "Service Now" lights are used to indicate a malfunction that the computer has detected in the vehicle's operation. The malfunctions can be related to the operating sensors or the Electronic Control Module (ECM). The service light will go out automatically if the trouble is cleared or intermittent.

The ECM, however will automatically store the trouble code until the diagnostic system is "Cleared".

CLEARING ECM TROUBLE CODES

Except Cadillac

With the ignition switch in the OFF position, disconnect battery voltage to the ECM for at least 30 seconds by performing 1 of the following:

1. Remove the ECM fuse from the fuse panel.
2. Disconnect the ECM pigtail.
3. Disconnect the negative battery cable.

NOTE: Disconnecting the negative battery cable should only be done as a last resort as it will

also erase the memories for the digital radio, digital clock, trip odometer etc.

Cadillac

1. Turn the key to the ON position.
2. Simultaneously press the OFF and HI buttons on the climate control panel until E.O.O appears in the readout.
3. To clear the Body Computer Module (BCM) codes, depress the OFF and LO buttons simultaneously until F.O.O appears.
4. After E.O.O or F.O.O is displayed, .7.0 will appear. With the .7.0 displayed turn the ignition OFF for at least 10 seconds before re-entering the diagnostic mode.

ENGINE MECHANICAL

NOTE: Disconnecting the negative battery cable on some vehicles may interfere with the functions of the on board computer systems and may require the computer to undergo a relearning process, once the negative battery cable is reconnected.

Engine Assembly

REMOVAL AND INSTALLATION

3.8L Engine

VIN L AND 1

1. Disconnect the negative battery cable. Using a scribing tool, match-mark the hood hinges and remove the hood.
2. Depressurize the fuel system.
3. Drain the coolant and the engine oil from the vehicle.
4. Remove the strut tower cross brace. Disconnect the windshield washer, radiator and heater supply hoses.
5. Disconnect the wiring to the starter. Disconnect the main wiring at the harness near the relay center.
6. Remove the drive belt(s). Disconnect the power steering pump and set off to the side.
7. Remove the air inlet duct and the air cleaner assembly. Disconnect the throttle cable from the linkage.

8. Disconnect the wiring harness connectors from the MAT sensor, the throttle position switch, the idle air control valve and the oxygen sensor.
9. Disconnect the ignition coil ground strap from the fender inner panel. Disconnect the fuel lines from the fuel rail and from the pressure regulator.
10. Disconnect the emission control hoses from the throttle body connections.
11. Disconnect the brake booster and heater control hoses from the vacuum connections.
12. Raise and safely support the vehicle.
13. Disconnect the exhaust pipe from the right side manifold and disconnect the vacuum lines from the cruise control and servo assembly.
14. Attach an engine lifting device to the engine and raise so it begins to support the engine.
15. Disconnect the air conditioner compressor and tie back away from the engine. If equipped with an engine oil cooler, disconnect the cooler lines.
16. Remove the front engine mount and remove the right front engine to transaxle bracket.
17. Support the transaxle and remove the engine to transaxle bolts. Remove the flywheel cover.
18. Remove the torque converter to flywheel bolts and use a scribe to mark the proper flywheel to torque converter relationship.
19. Separate the engine from the transaxle and remove the engine from the vehicle.

To install:
20. Install the engine in the vehicle.
21. Install the engine to transaxle bolts. Install the right front engine to transaxle bracket.
22. Install the front engine mount.
23. Install the torque converter to flywheel bolts, making sure flywheel and converter are aligned as before.
24. Install the flywheel cover and the oil cooler lines, if equipped.
25. Install the air conditioning compressor. Connect the cruise control and vacuum hoses at the servo.
26. Connect the exhaust pipe to the right side manifold.
27. Connect the wiring harness connectors to the MAT sensor, throttle position switch, idle air control valve and the oxygen sensor.
28. Connect the throttle cable to the linkage and to the mounting bracket. Install the air intake duct and the air cleaner.
29. Install the power steering pump and drive belt(s).

30. Connect the main wiring harness to the engine and battery connectors.

31. Connect the wiring to the starter and connect the windshield washer, radiator and heater supply hoses.

32. Fill the coolant to the proper level and refill the engine oil.

33. Connect the negative battery cable.

34. Start the engine and check for fluid or oil leakage.

4.9L Engine

1. Disconnect the negative battery cable. Drain the coolant into a clean container for reuse.

2. Remove the air cleaner. Using a scribing tool, matchmark the hood to the support brackets and remove the hose.

3. If equipped with air conditioning, perform the following procedures:
   a. Remove the hose strap from the right-strut tower.
   b. Remove the accumulator from its bracket and position it aside.
   c. Remove the canister hoses from the accumulator bracket.
   d. Remove the accumulator bracket from the wheel house.

4. Remove the cooling fans, the accessory drive belt, the radiator and heater hoses.

5. Label and disconnect the electrical connectors from the following items:
   a. Oil pressure switch
   b. Coolant temperature sensor
   c. Distributor
   d. EGR solenoid
   e. Engine temperature switch

6. Label and disconnect the cables from the following items:
   a. Accelerator
   b. Cruise control linkage
   c. Transaxle Throttle Valve (TV) cable

7. If equipped with cruise control, remove the diaphragm with the bracket attached and move it aside.

8. Remove the vacuum supply hose and the exhaust crossover pipe.

9. Disconnect the oil cooler lines from the oil filter adapter, the oil line cooler bracket from the transaxle and position them aside.

10. Remove the air cleaner mounting bracket.

11. Properly relieve the fuel system pressure. Disconnect the fuel lines from the throttle body. Remove the fuel line bracket from the transaxle and secure the fuel lines aside.

12. Remove the small vacuum line from the brake booster.

13. Label and disconnect the AIR solenoid electrical and hose connections. Remove the AIR valves with the bracket.

14. Label and disconnect the electrical connectors from the following:
   a. Idle Speed Control (ISC) motor
   b. Throttle Position Switch (TPS)
   c. Fuel injectors
   d. Manifold Air Temperature (MAT) sensor
   e. Oxygen sensor
   f. Electric Fuel Evaporation (EFE) grid
   g. Alternator bracket

15. Remove the power steering pump hose strap from the stud-headed bolt in front of the right cylinder head and the stud-headed bolt.

16. Remove the AIR pipe clip located near the No. 2 spark plug, if equipped.

17. Remove the power steering pump and belt tensioner with bracket attached; wire them aside.

18. Raise and safely support the vehicle.

19. Label and disconnect the electrical connectors from the starter and the ground wire from the cylinder block.

20. Remove the 2 flywheel covers. Remove the starter-to-engine bolts and the starter. Matchmark the flywheel-to-torque converter location. Remove the 3 flywheel-to-torque converter bolts and slide the converter back into the bell housing.

21. If equipped with air conditioning, perform the following procedures:
   a. Remove the compressor lower dust shield.
   b. Remove the right front wheel/tire assembly and outer wheelhouse plastic shield.
   c. Remove the compressor-to-bracket bolts and lower the compressor from the engine. Do not disconnect the refrigerant lines.

22. Remove the lower radiator hose.

23. From the lower right front of the engine and cradle, remove the driveline vibration damper with the brackets, if equipped, and the engine-to-transaxle bracket bolts. Pull the alternator wire with the plastic cover down and aside.

24. Remove the exhaust pipe-to-manifold bolts with the springs attached and the AIR pipe-to-converter bracket from the exhaust manifold stud.

NOTE: Be careful not to lose the springs when detaching the exhaust pipe.

25. Remove the lower right side bell housing-to-engine bolt. Lower the vehicle.

26. Using a vertical engine hoist, attach it to the engine and support it.

27. Remove the upper bell housing-to-engine bolts and left front engine mount bracket-to-engine bolts. Remove the engine from the vehicle.

To install:

28. Raise the transaxle with a separate jack to engage the engine.

29. Install the engine into the vehicle, using a suitable engine hoist. Engage the dowels on the block with the transaxle case.

30. Install the transaxle bell housing-to-engine mounting bolts.

31. Lower and remove the floor jack assembly from the transaxle.

32. Lower the engine, making sure it is seated on the mount properly.

33. Remove the engine hoist. Raise and safely support the vehicle.

34. Lower the right hand transaxle bell housing-to-engine bolt. Support the engine.

35. Install the left front engine mount bracket-to-engine bolts and the flexplate-to-converter bolts.

36. Replace the flexplate cover.

37. Install the starter motor and connect the electrical wires to the starter.

38. Connect the AIR pipe-to-converter bracket to the exhaust manifold stud.

39. Install the exhaust pipe to manifold bolts and spring.

40. Connect the alternator and install the plastic cover. Install the the right front engine-to-transaxle bracket and tighten the bolts to 30 ft. lbs. (41 Nm).

41. Install the lower radiator hose and replace the air conditioning compressor mounting bolts.

42. Install the air conditioning compressor lower dust shield and the outer wheel house plastic shield.

43. Install the right front tire and wheel assembly. Lower the vehicle.

44. Install the power steering pump and the belt tensioner. Replace the stud headed bolt.

45. Install the power steering hose strap to the stud headed bolt in front of the cylinder head.

46. Connect the electrical connectors to the following:
   a. Idle Speed Control (ISC) motor
   b. Throttle Position Switch (TPS)
   c. Fuel injectors
   d. Manifold Air Temperature (MAT) sensor
   e. Oxygen sensor

f. Electric Fuel Evaporator (EFE) grid

g. Alternator bracket

47. Replace the air valve and bracket. Connect the air solenoid electrical and hose connections.

48. Connect the vacuum line to the brake booster.

49. Connect the fuel lines at the throttle body and replace the fuel line bracket at the transaxle.

50. Replace the air cleaner mounting bracket and connect the oil cooler lines to the oil filter adapter.

51. Connect the oil cooler line bracket at the transaxle. Replace the exhaust crossover pipe.

52. Replace the cruise control diaphragm and connect the vacuum lines.

53. Connect the accelerator, cruise control and the transaxle throttle valve cables to the throttle lever.

54. Connect the wire connectors to the following:

a. Oil pressure switch

b. Coolant temperature sensor

c. Distributor

d. EGR solenoid

e. Engine temperature switch

55. Replace the accessory drive belt, heater hoses and upper radiator hose.

56. Install the cooling fans and connect the air conditioning accumulator bracket.

57. Install the air conditioning accumulator and connect the wires and hoses.

58. Install the hood assembly and replace the air cleaner.

59. Refill the engine coolant. Connect the negative battery cable.

60. Start the engine, allow it to reach normal operating temperatures and check for leaks.

Engine Mounts

REMOVAL AND INSTALLATION

3.8L Engine

1. Disconnect the negative battery cable.

2. Raise and support the vehicle safely.

3. Remove the engine mount through bolt. Using a vertical lifting device, attach it to the engine and raise the engine.

4. Remove the engine mount bolts and the mount.

To install:

5. Install the engine mount and the mount bolts.

6. Lower the engine into the engine mount. Install the engine mount through bolt.

7. Lower the vehicle.

8. Connect the negative battery cable.

4.9L Engine

RIGHT

1. Disconnect the negative battery cable and brace from the engine bracket to the engine.

2. Remove the nuts securing the engine bracket to the mount.

3. Raise and safely support the vehicle.

4. Support the vehicle with stands at each front frame horn.

5. Remove the nuts on the engine mount securing to the frame.

6. Remove the nuts securing the transaxle mount to the mount.

7. Remove the nuts securing the transaxle mount to the frame bracket.

8. Raise the engine using an engine support tool.

9. Raise the engine until the bracket is free of the engine mount. Remove the stud and the bolts that secure the bracket to the block. Remove the mount and bracket by pulling forward.

10. Remove the transaxle mounting bracket from the transaxle.

11. Remove the mount assembly.

To install:

12. Position the engine mount and bracket, in place between the transaxle and frame and secure the bracket to the transaxle with the 2 bolts and tighten to 34 ft. lbs. (46 Nm).

13. While lowering the engine, guide the motor mount into location and install the engine mount to frame and transaxle mount to frame bracket with the 2 nuts each and tighten to 22 ft. lbs. (30 Nm).

14. Install the nuts to the engine mount studs and the nuts to transaxle mount studs and tighten to 22 ft. lbs. (30 Nm).

15. Remove the brace from the engine bracket to engine.

16. Remove the stands and lower the hoist. Connect the negative battery cable.

LEFT

1. Raise the vehicle and support it safely. Disconnect the negative battery cable.

2. Support the vehicle with stands at each front frame horn.

3. Remove the nut securing the mount to the transaxle bracket and

nuts securing the mount to the frame.

4. Lift the engine using engine support tool.

5. Remove the bolts securing the bracket to the transaxle.

6. Raise the engine assembly until the brackets are free.

7. Remove the mount and bracket by pulling it upward.

To install:

8. Position the engine mount and bracket in place between the transaxle and frame. Tighten the bracket to 41 ft. lbs. (56 Nm) and nuts to 22 ft lbs. (30 Nm).

9. Lower the transaxle onto the mount until it is seated.

10. Install the nut securing the mount to the bracket and tighten to 22 ft. lbs. (30 Nm).

11. Connect the negative battery cable.

Cylinder Head

REMOVAL AND INSTALLATION

3.8L Engines

1. Disconnect the negative battery cable.

2. Remove the intake and exhaust manifolds.

3. Remove the valve cover.

4. Label and disconnect the ignition module wires, spark plug wires and alternator bracket. Remove air conditioning compressor bracket bolts.

5. Remove the power steering pump, tensioner assembly and the fuel line heat shield.

6. Remove the rocker arm assemblies, guide plate and the pushrods.

7. Remove the cylinder head bolts and remove the cylinder head.

8. Clean all gasket mating surfaces and the cylinder head bolt holes in the block.

To install:

9. Install the cylinder head gasket and head onto the block.

10. Install the cylinder head bolts and tighten as follows:

a. Tighten the cylinder head bolts, in sequence, to 35 ft. lbs. (47 Nm).

b. Rotate each bolt 130 degrees, in sequence.

c. Rotate the center 4 bolts an additional 30 degrees, in sequence.

11. Install the pushrods, guide plate and the rocker arm assemblies. Tighten the rocker arm pedestal bolts to 28 ft. lbs. (38 Nm).

12. Install the intake manifold, exhaust manifold and the valve covers.

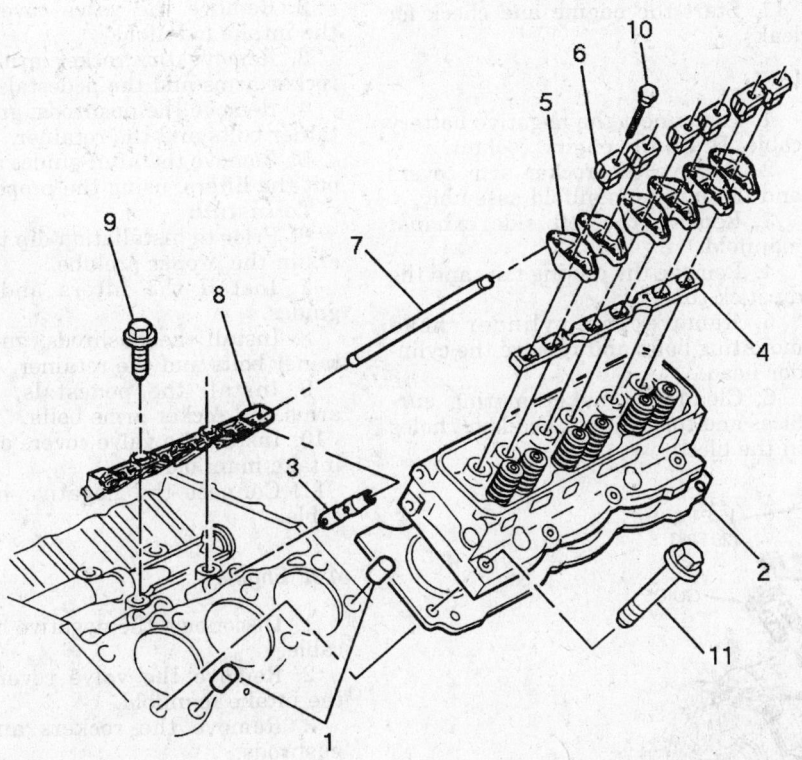

1. Dowel pin
2. Head gasket
3. Valve lifter
4. Pushrod guide
5. Rocker arm
6. Rocker arm bearing
7. Pushrod
8. Lifter guide retainer
9. Bolt
10. Bolt
11. Head bolt

8470G040

Cylinder head — 3.8L non–supercharged engine

1. Dowel pin
2. Head gasket
3. Valve lifter
4. Pivot retainer
5. Rocker arm
6. Rocker arm pivot
7. Pushrod
8. Lifter guide
9. Bolt
10. Bolt
11. Head bolt

8470G041

Cylinder head — 3.8L supercharged engine

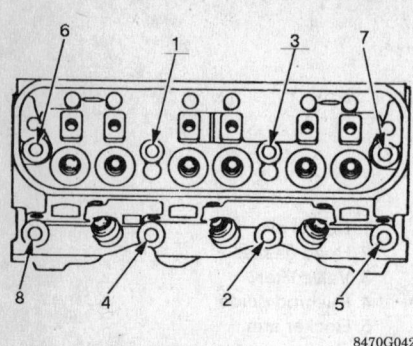

Cylinder head torque sequence — 3.8L engine

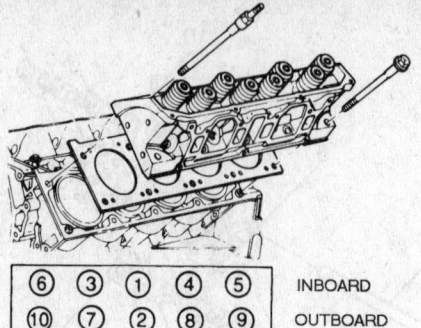

6	3	1	4	5	INBOARD
10	7	2	8	9	OUTBOARD

8470G044

Cylinder head torque sequence — 4.9L engine

13. Replace the air conditioning compressor bracket bolt and tighten to 52 ft. lbs. (71 Nm).

14. Install the alternator support bracket and replace the ignition module and spark plug wires.

15. Install the tensioner, power steering pump and the fuel line heat shield.

16. Connect the negative battery cable. Start the engine and check for leaks.

4.9L Engine

RIGHT

1. Disconnect the negative battery cable. Drain the coolant into a clean container for reuse. Properly relieve the fuel system pressure.

2. Remove the rocker arm covers and the intake manifold assembly.

3. Remove the right side exhaust manifold and disconnect the engine lift bracket and AIR pump bracket.

4. Remove the cylinder head bolts in the reverse order of the tightening sequence. Remove the cylinder head.

5. Clean all gasket mating surfaces and the cylinder head bolt holes in the block.

To install:

6. Install the cylinder head gasket and the cylinder head.

7. Tighten the cylinder head bolts as follows:

    a. Tighten the cylinder head bolts, in sequence, to 38 ft. lbs. (50 Nm).

    b. Tighten the cylinder head bolts, in sequence, to 68 ft. lbs. (90 Nm).

    c. Tighten cylinder head bolts 1, 3 and 4 to 90 ft. lbs. (120 Nm).

8. Install the engine lift bracket and the air pump bracket.

9. Install the exhaust manifold, intake manifold and the rocker arm covers.

10. Refill the engine coolant. Connect the negative battery cable.

11. Start the engine and check for leaks.

LEFT

1. Disconnect the negative battery cable. Drain the engine coolant.

2. Remove the rocker arm covers and the intake manifold assembly.

3. Remove the left side exhaust manifold.

4. Remove the cooling fans and the dipstick tube.

5. Remove the cylinder head mounting bolts and remove the cylinder head.

6. Clean all gasket mating surfaces and the cylinder head bolt holes in the block.

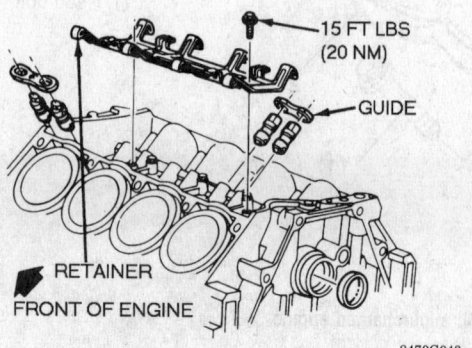

15 FT LBS (20 NM)

GUIDE

RETAINER

FRONT OF ENGINE

8470G043

Lifter guides and retainer — 4.9L engine

To install:

7. Install a new head gasket over the dowels on the cylinder block.

8. Install the cylinder head and tighten the bolts as follows:

    a. Tighten the cylinder head bolts, in sequence, to 38 ft. lbs. (50 Nm).

    b. Tighten the cylinder head bolts, in sequence, to 68 ft. lbs. (90 Nm).

    c. Tighten cylinder head bolts 1, 3 and 4 to 90 ft. lbs. (120 Nm).

9. Install the dipstick tube and replace the cooling fans.

10. Install the exhaust manifold, intake manifold and the rocker arm covers.

11. Refill the engine coolant. Connect the negative battery cable.

12. Start the engine and check for leaks.

Valve Lifters

REMOVAL AND INSTALLATION

3.8L Engine

1. Disconnect the negative battery cable.

2. Remove the valve covers and the intake manifold.

3. Remove the rocker arm bolts, rocker arms and the pedestals.

4. Remove the pushrods, guide retainer bolts and the retainer.

5. Remove the lifter guides and lift out the lifters, using the proper tool.

To install:

6. Prior to installation dip the lifters in the proper prelube.

7. Install the lifters and lifter guides.

8. Install the pushrods, guide retainer bolts and the retainer.

9. Install the pedestals, rocker arms and rocker arms bolts.

10. Install the valve covers and the intake manifold.

11. Connect the negative battery cable.

4.9L Engine

1. Disconnect the negative battery cable.

2. Remove the valve covers and the intake manifold.

3. Remove the rockers and the pushrods.

4. Disconnect the valve guide retainers.

5. Remove the valve lifter guides and pull out the lifters, using the proper tool.

To install:

6. Prior to installation dip the lifters in the proper prelube.

7. Install the valve lifters and lifter guides.

8. Connect the valve guide retainer. Tighten the retainer bolts to 15 ft. lbs.

9. Install the rockers and the pushrods.

10. Install the valve covers and the intake manifold.

11. Connect the negative battery cable.

Rocker Arms

REMOVAL AND INSTALLATION

3.8L Engines

RIGHT

1. Disconnect the negative battery cable. Remove the accessory drive belt.

2. Loosen the power steering pump bolts and slide the pump forward. Disconnect the power steering bracket.

3. Disconnect the EGR pipe and remove EGR valve and adapter from the throttle body.

4. Disconnect the spark plug wires and remove the rocker arm cover bolts and cover.

5. Remove the rocker arm pedestal retaining bolts and lift out the pedestal and rocker arm assembly.

To install:

6. Install the pedestal, rocker arm assembly and rocker arm pedestal retaining bolts. Tighten the pedestal bolts to 28 ft. lbs. (38 Nm).

7. Install the rocker arm cover and bolts. Tighten to 88 inch lbs. (10 Nm). Connect the spark plug wires.

8. Install the EGR valve and adapter to the throttle body. Connect the EGR pipe.

9. Connect the power steering bracket. Slide the power steering pump into position and install the bolts.

10. Install the serpentine drive belt. Connect the negative battery cable.

LEFT

1. Disconnect the negative battery cable. Remove the accessory drive belt.

2. Remove the alternator mounting bracket bolt and bracket.

3. Disconnect the spark plug wires. Remove the valve cover bolts and the valve cover.

4. Remove the rocker arm pedestal retaining bolts and lift out the pedestal and rocker arm assembly.

To install:

5. Install the rocker arm pedestal, rocker arm assembly and retaining bolts. Tighten to 28 ft. lbs. (38 Nm).

6. Install the valve cover and bolts. Tighten to 88 inch lbs. (10 Nm). Connect the spark plug wires.

7. Install the alternator mounting bracket and bolt.

8. Connect the negative battery cable.

4.9L Engine

RIGHT

1. Disconnect the negative battery cable. Remove the air cleaner and the AIR management valve with bracket, move the assembly aside.

2. From the throttle body, remove the Manifold Absolute Pressure (MAP) hose.

3. Remove the right side spark plug wires and conduit.

4. Remove the fuel vapor canister pipe bracket from the valve cover stay.

5. Drain the cooling system to a level below the thermostat housing. Remove the heater hose from the thermostat housing and move it aside.

6. Remove the brake booster vacuum hose from the intake manifold.

7. Remove the rocker arm cover-to-cylinder screws, the cover and the gasket/seals. Discard the gasket.

8. Remove the rocker arm pivot-to-rocker arm support bolts, the pivots and the rocker arms.

9. If necessary, remove the rocker arm support-to-cylinder head nuts/bolts and the support.

10. Clean the gasket mounting surfaces. Inspect the parts for wear and/or damage and replace the parts, if necessary.

To install:

11. Lubricate the parts with clean engine oil, use a new gasket and coat both sides with RTV sealant, install RTV sealant between the intake manifold-to-cylinder head mating surfaces.

12. Install the rocker arms and pivots to the rocker arm support. Tighten the pivot bolts to 22 ft. lbs. (30 Nm).

13. Install the rocker arm support and place each pushrod into the rocker arm seat.

14. Install the rocker arm support retaining nuts, tighten to 37 ft. lbs. (50 Nm).

15. Install the rocker arm support retaining bolts, tighten to 7 ft. lbs. (9 Nm).

16. Install the rocker arm cover seals and place the molded seal into the groove in the rocker arm cover.

17. Install the rocker arm cover and tighten the mounting screws to 8 ft. lbs. (11 Nm).

18. Connect the brake booster vacuum hose and the EECS pipe bracket.

19. Install the spark plug wires and conduit. Connect the MAP hose to the throttle body.

20. Install the air management and bracket assembly.

21. Replace the heater hose and air cleaner assembly.

22. Connect the negative battery cable. Start the engine and check for leaks.

LEFT

1. Disconnect the negative battery cable. Remove the air cleaner, the PCV valve, the throttle return spring and the serpentine drive belt.

2. Loosen the lower power steering pump bracket nuts.

3. Remove the power steering pump, the belt tensioner, the bracket-to-engine bolts and the bracket. Move the power steering pump assembly toward the front of the vehicle; do not disconnect the pressure hose.

4. Remove the left side spark plug wires and conduit.

5. Remove the rocker arm cover-to-cylinder screws, the cover and the gasket/seals. Discard the gasket.

6. Remove the rocker arm pivot-to-rocker arm support bolts, the pivots and the rocker arms.

7. If necessary, remove the rocker arm support-to-cylinder head nuts/bolts and the support.

8. Clean the gasket mounting surfaces. Inspect the parts for wear and/or damage and replace the parts, if necessary.

To install:

9. Lubricate the parts with clean engine oil, use a new gasket, coat both sides with RTV sealant, install RTV sealant between the intake manifold-to-cylinder head mating surfaces.

10. Install the rocker arms and pivots to the rocker arm support. Tighten the pivot bolts to 22 ft. lbs. (30 Nm).

11. Install the rocker arm support and place each pushrod into the rocker arm seat.

12. Install the rocker arm support retaining nuts, tighten to 37 ft. lbs. (50 Nm).

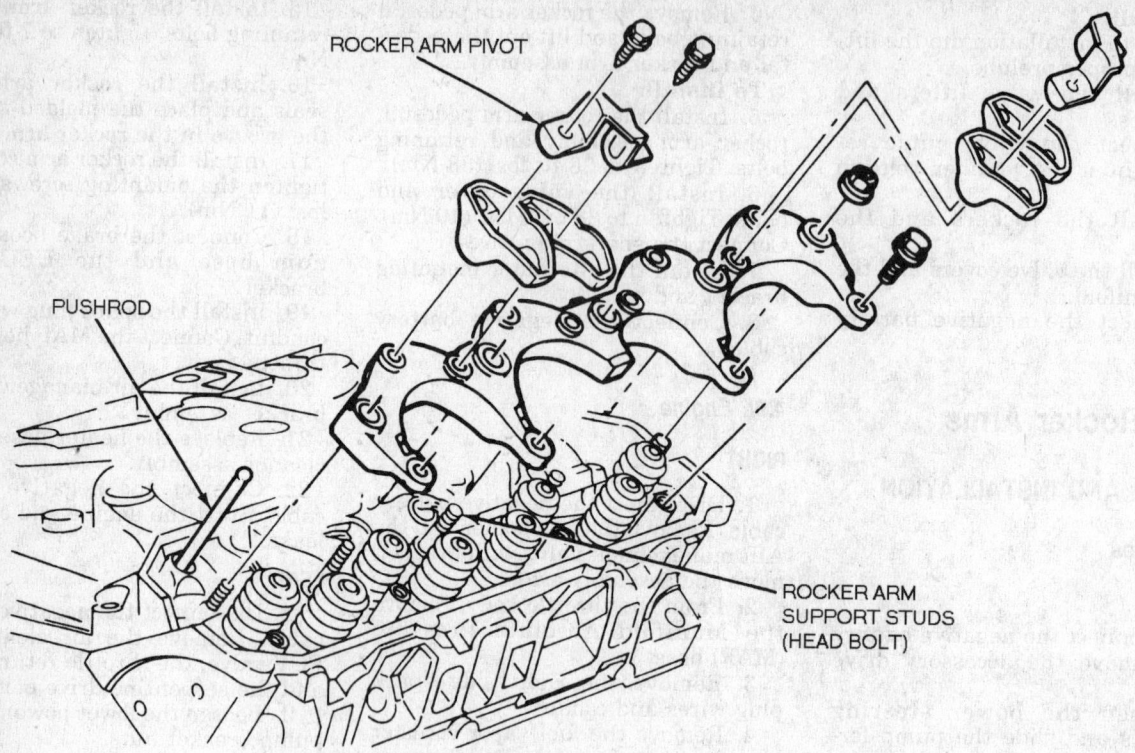

Rocker arm assembly — 4.9L engine

8470G045

13. Install the rocker arm support retaining bolts, tighten to 7 ft. lbs. (9 Nm).

14. Install the rocker arm cover seals and place the molded seal into the groove in the rocker arm cover.

15. Install the rocker arm cover and tighten the mounting screws to 8 ft. lbs. (11 Nm).

16. Install the spark plug wires and conduit.

17. Install the power steering pump, belt tensioner and bracket assembly. Replace the accessory drive belt.

18. Install the throttle return spring and the PCV valve.

19. Install the air cleaner and connect the negative battery cable.

20. Start the engine and check for leaks.

Intake Manifold

REMOVAL AND INSTALLATION

3.8L (VIN 1 and L) Engines

1. Disconnect the negative battery cable. Relieve the fuel system pressure.

2. Remove the fuel injector sight shield and the air intake duct.

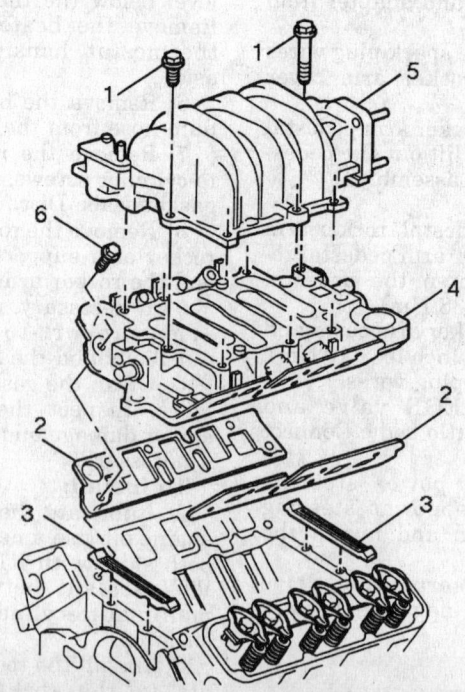

1. Bolt, intake manifold upper
2. Intake manifold gasket
3. Intake manifold seal
4. Intake manifold lower
5. Intake manifold upper
6. Bolt, intake manifold lower

8470G050

Intake manifold and gaskets — 3.8L (VIN 1 and L) engines

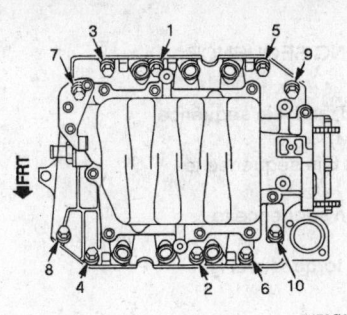

8470G051

**Intake manifold bolt torque sequence —
3.8L (VIN 1 and L) engines**

3. Remove and tag the right side spark plug wires. Remove the fuel rail assembly.

4. Remove the exhaust crossover heat shield.

5. Remove the cable bracket to the cylinder head mounting bolt.

6. Remove the power steering pump support bracket. Remove the alternator bracket and move the alternator out of the way.

7. Remove the heater pipes and bypass hose.

8. Remove the intake manifold bolts and the intake manifold assembly.

NOTE: On the supercharged engine (VIN 1), the supercharger does not have to be removed when removing the intake manifold. It may be left together as a complete assembly.

To install:

9. Install the intake manifold bolts and tighten the bolts to 88 inch lbs. (10 Nm) twice in the proper sequence.

10. Connect the bypass hose and the heater pipe.

11. Install the alternator bracket and return the alternator to it's proper position.

12. Install the power steering pump support bracket. Install the cable bracket to the cylinder head.

13. Install the exhaust crossover heat shield and the fuel rail.

14. Install the right side spark plug wires and install the fuel injector sight shield and air intake duct.

15. Connect the negative battery cable.

4.9L Engine

1. Disconnect the negative terminal from the battery. Drain the cooling system to a level below the intake manifold. Disconnect the upper radiator hose from the thermostat housing.

2. Remove the air cleaner and the serpentine drive belt. Label and disconnect the spark plug wires from the spark plugs.

3. Remove the upper power steering pump bracket-to-engine bolts and loosen the lower nuts.

4. Disconnect the following electrical connections and position the wiring harness aside: distributor, oil pressure switch, EGR solenoid, coolant sensor, mass airflow temperature sensor, throttle position sensor, 4-way connector at the distributor, electric fuel evaporator grid, idle speed control motor and fuel injectors.

5. From the throttle lever, disconnect the accelerator, cruise control, if equipped, and transaxle TV cables.

6. Using a shop rag at the fuel line Schraeder valve (test port), bleed off the fuel pressure. Disconnect the fuel inlet and return lines from the throttle body. From the transaxle, remove the fuel line brackets and move the lines aside; disconnect the modulator vacuum line.

7. Disconnect the heater hose from the nipple at the rear of the intake manifold.

8. From the intake manifold, remove the cruise control bracket, if equipped. Remove the vacuum line from the left rear engine lift bracket and the throttle body.

9. Disconnect the electrical connectors from the alternator and AIR management solenoid. Remove the alternator, the idler pulley, the AIR management valve/bracket and EGR solenoid/bracket. Disconnect the hose from the MAP hose.

10. From the right cylinder head, remove the power steering pipe and the AIR pipe. Raise and safely support the vehicle.

11. Drain the engine oil and remove the oil filter. Lower the vehicle.

12. Remove the distributor. Remove both rocker arm covers. Remove the rocker arm support with the rocker arms intact by first alternately and evenly removing the 4 bolts followed by the 5 nuts. Keep the pushrods in sequence so they may be reassembled in their original positions.

13. If equipped with air conditioning, partially remove the compressor; do not discharge the system. Remove the vacuum harness connections from the TVS at the rear of the intake manifold.

14. Remove the intake manifold bolts and remove the 2 bolts securing the lower thermostat housing to the front cover. Remove the engine lift brackets or bend them aside.

15. Remove the intake manifold and lower the thermostat housing as an assembly by lifting it straight up off the dowels.

16. Clean the gasket mounting surfaces.

To install:

17. Install new gaskets and apply the proper RTV sealant to the 4 corners where the end seals meet.

18. Install the intake manifold, using new gaskets.

19. Tighten the mounting bolts as follows:

   a. Torque the No. 1–4 bolts, in sequence, to 8 ft. lbs. (12 Nm).

   b. Torque the No. 5–16 bolts, in sequence, to 8 ft. lbs. (12 Nm).

   c. Retorque all bolts, in sequence, to 12 ft. lbs. (16 Nm).

   d. Repeat Step c until torque level is maintained.

20. Install the right side engine lift brackets. Install the alternator and idler pulley mounting bracket and replace the brackets at the right cylinder head.

21. Install the pushrods and the rocker arm support assemblies.

22. Install the rocker arm covers, using new seals.

23. Replace the EGR valve and bracket assembly. Connect the MAP hose.

24. Connect the wire connectors at the ISC motor, TPS, the fuel injectors and the MAT sensor.

25. Connect the air management wires, valves and the bracket assembly.

26. Install the alternator and connect the electrical wires.

27. Install the belt tensioner, power steering pump and bracket assembly.

28. Connect the transaxle modulator vacuum line and the vacuum supply line at the throttle body.

29. Install the vacuum line bracket at the left rear engine lift bracket.

30. Install the cruise control servo bracket and connect the fuel lines at the throttle body. Connect the fuel line brackets at the transaxle.

31. Replace the upper radiator hose.

32. Connect the transmission TV, cruise control and accelerator cables at the throttle body.

33. Install the distributor cap, wires and conduit.

34. Connect the wire connectors at the distributor, oil pressure switch, coolant sensor and the EGR solenoid.

35. Replace the heater hose at the thermostat housing.

36. Raise and support the vehicle safely. Replace the oil filter and tighten the oil drain plug.

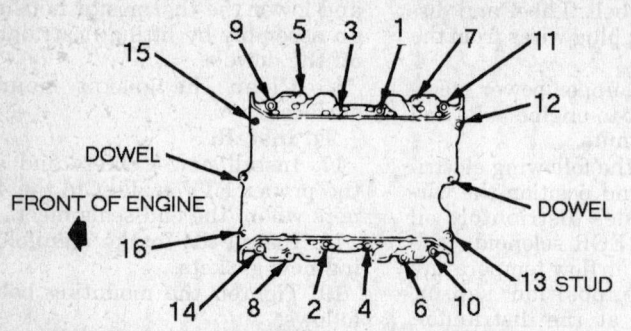

1. Tighten bolts 1, 2, 3, and 4 in sequence to 8 FT LBS (12 NM)
2. Tighten bolts 5 thru 6 in sequence to 8 FT LBS (12 NM)
3. Retighten all bolts in sequence to 12 FT LBS (16 NM)
4. Repeat Step 3 until torque level is maintained.

BOLT POSITION	BOLT LENGTH (MM)	BOLT POSITION	BOLT LENGTH (MM)
1	55	9	40
2	55	10	40
3	55	11	40
4	55	12	55
5	30	13	40 W/Studhead
6	30	14	40
7	30	15	55
8	30	16	40

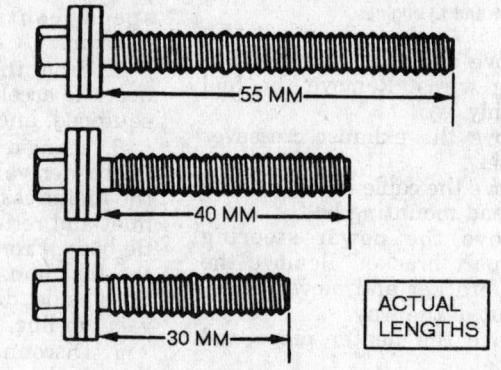

8470G052

Intake manifold bolt size and torque sequence — 4.9L engine

37. Install the upper left side power steering pump bracket bolts. Replace the accessory drive belt.

38. Install the air cleaner assembly and refill the cooling system.

39. Connect the negative battery cable. Start the engine and allow it to reach normal operating temperatures and check for leaks.

Exhaust Manifold

REMOVAL AND INSTALLATION

3.8L Engine

RIGHT

1. Disconnect the negative battery cable.

2. If necessary, disconnect the Mass Air Flow (MAF) sensor, air intake duct, the crankcase ventilation pipe and the IAC connector from the throttle body.

3. Label and disconnect the wires from the spark plugs. Disconnect the oxygen sensor lead.

4. If equipped, disconnect the heater inlet pipe from the manifold stud. If equipped, remove the transaxle oil indicator tube.

5. Remove the exhaust crossover pipe-to-exhaust manifold bolts and

the pipe. Disconnect the alternator bracket, if necessary.

6. Raise and support the vehicle safely. Remove the exhaust pipe-to-manifold bolts, the exhaust manifold-to-cylinder head bolts and the manifold.

7. Remove the EGR pipe from the exhaust manifold.

8. Clean the gasket mounting surfaces.

To install:

9. Replace the EGR pipe to the exhaust manifold.

10. Install the exhaust manifold, using a new gasket. Tighten the mounting studs to 37–41 ft. lbs. (50–56 Nm).

11. Lower the vehicle. Connect the alternator bracket, if necessary.

12. Install the crossover pipe and replace the exhaust manifold-to-cylinder bolts.

13. If equipped, replace the transaxle oil indicator tube. Connect the heater inlet pipe to the manifold, if equipped.

14. Connect the oxygen sensor lead and the spark plug wires.

15. If removed, connect the Mass Air Flow sensor, air intake duct, the crankcase ventilation pipe and the IAC connector from the throttle body.

16. Connect the negative battery cable. Start the engine and check for leaks.

LEFT—NON-SUPERCHARGED

1. Disconnect the negative battery cable. If necessary, remove the Mass Air Flow sensor, air intake duct and crankcase ventilation pipe.

2. Remove the exhaust crossover pipe-to-exhaust manifold bolts. Label and disconnect the spark plug wires.

3. Remove the exhaust manifold-to-cylinder head bolts and the manifold.

NOTE: It may be necessary to remove the oil dipstick tube to provide additional clearance.

To install:

4. Clean the gasket mounting surfaces and install a new gasket.

5. Install the exhaust manifold and tighten the manifold mounting studs to 37–41 ft. lbs. (50–56 Nm).

6. Connect the spark plug wires. Install the exhaust crossover pipe-to-exhaust manifold bolts.

7. If removed, install the Mass Air Flow sensor, air intake duct and crankcase ventilation pipe.

8. Connect the negative battery cable.

9. Start the engine and check for exhaust leaks.

LEFT–SUPERCHARGED

1. Disconnect the negative battery cable.

2. Remove the 2 flange bolts and the manifold to bracket nut.

3. Remove the manifold to engine studs and remove the manifold.

To install:

4. Clean the gasket mounting surfaces and install a new gasket.

5. Install the exhaust manifold and tighten the manifold mounting studs to 37–41 ft. lbs. (50–56 Nm).

6. Install the manifold to bracket nut and the flange gasket. Install the flange bolts.

7. Connect the negative battery cable.

8. Start the engine and check for exhaust leaks.

4.9L Engine

RIGHT

1. Disconnect the negative battery cable. Remove the air cleaner.

2. Remove the exhaust crossover pipe. Disconnect the oxygen and coolant temperature sensors.

3. Remove the catalytic converter-to-AIR pipe clip bolt. Remove the upper manifold-to-cylinder head bolts. Raise and safely support the vehicle.

4. Disconnect the converter air pipe bracket from the stud and remove the converter-to-manifold exhaust pipe.

5. Support the engine cradle with screw jacks and remove the rear cradle bolts. Loosen the front cradle bolts and slightly lower the engine cradle.

6. Remove the remaining exhaust manifold-to-cylinder head bolts, the AIR pipe and the manifold.

7. Clean the gasket mounting surfaces.

To install:

8. Install the exhaust manifold and replace the AIR pipe. Tighten the manifold mounting bolts to 16–18 ft. lbs.

9. Install the manifold-to-converter exhaust pipe and replace the converter air pipe bracket to the stud.

10. Raise the engine cradle and install the rear cradle bolts. Tighten to 75 ft. lbs (102 Nm).

11. Lower the vehicle. Replace the upper manifold-to-cylinder head bolts.

12. Replace the converter air pipe to AIR pipe clip bolt.

13. Connect the coolant temperature and oxygen sensor connectors. Replace the exhaust crossover pipe.

14. Replace the air cleaner and connect the negative battery cable.

15. Start the engine and check for leaks.

LEFT

1. Disconnect the negative battery cable. Remove the cooling fan(s) and the exhaust crossover pipe.

2. Remove the serpentine drive belt and the AIR pump pivot bolt.

3. Remove the belt tensioner and the power steering pump bracket.

4. Remove the exhaust manifold-to-cylinder head bolts, the AIR pipe and the manifold.

To install:

5. Clean the gasket mounting surfaces.

6. Install the manifold, AIR pipe and exhaust manifold-to-cylinder head bolts. Tighten to 16–18 ft. lbs. (22–24 Nm).

7. Install the belt tensioner and the power steering pump brace.

8. Install the AIR pump pivot bolt and the serpentine drive belt.

9. Install both cooling fans and the exhaust crossover pipe.

10. Connect the negative battery cable.

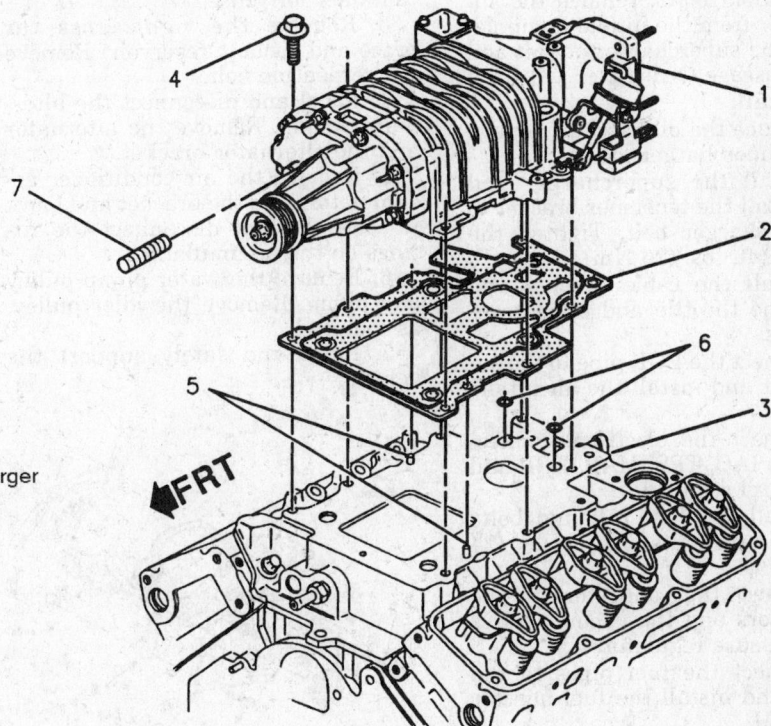

1. Supercharger
2. Gasket, supercharger
3. Lower intake manifold
4. Bolts, supercharger (8)
5. Locator pins
6. O-rings, coolant passage (2)
7. Stud, tensioner bracket to supercharger

8470G056

Supercharger assembly

Supercharger

REMOVAL AND INSTALLATION

3.8L Engine (VIN 1)

1. Disconnect the negative battery cable.

2. Remove the accessory drive belt from the supercharger pulley.

3. Relieve the fuel pressure and remove the fuel injector sight shield.

4. Disconnect the fuel pipes from the fuel rail and vacuum hose at the pressure regulator.

5. Disconnect the electrical connectors from the fuel injectors and remove the fuel rail mounting bolts. Remove the fuel rail with the injectors intact.

6. Disconnect the electrical connectors at the IAC, TPS, MAF, EGR and boost control solenoid. Lay the wiring harness aside.

7. Remove the air intake duct and remove the EGR pipe from the supercharger.

8. Disconnect the throttle cable and the cruise control cable. Remove the cable bracket.

9. Remove the tensioner bracket to supercharger mounting stud.

10. Remove the supercharger to intake manifold bolts, remove the supercharger from the intake manifold. Remove the supercharger gasket and coolant passage O-rings.

To install:

11. Replace the oil passage O-rings and the supercharger gasket.

12. Install the supercharger and bolts. Install the tensioner bracket to the supercharger bolt. Tighten the bolts to 19 ft. lbs. (26 Nm).

13. Install the cable bracket and connect the throttle and cruise control cables.

14. Connect the EGR pipe to the supercharger and install the air intake duct.

15. Connect the electrical connectors to the IAC, TPS, MAF, EGR and boost control solenoid.

16. Install the fuel rail and bolts and tighten the bolts to 15 ft. lbs. (24 Nm).

17. Connect the connectors to the fuel injectors and the vacuum hoses at the pressure regulator.

18. Connect the fuel pipes to the fuel rail and install the fuel injector sight shield.

19. Install the accessory drive belt to the supercharger and connect the negative battery cable.

Timing Chain Front Cover

REMOVAL AND INSTALLATION

3.8L Engines

1. Disconnect the negative battery cable. Remove the drive belt.

2. Remove the crankshaft pulley using tool J38197 or equivalent.

3. Remove the sensor shield.

4. Remove the oil pan to front cover bolts.

5. Remove the front cover attaching bolts and remove the cover.

To install:

6. Install the front cover and the attaching bolts. Tighten the bolts to 22 ft. lbs. (30 Nm).

7. Install the oil pan to front cover bolts and tighten to 124 inch lbs. (14 Nm).

8. Adjust the crankshaft sensor using tool J37087 or equivalent.

9. Install the sensor shield and install the pulley and the bolt. Tighten the bolt to 105 ft. lbs. (140 Nm) + 56 degrees turn.

10. Install the drive belt and connect the negative battery cable.

4.9L Engine

1. Disconnect the negative battery cable. Remove the air cleaner.

2. Drain the coolant into a clean container for reuse.

3. Remove the right cross car brace and coolant reservoir. Remove the serpentine belt.

4. Label and disconnect the alternator wiring. Remove the alternator and the alternator bracket.

5. Remove the air conditioner accumulator from the bracket and move it aside. Do not disconnect the fittings on the accumulator.

6. Remove the water pump pulley and pump. Remove the idler pulley, as required.

7. Raise and safely support the vehicle.

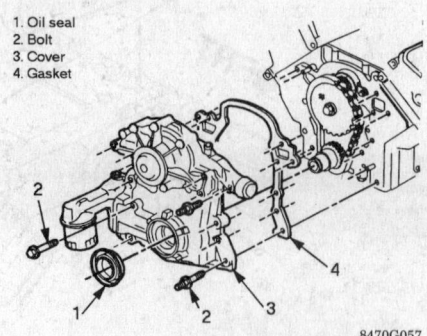

1. Oil seal
2. Bolt
3. Cover
4. Gasket

8470G057

Front cover assembly — 3.8L engine

8. Remove the crankshaft pulley-to-crankshaft pulley bolt. Attach a puller to the crankshaft damper/pulley; using the center bolt, press the crankshaft damper/pulley from the crankshaft.

9. Remove the front cover-to-engine bolts, the oil pan-to-front cover bolts and the front cover.

10. Clean the gasket mounting surfaces.

To install:

11. Install the timing cover and tighten the mounting bolts to 15 ft. lbs. (20 Nm).

12. Install the crankshaft damper and tighten the bolt to 18 ft. lbs. (24 Nm).

13. Lower the vehicle. Replace the water pump and pulley.

14. If removed, install the idler pulley. Install the serpentine belt.

15. Connect the alternator wiring and install the alternator and bracket.

16. Replace the air conditioner accumulator and connect the bracket.

17. Replace the air cleaner and refill the cooling system.

18. Connect the negative battery cable. Start the engine and check for leaks.

Front Cover Oil Seal

REPLACEMENT

3.8L Engine

1. Disconnect the negative battery cable.

2. Remove the serpentine drive belt. Remove the crankshaft balancer-to-crankshaft bolt.

3. Using a small prybar, pry the oil seal from the front cover. Be careful not to damage the sealing surfaces.

To install:

4. Clean the oil seal mounting surface. Using the proper lubricant coat the outside of the seal and the crankshaft balancer.

5. Using the oil seal installation tool, drive the new seal into the front cover until it seats.

6. Install the crankshaft balancer-to-crankshaft bolts. On 1992–93 models tighten to 105 ft. lbs. (140 Nm) + 56 degrees turn. Install the serpentine drive belt.

7. Connect the negative battery cable.

4.9L Engine

1. Disconnect the negative battery cable. Remove the serpentine belt.

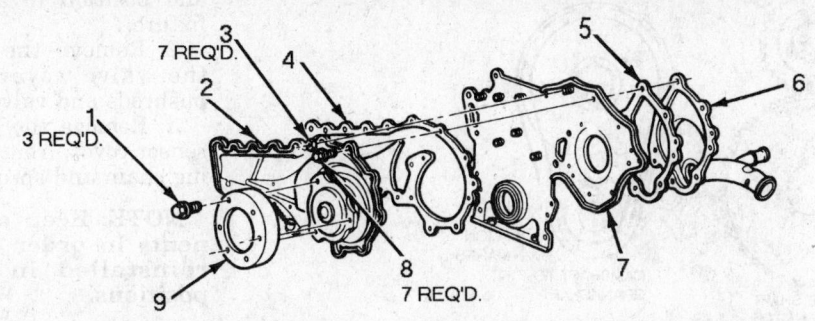

7 REQ'D.
3 REQ'D.
7 REQ'D.

4 REQ'D.
MARKED "B"

2 REQ'D.

"B"

"A"

"A"

"A"

4 REQ'D.
MARKED "A"

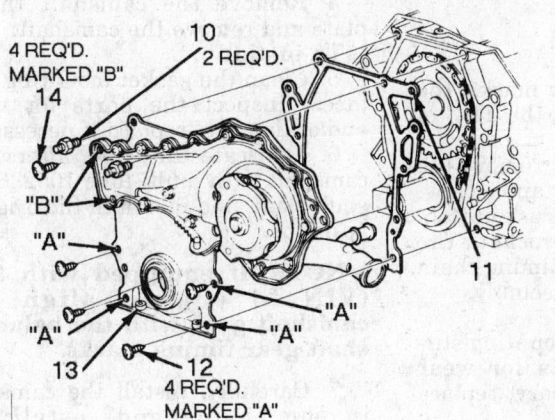

1. Bolt	8. Bolt
2. Water pump assembly	9. Water pump pulley
3. Nut	10. Stud headed bolt
4. Water pump gasket	11. Front cover gasket
5. Inlet gasket	12. Torx® screw
6. Inlet	13. Front cover/water pump/inlet assembly
7. Front cover	14. Torx® screw

8470G061

Front cover assembly — 4.9L engine

2. Remove the crankshaft pulley-to-crankshaft pulley bolt.

3. Attach a puller tool to the crankshaft pulley/damper. Using the center bolt, press the crankshaft pulley/damper from the crankshaft.

4. Using the oil seal removal tools, press the oil seal from the front cover. Clean the oil seal mounting surface.

To install:

5. Lubricate the new seal with engine oil. Using a hammer and an oil seal installation tool, drive the new oil seal into the front cover until it seats.

6. Install the crankshaft pulley/damper to the crankshaft. Tighten the crankshaft pulley-to-crankshaft bolt to 18 ft. lbs. (24 Nm).

7. Install the serpentine belt.

8. Connect the negative battery cable.

Timing Chain and Sprockets

REMOVAL AND INSTALLATION

3.8L Engine

1. Disconnect the negative battery cable. Remove the front cover.

2. Remove the button and spring/damper assembly from the

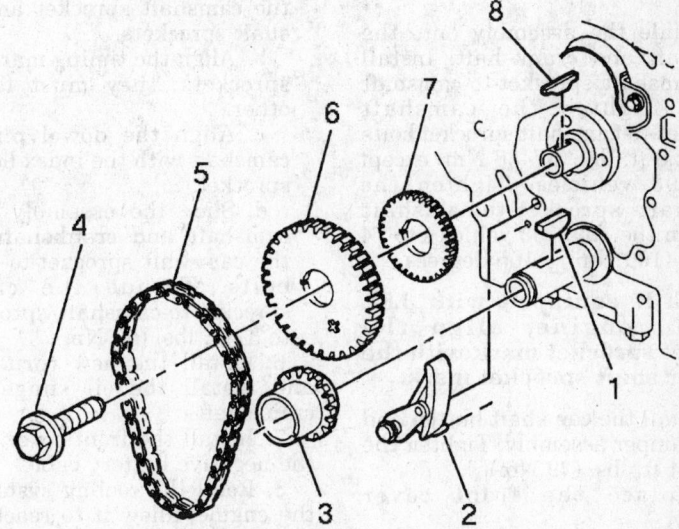

1. Key, crankshaft	5. Timing Chain
2. Damper assembly	6. Camshaft sprocket
3. Crankshaft sprocket	7. Camshaft gear
4. Bolt	8. Key, camshaft

8470G058

Timing chain and sprockets — 3.8L engine

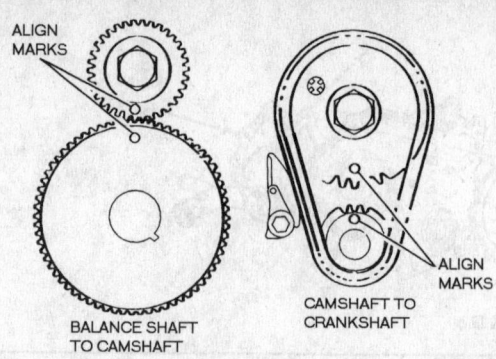

ALIGN MARKS

BALANCE SHAFT TO CAMSHAFT

ALIGN MARKS

CAMSHAFT TO CRANKSHAFT

8470G059

Timing chain/sprocket/balancer alignment — 3.8L engine

center of the camshaft. Align the marks of the timing sprockets as they must be close together.

3. Remove the camshaft sprocket bolts, the sprocket and the timing chain.

4. Remove the crankshaft sprocket. Clean the gasket mounting surfaces.

To install:

5. Install the timing chain and sprockets by performing the following:

   a. Assemble the timing chain on the camshaft sprocket and crankshaft sprockets.

   b. Align the marks on the sprockets; they must face each other.

   c. Slide the assembly onto the camshaft and crankshaft. Install the camshaft sprocket-to-camshaft bolts. Tighten the camshaft sprocket-to-camshaft sprocket bolts to 27–28 ft. lbs. (37–38 Nm) except 1992–93 vehicles. Tighten the camshaft sprocket-to-camshaft bolts on the 1992–93 vehicles to 74 ft. lbs. (100 Nm) + 105 degrees.

NOTE: If equipped with 3.8L (VIN L) engine, align the camshaft sprocket mark with the balancer shaft sprocket mark.

6. Install the camshaft button and spring/damper assembly. Tighten the bolt to 14 ft. lbs. (19 Nm).

7. Replace the front cover assembly.

8. Connect the negative battery cable.

9. Refill the cooling system. Start the engine, allow it to reach normal operating temperatures and check for leaks.

4.9L Engine

1. Disconnect the negative battery cable. Remove the front cover.

2. Remove the oil slinger from the crankshaft. Rotate the engine to

align the sprocket timing marks; the No. 1 cylinder will be on the TDC of its compression stroke.

3. From the camshaft, remove the camshaft thrust button and screw. Discard the camshaft thrust button. Slide the camshaft sprocket, the crankshaft sprocket and timing chain from the engine as an assembly.

To install:

4. Clean the gasket mounting surfaces. Inspect the parts for wear and/or damage; if necessary, replace the parts.

5. Install the timing chain and sprockets by performing the following:

   a. Assemble the timing chain on the camshaft sprocket and crankshaft sprockets.

   b. Align the timing marks on the sprockets; they must face each other.

   c. Align the dowel pin in the camshaft with the index hole in the sprocket.

   d. Slide the assembly onto the camshaft and crankshaft. Install the camshaft sprocket-to-camshaft bolts. Torque the camshaft sprocket-to-camshaft sprocket bolt to 37 ft. lbs. (50 Nm).

6. Install the new thrust button and install the oil slinger to the crankshaft.

7. Install the front cover. Connect the negative battery cable.

8. Refill the cooling system. Start the engine, allow it to reach normal operating temperatures and check for leaks.

Camshaft

REMOVAL AND INSTALLATION

3.8L Engine

1. Disconnect the negative battery cable. Remove the engine assembly

and position in a suitable holding fixture.

2. Remove the intake manifold, the valve covers, rocker arms, pushrods and valve lifters.

3. Remove the crankshaft pulley, sensor cover, front timing cover, timing chain and sprockets.

NOTE: Keep all valve components in order so they may be reinstalled in their original positions.

4. Remove the camshaft thrust plate and remove the camshaft.

To install:

5. Clean the gasket mounting surfaces. Inspect the parts for wear and/or damage, replace if necessary.

6. Lubricate the valve lifters and camshaft with multi-lube 1052365 or equivalent, and install in the original positions.

NOTE: If equipped with 3.8L (VIN L) engine, align the camshaft gear with the balancer shaft gear timing marks.

7. Carefully, install the camshaft in the engine and install the camshaft thrust plate.

8. Install the timing chain and sprockets and install the front timing cover.

9. Install the crankshaft sensor cover and crankshaft pulley.

10. Install the valve lifters, pushrods, and rocker arms.

11. Install the valve covers and install the intake manifold.

12. Install the engine to the vehicle and connect the negative battery cable.

4.9L Engine

1. Disconnect the negative battery cable. Remove the engine assembly and position in a suitable holding fixture.

2. Remove the intake manifold and the timing chain and remove the valve lifters.

NOTE: Keep all valve components in order so they may be reinstalled in their original positions.

3. Carefully slide the camshaft out from the front of the engine. Be sure not to damage the camshaft bearings.

To install:

4. Clean the gasket mounting surfaces. Inspect the parts for wear and/or damage; if necessary, replace the parts.

5. Lubricate the camshaft and carefully install in the engine. Tem-

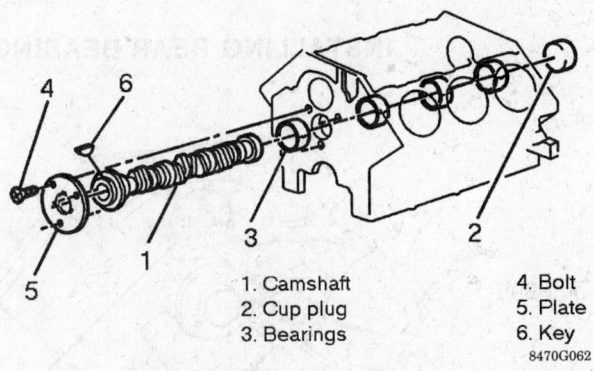

Camshaft and timing chain alignment — 4.9L engine

1. Camshaft
2. Cup plug
3. Bearings
4. Bolt
5. Plate
6. Key

Camshaft assembly — 3.8L engine

porarily install cam sprocket to the camshaft to act as a handle.

NOTE: If a new camshaft is to be installed, new lifters and a distributor drive gear must also be installed.

6. Install the lifters, timing chain and intake manifold.
7. Install the engine in the vehicle.
8. Connect the negative battery cable.
9. Fill cooling system and check for leaks. Start the engine and allow to come to normal operating temperature. Recheck for leaks. Top-up coolant.

Balance Shaft

REMOVAL AND INSTALLATION

3.8L Engine

1. Disconnect the negative battery cable. Remove the engine and secure it to a workstand.
2. Remove the flywheel-to-crankshaft bolts and remove the flywheel.
3. Remove the timing chain cover-to-engine bolts and the cover.
4. Remove the camshaft sprocket-to-camshaft gear bolts, the sprocket, the timing chain and the gear.

5. To remove the balance shaft, perform the following procedures:
   a. Remove the balance shaft gear-to-shaft bolt and the gear.
   b. Remove the balance shaft retainer-to-engine bolts and the retainer.
   c. Using the slide hammer tool, pull the balance shaft from the front of the engine.
To install:
6. If replacing the rear balance shaft bearing, perform the following:
   a. Drive the rear plug from the engine.
   b. Using the camshaft remover/installer tool, press the rear bearing from the rear of the engine.
   c. Dip the new bearing in clean engine oil.
   d. Using the balance shaft rear bearing installer tool, press the new rear bearing into the rear of the engine.
   e. Install the rear cup plug.
7. Using the balance shaft installer tool, screw it into the balance shaft and install the shaft into the engine; remove the installer tool.
8. Clean the gasket mounting surfaces. Inspect the parts for wear and/or damage; replace the parts, if necessary.
9. Install the balance shaft retainer. Torque the balance shaft re-

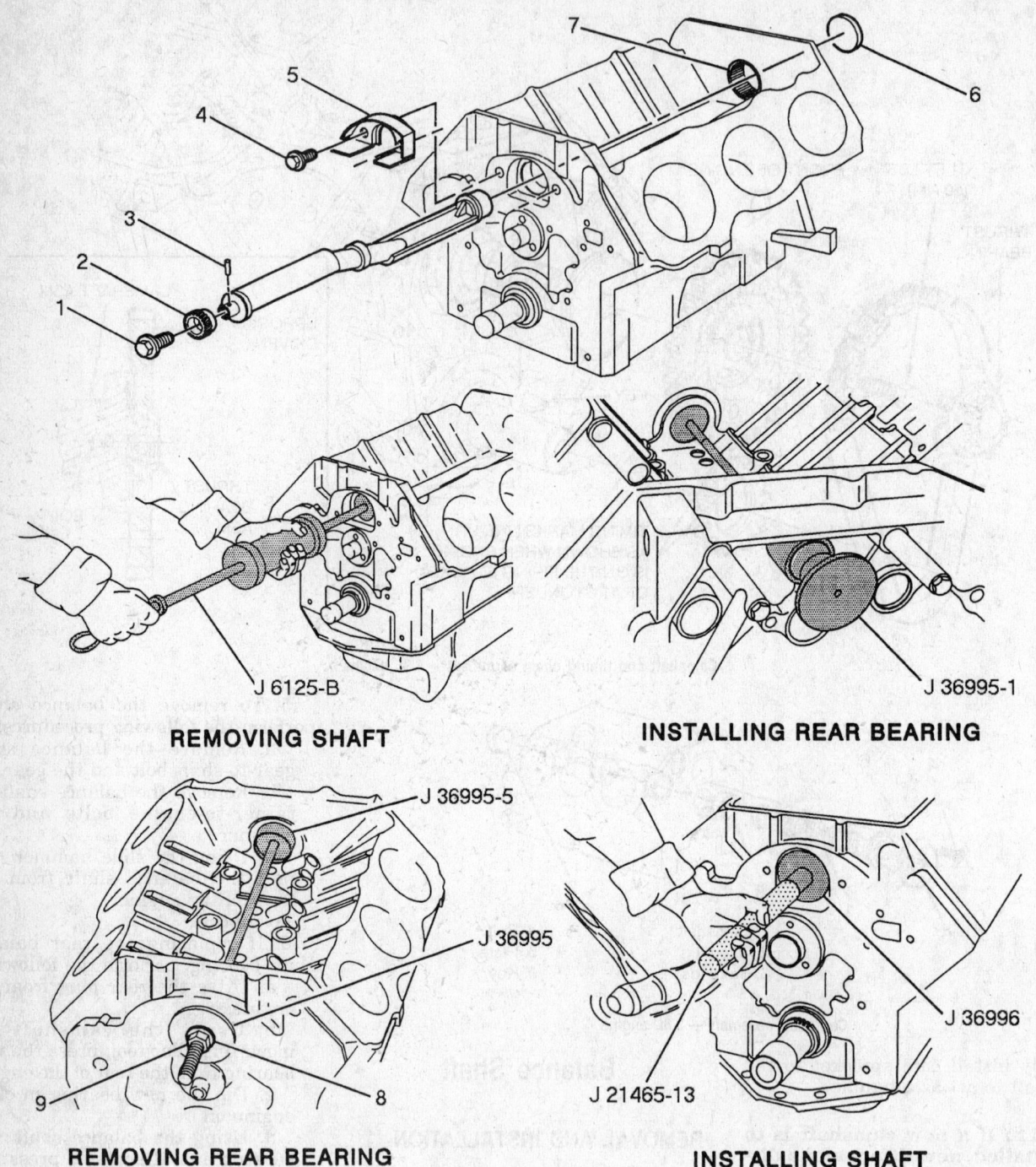

J 6125-B

REMOVING SHAFT

J 36995-1

INSTALLING REAR BEARING

J 36995-5

J 36995

9   8

REMOVING REAR BEARING

J 36996

J 21465-13

INSTALLING SHAFT

1. Bolt
2. Balance
   shaft gear
3. Pin
4. Bolt
5. Retainer
6. Plug
7. Bearing
8. Washer
9. Nut

8470G063

Balance shaft service — 3.8L engine

tainer-to-engine bolts to 27 ft. lbs. (37 Nm).

10. Align the balance shaft gear with the camshaft gear timing marks. Install the balance shaft gear onto the balance shaft. Torque the balance gear-to-balance shaft bolt to 14 ft. lbs (19 Nm), then using a torque angle meter tool, rotate another 35 degrees.

11. Align the marks on the balance shaft gear and the camshaft gear by turning the balance shaft.

12. Turn the crankshaft so the No. 1 piston is at TDC.

13. Install the timing chain and sprocket.

14. Replace the balance shaft front bearing retainer and bolts. Tighten the bolts to 61 ft. lbs. (83 Nm).

15. Install the front timing cover and the lifter guide retainer.

16. Install the intake manifold and flywheel assembly. Tighten the flywheel bolts to 61 ft. lbs. (83 Nm).

17. Install the engine assembly and connect the negative battery cable. Start the engine and check for leaks.

Piston and Connecting Rod

Positioning

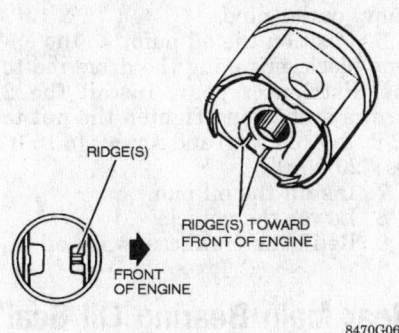

RIDGE(S)

RIDGE(S) TOWARD FRONT OF ENGINE

FRONT OF ENGINE

8470G064

Piston installation direction — 3.8L and 4.9L engines

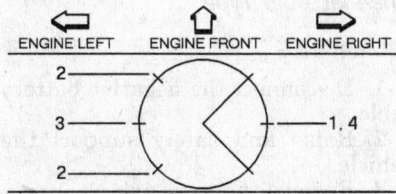

ENGINE LEFT ENGINE FRONT ENGINE RIGHT

2

3 ———————————— 1, 4

2

1. Oil ring spacer gap
   (tang in hole or slot with arc)
2. Oil ring rail gaps
3. 2nd compression ring gap
4. Top compression ring gap

8470G065

Piston ring gap location — 3.8L engine

ENGINE LUBRICATION

Oil Pan

REMOVAL AND INSTALLATION

3.8L Engine

1. Disconnect the negative battery cable. Raise and safely support the vehicle.

2. Drain the crankcase and remove the transaxle converter cover.

3. Remove the oil filter and the starter motor.

4. Remove the oil pan-to-engine bolts and the oil pan.

To install:

5. Clean the gasket mounting surfaces.

6. Install the oil pan and the oil pan-to-engine bolts. Tighten bolts according to 124 inch lbs. (14 Nm).

7. Install a new oil filter and the starter motor.

8. Install the transaxle converter cover.

9. Lower the vehicle.

10. Fill the crankcase with oil.

11. Connect the negative battery cable.

4.9L Engine

1. Disconnect the negative battery cable. Raise and safely support the vehicle.

2. Drain the crankcase and remove the oil filter. Remove the flywheel cover.

3. Remove the oil pan-to-engine bolts and the oil pan.

NOTE: If the pan is difficult to remove, lightly tap the edges with a plastic hammer.

To install:

4. Clean the gasket mounting surfaces.

5. Install a new oil pan gasket. Install the oil pan to the engine. Tighten the oil pan-to-engine bolts to 14 ft. lbs. (18 Nm).

6. Install the flywheel inspection cover.

7. Install a new oil filter.

8. Lower the vehicle.

9. Refill the crankcase with oil.

10. Connect the negative battery cable.

11. Start the engine and check for leaks.

Oil Pump

REMOVAL AND INSTALLATION

3.8L Engine

1. Disconnect the negative battery cable. Remove the front cover from the engine.

2. Remove the oil filter adapter, pressure regulator valve and spring.

3. Remove the oil pump cover-to-front cover screws and the cover. Remove the inner and outer pump gears.

To install:

4. Using petroleum jelly, pack the pump and assemble the gears in the housing. Tighten the oil pump cover-to-front cover screws to 97 inch lbs. (11 Nm).

5. Install the pressure regulator spring and valve. Install the oil filter adapter.

6. Install the front cover to the engine.

7. Connect the negative battery cable.

Engine

1. Disconnect the negative battery cable. Raise and safely support the vehicle.

2. Drain the crankcase. Remove the oil pan mounting bolts and remove the oil pan.

3. Remove the oil pump-to-engine screws/nut and the oil pump from the engine.

To install:

4. Clean the mounting surfaces. Install the pump assembly and tighten the mounting screws to 15 ft. lbs. (20 Nm) and the nut to 22 ft. lbs. (30 Nm).

5. Install a new oil pan gasket. Install the oil pan and bolts.

6. Lower the vehicle.

7. Connect the negative battery cable.

8. Refill the crankcase start the engine and check for leaks.

Checking

3.8L Engine

1. Remove the front cover from the engine.

2. Remove the oil filter adapter, pressure regulator valve and spring.

3. Remove the oil pump cover-to-front cover screws and the cover. Remove the inner and outer pump gears.

4. Check the oil pump gears for:

   a. Inner gear tip clearance — 0.006 inch (0.015mm)

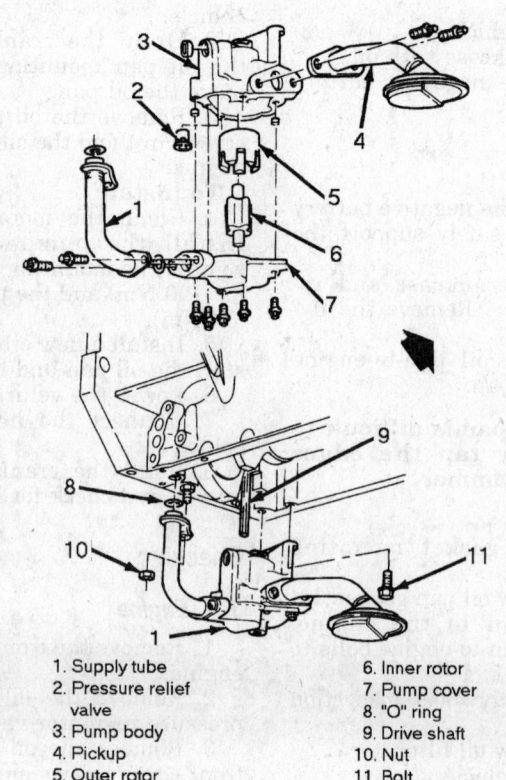

1. Pump outer gear
2. Pump inner gear
3. Oil pump cover
4. Screw
5. Front cover

8470G067

Oil pump and housing — 3.8L engine

1. Supply tube
2. Pressure relief valve
3. Pump body
4. Pickup
5. Outer rotor
6. Inner rotor
7. Pump cover
8. "O" ring
9. Drive shaft
10. Nut
11. Bolt

8470G068

Oil pump and housing — 4.9L engine

b. Outer gear diameter clearance — 0.008–0.015 inch (0.203–0.381mm)

c. Gear end clearance — 0.001–0.0035 inch (0.025–0.0.089mm)

d. Pressure regulator valve-to-bore clearance — 0.0015–0.003 inch (0.038–0.076mm)

To install:

5. Install the inner and outer pump gears. Install the oil pump cover-to-front cover screws and the cover.

6. Install the oil filter adapter, pressure regulator valve and spring.

7. Install the front cover from the engine.

4.9L Engine

1. Raise and support the vehicle safely.

2. Remove the oil pump assembly and the screws mounting the pump cover to the housing.

3. Remove the oil pressure regulator spring from the bore in the housing. Check the free length of the regulator spring, should be 2.57–2.69 inches. A force of 9.3–10.5 lbs. should be required to compress the spring to 1.46 inch (37.08mm).

To install:

4. Assemble the oil pump.

5. Replace the O-ring at the oil pump outlet pipe.

6. Position the oil pump to the engine block, engaging the drive rod to the distributor gear. Install the 2 screws and 1 nut. Tighten the nut to 22 ft. lbs. (30 Nm) and screws to 15 ft. lbs. (20 Nm).

7. Install the oil pan.

8. Lower the vehicle.

9. Refill the crankcase with oil.

Rear Main Bearing Oil Seal

REMOVAL AND INSTALLATION

One-Piece Lip Type

3.8L ENGINES

1. Disconnect the negative battery cable.

2. Raise and safely support the vehicle.

3. Remove the transaxle.

4. Remove the flywheel.

5. Insert a suitable prying tool through the dust lip and pry the seal out by moving the handle of the tool toward the end of the crankshaft pi-

lot. Repeat the process, as required, around the seal until it is removed.

NOTE: Use care when prying out the seal to avoid damage to the OD and chamfer of the crankshaft.

To install:

6. Apply engine oil to the ID and OD of the new seal. Slide the new seal over the mandrel until the back of the seal bottoms squarely against the collar of the tool.

7. Align the dowel pin of the installation tool with the dowel pin in the crankshaft and attach the tool to the crankshaft by hand or by tightening the attaching screw to 60 inch lbs. (5 Nm).

8. Turn the T-handle of the tool so the collar pushes the seal into the bore. Continue turning until the collar is tight against the case. This will ensure that the seal is seated properly.

9. Loosen the T-handle of the tool until it comes to a stop. This will ensure that the collar will be in the proper position for install another new seal.

10. Remove the attaching screws.

11. Install the flywheel.

12. Install the transaxle.

13. Lower the vehicle.

14. Connect the negative battery cable.

4.9L ENGINE

1. Raise and safely support the vehicle.

2. Remove the transaxle assembly. Remove the flexplate from the crankshaft.

3. Using the proper tool J26868 or equivalent, pry out the old seal from the rear of the engine.

To install:

4. Lubricate the new seal with wheel bearing grease and install on the crankshaft with the spring facing inside the engine.

5. Press the seal into position, using the proper tool J34604 or equivalent.

NOTE: The seal should be flush with the block. It is necessary to use the proper tool because the seal must be installed square or an oil leak could result.

6. Install the flexplate to the crankshaft.

7. Install the transaxle assembly.

8. Lower the vehicle.

AUTOMATIC TRANSAXLE

Transaxle Assembly

REMOVAL AND INSTALLATION

3.8L Engine with 4T60/4T60E Transaxle

1. Disconnect the negative terminal from the battery. Disconnect the wire connector at the Mass Air Flow sensor, if equipped.

2. Remove the cross brace to strut towers, if equipped. Reinstall the inboard strut nut.

3. Remove the air intake duct.

4. Disconnect the cruise control assembly and the the shift control linkage.

5. Label and disconnect the following:
   a. Transaxle neutral start and backup lamp switch
   b. Transaxle electrical connector
   c. Vehicle speed sensor and fuel pipe retainers
   d. Vacuum modulator hose at the modulator

6. Remove the top transaxle-to-engine block bolts and install an engine support fixture.

7. Raise and safely support the vehicle. Remove both front tire and wheel assemblies and turn the steering wheel to the full left position.

8. Remove the right front ball joint nut and separate the control arm from the steering knuckle.

9. Remove the right halfshaft.

NOTE: Be careful not to allow the halfshaft splines to contact any portion of the lip seal.

10. Using a medium prybar, remove the left halfshaft. Be careful not to damage the pan. Install halfshaft boot seal protectors.

11. Remove the bolts at the transaxle and the nuts at the cradle member. Remove the left front transaxle mount.

12. Remove the right front mount-to-cradle nuts. Remove the left rear transaxle mount-to-transaxle bolts.

13. Remove the torque strut bracket from the transaxle.

14. Remove the left rear transaxle mount. Remove the transaxle brace from the engine bracket.

15. Remove the stabilizer shaft link to control arm bolt.

16. Remove the flywheel cover, matchmark the flywheel-to-torque converter and remove the flywheel-to-converter bolts.

NOTE: Be sure to matchmark the flywheel-to-converter relationship for proper alignment upon reassembly.

17. Remove the rear frame member-to-front cradle dog leg.

18. Remove the front left cradle-to-body bolt and the front cradle dog leg-to-right cradle member bolts.

19. Install a transaxle support fixture into position.

20. Remove the cradle assembly by swinging it aside and supporting it with jackstand.

21. Disconnect and plug the oil cooler lines at the transaxle.

NOTE: One bolt located between the transaxle and the engine block is installed in the opposite direction.

22. Remove the remaining lower transaxle-to-engine bolts and lower the transaxle from the vehicle.

To install:

23. Install the transaxle into the vehicle using the dowel pin as guide. Tighten the bolts to 55 ft. lbs. (75 Nm).

24. Connect the oil cooler lines and remove the support fixture.

25. Install the front left cradle-to-body bolts and replace the rear cradle-to-front cradle dog leg.

26. Install the flywheel and tighten the bolts to 46 ft. lbs. (62 Nm). Replace the flywheel cover and tighten the bolts to 136 inch lbs. (15 Nm).

27. Install the right rear transaxle mount. Replace the engine support bracket-to-transaxle case bolts and tighten to 40 ft. lbs. (54 Nm).

28. Install the right front mount-to-cradle nuts. Replace the left rear transaxle mount-to-transaxle bolts and tighten to 30 ft. lbs. (41 Nm).

29. Replace the bolts at the transaxle and the nuts at the cradle member. Replace the left front transaxle mount and tighten the bolts to 40 ft. lbs. (54 Nm).

30. Install both halfshafts.

31. Connect the control arm to the steering knuckle and tighten the right front ball joint nut.

32. Install the tire and wheel assemblies. Lower the vehicle.

33. Install the top transaxle-to-engine block bolts and remove the engine support fixture.

34. Connect the following:
   a. Park/Neutral switch
   b. Torque converter clutch

c. Vehicle speed sensor and fuel pipe retainers

d. Vacuum modulator hose at the modulator

35. Connect the cruise control assembly and the the shift control linkage.

36. Replace the air intake duct and install the cross brace to strut towers, if equipped.

37. Connect the wire connector at the Mass Air Flow sensor, if equipped.

38. Connect the negative battery cable.

4.9L Engine with 4T60E Transaxle

1. Disconnect the negative terminal from the battery. Remove the air cleaner and the TV cable.

2. Disconnect the shift cable and remove the bracket.

3. Disconnect all of the electrical connectors between the transaxle and engine.

4. Remove the engine harness bracket.

5. Disconnect the engine oil cooler line, vacuum hose. Remove the fuel line bracket.

6. Remove the vacuum modulator, transaxle filler tube and mounting bracket.

7. Remove the upper bell housing-to-engine bolts and studs.

8. Install an engine support device.

9. Raise and support the vehicle safely. Remove both front wheels.

10. Remove both side stabilizer link bolts, ball joint cotter pins and nuts. Separate both ball joints from the steering knuckles. Remove both drive axles from the hubs and then from the transaxle.

11. Remove the air conditioning splash shield, right and left wheelhouse splash shields.

12. Return the power steering return line bracket and ABS pump from the bracket.

13. Remove the flywheel splash shield. Matchmark the torque converter-to-flywheel and remove the converter-to-flywheel bolts.

14. Disconnect the power steering line and trans line.

15. Remove the right and left cradle mount bolts and the right side motor mount nuts.

16. Separate the right front corner of the cradle from the cradle. Remove the cradle insulator bolt and remove the left cradle member.

17. Using a floor jack, position it under the transaxle and remove the

bracket assembly from the transaxle mount bracket.

18. Remove the engine to transaxle and to left side transaxle brackets.

NOTE: To reach the last bell housing bolt, use a 3 in. socket wrench extension through the right wheel arch opening.

19. Remove the 2 lower bell housing bolts and remove the transaxle assembly.

To install:

20. Install the transaxle assembly and replace the lower bell housing bolts. Tighten the bolts to 55 ft. lbs. (75 Nm).

21. Replace the converter-to-flexplate bolts and tighten to 46 ft. lbs. (62 Nm). Install the flexplate splash shield.

22. Connect the oil cooler lines at the transaxle case.

23. Install the extension housing-to-engine support bracket. Replace the left front cradle assembly.

24. Replace both the right and left side cradle mount bolts and motor mount nuts.

25. Connect the power steering line and trans lines. Install the power steering return line bracket and ABS pump.

26. Install both drive axles. Fully seat by inserting the proper tool in the groove on the joint housing and tap until the joints are seated.

27. Connect the lower ball joint to the steering knuckle and replace the left and right front transaxle mount-to-cradle attachments. Tighten the nuts to 23 ft. lbs. (31 Nm).

28. Replace both front tire and wheel assemblies. Lower the vehicle.

29. Replace the upper bell housing-to-engine bolts/studs and tighten to 55 ft. lbs. (75 Nm).

30. Connect the electrical connectors and connect the shift linkage to the transaxle. Remove the engine support fixture tool.

31. Replace the air cleaner and the TV cable.

32. Connect the negative battery cable. Check the fluid levels and start the engine and check for leaks.

SHIFT LINKAGE ADJUSTMENT

1. Position the shift lever in the **N** position.

2. Raise and safely support the vehicle.

3. Push the tab on the cable adjuster to adjust the cable in the cable mounting bracket on 3.8L and 4.9L engines.

4. Lower the vehicle.

THROTTLE LINKAGE ADJUSTMENT

1. Stop the engine. Raise and safely support the vehicle.

NOTE: Check the throttle body for full travel prior to any adjustments.

2. Depress and hold-down the metal readjust tab at the engine end of the TV cable.

3. Move the slider until it stops against the fitting.

4. Release the adjustment tab.

5. Rotate the throttle lever to the full travel position.

6. The slider must move toward the lever when the lever is rotated to it's full travel position.

DRIVE AXLE

Halfshaft

REMOVAL AND INSTALLATION

NOTE: Use care when removing the halfshaft. Tri-pots can be damaged if the halfshaft is overextended.

1. Raise and safely support the vehicle. Remove the tire and wheel assembly.

2. Use a halfshaft boot seal protector tool and install it onto the seal.

3. Insert drift into rotor and caliper to prevent rotor from turning.

4. Remove hub nut and washer using a hub nut socket tool.

5. Remove the lower ball joint cotter pin and nut and loosen the joint using a ball joint separator tool. If removing the right halfshaft, turn the wheel to the left, if removing the left halfshaft turn the wheel to the right.

6. With a prybar between the suspension support and the lower control arm, separate the joint.

7. Pull out on the lower knuckle area and with a plastic or rubber mallet strike the end of the axle shaft to disengage the axle from the hub and bearing. The shaft nut can be partially installed to protect the threads.

8. Separate the hub and bearing assembly from the halfshaft and move the strut and knuckle assembly rearward. Remove the inner joint from the transaxle using the proper

tool from the intermediate shaft, if equipped.

NOTE: If equipped with the anti-lock brake system, care must be used to prevent damage to the toothed sensor ring on the half-shaft and the wheel speed sensor on the steering knuckle.

To install:

9. Seat the halfshaft into the transaxle by placing the proper tool into the groove on the joint housing and tapping until seated.

10. Verify the halfshaft is seated into the transaxle by grasping on the housing and pulling outboard. Do not pull on the halfshaft.

11. Install the halfshaft into the hub and bearing assembly.

12. Install the lower ball joint to the knuckle. Tighten the nut to 41 ft. lbs. (56 Nm) minimum and to 50 ft. lbs. (68 Nm) maximum to install the cotter pin.

13. Install the cotter pin.

14. Install the washer and new shaft nut.

15. Insert drift into rotor and caliper to prevent rotor from turning.

16. Torque the shaft nut to 185 ft. lbs. (251 Nm).

17. Remove the boot protector.

18. Install the tire and wheel assembly. Lower the vehicle.

CV-Boot

REMOVAL AND INSTALLATION

Inner Boot

1. Raise and support the vehicle safely. Remove the halfshaft.

2. Remove the joint assembly retaining ring and the joint assembly.

3. Remove the bearing race retaining ring and the seal retainer.

4. Remove the inner seal retainer clamp and the inner joint seal.

To install:

5. Pack the joint with grease.

6. Install the inner seal retainer clamp.

7. Install the seal retainer and bearing race retaining ring.

8. Install the joint assembly and joint assembly retaining ring.

9. Install the halfshaft.

10. Lower the vehicle.

Outer Boot

1. Raise and support the vehicle safely. Remove the halfshaft.

2. Using a brass drift, lightly tap around the seal retainer to loosen it. Remove the seal retainer.

3. Remove the seal retainer clamp and discard.

4. Using snapring pliers, remove the race retaining ring from the halfshaft.

5. Pull the outer joint assembly and the outboard seal away from the halfshaft.

To install:

6. Pack the joint with grease.

7. Install the outboard seal and outer joint assembly on the halfshaft.

8. Install the race retaining ring on the halfshaft.

9. Install a new seal retainer clamp.

10. Install the halfshaft.

11. Lower the vehicle.

Front Wheel Hub, Knuckle and Bearings

REMOVAL AND INSTALLATION

1. Raise and support the vehicle safely. Place a suitable jacking device under the control arm and lower the vehicle slightly to rest the weight of the vehicle on the control arm.

2. Remove the tire and wheel assembly. Remove the caliper bolts, remove and support the caliper aside.

3. Remove the rotor and using the proper tool, separate the hub from the halfshaft.

4. Remove the hub and bearing retaining bolts, shield, hub and bearing assembly and the O-ring.

5. Disconnect the ball joint from the steering knuckle, using the proper tool.

6. Remove the halfshaft assembly and tap the seal from the steering knuckle. Remove the steering knuckle from the hub.

NOTE: The hub and bearing are replaced only as an assembly.

To install:

7. Install a new hub and bearing seal in the steering knuckle with the proper seal installer tool. Install the steering knuckle to the strut.

8. Lubricate the hub and bearing with grease and install the halfshaft.

9. Connect the ball joint to the steering knuckle and insert a new O-ring around the hub and bearing assembly.

10. Install the hub and bearing assembly into the steering knuckle. Tighten the bolts to 75 ft. lbs. (101 Nm).

11. Install the rotor and caliper assembly. Tighten the caliper bolts to 38 ft. lbs. (52 Nm).

12. Install the shaft washer and nut. Tighten the nut to 180 ft. lbs. (244 Nm).

13. Install the tire and wheel assembly.

14. Lower the vehicle.

STEERING

Steering Wheel

— CAUTION —

Some vehicles are equipped with the Supplemental Inflatable Restraint or air bag system. The air bag system must be disabled before performing service on or around the air bag, instrument panel components, wiring and sensors. Failure to follow safety and disabling procedures could result in accidental air bag deployment, possible personal injury and unnecessary air bag system repairs.

REMOVAL AND INSTALLATION

Without SIR System

1. Disconnect the negative battery cable.

2. Remove the screws holding the steering pad.

3. Remove the steering pad and disconnect the horn lead.

4. Remove the retainer and nut.

5. Remove the steering wheel, using the proper tool.

To install:

6. Install the steering wheel. Tighten the steering shaft nut to 30 ft. lbs. (41 Nm).

7. Install the retainer and nut.

8. Connect the horn lead and install the steering pad.

9. Install the screws holding the steering pad.

10. Connect the negative battery cable.

With SIR System

1. Disconnect the negative battery cable.

2. Disable the SIR system.

3. Remove the inflator module by performing the following:

   a. Remove the inflator module attaching screws from the back of the steering wheel.

   b. Lift the inflator module from the steering wheel.

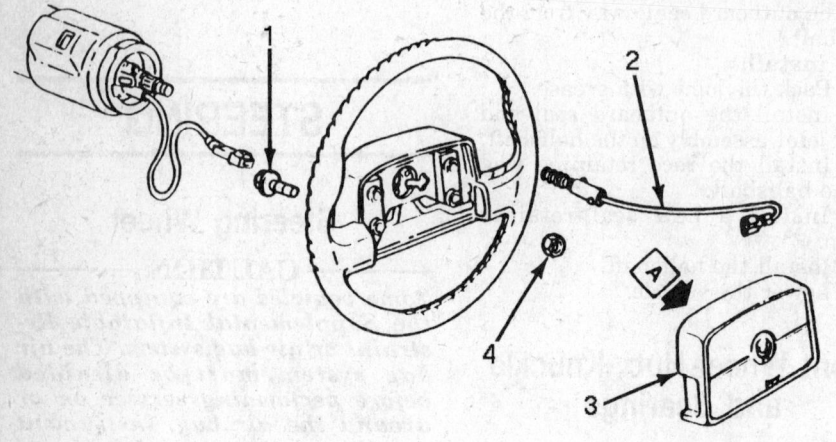

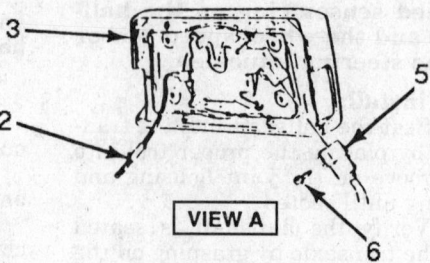

VIEW A

1. Bolt; 25 LB IN (2.8 NM)
2. Horn lead wire
3. Inflator module
4. Lock nut; 30 LB FT (41 NM)
5. SIR coil assembly lead
6. Connector position assurance (CPA)

8470G074

Steering wheel and inflator module — 1992–93 Cadillac

c. Push down and twist the horn lead out of the cam tower.

d. Remove the CPA retainer and coil assembly connector from the inflator module.

4. Remove the hexagonal steering wheel locknut.

5. Mark the steering shaft and steering wheel to ensure proper alignment during installation.

6. Remove the steering wheel, using a suitable puller.

To install:

7. Feed the SIR coil assembly lead through the slot in the steering wheel.

8. Align the mark on the steering wheel with the mark on the shaft.

9. Install the steering wheel.

10. Install the hexagonal steering wheel locknut. Tighten to 30 ft. lbs. (41 Nm).

11. Install the inflator module by performing the following:

a. Feed the horn lead into the cam tower.

b. Connect the coil assembly connector and CPA retainer to the inflator module.

c. Install the inflator module to the steering wheel. Ensure that the inflator module is properly aligned with the steering wheel and that

the wires behind the module are not pinched during installation.

d. Install the inflator module attaching screws to the back of the steering wheel.

12. Enable the SIR system.

13. Connect the negative battery cable.

Steering Column

REMOVAL AND INSTALLATION

Except Cadillac

1. Disconnect the negative battery cable. If equipped with SIR, disable the system.

2. Remove the lower instrument panel trim plates. Remove the left side sound insulator panel.

3. Remove the shift indicator cable from the shift boot.

4. Label and disconnect the electrical connectors from the steering column. Remove the steering column-to-dash bolts.

5. Remove the steering shaft-to-intermediate shaft bolt and the steering column from the vehicle.

To install:

6. Install the steering column to the vehicle and steering shaft-to-intermediate shaft bolt.

7. Install the steering column-to-dash bolts. Connect the electrical connectors to the steering column.

8. Install the shift indicator cable to the shift bowl.

9. Install the lower instrument panel trim plates. Install the left side sound insulator panel.

10. Enable the SIR system. Connect the negative battery cable.

Cadillac

1. Disconnect the negative battery cable.

2. If equipped, disable the SIR system and remove the inflator module.

3. Remove the steering column trim plate.

4. Remove the retaining filler, the column reinforcement plate and disconnect the electrical connections. Remove the shift control cable at the actuator.

5. Remove the bolts securing the seal assembly and the bolt from the upper knuckle of the intermediate steering shaft.

6. Disconnect the lower brace assembly and the lower support bracket.

7. Remove the bolts securing the column to the upper support and remove the column assembly.

To install:

8. Install the column assembly. Install the bolts securing the column to the upper support.

9. Connect the lower brace assembly and the lower support bracket.

10. Install the bolts securing the seal assembly and the bolt to the upper knuckle of the intermediate steering shaft.

11. Install the retaining filler, the column reinforcement plate and connect the electrical connections. Install the shift control cable at the actuator.

12. Install the steering column trim plate.

13. If equipped with SIR, install the inflator module and enable the SIR system.

14. Connect the negative battery cable.

Power Steering Rack

ADJUSTMENT

Rack Bearing Preload

1. Loosen the adjuster plug locknut and turn the adjuster plug clockwise until it bottoms in the housing. Then back off 50–70 degrees which is approximately one flat.

2. Raise and support the vehicle safely to make the proper adjustments. Be sure the steering wheel returns freely to the center position after the adjustment.

3. Tighten the locknut to the adjuster plug to 50 ft. lbs.

REMOVAL AND INSTALLATION

1. Raise and safely support the vehicle. Allow the front suspension to hang freely. Disconnect the pressure lines from the steering gear and drain the excess fluid into a container. Be sure to plug the openings.

2. Move the intermediate shaft cover upward and remove the intermediate shaft-to-stub shaft pinch bolt. Remove both front tire and wheel assemblies.

3. Disconnect the tie rod ends from the steering knuckles. Remove the line retainer, outlet and pressure hoses.

4. Remove the rack/pinion assembly-to-chassis bolts.

5. Loosen the front engine cradle mounting bolts and the lower the rear of the cradle about 3 inches, if necessary. Remove the rack and pinion assembly.

To install:

6. Install the rack and pinion assembly into the vehicle. Raise the front engine cradle into position and tighten the attaching bolts.

7. Install the rack/pinion assembly-to-chassis bolts. Tighten the rack mounting bolts to 50 ft. lbs. (68 Nm).

8. Connect the tie rod ends to the steering knuckles. Tighten the tie rod end nut to 35–52 ft. lbs. (47–71 Nm). Install the line retainer, outlet and pressure hoses.

9. Install the intermediate shaft-to-stub shaft pinch bolt. Move the intermediate shaft cover upward into position. Install both front tire and wheel assemblies.

10. Refill the power steering pump reservoir.

11. Bleed the power steering system and check for leaks.

12. Lower the vehicle.

13. Check and/or adjust the front wheel alignment.

Power Steering Pump

REMOVAL AND INSTALLATION

3.8L Engine

1. Disconnect the negative battery cable.

2. Remove the serpentine drive belt and disconnect the pressure and return hoses.

3. Remove the power steering pump mounting bolts.

4. Remove the pump assembly. Transfer the pulley as necessary.

To install:

5. Install the pump assembly.

6. Remove the power steering pump mounting bolts.

7. Remove the drive belt and disconnect the pressure and return hoses.

8. Connect the negative battery cable.

9. Install the serpentine drive belt and bleed the power steering system.

4.9L Engine

1. Disconnect the negative battery cable.

2. Remove the serpentine drive belt and the power steering pump pulley, using the proper tool.

3. Disconnect and plug the high pressure and feed lines from the pump. Remove the belt tensioner, as required.

4. Remove the power steering pump-to-bracket bolts and the pump.

To install:

5. Install the power steering pump-to-bracket bolts and the pump. Tighten the power steering pump mounting bolts to 18 ft. lbs. (24 Nm).

6. Connect the high pressure and feed lines to the pump. If removed, install the belt tensioner.

7. Install the power steering pump pulley and the serpentine drive belt.

8. Refill the power steering pump reservoir. Bleed the power steering system.

9. Connect the negative battery cable.

BELT ADJUSTMENT

The serpentine is self adjusting within the tensioner operating limits.

SYSTEM BLEEDING

1. Raise and support the vehicle safely. Fill the fluid reservoir.

2. Bleed the system by turning the wheels from side to side, without reaching the stop at either end. Keep the fluid level at the FULL COLD mark. Continue this until the air is eliminated from the fluid.

3. Start the engine and run at fast idle. Recheck the fluid level.

4. Return the wheels to the center position and lower the vehicle.

5. Recheck the fluid level.

Tie Rod Ends

REMOVAL AND INSTALLATION

1. Raise and safely support the vehicle.

2. Remove the cotter pin and loosen the jam nut from the outer tie rod end.

3. Disconnect the outer tie rod end from the steering knuckle, using the proper tool.

4. Matchmark the threads and disconnect the outer tie rod end from the inner tie rod. Remove the tie rod end.

5. Install the tie rod end to the matchmarks on the inner tie rod.

To install:

6. Install the tie rod end to the matchmarks on the inner tie rod. Tighten the hex nut to 35–45 ft. lbs. (47–61 Nm).

7. Connect the outer tie rod end to the steering knuckle.

8. Tighten the jam nut on the outer tie rod end. Install a new cotter pin.

9. Lower the vehicle.

BRAKES

Master Cylinder

REMOVAL AND INSTALLATION

1. Disconnect the negative battery cable and, if equipped, the electrical connector from the level sensor unit.

NOTE: If equipped with Anti-lock Brake System (ABS), ensure that the hydraulic accumulator is fully depressurized before disconnecting any hydraulic lines, hoses or fittings.

2. Disconnect and plug hydraulic lines from the master cylinder.
3. Remove the mounting bolts and the master cylinder assembly.
To install:
4. Install the master cylinder assembly and mounting bolts.
5. Connect the hydraulic lines to the master cylinder.
6. Connect the negative battery cable and, if equipped, the electrical connector to the level sensor unit.
7. Refill the master cylinder with clean brake fluid. Bleed the brake system.

Proportioning Valve

REMOVAL AND INSTALLATION

1. Disconnect the negative battery cable.

NOTE: If equipped with Anti-lock Brake System (ABS), ensure that the hydraulic accumulator is fully depressurized before disconnecting any hydraulic lines, hoses or fittings.

2. Disconnect and plug the brake lines at the master cylinder on the non-ABS models. On ABS equipped models, disconnect the front brake line from the proportioner valve and plug.
3. Remove the proportioner valve and O-ring assembly.
To install:
4. Install new O-rings on the proportioner valve.
5. Install the new valve(s) into the master cylinder on non-ABS system. If equipped with ABS, install the new valve(s) to brake lines.
6. Refill the master cylinder and bleed the brake system.
7. Connect the negative battery cable.

Power Brake Booster

REMOVAL AND INSTALLATION

1. Disconnect the negative battery cable.
2. From inside the vehicle, detach the brake pushrod from the brake pedal.
3. Remove the master cylinder-to-power brake booster bolts and move the master cylinder aside.
4. Disconnect the vacuum hose from the power brake booster.
5. Remove the power brake booster-to-cowl nuts and the booster.
To install:
6. Install the booster and the power brake booster-to-cowl nuts.
7. Connect the vacuum hose to the power brake booster.
8. Move the master cylinder into position and install the master cylinder-to-power brake booster bolts.
9. From inside the vehicle, attach the brake pushrod to the brake pedal.
10. Connect the negative battery cable.

Brake Caliper

REMOVAL AND INSTALLATION

NOTE: If equipped with Anti-lock Brake System (ABS), ensure that the hydraulic accumulator is fully depressurized before disconnecting any hydraulic lines, hoses or fittings.

1. Raise and safely support the vehicle. Remove the tire and wheel assembly.
2. Push the piston into caliper, using the proper tool, to provide clearance between the pad and the rotor.
3. Disconnect and plug the brake line and remove the mounting bolts and sleeves.
4. Remove the caliper from the rotor and the mounting bracket.
To install:
5. Install the caliper onto the rotor and mounting bracket.
6. Connect the brake line to the caliper.
7. Install the caliper mounting nuts and sleeves. Tighten the caliper mounting bolts to 38 ft. lbs. (52 Nm).
8. With the caliper mounting bolts tight, ensure that the brake line fitting is tight.
9. Install the tire and wheel assembly.
10. Lower the vehicle.
11. Check the brake fluid level in the reservoir.

12. Before starting the engine, depress the brake pedal until the pedal is firm. Bleed the brake system, as required.
13. Recheck the master cylinder fluid level.

Disc Brake Pads

REMOVAL AND INSTALLATION

1. If the brake pads are to be replaced, use a syringe or similar tool to remove the brake fluid from the master cylinder reservoir until it is approximately $\frac{1}{3}$–$\frac{1}{2}$ full.
2. Raise and safely support the vehicle. Remove the tire and wheel assembly.
3. Remove the caliper from the rotor and support the caliper out of the way.
4. Remove the brake pads from the caliper.
5. Using a C-clamp, press the piston into caliper to provide additional clearance between the pad and rotor for the new pads.
To install:
6. Install new bushings into the grooves in the mounting bolt holes. Install the inboard pad by snapping the retainer spring into the piston.
7. Install the outboard pad with the back of the pad flat against the caliper.
8. Install the caliper to the rotor. Install the caliper attaching bolts.
9. Install the tire and wheel assembly.
10. Check the brake fluid level in the master cylinder reservoir. Top-up as necessary.
11. Before starting the engine, slowly depress the brake pedal until the pedal is firm. Bleed the brake system, as required.
12. Recheck the master cylinder fluid level.

Brake Rotor

REMOVAL AND INSTALLATION

1. Raise and safely support the vehicle. Remove the tire and wheel assembly.
2. Remove the caliper from the rotor. Support the caliper aside using a length of wire. Do not allow the caliper to hang by the brake hose unsupported.
3. Remove the shaft nut and washer and remove the rotor assembly.

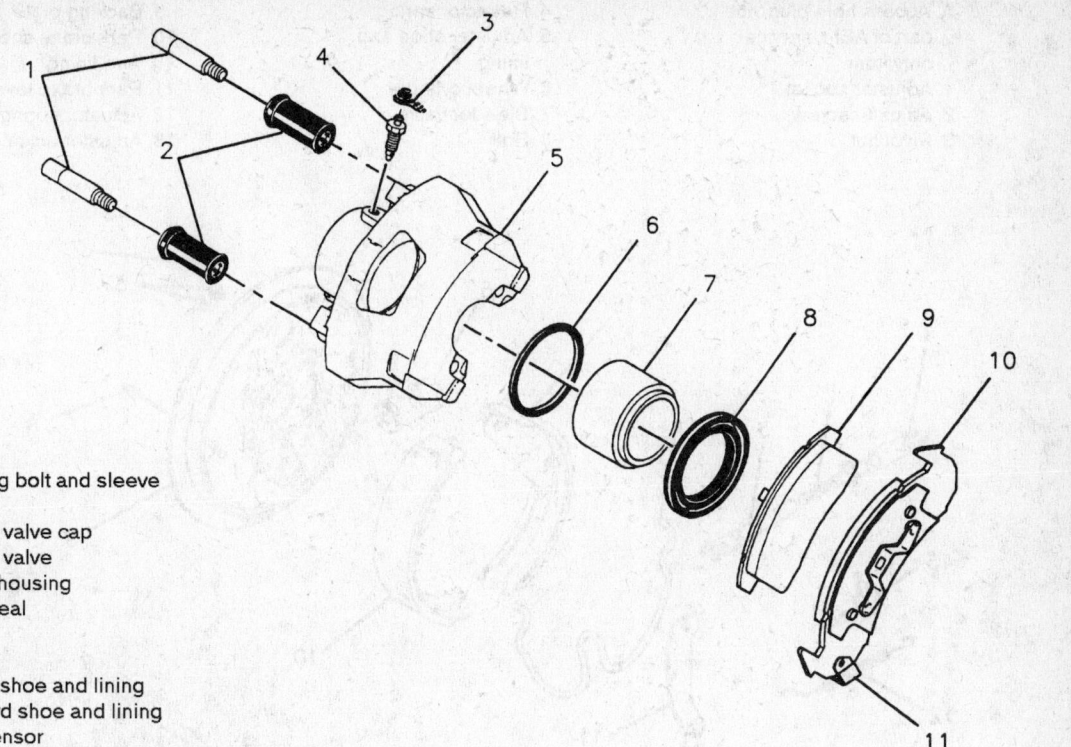

1. Mounting bolt and sleeve
2. Bushing
3. Bleeder valve cap
4. Bleeder valve
5. Caliper housing
6. Piston seal
7. Piston
8. Boot
9. Inboard shoe and lining
10. Outboard shoe and lining
11. Wear sensor

8470G075

Front brake caliper components

To install:
4. Install the rotor to the hub assembly. Tighten the shaft nut to 70 ft. lbs. (95 Nm).
5. Install the caliper.
6. Install the tire and wheel assembly.
7. Lower the vehicle.

Brake Drums

REMOVAL AND INSTALLATION

1. Raise and safely support the vehicle.
2. Matchmark the wheel to the hub flange.
3. Remove the tire and wheel assembly. Matchmark the drum to the hub flange.
4. Remove the brake drum assembly. Make sure the parking brake is released.
To install:
5. Install the brake drum.
6. Install the tire and wheel assembly.
7. Lower the vehicle.

Brake Shoes

REMOVAL AND INSTALLATION

1. Raise and safely support the vehicle. Remove the brake drum assembly.
2. Remove the actuator and the upper return spring with the proper tools.
3. Disconnect the spring connecting link, adjuster actuator and the hold-down washer.
4. Remove the hold-down springs and the pins. Disconnect the brake shoes from the parking brake cable.
5. Remove the brake shoe and lining assemblies.
To install:
6. Install the brake shoe and lining assemblies.
7. Connect the brake shoes to the parking brake cable. Install the brake shoe hold-down pins and springs.
8. Connect the hold-down washer, adjuster actuator and spring connecting link.
9. Install the upper return springs and actuator.
10. Install the brake drum.

11. Install the tire and wheel assembly.
12. Adjust the brakes.
13. Lower the vehicle and road test.

Wheel Cylinder

REMOVAL AND INSTALLATION

1. Raise and safely support the vehicle. Remove the rear drum assembly.
2. Remove the brake shoe and lining assembly.
3. Disconnect and plug the inlet line. Remove the mounting screws and lockwashers.
4. Remove the wheel cylinder assembly.
To install:
5. Install the wheel cylinder assembly.
6. Install the mounting screws and lockwashers.
7. Install the brake shoe and lining assembly.
8. Install the brake drum.
9. Bleed the brake system. Check the brake fluid level in the master cylinder frequently while bleeding the system.
10. Lower the vehicle.

A. Access hole plug; not
   part of ASM; service
   only item
1. Adjuster socket
2. Adjuster screw
3. Pivot nut

4. Retractor spring
5. Adjuster shoe and
   lining
6. Wheel cylinder
7. Bleeder valve
8. Bolt

9. Backing plate
10. Park brake shoe
    and lining
11. Park brake lever
12. Actuator spring
13. Adjuster actuator

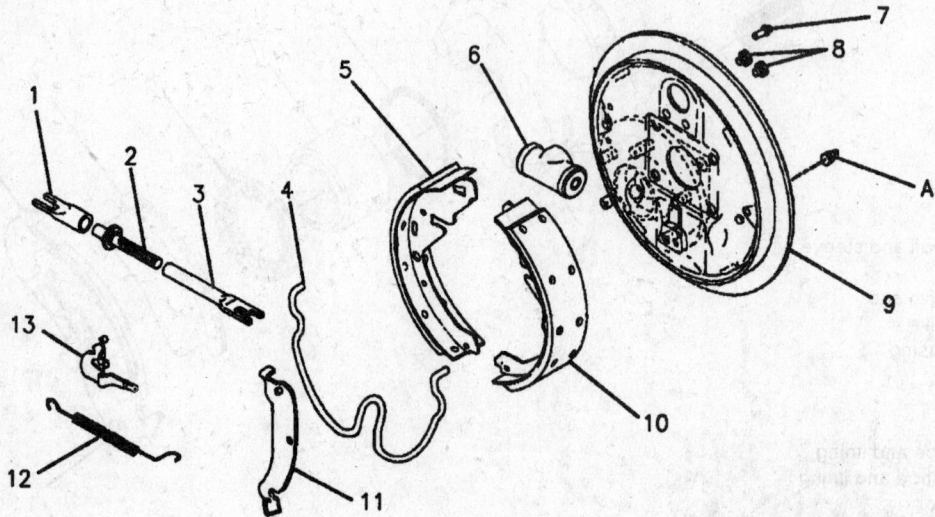

8470G076

Rear drum brake components

Parking Brake Cable

ADJUSTMENT

1. Adjust the rear brakes.
2. Apply and release the parking brake 6 times to 10 clicks. Release the park brake pedal.
3. Raise and support the vehicle safely. Remove the access plug.
4. Adjust the park brake cable until a ⅛ drill can be inserted through the access hole into the space between the shoe web and the park brake lever.
5. Check for free wheel rotation. Replace the access plug.
6. Lower the vehicle.

REMOVAL AND INSTALLATION

Front

1. Raise and safely support the vehicle.
2. Loosen the equalizer assembly at the front parking brake cable. Remove the front parking brake cable from the equalizer assembly.
3. Disconnect the cable casing retaining nut at the underbody. Remove the cable casing and cable from the control assembly.

To install:

4. Install the cable casing and cable to the control assembly. Connect the cable casing retaining nut at the underbody. Tighten the casing retaining nut to 22 ft. lbs. (30 Nm).
5. Install the front parking brake cable to the equalizer assembly. Tighten the equalizer assembly at the front parking brake cable.
6. Adjust the cable.
7. Lower the vehicle.

Intermediate

1. Raise and safely support the vehicle.
2. Disconnect the intermediate brake cable from the adjuster.
3. Remove the clip from the brake pipe retainer and cable and remove the cable from the rear equalizer.
4. Remove the cable from the bracket and from the brake pipe retainers.

To install:

5. Install the cable into the brake pipe retainers and snap the cable into the bracket.
6. Install the cable through the top support hole in the underbody.
7. Connect the left and right rear cables to the intermediate cable, utilizing the equalizer.

8. Install the clip around the cable and the brake pipe retainer and tighten the bolt to 17 inch lbs. (3 Nm).
9. Connect the cable to the adjuster and adjust the cable as necessary.
10. Lower the vehicle.

Rear

1. Raise and safely support the vehicle. Remove the tire and wheel assembly.
2. Remove the brake drum and insert the proper tool between the brake shoe and the top part of the actuator bracket.
3. Push the bracket to the front and release the top adjuster bracket rod.
4. Remove the rear hold-down spring, actuator lever and the lever return spring.
5. Disconnect the adjuster screw spring and remove the top rear brake shoe return spring.
6. Disconnect the parking brake cable from the parking brake lever.
7. Depress the conduit fitting retaining tangs and remove the conduit fitting from the backing plate.
8. Remove the left rear cable by backing off the equalizer nut and dis-

connecting the conduit from the under body bracket.

9. Remove the right rear cable by disconnecting the cable end button from the connector and remove the conduit fitting from the axle bracket.

To install:

10. Install the right rear cable by connecting the conduit fitting to the axle bracket and cable end button to the connector.

11. Install the left rear cable by connecting the conduit fitting to the axle bracket and the left cable to the equalizer nut. Connect the conduit fitting the underbody bracket.

12. Install the conduit fitting to the backing plate and connect the parking brake cable to the parking brake lever.

13. Install the top brake shoe return spring and the adjuster screw spring.

14. Replace the lever return spring, actuator lever and the rear hold-down spring.

15. Install the top adjuster bracket rod. Replace the brake drum assembly.

16. Install the tire and wheel assembly. Adjust the parking brake cable.

17. Lower the vehicle.

Brake System Bleeding

1. Fill the master cylinder reservoirs with brake fluid. Keep the level at least ½ full during the bleeding operation.

2. Disconnect and plug the brake lines. Fill the master cylinder until fluid begins to flow from the front pipe connector port.

3. Connect the brake lines to the master cylinder and tighten.

4. Depress the brake pedal slowly one time and hold, tighten the connection and then release the brake pedal slowly. Wait 15 seconds.

5. Repeat the sequence until all the air has been removed from the master cylinder bore.

6. After all the air has been removed from the front connections repeat the same procedure at the rear connections of the master cylinder.

7. Individual wheel cylinders and calipers are bled only after all the air has been removed from the master cylinder.

8. To bleed the caliper or the wheel cylinder perform the following:

a. Fill the master cylinder reservoirs with brake fluid. Keep the level at least ½ full during the bleeding operation.

b. Raise and support the vehicle safely. Attach a transparent tube over the bleeder screw.

c. Using an assistant, depress the brake pedal slowly, one time and hold.

d. Loosen the bleeder valve to purge the air from the cylinder.

e. Tighten the bleeder screw and slowly release the brake pedal. Wait 15 seconds.

f. Repeat this sequence until all the air is removed. The bleeding sequence is R/R, L/F, L/R and R/F.

g. Lower the vehicle and refill the master cylinder.

Anti-Lock Brake System Service

PRECAUTION

Failure to observe the following precautions may result in system damage.

- Before performing electric arc welding on the vehicle, disconnect the Electronic Brake Control Module (EBCM) and the hydraulic modulator connectors.

- When performing painting work on the vehicle, do not expose the Electronic Brake Control Module (EBCM) to temperatures in excess of 185°F (85°C) for longer than 2 hrs. The system may be exposed to temperatures up to 200°F (95°C) for less than 15 min.

- Never disconnect or connect the Electronic Brake Control Module (EBCM) or hydraulic modulator connectors with the ignition switch ON.

- Never disassemble any component of the Anti-Lock Brake System (ABS) which is designated non-serviceable; the component must be replaced as an assembly.

- When filling the master cylinder, always use Delco Supreme 11 brake fluid or equivalent, which meets DOT-3 specifications; petroleum base fluid will destroy the rubber parts.

RELIEVING ANTI-LOCK BRAKE SYSTEM PRESSURE

1. Disconnect the negative battery cable. Turn the ignition to the **OFF** position.

2. Pump the brake pedal a minimum of 25 times.

3. When a definite increase in pedal effort is felt, stroke the pedal a few more times.

4. This should relieve all the hydraulic pressure from the system.

Pressure Modulator Valve (PMV) Assembly

REMOVAL AND INSTALLATION

1. Disconnect the negative battery cable and remove the air cleaner assembly.

2. Disconnect the PMV electrical connectors.

3. Remove the clamp on the PMV reservoir and disconnect the hose. Plug the hose to prevent loss of brake fluid.

4. Disconnect the brake lines from the PMV assembly.

5. Raise and safely support the vehicle. Remove the lower PMV assembly bolt. Lower the vehicle.

6. Remove the upper PMV assembly bolts and remove the PMV assembly from the vehicle.

To install:

7. Install the PMV assembly to the vehicle. Install the bolts and tighten the bolts to 20 ft. lbs. (27 Nm).

8. Install the lower PMV assembly bolt and tighten to 20 ft. lbs. (27 Nm).

9. Connect the brake lines to the PMV assembly and tighten to 11 ft. lbs. (15 Nm).

10. Connect the reservoir hose to the PMV reservoir and install the clamp.

11. Connect the electrical connectors to the PMV assembly.

12. Connect the negative battery cable and install the air cleaner assembly.

13. Fill the brake reservoir. Bleed the brake system.

Electronic Brake Control Module (EBCM)

REMOVAL AND INSTALLATION

1. Disconnect the negative battery cable.

2. Lower the lower dash panel and disconnect the EBCM module from the bracket..

3. Disconnect the EBCM connector and remove the EBCM module.

To install:

4. Install the EBCM module and connect the EBCM electrical connector.

5. Connect the EBCM to the bracket and install the lower dash panel.

6. Connect the negative battery cable.

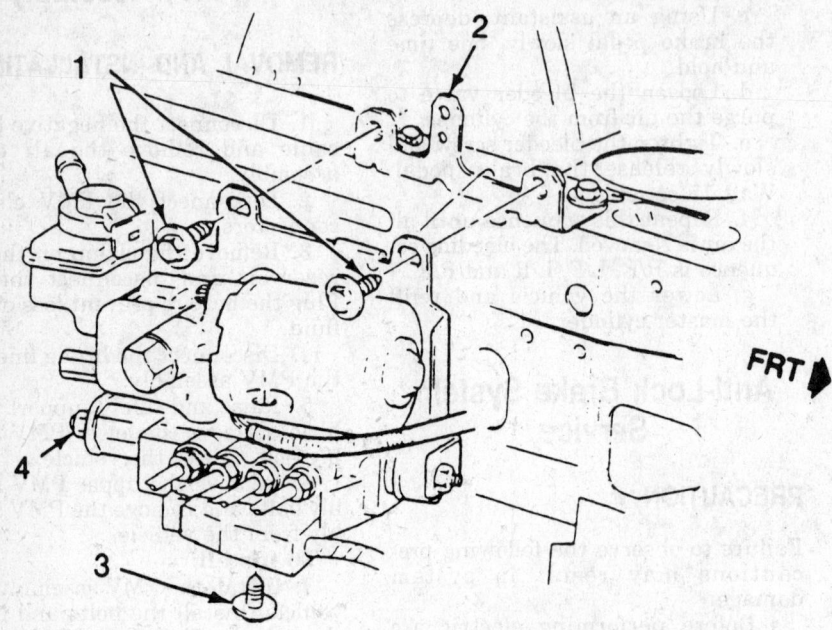

1. Bolt
2. Side rail bracket
3. Bolt
4. Pressure Modulator Valve (PMV) assembly

8569G001

Pressure Modulator Valve (PMV) assembly

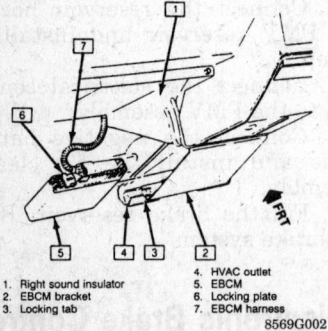

1. Right sound insulator
2. EBCM bracket
3. Locking tab
4. EBCM
5. Locking plate
6. EBCM harness
7.

8569G002

Location of the Electronic Brake Control Module (EBCM) — Cadillac equipped with ABS

Wheel Speed Sensors

REMOVAL AND INSTALLATION

Front

1. Disconnect the negative battery cable.
2. Raise and safely support the vehicle. Remove the wheel and tire assembly.
3. Disconnect the wheel speed sensor electrical connector.
4. Remove the front hub and bearing assembly.

5. Pry the wheel speed sensor slinger off, using a prybar. Discard the old slinger.
6. Remove the sensor by gently prying the bearing assembly off.

To install:
7. Apply a locking fixture to the groove in the outer diameter of the bearing hub.
8. Using tool J-38764 or equivalent and a press, install the sensor.
9. Install the hub and bearing assembly and connect the sensor connector.
10. Install the wheel and tire assembly and lower the vehicle.
11. Connect the negative battery cable.

Rear

1. Disconnect the negative battery cable.
2. Raise and safely support the vehicle. Remove the wheel and tire assembly.
3. Disconnect the wheel speed sensor electrical connector.
4. Remove the rear hub and bearing assembly.
5. Remove the Torx screws and remove the sensor.

To install:
6. Install the sensor with O-ring intact.
7. Install the Torx screws and tighten to 33 inch lbs. (3.7 Nm).
8. Install the hub and bearing assembly.
9. Connect the wheel speed sensor electrical connector.
10. Install the wheel and tire assembly and lower the vehicle.
11. Connect the negative battery cable.

FRONT SUSPENSION

MacPherson Strut

REMOVAL AND INSTALLATION

1. Loosen the bar assembly through bolts.
2. Disconnect the 3 mounting nuts from the top of the strut assembly.
3. Raise and safely support the vehicle. Position a jackstand under the engine cradle and lower the vehicle so the weight of the vehicle rests on

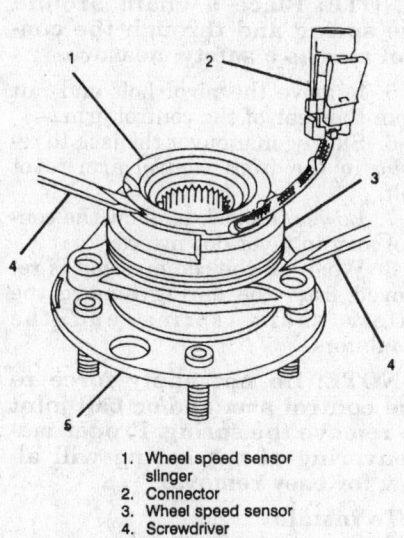

1. Wheel speed sensor slinger
2. Connector
3. Wheel speed sensor
4. Screwdriver
5. Hub and bearing assembly

8569G003

Front Wheel Speed Sensor

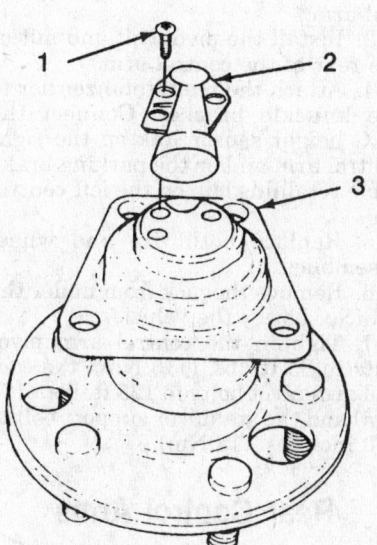

1. Screw
2. Wheel speed sensor
3. Hub

8569G004

Rear Wheel Speed Sensor

the a jackstand and not the control arms.

4. Remove the tire and wheel assemblies. If equipped with ABS, disconnect the front sensor.

5. Disconnect the brake line bracket from the strut assembly. Remove the strut-to-steering knuckle bolts.

6. Remove the strut assembly from the vehicle.

To install:

7. Install the strut assembly.

8. Install the strut-to-steering knuckle bolts. Connect the brake line bracket to the strut assembly.

9. If equipped with ABS, connect the front sensor. Install the tire and wheel assemblies.

10. Remove the jackstand. Lower the vehicle.

11. Connect the mounting nuts to the top of the strut assembly.

Strut Cartridge

REMOVAL AND INSTALLATION

1. Install the strut assembly to a strut compressor.

2. Turn the compressor so that the spring becomes compressed.

3. Hold the strut shaft from turning and remove the 24mm strut nut.

4. Install special rod J34013-38 to the strut shaft and guide the strut out of the assembly while loosening the spring compressor.

5. Remove the strut cartridge from the assembly.

To install:

6. Install the strut to the strut compressor/spring assembly.

7. Start turning the compressor screw clockwise to compress the spring while guiding the shaft through the mounting hole.

8. Tighten the mounting nut to 55 ft. lbs. (75 Nm) while holding the strut shaft.

Lower Ball Joints

INSPECTION

1. Raise and support the vehicle safely. Position a jackstand under the engine cradle and lower the vehicle so the weight of the vehicle rests on the a jackstand and not the control arms.

2. Grasp the wheel at the top and the bottom and shake the wheel in and out.

3. If the is any movement of the steering knuckle in relation the con-

trol arm, the ball joints are defective and must be replaced.

REMOVAL AND INSTALLATION

1. Raise and safely support the vehicle. Position a jackstand under the engine cradle and lower the vehicle so the weight of the vehicle rests on the jackstand and not the control arms.

2. Remove the tire and wheel assembly.

3. Disconnect the ball joint from the steering knuckle, using the proper tool.

4. Drill out the rivets retaining the ball joint and loosen the stabilizer shaft bushing assembly nut.

5. Remove the ball joint from the steering knuckle and the control arm.

To install:

6. Install the ball joint to the steering knuckle and the control arm.

7. Install the 3 ball joint bolts facing down. Tighten nuts to 50 ft. lbs. (68 Nm). Tighten the stabilizer shaft bushing assembly nut to 13 ft. lbs. (17 Nm).

8. Connect the ball joint to the steering knuckle. Install a new cotter pin.

9. Install the tire and wheel assembly.

10. Lower the vehicle.

Lower Control Arms

REMOVAL AND INSTALLATION

1. Raise and safely support the vehicle. Position a jackstand under the engine cradle and lower the vehicle so the weight of the vehicle rests on the jackstand and not the control arms.

2. Remove the tire and wheel assembly. Disconnect the stabilizer shaft-to-control arm bolt.

3. Remove the ball joint from the steering knuckle and the control arm.

4. Remove the control arm mounting bolts and remove the control arm from the engine cradle.

To install:

5. Install the control arm to the engine cradle. Do not tighten the control arm bolts at this time.

6. Install the stabilizer shaft bushings and connect the ball joint to the steering knuckle.

7. Raise the vehicle so the weight of the vehicle is supported by the control arm.

NOTE: The weight of the vehicle must be supported by the control arms when tightening the control arm mounting nuts.

8. Tighten the rear control arm mounting nut to 90 ft. lbs. (122 Nm) and the front mounting nut to 140 ft. lbs. (190 Nm).

9. Install the ball joint to the control arm and tighten the nut to 37 ft. lbs. (50 Nm).

10. Replace the tire and wheel assemblies.

11. Raise the vehicle and remove the jackstand.

12. Lower the vehicle.

Sway Bar

REMOVAL AND INSTALLATION

1. Raise and safely support the vehicle. Position a jackstand under the engine cradle and lower the vehicle so the weight of the vehicle rests on the jackstand and not the control arms.

2. Remove the tire and wheel assemblies.

3. Remove the bolts connecting the stabilizer bar bushings to the control arms.

4. Remove the stabilizer bar mounting bolts. Matchmark and disconnect the tie rod ends from the steering knuckles.

5. Disconnect the exhaust pipe from the exhaust manifold and turn the passenger side strut assembly completely to the right.

6. Slide the stabilizer bar over the steering knuckle and pull down until the stabilizer bar clears the frame.

7. Remove the stabilizer bar from the vehicle.

To install:

8. Install the stabilizer bar over the steering knuckle.

9. Raise the stabilizer bar over the frame and slide into position.

10. Loosely, install the stabilizer bar mount bushings, brackets and bolts.

11. Install the tie rod ends to the steering knuckles, tighten the nuts to 52 ft. lbs. (71 Nm). Tighten the stabilizer bar mounting bolts to 37 ft. lbs. (50 Nm).

12. Connect the exhaust pipe to the exhaust manifold and tighten the bolts to 15 ft. lbs. (20 Nm).

13. Replace the tire and wheel assemblies.

14. Raise the vehicle and remove the jackstands.

15. Lower the vehicle.

REAR SUSPENSION

MacPherson Strut

REMOVAL AND INSTALLATION

1. Raise and safely support the vehicle.

2. Remove the trunk side cover. Remove the tire and wheel assemblies.

3. Support the control arm with a suitable jack.

4. Disconnect the Electronic Level Control (ELC) air tube and separate from the strut air tube, if equipped. If equipped with Computer Command Ride (CCR), disconnect the strut electrical connector from the harness.

5. Disconnect the strut tower mounting nuts. The nuts are located inside the trunk.

6. Remove the strut anchor bolts, washers and nuts from the steering knuckle and bracket.

7. Remove the strut assembly from the vehicle.

To install:

8. Install the strut assembly and connect the upper strut mounting nuts.

9. Replace the strut anchor bolts, washer, knuckle bracket and nuts.

10. Connect the ELC tube or CCR connector if equipped.

11. Tighten the upper mount nuts to 35 ft. lbs. (47 Nm) and the strut-to-knuckle nuts to 140 ft. lbs. (190 Nm).

12. Replace the tire and wheel assemblies. Remove the jack from under the vehicle.

13. Replace the trunk side cover and lower the vehicle.

Coil Springs

REMOVAL AND INSTALLATION

1. Raise and support the vehicle safely. Support the vehicle so the control arms hang free.

2. Remove both tire and wheel assemblies.

3. Disconnect the ELC height sensor on the right control arm and/or the parking brake cable retaining clip on the left control arm.

4. Place a proper tool and jack into position and remove the tension from the control arm pivot bolts.

NOTE: Place a chain around the spring and through the control arm as a safety measure.

5. Remove the pivot bolt and nut from the rear of the control arm.

6. Slowly, maneuver the jack to relieve in the front control arm pivot bolt.

7. Lower the jack to allow the control arm to pivot downward.

8. When all the compression is removed from the spring remove the safety chain, spring and the insulators.

NOTE: Do not apply force to the control arm and/or ball joint to remove the spring. Proper maneuvering of the spring will allow for easy removal.

To install:

9. Snap the upper insulator on the spring prior to installation.

10. Position the lower insulator and spring in the vehicle. Install the coil springs so the upper end of the springs are positioned properly.

11. Raise the control arm into position, using the proper tools.

12. Slowly, maneuver the jack to permit the installation of the pivot bolt and nut at the front of the control arm.

13. Install the pivot bolt and nut at the rear of the control arm.

14. Attach the rear stabilizer bar to the knuckle bracket. Connect the ELC height sensor link on the right control arm and/or the parking brake cable retaining clip on the left control arm.

15. Replace both tire and wheel assemblies.

16. Remove the jack from under the vehicle. Lower the vehicle.

17. Tighten the control arm pivot nuts to 85 ft. lbs. (115 Nm), the control arm pivot bolts to 125 ft. lbs. (170 Nm) and the stabilizer support bolt to 160 inch lbs. (18 Nm).

Rear Control Arms

REMOVAL AND INSTALLATION

1. Raise and support the vehicle safely. Remove the tire and wheel assembly.

2. If equipped, disconnect the ELC height sensor on the right control arm and/or the parking brake cable retaining clip on the left control arm.

3. Disconnect the suspension adjustment link retaining nut and sepa-

rate the link assembly from the control arm.

4. Remove the ball stud and the castellated nut. Turn over and install with the flat portion facing up. Do not tighten.

5. Separate the knuckle from the ball stud, using the proper tool. Remove the control arm.

To install:

6. Install the control arm. Connect the knuckle to the ball stud. Install the castellated nut.

7. Connect the link assembly to the control arm. Connect the suspension adjustment link retaining nut.

8. If equipped, connect the ELC height sensor on the right control arm and/or the parking brake cable retaining clip on the left control arm.

9. Install the tire and wheel assembly.

10. Lower the vehicle.

11. Tighten the control arm pivot nuts to 85 ft. lbs. (115 Nm) and the pivot bolts to 125 ft. lbs. (170 Nm). Tighten the pivot nuts and bolts with the vehicle unsupported and the wheels at normal height.

Rear Wheel Bearings

REMOVAL AND INSTALLATION

1. Raise and support the vehicle safely. Remove the tire and wheel assembly.

2. Remove the brake drum from the vehicle.

3. Remove the hub and bearing assembly from the axle.

NOTE: The bolts that attach the hub and bearing assembly also support the brake assembly. Do not let the brake line support the brake assembly.

4. Remove the wheel bearings.

To install:

5. Install the wheel bearings.

6. Install the hub and bearing assembly to the axle. Tighten the hub and bearing bolts to 52 ft. lbs. (71 Nm).

7. Install the brake drum.

8. Install the tire and wheel assembly.

9. Lower the vehicle.

GM "E, K AND V" BODY

Front Wheel Drive

CADILLAC—DeVille, Concours, Eldorado, Seville **BUICK**—Allante, Riviera **OLDSMOBILE**—Toronado

13

FIRING ORDER

NOTE: To avoid confusion, always replace spark plug wires one at a time.

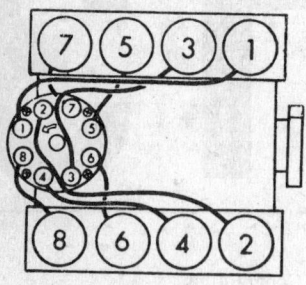

8470H004

4.5L and 4.9L Engines
Engine Firing Order:
1-8-4-3-6-5-7-2
Distributor Rotation:
Counterclockwise

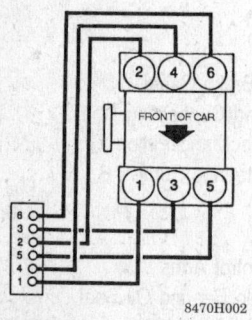

8470H002

3.8L Engine
Engine Firing Order:
1-6-5-4-3-2
Distributorless Ignition System

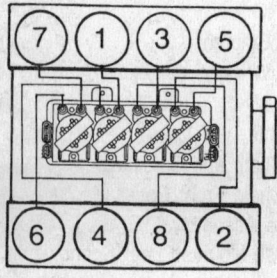

8470H003

4.6L Engines
Engine Firing Order:
1-2-7-3-4-5-6-8
Distributorless Ignition System

ENGINE ELECTRICAL

NOTE: Disconnecting the negative battery cable on some vehicles may interfere with the functions of the on board computer systems and may require the computer to undergo a relearning process, once the negative battery cable is reconnected.

Distributor

The High Energy Ignition (HEI) distributor with Electronic Spark Timing (EST) easily identified by the presence of a 6 terminal ECM connector.

REMOVAL

1. Disconnect the negative battery cable.
2. Set No. 1 cylinder to TDC of its compression stroke.
3. Remove distributor appearance cover and retainer, if equipped.
4. Remove ignition switch battery feed wire from distributor cap. Remove coil connectors from cap.

NOTE: Do not use a prybar to release locking tabs.

5. Remove 4 bolts from distributor cap and move cap aside. Note the positioning of the cap upon removal and reinstall in same position.
6. Remove 6 terminal ECM harness from distributor. Matchmark the rotor-to-housing and the housing-to-engine.
7. Remove distributor clamp nut and hold-down nut. Use special tool J-29791 or equivalent, to remove hold-down nut.
8. Note the position of rotor, then pull distributor up until rotor just stops turning counterclockwise and again note position of rotor. Remove distributor.

INSTALLATION

Timing Not Disturbed

1. Insert the distributor into the engine, making sure the tip of the rotor is aligned with the alignment marks on the distributor housing and the engine.
2. Make sure the oil pump intermediate driveshaft is properly seated in the oil pump.

3. Install the distributor lock but do not tighten.
4. Connect the electrical harness connector(s) to the distributor, then, install distributor cap.
5. Start the engine and allow to come to normal operating temperature. Check and/or adjust the timing.

Timing Disturbed

1. Remove the No. 1 cylinder spark plug and place a finger over the hole. Using a wrench on the crankshaft pulley bolt, slowly turn the engine until compression is felt.
2. Align the timing marks so No. 1 cylinder is on TDC of the compression stroke.
3. Position the distributor in the engine with the rotor at No. 1 firing position. Make sure the oil pump intermediate driveshaft is properly seated in the oil pump.
4. Install the distributor retainer and lock bolt, tighten the lock bolt.
5. Reconnect the electrical harness connector(s) to the distributor and install distributor cap.
6. Start the engine and allow to come to normal operating temperature. Check and/or adjust the timing.

Distributorless Ignition System

The Computer Controlled Coil Ignition (C₃I) system uses an ignition coil pack, ignition module, dual crankshaft sensor and associated wiring.

REMOVAL AND INSTALLATION

Ignition Coil

3.8L ENGINE

1. Disconnect the negative battery cable.
2. Label and disconnect the spark plug wires.
3. Remove the 2 screws securing the individual coil pack to the ignition module.
4. Remove the coil assembly.
To install:
5. Install the coil assembly.
6. Install the 2 screws and tighten to 40 inch lbs. (4–5 Nm).
7. Connect the spark plug wires.
8. Connect the negative battery cable.

4.5L AND 4.9L ENGINES

1. Disconnect the negative battery cable.

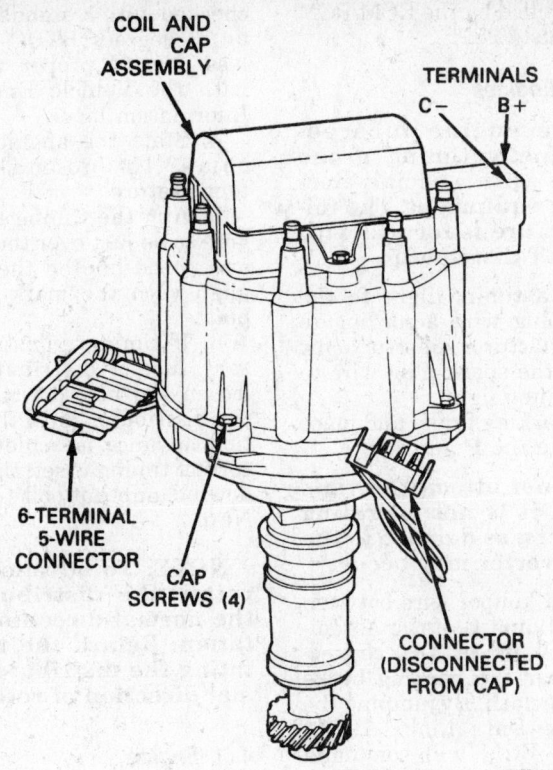

COIL AND CAP ASSEMBLY

TERMINALS
C− B+

6-TERMINAL 5-WIRE CONNECTOR

CAP SCREWS (4)

CONNECTOR (DISCONNECTED FROM CAP)

8470H005

Distributor assembly with coil in cap

2. Disconnect the battery lead wire and coil connections from the cap.

3. Remove the 2 coil cover attaching screws and remove the cover.

4. Remove the coil attaching screws and remove coil and leads from the cap.

To install:

5. Connect the coil leads to the cap.

6. Install the 4 coil attaching screws and install the coil cover and attaching screws.

7. Connect the battery feed wire and coil connection to the cap. Connect the negative battery cable.

4.6L (VIN 9 AND Y) ENGINES

1. Disconnect the negative battery cable.

2. Disconnect the spark plug wires and disconnect the electrical connectors at the ignition control module assembly.

3. Remove the 4 bolts that retain the ignition control module to the rear camshaft cover.

4. Remove the ignition control module assembly from the vehicle and remove the coil retaining bolts from the coil. Separate the ignition coil from the module assembly.

To install:

5. Install the coil to the ignition control module assembly. Install the mounting bolts.

6. Install the ignition control module assembly to the rear camshaft cover and install the mounting bolts.

7. Connect the electrical connectors, spark plug wires and connect the negative battery cable.

Ignition Module

3.8L ENGINE

1. Disconnect the negative battery cable.

2. Remove 14-way connector at ignition module.

3. Label and disconnect the spark plug wires at coil assembly.

4. Remove nuts and washers (3) securing ignition module assembly to bracket.

5. Remove 6 screws securing coil assembly to ignition module.

6. Note lead colors and mark for reassembly.

7. Disconnect connectors between coil and ignition module.

8. Remove ignition module.

To install:

9. Install coil and connectors to ignition module.

10. Install 6 screws and tighten to 27 inch lbs. (3 Nm).

11. Install nuts and washers securing assembly to bracket.

12. Install plug wires.

13. Connect 14-way connector to module.

14. Connect the negative battery cable.

4.5L AND 4.9L ENGINES

1. Disconnect the negative battery cable.

2. Remove the distributor cap from the distributor and remove the rotor.

3. Remove the module attaching screws, remove the shield and lift module up.

4. Note color code on leads to module for reassembly. Disconnect the leads from the module.

To install:

5. Connect the leads to the module, observing the color coded wiring.

6. Install the module shield and module attaching screws.

7. Install the rotor and the cap.

8. Connect the negative battery cable.

4.6L (VIN 9 AND Y) ENGINES

1. Disconnect the negative battery cable.

2. Disconnect the spark plug wires and disconnect the electrical connectors at the ignition control module assembly.

3. Remove the 4 bolts that retain the ignition control module to the rear camshaft cover.

4. Remove the ignition control module assembly from the vehicle.

To install:

5. Install the ignition control module assembly to the rear camshaft cover and install the mounting bolts.

6. Connect the electrical connectors and the spark plug wires.

7. Connect the negative battery cable.

Crankshaft Sensor

EXCEPT 4.6L ENGINE

1. Disconnect the negative battery cable.

2. Remove nuts holding vibration damper support to ignition module bracket and vibration damper to engine bracket.

3. Remove support.

4. Remove bolts holding bracket to front of engine.

5. Remove nut from vibration damper to engine cradle.

6. Remove vibration damper and support assembly.

7. Remove serpentine belt from crankshaft pulley.

8. Raise and safely support the vehicle.

9. Remove right front tire and wheel assembly.

10. Remove right inner fender access cover.

11. Remove crankshaft harmonic balancer retaining bolt using 28mm socket.

12. Remove crankshaft harmonic balancer.

13. Disconnect sensor electrical connector.

14. Remove sensor and pedestal from block face.

15. Remove sensor from pedestal.

To install:

16. Loosely install crankshaft sensor on pedestal.

17. Position sensor with pedestal attached on special tool J–37089.

18. Position special tool on crankshaft.

19. Install bolts to hold pedestal to block face. Tighten to 14–28 ft. lbs. (20–40 Nm).

20. Tighten pedestal pinch bolt to 36–40 ft. lbs. (4–4.5 Nm).

21. Remove special tool J–37089.

22. Place special tool J–37089 on harmonic balancer and turn. If any vane of the harmonic balancer touches the tool, replace the balancer assembly.

23. Install balancer on crankshaft.

24. Tighten crankshaft bolt to 200–239 ft. lbs. (270–315 Nm).

25. Install inner fender shield.

26. Install tire and wheel assembly and tighten to 100 ft. lbs. (140 Nm).

27. Connect the negative battery cable.

4.6L ENGINE

1. Disconnect the electrical connector.

2. Remove the retaining bolt and remove the sensor.

3. Installation is the reverse of the removal procedure.

Ignition Timing

ADJUSTMENT

NOTE: Always consult the Vehicle Emission Control Information label in the engine compartment before adjusting timing. If the underhood sticker differs from the following procedures, follow the sticker.

3.8L Engine

The 3.8L engines are equipped with a C_3I ignition system which does not incorporate a distributor. Ignition timing is controlled by the ECM/PCM and is not adjustable.

4.5L and 4.9L Engines

NOTE: The engine incorporates a magnetic timing probe hole for use with special electronic timing equipment. The following procedure is for use with the HEI — EST distributor.

1. Connect a timing light to the No. 1 spark plug wire according to the light manufacturer's instructions. Do not pierce the spark plug wire to connect the timing light.

2. Set the parking brake and place the transaxle in the **P** position.

NOTE: Do not attempt to time the engine if it is not operating on all cylinders, as damage to the catalytic converter may occur.

3. Connect a jumper wire between pins **A** (ground) and **B** of the Assembly Line Data Link (ALDL) connector, located near the parking brake pedal under the dash. By jumping the Assembly Line Data Link (ALDL) connector, the ECM will command the BCM to display a SET TIMING message on the Climate Control Driver Information Panel (CCDIC). The engine will now operate at base timing. The timing can now be checked with a standard timing light at 10 degrees BTDC at 900 rpm or less. Verify proper timing setting with the Vehicle Emission Control Information label.

4. Start the engine and allow to come to normal operating temperature.

5. Aim the timing light at the degree scale just over the harmonic balancer; the line on the pulley should align with the mark on the timing plate.

6. If timing adjustment is necessary, use a distributor wrench to loosen the hold-down clamp. Rotate the distributor until the desired ignition advance is achieved. When the correct timing is set, tighten the hold-down clamp nut/bolt to 20 ft. lbs. (27 Nm).

NOTE: To advance the timing, rotate the distributor opposite the normal direction of rotor rotation. Retard the timing by rotating the distributor in the normal direction of rotor rotation.

4.6L Engine

The 4.6L engine is equipped with the NORTHSTAR ignition system which does not incorporate a distributor. Ignition timing is controlled by the ig-

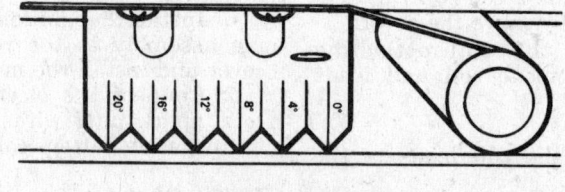

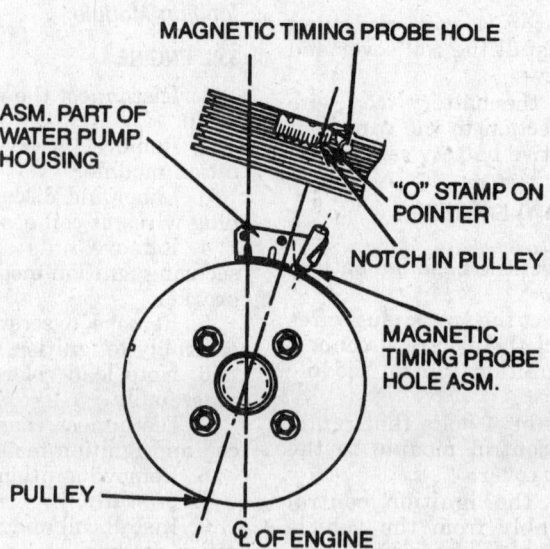

MAGNETIC TIMING PROBE HOLE

ASM. PART OF WATER PUMP HOUSING

"O" STAMP ON POINTER

NOTCH IN PULLEY

MAGNETIC TIMING PROBE HOLE ASM.

PULLEY

℄ OF ENGINE

8470H006

Timing marks and magnetic timing probe hole

nition control module and is not adjustable.

Alternator

PRECAUTIONS

Several precautions must be observed with alternator equipped vehicles to avoid damage to the unit.

• If the battery is removed for any reason, make sure it is reconnected with the correct polarity. Reversing the battery connections may result in damage to the one-way rectifiers.

• When utilizing a booster battery as a starting aid, always connect the positive to positive terminals and the negative terminal from the booster battery to a good engine ground on the vehicle being started.

• Never use a fast charger as a booster to start vehicles.

• Disconnect the battery cables when charging the battery with a fast charger.

• Never attempt to polarize the alternator.

• Do not use test lights of more than 12 volts when checking diode continuity.

• Do not short across or ground any of the alternator terminals.

• The polarity of the battery, alternator and regulator must be matched and considered before making any electrical connections within the system.

• Never separate the alternator on an open circuit. Make sure all connections within the circuit are clean and tight.

• Disconnect the battery ground terminal when performing any service on electrical components.

• Disconnect the battery if arc welding is to be done on the vehicle.

BELT TENSION ADJUSTMENT

All accessories are driven by a single serpentine belt. The tension is maintained automatically by a spring-loaded tensioner. Periodic adjustment is not required.

Belt tension can be checked using a suitable belt tension gauge. The tensioner should maintain approximately 110 lbs. (490 N) of tension throughout its functional travel. If the tension is below specification and the tensioner is resting on the maximum travel stop, replace the serpentine belt.

REMOVAL AND INSTALLATION

Except 4.6L Engine

1. Disconnect the negative battery cable.
2. Label and disconnect the electrical connectors from the back of the alternator.
3. Release the tension from the drive belt and remove the belt from the alternator pulley. Do not remove the belt from any other pulleys.
4. Remove the alternator-to-bracket bolts and the alternator from the vehicle. If necessary, disconnect the ABS ground strap.

To install:

5. Install alternator on vehicle.
6. Reposition drive belt on alternator pulley.
7. Install electrical connectors.
8. Connect negative battery cable.

4.6L Engine

1. Disconnect the negative battery cable.
2. Remove the headlight cover and radiator shroud.
3. Remove the air cleaner assembly and the left engine torque strut.
4. Disconnect the upper trans oil cooler line.
5. Remove the right and left cooling fan.
6. Remove the serpentine belt from the alternator pulley.
7. Remove the top and lower front alternator mounting bolts.
8. Disconnect the harness connector and the output cable from the alternator.
9. Remove the 2 bolts from the alternator bracket to alternator.

NOTE: The bolt nearest the exhaust manifold cannot be fully removed but can be pulled out enough to remove the alternator.

10. Remove the A/C splash shield from the cradle.
11. Remove the access panel from the bottom side of the radiator support.
12. Remove the engine harness clip from the cradle.
13. Remove the alternator from the vehicle.

To install:

14. Install the alternator to the mounting bracket and hand tighten the 2 rear bolts.
15. Connect the engine harness clip to the cradle.
16. Install the access panel to the lower radiator support.
17. Install the A/C splash shield to the cradle.

18. Connect the alternator electrical connectors.
19. Tighten the mounting bolts to 36 ft. lbs. (47 Nm).
20. Rotate the drive belt tensioner and install the drive belt around the pulley. Check the pulley alignment.
21. Install the cooling fans and connect the upper trans oil cooler line.
22. Install the left engine torque strut and air cleaner.
23. Install the headlight cover and radiator shroud.
24. Connect the negative battery cable.

Starter

REMOVAL AND INSTALLATION

Except 4.6L Engine

1. Disconnect the negative battery cable.
2. Raise and safely support the vehicle.
3. If equipped, remove the starter motor shield.
4. Remove the 4 flywheel inspection cover bolts, as required.
5. Disconnect the solenoid wires and battery cables.
6. Remove starter motor mounting bolts and stud.

NOTE: If the starter is mounted using shims, note their position prior to removal and ensure that they are repositioned properly upon installation.

To install:

7. Install starter motor mounting bolts and stud. Tighten to 32 ft. lbs. (43 Nm).
8. If removed, install the 4 flywheel inspection cover bolts.
9. Connect solenoid wires and battery cable to the starter.
10. If equipped, install starter motor shield.
11. Lower the vehicle.
12. Connect the negative battery cable.

4.6L Engine

1. Disconnect both battery cables from the battery.
2. Mark and disconnect the front bank of spark plug wires.
3. Remove the air intake duct from the throttle body.
4. Disconnect the electrical connectors from the intake manifold assembly.
5. Mark and disconnect the vacuum hoses from the brake vacuum booster, fuel pipe bundle and body.

6. Disconnect the PCV hoses at the intake manifold.

7. Disconnect the accelerator cable from the throttle body and position it aside.

8. Properly relieve the fuel system pressure.

9. Disconnect the fuel pipe connectors at the fuel pipe bundle assembly.

10. Remove the EVAP solenoid bracket at the right/rear cam cover.

11. Move the transaxle range control cable away from the cruise control servo unit.

12. Disconnect the coolant hoses from the throttle body and coolant reservoir. Immediately plug the hoses.

13. Remove the 4 intake bolts and lift the intake manifold/throttle body assembly out and off the engine.

14. Remove the solenoid **S** terminal nut and battery cable nut.

15. Remove the starter motor mounting nuts and remove the starter.

To install:

16. Before installing the starter to the engine, securely tighten the inner nuts on the terminals.

17. Connect the cables to the starter and install the starter to the engine. Tighten the mounting bolts to 22 ft. lbs. (30 Nm).

18. Install the intake manifold/throttle body assembly and tighten the 4 bolts in the proper procedure.

19. Connect the coolant hoses to the throttle body and the coolant reservoir.

20. Reposition and attach the transaxle range control cable to the cruise control bracket.

21. Install the EVAP solenoid bracket to the rear/right cam cover.

22. Connect the fuel lines to the fuel pipe cluster.

23. Connect the accelerator cable to the throttle body.

24. Connect the vacuum hoses, the PCV hose and the electrical connectors.

25. Install the air intake duct.

26. Connect the spark plug wires and the battery cables.

CHASSIS ELECTRICAL

Air Bag

CAUTION

Some vehicles are equipped with the Supplemental Inflatable Restraint (SIR) or air bag system. The SIR system must be disabled before performing service on or around SIR system components, steering column, instrument panel components, wiring and sensors. Failure to follow safety and disabling procedures could result in accidental air bag deployment, possible personal injury and unnecessary SIR system repairs.

PRECAUTIONS

Several precautions must be observed when handling the inflator module to avoid accidental deployment and possible personal injury.

• Never carry the inflator module by the wires or connector on the underside of the module.

• When carrying a live inflator module, hold securely with both hands, and ensure that the bag and trim cover are pointed away.

• Place the inflator module on a bench or other surface with the bag and trim cover facing up.

• With the inflator module on the bench, never place anything on or close to the module which may be thrown in the event of an accidental deployment.

DISARMING

1. Disconnect the negative battery cable.
2. Remove the SIR fuse from the fuse panel.
3. Remove the left side sound insulator.
4. Remove the Connector Positive Assurance (CPA) from the yellow 2-way SIR harness connector at the base of the steering column and separate the connector.

ARMING

1. Connect the yellow 2-way SIR connector at the base of the steering column and insert the Connect Positive Assurance (CPA).

2. Install the left side sound insulator.
3. Install the SIR fuse in the fuse panel.
4. Connect the negative battery cable.

REMOVAL AND INSTALLATION

Inflator Module

1. Disconnect the negative battery cable. Disarm the SIR system.

NOTE: Rotate the steering wheel so the access holes on the back of the steering wheel are at the 12 and 6 o'clock positions. This will allow tool access and reduce the possibility of marring the steering column cover.

2. Remove the 4 bolts from the back of the inflator module. Remove the inflator module from the steering wheel.

3. Disconnect the horn contact by pushing slightly and twisting counterclockwise.

4. If equipped with steering wheel controls, disconnect the steering wheel switch assembly connector from the steering column coil connector.

5. Disconnect the coil assembly from the inflator module.

To install:

6. If equipped, with the ignition switch in the **OFF** position, connect the steering wheel switch assembly connector to the coil connector.

7. Connect the horn contact. Connect the coil assembly connector.

NOTE: Ensure that no wires at the back of the inflator module are pinched when aligning the inflator module to the steering wheel.

8. Install the inflator module and the 4 attaching bolts. Arm the SIR system. Connect the negative battery cable.

Heater Blower Motor

REMOVAL AND INSTALLATION

Riviera

1. Disconnect the negative battery cable.
2. Remove cowl cross-tower brace; 2 nuts each side. Remove both cowl relay center bracket nuts and position aside.
3. Remove blower motor electrical connector, cooling hose and mounting

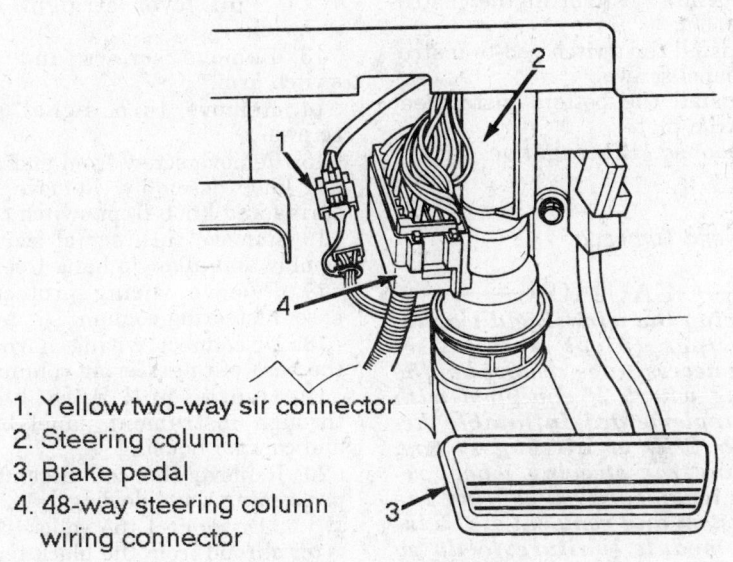

1. Yellow two-way sir connector
2. Steering column
3. Brake pedal
4. 48-way steering column wiring connector

8470H013

Yellow air bag harness connector

screws. Tilt blower motor in case and detach fan from motor.

4. Remove blower motor from case. Remove fan from case.

To install:

5. Install the fan to the case. Install the blower motor to case.

6. Tilt blower motor in case and attach fan to motor. Install blower motor mounting screws, electrical connector and cooling hose.

7. Install both cowl relay center bracket nuts. Install cowl cross-tower brace. Connect the negative battery cable.

Allante

1. Disconnect the negative battery cable. Remove the cross-tower brace.

2. Partially remove the upper intake manifold by performing the following procedures:

   a. Remove both right rear EGR pipe bolts.

   b. Remove the right rear transaxle dipstick bolt.

   c. Remove the right rear bracket bolt.

   d. Remove the right rear lower intake manifold nuts.

   e. Position the upper intake manifold aside.

3. Remove the electrical harness bracket and disconnect the electrical

connector. Remove the cooling hose, the mounting screws and the blower motor.

To install:

4. Install the blower motor, mounting screws and cooling hose. Install the electrical harness bracket and connect the electrical connector.

5. Install the upper intake manifold by performing the following procedures:

   a. Place the upper intake manifold into position.

   b. Install the right rear lower intake manifold nuts.

   c. Install the right rear bracket bolt.

   d. Install the right rear transaxle dipstick bolt.

   e. Install both right rear EGR pipe bolts.

6. Install the cross-tower brace. Connect the negative battery cable.

Eldorado and Seville

1. Disconnect the negative battery cable.

2. Remove the relay center bracket nuts and move the bracket aside. Remove the air cleaner assembly and the cross-tower brace.

3. Disconnect the electrical harness support bracket. Remove the MAP sensor bracket.

4. Label and disconnect the electrical wiring connectors. Remove the cooling hose and mounting screws.

5. Tilt the blower motor in the case and remove the fan from the blower motor.

NOTE: Be careful not to bend the fan upon removal as a fan imbalance could result after reassembly.

6. Remove the blower motor and fan assembly from the vehicle.

To install:

7. Install the blower motor and fan assembly to the vehicle. Tilt the blower motor in the case and install the fan to the blower motor.

8. Install the cooling hose and mounting screws. Connect the electrical wiring connectors. Install the MAP sensor bracket.

9. Connect the electrical harness support bracket. Install the air cleaner assembly and the cross-tower brace.

10. Install the relay center bracket nuts. Connect the negative battery cable.

Toronado

1. Disconnect the negative battery cable.

2. Remove the cowl cross-tower brace; 2 nuts each side. Remove both cowl relay center bracket nuts and position aside.

3. Remove blower motor electrical connector, cooling hose and mounting screws. Tilt blower motor in case and detach fan from motor.

4. Remove blower motor from case. Remove fan from case.

To install:

5. Install fan to case. Install blower motor to case.

6. Tilt blower motor in case and attach fan to motor. Install blower motor mounting screws, electrical connector and cooling hose.

7. Install both cowl relay center bracket nuts. Install cowl cross-tower brace.

8. Connect the negative battery cable.

Windshield Wiper Motor

REMOVAL AND INSTALLATION

1. Disconnect the negative battery cable. Remove both wiper arms.

2. Remove the A/C pipe shroud if required.

3. Remove the cowl cover.

4. Remove the wiper arm drive link from the crank arm.

5. Disconnect the electrical connectors.

6. Remove the wiper motor-to-chassis bolts and the motor; guide the crank arm through the hole.

To install:

7. Guide the crank arm through the hole and install the wiper motor and the motor-to-chassis bolts.

8. If removed, install the air conditioning pipe shroud bracket.

9. Connect the electrical connectors.

10. Install the wiper arm drive link from the crank arm.

11. Install the cowl cover.

12. Connect the negative battery cable.

13. Verify proper wiper motor operation.

Windshield Wiper Switch

REMOVAL AND INSTALLATION

Eldorado and Seville

The windshield wiper switch is attached to switch pod, located on the instrument panel to the right side of the steering wheel.

1. Disconnect the negative battery cable.

2. Remove the switch trim panel from the instrument panel.

3. Remove the switch-to-instrument panel screws.

4. Pull the switch outward and disconnect the electrical connectors from the rear of the switch.

To install:

5. Connect the electrical connectors to the rear of the switch and push the switch into position.

6. Install the switch-to-instrument panel screws.

7. Install the switch trim panel to the instrument panel

8. Connect the negative battery cable.

Allante

The windshield wiper switch is attached to switch pod, located on the instrument panel to the right side of the steering wheel.

1. Disconnect the negative battery cable.

2. Remove the bottom instrument panel trim plate.

3. Remove the switch pod-to-instrument panel screws, pull the pod outward and disconnect the electrical connectors. Remove the switch pod from the vehicle.

To install:

4. Connect the electrical connectors to the back of the pod and push the pod into position in the instrument panel.

5. Install the switch pod-to-instrument panel screws.

6. Install the bottom instrument panel trim plate.

7. Connect the negative battery cable.

Riviera and Toronado

───────── CAUTION ─────────
Replacing the windshield washer and wiper (pivot and pulse) switch necessitates removal of the steering wheel. If equipped with the Supplemental Inflatable Restraint (SIR) or air bag system, removing the steering wheel requires temporarily disabling the SIR system and removal of the inflator module. Failure to do so could result in accidental deployment of the air bag, possible personal injury and unnecessary SIR system repairs.

1. Disconnect the negative battery cable.

2. Place the ignition switch in the **LOCK** position to prevent un-centering of the coil assembly ring.

3. If equipped, disable the SIR system. Remove the inflator module.

4. Remove the steering wheel.

5. Remove coil assembly retaining ring.

6. Remove coil assembly from shaft end, allowing coil to hang freely.

NOTE: Coil assembly will become uncentered if the steering column is separated from steering gear and is allowed to rotate or if the centering spring is depressed, allowing hub to rotate while coil is removed from column.

7. Remove wave washer.

8. Remove shaft lock retaining ring using special tool J–23653–C to depress shaft lock.

9. Remove shaft lock.

10. Remove turn signal cancelling cam assembly.

11. Remove upper bearing spring, inner race seat and inner race.

12. Remove multi-function lever by performing the following:

   a. Ensure that the switch is in the **OFF** position before removing the access cover from steering wheel.

   b. Remove cruise control connector from lever. Note position of connector when installed in column.

   c. Pull lever straight out of switch.

13. Remove screws and signal switch arm.

14. Remove turn signal switch screws.

15. Remove screw from end of hazard knob assembly. Remove button spring and knob from switch cavity.

16. Remove turn signal switch assembly and allow to hang freely.

17. Remove wiring protector at base of steering column.

18. Disconnect wiring harness at the base of the steering column.

19. Gently pull wire harness through instrument panel bracket and column housing.

20. Remove the coil assembly by performing the following:

   a. Disconnect the yellow connector shroud from the black terminal connector.

   b. Remove the wiring protector.

   c. Attach a length of wire to the black terminal connector to aid in reassembly.

   d. Gently pull the wire through the instrument panel bracket and column housing.

21. Remove the key from the pass key lock cylinder set.

22. Remove the buzzer switch assembly and buzzer switch retaining clip using a paper clip.

23. Reinsert the key in the pass key lock cylinder. Place the key in the **LOCK** position.

24. Remove the pass key lock cylinder by performing the following:

   a. Disconnect the terminal connector.

   b. Remove the wiring protector.

   c. Attach a length of wire to the terminal connector to aid in reassembly.

   d. Gently pull the wire through the instrument panel bracket and column housing.

25. Remove the lock housing cover screws. Remove the lock housing cover assembly.

26. Remove the tilt lever by gripping firmly and turning counterclockwise to remove from the steering column.

27. Remove the base plate and dimmer switch rod actuator.

28. Gently pull the pivot and pulse (wiper/washer) switch wire harness through the instrument panel bracket and column housing.

29. Remove the switch actuator pivot pin.

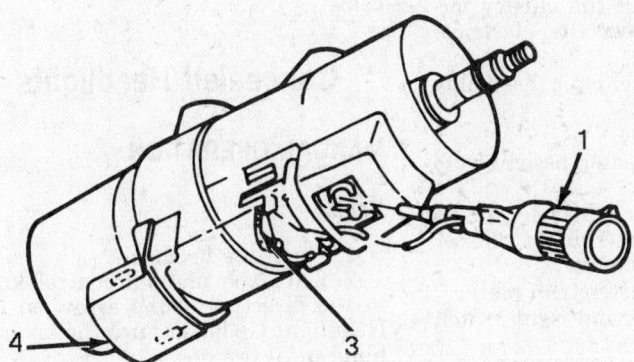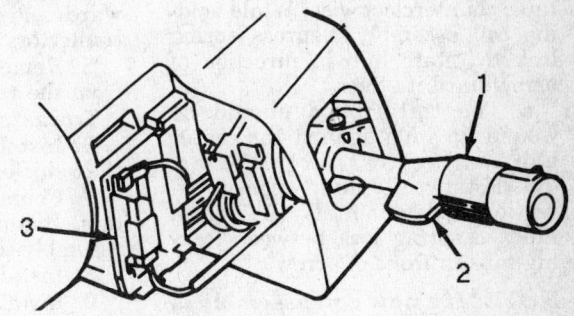

1. Multi-funtion turn signal lever
2. "Wash" paddle
3. Cruise control wire connection
4. Access cover

8470H016

Multi-function switch assembly — Riviera and Toronado

30. Remove the pivot and pulse switch assembly.

To install:

31. Install the pivot and pulse switch assembly to the cover.

32. Install the switch actuator pivot pin to the switch and cover.

33. Feed the pivot and pulse connector through the column housing and instrument panel bracket.

34. Connect the dimmer switch rod actuator to the base plate.

35. Install the base plate to the lock housing cover assembly.

NOTE: The bottom edge of the dimmer switch rod actuator should rest on the bend in the dimmer switch rod.

36. Install the lock housing cover assembly.

37. Install the multi-function lever by performing the following:

a. Plug the multi-function lever connector and cruise control wire together and mount on the base plate.

b. With the **WASH** paddle loose on the shaft, align the shaft with the switch notch and insert the shaft only.

c. Rotate the **WASH** paddle into position and push into the switch

d. Push on the knob to seat the lever into the switch.

38. Install the housing cover end cap. Install the screws and tighten the screw in the 12 o'clock position 1st, the screw in the 8 o'clock position 2nd and the screw in the 3 o'clock position 3rd. Tighten in the same sequence to 80 inch lbs. (9 Nm).

39. Install the pass key lock cylinder.

40. Install the lock retaining screw. Tighten to 22 inch lbs. (2.5 Nm).

41. Place the key in the **RUN** position.

42. Install the buzzer switch assembly and clip.

43. Route wiring assembly for the turn signal switch through column housing and instrument panel bracket.

44. Connect wiring assembly to connector at base of the steering column.

45. Connect coil assembly wire harness through column housing and instrument panel bracket. Allow coil to hang freely.

46. Install turn signal switch assembly and screws. Tighten to 30 inch lbs. (3.4 Nm).

47. Connect the yellow connector shroud to the black terminal connector.

48. Install wiring protector.

49. Install signal switch arm and screws. Tighten to 20.4 inch lbs. (2.3 Nm).

50. Install hazard knob, spring and button to hazard warning switch cavity. Install switch screw; drive in fully. Do not strip.

51. Install inner race, upper bearing inner race seat and upper bearing spring.

52. Install turn signal cancelling cam assembly.

53. Install shaft lock.

NOTE: Inspect shaft lock retaining ring for damage or deformation. If damaged or deformed, replace with new retaining ring.

54. Install shaft lock retaining ring. Align to block tooth on shaft using special tool J–23653–C to depress shaft lock. Ring must be firmly seated in groove on shaft.

NOTE: Set steering shaft so block teeth on upper steering shaft are at the 12 o'clock and 6 o'clock positions. The alignment mark at the end of the shaft should be at the 12 o'clock position and vehicle wheels straight-ahead. Set the ignition switch to the LOCK position to ensure no damage occurs to the coil assembly.

55. Ensure coil assembly hub is centered by performing the following:

a. Hold coil assembly with clear bottom up to see coil ribbon.

b. There are 2 styles of coils. One rotates clockwise and the other rotates counterclockwise. While holding coil assembly, depress spring lock to rotate hub in direction of arrow until it stops.

c. The coil ribbon should be wound up snug against the center hub.

d. Rotate coil hub in opposite direction approximately 2½ turns. Release spring lock between locking tabs in front of arrow.

NOTE: If a new coil assembly is being installed, assemble the pre-centered coil assembly to column. Remove centering tab and dispose.

56. Install wave washer.

57. Install coil assembly using horn tower on cancelling cam assembly inner ring and projections on outer ring for alignment.

58. Install coil assembly retaining ring. Ring must be firmly seated in groove on shaft.

NOTE: Gently pull lower coil assembly wire to remove any wire kinks that may be inside column assembly.

59. Install steering wheel.

60. Install inflator module and enable SIR system.

61. Connect the negative battery cable.

Instrument Cluster

REMOVAL AND INSTALLATION

Riviera

1. Disconnect the negative battery cable.

2. Remove the center, left and right trim covers.

3. Remove the instrument cluster-to-dash screws, then, pull the cluster straight out of the housing.

To install:

4. Place the instrument cluster into position and install the instrument cluster-to-dash screws.

5. Install the center, left and right trim covers.

6. Connect the negative battery cable.

Allante

1. Disconnect the negative battery cable.

2. Remove the left and right switch pod trim plates.

3. Remove the cluster trim plate screws and remove the plate.

4. Remove the cluster assembly-to-dash screws, pull the cluster forward and disconnect the electrical connectors.

5. Remove the cluster assembly from the vehicle.

To install:

6. Install the cluster assembly to the vehicle.

7. Connect the electrical connectors. Install the instrument cluster assembly-to-dash screws.

8. Install the cluster trim plate.

9. Install the left and right switch pod trim plates.

10. Connect the negative battery cable.

Eldorado and Seville

1. Disconnect the negative battery cable. Remove the **A5** and **B5** fuses from the rear fuse compartment. Remove the **A3** fuse from the engine fuse compartment.

2. Remove the upper trim panel.

3. Disconnect the 2 electrical connectors located on top of the instrument cluster.

4. Remove the 4 screws that secure the cluster to the panel.

5. If equipped with digital cluster, raise the cluster and remove the 2 screws that secure the PRNDL mechanism.

6. Remove the cluster.

To install:

7. Align the instrument cluster with the panel.

8. Install the 2 screws that secure the PRNDL mechanism. (Digital cluster only).

9. Install the 4 cluster retaining screws and connect the 2 electrical connectors at the top of the cluster.

10. Install the upper trim panel and replace the fuses. Connect the negative battery cable.

Toronado

1. Disconnect the negative battery cable.

2. Remove instrument panel cluster trim plate.

3. Remove screws retaining cluster to instrument panel.

4. Pull cluster out and disengage electrical connector.

To install:

5. Place the instrument cluster into position and engage the electrical connector.

6. Install the screws retaining the cluster to instrument panel.

7. Install the instrument cluster panel trim plate.

8. Connect the negative battery cable.

Concealed Headlights

MANUAL OPERATION

Reatta

1. Open the hood.

2. Turn the manual control knob in the direction of the arrow on the Headlight Up label. Turn the knob by hand until it stops.

3. Close the hood and check headlight operation.

Toronado

1. Disconnect 3-way headlight door actuator connector.

2. Remove protective cover from the knob.

3. Rotate the knob clockwise until the headlight doors open.

4. To close the doors, rotate the knob counterclockwise until the headlight doors close.

5. Install protective cover over knob.

6. Connect 3-way headlight door actuator connectors.

Headlight Switch

REMOVAL AND INSTALLATION

The headlight switch is located on the left side of the instrument panel.

1. Remove the left trim plate screws and the trim plate, if equipped.

2. If equipped, remove the left air vent.

3. Remove the headlight switch screws, pull the switch forward and disconnect the electrical connectors or the fiber optic lead, if equipped.

4. Remove the headlight switch/switch pod.

To install:

5. Connect the electrical connectors or fiber optic lead, if equipped, to the headlight switch.

6. Push the switch/switch pod into position and install the headlight attaching screws.

7. Install the left air vent, if equipped.

8. Install the left trim plate and attaching screws.

Dimmer Switch

The dimmer switch is attached to the lower steering column jacket. It is activated by a rod attached to the multi-function lever.

REMOVAL AND INSTALLATION

1. Disconnect the negative battery cable. Remove the left side sound insulator panel.
2. If necessary, remove the lower steering column trim cover.
3. Disconnect the electrical connector from the dimmer switch.
4. Remove the dimmer switch-to-steering column screws and the dimmer switch.
   To install:
5. Position the actuator rod into the dimmer switch hole and install the dimmer switch-to-steering column screws.
6. Connect the electrical connector to the dimmer switch.
7. Adjust the dimmer switch by depressing the switch slightly and inserting a $3/32$ in. drill bit into the adjusting hole. Push the switch up to remove any play and tighten the dimmer switch adjusting screw.
8. If removed, install the lower steering column trim cover.
9. Install the left side sound insulator panel.
10. Connect the negative battery cable.

Turn Signal Switch

─────── CAUTION ───────
Replacing the turn signal switch requires removal of the steering wheel. If equipped with the Supplemental Inflatable Restraint (SIR) system, removing the steering wheel requires temporarily disabling the SIR system and removal of the inflator module. Failure to do so could result in accidental deployment of the air bag, possible personal injury and unnecessary SIR system repairs.

REMOVAL AND INSTALLATION

1. Disconnect the negative battery cable.
2. Place the ignition switch in the **LOCK** position to prevent un-centering of the coil assembly ring.
3. If equipped, disable the SIR system. Remove the inflator module.

4. Remove the steering wheel.
5. Remove coil assembly retaining ring.
6. Remove coil assembly from shaft end, allowing coil to hang freely.

NOTE: Coil assembly will become uncentered if the steering column is separated from steering gear and is allowed to rotate or if the centering spring is depressed, allowing hub to rotate while coil is removed from column.

7. Remove wave washer.
8. Remove shaft lock retaining ring using special tool J–23653–C to depress shaft lock.
9. Remove shaft lock.
10. Remove turn signal cancelling cam assembly.
11. Remove upper bearing spring, inner race seat and inner race.
12. Remove multi-function lever by performing the following:
    a. Ensure that the switch is in the **OFF** position before access cover from steering wheel.
    b. Remove cruise control connector from lever. Note position of connector when installed in column.
    c. Pull lever straight out of switch.
13. Remove screws and signal switch arm.
14. Remove turn signal switch screws.
15. Remove screw from end of hazard knob assembly. Remove button spring and knob from switch cavity.
16. Remove turn signal switch assembly and allow to hang freely.
17. Remove wiring protector at base of steering column.
18. Disconnect wiring harness at the base of the steering column.
19. Gently pull wire harness through instrument panel bracket and column housing.
    To install:
20. Route wiring assembly for new switch through column housing and instrument panel bracket.
21. Connect wiring assembly to connector at base of the steering column.
22. Connect coil assembly wire harness through column housing and instrument panel bracket. Allow coil to hang freely.
23. Install turn signal switch assembly and screws. Tighten to 30 inch lbs. (3.4 Nm).
24. Install wiring protector.
25. Install signal switch arm and screws. Tighten to 20.4 inch lbs. (2.3 Nm).

26. Install hazard knob, spring and button to hazard warning switch cavity. Install switch screw; drive in fully. Do not strip.
27. Install multi-function lever by performing the following:

NOTE: Ensure that the switch is in the OFF position before installation.

   a. Install lever electrical connectors.
   b. With WASH paddle loose on the metal shaft, align shaft with the switch notch and insert shaft only.
   c. Rotate WASH paddle into position and push into switch.
   d. Push on the knob to seat lever into switch.
   e. Install cruise control connector.
   f. Install access cover onto steering column.
28. Install inner race, upper bearing inner race seat and upper bearing spring.
29. Install turn signal cancelling cam assembly.
30. Install shaft lock.

NOTE: Inspect shaft lock retaining ring for damage or deformation. If damaged or deformed, replace with new retaining ring.

31. Install shaft lock retaining ring. Align to block tooth on shaft using special tool J–23653–C to depress shaft lock. Ring must be firmly seated in groove on shaft.

NOTE: Set steering shaft so block teeth on upper steering shaft are at the 12 o'clock and 6 o'clock positions. The alignment mark at the end of the shaft should be at the 12 o'clock position and vehicle wheels straight-ahead. Set the ignition switch to the LOCK position to ensure no damage occurs to the coil assembly.

32. Ensure coil assembly hub is centered by performing the following:
    a. Hold coil assembly with clear bottom up to see coil ribbon.
    b. There are 2 styles of coils. One rotates clockwise and the other rotates counterclockwise. While holding coil assembly, depress spring lock to rotate hub in direction of arrow until it stops.
    c. The coil ribbon should be wound up snug against the center hub.
    d. Rotate coil hub in opposite direction approximately $2\frac{1}{2}$ turns.

Release spring lock between locking tabs in front of arrow.

NOTE: If a new coil assembly is being installed, assemble the pre-centered coil assembly to column. Remove centering tab and dispose.

33. Install wave washer.
34. Install coil assembly using horn tower on cancelling cam assembly inner ring and projections on outer ring for alignment.
35. Install coil assembly retaining ring. Ring must be firmly seated in groove on shaft.

NOTE: Gently pull lower coil assembly wire to remove any wire kinks that may be inside column assembly.

36. Install steering wheel.
37. Install inflator module and enable SIR system.
38. Connect the negative battery cable.

Ignition Lock

CAUTION
Replacing the ignition lock assembly necessitates removal of the steering wheel. If equipped with the Supplemental Inflatable Restraint (SIR) system (air bag), removing the steering wheel and inflator module requires temporarily disabling the SIR system and removal of the inflator module. Failure to do so could result in accidental deployment of the air bag and possible personal injury.

REMOVAL AND INSTALLATION

1. Disconnect the negative battery cable.
2. Place the ignition switch in the **LOCK** position to prevent un-centering of the coil assembly ring.
3. Disable the SIR system and remove the inflator module (air bag), if equipped.
4. Remove the steering wheel.
5. Remove the combination switch assembly and allow to hang freely. Do not remove wiring harness and connector from steering column.
6. Remove key from pass key lock cylinder set.
7. Disconnect buzzer switch assembly.
8. Reinsert key in pass key lock cylinder. Turn key to **LOCK** position.
9. Remove lock retaining screw.

10. Disconnect pass key lock cylinder terminal connector.
11. Remove wiring protector.
12. Attach a length of mechanics wire to terminal connector to aid in reassembly.
13. Gently pull wire through instrument panel bracket and column housing.
14. Remove pass key lock cylinder.
To install:

NOTE: Route wire from lock cylinder through steering column using mechanics wire. Rotate panel clip 360 degrees and snap clip into hole in housing. Failure to do so may result in component damage or malfunction of pass key lock cylinder.

15. Install pass key lock cylinder.
16. Gently pull lower lock cylinder wire to remove any wire kinks that may be inside column assembly.
17. Install lock retaining screw. Tighten to 22 inch lbs. (2.5 Nm).
18. Turn key to **RUN** position.
19. Install buzzer switch assembly.
20. Install combination switch.
21. Install inflator module. Enable SIR system.
22. Install steering wheel.
23. Connect negative battery cable.

Ignition Switch

REMOVAL AND INSTALLATION

The ignition switch is hard-wired. The wiring harness with the column harness connector must be replaced with the ignition switch. Do not splice the new switch to the existing column wiring harness.
1. Disconnect the negative battery cable.
2. Remove the lower left sound insulator and the instrument panel steering column cover.
3. Remove the ignition switch wire protector and the switch-to-column screws.
4. Disconnect the ignition and turn signal switch column harness connectors from the dash connector.
5. Disconnect the turn signal harness connector from the column harness connector.
6. Remove the steering column bolts and nuts and gently lower steering column to the seat.
7. Remove the ignition switch assembly with the switch, harness and connector.

To install:
8. Install the ignition switch assembly with the harness and connector.
9. Raise the steering column into position and install the bolts and nuts.
10. Connect the turn signal harness connector to the column harness connector.
11. Connect the ignition and turn signal switch column harness connectors to the dash connector.
12. Install the ignition switch wire protector and the switch-to-column screws.
13. Install the lower left sound insulator and the instrument panel steering column cover.
14. Connect the negative battery cable.

Brake Light Switch

ADJUSTMENT

NOTE: When the brake pedal is in the fully released position, the brake light switch plunger should be fully depressed against the pedal arm. The switch is adjusted by moving it in or out.

1. Remove the brake light switch from the brake pedal bracket.
2. Insert the switch into the retainer until the switch body seats on the tube clip.
3. Pull the brake pedal rearward against the internal pedal stop.

NOTE: The switch will be moved in the retainer resulting in proper adjustment.

4. When no further adjustment clicks are heard and the brake lights remain **OFF**, the brake light switch will be properly seated.

REMOVAL AND INSTALLATION

1. Disconnect the negative battery cable. Remove the underdash hush panel, if equipped.
2. Locate the brake light switch on the brake pedal bracket.
3. Remove the tubular retaining clip or switch retainer.
4. Remove the brake light switch electrical connectors.
5. Remove the switch assembly from the vehicle.
To install:
6. Install the switch assembly to the vehicle.
7. Connect the brake light switch electrical connectors.

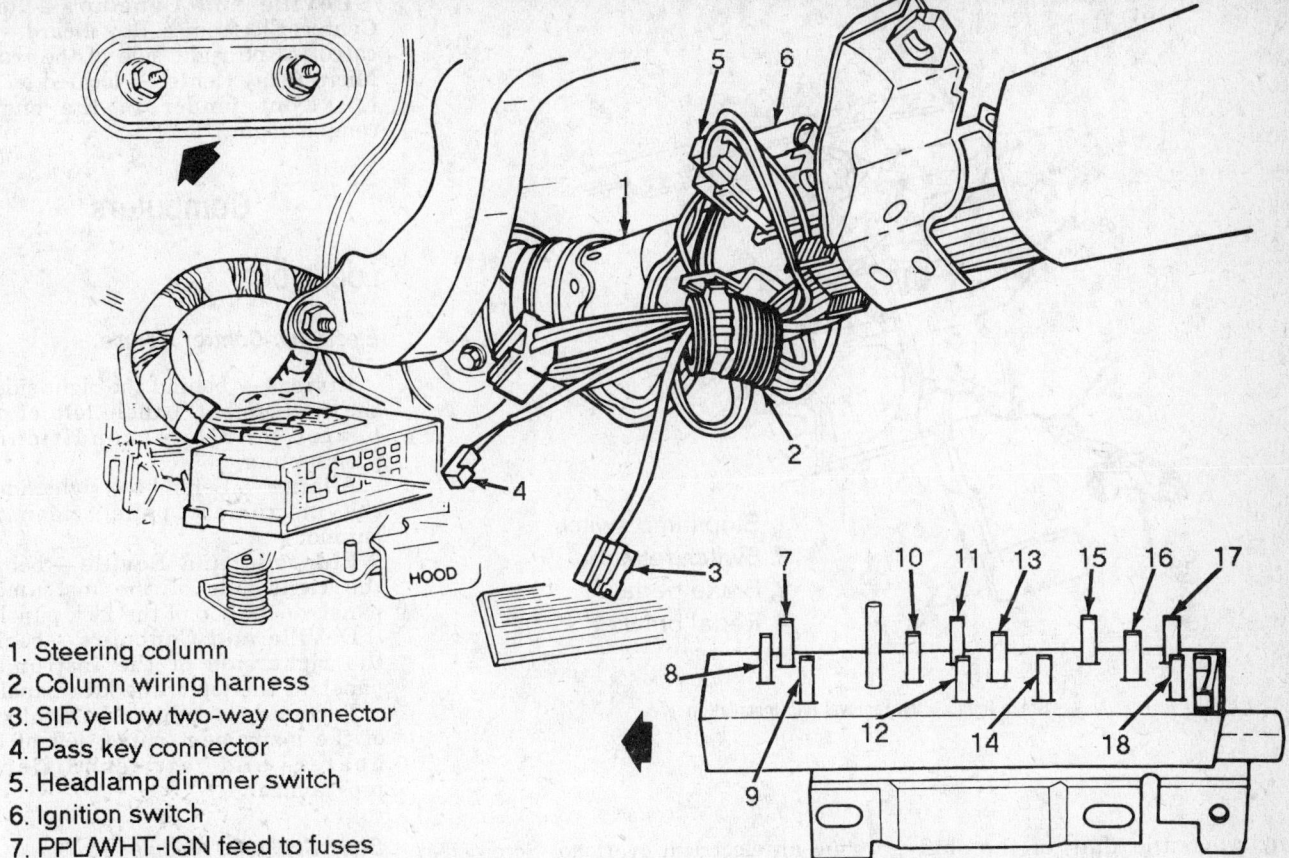

1. Steering column
2. Column wiring harness
3. SIR yellow two-way connector
4. Pass key connector
5. Headlamp dimmer switch
6. Ignition switch
7. PPL/WHT-IGN feed to fuses
   8, 9 and 10; hot in run
8. Red/Blk-Battery feed to ignition switch
9. DK Blue/White-ignition feed to fuses
   18 and 19; hot in run & start
10. DK Green-ground to twilight crank relay;
    grounded in bulb test & start
11. ORN- ignition feed to fuse 6; hot in run
12. Tan/Wht-ground to IPC brake indicator
    bulb check; grounded in bulb test & start

13. Red-battery feed to ignition switch
14. BRN-ignition feed to fuses 11 & 12;
    hot in accessory & run
15. Not used
16. Red-battery feed to ignition switch
17. Yellow-ignition feed to start solenoid
18. Pink-ignition feed to interior & underhood
    relay centers; hot in run; bulb test & start

8470H022

Ignition switch and steering column wiring

8. Install the tubular retaining clip or switch retainer.
9. Connect the negative battery cable.
10. Adjust brake light switch.

Neutral Safety Switch

ADJUSTMENT

1. Place transaxle shift lever in **N**.
2. Loosen switch attaching screws.
3. Rotate switch on shifter assembly to align service adjustment slots.
4. Insert ³/32 in. (2.34mm) max. diameter gauge pin or drill bit to a depth of ⁵/32 in. (12mm).

5. Tighten 2 attaching screws to 20 ft. lbs. (27 Nm).
6. Remove gauge pin.
7. Ensure that engine will start only in **P** and **N** positions. If engine will start in any other position, readjust switch.

REMOVAL AND INSTALLATION

All neutral safety/backup light switches come with a small plastic alignment pin installed. Leave this pin in place.
1. Place the shifter assembly in the **N** position.
2. Remove the shifter lever-to-switch nut and the lever.

3. Disconnect the electrical connector from the neutral safety/backup light switch.
4. Remove the neutral safety/backup light switch-to-transaxle bolts and the switch from the vehicle.
   To install:
5. Position the shifter shaft in the **N** position.

NOTE: If using an old switch or the plastic pin (new switch) is broken, install a ³/32 in. pin gauge (drill bit) into the neutral safety/backup light switch; the switch is locked into its neutral position.

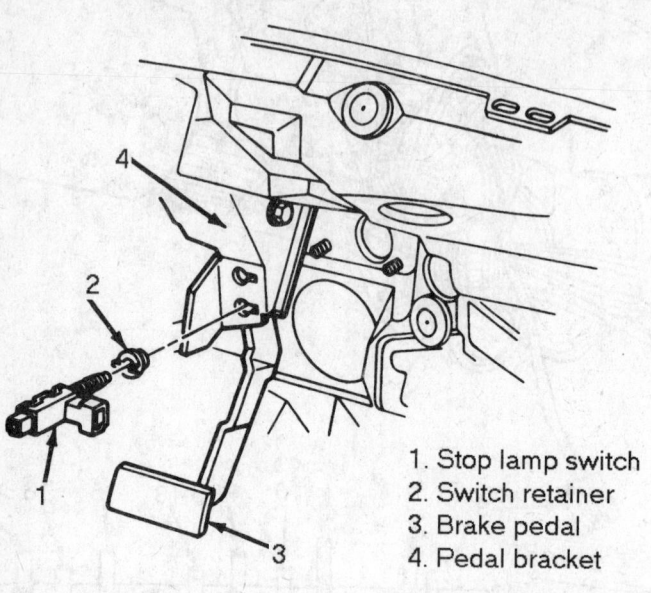

1. Stop lamp switch
2. Switch retainer
3. Brake pedal
4. Pedal bracket

8470H023

Brake light switch removal and installation

6. Align the flats of the shifter shaft and the neutral safety/backup light, then, align the switch-to-tang on the transaxle. Tighten the switch-to-transaxle bolts to 22 ft. lbs. Remove the pin gauge.

7. To complete installation, reverse the removal procedures. Make sure the engine starts only in the **P** and **N** positions.

Fuses, Circuit Breakers and Relays

LOCATION

Fuse Panels

Toronado — located in the glove box.

Riviera — located at the front left side of the console.

Allante — located at the center console, under the ashtray.

Eldorado and Seville — located in the glove box.

DeVille and Concours — located in the engine compartment.

Circuit Breakers

A circuit breaker is an electrical switch which breaks the circuit during an electrical overload. Some circuit breakers are designed to automatically reset after a specified period of time. Others must be manually reset after the electrical malfunction causing the overload has been corrected.

The majority of circuit breakers can be found in the fuse panel. some, however, are installed in-line near the device they are intended to protect.

Relays

Relays are generally mounted in the vicinity of the device(s) they are intended to control. On the vehicles listed below, there is an Interior Relay Center (IRC).

Riviera — below center of the instrument panel, right front of console.

Eldorado and Seville — behind the right side of the instrument panel, below the glove box, for 1992–93. Relay Center Electronics Bay Board — located in the right side of the trunk, for 1994–96. Micro Relay Center — located on the left front fender in the engine compartment, for 1994–96.

Toronado — behind the right side of the instrument panel, behind the instrument panel compartment.

DeVille and Concours — Relay Center Electronics Bay Board — located in the right side of the trunk. Micro Relay Center — located on the left front fender in the engine compartment.

Computers

LOCATION

Electronic Control Module

Riviera — behind the right side of the instrument panel, left of the heater and air conditioning programmer.

Allante — Behind the right side of the instrument panel, near the shroud.

Eldorado and Seville — behind the right side of the instrument panel, at the top of the kick panel.

DeVille and Concours — behind the right side of the instrument panel, at the top of the kick panel.

Toronado — behind the right side of the instrument panel, left of the heater and air conditioner programmer.

Body Computer Module

Riviera — behind the upper right side of the instrument panel, behind the glove box.

Allante — behind the center of the instrument panel.

Eldorado and Seville — behind the instrument panel, behind the glove box.

Toronado — behind the instrument panel, above and right of the fuse panel.

DeVille and Concours — at the right side of the engine compartment at the fender well.

Turn Signal/Hazard Flashers

LOCATION

Rivera — right side of the steering column.

Allante — the turn signals and hazard warning lights are controlled by the Body Computer Module (BCM). Therefore, individual turn signal and hazard flasher units are not used.

Eldorado and Seville — behind the center of the instrument panel, below the radio.

Toronado — behind the instrument panel, right side of the steering column support.

DeVille and Concours — at the right side of the engine compartment at the fender well.

Cruise Control

ADJUSTMENT

Riviera and Toronado

With the engine OFF, adjust the cable or rod length to obtain the minimum slack.

Allante, Eldorado and Seville

1. With the engine **OFF**, ensure that the idle speed motor has retracted until the throttle body lever contacts the minimum throttle angle adjusting screw.
2. Select the servo blade hole that will result in minimum cable slack.

ENGINE COOLING

Radiator

REMOVAL AND INSTALLATION

Riviera

1. Disconnect the negative battery cable.
2. Drain coolant from radiator.
3. Remove plastic radiator support cover.
4. Remove engine-to-radiator torque strut.
5. Remove the rear cooling fan.
6. Remove coolant reservoir hose at filler neck.

1. Cruise control cable
2. Throttle cable
3. Engine harness
4. Throttle valve cable

8569Z039

Adjusting the cruise control cable — Riviera and Toronado

7. Remove upper and lower radiator hoses from radiator.
8. Remove transaxle oil cooler lines at radiator.
9. Remove radiator top support, 3 remaining bolts with torque strut removed.
10. Remove radiator from vehicle; lift radiator straight up and out.

To install:

11. Install radiator in vehicle.
12. Install radiator top support, securing with 3 retaining bolts. Tighten to 18 ft. lbs. (25 Nm).
13. Connect oil cooler lines at radiator. Tighten to 20 ft. lbs. (27 Nm).

14. Install upper and lower radiator hoses to radiator, securing hose clamps.
15. Connect reservoir hose at filler neck, securing hose clamp.
16. Install rear cooling fan.
17. Install engine-to-radiator torque strut and 2 remaining strut/radiator support retaining bolts. Tighten radiator support retaining bolts to 18 ft. lbs. (25 Nm).
18. Install plastic radiator support cover.
19. Fill radiator with coolant.
20. Connect negative battery cable.
21. Start engine and check for leaks. Check transaxle fluid level and add, as necessary. Allow engine to come to normal operating temperature and check again for leaks.

Allante, Eldorado and Seville

1. Disconnect the negative battery cable.
2. Drain cooling system.
3. Remove the plastic radiator support cover.
4. Remove right and left cooling fans. On Eldorado and Seville remove rear cooling fan.
5. Disconnect coolant reservoir hose at filler neck.
6. Remove upper and lower radiator hoses from radiator.

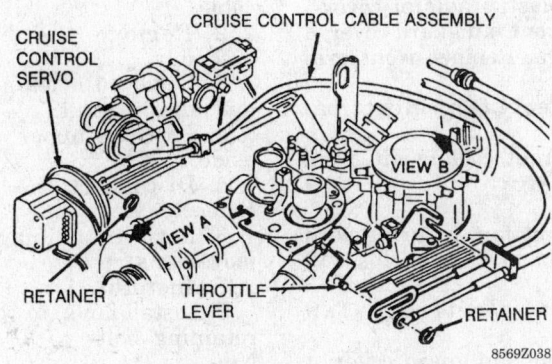

8569Z038

Adjusting the cruise control cable — Allante, Eldorado and Seville

7. Remove engine oil cooler lines and transaxle oil cooler lines from the radiator.

8. Remove the radiator top support.

9. Remove radiator from vehicle, lifting radiator straight up and out.

To install:

10. Install radiator in vehicle.

11. Install radiator top support. Tighten radiator support retaining bolts to 18 ft. lbs. (25 Nm).

12. Connect transaxle oil cooler lines at radiator. Tighten to 20 ft. lbs. (27 Nm).

13. Connect oil cooler lines at radiator. Tighten to 13 ft. lbs. (18 Nm).

14. Install upper and lower radiator hoses to radiator securing hose clamps.

15. Connect coolant reservoir hose at filler neck.

16. Install cooling fan(s) and plastic radiator support cover.

17. Fill cooling system.

18. Connect negative battery cable.

19. Start engine and check for leaks. Check transaxle fluid level and add, as necessary. Allow engine to come to normal operating temperature and check again for leaks.

Toronado

1. Disconnect the negative battery cable.

2. Drain cooling system.

3. Remove plastic radiator support cover.

4. Remove engine-to-radiator torque strut.

5. Remove rear cooling fan.

6. Remove upper air cleaner duct and/or silencer, as necessary.

7. Remove coolant reservoir hose at filler neck.

8. Remove upper and lower radiator hoses from radiator.

9. Remove transaxle oil cooler lines.

10. Remove radiator top support, 3 remaining bolts with torque strut removed.

11. Remove radiator from vehicle, lifting straight up and out.

To install:

12. Install radiator in vehicle.

13. Install radiator top support, securing with 3 retaining bolts.

14. Connect transaxle oil cooler lines at radiator. Tighten to 20 ft. lbs. (27 Nm).

15. Connect upper and lower radiator hoses to radiator, securing with clamps.

16. Connect coolant reservoir hose at filler neck, securing with hose clamp.

17. Install rear cooling fan.

18. Install upper air cleaner duct and/or silencer, if removed.

19. Install engine-to-radiator torque strut and 2 remaining strut/radiator support retaining bolts. Tighten to 18 ft. lbs. (25 Nm).

20. Install plastic radiator support cover.

21. Fill cooling system.

22. Connect negative battery cable.

23. Start engine and check for leaks. Check transaxle fluid level and add, as necessary. Allow engine to come to normal operating temperature and check again for leaks.

Electric Cooling Fan

TESTING

1. Check fuse or circuit breaker for power to cooling fan motor.

2. Remove connector(s) at cooling fan motor(s). Connect jumper wire and apply battery voltage to the positive terminal of the cooling fan motor.

3. Using and ohmmeter, check for continuity in cooling fan motor.

NOTE: Remove the cooling fan connector at the fan motor before performing continuity checks. Perform continuity check of the motor windings only. The cooling fan control circuit is connected electrically to the ECM through the cooling fan relay center. Ohmmeter battery voltage must not be applied to the ECM.

4. Ensure proper continuity of cooling fan motor ground circuit at chassis ground connector.

REMOVAL AND INSTALLATION

Riviera

FRONT FAN

1. Disconnect the negative battery cable.

2. Remove plastic radiator cover.

3. Remove front fan guard cover; 4 clips for Riviera. Remove front grill on Reatta.

4. Disconnect fan electrical connector.

5. Remove front cooling fan from vehicle.

To install:

6. Install front fan, securing with 3 bolts. Tighten to 89 inch lbs. (10 Nm).

7. Connect electrical fan connector.

8. Install front fan guard cover; 4 clips for Riviera. Install front grille on Reatta.

9. Install plastic radiator cover.

10. Connect negative battery cable.

REAR FAN

1. Disconnect the negative battery cable.

2. Remove upper engine-to-radiator support torque strut.

3. Disconnect fan electrical connector.

4. Remove 2 upper and 2 lower retaining bolts and remove fan from vehicle.

To install:

5. Install fan to vehicle, securing with 4 bolts. Tighten to 89 inch lbs. (10 Nm).

6. Connect fan electrical connector.

7. Install upper engine-to-radiator mounting bolts. Tighten to 18 ft. lbs. (25 Nm).

8. Connect negative battery cable.

1992 Allante

RIGHT OR LEFT FAN

1. Disconnect the negative battery cable.

2. Disconnect fan electrical connector.

3. For the left side fan, remove upper engine-to-radiator support torque strut; 4 bolts from radiator support.

4. Remove fan retaining bolts and remove fan from vehicle.

To install:

5. Install fan to vehicle. Tighten retaining bolts to 88 inch lbs. (10 Nm).

6. Connect fan electrical connector.

7. For the left side fan, install upper engine-to-radiator support torque strut. Tighten to 17 ft. lbs. (23 Nm).

8. Connect negative battery cable.

1993 Allante

RIGHT OR LEFT FAN

1. Disconnect the negative battery cable.

2. Remove the beauty panel assembly.

3. Remove the left side engine torque support strut.

4. Position upper radiator hose aside.

5. Disconnect the fan electrical connector.

6. Remove retaining bolts and remove fan(s).

To install:

7. Install fan(s) to vehicle. Tighten retaining bolts to 88 inch lbs. (10 Nm).

8. Connect fan electrical connector.

9. Reposition upper radiator hose and install left side engine torque strut.

10. Install beauty panel assembly and connect the negative battery cable.

Eldorado and Seville

4.5L AND 4.9L ENGINES — FRONT FAN

1. Disconnect the negative battery cable.
2. Remove radiator cover panel.
3. Disconnect electrical connector.
4. Remove the right headlight bracket.
5. Remove fan retaining bolts and remove fan from vehicle.
   To install:
6. Install fan to vehicle. Tighten to 88 inch lbs. (10 Nm).
7. Connect electrical connector.
8. Install right headlight.
9. Install radiator cover panel.
10. Connect negative battery cable.

4.5L AND 4.9L ENGINES — REAR FAN

1. Disconnect the negative battery cable.
2. Disconnect fan electrical connector.
3. Remove upper engine-to-radiator support torque strut and oil cooler line bracket from fan.
4. Remove fan retaining bolts and remove fan from vehicle.
   To install:
5. Install fan in vehicle. Tighten bolts to 97 inch lbs. (11 Nm).
6. Connect electrical connector.
7. Connect upper engine-to-radiator support torque strut and oil cooler line bracket to fan. Tighten torque strut-to-radiator mounting bolts to 17 ft. lbs. (23 Nm).
8. Connect negative battery cable.

4.6L ENGINE

1. Disconnect the negative battery cable.
2. Remove the beauty panel assembly.
3. Remove the left side engine torque support strut.
4. Position upper radiator hose out of the way.
5. Disconnect the fan electrical connector.
6. Remove retaining bolts and remove fan(s).
   To install:
7. Install fan(s) to vehicle. Tighten retaining bolts to 88 inch lbs. (10 Nm).
8. Connect fan electrical connector.
9. Reposition upper radiator hose and install left side engine torque strut.

10. Install beauty panel assembly and connect the negative battery cable.

Toronado

FRONT FAN

1. Disconnect the negative battery cable.
2. Remove plastic radiator cover.
3. Disconnect electrical connector.
4. Remove fan retaining bolts and remove fan from vehicle.
   To install:
5. Install fan in vehicle. Tighten bolts to 89 inch lbs. (10 Nm).
6. Connect electrical connector.
7. Install plastic radiator cover.
8. Connect negative battery cable.

REAR FAN

1. Disconnect the negative battery cable.
2. Remove the upper engine-to-radiator support torque strut.
3. Disconnect the fan electrical connector.
4. Remove the fan attaching bolts and remove the fan assembly from the vehicle.
   To install:
5. Install the fan assembly and 4 attaching bolts. Tighten to 89 inch lbs. (10 Nm).
6. Connect the fan electrical connector.
7. Install the upper engine-to-radiator support torque strut. Tighten bolts to 18 ft. lbs. (25 Nm).
8. Connect the negative battery cable.

Heater Core

REMOVAL AND INSTALLATION

Riviera

1. Disconnect the negative battery cable.
2. Drain the engine coolant into a clean container for reuse.
3. If equipped, disarm the SIR system.
4. Remove the console and instrument panel.
5. Remove air conditioner programmer attaching screws. Disconnect the programmer electrical connectors. Remove the programmer.
6. Disconnect the BCM electrical connectors. Remove the BCM and mounting bracket.
7. Disconnect the ECM electrical connectors. Remove the ECM and mounting bracket.
8. Remove the heater core cover from housing.

9. Disconnect inlet and outlet heater hoses from heater core.
10. Remove 2 heater retaining screws. Remove heater core from vehicle.
    To install:
11. Install heater core to heater case, securing with 2 screws. Connect inlet and outlet heater hoses to heater core. Install the heater core cover.
12. Install ECM mounting bracket and ECM. Connect the ECM electrical connectors. Install the ECM attaching screws.
13. Install ECM mounting bracket and ECM. Connect the ECM electrical connectors. Install the ECM attaching screws.
14. Install air conditioner programmer. Connect the programmer electrical connectors. Install the programmer attaching screws. Check adjustment of the programmer.
15. Install instrument panel and console. If equipped, arm the SIR system. Connect the negative battery cable.
16. Fill cooling system and check for leaks. Start the engine and allow to come to normal operating temperature. Recheck for leaks. Top-up coolant.

Allante

1. Disconnect the negative battery cable. Drain the cooling system to a level below the heater core.
2. Remove the glove box screws. Label and disconnect the electrical connectors from the glove box.
3. Remove the glove box assembly from the vehicle. Remove the lower sound insulator to gain working clearance. Remove the radio.
4. Remove the air conditioning programmer, the Electronic Control Module (ECM) screws and the ECM.
5. Remove the module assembly heater core cover. Disconnect the hoses from the heater core. Remove the heater core screws and the heater core.
   To install:
6. Install the heater core in the vehicle. Install the module assembly heater core cover. Connect hoses to the heater core.
7. Install ECM bracket, ECM and electrical connectors. Install the air conditioning programmer. Check adjustment of the programmer.
8. Install the radio and lower sound insulator. Install the glove box assembly and the glove box electrical connectors. Fill the cooling system.
9. Start the engine and check for coolant leaks. Allow the engine to

come to normal operating temperature. Recheck for coolant leaks.

Eldorado and Seville

1. Disconnect the negative battery cable. Drain the cooling system to a level below the heater core.
2. Remove the glove box screws. Label and disconnect the electrical connectors from the glove box.
3. Remove the glove box assembly from the vehicle. Remove the lower sound insulator to gain working clearance.
4. Remove the air conditioner programmer, the Electronic Control Module (ECM) screws and the ECM.
5. Remove the module assembly heater core cover. Disconnect the hoses from the heater core. Remove the heater core screws and the heater core.

To install:

6. Install the heater core in vehicle. Connect hoses to heater core. Install module assembly heater core cover.
7. Install the air conditioner programmer and the ECM. Check adjustment of the programmer.
8. Install the lower sound insulator. Install the glove box assembly to vehicle. Connect the electrical connectors to the glove box.
9. Fill cooling system. Start engine and check for coolant leaks. Allow the engine to come to normal operating temperature. Recheck for coolant leaks.

Toronado

1. Disconnect the negative battery cable. Drain the engine coolant into a clean container for reuse.
2. If equipped, disarm the SIR system. Remove console and instrument panel.
3. Remove air conditioner programmer attaching screws. Disconnect the programmer electrical connectors. Remove the programmer.
4. Disconnect the BCM electrical connectors. Remove the BCM and mounting bracket.
5. Disconnect the ECM electrical connectors. Remove the ECM and mounting bracket.
6. Remove the heater core cover from the housing. Disconnect inlet and outlet heater hoses from heater core.
7. Remove 2 heater retaining screws. Remove the heater core from the vehicle.

To install:

8. Install the heater core to the heater case, securing with 2 screws. Connect inlet and outlet heater hoses to heater core. Install heater core cover.
9. Install ECM mounting bracket and ECM. Connect the ECM electrical connectors. Install the ECM attaching screws.
10. Install BCM mounting bracket and BCM. Connect the BCM electrical connectors. Install the BCM attaching screws.
11. Install the air conditioner programmer. Connect the programmer electrical connectors. Install the programmer attaching screws. Check adjustment of the programmer.
12. Install the instrument panel and console. If equipped, arm the SIR system. Connect the negative battery cable.
13. Fill the cooling system and check for leaks. Start the engine and allow to come to normal operating temperature. Recheck for leaks. Top-up coolant.

Air Conditioner Programmer

ADJUSTMENT

1. Remove the right side sound insulator and glove box.
2. On the temperature control panel, set the temperature for 90°F, allow 1–2 minutes for the programmer arm to travel to its maximum heat position.
3. Disconnect the threaded rod from the plastic retainer on the programmer output arm.
4. To check the air mixture valve for free travel, push the valve to the maximum air conditioning position and check for binding.
5. Place the pre-load air mixture valve in the maximum heat position; pull on the threaded rod to ensure the valve is seating. The programmer arm should be in the maximum heat position.
6. To avoid influencing the programmer arm or air mixture valve position, carefully snap the threaded rod into the plastic retainer.
7. Adjust the temperature setting to 60°F, then, check to verify the programmer arm and air mixture valve travel to the maximum air conditioning position.

Water Pump

REMOVAL AND INSTALLATION

3.8L Engine

1. Disconnect the negative battery cable.
2. Position a drain pan under the radiator, open the drain cock and drain the cooling system.
3. Disconnect the hoses from the water pump.
4. Remove the serpentine drive belt.
5. Remove the water pump pulley bolts and the pulley.

NOTE: The long bolt is removed through the access hole provided in the body side rail.

6. Remove the water pump-to-engine bolts and the pump.

To install:

7. Clean the gasket mounting surfaces.
8. Install the water pump using a new gasket.
9. Tighten the water pump-to-engine long bolts to 29 ft. lbs. (39 Nm) and the short bolts to 97 inch lbs. (11 Nm).
10. Connect the hoses to the water pump.
11. Install the serpentine drive belt.
12. Connect the negative battery cable.
13. Fill cooling system and check for leaks. Start the engine and allow to come to normal operating temperature. Recheck for leaks. Top-up coolant.

NOTE: Because the radiator is made of aluminum and plastic, make sure the antifreeze solution is approved for use in cooling systems with a high aluminum content. GM recommends the use of a supplement/sealant 3634621 or equivalent, specifically designed for use in aluminum engines to protect the engine from damage.

4.5L and 4.9L Engines

1. Disconnect the negative battery cable.
2. Drain the engine coolant into a clean container for reuse.
3. Remove the air filter assembly. Disconnect and remove the coolant recovery tank.
4. Disconnect and remove the cross brace.
5. Remove the water pulley bolts.

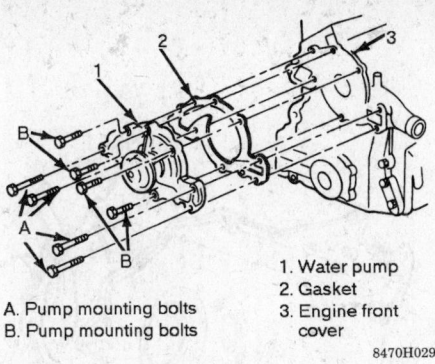

1. Water pump
2. Gasket
3. Engine front cover

A. Pump mounting bolts
B. Pump mounting bolts

8470H029

Water pump mounting — 3.8L engine

6. Remove the serpentine drive belt and the water pump pulley.

7. Remove the water pump-to-engine bolts and the pump.

To install:

8. Clean the gasket mounting surfaces.

9. Place a new gasket over the water pump studs.

10. Install the water pump. Tighten the water pump bolts as follows:

Water pump-to-engine Torx® bolts–30 ft. lbs. (40 Nm)

Water pump-to-engine stud nuts–5 ft. lbs. (7 Nm)

Hex head bolts–30 ft. lbs. (40 Nm)

Remaining hex head bolts–5 ft. lbs. (7 Nm).

11. Install the water pump pulley. Install the water pump pulley bolts finger-tight.

12. Install the serpentine drive belt.

13. Tighten the water pump pulley bolts to 22 ft. lbs. (30 Nm).

14. Install the cross brace.

15. Install the connect the coolant recovery tank. Install the air filter assembly.

16. Connect the negative battery cable.

17. Fill cooling system and check for leaks. Start the engine and allow to come to normal operating temperature. Recheck for leaks. Top-up coolant.

NOTE: Because the engine block and radiator are aluminum, make sure the antifreeze solution is approved for use in cooling systems with a high aluminum content. GM recommends the use of a supplement/sealant 3634621 or equivalent, specifically designed for use in aluminum engines to protect the engine from damage.

4.6L Engine

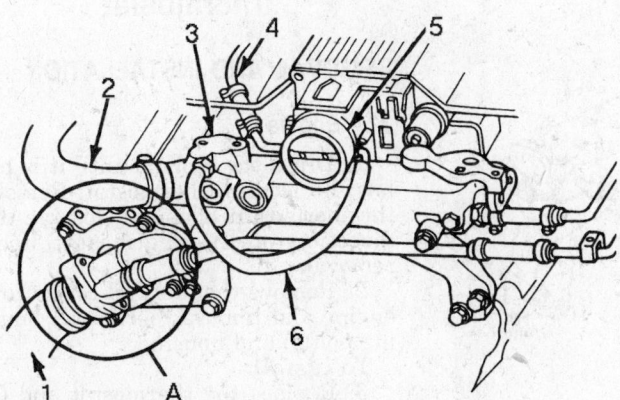

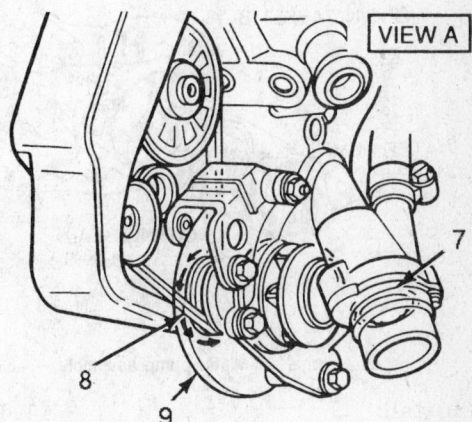

VIEW A

1. Lower radiator hose to water pump
2. Upper radiator hose return to radiator
3. Crossover
4. To surge tank
5. Throttle body
6. Crossover hose to throttle body
7. Thermostat
8. Water pump rotation
9. Crosssover

8470H032

Water pump and coolant crossover assemblies — 4.6L engine

1. Disconnect the negative battery cable.

2. Drain the engine coolant into a clean container for reuse.

3. Remove the air cleaner assembly.

4. Remove the water pump pulley bolts.

5. Remove the water pump drive belt and the water pump pulley.

6. Remove the water pump-to-engine bolts and the pump.

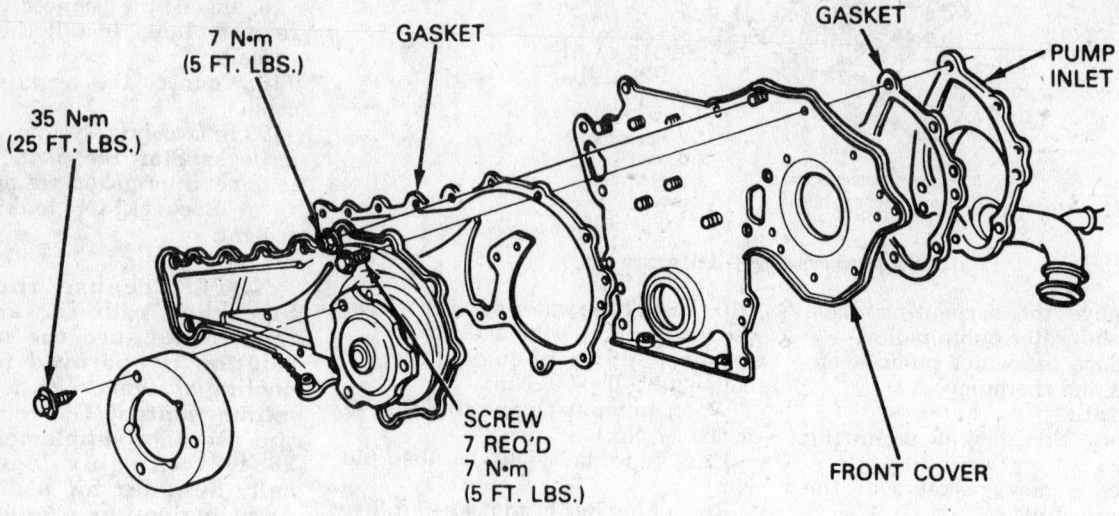

7 N•m
(5 FT. LBS.)

GASKET

GASKET

PUMP INLET

35 N•m
(25 FT. LBS.)

SCREW
7 REQ'D
7 N•m
(5 FT. LBS.)

FRONT COVER

8470H030

Water pump assembly — 4.5L and 4.9L engines

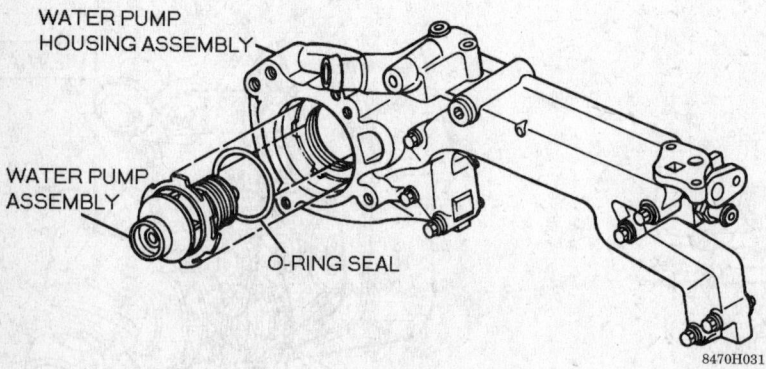

WATER PUMP
HOUSING ASSEMBLY

WATER PUMP
ASSEMBLY

O-RING SEAL

8470H031

Water pump assembly — 4.6L engine

To install:

7. Clean the gasket mounting surfaces.

8. Place a new gasket over the water pump studs.

9. Install the water pump and tighten the housing bolts to 5 ft. lbs. (7 Nm).

10. Install the water pump pulley. Install the water pump pulley bolts finger-tight.

11. Install the drive belt.

12. Tighten the water pump pulley bolts to 22 ft. lbs. (30 Nm).

13. Install the air cleaner assembly.

14. Connect the negative battery cable.

15. Fill cooling system and check for leaks. Start the engine and allow to come to normal operating temperature. Recheck for leaks. Top-up coolant.

NOTE: Because the engine block and radiator are aluminum, make sure the antifreeze solution is approved for use in cooling systems with a high aluminum content. GM recommends the use of a supplement/sealant 3634621 or equivalent, specifically designed for use in aluminum engines to protect the engine from damage.

Thermostat

REMOVAL AND INSTALLATION

3.8L Engine

1. Drain the coolant until it is below the level of thermostat. Remove the thermostat housing. Observe the direction of the thermostat upon removal.

2. Remove the fuel rail cover from engine and remove thermostat housing bolt(s) and housing.

To install:

3. Replace the thermostat and O-ring ensuring the proper direction of new thermostat.

4. Install the thermostat housing and bolt(s) and tighten the bolt(s) to 10 ft. lbs. (14 Nm).

5. Refill cooling system to proper level with a 50/50 mixture of water and ethylene glycol antifreeze.

6. Start engine and check for coolant leaks. Allow engine to come to normal operating temperature. Recheck for coolant leaks.

4.5L, 4.6L and 4.9L Engines

1. Drain coolant to a level below the thermostat housing.

2. Remove 2 bolts securing upper thermostat housing to lower housing.

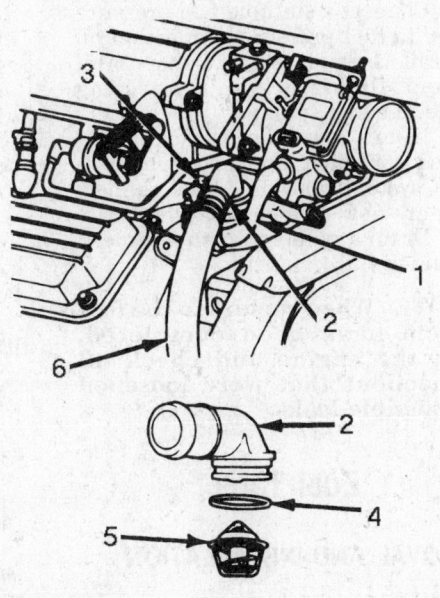

1. Throttle body inlet coolant hose
2. Manifold coolant outlet
3. Bolt
4. O-Ring
5. Thermostat
6. Radiator

8470H033

Throttle body coolant hoses and thermostat — 3.8L engine

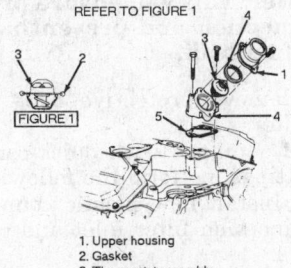

REFER TO FIGURE 1

FIGURE 1

1. Upper housing
2. Gasket
3. Thermostat assembly
4. Lower housing
5. Gasket

8470H034

Thermostat and housing — 4.5L and 4.9L engines

3. Remove upper thermostat housing.

4. Remove thermostat and O-ring from lower housing.

To install:

5. Install thermostat and a new O-ring to lower housing.

6. Install upper thermostat housing to lower housing. Tighten thermostat housing bolts to 20 ft. lbs. (27 Nm).

7. Refill cooling system using a 50/50 mixture of water and ethylene glycol antifreeze.

8. Start engine and check for coolant leaks. Allow engine to come to normal operating temperature. Recheck for coolant leaks.

COOLING SYSTEM BLEEDING

1. With the cooling system completely drained, fill the system with at least a 50/50 mixture of ethylene glycol antifreeze and water but no more than a 70/30 mixture of water to antifreeze.

2. Fill the radiator to just below the filler neck. Fill the coolant recovery reservoir to the COLD FILL mark.

3. Run the engine with the radiator cap removed until normal operating temperature is reached, with the radiator inlet hose hot.

4. With the engine idling, add coolant to the radiator until it reaches the bottom of the filler neck.

5. Position the heating system controls on maximum; allowing coolant to circulate through the heater core.

6. Check the coolant level again and add, as necessary.

7. Install the radiator cap.

1. Thermostat
2. Thermostat housing
3. Coolant pump inlet
4. Thermostat by-pass hose

8470H035

Thermostat and housing — 4.6L engine

FUEL SYSTEM

Fuel System Service Precautions

Safety is the most important factor when performing not only fuel system maintenance but any type of maintenance. Failure to conduct maintenance and repairs in a safe manner may result in serious personal injury or death. Maintenance and testing of the vehicle's fuel system components can be accomplished safely and effectively by adhering to the following rules and guidelines.

• To avoid the possibility of fire and personal injury, always disconnect the negative battery cable unless the repair or test procedure requires that battery voltage be applied.

• Always relieve the fuel system pressure prior to disconnecting any fuel system component (injector, fuel rail, pressure regulator, etc.), fitting or fuel line connection. Exercise extreme caution whenever relieving fuel system pressure to avoid exposing skin, face and eyes to fuel spray. Please be advised that fuel under pressure may penetrate the skin or any part of the body that it contacts.

• Always place a shop towel or cloth around the fitting or connection prior to loosening to absorb any excess fuel due to spillage. Ensure that all fuel spillage (should it occur) is quickly removed from engine surfaces. Ensure that all fuel soaked cloths or towels are deposited into a suitable waste container.

• Always keep a dry chemical (Class B) fire extinguisher near the work area.

• Do not allow fuel spray or fuel vapors to come into contact with a spark or open flame.

• Always use a backup wrench when loosing and tightening fuel line connection fittings. This will prevent unnecessary stress and torsion to fuel line piping. Always follow the proper torque specifications.

• Always replace worn fuel fitting O-rings with new. Do not substitute fuel hose or equivalent where fuel pipe is installed.

RELIEVING FUEL SYSTEM PRESSURE

1. Disconnect the negative battery cable.

2. Loosen fuel filler cap to relieve tank vapor pressure. Do not tighten until service has been completed.

3. Connect a suitable fuel pressure gauge to fuel pressure connection on fuel rail assembly. Wrap a shop towel around fitting while connecting gauge to avoid spillage.

4. Install bleed hose into an approved container and open valve to bleed system pressure. Fuel connections are now safe for servicing.

5. Drain any fuel into an approved container.

NOTE: When repairs to the fuel system have been completed, start the engine and check all connections that were loosened for possible leaks.

Fuel Tank

REMOVAL AND INSTALLATION

1. Disconnect the negative battery cable. Relieve the fuel system pressure.

2. Drain all fuel from the tank into a proper container.

3. Disconnect the sender assembly wires, tank filler and the vent hoses.

4. Disconnect the fuel pipe quick connectors.

5. Have an assistant support the fuel tank and disconnect the 2 tank retaining straps.

6. Disconnect the exhaust at the rear hanger and remove the tank from the vehicle.

To install:

7. Install the fuel tank to the vehicle and install the 2 retaining straps.

8. Raise the exhaust and connect the rear hanger.

9. Connect the fuel pipe quick connectors.

10. Connect the sender wires, the tank filler and vent hoses.

11. Refill the tank with fuel and connect the negative battery cable.

12. Inspect for any fuel leakage.

Fuel Filter

REMOVAL AND INSTALLATION

1. Disconnect the negative battery cable.

2. Relieve fuel system pressure.

3. Raise and safely support the vehicle.

4. Remove bolt retaining fuel filter bracket or open fuel filter bracket release tabs, as required.

5. If equipped with quick-connect fuel fittings, perform the following procedures:

a. Grasp filter and 1 fuel line fitting. Twist quick-connect fitting 1/4 turn in each direction to loosen any dirt within fitting. Repeat for other fuel line fitting.

b. Using compressed air, blow out dirt from quick-connect fittings at both ends of fuel filter.

c. Remove quick-connect fittings by squeezing plastic tabs of male end connector and pull connection apart. Repeat for other fitting.

6. If equipped with threaded fuel fittings, perform the following:

a. Using a backup wrench on fuel filter, loosen fuel line retaining nut. Repeat for other fuel line fitting.

b. Using compressed air, blow out dirt from fuel line fittings at both ends of fuel filter.

c. Back off nut completely so fuel line can be separated from filter at both ends.

7. Remove fuel filter.

To install:

NOTE: Before installing a new filter, always apply a few drops of clean engine oil to both ends of the filter. This will ensure proper reconnection and prevent a possible fuel leak.

8. Remove protective caps from new filter.

9. If equipped with quick-connect fuel fittings, perform the following:

a. Install new plastic connector retainers on filter inlet and outlet tubes.

b. Install filter in retainer noting direction of flow indicated on filter.

c. Install quick-connect fittings by pushing connectors together to cause the retaining tabs/fingers to snap into place.

NOTE: Once installed, pull on both ends of each connection to make sure connection is secure.

10. If equipped with threaded fuel fittings, install new O-ring seals, install fuel lines into the filter.

NOTE: Use backup wrench when installing fuel lines into new filter to prevent filter O-ring or fuel line damage.

11. Install fuel filter into retainer and engage bracket tabs or install retainer bracket bolt, as required.

12. Lower vehicle.

13. Tighten fuel filler cap.

14. Connect negative battery cable.

NOTE: Before cranking the engine, turn ignition switch to the ON position for 2 seconds, then turn switch OFF for 5 seconds. Again turn ignition switch to ON position and check for fuel leaks.

Electric Fuel Pump

The fuel pump is mounted in the tank and is part of the fuel tank meter assembly. The tank must be removed from the vehicle in order to service the fuel pump and fuel tank meter assembly.

PRESSURE TESTING

1. Connect a suitable fuel pressure gauge to the fuel pressure test fitting on the fuel rail assembly. Wrap a shop towel around the fuel pressure tap to absorb any fuel leakage that may occur when installing the gauge.
2. Turn ignition switch to the **ON** position. Check to see that pressure is within specification.
3. Turn ignition switch **OFF**. Pressure should not leak down with fuel pump **OFF**.
4. Pressure at idle should be 3–10 psi (21–69 kPa) lower than static pressure.

REMOVAL AND INSTALLATION

1. Disconnect the negative battery cable.
2. Relieve fuel system pressure.
3. Remove fuel filler cap to release fuel tank vapors. Leave cap off until repairs are completed.

─────── **CAUTION** ───────
Gasoline fuel vapors are extremely flammable. Ensure that fuel is stored in a container that can be properly sealed. Never store fuel in an open container. Store container in a safe place away from heat.
──────────────────────────

4. Remove fuel tank by performing the following:
  a. Drain fuel from the tank into an approved container for storage.
  b. Raise and safely support the vehicle.
  c. Remove rear stabilizer bar at links, pivot bar downward.
  d. Remove hoses and pipes from tank unit.
  e. Remove hoses at tank from filler and vent pipe.
  f. Disconnect tank unit harness from rear body harness.

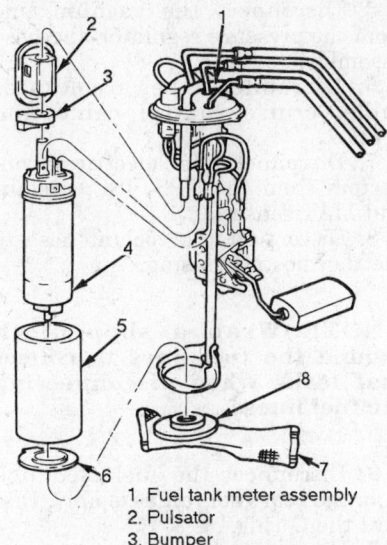

1. Fuel tank meter assembly
2. Pulsator
3. Bumper
4. Fuel pump
5. Sound isolator sleeve
6. Sound insulator
7. Filter strainer
8. Deflector

8470H037

Fuel pump unit

  g. Support fuel tank and disconnect 2 fuel tank retaining straps.
  h. Remove tank from vehicle.
5. Remove sending unit, gasket and pump assembly by turning cam lock ring counterclockwise. Lift assembly from fuel tank and remove fuel pump from fuel tank sending unit.
6. Pull fuel pump up into attaching hose while pulling outward away from bottom support. Take care to prevent damage to rubber insulator and strainer during removal. After pump assembly is clear of bottom support, pull pump assembly out of rubber connector for removal.

To install:
7. Push fuel pump assembly into attaching hose.
8. Install fuel tank sending unit and pump assembly into tank assembly. Use new O-ring seal during reassembly.
9. Install cam lock over assembly and lock by turning clockwise.
10. Support tank and position in vehicle. Install tank straps and secure with retaining bolts. Tighten to 25 ft. lbs. (33 Nm).
11. Connect tank unit harness to body harness.
12. Connect hoses to filler and vent pipes. Tighten clamps.

13. Connect hoses and pipes to tank unit.
14. Connect rear stabilizer bar to links. Tighten bolts to 42 ft. lbs. (58 Nm).
15. Lower vehicle.
16. Refill tank and install filler cap.
17. Connect negative battery cable.
18. Start engine and check for leaks.

Fuel Injection

IDLE SPEED ADJUSTMENT

Idle speed is automatically controlled by the ECM. Periodic adjustments are not required.

IDLE MIXTURE ADJUSTMENT

Idle mixture is automatically maintained by the ECM. Periodic adjustments are not required.

Fuel Rail

REMOVAL AND INSTALLATION

Riviera and Toronado

1. Disconnect the negative battery cable.
2. Properly relieve the fuel system pressure.
3. Using a shop towel to catch any fuel, disconnect the fuel supply and return lines from the fuel rail inlet and outlet. Use a backup wrench to avoid twisting the fittings on the fuel rail.
4. Disconnect the fuel injector electrical connectors.
5. Disconnect the vacuum line from the pressure regulator.
6. Remove the 4 bolts attaching the fuel rail assembly to the intake manifold.
7. Carefully, remove the fuel rail assembly from the intake manifold.

NOTE: With the fuel rail removed, cover the injector openings to prevent the entry of dirt and other contaminants.

To install:
8. Install the new injector O-rings. Lubricate lightly with engine oil.
9. Carefully, install the fuel rail to the intake manifold. Seat each injector by hand.
10. Install the 4 bolts attaching the fuel rail to the intake manifold. Tighten to 7–14 ft. lbs. (10–20 Nm).
11. Connect the fuel supply and return lines to the fuel rail.

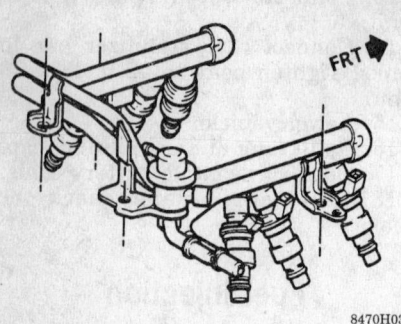

Fuel rail and injectors — 3.8L engine

12. Connect the fuel injector electrical connectors.

13. Connect the vacuum line to the fuel pressure regulator.

14. Connect the negative battery cable.

15. Start the engine and check for fuel leaks.

Allante, Eldorado and Seville

4.5L AND 4.9L ENGINES

1. Disconnect the negative battery cable.

2. Remove the air cleaner.

3. Properly relieve the fuel system pressure.

4. Remove the power steering pump.

5. Disconnect the vacuum line from the pressure regulator and base assembly.

6. Disconnect the accelerator cable, cruise control cable and bracket.

7. Disconnect the electrical connectors from the TPS, ISC, coolant and MAT sensors.

8. Disconnect the coolant hose to the thermostat housing.

NOTE: Wrap a shop cloth around the fuel lines to collect that leaks when disconnecting the fuel lines.

9. Disconnect the fuel feed line from the rear fuel rail assembly. Discard the O-ring.

10. Disconnect the fuel return line. Discard the O-ring.

11. Disconnect the EGR vacuum lines and remove the EGR valve.

12. Remove the 5 fuel rail support bracket attaching bolts.

13. Disconnect the front and rear fuel rail electrical connectors.

14. Carefully, remove the fuel rail from the intake manifold.

15. Remove the lower O-ring seal from the injectors and discard.

To install:

16. Install new injector O-rings. Lubricate lightly with engine oil.

17. Carefully, install the fuel rail assembly to the intake manifold.

18. Install the 5 fuel rail attaching bolts. Tighten to 18 ft. lbs. (24 Nm).

19. Connect the front and rear fuel rail electrical connectors.

20. Install the EGR valve and connect the vacuum lines.

21. Install new fuel feed line O-rings. Lubricate O-rings with petroleum based grease. Connect the fuel feed line. Using a backup wrench, tighten to 22 ft. lbs. (30 Nm).

22. Install new fuel return line O-rings. Lubricate O-rings with petroleum based grease. Connect the fuel return line. Using a backup wrench, tighten to 22 ft. lbs. (30 Nm).

23. Connect the coolant hose to the thermostat housing.

24. Connect the electrical connectors to the TPS, ISC, coolant and MAT sensors.

25. Connect the accelerator cable, and cruise control cable and bracket.

26. Connect the vacuum line to the pressure regulator and base assembly.

27. Install the power steering pump.

28. Install the air cleaner.

1. Injector assembly
2. Front fuel rail assembly
3. Rear fuel rail assembly
4. Pressure regulator and base assembly
5. Fuel return tube
6. Fuel crossover tube
7. Front wiring (rail) assembly
8. Rear wiring (rail) assembly

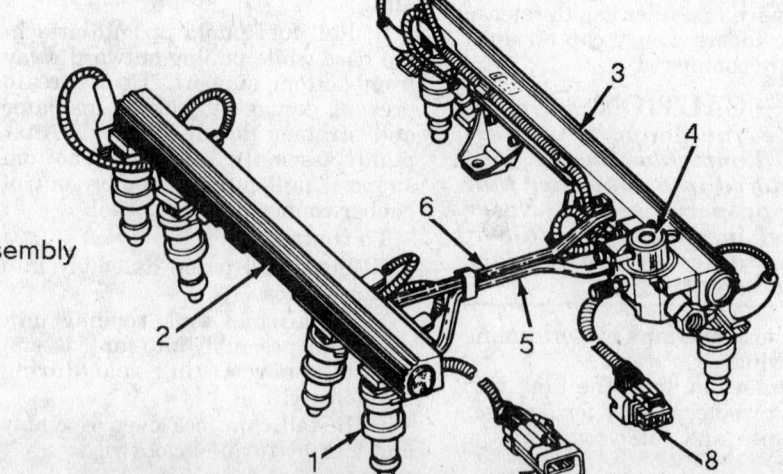

Fuel rail and injectors — 4.5L and 4.9L engines

29. Connect the negative battery cable.

30. Start the engine and check for fuel leaks.

4.6L ENGINE

1. Disconnect the negative battery cable.

2. Disconnect the number **1** and **2** fuel pump relays.

3. Properly relieve the fuel system pressure.

4. Remove the intake manifold top cover assembly.

5. Disconnect the intake manifold electrical connectors.

6. Remove the fuel rail assembly with the injectors intact from the intake manifold.

7. Separate the fuel injector from the fuel rail.

NOTE: Wrap a shop cloth around the fuel lines to collect that leaks when disconnecting the fuel lines.

8. Remove the O-ring seals from the injectors and discard.

To install:

9. Install new injector O-rings. Lubricate lightly with engine oil.

10. Connect the injector(s) to the fuel rail assembly.

11. Carefully, install the fuel rail assembly to the intake manifold.

12. Install the intake manifold cover and tighten the bolts in proper sequence to 106 inch lbs. (12 Nm).

13. Connect the negative battery cable.

14. Start the engine and check for fuel leaks.

Fuel Injector

REMOVAL AND INSTALLATION

NOTE: Care must be taken when removing injectors to prevent damage to the electrical connector pins on the injector and the nozzle. The injectors are serviced as a complete assembly only. Injectors are an electrical component and should not be immersed in any type of cleaner.

Sequential Fuel Injection (SFI)

1. Disconnect the negative battery cable.

2. Properly relieve the fuel pressure.

3. Remove the fuel rail.

4. On Allante, Eldorado and Seville, disconnect the injector electrical connector by pushing in the wire connector clip while pulling the connector body away from the injector.

5. Remove the injector retainer clip from the injector.

6. Separate the injector from the fuel rail.

7. Remove the injector O-rings and discard.

To install:

8. Lubricate new injector O-rings lightly and install on the injector.

9. If supplied, install new injector clip on the injector.

10. Install the fuel injector assembly into the fuel rail socket.

NOTE: On Allante, Eldorado and Seville, the electrical connectors should be facing the front of the engine for injectors 1–4 and the rear of the engine for injectors 5–8.

11. Connect the electrical connector to the injector assembly.

12. Install the fuel rail assembly.

13. Connect the negative battery cable.

14. Start the engine and check for fuel leaks.

Throttle Body Injection (TBI)

1. Disconnect the negative battery cable. Remove the air cleaner.

2. Properly relieve the fuel system pressure.

3. Disconnect the electrical connector from the fuel injector(s) by squeezing both tabs together and pulling it straight up.

4. Remove the fuel meter cover-to-throttle body screws and the cover; be sure to note the position of the short screws. Allow the gasket to remain in place to prevent damage to the casting housing.

5. Using a small prybar and a ¼ in. rod, pry the fuel injector(s) from the throttle body; discard the O-rings.

To install:

6. Lubricate the new small O-ring with clean Dexron®II automatic transmission fluid. Push the new small O-ring onto the nozzle end of the injector pressing the ring up against the injector fuel filter.

7. Install the steel backup washer into the recess of the fuel meter body.

8. Lubricate the new large O-ring with clean Dexron®II automatic transmission fluid. Install the O-ring directly above the backup washer, pressing the O-ring down into the cavity recess. O-ring is located properly when it is flush with the fuel meter body casting surface.

NOTE: Do not attempt to reverse this procedure and install the backup washer and O-ring after the injector is located in the cavity. To do so will prevent the seating of the O-ring in the cavity recess which may result in a fuel leak.

9. Install the injector using a pushing/twisting motion to center the nozzle O-ring in the bottom of the injector cavity. Align the raised lug on the injector base with the notch cast into the fuel meter body. Push down on the injector making sure it is fully seated in the cavity. The injector installation is correct with the lug seated in the notch and the electrical terminals parallel to the throttle shaft in the throttle body.

10. Install the fuel meter cover.

11. Connect the injector electrical connector.

12. Install the air cleaner.

13. Connect the negative battery cable.

14. Start the engine and check for fuel leaks.

EMISSION CONTROLS

Emission Warning Lamps

The dash mounted Service Engine Soon and Service Vehicle Soon lights are used to indicate a malfunction that the computer has detected in the vehicle's operation. The malfunctions can be related to the operating sensors or the Electronic Control Module (ECM). The service light will go out automatically if the trouble is cleared or intermittent.

The ECM, however will automatically store the trouble code until the diagnostic system is Cleared.

CLEARING ECM TROUBLE CODES

Except Allante, Eldorado and Seville

With the ignition switch in the **OFF** position, disconnect battery voltage to the ECM for at least 30 seconds by performing 1 of the following:

1. Remove the ECM fuse from the fuse panel.

2. Disconnect the ECM pigtail.

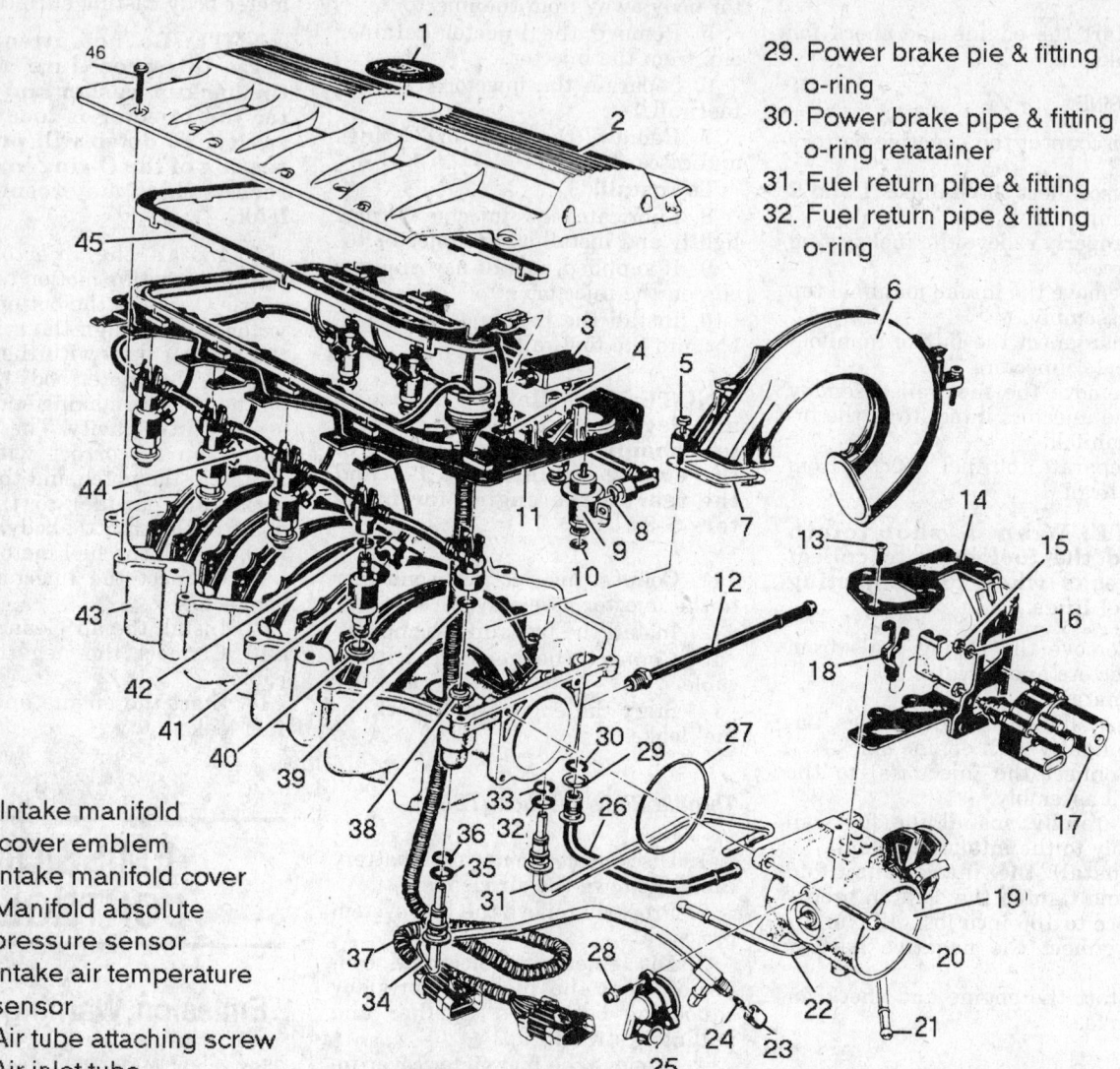

29. Power brake pie & fitting
    o-ring
30. Power brake pipe & fitting
    o-ring retatainer
31. Fuel return pipe & fitting
32. Fuel return pipe & fitting
    o-ring

1. Intake manifold
   cover emblem
2. Intake manifold cover
3. Manifold absolute
   pressure sensor
4. Intake air temperature
   sensor
5. Air tube attaching screw
6. Air inlet tube
7. Air inlet to manifold
   seal
8. Fuel return line o-ring
9. Fuel pressure regulator
10. Fuel return tube o-ring
11. Intake manifold cover
    gasket
12. PCV tube
13. ISC bracket attaching
    screw
14. ISC bracket
15. ISC motor attaching nut
16. ISC motor attaching
    lockwasher
17. ISC motor

18. Fuel tube clamp
19. Throttle body
20. Throttle body attaching
    bolt
21. Coolant outlet tube
22. Coolant inlet tube
23. Fuel pressure
    connection cap
24. Valve core
25. Throttle position sensor
26. TP sensor attaching
    screw
27. Throttle body to manifold
    o-ring
28. Power brake pipe & fitting

33. Fuel return pipe o-ring
    retainer
34. Fuel inlet pipe & fitting
35. Fuel inlet pipe & fitting o-ring
36. Fuel inlet pipe o-ring retainer
37. Wiring harness
38. Fuel inlet o-ring retainer
39. Fuel inlet fitting o-ring
40. Injector lower seal
41. Port fuel injector
42. Injector upper seal
43. Intake manifold housing
44. Fuel rail
45. Wiring harness cover
46. Intake manifold cover bolt

8470H041

Intake manifold, fuel rail and injectors — 4.6L engine

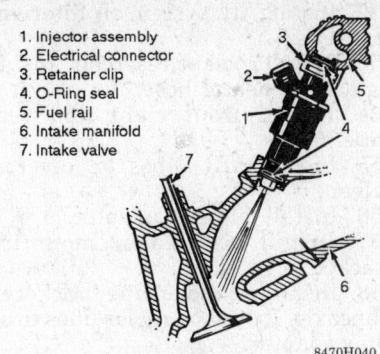

1. Injector assembly
2. Electrical connector
3. Retainer clip
4. O-Ring seal
5. Fuel rail
6. Intake manifold
7. Intake valve

8470H040

PFI fuel injector

3. Disconnect the negative battery cable.

NOTE: Disconnecting the negative battery cable should only be done as a last resort as it will also erase the memories for the digital radio, digital clock, trip odometer etc.

Allante, Eldorado and Seville

1. Turn the key to the **ON** position.
2. Simultaneously press the **OFF** and **HI** buttons on the climate control panel until CODES CLEAR appears in the readout.
3. To clear the Body Computer Module (BCM) codes, depress the **OFF** and **LO** buttons simultaneously until CODES CLEAR appears.

ENGINE MECHANICAL

NOTE: Disconnecting the negative battery cable on some vehicles may interfere with the functions of the on board computer systems and may require the computer to undergo a relearning process, once the negative battery cable is reconnected.

Engine Assembly

REMOVAL AND INSTALLATION

Riviera and Toronado

3.8L ENGINE

1. Matchmark the hood hinge-to-hood and remove the hood.
2. Properly relieve the fuel pressure and disconnect the fuel lines from the fuel rail.

3. Disconnect the negative battery cable. Drain the coolant and the engine oil.
4. Disconnect the windshield washer, radiator and heater supply hoses.
5. Disconnect the wiring to the starter and to the engine and battery connectors located near the relay center.
6. Remove the accessory drive belt. Remove the power steering pump from the brackets and set aside.
7. Remove the air flow duct and air cleaner assembly.
8. Remove the throttle cable from the throttle linkage mounting bracket.
9. Disconnect the mat sensor, throttle position switch, idle air control valve and the oxygen sensor connectors.
10. Disconnect the ignition coil ground strap from the fender inner panel.
11. Disconnect the fuel feed and return pipes from the fuel rail and the fuel pressure regulator.
12. Disconnect the emission control canister hoses from the throttle body connections.
13. Disconnect the brake booster, heater control, cruise control and servo vacuum hoses.
14. Raise and safely support the vehicle.
15. Remove the exhaust pipe from the right manifold.
16. Using a vertical lifting device, secure it to the engine and support its weight.
17. Disconnect the air conditioning compressor from the mounts and secure it aside.
18. Remove the left front engine mount and the right front engine to transaxle bracket.
19. Remove the torque strut assembly and front engine to frame stabilizer.
20. Place a jack or other support under the transaxle and remove the engine to transaxle bolts.
21. Remove the flywheel cover. Matchmark the torque converter-to-flywheel for alignment purposes. Remove the torque converter-to-flywheel bolts and slide the torque converter rearward.
22. Disconnect and move aside any electrical harness connectors which may be in the way.
23. Lift the engine assembly from the vehicle and attach it to a work stand.

To install:
24. Install engine assembly in vehicle. Install upper engine-to-transaxle bolts.
25. Install the right front engine to transaxle bracket and left front engine mount.
26. Install the front engine to frame stabilizer.
27. Install the torque converter-to-flywheel bolts aligning marks made during removal. Tighten to 46 ft. lbs. (62 Nm). Install flywheel cover.
28. Install the air conditioner compressor and connect the cruise control vacuum hoses to the servo unit.
29. Connect the exhaust pipe to the manifold. Connect the wiring harness connectors to the mat sensor, throttle position switch, idle air control valve, and the oxygen sensor.
30. Connect the throttle cable to the linkage. Install the air flow duct and air cleaner assembly.
31. Install the power steering pump to the engine.
32. Connect the main wiring harness connectors behind the relay housing.
33. Connect the wiring to the starter. Connect the windshield washer, radiator and heater supply hoses.
34. Add coolant and engine oil.
35. Connect the negative battery cable.
36. Install the hood at matchmarks made during removal.
37. Start the engine and check for fuel, coolant and transaxle leaks.

Allante

1992

1. Disconnect the negative battery cable. Properly relieve the fuel system pressure. Position a drain pan under the radiator, open the drain cock and drain the cooling system.
2. Remove the air cleaner. Matchmark the hood hinge-to-hood position and remove the hood.
3. Remove the cooling fans and the accessory drive belt.
4. Remove the upper intake manifold. Remove the upper radiator hose and disconnect the heater hose from the thermostat housing.
5. Disconnect the following electrical connectors and position aside:
   a. Oil pressure sending unit
   b. Coolant temperature sensor
   c. Distributor
   d. EGR solenoid
   e. Engine temperature switch
   f. Idle speed control
   g. Throttle position sensor
   h. Injector electrical connections
   i. MAT sensor

  j. Oxygen sensor

  k. Throttle body base warmer

  l. Alternator

  m. Ground wires at the alternator mounting bracket

6. Disconnect the accelerator, the cruise control and the transaxle throttle valve cables from the throttle lever.

7. Disconnect the cruise control diaphragm/bracket and move them aside.

8. Disconnect the transaxle oil cooler lines from the radiator. Remove the radiator.

9. Disconnect and remove the oil cooler lines from the oil filter adapter.

10. Remove the oil cooler lines-to-transaxle bracket.

11. Remove the air cleaner bracket and the oil filter adapter.

12. Disconnect the air injection tubes from the diverter valve.

13. Remove the cross brace.

14. Remove the right front heater hose and the coolant reservoir.

15. Remove the Air Injection Reactor (AIR) filter and bracket.

16. Remove the power steering line brace from the right cylinder head. Remove the pump and belt tensioner as an assembly and position them forward of the engine.

17. Properly discharge and recover the refrigerant from the air conditioning system and remove the air conditioning lines from the accumulator and condenser.

18. Disconnect supply and return fuel lines from the fuel rail. Remove the fuel line bracket from the transaxle and move the fuel lines aside.

19. Raise and safely support the vehicle.

20. Label and disconnect the electrical connectors from the starter. Disconnect any ground wires still connected to the engine.

21. Disconnect the oxygen sensor wire and remove the oxygen sensors.

22. Disconnect and remove the exhaust Y-pipe. Remove the starter-to-engine bolts and the starter.

23. Remove the torque converter covers. Matchmark the torque converter-to-flywheel and remove the flywheel-to-torque converter bolts.

24. Remove the air conditioning compressor lower dust shield, the right front tire and the outer wheel house plastic shield.

25. Remove the right rear transaxle-to-engine mount bolt, the front engine mount nuts and the right rear transaxle mount bolts.

26. Remove the alternator. Remove the oxygen sensor wires. Remove the

heater bypass bracket from the right side of the vehicle.

27. Remove the right side engine brace and lower the vehicle to the ground.

28. Remove the engine-to-transaxle bolts. The bolts are accessible from the top.

29. Connect a chain from a lifting crane down to both lift points on top of the engine and ensure it is secure. Lift the engine out of the vehicle.

To install:

30. Situate a floor jack under the transaxle and raise it slightly so it will align with the engine. Lower the engine into the engine compartment and engage the dowels that are on the engine block with the corresponding holes in the transaxle.

31. Install the upper transaxle-to-engine bolts. Lower the engine, directing it squarely onto the mounts. Remove the lifting equipment.

NOTE: Ensure that converter is properly positioned to the flexplate and engaged in the front pump of the transaxle.

32. Install 5 upper transaxle bellhousing-to-engine bolts.

33. Lower floor jack and remove from transaxle.

34. Lower engine making sure it is properly seated on mounts.

35. Remove lifting equipment. Raise and safely support the vehicle.

36. Install right side engine brace.

37. Remove engine support.

38. Install alternator and oxygen sensor wires and heater bypass bracket to right side of vehicle.

39. Install front engine mount nuts and right rear transaxle mounting bolts.

40. Connect oil level sensor at oil pan and both oxygen sensors.

41. Install right rear transaxle-to-engine mounting bolt.

42. Install outer wheel house plastic shield.

43. Install right front tire and wheel assembly.

44. Install air conditioning compressor lower dust shield.

45. Install 3 flexplate-to-converter bolts. Install flexplate cover.

46. Install starter. Install exhaust Y pipe.

47. Install electrical connectors at starter and ground wires to block.

48. Lower vehicle.

49. Install fuel line bracket. Install fuel lines at fuel rail.

50. Install air conditioning lines to accumulator and condenser.

51. Install power steering pump and tensioner. Install power steering line brace on right cylinder head.

52. Install AIR system air filter and bracket.

53. Install coolant reservoir. Install right front heater hose.

54. Install front right and rear cross braces.

55. Install AIR tubes on diverter valve.

56. Install oil filter adapter.

57. Install air cleaner mounting bracket.

58. Install oil cooler line bracket at transaxle. Install oil cooler lines to oil filter adapter.

59. Install radiator. Install engine oil and transaxle oil cooler lines to radiator.

60. Connect cruise control diaphragm with bracket.

61. Install the following wiring connectors:

  a. Injectors

  b. Ground wires at alternator bracket

  c. Oil pressure switch

  d. Coolant temperature sensor

  e. Distributor

  f. Engine temperature switch

62. Connect cables from throttle lever including: accelerator, cruise control and transaxle throttle valve.

63. Install accessory drive belt.

64. Install upper radiator hose and heater hose to thermostat housing.

65. Install cooling fan.

66. Install air conditioning accumulator hose brace.

67. Install vehicle hood.

68. Install air cleaner. Install engine coolant. Connect negative battery cable.

69. Evacuate, recharge and leak test the air conditioning system.

70. Start engine and check for oil, coolant and transaxle leaks.

1993

1. Disconnect the negative battery cable. Remove the air cleaner inlet duct.

2. Matchmark the hood hinge-to-hood and remove the hood.

3. Drain the coolant from the radiator.

4. Remove the left and right torque struts. Install the left front strut bolt back into the bracket.

5. Disconnect the radiator hoses at the water crossover. Remove both cooling fans from the engine.

6. Remove the serpentine accessory drive belt.

7. Disconnect the cruise control servo connections and the ISC motor electrical connector.

8. Disconnect the throttle cable from the throttle body cam. Disconnect the shift cable from the

park/neutral switch. Remove the cable bracket at the transaxle.

9. Remove the park/neutral switch and disconnect the power brake vacuum hose.

10. At the rear of the right head, disconnect the cylinder head temperature switch.

11. Remove the bellhousing bolts.

12. Remove the ignition coils and remove the spark plug wires.

13. Raise and safely support the vehicle.

14. Remove the oil pan-to-transmission brace. Remove the torque converter splash shield and the 4 converter-to-flywheel bolts.

15. Disconnect the oil cooler lines from the oil filter adapter.

16. Remove the A/C compressor mounting bolts and disconnect the electrical connectors. Move compressor out of way.

17. Disconnect the electrical connectors from the left side of the engine and move the harness from behind the exhaust manifold.

18. Remove the 2 nuts that secure the motor mount to the engine cradle front crossmember.

19. Remove the exhaust Y-pipe and remove the right front wheel.

20. Remove the crankcase to transmission bracket at the transmission tail shaft. Disconnect the knock sensor.

21. Remove the bolt from the transmission to the cylinder head brace at the cylinder head.

22. Lower the vehicle. Disconnect the fuel inlet and fuel return lines using special tool J-37088 or equivalent.

23. Disconnect the injector harness connector and the hoses from the coolant reservoir. Remove the reservoir.

24. Disconnect the cam position sensor. Disconnect the heater hoses from the water pipes at the front of the right cylinder head.

25. Disconnect the battery cable from the junction block and remove the retainer at the cylinder head.

26. Disconnect the starter cable from the junction block.

27. Disconnect the power steering pump pressure and return lines at the pump. Return power steering line retainer from the right front of the crankcase.

28. Disconnect the rear oxygen sensor.

29. Remove the 3 screws securing the wiring harness retainer to right cam cover and position harness aside.

30. Connect an engine lifting device to the engine using the support hooks

at left and right rear of engine. The torque strut bracket at the left front of the engine should be used as a 3rd lifting hook.

31. Carefully remove the engine from the vehicle.

To install:

32. Lower the engine into the vehicle. Remove the lifting device.

33. Install the 4 bellhousing bolts and tighten to 75 ft. lbs. (100 Nm).

34. Raise and safely support the vehicle.

35. Install 2 nuts to the motor mount at the front cradle crossmember. Do not fully tighten.

36. Install bolt to the cylinder head for transmission brace. Do not fully tighten.

37. Install the transmission to crankcase bracket with the 4 bolts. Do not fully tighten the bolts.

38. Tighten the motor mount to cradle crossmember bolts to 30 ft. lbs. (40 Nm). Tighten the transmission brace bolt and transmission to crankcase bolts to 45 ft. lbs. (60 Nm).

39. Install the right front wheel and connect the knock sensor.

40. Install the exhaust Y-pipe.

41. Install the 4 torque converter to flywheel bolts and tighten to 45 ft. lbs. (60 Nm).

42. Install the converter splash shield and install the transmission to oil pan brace. Tighten the bolt to 35 ft. lbs. (50 Nm).

43. Position the A/C compressor in place and install the mounting bolts.

44. Route the electrical harness along the left side of the engine and connect the connectors.

45. Connect the oil cooler lines to the oil filter adapter.

46. Lower the vehicle.

47. Secure the wiring harness to the right cam cover with the 3 screws.

48. Connect the rear oxygen sensor and connect the cam position sensor.

49. Connect the power steering hoses to the pump and secure the return line to the crankcase.

50. Connect the heater hoses to the water pipes.

51. Connect the starter and battery cables at the junction box. Secure battery cable with retainer.

52. Connect and install the coolant reservoir.

53. Install coils and secure with 4 screws.

54. Install the serpentine drive belt and connect the injector harness to the FIS harness.

55. Connect the fuel line connectors. Connect the cylinder head tem-

perature switch to the rear of the right head.

56. Connect the power brake vacuum line.

57. Install the park/neutral switch and shift cable. Adjust switch if necessary.

58. Install the cruise servo and connect the ISC motor.

59. Connect the throttle cable and install both cooling fans.

60. Connect the radiator hoses to the water crossover.

61. Install the torque struts and adjust the preload to zero.

62. Connect the negative battery cable.

63. Refill the engine with coolant. Install the hood and install the air cleaner.

64. Start engine and check for oil, coolant and transaxle leaks.

Eldorado and Seville

4.5L AND 4.9L ENGINES

1. Disconnect the negative battery cable. Properly relieve the fuel system pressure. Position a drain pan under the radiator, open the drain cock and drain the cooling system.

2. Remove the air cleaner. Matchmark the hood hinge-to-hood and remove the hood.

3. Remove the cooling fan and the accessory drive belt.

4. Remove the upper radiator hose and disconnect the heater hose from the thermostat housing.

5. Disconnect the following electrical connectors, if equipped and position the wires aside:
   a. Oil pressure sending unit
   b. Coolant temperature sensor
   c. Distributor
   d. EGR solenoid
   e. Engine temperature switch
   f. Idle speed control
   g. Throttle position sensor
   h. Injector electrical connections
   i. MAT sensor
   j. Oxygen sensor
   k. Throttle body base warmer
   l. Alternator
   m. Ground wires at the alternator mounting bracket

6. Disconnect the accelerator, the cruise control and the transaxle throttle valve cables from the throttle lever.

7. Disconnect the cruise control diaphragm/bracket and move them aside.

8. Disconnect the transaxle oil cooler lines from the radiator. Remove the radiator.

9. Disconnect and remove the oil cooler lines from the oil filter adapter.

10. Remove the oil cooler lines-to-transaxle bracket.

11. Remove the air cleaner bracket and the oil filter housing adapter.

12. If equipped, disconnect the air injection tubes from the diverter valve.

13. Remove the right front and right rear body braces.

14. Remove the right front heater hose and the coolant reservoir.

15. If equipped, remove the Air Injection Reactor (AIR) filter box and bracket. Remove the idler pulley for the accessory drive belt.

16. Remove the power steering line brace from the right cylinder head. Remove the pump and belt tensioner as an assembly and position them forward of the engine.

17. Properly discharge and recover the refrigerant from the air conditioning system and remove the air conditioning lines from the accumulator and condenser.

18. Disconnect supply and return fuel lines from the throttle body. Remove the fuel line bracket from the transaxle and move the fuel lines aside.

19. Remove the EGR lines and brackets. Remove the vacuum modulator line and the fuel filter; reposition them aside.

20. Raise and safely support the vehicle.

21. Remove the starter heat shield. Label and disconnect the electrical connectors from the starter. Disconnect any ground wires still connected to the engine.

22. Disconnect and remove the exhaust crossover pipe. Remove the starter-to-engine bolts and the starter.

23. Remove the torque converter covers. Matchmark the torque converter-to-flywheel and remove the flywheel-to-torque converter bolts.

24. Remove the air conditioning compressor lower dust shield, the right front tire and the outer wheel house plastic shield.

25. Remove the right rear transaxle-to-engine mount bolt and the lower engine mounting damper nut.

26. Remove the front engine mount nuts and the right rear transaxle mount nuts.

27. Remove the alternator. Remove the oxygen sensor wires. Remove the heater bypass bracket from the right side of the vehicle.

28. Remove the right side engine brace and lower the vehicle to the ground.

29. Remove the engine-to-transaxle bolts. The bolts are accessible from the top.

30. Run a chain from a lifting crane down to both lift points on top of the engine and ensure it is secure. Lift the engine out of the vehicle.

To install:

31. Situate a floor jack under the transaxle and raise it slightly so it will align with the engine. Lower the engine into the engine compartment and engage the dowels on the engine block with the corresponding holes in the transaxle.

NOTE: Ensure that converter is properly positioned to the flexplate and engaged in the front pump of transaxle.

32. Install upper 5 transaxle bellhousing-to-engine bolts.

33. Lower floor jack and remove from transaxle.

34. Lower engine making sure it is seated on the mount properly.

35. Remove lifting equipment.

36. Raise and safely support the vehicle.

37. Support the engine. Install right side engine brace. Remove engine support.

38. Install alternator and oxygen sensor wires and heater bypass bracket to right side of vehicle.

39. Install front engine mount nuts and right rear transaxle mount bolts.

40. Install lower engine damper nut.

41. Install right rear transaxle-to-engine mounting bolt.

42. Install outer wheel house plastic shield.

43. Install right front tire and wheel assembly.

44. Install air conditioner compressor lower dust shield.

45. Install 3 flexplate-to-converter bolts. Install 2 flexplate covers.

46. Install starter to engine and connect electrical connectors. Install engine ground connectors.

47. Install exhaust crossover pipe.

48. Install starter heat shield.

49. Lower vehicle.

50. Install vacuum modulator line and vacuum hose to power brake booster.

51. Install EGR lines and bracket.

52. Install fuel line bracket at transaxle. Install fuel lines at throttle body.

53. Install air conditioning lines to accumulator and condenser.

54. Install power steering pump and tensioner. Install power steering line brace on right cylinder head.

55. If equipped, install A.I.R. system air filter and bracket.

56. Install coolant reservoir. Install right front heater hose.

57. Install front right and rear cross braces.

58. If equipped, install A.I.R. tubes on diverter valve.

59. Install oil filter adapter.

60. Install air cleaner mounting bracket.

61. Install oil cooler line bracket at transaxle. Install oil cooler lines to oil filter adapter.

62. Install radiator. Install engine oil and transaxle oil cooler lines to radiator.

63. Connect cruise control diaphragm with bracket.

64. Install the following wiring connectors:
   a. ISC
   b. TPS
   c. Injectors
   d. MAT sensor
   e. Oxygen sensor
   f. Electric EFE grid
   g. Ground wires at alternator bracket
   h. Oil pressure switch
   i. Coolant temperature sensor
   j. Distributor
   k. EGR solenoid
   l. Engine temperature switch

65. Connect cables from throttle lever including: accelerator, cruise control and transaxle throttle valve.

66. Install accessory drive belt.

67. Install upper radiator hose and heater hose to thermostat housing.

68. Install cooling fan.

69. Install air conditioning accumulator hose brace.

70. Install vehicle hood.

71. Install air cleaner. Install engine coolant. Connect negative battery cable.

72. Evacuate, recharge and leak test the air conditioning system.

73. Start engine and check for oil, coolant and transaxle leaks.

4.6L ENGINE

1. Disconnect the negative battery cable. Remove the air cleaner inlet duct.

2. Matchmark the hood hinge-to-hood and remove the hood.

3. Drain the coolant from the radiator.

4. Remove the left and right torque struts. Install the left front strut bolt back into the bracket.

5. Disconnect the radiator hoses at the water crossover. Remove both cooling fans from the engine.

6. Remove the serpentine accessory drive belt.

7. Disconnect the cruise control servo connections and the ISC motor electrical connector.

8. Disconnect the throttle cable from the throttle body cam. Disconnect the shift cable from the park/neutral switch. Remove the cable bracket at the transaxle.

9. Remove the park/neutral switch and disconnect the power brake vacuum hose.

10. At the rear of the right head, disconnect the cylinder head temperature switch.

11. Remove the bellhousing bolts.

12. Remove the ignition coils and remove the spark plug wires.

13. Raise and safely support the vehicle.

14. Remove the oil pan-to-transmission brace. Remove the torque converter splash shield and the 4 converter-to-flywheel bolts.

15. Disconnect the oil cooler lines from the oil filter adapter.

16. Remove the A/C compressor mounting bolts and disconnect the electrical connectors. Move compressor aside.

17. Disconnect the electrical connectors from the left side of the engine and move the harness from behind the exhaust manifold.

18. Remove the 2 nuts that secure the motor mount to the engine cradle front crossmember.

19. Remove the exhaust Y-pipe and remove the right front wheel.

20. Remove the crankcase to transmission bracket at the transmission tail shaft. Disconnect the knock sensor.

21. Remove the bolt from the transmission to the cylinder head brace at the cylinder head.

22. Lower the vehicle. Disconnect the fuel inlet and fuel return lines using special tool J37088 or equivalent.

23. Disconnect the injector harness connector and the hoses from the coolant reservoir. Remove the reservoir.

24. Disconnect the cam position sensor. Disconnect the heater hoses from the water pipes at the front of the right cylinder head.

25. Disconnect the battery cable from the junction block and remove the retainer at the cylinder head.

26. Disconnect the starter cable from the junction block.

27. Disconnect the power steering pump pressure and return lines at the pump. Return power steering line retainer from the right front of the crankcase.

28. Disconnect the rear oxygen sensor.

29. Remove the 3 screws securing the wiring harness retainer to right

cam cover and position harness out of the way.

30. Connect an engine lifting device to the engine using the support hooks at left and right rear of engine. The torque strut bracket at the left front of the engine should be used as a 3rd lifting hook.

31. Carefully remove the engine from the vehicle.

To install:

32. Lower the engine into the vehicle. Remove the lifting device.

33. Install the 4 bellhousing bolts and tighten to 75 ft. lbs. (100 Nm).

34. Raise and safely support the vehicle.

35. Install 2 nuts to the motor mount at the front cradle crossmember. Do not fully tighten.

36. Install bolt to the cylinder head for transmission brace. Do not fully tighten.

37. Install the transmission to crankcase bracket with the 4 bolts. Do not fully tighten the bolts.

38. Tighten the motor mount to cradle crossmember bolts to 30 ft. lbs. (40 Nm). Tighten the transmission brace bolt and transmission to crankcase bolts to 45 ft. lbs. (60 Nm).

39. Install the right front wheel and connect the knock sensor.

40. Install the exhaust Y-pipe.

41. Install the 4 torque converter to flywheel bolts and tighten to 45 ft. lbs. (60 Nm).

42. Install the converter splash shield and install the transmission to oil pan brace. Tighten the bolt to 35 ft. lbs. (50 Nm).

43. Position the A/C compressor in place and install the mounting bolts.

44. Route the electrical harness along the left side of the engine and connect the connectors.

45. Connect the oil cooler lines to the oil filter adapter.

46. Lower the vehicle.

47. Secure the wiring harness to the right cam cover with the 3 screws.

48. Connect the rear oxygen sensor and connect the cam position sensor.

49. Connect the power steering hoses to the pump and secure the return line to the crankcase.

50. Connect the heater hoses to the water pipes.

51. Connect the starter and battery cables at the junction box. Secure battery cable with retainer.

52. Connect and install the coolant reservoir.

53. Install coils and secure with 4 screws.

54. Install the serpentine drive belt and connect the injector harness to the FIS harness.

55. Connect the fuel line connectors. Connect the cylinder head temperature switch to the rear of the right head.

56. Connect the power brake vacuum line.

57. Install the park/neutral switch and shift cable. Adjust switch if necessary.

58. Install the cruise servo and connect the ISC motor.

59. Connect the throttle cable and install both cooling fans.

60. Connect the radiator hoses to the water crossover.

61. Install the torque struts and adjust the preload to zero.

62. Connect the negative battery cable.

63. Refill the engine with coolant. Install the hood and install the air cleaner.

64. Start engine and check for oil, coolant and transaxle leaks.

Engine Mounts

REMOVAL AND INSTALLATION

Riviera and Toronado

1. Disconnect the negative battery cable.

2. Safely support the engine using a suitable engine holding fixture.

3. Raise and safely support the vehicle.

4. Remove the engine mount bracket nuts.

5. Raise the engine slightly.

6. Remove the engine mount retaining bolts. Remove the engine mount.

To install:

7. Install the engine mount and mount retaining bolts.

8. Lower the engine.

9. Install the engine mount bracket nuts.

10. Lower the vehicle.

11. Remove the engine holding fixture.

12. Connect the negative battery cable.

1992 Allante

RIGHT SIDE ENGINE AND TRANSAXLE MOUNT

1. Disconnect the negative battery cable.

2. Raise and safely support the vehicle.

3. Remove 2 heat shield screws.

4. Remove screw from engine mount brace at engine mount bracket.

5. Loosen nut at top of brace to exhaust manifold and position brace aside.

6. Support the engine with a transaxle jack.

7. Remove 2 screws securing mount bracket to transaxle.

8. Remove 4 nuts at top and bottom of mount.

9. Raise engine with transaxle jack.

10. Remove mount.

To install:

11. Position transaxle mount and bracket in place between transaxle and frame. Secure bracket to transaxle with 2 bolts. Tighten to 50 ft. lbs. (70 Nm).

12. Guide engine mount into location while lowering engine and lower the engine.

13. Install mount to frame and transaxle bracket with 2 nuts each. Tighten to 30 ft. lbs. (40 Nm).

14. Install brace from bracket to engine. Tighten to 25 ft. lbs. (35 Nm).

15. Install heat shield.

16. Remove transaxle jack and lower hoist.

LEFT SIDE ENGINE MOUNT

1. Disconnect the negative battery cable.

2. Remove air cleaner assembly.

3. Remove serpentine belt.

4. Properly discharge and recover the refrigerant from the air conditioning system.

5. Lower center exhaust manifold nuts.

6. Raise and safely support the vehicle.

7. Remove right side engine compartment splash shield. Remove air conditioning splash shield.

8. Remove 2 air conditioning compressor brackets. Remove air conditioning compressor.

9. Remove engine mount bracket bolts from engine block and cradle.

10. Raise engine with transaxle jack and remove mount and bracket.

To install:

11. Place mount in vise and position mount bracket onto mount. Tighten 2 nuts to 30 ft. lbs. (40 Nm).

12. Install engine mount and bracket through right side wheel well.

13. Install engine mount bracket bolts to engine block. Tighten to 50 ft. lbs. (70 Nm).

14. Install engine mount to cradle nuts. Tighten to 30 ft. lbs. (40 Nm).

15. Install air conditioning compressor. Install 2 air conditioning compressor brackets.

16. Install air conditioning splash shield. Install right side engine compartment splash shield.

17. Lower vehicle.

18. Install lower center exhaust manifold nut.

19. Install serpentine belt.

20. Connect negative battery cable.

21. Install air cleaner assembly.

22. Evacuate, recharge and leak test the air conditioning system.

Allante, Seville and Eldorado With 4.6L Engine

FRONT ENGINE MOUNT

1. Disconnect the negative battery cable and remove right side cooling fan.

2. Remove left side cooling fan.

3. Remove the right and left torque struts.

4. Install an engine support fixture, J-28467-A or equivalent. Connect only one support at left rear engine bracket.

5. Raise and safely support the vehicle.

6. Remove the 2 nuts that secure the motor mount to the engine cradle.

7. Remove the 2 bolts that secure the motor mount bracket to the crankcase.

8. Lower the vehicle.

9. Remove the 2 bolts that secure the motor mount bracket to the cylinder head. Remove the 2 nuts that secure the motor mount to the bracket.

10. Raise engine by tightening support chain. Separate mount and bracket and remove mount.

To install:

11. Position the motor mount and bracket into position at front of engine.

12. Install the 2 nuts that secure the mount to the bracket. Do not fully tighten the nuts.

13. Install the 2 bolts securing the mount bracket to the cylinder head. Do not fully tighten the bolts.

14. Lower the engine and guide the motor mount studs into the engine cradle.

15. Raise and safely support the vehicle.

16. Install the 2 bolts securing the mount bracket to the crankcase. Tighten the bolts to 25 ft. lbs. (30 Nm).

17. Install the 2 nuts securing the motor mount to the cradle and tighten to 25 ft. lbs. (30 Nm).

18. Lower the vehicle.

19. Torque the 2 mount bracket to cylinder head bolts to 25 ft. lbs. (30 Nm).

20. Remove the engine support fixture.

21. Install the 2 nuts securing the motor mount to the bracket and tighten to 25 ft. lbs. (30 Nm).

22. Tighten the 2 nuts that secure the mount to the engine cradle to 25 ft. lbs. (30 Nm).

23. Install the 2 torque struts and set to zero preload.

24. Install both cooling fans and connect the negative battery cable.

Eldorado and Seville With 4.5L and 4.9L Engines

RIGHT SIDE ENGINE AND TRANSAXLE MOUNT

1. Disconnect the negative battery cable.

2. Remove the brace from the engine bracket to engine.

3. Remove 2 engine bracket-to-mount nuts.

4. Raise and safely support the vehicle.

5. Remove 2 nuts securing the engine mount to the frame. Remove 2 nuts securing transaxle bracket to mount. Remove 2 nuts securing the transaxle mount to the frame bracket.

6. Using the engine support tool, raise the engine.

7. Raise the engine slowly until the bracket is free from the engine and transaxle mount. Remove the bracket-to-block stud and bolts. Remove the mount and bracket by pulling forward.

8. Remove the transaxle mounting bracket from the transaxle. Remove the mount assembly.

To install:

9. Position engine mount and bracket in place between cylinder block and frame. Secure bracket to block with 1 stud and 2 bolts. Tighten to 34 ft. lbs. (46 Nm).

10. Position transaxle mount and bracket in place between transaxle and frame. Secure bracket to transaxle with 2 bolts. Tighten to 34 ft. lbs. (46 Nm).

NOTE: Guide engine mount into location while lowering engine.

11. Lower engine.

12. Install engine mount to frame and transaxle mount to frame bracket with 2 nuts. Tighten to 22 ft. lbs. (31 Nm).

13. Install 2 nuts to engine mount studs and 2 nuts to transaxle mount studs. Tighten to 22 ft. lbs. (31 Nm).

14. Remove brace from engine bracket to engine.

15. Remove stands and lower vehicle.

16. Connect negative battery cable.

LEFT SIDE ENGINE MOUNT

1. Disconnect the negative battery cable. Remove the air cleaner assembly.

2. Remove the serpentine belt. Properly discharge and recover the refrigerant from the air conditioning system.

3. Install the engine support tool.

4. Remove the lower center exhaust manifold nut and top nut of the engine damper.

5. Raise and safely support the vehicle.

6. Remove the right side engine compartment splash shield and air conditioning splash shield.

7. Remove the engine damper. Remove both air conditioning compressor brackets. Remove the air conditioning compressor.

8. Remove the water pipe bracket bolt.

9. Remove the engine mount bracket bolts from the engine block and cradle. Remove the engine mount and bracket through the right side wheel well.

To install:

10. Place mount in vice and position mount bracket onto mount. Tighten 2 nuts to 31 ft. lbs. (41 Nm).

11. Install engine mount and bracket through right wheel well.

12. Install engine mount bracket bolts to engine block. Tighten to 50 ft. lbs. (68 Nm).

13. Install engine mount to cradle nuts. Tighten bolts to 31 ft. lbs. (41 Nm).

14. Install water pipe bracket bolt.

15. Install air conditioning compressor brackets.

16. Install engine damper.

17. Install air conditioning compressor splash shield.

18. Install right side engine compartment splash shield.

19. Lower vehicle.

20. Install lower center exhaust manifold nut and top nut on engine damper.

21. Remove engine support tool.

22. Install serpentine belt.

23. Connect negative battery cable.

24. Install air cleaner assembly.

25. Evacuate, recharge and leak test the air conditioning system.

Cylinder Head

REMOVAL AND INSTALLATION

3.8L Engine

1. Disconnect the negative battery cable.

2. Remove the intake and exhaust manifolds.

3. Remove the valve cover.

4. If removing the front (left) side cylinder head, perform the following:

   a. Remove the C$_3$I and spark plug wires.

   b. Remove the alternator bracket.

   c. Remove 1 air conditioning compressor bracket bolt.

5. If removing the rear (right) side cylinder head, perform the following:

   a. Remove the power steering pump.

   b. Remove the belt tensioner assembly.

   c. Remove fuel line heat shield.

6. Remove rocker arm assemblies, guide plate and pushrods.

7. Remove cylinder head bolts and cylinder head.

NOTE: Clean all gasket mating surfaces and cylinder head bolt holes in block.

To install:

8. Clean threads in block using an appropriate tap.

9. Install cylinder head gasket on block.

10. Apply an appropriate sealant to cylinder head bolt threads. Install cylinder head bolts.

11. Tighten cylinder head bolts using the following steps:

   a. Tighten each cylinder head bolt to 35 ft. lbs. (47 Nm) following the proper sequence.

   b. Rotate each bolt 130 degrees, in sequence, using an appropriate torque angle meter.

   c. Rotate each bolt an additional 30 degrees, in sequence, using torque angle meter.

12. Install pushrods, guide plate and rocker arm assemblies.

13. Apply an appropriate high temperature, high strength thread sealant compound to the rocker arm pedestal bolts. Tighten to 28 ft. lbs. (38 Nm).

14. Install intake manifold.

15. Install valve cover.

16. Install exhaust manifold.

17. If the front (left) side cylinder head was removed, perform the following:

   a. Install air conditioning compressor bracket bolt. Tighten to 52 ft. lbs. (80 Nm).

   b. Install alternator support bracket to cylinder head.

   c. Install alternator.

   d. Install C$_3$I and spark plug wires.

18. If the rear (right) side cylinder head was removed, perform the following:

   a. Install belt tensioner assembly.

   b. Install power steering pump.

   c. Install fuel line heat shield.

19. Connect negative battery cable.

20. Start engine and check for coolant, oil and fuel leaks. Allow engine to come to normal operating temperature and recheck for leaks.

4.5L and 4.9L Engines

RIGHT SIDE

1. Disconnect the negative battery cable. Drain the engine coolant.

2. Remove rocker arm covers.

3. Remove the lower intake and right side exhaust manifolds.

4. Remove engine lift bracket and oil dipstick tube.

5. Reposition AIR bracket.

6. Remove 10 cylinder head bolts.

7. Remove cylinder head.

To install:

NOTE: Clean sealing surfaces of cylinder head, block and liners. Clean cylinder head bolt holes with an appropriate tap. Ensure that bolt holes are free of shavings, oil and coolant.

8. Install new head gasket over dowels on cylinder block with either side facing up.

9. Install cylinder head.

10. Apply an appropriate lubricant to the threads of the head bolts. Install cylinder head bolts finger-tight.

11. Tighten cylinder head bolts, in sequence, to 38 ft. lbs. (50 Nm).

12. Tighten cylinder head bolts, in sequence, to 68 ft. lbs. (90 Nm).

13. Tighten No. 1, 3 and 4 cylinder head bolts to 90 ft. lbs. (120 Nm).

14. Install engine lift bracket and AIR bracket.

15. Install lower intake and right side exhaust manifolds.

16. Install rocker arm covers.

17. Fill cooling system.

18. Connect negative battery cable.

19. Start engine and check for coolant, oil and fuel leaks. Allow engine to come to normal operating temperature and recheck for leaks.

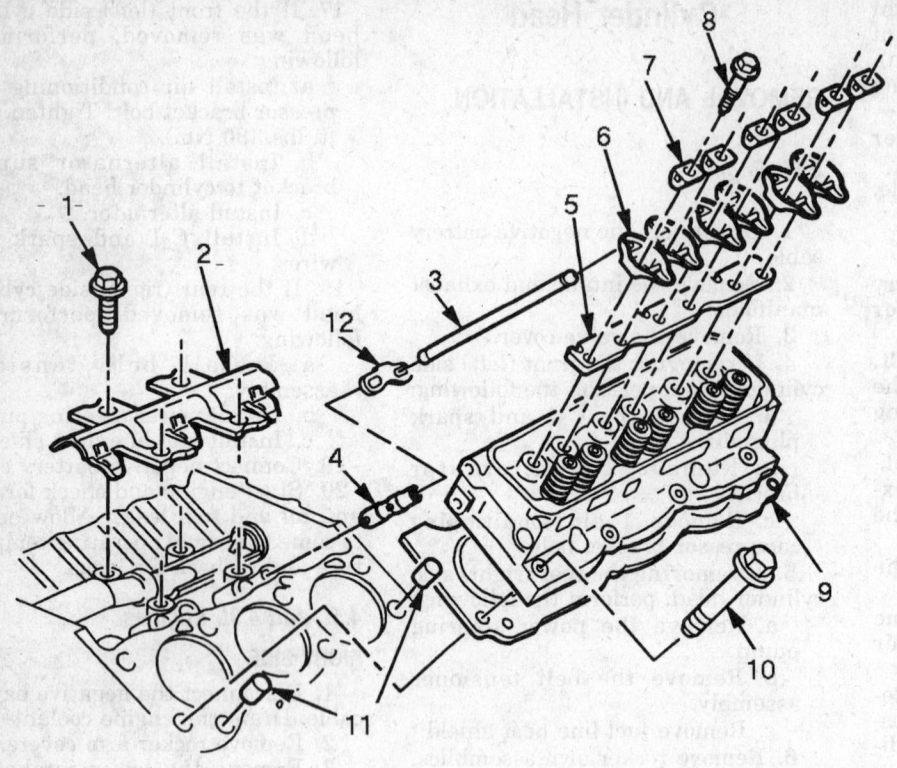

1. Bolt
2. Lifter guide
3. Pushrod
4. Valve lifter
5. Pushrod guide
6. Rocker arm
7. Rocker arm pivot
8. Bolt
9. Head gasket
10. Head bolt
11. Dowel pin
12. Lifter guide

8470H043

Cylinder head and valve train assembly — 3.8L engine

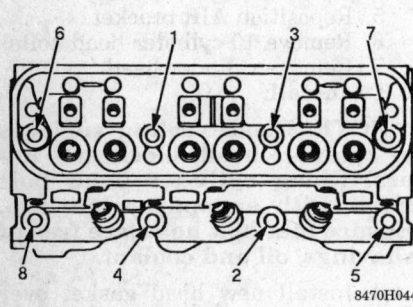

8470H044

Cylinder head bolt torque sequence — 3.8L engine

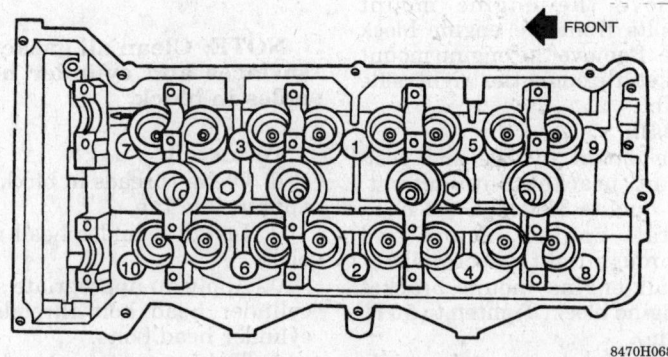

8470H068

Cylinder head torque sequence — 4.6L engine

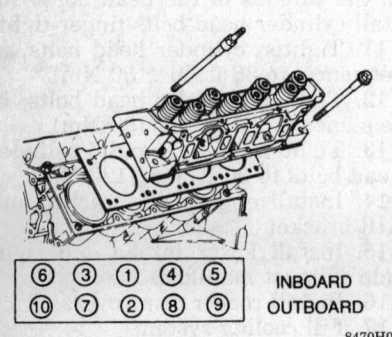

INBOARD

OUTBOARD

8470H045

Cylinder head torque sequence — 4.9L engine

LEFT SIDE

1. Disconnect the negative battery cable.
2. Drain the cooling system.
3. Remove the rocker arm covers.
4. Remove the intake manifold-to-engine bolts and intake manifold.
5. Disconnect the exhaust manifold crossover pipe, the exhaust pipe-to-exhaust manifold bolts, the exhaust manifold-to-cylinder head bolts and the exhaust manifold.
6. Remove the engine lifting bracket and the dipstick tube.

7. Remove the AIR bracket-to-engine bolts and move the bracket aside.
8. Remove the cylinder head-to-engine bolts and the cylinder head.
To install:
9. Clean the gasket mounting surfaces.
10. Install new head gasket over dowels on cylinder block with either side facing up.
11. Install cylinder head.
12. Apply a suitable lubricant to the cylinder head bolt threads.
13. Install cylinder head bolts finger-tight.

14. Tighten bolts, in sequence, to 38 ft. lbs. (50 Nm).

15. Tighten cylinder head bolts, in sequence, to 68 ft. lbs. (90 Nm).

16. Tighten No. 1, 3 and 4 cylinder head bolts to 90 ft. lbs. (120 Nm).

17. Install AIR bracket. Install dipstick tube and engine lift bracket.

18. Install exhaust manifold. Install lower intake manifold.

19. Install rocker arm covers.

20. Fill cooling system.

21. Connect negative battery cable.

22. Start engine and check for coolant, oil and fuel leaks. Allow engine to come to normal operating temperature and recheck for leaks.

4.6L Engine

1. Disconnect the negative battery cable.

2. Remove the engine from the vehicle.

3. Remove the intake manifold, the cam covers, the harmonic balancer, the front timing cover and the oil pump as described elsewhere in this section.

4. For the cylinder head that is being removed, do the following:

a. Remove the chain tensioner from the timing chain for the cylinder head that is being removed.

b. Remove the cam sprockets from the head that is being removed. Leave the timing chain in the case.

5. Remove the timing chain guides, these can be accessed through the plugs at the front of the cylinder head.

6. Remove the water crossover and the exhaust manifold.

7. Remove the cylinder head bolts.

8. Remove the cylinder head and the gasket.

NOTE: Do not rest the cylinder head on a flat surface with the cylinder face down. When the camshafts remain in the cylinder head, some valves will remain open and may be damaged.

To install:

9. Install a new cylinder head gasket.

10. Coat the cylinder head bolts with engine oil and install the cylinder head and the head bolts.

11. Tighten the cylinder head bolts in the following sequence:

a. The 10 longer bolts to 22 ft. lbs. (30 Nm) plus an additional 90 degree turn in the sequence.

b. Rotate the 10 bolts an additional 90 degree turn.

c. Tighten the 3 shorter bolts to 10 ft. lbs (16 Nm).

12. Install the camshafts to the engine.

13. Properly set the camshaft timing.

14. Install the camshaft guide bolt access hole plugs into the cylinder head.

15. Install the cam covers and the oil pump.

16. Install the front cover and the harmonic balancer.

17. Install the intake manifold and the water crossover.

18. Install the exhaust manifold, tighten the manifold nuts to 25 ft. lbs. (30 Nm) or the manifold bolts to 20 ft. lbs. (25 Nm).

19. Install the engine to the vehicle.

Valve Lifters

REMOVAL AND INSTALLATION

NOTE: When disassembling valve train components, ensure that all parts are kept in order so they can be reinstalled in their original locations and with the same mating surfaces.

1. Disconnect the negative battery cable. Remove the intake manifold.

2. Remove the rocker arm cover and discard the old gasket.

3. Remove the rocker arm assemblies. Remove the pushrods.

4. Remove the lifter guide retainer bolts and retainer.

5. Remove the lifter retainers.

6. Using the valve lifter removal tool, remove the valve lifters.

To install:

7. Clean the gasket mounting surfaces.

8. Lubricate the lifters with clean engine oil, use new gaskets and/or sealant.

9. Install the valve lifters.

10. Install the lifter guide, retainer and retainer bolts.

11. Install the pushrods. Install the rocker arm assemblies.

12. Install the rocker arm cover.

13. Install the intake manifold.

14. Connect the negative battery cable.

Valve Lash

All engines use hydraulic lifters which are non-adjustable. Hydraulic valve lifters keep all parts of the valve train in constant contact and adjust automatically to maintain **0** lash under all operating conditions.

Rocker Arms

REMOVAL AND INSTALLATION

3.8L Engine

1. Disconnect the negative battery cable. Remove the rocker arm cover nuts, washers, seals, the cover and gasket, discard the gasket.

2. Remove the rocker arm pivot-to-cylinder head bolts, the pivots, the rocker arms and the pushrod guide.

NOTE: Be sure to keep the parts in order for reassembly purposes.

3. Clean the gasket mounting surfaces.

4. Install the pushrod guide, rocker arms, pivots and rocker arm pivot-to-cylinder head bolts. Tighten to 28 ft. lbs. (38 Nm).

5. Install the rocker arm cover using a new gasket.

6. Connect the negative battery cable.

4.5L and 4.9L Engines

1. Disconnect the negative battery cable. Remove the rocker arm cover.

2. Remove the rocker arm support-to-cylinder head bolts.

3. Remove the rocker arm support-to-cylinder head stud nuts.

NOTE: This method of removal is preferred as the pivot assemblies may be damaged if the pivot bolt torque is not removed evenly against the valve spring tension.

4. Place the rocker arm support in a vise and remove the rocker arm pivot-to-rocker arm support bolts.

To install:

5. Lubricate all parts with axle lube 1052271 or equivalent, and reverse the removal procedures. Tighten the rocker arm pivot-to-rocker arm support bolts to 22 ft. lbs. (30 Nm).

NOTE: The pivot bolts are self-tapping.

6. Position the pushrod into the seat of each rocker arm and loosely install the retaining nuts.

7. Recheck the pushrods for being seated correctly. Tighten the nuts alternately and evenly, checking the position of the pushrods while tightening.

8. When the nuts have been seated and the pushrods are correct, tighten the rocker arm support-to-cylinder head nuts to 37 ft. lbs. (50 Nm) and the bolts to 7 ft. lbs. (10 Nm).

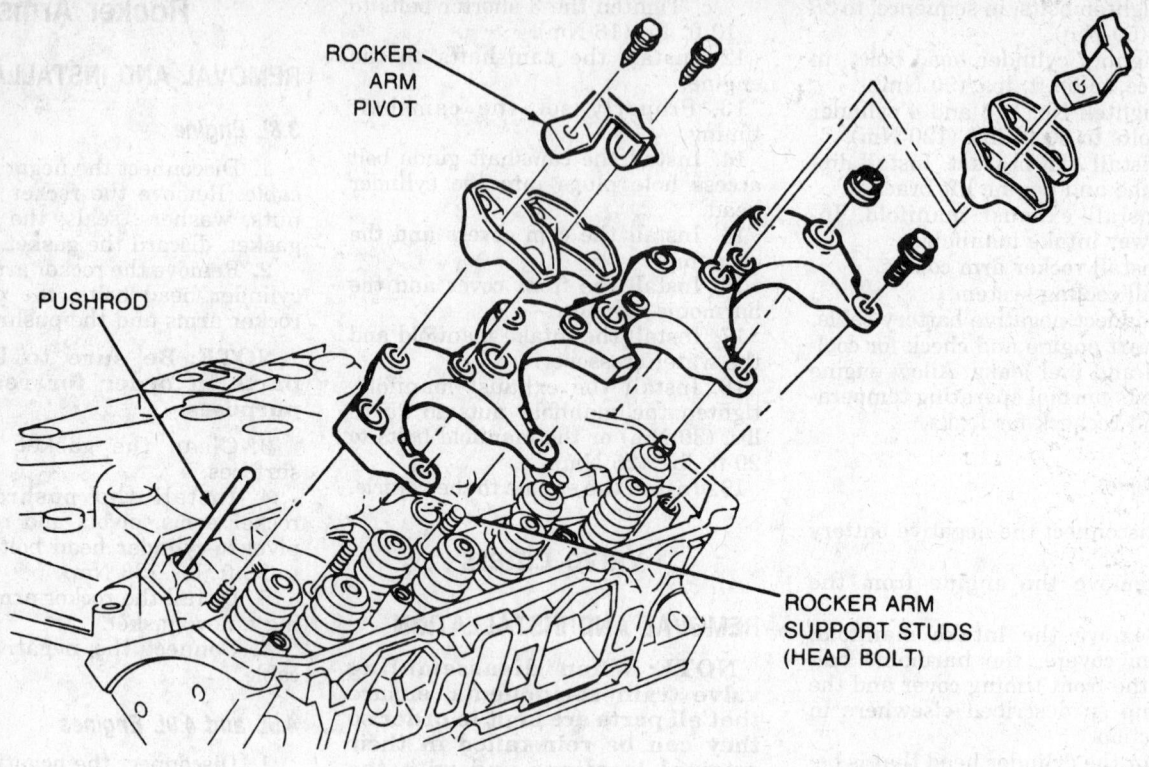

ROCKER ARM PIVOT

PUSHROD

ROCKER ARM SUPPORT STUDS (HEAD BOLT)

8470H050

Rocker arm support, arms and pivots — 4.9L engine

9. Install the rocker arm cover.
10. Connect the negative battery cable.

Intake Manifold

REMOVAL AND INSTALLATION

Riviera and Toronado

1. Disconnect the negative battery cable and remove plastic engine cover/fuel injector sight shield.
2. Remove the air intake duct. Tag and disconnect the right side spark plug wires.
3. Remove the fuel rail assembly.
4. Remove the exhaust crossover heat shield and the cable bracket to cylinder head mounting bolt.
5. Remove the power steering pump support bracket and loosen the alternator. Move alternator aside.
6. Remove the alternator bracket.
7. Disconnect the heater pipes and bypass hose.
8. Remove the intake manifold bolts and remove the manifold from the vehicle.
To install:
9. Clean the gasket mounting surfaces.
10. Using new gaskets and sealant 1234536 or equivalent, on the ends

of the manifold seals, install the intake manifold. Tighten the intake manifold bolts, in sequence, to 88 inch lbs. (10 Nm) twice.
11. Connect the bypass and heater hoses.
12. Install the alternator bracket and return the alternator to the proper position.
13. Install the power steering pump support bracket.
14. Install the cable bracket to cylinder head mounting bolt.
15. Install the exhaust crossover heat shield and the fuel rail.
16. Connect the right side spark plug wires and install the air intake duct.
17. Install the plastic engine cover/injector sight shield and connect the negative battery cable.

Eldorado and Seville With 4.5L and 4.9L Engines

1. Disconnect the negative battery cable. Relieve fuel system pressure. Drain the cooling system to a level below the intake manifold. Remove the coolant reservoir. Disconnect the upper radiator hose from the thermostat housing.
2. Remove the air cleaner and the serpentine drive belt. Label and dis-

connect the spark plug wires from the spark plugs.
3. Remove the cross brace.
4. Remove power steering pump and tensioner bracket assembly and reposition toward the front of engine.
5. Remove alternator and bracket.
6. Remove cruise control servo with bracket and throttle valve cables and position aside.
7. Disconnect wire connections and reposition:
   a. Distributor
   b. Oil pressure switch
   c. Coolant temperature sensor
   d. EGR solenoid
   e. ISC motor
   f. Throttle position switch
   g. If equipped, electric EFE grid
   h. Injectors
   i. MAT sensor
8. If equipped, disconnect the MAP hoses. Remove upper radiator hose and heater hose. Remove air conditioning hose bracket.
9. Disconnect spark plug wire protectors and reposition cap.
10. Mark the distributor rotor position and remove distributor.

NOTE: Do not crank or in any other way rotate crankshaft with the distributor removed.

11. Disconnect fuel and vacuum lines from the throttle body. Discon-

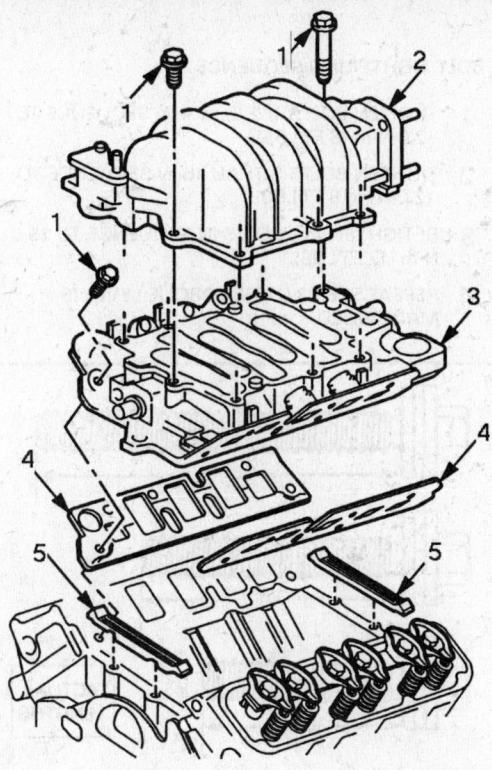

1. Bolt
2. Intake manifold upper
3. Intake manifold lower
4. Intake manifold gasket
5. Intake manifold seal

8470H046

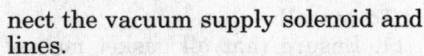

Intake manifold and gaskets — 3.8L engine

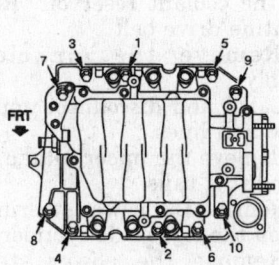

8470H047

Intake manifold bolt torque sequence — 3.8L engine

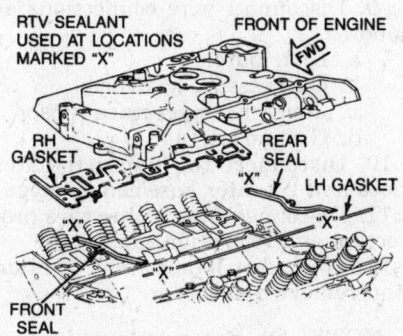

8470H048

Intake manifold and gaskets — 4.9L engine

nect the vacuum supply solenoid and lines.

12. Remove valve covers. Remove rocker arms and pushrods.

NOTE: Pushrods should be marked or retained in sequence so they may be reinstalled in their original positions.

13. Remove the right front and rear lift brackets. Remove intake manifold bolts and remove intake manifold, gaskets and seals. Discard gaskets and seals.

14. Clean sealing surfaces of intake manifold, cylinder head and cylinder block.

To install:

15. Install new end seals. Use RTV at 4 corners where end seals will meet side gaskets.

16. Install new intake to cylinder head gaskets. Use RTV at 4 corners of end seals.

17. Tighten the intake manifold bolts by performing the following:

   a. Tighten bolts 1, 2, 3 and 4, in sequence, to 8 ft. lbs. (12 Nm).

   b. Tighten bolts 5 thru 16, in sequence, to 8 ft. lbs. (12 Nm).

   c. Retighten all bolts, in sequence, to 12 ft. lbs. (16 Nm).

   d. Repeat Step c until torque level is maintained.

18. Install pushrods and rocker arm assembly.

19. Install valve covers. Install vacuum supply solenoid and lines. Install fuel and vacuum lines to throttle body.

20. Install distributor in original position. Install distributor cap and wire protectors.

21. Install air conditioning hose bracket.

22. Install upper radiator hose and heater hose. If equipped, connect the MAP hoses.

23. Connect following wire connectors:

   a. Distributor
   b. Oil pressure switch
   c. Coolant temperature sensor
   d. EGR solenoid
   e. ISC motor
   f. Throttle position switch
   g. If equipped, electric EFE grid
   h. Injectors
   i. MAT sensor

24. Install cruise control servo and throttle valve cables.

25. Install alternator bracket and alternator.

26. Install power steering pump and tensioner assembly. Install power steering line brace to right side cylinder head.

27. Install serpentine drive belt. Install coolant reservoir.

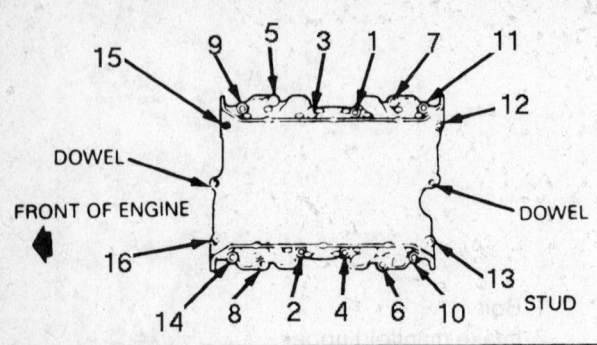

BOLT TIGHTENING SEQUENCE

1. TIGHTEN BOLTS 1, 2, 3, & 4 IN SEQUENCE TO 12.0 N·m (8 FT-LBS).

2. TIGHTEN BOLTS 5 THRU 16 IN SEQUENCE TO 12.0 N·m (8 FT-LBS).

3. RETIGHTEN ALL BOLTS IN SEQUENCE TO 16.0 N·m (12 FT-LBS).

4. REPEAT STEP 3 UNTIL TORQUE LEVEL IS MAINTAINED.

BOLT POSITION	BOLT LENGTH (MM)	BOLT POSITION	BOLT LENGTH (MM)
1	55	9	40
2	55	10	40
3	55	11	40
4	55	12	55
5	30	13	40 W'Studhead
6	30	14	40
7	30	15	55
8	30	16	40

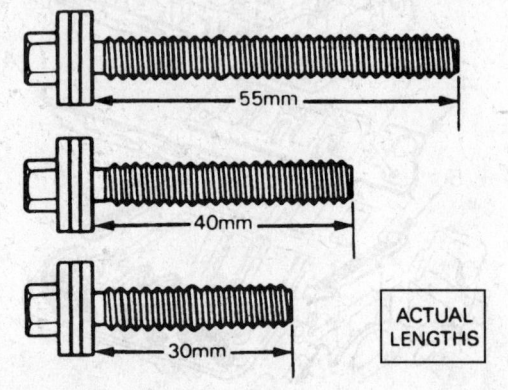

8470H049

Intake manifold bolt size and torque sequence — 4.9L engine

28. Install cross brace.
29. Fill cooling system.
30. Install air cleaner assembly.
31. Connect negative battery cable.
32. Start engine and check for coolant, oil and fuel leaks. Allow engine to come to normal operating temperature and recheck for leaks.

Allante — 1992

UPPER INTAKE MANIFOLD

1. Disconnect the negative battery cable.
2. Shock tower support bracket, as required.
3. Label and disconnect vacuum hoses.
4. Remove the transmission dipstick tube bolt.
5. Disconnect the MAT sensor electrical connector.
6. Remove the rear upper intake manifold support.
7. Remove the throttle body assembly from the upper intake manifold and discard the gasket.
8. Remove the throttle heater assembly and discard the gasket.
9. Remove the 4 upper intake manifold attaching nuts.
10. Remove the upper intake manifold and discard the gasket.

To install:

11. Ensure that all gasket mating surfaces are free of old gasket material.
12. Install a new upper intake-to-lower intake gasket.
13. Install the upper intake manifold and attaching nuts. Tighten to 15 ft. lbs. (20 Nm).
14. Install a new throttle heater gasket. Install the throttle heater assembly.
15. Install a new throttle body gasket. Install the throttle body to the upper intake manifold. Tighten throttle body attaching bolts to 15 ft. lbs. (20 Nm).
16. Install the rear upper intake manifold support.
17. Connect the MAT sensor electrical connector.
18. Install the transmission dipstick tube bolt.
19. Connect all vacuum lines.
20. If removed, install the shock tower support bracket.
21. Connect the negative battery cable.

LOWER INTAKE MANIFOLD

1. Disconnect the negative battery cable. Relieve fuel system pressure. Drain the cooling system to a level below the lower intake manifold. Re-move the coolant reservoir. Remove serpentine drive belt.
2. Remove the air cleaner assembly.
3. Label and disconnect appropriate vacuum lines.
4. Remove the upper intake manifold and fuel rails.
5. Remove the power steering line brace on the right side cylinder head.
6. Remove the power steering pump and tensioner bracket assembly and reposition toward the front of the engine.
7. Remove alternator with bracket and idler pulley.
8. Remove cruise control servo with bracket and cables. Reposition aside.
9. Disconnect wire connections as follows:
    a. Distributor
    b. Oil pressure switches
    c. Coolant temperature sensor
    d. Ground wires
10. Disconnect the upper radiator hose and 2 heater hose connections.
11. Disconnect spark plug wire protectors and reposition cap.
12. Mark distributor rotor position and remove distributor.

NOTE: Do not crank or in any other way rotate crankshaft with the distributor removed.

13. Remove valve covers. Remove rocker arms and pushrods.

NOTE: Pushrods should be marked or retained in sequence so they may be reinstalled in their original positions.

14. Remove intake manifold bolts and remove intake manifold, gaskets and seals. Discard gaskets and seals.
15. Clean sealing surfaces of intake manifold, cylinder head and cylinder block.

To install:

16. Install new end seals. Use RTV 1052915 or equivalent, at the 4 corners where end seals meet side gaskets.
17. Install new intake to cylinder head gaskets. Use RTV at 4 corners of end seals.
18. Tighten the intake manifold bolts by performing the following:

   a. Tighten bolts 1, 2, 3 and 4, in sequence, to 8 ft. lbs. (12 Nm).

   b. Tighten bolts 5 thru 16, in sequence, to 8 ft. lbs. (12 Nm).

   c. Retighten all bolts, in sequence, to 12 ft. lbs. (16 Nm).

   d. Repeat Step c until torque level is maintained.

19. Install pushrods and rocker arm assembly.
20. Install valve covers.
21. Install distributor in original position. Install distributor cap and wire protectors.
22. Install air conditioning hose bracket.
23. Install upper radiator hose and heater hose.
24. Connect following wire connectors:

   a. Distributor

   b. Oil pressure switch

   c. Coolant temperature sensor

   d. Ground wires

25. Install cruise control servo and throttle valve cables.
26. Install alternator bracket and alternator.
27. Install power steering line brace to right side cylinder head. Install power steering pump and tensioner assembly.
28. Install serpentine drive belt. Install coolant reservoir.
29. Install fuel rail assembly and upper intake manifold to the lower intake manifold.
30. Connect vacuum lines.
31. Install heater assembly and gasket.
32. Install accelerator, cruise control and throttle valve cables.
33. Fill cooling system.
34. Install air cleaner assembly.
35. Connect negative battery cable.

36. Start engine and check for coolant, oil and fuel leaks. Allow engine to come to normal operating temperature and recheck for leaks.

1993 Allante and 1993–96 Eldorado/Seville With 4.6L Engine

1. Disconnect the negative battery cable.
2. Remove the air intake duct from the throttle body.
3. Wrap a shop towel around the coolant hoses and disconnect the hoses from the throttle body and the coolant reservoir. Plug the hoses.
4. Disconnect the intake manifold electrical connectors.
5. Label and disconnect vacuum hoses.
6. Disconnect the PCV hose at the intake manifold.
7. Disconnect the accelerator cable from the throttle body and position it aside.
8. Properly relieve the fuel system pressure.
9. Disconnect the fuel line quick connectors at the fuel pipe bundle in the engine compartment.
10. Remove the EVAP solenoid bracket at the rear cam cover.
11. Move the transaxle range cable away from the cruise control servo.
12. Remove the 4 intake manifold attaching nuts and lift the intake manifold with the throttle body out of the engine compartment.
13. Remove the intake manifold seals and spacers at the cylinder heads.

To install:

14. Replace the intake manifold seals and spacers at the cylinder heads.
15. Install the intake manifold with the throttle body onto the engine.
16. Install the 4 bolts and tighten the bolts in sequence to 71 inch lbs. (8 Nm).
17. Connect the coolant hoses at the throttle body and the coolant reservoir. Add coolant if necessary.
18. Reposition the transaxle range control cable into place at the cruise control bracket.
19. Install the EVAP solenoid bracket to the rear of the cam cover.
20. Connect the fuel pipe quick connectors at the fuel pipe bundle in the engine compartment.
21. Connect the accelerator cable to the throttle body.
22. Connect all vacuum lines and the PCV hose.
23. Connect the electrical connectors for the intake manifold.
24. Install the air intake duct to the throttle body.

25. Connect the negative battery cable.

Exhaust Manifold

REMOVAL AND INSTALLATION

3.8L Engine

LEFT SIDE

1. Disconnect the negative battery cable.
2. Remove the engine strut.
3. Remove the 2 bolts attaching the exhaust crossover pipe-to-exhaust manifold.
4. Remove the cooling fan assembly, as required.
5. Label and disconnect the spark plug wires.
6. Remove the oil dipstick tube to provide access to the manifold bolts, as required.
7. Remove the exhaust manifold-to-cylinder head bolts and the manifold.

To install:

8. Install the exhaust manifold gasket. Tighten the exhaust manifold-to-cylinder head bolts to 41 ft. lbs. (55 Nm).
9. If removed, install the oil dipstick tube.
10. Connect the spark plug wires.
11. If removed, install the cooling fan assembly.
12. Install the 2 exhaust crossover pipe-to-exhaust manifold attaching bolts. Tighten the exhaust crossover pipe-to-manifold bolts to 22 ft. lbs. (30 Nm).
13. Install the engine strut.
14. Connect the negative battery cable. Start the engine and check for exhaust leaks.

RIGHT SIDE

1. Disconnect the negative battery cable.
2. Label and disconnect the spark plug wires.
3. Remove the throttle cable bracket.
4. Remove the crossover pipe heat shield.
5. Remove the transaxle oil level indicator and indicator tube.
6. Disconnect the oxygen sensor lead.
7. Remove the 2 bolts attaching the exhaust crossover pipe to the manifold.
8. Remove the plastic vacuum tank mounted on the cowl, as required.
9. Remove the EGR pipe, as required.

10. Remove the 2 upper heat shield screws, as required.

11. Remove the upper exhaust manifold bolts.

12. Raise and safely support the vehicle.

13. Remove the 2 lower heat shield screws, as required.

14. Remove the lower exhaust manifold bolts.

15. Remove the front exhaust pipe-to-exhaust manifold attaching nuts.

16. Disconnect the front exhaust pipe from the exhaust manifold.

17. Lower the vehicle.

18. Remove the engine lift bracket.

19. Remove the exhaust manifold nuts and remove the manifold.

To install:

20. Install the exhaust manifold and manifold nuts. Tighten to 41 ft. lbs. (55 Nm).

21. Install the engine lift bracket.

22. Raise and safely support the vehicle.

23. Connect the front exhaust pipe to the exhaust manifold.

24. Install the front exhaust pipe-to-exhaust manifold attaching nuts.

25. Install the lower exhaust manifold bolts.

26. If removed, install the 2 lower heat shield screws.

27. Lower the vehicle.

28. Install the upper exhaust manifold bolts.

29. If removed, install the 2 upper heat shield screws.

30. If removed, install the EGR pipe.

31. If removed, install the plastic vacuum tank mounted on the cowl.

32. Install the 2 bolts attaching the exhaust crossover pipe to the manifold.

33. Connect the oxygen sensor lead.

34. Install the transaxle oil level indicator and indicator tube.

35. Install the crossover pipe heat shield.

36. Install the throttle cable bracket.

37. Connect the spark plug wires.

38. Connect the negative battery cable.

4.5L and 4.9L Engines

LEFT SIDE

1. Disconnect the negative battery cable.

2. Remove the air cleaner.

3. Remove the AIR pipe from the AIR pump and position aside.

4. Remove the starter shield.

5. Remove the serpentine belt.

6. Remove the power steering pump and tensioner bracket covering the manifold.

7. Remove both cooling fans.

8. Label and disconnect the spark plug wires.

9. Raise and safely support the vehicle.

10. Remove the exhaust Y-pipe and the air conditioning-to-manifold brace.

11. Remove the exhaust manifold-to-cylinder head bolts. Remove the exhaust manifold.

To install:

12. Clean the gasket mounting surfaces.

13. Apply graphite dry film lubricant to the exhaust manifold sealing surface.

14. Install the exhaust manifold to the cylinder head. Install the 7 attaching bolts and tighten to 16 ft. lbs. (20 Nm).

15. Install the exhaust Y-pipe and the air conditioning-to-manifold brace.

16. Lower the vehicle.

17. Connect the spark plug wires.

18. Install both cooling fans.

19. Install the power steering pump and tensioner bracket covering the manifold.

20. Install the serpentine belt.

21. Install the starter shield.

22. Install the AIR pipe to the AIR pump.

23. Install the air cleaner.

24. Connect the negative battery cable.

RIGHT SIDE

1. Disconnect the negative battery cable. Remove the air cleaner.

2. Remove the EGR pipe from the manifold, as required. Remove 2 heat shield screws.

3. Raise and safely support the vehicle.

4. Disconnect the Y-pipe from the manifold.

5. Remove the engine mount brace from the front of the manifold.

6. Disconnect the oxygen sensor wire. Remove heat shield.

7. Support engine cradle with screw jacks and remove rear cradle bolts on both sides. Loosen front cradle bolts. Slightly lower engine cradle.

8. Remove the exhaust manifold-to-cylinder head bolts and the manifold.

To install:

9. Clean the gasket mounting surfaces.

10. Apply graphite dry film lubricant to the exhaust manifold sealing surface.

11. Install the exhaust manifold to the cylinder head. Install the 7 at-taching bolts and tighten to 16 ft. lbs. (20 Nm).

12. Install the heat shield.

13. Connect the oxygen sensor wire.

14. Install the engine brace on the right side of the manifold.

15. Raise the engine cradle and install the rear bolts. Tighten all mounting bolts to 75 ft. lbs. (100 Nm).

16. Install the exhaust crossover pipe.

17. Lower the vehicle.

18. Install the 2 heat shield screws.

19. Install the air cleaner.

20. Connect the negative battery cable.

4.6L Engine

LEFT SIDE

1. Disconnect the negative battery cable. Remove the left side motor mount and bracket.

2. Remove the rear alternator bracket.

3. Remove the 2 bolts at the manifold outlet flange.

4. Disconnect the oxygen sensor.

5. Remove the exhaust manifold from the cylinder head and remove the manifold.

6. Remove the gasket. Remove the oxygen sensor from the manifold.

To install:

7. Install gasket to the manifold. Insert 2 screws to hold gasket in place.

8. Insert outlet pipe partially into exhaust crossover pipe to install exhaust manifold. Move manifold into position.

9. Tighten the manifold bolts to 20 ft. lbs. (25 Nm).

10. Coat the oxygen sensor threads with Hi temperature anti-seize compound and install the sensor. Tighten sensor nut to 30 ft. lbs. (40 Nm).

11. Connect the oxygen sensor connector and install the rear alternator bracket. Tighten the crankcase bolts to 40 ft. lbs. (60 Nm) and the alternator bolts to 25 ft. lbs. (30 Nm).

12. Install the motor mount and bracket.

13. Install 2 new bolts at the manifold outlet flange and tighten to 35 ft. lbs. (50 Nm).

14. Connect the negative battery cable.

RIGHT SIDE

1. Disconnect the negative battery cable.

2. Disconnect the rear oxygen sensor at the rear of the right cam cover. Disconnect the harness clip.

3. Raise and safely support the vehicle.

4. Disconnect the Y-pipe from the front of the catalytic converter.

5. Disconnect the suspension position sensor at lower control arm from both sides.

6. Place a support below the rear cross member of the engine cradle and remove the 4 cradle to body bolts.

7. Lower the rear of the engine cradle and disconnect the Y-pipe from the exhaust crossover and from the manifold.

8. Remove the manifold nuts and remove the manifold.

9. Remove the gasket from the manifold. Replace if damaged. Remove the oxygen sensor from the manifold as necessary.

To install:

10. Coat oxygen sensor threads with hi-temperature anti-seize compound. Tighten sensor to 30 ft. lbs. (40 Nm).

11. Install gasket, manifold and nuts. Tighten nuts to 25 ft. lbs. (30 Nm).

12. Install exhaust Y-pipe and install 4 new bolts. Tighten the bolts to 45 ft. lbs. (60 Nm).

13. Raise engine cradle into position and tighten the bolts to 75 ft. lbs. (100 Nm).

14. Connect the exhaust Y-pipe to the catalytic converter and tighten 2 new bolts to 35 ft. lbs. (50 Nm).

15. Connect the suspension position sensors to the lower control arms.

16. Lower the vehicle and connect the oxygen sensor. Install the harness retainer.

17. Connect the negative battery cable.

Timing Chain Front Cover

REMOVAL AND INSTALLATION

3.8L Engine

1. Disconnect the negative battery cable.

2. Drain the cooling system. Remove the lower radiator hose and the coolant bypass hose from the timing case cover. Remove the heater pipes.

3. Remove the serpentine drive belt and the water pump pulley.

4. Raise and safely support the vehicle.

5. Remove right front tire and wheel assembly.

6. Remove the inner splash shield.

7. Remove the front engine-to-frame stabilizer and bracket, as required.

8. Remove the crankshaft balancer bolt/washer and the balancer.

9. Remove the sensor shield.

10. Disconnect the electrical connectors from the crankshaft sensor, the camshaft sensor and the oil pressure switch.

11. Remove the oil pan-to-timing case cover bolts, the timing case cover-to-engine bolts and the cover.

To install:

12. Clean the gasket mounting surfaces.

13. Install a new gasket and apply sealant 1052080 or equivalent. Install the front cover.

14. Install the oil pan-to-timing case cover bolts. Tighten to 124 inch lbs. (14 Nm). Install the timing case cover-to-engine bolts. Tighten to 22 ft. lbs. (30 Nm).

15. Connect the electrical connectors to the crankshaft sensor, the camshaft sensor and the oil pressure switch.

16. Install the sensor shield.

17. Install the crankshaft balancer bolt/washer and the balancer.

18. If removed, install the front engine-to-frame stabilizer and bracket.

19. Install the inner splash shield.

20. Install right front tire and wheel assembly.

21. Lower the vehicle.

22. Install the water pump pulley and serpentine drive belt.

23. Install the lower radiator hose and the coolant bypass hose to the timing case cover. Install the heater pipes.

24. Connect the negative battery cable.

25. Fill cooling system and check for leaks. Start the engine and allow to come to normal operating temperature. Recheck for leaks. Top-up coolant.

4.5L and 4.9L Engines

1. Disconnect the negative battery cable.

2. Drain the cooling system. Remove the air cleaner.

3. Remove the serpentine belt.

4. Remove the cross-car brace and coolant reservoir.

5. Remove the AIR air filter and bracket, if equipped.

6. Remove the water pump pulley bolts and the pulley. Remove the water pump from the vehicle.

7. Raise and safely support the vehicle.

8. Remove the crankshaft damper by performing the following:

   a. Remove the crankshaft damper-to-crankshaft bolt.

NOTE: The use of shop air, applied to a cylinder on its compression stroke, may be required to prevent the crankshaft from turning while removing the crankshaft damper bolt. Remove a spark plug and rotate the crankshaft until that cylinder is on its compression stroke. Install the appropriate adapter finger-tight into the spark plug hole and apply shop air to the cylinder.

   b. Attach a wheel puller to the crankshaft damper.

   c. Using a pilot between the crankshaft and the center bolt, press the crankshaft damper from the crankshaft.

   d. Remove the Woodruff® key from the crankshaft.

9. Remove the timing case cover-to-engine bolts, the oil pan-to-timing case cover bolts and the cover.

To install:

10. Clean the gasket mounting surfaces.

11. To avoid oil leakage, apply RTV sealer according to the following:

   a. Apply a bead of RTV on the front cover lip on the oil pan sealing surface. Ensure that this bead is placed along the front cover lip behind the 2 oil pan-to-front cover bolts.

   b. Apply a ¼ in. bead of RTV on the oil pan where the oil pan, block and front cover join.

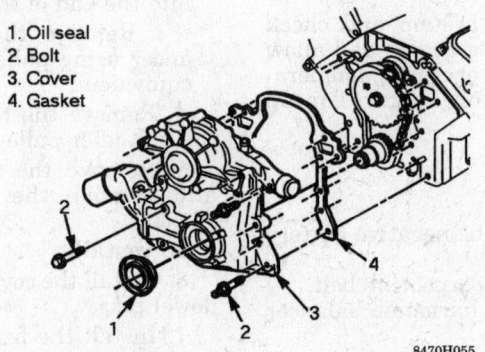

1. Oil seal
2. Bolt
3. Cover
4. Gasket

8470H055

Front cover assembly — 3.8L engine

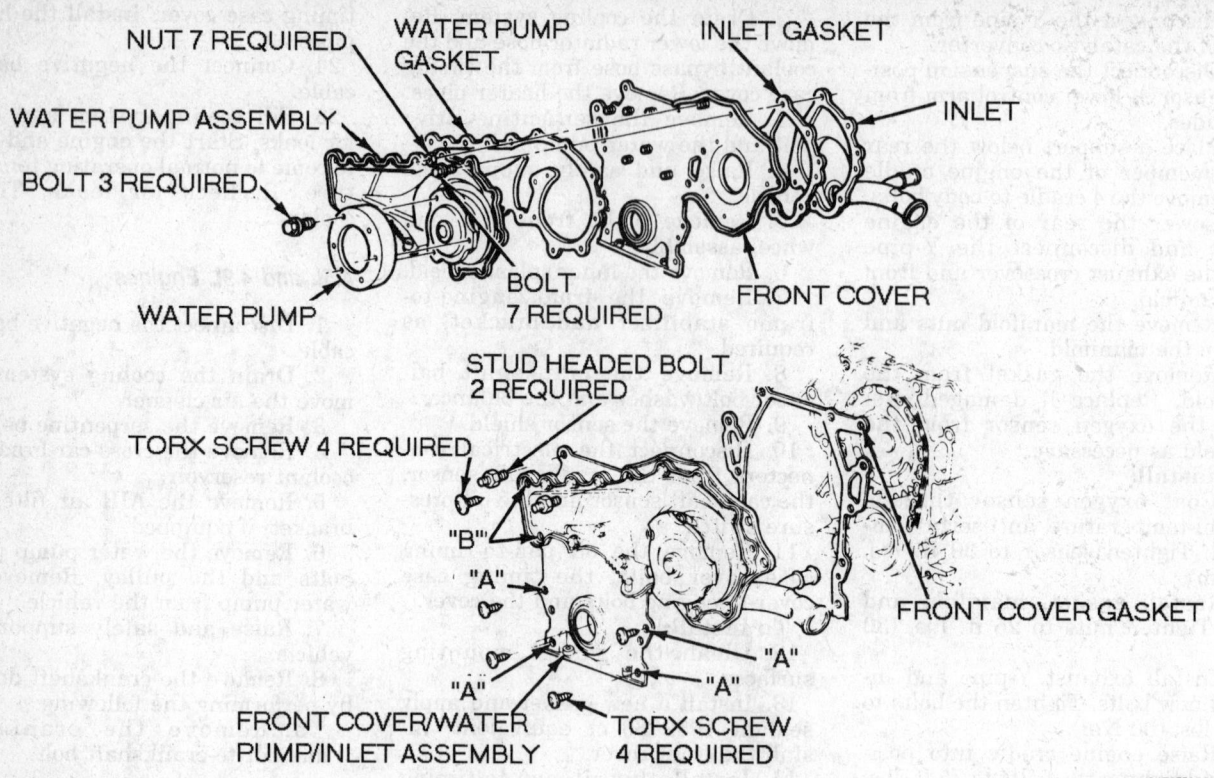

Front cover assembly — 4.9L engine

8470H056

c. Remove any excess RTV that is squeezed out of the sealing area.

12. Install the front cover.

13. Install the crankshaft damper by performing the following:

a. Lubricate the bore of the hub and the inside diameter of the seal with EP lubricant.

b. Install the Woodruff® key in the key slot in the crankshaft.

c. Position the damper on the crankshaft, lining up the key slot with the key.

d. Thread the installer into the end of the crankshaft. Position the thrust bearing with the inner race forward, washer next and installer nut last.

e. Install the damper on the crankshaft by tightening the installer nut.

NOTE: The use of compressed air, applied to a cylinder on its compression stroke, may be required to prevent the crankshaft from turning while installing the crankshaft damper bolt. Remove a spark plug and rotate the crankshaft until that cylinder is on its compression stroke. Install an adapter finger-tight into the spark plug hole and apply shop air to the cylinder.

f. Tighten nut until the hub bottoms out on the crankshaft. Tighten the nut to 60–65 ft. lbs. (80–90 Nm) to fully seat the balancer and timing gear. Remove the installer and reinstall the bolt and washer into the crankshaft. Tighten to 60–65 ft. lbs. (80–90 Nm).

g. Exhaust the compressed air to the cylinder, remove the adapter and reinstall the spark plug.

14. Lower the vehicle.

15. Install the water pump.

16. Install the water pump pulley.

17. Install the serpentine belt.

18. Install the coolant reservoir and cross-car brace.

19. Connect the negative battery cable.

20. Fill cooling system and check for leaks. Start the engine and allow to come to normal operating temperature. Recheck for leaks. Top-up coolant.

4.6L Engine

1. Disconnect the negative battery cable.

2. Remove the serpentine belt.

3. Remove the harmonic balancer as follows:

a. Release tension from the accessory drive belt.

b. Raise and safely support the vehicle, remove the right front wheel.

c. Remove the splash shields from the wheelhouse and remove the brace between the oil pan and the transmission case.

d. Install the flywheel holder tool J-39411 or equivalent and remove the balancer bolt.

e. Support the engine cradle and remove the 3 bolts from the right side of the cradle.

f. Disconnect the RSS sensor from the right lower control arm.

g. Lower the engine cradle enough for clearance of puller tool.

h. Install pilot tool J-39344-2 into the end of the crankshaft.

i. Remove the harmonic balancer using puller tool J-38416 or equivalent.

4. Remove the belt tensioner and the belt idler pulley.

5. Remove the front cover bolts and remove the cover with the gasket.

To install:

6. Install the cover gasket over the dowel pins.

7. Install the front cover over the dowel pins and tighten the cover screws to 7 ft. lbs. (10 Nm).

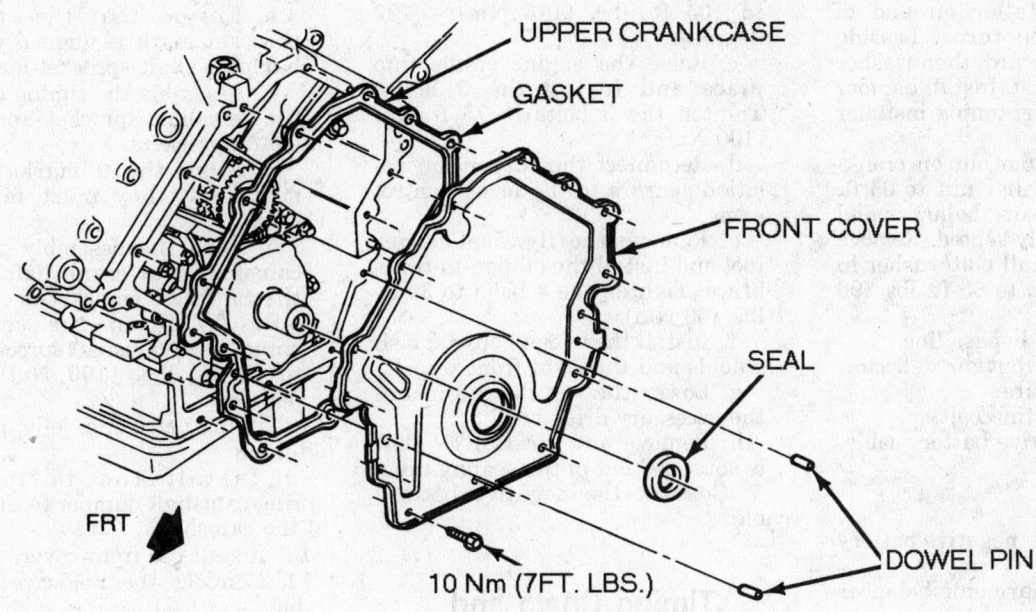

UPPER CRANKCASE

GASKET

FRONT COVER

SEAL

DOWEL PIN

10 Nm (7FT. LBS.)

8470H057

Front cover — 4.6L engine

8. Install the idler pulley and the belt tensioner. Tighten both to 35 ft. lbs. (50 Nm).

9. Install the harmonic balancer as follows:

a. Position the balancer to the crankshaft and using tool J-39344 or equivalent install the balancer.

b. Clean the balancer bolt threads and apply oil to the threads. Tighten the balancer bolt to 105 ft. lbs. (145 Nm) + 120 degrees.

c. Raise the engine cradle into place and install the 3 bolts. Tighten the 3 bolts to 75 ft. lbs. (100 Nm).

d. Reconnect the suspension position sensors to the lower control arms.

e. Remove the flywheel holder tool and install the oil pan-to-trans brace. Tighten the 4 bolts to 35 ft. lbs. (50 Nm).

f. Install the wheel house splash shields and the right front wheel.

g. Lower the vehicle and install the accessory drive belt.

h. Remove any excess RTV that is squeezed out of the sealing area.

10. Install the serpentine drive belt and connect the negative battery cable.

Front Cover Oil Seal

REPLACEMENT

3.8L Engine

1. Disconnect the negative battery cable.
2. Remove the serpentine drive belt.
3. Remove the crankshaft balancer-to-crankshaft bolts.
4. Using a small prybar, pry the oil seal from the timing case cover; be careful not to damage the sealing surfaces.

To install:

5. Clean the oil seal mounting surface.
6. Using GM lubricant 1050169 or equivalent, coat the outside of the seal and the crankshaft balancer.
7. Using an appropriate oil seal installation tool, press the new seal into the timing case cover until it seats.
8. Install the crankshaft balancer-to-crankshaft bolt and tighten the crankshaft balancer-to-crankshaft bolt to 105 ft. lbs. (140 Nm).
9. Install the serpentine drive belt.
10. Connect the negative battery cable.

4.5L and 4.9L Engines

1. Disconnect the negative battery cable.
2. Remove the serpentine belt.
3. Raise and safely support the vehicle.
4. Remove right front tire. Remove right front air deflector.
5. Loosen and reposition the heater bypass line.
6. Remove the crankshaft pulley-to-crankshaft pulley bolt. Attach a wheel puller to the crankshaft pulley. Using a pilot between the crankshaft and the center bolt, press the crankshaft pulley from the crankshaft. Remove the Woodruff® key from the crankshaft.
7. Using a small prybar, pry the oil seal from the timing case cover, discard it.

To install:

8. Clean the oil seal mounting surface. Lubricate the new seal with engine oil.
9. Using a hammer and the oil seal installation tool, drive the new oil seal into the timing case cover until it seats.
10. Lubricate bore of hub and inside diameter of seal with EP lubricant to prevent seizure to crankshaft and provide lubrication of oil seal lip.

11. Position damper on crankshaft, lining up key slot in hub with key on crankshaft.

12. Position installer on end of crankshaft. Position thrust bearing with inner race forward, then washer and installer nut last. Install damper on crankshaft by tightening installer nut.

13. Hub will bottom out on crankshaft. Tighten installer nut to 65 ft. lbs. (90 Nm) to ensure balancer and timing gear are fully seated. Remove installer and reinstall bolt/washer in crankshaft. Tighten to 65 ft. lbs. (90 Nm).

14. Install heater bypass line.

15. Install right front air deflector. Install right front tire.

16. Install serpentine belt.

17. Connect negative battery cable.

4.6L Engine

1. Disconnect the negative battery cable.

2. Remove the harmonic balancer as follows:

a. Release tension from the accessory drive belt.

b. Raise and safely support the vehicle, remove the right front wheel.

c. Remove the splash shields from the wheelhouse and remove the brace between the oil pan and the transmission case.

d. Install the flywheel holder tool J-39411 or equivalent, and remove the balancer bolt.

e. Support the engine cradle and remove the 3 bolts from the right side of the cradle.

f. Disconnect the RSS sensor from the right lower control arm.

g. Lower the engine cradle enough for clearance of puller tool.

h. Install pilot tool J-39344-2 into the end of the crankshaft.

i. Remove the harmonic balancer using puller tool J-38416 or equivalent.

3. Using a small prybar, pry the oil seal out of the bore. Use caution not to damage the bore. Discard the old oil seal.

To install:

4. Clean the oil seal mounting surface. Lubricate the new seal with engine oil.

5. Install the new seal to the front cover, using seal installer tool J-38818 and harmonic balancer installation tool J39344 or equivalents.

6. Install the harmonic balancer as follows:

a. Position the balancer to the crankshaft and using tool J-39344 or equivalent install the balancer.

b. Clean the balancer bolt threads and apply oil to the threads. Tighten the balancer bolt to 105 ft. lbs. (145 Nm) + 120 degrees.

c. Raise the engine cradle into place and install the 3 bolts. Tighten the 3 bolts to 75 ft. lbs. (100 Nm).

d. Reconnect the suspension position sensors to the lower control arms.

e. Remove the flywheel holder tool and install the oil pan-to-trans brace. Tighten the 4 bolts to 35 ft. lbs. (50 Nm).

f. Install the wheel house splash shields and the right front wheel.

g. Lower the vehicle and install the accessory drive belt.

h. Remove any excess RTV that is squeezed out of the sealing area.

7. Connect the negative battery cable.

Timing Chain and Sprockets

REMOVAL AND INSTALLATION

3.8L Engine

1. Disconnect the negative battery cable. Remove the front cover.

2. Rotate the crankshaft to align the marks of the timing sprockets.

3. Remove the button and spring or damper from the center of the camshaft.

4. Remove the camshaft sprocket bolts, the sprocket and the timing chain.

5. Remove the crankshaft sprocket and the Woodruff® key.

To install:

6. Clean the gasket mounting surfaces. Inspect the parts for wear and/or damage. Replace as required.

7. Install the timing chain and sprockets by performing the following:

a. Ensure that the camshaft sprocket mark is aligned with the balancer shaft sprocket mark.

b. Assemble the timing chain on the camshaft sprocket and crankshaft sprockets.

c. Align the **0** marks on the sprockets; they must face each other.

d. Slide the assembly onto the camshaft and crankshaft. Install the camshaft sprocket-to-camshaft bolts. Tighten the camshaft sprocket-to-camshaft sprocket bolts to 74 ft. lbs. (100 Nm) + 105 degrees.

8. Using petroleum jelly, pack the oil pump.

9. Install the button and spring/camshaft damper to the center of the camshaft.

10. Install the front cover.

11. Connect the negative battery cable.

12. Fill cooling system and check for leaks. Start the engine and allow to come to normal operating temperature. Recheck for leaks. Top-up coolant.

4.5L and 4.9L Engines

1. Disconnect the negative battery cable. Drain the cooling system.

2. Remove engine front cover.

3. Remove oil slinger from crankshaft.

4. Rotate the engine until the crankshaft and camshaft timing marks are aligned.

5. Remove thrust button and screw securing camshaft sprocket to camshaft. Discard thrust button.

6. Remove camshaft and crankshaft sprockets with chain attached.

To install:

7. If timing was disturbed, rotate crankshaft until timing mark on

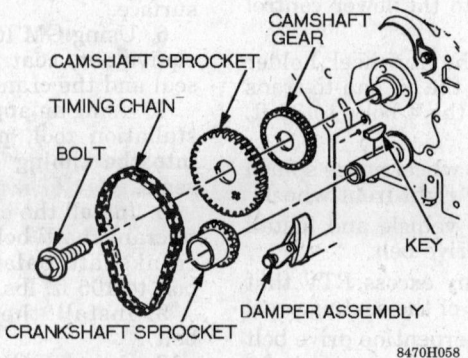

Timing chain assembly — 3.8L engine

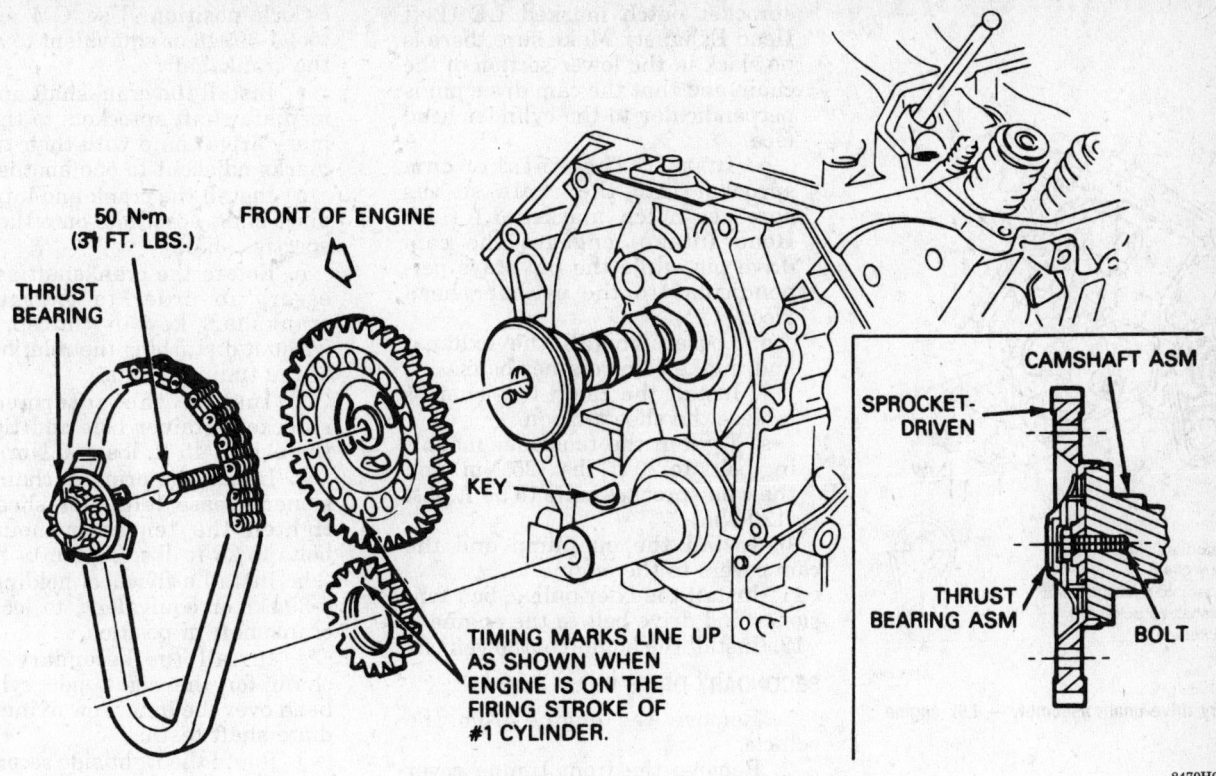

50 N·m
(3? FT. LBS.)

FRONT OF ENGINE

THRUST BEARING

KEY

TIMING MARKS LINE UP AS SHOWN WHEN ENGINE IS ON THE FIRING STROKE OF #1 CYLINDER.

CAMSHAFT ASM

SPROCKET-DRIVEN

THRUST BEARING ASM

BOLT

8470H059

Timing chain/timing marks — 4.9L engine

crank sprocket is positioned straight up.

8. Install timing chain over camshaft sprocket.

9. Install cam sprocket, crank sprocket and timing chain over crankshaft, ensuring that timing marks are aligned.

10. Move camshaft until the dowel pin mates with the index hole in the sprocket.

11. Hold camshaft sprocket in position against end of camshaft and press sprocket onto camshaft by hand, being sure index pin in camshaft is aligned with index hole in sprocket.

12. Install screw securing camshaft sprocket to camshaft. Tighten to 36 ft. lbs. (48 Nm).

NOTE: It may be necessary to keep the engine from rotating while setting the torque.

13. Install new thrust button.

14. Install oil slinger on crankshaft with smaller end of slinger against crankshaft sprocket.

15. Install engine front cover.

16. Connect negative battery cable.

4.6L Engine

NOTE: The 4.6L engine has a camshaft primary drive chain and a camshaft secondary drive chain.

PRIMARY DRIVE CHAIN

1. Remove the engine from the vehicle and install to a suitable engine holding stand.

2. Remove the serpentine drive belt, idler pulley and belt tensioner.

3. Remove the front cover assembly and the oil pump assembly from the engine.

4. Remove the cam covers from the engine.

5. Remove the 3 timing chain tensioners.

6. Remove the 4 camshaft sprocket bolts from all 4 camshafts and remove all sprockets.

7. Remove the secondary drive chains from around the immediate shaft sprocket.

8. Remove 1 bolt from the shaft sprocket and slide the gears and the primary drive chain off the crankshaft and immediate shaft.

To install:

9. Install the timing chains and reset the camshaft timing as described in the following procedure:

a. Install the secondary and primary chain guides, if previously removed.

b. Rotate the crankshaft until the sprocket drive key is in the 1 o'clock position. Use GM special tool J-39946 or equivalent to rotate the crankshaft.

c. Install the crankshaft and immediate shaft sprockets to the primary drive chain with their timing marks adjacent to one another.

d. Install the crank and intermediate shaft sprockets onto their respective shafts.

e. Rotate the crankshaft as necessary in order to engage the crankshaft key in the sprocket without disturbing the relationship of the timing marks.

f. Install the intermediate sprocket retainer bolt and tighten the bolt to 45 ft. lbs. (60 Nm).

g. Install the primary chain tensioner/release tensioner shoe and tighten the tensioner mounting bolts to 20 ft. lbs. (25 Nm).

h. Install a flywheel holding tool (J-39411 or equivalent) to lock the crankshaft in position.

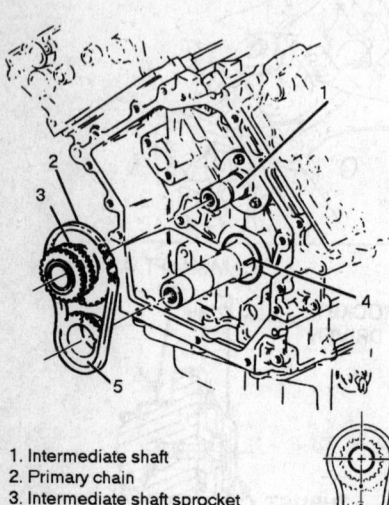

1. Intermediate shaft
2. Primary chain
3. Intermediate shaft sprocket
4. Crankshaft sprocket key
5. Sprocket

8470H060

Primary drive chain assembly — 4.6L engine

i. Install the secondary drive chain for the right side cylinder head over the inner row of intermediate shaft teeth.

j. Route the right side secondary drive chain over the chain guide and install the exhaust cam sprocket to the chain so the camshaft drive pin engages the sprocket notch marked **RE** (Right Head Exhaust). Make sure there is no slack in the lower section of the chain and that the cam drive pin is perpendicular to the cylinder head face.

k. Install the intake cam sprocket into the chain so the sprocket notch marked **RI** (Right Head Intake) engages the cam drive pin while the pin stays perpendicular to the cylinder head face.

l. Loosely install the exhaust and intake cam retainer bolts.

m. Install the chain tensioner or release the shoe tension.

n. Tighten the tensioner mounting bolts to 20 ft. lbs. (25 Nm) and the cam sprocket bolts to 90 ft. lbs. (120 Nm).

o. Route the left side secondary drive chain over the chain guide and install the exhaust cam sprocket to the chain so the camshaft drive pin engages the

sprocket notch marked **LE** (Left Head Exhaust). Make sure there is no slack in the lower section of the chain and that the cam drive pin is perpendicular to the cylinder head face.

p. Install the intake cam sprocket into the chain so the sprocket notch marked **LI** (Left Head Intake) engages the cam drive pin while the pin stays perpendicular to the cylinder head face.

q. Loosely install the exhaust and intake cam retainer bolts.

r. Install the chain tensioner or release the shoe tension.

s. Tighten the tensioner mounting bolts to 20 ft. lbs. (25 Nm) and the cam sprocket bolts to 90 ft. lbs. (120 Nm).

10. Install the oil pump and the cam covers to the engine.

11. Install the idler pulley, belt tensioner and drive belt to the engine.

12. Install the engine to the vehicle.

SECONDARY DRIVE CHAIN

1. Remove the engine from the vehicle.

2. Remove the front timing cover assembly.

3. Remove the left side cam cover assembly.

4. Remove the left side secondary chain tensioner.

5. Remove the left side chain guide. Access to the upper chain guide mounting bolt can be achieved by way of the hole in the cylinder head that is covered with a plastic plug.

6. Remove the left side cam sprocket bolts and sprockets.

7. Remove the left side secondary drive chain.

8. Remove the right side cam cover assembly.

9. Remove the right side secondary chain tensioner.

10. Remove the right side chain guide. Access to the upper chain guide mounting bolt can be achieved by way of the hole in the cylinder head that is covered with a plastic plug.

11. Remove the right side cam sprocket bolts and sprockets.

12. Remove the right side secondary drive chain.

To install:

13. Install the timing chains and reset the camshaft timing as described in the following procedure:

a. Install the secondary and primary chain guides, if previously removed.

b. Rotate the crankshaft until the sprocket drive key is in the 1

o'clock position. Use GM special tool J-39946 or equivalent to rotate the crankshaft.

c. Install the crankshaft and immediate shaft sprockets to the primary drive chain with their timing marks adjacent to one another.

d. Install the crank and intermediate shaft sprockets onto their respective shafts.

e. Rotate the crankshaft as necessary in order to engage the crankshaft key in the sprocket without disturbing the relationship of the timing marks.

f. Install the intermediate sprocket retainer bolt and tighten the bolt to 45 ft. lbs. (60 Nm).

g. Install the primary chain tensioner/release tensioner shoe and tighten the tensioner mounting bolts to 20 ft. lbs. (25 Nm).

h. Install a flywheel holding tool J-39411 or equivalent, to lock the crankshaft in position.

i. Install the secondary drive chain for the right side cylinder head over the inner row of intermediate shaft teeth.

j. Route the right side secondary drive chain over the chain guide and install the exhaust cam sprocket to the chain so the camshaft drive pin engages the sprocket notch marked **RE** (Right Head Exhaust). Make sure there is no slack in the lower section of the chain and that the cam drive pin is perpendicular to the cylinder head face.

k. Install the intake cam sprocket into the chain so the sprocket notch marked **RI** (Right Head Intake) engages the cam drive pin while the pin stays perpendicular to the cylinder head face.

l. Loosely install the exhaust and intake cam retainer bolts.

m. Install the chain tensioner or release the shoe tension.

n. Tighten the tensioner mounting bolts to 20 ft. lbs. (25 Nm) and the cam sprocket bolts to 90 ft. lbs. (120 Nm).

o. Route the left side secondary drive chain over the chain guide and install the exhaust cam sprocket to the chain so the camshaft drive pin engages the sprocket notch marked **LE** (Left Head Exhaust). Make sure there is no slack in the lower section of the chain and that the cam drive pin is perpendicular to the cylinder head face.

p. Install the intake cam sprocket into the chain so the

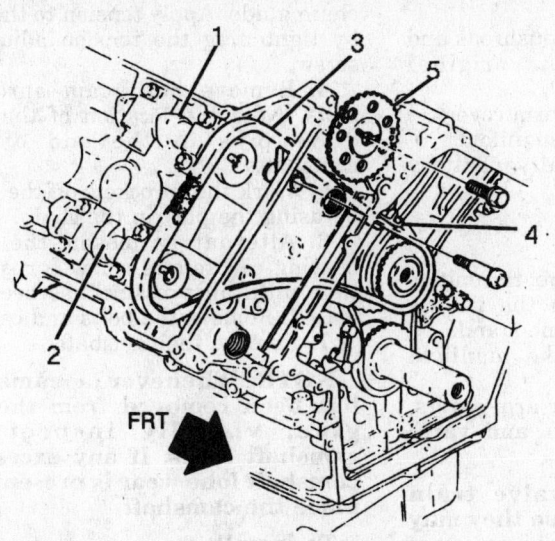

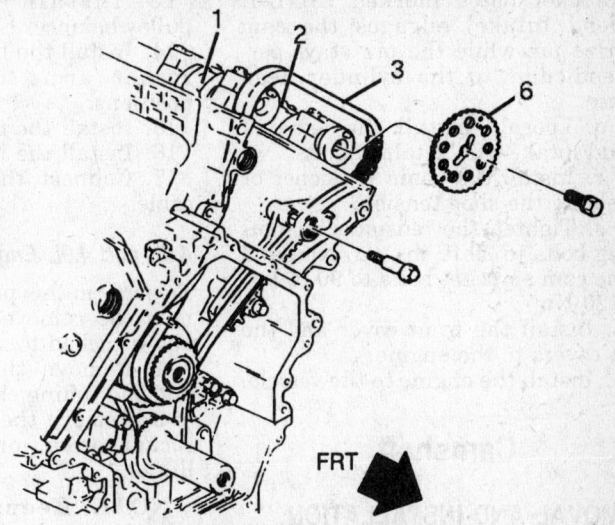

1. Intake camshaft
2. Exhaust camshaft
3. Secondary cam drive chain
4. Chain guide

5. RH sprocket-install cam pin in
   RE slot for exhaust position;
   RI slot for intake position
6. LH sprocket-install cam pin in
   LE slot for exhaust position;
   LI slot for ontake position

8470H061

Secondary drive chain — 4.6L engine

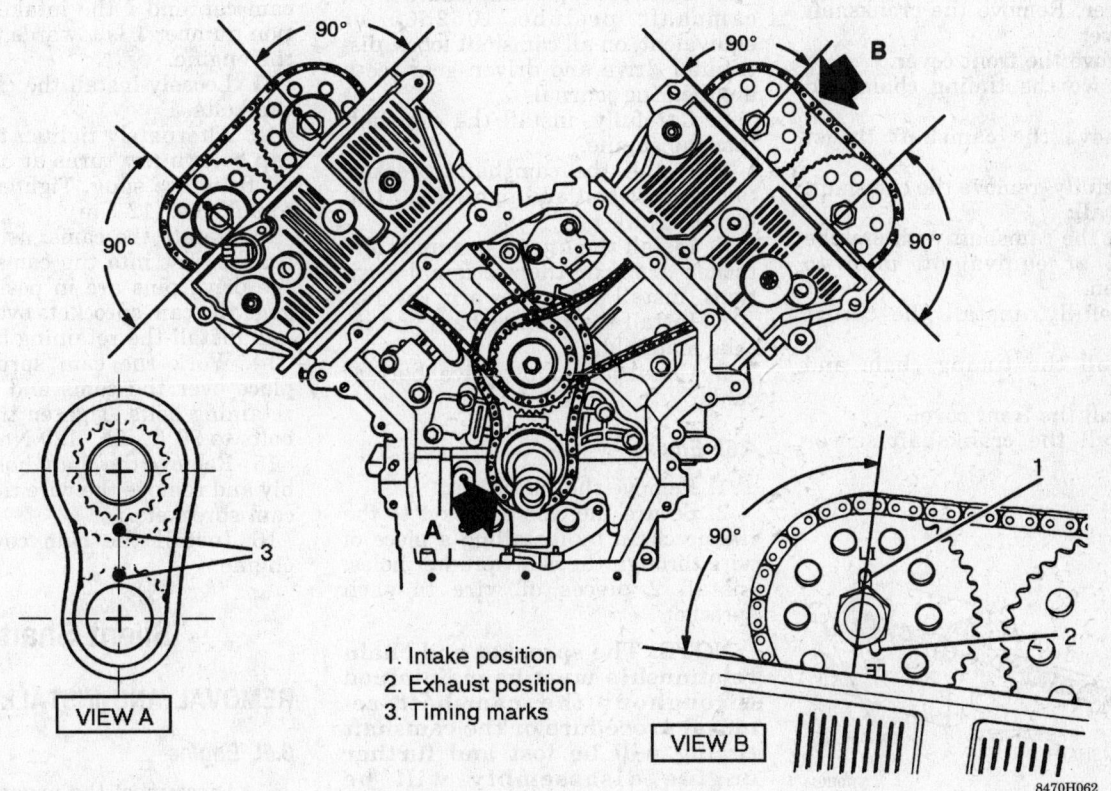

1. Intake position
2. Exhaust position
3. Timing marks

8470H062

Setting the camshaft timing — 4.6L engine

sprocket notch marked **LI** (Left Head Intake) engages the cam drive pin while the pin stays perpendicular to the cylinder head face.

q. Loosely install the exhaust and intake cam retainer bolts.

r. Install the chain tensioner or release the shoe tension.

s. Tighten the tensioner mounting bolts to 20 ft. lbs. (25 Nm) and the cam sprocket bolts to 90 ft. lbs. (120 Nm).

14. Install the front cover and the cam covers to the engine.

15. Install the engine to the vehicle.

Camshaft

REMOVAL AND INSTALLATION

3.8L Engine

1. Remove the intake manifold.
2. Remove the rocker arm covers, rocker arms, pushrods and lifters.

NOTE: Keep all valve train components in order so they may be reinstalled in their original positions.

3. Remove the crankshaft pulley/balancer. Remove the crankshaft sensor cover.
4. Remove the front cover.
5. Remove the timing chain and sprockets.
6. Remove the camshaft thrust plate.
7. Carefully, remove the camshaft.
To install:
8. Coat the camshaft with prelube 10423565 or equivalent, prior to installation.
9. Carefully, install the thrust plate.
10. Install the timing chain and sprockets.
11. Install the front cover.
12. Install the crankshaft sensor cover.

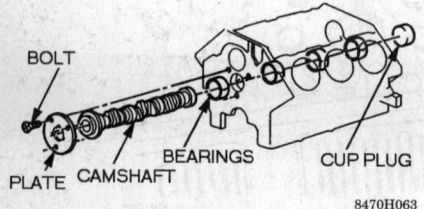

Camshaft assembly — 3.8L engine

13. Install the crankshaft pulley/balancer.
14. Install the lifters, pushrods and rocker arms in their original positions.
15. Install the rocker arm covers.
16. Install the intake manifold.
17. Connect the negative battery cable.

4.5L and 4.9L Engines
To perform this procedure, the engine must be removed from the vehicle and attached to an engine stand.
1. Remove the intake manifold and the timing chain.
2. Remove the rocker arm covers, rocker arms, pushrods and valve lifters.

NOTE: Keep all valve train components in order so they may be reinstalled in their original positions.

3. Carefully slide the camshaft out from the front of the engine.
To install:

NOTE: If a new camshaft is to be installed, new lifters and a distributor drive gear must also be installed.

4. Lubricate the camshaft with camshaft prelube 1052365 or equivalent, on all camshaft lobes, distributor drive and driven gear teeth and bearing journals.
5. Carefully, install the camshaft into the engine.
6. Install the camshaft sprocket-to-camshaft bolt and tighten to 31 ft. lbs. (50 Nm).
7. Install the lifters, pushrods and rocker arms in their original positions. Install the rocker arm covers.
8. Install the timing chain and intake manifold.
9. Connect the negative battery cable.

4.6L Engine
1. Remove the cam cover.
2. Secure the cam sprocket to the timing chain by installing a piece of wire through the cam sprocket holes. Install 2 pieces of wire to each sprocket.

NOTE: The sprocket and chain relationship must be maintained throughout the camshaft removal procedure or the camshaft timing will be lost and further engine disassembly will be required.

3. From behind the sprockets, install the cam chain holder, J-38815 or equivalent, so it is positioned be-

tween the chain tensioner and the chain guide. Apply tension to the tool by tightening the tension adjusting screw.
4. Remove both cam sprocket bolts. Note the location of the cam drive pins in the end of the camshafts.
5. Work the sprockets off the cams by using the play in the chain.
6. Alternately loosen the cam bearing cap screws a few turns at a time until all pressure has been released. Remove the bolts and caps.
7. Remove the camshaft.

NOTE: Whenever a camshaft has been removed from the engine, visually inspect all camshaft lobes. If any excessive camshaft lobe wear is present, replace the camshaft.

To install:
8. Apply camshaft prelube 1052365 or equivalent to the face of each cam lobe.
9. Install the camshaft to the engine.
10. Position the cam bearing caps to the cylinder head. Each cap is identified for position and direction. The arrow points toward the front of the engine. **E** indicates the exhaust cam cap and **I** the intake cap. Position number **1** is towards the front of the engine.
11. Loosely install the cam bearing cap bolts.
12. Alternately tighten the bearing cap bolts a few turns at a time until all bolts are snug. Tighten the bolts to 9 ft. lbs. (12 Nm).
13. Rotate the cams, using the hex that is cast into the camshaft, until the drive pins are in position to engage the cam sprockets over the cams and install the retaining bolts.
14. Work the cam sprockets into place over the cams and install the retaining bolts. Tighten the sprocket bolts to 90 ft. lbs. (120 Nm).
15. Remove the chain holder assembly and remove the wire ties from the cam sprockets.
16. Install the cam cover to the engine.

Silent Shaft

REMOVAL AND INSTALLATION

3.8L Engine
1. Disconnect the negative battery cable. Remove the engine and secure it to a workstand.
2. Remove the flywheel-to-crankshaft bolts and the flywheel.

3. Remove the intake manifold.

4. Remove the lifter guide retainer.

5. Remove the front cover-to-engine bolts and front cover.

6. Remove the camshaft sprocket-to-camshaft gear bolts, the sprocket, the timing chain and the gear.

7. To remove the balance shaft, perform the following:

   a. Remove the balance shaft gear-to-shaft bolt and the gear.

   b. Remove the balance shaft retainer-to-engine bolts and the retainer.

   c. Using the slide hammer tool, pull the balance shaft from the front of the engine.

8. If replacing the rear balance shaft bearing, perform the following procedures:

   a. Drive the rear plug from the engine.

   b. Using the camshaft remover/installer tool, press the rear bearing from the rear of the engine.

   c. Dip the new bearing in clean engine oil.

   d. Using the balance shaft rear bearing installer tool, press the new rear bearing into the rear of the engine.

   e. Install the rear cup plug.

To install:

9. Using the balance shaft installer tool, screw it into the balance shaft and install the shaft into the engine. Remove the installer.

10. Turn the camshaft with the camshaft sprocket temporarily installed, so the timing mark is straight down.

11. With the camshaft sprocket and the camshaft gear removed, turn the balance shaft so the timing mark on the gear points straight down.

12. Align the marks on the balance shaft gear and camshaft gear by turning the balance shaft. Install the camshaft gear.

13. Turn the crankshaft so No. 1 piston is on TDC.

14. Install the timing chain and camshaft sprocket.

15. Install the balance shaft front bearing retainer and bolts. Tighten to 22 ft. lbs. (30 Nm).

16. Install the front cover.

17. Install the lifter guide retainer.

18. Install the intake manifold.

19. Install the flywheel. Tighten the attaching bolt to 11 ft. lbs. (15 Nm) + 50 degrees.

20. Install the engine and connect the negative battery cable.

Piston and Connecting Rod

POSITIONING

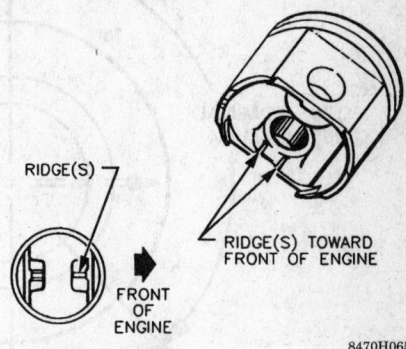

Piston installation direction — 3.8L engine

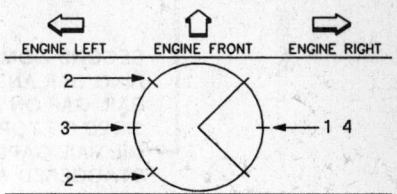

1. Oil ring spacer gap
2. Oil ring rail gaps
3. 2nd compression ring gap
4. Top compression ring gap

Piston ring gap location — 3.8L engine

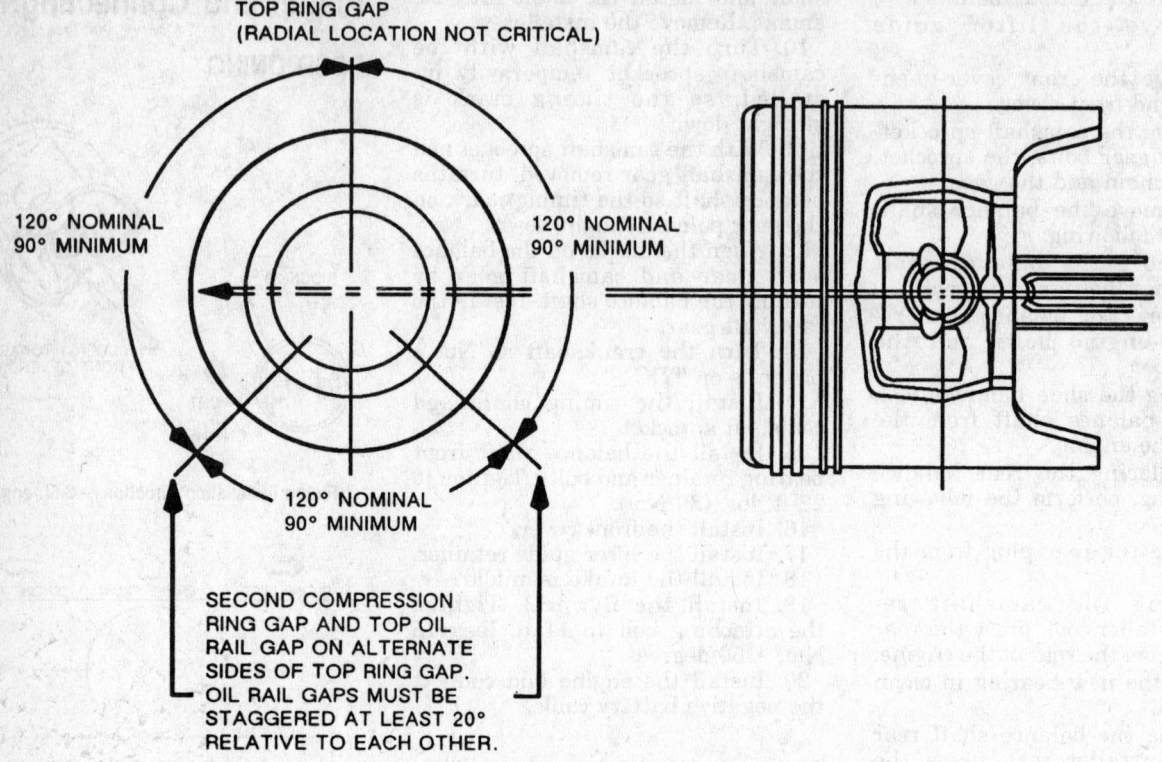

Piston ring orientation — 4.9L engine

8470H067

ENGINE LUBRICATION

Oil Pan

REMOVAL AND INSTALLATION

3.8L Engine

1. Disconnect the negative battery cable.
2. Raise and safely support the vehicle.
3. Drain the crankcase.
4. Disconnect the oil level sensor connector.
5. Remove the oil pan retaining bolts and remove the oil pan.
To install:
6. Clean the gasket mounting surfaces and install a new gasket to the pan.
7. Install the oil pan and oil pan-to-engine bolts. Tighten to 124 inch lbs. (14 Nm).
8. Connect the oil level sensor connector.
9. Fill the crankcase.
10. Lower the vehicle.

11. Connect the negative battery cable.

4.5L and 4.9L Engines

1992 ALLANTE

1. Disconnect the negative battery cable.
2. Raise and safely support the vehicle.
3. Drain the crankcase. Disconnect the oil level sensor, if equipped.
4. Remove the flywheel covers.
5. Remove the exhaust Y-pipe.
6. Remove the oil pan-to-engine bolts/nuts and the oil pan.
To install:
7. Clean the gasket mounting surfaces.

NOTE: Apply a ¼ in. bead of RTV at the rear main bearing cap and front cover to block joints.

8. Install the oil pan and oil pan-to-engine bolts/nuts. Tighten to 14 ft. lbs. (18 Nm).
9. Install the flywheel covers.
10. Install the exhaust Y-pipe.
11. If equipped, connect the oil level sensor.
12. Lower the vehicle.
13. Fill the crankcase.
14. Connect the negative battery cable.

ELDORADO AND SEVILLE

1. Disconnect the negative battery cable. Raise and safely support the vehicle. Drain the crankcase.
2. Remove the 2 torque converter/flywheel covers from the lower side of the transaxle.
3. Remove the exhaust crossunder pipe and reposition.
4. Remove the oil pan-to-engine bolts and the oil pan.
To install:
5. Clean the gasket mounting surfaces.

NOTE: Apply a ¼ in. bead of RTV at the rear main bearing cap and front cover to block joints.

6. Install the oil pan and oil pan-to-engine bolts. Tighten to 14 ft. lbs. (18 Nm).
7. Install the exhaust crossunder pipe.
8. Install the 2 torque converter/flywheel covers.
9. Lower the vehicle.
10. Fill the crankcase.
11. Connect the negative battery cable.

4.6L Engine

1. Remove the engine from the vehicle and place it on the stand.

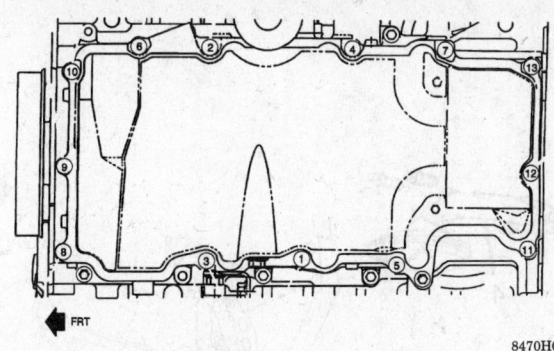

8470H072

Oil pan bolt torque sequence — 4.6L engine

2. Completely drain the oil from the oil pan.

3. Remove the 13 oil pan bolts and remove the oil pan assembly.

To install:

4. The oil pan gasket may be re-used if it is not damaged. Do not remove the gasket from the oil pan groove, unless it is being replaced.

5. Position the oil pan to the crankcase.

6. Install the 13 oil pan bolts and tighten to 9 ft. lbs. (10 Nm) In the proper sequence.

7. Install the engine to the vehicle and refill the oil to the proper level.

Oil Pump

REMOVAL AND INSTALLATION

3.8L Engine

The oil pump is located in the bottom of the front cover. The oil pump is an integral part of the front cover with the crankshaft passing through the pump.

1. Disconnect the negative battery cable. Remove the front cover.

2. Clean the gasket mounting surfaces.

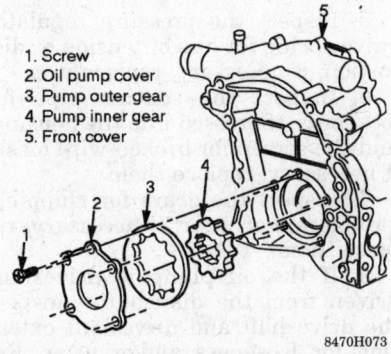

1. Screw
2. Oil pump cover
3. Pump outer gear
4. Pump inner gear
5. Front cover

8470H073

Oil pump and housing — 3.8L engine

3. To inspect the pump gears, perform the following:

   a. Remove the oil pump cover-to-front cover screws and the cover.

   b. Remove the inner and outer pump gears.

   c. Using solvent, clean the gears.

   d. Inspect the gears for wear and/or damage; if necessary, replace the parts.

To install:

4. Using petroleum jelly, pack the pump and reinstall the parts. Tighten the oil pump cover-to-front cover screws to 22 ft. lbs. (30 Nm).

NOTE: The oil pump must be primed this way or no pressure will be produced when the engine is started.

5. Install the front cover.

6. Connect the negative battery cable.

7. Check and/or refill the oil level in the crankcase. Replace the oil filter. Start the engine and check for leaks.

4.5L and 4.9L Engines

1. Disconnect the negative battery cable. Remove the oil pan.

2. Remove the oil pump-to-engine screws/nut and the oil pump from the engine.

3. To disassemble, remove the oil pump cover-to-housing screws, slide the driveshaft, drive gear and driven gear from the pump housing.

4. Remove the oil pressure regulator valve and spring from the bore in the housing assembly.

5. Inspect the oil pressure regulator valve for nicks and burrs.

6. Measure the free length of the regulator valve spring. It should be 2.57–2.69 in. (65.28–68.32mm).

7. Inspect the drive gear and driven gear for nicks and burrs.

To install:

8. Assemble the pump drive gear over the driveshaft so the retaining

ring is inside the gear. Position the drive gear over the pump housing shaft closest to the pressure regulator bore.

9. Slide the driven gear over the remaining shaft in the pump housing, meshing the driven gear with the drive gear.

10. Install the oil pressure regulator spring and valve in the bore of the pump housing assembly.

11. Install the pump cover-to-pump housing screws to 5 ft. lbs. (7 Nm), the oil pump-to-engine screws to 15 ft. lbs. (20 Nm) and nut to 22 ft. lbs. (30 Nm).

12. Install the oil pan.

13. Connect the negative battery cable.

4.6L Engine

The oil pump is located behind the front cover.

1. Disconnect the negative battery cable. Remove the front cover.

2. Remove the 3 oil pump mounting bolts and remove the oil pump and drive spacer.

3. To inspect the pump gears, perform the following:

   a. Remove the drive spacer from the housing. Remove the 2 screws that hold the pump housing halves together.

   b. Remove the inner and outer rotors from the pump housing. Remove the pressure relief valve.

   c. Using solvent, clean the gears.

   d. Inspect the gears for wear and/or damage; if necessary, replace the parts.

To install:

4. Install the inner and outer pump rotors to the housing. Install the pressure relief valve assembly.

5. Assemble the housing and the cover over the locating dowel pin.

6. Insert a ⅜ inch drill into the oil pump mounting hole to aid in the alignment of the housing and the cover. Tighten the cover screws to 9 ft. lbs. (12 Nm).

7. Install the oil pump drive spacer to the oil pump from the rear so the drive flat engages the pump rotor.

8. Install the oil pump over the crankshaft and loosely install the mounting screws. Hold the pump in, in the furthest position while fully tightening the screws to 7 ft. lbs. (10 Nm) plus 35 degree turn.

9. Install the front engine cover.

10. Connect the negative battery cable.

11. Check and/or refill the oil level in the crankcase. Replace the oil fil-

1. Supply tube
2. Pressure relief valve
3. Pump body
4. Pickup
5. Outer rotor
6. Inner rotor
7. Pump cover
8. "O" ring
9. Drive shaft
10. Nut
11. Bolt

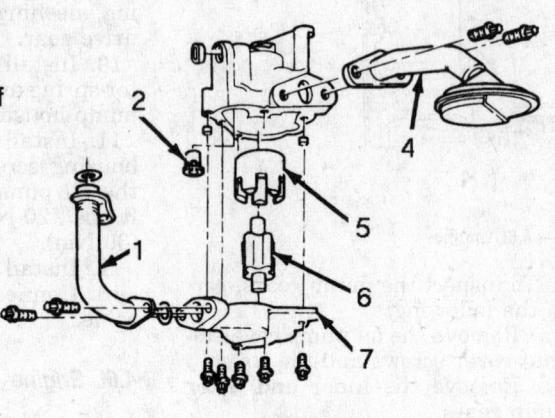

Oil pump assembly — 4.9L engine

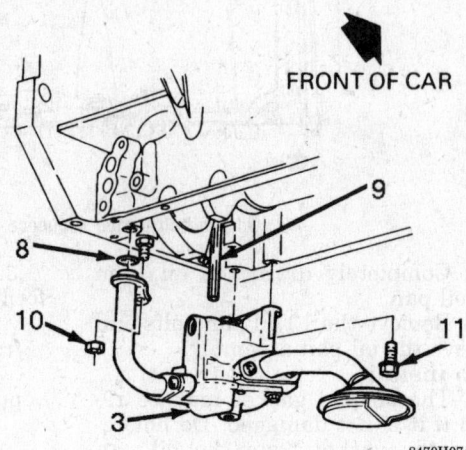

FRONT OF CAR

8470H074

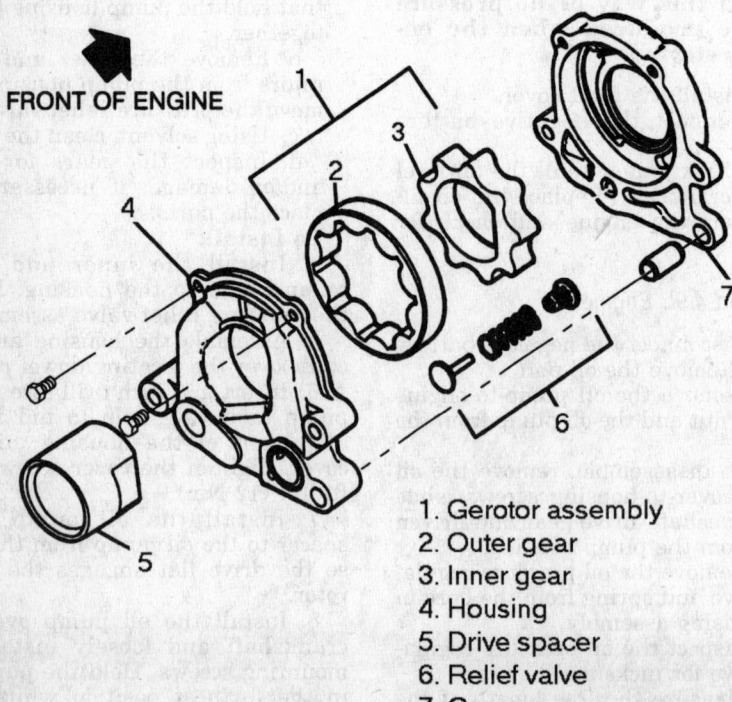

FRONT OF ENGINE

1. Gerotor assembly
2. Outer gear
3. Inner gear
4. Housing
5. Drive spacer
6. Relief valve
7. Cover

8470H076

Oil pump exploded view — Eldorado/Seville with 4.6L engine

ter. Start the engine and check for leaks.

CHECKING

1. If foreign matter is present, determine it's source.

2. Check the pump cover and housing for cracks, scoring and/or damage; if necessary, replace the housing(s).

3. Inspect the idler gear shaft for looseness in the housing; if necessary, replace the pump or timing chain, depending on the model.

4. Inspect the pressure regulator valve for scoring or sticking; if burrs are present, remove them with an oil stone.

5. Inspect the pressure regulator valve spring for loss of tension or distortion; if necessary, replace it.

6. Inspect the suction pipe for looseness, if pressed into the housing, and the screen for broken wire mesh; if necessary, replace them.

7. Inspect the gears for chipping, galling and/or wear; if necessary, replace them.

8. If the oil pump is driveshaft driven from the distributor, inspect the driveshaft and driveshaft extension for looseness and/or wear. Replace as required.

Rear Main Bearing Oil Seal

REMOVAL AND INSTALLATION

3.8L, 4.5L, 4.6L and 4.9L Engines

NOTE: To perform this procedure, use a seal removal tool and a seal installer tool.

1. Disconnect the negative battery cable. Remove the transaxle.
2. Unbolt and remove the flexplate from the rear end of the crankshaft.
3. Using a seal removal tool, remove the old seal. Thoroughly clean the seal bore of any left over seal material with a clean rag.
To install:
4. Lubricate the lip of the new seal with wheel bearing grease. Position it over the crankshaft and into the seal bore with the spring facing inside the engine.
5. Using a seal installer tool, press the seal into place. The seal must be square and flush with the block to 1mm indented.
6. Install the flexplate and tighten according to the following:
   a. On Allante and Eldorado/Seville, tighten the flexplate-to-crankshaft bolts to 70 ft. lbs. (95 Nm).

b. On the 3.8L engine, tighten the flexplate-to-crankshaft bolts to 61 ft. lbs. (82 Nm).
7. Install the transaxle.
8. Connect the negative battery cable.

AUTOMATIC TRANSAXLE

Transaxle Assembly

REMOVAL AND INSTALLATION

Riviera and Toronado

1. Disconnect the negative battery cable. Remove the air intake duct.
2. Disconnect the Throttle Valve (TV) cable from the transaxle and the throttle body. Disconnect the cruise control servo and cable.
3. Remove the exhaust pipe crossover.
4. Disconnect the shift control linkage lever from the manual shaft and the mounting bracket from the transaxle.

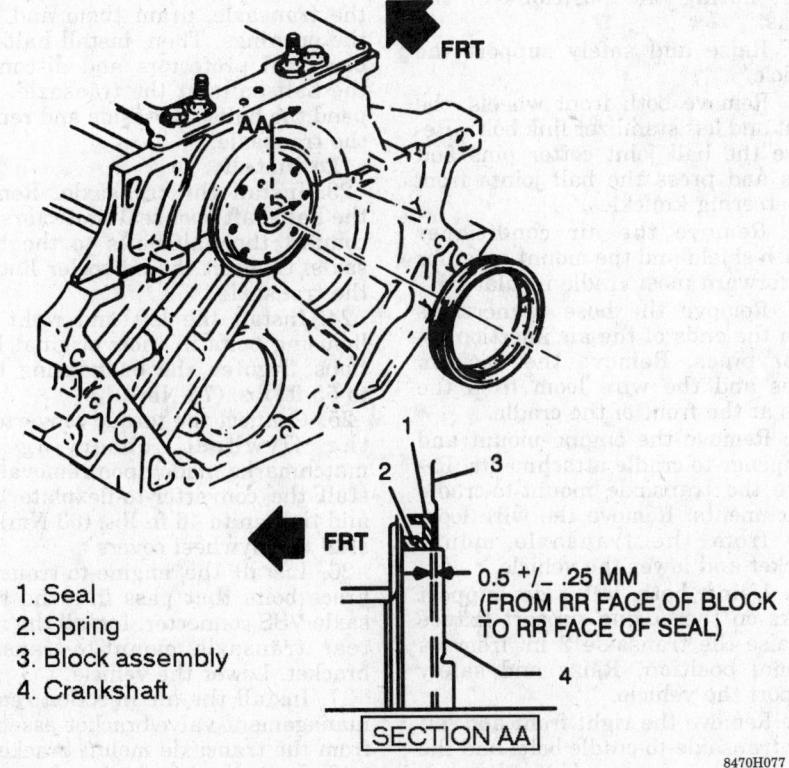

1. Seal
2. Spring
3. Block assembly
4. Crankshaft

0.5 +/_ .25 MM
(FROM RR FACE OF BLOCK
TO RR FACE OF SEAL)

SECTION AA

8470H077

Rear main seal assembly — Eldorado/Seville with 4.6L engine

5. Disconnect the electrical harness connectors from the neutral start/backup light switch, the Torque Converter Clutch (TCC) and the Vehicle Speed Sensor (VSS).
6. Disconnect the hose from the vacuum modulator.
7. Remove the upper transaxle-to-engine bolts.
8. Using the engine support fixture tool, attach it to the engine, turn the wing nuts to relieve the tension on the engine cradle and mounts.
9. Turn the steering wheel to the full left position.
10. Raise and safely support the vehicle. Remove both from wheel assemblies.
11. Using the halfshaft seal protector tool, install one on each halfshaft. Remove both front ball joint-to-steering knuckle nuts and separate the control arms from the steering knuckles.
12. Using a medium prybar, pry the halfshaft from the transaxle and support it on a wire. Do not remove the halfshaft from the steering knuckle.

NOTE: When removing the halfshaft, be careful not to damage the seal lips.

13. Remove the right rear transaxle-to-frame nuts, the left rear transaxle mount-to-transaxle bolts and the right rear transaxle mount.
14. Remove the stabilizer shaft from the left control arm.
15. Remove the flywheel cover bolts and the cover.
16. Matchmark the torque converter-to-flywheel bolts for reinstallation purposes. Remove the torque converter-to-flywheel bolts and push the torque converter back into the transaxle.
17. Remove the partial frame-to-main frame bolts, the partial frame-to-body bolts and the partial frame.
18. Disconnect and plug the oil cooler tubes from the transaxle.
19. Remove the lower transaxle-to-engine bolts.

NOTE: One bolt is located between the engine and the transaxle case and is positioned in the opposite direction.

20. Lower the transaxle from the vehicle. Be careful not to damage the hoses, lines and wiring.
To install:
21. Raise transaxle into position. Install the lower transaxle bolts.

NOTE: Make sure the opposite-facing bolt is reinstalled in the proper direction.

22. Unplug and connect the oil cooler tubes to the transaxle.

23. Install the partial frame. Secure with the partial frame-to-body and the partial frame-to-main frame bolts.

24. Install the torque converter observing matchmarks made on disassembly and secure with torque converter-to-flywheel bolts. Tighten to 46 ft. lbs. (62 Nm). Install flywheel cover and secure with flywheel cover bolts.

25. Install left control arm and stabilizer shaft.

26. Install right rear transaxle mount, right rear transaxle-to-frame nuts and the left rear transaxle mount-to-frame nuts.

27. Install halfshaft into transaxle.

NOTE: When installing half-shafts, be sure not to damage seals.

28. Connect the control arms to the transaxle and secure with both front ball joint-to-steering knuckle nuts.

29. Install both wheel and tire assemblies.

30. Lower the vehicle.

31. Remove engine support fixture tool.

32. Install the upper transaxle-to-engine bolts.

33. Connect vacuum modulator hose.

34. Connect electrical harness connectors to neutral start/backup light switch, Torque Converter Clutch (TCC) and the Vehicle Speed Sensor (VSS).

35. Connect shift control linkage lever to manual shaft and mounting bracket to transaxle.

36. Install exhaust crossover pipe.

37. Connect Throttle Valve (TV) cable to the transaxle and throttle body. Connect cruise control servo.

38. Install air intake duct. Connect negative battery cable.

39. Start engine and check for transaxle leaks. Refill as necessary.

Allante, Eldorado and Seville With 4.5L and 4.9L Engines

1. Disconnect the negative battery cable. Remove the air cleaner assembly. Disconnect the transaxle throttle valve cable.

2. Remove the cruise control servo and bracket assembly. Disconnect the electrical connectors going to the distributor, oil pressure sending unit and transaxle.

3. Remove the bracket for the engine oil cooler lines.

4. Remove the shift linkage bracket from the transaxle and the

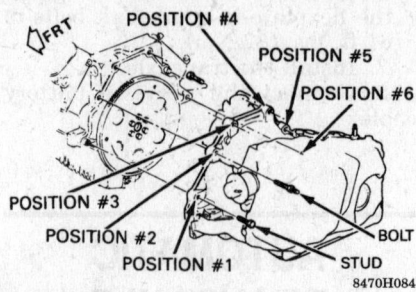

Transaxle case to engine mounting — Eldorado and Seville with 4.9L engine

manual shift lever from the manual shift shaft; leave the cable attached to the lever and bracket.

5. Remove the fuel line bracket and disconnect the neutral safety switch connector.

6. Remove the vacuum modulator.

7. Remove the throttle valve cable support bracket and engine oil cooler line bracket. Remove the bellhousing bolts except the left and right side bolts; note the bolt lengths and positions.

8. Remove the air injection reactor crossover pipe fitting and reposition the pipe. Remove the radiator hose bracket and transaxle mount-to-bracket nuts.

9. Install an engine support fixture, noting the positions of the hooks.

10. Raise and safely support the vehicle.

11. Remove both front wheels, the right and left stabilizer link bolts. Remove the ball joint cotter pins and nuts and press the ball joints from the steering knuckles.

12. Remove the air conditioner splash shield and the mount cover for the forward most cradle insulator.

13. Remove the hose connections from the ends of the air injection reactor pipes. Remove the vacuum hoses and the wire loom from the clips at the front of the cradle.

14. Remove the engine mount and dampener-to-cradle attachments. Remove the transaxle mount-to-cradle attachments. Remove the wire loom clip from the transaxle mount bracket and lower the vehicle.

15. Using both left side support hooks on the engine support fixture to raise the transaxle 2 in. from its normal position. Raise and safely support the vehicle.

16. Remove the right front and left rear transaxle-to-cradle bolts and the left stabilizer mount bolts. Remove the foremost cradle mount insulator

bolt and the left cradle member, separate the right front corner 1st.

17. Remove the air injection reactor management valve/bracket assembly from the transaxle mount bracket and reposition the bracket to the transaxle stud bolts.

18. Lower the vehicle. Lower the transaxle to its normal position to gain access to the transaxle mounting bracket. Remove the mounting bracket.

19. Raise and safely support the vehicle. Remove the right rear transaxle mount-to-transaxle bracket. Remove the engine-to-transaxle brace bolts that pass into the transaxle VSS connector.

20. Mark the relationship between torque converter and flexplate for reassembly in the same position. Remove the flywheel covers, then, remove the torque converter bolts, rotating the crankshaft with a socket wrench as necessary to gain access. Position a jack under the transaxle to support it.

21. Remove the left and right bellhousing bolts; note the bolt lengths and positions.

NOTE: Access may be gained through the right wheelhouse opening to remove the bolt on the right side; use a 3 foot long socket extension to reach it.

22. Disconnect the oil cooler lines at the transaxle, drain them and plug the openings. Then, install halfshaft boot seal protectors and disconnect the halfshafts at the transaxle. Suspend the halfshafts aside and remove the transaxle.

To install:

23. Install the transaxle. Remove the halfshaft boot seal protectors and connect the halfshafts to the transaxle. Connect the oil cooler lines at the transaxle.

24. Install the left and right bellhousing bolts in their original locations. Tighten the bellhousing bolts to 55 ft. lbs. (75 Nm).

25. Connect the torque converter to the flywheel, observing the matchmarks made upon removal. Install the converter-to-flexplate bolts and tighten to 46 ft. lbs. (63 Nm). Install the flywheel covers.

26. Install the engine-to-transaxle brace bolts that pass into the transaxle VSS connector. Install the right rear transaxle mount-to-transaxle bracket. Lower the vehicle.

27. Install the air injection reactor management valve/bracket assembly from the transaxle mount bracket.

28. Install the foremost cradle mount insulator bolt and the left cra-

dle member. Install the right front and left rear transaxle-to-cradle bolts and the left stabilizer mount bolts.

29. Install the engine mount and dampener-to-cradle attachments. Install the transaxle mount-to-cradle attachments. Install the wire loom clip from the transaxle mount bracket and lower the vehicle.

30. Install the hose connections to the ends of the AIR pipes. Install the vacuum hoses and the wire loom to the clips at the front of the cradle.

31. Install the air conditioner splash shield and the mount cover for the forward most cradle insulator.

32. Install the ball joint cotter pins and nuts and press the ball joints to the steering knuckles. Tighten the ball joint nuts to 81 ft. lbs. (110 Nm). Install both front wheels, the right and left stabilizer link bolts.

33. Lower the vehicle.

34. Remove the engine support fixture.

35. Install the air injection reactor crossover pipe fitting and reposition the pipe. Install the radiator hose bracket and transaxle mount-to-bracket nuts.

36. Install the throttle valve cable support bracket and engine oil cooler line bracket. Install the bellhousing bolts. Tighten the bellhousing bolts to 55 ft. lbs. (75 Nm).

37. Install the vacuum modulator.

38. Install the fuel line bracket and connect the neutral safety switch connector.

39. Install the shift linkage bracket to the transaxle and the manual shift lever to the manual shift shaft.

40. Install the bracket for the engine oil cooler lines.

41. Install the cruise control servo and bracket assembly. Connect the electrical connectors going to the distributor, oil pressure sending unit and transaxle.

42. Install the air cleaner assembly. Disconnect the transaxle throttle valve cable. Connect the negative battery cable.

43. Adjust the transaxle valve cable and the shift linkage. Refill the transaxle to the proper level. Start engine and allow to come to normal operating temperature. Check transaxle fluid level and adjust as necessary.

Allante, Seville and Eldorado with 4.6L Engine

1. Disconnect the negative battery cable.

2. Remove the air cleaner and disconnect the range control cable and bracket at the transaxle.

3. Disconnect the manual shaft lever and the transaxle range switch.

4. Install an engine support fixture tool J-28467 or equivalent, to the vehicle. Load the fixture so it begins to take the weight off the engine mounts.

5. Raise and safely support the vehicle.

6. Remove both front tires and wheels and remove both wheel opening splash shields.

7. Disconnect the electrical connectors at the 2 transaxle connectors, at the speed sensor connector and at the power steering gear connector.

8. Disconnect and plug the power steering pressure hose and return hose at the steering gear and the auxiliary cooler.

9. Rotate the steering shaft so the steering stub shaft clamp bolt is accessible from the left wheel opening. Remove the clamp bolt and disconnect the shaft from the steering gear.

NOTE: Do not turn the steering wheel after disconnecting the shaft from the steering gear. If the wheel is turned the SRS system may be disturbed.

10. Disconnect both front suspension sensors from the lower control arms and move them aside.

11. Remove both stabilizer links from the steering knuckles.

12. Remove the tie rod cotter pins and nuts and separate the tie rods from the steering knuckles.

13. Remove the lower ball joint cotter pins and nuts and separate the ball joints from the steering knuckles.

14. Remove the drive axle nuts and separate the drive axles from the hubs.

15. Remove the drive axles from the transaxle.

16. Remove the splash shield from the frame and remove the ABS modulator from the bracket and support it.

17. Remove the engine oil pan to transaxle bracket and remove the torque converter cover.

18. Mark the flywheel-to-converter positioning for assembly purposes. Remove the flywheel-to-converter bolts.

19. Disconnect the transaxle cooler lines from the transaxle.

20. Remove the left and right transaxle mount nuts and the right engine mount nuts at the frame.

21. Support the frame and remove the 6 frame mount bolts.

22. Lower the frame and/or raise the vehicle with steering gear intact.

23. Remove the left and right transaxle mounts and brackets from the transaxle.

24. Remove the engine-to-transaxle bracket.

25. Install a transmission jack to the transaxle.

26. Remove the engine-to-transaxle bolts and lower the transaxle out of the vehicle.

To install:

27. Raise the transmission jack until the transaxle is in place.

28. Install the engine to transaxle bolts and tighten the bolts to 35 ft. lbs. (47 Nm).

29. Install the right and left engine-to-transaxle brackets and mounts and tighten the bolts and nuts to 35 ft. lbs. (47 Nm).

30. Raise the frame and/or lower the vehicle while aligning the studs and the bolt holes.

31. Install the left side No. 2 bolt into the body and then the No. 1 bolt.

32. Install the remaining bolts and tighten all to 74 ft. lbs. (100 Nm).

33. Install the right and left transaxle mount nuts and right engine mount nuts at the frame. Torque the nuts to 35 ft. lbs. (47 Nm).

34. Connect the transaxle cooler pipe fittings to the transaxle. Tighten the fittings to 16 ft. lbs. (22 Nm).

35. Align the flywheel to it's proper position and tighten the flywheel-to-converter bolts to 35 ft. lbs. (47 Nm).

36. Install the torque converter cover and tighten the bolt to 106 in. lbs. (12 Nm).

37. Install the engine oil pan-to-transaxle bracket and tighten the bolts to 35 ft. lbs. (47 Nm).

38. Install the ABS modulator to the bracket and install the A/C splash shield to the frame.

39. Install both drive axles into the transaxle and into the hubs. Tighten both drive axle nuts to 110 ft. lbs. (145 Nm).

40. Install both lower ball joints into the steering knuckles and install both joint nuts and cotter pins.

41. Install both tie rods into the steering knuckles and install both tie rod nuts and cotter pins.

42. Install both stabilizer links to the steering knuckles and tighten the nuts to 49 ft. lbs. (65 Nm).

43. Connect both front suspension position sensors to the lower control arms.

44. Connect the steering intermediate shaft to the steering gear install the clamp bolt. Tighten the bolt to 35 ft. lbs. (47 Nm).

45. Connect the power steering return and pressure hoses. Tighten the pressure fitting to 20 ft. lbs. (27 Nm).

46. Connect the electrical connectors for the transaxle (2), for the speed sensor and for the power steering gear.

47. Install both front wheel shields and install both front wheels.

48. Lower the vehicle and remove the engine support fixture.

49. Connect the manual shaft lever and neutral start switch.

50. Adjust the transaxle range switch as needed.

51. Connect the range control cable and bracket at the transaxle. Tighten the bolts to 106 in. lbs. (12 Nm).

52. Install the air cleaner and connect the negative battery cable.

53. Check front suspension alignment and reset transaxle adapts.

54. Reset the transaxle oil life indicator.

SHIFT LINKAGE ADJUSTMENT

440-T4 Transaxle

1. Place the console shift lever in the **N** position.

2. Loosen the cable end pin nut at the transaxle lever arm.

3. Position the transaxle linkage lever arm in **N**. Locate the neutral position by rotating the transaxle lever arm clockwise from the **P** position, through **R** to **N**. Verify the console shift lever is in **N**.

4. Hold the shift lever in **N** and tighten the cable end pin nut. Tighten the nut to 20 ft. lbs. (27 Nm).

4T60 and 4T60E Transaxles

1. Move the shift lever to the **N** position. Neutral can be found by rotating the selector shaft clockwise from **P** through **R** to **N**.

2. Place the shift control assembly in **N**.

3. Push the cable adjuster tab to adjust the cable in the cable mounting bracket.

4T80E Transaxle

1. Pry the lock button on the range control cable to the unlocked position.

2. Place the transaxle range control in the **N** position.

3. Move the transaxle manual shaft into the **N** position.

4. Depress the lock button on the range control cable into the locked position.

THROTTLE LINKAGE ADJUSTMENT

1. With the engine stopped, depress the accelerator pedal fully and have an assistant check the throttle body for wide open throttle.

NOTE: If the throttle body cannot achieve full throttle, repair the accelerator system.

2. At the engine end of the TV cable, depress and hold-down the metal readjust tab, move the slider until it stops against the fitting and release the readjustment tab.

3. Rotate the throttle lever, by hand, to it's full travel position.

4. The slider must move, ratchet, toward the lever when the lever is rotated to it's full travel position.

DRIVE AXLE

Halfshaft

REMOVAL AND INSTALLATION

1. Remove the hub nut and washer.

2. Raise and safely support the vehicle. Remove the front wheel.

3. Remove the brake caliper and rotor.

4. Remove the stabilizer link from the control arm.

5. Remove the tie rod end-to-steering knuckle cotter pin and nut. Using a ball joint removal tool, separate the tie rod end from the steering knuckle.

6. Remove the lower ball joint-to-steering knuckle cotter pin and nut. Using a ball joint removal tool, separate the lower ball joint from the steering knuckle.

7. Using a prybar and a wooden block, pry the halfshaft from the transaxle and suspend it on a wire.

NOTE: When removing the halfshaft, be careful not to allow the shaft to drop causing damage to the CV-joints. Do not allow the halfshaft to overextended because the Tri-Pot (S-plan) joint can disengage from the bearing blocks.

8. Using the halfshaft removal tool, press the halfshaft from the

steering knuckle hub and remove it from the vehicle.

NOTE: If equipped with an anti-lock brake system, be careful not to damage the toothed sensor ring (on halfshaft) and the wheel speed sensor (on steering knuckle).

To install:

9. Install the drive axle into the transaxle. Verify that the drive axle snapring is properly seated by grasping the housing and pulling outboard.

NOTE: Do not pull on the drive axle.

10. Install the outer end of the drive axle into the hub and bearing assembly.

11. Install the lower ball joint stud to the steering knuckle.

12. Install the washer and new torque prevailing nut. Tighten to 183 ft. lbs. (245 Nm).

NOTE: To keep the halfshaft from turning, place a small drift pin into one of the rotor's slots.

13. Install the stabilizer link to the control arm.

14. Install the brake caliper and rotor.

15. Install the front wheel. Lower the vehicle

CV-Boot

REPLACEMENT

Inner (Inboard)

1. Disconnect the negative battery cable.

2. Raise and safely support the vehicle. Remove the front wheels.

3. Remove the outer boot assembly.

4. Remove the boot retaining clamps and the spacer ring.

5. Slide the halfshaft and the spider bearing assembly out of the tripot housing. Install the spider retainer onto the spider bearing assembly.

6. Remove the spider assembly and the boot from the halfshaft.

To install:

7. Pack the new boot with grease. Install the boot and spider assembly to the halfshaft.

8. Install the spider retainer onto the spider bearing assembly. Slide the halfshaft and the spider bearing assembly into the tri-pot housing.

9. Install the boot retaining clamps and the spacer ring.

10. Install the outer boot assembly.

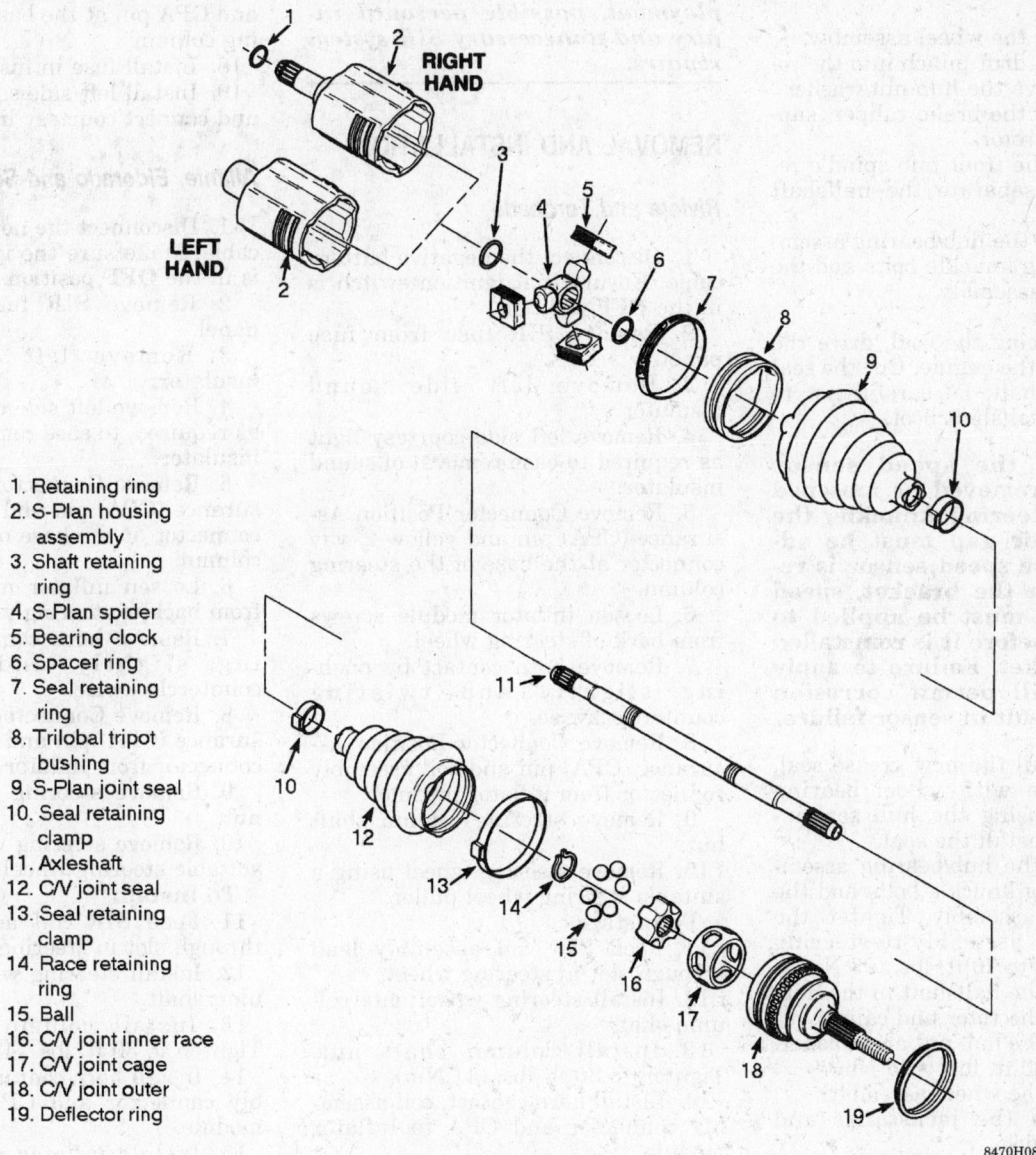

1. Retaining ring
2. S-Plan housing assembly
3. Shaft retaining ring
4. S-Plan spider
5. Bearing clock
6. Spacer ring
7. Seal retaining ring
8. Trilobal tripot bushing
9. S-Plan joint seal
10. Seal retaining clamp
11. Axleshaft
12. C/V joint seal
13. Seal retaining clamp
14. Race retaining ring
15. Ball
16. C/V joint inner race
17. C/V joint cage
18. C/V joint outer
19. Deflector ring

8470H089

Drive axle exploded view

11. Install the front wheels. Lower the vehicle.

12. Connect the negative battery cable.

Outer (Outboard)

1. Disconnect the negative battery cable.

2. Raise and safely support the vehicle. Remove the front wheels.

3. Remove the brake caliper and support on a wire. Remove the rotor.

4. Slide the outer CV-joint assembly off the halfshaft.

5. Remove the bearing retaining ring, the boot retainer, the clamp and the outer boot.

To install:

6. Pack the new boot with grease. Install the bearing retaining ring, the boot retainer, the clamp and the outer boot.

7. Slide the outer CV-joint assembly onto the halfshaft.

8. Install the rotor. Install the brake caliper.

9. Install the front wheels.

10. Connect the negative battery cable.

Front Wheel Hub, Spindle and Bearing

NOTE: The bearings are preadjusted and require no lubrication, maintenance or adjustment. There are darkened areas on the bearing assembly which are the result of a heat treating process.

REMOVAL AND INSTALLATION

1. Raise and safely support the vehicle.

2. Place jackstands under the cradle and lower the vehicle slightly so

the weight of the vehicle rests on the jackstands and not on the control arms.

3. Remove the wheel assembly.

4. Insert a drift punch into the rotor and remove the hub nut/washer.

5. Remove the brake caliper, support and the rotor.

6. Using the front hub spindle remover tool, separate the halfshaft from the hub.

7. Remove the hub/bearing assembly-to-steering knuckle bolts and the hub/bearing assembly.

To install:

8. If replacing the seal, drive the seal towards the engine. Cut the seal off the halfshaft; be careful not to damage the halfshaft boot.

NOTE: If the speed sensor bracket is removed or loosened from the steering knuckle, the speed sensor gap must be adjusted. If the speed sensor is removed from the bracket, speed sensor wax must be applied to the sensor before it is reinstalled in the bracket. Failure to apply the wax will permit corrosion and may result in sensor failure.

9. To install the new grease seal, lubricate the with wheel bearing grease and using the hub seal installer tool, install the seal.

10. Install the hub/bearing assembly-to-steering knuckle bolts and the hub/bearing assembly. Tighten the hub/bearing assembly-to-steering knuckle bolts to 70 ft. lbs. (95 Nm).

11. Install the halfshaft to the hub.

12. Install the rotor and caliper.

13. Install the hub nut and washer. Tighten to 183 ft. lbs. (245 Nm).

14. Install the wheel assembly.

15. Remove the jackstands and lower the vehicle.

STEERING

Steering Wheel

— CAUTION —

Some vehicles are equipped with the Supplemental Inflatable Restraint (SIR) or air bag system. The SIR system must be disabled before performing service on or around SIR system components, steering column, instrument panel components, wiring and sensors. Failure to follow safety and disabling procedures could result in accidental air bag deployment, possible personal injury and unnecessary SIR system repairs.

REMOVAL AND INSTALLATION

Riviera and Toronado

1. Disconnect the negative battery cable. Ensure that ignition switch is in the **OFF** position.

2. Remove SIR fuse from fuse panel.

3. Remove left side sound insulator.

4. Remove left side courtesy light as required to ease removal of sound insulator.

5. Remove Connector Position Assurance (CPA) pin and yellow 2 way connector at the base of the steering column.

6. Loosen inflator module screws from back of steering wheel.

7. Remove horn contact by pushing slightly and twisting counterclockwise.

8. Remove Connector Position Assurance (CPA) pin and coil assembly connector from inflator module.

9. Remove steering column shaft nut.

10. Remove steering wheel using a suitable steering wheel puller.

To install:

11. Feed SIR coil assembly lead through slot in steering wheel.

12. Install steering wheel onto column shaft.

13. Install column shaft nut. Tighten to 30 ft. lbs. (41 Nm).

14. Install horn contact, coil assembly connector and CPA to inflator module.

15. Install inflator module onto steering wheel, securing with 4 screws behind steering wheel. Tighten to 27 inch lbs. (3 Nm).

16. Connect negative battery cable.

17. Connect yellow 2 way connector and CPA pin at the base of the steering column.

18. Install fuse in fuse panel.

19. Install left side sound insulator and connect courtesy light.

Allante, Eldorado and Seville

1. Disconnect the negative battery cable. Make sure the ignition switch is in the **OFF** position.

2. Remove SIR fuse from fuse panel.

3. Remove left side sound insulator.

4. Remove left side courtesy light, as required, to ease removal of sound insulator.

5. Remove Connector Position Assurance (CPA) pin and yellow 2 way connector at the base of the steering column.

6. Loosen inflator module screws from back of steering wheel.

7. Remove horn contact by pushing slightly and twisting counterclockwise.

8. Remove Connector Position Assurance (CPA) pin and coil assembly connector from inflator module.

9. Remove steering column shaft nut.

10. Remove steering wheel using a suitable steering wheel puller.

To install:

11. Feed SIR coil assembly lead through slot in steering wheel.

12. Install steering wheel onto column shaft.

13. Install column shaft nut. Tighten to 30 ft. lbs. (41 Nm).

14. Install horn contact, coil assembly connector and CPA to inflator module.

15. Install inflator module onto steering wheel, securing with 4 screws behind steering wheel. Tighten to 27 inch lbs. (3 Nm).

16. Connect negative battery cable.

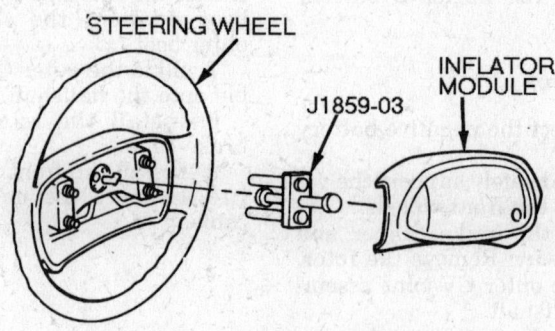

Steering wheel removal — Riviera shown

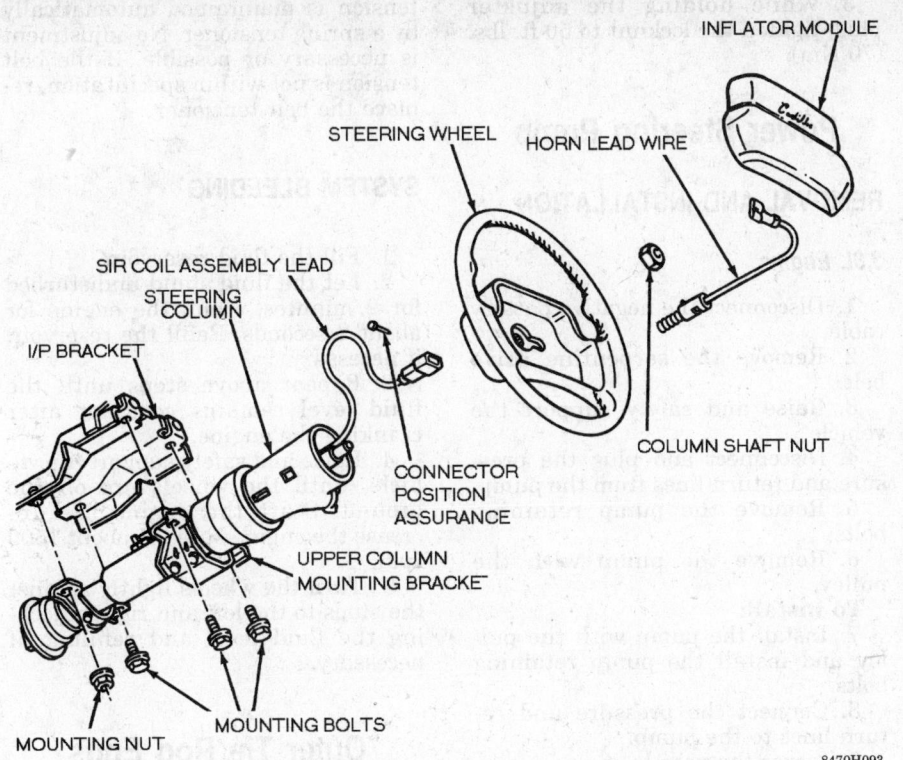

INFLATOR MODULE

STEERING WHEEL

HORN LEAD WIRE

SIR COIL ASSEMBLY LEAD

STEERING COLUMN

I/P BRACKET

CONNECTOR POSITION ASSURANCE

COLUMN SHAFT NUT

UPPER COLUMN MOUNTING BRACKET

MOUNTING NUT

MOUNTING BOLTS

8470H093

Steering wheel and column assembly with SIR (Air bag) — 1993 Allante shown

17. Connect yellow 2 way connector and CPA pin at the base of the steering column.

18. Install fuse in fuse panel.

19. Install left side sound insulator and connect courtesy light, if removed.

Steering Column

REMOVAL AND INSTALLATION

Riviera and Toronado

1. Disconnect the negative battery cable.

2. Remove the left side sound insulator.

3. Remove the steering column trim cover.

4. Label and disconnect the electrical connectors from the steering column. Remove the wiring harness protector.

5. Remove the park lock cable from the ignition switch, if equipped.

6. Remove the lower column mounting bolts.

NOTE: On the Toronado, remove the pinch bolt.

7. If equipped with a column shifter, disconnect the shift linkage at the column.

8. Remove the upper steering column-to-instrument panel bolts and the column assembly from the vehicle.

To install:

9. Install the column assembly to the vehicle. Install the upper steering column-to-instrument panel bolts. Install the lower steering column-to-instrument panel bolts. Tighten the column bolts to 20 ft. lbs. (27 Nm).

NOTE: Failure to install the upper bolts first may result in a cracked lower bearing casting.

10. If equipped with a column shifter, connect the shift linkage to the column.

11. Install the lower column mounting bolts.

12. On the Toronado, install the pinch bolt.

13. Install the park lock cable to the ignition switch, if equipped.

14. Connect the electrical connectors to the steering column. Install the wiring harness protector.

15. Install the steering column trim cover.

16. Install the left side sound insulator.

17. Connect the negative battery cable.

Allante, Eldorado and Seville

1. Disconnect the negative battery cable. Ensure that ignition switch is in the **OFF** position.

2. Remove SIR fuse from fuse panel.

3. Remove left side sound insulator.

4. Remove left side courtesy light, as required, to ease removal of sound insulator.

5. Remove Connector Position Assurance (CPA) pin and yellow 2 way connector at the base of the steering column.

6. On Eldorado and Seville, remove center trim plate and instrument panel steering column reinforcing plate.

7. Remove knee bolster.

8. Disconnect ignition wiring connector and multi-function connector.

9. Remove pinch bolt from intermediate shaft.

10. Remove lower support bracket from vehicle. Remove upper column support from instrument panel and remove column from vehicle.

To install:

11. Install steering column into vehicle; support at upper bracket with 2 bolts. Do not tighten fully at this time.

12. Install column lower support bracket to vehicle. Do not tighten fully at this time.

13. Install steering column intermediate shaft to steering rack.

14. Install pinch bolt to intermediate shaft. Tighten pinch bolt and nut to 35 ft. lbs. (47 Nm). Tighten upper and lower column support nut and bolts to 20 ft. lbs. (27 Nm). Tighten lower support bracket-to-column screws to 12 ft. lbs. (16 Nm).

15. Connect multi-function switch connector and ignition wiring connector.

16. On Eldorado and Seville, install instrument panel steering column reinforcement plate and center trim plate.

17. Install knee bolster.

18. Connect negative battery cable.

19. Connect yellow 2 way connector and CPA pin at the base of the steering column.

20. Install fuse in fuse panel.

21. Install left side sound insulator and connect courtesy light, if removed.

Power Rack and Pinion

REMOVAL AND INSTALLATION

1. Disconnect the negative battery cable.
2. Raise and safely support the vehicle.
3. Remove both front tire and wheel assemblies.
4. Remove the intermediate shaft lower pinch bolt.
5. Remove the tie rod ends from the steering knuckles.
6. Remove the line retainer. Disconnect and plug the return and pressure hose from the steering rack and pinion.
7. Label and disconnect the electrical connection at the idle speed power steering switch.
8. Remove the rack and pinion assembly retaining bolts. Remove the rack and pinion assembly.

To install:

9. Install the rack and pinion assembly. Install the rack and pinion assembly attaching bolts. Tighten to 50 ft. lbs. (68 Nm).
10. Connect the electrical connection to the idle speed power steering switch.
11. Connect the return and pressure hose to the steering rack and pinion assembly. Install the line retainer.
12. Install the tie rod ends to the steering knuckles. Tighten nuts to 33 ft. lbs. (45 Nm).
13. Install the intermediate shaft lower pinch bolt. Tighten to 30 ft. lbs. (41 Nm).
14. Install both front tire and wheel assemblies.
15. Lower the vehicle.
16. Connect the negative battery cable.
17. Bleed the power steering system and check for leaks.

ADJUSTMENT

Rack Bearing Preload

NOTE: Make adjustment with front wheels raised and steering wheel centered. Be sure to check returnability of steering wheel to center after adjustment.

1. Disconnect the negative battery cable. Loosen the adjuster plug locknut.
2. Turn the adjuster plug clockwise until it bottoms and back it off 50–70 degrees.

3. While holding the adjuster plug, tighten the locknut to 50 ft. lbs. (70 Nm).

Power Steering Pump

REMOVAL AND INSTALLATION

3.8L Engine

1. Disconnect the negative battery cable.
2. Remove the serpentine drive belt.
3. Raise and safely support the vehicle.
4. Disconnect and plug the pressure and return lines from the pump.
5. Remove the pump retaining bolts.
6. Remove the pump with the pulley.

To install:

7. Install the pump with the pulley and install the pump retaining bolts.
8. Connect the pressure and return lines to the pump.
9. Lower the vehicle.
10. Install the serpentine drive belt.
11. Connect the negative battery cable.
12. Refill the power steering pump reservoir. Bleed the power steering system.

4.5L, 4.6L and 4.9L Engines

1. Disconnect the negative battery cable.
2. Remove the serpentine drive belt, the power steering pump pulley.
3. Disconnect and plug the high pressure and feed lines from the pump.
4. Remove the power steering pump-to-bracket bolts and the pump.

To install:

5. Install the pump and the power steering pump-to-bracket bolts. Tighten to 30 ft. lbs. (41 Nm).
6. Connect the high pressure and feed lines to the pump.
7. Install the power steering pump pulley and the serpentine drive belt.
8. Connect the negative battery cable.
9. Refill the power steering pump reservoir. Bleed the power steering system.

BELT ADJUSTMENT

All accessories are driven by a single serpentine belt. The serpentine belt tension is maintained automatically by a spring tensioner. No adjustment is necessary or possible. If the belt tension is not within specification, replace the belt tensioner.

SYSTEM BLEEDING

1. Fill the fluid reservoir.
2. Let the fluid stand undisturbed for 2 minutes, crank the engine for about 2 seconds. Refill the reservoir, if necessary.
3. Repeat above steps until the fluid level remains constant after cranking the engine.
4. Raise and safely support the vehicle, until the wheels are off the ground. Start the engine and increase the engine speed to about 1500 rpm.
5. Turn the wheels lightly against the stops to the left and right, checking the fluid level and refilling, if necessary.

Outer Tie Rod Ends

REMOVAL AND INSTALLATION

1. Disconnect the negative battery cable.
2. Raise and safely support the vehicle.
3. Remove cotter pin and hex slotted nut from outer tie rod assembly. Loosen jam nut.
4. Disconnect outer tie rod from steering knuckle using a suitable steering linkage separator tool.
5. Remove outer tie rod from inner tie rod.

To install:

6. Install outer tie rod assembly to inner tie rod. Do not tighten jam nut.
7. Connect outer tie rod to steering knuckle, hex slotted nut to outer tie rod stud. Tighten hex slotted nut to 35 ft. lbs. (50 Nm). Check for cotter pin slot alignment. Maximum torque is 45 ft. lbs. (60 Nm) to align slot. Do not back off for cotter pin insertion.
8. Install cotter pin into hole in tie rod stud.
9. Check toe and adjust by turning inner tie rod.

NOTE: Be sure rack and pinion boot is not twisted or puckered during toe adjustment.

10. Tighten jam nut against outer tie rod to 50 ft. lbs. (70 Nm).

BRAKES

Master Cylinder

REMOVAL AND INSTALLATION

1. Disconnect the negative battery cable.
2. If equipped with ABS, relieve the brake system pressure.
3. If equipped with a fluid level sensor, disconnect the electrical connector.
4. Disconnect and plug hydraulic lines. Drain the master cylinder.
5. Remove the master cylinder-to-power brake booster nuts and the master cylinder.
To install:
6. Install the master cylinder. Install the master cylinder-to-power brake booster nuts. Tighten the mounting nuts to 26 ft. lbs. (35 Nm).
7. Connect the hydraulic lines to the master cylinder.
8. If equipped with a fluid level sensor, connect the electrical connector.
9. Refill the master cylinder and bleed the system.
10. Connect the negative battery cable.

Proportioning Valve

REMOVAL AND INSTALLATION

Diagonal Split System

NOTE: Individual proportioning valves are installed on the master cylinder outlets.

1. Disconnect the negative battery cable. Disconnect and plug the fluid lines from the proportioning valves.
2. Remove the proportioning valves and O-rings from the master cylinder.
To install:
3. Replace the O-rings and install the proportioning valves. Tighten the proportioning valve-to-master cylinder to 18–30 ft. lbs. (24–41 Nm). Refill the master cylinder reservoir with clean brake fluid. Bleed the brake system.

Teves® Anti-lock System

The Teves system uses a single proportioning valve located near the left

rear wheel. The valve is not to be disassembled.
1. Disconnect the negative battery cable. Turn the ignition switch **OFF** throughout this procedure.
2. Using at least 50 lbs. (68 Nm) pressure on the brake pedal, depress the pedal at least 25 times; a noticeable change in pedal pressure will be noticed when the accumulator is discharged.
3. Disconnect the fluid lines from the proportioning valve and the valve from the vehicle.
To install:
4. Install the new proportioning valve and connect the brake fluid lines.
5. Bleed the brake system.
6. Connect the negative battery cable.

Bosch III® System

The Bosch III system uses individual proportioning valves installed to the master cylinder. The valves are not to be disassembled.
1. Disconnect the negative battery cable. Turn the ignition switch **OFF** throughout this procedure.
2. Using at least 50 lbs. pressure on the brake pedal, depress the pedal at least 25 times; a noticeable change in pedal pressure will be noticed when the accumulator is discharged.
3. Disconnect and plug the fluid line(s) from the proportioning valve(s).
4. Remove the proportioning valve(s) from the hydraulic unit.
To install:
5. Install the proportioning valve(s) to the hydraulic unit. Tighten the proportioning valve(s)-to-hydraulic unit to 11 ft. lbs. (15 Nm).
6. Connect the fluid line(s) to the proportioning valve(s).
7. Bleed the brake system.
8. Connect the negative battery cable.

Bosch 2U® Anti-lock System

The Bosch 2U system uses 2 proportioning valves located in-line on both sides of the vehicle. The valve is not to be disassembled.
1. Disconnect the negative battery cable. Turn the ignition switch **OFF** throughout this procedure.
2. Using at least 50 lbs. (68 Nm) pressure on the brake pedal, depress the pedal at least 25 times; a noticeable change in pedal pressure will be noticed when the accumulator is discharged.

3. Disconnect the fluid lines from the proportioning valves and the valves from the vehicle.
To install:
4. Install the new proportioning valves and connect the brake fluid lines.
5. Bleed the brake system.
6. Connect the negative battery cable.

Power Brake Booster

REMOVAL AND INSTALLATION

1. Disconnect the negative battery cable. Remove the master cylinder-to-power booster nuts and move the master cylinder aside.
2. From inside the vehicle, detach the brake pushrod from the brake pedal.
3. Detach the vacuum hose at the vacuum cylinder.
4. Remove the nuts from the mounting studs which hold the unit to the dash panel. Remove the unit and clean it prior to installation.
To install:
5. Install the power brake booster and nuts to the mounting studs which hold the unit to the dash panel. Tighten the power booster-to-cowl nuts to 28 ft. lbs. (38 Nm).
6. Attach the vacuum hose to the vacuum cylinder.
7. From inside the vehicle, attach the brake pushrod to the brake pedal.
8. Install the master cylinder and master cylinder-to-power booster nuts. Tighten the master cylinder-to-power booster nuts to 28 ft. lbs. (38 Nm).
9. Connect the negative battery cable.
10. Bleed the brake system.

Brake Caliper

REMOVAL AND INSTALLATION

Front

1. Remove ⅔ of brake fluid from master cylinder assembly.
2. Raise and safely support the vehicle. Mark the relationship of the wheel to axle flange.
3. Remove wheel. Reinstall 2 wheel nuts to retain rotor.
4. Remove bolt attaching inlet fitting. Plug openings in caliper and pipe to prevent fluid loss and contamination.
5. Remove mounting bolts.
6. Remove caliper from rotor and mounting bracket.

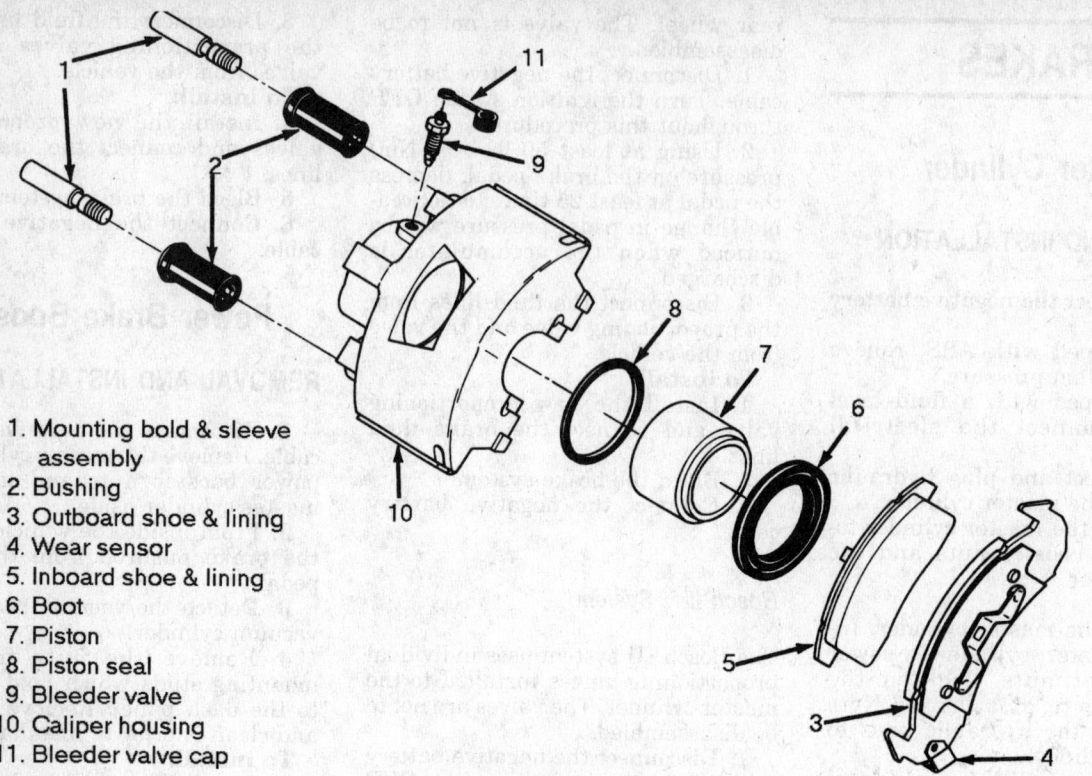

1. Mounting bold & sleeve assembly
2. Bushing
3. Outboard shoe & lining
4. Wear sensor
5. Inboard shoe & lining
6. Boot
7. Piston
8. Piston seal
9. Bleeder valve
10. Caliper housing
11. Bleeder valve cap

8470H099

Front brake caliper assembly — Riviera shown

To install:

7. Install caliper over rotor in mounting bracket. Ensure that the bolt boots are in place.

8. Lubricate entire shaft of mounting bolts with silicone grease. Tighten the mounting bolts to 38 ft. lbs. (51 Nm).

9. Connect inlet fitting and tighten fitting to 33 ft. lbs. (45 Nm).

10. Remove wheel nuts securing rotor to hub. Install wheels and tires, aligning previous marks.

11. Lower vehicle.

12. Tighten wheel nuts to 100 ft. lbs. (140 Nm).

13. Fill master cylinder to proper level with clean brake fluid.

14. Bleed caliper.

Rear

1. Raise and safely support the vehicle.

2. Remove wheel from the vehicle.

3. Disconnect the brake hose from the caliper. Plug the brake hose and the caliper.

4. Disconnect the parking brake cable from the lever.

5. Remove the bolt and washer that attach the cable support bracket to the caliper.

6. Remove the sleeve bolt and remove the caliper by sliding off the pin.

To install:

7. Install caliper to original position. Make sure the boot and brake pads are in the proper position.

8. Install the sleeve bolt and tighten the bolt 20 ft. lbs. (27 Nm).

9. Install the cable support bracket and tighten the bolt to 32 ft. lbs. (43 Nm).

10. Connect the end of the brake cable to the lever.

11. Connect the brake hose to the caliper and bleed the system.

12. Install the wheels to the vehicle and lower the vehicle.

13. Pump the brakes 3 times to properly seat the brake pads.

Disc Brake Pads

REMOVAL AND INSTALLATION

1. Remove disc brake caliper from mounting bracket and support with a length of wire or remove sleeve bolt and rotate caliper up and out of the way to remove shoes. Do not allow caliper to hang by the brake line unsupported.

2. Remove outboard shoe and lining. Use a suitable tool to disengage shoe springs from holes in caliper housing.

3. Remove inboard shoe and lining, unsnapping shoe spring from piston.

4. If installing new shoe and linings, bottom piston in caliper bore using large pliers. Take care not to damage piston or piston boot.

5. Remove bushings from mounting bolt holes in bracket.

To install:

6. Install new bushings to mounting bolt holes in bracket. Lubricate bushings with silicone grease before installation.

7. Install inboard shoe and lining by snapping shoe retainer spring into piston. Shoe retainer spring is already staked to the inboard shoe. Shoe must lay flat against piston.

8. Install outboard shoe and lining by snapping shoe springs into holes in caliper housing. Wear sensor should be at the trailing edge of shoe during forward wheel rotation. Back of shoe must lay flat against caliper.

9. Install caliper.

10. Apply approximately 175 lbs. (778 N) of force 3 times to brake pedal to seat linings.

Brake Rotor

REMOVAL AND INSTALLATION

1. Remove disc brake caliper from mounting bracket and support with a length of mechanics wire. Do not allow caliper to hang by the brake line unsupported.
2. Remove 2 bolts retaining caliper mounting bracket, remove bracket and set aside.
3. Remove brake rotor taking care not to damage wheel nut threads.

To install:

4. Install the brake rotor.
5. Install the caliper mounting bracket and the 2 retaining bolts.
6. Install the caliper to the mounting bracket.

Parking Brake Cable

ADJUSTMENT

1. Lube the cables at the underbody rub points and at the equalizer hooks. Set and release the parking brake several times and check for free movement of all cables.

NOTE: With the ignition switch turned ON, the parking brake warning light should be OFF.

2. Set the parking brake pedal in the fully released position, raise and safely support the vehicle.
3. Hold the brake cable stud and tighten the equalizer nut until all cable slack is removed. Make sure the caliper levers are against the stops on the caliper housing; if not, loosen the cable until they are.
4. Operate the parking brake pedal several times to check the adjustment; the pedal should become firm after 3½ strokes.
5. Lower the vehicle and check that the caliper levers are still on their stops. If not, back off the parking brake adjuster until they are.

REMOVAL AND INSTALLATION

The parking brake cable system consists of 4 separate cables: front, intermediate, left and right. The front and intermediate cables are joined at the adjuster screw. The left and right cables are joined to the intermediate cable through an equalizer.

1. Ensure that the parking brake is fully released.

2. Release the cable adjustment enough to allow removal of the desired cable(s).

NOTE: To prevent damage to threaded parking brake adjusting rod clean the exposed threads on each side of the nut and lubricate threads on the adjusting rod before turning the nut.

3. Remove old cable(s) and connect replacement cable(s).
4. Adjust new cable and check operation of parking brake.

BRAKE SYSTEM BLEEDING

Diagonal Split System

MASTER CYLINDER

1. Refill the master cylinder reservoir.
2. Push the plunger several times to force fluid into the piston.
3. Continue pumping the plunger until the fluid is free of the air bubbles.
4. Plug the outlet ports and install the master cylinder.

COMPLETE SYSTEM

1. Fill the master cylinder with fresh brake fluid. Check the level often during the procedure.
2. Starting with the right rear wheel, remove the protective cap from the bleeder, if equipped, and place where it will not be lost. Clean the bleed screw.

CAUTION

When bleeding the brakes, keep face away from the brake area. Spewing fluid may cause facial and/or visual damage. Do not allow brake fluid to spill on the vehicle's finish; it will remove the paint.

---

3. If the system is empty, the most efficient way to get fluid down to the wheel is to loosen the bleeder about ½–¾ turn, place a finger firmly over the bleeder and have a helper pump the brakes slowly until fluid comes out the bleeder. Once fluid is at the bleeder, close it before the pedal is released inside the vehicle.

NOTE: If the pedal is pumped rapidly, the fluid will churn and create small air bubbles, which are difficult to remove from the system. These air bubbles will eventually congregate resulting in a spongy pedal.

4. Once fluid has been pumped to the caliper or wheel cylinder, open

the bleed screw again, have the helper press the brake pedal to the floor, lock the bleeder and have the helper slowly release the pedal. Wait 15 seconds and repeat the procedure (including the 15 second wait) until no more air comes out of the bleeder upon application of the brake pedal. Remember to close the bleeder before the pedal is released inside the vehicle each time the bleeder is opened. If not, air will be induced into the system.

5. If a helper is not available, connect a small hose to the bleeder, place the end in a container of brake fluid and proceed to pump the pedal from inside the vehicle until no more air comes out the bleeder. The hose will prevent air from entering the system.

6. Repeat the procedure on remaining wheel cylinders in order:
   a. Left front
   b. Left rear
   c. Right front

7. Hydraulic brake systems must be totally flushed if the fluid becomes contaminated with water, dirt or other corrosive chemicals. To flush, bleed the entire system until all fluid has been replaced with the correct type of new fluid.

8. Install the bleeder cap(s) on the bleeder to keep dirt out. Always road test the vehicle after brake work of any kind is done.

Teves® Anti-lock Brake System

FRONT BRAKES

1. Turn the ignition switch **OFF** throughout this procedure.
2. Using at least 50 lbs. pressure on the brake pedal, depress the pedal at least 25 times; a noticeable change in pedal pressure will be noticed when the accumulator is discharged.
3. Remove the reservoir cap. Check and/or refill the master cylinder reservoir.
4. Using the bleeder adapter tool, install it onto the fluid reservoir.
5. Attach a diaphragm type pressure bleeder to the adapter and charge the bleeder to 20 psi.
6. Using a transparent vinyl tube, connect it to either front wheel caliper and insert the other end in a beaker ½ full of clean brake fluid.
7. Open the bleeder valve ½–¾ turn and purge the caliper until bubble free fluid flows from the hose.
8. Tighten the bleeder screw and remove the bleeder equipment.
9. Turn the ignition switch **ON** and allow the pump to charge the accumulator.
10. After bleeding, inspect the pedal for sponginess and the brake

warning light for unbalanced pressure; if either of the conditions exist, repeat the bleeding procedure.

REAR BRAKES

1. Turn the ignition switch **OFF**.
2. Using at least 50 lbs. pressure on the brake pedal, depress the pedal at least 25 times; a noticeable change in pedal pressure will be noticed when the accumulator is discharged.
3. Check and/or refill the master cylinder reservoir.
4. Turn the ignition switch **ON** and allow the system to charge.

NOTE: The pump will turn OFF when the system is charged.

5. Using a transparent vinyl tube, connect it to a rear wheel bleeder valve and insert the other end in a beaker ½ full of clean brake fluid.
6. Open the bleeder valve ½-¾ turn and slightly depress the brake pedal for at least 10 seconds or until air is removed from the brake system. Close the bleeder valve.

NOTE: It is a good idea to check the fluid level several times during the bleeding operation. Remember, depressurize the system before checking the reservoir fluid.

7. Repeat the bleeding procedure for the other rear wheel.
8. After bleeding, inspect the pedal for sponginess and the brake warning light for unbalanced pressure; if either of the conditions exist, repeat the bleeding procedure.

Bosch® III Anti-lock Brake System

1. Turn the ignition switch **OFF**.
2. Using at least 50 lbs. pressure on the brake pedal, depress the pedal at least 25 times; a noticeable change in pedal pressure will be noticed when the accumulator is discharged.
3. Check and/or refill the reservoir to the full mark.
4. Using a transparent vinyl hose, connect it to a pump bleeder screw and insert the other end in a beaker ½ full of clean brake fluid.
5. Loosen the bleeder screw ½-¾ turn. Turn the ignition switch **ON**; the pump should run forcing fluid from the hose. When the fluid becomes bubble-free, turn the ignition switch **OFF**, tighten the bleeder screw.
6. Move the transparent vinyl hose to the hydraulic unit bleeder screw. Loosen the bleeder screw ½-¾ turn. Turn the ignition switch **ON**; the pump should run forcing fluid from the hose. When the fluid be-

comes bubble-free, turn the ignition switch **OFF**, tighten the bleeder screw.
7. Disconnect the bleeder hose.
8. Turn the ignition switch **ON** and allow the hydraulic unit to charge; the pump should turn **OFF** after 30 seconds.

Bosch® 2U Anti-lock Brake System

1. Turn the ignition switch **OFF**.
2. Using at least 50 lbs. pressure on the brake pedal, depress the pedal at least 25 times; a noticeable change in pedal pressure will be noticed when the accumulator is discharged.
3. Check and/or refill the reservoir to the full mark.
4. Using a transparent vinyl hose, connect it to a pump bleeder screw and insert the other end in a beaker ½ full of clean brake fluid.
5. Loosen the bleeder screw ½-¾ turn. Turn the ignition switch **ON**; the pump should run forcing fluid from the hose. When the fluid becomes bubble-free, turn the ignition switch **OFF**, tighten the bleeder screw.
6. Move the transparent vinyl hose to the hydraulic unit bleeder screw. Loosen the bleeder screw ½-¾ turn. Turn the ignition switch **ON**; the pump should run forcing fluid from the hose. When the fluid becomes bubble-free, turn the ignition switch **OFF**, tighten the bleeder screw.
7. Disconnect the bleeder hose.
8. Turn the ignition switch **ON** and allow the hydraulic unit to charge; the pump should turn **OFF** after 30 seconds.

Anti-Lock Brake System Service

PRECAUTIONS

Failure to observe the following precautions may result in system damage.
• Before performing electric arc welding on the vehicle, disconnect the Electronic Brake Control Module (EBCM) and the hydraulic modulator connectors.
• When performing painting work on the vehicle, do not expose the Electronic Brake Control Module (EBCM) to temperatures in excess of 185°F (85°C) for longer than 2 hrs. The system may be exposed to temperatures up to 200°F (95°C) for less than 15 min.

• Never disconnect or connect the Electronic Brake Control Module (EBCM) or hydraulic modulator connectors with the ignition switch ON.
• Never disassemble any component of the Anti-Lock Brake System (ABS) which is designated non-serviceable; the component must be replaced as an assembly.
• When filling the master cylinder, always use Delco Supreme 11 brake fluid or equivalent, which meets DOT-3 specifications; petroleum base fluid will destroy the rubber parts.

RELIEVING ANTI-LOCK BRAKE SYSTEM PRESSURE

NOTE: Unless otherwise specified, the hydraulic accumulator should be depressurized before disassembling any portion of the hydraulic system.

1. With the ignition switch in the **OFF** position, sensor block connector disconnected from the hydraulic unit or the negative battery cable disconnected, pump the brake pedal a minimum of 25 times using approximately 50 lbs. of pedal force. When a noticeable change in pedal feel occurs, the accumulator is discharged.
2. When a definite increase in pedal effort is felt, stroke the pedal a few additional times.

Hydraulic Modulator

REMOVAL AND INSTALLATION

Teves System

NOTE: The hydraulic accumulator is under pressure and must be depressurized before attempting to dismantle the system.

1. Disconnect the negative battery cable. Firmly apply the parking brake.
2. Using at least 50 lbs. pressure on the brake pedal, depress the pedal at least 20 times; a noticeable change in pedal pressure will be noticed when the accumulator is discharged.
3. Disconnect the electrical connectors from the hydraulic brake unit.
4. Remove the pump-to-hydraulic unit bolt and move the unit aside to gain access to the hydraulic lines.
5. Using a backup wrench, disconnect the hydraulic lines from the hydraulic unit.
6. From under the dash, disconnect the pushrod from the brake pedal.

7. Move the dust boot forward, past the pushrod hex and unscrew both pushrod halves.

8. Remove the hydraulic unit-to-pushrod bracket bolts and separate the hydraulic unit from the pushrod bracket; half of the pushrod will remain locked in the hydraulic unit.

9. Disassemble the master cylinder from the hydraulic unit.

To install:

10. Assemble the master cylinder to the hydraulic unit.

11. Install the hydraulic unit to the pushrod bracket and install the hydraulic unit-to-pushrod bracket bolts. Tighten the hydraulic unit-to-pushrod bracket bolts to 37 ft. lbs. (50 Nm).

12. Install the pushrod halves and move the dust boot into position. From under the dash, connect the pushrod to the brake pedal.

13. Using a backup wrench, connect the hydraulic lines to the hydraulic unit. Install the hydraulic unit and pump-to-hydraulic unit bolt.

14. Connect the electrical connectors to the hydraulic brake unit. Bleed the brake system.

15. Release the parking brake. Connect the negative battery cable.

Bosch III System

NOTE: The hydraulic accumulator is under pressure and must be depressurized before attempting to dismantle the system.

1. Disconnect the negative battery cable. Firmly apply the parking brake.

2. Using at least 50 lbs. pressure on the brake pedal, depress the pedal at least 20 times; a noticeable change in pedal pressure will be noticed when the accumulator is discharged.

3. On Allante, remove the air intake duct from the air cleaner and the throttle body, as required.

4. Remove the cross brace. Disconnect the electrical connectors from the hydraulic brake unit and the pump motor. Using a siphon, remove as much fluid from the reservoir as possible.

5. Remove the pressure hose fitting (banjo bolt) from the hydraulic unit; be careful not to drop the fitting washers. Disconnect the return hose from the reservoir fitting.

6. Using a backup wrench, disconnect the hydraulic lines from the hydraulic unit.

7. From under the dash, remove the driver's side sound insulator panel. From the pedal hub pin, re-

move the pushrod retainer and the foam washer.

8. From the engine compartment, remove the hydraulic unit-to-mounting adapter nuts.

9. Move the hydraulic unit to disengage the pushrod-to-pedal hub pin. Remove the hydraulic unit from the vehicle.

To install:

10. Install the hydraulic unit to the vehicle. Move the hydraulic unit to engage the pushrod-to-pedal hub pin.

11. Install the hydraulic unit-to-mounting adapter nuts. Tighten the hydraulic unit-to-mounting bracket nuts to 20 ft. lbs. (27 Nm).

12. From under the dash, install the pushrod retainer and the foam washer. Install the driver's side sound insulator panel.

13. In the engine compartment, connect the hydraulic lines to the hydraulic unit, using a backup wrench.

14. Install the pressure hose fitting (banjo bolt) to the hydraulic unit. Connect the return hose to the reservoir fitting.

15. Connect the electrical connectors to the hydraulic brake unit and the pump motor. Refill the reservoir to the **FULL** mark.

16. Turn the ignition **ON** and allow the pump to charge the hydraulic ac-

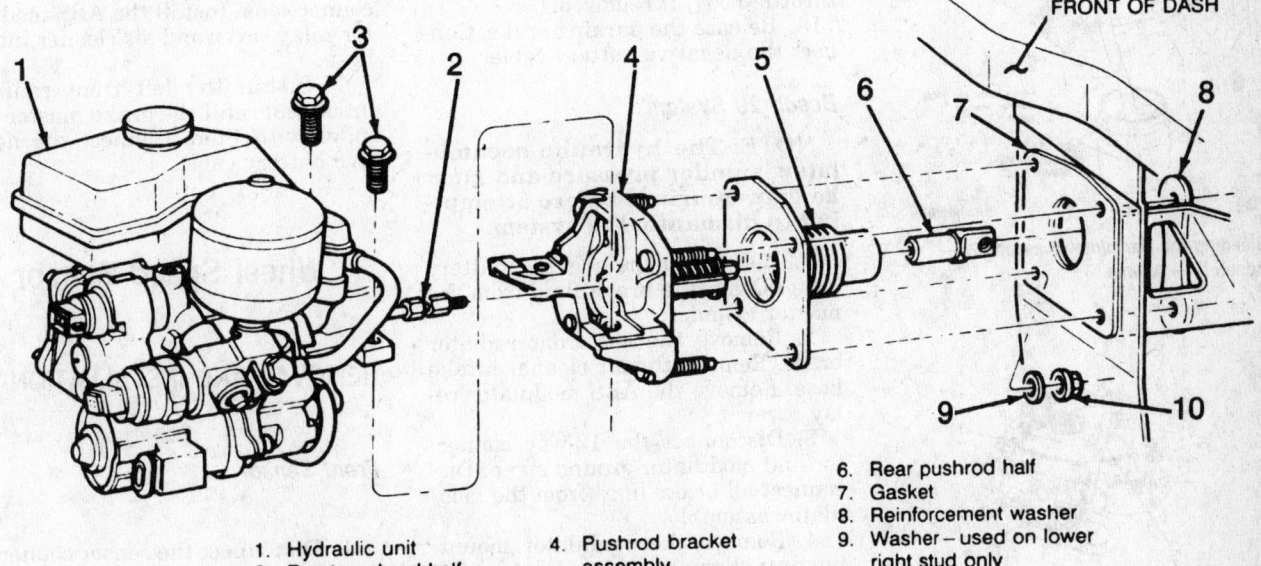

1. Hydraulic unit
2. Front pushrod half
3. Bolts – 37 ft. lbs.
4. Pushrod bracket assembly
5. Rubber boot
6. Rear pushrod half
7. Gasket
8. Reinforcement washer
9. Washer – used on lower right stud only
10. Nuts – 15 ft. lbs.

8569H001

Exploded view of the anti-lock brake system hydraulic unit — Teves — except Allante

1. Hydraulic unit
2. Nuts - 20 ft. lbs.
3. Mounting adapter
4. Front of dash
5. Nuts - 15 ft. lbs.

8569H002

View of the anti-lock brake system hydraulic unit and mounting bracket — Bosch III — Allante

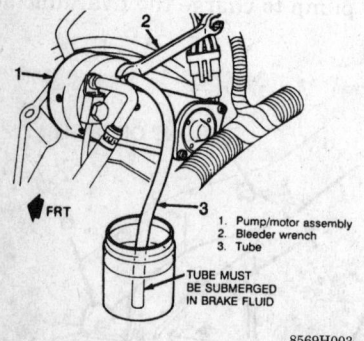

1. Pump/motor assembly
2. Bleeder wrench
3. Tube

TUBE MUST
BE SUBMERGED
IN BRAKE FLUID

8569H003

Bleeding the pump/motor assembly — Bosch III — Allante

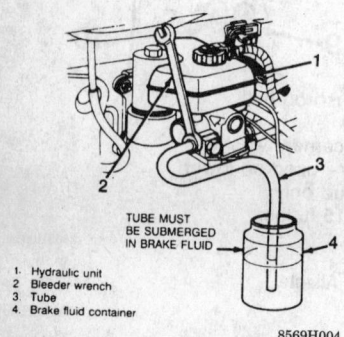

TUBE MUST
BE SUBMERGED
IN BRAKE FLUID

1. Hydraulic unit
2. Bleeder wrench
3. Tube
4. Brake fluid container

8569H004

Bleeding the hydraulic unit — Bosch III — Allante

cumulator. Bleed the brake system. Install the cross brace.

17. On Allante, install the air intake duct to the air cleaner and the throttle body, if removed.

18. Release the parking brake. Connect the negative battery cable.

Bosch 2U System

NOTE: The hydraulic accumulator is under pressure and must be depressurized before attempting to dismantle the system.

1. Disconnect the negative battery cable. Drain the brake fluid from the master cylinder.

2. Remove the left front radiator brace. Remove the air cleaner intake hose. Remove the ABS modulator relay cover.

3. Disconnect the 12-way connector and modulator ground strap. Disconnect all brake lines from the modulator assembly.

4. Remove the modulator mounting nuts. Remove the modulator from the mounting bracket; be careful not to drip fluid onto any painted surfaces. Remove the mounting insulators from the modulator.

To install:

5. Install the mounting insulators to the modulator. Install the hydraulic modulator to the mounting

bracket and install the mounting nuts.

6. Connect the brake lines to the modulator and connect the electrical connections. Install the ABS modulator relay cover and air cleaner intake hose.

7. Install the left front radiator brace and refill the brake master cylinder with fluid. Connect the negative battery cable.

Wheel Speed Sensor

REMOVAL AND INSTALLATION

Front Sensor

1. Disconnect the sensor connector from underhood area near strut tower. Raise and safely support the vehicle.

2. Disengage the sensor cable grommet from the wheel house pass-through hole and remove sensor cable from retainers.

3. Remove sensor mounting bolts and remove sensor from vehicle.

To install:

4. Route sensor cable and install retainers. Install wheel-house pass-through grommet.

NOTE: Proper installation of wheel speed sensor cables is critical to continued system operation. Be sure cables are installed in retainers. Failure to install cables in retainers properly may result in contact with moving parts and/or over-extension of cables, resulting in circuit damage.

5. Position sensor in knuckle and install mounting bolt. Tighten mounting bolt to 9 ft. lbs. (12 Nm).

NOTE: If the wheel speed sensor is removed or replaced, the sensor body must be coated with a suitable anti-corrosion compound where the sensor comes in contact with the knuckle.

6. Lower the vehicle. Connect the wheel speed sensor connector underhood.

Rear Sensor

1. Raise and safely support the vehicle.
2. Disengage the sensor connector and remove sensor cable from retainer brackets.
3. Remove sensor mounting bolts and remove sensor from vehicle.

To install:

4. Position sensor in knuckle and install mounting bolt. Tighten mounting bolt to 9 ft. lbs. (12 Nm).

NOTE: If the wheel speed sensor is removed or replaced, the sensor body must be coated with a suitable anti-corrosion compound where the sensor comes in contact with the knuckle.

5. Install the wheel speed sensor cable in the retainers.
6. Connect the wheel speed sensor connector. Lower the vehicle.

Electronic Brake Control Module (EBCM)

REMOVAL AND INSTALLATION

Except Allante

1. Disconnect the negative battery cable. Open trunk lid. Remove left trunk carpet trim.
2. Remove velcro-attached cover concealing the EBCM.
3. Disconnect the EBCM connector. Remove the EBCM.

To install:

4. Install the EBC Connect the EBCM connector.
5. Install the velcro-attached cover concealing the EBCM.
6. Install the left truck carpet trim. Close the trunk lid.
7. Connect the negative battery cable.

Allante

1. Disconnect the negative battery cable. Remove the driver's side insulator panel.
2. Remove the EBCM connector by disengaging retainer and rotating connector toward the driver's seat.
3. Remove the EBCM retaining bolts.
4. Disengage the EBCM from the mounting bracket and remove from vehicle.

To install:

5. Position the EBCM in the mounting bracket and install the retaining bolts.
6. Install the EBCM connector. Install the driver's side sound insulator panel.
7. Connect the negative battery cable.

FRONT SUSPENSION

MacPherson Strut

REMOVAL AND INSTALLATION

1. Disconnect the negative battery cable.
2. Remove nut(s) attaching top of strut assembly to body.
3. If equipped, disconnect electrical connector from top of strut.
4. Raise and safely support the vehicle.
5. Remove tire and wheel assembly.

NOTE: Whenever working near the halfshafts, care must be taken to prevent inner Tri-Pot joints from being overextended. Overextension of the joint could result in separation of internal components which could go undetected and result in failure of the joint. Care should be taken to avoid scratching or cracking the spring coating when handling the front suspension coil spring. Damage to the spring coating could result in premature failure.

6. In order to reassemble the knuckle and strut in the same relationship, make the following scribe marks:

a. Using a sharp tool, scribe the inboard surface of the strut along the upper knuckle radius.
b. Scribe the knuckle along the lower curve of the strut.
c. Scribe mark across the strut and knuckle interface.

7. Remove brake line bracket from strut.
8. Remove stabilizer link from strut.
9. Remove strut-to-knuckle bolts and support knuckle with wire.
10. Remove strut from vehicle.

To install:

11. Install strut while aligning scribe marks.
12. Install strut-to-knuckle bolts.
13. Install stabilizer link to strut.
14. Install brake line bracket to strut.
15. Install nuts attaching top of strut to body. Tighten stabilizer link nuts to 48 ft. lbs. (65 Nm). Tighten strut assembly-to-body nuts to 18 ft. lbs. (24 Nm). Tighten steering knuckle-to-strut nuts to 140 ft. lbs. (190 Nm).
16. Install tire and wheel assembly.
17. Lower vehicle.
18. Tighten wheel mounting nuts to 100 ft. lbs. (140 Nm).
19. If equipped, connect electrical connector to top of strut.
20. Connect negative battery cable.

Strut Cartridge

REMOVAL AND INSTALLATION

1. Install the strut assembly to a strut compressor.
2. Turn the compressor so the spring becomes compressed.
3. Hold the strut shaft from turning and remove the 24mm strut nut.
4. Install special rod J-34013-38 to the strut shaft and guide the strut out of the assembly while loosening the spring compressor.
5. Remove the strut cartridge from the assembly.

To install:

6. Install the strut to the strut compressor/spring assembly.
7. Start turning the compressor screw clockwise to compress the spring while guiding the shaft through the mounting hole.

8. Tighten the mounting nut to 55 ft. lbs. (75 Nm) while holding the strut shaft.

Lower Ball Joints

INSPECTION

1. Raise and safely support the vehicle. Install jackstands under both lower control arms as far outboard as possible.
2. Lower the vehicle onto the jackstands so the downward tension exerted by the stabilizer bar is relieved.
3. Install a dial indicator and clamp the assembly to the lower control arm.
4. Position the dial indicator plunger tip against the knuckle arm. Zero the dial indicator gauge.
5. Measure the axial travel of the knuckle arm with respect to the control arm, by raising and lowering the wheel using a prybar under the center of the tire.
6. During the measurement, if the axial travel of the control arm is 0.030 in. or more, relative to the knuckle arm, the ball joint should be replaced.

REMOVAL AND INSTALLATION

1. Raise and safely support the vehicle.
2. Place jackstands under cradle and lower vehicle slightly so weight of the vehicle rests on the jackstands and not on the control arms.
3. Remove tire and wheel assembly.
4. Install a suitable outer CV-joint boot protector.
5. Remove stabilizer bar insulators, retainers, spacer and bolt.
6. Remove ball joint from knuckle.

NOTE: If equipped with anti-lock brakes, ensure that there is enough clearance between the

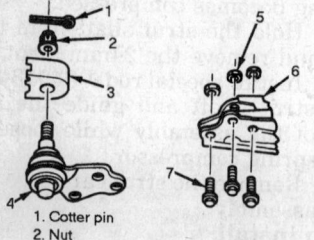

1. Cotter pin
2. Nut
3. Steering knuckle
4. Service ball joint
5. Ball joint mounting nuts 68 Nm (50ft. lbs.)
6. Control arm
7. Ball joint mounting bolts must face up

8470H105

Lower ball joint assembly

ball joint stud and speed sensor ring; if not, remove the halfshaft hub nut. Install special tool J-28733 or equivalent halfshaft remover. Tighten tool until halfshaft moves inboard enough to provide clearance for ball joint removal.

7. Drill out 3 rivets retaining ball joint starting with ¼ in. drill bit and finishing with ½ in. drill bit.
8. Remove ball joint.
To install:
9. Install new ball joint into control arm.
10. Install ball joint bolts.
11. Connect ball joint to knuckle. Tighten ball joint bolts to 50 ft. lbs. (68 Nm). Tighten ball joint nut to 7 ft. lbs. (10 Nm). Tighten nut an additional ½ turn (3 flats.)

NOTE: When tightening nut, a minimum torque of 48 ft. lbs. (65 Nm) must be obtained. If 48 ft. lbs. (65 Nm) is not obtained, inspect for stripped threads. If threads are satisfactory, replace ball joint and knuckle. If required, turn the nut up to an additional ¼ turn to allow for installation of the cotter pin. Bend both ends of the cotter pin.

12. If removed, tighten the hub nut to 183 ft. lbs. (245 Nm), to assure proper bearing clamp load.
13. Remove CV-joint boot protector.
14. Install tire and wheel assembly.
15. Raise vehicle enough to allow removal or jackstands.
16. Lower vehicle. Tighten wheel nuts to 100 ft. lbs. (140 Nm).

Lower Control Arms

REMOVAL AND INSTALLATION

1. Raise and safely support the vehicle.
2. Place jackstands under cradle and lower vehicle slightly so weight of the vehicle rests on the jackstands and not the control arms.
3. Remove the tire and wheel assembly.

NOTE: Care must be taken not to overextend Tri-Pot joints. Overextension of the joint could result in separation of internal components which could go undetected and result in failure of the joint.

4. If equipped, disconnect the Road Sensing Suspension position sensor and install a suitable CV-joint boot protector.

5. Remove stabilizer shaft insulator, retainers, spacer and bolt to control arm.
6. Lower ball joint from knuckle.
7. Remove control arm bushing bolt and front nut, retainer and insulator.
8. Remove control arm from frame.
To install:
9. Connect control arm to frame.
10. Install control arm bushing bolt and front nut, retainer and insulator. Do not tighten at this time.
11. Connect lower ball joint to knuckle.
12. Install stabilizer shaft insulator, retainers, spacer and bolt. Tighten stabilizer shaft nut and bolt to 13 ft. lbs. (17 Nm).

NOTE: Tighten ball joint nut to 7 ft. lbs. (10 Nm). Tighten nut an additional ½ turn (3 flats). When tightening nut a minimum torque of 48 ft. lbs. (65 Nm) must be obtained. If 48 ft. lbs. (65 Nm) is not obtained, inspect for stripped threads. If threads are satisfactory, replace ball joint and knuckle. If required, turn the nut up to an additional ¼ of a turn to allow for installation of the cotter pin. Bend both ends of the cotter pin.

13. Remove outer CV-joint boot protector and connect the Road Sensing Suspension position sensor.
14. Install tire and wheel assembly.
15. Raise vehicle slightly so weight of vehicle is supported by the control arms. Tighten control arm bushing bolt to 100 ft. lbs. (140 Nm) or nut to 91 ft. lbs. (123 Nm). Tighten retainer to 52 ft. lbs. (70 Nm).
16. Remove jackstands and lower vehicle.
17. Tighten wheel nuts to 100 ft. lbs. (140 Nm).

Sway Bar

REMOVAL AND INSTALLATION

1. Disconnect the negative battery cable.
2. Raise and safely support the vehicle.
3. Place jackstands under cradle and lower vehicle slightly so the weight of the vehicle rests on the jackstands and not on the control arms.
4. Remove right side wheel assembly.
5. Remove left and right insulators, retainers, spacers and bolts.

6. Remove left and right bracket bolts, brackets and insulators.

7. Remove exhaust pipe from rear manifold and move pipe up.

8. Remove stabilizer shaft.

To install:

9. Install stabilizer shaft.

10. Install exhaust pipe to rear manifold.

11. Install left and right insulators, brackets and loosely install bolts.

12. Install left and right insulators, retainers, spacers and bolts.

13. Center stabilizer on frame and check clearance. Tighten bracket to frame bolts to 33 ft. lbs. (45 Nm). Tighten nuts to 13 ft. lbs. (17 Nm).

14. Raise vehicle enough to allow for removal of jackstands.

15. Lower vehicle. Tighten wheel nuts to 100 ft. lbs. (140 Nm).

REAR SUSPENSION

MacPherson Strut

REMOVAL AND INSTALLATION

1. Disconnect the negative battery cable.

2. Raise and safely support the vehicle.

3. Reinstall 2 wheel nuts to hold rotor on hub and bearing assembly.

4. Remove brake caliper and support with a length of wire.

NOTE: Do not allow caliper to hang by the brake hose unsupported.

5. Loosen knuckle pivot bolt on outboard end of control arm. Do not remove.

6. Remove upper strut rod cap, mounting nut, retainer and insulator.

7. Compress strut by hand and remove lower insulator.

8. Rotate strut and knuckle assembly outward by pivoting on knuckle pivot bolt.

9. Remove knuckle pinch bolt.

10. Remove strut from knuckle.

To install:

11. Position strut in knuckle. Strut must by fully seated in knuckle with tang on strut bottomed in knuckle slot.

12. Install knuckle pinch bolt. Tighten to 44 ft. lbs. (60 Nm).

13. Install lower insulator on strut and position strut rod in suspension support.

14. Install upper strut insulator, retainer and nut. Tighten upper strut nut to 65 ft. lbs. (88 Nm). Tighten knuckle pivot bolt to 59 ft. lbs. (80 Nm).

15. Install strut rod cap.

16. Install caliper and new caliper bracket mounting bolts.

17. Remove 2 wheel nuts previously installed to retain rotor.

18. Install wheel and tire assembly.

19. Lower vehicle. Tighten wheel nuts to 100 ft. lbs. (140 Nm).

Transverse-Mounted Leaf Spring

REMOVAL AND INSTALLATION

NOTE: Removal and Installation of the transverse-mounted rear spring requires disassembly of either the left or right suspension while leaving the other side intact. The spring may be removed from either side of the vehicle.

1. Disconnect the negative battery cable.

2. Raise and safely support the vehicle.

3. Remove tire and wheel assembly.

4. Disconnect height sensor link, if disassembling left control arm.

5. Remove stabilizer shaft mounting bolt at strut, if equipped with stabilizer.

6. Reinstall 2 wheel nuts to hold rotor on hub and bearing assembly.

7. Remove brake caliper and support with a length of wire.

NOTE: Do not allow caliper to hang by the brake hose unsupported.

8. Loosen knuckle pivot bolt on outboard end of control arm. Do not remove pivot bolt.

9. Support outboard end of control arm with a suitable lifting device to slightly compress spring.

10. Remove strut rod cap, mounting nut, retainer and upper insulator.

11. Slowly remove lifting device to relieve spring pressure.

12. Compress strut by hand and remove lower insulator.

13. Remove wheel speed sensor, if equipped with anti-lock brakes.

14. Remove inner control arm nuts.

15. While supporting the knuckle and control arm, remove inner control arm bolts and remove the control arm, knuckle, strut, hub and bearing and rotor from vehicle as an assembly.

16. Place a jackstand under the outboard end of spring.

17. Lower the vehicle so the weight loads the spring downward on jackstand.

18. Remove the 3 spring retainer bolts, retainer and lower insulator from retainer nearest the supported end of spring.

19. Slowly raise vehicle, allowing spring to deflect downward until spring no longer exerts force on the lifting device. Remove lifting device.

20. Remove spring retainer bolts, retainer and lower insulator from retainer on opposite side of vehicle.

21. Withdrawal spring from rear suspension support through disassembled side of vehicle suspension.

22. Remove upper spring insulators, as required.

NOTE: Inspect all spring insulators, insulator locating pads, retainers and control arm contact pads for cuts, cracks, tears or other damage. Replace worn or damaged parts.

To install:

23. Install spring insulators which were previously removed. Ensure that molded arrow on the insulator points toward the centerline of the vehicle when installing upper outboard insulators. Tighten center and upper outboard insulator nuts to 21 ft. lbs. (28 Nm).

NOTE: When positioning spring in suspension support, outboard and center insulator locating bands must be centered on spring insulators. Failure to position spring correctly may result in reduced vehicle handling characteristics.

24. With spring properly located, install lower insulator and spring retainer on side of vehicle opposite the disassembled portion of suspension.

25. Place suitable lifting device under free end of spring.

26. Lower vehicle, allowing weight to load spring and deflect free end of spring into position in suspension support.

27. Install lower insulator and spring retainer on disassembled side of suspension support. Tighten spring retainer bolts to 21 ft. lbs. (28 Nm).

28. Raise the vehicle and remove spring lifting device.

29. Position the assembled control arm, knuckle, strut, hub and bearing and rotor assembly in suspension support and install inner control arm bolts and nuts. Do not tighten at this time.

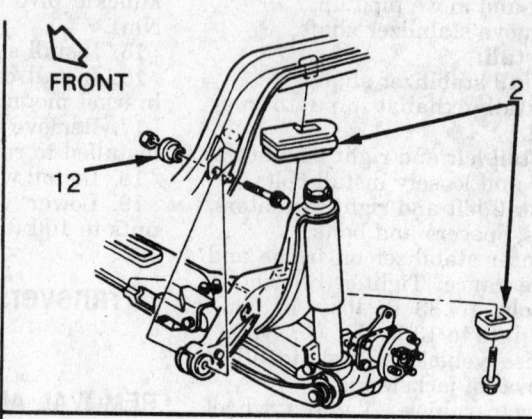

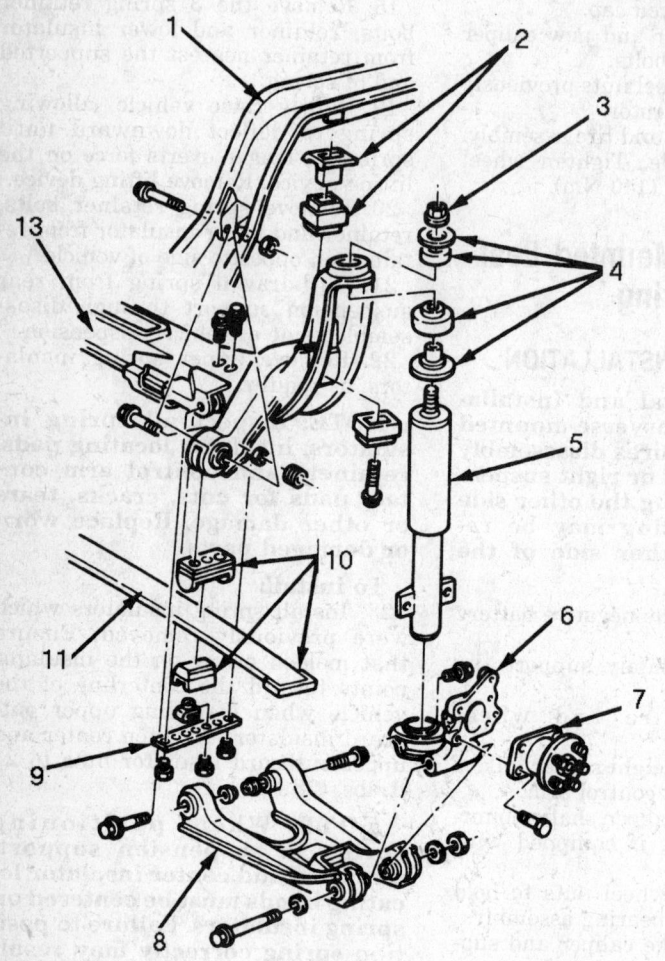

1. Underbody assembly
2. Suspension support insulators
3. Upper strut mounting nut
4. Strut mount insulators
5. Strut
6. Knuckle
7. Hub and bearing assembly
8. Control arm
9. Spring retainer
10. Spring insulators
11. Single leaf spring
12. Spacer left side only
13. Suspension support

8470H106

Rear suspension components

30. Connect wheel sensor, if equipped with anti-lock brakes.
31. Install lower strut insulator and position strut rod in suspension support assembly.
32. Position suitable lifting under outboard end of lower control arm to slightly compress spring.
33. Install strut insulator, retainer and nut. Tighten upper strut nut to 65 ft. lbs. (88 Nm). Tighten knuckle pivot bolt to 59 ft. lbs. (80 Nm). Tighten inner control arm bolts to 66 ft. lbs. (90 Nm).
34. Remove lifting device.
35. Install strut rod cap.
36. Install stabilizer shaft mounting bolt, if equipped with stabilizer.

Tighten stabilizer shaft mounting bolt to 43 ft. lbs. (58 Nm).
37. Remove 2 wheel nuts previously installed to retain motor.
38. Install caliper and new caliper mounting bracket bolts. Tighten caliper mounting bracket bolts to 83 ft. lbs. (113 Nm).
39. Connect height sensor link, if left side of suspension was disassembled.
40. Install wheel and tire assembly.
41. Lower vehicle. Tighten wheel nuts to 100 ft. lbs. (140 Nm).

NOTE: Vehicle must have rear wheel alignment performed after removal and installation of rear spring.

Rear Control Arms

REMOVAL AND INSTALLATION

Except 1993 Allante

1. Disconnect the negative battery cable.
2. Raise and safely support the vehicle.
3. Remove wheel and tire assembly.
4. If equipped with anti-lock brakes, remove speed sensor from knuckle.
5. Reinstall 2 wheel nuts to hold rotor on hub and bearing assembly.

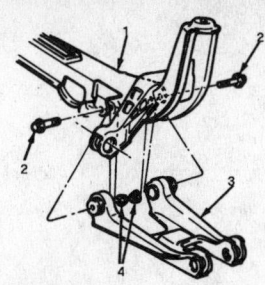

1. Suspension support
2. Inner control arm bolts
3. Control arm
4. Nuts 90Nm (66 ft. lbs.)

8470H108

Rear control arm mounting

6. Remove brake caliper and support with a length of wire.

NOTE: Do not allow caliper to hang by the brake hose unsupported.

7. Disconnect electrical connector from top of strut. Loosen knuckle pivot bolt on outboard end of control arm. Do not remove.
8. Support the outboard end of the control arm with a jackstand to slightly compress the spring.
9. Remove upper strut rod cap, mounting nut, retainer and insulator.
10. Slowly remove the jackstand to relieve the spring pressure.
11. Compress strut by hand and remove lower insulator.
12. While supporting the knuckle, remove knuckle pivot bolt and remove the knuckle, strut, hub, bearing and rotor from the vehicle as an assembly.
13. Remove both inner control arm bolts and remove control arm from vehicle.
   To install:
14. Position control arm in vehicle and install both inner control arm bolts. Do not tighten bolts at this time.
15. Position the assembled knuckle, strut, hub and bearing and rotor assembly in control arm and install knuckle pivot bolt. Do not tighten bolt at this time.
16. Install lower strut insulator and position strut rod in suspension support.
17. Position a jackstand under the outboard end of the lower control arm to slightly compress the spring.
18. Install upper strut insulator, retainer and nut. Tighten upper strut nut to 55 ft. lbs. (75 Nm). Tighten knuckle pivot bolt to 59 ft. lbs. (80 Nm). Tighten inner control arm bolts to 66 ft. lbs. (90 Nm).
19. Install strut rod cap.
20. Remove 2 wheel nuts previously installed to retain rotor.

21. Install caliper and new caliper bracket mounting bolts.
22. If equipped, install speed sensor to knuckle.
23. Install wheel and tire assembly.
24. Lower vehicle. Tighten wheel nuts to 100 ft. lbs. (140 Nm).

1993 Allante

LOWER

1. Raise and safely support the vehicle.
2. Remove the wheel and tire assembly.
3. Support the inboard end of the lower control arm with a jackstand.
4. Remove the stabilizer link lower attachment.
5. Disconnect the shock absorber lower attachment.
6. Remove the inboard lower control arm nuts and bolts.
7. Slowly lower the jackstand to relieve the spring pressure.
8. Pull lower control arm to remove the spring and remove the outboard bolt.
9. Remove the control arm from the vehicle.
   To install:
10. Install the lower control arm to the vehicle and install the outboard control arm bolt and nut. Tighten the outer nut to 75 ft. lbs. (102 Nm).
11. Install the spring and the insulators and position the jackstand under the lower control arm. Raise the jackstand to slightly compress the spring.
12. Insert the inboard lower control arm bolts and nuts.
13. Install the shock absorber lower attachment and the stabilizer link lower attachment.
14. Remove the jackstand and place under the lower control arm to bring the suspension into the proper position.
15. Tighten the stabilizer link lower nut to 44 ft. lbs. (60 Nm), the shock absorber lower nut to 75 ft. lbs. (102 Nm) and the lower control arm inner nuts to 75 ft. lbs. (102 Nm).
16. Install the wheel and lower the vehicle.
17. Rear wheel alignment must be done if control arm fasteners were loosened.

UPPER

1. Raise and safely support the vehicle.
2. Remove the wheel.
3. Disconnect the Road Sensing Suspension position sensor and bracket from the shock tower.
4. Remove the inner and outer control arm bolts.

5. Remove the control arm up and over the shock tower to remove from the vehicle.
   To install:
6. Install the control arm over the shock tower.
7. Install the inner and outer control arm bolts.
8. Place a jackstand under the outboard end of the lower control arm to bring the suspension to the proper position.
9. Tighten the upper control arm inner and outer nuts to 42 ft. lbs. (57 Nm).
10. Connect the Road Sensing Suspension position sensor bracket and sensor.
11. Install the wheel and tire and lower the vehicle.

Rear Wheel Bearings

REMOVAL AND INSTALLATION

1. Disconnect the negative battery cable.
2. Raise and safely support the vehicle.
3. Remove wheel and tire assembly.
4. If equipped with anti-lock brakes, remove speed sensor from knuckle.
5. Reinstall 2 wheel nuts to hold rotor on hub and bearing assembly.
6. Remove brake caliper and support with a length of wire.

NOTE: Do not allow caliper to hang by the brake hose unsupported.

7. Remove rotor.
8. Remove 4 hub mounting bolts.
9. Remove hub and bearing assembly.
   To install:
10. Position hub and bearing assembly on knuckle.
11. Install 4 hub mounting bolts. Tighten to 52 ft. lbs. (70 Nm).
12. Install rotor.
13. Install caliper and new caliper bracket mounting bolts. Tighten to 83 ft. lbs. (113 Nm).
14. Install wheel and tire assembly.
15. Lower vehicle. Tighten wheel nuts to 100 ft. lbs. (140 Nm).

ADJUSTMENT

The hub and bearing are installed as an assembly. No periodic adjustment is required. If the bearing is found to have excessive play, the assembly must be replaced.

GM "J" BODY

Front Wheel Drive

CHEVROLET—Cavalier PONTIAC—Sunbird

14

FIRING ORDERS

NOTE: To avoid confusion, always replace spark plug wires one at a time.

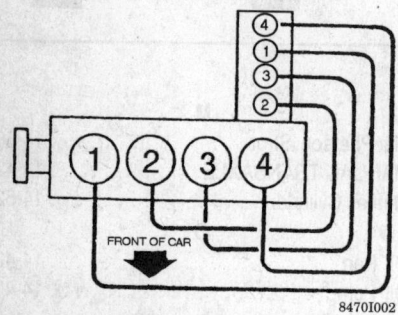

84701002

2.0L and 2.2L Engines
Engine Firing Order: 1-3-4-2
Distributorless Ignition System

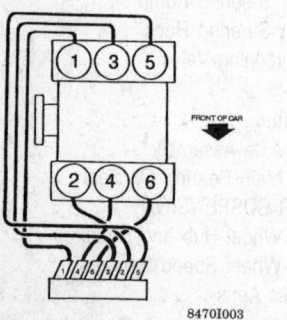

84701003

3.1L Engine
Engine Firing Order:
1-2-3-4-5-6
Distributorless Ignition
System

ENGINE ELECTRICAL

NOTE: Disconnecting the negative battery cable on some vehicles may interfere with the functions of the on-board computer systems and may require the computer to undergo a relearning process, once the negative battery cable is reconnected.

Distributorless Ignition System

REMOVAL AND INSTALLATION

DIS Ignition Module Assembly

1. Disconnect the negative battery cable.
2. Unplug the electrical connectors from the DIS assembly.
3. Mark the location of the spark plug wires on the DIS assembly, then remove the secondary wires from the module coil towers.
4. Remove the DIS assembly mounting bolts, then remove the assembly from the block.

NOTE: On all vehicles, except the Sunbird equipped with the 2.0L engine, the ignition coils may be replaced separately. Simply remove the coil mounting bolts and separate the coil from the assembly. This may be performed with the module on or off the engine. Upon installation, tighten the coil retaining bolts to 40 inch lbs. (4.5 Nm); be careful not to overtighten the retainers.

To install:
5. Install the DIS assembly on the block. Tighten the assembly bolts to 89 inch lbs. (10 Nm) for the 2.0L engine, 15–22 ft. lbs. (20–30 Nm) for the 2.2L engine or 19 ft. lbs. (25 Nm) for the 3.1L engine.
6. Reconnect the plug wires to their proper coil towers, as noted during removal.
7. Connect the DIS assembly wiring.
8. Connect the negative battery cable.
9. If equipped with 3.1L engine, perform the idle learn procedure to allow the ECM memory to be updated with the correct IAC valve pintle position and provide for a stable idle speed.
   a. Install a Tech 1 or equivalent, scan tool.
   b. Turn the ignition to the ON position, engine not running.
   c. Select IAC SYSTEM, then IDLE LEARN in the MISC TEST mode.
   d. Place the transaxle in N or P, then proceed with idle learn as directed by the scan tool.

Crankshaft Sensor

1992 2.0L ENGINE

1. Disconnect the negative battery cable.

2. Remove the serpentine drive belt and the timing belt cover from the front of the engine.
3. Remove the sensor retainer, then unplug the wiring harness from the sensor.
4. Remove the sensor from the engine block.

To install:
5. Inspect the sensor O-ring and replace, if damaged.
6. Lube the sensor O-ring with clean engine oil, then install the sensor into the block.
7. Install the sensor retainer and tighten to 20 inch lbs. (2.3 Nm).
8. Connect the wiring harness to the sensor.
9. Install the timing belt cover and the serpentine drive belt.
10. Connect the negative battery cable.

1993–96 2.0L ENGINE

1. Disconnect the negative battery cable, then raise and support the vehicle safely.
2. Remove the retaining bolt, then withdraw the sensor from the engine block.
3. Remove the 2 nuts from the lower power steering bracket.
4. Lower the vehicle and remove the serpentine drive belt.
5. Remove the 4 bolts and 2 nuts securing the alternator, hinge and crankcase ventilation tube, then position the components aside.
6. Remove the 3 bolts from the upper power steering bracket and the remaining bolts from the lower bracket, then position the pump assembly aside.
7. Remove the timing belt cover.
8. Unplug the crankshaft position sensor wiring harness and cut the tie strap.
9. Feed the harness behind the timing plate, then remove the harness and sensor.

To install:
10. Raise and support the vehicle safely, then install the sensor into the engine and tighten the retaining bolt.
11. Feed the harness through the A/C compressor mount, then lower the vehicle.
12. Feed the harness behind the timing plate.
13. Connect the harness at the rear of the engine and install the tie strap.
14. Install the timing cover and secure using the fasteners.
15. Position the power steering pump assembly, then install the 2 top bolts for the lower bracket.
16. Position the alternator, along with the hinge and crankcase ventila-

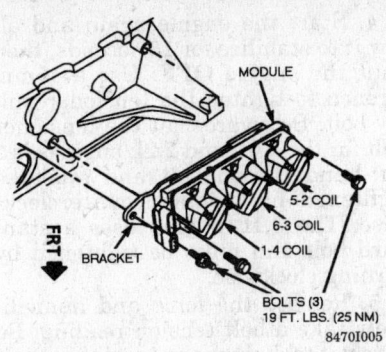

DIS ignition module and coil pack assembly — 3.1L engine

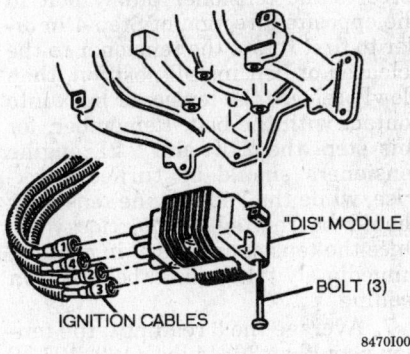

DIS ignition module — 2.0L engine

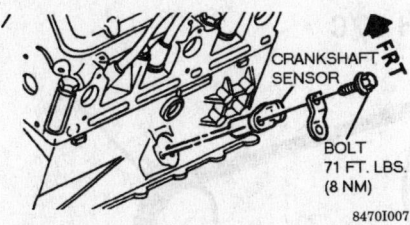

Crankshaft sensor mounting — 3.1L engine

tion tube, then secure using the bolts and nuts.

17. Raise and support the vehicle safely, then install the lower power steering bracket nuts.

18. Lower the vehicle, then install the serpentine drive belt.

19. Connect the sensor to engine harness.

20. Connect the negative battery cable.

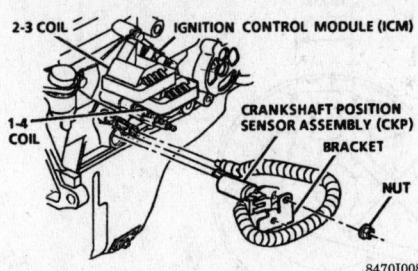

Ignition coil and crankshaft position sensor mounting — 2.2L engine

EXCEPT 2.0L ENGINE

1. Disconnect the negative battery cable.

2. Unplug the wiring harness from the sensor.

3. Remove the sensor-to-block bolt, then remove the sensor from the engine.

To install:

4. Inspect the sensor O-ring and replace, if damaged.

5. Lube the sensor O-ring with clean engine oil, then install the sensor into the block.

6. Tighten the sensor bolt to 71 inch lbs. (8 Nm), except for 1992 2.2L engines which should be tightened to 53–107 inch lbs. (6–12 Nm).

7. Connect the sensor harness plug.

8. Connect the negative battery cable.

Ignition Timing

ADJUSTMENT

All DIS Engines

The Electronic Control Module (ECM) for engines equipped with a distributorless ignition system electronically controls engine timing advance or retard. No adjustments are necessary or possible.

Alternator

PRECAUTIONS

Several precautions must be observed with alternator equipped vehicles to avoid damage to the unit.

• If the battery is removed for any reason, make sure it is reconnected with the correct polarity. Reversing the battery connections may result in damage to the one-way rectifiers.

• When utilizing a booster battery as a starting aid, always connect the positive to positive terminals and the negative terminal from the booster battery to a good engine ground on the vehicle being started.

• Never use a fast charger as a booster to start vehicles.

• Disconnect the battery cables when charging the battery with a fast charger.

• Never attempt to polarize the alternator.

• Do not use test lamps of more than 12 volts when checking diode continuity.

• Do not short across or ground any of the alternator terminals.

• The polarity of the battery, alternator and regulator must be matched and considered before making any electrical connections within the system.

• Never operate the alternator on an open circuit. Make sure all connections within the circuit are clean and tight.

• Disconnect the battery ground terminal when performing any service on electrical components.

• Disconnect the battery if arc welding is to be done on the vehicle.

BELT TENSION ADJUSTMENT

V-Belts

If equipped with 2.0L engine, the air conditioner compressor is driven by a separate V-belt (all other accessories utilize a self-adjusting serpentine drive belt). Using a belt tension gauge, adjust the air conditioner belt to 225 lbs. (1000 N) for a new belt or 115 lbs. (525 N) for a used belt.

Serpentine Belts

Serpentine belt tension is automatically adjusted by a spring loaded belt tensioner assembly, on which the belt is routed. The belt may be removed by rotating the tensioner using an appropriately sized wrench or breaker bar, depending on the particular engine. For the 2.0L engine, use a 19mm socket or wrench to pivot the tensioner. For the 2.2L engine a 15mm socket or wrench, and for the 3.1L engine, a ½ in. breaker bar, should be used to pivot the tensioner. Belt tension may be visually checked using the indicator mark(s) of the belt tensioner. If the indicator mark is not within specification, either the

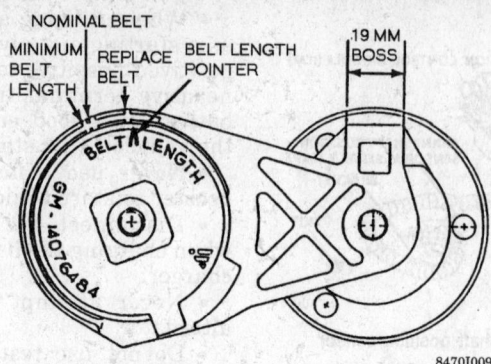

NOMINAL BELT
MINIMUM BELT LENGTH
REPLACE BELT
BELT LENGTH POINTER
19 MM BOSS
BELT LENGTH
GM. 14076484

84701009

Serpentine drive belt tensioner operating range

belt or the tensioner is worn and must be replaced.

NOTE: To remove or install the serpentine drive belt, push and rotate the tensioner using a wrench or breaker bar. Care must always be taken to avoid twisting or bending the tensioner when applying torque.

CHECKING SERPENTINE BELT TENSION

1. Inspect the tensioner to see if the belt is within normal operating range. The belt should be replaced if the tensioner shows it is out of specification. If the tensioner markings indicate the belt is good, but a problem is still suspected, proceed with the test.

2. Make sure all accessories are turned OFF, then start the engine and warm to normal operating temperature.

3. Once the engine is properly warmed, shut the engine OFF and immediately check the belt tension using J-23600-B or an equivalent belt tension gauge. On the 2.0L engine, check tension between alternator and the crankshaft. For the 2.2L and 3.1L engines, check tension between the alternator and the power steering pump. Record the readings and proceed.

4. Start the engine again and allow it to stabilize for 15 seconds, then shut the engine OFF. Use a 15mm wrench to tighten the tensioner pulley bolt. Be aware that the tensioner bolt for the 2.0L and 2.2L engines is a left-hand thread bolt and must be tightened by turning counterclockwise. The 3.1L engine uses a standard bolt and must be tightened by turning clockwise.

5. Release the force and immediately take a belt tension reading. Be sure not to disturb the tensioner position before taking the reading.

6. Using the same wrench, apply force to the tensioner pulley bolt in the opposite direction of Step 4 in order to first rotate the tensioner to the released or belt install position, then slowly release the tensioner back into contact with the belt. Remember, for this step, the 2.0L and 2.2L engine tensioners should be turned clockwise, while the 3.1L engine tensioner should be rotated counterclockwise. Once the tensioner is back in contact, immediately take a final belt tension reading.

7. Average the 3 readings, the tension should be 36–44 lbs. (160–195 N) for the 2.0L engine, 63–77 lbs. (280–342 N) for the 2.2L engine or 50–70 lbs. (225–315 N) for the 3.1L engine. If tension is incorrect, but the

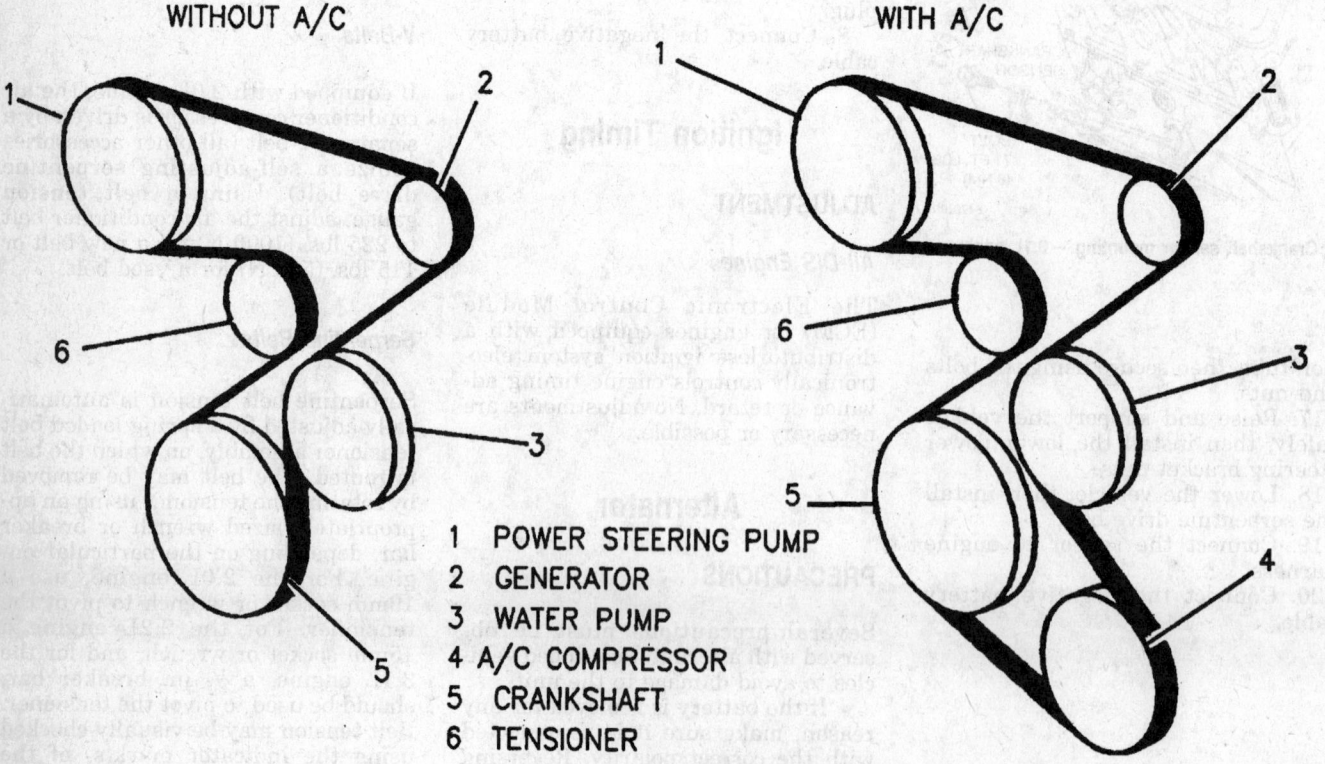

WITHOUT A/C   WITH A/C

1 POWER STEERING PUMP
2 GENERATOR
3 WATER PUMP
4 A/C COMPRESSOR
5 CRANKSHAFT
6 TENSIONER

84701010

Serpentine drive belt routing — 2.0L engine

Serpentine drive belt tensioner installation — 3.1L engine

TENSIONER

BOLT

TO RELEASE TENSION

NOMINAL BELT

REPLACE BELT

INSTALL BELT

INDICATOR MARK

VIEW A

THE INDICATOR MARK ON THE MOVEABLE PORTION OF THE TENSIONER MUST BE WITHIN THE LIMITS OF THE SLOTTED AREA ON THE STATIONARY PORTION OF THE TENSIONER. ANY READING OUTSIDE THESE LIMITS INDICATES EITHER A DEFECTIVE BELT OR TENSIONER.

8470I011

tensioner markings do not indicate a problem (the belt is within the tensioner marking range), the tensioner must be replaced.

REMOVAL AND INSTALLATION

1. Disconnect the negative battery cable.
2. Disconnect and tag the alternator wiring at the rear of the alternator.
3. Release the serpentine drive belt by pivoting the belt tensioner using a wrench or breaker bar, then remove the belt from the alternator pulley.
4. Support the alternator and remove the through-bolts retaining the alternator to the bracket(s).
5. Remove the alternator from the engine.
   To install:
6. Position the alternator in the mounts and install the bolts. Tighten the bolts which thread into the alternator to 18 ft. lbs. (25 Nm) and the bolts/nuts which pass through the alternator to 37 ft. lbs. (50 Nm).
7. Pivot the belt tensioner, position the belt over the alternator pulley and gently pivot the tensioner back into contact with the belt.

8. Connect the alternator wiring, then connect the negative battery cable.

Starter

REMOVAL AND INSTALLATION

Except 2.0L Engine

1. Disconnect the negative battery cable, then raise and support the vehicle safely.
2. For the 2.2L engine, remove the rear starter support bracket.
3. Support the starter and remove the 2 starter-to-engine bolts.
4. Carefully lower the starter until the electrical terminals may be reached, then support the starter and disconnect the solenoid electrical connections. Be sure to note and/or tag all wires for proper installation.
5. Remove the starter from the vehicle. If present, note the location and number of any shims.
6. Raise the starter sufficiently to install the electrical connections to the solenoid, then position any shims which were removed and install the starter.
7. Tighten the starter mounting bolts to 32 ft. lbs. (43 Nm).
8. On the 2.2L engine, install the rear support bracket. Tighten the bracket bolt to 9 ft. lbs. (12 Nm) for the 1992 vehicles or 24 ft. lbs. (32 Nm) for 1993–96 vehicles. Tighten the bracket nuts to 24 ft. lbs. (32 Nm) for 1992 vehicles or 75 inch lbs. (8.5 Nm) for 1993–96 vehicles.
9. Connect the negative battery cable and check starter operation.

2.0L Engine

MANUAL TRANSAXLE

1. Disconnect the negative battery cable.
2. Remove the wire loom strap from the upper starter bolt.
3. Disconnect the shift and selector cables at the external selector lever.
4. Remove the upper and lower transaxle control lever cable bracket and cables.
5. Remove the drive axle support brace.
6. Unplug or remove the starter electrical connectors.
7. Remove the starter from the vehicle.
   To install:
8. Install the starter. Tighten the starter mounting flange bolts to 37 ft.

lbs. (50 Nm), the bracket bolt to 20 ft. lbs. (27 Nm) and the bracket nuts to 27 inch lbs. (3 Nm).
9. Install the starter electrical connectors.
10. Install the drive axle support brace.
11. Install the upper and lower transaxle control lever cable bracket and cables.
12. Connect the shift and selector lever cable bracket and cable.
13. Install the wire loom strap to the upper starter bolt.
14. Connect the negative battery cable.

AUTOMATIC TRANSAXLE

1. Disconnect the negative battery cable.
2. Remove the blower motor.
3. Disconnect the starter electrical connectors.
4. Remove the rear starter brace.
5. Remove the wire loom from the upper starter bolt.
6. Remove the upper starter bolt.
7. Remove the lower starter bolt.
8. Remove the starter motor from the vehicle through the blower motor opening.
   To install:
9. Install the starter motor through the blower motor opening.
10. Install the lower starter bolt.
11. With the help of an assistant, install the upper starter bolt.
12. Install the wire loom to the upper starter bolt.
13. Install the rear starter brace.
14. Install the motor electrical connectors.
15. Install the blower motor.
16. Connect the negative battery cable.

CHASSIS ELECTRICAL

Heater Blower Motor

REMOVAL AND INSTALLATION

2.0L and 2.2L Engines

1. Disconnect the negative battery cable.
2. Mark and remove the electrical connections at the blower motor.
3. Remove the blower motor cooling tube.

4. Remove the blower motor retaining screws. Remove the blower motor fan.

NOTE: The blower motor and fan are serviced as an assembly.

To install:

5. Install the blower motor and fan assembly in the correct position.

6. Install and tighten evenly the fan assembly retaining screws.

7. Install the blower motor cooling tube.

8. Connect the electrical connections and reconnect the negative battery cable. Check the blower motor operation in all speeds.

3.1L Engine

1. Disconnect the negative battery cable.

2. Remove the tower to tower brace. Mark and remove the electrical connections at the blower motor.

3. Remove the blower motor cooling tube.

4. Remove the alternator assembly.

5. Remove the blower motor retaining screws. Remove the blower motor assembly.

NOTE: The blower motor and fan are serviced as an assembly.

To install:

6. Install the blower motor and fan assembly in the correct position.

7. Install and tighten evenly the fan assembly retaining screws.

8. Install the alternator assembly. Adjust the drive belt.

9. Install the blower motor cooling tube.

10. Connect the electrical connections and install the tower to tower brace.

11. Reconnect the negative battery cable. Check the blower motor operation in all speeds.

Windshield Wiper Motor

REMOVAL AND INSTALLATION

1. Disconnect the negative battery cable.

2. Remove the wiper arm and blade assemblies, then remove the shroud top vent grille.

3. Disconnect the drive link from the wiper motor crank arm.

4. Unplug the wiring harness from the wiper motor.

5. Remove the mounting bolts, rotate the motor up and remove the motor by guiding the crank arm through the opening. Inspect the motor gas-

ket, if damaged remove and discard the gasket from the rear of the motor.

To install:

6. Make sure the gasket is positioned on the motor, then guide the crank arm through the opening in the body and install the mounting bolts. Tighten the bolts to 80 inch lbs. (9 Nm).

7. Install the wiring harness connector to the motor.

8. With the motor in the park position, press the drive link socket into engagement with the crank arm ball.

9. Install the shroud top vent grille and the wiper arms assemblies.

10. Connect the negative battery cable.

11. Check the operation of the wiper system.

Windshield Wiper Switch

REMOVAL AND INSTALLATION

Cavalier

1. Disconnect the negative battery cable.

2. Remove the steering wheel from the column.

3. If applicable, remove the tilt lever from the steering column.

4. Remove the upper steering column cover attaching screws, then remove the upper steering column.

5. Remove the lower steering column attaching screws. Remove the lower steering column cover.

6. Remove the wiper and washer switch attaching screws.

7. Depress the locking tab(s), then remove all electrical connectors from the switch and remove the switch from the vehicle.

To install:

8. Position the switch and install the wiring harness electrical connector(s).

9. Install the switch attaching screws and tighten to 49 inch lbs. (5.5 Nm).

10. If applicable, connect the rose bud fastener to the jacket assembly.

11. Install the lower steering column cover and attaching screws. Tighten to 49 inch lbs. (5.5 Nm).

12. Install the upper steering column cover and attaching screws. Tighten to 49 inch lbs. (5.5 Nm).

13. If removed, install the tilt lever to the column.

14. Install the steering wheel onto the steering shaft. Install the hexagonal retaining nut and tighten to 30 ft. lbs. (41 Nm) except for 1993–96 vehicles whose nuts should be tightened to 37 ft. lbs. (50 Nm).

15. Connect the negative battery cable.

Sunbird

1. Disconnect the negative battery cable.

2. Remove the right side trim plate from the instrument panel. To remove the trim plate, remove the 4 screws and 1 or 2 nuts. If equipped with a console, loosen the housing bracket sufficiently to pivot it downward for clearance. Carefully pry the trim plate from of the instrument panel.

3. Remove the attaching screw from the wiper switch housing.

4. Unplug the windshield wiper switch electrical connector, then remove the switch from the vehicle.

To install:

5. Install the wiring harness electrical connector to the wiper switch.

6. Position the switch to the instrument panel and install the attaching screw.

7. Install the right side trim plate to the instrument panel. Tighten the retaining screws to 5 ft. lbs. (7 Nm) and the nuts to 8 ft. lbs. (10 Nm).

8. Connect the negative battery cable.

Instrument Cluster

REMOVAL AND INSTALLATION

The only serviceable instrument cluster components are the bulbs and sockets;. a damaged cluster must be removed as an assembly and repaired by an authorized source or replaced.

Cavalier

1. Disconnect the negative battery cable.

2. Remove the 4 screws from the steering column opening filler. Pull downward on the filler panel in order to disengage the clips, then remove the filler from the vehicle.

3. Remove the 2 screws from the bottom of the instrument cluster trim extension; it will be necessary to pull down slightly on the column seal to expose the screws. Pull the extension rearward to access the interior lamp control and instrument panel dimmer switch connectors. Unplug the wiring harness from the switches and remove the cluster extension from the vehicle.

4. Remove the 2 retaining screws from the top of the instrument cluster assembly, then pull the cluster

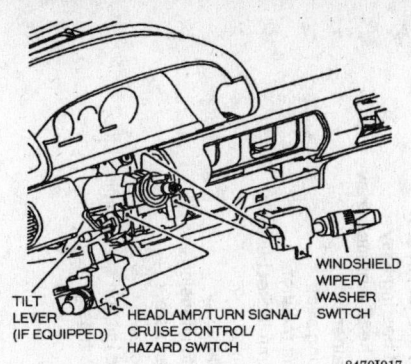

Steering column switches and tilt lever

rearward and remove it from the vehicle.

To install:

5. Position the cluster assembly in the vehicle and install it to the instrument panel. Tighten the cluster retaining screws to 19 inch lbs. (2 Nm).

6. Install the wiring harness connectors and position the cluster extension, then secure using the retaining screws. Make sure the steering column seal is properly positioned.

7. Position the steering column opening filler and push upward to engage the clips, then secure the filler using the retaining screws.

8. Connect the negative battery cable.

Sunbird

1. Disconnect the negative battery cable.

2. Gently pry the steering column opening filler downward and from the retaining clips, then remove the filler from the vehicle.

3. Remove the 2 attaching screws from the left trim plate, then gently pry the plate from the instrument panel.

4. Remove the right side trim plate from the instrument panel. To remove the trim plate, remove the 4 screws and 1 or 2 nuts. If equipped with a console, loosen the housing bracket sufficiently to pivot it downward for clearance. Carefully pry the trim plate from the instrument panel.

5. Remove the left hand console trim plate by gently prying it outward.

6. Remove the 4 attaching screws the instrument cluster assembly, then pull the cluster rearward and remove it from the vehicle.

To install:

7. Position the cluster assembly in the vehicle and install it to the in-strument panel. Tighten the cluster retaining screws to 12 inch lbs. (1.4 Nm).

8. Install the left console trim plate, then position the right side trim plate to the instrument panel. Install the right trim plate into the clips, then install the fasteners. Tighten the retaining screws to 5 ft. lbs. (7 Nm) and the nuts to 8 ft. lbs. (10 Nm).

9. Install the left trim plate to the instrument panel and clips, then install the 2 retaining screws and tighten to 5 ft. lbs. (7 Nm).

10. Position the steering column opening filler and push upward to engage the retaining clips.

11. Connect the negative battery cable.

Speedometer

A damaged cluster, must be replaced or sent to an authorized repair center.

REMOVAL AND INSTALLATION

1. Disconnect the negative battery cable.

2. Remove the speedometer cluster from instrument panel.

3. Remove cluster lens and face plate.

4. Remove screws securing speedometer to the cluster assembly, then remove the speedometer.

To install:

5. Install the speedometer into the cluster and secure using the screws.

6. Install cluster face plate and lens.

7. Install speedometer cluster to the instrument panel.

8. Connect the negative battery cable.

Headlight Switch

REMOVAL AND INSTALLATION

Cavalier models utilize a combination switch mounted to the left side of the steering column. This combination switch performs the functions of the headlight, headlight dimmer, turn signal and, if applicable, cruise control switches.

Sunbird

1. Disconnect the negative battery cable.

2. Remove the steering column filler panel.

3. Remove the 2 attaching screws from the left trim plate, then gently pry the plate from the instrument panel.

4. Remove the attaching screw from the headlight switch housing.

5. Unplug the headlight switch electrical connector, then remove the switch from the vehicle.

To install:

6. Connect the wiring harness to the headlight switch.

7. Install the headlight switch to the instrument panel and housing, then install the retaining screw. Make sure the screw is fully tightened, but not stripped.

8. Install the left side trim plate and tighten the retaining screws to 5 ft. lbs. (7 Nm), then install the left sound insulator or the steering column filler panel, as applicable.

9. Connect the negative battery cable.

Dimmer Switch

REMOVAL AND INSTALLATION

Sunbird

1. Disconnect the negative battery cable. For 1993–94 vehicles, remove the steering wheel from the vehicle.

2. Inspect the lower steering column for access to the switch assembly. If necessary, remove trim plates or components to ease access to the switch.

3. Remove the retaining screw and nut from the dimmer switch assembly.

4. Free the dimmer switch from the actuator rod, unplug the wiring harness from the switch terminal and remove the switch from the vehicle.

To install:

5. Position the switch assembly to the actuator rod, then install and finger-tighten the retainers.

6. Adjust the dimmer switch by inserting a ³⁄₃₂ in. drill bit into the adjusting hole and positioning the switch to the steering column. Push the switch up against the rod and the drill bit to remove any play and tighten the dimmer switch retainers to 35 inch lbs. (4 Nm), then remove the drill bit.

7. Connect the wiring harness to the dimmer switch assembly.

8. Connect the negative battery cable.

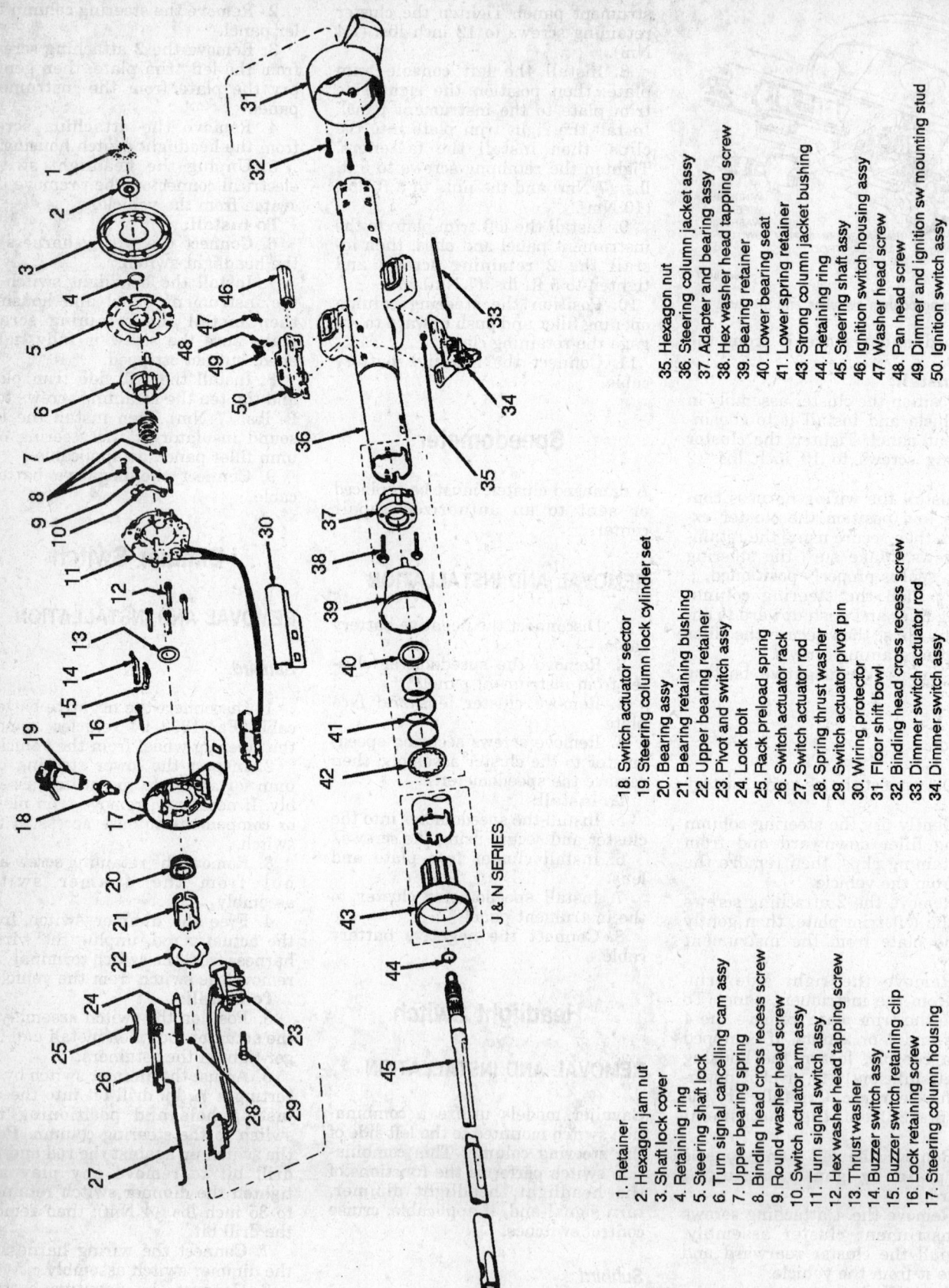

35. Hexagon nut
36. Steering column jacket assy
37. Adapter and bearing assy
38. Hex washer head tapping screw
39. Bearing retainer
40. Lower bearing seat
41. Lower spring retainer
42. Strong column jacket bushing
43. Strong column jacket bushing
44. Retaining ring
45. Steering shaft assy
46. Ignition switch housing assy
47. Washer head screw
48. Pan head screw
49. Dimmer and ignition sw mounting stud
50. Ignition switch assy

18. Switch actuator sector
19. Steering column lock cylinder set
20. Bearing assy
21. Bearing retaining bushing
22. Upper bearing retainer
23. Pivot and switch assy
24. Lock bolt
25. Rack preload spring
26. Switch actuator rack
27. Switch actuator rod
28. Spring thrust washer
29. Switch actuator pivot pin
30. Wiring protector
31. Floor shift bowl
32. Binding head cross recess screw
33. Dimmer switch actuator rod
34. Dimmer switch assy

1. Retainer
2. Hexagon jam nut
3. Shaft lock cover
4. Retaining ring
5. Steering shaft lock
6. Turn signal cancelling cam assy
7. Upper bearing spring
8. Binding head cross recess screw
9. Round washer head screw
10. Switch actuator arm assy
11. Turn signal switch assy
12. Hex washer head tapping screw
13. Thrust washer
14. Buzzer switch assy
15. Buzzer switch retaining clip
16. Lock retaining screw
17. Steering column housing

J & N SERIES

Standard steering column components — 1991 Sunbird — 1992–94 Sunbird similar

84701019

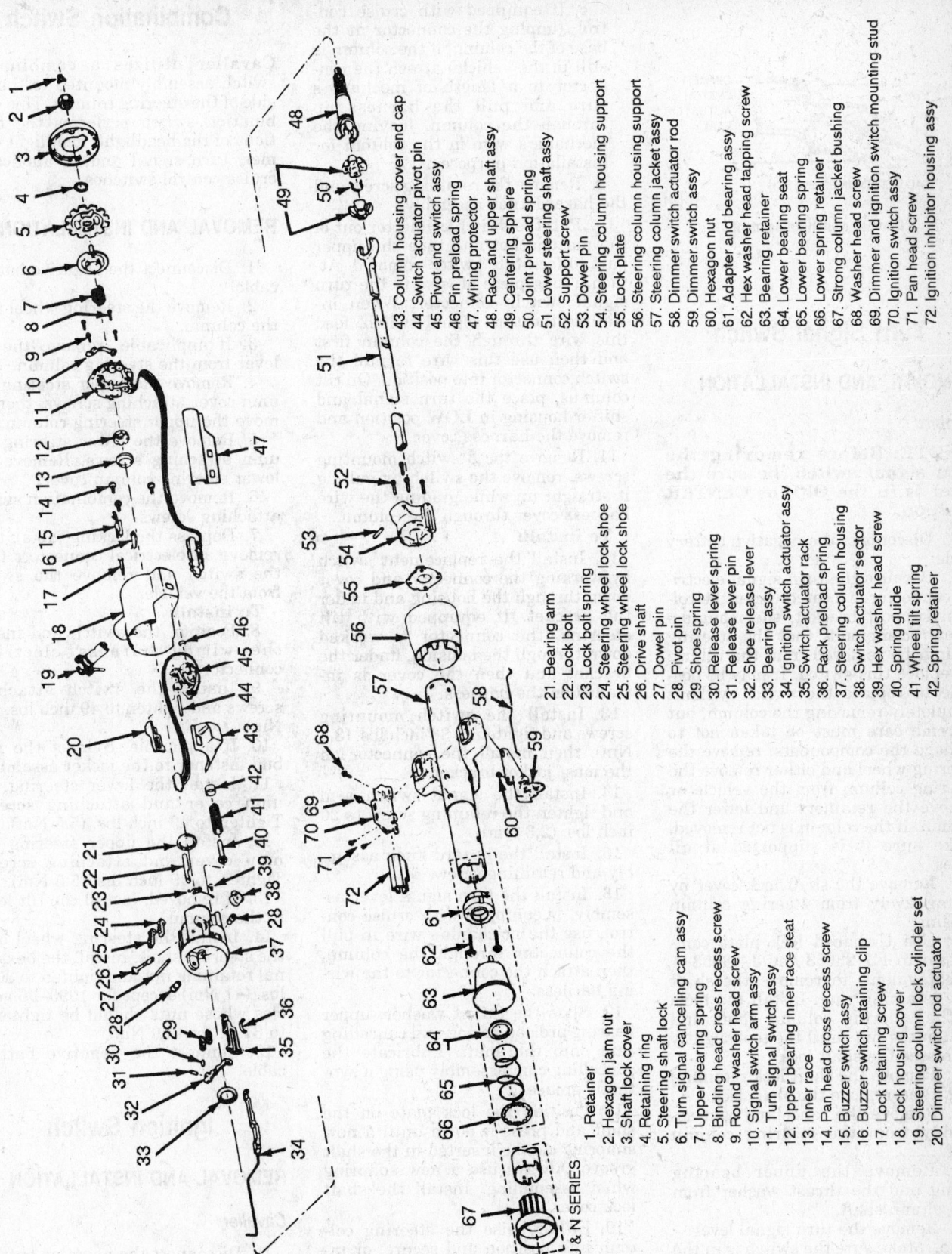

1. Retainer
2. Hexagon jam nut
3. Shaft lock cover
4. Retaining ring
5. Steering shaft lock
6. Turn signal cancelling cam assy
7. Upper bearing spring
8. Binding head cross recess screw
9. Round washer head screw
10. Signal switch arm assy
11. Turn signal switch assy
12. Upper bearing inner race seat
13. Inner race
14. Pan head cross recess screw
15. Buzzer switch assy
16. Buzzer switch retaining clip
17. Lock retaining screw
18. Lock housing cover
19. Steering column lock cylinder set
20. Dimmer switch rod actuator

21. Bearing arm
22. Lock bolt
23. Lock bolt spring
24. Steering wheel lock shoe
25. Steering wheel lock shoe
26. Drive shaft
27. Dowel pin
28. Pivot pin
29. Shoe spring
30. Release lever spring
31. Release lever pin
32. Shoe release lever
33. Bearing assy
34. Ignition switch actuator assy
35. Switch actuator rack
36. Rack preload spring
37. Steering column housing
38. Switch actuator sector
39. Hex washer head screw
40. Spring guide
41. Wheel tilt spring
42. Spring retainer

43. Column housing cover end cap
44. Switch actuator pivot pin
45. Pivot and switch assy
46. Pin preload spring
47. Wiring protector
48. Race and upper shaft assy
49. Centering sphere
50. Joint preload spring
51. Lower steering shaft assy
52. Support screw
53. Dowel pin
54. Steering column housing support
55. Lock plate
56. Steering column housing support
57. Steering column jacket assy
58. Dimmer switch actuator rod
59. Dimmer switch assy
60. Hexagon nut
61. Adapter and bearing assy
62. Hex washer head tapping screw
63. Bearing retainer
64. Lower bearing seat
65. Lower bearing spring
66. Lower spring retainer
67. Strong column jacket bushing
68. Washer head screw
69. Dimmer and ignition switch mounting stud
70. Ignition switch assy
71. Pan head screw
72. Ignition inhibitor housing assy

J & N SERIES

Tilt steering column components — 1991 Sunbird — 1992–94 Sunbird similar

84701020

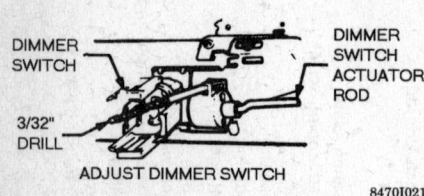

Dimmer switch adjustment

Turn Signal Switch

REMOVAL AND INSTALLATION

Sunbird

NOTE: Before removing the turn signal switch, be sure the lever is in the OFF or CENTER position.

1. Disconnect the negative battery cable.

2. Because the turn signal electrical connector is located under the column support bracket, the manufacturer recommends that the steering column be removed from the vehicle to replace this switch. It may be possible to replace the switch without completely removing the column, but extreme care must be taken not to damage the components. remove the steering wheel and either remove the steering column from the vehicle or remove the retainers and lower the column. If the column is not removed, make sure it is supported at all times.

3. Remove the shaft lock cover by prying away from steering column housing.

4. Use U-shaped lock plate compressor tool J–23653 and J–23653–4, or equivalent, to remove the shaft lock retaining ring. Install the tools to the steering column shaft and tighten the nut until the tool slightly depresses the shaft lock.

5. Remove the shaft lock retaining ring, then remove the shaft lock.

6. Remove the cancelling cam assembly from the steering column shaft.

7. Remove the upper bearing spring and the thrust washer from the column shaft.

8. Remove the turn signal lever.

  a. Make sure the switch is in the center or **OFF** position.

  b. Pull the lever straight out of the turn signal switch.

c. If equipped with cruise control, (unplug the connector at the base of the column, if the column is still in the vehicle) attach the connector to a length of mechanic's wire and pull the harness up through the column, leaving the mechanic's wire in the column for installation purposes.

9. Remove the retaining screw and the hazard knob assembly.

10. Pull the switch connector out of the mast jacket and tape the upper part to facilitate switch removal. Attach a long piece of wire to the turn signal switch connector. When installing the turn signal switch, feed this wire through the column first and then use this wire to pull the switch connector into position. On tilt columns, place the turn signal and shifter housing in **LOW** position and remove the harness cover.

11. Remove the 3 switch mounting screws. remove the switch by pulling it straight up while guiding the wire harness cover through the column.

To install:

12. Install the replacement switch by working the connector and cover down through the housing and under the bracket. If equipped with tilt steering, the connector is worked down through the housing, under the bracket and then the cover is installed on the harness.

13. Install the switch mounting screws and tighten to 30 inch lbs. (3.4 Nm), then install the connector on the mast jacket bracket.

14. Install the signal switch arm and tighten the retaining screw to 20 inch lbs. (2.3 Nm).

15. Install the hazard knob assembly and retaining screw.

16. Install the turn signal lever assembly. If equipped with cruise control, use the mechanic's wire to pull the connector through the column, then attach the connector to the wiring harness.

17. Slide the thrust washer, upper bearing preload spring and cancelling cam onto the shaft. Lubricate the cancelling cam assembly using a synthetic grease.

18. Position the lock plate on the shaft and press it down until a new snapring can be inserted in the shaft groove. Always use a new snapring when assembling. Install the shaft lock cover.

19. Either raise the steering column into position and secure, or install the column into the vehicle.

20. Install the steering wheel and connect the negative battery cable.

Combination Switch

Cavalier utilizes a combination switch assembly mounted to the left side of the steering column. This combination switch performs the functions of the headlight, headlight dimmer, turn signal and, if applicable, cruise control switches.

REMOVAL AND INSTALLATION

1. Disconnect the negative battery cable.

2. Remove the steering wheel from the column.

3. If applicable, remove the tilt lever from the steering column.

4. Remove the upper steering column cover attaching screws, then remove the upper steering column.

5. Remove the lower steering column attaching screws. Remove the lower steering column cover.

6. Remove the combination switch attaching screws.

7. Depress the locking tab(s), then remove all electrical connectors from the switch and remove the switch from the vehicle.

To install:

8. Position the switch and install the wiring harness electrical connector(s).

9. Install the switch attaching screws and tighten to 49 inch lbs. (5.5 Nm).

10. If applicable, connect the rose bud fastener to the jacket assembly.

11. Install the lower steering column cover and attaching screws. Tighten to 49 inch lbs. (5.5 Nm).

12. Install the upper steering column cover and attaching screws. Tighten to 49 inch lbs. (5.5 Nm).

13. If removed, install the tilt lever to the column.

14. Install the steering wheel onto the steering shaft. Install the hexagonal retaining nut and tighten to 30 ft. lbs. (41 Nm) except for 1993–96 vehicles whose nuts should be tightened to 37 ft. lbs. (50 Nm).

15. Connect the negative battery cable.

Ignition Switch

REMOVAL AND INSTALLATION

Cavalier

1. Disconnect the negative battery cable.

2. Remove the steering wheel from the column.

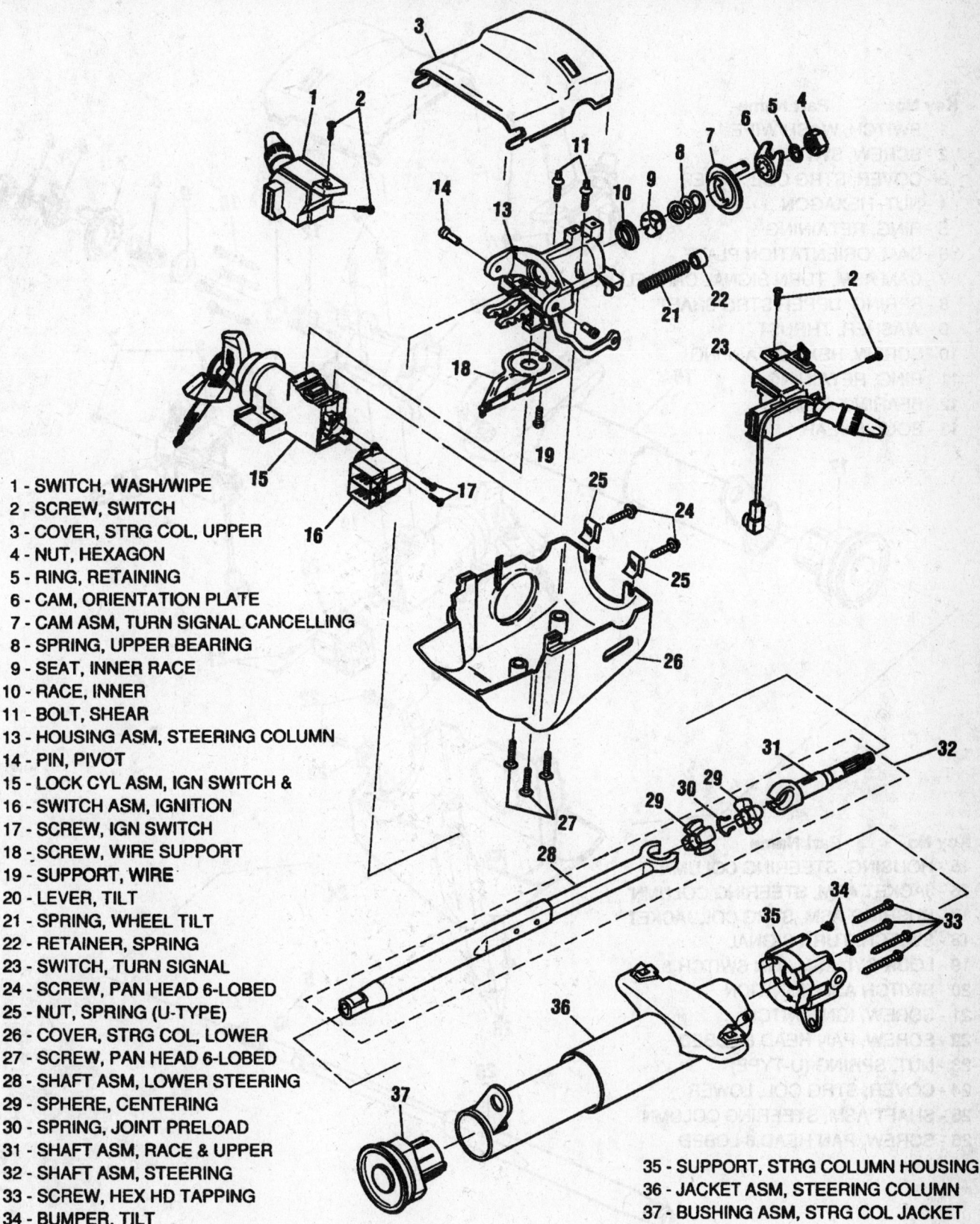

1 - SWITCH, WASH/WIPE
2 - SCREW, SWITCH
3 - COVER, STRG COL, UPPER
4 - NUT, HEXAGON
5 - RING, RETAINING
6 - CAM, ORIENTATION PLATE
7 - CAM ASM, TURN SIGNAL CANCELLING
8 - SPRING, UPPER BEARING
9 - SEAT, INNER RACE
10 - RACE, INNER
11 - BOLT, SHEAR
13 - HOUSING ASM, STEERING COLUMN
14 - PIN, PIVOT
15 - LOCK CYL ASM, IGN SWITCH &
16 - SWITCH ASM, IGNITION
17 - SCREW, IGN SWITCH
18 - SCREW, WIRE SUPPORT
19 - SUPPORT, WIRE
20 - LEVER, TILT
21 - SPRING, WHEEL TILT
22 - RETAINER, SPRING
23 - SWITCH, TURN SIGNAL
24 - SCREW, PAN HEAD 6-LOBED
25 - NUT, SPRING (U-TYPE)
26 - COVER, STRG COL, LOWER
27 - SCREW, PAN HEAD 6-LOBED
28 - SHAFT ASM, LOWER STEERING
29 - SPHERE, CENTERING
30 - SPRING, JOINT PRELOAD
31 - SHAFT ASM, RACE & UPPER
32 - SHAFT ASM, STEERING
33 - SCREW, HEX HD TAPPING
34 - BUMPER, TILT

35 - SUPPORT, STRG COLUMN HOUSING
36 - JACKET ASM, STEERING COLUMN
37 - BUSHING ASM, STRG COL JACKET

84701022

Exploded view of the tilt steering column — Cavalier

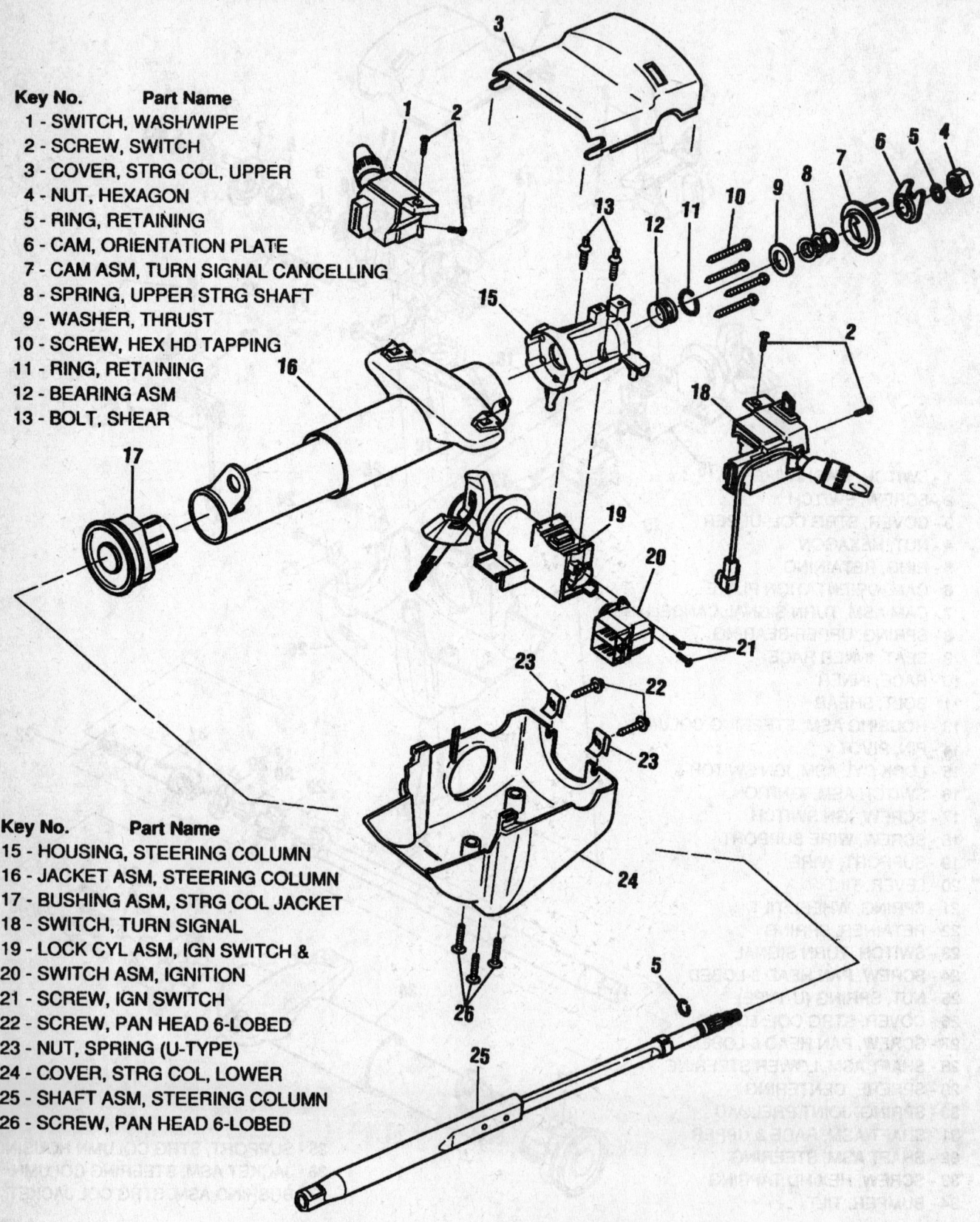

Key No.   Part Name
1 - SWITCH, WASH/WIPE
2 - SCREW, SWITCH
3 - COVER, STRG COL, UPPER
4 - NUT, HEXAGON
5 - RING, RETAINING
6 - CAM, ORIENTATION PLATE
7 - CAM ASM, TURN SIGNAL CANCELLING
8 - SPRING, UPPER STRG SHAFT
9 - WASHER, THRUST
10 - SCREW, HEX HD TAPPING
11 - RING, RETAINING
12 - BEARING ASM
13 - BOLT, SHEAR

Key No.   Part Name
15 - HOUSING, STEERING COLUMN
16 - JACKET ASM, STEERING COLUMN
17 - BUSHING ASM, STRG COL JACKET
18 - SWITCH, TURN SIGNAL
19 - LOCK CYL ASM, IGN SWITCH &
20 - SWITCH ASM, IGNITION
21 - SCREW, IGN SWITCH
22 - SCREW, PAN HEAD 6-LOBED
23 - NUT, SPRING (U-TYPE)
24 - COVER, STRG COL, LOWER
25 - SHAFT ASM, STEERING COLUMN
26 - SCREW, PAN HEAD 6-LOBED

84701023

Exploded view of the standard steering column — Cavalier

3. If applicable, remove the tilt lever from the steering column.

4. Remove the upper steering column cover attaching screws, then remove the upper steering column.

5. Remove the lower steering column attaching screws. Remove the lower steering column cover.

6. Make sure the shift lever is in the **PARK** position and the ignition is **OFF** with the key is removed.

7. Remove the ignition switch retaining screws, then unplug the switch electrical connectors and remove the switch from the vehicle.

To install:

8. Make sure the shift lever and ignition lock cylinder have not been moved, then position the switch and install the wiring harness electrical connector(s).

9. Install the switch attaching screws and tighten to 25 inch lbs. (2.8 Nm).

10. If applicable, connect the rose bud fastener to the jacket assembly.

11. Install the lower steering column cover and attaching screws. Tighten to 49 inch lbs. (5.5 Nm).

12. Install the upper steering column cover and attaching screws. Tighten to 49 inch lbs. (5.5 Nm).

13. If removed, install the tilt lever to the column.

14. Install the steering wheel onto the steering shaft. Install the hexagonal retaining nut and tighten to 30 ft. lbs. (41 Nm) except for 1993–96 vehicles whose nuts should be tightened to 37 ft. lbs. (50 Nm).

15. Connect the negative battery cable.

Sunbird

1. Disconnect the negative battery cable. For 1993–94 vehicles, remove the steering wheel from the vehicle.

2. Inspect the lower steering column for access to the switch assembly. If necessary, remove trim plates or components to ease access to the switch.

3. Remove the retaining screw and nut from the dimmer switch assembly.

4. Free the dimmer switch from the actuator rod, then remove the dimmer and ignition switch mounting stud.

5. If present, remove the 2 cross recess screws. Remove the ignition switch from the actuator assembly. Unplug the wiring harness and remove the switch from the vehicle.

To install:

6. Position the ignition switch to the actuator assembly, move the switch slider to the extreme right,

then move the slider 1 detent to the left into the off lock position.

7. If applicable, install the 2 cross recess screws and tighten to 30 inch lbs. (3.4 Nm).

8. Install the mounting stud and tighten to 35 inch lbs. (4 Nm).

9. Position the dimmer switch assembly to the actuator rod, then install and finger-tighten the retainers.

10. Adjust the dimmer switch by inserting a $\frac{3}{32}$ in. drill bit into the adjusting hole and positioning the switch to the steering column. Push the switch up against the rod and the drill bit to remove any play and tighten the dimmer switch retainers to 35 inch lbs. (4 Nm), then remove the drill bit.

11. Connect the wiring harness to the dimmer switch assembly.

12. Connect the negative battery cable.

Ignition Lock Cylinder

REMOVAL AND INSTALLATION

Sunbird

1. Disconnect the negative battery cable.

2. Remove the steering wheel.

3. Remove the turn signal switch from the steering column and allow it to hang from the wiring harness.

4. Make sure the ignition is in the lock position, then remove the key from the lock cylinder. Remove the buzzer switch assembly, reinsert the key, remove the retaining screw, then remove the lock cylinder assembly from the vehicle.

NOTE: Use extreme caution when removing the lock cylinder retaining screw. If the screw is dropped during removal, it could fall into the column, requiring complete column disassembly to retrieve the screw.

To install:

5. Align the lock cylinder set with the steering column housing.

6. Push the lock all the way in.

7. Install the cylinder retaining screw and tighten to 40 inch lbs. (4.5 Nm), except for 1993–94 vehicles which should be tightened to 22 inch lbs. (2.5 Nm).

8. With the key still in the same position as during removal, install the buzzer switch.

9. Install the turn signal switch.

10. Install the steering wheel.

11. Connect the negative battery cable.

Cavalier

1. Disconnect the negative battery cable.

2. Remove the steering column from the vehicle.

3. Turn the ignition key to the **RUN** position and, if applicable, place the shift lock cable lever in the **PARK** position.

4. Drill off the heads of the lock cylinder assembly shear bolts using a $\frac{1}{4}$ in. (6.5mm) drill bit.

5. Remove the lock cylinder housing assembly from the steering column.

6. Using a pair of locking pliers, remove the threaded ends of the shear bolts.

To install:

7. Thoroughly clean all metal shavings from the steering column assembly.

8. Place the lock cylinder key in the **RUN** position, then install the cylinder housing to the steering column assembly. Tighten the shear bolts until the head separates from the rest of the body, this should occur at approximately 97 inch lbs. (11 Nm) of torque.

9. Install the steering column to the vehicle.

10. Connect the negative battery cable.

Brake Light Switch

ADJUSTMENT

The brake light switch, located on the pedal bracket is self-adjusting. If incorrect adjustment is suspected, fully seat the switch in the tube mounted to the bracket, then pull the brake pedal fully upwards; against the switch. Audible clicks should be heard and the threads of the switch seat in the proper position. If the switch cannot be adjusted, it or the support tube must be replaced.

REMOVAL AND INSTALLATION

The brake light and, if applicable, TCC/cruise control (automatic transaxle) or cruise control vacuum switch (manual transaxle) are located on the brake pedal mounting bracket and are adjusted in an identical manner.

1. If necessary, remove the sound insulator panel for switch access.

2. Remove the wiring from switch and pull the switch from the bracket.

3. To install, insert the retaining tubular clip in the bracket on the pedal assembly.

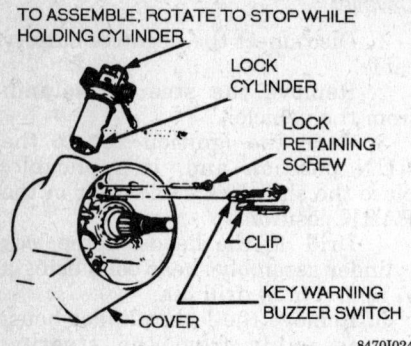

TO ASSEMBLE, ROTATE TO STOP WHILE HOLDING CYLINDER

LOCK CYLINDER

LOCK RETAINING SCREW

CLIP

KEY WARNING BUZZER SWITCH

COVER

8470I024

Lock cylinder installation — Sunbird

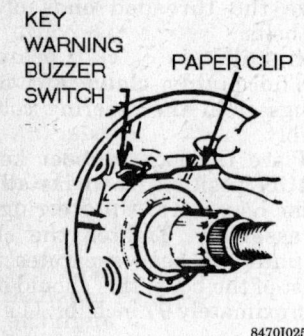

KEY WARNING BUZZER SWITCH

PAPER CLIP

8470I025

Removing the warning buzzer switch — Sunbird

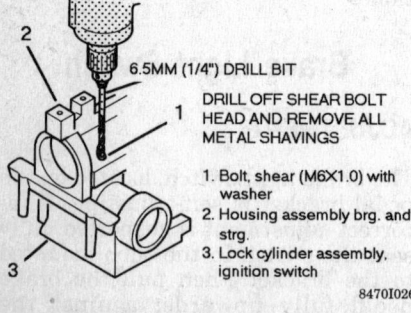

6.5MM (1/4") DRILL BIT

DRILL OFF SHEAR BOLT HEAD AND REMOVE ALL METAL SHAVINGS

1. Bolt, shear (M6X1.0) with washer
2. Housing assembly brg. and strg.
3. Lock cylinder assembly, ignition switch

8470I026

Drill the heads from the ignition lock cylinder housing shear bolts in order to remove the housing from the steering column

4. With the pedal depressed, insert the switch into the tubular clip until the switch body seats on clip.

5. Grasp the brake pedal and pull upward against the bracket and switch, until the pedal is in the fully released position and the switch has adjusted itself.

NOTE: Audible clicks can be heard as threaded portion of switch is pushed through the clip and adjusted by the brake pedal.

6. Connect the switch wiring harness, then confirm proper switch operation.

7. If removed, install the sound insulator panel.

Clutch Switch

The clutch start switch is used on vehicles equipped with a manual transaxle. The switch prevents the engine from starting unless the clutch pedal is depressed.

ADJUSTMENT

The clutch switch is mounted to a stud located below the clutch pedal bracket. When the pedal is fully depressed, the pedal will depress the switch and close the starter circuit. Adjustment should not be necessary if the switch is properly installed. Make sure the retainers are properly tightened and that the clutch pedal assembly is not bent or damaged. Switch interference could also come from carpeting or floor mats that cock the switch or prevent the clutch pedal from making contact with the switch.

REMOVAL AND INSTALLATION

1. Disconnect the negative battery cable.

2. Unplug the wiring harness connector from the switch.

3. Remove the switch and instrument panel harness retaining nuts, then reposition the harness and remove the switch from the mounting studs.

To install:

4. Install the switch and the instrument panel harness over the mounting studs, then secure using the nuts.

5. Install wiring harness electrical connector to the clutch switch.

6. Connect the negative battery cable.

Neutral Safety Switch

The neutral safety system for all vehicles equipped with an automatic transaxle takes 2 forms. Vehicles are equipped with a neutral safety switch which will prevent engine starting unless the transaxle is in **P** or **N**. In addition to this, vehicles are equipped with a floor shift mechanical lockout that physically prevents

the shifter from moving out of **P** if the lock cylinder is in the locked position, or conversely, prevents the key from turning to lock if the transaxle is in **N**.

The floor shift mechanical park lock system uses a flexible cable actuator which is attached at one end to the shift lever and the other end is attached to the column mounted ignition switch where it actuates a locking pin. The locking pin engages an ignition switch sliding contact when the shift lever is in **R**, **N** or **D** and does not allow the ignition switch slider to move to the **LOCK** position. When the shift lever is in **P**, the pin disengages from the slider and allows it to move to the **LOCK** position.

ADJUSTMENT

1. Place the transmission shifter in the **N** notch in the detent plate.

2. Loosen the attaching screws.

3. Insert a $^3/_{32}$ in. (2.34mm) drill bit or gauge pin into the adjustment hole, then rotate the switch until the gauge pin drops to a depth of $^9/_{64}$ in. (9mm).

4. Tighten the attaching screws to 18 ft. lbs. (24 Nm).

5. Remove the gauge pin and verify that the engine will only start in **P** or **N**.

REMOVAL AND INSTALLATION

1. Disconnect the negative battery cable.

2. Disconnect the shift linkage.

3. Unplug the switch electrical connector.

4. Remove the attaching bolts.

5. Remove the switch assembly.

To install:

6. Place the shift shaft in the **N** position.

7. Align the flats of the shift shaft with the switch.

8. If installing a new switch, the component should be pinned in the proper position making adjustment unnecessary; install the switch and tighten the attaching screws to 18 ft. lbs. (24 Nm).

9. If installing an old switch or a new switch which has been rotated, breaking the plastic pin and moving the switch out of adjustment, loosely install the switch. Adjust the switch and secure using the retaining bolts.

10. Verify that the engine will only start with the transmission selector in the **P** or **N** position.

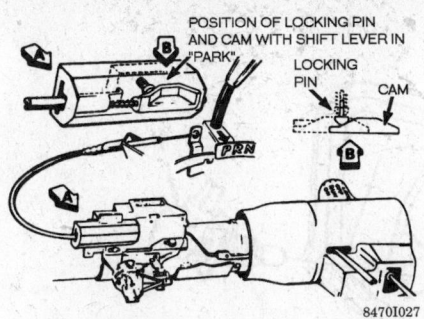

Floor shift mechanical park lock mechanism

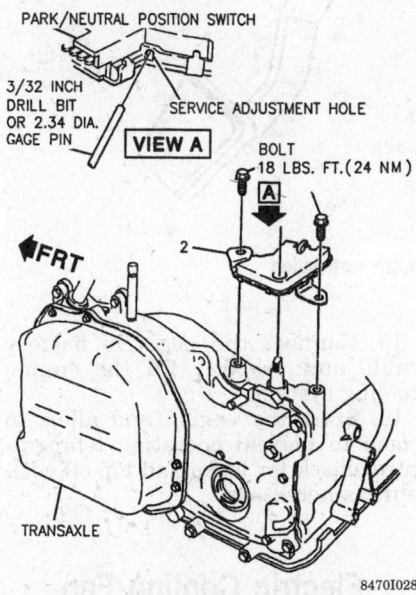

Neutral safety switch installation

Fuses, Circuit Breakers and Relays

LOCATION

Fusible Links

Fusible links are used to prevent major wire harness damage in the event of short circuit or an overload condition in the wiring circuits which are normally not fused, due to carrying high amperage loads or because of their locations within the wiring harness. Each fusible link is of a fixed value for a specific electrical load and should a link fail, the cause of failure must be determined and repaired prior to installing a new fusible link of the same value. Fusible links are located in the engine harness at the starter solenoid and the left hand front of the dash at the battery junction block.

Circuit Breakers

Circuit breakers are used along with the fusible links to protect the various components of the electrical system, such as headlights, the windshield wipers and electric windows. The circuit breakers are located either in the switch or mounted on or near the lower lip of the instrument panel, to the right or left of the steering column.

Fuse Panels

The fuse panel is located on the left side of the vehicle. It is under the instrument panel assembly. In order to gain access to the fuse panel, it may be necessary to first remove the under dash padding.

Convenience Center and Relays

The convenience center is located on the underside of the instrument panel near the fuse panel. It provides a central location for various relays, hazard flasher units and buzzers. All units are easily replaced with plug-in modules.

Computer

LOCATION

The Electronic Control Module (ECM) is located on the right side of the vehicle. It is positioned in front of the right side kick panel. In order to gain access to the assembly, remove the trim panel.

Flashers

LOCATION

Turn Signal Flasher

The turn signal flasher is located directly under the steering column of the vehicle. It is secured in place by means of a plastic retainer. In order to gain access to the component, it may be necessary to remove the underdash padding panel.

Hazard Flasher

The hazard flasher is located in the fuse block. It is positioned on the lower right side corner of the fuse block assembly. In order to gain access to the turn signal flasher, it may be necessary to first remove the under dash padding.

Cruise Control

ADJUSTMENT

Release Switch and Valve

1. Depress the brake pedal and insert the vacuum release valve into the retainer until a click is heard indication that the valve switch is seated.
2. Allow the brake pedal to travel rearward to the positive stop.
3. The valve switch will be moved through the retainer into the proper position.

NOTE: Audible clicks can be heard as threaded position of switch is pushed through the clip toward the brake pedal. Vacuum release valve and stoplight switch are self-adjusting.

Servo Cable

1. Install the cable into the engine bracket. Route the cable assembly to the servo bracket.
2. Pull the servo end of the cable towards the servo assembly without moving the throttle lever.
3. Align the pin in the end of the cable with 1 of the holes in the servo assembly tab.
4. Insert the cable pin into 1 of the 6 holes in the servo bracket. Install the retainer.

NOTE: Do not stretch the cable to make a certain connection as this will prevent the engine from returning to idle. Use the next closest hole.

ENGINE COOLING

Radiator

REMOVAL AND INSTALLATION

1. Disconnect the negative battery cable, then drain the engine cooling system into a clean container.

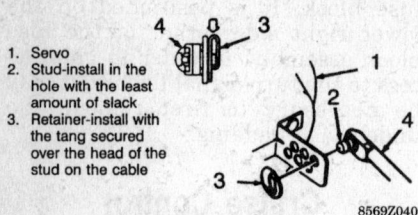

1. Servo
2. Stud-install in the hole with the least amount of slack
3. Retainer-install with the tang secured over the head of the stud on the cable

8569Z040

Servo cable adjustment

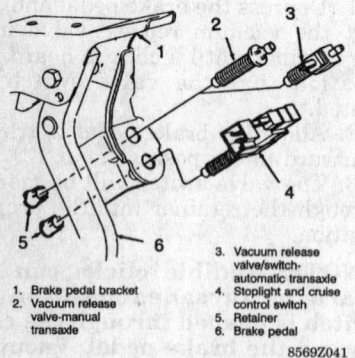

3. Vacuum release valve/switch-automatic transaxle
4. Stoplight and cruise control switch
5. Retainer
6. Brake pedal

1. Brake pedal bracket
2. Vacuum release valve-manual transaxle

8569Z041

Cruise control vacuum/switch installation

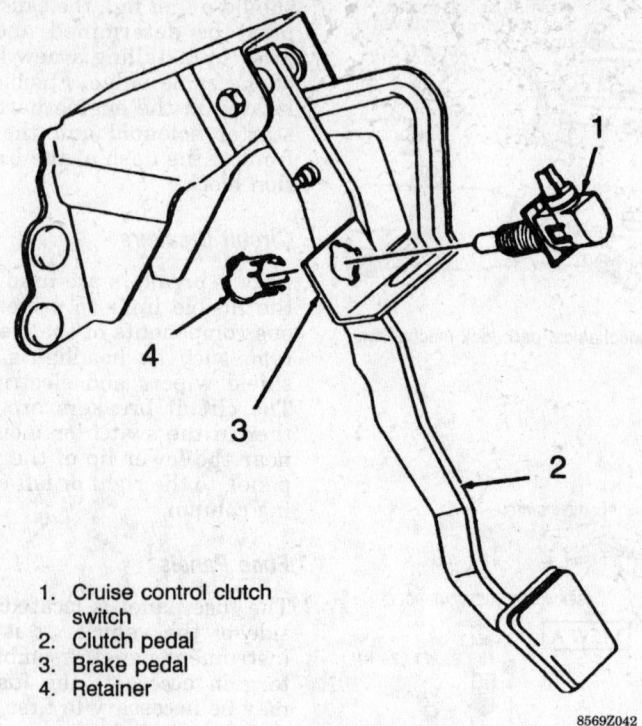

1. Cruise control clutch switch
2. Clutch pedal
3. Brake pedal
4. Retainer

8569Z042

Cruise control clutch switch installation

2. Remove the wiring harness from the fan frame, then unplug the electrical lead from the fan motor.

3. Remove the fan attaching bolts and remove the fan assembly from the vehicle.

4. Scribe matchmarks around the hood latch location, then remove the latch from the radiator support. For 1993–96 vehicles, remove the radiator cooling air intake duct/splash shield assembly.

5. Disconnect the upper and lower radiator hoses and the coolant recovery hose from the radiator.

6. For automatic transaxle vehicles, disconnect the transaxle fluid cooler lines from the radiator and wire them out of the way. If equipped with A/C, remove the 4 radiator-to-condenser bolts and the radiator-to-refrigerant line clamp bolt.

7. Remove the radiator-to-radiator support attaching bolts and clamps, then remove the radiator assembly from the vehicle.

To install:

8. Place the radiator in the vehicle so the bottom is located in the lower mounting pads. Install and tighten

the attaching bolts and clamps. The bolts should be tightened until they are fully seated, but not stripped. For 1993–96 vehicles, tighten the retaining bolts to 89 inch lbs. (10 Nm).

9. In applicable, install the radiator-to-condenser attaching bolts and the refrigerant line clamp bolt. For vehicles equipped with an automatic transaxle, connect the transaxle oil cooler lines and tighten the fittings to 20 ft. lbs. (27 Nm) for vehicles with a standard radiator assembly or to 15 ft. lbs. (20 Nm) for vehicles with an aluminum radiator assembly.

10. Connect the upper and lower radiator hoses and the coolant recovery hose to the radiator.

11. If removed, install the air inlet duct/splash shield assembly.

12. Install the hood latch to the radiator support, aligning the matchmarks scribed during removal.

13. Install the fan assembly to the vehicle; if used, make sure the bottom leg of the frame fits into the rubber grommet on the lower radiator support. Secure the assembly using the attaching bolts.

14. Position the fan wiring harness to the assembly and connect the fan motor electrical lead.

15. Connect the negative battery cable and properly fill the engine cooling system.

16. Start the engine and allow to come to normal operating temperature, check for leaks and top-off coolant, as necessary.

Electric Cooling Fan

The coolant fan relay is activated by the Electronic Control Module (ECM) when the coolant temperature sensor recognizes temperature readings above 220°F (106°C). In most cases the coolant fan is also activated if a coolant temperature sensor failure is detected (Code 14 or 15) or if the ECM is in the backup mode. The ECM will activate the cooling fan relay when the air conditioning is turned ON and the low pressure switch is closed.

NOTE: The ECM controls the cooling fan relay by grounding terminal 85 (DK GRN/WHT wire). Power that is always supplied to the relay through terminal 30 (RED wire) is then applied to the cooling fan through terminal 87 (BLK/RED wire).

TESTING

NOTE: If the fan does not run while connected to the electrical wiring connector, inspect for a defective coolant temperature switch or air conditioning relay, if equipped. Always check body wiring for frayed or loose connections.

1. Unplug the electrical wiring connector from the electric cooling fan.
2. Using a 14 gauge jumper wire, connect it between the fan and the positive battery terminal; the fan should run.
3. If the fan does not run when connected to the jumper wire, replace the fan assembly.

REMOVAL AND INSTALLATION

Except 3.1L Engine

1. Disconnect the negative battery cable.
2. Remove the air cleaner duct.
3. Unplug the wiring harness from the motor, then remove the harness from the frame assembly.
4. Remove the fan assembly retaining bolts, then remove the fan and motor assembly from the vehicle.
   To install:
5. Install the fan and motor assembly, then tighten the retaining bolts to 89 inch lbs. (10 Nm).
6. Position the wiring harness to the fan frame, then install the harness connector to the motor terminal.
7. Install the air cleaner duct and connect the negative battery cable.

3.1L Engine

1. Disconnect the negative battery cable and drain the engine coolant to a level below the upper radiator hose.
2. Remove the air cleaner duct, then remove the air cleaner assembly.
3. Scribe matchmarks around the hood latch location, then remove the latch from the radiator support.
4. Disconnect the upper radiator (inlet) hose from the radiator and position it aside.
5. If equipped, disconnect the automatic transaxle fluid cooler lines from the radiator and position aside.
6. Unplug the wiring harness from the fan and motor assembly.
7. Remove the fan assembly retaining bolts, then remove the fan and motor assembly from the radiator support and the vehicle.

To install:
8. Install the fan and motor assembly, then tighten the retaining bolts to 89 inch lbs. (10 Nm).
9. Install the harness connector to the fan motor terminal
10. If applicable, connect the automatic transaxle fluid cooler lines to the radiator and tighten the fittings to 20 ft. lbs. (27 Nm) for vehicles with a standard radiator assembly or to 15 ft. lbs. (20 Nm) for vehicles with an aluminum radiator assembly
11. Connect the radiator inlet hose.
12. Install the hood latch to the radiator support, aligning the matchmarks scribed during removal.
13. Install the air cleaner assembly and the air duct.
14. Connect the negative battery cable and properly fill the engine cooling system.

Heater Core

REMOVAL AND INSTALLATION

Without Air Conditioning

1. Disconnect the negative battery cable and drain the cooling system.
2. Remove the heater hoses at the heater core. Remove the heater outlet deflector.
3. Remove the heater core cover retaining screws. Remove the heater core cover.
4. Remove the heater core retaining straps and remove the heater core.
   To install:
5. Install the new heater core and remaining straps.
6. Install the heater outlet deflector and heater core cover. Connect the heater hoses to the core.
7. Fill and bleed the cooling system. Check for leaks and the heater operation.

With Air Conditioning

1. Disconnect the negative battery cable and drain the cooling system. Raise and safely support the vehicle.
2. Disconnect the drain tube from the heater case. Remove the rear lateral transaxle support. Remove the heater hoses and the drain tube from the housing.
3. Lower the vehicle. Remove the right and left hush panels, steering column trim cover, heater outlet duct and glove box.
4. Remove the heater core cover. Pull the cover straight to the rear so it does not damage the drain tube.

5. Remove the heater core clamps and remove the heater core.
   To install:
6. Install the heater core and clamps. Install the heater core cover using care not to damage the drain tube.
7. Install the glove box, heater outlet duct, steering column trim cover and hush panels. Raise and safely support the vehicle.
8. Connect the heater hoses and the drain tube to the case. Install the rear transaxle lateral support.
9. Lower the vehicle, fill the cooling system and connect the negative battery cable.
10. Check the heater operation and bleed the cooling system. Check for leaks.

Water Pump

REMOVAL AND INSTALLATION

Except 2.0L Engine

1. Disconnect the negative battery cable and drain the cooling system.
2. Remove the serpentine drive belt.
3. For the 2.2L engine, remove the alternator and bracket.
4. Remove the bolts from the water pump pulley, then remove the pulley from the pump.
5. Remove the pump mounting bolts, then remove the pump from the engine. Thoroughly clean the sealing surfaces.
   To install:
6. Coat the 3.1L engine pump retaining bolts with a suitable pipe sealant. While the sealer is still wet, install the pump using a new gasket and tighten the bolts to 18 ft. lbs. (25 Nm) on 2.2L engine or to 89 inch lbs. (10 Nm) on 3.1L engine.
7. Install the water pump pulley and tighten the mounting bolts to 22 ft. lbs. (30 Nm) for 2.2L engine or to 15 ft. lbs. (21 Nm) for 3.1L engine.
8. If removed, install the alternator and bracket.
9. Install the serpentine drive belt.
10. Connect the negative battery cable.
11. Fill cooling system and check for leaks. Start the engine and allow to come to normal operating temperature. Recheck for leaks and top-off the coolant.

2.0L Engine

1. Disconnect negative battery cable and drain the cooling system.

2. Remove timing belt.

3. Remove the timing belt rear protective covers.

4. Disconnect the hose from the water pump, then remove the retaining bolts, water pump and seal ring from the engine.

To install:

5. Install the water pump using a new pump seal ring, then secure with the attaching bolts. Tighten the water pump bolts to 18 ft. lbs. (25 Nm).

6. Install the rear protective covers, then install the timing belt.

7. Connect the negative battery cable.

8. Fill cooling system and check for leaks. Start the engine and allow to come to normal operating temperature. Recheck for leaks and top-off the coolant.

Thermostat

REMOVAL AND INSTALLATION

Except 2.0L Engine

The thermostat is located inside a housing which is either located on the intake manifold for 3.1L engine or on the end of the cylinder head for 2.2L engine. It is not necessary to remove the radiator hose from the housing when removing the thermostat.

1. Disconnect the negative battery cable and drain the cooling system to a level below the thermostat housing.

2. Remove the air cleaner.

3. Remove the retaining nut and bolt from the housing, then separate the housing cover from the intake manifold or the cylinder head thermostat housing.

4. Lift out the thermostat.

To install:

5. Thoroughly clean the mating surfaces.

6. Insert the new thermostat, spring end down or inward, then position the housing cover over the thermostat.

7. Tighten the housing retainers to 18 ft. lbs. (25 Nm) on 3.1L engine or 89 inch lbs. (10 Nm) on 2.2L engine.

8. Connect the negative battery cable.

9. Fill cooling system and check for leaks. Start the engine and allow to come to normal operating temperature. Recheck for leaks and top-off coolant, as necessary.

2.0L Engine

NOTE: The engine must be COLD for this procedure.

1. Disconnect the negative battery cable and drain the coolant to a level below the thermostat.

2. Remove the thermostat housing cap.

3. Grasp the handle of the thermostat assembly and gently pull upward.

4. If present, clean the thermostat housing O-ring.

To install:

5. If equipped, make sure the O-ring is properly positioned.

6. Install the thermostat into the housing, pushing down to ensure that the thermostat is firmly seated.

7. Replace the thermostat housing cap.

8. Connect the negative battery cable and top-off the cooling system.

Cooling System Bleeding

After working on the cooling system, even to replace the thermostat, it must be bled. Air trapped in the system will prevent proper filling and leave the radiator coolant level low, causing a risk of overheating.

1. Make sure the radiator drain cock is closed and, if removed, that the block drain plugs are installed.

2. Fill the cooling system through the reservoir tank or the radiator until the FULL COLD mark is reached. Be sure to use a solution which is 50–70 percent ethylene glycol antifreeze and the balance water.

3. For the 2.0L engine, remove the thermostat cap and fill the coolant to a level just below the housing cap seat.

4. Install the radiator, surge and/or thermostat housing caps.

5. Start the engine and allow it to run until normal operating temperature is reached and the upper radiator hose becomes hot. Stop the engine and observe the coolant level in the surge tank. The coolant should now be at the FULL or FULL HOT line.

6. Allow the engine to cool until the ambient temperature is reached, then check the coolant level, it should be at or above the FULL COLD line. If necessary, add coolant to top-off the system.

FUEL SYSTEM

Fuel System Service Precautions

Safety is the most important factor when performing not only fuel system maintenance, but any type of service. Failure to conduct maintenance and repairs in a safe manner may result in serious personal injury or death. Maintenance and testing of the vehicle's fuel system components can be accomplished safely and effectively by adhering to the following rules and guidelines.

• Always disconnect the negative battery cable before opening the fuel system fittings, unless the repair or test procedure requires that battery voltage be applied. This will prevent excessive fuel spillage if the ignition switch is accidentally turned **ON** while fuel fittings are still disconnected.

• Always relieve the fuel system pressure prior to disconnecting any fuel system fitting or connection.

• Exercise extreme caution whenever relieving fuel system pressure to avoid exposing skin, face and eyes to fuel spray. Fuel under pressure may penetrate the skin or any part of the body that it contacts.

• Always place a shop towel around a fitting or connection prior to loosening in order to absorb any fuel spillage. Ensure that all spilled fuel is quickly removed from engine surfaces. Ensure that all fuel soaked rags are deposited into a suitable waste container.

• Always keep a dry chemical (Class B) fire extinguisher near the work area.

• Ventilate the work area properly and pay attention to where the fumes go. Do not allow fuel vapors to come into contact with a source of ignition.

• Always use a backup wrench when loosening and tightening fuel line connection fittings. This will prevent unnecessary stress to fuel line piping. Always follow the proper torque specifications.

• Always replace worn fuel fitting O-rings. Do not substitute fuel hose where metal fuel pipe is normally installed.

RELIEVING FUEL SYSTEM PRESSURE

The fuel delivery pipe is under high pressure even after the engine is stopped. Direct removal of the fuel line, may result in dangerous fuel spray. Make sure to release the fuel pressure according to the following procedures:

2.2L and 2.0L Engines

1. Disconnect the negative battery cable.
2. Release the fuel vapor pressure in the fuel tank by momentarily removing the tank filler cap.
3. Remove the fuel pump fuse from the fuse box.
4. Start the engine and allow it to run until the fuel in the pipes runs out.
5. Once the engine stops, crank it a few times with the starter for about 3 seconds to dissipate any remaining fuel in the lines.
6. If the fuel pressure can't be released in the above manner because the engine failed to run, disconnect the negative battery cable, cover the union bolt of the fuel line with a shop towel and loosen the union bolt slowly to gradually release the fuel pressure.
7. Once the tests or repairs are completed, prime the fuel system by cycling the ignition switch **ON** for 2 seconds, **OFF** for 10 seconds and then **ON** again. Repeat, if necessary to build system pressure.

3.1L Engine

1. Disconnect the negative battery cable.
2. Release the fuel vapor pressure in the fuel tank by momentarily removing the tank filler cap.
3. Connect J–34730–1 or equivalent fuel pressure gauge, to the fuel pressure connection located on the end of the fuel rail assembly. Wrap a cloth around the fitting to absorb any fuel leakage.
4. Install the bleed hose into an approved container and open the valve to bleed system pressure.
5. Once the tests or repairs are completed, prime the fuel system by cycling the ignition switch **ON** for 2 seconds, **OFF** for 10 seconds and then **ON** again. Repeat, if necessary to build system pressure.

Fuel Tank

REMOVAL AND INSTALLATION

1. Relieve the fuel system pressure, then disconnect the negative battery cable.
2. Drain the fuel tank using a hand pump.
3. Raise and support the vehicle safely.
4. Unplug the wiring harness from the fuel pump assembly. Check the harness for a ground wire retaining screw and remove it from the underbody, if present.
5. Remove the muffler hanger bolts and disconnect the rubber exhaust hangers, then allow the exhaust to rest on the rear axle assembly.
6. Disconnect the hoses from the fuel pump assembly. Remove the nylon quick-connect fittings by grasping the fitting and giving 1/4 turn in either directions to loosen any dirt, then use compressed air and safety glasses to blow dirt from the fitting. Squeeze the plastic tabs of the male connector and pull the fitting apart.
7. Disconnect the hoses at the tank from the filler, vent and vapor pipes.
8. With the help of an assistant, support the fuel tank assembly and disconnect the 2 retaining straps.
9. Carefully lower the tank assembly and remove it from the vehicle. Make sure neither the wiring harness nor any hoses are caught on the assembly as it is lowered. If necessary, remove sound insulators and the fuel pump assembly from the tank for service.
To install:
10. If removed, install the fuel pump assembly and the sound insulators.
11. Raise the fuel tank assembly into position and secure using the retaining straps. Tighten the retaining bolts to 25 ft. lbs. (33 Nm) and/or the nuts to 108 inch lbs. (12 Nm).
12. Connect the hoses to the filler, vent and vapor pipes.
13. Install the hoses to the fuel pump assembly. Install the quick-connect fitting, by first applying a few drops of clean engine oil the male end of the fitting, then push the connectors together until the retaining tabs snap into place. Gently tug on either side of the fitting to assure proper connection.

14. Install the exhaust rubber hangers, then secure the muffler using the retaining bolts and tighten to 11 ft. lbs. (15 Nm).
15. Install the wiring harness connector to the fuel pump assembly, and if used, install the ground lead to the underbody.
16. Lower the vehicle and fill the fuel tank.
17. Connect the negative battery cable and pressurize the fuel system by cycling the ignition, then check for leaks.

Fuel Filter

REMOVAL AND INSTALLATION

The fuel filter is located under the rear of the vehicle near the fuel tank.
1. Relieve the fuel system pressure and disconnect the negative battery cable.
2. Raise and support the vehicle safely.
3. Using a backup wrench to prevent fuel line damage, loosen the line nut fitting and disconnect the fuel line from the filter.
4. Remove the nylon quick-connect fitting by grasping the fitting and giving 1/4 turn in either directions to loosen any dirt, then use compressed air and safety glasses to blow dirt from the fitting. Squeeze the plastic tabs of the male connector and pull the fitting apart.
5. Note the filter's position for installation purposes, then remove the filter from the vehicle.
To install:
6. Install the new filter facing in the proper position as noted during removal. Make sure any protective caps are removed from the new filter and that new plastic connector retainers are installed on the filter inlet tube.
7. Install the quick-connect fitting, by first applying a few drops of clean engine oil the male end of the fitting, then push the connectors together until the retaining tabs snap into place. Gently tug on either side of the fitting to assure proper connection.
8. Connect the fuel line to the filter, using a new O-ring seal. Tighten the fuel line to 20 ft. lbs. (27 Nm) using a backup wrench to prevent damage.
9. Lower the vehicle.
10. Connect the negative battery cable, then prime the fuel system, start the engine and check for leaks.

Electric Fuel Pump

PRESSURE TESTING

1. Properly relieve the fuel system pressure. For the 3.1L engine, leave the pressure gauge attached to the fuel pressure port located on the end of the fuel rail assembly.

2. Except for the 3.1L engine, connect a fuel gauge inline between the fuel filter and the fuel rail assembly.

3. Cycle the ignition to build system pressure. With ignition **ON** pump pressure should be 41–47 psi.

4. Start and run the engine at idle. With the engine is idling, pressure should drop 3–10 psi.

NOTE: The application of vacuum to the pressure regulator should result in a fuel pressure drop.

5. When the test is complete, release the fuel system pressure and remove the pressure gauge. If applicable, reconnect the fuel filter-to-fuel rail line.

REMOVAL AND INSTALLATION

The electric fuel pump is located in the fuel tank.

1. Relieve the fuel system pressure and disconnect the negative battery cable.

2. Drain the fuel tank, then raise and support the vehicle safely.

3. Remove the fuel tank from the vehicle.

4. Apply pressure on the spring loaded fuel pump assembly and remove the snapring from the slots in the retainer.

5. Slowly release the pressure on the assembly, and remove it from the fuel tank. Be aware that the reservoir bucket will retain some fuel and the assembly must be tilted in order to prevent damage to the float.

6. Carefully pour the fuel from the reservoir into an approved container, then remove and discard the pump assembly O-ring.

7. Remove the external fuel strainer, then remove the Connector Position Assurance (CPA) device and unplug the electrical connector.

8. Gently release the tabs on the sides of the fuel pump-to-cover assembly. Squeeze the sides of the reservoir, releasing the tab opposite the fuel lever sensor first, then move clockwise to release the 2nd and 3rd tabs in the same manner.

9. Lift the cover assembly sufficiently to unplug the pump electrical connector, then rotate the baffle counterclockwise and remove the baffle/pump assembly from the retainer.

10. Slide the pump outlet from the slot and remove the fuel pump seal/dampener.

To install:

11. Install the pump seal/dampener assembly, then slide the pump outlet into the slot.

12. Make sure the wiring is properly routed and/or connected, as applicable. Install the pump and baffle assembly onto the reservoir retainer and turn clockwise until seated.

13. Lower the retainer assembly partially into the reservoir, aligning all 3 sleeve tabs, then press the retainer onto the reservoir until firmly seated.

14. Install the fuel pump connector and the CPA device, then install the new pump strainer.

15. Position a new O-ring onto the fuel tank, then install the pump assembly to the tank while aligning the front of the pump with the slot on the front of the retainer snapring.

16. Carefully apply pressure to the top of the pump assembly until it aligns flush with the tank retainer, then install the snapring into the slots, making sure it is fully seated.

17. Install the fuel tank assembly into the vehicle.

18. Lower the vehicle and fill the fuel tank, then install the filler cap.

19. Connect the negative battery cable and prime the fuel system by cycling the ignition without starting the engine.

Fuel Injection

IDLE SPEED AND MIXTURE ADJUSTMENT

Idle speed and mixture are controlled by the Electronic Control Module (ECM). No adjustments are necessary.

Fuel Injector

REMOVAL AND INSTALLATION

NOTE: Use care in removing injectors to prevent damage to the electrical pins on top of each injector. Because fuel injectors are electrical components, do not immerse then in any type of cleaner or solvent.

MFI Systems

2.0L ENGINE

1. Relieve fuel system pressure and disconnect the negative battery cable.

2. Remove the air cleaner cover and air intake duct.

3. Partially drain the cooling system so the coolant hoses can be disconnected to the throttle body, but do not attempt to disconnect the coolant hoses at this time.

4. Label and disconnect the wiring and the vacuum hose from the throttle body. Disconnect the throttle cables.

5. Remove the attaching bolts and separate the throttle body from the manifold, then disconnect the coolant hoses and vacuum line from the bottom of the throttle body.

6. Remove the throttle body from the engine, then remove and discard the old gasket.

7. Remove the PCV and breather hoses from the camshaft cover.

8. Label and disconnect the wiring from the EGR and canister purge solenoids, and the MAP sensor. Label and disconnect the vacuum hoses.

9. Remove the canister purge and EGR solenoid along with their brackets. Remove the MAP sensor.

10. Disconnect the wiring from the injector terminals.

11. Remove the fuel inlet pipe retainer attaching screw, then remove the retainer. Disconnect the fuel supply and return lines from the fuel rail. Discard the old O-ring. Be sure to use a backup wrench on the pressure regulator fitting to prevent damage.

12. Remove the attaching bolts, then carefully remove the fuel rail assembly along with the fuel injectors from the engine.

13. Remove the retaining clip from each injector, then remove the injectors from the rail. Remove and discard to O-rings from each injector.

To install:

14. Lubricate the new injector O-rings with clean engine oil and assemble the injectors to the fuel rail. Make sure the electrical connector is facing inward towards the intake manifold and install new injector retainer clips.

15. Install the fuel rail assembly to the engine and tighten the retaining bolts to 19 ft. lbs. (26 Nm).

16. Position a new O-ring coated with clean engine oil and install the fuel supply line. Install the retainer and the attaching screw, then tighten the screw to 53 inch lbs. (6 Nm).

17. Connect the fuel return line and tighten the fitting to 15 ft. lbs. (20 Nm). Use a backup wrench on the pressure regulator fitting to prevent damage.

18. Install the wiring harness connectors to the injector wiring terminals.

19. Install the MAP sensor, then install the EGR and purge valve solenoids (with brackets). Tighten the MAP sensor retainer to 27 inch lbs. (3 Nm) and the solenoid bracket retaining screws to 37 inch lbs. (50 Nm). Connect the wiring and vacuum lines.

20. Install the PCV and breather hoses to the camshaft cover.

21. Connect the vacuum hose and the coolant hoses to the bottom of the throttle body, then position the assembly against the manifold using a new gasket. Install the throttle body retaining bolts and tighten to 11 ft. lbs. (15 Nm).

22. Connect the throttle body wiring, control cables and the vacuum line.

23. Fill the cooling system and connect the negative battery cable.

24. Cycle the ignition to build system pressure and check for leaks.

25. Turn the ignition **OFF**, then install the air cleaner cover and intake duct.

2.2L ENGINE

1. Relieve the fuel system pressure.

2. Disconnect the negative battery cable.

3. Remove the upper intake manifold assembly:

   a. Remove the air intake duct.

   b. Remove the cable shield from the accelerator cable bracket, then disconnect the throttle control cables.

   c. Label and disconnect the wiring and vacuum hoses from the upper manifold.

   d. Remove the attaching bolts and nuts, then remove the throttle cable bracket and position aside.

   e. Remove the bolts and studs, then remove the upper intake manifold assembly. Remove and discard the gasket from the mating surface.

4. Remove the retaining nut and bracket, then disconnect the fuel return line from the pressure regulator.

5. Disconnect the vacuum line and remove the pressure regulator.

6. Remove the screws and carefully slide the injector retaining bracket off. Do not attempt to remove

the injectors with the bracket or the injectors could be damaged.

7. Unplug the wiring harness from the injector terminals.

8. Pull the injectors out of the intake manifold and discard the O-rings. Make sure the lower O-ring does not stay in the manifold or the injector will not seat properly when installed.

To install:

9. Lubricate the new injector O-rings with clean engine oil and install them onto the injectors.

10. Look into the injector mounting hole in the manifold and make sure the old O-ring is not still there. Fit each injector into it's hole with the electrical connector facing the engine.

11. Carefully install the injector retaining bracket, aligning injector retaining slots and the regulator with the bracket slots. Start, but do not tighten the screws.

12. Connect the injector wiring.

13. Lubricate and install a new O-ring onto the pressure regulator and install the regulator.

14. Apply thread locking compound to the injector bracket screws and the pressure regulator screws, then install and torque them all to 31 inch lbs. (3.5 Nm).

15. Use a new gasket and install the upper intake manifold. Torque the bolts to 22 ft. lbs. (30 Nm).

16. Install the throttle cable bracket but do not tighten the bolts yet. To adjust the position of the bracket:

   a. If the bracket is equipped with a cross brace, no adjustment is required.

   b. Hold a steel rule against the throttle body bore with one end against the bracket.

   c. Adjust the gap between the bracket and the bore to 3/8 in. (10mm).

   d. Tighten the upper bracket bolt or nut first, then the remaining fasteners to 18 ft. lbs. (25 Nm).

   e. Install the cable shield to the bracket.

17. Connect the throttle cables, wiring and hoses and install all remaining components.

18. Connect the negative battery cable, run the engine and check for leaks.

3.1L ENGINE

NOTE: The fuel rail is removed as an assembly, then the injectors can be removed.

1. Disconnect the negative battery cable and relieve the fuel system pressure.

2. Remove the upper intake manifold plenum:

   a. Tag and disconnect the vacuum lines. Remove the EGR-to-plenum retaining nuts.

   b. Remove the 2 throttle body retaining bolts, then remove the throttle body from the manifold. Remove and discard the gasket from the mating surface.

   c. Remove the throttle cable bracket bolts, then remove the ignition wire plastic shield bolts.

   d. Remove the plenum bolts, then remove the plenum. Remove and discard the gaskets from the mating surfaces.

3. Remove the fuel line bracket bolt, then disconnect the fuel lines from the rail assembly using a backup wrench to prevent rail damage. Remove and discard the O-rings from the fuel lines.

4. Unplug the vacuum hose from the pressure regulator, then remove the fuel rail retaining bolts. Remove the fuel rail assembly.

5. Remove and discard the injector retaining clip, then separate the fuel injector from the fuel rail. Remove and discard the old O-rings from the injectors.

To install:

6. Replace the injector O-rings and lubricate using clean engine oil.

7. Install the fuel injector to the fuel rail assembly and secure using a new retainer clip.

8. Position the fuel rail assembly over the intake manifold, tilt to allow injector installation, then install the fuel rail and secure using the retaining bolts. Tighten the fuel rail retaining bolts to 88 inch lbs. (10 Nm).

9. Install the wiring harness connectors to the fuel injector terminals, then connect the vacuum line to the pressure regulator.

10. Install new O-rings to the fuel lines, then connect the lines and tighten the nuts to 17 ft. lbs. (23 Nm), using a backup wrench to prevent damage.

11. Temporarily connect the negative battery cable and cycle the ignition without starting the engine in order to build system pressure. Check for leaks, then disconnect the negative battery cable.

12. Install the upper intake manifold plenum assembly using new gaskets and tighten the bolts to 88 inch lbs. (10 Nm). Install the ignition wire plastic shield bolts.

13. Install the throttle body using a new gasket and tighten the retaining bolts to 18 ft. lbs. (25 Nm). Install the

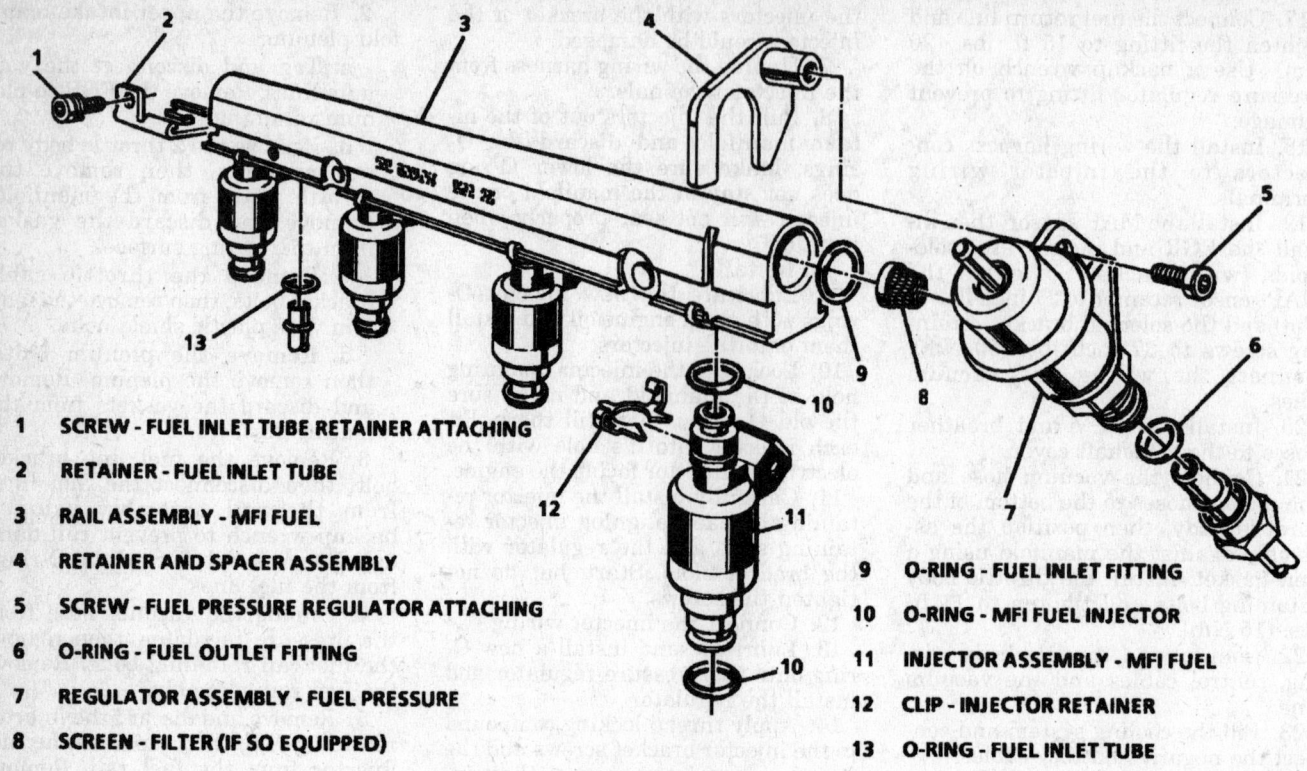

1   SCREW - FUEL INLET TUBE RETAINER ATTACHING

2   RETAINER - FUEL INLET TUBE

3   RAIL ASSEMBLY - MFI FUEL

4   RETAINER AND SPACER ASSEMBLY

5   SCREW - FUEL PRESSURE REGULATOR ATTACHING

6   O-RING - FUEL OUTLET FITTING

7   REGULATOR ASSEMBLY - FUEL PRESSURE

8   SCREEN - FILTER (IF SO EQUIPPED)

9   O-RING - FUEL INLET FITTING

10   O-RING - MFI FUEL INJECTOR

11   INJECTOR ASSEMBLY - MFI FUEL

12   CLIP - INJECTOR RETAINER

13   O-RING - FUEL INLET TUBE

84701034

Exploded view of the fuel rail assembly — 2.2L engine

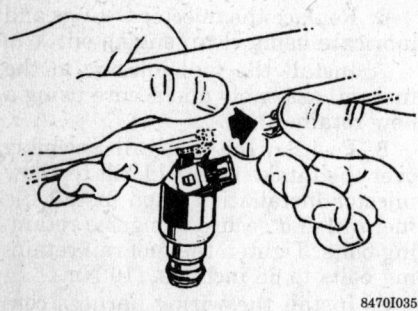

84701035

Removing the fuel injector from the rail — 2.2L engine

EGR nuts, the throttle cable bracket bolts and the vacuum lines.

14. Connect the negative battery cable.

EMISSION CONTROLS

Emission Warning Lamps

The CHECK ENGINE light located in the instrument cluster serves 2 main functions:

1. The lamp indicates when a problem has occurred and that the vehicle should be taken for service as soon as reasonably possible.

2. The light may be used by technicians to monitor diagnostic trouble codes and/or open/closed loop engine operation, whenever the system is placed in the diagnostic mode.

To verify proper operation of the bulb and wiring, the lamp will illuminate when the ignition is first turned ON, but the engine is not running. If the system is operating properly, the lamp will turn OFF once the engine is started.

If the CHECK ENGINE light remains lit once the engine is started, the self-diagnostic system has detected a problem. If the problem goes away, the light will extinguish in 10 seconds (in most cases), but a diagnostic trouble code will remain in the ECM memory.

RESETTING

NOTE: In order to prevent damage to the ECM, the key must be OFF when connecting or disconnecting power to the ECM.

After repairs are made to the faulty system(s), it is necessary to make sure the ECM memory is cleared of any old diagnostic trouble codes. Removing the battery voltage to the ECM for a minimum of 30 seconds will clear all codes. This may be accomplished in various ways depending on how the vehicle is equipped. The ECM harness power feed may be disconnected at the positive battery terminal "pigtail." The fuse may be removed from the inline fuse holder which originates at the positive battery connection or from fuse block, as applicable. Also, the negative battery cable may be disconnected, but other on-board data such as the clock or radio presets will also be lost.

ECM LEARNING ABILITY

The ECM has a "learning" ability which allows it to make corrections for minor variations in the fuel system, in order to improve driveability. If the battery is disconnected to clear diagnostic codes or for safety during repairs, the "learning" process will reset and must begin again. A change may be noted in the vehicle's performance while the learning process begins. To "teach" the vehicle, make sure the engine is at normal operating temperature, then drive the vehicle at part throttle, with moderate acceleration and idle conditions, until normal performance returns.

ENGINE MECHANICAL

NOTE: Disconnecting the negative battery cable on some vehicles may interfere with the functions of the on-board computer systems and may require the computer to undergo a relearning process, once the negative battery cable is reconnected.

Engine Assembly

REMOVAL AND INSTALLATION

2.0L Engine

NOTE: This procedure requires a powertrain dolly and wooden boards to support the engine/transaxle assembly when they are removed from the bottom of the vehicle.

1. Relieve fuel system pressure, then disconnect the negative battery cable and the engine ground wire. Disconnect the positive battery cable, then remove the battery from the vehicle.
2. Drain the cooling system into a clean container for reuse. If equipped, discharge the A/C system using a suitable recovery system.
3. Remove the air cleaner assembly.
4. Remove the coolant hoses, as necessary for access, then remove the cooling fan assembly.
5. Unplug the engine electrical harness at bulkhead.
6. Unplug the electrical connector at brake cylinder.
7. Disconnect the air conditioner relay cluster switches.
8. Unplug the wiper motor electrical connector.

9. Unplug the cooling fan, relay and ground wires.
10. Unplug the ECM harness, then pull the harness through the bulkhead.
11. Disconnect the engine coolant temperature switch at the thermostat housing.
12. Disconnect the throttle body, MAP sensor and EVAP canister vacuum hoses.
13. Disconnect the throttle cable(s) from the bracket and the throttle body, then disconnect the shift control cable at the transaxle.
14. Disconnect the power steering return hose at the pump.
15. Raise and support the vehicle safely.
16. Unplug the VSS connector at the PM generator and/or the speedometer cable at the transaxle.
17. Disconnect the exhaust pipe at the exhaust manifold and exhaust hangers and swing aside.
18. Disconnect the hoses from the heater core.
19. Disconnect the fuel lines.
20. If equipped with automatic transaxle, disconnect the fluid cooler lines from the radiator.
21. Remove the front wheels.
22. Remove the brake calipers and support using a length of wire.
23. If equipped with A/C, unplug the wiring connectors from the compressor. Make sure the refrigerant has been properly recovered, then disconnect the refrigerant lines from the compressor.

NOTE: Cap the refrigerant lines when opening the system to prevent the entry of dirt or moisture and in order to prevent the loss of refrigerant lubricant.

24. Remove the suspension support bolts as follows:
    a. Remove the 2 center bolts on each side.
    b. Remove 1 bolt at each end.
    c. Loosen the remaining bolt.

NOTE: Properly support the vehicle, engine and transaxle during the following steps.

25. If equipped with automatic transaxle, disconnect the lateral strut at the rear of the transaxle.
26. Disconnect the transaxle strut from the front of the transaxle.
27. Support the front of the vehicle with stands under the radiator core support.
28. Reposition the jack to the rear of the cowl with 4 x 4 x 6 in. timber spanning the vehicle width.
29. Raise the vehicle enough to remove the jackstands.

30. Position the dolly under the engine and transaxle with three 4 x 4 x 12 in. blocks as support.
31. Lower the vehicle onto the dolly lightly.
32. Remove the remaining bolt at each end of the right and left front suspension supports.
33. Remove the long mount-to-bracket bolt from the transaxle.
34. Remove the 2 mount-to-bracket bolts from the front engine mount.
35. Remove the 2 mount-to-bracket nuts and reinforcement bracket from the rear engine mount.
36. Carefully scribe the position of the strut on the hub to preserve the camber adjustment. Remove the 2 knuckle-to-strut bolts on each side.
37. Raise the vehicle leaving the engine, transaxle and suspension on the dolly.
38. Separate the engine and transaxle.

To install:
39. With the aid of an assistant, assemble the engine and transaxle. Tighten the engine-to-transaxle bolts and nuts to 55 ft. lbs. (75 Nm). Position the engine and transaxle assembly in the vehicle.
40. Install the 1 long mount-to-bracket bolt at the transaxle. Install the nut and tighten to 83 ft. lbs. (113 Nm).

NOTE: The engine mount bolts must be cleaned of all thread sealant, then recoated with Loctite® or equivalent before installation.

41. Install the 2 rear engine mount-to-bracket bolts and tighten to 38 ft. lbs. (52 Nm).
42. Install the 2 mount-to-bracket bolts at the front engine mount and tighten to 61 ft. lbs. (83 Nm).
43. Loosely install the bolt at each end of the right and left front suspension supports.
44. Install the knuckle-to-strut bolts. Align the scribe marks made during removal. Tighten the nuts to 133 ft. lbs. (180 Nm).
45. Raise the vehicle and remove the dolly. Using jackstands, remove the 6 in. timber and move the hoist to the front.
46. Install the remaining bolts in the right and left front suspension supports. Tighten to 65 ft. lbs. (88 Nm).
47. Connect the front and rear transaxle and tighten the retainers to 38 ft. lbs. (52 Nm).
48. Install the electrical wiring connectors to the compressor, if equipped.
49. Install the brake calipers.

50. Install the front wheels.
51. If equipped with automatic transaxle, connect the cooler lines to the radiator.
52. Connect the fuel lines.
53. Connect the hoses to the heater core.
54. Connect the exhaust pipe to the exhaust manifold and hangers.
55. Install the VSS connector and/or the speedometer cable at the transaxle.
56. Lower the vehicle.
57. Connect the power steering return hose to the pump.
58. Connect the power steering cut-off switch.
59. Connect the transaxle shift cable.
60. Connect the throttle cable(s) to the bracket and throttle body.
61. Connect the vacuum hoses to the MAP sensor, canister and throttle body.
62. Install the electrical connector to the temperature switch at the thermostat housing.
63. Pull the ECM harness through the bulkhead and install the ECM connector.
64. Connect the air conditioner relay cluster switches.
65. Install the wiper motor electrical connector.
66. Install the cooling fan, relay and ground.
67. Install the electrical connector to the brake cylinder.
68. Install engine harness bulkhead connectors.
69. Install the cooling fan assembly, then connect the radiator hose. Install the air cleaner assembly.
70. Replace the compressor fitting O-rings. Lubricate the O-rings with refrigerant oil. Connect the air conditioner refrigerant lines.
71. Install the battery to the vehicle, then connect the positive battery cable followed by the negative battery cable.
72. Fill cooling system and check for leaks. Start the engine and allow it to warm until normal operating temperature is reached, then top-off the coolant.
73. If equipped, evacuate, recharge and leak test the air conditioning system.
74. Recheck for coolant, fuel, oil and transaxle fluid for proper levels or leaks.

2.2L Engine

1. Relieve fuel system pressure, then disconnect the negative battery cable and the engine ground wire. Disconnect the positive battery cable,

then remove the battery from the vehicle.
2. Drain the cooling system into a clean container for reuse. If equipped, discharge the A/C system using a suitable recovery system.
3. Disconnect the hood lamp wiring. Scribe alignment marks on the hood/hinges, then remove the fasteners and, with the aid of an assistant, remove the hood from the vehicle.
4. Remove the throttle body air intake duct, then if equipped, remove the rear sight shields.
5. Remove the battery, then remove the air cleaner housing.
6. Remove the upper radiator hose, then disconnect the brake booster vacuum hose.
7. Remove the alternator top brace and wiring.
8. Disconnect the upper engine wiring harness from the engine.
9. If equipped with A/C, make sure the refrigerant has been properly recovered, then disconnect the refrigerant lines from the compressor.

NOTE: Cap the refrigerant lines when opening the system to prevent the entry of dirt or moisture and in order to prevent the loss of refrigerant lubricant.

10. Raise and support the vehicle safely, then remove the engine splash shield.
11. Remove the exhaust system assembly.
12. Disconnect the lower engine wiring.
13. Remove the flywheel inspection cover, then remove the front wheels from the vehicle.
14. Remove the lower radiator hose, then disconnect the heater hoses from the heater core.
15. Remove the calipers from the steering knuckles, then support the calipers using mechanic's wire in order to prevent damaging the brake lines.
16. Disconnect the tie rods from the struts.
17. Lower the vehicle, then remove the clutch slave cylinder from the transaxle assembly.
18. Disconnect the fuel lines.
19. Disconnect the linkage from the transaxle assembly.
20. Remove the accelerator and, if applicable, the cruise control and/or automatic transaxle throttle valve cables from the throttle body.
21. If equipped with an automatic transaxle, remove the fluid cooler lines from the transaxle.
22. Remove the power steering pump hoses from the pump assembly.

23. Remove the 4 suspension bolts from the center carriage.
24. Align an engine support dolly under the vehicle's suspension supports, engine and transaxle, then carefully lower the vehicle to the dolly. Place additional support under the engine.
25. Support the rear of the vehicle.
26. Remove the upper transaxle mount.
27. Remove the upper strut bolts and nuts.
28. Remove the front and rear engine mounts.
29. Remove the 4 suspension bolts from the rear carriage, then remove the 4 bolts from the front carriage.
30. Wire the front carriage support bolt holes together in order to prevent axle separation.
31. Raise the vehicle, leaving the engine, transaxle and suspension on the dolly.
32. If necessary, remove the engine from the transaxle assembly.

To install:
33. With the aid of an assistant, assemble the engine and transaxle. Tighten the engine-to-transaxle bolts and nuts to 55 ft. lbs. (75 Nm). Position the engine and transaxle assembly in the vehicle.
34. Install the front, center and rear suspension carriage bolts and tighten to 66 ft. lbs. (90 Nm).

NOTE: The engine mount bolts must be cleaned of all thread sealant, then recoated with Loctite® or equivalent before installation.

35. Loosely install the transaxle mount, followed by the rear, then the front engine mounts. Tighten the transaxle mount bolt(s) to 38 ft. lbs. (52 Nm), then tighten the rear mount bolts to 38 ft. lbs. (52 Nm) and the front engine mount bolts to 61 ft. lbs. (83 Nm).
36. Connect the power steering hoses to the pump assembly.
37. Connect the accelerator, cruise control and/or throttle valve cables to the throttle body, as applicable.
38. If equipped, connect the automatic transaxle fluid cooler lines.
39. Install the transaxle linkage.
40. Connect the fuel lines.
41. Install the clutch slave cylinder assembly to the transaxle.
42. Raise and support the vehicle safely, then connect the tie rods.
43. Remove the wire supports and install the calipers to the steering knuckles.
44. Connect the heater hoses to the heater core, then install the lower radiator hose.

45. If removed, install the A/C compressor assembly to the engine.

46. Install the flywheel inspection cover and the engine splash shield.

47. Install the front wheels and lower the vehicle.

48. Connect the upper engine wiring.

49. Replace the compressor fitting O-rings. Lubricate the O-rings with refrigerant oil. Connect the air conditioner refrigerant lines.

50. Install the alternator top brace and connect the wiring.

51. Connect the brake booster vacuum hose, then install the upper radiator hose.

52. Install the upper strut bolts and nuts, then raise and support the vehicle safely.

53. Install the lower engine wiring.

54. Install the exhaust assembly, then lower the vehicle.

55. Install the air cleaner and the throttle body air intake duct.

56. Install the battery to the vehicle, then connect the positive battery cable followed by the negative battery cable.

57. Fill cooling system and check for leaks. Start the engine and allow it to warm until normal operating temperature is reached, then top-off the coolant.

58. With the help of an assistant, align the marks made earlier and install the hood to the vehicle, then connect the hood lamp wiring.

59. If equipped, evacuate, recharge and leak test the air conditioning system.

60. Recheck for coolant, fuel, oil and transaxle fluid for proper levels or leaks.

3.1L Engine

NOTE: Unlike the 4 cylinder engines found in the J-body vehicles, the 3.1L engine is removed from the top of the vehicle.

1. Remove the air cleaner and duct assembly.

2. Relieve fuel system pressure, then disconnect the negative battery cable and the engine ground wire. Disconnect the positive battery cable, then remove the battery from the vehicle.

3. Drain the cooling system into a clean container for reuse. If equipped, discharge the A/C system using a suitable recovery system.

4. Remove the exhaust manifold crossover assembly.

5. Remove the serpentine drive belt, then remove the tensioner from the front of the engine. If equipped, remove the idler from the engine.

6. Disconnect the radiator hoses from the engine, then disconnect the cables from the plenum cable bracket.

7. Remove the alternator from the engine.

8. Tag and disconnect the wiring harness at the engine.

9. Disconnect the fuel lines, then remove the coolant bypass and overflow hoses from the engine.

10. Install J–28467–A, or an equivalent engine support fixture, to the engine assembly.

11. Raise the vehicle and support it safely.

12. Remove the right inner fender splash shield, then remove the flywheel cover.

13. Remove the starter assembly from the engine.

14. If equipped, make sure the refrigerant has been properly recovered, then remove the A/C compressor from the engine.

15. Disconnect the exhaust pipe from the rear of the exhaust manifold.

16. Remove the flywheel-to-torque converter bolts.

17. Remove the engine mounts from the vehicle.

18. If equipped with a manual transaxle, disconnect the intermediate shaft bracket from the engine.

19. Disconnect the shift cable bracket at the transaxle, then remove the lower bellhousing-to-engine bolts.

20. Lower the vehicle, then remove the heater hoses.

21. Install an engine lifting device, then remove the engine support fixture.

22. Support the transaxle, then remove the remaining transaxle-to-engine bolts.

NOTE: Although it is not necessary to remove the hood from the engine compartment, it may be easier to remove the engine if done. Using an awl, scribe marks around the hood hinges to help aid correct hood alignment upon installation.

23. Remove the engine assembly from the vehicle.

To install:

24. Lower the engine assembly into position in the vehicle.

25. Install the engine support fixture, then remove the lifting device.

26. Install the upper transaxle-to-engine bolts and tighten to 55 ft. lbs. (75 Nm).

27. Install the heater hoses, then raise and support the vehicle safely.

28. Install and tighten the lower transaxle bolts to 55 ft. lbs. (75 Nm).

29. Connect the shift cable bracket to the transaxle.

30. If equipped with a manual transaxle, install the intermediate shaft bracket to the engine.

31. Install the engine mounts to the vehicle.

32. Install the flywheel-to-converter bolts and tighten to 52 ft. lbs. (70 Nm).

33. Reconnect the exhaust pipe to the rear of the manifold, then install the air conditioning compressor.

34. Install the starter assembly to the engine, then install the flywheel cover.

35. Install the right inner fender splash shield, then lower the vehicle and remove the engine support fixture.

36. Connect the coolant bypass and overflow hoses to the engine.

37. Connect the fuel lines.

38. Connect the wiring harness to the engine, then install the alternator assembly.

39. Install the cables to the bracket on the plenum, then connect the radiator hoses.

40. If equipped, install the idler.

41. Install the drive belt tensioner assembly, then install the serpentine belt to the front of the engine.

42. Install the exhaust manifold crossover assembly.

43. Install the battery to the vehicle, then connect the positive battery cable followed by the negative battery cable.

44. Install the air cleaner and duct assembly.

45. Fill cooling system and check for leaks. Start the engine and allow it to warm until normal operating temperature is reached, then top-off the coolant.

46. If equipped, evacuate, recharge and leak test the air conditioning system.

47. Recheck for coolant, fuel, oil and transaxle fluid for proper levels or leaks.

Engine Mounts

REMOVAL AND INSTALLATION

Front

1. Disconnect the negative battery cable.

2. For the 2.0L and the 2.2L engines, install J–28467–A, or an equivalent engine support fixture and adapter. Remove the engine weight from the mount using the fixture.

3. Remove the mount-to-body and/or bracket bolts:

a. For the 2.0L engine, remove the 2 mount-to-bracket bolts, followed by the 2 top mount bolts.

b. For the 2.2L engine, remove the 2 upper mount-to-body bolts, then remove the 2 mount-to-bracket bolts.

c. For the 3.1L engine, remove the mount-to-body bracket bolts, followed by the upper mount-to-engine bracket bolt.

4. Raise the vehicle and support safely. For the 3.1L engine, place a support under the engine assembly.

5. Except for the 2.0L engine, remove the inner fender splash shield.

6. Remove the lower mount-to-body or body bracket bolt, then for the 3.1L engine, remove the lower engine mount-to-engine bracket bolt.

7. Remove the engine mount.

To install:

8. Thoroughly clean the threads of all the fasteners of any remaining threadlocking material. Before installation, each fastener should be coated with Loctite®, or an equivalent threadlock.

9. Position the engine mount in the vehicle.

10. Install and tighten the lower engine mount bolt(s). For the 3.1L engine, lower the engine into position, loading the mount, by removing the engine support from under the vehicle:

a. For the 2.0L engine, tighten the lower mount bolt to 46 ft. lbs. (63 Nm).

b. For the 2.2L engine, tighten the mount-to-body bolt to 61 ft. lbs. (83 Nm).

c. For the 3.1L engine, tighten the lower engine mount-to-bracket bolt to 50 ft. lbs. (68 Nm) for 1992 vehicles or to 61 ft. lbs. (83 Nm) for 1993–96 vehicles. Then install and tighten the lower mount-to-body bracket bolt to 61 ft. lbs. (83 Nm) for 1992 vehicles or to 46 ft. lbs. (63 Nm) for 1993–96 vehicles.

11. Except for the 2.0L engine, install the inner fender splash shield.

12. Lower the vehicle.

13. Install the mount-to-body and or bracket bolts:

a. For the 2.0L engine, tighten the 2 top mount bolts to 54 ft. lbs. (73 Nm) for 1992 vehicles or to 46 ft. lbs. (63 Nm) for 1993–96 vehicles, then tighten the 2 mount-to-bracket bolts to 50 ft. lbs. (68 Nm) for 1992 vehicles or to 61 ft. lbs. (83 Nm) for 1993–96 vehicles.

b. For the 2.2L engine, tighten the 1 or 2 mount-to-bracket bolts (as applicable) to 50 ft. lbs. (68 Nm), then tighten the 2 upper mount-to-body bolts 50 ft. lbs. (68 Nm).

c. For the 3.1L engine, tighten the upper mount-to-engine bracket bolt to 50 ft. lbs. (68 Nm) for 1992 vehicles or to 61 ft. lbs. (83 Nm) for 1993–96 vehicles, then tighten the mount-to-body bracket bolts to 54 ft. lbs. (73 Nm) for 1992 vehicles or to 46 ft. lbs. (63 Nm) for 1993–96 vehicles.

14. For the 2.0L and the 2.2L engines, carefully lower the engine weight completely onto the mounts, then remove the engine support fixture and adapter.

15. Connect the negative battery cable.

Rear

1. Disconnect the negative battery cable.

2. For the 2.0L and the 2.2L engines, install J–28467–A, or an equivalent engine support fixture and adapter. Remove the engine weight from the mount using the fixture.

3. For the 2.0L engine, remove the 2 mount-to-bracket bolts.

4. Raise and support the vehicle safely.

5. For the 3.1L engine, position an engine support to unload the engine mount.

6. Remove the engine mounting nuts and, if applicable, bolts. Remove the engine mount and, for the 2.0L engine, the reinforcement.

To install:

7. Thoroughly clean the threads of all the fasteners of any remaining threadlocking material. Before installation, each fastener should be coated with Loctite®, or an equivalent threadlock.

8. Position the engine mount in the vehicle.

9. Install and tighten the engine mount fasteners, except for the 2.0L engine mount-to-bracket bolts:

a. For the 2.0L engine, tighten the nuts to 18 ft. lbs. (24 Nm) except for on 1993–96 vehicles which should be tightened to 38 ft. lbs. (52 Nm).

b. For the 2.2L engine, tighten the nuts to 18 ft. lbs. (24 Nm) and the bolts to 40 ft. lbs. (54 Nm).

c. For the 3.1L engine, tighten the nuts to 17 ft. lbs. (23 Nm) and the bolts to 40 ft. lbs. (54 Nm) except for 1993–96 vehicles which should be tightened to 38 ft. lbs. (52 Nm).

10. For the 3.1L engine, carefully lower the engine and remove the support.

11. Lower the vehicle.

12. For the 2.0L engine, install the 2 mount-to-bracket bolts and tighten to 40 ft. lbs. (54 Nm) except for 1993–96 vehicles which should be tightened to 38 ft. lbs. (52 Nm).

13. For the 2.0L and the 2.2L engines, lower the engine weight onto the mounts and remove the engine support fixture.

14. Connect the negative battery cable.

Cylinder Head

REMOVAL AND INSTALLATION

2.0L Engine

NOTE: Cylinder head gasket replacement is necessary any time the camshaft carrier/cylinder head bolts are loosened. Do not attempt to remove the camshaft carrier and install again without replacing the cylinder head gasket. The head bolts should only be loosened when cold. New head bolts should be used every time camshaft carrier/cylinder head or gasket are replaced.

1. Relieve the fuel system pressure, then disconnect the negative battery cable.

2. Remove the air cleaner assembly and drain the cooling system into a clean container for possible reuse.

3. Remove the coolant reservoir tank.

4. Disconnect the EVAP canister vapor pipe assembly.

5. Remove the serpentine drive belt.

6. Remove the timing belt front cover upper bolts and nuts, then loosen the serpentine belt tensioner and pivot it aside.

7. Raise and support the vehicle safely, then remove the right inner fender and right lower splash shields.

8. If equipped, remove the air conditioning V-belt.

9. Remove the crankshaft pulley and the flywheel inspection cover, then remove the timing belt front cover lower bolts and the cover assembly.

10. Align the timing marks.

11. Loosen the water pump, then release the timing belt tension using J–33039–A, or an equivalent tool. Remove the timing belt.

12. Disconnect the exhaust pipe from the manifold.

13. Lower the vehicle, then remove the bolts and the rear timing belt cover from the engine.

14. Disconnect the PCV hose, then tag and unplug the electrical connections from the intake manifold and the cylinder head.

15. Remove the exhaust manifold bolts, then remove the manifold.

16. Remove the power steering pump pressure and return hoses, then remove the alternator, bracket and power steering pump, as an assembly.

17. Remove the front and rear engine lift brackets.

18. Remove the coil assembly.

19. Remove the breather tube and bracket.

20. Disconnect the fuel lines, then tag and remove the hoses from the cylinder head and intake manifold.

21. Disconnect the radiator and coolant hoses from the cylinder head.

22. Remove the cylinder head/camshaft carrier bolts in the proper sequence, working clockwise from the end blots inward to the center bolts.

23. Remove the camshaft carrier.

24. Remove the rocker arms, lash compensators and the thrust pieces.

25. Remove the cylinder head and, if necessary, disconnect the intake manifold.

To install

26. Thoroughly clean the gasket mating surfaces of any remaining gasket material and of oils. Make sure the cylinder block threads are clean and free of dirt or foreign material.

27. Apply a continuous 3mm bead of gasket sealant to the mating surface of the camshaft carrier.

28. If removed, install the intake and/or exhaust manifolds to the cylinder head, then position the head onto the block using a new gasket.

29. Install the valve lash compensators, thrust pieces and rocker arms.

30. Position the camshaft carrier over the cylinder head, then install the bolts and tighten in the proper sequence to 18 ft. lbs. (25 Nm). For 1992 vehicles, reverse the bolt removal sequence, while for 1993-96 vehicles, follow the removal sequence. Using a torque angle gauge, tighten the bolts first to specification, then in 3 additional passes of 60 degrees each to a total torque of 18 ft. lbs. (25 Nm) and 180 degrees.

31. Install the oil level indicator and breather tube.

32. Connect the radiator hoses and coolant lines.

33. Install the wiring and the vacuum hoses to the cylinder head and intake manifold assemblies.

34. Connect the fuel lines.

35. Install the accelerator linkage and bracket.

36. Install the coil assembly. If applicable and removed, install the distributor cap and wires.

37. Install the power steering pump, bracket and alternator assembly.

38. If applicable, install the exhaust manifold turbo assembly.

39. Install the camshaft carrier cover, then connect the PCV valve hose.

40. Install the rear timing belt cover, followed by the EVAP canister vapor pipe assembly.

41. Raise and support the vehicle safely.

42. Connect the exhaust pipe to the manifold.

43. Install the timing belt and adjust the tension, then install the timing belt cover and secure using the lower bolts.

44. Install the crankshaft pulley, then if equipped, install the air conditioning V-belt.

45. Install the splash shields and the flywheel inspection cover.

46. Lower the vehicle, then position and secure the serpentine belt tensioner.

47. Install and secure the timing belt front cover upper bolts.

48. Install the serpentine drive belt, then install the coolant recovery tank.

49. Install the air cleaner assembly and connect the negative battery cable.

50. Fill the engine cooling system, then start and warm the engine to normal operating temperature. If necessary, top-off the coolant.

51. With the engine at normal operating temperature tighten the cylinder head/camshaft carrier bolts in the proper sequence an additional 30-50 degrees.

2.2L Engine

NOTE: The engine must be cold before removing the cylinder head. Always release the fuel pressure before starting repair.

1. Relieve the fuel system pressure, then disconnect the negative battery cable.

2. Remove the air cleaner/inlet duct assembly and drain the cooling system into a clean container for possible reuse.

3. Tag and unplug the vacuum lines and wiring harness connectors.

4. Disconnect the accelerator linkage from the throttle body.

5. Remove the coolant reservoir, then remove the serpentine drive belt.

6. Remove the alternator, then remove the power steering pump. It may be possible to remove the pump from the engine with the lines connected and reposition the pump in the engine compartment to avoid needing to bleed the power steering system upon installation.

7. Remove the serpentine belt tensioner assembly.

8. Tag and disconnect the secondary ignition wires from the spark plugs.

9. Disconnect the EVAP canister purge line located beneath the manifold.

10. Disconnect the upper radiator hose, then remove the heater hoses from the manifold.

11. Disconnect the throttle body cables from the bracket, then remove the coolant inlet hose from the cylinder head.

12. Remove the intake manifold brace from the power steering pump bracket.

13. Disconnect the fuel lines.

14. Remove the rocker arm cover, then remove the rocker arms and pushrods.

NOTE: Whenever valve train components, such as rocker arms and pushrods, are removed from the cylinder head, they should be tagged or arranged for identification purposes. Valve train components must always be installed in their original locations and with the same mating surfaces to assure valve train integrity.

15. Remove the secondary ignition cable bracket, followed by the engine lift bracket.

16. Disconnect the exhaust pipe from the manifold.

17. Remove the head bolts, then for automatic transaxle equipped vehicles, remove the transaxle fluid level indicator bracket.

18. Remove the cylinder head assembly from the block.

To install:

19. Thoroughly clean the gasket mating surfaces of remaining gasket material and/or oil. Make sure the surfaces are clean and dry prior to assembly. Do not use sealant on the cylinder head gasket mating surface.

20. Position the new cylinder head gasket over the dowel pins on the

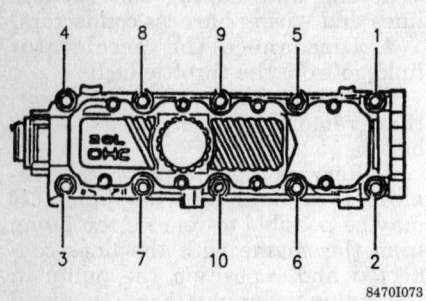

Cylinder head/camshaft carrier bolt removal sequence — 2.0L engine

8470I073

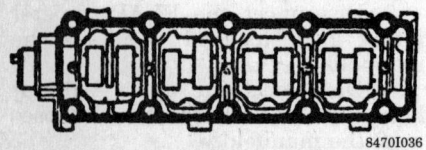

Apply a continuous 3mm bead of gasket sealant to the camshaft carrier surface prior to installation — 2.0L engine

8470I036

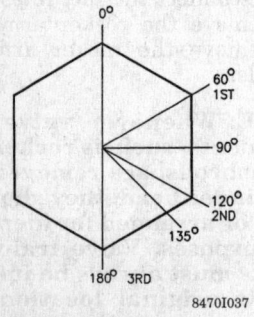

8470I037

Tighten the cylinder head/camshaft carrier bolts an additional 180 degrees in 3 passes — 2.0L engine

block, then carefully lower the cylinder head into place.

21. Install and finger-tighten the cylinder head bolts.

22. Tighten the bolts in sequence to the proper specification. Tighten the long bolts to 46 ft. lbs. (63 Nm) and the short bolts to 43 ft. lbs. (58 Nm). Then using a torque angle gauge, tighten all bolts (in sequence) an additional 90 degrees.

23. Connect the throttle body cables, then install the transaxle fluid level indicator bracket.

24. Install the engine left bracket, followed by the secondary ignition cable bracket.

25. Install the rocker arms and pushrods, followed by the rocker arm cover.

26. Connect the fuel lines, followed by the vacuum hoses and the electrical wiring connectors.

27. Install the intake manifold brace.

28. Install the coolant inlet hose to the cylinder head, then install the heater hoses and the upper radiator hose.

29. Connect the secondary ignition wires to the spark plugs.

30. Install the serpentine belt tensioner.

31. Install the power steering pump assembly, then install the alternator.

32. Install the serpentine drive belt.

33. Install the coolant reservoir, then install the air cleaner/duct assembly.

34. Raise and support the vehicle, then connect the exhaust pipe to the manifold. Lower the vehicle.

35. Connect the negative battery cable and fill the engine cooling system.

36. Check the engine oil and add, if necessary.

37. Start the engine and allow it to come to normal operating temperature, then check for leaks.

3.1L Engine

LEFT SIDE

1. Relieve the fuel system pressure and disconnect the negative battery cable.

2. Drain the engine coolant into a clean container for possible reuse and remove the air cleaner assembly.

3. Remove the rocker cover from the cylinder head.

4. Remove the intake manifold and plenum assembly.

5. Disconnect the exhaust crossover.

6. Remove the left exhaust manifold assembly.

7. Disconnect the oil level indicator tube and bracket assembly.

8. Tag and disconnect the secondary ignition wires from the spark plugs.

9. Loosen the rocker arms nuts sufficiently to remove the pushrods. Remove the pushrods and tag or arrange them for identification so they may be installed in the same locations from which they were removed.

10. Starting with the outer bolts and moving gradually inward, remove the cylinder head bolts.

11. Remove the cylinder head from the engine block.

12. Clean and inspect the surfaces of the cylinder head, block and intake manifold. Clean the threads in the block and the threads on the bolts. Make sure the gasket surfaces are clean and free of dirt or oil.

To install:

13. Align the new gasket over the dowels on the block with the note **THIS SIDE UP** facing the cylinder head.

14. Install the cylinder head assembly over the gasket and onto the dowels.

15. Coat the cylinder head bolts with a proper sealer and install the bolts hand-tight.

16. Tighten the bolts, in the correct sequence, to 33 ft. lbs. (45 Nm), then rotate an additional 90 degrees (1/4 turn).

17. Install the pushrods into the same locations from which they were removed. Note that the intake pushrods are marked orange and are approximately 6 in. long, while the exhaust pushrods are marked blue and are 6⅜ in. long.

18. Install the rocker arms and tighten to 18 ft. lbs. (25 Nm).

19. Install the intake manifold and plenum assembly using a new gasket, then tighten the bolts evenly to 88 inch lbs. (10 Nm).

20. Install the rocker cover to the cylinder head.

21. Install the oil level dipstick tube assembly.

22. Connect the ignition wires to the spark plugs.

23. Install the exhaust manifold, then connect the crossover pipe.

24. Connect the negative battery cable, then fill the engine cooling system and check for leaks.

25. Install the air cleaner assembly, then start the engine and run it at idle until normal operating temperature is reached. Recheck for leaks and top-off the coolant, as necessary.

RIGHT SIDE

1. Relieve the fuel system pressure and disconnect the negative battery cable.

2. Drain the engine coolant into a clean container for possible reuse and remove the air cleaner assembly.

3. Tag and disconnect the secondary ignition wires from the spark plugs.

4. Remove the right exhaust manifold assembly.

5. Remove the rocker cover from the cylinder head.

6. Remove the intake manifold and plenum assembly.

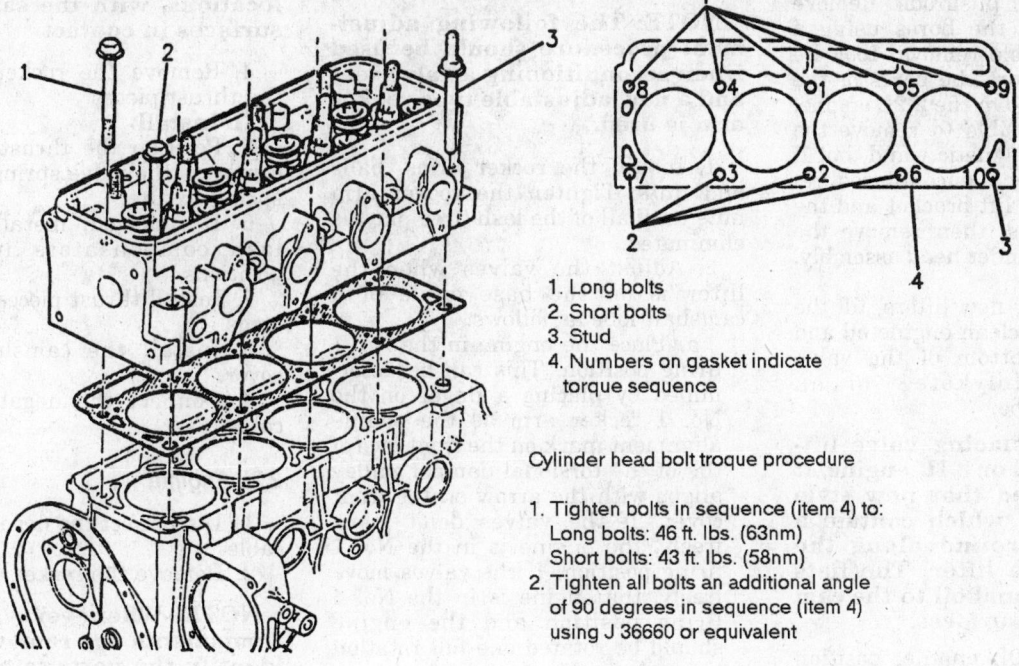

1. Long bolts
2. Short bolts
3. Stud
4. Numbers on gasket indicate torque sequence

Cylinder head bolt troque procedure

1. Tighten bolts in sequence (item 4) to:
   Long bolts: 46 ft. lbs. (63nm)
   Short bolts: 43 ft. lbs. (58nm)
2. Tighten all bolts an additional angle of 90 degrees in sequence (item 4) using J 36660 or equivalent

8470I038

2.2L engine cylinder head bolt torque sequence

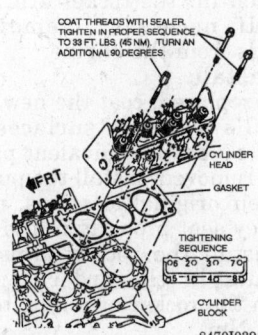

Cylinder head installation and torque sequence — 3.1L engine

8470I039

7. Loosen the rocker arms nuts sufficiently to remove the pushrods. Remove the pushrods and tag or arrange them for identification so they may be installed in the same locations from which they were removed.

8. Starting with the outer bolts and moving gradually inward, remove the cylinder head bolts.

9. Remove the cylinder head from the engine block.

10. Clean and inspect the surfaces of the cylinder head, block and intake manifold. Clean the threads in the block and the threads on the bolts.

Make sure the gasket surfaces are clean and free of dirt or oil.

To install:

11. Align the new gasket over the dowels on the block with the note **THIS SIDE UP** facing the cylinder head.

12. Install the cylinder head assembly over the gasket and onto the dowels.

13. Coat the cylinder head bolts with a proper sealer and install the bolts hand-tight.

14. Tighten the bolts, in the correct sequence, to 33 ft. lbs. (45 Nm), then rotate an additional 90 degree (1/4 turn).

15. Install the pushrods into the same locations from which they were removed. Note that the intake pushrods are marked orange and are approximately 6 in. long, while the exhaust pushrods are marked blue and are 6 3/8 in. long.

16. Install the rocker arms and tighten to 18 ft. lbs. (25 Nm).

17. Install the intake manifold and plenum assembly using a new gasket, then tighten the bolts evenly to 88 inch lbs. (10 Nm).

18. Install the rocker cover to the cylinder head.

19. Install the exhaust manifold.

20. Connect the ignition wires to the spark plugs.

21. Connect the negative battery cable, then fill the engine cooling system and check for leaks.

22. Install the air cleaner assembly, then start the engine and run it at idle until normal operating temperature is reached. Recheck for leaks and top-off the coolant, as necessary.

Valve Lifters

REMOVAL AND INSTALLATION

1. Disconnect the negative battery cable.

2. For the 3.1L engine, remove the intake manifold.

3. Remove the rocker arm or camshaft cover.

4. For the 2.0L engine, compress the valves and springs using J–33302-25 or an equivalent compressing fixture, then remove the rocker arms, thrust pieces and the valve lifters.

NOTE: Whenever valve train components are removed, tag or identify the parts to assure that they are reinstalled in the same locations, with the same mating surfaces in contact.

5. Except for the 2.0L engine, loosen the rocker arm holding nut

and turn the rocker arm to the side, then remove the pushrods. Remove the lifters from the bores using a magnet or suitable removal tool. Be careful not to score the bores or the lifter assemblies. On the 2.2L engine, it should be possible to remove the lifters using a magnetic wand, but if extreme difficulty is encountered, remove the engine lift bracket and the spark plug wires, then remove the bolts and the cylinder head assembly.

To install:

6. If installing new lifters, fill the assemblies with clean engine oil and lubricate the bottom of the valve lifter with Molykote® or an equivalent prelube.

NOTE: If replacing valve lifters for the 2.2L or 3.1L engine, it is recommended that new style lifters be used which contain a narrow flat ground along the lower ¾ of the lifter. The flats provide additional oil to the cam lobe and lifter surfaces.

7. For the 2.0L engine, position the thrust pieces and compress the valve springs, then install the lifters followed by the thrust pieces and rocker arms.

8. Except for the 2.0L engine, install the lifters into their bores. If removed for lifter access on the 2.2L engine, install the cylinder head assembly. Install the pushrods, making sure they are properly seated in the lifters, then move the rocker arm into position. Tighten the rocker arm nuts to 22 ft. lbs. (30 Nm) for 2.2L engine or to 18 ft. lbs. (25 Nm) for the 3.1L engine.

NOTE: Certain 3.1L engines may be equipped with both normal and oversized lifters. The bores of these lifters should be marked with a dab or white paint and/or stamped "0.25 OS" to signify 0.25mm oversized.

9. Install the rocker arm or camshaft cover.

10. For the 3.1L engine, install the intake manifold.

11. Connect the negative battery cable.

Valve Lash

ADJUSTMENT

All engines are originally equipped with hydraulic valve lifters. No adjustment is necessary. The 3.1L engine replacement rocker arm stud is adjustable and the adjustment can be performed as listed below.

3.1L Engine

NOTE: The following adjustment procedure should be used when reconditioning a valve seat and a new adjustable type rocker arm is used.

1. Install the rocker arms, balls and nuts. Tighten the rocker arm nuts until all of the lash (free-play) is eliminated.

2. Adjust the valves when the lifter is on the base circle of a camshaft lobe as follows:

   a. Place the engine in the No. 1 firing position. This can be determined by placing a finger on the No. 1 rocker arm as the engine alignment mark on the front face of the of the torsional damper pulley aligns with the arrow on the front cover. If the valves don't move freely, the engine is in the No. 1 firing position. If the valves move freely, the engine is in the No. 4 firing position and the engine should be rotated one full rotation to reach the No. 1 position.

   b. With the engine TDC on the No. 1 cylinder, adjust the following valves:

   • Exhaust — 1, 2, 3
   • Intake — 1, 5, 6

   c. Loosen the adjusting nut several turns backwards and then tighten until all lash (free-play) is removed. After all of the valve lash is removed turn the nut an additional 1½ turns; this will center the lifter plunger.

   d. Turn the engine 1 complete revolution until the timing tab and the alignment mark are again aligned; this will place the engine in the No. 4 firing position.

   e. With the engine TDC on the No. 4 cylinder, adjust the following valves:

   • Exhaust — 4, 5, 6
   • Intake — 2, 3, 4

Rocker Arms

REMOVAL AND INSTALLATION

2.0L Engine

1. Disconnect the negative battery cable.

2. Remove camshaft carrier cover.

3. Compress the valve springs using J-33302-25 or equivalent an equivalent spring fixture.

NOTE: Whenever valve train components are removed, tag or identify the parts to assure that

they are reinstalled in the same locations, with the same mating surfaces in contact.

4. Remove the rocker arms and the thrust pieces.

To install:

5. Position the thrust pieces and compress the valve springs using the spring fixture.

6. If removed, install the valve lash compensators in original positions.

7. Install thrust pieces and rocker arms.

8. Install the camshaft carrier cover.

9. Connect the negative battery cable.

2.2L Engine

1. Disconnect the negative battery cable.

2. Remove the rocker arm cover.

NOTE: Whenever valve train components are removed, tag or identify the parts to assure that they are reinstalled in the same locations, with the same mating surfaces in contact.

3. Remove the rocker arm nut and ball, then lift the rocker arm off the stud. If necessary, remove the pushrods from the engine.

To install:

4. If replaced, coat the new rocker arm/balls bearing surfaces with Molykote® or an equivalent prelube.

5. If removed, install the pushrods into their original locations, making sure they seat properly in the lifter.

6. Install the rocker arms, balls and nuts in the order removed. Tighten the rocker arm nuts to 22 ft. lbs. (30 Nm).

7. Install the rocker arm cover.

8. Connect the negative battery cable.

3.1L Engine

1. Disconnect the negative battery cable.

2. Remove the rocker arm covers.

NOTE: Whenever valve train components are removed, tag or identify the parts to assure that they are reinstalled in the same locations, with the same mating surfaces in contact.

3. Remove the rocker arm nuts, followed by the rocker arm pivot balls and rocker arms.

4. If necessary, remove the pushrods from the cylinder head bores.

To install:

5. If removed, install the pushrods into the same locations from which they were removed. Note that the intake pushrods are marked orange and are approximately 6 in. long, while the longer exhaust pushrods are marked blue and are 6 ³/₈ in. long.

6. If replaced, coat the new rocker arm/balls bearing surfaces with Molykote® or an equivalent prelube.

7. Install the rocker arms and pivot balls, then install the nuts and tighten to 18 ft. lbs. (25 Nm).

8. Install the rocker arm covers.

9. Connect the negative battery cable.

Intake Manifold

REMOVAL AND INSTALLATION

2.0L Engine

1. Relieve the fuel fuel system pressure, then disconnect the negative battery cable.

2. Disconnect the air cleaner duct from the intake manifold, then remove the electronic ignition unit.

3. Drain the engine cooling system into a clean container for possible reuse.

4. Disconnect the coolant and vacuum hoses from the throttle body. Be sure to tag the vacuum hoses for installation purposes.

5. Remove the throttle body, then discard the old gasket.

6. Remove the fuel injector/fuel rail assembly.

7. Remove the EGR valve from the intake manifold, then disconnect the PCV hose.

8. Remove the alternator and bracket from the camshaft carrier.

9. Disconnect the power steering bracket from the intake, then remove the pump and bracket assembly from the engine. Position the assembly aside, making sure not to kink or damage the pump hoses.

10. Remove the ECM wiring harness for access to the lower manifold retainers.

11. Remove the manifold retaining nuts, then remove the manifold from the vehicle. Remove and discard the old gasket form the mating surfaces.

To install:

12. Thoroughly clean the gasket mating surfaces.

13. Position a new gasket, then install the intake manifold to the cylinder head. Install the retaining nuts with washers and tighten to 16 ft. lbs. (22 Nm) in the proper sequence (working outward from the center of the manifold).

14. Install the ECM wiring harness.

15. Position and secure the power steering pump and bracket assembly.

16. Install the alternator and bracket.

17. Install the EGR valve and tighten the retaining bolts to 16 ft. lbs. (22 Nm).

18. Install the throttle body using a new gasket. Tighten the retaining bolts to 11 ft. lbs. (15 Nm).

19. Connect the coolant and vacuum hoses to the throttle body, then install the PCV hose.

20. Install the electronic ignition unit.

21. Fill the engine cooling system and install the air cleaner duct.

22. Connect the negative battery cable, then start the engine and check for leaks.

2.2L Engine

1. Relieve the fuel fuel system pressure, then disconnect the negative battery cable.

2. Remove the air intake duct .

3. Drain the coolant into a clean container for possible reuse.

4. Tag and remove the vacuum lines and wires as necessary.

5. Disconnect the throttle linkage.

6. Remove the power steering pump assembly and position aside being careful not to kink or damage the pump hoses.

7. Disconnect the MAP sensor and the EGR solenoid valve.

8. Remove the retainers and the upper intake manifold assembly.

9. Disconnect the EGR valve injector.

10. Remove the fuel injector retainer bracket, regulator and injectors.

11. Raise and support the vehicle safely.

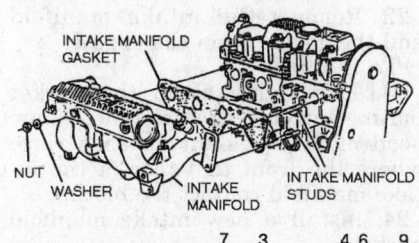

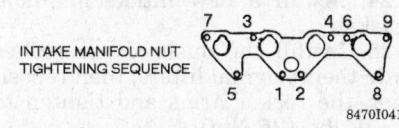

Intake manifold tightening sequence — 2.0L engine

12. Disconnect the accelerator and TV cables and cable bracket.

13. Remove the 6 lower intake manifold nuts.

14. Lower the vehicle.

15. Remove the upper retainers, then remove the intake manifold from the engine. Remove and discard the old gasket from the mating surface.

To install:

16. Install the manifold to the engine using a new gasket.

17. Loosely install the upper manifold retainers.

18. Raise and safely support the vehicle.

19. Loosely install the lower manifold retainers.

20. Tighten the nuts in the correct sequence (working from the center outward) to 22 ft. lbs. (30 Nm).

21. Lower the vehicle and install the EGR injector. Position the port facing directly upwards towards the throttle body.

22. Install the upper intake manifold assembly.

23. Install the MAP sensor and EGR solenoid valve.

24. Install the accelerator cable bracket and throttle linkage. Tighten the cable bracket bolts to 18 inch lbs. (25 Nm).

25. Connect the vacuum lines and wires.

26. Position and secure the power steering pump assembly.

27. Install the air cleaner or duct assembly.

28. Connect the negative battery cable, then fill cooling system and check for leaks.

29. Start and run the engine, allowing it to come to normal operating temperature. Recheck for leaks and top-off coolant, as necessary.

3.1L Engine

1. Relieve the fuel system pressure, then disconnect the negative battery cable.

2. Drain the engine cooling system into a clean container for possible reuse.

3. Remove the air cleaner assembly and disconnect the cables from the throttle body.

4. Disconnect the brake vacuum pipe from the plenum, then remove the throttle body from the plenum assembly.

5. Remove the EGR valve from the plenum.

6. Disconnect the wiring harness from the plenum, then remove the plenum from the engine.

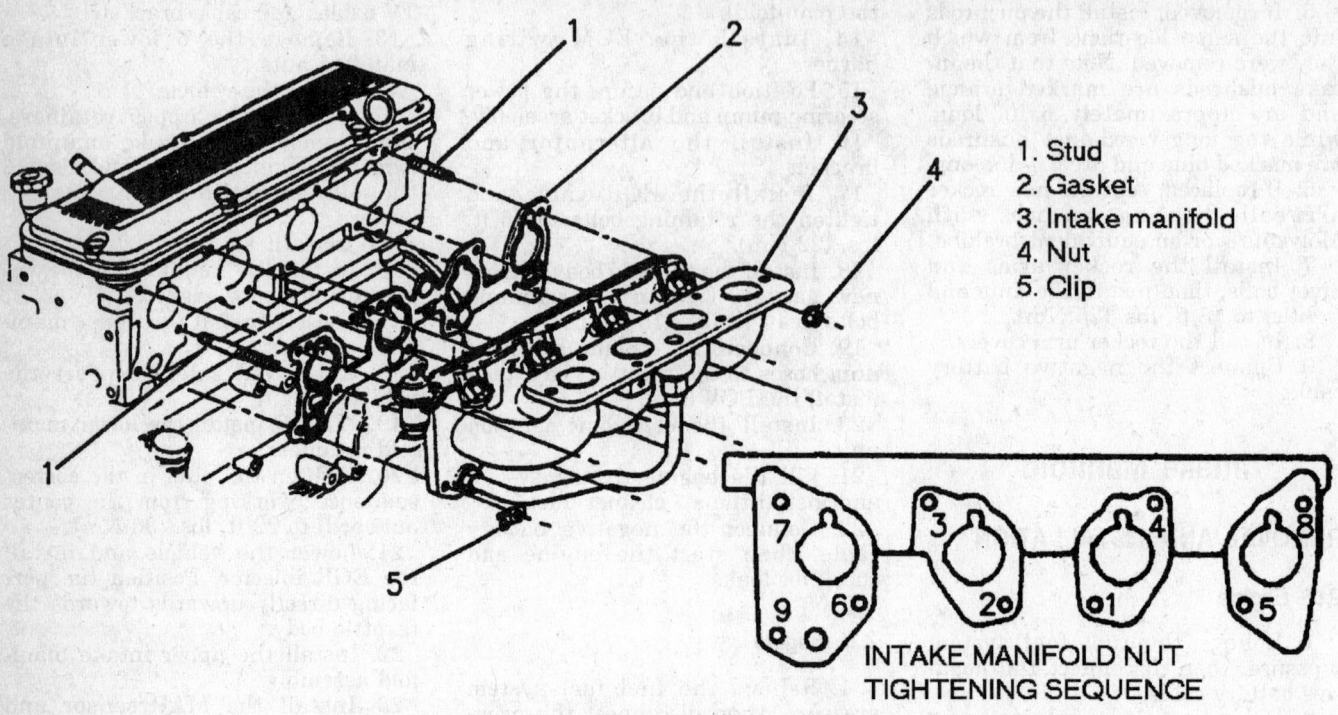

1. Stud
2. Gasket
3. Intake manifold
4. Nut
5. Clip

INTAKE MANIFOLD NUT
TIGHTENING SEQUENCE

84701042

Intake manifold tightening sequence — 2.2L engine

7. Disconnect the fuel lines from the rail assembly.

8. Remove the serpentine drive belt from the engine, then remove the alternator.

9. Disconnect the power steering lines from the alternator bracket, then remove the power steering pump retaining bolts and support the pump assembly aside.

10. Unplug the wiring harness connectors from the fuel injectors, then remove the retainers and the fuel rail assembly.

11. Remove the wires from the intake manifold.

12. Disconnect the heater pipe at the water pump and the cylinder head.

13. Remove the front valve cover from the engine.

14. Disconnect the PCV hose, then remove the alternator brace and bracket.

15. Remove the rear valve cover from the engine.

16. Disconnect the upper radiator hose, then tag and disconnect any wiring, as necessary.

17. Remove the engine coolant temperature sensor.

18. Remove the fuel lines from the bracket, then remove the throttle body heater hose.

19. Disconnect the heater pipe from the intake manifold.

20. Remove the manifold bolts, noting the positioning of the washers on the center bolts.

21. Loosen the rocker arms and remove the pushrods. Tag or arrange the pushrods for assembly in the same locations from which they were removed. Note the intake and exhaust pushrods are of different lengths.

NOTE: Whenever valve train components are removed, tag or identify the parts to assure that they are reinstalled in the same locations, with the same mating surfaces in contact.

22. Remove the intake manifold and the gasket from the engine.
To install:
23. Thoroughly clean the gasket mating surfaces, then place a 2–3mm bead of RTV sealant on each ridge where the front and rear of the intake manifold contact the block.

24. Install a new intake manifold gasket.

25. Install the pushrod assemblies into their original lifters, then reposition the rocker arms and tighten to 18 ft. lbs. (25 Nm).

26. Install the intake manifold to the engine and tighten the retaining bolts in proper sequence to 15 ft. lbs. (20 Nm) and then in a second pass to 24 ft. lbs. (33 Nm).

27. Install the heater pipe to the manifold, then install the throttle body heater hose.

28. Install the engine coolant temperature sensor.

29. Install the wiring harness connectors, as necessary.

30. Install the upper radiator hose.

31. Install the rear valve cover, then install the alternator bracket and brace.

32. Connect the PCV hose, then install the front valve cover.

33. Connect the heater pipe to the water pump and the cylinder head.

34. Install the plug wires.

35. Install the fuel rail, then connect the wiring harness to the injector terminals.

36. Install the power steering pump, then connect the line to the alternator bracket.

37. Install the alternator.

38. Connect the fuel lines to the rail assembly, then to the bracket.

39. Install the serpentine drive belt.

40. Install the plenum and tighten the retainers to 88 inch lbs. (10 Nm), then install the plug harness.

41. Install the EGR valve.

42. Install the throttle body.

43. Install the air intake duct, the cable bracket and the brake vacuum pipe.

44. Install the cables to the throttle body, then connect the negative battery cable.

45. Fill the engine cooling system, then start the engine and check for leaks.

Exhaust Manifold

REMOVAL AND INSTALLATION

2.0L Engine

1. Disconnect the negative battery cable.

2. Tag and disconnect the spark plug wires.

3. Loosen the fasteners and disconnect the exhaust pipe from the manifold.

4. Remove exhaust manifold retaining nuts, then remove the manifold from the engine. Remove and discard the old gasket from the mating surfaces.

To install:

5. Install the exhaust manifold using a new gasket. Tighten the exhaust manifold nuts to 16 ft. lbs. (22 Nm).

NOTE: Tighten the center exhaust manifold retaining nuts prior to tightening the outer nuts.

6. Position the exhaust pipe to the manifold and secure using the retainers. Tighten the pipe retaining nuts to 26 ft. lbs. (35 Nm).

7. If unplugged, connect the wiring harness to the oxygen sensor terminal.

8. Connect the spark plug wires.

9. Connect the negative battery cable.

2.2L Engine

1. Disconnect the negative battery cable.

2. Unplug the wiring harness from the oxygen sensor.

3. Remove the serpentine drive belt.

4. Remove the alternator.

5. Raise and support the vehicle safely.

6. Remove the retainers and separate the exhaust pipe from the manifold.

7. Lower the vehicle and remove the oil fill tube.

8. Remove the manifold retaining nuts, then remove the manifold from the cylinder head. Remove and discard the gasket from the mating surfaces.

To install:

9. Install the manifold to the cylinder head using a new gasket. Tighten the retaining nuts to 115 inch lbs. (13 Nm).

10. Raise and support the vehicle safely, then install the exhaust pipe to the manifold. Tighten the retaining nuts to 19 ft. lbs. (25 Nm), then lower the vehicle.

11. Install the alternator and the serpentine drive belt.

12. Install the oil fill tube.

13. Connect the wiring harness to the oxygen sensor.

14. Connect the negative battery cable.

3.1L Engine

LEFT SIDE

1. Disconnect the negative battery cable and remove the air cleaner assembly.

2. Drain the engine cooling system and remove the coolant bypass pipe.

3. Remove the exhaust heat shield.

4. Remove the exhaust crossover pipe from the manifold.

5. Remove the exhaust manifold bolts.

6. Remove the exhaust manifold, then remove and discard the gasket from the mating surface.

To install:

7. Loosely install the exhaust manifold using a new gasket.

8. Install the crossover pipe to the manifold.

9. Tighten the manifold retaining bolts to 19 ft. lbs. (25 Nm) except for 1993–96 engines which should be tightened to 21 ft. lbs. (28 Nm).

10. Install the engine heat shield and tighten the nuts to 89 inch lbs. (10 Nm).

11. Install the coolant bypass pipe.

12. Install the air cleaner assembly and connect the negative battery cable.

13. Fill the engine cooling system, then start the engine and check for leaks.

RIGHT SIDE

1. Disconnect the negative battery cable.

2. Remove the air cleaner assembly.

3. Raise and support the vehicle safely and, if equipped, remove the heat shield. Disconnect the exhaust pipe at the crossover and lower the vehicle.

4. Disconnect the crossover pipe from the manifold.

5. Remove the EGR pipe.

6. Unplug the wiring harness from the oxygen sensor.

7. Remove the exhaust manifold bolts, then remove the manifold from the cylinder head. Remove and discard the old gasket from the mating surface.

To install:

8. Install the exhaust manifold using a new gasket, then loosely install the bolts to retain the assembly.

9. Connect the crossover to the manifold.

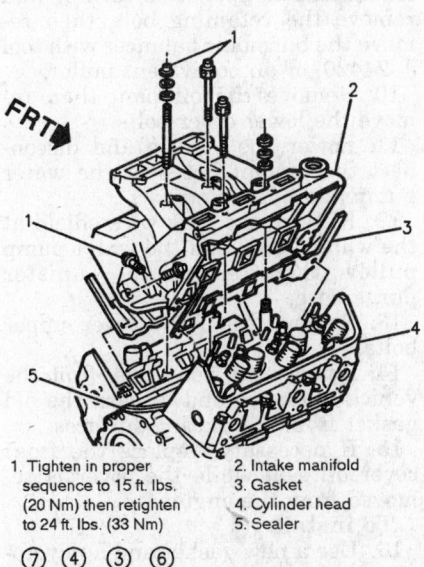

FRT

1. Tighten in proper sequence to 15 ft. lbs. (20 Nm) then retighten to 24 ft. lbs. (33 Nm)

2. Intake manifold
3. Gasket
4. Cylinder head
5. Sealer

⑦ ④ ③ ⑥
⑧ ① ② ⑤

84701043

Intake manifold installation and tightening sequence — 3.1L engine

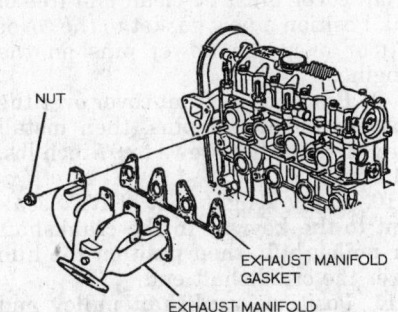

NUT

EXHAUST MANIFOLD GASKET

EXHAUST MANIFOLD

TORQUE NO. 2 AND NO. 3 MANIFOLD RUNNERS PRIOR TO NO. 1 AND NO. 4.

84701044

Exhaust manifold — 2.0L engine

10. Tighten the manifold retaining bolts to 19 ft. lbs. (25 Nm) except for 1993–96 engines which should be tightened to 21 ft. lbs. (28 Nm).

11. Install the wiring harness to the oxygen sensor terminals.

12. Connect the EGR pipe.

13. Raise and support the vehicle safely, then install the exhaust pipe to the crossover. If equipped, install the heat shield and tighten the retaining nuts to 89 inch lbs. (10 Nm).

14. Lower the vehicle and install the air cleaner assembly.

15. Connect the negative battery cable.

Turbocharger

REMOVAL AND INSTALLATION

1. Disconnect the negative battery cable.

2. Raise and safely support the vehicle.

3. Remove the lower fan retaining screw.

4. Disconnect the exhaust pipe at the turbocharger.

5. Remove air conditioning rear support bracket.

6. Remove the turbocharger support bracket from the engine.

7. Disconnect the oil drain and water return pipes at turbo.

8. Lower the vehicle and remove coolant recovery pipe.

9. Remove induction tube, coolant fan and oxygen sensor.

10. Disconnect the oil and water feed pipes.

11. Remove the air intake duct and vacuum hose at the actuator.

12. Remove the exhaust manifold retaining nuts, remove the turbocharger and manifold as an assembly.

13. Remove the turbocharger from exhaust manifold.

To install:

14. Install the turbocharger to the exhaust manifold and tighten the bolts to 18 ft. lbs. (24 Nm).

15. Install a new manifold gasket and install the manifold in position on the block. Tighten the bolts to 16 ft. lbs. (22 Nm).

16. Install the oil feed lines and the oil feed/return lines.

17. Install the oxygen sensor, then connect the air intake duct and vacuum hose to the actuator.

18. Install the cooling fan and upper screws.

19. Install the induction tube and the coolant recovery pipe.

20. Raise and support the vehicle safely, then install the turbo support and air conditioning rear support brackets.

21. Install the oil drain hose and the lower fan screw.

22. Connect the exhaust pipe and lower the vehicle.

23. Check fluid levels and make sure all turbocharger connections are properly fastened.

24. Connect the negative battery cable.

Timing Chain Front Cover

REMOVAL AND INSTALLATION

2.2L Engine

NOTE: The following procedure requires the use of a crankshaft hub installation tool J–35468 and crankshaft puller J–24420–B or their equivalents.

1. Disconnect the negative battery cable.

2. Remove the serpentine drive belt and the belt tensioner from the front of the engine.

3. Raise and support the vehicle safely.

4. Although not absolutely necessary, removal of the right front inner fender splash shield will facilitate access to the front cover.

5. Remove the oil pan.

6. Remove the center bolt from the crankshaft pulley, then remove the side pulley retaining bolts, remove the pulley. Using puller tool J–24420–B or equivalent, remove hub from the crankshaft.

7. Remove the front cover-to-block bolts and remove the front cover. If the front cover is difficult to remove, use a rubber mallet to break and loosen the seal.

To install:

8. The surfaces of the block and front cover must be clean and free of oil. Position a new gasket to the cover lip or over the dowel pins on the engine.

9. Position the front cover over the gasket and dowel pins, then install and tighten the screws to 97 inch lbs. (11 Nm).

10. Apply a light coat of RTV sealant to the keyway in the crankshaft or pulley hub, then position the hub over the crankshaft end.

11. Position crankshaft pulley and thread at least ¼ in. (6mm) of the hub installer tool threads (J–29113 or equivalent) into the end of the crankshaft. Using the tool, pull the crank-

shaft pulley into position over the crankshaft hub. Tighten the pulley bolts to 37 ft. lbs. (50 Nm) and the hub bolt to 77 ft. lbs. (105 Nm).

12. Install the oil pan.

13. If removed, install the right front inner fender splash shield.

14. Lower the vehicle.

15. Install the belt tensioner, then install the serpentine drive belt.

16. Fill the engine crankcase and the engine cooling system, then connect the negative battery cable.

3.1L Engine

1. Disconnect the negative battery cable.

2. Drain the cooling system and remove the coolant recovery tank from the vehicle.

3. Remove the serpentine belt and adjusting pulley.

4. Remove the alternator assembly from the vehicle.

5. Remove the power steering pump from the engine and position aside with the hoses still attached. Be careful not to kink or damage the hoses.

6. Raise the vehicle and support it safely.

7. Remove the inner fender splash shield.

8. Remove the flywheel cover, then remove the starter assembly from the vehicle.

9. Have an assistant hold the crankshaft damper from turning and remove the retaining bolt, then remove the harmonic balancer with tool J–24420, or an equivalent puller.

10. Remove the oil pan, then remove the lower cover bolts.

11. Lower the vehicle and disconnect the coolant hoses at the water pump and bypass pipe.

12. Remove the plug wire shield at the water pump and the water pump pulley, then remove the canister purge hose.

13. Remove the front cover upper bolts.

14. Remove the front cover from the vehicle. Remove and discard the old gasket from the mating surfaces.

15. If necessary, replace the front cover oil seal while the cover is removed from the engine.

To install:

16. Use a new gasket and apply apply a bead of RTV sealer to the front cover gasket surface from ½ way through the lower bolt holes to the bottom of the gasket.

17. Install the front cover and tighten the upper bolts to 20–28 ft. lbs. (27–38 Nm) for 1992 vehicles, or to 15 ft. lbs. (21 Nm) for 1993–96 ve-

hicles. Then for 1993–96 vehicles, tighten the 4 longer upper bolts to 35 ft. lbs. (45 Nm). The 4 bolts should be the upper bolts, but not the 2 top most centered bolts.

18. Raise and safely support the vehicle, then install the oil pan.

19. Install the lower front cover bolts and tighten to 20–28 ft. lbs. (27–38 Nm) for 1992 vehicles, or to 15 ft. lbs. (21 Nm) for 1993–96 vehicles.

20. Position the crankshaft balancer over the crankshaft key, then use J–29113 or an equivalent installer, to pull the balancer fully onto the crankshaft. Have an assistant keep the balancer from turning and install the retaining bolt. Tighten the bolt to 76 ft. lbs. (103 Nm).

21. Install the starter and the flywheel cover.

22. Install the inner splash shield and lower the vehicle.

23. Install the coolant hoses and the canister purge hose.

24. Install the plug wire shield to the water pump and the water pump pulley.

25. Position and secure the power steering pump.

26. Install the alternator, then install the belt tensioner and the serpentine drive belt.

27. Refill the engine crankcase and the engine cooling system, then connect the negative battery cable.

Front Cover Oil Seal

REPLACEMENT

2.2L and 3.1L Engines

The oil seal can be replaced with the front cover either on or off the engine.

1. If the front cover is still on the engine,

    a. For the 3.1L engine, raise and support the vehicle safely, then remove the right front tire and the inner fender splash shield.

    b. Remove the crankshaft pulley and hub. Remove the side and/or center pulley retaining bolts, remove the pulley and use a puller to remove the hub from the crankshaft.

    c. For the 3.1L engine, the key may be removed from the crankshaft to prevent interference with the new seal.

2. Pry the seal from the front cover using a small suitable tool and being careful not to distort the seal mating surfaces.

To install:

3. Lubricate the new seal with clean engine oil, then install the new

seal so the lip side, is towards the engine.

4. Using J–35468, or an equivalent front cover aligner and oil seal installer, press the new seal into position.

5. If the front cover is still on the engine, install the crankshaft hub and pulley.

6. For the 3.1L engine, install the splash shield and right front tire, then lower the vehicle.

Timing Chain and Sprockets

REMOVAL AND INSTALLATION

2.2L Engine

1. Disconnect the negative battery cable.

2. Remove the timing chain front cover from the engine.

3. Turn the engine until he marks on the camshaft and crankshaft sprockets are facing each other in alignment.

4. Loosen the timing chain tensioner upper bolt, then loosen the torx bolt as far as possible, without actually removing it.

5. Remove the camshaft sprocket bolt, then remove the sprocket and chain together. If the sprocket does not slide from the camshaft easily, a light blow with a rubber faced mallet at the lower edge of the sprocket should help to loosen it.

6. Using J–22888–20 or equivalent gear puller, remove the crankshaft sprocket from the engine.

To install:

7. Press the new crankshaft sprocket onto the crankshaft using crankshaft sprocket installer J–5590 or equivalent.

NOTE: Ensure that the sprocket is fully seated against the crankshaft.

8. Compress the tensioner spring, then insert a cotter pin or nail, into the hole to retain the tensioner.

9. Align the crankshaft and camshaft timing marks with the tabs on the chain tensioner.

10. Install the timing chain over the camshaft sprocket and around the crankshaft sprocket. Make sure the marks on the 2 sprockets are in alignment. Lubricate the gear and chains with clean engine oil.

11. Align the dowel in the camshaft with the dowel hole in the sprocket and install the sprocket onto the camshaft. Use the mounting bolt to

draw the sprocket onto the camshaft and tighten to 77 ft. lbs. (105 Nm).

12. Tighten the tensioner bolt to 18 ft. lbs. (24 Nm), then remove the timing chain pin.

13. Install the timing chain front cover.

14. Connect the negative battery cable.

3.1L Engine

1. Disconnect the negative battery cable.

2. Remove the timing chain front cover.

3. Position the No. 1 piston at **TDC** with the marks on the crankshaft and camshaft sprockets aligned at the top of each gear.

4. Remove the camshaft sprocket retaining bolts.

5. Remove the camshaft sprocket and chain from the front of the engine.

NOTE: If the sprocket does not move freely from the camshaft, a light blow using a plastic mallet on the lower edge of the sprocket should dislodge it.

6. Remove the crankshaft sprocket. If necessary, use a sprocket puller to free the sprocket from the engine.

To install:

7. Position the crankshaft sprocket and pull into position using an installation tool.

8. Apply Molykote® or equivalent, to the sprocket thrust surface.

9. Hold the sprocket with the chain hanging and align the timing marks on the camshaft and crankshaft sprockets.

10. Align the dowel in the camshaft with the dowel hole in the camshaft sprocket.

11. Draw the camshaft sprocket onto the camshaft using the mounting bolts. Tighten to 21 ft. lbs. (28 Nm).

12. Lubricate the timing chain with engine oil.

13. Install the timing chain front cover.

14. Connect the negative battery cable.

Timing Belt Front Cover

REMOVAL AND INSTALLATION

2.0L Engine

1. Disconnect the negative battery cable.

2. Remove the serpentine belt.

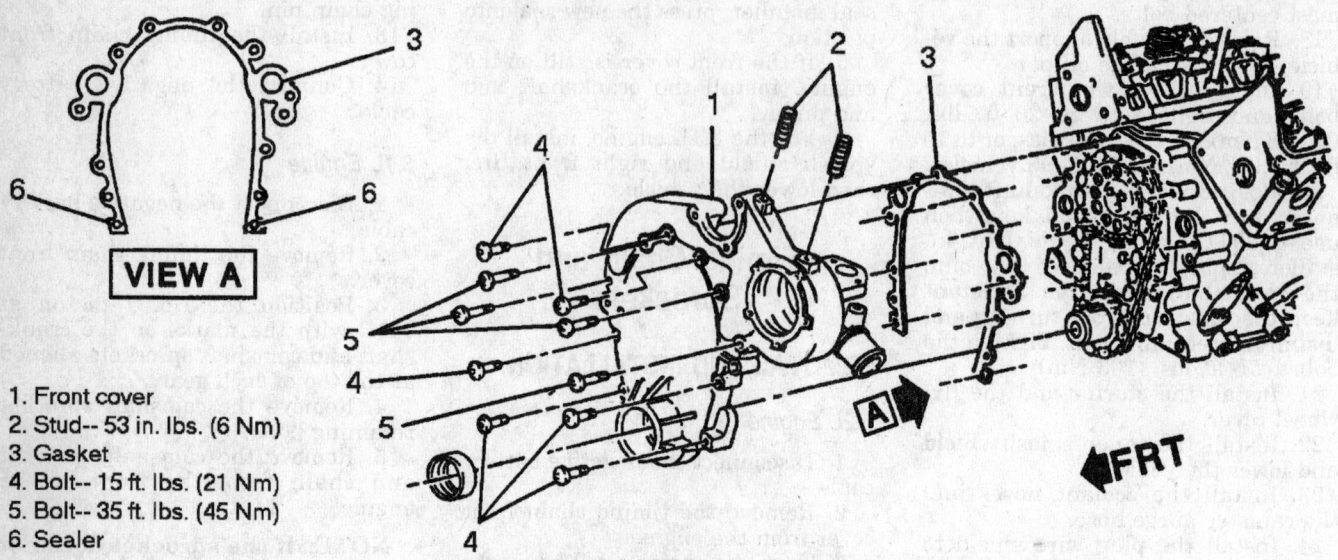

VIEW A

1. Front cover
2. Stud-- 53 in. lbs. (6 Nm)
3. Gasket
4. Bolt-- 15 ft. lbs. (21 Nm)
5. Bolt-- 35 ft. lbs. (45 Nm)
6. Sealer

8470I045

Timing chain front cover assembly — 3.1L engine

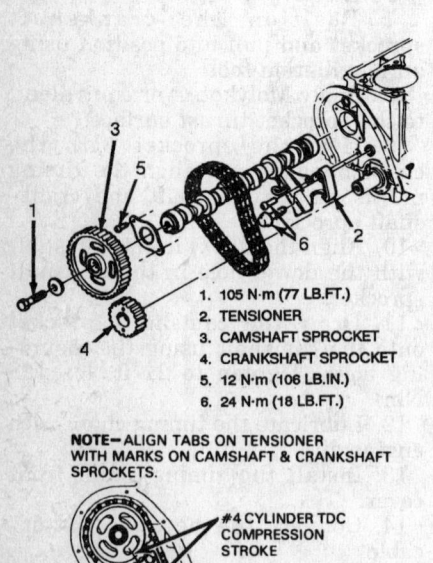

1. 105 N·m (77 LB.FT.)
2. TENSIONER
3. CAMSHAFT SPROCKET
4. CRANKSHAFT SPROCKET
5. 12 N·m (106 LB.IN.)
6. 24 N·m (18 LB.FT.)

NOTE—ALIGN TABS ON TENSIONER WITH MARKS ON CAMSHAFT & CRANKSHAFT SPROCKETS.

#4 CYLINDER TDC COMPRESSION STROKE

8470I046

Exploded view of the timing chain assembly — 2.2L engine

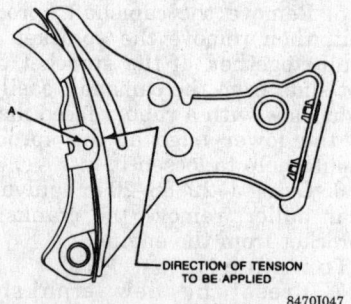

DIRECTION OF TENSION TO BE APPLIED

8470I047

Compress the tensioner spring, then insert a cotter pin or nail into the hole to hold the tension from the timing chain — 2.2L engine

3. Loosen the drive belt tensioner bolt and the tensioner will swing downward. If necessary, remove the bolt and tensioner from the engine.

4. Remove the cover attaching bolts, then remove the timing belt cover from the engine.

To install:

5. Install the timing belt cover and attaching bolts. Tighten to 62 inch lbs. (7 Nm).

6. Pivot or install the the timing belt tensioner into position and tighten the retaining bolt to 35 ft. lbs. (48 Nm).

7. Install the serpentine belt.

8. Connect the negative battery cable.

CRANKSHAFT OIL SEAL REPLACEMENT

2.0L Engine

1. Remove the timing belt front cover from the vehicle.

2. Remove the crankshaft sprocket.

3. Remove the crankshaft key and rear thrust washer.

4. Remove the timing belt tensioner assembly, then remove the retaining bolts and the rear timing cover.

5. Pry the front oil seal from the engine using a small suitable prytool.

To install:

6. Place the protective sleeve of special tool set J–33083, seal installer or equivalent, onto the crankshaft.

7. Lubricate the lip of the new seal. Using special tool J–33083, install the seal.

8. Remove the protective sleeve.

9. Install the timing belt rear cover and the timing belt tensioner to the engine.

10. Install the rear thrust washer and key on the crankshaft.

11. Install the crankshaft sprocket.

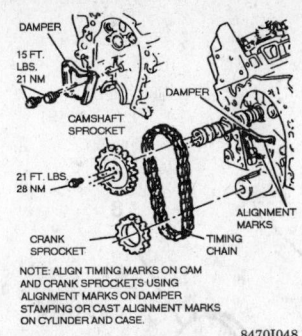

Timing chain and sprocket installation — 3.1L engine

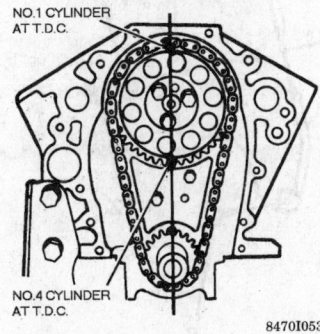

Align the proper timing marks when installing the timing chain — 3.1L engine

Timing Belt and Tensioner

REMOVAL AND INSTALLATION

2.0L Engine

1. Disconnect the negative battery cable and drain the engine cooling system to a level below the water pump.
2. Remove the coolant reservoir tank.
3. Remove the serpentine belt from the engine. Remove the fuel vapor pipe assembly.
4. Remove the timing belt front cover from the engine.
5. Turn the engine to align the timing marks on the gears with the marks on the timing belt rear cover.
6. Loosen the water pump bolts and release timing belt tension with tension adjusting tool J–33039 or equivalent. If equipped, remove the A/C drive belt.
7. Raise and support the vehicle safely, then remove the right splash shield.
8. Remove the pulley retaining bolt, then remove the pulley from the end of the crankshaft.

9. Lower the vehicle and remove the timing belt. If necessary, remove the retainers and the belt tensioner from the engine.

To install:

10. If removed, install the timing belt tensioner and tighten the retainers to 18 ft. lbs. (25 Nm).
11. If necessary, turn the crankshaft and/or the camshaft gears clockwise to align the timing marks on the gears with the timing marks on the rear cover.
12. Install the timing belt, making sure the portion between the camshaft gear and crankcase gear is in tension.
13. Using tool J–33039 or equivalent, turn the water pump eccentric clockwise until the tensioner contacts the high torque stop. Tighten the water pump screws slightly.
14. Turn the engine clockwise 720 degrees using the crankshaft gear bolt in order to fully seat the belt into the gear teeth.
15. Turn the water pump eccentric counterclockwise until the hole in the tensioner arm is aligned with the hole in the base. In order for the holes to properly align, the engine must be at or near room temperature of 68°F (20°C).
16. Tighten the water pump screws to 18 ft. lbs. (25 Nm) while checking that the tensioner holes remain as adjusted in the prior step.
17. Raise and support the vehicle safely, then install the crankshaft pulley. Coat the pulley retainer bolt threads with Loctite® 242, or equivalent threadlock. Install the retainer and tighten to 15 ft. lbs. (21 Nm).
18. Install the right splash shield and lower the vehicle.
19. Install the front timing cover assembly, then if removed, install the fuel vapor pipes.
20. Install the serpentine belt and, if equipped, the A/C drive belt. Install the coolant reservoir.
21. Connect the negative battery cable and properly fill the engine cooling system.

Timing Sprockets

REMOVAL AND INSTALLATION

Camshaft Sprocket

1. Disconnect the negative battery cable.
2. Remove the camshaft carrier cover.

3. Remove the timing belt.
4. Hold the camshaft with an open end wrench on the flats provided and remove the sprocket bolt, washer and sprocket.

To install:

5. Install the sprocket, retaining bolt and washer with the mark on the sprocket lined up with the mark on the rear timing belt cover. Tighten the retaining bolt to 33 ft. lbs. (45 Nm).
6. Install the timing belt.
7. Install the camshaft carrier cover.
8. Connect the negative battery cable.

Crankshaft Sprocket

1. Disconnect the negative battery cable.
2. Remove the timing belt.
3. Remove the bolt and retaining washer, then remove the crankshaft sprocket from the vehicle. Be sure to use J–37096 or an equivalent flywheel holder to prevent the engine from turning.

To install:

4. Install the sprocket over the key on the end of the crankshaft.
5. Install the thrust washer and attaching bolt, then tighten the bolt to 114 ft. lbs. (155 Nm) using a suitable flywheel holder to prevent the engine from turning.
6. Install the timing belt.
7. Connect the negative battery cable.

Camshaft

REMOVAL AND INSTALLATION

2.0L Engine

1. Disconnect the negative battery cable.
2. Remove the rocker arms and the valve lash compensators.

NOTE: Whenever valve train components are removed, tag or identify the parts to assure that they are reinstalled in the same locations, with the same mating surfaces in contact.

3. Remove the camshaft sprocket.
4. Remove the washer fluid container. If equipped, matchmark and remove the distributor assembly from the camshaft carrier.
5. Remove the rear cam cover.
6. Remove the camshaft thrust plate from rear of camshaft carrier.
7. Slide the camshaft rearward and remove it from the carrier.

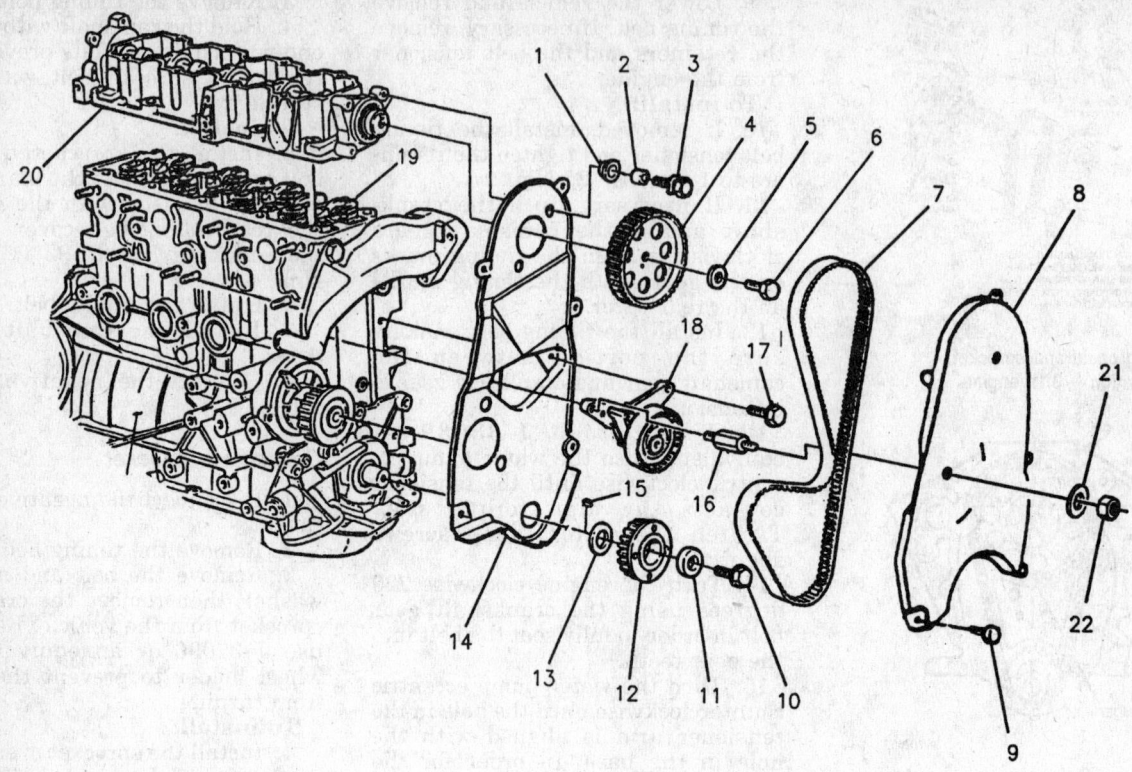

1	GROMMET	12	CRANKSHAFT SPROCKET
2	SLEEVE	13	WASHER
3	BOLT – 10 N·m (89 LBS. IN.)	14	REAR COVER
4	CAMSHAFT SPROCKET	15	KEYWAY
5	WASHER	16	STUD – 48 N·m (35 LBS. FT.)
6	BOLT – 45 N·m (22 LBS. FT.)	17	BOLT – 48 N·m (35 LBS. FT.)
7	TIMING BELT	18	TENSIONER
8	FRONT COVER	19	ENGINE
9	BOLT – 9 N·m (80 MLBS. IN.)	20	CAMSHAFT
10	BOLT – 155 N·m (144 LBS. FT.)	21	WASHER
11	WASHER	22	NUT

84701049

Exploded view of the timing covers, gears and belt assembly — 2.0L engine

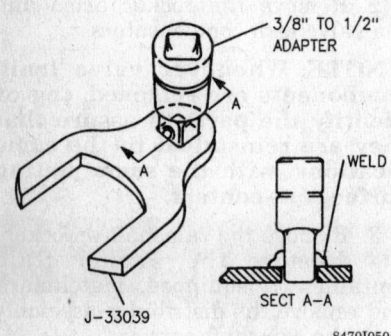

3/8" TO 1/2" ADAPTER

A

A

WELD

SECT A–A

J–33039

84701050

The timing belt tension adjuster may be made or modified to suit the engine

To install:

8. Hand install a new oil seal to the front of the camshaft carrier.

9. Carefully slide the camshaft into the carrier.

NOTE: Take care not to damage the carrier front oil seal when installing the camshaft.

10. Install the camshaft thrust plate retaining bolts. Tighten bolts to 71 inch lbs. (8 Nm).

11. Check the camshaft endplay, which should be within 0.016–0.064 in. (0.04–0.16mm).

12. Install the distributor or the rear cam cover, as applicable.

13. Install the washer fluid container.

14. Install the camshaft sprocket.

15. Install the rocker arms and valve lash components, then connect the negative battery cable.

2.2L Engine

This procedure requires that the engine be removed from the vehicle in order to provide the necessary access for camshaft removal and installation.

1. Remove the engine assembly from the vehicle, then mount the engine on a work stand.

2. Remove the serpentine drive belt from the engine.

3. Remove the alternator and brackets.

4. Remove the power steering pump assembly, then remove the serpentine belt tensioner.

5. Remove the water pump pulley.

6. Drain the engine oil and remove the filter.

7. Remove the crankshaft pulley, then remove the crankshaft hub.

8. Remove the rocker cover, then remove the rocker arms and pushrods.

NOTE: Whenever valve train components are removed, tag or identify the parts to assure that they are reinstalled in the same locations, with the same mating surfaces in contact.

9. Remove the hydraulic valve lifters.

10. Remove the engine front cover, timing chain and sprockets and tensioner.

11. Remove the oil pump drive.

12. Carefully remove the camshaft thrust plate.

13. Carefully slide the camshaft from the engine, making sure not to damage the camshaft bearings.

To install:

14. Coat the lobes and journals of the camshaft using prelube, then carefully slide the camshaft into the engine.

15. Install the thrust plate and tighten the retaining bolts to 106 inch lbs. (12 Nm).

16. Install the tensioner, timing chain and sprockets, then install the timing chain front cover.

17. Install the lifters. If the camshaft was replaced, new lifters must be installed to assure proper cam life. Certain lifters may be oversized, look for markings on the lifter bores.

18. Install the oil pump drive.

19. Install the rocker arms and pushrods, then install the rocker covers.

20. Install the crankshaft hub, then install the pulley.

21. Install the water pump.

22. Install the serpentine belt tensioner.

23. Install the power steering pump, then install the alternator and brackets.

24. Install the serpentine drive belt.

25. Install the engine to the vehicle.

26. Properly fill the engine crankcase and install a new oil filter.

3.1L Engine

This procedure requires that the engine be removed from the vehicle in order to provide the necessary access for camshaft removal and installation.

1. Remove the engine assembly from the vehicle, then mount the engine on a work stand.

2. Remove the hydraulic valve lifters from the engine.

NOTE: Whenever valve train components are removed, tag or identify the parts to assure that they are reinstalled in the same locations, with the same mating surfaces in contact.

3. Remove the timing chain front cover.

4. Remove the timing chain and camshaft sprocket.

5. Carefully slide the camshaft out from the front of the engine, making sure not to damage the camshaft bearings.

To install:

6. If installing a new camshaft, coat the lobes and journals of the camshaft using prelube. If installing the original camshaft, lubricate the journals and lobes with clean engine oil.

7. Carefully slide the camshaft into the engine.

8. Install the timing chain and camshaft sprocket.

9. Install the timing chain front cover.

10. Install the lifters. If the camshaft was replaced, new lifters must be installed to assure proper cam life. Certain lifters may be oversized, look for markings on the lifter bores.

11. Install the engine assembly to the vehicle.

12. Connect the negative battery cable.

Piston and Connecting Rod

POSITIONING

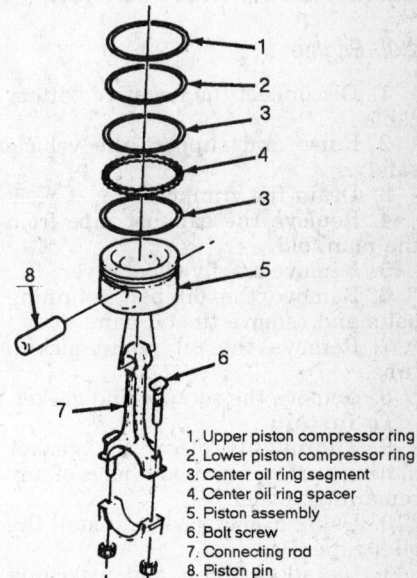

1. Upper piston compressor ring
2. Lower piston compressor ring
3. Center oil ring segment
4. Center oil ring spacer
5. Piston assembly
6. Bolt screw
7. Connecting rod
8. Piston pin

8470I051

Exploded view of the piston and connecting rod assembly

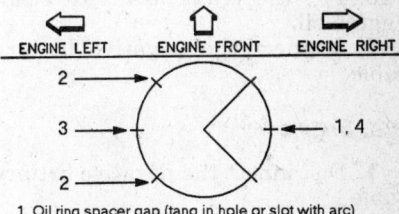

1. Oil ring spacer gap (tang in hole or slot with arc)
2. Oil ring rail gaps
3. No. 2 compression ring gap
4. Top compression ring gap

8470I052

Piston ring gap locations

ENGINE LUBRICATION

Oil Pan

REMOVAL AND INSTALLATION

2.0L Engine

1. Disconnect the negative battery cable.
2. Raise and support the vehicle safely.
3. Drain the crankcase.
4. Remove the exhaust pipe from the manifold.
5. Remove the flywheel cover.
6. Remove the oil pan retaining bolts and remove the oil pan.
7. Remove the oil pump pickup tube.
8. Remove the scraper and gasket.
To install:
9. Thoroughly clean the gasket mating surfaces and bolt holes of any remaining sealer.
10. Using a new gasket, install the oil scraper.
11. Install the pan and attaching bolts with Loctite®. Tighten the oil pan bolts to 97 inch lbs. (11 Nm).
12. Install the oil pan plug and tighten to 33 ft. lbs. (45 Nm).
13. Install the flywheel cover.
14. Connect the exhaust pipe to the manifold.
15. Lower the vehicle.
16. Fill the crankcase with clean engine oil.
17. Connect the negative battery cable.

2.2L Engine

1. Disconnect the negative battery cable.
2. Raise and support the vehicle safely, then drain the crankcase.
3. Disconnect the exhaust pipe from the manifold, access may be easier from the bottom of the engine.
4. Remove the starter bracket from the block and either support the assembly aside or remove it from the engine.
5. Remove the flywheel cover.
6. Remove the oil pan retaining nuts and/or bolts, then remove the oil pan assembly from the engine.
To install:

NOTE: **Prior to oil pan installation, check the sealing surfaces on the pan, cylinder block and**

front cover are clean and free of oil. If installing the old oil pan, be sure all old RTV has been removed.

7. Apply a ⅛ in. bead of RTV sealant to the oil pan side and front sealing surfaces. Use a new oil pan rear seal and position the pan to the engine. Install the retainers and tighten to tighten to 71 inch lbs. (6 Nm).
8. If removed, install the adaptor and oil filter to the engine and/or secure the right support in position using the retaining bolts.
9. Install the flywheel cover and the starter assembly.
10. If easier from below the vehicle, connect the exhaust pipe at the manifold.
11. Lower the vehicle and fill the engine cooling system.
12. If not done already, connect the pipe to the exhaust manifold.
13. Connect the negative battery cable.

3.1L Engine

1. Disconnect the negative battery cable.
2. Remove the serpentine belt and the tensioner.
3. Support the engine with tool J–28467 or an equivalent engine support fixture.
4. Raise and support the vehicle safely, then drain the engine oil from the crankcase.
5. Remove the starter assembly from the vehicle.
6. For 1992 vehicles, remove the outboard flywheel/starter plastic shield followed by the inboard metal shield.
7. For 1993–96 vehicles, remove the flywheel inspection cover.
8. Remove the engine-to-frame mount retaining nuts.
9. Lower the vehicle.
10. Remove the right tire and wheel assembly, then remove the right inner fender splash shield.
11. Remove the oil pan retaining bolts and nuts, then remove the oil pan.
To install:
12. Clean the gasket mating surfaces.
13. Install a new gasket on the oil pan. Apply silicon sealer to the portion of the pan that contacts the rear of the block.
14. Install the oil pan and secure using the retaining nuts. Tighten the nuts to 89 inch lbs. (10 Nm).
15. Install the oil pan retaining bolts. Tighten the rear bolts to 18 ft.

lbs. (24 Nm) and the remaining bolts to 89 inch lbs. (10 Nm).
16. Install the right inner fender splash shield.
17. Install the engine to frame mounting nuts.
18. Install the flywheel cover(s).
19. Install the starter assembly, then if removed, install the oil filter.
20. Lower the vehicle and remove the engine support fixture.
21. Fill the crankcase with oil, then install the belt tensioner and the serpentine drive belt.
22. Connect the negative battery cable.

Oil Pump

REMOVAL AND INSTALLATION

2.0L Engine

1. Disconnect the negative battery cable.
2. Remove the crankshaft sprocket from the engine.
3. Remove the timing belt rear cover.
4. Unplug the oil pressure switch connector.
5. Remove the oil pan from the vehicle.
6. Remove the oil filter.
7. Remove the crankshaft sprocket key and washer.
8. Unbolt and remove the oil pickup tube.
9. Unbolt and remove the oil pump.
10. Pry out the front crankshaft seal using a small suitable pry tool. Be careful not to score the sealing surfaces.
To install:
11. Install the pump using a new gasket and tighten the attaching bolts to 62 inch lbs. (7 Nm).
12. Install the pickup tube and support with a new O-ring.
13. Install the oil pan.
14. Using seal installer J–33083 or equivalent tool, draw a new front oil seal into position.
15. Install a new oil filter.
16. Install the wiring harness to the oil pressure switch connector.
17. Install the rear timing belt cover.
18. Install the crankshaft sprocket.
19. Connect the negative battery cable and start the engine to check for immediate oil pressure build-up. If oil pressure does not appear, turn the ignition **OFF** right away to avoid excessive engine damage.

2.2L Engine

1. Disconnect the negative battery cable.
2. Remove the oil pan from the engine.
3. Remove the pump-to-rear main bearing cap attaching bolts and carefully lower the pump, extension shaft and retainer.
4. Remove the extension shaft and retainer from the assembly, being careful not to crack the retainer.
   To install:

NOTE: Heat the retainer in hot water prior to assembling the extension shaft.

5. Carefully install extension shaft to the oil pump. Make sure the retainer does not crack during installation.

NOTE: To ensure immediate oil pressure on start-up, the oil pump gear cavity should be packed with petroleum jelly.

6. Install the pump assembly to the rear bearing cap and bolt. Tighten to 32 ft. lbs. (43 Nm).
7. Install the oil pan.
8. Fill the crankcase with clean engine oil.
9. Connect the negative battery cable and start the engine to check for immediate oil pressure build-up. If oil pressure does not appear, turn the ignition **OFF** right away to avoid excessive engine damage.

3.1L Engine

1. Disconnect the negative battery cable.
2. Remove the oil pan from the vehicle.
3. Remove the pump retainer from the rear bearing cap, then carefully lower the pump and extension shaft from the engine.
   To install:
4. Install the oil pump and extension shaft.
5. Engage the drive shaft extension into the drive gear.
6. Secure the pump to the rear bearing cap and tighten the bolt to 30 ft. lbs. (41 Nm).
7. Install the oil pan.
8. Fill the crankcase with clean oil.
9. Connect the negative battery cable and start the engine to check for immediate oil pressure build-up. If oil pressure does not appear, turn the ignition **OFF** right away to avoid excessive engine damage.

CHECKING

1. Drain the oil from the pump and remove the pump cover.
2. Measure the pump gear lash using a feeler gauge. It should be 0.0037–0.0077 in. (0.094–0.195mm).
3. Measure the gear side clearance:
   a. For the 2.0L engine, body clearance to the outer gear should be 0.004–0.007 in. (0.11–0.19mm); inner gear-to-crescent should be 0.007–0.010 in. (0.18–0.26mm) and the outer gear-to-crescent should be 0.004–0.009 in. (0.11–0.24mm).
   b. For the 2.2L engine, drive gear and idler gear side clearance should be 0.0015–0.0040 in. (0.038–0.102mm).
   c. For the 3.2L engine, side clearance should be 0.003–0.004 in. (0.08–0.10mm).
4. Measure the gear end clearance between the gears and the pump cover:
   a. For the 2.0L engine, end clearance should be 0.001–0.004 in. (0.03–0.10mm).
   b. For the 2.2L engine, clearance should be 0.002–0.007 in. (0.05–0.18mm).
   c. For the 3.2L engine, clearance should be 0.002–0.006 in. (0.050–0.152mm).
5. Measure the pump gear pocket depth and diameter:
   a. For the 2.0L engine, the pocket depth should be 0.395–0.397 in. (10.03–10.08mm), while the inner pocket diameter should be 3.231–3.234 in. (82.07–82.15mm) and the outer pocket diameter should be 1.614–1.615 in. (41.000–41.025mm).
   b. For the 2.2L engine, depth should be 1.195–1.198 in. (30.36–30.44mm) and the diameter should be 1.503–1.506 in. (38.18–38.25mm).
   c. For the 3.1L engine, depth should be 1.202–1.205 in. (30.53–30.61mm) and the diameter should be 1.504–1.506 in. (38.202–38.252mm).
6. Lubricate all internal parts with engine oil during reassembly and install the pump gears.

NOTE: To ensure immediate oil pressure on start-up, the oil pump gear cavity should be packed with petroleum jelly.

7. Install the cover and gasket and tighten the pump cover bolts to 89 inch lbs. (10 Nm).

NOTE: Use only original equipment gaskets. The gasket thickness is critical to proper functioning of the pump.

Rear Main Bearing Oil Seal

REMOVAL AND INSTALLATION

2.0L Engine

NOTE: The rear main bearing oil seal is a 1 piece unit and can be replaced without the removal of the oil pan or crankshaft.

1. Disconnect the negative battery cable.
2. Remove the transaxle assembly from the vehicle.
3. If equipped with a manual transaxle, remove the pressure plate and clutch disc.
4. Remove the flywheel/flexplate-to-crankshaft bolts and the flywheel/flexplate. If equipped with a manual transaxle, discard the old bolts.

NOTE: Flywheel bolts cannot be reused.

5. Pry the old seal from the rear of the engine using a small pry tool. Be careful not to damage the crankshaft surface.
   To install:
6. Clean the block and crankshaft-to-seal mating surfaces.
7. Lubricate the outside of the seal to aid installation and press the seal evenly into the retainer using J–36227, or an equivalent seal installation tool.
8. If equipped with automatic transaxle, install the flexplate and attaching bolts. Tighten the bolts to 48 ft. lbs. (65 Nm). Flexplate bolts may be reused.
9. If equipped with manual transaxle, install the flywheel using new bolts. Tighten to 48 ft. lbs. (65 Nm), then tighten the bolts and additional 30 degrees.
10. If equipped with manual transaxle, install the pressure plate and disc.
11. Install the transaxle.
12. Connect the negative battery cable.

2.2L and 3.1L Engines

1. Disconnect the negative battery cable.
2. For the 3.1L engine, install an engine support fixture.

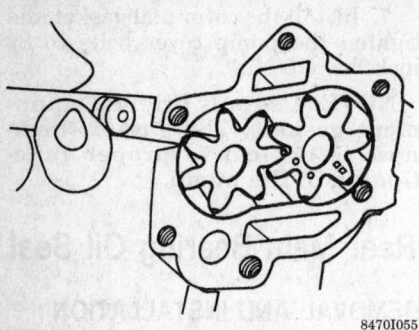

Measuring pump gear side clearance — 2.2L and 3.1L engines — 2.0L similar

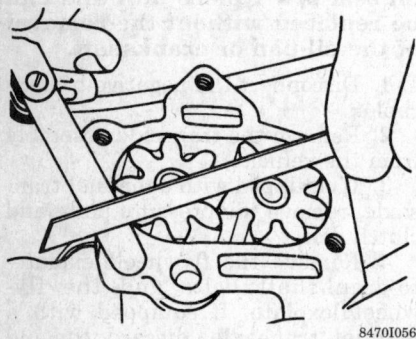

Measuring gear end clearance — 2.2L and 3.1L engines — 2.0L similar

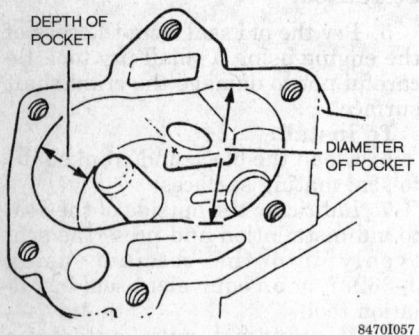

Measuring pump gear pocket dimensions — 2.2L and 3.1L engines — 2.0L similar

3. Remove the transaxle assembly.

4. Remove the right underside splash shield for access.

5. If equipped with a manual transaxle, matchmark the relationship between the pressure plate and flywheel, then remove the pressure plate and clutch disc.

6. Remove the flywheel/flexplate. For the 3.1L engine equipped with an automatic transaxle, remove the retainer along with the flexplate.

7. Carefully insert a small pry tool through the seal dust lip and work the seal free of the engine. Make sure not to damage the sealing surfaces of the crankshaft and block seal retainer.

To install:

8. Clean the cylinder block and crankshaft sealing surface. Inspect the crankshaft for damage.

9. Coat the seal and engine mating surface with clean engine oil.

10. Press the new seal into the retainer until fully seated using J–34686, or an equivalent seal installation tool.

11. Install the flywheel/flexplate using Loctite® 271, or an equivalent threadlock on the bolt threads. Tighten the bolts evenly to specification.

12. If equipped with a manual transaxle, install the clutch and pressure plate assembly, aligning the matchmarks with the flywheel made during removal.

13. Install the transaxle assembly.

14. If applicable, remove the engine support fixture.

15. Connect the negative battery cable.

MANUAL TRANSAXLE

Transaxle Assembly

REMOVAL AND INSTALLATION

2.0L and 2.2L Engines

The 4 cylinder engines may be equipped with either an Isuzu built or Hydra-matic® built manual transaxle.

1. Disconnect the negative battery cable.

2. Install an engine holding bar so one end is supported on the radiator support and the other toward the center of a cross-bar whose ends rest on the strut towers. Use padding and be careful not to damage the paint or body work with the bars. Attach a lifting hook to the engine lift ring and to the bar and raise the engine enough to take the pressure off the motor mounts.

NOTE: If a lifting bar and hook is not available, a chain hoist can be used, however, during the procedure the vehicle must be raised, at which time the chain hoist must be adjusted to keep tension on the engine/transaxle assembly.

3. Remove the left sound insulator, then disconnect the clutch master cylinder pushrod from the clutch pedal.

4. Except for Isuzu transaxles, remove the air cleaner and duct assembly.

5. Disconnect the clutch slave cylinder from the transaxle support bracket and support it aside.

6. For the Isuzu transaxles, disconnect the wiring harness at the mount bracket, then remove the transaxle mount attaching bolts.

7. Except for Isuzu transaxle, remove the transaxle mount through-bolt.

8. Remove the transaxle mount bracket.

9. Disconnect the shift cables and retaining clamp or linkage from the transaxle.

10. For Isuzu transaxles, remove the ground cables from the transaxle mounting studs, then unplug the backup lamp wiring harness from the switch terminal.

11. Except for Isuzu transaxles, remove the transaxle vent tube, then remove the upper transaxle-to-engine bolts.

12. Raise the vehicle and support the vehicle safely.

13. Remove the front tire and wheel assemblies, then remove the left front inner splash shield.

14. Remove the transaxle strut and bracket.

15. Except for Isuzu transaxles, disconnect the 2 exhaust manifold bolts and drain the transaxle.

16. Remove the flywheel cover.

17. Disconnect the speedometer cable or the speed sensor at the transaxle.

18. Remove the left and right drive axle nuts, then remove the left and right ball joint nuts.

19. Disconnect the left and right stabilizer links.

20. Remove the drive axles, then remove the left side U-bolt from the stabilizer bar. If difficulty is encountered removing the intermediate shaft, support it and guide it free of the transaxle, as the assembly is lowered from the engine.

21. Remove the left suspension support attaching bolts.

22. Position a jack under the transaxle case, remove the remaining transaxle-to-engine mounting bolts, then remove the transaxle by sliding it away from the engine. Carefully lower the jack and, if still installed, guide the intermediate shaft out the transaxle.

To install:

23. Raise the transaxle into position using the jack assembly. If it was necessary to partially lower the transaxle before removing the intermediate shaft, guide the shaft into its bore as the transaxle is being raised.

24. Install the accessible transaxle attaching bolts and tighten to 55 ft. lbs. (75 Nm).

25. Install the flywheel housing cover and tighten the retainers to 89 inch lbs. (10 Nm).

26. Install the left suspension support bolts, then install the left U-bolt to the stabilizer bar.

27. Install the left and right drive axles, then install and tighten the drive axle nuts.

28. Install the left and right ball joint nuts, followed by the stabilizer link nuts. Tighten the link nuts to 10 ft. lbs. (17 Nm).

29. Connect the speedometer cable or the speed sensor connector to the transaxle.

30. Except for Isuzu transaxles, install the 2 exhaust manifold bolts.

31. Install the transaxle strut bracket followed by the strut and tighten the retainers to 38 ft. lbs. (58 Nm).

32. Install the inner splash shield, then install the front wheel assemblies.

33. Lower the vehicle. For the Isuzu transaxles, connect the ground cables to the transaxle mounting studs, then install the wiring to the backup lamp switch.

34. Install and tighten any remaining upper transaxle-to-engine mounting bolts which were not installed earlier.

35. Except for the Isuzu transaxles, install the vent tube and the shift cables.

36. Install the clutch slave cylinder to the transaxle support bracket and tighten the retainers evenly to prevent cylinder damage. Then inside the vehicle, connect the cylinder pushrod to the clutch pedal and install the left sound insulator.

37. Install the transaxle mount bracket attaching bolts and tighten to 55 ft. lbs. (75 Nm), then install the mount using the nuts and bolts. When installing the bolts, check the alignment bolt at the engine mount. If excessive effort is required to remove the alignment bolt, realign the powertrain components, then tighten the nuts to 23 ft. lbs. (31 Nm) and the bolts to 38 ft. lbs. (52 Nm), then remove the alignment bolt.

38. For the Isuzu transaxles, connect the wiring harness to the transaxle bracket.

39. Remove the engine support fixture, then, if not done already connect the shift cables and linkage.

40. Fill the transaxle assembly using a proper synchromesh transaxle fluid, then connect the negative battery cable.

3.1L Engine

1. Disconnect the negative battery cable.

2. Install an engine holding bar so one end is supported on the radiator support and the other toward the center of a cross-bar whose ends rest on the strut towers. Use padding and be careful not to damage the paint or body work with the bars. Attach a lifting hook to the engine lift ring and to the bar and raise the engine enough to take the pressure off the motor mounts.

— CAUTION —

If a lifting bar and hook is not available, a chain hoist can be used, however, during the procedure the vehicle must be raised, at which time the chain hoist must be adjusted to keep tension on the engine/transaxle assembly.

3. For 1992 vehicles, remove the left sound insulator, then disconnect the clutch master cylinder pushrod from the clutch pedal.

4. Remove the air cleaner and bracket/duct assembly; then, remove the battery from the vehicle.

5. Disconnect the clutch slave cylinder from the transaxle bracket and support aside (1992 vehicles) or disconnect the clutch master cylinder hydraulic line from the slave cylinder and plug the opening to prevent excessive fluid loss or contamination (1993–96 vehicles).

6. Disconnect the shift cables from the transaxle.

7. Remove the 4 top transaxle-to-engine bolts.

8. Remove the transaxle mount and bracket.

9. Properly discharge the A/C system using a refrigerant recovery station.

10. Raise the vehicle and support the vehicle safely.

11. Remove the front tire and wheel assemblies, then remove the left front inner splash shield.

12. Remove both drive axle nuts, then remove the left and right ball joint nuts.

13. Disconnect the left and right stabilizer links .

14. Remove the drive axles, then remove the intermediate shaft and housing. If difficulty is encountered removing the intermediate shaft, support it and guide it free of the transaxle, as the assembly is lowered from the engine.

15. Remove the evaporator-to-accumulator lines.

16. Unplug the wire connectors from the vehicle speed sensor and the backup lamp switch.

17. Drain the transaxle assembly, then remove the strut bracket-to-transaxle bolts.

18. Remove the flywheel inspection cover, then remove the shift linkage bracket.

19. Unplug the necessary vacuum connections, then remove the ground wires from the lower bellhousing bolts.

20. Remove the U-bolt from the left side of the stabilizer bar.

21. Remove the left side suspension attaching bolts.

22. Position a jack under the transaxle case, remove the remaining transaxle-to-engine mounting bolts, then remove the transaxle by sliding it away from the engine. Carefully lower the jack and, if still installed, guide the intermediate shaft out the transaxle.

To install:

23. Raise the transaxle into position using the jack assembly. If it was necessary to partially lower the transaxle before removing the intermediate shaft, guide the shaft into its bore as the transaxle is being raised.

24. Install the accessible lower transaxle attaching bolts and tighten to 55 ft. lbs. (75 Nm).

25. Install the flywheel housing cover and tighten the retainers to 89 inch lbs. (10 Nm).

26. Install the left suspension support bolts, then install strut bracket and bolts to the transaxle. Tighten the strut bracket bolts to 40 ft. lbs. (54 Nm). Install the left U-bolt to the stabilizer bar.

27. Install the evaporator-to-accumulator lines.

28. Install the vacuum connections, then connect the ground wires to the transaxle studs.

29. If not done already, install the intermediate shaft and housing.

30. Install the left and right drive axles, then install and tighten the drive axle nuts.

31. Install the left and right ball joint nuts, followed by the stabilizer

link nuts. Tighten the link nuts to 10 ft. lbs. (17 Nm).

32. Install the inner splash shield and the front tire and wheel assemblies

33. Lower the vehicle.

34. Install the upper transaxle mount and bracket. Tighten the nuts to 23 ft. lbs. (31 Nm) and the bolts to 38 ft. lbs. (52 Nm).

35. Remove the engine support.

36. Install the upper transaxle bolts and tighten to 55 ft. lbs. (75 Nm).

37. If removed, install the clutch slave cylinder to the transaxle support bracket and tighten the retainers evenly to prevent cylinder damage. Uncap and connect the clutch master cylinder line the hydraulic slave cylinder. Then inside the vehicle, if disconnected, install the cylinder pushrod to the clutch pedal and install the left sound insulator.

38. Install the exhaust crossover pipe.

39. Install the wiring harness connectors to the backup lamp switch and the vehicle speed sensor.

40. Install the shift cables to the transaxle.

41. Install the battery to the vehicle.

42. Remove the engine support, then install the air cleaner and duct assembly.

43. Fill the transaxle assembly using a proper synchromesh transaxle fluid.

44. Connect the negative battery cable. Properly evacuate and charge the A/C system.

CLUTCH

Clutch Assembly

——— CAUTION ———
The clutch plate contains asbestos, which has been determined to be a cancer causing agent. Never clean the clutch surfaces with compressed air. Avoid inhaling any dust from any clutch surface.

REMOVAL AND INSTALLATION

1. Disconnect the negative battery cable.

——— WARNING ———
Whenever the clutch slave cylinder is removed from the transaxle, the pushrod must first be disconnected from the clutch pedal. This is necessary to prevent the cylinder from becoming permanently damaged should the pedal be depressed with the cylinder removed from the transaxle.

2. Except for the 1993–96 3.1L engine, remove the left sound insulator and disconnect the actuator pushrod from the clutch pedal.

3. Remove the transaxle assembly from the vehicle.

4. Loosen the pressure plate attaching bolts 1 turn at a time until spring tension is relieved.

5. Support the pressure plate and remove the bolts, then remove the pressure plate and the clutch disc.

To install:

6. Inspect the flywheel, pressure plate, clutch disc, release bearing and the clutch fork for wear. Do not attempt to disassembly the pressure plate assembly.

7. Clean the flywheel mating surfaces. Position the clutch disc and pressure plate into the installed position and support with a dummy shaft or clutch aligning tool.

NOTE: The flywheel and pressure plate must be installed correctly. The HEAVY SIDE of the flywheel is marked with an X, this must face the pressure plate's LIGHT SIDE which is marked with paint. The clutch disc is installed with damper springs offset towards the transaxle and with the side marked FLYWHEEL SIDE toward the engine.

8. Install the pressure plate-to-flywheel bolts. Bolts should be tightened in a criss-cross pattern starting at the upper right of the cover assembly. Seat bolts 1, 2, and 3 first, then seat bolts 4, 5 and 6. Tighten all bolts using the same pattern to 12 ft. lbs. (16 Nm), then tighten the bolts in the same pattern to 18 ft. lbs. (24 Nm), except for bolts on 2.0L engines which should be tightened to 22 ft. lbs. (30 Nm). Finally, tighten bolts using the same pattern an additional 30 degrees.

9. Lubricate the outside grooves and the inside recess of the release bearing with high temperature

grease. Wipe off any excess. Install the release bearing.

10. Install the transaxle.

11. If removed, connect the clutch master cylinder pushrod to the clutch pedal, then install the left sound insulator.

12. Connect the negative battery cable.

PEDAL HEIGHT/FREE-PLAY ADJUSTMENT

These vehicles use an hydraulic clutch system which provides automatic clutch adjustment. No adjustment of the clutch linkage or pedal height is required.

Clutch Master/Slave Cylinder Assembly

REMOVAL AND INSTALLATION

2.0L and 2.2L Engines

The clutch hydraulic system is serviced as a complete unit. Individual components of the system are not available separately.

1. Disconnect the negative battery cable.

——— WARNING ———
Whenever the clutch slave cylinder is removed from the transaxle, the pushrod must first be disconnected from the clutch pedal. This is necessary to prevent the cylinder from becoming permanently damaged should the pedal be depressed with the cylinder removed from the transaxle.

2. Remove the left sound insulator and disconnect the actuator pushrod from the clutch pedal.

3. Remove the clutch master cylinder-to-cowl brace nuts. If equipped, disconnect the remote reservoir from the clutch master cylinder.

4. Remove the slave cylinder retaining nuts and separate the slave cylinder from the transaxle. Remove the clutch master cylinder from the cowl brace, then remove the hydraulic system from the vehicle as a unit.

To install:

5. Install the clutch slave/master cylinder assembly into the vehicle as a unit. Install the slave cylinder to the transaxle and secure using the

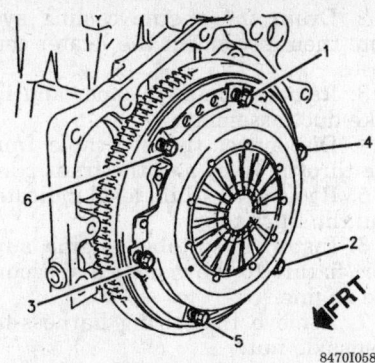

84701058

Pressure plate bolt torque sequence

attaching nuts. Tighten the nuts evenly to 16 ft. lbs. (22 Nm).

NOTE: Do not remove the plastic pushrod retainer from a new slave cylinder. The strap will break on the first clutch pedal application.

6. Install the clutch master cylinder to the cowl and tighten the retaining nuts evenly to 15 ft. lbs. (21 Nm).

7. If equipped, connect the remote reservoir to the clutch master cylinder.

8. Connect the master cylinder pushrod to the clutch pedal. If installing a new assembly, remove the clutch pushrod restrictor from the assembly before connecting it to the clutch pedal.

9. Install the left side sound insulator panel.

10. Connect the negative battery cable.

11. Check, and if necessary, bleed the hydraulic system.

3.1L Engine

The 1992 vehicles equipped with the 3.1L engine utilize a 1-piece slave cylinder/clutch master cylinder assembly. On these vehicles, the assembly must be replaced as a unit and the slave cylinder is attached to the transaxle using retainers.

The 1993–96 vehicles equipped with the 3.1L engine utilize a 2-piece clutch release hydraulic system. The clutch master cylinder is easily replaceable after some engine compartment components are removed for access purposes. The slave cylinder however, is mounted on the input shaft from within the bellhousing. To replace the slave cylinder, the transaxle must be separated from the engine and removed from the vehicle.

1. Disconnect the negative battery cable, followed by the positive cable.

2. Remove the air intake duct from the air cleaner assembly, then remove left fender brace and the battery from the vehicle.

3. Unplug the IAT sensor at the air cleaner, then disconnect the mass air flow sensor lead.

4. Remove the PCV pipe retaining clamp from the air intake duct, then remove the air intake duct-to-throttle body clamp.

5. Remove the mass air flow sensor retaining bolt, then remove the air cleaner bracket bolts at the battery tray.

6. Remove the air cleaner, mass air flow sensor and the air intake duct as an assembly.

7. Unplug the wiring harness from the washer bottle, then remove the bolts and the bottle from the vehicle.

8. If equipped, remove the cruise control mounting bracket nuts from the strut tower.

————— **WARNING** —————

Whenever the clutch slave cylinder is removed from the transaxle, the pushrod must first be disconnected from the clutch pedal. This is necessary to prevent the cylinder from becoming permanently damaged should the pedal be depressed with the cylinder removed from the transaxle.

9. Remove the left sound insulator and disconnect the actuator pushrod from the clutch pedal.

10. Remove the clutch master cylinder-to-cowl brace nuts.

11. For 1992 vehicles:

a. If equipped, remove the remote reservoir from the clutch master cylinder.

b. Remove the slave cylinder retainers at the transaxle assembly, then carefully withdraw the cylinder.

c. Remove the slave cylinder/clutch master cylinder assembly from the vehicle as a unit.

12. For 1993–96 vehicles:

a. Remove the clutch master cylinder line from the slave cylinder at the quick disconnect fitting. Move the fitting release slide inward and separate the lines. Remove the clutch master cylinder assembly from the vehicle.

b. If slave cylinder removal is necessary, remove the transaxle from the vehicle.

c. Remove the slave cylinder from the input shaft and bellhousing.

To install:

13. For 1993–96 vehicles:

a. Install the slave cylinder to the input shaft and bellhousing.

b. Install the transaxle to the vehicle.

c. Position the clutch master cylinder to the vehicle and install the hydraulic line to the slave cylinder at the quick connect fitting.

d. Install the clutch master cylinder retaining nuts and tighten evenly to 15 ft. lbs. (21 Nm).

14. For 1992 vehicles:

a. Position the slave cylinder/clutch master cylinder assembly to the vehicle as a unit.

NOTE: Do not remove the plastic pushrod retainer from a new slave cylinder. The strap will break on the first clutch pedal application.

b. Install the slave cylinder to the transaxle assembly, then install the retainers and tighten evenly to 16 ft. lbs. (22 Nm).

c. Install the clutch master cylinder assembly to the dash and tighten the retainers evenly to 15 ft. lbs. (21 Nm).

d. If equipped, install the remote reservoir to the clutch master cylinder.

15. Connect the master cylinder pushrod to the clutch pedal. If installing a new assembly, remove the clutch pushrod restrictor from the assembly before connecting it to the clutch pedal.

16. Check and, if necessary, adjust the cruise control switch at the clutch pedal.

17. Install the left side sound insulator panel.

18. Check, and if necessary, bleed the hydraulic system. 1993–96 vehicles must have the system bled, as the master cylinder-to-slave cylinder line was disconnected.

19. Install the washer bottle and the electrical connector.

20. Install the air cleaner, mass air flow sensor and the air intake duct assembly.

21. Install the air cleaner bracket mounting bolts, then install the mass air flow sensor mounting bolt.

22. Secure the air intake duct to the throttle body, then secure the PCV pipe to the duct using the clamps.

23. Install the wiring harness connectors to the mass air flow and the intake air temperature sensors.

24. Install the battery and the left fender brace.

25. Connect the positive battery cable, followed by the negative battery cable.

26. Connect the air intake duct to the air cleaner assembly.

Hydraulic Clutch System Bleeding

There are 2 possible methods of bleeding the hydraulic clutch system depending on whether or not the system contains a bleed screw. To determine which method to use, locate the slave cylinder located on the transaxle and look for a bleed screw next to the hydraulic inlet connection. If no bleed screw is present, the slave cylinder must be removed from the transaxle, follow the appropriate procedure.

WITHOUT BLEED SCREW

——————— WARNING ———————
Whenever the clutch slave cylinder is removed from the transaxle, the pushrod must first be disconnected from the clutch pedal. This is necessary to prevent the cylinder from becoming permanently damaged should the pedal be depressed with the cylinder removed from the transaxle.

1. Remove the left sound insulator and disconnect the actuator pushrod from the clutch pedal.
2. Remove the slave cylinder from the transaxle.
3. Loosen the clutch master cylinder mounting nuts out to the end of the studs, but do not remove them or the master cylinder.
4. Remove the clutch fluid reservoir cap and diaphragm. Be sure the clean the cap and surrounding area before removal in order to prevent fluid contamination.
5. Measure the slave cylinder pushrod, then depress the pushrod 0.787 in. (20mm) into the bore. Hold the pushrod in the depressed position and reinstall the reservoir cap with diaphragm.
6. Hold the slave cylinder vertically with the pushrod end facing down and at a level lower than the master cylinder and reservoir, then release the pushrod.
7. Depress the pushrod into the bore with short 0.39 in. (10mm) strokes while peering through the reservoir sides for bubbles. Continue to cycle the pushrod until air bubbles fail to appear in the reservoir
8. Install the slave cylinder to the transaxle.

9. Secure the master cylinder to the cowl bracket by evenly tightening the nuts to 15 ft. lbs. (21 Nm).
10. Inspect the clutch fluid reservoir and top-off, if necessary, using DOT 3 fluid.
11. Connect the clutch master cylinder pushrod to the clutch pedal, then install the left sound insulator.
12. Start the engine and push the clutch to the floor, then wait about 10 seconds and select the reverse gear. There should be no gear clashing. If the gears grate, the hydraulic system may still contain air and should be bled again.

WITH BLEED SCREW

1. Clean dirt and grease from the cap reservoir to ensure no foreign substances enter the system.
2. Remove the cap and diaphragm, then fill reservoir to the top with approved brake fluid only.

NOTE: Brake fluid must be certified to DOT 3 specification.

3. Fully loosen the bleed screw located on the slave cylinder body, next to the hydraulic inlet connection.
4. Fluid will now begin to move from the master cylinder, down the tube, to the slave cylinder. The reservoir must be kept full at all times in order to accomplish an efficient gravity fill.
5. When the slave cylinder is full, a steady stream of fluid will come from the slave outlet. At this point the system should be free of air bubbles; tighten the bleed screw to 18 inch lbs. (2 Nm).
6. Install the reservoir cap and diaphragm.
7. Start the engine and push the clutch to the floor, then wait about 10 seconds and select the reverse gear. There should be no gear clashing. If the gears grate, the hydraulic system may still contain air and should be bled again.

AUTOMATIC TRANSAXLE

Transaxle Assembly

REMOVAL AND INSTALLATION

1. Disconnect the negative terminal from the battery.

2. Drain the engine cooling system, then disconnect the heater core hoses.
3. Remove the air cleaner and intake duct assembly.
4. Disconnect the TV cable from the throttle lever and the transaxle.
5. Remove the fluid level indicator and the filler tube.
6. Install a suitable engine support fixture to the vehicle and secure the engine.
7. Remove the wiring harness-to-transaxle nut.
8. Label and unplug the wires for the speed sensor, TCC connector and the neutral safety/backup lamp switch.

NOTE: Be careful when unplugging/installing T-latch style connectors. Care must be taken for the proper reassembly of both the connector and T-latch in order to prevent intermittent loss of switch function.

9. Disconnect the shift linkage from the transaxle assembly.
10. Remove the 2 upper transaxle-to-engine bolts, then remove the left upper transaxle mount and bracket assembly.
11. Remove the rubber hose from the transaxle-to-vent pipe, then remove the remaining upper transaxle-to-engine bolts.
12. Raise and support the vehicle safely.
13. Remove the front wheel assemblies, then drain the transaxle fluid.
14. Remove both ball joints from the control arms.
15. Using modified J–34754, or equivalent halfshaft seal protector tools, install one on each halfshaft to protect the seal from damage and the joint from possible failure.
16. Using care not to damage the halfshaft boots, disconnect the halfshafts from the transaxle.
17. Remove the engine-to-transaxle brace.
18. Remove the transaxle mounting strut.
19. Remove the left stabilizer shaft link pin bolt, then remove the left shaft frame bushing clamp nuts. Remove the left suspension support assembly.
20. For the 2.2L and 3.1L engines, disconnect the exhaust pipe or front exhaust pipe, as applicable, from the manifold.
21. If applicable, disconnect the speedometer cable from the transaxle.
22. Remove the start assembly, then remove the transaxle converter cover.

23. Matchmark the converter to the flywheel for assembly purposes, then remove the torque converter bolts.

24. Disconnect the transaxle cooler pipes, then plug the lines to prevent system contamination or excessive fluid loss.

25. Remove the transaxle-to-engine support bracket.

26. Position and secure a transaxle jack to the transaxle, then remove the remaining transaxle-to-engine bolts.

27. Carefully separate the transaxle from the engine, then remove the transaxle from the vehicle, making sure the torque converter does not fall.

NOTE: The transaxle cooler and lines should be flushed any time the transaxle is removed for overhaul or to replace the pump, case or converter.

To install:

28. Put a small amount of grease on the pilot hub of the converter and make sure the converter is properly engaged with the pump.

29. Raise the transaxle to the engine and install the lower transaxle mounting bolts. Tighten the bolts to 55 ft. lbs. (75 Nm) and remove the jack.

30. Install the transaxle-to-engine support bracket. In order to prevent shake at idle and harsh engagement, be sure to center the bolt in the left rear transaxle mount slot-to-body.

31. Unplug and install the transaxle fluid cooler lines.

32. Align the converter with the marks made previously on the flywheel, then secure using the retaining bolts. Hand start and tighten the net slot bolt to 46 ft. lbs. (62 Nm) first, then hand start and tighten the 2 remaining bolts to the same specification. Install the converter cover.

33. Install the starter assembly to the engine.

34. If applicable, connect the speedometer cable.

35. If removed, connect the exhaust pipe to the manifold.

36. Install the left suspension support assembly, followed by the stabilizer shaft frame bushing nuts and the link pin bolt.

37. Install the transaxle mounting strut, then if applicable, install the engine-to-transaxle brace.

38. Install the drive axles and remove the boot protectors.

39. Install the ball joints to the control arms.

40. Install the wheel assemblies, then lower the vehicle.

41. Install and torque the upper transaxle-to-engine bolts.

42. Install the left side transaxle mount, then connect the shift linkage to the transaxle.

43. Install the wiring harness connectors to the speed sensor, TCC connector terminal and the neutral safety/backup lamp switch.

44. Position the wiring harness to the transaxle and secure using the nut.

45. Remove the engine support fixture, then install the fluid level indicator and fill tube.

46. Connect the TV cable to the transaxle and to the throttle lever, then install the rubber hose to the vent pipe.

47. Install the air cleaner assembly and intake duct.

48. Connect the heater core hoses, then fill the cooling system.

49. Fill the transaxle using automatic transaxle fluid, then connect the negative battery cable.

50. Start and run the engine to check for leaks, then check for proper fluid levels.

51. Check and adjust the shift and TV cables.

SHIFT CONTROL CABLE ADJUSTMENT

1. Place the shift lever in the **N**.

NOTE: Neutral can be found by rotating the transaxle selector shaft counterclockwise from P through R to N.

2. Loosely attach the cable to the transaxle shift lever using the nut. Assemble the cable to the cable bracket and to shift lever.

NOTE: The lever must be held out of P when torquing the nut.

3. Tighten the cable-to-transaxle shift lever nut to 15 ft. lbs. (20 Nm).

THROTTLE VALVE (TV) CABLE ADJUSTMENT

Setting of the TV cable must be done by rotating the throttle lever at the carburetor or throttle body. Do not use the accelerator pedal to rotate the throttle lever.

1. With the engine OFF, depress and hold the reset tab at the engine end of the TV cable.

2. Move the slider back through the fitting in the direction away from the cable actuating lever until it stops against the fitting.

3. Release the reset tab.

4. Rotate the throttle lever to its full travel.

5. The slider must move (ratchet) toward the lever when the lever is rotated to its full travel position.

6. Recheck after the engine is hot and road test the vehicle.

DRIVE AXLE

Halfshaft

REMOVAL AND INSTALLATION

NOTE: Care must be exercised not to allow CV or tri-pot joints to become overextended. Over extending the joint could result in separation of internal components.

1. Disconnect the negative battery cable, then raise and support the vehicle safely. Do not support under lower control arms.

2. Remove the front tire and wheel assemblies.

NOTE: Install J–34754, or a equivalent halfshaft seal boot protectors, on the outer drive seal. If a seal protecting tool is not available, the manufacturer recommends that shop towels be positioned to protect the seal.

3. Insert a drift or small prybar into the caliper and rotor to prevent the rotor from turning, then remove the halfshaft nut and washer.

4. Remove the cotter pin and nut from the lower ball joint, then use a ball joint separator tool to loosen the joint. Turn the steering wheel fully in the direction opposite the shaft which is being removed. For example, if removing the left shaft, turn the steering wheel full lock to the right.

5. Separate the ball joint using a prybar between the suspension support and the lower control arm.

6. Separate the hub and bearing assembly from the halfshaft using J–28773, or an equivalent hub spindle removal tool. Tighten the forcing screw until the axle splines are just loose, then separate the halfshaft and move the strut and knuckle assembly rearward.

7. Using a halfshaft remover such as J–28468 or equivalent and a slide hammer assembly, remove the halfshaft from the transaxle.

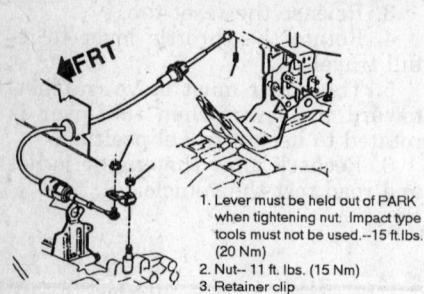

1. Lever must be held out of PARK when tightening nut. Impact type tools must not be used.--15 ft.lbs. (20 Nm)
2. Nut-- 11 ft. lbs. (15 Nm)
3. Retainer clip
4. Floorshift assembly

8470I059

Shift cable adjustment

To install:

8. To install the halfshaft, start the splines of the halfshaft into the transaxle or intermediate shaft, then position a non-ferrous drift into the groove on the joint housing and tap until seated. Be careful not to damage the axle seal or dislodge the seal garter spring.

9. Verify that the halfshaft is seated into the transaxle by grasping on the housing and pulling outboard.

10. Install the halfshaft to hub and bearing assembly.

11. Install the lower ball joint to the steering knuckle. Tighten the ball joint-to-steering knuckle nut to 41 ft. lbs. (56 Nm) for 1992 vehicles or to 48 ft. lbs. (65 Nm) for 1993–96 vehicles, then install a cotter pin. Do not loosen from the torque value to install a cotter. If necessary, tighten the nut additionally, but do not exceed a maximum torque of 50 ft. lbs. (65 Nm) for 1992 vehicles or to 63 ft. lbs. (85 Nm) for 1993–96 vehicles.

12. Install the washer and new driveshaft nut. Have an assistant insert a prybar to prevent the rotor from turning, then tighten the new axle shaft nut to 192 ft. lbs. (260 Nm).

13. Install the front tire and wheel assemblies.

14. Lower the vehicle and connect the negative battery cable.

CV-Boot

REMOVAL AND INSTALLATION

Outer

1. Remove the halfshaft assembly.
2. Use a side cutter to remove the large seal retaining clamp from the joint, then discard the clamp pieces.
3. Remove the small seal retaining clamp from the shaft, also using the side cutter, then discard the clamp.
4. Separate the joint seal from the race at the large diameter, then slide the seal way from the joint and along the shaft.
5. Wipe the grease from the face of the inner race, then spread the ears of the race retaining ring using a pair of snapring pliers. Remove the joint assembly from the halfshaft.
6. Remove the seal from the shaft.
7. If necessary, disassemble the CV-joint for inspection/repair purposes. If not disassembled, thoroughly clean the components of all old grease.

To install:

8. If disassembled, prepare the CV-joint assembly for installation.
9. Clean the splines of the shaft and the CV-joint with solvent, then repack the joint. Install a new retaining ring inside the joint.

NOTE: When repacking CV-joint, make sure to add grease to axle boot.

10. Position the small seal clamp onto the seal, then slide them onto the shaft and position the neck of the seal in the shaft groove. Using a torque wrench and J-35910, or an equivalent seal clamp tool, crimp the retaining clamp to 100 ft. lbs. (136 Nm).

11. Push the CV-joint onto the axle shaft until the retaining ring is seated in the axle shaft groove.

12. Slide the large diameter of the seal along with the large seal retaining clamp in place over the outside of the CV-joint race, then locate the seal lip in the groove on the race.

NOTE: The seal must not be dimpled, stretched or in any way out of shape. If the seal in not correctly shaped, equalize pressure in the seal and shape by hand.

13. Using the seal clamp tool and a torque wrench, crimp the large clamp to 130 ft. lbs. (176 Nm).

14. Install the halfshaft assembly.

Inner

There are 2 types of inner joints used on the vehicles. Either a cross groove joint or a tripot/free-motion joint. The tripot joint may be disassembled for service, while the cross groove joint must be replaced as an assembly. The easiest way to tell the difference between the assemblies is with the seal removed. The tripot joints utilize a spider assembly, while the cross groove joint uses a chrome allow ball bearing/cage assembly.

CROSS GROOVE JOINT

1. Remove the halfshaft assembly.
2. Use a side cutter to remove the large seal retaining clamp from the C/G-joint, then discard the clamp pieces.
3. Remove the small seal retaining clamp from the shaft, also using the side cutter, then discard the clamp.
4. Separate the joint seal from the race at the large diameter, then slide the seal way from the joint and along the shaft.
5. Wipe the grease from the face of the inner race, then spread the ears of the race retaining ring using a pair of snapring pliers. Remove the joint assembly from the halfshaft.
6. Remove the seal from the shaft.
7. Thoroughly clean the components of all old grease. Because of the precision grinding and selected dimensional component fits, disassembly of the C/G-joint is not recommended.

To install:

8. Clean the splines of the shaft and the C/G-joint with solvent, then repack the joint.

NOTE: When repacking C/G-joint, make sure to add grease to axle boot.

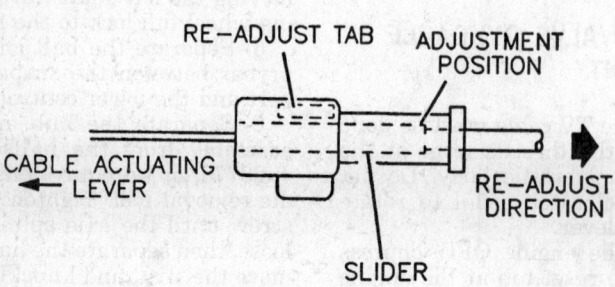

RE–ADJUST TAB   ADJUSTMENT POSITION

CABLE ACTUATING LEVER   RE–ADJUST DIRECTION

SLIDER

8470I060

TV cable adjustment

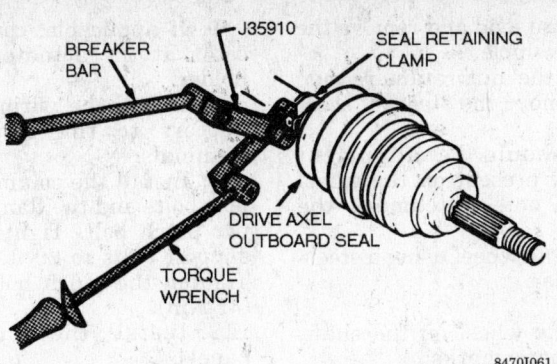

Crimping the CV-joint seal to specification

9. Position the small seal clamp onto the seal, then slide them onto the shaft and position the neck of the seal in the shaft groove. Using a torque wrench and J–35910, or an equivalent seal clamp tool, crimp the retaining clamp to 100 ft. lbs. (136 Nm).

10. Position the new large seal retaining clamp onto the seal, but do not crimp at this time.

11. Push the C/G-joint onto the axle shaft until the retaining ring is seated in the axle shaft groove.

12. Slide the large diameter of the seal along with the large seal retaining clamp in place over the outside of the C/G-joint, then locate the seal lip in the groove on the ball retainer.

NOTE: The seal must not be dimpled, stretched or in any way out of shape. If the seal in not correctly shaped, equalize pressure in the seal and shape by hand. A small blunt tool may be inserted under the large seal opening to help shape the seal, but be very careful not to puncture and ruin the seal.

13. Pull the joint outward slightly to achieve the proper dimension of 5¼ in. (133mm) between the seal clamps. Using the seal clamp tool and a torque wrench, crimp the large clamp to 130 ft. lbs. (176 Nm). The seal, race and large clamp must remain in alignment while crimping.

14. Install the halfshaft assembly.

TRIPOT/FREE-MOTION JOINT

1. Remove the halfshaft assembly.

2. Use a side cutter to remove the large seal retaining clamp from the joint, then discard the clamp pieces.

NOTE: When cutting the seal clamps, use care not to cut through the seal and damage the sealing surface of the tri-pot outer housing or trilobal bushing.

3. Remove the small seal retaining clamp from the shaft, also using the side cutter, then discard the clamp.

4. Separate the joint seal from the trilobal bushing at the large diameter, then slide the seal way from the joint and along the shaft.

5. Remove the housing from the spider and the shaft, then spread the ears of the spacer retaining ring (inboard of the tripot spider) using a pair of snapring pliers. Slide the spacer ring and spider back on the axle shaft for access to the shaft retaining ring.

6. Remove the shaft retaining ring from the axle shaft groove, then slide the spider assembly from the shaft. Handle the spider carefully as the tripot balls and needle rollers may separate from the spider trunnions.

7. Remove the trilobal bushing from the housing, then remove the spacer ring and the seal from the shaft.

8. If necessary, disassemble the tripot spider for inspection/repair purposes. If not disassembled, thoroughly clean the components of all old grease.

To install:

9. If disassembled, prepare the tripot spider assembly for installation.

10. Position the small seal clamp onto the seal, then slide them onto the shaft and position the neck of the seal in the shaft groove. Using a torque wrench and J–35910, or an equivalent seal clamp tool, crimp the retaining clamp to 100 ft. lbs. (136 Nm).

11. Install the spacer ring onto the shaft, past the 2nd shaft groove, then slide the spider assembly past its installation point and against the spacer ring. The counterbored face of the spider must face the end of the shaft.

12. Install the shaft retaining ring in the outer axle shaft groove, then slide the spider towards the end of the shaft and seat the spacer ring in the groove.

13. Place grease in both the seal and the housing. If a service kit is being used, divide the provided grease equally between the seal and housing.

14. Install the trilobal bushing to the housing, then position the new large clamp on the seal.

15. Slide the large diameter of the seal along with the large seal retaining clamp in place over the outside of the trilobal bushing, then locate the seal lip in the groove.

NOTE: The seal must not be dimpled, stretched or in any way out of shape. If the seal in not correctly shaped, equalize pressure in the seal and shape by hand. A small blunt tool may be inserted under the large seal opening to help shape the seal, but be very careful not to puncture and ruin the seal.

16. Pull the joint outward slightly to achieve the proper dimension of 7½ in. (190.5mm) from the small seal clamp to the top of the housing. Using a seal clamp tool, crimp the large clamp in position. The seal, housing and large clamp must remain in alignment while crimping.

17. Install the halfshaft assembly.

Front Wheel Hub and Bearings

REMOVAL AND INSTALLATION

1. If equipped with ABS, disconnect the negative battery cable.

2. Raise and support the vehicle safely, then remove the front wheel.

3. Install a boot cover protector to prevent CV-joint seal damage, then remove the drive axle. On some vehicles, it may be possible to disconnect the drive axle from the steering knuckle only (not from the transaxle) and support it out of the way, at a slight downward angle.

4. Remove the brake caliper bolts, then remove the caliper and support from the suspension using a length of wire.

NOTE: Do not allow the brake caliper to hang by the brake hose unsupported.

5. Remove the rotor.

6. Remove the 3 hub and bearing attaching bolts.

7. Separate the hub and bearing assembly, along with the slash shield

(if equipped) from the steering knuckle.

8. Remove the inner knuckle seal using brass drift pin or equivalent.

To install:

9. Install the hub and bearing assembly to the steering knuckle. If applicable, position the splash shield. Install the bolts and tighten to 70 ft. lbs. (95 Nm).

10. Lubricate the inside diameter of the seal lips and completely fill the cavity between the assembly and seal with chassis grease then, install the new hub and bearing seal into the steering knuckle using J–22388 or an equivalent seal installer.

11. Install the brake rotor, then remove the caliper support and install the caliper to the steering knuckle.

12. Install the drive axle to the vehicle and/or the hub and bearing assembly. Remove the boot protectors once installed.

13. Install the front wheel and lower the vehicle.

14. If applicable, connect the negative battery cable.

STEERING

Steering Wheel

REMOVAL AND INSTALLATION

1. Disconnect the negative battery cable.

2. Check the pad for retaining screws, some models will contain 2 pad screws, and if present remove them to allow for horn/steering pad removal.

3. Carefully pry the pad upward and remove from the steering wheel.

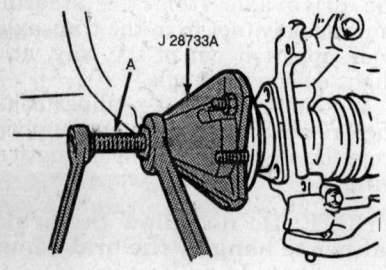

J 28733A

A. Turn forcing screw until axle splines are just loose

84701062

Separate the drive axle from the hub and bearing assembly using a press separator tool

Unplug the horn lead and remove the pad from the vehicle.

4. Remove the nut retainer, then loosen and remove the steering shaft nut.

5. There should be alignment marks already present on the wheel and shaft. If not, matchmark the parts.

6. Remove the wheel using a steering wheel puller.

To install:

7. Install the wheel on the shaft, aligning the matchmarks.

8. Install the shaft nut and tighten to 30 ft. lbs. (41 Nm), except for 1993–96 vehicles which should be tightened to 37 ft. lbs. (50 Nm).

9. Install the retainer.

10. Install the horn lead connector, then install the pad. If applicable, install the pad retaining screws.

11. Connect the negative battery cable.

Steering Column

REMOVAL AND INSTALLATION

———— **WARNING** ————

Once removed from the vehicle, the steering column is extremely susceptible to damage. Dropping the column assembly on its end could collapse the steering shaft or loosen the plastic injections which maintain column rigidity. If it is necessary to remove the steering wheel, use a standard wheel puller. Under no condition should the end of the shaft be hammered upon, as hammering could also loosen or break the plastic injections.

1. Disconnect the negative battery cable.

2. If column repairs are to be made, remove the steering wheel.

3. Remove the sound insulator panels, as necessary for access to the steering column retaining bolts.

4. Remove the steering shaft-to-flange and steering coupling pinch bolt, then remove the column bracket support bolts.

5. Unplug the harness connectors from the column.

6. If equipped with a column shift, disconnect the indicator cable.

7. Lower the column to clear the mounting bracket, then carefully remove it from the vehicle.

To install:

8. Position the steering column in the vehicle.

9. If applicable, connect the shift cable at the actuator and housing holder.

10. Install the wiring harness connectors to the column harness terminals.

11. Install the column bracket support bolts and the flange/coupling upper pinch bolt. Tighten the bracket support bolts to 20 ft. lbs. (27 Nm). Tighten the pinch bolt to 30 ft. lbs. (41 Nm).

12. Install the sound insulator panels.

13. If column repairs were made, install the steering wheel.

NOTE: Some vehicles equipped with tilt steering columns may experience a squeaking noise when turning the steering wheel in a tilted position. This can be caused by insufficient grease in the tilting mechanism.

14. Disconnect the negative battery cable.

Power Steering Rack

REMOVAL AND INSTALLATION

1. Disconnect the negative battery cable.

2. Remove the left sound insulator for access, then remove the upper pinch bolt from the coupling assembly.

3. If applicable, remove the line retainer. For 1993–96 vehicles, loosen the retainers and move the power brake booster away from the cowl wall, leaving the master cylinder attached.

4. Raise and support the vehicle safely.

5. Remove both front wheel assemblies, except for 1993–96 vehicles on which only the left front wheel need be removed.

6. Disconnect the tie rod ends from the struts using J–24319–01, or an equivalent puller, then lower the vehicle sufficiently for underhood access.

7. Remove the left and right mounting clamps, then position a drain pan and disconnect the inlet and outlet pipes from the assembly.

8. Move the rack assembly forward and remove the lower pinch bolt from the flange coupling assembly, then remove the coupling from the rack.

9. Remove the dash seal from the rack, then remove the rack assembly through the left wheel opening.

To install:

10. Install the rack assembly through the left wheel opening, then position the dash seal and move the gear forward into contact with the coupling.

11. Install the lower pinch bolts and tighten to 30 ft. lbs. (41 Nm).

12. Install the pump lines to the gear and tighten the fittings to 20 ft. lbs. (27 Nm).

13. Hand start the rack clamp nuts, then tighten the nuts to specification beginning with the left side clamp nut. Tighten the nuts to 22 ft. lbs. (30 Nm).

14. Raise the vehicle sufficiently for under vehicle access, then connect the tie rods ends to the struts. Tighten the nuts and install new cotter pins.

15. Install the front tire and wheel assemblies or the left wheel assembly, as applicable. If removed, install the line retainer.

16. Lower the vehicle, then install the upper pinch bolt and tighten to 30 ft. lbs. (41 Nm). Install the left sound insulator panel.

17. Connect the negative battery cable, then fill and bleed the power steering system.

18. Check and adjust the toe setting, as required.

Power Steering Pump

REMOVAL AND INSTALLATION

1. Disconnect the negative battery cable.

2. Remove the serpentine drive belt.

3. Loosen the line clamp and/or line fittings, then disconnect the inlet and outlet lines from the pump. Have a drain pan and some rags handy to catch the escaping power steering fluid. Plug the lines to prevent system contamination or excessive fluid loss.

4. Remove the 3 pump-to-bracket bolts, then remove the pump from the engine.

5. If necessary, use a puller to remove the pump pulley.

To install:

6. If removed, install the pump pulley using an installer tool. Do not use an arbor press to install the pulley.

7. Install the pump assembly to the engine and tighten the retaining bolts:

　a. For the 2.0L engine, tighten the retaining bolts to 20 ft. lbs. (27 Nm).

　b. For the 2.2L engine, tighten the lower center bolt, followed by the upper side bolts to 22 ft. lbs. (30 Nm).

　c. For the 3.1L engine, tighten the retaining bolts to 18 ft. lbs. (25 Nm) for 1992 vehicles or to 22 ft. lbs. (30 Nm) for 1993–96 vehicles.

8. Unplug and install the lines to the pump, then tighten the fitting(s) to 20 ft. lbs. (27 Nm) and, if applicable the outlet hose clamp to 18–22 inch lbs. (2–2.5 Nm).

9. Install the serpentine drive belt.

10. Disconnect the negative battery cable, then bleed the power steering system.

BELT ADJUSTMENT

Serpentine belt tension is automatically adjusted by a spring loaded belt tensioner assembly, on which the belt is routed. The belt may be removed by rotating the tensioner using an appropriately sized wrench or breaker bar, depending on the particular engine. For the 2.0L engine, use a 19mm socket or wrench to pivot the tensioner. For the 2.2L engine a 15mm socket or wrench, and for the 3.1L engine, a ½ in. breaker bar, should be used to pivot the tensioner. Belt tension may be visually checked using the indicator mark(s) of the belt tensioner. If the indicator mark is not within specification, either the belt or the tensioner is worn and must be replaced.

NOTE: To remove or install the serpentine drive belt, push and rotate the tensioner using a wrench or breaker bar. Care must always be taken to avoid twisting or bending the tensioner when applying torque.

Checking Serpentine Belt Tension

1. Inspect the tensioner to see if the belt is within normal operating range. The belt should be replaced if the tensioner shows it is out of specification. If the tensioner markings indicate the belt is good, but a problem is still suspected, proceed with the test.

2. Make sure all accessories are turned OFF, then start the engine and warm to normal operating temperature.

3. Once the engine is properly warmed, shut the engine OFF and immediately check the belt tension using J–23600-B or an equivalent belt tension gauge. On the 2.0L engine, check tension between alternator and the crankshaft. For the 2.2L and 3.1L engines, check tension between the alternator and the power steering pump. Record the readings and proceed.

4. Start the engine again and allow it to stabilize for 15 seconds, then shut the engine OFF. Use a 15mm wrench to tighten the tensioner pulley bolt. Be aware that the tensioner bolt for the 2.0L and 2.2L engines is a left-hand thread bolt and must be tightened by turning counterclockwise. The 3.1L engine uses a standard bolt and must be tightened by turning clockwise.

5. Release the force and immediately take a belt tension reading. Be sure not to disturb the tensioner position before taking the reading.

6. Using the same wrench, apply force to the tensioner pulley bolt in the opposite direction of Step 4 in order to first rotate the tensioner to the released or belt install position, then slowly release the tensioner back into contact with the belt. Remember, for this step, the 2.0L and 2.2L engine tensioners should be turned clockwise, while the 3.1L engine tensioner should be rotated counterclockwise. Once the tensioner is back in contact, immediately take a final belt tension reading.

7. Average the 3 readings, the tension should be 36–44 lbs. (160–195 N) for the 2.0L engine, 63–77 lbs. (280–342 N) for the 2.2L engine, or 50–70 lbs. (225–315 N) for the 3.1L engine. If tension is incorrect, but the tensioner markings do not indicate a problem (the belt is within the tensioner marking range), the tensioner must be replaced.

SYSTEM BLEEDING

1. Raise the front of the vehicle and support safely with the front wheels off the ground.

2. With the wheels turned all the way to the left, add power steering fluid until the level reaches FULL COLD mark on the fluid level indicator.

3. Begin bleeding air from the system by tuning the wheels from side to side, without hitting the stops. It may require several passes to remove air from the system. Keep the fluid level to the FULL COLD mark.

NOTE: Power steering fluid which is contaminated with air will normally have a tan appearance.

4. Start the engine and check the fluid level at fast idle. Add fluid, if

necessary, to bring the level up to the **FULL COLD** mark.

5. Return the wheels to the center position and lower the vehicle to the ground while continuing to run the engine for 2–3 minutes.

6. Road test the vehicle to check steering function, then recheck the fluid level with the system at its normal operating temperature. Fluid should be at the **FULL HOT** mark. If necessary, add fluid to bring the level up to the mark.

Tie Rod Ends

REMOVAL AND INSTALLATION

1. Remove the cotter pin, then loosen and remove the slotted hex nut from the outer tie rod ball stud.

2. Loosen the outer tie rod pinch bolt.

3. Using J-24319-01, or an equivalent steering linkage puller, separate the outer tie rod end from the steering knuckle.

4. Unscrew the outer tie rod end from the tie rod adjuster. For assembly purposes, either scribe alignment marks (if the part is to be reused) before unthreading the tie rod, or count the number of turns required before they are disconnected.

To install:

5. Install the tie rod end, either threading it onto the adjuster using the same number of turns as counted during removal or aligning the scribe marks made earlier. Make sure the tie rod adjuster is centered between the inner and outer tie rod, with an equal number of threads exposed on both sides of the adjuster nut. If necessary, reposition the adjuster, but an equal number of turns made inward on 1 tie rod must be matched by outward turns on the other tie rod.

6. Position the tie rod into the steering knuckle, then install the slotted hex nut. Tighten the nut to 35 ft. lbs. (50 Nm) and install a cotter pin. If necessary, tighten the nut additionally in order to align a slot with the stud hole, but DO NOT loosen the nut from the initial torque. Final torque to align the hex nut slot must not exceed 50 ft. lbs. (68 Nm).

7. Check front end alignment and adjust toe, as necessary.

BRAKES

Master Cylinder

REMOVAL AND INSTALLATION

With Anti-Lock Brakes

The master cylinder for ABS equipped vehicles is part of the ABS hydraulic modulator/master cylinder assembly and must be removed as a single unit, then separated for service.

Proportioning Valve

REMOVAL AND INSTALLATION

1. Remove the master cylinder or the ABS hydraulic modulator/master cylinder assembly from the vehicle, as applicable.

2. If equipped with ABS, separate the master cylinder from the hydraulic modulator.

3. Clean the reservoir cap using a shop cloth, then remove the cap. Inspect the cap and diaphragm for cuts, cracks, nicks and deformation. Replace damaged parts, as necessary.

4. Drain the master cylinder reservoir of brake fluid, then clamp the master cylinder in a vise by the flange. Do not clamp the cylinder body or the assembly may be damaged.

5. Drive out the spring pins retaining the reservoir using a ⅛ in. punch. Be careful not to damage the reservoir or the cylinder body when driving out the pins.

6. Remove the reservoir from the cylinder body by pulling the reservoir straight up and away from the body.

7. Remove and discard the old reservoir-to-body O-rings.

8. Loosen and remove the 2 proportioner valve caps from the top rear side of the cylinder body. Remove and discard the old cap O-rings.

9. Remove the valve piston springs, then use a pair of needle nose pliers to remove the valve pistons. Be careful not to scratch or damage the piston stems.

10. Remove the proportioner valve seals from the pistons.

11. Clean all parts in denatured alcohol, then dry with unlubricated compressed air. Inspect and replace components, as necessary.

To install:

12. Lubricate the new proportioner valve cap O-rings and the valve seals using silicone grease, then lubricate the proportioner valve pistons.

13. Install the new valve seals on the pistons with the seal lips facing upward toward the valve cap, then install the pistons and seals into the cylinder body bores.

14. Install the valve springs over the pistons, then install the caps using the new O-rings. Tighten the caps to 20 ft. lbs. (27 Nm).

15. Lubricate the new reservoir O-rings and the reservoir flanges using clean brake fluid, then position the new O-rings into the reservoir grooves. The O-rings must be properly seated.

16. Install the reservoir to the cylinder by pressing straight down using hand pressure.

17. Drive the spring pins into position to retain the reservoir.

18. If equipped with ABS, install the master cylinder to the hydraulic modulator.

19. Install the master cylinder or the hydraulic modulator/master cylinder assembly to the vehicle.

20. Properly bleed the brake system.

Power Brake Booster

REMOVAL AND INSTALLATION

1. Remove the master cylinder from the booster and position the master cylinder aside. It is not necessary to disconnect the lines from the master cylinder or ABS hydraulic modulator/master cylinder assembly.

2. Unplug the hose from the vacuum check valve.

3. Remove the booster attaching nuts, then til the booster assembly slightly to facilitate removal of the pushrod.

4. Work the pushrod from the brake pedal clevis pin, being careful not to place undue side pressure on the pushrod.

5. Remove the booster assembly from the vehicle.

To install:

6. Position the booster assembly in the vehicle, then tilt slightly to work the pushrod onto the pedal clevis pin. Be careful not to place excessive side stress on the pushrod.

7. Install the booster to the firewall and tighten the mounting nuts to 20 ft. lbs. (27 Nm).

8. Connect the vacuum hose to the booster vacuum check valve.

9. Reposition and install the master cylinder or ABS hydraulic modulator/master cylinder assembly to the brake booster.

10. If brake lines were disconnected, then bleed the brake system.

Brake Caliper

REMOVAL AND INSTALLATION

1. Remove up to ⅔ of the brake fluid from the master cylinder.

2. Raise and support the vehicle safely.

3. Matchmark, then remove the wheel and tire assembly. Reinstall 2 nuts to retain the rotor on the hub and bearing assembly.

4. Position a large C-clamp over the back of the outboard brake shoe and top of the caliper housing, then slowly tighten the clamp to bottom the piston in the caliper bore. This provides clearance between the linings and rotor.

5. If the caliper is being completely removed from the vehicle for replacement or overhaul, remove the bolt attaching the inlet fitting. Plug the caliper and line openings to prevent system contamination and excessive fluid loss.

6. Remove the caliper mounting bolts and sleeve assemblies.

7. Remove the caliper from the rotor and mounting bracket.

8. If only the brake pads are being replaced, suspend the caliper with a wire hook from the strut.

To install:

9. Liberally coat the inside diameter of the bushings with silicone grease.

10. Install the caliper over the rotor and to the mounting bracket.

11. Install the mounting bolt and sleeve assemblies, then tighten the bolts to 38 ft. lbs. (52 Nm).

12. If the caliper was removed for overhaul or replacement, remove the plugs, then install the inlet fitting and tighten to 32 ft. lbs. (44 Nm).

13. Remove the wheel nuts securing the rotor to the hub.

14. Install the wheel and tire assembly, then lower the vehicle and fill the master cylinder.

15. Bleed the system if the caliper inlet fitting was removed and recheck fluid level.

Disc Brake Pads

REMOVAL AND INSTALLATION

1. Raise and support the vehicle safely, then remove the tire and wheel assemblies.

2. Remove the calipers from the rotors and mounting brackets, then support the calipers from the strut using a hook or length of mechanic's wire. Do not allow the brake hose to become kinked or stretched. Make sure the caliper piston is completely depressed and the boot is flat. If necessary, lift the inner edge of the boot and press out any trapped air.

3. Remove the brake pads using adjustable pliers or a small pry tool to disengage the buttons on the pad or straighten the bent over pad tabs.

4. Remove the caliper bushings from the mounting bolt holes.

To install:

5. Lubricate the inside diameter of the caliper bolt bushings with silicone grease.

6. Install the inboard pads into the calipers and snap the retaining springs into position on each piston inner diameter. The pads must lay flat on the pistons. Check to make sure the pads are NOT touching the piston boots. If necessary, remove and reposition the lining or the boot to prevent contact.

7. Install the outboard pads to each assembly with the wear sensor at the leading edge of the pad. During forward wheel rotation, the back of the pads must lay flat against the calipers.

8. Remove each caliper support, and install the calipers to the rotors and mounting brackets. Install the mounting bolt and sleeve assemblies, then tighten the bolts to 38 ft. lbs. (52 Nm).

9. If the pads are equipped with retaining tabs, firmly apply the brake pedal 3 times, then clinch the outboard pad retaining tabs using a small prybar to bend the tabs. The outboard pad should be locked in a fixed position.

10. Install the tire and wheel assemblies, then lower the vehicle. If not done already, apply the brake pedal a few times to seat the pads.

Brake Rotor

REMOVAL AND INSTALLATION

1. Raise and support the vehicle safely.

2. Remove the wheel and tire assembly.

3. Remove the caliper from the rotor and mounting bracket, then support the caliper from the strut using a hook or length of mechanic's wire.

4. Remove the rotor from the hub and bearing assembly.

To install:

5. Reposition the rotor to the hub and bearing assembly.

6. Install the caliper to the rotor and mounting bracket. Install the mounting bolt and sleeve assemblies, then tighten the bolts to 38 ft. lbs. (52 Nm).

7. Install the tire and wheel assembly, then lower the vehicle.

Brake Drums

REMOVAL AND INSTALLATION

1. Raise and support the vehicle safely.

2. Remove the tire and wheel assembly.

3. Mark the relationship of the drum to the axle flange.

4. Remove the brake drum. If the drum is difficult to remove, check to make sure the parking brake is off and that the brake adjuster is not turned all the way out. If necessary, use a rubber mallet to tap gently on the outer rim of the drum and/or around the inner drum diameter by the spindle.

To install:

5. Measure the drum inner diameter using a brake micrometer, then turn the adjuster star wheel to position the brake shoe outer diameter at 0.030 in. (0.76mm) less then the drum inner diameter.

6. Install the brake drum aligning the matchmarks made during removal.

7. Install the tire and wheel assembly.

8. Lower the vehicle.

Brake Shoes

REMOVAL AND INSTALLATION

1. Raise and support the vehicle safely.

2. Remove the wheel and tire assemblies.

3. Remove the brake drum, if the drum is hard to remove, check to make sure the parking brake is off and the brake adjuster is not turned all the way out. If necessary, use a rubber mallet to tap gently on the

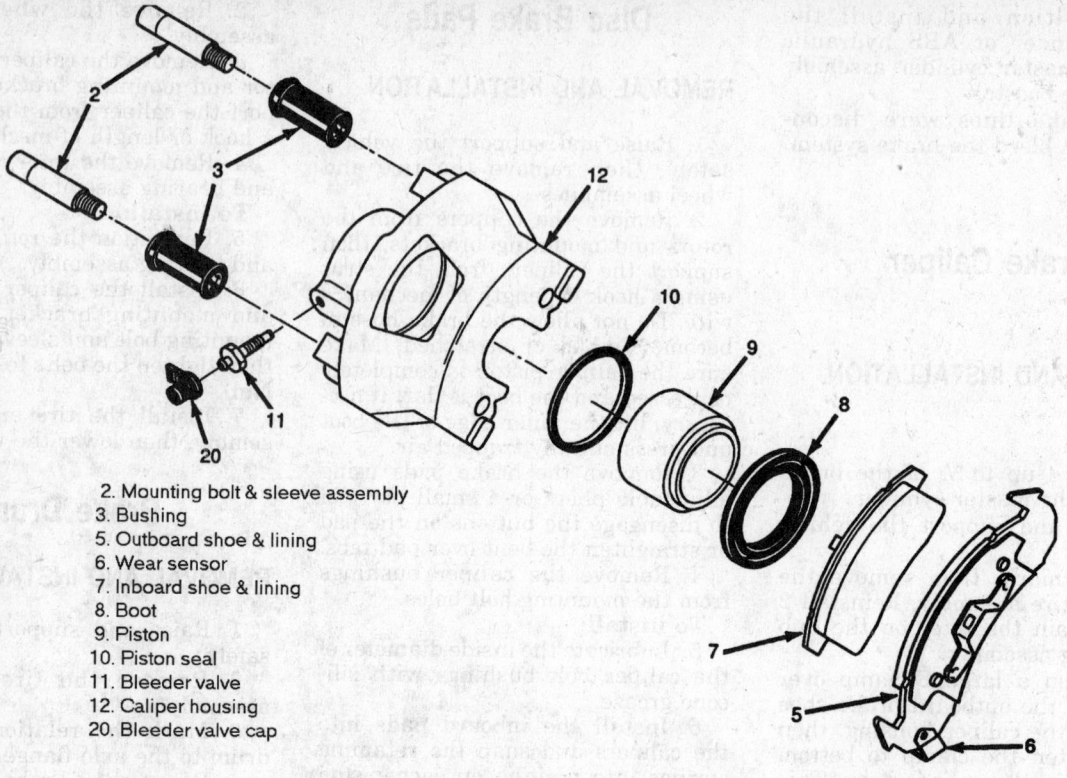

2. Mounting bolt & sleeve assembly
3. Bushing
5. Outboard shoe & lining
6. Wear sensor
7. Inboard shoe & lining
8. Boot
9. Piston
10. Piston seal
11. Bleeder valve
12. Caliper housing
20. Bleeder valve cap

84701066

Exploded view of the brake caliper assembly, but bleed valve relocated to top of caliper

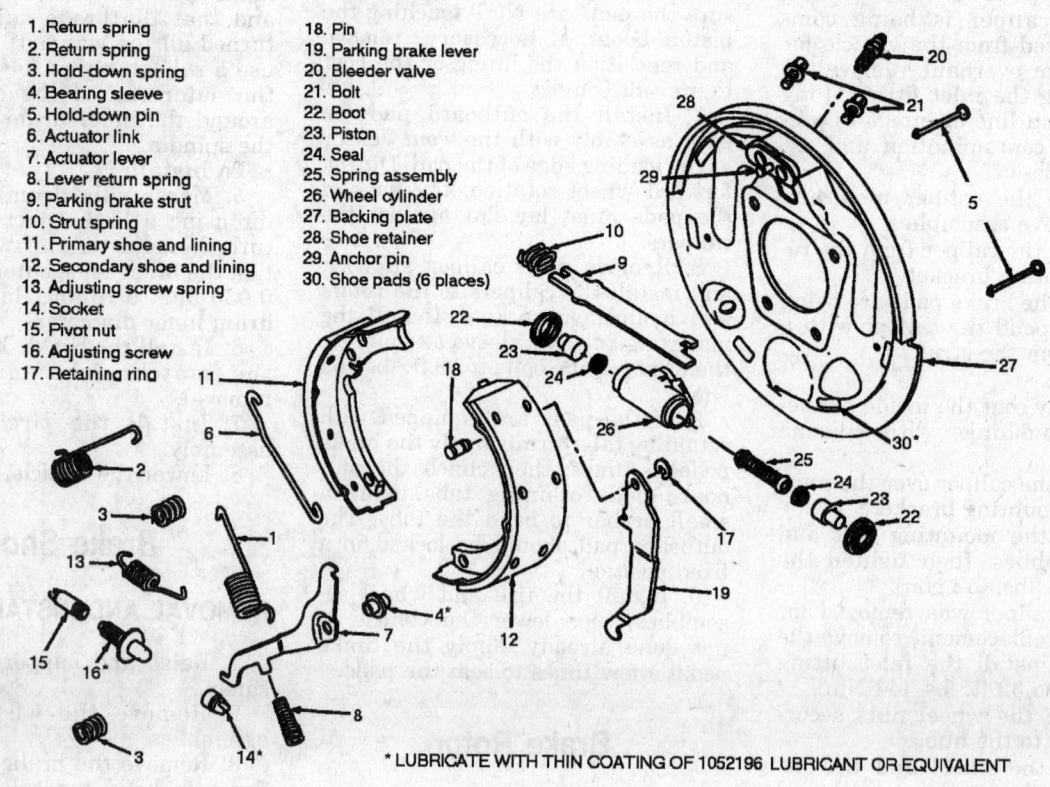

1. Return spring
2. Return spring
3. Hold-down spring
4. Bearing sleeve
5. Hold-down pin
6. Actuator link
7. Actuator lever
8. Lever return spring
9. Parking brake strut
10. Strut spring
11. Primary shoe and lining
12. Secondary shoe and lining
13. Adjusting screw spring
14. Socket
15. Pivot nut
16. Adjusting screw
17. Retaining ring
18. Pin
19. Parking brake lever
20. Bleeder valve
21. Bolt
22. Boot
23. Piston
24. Seal
25. Spring assembly
26. Wheel cylinder
27. Backing plate
28. Shoe retainer
29. Anchor pin
30. Shoe pads (6 places)

* LUBRICATE WITH THIN COATING OF 1052196 LUBRICANT OR EQUIVALENT

84701067

Exploded view of the drum brake components

outer rim of the drum and/or around the inner drum diameter by the spindle.

4. Remove the return springs, using brake spring pliers.

5. Remove the hold-down springs and pins.

6. Remove the actuator link while lifting up on the actuator lever.

7. Remove the actuator lever, lever return spring and bearing sleeve.

8. Remove the parking brake strut and strut spring.

9. Remove the brake shoes, after removing the parking brake cable from the shoe.

10. Remove the adjusting screw assembly and spring. Remove the retaining ring, pin and parking brake lever from the secondary shoe. The adjusting screw should be disassembled and thoroughly cleaned. Replace any parts which are worn, damaged or of doubtful strength.

To install:

11. Lubricate and assembly the brake adjusting screw.

12. Install the parking brake lever on the secondary shoe with the pin and retaining ring.

13. Install the adjusting screw and spring assembly.

14. Install the brake shoe assemblies after installing and positioning the parking brake cable.

15. Install the parking brake strut and strut spring by spreading the shoes apart. The end without the strut spring should engage the parking brake lever and secondary shoe. The end with the strut spring should engage the primary shoe.

16. Install the bearing sleeve, actuator lever and lever return spring. The bearing sleeve should be positioned between the shoe and actuator lever.

17. Install the hold-down pins and springs, then install the actuator link on the anchor pin.

18. Install the actuator link into the actuator lever while holding up on the lever.

19. Install the shoe return springs.

20. Measure the drum inner diameter using a brake micrometer, then turn the adjuster star wheel to position the brake shoe outer diameter at 0.030 in. (0.76mm) less then the drum inner diameter.

21. Install the brake drum aligning the matchmarks made during removal.

22. Install the wheel and tire assemblies.

23. Lower the vehicle and apply the brakes repeatedly.

24. Complete brake adjustment by making several alternate forward and reverse stops applying firm force to the brake pedal. Repeat until ample pedal reserve is obtained.

Wheel Cylinder

REMOVAL AND INSTALLATION

1. Raise and support the vehicle safely.

2. Remove the rear wheel and brake drum assembly.

3. Remove the rear brake shoes and components, as necessary to access the wheel cylinder.

4. Clean the area surrounding the wheel cylinder and brake line fitting, then disconnect the hydraulic line from the wheel cylinder. Plug the line to prevent system contamination or excessive fluid loss.

5. Use a #6 socket to remove the 2 Torx® screws and remove the wheel cylinder from the backing plate. If necessary, loosen the hub assembly bolts to provide access for cylinder removal.

To install:

6. Position the wheel cylinder and hold it in place using a wooden block placed between the the wheel cylinder and the axle flange.

7. Install the Torx® screws and torque to 15 ft. lbs. (20 Nm).

8. If loosened for access, tighten the hub assembly bolts.

9. Remove the plug from the brake hydraulic line, then install the line and torque the flare nut to 12 ft. lbs. (16 Nm) for 1992 vehicles or to 17 ft. lbs. (23 Nm) for 1993–96 vehicles.

10. Install the rear brake shoes and components, then adjust the brakes and install the drum.

11. Bleed the brake system.

12. Install the wheel assembly and lower the vehicle.

Parking Brake Cable

ADJUSTMENT

1. Disconnect the negative battery cable.

2. Raise and support the vehicle safely, with both rear wheels off the ground.

3. Pull the parking brake hand lever upward exactly 5 ratchet clicks.

If equipped with a foot pedal, depress the brake 2 ratchet clicks.

NOTE: To prevent damage to the threaded adjusting rod, thoroughly clean and lubricate the threads before turning the adjusting nut.

4. Tighten the adjusting nut until the left rear wheel can just be turned backward using 2 hands but is locked when forward rotation is attempted.

5. Release the parking brake, then rotate the rear wheels, there should be no brake drag.

6. Lower the vehicle.

REMOVAL AND INSTALLATION

Front

1. Raise and support the vehicle safely.

2. Loosen the parking brake cable equalizer or adjuster nut.

3. Lower the vehicle, then remove the center console.

4. Disconnect the parking brake cable from the lever.

5. Remove the cable retaining nut and the bracket securing the front cable to the floor panel.

6. Raise and support the vehicle safely, then loosen the catalytic converter shield and remove the parking brake cable from the body.

––––––– **CAUTION** –––––––

Use extreme care when working around the catalytic converter to avoid burns. If the engine was run recently, the exhaust components may be VERY hot.

7. Disconnect the cable from the equalizer and remove the cable from the guide and the underbody clips.

To install:

8. Install the cable to the guide and the underbody clips and connect the cable to the equalizer.

9. Install the parking brake cable to the body, then tighten the catalytic converter shield.

10. Lower the vehicle, then install the cable retaining nut and the bracket securing the front cable to the floor panel.

11. Connect the parking brake cable to the lever.

12. Install the center console.

13. Adjust the parking brake.

14. Lower the vehicle.

Rear

1. Raise and support the vehicle safely

2. Back off the equalizer nut until the cable tension is eliminated. If re-

moving the left cable, the threaded rod must be separated completely.

3. Remove the wheel assembly and brake drum.

4. Insert a small prybar or equivalent, between the brake shoe and the top part of the brake adjuster bracket. Push the bracket to the front and release the top adjuster bracket rod.

5. Remove the rear hold-down spring, actuator lever and the lever return spring.

6. Remove the adjuster screw spring.

7. Remove the top rear brake shoe return spring.

8. Unhook the parking brake cable from the parking brake lever.

9. Depress the conduit fitting retaining tangs and remove the conduit fitting from the backing plate.

10. Remove the cable end button from the connector, if applicable.

11. Depress the conduit fitting retaining tangs and remove the conduit fitting from the axle bracket.

To install:

12. Install the conduit fitting to the axle bracket, engaging the retaining tangs.

13. If applicable, install the cable end button to the connector.

14. Install the conduit fitting to the backing plate.

15. Connect the parking brake cable to the parking brake lever.

16. Install the top rear brake shoe return spring.

17. Install the adjuster screw spring.

18. Install the lever return spring, actuator lever and rear hold-down spring.

19. Connect the top adjuster bracket rod.

20. Install the wheel assembly and brake drum.

21. Adjust the parking brake.

22. Lower the vehicle.

Brake System Bleeding

The brake system must be bled when any brake line is disconnected and/or there is air in the system.

NOTE: Never bleed a wheel cylinder when a drum is removed.

Anti-Lock Brake System Service

Beginning with the 1992 model year, ABS-VI became standard equipment on the Cavalier and Sunbird. When activated, the system minimizes the chances of wheel lock-up by reducing hydraulic pressure to one or both front calipers and/or to both rear wheel cylinders as a pair. This is done by moving displacement pistons up or down to operate check valves in the modulator assembly. When the pistons are all the way up, the check valves are open and the system operates in normal braking mode. The pistons are operated by 3 motors and a gear train, all housed in the hydraulic modulator assembly. This system does not include a hydraulic pump or high pressure chamber. It cannot increase hydraulic pressure above master cylinder pressure or apply the brakes by itself.

If the amber ABS warning light on the instrument panel is flashing while driving, ABS operation may still be possible but the system requires service. If the light stays **ON**, a problem exists and the system will not function. Normal braking of course, is still available as long as the red brake warning light is **OFF**. If either light is **ON**, first check the fluid level.

Initializing the System

Before bleeding the ABS hydraulic brake system, the hydraulic modulator/master cylinder assembly must be initialized. During initialization, the electrical motors are run up to the top of their travel (normal braking) to uncover system check valves. In this position, air may be properly bled from all points in the system.

Without Scan Tool

1. Start the engine and run at idle for more than 10 seconds without touching the brake pedal.

2. If the ABS warning light turns **OFF**, the system is initialized. Bleed the entire system according to procedure. If the ABS warning light stays **ON**, there is another problem with the system that requires use of a diagnostic scan tool.

With Scan Tool

1. If the ABS warning light stays **ON** after the engine is started and run for at least 10 seconds, the system must be manually initialized using the scan tool, before brake bleeding can occur. Connect the Scan tool and enter manual control function.

2. Make sure the enable relay is **ON** and "apply" the front and rear motors.

3. The ABS light on the instrument panel should be **OFF**. The brakes can now be bled manually or with a power bleeder.

4. If the warning light remains, the scan tool should be used to retrieve diagnostic trouble codes and the system should be repaired.

Brake System Bleeding

NOTE: Bleeding the master cylinder/modulator requires initializing the system, setting the displacement pistons to the top of the modulator cylinders. If there is a problem with the system and the ABS warning light stays ON, the system cannot be bled.

With Pressure Bleeder

1. Initialize the ABS modulator pistons and check the fluid level in the reservoir.

2. Connect a diaphragm type pressure bleeder to the brake fluid reservoir.

3. Install 1 end of a clean plastic bleeder hose to the rearward bleeder valve on the hydraulic modulator/master cylinder assembly, then submerge the other end of the tube in a container clean brake fluid.

4. Pressurize the system to 5–10 psi. (35–70 kPa) and wait for approximately 30 seconds, then check for leaks.

5. Once it is determined that the system is secure, increase the pressure to 30–35 psi. (205–240 kPa).

6. Slowly open the rear bleeder on the hydraulic modulator assembly. When no air is seen in the fluid flow, close the bleeder and tighten to 80 inch lbs. (9 Nm). Repeat this until all fluid flows without air bubbles.

7. Check the fluid level, then switch the clear brake line to the front bleeder valve and repeat Step 6 at the front bleeder.

8. Check the fluid level, then position shop rags under the modulator pipe fittings to catch any escaping brake fluid. Loosen the forward brake pipe nut just a crack and check for air in the escaping fluid. When air flow ceases, immediately tighten the nut to 18 ft. lbs. (24 Nm). Repeat the step for each of the 3 remaining brake pipes.

9. Check the fluid level and use the same procedure as used on the modulator bleeder valves to bleed the wheel brakes in the following order:

   a. Right rear

   b. Left rear

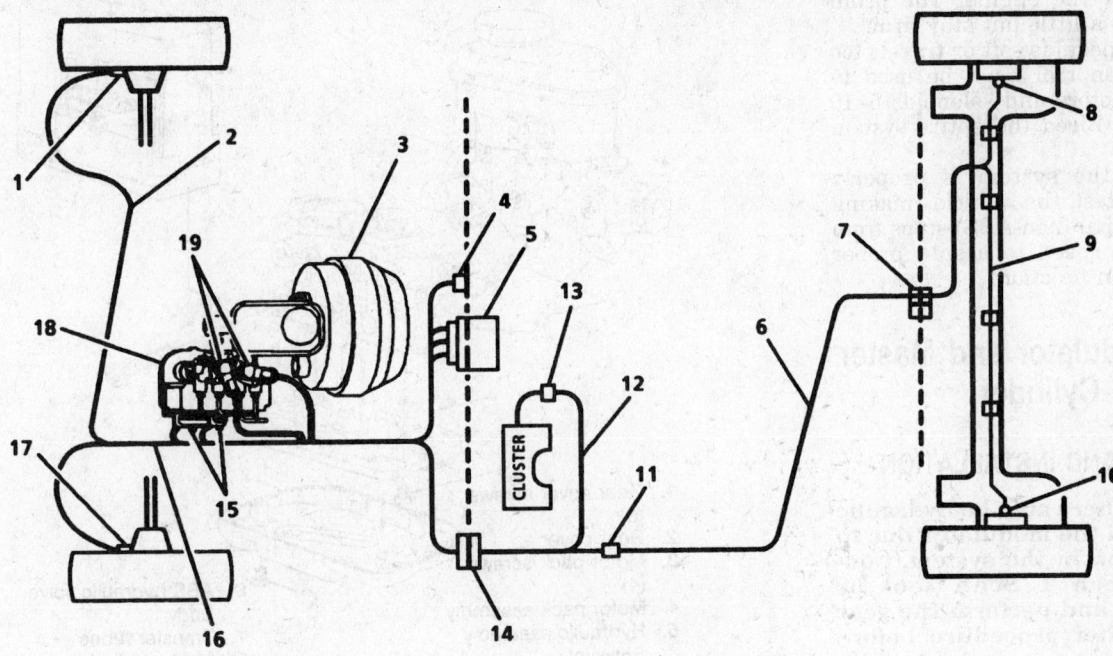

1. Right front wheel speed sensor
2. Engine harness sensor branch
3. Master cylinder
4. ABS relay
5. Electronic brake control module
6. Body extension harness
7. Rear body pass thru connector
8. Right rear wheel speed sensor
9. Rear axle harness
10. Left rear wheel speed sensor
11. Body connector
12. L/P harness
13. Lamp driver module
14. Bulkhead connector
15. ABS motor/EMB connector
16. Engine harness sensor branch
17. Left front wheel speed sensor
18. ABS hydraulic modulator assembly
19. Isolation solenoids

84701070

Anti-Lock Brake System component locations and control schematic

c. Right front
d. Left front

10. After bleeding the brakes, turn the ignition switch **ON** and step on the brake pedal. If the pedal feels firm and does not have excessive travel, start the engine. The pedal should drop a little but stay firm.

11. If the pedal is soft or travels too far, the Scan tool must be used to cycle the motors and solenoids 5–10 times each. Bleed the entire system again.

12. Once the system is properly bled, road test the vehicle, making several normal (non-ABS) stops from a moderate speed to assure proper brake system function.

Without Pressure Bleeder

1. Initialize the ABS modulator pistons and check the fluid level in the reservoir.

2. Connect a clear tube to the rear modulator bleeder valve and submerge the other end of the tube into a container of clean brake fluid.

3. Slowly open the bleeder $1/2$–$3/4$ turn, then have an assistant slowly depress the brake pedal and hold until fluid begins to flow. Close the bleeder and release the brake pedal, then wait 5 seconds. Repeat the step, including the 5 second pause, until there is no air at the rear bleeder.

4. Check the fluid level and repeat the procedure at the front bleeder.

5. Once the modulator/master cylinder assembly has been initially bled, it is sufficiently full to bleed the system hydraulic low points (wheel fittings). Check the fluid level and use the tube to bleed the wheel brakes in the following order:
   a. Right rear
   b. Left rear
   c. Right front
   d. Left front

6. To assure the modulator/master cylinder assembly is completely free of air, repeat the bleeding procedure at the rear, then front bleeder valves on the assembly.

7. After bleeding the brakes, turn the ignition switch **ON** and step on

the brake pedal. If the pedal feels firm and does not have excessive travel, start the engine. The pedal should drop a little but stay firm.

8. If the pedal is soft or travels too far, the Scan tool must be used to cycle the motors and solenoids 5–10 times each. Bleed the entire system again.

9. Once the system is properly bled, road test the vehicle, making several normal (non-ABS) stops from a moderate speed to assure proper brake system function.

ABS Modulator and Master Cylinder

REMOVAL AND INSTALLATION

NOTE: There may be hydraulic pressure in the modulator due to gear tension in the system. Connect a Tech 1 Scan tool or equivalent and perform the gear tension relief procedure before disconnecting any hydraulic lines.

1. Relieve the gear system pressure in the modulator assembly.
2. Disconnect the modulator and fluid sensor wiring.
3. Disconnect the hydraulic lines. Do not allow fluid to contact the electrical connectors or get into the motor pack. Plug lines.
4. Remove the 2 nuts and remove the ABS modulator/master cylinder assembly from the brake booster.
5. Installation is the reverse of removal. Torque the nuts to 20 ft. lbs. (27 Nm).

Fluid Level Sensor

The sensor is mounted low on the left side of the reservoir and can be removed with needle-nose pliers.

Front Wheel Speed Sensors

REMOVAL AND INSTALLATION

1. The sensor is mounted to the steering knuckle. Disconnect the wiring from the sensor.
2. Remove the bolt to remove the sensor. If the locating pin on the sensor will not pull out of the locating hole easily, remove the brake rotor and carefully tap it out with a punch.

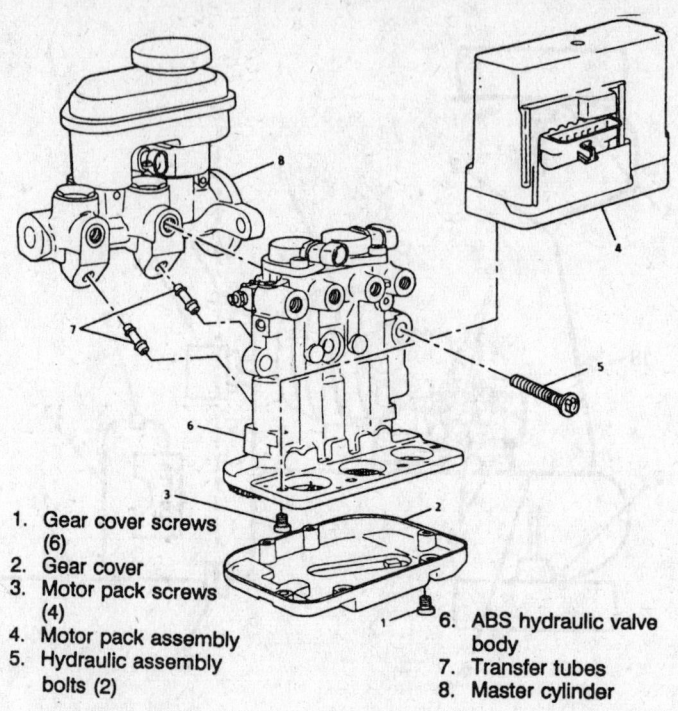

1. Gear cover screws (6)
2. Gear cover
3. Motor pack screws (4)
4. Motor pack assembly
5. Hydraulic assembly bolts (2)
6. ABS hydraulic valve body
7. Transfer tubes
8. Master cylinder

85691001

ABS hydraulic modulator and master cylinder assembly

3. When installing the sensor, make sure the locating pin hole is clean and the sensor fits flush against the steering knuckle. Do not enlarge the pin hole.

Rear Wheel Speed Sensors

REMOVAL AND INSTALLATION

1. The sensor, rear wheel hub and bearing are all a single assembly. Raise and safely support the vehicle and remove the rear wheel.
2. Remove the brake drum.
3. Remove the nuts and bolts to remove the rear hub assembly. The top bolt will not quite clear the brake shoe until the assembly is partially out.
4. Unplug the sensor connector. The backing plate is now held in place only by the metal brake line. Be careful not to damage the brake line.
5. Installation is the reverse of removal. Torque the bolts to 37 ft. lbs. (50 Nm).

FRONT SUSPENSION

MacPherson Strut

REMOVAL AND INSTALLATION

NOTE: Before removing front suspension components, their positions should be marked so they may be assembled correctly.

1. Remove the 3 strut-to-body fasteners from the top of the strut assembly.
2. Raise and support the vehicle safely.
3. Position jackstands under the front suspension support and lower the vehicle slightly so the weight rests on jackstands.
4. Remove the front wheel and tire assembly, then for 1993–96 vehicles, disconnect the brake line bracket.

NOTE: Drive axle boot protectors should be used any time service is performed neat the axle joints. Failure to observe this could result in interior joint or boot damage and possible joint failure.

5. Remove the cotter pin and slotted nut, then separate the tie rod from the strut assembly using tool J–24319 or equivalent tie rod end puller.

6. Scribe matchmarks for the strut flange on the steering knuckle, then remove the strut-to-steering knuckle nuts and/or bolts.

NOTE: Support steering knuckle to prevent axle joint overextension and to keep tension from being applied to brake hose.

7. Remove the strut assembly from the vehicle. Care should be taken to avoid chipping or cracking the spring coating when handling the front suspension coil spring assembly.

To install:

8. Position the strut assembly to the vehicle and loosely install the upper mounting fasteners to hold the assembly.

9. Align the matchmarks made during removal, then install the strut-to-steering knuckle bolts and tighten to 133 ft. lbs. (180 Nm).

10. Position the tie rod into the steering knuckle, then install the slotted hex nut. Tighten the nut to 35 ft. lbs. (50 Nm) and install a cotter pin. If necessary, tighten the nut additionally in order to align a slot with the stud hole, but DO NOT loosen the nut from the initial torque. Final torque to align the hex nut slot must not exceed 50 ft. lbs. (68 Nm).

11. Tighten the upper strut-to-body fasteners to 18 ft. lbs. (25 Nm).

12. Connect the brake line bracket, then remove the drive axle boot protectors.

13. Raise the vehicle and remove the jackstands, then install the tire and wheel assembly and lower the vehicle.

14. Check and/or adjust the front end alignment.

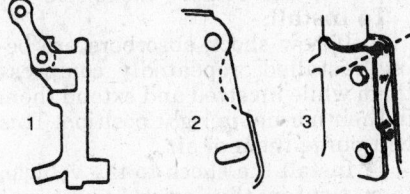

1. Scribe knuckle along lower outboard strut radius
2. Scribe strut flange on inboard side along curve of knuckle
3. Scribe across strut/knuckle interface

8470I072

Scribing alignment marks for the strut and steering knuckle

Strut Cartridge Replacement

1. Remove the strut from the vehicle, then mount it into a suitable strut compressor and holding fixture.

2. Compress the strut approximately ½ of its height after the initial contact with the top cap.

————— **WARNING** —————
When compressing the strut assembly, never bottom the spring or dampener rod or damage may occur.

3. Remove the nut from the strut dampener shaft, then position a guiding rod onto the top of the shaft.

4. Use the rod to guide the dampener shaft straight downward through the bearing cap, while carefully decompressing the spring. Remove the components from the assembly.

5. If removed, install the bearing cap into the strut compressor.

6. Mount the strut into the compressor, using the locking pin only, then extend the dampener shaft and install tool clamp onto the shaft.

7. Install the spring over the dampener and swing the assembly upward so the upper locking pin can be installed.

8. Install the upper insulator, shield, bumper and upper spring seat. Make sure the seat flat is facing in the same direction as the centerline of the strut assembly spindle.

9. Install an alignment rod and turn the tool forcing screw while the rod centers the shaft assembly. When the threads on the dampener shaft are visible, remove the alignment rod and install the shaft nut.

10. While holding the dampener shaft using a socket, tighten the assembly retaining nut to 65 ft. lbs. (85 Nm).

11. Remove the clamp, and remove the strut assembly from the fixture.

12. Install the strut assembly to the vehicle.

Lower Ball Joint

INSPECTION

1. Raise and support the vehicle safely, allowing the front suspension to hang free.

2. Grasp the wheel at the top and bottom, shake it in an "in-and-out" motion. Check for any horizontal movement of the steering knuckle relative to the lower control arm. Re-

place the ball joint if such movement is noted.

3. The ball stud must be tight in the knuckle boss. Shake the wheel and check for movement of the stud end or castellated nut. A loose nut may be an indication of a bent stud or worn hole. If the knuckle boss is worn, the steering knuckle must also be replaced.

4. If the ball stud is disconnected from the steering knuckle and any looseness is detected or if the ball stud can be twisted in its socket using finger pressure, replace the ball joint.

REMOVAL AND INSTALLATION

NOTE: This procedure requires the use of a special ball joint separator tool. The Mac-Pherson strut suspension design does not use an upper ball joint.

1. Raise and support the vehicle safely, then remove the wheel assembly.

2. Position jackstands under the suspension supports and lower the vehicle so the weight rests on the jackstands and not the control arms.

————— **WARNING** —————
Drive axle boot protectors should be used any time service is performed neat the axle joints. Failure to observe this could result in interior joint or boot damage and possible joint failure.

3. Remove the cotter pin and slotted nut from the ball joint stud.

4. Remove the ball joint from the steering knuckle using J–38892, or an equivalent ball joint separator.

5. Use a ⅛ in. (3mm) drill bit to drill a pilot hole through the center of each of the 3 ball joint rivets.

6. Use a ½ in. (6mm) drill bit to drill completely through the rivet.

7. Drive the rivets from the suspension using a hammer and punch.

8. Loosen the stabilizer shaft clamp nuts, then remove the nut attaching the link to the stabilizer shaft.

9. Remove the ball joint from the steering knuckle and control arm.

To install:

10. Install the new ball joint into the control arm, then secure using the 3 bolts and nuts supplied with the replacement joint.

11. Position the ball joint stud through the steering knuckle, then install the ball joint nut.

12. Tighten the stabilizer shaft clamp nuts to 16 ft. lbs. (22 Nm), then install the slotted hex nut.

Tighten the nut to 41 ft. lbs. (55 Nm) and install a cotter pin. If necessary, tighten the nut additionally in order to align a slot with the stud hole, but DO NOT loosen the nut from the initial torque. Final torque to align the hex nut slot must not exceed 50 ft. lbs. (65 Nm). Once tightened, do not loosen the nut at any time during the installation procedure.

13. Install the nut attaching the stabilizer link to the shaft, then tighten to 13 ft. lbs. (17 Nm).

14. Install the tire and wheel assembly, then remove the jackstands and lower the vehicle.

15. Check the toe setting and adjust, as necessary.

Lower Control Arms

REMOVAL AND INSTALLATION

1. Raise and support the vehicle safely, then remove the wheel assembly.

2. Position jackstands under the suspension supports and lower the vehicle so the weight rests on the jackstands and not the control arms.

——— WARNING ———
Drive axle boot protectors should be used any time service is performed neat the axle joints. Failure to observe this could result in interior joint or boot damage and possible joint failure.

3. Disconnect the stabilizer bar from the control arm and/or support.

4. Remove the cotter pin and slotted nut from the ball joint stud, then remove the ball joint from the steering knuckle using J–38892, or an equivalent ball joint separator.

5. Remove the 2 control arm-to-support bolts, then remove the control arm from the vehicle.

6. If control arm support bar removal is necessary, unscrew the mounting bolts and remove the support.

To install:

7. If the control arm support bar was removed, install the support and secure by loosely installing the mounting bolts, starting with the center retainers.

8. Position the ball joint in the steering knuckle, then loosely install the control arm using the 2 arm-to-support bolts.

9. If removed, install the stabilizer shaft clamp-to-suspension support nuts.

10. Install the slotted hex nut to the ball joint stud. Tighten the nut to 41

ft. lbs. (55 Nm) and install a cotter pin. If necessary, tighten the nut additionally in order to align a slot with the stud hole, but DO NOT loosen the nut from the initial torque. Final torque to align the hex nut slot must not exceed 50 ft. lbs. (65 Nm).

11. If removed, install the nuts attaching the stabilizer link to the stabilizer shaft.

12. Install the wheel assembly and lower the vehicle so the suspension is at normal curb height, then tighten the suspension support and/or the control arm bolts. For the suspension support, first tighten the center bolts to 66 ft. lbs. (90 Nm), then tighten the front bolts followed by the rear bolts to 65 ft. lbs. (88 Nm). After the suspension support is secure, tighten the control arm bolts to 61 ft. lbs. (83 Nm).

13. Check the toe and adjust, as necessary.

Stabilizer Bar

REMOVAL AND INSTALLATION

1. Raise and support the vehicle safely, allowing the front suspension hang freely.

2. Remove the front tire and wheel assemblies.

3. Remove the nuts attaching the stabilizer shafts to the stabilizer link bolts and the control arms.

4. Remove the clamps attaching the stabilizer shaft to the suspension support assemblies.

5. Loosen the front bolts, then remove the rear and center bolts from the support assemblies. Lower the suspension supports sufficiently to remove the stabilizer shaft.

6. Remove the stabilizer shaft with grommets and insulators.

To install:

7. Install the stabilizer shaft with grommets and insulators.

8. Install the shaft-to-support clamps, then hand-tighten the retainers.

9. Raise the support assemblies into position and hand-tighten the bolts.

10. Install the nuts attaching the stabilizer shafts to the control arm link bolts, then tighten the nuts to 13 ft. lbs. (17 Nm).

11. Tighten the suspension support and stabilizer clamp retainers. For the suspension support, first tighten the center bolts to 66 ft. lbs. (90 Nm), then tighten the front bolts followed by the rear bolts to 65 ft. lbs. (88 Nm). After the suspension support is

secure, tighten the stabilizer clamp retainers to 16 ft. lbs. (22 Nm).

12. Install the front tire and wheel assemblies.

13. Lower the vehicle.

14. Check the toe and adjust, as necessary.

Front Wheel Bearings

For front wheel hub and bearing procedures, refer to the Drive Axle section.

REAR SUSPENSION

Shock Absorbers

REMOVAL AND INSTALLATION

——— WARNING ———
Both shock absorbers should not be removed at the same time if the vehicle is to be raised without supporting the rear axle. Suspending the rear axle at full length could result in damage to the brake pipes and hoses.

1. Open the rear trunk lid, then remove the shock absorber upper cover.

2. Loosen and remove the shock upper mounting nut.

3. Raise and support the vehicle safely to a convenient working height. If possible, support the rear axle while lifting and supporting the vehicle, so the shock absorbers are not at their full length of travel. It is not necessary to remove the weight of the vehicle from the shock absorbers in order to remove them, the vehicle can be left on the ground, if preferred.

4. Remove the lower attaching nut and bolt, then remove the shock.

To install:

5. If new shock absorbers are being installed, repeatedly compress them while inverted and extend them in their normal upright position. This will purge them of air.

6. Install the shock to the vehicle, then tighten the lower mount nut and bolt to 35 ft. lbs. (47 Nm).

7. Lower the vehicle and, if separate, the rear axle support.

8. Install the upper shock mounting nut and tighten to 21 ft. lbs. (29 Nm).

9. Install the shock absorber upper cover and close the trunk.

Coil Springs

REMOVAL AND INSTALLATION

---------- CAUTION ----------

The coil springs are under a considerable amount of tension. Be very careful when removing or installing them; if spring pressure is released suddenly, it could exert enough force to cause very serious injuries.

1. Raise and support the vehicle safely, if possible, raise the vehicle by the frame leaving the rear suspension free.
2. Support the rear axle using a jack so it can be raised and lowered.
3. Remove the tire and wheel assemblies.
4. Remove the left and right brake hose attaching brackets, allowing the hoses to hang freely. Do not disconnect the hoses.
5. Remove both shock absorber lower attaching bolts from the axle.
6. Carefully lower the axle, then remove the coil springs and/or insulators.

To install:

7. Position the upper spring insulators to the body using adhesive to hold them in position during assembly.
8. Position the springs and insulators in the seats and raise the axle. Make sure the ends of the upper coil in the spring are positioned in the seat and within 9/16 in. (15mm) of the spring stop.
9. Loosely install the lower shock absorber fasteners. Either lower the vehicle or position the lift and jacks so the suspension is at normal trim height, then tighten the shock absorber lower fasteners to 35 ft. lbs. (47 Nm).
10. Install the brake line brackets and tighten the screws to 97 inch lbs. (11 Nm).
11. If not done already, install the tire and wheel assemblies, then lower the vehicle.

Rear Wheel Hub and Bearings

REMOVAL AND INSTALLATION

1. If equipped with ABS brakes, disconnect the negative battery cable.
2. Raise and support the vehicle safely.
3. Remove the wheel and tire assembly.
4. Remove the brake drum.

---------- WARNING ----------

Avoid hammering on the brake drum for removal; damage to the bearing could result.

5. If equipped, unplug the electrical wiring harness from the ABS wheel speed sensor.
6. Turn the hub to align the large access hole with each of the fasteners. Remove the 4 hub and bearing retaining bolts, then remove the assembly from the axle. The top rear attaching bolt will not clear the brake shoe when removing the hub and bearing assembly. Partially remove the hub and bearing assembly prior to removing this bolt.

To install:

7. If equipped with ABS, install the wiring harness connector to the hub and bearing assembly.
8. Position the hub assembly and secure using the 4 retaining bolts. Tighten the bolts to 37 ft. lbs. (50 Nm).
9. Install the brake drum.
10. Install the wheel and tire assembly.
11. Lower the vehicle.
12. If applicable, connect the negative battery cable.

Rear Axle Assembly

REMOVAL AND INSTALLATION

1. Raise and support the vehicle safely. Raise the vehicle by the frame leaving the rear suspension free.
2. Support the rear axle using a jack so it can be raised and lowered.
3. If equipped, remove the stabilizer shaft from the axle assembly.
4. Remove the tire and wheel assemblies.
5. Disconnect the brake pipe from the brackets on the axle assembly, to make sure the axle is not supported by the brake lines at any point during the procedure.
6. Remove both shock absorber lower attaching bolts from the axle.
7. Carefully lower the axle, then remove the coil springs and/or insulators.
8. Remove the parking brake cable from the equalizer unit and from the axle or wheel assembly.
9. If equipped, unplug the ABS wiring connector and the mount clip located near the fuel tank.
10. Disconnect the left and right brake lines. Plug the lines to prevent system contamination or excessive fluid loss.
11. If applicable, remove the control arm bolts from the underbody brackets.
12. Carefully lower the axle assembly from the vehicle.

To install:

13. Secure the axle assembly on a jack and carefully raise it into position on the vehicle.
14. If applicable, install the control arm-to-underbody bracket bolts. With the weight on the vehicle, the fasteners should be tightened to 61 ft. lbs. (83 Nm).
15. Remove the plugs and connect the brake lines. If applicable, install the ABS wiring harness connector and mount clip.
16. Connect the parking brake cable to the axle or wheel and the cable equalizer.
17. Position the upper spring insulators to the body using adhesive to hold them in position during assembly.
18. Position the springs and insulators in the seats and raise the axle. Make sure the ends of the upper coil in the spring are positioned in the seat and within 9/16 in. (15mm) of the spring stop.
19. Loosely install the lower shock absorber fasteners. Either lower the vehicle or position the lift and jacks so the suspension is at normal trim height, then tighten the shock absorber lower fasteners to 35 ft. lbs. (47 Nm).
20. Install the brake line brackets and tighten the screws to 97 inch lbs. (11 Nm).
21. If not done already, install the tire and wheel assemblies, then lower the vehicle.
22. Bleed the rear brake system and adjust the parking brake cable.

1. Cover
2. Module assembly
3. Bolt/screw
4. Bolt/screw
5. Harness assembly
6. Coil assembly
7. Housing assembly
8. Ignition coil housing cover
9. Connector
10. Boot
11. Retainer
12. Ignition coil spacer
13. Ignition coil contact
14. Ignition coil term seal

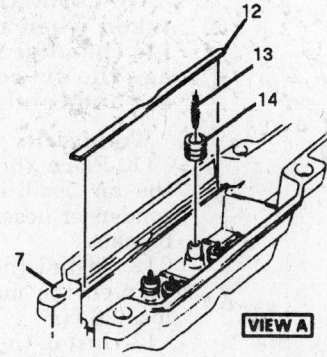

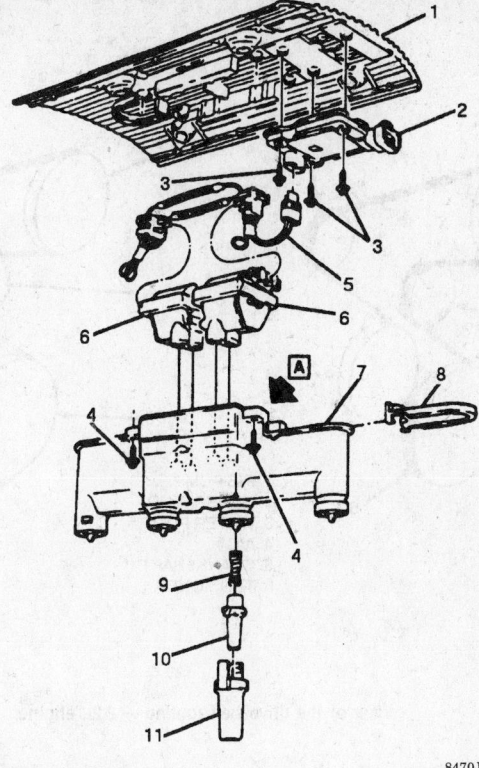

VIEW A

8470J010

Exploded view of the IDIS ignition system

Alternator

PRECAUTIONS

Several precautions must be observed with alternator equipped vehicles to avoid damage to the unit.

• If the battery is removed for any reason, make sure it is reconnected with the correct polarity. Reversing the battery connections may result in damage to the one-way rectifiers.

• When utilizing a booster battery as a starting aid, always connect the positive to positive terminals and the negative terminal from the booster battery to a good engine ground on the vehicle being started.

• Never use a fast charger as a booster to start vehicles.

• Disconnect the battery cables when charging the battery with a fast charger.

• Never attempt to polarize the alternator.

• When checking diode continuity, ensure the tester does not exceed 12 volts.

• Do not short across or ground any of the alternator terminals.

• The polarity of the battery, alternator and regulator must be matched and considered before making any electrical connections within the system.

• Never separate the alternator on an open circuit. Make sure all connections within the circuit are clean and tight.

• Disconnect the battery ground terminal when performing any service on electrical components.

• Disconnect the battery if arc welding is to be done on the vehicle.

BELT TENSION ADJUSTMENT

A single (serpentine) belt is used to drive all engine mounted components. Drive belt tension is maintained by a spring loaded tensioner.

The serpentine drive belt may be removed or installed by rotating the tensioner using a 15mm socket for the 2.2L and 3.1L engines. Use a 13mm open end wrench for the 2.3L engine. This will eliminate the belt tension and will allow the belt to be removed or installed.

CAUTION

To avoid personal injury when rotating the serpentine belt tensioner on the 2.3L engine, be sure to use a tight fitting 13mm wrench at least 24 inches long.

NOTE: The drive belt tensioner can control belt tension over a wide range of belt lengths; however, there are limits to the tensioner's ability to compensate for various belt lengths. Installing the wrong size belt and using the tensioner outside of it's operating range can result in poor tension control and/or damage to the tensioner, belt and driven components.

REMOVAL AND INSTALLATION

Except 2.3L Engine

1. Disconnect the negative battery cable.
2. Remove the serpentine drive belt.
3. Label and disconnect the electrical connectors from the back of the alternator.
4. Remove the alternator mounting bolts.
5. Remove the alternator-to-bracket bolts and the alternator.
To install:
6. Position the alternator to the the mounting bracket and install the attaching bolts.
7. Connect the alternator electrical connectors to the rear of the alternator.

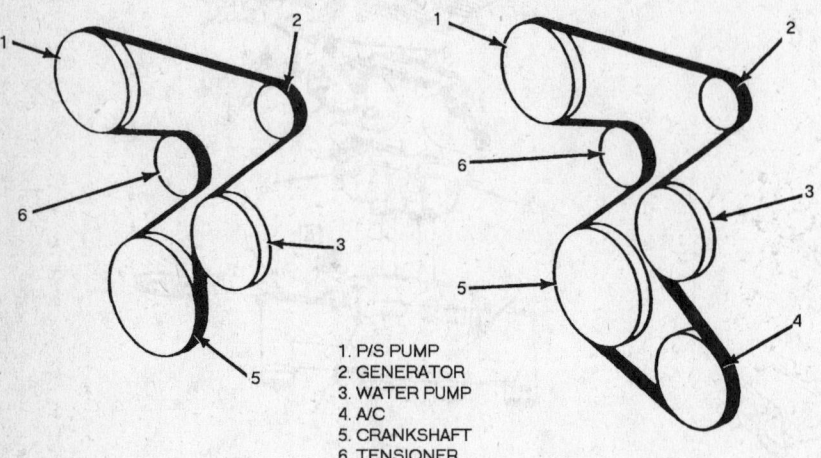

1. P/S PUMP
2. GENERATOR
3. WATER PUMP
4. A/C
5. CRANKSHAFT
6. TENSIONER

8470J011

View of the drive belt routing — 2.2L engine

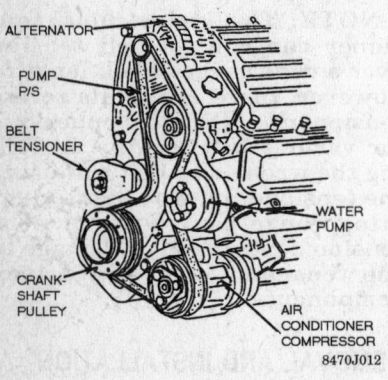

8470J012

View of the drive belt routing — 3.1L engine

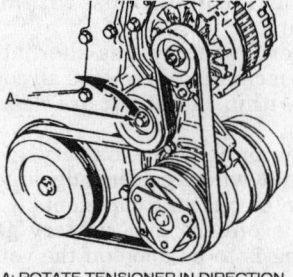

A: ROTATE TENSIONER IN DIRECTION OF ARROW TO REMOVE OR INSTALL BELT.

8470J013

View of the drive belt routing — 2.3L engine

8. Install the serpentine drive belt.

9. Connect the negative battery cable.

10. Start the engine and perform a charging system test.

?L Engine

?. Disconnect the negative battery cable.

?. Remove the serpentine drive belt.

CAUTION

To avoid personal injury when rotating the serpentine belt tensioner, be sure to use a tight fitting 13mm wrench at least 24 inches long.

3. Remove the coolant and washer reservoir attaching screws.

4. Disconnect the washer pump electrical connector and position the reservoir to the side.

5. Remove the air conditioner line rail clip.

6. Disconnect the 2 vacuum lines at the front of the engine and remove

vacuum harness attaching bracket, as required.

7. Disconnect and tag electrical connections from injector harness and alternator.

8. Remove the rear alternator mounting bolts.

9. Remove the front alternator mounting bolt and engine harness clip.

10. Carefully remove the alternator from between the mounting bracket and the air conditioning and condenser hose.

NOTE: Extreme care must be taken when removing or installing the alternator as not to damage the air conditioner compressor and condenser hoses.

To install:

11. Place the alternator between the air conditioner compressor and condenser hoses and install it on the bracket.

12. Install the rear mounting bolt. Tighten the mounting bolt to 19 ft. lbs. (26 Nm).

13. Install the front mounting bolts. Tighten the upper mounting bolt to 37 ft. lbs. (50 Nm) and the lower mounting bolt to 19 ft. lbs. (26 Nm).

14. Install the serpentine drive belt.

CAUTION

To avoid personal injury when rotating the serpentine belt tensioner, be sure to use a tight fitting 13mm wrench at least 24 inches long.

15. Install the air conditioner rail clip.

16. Connect the washer pump electrical connector.

17. Install the coolant and washer pump reservoir.

18. Connect the electrical connections for the alternator and injector harness.

19. If removed, install the vacuum harness attaching bracket and connect the vacuum lines at the front of the engine.

20. Connect the negative battery cable.

21. Start the engine and perform a charging system test.

Starter

REMOVAL AND INSTALLATION

2.2L Engine

1. Disconnect the negative battery cable.

2. Raise and safely support the vehicle.

3. Disconnect the starter motor wiring.

4. Remove the wiring clamp at the support bracket.

5. Remove the 1 bolt between the support bracket and the engine.

6. Remove the 2 bolts from the starter motor and remove the starter with the shims (if used).

To install:

7. Install the shims (if used) and the starter motor. Install the 2 bolts and tighten to 32 ft. lbs. (43 Nm).

8. Install the support bracket bolt and tighten to 24 ft. lbs. (32 Nm).

9. Install the wiring clamp to the support bracket and tighten the bolt to 106 inch lbs. (12 Nm).

10. Connect the starter motor wiring and lower the vehicle.

11. Connect the negative battery cable.

3.1L Engine

1. Disconnect the negative battery cable.

2. Raise and safely support the vehicle.

3. Remove the starter motor to engine bolts.

4. Lower the starter and disconnect the starter leads while supporting the starter.

5. Remove the starter from the vehicle.

To install:

6. Install the starter to the vehicle and connect the electrical leads while supporting the starter.

7. Install the starter motor mounting bolts and tighten to 32 ft. lbs. (43 Nm).

8. Lower the vehicle and connect the negative battery cable.

2.3L Engine

1. Disconnect the negative battery cable.

2. If necessary, remove the air induction tubing.

3. Raise and safely support the vehicle. Remove the oil filter.

4. Remove the starter mounting bolts.

5. Position starter aside to gain access to the wiring. Disconnect the starter wiring.

6. Remove the starter from the vehicle.

To install:

7. Connect the wiring to the starter and position the starter to the engine.

8. Install the upper and lower mounting bolts and tighten to 74 ft. lbs. (100 Nm).

9. Install the oil filter and connect the air induction tubing, if disconnected.

10. Lower the vehicle.

11. Connect the negative battery cable, refill the engine with oil and check for leaks.

CHASSIS ELECTRICAL

Air Bag

—— CAUTION ——

Some vehicles are equipped with the Supplemental Inflatable Restraint (SIR) or air bag system. The SIR system must be disabled before performing service on or around SIR system components, steering column, instrument panel components, wiring and sensors. Failure to follow safety and disabling procedures could result in accidental air bag deployment, possible personal injury and unnecessary SIR system repairs.

PRECAUTIONS

Several precautions must be observed when handling the inflator module to avoid accidental deployment and possible personal injury.

• Never carry the inflator module by the wires or connector on the underside of the module.

• When carrying a live inflator module, hold securely with both hands, and ensure that the bag and trim cover are pointed away.

• Place the inflator module on a bench or other surface with the bag and trim cover facing up.

• When the inflator module is on the bench, never place anything on or close to the module which may be thrown in the event of an accidental deployment.

DISARMING

1. Disconnect the negative battery cable.

2. Remove the SIR fuse (No. 3) from the fuse panel.

3. Remove the left side sound insulator.

4. Remove the Connector Positive Assurance (CPA) from the yellow 2-way SIR harness connector at the base of the steering column and separate the connector.

ARMING

1. Turn the ignition switch to the **OFF** position.

2. Connect the yellow 2-way SIR connector at the base of the steering column and insert the Connect Positive Assurance (CPA).

3. Install the left side sound insulator.

4. Install the SIR fuse in the fuse panel.

5. Connect the negative battery cable.

REMOVAL AND INSTALLATION

Inflator Module

1. Disconnect the negative battery cable.

2. Disarm the SIR system.

NOTE: Rotate the steering wheel so the access holes on the back of the steering wheel are at the 12 and 6 o'clock positions. This will allow tool access and reduce the possibility of marring the steering column cover.

3. Remove the 4 screws from the back of the inflator module.

4. Remove the inflator module from the steering wheel.

5. Remove the Connector Positive Assurance (CPA) from the inflator module electrical connector and disconnect the connector.

To install:

6. Connect the coil assembly connector. Install the CPA into the connector.

NOTE: Ensure that no wires at the back of the inflator module are pinched when aligning the inflator module to the steering wheel.

7. Install the inflator module and the 4 attaching bolts.

8. Arm the SIR system.

9. Connect the negative battery cable.

CENTERING THE COIL ASSEMBLY

In the event the coil becomes uncentered, perform the following:

1. With the steering wheel removed, remove the coil assembly from the steering column.

2. Hold the coil assembly with the clear bottom up in order to see the coil ribbon.

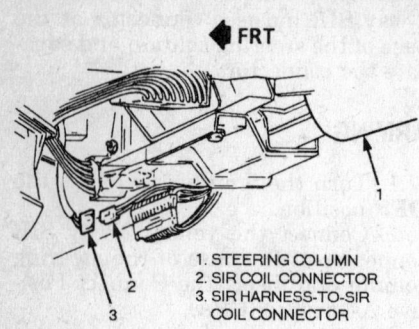

◄ FRT

1. STEERING COLUMN
2. SIR COIL CONNECTOR
3. SIR HARNESS-TO-SIR COIL CONNECTOR

8470J020

Location of yellow SIR harness connector

3. There are 2 styles of coils: one rotates clockwise and the other rotates counterclockwise.

4. While holding the coil assembly, depress the spring lock to rotate the hub in the direction of the arrow until it stops. The coil ribbon should be wound up snug against the center hub.

5. Rotate the coil hub in the opposite direction approximately 2½ turns.

6. Release the spring lock between the locking tabs adjacent to the arrow.

Heater Blower Motor

REMOVAL AND INSTALLATION

1. Disconnect the negative battery cable.

2. Disconnect the electrical connections from the blower motor and resistor.

3. Remove the plastic water shield from the right side of the cowl, if equipped.

4. If equipped with the 3.1L engine, it may be necessary to remove the alternator.

5. Remove the blower motor cooling hose.

6. Remove the blower attaching screws and pull the blower motor from the cowl.

7. Remove the fan attaching nut and the fan from the motor.

To install:

8. Install the fan on the new blower motor with the opening facing away from the motor and install the attaching nut.

9. Position the blower motor assembly to the cowl and install the attaching screws.

10. Install the blower motor cooling hose.

11. If equipped with the 3.1L engine, install the alternator, if removed.

12. Install the plastic water shield on the right side of the cowl, if equipped.

13. Connect the electrical connections to the blower motor and resistor.

14. Connect the negative battery cable.

Windshield Wiper Motor

REMOVAL AND INSTALLATION

1. Disconnect the negative battery cable.

2. Remove the left and right side wiper arms.

3. Loosen the drive link adjusting screws and disconnect the wiper motor drive link from the crank arm.

4. Disconnect the electrical connectors and washer hoses.

5. Remove the wiper motor-to-chassis bolts and the wiper motor by guiding the crank arm through the hole.

6. Remove the crank arm from the motor.

To install:

7. Install the crank arm on the new wiper motor shaft and install the attaching nut.

8. Install the wiper motor while guiding the crank arm through cowl opening.

9. Install the wiper motor to the chassis and install the attaching bolts.

10. Connect the blower motor electrical connectors to the wiper harness connectors and connect the washer hoses.

11. Connect the wiper arm drive link to the crank arm.

12. Install the top vent screen shroud in place to the cowl area.

13. Install the left and right wiper arms.

14. Connect the negative battery cable.

Windshield Wiper Switch

REMOVAL AND INSTALLATION

1. Disconnect the negative battery cable.

2. Remove the instrument cluster bezel.

3. Squeeze the small knob at the side and pull straight out.

4. Insert a small flat blade into the slots adjacent to the center of the inner knob to disengage the knob from the switch.

5. Remove the screws attaching the switch to the bezel.

6. Remove the switch.

To install:

7. Install the switch to the bezel. Install the attaching screws.

8. Position the inner knob on the switch. Ensure the tabs are lined up with the slots and press to secure the knob.

9. Position the outer knob on the switch and align the D-shaped hole in the knob to the shaft on the switch and press to secure the knob.

10. Install the instrument cluster bezel.

11. Connect the negative battery cable.

Instrument Cluster Bezel

REMOVAL AND INSTALLATION

1. Disconnect the negative battery cable.

2. Remove the bezel-to-instrument panel screws.

3. Pull the bezel to the rear to disengage the retaining clips.

4. Disconnect the headlight and windshield wiper switch electrical connectors.

5. If removing the switches, remove the screws attaching the switches to the bezel.

6. Remove the clips, as required.

To install:

7. If removed, install the clips to the bezel.

8. If removed, install the headlight and windshield wiper switches to the bezel and install the attaching screws.

9. Install the switch knobs.

10. Connect the electrical connectors.

11. Position the bezel and press in to engage the retaining clips.

12. Install the instrument panel-to-bezel screws.

13. Connect the negative battery cable.

Instrument Cluster

REMOVAL AND INSTALLATION

The speedometer and gauge cluster are replaced as an assembly.

NOTE: Whenever working on any electronic equipment, make sure to have a clean, static free environment in which to work. Always cover the work surface with a mat that is grounded and static free. Static electricity from walking across the floor or sliding across a vehicle's seat is enough to damage any equipment.

1. Disconnect the negative battery cable.
2. Remove the instrument cluster bezel.
3. Remove the instrument cluster-to-instrument panel attaching screws.
4. Remove the instrument cluster. The electrical connector will release as the cluster is removed.
To install:
5. Carefully, install the instrument cluster. The electrical connector will align and engage as the cluster is pushed into position.
6. Install the instrument cluster bezel.
7. Connect the negative battery cable.

Headlight Switch

REMOVAL AND INSTALLATION

1. Disconnect the negative battery cable.
2. Remove the instrument cluster bezel.
3. Squeeze the small knob at the side and pull straight out.
4. Insert a small flat blade into the slots adjacent to the center of the inner knob to disengage the knob from the switch.
5. Remove the screws attaching the switch to the bezel.
6. Remove the switch.
To install:
7. Install the switch to the bezel. Install the attaching screws.
8. Position the inner knob on the switch. Ensure the tabs are lined up with the slots and press to secure the knob.
9. Position the outer knob on the switch and align the D-shaped hole in the knob to the shaft on the switch and press to secure the knob.

10. Install the instrument cluster bezel.
11. Connect the negative battery cable.

Dimmer Switch

REMOVAL AND INSTALLATION

1. Disconnect the negative battery cable.
2. Disable the Supplemental Inflatable Restraint (SIR) system.
3. Place the ignition switch in the **OFF-LOCK** position.
4. Remove the left side sound insulator panel.
5. Remove the bolts from the lower steering column support.
6. Remove the flange and coupling pinch bolt.
7. Remove the upper and lower bolts from the upper steering column support.
8. Disconnect the dimmer and ignition switch electrical connectors.
9. Lower the steering column.
10. Remove the hexagonal nut and bolt/screw attaching the dimmer switch.

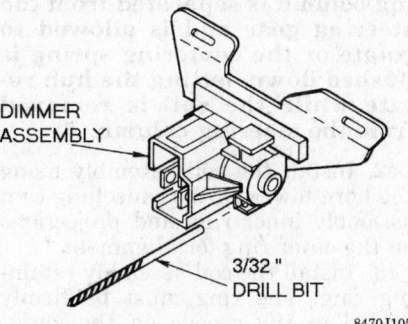

Adjusting the dimmer switch — 1993 shown

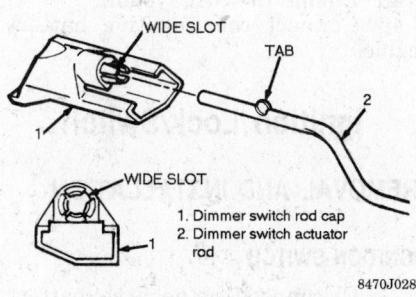

1. Dimmer switch rod cap
2. Dimmer switch actuator rod

Dimmer switch rod installation

11. Disengage the dimmer switch actuator from the switch and remove the switch.
To install:
12. Ensure the ignition switch is in the **OFF-LOCK** position.
13. Engage the dimmer switch actuator rod in the dimmer switch and position the dimmer switch on the mounting stud.
14. Install the nut and bolt/screw. Do not tighten.
15. Adjust the dimmer switch by inserting a 3/32 in. drill bit or a 2.34mm diameter gauge pin into the adjustment hole in the dimmer switch. Push the switch against the actuator rod to remove all the lash.
16. Tighten the nut and screw to 35 inch lbs. (4 Nm).
17. Remove the adjustment tool from the dimmer switch.
18. Support the steering column and install the column into the flange and coupling assembly.
19. Connect the dimmer and ignition switch electrical connectors.
20. Raise the column into position and loosely install the lower bolts to the upper steering column support bracket.
21. Install the lower steering column support bracket bolts. Tighten to 22 ft. lbs. (30 Nm).
22. Install the upper bolts to the upper steering column support bracket. Tighten the upper and lower bolts to 21 ft. lbs. (28 Nm).
23. Install the flange and coupling assembly pinch bolt. Tighten to 30 ft. lbs. (41 Nm).
24. Install the right side sound insulator panel.
25. Enable the SIR system.
26. Connect the negative battery cable.

Turn Signal Switch

REMOVAL AND INSTALLATION

1. Disconnect the negative battery cable.
2. Disable the SIR system.
3. Remove the steering wheel.
4. Remove the coil assembly retaining ring.
5. Lift the coil assembly from the end of the steering shaft and allow coil to hang freely.
6. Remove the wave washer.
7. If equipped with a standard column, remove the spacer shaft lock.
8. Remove the shaft lock retaining ring using tool J–23653–C or equivalent, to compress the shaft lock.

9. Pry off the retaining ring.

10. Remove the shaft lock.

11. Remove the turn signal cancelling cam assembly.

12. Remove the upper bearing spring.

13. Position the turn signal lever to the right turn position.

14. Remove the multi-function lever by performing the following:

a. Ensure the lever is in the center or **OFF** position.

b. If equipped with cruise control, disconnect the cruise control connector from the steering column assembly.

c. Pull the lever straight out of the turn signal switch.

15. Remove the hazard knob assembly.

16. Remove the screw and signal switch arm. If equipped with tilt column and cruise control, allow the switch arm to hang freely.

17. Remove the turn signal switch screws. Allow the switch to hang freely.

18. Disconnect the turn signal/hazard switch assembly terminal from the instrument panel harness.

19. If equipped with tilt column, disconnect the buzzer switch assembly terminals from the turn signal/hazard assembly connector. Remove the tan/black wire lead from cavity E and the light green wire from the cavity F.

20. Remove the upper steering column bolts.

21. Remove the wiring protector.

22. Connect a length of wire to the turn signal/hazard assembly terminal connector to aid in reassembly.

23. Gently pull the wire harness through the steering column housing shroud, steering column housing and lock assembly cover.

24. Disconnect the wire from the connector.

To install:

25. Connect the wire to the turn signal/hazard switch assembly connector.

26. Gently pull the connector through the steering column housing shroud, steering column housing and lock assembly cover.

27. Remove the wire.

28. Install the wiring protector.

29. If disconnected, connect the buzzer switch terminals to the turn signal/hazard switch assembly connector. Insert the tan/black wire lead into cavity E and the light green wire into cavity F.

30. Connect the turn signal/hazard switch assembly connector to the instrument panel harness.

31. Install the steering column support bracket bolts to the steering column. Tighten to 22 ft. lbs. (30 Nm).

32. Install the steering column upper support bolts. Tighten to 20 ft. lbs. (28 Nm).

33. Install the turn signal switch assembly and attaching screws. Tighten to 20 inch lbs. (2.3 Nm).

34. Install the hazard knob assembly.

35. Install the multi-function lever by performing the following:

a. Align the tab on the turn signal switch with the notch in the pivot of the turn signal switch.

b. Push the lever into the turn signal switch.

c. If equipped with cruise control, connect the connector to the steering column assembly.

36. Install the turn signal cancelling cam assembly. Lubricate with a synthetic grease.

37. Install the shaft lock.

38. Install the shaft lock retaining ring, aligning the block tooth on the shaft. Use tool J–23653–C to compress the shaft lock.

39. If equipped with a standard column, install the spacer shaft lock.

40. Install the wave washer.

41. Ensure the coil assembly is centered.

NOTE: The coil assembly will become uncentered if the steering column is separated from the steering gear and is allowed to rotate or the centering spring is pushed down, letting the hub rotate while the coil is removed from the steering column.

42. Install the coil assembly using the horn tower on the cancelling cam assembly inner ring and projections on the outer ring for alignment.

43. Install the coil assembly retaining ring. The ring must be firmly seated in the groove on the shaft. Gently pull the lower coil assembly wire to remove any wire kinks that may be inside the column.

44. Install the steering wheel.

45. Enable the SIR system.

46. Connect the negative battery cable.

Ignition Lock/Switch

REMOVAL AND INSTALLATION

IGNITION SWITCH

1. Disconnect the negative battery cable.

2. Disable the SIR system.

3. Place the ignition switch in the **OFF-LOCK** position.

4. Remove the left side sound insulator panel.

5. Remove the bolts from the lower steering column support.

6. Remove the flange and coupling pinch bolt.

7. Remove the upper and lower bolts from the upper steering column support.

8. Disconnect the dimmer and ignition switch electrical connectors.

9. Lower the steering column.

10. Remove the hexagonal nut and bolt/screw attaching the dimmer switch.

11. Disengage the dimmer switch actuator from the switch and remove the switch.

12. Remove the ignition switch stud.

13. Disconnect the ignition switch actuator rod.

14. Disconnect the park lock cable from the ignition switch.

15. Remove the ignition switch.

To install:

16. Ensure the ignition switch is in the **OFF-LOCK** position.

17. Adjust the ignition switch by performing the following:

a. Place the ignition switch slider in the far left position and move back 1 detent to the right of the **OFF-LOCK** position.

b. Insert a ³/₃₂ in. drill bit or a 2.34mm diameter gauge pin into the adjustment hole in the ignition switch to hold the switch slider in the proper position during installation.

18. Connect the park lock switch to the ignition switch.

19. Connect the ignition switch actuator rod.

20. Install the ignition switch mounting stud. Tighten to 35 inch lbs. (4 Nm).

21. Remove the adjustment tool from the ignition switch.

22. Engage the dimmer switch actuator rod in the dimmer switch and position the dimmer switch on the mounting stud.

23. Install the nut and bolt/screw. Do not tighten.

24. Adjust the dimmer switch by inserting a ³/₃₂ in. drill bit or a 2.34mm diameter gauge pin into the adjustment hole in the dimmer switch. Push the switch against the actuator rod to remove all the lash.

25. Tighten the nut and screw to 35 inch lbs. (4 Nm).

26. Remove the adjustment tool from the dimmer switch.

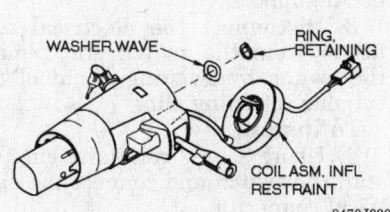

SIR coil assembly installation

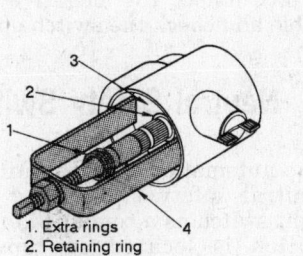

1. Extra rings
2. Retaining ring
3. Shaft lock
4. Shaft lock retaining ring compressor

8470J031

Shaft lock retaining ring removal — SIR equipped steering column

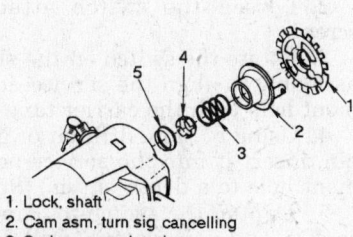

1. Lock, shaft
2. Cam asm, turn sig cancelling
3. Spring, upper bearing
4. Seat, upper bearing inner race
5. Race, inner

8470J032

Lock plate steering column assembly

27. Support the steering column and install the column into the flange and coupling assembly.

28. Connect the dimmer and ignition switch electrical connectors.

29. Raise the column into position and loosely install the lower bolts to the upper steering column support bracket.

30. Install the lower steering column support bracket bolts. Tighten to 22 ft. lbs. (30 Nm).

31. Install the upper bolts to the upper steering column support bracket. Tighten the upper and lower bolts to 21 ft. lbs. (28 Nm).

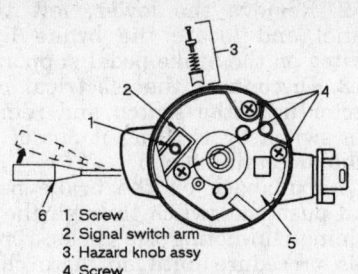

6 1. Screw
   2. Signal switch arm
   3. Hazard knob assy
   4. Screw
   5. Turn signal/hazard switch assy
   6. Multi-function turn signal lever

8470J033

Turn signal switch assembly and component locations — tilt column shown

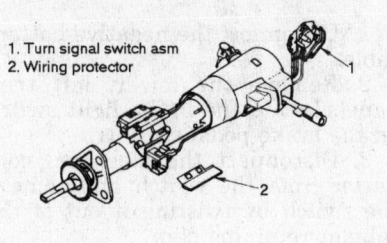

1. Turn signal switch asm
2. Wiring protector

8470J106

Turn signal switch removal — tilt column shown

32. Install the flange and coupling assembly pinch bolt. Tighten to 30 ft. lbs. (41 Nm).

33. Install the right side sound insulator panel.

34. Enable the SIR system.

35. Connect the negative battery cable.

LOCK CYLINDER

1. Disconnect the negative battery cable.

2. Disable the SIR system.

3. Remove the steering wheel.

4. Remove the coil assembly retaining ring.

5. Lift the coil assembly from the end of the steering shaft and allow coil to hang freely.

6. Remove the wave washer.

7. If equipped with a standard column, remove the spacer shaft lock.

8. Remove the shaft lock retaining ring using tool J-23653-C or equivalent, to compress the shaft lock.

9. Pry off the retaining ring.

10. Remove the shaft lock.

11. Remove the turn signal cancelling cam assembly.

12. Remove the upper bearing spring.

13. Position the turn signal lever to the right turn position.

14. Remove the multi-function lever by performing the following:

   a. Ensure the lever is in the center or **OFF** position.

   b. If equipped with cruise control, disconnect the cruise control connector from the steering column assembly.

   c. Pull the lever straight out of the turn signal switch.

15. Remove the hazard knob assembly.

16. Remove the screw and signal switch arm. If equipped with tilt column and cruise control, allow the switch arm to hang freely.

17. Remove the turn signal switch screws. Allow the switch to hang freely.

18. Disconnect the turn signal/hazard switch assembly terminal from the instrument panel harness.

19. If equipped with tilt column, disconnect the buzzer switch assembly terminals from the turn signal/hazard assembly connector. Remove the tan/black wire lead from cavity E and the light green wire from the cavity F.

20. Remove the upper steering column bolts.

21. Remove the wiring protector.

22. Connect a length of wire to the turn signal/hazard assembly terminal connector to aid in reassembly.

23. Gently pull the wire harness through the steering column housing shroud, steering column housing and lock assembly cover.

24. Disconnect the wire from the connector.

25. Ensure the lock cylinder is in the **LOCK** position. Remove the lock cylinder attaching screw.

26. Remove the lock cylinder.

To install:

27. Install the lock cylinder and attaching screw. Tighten to 40 inch lbs. (4 Nm).

28. Turn the ignition key to **RUN** position.

29. Install the buzzer swit

30. Connect the wire t signal/hazard switc connector.

31. Gently pull through the steer shroud, steerin lock assembly

32. Remov

33. Inst

34. I buzz sig r int into

35. Connect the turn signal/hazard switch assembly connector to the instrument panel harness.

36. Install the steering column support bracket bolts to the steering column. Tighten to 22 ft. lbs. (30 Nm).

37. Install the steering column upper support bolts. Tighten to 20 ft. lbs. (28 Nm).

38. Install the turn signal switch assembly and attaching screws. Tighten to 20 inch lbs. (2 Nm).

39. Install the hazard knob assembly.

40. Install the multi-function lever by performing the following:

a. Align the tab on the turn signal switch with the notch in the pivot of the turn signal switch.

b. Push the lever into the turn signal switch.

c. If equipped with cruise control, connect the connector to the steering column assembly.

41. Install the turn signal cancelling cam assembly. Lubricate with a synthetic grease.

42. Install the shaft lock.

43. Install the shaft lock retaining ring, lining up to block tooth on the shaft. Use tool J–23653–C to compress the shaft lock.

44. If equipped with a standard column, install the spacer shaft lock.

45. Install the wave washer.

46. Ensure the coil assembly is centered.

NOTE: The coil assembly will become uncentered if the steering column is separated from the steering gear and is allowed to rotate or the centering spring is pushed down, letting the hub rotate while the coil is removed from the steering column.

47. Install the coil assembly using the horn tower on the cancelling cam assembly inner ring and projections on the outer ring for alignment.

48. Install the coil assembly retaining ring. The ring must be firmly seated in the groove on the shaft. Gently pull the lower coil assembly wire to remove any wire kinks that may be inside the column.

Install the steering wheel.

Enable the SIR system.

Connect the negative battery

ake Light Switch

ENT

ect the negative battery

2. Remove the lower, left trim panel and locate the brake light switch on the brake pedal support.

3. Disconnect the electrical connector from the switch and remove the switch by twisting it out of the tubular retaining clip.

4. Pull back on the brake pedal and push the switch through the retaining clip noting the clicks; repeat this procedure until no more clicks can be heard.

5. Connect the electrical connector to the switch.

6. Connect the negative battery cable and check the switch operation.

REMOVAL AND INSTALLATION

1. Disconnect the negative battery cable.

2. Remove the lower, left trim panel. Locate the brake light switch on the brake pedal support.

3. Disconnect the electrical connector from the switch and remove the switch by twisting it out of the tubular retaining clip.

To install:

4. Using a new retaining clip, install the switch and connect the electrical connector.

5. To adjust the switch, pull back on the brake pedal, push the switch through the retaining clip noting the clicks; repeat this procedure until no more clicks can be heard.

6. Connect the negative battery cable and check the switch operation.

Clutch Switch

ADJUSTMENT

1. Disconnect the negative battery cable.

2. Remove the lower, left trim panel and locate the switch on the clutch pedal support.

3. Disconnect the electrical connector from the switch and remove the switch by twisting it out of the tubular retaining clip.

4. Pull back on the clutch pedal and push the switch through the retaining clip noting the clicks; repeat this procedure until no more clicks can be heard.

5. Connect the electrical connector to the switch.

6. Connect the negative battery cable and check the switch operation.

REMOVAL AND INSTALLATION

1. Disconnect the negative battery cable.

2. Remove the lower, left trim panel. Locate the switch on the clutch pedal support.

3. Disconnect the electrical connector from the switch and remove the switch by twisting it out of the tubular retaining clip.

To install:

4. Using a new retaining clip, install the switch and connect the electrical connector.

5. To adjust the switch, pull back on the clutch pedal, push the switch through the retaining clip noting the clicks; repeat this procedure until no more clicks can be heard.

6. Connect the negative battery cable and check the switch operation.

Neutral Safety Switch

The automatic transaxle utilizes the neutral safety switch and backup light switch as a combined unit. This switch is located on top of the transaxle.

ADJUSTMENT

1. Disconnect the negative battery cable.

2. Loosen the switch attaching screws.

3. Rotate the switch on the shifter assembly to align the service adjustment hole with the carrier tang hole.

4. Using a 3/32 in. drill bit or gauge pin, insert it into the service adjustment hole to a depth of 3/8 in. (9mm).

5. Tighten the switch-to-transaxle screws and remove the drill bit or gauge pin.

6. Connect the negative battery cable and test the switch operation.

REMOVAL AND INSTALLATION

1. Disconnect the negative battery cable and the electrical connector from the switch.

2. Remove the switch-to-transaxle screws and the switch.

To install:

3. Place the transaxle shift control lever in the **N** notch in the detent plate.

4. Position the switch onto the transaxle and install the screws loosely.

5. Perform a switch adjustment.

6. Connect the negative battery cable.

7. Start the engine and check the switch operation.

Backup Light Switch

The backup light switch applies to the manual transaxle only and is located on top of the transaxle.

REMOVAL AND INSTALLATION

1. Disconnect the negative battery cable.
2. Disconnect the electrical connector at the switch.
3. Screw the backup light switch out of the transaxle.
To install:
4. Prior to installing the switch, apply an approved thread sealant to the threads of the new switch.
5. Thread the backup light switch into the transaxle.
6. Tighten the switch to 84 inch lbs. (9 Nm) and connect the electrical connector.
7. Connect the negative battery cable.

Fuses, Circuit Breakers and Relays

LOCATION

Fuse Panel

The fuse panel is located on the left side of the instrument panel assembly. In order to gain access to the fuse panel, it is necessary to first remove the lower trim panel.

Fusible Links

Fusible Links A and E — located rear of the engine compartment, at the battery junction box.
Fusible Links B, C and D — located at the front section of the engine at the starter solenoid.
Fusible Link F — located on the left side of the engine compartment near the battery.

Circuit Breakers

Circuit breakers No. 12 and No 15 are located in fuse block.

Relays

The coolant fan, air conditioning compressor, air conditioning high blower speed and fuel pump relays are all located in the engine compartment mounted to the center of the firewall on the relay bracket.

Computers

LOCATION

The electronic control module is located on the right side of the vehicle. It is positioned up behind the glove box. In order to gain access to the electronic control module, remove the right side trim panel and/or glove box assembly.

Flashers

LOCATION

Turn Signal Flasher — located behind the lower left side of the instrument panel on the steering column.
Hazard Signal Flasher — located behind the lower left side of the instrument panel on the steering column.

Cruise Control

ADJUSTMENT

Control Cable

1. With the servo cable installed on the brackets, place the cable over the stud on the servo lever so the stud engages the slot in the cable end.
2. Connect the cable to the throttle lever and release the lever.
3. Pull the servo end of the cable towards the servo as far as possible without moving the throttle.
4. Attach the cable to the servo in the closest alignment holes without moving the throttle.

NOTE: Do not stretch the cable to attach it to the servo. This will not allow the engine to return to idle.

5. The cable is now adjusted properly.
6. Start the engine and turn **ON** the speed control main switch.
7. Drive the vehicle above 25 mph.
8. Engage the speed control and check the following functions: ser, disengage, coast and resume.

Brake Pedal Release Switch

The brake pedal release switch is located at the top of the brake pedal, directly above the brake pedal switch.
1. Remove the lower steering column cover.

2. Pull the brake pedal release switch from the mounting bracket.
3. Depress the brake pedal and insert the brake pedal release switch into the tubular retainer bracket until it seats on the retainer.

NOTE: Clicks can be heard as the threaded portion of the valve passes through the retainer toward the brake pedal.

4. Pull the brake pedal rearward against the pedal stop until audible clicks can no longer be heard.
5. Release the brake pedal and again, pull the pedal rearward to make sure no more clicks can be heard.
6. Install the lower steering column panel.

Clutch Pedal Release Switch

The clutch pedal release switch is located at the top of the clutch pedal.
1. Remove the lower steering column cover.
2. Pull the clutch pedal release switch from the mounting bracket.
3. Depress the clutch pedal and insert the clutch pedal release switch into the tubular retainer bracket until it seats on the retainer.

NOTE: Clicks can be heard as the threaded portion of the valve passes through the retainer toward the clutch pedal.

4. Pull the clutch pedal rearward against the pedal stop until audible clicks can no longer be heard.
5. Release the clutch pedal and again, pull the pedal rearward to make sure no more clicks can be heard.
6. Reinstall the lower steering column panel.

ENGINE COOLING

Radiator

REMOVAL AND INSTALLATION

——— **CAUTION** ———
Before attempting any work on the cooling system, allow the engine to first cool sufficiently. To avoid personal injury, do not remove the radiator cap while the engine is at or above normal operation temperature.

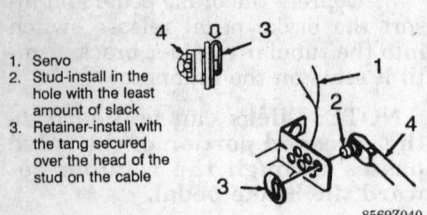

1. Servo
2. Stud-install in the hole with the least amount of slack
3. Retainer-install with the tang secured over the head of the stud on the cable

8569Z040

Servo cable adjustment

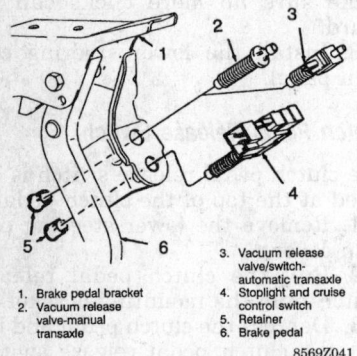

1. Brake pedal bracket
2. Vacuum release valve/switch-manual transaxle
3. Vacuum release valve/switch-automatic transaxle
4. Stoplight and cruise control switch
5. Retainer
6. Brake pedal

8569Z041

Cruise control vacuum valve/switch installation

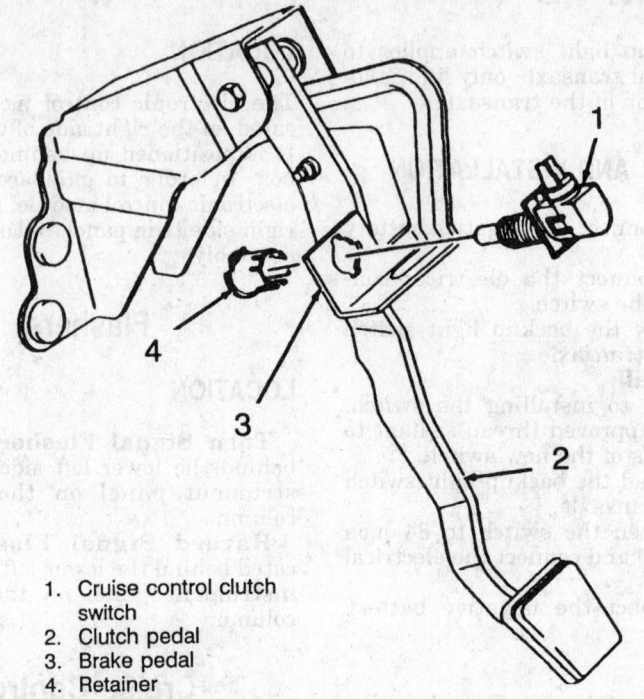

1. Cruise control clutch switch
2. Clutch pedal
3. Brake pedal
4. Retainer

8569Z042

Cruise control clutch switch installation

1. Disconnect the negative battery cable. Remove the battery on 3.1L engine.

2. Remove the air cleaner assembly.

3. Drain the engine coolant into a clean container for reuse.

4. Disconnect the electrical connection from the electric fan.

5. Remove the fan-to-chassis mounting bolts and remove the fan assembly.

6. Disconnect the radiator upper and lower hoses at the radiator end.

7. If equipped with an automatic transaxle, disconnect the transaxle cooler lines and plug.

8. If equipped with A/C, disconnect the condenser line retaining clip.

9. Remove the upper radiator mounting bolts.

10. Remove the condenser-to-radiator mounting bolts.

11. Carefully lift the radiator out.

To install:

12. Install the radiator in the vehicle.

13. Install the condenser-to-radiator mounting bolts.

14. Install the upper radiator mounting bolts.

15. Tighten the radiator mounting bolts to 90 inch lbs. (10 Nm).

16. If equipped with an automatic transaxle, connect the transaxle cooler lines.

17. Connect the radiator upper and lower hoses at the radiator end.

18. Install the fan assembly and the fan-to-chassis mounting bolts.

19. Connect the electrical connection to the electric fan.

20. Connect the negative battery cable. Install the battery to the 3.1L engine.

21. Fill cooling system and check for leaks. Start the engine and allow to come to normal operating temperature. Recheck for leaks. Top-up coolant.

22. Install the air cleaner assembly.

Electric Cooling Fan

TESTING

Coolant Temperature Switch

The coolant temperature switch is located at the left side of the engine on the coolant outlet on the 2.2L engine. On the left rear of side of the engine on the 2.3L engine or on the top left side of the engine on the 3.1L engine.

1. Drain the cooling system to a level below the coolant temperature switch.

2. Disconnect the electrical connector and remove the switch.

3. Using an ohmmeter, connect it's leads to the switch and submerge the tip of the switch in a container of water.

4. Heat the water to at least 230°F (108°C); the switch should close and cause the ohmmeter to show conductivity.

5. Allow the switch to cool to at least 220°F (101°C); the switch should open and cause the ohmmeter to show no conductivity.

6. If the switch does respond accordingly, replace it.

Coolant Fan Pressure Switch

If equipped with air conditioning, the coolant fan pressure switch is located on the refrigerant line at the front, right side of the engine compartment.

When the air conditioning switch is turned **ON** and the low pressure switch is CLOSED, the cooling fan will turn ON.

Electric Fan Relay

The electric fan relay is located at the center, front of the dash on the relay block.

The ECM reads the sensor information and sends an electrical impulse to the relay's primary circuit causing the cooling fan to turn ON.

REMOVAL AND INSTALLATION

1. Disconnect the negative battery cable.
2. Disconnect the electrical wiring harness from the cooling fan frame.
3. Remove the fan assembly from the radiator support.

To install:

4. Install the fan assembly to the radiator support. Tighten the fan assembly-to-radiator support bolts to 7 ft. lbs. (10 Nm).
5. Connect the cooling fan electrical connector.
6. Connect the negative battery cable.

Heater Core

REMOVAL AND INSTALLATION

1. Disable the SIR system.
2. Disconnect the negative battery cable and remove the radio from the vehicle.
3. Gaining access through the radio opening, release the heater core cover clips.

4. Remove the heater floor outlet screws and turn the outlet clockwise and to the right to release.
5. Drain the engine coolant into a clean container for reuse.
6. Raise and safely support the vehicle.
7. Disconnect the heater hoses from the heater core and drain the tube elbow from the heater core cover.
8. Lower the vehicle and remove the heater core cover screws and the heater core cover.
9. Remove the heater core screws and clamps and remove the heater core from the vehicle.

To install:

10. Position the heater core in place and install the core straps and screws. Tighten the screws to 12 inch lbs. (1.4 Nm).
11. Install the heater core cover and screws.
12. Reach through the radio opening and position the heater core cover under the clips.
13. Install the radio.
14. Install the floor outlet and screws.
15. Raise and safely support the vehicle.
16. Connect the heater hoses to the heater core and lower the vehicle.

17. Fill the cooling system with coolant and connect the negative battery cable.
18. Enable the SIR system.

Water Pump

REMOVAL AND INSTALLATION

Except 2.3L Engine

1. Disconnect the negative battery cable.
2. Drain the engine coolant into a clean container for reuse.
3. Remove the serpentine drive belt.
4. If equipped with the 3.1L engine, remove the radiator hoses and heater hoses.
5. Remove the water pump pulley bolts and the pulley.
6. Remove the water pump-to-engine bolts and the pump.

To install:

7. Clean the gasket mounting surfaces.
8. Install the water pump and the water pump attaching bolts. Tighten the water pump-to-engine bolts to 14–22 ft. lbs. (19–30 Nm) on the 2.2L engine or to 6–9 ft. lbs. (8–12 Nm) on the 3.1L engine.

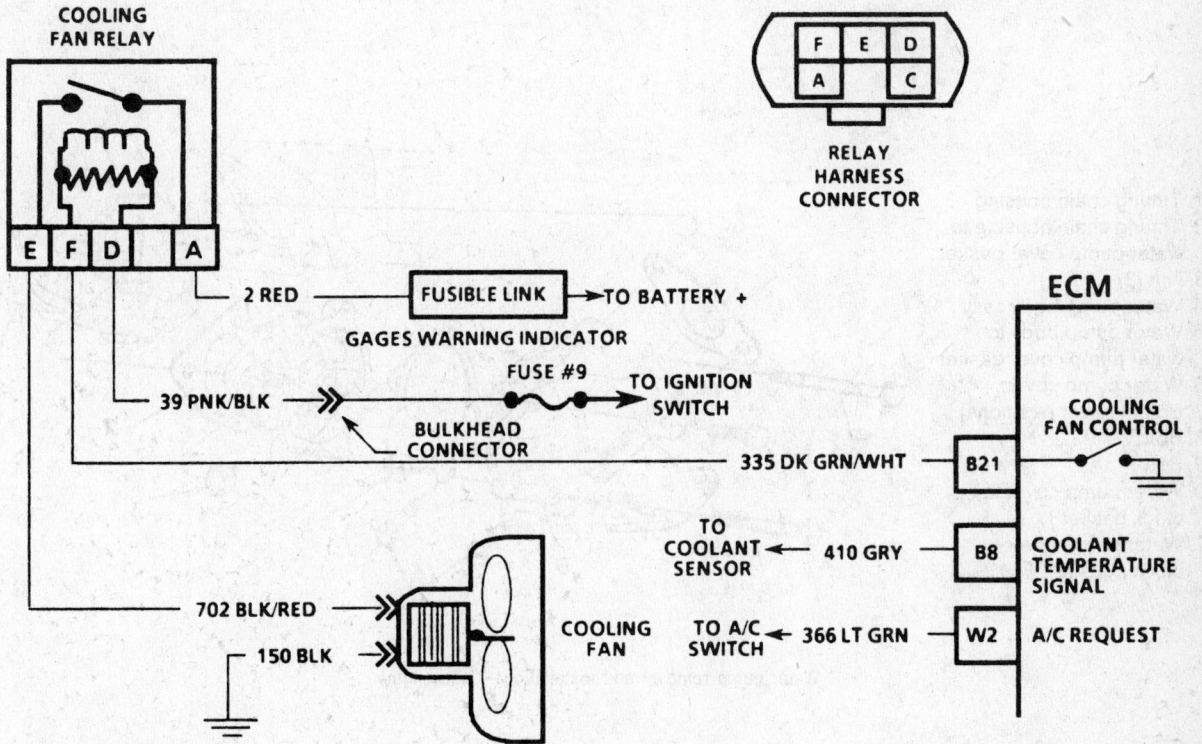

Schematic of the cooling fan system

8470J044

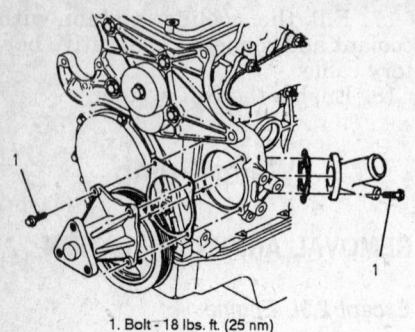

1. Bolt - 18 lbs. ft. (25 nm)

8470J047

Water pump installation — 2.2L engines

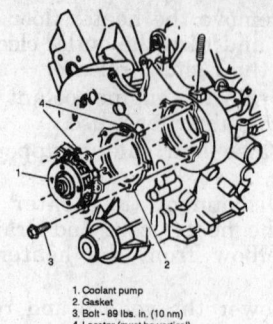

1. Coolant pump
2. Gasket
3. Bolt - 89 lbs. in. (10 nm)
4. Locator (must be vertical)

8470J049

Water pump installation — 3.1L engines

9. Install the water pump pulley and attaching bolts.

10. If equipped with the 3.1L engine, install the radiator hoses and heater hoses.

11. Install the serpentine drive belt.

12. Connect the negative battery cable.

13. Fill cooling system and check for leaks. Start the engine and allow to come to normal operating temperature. Recheck for leaks. Top-up coolant.

2.3L Engine

1. Disconnect the negative battery cable.

2. Drain the engine coolant into a clean container for reuse.

NOTE: Remove the heater hose from the thermostat housing for additional draining.

3. Disconnect the oxygen sensor connector.

4. Remove the upper and lower exhaust manifold heat shield attaching bolts and remove the shields.

5. Remove the exhaust manifold brace-to-manifold attaching bolt.

6. Using a 13mm box wrench, loosen the exhaust pipe-to-manifold spring bolts from the engine compartment.

7. Raise and safely support the vehicle.

8. Remove the bolts from the exhaust flange using a 7/32 in. (5.5mm) socket an 1 bolt rotate clockwise first.

NOTE: Rotating the bolt clockwise is necessary to relieve the spring pressure from 1st bolt prior to removing the 2nd bolt otherwise the exhaust pipe will twist and bind the bolt as it is removed.

9. Thread the bolt with the least amount of pressure on it out 4 turns.

10. Position the other bolt so it can be turned all the way out of the exhaust pipe flange.

11. Return to the 1st bolt and rotate it the rest of the way out.

12. Pull the exhaust pipe back from the exhaust manifold.

13. Remove the radiator outlet pipe from the oil pan and transaxle.

14. Remove the exhaust manifold brace.

15. Pull down on the radiator outlet pipe to disengage it from the water pump.

16. Lower the vehicle.

17. Remove the exhaust manifold-to-cylinder head attaching nuts.

18. Remove the exhaust manifold, seals and gaskets.

1. Timing chain housing
2. Timing chain housing to water pump cover gasket
3. Nut (3)
4. Water pump body assy
5. Water pump body to water pump cover gasket
6. Water pump cover
7. Bolt (3 lower positions)
8. Bolt
9. Bolt
10. Water pump cover to block gasket
11. Water pump cover to block bolts (2)

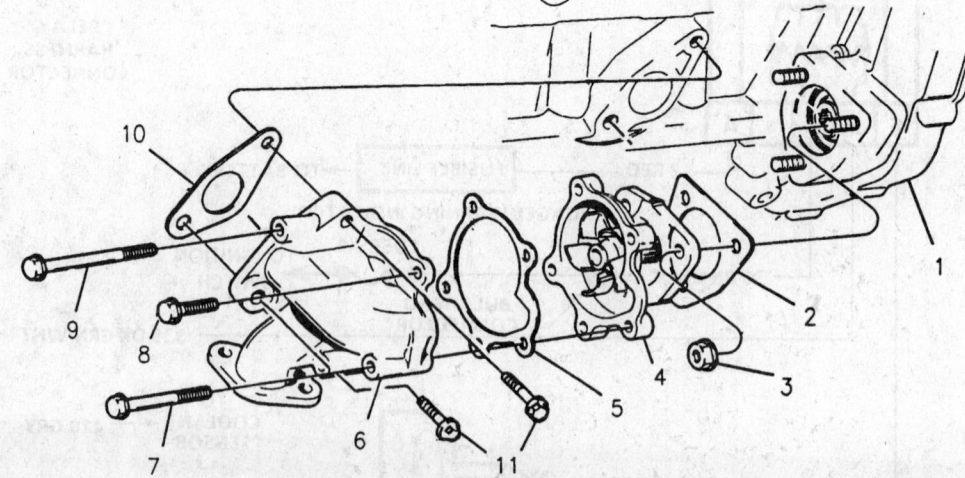

8470J048

Water pump removal and installation — 2.3L engine

19. Remove the water pump cover-to-engine attaching bolts.

20. Remove the water pump-to-timing chain housing attaching nuts.

21. Remove the water pump and cover assembly from the engine.

22. Remove the water pump cover-to-radiator pump assembly.

To install:

NOTE: **Before installing the water pump it is important to first read over the entire procedure. Pay special attention to the tightening sequence, to avoid part damage and to insure proper sealing.**

23. Clean all mating surfaces thoroughly and use new gaskets.

24. Position the water pump cover to the radiator pump assembly and install the attaching bolts. Do not tighten.

25. Lubricate the splines of the radiator pump drive with the an approved chassis grease and install the pump and cover assembly.

26. Install the pump cover-to-engine attaching bolts. Do not tighten.

27. Install the timing chain housing nuts. Do not tighten.

28. Lubricate the O-ring on the radiator outlet pipe with a solution of antifreeze and slide the pipe into the radiator pump cover. Install the attaching bolts. Do not tighten.

29. Tighten the bolts and nuts in following order:

    a. Pump assembly-to-timing chain housing nuts — 19 ft. lbs. (26 Nm).

    b. Water pump-to-pump cover assembly — 106 inch lbs. (12 Nm).

    c. Water Pump cover-to-engine (tighten the bottom bolt first) — 19 ft. lbs. (26 Nm).

    d. Radiator outlet pipe assembly-to-pump cover — 125 ft. lbs. (14 Nm).

30. Install the exhaust manifold with new gaskets.

31. Install the exhaust manifold-to-cylinder head attaching nuts. Tighten the attaching nuts in sequence to 22 ft. lbs. (30 Nm).

32. Raise and safely support the vehicle.

33. Seat the exhaust manifold bolts into the exhaust pipe flange.

34. Using a 7/32 in. (5.5mm) socket start both bolts. Rotate the bolts counterclockwise.

35. Turn both bolts in evenly to avoid cocking the exhaust pipe and binding the bolts. Turn the bolts in until fully seated.

36. Install the radiator outlet pipe to the transaxle and to the oil pan and install the exhaust manifold brace.

37. Lower the vehicle.

38. Install the exhaust manifold brace-to-manifold attaching bolt.

39. Using a 13mm wrench, tighten the exhaust pipe-to-manifold nuts to 22 ft. lbs. (30 Nm).

40. Install the lower heat shields.

41. Connect the oxygen connector to the oxygen sensor.

42. Connect the negative battery cable.

43. Fill cooling system and check for leaks. Start the engine and allow to come to normal operating temperature. Recheck for leaks. Top-up coolant.

Thermostat

REMOVAL AND INSTALLATION

1. Disconnect the negative battery cable.

2. Remove the air cleaner assembly.

3. Drain the engine coolant level below the thermostat housing.

4. Remove the upper radiator hose from the thermostat water outlet and position it to the side.

5. On the 2.3L engine, remove the heater and throttle body coolant hoses from the thermostat housing and disconnect the electrical connector from the coolant temperature sensor.

6. Remove the thermostat attaching bolts.

7. Remove the thermostat housing gasket and thermostat.

To install:

8. Thoroughly clean the mating surfaces of the engine and thermostat.

9. Install the new thermostat, gasket and housing, being careful not to allow the thermostat to slip out of position.

10. Install the attaching bolts and tighten to 6–9 ft. lbs. (8–12 Nm) for the 2.2L engine, 15–22 ft. lbs. (20–30 Nm) for the 3.1L engines or 19 ft. lbs. (26 Nm) for the 2.3L engine.

11. On 2.3L engine, connect the heater and throttle body coolant hoses the thermostat housing and connect the coolant temperature sensor connector.

12. Connect the upper radiator hose to the thermostat housing water outlet.

13. Refill and bleed the cooling system. Start the engine, allow it to reach normal operating temperature and check for leaks.

14. Allow time for the thermostat to open, recheck the coolant level and top up, as required.

Cooling System Bleeding

After working on the cooling system, even to replace the thermostat, the system must be bled. Air trapped in the system will prevent proper coolant circulation and leave the system coolant level low, causing a risk of overheating.

1. To bleed the system, start with the system cool, the radiator cap off and the radiator filled to about an inch below the filler neck.

2. Start the engine and run it at slightly above normal idle speed. This will insure adequate circulation. If air bubbles appear and the coolant level drops, fill the system with a mixture of anti-freeze and water to bring the level back to the proper level.

3. Run the engine this way until the thermostat opens. When this happens, the coolant will move abruptly across the top of the radiator and the temperature of the upper radiator tank and upper radiator hose will rise suddenly.

4. At this point, air is often expelled and the level may drop quite a bit. Keep refilling the system until the level is near the top of the radiator and remains constant.

5. If the vehicle has an overflow tank, fill the radiator up to the top of the filler neck and check the coolant the level in the overflow tank.

FUEL SYSTEM

Fuel System Service Precautions

Safety is the most important factor when performing not only fuel system maintenance but any type of maintenance. Failure to conduct maintenance and repairs in a safe manner may result in serious personal injury or death. Maintenance and testing of the vehicle's fuel system components can be accomplished safely and effectively by adhering to the following rules and guidelines.

• To avoid the possibility of fire and personal injury, always disconnect the negative battery cable unless the repair or test procedure requires that battery voltage be applied.

• Always relieve the fuel system pressure prior to disconnecting any fuel system component (injector, fuel rail, pressure regulator, etc.), fitting or fuel line connection. Exercise extreme caution whenever relieving fuel system pressure to avoid exposing skin, face and eyes to fuel spray. Please be advised that fuel under pressure may penetrate the skin or any part of the body that it contacts.

• Always place a shop towel or cloth around the fitting or connection prior to loosening to absorb any excess fuel due to spillage. Ensure that all fuel spillage (should it occur) is quickly removed from engine surfaces. Ensure that all fuel soaked cloths or towels are deposited into a suitable waste container.

• Always keep a dry chemical (Class B) fire extinguisher near the work area.

• Do not allow fuel spray or fuel vapors to come into contact with a spark or open flame.

• Always use a backup wrench when loosening and tightening fuel line connection fittings. This will prevent unnecessary torsional stress to fuel line piping. Always follow the proper torque specifications.

• Always replace worn fuel fitting O-rings with new. Do not substitute fuel hose or equivalent where fuel pipe is installed.

RELIEVING FUEL SYSTEM PRESSURE

Throttle Body Injection

1. Disconnect the negative battery cable.
2. Remove the fuel filler cap to relieve tank vapor pressure.
3. Wrap a shop towel around the fuel line fitting.
4. Open the fuel line and absorb any excess fuel remaining in the line.
5. When the line fitting is reconnected, use a new O-ring.

Port Fuel Injection

EXCEPT 2.3L ENGINE

1. Disconnect the negative battery cable.
2. Remove the fuel filler cap to relieve tank vapor pressure.

3. Connect a fuel gauge to the fuel pressure test fitting.

NOTE: Be sure to wrap a shop cloth around the fuel line fitting when connecting the fuel gauge tool to the fuel pressure connector.

4. Place the bleeder hose and shop cloth in an approved fuel container. Open the pressure valve to bleed the fuel pressure from the system.
5. After the fuel pressure is bled, retighten the fuel pressure valve.

2.3L ENGINE

1. Loosen the fuel filler cap to relieve the tank pressure.
2. Raise and safely support the vehicle.
3. Disconnect the fuel pump electrical connector.
4. Lower the vehicle.
5. Start the engine and run until the fuel supply remaining in the fuel lines is consumed. Engage the starter for several seconds to assure relief of any remaining pressure.
6. Raise and safely support the vehicle.
7. Connect the fuel pump electrical connector.
8. Lower the vehicle.
9. Disconnect the negative battery cable to avoid possible fuel discharge if an accidental attempt is made to start the engine.

Fuel Filter

REMOVAL AND INSTALLATION

An inline fuel filter is used on all engines. It is located on a frame crossmember near the rear of the vehicle.

Threaded Fuel Line Fitting

1. Relieve the fuel system pressure.
2. Raise and safely support the vehicle.
3. Using a backup wrench, remove the fuel line fittings from the fuel filter.
4. Remove the fuel filter-to-crossmember screws and the filter from the vehicle.
To install:
5. Install the fuel filter and the attaching screws.
6. Replace the fuel filter O-rings.
7. Connect the fuel lines. Using a backup wrench, tighten the fuel line fittings to 22 ft. lbs. (30 Nm).
8. Lower the vehicle.
9. Connect the negative battery cable.

Quick-Connect Fitting

1. Disconnect the negative battery cable.
2. Relieve the fuel system pressure.
3. Raise and safely support the vehicle.
4. Remove the fuel filter attaching screw.

NOTE: If the nylon fuel feed or return connecting lines become kinked and cannot be straightened, they must be replaced.

5. Grasp the filter and 1 nylon fuel connecting line fitting. Twist the quick-connect fitting ¼ turn in each direction to loosen any dirt within the fitting. Repeat for the other nylon fuel connecting line fitting.
6. Using compressed air, blow out any accumulated dirt from the quick-connect fittings at both ends of the fuel filter.
7. Squeeze the plastic tabs of the male end connector and pull connection apart. Repeat for the other fitting.
8. Remove the fuel filter.
To install:
9. Apply a few drops of clean engine oil to the male tube ends of the filter.
10. Remove the protective caps from the new filter.
11. Install new plastic connector retainers on the filter inlet and outlet tubes.
12. Push the connectors together to cause the retaining tabs/fingers to snap into place.
13. Once installed, pull on both ends of each connection to ensure they are secure.
14. Place the fuel filter into position and install the attaching screw.
15. Tighten the fuel filler cap.
16. Connect the negative battery cable.

Electric Fuel Pump

PRESSURE TESTING

PFI System

1. Relieve the fuel system pressure.
2. Using a fuel pressure gauge tool, connect it to the fuel pressure connection fitting on the fuel rail.
3. Using a clean shop cloth, wrap it around the fitting to catch any fuel leakage when connecting the gauge.
4. Turn the ignition ON and read the fuel pressure on the gauge, it should be 37–43 psi.

5. Start the engine and again note the fuel pressure on the gauge.

6. With the engine idling, the fuel pressure should be 33–40 psi. This idle pressure will vary somewhat depending on barometric pressure but it should be lower.

7. Relieve the fuel system pressure and disconnect the gauge.

REMOVAL AND INSTALLATION

The fuel pump is located in the fuel tank. Removal and installation procedures require the fuel tank to be removed from the vehicle.

─────── **CAUTION** ───────

The fuel system pressure must be relieved before attempting any service procedures. Use caution to avoid the risk of fire by disposing of any fuel and fuel soaked rags properly.

───────────────────────

1. Relieve the fuel pressure.
2. Disconnect the negative battery cable.
3. Using a siphon hose and pump, drain the fuel from the fuel tank.
4. Raise and safely support the vehicle.
5. Support the fuel tank and disconnect the retaining straps.
6. Lower the tank enough to disconnect the sending unit wire, the hoses and the ground strap. Remove the fuel tank from the vehicle.
7. Using a locking cam tool, remove the sending unit retaining cam from the fuel tank.
8. Remove the fuel pump and sending unit assembly from the tank. Remove and discard the O-ring gasket.

To install:

9. Install a new O-ring and gasket. Carefully install the fuel pump and sending unit assembly into the fuel tank.
10. Install the retaining cam and lock and secure the sending unit in place to the fuel tank.
11. Raise the tank in position to connect the sending unit wire, the hoses and the ground strap. Install the tank retaining straps and secure the tank in place.
12. Lower the vehicle and refill the tank with fuel.
13. Connect the negative battery cable. Turn the ignition switch to the **ON** position, to restore system pressure.
14. Start the engine and check for fuel leaks.

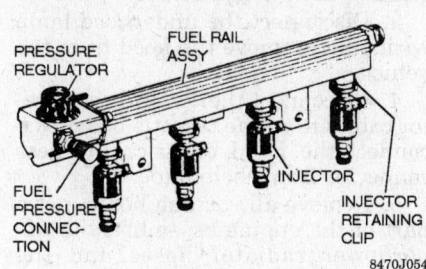

Fuel rail assembly — 2.3L engine

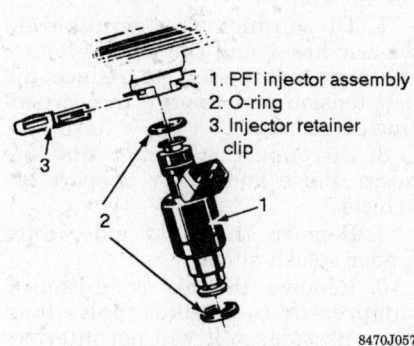

1. PFI injector assembly
2. O-ring
3. Injector retainer clip

8470J057

Fuel injector to fuel rail mounting

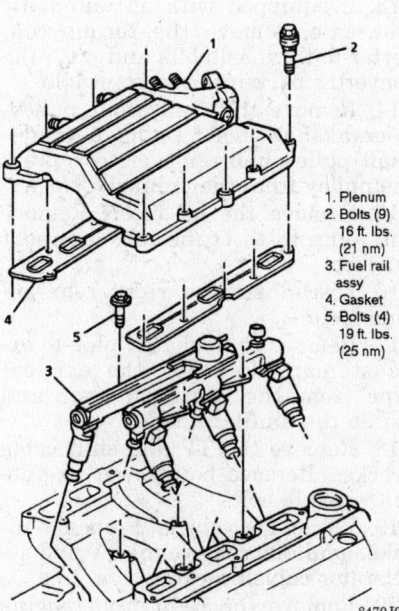

1. Plenum
2. Bolts (9) 16 ft. lbs. (21 nm)
3. Fuel rail assy
4. Gasket
5. Bolts (4) 19 ft. lbs. (25 nm)

8470J055

Fuel rail assembly — 3.1L engine

Fuel Injection

Port Fuel Injection (PFI)

This system uses Bosch fuel injectors, 1 at each intake port. The injectors are mounted on a fuel rail and are activated by a signal from the Electronic Control Module (ECM). The injector is a solenoid operated valve which remains open depending on the width of the electronic pulses, length of the signal from the ECM; the longer the open time, the more fuel is injected. In this manner, the air/fuel mixture can be precisely controlled for maximum performance with minimum emissions. A pressure regulator maintains 28–36 psi in the fuel line to the injectors and the excess fuel is fed back to the tank.

IDLE SPEED AND IDLE MIXTURE ADJUSTMENT

Idle speed and mixture are controlled by the Electronic Control Module (ECM). No adjustments are possible.

Fuel Injector

REMOVAL AND INSTALLATION

2.2L, 2.3L and 3.1L Engines

1. Relieve the fuel system pressure.
2. Disconnect the negative battery cable.
3. Disconnect the fuel line from the fuel rail.
4. Remove the fuel rail-to-intake manifold bolts and the fuel rail assembly from the intake manifold.

NOTE: When removing the fuel rail, the fuel injectors will pull straight out of the intake manifold.

5. Remove the fuel injector-to-fuel rail retaining clips and the injectors from the fuel rail.

To install:

6. Replace the O-rings on the fuel injectors.
7. Install the injectors to the fuel rail and fuel injector-to-fuel rail retaining clips.
8. Install the fuel rail assembly to the intake manifold and the fuel rail-to-intake manifold bolts.
9. Connect the fuel line to the fuel rail.
10. Connect the negative battery cable.

EMISSION CONTROLS

Emission Warning Lamps

RESETTING

When the ECM finds a problem, the Service Engine Soon light will turn ON and a trouble code will be recorded in the ECM memory. If the problem is intermittent, the Service Engine Soon light will light go out after 10 seconds, when the fault goes away. However, the trouble code will stay in the ECM memory until the battery voltage to the ECM is removed. Removing the battery voltage for 10 seconds will clear all stored trouble codes. This is done by disconnecting the ECM harness from the positive battery pigtail for 30 seconds with the ignition **OFF** or by disconnecting the ECM fuse, designated ECM or ECM/BAT, from the fuse holder.

NOTE: To prevent ECM damage, the ignition switch must be OFF when disconnecting or reconnecting power to ECM (for example battery cable, ECM pigtail, ECM fuse, jumper cables, etc.).

ENGINE MECHANICAL

NOTE: Disconnecting the negative battery cable on some vehicles may interfere with the functions of the on board computer systems and may require the computer to undergo a relearning process, once the negative battery cable is reconnected.

Engine Assembly

REMOVAL AND INSTALLATION

2.3L Engines

1. Relieve the fuel system pressure. Disconnect the battery cables (negative cable first). Remove the battery from the vehicle.
2. Position a clean drain pan under the radiator, open the drain cock and drain the cooling system. Remove the air intake hose.
3. Disconnect the underhood lamp wiring and remove the hood from the vehicle.
4. Disconnect the TV and accelerator cables from the throttle body. Disconnect the ECM electrical harness connector from the engine.
5. Remove all vacuum hoses, not a part of the engine assembly, the upper/lower radiator hoses and the heater hoses from the engine.
6. Remove the heat shield from the exhaust manifold. Disconnect and label the engine wiring harness from the firewall.
7. Disconnect the windshield washer hoses and the bottle. Rotate the tensioner pulley, to reduce the belt tension and remove the serpentine drive belt.
8. Disconnect and plug the fuel hoses. Raise and safely support the vehicle.
9. Remove the right side inner fender splash shield.
10. Remove the air conditioning compressor-to-bracket bolts and move it aside, so it will not interfere with the engine removal; do not disconnect the refrigerant lines.
11. Remove the flywheel splash shield. Label and disconnect electrical wires from the starter.
12. Remove the front starter brace, the starter-to-engine bolts and the starter.
13. If equipped with an automatic transaxle, remove the torque converter-to-flywheel bolts and push the converter back into the transaxle.
14. Remove the crankshaft pulley-to-crankshaft bolt. Using a crankshaft pulley hub remover tool, press the pulley from the crankshaft.
15. Remove the oil filter. Remove the engine-to-transaxle support bracket.
16. Disconnect the right rear engine mount.
17. Remove the exhaust pipe-to-exhaust manifold bolts, the exhaust pipe from the center hanger and loosen the muffler hanger.
18. Remove the TV and shift cable bracket. Remove both lower engine-to-transaxle bolts.
19. Lower the vehicle. From the intake manifold, remove the TV and accelerator cable bracket.
20. Remove the right front engine mount nuts. Disconnect the electrical connectors. Remove the alternator-to-bracket bolts and the alternator.
21. Remove the master cylinder-to-booster nuts, move the master cylinder and support it aside; do not disconnect the brake lines.
22. Using a vertical lifting device, install to the engine and lift it slightly.
23. Remove the right front engine mount bracket. Remove the remaining engine-to-transaxle bolts.
24. Remove the power steering pump-to-engine bolts and move it aside; do not disconnect the high pressure hoses.
25. Carefully lift and remove the engine from the vehicle.

To install:
26. Secure the engine on a engine suitable lifting device.
27. Support the transaxle with floor jack.
28. Carefully lower the engine into the vehicle, aligning it to the transaxle.
29. Install the engine-to-transaxle bolts. Install the right front engine mount bracket and attaching nuts.
30. Install the right rear engine mount and attaching bolts.
31. Install the engine-to-transaxle support bracket and attaching bolts.
32. Lower the transaxle jack and remove it from the vehicle.
33. Install the power steering pump and pump-to-engine attaching bolts.
34. Install the master cylinder and the master cylinder-to-booster attaching nuts.
35. Install the alternator, bracket and attaching bolts. Connect the electrical connectors to the alternator.
36. Install the TV and accelerator cable bracket.
37. Install the TV and shift cable bracket.
38. Raise and safely support the vehicle.
39. Install the exhaust pipe to the exhaust manifold and install the center hanger. Install the exhaust pipe-to-exhaust manifold attaching bolts.
40. Install the oil filter.
41. Install the crankshaft pulley on the crankshaft and install the pulley-to-crankshaft attaching bolt.
42. If equipped with an automatic transaxle, install the torque converter-to-flywheel attaching bolts.
43. Install the starter, front starter brace and the starter-to-engine attaching bolts.
44. Connect the electrical wires to the starter.
45. Install the flywheel splash shield.
46. Lower the vehicle.
47. Install the air conditioning compressor, with the refrigerant lines at-

tached. Install the air conditioning compressor-to-bracket bolts.

48. Install the right side inner fender splash shield.

49. Connect the fuel hoses.

50. Install the windshield washer bottle and connect the washer hoses.

51. Rotate the tensioner pulley and install the serpentine drive belt.

52. Install the heat shield to the exhaust manifold. Connect the engine wiring harness to the firewall.

53. Install all vacuum hoses, the upper and lower radiator hoses and heater hoses to the engine.

54. Connect the TV and accelerator cables to the throttle body.

55. Connect the ECM electrical harness connector to the engine.

56. Install the air intake hose and install the hood.

57. Close the radiator pet cock and refill the cooling system.

58. Install the battery and secure it in place. Connect the battery cables (the negative cable first).

59. Start the engine, allow it to reach normal operating temperatures and check for leaks.

2.2L Engine

1. Disconnect the negative battery cable.

2. Relieve the fuel system pressure and drain the cooling system.

3. Disconnect the underhood lamp wiring and remove the hood from the vehicle.

4. Remove the throttle body duct and on the GTZ model, remove the rear firewall cover shield.

5. Remove the battery and the air cleaner housing.

6. Disconnect the upper radiator hose and the brake booster vacuum hose.

7. Remove the upper alternator brace and disconnect the wiring.

8. Disconnect the upper engine harness from the engine.

9. Properly discharge the A/C system and disconnect the compressor-to-condenser and accumulator lines.

10. Raise and safely support the vehicle and remove the engine splash shield.

11. Remove the exhaust system from the vehicle.

12. Disconnect the lower engine wiring.

13. Remove the flywheel inspection cover and remove the front wheels from the vehicle.

14. Remove the lower radiator hose and remove the heater hoses from the heater core.

15. Remove the brake calipers from the discs and support them.

16. Disconnect the tie rods from the struts and lower the vehicle.

17. Remove the clutch slave cylinder.

18. Disconnect the fuel lines.

19. Disconnect the transaxle linkage at the transaxle and disconnect the following cables:
   a. Accelerator cable
   b. Cruise control cable
   c. TV cable (automatic only)

20. Disconnect the transaxle cooling lines from the transaxle (automatic only).

21. Disconnect the power steering hoses from the power steering pump and raise the vehicle.

22. Remove the 4 center support bolts and align and support the engine with the dolly/support fixture.

23. Support the rear of the vehicle and remove the transaxle mount.

24. Remove the upper strut bolts and nuts.

25. Remove the right side engine mount and mount strut.

26. Remove the 4 front and the 4 rear suspension support bolts.

27. Install wire to the front suspension support bolt holes to prevent axle separation.

28. Raise the vehicle and remove the engine and transaxle assembly on the dolly.

To install:

29. Lower the vehicle and raise the engine and transaxle assembly into place.

30. Install the suspension support bolts.

31. Install the transaxle mount, the right engine mount and the engine mount strut. Do not tighten until all 3 are installed.

32. Connect the following:
   a. Power steering hoses
   b. Accelerator cable
   c. Cruise control cable
   d. TV cable
   e. Transaxle cooling lines
   f. Transaxle linkage
   g. Fuel lines

33. Install the clutch slave cylinder and raise the vehicle.

34. Install the tie rods and brake calipers.

35. Connect the heater hoses and lower radiator hoses.

36. Install the A/C compressor to the vehicle.

37. Install the flywheel inspection cover and engine splash shield.

38. Install the front wheels and lower the vehicle.

39. Connect the upper engine wiring and install the A/C condenser and accumulator lines.

40. Connect the brake booster vacuum hose.

41. Install the alternator top brace and connect the wiring.

42. Connect the upper radiator hose and install the upper strut bolts and nuts.

43. Raise the vehicle and connect the lower engine wiring.

44. Install the exhaust system to the vehicle and lower the vehicle.

45. Install the throttle body and the air cleaner. Properly charge the A/C system.

46. Check and adjust the wheel alignment if necessary.

47. Install the hood to the vehicle and connect the hood lamp wiring.

48. Install the rear firewall shield/cover (GTZ only).

49. Install the battery and connect the cables.

3.1L Engine

1. Relieve the fuel pressure. Disconnect the battery cables (negative cable first). Remove the battery from the vehicle.

2. Remove the air cleaner, the air inlet hose and the mass air flow sensor.

3. Position a clean drain pan under the radiator, open the drain cock and drain the cooling system. Remove the exhaust manifold crossover assembly bolts and separate the assembly from the exhaust manifolds.

4. Remove the serpentine belt tensioner and the drive belt. Remove the power steering pump-to-bracket bolts and support the pump aside.

5. Disconnect the radiator hose from the engine.

6. Disconnect the TV and accelerator cables from the throttle valve bracket on the plenum.

7. Disconnect the electrical connectors. Remove the alternator-to-bracket bolts and the alternator. Label and disconnect the electrical wiring harness from the engine.

8. Disconnect and plug the fuel hoses. Remove the coolant overflow and bypass hoses from the engine.

9. From the charcoal canister, disconnect the purge hose. Label and disconnect all the necessary vacuum hoses.

10. Using a engine holding fixture tool, support the engine.

11. Raise and safely support the vehicle.

12. Remove the right inner fender splash shield. Remove the crankshaft pulley-to-crankshaft bolt. Using a wheel puller, press the crankshaft pulley from the crankshaft.

13. Remove the flywheel cover. Label and disconnect the starter wires. Remove the starter-to-engine bolts and the starter.

14. Disconnect the wires from the oil pressure sending unit.

15. Remove the air conditioning compressor-to-bracket bolts and the bracket-to-engine bolts. Support the compressor so it will not interfere with the engine; do not disconnect the refrigerant lines.

16. Disconnect the exhaust pipe from the rear of the exhaust manifold.

17. If equipped with an automatic transaxle, remove the torque converter-to-flywheel bolts and push the converter into the transaxle.

18. Remove the front and rear engine mount bolts along with the mount brackets.

19. Remove the intermediate shaft bracket from the engine.

20. Disconnect the shifter cable from the transaxle.

21. Remove the lower engine-to-transaxle bolts and lower the vehicle.

22. Disconnect the heater hoses from the engine.

23. Using an vertical engine lift, install it to the engine and lift it slightly. Remove the engine holding fixture. Using a floor jack, support the transaxle.

24. Remove the upper engine-to-transaxle bolts. Remove the front engine mount bolts and transaxle mounting bracket.

25. Remove the engine from the vehicle.

To install:

26. Secure the engine on a engine suitable lifting device.

27. Carefully lower the engine into the vehicle, aligning it to the transaxle.

28. Install the upper engine-to-transaxle bolts. Tighten bolts to 55 ft. lbs. (75 Nm).

29. Install the transaxle mount bracket and front engine mount attaching bolts. Tighten the bolts to 65 ft. lbs. (88 Nm).

30. Using a floor jack, support the transaxle and remove the engine lifting device from the engine.

31. Install the lower engine-to-transaxle.

32. Connect the heater hoses to the engine.

33. Connect the shifter cable to the transaxle.

34. Install the intermediate shaft bracket to the engine.

35. Install the front and rear engine mount bolts along with the mount brackets.

36. Lower the jack and remove it from the transaxle.

37. Raise the vehicle and support it safely.

38. If equipped with an automatic transaxle, install the torque converter-to-flywheel bolts.

39. Install the flywheel cover and attaching bolts.

40. Connect the exhaust pipe to the the exhaust manifold and install the attaching bolts.

41. Lower the vehicle.

42. Position the air conditioning compressor, with the lines attached, in place and install the compressor-to-bracket bolts.

43. Install the compressor bracket-to-engine bolts.

44. Connect the wires to the oil pressure sending unit.

45. Connect the starter wires. Position the starter in place and install the starter-to-engine bolts.

46. Install the crankshaft pulley and install the pulley-to-crankshaft bolt. Install the right inner fender splash shield.

47. Connect the purge hose to the charcoal canister. Connect all the necessary vacuum hoses.

48. Connect the coolant overflow and bypass hoses to the engine.

49. Connect the fuel delivery hoses to the engine.

50. Position the alternator in place and install the alternator-to-bracket bolts. Connect the electrical connectors to the alternator.

51. Connect all electrical wiring harnesses to the engine.

52. Connect the TV and accelerator cables to the throttle valve bracket on the plenum.

53. Connect the radiator hoses to the engine.

54. Install the serpentine belt tensioner and the drive belt.

55. Position the power steering pump in place and install the power steering pump-to-bracket bolts.

56. Connect the crossover pipe to the exhaust manifold and install the attaching bolts.

57. Install the air cleaner, air inlet hose and the mass air flow sensor.

58. Close the radiator cock and refill the cooling system.

59. Install the battery and secure it in place. Connect the battery cables (the negative cable last).

60. Start the engine, allow it to reach normal operating temperatures and check for leaks.

Engine Mounts

REMOVAL AND INSTALLATION

Front

1. Disconnect the negative battery cable.

2. Install an engine holding fixture tool and support the engine.

3. Remove the upper mount-to-body bracket bolts.

4. Remove the engine mount-to-engine mount bracket bolts.

5. Raise and safely support the vehicle.

6. Remove the right side inner fender shield.

7. Remove the lower engine mount-to-body bracket bolt.

8. Remove the engine mount.

To install:

9. Install the lower engine mount and the mount-to-body bracket bolt. Tighten to 50 ft. lbs. (68 Nm).

10. Install the engine mount through bolts. Tighten to 35 ft. lbs. (47 Nm).

11. Install the left side inner fender shield.

12. Lower the vehicle.

13. Install the upper engine mount-to-body bracket bolt. Tighten to 50 ft. lbs. (68 Nm).

14. Remove the engine holding fixture tool.

15. Lower the vehicle.

16. Connect the negative battery cable.

Rear

1. Disconnect the negative battery cable.

2. Install an engine holding fixture tool and support the engine.

3. Raise and safely support the vehicle.

4. Remove the engine mount nuts/bolts and the engine mount.

To install:

5. Install the engine mount and the engine mount nuts/bolts. Tighten the mounting bolts to 50 ft. lbs. (68 Nm) and nuts to 18 ft. lbs. (24 Nm).

6. Lower the vehicle.

7. Remove the engine holding fixture.

8. Connect the negative battery cable.

Cylinder Head

REMOVAL AND INSTALLATION

2.2L Engine

1. Relieve the fuel system pressure and disconnect the negative battery cable.
2. Remove the air inlet duct and properly drain the coolant from the cooling system.
3. Disconnect the vacuum lines and electrical connections. Disconnect the accelerator linkage.
4. Remove the coolant reservoir and the serpentine belt.
5. Remove the alternator and the power steering pump.
6. Remove the belt tensioner and the secondary ignition wires.
7. Disconnect the following:
   a. Canister purge line (below the manifold)
   b. Upper radiator hose
   c. Throttle body cables from the bracket
   d. Coolant inlet hose
   e. Fuel lines
8. Remove the intake manifold brace and the valve cover.
9. Remove the rocker arms and pushrods. Keep in order for easier installation.
10. Remove the secondary ignition cable bracket and the engine lift bracket.
11. Remove the exhaust pipe and the head bolts.
12. If equipped with an automatic transaxle, remove the trans fluid level indicator bracket.
13. Remove the cylinder head from the vehicle.

NOTE: Clean all gasket surfaces with plastic or wood scraper. Do not use any sealing material.

To install:
14. Install the cylinder head gasket over the dowel pins and carefully install the head onto the pins and the gasket.
15. Install the cylinder head bolts finger tight and then following the proper sequence tighten the long bolts to 46 ft. lbs. (63 Nm) and the short bolts to 43 ft. lbs. (58 Nm).
16. Tighten all bolts an additional 90 degrees in sequence.
17. Install the throttle body cables and the trans fluid level indicator bracket bolt.
18. Install the engine lift bracket and the secondary ignition cable bracket.

19. Install the rocker arms and the pushrods and install the valve cover.
20. Connect the vacuum lines, fuel lines and electrical connectors.
21. Connect the coolant inlet hose and install the intake manifold brace.
22. Install the upper radiator hose and connect the secondary ignition wires.
23. Install the belt tensioner and the power steering pump.
24. Install the alternator and the serpentine drive belt.
25. Install the coolant reservoir and the air cleaner assembly.
26. Raise the vehicle and connect the exhaust pipe.
27. Lower the vehicle and refill the coolant to the proper level.
28. Inspect for leaks and connect the negative battery cable.

2.3L Engine

1. Relieve the fuel system pressure. Disconnect the negative battery cable. Drain the engine coolant into a clean container for reuse.
2. Disconnect heater inlet and throttle body heater hoses from water outlet. Disconnect upper radiator hose from water outlet.
3. Remove exhaust manifold.
4. Remove intake and exhaust camshaft housings.
5. Remove oil cap and dipstick. Pull oil fill tube upward to unseat from block.
6. Disconnect and tag injector harness electrical connector.
7. Disconnect throttle body to air cleaner duct. Remove throttle cable and bracket and position aside.
8. Remove throttle body from intake manifold with electrical harness, hoses, cable attached and position aside.
9. Disconnect and tag MAP sensor vacuum hose from intake manifold.
10. Remove intake manifold bracket to block bolt.
11. Disconnect and tag 2 coolant sensor connections.
12. Remove cylinder head to block bolts.

NOTE: When removing cylinder head to block bolts follow reverse of tighten sequence.

13. Remove cylinder head and gasket.

NOTE: Clean all gasket surfaces with plastic or wood scraper. Do not use any sealing material.

To install:
14. Install the cylinder head gasket to the cylinder block and carefully position the cylinder head in place.
15. Coat the head bolt threads with clean engine oil and allow the oil to drain off before installing.
16. Tighten the cylinder head bolts in sequence.
17. Install the intake manifold-to-block bracket bolt and bracket.
18. Connect the MAP sensor vacuum hose to the intake manifold.
19. Install the throttle body on the intake manifold with electrical harness, hoses and cable attached.
20. Connect the throttle body-to-air cleaner duct. Install the throttle cable and bracket.
21. Connect the injector harness electrical connector.
22. Connect the 2 coolant sensor connections.
23. Install the oil cap and dipstick. Install the oil fill tube into the block.
24. Install the exhaust and intake camshaft housings.
25. Install the exhaust manifold.
26. Connect the heater inlet and throttle body heater hoses to the water outlet. Connect the upper radiator hose to the water outlet.
27. Fill the cooling system and connect the negative battery cable.
28. Start the engine, allow it to reach operating temperature and check for leaks.

3.1L Engine

LEFT SIDE

1. Relieve the fuel pressure.
2. Disconnect the negative battery cable and remove the air cleaner assembly.
3. Place a drain pan under the radiator and drain the cooling system.
4. Remove the rocker cover attaching bolts and remove rocker cover.
5. Remove the intake manifold-to-cylinder head bolts and the remove the intake manifold.
6. Remove the fuel plenum and fuel rail assembles.
7. Disconnect the exhaust crossover from the right exhaust manifold.
8. Disconnect the oil level indicator tube bracket.
9. Loosen the rocker arms nuts, turn the rocker arms and remove the pushrods.

NOTE: Be sure to keep the parts in order for installation purposes.

10. Remove the cylinder head-to-engine bolts; start with the outer bolts and work toward the center. Re-

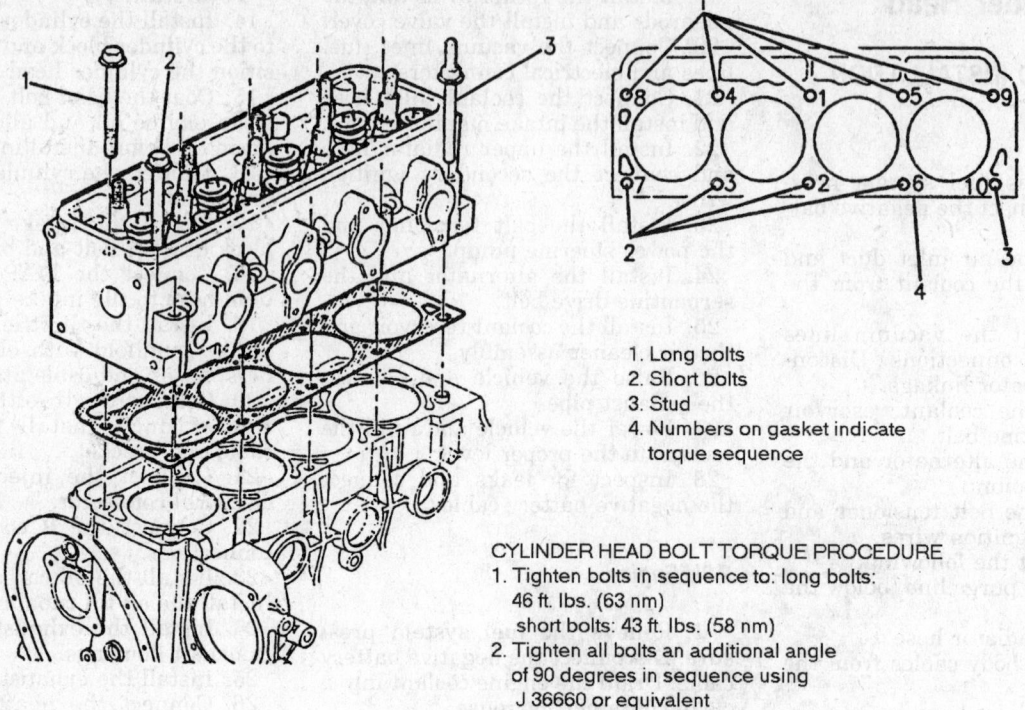

1. Long bolts
2. Short bolts
3. Stud
4. Numbers on gasket indicate torque sequence

CYLINDER HEAD BOLT TORQUE PROCEDURE
1. Tighten bolts in sequence to: long bolts:
   46 ft. lbs. (63 nm)
   short bolts: 43 ft. lbs. (58 nm)
2. Tighten all bolts an additional angle
   of 90 degrees in sequence using
   J 36660 or equivalent

8470J058

2.2L engine cylinder head torque sequence

USE THE TIGHTENING PROCEDURE
DETAILED IN THE TEXT

BOLTS 1 THROUGH 6 – 25 N·m (18 LBS. FT.) PLUS 90°
BOLTS 7 AND 8 – 30 N·m (22 LBS. FT.) PLUS 60°
BOLTS 9 AND 10 – 35 N·m (26 LBS. FT.) PLUS 60°

8470J107

2.3L engine cylinder head torque sequence (1993–96)

USE THE TIGHTENING PROCEDURE
DETAILED IN THE TEXT

BOLTS 1 THROUGH 6 - 35 N·m (26 LBS. FT.)
BOLT 7 AND 8 - 20 N·m (15 LBS. FT.)
BOLTS 9 AND 10 - 30 N·m (22 LBS. FT.)

8470J059

2.3L engine cylinder head torque sequence (1992)

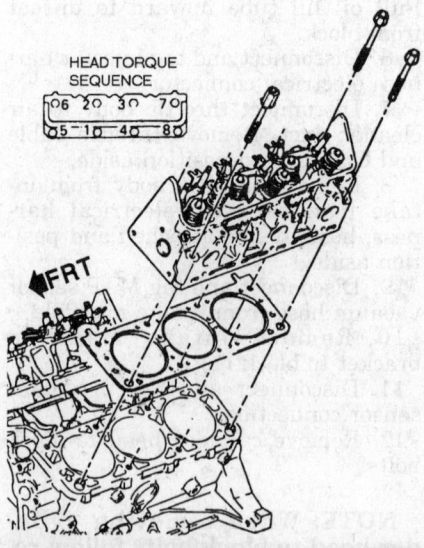

HEAD TORQUE SEQUENCE

8470J061

Cylinder head bolt torque sequence — 3.1L engine

move the cylinder head with the exhaust manifold.

To install:

11. Clean the gasket mounting surfaces. Inspect the surfaces of the cylinder head, block and intake manifold damage and/or warpage. Clean the threaded holes in the block and the cylinder head bolt threads.

12. Using new gaskets, align the new cylinder head gasket over the dowels on the block with the note **This Side Up** facing the cylinder head.

13. Install the cylinder head and exhaust manifold crossover assembly on the engine.

14. Coat the cylinder head bolt threads with engine oil and install the hand tight.

15. Using the proper torque sequence, tighten the bolts to 33 ft. lbs. (45 Nm). After all bolts are torqued to 33 ft. lbs. (45 Nm), rotate the torque wrench another 90 degrees or 1/4 turn. This will apply the correct torque to the bolts.

16. Install the pushrods in the same order that they were removed. Tighten the rocker arm nuts to 14–20 ft. lbs. (19–27 Nm).

17. Install the intake manifold using a new gasket and following the correct sequence, tighten the bolts to

24 ft. lbs. (33 Nm) and nuts to 18 ft. lbs. (24 Nm).

18. Install the fuel plenum and fuel rail. Tighten the plenum bolts to 16 ft. lbs. (22 Nm).

19. Connect the exhaust crossover to the right exhaust manifold.

20. Connect the oil level indicator tube bracket.

21. Refill the cooling system. Connect the negative battery cable.

22. Operate the engine until normal operating temperatures are reached and check for leaks.

RIGHT SIDE

1. Relieve the fuel pressure. Disconnect the negative battery cable. Drain the cooling system and remove the air cleaner.

2. Raise and safely support the vehicle. Remove the exhaust manifold-to-exhaust pipe bolts and separate the pipe from the manifold.

3. Lower the vehicle. Remove the exhaust manifold-to-cylinder head bolts and exhaust manifold.

4. Remove the rocker arm cover. Remove the intake manifold-to-cylinder head bolts and the intake manifold.

5. Loosen the rocker arms nuts, turn the rocker arms and remove the pushrods.

NOTE: Be sure to keep the components in order for reassembly purposes.

6. Remove the cylinder head-to-engine bolts, starting with the outer bolts, working towards the center of the head.

7. Lift the cylinder head from the engine.

To install:

8. Clean the gasket mounting surfaces. Inspect the parts for damage and/or warpage; if necessary, machine or replace the parts.

9. Clean the engine block's threaded holes and the cylinder head bolt threads.

10. Using new gaskets, reverse the removal procedures. Using sealant, coat the cylinder head bolts and install the bolts hand tight.

11. Using the torquing sequence, tighten the bolts to 33 ft. lbs. (45 Nm). After all bolts are torqued to 33 ft. lbs. (45 Nm), rotate the torque wrench another 90 degrees or ¼ turn; this will apply the correct torque to the bolts.

12. Install the pushrods in the same order as they were removed. Tighten the rocker arm nuts to 14–20 ft. lbs. (19–27 Nm).

13. Follow the torquing sequence, use a new gasket and install the intake manifold.

14. Install the exhaust manifold and exhaust manifold-to-cylinder head bolts.

15. Raise the vehicle and support it safely.

16. Connect the exhaust pipe to the exhaust manifold and install the exhaust manifold-to-exhaust pipe bolts.

17. Lower the vehicle. Refill the cooling system.

18. Connect the negative battery cable. Start the engine, allow it to reach normal operating temperatures and check for leaks.

Valve Lifters

REMOVAL AND INSTALLATION

2.2L Engines

1. Disconnect the negative battery cable. Remove the rocker arm cover.

2. Loosen the rocker arms nuts enough to move the rocker arms aside and remove the pushrods.

3. Using a valve lifter remover tool, remove the lifters from the engine.

To install:

4. Using Molykote® or equivalent, coat the base of the new lifters. Using a valve lifter remover tool, install the lifters into the engine.

5. Install the pushrods and reposition the rocker arms. Tighten the rocker arm nuts to 22 ft. lbs. (30 Nm).

6. Install the rocker arm cover. Tighten the rocker arm cover bolts to 8 ft. lbs. (11 Nm).

7. Connect the negative battery cable.

2.3L Engine

The valve train consists of 2 chain driven overhead camshafts with direct acting lifters, therefore, camshaft removal is necessary in order to gain access to the lifters. Once the camshafts are removed from their mountings the valve lifters can be removed from their bores.

3.1L Engine

1. Disconnect the negative battery cable.

2. Drain the cooling system.

3. Remove the rocker arm covers and intake manifold.

4. Loosen the rocker arm nuts enough to move the rocker arms aside and remove the pushrods.

5. Remove the lifters from the engine.

To install:

6. Using Molykote® or equivalent, coat the base of the new lifters and install them into the engine.

7. Install the pushrods and the reposition the rocker arms. Tighten the rocker arm nuts to 18 ft. lbs. (25 Nm).

8. Install the rocker arm covers.

9. Install the intake manifold. Tighten the intake manifold-to-cylinder head bolts to 20 ft. lbs. (27 Nm).

10. Connect the negative battery cable.

Valve Lash

ADJUSTMENT

The 2.2L and 3.1L engines are originally equipped with hydraulic valve lifters. Hydraulic valve lifters are used in the 2.2L and 3.1L engines and are not adjustable. The 3.1L engine replacement rocker arm stud is adjustable and the adjustment can be performed as listed below. If valve system noise is present, check the torque on the rocker arm nuts. The correct torque is 7–11 ft. lbs. (9–15 Nm) for the 2.2L engines or 14–20 ft. lbs. (19–27 Nm) for the 3.1L engine. If noise is still present, check the condition of the camshaft, lifters, rocker arms, pushrods and valves.

On the 2.3L engine, direct acting hydraulic valve lifters are used. The valve lifter body includes a harden iron contact foot bonded to a steel shell. These lifters are not serviceable or adjustable.

3.1L Engine

NOTE: The following adjustment procedure should be used when reconditioning a valve seat and a new adjustable type rocker arm is used.

1. Install the rocker arms, balls and nuts. Tighten the rocker arm nuts until all of the lash (freeplay) is eliminated.

2. Adjust the valves when the lifter is on the base circle of a camshaft lobe as follows:

a. Place the engine in the number 1 firing position. This can be determined by placing a finger on the number 1 rocker arm as the engine alignment mark on the front face of the of the torsional dampener pulley aligns with the arrow on the front cover. If the valves don't move freely, the engine is in the number 1 firing position. If the valves move freely, the engine is in the number 4 firing position and the engine should be rotated 1 full rotation to reach the number 1 position.

b. With the engine in the number 1 firing order, adjust the following valves:

- Exhaust — 1, 2, 3
- Intake — 1, 5, 6

c. Loosen the adjusting nut several turns backwards and then tighten until all lash (freeplay) is removed. After all of the valve lash is removed turn the nut an additional 1 ½ turns, this will center the lifter plunger.

d. Turn the engine 1 complete revolution until the timing tab and the alignment mark are again aligned, this will place the engine in the number 4 firing position.

e. With the engine in the number 4 firing order, adjust the following valves:

- Exhaust — 4, 5, 6
- Intake — 2, 3, 4

Rocker Arms

REMOVAL AND INSTALLATION

2.2L Engine

1. Disconnect the negative battery cable. Remove the air hose from the TBI unit and the air cleaner.
2. Remove the intake manifold-to-rocker cover hose.
3. Remove the rocker arm cover bolts and the cover.
4. Remove the rocker arm nuts and the rocker arms.

NOTE: Be sure to keep the components in order for installation purposes.

To install:
5. Install the rocker arms and rocker arm nuts. Tighten to 22 ft. lbs. (30 Nm).
6. Install the rocker arm cover.
7. Connect the intake manifold-to-rocker cover.
8. Connect the hose to the TBI unit and air cleaner.
9. Connect the negative battery cable.

2.3L Engine

The valve train consists of 2 chain driven overhead camshafts with direct acting lifters.

3.1L Engine

LEFT SIDE

1. Disconnect the negative battery cable. Disconnect the bracket tube from the rocker cover.

2. Remove the spark plug wire cover. Drain the cooling system and remove the heater hose from the filler neck.
3. Remove the rocker arm cover-to-cylinder head bolts and the rocker cover.

NOTE: If the rocker arm cover will not lift off the cylinder head easily, strike the end with the palm of the hand or a rubber mallet.

4. Remove the rocker arm nuts and the rocker arms; be sure to keep the components in order for installation purposes.

To install:
5. Clean the gasket mounting surfaces.
6. Install the rocker arms and rocker arm nuts. Tighten to 14–20 ft. lbs. (19–27 Nm).
7. Install the rocker cover.
8. Install the spark plug wire cover.
9. Connect the negative battery cable.
10. Fill cooling system and check for leaks. Start the engine and allow to come to normal operating temperature. Recheck for leaks. Top-up coolant.

RIGHT SIDE

1. Disconnect the negative battery cable. Disconnect the brake booster vacuum line from the bracket.
2. Disconnect the cable bracket from the plenum.
3. Disconnect the vacuum line bracket from the cable bracket.
4. Disconnect the lines from the alternator brace stud.
5. Remove the rear alternator brace and the serpentine drive belt.
6. Remove the alternator and support it aside.
7. Remove the PCV valve.
8. Loosen the alternator bracket.
9. Disconnect the spark plug wires from the spark plugs. Remove the rocker cover-to-cylinder head bolts and the rocker cover.

NOTE: If the rocker arm cover will not lift off the cylinder head easily, strike the end with the palm of the hand or a rubber mallet.

10. Remove the rocker arm nuts and the rocker arms; be sure to keep the components in order for installation purposes.

To install:
11. Clean the gasket mounting surfaces.

12. Install the rocker arm and rocker arm nuts. Tighten the rocker arm nuts to 14–20 ft. lbs. (19–27 Nm).
13. Install the rocker cover and the rocker cover-to-cylinder head bolts. Connect the spark plug wires to the spark plugs.
14. Tighten the alternator bracket.
15. Install the PCV valve.
16. Install the alternator.
17. Install the rear alternator brace and the serpentine drive belt.
18. Connect the lines to the alternator brace stud.
19. Connect the vacuum line bracket to the cable bracket.
20. Connect the cable bracket to the plenum.
21. Connect the brake booster vacuum line to the bracket.
22. Connect the negative battery cable.

Intake Manifold

REMOVAL AND INSTALLATION

2.2L Engine

1. Disconnect the negative battery cable. Relieve the fuel pressure. Remove the TBI cover and if necessary, remove the air cleaner.
2. Drain the cooling system. Label and disconnect the vacuum lines and electrical connectors from the intake manifold.
3. Disconnect and plug the fuel line.
4. Disconnect the TBI linkage. Remove the throttle body-to-intake manifold bolts and the throttle body.
5. Remove the serpentine drive belt. Remove the power steering pump-to-bracket bolts and support the pump aside; do not disconnect the pressure hoses.
6. Raise and safely support the vehicle.
7. Disconnect the TV cable, accelerator cable and brackets.
8. Disconnect the heater hose from the bottom of the intake manifold. Lower the vehicle.
9. Remove the intake manifold-to-cylinder head nuts/bolts and the manifold.

To install:
10. Clean the gasket mounting surfaces. Install new intake manifold gaskets.
11. Install the intake manifold and the intake manifold-to-cylinder head nuts/bolts. Tighten the intake manifold-to-cylinder heads bolts, in the proper sequence to 15–22 ft. lbs. (20–30 Nm).

12. Raise and safely support the vehicle.

13. Connect the heater hose to the bottom of the intake manifold.

14. Connect the TV cable, accelerator cable and brackets.

15. Lower the vehicle.

16. Install the serpentine drive belt. Install the power steering pump-to-bracket bolts and support the pump aside; do not disconnect the pressure hoses.

17. Install the throttle body-to-intake manifold bolts and the throttle body. Connect the TBI linkage.

18. Connect the fuel line.

19. Connect the vacuum lines and electrical connectors to the intake manifold.

20. Install the TBI cover and the air cleaner assembly, if removed.

21. Connect the negative battery cable.

22. Fill cooling system and check for leaks. Start the engine and allow to come to normal operating temperature. Recheck for leaks. Top-up coolant.

2.3L Engine

1. Disconnect the negative battery cable.

2. Drain the coolant to the proper level.

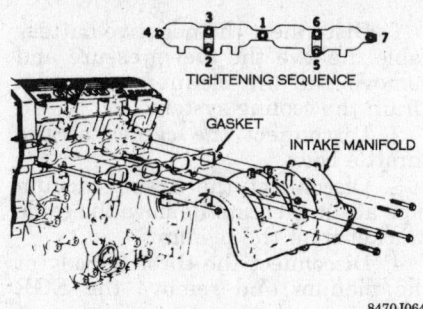

Intake manifold installation — 2.3L engine

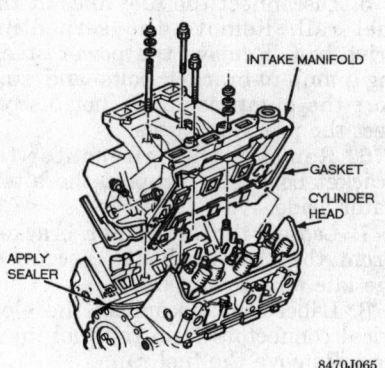

Intake manifold installation — 3.1L engine

3. Disconnect the following:

a. Vacuum hose from the MAP sensor

b. Electrical connector from the MAP sensor

c. Electrical connector from the MAT sensor

d. Electrical connector from the purge solenoid

e. Fuel injector harness connectors

4. Disconnect the vacuum hoses from the intake manifold and the hose at the fuel regulator and purge solenoid to canister.

5. Disconnect the throttle body to the air cleaner duct and the vent tube to the air cleaner duct.

6. Remove the throttle cable bracket and remove the power brake vacuum hose, including the retaining bracket to power steering bracket and position it to the side.

7. Disconnect the coolant lines from the throttle body and remove the oil/air separator bolts and hoses. Leave the hoses attached to the separator, disconnect from the oil fill, chain housing and the intake manifold. Remove as an assembly.

8. Remove the oil fill cap and oil level indicator stick.

9. Pull the oil tube fill upward to unseat from block and remove.

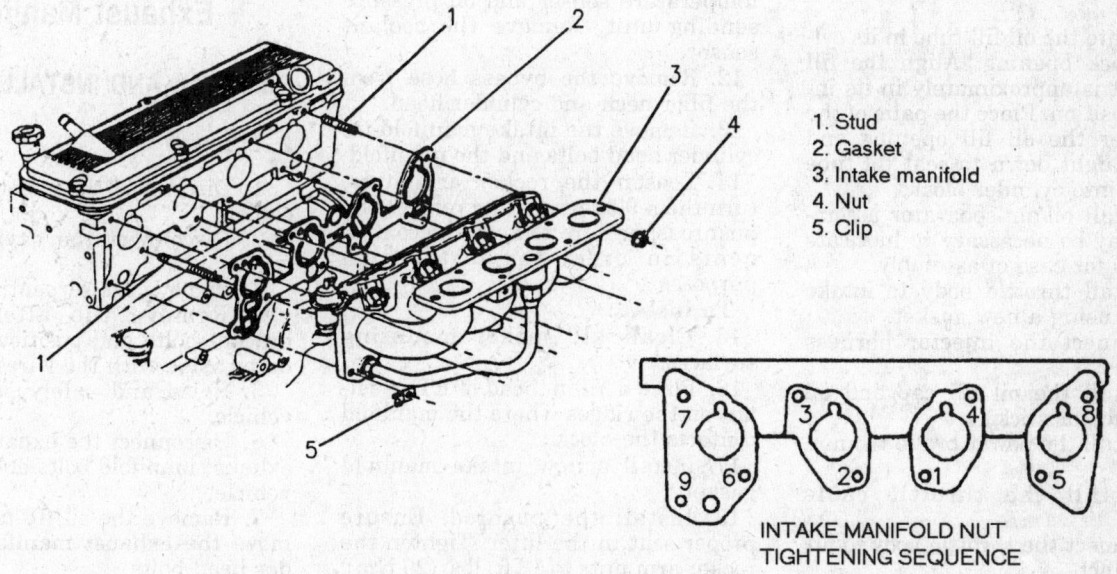

1. Stud
2. Gasket
3. Intake manifold
4. Nut
5. Clip

INTAKE MANIFOLD NUT TIGHTENING SEQUENCE

Intake manifold installation — 2.2L engine

10. Disconnect the injector harness connector.

11. Remove the fill tube out top, rotating as necessary to gain clearance for the oil/air separator nipple between the intake tubes and fuel rail electrical harness.

12. Remove the intake manifold support bracket bolts and nut. Remove the intake manifold attaching nuts and bolts.

13. Remove the intake manifold.

NOTE: Intake manifold mounting hole closest to chain housing is slotted for additional clearance.

To install:

14. Install the intake manifold and gasket. Tightening the intake manifold bolts/nuts in sequence and to 18 ft. lbs. (25 Nm). Tighten intake manifold brace and retainers hand tight. Tighten to specifications in the following sequence:
   a. Nut to stud bolt — 18 ft. lbs. (25 Nm).
   b. Bolt to intake manifold — 40 ft. lbs. (55 Nm).
   c. Bolt to cylinder block — 40 ft. lbs. (55 Nm).

15. Lubricate a new oil fill tube ring seal with engine oil. Install the tube between No. 1 and 2 intake tubes. Rotate as necessary to gain clearance for oil/air separator nipple on fill tube.

16. Locate the oil fill tube in its cylinder block opening. Align the fill tube so it is approximately in its installed position. Place the palm of the hand over the oil fill opening and press straight down to seat fill tube and seal into cylinder block.

17. Install oil/air separator assembly, it may be necessary to lubricate the hoses for ease of assembly.

18. Install throttle body to intake manifold using a new gasket.

19. Connect the injector harness connector.

20. Install the oil fill cap and oil level indicator stick.

21. Install the power brake vacuum hose.

22. Install the throttle cable bracket.

23. Connect the throttle body to air cleaner duct.

24. Install the coolant recovery tank, vacuum hose and electrical connector to the MAP sensor and to the MAT sensor.

25. Connect the negative battery cable.

3.1L Engine

1. Disconnect the negative battery cable. Relieve the fuel pressure and remove the air cleaner assembly. Drain the cooling system.

2. Disconnect the cables at the throttle body.

3. Disconnect the brake vacuum pipe at the plenum. Remove the cable bracket from the plenum.

4. Disconnect the throttle body at the plenum and remove the EGR valve from the plenum. Disconnect the harness at the plenum and remove the plenum assembly.

5. Disconnect the fuel lines at the fuel rail. Remove the serpentine drive belt. Remove the power steering pump-to-bracket bolts and support the pump aside; do not disconnect the pressure hoses.

6. Remove the alternator-to-bracket bolts and support the alternator aside.

7. Loosen the alternator bracket. From the throttle body, disconnect the idle air vacuum hose.

8. Label and disconnect the electrical connectors from the fuel injectors. Remove the fuel rail.

9. Remove the plug wires at the intake.

10. Remove both rocker arm cover-to-cylinder head bolts and the covers. Remove the radiator hose from the thermostat housing.

11. Label and disconnect the electrical connectors from the coolant temperature sensor and oil pressure sending unit. Remove the coolant sensor.

12. Remove the bypass hose from the filler neck and cylinder head.

13. Remove the intake manifold-to-cylinder head bolts and the manifold.

14. Loosen the rocker arm nuts, turn them 90 degrees and remove the pushrods; be sure to keep the components in order for installation purposes.

To install:

15. Clean all gasket mounting surfaces.

16. Place a 3/16 in. bead of RTV sealant on the ridges where the manifold contacts the block.

17. Install a new intake manifold gasket.

18. Install the pushrod. Ensure proper seat in the lifter. Tighten the rocker arm nuts to 18 ft. lbs. (25 Nm).

19. Install the intake manifold and intake manifold bolts. Tighten the intake manifold-to-cylinder head bolts, following the torquing sequence, to 15 ft. lbs. (20 Nm) and retighten to 24 ft. lbs. (33 Nm).

20. Connect the bypass hose to the filler neck and cylinder head.

21. Install the coolant sensor. Connect the electrical connectors to the coolant temperature sensor and oil pressure sending unit.

22. Install both rocker arm covers and rocker arm cover-to-cylinder head bolts. Install the radiator hose to the thermostat housing.

23. Connect the runners. Install the breather tube.

24. Install the fuel rail. Connect the electrical connectors to the fuel injectors.

25. Install the alternator and the alternator-to-bracket bolts.

26. Connect the idle air vacuum hose to the throttle body.

27. Install the power steering pump-to-bracket bolts. Install the serpentine drive belt.

28. Install the plenum and the plenum-to-intake manifold bolts. Connect the fuel lines and return pipes at the fuel rail.

29. Install the throttle body-to-plenum bolts and the throttle body. Install the EGR valve.

30. Connect the cables to the plenum.

31. Connect the negative battery cable.

32. Fill cooling system and check for leaks. Start the engine and allow to come to normal operating temperature. Recheck for leaks. Top-up coolant.

Exhaust Manifold

REMOVAL AND INSTALLATION

2.2L Engine

1. Disconnect the negative battery cable.

2. Disconnect the oxygen sensor wire.

3. Remove the serpentine belt.

4. Remove the alternator-to-bracket bolts and position the alternator aside with the wires attached.

5. Raise and safely support the vehicle.

6. Disconnect the exhaust pipe-to-exhaust manifold bolts and lower the vehicle.

7. Remove the oil fill tube and remove the exhaust manifold-to-cylinder head bolts.

8. Remove the exhaust manifold from the exhaust pipe flange and the manifold from the vehicle.

To install:

9. Clean the gasket mounting surfaces.

10. Using new gaskets, install the exhaust manifold and connect to the exhaust pipe flange. Tighten the exhaust manifold-to-cylinder head nuts to 3–11 ft. lbs. (4–15) Nm and bolts to 6–13 ft. lbs. (8–18 Nm).

11. Raise and safely support the vehicle.

12. Install the exhaust pipe-to-exhaust manifold bolts and lower the vehicle.

13. Install the alternator and the alternator-to-bracket bolts.

14. Install the serpentine belt.

15. Install the oil fill tube and connect the oxygen sensor wire.

16. Connect the negative battery cable.

2.3L Engine

1. Disconnect the negative battery cable and oxygen sensor connector.

2. Remove upper and lower exhaust manifold heat shields.

3. Remove exhaust manifold brace to manifold bolt.

4. Break loose the manifold to exhaust pipe spring loaded bolts using a 13mm box wrench.

5. Raise and support vehicle safely.

6. Remove the manifold-to-exhaust pipe bolts from the exhaust pipe flange, using a 7/32 in. (5.5mm) socket. Rotate clockwise as if tightening a bolt with right hand threads or removing a bolt with left hand threads. It is necessary to relieve the spring pressure from 1 bolt prior to removing the second bolt. If the spring pressure is not relieved, it will cause the exhaust pipe to twist and bind the bolt as it is removed. Relieve the spring pressure by:

  a. Thread 1 bolt out 4 turns.

  b. Move to the other bolt and turn it all the way out of the exhaust pipe flange.

  c. Return to the first bolt and rotate it the rest of the way out of the exhaust pipe flange.

7. Pull down and back on the exhaust pipe to disengage it from the exhaust manifold bolts.

8. Lower vehicle.

9. Remove exhaust manifold to cylinder head attaching nuts and remove exhaust manifold.

To install:

10. Clean all sealing surfaces. Install a new exhaust manifold gasket, the exhaust manifold and the exhaust manifold-to-cylinder head attaching nuts. Tighten, in sequence, to 31 ft. lbs. (42 Nm).

11. Raise and safely support the vehicle.

12. Connect the exhaust pipe to the exhaust manifold flange.

13. Install the manifold to exhaust pipe bolts to the exhaust pipe flange. Tighten to 22 ft. lbs. (30 Nm). Turn the nuts evenly to prevent binding.

14. Lower the vehicle.

15. Install the exhaust manifold brace-to-manifold bolt. Tighten to 19 ft. lbs. (26 Nm).

16. Install upper and lower exhaust manifold heat shields.

17. Connect the oxygen sensor connector.

18. Connect the negative battery cable.

3.1L Engines

LEFT SIDE

1. Disconnect the negative battery cable. Drain the cooling system.

2. Remove the air cleaner, air inlet hose and the mass air flow sensor.

3. Remove the coolant bypass pipe and coolant fan. Remove the manifold heat shield.

4. Disconnect the exhaust manifold crossover assembly at the right manifold.

5. Remove the exhaust manifold-to-cylinder head attaching bolts.

6. Remove the exhaust manifold with the crossover assembly.

To install:

7. Clean the gasket mounting surfaces.

8. Install the exhaust manifold with the crossover assembly. Tighten the exhaust manifold-to-cylinder head bolts to 19 ft. lbs. (26 Nm).

9. Connect the exhaust manifold crossover assembly to the right manifold.

10. Install the coolant bypass pipe. Install the manifold heat shield.

11. Install the mass air flow sensor, air inlet hose and air cleaner.

12. Connect the negative battery cable.

13. Fill cooling system and check for leaks. Start the engine and allow to come to normal operating temperature. Check for exhaust leaks and recheck for coolant leaks. Top-up coolant.

RIGHT SIDE

1. Remove the air cleaner assembly and disconnect the negative battery cable.

2. Raise and safely support the vehicle.

3. Remove the heat shield.

4. Remove the exhaust pipe-to-exhaust manifold bolts and the crossover pipe-to-exhaust manifold bolts.

5. Remove the EGR pipe-to-exhaust manifold bolts and the pipe.

6. Remove the accelerator cables and TV cables. Disconnect the oxygen sensor wire.

7. Remove the exhaust manifold-to-cylinder head bolts and the exhaust manifold from the vehicle.

To install:

8. Clean the gasket mounting surfaces.

9. Install the exhaust manifold and exhaust manifold-to-cylinder head bolts. Tighten the exhaust manifold-to-cylinder head bolts to 19 ft. lbs. (26 Nm) and the crossover pipe bolts to 25 ft. lbs. (34 Nm).

10. Connect the oxygen sensor wire.

11. Install the EGR pipe and the EGR pipe-to-exhaust manifold bolts.

12. Install the exhaust pipe-to-exhaust manifold bolts and the crossover pipe-to-exhaust manifold bolts.

13. Install the heat shield.

14. Lower the vehicle.

15. Connect the negative battery cable. Start the engine and check for leaks.

Timing Chain Front Cover

REMOVAL AND INSTALLATION

2.2L Engines

1. Disconnect the negative battery cable.

2. Raise and safely support the vehicle.

3. Drain the engine oil and remove the oil pan.

4. Lower the vehicle.

5. Remove the serpentine belt and the belt tensioner.

6. Remove the crankshaft pulley attaching bolt. Using a crankshaft pulley puller tool, remove the crankshaft pulley.

7. Remove the timing case cover bolts. Tap the cover with a rubber mallet and remove the cover.

To install:

8. Clean gasket mounting surfaces.

9. Using new gaskets, install the timing case cover over the dowels on the block and reverse the removal procedures. Tighten the timing case cover-to-engine bolts to 97 inch lbs. (11 Nm).

10. Using a crankshaft pulley installer tool, press the pulley onto the crankshaft. Tighten the crankshaft pulley bolt to 66–88 ft. lbs. (89–119 Nm).

11. Install the belt tensioner and serpentine belt.

12. Raise and safely support the vehicle.

13. Install the oil pan.

14. Lower the vehicle.

15. Fill the crankcase with oil to specification.

16. Connect the negative battery cable.

17. Start the engine and check for leaks.

18. Stop the engine, allow to stand for several minutes and check oil level.

2.3L Engine

1. Disconnect the negative battery cable from the battery. Remove coolant recovery reservoir.

2. Remove the serpentine drive belt.

NOTE: To avoid personal injury when rotating the serpentine belt tensioner, use a 13mm wrench that is at least 24 inches long.

3. Remove upper cover fasteners.

4. Raise and safely support the vehicle.

5. Remove right front wheel assembly.

6. Remove right lower splash shield.

7. Remove crankshaft balancer assembly.

8. Remove lower cover fasteners and lower vehicle.

9. Remove the front cover.

To install:

10. Install the front cover using new gaskets. Tighten to 106 inch lbs. (12 Nm).

11. Raise and safely support the vehicle. Install the remaining front cover bolts. Tighten to 106 inch lbs. (12 Nm).

12. Install crankshaft balancer assembly. Tighten the attaching bolt and washer for balancer assembly to 74 ft. lbs. (100 Nm).

NOTE: The automatic transaxle crankshaft balancer must not be installed on a manual transaxle engine.

13. Install right lower splash shield.

14. Install right front wheel assembly.

15. Lower the vehicle.

16. Install upper cover fasteners.

17. Install the serpentine drive belt.

NOTE: To avoid personal injury when rotating the serpentine belt tensioner, use a 13mm wrench that is at least 24 inches long.

18. Install coolant recovery reservoir.

19. Connect the negative battery cable.

3.1L Engine

1. Disconnect the negative battery cable. Drain the cooling system.

2. Remove the coolant reservoir.

3. Remove the serpentine belt and the belt tensioner.

4. Remove the power steering pump-to-bracket bolts and support it aside; do not disconnect the pressure hoses.

5. Raise and safely support the vehicle.

6. Remove the right side inner fender splash shield and the flywheel dust cover.

7. Using a crankshaft pulley puller tool, remove the crankshaft damper.

8. Remove the serpentine belt idler pulley.

9. Remove the oil pan and remove the lower cover bolts.

10. Lower the vehicle. Disconnect the radiator hose from the water pump.

11. Disconnect the bypass pipe at the front cover.

12. Disconnect the canister purge hose.

13. Remove the upper timing chain cover-to-engine bolts and the timing cover.

To install:

14. Clean gasket mounting surfaces.

15. Using silicone sealant and a new gasket, apply a thin bead to the front cover mating surface, install the timing case cover to the engine.

16. Raise and safely support the vehicle and install the oil pan.

17. Install the lower cover bolts.

18. Install the serpentine belt pulley and the crankshaft balancer.

19. Install the flywheel cover and the inner splash shield.

20. Lower the vehicle and connect the water pump hose, the bypass pipe and the canister purge hose.

21. Install the power steering pump.

22. Install the drive belt tensioner and install the serpentine belt to the vehicle.

23. Install the coolant reservoir. Fill the cooling system and connect the negative battery cable.

24. Start the engine and inspect for leaks.

Front Cover Oil Seal

REPLACEMENT

2.2L Engine

1. Disconnect the negative battery cable. Remove the serpentine belt.

2. Raise and safely support the vehicle. Remove the right front wheel and tire assembly.

3. Remove the inner fender splash shield.

4. Remove the crankshaft pulley bolt.

5. Using a crankshaft pulley puller tool, remove the crankshaft pulley.

6. Using a small prybar, pry the oil seal from the front cover.

NOTE: Use care not to damage the seal seat or the crankshaft while removing or installing the seal. Inspect the sealing surface of the crankshaft for grooves or other wear.

To install:

7. Using an oil seal centering tool, drive the new seal into the cover with the lip facing towards the engine.

8. Install a crankshaft pulley installer tool, onto the crankshaft pulley and press the pulley onto the crankshaft. Install the pulley bolt and tighten to 66–88 ft. lbs. (89–119 Nm).

9. Remove the inner fender splash shield.

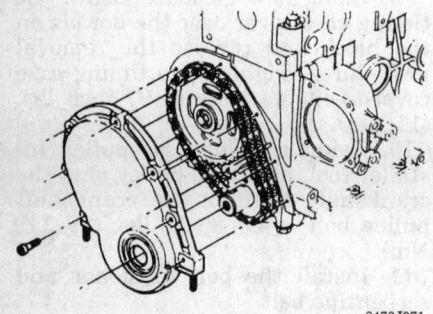

Front cover installation — 2.2L engines

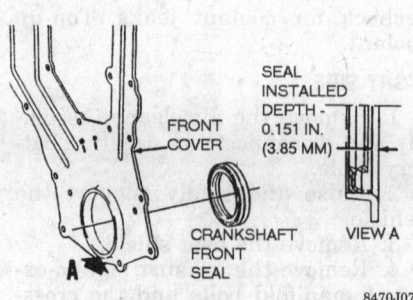

Front cover installation — 2.3L engine

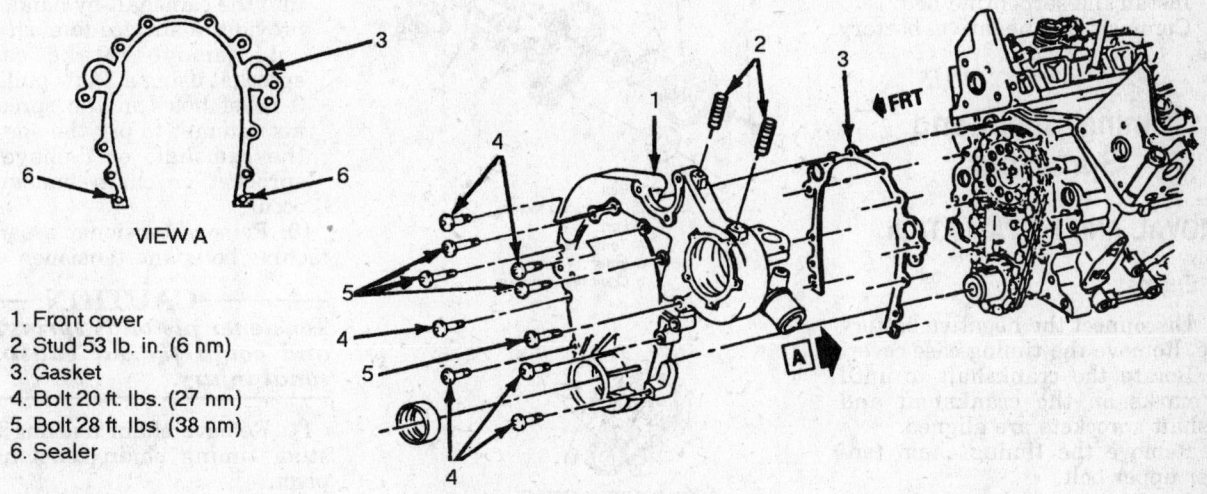

1. Front cover
2. Stud 53 lb. in. (6 nm)
3. Gasket
4. Bolt 20 ft. lbs. (27 nm)
5. Bolt 28 ft. lbs. (38 nm)
6. Sealer

VIEW A

8470J073

Front cover installation — 3.1L engine

10. Remove the right front wheel and tire assembly.
11. Lower the vehicle.
12. Install the serpentine belt.
13. Connect the negative battery cable.

2.3L Engine

1. Disconnect the negative battery cable from the battery. Remove coolant recovery reservoir.
2. Remove the serpentine drive belt.

NOTE: To avoid personal injury when rotating the serpentine belt tensioner, use a 13mm wrench that is at least 24 inches long.

3. Remove upper cover attaching bolts.
4. Raise vehicle and support it safely.
5. Remove right front wheel assembly.
6. Remove right lower splash shield.
7. Remove crankshaft balancer assembly.
8. Remove lower cover attaching bolts and lower the vehicle.
9. Remove the front cover.

To install:
10. Install the front cover. Tighten the front cover attaching bolts to 106 inch lbs. (12 Nm).
11. Raise and safely support the vehicle.
12. Install lower cover attaching bolts.
13. Install crankshaft balancer assembly. Tighten attaching bolt and washer for balancer assembly to 74 ft. lbs. (100 Nm).

NOTE: The automatic transaxle crankshaft balancer must not be installed on a manual transaxle engine.

14. Install right lower splash shield.
15. Install right front wheel assembly.
16. Lower the vehicle.
17. Install upper cover attaching bolts.
18. Install the serpentine drive belt.

NOTE: To avoid personal injury when rotating the serpentine belt tensioner, use a 13mm wrench that is at least 24 inches long.

19. Install coolant recovery reservoir.

20. Connect the negative battery cable.

3.1L Engine

1. Disconnect the negative battery cable. Remove the serpentine belt.
2. Raise and safely support the vehicle. Remove the right front wheel and remove the right side inner fender splash shield.
3. Remove the damper attaching bolt.
4. Using a crankshaft pulley puller tool, press the damper pulley from the crankshaft.
5. Remove the key from the keyway.
6. Using a small prybar, pry out the seal in the front cover.

NOTE: Use care not to damage the seal seat or the crankshaft while removing or installing the seal. Inspect the crankshaft seal surface for signs of grooves or wear.

To install:
7. Using a seal installer tool, drive the new seal in the cover with the lip facing towards the engine.
8. Install the key to the keyway.
9. Using a crankshaft pulley installer tool, press the crankshaft pulley onto the crankshaft. Tighten the

damper bolt to 67–85 ft. lbs. (90–115 Nm).

10. Install the right side inner fender splash shield and the right front wheel. Lower the vehicle.

11. Install the serpentine belt.

12. Connect the negative battery cable.

Timing Chain and Sprockets

REMOVAL AND INSTALLATION

2.2L Engine

1. Disconnect the negative battery cable. Remove the timing case cover.

2. Rotate the crankshaft to until the marks on the crankshaft and camshaft sprockets are aligned.

3. Remove the timing chain tensioner upper bolt.

4. Loosen the timing chain tensioner nut as far as possible but do not remove the nut.

5. Remove the timing chain and camshaft sprocket.

6. Using a gear puller, remove the crankshaft sprocket.

To install:

7. Before installing the camshaft sprocket, lubricate the thrust side with Molykote® or equivalent. Using a sprocket installer tool, install the crankshaft sprocket.

8. Align the camshaft sprocket mark with the crankshaft sprocket marks. Install the timing chain and camshaft sprocket.

9. Press the camshaft sprocket onto the camshaft using the camshaft sprocket bolt. Tighten the camshaft sprocket bolt to 66–88 ft. lbs. (89–119 Nm).

10. Align the tabs on the tensioner with the marks on the camshaft and crankshaft sprockets and tighten the tensioner.

11. Install the timing case cover.

12. Connect the negative battery cable.

2.3L Engine

NOTE: Prior to removing the timing chain, review the entire procedure.

1. Disconnect the negative battery cable.

2. Remove front engine cover and crankshaft oil slinger.

3. Rotate the crankshaft clockwise, as viewed from front of engine/normal rotation until the camshaft sprockets' timing dowel pin holes line up with the holes in the

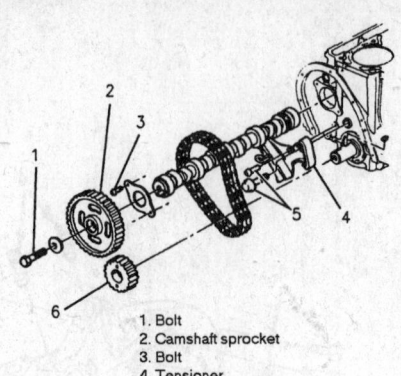

1. Bolt
2. Camshaft sprocket
3. Bolt
4. Tensioner
5. Bolts
6. Crankshaft sprocket

A. Align tabs on tensioner with marks on camshaft and crankshaft sprockets.

8470J074

Timing chain and sprockets installation — 2.2L engines

timing chain housing. The mark on the crankshaft sprocket should line up with the mark on the cylinder block. The crankshaft sprocket keyway should point upwards and line up with the centerline of the cylinder bores. This is the timed position.

4. Remove 3 timing chain guides.

5. Raise vehicle and support in safely.

6. Gently pry off timing chain tensioner spring retainer and remove spring.

NOTE: Two styles of tensioner are used. One with a spring post, early production and 1 without a spring post, late production. Both styles are identical in operation and are interchangeable.

7. Remove timing chain tensioner shoe retainer.

8. Make sure all the slack in the timing chain is above the tensioner assembly; remove the chain tensioner shoe. The timing chain must be disengaged from the wear grooves in the tensioner shoe in order to remove the shoe. Slide a prybar under the timing chain while pulling shoe outward.

9. If difficulty is encountered removing chain tensioner shoe, proceed as follows:

a. Lower the vehicle.

b. Hold the intake camshaft sprocket with a holding tool and remove the sprocket bolt and washer.

c. Remove the washer from the bolt and re-thread the bolt back into the camshaft by hand, the bolt provides a surface to push against.

d. Remove intake camshaft sprocket using a 3-jaw puller in the 3 relief holes in the sprocket. Do not attempt to pry the sprocket off the camshaft or damage to the sprocket or chain housing could occur.

10. Remove tensioner assembly attaching bolts and tensioner.

— CAUTION —
Tensioner piston is spring loaded and could fly out causing personal injury.

11. Remove chain housing to block stud, timing chain tensioner shoe pivot.

12. Remove timing chain.

NOTE: Failure to follow this procedure could result in severe engine damage.

To install:

13. Tighten intake camshaft sprocket attaching bolt and washer, to specification while holding sprocket in place.

14. Install a special tool through holes in camshaft sprockets into holes in timing chain housing, this positions the camshafts for correct timing.

15. If the camshafts are out of position and must be rotated more than 1/8 turn in order to install the alignment dowel pins, perform the following:

a. The crankshaft must be rotated 90 degrees clockwise off TDC in order to give the valves adequate clearance to open.

b. Once the camshafts are in position and the dowels installed, rotate the crankshaft counterclockwise back to top dead center. Do not rotate the crankshaft clockwise to TDC, valve or piston damage could occur.

16. Install timing chain over exhaust camshaft sprocket, around idler sprocket and around crankshaft sprocket.

17. Remove the alignment dowel pin from the intake camshaft. Using a dowel pin remover tool rotate the intake camshaft sprocket counterclockwise enough to slide the timing chain over the intake camshaft sprocket. Release the camshaft sprocket wrench. The length of chain between the 2 camshaft sprockets

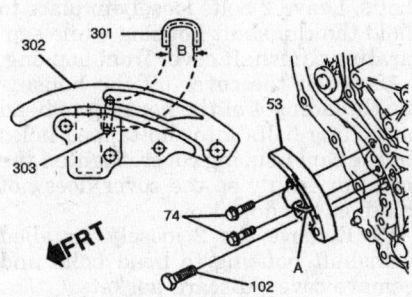

A. After installation, remove anti-release from tensioner asm. To release tensioner
B. 1/2 inch (13mm)
53. Timing chain tensioner and shoe assembly
74. Bolts - 89 lbs in (10 nm)
120. Bolt - 19 lbs ft (26 nm)
301. Anti-release keeper - fabricated from heavy gage wire or steel rod
302. Blade
303. Reset access hole

8470J076

Timing chain tensioner installation — 2.3L engine

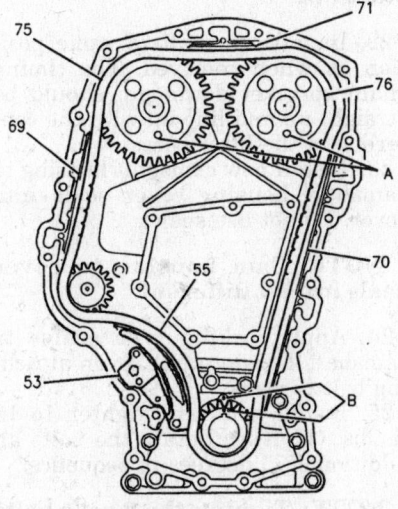

A. Camshaft timing alignment pin location
B. Crankshaft gear timing mark
53. Shoe assembly timing chain tensioner
55. Timing chain
69. Guide - R.H. timing chain
70. Guide - L.H. timing chain
71. Guide - upper timing chain
75. Sprocket - exhaust camshaft
76. Sprocket - intake camshaft

8470J077

Timing chain installation — 2.3L engine

NOTE - ALIGN TIMING MARKS ON CAM AND CRANK SPROCKETS USING ALIGNMENT MARKS ON DAMPER STAMPING OR CAST ALIGNMENT MARKS ON CYL. AND CASE.

1. Timing chain	5.	21 ft. lbs.
2. Crank sprocket		(28 nm)
3. Camshaft sprocket	6.	15 ft. lbs.
4. Damper		(21 nm)

8470J078

Timing chain and sprocket installation — 3.1L engine

will tighten. If properly timed, the intake camshaft alignment dowel pin should slide in easily. If the dowel pin does not fully index, the camshafts are not timed correctly and the procedure must be repeated.

18. Leave the alignment dowel pins installed.

19. With slack removed from chain between intake camshaft sprocket and crankshaft sprocket, the timing marks on the crankshaft and the cylinder block should be aligned. If marks are not aligned, move the chain 1 tooth forward or rearward, remove slack and recheck marks.

20. Tighten chain housing to block stud, timing chain tensioner shoe pivot. Stud is installed under the timing chain. Tighten to 19 ft. lbs. (26 Nm).

21. Reload timing chain tensioner assembly to its zero position as follows:

a. Assemble restraint cylinder, spring and nylon plug into plunger. Index slot in restraint cylinder with peg in plunger. While rotating the restraint cylinder clockwise, push the restraint cylinder into the plunger until it bottoms. Keep rotating the restraint cylinder clockwise but allow the spring to push it out of the plunger. The pin in the

plunger will lock the restraint in the loaded position.

b. Install a special plunger installer tool into plunger assembly.

c. Install plunger assembly into tensioner body with the long end toward the crankshaft when installed.

22. Install tensioner assembly to chain housing. Recheck plunger assembly installation. It is correctly installed when the long end is toward the crankshaft.

23. Install and tighten timing chain tensioner bolts and tighten to 10 ft. lbs. (14 Nm).

24. Install tensioner shoe and tensioner shoe retainer.

25. Remove the special tool from the plunger and squeeze plunger assembly into tensioner body to unload the plunger assembly.

26. Lower vehicle enough to reach and remove the alignment dowel pins. Rotate crankshaft clockwise 2 full rotations. Align crankshaft timing mark with mark on cylinder block and reinstall alignment dowel pins. Alignment dowel pins will slide in easily if engine is timed correctly.

NOTE: If the engine is not correctly timed, severe engine damage could occur.

27. Install 3 timing chain guides and crankshaft oil slinger.

28. Install engine front cover.

29. Connect the negative battery cable. Start engine and check for oil leaks.

3.1L Engine

1. Disconnect the negative battery cable. Remove the front cover.

2. Rotate the crankshaft to position the No. 1 piston at TDC with the crankshaft and camshaft sprockets aligned.

NOTE: When the camshaft and crankshaft marks are aligned, the No. 4 piston is on the TDC of its compression stroke.

3. Remove the camshaft sprocket bolts, the sprocket and the timing chain.

4. Remove the crankshaft sprocket.

To install:

5. Before installing the sprockets, apply Molykote® or equivalent, to the thrust face of the sprocket(s).

6. Install the sprocket on the crankshaft.

7. Hold the camshaft sprocket with the chain hanging down. Align the marks on the camshaft and crankshaft sprockets.

8. Align the dowel in the camshaft with the sprocket. Install the sprocket and timing chain using a camshaft bolt to pull the sprocket into position.

9. Tighten the camshaft bolts to 15–20 ft. lbs. (20–27 Nm).

10. Lubricate the new timing chain with clean engine oil.

11. Install the front cover.

12. Connect the negative battery cable. Start the engine and check for leaks.

Camshaft

REMOVAL AND INSTALLATION

2.2L Engine

1. Relieve the fuel pressure. Disconnect the negative battery cable. Remove the engine and attach it to an engine stand.

2. Remove the timing chain and sprocket from the engine.

3. Drain the engine oil and remove the oil filter.

4. Remove the rocker cover. Loosen the rocker arms and turn the rocker arms 90 degrees. Remove the pushrods and lifters; note the position of the valve train components for reassembly purposes.

5. Remove the oil pump drive.

6. Remove the camshaft thrust plate-to-engine bolts and carefully pull the camshaft from the engine.

NOTE: Use care when removing and installing the camshaft; do not damage the camshaft bearings or the bearing surfaces on the camshaft.

To install:
7. Clean gasket mounting surfaces.

8. Lubricate the lobes of the new camshaft and insert the camshaft into the engine.

NOTE: If a new camshaft is being installed, replace the lifters. Reused lifters must be reinstalled on the same camshaft and lobe location in which they were originally installed.

9. Align the marks on the camshaft and crankshaft sprockets. Install the timing chain and sprocket.

10. Install the oil pump drive.

11. Install the lifters, pushrods and reposition the rocker arms. Tighten the rocker arm nuts to 11–18 ft. lbs. (15–24 Nm).

12. Install the rocker covers.

13. Install the timing chain and sprockets to the engine.

14. Install the engine.

15. Install the oil filter and add engine oil to specification.

16. Connect the negative battery cable.

2.3L Engine

INTAKE CAMSHAFT

NOTE: Any time the camshaft housing to cylinder head bolts are loosened or removed, the camshaft housing to cylinder head gasket must be replaced.

1. Relieve the fuel system pressure. Disconnect the negative battery cable.

2. Remove ignition coil and module assembly electrical connections mark or tag, if necessary.

3. Remove 4 ignition coil and module assembly to camshaft housing bolts and remove assembly by pulling straight up. Use a special spark plug boot wire remover tool to remove connector assemblies if stuck to the spark plugs.

4. Remove the idle speed power steering pressure switch connector.

5. Loosen 3 power steering pump pivot bolts and remove drive belt.

6. Disconnect the 2 rear power steering pump bracket to transaxle bolts.

7. Remove the front power steering pump bracket to cylinder block bolt.

8. Disconnect the power steering pump assembly and position aside.

9. Using special tools remove power steering pump drive pulley from intake camshaft.

10. Remove oil/air separator bolts and hoses. Leave the hoses attached to the separator, disconnect from the oil fill, chain housing and intake manifold. Remove as an assembly.

11. Remove vacuum line from fuel pressure regulator and fuel injector harness connector.

12. Disconnect fuel line retaining clamp from bracket on top of intake camshaft housing.

13. Remove fuel rail to camshaft housing attaching bolts.

14. Remove fuel rail from cylinder head. Cover injector openings in cylinder head and cover injector nozzles. Leave fuel lines attached and position fuel rail aside.

15. Disconnect timing chain and housing but do not remove from the engine.

16. Remove intake camshaft housing cover to camshaft housing attaching bolts.

17. Remove intake camshaft housing to cylinder head attaching bolts.

Use the reverse of the tightening procedure when loosening camshaft housing to cylinder head attaching bolts. Leave 2 bolts loosely in place to hold the camshaft housing while separating camshaft cover from housing.

18. Push the cover off the housing by threading 4 of the housing to head attaching bolts into the tapped holes in the cam housing cover. Tighten the bolts in evenly so the cover does not bind on the dowel pins.

19. Remove the 2 loosely installed camshaft housing to head bolts and remove cover, discard gaskets.

20. Note the position of the chain sprocket dowel pin for reassembly. Remove camshaft being careful not to damage the camshaft oil seal from camshaft or journals.

21. Remove intake camshaft oil seal from camshaft and discard seal. This seal must be replaced any time the housing and cover are separated.

To install:

NOTE: If the camshaft is being replaced, the lifters must also be replaced. Lube camshaft lobes, journals and lifters with camshaft and lifter prelube. The camshaft lobes and journals must be adequately lubricated or engine damage could occur upon start up.

22. Install camshaft in same position as when removed. The timing chain sprocket dowel pin should be straight up and line up with the centerline of the lifter bores.

23. Install new camshaft housing to camshaft housing cover seals into cover. Do not use sealer.

NOTE: Cam housing to cover seals are all different.

24. Apply locking type sealer to camshaft housing and cover attaching bolt threads.

25. Install bolts and tighten to 11 ft. lbs. (15 Nm). Rotate the bolts an additional 75 degrees in sequence.

NOTE: Tighten the 2 rear bolts that hold fuel pipe to camshaft housing to 11 ft. lbs. (15 Nm), then rotate the bolts an additional 25 degrees.

26. Install timing chain housing and timing chain.

27. Uncover fuel injectors and install new fuel injector ring seals lubed with engine oil.

28. Install fuel rail to cylinder head.

29. Install fuel rail to camshaft housing attaching bolts.

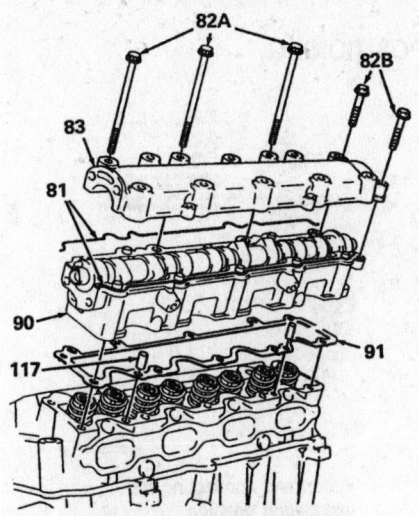

81. Seals, camshaft housing to camshaft
     housing cover (each seal is different)
82A. Bolt, camshaft housing to cylinder head
82B. Bolt, camshaft housing cover to camshaft
     housing
83. Camshaft cover
90. Camshaft housing (intake shown)
91. Gasket, camshaft housing to cylinder head
117. Dowel pin (2)

8470J079

Camshaft housing assembly — 2.3L engine

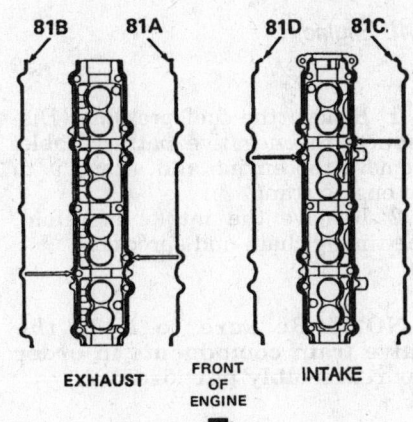

81A. SEAL-INNER (EXHAUST, RED)
81B. SEAL-OUTER (EXHAUST, RED)
81C. SEAL-OUTER (INTAKE, BLUE)
81D. SEAL-INNER (INTAKE, BLUE)

8470J081

Camshaft cover seals — 2.3L engine

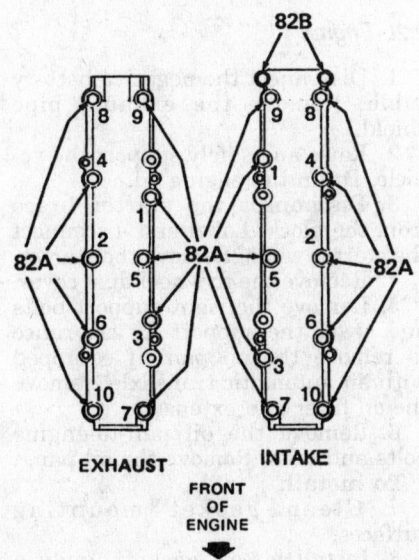

8470J080

Camshaft housing bolt torque sequence — 2.3L engine

30. Connect fuel line retaining clamp to bracket on top of intake camshaft housing.

31. Install vacuum line to fuel pressure regulator and fuel injector harness connector.

32. Install oil/air separator bolts and hoses.

33. Install power steering pump drive pulley to intake camshaft.

34. Install the power steering pump assembly.

35. Install the front power steering pump bracket to cylinder block bolt.

36. Connect the 2 rear power steering pump bracket to transaxle bolts.

37. Tighten the 3 power steering pump pivot bolts and install serpentine belt.

38. Connect the idle speed power steering pressure switch connector.

39. Install ignition module assembly and the 4 ignition coil and module assembly to camshaft housing bolts.

NOTE: Clean any loose lubricant that is present on the ignition coil and module assembly to camshaft housing bolts. Apply Loctite® 592 or equivalent onto the ignition coil and module assembly to camshaft housing bolts. Install the bolts and tighten to 13 ft. lbs. (18 Nm).

40. Connect ignition coil and module assembly electrical connectors.

41. Connect the negative battery cable.

EXHAUST CAMSHAFT

NOTE: Any time the camshaft housing to cylinder head bolts are loosened or removed the camshaft housing to cylinder head gasket must be replaced.

1. Relieve the fuel system pressure. Disconnect the negative battery cable.

2. Remove electrical connection from ignition coil and module assembly.

3. Remove 4 ignition coil and module assembly to camshaft housing bolts and remove assembly by pulling straight up. Use a special tool to remove connector assembly if stuck to the spark plugs.

4. Remove electrical connection from oil pressure switch.

5. Remove transaxle fluid level indicator tube assembly from exhaust camshaft cover and position aside.

6. Remove exhaust camshaft cover and gasket.

7. Disconnect timing chain and housing but do not remove from the engine.

8. Remove exhaust camshaft housing to cylinder head bolts. Use the reverse of the tightening procedure when loosening camshaft housing while separating camshaft cover from housing.

9. Push the cover off the housing by threading 4 of the housing to head attaching bolts into the tapped holes in the camshaft cover. Tighten the bolts in evenly so the cover does not bind on the dowel pins.

10. Remove the 2 loosely installed camshaft housing to cylinder head bolts and remove cover, discard gaskets.

11. Loosely reinstall 1 camshaft housing to cylinder head bolt to hold the camshaft housing in place during camshaft and lifter removal.

12. Note the position of the chain sprocket dowel pin for reassembly. Remove camshaft being careful not to damage the camshaft or journals.

13. If removing the camshaft housing, remove the valve lifters. Keep the lifters in order so they can be reinstalled in the same location.

14. Remove the camshaft housing and gasket.

To install:

15. Install the camshaft housing and gasket.

16. Loosely install one camshaft housing-to-cylinder head bolt to hold the housing in place.

NOTE: Used lifters must be returned to their original position in the camshaft. If the camshaft is being replaced, the lifters must also be replaced. Lube camshaft lobe, journals and lifters with camshaft and lifter prelube. The camshaft lobes and journals must be adequately lubricated or engine damage could occur upon start up.

17. Install the lifters into the lifter bores.
18. Install camshaft in same position as when removed. The timing chain sprocket dowel pin should be straight up and line up with the centerline of the lifter bores.
19. Install new camshaft housing-to-camshaft housing cover seals into cover, no sealer is needed.

NOTE: Cam housing to cover seals are all different.

20. Remove the bolt holding the housing in place. Apply locking type sealer to camshaft housing and cover attaching bolt threads.
21. Install camshaft housing cover to camshaft housing.
22. Install bolts and tighten in sequence to 11 ft. lbs. (15 Nm), then rotate an additional 75 degrees in sequence.
23. Install timing chain housing and timing chain.
24. Install exhaust camshaft housing cover and new gasket and tighten to 10 ft. lbs. (14 Nm).
25. Connect the oil pressure switch electrical connector.
26. Reinstall any spark plug boot connector that was stuck to a spark plug back onto the ignition coil assembly.
27. Locate the ignition coil and module assembly over the spark plugs and push straight down.

NOTE: Clean any loose lubricant that is present on the ignition coil and module assembly to camshaft housing bolts.

28. Apply Loctite® 592 or equivalent to the ignition coil and module assembly to camshaft housing bolts. Install and hand start the ignition coil and module assembly bolts. Tighten to 15 ft. lbs. (20 Nm).
29. Connect the ignition coil and module assembly electrical connectors.

30. Connect the negative battery cable.

3.1L Engine

1. Relieve the fuel pressure. Disconnect the negative battery cable. Remove the engine and attach it to an engine stand.
2. Remove the intake manifold, the timing chain and sprockets.

NOTE: Be sure to keep the valve train components in order for reassembly purposes.

3. Remove the valve lifters.
4. Carefully pull the camshaft from the front of the engine.

NOTE: The camshaft journals are all the same size. Use extreme care when removing or installing the camshaft not to damage the camshaft bearings or the bearing journals of the camshaft.

To install:
5. Clean gasket mounting surfaces.
6. If installing a new camshaft, lubricate the camshaft lobes and insert the camshaft in the engine.

NOTE: If a new camshaft is being used, replace all of the lifters. Used lifters can only be used on the camshaft that they were originally installed with; provided they are installed in the exact same position they were removed.

7. Align the camshaft and crankshaft sprocket marks. Install the timing chain and sprocket.
8. Install the front cover and valve train components. Tighten the rocker arm nuts to 14–20 ft. lbs. (19–27 Nm).
9. Install the intake manifold.
10. Install the engine in the vehicle.
11. Connect the negative battery cable.
12. Fill cooling system and check for leaks. Start the engine and allow to come to normal operating temperature. Recheck for leaks. Top-up coolant.

Piston and Connecting Rod

POSITIONING

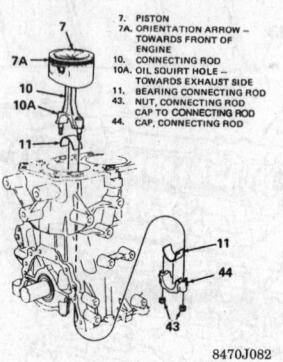

7. PISTON
7A. ORIENTATION ARROW – TOWARDS FRONT OF ENGINE
10. CONNECTING ROD
10A. OIL SQUIRT HOLE – TOWARDS EXHAUST SIDE
11. BEARING CONNECTING ROD
43. NUT, CONNECTING ROD CAP TO CONNECTING ROD
44. CAP, CONNECTING ROD

8470J082

Piston and connecting rod installation position

ENGINE LUBRICATION

Oil Pan

REMOVAL AND INSTALLATION

2.2L Engine

1. Disconnect the negative battery cable. Remove the exhaust pipe shield.
2. Raise and safely support the vehicle. Drain the engine oil.
3. Disconnect the starter brace from the block. Label and disconnect the starter wires. Remove the starter.
4. Remove the flywheel dust cover.
5. Remove the right support bolts and lower the support for clearance to remove the oil pan. If equipped with an automatic transaxle, remove the oil filter and extension.
6. Remove the oil pan-to-engine bolts and nuts. Remove the oil pan.
To install:
7. Clean gasket mounting surfaces.
8. Install a new gasket. Apply a small bead of RTV sealant to the oil pan-to-engine block sealing surface. Apply a thin layer of RTV sealant on the ends of the oil pan rear seal.
9. Install the oil pan and attaching bolts. Tighten the oil pan-to-engine bolts to 6 ft. lbs. (8 Nm).
10. If removed, install the oil filter and extension.

11. Install the starter. Connect the electrical connectors. Install the starter brace to the block.

12. Install the flywheel cover and lower the vehicle.

13. Connect the negative battery cable.

14. Refill the engine with the clean engine oil. Start the engine and check for leaks.

2.3L Engine

1. Disconnect the negative battery cable.

2. Raise and support the vehicle safely.

3. Drain the oil and the cooling system.

4. Remove the flywheel inspection cover and remove the right front wheel.

5. Remove the splash shield-to-suspension support bolt.

6. Release tension from the serpentine drive belt. Remove the engine mount strut and strut bracket.

7. Remove the A/C compressor from the bracket and support it out of the way.

8. Remove the radiator and air conditioning outlet pipes from the suspension supports.

9. Remove the exhaust manifold brace.

10. Remove the oil pan to flywheel cover bolt and nut and remove the flywheel cover stud.

11. Remove the radiator outlet pipe from the lower radiator hose and from the oil pan.

12. Disconnect the oil level sensor wire, if equipped.

13. Remove the oil pan bolts. Remove the oil pan from the engine.

To install:

14. Install the oil pan to the engine. Install the oil pan bolts. Tighten the chain housing and carrier seal bolts to 106 inch lbs. (12 Nm). Tighten the oil pan-to-block bolts to 17 ft. lbs. (23 Nm).

15. Install the spacer and install the stud.

16. Install the oil pan-to-transaxle nut and tighten to 41 ft. lbs. (56 Nm).

17. Connect the oil level sensor wire.

18. Connect the radiator outlet pipes and the air conditioning pipes.

19. Install the exhaust manifold brace.

20. Install the engine mount strut bracket and install the A/C compressor. Install the engine mount strut.

21. Apply tension to the serpentine drive belt and install the right splash shield.

22. Install the right front wheel and the flywheel cover. Lower the vehicle.

23. Fill the crankcase with oil to specification and fill the cooling system.

24. Connect the negative battery cable. Start the engine and check for leaks.

25. Turn the engine OFF and allow to stand. Check oil level, add as necessary.

3.1L Engine

1. Disconnect the negative battery cable.

2. Raise and safely support the vehicle. Drain the engine oil.

3. Remove the flywheel dust cover and the oil filter.

4. Label and disconnect the starter wires. Remove the starter.

5. Remove the oil pan-to-engine nuts/bolts and the oil pan.

To install:

6. Clean gasket mounting surfaces.

7. Install a new gasket. Install the oil pan and attaching bolts. Tighten the oil pan nuts to 6–9 ft. lbs. (8–12 Nm) or bolts to 15–22 ft. lbs. (20–30 Nm).

8. Install the starter. Connect the electrical connectors.

9. Install the flywheel dust cover.

10. Install a new oil filter.

11. Lower the vehicle.

12. Fill the crankcase with oil to specification.

13. Connect the negative battery cable. Start the engine and check for leaks.

14. Turn the engine OFF and allow to stand. Check oil level, add as necessary.

Oil Pump

REMOVAL AND INSTALLATION

Except 2.3L Engine

1. Disconnect the negative battery cable. Raise and safely support the vehicle. Drain the engine oil.

2. Remove the oil pan-to-engine bolts and the oil pan.

3. Remove the oil pump-to-rear main bearing cap bolt, the oil pump and extension shaft.

To install:

4. Install the extension shaft, oil pump and pump-to-rear main cap bolt. Tighten the oil pump-to-bearing cap bolt to 25–38 ft. lbs. (34–52 Nm) and the upper oil pump drive bolt to 14–22 ft. lbs. (19–30 Nm), on the 2.2L

engine or to 25–38 ft. lbs. (34–52 Nm) on the 3.1L engine.

5. Install the oil pan and attaching bolts.

6. Lower the vehicle.

7. Fill the crankcase with oil to specification.

8. Connect the negative battery cable. Start the engine and check oil pressure and check for leaks.

9. Turn the engine OFF and allow to stand. Check oil level, add as necessary.

2.3L Engine

1. Disconnect the negative battery cable.

2. Raise and support the vehicle safely.

3. Remove the attaching bolts and the oil pan.

4. Remove the oil pump assembly retainers and bolts.

5. Remove the oil pump assembly and shims if equipped.

NOTE: Oil pump drive gear backlash must be checked when any of the following components are replaced: oil pump assembly, oil pump drive gear, crankshaft and cylinder block.

To install:
6. Check and adjust oil pump drive gear backlash as follows:

a. With oil pump assembly off engine, remove 3 attaching bolts and separate the driven gear cover and screen assembly from the oil pump.

b. Install the oil pump on the block using the original shims. Tighten the bolts to 33 ft. lbs. (45 Nm).

c. Install the dial indicator assembly to measure backlash between oil pump to drive gear.

d. Record oil pump drive to driven gear backlash correct backlash clearance is 0.0091–0.0201 in. (0.23–0.51mm). When taking measurement crankshaft cannot move.

e. Remove oil pump from block reinstall driven gear cover and screen assembly to pump and tighten to 106 inch lbs. (12 Nm).

f. Reinstall the pump assembly on block. Tighten oil pump-to-block bolts 33 ft. lbs. (45 Nm).

7. Install the oil pump assembly, including shims if removed.

8. Tighten oil pump to block bolts to 33 ft. lbs. (45 Nm).

9. Install the oil pan and attaching bolts.

10. Lower the vehicle.

11. Fill the crankcase with oil to specification.

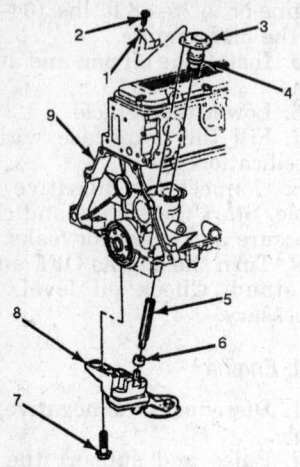

1. Bracket
2. Bolt
3. Oil pump drive assembly
4. O-ring
5. Shaft
6. Retainer; heat and water soak prior to installation
7. Bolt
8. Oil pump
9. Cylinder block

8470J108

Exploded view of the oil pump — 2.2L engine

12. Connect the negative battery cable. Start the engine and check oil pressure and check for leaks.
13. Turn the engine OFF and allow to stand. Check oil level, add as necessary.

CHECKING

1. If foreign matter is present, determine it's source.
2. Check the pump cover and housing for cracks, scoring and/or damage; if necessary, replace the housings.
3. Inspect the idler gear shaft for looseness in the housing; if necessary, replace the pump or timing chain, depending on the model.
4. Inspect the pressure regulator valve for scoring or sticking; if burrs are present, remove them with an oil stone.
5. Inspect the pressure regulator valve spring for loss of tension or distortion; if necessary, replace it.
6. Inspect the suction pipe for looseness, if pressed into the housing and the screen for broken wire mesh; if necessary, replace them.
7. Inspect the gears for chipping, galling and/or wear; if necessary, replace them.

8. Inspect the driveshaft and driveshaft extension for looseness and/or wear; if necessary, replace them.

Rear Main Bearing Oil Seal

REMOVAL AND INSTALLATION

NOTE: This procedure should only be performed by using rear crankshaft seal installer tool J–34686 for 2.2L or 3.1L engines or J–36005 for the 2.3L engine or equivalent.

1. Disconnect the negative battery cable. Remove the transaxle.
2. If equipped with a manual transaxle, matchmark and remove the clutch/flywheel assembly. If equipped with an automatic transaxle, remove the flywheel.
3. Using a small prybar, pry the rear main seal from the engine.

NOTE: Use care when removing or installing the seal to avoid damage to the crankshaft sealing surface. If equipped with a manual transaxle, inspect the condition of the clutch to insure that the clutch was not damaged by oil loss from the rear main seal.

To install:
4. To install the rear main oil seal, perform the following procedures:
   a. Lubricate the seal bore and seal surface with engine oil.
   b. Using a seal installation tool, press the new rear oil seal into the engine. The seal must fit squarely against the back of the tool.
   c. Align the dowel pin of the tool with the dowel pin in the crankshaft and tighten the attaching screws on the tool to 2–5 ft. lbs. (3–7 Nm).
   d. Tighten the T-handle of the tool to push the seal into the seal bore.
   e. Loosen the T-handle. Remove the attaching screws and tool.
   f. Check the seal to make sure it is seated squarely in the bore.
5. Install the flywheel. Tighten the flywheel-to-crankshaft bolts to 45–59 ft. lbs. (61–80 Nm) for automatic transaxles or to 47–63 ft. lbs. (64–85 Nm) for manual transaxles.
6. Lower the vehicle and connect the negative battery cable.
7. Start the engine and check for leaks.

MANUAL TRANSAXLE

Transaxle Assembly

REMOVAL AND INSTALLATION

NOTE: Before performing any maintenance that requires the removal of the slave cylinder, transaxle or clutch housing, the clutch master cylinder pushrod must first be disconnected from the clutch pedal. Failure to disconnect the pushrod will result in permanent damage to the slave cylinder if the clutch pedal is depressed with the slave cylinder disconnected.

Muncie 5TM40/NVT550

1. Disconnect the negative battery cable and remove the battery.
2. Using an engine support fixture tool and an adapter, install them on the engine and raise the engine enough to take the engine weight off the engine mounts.
3. Remove the left side sound insulator.
4. Disconnect the clutch master cylinder pushrod from the clutch pedal.
5. Remove the air cleaner and duct assembly.
6. Disconnect the clutch slave cylinder-to-transaxle support bolts and position the cylinder aside.
7. Remove the transaxle-to-mount through bolt.
8. Raise and safely support the vehicle.
9. Remove both exhaust crossover bolts at the right side manifold.
10. Lower the vehicle. Remove the left side exhaust manifold.
11. Disconnect the transaxle mounting bracket.
12. Disconnect the shifter cables.
13. Remove the upper transaxle-to-engine bolts.
14. Raise and safely support the vehicle.
15. Remove the left front wheel and tire assembly and the left side inner splash shield.
16. Remove the transaxle strut and bracket.
17. Place a drain pan under the transaxle, remove the drain plug and drain the fluid from the transaxle.
18. Remove the clutch housing cover bolts.

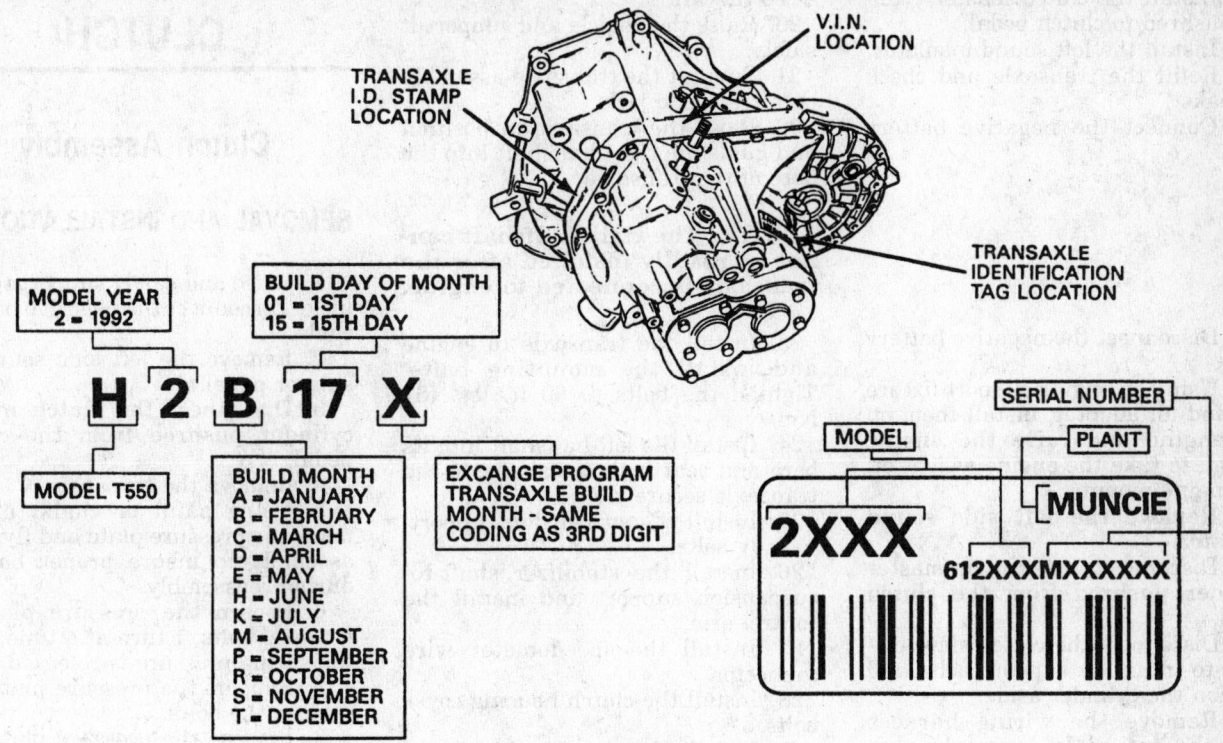

MODEL YEAR
2 = 1992

BUILD DAY OF MONTH
01 – 1ST DAY
15 – 15TH DAY

H 2 B 17 X

MODEL T550

BUILD MONTH
A = JANUARY
B = FEBRUARY
C = MARCH
D = APRIL
E = MAY
H = JUNE
K = JULY
M = AUGUST
P = SEPTEMBER
R = OCTOBER
S = NOVEMBER
T = DECEMBER

EXCANGE PROGRAM
TRANSAXLE BUILD
MONTH – SAME
CODING AS 3RD DIGIT

TRANSAXLE
I.D. STAMP
LOCATION

V.I.N.
LOCATION

TRANSAXLE
IDENTIFICATION
TAG LOCATION

SERIAL NUMBER

MODEL

PLANT

2XXX

MUNCIE

612XXXMXXXXXX

8470J086

Transaxle identification — Muncie manual transaxle

ISUZU 5-SPEED TRANSAXLE

TRANSAXLE I.D.
NAMEPLATE

5 0 0 0 0 0 1

SEQUENCE NUMBER
LAST NUMBER OF CALENDAR YEAR

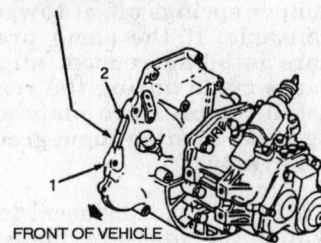

FRONT OF VEHICLE

1. VIN location
2. Optional VIN location

8470J087

Transaxle identification — Isuzu manual transaxle

19. Disconnect the speedometer wire.
20. From the left suspension support and control arm, disconnect the stabilizer shaft.
21. Remove the left suspension support mounting bolts and move the support aside.
22. Disconnect both halfshafts from the transaxle and remove the left halfshaft from the vehicle.
23. Using a transmission jack, attach it to and support the transaxle.
24. Remove the remaining transaxle-to-engine bolts.
25. Slide the transaxle away from the engine, lower it and remove the right side halfshaft.
    To install:
26. Raise the vehicle and support it safely.
27. Support the transaxle assembly on a transaxle jack.
28. Raise the transaxle in position and guide the right halfshaft into the bore of the transaxle.

NOTE: The right halfshaft cannot be readily installed after the transaxle is connected to engine.

29. Install the transaxle to engine and install the mounting bolts. Tighten the bolts to 60 ft. lbs. (81 Nm).

30. Install the left halfshaft into its bore and seat both halfshafts to the transaxle securely.
31. Install the suspension support-to-body bolts.
32. Install the stabilizer shaft-to-suspension support and install the control arm.
33. Install the speedometer wire connector.
34. Install the clutch housing cover bolts.
35. Install the strut bracket to transaxle and install the strut.
36. Install the inner splash shield.
37. Tire and wheel assembly and lower the vehicle.
38. Install the upper transaxle-to-engine bolts.
39. Connect the shift cables.
40. Install left side exhaust manifold.
41. Raise vehicle and support it safely.
42. Install both exhaust crossover bolts at the right side manifold.
43. Lower the vehicle.
44. Install the transaxle-to-mount through bolt.
45. Install the clutch slave cylinder to the support bracket.
46. Install the air cleaner and air intake duct assembly.
47. Remove engine support fixture.

48. Install the clutch master cylinder pushrod to clutch pedal.
49. Install the left sound insulator.
50. Refill the transaxle and check for leaks.
51. Connect the negative battery cable.

Isuzu

1. Disconnect the negative battery cable.
2. Using an engine support fixture tool and an adapter, install them on the engine and raise the engine enough to take the engine weight off the engine mounts.
3. Remove the left side sound insulator.
4. Disconnect the clutch master cylinder pushrod from the clutch pedal.
5. Disconnect the clutch slave cylinder-to-transaxle support bolts and position the cylinder aside.
6. Remove the wiring harness from the transaxle mount bracket and the shift wire electrical connector.
7. Remove the transaxle-to-mount bolts and the transaxle mount bracket-to-chassis nuts/bolts.
8. Disconnect the shift cables and remove the retaining clamp from the transaxle. Remove the ground cables from the transaxle mounting studs.
9. Raise and safely support the vehicle.
10. Remove the front wheel and tire assemblies and the left side inner splash shield.
11. Remove the transaxle front strut and bracket.
12. Remove the clutch housing cover bolts. Disconnect the speedometer wire connector.
13. From the left suspension support and control arm, disconnect the stabilizer shaft.
14. Remove the left suspension support mounting bolts and move the support aside.
15. Disconnect both halfshafts from the transaxle and remove the left halfshaft from the vehicle.
16. Place a drain pan under the transaxle, remove the drain plug and drain the fluid from the transaxle.
17. Using a transmission jack, attach it to and support the transaxle.
18. Remove the transaxle-to-engine bolts.
19. Slide the transaxle away from the engine, lower it and remove the right side halfshaft.

To install:
20. Raise the vehicle and support it safely.
21. Support the transaxle assembly on a transaxle jack.
22. Raise the transaxle in position and guide the right halfshaft into the bore of the transaxle.

NOTE: The right halfshaft cannot be readily installed after the transaxle is connected to engine.

23. Install the transaxle to engine and install the mounting bolts. Tighten the bolts to 60 ft. lbs. (81 Nm).
24. Install the left halfshaft into its bore and seat both halfshafts to the transaxle securely.
25. Install the suspension support-to-body bolts.
26. Install the stabilizer shaft-to-suspension support and install the control arm.
27. Install the speedometer wire connector.
28. Install the clutch housing cover bolts.
29. Install the front strut bracket to transaxle and install the front strut.
30. Install the inner splash shield.
31. Install the tire and wheel assembly and lower the vehicle.
32. Install the ground cables at the mounting studs.
33. Install the electrical connections for the shift light.
34. Install the slave cylinder to the transaxle bracket aligning the pushrod into the pocket of the clutch release lever. Install the attaching nuts and tighten evenly to prevent damage to the cylinder.
35. Install the transaxle mount bracket.
36. Install the transaxle mount to the side frame and install the attaching bolts.
37. Connect the wire harness at the mount bracket.
38. Remove the engine support.
39. Install the shift cables.
40. Refill the transaxle and check for leaks.
41. Connect the negative battery cable.

LINKAGE ADJUSTMENT

No adjustments are possible on the manual transaxle shifting cables or linkage. If the transaxle is not engaging completely, check for stretched cables or broken shifter components or a faulty transaxle.

CLUTCH

Clutch Assembly

REMOVAL AND INSTALLATION

1. Raise and safely support the vehicle. Disconnect the negative battery cable.
2. Remove the left side sound insulator panel.
3. Disconnect the clutch master cylinder pushrod from the clutch pedal.
4. Remove the transaxle.
5. Using paint or chalk, match-mark the pressure plate and flywheel assembly to insure proper balance during reassembly.
6. Loosen the pressure plate-to-flywheel bolts, 1 turn at a time, until the spring pressure is released.
7. Support the pressure plate and remove the bolts.
8. Remove the pressure plate and disc assembly; be sure to note the flywheel side of the clutch disc.
9. Clean and inspect the clutch assembly, flywheel, release bearing, clutch fork and pivot shaft for signs of wear. Replace any necessary parts.
To install:
10. Position the clutch disc and pressure plate in the appropriate position, support the assembly with an alignment tool.

NOTE: Ensure the clutch disc is facing the same direction it was when removed. The driven plate is installed with the damper springs offset toward the transaxle. If the same pressure plate is being reused, align the marks made during the removal, install the pressure plate attaching bolts. Tighten them gradually and evenly.

11. Remove the alignment tool and tighten the pressure plate-to-flywheel bolts to 15 ft. lbs. (20 Nm). Lightly lubricate the clutch fork ends. Fill the recess ends of the release bearing with grease. Lubricate the spline input shaft with a light coat of grease.

NOTE: On 5-speed Isuzu transaxles, ensure the bearing pads are located on the fork ends and both spring ends are in the fork holes with the spring completely seated in the bearing groove.

12. Install the transaxle in the vehicle.

NOTE: The clutch lever must not be moved towards the flywheel until the transaxle is bolted to the engine. Damage to the transaxle, release bearing and clutch fork could occur if this is not followed.

13. Connect the clutch master cylinder pushrod to the clutch pedal.

14. Install the left side sound insulator.

15. Connect the negative battery cable.

PEDAL HEIGHT/FREE-PLAY ADJUSTMENT

Push the clutch pedal all the way to the floor; the distance of travel should be 6.4 ± 0.5 in. (163 ± 13mm). If the measurement is not correct check the following areas:

• Clutch pedal assembly distorted
• Incorrect clutch master cylinder pushrod length
• Dash mat under the neutral start switch
• Mislocated neutral start switch

Clutch Master and Slave Cylinder

A hydraulic clutch mechanism is used on all clutch equipped vehicles. This mechanism uses a clutch master cylinder with a remote reservoir and a slave cylinder connected to the master cylinder. Whenever the system is disconnected for repair or replacement, the clutch system must be bled to insure proper operation.

REMOVAL AND INSTALLATION

The clutch master and slave cylinders are removed from the vehicle as an assembly. After installation the clutch hydraulic system must be bled.

1. Disconnect the negative battery cable.
2. From inside the vehicle, remove the left side sound insulator.

NOTE: If equipped with a 3.1L engine, remove the air cleaner, the mass air flow sensor and the air intake duct as an assembly.

3. Disconnect the clutch master cylinder pushrod from the clutch master cylinder.
4. From the front of the dash, remove the trim cover.

5. Remove the clutch master cylinder-to-clutch pedal bracket nuts and the remote reservoir-to-chassis screws.
6. Remove the slave cylinder-to-transaxle nuts and the slave cylinder.
7. Remove the hydraulic system (as a unit) from the vehicle.

To install:

8. Install the slave cylinder-to-transaxle support, align the pushrod to the clutch fork outer lever pocket. Tighten the slave cylinder-to-transaxle support nuts to 14–20 ft. lbs. (19–27 Nm).

NOTE: If installing a new clutch hydraulic system, do not break the pushrod plastic retainer; the straps will break on the first pedal application.

9. Install the master cylinder-to-clutch pedal bracket. Tighten the nuts evenly, to prevent damaging the master cylinder, to 15–20 ft. lbs. (20–27 Nm). Remove the pedal restrictor from the pushrod. Lubricate the pushrod bushing on the clutch pedal; if the bushing is cracked or worn, replace it.
10. If equipped with cruise control, check the switch adjustment at the clutch pedal bracket.

NOTE: When adjusting the cruise control switch, do not exert more than 20 lbs. of upward force on the clutch pedal pad for damage to the master cylinder pushrod retaining rod can result.

11. Depress the clutch pedal several times to break the plastic retaining straps; do not remove the plastic button from the end of the pushrod.

NOTE: If equipped with a 3.1L engine, install the air cleaner, the mass air flow sensor and the air intake duct as an assembly.

12. Install the left side sound insulator.
13. Connect the negative battery cable.
14. If necessary, bleed the clutch hydraulic system.

Hydraulic Clutch System Bleeding

PROCEDURE

1. Disconnect the slave cylinder from the transaxle.
2. Loosen the master cylinder mounting attaching nuts. Do not remove the master cylinder.

3. Remove any dirt or grease around the reservoir cap so dirt cannot enter the system. Fill the reservoir with an approved DOT 3 brake fluid.
4. Depress the hydraulic actuator cylinder pushrod approximately 0.787 in. (20.0mm) into the slave cylinder bore and hold.
5. install the diaphragm and cap on the reservoir while holding the slave cylinder pushrod.
6. Release the slave cylinder pushrod.
7. Hold the slave cylinder vertically with the pushrod end facing the ground.

NOTE: The slave cylinder should be lower than the master cylinder.

8. Press the pushrod into the slave cylinder bore with short 0.390 in. (10.0mm) strokes.
9. Observe the reservoir for air bubbles. Continue until air bubbles no longer enter the reservoir.
10. Connect the slave cylinder to the transaxle.
11. Tighten the master cylinder attaching nuts.
12. Top-up the clutch master cylinder reservoir.
13. To test the system, start the engine and push the clutch pedal to the floor. Wait 10 seconds and select reverse gear. There should be no gear clash. If clash is present, air may still be present in the system. Repeat bleeding procedure.

AUTOMATIC TRANSAXLE

Transaxle Assembly

REMOVAL AND INSTALLATION

2.2L and 2.3L Engines

1. Disconnect the negative battery cable. Remove the air cleaner and air intake assembly.
2. Disconnect the TV cable from the throttle lever and the transaxle.
3. Remove the fluid level indicator and the filler tube.
4. Using an engine support fixture tool and an adapter, install them onto the engine.
5. Remove the wiring harness-to-transaxle nut.

15 GM "L" BODY CORSICA, BERETTA

6. Label and disconnect the electrical connectors for the speed sensor, TCC connector and the neutral safety/backup light switch.

7. Disconnect the shift linkage from the transaxle.

8. Remove the upper transaxle-to-engine bolts, the transaxle mount and bracket assembly.

9. Disconnect the rubber hose that runs from the transaxle to the vent pipe.

10. Raise and safely support the vehicle.

11. Remove the front wheels and tire assemblies.

12. Disconnect the shift linkage and bracket from the transaxle.

13. Remove the left side splash shield.

14. Using a modified halfshaft boot protector tool, install 1 on each halfshaft to protect the boot from damage and the joint from possible failure.

15. Using care not to damage the halfshaft boots, disconnect the halfshafts from the transaxle.

16. Remove the transaxle strut. Remove the left side stabilizer link pin bolt and bushing clamp nuts from the support.

17. Remove the left frame support bolts and move it aside.

18. Disconnect the speedometer wire from the transaxle.

19. Remove the transaxle converter cover and matchmark the torque converter-to-flywheel for reassembly.

20. Disconnect and plug the transaxle cooler pipes.

21. Remove the transaxle-to-engine support.

22. Using a transmission jack, position and secure the jack to the transaxle. Remove the remaining transaxle-to-engine bolts.

23. Making sure the torque converter does not fall out, remove the transaxle from the vehicle.

NOTE: The transaxle cooler and lines should be flushed any time the transaxle is removed for overhaul or replacing the pump, case or converter.

To install:

24. Put a small amount of grease on the pilot hub of the converter and make sure the converter is properly engaged with the pump.

25. Raise the transaxle to the engine while guiding the right side halfshaft into the transaxle.

26. Install the lower transaxle mounting bolts and remove the jack.

27. Align the converter with the matchmarks on the flywheel and install the bolts hand tight.

28. Tighten the converter bolts to 46 ft. lbs. (62 Nm); retighten the first bolt after the others.

29. Connect the transaxle cooler pipes.

30. Connect the speedometer wire to the transaxle.

31. Install the left frame support bolts.

32. Install the left side stabilizer link pin bolt and bushing clamp nuts to the support. Install the transaxle strut.

33. Connect the halfshafts to the transaxle.

34. Remove the halfshaft boot protector.

35. Install the left side splash shield.

36. Connect the shift linkage and bracket to the transaxle.

37. Install the front wheels and tire assemblies.

38. Lower the vehicle.

39. Connect the rubber hose that runs from the transaxle to the vent pipe.

40. Install the upper transaxle-to-engine bolts, the transaxle mount and bracket assembly.

41. Connect the shift linkage to the transaxle.

42. Connect the electrical connectors for the speed sensor, TCC connector and the neutral safety/backup light switch.

43. Install the wiring harness-to-transaxle nut.

44. Remove the engine support fixture tool and an adapter.

45. Install the fluid level indicator and the filler tube.

46. Connect the TV cable to the throttle lever and the transaxle.

47. Install the air cleaner and air intake assembly.

48. Connect the negative battery cable. Check the fluid level when finished.

3.1L Engine

1. Disconnect the negative battery cable. Remove the air cleaner, bracket, Mass Air Flow (MAF) sensor and air tube as an assembly.

2. Disconnect the exhaust crossover from the right side manifold and remove the left side exhaust manifold. Raise and support the manifold/crossover assembly.

3. Disconnect the TV cable from the throttle lever and the transaxle.

4. Remove the vent hose and the shift cable from the transaxle.

5. Remove the fluid level indicator and the filler tube.

6. Using an engine support fixture tool and an adapter, install them on the engine.

7. Remove the wiring harness-to-transaxle nut.

8. Label and disconnect the wires for the speed sensor, TCC connector and the neutral safety/backup light switch.

9. Remove the upper transaxle-to-engine bolts.

10. Remove the transaxle-to-mount through bolt, the transaxle mount bracket and the mount.

11. Raise and safely support the vehicle.

12. Remove the front wheel and tire assemblies.

13. Disconnect the shift cable bracket from the transaxle.

14. Remove the left side splash shield.

15. Using a modified halfshaft boot protector tool, install 1 on each halfshaft to protect the boot from damage and the joint from possible failure.

16. Using care not to damage the halfshaft boots, disconnect the halfshafts from the transaxle.

17. Remove the torsional and lateral strut from the transaxle. Remove the left side stabilizer link pin bolt.

18. Remove the left frame support bolts and move it aside.

19. Disconnect the speedometer wire from the transaxle.

20. Remove the transaxle converter cover and matchmark the converter-to-flywheel for assembly.

21. Disconnect and plug the transaxle cooler pipes.

22. Remove the transaxle-to-engine support.

23. Using a transmission jack, position and secure it to the transaxle. Remove the remaining transaxle-to-engine bolts.

24. Make sure the torque converter does not fall out and remove the transaxle from the vehicle.

NOTE: The transaxle cooler and lines should be flushed any time the transaxle is removed for overhaul, to replace the pump, case or converter.

To install:

25. Put a small amount of grease on the pilot hub of the converter and make sure the converter is properly engaged with the pump.

26. Raise the transaxle to the engine while guiding the right side halfshaft into the transaxle.

27. Install the lower transaxle mounting bolts and Install the jack.

28. Align the converter with the matchmarks on the flywheel and install the bolts hand tight.

29. Tighten the converter bolts to 46 ft. lbs. (62 Nm); retighten the first bolt after the others.

30. Connect the transaxle cooler pipes.

31. Connect the speedometer wire to the transaxle.

32. Install the left frame support bolts.

33. Install the left side stabilizer link pin bolt. Install the torsional and lateral strut to the transaxle.

34. Connect the halfshafts to the transaxle.

35. Remove the boot protectors.

36. Install the left side splash shield.

37. Connect the shift cable bracket to the transaxle.

38. Install the front wheel and tire assemblies.

39. Lower the vehicle.

40. Install the transaxle-to-mount through bolt, the transaxle mount bracket and the mount.

41. Install the upper transaxle-to-engine bolts.

42. Connect the wires for the speed sensor, TCC connector and the neutral safety/backup light switch.

43. Install the wiring harness-to-transaxle nut.

44. Remove the engine support fixture tool.

45. Install the fluid level indicator and the filler tube.

46. Install the vent hose and the shift cable to the transaxle.

47. Connect the TV cable to the throttle lever and the transaxle.

48. Install the left side exhaust manifold. Connect the exhaust crossover to the right side manifold.

49. Install the air cleaner, bracket, Mass Air Flow (MAF) sensor and air tube as an assembly.

50. Connect the negative battery cable. Check the fluid level when finished.

SHIFT CONTROL LINKAGE ADJUSTMENT

1. Loosen the cable-to-transaxle shift lever nut so the cable is free.

2. Position the gear shift selector and the transaxle shift lever into the **N** position.

3. While holding transaxle's shift lever out of the **P** position, tighten the shift cable-to-shift lever nut to 11 ft. lbs. (15 Nm) for floor shift or 15 ft. lbs. (20 Nm) for column shift.

THROTTLE VALVE ADJUSTMENT

1. Turn the engine **OFF**.

2. At the end of the TV cable (engine side), depress and hold down the cable's metal readjustment tab.

3. Move the slider until it stops against the fitting and release the readjustment tab.

4. Rotate the throttle lever (by hand) to it's full travel position; the TV slider should move (ratchet) toward the lever when the lever. Release the TV.

5. After adjustment, make sure the cable moves freely and road test the vehicle.

NOTE: Even if the cable appears to function properly when the engine is cold or stopped, recheck it after the engine is hot.

Park/Neutral and Backup Light Switch

The switch assembly is located on top of the transaxle.

1. Place the transaxle's shift control lever in the **N** notch in the detent plate.

2. Loosen the switch-to-transaxle screws.

3. Rotate the switch on the shifter assembly to align the service adjustment hole with the carrier tang hole.

4. Using a 3/32 in. drill bit or gauge pin, insert it into the service adjustment hole to a depth of 3/8in. (9mm).

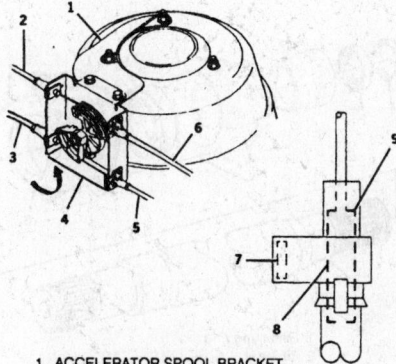

1. ACCELERATOR SPOOL BRACKET
2. ACCELERATOR CONTROL CABLE
3. THROTTLE VALVE CABLE
4. ACCELERATOR CABLE SPOOL ASSEMBLY
5. CRUISE CONTROL SERVO CABLE
6. THROTTLE BODY CABLE
7. RE-ADJUST BUTTON
8. SLIDER
9. ADJUSTED POSITION

8470J089

View of the Throttle Valve (TV) cable adjuster — 2.3L (VIN A)

5. Tighten the switch-to-transaxle screws and remove the drill bit or gauge pin.

DRIVE AXLE

Halfshaft

REMOVAL AND INSTALLATION

If equipped with an automatic transaxle, the inner joint on the right side halfshaft uses a male spline that locks into the transaxle gears. The left side halfshaft uses a female spline that is installed over the stub shaft on the transaxle.

An intermediate shaft is installed between the transaxle and the right halfshaft.

Except Intermediate Shaft

1. With the weight of the vehicle on the tires, loosen the hub nut.

2. Raise and safely support the vehicle.

3. Remove the hub nut.

4. Install boot protectors on the boots.

5. Remove the brake caliper with the line attached and support it (on a wire) aside; do not allow the caliper to hang from the line.

6. Remove the brake rotor and caliper mounting bracket.

7. Remove the strut to steering knuckle bolts. Pull the steering knuckle out of the strut bracket.

8. Using a halfshaft removal tool and an extension, remove the halfshafts from the transaxle and support them safely.

9. Using a spindle remover tool, remove the halfshaft from the hub and bearing.

To install:

10. Loosely place the halfshaft on the transaxle and in the hub and bearing.

11. Properly position the steering knuckle to the strut bracket and install the bolt. Tighten the bolts to 133 ft. lbs. (181 Nm).

12. Install the brake rotor, caliper bracket and caliper. Place a holding device in the rotor to prevent it from turning.

13. Install the hub nut and washer. Tighten the nut to 71 ft. lbs. (96 Nm).

14. Seat the halfshafts into the transaxle using a prybar on the groove on the inner retainer.

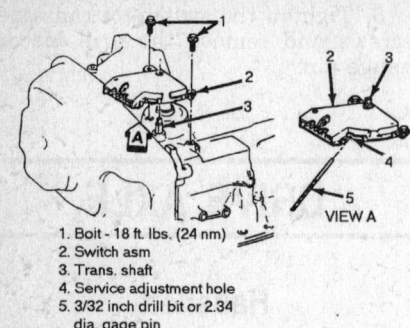

1. Bolt - 18 ft. lbs. (24 nm)
2. Switch asm
3. Trans. shaft
4. Service adjustment hole
5. 3/32 inch drill bit or 2.34 dia. gage pin

8470J090

Park/neutral and reverse light switch

15. Verify that the shafts are seated by grasping the CV-joint and pulling outwards; do not grasp the shaft. If the snapring is seated, the halfshaft will remain in place.

16. Remove the boot protectors.

17. Lower the vehicle.

18. When the vehicle is lowered with the weight on the wheels, tighten the hub nut to 191 ft. lbs. (259 Nm).

Intermediate Shaft

1. Raise and safely support the vehicle. Remove the front right wheel and tire assembly.

2. Drain the transaxle.

3. Using a modified boot protector, place it over the outer boot.

4. Remove the stabilizer bar from the right control arm.

5. Remove the right ball joint-to-steering knuckle cotter pin and nut. Using a ball joint remover tool, separate the ball joint from the steering knuckle.

6. Pull the steering knuckle outward and separate the halfshaft from the intermediate shaft.

7. Remove the intermediate shaft housing-to-bracket bolts and the lower bracket-to-engine bolt. Loosen the upper bracket-to-engine bolt and swing the bracket aside.

8. Remove the intermediate shaft housing-to-transaxle bolts, disengage the housing from the transaxle and remove the intermediate shaft assembly.

To install:

9. Lubricate the intermediate shaft splines with grease and install the intermediate shaft. Tighten the intermediate shaft housing-to-transaxle bolts to 18 ft. lbs. (25 Nm), the intermediate shaft housing-to-bracket bolts to 37 ft. lbs. (50 Nm) and the bracket-to-engine bolts to 37 ft. lbs. (50 Nm).

10. Install the intermediate shaft housing-to-bracket bolts and the lower bracket-to-engine bolt.

11. Connect the halfshaft to the intermediate shaft.

12. Connect the ball joint to the steering knuckle. Install the ball joint-to-steering knuckle nut and cotter pin.

13. Install the stabilizer bar to the right control arm.

14. Remove the boot protector.

15. Install the right front tire and wheel assembly.

16. Lower the vehicle.

17. Refill the transaxle.

18. Start the engine and allow to come to normal operating temperature. Check the automatic transaxle fluid level. Top-up as necessary.

CV-Boot

REMOVAL AND INSTALLATION

Inner

1. Remove the halfshaft.

2. Cut the seal retaining clamps.

3. Using a pair of snapring pliers, remove the retaining ring from the shaft and remove the spider assembly.

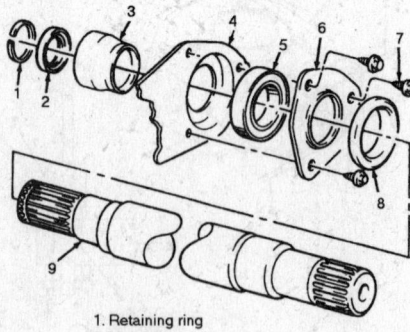

1. Retaining ring
2. Lip seal
3. Outer slinger
4. Support
5. Bearing
6. Retainer
7. Screw - 9 ft. lbs. (12 nm)
8. Inner slinger
9. Shaft

8470J092

Exploded view of the intermediate shaft

4. Remove the old boot from the shaft.

To install:

5. Using solvent, clean the splines of the shaft and repack the joint.

6. Install the inner boot clamp first and the new boot second.

7. Push the CV-joint assembly onto the shaft until the retaining ring is seated on the shaft.

8. Slide the boot onto the joint. Install both the inner and outer clamps.

9. Install the halfshaft.

Outer

1. Remove the halfshaft from the vehicle.

2. Cut off the boot retaining clamps and discard them. Remove the old boot.

3. If equipped with a deflector ring, use a brass drift and carefully tap it off.

4. Using a pair of snapring pliers, spread the retaining ring inside the outer CV-joint and tap the joint off the halfshaft.

To install:

5. Using solvent, clean the splines of the halfshaft and the CV-joint and repack the joint. Install a new retaining ring inside the joint.

6. Install the inner boot clamp first, the new boot second.

7. Push the joint assembly onto the halfshaft until the ring is seated on the shaft.

8. Slide the boot onto the joint and install the clamps on both the inner and outer part of the boot.

9. Install the halfshaft.

Front Wheel Hub, Knuckle and Bearings

REMOVAL AND INSTALLATION

The hub and bearing are replaced as an assembly only.

1. With the vehicle weight on the tires, loosen the hub nut.

2. Raise and safely support the vehicle. Remove the wheel and tire assembly.

3. Install a boot cover over the outer CV-joint boot.

4. Remove the hub nut. Remove the brake caliper and support it aside (on a wire); do not allow the caliper to hang on the brake line.

5. Remove the hub and bearing mounting bolts.

6. Remove the brake rotor splash shield.

7. Using a hub puller tool, press the hub and bearing from the halfshaft.

8. Disconnect the stabilizer link from the lower control arm.

9. Remove the cotter pin and the ball joint-to-knuckle attaching nut.

10. Disconnect the ball joint from the steering knuckle, using a ball joint separator tool.

11. Remove the halfshaft from the knuckle and support it aside.

12. Matchmark the strut in relationship to the knuckle, for alignment purposes and remove the strut-to-knuckle attaching nuts.

13. Remove the knuckle from the strut.

14. Using a brass drift, remove the inner knuckle seal.

To install:

15. Clean and inspect the steering knuckle bore and the bearing mating surfaces.

16. Using a seal driver tool, install it into the steering knuckle; be sure to lubricate the new seal and the bearing with a high temperature wheel bearing grease.

17. Connect the ball joint to the knuckle and install the ball joint-to-knuckle attaching nut, hand tight.

18. Position the knuckle to the strut and install the attaching bolts. Align the matchmarks and tighten the attaching bolts to 129 ft. lbs. (175 Nm). Tighten the ball joint-to-knuckle attaching nut to 55 ft. lbs (75 Nm).

19. Install a new O-ring between the bearing and knuckle assembly.

20. Install the splash shield, hub/bearing assembly, to the knuckle and install the attaching bolts. Tighten the attaching bolts to 67 ft. lbs. (90 Nm).

21. Remove the boot cover from the outer CV-joint boot and slide the halfshaft into the knuckle assembly.

22. Install the hub washer and attaching nut, (use and new nut) on the halfshaft. Tighten the attaching nut to 71 ft. lbs. (100 Nm).

23. Connect the stabilizer link to the lower control arm.

24. Install the brake rotor, caliper and the wheel/tire assembly.

25. Lower the vehicle and tighten the hub nut to 191 ft. lbs. (259 Nm).

STEERING

Steering Wheel

REMOVAL AND INSTALLATION

1. Disconnect the negative battery cable.

2. If equipped with SIR, disable the system and remove the inflator module.

3. Without SIR, remove the horn cover-to-steering wheel screws.

4. Disconnect the horn electrical connector from the steering wheel and remove the horn contact.

5. Remove the steering wheel-to-column retainer, nut, washer.

6. Mark the steering wheel alignment with the steering shaft for installation purposes.

7. Using a steering wheel puller, press the steering wheel from the steering column.

NOTE: Under no circumstances should the steering wheel or shaft be hammered on. Sharp blows to the steering column could loosen the plastic injections which maintain column rigidity.

To install:

8. If equipped with SIR, feed the coil assembly connector through the steering wheel.

9. Align the matchmarks made during removal and install the steering wheel.

10. Align the steering wheel with the turn signal cancelling cam assembly.

11. Install the hexagon locking nut. Tighten the steering wheel nut to 31 ft. lbs. (42 Nm).

12. If equipped with SIR, install the inflator module and enable the system.

13. Connect the negative battery cable.

Steering Column

REMOVAL AND INSTALLATION

1. Disconnect the negative battery cable.

2. Remove the left side sound insulator.

3. Disconnect the combination switch electrical connector.

4. If equipped, disable the SIR system.

5. Disconnect the ignition and dimmer switch connectors and if equipped, disconnect the cruise switch terminal connection.

6. Remove the steering column support bracket bolts.

7. Remove the flange and coupling pinch bolt.

8. Remove the upper and lower steering column support bolts.

9. Disconnect the dimmer switch and turn signal switch electrical connectors.

10. If equipped with park lock, remove the park lock cable from the ignition switch.

NOTE: If equipped with park lock, the park lock cable must be disconnected by pressing the locking tab at the ignition switch inhibitor before removing the column from the vehicle.

11. Remove the steering column assembly from the vehicle.

To install:

12. Position the steering column in the vehicle.

13. Connect the park lock cable to the ignition switch.

14. Connect the electrical connectors.

15. Position the steering column into the flange and coupling assembly.

16. Install the lower steering column support bolts. Tighten to 21 ft. lbs. (28 Nm).

17. Install the steering column support bracket-to-steering column bolts. Tighten to 22 ft. lbs. (30 Nm).

18. Install the upper steering column support bolts. Tighten to 21 ft. lbs. (28 Nm).

19. Install the flange coupling pinch bolt. Tighten to 30 ft. lbs. (41 Nm).

20. Connect the hazard/turn signal switch electrical connectors.

21. If equipped, connect the cruise control electrical connector.

22. If equipped, enable the SIR system.

23. Install the left side sound insulator.

24. Connect the negative battery cable.

Power Steering Rack

ADJUSTMENT

1. Disconnect the negative battery cable. Raise and safely support the vehicle.

2. With the front tires off the ground, loosen the locknut on the bottom of the steering rack.

3. Turn the adjuster plug clockwise until it bottoms out in the housing.

4. Turn the adjuster plug in the opposite direction 50–70 degrees.

5. While holding the adjuster plug, tighten the locknut to 50 ft. lbs. (68 Nm).

NOTE: If the adjuster plug is not held, damage to the pinion teeth on the steering rack may occur.

6. Check to make sure the steering wheel returns to center.

REMOVAL AND INSTALLATION

1. Disconnect the negative battery cable. From inside the vehicle, remove the left side lower sound insulator.

2. Remove the upper steering shaft-to-steering rack coupling pinch bolt.

3. Place a drain pan under the steering gear and disconnect the pressure lines from the steering gear.

4. Raise and safely support the vehicle.

5. Remove both front wheel and tire assemblies.

6. Using a ball joint remover, disconnect the tie rod ends from the steering knuckles.

7. Lower the vehicle.

8. Remove both steering gear-to-chassis clamps.

9. Slide the steering gear forward and remove the lower steering shaft-to-steering rack coupling pinch bolt.

10. From the firewall, disconnect the coupling and seal from the steering gear.

11. Raise and safely support the vehicle.

12. Through the left wheel opening, remove the steering gear with the tie rods.

To install:

13. Installation is the reverse of the removal procedures. Lower the vehicle.

14. Tighten the steering gear-to-chassis clamp bolts to 28 ft. lbs. (38 Nm), the tie rod nut to 44 ft. lbs. (60 Nm) and the fluid lines to 18 ft. lbs. (24 Nm).

15. Refill power steering pump reservoir and bleed the power steering system. Connect the negative battery cable.

16. Check and adjust the front end alignment as required.

Power Steering Pump

REMOVAL AND INSTALLATION

1. Disconnect the negative battery cable.

2. Remove the pressure and return hoses from the pump and drain the system into a suitable container.

3. Cap the fittings at the pump.

4. Remove the serpentine belt.

5. Locate the pump attaching bolts through the pulley and remove the bolts.

6. Remove the pump assembly.

To install:

7. Installation is the reverse of the removal procedures.

8. Tighten the power steering pump bolts to 20 ft. lbs. (27 Nm).

9. Refill power steering pump reservoir and bleed the system.

10. Connect the negative battery cable.

BELT ADJUSTMENT

1. Install a belt tension gauge on the power steering belt.

2. Loosen pump adjustment bolts.

3. Tighten the front bracket-to-engine bolt **A** to 9 inch lbs. (1 Nm).

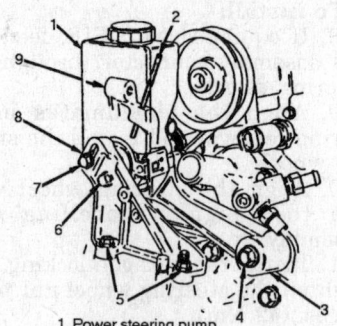

1. Power steering pump
2. Adjustment stud
3. Front adjusting bracket
4. Bolt - 67 ft. lbs. (91 nm)
5. Bolt - 20 ft. lbs. (54 nm)
6. Bolt - 20 ft. lbs. (27 nm)
7. Bolt - 20 ft. lbs. (27 nm)
8. Rear adjusting bracket
9. Pump front support

To Adjust:
A. Loosen adjusting bolts
B. Set belt tension
C. Tighten bolt 4
D. Tighten bolt 6
E. Tighten bolt 7
F. Tighten bolts 5
G. Tighten stud 2 to 53 lbs. in. (5 nm)

8470J097

Adjusting the power steering belt tension — 2.3L engine

4. Set the belt tension by turning adjustment stud.

NOTE: The adjustment bolts are all tighten to different torque specifications. Tighten each bolt as follows:

5. Tighten adjustment bolts **A** to 67 ft. lbs. (91 Nm), bolts **B** to 19 ft. lbs. (26 Nm) and bolts **C** to 40 ft. lbs. (54 Nm).

6. Start engine and run it for a minimum of 2 minutes. Re-adjust the belt tension.

SYSTEM BLEEDING

NOTE: Automatic transmission fluid is not compatible with the seals and hoses of the power steering system. Under no circumstances should automatic transmission fluid be used in place of power steering fluid in this system.

1. With the engine turned **OFF**, turn the wheels all the way to the left.

2. Fill the reservoir with power steering fluid until the level is at the **COLD** mark on the reservoir.

3. Start and operate the engine at fast idle for 15 seconds. Turn the engine **OFF**.

4. Recheck the fluid level and fill it to the **COLD** mark.

5. Start the engine and bleed the system by turning the wheels in both directions slowly to the stops.

6. Stop the engine and check the fluid. Fluid that still has air in it will be a light tan color.

7. Repeat this procedure until all air is removed from the system.

BRAKES

Master Cylinder

REMOVAL AND INSTALLATION

1. Disconnect the electrical connector from the fluid level sensor and the connectors from both solenoids.

2. Disconnect the 3 pin and 6 pin motor pack electrical connectors

3. Disconnect the brake lines from the master cylinder and from the modulator assembly. Plug the lines.

4. Remove the master cylinder mounting nuts and remove the master cylinder and modulator assembly.

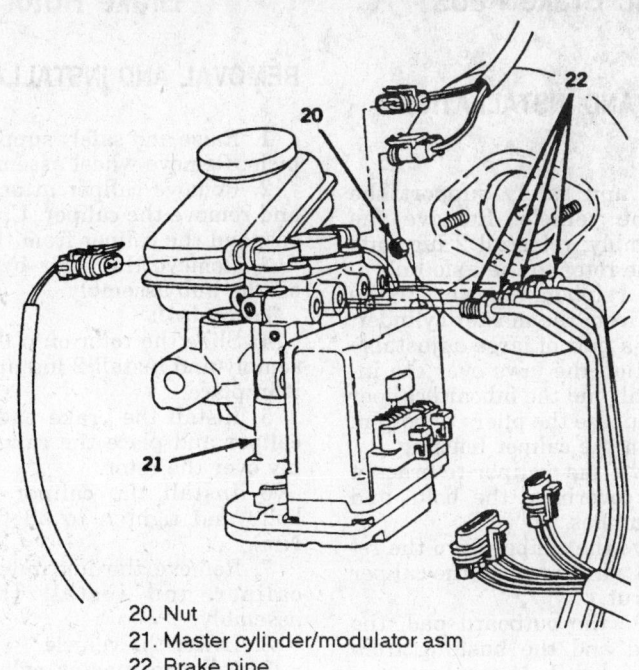

20. Nut
21. Master cylinder/modulator asm
22. Brake pipe

8470J099

Master cylinder

To install:

5. Install the master cylinder and modulator assembly to the vehicle and install the mounting nuts. Tighten the mounting nuts to 20 ft. lbs. (27 Nm).

6. Connect the brake lines to the master cylinder and the modulator. Tighten the nuts to 15 ft. lbs. (20 Nm).

7. Connect the electrical connectors.

8. Fill the master cylinder with brake fluid to the proper level and bleed the brake system as necessary.

BENCH BLEEDING

This procedure is used to bench bleed the master cylinder.

1. Refill the master cylinder reservoir.

2. Push the plunger several times to force fluid into the piston.

3. Continue pumping the plunger until the fluid is free of the air bubbles.

4. Plug the outlet ports and install the master cylinder.

Proportioning Valve

REMOVAL AND INSTALLATION

NOTE: It is necessary to remove the master cylinder in order to remove the proportioning valve. Bleed the brake system when finished.

1. Disconnect the negative battery cable.

2. Remove the master cylinder from the vehicle.

3. Remove the proportioning valve cap on the master cylinder.

4. Remove and discard the O-rings.

5. Remove the springs, the proportioning valve pistons and the seals from the valves.

6. Inspect the valves for corrosion or abnormal wear, replace as required.

7. Clean all parts in denatured alcohol or an equivalent. Dry all parts with air before reassembling.

To install:

8. Assemble the springs, proportioning valve pistons and the seals on the valves.

9. Install new O-ring seals.

10. Install the proportioning valve cap on the master cylinder.

11. Tighten the caps to 20 ft. lbs. (27 Nm). Refill the reservoir and bleed the brake system.

12. Install the master cylinder to the vehicle and connect the negative battery cable.

Power Brake Booster

REMOVAL AND INSTALLATION

1. Disconnect the negative battery cable. Remove the master cylinder.

NOTE: Place the master cylinder in an upright position to prevent fluid loss.

2. Remove the lower-left trim panel inside the vehicle and disconnect the brake pedal-to-booster pushrod from the brake pedal.

3. Disconnect the vacuum line from the booster.

4. Remove the brake booster mounting nuts and the booster.

To install:

5. Installation is the reverse of the removal procedures. Tighten the master cylinder-to-power booster to 20 ft. lbs. (27 Nm) and the power booster mounting nuts to 20 ft. lbs. (27 Nm).

6. Bleed the brake system. Connect the negative battery cable.

Brake Caliper

REMOVAL AND INSTALLATION

1. Disconnect the negative battery cable.

2. Remove half of the brake fluid from the master cylinder.

3. Raise and support the vehicle safely and remove the wheel assembly.

NOTE: Remove the brake hose attaching bolt, only if the caliper is going to be overhauled or replaced.

4. Position a large C-clamp over the caliper with the screw end against the outboard brake pad. Tighten the clamp until the caliper piston is pushed out enough to bottom the piston.

5. Remove the C-clamp. Remove the caliper guide pins and lift the caliper off the rotor.

6. Support the caliper so there is no strain on the brake hose.

7. Press the inboard pad outward and remove it from the caliper.

8. Remove and discard the O-ring bushings and steel sleeves, new parts are to be installed.

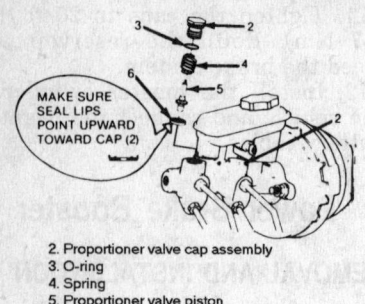

2. Proportioner valve cap assembly
3. O-ring
4. Spring
5. Proportioner valve piston
6. Proportioner valve seal

8470J100

Proportioning valve installation

9. Check the condition of the rotor. If rotor measurements exceed manufacturer's specifications or has mild scoring, machine the rotor.
To install:
10. Lubricate and install the O-ring bushings. Install the sleeves by pressing them through the O-rings until the sleeve end on the pad side is flush with caliper ear.
11. Position the inboard pads so the pad contacts the piston and the support spring ends. The inboard and outboard pads are similar but not interchangeable.
12. Press down on the ears at the top of the inboard pad until the pad lies flat and the spring ends are just inside the lower edge of the pad.
13. Position the outboard pad with the ears toward the positioning pin holes and the tab on the inner edge of the pad resting in the notch in the edge of the caliper. Bend the ears to provide a slight interference fit in the caliper.
14. Press the outboard pad tightly into position and clinch the ears of the outboard pad over the outboard caliper half.
15. Position the caliper over the rotor.
16. Install the caliper over the rotor.
17. Install the caliper mounting bolts and tighten to 38 ft. lbs. (51 Nm).
18. If the brake hose attaching nut was disconnected, reconnect it and tighten to 33 ft. lbs. (45 Nm).
19. Install the wheel assembly and lower the vehicle.
20. Fill the master cylinder with brake fluid and bleed the system.
21. Connect the negative battery cable.

Disc Brake Pads

REMOVAL AND INSTALLATION

1. Raise and safely support the front of the vehicle. Remove the wheel assembly; reinstall 2 lug nuts to retain the rotor to the axle hub.
2. Using a siphon, remove 1/3 of the brake fluid from the master cylinder.
3. Using a pair of large adjustable pliers, position the jaws over the inboard pad tab and the inboard caliper housing. Squeeze the pliers to bottom the piston in the caliper housing.
4. Remove the caliper-to-bracket boots, bolt coverings, the bolts and sleeve assemblies.
5. Remove the caliper from the rotor. Using a wire, suspend the caliper from the strut.
6. Remove the outboard pad, the inboard pad and the bushing from the mounting bolt hole groves.
To install:
7. Using silicone grease, lubricate the new mounting bolt bushings and install them in the holes.
8. Install the retainer spring onto the inboard pad and the pad into the caliper by snapring the retaining spring into the piston; the inboard pad must lay flat against the piston.

NOTE: On some models, the retaining spring is already staked to the inboard pad.

9. Install the outboard pad with the wear sensor at the leading edge of the forward wheel rotating; the pad must lay flat against the caliper.
10. Position the caliper assembly over the rotor in the mounting bracket. Tighten the caliper-to-bracket bolts to 38 ft. lbs. (51 Nm).
11. Using a small prybar, position it between the outboard pad and the rotor hub to hold the pad in position. Have an assistant, apply approximately 50 lbs. pressure on the brake pedal.
12. While the assistant is applying pressure, position a ball peen hammer on the outboard pad tab and tap it with another hammer to drive the tab downward to a 45 degree angle to lock the pad into position.
13. Remove the 2 rotor-to-wheel hub nuts and install the wheel.
14. Lower the vehicle. Refill the master cylinder reservoir and road test the vehicle.

Brake Rotor

REMOVAL AND INSTALLATION

1. Raise and safely support the vehicle. Remove wheel assembly.
2. Remove caliper attaching bolts and remove the caliper. Using a wire suspend the caliper from the strut.
3. Remove the rotor by sliding it off the hub assembly.
To install:
4. Slide the rotor onto the hub assembly and install 2 lug nuts to hold it in place.
5. Install the brake pads into the caliper and place the caliper assembly over the rotor.
6. Install the caliper mounting bolts and tighten to 38 ft. lbs. (51 Nm).
7. Remove the lug nuts from the caliper and install the wheel assembly.
8. Lower the vehicle.
9. Fill the master cylinder with brake fluid.
10. Depress the brake pedal 3–4 times to seat the brake linings and to restore pressure in the system.

Brake Drums

REMOVAL AND INSTALLATION

1. Raise and safely support the vehicle.
2. Remove the wheel assembly.
3. Remove the brake drum from the spindle.
To install:
4. Using a brake adjusting tool, adjust the brake shoe to 0.50 in. (1.27mm) less than the brake drum diameter. Install the brake drum to the axle.
5. Install the wheel assembly and lower the vehicle.

Brake Shoes

REMOVAL AND INSTALLATION

1. Raise and safely support the vehicle. Remove the wheel assembly.
2. If the brake drum is difficult to remove, perform the following procedures:
   a. Make sure the parking brake is released.
   b. Back off the parking brake cable adjustment.

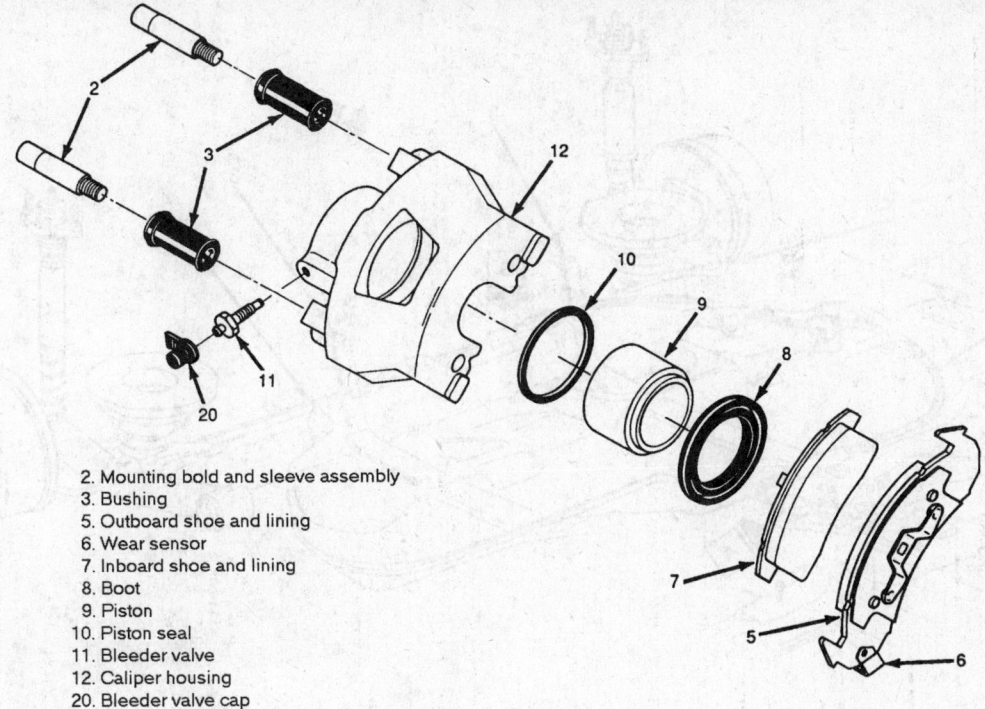

2. Mounting bold and sleeve assembly
3. Bushing
5. Outboard shoe and lining
6. Wear sensor
7. Inboard shoe and lining
8. Boot
9. Piston
10. Piston seal
11. Bleeder valve
12. Caliper housing
20. Bleeder valve cap

8470J101

Exploded view of the brake caliper assembly

c. Remove the adjusting hole knockout plate and back off the adjusting screw.

NOTE: On some drum designs, the knockout plate must be drilled out using a 7/16 in. (11mm) drill bit. A rubber adjusting hole cover is available for installation purposes.

d. Using a rubber mallet, tap the drum from the spindle.

3. Remove the return springs, the hold-down springs and the lever pivot. While lifting up on the actuator lever, remove the actuator link.

4. Remove the actuator lever, the lever return spring, the parking brake strut and the strut spring.

5. Disconnect the parking brake cable and remove the primary brake shoe.

6. Remove the adjusting screw, the spring, the retaining ring, the pin, the parking brake lever and the secondary shoe.

7. If any parts are of doubtful strength or quality, due to discoloration from heat, stress or wear, replace them.

To install:

8. Clean all of the parts in denatured alcohol. Lubricate the necessary parts.

9. To install, reverse the removal procedures and install all of the parts, except the brake drum.

10. Using a brake adjusting tool, adjust the brake shoe to 0.50 in. (1.27mm) less than the brake drum diameter. Install the brake drum.

11. To complete the installation, reverse the removal procedures. Road test the vehicle.

Wheel Cylinder

REMOVAL AND INSTALLATION

1. Raise and safely support the vehicle. Remove the wheel assembly and brake drum Remove the brake shoes and attaching hardware.

2. Clean any dirt from around the wheel cylinder.

3. Disconnect and plug the brake line from the wheel cylinder.

4. Remove the wheel cylinder-to-backing plate bolt and lockwasher.

5. Remove the wheel cylinder.

To install:

6. Apply a liquid gasket to the shoulder of the wheel cylinder that faces the backing plate and reverse the removal procedures. Tighten the wheel cylinder-to-backing plate bolt to 15 ft. lbs. (20 Nm) and the brake

line-to-wheel cylinder to 12 ft. lbs. (17 Nm).

7. Bleed the brake system. Lower the vehicle and check the brake operation.

Parking Brake Cable

ADJUSTMENT

1. Apply and release the parking brake lever (10 clicks) at least 6 times. Apply the parking brake lever 5 clicks or if floor mounted parking brake, apply pedal 2 clicks.

2. Raise and safely support the vehicle.

3. Locate the access hole in the backing plate and adjust the parking brake cable until the right rear wheel can be turned rearward but is locked when attempting to turn forward.

4. Release the parking brake and check to see if both wheels turn freely by hand.

5. Lower the vehicle.

REMOVAL AND INSTALLATION

Front Cable

1. Raise and safely support the vehicle.

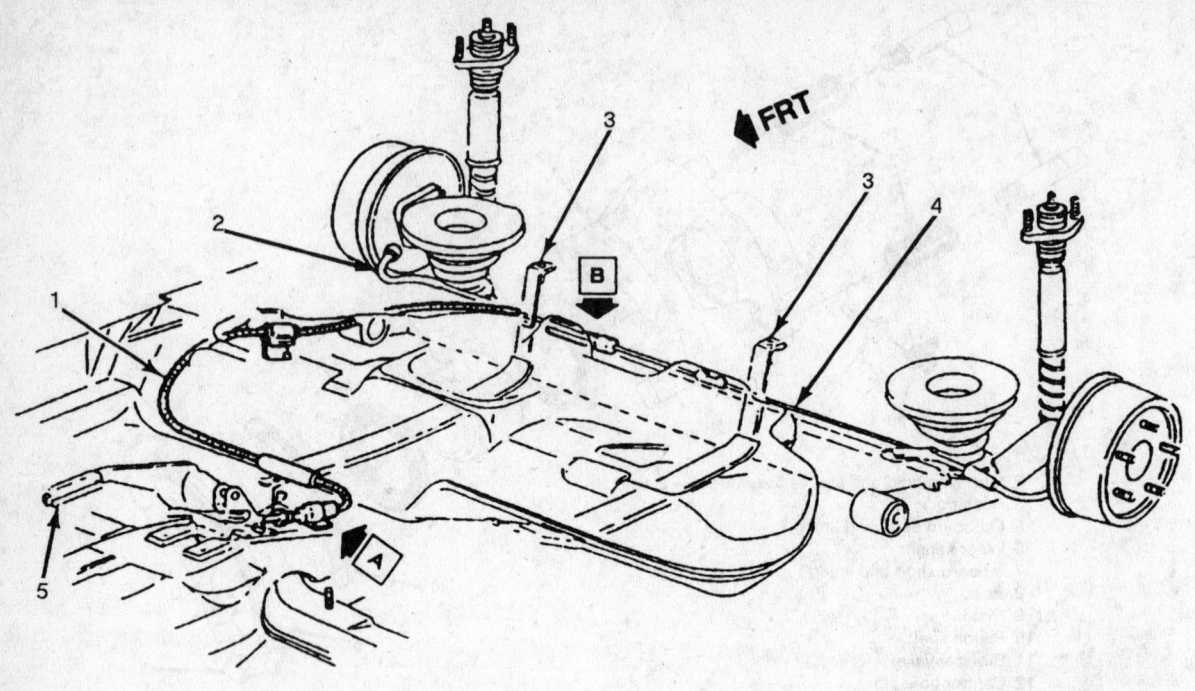

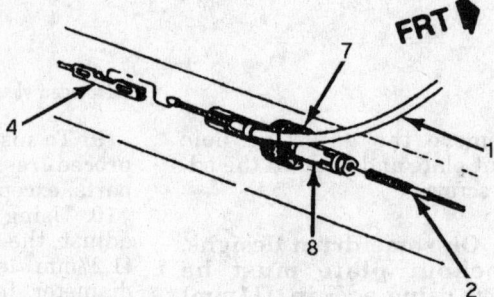

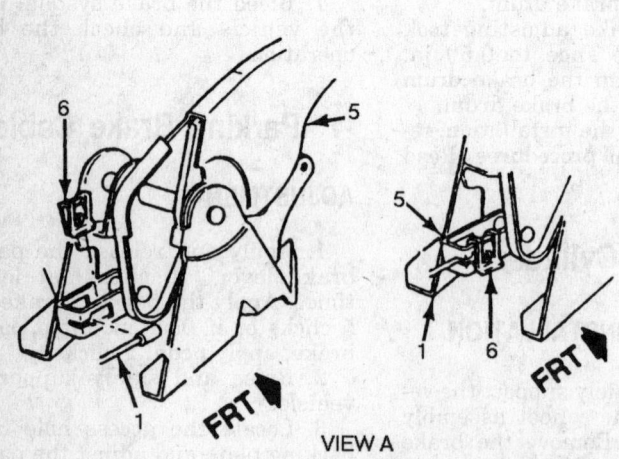

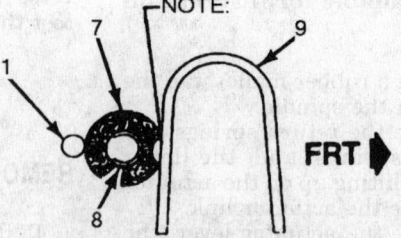

VIEW A

1. Front parking brake cable
2. Right rear parking brake cable
3. Fuel tank strap
4. Left rear parking brake cable
5. Parking brake lever
6. Cable retainer
7. Insulator
8. Equalizer
9. Axle assembly

NOTE: Notch in insulator to be installed opposite front park brake cable.

VIEW B

8470J102

Exploded view of the parking brake cable assembly

2. Loosen but do not remove the equalizer nut.

3. Remove the console.

4. Disconnect the parking brake cable from the lever.

5. Remove the cable retaining nut that secures the cable to the floor panel.

6. Loosen the catalytic converter shield and disconnect the brake cable from the body.

7. Disconnect the cable from the equalizer, from the guides and from the underbody clips.

To install:

8. Connect the cable to the equalizer, to the guides and secure with the underbody clips.

9. Connect the the cable to the underbody and tighten the catalytic converter shield.

10. Install the cable retaining nut that secures the cable to the floor panel.

11. Connect the cable to the lever.

12. Install the console and adjust the cable as necessary.

13. Lower the vehicle.

Rear Cable

1. Raise and safely support the vehicle.

2. Loosen the equalizer nut until the cable tension is released.

3. Remove the tire/wheel assembly and the brake drum.

4. Place a prybar between the brake shoe and the top part of the brake adjuster bracket.

5. Release the top adjuster bracket by pushing the bracket to the front.

6. Remove the following:

a. Hold-down spring
b. Actuator lever
c. Lever return spring
d. Adjuster screw spring
e. Top rear brake shoe return spring

7. Disconnect the parking brake cable from the parking brake lever.

8. Disconnect the conduit fitting from the backing plate while depressing the retaining tangs.

9. Remove the cable end button from the right side connector.

10. Disconnect the conduit fitting from the axle bracket while depressing the retaining tangs.

To install:

11. Connect the conduit fitting to the axle bracket.

12. Connect the cable end button to the connector on the right side.

13. Connect the conduit fitting to the backing plate.

14. Install the parking brake cable to the parking brake lever.

15. Install the top rear brake shoe return spring and the adjuster screw spring.

16. Install the lever return spring, the actuator lever and the rear hold-down spring.

17. Install the top adjuster bracket rod.

18. Install the brake drum and the tire/wheel.

19. Adjust the brake cable as necessary and lower the vehicle.

Brake System Bleeding

PROCEDURE

1. Clean the bleeder screw at each wheel.

2. Attach a small rubber hose to the bleed screw and place the end in a clear container of fresh brake fluid.

3. Fill the master cylinder reservoir with fresh brake fluid. The master cylinder reservoir level should be checked and filled often during the bleeding procedure.

4. Have an assistant slowly pump the brake pedal and hold the pressure.

5. Open the bleeder screw about 1/4 turn. The pedal should fall to the floor as air and fluid are pushed out. Close the bleeder screw while the assistant holds the pedal to the floor. Slowly release the pedal and wait 15 seconds. Repeat the process until no more air bubbles are forced from the system when the brake pedal is applied. It may be necessary to repeat this 10 or more times to get all of the air from the system.

6. Repeat this procedure on the remaining wheel cylinders and calipers. Make sure the master cylinder does not run out of brake fluid.

NOTE: Wait 15 seconds between each bleeding and do not pump the pedal rapidly. Rapid pumping of the brake pedal pushes the master cylinder secondary piston down the bore in a manner that makes it difficult to bleed the system.

7. Check the brake pedal and system for proper operation. Repeat the entire bleeding procedure if necessary. Check the fluid level when finished.

Anti-Lock Brake System Service

PRECAUTIONS

Failure to observe the following precautions may result in system damage.

• Before performing electric arc welding on the vehicle, disconnect the Electronic Brake Control Module (EBCM) and the hydraulic modulator connectors.

• When performing painting work on the vehicle, do not expose the Electronic Brake Control Module (EBCM) to temperatures in excess of 185°F (85°C) for longer than 2 hours. The system may be exposed to temperatures up to 200°F (95°C) for less than 15 minutes.

• Never disconnect or connect the Electronic Brake Control Module (EBCM) or hydraulic modulator connectors with the ignition switch ON.

• Never disassemble any component of the Anti-Lock Brake System (ABS) which is designated non-serviceable; the component must be replaced as an assembly.

• When filling the master cylinder, always use Delco Supreme 11 brake fluid or equivalent, which meets DOT-3 specifications; petroleum base fluid will destroy the rubber parts.

The anti-lock brake system that is utilized on the Beretta and the Corsica is the GM ABS VI® system. The system consists of a motor pack assembly which is connected directly to the master cylinder and vacuum booster unit and individual wheel speed sensors.

ABS Motor Pack Assembly

REMOVAL AND INSTALLATION

1. Disconnect the negative battery cable.

2. Remove the master cylinder assembly from the vehicle.

3. Remove the 6 attaching Torx® bolts and remove the motor pack assembly.

4. Installation is the reverse of removal. Tighten the Torx® bolts to 27 inch lbs. (3 Nm).

ABS Hydraulic Modulator Assembly

REMOVAL AND INSTALLATION

1. Disconnect the negative battery cable.
2. Remove the master cylinder assembly from the vehicle.
3. Remove the 6 attaching Torx® bolts and remove the motor pack assembly.
4. Remove the 2 modulator-to-master cylinder through bolts and separate the modulator from the master cylinder.
5. Installation is the reverse of the removal. Tighten the 2 thru bolts to 12 ft. lbs. (16 Nm) and the Torx® bolts to 27 inch lbs. (3 Nm).

Wheel Speed Sensor

REMOVAL AND INSTALLATION

Front Sensor

1. Disconnect sensor connector from underhood area near strut tower.
2. Raise and safely support the vehicle.
3. Remove the wheel speed sensor retaining bolt.
4. Slide the sensor out of the knuckle. If sensor will not slide out, remove the brake rotor and push sensor out from back side of knuckle.
5. Installation is the reverse of the removal. Tighten the retaining bolt to 106 inch lbs. (12 Nm).

Rear Sensor

1. Raise and safely support the vehicle.
2. Remove the rear wheel and tire assembly.
3. Remove the rear brake drum and disconnect the sensor electrical connector.
4. Remove the bolts and nuts that attach the rear wheel bearing and sped sensor and remove the assemblies.
5. Installation is the reverse of the removal. Tighten the bolts to 38 ft. lbs. (52 Nm).

FRONT SUSPENSION

MacPherson Strut

REMOVAL AND INSTALLATION

1. Disconnect the upper strut-to-body attaching bolts.
2. Raise and safely support the vehicle. Allow the suspension to hang free. Remove the wheel assembly. Install a halfshaft boot protector.
3. Remove the cotter pin and tie rod attaching nut. Using a tie rod separator tool, separate the tie rod from the strut.
4. Support the steering knuckle to prevent tension from being applied to the brake line.
5. Matchmark the strut in relationship to the knuckle and remove both strut-to-knuckle attaching bolts. Remove the strut assembly from the vehicle.
To install:
6. Installation is the reverse of the removal procedures. When installing the mounting bolts be sure to place the flats of the bolts in the horizontal position.
7. Tighten the strut-to-knuckle bolts to 129 ft. lbs. (175 Nm) and the upper strut-to-body attaching bolts to 18 ft. lbs. (25 Nm).
8. Lower the vehicle. Check and adjust the alignment as required.

MacPherson Strut Cartridge

REMOVAL AND INSTALLATION

1. Install the strut assembly to a strut compressor.
2. Turn the compressor so that the spring becomes compressed.
3. Hold the strut shaft from turning and remove the 24mm strut nut.
4. Install special rod J34013-38 to the strut shaft and guide the strut out of the assembly while loosening the spring compressor.
5. Remove the strut cartridge from the assembly.
To install:
6. Install the strut to the strut compressor/spring assembly.
7. Start turning the compressor screw clockwise to compress the spring while guiding the shaft through the mounting hole.
8. Tighten the mounting nut to 55 ft. lbs. (75 Nm) while holding the strut shaft.

Lower Ball Joints

INSPECTION

1. Raise and safely support the vehicle; be sure the weight of the vehicle does not rest on the lower control arm assemblies.
2. With the ball joint installed to the steering knuckle, grasp the top and bottom of the wheel, then move the wheel using an in and out shaking motion. Observe any movement between the steering knuckle and the control arm. If movement exists, replace the ball joint.

REMOVAL AND INSTALLATION

1. Raise and safely support the vehicle and remove the wheel assembly.
2. If no countersink is found on the lower side of the rivets, carefully locate the center of the rivet body and mark it using a punch.
3. Properly drill out the rivets of the ball joint assembly. Using a ball joint separator tool, separate the ball joint from the steering knuckle.
4. Disconnect the stabilizer bar from the lower control arm. Remove the ball joint from the vehicle.
To install:
5. Installation is the reverse of the removal procedures.
6. Attach the ball joint the lower control arm with the attaching bolts and nuts. Tighten the attaching bolts and nuts to 50 ft. lbs. (68 Nm).
7. Lower the vehicle. Check and align the front end as required.

Lower Control Arms

REMOVAL AND INSTALLATION

1. Raise and safely support the vehicle and remove the wheel assembly.
2. Disconnect the stabilizer bar from the lower control arm assembly. Using a ball joint separator tool, separate the ball joint from the steering knuckle.
3. Remove the lower control arm attaching bolts and remove the lower control arm from the vehicle.
To install:
4. Installation is the reverse of the removal procedures. Tighten the lower control arm bolts to 63 ft. lbs. (85 Nm). Tighten the ball joint-to-knuckle attaching nut to 55 ft. lbs. (75 Nm). Check and align the front end as required.

Sway Bar

REMOVAL AND INSTALLATION

1. Open the hood and install an engine support tool. Raise and safely support the vehicle; allow the suspension to hang free. Remove the left front wheel assembly.

2. Disconnect the stabilizer link bolts and nuts from the control arms. Disconnect the stabilizer shaft from the support assemblies.

3. Loosen the front bolts and remove the bolts from the rear and center of the support assemblies, allowing the supports to be lowered enough to remove the stabilizer bar assembly. Remove the assembly from the vehicle.

To install:

4. Installation is the reverse of the removal procedures. Loosely assemble all components while insuring that the stabilizer bar is centered, side-to-side. Tighten the stabilizer bar support assemblies to 14 ft. lbs. (19 Nm). Tighten the stabilizer link bolts and nuts 14 ft. lbs. (19 Nm).

5. Lower the vehicle.

REAR SUSPENSION

Shock Absorbers

REMOVAL AND INSTALLATION

1. Open the trunk and remove the shock absorber trim cover, if equipped. Remove the upper shock absorber attaching bolt. Remove each shock absorber separately when both assemblies are being replaced.

2. Raise and safely support the vehicle and the rear axle assembly.

3. Remove the lower shock attaching bolts. Remove the shock absorber from the vehicle.

To install:

4. Installation is the reverse of the removal procedures. Tighten the lower shock attaching bolt to 35 ft. lbs. (48 Nm) and the upper shock attaching bolt to 22 ft. lbs. (30 Nm).

Coil Springs

REMOVAL AND INSTALLATION

1. Raise and safely support the vehicle under the rear control arms. Support the rear axle assembly with and jack.

2. Remove the wheel assembly. Remove the right and left brake line bracket attaching screws from the body and allow the brake line to hang free.

3. Remove the shock absorber lower attaching bolts. Lower the rear axle assembly to remove the coil springs. Do not allow the axle assembly to hang unsupported in this position.

To install:

4. Installation is the reverse of the removal procedures. Before installing the coil springs it is necessary to install the insulators to the body using adhesive.

5. Position the spring and insulator in the spring seat and raise the axle. The upper ends of the coil must be positioned properly in the seat of the body.

6. Tighten the shock absorber lower attaching bolts to 21 ft. lbs. (28 Nm).

7. Install the wheel assemblies and lower the vehicle.

Stabilizer Bar

REMOVAL AND INSTALLATION

1. Raise and safely support the vehicle.

2. Remove the nuts and bolts at both axle and control arm attachments.

3. Remove the bracket. Remove the insulator and the stabilizer bar assembly assembly.

To install:

4. Installation is the reverse of the removal procedures. Tighten the bracket-to-axle bolts to 13 ft. lbs. (18 Nm) and the bracket-to-control arm bolts to 16 ft. lbs. (22 Nm).

Rear Wheel Bearings

REMOVAL AND INSTALLATION

The rear wheel hub and bearing are replaced as an assembly only.

1. Raise and safely support the vehicle.

2. Remove the wheel and tire assembly and the brake drum.

3. Remove the hub/bearing assembly-to-rear axle nuts/bolts.

NOTE: The top mounting bolt will not clear the brake shoe when removing the hub and bearing. The hub and bearing must be partially removed while the top bolt is being turned out.

To install:

4. To install, insert and turn the top bolt in while installing the hub and bearing. Install the attaching bolts.

5. Tighten the hub/bearing assembly-to-rear axle nuts/bolts to 38 ft. lbs. (52 Nm).

6. Install the brake drum and wheel and tire assembly.

Rear Axle Assembly

REMOVAL AND INSTALLATION

1. Raise and safely support the vehicle under the rear control arms. Support the rear axle assembly with and jack.

2. Remove the wheel assembly. Remove the right and left brake line bracket attaching screws from the body and allow the brake line to hang free.

3. Remove the stabilizer bar brackets. Remove the insulator and the stabilizer bar assembly.

4. Remove the shock absorber lower attaching bolts. Lower the rear axle assembly to remove the coil springs. Do not allow the axle assembly to hang in this position.

5. Remove the control arm attaching bolts from the underbody bracket and lower the axle.

6. Remove the hub attaching bolts an remove the hub, bearing and backing plate assembly.

NOTE: Be careful not to drop the hub/bearing assembly, damage to the bearing could result.

To install:

7. Install the backing plate and hub/bearing assembly to the rear axle assembly. Install the attaching bolts and nuts and tighten to 38 ft. lbs. (52 Nm).

8. Install the stabilizer bar to the rear axle assembly and install the attaching nuts and bolts. Tighten the bracket-to-axle bolts to 13 ft. lbs. (18 Nm) and the bracket-to-control arm bolts to 16 ft. lbs. (22 Nm).

9. Secure the axle assembly on a transmission jack and raise it into position.

10. Install the control arms to the underbody bracket and install the mounting nuts and bolts. Do not tighten the bolts at this time. The

bolts must be tightened at curb height.

NOTE: The control arm mounting bolts must be install from the inboard side.

11. Connect the brake line connections and install the brake cable to the rear axle assembly.

12. Position the springs and insulators in the spring seat and raise the axle. The upper ends of the coil must be positioned properly in the seat of the body.

13. Connect the shock absorber at the lower end and install attaching bolt. Tighten the attaching bolt to 35 ft. lbs. (48 Nm).

14. Connect the parking brake to the guide hook. Adjust the cable as required.

15. Bleed the brake system and refill the reservoir. Adjust the brakes as required.

16. Lower the axle to curb height and tighten the axle-to-body mounting bolts. Tighten the bolts to 66 ft. lbs. (90 Nm).

17. Install the wheel assemblies and lower the vehicle. Tighten the lug nuts to 100 ft. lbs. (140 Nm).

FIRING ORDERS

NOTE: To avoid confusion, always replace spark plug wires one at a time.

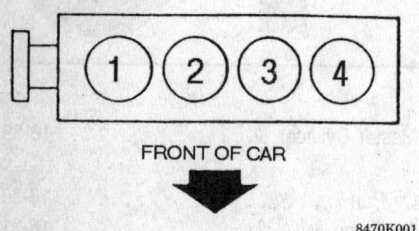

FRONT OF CAR

8470K001

2.3L Engine
Engine Firing Order: 1–3–4–2
Distributorless Ignition System

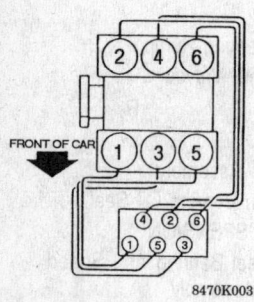

FRONT OF CAR

8470K003

3.1L and 3.3L Engines
3.1L Engine Firing Order:
1–2–3–4–5–6
3.3L Engine Firing Order:
1–6–5–4–3–2
Distributorless Ignition System

ENGINE ELECTRICAL

NOTE: Disconnecting the negative battery cable on some vehicles may interfere with the functions of the on board computer systems and may require the computer to undergo a relearning process, once the negative battery cable is reconnected.

Distributorless Ignition System

REMOVAL AND INSTALLATION

2.3L Engine

ELECTRONIC IGNITION MODULE ASSEMBLY

1. Disconnect the negative battery cable.
2. Disconnect the ignition module assembly harness connector.
3. Remove the bolts that fasten the assembly to the camshaft housing.
4. Remove the assembly. If the boots adhere to the spark plugs, remove them by twisting and pulling up on the retainers.

To install:

5. Install the boots and retainers to the housing, if they were separated during removal.
6. Align the spark plug boots with the plugs and place the assembly on the camshaft housing.
7. Install the mounting bolts and tighten to 15 ft. lbs. (20 Nm).
8. Connect the harness connector.
9. Connect the negative battery cable and check for proper operation.

IGNITION COILS

1. Disconnect the negative battery cable.
2. Remove the Integrated Direct Ignition (IDI) assembly.
3. Remove the housing to cover screws and remove the cover.
4. Disconnect the coil harness connectors.
5. Remove the coil(s), contact(s) and seal(s) from the cover.

To install:

6. Install the coil(s) to the cover and connect the connectors.
7. Install new seal(s) to the housing. Using petroleum jelly to retain, install the contact(s) to the housing.
8. Assemble the cover to the housing, install the screws and tighten to 35 inch lbs. (4 Nm).
9. Install the Integrated Direct Ignition (IDI) assembly.
10. Connect the negative battery cable and check for proper operation.

IGNITION MODULE

1. Disconnect the negative battery cable.
2. Remove the Integrated Direct Ignition (IDI) assembly.
3. Remove the housing to cover screws and remove the cover.
4. Disconnect the coil harness connector from the ignition module.

5. Remove the screws that fasten the module to the cover and remove the module from the cover. Do not wipe the heat-protective grease away from the module if it is being reused.

To install:

6. If a new module is used, spread the grease included with the package on the metal face of the module and on the module's seat on the cover.
7. Install the module to the cover and connect the harness connector.
8. Assemble the cover to the housing, install the screws and tighten to 35 inch lbs. (4 Nm).
9. Install the Integrated Direct Ignition (IDI) assembly.
10. Connect the negative battery cable and check for proper operation.

CRANKSHAFT SENSOR

1. Disconnect the negative battery cable.
2. Disconnect the connector from the sensor.
3. Remove the attaching bolt and remove the sensor from the engine.

To install:

4. Inspect the O-ring for damage and replace, if necessary.
5. Lubricate the O-ring with oil and install the sensor to its bore in the engine.
6. Install the attaching bolt and tighten to 88 inch lbs. (10 Nm).
7. Connect the sensor electrical connector.
8. Connect the negative battery cable.

3.1L and 3.3L Engines

C³I COILS AND MODULE ASSEMBLY

1. Disconnect the negative battery cable.
2. Disconnect the 14-way connector from the module.
3. Label and remove the spark plug wires from the assembly.
4. Remove the fasteners securing the assembly to its mounting bracket and remove the assembly.

To install:

5. Install the assembly to the bracket and install the fasteners.
6. Connect the spark plug wires and the harness connector.
7. Connect the negative battery cable and check the for proper operation.

IGNITION COILS

1. Disconnect the negative battery cable.
2. Disconnect the spark plug wires.
3. Remove the screws and remove the coil(s) or coil pack from the igni-

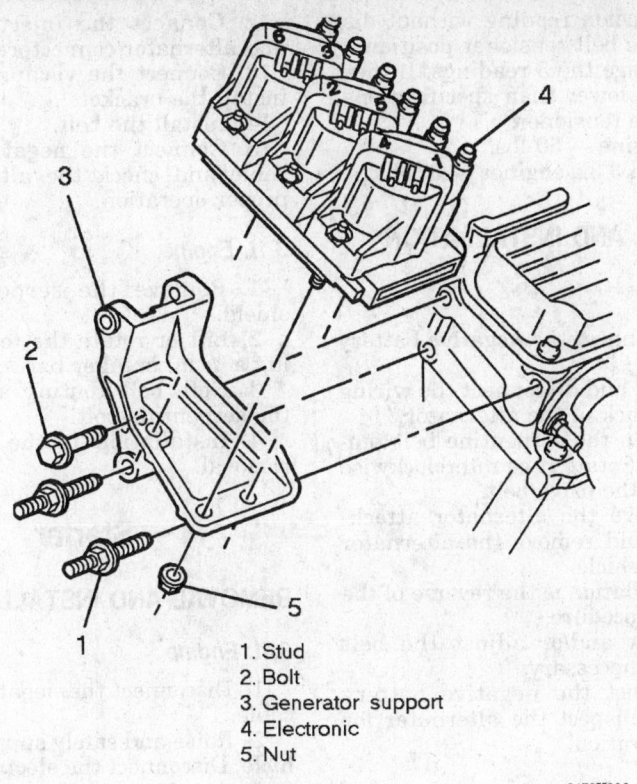

1. Stud
2. Bolt
3. Generator support
4. Electronic
5. Nut

8470K006

C³I ignition coil pack

tion module. Disconnect the coil to module connector, if equipped.

To install:

4. Connect the harness connector.
5. Install the coil(s) or coil pack to the ignition module and install the attaching screws.
6. Connect the spark plug wires.
7. Connect the negative battery cable and check for proper operation.

CRANKSHAFT SENSOR

The 3.1L engine is equipped with 2 separate crankshaft sensors. The 3X crankshaft sensor is mounted to the side of the engine block, above the oil pan flange and the 24X crankshaft sensor is mounted to the front timing cover, under the harmonic balancer.

24X Crankshaft Sensor

1. Disconnect the negative battery cable.
2. Remove the serpentine belt.
3. Raise and safely support the vehicle.
4. Remove the right front wheel and splash shield.
5. Remove the harmonic balancer.
6. Disconnect the sensor electrical connector.
7. Remove the sensor and pedestal from the engine and remove the sensor from the pedestal.

To install:

8. Loosely install the sensor to the pedestal.
9. Attach special aligning tool J–37089 or equivalent, to the assembly. Slide the tool over the crankshaft and tighten the pedestal to engine screws to 22 ft. lbs. (30 Nm). Tighten the pedestal pinch bolt to 30–35 inch lbs. (3–4 Nm).
10. Remove tool J–37089 from the crankshaft and place on the harmonic balancer and turn. If any vane of the harmonic balancer touches the tool, replace the balancer assembly.
11. Install the harmonic balancer to the crankshaft and tighten the attaching bolt to 219 ft. lbs. (300 Nm).
12. Connect the sensor connector.
13. Install the splash shield and wheel.
14. Lower the vehicle and install the serpentine belt.
15. Connect the negative battery cable and check for proper operation.

3X Crankshaft Sensor

NOTE: The 3X crankshaft sensor is mounted to the side of the engine block, above the oil pan flange. For the 3.1L engine with manual transaxle, the 3X crankshaft sensor is easily accessed from beneath the vehicle. For the

3.1L engine with automatic transaxle, the rack and pinion heatshield and catalytic converter intermediate exhaust assembly must be removed.

1. Disconnect the negative battery terminal.
2. Disconnect the sensor electrical connector.
3. Remove the sensor bolt and sensor from the engine.
4. Install a new O-ring and lubricate with engine oil. Install the bolt and torque to 88 inch lbs. (10 Nm).
5. Connect the negative battery terminal and check for proper operation.

Ignition Timing

ADJUSTMENT

NOTE: Distributorless ignition systems do not give provisions for setting ignition timing.

Alternator

PRECAUTIONS

Several precautions must be observed with alternator-equipped vehicles to avoid damage to the unit.

• If the battery is removed for any reason, make sure it is reconnected with the correct polarity. Reversing the battery connections may result in damage to the rectifiers.
• When utilizing a booster battery as a starting aid, always connect the positive to positive terminals and the negative terminal from the booster battery to a good engine ground on the vehicle being started.
• Never use a fast charger as a booster to start vehicles.
• Disconnect the battery cables when charging the battery with a fast charger.
• Never attempt to polarize the alternator.
• Do not use a tester of of greater than 12 volts when checking diode continuity.
• Do not short across or ground any of the alternator terminals.
• The polarity of the battery, alternator and regulator must be matched and considered before making any electrical connections within the system.
• Never separate the alternator on an open circuit. Make sure all connections within the circuit are clean and tight.

• Disconnect the battery ground terminal when performing any service on electrical components.
• Disconnect the battery if arc welding is to be done on the vehicle.
• Never disconnect the battery with the engine running.

BELT TENSION ADJUSTMENT

V-Belt

1. Disconnect the negative battery cable.
2. Loosen the alternator mounting bolts.
3. Using a standard belt tension gauge, install it to the center of the longest span of the drive belt.
4. Use a medium prybar or the adjustment lug on the alternator housing to move the alternator. When the drive belt tension is 90–100 lbs. for a used belt or 165–175 lbs. for a new belt, tighten the alternator mounting bolts.
5. Connect the negative battery cable.

Serpentine Belt

A single serpentine belt may be used to drive engine-mounted accessories. Drive belt tension is maintained by a spring loaded tensioner. The drive belt tensioner can control belt tension over a broad range belt lengths, however, there are limits to the tensioner's ability to compensate.

1. Disconnect the negative battery cable.
2. Inspect tensioner markings to see if the belt is within operating lengths. Replace the belt if the belt is excessively worn or is outside of the tensioner's operating range.
3. Run the engine until operating temperature is reached. Be sure all accessories are OFF. Turn the engine OFF and read the belt tension using a belt tension gauge tool placed halfway between the alternator and the air conditioning compressor. If not equipped with air conditioning, read the tension between the power steering pump and crankshaft pulley. Remove the tool.
4. Run the engine for 15 seconds and turn OFF. Using a box-end wrench, apply clockwise force to tighten to the tensioner pulley bolt. Release the force and immediately take a tension reading without disturbing belt tensioner position.
5. Using the same wrench, apply a counterclockwise force to the tensioner pulley bolt and raise the pulley to its fully raised position. Slowly lower the pulley to engage the belt.

Take a tension reading without disturbing the belt tensioner position.
6. Average the 3 readings. If their average is lower than specifications, replace the tensioner:
   2.3L engine — 50 lbs.
   3.1L and 3.3L engines — 67 lbs.

REMOVAL AND INSTALLATION

3.3L Engine

1. Disconnect the negative battery cable.
2. Label and disconnect the wiring from the back of the alternator.
3. Loosen the serpentine belt tensioner and rotate it counterclockwise to remove the drive belt.
4. Remove the alternator attaching bolts and remove the alternator from the vehicle.
5. Installation is the reverse of the removal procedure.
6. Check and/or adjust the belt tension as necessary.
7. Connect the negative battery cable and inspect the alternator for proper operation.

2.3L Engine

1. Disconnect the negative battery cable.
2. Using a 13mm wrench that is at least 24 in. long, loosen the tensioner pulley bolt, rotate the tensioner counterclockwise and remove the belt from the alternator pulley.
3. Label and disconnect the vacuum lines at the front of engine and remove the attaching bracket.
4. Label and disconnect the injector harness and alternator connectors.
5. Remove the 2 rear alternator mounting bolts.
6. Remove the front alternator bolt and engine harness clip.

NOTE: Care must be taken during removal and installation not to damage the air conditioning hoses.

7. Remove the alternator by manipulating it between the engine lifting eyelet and the air conditioning hoses.
To install:
8. Position the alternator on the engine.
9. Install the front mounting bolt loosely and install the clip.
10. Install the 2 rear mounting bolts and tighten to 37 ft. lbs. (50 Nm).
11. Tighten the front mounting bolt to 20 ft. lbs. (26 Nm).

12. Connect the injector harness and alternator connectors.
13. Connect the vacuum lines and install the bracket.
14. Install the belt.
15. Connect the negative battery cable and check the alternator for proper operation.

3.1L Engine

1. Remove the serpentine belt shield.
2. Lift or rotate the tensioner using a 3/8 in. breaker bar.
3. Note belt routing and remove the serpentine belt.
4. Installation is the reverse of removal.

Starter

REMOVAL AND INSTALLATION

3.3L Engine

1. Disconnect the negative battery cable.
2. Raise and safely support the vehicle. Disconnect the electrical wiring from the starter.
3. Remove the dust cover bolts and pull the dust cover back to gain access to the front starter bolt and remove the front starter bolt.
4. Remove the rear support bracket.
5. Pull the rear dust cover back to gain access to the rear starter bolt and remove the rear bolt.
6. Note the number and location of any shims.
7. Push the dust cover back into place and remove the starter from the vehicle.
To install:
8. Install the starter to the engine block along with any necessary shims.
9. Tighten the starter bolts to 30–35 ft. lbs. (41–47 Nm).
10. Install the dust cover and connect the wiring.
11. Connect the electrical connectors and the negative battery cable.

2.3L Engine

1. Disconnect the negative battery cable. Remove the air induction tube, if necessary.
2. Remove the cooling fan assembly.
3. Remove the oil filter, if necessary.
4. Remove the intake manifold brace, if equipped.
5. Remove the mounting bolts; some engines may have 3 starter

mounting bolts. Pull the starter out of the hole and move toward the front of the vehicle.

6. Disconnect the wiring from the starter.

7. Remove the starter by lifting it between the intake manifold and the radiator.

To install:

8. Lower the starter between the intake manifold and radiator and connect the wiring to the solenoid.

9. Rotate the starter into installation position and install the mounting bolts. Tighten to 74 ft. lbs. (100 Nm).

10. Install the intake manifold brace and oil filter.

11. Install the cooling fan assembly and air induction tube, if removed.

12. Connect the negative battery cable and check the starter for proper operation.

3.1L Engine

1. Disconnect the negative battery cable.

2. Raise the vehicle and safely support.

3. Disconnect the engine wiring harness from the front of the frame.

4. Remove the inspection cover and electrical connections from the starter.

5. Remove the starter bolt and starter. Save any shims that are removed.

To install:

6. Connect the solenoid battery and S terminals. Torque the battery nut to 12 ft. lbs. (16 Nm) and the S terminal nut to 27 inch lbs. (3 Nm).

7. Install the starter bolts and torque to 32 ft. lbs. (43 Nm). Install the remaining components.

CHASSIS ELECTRICAL

Air Bag

DISARMING

1994–96

NOTE: Before attempting any repair procedure that is located in the area of an air bag sensor or wire harness, it is recommended that the air bag system be disarmed. Failure to disarm the air

bag system may result in accidental deployment of the air bag module and possible personal injury.

To disarm the air bag system, disconnect the negative battery cable, remove the underdash Supplemental Inflatable Restraint (SIR) fuse, and disconnect the yellow 2 way connector at the base of the steering column.

Heater Blower Motor

REMOVAL AND INSTALLATION

1. Disconnect the negative battery cable.

2. If equipped with the 3.3L engine, remove the power steering retaining pump bolts and position the pump out of the way.

3. Disconnect the electrical connectors from the blower motor.

4. Cut the blower case following the marks indicated on the case.

NOTE: Cover is 1/8 inch (2mm) thick. Do not cut much deeper or damage may result to the cooling tube.

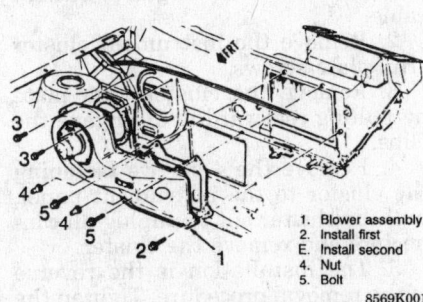

1. Blower assembly
2. Install first
E. Install second
4. Nut
5. Bolt

8569K001

Blower case and motor assembly

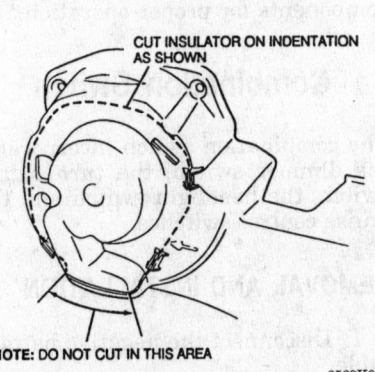

CUT INSULATOR ON INDENTATION AS SHOWN

NOTE: DO NOT CUT IN THIS AREA

8569K002

Blower motor case cut diagram

5. Swing the cut portion of the cover down and disconnect the blower motor cooling tube.

6. Remove the blower motor retaining screws and remove the blower motor.

To install:

7. Install the blower motor and mounting screws.

8. Install the blower motor cooling tube.

9. Install the blower motor cover and secure with retaining clips.

10. Connect the electrical connectors to the blower motor.

11. Install the power steering pump to the 3.3L engine.

12. Connect the negative battery cable.

Windshield Wiper Motor

REMOVAL AND INSTALLATION

1. Disconnect the negative battery cable.

2. Remove the wiper arm assembly(s) and cowl cover/panel, if necessary.

3. Remove the wiper arm drive link from the crank arm.

4. Disconnect the connectors from the motor.

5. Remove the wiper motor attaching bolts.

6. Remove the wiper motor and crank arm by guiding the assembly through the access hole in the upper shroud panel.

To install:

7. Install the wiper motor while guiding the crank arm through the hole.

8. Install the wiper motor attaching bolts and tighten to 80 inch lbs. (9 Nm)

9. Connect the electrical connectors.

10. Connect the wiper arm drive link to the motor crank arm.

11. Install the cowl cover/panel assembly.

12. Install the wiper arm/blade assemblies and connect the negative battery cable.

Windshield Wiper Switch

REMOVAL AND INSTALLATION

1. Disconnect the negative battery cable.

2. Remove the horn pad and the steering wheel from the vehicle.

3. Remove the tilt lever from the column, if equipped. This can be done

by turning the lever counterclockwise and pulling outward with locking pliers.

4. Remove the upper and lower steering column covers.

5. Remove the dampener assembly.

6. Remove the multi-function switch screw and remove the switch assembly.

7. Remove the turn signal switch assembly.

To install:

8. Install the turn signal and headlight switches.

9. Install the dampener assembly.

10. Install the upper and lower steering column covers.

11. If equipped with tilt wheel, install the tilt lever to the column.

12. Install the steering wheel and install the horn pad.

13. Connect the negative battery cable.

Instrument Cluster

REMOVAL AND INSTALLATION

Achieva

1. Disconnect the negative battery cable.

2. Remove the instrument cluster trim plate screws.

3. Remove the cluster trim plate by pulling rearward to disengage the clips.

4. Remove the 4 screws fastening the cluster to the instrument panel, pull the cluster out to unplug all connectors and remove the cluster.

5. The installation is the reverse of the removal procedure. Tighten the screws to 17 inch lbs. (2 Nm).

6. Connect the negative battery cable and check all cluster-related components for proper operation.

Grand Am

1. Disconnect the negative battery cable.

2. Remove the left sound insulator from below the dashboard.

3. Remove the steering column filler.

4. Remove the driver's side air deflectors by gently pulling rearward.

5. Remove the instrument panel cover by alternately prying upward on the left and right retaining clips.

6. Remove the fuse cover and remove the left instrument panel trim plate screws. Remove the left side trim plate.

7. Remove the upper glove compartment by opening the compart-

ment door and removing the attaching screws.

8. Remove the lower glove compartment by removing the compartment door and then removing the attaching screws.

9. Remove the right side instrument panel cluster trim plate screws and pull trim plate rearward to disengage the clips. Remove the trim plate.

10. Remove the cluster mounting screws and pull cluster out to disconnect the electrical connectors.

11. Remove the cluster from the vehicle.

To install:

12. Install the instrument cluster to the vehicle and tighten the screws to 17 inch lbs. (2 Nm).

13. Install the right side instrument panel trim plate.

14. Install the upper and lower glove compartments.

15. Install the left side instrument panel trim plate.

16. Install the instrument panel cover.

17. Install the steering column filler.

18. Install the left sound insulator.

19. Connect the negative battery cable.

Skylark

1. Disconnect the negative battery cable.

2. Remove the instrument cluster trim plate screws.

3. Remove the cluster trim plate by pulling rearward to disengage the clips.

4. Remove the 4 screws fastening the cluster to the instrument panel, pull the cluster out to unplug all connectors and remove the cluster.

5. The installation is the reverse of the removal procedure. Tighten the screws to 17 inch lbs. (2 Nm).

6. Connect the negative battery cable and check all cluster-related components for proper operation.

Combination Switch

The combination switch incorporates the dimmer switch, the turn signal switch, the headlight switch and the cruise control switches.

REMOVAL AND INSTALLATION

1. Disconnect the negative battery cable.

2. Remove the horn pad and the steering wheel from the vehicle.

3. Remove the tilt lever from the column, if equipped. This can be done by turning the lever counterclockwise and pulling outward with locking pliers.

4. Remove the upper and lower steering column covers.

5. Remove the dampener assembly.

6. Remove the combination switch screw and remove the switch assembly.

To install:

7. Install the combination switch.

8. Install the dampener assembly.

9. Install the upper and lower steering column covers.

10. If equipped with tilt wheel, install the tilt lever to the column.

11. Install the steering wheel and install the horn pad.

12. Connect the negative battery cable.

Ignition Lock Cylinder

REMOVAL AND INSTALLATION

1. Disconnect the negative battery cable.

2. Remove the left side instrument panel sound insulator from below the dashboard.

3. Remove the lower steering column filler panel.

4. Remove the horn pad and remove the steering wheel.

5. Remove the tilt lever, if equipped.

6. Remove the upper and lower steering column covers.

7. Disconnect the headlight and windshield wiper switch electrical connectors.

8. Disconnect the park lock/brake transaxle shift interlock cable from the ignition switch.

9. Remove the upper flexible column bolt and the column bracket support bolts.

10. Disconnect the attaching electrical connectors and remove the steering column from the vehicle.

11. Turn the key to the **RUN** position and shift the shifter into **P**.

12. Using a ¼ inch (6.5mm) drill bit, drill off the heads of the shear bolts that attach the lock cylinder housing.

13. Remove the lock cylinder housing from the vehicle.

14. Remove the remainder of the shear bolts from the housing.

To install:

15. Install the lock cylinder and install the shear bolts. Tighten the shear bolts until the heads separate.

16. Install the steering column to the vehicle. Tighten the bracket support bolts to 22 ft. lbs. (30 Nm) and the upper pinch bolt to 29 ft. lbs. (40 Nm).

17. Install the park lock/brake transaxle shift interlock cable to the ignition switch.

18. Connect the headlight switch connector and the windshield wiper switch connector.

19. Install the upper and lower steering column covers. Install the tilt lever, if equipped.

20. Install the steering wheel and the horn pad.

21. Install the lower steering column filler panel and the left side sound insulator.

22. Connect the negative battery cable.

Ignition Switch

REMOVAL AND INSTALLATION

1. Disconnect the negative battery cable.

2. Remove the steering wheel pad and remove the steering wheel.

3. Place the vehicle in **P** and remove the key.

4. Remove the steering wheel covers.

5. Remove the ignition switch screws and remove the switch.

6. Disconnect the electrical connector from the switch.

To install:

7. Connect the electrical connector to the switch.

8. Install the ignition switch to the lock cylinder housing and secure with the screws. Tighten the screws to 21 inch lbs. (2.4 Nm).

9. Install the steering wheel, horn pad and the steering wheel covers.

10. Connect the negative battery cable.

Brake Light Switch

REMOVAL AND INSTALLATION

1. Disconnect the negative battery cable.

2. Remove the left sound insulator.

3. Disconnect the wiring from the switch.

4. Pull the switch out of the retainer in the bracket.

To install:

5. Install the retainer in the bracket, at the underside of the bracket.

6. Depress the brake pedal and insert the switch into the retainer until the switch seats. Allow the pedal to return.

7. Connect the connector.

8. To adjust the switch, pull the pedal up against the switch until no more clicks are heard. The switch will automatically move up in the retainer providing adjustment. Repeat a few times to ensure that the switch is properly adjusted.

9. Connect the negative battery cable and check the switch for proper operation.

Clutch Switch

REMOVAL AND INSTALLATION

Cruise Control Release Switch

1. Disconnect the negative battery cable.

2. Remove the left sound insulator.

3. Disconnect the wiring from the switch.

4. Pull the switch out of the retainer in the bracket.

To install:

5. Install the retainer in the bracket, from the underside of the bracket.

6. Depress the clutch pedal and insert the switch into the retainer until the switch seats. Allow the pedal to return.

7. Connect the connector.

8. To adjust the switch, pull the pedal up against the switch until no more clicks are heard. The switch will automatically move up in the retainer providing adjustment. Repeat a few times to ensure that the switch is properly adjusted.

9. Connect the negative battery cable and check the switch for proper operation.

Neutral Start Switch

1. Disconnect the negative battery cable.

2. Remove the left sound insulator and disconnect the wiring from the switch.

3. Remove the attaching nuts.

4. Remove the switch.

5. The installation is the reverse of the removal procedure.

6. Connect the negative battery cable and check the switch for proper operation.

Neutral Safety Switch

ADJUSTMENT

1. Place the shifter in the **N** detent.

2. The switch is located on the shift shaft on the top of the automatic transaxle. Loosen the switch attaching bolts.

3. Rotate the switch on the shifter assembly to align the service adjustment hole with the carrier tang hole.

4. Insert a $^3/_{32}$ in. maximum diameter gauge pin into the hole to a depth of $^5/_8$ in.

5. Tighten the mounting bolts and remove the pin.

REMOVAL AND INSTALLATION

1. Disconnect the negative battery cable. Place the shifter in the **N** detent.

2. Disconnect the shifter linkage.

3. Disconnect the switch.

4. Remove the mounting bolts and remove the switch from the transaxle.

To install:

5. If not already done, place the shifter shaft in the **N** detent.

6. Align the flats of the shift shaft with those of the switch.

7. If replacing the switch, tighten the installation bolts and remove the pre-installed alignment pin.

8. If reusing the old switch, install the mounting bolts loosely and adjust the switch.

9. Connect the negative battery cable and check the switch for proper operation. The reverse lights should come ON when the transaxle is shifted into **R**. If the engine can be started in any gear except **P** or **N**, readjust the switch.

Fuses, Circuit Breakers and Relays

LOCATION

Fuses and Circuit Breakers

The fuse block, which contains the fuses and the circuit breakers for the power accessories, is located on the lower left side of the instrument panel, behind an access door.

Relays

Horn Relay — located in the convenience center near the fuse on all vehicles.

Power Antenna Relay — located on the right side of the instrument panel, below the speaker.

Rear Window Defogger Relay — located on the right side of the instrument panel on all vehicles.

Fuel Pump Relay — located in the engine compartment on the relay bracket on the firewall. This relay is closest to the blower.

A/C Compressor Cut Out Relay — located in the engine compartment on the relay bracket on the firewall. This relay is next to the fuel pump relay.

Cooling Fan Relay — located in the engine compartment on the relay bracket on the firewall. This relay is next to the blower speed relay.

Blower Speed Relay — located in the engine compartment on the relay bracket on the firewall. This relay is closest to the master cylinder.

Electronic Brake Control Relay — located in the engine compartment on the relay bracket on the firewall.

Fog Light Relay — located in the engine compartment on the relay bracket on the firewall.

Ignition Key, Seat Belt, Light and Turn Signal Warning Alarm — located in the convenience center near the fuse block in all vehicles.

Cruise Control Module — mounted to a bracket on the left side of the instrument panel.

Instrument Panel Light Dimmer Module — located on the lower left tie bar on all vehicles.

ABS Enable Relay — located on the engine compartment side of the firewall, inside of the relay bracket and to the right.

Flashers

LOCATION

Turn Signal Flasher — located at the instrument panel near the fuse block.

Hazard Flasher — located in the convenience center, near the fuse block.

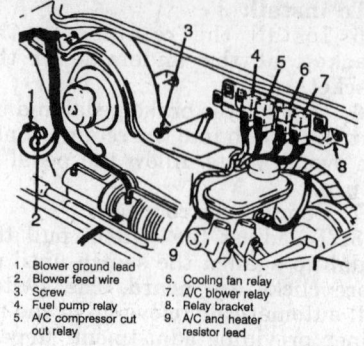

1. Blower ground lead
2. Blower feed wire
3. Screw
4. Fuel pump relay
5. A/C compressor cut out relay
6. Cooling fan relay
7. A/C blower relay
8. Relay bracket
9. A/C and heater resistor lead

8569Z043

Firewall mounted relay identification

Computer

LOCATION

The ECM is located on the right side of the instrument panel.

Cruise Control

ADJUSTMENT

1. Make sure the throttle lever is in the idle position with the engine OFF.
2. Pull the servo assembly end of the cable toward the servo without moving the throttle lever.
3. If 1 of the 6 holes in the servo assembly tab aligns with the cable pin, connect the pin to the tab and install the retainer with the tang over the stud.
4. If the pin does not align with a hole, install it to the next hole closest to the throttle lever and install the retainer.
5. Make sure the cable is not stretched in such a way that the throttle lever has been moved of its idle position.

ENGINE COOLING

Radiator

REMOVAL AND INSTALLATION

1. Disconnect the negative battery cable.
2. Drain the cooling system into a proper container.
3. Remove the air intake duct assembly.

4. Disconnect the upper transaxle cooler line and the upper radiator hose.
5. Remove the lower transaxle cooler line.
6. Disconnect the cooling fan electrical connector and remove the fan.
7. Remove the splash shield from below the lower radiator hose and remove the lower radiator hose.
8. Remove the condenser line retaining clip and remove the condenser to radiator bolts.
9. Remove the coolant surge tank hose.
10. Remove the radiator retaining bolts and remove the radiator from the vehicle.

To install:

11. Install the radiator to the vehicle and install the retaining bolts. Tighten the bolts to 90 inch lbs. (10 Nm).
12. Install the coolant surge tank hose.
13. Install the condenser to radiator bolts and install the condenser line retaining clip.
14. Install the lower radiator hose to the radiator.
15. Install the splash guard below the lower radiator hose.
16. Install the cooling fan and retaining bolt(s). Connect the fan electrical connector.
17. Install the lower transaxle cooler line, upper radiator hose and the upper transaxle cooler line.
18. Install the air intake duct assembly.
19. Fill the cooling system to the proper level and inspect for leaks.
20. Connect the negative battery cable and run the vehicle until the thermostat opens.
21. After engine has cooled, check the coolant level.

Electric Cooling Fan

— **CAUTION** —

The cooling fan can turn ON at any time. To avoid personal injury, ensure the ignition key is in the OFF position and use caution when working on or near the electric cooling fan.

TESTING

1. Check fuse or circuit breaker for power to cooling fan motor.
2. Remove connector(s) at cooling fan motor(s). Connect jumper wires to the connector on the cooling fan: 1 to a solid ground and the other to the

positive battery terminal. The motor should run.

3. Using an ohmmeter, check for continuity in cooling fan motor.

NOTE: Remove the cooling fan connector at the fan motor before performing continuity checks. Perform continuity check of the motor windings only. The cooling fan control circuit is connected electrically to the ECM through the cooling fan relay. Ohmmeter battery voltage must not be applied to the ECM.

4. Ensure continuity of cooling fan motor ground circuit at chassis ground connector.

REMOVAL AND INSTALLATION

2.3L Engine

1. Disconnect the negative battery cable.

2. Remove the air intake duct assembly.

3. Remove the coolant fan mounting bolt and disconnect the coolant fan electrical connector.

4. Remove the fan assembly through the bottom.

5. Installation is the reverse of the removal procedure. Tighten the coolant fan mounting bolt to 8 ft. lbs. (11 Nm).

3.1L and 3.3L Engines

1. Disconnect the negative battery cable.

2. Remove the air intake duct to the air cleaner assembly.

3. Partially drain the cooling system.

4. Remove the top radiator hose from the vehicle.

5. Disconnect the wiring harness from the motor and from the fan frame.

6. Remove the fan guard and the hose support, if necessary.

7. Remove the fan assembly from the vehicle.

To install:

8. Install the fan to the radiator support.

9. Install the fan guard and hose support, if removed.

10. Connect the wiring harness and install the top radiator hose to the radiator.

11. Fill the cooling system to the proper level.

12. Install the air intake duct assembly.

13. Connect the negative battery cable.

Heater Core

REMOVAL AND INSTALLATION

1. Disconnect the negative battery cable. Drain the engine coolant into a clean container for reuse.

2. Raise and safely support the vehicle. Remove the rear lateral transaxle strut mount, if necessary.

3. Remove the drain tube and disconnect the heater hoses from the core tubes. Lower the vehicle.

4. Remove the sound insulators, console, console extensions and/or steering column filler, as required.

5. Remove the floor or console outlet ductwork and hoses.

6. Remove the heater core cover. Remove the heater core mounting clamps and remove the heater core.

To install:

7. Install the heater core and clamps. Install the heater core cover. Install the outlet hoses and ducts.

8. Install the sound insulators, console, console extensions and/or steering column filler.

9. Raise and safely support the vehicle. Install the drain tube and connect the heater hoses to the core tubes.

10. Install the rear lateral transaxle strut mount, it removed. Lower the vehicle. Connect the negative battery cable.

11. Fill cooling system and check for leaks. Start the engine and allow to come to normal operating temperature. Recheck for leaks. Top-up coolant.

Water Pump

REMOVAL AND INSTALLATION

2.3L Engine

1. Disconnect the negative battery cable and oxygen sensor connector.

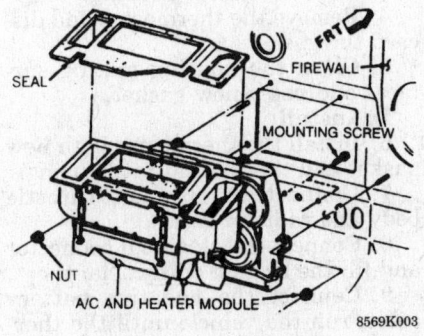

Removing the heater case

2. Drain the engine coolant into a clean container for reuse. Remove the heater hose from the thermostat housing for more complete coolant drain.

3. Remove upper and lower exhaust manifold heatshields.

4. Remove the bolt that attaches the exhaust manifold brace to the manifold.

5. Break loose the manifold to exhaust pipe spring loaded bolts using a 13mm box wrench.

6. Raise and safely support the vehicle.

NOTE: It is necessary to relieve the spring pressure from 1 bolt prior to removing the second bolt. If the spring pressure is not relieved, it will cause the exhaust pipe to twist and bind up the bolt as it is removed.

7. Remove the manifold-to-exhaust pipe bolts from the exhaust pipe flange as follows:
   a. Unscrew either bolt clockwise 4 turns.
   b. Remove the other bolt.
   c. Remove the first bolt.

8. Pull down and back on the exhaust pipe to disengage it from the manifold bolts.

9. Remove the radiator outlet pipe from the oil pan and transaxle. If equipped with a manual transaxle, remove the exhaust manifold brace. Leave the lower radiator hose attached and pull down on the outlet pipe to remove it from the water pump.

10. Lower the vehicle.

11. Remove the exhaust manifold, seals and gaskets.

12. Loosen and reposition the rear engine mount and bracket for clearance, as required.

13. Remove the water pump mounting bolts and nuts. Remove the water pump and cover assembly and separate the 2 pieces.

To install:

14. Thoroughly clean and dry all mounting surfaces, bolts and bolt holes. Using a new gasket, install the water pump to the cover and tighten the bolts finger-tight.

15. Lubricate the splines of the water pump with clean grease and install the assembly to the engine using new gaskets. Install the mounting bolts and nuts finger-tight.

16. Lubricate the radiator outlet pipe O-ring with antifreeze and install to the water pump with the bolts finger-tight.

17. With all gaps closed, tighten the bolts, in the following sequence, to the proper values:

   a. Pump assembly-to-chain housing nuts — 19 ft. lbs. (26 Nm).

   b. Pump cover-to-pump assembly — 106 inch lbs. (12 Nm).

   c. Cover-to-block, bottom bolt first — 19 ft. lbs. (26 Nm).

   d. Radiator outlet pipe assembly-to-pump cover — 125 inch lbs. (14 Nm).

18. Install the exhaust manifold.

19. Raise and safely support the vehicle.

20. Install the exhaust pipe flange bolts evenly and gradually to avoid binding.

21. Connect the radiator outlet pipe to the transaxle and oil pan. Install the exhaust manifold brace, if removed. Lower the vehicle.

22. Install the bolt that attaches the exhaust manifold brace to the manifold.

23. Install the heatshields.

24. Connect the oxygen sensor connector.

25. Fill the radiator with coolant until it comes out the heater hose outlet at the thermostat housing. Then connect the heater hose.

26. Connect the negative battery cable, run the vehicle until the thermostat opens, fill the radiator and recovery tank completely.

27. Once the vehicle has cooled, recheck the coolant level.

3.1L Engine

1. Disconnect the negative battery cable.

2. Drain cooling system.

3. Remove the serpentine drive belt.

4. Remove the pulley bolts and pulley.

5. Remove the water pump retaining bolts and water pump.

6. Installation is the reverse of removal. Clean the gasket mating sur-

1 GASKET, WATER PUMP
2 PUMP ASSEMBLY, WATER
3 BOLT/SCREW, WATER PUMP

8569y001

Water pump assembly — 3.1L engine

faces, torque the pump retaining bolts to 18 ft. lbs. (25 Nm) and pulley bolts to 22 ft. lbs. (30 Nm).

3.3L Engine

1. Disconnect the negative battery cable.

2. Drain the engine coolant into a clean container for reuse.

3. Remove the serpentine belt.

4. Remove the idler pulley bolt.

5. Remove the water pump pulley bolts and remove the pulley.

6. Remove the water pump mounting bolts and remove the pump.

To install:

7. Thoroughly clean and dry the mounting surfaces, bolts and bolt holes.

8. Using a new gasket, install the water pump to the engine and tighten pump-to-front cover bolts to 97 inch lbs. (11 Nm) and the pump-to-block bolts to 29 ft. lbs. (39 Nm).

9. Install the water pump pulley and tighten the bolts to 115 inch lbs. (13 Nm).

10. Install the idler pulley bolt.

11. Install the serpentine belt.

12. Fill the system with coolant.

13. Connect the negative battery cable, run the vehicle until the thermostat opens, fill the radiator and recovery tank completely.

14. Once the vehicle has cooled, recheck the coolant level.

Thermostat

REMOVAL AND INSTALLATION

Except 3.1L Engine

1. Disconnect the negative battery cable. Drain the coolant down to thermostat level or below.

2. Remove the air cleaner assembly, as required..

3. Disconnect the hose(s) and remove the thermostat housing.

4. Remove the thermostat and discard the gasket.

5. Clean the housing mating surfaces and use a new gasket.

To install:

6. Install the thermostat with new gasket and the thermostat housing.

7. Connect the heater, throttle body and radiator hoses.

8. Connect the electrical connector and fill the system with coolant.

9. Connect the negative battery cable, run the vehicle until the thermostat opens, fill the radiator and recovery tank completely.

3.1L Engine

1. Disconnect the negative battery cable. Drain the cooling system.

2. Remove the radiator hose from the water outlet.

3. Remove the outlet nuts, outlet and thermostat.

To install:

4. Clean mating surfaces thoroughly. Apply a ⅛ inch (3mm) bead of suitable RTV sealant in the groove of the water outlet.

5. Install the thermostat with the spring toward the engine. Install the water outlet. Torque bolts to 89 inch lbs. (10 Nm).

6. Connect the negative battery cable.

7. Fill cooling system and check for leaks. Start the engine and allow it to come to normal operating temperature. Check for leaks. Fill coolant to proper level.

COOLING SYSTEM BLEEDING

To insure complete filling of the cooling system, it is necessary to bleed the system.

1. Disconnect the negative battery cable.

2. Park vehicle on level surface.

3. Remove thermostat housing cap and thermostat or open bleed vents as necessary.

4. Fill cooling system with coolant to base of radiator neck .

5. Reinstall or replace the thermostat and housing and close air vents.

6. Fill coolant reservoir to proper level with ethylene glycol/water mixture.

7. Reconnect negative battery cable. Start vehicle and let engine reach operating temperature adding coolant as needed. Check the cooling system for leaks.

FUEL SYSTEM

Fuel System Service Precautions

Safety is the most important factor when performing not only fuel system maintenance but any type of maintenance. Failure to conduct maintenance and repairs in a safe manner may result in serious personal injury or death. Maintenance and testing of the vehicle's fuel system components can be accomplished

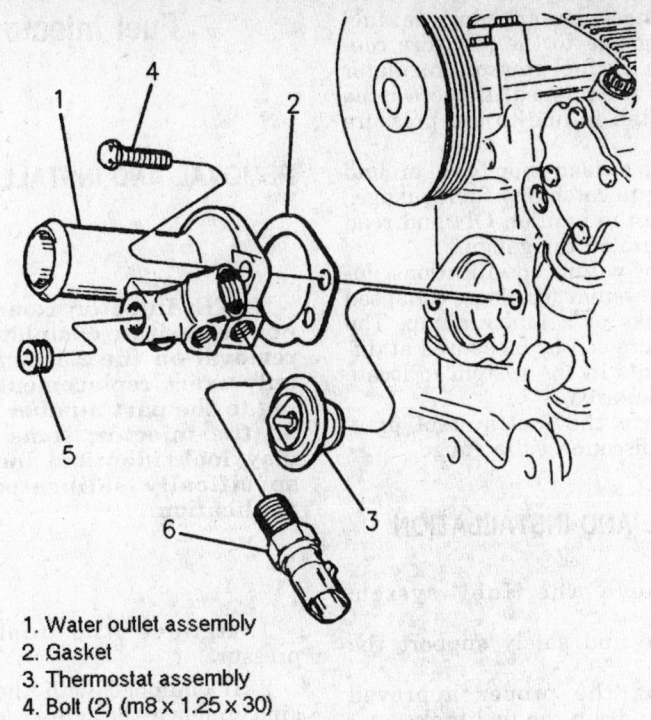

1. Water outlet assembly
2. Gasket
3. Thermostat assembly
4. Bolt (2) (m8 x 1.25 x 30)
5. Wate routlet plug
6. Coolant sensor

8470K019

Thermostat assembly — 2.3L engine

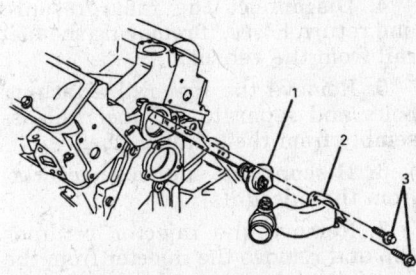

1 THERMOSTAT ASSEMBLY, ENGINE COOLANT
2 OUTLET ASSEMBLY, WATER
3 BOLT/SCREW, WATER OUTLET

8569y002

Thermostat assembly — 3.1L engine

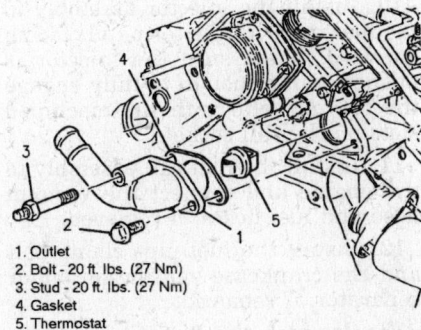

1. Outlet
2. Bolt - 20 ft. lbs. (27 Nm)
3. Stud - 20 ft. lbs. (27 Nm)
4. Gasket
5. Thermostat

8470K020

Thermostat assembly — 3.3L engine

safely and effectively by adhering to the following rules and guidelines.

• To avoid the possibility of fire and personal injury, always disconnect the negative battery cable unless the repair or test procedure requires that battery voltage be applied.

• Always relieve the fuel system pressure prior to disconnecting any fuel system component (injector, fuel rail, pressure regulator, etc.), fitting or fuel line connection. Exercise extreme caution whenever relieving fuel system pressure to avoid exposing skin, face and eyes to fuel spray. Please be advised that fuel under pressure may penetrate the skin or any part of the body that it contacts.

• Always place a shop towel or cloth around the fitting or connection prior to loosening to absorb any excess fuel due to spillage. Ensure that all fuel spillage (should it occur) is quickly removed from engine surfaces. Ensure that all fuel soaked cloths or towels are deposited into a suitable waste container.

• Always keep a dry chemical (Class B) fire extinguisher near the work area.

• Do not allow fuel spray or fuel vapors to come into contact with a spark or open flame.

• Always use a backup wrench when loosening and tightening fuel line connection fittings. This will prevent unnecessary stress and torsion to fuel line piping. Always follow the proper torque specifications.

• Always replace worn fuel fitting O-rings with new. Do not substitute fuel hose or equivalent where fuel pipe is installed.

RELIEVING FUEL SYSTEM PRESSURE

2.3L Engine

1. Loosen the fuel filler cap.
2. Remove the fuse marked fuel pump from the fuse block or disconnect the harness connector at the tank.
3. Start the engine and run at idle until it stalls.
4. Crank the engine for an additional 3 seconds to make sure all of the fuel pressure is exhausted from the fuel lines.
5. Turn the ignition switch **OFF**, disconnect the negative battery cable and reinstall the fuel pump fuse or connect the connector at the tank.
6. Tighten the filler cap.

3.3L Engine

1. Disconnect the negative battery cable.
2. Loosen the fuel filler cap.
3. Install a fuel pressure gauge to the fuel pressure connection on the fuel pressure regulator assembly. Wrap a shop towel around the connection to avoid any fuel spray.
4. Install the bleed hose into an approved container and open the valve to bleed the fuel pressure.
5. Drain any residual fuel in the gauge into the container.
6. Tighten the filler cap.

Fuel Tank

REMOVAL AND INSTALLATION

1. Disconnect the negative battery cable.
2. Drain the fuel tank into a proper container.
3. Raise and safely support the vehicle.
4. Disconnect the fuel sender connector.
5. Remove the ground wire screw and the muffler hanger bolt.
6. Remove the rubber exhaust hangers and allow the exhaust pipe to rest against the rear axle.

7. Disconnect all hoses at the fuel tank.

8. With the aid of an assistant, support the fuel tank and disconnect the 2 fuel tank retaining straps.

9. Lower the tank away from the vehicle. Make sure all hoses and electrical connectors are disconnected.

To install:

10. With the aid of an assistant raise the fuel tank up and into position.

11. Install the fuel tank retaining straps and tighten the bolts to 25 ft. lbs. (33 Nm).

12. Connect the hoses and connectors to the fuel tank.

13. Install the rubber exhaust hangers and install the muffler hanger bolt.

14. Connect the ground lead to the underbody.

15. Connect the fuel tank sender electrical connector.

16. Lower the vehicle and refill the fuel tank.

17. Connect the negative battery cable.

18. Turn the ignition to **ON** for 2 seconds and then **OFF** for 10 seconds. Repeat the procedure and then inspect fuel system for leaks.

19. Turn the ignition **ON** and check fuel gauge operation.

Fuel Filter

The fuel filter is located near the rear of the vehicle, forward of the fuel tank.

REMOVAL AND INSTALLATION

1. Relieve the fuel system pressure.

2. Raise and safely support the vehicle.

3. Using a backup wrench, remove the fuel line fittings from the fuel filter.

4. Remove the fuel filter mounting screws and remove the filter from the vehicle.

5. The installation is the reverse of the removal procedure. Replace the O-rings. Tighten the fuel line-to-filter connectors to 22 ft. lbs. (30 Nm).

Electric Fuel Pump

PRESSURE TESTING

1. Relieve the fuel system pressure.

2. Connect an appropriate fuel pressure gauge to the pressure connection on the fuel pressure regulator assembly, if equipped. If there is no valve, install in-line to the pressure line.

3. Wrap a clean shop towel around the fitting to catch any fuel leakage.

4. Turn the ignition **ON** and read the pressure on the gauge.

5. If not within specifications, inspect the system for clogs, collapsed hoses, kinks or a faulty pump. The fuel pressure can be measured at different points in the system to locate the problem area.

6. Relieve the fuel system pressure and disconnect the gauge.

REMOVAL AND INSTALLATION

1. Relieve the fuel system pressure.

2. Raise and safely support the vehicle.

3. Using the proper approved equipment, drain the fuel tank.

4. Disconnect all wiring and hoses from the tank.

5. Place a transmission jack under the center of the tank and apply slight pressure. Remove the tank straps.

6. Remove the fuel tank from the vehicle.

7. Remove the snapring from the top of the pump/sending unit assembly and remove the assembly.

8. Disassemble the unit to separate the pump itself from the assembly.

To install:

9. Push the fuel pump onto the attaching hose and install the filter on the end of the pump.

10. Install a new tank seal O-ring to the pump.

11. Install the pump into the tank and install the snapring.

12. Install the fuel tank.

13. Connect the negative battery cable, start the engine and check for leaks.

Fuel Injection

IDLE SPEED ADJUSTMENT

The idle speed and mixture are controlled by the ECM, which receives data from various sensors and switches within the fuel injection system. Adjustments are preset at the factory and not adjustable.

Fuel Injector

REMOVAL AND INSTALLATION

NOTE: Injector removal does not necessitate complete fuel rail removal on the 2.3L engine. Use only exact replacements according to the part number inscribed on the injector; some injectors may look identical but each is specifically calibrated for its application.

1. Relieve the fuel system pressure.

2. If equipped with the 2.3L engine, remove the crankcase ventilation oil/air separator and the fuel pipe clamp bolt.

3. Disconnect the vacuum hose from the pressure regulator.

4. Disconnect the fuel pressure and return hoses, if removing the fuel rail from the vehicle.

5. Remove the fuel rail attaching bolts and separate the fuel rail assembly from the cylinder head.

6. Disconnect the connector(s) from the injector(s).

7. Remove the injector retainer clip and remove the injector from the fuel rail assembly.

To install:

8. Lubricate the new injector O-rings with clean engine oil and install to the injector.

9. Install a new retainer clip to the injector so the opening of the clip faces the injector's terminals.

10. Install the injector assembly to the fuel rail with the terminals facing outward. Make sure the injector is pushed in far enough to fully engage the retainer clip with the machined slots on the rail socket.

11. Install the fuel rail assembly to the engine and connect the vacuum hose and fuel hoses, if removed.

12. Install the fuel pipe clamp bolt and the crankcase ventilation oil/air separator, if removed.

13. Connect the negative battery cable, start the engine and check for fuel leaks.

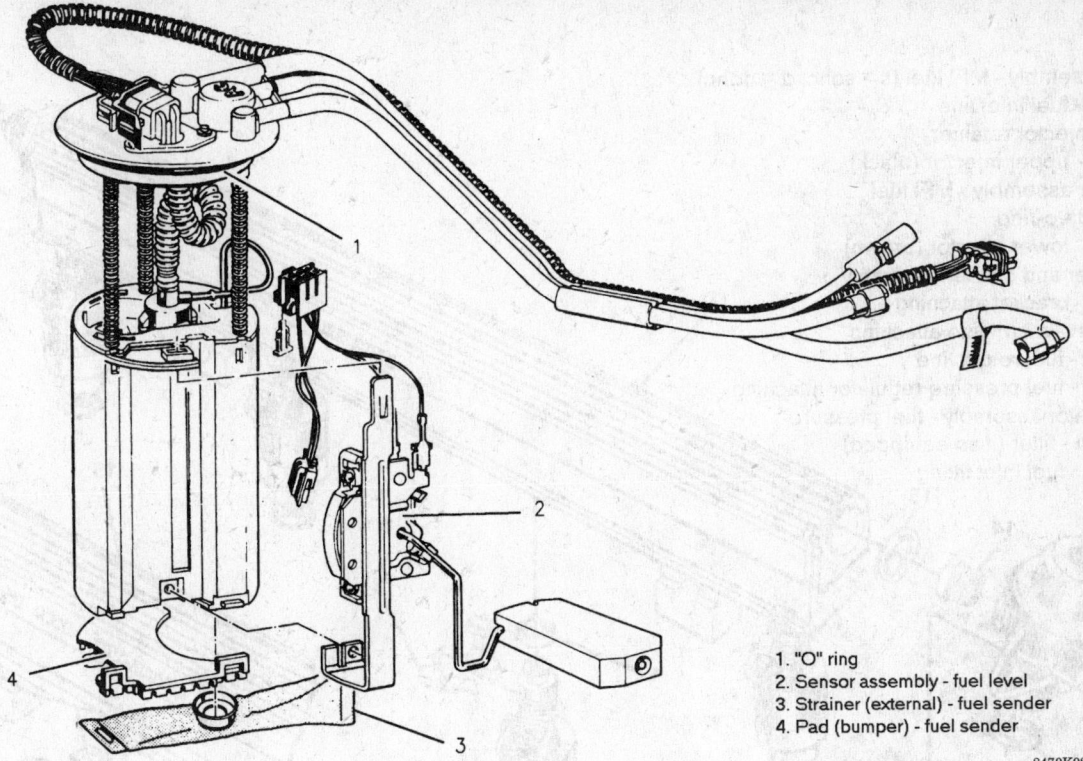

1. "O" ring
2. Sensor assembly - fuel level
3. Strainer (external) - fuel sender
4. Pad (bumper) - fuel sender

8470K021

Fuel pump/sending unit assembly

ENGINE MECHANICAL

NOTE: Disconnecting the negative battery cable on some vehicles may interfere with the functions of the on board computer systems and may require the computer to undergo a relearning process, once the negative battery cable is reconnected.

Engine Assembly

REMOVAL AND INSTALLATION

2.3L Engine

1. Relieve the fuel system pressure.
2. Disconnect both battery cables and ground straps from the front engine mount bracket and the transaxle. Drain the cooling system and remove the cooling fan.
3. Drain the cooling system and remove the cooling fan.
4. Remove the air cleaner duct.
5. Disconnect the heater and radiator hoses from the thermostat housing.

6. Properly discharge the air conditioning system and disconnect the hoses from the compressor.
7. Remove the upper radiator support.
8. Disconnect the 2 vacuum hoses from the front of the engine.
9. Label and disconnect all electrical connectors from engine and transaxle mounted devices.
10. Disconnect the wires at the starter solenoid.
11. Disconnect the power brake vacuum hose from the throttle body.
12. Disconnect the throttle cable and remove the bracket.
13. Remove the power steering pump bracket and lay the pump aside with the lines attached.
14. Disconnect and plug the fuel lines.
15. If equipped with a manual transaxle, disconnect the shifter cables and the clutch actuator cylinder.
16. If equipped with an automatic transaxle, disconnect the shift and TV cables.
17. Disconnect the transaxle and engine oil cooler pipes, if equipped.
18. Remove the exhaust manifold and heatshield.
19. Remove the lower radiator hose and front engine mount.
20. Install engine support fixture tool J–28467–A or equivalent.

21. Raise and safely support the vehicle.
22. Remove the wheels, right side splash shield and radiator air deflector.
23. Separate the ball joints from the steering knuckles.
24. Using the proper equipment, support the suspension supports, crossmember and stabilizer shaft. Remove the attaching bolts and remove as an assembly.
25. Disconnect the heater hose from the radiator outlet pipe.
26. Remove the halfshafts from the transaxle.
27. Remove the nut from the transaxle mount through bolt.
28. Remove the nut from the rear engine mount through bolt.
29. Remove the rear engine mount body bracket.
30. Position a suitable support fixture below the engine/transaxle assembly and lower the vehicle so the weight of the engine/transaxle assembly is on the support fixture.
31. Remove the transaxle mount through bolt.
32. Mark the threads on fixture tool J–28467–A so the setting can be duplicated when installing the engine/transaxle assembly. Remove the fixture.

1. Rail assembly - MFI fuel (s = sohc; d = dohc)
2. O-ring - fuel inlet line
3. Clip - injector retainer
4. O-ring - upper injector (black)
5. Injector assembly - MFI fuel
6. Backup - o-ring
7. O-ring - lower injector (brown)
8. Retainer and spacer assembly
9. Screw - bracket attaching
10. Bracket - return line attaching
11. O-ring - fuel return line
12. Screw - fuel pressure regulator attaching
13. Regulator assembly - fuel pressure
14. Screen - filter (if so equipped)
15. O-ring - fuel inlet fitting

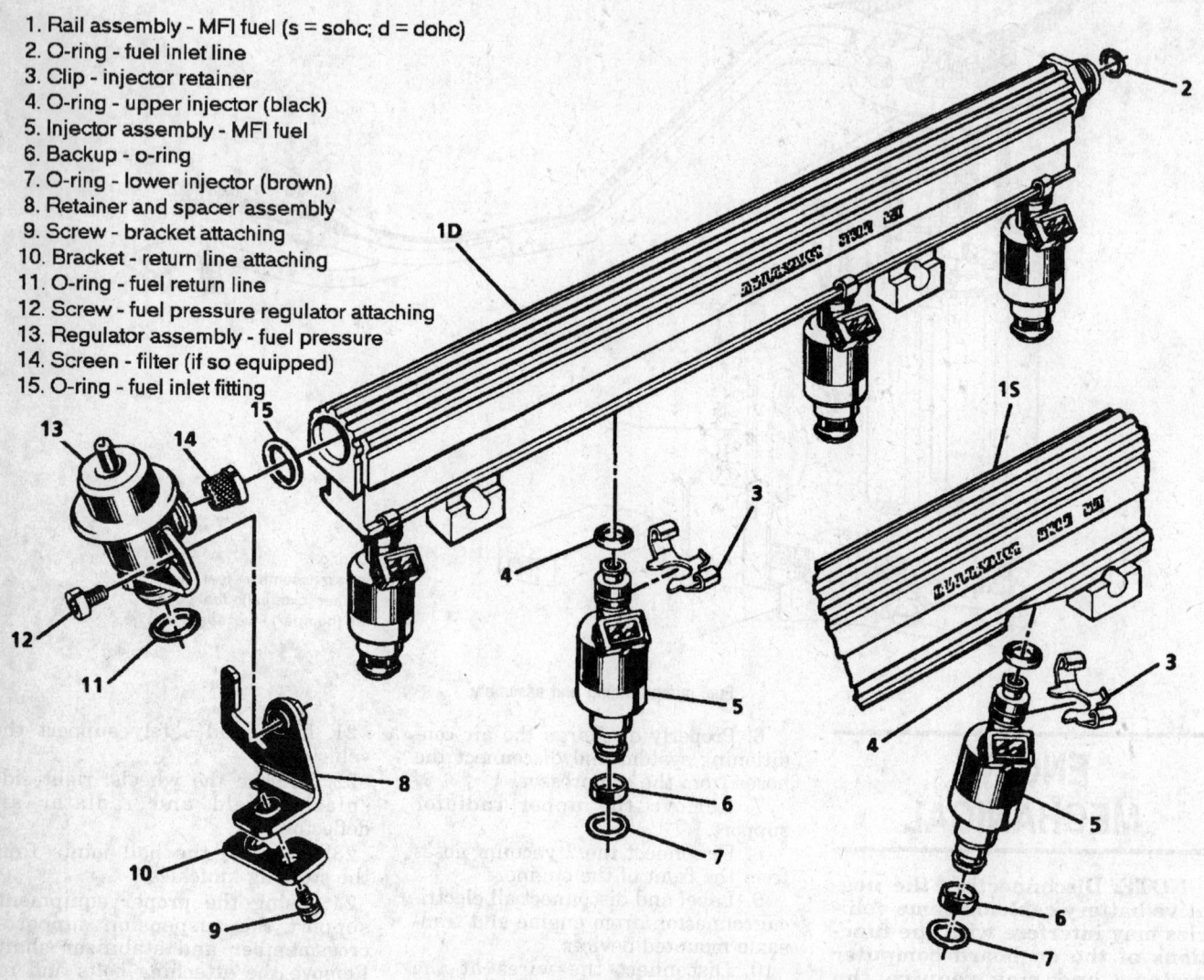

Fuel rail assembly and fuel injectors — 2.3L engine

8470K022

33. Move the engine/transaxle assembly rearward and slowly raise the vehicle from the engine/transaxle assembly.

NOTE: Many of the bellhousing bolts are of different lengths; note their locations before removing. It is imperative that these bolts go back in their original locations when assembling the engine and transaxle or engine damage could result.

34. Separate the engine from the transaxle.

To install:

35. Assemble the engine to the transaxle. If equipped with an automatic transaxle, thoroughly clean and dry the torque converter bolts and bolt holes, apply thread locking compound to the threads and tighten the bolts to 46 ft. lbs. (63 Nm). If equipped with a manual transaxle, tighten the clutch cover bolts to 22 ft. lbs. (30 Nm).

36. Raise and safely support the vehicle. Position the engine/transaxle assembly and lower the vehicle over the assembly until the transaxle mount is indexed, then install the bolt.

37. Install the engine support fixture and adjust to previously indexed setting. Raise the vehicle off the support fixture.

38. Install the rear mount to body bracket and tighten the bolts to 55 ft. lbs. (75 Nm).

39. Install the rear mount nut and tighten to 55 ft. lbs. (75 Nm).

40. Install the transaxle mount through bolt and tighten the nut to 55 ft. lbs. (75 Nm). Tighten so equal gaps are maintained.

41. Install the halfshafts.

42. Connect the heater hose to the the radiator outlet pipe.

43. Install the suspension supports, crossmember and stabilizer shaft assembly. Tighten the center bolts first, then front, then rear, to 65 ft. lbs. (90 Nm).

44. Install the ball joints and tighten the nuts to a maximum of 50 ft. lbs. (68 Nm).

45. Install the radiator air deflector and splash shield.

46. Install the wheels and lower the vehicle.

47. Install the front engine mount nut and tighten to 41 ft. lbs. (56 Nm). Remove the engine support fixture. Connect the lower radiator hose.

48. Install the exhaust manifold and heatshield.

49. Connect the transaxle and engine oil cooler pipes, if equipped.

50. If equipped with a manual transaxle, connect the shifter cables and the clutch actuator cylinder.

51. If equipped with an automatic transaxle, connect the shift and TV cables.

52. Connect the fuel lines.

53. Install the power steering pump and related parts.

54. Connect the throttle cable and install the bracket.

55. Connect the power brake vacuum hose to the throttle body.

56. Connect the starter wires.

57. Connect all electrical connectors and cables to the proper engine and transaxle-mounted devices.

58. Connect the 2 vacuum hoses at the front of the engine.

59. Install the upper radiator support.

60. Using new seals, connect the air conditioning hoses to the compressor.

61. Connect the heater and radiator hoses at the thermostat housing.

62. Install the air cleaner duct.

63. Fill all fluids to their proper levels.

64. Connect the battery cables, start the engine and check for leaks.

3.1L Engine

1. Disconnect the battery cables and remove the air cleaner assembly.

2. Scribe the bolt locations and remove the hood with the help of an assistant.

3. Remove the heater and radiator hoses from the engine. Remove the engine torque strut at the radiator support.

4. Remove the serpentine belt from the engine.

5. Relieve the fuel system pressure. Disconnect the throttle body bracket, cables and fuel and coolant hoses.

6. Label and disconnect the electrical connections from the engine.

7. Label and disconnect the vacuum lines from the engine.

8. Disconnect the power steering lines and remove the power steering brace.

9. Remove the coolant reservoir and 2 upper A/C compressor upper bolts.

10. Disconnect the electrical connectors from the transaxle.

11. Remove the 4 upper transaxle-to-engine mounting bolts.

12. Raise the vehicle and safely support.

13. Disconnect the exhaust pipe from the manifold.

14. Remove the oil drip shield, flywheel cover and starter motor.

15. Disconnect all electrical connections from the engine.

16. Remove the flywheel-to-converter bolts.

17. Remove the A/C compressor and position aside. Do not disconnect the refrigerant lines.

18. Install a transaxle support bracket and remove the remaining transaxle bolts.

19. Remove the engine mounts and 2 remaining transaxle bolts.

20. Lower the vehicle install an approved engine lifting device.

21. Remove the engine assembly slowly and check that all components are disconnected and free from obstruction. Place the engine on a work stand.

To install:

22. Lower the engine into the vehicle and start 2 transaxle-to-engine bolts.

23. Remove the transaxle support tool.

24. Install the remaining transaxle bolts.

25. Install the engine mounts, transaxle support bracket and bolts.

26. Position the A/C compressor and tighten the bolts.

27. Install the flywheel-to-converter bolts and torque to 53 ft. lbs. (71 Nm).

28. Connect the engine grounds to the transaxle mounting bolts. Connect all accessible electrical connectors to the engine.

29. Install the starter motor, flywheel cover and oil drip shield.

30. Install the exhaust pipe-to-manifold and torque to 18 ft. lbs. (25 Nm).

31. Install the upper A/C compressor bolts, coolant reservoir and power steering brace and lines.

32. Connect all vacuum and electrical connections to the engine.

33. Connect the fuel lines and install the throttle body bracket and cable.

34. Connect the heater and radiator hoses.

35. Install the serpentine belt.

36. With the help of an assistant, install the hood to its original position.

37. Connect the battery cables, refill all engine fluids to the proper level and install the air cleaner.

38. Start the engine and check for leaks.

3.3L Engine

1. Remove the hood from the vehicle and cover the fenders.

2. Install engine support/lift device J–28467–A or equivalent to the engine.

3. Depressurize the fuel system and disconnect the fuel lines from the fuel rail.

4. Disconnect the negative battery cable.

5. Drain the cooling system.

6. Disconnect the radiator and heater hoses.

7. Remove the cooling fan assembly.

8. Remove the air intake duct from the throttle body.

9. Disconnect the vacuum lines from the brake power booster and from the evaporative purge canister.

10. Disconnect the cable bracket and the cables from the throttle body.

11. Remove the accessory drive belt.

12. Remove the power steering pump bolts and place the pump aside, out of the way.

13. Disconnect all electrical connectors.

14. Remove the upper transaxle-to-engine bolts.

15. Raise and safely support the vehicle.

16. Remove the A/C compressor bolts and position aside, out of the way.

17. Remove the right engine mount and the torque strut.

18. Remove the flywheel dust cover. Use a scribe to mark the relationship of the flywheel to the converter and remove the flywheel-to-converter bolts.

19. Remove the lower engine to transaxle bolts.

20. Lower the vehicle away from the engine.

To install:

21. Lower the engine into the engine compartment. Align the engine

mounts and install the bolts. Tighten the bolts to their proper values:

Front engine mount strut-to-support — 89 ft. lbs. (120 Nm)

A/C compressor bracket assembly bolts — 66 ft. lbs. (90 Nm)

Engine mount strut bracket-to-A/C compressor bracket — 37 ft. lbs. (50 Nm)

22. Align the flywheel to the converter and install the bolts. Tighten the bolts twice to 46 ft. lbs. (63 Nm).
23. Install the flywheel dust cover.
24. Install the right engine mount and torque strut.
25. Install the A/C compressor.
26. Lower the vehicle and install the upper engine-to-transaxle bolts.
27. Connect the electrical connections.
28. Install the power steering pump and accessory drive belt.
29. Connect the cable bracket and cables to the throttle body.
30. Connect the vacuum lines and install the air intake duct.
31. Install the cooling fan and radiator and heater hoses.
32. Refill the cooling system with the proper coolant and connect the fuel lines.
33. Connect the negative battery cable and install the hood.

Engine Mounts

REMOVAL AND INSTALLATION

1. Disconnect the negative battery cable.
2. Matchmark the engine mount to its mounting location.
3. Raise and safely support the vehicle, as required. Using the proper equipment, support the weight of the engine.
4. Remove all bolts and nuts that attach the mount to the engine, transaxle or body and remove the mount assembly from the vehicle.
5. Remove the through bolt and separate the insulator from the bracket, as required.
6. The installation is the reverse of the removal procedure. Make sure the matchmarks are aligned before tightening bolts.

Cylinder Head

REMOVAL AND INSTALLATION

2.3L Engine

1. Relieve the fuel system pressure. Disconnect the negative battery cable and drain cooling system.

2. Disconnect heater inlet and throttle body heater hoses from water outlet. Disconnect the upper radiator hose from the water outlet.
3. Remove the exhaust manifold.
4. Remove the intake and exhaust camshaft housings.
5. Remove the oil cap and dipstick. Pull oil fill tube upward to unseat from block.
6. Label and disconnect the injector harness electrical connector.
7. Disconnect the throttle body air intake duct. Disconnect the cables and bracket and position aside.
8. Remove the throttle body from the intake manifold.
9. Matchmark and disconnect the vacuum hose from intake manifold.
10. Remove intake manifold bracket-to-block bolt.
11. Disconnect the coolant sensor connectors.
12. Remove the cylinder head bolts in reverse order of the installation sequence.
13. Remove the cylinder head and gasket. Inspect the oil flow check valve for freedom of movement.

To install:
14. Thoroughly clean and dry all bolts, bolt holes and mating surfaces. Inspect the head bolts for any damage and replace, if necessary.
15. Install the cylinder head gasket to the cylinder block and carefully position the cylinder head in place.
16. Coat the head bolt threads with clean engine oil and allow the oil to drain off before installing.
17. Tighten the cylinder head bolts in sequence as follows:

Step 1 — Tighten head bolts 1 through 6 to 26 ft. lbs. (35 Nm).

Step 2 — Tighten head bolts 7 and 8 to 15 ft. lbs. (20 Nm).

Step 3 — Tighten head bolts 9 and 10 to 22 ft. lbs. (30 Nm).
18. Install the intake manifold bracket.
19. Connect the MAP sensor vacuum hose to the intake manifold.
20. Install the throttle body to the intake manifold.
21. Connect the throttle body air intake duct. Install the throttle cable and bracket.
22. Connect the injector harness electrical connector.
23. Connect the 2 coolant sensor connections.
24. Install the oil cap and dipstick. Install the oil fill tube into the block.
25. Install the exhaust and intake camshaft housings.
26. Install the exhaust manifold.
27. Connect the heater inlet and throttle body heater hoses to the

water outlet. Connect the upper radiator hose to the water outlet.
28. Fill all fluids to their proper levels.
29. Connect the battery cable, start the engine and check for leaks.

3.1L Engine

LEFT SIDE (FRONT)

1. Drain and recover the A/C refrigerant. Disconnect the battery cables.
2. Remove the intake manifold assembly.
3. Remove the exhaust crossover pipe. Label and disconnect the spark plug wires.
4. Remove the rocker arm covers, rocker arms and pushrods. Label these components for correct installation.
5. Remove the air level indicator and tube.
6. Remove the A/C compressor bolts from the top.
7. Raise the vehicle and support safely.
8. Disconnect the A/C compressor hoses. Remove the bolts, electrical connectors and compressor.
9. Remove the A/C compressor lower brackets.
10. Lower the vehicle and remove the A/C compressor upper brackets.
11. Remove the cylinder head bolts, cylinder head and gasket.
12. Clean all mating surfaces and check for warpage.

To install:
13. Place the gasket on the block with the "This Side Up" showing. Install the cylinder head and bolts.
14. Torque the head bolts in sequence to 33 ft. lbs. (45 Nm) and then another 90 degrees torquing angle.
15. Install the compressor bracket and upper bolts.
16. Raise the vehicle and support safely.
17. Install the A/C compressor lower brackets.
18. Install the compressor. Connect the A/C compressor hoses and electrical connectors.
19. Install the air level indicator and tube.
20. Install the rocker arm covers, rocker arms and pushrods.
21. Install the exhaust crossover pipe. Connect the spark plug wires.
22. Install the intake manifold assembly.
23. Refill and recharge the A/C refrigerant. Connect the battery cables.

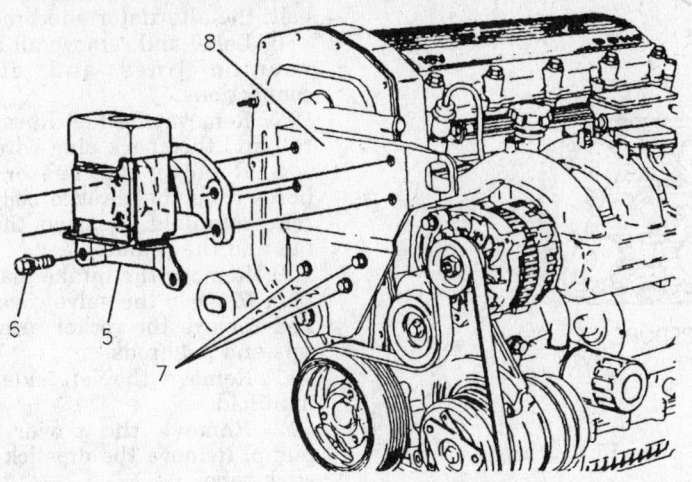

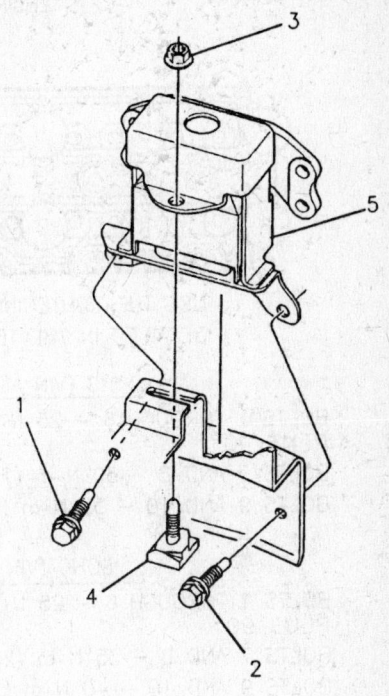

1. Bolt - 42 ft. lbs. (66 Nm) (tighten first)
2. Bolt - 42 ft. lbs. (66 Nm) (tighten second)
3. Nut - 31 ft. lbs. (42 Nm) (tighten last)
4. Bolt
5. Right engine mount
6. Bolts - 46 ft. lbs. (62 Nm)
7. Bolts - 37 ft. lbs. (50 Nm) + Turn 180°
8. Engine mount bracket

8470K023

Right side engine mount — 2.3L engine

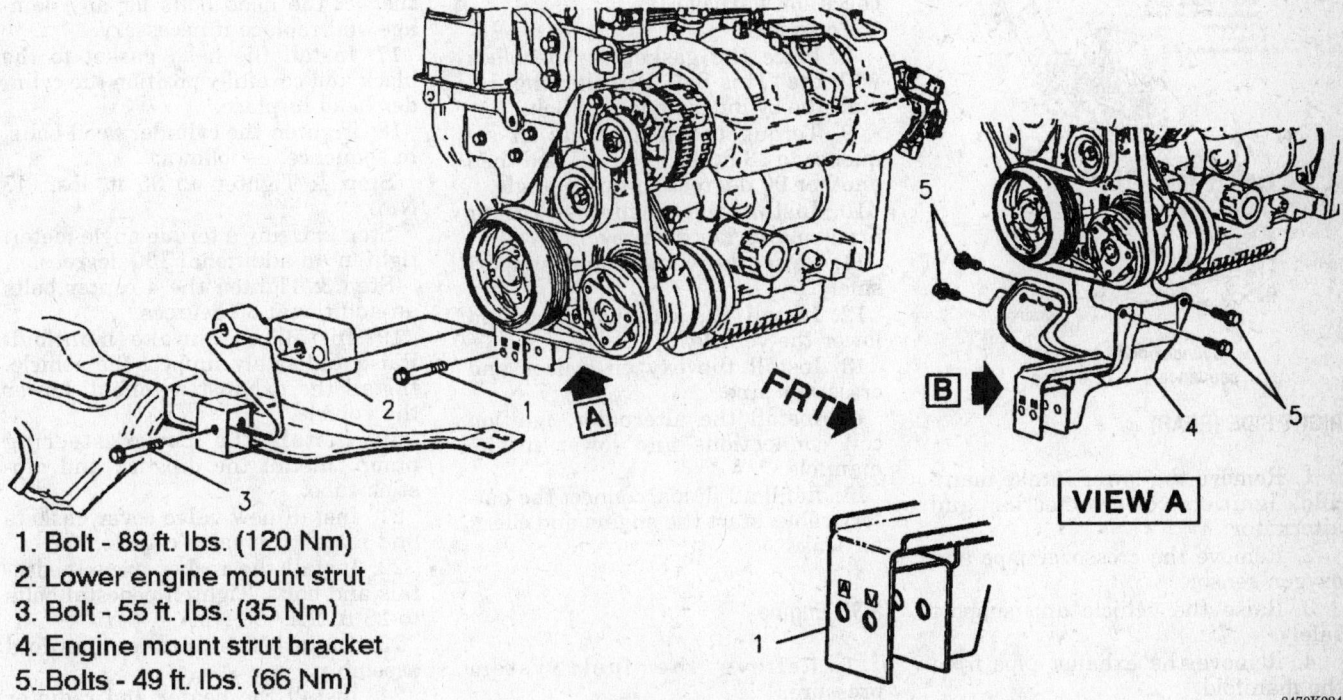

1. Bolt - 89 ft. lbs. (120 Nm)
2. Lower engine mount strut
3. Bolt - 55 ft. lbs. (35 Nm)
4. Engine mount strut bracket
5. Bolts - 49 ft. lbs. (66 Nm)

8470K024

Engine mount strut and bracket — 2.3L engine

FRONT
OF
ENGINE

USE THE TIGHTENING PROCEDURE
DETAILED IN THE TEXT.

DOHC (VIN A & D)

BOLTS 1 THROUGH 6 — 25 N·m (18 LBS. FT.)
PLUS 90°
BOLTS 7 AND 8 — 30 N·m (22 LBS. FT.) PLUS 60°
BOLTS 9 AND 10 — 35 N·m (26 LBS. FT.) PLUS 60°

SOHC (VIN 3)

BOLTS 1 THROUGH 6 — 25 N·m (18 LBS. FT.)
PLUS 90°
BOLTS 7 AND 8 — 35 N·m (26 LBS. FT.) PLUS 60°
BOLTS 9 AND 10 — 40 N·m (30 LBS. FT.) PLUS 60°

8470K028

Cylinder head bolt torque sequence — 2.3L engine

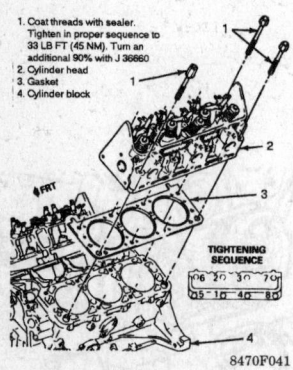

1. Coat threads with sealer. Tighten in proper sequence to 33 LB FT (45 NM). Turn an additional 90% with J 36660
2. Cylinder head
3. Gasket
4. Cylinder block

TIGHTENING SEQUENCE

8470F041

Cylinder head torque
sequence — 3.1L engine

RIGHT SIDE (REAR)

1. Remove the lower intake manifold, ignition coil connection and alternator.
2. Remove the crossover pipe and oxygen sensor.
3. Raise the vehicle and support safely.
4. Remove the exhaust pipe from the manifold.
5. Lower the vehicle and remove the rocker cover, rocker arms and pushrods. Label these components for proper installation.
6. Remove the cylinder head bolts, cylinder head and gasket.

7. Clean all mating surfaces and check for warpage.
To install:
8. Place the gasket on the block with the "This Side Up" showing. Install the cylinder head and bolts.
9. Torque the head bolts in sequence to 33 ft. lbs. (45 Nm) and then another 90 degrees torquing angle.
10. Install the pushrods, rocker arms and rocker arm cover.
11. Raise the vehicle and support safely.
12. Install the exhaust pipe and lower the vehicle.
13. Install the oxygen sensor and crossover pipe.
14. Install the alternator, ignition coil connections and lower intake manifold.
15. Refill all fluids, connect the battery cable, start the engine and check for leaks.

3.3L Engine

1. Relieve the fuel system pressure.
2. Disconnect the negative battery cable and drain the coolant.
3. Remove the mass air flow sensor and the air intake duct.
4. Remove C³I ignition module and wiring.

5. Remove the serpentine drive belt, the alternator and bracket.
6. Label and remove all necessary vacuum lines and electrical connections.
7. Remove the fuel lines, the fuel rail and the spark plug wires.
8. Remove the heater/radiator hoses from the throttle body and intake manifold. Remove the cooling fan and the radiator.
9. Remove the intake manifold.
10. Remove the valve covers. Label and remove the rocker arms, pedestals and pushrods.
11. Remove the left side exhaust manifold.
12. Remove the power steering pump. Remove the dipstick and dipstick tube.
13. Remove the left side head bolts in reverse order of the installation sequence and lift the left cylinder head from the engine.
14. Raise and safely support the vehicle. Remove the right exhaust manifold-to-engine bolts.
15. Remove the right cylinder head-to-engine bolts in reverse of the installation sequence and lift the right cylinder head from the engine.
To install:
16. Thoroughly clean and dry all bolts, bolt holes and mating surfaces. Inspect the head bolts for any damage and replace if necessary.
17. Install the head gasket to the block and carefully position the cylinder head in place.
18. Tighten the cylinder head bolts, in sequence, as follows:
Step 1: Tighten to 35 ft. lbs. (47 Nm).
Step 2: Using a torque angle meter, tighten an additional 130 degrees.
Step 3: Tighten the 4 center bolts an additional 30 degrees.
19. Install the intake manifold. Raise and safely support the vehicle. Install the exhaust manifold. Lower the vehicle.
20. Install the power steering pump. Install the dipstick and dipstick tube.
21. Install new valve cover gaskets and install the valve covers.
22. Install the rocker arms, pedestals and bolts. Tighten pedestal bolts to 28 ft. lbs. (38 Nm).
23. Install the intake manifold assembly.
24. Install the heater and radiator hoses to the throttle body and intake manifold.
25. Install the cooling fan and the radiator.
26. Install the fuel lines, the fuel rail and the spark plug wires.

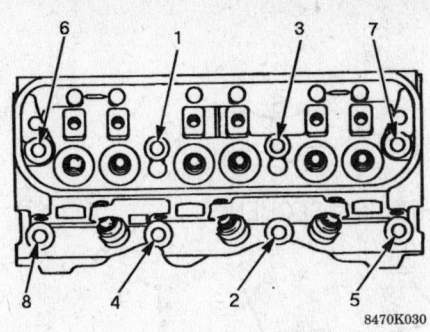

Cylinder head bolt torque sequence — 3.3L engine

8470K030

27. Install all vacuum lines and electrical connections.

28. Install the serpentine drive belt, the alternator and bracket.

29. Install the C³I ignition module and wiring.

30. Install the mass air flow sensor and the air intake duct.

31. Fill all fluids to their proper levels.

32. Connect the battery cable, start the engine and check for leaks.

Valve Lifters

REMOVAL AND INSTALLATION

2.3L Engine

1. Disconnect the negative battery cable.

2. Remove the valve covers and proceed to remove camshafts.

3. Remove the lifters from their bores.

4. The installation is the reverse of the removal procedure. Soak the lifters in clean engine oil prior to installation.

5. Connect the negative battery cable and check the lifters for proper operation.

3.1L and 3.3L Engine

1. Relieve the fuel system pressure.

2. Disconnect the negative battery terminal.

3. Disconnect and remove the fuel rail and the throttle body from the intake manifold.

4. Drain the cooling system.

5. Remove valve covers and the intake manifold.

6. Remove the rocker arms, pedestals and pushrods. Keep these components in order for proper installation.

7. Remove the valve lifters.

To install:

8. Soak the lifters in clean engine oil prior to installation.

9. Clean all gasket surfaces and valve train parts.

10. Assemble the lifters, guides, retainers, pushrods and rocker arms.

11. Apply a thread locking compound to the rocker arm bolts and tighten to 28 ft. lbs. (38 Nm).

12. Install the intake manifold and gaskets.

13. Install the valve covers and gaskets.

14. Install the fuel rail assembly.

15. Refill the coolant to the proper level and connect the negative battery cable.

Valve Lash

ADJUSTMENT

All engines are originally equipped with hydraulic valve lifters. No adjustment is necessary. The 3.1L engine replacement rocker arm stud is adjustable and the adjustment can be performed as listed below.

3.1L Engine

NOTE: The following adjustment procedure should be used when reconditioning a valve seat and a new adjustable type rocker arm is used.

1. Install the rocker arms, balls and nuts. Tighten the rocker arm nuts until all of the lash (free-play) is eliminated.

2. Adjust the valves when the lifter is on the base circle of a camshaft lobe as follows:

a. Place the engine in the No. 1 firing position. This can be determined by placing a finger on the No. 1 rocker arm as the engine alignment mark on the front face of the of the torsional damper pulley aligns with the arrow on the front cover. If the valves don't move freely, the engine is in the No. 1 firing position. If the valves move freely, the engine is in the No. 4 firing position and the engine should be rotated one full rotation to reach the No. 1 position.

b. With the engine TDC on the No. 1 cylinder, adjust the following valves:

- Exhaust — 1, 2, 3
- Intake — 1, 5, 6

c. Loosen the adjusting nut several turns backwards and then tighten until all lash (free-play) is removed. After all of the valve lash is removed turn the nut an additional 1½ turns; this will center the lifter plunger.

d. Turn the engine 1 complete revolution until the timing tab and the alignment mark are again aligned; this will place the engine in the No. 4 firing position.

e. With the engine TDC on the No. 4 cylinder, adjust the following valves:

- Exhaust — 4, 5, 6
- Intake — 2, 3, 4

All engines are originally equipped with hydraulic valve lifters. No adjustment is necessary.

Rocker Arms

REMOVAL AND INSTALLATION

3.1L Engine

1. Remove the rocker cover.

2. Label all components for correct installation.

NOTE: The intake and exhaust pushrods are of different lengths. The exhaust pushrods are longer than the intake rod. Intake rods are marked orange and are 6 inches long. The exhaust rods are blue and are 6⅜ inches long.

3. Remove the rocker arm pivot balls, rocker arms, studs and pushrods.

4. Install the pushrods to there proper location.

5. Install the studs, rocker arms, rocker arm pivot balls and nuts.

6. Adjust the valve lash if any components were replaced. Torque the rocker arm nuts to 18 ft. lbs. (24 Nm) if no components were replaced. Install the rocker arm cover.

7. Refill the fluids, start the engine and check for valve train noise. Any noise should go away after the engine is warm and driven a few miles at various engine speeds.

3.3L Engine

LEFT/FRONT HEAD

1. Relieve the fuel system pressure.

2. Disconnect the negative battery cable.

3. Disconnect all electrical components and vacuum hoses which prevent access to the valve cover bolts.

4. Remove the serpentine drive belt.

5. Remove the alternator brace bolt and remove the alternator belt.

6. Remove the spark plug wire harness.

7. Remove the valve cover.

8. Remove the rocker arm pedestal-to-cylinder head bolts, the rocker arm and pedestal assembly.

To install:

9. Install the rocker arm and pedestal assembly. Apply a thread locking compound to the bolt threads and tighten the rocker arm pedestal bolts to 28 ft. lbs. (38 Nm).

10. Install the valve cover and spark plug wire harness.

11. Install the alternator belt and tighten the brace bolt.

12. Install the serpentine drive belt.

13. Connect any vacuum lines and electrical connectors that were disconnected.

14. Connect the negative battery cable and check for proper operation.

RIGHT/REAR HEAD

1. Relieve the fuel system pressure.

2. Disconnect the negative battery terminal.

3. Remove the serpentine drive belt.

4. Loosen the power steering pump bolts and slide the pump forward.

5. Remove the power steering braces.

6. Remove the spark plug wires from the spark plugs.

7. Remove the valve cover.

8. Remove the rocker arm pedestal-to-cylinder head bolts. Remove the rocker arm and pedestal assembly.

To install:

9. Install the rocker arm and pedestal assembly.

10. Apply a thread locking compound to the bolt threads and tighten the rocker arm pedestal bolts to 28 ft. lbs. (38 Nm).

11. Install the valve cover and connect the spark plug wires to the spark plugs.

12. Install the power steering pump to it's proper position and tighten the bolts. Install the power steering brace.

13. Install the serpentine drive belt.

14. Refill the cooling system. Connect the battery cable and check for proper operation.

Intake Manifold

REMOVAL AND INSTALLATION

2.3L Engine

1. Disconnect the negative battery cable.

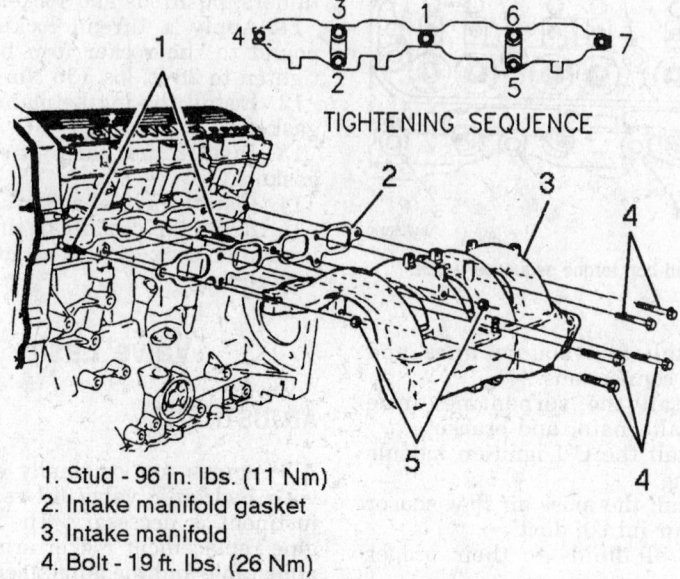

1. Stud - 96 in. lbs. (11 Nm)
2. Intake manifold gasket
3. Intake manifold
4. Bolt - 19 ft. lbs. (26 Nm)
5. Nut - 19 ft. lbs. (26 Nm)

8470K031

Intake manifold installation — 2.3L engine

2. Remove the coolant fan shroud, vacuum hose and electrical connector from the MAP sensor.

3. Disconnect the throttle body to air cleaner duct.

4. Remove the throttle cable bracket.

5. Remove the power brake vacuum hose, including the attaching bracket to power steering bracket and position it aside.

6. Remove the throttle body from the intake manifold with electrical harness, coolant hoses, vacuum hoses and throttle cable attached. Position these components aside.

7. Remove the oil/air separator bolts and hoses. Leave the hoses attached to the separator, disconnect from the oil fill, chain housing and the intake manifold. Remove as an assembly.

8. Remove the oil fill cap and oil level indicator stick.

9. Pull the oil tube fill upward to unseat from block and remove.

10. Disconnect the injector harness connector.

11. Remove the fill tube, rotating as necessary to gain clearance for the oil/air separator nipple between the intake tubes and fuel rail electrical harness.

12. Remove the intake manifold support bracket bolts and nut. Remove the intake manifold attaching nuts and bolts.

13. Remove the intake manifold.

To install:

14. Thoroughly clean and dry the mating surfaces. Install new gaskets and place the intake manifold in position.

15. Tighten the intake manifold bolts/nuts, in sequence, to 18 ft. lbs. (25 Nm). Tighten intake manifold brace and retainers hand tight. Tighten to specifications in the following order:

a. Nut-to-stud bolt — 18 ft. lbs. (25 Nm).

b. Bolt-to-intake manifold — 40 ft. lbs. (55 Nm).

c. Bolt-to-cylinder block — 40 ft. lbs. (55 Nm).

16. Lubricate a new oil fill tube ring seal with engine oil and install tube between No. 1 and 2 intake tubes. Rotate as necessary to gain clearance for oil/air separator nipple on fill tube.

17. Locate the oil fill tube in its cylinder block opening. Align the fill tube so it is approximately in its installed position. Press straight down to seat fill tube and seal into cylinder block.

18. Lubricate the hoses and install the oil/air separator assembly. Install

the throttle body to intake manifold using a new gasket.

19. Install the power brake vacuum hose and the attaching bracket to power steering bracket.

20. Install the throttle cable bracket.

21. Connect the throttle body to air cleaner duct.

22. Install the coolant fan shroud, vacuum hose and electrical connector to the MAP sensor.

23. Fill all fluids to their proper levels.

24. Connect the negative battery cable and check for leaks.

3.1L Engine

UPPER MANIFOLD

1. Disconnect the negative battery cable, drain the cooling system and remove the air cleaner.

2. Remove the throttle control cables, fuel lines and brackets from the manifold and throttle body.

3. Disconnect the vacuum lines from the upper intake manifold.

4. Remove the EGR valve and position the heater inlet hose out of the way.

5. Remove the ignition coil nuts and bolts.

6. Remove the power steering line clip from the alternator brace.

7. Remove the alternator brackets and disconnect the electrical connections from the throttle body.

8. Remove the upper intake manifold bolts and manifold from the throttle body.

9. Clean all gasket mating surfaces and sealing surfaces.

   To install:

10. Apply a 2–3mm bead of Ultra Black RTV sealer on each ridge where the front and rear of the intake manifold contact the cylinder head.

11. Install a new gasket, upper manifold and bolts. Torque the bolts to 18 ft. lbs. (25 Nm).

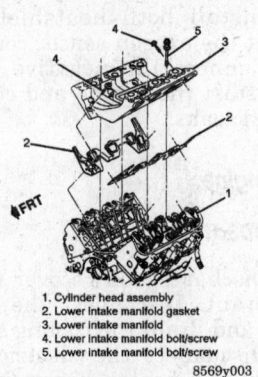

1. Cylinder head assembly
2. Lower intake manifold gasket
3. Lower intake manifold
4. Lower intake manifold bolt/screw
5. Lower intake manifold bolt/screw

8569y003

Intake manifold — 3.1L engine

12. Connect all vacuum and electrical connections.

13. Install the alternator brackets, power steering line clip and ignition coil fasteners.

14. Properly position heater inlet pipe hose clamps.

15. Install the EGR valve, control cable bracket, fuel lines, throttle cables and air cleaner.

16. Refill the cooling system, connect the battery cable, start the engine and check for leaks.

LOWER MANIFOLD

1. Disconnect the negative battery cable, drain the cooling system and remove the air cleaner.

2. Relieve the fuel pressure and remove the upper intake manifold.

3. Disconnect the fuel lines and remove the fuel rail.

4. Disconnect the coolant hoses and remove the serpentine belt.

5. Remove the alternator brackets and power steering pump.

6. Disconnect the upper radiator hose and heater hose from the thermostat housing.

7. Remove the ignition coil and engine torque strut.

8. Remove the rocker cover, lower manifold bolts and manifold.

   To install:

9. Clean the gasket mating surfaces.

10. Apply a 2–3mm bead of Ultra Black RTV sealer on each ridge where the manifold contacts the engine block.

11. Install a new gasket, lower manifold and bolts. Torque the bolts to 116 inch lbs. (13 Nm).

12. Connect all vacuum and electrical connections.

13. Install the rocker covers, engine torque strut and ignition coils.

14. Install the heater hose, radiator hose, power steering pump, alternator brackets and serpentine belt.

15. Install the fuel rail and connect the coolant hose and fuel lines.

16. Install the upper intake manifold.

17. Refill the cooling system, connect the battery cable, start the engine and check for leaks.

3.3L Engine

1. Relieve the fuel system pressure.

2. Disconnect the negative battery cable.

3. Drain the coolant and remove the air intake duct.

4. Remove the serpentine drive belt, alternator and bracket.

5. Remove the power steering pump braces and the coolant bypass hose.

6. Label and remove all the necessary vacuum and electrical wiring connectors.

7. Remove the throttle, cruise control and TV cables from the throttle body assembly.

8. Disconnect the heater hoses from the throttle body.

9. Remove the upper radiator hose from the intake manifold.

10. Remove the fuel lines, the fuel rail and the fuel injectors. Label and disconnect the spark plug wires.

11. Remove the intake manifold mounting bolts and remove the intake manifold.

   To install:

12. Thoroughly clean and dry all mating surfaces. Apply sealer to the 4 head-to-block corners.

13. Apply thread lock compound to the threads and tighten to 88 inch lbs. (10 Nm).

14. Install the fuel injectors, rail and lines. Connect the spark plug wires.

15. Connect the heater hoses to the throttle body.

16. Install the upper radiator hose to the intake manifold.

17. Connect the throttle, cruise control and TV cables to the throttle body assembly.

18. Connect all remaining vacuum and electrical wiring connectors.

19. Install the power steering pump braces.

20. Install the alternator, bracket and serpentine drive belt.

21. Connect the mass air flow sensor, if equipped. Install the air intake duct.

22. Fill all fluids to their proper levels.

23. Connect the negative battery cable and check for leaks.

Exhaust Manifold

REMOVAL AND INSTALLATION

2.3L Engine

1. Disconnect the negative battery cable and oxygen sensor connector.

2. Remove upper and lower exhaust manifold heatshields.

3. Remove the bolt that attaches the exhaust manifold brace to the manifold.

4. Break loose the manifold-to-exhaust pipe spring loaded bolts using a 13mm box wrench.

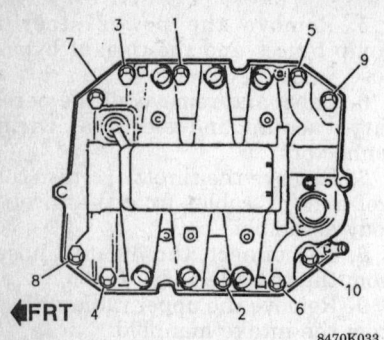

8470K033

Intake manifold bolt torque sequence — 3.3L engine

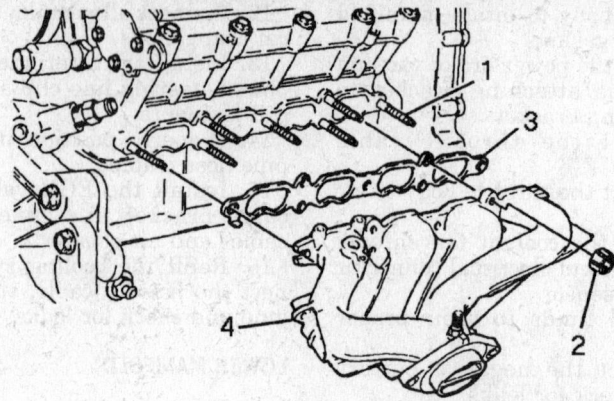

(HEAT SHIELD REMOVED FOR ILLUSTRATION PURPOSES)

TIGHTENING SEQUENCE

1. Stud - 106 in. lbs. (12 Nm)
2. Nut (7) - 31 ft. lbs. (42 Nm)
3. Gasket
4. Manifold assembly

8470K035

Exhaust manifold and gasket — 2.3L engine

5. Raise and safely support the vehicle.

NOTE: It is necessary to relieve the spring pressure from 1 bolt prior to removing the second bolt. If the spring pressure is not relieved it will cause the exhaust pipe to twist and bind up the bolt as it is removed.

6. Remove the manifold to exhaust pipe bolts from the exhaust pipe flange as follows:

   a. Unscrew either bolt clockwise 4 turns.

   b. Remove the other bolt.

   c. Remove the first bolt.

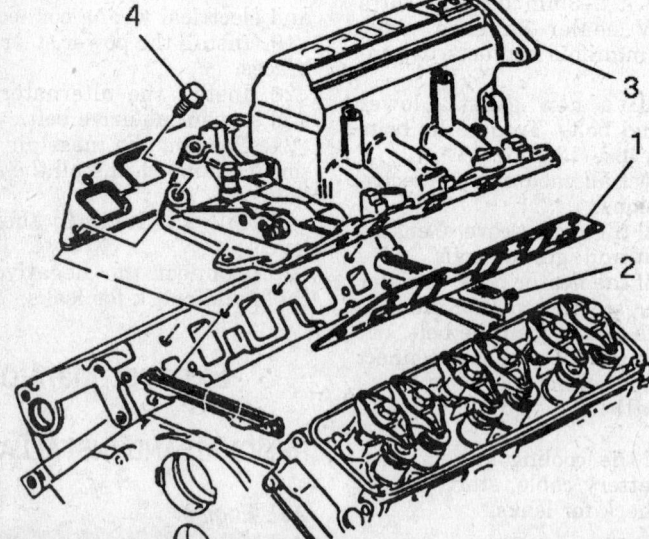

1. Intake manifold gasket
2. Intake manifold seal
3. Intake manifold
4. Bolt 88 in. lbs. (10 Nm)
   Tighten twice in given sequence. Apply p/n 1052624 to bolts before assembly

8470K034

Intake manifold assembly — 3.3L engine

7. Pull down and back on the exhaust pipe to disengage it from the exhaust manifold bolts.

8. Lower the vehicle.

9. Remove the exhaust manifold mounting bolts and remove the manifold.

To install:

10. Install the exhaust manifold, lower heatshield and new gaskets.

11. Tighten the cylinder head retaining nuts, in sequence, to 31 ft. lbs. (42 Nm).

12. Raise the vehicle install the exhaust manifold brace-to-manifold bolt.

13. Install the exhaust pipe flange bolts evenly and gradually to avoid binding.

14. Install both heatshields and connect the oxygen sensor connector.

15. Connect the negative battery cable, start the engine and check for exhaust leaks.

3.1L Engine

LEFT SIDE (FRONT)

1. Discharge and recover the A/C refrigerant. Disconnect the battery cables and drain the cooling system.

2. Disconnect the electrical connectors and heater hoses from the throttle body.

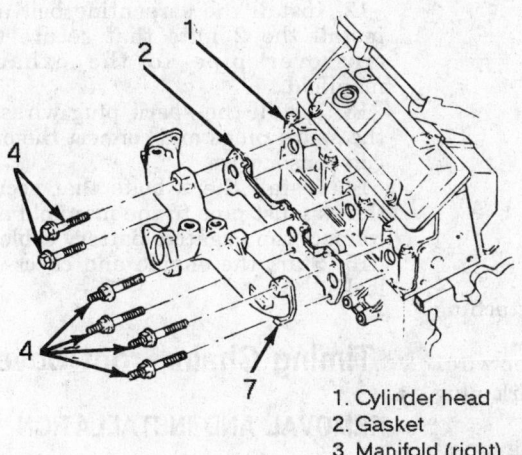

1. Cylinder head
2. Gasket
3. Manifold (right)
4. 18 LB FT (25 NM)
5. 89 LB IN (10 NM)
6. Heat shield
7. Manifold (left)

8470F050

Exhaust manifold — 3.1L engine

3. Relieve the fuel pressure and remove the throttle body.

4. Disconnect the fuel lines and coolant hoses.

5. Remove the crossover heatshield, crossover pipe and engine strut.

6. Remove the 2 top A/C compressor and bracket bolts.

7. Raise the vehicle and support safely.

8. Disconnect the A/C hoses and electrical connectors from the compressor.

9. Remove the lower A/C compressor bolts and compressor. Remove the lower bracket bolts and bracket.

10. Lower the vehicle

11. Remove the exhaust manifold heatshield, manifold nuts and manifold.

To install:

12. Clean the gasket mating surfaces.

13. Install the gasket, manifold and nuts. Torque the nuts to 18 ft. lbs. (25 Nm). Install the heatshield.

14. Raise the vehicle and support safely.

15. Install the A/C bracket and compressor. Connect the A/C hoses and electrical connectors to the compressor. Use new sealing washers.

16. Lower the vehicle and install the upper A/C bracket and compressor bolts.

17. Install the engine torque strut, crossover pipe, heatshield and coolant hoses.

18. Connect the fuel lines and install the throttle body.

19. Refill the cooling system, evacuate the A/C system, start the engine and check for leaks.

RIGHT SIDE (REAR)

1. Drain the cooling system and disconnect the negative battery terminal.

2. Remove the throttle body.

3. Disconnect the radiator hose from the thermostat housing.

4. Remove the EGR tube.

5. Relieve the fuel pressure and disconnect the fuel lines.

6. Remove the crossover heatshield, crossover and oxygen sensor.

7. Remove the heatshield bolt from the top of the exhaust manifold.

8. Raise the vehicle and support safely.

9. Remove the exhaust pipe at the converter.

10. Remove the transaxle oil fill tube.

11. Remove the heatshield, manifold nuts and manifold.

To install:

12. Clean the gasket mating surfaces.

13. Install the gasket, manifold and nuts. Torque the nuts to 12 ft. lbs. (16 Nm). Install the heatshield.

14. Install the transaxle fill tube, exhaust pipe and lower the vehicle.

15. Install the heatshield top bolts, oxygen sensor, crossover pipe and heatshield.

16. Connect the fuel lines, EGR tube and radiator hose.

17. Install the throttle body.

18. Refill the cooling system and connect the battery cable. Start the engine and check for leaks.

3.3L Engine

LEFT/FRONT MANIFOLD

1. Disconnect the negative battery cable.

2. Disconnect air cleaner mounting bolts.

3. Remove the bolts attaching the exhaust crossover pipe to the manifold.

4. Disconnect the spark plug wires.

5. Remove the cooling fan.

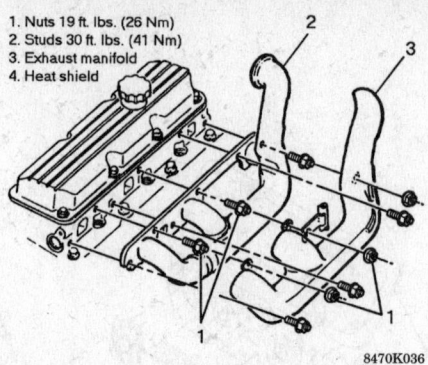

1. Nuts 19 ft. lbs. (26 Nm)
2. Studs 30 ft. lbs. (41 Nm)
3. Exhaust manifold
4. Heat shield

8470K036

Left/front exhaust manifold — 3.3L engine

6. Remove the mounting bolts and remove the manifold.

NOTE: The oil dipstick tube may have to be removed to provide access to the manifold bolts.

7. The installation is the reverse of the removal procedure. Tighten the mounting bolts to 30 ft. lbs. (41 Nm) and the nuts to 19 ft. lbs. (26 Nm).
8. Connect the negative battery cable and check for leaks.

RIGHT/REAR MANIFOLD

1. Disconnect the negative battery cable.

1. Studs 30 ft. lbs. (41 Nm)
2. Exhaust manifold heat shield
3. Exhaust manifold
4. Oxygen sensor
5. Nuts 19 ft. lbs. (26 Nm)

8470K037

Right/rear exhaust manifold — 3.3L engine

2. Remove the 2 bolts attaching exhaust pipe to manifold.
3. Disconnect oxygen sensor wire.
4. Disconnect and tag spark plug wires.
5. Remove 2 nuts attaching cross-over pipe to manifold.
6. Remove serpentine belt.
7. Remove power steering pump.
8. Remove heater hose from tube, heatshield and C$_3$I bracket nuts, if necessary.
9. Remove the bolts attaching the manifold to cylinder head.
To install:
10. Install the manifold to the cylinder head and tighten the mounting

bolts to 30 ft. lbs. (41 Nm) and the nuts to 19 ft. lbs. (26 Nm).
11. Install the heater hose to the tube, if removed and install the power steering pump.
12. Install the serpentine belt and install the 2 nuts that secure the crossover pipe to the exhaust manifold.
13. Install the spark plug wires to the spark plugs and connect the oxygen sensor wire.
14. Install the 2 bolts that secure the exhaust pipe to the manifold and connect the negative battery cable.
15. Start the engine and check for leaks.

Timing Chain Front Cover

REMOVAL AND INSTALLATION

2.3L Engine

1. Disconnect the negative battery cable. Remove the coolant recovery reservoir.
2. Remove the serpentine drive belt using a 13mm wrench that is at least 24 in. long.
3. Remove upper cover fasteners.
4. Raise and safely support the vehicle.
5. Remove the right front wheel assembly and lower splash shield.
6. Remove the crankshaft balancer assembly.

NOTE: Do not install an automatic transaxle-equipped engine balancer on a manual transaxle equipped engine or vice-versa.

7. Remove lower cover fasteners and lower the vehicle.
8. Remove the front cover.
9. The installation is the reverse of the removal procedure. Tighten the balancer attaching bolt to 74 ft. lbs. (100 Nm).

3.1L Engine

1. Disconnect the negative battery terminal.
2. Drain the engine oil and remove the oil pan.
3. Drain the cooling system and remove the serpentine belt.
4. Remove the alternator brackets, power steering pump and belt tensioner.
5. Remove the coolant bypass adapter and coolant hose from the water pump.
6. Remove the crankshaft balancer and knock sensor.
7. Remove the front cover bolts, front cover and gasket.

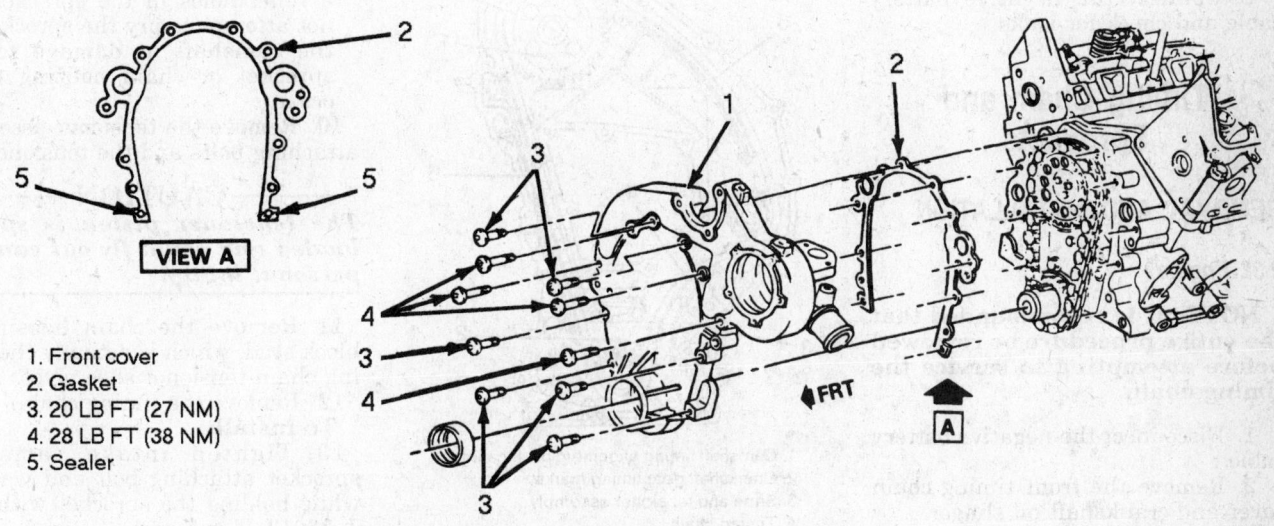

1. Front cover
2. Gasket
3. 20 LB FT (27 NM)
4. 28 LB FT (38 NM)
5. Sealer

8470F055

Timing chain front cover/water pump assembly — 3.1L Engine

To install:

8. Clean the gasket mating surfaces and apply a ⅛ in. (3mm) bead of silicone sealer to the oil pan, engine block and front cover.

9. Install the front cover bolts, front cover and gasket. Torque the small bolts to 15 ft. lbs. (21 Nm) and the large bolts to 41 ft. lbs. (55 Nm).

10. Install the crankshaft balancer and knock sensor.

11. Install the coolant bypass adapter and coolant hose to the water pump.

12. Install the alternator brackets, power steering pump and belt tensioner.

13. Refill the cooling system and install the serpentine belt.

14. Install the oil pan and refill the engine oil.

15. Connect the negative battery terminal, start the engine and check for leaks.

3.3L Engine

1. Disconnect the negative battery cable and drain the engine coolant.

2. Remove the accessory drive belt and remove the heater pipes.

3. Remove the lower radiator hose and coolant bypass hose from the cover.

4. Raise and safely support the vehicle. Remove the right front wheel assembly and the right inner fender splash shield.

5. Remove the torque converter cover.

6. Hold the flywheel in place, using a flywheel holding device J–37096 or equivalent, and remove the balancer bolt and balancer assembly.

7. Remove the crankshaft sensor shield and disconnect the following electrical connectors:

   a. Crankshaft sensor
   b. Camshaft sensor
   c. Oil pressure sender

8. Remove the oil pan to the front cover bolts.

9. Remove the front cover attaching bolts and remove the cover.

To install:

10. Install the gasket to the cylinder block and install the front cover and attaching bolts. Apply thread locking compound to the bolts and tighten the bolts to 22 ft. lbs. (30 Nm).

11. Install the oil pan-to-front cover bolts and tighten to 88 inch lbs. (10 Nm).

12. Connect the electrical connections.

13. If necessary, adjust the crankshaft sensor.

14. Install the crankshaft sensor shield.

15. Install the crankshaft balancer and bolt and tighten to 110 ft. lbs. (150 Nm) plus 76 degrees.

16. Install the torque converter cover and inner fender splash shield.

17. Install the right front wheel to the vehicle and lower the vehicle.

18. Install the coolant bypass hose, lower radiator hose and heater pipes.

19. Install the accessory drive belt and fill the cooling system.

20. Connect the negative battery cable and check for leaks.

Front Cover Oil Seal

REPLACEMENT

1. Disconnect the negative battery cable.

2. Remove the front cover.

3. Using a small prybar, pry out the old oil seal.

NOTE: Use care to avoid damage to seal bore or seal contact surfaces.

4. Thoroughly clean and dry the oil seal mounting surface.

5. Use the appropriate installation tool and drive the oil seal into the front cover.

6. Lubricate balancer and seal lip with clean engine oil.

7. The installation is the reverse of the removal procedure.

8. Connect the negative battery cable and check for leaks.

Timing Chain and Sprockets

REMOVAL AND INSTALLATION

2.3L Engine

NOTE: It is recommended that the entire procedure be reviewed before attempting to service the timing chain.

1. Disconnect the negative battery cable.

2. Remove the front timing chain cover and crankshaft oil slinger.

3. Looking from the front of the engine, rotate the crankshaft clockwise, (normal rotation) until the camshaft sprocket's timing dowel pin holes align with the holes in the timing chain housing. The mark on the crankshaft sprocket should align with the mark on the cylinder block. The crankshaft sprocket keyway should point upwards and align with

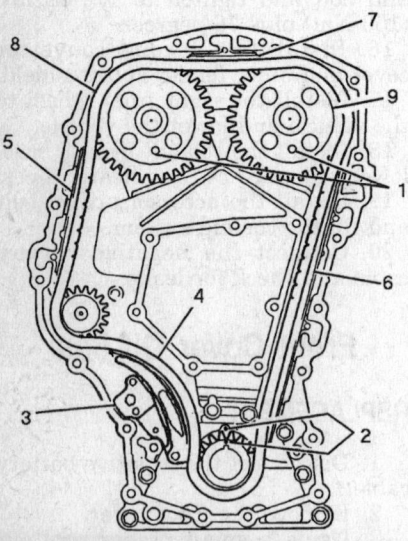

1. Camshaft timing alignment pin location
2. Crankshaft gear timing mark
3. Shoe assembly timing chain tensioner
4. Timing chain
5. Guide - R. H. timing chain
6. Guide - L. H. timing chain
7. Guide - upper timing chain
8. Sprocket - Exhaust camshaft
9. Sprocket - intake camshaft

8470K040

Timing chain assembly — 2.3L DOHC engine

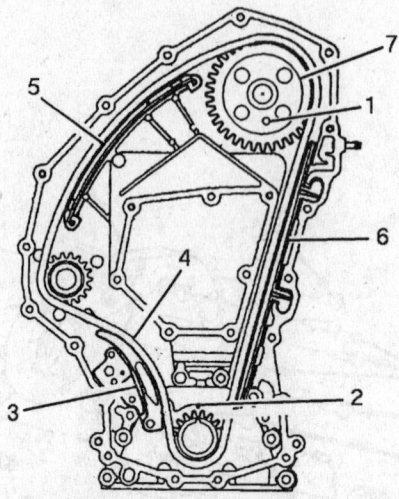

1. Camshaft timing alignment pin locations
2. Crankshaft gear timing marks
3. Shoe and tensioner assembly
4. Timing chain
5. Guide - R.H. timing chain
6. Guide - L. H. timing chain
7. Camshaft sprocket

8470K041

Timing chain assembly — 2.3L SOHC engine

the centerline of the cylinder bores. This is the normal timed position.

4. Remove the timing chain guides.

5. Raise and safely support the vehicle.

6. Gently pry off timing chain tensioner spring retainer and remove spring.

NOTE: Two styles of tensioner are used. Early production engines will have a spring post and late production ones will not. Both styles are identical in operation and are interchangeable.

7. Remove the timing chain tensioner shoe retainer.

8. Make sure all the slack in the timing chain is above the tensioner assembly; remove the chain tensioner shoe. The timing chain must be disengaged from the wear grooves in the tensioner shoe in order to remove the shoe. Slide a prybar under the timing chain while pulling shoe outward.

9. If difficulty is encountered removing chain tensioner shoe, proceed as follows:

a. Lower the vehicle.

b. Hold the intake camshaft sprocket with a holding tool and remove the sprocket bolt and washer.

c. Remove the washer from the bolt and re-thread the bolt back

into the camshaft by hand, the bolt provides a surface to push against.

d. Remove intake camshaft sprocket using a 3-jaw puller in the 3 relief holes in the sprocket. Do not attempt to pry the sprocket off the camshaft or damage to the sprocket or chain housing could occur.

10. Remove the tensioner assembly attaching bolts and the tensioner.

CAUTION
The tensioner piston is spring loaded and could fly out causing personal injury.

11. Remove the chain housing to block stud, which is actually the timing chain tensioner shoe pivot.

12. Remove the timing chain.

To install:

13. Tighten intake camshaft sprocket attaching bolt and washer, while holding the sprocket with tool J–36013, if removed.

14. Install the special tool through holes in camshaft sprockets into holes in timing chain housing. This positions the camshafts for correct timing.

15. If the camshafts are out of position and must be rotated more than ⅛ turn in order to install the alignment dowel pins:

a. The crankshaft must be rotated 90 degrees clockwise off TDC in order to give the valves adequate clearance to open.

b. Once the camshafts are in position and the dowels installed, rotate the crankshaft counterclockwise back to TDC. Do not rotate the crankshaft clockwise to TDC or valve and piston damage could occur.

16. Install the timing chain over the exhaust camshaft sprocket, around the idler sprocket and around the crankshaft sprocket.

17. Remove the alignment dowel pin from the intake camshaft. Using a dowel pin remover tool, rotate the intake camshaft sprocket counterclockwise enough to slide the timing chain over the intake camshaft sprocket. Release the camshaft sprocket wrench. The length of chain between the 2 camshaft sprockets will tighten. If properly timed, the intake camshaft alignment dowel pin should slide in easily. If the dowel pin does not fully index, the camshafts are not timed correctly and the procedure must be repeated.

18. Leave the alignment dowel pins installed.

19. With slack removed from chain between intake camshaft sprocket

and crankshaft sprocket, the timing marks on the crankshaft and the cylinder block should be aligned. If marks are not aligned, move the chain 1 tooth forward or rearward, remove slack and recheck marks.

20. Tighten the chain housing to block stud. The stud is installed under the timing chain. Tighten to 19 ft. lbs. (26 Nm).

21. Reload timing chain tensioner assembly to its position as follows:

a. Assemble restraint cylinder, spring and nylon plug into plunger. Index slot in restraint cylinder with peg in plunger. While rotating the restraint cylinder clockwise, push the restraint cylinder into the plunger until it bottoms. Keep rotating the restraint cylinder clockwise but allow the spring to push it out of the plunger. The pin in the plunger will lock the restraint in the loaded position.

b. Install tool J–36589 or equivalent, onto plunger assembly.

c. Install plunger assembly into tensioner body with the long end toward the crankshaft when installed.

22. Install the tensioner assembly to the chain housing. Recheck plunger assembly installation. It is correctly installed when the long end is toward the crankshaft.

23. Install and tighten timing chain tensioner bolts and tighten to 10 ft. lbs. (14 Nm).

24. Install the tensioner shoe and tensioner shoe retainer. Remove special tool J–36589 and squeeze plunger assembly into the tensioner body to unload the plunger assembly.

25. Lower vehicle and remove the alignment dowel pins. Rotate crankshaft clockwise 2 full rotations. Align crankshaft timing mark with mark on cylinder block and reinstall alignment dowel pins. Alignment dowel pins will slide in easily if engine is timed correctly.

NOTE: If the engine is not correctly timed, severe engine damage could occur.

26. Install 3 timing chain guides and crankshaft oil slinger.

27. Install the timing chain front cover.

28. Connect the negative battery cable and check for leaks.

3.3L Engine

1. Disconnect the negative battery cable.

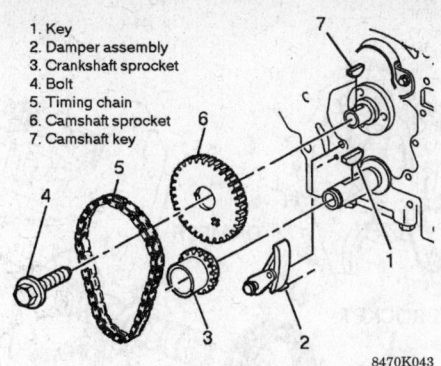

1. Key
2. Damper assembly
3. Crankshaft sprocket
4. Bolt
5. Timing chain
6. Camshaft sprocket
7. Camshaft key

8470K043

Timing chain assembly — 3.3L engine

2. Drain the cooling system. Disconnect the cooling hose from the water pump.

3. Raise and safely support the vehicle.

4. Remove the inner fender splash shield.

5. Remove the serpentine drive belt.

6. Remove the crankshaft pulley bolt and slide the pulley from the crankshaft.

7. Remove the front cover.

8. Rotate the crankshaft to align the timing marks on the sprockets. Remove the chain dampener assembly.

9. Remove the camshaft sprocket-to-camshaft bolt(s), remove the camshaft sprocket and chain and thrust bearing.

10. Remove the crankshaft gear by sliding it forward.

11. Clean the gasket mounting surfaces. Inspect the timing chain and the sprockets for damage and/or wear and replace damaged parts.

12. Position the crankshaft so the No. 1 piston is at TDC of its compression stroke.

13. Temporarily install the gear on the camshaft and position the camshaft so the timing mark on the gear is pointing straight down.

14. Assemble the timing chain to the gears so the timing marks are aligned, mark-to-mark.

15. Install the camshaft sprocket attaching bolt(s).

16. Install the camshaft thrust bearing, if not already done.

17. Install the timing chain dampener.

18. Install the front cover and all related parts.

19. Connect the negative battery cable and check for leaks.

3.1L Engine

1. Relieve the pressure in the fuel system before disconnecting any fuel line connections. Disconnect the negative battery cable.

2. Remove the crankcase front cover.

3. Place the No. 1 piston at TDC with the marks on the camshaft and crankshaft sprockets aligned.

4. Remove the camshaft sprocket and chain.

NOTE: If the sprocket does not come off easily, a light blow with a plastic mallet on the lower edge of the sprocket should dislodge the sprocket.

5. Remove the crankshaft sprocket.

To install:

6. Install the crankshaft sprocket. Apply Molykote® or equivalent, to the sprocket thrust surface.

7. Hold the sprocket with the chain hanging down and align the marks on the camshaft and crankshaft sprockets.

8. Align the dowel in the camshaft with the dowel hole in the camshaft sprocket.

9. Draw the camshaft sprocket onto the camshaft using the mounting bolts. Tighten the camshaft sprocket mounting bolts to 18 ft. lbs. (25 Nm).

10. Lubricate the timing chain with engine oil. Install the crankcase front cover. Connect battery negative cable.

Camshaft

REMOVAL AND INSTALLATION

2.3L Engine

DOHC INTAKE AND SOHC CAMSHAFT

NOTE: Any time the camshaft housing-to-cylinder head bolts are loosened or removed, the camshaft housing-to-cylinder head gasket must be replaced.

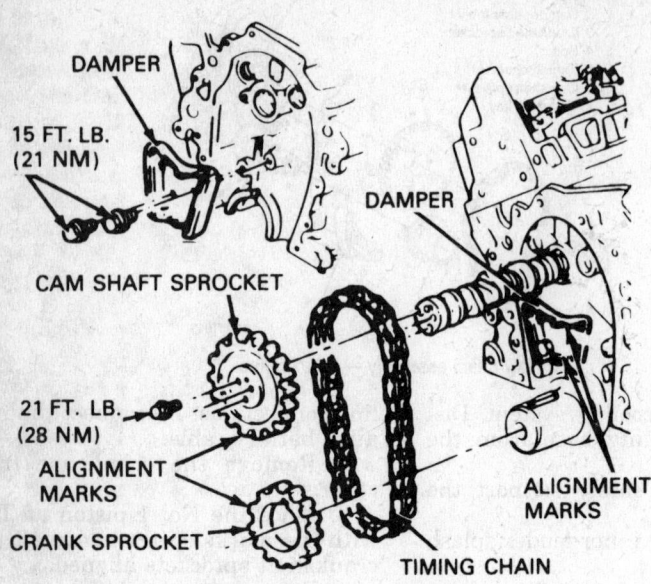

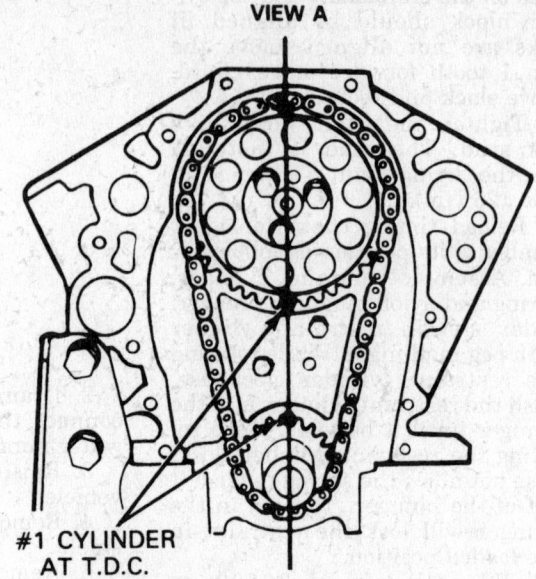

VIEW A

#1 CYLINDER
AT T.D.C.

NOTE—CAMSHAFT SPROCKET MARK
AT 6 O'CLOCK
CRANKSHAFT SPROCKET MARK
AT 12 O'CLOCK

8470M084

NOTE—ALIGN TIMING MARKS ON CAM
& CRANK SPROCKETS USING ALIGNMENT
MARKS ON DAMPER STAMPING OR CAST
ALIGNMENT MARKS ON CYL & CASE

Timing chain and sprockets — 3.1L engine

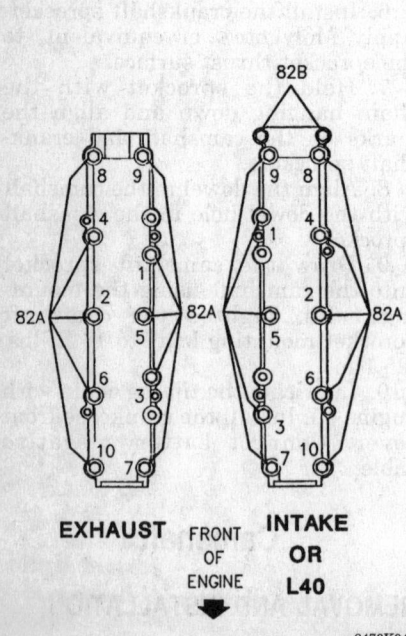

EXHAUST FRONT
OF
ENGINE

INTAKE
OR
L40

8470K044

Camshaft housing bolt torque sequence — 2.3L engine

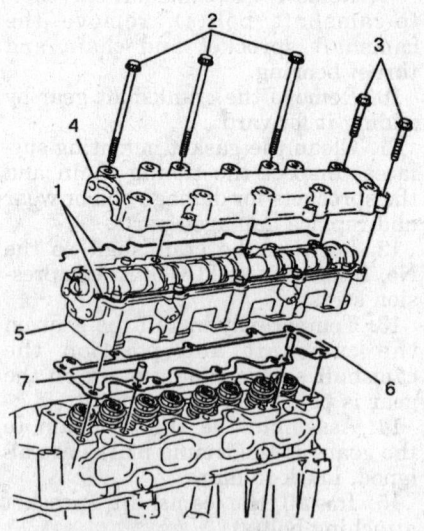

1. Seals - camshaft housing to camshaft
2. Bolt - camshaft housing to cylinder head 11 ft. lbs. (15 Nm) plus turn 90°
3. Bolt - camshaft housing cover to camshaft housing - 11 ft. lbs. (15 Nm) plus turn 30°
4. Cover - camshaft
5. Camshaft housing (intake shown)
6. Gasket - camshaft housing to cylinder head
7. Dowel pin (2)

8470K045

Camshaft housing, cover and gaskets — 2.3L engine

1. Relieve the fuel system pressure. Disconnect the negative battery cable.

2. Label and disconnect the ignition coil and module assembly electrical connections.

3. Remove the ignition coil and module assembly-to-camshaft housing bolts and remove assembly by pulling straight up. Use a special spark plug boot wire remover tool to remove connector assemblies, if they are stuck to the spark plugs.

4. Remove the idle speed power steering pressure switch connector.

5. Loosen 3 power steering pump pivot bolts and remove drive belt.

6. Disconnect the 2 rear power steering pump bracket to transaxle bolts.

7. Remove the front power steering pump bracket-to-cylinder block bolt.

8. Disconnect the power steering pump assembly and position aside.

9. Using the special tool, remove the power steering pump drive pulley from the intake camshaft.

10. Remove oil/air separator bolts and hoses. Leave the hoses attached to the separator, disconnect from the oil fill, chain housing and intake manifold. Remove as an assembly.

11. Remove vacuum line from fuel pressure regulator and disconnect the fuel injector harness connector.

12. Disconnect fuel line attaching clamp from bracket on top of intake camshaft housing.

13. Remove fuel rail-to-camshaft housing attaching bolts.

14. Remove the fuel rail from the cylinder head. Cover injector openings in cylinder head and cover injector nozzles. Leave fuel lines attached and position fuel rail aside.

15. Disconnect the timing chain and housing, but do not remove from the engine.

16. Remove intake camshaft housing cover-to-camshaft housing attaching bolts.

17. Remove the intake camshaft housing-to-cylinder head attaching bolts. Use the reverse of the tightening sequence when loosening camshaft housing to cylinder head attaching bolts. Leave 2 bolts loosely in place to hold the camshaft housing while separating camshaft cover from housing.

18. Push the cover off the housing by threading 4 of the housing to head attaching bolts into the tapped holes in the cam housing cover. Tighten the bolts in evenly so the cover does not bind on the dowel pins.

19. Remove the 2 loosely installed camshaft housing to head bolts and remove the cover. Discard the gaskets.

20. Note the position of the chain sprocket dowel pin for reassembly. Remove the camshaft carefully; do not damage the camshaft oil seal.

21. Remove intake camshaft oil seal from camshaft and discard seal. This seal must be replaced any time the housing and cover are separated.

22. Remove the camshaft carrier from the cylinder head and remove the gasket.

To install:

23. Thoroughly clean the mating surfaces of the camshaft carrier and the cylinder head, bolts and bolt holes. Install a new gasket and place the housing on the head. Install 1 bolt loosely to hold in place.

24. Install the lifters into their bores. If the camshaft is being replaced, the lifters must also be replaced. Lubricate camshaft lobes, journals and lifters with camshaft and lifter prelube. The camshaft lobes and journals must be adequately lubricated or engine damage could occur upon start up.

25. Install the camshaft in the same position as when removed. The

timing chain sprocket dowel pin should be straight up and align with the centerline of the lifter bores.

26. Install new camshaft housing to camshaft housing cover seals into cover; do not use sealer. Make sure the correct color seal is placed in each groove. Install the cover to the housing.

27. Apply thread locking compound to the camshaft housing and cover attaching bolt threads.

28. Install bolts and tighten to 11 ft. lbs. (15 Nm). Rotate the bolts, except the 2 rear bolts that hold the fuel pipe to the camshaft housing, an additional 75 degrees, in sequence. Tighten the excepted bolts to 16 ft. lbs. (15 Nm), then rotate an additional 25 degrees.

29. Install timing chain housing and timing chain.

30. Uncover fuel injectors and install new fuel injector O-ring seals lubricated with oil. Install the fuel rail.

31. Install the fuel line attaching clamp and retainer to bracket on top of the intake camshaft housing.

32. Connect the vacuum line to the fuel pressure regulator.

33. Connect the fuel injectors harness connector.

34. Install the oil/air separator assembly.

35. Lubricate the inner sealing surface of the intake camshaft seal with oil and install the seal to the housing.

36. Install the power steering pump pulley onto the intake camshaft.

37. Install the power steering pump assembly and drive belt.

38. Connect the idle speed power steering pressure switch connector.

39. Clean any loose lubricant that is present on the ignition coil and module assembly to camshaft housing bolts. Apply Loctite® or equivalent, onto the ignition coil and module assembly to camshaft housing bolts. Install the bolts and tighten to 13 ft. lbs. (18 Nm).

40. Connect the electrical connectors to ignition coil and module assembly.

41. Connect the negative battery cable and road test the vehicle. Check for leaks.

EXHAUST CAMSHAFT

NOTE: Any time the camshaft housing to cylinder head bolts are loosened or removed the camshaft housing to cylinder head gasket must be replaced.

1. Relieve the fuel system pressure. Disconnect the negative battery cable.

2. Label and disconnect the ignition coil and module assembly electrical connections.

3. Remove the ignition coil and module assembly to camshaft housing bolts and remove assembly by pulling straight up. Use a special tool to remove connector assemblies if they have stuck to the spark plugs.

4. Remove the idle speed power steering pressure switch connector.

5. Remove the transaxle fluid level indicator tube assembly from exhaust camshaft cover and position aside.

6. Remove exhaust camshaft cover and gasket.

7. Disconnect the timing chain and housing, but do not remove from the engine.

8. Remove exhaust camshaft housing to cylinder head bolts. Use the reverse of the tightening procedure when loosening camshaft housing while separating camshaft cover from housing.

9. Push the cover off the housing by threading 4 of the housing to head attaching bolts into the tapped holes in the camshaft cover. Tighten the bolts in evenly so the cover does not bind on the dowel pins.

10. Remove the 2 loosely installed camshaft housing to cylinder head bolts and remove cover, discard gaskets.

11. Loosely reinstall 1 camshaft housing-to-cylinder head bolt to retain the housing during camshaft and lifter removal.

12. Note the position of the chain sprocket dowel pin for reassembly. Remove camshaft being careful not to damage the camshaft or journals.

13. Remove the camshaft carrier from the cylinder head and remove the gasket.

To install:

14. Thoroughly clean the mating surfaces of the camshaft carrier and the cylinder head, bolts and bolt holes. Install a new gasket and place the housing on the head. Install 1 bolt loosely to hold in place.

15. Install the lifters into their bores. If the camshaft is being replaced, the lifters must also be replaced. Lubricate camshaft lobes, journals and lifters with camshaft and lifter prelube. The camshaft lobes and journals must be adequately lubricated or engine damage could occur upon start up.

16. Install camshaft in same position as when removed. The timing chain sprocket dowel pin should be straight up and align with the centerline of the lifter bores.

17. Install new camshaft housing to camshaft housing cover seals into cover; do not use sealer. Make sure the correct color seal is placed in each groove. Install the cover to the housing.

18. Apply thread locking compound to the camshaft housing and cover attaching bolt threads.

19. Install bolts and tighten, in sequence, to 11 ft. lbs. (15 Nm). Then rotate the bolts an additional 75 degrees, in sequence.

20. Install timing chain housing and timing chain.

21. Install the transaxle fluid level indicator tube assembly to exhaust camshaft cover.

22. Connect the idle speed power steering pressure switch connector.

23. Clean any loose lubricant that is present on the ignition coil and module assembly to camshaft housing bolts. Apply Loctite® or equivalent, onto the ignition coil and module assembly to camshaft housing bolts. Install the bolts and tighten to 13 ft. lbs. (18 Nm).

24. Connect the electrical connectors to ignition coil and module assembly.

25. Connect the negative battery cable and road test the vehicle. Check for leaks.

3.1L and 3.3L Engines

1. Disconnect the negative battery cable. Relieve the fuel system pressure before disconnecting any fuel lines. Remove the engine from the vehicle and secure to a suitable holding fixture.

2. Remove the intake manifold.

3. Remove the valve covers, rocker arm assemblies, pushrods and lifters. Keep all parts in order for reassembly.

4. Remove the crankshaft balancer from the crankshaft.

5. Remove the crankshaft sensor shield and the front cover.

6. Rotate the crankshaft to align the timing marks on the timing sprockets. Remove the camshaft sprocket and the timing chain.

7. Remove the camshaft retainer bolts/thrust plate and slide the camshaft forward out of the engine. Take care not to damage the bearings while removing the camshaft.

To install:

8. Install the camshaft to the engine and install the retainer bolts/thrust plate. Coat all parts with a liberal amount of clean engine oil supplement before installing.

9. Install the timing chain and sprockets.

10. Install the front cover and crankshaft sensor shield.

11. Install the crankshaft balancer and valve lifters.

12. Install the pushrods, rocker arms and the valve covers.

13. Install the intake manifold.

14. Install the engine to the vehicle.

15. Connect the negative battery cable and check for leaks.

Piston and Connecting Rod

POSITIONING

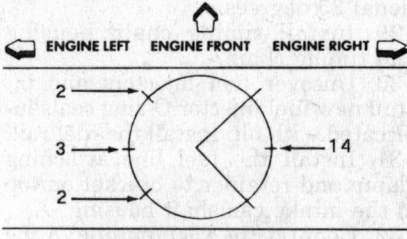

1. Oil ring spacer gap (tang in hole or slot with ARC)
2. Oil ring rail gaps
3. 2nd compression ring gap
4. Top compression ring gap

8470F067

Piston ring gap locations — 3.1L engine

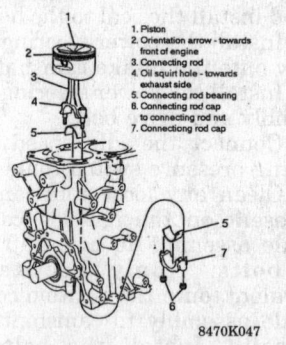

1. Piston
2. Orientation arrow - towards front of engine
3. Connecting rod
4. Oil squirt hole - towards exhaust side
5. Connecting rod bearing
6. Connecting rod cap to connecting rod nut
7. Connecting rod cap

8470K047

Piston and connecting rod installation — 2.3L engine

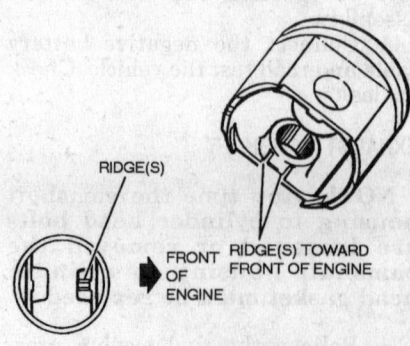

RIDGE(S)

FRONT OF ENGINE

RIDGE(S) TOWARD FRONT OF ENGINE

8470K048

Piston installation direction — 3.3L engine

ENGINE LUBRICATION

Oil Pan

REMOVAL AND INSTALLATION

2.3L Engine

1. Disconnect the negative battery cable. Raise and safely support the vehicle.

2. Remove the flywheel inspection cover.

3. Remove the splash shield-to-suspension support bolt. Remove the exhaust manifold brace, if equipped.

4. Remove the radiator outlet pipe-to-oil pan bolt.

5. Remove the transaxle-to-oil pan nut and stud using a 7mm socket.

6. Gently pry the spacer out from between oil pan and transaxle.

7. Remove the oil pan bolts. Rotate the crankshaft, if necessary and remove the oil pan and gasket from the engine.

8. Inspect the silicone strips across the top of the aluminum carrier at the oil pan-cylinder block-seal housing 3-way joint. If damaged, these strips must be repaired with silicone sealer. Use only enough sealer to restore the strips to their original dimension; too much sealer could cause leakage.

To install:

9. Thoroughly clean and dry the mating surfaces, bolts and bolt holes. Install the oil pan with a new gasket; do not uses sealer on the gasket. Loosely install the pan bolts.

10. Place the spacer in its approximate installed position but allow clearance to tighten the pan bolt above it.

11. Tighten the pan to block bolts to 17 ft. lbs. (24 Nm) and the remaining bolts to 106 inch lbs. (12 Nm).

12. Install the spacer and stud.

13. Install the oil pan transaxle nut and bolt.

14. Install the slash shield to suspension support.

15. Install the radiator outlet pipe bolt.

16. Install the exhaust manifold brace, if removed.

17. Install the flywheel inspection cover.

18. Fill the crankcase with the proper oil.

19. Connect the negative battery cable and check for leaks.

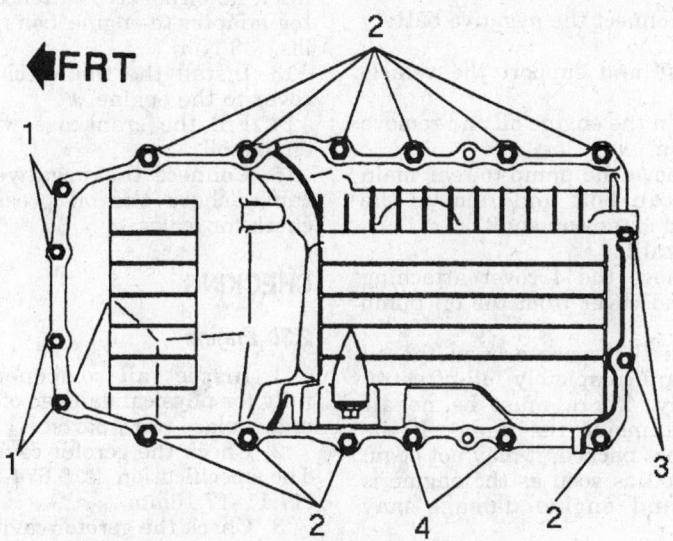

1. Bolt (4) (m6 × 1.0 × 25) - 106 ft. lbs. (12 Nm)
2. Bolt (10) (m8 × 1.25 × 22) - 18 ft. lbs. (24 Nm)
3. Bolt (10) (m6 × 1.0 × 25) - 106 ft. lbs. (12Nm)
4. Stud or bolt (2) (m8 × 1.25 × 22) - 19 ft. lbs. (19 Nm)

8470K049

Oil pan mounting bolts — 2.3L engine

3.1L Engine

NOTE: Special GM tools, engine support fixture J–28467A, engine support adapter leg J–36462 and torque wrench adapter J–39505 are needed to perform the oil pan removal and installation.

1. Disconnect the negative battery cable and drain the engine oil.
2. Remove the torque strut bolt. Raise the vehicle and support safely.
3. Remove the oil drip shield and engine mounts. Support the engine using a suitable jack.
4. Remove the transaxle mount nuts and exhaust pipe from the manifold.
5. Raise the engine using tools J–28467–A and J–36462.
6. Lower the vehicle. Place jackstands under the frame at the front and rear center crossmembers.
7. Loosen but do not remove the rear frame bolts.
8. Remove the front frame bolts and lower front of frame.
9. Remove the front engine mount bracket bolts, bracket and mount.
10. Remove the starter motor and electrical brackets at the oil pan.
11. Remove the oil pan bolts and oil pan. The side bolts need to be re-

moved with tool J–39505, or equivalent

To install:

12. Clean the gasket mating surfaces. Apply a bead of Ultra Black RTV sealer on the oil pan gasket tabs that insert into the gasket groove of the outer surface on the rear main bearing cap.
13. Install a new gasket, oil pan and bolts. Torque the side bolts to 37 ft. lbs. (50 Nm) with special tool J–39505. Torque the bottom bolts to 18 ft. lbs. (25 Nm).
14. Install the electrical brackets, starter motor and engine mount/bracket.
15. Raise the frame to proper position using new frame bolts. Remove the jackstands.
16. Raise the vehicle and support safely. Lower the engine to the correct position using engine support tools.
17. Install the exhaust pipe, transaxle mount, engine mount and oil drip shield.
18. Lower the vehicle and fill the engine with the proper amount of oil.
19. Install the torque strut bolt and remove the engine support fixture tools. Recheck the engine oil level, start the engine and check for leaks.

3.3L Engine

1. Disconnect the negative battery cable.
2. Raise and safely support the vehicle.
3. Drain the engine oil and remove the oil filter.
4. Remove the lower flap and the splash shield.
5. Remove the crankshaft pulley and the crank sensor cover.
6. Disconnect the air conditioning compressor electrical connector and remove the compressor from the bracket and support the compressor off to the side.
7. Remove the bolts from the right front suspension support.
8. Loosen all the remaining suspension support bolts to the point that the supports actually drop 1.5 inches (38mm).
9. Disconnect the oil level sensor from the oil pan, if equipped.
10. Remove the transaxle converter cover.
11. Remove the oil pan retaining bolts and remove the oil pan.

NOTE: It may be necessary to move the air conditioning line out of the way for added clearance when removing the oil pan.

12. Discard the old oil pan gasket.
To install:
13. Install a new gasket to the oil pan and install the oil pan to the engine block.
14. Tighten the oil pan bolts to 124 inch lbs. (14 Nm).
15. Install the oil sensor to the oil pan.
16. Tighten the suspension support bolts and install the right front support bolts.
17. Install the air conditioning compressor and hose support.
18. Connect the compressor electrical connector.
19. Install the crank sensor cover and the crankshaft pulley.
20. Install the lower flap, splash shield and the transaxle converter cover.
21. Lower the vehicle, refill the engine with oil and connect the negative battery cable.

Oil Pump

REMOVAL AND INSTALLATION

2.3L Engine

1. Disconnect the negative battery cable.

2. Raise and safely support the vehicle.

3. Drain the engine oil and remove the oil pan.

4. Remove the oil pump attaching bolts and nut.

5. Remove the oil pump assembly, shims if equipped and screen.

To install:

6. With the oil pump assembly off the engine, remove 3 attaching bolts and separate the driven gear cover and screen assembly from the oil pump.

7. Install the oil pump on the block using the original shims, if equipped. Tighten the bolts to 40 ft. lbs. (54 Nm).

8. Mount a dial indicator assembly to measure backlash between oil pump to drive gear.

9. Record oil pump drive to driven gear backlash. Proper backlash is 0.010–0.018 in. When measuring, do not allow the crankshaft to move.

10. If equipped with shims, remove shims to decrease clearance and add shims to increase clearance. If no shims were present, replace the assembly if proper backlash cannot be obtained.

11. When the proper clearance is reached, rotate crankshaft ½ turn and recheck clearance.

12. Remove oil pump from block, fill the cavity with petroleum jelly and reinstall driven gear cover and screen assembly to pump. Tighten the bolts to 106 inch lbs. (13 Nm).

13. Reinstall the pump assembly to the block. Tighten oil pump-to-block bolts to the proper torque specifications.

14. Install the oil pan.

15. Fill the crankcase with the proper oil.

16. Connect the negative battery cable, check the oil pressure and check for leaks.

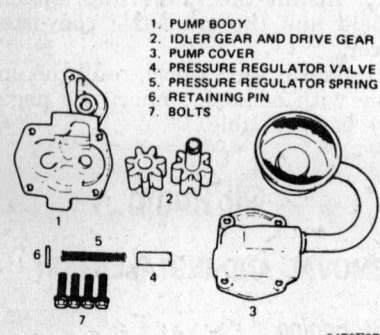

1. PUMP BODY
2. IDLER GEAR AND DRIVE GEAR
3. PUMP COVER
4. PRESSURE REGULATOR VALVE
5. PRESSURE REGULATOR SPRING
6. RETAINING PIN
7. BOLTS

8470F079

Exploded view of the oil pump assembly — 3.1L engine

3.1L Engine

1. Disconnect the negative battery cable.

2. Raise and support the vehicle safely.

3. Drain the engine oil and remove the oil pan.

4. Remove the pump-to-rear main bearing cap bolt and remove the pump and extension shaft.

To install:

5. Remove the 4 cover attaching screws and cover from the oil pump assembly.

6. Pack the space around the oil pump gears completely full of petroleum jelly. There must be no air space left inside the pump. If the pump is not packed, it may not begin to pump oil as soon as the engine is started and engine damage may result.

7. Assemble the pump and extension shaft with retainer to rear main bearing cap, aligning the top end of the extension shaft with the lower end of the drive gear.

8. Install the pump-to-the rear bearing cap bolt. Tighten to 30 ft. lbs. (40 Nm).

9. Install the oil pan. Torque the rear pan bolts to 18 ft. lbs. (25 Nm), all others for the 3.1L (VIN T) engine to 71 inch lbs. (8 Nm) or 18 ft. lbs. (25 Nm) for the 3.1L engine.

10. Lower the vehicle.

11. Fill the crankcase with oil.

12. Connect the negative battery cable.

3.3L Engine

1. Disconnect the negative battery cable.

2. Remove the timing chain front cover.

3. Raise and safely support vehicle.

4. Drain the engine oil. Lower the vehicle.

5. Remove the oil filter adapter, the pressure regulator valve and the valve spring.

6. Remove the oil pump cover-to-oil pump screws and remove the cover.

7. Remove the oil pump gears.

To install:

8. Lubricate the oil pump gears with clean engine oil.

9. Pack the pump cavity with petroleum jelly.

10. Install the oil pump cover screws using a new gasket and tighten to 97 inch lbs. (11 Nm).

11. Install the pressure regulator spring and valve.

12. Install the oil filter adaptor using a new gasket. Tighten the oil filter adapter-to-engine bolts to 24 ft. lbs. (33 Nm).

13. Install the timing chain front cover to the engine.

14. Fill the crankcase with clean engine oil.

15. Connect the negative battery cable, check the oil pressure and check for leaks.

CHECKING

2.3L Engine

1. Inspect all components carefully for physical damage of any type and replace worn parts.

2. Check the gerotor cavity depth. The specification is 0.674–0.676 in. (17.11–17.16mm).

3. Check the gerotor cavity diameter. The specification is 2.127–2.129 in. (53.95–54.00mm).

4. Check the inner gerotor tip clearance. The maximum clearance is 0.006 in. (15mm).

5. Check the outer gerotor diameter clearance. The specification is 0.010–0.014 in. (0.254–0.354mm).

3.1L Engine

1. Inspect all components carefully for physical damage of any type and replace worn parts.

2. Check the gear backlash. The specification is 0.0037–0.0077 in. (0.094–0.195mm).

3. Check the gear pocket depth. The specification is 1.202–1.204 in. (30.52–30.58mm).

4. Check the gear pocket diameter. The maximum clearance is 1.503–1.505 in. (38.176–38.226mm).

5. Check the gear side clearance. The specification is 0.001–0.003 in. (0.038–0.088mm).

6. Check the gear end clearance. The specification is 0.002–0.005 in. (0.040–0.125mm).

7. Check the relief valve-to-bore clearance. The specification is 0.0015–0.0035 in. (0.038–0.089mm).

3.3L Engine

1. Inspect all components carefully for physical damage of any type and replace worn parts.

2. Check the gear pocket depth. The specification is 0.461–0.463 in. (11.71–11.75mm).

3. Check the gear pocket diameter. The specification is 3.508–3.512 in. (89.10–89.20mm).

4. Check the inner gear tip clearance. The maximum clearance is 0.006 in. (0.152mm).

5. Check the outer gear diameter clearance. The specification is 0.008–0.015 in. (0.025–0.089mm).

Rear Main Bearing Oil Seal

REMOVAL AND INSTALLATION

2.3L Engine

1. Disconnect the negative battery cable.

2. Remove the transaxle.

3. If equipped with a manual transaxle, remove the pressure plate and clutch disc.

4. Remove the flywheel-to-crankshaft bolts and the flywheel.

5. Remove the oil pan-to-seal housing bolts and the block-to-seal housing bolts.

6. Remove the seal housing from the engine.

7. Place 2 blocks of equal thickness on a flat surface and position the seal housing on the 2 blocks. Remove the seal from the housing.

To install:

8. Press the new seal into the housing, using tool J36005 or equivalent.

9. Position the new seal housing to the block over the dowel alignment pins.

10. Lube the lip of the crankshaft seal with engine oil and install the seal housing assembly.

11. Tighten the seal housing-to-block bolts to 106 inch lbs. (12 Nm).

12. Tighten the oil pan-to-seal housing bolts to 106 inch lbs. (12 Nm).

13. Install the flywheel. Tighten the bolts evenly to specification.

14. If equipped with manual transaxle, install the clutch, pressure plate and clutch cover.

15. Install the transaxle to the vehicle and connect the negative battery cable.

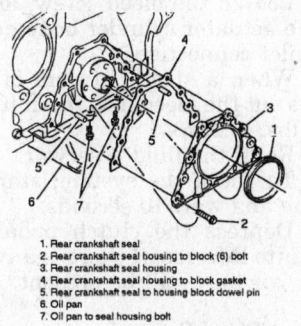

1. Rear crankshaft seal
2. Rear crankshaft seal housing to block (6) bolt
3. Rear crankshaft seal housing to block gasket
4. Rear crankshaft seal housing to block gasket
5. Rear crankshaft seal to housing block dowel pin
6. Oil pan
7. Oil pan to seal housing bolt

8470K054

Rear main crankshaft seal and housing — 2.3L engine

16. Start the engine and check for leaks.

3.1 and 3.3L Engines

1. Disconnect the negative battery cable.

2. Raise and safely support the vehicle and remove the transaxle from the vehicle.

3. Remove the flywheel from the vehicle.

4. Carefully pry the seal out using a flat bladed prybar.

5. Inspect the inside diameter of the bore for nicks, burrs or scratches.

6. Apply clean engine oil to outside diameter of the new seal.

7. Using a rear seal installation tool J-38196 or equivalent, install the seal.

8. Install the flywheel and install the transaxle.

9. Lower the vehicle and connect the negative battery cable.

MANUAL TRANSAXLE

Transaxle Assembly

REMOVAL AND INSTALLATION

1. Disconnect the negative battery cable from the battery and transaxle. Remove air ducts and tubes, etc. to gain access to transaxle mounting bolts.

2. Remove the power steering pump and brackets and position aside, if necessary.

3. Attach an engine support fixture to the engine and raise the engine enough to take the pressure off the engine mounts.

NOTE: If a lifting bar is not available, a chain hoist can be used. However, during the removal procedure the vehicle must be raised and the chain hoist adjusted to keep tension on the engine/transaxle assembly.

4. Remove the left side steering column opening filler from inside the vehicle.

5. Disconnect the clutch master cylinder pushrod from the clutch pedal.

6. Disconnect the clutch slave cylinder from the transaxle support bracket and move it aside.

7. Remove the transaxle mount-to-transaxle bolts. Discard the bolts attaching the mount to the side frame. New bolts must be used upon installation.

8. Remove the transaxle mount bracket attaching bolts and nuts. Remove the upper transaxle to engine bolts.

9. Remove the transaxle vent tube and disconnect the reverse light switch.

10. Disconnect the shift cables and retaining clips from the transaxle.

11. Raise and safely support the vehicle.

12. Remove the left front wheel assembly.

13. Remove the left front inner splash shield. Drain the transaxle oil.

14. Remove the transaxle strut and bracket, if equipped.

15. Remove the flywheel housing cover bolts.

16. Disconnect the speedometer cable or sensor from the transaxle.

17. If equipped with a 2.3L engine, remove the radiator outlet pipe support bolt from transaxle.

18. Disconnect the stabilizer bar from the left suspension support and control arm.

19. Disconnect the ball joint-to-steering knuckle nut and separate the ball joint from the steering knuckle.

20. Remove the left suspension support attaching bolts, the support and control arm as an assembly.

21. Use boot protectors and disengage the halfshafts from the transaxle. Remove the left halfshaft from the transaxle.

22. Remove engine mount components and remaining transaxle mount bolts, as required.

23. Position a transmission jack under and secure to the transaxle case. Remove the remaining transaxle-to-engine mounting bolts.

24. Remove the transaxle by sliding it toward the driver's side, away from the engine. Carefully lower the jack, guiding the right or intermediate shaft out of the transaxle. Lower the engine to aid the operation, if necessary.

To install:

25. Install the transaxle into position. As the transaxle is being installed, guide the right halfshaft into place. Lower the engine to its installation position.

26. Connect the negative battery cable to the transaxle case.

27. Install engine mount components and remaining transaxle

mount bolts. Install the flywheel cover(s).

28. Remove the support jack when the transaxle is securely mounted.

29. Install the left halfshaft.

30. Install the left suspension support.

31. Install the engine mount cross-member nuts, if removed.

32. Connect the stabilizer bar to the left suspension support and control arm.

33. Install the radiator outlet pipe support bolt, if equipped.

34. Connect the speedometer cable or sensor.

35. Install the transaxle bracket and strut, if equipped.

36. Install the splash shield and wheel. Lower the vehicle.

37. Connect the shift cables and install the retaining clips.

38. Install the transaxle vent tube and connect the reverse light switch connector.

39. Install the upper transaxle to engine bolts. Install the transaxle mount bracket attaching bolts and nuts.

40. Install the new transaxle mount-to-transaxle bolts.

41. Connect the clutch slave cylinder to the support bracket.

42. Connect the clutch master cylinder pushrod to the clutch pedal.

43. Install the steering column opening filler panel.

44. Remove the engine support tool.

45. Install the power steering pump and brackets, if they were removed.

46. Install air ducts, etc. that were removed.

47. Fill the transaxle with the proper fluid.

48. Connect the negative battery cable and check the transaxle for proper operation.

CLUTCH

Clutch Assembly

REMOVAL AND INSTALLATION

1. Disconnect the negative battery cable.

2. Remove the sound insulator panel from inside of the vehicle and disconnect the clutch master cylinder pushrod from the clutch pedal.

3. Remove the transaxle from the vehicle.

4. If reinstalling old parts, match-mark the clutch/pressure plate cover and flywheel. Insert a clutch plate alignment tool into the clutch disc hub.

5. Loosen the flywheel to pressure plate bolts gradually and evenly to avoid warpage.

6. Remove the pressure plate/clutch assembly from the flywheel.

7. Inspect the flywheel for excessive scores or cracks and replace if damaged. If the flywheel appears to be OK, sand the flywheel.

8. Sparingly apply anti-seize compound to the input shaft and clutch disc splines. Install a new release bearing.

To install:

9. Install the clutch disc and the pressure plate. Align with a clutch disc alignment tool and loosely tighten the pressure plate bolts to center the disc.

10. Tighten bolts 1, 2 and 3 to 12 ft. lbs. (16 Nm) and then bolts 4, 5 and 6 to 12 ft. lbs. (16 Nm).

11. Tighten all the bolts in order to 15 ft. lbs. (20 Nm) plus an additional 30 degrees.

12. Install the transaxle.

13. Connect the pushrod to the clutch pedal and install the sound insulator.

14. Connect the negative battery cable and check the clutch and reverse lights for proper operation.

Clutch Master and Slave Cylinders

REMOVAL AND INSTALLATION

1. Disconnect the negative battery cable.

2. Remove the steering column opening filler/sound insulator from inside the vehicle.

3. Disconnect the clutch master cylinder pushrod from the clutch pedal.

4. Remove the clutch master cylinder attaching nuts at the front of the dash and disconnect the remote fluid reservoir, if equipped.

5. Remove the actuator cylinder attaching nuts at the transaxle.

6. Remove the hydraulic actuating system as an assembly.

To install:

7. Bleed the system, if necessary.

8. Install the actuator cylinder to the transaxle, aligning the pushrod into the pocket on the lever. Tighten the attaching nuts evenly to prevent damage.

NOTE: New actuators are packaged with plastic straps to retain the pushrod. Do not break the strap off; it will break upon the first clutch application.

9. Install the master cylinder. Tighten the attaching nuts evenly to prevent damage. Connect the remote fluid reservoir, if equipped. If equipped with a bleed screw and bleeding is necessary, bleed the system.

10. Remove the pushrod restrictor from the master cylinder pushrod. Lubricate the bushing on the clutch pedal. Connect the pushrod to the pedal and install the retaining clip. Make sure the cruise control switch is operating properly.

NOTE: When adjusting the cruise control switch, do not use a force of more than 20 lbs. to pull the pedal up, or damage to the master cylinder pushrod retaining ring could result.

11. Install the steering column opening filler from inside the vehicle.

12. Push the clutch pedal down a few times. This will break the plastic straps on the actuator.

13. Connect the negative battery cable and check for proper operation.

ADJUSTMENT

The hydraulic system used provides automatic clutch adjustment, therefore no adjustment to any portion of the system is required.

HYDRAULIC CLUTCH SYSTEM BLEEDING

With Bleed Screw

1. Make sure the reservoir is full of DOT 3 fluid and is kept topped off throughout this procedure.

2. Loosen the bleed screw, located on the actuator cylinder body next to the inlet connection.

3. When a steady stream of fluid comes out the bleeder, tighten it to 17 inch lbs. (2 Nm).

4. Refill the fluid reservoir.

5. To check the system, start the engine and wait 10 seconds.

6. Depress the clutch pedal and shift into Reverse. If there is any gear clash, air may still be present.

Without Bleed Screw

1. Remove the actuator cylinder from the transaxle.

2. Loosen the master cylinder attaching nuts to the ends of the studs.

3. Remove the reservoir cap and diaphragm.

4. Depress the actuator cylinder pushrod about ¾ in. into its bore and hold the position.

5. Install the reservoir diaphragm and cap while holding the actuator pushrod.

6. Release the pushrod when the diaphragm and cap are properly installed.

7. With the actuator lower than the master cylinder, hold the actuator vertically with the pushrod end facing the ground.

8. Press the actuator pushrod into its bore with ½ in. strokes. Check the reservoir for bubbles. Continue until no bubbles enter the reservoir.

9. Install the master cylinder and actuator.

10. Refill the fluid reservoir.

11. To check the system, start the engine and wait 10 seconds.

12. Depress the clutch pedal and shift into reverse. If there is any gear clash, air may still be present.

AUTOMATIC TRANSAXLE

Transaxle Assembly

REMOVAL AND INSTALLATION

Except Turbo Hydro-Matic 4T60-E Transaxle

1. Disconnect the negative battery cable. If necessary, drain the coolant and disconnect the heater core hoses.

2. Remove the air cleaner assembly. If equipped with a 3.3L engine, remove the mass air flow sensor and air intake duct.

3. Disconnect the throttle valve cable from the throttle lever and the transaxle.

4. If equipped with a 2.3L engine, remove the power steering pump and bracket and position it aside.

5. Remove the transaxle dipstick and tube.

6. Install an engine support tool. Insert a ¼ x 2 inch bolt in the hole at the front right motor mount to maintain driveline alignment.

7. Remove the wiring harness-to-transaxle nut. Disconnect the wiring connectors from the speed sensor,

TCC connector, neutral safety switch and reverse light switch.

8. Disconnect the shift linkage from the transaxle.

9. Remove the upper 2 transaxle-to-engine bolts and the upper left transaxle mount along with the bracket assembly.

10. Remove the rubber hose from the transaxle vent pipe. Remove the remaining upper engine-to-transaxle bolts.

11. Raise and safely support the vehicle. Remove both front wheels.

12. If equipped with a 2.3L engine, remove both lower ball joints and stabilizer shafts links.

13. Drain the transaxle fluid.

14. Remove the shift linkage bracket from the transaxle.

15. Install a halfshaft boot seal protector on the inner seals.

NOTE: Some vehicles may use a gray silicone boot on the inboard axle joint. Use boot protector tool on these boots. All other boots are made from a black thermo-plastic material and do not require the use of a boot seal protector.

16. Remove both ball joint-to-control arm nuts and separate the ball joints from the control arms.

17. Remove both halfshafts and support them with a cord or wire.

18. Remove the transaxle mounting strut/brace.

19. Remove the left stabilizer bar link pin bolt, left frame bushing clamp nuts and left frame support assembly.

20. Remove the torque converter cover. Matchmark the flexplate and torque converter for installation purposes. Remove the torque converter-to-flexplate bolts.

21. Disconnect and plug the transaxle oil cooler lines.

22. Remove the transaxle-to-engine support bracket and install the transaxle removal jack.

23. Remove the remaining transaxle-to-engine attaching bolts and the transaxle from the vehicle.

To install:

24. Secure the transaxle to the jack.

25. Apply a small amount of grease on the torque converter hub and seat in the oil pump.

26. Position the transaxle in the vehicle and install the lower engine to transaxle bolts.

27. Install the transaxle to engine support bracket. Once the transaxle is securely held in place, remove the jack. Connect the cooler lines.

28. Install the torque converter bolts and tighten to specification.

29. Install the torque converter cover.

30. Install the left frame support assembly.

31. Install the left stabilizer shaft frame bushing nuts and link pin bolt.

32. Install the transaxle mounting strut.

33. Install the halfshafts. Install the ball joints.

34. Install the shift linkage bracket to the transaxle.

35. Install the wheels and lower the vehicle.

36. Install the upper transaxle to engine bolts.

37. Install the left side transaxle mount.

38. Connect the shift linkage to the transaxle.

39. Connect the wiring connectors to their switches on the transaxle.

40. Remove the ¼ x 2 in. bolt that was placed in the hole at the front right motor mount to maintain driveline alignment. Remove an engine support tool.

41. Replace the O-ring, lubricate it and install the dipstick tube and dipstick.

42. Install the TV cable and rubber vent tube.

43. Install the air cleaner assembly and air tubes.

44. Connect the heater hoses, if disconnected.

45. Fill all fluids to their proper levels. Adjust cables as required.

46. Connect the negative battery cable and check the transaxle for proper operation and leaks.

Turbo Hydro-Matic 4T60-E Transaxle

NOTE: Special tools needed for this procedure: engine support fixture J-28467A, oil cooler and line flusher J-35944A, oil cooler and line flusher adapter J-36462 and axle seal protector J-37292B.

1. Disconnect the negative battery cable and remove the air cleaner.

2. Remove the engine torque strut from the engine.

3. Disconnect the shift control cable and remove the bracket from the transaxle case lever.

4. Disconnect the TCC switch connector and vacuum hose.

5. Remove the upper transaxle mounting bolts and install engine support fixture tool J-28467A.

6. Raise the vehicle and support safely. Remove the front tire assemblies and engine splash shields.

7. Remove the pinch bolts from the controls arms and steering shaft.

8. Remove the stabilizer shaft nuts and brackets from the frame.

Separate the stabilizer from the control arm.

9. Use a 7/16 inch drill bit to drill through the 2 spot welds located between the front and rear holes of the left front stabilizer shaft mounting.

10. Remove the front and rear transaxle mounting nuts. Disconnect the power steering cooler line bolts.

11. Disconnect the engine wiring harness from the frame.

12. Remove the right frame-to-left frame retaining bolt. Position jackstands under the frame for support.

13. Loosen the 2 right frame mounts and discard bolts. Remove the 2 left frame bolts from the frame.

14. Remove the left frame with the help of an assistant.

15. Disconnect the right lower ball joint from the steering knuckle.

16. Remove the transaxle support bracket bolts from the transaxle.

17. Disconnect the power steering cooler line support and remove the torque converter cover.

18. Remove the starter motor and torque converter bolts.

19. Remove the transaxle mount bolts and mount from the case.

20. Disconnect all electrical connectors from the transaxle.

21. Remove both halfshafts from the transaxle and install the protective covers J–37292B, or equivalent.

22. Install a suitable transaxle jack.

23. Disconnect the oil cooler lines and plug openings.

24. Remove the remaining transaxle bolts and transaxle. Remove slowly to check for components not disconnected or hanging up.

To install:

25. Place the transaxle on the jack and move into position. Install the front bolt and torque to 55 ft. lbs. (75 Nm).

26. Connect the cooler lines and remove the transaxle jack.

27. Connect all electrical, vacuum and cable connections to the lower portion of the transaxle.

28. Install the halfshafts into the transaxle and make sure they are seated properly.

29. Install the transaxle mount and torque to 41 ft. lbs. (55 Nm).

30. Install the torque converter bolts and torque to 47 ft. lbs. (63 Nm). Retorque again using same pattern.

31. Install the starter motor, converter cover, power steering cooler line and transaxle support bracket.

32. Install the pinch bolts to the control arms. Install the right and left frame assembly and torque the bolts to 40 ft. lbs. (54 Nm).

33. Install the jackstands and the remainder of the right and left frame bolts.

34. Install the transaxle rear nuts and torque to 24 ft. lbs. (33 Nm).

35. Install the stabilizer bar bolts and torque to 30 ft. lbs. (44 Nm).

36. Install the steering shaft pinch bolt.

37. Install the engine splash shields, front wheels and remove the engine support fixture.

38. Install the upper transaxle bolts and ground wires. Torque bolts to 55 ft. lbs. (75 Nm).

39. Install the engine torque strut and air cleaner.

40. Connect the battery cable, refill the transaxle fluid, start the engine and check for leaks.

TV CABLE ADJUSTMENT

Except 2.3L Engine

1. Disconnect the negative battery cable.

2. Depress and hold the adjustment tap at the TV cable adjuster.

3. Release the throttle lever by hand to its full travel position.

4. The slider must move toward the lever when the lever is rotated to the full travel position.

5. Inspect the cable for freedom of movement. The cable may appear to function properly with the engine stopped and cold. Recheck the cable after the engine is warm.

6. Road test the vehicle and check for proper shifting.

2.3L Engine

1. Disconnect the negative battery cable.

2. Rotate the TV cable adjuster body at the transaxle 90 degrees and pull the cable conduit out until the slider mechanism contacts the stop.

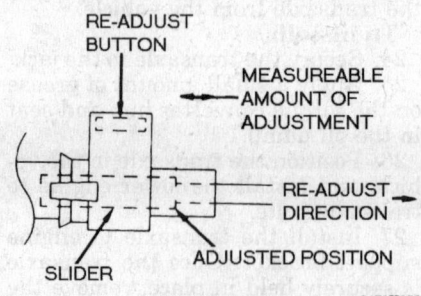

TV cable setting

8470K059

3. Rotate the adjuster body back to the original position.

4. Using a torque wrench, rotate the TV cable adjuster until 75 inch lbs. (9 Nm) is reached.

5. Road test the vehicle and check for proper shifting.

SHIFT CABLE ADJUSTMENT

1. Place the selector in the **N** detent.

2. Raise the locking tab on the cable adjuster.

3. Place the shift control assembly on the transaxle in the neutral position.

4. Push the locking tab back into position.

DRIVE AXLE

Halfshaft

REMOVAL AND INSTALLATION

NOTE: If equipped with Tri-pot joints, care must be exercised not to allow joints to become overextended. Overextending the joint could result in separation of internal components.

1. Disconnect the negative battery cable.

2. Raise and safely support the vehicle.

3. Remove the wheels.

4. Install the halfshaft seal protector on the outer joint.

5. Remove the shaft nut and washer.

6. Remove the ball joint attaching nut and separate the control arm from the steering knuckle. Remove the stabilizer shaft, if necessary.

7. Pull out on lower knuckle area. Using a plastic or rubber mallet, strike the end of the halfshaft to disengage it from the hub and bearing assembly.

8. Separate the halfshaft from the hub and bearing assembly and move the strut assembly rearward.

9. Remove the inner joint from the transaxle or intermediate shaft using the slide hammer tool.

10. To remove the intermediate shaft, remove the rear engine mount through bolt. Then remove the intermediate shaft bracket bolts and remove the assembly.

To install:

11. Install the seal protector to the transaxle. Install the intermediate shaft, if removed. Tighten the bracket bolts to 35 ft. lbs. (47 Nm).

12. Drive the halfshaft into the transaxle or intermediate shaft by placing a suitable tool into the groove on the joint housing and tapping until seated. Be careful not to damage the axle seal or spring. Verify that the axle is seated by grasping the inner joint housing and pulling outboard.

13. Install the axle to the hub and bearing assembly.

14. Install the washer and nut and tighten to 185 ft. lbs. (260 Nm).

15. Install the ball joint to the steering knuckle. Install the stabilizer shaft, if removed.

16. Remove the seal protectors.

17. Install the wheels.

18. Connect the negative battery cable and check for proper operation.

CV-Boot

REMOVAL AND INSTALLATION

1. Disconnect the negative battery cable. Raise and safely support the vehicle. Remove the halfshaft assembly.

2. Remove the steel deflector ring by using brass drift to tap it off. If rubber ring is used, slide it off.

3. Cut the seal's retaining clamps and lift the boot up to gain access to retaining ring.

4. Remove the snapring and remove the joint from the shaft.

5. Slide the boot off shaft.

To install:

6. Clean the splines of the shaft and the CV-joint.

7. Install the clamp and boot onto the shaft. Fill the boot with amount of grease specified.

8. Install the joint to the shaft and install a new retaining ring.

9. Crimp the outer clamp securely in the groove.

10. Install the steel deflector ring or rubber ring.

11. Install the halfshaft assembly.

12. Connect the negative battery cable and check for proper operation.

Front Wheel Hub, Knuckle and Bearing

REMOVAL AND INSTALLATION

1. Raise and safely support the vehicle.

2. Remove the front wheel assemblies.

3. Install a halfshaft boot seal protector tool on the outer CV-joints and a halfshaft boot seal protector tool on the inner Tri-pot joints.

4. Insert a long punch through the caliper and into a rotor vent to keep it from turning.

5. Clean the shaft threads and lubricate them with a thread lubricant.

6. Remove the hub nut and washer.

7. Remove the caliper-to-steering knuckle bolts and support the caliper on a wire aside.

8. Remove the rotor.

9. Remove the halfshaft from the hub and bearing assembly.

10. Remove the 3 hub bolts, the shield and the hub and bearing assembly. Remove the bearing seal from the knuckle.

11. To remove the steering knuckle, perform the following procedures:

    a. At the ball joint-to-steering knuckle and the tie-rod-to-steering knuckle intersections, remove the cotter pins and nuts.

    b. Using a ball joint removal tool, separate the ball joint and the tie-rod end from the steering knuckle.

    c. Matchmark the strut to the knuckle. While supporting the steering knuckle, remove the steering knuckle-to-strut bolts and the steering knuckle from the vehicle.

To install:

12. Install the steering knuckle and all attaching bolts. Tighten the bolts to their proper torques:

    a. Align the matchmarks and tighten the steering knuckle-to-strut bolts to 140 ft. lbs. (190 Nm).

    b. Tighten the ball joint-to-steering knuckle nut to 55–65 ft. lbs. (75–88 Nm) and install a new cotter pin.

    c. Tighten the tie-rod-to-steering knuckle nut to 35 ft. lbs. (47 Nm) and install a new cotter pin.

13. Install a new seal to the knuckle.

14. If reinstalling the original assembly, replace the O-ring. Install the hub and bearing assembly, shield and bolts. Tighten the bolts to 70 ft. lbs. (95 Nm).

15. Install the halfshaft and brake parts.

16. Install the wheels.

17. Check and adjust front end alignment, as required.

STEERING

Steering Wheel

REMOVAL AND INSTALLATION

1. Disconnect the negative battery cable.

2. Remove the 2 screws that retain the steering pad, if equipped.

3. Disconnect the horn lead and remove the horn pad.

4. Remove the retainer, nut and dampener, if equipped.

5. Matchmark the steering wheel to the shaft and remove the steering wheel from the vehicle.

6. The installation is the reverse of the removal procedure. Tighten the attaching nut to 30 ft. lbs. (41 Nm).

Steering Column

REMOVAL AND INSTALLATION

1. Disconnect the negative battery cable.

2. Remove the steering wheel.

3. Remove the steering column-to-intermediate shaft coupling pinch bolt. Remove the safety strap and bolt, if equipped.

4. Remove the steering column trim shrouds and column covers.

5. If equipped, remove the tilt lever.

6. Disconnect all wiring harness connectors. Remove the dust boot mounting screws and steering column-to-dash bracket bolts.

7. Lower the column to clear the mounting bracket and carefully remove from the vehicle.

To install:

8. Install the column assembly and install the column bracket support bolts and the upper pinch bolt.

9. Tighten the column bracket support bolts to 22 ft. lbs. (30 Nm) and the upper pinch bolt to 29 ft. lbs. (40 Nm).

10. Connect the park lock/brake transaxle shift interlock cable to the ignition switch.

11. Connect the electrical connectors.

12. Install the upper and lower steering column covers and install the tilt lever, if equipped.

13. Install the steering wheel and the horn pad.

14. Install the lower steering column filler and left sound insulator.

15. Connect the negative battery cable and check all column mounted switches, accessories and the vehicle's steering mechanism for proper operation.

Power Rack and Pinion Steering Gear

ADJUSTMENT

Rack Bearing Preload

1. Center the steering wheel. Raise and safely support the vehicle.

2. Loosen the locknut and turn the adjuster plug clockwise until it bottoms in the housing. Then back off about 1/8 turn and tighten the locknut while holding the position of the adjuster plug.

3. Check the steering for ability to return to center after the adjustment has been completed.

REMOVAL AND INSTALLATION

1. Disconnect the negative battery cable. Remove the left side sound insulator.

2. Disconnect the upper pinch bolt on the steering coupling assembly.

3. Disconnect the clamp nuts.

4. Raise and safely support the vehicle. Remove both front wheel assemblies.

5. Remove the clamp nut and the fluid line retainer.

6. Remove the tie rod end-to-steering knuckle cotter pin and castle nut. Using a puller tool, disconnect the tie rod ends from the steering knuckles.

7. Lower the vehicle.

8. Disconnect and plug the fluid lines from the power steering rack.

9. Remove the mounting clamps. Move the steering rack forward and remove the lower pinch bolt on the coupling assembly.

10. Disconnect the coupling from the steering rack.

11. Remove the rack and pinion assembly with the dash seal through the left wheel opening.

To install:

12. If the studs were removed with the mounting clamps, reinstall the studs into the cowl. If the stud is being reused, use Loctite® to secure the threads.

13. Slide the rack and pinion assembly through the left side wheel housing opening and secure the dash seal.

14. Move the assembly forward and install the coupling.

15. Install the lower pinch bolt and tighten to 29 ft. lbs. (40 Nm).

16. Connect the fluid lines.

17. Install the clamp nuts. Tighten the left side clamp first, then tighten the right side. Raise and safely support the vehicle.

18. Connect the tie rod ends to the steering knuckle, tighten the nut to 35 ft. lbs. (47 Nm) and install a new cotter pin. Install the wheels.

19. Install the line retainer and lower the vehicle.

20. Install the upper pinch bolt on the coupling assembly. Tighten to 29 ft. lbs. (40 Nm).

21. Install the sound insulator.

22. Fill the power steering pump with fluid and bleed the system.

23. Connect the negative battery cable and check the rack for proper operation and leaks.

24. Check and adjust front end alignment, as required.

Power Steering Pump

REMOVAL AND INSTALLATION

2.3L Engine

1. Disconnect the negative battery cable.

2. Disconnect the pressure and return lines from the pump.

3. Remove the rear bracket to pump bolts.

4. Remove the drive belt and position aside.

5. Remove the rear bracket to transaxle bolts.

6. Remove the front bracket to engine bolt.

7. Remove the pump and bracket as an assembly.

8. Transfer pulley and bracket, as necessary.

9. The installation is the reverse of the removal procedure.

10. Fill the power steering pump with fluid and bleed the system.

11. Connect the negative battery cable and check the pump for proper operation and leaks.

3.3L Engine

1. Disconnect the negative battery cable.

2. Remove the serpentine drive belt.

3. Remove the power steering pump-to-engine bolts.

4. Pull the pump forward and disconnect the pressure lines.

5. Remove the pump and transfer the pulley, as necessary.

To install:

6. Connect the power steering lines to the pump.

7. Install the pump to the bracket and install the bolts. Tighten the bolts to 18 ft. lbs. (25 Nm).

8. Install the belt and adjust the drive belt tension.

9. Fill the power steering pump with fluid and bleed the system.

10. Connect the negative battery cable and check the pump for proper operation and leaks.

BELT ADJUSTMENT

NOTE: Serpentine belt driven power steering pumps do not require adjustment. If the belt is stretched beyond usable limits, replace it.

1. Place the appropriate gauge on the belt and measure the tension; specifications are: new and used belt — 110 lbs. for 2.3L engine.

2. If the tension is not at specifications, loosen the mounting bolts and move the pump or turn the adjustment stud.

3. Tighten the mounting bolts while holding the adjusted position of the pump.

4. Run the engine for 2 minutes and recheck the tension.

SYSTEM BLEEDING

1. Raise the vehicle so the wheels are off the ground. Turn the wheels all the way to the left. Add power steering fluid to the **COLD** or **FULL COLD** mark on the fluid level indicator.

2. Start the engine and check the fluid level at fast idle. Add fluid, if necessary to bring the level up to the mark.

3. Bleed air from the system by turning the wheels from side-to-side without hitting the stops. Keep the fluid level at the **COLD** or **FULL COLD** mark. Fluid with air in it has a tan appearance.

4. Return the wheels to the center position and continue running the engine for 2–3 minutes.

5. Lower the vehicle and road test to check steering function and recheck the fluid level with the system at its normal operating temperature. Fluid should be at the **HOT** mark when finished.

Tie Rod Ends

REMOVAL AND INSTALLATION

Inner Tie Rod

1. Disconnect the negative battery cable. Remove the rack and pinion gear from the vehicle.
2. Remove the lock plate from the inner tie rod bolts.
3. If removing both tie rods, remove both bolts, the bolt support plate and 1 of the tie rod assemblies. Reinstall the removed tie rod's bolt to keep inner parts of the rack aligned. Remove the remaining tie rod.
4. If only removing 1 tie rod, slide the assembly out from between the support plate and the center housing cover washer.

To install:

5. Install the center housing cover washer fitted into the rack and pinion boot.
6. Install the inner tie rod bolts through the holes in the bolt support plate, inner pivot bushing, center housing cover washer, rack housing and into the threaded holes.
7. Tighten the bolts to 65 ft. lbs. (90 Nm).
8. Install a new lock plate with its notches over the bolt flats.
9. Install the rack and pinion gear.
10. Fill the power steering pump with fluid and bleed the system.
11. Connect the negative battery cable and check the rack for proper operation and leaks.

Outer Tie Rod

1. Disconnect the negative battery cable.
2. Remove the cotter pin and the nut from the tie rod ball stud at the steering knuckle.
3. Loosen the pinch bolts.
4. Using the proper tools, separate the tie rod taper from the steering knuckle.
5. Remove the tie rod from the adjuster.
6. The installation is the reverse of the removal procedure.
7. Perform a front end alignment.

BRAKES

Master Cylinder

REMOVAL AND INSTALLATION

1. Disconnect the negative cable and the electrical connector from the fluid level sensor.
2. Disconnect the electrical connectors from both solenoids.
3. Disconnect the 3-pin and 6-pin motor pack electrical connectors.
4. Disconnect the brake pipe tube nuts from the master cylinder and from the modulator assembly.
5. Plug the brake lines to prevent brake fluid loss.
6. Remove the master cylinder mounting nuts.
7. Remove the master cylinder and the modulator assembly.

To install:

8. Install the master cylinder and the modulator assembly to the power booster.
9. Tighten the master cylinder and modulator assembly mounting nuts to 20 ft. lbs. (27 Nm).
10. Connect the brake lines to the master cylinder and to the modulator assembly. Tighten the nuts to 15 ft. lbs. (20 Nm).
11. Connect the electrical connectors to the fluid level sensor and to both solenoids.
12. Connect the 3-pin and 6-pin electrical connectors to the motor pack.
13. Refill the master cylinder with brake fluid and bleed the system if necessary.
14. Connect the negative battery cable.

Proportioner Valves

REMOVAL AND INSTALLATION

1. Disconnect the negative battery cable.
2. Remove the retaining roll pins and remove the fluid reservoir from the cylinder, if necessary.
3. Remove the proportioner valve cap assemblies.
4. Remove the O-rings.
5. Remove the springs.
6. Carefully remove the proportioner valve pistons.
7. Remove the seals from the pistons.

To install:

8. Thoroughly clean and dry all parts.
9. Lubricate the new piston seals with the silicone grease included in the repair kit or brake assembly fluid. Install to the pistons with the seal lips facing upward toward the cap assembly.
10. Lubricate the stem of the pistons and install to their bores.
11. Install the springs.
12. Lubricate and install the new O-rings in their grooves in the cap assemblies.
13. Install the caps to the master cylinder and tighten to 20 ft. lbs. (27 Nm).
14. Install the reservoir, if removed.
15. Fill the reservoir with brake fluid.
16. Connect the negative battery cable and check the brakes for proper operation.

Power Brake Booster

REMOVAL AND INSTALLATION

1. Disconnect the negative battery cable.
2. Disconnect the vacuum hose(s) from the booster.
3. Remove the master cylinder and if equipped, remove the modulator assembly.
4. From inside of the vehicle, remove the booster pushrod from the brake pedal.
5. Remove the nuts that attach the booster to the dash panel and remove it from the vehicle.
6. Transfer the necessary parts to the new booster.
7. The installation is the reverse of the removal procedure.
8. Connect the negative battery cable and check the brakes for proper operation.

Brake Caliper

REMOVAL AND INSTALLATION

1. Raise and safely support the vehicle.
2. Remove the tire and wheel assembly.
3. Push the piston completely into its bore for clearance.
4. Remove the bolt that attaches the brake hose from the caliper. Plug the hose and the caliper to prevent fluid loss.

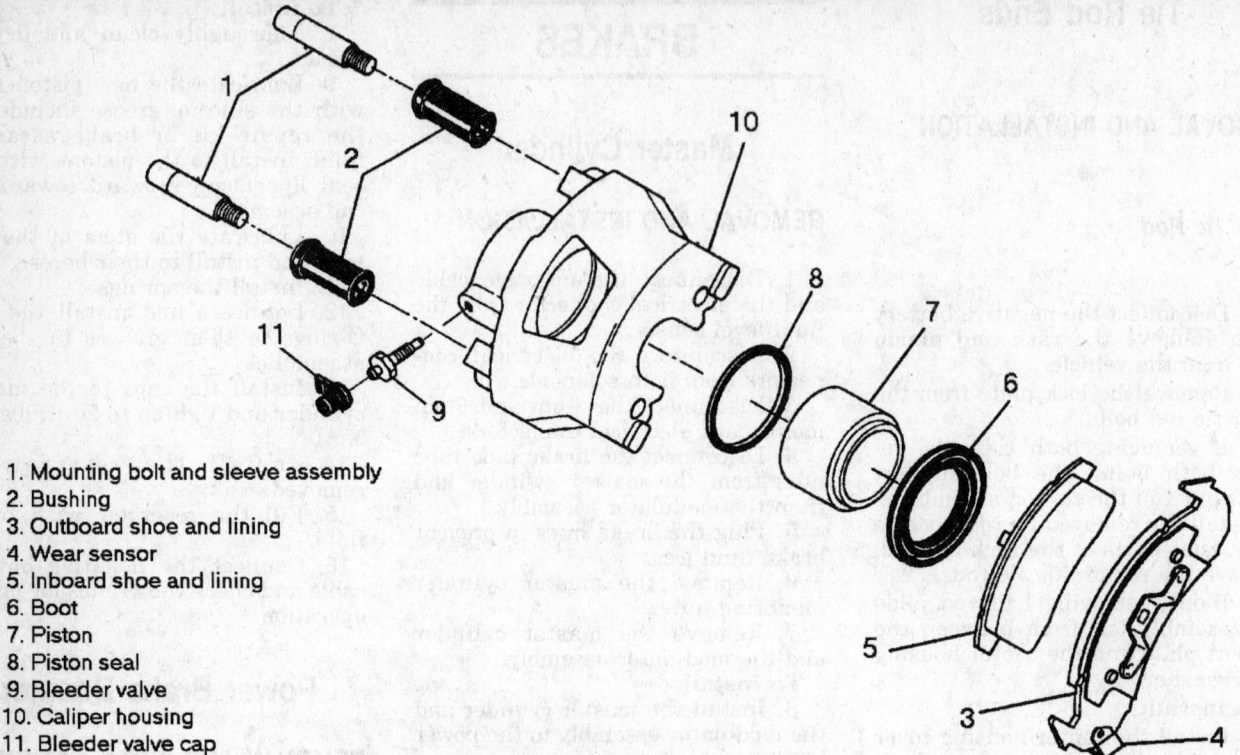

1. Mounting bolt and sleeve assembly
2. Bushing
3. Outboard shoe and lining
4. Wear sensor
5. Inboard shoe and lining
6. Boot
7. Piston
8. Piston seal
9. Bleeder valve
10. Caliper housing
11. Bleeder valve cap

8470K070

Front disc brake caliper assembly

5. Remove the caliper mounting bolt and sleeve assemblies.
6. Lift the caliper off the rotor.
To install:
7. Install the brake hose to the caliper using new copper washers.
8. Position the caliper over the rotor so the caliper engages the adaptor correctly. Lubricate and install the sleeves and bolts. Tighten to 38 ft. lbs. (51 Nm).
9. Connect the brake line inlet fitting and tighten the fitting to 33 ft. lbs. (45 Nm).
10. Install the tire and wheel assembly.
11. Fill the master cylinder and bleed the brakes.

Disc Brake Pads

REMOVAL AND INSTALLATION

1. Remove some of the fluid from the master cylinder. Raise and safely support the vehicle.
2. Remove the tire and wheel assembly.
3. Bottom the piston in its bore for clearance.
4. Remove the caliper mounting bolt and sleeve assemblies.
5. Lift the caliper off the rotor.

6. Remove the pads from the caliper.
To install:
7. Use a large C-clamp to compress the piston back into the caliper bore.
8. Install the pads and anti-rattle clip to the caliper. Adjust the bent-over tabs for a tight fit.
9. Position the caliper over the rotor so the caliper engages the adaptor correctly. Lubricate and install the sleeves and bolts. Tighten to 38 ft. lbs. (51 Nm).
10. Install the tire and wheel assembly.
11. Fill the master cylinder and check the brakes for proper operation.

Brake Rotor

REMOVAL AND INSTALLATION

1. Raise and safely support the vehicle. Remove the tire and wheel assembly.
2. Remove the caliper and brake pads.
3. Remove the rotor from the hub.
4. The installation is the reverse of the removal procedure.

Brake Drums

REMOVAL AND INSTALLATION

1. Raise and safely support the vehicle.
2. Remove the wheel and tire assembly.
3. Remove the drum. If the drum is difficult to remove, remove the plug from the rear of the backing plate and push the self-adjuster lever away from the star wheel. Rotate the star wheel to retract the shoes.
4. The installation is the reverse of the removal procedure.
5. Adjust the brakes as required.

Brake Shoes

NOTE: If unsure of spring positioning, finish one side before starting the other and use the untouched side as a guide.

REMOVAL AND INSTALLATION

1. Remove the wheels and drums. Remove the primary and secondary shoe return springs from the anchor pin but leave them installed on the shoes.
2. Lift on the adjuster lever and remove the adjuster cable. Remove

1. Return spring
2. Return spring
3. Hold down spring
4. Bearing sleeve
5. Hold- down pin
6. Actuator link
7. Actuator lever
8. Lever return spring
9. Parking brake strut
10. Strut spring
11. Primary shoe and lining
12. Secondary shoe and lining
13. Adjusting screw spring
14. Socket
15. Pivot nut
16. Adjusting screw
17. Retaining ring
18. Pin
19. Parking brake lever
20. Bleeder valve
21. Bolt
22. Boot
23. Piston
24. Seal
25. Spring assembly
26. Wheel cylinder
27. Backing plate
28. Shoe retainer
29. Anchor pin
30. Shoe pads (6 places)

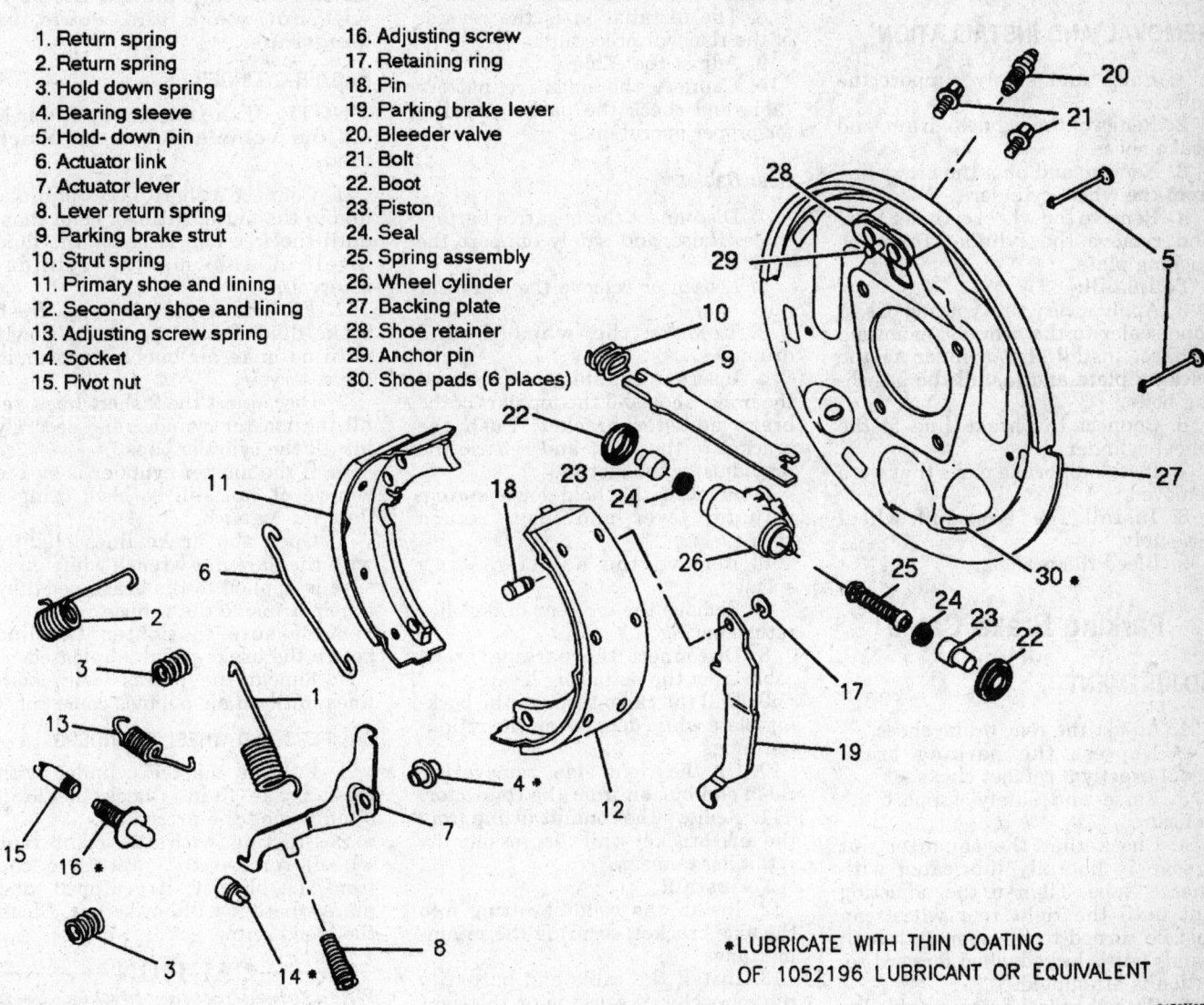

*LUBRICATE WITH THIN COATING
OF 1052196 LUBRICANT OR EQUIVALENT

8470K072

Rear drum brake assembly

the actuating lever link and pawl return spring.

3. Remove the hold-down pin return springs and cups. Remove the parking brake strut and spring. Remove the actuating lever and pawl.

4. Remove the shoes, held together by the lower spring, while separating the parking brake actuating lever from the shoe with a twisting motion.

5. Lift the wheel cylinder dust boots and inspect for fluid leakage.

6. Thoroughly clean and dry the backing plate.

To install:

7. Remove, clean and dry all parts still on the old shoes. Lubricate the star wheel shaft threads and transfer all the parts to the new shoes in their proper locations.

8. To prepare the backing plate, lubricate the bosses, anchor pin and parking brake actuating lever pivot surface lightly with the brake-compatible lubricant.

9. Spread the shoes apart, engage the parking brake actuating lever and position them on the backing plate so the wheel cylinder pins engage properly and the anchor pin holds the shoes up.

10. Install the parking brake strut and the hold-down pin assemblies.

Install the actuating lever with the hold-down pin assembly.

11. Install the anchor plate. Lubricate the sliding surface of the adjuster cable plate and install the adjuster cable.

12. Install the shoe return spring opposite the cable, then the remaining spring. Install the actuating lever link, the shoe return springs and assemble the pawl and return spring.

13. Adjust the star wheel.

14. Remove any grease from the linings and install the drum.

15. Complete the brake adjustment with the wheels installed and adjust the parking brake cable.

Wheel Cylinder

REMOVAL AND INSTALLATION

1. Raise and safely support the vehicle.
2. Remove the wheel, drum and brake shoes.
3. Remove and plug the brake line from the wheel cylinder.
4. Remove the wheel cylinder bolts and remove the cylinder from the backing plate.
To install:
5. Apply a very thin coating of silicone sealer to the cylinder mounting surface, install the cylinder to the backing plate and install the attaching bolts.
6. Connect the brake line to the wheel cylinder.
7. Install all brake parts that were removed.
8. Install the tire and wheel assembly.
9. Bleed the brakes.

Parking Brake Cable

ADJUSTMENT

1. Adjust the rear brake shoes.
2. Depress the parking brake pedal exactly 3 ratchet clicks.
3. Raise and safely support the vehicle.
4. Check that the equalizer nut groove is liberally lubricated with chassis lube. Tighten the adjusting nut until the right rear wheel can just be turned to the rear with both hands but is locked when forward rotation is attempted.
5. With the mechanism totally disengaged, both rear wheels should turn freely in either direction with no brake drag. Do not adjust the parking brake so tightly as to cause brake drag.

REMOVAL AND INSTALLATION

Front Cable

1. Disconnect the negative battery cable. Raise and safely support the vehicle.
2. Loosen and remove the equalizer nut. Lower the vehicle.
3. Remove the console.
4. Disconnect the parking brake cable from the lever.
5. Remove the nut that secures the front cable to the floor pan.
6. Loosen the catalytic converter shield and the parking brake cable from the body, if necessary.

7. Remove the cable from the equalizer, guide and underbody clips.
8. The installation is the reverse of the removal procedure.
9. Adjust the cable.
10. Connect the negative battery cable and check the parking brakes for proper operation.

Rear Cables

1. Disconnect the negative battery cable. Raise and safely support the vehicle.
2. Loosen or remove the equalizer nut.
3. Remove the wheel(s) and drum(s).
4. Insert a suitable tool between the brake shoe and the top part of the brake adjuster bracket. Push the bracket to the front and release the top adjuster bracket rod.
5. Remove the hold-down spring, actuator lever and lever return spring.
6. Remove the adjuster screw spring.
7. Remove the top rear brake shoe return spring.
8. Disconnect the parking brake cable from the actuating lever.
9. Pull the cable through the backing plate while depressing the retaining tangs.
10. On the right side, remove the cable end button from the connector.
11. Remove the conduit fitting from the axle bracket while depressing the retaining tangs.
To install:
12. Install the conduit fitting into the axle bracket, securing the retaining tangs.
13. Install the cable end button to the connector, if working on the right side.
14. Click the cable assembly into the backing plate.
15. Connect the cable to the actuating lever.
16. Assemble the rear brake components.
17. Install the drum(s) and wheel(s).
18. Adjust the rear brakes and parking brake cable.
19. Connect the negative battery cable and check the parking brakes for proper operation.

BRAKE SYSTEM BLEEDING

Except Anti-lock Brakes

NOTE: If using a pressure bleeder, follow the instructions furnished with the unit and choose the correct adapter for

the application. Do not substitute an adapter that almost fits as it will not work and could be dangerous.

MASTER CYLINDER

NOTE: If the master cylinder is off the vehicle it can be bench bled.

1. Connect 2 short pieces of brake line to the outlet fittings, bend them until the free end is below the fluid level in the master cylinder reservoirs.
2. Fill the reservoir with fresh brake fluid. Pump the piston slowly until no more air bubbles appear in the reservoirs.
3. Disconnect the 2 short lines, refill the master cylinder and securely install the cylinder caps.
4. If the master cylinder is on the vehicle, it can still be bled, using a flare nut wrench.
5. Open the brake lines slightly with the flare nut wrench while pressure is applied to the brake pedal by a helper inside the vehicle.
6. Be sure to tighten the line before the brake pedal is released.
7. Repeat the process with both lines until no air bubbles come out.

CALIPERS AND WHEEL CYLINDERS

1. Fill the master cylinder with fresh brake fluid. Check the level often during the procedure.
2. Starting with the right rear wheel, remove the protective cap from the bleeder, if equipped, and place where it will not be lost. Clean the bleed screw.

——— CAUTION ———
When bleeding the brakes, keep face away from the brake area. Spewing fluid may cause facial and/or visual damage. Do not allow brake fluid to spill on the car's finish; it will remove the paint.

3. If the system is empty, the most efficient way to get fluid down to the wheel is to loosen the bleeder about 1/2–3/4 turn, place a finger firmly over the bleeder and have a helper pump the brakes slowly until fluid comes out the bleeder. Once fluid is at the bleeder, close it before the pedal is released inside the vehicle.

NOTE: If the pedal is pumped rapidly, the fluid will churn and create small air bubbles, which are almost impossible to remove from the system. These air bubbles will eventually congregate and a spongy pedal will result.

4. Once fluid has been pumped to the caliper or wheel cylinder, open the bleed screw again, have the helper press the brake pedal to the floor, lock the bleeder and have the helper slowly release the pedal. Wait 15 seconds and repeat the procedure (including the 15 second wait) until no more air comes out of the bleeder upon application of the brake pedal. Remember to close the bleeder before the pedal is released inside the vehicle each time the bleeder is opened. If not, air will be induced into the system.

5. If a helper is not available, connect a small hose to the bleeder, place the end in a container of brake fluid and proceed to pump the pedal from inside the vehicle until no more air comes out the bleeder. The hose will prevent air from entering the system.

6. Repeat the procedure on remaining wheel cylinders in order:
   a. Left front
   b. Left rear
   c. Right front

7. Hydraulic brake systems must be totally flushed if the fluid becomes contaminated with water, dirt or other corrosive chemicals. To flush, bleed the entire system until all fluid has been replaced with the correct type of new fluid.

8. Install the bleeder cap(s), if equipped, on the bleeder to keep dirt out. Always road test the vehicle after brake work of any kind is done.

Anti-lock Brakes

BRAKE CONTROL ASSEMBLY

NOTE: Only use brake fluid from a sealed container which meets DOT 3 specifications.

1. Clean the area around the master cylinder cap.
2. Check fluid level in master cylinder reservoir and top-off, as necessary. Check fluid level frequently during bleeding procedure.
3. Attach a bleeder hose to the rear bleeder valve on the brake control assembly. Slowly open the bleeder valve.
4. Depress the brake pedal slowly until fluid begins to flow.
5. Close the valve and release the brake pedal.
6. Repeat for the front bleeder valve on the brake control assembly.

NOTE: When fluid flows from both bleeder valves, the brake control assembly is sufficiently full of fluid. However, it may not be completely purged of air. Bleed the individual wheel cali-

pers/cylinders and return to the control assembly to purge the remaining air.

WHEEL CALIPERS/CYLINDERS

NOTE: Prior to bleeding the rear brakes, the rear displacement cylinder must be returned to the top-most position. This can be accomplished using the Tech I Scan tool, T-100 (CAMS) or equivalent, by entering the manual control function and applying the rear motor. If a Tech I or T-100 are unavailable, bleed the front brakes. Ensure the pedal is firm. Carefully drive the vehicle to a speed above 4 mph to cause the ABS system to initialize. This will return the rear displacement cylinder to the top-most position.

1. Clean the area around the master cylinder cap.
2. Check fluid level in master cylinder reservoir and top-off, as necessary. Check fluid level frequently during bleeding procedure.
3. Raise and safely support the vehicle.
4. Attach a bleeder hose to the bleeder valve of the right rear wheel and submerge the opposite hose in a clean container partially filled with brake fluid.
5. Open the bleeder valve.
6. Slowly depress the brake pedal.
7. Close the bleeder valve and release the brake pedal.
8. Wait 5 seconds.
9. Repeat Steps 5–8 until the pedal begins to feel firm and no air bubbles appear in the bleeder hose.
10. Repeat Steps 5–9, until the pedal is firm and no air bubbles appear in the brake hose, for the remaining wheels in the following order:
    a. Left rear
    b. Right front
    c. Left front.
11. Lower the vehicle.

Anti-Lock Brake System Service

PRECAUTION

Failure to observe the following precautions may result in system damage.
• Before performing electric arc welding on the vehicle, disconnect the Electronic Brake Control Module (EBCM) and the hydraulic modulator connectors.

• When performing painting work on the vehicle, do not expose the Electronic Brake Control Module (EBCM) to temperatures in excess of 185°F (85°C) for longer than 2 hours. The system may be exposed to temperatures up to 200°F (95°C) for less than 15 minutes.
• Never disconnect or connect the Electronic Brake Control Module (EBCM) or hydraulic modulator connectors with the ignition switch **ON**.
• Never disassemble any component of the Anti-Lock Brake System (ABS) which is designated non-serviceable; the component must be replaced as an assembly.
• When filling the master cylinder, always use Delco Supreme 11 brake fluid or equivalent, which meets DOT-3 specifications; petroleum base fluid will destroy the rubber parts.

ABS Hydraulic Modulator Assembly

REMOVAL AND INSTALLATION

———— **CAUTION** ————
To avoid personal injury, use the Tech I Scan tool to relieve the gear tension in the hydraulic modulator. This procedure must be performed prior to removal of the brake control and motor assembly.

1. Disconnect the negative battery cable.
2. Disconnect the 2 solenoid electrical connectors and the fluid level sensor connector.
3. Disconnect the 6-pin and 3-pin motor pack electrical connectors.
4. Wrap a shop towel around the hydraulic brake lines and disconnect the 4 brake lines from the modulator.

NOTE: Cap the disconnected lines to prevent the loss of fluid and the entry of moisture and contaminants.

5. Remove the 2 nuts attaching the ABS hydraulic modulator assembly to the vacuum booster.
6. Remove the ABS hydraulic modulator assembly from the vehicle.
To install:
7. Install the ABS hydraulic modulator assembly to the vehicle. Install the 2 attaching nuts and tighten to 20 ft. lbs. (27 Nm).
8. Connect the 4 brake pipes to the modulator assembly. Tighten to 14 ft. lbs. (17 Nm).

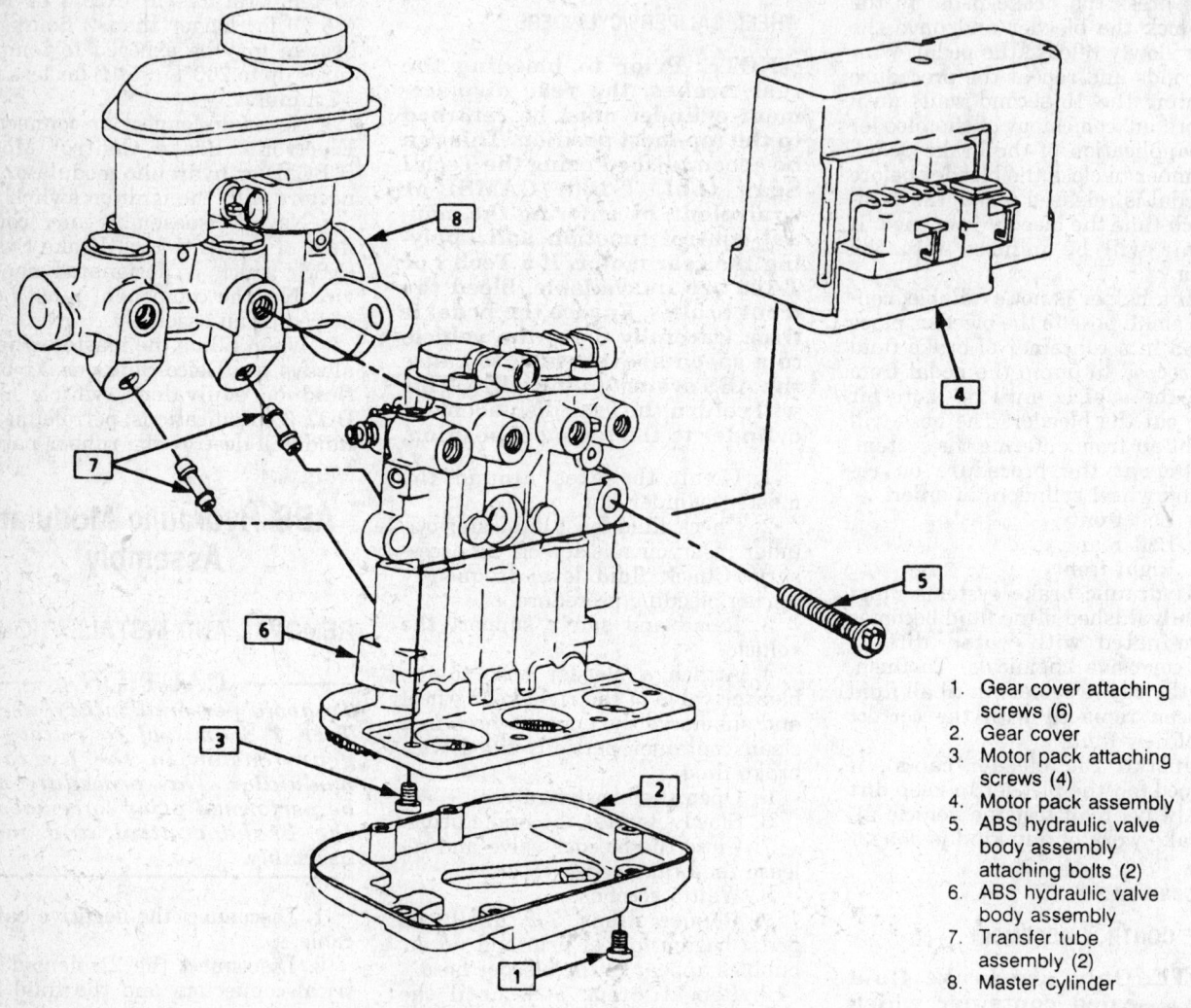

1. Gear cover attaching screws (6)
2. Gear cover
3. Motor pack attaching screws (4)
4. Motor pack assembly
5. ABS hydraulic valve body assembly attaching bolts (2)
6. ABS hydraulic valve body assembly
7. Transfer tube assembly (2)
8. Master cylinder

8569K004

ABS-VI hydraulic modulator assembly components

9. Connect the 6-pin and 3-pin electrical connectors and the fluid level sensor connector.
10. Properly bleed the system.
11. Connect the negative battery cable.

Brake Control Solenoid Assembly

REMOVAL AND INSTALLATION

1. Disconnect the negative battery cable.
2. Disconnect the solenoid electrical connector.

3. Remove the Torx® head bolts.
4. Remove the solenoid assembly.

To install:

5. Lubricate the O-rings on the new solenoid with clean brake fluid.

6. Position the solenoid so the connectors face each other.

7. Press down firmly by hand until the solenoid assembly flange seats on the modulator assembly.

8. Install the Torx® head bolts. Tighten to 39 inch lbs. (5 Nm).

9. Connect the solenoid electrical connector.

10. Properly bleed the brake system.

11. Connect the negative battery cable.

Front Wheel Speed Sensor

REMOVAL AND INSTALLATION

1. Disconnect the negative battery cable.
2. Raise and safely support the vehicle.
3. Disconnect the front sensor electrical connector.
4. Remove the Torx® bolt.
5. Remove the front wheel speed sensor.

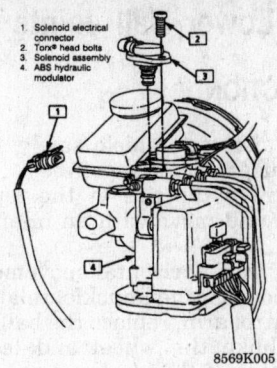

1. Solenoid electrical connector
2. Torx® head bolts
3. Solenoid assembly
4. ABS hydraulic modulator

8569K005

Brake control solenoid removal

To install:

6. Install the front wheel speed sensor on the mounting bracket.

NOTE: Ensure the front wheel speed sensor is properly aligned and lays flat against the bracket bosses.

7. Install the Torx® bolt. Tighten to 106 inch lbs. (12 Nm).
8. Connect the front sensor electrical connector.
9. Lower the vehicle.
10. Connect the negative battery cable.

Rear Wheel Bearing And Speed Sensor Assembly

REMOVAL AND INSTALLATION

NOTE: The rear integral wheel bearing and sensor assembly must be replaced as a unit.

1. Disconnect the negative battery cable. Raise and safely support the vehicle.
2. Remove the rear wheel. Remove the brake drum.
3. Disconnect the rear sensor electrical connector.
4. Remove the bolts and nuts attaching the rear wheel bearing and speed sensor assembly to the backing plate.

NOTE: With the rear wheel bearing and speed sensor attaching bolts and nuts removed, the drum brake assembly is supported only by the brake line connection. To avoid bending or damage to the brake line, do not bump or exert force on the assembly.

5. Remove the rear wheel bearing and speed sensor assembly.

To install:

6. Install the rear wheel bearing and speed sensor assembly by aligning the bolt hoses in the wheel bearing and speed sensor assembly, drum brake assembly and rear suspension bracket. Install the attaching bolts and nuts. Tighten to 37 ft. lbs. (50 Nm).
7. Connect the rear speed sensor electrical connector.
8. Install the brake drum. Install the rear wheel.
9. Lower the vehicle. Connect the negative battery cable.

FRONT SUSPENSION

MacPherson Strut

REMOVAL AND INSTALLATION

1. Remove the mounting nuts from the shock tower under the hood.
2. Raise and safely support the vehicle. Remove the wheel.

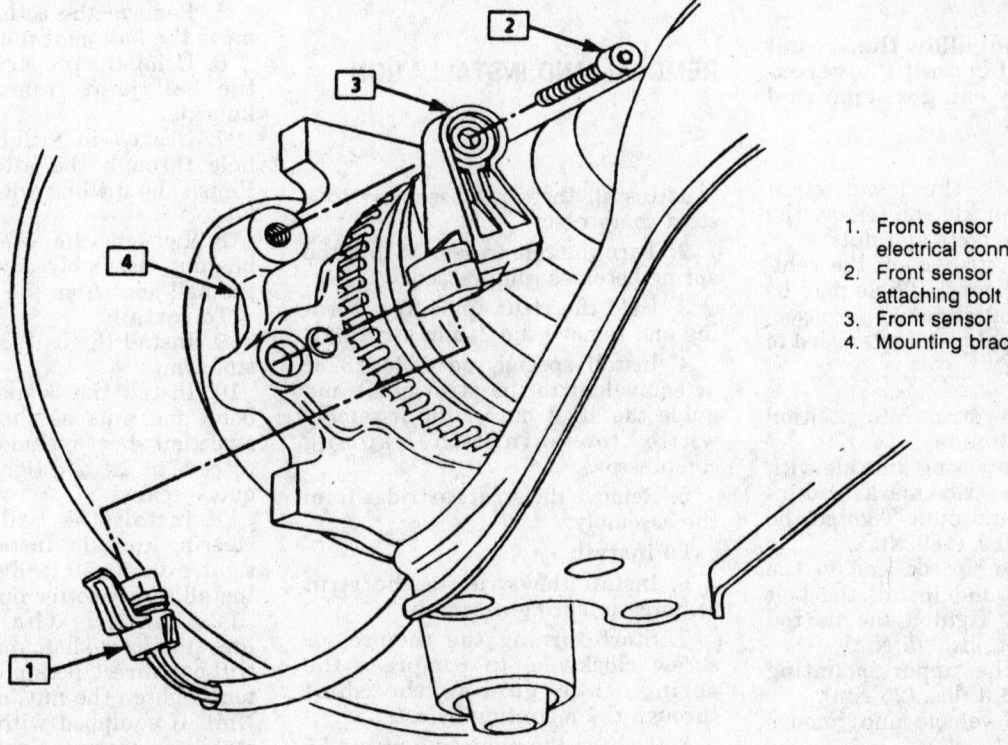

1. Front sensor electrical connector
2. Front sensor attaching bolt
3. Front sensor
4. Mounting bracket

8569K006

Front wheel speed sensor removal

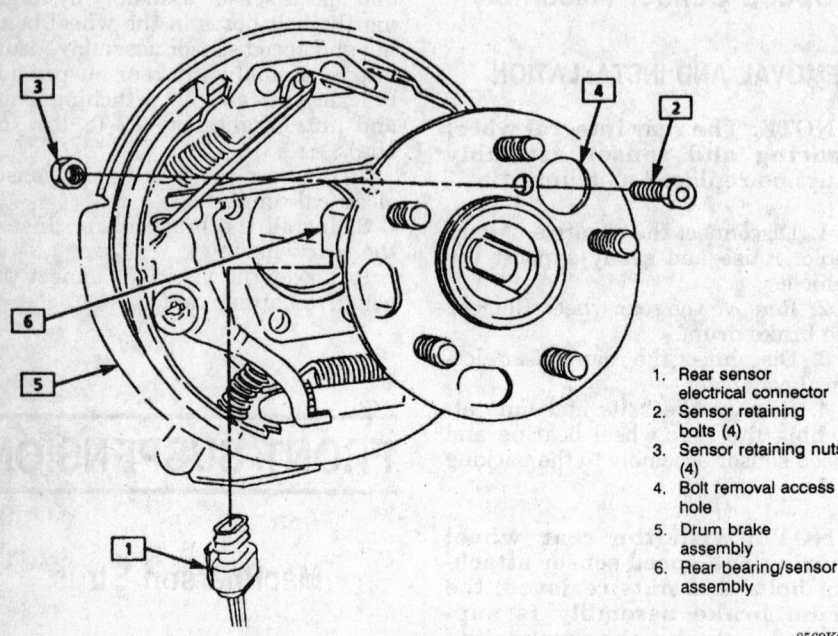

1. Rear sensor electrical connector
2. Sensor retaining bolts (4)
3. Sensor retaining nuts (4)
4. Bolt removal access hole
5. Drum brake assembly
6. Rear bearing/sensor assembly

8569K007

Rear wheel speed sensor removal

3. Place jackstands under the front suspension to support the vehicle's weight.

NOTE: Do not allow the Tri-pot joints from becoming overextended or they can get separated and damaged.

4. Matchmark the lower strut mount to the knuckle and remove the strut to knuckle bolts and nuts.
5. While the strut is off the vehicle, the lower mounting hole may be elongated for alignment purposes. Paint any exposed metal afterward to prevent rusting.
To install:
6. Install the strut into position and install the 3 nuts.
7. Align the steering knuckle with the strut flange scribe marks and install the bolts and nuts. Tighten the nuts to 133 ft. lbs. (180 Nm).
8. Install the tie rod end to the strut assembly and install the bolt and cotter pin. Tighten the tie rod end bolt to 55 ft. lbs. (75 Nm).
9. Tighten the upper mounting strut nuts to 18 ft. lbs. (25 Nm).
10. Raise the vehicle and remove the jackstands.
11. Install the tire/wheel(s) and check the front end alignment.

Strut Cartridge

REMOVAL AND INSTALLATION

1. Install the strut assembly to a strut compressor.
2. Turn the compressor so that the spring becomes compressed.
3. Hold the strut shaft from turning and remove the 24mm strut nut.
4. Install special rod J–34013–38 or equivalent to the strut shaft and guide the strut out of the assembly while loosening the spring compressor.
5. Remove the strut cartridge from the assembly.
To install:
6. Install the strut to the strut compressor/spring assembly.
7. Start turning the compressor screw clockwise to compress the spring while guiding the shaft through the mounting hole.
8. Tighten the mounting nut to 55 ft. lbs. (75 Nm) while holding the strut shaft.

Lower Ball Joints

INSPECTION

1. Raise the vehicle safely so the front suspension hangs free.
2. Grasp the tire at the top and bottom and move with an in-and-out motion.
3. If any horizontal movement is detected from the knuckle, relative to the control arm, replace the ball joint.
4. Shake the wheel and feel for movement of the stud end or castellated nut at the knuckle boss.
5. Check the nut for loose torque. A loose nut may indicate a bent stud or expanded hole in the knuckle.
6. Replace all parts found to be worn or damaged.

REMOVAL AND INSTALLATION

1. Raise and safely support the vehicle.
2. The control arms must not be supporting the vehicle's weight.

NOTE: Do not allow the Tri-pot joints from becoming overextended or they can get separated and damaged.

3. Remove the wheel.
4. Install inner drive joint seal protector J–34754 or equivalent.
5. Remove the cotter pin and remove the ball joint nut.
6. Using the proper tools, separate the ball joint from the steering knuckle.
7. Use a ⅛ in. drill bit, drill a pilot hole through the attaching rivets. Finish the drilling with a ½ in. drill bit.
8. Loosen the stabilizer shaft bushing assembly nut and remove the ball joint from the control arm.
To install:
9. Install the ball joint to the control arm.
10. Install the 3 special ball joint bolts and nuts as shown in the instruction sheet included with the replacement kit and tighten to the torque specified.
11. Install the ball stud to the steering knuckle. Install the nut and tighten to 40–50 ft. lbs. (55–65 Nm). Install a new cotter pin.
12. Install the stabilizer link/stabilizer shaft nut. If equipped without direct acting stabilizer system, tighten the nut to 13 ft. lbs. (17 Nm). If equipped with direct acting stabilizer system, tighten the nut to 70 ft. lbs. (95 Nm).
13. Install the wheel.

14. Perform a front end alignment and road test the vehicle.

Lower Control Arms

REMOVAL AND INSTALLATION

1. Raise and safely support the vehicle. Remove the tire and wheel assembly.
2. Remove the nut attaching the stabilizer shaft to the stabilizer link and the nuts attaching the stabilizer shaft clamp to the suspension support. Remove the stabilizer shaft.

NOTE: Do not allow the Tri-pot joints from becoming overextended or they can get separated and damaged.

3. Remove the ball joint stud attaching nut.
4. Pry the lower control arm from the steering knuckle.
5. Remove the control arm-to-suspension support bolts and nuts.
6. Remove the control arm from the vehicle.
7. Transfer reusable parts to the new control arm.
To install:
8. Install the control arm to the vehicle and loosely install the attaching bolts.
9. Install the suspension support into position and guide the ball joint into position. Loosely install the bolts.
10. Install the nuts attaching the stabilizer shaft clamp to the suspension support. Tighten the nuts to 17 ft. lbs. (23 Nm).
11. Install the ball joint-to-steering knuckle nut and tighten to 26 ft. lbs. (35 Nm) plus 60 degrees.
12. Install the stabilizer link to stabilizer shaft nut and tighten the nut as follows:
   a. If equipped with direct acting stabilizer system, tighten nut to 70 ft. lbs. (95 Nm).
   b. If not equipped with direct acting stabilizer system, tighten nut to 13 ft. lbs. (17 Nm).
13. Install the tire/wheel assembly and lower the vehicle so the full weight of the vehicle is on the ground.
14. Torque the suspension support bolts as follows:
   a. Torque the center bolts to 66 ft. lbs. (90 Nm).
   b. Torque the front bolts to 65 ft. lbs. (88 Nm).
   c. Torque the rear bolts to 65 ft. lbs. (88 Nm).

15. Torque the control arm attaching bolts to 61 ft. lbs. (83 Nm).
16. Perform a front end alignment.

Stabilizer Link

REMOVAL AND INSTALLATION

1. Remove the stabilizer link to the stabilizer shaft nut.
2. If equipped with direct acting stabilizer system, remove the stabilizer link to the strut bracket nut, and remove the stabilizer link.
3. Remove the bolt, insulators, spacer and washers from vehicles not equipped with direct acting stabilizer system, and remove the stabilizer link.
4. Installation is the reverse of removal.
5. If equipped with the direct acting suspension system, tighten the nut to 70 ft. lbs. (95 Nm).
6. If not equipped with the direct acting suspension system, tighten the nut to 13 ft. lbs. (17 Nm).
7. Tighten the stabilizer link-to-strut bracket nut to 70 ft. lbs. (95 Nm).

Stabilizer Shaft

REMOVAL AND INSTALLATION

1. Raise and safely support the vehicle.
2. Remove the front tire/wheel assemblies.
3. Remove the nuts attaching the stabilizer shafts to the stabilizer links.
4. Support the suspension with jackstands and remove the clamps attaching the stabilizer shaft to the stabilizer links.
5. Remove the rear and center suspension support assemblies and loosen the front bolts.
6. Remove the stabilizer shaft with the insulators.
To install:
7. Install the stabilizer shaft with the insulators. Install the clamps and hand tighten.
8. Install the suspension support assemblies into position and hand tighten the bolts. Remove the jackstands.
9. Install the nuts that attach the stabilizer shaft to the stabilizer links. Tighten the nuts as follows:
   a. If equipped with direct acting stabilizer system, tighten nut to 70 ft. lbs. (95 Nm).

   b. If not equipped with direct acting stabilizer system, tighten nut to 13 ft. lbs. (17 Nm).
10. Torque the suspension support bolts as follows:
   a. Torque the center bolts to 66 ft. lbs. (90 Nm).
   b. Torque the front bolts to 65 ft. lbs. (88 Nm).
   c. Torque the rear bolts to 65 ft. lbs. (88 Nm).
   d. Torque the stabilizer shaft to the support assembly nuts to 16 ft. lbs. (22 Nm).
   e. Torque the stabilizer shaft-to-control arm nuts to 13 ft. lbs. (17 Nm).
   f. Torque the clamp nuts to 17 ft. lbs. (23 Nm).
11. Install the front wheel/tire assemblies.
12. Check the front end alignment.

REAR SUSPENSION

Shock Absorbers

REMOVAL AND INSTALLATION

1. Disconnect the negative battery cable.
2. Open the deck lid and remove the trim cover.
3. Remove the upper shock attaching nut. Remove 1 shock at a time if removing both.
4. Raise and safely support the vehicle.
5. Remove the lower mounting bolt.
6. Remove the shock from the vehicle.
7. The installation is the reverse of the removal procedure.

Coil Springs

REMOVAL AND INSTALLATION

1. Raise and safely support the vehicle.
2. Using the proper equipment, support the weight of the rear axle. Disconnect the brake lines from the rear axle.
3. Remove the bolts that attach the shock to the lower mounting bracket.
4. Lower the axle and remove the coil spring from the vehicle.
5. The installation is the reverse of the removal procedure.

Rear Wheel Bearings

The hub and bearing assemblies are sealed units and are non-serviceable. If the assembly is damaged, the complete unit must be replaced.

REMOVAL AND INSTALLATION

1. Disconnect the negative battery cable.
2. Raise and support the vehicle safely.
3. Remove the rear wheel, caliper, bracket and rotor.
4. Loosen the 4 hub/bearing-to-knuckle attaching bolts.
5. Remove the hub/bearing assembly.
   To install:
6. Install the hub/bearing assembly onto the knuckle. Install the 4 attaching bolts and torque to 52 ft. lbs. (70 Nm).
7. Install the rotor, caliper and bracket.
8. Install the rear wheel and torque the lug nut to 100 ft. lbs. (135 Nm).

9. Lower the vehicle and connect the negative battery cable.

Rear Axle Assembly

REMOVAL AND INSTALLATION

1. Raise the vehicle safely under the control arms.
2. If equipped, remove the stabilizer bar from the axle assembly.
3. Remove the wheel assemblies and support the rear axle with jackstands.
4. Remove the lower shock absorber-to-axle assembly nuts/bolts and separate the shock absorbers from the rear axle assembly.
5. Disconnect the parking brake cable at the equalizer and at the right rear wheel assembly.
6. Disconnect the ABS wiring connector, if equipped with anti-lock brakes, along with the clip, located near the fuel tank.
7. Disconnect the brake lines from the rear axle assembly; be sure the assembly is not suspended by the brake lines.

8. Lower the rear axle assembly and remove the coil spring. Transfer all reusable parts to the new assembly.
   To install:
9. Install the rear axle and loosely install the attaching bolts.
10. Connect the right and left brake lines.
11. Connect the ABS wiring connector and mount clip.
12. Connect the parking brake cable.
13. Install the upper and lower insulators.
14. Install both springs and raise the axle assembly into place.
15. Install the lower shock absorber mount bolts and nuts and tighten to 35 ft. lbs. (47 Nm).
16. Install the left and right side brake line bracket mount bolts and tighten the screws to 8 ft. lbs. (11 Nm).
17. Install the tire/wheel assemblies and remove the jackstands from under the axle.
18. Lower the vehicle and bleed the rear brake system.
19. Adjust the parking brake, if necessary.

GM "W" BODY
Front Wheel Drive
OLDSMOBILE—CUTLASS SUPREME **PONTIAC**—GRAND PRIX
CHEVROLET—LUMINA **BUICK**—REGAL

17

FIRING ORDERS

NOTE: To avoid confusion, always replace spark plug wires one at a time.

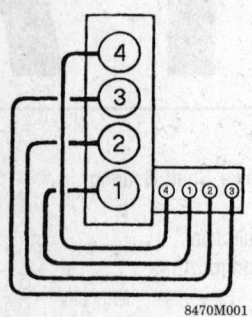

8470M001

**2.2L and 2.5L Engines
Engine Firing Order:
1–3–4–2
Distributorless Ignition
System**

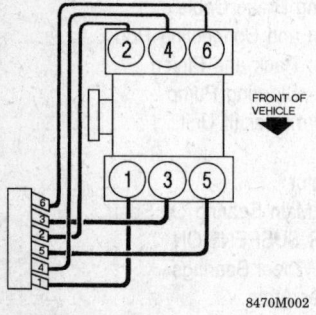

8470M002

**3.8L Engine
Engine Firing Order: 1–6–5–4–3–2
Distributorless Ignition System**

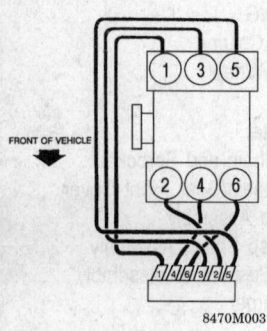

8470M003

**3.1L and 3.4L Engine
Engine Firing Order:
1–2–3–4–5–6
Distributorless Ignition
System**

ENGINE ELECTRICAL

NOTE: Disconnecting the negative battery cable on some vehicles may interfere with the functions of the on board computer systems and may require the computer to undergo a relearning process, once the negative battery cable is reconnected.

Distributorless Ignition System

REMOVAL AND INSTALLATION

Ignition Coil

2.2L ENGINE

1. Disconnect the negative battery cable.
2. Disconnect the ignition coil electrical connectors.
3. Disconnect the spark plug wires, noting the original position for installation purposes.
4. Remove the 3 ignition coil to block bolts and remove the coil assembly from the engine.
To install:
5. Install the ignition coil to the engine block and install the 3 mounting bolts.
6. Tighten the 3 mounting bolts to 15–22 ft. lbs. (20–30 Nm).
7. Connect the proper spark plug cables to the appropriate coil.
8. Connect the ignition coil electrical connectors and the negative battery cable.

2.5L, 3.1L AND 3.4L ENGINES

1. Disconnect the negative battery cable.
2. Raise and safely support the vehicle.

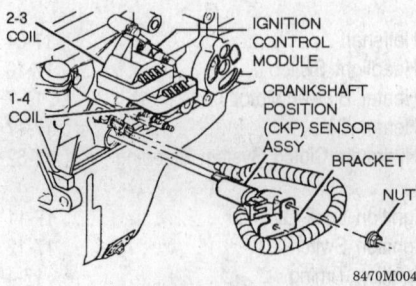

8470M004

Ignition coil assembly and CKP sensor — 2.2L engine

3. Label each spark plug wire for proper installation.
4. Remove the spark plug wires from the ignition coils.
5. Remove the DIS electrical connectors.
6. Remove the 3 DIS assembly to block bolts.
7. Remove the DIS assembly from the engine.
8. Remove coil retaining nuts for coil(s) to be replaced.
9. Remove coil(s) from DIS assembly and replace as required.
To install:
10. Install coil retaining nuts and torque to 40 inch lbs. (4.5 Nm).

NOTE: Before installing DIS assembly to block on 2.5L engine inspect crankshaft sensor O-ring for wear, cracks or leakage. Replace if necessary. Lube new O-ring with engine oil before installing.

11. Install DIS assembly to block and torque to 20 ft. lbs. (27 Nm).
12. Install the spark plug wires and electrical connectors.
13. Reconnect negative battery cable.

3.8L ENGINE

1. Disconnect negative battery cable.
2. Label and disconnect spark plug wires.
3. Remove 2 screws securing coil to ignition module.
4. Remove coil(s) from module.
5. Install coil using 2 screws, torque to 40 inch lbs.
6. Reconnect spark plug wires and negative battery cable.

Ignition Module

2.2L ENGINE

1. Disconnect the negative battery cable.
2. Remove the ignition coil(s) from the engine.
3. Remove the coil(s) and the module from the assembly plate.
To install:
4. Install the module to the assembly plate.
5. Install the coil(s) to the assembly plate.
6. Install the coil assembly to the engine.
7. Connect the negative battery cable.

2.5L ENGINE

1. Disconnect the negative battery cable.
2. Label each spark plug wire for proper installation.

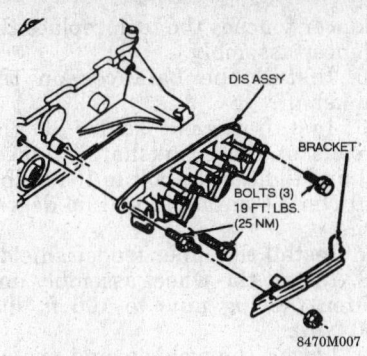

Coil and module assembly mounting — 3.1L engine

3. Remove the spark plug and module electrical connectors from the DIS assembly.

4. Remove the 3 DIS assembly-to-engine attaching bolts.

NOTE: Be careful not to damage the crankshaft sensor and module terminals when pulling the DIS assemblies from the engine. Pull slowly and carefully away from the engine.

5. Remove the DIS assembly from the engine.

6. Remove the coils from the DIS assembly.

7. Remove the module from assembly plate.

To install:

8. Carefully engage the sensor to module terminals and install module assembly to plate.

9. Reinstall coils, torque screws to 45 inch lbs. (5 Nm).

10. Install the DIS assembly and torque bolts to 20 ft. lbs. (27 Nm).

11. Reconnect the spark plugs and module electrical connectors to their original positions.

3.1L (VIN T) AND 3.4L ENGINES

1. Disconnect the negative battery cable.

2. Raise the vehicle and support safely.

3. Label each spark plug wire for proper installation.

4. Remove the spark plug and module electrical connectors from the DIS assembly.

5. Remove the 3 DIS assembly attaching bolts.

6. Remove the DIS assembly from the engine.

7. Remove the coils from the DIS assembly. Remove the module from assembly plate.

To install:

8. Install the module to the assembly plate.

9. Install the coil assemblies to the module and torque the screws to 45 inch lbs. (5 Nm).

10. Install the DIS assembly and attaching bolts to the engine and torque to 20 ft. lbs. (27 Nm).

11. Reconnect the spark plug and module electrical connectors to their original positions.

12. Reconnect the negative battery cable.

3.1L (VIN M) AND 3.8L ENGINES

1. Disconnect the negative battery cable.

2. Disconnect the 14-way connector at the ignition module.

3. Disconnect and label the spark plug wires.

4. Remove the 6 screws securing the coil assemblies to the ignition module and disconnect the coils from the module.

5. Remove the 3 nuts and washers securing the ignition module assembly to the bracket and remove the module.

To install:

6. Install the coils onto the module and tighten the 6 retaining screws to 40 inch lbs.

7. Install the 3 nuts and washers securing the ignition module assembly to the bracket and tighten to 70 inch lbs.

8. Connect the spark plug wires.

9. Connect the 14-way connector to the ignition module.

10. Reconnect negative battery cable.

Crankshaft Sensor

2.2L ENGINE

1. Disconnect the negative battery cable.

2. Disconnect the sensor harness connector from the module.

3. Remove the sensor to engine block bolt and remove the sensor.

To install:

4. Install the sensor to the engine block and install the mounting bolt. Tighten the mounting bolt to 71 inch lbs. (8 Nm).

5. Connect the module electrical connector and the negative battery cable.

2.5L ENGINE

1. Disconnect the negative battery cable.

2. Remove the Direct Ignition System (DIS) assembly.

3. After the DIS assembly has been removed from the vehicle, remove the 2 crankshaft sensor retaining screws.

NOTE: Be careful not to damage the crankshaft and module terminals when pulling the coil assemblies from the engine. Pull slowly and carefully away from the engine.

4. Remove the crankshaft sensor from the DIS assembly.

To install:

5. Inspect the sensor O-ring for wear, leakage or cracks. Replace if necessary.

6. Lubricate the new O-ring seal with engine oil before installing.

7. Install the crankshaft sensor onto the DIS assembly and torque the 2 attaching screws to 20 inch lbs. (2.3 Nm).

NOTE: Use extreme care when installing the crankshaft sensor on the DIS assembly so the sensor terminals are not damaged.

8. Position the DIS assembly onto the engine. Torque the 3 attaching bolts to 9 ft. lbs. (12.2 Nm).

9. Reconnect the spark plug wires and module electrical connectors in their original positions. Reconnect the negative battery cable.

3.1L (VIN T) AND 3.4L ENGINES

1. Disconnect the negative battery cable.

2. If equipped with 3.4L engine and automatic transaxle, remove the rack and pinion heat shield and the exhaust system converter pipe assembly to gain access to the sensor.

3. Remove the sensor electrical connector.

4. Remove the sensor attaching bolts (2) and sensor from the engine.

5. Inspect the sensor O-ring for wear, cracks or leakage and replace, if necessary. Lube new O-ring with engine oil before installing.

To install:

6. Install the sensor and attaching bolt, torque the bolt to 88 inch lbs. (10 Nm).

7. Connect the sensor electrical connector and negative battery cable.

3.1L (VIN M) ENGINE, 24X CRANKSHAFT SENSOR

NOTE: The 3.1L (VIN M) engine is equipped with 2 separate crankshaft sensors. The 3X crankshaft sensor is mounted to the side of the engine block, above the oil pan flange and the 24X crankshaft sensor is mounted to the front timing cover, under the harmonic balancer.

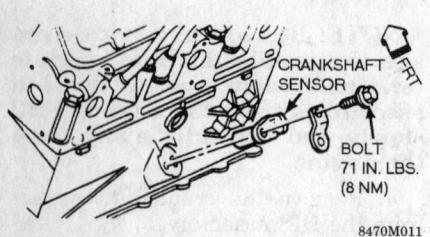

Crankshaft sensor assembly — 3.1L engine shown

1. Disconnect battery negative cable.

2. Disconnect serpentine belt from crankshaft pulley.

3. Raise and safely support the vehicle.

4. Remove right front tire and wheel assembly, then the inner fender access cover.

5. Remove crankshaft harmonic balancer retaining bolt and crankshaft harmonic balancer.

6. Disconnect electrical connector from sensor, remove the foreign object deflector and remove the crankshaft sensor from the vehicle.

To install:

7. Loosely install the crankshaft sensor on the pedestal.

8. Position the sensor with the pedestal attached on special tool J-37089.

9. Position the tool on the crankshaft.

10. Install the bolts to hold the pedestal to the block face. Tighten to 18–26 ft. lbs. (25–35 Nm).

11. Tighten the pedestal pinch bolt to 26–44 inch lbs. (3–5 Nm).

12. Remove special tool J-37089 and install the foreign object deflector.

13. Place special tool J-37089 on the harmonic balancer and turn. If any vane of the harmonic balancer touches the tool, replace the balancer assembly.

14. Install the balancer on the crankshaft and install the crankshaft balancer bolt. Tighten to 104 ft. lbs. + 56 degrees (140 Nm + 56 degrees).

15. Install the inner fender shield.

16. Install the tire and wheel assembly. Tighten to 100 ft. lbs. (140 Nm).

17. Lower the vehicle.

18. Install the serpentine belt.

19. Connect the negative battery cable.

3.1L (VIN M) ENGINE, 3X CRANKSHAFT SENSOR

NOTE: The 3X crankshaft sensor is mounted to the side of the engine block, above the oil pan flange. For the 3.1L engine with manual transaxle, the 3X crankshaft sensor is easily accessed from beneath the vehicle. For the 3.1L engine with automatic transaxle, the rack and pinion heatshield and catalytic converter intermediate exhaust assembly must be removed.

1. Disconnect the negative battery terminal.

2. Disconnect the sensor electrical connector.

3. Remove the sensor bolt and sensor from the engine.

4. Install a new O-ring and lubricate with engine oil. Install the bolt and torque to 88 inch lbs. (10 Nm).

5. Connect the negative battery terminal and check for proper operation.

3.8L ENGINE

1. Disconnect the negative battery cable and remove the serpentine belt assembly.

2. Raise and support the vehicle safely.

3. Remove the right front wheel assembly.

4. Remove the right inner fender access cover.

5. Remove the crankshaft harmonic balancer retaining bolt and remove the balancer, using tool J-38197 or equivalent.

6. Remove the foreign object deflector.

7. Disconnect the sensor electrical connector.

8. Remove the sensor and pedestal from the block face and remove the sensor from the pedestal.

To install:

9. Loosely install the crankshaft sensor on the pedestal.

10. Position the sensor with the pedestal attached on tool J-37089 or equivalent, and position tool on the crankshaft.

11. Install the bolts to hold the pedestal to the block face and tighten to 14–28 ft. lbs. (20–40 Nm).

12. Torque the pedestal pinch bolt to 36–40 inch lbs. (4–4.5 Nm).

13. Remove the special tool and install the foreign object deflector.

14. Place tool J-37089 or equivalent, on the harmonic balancer and turn. If any vane of the harmonic

balancer touches the tool, replace the balancer assembly.

15. Install the balancer on the crankshaft.

16. Install thread sealer to the threads of the crankshaft balancer bolt and tighten the bolt to 104 ft. lbs. (140 Nm), + an additional 56 degree turn.

17. Install the inner fender shield.

18. Install the wheel assembly and tighten the lug nuts to 100 ft. lbs. (140 Nm).

19. Lower the vehicle and install the serpentine belt.

Ignition Timing

ADJUSTMENT

Because the reluctor is an integral part of the crankshaft and the crankshaft sensor is mounted in a fixed position, timing adjustment is not possible.

Alternator

PRECAUTIONS

Several precautions must be observed with alternator equipped vehicles to avoid damage to the unit.

• If the battery is removed for any reason, make sure it is reconnected with the correct polarity. Reversing the battery connections may result in damage to the 1-way rectifiers.

• When utilizing a booster battery as a starting aid, always connect the positive to positive terminals and the negative terminal from the booster battery to a good engine ground on the vehicle being started.

• Never use a fast charger as a booster to start vehicles.

• Disconnect the battery cables when charging the battery with a fast charger.

• Never attempt to polarize the alternator.

• Do not use test lights of more than 12 volts when checking diode continuity.

• Do not short across or ground any of the alternator terminals.

• The polarity of the battery, alternator and regulator must be matched and considered before making any electrical connections within the system.

• Never unplug the alternator on an open circuit. Make sure all connections within the circuit are clean and tight.

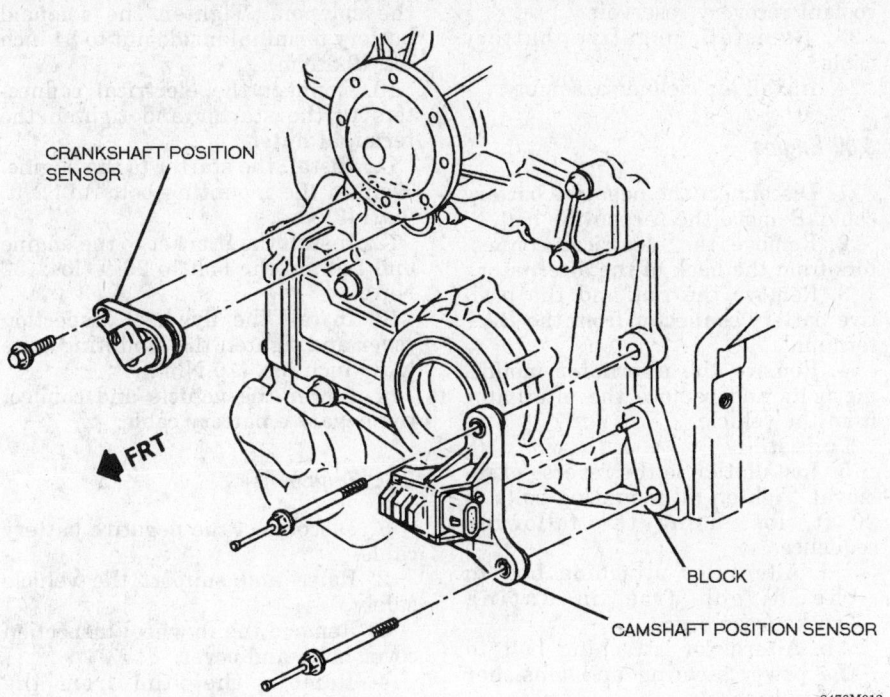

CRANKSHAFT POSITION SENSOR

FRT

BLOCK

CAMSHAFT POSITION SENSOR

8470M012

Camshaft and crankshaft sensor installation — 3.8L engine

• Disconnect the battery ground terminal when performing any service on electrical components.

• Disconnect the battery if arc welding is to be done on the vehicle.

BELT TENSION ADJUSTMENT

A single serpentine belt is used to drive all engine mounted components. Drive belt tension is maintained by a spring loaded tensioner.

NOTE: The drive belt tensioner can control the belt tension over a wide range of belt lengths; however, there are limits to the tensioner's ability to compensate for various belt lengths. Installing the wrong size belt and using the tensioner outside of its operating range can result in poor tension control and damage to the tensioner, drive belt and driven components.

REMOVAL AND INSTALLATION

2.2L Engine

1. Disconnect the negative battery cable.
2. Remove the serpentine drive belt by doing the following:
   a. Remove the coolant reservoir.

   b. Rotate the tensioner clockwise with a 15mm wrench and slide the belt off the alternator pulley.

   c. Release the tensioner and remove the belt.

3. Remove the rear bracket and heat shield nuts from the exhaust manifold.
4. Remove the rear bracket and heat shield bolts from the engine block, near the water pump.
5. Remove the rear bracket and heat shield nut at the alternator and remove the bracket and heat shield assembly.
6. Label and disconnect the electrical connections from the alternator.
7. Remove the front alternator attaching bolts and remove the alternator from the engine.
To install:
8. Install the alternator and tighten the front mounting bolts as follows:
   a. Long bolt — 37 ft. lbs. (50 Nm).
   b. Short bolt — 18 ft. lbs. (25 Nm).
9. Connect the electrical connectors to the alternator.
10. Install the rear bracket/heat shield and install the alternator mounting bolt. Tighten the mounting bolt to 70 inch lbs. (8 Nm).

11. Install the rear bracket/heat shield to engine block bolts, located near the water pump. Tighten the bolts to 63 ft. lbs. (83 Nm).
12. Install the rear bracket/heat shield to exhaust manifold nuts. Tighten the nuts to 37 ft. lbs. (50 Nm).
13. Install the serpentine belt and connect the negative battery cable.

2.5L Engine

1. Disconnect the negative battery cable.
2. Remove the serpentine belt.
3. Remove the electrical connectors from the back of the alternator.
4. Remove the rear attaching bolt first, then the front attaching bolt and heat shield.
5. Remove the alternator assembly carefully making sure all wires are disconnected.
To install:
6. Position the alternator into the mounting bracket.
7. Install the front and rear mounting bolts but do not tighten.
8. Install the heat shield with the rear mounting bolts.
9. Install the electrical connectors and tighten the battery cable nut.
10. Torque the mounting bolts to 18 ft. lbs. (25 Nm).
11. Install the serpentine belt.
12. Reconnect the negative battery cable.

3.1L (VIN M) Engine

1. Remove the serpentine belt shield.
2. Lift or rotate the tensioner using a 3/8 in. breaker bar.
3. Note belt routing and remove the serpentine belt.
4. Installation is the reverse of removal.

3.1L (VIN T) Engine

1. Disconnect the negative battery cable. Remove the air cleaner assembly.
2. Remove the serpentine belt.
3. Remove the electrical connectors from the back of the alternator.
4. Remove the rear and front attaching bolts and the bolt from brace to alternator.
5. Remove the alternator assembly carefully making sure all wires are disconnected.

NOTE: If alternator brace is removed, studs must be retightened before installation or damage to the brace may result.

To install:

6. Position the alternator into the mounting bracket.

7. Install brace to alternator bolt but do not tighten.

8. Install the front and rear mounting bolts. Torque the mounting bolts as follows:

    a. Long bolt to 35 ft. lbs. (47 Nm)

    b. Short bolt to 18 ft. lbs. (25 Nm)

    c. Bracket bolt to 18 ft. lbs. (25 Nm)

9. Check that tightening of the brace bolts did not bind alternator.

10. Install the electrical connectors and tighten the battery cable nut.

11. Install the serpentine belt.

12. Install the air cleaner and negative battery cable.

3.4L Engine

1. Disconnect the negative battery cable.

2. Remove air cleaner assembly.

3. Remove coolant recovery reservoir and set aside.

4. Remove serpentine belt.

5. Raise and safely support vehicle.

6. Remove power steering pipe retaining clip nut from upper alternator stud and remove alternator stud.

7. Remove right front tire and wheel assembly.

8. Separate lower ball joint from lower control arm.

9. Remove halfshaft from transaxle.

10. Remove right hand engine splash shield.

11. Disconnect connectors and wires from alternator.

12. Remove brace bolt from alternator and loosen brace at engine block.

13. Remove alternator lower mounting bolt and alternator.

To install:

14. Install alternator and loosely install all mounting bolts. If replacement alternator does not fit into mounts, remove adhesive-backed shim from rear of alternator bracket.

15. Tighten alternator lower mounting bolts to 61 ft. lbs. (83 Nm).

16. Install connectors and wires to alternator.

17. Install right hand engine splash shield.

18. Reinstall halfshaft.

19. Install lower ball joint to lower control arm.

20. Reinstall tire and wheel assembly and lower vehicle.

21. Install upper alternator stud and power steering pipe retaining clip nut.

22. Reinstall serpentine belt and coolant recovery reservoir.

23. Reinstall negative battery cable.

24. Install air cleaner assembly.

3.8L Engine

1. Disconnect the negative battery cable. Remove the serpentine belt.

2. Remove the electrical connectors from the back of the alternator.

3. Remove the nut and the positive battery connector from the **BAT** terminal.

4. Remove the alternator mounting bolts and remove the alternator from the vehicle.

To install:

5. Installation is the reverse of removal. Tighten all mounting bolts to 20 ft. lbs. using the following sequence:

    a. Alternator attaching bolt to the direct fire mounting bracket/rear brace.

    b. Alternator attaching bolt to the power steering and tensioner pulley bracket.

    c. Alternator brace bolt to engine.

NOTE: Make sure tightening bolts does not bind alternator.

Starter

REMOVAL AND INSTALLATION

2.2L Engine

1. Disconnect the negative battery cable.

2. Raise and safely support the vehicle.

3. Remove the bolts from the flywheel inspection cover and remove the cover.

4. Disconnect the starter electrical connectors.

5. Remove the stud from the bracket.

6. Remove the mounting bolts from the starter and remove the starter from the engine.

7. Remove the bracket from the starter.

To install:

8. Install the bracket to the starter. Tighten the nuts to 80 inch lbs. (9 Nm).

NOTE: Make sure the electrical terminals are tight on the solenoid battery terminal. If the terminals are loose, starter motor failure may occur.

9. Secure the electrical terminal to the solenoid. Tighten the solenoid battery terminal inside nut to 84 inch lbs. (9.5 Nm).

10. Connect the electrical connectors to the starter and tighten the terminal nuts.

11. Install the starter to the engine. Tighten the mounting bolts to 32 ft. lbs. (43 Nm).

12. Install the bracket to the engine and tighten the bolt to 26 ft. lbs. (32 Nm).

13. Install the flywheel inspection cover and tighten the mounting bolts to 89 inch lbs. (10 Nm).

14. Lower the vehicle and connect the negative battery cable.

2.5L Engine

1. Disconnect the negative battery cable.

2. Raise and support the vehicle safely.

3. Remove the flywheel inspection cover bolts and cover.

4. Remove the stud from the starter support bracket.

5. Remove the 2 starter mounting bolts and shim, if equipped.

6. Remove the starter motor. Be careful not to damage the starter wires by letting the starter hang.

7. While holding the starter motor, disconnect the starter electrical connectors from the starter solenoid.

8. Remove the starter from the rear bracket.

To install:

9. Install the support bracket to the starter.

10. Install the starter adjustment shims, if equipped.

11. Position the starter to the engine mounting flange and torque the bolts to 32 ft. lbs. (43 Nm).

12. Install the bracket-to-engine and torque the stud to 18 ft. lbs. (25 Nm).

13. Install the inspection cover.

14. Lower the vehicle and connect the starter electrical wires. Reconnect the negative battery cable.

3.1L (VIN T) and 3.4L Engines

1. Remove the air cleaner.

2. Disconnect the negative battery cable.

3. Raise the vehicle and support it safely. Disconnect the electrical connectors from the DIS module and the engine oil pressure sensor.

4. If equipped with an engine oil cooler, position a drain pan under the engine and remove the engine oil and oil filter. Remove the oil cooler

adapter stud and position the oil cooler aside.

NOTE: It is not necessary to open the cooling system to position the oil cooler aside.

5. If equipped with 3.1L engine, remove the nut from the brace at the air conditioning compressor, nut from the brace at the engine and the brace.
6. Remove the flywheel inspection cover.
7. Remove the starter bolts and shims, if equipped. Do not let the starter hang from the starter wires.
8. Remove the starter wires from the solenoid and remove the starter.

To install:
9. While supporting the starter, connect the starter wires at the solenoid.
10. Install the starter motor-to-engine mount with the shims, if equipped, and the mounting bolts. Torque the bolts to 32 ft. lbs. (43 Nm).
11. If equipped with an engine oil cooler, reposition the hose next to the starter motor, install the oil filter and refill the engine with the proper amount of engine oil.
12. Install the flywheel inspection cover and tighten the bolts.
13. Install the starter support brace to the air conditioning compressor and torque the nut to 23 ft. lbs. (31 Nm).
14. Lower the vehicle, reconnect the negative battery cable and install the air cleaner assembly.

3.1L (VIN M) Engine

1. Disconnect the negative battery cable.
2. Raise the vehicle and safely support.
3. Disconnect the engine wiring harness from the front of the frame.
4. Remove the inspection cover and electrical connections from the starter.
5. Remove the starter bolt and starter. Save any shims that are removed.

To install:
6. Connect the solenoid battery and S terminals. Torque the battery nut to 12 ft. lbs. (16 Nm) and the S terminal nut to 27 inch lbs. (3 Nm).
7. Install the starter bolts and torque to 32 ft. lbs. (43 Nm). Install the remaining components.

3.8L Engine

1. Disconnect the negative battery cable.
2. If necessary, remove the right side cooling fan.

3. Remove the serpentine drive belt.
4. Disconnect the air conditioning compressor upper support brace and lay the compressor in the fan opening.
5. Raise and support the vehicle safely.
6. Disconnect the engine oil cooler lines at the flex connector.
7. Remove the flywheel inspection cover.
8. Remove the starter motor retaining bolts and remove the starter motor and shims, if used.
9. Disconnect the starter motor wiring and remove the starter from the vehicle.

To install:
10. Position the starter motor and shims, if used, to the engine and tighten the mounting bolts to 32 ft. lbs. (43 Nm).
11. Connect the electrical connectors to the starter terminals and tighten the battery nut to 80 inch lbs. and the S terminal nut to 27 inch lbs. (3 Nm).
12. Install the flywheel inspection cover. Tighten to 89 inch lbs. (10 Nm).
13. Connect the engine oil cooler lines at the flex connector.
14. Lower the vehicle and install the air conditioner compressor.
15. Install the serpentine drive belt, cooling fan and negative battery cable.

CHASSIS ELECTRICAL

Heater Blower Motor

REMOVAL AND INSTALLATION

1. Disconnect the negative battery cable.
2. Remove the mounting screws and the sound insulator from under the right side of the instrument panel.
3. Remove the convenience center rear screws, loosen the front screws and slide the convenience center out of the vehicle.
4. Grasp the carpet at the top side and pull forward.
5. Disconnect the electrical connections from the blower motor and resistor.

6. Remove the plastic water shield from the right side of the cowl, if equipped.
7. Remove the blower motor-to-chassis screws and the blower motor.
8. Remove the cage retaining nut and the cage (old style).

NOTE: Some of the new style blower cages are plastic welded to the motor shaft. Use a hot knife to cut a slot in the cage shaft sleeve in 3 places. Cut through the plastic material from the dome to the end of the shaft until the cage splits from the shaft.

To install:
9. Install the cage on the new blower motor with the opening facing away from the motor.
10. Install the blower motor and screws. Install the sound insulator and connect the electrical leads to the motor and resistor.
11. Install the water shield to the cowl. Reinstall the carpet at the cowl.
12. Install the convenience center and secure retainer screws.
13. Install the sound insulator panel and connect the negative battery cable.

Windshield Wiper Motor

REMOVAL AND INSTALLATION

Except 1991 Lumina

1. Disconnect the negative battery cable.
2. Remove wiper module from vehicle, if equipped, as follows:
   a. Raise the hood. Disconnect the washer hoses and remove protective cap and nut from each wiper arm. Lift each wiper arm and insert a pin or pop rivet completely through the 2 holes located next to the pivot of arm. Then lift the arm off transmission shaft using a rocking motion.

NOTE: Remove metal shavings from knurls of transmission linkage shaft using a wire brush.

   b. Remove the screws retaining the cowl cover. Lower the hood partially and remove the cowl cover.
   c. Remove the air inlet panel and underhood light switch, if equipped.

NOTE: Attach holding wire to upper portion of switch before removing retaining nut or switch will fall between panels.

d. Disconnect 2 wiring harness connectors from motor, and washer hose at bulkhead.

e. Position crank arm to inner wipe position, remove 3 screws from bellcrank housing, lower transmission and remove.

3. Remove crank arm from motor.

NOTE: Do not remove the crank arm from the transmission because the factory has preset the adjustment. The crank arm must be removed from the motor only.

4. Remove 3 screws retaining the motor and remove the motor.

To install:

5. Attach the motor to the module assembly.

6. Install the crank arm and nut. Tighten to 25–38 ft. lbs. (34–51 Nm).

7. Attach the bellcrank to module assembly and install the wire connectors washer hose, air inlet panel and light switch.

8. Install cowl cover, wiper arms, washer hoses and nuts with protective caps.

9. Connect the negative battery cable and check the operation of the wiper motor.

Windshield Wiper Switch

REMOVAL AND INSTALLATION

The wiper/washer switch is mounted on the steering column.

1. Disconnect the negative battery cable.

2. Remove the steering wheel horn pad, wheel retaining nut and steering wheel.

3. Remove the turn signal cancelling cam assembly, if required.

4. Remove the wiring protector around the instrument panel opening and the switch retaining screws.

5. To aid in switch removal, pull the bottom of the switch rearward first and then remove. Disconnect the electrical connector.

To install:

6. Install the switch assembly. Install the wiring protector around the instrument panel opening, covering all wires.

7. Install the steering column housing cover and torque the screws to 35 inch lbs. (4 Nm).

8. Install the hazard knob and lubricate the bottom side of the cancelling cam with lithium grease.

9. Install the steering wheel and torque the shaft nut to 30 ft. lbs. (41 Nm).

10. Connect the negative battery cable and check steering column operations.

Instrument Cluster

REMOVAL AND INSTALLATION

Cutlass Supreme

1. Disconnect the negative battery cable.

2. Remove screws at top of the trim plate.

3. Pull the bottom of the trim plate out to release the spring clips and remove panel from the vehicle.

4. Disconnect the **PRNDL** cable, if equipped.

5. Remove the screws retaining the instrument cluster and pull the cluster forward slightly. Disconnect the electrical connectors.

6. Remove the cluster assembly from the instrument panel.

To install:

7. Position the cluster at the instrument panel and connect the electrical harness connectors. Install the cluster assembly into the carrier.

8. Connect the **PRNDL** cable, if equipped.

9. Secure cluster in place with the retainer bolts tightened to 18 inch lbs. (2 Nm).

10. Install the cluster trim panel. Connect the negative battery cable and check all gauges for proper operation.

11. If removed, install the air cleaner assembly.

1992 Grand Prix, Lumina and Regal

1. Remove the air cleaner assembly. Disconnect the negative battery cable.

2. Remove the instrument panel pad from the vehicle as follows:

a. Disconnect daytime running lamp sensor connector, if equipped.

b. If equipped, remove 1 screw under each speaker grille.

c. Remove 5 screws under lower edge of the instrument panel pad.

d. Remove pad by lifting the front, pulling rearward to release, then lifting pad up and out.

3. Remove the cluster trim plate and screws retaining the instrument cluster.

4. Pull the cluster forward, disconnect the electrical connectors and the **PRNDL** cable if equipped. Remove the cluster assembly from the vehicle.

To install:

5. Install the cluster to the instrument panel. Connect the electrical leads and **PRNDL** cable.

6. Install the upper panel pad.

7. Install the cluster trim panel.

8. Connect the negative battery cable and install the air cleaner assembly. Check all gauges for proper operation.

1993–96 Grand Prix

1. Remove the air cleaner assembly. Disconnect the negative battery cable.

2. If equipped with the Head–up Display (HUD) assembly, remove the HUD retaining screws and lift the assembly away from the cluster. Be careful not to bend or kink the HUD cable.

3. Remove the instrument panel lower compartment.

4. Remove the instrument panel pad cover as follows:

a. Remove the 1 screw above the lower compartment.

b. Remove the screws at the top of the instrument cluster trim plate.

c. Remove pad by lifting the front, pulling rearward to release, then lifting pad up and out.

d. Disconnect the speaker wire connector and if equipped, disconnect the daytime running light sensor connector.

5. If equipped with HUD, remove the mounting bracket.

6. Remove the instrument cluster trim panel. Remove the shift indicator cable from the bracket and the lever.

7. Remove the bolts/screws retaining the instrument cluster.

8. Pull the cluster forward, disconnect the electrical connectors. Remove the cluster assembly from the vehicle.

To install:

9. Install the cluster to the instrument panel. Connect the electrical leads.

10. Install the 4 mounting bolts/screws and tighten to 18 inch lbs. (2 Nm).

11. Connect the shift indicator cable at the bracket and the lever.

12. Install the instrument trim panel.

13. If equipped with HUD, install the HUD mounting bracket.

14. Install the instrument panel pad cover as follows:

a. Connect the speaker wire connector and the daytime running light sensor, if equipped.

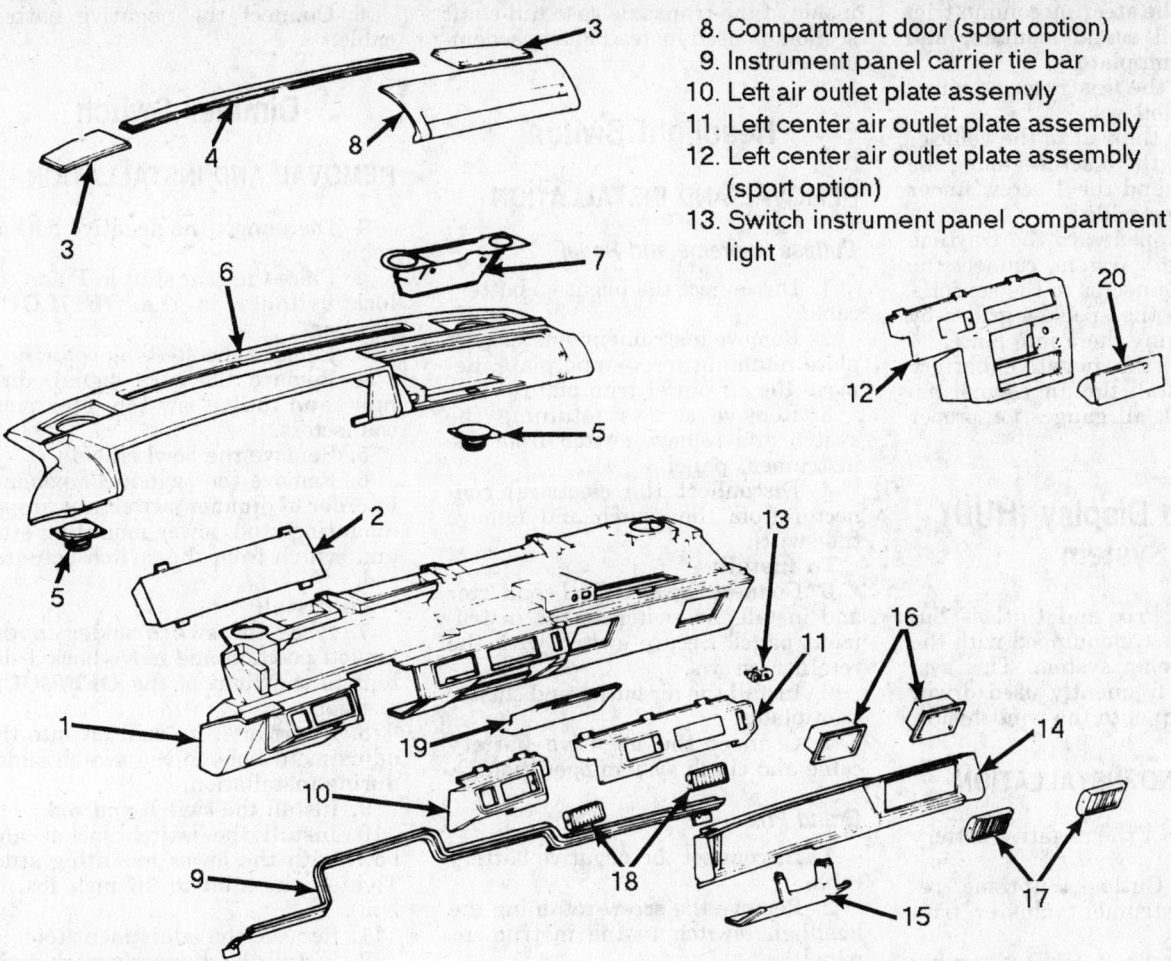

8. Compartment door (sport option)
9. Instrument panel carrier tie bar
10. Left air outlet plate assemvly
11. Left center air outlet plate assembly
12. Left center air outlet plate assembly (sport option)
13. Switch instrument panel compartment light

1. Instrument panel carrier
2. Instrument cluster
3. Sparaker covers
4. Defroster grille
5. Speaker
6. Instrument panel upper pad
7. Lower compartment

14. Instrument cluster trim plate
15. Steering column lower filler
16. Right and right center air outlet housings
17. Right and right center air outlet grilles
18. Left and left center air outlet grilles
19. Ashtray
20. Ashtray (sport option)

8470M014

Exploded view of the instrument panel without HUD system

b. Install the pad and push firmly towards the front of the vehicle to engage the clips.

c. Push down on the edge of the pad nearest the seats to engage the front clips.

d. Install the cluster trim plate mounting screws.

e. Install the lower compartment assembly.

f. Install the HUD unit and secure with the mounting screws.

15. Connect the negative battery cable and install the air cleaner assembly. Check all gauges for proper operation.

1993–96 Lumina and Regal

1. Remove the air cleaner assembly. Disconnect the negative battery cable.

2. Remove the instrument panel pad from the vehicle as follows:

a. Disconnect daytime running lamp sensor connector, if equipped.

b. Remove the speaker grilles by gently prying upward. Remove 1 screw under each speaker grille.

c. Remove 5 screws under lower edge of the instrument panel pad.

d. Remove pad by lifting the front, pulling rearward to release, then lifting pad up and out.

3. Remove the cluster trim plate.

4. Remove the left sound insulator and the steering column trim panel.

5. Disconnect the shift control cable from the bracket and the lever. Remove the shift indicator cable.

6. Remove the cluster retaining bolts. Pull the cluster forward and disconnect the electrical connectors. Remove the cluster assembly from the vehicle.

To install:

7. Install the cluster to the instrument panel. Connect the electrical leads. Install the mounting bolts.

8. Install the shift indicator cable. Install the shift control cable to the bracket and to the lever.

9. Install the steering column trim panel, the left sound insulator and the cluster trim plate.

10. Install the instrument panel pad cover as follows:

a. Install the pad to the vehicle.

b. Install the 5 screws along the lower edge and the 1 screw under each speaker grille.

c. If equipped with the Daytime running light system, connect the electrical connector to the sensor.

d. Install the speaker grilles by firmly pushing them into place.

11. Connect the negative battery cable and install the air cleaner assembly. Check all gauges for proper operation.

Head-Up Display (HUD) System

Some Grand Prix and Cutlass Supreme models are equipped with the Head-Up Display system. This system displays frequently used driver information up onto the windshield.

REMOVAL AND INSTALLATION

1. Disconnect the negative battery cable.

2. On the Cutlass Supreme, remove the instrument cluster trim bezel.

3. Remove the 2 HUD assembly retaining screws.

4. Disconnect the HUD unit electrical connector and remove the HUD unit.

To install:

5. Connect the HUD unit electrical connector.

6. Install the HUD unit to the dash by first inserting the tab into the mounting bracket front slot.

7. Install the 2 HUD mounting screws.

8. On the Cutlass Supreme, install the instrument cluster trim bezel and rotate the adjuster thumb wheel in the UP direction to remove the HUD unit from the load position.

9. On the Grand Prix, slide the adjuster control toward the driver to release it from the load position.

Speedometer

The speedometer and gauges are serviced as a unit. Removal of the instrument cluster is necessary in order to gain access to the circuit board that controls the gauges. An electronic speed sensor, mounted on the

inside of the transaxle case tail shaft section, is used instead of a speedometer cable.

Headlight Switch

REMOVAL AND INSTALLATION

Cutlass Supreme and Regal

1. Disconnect the negative battery cable.

2. Remove instrument cluster trim plate retaining screws and plate. Remove the air outlet trim plate.

3. Remove screws retaining the switch and remove switch from the instrument panel.

4. Disconnect the electrical connector from the switch and remove the switch.

To install:

5. Connect the electrical connector and install the switch in the instrument panel. Secure switch with the retainer screws.

6. Install the air outlet and cluster trim plates.

7. Connect the negative battery cable and check system operation.

Grand Prix

1. Disconnect the negative battery cable.

2. Remove the screw retaining the headlight switch to the instrument panel.

3. Pull the top of the switch out to release the lower retaining clips and remove it from the instrument panel.

4. Disconnect the electrical connector and remove the switch from the vehicle.

To install:

5. Connect the electrical connector and install the switch in the instrument panel.

6. Secure switch in place using the fasteners.

7. Connect the negative battery cable and check system operation.

Lumina

1. Disconnect the negative battery cable.

2. Remove left instrument panel trim plate.

3. Remove retaining screws, disconnect the wire harness connector and remove the switch from the vehicle.

To install:

4. Connect the wire harness to the headlight switch.

5. Install the switch retaining screws and install the left instrument panel trim plate.

6. Connect the negative battery cable.

Dimmer Switch

REMOVAL AND INSTALLATION

1. Disconnect the negative battery cable.

2. Place the gear shift in **P** and the lock cylinder in the **OFF/LOCK** position.

3. Remove the steering column.

4. Remove the turn signal, dimmer and pulse switch electrical connectors.

5. Remove the bowl shield.

6. Remove the switch components in order of dimmer switch nut, upper mounting stud, lower mounting stud and switch from the switch actuator rod.

To install:

7. Place the switch slider in the far left position and move back 1 detent to the right of the **OFF/LOCK** position.

8. Insert a 3/32 in. drill bit into the adjustment hole on the switch slider during installation.

9. Install the switch and rod.

10. Install the switch jacket and bowl with the lower mounting stud. Tighten the stud to 36 inch lbs. (4 Nm).

11. Remove the adjustment tool.

12. Install the dimmer switch actuator rod with the tab first, through the hole in the instrument panel bracket and into the switch rod cap.

13. Install the dimmer switch and adjust using a 3/32 in. drill bit into the hole in the top. Remove all excess lash. Do not tighten at this time.

14. After adjustment has been made, tighten the dimmer switch nut and mounting stud to 36 inch lbs. (4 Nm). Remove the adjusting tool.

15. Install the column jacket, bowl and shield.

16. Connect the turn signal, pulse and dimmer switch electrical connectors.

17. Connect the negative battery cable.

Turn Signal Switch

REMOVAL AND INSTALLATION

NOTE: Tool J-35689-A or equivalent, is required to remove the terminals from the connector on the turn signal switch.

1. Disconnect the negative battery cable. Remove the steering wheel.

2. Pull the turn signal cancelling cam assembly from the steering shaft.

3. Remove the hazard warning knob-to-steering column screw and the knob.

NOTE: Before removing the turn signal assembly, position the turn signal lever so the turn signal assembly to steering column screws can all be removed.

4. Remove the long blue column housing cover-to-column housing bowl screw and the cover.

NOTE: If equipped with cruise control, disconnect the cruise control electrical connector.

5. Remove the turn signal lever-to-pivot assembly screw and the lever; 1 screw is in the front and the other screw is in the rear.

6. Remove the wiring protector from the opening in the instrument panel bracket and separate from the wires.

7. Disconnect the pivot and switch connector from the ignition and the dimmer switch.

8. Remove the pivot switch mounting screw and switch from the steering column.

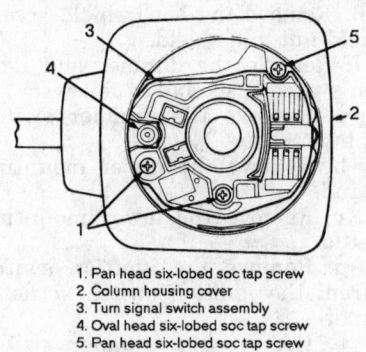

1. Pan head six-lobed soc tap screw
2. Column housing cover
3. Turn signal switch assembly
4. Oval head six-lobed soc tap screw
5. Pan head six-lobed soc tap screw

8470M019

Turn signal switch mounting

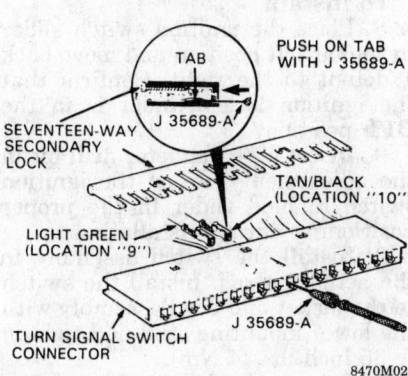

8470M020

Buzzer switch wire removal

9. Remove the turn signal switch mounting screws. Disconnect the electrical connector from the ignition and dimmer switch connector.

10. Using the terminal remover tool J-35689–A or equivalent, label and remove 2 wires connected to the buzzer switch, located in positions **9** and **10** from the turn signal switch harness connector.

11. Disconnect the turn signal interface module from the turn signal switch assembly, if equipped, as follows:

   a. Remove the tape and separate the module from the wire harness.

   b. Depress the tab on the connector and gently separate the module from the connector.

12. Remove the turn signal switch from the steering column.

   To install:

13. Install the turn signal switch to the steering column, torque the turn signal switch-to-steering column screws to 20–35 inch lbs. (2.3–4.0 Nm).

14. Install the wires for the buzzer switch assembly into positions **9** and **10** of the turn signal switch harness connector. The light green wire is to be inserted into terminal location **9** and the tan/black wire is to be inserted into terminal location **10**.

15. Install the turn signal interface module connector as follows:

   a. Install the module to the connector on the wire harness and snap into place.

   b. Position the module against the wiring harness and secure in place using tape.

16. Install the turn signal connector to the ignition and the dimmer switch connector and snap into place.

17. Install the pivot and pulse switch assembly. Secure switch with retainer screw tightened to 20 inch lbs. (2.3 Nm).

18. Connect the pivot switch connector to the ignition and dimmer switch connector and snap into place. Install the wiring protector and snap in place.

19. Install the shoe pin retainer cap and column housing cover.

20. Install the housing screw and tighten to 20 inch lbs. (2.3 Nm).

21. Install the hazard warning knob and secure in place.

22. Lubricate the bottom side of the cancelling cam with synthetic grease and install onto the steering column.

23. Install the steering wheel and tighten the jam nut to 30 ft. lbs. (41 Nm).

24. Connect the negative battery cable and check system for proper operation.

Ignition Lock Cylinder

REMOVAL AND INSTALLATION

Standard Column

1. Disconnect the negative terminal from the battery. Remove the left side lower trim panel.

2. Remove the steering column from the vehicle.

3. Remove the turn signal switch from the steering column.

4. Remove the 2 lower spring retainers and discard. Remove the lower bearing spring and lower bearing seat.

5. Remove the adapter screws, adapter and bearing assembly.

6. Place the ignition lock cylinder in **RUN** position. Place opening in retainer ring over flat on steering shaft. Remove retainer ring and discard.

7. Remove the thrust washer, upper bearing spring and the washer.

8. Remove the steering shaft from the lower end of the jacket and bowl assembly.

9. Remove the steering column housing mounting screws and housing from the column assembly. Remove the housing spacer.

10. Using a drift, remove the bearing from the housing and discard. Remove the housing circuit bridge.

11. Place the ignition lock in **OFF/LOCK** position and remove the key.

12. Remove the buzzer switch from the column by lifting the switch with a flat tipped tool and gently pulling on the wires.

13. Remove the lock retainer screw from the bowl assembly.

14. Remove the ignition lock cylinder.

   To install:

15. Placing the ignition key in **OFF** position and remove the key. Install the steering column lock set into the housing and secure with the lock retainer screw tightened to 62 inch lbs. (7 Nm).

16. Push the buzzer switch assembly down into the retaining bore until it bottoms and the plastic tab covers lock retainer screw.

17. Install the housing circuit bridge into housing with the clip notch over the housing lip.

18. Lubricate bearing with lithium grease. Press bearing into housing using a 1½ in. (38mm) socket until bottomed.

19. Install the housing spacer to the housing. Install steering column housing to the steering column and secure with housing screw tightened to 88 inch lbs. (10 Nm).

20. Turn the steering column lock cylinder to the **RUN** position. Insert steering shaft into the lower end of the jacket and bowl assembly until shaft rests against the bearing.

NOTE: The shaft, when properly installed, will extend 2.5 in. (63mm) beyond the highest surface of the steering column housing.

21. Install the thrust washer, upper bearing spring and thrust washer on the shaft.

22. Position a piece of shim stock around the shaft and slip a new retaining ring until it seats in the retainer ring groove in the shaft. Remove and discard the shim stock.

23. Install the adapter and lower bearing assembly. Install the adapter retainer screws and tighten to 26 inch lbs. (3 Nm).

24. Install the lower bearing seat and spring. Install 2 new lower spring retainers, compress the spring until retainers are positioned 1.14 in. (29mm) from the lower end of the steering shaft.

25. Install the steering column into the vehicle.

26. Install the park lock cable into the ignition switch inhibitor and snap into place.

27. Install the turn signal switch and remaining components.

28. Connect all electrical leads and lower trim panels.

29. Connect the negative battery cable and check for proper operation of the steering column and related components. Test drive vehicle and make sure the steering column does not bind during operation.

Tilt Column

1. Disconnect negative battery cable.

2. Remove the left side lower trim panel.

3. Remove the steering column from the vehicle.

4. Tilt the column up as far as it will go.

5. Insert a Phillips head screwdriver into the spring retainer, push down and turn to the left and remove the retainer, tilt wheel spring and the spring guide.

6. Remove the 2 lower spring retainers and discard.

7. Remove the lower bearing spring and seat. Remove the adapter

screws and remove the adapter and lower bearing assembly assembly.

8. Remove the pivot pins from the housing using tool J–21854–01 or equivalent.

9. Place the lock cylinder in the **RUN** position.

10. Pull the tilt lever and release the shaft and housing assembly and remove from the jacket and bowl assembly.

11. Place the lock cylinder in the **OFF/LOCK** position and remove the key.

12. Using a flat tipped tool, lift the tab on the buzzer switch and gently pull the switch from the housing.

13. Remove the lock retainer screw and the lock cylinder from the housing.

To install:

14. Place the ignition cylinder to **OFF/LOCK** position and remove the key. Install the steering column lock cylinder set into the housing. Install the lock retainer screw and tighten to 62 inch lbs. (7 Nm).

15. Push the buzzer switch assembly down into the retaining bore until it bottoms and the plastic tab covers lock retainer screw.

16. Insert the key into cylinder and turn to the **RUN** position. Install the shaft and housing assembly.

17. Lubricate the pivot pins with lithium grease. Install pins into the holes in the housing until the pins bottom.

18. Install the tilt lever if removed, and tilt the column to its most upward position.

19. Lubricate the tilt spring guide with lithium grease. Install the tilt spring guide into the tilt spring.

20. Install the guide and tilt springs into the housing as follows:

    a. Insert a Phillips head screwdriver into the opening of the spring retainer.

    b. Push down on the spring retainer and turn right to lock in place. Be sure the recess in the spring guide engages the round locking tab in the jacket and bowl assembly.

21. Install the adapter and lower bearing assembly. Install the adapter screw and tighten to 26 inch lbs. (3 Nm).

22. Install bearing seat and lower bearing spring. Install 2 new lower spring retainers, compress the spring until retainers are positioned 1.14 in. (29mm) from the lower end of the steering shaft.

23. Install the steering column into the car.

24. Install the park lock cable into the ignition switch inhibitor and snap into place.

25. Install the turn signal switch and remaining components.

26. Connect all electrical leads and lower trim panels.

27. Connect the negative battery cable and check for proper operation of the steering column and related components. Test drive vehicle and make sure the steering column does not bind during operation.

Ignition Switch

REMOVAL AND INSTALLATION

1. Disconnect negative battery cable.

2. Place the shifter assembly in **P** and the ignition cylinder in **OFF/LOCK**. Remove the ignition key from the cylinder.

3. Remove the steering column from the car.

4. Disconnect the turn signal switch connector from the ignition and dimmer switch assembly connector.

5. Remove the pivot and pulse switch connector from the ignition and dimmer switch assembly connector.

6. Remove the bowl shield screw, shield nut and shield.

7. Remove the dimmer and ignition switch assembly as follows:

    a. Remove the dimmer switch nut.

    b. Remove the upper mounting stud.

    c. Remove the lower mounting stud.

    d. Remove the ignition switch from the ignition switch actuator rod.

    e. Remove the dimmer switch actuator rod from the rod cap.

    f. Remove the switch assembly.

To install:

8. Place the ignition switch slider in the far left position and move back 1 detent to the right. Confirm that the ignition lock cylinder is in the **OFF** position.

9. Insert a $^3/_{32}$ diameter drill bit in the adjustment hole on the ignition switch to hold slider in the proper positioning during installation.

10. Install the switch assembly to the actuating rod. Install the switch to the jacket and bowl assembly with the lower mounting stud and tighten to 35 inch lbs. (4 Nm).

11. Remove the drill bit from the ignition switch. Install the dimmer

1. Hexagon jam nut
2. Spacer and cancelling cam assy
3. Pan head six-lobed soc tap screw
4. Column housing cover
5. Hazard warning knob
6. Oval head c/rec. screw
7. Turn signal switch assembly
8. Hsg shoe pin retainer cap
9. Shaft and housing assy
10. Pivot pin
11. Spring retainer
12. Wheel tilt spring
13. Tilt spring guide
14. Oval head six-lobed soc tap screw
15. Pivot and pulse switch assy
16. Wiring protector
17. Buzzer switch assembly
18. Lock retaining screw
19. Jacket and bowl assy
20. Strg column lock cylinder set
21. Hex washer hd tapping screw
22. Bowl shield
23. PRNDL adjuster assembly
24. Adapter and bearing assy
25. Hex washer hd tapping screw
26. Lower bearing seat
27. Lower bearing spring
28. Lower spring retainer
29. Oval head six-lobed soc tap screw
30. Tilt lever and bracket assembly
31. Column tilt bumper
32. Dimmer switch rod cap
33. Dimmer switch actuator rod
34. Hexagon nut
35. Dimmer switch actuator rod
36. Ignition switch assembly
37. E and C interface module assy
38. Ignition switch rod
39. Switch actuator rack
40. Pan head six-lobed soc tap screw
41. Shift lever seal

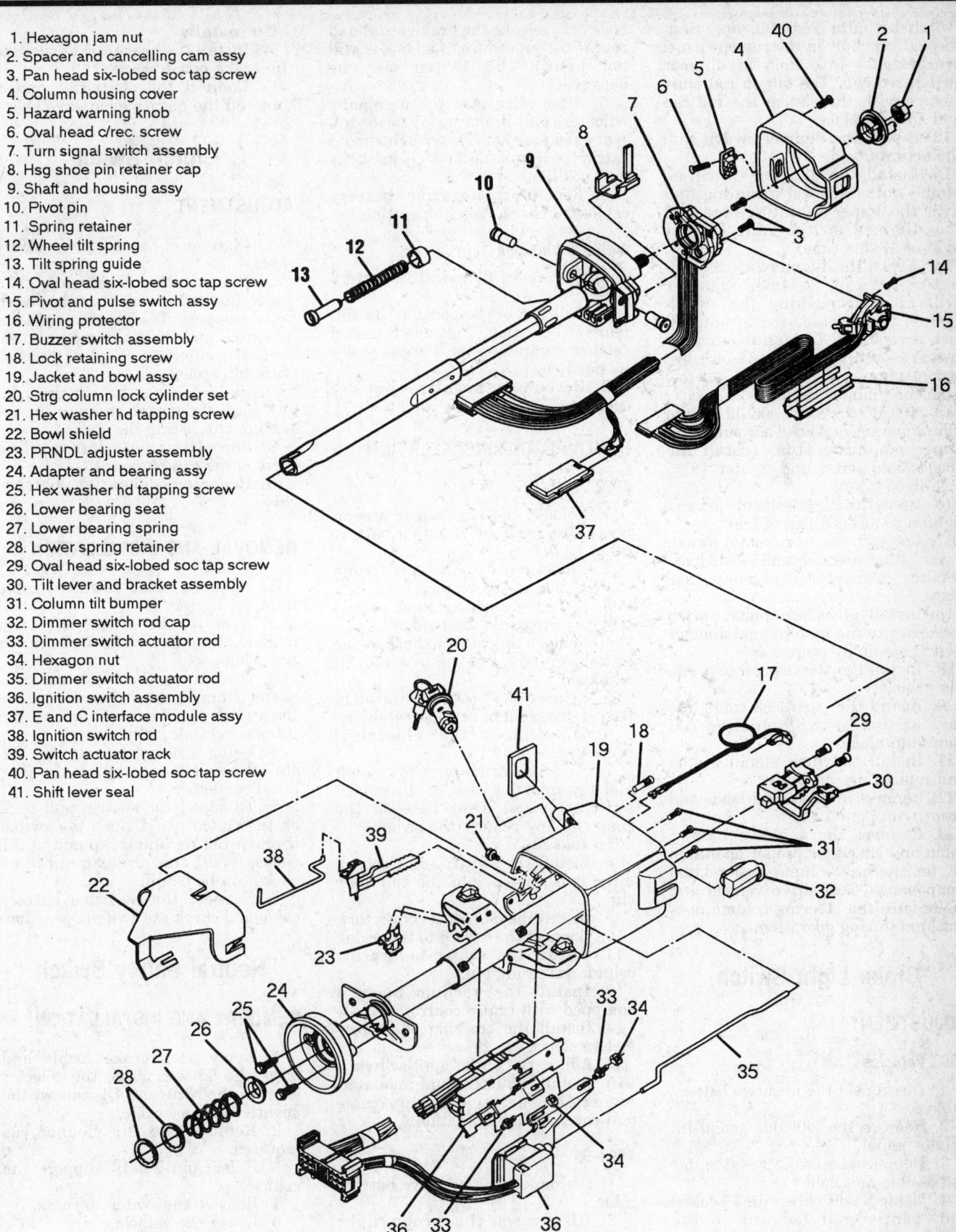

Tilt steering column assembly

8470M024

switch actuator rod, tab end first, through the hole in instrument panel bracket and into hole in dimmer switch rod cap. The tab on rod must engage with the slot in the rod cap and snap in place.

12. Install the dimmer switch onto the actuator rod.

13. Install the dimmer switch assembly onto the lower mounting stud with the upper mounting stud and the dimmer switch nut. Do not tighten at this time.

14. Adjust the dimmer switch by inserting a 3/32 in. (2.34mm) diameter drill bit and pushing the switch against the actuator rod to until all lash is removed. Tighten the dimmer switch mounting nuts to 35 inch lbs. (4 Nm). Remove the adjustment tool from the dimmer switch.

15. Install the bowl shield to the column jacket and bowl assembly and upper mounting stud. Install the bowl shield screw and tighten to 35 inch lbs. (4 Nm).

16. Install the bowl shield nut and tighten to 35 inch lbs. (4 Nm).

17. Connect the turn signal switch to the ignition and dimmer switch assembly connector and snap into place.

18. Install pivot and pulse switch connector to the ignition and dimmer switch assembly connector.

19. Install the steering column into the vehicle.

20. Install the park lock cable into the ignition switch inhibitor and snap into place.

21. Install the turn signal switch and remaining components.

22. Connect all electrical leads and lower trim panels.

23. Connect the negative battery cable and check for proper operation of the steering column and related components. Test drive vehicle and make sure the steering column does not bind during operation.

Brake Light Switch

ADJUSTMENT

1992 Vehicles

1. Disconnect the negative battery cable.

2. Remove the left side sound insulator panel.

3. Depress the brake pedal as far as possible and hold.

4. Using a stiff wire with a hooked end, gently pull forward on the switch set lever and listen for an audible click. This indicates the release of the automatic adjuster. If there is

NO click, release the brake pedal and repeat the procedure; if a click is still not heard, the switch may be defective.

5. After release of the automatic adjuster, pull brake pedal to its full rearward position. The switch should ratchet a minimum of 3 clicks to its new position.

6. Reconnect negative battery cable and check switch operation.

1993–96 Vehicles

1. Disconnect the negative battery cable.

2. Pull the brake pedal to its full rearward position. The switch should ratchet a minimum of 3 clicks to set its position.

3. Reconnect negative battery cable and check switch operation.

REMOVAL AND INSTALLATION

1992

1. Remove the air cleaner assembly. Disconnect the negative battery cable.

2. Remove the 3 fasteners from the left side insulator panel.

3. Slide the steering shaft protective cover towards the cowl.

4. Remove the vacuum hose at the cruise control cut off switch, if equipped.

5. Remove the brake light switch-to-steering column bracket retainer.

6. Disconnect the electrical connector.

7. Push the switch arm to the left and towards the cowl to disconnect switch-to-pedal arm. Release the snap clip and remove the switch.

To install:

8. Install the switch and push up until it is seated into the top snap clip.

9. Install the electrical connectors.

10. Connect the switch to the pedal.

11. Install the switch-to-steering column retaining pin.

12. Install the vacuum hose, if equipped with cruise control.

13. Install the steering shaft protective sleeve.

14. Adjust the brake light switch.

15. Install the left sound insulator, connect the negative battery cable and check switch operation.

1993–96

1. Disconnect the negative battery cable.

2. Disconnect the brake light switch electrical connector.

3. Remove the brake light switch from the brake pedal bracket.

To install:

4. Install the brake light switch to the brake pedal bracket.

5. Connect the electrical connectors and the negative battery cable.

Clutch Switch

ADJUSTMENT

1. Disconnect the negative battery cable.

2. Remove the lower, left trim panel. Locate the switch on the clutch pedal support. Disconnect connector at switch and check for good connection. If connection is good, proceed with adjustment.

3. Pull back on the clutch pedal and push the switch through the retaining clip noting the clicks.

4. Repeat this procedure until no more clicks can be heard.

5. Reconnect negative battery cable.

REMOVAL AND INSTALLATION

1. Disconnect the negative cable from the battery.

2. Remove the lower left trim panel. Locate the switch on the clutch pedal support.

3. Disconnect the electrical connector from the switch and remove the switch by twisting it out of the tubular retaining clip.

4. Using a new retaining clip, install the switch and connect the electrical connector.

5. To adjust the switch, pull back on the clutch pedal, push the switch through the retaining clip noting the clicks; repeat this procedure until no clicks can be heard.

6. Connect the negative battery cable and check the switch operation.

Neutral Safety Switch

REMOVAL AND INSTALLATION

1. Apply park brake firmly and block the wheels. Place the selector lever in the **N** detent. Disconnect the negative battery cable.

2. Remove the air cleaner, as required.

3. Raise and safely support the vehicle.

4. Remove the switch harness.

5. Lower the vehicle.

6. Remove the vacuum lines and electrical connectors from the cruise control servo, if equipped.

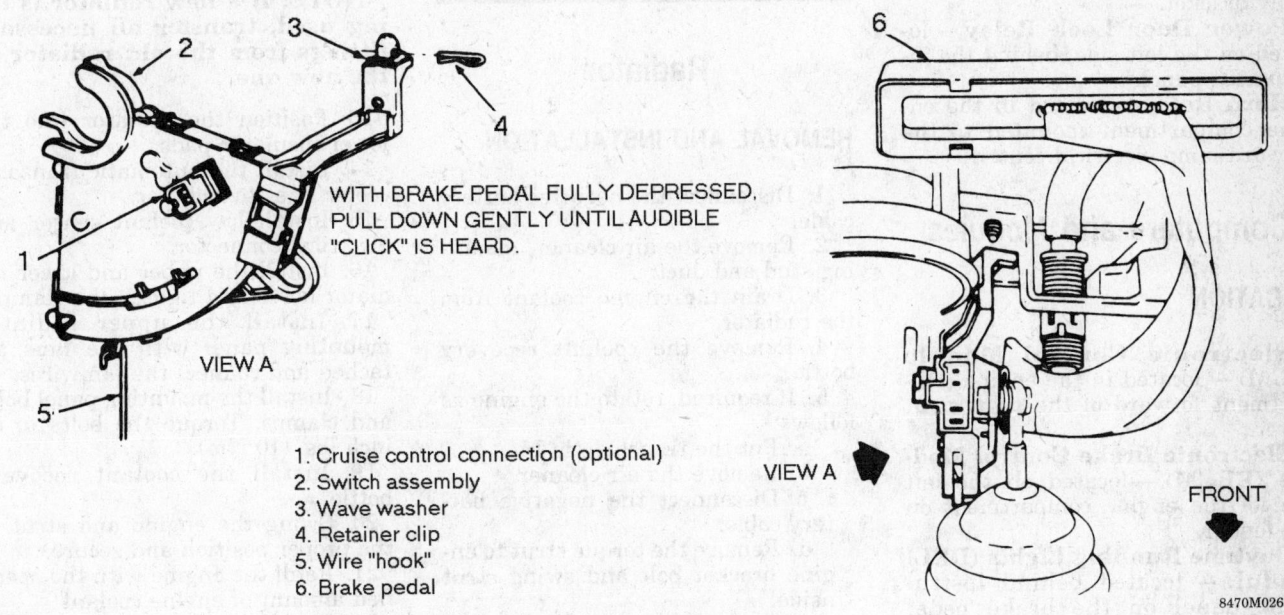

WITH BRAKE PEDAL FULLY DEPRESSED,
PULL DOWN GENTLY UNTIL AUDIBLE
"CLICK" IS HEARD.

VIEW A

VIEW A

FRONT

8470M026

1. Cruise control connection (optional)
2. Switch assembly
3. Wave washer
4. Retainer clip
5. Wire "hook"
6. Brake pedal

1992 Vehicle's brake light switch

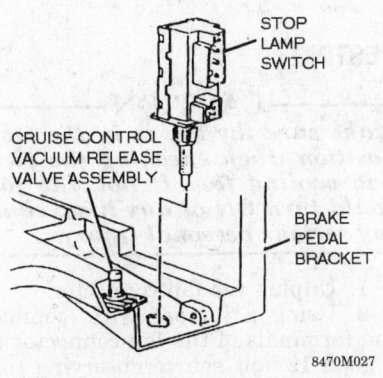

STOP LAMP SWITCH

CRUISE CONTROL VACUUM RELEASE VALVE ASSEMBLY

BRAKE PEDAL BRACKET

8470M027

1993–96 Vehicle's brake light switch

7. Remove the shift lever, cruise control servo and switch. Do not disconnect the lever from the cable.

To install:

8. Align the notch on the inner sleeve of the switch with the notch on the switch body.

9. Install the switch and tighten the bolts to 18 ft. lbs. (24 Nm).

10. Install the shift lever and tighten the nut to 15 ft. lbs. (20 Nm).

11. Raise and safely support the vehicle, connect the switch harness and lower the vehicle.

12. Install the cruise control servo, vacuum lines and electrical connectors, if equipped.

13. Install the air cleaner, as required and connect the negative battery cable.

14. After switch has been installed, verify that the engine will not start in any gear other than **P** or **N**. If engine will start in any other position, readjust switch and check again.

Fuses, Circuit Breakers and Relays

LOCATION

Fusible Links

Fusible links are in the following locations on the vehicle.

Starter solenoid terminal.
Wiring harness near the battery.
Electrical center in the engine compartment.

Fusible links are used to protect wiring in circuits that are not normally fused, such as the ignition circuit. In the event of an electrical overload, the fuse link will melt and create an open in the circuit. The fuse link is smaller than the wire it is to protect. The gauge size is marked on the insulation. The replacement fuse link must be the same size as the original link. To replace a damaged fuse link remove the wire section beyond the splice and splice the replacement link into the wiring harness.

Circuit Breakers

The majority of the circuit breakers are located in the fuse block. There are a few circuit breakers located in the convenience center, which is located under the right side of the instrument panel behind the right sound insulator.

Fuse Panel

The fuse panel is located on the right side of the instrument panel under the lower storage compartment on Cutlass Supreme or in the glove box on the remaining models.

Relays

Coolant Fan Relay — located in the engine compartment mounted to the right side of the firewall on the relay bracket.

Air Conditioner Compressor Relay — located in the engine compartment mounted to the right side of the firewall on the relay bracket.

High Blower Speed Relay — located in the engine compartment mounted to the right side of the firewall on the relay bracket.

Fuel Pump Relay — located in the engine compartment mounted to the right side of the firewall on the relay bracket.

Power Door Lock Relay — located on the left side, behind the instrument panel.

Horn Relay — located in the engine compartment mounted to the forward lamp electrical center.

Computers and Modules

LOCATION

Electronic Control Module (ECM) — located in the engine compartment forward of the right strut tower.

Electronic Brake Control Module (EBCM) — located on the left side of the engine compartment on the fender.

Daytime Running Lights (DRL) Module — located behind instrument panel on the brake pedal support.

Computer Controlled Coil Ignition (C₃I) Module — located on the right front of engine.

Flashers

LOCATION

Hazard Warning Flasher — in the convenience center located under the right side of the instrument panel behind the right sound insulator.

Turn Signal Flasher — located under the instrument panel to the right of the steering column.

Cruise Control

ADJUSTMENT

1. With the cable installed in the cable brackets, install cable end to throttle linkage.

2. Pull the servo end of the cable towards the servo as far as possible without moving the throttle.

3. Attach the cable to the servo in the closest alignment holes without moving the throttle.

NOTE: Do not stretch the cable to attach it to the servo. This will not allow the engine to return to idle.

4. Check the system operation and repeat the adjustment as necessary.

ENGINE COOLING

Radiator

REMOVAL AND INSTALLATION

1. Disconnect the negative battery cable.

2. Remove the air cleaner, mounting stud and duct.

3. Drain the engine coolant from the radiator.

4. Remove the coolant recovery bottle.

5. If required, rotate the engine as follows:

a. Put the transaxle in **N**.

b. Remove the air cleaner.

c. Disconnect the negative battery cable.

d. Remove the torque strut to engine bracket bolt and swing strut aside.

e. Replace the passenger side torque strut to engine bracket bolt in engine bracket.

f. Place a prybar in the bracket so it contacts the bracket and the bolt.

g. Rotate the engine by pulling forward on the prybar. Align the slave hole in the driver side torque strut to the engine bracket hole.

h. Retain the engine in this position using the torque strut to engine bracket bolt.

i. After repairs, pull forward on the prybar to take the weight off the torque strut to engine bracket bolt and remove bolt from the strut slave hole and engine bracket. Reverse the removal procedure. Tighten the strut to engine bracket bolt to 32 ft. lbs. (43 Nm).

NOTE: To prevent shearing of the rubber bushing, loosen the bolts on the engine strut before swinging the struts.

6. Remove the air intake resonator mounting nut, upper radiator mounting panel bolts and clamps.

7. Disconnect the cooling fan electrical connectors.

8. Remove the upper radiator mounting panel with the fans attached.

9. Remove the upper and lower radiator hoses.

10. Remove low coolant sensor and electrical connector, if used.

11. If equipped with automatic transaxle, disconnect the cooler lines from the radiator and plug.

12. Remove the radiator.

To install:

NOTE: If a new radiator is being used, transfer all necessary fittings from the old radiator to the new one.

13. Position the radiator into the lower insulator pads

14. Install the automatic transaxle cooler lines to radiator.

15. Install low coolant sensor and electrical connector.

16. Install the upper and lower radiator hoses and tighten the clamps.

17. Install the upper radiator mounting panel with the fans attached and connect the fan wires.

18. Install the mounting panel bolts and clamps. Torque the bolts to 89 inch lbs. (10 Nm).

19. Install the coolant recovery bottle.

20. Swing the engine and strut to the proper position and secure.

21. Refill the engine with the specified amount of engine coolant.

22. Install the air cleaner and negative battery cable. Start the engine and check for coolant leaks.

Electric Cooling Fan

TESTING

— CAUTION —
Make sure the key is in the OFF position when checking the electric cooling fan. If not, the fan could turn ON at any time, causing serious personal injury.

1. Unplug the fan connector.

2. Using a jumper wire, connect the terminals of the fan connector to a good 12 volt source observing correct polarity. The female terminal on the fan motor is normally the negative terminal.

3. The fan should come ON with the circuit completed and should run smoothly and free of vibrations.

4. If not, the fan is defective and should be replaced.

REMOVAL AND INSTALLATION

1. Disconnect the negative battery cable.

2. Remove coolant reservoir.

3. If required, rotate the engine as follows:

a. Put the transaxle in **N**.

b. Remove the air cleaner.

c. Disconnect the negative battery cable.

d. Remove the torque strut to engine bracket bolt and swing strut aside.

e. Replace the passenger side torque strut to engine bracket bolt in engine bracket.

f. Place a prybar in the bracket so it contacts the bracket and the bolt.

g. Rotate the engine by pulling forward on the prybar. Align the slave hole in the driver side torque strut to the engine bracket hole.

h. Retain the engine in this position using the torque strut to engine bracket bolt.

i. After repairs, pull forward on the prybar to take the weight off the torque strut to engine bracket bolt and remove bolt from the strut slave hole and engine bracket. Reverse the removal procedure. Tighten the strut to engine bracket bolt to 32 ft. lbs. (43 Nm).

NOTE: To prevent shearing of the rubber bushing, loosen the bolts on the engine strut before swinging the struts.

4. Disconnect the electrical wiring harness from the cooling fan frame.

5. Remove the fan assembly from the radiator support.

To install:

6. Install the fan assembly to the radiator support. Torque the fan assembly-to-radiator support bolts to 7 ft. lbs. (9.5 Nm). Attach electrical connector.

7. Install engine strut to proper position.

8. Reinstall coolant reservoir.

9. Attach the wiring harness and connect the negative battery cable.

Heater Core

REMOVAL AND INSTALLATION

Without Air Conditioning

1. Disconnect the negative battery cable.

2. Drain the cooling system.

3. Rotate the engine as follows:

   a. Put the transaxle in **N**.

   b. Remove the air cleaner.

   c. Disconnect the negative battery cable.

   d. Remove the torque strut to engine bracket bolt and swing strut aside.

   e. Replace the passenger side torque strut to engine bracket bolt in engine bracket.

   f. Place a prybar in the bracket so it contacts the bracket and the bolt.

g. Rotate the engine by pulling forward on the prybar. Align the slave hole in the driver's side torque strut to the engine bracket hole.

h. Retain the engine in this position using the torque strut to engine bracket bolt.

i. After repairs, pull forward on the prybar to take the weight off the torque strut to engine bracket bolt and remove bolt from the strut slave hole and engine bracket. Reverse the removal procedure. Tighten the strut to engine bracket bolt to 32 ft. lbs. (43 Nm).

NOTE: To prevent shearing of the rubber bushing, loosen the bolts on the engine strut before swinging the struts.

4. Remove the heater hose retaining nuts and the heater hose from core after loosening mubea clamps using tool J-38543 or equivalent.

5. Remove the right sound insulator panel and rear seat duct adapter.

6. Remove heater floor duct and lower left sound insulator panel.

7. Remove core cover screws and cover.

8. Remove core retaining bolts and core.

To install:

9. Install core and retaining bolts.

10. Install core cover and attaching screws.

11. Install lower left sound insulator panel, heater floor duct and rear seat duct adapter.

12. Reinstall right sound insulator panel.

13. Install heater hoses to core using mubea clamps and tool J-38543 or equivalent.

14. Reinstall heater hose retaining bracket nuts.

15. Refill with coolant using the proper solution and reconnect negative battery cable.

With Air Conditioning

1. Disconnect the negative battery cable.

2. Drain the cooling system.

3. Rotate the engine as follows:

   a. Put the transaxle in **N**.

   b. Remove the air cleaner.

   c. Disconnect the negative battery cable.

   d. Remove the torque strut to engine bracket bolt and swing strut aside.

   e. Replace the passenger side torque strut to engine bracket bolt in engine bracket.

f. Place a prybar in the bracket so it contacts the bracket and the bolt.

g. Rotate the engine by pulling forward on the prybar. Align the slave hole in the driver's side torque strut to the engine bracket hole.

h. Retain the engine in this position using the torque strut to engine bracket bolt.

i. After repairs, pull forward on the prybar to take the weight off the torque strut to engine bracket bolt and remove bolt from the strut slave hole and engine bracket. Reverse the removal procedure. Tighten the strut to engine bracket bolt to 32 ft. lbs. (43 Nm).

NOTE: To prevent shearing of the rubber bushing, loosen the bolts on the engine strut before swinging the struts.

4. Remove the upper firewall weatherstrip. Remove the upper secondary cowl and lower secondary cowl upper retaining nut.

5. Remove the heater hoses from the core.

6. Remove the heater core cover and remove the heater core.

To install:

7. Install the heater core and the heater core cover.

8. Install the sound insulator.

9. Attach the heater hoses to the core. Install the lower secondary cowl upper nut, the upper cowl and the weatherstrip.

10. Fill the cooling system and check for leaks. Connect the negative battery cable.

Water Pump

REMOVAL AND INSTALLATION

2.2L Engine

1. Disconnect the negative battery cable.

2. Drain the coolant from the cooling system.

3. Remove the serpentine drive belt as follows:

   a. Remove the coolant reservoir.

   b. Rotate the tensioner clockwise with a 15mm wrench and slide the belt off the alternator pulley.

   c. Release the tensioner and remove the belt.

4. Remove the water pump pulley attaching bolts and remove the water pump pulley.

5. Remove the alternator and the side bracket.

6. Disconnect the water pump hoses.

7. Remove the water pump attaching bolts and remove the water pump and the gasket.

To install:

8. Install the water pump and the water pump gasket. Install the water pump attaching bolts and tighten to 18 ft. lbs. (25 Nm).

9. Install the water pump pulley and tighten the pulley attaching bolts to 22 ft. lbs. (30 Nm).

10. Connect the water pump hoses.

11. Install the alternator and the alternator bracket.

12. Install the serpentine drive belt.

13. Refill the cooling system with coolant to the proper level.

14. Connect the negative battery cable and inspect for leaks.

2.5L Engine

1. Disconnect the negative battery cable.

2. Remove the alternator.

3. Remove the convenience center heat shield.

4. Drain about a gallon of engine coolant from the radiator. Enough to be below the water pump level.

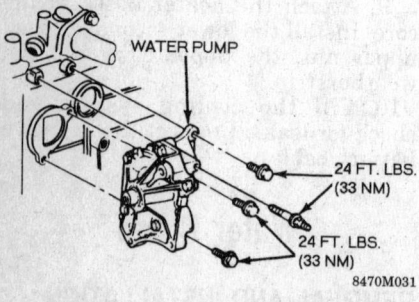

WATER PUMP

24 FT. LBS. (33 NM)

24 FT. LBS. (33 NM)

8470M031

Water pump mounting — 2.5L engine

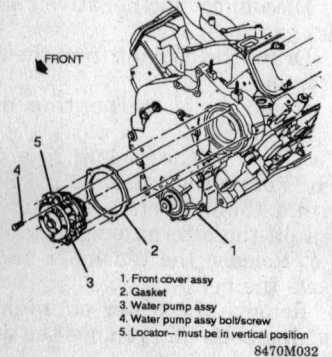

FRONT

1. Front cover assy
2. Gasket
3. Water pump assy
4. Water pump assy bolt/screw
5. Locator-- must be in vertical position

8470M032

Water pump mounting — 3.1L (VIN T) engine

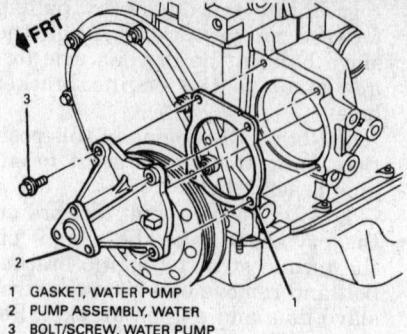

FRT

1 GASKET, WATER PUMP
2 PUMP ASSEMBLY, WATER
3 BOLT/SCREW, WATER PUMP

8569y001

Water pump assembly — 3.1L (VIN M) engine

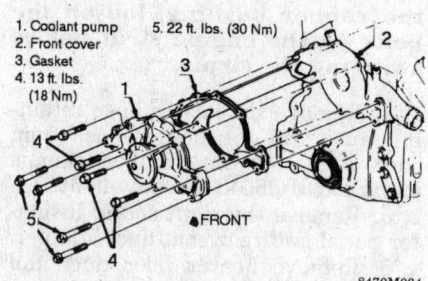

1. Coolant pump
2. Front cover
3. Gasket
4. 13 ft. lbs. (18 Nm)
5. 22 ft. lbs. (30 Nm)

FRONT

8470M034

Water pump mounting — 3.8L engine

5. Remove water pump-to-engine attaching bolts.

6. Remove the water pump and gasket.

7. Remove the pulley from the old pump, as required.

To install:

8. Clean the water pump mating surfaces.

9. Install the pump and pulley assembly onto the engine with a new gasket in place.

10. Install the water pump attaching bolts and torque to 24 ft. lbs. (33 Nm).

11. Apply sealer to the pump inlet and install. Install coolant pump inlet bolts and coolant pump hoses.

12. Install the convenience center heat shield, alternator and negative battery cable.

13. Refill the cooling system with the specified amount of engine coolant.

14. Start the engine and check for coolant leaks.

3.1L (VIN T) and 3.4L Engines

1. Disconnect the negative battery cable.

2. Remove the air cleaner assembly.

3. Drain about a gallon of engine coolant from the radiator. The level must be below the water pump level. If equipped with 3.4L engine, remove the coolant recovery tank.

4. Remove the serpentine belt.

5. Remove the pulley.

6. Remove water pump attaching bolts.

7. Remove the water pump and gasket.

To install:

8. Clean the water pump mounting surfaces.

9. Install the water pump with a new gasket in place.

10. Install the attaching bolts and torque to 89 inch lbs. (10 Nm).

11. Install the pulley, recovery tank and serpentine belt.

12. Refill the cooling system with the specified amount of engine coolant.

13. Connect the negative battery cable and the air cleaner assembly.

14. Start the engine and check for coolant leaks.

3.1L (VIN M) Engine

1. Disconnect the negative battery cable.

2. Drain cooling system.

3. Remove the serpentine drive belt.

4. Remove the pulley bolts and pulley.

5. Remove the water pump retaining bolts and water pump.

6. Installation is the reverse of removal. Clean the gasket mating surfaces, torque the pump retaining bolts to 18 ft. lbs. (25 Nm) and pulley bolts to 22 ft. lbs. (30 Nm).

3.8L Engine

1. Disconnect the negative battery cable.

2. Drain the engine coolant from the radiator.

3. Disconnect the coolant recovery reservoir.

4. Remove the serpentine belt.

NOTE: If more access is needed, remove the inner fender electrical cover.

5. Remove the pulley.

6. Remove water pump attaching bolts.

7. Remove the water pump and gasket.

To install:

8. Clean the water pump mounting surfaces.

9. Install the water pump with a new gasket.

10. Install the attaching bolts and torque the long bolts to 22 ft. lbs. (30

Nm) and the short bolts to 13 ft. lbs. (18 Nm).

11. Install the pulley and serpentine belt. Tighten the pulley to 115 inch lbs.

12. Reconnect the coolant recovery reservoir.

13. Refill the cooling system with the specified amount of engine coolant.

14. Install the negative battery cable.

15. Start the engine and check for coolant leaks.

Thermostat

REMOVAL AND INSTALLATION

2.2L Engine

1. Disconnect the negative battery cable.

2. Partially drain the cooling system.

3. Remove the 3 thermostat housing mounting nuts.

4. Remove the housing and the thermostat.

To install:

5. Completely clean all of the gasket material from the thermostat housing mating surfaces.

6. Install sealer and install the thermostat.

7. Install the thermostat housing and the 3 nuts.

8. Tighten the nuts to 89 inch lbs. (10 Nm).

9. Refill the coolant to the proper level and inspect for leaks.

2.5L Engine

1. Partially drain engine coolant from the radiator. Disconnect negative battery cable.

2. Remove the thermostat housing cap.

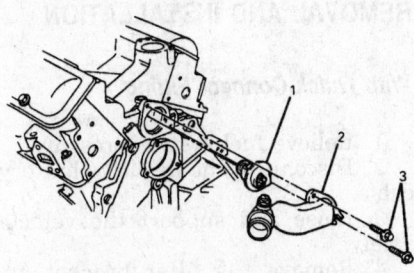

1 THERMOSTAT ASSEMBLY, ENGINE COOLANT
2 OUTLET ASSEMBLY, WATER
3 BOLT/SCREW, WATER OUTLET

8569y002

Thermostat assembly — 3.1L (VIN M) engine

3. Remove the thermostat by using the wire handle to lift it out of the housing.

To install:

4. Insert the thermostat and seal into the housing.

5. Install the thermostat housing cap and refill the engine with the proper amount of engine coolant. Reconnect negative battery cable.

6. Start engine and check for leaks.

3.1L (VIN T) and 3.4L Engines

1. Disconnect the negative battery cable. Drain 1 gallon of engine coolant from the radiator.

2. Remove the radiator hose from the water outlet.

3. Remove the water outlet attaching bolts and water outlet.

4. Remove the thermostat.

5. Clean the manifold water inlet and water outlet mating surfaces.

To install:

6. Position the thermostat into the inlet manifold.

7. Apply a 0.125 inch (3mm) bead of RTV sealer to the thermostat housing.

8. Install the water outlet to the inlet manifold. Torque the attaching bolts to 18 ft. lbs. (25 Nm).

9. Install the radiator hose to the water outlet housing.

10. Refill the engine with the specified engine coolant. Reconnect negative battery cable, start the engine and check for coolant leaks.

3.1L (VIN M) Engine

1. Disconnect the negative battery cable. Drain the cooling system.

2. Remove the radiator hose from the water outlet.

3. Remove the outlet nuts, outlet and thermostat.

To install:

4. Clean mating surfaces thoroughly. Apply a 1/8 inch (3mm) bead of suitable RTV sealant in the groove of the water outlet.

5. Install the thermostat with the spring toward the engine. Install the water outlet. Torque bolts to 89 inch lbs. (10 Nm).

6. Connect the negative battery cable.

7. Fill cooling system and check for leaks. Start the engine and allow it to come to normal operating temperature. Check for leaks. Fill coolant to proper level.

3.8L Engine

1. Drain about a 1/2 gallon of engine coolant from the radiator. Disconnect negative battery cable.

2. Remove the radiator hose from the water outlet.

3. Disconnect the electrical connections from the throttle body assembly.

4. Remove the water outlet attaching bolts and water outlet.

5. Remove the thermostat.

6. Clean the manifold water inlet and water outlet mating surfaces.

To install:

7. Position the thermostat into the intake manifold with a new gasket.

8. Install the water outlet to the intake manifold with RTV sealer. Torque the attaching bolts to 20 ft. lbs. (27 Nm).

9. Install the radiator hose to the water outlet housing.

10. Connect the electrical connections to the throttle body assembly.

11. Refill the engine with the specified engine coolant. Connect the negative battery cable, start the engine and check for coolant leaks.

COOLING SYSTEM BLEEDING

To insure complete filling of the cooling system, it is necessary to bleed the system.

1. Disconnect the negative battery cable.

2. Park vehicle on level surface.

3. Remove thermostat housing cap and thermostat or open bleed vents:

a. On 2.5L engine, remove the thermostat housing cap and thermostat.

b. On 3.1L engine, open the air bleed vents on the thermostat housing and the throttle body return pipe above coolant pump. Open vents 2–3 turns.

c. On 3.4L engine, open the air bleed vents on the thermostat housing and the heater coolant inlet pipe by the master brake cylinder. Open vents 2–3 turns.

d. On 3.8L engine, open air bleed vent on thermostat housing. Open 2–3 turns.

4. Fill cooling system with coolant to base of radiator neck .

5. Reinstall or replace the thermostat and housing and close air vents.

6. Fill coolant reservoir to proper level with ethylene glycol/water mixture.

7. Reconnect negative battery cable. Start vehicle and let engine reach operating temperature adding coolant as needed. Check the cooling system for leaks.

FUEL SYSTEM

Fuel System Service Precautions

Safety is the most important factor when performing not only fuel system maintenance but any type of maintenance. Failure to conduct maintenance and repairs in a safe manner may result in serious personal injury or death. Maintenance and testing of the vehicle's fuel system components can be accomplished safely and effectively by adhering to the following rules and guidelines.

• To avoid the possibility of fire and personal injury, always disconnect the negative battery cable unless the repair or test procedure requires that battery voltage be applied.

• Always relieve the fuel system pressure prior to disconnecting any fuel system component (injector, fuel rail, pressure regulator, etc.), fitting or fuel line connection. Exercise extreme caution whenever relieving fuel system pressure to avoid exposing skin, face and eyes to fuel spray. Please be advised that fuel under pressure may penetrate the skin or any part of the body that it contacts.

• Always place a shop towel or cloth around the fitting or connection prior to loosening to absorb any excess fuel due to spillage. Ensure that all fuel spillage (should it occur) is quickly removed from engine surfaces. Ensure that all fuel soaked cloths or towels are deposited into a suitable waste container.

• Always keep a dry chemical (Class B) fire extinguisher near the work area.

• Do not allow fuel spray or fuel vapors to come into contact with a spark or open flame.

• Always use a backup wrench when loosening and tightening fuel line connection fittings. This will prevent unnecessary stress and torsion to fuel line piping. Always follow the proper torque specifications.

• Always replace worn fuel fitting O-rings with new. Do not substitute fuel hose or equivalent where fuel pipe is installed.

RELIEVING FUEL SYSTEM PRESSURE

2.2L and 2.5L Engines

1. Remove the fuel filler cap.
2. Raise and safely support the vehicle.
3. Disconnect the fuel pump harness connector at the fuel pump electrical connector.
4. Lower the vehicle.
5. Start the engine and run until the engine stops due to the lack of fuel.
6. Crank the engine for 3 seconds to ensure all pressure is relieved.
7. Reconnect the fuel pump harness connector.
8. Disconnect the negative battery cable to prevent the build of fuel pressure in the event that the key accidentally is turned **ON**.

3.1L, 3.4L and 3.8L Engines

1. Disconnect the negative battery cable. Loosen fuel filler cap.
2. Connect fuel pressure gauge J–34730–1 or equivalent, to the fuel pressure connection.
3. Wrap a shop cloth around the fitting while connecting the gauge to catch any leaking fuel.
4. Install the bleed hose into an approved container and open the valve. Connect the negative battery cable.
5. When the repair to the fuel system is complete check all of the fittings for leaks.

Fuel Tank

REMOVAL AND INSTALLATION

------ **CAUTION** ------
To help avoid personal injury when vehicle is on a hoist, provide additional support for the vehicle on the opposite end from which components are being removed. This will reduce the possibility of the vehicle falling off the hoist.

If the nylon fuel feed system pressure or return pipe becomes kinked and cannot be straightened, they must be replaced.

1. Disconnect the negative battery cable.
2. Relieve fuel system pressure.
3. Raise and safely support vehicle.
4. Drain fuel from fuel tank.
5. Remove fuel filler vent hose from tank.

6. Remove rear fuel feed pipe from fuel filter and rear fuel return pipe assembly from return pipe and move aside.
7. Disconnect vapor hose from connection at front of tank.
8. Remove exhaust pipe heat shield bolts and shield. For more room between exhaust and tank, remove exhaust hangers (rubber). This will allow the exhaust to drop slightly.
9. Support tank and remove 2 front tank strap attaching bolts. Loosen rear bolts.
10. Lower tank slightly and disconnect electrical connector at meter and vapor hoses. Remove fuel tank from vehicle.
   To install:
11. With the aid of an assistant, position the tank in the vehicle. Install the tank straps and loosely install the front attaching bolts.
12. Connect the vapor hose, fuel sender electrical connector and retainer clips.
13. Tighten the rear fuel tank strap attaching bolts. Tighten all tank strap retainers to 35 ft. lbs. (47 Nm).
14. Connect the fuel filler hose to fuel tank.
15. Install the heat shield and secure with retainer screws.
16. Install the exhaust into the hangers, if removed.
17. Lower the vehicle. Add fuel and install the fuel filler cap.
18. Connect the negative battery cable.
19. Turn the ignition switch to the **ON** position for 2 seconds, then turn **OFF** for 10 seconds.
20. If equipped with 3.1L or 3.4L engines, perform the ECM idle learn procedure after the negative battery cable is connected.

Fuel Filter

REMOVAL AND INSTALLATION

With Quick-Connect Fitting

1. Relieve fuel system pressure.
2. Disconnect the negative battery cable.
3. Raise and support the vehicle safely.
4. Remove the filter bracket attaching screws and the filter bracket.
5. Disconnect the quick-connect fittings as follows:
   a. Grasp the filter and fuel line fitting. Twist the quick-connect fit-

ting ¼ turn in each direction to loosen any dirt within the fitting.

NOTE: Safety glasses should be worn when using compressed air or working with the fuel system, as flying dirt particles or fuel spray may cause eye injury.

b. Using compressed air, blow the dirt from the quick-connect fittings. Clean the filter connection and surrounding area before disconnecting to prevent possible contamination of the system.

c. Squeeze plastic tab on male end of connector and pull connection apart.

6. To reduce fuel spillage, place a shop towel over the fuel lines before disconnecting. Disconnect the fuel feed pipe nut from the fuel filter. Drain any fuel remaining in the filter into an approved gasoline container.

7. Inspect the fuel pipe O-ring for cuts, nicks or swelling and replace if necessary.

To install:

8. Apply a few drops of clean engine oil to the male tube end of the filter. Install a new plastic connector retainer on filter inlet.

9. Push the connectors together to cause the retaining tabs to snap into place. Once installed, pull on both ends of each connection to make sure they are secure.

10. Align the fuel filter on the frame and install the filter bracket attaching screws.

11. Install and tighten the fuel filter outlet nut to 22 ft. lbs. (30 Nm). Install and tighten the fuel filler cap.

12. Connect the negative battery cable. Turn the ignition **ON** for 2 seconds and then turn to **OFF** for 10 seconds. Again turn the key **ON** and check for fuel leaks.

13. If equipped with the 3.1L or 3.4L engine, perform the Idle Learn procedure to allow the ECM memory to be updated with the correct IAC valve pintle position for a stable idle speed.

a. Install a Tech 1 scan tool.

b. Turn the ignition to the **ON** position, engine not running.

c. Select IAC SYSTEM, then IDLE LEARN in the MISC TEST mode.

d. Proceed with idle learn as directed by the scan tool.

Except Quick Connect Fitting

1. Relieve fuel system pressure.
2. Disconnect the negative battery cable.
3. Raise and support the vehicle safely.

4. Disconnect the fuel lines from the filter.
5. Remove the clamp and filter from the vehicle.

To install:

6. Loosely install the new filter. Using new O-ring seals, install the fuel lines to the filter.

7. Use a backup wrench to prevent the filter from turning and O-ring damage. Torque the fittings to 16 ft. lbs. (22 Nm).

8. Secure the filter to the vehicle. Tighten fuel filler cap.

9. Reconnect the negative battery cable. Lower the vehicle and start the engine to check for fuel leaks.

Electric Fuel Pump

PRESSURE TESTING

2.5L Engine

1. With the ignition **OFF**, release the fuel pressure and check for fuel in the tank.

2. Connect a fuel pressure gauge J–29658–B or equivalent, to the service fitting. Jump the fuel pump test terminal to 12 volts using a fused jumper wire.

3. With the key in the **ON** position and engine NOT running, the pressure should be 26–32 psi (179–220 kPa).

4. Listen to the pump running in the tank. If the pump is running, check for obstructed fuel filter, lines or pressure regulator.

Except 2.5L Engine

1. Release the fuel system pressure. Wrap a shop towel around fuel pressure connector on the fuel rail to absorb any leakage that may occur when installing gauge.

2. Connect a fuel pressure gauge J–34730–1 or equivalent, to the service fitting.

3. With the ignition switch **ON** and engine NOT running, the fuel pump pressure should be 40–47 psi (280–325 kPa) and hold steady when the engine is turned OFF.

REMOVAL AND INSTALLATION

1. Release the fuel system pressure. Disconnect the negative battery cable.

2. Drain all fuel from the fuel tank.

3. Raise and safely support the vehicle. Support the fuel tank and remove the retaining straps.

4. Lower the fuel tank slightly and disconnect the fuel lines, hoses and the sending unit electrical connectors.

5. Remove the tank from the vehicle.

6. Remove the sending unit retaining cam using tool J–35731 or equivalent and remove the sending unit assembly from the tank.

7. Support the pump with 1 hand and grasp the strainer with the other hand. Rotate the strainer in 1 direction and pull off pump.

8. Disconnect the fuel pump electrical connector. Place the sender assembly upside down on a bench. Pull the fuel pump downward to remove from the mounting bracket, then tilt pump outward and remove from fuel pulse dampener.

9. Inspect the pump strainer. If the strainer is contaminated, the fuel tank must be flushed.

To install:

10. Install the rubber bumper and insulator onto the fuel pump, if removed. Position the fuel pump sender assembly upside down. Install the fuel pump between the fuel pulse dampener and mounting bracket. Connect the fuel pump electrical connector.

NOTE: Always install a new pump strainer when installing fuel pump.

11. Position new pump strainer on fuel pump and push on outer edge of ferrule until fully seated.

12. Install the sender assembly retainer cam using tool J–35731 or equivalent.

13. Replace O-ring on pump assembly and install the unit into the tank.

14. Raise the tank into position and attach all fuel lines, hoses and electrical connectors to the tank.

NOTE: If equipped with quick-connect fittings, lubricate the male tube ends with clean engine oil prior to connecting line fittings. This will insure proper reconnection and prevent a possible fuel leak.

15. Install the retaining straps. Tighten the tank retaining strap bolts to 35 ft. lbs. (47 Nm).

16. Lower the vehicle and refill the tank. Connect the negative battery cable.

17. Turn the ignition **ON** for 2 seconds, then turn ignition **OFF** and check for leaks. Start vehicle and recheck for leaks.

18. If equipped with the 3.1L or 3.4L engine, perform the idle learn procedure to allow the ECM memory

to be updated with the correct IAC valve pintle position for a stable idle speed.

Fuel Injection

IDLE SPEED ADJUSTMENT

Idle speed and mixture are electronically controlled by the ECM. No adjustments are possible.

Fuel Injector

REMOVAL AND INSTALLATION

2.2L Engine

1. Relieve the fuel system pressure and disconnect the negative battery cable.
2. Remove the upper manifold assembly as follows:
  a. Remove the air intake duct.
  b. Remove the accelerator cable splash shield from the bracket.
  c. Disconnect the accelerator, cruise and transaxle control cables.
  d. Disconnect the vacuum hose harness from the top of the air inlet.
  e. Disconnect the crankcase ventilation valve and power brake vacuum hoses from the vacuum tubes at the upper manifold. Position the hoses aside.
  f. Disconnect the electrical connectors at the MAP and TP sensors and the IAC valve.
  g. Remove the bolts and nuts that attach the throttle cable bracket. Move the cables and the bracket aside.
  h. Remove the bolts/studs that attach the upper manifold to the lower manifold.
  i. Remove the upper manifold and the gasket.
3. Remove the fuel line retaining bracket nut and remove the bracket. Move the fuel line away from the regulator.
4. Remove the fuel pressure regulator assembly.
5. Remove the fuel injector retainer bracket attaching screws and remove the retainer bracket by carefully sliding it off.
6. Disconnect the fuel injector electrical connectors and remove the injectors.

—————— CAUTION ——————

Make sure when the injector is removed the small O-ring does not remain in the lower manifold. If the old O-ring is left in place, the new injector will not seat properly and fuel leakage may occur.

To install:
7. Lubricate the new injector O-ring seals with clean engine oil and install to the injector assembly.

NOTE: Make sure the replacement injector is an identical part. The injectors from other systems may fit but are calibrated for different flow rates.

8. Install the fuel injector to the lower manifold assembly with the electrical connectors facing inward.
9. Carefully install the injector retainer bracket so the injector retaining slots and regulator are aligned with the bracket slots.
10. Connect the fuel injector electrical connectors and install the pressure regulator assembly.
11. Install the injector retainer bracket attaching screws.
12. Install the upper manifold assembly. Tighten the upper manifold mounting nuts/studs to 22 ft. lbs. (30 Nm).
13. Connect the accelerator cable bracket with the attaching nuts and bolts.
14. Tighten the fuel filler cap and connect the negative battery cable.

2.5L Engine

1. Release fuel system pressure. Disconnect the negative battery cable.
2. Remove the air intake duct and disconnect the electrical connector to the fuel injector.
3. Remove the injector screw and retainer.
4. Using a fulcrum, place a prybar under the ridge opposite the connector end and carefully pry the injector out of the cavity.
5. Remove the upper and lower O-rings from the injector and cavity.
6. Inspect the injector and fuel lines for dirt and contamination. If excess contamination is present, the fuel system will have to be flushed.

NOTE: Make sure the replacement injector is an identical part. The injectors from other model 700 systems may fit but are calibrated for different flow rates. Check the part number on the side of the throttle body.

To install:
7. Lubricate the new upper and lower O-rings with clean engine oil and place them on the injector. Make sure the upper O-ring is in the groove

and the lower one is flush against the filter.
8. Install the injector into the cavity by pushing straight into the fuel injector cavity.
9. Install the injector retainer and coat the screw with thread locking compound. Tighten the attaching screw to 27 inch lbs. (3.0 Nm).
10. Connect the injector electrical connector and negative battery cable.

3.1L Engine

1. Relieve the pressure in the fuel system.
2. Disconnect the negative terminal from the battery. Remove the air inlet tube.
3. Label and disconnect the vacuum lines from the plenum.
4. Remove the EGR valve from the plenum.
5. Remove the 2 throttle body-to-plenum bolts and the throttle body.
6. Remove the throttle cable bracket bolts. Disconnect the vacuum line from the fuel pressure regulator.
7. Remove the ignition wire shield.
8. Remove the plenum-to-intake manifold mounting bolts and the plenum.
9. Remove the fuel line bracket bolt and disconnect the fuel lines from the fuel rail. Wrap a rag around the lines to collect the excess fuel. Dispose of the rag properly.
10. Remove and discard the fuel line O-rings.
11. Disconnect the electrical connectors from the fuel injectors.
12. Remove the fuel rail assembly with the injectors.
13. Remove the fuel injector-to-fuel rail retaining clip, the fuel injectors and O-rings.

To install:
14. Install new O-rings on the spray tip of each injector and install to the rail. Secure the injector to the rail using the retainer clip. Make sure the open end of the clip faces towards the wire connector.
15. Lubricate the new O-rings on the fuel injector and install assembly on engine. Torque the fuel rail-to-intake manifold bolts to 8 ft. lbs. (10 Nm).
16. Connect the fuel lines to the fuel rail. Attach the electrical connectors to the injectors.
17. Install the plenum to manifold bolts and tighten and the plenum bolts to 16 ft. lbs. (22 Nm).
18. Install the throttle body to the plenum. Install the EGR valve. Reconnect all vacuum and electrical leads. Install the air inlet tube.

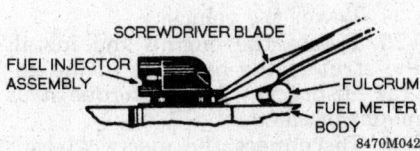

Fuel injector removal — 2.5L engine

19. Connect the negative battery cable.

3.4L Engine

1. Disconnect the negative battery cable. Relieve fuel system pressure.
2. Remove upper manifold assembly as follows:

   a. Drain cooling system below intake manifold.

   b. Disconnect throttle and cruise control cables from throttle lever. Remove air cleaner assembly and duct.

   c. Remove power brake and PCV vacuum hoses from upper manifold.

   d. Remove electrical connectors from IAC valve, TPS, MAP sensor and EGR valve.

   e. Disconnect the crankcase vent hose from the front of the camshaft cover. Disconnect the vacuum hose from the vacuum module located under the MAP sensor.

   f. Remove the bolts retaining the engine identification cover and remove the cover from the engine.

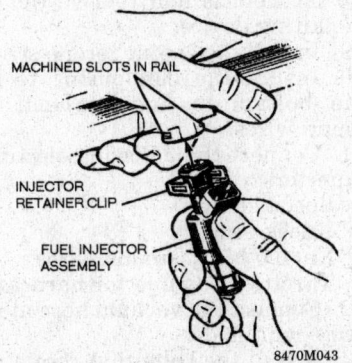

Installation of the fuel injector — 3.1L engine

g. Remove retaining bolts and EGR tube from adapter. Remove bolt retaining coolant tube to throttle cable bracket.

h. Remove fuel pipe retainer bolt, heater hoses, vacuum hoses and electrical connections from manifold.

i. Disconnect spark plug wires from 2 rear cylinders on both sides of engine. Label for proper installation.

j. Remove the upper manifold retaining bolts and rear mounting nuts and extract manifold from engine.

3. Disconnect the fuel supply lines at the fuel rail. Disconnect the vacuum lines at the fuel pressure regulator.

4. Remove the fuel rail retaining bolts. Disconnect the electrical harness connectors from each injector and remove the fuel rail assembly from the engine.

5. Remove the retaining clips from the injector and discard. Remove the injector. Remove and discard the O-ring located on both ends of the injector assembly.

To install:

6. Lubricate the new fuel injector O-rings with clean engine oil and install onto the fuel injector assembly. Install the injector to the fuel rail, pushing in far enough to engage the new retainer clips. Position open end of new injector retainer clip facing injector wire connector.

7. Attach rail to manifold and torque the fuel rail to manifold bolts to 88 inch lbs. (10.0 Nm).

8. Install upper manifold assembly reversing the removal steps above making sure to follow torque guide for fasteners:

   a. Upper manifold bolts to 18 ft. lbs. (24 Nm)

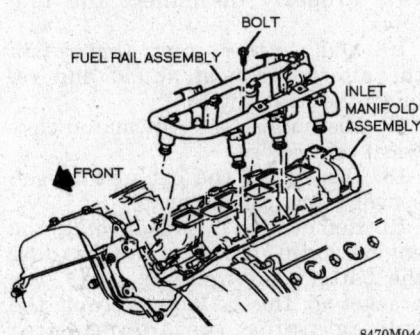

Fuel rail removal — 3.4L engine

b. Upper manifold nuts to 18 ft. lbs. (24 Nm)

c. Throttle cable bracket bolts to 18 ft. lbs. (24 Nm)

d. Fuel pipe nuts to 22 ft. lbs. (30 Nm)

e. Fuel rail attaching bolts to 88 inch lbs. (10 Nm)

f. EGR valve attaching bolts to 18 ft. lbs. (24 Nm)

9. Reconnect negative battery cable. Turn ignition **ON** for 3 seconds and the return to the **OFF** position. Check for fuel system for leaks. Refill cooling system, run engine until operating temperature is reached, check for coolant leaks and refill system as required.

3.8L Engine

1. Properly relieve the fuel system pressure. Remove the air cleaner assembly. Disconnect the negative battery cable.

2. Label and disconnect the fuel injector electrical connectors.

3. Disconnect the fuel feed and return lines at the fuel rail.

4. Disconnect the vacuum hose at the fuel pressure regulator.

5. Remove the fuel rail retaining bolts and remove the fuel rail assembly from the intake manifold.

6. Separate the injector from the fuel rail by removing the fuel injector retainer clip and pulling injector from the fuel rail pod.

To install:

7. Install new O-rings onto the fuel injector assembly. Lubricate the O-rings with clean oil to aid in installation.

8. Install the injector into the fuel rail pod and install retainer clip.

9. Lubricate the O-rings on the spray ends of the injectors and install the rail onto the intake manifold.

10. Install the fuel rail mounting bolts and tighten to 7–14 ft. lbs. (10–20 Nm).

11. Connect the electrical connections at each injector.

12. Apply a few drops of clean engine oil to the male end of the fuel rail inlet and outlet pipes. Connect the fuel feed and return lines.

13. Install the vacuum lines to the fuel pressure regulator.

14. Connect the negative battery cable. Turn ignition **ON** for 3 seconds and the return to the **OFF** position. Check for fuel system for leaks.

EMISSION CONTROLS

Emission Warning Lamps

Resetting

When the ECM finds a problem, the "Check Engine/Service Engine Soon" light will turn ON and a trouble code will be recorded in the ECM memory. If the problem is intermittent, the "Check Engine/Service Engine Soon" light turn OFF after 10 seconds, when the fault goes away. However, the trouble code will stay in the ECM memory until the battery voltage to the ECM is removed. Removing the battery voltage for 10 seconds will clear all stored trouble codes. This is done by disconnecting the ECM harness from the positive battery pigtail for 10 seconds with the ignition OFF or by disconnecting the ECM fuse, designated ECM or ECM/BAT, from the fuse holder.

NOTE: To prevent ECM damage, the ignition switch must be OFF when disconnecting or reconnecting power to ECM (for example battery cable, ECM pigtail, ECM fuse, jumper cables, etc.).

Whenever the battery is disconnected, if equipped with 3.1L or 3.4L engine, an idle learn procedure should be performed to allow the ECM memory to be updated with the correct IAC valve pintle position for a stable idle speed.
1. Place the transaxle in **N** or **P**.
2. Install a Tech 1 scan tool.
3. Turn the ignition to the **ON** position, engine not running.
4. Select IAC SYSTEM, then IDLE LEARN in the MISC TEST mode.
5. Proceed with idle learn as directed by the scan tool.

ENGINE MECHANICAL

Engine Assembly

REMOVAL AND INSTALLATION

2.2L Engine

1. Relieve the fuel system pressure and disconnect the negative battery cable.
2. Mark the position of the hood hinges to aid in installation. Remove the hood hinge bolts and the hood with aid from an assistant.
3. Remove the air cleaner and the duct assembly.
4. Drain the coolant into the drain pan.
5. Remove the engine torque strut assembly.
6. Remove the air intake silencer assembly.
7. Remove the coolant recovery reservoir.
8. Disconnect the upper radiator hose from the engine.
9. Remove the lower radiator hose at the water pump at the rear of the engine.
10. Disconnect the brake booster vacuum hose at the intake manifold.
11. Disconnect the throttle control cables at the throttle body.
12. Remove the serpentine drive belt.
13. Disconnect the electrical connection and the retaining screws at the right side engine cooling fan and fan.
14. Remove the power steering pump.
15. Properly disconnect the fuel lines.
16. Remove the screws that retain the alternator heat shield and remove the heat shield.
17. Disconnect the alternator electrical connectors.
18. Disconnect the exhaust oxygen sensor electrical connector.
19. Remove the nuts that retain the engine torque strut mount bracket, the battery cable/ground wires, the bracket at the bellhousing and the bolt retaining the torque strut bracket at the engine lift bracket.
20. Raise and safely support the vehicle.
21. Remove the flywheel inspection cover and remove the flywheel to torque converter retaining bolts.
22. Remove the engine mount to frame nuts.
23. Disconnect the front exhaust pipe from the exhaust manifold.
24. Lower the vehicle.
25. Rotate the engine and install the strut to the bolt hole in the engine lift bracket and the torque strut mount bracket.
26. Disconnect the electrical connections at the starter motor, including the ground wire.
27. Properly discharge the air conditioning system. Remove the bolts that retain the A/C compressor to the mount bracket and set the compressor aside.
28. Remove the bolts that retain the engine to the transaxle bracket at the bracket.
29. Disconnect the vacuum hose at the intake manifold.
30. Disconnect the following electrical connectors:
   • Speed sensor
   • Knock sensor
   • Engine block ground wires
   • Throttle body/injector harness
31. Remove the bellhousing to engine bolts/nuts and disconnect the ground wires.
32. Remove the engine torque struts.
33. Install an engine lifting/support device to the engine.
34. Begin lifting the engine out with the engine lifting device.
35. Disconnect the electrical connections at the electronic ignition module.
36. Completely remove the engine from the vehicle.
   To install:
37. Lower the engine into the vehicle and connect the electrical connections at the ignition module.
38. Completely lower the engine into the vehicle and remove the engine lifting device.
39. Install the engine torque struts.
40. Install the bellhousing to engine bolts/nuts and connect the ground wires.
41. Connect the following electrical connectors:
   • Speed sensor
   • Knock sensor
   • Engine block ground wires
   • Throttle body/injector harness
42. Connect the vacuum hose at the intake manifold.
43. Install the bolts that retain the engine to the transaxle bracket at the bracket.
44. Install the bolts that retain the A/C compressor to the mount bracket and properly recharge the air conditioning system.

45. Connect the electrical connections at the starter motor, including the ground wire.

46. Rotate the engine and remove the strut to the bolt hole in the engine lift bracket and the torque strut mount bracket.

47. Raise the vehicle.

48. Connect the front exhaust pipe to the exhaust manifold.

49. Install the engine mount to frame nuts.

50. Install the flywheel mounting bolts and the flywheel inspection cover.

51. Lower the vehicle.

52. Install the nuts that retain the engine torque strut mount bracket, the battery cable/ground wires, the bracket at the bellhousing and the bolt retaining the torque strut bracket at the engine lift bracket.

53. Connect the exhaust oxygen sensor electrical connector.

54. Connect the alternator electrical connectors.

55. Install the alternator heat shield and the screws that retain the alternator heat shield.

56. Connect the fuel lines and install the power steering pump.

57. Connect the electrical connection and the retaining screws at the right side engine cooling fan and fan.

58. Install the serpentine drive belt.

59. Connect the throttle control cables at the throttle body.

60. Connect the brake booster vacuum hose at the intake manifold.

61. Install the lower radiator hose at the water pump at the rear of the engine.

62. Connect the upper radiator hose to the engine and install the coolant recovery reservoir.

63. Install the air intake silencer assembly.

64. Install the engine torque strut assembly.

65. Refill the coolant to the proper level.

66. Install the air cleaner and the duct assembly.

67. With the aid of an assistant, install the hood while aligning the previously marked position.

68. Connect the negative battery cable.

2.5L Engine

1. Disconnect the negative battery cable.

2. Place drain pan under the radiator drain valve and drain the engine coolant.

3. Remove the air cleaner assembly. Release fuel system pressure.

4. Mark the hood hinges with a scribe and remove the hood assembly.

5. Mark and remove all engine wiring. Place all the wire assemblies aside.

6. Remove the vacuum, heater and radiator hoses labeling for location.

7. Remove the air conditioning compressor from the engine and place to the side with a piece of rope or wire. Do not disconnect the hoses from the compressor.

8. Remove the alternator and bracket.

9. Remove the engine torque strut.

10. Remove the throttle and transaxle linkage.

11. Remove the transaxle-to-engine bolts except the 2 upper bolts.

12. Raise the vehicle and support it safely.

13. Remove the engine mount-to-frame bolts.

14. Remove the exhaust pipe from the manifold.

15. Remove the torque converter-to-flywheel bolts.

16. Remove the starter motor.

17. Remove the power steering pump and attach to the inner fender with a piece of rope or wire. Do not disconnect the hoses.

18. Release fuel pressure, if not done prior, and remove the fuel lines at the throttle body assembly.

19. Remove the rear engine support bracket.

20. Support the transaxle assembly with a transaxle holding fixture.

21. Disconnect the transaxle from the engine and support with a jack.

22. Attach an appropriate engine lifting device securely to the engine.

23. Remove the engine assembly.

24. Place the engine on a workstand.

To install:

25. Place the engine assembly onto an appropriate lifting device.

26. With the aid of an assistant, install the engine into the vehicle.

27. Position the engine into the engine mounts and engage the transaxle with the engine.

28. Remove the engine lifting device.

29. Install the torque converter bolts and engine-to-transaxle mounting bolts. Torque the torque converter bolts to 55 ft. lbs. (75 Nm).

30. Remove the transaxle holding fixture.

31. Install the rear support bracket bolts.

32. Install the engine mount nuts and torque to 32 ft. lbs. (43 Nm).

33. Install the rear transaxle mount bracket bolts and torque to 35 ft. lbs. (47 Nm).

34. Install the fuel lines to the throttle body assembly.

35. Install the power steering pump.

36. Install the starter motor assembly.

37. Install the flywheel cover plate.

38. Install the exhaust pipe-to-manifold.

39. Install the engine torque strut.

40. Install the alternator and bracket.

41. Install the air conditioning compressor.

42. Install the heater, radiator and vacuum hoses.

43. Install the throttle and transaxle linkages.

44. Install and reconnect all engine wiring harnesses.

45. Install the hood assembly to its original position with an assistant.

46. Refill the cooling system with engine coolant.

47. Reconnect the negative battery cable.

48. Install the air cleaner assembly.

49. Inspect for proper fluid levels.

50. Recheck every procedure for proper reinstallation.

51. Start the vehicle and check for fluid leaks.

3.1L (VIN T) and 3.4L Engines

1. Remove the air cleaner and duct assembly.

2. Disconnect the negative battery cable.

3. Mark the hood hinges to ensure proper reinstallation. With the help of an assistant, remove the hood retaining bolt and remove hood from the vehicle.

4. Mark and remove all necessary engine wiring and place the harnesses aside.

5. Remove the throttle, TV and cruise control cables, if equipped, from the throttle body assembly.

6. Release the fuel pressure and remove the fuel lines at engine.

7. Remove the AIR pump and serpentine belt.

8. Position drain pan under the radiator drain valve and drain the engine coolant. Remove coolant recovery tank. Remove the cooling fans.

9. Remove the upper and lower radiator hoses and heater hose quick connect at intake manifold.

10. Discharge the air conditioning system using the appropriate equipment. Remove the air conditioning compressor mounting bolts at the front mounting bracket.

11. Remove the power steering pump and move to the side. Attach to the body with a piece of wire or rope. Do not disconnect the pump hoses.

12. Remove the heater hoses from the engine and move aside.

13. Remove the brake booster vacuum hose.

14. Remove the EGR hose from the exhaust manifold. Remove pipe from EGR valve, if equipped.

15. Raise the vehicle and support it safely.

16. Remove the air conditioning compressor from the engine and attach to the body with a piece of rope or wire. The factory recommends removal of the air conditioning manifold from compressor.

17. Remove the right front tire and wheel. Remove the right front splash shield.

18. Disconnect right ball joint nut and separate from control arm.

19. Remove halfshaft assembly. Disconnect any remaining electrical connectors at the back of the engine.

20. Remove the flywheel cover, starter motor and torque converter bolts. Matchmark the converter to driveplate to aid installation.

21. Remove the transaxle bracket and front engine mount nuts.

22. Remove the exhaust pipe and converter assembly from manifold.

23. Lower the vehicle.

24. Remove the torque struts.

25. Remove the exhaust crossover.

26. Disconnect the bulkhead electrical connector and quick connects near Electronic Control Module (ECM).

27. Disconnect the electrical connectors at the alternator assembly.

28. Support the transaxle with floor jack or equivalent.

29. Remove the remaining transaxle-to-engine bolts.

30. Attach an engine lifting device and remove the engine from the vehicle. Check for connected wires and hoses as the engine is coming out of the body.

31. Place the engine on a workstand.

To install:

32. With an assistant, install a lifting device onto the engine and position into the vehicle.

33. Remove the lifting device.

34. Install the transaxle-to-engine bolts.

35. Remove the transaxle support.

36. Reconnect the right crossover pipe-to-manifold clamp.

37. Reconnect the bulkhead electrical connector.

38. Reconnect electrical connector at ECM.

39. Install the left crossover pipe-to-manifold clamp.

40. Install the coolant recovery bottle and torque struts.

41. Raise the vehicle and support it safely.

42. Reinstall halfshaft assembly.

43. Reconnect ball joint to control arm.

44. Reinstall tire and wheel. Torque to 100 ft. lbs.

45. Reconnect ABS electrical connector if equipped.

46. Install the crossover pipe and converter assembly.

47. Install the front engine mount retaining nuts and torque to 32 ft. lbs. (43 Nm).

48. Install the transaxle bracket, torque converter bolts and starter motor.

49. Install the flywheel cover.

50. Install the air conditioning compressor to engine.

51. Lower the vehicle.

52. Install the EGR pipe and hose to valve.

53. Reconnect the brake booster vacuum supply, heater hoses and power steering pump.

54. Install the air conditioning compressor front mounting bracket bolts.

55. Install the radiator hoses and fans, serpentine and AIR pump belts. Recharge as required.

56. Reconnect the fuel lines. Install coolant recovery tank.

57. Install the throttle, TV and cruise control linkage to the throttle body.

58. Reconnect all necessary engine electrical and ground wiring.

59. Install the hood assembly with an assistant.

60. Reconnect the battery cables.

61. Turn the ignition **ON** for 3 seconds and then return to **OFF** position. Check for fuel leaks. Repeat this procedure a second time.

62. Install the air cleaner and duct assembly.

63. Recheck all procedures for proper reinstallation and correct if necessary.

64. Refill the engine with engine oil, coolant and transaxle fluid, if needed.

65. Inspect vehicle for fluid leaks before and after starting the engine.

66. Road test the vehicle and recheck for fluid leaks.

3.1L (VIN M) Engine

1. Disconnect the battery cables and remove the air cleaner assembly.

2. Scribe the bolt locations and remove the hood with the help of an assistant.

3. Remove the heater and radiator hoses from the engine. Remove the engine torque strut at the radiator support.

4. Remove the serpentine belt from the engine.

5. Relieve the fuel system pressure. Disconnect the throttle body bracket, cables and fuel and coolant hoses.

6. Label and disconnect the electrical connections from the engine.

7. Label and disconnect the vacuum lines from the engine.

8. Disconnect the power steering lines and remove the power steering brace.

9. Remove the coolant reservoir and 2 upper A/C compressor upper bolts.

10. Disconnect the electrical connectors from the transaxle.

11. Remove the 4 upper transaxle-to-engine mounting bolts.

12. Raise the vehicle and safely support.

13. Disconnect the exhaust pipe from the manifold.

14. Remove the oil drip shield, flywheel cover and starter motor.

15. Disconnect all electrical connections from the engine.

16. Remove the flywheel-to-converter bolts.

17. Remove the A/C compressor and position aside. Do not disconnect the refrigerant lines.

18. Install a transaxle support bracket and remove the remaining transaxle bolts.

19. Remove the engine mounts and 2 remaining transaxle bolts.

20. Lower the vehicle install an approved engine lifting device.

21. Remove the engine assembly slowly and check that all components are disconnected and free from obstruction. Place the engine on a work stand.

To install:

22. Lower the engine into the vehicle and start 2 transaxle-to-engine bolts.

23. Remove the transaxle support tool.

24. Install the remaining transaxle bolts.

25. Install the engine mounts, transaxle support bracket and bolts.

26. Position the A/C compressor and tighten the bolts.

27. Install the flywheel-to-converter bolts and torque to 53 ft. lbs. (71 Nm).

28. Connect the engine grounds to the transaxle mounting bolts. Connect all accessible electrical connectors to the engine.

29. Install the starter motor, flywheel cover and oil drip shield.

30. Install the exhaust pipe-to-manifold and torque to 18 ft. lbs. (25 Nm).

31. Install the upper A/C compressor bolts, coolant reservoir and power steering brace and lines.

32. Connect all vacuum and electrical connections to the engine.

33. Connect the fuel lines and install the throttle body bracket and cable.

34. Connect the heater and radiator hoses.

35. Install the serpentine belt.

36. With the help of an assistant, install the hood to its original position.

37. Connect the battery cables, refill all engine fluids to the proper level and install the air cleaner.

38. Start the engine and check for leaks.

3.8L Engine

1. Disconnect the negative battery cable.

2. Remove the air cleaner assembly.

3. Release the fuel system pressure.

4. Disconnect the fuel lines from the rail and mounting brackets.

5. Drain the engine coolant and remove the recovery bottle.

6. Remove the inner fender electrical cover and the fuel injector sight cover.

7. Disconnect the throttle cables from the throttle body and mounting bracket.

8. Remove the rear heat shield from the crossover pipe.

9. Remove the throttle cable mounting bracket and vacuum line as an assembly.

10. Disconnect the exhaust crossover from the manifolds.

11. Disconnect the engine torque strut bolt and strut from the engine.

12. Remove the right side engine cooling fan.

13. Disconnect the vacuum line to the transaxle module.

14. Remove the serpentine belt.

15. Remove the power steering pump and alternator assemblies.

16. Tag and disconnect all electrical connections from the engine.

17. Disconnect the upper and lower radiator, and heater hoses from the engine.

18. Remove the transaxle to engine bolts and ground wire harness.

19. Raise and support the vehicle safely.

20. Remove the right front wheel and inner splash shield.

21. Remove the flywheel cover, scribe a mark on the torque converter and flywheel and remove the flywheel to torque converter bolts.

22. Disconnect the wire harness clamps from the frame near the radiator.

23. Remove the air conditioner compressor from the bracket, lay aside and secure to the frame.

24. Disconnect the wires and remove the starter motor assembly.

25. Safely support the transaxle and remove the transaxle to engine bolt, through the wheel well, using a long extension.

26. Attach a lifting device and remove the engine mount to frame nuts.

27. Drain the engine oil and remove the oil filter.

28. Disconnect the oil cooler pipes from the hose connections.

29. Disconnect the exhaust pipe from the manifold.

30. Lower the vehicle and remove the engine assembly from the vehicle.

To install:

31. With an assistant, install a lifting device onto the engine and position into the vehicle.

32. Support the transaxle, install the transaxle-to-engine bolts and ground wire harness and torque to 46 ft. lbs. (62 Nm).

33. Install the heater and upper and lower radiator hoses to the engine.

34. Install all electrical connections to the engine.

35. Install the alternator, power steering pump and serpentine belt.

36. Install the vacuum line to the transaxle module.

37. Install the engine torque strut and bolt and torque to 41 ft. lbs. (56 Nm).

38. Install the exhaust crossover pipe.

39. Install the throttle cable mounting bracket and vacuum lines.

40. Install the heat shield to the crossover pipe and the throttle cables to the throttle body and mounting bracket.

41. Install the inner fender electrical cover and the coolant recovery bottle.

42. Install the fuel hoses to the fuel rail and mounting brackets.

43. Raise and support the vehicle safely.

44. Connect the front exhaust pipe to the manifold.

45. Install the oil filter and oil cooler pipes.

46. Install the engine mount nuts to the frame and torque to 32 ft. lbs. (43 Nm).

47. Install the transaxle to engine bolt through the wheel well and torque to 46 ft. lbs. (62 Nm).

48. Install the starter motor assembly and connect the electrical connectors.

49. Install the air conditioner compressor to the bracket.

50. Install the wire harness clamps to the frame near the radiator.

51. Align the scribe marks, install the torque converter to flywheel bolts and torque to 46 ft. lbs. (62 Nm).

52. Install the flywheel cover and the inner fender splash shield.

53. Install the right front wheel assembly and lower the vehicle.

54. Refill the cooling system and bleed the power steering system.

55. Install the right side cooling fan.

56. Install the fuel injector sight shield and the air cleaner assembly.

57. Connect the negative battery cable and install the hood.

58. Check and add fluids as required. Test drive vehicle and recheck for leaks and correct levels.

Engine Mounts

REMOVAL AND INSTALLATION

2.2L Engine

1. Disconnect the negative battery cable.

2. Remove the air cleaner duct assembly.

3. Remove the engine torque struts.

4. Install an engine lifting/support tools J–28467A, J–2846790, J–35953 and J–36462 or equivalent.

5. Raise and safely support the vehicle.

6. Remove the engine mount to chassis nuts and lower the vehicle.

7. Using the engine support device, raise the engine up off the mounts.

8. Raise the vehicle and remove the upper engine mount to bracket nuts.

9. Remove the engine mount.

To install:

10. Install the engine mount and secure with the engine mount to engine bracket nuts.

11. Tighten the nuts to 39 ft. lbs. (53 Nm).

12. Lower the vehicle and lower the engine.

13. Raise the vehicle and install the engine mount to chassis nuts.

14. Tighten the nuts to 39 ft. lbs (53 Nm).

15. Lower the vehicle and remove the engine lifting/support device.

16. Install the engine torque struts.

17. Install the air cleaner duct assembly and connect the negative battery cable.

2.5L Engine

1. Disconnect the negative battery cable.

2. Raise and safely support the vehicle.

3. Remove the engine-to-chassis nuts.

4. Disconnect the engine torque struts.

5. Install an engine support fixture J–28467–A or equivalent.

6. Remove the upper mount-to-engine bracket nuts and remove the mount.

To install:

7. Install the mount and mount-to-engine bracket. Tighten the nuts to 32 ft. lbs. (43 Nm).

8. Install and tighten the torque strut nuts to 32 ft. lbs. (43 Nm).

9. Lower the vehicle and remove the engine support fixture.

10. Reconnect negative battery cable.

3.1L Engine

1. Disconnect the negative battery cable. Raise and safely support the vehicle.

2. Remove the engine mount retaining nuts from below the cradle mounting bracket.

3. Raise the engine slightly to provide clearance and remove the engine mount-to-bracket nuts.

4. Remove the engine mount.

To install:

5. Install the mount in position and tighten the mount-to-bracket nuts to 32 ft. lbs. (43 Nm). Lower the engine into position.

6. Install the mounting bracket-to-cradle nuts and tighten to 63 ft. lbs. (85 Nm).

7. Lower the vehicle and connect the negative battery cable.

3.4L Engine

FRONT MOUNT

1. Disconnect the negative battery cable.

2. Remove the air cleaner assembly.

3. Remove the engine torque strut.

4. Position engine support tools J–284678–A, J–28647–90 and J–36462 or equivalents, to support engine.

5. Raise and safely support vehicle.

6. Remove right front tire and wheel assembly.

7. Remove right front engine splash shield and halfshaft splash shield.

8. Remove engine oil filter.

9. Remove engine mount nuts on frame.

10. Remove engine mount nuts on bracket.

11. Install halfshaft boot protector and raise engine. Remove mount.

To install:

12. Install mount in place and lower engine. Remove halfshaft boot protector.

13. Install engine mount nuts at bracket and tighten to 35 ft. lbs. (47 Nm).

14. Install engine mount nuts at frame and tighten to 32 ft. lbs. (43 Nm).

15. Install oil filter and right front splash shield.

16. Install right front wheel assembly.

17. Lower vehicle and remove engine supports.

18. Install engine torque strut, air cleaner assembly and negative battery cable.

REAR MOUNT

1. Disconnect the negative battery cable.

2. Remove the air cleaner assembly.

3. Remove the engine torque strut.

4. Position engine support tools J–284678–A, J–28647–90 and J–36462 or equivalents, to support engine.

5. Raise and safely support vehicle.

6. Remove right front tire and wheel assembly.

7. Remove right front engine splash shield and halfshaft splash shield.

8. Remove engine oil filter.

9. Remove engine mount nuts on frame.

10. Raise engine slightly. Remove rack and pinion mounting bolts and secure to frame.

11. Remove right ball joint at control arm. Install support under right side of frame.

12. Remove right frame mounting bolts, loosen left side frame mounting bolts and lower right side of frame 2–3 inches.

13. Install halfshaft boot protector. Remove upper engine mount nuts at mount. Remove mount.

To install:

14. Install mount in place.

15. Install upper engine mount nuts at mount.

16. Install halfshaft splash shield.

17. Raise right side frame. Install and tighten right side frame and left frame mounting bolts to 103 ft. lbs. (140 Nm).

18. Install right side ball joint and rack and pinion assembly.

19. Lower engine into position.

20. Install engine mount nuts at frame, torque to 32 ft. lbs. (43 Nm).

21. Install oil filter and right front splash shield. Remove halfshaft boot protector.

22. Install right front wheel assembly.

23. Lower vehicle and remove engine supports.

24. Install engine torque strut, air cleaner assembly and negative battery cable.

3.8L Engine

1. Disconnect the negative battery cable. Raise and safely support the vehicle.

2. Remove the mount retaining nuts from below the frame mounting bracket.

3. Raise the engine slightly to provide clearance and remove the engine mount-to-bracket nuts using engine support and lifting fixtures J–28467–A, J–28467–90 and J–35953 or equivalent.

4. Remove the engine mount nuts and the mounts.

To install:

5. Install the mount and attach to engine bracket. Once the engine is securely in place, remove the engine support and lifting fixtures.

6. Install the engine mount to frame nuts and torque to 32 ft. lbs. (43 Nm), the engine mount to frame nuts to 32 ft. lbs. (43 Nm) and the engine bracket to engine bolts to 70 ft. lbs. (95 Nm).

7. Connect the negative battery cable.

Cylinder Head

REMOVAL AND INSTALLATION

2.2L Engine

1. Relieve the fuel system pressure.

2. Disconnect the negative battery cable.

3. Remove the air cleaner assembly.

4. Drain the coolant from the cooling system into a suitable container.

5. Disconnect the vacuum lines and electrical connectors at the upper intake manifold assembly.

6. Disconnect the accelerator linkage at the upper intake manifold assembly.

7. Remove the serpentine drive belt tensioner assembly.

8. Disconnect the secondary ignition wires.

9. Disconnect the canister purge line beneath the manifold.

10. Disconnect the following hoses:
• Upper radiator hose
• Upper heater hose at the manifold
• Lower heater hose at the manifold
• Coolant inlet hose on the cylinder head

11. Disconnect the fuel lines.

12. Remove the rocker arms and the pushrods.

13. Remove the oil fill tube.

14. Remove the exhaust manifold.

15. Remove the lower intake manifold.

16. Remove the engine lift brackets.

17. Remove the cylinder head bolts and remove the cylinder head.

To install:
18. Clean all gasket mating surfaces with a plastic scraper and solvent. Remove all dirt from the bolts with a wire brush.

19. Check the cylinder head mating surface for flatness using a straight-edge and a feeler gauge. Replace the head, if the warpage exceeds 0.010 inch (0.25mm).

20. Check to see if the dowel pins are installed properly, replace, if necessary.

NOTE: To avoid damage, install new spark plugs after the cylinder head has been installed on the engine. In the meantime, plug the holes to prevent dirt from entering the combustion chamber during reinstallation.

21. Install the cylinder head gasket over the dowel pins on the cylinder block.

22. Carefully guide the cylinder head over the dowel pins and the gasket.

23. Install the cylinder head bolts finger-tight.

24. Tighten the cylinder head bolts to the following torque sequence in the order shown:
Long bolts — 46 ft. lbs. (63 Nm) + 90 degree turn.
Short bolts — 43 ft. lbs. (58 Nm) + 90 degree turn.

25. Install the engine lift brackets. Tighten the front bracket bolt to 41 ft. lbs. (55 Nm) and the rear bracket bolt to 32 ft. lbs. (43 Nm).

26. Install the lower intake manifold and the exhaust manifold.

27. Install the oil fill tube.

28. Install the rocker arms and push rods.

29. Connect the fuel lines and install the intake manifold brace.

30. Connect the coolant inlet hose to the cylinder head.

31. Install the lower and upper heater hose. Connect the upper radiator hose.

32. Connect the canister purge line under the manifold.

33. Connect the secondary ignition wires.

34. Install the serpentine drive belt tensioner.

35. Connect the accelerator linkage at the upper intake manifold assembly.

36. Connect the vacuum hoses and electrical connections to the upper intake manifold assembly.

37. Install the air cleaner and connect the negative battery cable.

2.5L Engine

1. Disconnect the negative battery cable.

2. Drain the cooling system.

3. Raise and safely support the vehicle.

4. Remove the exhaust pipe and oxygen sensor.

5. Lower the vehicle.

6. Remove the oil level indicator tube and auxiliary ground cable.

7. Remove the air cleaner assembly.

8. Disconnect the EFI electrical connections and vacuum hoses.

9. Release the fuel pressure. Remove the wiring connectors, throttle linkage and fuel lines.

10. Remove the heater hose from the intake manifold.

11. Remove the wiring connectors from the manifold and cylinder head.

12. Remove the vacuum hoses, serpentine belt and alternator bracket.

13. Remove the radiator hoses.

14. Remove the rocker arm cover.

15. Loosen the rocker arm nuts and move the rocker arms to the side enough to remove the pushrods.

16. Mark each pushrod and remove from the engine.

NOTE: Mark each valve train component to ensure that it is installed in the same location as removed.

17. Remove the cylinder head bolts.

18. Tap the sides of the cylinder head with a plastic hammer to dislodge the gasket. Remove the cylinder head with the intake and exhaust manifold still attached.

19. If the cylinder head has to be serviced or replaced, remove the intake manifold, exhaust manifold and remaining hardware.

To install:
20. Before installing, clean the gasket surfaces of the head and block.

21. Check the cylinder head for warpage using a straight-edge.

22. Match up the old head gasket with the new one to ensure the holes are exact. Install a new gasket over the dowel pins in the cylinder block.

23. Install the cylinder head in place over the dowel pins.

24. Coat the cylinder head bolt threads with sealing compound and install finger-tight.

25. Torque the cylinder head bolts, in sequence, in 3 steps.
   a. Torque all bolts to 18 ft. lbs. (26 Nm).
   b. Torque bolts "A" through "J" except "I" to 26 ft. lbs. (35 Nm). Torque bolt "I" to 18 ft. lbs. (24 Nm).
   c. Turn all bolts an additional 90 degree (¼ turn).

26. Install the pushrods, rocker arms and nuts (or bolts) in the same location as removed. Tighten the nuts (or bolts) to 24 ft. lbs. (32 Nm).

27. Install the rocker arm cover.

28. Install the radiator hoses, alternator bracket and serpentine belt.

29. Connect all intake manifold and cylinder head wiring.

30. Install the vacuum hoses and heater hose at manifold.

31. Install the wiring, throttle linkage and fuel lines to the throttle body assembly.

32. Install the oil level indicator tube-to-exhaust manifold.

33. Install the air cleaner assembly and refill the cooling system.

34. Raise and safely support the vehicle.

35. Install the exhaust pipe and oxygen sensor.

36. Lower the vehicle and connect the negative battery cable.

37. Start the engine and check for leaks.

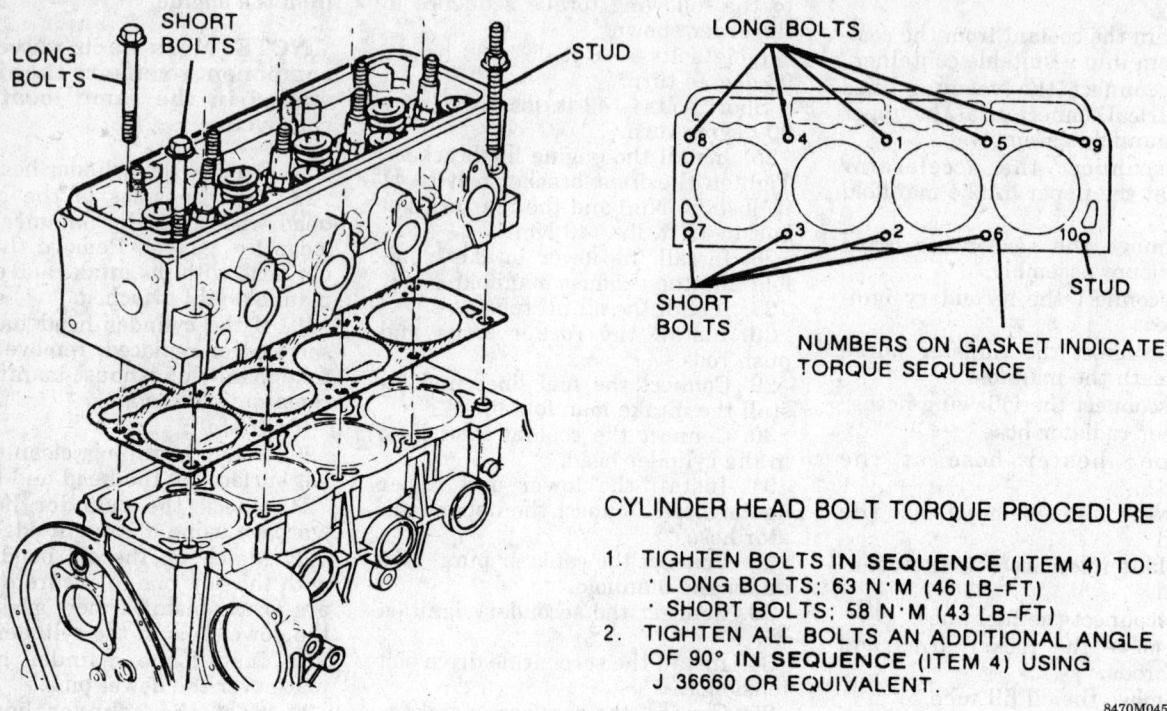

CYLINDER HEAD BOLT TORQUE PROCEDURE

1. TIGHTEN BOLTS IN **SEQUENCE** (ITEM 4) TO:
   · LONG BOLTS; 63 N·M (46 LB-FT)
   · SHORT BOLTS; 58 N·M (43 LB-FT)
2. TIGHTEN ALL BOLTS AN ADDITIONAL ANGLE OF 90° IN **SEQUENCE** (ITEM 4) USING J 36660 OR EQUIVALENT.

8470M045

Cylinder head bolt torque sequence — 2.2L engine

NOTE:
TIGHTEN ALL BOLTS IN PROPER SEQUENCE TO 18 FT. LBS. (25 NM) "A" THROUGH "J". TIGHTEN BOLTS "A" THROUGH "J" AGAIN (EXCEPT "I") TO 26 FT. LBS. (35 NM). TIGHTEN BOLT "I" TO 18 FT. LBS. (25 NM) FOLLOWING THE PROPER SEQUENCE. TIGHTEN ALL BOLTS 1/4 TURN OR 90 DEGREES.

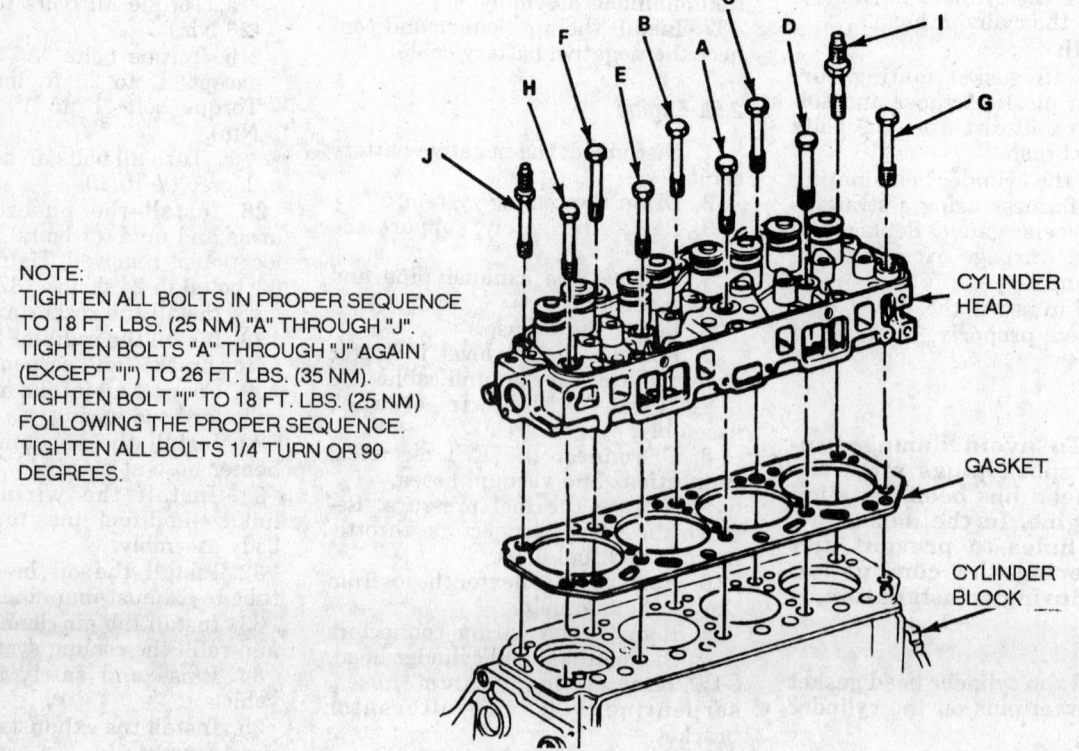

8470M047

Cylinder head bolt torque sequence — 2.5L engine

3.1L (VIN T) Engine

LEFT SIDE (FRONT)

1. Disconnect the negative battery cable. Drain the cooling system. Remove the rocker cover.

2. Remove the intake manifold-to-cylinder head bolts and the intake manifold.

3. Disconnect the exhaust crossover and manifold bolts and remove left exhaust manifold.

4. Disconnect the oil level indicator tube bracket.

5. Loosen the rocker arms nuts, turn the rocker arms and remove the pushrods. Intake and exhaust pushrods are different lengths and are color coded for identification; intake pushrods are marked orange and exhaust pushrods are marked blue in color.

NOTE: Be sure to keep the parts in order for installation purposes.

6. Remove spark plug wires.

7. Remove the cylinder head-to-engine bolts; start with the outer bolts and work toward the center. Remove the cylinder head with the exhaust manifold as an assembly.

To install:

8. Clean the gasket mounting surfaces. Inspect the surfaces of the cylinder head, block and intake manifold for damage or warpage. Clean the threaded holes in the block and the cylinder head bolt threads.

9. Use new gaskets, align the new cylinder head gasket over the dowels on the block with the note THIS SIDE UP facing the cylinder head.

10. Install the cylinder head and exhaust manifold crossover assembly on the engine.

11. Using GM sealant 1052080 or equivalent, coat the cylinder head bolts and install the bolts hand-tight.

12. Using the correct sequence, torque the bolts to 33 ft. lbs. (45 Nm). After all bolts are torqued to 33 ft. lbs. (45 Nm), rotate the torque wrench another 90 degrees or 1/4 turn. This will apply the correct torque to the bolts.

13. Install the pushrods in the same order that they were removed. Torque the rocker arm nuts to 14–20 ft. lbs. (19–27 Nm).

14. Install the intake manifold using a new gasket and following the correct sequence, torque the bolts to the correct specification.

15. Install the oil level indicator tube and install the rocker cover. Install the air inlet tube and spark plug wires.

COAT THREADS WITH SEALER
TIGHTEN IN PROPER SEQUENCE TO
45 N·m (33 LB. FT.). TURN
AN ADDITIONAL 90° WITH J 36660

FRT

CYLINDER
HEAD

GASKET

TIGHTENING
SEQUENCE

06 20 30 70
05 10 40 80

CYLINDER
BLOCK

8470M048

Cylinder head torque sequence — 3.1L engine

16. Reinstall engine strut bracket and exhaust manifold.

17. Connect the negative battery cable. Refill the cooling system. Start the engine and check for leaks.

RIGHT SIDE (REAR)

1. Disconnect the negative battery cable. Drain the cooling system. Remove air cleaner assembly. Remove the torque strut at engine.

2. Raise and safely support the vehicle. Remove the exhaust manifold-to-exhaust pipe bolts and separate the pipe from the manifold.

3. Disconnect the oxygen sensor harness connector. Lower the vehicle. Remove coolant recovery tank.

4. If more clearance is required, rotate the engine as follows:

  a. Put the transaxle in **N**.

  b. Remove the air cleaner.

  c. Disconnect the negative battery cable.

  d. Remove the torque strut to engine bracket bolt and swing strut aside.

  e. Replace the passenger side torque strut to engine bracket bolt in engine bracket.

  f. Place a prybar in the bracket so it contacts the bracket and the bolt.

  g. Rotate the engine by pulling forward on the prybar. Align the slave hole in the driver side torque strut to the engine bracket hole.

  h. Retain the engine in this position using the torque strut to engine bracket bolt.

NOTE: To prevent shearing of the rubber bushing, loosen the bolts on the engine strut before swinging the struts.

5. Remove the exhaust manifold-to-cylinder head bolts and the exhaust manifold from the engine.

6. Remove exhaust crossover heat shield and crossover pipe at right exhaust manifold.

7. Remove right side spark plug wires at cylinder head.

8. Remove the rocker arm cover. Remove the intake manifold-to-cylinder head bolts and the intake manifold.

9. Loosen the rocker arms nuts, turn the rocker arms and remove the pushrods. Intake and exhaust pushrods are different lengths and are color coded for identification; intake pushrods are marked orange and exhaust pushrods are marked blue in color.

NOTE: Be sure to keep the components in order for reassembly purposes.

10. Remove the cylinder head-to-engine bolts, starting with the outer bolts and working toward the center and the cylinder head.

To install:

11. Clean the gasket mounting surfaces. Inspect the parts for damage and/or warpage.

12. Clean the engine block's threaded holes and the cylinder head bolt threads.

13. Install new gasket on the alignment dowels with THIS SIDE UP facing the cylinder head.

14. Install the cylinder head onto the engine. Coat the cylinder head bolt threads with GM sealant 1052080 or equivalent, and install bolts hand-tight.

15. Following the proper torque sequence, tighten bolts to 33 ft. lbs. (45 Nm). After all bolts are torqued to 33 ft. lbs. (45 Nm), rotate the torque wrench an additional 90 degrees or 1/4 turn. This will apply the correct torque to the bolts.

16. Install the pushrods in the same order as they were removed. Torque the rocker arm nuts to 14–20 ft. lbs. (19–27 Nm).

17. Follow the torquing sequence, use a new gasket and install the intake manifold.

18. Return the engine to normal resting position as follows:

  a. Pull forward on the prybar to take the weight off the torque strut to engine bracket bolt.

  b. Remove bolt from the strut slave hole and engine bracket.

  c. Install engine torque strut and tighten the strut to engine bracket bolt to 32 ft. lbs. (43 Nm).

19. Install spark plug wires to cylinder head.

20. Install right side exhaust crossover pipe, heat shield and manifold.

21. Install exhaust pipe to manifold. Connect the oxygen sensor harness connector.

22. Install the oil level indicator tube and install the rocker cover. Install the air inlet tube.

23. Install coolant recovery tank. Refill the cooling system. Start the engine, allow it to reach normal operating temperatures and check for leaks.

3.1L (VIN M) Engine

LEFT SIDE (FRONT)

1. Drain and recover the A/C refrigerant. Disconnect the battery cables.

2. Remove the intake manifold assembly.

3. Remove the exhaust crossover pipe. Label and disconnect the spark plug wires.

4. Remove the rocker arm covers, rocker arms and pushrods. Label these components for correct installation.

5. Remove the air level indicator and tube.

6. Remove the A/C compressor bolts from the top.

7. Raise the vehicle and support safely.

8. Disconnect the A/C compressor hoses. Remove the bolts, electrical connectors and compressor.

9. Remove the A/C compressor lower brackets.

10. Lower the vehicle and remove the A/C compressor upper brackets.

11. Remove the cylinder head bolts, cylinder head and gasket.

12. Clean all mating surfaces and check for warpage.

To install:

13. Place the gasket on the block with the "This Side Up" showing. Install the cylinder head and bolts.

14. Torque the head bolts in sequence to 33 ft. lbs. (45 Nm) and then another 90 degrees torquing angle.

15. Install the compressor bracket and upper bolts.

16. Raise the vehicle and support safely.

17. Install the A/C compressor lower brackets.

18. Install the compressor. Connect the A/C compressor hoses and electrical connectors.

19. Install the air level indicator and tube.

20. Install the rocker arm covers, rocker arms and pushrods.

21. Install the exhaust crossover pipe. Connect the spark plug wires.

22. Install the intake manifold assembly.

23. Refill and recharge the A/C refrigerant. Connect the battery cables.

RIGHT SIDE (REAR)

1. Remove the lower intake manifold, ignition coil connection and alternator.

2. Remove the crossover pipe and oxygen sensor.

3. Raise the vehicle and support safely.

4. Remove the exhaust pipe from the manifold.

5. Lower the vehicle and remove the rocker cover, rocker arms and pushrods. Label these components for proper installation.

6. Remove the cylinder head bolts, cylinder head and gasket.

7. Clean all mating surfaces and check for warpage.

To install:

8. Place the gasket on the block with the "This Side Up" showing. Install the cylinder head and bolts.

9. Torque the head bolts in sequence to 33 ft. lbs. (45 Nm) and then another 90 degrees torquing angle.

10. Install the pushrods, rocker arms and rocker arm cover.

11. Raise the vehicle and support safely.

12. Install the exhaust pipe and lower the vehicle.

13. Install the oxygen sensor and crossover pipe.

14. Install the alternator, ignition coil connections and lower intake manifold.

15. Refill all fluids, connect the battery cable, start the engine and check for leaks.

3.4L Engine

LEFT SIDE (FRONT)

1. Disconnect the negative battery cable.

2. Drain cooling system. Remove intake manifold.

3. Remove left side cam carrier as follows:

   a. Disconnect oil/air breather hose from cam carrier cover. Remove spark plug wires from plugs and remove rear spark plug wire cover.

   b. Remove cam carrier cover bolts and lift off cover. Remove gasket and O-rings from cover.

   c. Remove secondary timing belt by removing secondary timing belt actuator and tensioner assembly and sliding belt from pulleys.

   d. Install 6 sections of fuel line hoses under camshaft and between lifters. This will hold lifters in the carrier. For this procedure use $3/16$ inch fuel line hose for exhaust valves and $5/32$ inch fuel line hose for the intake valves.

   e. Remove exhaust crossover pipe and torque strut.

   f. Remove torque strut bracket at engine.

   g. Remove cam carrier mounting bolts and nuts and remove cam carrier.

   h. Remove cam carrier gasket from cylinder head.

4. Remove front air hose on manual transaxle only.

5. Remove right cooling fan.

6. Remove exhaust mounting bolts and manifold.

7. Remove oil level indicator tube bolt and tube.

8. Disconnect electrical connector from temperature sending unit.

9. Remove cylinder head bolts and remove cylinder head.

To install:

10. Clean the gasket mounting surfaces. Inspect the parts for damage or warpage.

11. Clean the engine block threaded holes and the cylinder head bolt threads. Remove oil from threaded holes in block.

12. Install new cylinder head gasket to block with tabs between cylinders facing up.

13. Install cylinder head and bolts and torque in proper sequence. Tighten bolts to 33 ft. lbs. (45 Nm) + an additional $1/4$ turn.

14. Connect electrical connector to coolant temperature sending unit.

15. Install oil level tube and bolt. Tighten to 89 inch lbs. (10 Nm).

16. Install exhaust manifold and nuts. Tighten to 116 inch lbs. (13 Nm).

17. Install front air pipe, manual transaxle. Install cooling fan.

18. Install cam carrier following these steps:

   a. Install new gasket on cam carrier to cylinder mounting surface.

   b. Install cam hold-down tool J–38613 or equivalent, to carrier assembly.

   c. Install cam carrier to cylinder head. Install mounting bolts and nuts. Torque bolts and nuts to 18 ft. lbs. (24 Nm).

   d. Remove lifter hold-down hoses and cam hold-down tool.

   e. Install torque strut bracket to engine and install torque strut.

   f. Install engine crossover pipe.

   g. Install secondary timing belt and cam carrier cover.

19. Install intake manifold. Tighten bolts to 18 ft. lbs. (25 Nm).

20. Refill fluid levels as required. Connect negative battery cable.

21. Start vehicle and check for fluid leaks.

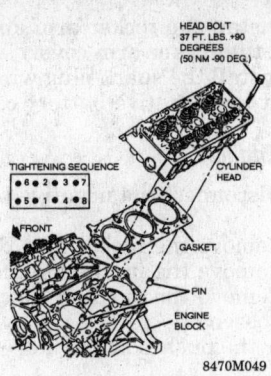

HEAD BOLT
37 FT. LBS. +90
DEGREES
(50 NM -90 DEG.)

TIGHTENING SEQUENCE

CYLINDER HEAD

FRONT

GASKET

PIN

ENGINE BLOCK

8470M049

**Cylinder head torque
sequence — 3.4L engine**

RIGHT SIDE (REAR)

1. Disconnect the negative battery cable.

2. Drain cooling system. Remove intake manifold.

3. Remove right side cam carrier as follows:

   a. Remove intake plenum and right timing belt cover.

   b. Remove right spark plug wires.

   c. Remove air/oil separator hose at cam carrier cover.

   d. Remove cam carrier cover bolts and lift of cover. Remove gasket and O-rings from cover.

   e. Remove secondary timing belt by removing secondary timing belt actuator and tensioner assembly and sliding belt from pulleys.

   f. Install 6 sections of fuel line hoses under camshaft and between lifters. This will hold lifters in carrier. For this procedure use 3/16 inch fuel line hose for exhaust valves and 5/32 inch fuel line hose for the intake valves.

   g. Remove exhaust crossover pipe and torque strut.

   h. Remove torque strut bracket at engine. Remove front engine lift hook.

   i. Remove cam carrier mounting bolts and nuts and remove cam carrier.

   j. Remove cam carrier gasket from cylinder head.

4. Raise and support vehicle safely.

5. Remove front exhaust pipe at manifold.

6. Remove rear air hose from air pipe on manual transaxle only.

7. Lower vehicle and disconnect electrical connector from oxygen sensor.

8. Remove rear timing belt tensioner bracket.

9. Remove cylinder head bolts and remove cylinder head.

To install:

10. Clean the gasket mounting surfaces. Inspect the parts for damage and/or warpage.

11. Clean the engine block threaded holes and the cylinder head bolt threads. Remove oil from threaded holes in block.

12. Install new cylinder head gasket to block with tabs between cylinders facing up.

13. Install cylinder head and bolts and torque in proper sequence. Tighten bolts to 33 ft. lbs. (45 Nm) + an additional 1/4 turn.

14. Install rear timing belt tensioner bracket.

15. Connect electrical connector to oxygen sensor.

16. Raise vehicle and support safely.

17. Connect rear air hose to air pipe for manual transaxle.

18. Install front exhaust pipe to manifold. Lower the vehicle.

19. Install cam carrier as follows:

   a. Install new gasket on cam carrier to cylinder mounting surface.

   b. Install cam hold-down tool J–38613 or equivalent, to carrier assembly.

   c. Install cam carrier to cylinder head. Install mounting bolts and nuts. Torque bolts and nuts to 18 ft. lbs. (25 Nm).

   d. Remove lifter hold-down hoses and cam hold-down tool.

   e. Install torque strut bracket to engine and install torque strut.

   f. Install engine crossover pipe and engine lift hook.

   g. Install secondary timing belt and cam carrier cover.

   h. Install spark plug wires and cover.

20. Install intake manifold. Torque bolts to 18 ft. lbs. (25 Nm).

21. Refill fluid levels as required. Connect negative battery cable.

22. Start vehicle and check for fluid leaks.

3.8L Engine

LEFT SIDE (FRONT)

1. Disconnect the negative battery cable and remove the air cleaner assembly.

2. Drain the cooling system and remove the intake manifold.

3. Remove the valve covers and remove the rocker arm assemblies.

4. Disconnect the torque strut from the bracket at cylinder head.

5. Disconnect the vacuum line from the transaxle.

6. Remove the left exhaust manifold.

7. Disconnect the spark plug wires and remove the spark plugs.

8. Remove the alternator front mount bracket and ignition module with bracket.

9. Remove the cylinder head bolts and remove the cylinder head.

10. Clean all gasket mating surfaces and the cylinder head bolt holes in the block.

To install:

11. Place the cylinder head gasket on the engine block dowels with the note THIS SIDE UP facing the cylinder head and the arrow facing the front of the engine.

12. Install the cylinder head bolts and tighten as follows:

   a. Tighten the cylinder head bolts, in sequence, to 35 ft. lbs. (47 Nm).

   b. Rotate each bolt 130 degrees, in sequence.

   c. Rotate the center 4 bolts an additional 30 degrees, in sequence.

13. Install the rocker arm assemblies and valve covers.

14. Install the intake and exhaust manifolds.

15. Install the alternator front mount bracket and ignition module with bracket and torque the bolts to 37 ft. lbs. (50 Nm).

16. Install the spark plugs and wires.

17. Install the torque strut to the bracket, at the head and torque to 41 ft. lbs. (56 Nm).

18. Fill the cooling system, connect the negative battery cable and install the air cleaner assembly.

RIGHT SIDE (REAR)

1. Disconnect the negative battery cable and remove the air cleaner assembly.

2. Drain the cooling system and disconnect the exhaust crossover pipe.

3. Remove the intake manifold.

4. Raise and support the vehicle safely.

5. Disconnect the front exhaust pipe from the manifold.

6. Remove the valve covers.

7. Remove the belt tensioner pulley.

8. Disconnect the heater hose from the engine.

9. Remove the power steering pump mounting bracket and lay the pump aside.

10. Remove the spark plug wires and remove the spark plugs.

11. Disconnect the exhaust manifold and leave in place.

12. Disconnect the electrical connection from the oxygen sensor.

13. Remove the rocker arm assemblies.

14. Remove the cylinder head bolts and remove the cylinder head.

15. Clean all gasket mating surfaces and the cylinder head bolt holes in the block.

To install:

16. Place the cylinder head gasket on the engine block dowels with the note THIS SIDE UP facing the cylinder head and the arrow facing the front of the engine.

17. Install the cylinder head bolts and tighten as follows:

a. Tighten the cylinder head bolts, in sequence, to 35 ft. lbs. (47 Nm).

b. Rotate each bolt 130 degrees, in sequence.

c. Rotate the center 4 bolts an additional 30 degrees, in sequence.

18. Connect the electrical connection to the oxygen sensor.

19. Install the exhaust manifold and intake manifold.

20. Install the rocker arm assemblies.

21. Install the valve cover.

22. Install the spark plugs and wires.

23. Install the power steering pump bracket and torque the bolts to 37 ft. lbs. (50 Nm).

24. Install the belt tensioner pulley.

25. Install the heater hose to the engine.

26. Install the exhaust crossover pipe.

27. Raise and support the vehicle safely.

28. Install the front exhaust pipe to the manifold and lower the vehicle.

29. Fill the cooling system, connect the negative battery cable and install the air cleaner assembly.

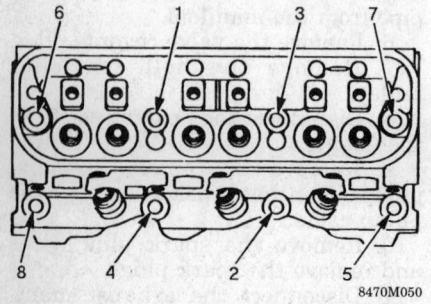

8470M050

Cylinder head bolt torque sequence — 3.8L engine

Valve Lifters

REMOVAL AND INSTALLATION

2.2L Engine

1. Disconnect the negative battery cable.

2. Mark the location of the spark plug wires and disconnect the spark plug wires from the spark plugs.

3. Remove the valve rocker arm cover.

4. Loosen the rocker arm nuts and swing the rocker arm aside.

5. Remove the pushrod assembly.

6. Remove the engine lift bracket from the rear of the engine.

7. Route the spark plug wires aside from behind the lower intake manifold.

8. Remove the cylinder head bolts and studs.

9. With the aid of an assistant remove the cylinder head with the exhaust and intake manifold attached.

10. Remove the cylinder head gasket and remove the valve lifters.

To install:

NOTE: The lifter foot is designed to be slightly convex. This should be checked by holding a straight-edge to the surface. While shining a light source, look for a slight gap in the surface. If the lifter foot is worn to the point of being flat or grooved, it MUST be replaced.

11. If new lifters are being installed, coat the foot of the valve lifters with GM camshaft assembly lube 1052365 or equivalent prior to installation.

12. Install the valve lifter(s).

13. Install a new head gasket into position.

14. Install the cylinder head gasket over the dowel pins on the cylinder block.

15. Carefully guide the cylinder head over the dowel pins and the gasket.

16. Install the cylinder head bolts finger-tight.

17. Tighten the cylinder head bolts to the following torque sequence:

Long bolts — 46 ft. lbs. (63 Nm) + 90 degree turn.

Short bolts — 43 ft. lbs. (58 Nm) + 90 degree turn.

18. Install the engine lift bracket to the rear of the engine.

19. Route the spark plug wires up through the lower intake manifold.

20. Install the pushrods making sure they properly seat in the lifters.

21. Install the rocker arm and nut. Install the rocker arm cover.

22. Install the spark plug wires and connect the negative battery cable.

2.5L Engine

1. Disconnect the negative battery cable.

2. Remove the rocker arm cover.

3. Remove the intake manifold.

4. Remove the pushrod cover.

5. Loosen the rocker arms, rotate to clear the pushrods and move to the side.

6. Mark and remove the pushrods, retainer and lifter guides.

7. Mark and remove the lifters.

NOTE: Mark each valve component location for reassembly.

8. Lubricate all bearing surfaces and lifters with clean engine oil.

To install:

9. Install the lifters, lifter guides, retainers and pushrods in their original position.

10. Position the rocker arms over the pushrods and tighten the rocker arm nuts to 24 ft. lbs. (32 Nm) with the lifter at the base circle of the camshaft.

11. Install the pushrod cover, intake manifold and rocker arm cover.

12. Connect the negative battery cable. Start the engine and check for proper operation and fluid leaks.

3.1L Engine

1. Disconnect negative battery cable.

2. Drain the cooling system.

3. Remove the rocker arm covers and intake manifold from the engine.

4. Loosen the rocker arms nuts enough to move the rocker arms aside and remove the pushrods.

NOTE: The pushrods used on the 3.1L engine are different lengths. The intake pushrods are 6 in. long and are orange in color. The exhaust pushrods are blue in color and are 6 3/8 in. long. Label pushrods so they can be installed in their original positions during assembly. Some 3.1L engines may contain oversized lifters. Where oversized lifters are used, the cylinder case will be marked with white paint or 0.25mm will be stamped on the lifter boss. If replacement of the lifter is required, use the correct size lifters with a narrow flat ground along the lower 3/4 of lifter. This flat will allow for additional oil to flow to the cam lobe and the lifter surfaces.

5. Remove the lifters from the engine keeping in order or removal. If original lifter is being reused, it is essential that they be installed in their original position.

To install:

6. Using Molykote® or equivalent, coat the base of the new lifters and install them into the engine.

7. Position the pushrods and the rocker arms correctly into their original positions. Torque the rocker arm nuts to 18 ft. lbs. (25 Nm).

8. Install the intake manifold and tighten the intake manifold-to-cylinder head bolts to specification following the torque sequence.

9. Install the rocker cover.

10. Connect the negative battery cable and fill the cooling system. Start the engine, check for proper operation and fluid leaks.

3.4L Engine

LEFT SIDE (FRONT)

1. Disconnect the negative battery cable. Drain the cooling system.

2. Remove left side cam carrier as follows:

   a. Disconnect oil/air breather hose from cam carrier cover. Remove spark plug wires from plugs and remove rear spark plug wire cover.

   b. Remove cam carrier cover bolts and lift off cover. Remove gasket and O-rings from cover.

   c. Remove secondary timing belt by removing secondary timing belt actuator and tensioner assembly and sliding belt from pulleys.

   d. Install 6 sections of fuel line hoses under camshaft and between lifters. This will hold lifters in the carrier. For this procedure use $\frac{3}{16}$ in. fuel line hose for exhaust valves and $\frac{5}{32}$ in. fuel line hose for the intake valves.

   e. Remove exhaust crossover pipe and torque strut.

   f. Remove torque strut bracket at engine.

   g. Remove cam carrier mounting bolts and nuts and remove cam carrier.

   h. Remove cam carrier gasket from cylinder head.

3. Remove the 6 lifter hold-down hoses. Remove the lifters.

NOTE: Valve lifters must be kept in order so they can be installed in their original position.

To install:

4. Lubricate lifters with clean engine oil and install lifters into original position.

5. Install lifter hold-down hoses to cam carrier.

6. Install cam carrier following these steps:

   a. Install new gasket on cam carrier to cylinder mounting surface.

   b. Install cam hold-down tool J–38613 or equivalent, to carrier assembly.

   c. Install cam carrier to cylinder head. Install mounting bolts and nuts. Torque bolts and nuts to 18 ft. lbs.

   d. Remove lifter hold-down hoses and cam hold-down tool.

   e. Install torque strut bracket to engine and install torque strut.

   f. Install engine crossover pipe.

   g. Install secondary timing belt and cam carrier cover.

   h. Reconnect spark plug cover and wires.

   i. Connect breather hose to cam carrier cover.

7. Add fluids as required, reconnect negative battery cable. Start engine and recheck for leaks.

RIGHT SIDE (REAR)

1. Disconnect the negative battery cable. Drain cooling system.

2. Remove right side cam carrier as follows:

   a. Remove intake plenum and right timing belt cover.

   b. Remove right spark plug wires.

   c. Remove air/oil separator hose at cam carrier cover.

   d. Remove cam carrier cover bolts and lift of cover. Remove gasket and O-rings from cover.

   e. Remove secondary timing belt by removing secondary timing belt actuator and tensioner assembly and sliding belt from pulleys.

   f. Install 6 sections of fuel line hoses under camshaft and between lifters. This will hold lifters in carrier. For this procedure use $\frac{3}{16}$ in. fuel line hose for exhaust valves and $\frac{5}{32}$ in. fuel line hose for the intake valves.

   g. Remove exhaust crossover pipe and torque strut.

   h. Remove torque strut bracket at engine. Remove front engine lift hook.

   i. Remove cam carrier mounting bolts and nuts and remove cam carrier.

   j. Remove cam carrier gasket from cylinder head.

3. Remove 6 lifter hold-down hoses.

4. Remove lifters keeping in order of removal.

NOTE: Valve lifters must be kept in order so they can be installed in their original position.

To install:

5. Lubricate lifters with clean engine oil and install lifters into original position.

6. Install lifter hold-down hoses to cam carrier.

7. Install cam carrier following these steps:

   a. Install new gasket on cam carrier to cylinder mounting surface.

   b. Install cam hold-down tool J–38613 or equivalent, to carrier assembly.

   c. Install cam carrier to cylinder head. Install mounting bolts and nuts. Torque bolts and nuts to 18 ft. lbs.

   d. Remove lifter hold-down hoses and cam hold-down tool.

   e. Install torque strut bracket to engine and install torque strut.

   f. Install engine crossover pipe and engine lift hook.

   g. Install secondary timing belt and cam carrier cover.

   h. Install spark plug wires and cover.

8. Add fluids as required. Connect negative battery cable. Start engine and check for fluid leaks.

3.8L Engine

1. Disconnect negative battery cable.

2. Drain the cooling system.

3. Remove the rocker arm covers and intake manifold.

4. Remove the rocker arm assemblies.

5. Remove the guide retainer bolts and retainer.

NOTE: Be sure to keep all valve train components in order so they can be reinstalled in their original locations and with the same mating surfaces as when removed.

6. Remove the valve lifter guides and the valve lifters keeping in order of removal.

To install:

7. Prelube (dip) the valve lifters with oil before installation.

8. Install the lifter guides, guide retainers and bolts and torque to 22 ft. lbs. (30 Nm).

9. Install the rocker arm assemblies, intake manifold and valve covers.

10. Fill the cooling system and connect the negative battery cable. Start

the engine and check for proper operation and fluid leaks.

Valve Lash

ADJUSTMENT

All engines are originally equipped with hydraulic valve lifters. No adjustment is necessary. The 3.1L engine replacement rocker arm stud is adjustable and the adjustment can be performed as listed below.

3.1L Engine

NOTE: The following adjustment procedure should be used when reconditioning a valve seat and a new adjustable type rocker arm is used.

1. Install the rocker arms, balls and nuts. Tighten the rocker arm nuts until all of the lash (free-play) is eliminated.
2. Adjust the valves when the lifter is on the base circle of a camshaft lobe as follows:
   a. Place the engine in the No. 1 firing position. This can be determined by placing a finger on the No. 1 rocker arm as the engine alignment mark on the front face of the of the torsional damper pulley aligns with the arrow on the front cover. If the valves don't move freely, the engine is in the No. 1 firing position. If the valves move freely, the engine is in the No. 4 firing position and the engine should be rotated one full rotation to reach the No. 1 position.
   b. With the engine TDC on the No. 1 cylinder, adjust the following valves:
      • Exhaust — 1, 2, 3
      • Intake — 1, 5, 6
   c. Loosen the adjusting nut several turns backwards and then tighten until all lash (free-play) is removed. After all of the valve lash is removed turn the nut an additional 1½ turns; this will center the lifter plunger.
   d. Turn the engine 1 complete revolution until the timing tab and the alignment mark are again aligned; this will place the engine in the No. 4 firing position.
   e. With the engine TDC on the No. 4 cylinder, adjust the following valves:
      • Exhaust — 4, 5, 6
      • Intake — 2, 3, 4

Rocker Arms

NOTE: Some engines have pushrods of different lengths. If the pushrods are of different lengths, the pushrods are color coded. Over time the color may wear off the pushrods. The intake pushrods are orange and measure 6 inches long. The exhaust pushrods are blue and measure 6⅜ inches long.

REMOVAL AND INSTALLATION

2.2L Engine

1. Disconnect the negative battery cable.
2. Remove the valve rocker arm cover.
3. Remove the rocker arm nut and remove the rocker arm and ball.
4. Place the components in the order of removal for installation purposes.

To install:

NOTE: If new rocker arms are being installed, coat the bearing surfaces of the rocker arms with GM camshaft assembly lube 1052365 or equivalent.

5. Install the pushrods, making sure they are properly seated in their lifters.
6. Install the rocker arm and the ball.
7. Apply GM Dri-Slide Moly lubricant 1052948 or equivalent to the threads of the studs.
8. Install the rocker arm nuts and tighten to 22 ft. lbs. (30 Nm).
9. Install the valve rocker arm cover assembly and connect the negative battery cable.

2.5L Engine

1. Disconnect the negative battery cable.
2. Remove the rocker arm cover.
3. Remove the rocker arm bolt and ball.
4. Remove the rocker arm and guide.

NOTE: Mark all valve components so they are reinstalled in their original location. The pushrods are of different lengths and must be installed in their original locations.

5. If removed, install the pushrod through the cylinder head and into the lifter seat.
6. Install the guide, rocker arm, ball and bolt. Tighten the rocker arm bolts to 24 ft. lbs. (32 Nm)

7. Install the rocker arm cover and connect the negative battery cable.

3.1L (VIN T) Engine

LEFT SIDE

1. Disconnect the negative battery cable. Remove the air cleaner assembly.
2. Remove the ignition wire clamps from coolant tube. Disconnect the bracket tube from the rocker cover.
3. Remove the spark plug wire cover. Drain the cooling system and remove the heater hose from the filler neck. Remove the coolant hose at the coolant pump and the coolant tube.
4. Remove the rocker arm cover-to-cylinder head bolts and the rocker cover.

NOTE: If the rocker arm cover will not lift off the cylinder head easily, strike the end with the palm of the hand or a rubber mallet.

5. Remove the rocker arm nuts and remove the rocker arms, keep the components in order for installation purposes.
6. Clean the gasket mounting surfaces.
7. To install rocker arms torque the rocker arm nuts to 18–20 ft. lbs. (25–27 Nm).
8. To install new rocker cover gaskets apply a bead of sealant, GM 1052917 or equivalent, to the rocker cover and position on head.
9. Install the spark plug wire cover. Install EGR valve, if removed.
10. Attach the heater hose to the filler neck. Attach the coolant hose at the coolant pump. Fill the cooling system.
11. Install negative battery cable and air cleaner assembly. Start vehicle and check for leaks.

RIGHT SIDE

1. Disconnect the negative battery cable. Disconnect the brake booster vacuum line from the bracket.
2. Disconnect the cable bracket from the plenum. Disconnect throttle, cruise control and transaxle cable from throttle body.
3. Drain cooling system and remove coolant hose at throttle body. Remove coolant recovery tank.
4. Remove serpentine belt. Remove EGR tube at crossover pipe and disconnect crossover pipe from exhaust pipe.
5. Disconnect the vacuum line bracket from the cable bracket.
6. Disconnect the lines from the alternator brace stud.

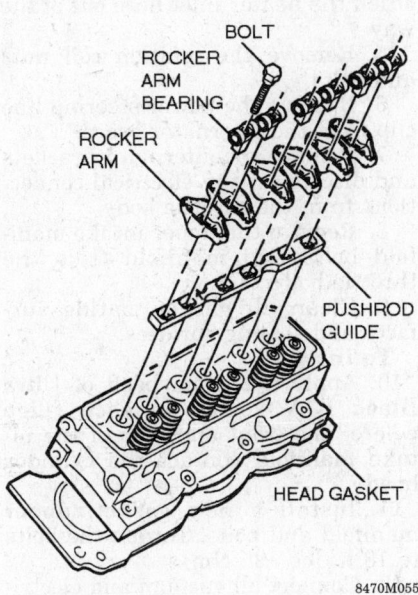

Rocker arm installation — 3.8L engine

8470M055

7. Remove the rear alternator brace and the serpentine drive belt.

8. Remove the alternator and position aside.

9. Remove the PCV valve.

10. Loosen the alternator bracket.

11. Disconnect the spark plug wires from the spark plugs. Remove the rocker cover-to-cylinder head bolts and the rocker cover.

NOTE: If the rocker arm cover will not lift off the cylinder head easily, strike the end with the palm of the hand or a rubber mallet.

12. Remove the rocker arm nuts and the rocker arms; be sure to keep the components in order for installation purposes.

To install:

13. Clean the gasket mounting surfaces.

14. Install rocker assembly and torque nuts to 18 ft. lbs. (25 Nm).

15. To install, use new rocker cover gaskets apply a bead of sealant, GM 1052917 or equivalent, to the rocker cover and torque cover bolts to 89 inch lbs. (10 Nm).

16. Install the spark plug wire cover and attach the heater hose to the filler neck. Install coolant recovery tank and hose at throttle body. Fill the cooling system.

17. Reconnect exhaust crossover pipe and exhaust pipe.

18. Install the serpentine drive belt.

19. Install throttle, transaxle and cruise control cables to throttle body and resecure cable bracket.

20. Refasten all electrical and vacuum connection.

21. Install negative battery cable and air cleaner assembly and start engine. Check for fluid leaks.

3.1L (VIN M) Engine

1. Remove the rocker cover.

2. Label all components for correct installation.

NOTE: The intake and exhaust pushrods are of different lengths. The exhaust pushrods are longer than the intake rod. Intake rods are marked orange and are 6 inches long. The exhaust rods are blue and are 6 ⅜ inches long.

3. Remove the rocker arm pivot balls, rocker arms, studs and pushrods.

4. Install the pushrods to there proper location.

5. Install the studs, rocker arms, rocker arm pivot balls and nuts.

6. Adjust the valve lash if any components were replaced. Torque the rocker arm nuts to 18 ft. lbs. (24 Nm) if no components were replaced. Install the rocker arm cover.

7. Refill the fluids, start the engine and check for valve train noise. Any noise should go away after the engine is warm and driven a few miles at various engine speeds.

3.8L Engine

1. Disconnect the negative battery cable.

2. Remove the valve cover.

3. Remove the rocker arm pedestal retaining bolts and remove the pedestal and rocker arm assembly.

4. Remove the pushrods keeping in order of removal.

NOTE: Store components in order so they can be reassembled in the same location.

To install:

5. Install the pushrods and make sure they seat in the lifter.

6. Apply a thread lock compound to the bolt threads before reassembly.

7. Install the pedestal and rocker arm assemblies and tighten the retaining bolts to 28 ft. lbs. (38 Nm).

8. Install the valve covers and connect the negative battery cable.

9. Start engine and check for fluid leaks.

Intake Manifold

REMOVAL AND INSTALLATION

2.2L Engine

1. Properly relieve the fuel system pressure.

2. Disconnect the negative battery cable.

3. Remove the air cleaner assembly.

4. Drain the coolant into a suitable container.

5. Remove the serpentine drive belt.

6. Remove the power steering pump mounting bolts. Do not disconnect the power steering fluid lines. Set the power steering pump aside.

7. Disconnect the vacuum lines and electrical connectors as necessary.

8. Remove the accelerator cable bracket.

9. Remove the MAP sensor and the EGR solenoid valve assembly.

10. Remove the upper intake manifold assembly.

11. Remove the EGR valve injector assembly.

12. Remove the fuel injector retainer bracket, the regulator and the fuel injectors.

13. Remove the manifold mounting nuts.

14. Remove the lower intake manifold and the gasket.

15. Clean the mating surfaces of the cylinder head and the manifold of all gasket material.

16. Clean the EGR passages of excessive carbon deposits.

17. Inspect the manifold for cracks, broken flanges and gasket surface damage.

To install:

18. Install the gasket and the lower intake manifold.

19. Install the manifold nuts and tighten the nuts to 22 ft. lbs. (30 Nm) in the proper sequence.

20. Install the fuel injector retainer bracket, the regulator and the fuel injectors.

21. Tighten the retainer bracket bolt/screw to 31 inch lbs. (3.5 Nm).

22. Install the EGR valve injector so the port is facing directly towards the throttle body.

23. Install the upper intake manifold and tighten the nuts to 22 ft. lbs. (30 Nm).

24. Install the EGR solenoid valve and the MAP sensor and seal.

25. Install the accelerator cable bracket and tighten the bolts to 18 ft.

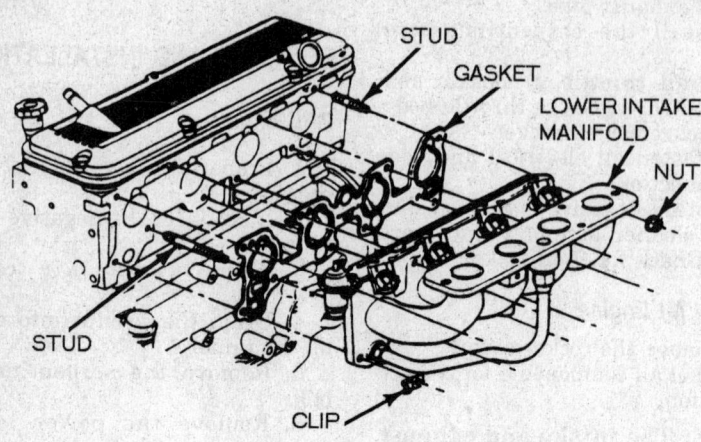

INTAKE MANIFOLD NUT
TIGHTENING SEQUENCE

8470M057

Lower intake manifold assembly — 2.2L engine

lbs. (25 Nm) and the nut to 22 ft. lbs. (30 Nm).

26. Connect the vacuum lines and the electrical wires.

27. Install the power steering pump.

28. Refill the cooling system.

29. Install the air cleaner assembly and connect the negative battery cable.

2.5L Engine

1. Disconnect the negative battery cable.

2. Remove the air cleaner assembly.

3. Remove the PCV valve and hose at the throttle body assembly.

4. Drain the engine coolant at the radiator.

5. Release the fuel pressure and remove the fuel lines from the throttle body.

6. Remove the vacuum lines and brake booster hose from the throttle body.

7. Remove all linkage and wiring from the TBI assembly.

8. Remove the power steering pump and position aside.

9. Remove the heater hose.

10. Remove the 7 intake manifold retaining bolts and the manifold.

To install:

11. Clean all gasket surfaces on the cylinder head and intake manifold.

12. Install the intake manifold with a new gasket.

13. Install all the retaining bolts and washers hand-tight.

14. Tighten the bolts, in proper sequence, to 25 ft. lbs. (34 Nm)

15. Install power steering pump assembly and tighten bolts to 20 ft. lbs. (27 Nm).

16. Install all heater hoses, vacuum hoses, throttle linkages and wiring.

17. Install the fuel lines using new O-rings at each connection.

18. Install the PCV valve and hose to the TBI assembly.

19. Refill the engine coolant.

20. Install the air cleaner assembly and connect the negative battery cable.

21. Start the engine and check for fluid leaks.

3.1L (VIN M) Engine

UPPER MANIFOLD

1. Disconnect the negative battery cable, drain the cooling system and remove the air cleaner.

2. Remove the throttle control cables, fuel lines and brackets from the manifold and throttle body.

3. Disconnect the vacuum lines from the upper intake manifold.

4. Remove the EGR valve and position the heater inlet hose out of the way.

5. Remove the ignition coil nuts and bolts.

6. Remove the power steering line clip from the alternator brace.

7. Remove the alternator brackets and disconnect the electrical connections from the throttle body.

8. Remove the upper intake manifold bolts and manifold from the throttle body.

9. Clean all gasket mating surfaces and sealing surfaces.

To install:

10. Apply a 2–3mm bead of Ultra Black RTV sealer on each ridge where the front and rear of the intake manifold contact the cylinder head.

11. Install a new gasket, upper manifold and bolts. Torque the bolts to 18 ft. lbs. (25 Nm).

12. Connect all vacuum and electrical connections.

13. Install the alternator brackets, power steering line clip and ignition coil fasteners.

14. Properly position heater inlet pipe hose clamps.

15. Install the EGR valve, control cable bracket, fuel lines, throttle cables and air cleaner.

16. Refill the cooling system, connect the battery cable, start the engine and check for leaks.

LOWER MANIFOLD

1. Disconnect the negative battery cable, drain the cooling system and remove the air cleaner.

2. Relieve the fuel pressure and remove the upper intake manifold.

3. Disconnect the fuel lines and remove the fuel rail.

4. Disconnect the coolant hoses and remove the serpentine belt.

5. Remove the alternator brackets and power steering pump.

6. Disconnect the upper radiator hose and heater hose from the thermostat housing.

7. Remove the ignition coil and engine torque strut.

8. Remove the rocker cover, lower manifold bolts and manifold.

To install:

9. Clean the gasket mating surfaces.

10. Apply a 2–3mm bead of Ultra Black RTV sealer on each ridge where the manifold contacts the engine block.

11. Install a new gasket, lower manifold and bolts. Torque the bolts to 116 inch lbs. (13 Nm).

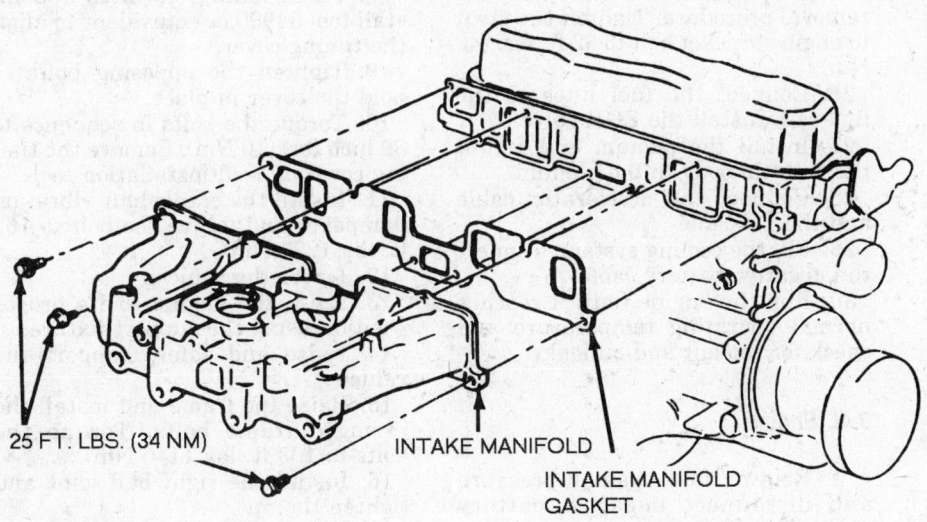

25 FT. LBS. (34 NM)

INTAKE MANIFOLD

INTAKE MANIFOLD
GASKET

TIGHTENING SEQUENCE

8470M059

Intake manifold installation — 2.5L engine

12. Connect all vacuum and electrical connections.

13. Install the rocker covers, engine torque strut and ignition coils

14. Install the heater hose, radiator hose, power steering pump, alternator brackets and serpentine belt.

15. Install the fuel rail and connect the coolant hose and fuel lines.

16. Install the upper intake manifold.

17. Refill the cooling system, connect the battery cable, start the engine and check for leaks.

3.1L (VIN T) Engine

1. Disconnect the negative battery cable. Drain the cooling system. Relieve fuel system pressure.

2. Disconnect the TV and accelerator cables from the plenum.

3. Remove the throttle body-to-plenum bolts and the throttle body. Remove the EGR valve.

4. Remove the plenum-to-intake manifold bolts and the plenum. Disconnect and plug the fuel lines and return pipes at the fuel rail.

5. Remove the serpentine drive belt. Remove the power steering pump-to-bracket bolts and support the pump aside; do not disconnect the pressure hoses.

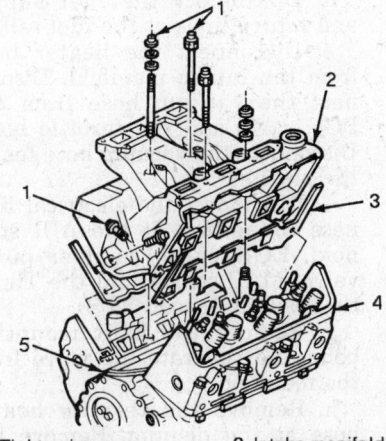

1. Tighten in proper sequence to 15 ft. lbs. (20 Nm), then retighten to 24 ft. lbs. (33 Nm)

⑦ ④ ③ ⑥
⑧ ① ② ⑤

2. Intake manifold
3. Gasket
4. Cylinder head
5. Sealer

8470M060

Intake manifold installation — 3.1L (VIN T) engine

6. Rotate the engine as follows:

a. Put the transaxle in **N**.

b. Remove the air cleaner.

c. Disconnect the negative battery cable.

d. Remove the torque strut to engine bracket bolt and swing strut aside.

e. Replace the passenger side torque strut to engine bracket bolt in engine bracket.

f. Place a prybar in the bracket so it contacts the bracket and the bolt.

g. Rotate the engine by pulling forward on the prybar. Align the slave hole in the driver side torque strut to the engine bracket hole.

h. Retain the engine in this position using the torque strut to engine bracket bolt.

NOTE: To prevent shearing of the rubber bushing, loosen the bolts on the engine strut before swinging the struts.

7. Remove the alternator-to-bracket bolts and support the alternator aside.

8. Loosen the alternator bracket. Disconnect the idle air vacuum hose from the throttle body.

9. Label and disconnect the electrical connectors from the fuel injectors. Remove the fuel rail.

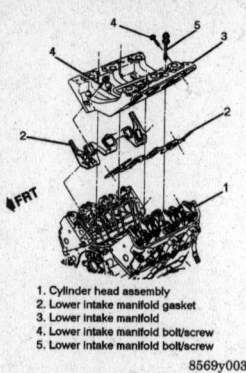

1. Cylinder head assembly
2. Lower intake manifold gasket
3. Lower intake manifold
4. Lower intake manifold bolt/screw
5. Lower intake manifold bolt/screw

8569y003

Intake manifold — 3.1L (VIN M) engine

10. Remove the breather tube. Disconnect the runners.

11. Remove both rocker arm cover-to-cylinder head bolts and the covers. Remove the radiator hose from the thermostat housing.

12. Label and disconnect the electrical connectors from the coolant temperature sensor and oil pressure sending unit. Remove the coolant sensor.

13. Remove the bypass hose from the filler neck and cylinder head. Remove top radiator hose.

14. Remove the intake manifold-to-cylinder head bolts and the manifold.

15. Loosen the rocker arm nuts, turn them 90 degrees and remove the pushrods; be sure to keep the components in order for installation purposes.

16. Clean all of the gasket mounting surfaces.

To install:

17. Place a bead of RTV sealer or equivalent on each ridge where the intake manifold and block meet. Install the intake manifold gasket in place on the block.

18. Install the pushrods and reposition the rocker arms, tighten the rocker arm nuts to 18 ft. lbs. (25 Nm).

19. Mount the intake manifold on the engine and tighten the bolts to 23 ft. lbs. (29 Nm) following the tightening sequence.

20. Connect the heater inlet pipe to the manifold. Install and connect the coolant sensor.

21. Attach the radiator hoses. Connect the wire at the oil sending switch.

22. Install the rocker covers, tighten the retaining bolts to 90 inch lbs. (10 Nm).

23. Install the runners, breather tube, fuel rail and connect the wires at the fuel injectors.

24. Install the alternator bracket and the alternator. Install the power steering pump.

25. After repairs, pull forward on the prybar to take the weight off the torque strut to engine bracket bolt and remove bolt from the strut slave hole and engine bracket. Reverse the removal procedure. Tighten the strut to engine bracket bolt to 32 ft. lbs. (43 Nm).

26. Connect the fuel lines to the fuel rail. Install the EGR valve.

27. Install the plenum and mount the throttle body to the plenum.

28. Connect the accelerator cable and the TV cable.

29. Fill the cooling system. Connect the negative battery cable.

30. Run the engine until it reaches normal operating temperature and check for coolant and oil leaks.

3.4L Engine

1. Relieve fuel system pressure and disconnect negative battery cable.

2. Drain the cooling system.

3. Remove the intake plenum as follows:

a. Remove the air cleaner assembly.

b. Remove the control cables from the throttle body.

c. Remove the fuel rail cover bolts and the fuel rail from the engine.

d. Disconnect the fuel supply and return lines at the fuel rail.

e. Disconnect the heater hose from the intake manifold. Disconnect the vacuum hose from the PCV valve and the throttle body. Disconnect the vacuum hose tee on the plenum.

f. Disconnect the electrical harness connectors at the AIR solenoid, EGR valve, canister purge valve, MAP sensor and the Throttle Position Sensor (TPS).

g. Remove the EGR mounting bolts and separate the valve from the manifold.

h. Remove the throttle heater hose at the plenum. Remove the fuel line bracket at the throttle body plenum.

i. Remove the nuts from the plenum support bracket. Remove the plenum mounting bolts and the intake plenum from the engine.

4. Remove fuel rail from the engine.

5. Remove the radiator hose from the thermostat housing. Disconnect the electrical connector at the temperature sensor.

6. Remove the heater pipe nut at the throttle body.

7. Remove intake manifold mounting bolts and manifold from the engine.

To install:

8. Clean mating surfaces and install tool 34995 or equivalent to align the timing cover.

9. Tighten the opposing bolts to hold the cover in place.

10. Torque the bolts in sequence to 89 inch lbs. (10 Nm). Remove the timing cover oil seal installation tool.

11. Install the crankshaft vibration dampener and torque the bolt to 162 ft. lbs. (220 Nm).

12. Lower the vehicle.

13. Raise the engine to its proper position using the support fixture.

14. Raise and safely support the vehicle.

15. Raise the frame and install the removed frame bolts. Torque the bolts to 103 ft. lbs. (140 Nm).

16. Install the right ball joint and tighten the nut.

17. Install the right front tire, torque the lug nuts to 100 ft. lbs. (136 Nm) and lower the vehicle.

18. Remove the engine support fixture.

19. Install the torque strut and bolt to the cylinder head bracket.

20. Install the serpentine belt, connect the negative battery cable and check for oil leaks.

3.8L Engine

1. Relieve the fuel system pressure.

2. Disconnect the negative battery cable. Place a clean drain pan under the radiator, open the drain cock and drain the cooling system.

3. Remove the air cleaner assembly and the fuel injector sight shield.

4. Disconnect the cables from the throttle body and mount bracket.

5. Remove the coolant recovery reservoir.

6. Remove the inner fender electrical cover on the right side.

7. Remove the right rear crossover pipe heat shield.

8. Disconnect the fuel lines from the fuel rail and from the cable bracket.

9. Remove the alternator and brace and position aside.

10. Remove the throttle body cable mounting bracket with the vacuum lines and disconnect the vacuum lines.

11. Tag and disconnect the electrical connections at the throttle body and both banks of fuel injectors.

12. Disconnect the vacuum hoses from the canister purge solenoid

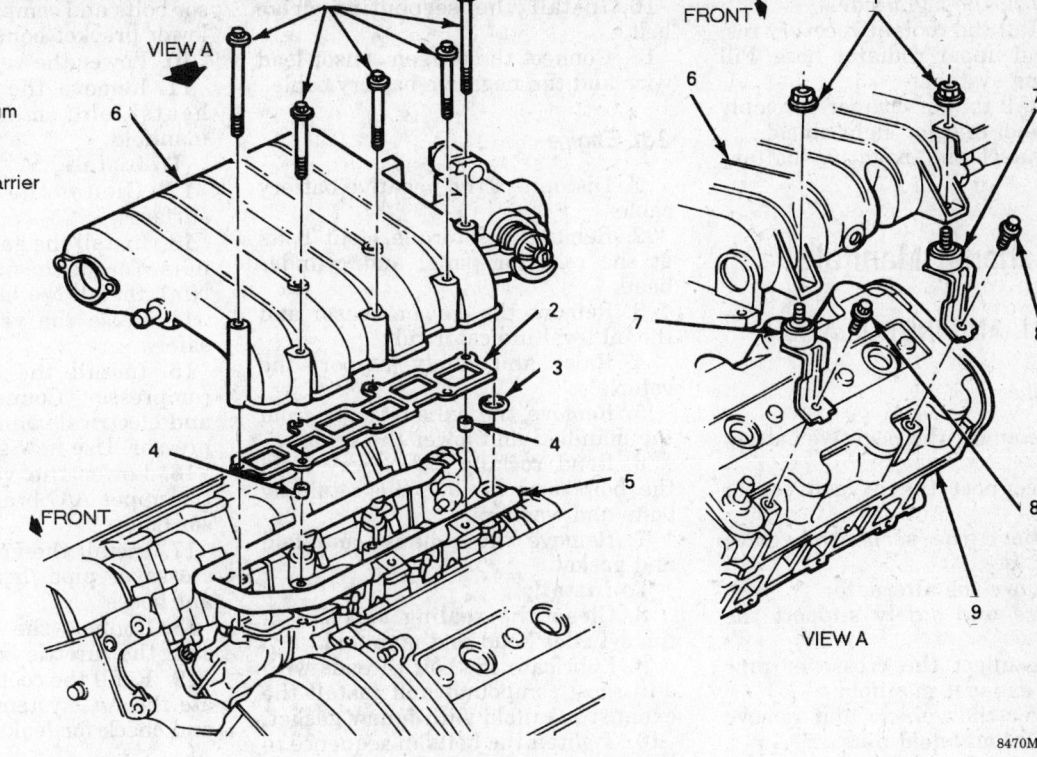

1. Bolt
2. Gasket
3. Seal
4. Pin
5. Fuel rail
6. Intake plenum
7. Bracket
8. Bolt
9. Camshaft carrier

VIEW A

FRONT

FRONT

VIEW A

8470M061

Upper intake manifold assembly — 3.4L engine

valve, transaxle module and intake connection.

13. Disconnect the power steering pump and move forward. Remove the belt tensioner pulley from the mounting bracket.

14. Disconnect the spark plug wires and lay aside.

15. Disconnect the coolant bypass hose from the intake manifold.

16. Disconnect the solenoid valve mounting bracket and power steering support brace from the intake manifold.

17. Disconnect the heater pipes from the intake and front cover.

18. Disconnect the alternator support brace from the intake.

19. Disconnect the upper radiator hose from the housing.

20. Remove the thermostat housing and thermostat from the intake.

21. Disconnect the electrical connector from the temperature sensor and sensor switch.

22. Remove the intake manifold bolts and manifold as an assembly from the vehicle.

23. Remove the upper intake manifold as follows:

   a. Remove the fuel injectors from the manifold.

   b. Remove the coolant sensor switch.

c. Remove the manifold end covers.

d. Remove the upper intake manifold and the throttle body from the manifold.

To install:

24. Clean all gasket material from the manifold mating surfaces.

25. Apply a bead of Loctite® Instant Gasket Eliminator or equivalent, to the lower manifold mating surfaces making sure to circle all bolt holes.

26. Install upper intake manifold onto the lower manifold and install bolts tightening to 22 ft. lbs. (30 Nm).

27. Install the manifold end cap covers and the coolant sensor switch.

28. Install the fuel injectors and rail to the manifold.

29. Install intake manifold gaskets to the engine. Apply sealer to ends of intake manifold seals. Install intake manifold assembly.

30. Apply thread lock compound to the intake manifold bolt threads and install. Tighten the manifold bolts to 88 inch lbs. (10 Nm), twice following the torque sequence.

31. Install the electrical connector at the temperature sensor switch at intake.

32. Install the thermostat housing and thermostat with a new gasket.

33. Connect the alternator support brace to the intake.

34. Connect the solenoid valve mounting bracket and power steering support brace to the intake manifold.

35. Connect the heater pipes to the intake and front cover.

36. Connect the coolant bypass hose to the intake manifold.

37. Install the power steering pump support bracket and torque to 37 ft. lbs. (49 Nm).

38. Install the spark plug wires on both sides.

39. Install the belt tensioner pulley and tighten to 33 ft. lbs. (45 Nm).

40. Install the power steering pump.

41. Connect the vacuum hoses to the canister purge solenoid valve and transaxle module and intake connection.

42. Connect the electrical connections at the throttle body and both banks of fuel injectors.

43. Install the alternator and brace.

44. Connect the throttle body cable mounting bracket with the vacuum lines.

45. Install the right rear crossover pipe heat shield.

46. Install the cables to the throttle body.

47. Connect the fuel lines to the fuel rail and mount bracket.

48. Install the inner fender electrical cover on the right side.

49. Install the coolant recovery reservoir and upper radiator hose. Fill the cooling system.

50. Install the air cleaner assembly and the fuel injector sight shield.

51. Connect the negative battery cable.

Exhaust Manifold

REMOVAL AND INSTALLATION

2.2L Engine

1. Disconnect the negative battery cable.

2. Disconnect the oxygen sensor lead wire.

3. Remove the serpentine drive belt.

4. Remove the alternator.

5. Raise and safely support the vehicle.

6. Disconnect the crossover pipe from the exhaust manifold.

7. Lower the vehicle and remove the exhaust manifold nuts.

8. Remove the oil fill tube and the dipstick.

9. Remove the exhaust manifold and the gasket.

To install:

10. Clean all mating surfaces of the cylinder head and the manifold. Inspect the manifold for cracks, broken flanges and gasket surface damage.

11. If installing a new exhaust manifold, install the oxygen sensor to the manifold.

12. Install the exhaust manifold gasket and install the exhaust manifold. Tighten the mounting nuts to 115 inch lbs. (13 Nm).

13. Install the oil fill tube and the dipstick.

14. Raise the vehicle and connect the crossover pipe to the exhaust manifold.

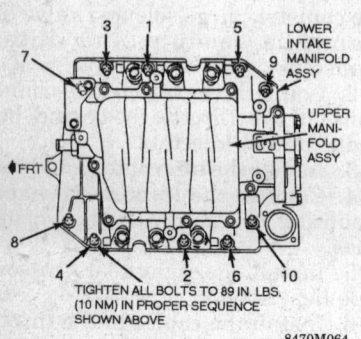

TIGHTEN ALL BOLTS TO 89 IN. LBS. (10 NM) IN PROPER SEQUENCE SHOWN ABOVE

8470M064

Intake manifold assembly bolt torque sequence — 3.8L engine

15. Lower the vehicle.

16. Install the serpentine drive belt.

17. Connect the oxygen sensor lead wire and the negative battery cable.

2.5L Engine

1. Disconnect the negative battery cable.

2. Remove the torque strut bolts at the radiator panel and cylinder head.

3. Remove the oxygen sensor and the oil level indicator tube.

4. Raise and safely support the vehicle.

5. Remove the exhaust pipe from the manifold and lower the vehicle.

6. Bend rocking tabs away from the bolts and remove the retaining bolts and washers.

7. Remove the exhaust manifold and gasket.

To install:

8. Clean the sealing surfaces of the cylinder head and manifold.

9. Lubricate the bolt threads with anti-seize compound and install the exhaust manifold with a new gasket.

10. Tighten the bolts in sequence to the appropriate torque.

11. Bend the locking tabs against the bolts.

12. Raise and support the vehicle safely.

13. Install the exhaust pipe to the manifold and lower the vehicle.

14. Install the oil level indicator tube, oxygen sensor and torque rod bracket at the cylinder head and radiator support.

15. Connect the negative battery cable.

3.1L (VIN M) Engine

LEFT SIDE (FRONT)

1. Discharge and recover the A/C refrigerant. Disconnect the battery cables and drain the cooling system.

2. Disconnect the electrical connectors and heater hoses from the throttle body.

3. Relieve the fuel pressure and remove the throttle body.

4. Disconnect the fuel lines and coolant hoses.

5. Remove the crossover heatshield, crossover pipe and engine strut.

6. Remove the 2 top A/C compressor and bracket bolts.

7. Raise the vehicle and support safely.

8. Disconnect the A/C hoses and electrical connectors from the compressor.

9. Remove the lower A/C compressor bolts and compressor. Remove the lower bracket bolts and bracket.

10. Lower the vehicle

11. Remove the exhaust manifold heatshield, manifold nuts and manifold.

To install:

12. Clean the gasket mating surfaces.

13. Install the gasket, manifold and nuts. Torque the nuts to 18 ft. lbs. (25 Nm). Install the heatshield.

14. Raise the vehicle and support safely.

15. Install the A/C bracket and compressor. Connect the A/C hoses and electrical connectors to the compressor. Use new sealing washers.

16. Lower the vehicle and install the upper A/C bracket and compressor bolts.

17. Install the engine torque strut, crossover pipe, heatshield and coolant hoses.

18. Connect the fuel lines and install the throttle body.

19. Refill the cooling system, evacuate the A/C system, start the engine and check for leaks.

RIGHT SIDE (REAR)

1. Drain the cooling system and disconnect the negative battery terminal.

2. Remove the throttle body.

3. Disconnect the radiator hose from the thermostat housing.

4. Remove the EGR tube.

5. Relieve the fuel pressure and disconnect the fuel lines.

6. Remove the crossover heatshield, crossover and oxygen sensor.

7. Remove the heatshield bolt from the top of the exhaust manifold.

8. Raise the vehicle and support safely.

9. Remove the exhaust pipe at the converter.

10. Remove the transaxle oil fill tube.

11. Remove the heatshield, manifold nuts and manifold.

To install:

12. Clean the gasket mating surfaces.

13. Install the gasket, manifold and nuts. Torque the nuts to 12 ft. lbs. (16 Nm). Install the heatshield.

14. Install the transaxle fill tube, exhaust pipe and lower the vehicle.

15. Install the heatshield top bolts, oxygen sensor, crossover pipe and heatshield.

16. Connect the fuel lines, EGR tube and radiator hose.

17. Install the throttle body.

BOLT TIGHTENING SEQUENCE: TIGHTEN BOLT POSITION NUMBER IN SEQUENCE AS FOLLOWS: 3-5-6-2-1-7-4 OR BY USING ALPHA GROUPS "A" AND "B". "A" BEING FIRST AND "B" LAST OR SIMULTANEOUS GANG DRIVE.

NOTE:
WHEN INSTALLING LOCK TABS ON EXHAUST MANIFOLD ONE EAR MUST BE BENT AGAINST FLAT OF HEX TO PREVENT ROTATION. (ANY ONE OF THE THREE EARS MAY BE USED).

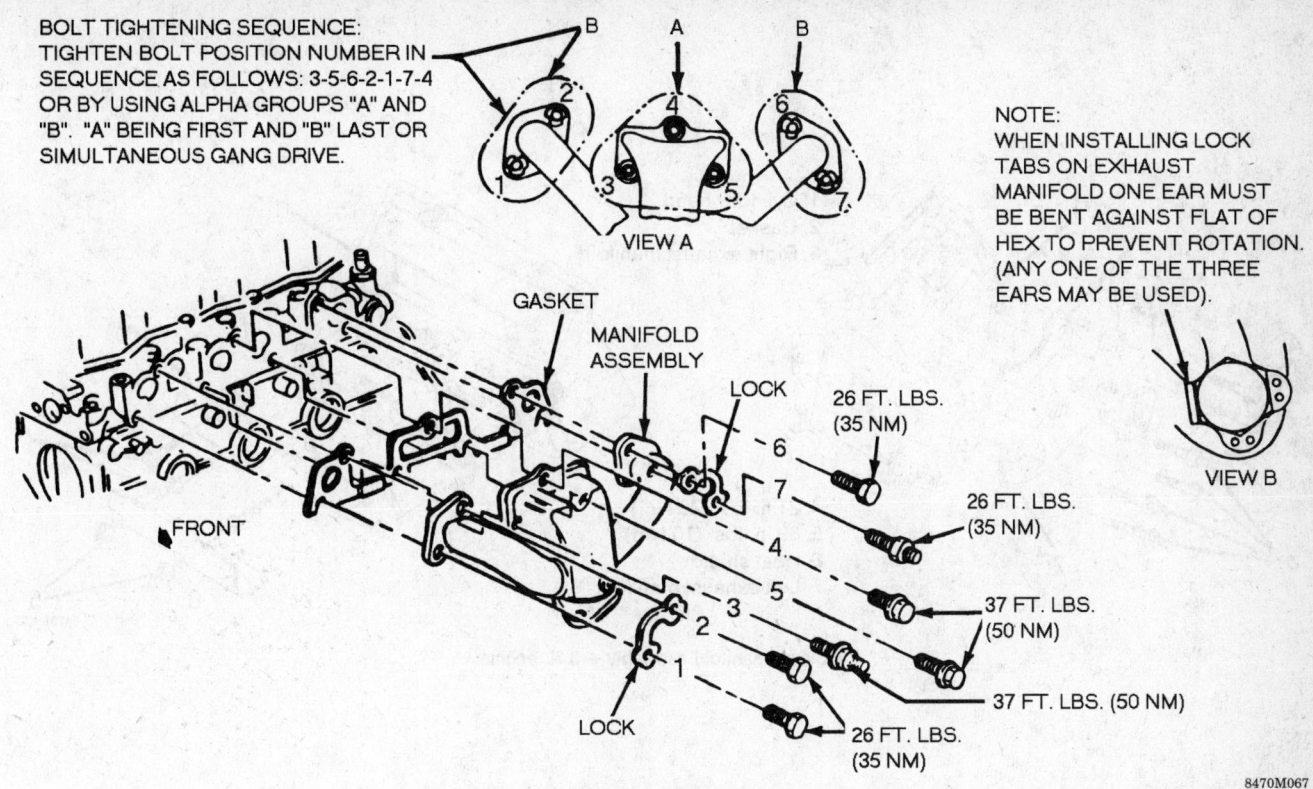

Exhaust manifold assembly — 2.5L engine

3.1L (VIN T) Engine

LEFT SIDE

1. Disconnect the negative battery cable.
2. Remove the coolant recovery bottle.
3. Relieve the accessory drive belt tension and remove the belt.
4. Remove the air conditioner compressor mounting bolts and support the compressor aside.
5. Remove the right side engine torque strut. Remove the bolts retaining the air conditioner compressor and torque strut mounting bracket, remove the bracket.
6. Remove the heat shield and crossover pipe at the manifold.
7. Remove the exhaust manifold mounting bolts and remove the manifold.
To install:
8. Clean the gasket mounting surfaces.
9. Install the exhaust manifold to the engine, loosely install the mounting bolts.
10. Install the exhaust crossover pipe. Tighten the exhaust manifold bolts to 18 ft. lbs. (25 Nm)

18. Refill the cooling system and connect the battery cable. Start the engine and check for leaks.

11. Attach the heat shield. Install the air conditioner and torque strut mounting bracket.
12. Install the torque strut. Mount the air conditioner compressor and install the accessory drive belt.
13. Install the coolant recovery bottle and connect the negative battery cable.

RIGHT SIDE

1. Disconnect the negative battery cable.
2. Raise and safely support the vehicle.
3. Remove the exhaust pipe at the crossover. Lower the vehicle.
4. Remove the coolant recovery bottle.
5. Rotate the engine as follows:
   a. Put the transaxle in **N**.
   b. Remove the air cleaner.
   c. Disconnect the negative battery cable.
   d. Remove the torque strut to engine bracket bolt and swing strut aside.
   e. Replace the passenger side torque strut to engine bracket bolt in engine bracket.
   f. Place a prybar in the bracket so it contacts the bracket and the bolt.
   g. Rotate the engine by pulling forward on the prybar. Align the

slave hole in the driver side torque strut to the engine bracket hole.
   h. Retain the engine in this position using the torque strut to engine bracket bolt.

NOTE: To prevent shearing of the rubber bushing, loosen the bolts on the engine strut before swinging the struts.

6. Remove the air cleaner, breather, mass air flow sensor and heat shield.
7. Remove the crossover at the manifold. Disconnect the accelerator and TV cables.
8. Remove the manifold mounting bolts and remove the manifold. Clean the manifold mounting surfaces.
To install:
9. Install the exhaust manifold and loosely install the mounting bolts.
10. Attach the crossover at the manifold. Tighten the manifold mounting bolts to 18 ft. lbs. (25 Nm).
11. Connect the accelerator and TV cables.
12. Attach the air cleaner, breather and mass air flow sensor.
13. Position the engine in it's normal resting position as follows:
   a. Pull forward on the prybar to take the weight off the torque strut to engine bracket bolt.

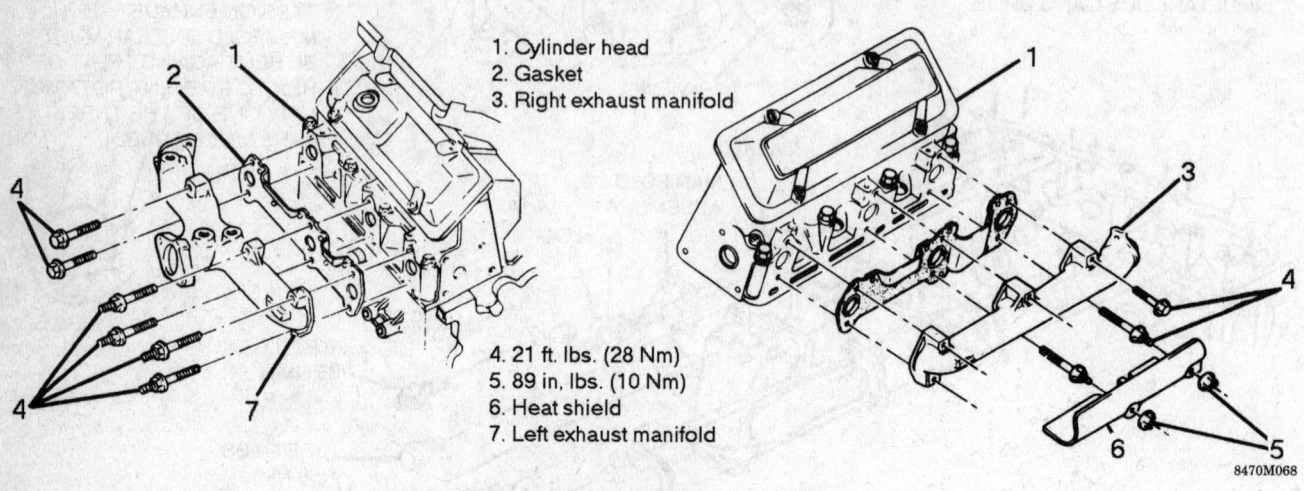

1. Cylinder head
2. Gasket
3. Right exhaust manifold

4. 21 ft. lbs. (28 Nm)
5. 89 in, lbs. (10 Nm)
6. Heat shield
7. Left exhaust manifold

8470M068

Exhaust manifold assembly — 3.1L engine

b. Remove bolt from the strut slave hole and engine bracket.

c. Position the strut to the engine and tighten the strut to engine bracket bolt to 32 ft. lbs. (43 Nm).

14. Install the coolant recovery bottle.

15. Raise and safely support the vehicle. Install the exhaust pipe to the crossover.

16. Lower the vehicle. Connect the negative battery cable.

3.4L Engine

LEFT SIDE (FRONT)

1. Remove air cleaner assembly. Disconnect the negative battery cable.

2. Remove exhaust crossover.

3. Remove the engine torque strut bracket at frame and position aside.

4. Remove upper radiator shroud. Remove the cooling fan assembly.

5. Remove front hose from air pipe for manual transaxle only.

6. Remove exhaust retaining nuts and manifold. Remove old gasket and discard.

To install:

7. Install a new gasket, manifold and heat shields onto the engine.

8. Install manifold nuts and torque to 115 inch lbs. (13 Nm).

9. Install cooling fan, radiator shroud and torque strut into position and secure.

10. Install exhaust crossover. Install negative battery cable and air cleaner assembly.

RIGHT SIDE (REAR) WITH AUTOMATIC TRANSAXLE

1. Disconnect the negative battery cable.

2. Remove right side cam carrier as follows:

   a. Remove intake plenum and right timing belt cover.

   b. Remove right spark plug wires.

   c. Remove air/oil separator hose at cam carrier cover.

   d. Remove cam carrier cover bolts and lift of cover. Remove gasket and O-rings from cover.

   e. Remove secondary timing belt by removing secondary timing belt actuator and tensioner assembly and sliding belt from pulleys.

   f. Install 6 sections of fuel line hoses under camshaft and between lifters. This will hold lifters in carrier.

   g. Remove exhaust crossover pipe and torque strut.

   h. Remove torque strut bracket at engine. Remove front engine lift hook.

   i. Remove cam carrier mounting bolts and nuts and remove cam carrier.

   j. Remove cam carrier gasket from cylinder head.

3. Remove exhaust manifold to crossover pipe nuts and the crossover pipe.

4. Raise and safely support vehicle.

5. Remove front exhaust pipe at manifold. Lower vehicle.

6. Remove electrical connector from oxygen sensor.

7. Remove exhaust manifold nuts, heat shield and manifold.

To install:

8. Clean all mating surfaces, install manifold gasket and heat shields.

9. Install exhaust manifold. Torque nuts to 116 inch lbs. (13 Nm).

10. Install electrical connector at oxygen sensor.

11. Raise and safely support vehicle.

12. Install exhaust pipe at manifold. Lower vehicle.

13. Install exhaust crossover pipe.

14. Install right cam carrier as follows:

   a. Install new gasket on cam carrier to cylinder mounting surface.

b. Install cam hold-down tool J–38613 or equivalent, to carrier assembly.

c. Install cam carrier to cylinder head. Install mounting bolts and nuts. Torque bolts and nuts to 18 ft. lbs.

d. Remove lifter hold-down hoses and cam hold-down tool.

e. Install torque strut bracket to engine and install torque strut.

f. Install engine crossover pipe and engine lift hook.

g. Install secondary timing belt and cam carrier cover and gasket.

h. Install spark plug wires and cover.

15. Reconnect negative battery cable.

RIGHT SIDE (REAR) WITH MANUAL TRANSAXLE

1. Disconnect the negative battery cable. Remove the air cleaner assembly.
2. Remove exhaust crossover.
3. Raise and safely support vehicle.
4. Remove exhaust pipe and converter assembly. Remove oxygen sensor connector.
5. Remove EGR pipe at manifold and manifold heat shields.
6. Remove exhaust manifold retaining nuts, manifold and gasket from the engine.

To install:

7. Install gasket and manifold to the engine. Torque retaining nuts to 116 inch lbs. (13 Nm).
8. Install EGR pipe and heat shields to exhaust manifold.
9. Install electrical connector at oxygen sensor.
10. Install exhaust pipe to manifold and lower vehicle.
11. Install exhaust crossover and negative battery cable.
12. Start the engine and check for leaks.

3.8L Engine

LEFT SIDE (FRONT)

1. Disconnect the negative battery cable.
2. Remove the air cleaner assembly and disconnect the spark plug wires.
3. Disconnect the exhaust crossover pipe.
4. Remove the oil level indicator and tube from the manifold.
5. Disconnect the engine lift bracket and the air conditioner compressor support brace.
6. Remove the exhaust manifold.

To install:

7. Clean the mating surfaces and loosely install the exhaust manifold and retaining bolts.
8. Install the crossover pipe to the manifold and support bracket.
9. Tighten the manifold retaining bolts to 38 ft. lbs. (52 Nm).
10. Install the engine lift bracket and the air conditioner compressor support brace.
11. Install the oil level indicator and tube to the manifold.
12. Install the air cleaner assembly and connect the spark plug wires.
13. Connect the negative battery cable.

RIGHT SIDE (REAR)

1. Disconnect the negative battery cable. Remove the fuel injector sight shield.
2. Remove the coolant recovery reservoir. Disconnect the exhaust crossover pipe.
3. Remove the air cleaner assembly and disconnect the spark plug wires.
4. Remove the oil level indicator and tube from the manifold.
5. Disconnect the oxygen sensor electrical connector.
6. Disconnect the engine torque strut and bolt from the engine.
7. Remove the engine lift bracket from the engine.
8. Remove the spark plugs from the right side rear bank.
9. Raise and support the vehicle safely.
10. Remove the front exhaust pipe and the converter from the vehicle.
11. Remove the right rear engine mount to frame nuts and lower the engine.
12. Use a floor jack and raise and support safely the right rear corner of the engine for access.
13. Remove the exhaust manifold retaining bolts and remove the exhaust manifold.

To install:

14. Clean the mating surfaces and loosely install the exhaust manifold and retaining bolts.
15. Install the crossover pipe to the manifold and support bracket.
16. Tighten the manifold retaining bolts to 38 ft. lbs. (52 Nm).
17. Lower the engine and remove the floor jack.
18. Raise and support the vehicle safely.
19. Install the front exhaust pipe and the converter.
20. Install the right rear engine mount to frame nuts and lower the engine.

21. Tighten the crossover bolts.
22. Install the spark plugs to the right side rear bank.
23. Install the engine lift bracket to the engine.
24. Connect the oxygen sensor electrical connector.
25. Connect the engine torque strut and bolt to the engine and torque to 35 ft. lbs. (47 Nm).
26. Install the oil level indicator and tube to the manifold.
27. Install the air cleaner assembly, injector sight shield and connect the spark plug wires.
28. Connect the negative battery cable.

Turbocharger

REMOVAL AND INSTALLATION

3.1L Engine

1. Disconnect the negative battery cable.
2. Drain the coolant from the radiator.
3. Remove the intercooler to intake manifold duct attaching bolt at the thermostat housing and remove the intercooler to intake manifold duct.
4. Disconnect the air cleaner to turbocharger duct at the turbo.
5. Disconnect the air cleaner inlet duct.
6. Remove the air cleaner and duct assembly.
7. Disconnect the turbocharger to intercooler duct at the turbocharger.
8. Remove the turbocharger heat covers.
9. Disconnect the oxygen sensor electrical connector and remove the oxygen sensor.
10. Disconnect the turbo water and oil lines at the turbocharger.
11. Disconnect the vacuum lines at the turbocharger compressor outlet and actuator assembly.
12. Disconnect the actuator arm from the wastegate.
13. Disconnect the wastegate actuator from the turbocharger.
14. Remove the cruise control servo and set aside.
15. Disconnect the turbocharger downpipe at the turbocharger.
16. Disconnect the water supply clamp and rubber hose.
17. Disconnect the turbocharger drain hose at the drain pipe.
18. Remove the turbocharger to exhaust crossover attaching bolts and remove the turbocharger from the engine.

To install:

19. Install the turbocharger to the engine compartment and tighten the turbocharger to exhaust crossover bolts to 17 ft. lbs. (23 Nm).

20. Connect the turbocharger drain hose at the drain pipe.

21. Connect the the water supply clamp and rubber hose.

22. Connect the turbocharger downpipe at the turbocharger and tighten to 17 ft. lbs. (23 Nm).

23. Install the cruise control servo.

24. Connect the wastegate actuator to the turbocharger.

25. Connect the actuator arm to the wastegate.

26. Connect the vacuum lines at the turbocharger compressor outlet and actuator assembly.

27. Connect the turbo water line and tighten to 21 ft. lbs. (28 Nm).

28. Connect the oil line at the turbocharger and tighten to 15 ft. lbs. (20 Nm).

29. Install the oxygen sensor and tighten to 31 ft. lbs. (42 Nm). Install the electrical connector.

30. Install the turbocharger heat covers.

31. Connect the turbocharger to intercooler duct at the turbocharger.

32. Install the air cleaner and duct assembly.

33. Install the air cleaner to turbocharger duct at the turbo.

34. Install the intercooler to intake manifold duct attaching bolt at the thermostat housing and tighten to 17 ft. lbs. (23 Nm).

35. Fill the radiator with coolant.

36. Connect the negative battery cable.

NOTE: Prime the turbocharger with oil before running the engine. Crank the engine with the fuel pump fuse removed until normal operating oil pressure is achieved.

37. Perform the idle learn procedure to allow the ECM memory to be updated with the correct IAC valve pintle position and provide for a stable idle speed.

a. Install a Tech 1 scan tool.

b. Turn the ignition to the **ON** position, engine not running.

c. Select IAC SYSTEM, then IDLE LEARN in the MISC TEST mode.

d. Proceed with idle learn as directed by the scan tool.

Timing Chain/Gear Front Cover

REMOVAL AND INSTALLATION

2.2L Engine

1. Disconnect the negative battery cable.

2. Remove the electrical center side cover.

3. Remove the serpentine drive belt tensioner, bracket and the belt.

4. Drain the engine oil and remove the oil pan.

5. Remove the crankshaft pulley and the pulley hub.

6. Remove the front cover bolts and remove the front cover. To loosen the cover it may be necessary to tap on the cover with a rubber mallet.

To install:

7. Clean the sealing surface of the engine block and the cover. Install a new gasket.

8. Install the front cover over the dowel pins. Install the front cover bolts and tighten them to 97 inch lbs. (11 Nm).

9. Install the crankshaft pulley hub and the crankshaft pulley.

10. Install the oil pan and refill the engine oil to the proper level.

11. Install the serpentine drive belt tensioner, bracket and the belt.

12. Install the electrical center side cover and connect the negative battery cable.

2.5L Engine

1992

1. Disconnect negative battery cable.

2. Remove the accessory drive belt and tensioner.

3. Raise and safely support the vehicle.

4. Remove the flywheel cover, right front tire and right side engine splash shield.

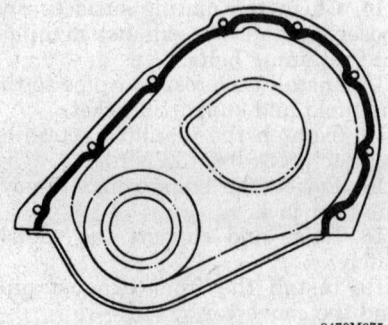

Front cover sealer application — 1992 2.5L engine

8470M075

5. Install appropriate tool to prevent flywheel from turning. Remove the crankshaft pulley bolt and washer.

6. Using tool J–24420B or equivalent, remove the crankshaft pulley.

7. Remove the crankshaft key so it won't get lost. Remove the front cover retaining screws. Lower the vehicle.

8. Remove the front cover from the engine.

9. Clean all gasket material from all mating surfaces. Apply degreaser to all sealing surfaces.

To install:

10. Apply a ³⁄₈ in. by ³⁄₁₆ in. thick bead of sealer to the joint at the oil pan and front cover. Apply a ¼ in. by ⅛ in. bead of sealer to the front cover at block mating surfaces.

11. Install alignment tool J–34995 in the front cover oil seal. Install front cover to the engine and partially tighten 2 opposing cover screws while leaving the alignment tool in place.

12. Raise and safely support the vehicle. Tighten the remaining cover bolts to 89 inch lbs. (10 Nm). Remove the alignment tool.

13. Install the crankshaft pulley using tool J–29113 or equivalent, making sure to put key in nose of crankshaft prior to installation.

14. Install washer and bolt into crankshaft and tighten to 162 ft. lbs. (220 Nm) while holding flywheel from turning using appropriate tool.

15. Install the right front tire, splash shield and flywheel cover.

16. Lower the vehicle and install the serpentine belt.

17. Reconnect the negative battery cable.

3.1L (VIN M) Engine

1. Disconnect the negative battery terminal.

2. Drain the engine oil and remove the oil pan.

3. Drain the cooling system and remove the serpentine belt.

4. Remove the alternator brackets, power steering pump and belt tensioner.

5. Remove the coolant bypass adapter and coolant hose from the water pump.

6. Remove the crankshaft balancer and knock sensor.

7. Remove the front cover bolts, front cover and gasket.

To install:

8. Clean the gasket mating surfaces and apply a ⅛ in. (3mm) bead of silicone sealer to the oil pan, engine block and front cover.

9. Install the front cover bolts, front cover and gasket. Torque the small bolts to 15 ft. lbs. (21 Nm) and the large bolts to 41 ft. lbs. (55 Nm).

10. Install the crankshaft balancer and knock sensor.

11. Install the coolant bypass adapter and coolant hose to the water pump.

12. Install the alternator brackets, power steering pump and belt tensioner.

13. Refill the cooling system and install the serpentine belt.

14. Install the oil pan and refill the engine oil.

15. Connect the negative battery terminal, start the engine and check for leaks.

3.1L (VIN T) Engine

1. Disconnect the negative terminal from the battery. Drain the cooling system.

2. Remove the serpentine belt and the belt tensioner.

3. Remove the alternator-to-bracket bolts and remove the alternator, with the wires attached, support it aside.

4. Remove the power steering pump-to-bracket bolts and support it aside. Do not disconnect the pressure hoses.

5. Raise and safely support the vehicle.

6. Remove the right side inner fender splash shield. Remove the flywheel dust cover.

7. Remove the crankshaft pulley and damper using the appropriate puller.

8. Label and disconnect the starter wires, remove the starter.

9. Drain the engine oil and remove the oil pan. Remove the lower front cover bolts.

10. Lower the vehicle. Disconnect the radiator hose from the water pump.

11. Disconnect the heater hose from the cooling system filler pipe.

12. Remove the bypass and overflow hoses.

13. Remove the upper front cover-to-engine bolts.

14. Remove the front cover.

15. Clean front cover mounting surfaces.

To install:

16. Apply a thin bead of silicone sealant on the front cover mating surface and using a new gasket, install the front cover on the engine with the top bolts to hold it in place.

17. Raise and safely support the vehicle.

18. Install the oil pan. Install the lower front cover bolts, tighten all of the front cover bolts to 26–35 ft. lbs. (35–48 Nm).

19. Install the serpentine belt and idler pulley. Install the damper on the engine using tool J–29113 or equivalent. Install the starter.

20. Install the inner fender splash shield. Lower the vehicle.

21. Attach the radiator hose too the water pump and attach the heater hoses.

22. Install the power steering pump and the alternator.

23. Attach the spark plug wire shield. Fill the cooling system.

24. Connect the negative battery cable. Check for coolant and oil leaks.

3.4L Engine

1. Disconnect the negative battery cable.

2. Remove secondary timing belt tensioner mounting bracket and gasket by removing tensioner pulley and mounting bracket bolts.

3. Remove secondary timing belt idler pulleys.

4. Remove the front engine lift hook.

5. Remove engine torque strut mount bracket to frame bolts and position strut aside.

6. Remove the upper radiator support, cooling fan bolts and cooling fans.

7. Drain cooling system and remove lower radiator hose from coolant pump inlet pipe. Remove both cooling fans.

8. Remove coolant hoses at the water pump and the heater pipe bracket retainer bolts at frame.

9. If equipped with manual transaxle, remove the air hose at the front exhaust pipe.

10. Remove the heater pipe retaining screws at the frame.

11. Raise and safely support vehicle. Remove right front tire and wheel assembly. Remove right splash shield.

12. Remove crankshaft pulley and damper. Remove oil filter.

13. Remove air conditioner compressor mounting bracket bolts. Remove the air conditioning compressor and set compressor aside.

14. Remove the starter motor and position aside.

15. Remove the torsional damper.

16. Remove the alternator and position aside. Remove the rear alternator bracket. Lower vehicle.

17. Disconnect and relocate the engine oil cooler assembly as required.

18. Remove the front oil pan retainer bolts and nuts. Loosen the remaining oil pan mounting bolts.

19. Remove the lower front cover mounting bolts.

20. Remove the timing belt drive sprocket retaining bolt and extract sprocket using tool J–38616 or equivalent.

21. Remove the forward lamp relay center screw and position relay center aside.

22. Remove coolant pump pulley.

23. Remove upper front cover bolts and the front cover. Remove the old gasket and clean mating surfaces of front cover and block.

To install:

24. Apply GM sealer 1052080 or equivalent, to lower edges of the sealing surface of the front cover and install. Apply thread sealant to large bolts and tighten cover into place.

25. Install coolant pump pulley. Install oil cooler coolant hose to front cover.

26. Install forward light relay center and upper alternator retaining bolts.

27. Install the drive belt sprocket and retaining bolt.

28. Raise and safely support vehicle.

29. Install starter motor.

30. Reinstall halfshaft and rear alternator bracket.

31. Install lower front cover bolts. Tighten lower cover bolts to 18 ft. lbs. (25 Nm). Install air conditioning compressor mounting bolts.

32. Install oil filter, crankshaft damper and crankshaft pulley.

33. Install right side splash shield and wheel assembly. Lower vehicle.

34. Tighten upper front cover small bolts to 18 ft. lbs. (25 Nm) and the front cover large bolts to 35 ft. lbs. (47 Nm).

35. Install heater hoses at front cover, lower radiator hose to coolant pump and add coolant to correct level.

36. Install retainer screws into heater pipe bracket.

37. Install both radiator fans, upper radiator support and torque strut to frame bolts.

38. Install front engine lift hook and secondary timing belt idler pulley.

39. Install secondary timing belt tensioner mounting bracket tightening bolts to 37 ft. lbs. (50 Nm).

40. Reconnect negative battery cable.

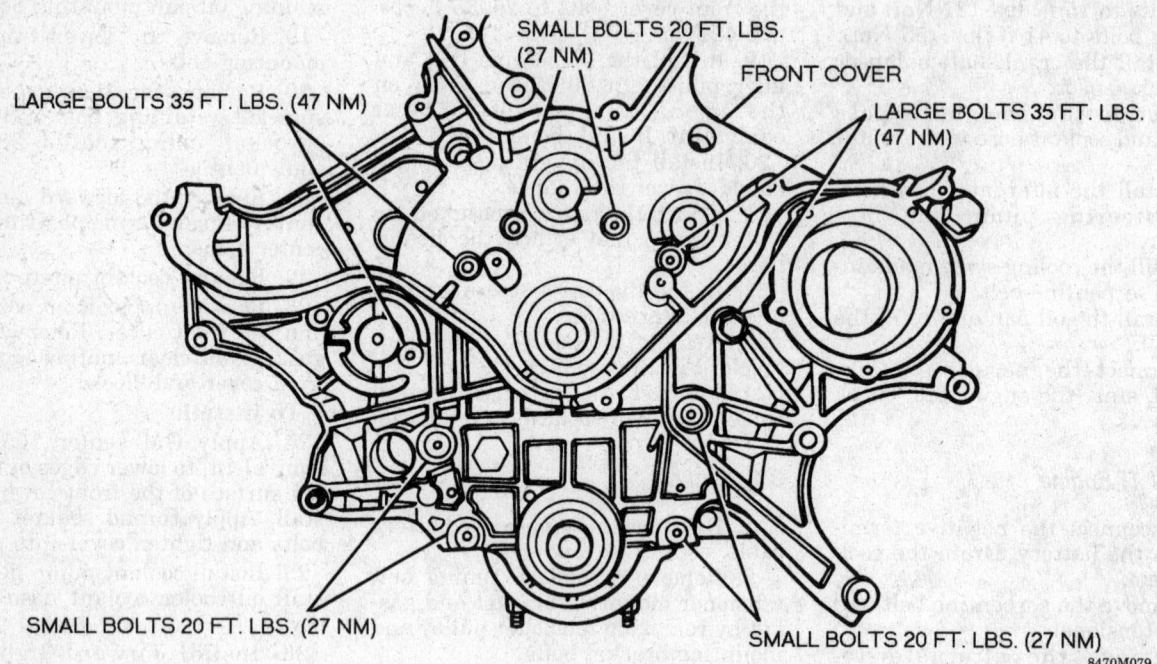

LARGE BOLTS 35 FT. LBS. (47 NM)

SMALL BOLTS 20 FT. LBS. (27 NM)

FRONT COVER

LARGE BOLTS 35 FT. LBS. (47 NM)

SMALL BOLTS 20 FT. LBS. (27 NM)

SMALL BOLTS 20 FT. LBS. (27 NM)

8470M079

Front cover assembly bolt locations — 3.4L engine.

3.8L Engine

1. Disconnect the negative battery cable.
2. Remove the crankshaft balancer.
3. Remove the crankshaft sensor cover.
4. Disconnect the electrical connections at the camshaft, crankshaft and oil pressure sensors.
5. Raise and support the vehicle safely.
6. Drain the engine oil and remove the oil pan to front cover bolts.
7. Remove the oil filter and disconnect the oil cooler pipes from the oil filter adapter housing.

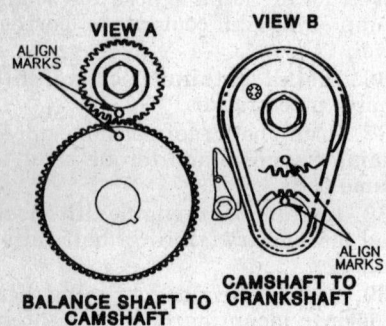

VIEW A

ALIGN MARKS

VIEW B

ALIGN MARKS

ALIGN MARKS

BALANCE SHAFT TO CAMSHAFT

CAMSHAFT TO CRANKSHAFT

8470MA79

Timing balancer shaft and camshaft marks — 3.8L engine

8. Lower the vehicle and drain the cooling system.
9. Remove the alternator and brace.
10. Disconnect the heater hoses and pipe and the bypass hose from the cover.
11. Disconnect the lower radiator hose.
12. Remove the coolant pump pulley.
13. Remove the front cover attaching bolts and cover with the oil filter adapter as an assembly.
14. Remove the oil filter adapter housing.
15. Remove the oil pressure valve, spring and oil pump from the front cover.
16. Remove the coolant pump from the front cover.
17. Pry the oil seal out of the cover using a prying tool.
   To install:

NOTE: The oil pan bolts can be loosened and the pan dropped slightly for front cover clearance. If the oil pan gasket is excessively swollen, the oil pan must be removed and the gasket replaced.

18. Clean the mating surfaces of the front cover and cylinder block with a degreaser.

19. Install the oil filter and adapter housing with the oil pressure valve and spring to the cover. Tighten the bolts to 24 ft. lbs. (33 Nm).
20. Install the oil pump assembly to the cover.
21. Use a new gasket, apply sealer to the bolt threads and install the coolant pump to the front cover.
22. Lubricate a new front cover oil seal with clean engine oil and install it to the front cover, using tool J–35354 or equivalent. Use the crankshaft balancer bolt with the tool and tighten the bolt until the seal is seated in the cover. Remove the tool.
23. Install the front cover to the engine and install the upper cover bolts. Tighten the upper cover bolts to 124 inch lbs. (14 Nm).
24. Install the crankshaft sensor and adjust, using tool J–37089 or equivalent.
25. Install the sensor cover and electrical connections.
26. Install the crankshaft balancer.
27. Install the oil cooler lines and the oil filter.
28. Lower the vehicle and install the coolant pump pulley.
29. Install the lower radiator hose, bypass hose and heater hoses.
30. Install the alternator and brace.
31. Add engine coolant, oil and connect the negative battery cable.

Front Cover Oil Seal

REPLACEMENT

1. Disconnect the negative terminal from the battery. Remove the serpentine belt.
2. Raise and safely support the vehicle. Remove the right side inner fender splash shield.
3. Remove the damper retaining bolt.
4. Using the appropriate tools, remove the damper pulley from the crankshaft.
5. Using a small prybar, pry out the seal in the front cover.

NOTE: Use care not to damage the seal seat or the crankshaft while removing or installing the seal. Inspect the crankshaft seal surface for signs of wear.

6. Coat the new seal with oil. Using a seal installer tool, drive the new seal in the cover with the lip facing towards the engine.
7. Press the crankshaft pulley onto the crankshaft, using the appropriate tools. Torque the damper bolt to 76 ft. lbs. (103 Nm) for 3.1L engines, 78 ft. lbs (106 Nm) for 3.4L engine, 162 ft. lbs. (220 Nm) for 2.5L engine or 105 ft. lbs. + an additional 56 degree turn for 3.8L engine.
8. Install the inner fender splash shield. Lower the vehicle.
9. Install the serpentine belt.
10. Connect the negative battery cable. Run the engine to normal operating temperature and check for leaks.

Timing Chain and Sprockets

REMOVAL AND INSTALLATION

2.2L Engine

1. Disconnect the negative battery cable.
2. Remove the front timing chain cover.
3. Align the marks on the camshaft sprocket and the crankshaft sprocket.
4. Remove the timing chain tensioner upper bolt.
5. Loosen the timing chain tensioner Torx® bolt but do not remove it.
6. Remove the camshaft sprocket and the timing chain.
7. Using GM tool J–22888–20 or equivalent, remove the crankshaft sprocket.

To install:
8. Using GM tool J–22888–20 or equivalent, install the crankshaft sprocket. Make sure the sprocket is fully seated against the crankshaft.
9. Compress the tensioner spring and insert a nail or cotter pin into the tensioner hole to hold it in place.
10. Align the crankshaft and camshaft timing marks with the tabs on the tensioner.
11. Install the tensioner bolt.
12. Install the timing chain onto the camshaft and crankshaft sprocket.
13. Align the camshaft dowel with the dowel hole in the camshaft sprocket and install the sprocket.
14. By hand, fully seat the camshaft sprocket to the camshaft.
15. Tighten the timing chain tensioner to 18 ft. lbs. (24 Nm) and the camshaft sprocket bolt to 77 ft. lbs. (105 Nm).
16. Remove the pin or nail from the timing chain tensioner.
17. Install the timing chain cover and connect the negative battery cable.

2.5L Engine

1992

1. Disconnect negative battery cable.
2. Remove the front cover as follows:
   a. Remove the accessory drive belt and tensioner.
   b. Raise and safely support the vehicle. Remove the flywheel cover, right front tire and right side engine splash shield.
   c. Install appropriate tool to prevent flywheel from turning. Remove the crankshaft pulley bolt and washer. Using tool J–24420B or equivalent, remove the crankshaft pulley.
   d. Remove the crankshaft key so it won't get lost. Remove the front

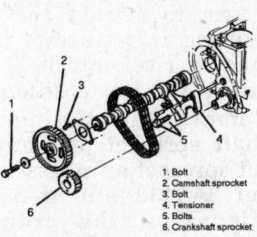

ALIGN TABS ON TENSIONER WITH MARKS ON CAMSHAFT AND CRANKSHAFT SPROCKETS

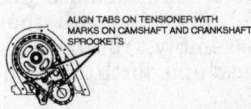

8470M081

Timing chain and sprockets — 2.2L engine

1. Bolt
2. Camshaft sprocket
3. Bolt
4. Tensioner
5. Bolts
6. Crankshaft sprocket

cover retaining screws. Lower the vehicle.
   e. Remove the front cover from the engine.
3. Position the engine at TDC so timing marks on the camshaft and crankshaft are in alignment.
4. Retract the timing chain tensioner and hold it in retract position with an appropriate size cotter pin or rivet.
5. Remove the camshaft bolt. Remove the timing chain and sprocket from the front of the engine.
6. Clean timing chain and sprocket and check for damage or excess wear, replace components as required.

To install:
7. Install timing chain and sprocket making sure timing marks on both the camshaft and the crankshaft are in alignment.
8. Install the camshaft gear retainer bolt and washer. Tighten the bolt to 43 ft. lbs. (58 Nm).
9. Remove the cotter pin or rivet holding the tensioner in the retracted position.
10. Install the front cover to the engine as follows:
   a. Apply a ⅜ in. by 3/16 in. thick bead of sealer to the joint at the oil pan and front cover. Apply a ¼ in. by ⅛ in. bead of sealer to the front cover at block mating surfaces.
   b. Install alignment tool J–34995 in the front cover oil seal. Install front cover to the engine and partially tighten 2 opposing cover screws while leaving the alignment tool in place.
   c. Raise and safely support the vehicle. Tighten the remaining cover bolts to 89 inch lbs. (10 Nm). Remove the alignment tool.
   d. Install the crankshaft pulley using tool J–29113 or equivalent, making sure to put key in nose of crankshaft prior to installation.
   e. Install washer and bolt into crankshaft and tighten to 162 ft. lbs. (220 Nm) while holding flywheel from turning using appropriate tool.
   f. Install the right front tire, splash shield and flywheel cover.
   g. Lower the vehicle and install the serpentine belt tensioner and belt.
   h. Reconnect the negative battery cable.
11. Start the engine and check for leaks.

3.1L Engine

1. Disconnect the negative battery cable.

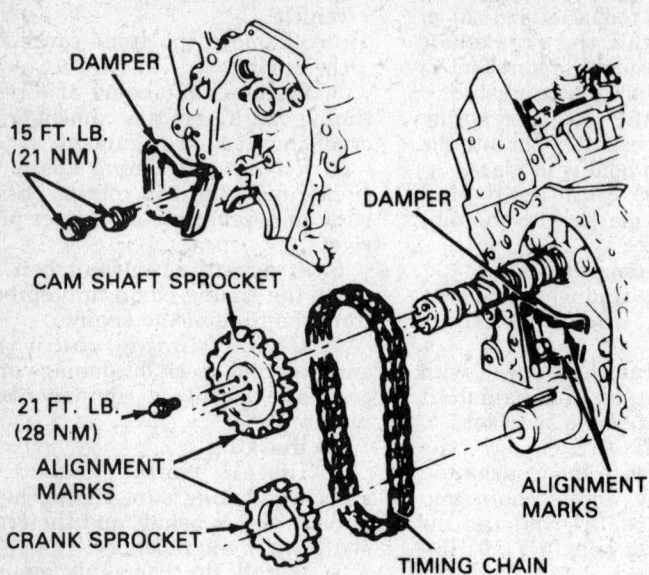

DAMPER

15 FT. LB.
(21 NM)

CAM SHAFT SPROCKET

DAMPER

21 FT. LB.
(28 NM)

ALIGNMENT
MARKS

CRANK SPROCKET

ALIGNMENT
MARKS

TIMING CHAIN

NOTE—ALIGN TIMING MARKS ON CAM
& CRANK SPROCKETS USING ALIGNMENT
MARKS ON DAMPER STAMPING OR CAST
ALIGNMENT MARKS ON CYL & CASE

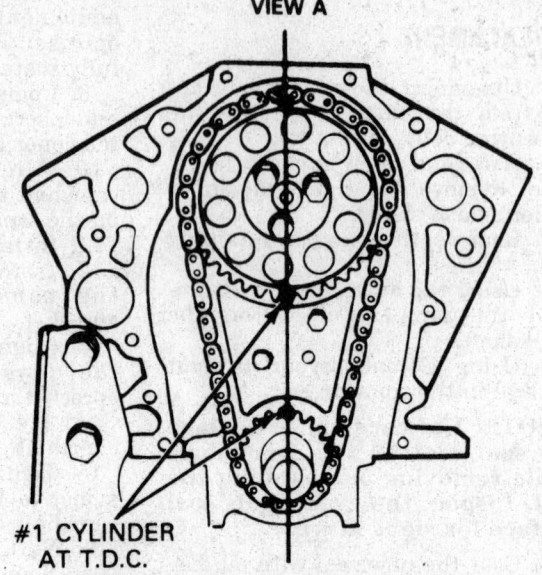

VIEW A

#1 CYLINDER
AT T.D.C.

NOTE—CAMSHAFT SPROCKET MARK
AT 6 O'CLOCK
CRANKSHAFT SPROCKET MARK
AT 12 O'CLOCK

8470M084

Timing chain and sprockets — 3.1L engine, 3.4L engine similar

2. Remove the front cover assembly.

3. Place the No. 1 piston at TDC with the marks on the crankshaft and the camshaft aligned.

4. Remove the camshaft sprocket and the timing chain.

NOTE: If the camshaft sprocket does not come off easily, a light blow on the lower edge of the sprocket with a rubber mallet should loosen the sprocket.

5. Remove the crankshaft sprocket using a prybar.

To install:

6. Install the crankshaft sprocket. Apply a coat of Molykote® or equivalent, to the sprocket thrust surface.

7. Hold the camshaft sprocket with the chain hanging down and align the marks on the camshaft and crankshaft sprockets.

8. Align the dowel in the camshaft with the dowel hole in the camshaft sprocket. Install the camshaft sprocket and chain, use the camshaft sprocket bolts to draw the sprocket on to the camshaft. Tighten the sprocket bolts to 18 ft. lbs. (25 Nm).

9. Lubricate the timing chain with engine oil. Install the front cover assembly.

3.4L Engine

1. Disconnect the negative battery cable.

2. Remove the engine front cover.

3. Mark the position of the crankshaft and the intermediate shaft sprockets on the timing chain.

4. Remove the timing chain tensioner bolts and tensioner from the engine.

5. Raise and safely support the vehicle. Retract timing chain tensioner shoe by using J–33875 or equivalent, on both sides of the tensioner and pulling on the through pin in the tensioner arm to retract the spring. While spring is retracted, insert a cotter pin or rivet into hole in tensioner to hold in this position.

6. Remove the timing chain, crankshaft sprocket and intermediate shaft sprocket as an assembly using tool J–8433 and J–38611 or equivalent, on the crankshaft sprocket. If intermediate gear does not slide off easily with the timing chain assembly, rotate the crankshaft back and forth to help loosen the fit.

7. Inspect the crankshaft alignment key for burrs or marks that could affect assembly.

To install:

8. Make sure the crankshaft key is installed and fully seated. Retract the chain tensioner by compressing the spring in the retractor assembly and inserting a cotter pin or rivet into the hole to hold in this position.

NOTE: The large chamfer and counterbore of the crankshaft sprocket are installed towards the crankshaft. The intermediate sprocket spline sockets are installed away from the case.

9. Slip both sprockets and chain over proper shaft and engage slot in key. Intermediate shaft may move against the rear cover. Slide sprocket and chain assembly on shafts maintaining parallel alignment of sprockets. Make sure the snubber or tensioner blade do not become caught, misaligned or dislodged. For the final 8mm, press the crankshaft sprocket on crankshaft using J–38612 or equivalent.

10. Verify timing of the engine was maintained.

11. Pull the retainer pin from the tensioner.

12. Install the front cover.

13. Reconnect the negative battery cable.

3.8L Engine

1. Disconnect the negative battery cable.
2. Remove the front cover assembly.
3. Align the timing marks on the sprockets and remove the timing chain damper.
4. Remove the camshaft sprocket bolts, camshaft sprocket and chain.
5. Remove the crankshaft sprocket by applying a light blow on the lower edge of the sprocket with a plastic mallet.

To install:

6. If the pistons have been moved in the engine, do the following:

a. Turn the crankshaft so the No. 1 piston is at Top Dead Center (TDC).

b. Turn the camshaft with the sprocket temporarily installed, so timing mark is straight down.

7. Assemble the timing chain on the sprockets with the timing marks facing each other.
8. Install the timing chain and sprockets and tighten the camshaft sprocket bolts to 74 ft. lbs. (100 Nm) + an additional 105 degree turn.
9. Install the timing chain damper and tighten the bolt to 14 ft. lbs. (19 Nm).
10. Rotate the engine 2 revolutions and make sure the marks are aligned correctly.
11. Install the front cover assembly.
12. Connect the negative battery cable.

Secondary Timing Belt Cover

REMOVAL AND INSTALLATION

3.4L Engine

RIGHT SIDE

1. Disconnect negative battery cable.
2. Remove retaining bolts and remove cover.
3. To install, position cover on front of engine and install retaining bolts. Torque bolts to 89 inch lbs. (10 Nm).

LEFT SIDE

1. Disconnect the negative battery cable.
2. Remove spark plug wire cover.
3. Remove retaining bolts and cover.
4. To install, position cover on engine and secure with retaining bolts. Torque bolts to 89 inch lbs. (10 Nm).

5. Install spark plug wire cover and connect the negative battery cable.

CENTER COVER

1. Disconnect the negative battery cable.
2. Disconnect Electronic Control Module (ECM) harness cover.
3. Remove serpentine belt tensioner.
4. Remove right and left side timing belt covers.
5. Remove power steering pipe retaining clip nut at alternator stud.
6. Remove center timing belt cover bolts and remove cover.

To install:

7. Install cover on engine and secure with retainer bolts. Torque bolts to 89 inch lbs. (10 Nm).
8. Reinstall power steering pipe retaining clip nut to alternator stud.
9. Install right and left side covers. Install serpentine belt.
10. Install Electronic Control Module (ECM) harness cover. Reconnect negative battery cable.

Secondary Timing Belt and Tensioner

ADJUSTMENT

3.4L Engine

Belt tension is set and maintained by fully automatic tensioners. No adjustment is required.

REMOVAL AND INSTALLATION

3.4L Engine

1. Disconnect the negative battery cable. Remove the serpentine belt.
2. Remove secondary timing belt actuator as follows:

a. Remove the power steering pump and set aside. If more clearance is required, siphon the fluid from the pump and remove pump from the vehicle.

b. Remove the center secondary timing belt cover.

c. Turn the crankshaft to position No. 1 cylinder at TDC. In this position all timing marks should be in alignment.

d. Loosely clamp the 2 cam sprockets on each side of the engine together using clamping pliers or equivalent. Hold the belt to the right hand exhaust sprocket with a C-clamp and a wide pad on belt. Do not mar cam sprockets with clamping device.

e. Remove the tensioner side plate retainer bolts from the tensioner and remove the side plate from the actuator and base.

f. Rotate actuator assembly around the arm pivot and out of the mounting base. Removal of the tensioner from the base allows it to extend to its maximum travel.

g. Set the actuator on table in vertical position to allow oil to drain to boot end for at least 5 minutes prior to refilling.

NOTE: The actuator assembly uses a tapered bushing between the actuator and mounting base. Do not loosen or damage the bushing when removing the tensioner assembly.

h. Straighten out a standard paper clip to a minimum straight length of 1.85 in. (47mm). Form a double loop in the bent end of the paper clip.

i. Remove the rubber end plug from the rear of the tensioner assembly. Oil may escape the tensioner. Hold tensioner in hand at vertical position with the plug end at the top and the tip pointing down. Do not remove the vent plug.

j. Push the paper clip through the center hole in the vent plug and into the pilot hole. Insert a small screwdriver into the screw slot inside the end of the tensioner.

k. Retract the tensioner plunger by rotating the screw in a clockwise direction while pushing the rod tip against a table top, until fully retracted.

l. Rotate the screw slot to align with the vent hole and push the straight section of wire into the screw slot to retain the plunger in the retracted position.

m. If tensioner oil has been lost, fill the tensioner with SAE 5W-30 synthetic engine oil through the end hole. Fill to bottom of plug hole only when the plunger is fully retracted and the lock pin is installed.

3. If the secondary timing belt is to be reused, mark direction of rotation for reference during installation.
4. Remove tensioner and pulley arm assembly.
5. Remove timing belt by sliding it off the pulleys. Do not bend, twist or kink belt or damage to the belt may occur.

To install:

6. Make sure the timing reference marks on all sprockets are properly aligned.

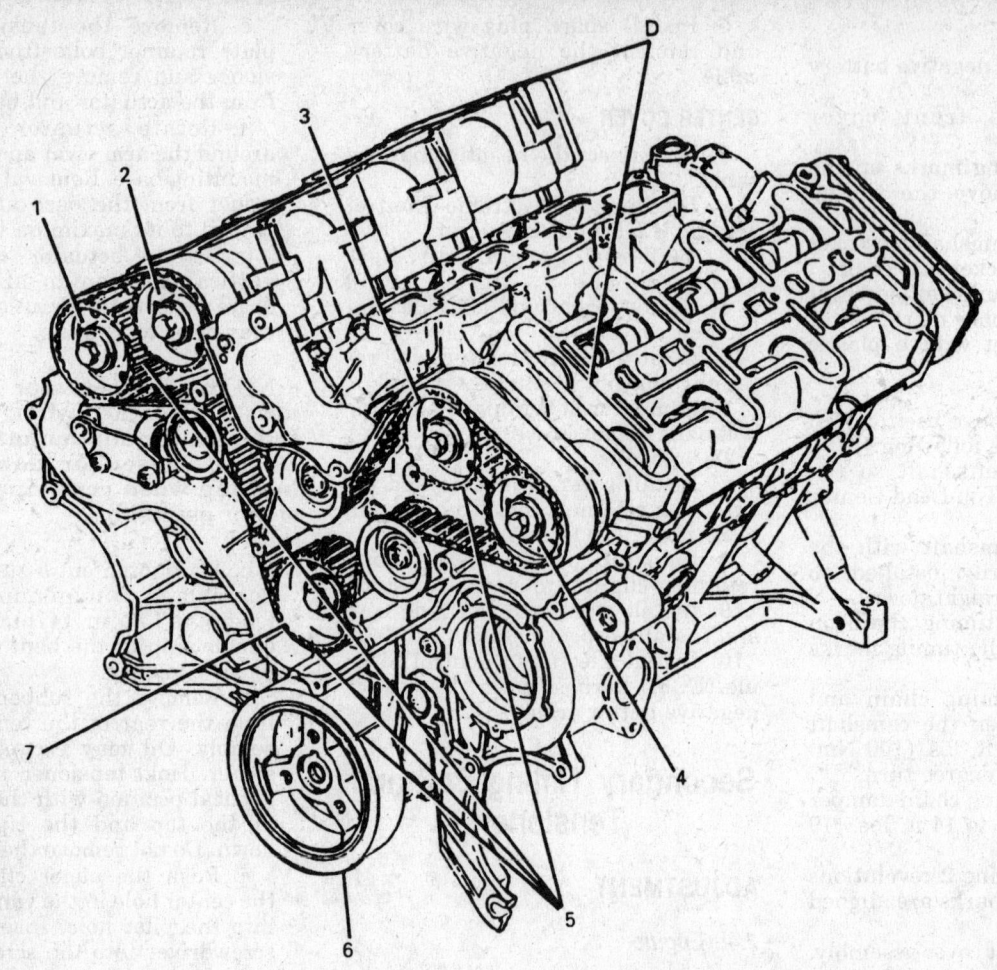

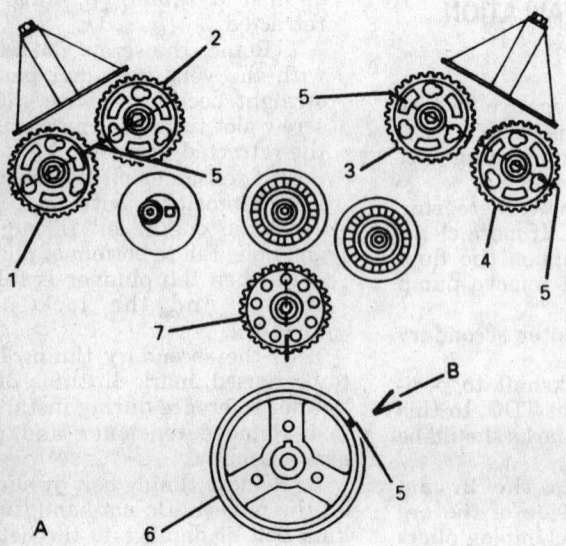

A LOCATION OF TIMING MARKS WITH CAM HOLD DOWN
   TOOLS J 38613 INSTALLED
B FRONT COVER TIMING MARK
C LOCATION OF TIMING MARKS WITH DRIVE BELT IN-
   STALLED
D LOCATION WHERE CAM HOLD DOWN TOOLS ARE
   INSTALLED

1 RH EXHAUST CAMSHAFT SPROCKET
2 RH INTAKE CAMSHAFT SPROCKET
3 LH INTAKE CAMSHAFT SPROCKET
4 LH EXHAUST CAMSHAFT SPROCKET
5 PERMANENT MARKS PAINTED DOTS REMOVE PREVIOUS
   MARKS IF TIMING IS BEING CHANGED AND MARK AGAIN
   IN THESE LOCATIONS
6 TORSIONAL DAMPER
7 INTERMEDIATE SHAFT SPROCKET

NOTE: THIS TDC #1 EXHAUST.
INTERMEDIATE SHAFT BELT
SPROCKET TIMING MARK IS
AT 6 O'CLOCK (POINTING
TOWARDS DRAIN NOTCH)

8470MA84

Timing belt assembly with timing marks — 3.4L engine

7. Install the actuator and side plate as follows:

    a. Install the rubber end plug to the rear of the actuator assembly, if not already done. The cap will snap into place and be flush against the case.

    b. Install the actuator bushing into the side plate. Install the actuator assembly into the mounting base by inserting tapered trunnion of tensioner into machined hole of the bushing in the bracket and installing the side plate bolts. Tighten the side plate bolts to 18 ft. lbs. (25 Nm).

8. Position the timing belt onto the engine by routing it around all sprockets and idlers as follows:

    a. Start with the intermediate cam sprocket and work counterclockwise.

    b. Make sure the belt is installed in the direction of rotation.

    c. Engage teeth into all sprockets, place rubber hose behind belt at intermediate sprocket and accumulate slack at the tensioner.

9. Install tension pulley to mounting base. Use tape or cup plug to hold pivot tube in pulley or pivot may fall out. After starting pivot bolt, rotate arm counterclockwise to position the square lug at the 6 o'clock position. Tighten the bolt to 37 ft. lbs. (50 Nm). Inspect the actuator assembly to assure it is free and will rotate under its own weight.

NOTE: The arm busing and pivot must be clean and not lubricated.

10. Gently rotate the tensioner pulley counterclockwise into the belt using the cast square lug on body and engage ball end of the actuator into socket on pulley arm.

11. Remove tensioner lock pin allowing tensioner shaft to extend and the pulley to move into the belt. Remove any belt holding devices still in place.

12. Rotate the tensioner pulley counterclockwise applying 12–15 ft. lbs. torque. This will set the initial tension on the belt.

13. Rotate the engine in direction of rotation, clockwise, 3 times to seat belt. Check the sprocket reference marks during final rotation to TDC. Do not allow crankshaft to spring back or reverse direction of rotation.

14. Install the secondary timing belt covers.

15. Install the power steering pump and serpentine belt.

16. Reconnect the negative battery cable.

Camshaft Sprocket

REMOVAL AND INSTALLATION

2.2L Engine

1. Disconnect the negative battery cable.

2. Remove the front timing chain cover.

3. Align the marks on the camshaft sprocket and the crankshaft sprocket.

4. Remove the timing chain tensioner upper bolt.

5. Loosen the timing chain tensioner Torx® bolt but do not remove it.

6. Remove the camshaft sprocket and the timing chain.

To install:

7. Compress the tensioner spring and insert a nail or cotter pin into the tensioner hole to hold it in place.

8. Align the crankshaft and camshaft timing marks with the tabs on the tensioner.

9. Install the tensioner bolt.

10. Install the timing chain onto the camshaft and crankshaft sprocket.

11. Align the camshaft dowel with the dowel hole in the camshaft sprocket and install the sprocket.

12. By hand, fully seat the camshaft sprocket to the camshaft.

13. Tighten the timing chain tensioner to 18 ft. lbs. (24 Nm) and the camshaft sprocket bolt to 77 ft. lbs. (105 Nm).

14. Remove the pin or nail from the timing chain tensioner.

15. Install the timing chain cover and connect the negative battery cable.

3.4L Engine

1. Release the fuel system pressure. Disconnect negative battery cable.

2. Remove the front and rear camshaft covers. Remove the secondary timing belt.

3. Rotate the camshaft so the flats on the cam to be serviced are face up. Remove oil from cam hold-down tool hole in the carrier and install tool J–38616 or equivalent, tightening the bolt to 22 ft. lbs. (30 Nm).

4. Remove the camshaft sprocket bolt and washer while holding the camshaft from turning using tool J–38613 and J–38614 or equivalent.

5. Remove the sprocket using tool J–38616. Remove flat ring from the sprocket bore.

To install:

6. Install new flat ring to large bore of sprocket. Wipe the nose of the camshaft with a light coat of oil.

7. Install the sprocket onto the camshaft. Lightly oil new lock ring and insert ring far enough into the sprocket to minimize tipping.

8. Lightly oil the camshaft sprocket bolt threads and washer before using. Thread bolt and washer into the camshaft finger-tight, then loosen bolt ½ turn.

9. Check sprocket for binding by rotating it around the shaft. If binding occurs, check for foreign material or burrs.

10. Install secondary timing belt and set camshaft timing.

Camshaft

REMOVAL AND INSTALLATION

2.2L Engine

NOTE: For the removal of the camshaft, the engine assembly must be removed from the vehicle.

1. Disconnect the negative battery cable.

2. Remove the engine assembly from the vehicle and mount the engine on a stand.

3. Remove the rocker arm cover, the rocker arms and pushrods.

4. Remove the pushrod cover and valve lifters. Mark the location of the valve lifters for installation purposes. The lifters must be reinstalled to the same bores from which they were removed.

5. Remove the front cover assembly.

6. Remove the cam sprocket, timing chain and tensioner.

7. Remove the oil pump drive as follows:

    a. Properly drain the oil from the engine.

    b. Remove the oil pan.

    c. Remove the oil pump from the engine.

    d. Remove the oil pump drive retaining bolt.

    e. Remove the oil pump drive by lifting and turning.

8. Remove the camshaft thrust plate.

9. Carefully remove the camshaft.

To install:

10. Install the camshaft and the camshaft thrust plate.

11. Tighten the thrust plate bolts to 106 inch lbs. (12 Nm).

12. Install the timing chain and sprockets.

13. Install the front cover and the valve lifters.

NOTE: If a new camshaft is being installed, ALL of the valve lifters must be replaced.

14. Install the oil pump drive and the oil pump.

15. Install the rocker arm and the pushrod.

16. Install the engine to the vehicle.

17. Connect the negative battery cable.

2.5L Engine

1992

NOTE: For the removal of the camshaft, the engine assembly must be removed from the vehicle.

1. Disconnect the negative battery cable.

2. Remove the engine assembly from the vehicle.

3. Remove the rocker arm cover and pushrods.

4. Remove the pushrod cover and valve lifters.

5. Remove the serpentine belt, crankshaft pulleys and vibration dampener.

6. Remove the front cover.

7. Remove the timing chain and sprockets from the engine.

8. Remove the camshaft thrust plate.

NOTE: The camshaft journals are the same diameter. Care must be taken when removing the camshaft to avoid damage to the cam bearings.

9. Carefully slide the camshaft and gear through the front of the block.

To install:

10. Lubricate the camshaft journals with Engine Oil Supplement (E.O.S) or equivalent, and carefully install the camshaft into the engine block by rotating and pushing forward until seated.

11. Install the camshaft thrust plate and tighten bolts to 89 inch lbs. (10 Nm).

12. Install the timing chain and sprockets. Tighten the camshaft sprocket to 43 ft. lbs. (58 Nm).

13. Install the pushrod cover and the valve lifters.

14. Install the rocker arm cover and pushrods.

15. Install the engine into the vehicle.

16. Refill all necessary fluids.

17. Start the engine and check for leaks.

3.1L and 3.8L Engines

NOTE: For the removal of the camshaft, the engine assembly must be removed from the vehicle.

1. Position the engine so No. 1 piston is at TDC of its compression stroke. Remove the engine assembly from the vehicle.

2. Remove the valve lifters from the engine.

3. Remove the front cover assembly, timing chain and sprockets.

4. Remove the camshaft thrust plate. Remove the camshaft by sliding it from the block.

To install:

5. Coat the camshaft journals with engine oil. Coat the camshaft lobes with GM Engine Oil Supplement (E.O.S) or equivalent.

6. Slide the camshaft into the block. Install the thrust plate and tighten the bolts to 11 ft. lbs. (15 Nm).

7. Install the timing chain and sprockets making sure to align the timing marks.

8. Install the front cover assembly. Install the valve lifters.

9. Install the engine assembly into the vehicle. Fill all fluids to the appropriate levels.

10. Run the engine and check for leaks.

3.4L Engine

LEFT SIDE

1. Disconnect the negative battery cable.

2. Drain cooling system.

3. Remove left side cam carrier as follows:

   a. Disconnect oil/air breather hose from cam carrier cover. Remove spark plug wires from plugs and remove rear spark plug wire cover.

   b. Remove cam carrier cover bolts and lift off cover. Remove gasket and O-rings from cover.

   c. Remove secondary timing belt by removing secondary timing belt actuator and tensioner assembly and sliding belt from pulleys.

   d. Install 6 sections of fuel line hoses under camshaft and between lifters. This will hold lifters in the carrier. For this procedure use $\frac{3}{16}$ inch fuel line hose for exhaust valves and $\frac{5}{32}$ inch fuel line hose for the intake valves.

   e. Remove exhaust crossover pipe and torque strut.

   f. Remove torque strut bracket at engine.

   g. Remove cam carrier mounting bolts and nuts and remove cam carrier.

   h. Remove cam carrier gasket from cylinder head.

4. Remove the 6 lifter hold-down hoses. Remove the lifters.

5. Install cam hold-down tool J–38613 or equivalent, in place and remove cam sprockets.

6. Remove cam carrier end caps and retainer plate bolts and plate.

7. Remove camshaft hold-down tool and carefully remove camshaft out the back of the carrier.

To install:

8. Coat camshaft lobes and journals with clean engine oil and install camshaft into carrier. Install retaining plate and bolts and tighten to 89 inch lbs. (10 Nm). Install cam carrier end caps.

9. Install camshaft sprocket.

10. Install cam hold-down tool.

11. Lubricate lifters with clean engine oil and install lifters into original position.

12. Install lifter hold-down hoses to cam carrier. Adjust cam timing.

13. Install cam carrier following these steps:

   a. Install new gasket on cam carrier to cylinder mounting surface.

   b. Install cam hold-down tool J–38613 or equivalent, to carrier assembly.

   c. Install cam carrier to cylinder head. Install mounting bolts and nuts. Torque bolts and nuts to 18 ft. lbs. (25 Nm).

   d. Remove lifter hold-down hoses and cam hold-down tool.

   e. Install torque strut bracket to engine and install torque strut.

   f. Install engine crossover pipe.

   g. Install secondary timing belt and cam carrier cover.

   h. Reconnect spark plug cover and wires.

   i. Connect breather hose to cam carrier cover.

14. Add fluids as required and reconnect negative battery cable. Start engine and recheck for leaks.

RIGHT SIDE (REAR)

1. Disconnect the negative battery cable. Drain cooling system.

2. Remove right side cam carrier as follows:

   a. Remove intake plenum and right timing belt cover.

   b. Remove right spark plug wires.

   c. Remove air/oil separator hose at cam carrier cover.

d. Remove cam carrier cover bolts and lift of cover. Remove gasket and O-rings from cover.

e. Remove secondary timing belt by removing secondary timing belt actuator and tensioner assembly and sliding belt from pulleys.

f. Install 6 sections of fuel line hoses under camshaft and between lifters. This will hold lifters in carrier. For this procedure use 3/16 inch fuel line hose for exhaust valves and 5/32 inch fuel line hose for the intake valves.

g. Remove exhaust crossover pipe and torque strut.

h. Remove torque strut bracket at engine. Remove front engine lift hook.

i. Remove cam carrier mounting bolts and nuts and remove cam carrier.

j. Remove cam carrier gasket from cylinder head.

3. Remove 6 lifter hold-down hoses.

4. Remove lifters.

5. Install cam hold-down tool J–38613 or equivalent, and remove cam sprocket.

6. Remove cam carrier end caps and retainer plate. Remove cam hold-down tool and slide camshaft out rear of carrier.

To install:

7. Lubricate camshaft lobes and journals with clean engine oil and slide into cam carrier. Install retainer plate and bolts and tighten bolts to 89 inch lbs. (10 Nm).

8. Install cam carrier end caps and cam sprockets.

9. Install camshaft carrier hold-down tool and adjust cam timing.

10. Lubricate lifters with clean engine oil and install lifters into original position.

11. Install lifter hold-down hoses to cam carrier.

12. Install cam carrier following these steps:

a. Install new gasket on cam carrier to cylinder mounting surface.

b. Install cam hold-down tool J–38613 or equivalent, to carrier assembly.

c. Install cam carrier to cylinder head. Install mounting bolts and nuts. Torque bolts and nuts to 18 ft. lbs.

d. Install lifter hold-down hoses and cam hold-down tool.

e. Install torque strut bracket to engine and install torque strut.

f. Install engine crossover pipe and engine lift hook.

g. Install secondary timing belt and cam carrier cover.

h. Install spark plug wires and cover.

13. Add fluids as required and connect negative battery cable. Start engine and check for fluid leaks.

Balance Shaft/Intermediate Shaft

REMOVAL AND INSTALLATION

3.4L Engine

INTERMEDIATE SHAFT

1. Disconnect the negative battery cable.

2. Remove engine from vehicle.

3. Remove right side cylinder head and oil pump drive assembly.

4. Remove the timing chain assembly.

5. Remove thrust plate screws and plate.

6. Remove the intermediate shaft using care not to damage journals or bearings.

To install:

7. Lubricate intermediate shaft journals and gear with engine oil. Install shaft, thrust plate and retainer screws. Tighten screws to 89 inch lbs. (10 Nm).

8. Replace O-ring after sprocket is installed and install timing chain and gear assembly.

9. Install oil pump drive assembly and cylinder head onto the cylinder block.

10. Install engine assembly into the vehicle. Fill fluids to the appropriate level, start the engine and check for leaks.

3.8L Engine

BALANCE SHAFT

1. Disconnect the negative battery cable. Remove the engine and secure to workstand.

2. Remove the flywheel-to-crankshaft bolts and the flywheel from the engine.

3. Remove the intake manifold from the engine.

4. Remove the lifter guide retainer bolt and retainer.

5. Remove the engine front cover.

6. Remove the balance shaft drive gear bolt.

7. Remove the camshaft sprocket and timing chain.

8. Remove the balance shaft retainer bolts, retainer and gear.

9. Using tool J–6125B or equivalent, remove the balance shaft from the engine.

10. If replacing the rear balance shaft bearing, perform the following procedures:

a. Drive the rear plug from the engine.

b. Using the camshaft remover/installer tool, press the rear bearing from the rear of the engine.

NOTE: The balance shaft and bearings are serviced as a complete package.

To install:

11. Dip bearing in clean engine oil and install into the engine using tool J–36995–5 or equivalent. Make sure the bearing with the rolled edge faces into the engine and the manufacturer's markings face the flywheel side.

12. Dip the front balance shaft bearing in clean engine oil. Install the balance shaft into the engine block using tool J–36996 or equivalent. Torque the balance shaft retainer-to-engine bolts to 27 ft. lbs. (37 Nm).

13. Coat the threads of the balance shaft drive gear bolt with thread lock compound. Install the balance shaft drive gear and bolt and tighten to 15 ft. lbs. (20 Nm). Then rotate the bolt an additional 35 degrees.

14. Install the balance shaft rear plug.

15. Align the marks on the balance shaft gear and the camshaft gear by turning the balance shaft. Turn the crankshaft so the No. 1 piston is at TDC. Install the timing chain and sprocket.

16. Replace the balance shaft front bearing retainer and bolts. Tighten the bolts to 26 ft. lbs. (35 Nm).

17. Install the front timing cover and lifter guide retainer. Tighten the lifter guide retainer bolts to 22 ft. lbs. (35 Nm).

18. Install the intake manifold and flywheel assembly. Tighten the flywheel bolts to 11 ft. lbs., + an additional 50 degrees.

19. Install the engine assembly into the vehicle and connect the negative battery cable. Start the engine and check for leaks.

Piston and Connecting Rod

POSITIONING

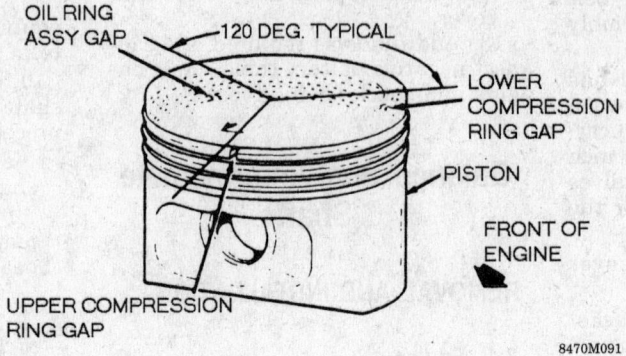

Piston ring end gap positioning — 2.2L engine

8470M091

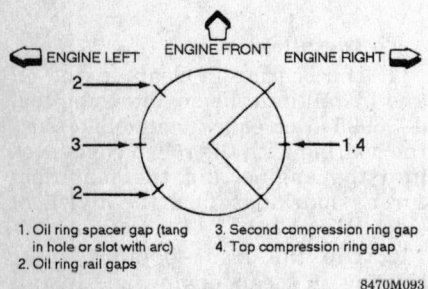

1. Oil ring spacer gap (tang in hole or slot with arc)
2. Oil ring rail gaps
3. Second compression ring gap
4. Top compression ring gap

8470M093

Piston ring gap locations — 2.5L, 3.1L, 3.4L and 3.8L engines

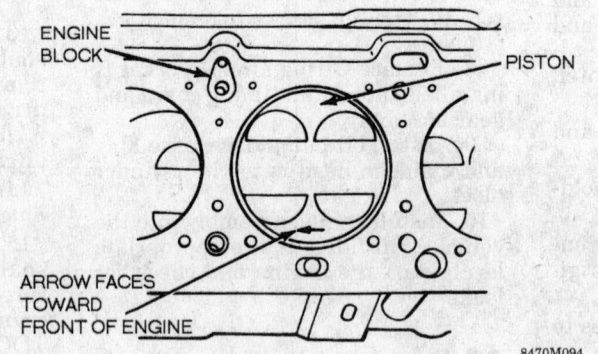

Piston positioning — 3.4L engine

8470M094

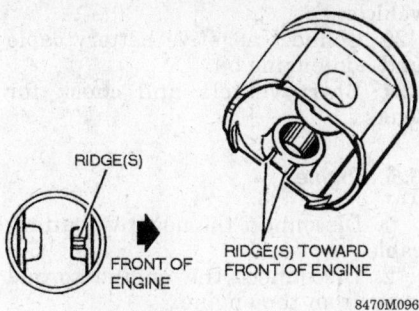

RIDGE(S)

FRONT OF ENGINE

RIDGE(S) TOWARD FRONT OF ENGINE

8470M096

Piston positioning — 3.8L engine

ENGINE LUBRICATION

Oil Pan

REMOVAL AND INSTALLATION

2.2L Engine

1. Disconnect the negative battery cable.
2. Raise and safely support the vehicle.
3. Drain the oil from the crankcase into a suitable container.
4. Remove the starter bracket at the block. Remove the starter and set it aside.
5. Remove the flywheel inspection cover.
6. Remove the oil filter, making sure the filter gasket is intact.
7. Remove the oil pan bolts and nuts and remove the oil pan.

To install:

8. Thoroughly clean and dry the mating surfaces, bolts and bolt holes.
9. Install a 2mm bead of RTV sealer to the diameter of the oil pan sealing flanges and to the surface which fits to the engine front cover.
10. Install a new rear oil pan gasket and apply a thin coat of RTV sealer. Install the oil pan to the engine and secure with the bolts and nuts.
11. Tighten the oil pan bolts and nuts to 124 inch lbs. (14 Nm).
12. Install the oil filter after first lubricating the oil filter gasket with fresh engine oil.
13. Install the starter and the starter bracket.
14. Lower the vehicle and refill the engine with oil to the proper level.

15. Connect the negative battery cable.

2.5L Engine

1. Disconnect the negative battery cable.
2. Remove the coolant recovery bottle, engine torque strut, air cleaner and the air inlet.
3. Remove the serpentine belt, loosen and move the air conditioning compressor from the bracket.
4. Remove the oil level indicator and fill tube.
5. Support the engine using an engine support tool J–28467–A and J–36462.
6. Raise and safely support the vehicle, drain the engine oil and remove the oil filter.
7. Remove the starter motor and flywheel cover. Turn the front wheels to full right travel.
8. Remove the engine wiring harness retainers under the oil pan on the right and left sides.
9. Remove the right engine splash shield, front engine mount bracket bolts and nuts.
10. Remove the transaxle mount nuts.
11. Using the engine support fixture tool J–28467–A and J–36462, raise the engine about 2 in.
12. Remove the front engine mount, bracket and loosen the frame bolts.
13. Remove the oil pan retaining bolts and oil pan.

To install:

14. Clean all gasket surfaces and apply RTV sealer to the oil pan and engine surfaces.
15. Install the oil pan and retaining bolts and tighten to 89 inch lbs. (10 Nm).
16. Install the frame bolts and tighten to 103 ft. lbs. (140 Nm).
17. Install the engine mount, bracket, lower the engine into position and install the transaxle mount nuts.
18. Install the engine mount nuts and bracket bolts.
19. Install the engine splash shield, wiring harness to the oil pan, flywheel cover and the starter motor.
20. Lower the vehicle and remove the engine support fixtures.
21. Install the oil level indicator and tube assembly.
22. Reinstall the air conditioning compressor to original location and serpentine belt.
23. Install the air inlet, air cleaner, torque strut and coolant recovery bottle.
24. Connect the negative battery cable and fill the engine with oil.

25. Start the engine and allow to reach normal operating temperature. Check for leaks.

3.1L (VIN M) Engine

NOTE: Special GM tools, engine support fixture J–28467A, engine support adapter leg J–36462 and torque wrench adapter J–39505 are needed to perform the oil pan removal and installation.

1. Disconnect the negative battery cable and drain the engine oil.
2. Remove the torque strut bolt. Raise the vehicle and support safely.
3. Remove the oil drip shield and engine mounts. Support the engine using a suitable jack.
4. Remove the transaxle mount nuts and exhaust pipe from the manifold.
5. Raise the engine using tools J–28467–A and J–36462.
6. Lower the vehicle. Place jackstands under the frame at the front and rear center crossmembers.
7. Loosen but do not remove the rear frame bolts.
8. Remove the front frame bolts and lower front of frame.
9. Remove the front engine mount bracket bolts, bracket and mount.
10. Remove the starter motor and electrical brackets at the oil pan.
11. Remove the oil pan bolts and oil pan. The side bolts need to be removed with tool J–39505, or equivalent

To install:

12. Clean the gasket mating surfaces. Apply a bead of Ultra Black RTV sealer on the oil pan gasket tabs that insert into the gasket groove of the outer surface on the rear main bearing cap.
13. Install a new gasket, oil pan and bolts. Torque the side bolts to 37 ft. lbs. (50 Nm) with special tool J–39505. Torque the bottom bolts to 18 ft. lbs. (25 Nm).
14. Install the electrical brackets, starter motor and engine mount/bracket.
15. Raise the frame to proper position using new frame bolts. Remove the jackstands.
16. Raise the vehicle and support safely. Lower the engine to the correct position using engine support tools.
17. Install the exhaust pipe, transaxle mount, engine mount and oil drip shield.
18. Lower the vehicle and fill the engine with the proper amount of oil.
19. Install the torque strut bolt and remove the engine support fixture

tools. Recheck the engine oil level, start the engine and check for leaks.

3.1L (VIN T) Engine

1. Disconnect the negative battery cable.
2. Remove the serpentine belt and the tensioner.
3. Support the engine with tool J–28467 or equivalent.
4. Raise and safely support the vehicle. Drain the engine oil.
5. Remove the right tire and wheel assembly. Remove the right inner fender splash shield.
6. Remove the steering gear pinch bolt. Remove the transaxle mount retaining bolts.

CAUTION

Failure to disconnect intermediate shaft from rack and pinion stub shaft can result in damage to the steering gear and/or intermediate shaft. This could cause a loss of steering control which could result in personal injury.
---

7. Remove the engine-to-cradle mounting nuts. Remove the front engine collar bracket from the block.
8. Remove the starter shield and the flywheel cover. Remove the starter.
9. Loosen, but do not remove the rear engine cradle bolts. Remove electrical connector at DIS sensor.
10. Remove the front cradle bolts and lower front of frame. Remove the oil pan retaining bolts and nuts. Remove the oil pan.
To install:
11. Clean the gasket mating surfaces.
12. Install a new gasket on the oil pan. Apply silicone sealer to the portion of the pan that contacts the rear of the block.
13. Install the oil pan, nuts and retaining bolts. Tighten rear bolts to 18 ft. lbs. (18–25 Nm) and remaining nuts and bolts to 89 inch lbs. (10 Nm).
14. Install the frame to the vehicle and loosely install new mounting bolts. Align the frame by inserting 2 pins 0.74 in. (19mm) in diameter by 8.0 in. (203mm) long in the alignment holes on the right side of the frame. Tighten the right side bolts with alignment pins in place to 103 ft. lbs. (140 Nm). Then tighten the remaining bolts to the same torque. Install and tighten the engine to engine bracket bolts.
15. Connect the DIS connector. Install the starter and the heat shield. Install the flywheel inspection cover.

16. Install the steering pinch bolt. Install the right inner fender splash shield and tire assembly. Lower the vehicle.
17. Once engine is securely fastened in the vehicle, remove the engine support tool. Install the serpentine belt and tensioner.
18. Fill the crankcase to the correct level. Connect the negative battery cable. Run the engine to normal operating temperature and check for leaks.

3.4L Engine

1. Disconnect the negative battery cable.
2. Raise and safely support vehicle. Drain engine oil.
3. Remove right front wheel assembly and steering gear heat shield.
4. Remove steering gear retaining bolts and support steering gear to body.
5. Separate right and left lower ball joints from the lower control arms.
6. Disconnect power steering cooler line clamps at frame.
7. Support frame and remove engine mount nuts at frame. Remove the engine oil filter.
8. Remove frame retaining bolts and remove frame assembly.
9. Remove the oil filter, starter assembly and flywheel cover. Disconnect the fluid lines at the oil cooler.
10. Remove the oil pan retaining nuts and bolts. Remove the oil pan from the vehicle.
11. Clean all gasket material from the oil pan flanges, oil pan rail, front cover, rear main bearing cap and threaded holes.
To install:
12. Install new gasket adding sealer next to the rear main bearing cap. Install the oil pan to the block and secure using the retainers. Tighten the rear bolts to 18 ft. lbs. (25 Nm), the nuts to 89 inch lbs. (10 Nm) and the remaining bolts to 89 inch lbs. (10 Nm).
13. Install flywheel cover and starter motor.
14. Install frame assembly and secure all bolts.
15. Install engine mount nuts at frame. Remove frame support.
16. Install power steering cooler lines at frame.
17. Install lower ball joints. Install steering gear to steering gear mounts.
18. Install steering gear retainer bolts and heat shield.

19. Install tire assembly and lower vehicle.
20. Connect negative battery cable and add engine oil.
21. Start vehicle and check for leaks.

3.8L Engine

1. Disconnect the negative battery cable.
2. Disconnect the engine torque strut from the engine.
3. Raise and support the vehicle safely.
4. Disconnect the front exhaust pipe from the manifold.
5. Remove the right front wheel and inner fender splash shield.
6. Drain the engine oil and remove the oil filter.
7. Disconnect the oil cooler pipes and allow to hang loose for access.
8. Remove both front engine mounts from frame.
9. Remove the flywheel cover.
10. Raise the engine assembly slightly using the proper equipment and remove the oil pan retaining bolts.
11. Lower the oil pan and disconnect the oil pump screen assembly.
12. Remove the oil pan and pump screen assembly.
To install:
13. Clean the gasket mating surfaces.
14. Use a new oil pan gasket and install the oil pan and screen assembly to the engine.

NOTE: If the rear main bearing cap is being installed, then RTV sealant must be placed on the oil pan gasket tabs that insert into the gasket groove of the outer surface on the rear main bearing cap.

15. Tighten the screen assembly bolts to 115 inch lbs. and the oil pan retaining bolts to 124 inch lbs. (13 Nm). Do not overtighten.
16. Lower the engine and install the transaxle converter cover.
17. Install the engine mount nuts to the frame and tighten to 32 ft. lbs. (44 Nm).
18. Install the oil cooler pipes and oil filter.
19. Install the inner fender splash shield and wheel assembly.
20. Install the front exhaust pipe to the manifold.
21. Lower the vehicle and install the engine torque strut to the engine.
22. Fill with engine oil and connect the negative battery cable.

Oil Pump

REMOVAL AND INSTALLATION

2.2L Engine

1. Disconnect the negative battery cable.
2. Raise and support the vehicle safely.
3. Drain the engine oil and remove the oil pan.
4. Remove the oil pump retaining bolt from the rear main bearing cap.
5. Remove the oil pump assembly and the extension shaft. Remove the extension shaft and retainer, being careful not to crack the retainer.

To install:

6. Install the retainer in a container of hot water to raise the temperature. This will ease the installation of the extension to the oil pump.
7. Install the extension to the oil pump. Make sure the retainer does not crack upon installation.
8. Install the oil pump to the rear bearing cap and install the mounting bolt. Tighten the bolt to 32 ft. lbs. (43 Nm).
9. Install the oil pan, lower the vehicle and connect the negative battery cable.

2.5L, 3.1L and 3.4L Engines

NOTE: On the 2.5L engine, the force balancer assembly does not have to be removed to service the oil pump or pressure regulator assemblies.

1. Disconnect the negative battery cable.
2. Raise and safely support the vehicle.
3. Drain the engine oil.
4. Remove the oil pan.
5. On 3.4L engine, remove the oil pan baffle by extracting the nuts and rotating the oil pickup tube aside.
6. Remove the oil pump retaining bolts and remove the oil pump and pump driveshaft.

To install:

7. Install the oil pump and pump driveshaft. Tighten the oil pump mounting bolts to 30 ft. lbs. (41 Nm) for the 3.1L engines, 40 ft. lbs. (54 Nm) for 3.4L engine or to 89 inch lbs. (10 Nm) for 2.5L engine.
8. Install oil pan baffle, if equipped, and tighten nuts to 18 ft. lbs. (24 Nm). Install oil pan. Lower the vehicle.
9. Fill the crankcase to the correct level with oil. Run the vehicle and check for leaks.

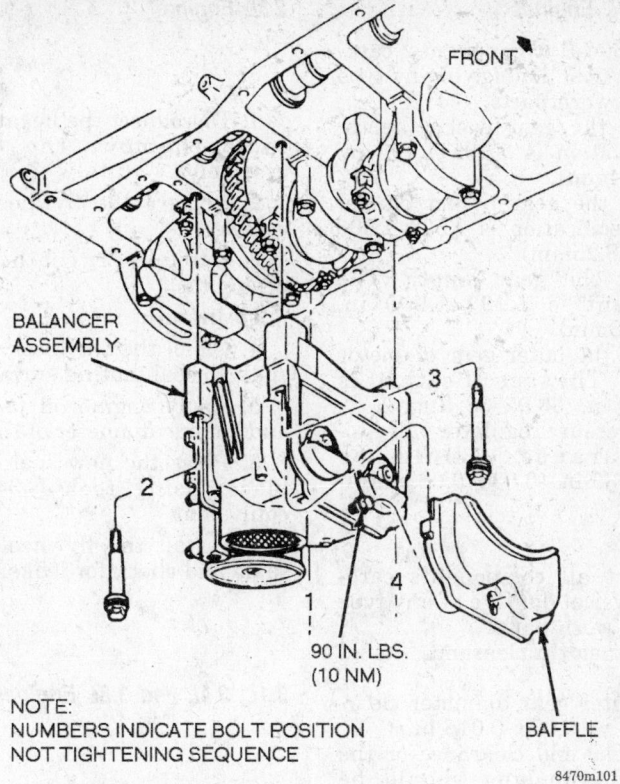

Crankshaft force balancer and oil pump assembly — 2.5L engine

NOTE:
NUMBERS INDICATE BOLT POSITION
NOT TIGHTENING SEQUENCE

8470m101

3.8L Engine

1. Disconnect the negative battery cable.
2. Raise and safely support the vehicle.
3. Drain the engine oil.
4. Remove the front cover assembly.
5. Remove the oil filter adapter, pressure regulator valve and spring.
6. Remove the oil pump cover attaching screws and remove the cover.
7. Remove the oil pump gears.

To install:

8. Lubricate the gears with petroleum jelly and install the gears into the housing.
9. Pack the gear cavity with petroleum jelly after the gears have been installed in the housing.
10. Install the oil pump cover and screws and tighten to 97 inch lbs. (11 Nm).
11. Install the oil filter adapter with new gasket, pressure regulator valve and spring.
12. Install the front cover assembly.
13. Fill with clean engine oil and test oil pressure.

NOTE: Running the engine without measurable oil pressure will cause extensive damage.

CHECKING

2.2L Engine

1. Inspect all components carefully for physical damage of any type and replace worn parts where necessary.
2. Check the oil pump gear pocket depth. The specification is 1.195–1.980 in. (30.36–30.44mm).
3. Check the oil pump gear pocket diameter. The specification is 1.503–1.506 in. (38.18–38.25mm).
4. Check the oil pump gear lash clearance. The clearance specification is 0.004–0.008 in. (0.094–0.195mm).
5. Check the oil pump gear side clearance. The specification is 0.0015–0.004 in. (0.038–0.102mm).

2.5L Engine

1. Inspect all components carefully for physical damage of any type and replace worn parts.
2. Check the case cavity depth. The specification is 0.514–0.516 in. (13.05–13.10mm).
3. Check the gear lash. The specification is 0.009–0.015 in. (0.23–0.38mm).
4. Check the clearance of both gears. The maximum clearance is 0.004 in. (0.10mm).

3.1L and 3.4L Engines

1. Inspect all components carefully for physical damage of any type and replace worn parts.

2. Check the gear pocket depth. The specification is 1.195–1.198 in. (30.36–30.44mm).

3. Check the gear pocket diameter. The specification is 1.503–1.506 in. (38.18–38.25mm).

4. Check the gear length. The measurement is 1.199–1.200 in. (30.45–30.48mm).

5. Check the outer gear diameter clearance. The specification is 1.498–1.500 in. (38.05–38.10mm).

6. The pressure regulator valve-to-bore clearance should be 0.0015–0.0035 in. (0.038–0.089mm).

3.8L Engine

1. Inspect all components carefully for physical damage of any type and replace worn parts.

2. The inner tip clearance should be 0.006 in.

3. The outer gear diameter clearance should be 0.008–0.015 in.

4. The gear end clearance or the drop in the housing should be 0.001–0.0035 in.

5. The pressure regulator valve-to-bore clearance should be 0.0015–0.003 in.

Rear Main Bearing Oil Seal

REMOVAL AND INSTALLATION

2.2L Engine

1. Disconnect the negative battery cable. Remove the transaxle from the vehicle.

2. Remove the flywheel.

3. Remove the seal by inserting a seal remover or prybar in through the dust lip. Carefully pry the seal out by moving the tool around the perimeter of the seal.

NOTE: Care must be taken not to damage the crankshaft seal surface with the removal tool.

To install:

4. Inspect the crankshaft for nicks or burrs on the seal contact surface.

5. Lubricate the seal bore to seal the surface with engine oil.

6. Install the new seal using GM crankshaft seal assembly tool J34686 or equivalent.

7. Install the flywheel.

8. Install the transaxle to the vehicle and connect the negative battery cable.

2.5L Engine

1. Disconnect the negative battery cable. Remove the transaxle assembly.

2. Remove the flywheel from the vehicle.

3. Carefully pry out the seal, using prying tool.

To install:

4. Clean the the block and crankshaft to seal mating surfaces.

5. Apply engine oil to the inside and outside diameter of the new seal.

6. Press the new seal evenly into place, using tool J–34924–A or equivalent.

7. Install the flywheel and transaxle and check for leaks.

3.1L, 3.4L and 3.8L Engines

NOTE: These engines use a round rear oil seal that requires removal of the transaxle and flywheel.

1. Support the engine with tool J–28467 or equivalent. Raise and safely support the vehicle.

2. Remove the transaxle assembly. Remove the flywheel.

3. Using a small prybar or equivalent, insert it through the dust lip at an angle and pry the old seal from the block.

4. Inspect the seal bore and the crankshaft end for any damage.

5. Coat the inside lip of the seal with engine oil and install on the seal installation tool J–34686 or equivalent.

6. Align the dowel pin of the tool with the dowel pin of the crankshaft. Install the tool on the crankshaft and turn the wing nut until the tool and seal are fully seated on the crankshaft.

7. Loosen the wing nut and remove the tool. Check the seal to make sure it is properly seated.

8. Install the flywheel and the transaxle.

9. Remove the engine support tool. Run the engine and check for leaks.

MANUAL TRANSAXLE

Transaxle Assembly

REMOVAL AND INSTALLATION

NOTE: Before performing any maintenance that requires the removal of the slave cylinder, transaxle or clutch housing, the clutch master cylinder pushrod must first be disconnected from the clutch pedal. Failure to disconnect the pushrod will result in permanent damage to the slave cylinder if the clutch pedal is depressed with the slave cylinder disconnected.

1. Disconnect the negative battery cable.

2. Install the engine support tool J–28467 or equivalent.

3. Remove the air cleaner housing and intake tube. Disconnect the clutch slave cylinder from the transaxle.

4. Disconnect the electrical connection at the speed sensor assembly. Disconnect the clutch and shift cables from the transaxle.

5. Remove the exhaust crossover pipe at the left manifold and remove the EGR tube from the crossover.

6. Loosen the crossover-to-right exhaust manifold clamp and move the crossover pipe to gain access to the transaxle bolts for V6 engine.

7. Remove the 2 upper transaxle mounting bolts and remove the 2 upper mounting studs. Leave 1 bottom bolt and stud attached.

8. Disconnect the electrical connection at the backup light switch. Raise and safely support the vehicle. Disconnect the speed sensor wire harness.

9. Drain the transaxle fluid. Remove the clutch housing cover. Remove both front tire assemblies.

10. Remove the inner fender splash shields from both side of the vehicle. Disconnect the power steering lines from the frame.

11. Remove the rack and pinion heat shield and remove the rack and pinion from the frame.

12. Disconnect the right and left ball joints. Remove the upper transaxle mount retaining bolts. Remove the lower engine mount retaining nuts.

13. Remove the sub-frame retaining bolts and remove the sub-frame

from the vehicle. Remove the starter and support it aside.

14. Remove the right and left half-shafts from the transaxle. Support the halfshafts to the frame with wire to prevent damage to the CV-joints. Support the transaxle and remove the remaining bolt and stud. Remove the transaxle from the vehicle.

To install:

15. Align the transaxle with the engine and install. Install the lower transaxle-to-engine mounting bolt and stud, tightening to 55 ft. lbs. (75 Nm).

16. Install the starter assembly. Install the left and right halfshaft.

17. Install the sub-frame and retaining bolts. Install the lower engine mount retaining nuts.

18. Install the upper transaxle retaining bolts, tightening to 55 ft. lbs. (75 Nm). Install the right and left ball joints to the steering knuckles.

19. Install the rack and pinion, heat shield and lines to the frame. Install the right and left inner fender splash shields.

20. Install the clutch housing cover, tighten the screws to 115 inch lbs. (13 Nm). Lower the vehicle.

21. Attach the crossover pipe to the manifolds and attach the EGR pipe to the crossover.

22. Attach the shift and clutch cables to the transaxle. Connect all of the electrical connectors. Install the air cleaner housing and tube. Remove the engine support tool.

23. Fill the transaxle with fluid. Connect the negative battery cable.

LINKAGE ADJUSTMENT

The shift control and cables are preset at the factory and require no adjustments.

CLUTCH

Clutch Assembly

REMOVAL AND INSTALLATION

NOTE: Before any service that requires removal of the slave cylinder, the master cylinder pushrod must be disconnected from the clutch pedal and the connection in the hydraulic lines must be separated using tool J–36221 or equivalent. If not dis-

connected, permanent damage to the slave cylinder will occur if the clutch pedal is depressed while the system is not resisted by clutch loads.

1. Disconnect the negative terminal from the battery.

2. From inside the vehicle, remove the sound insulator panel.

3. Disconnect the clutch master cylinder pushrod from the clutch pedal and disconnect the quick connect fitting in the hydraulic line. Remove the actuator from the transaxle housing.

4. Remove the transaxle.

5. With the transaxle removed, matchmark the pressure plate and flywheel assembly to insure proper balance during reassembly.

6. Loosen the pressure plate-to-flywheel bolts, a few turns at a time, until the spring pressure is removed.

7. Support the pressure plate and remove the bolts.

8. Remove the pressure plate and disc assembly; be sure to note the flywheel side of the clutch disc.

To install:

9. Clean and inspect the clutch assembly, flywheel, release bearing, clutch fork and pivot shaft for signs of wear. Replace any necessary parts.

10. Position the clutch disc and pressure plate in the appropriate position, support the assembly with the appropriate alignment tools.

NOTE: Make sure the clutch disc is facing the right direction. If the same pressure plate is being reused, align the marks made during removal and install, install the pressure plate retaining bolts and tighten them gradually and evenly.

11. With the alignment tool installed, tighten the clutch plate assembly mounting bolts until the plate contacts the flywheel. At this point the plate position can still adjusted.

12. Gradually turn each bolt down about ½ turn at a time tightening in an alternating sequence.

13. Using tool J–36660, torque the bolts to 15 ft. lbs. (20 Nm) in an alternating sequence. Then rotate the bolts an additional 30 degrees in the same tightening sequence. Remove the alignment tool.

14. Lightly lubricate the clutch fork ends. Fill the recess ends of the release bearing with grease. Lubricate the input shaft with a light coat of grease.

15. Install the transaxle assembly into the vehicle.

16. Install the clutch master cylinder pushrod and install the sound insulator panel.

NOTE: The clutch lever must not be moved towards the flywheel until the transaxle is bolted to the engine. Damage to the transaxle, release bearing and clutch fork could occur if this is not followed.

17. Connect the negative battery cable. Bleed the clutch system and check the clutch operation.

PEDAL HEIGHT/FREE-PLAY ADJUSTMENT

The clutch system is a hydraulic linkage system that provides automatic clutch adjustment and determines the clutch pedal position. No adjustment of clutch linkage or pedal position is required or possible.

Clutch Master Cylinder, Actuator and Reservoir

REMOVAL AND INSTALLATION

NOTE: The factory hydraulic system is serviced as a single assembly. Replacement hydraulic assemblies are pre-filled with fluid and do not require bleeding. Individual components of the system are not available separately from GM.

1. Disconnect the negative battery cable.

2. Remove the sound insulator inside the vehicle and disconnect the master cylinder pushrod at the clutch pedal.

3. Remove the left upper secondary cowl panel.

4. Remove the 2 master cylinder reservoir-to-strut tower retaining nuts.

5. Remove the anti-rotation screw located next to the master cylinder flange at the pedal support plate.

6. Using wrench flats on the front end of the master cylinder body, twist the cylinder counterclockwise to release the twist lock attachment-to-plate. Do not torque the hose connection on top of the cylinder body, damage may occur.

7. Remove the 2 actuator-to-transaxle retaining nuts and actuator assembly.

8. Pull the master cylinder with the pushrod attached forward out of the pedal plate. Lift the reservoir off the strut tower studs and remove the

3 components as a complete assembly.

To install:

9. Install the master cylinder into the opening in the pedal plate and rotate 45 degrees by applying torque on the wrench flats only.

10. Install the anti-rotation screw.

11. Install the fluid reservoir-to-strut tower and torque the retaining nuts to 36 inch lbs. (4 Nm).

12. Install a new pushrod bushing and lubricate before installation.

13. Install the master cylinder pushrod-to-clutch pedal.

14. Install the clutch actuator-to-transaxle.

15. Press the clutch pedal down several times to ensure proper operation. Adjust cruise control switch if equipped.

16. Install the left upper secondary cowl panel, sound insulator and connect the negative battery cable.

Clutch Slave Cylinder

REMOVAL AND INSTALLATION

1. Disconnect the negative battery cable.

2. Remove the sound insulator inside the vehicle and disconnect the master cylinder pushrod at the clutch pedal.

3. Remove 2 bolts holding canister to transaxle. Remove 2 actuator retainer nuts and remove actuator from transaxle housing.

To install:

4. Position canister mounting bracket and bolts to transaxle assembly and secure retaining bolts to 28 ft. lbs. (38 Nm).

5. Install actuator to housing studs with pushrods centered in pocket of lever in housing. Install actuator retainer nuts to 18 ft. lbs. (25 Nm).

6. Install a new pushrod bushing and lubricate before installation.

7. Install the master cylinder pushrod-to-clutch pedal.

8. Install the clutch actuator-to-transaxle.

9. Press the clutch pedal down several times to ensure proper operation. Adjust cruise control switch if equipped.

10. Install the left upper secondary cowl panel, sound insulator and connect the negative battery cable.

Hydraulic Clutch System Bleeding

1. Disconnect the negative battery cable.

2. Disconnect quick connect fittings in clutch hydraulic line. Insert J–36221 or equivalent hydraulic line separator tool and depress plastic sleeve to separate connection.

3. Remove cap and diaphragm and fill reservoir with DOT 3 brake fluid.

4. Remove left hand upper secondary cowl.

5. Remove air from supply hose by squeezing it until no more air bubbles are seen in reservoir.

6. Pump clutch pedal slowly until slight pressure is observed. Hold pressure on pedal and depress internal valve on quick connect fitting.

7. Repeat Step 6 until pedal is firm and no bubbles are seen.

8. Reconnect clutch hydraulic line. Refill clutch system and replace reservoir cap. Reconnect battery cable.

AUTOMATIC TRANSAXLE

Transaxle Assembly

REMOVAL AND INSTALLATION

Except Turbo Hydro–Matic 4T60–E

1. Disconnect the negative battery cable. Remove the air cleaner, coolant reservoir, Mass Air Flow (MAF) sensor and air tube as an assembly.

2. Disconnect both torque struts from the engine. Remove the left torque strut bracket. Disconnect the oil cooler lines at the transaxle.

3. Disconnect the shift control cable, TV cable from the throttle lever and the transaxle.

4. Remove the vent hose from the transaxle. Remove the fluid level indicator and the filler tube.

5. Using a engine support fixture tool J–28467 or equivalent and the adapter tool J–35953 or equivalent, install them on the engine.

6. Remove the wiring harness-to-transaxle nut.

7. Label and disconnect the wires for the speed sensor, TCC connector and the neutral safety/backup light switch.

8. Remove the upper transaxle-to-engine bolts.

9. Remove the transaxle-to-mount through bolt, the transaxle mount bracket and the mount.

10. Raise and safely support the vehicle. Remove the front wheel assemblies.

11. Disconnect the shift cable bracket from the transaxle. Remove the transaxle fill tube.

12. Remove the caliper assemblies and the rotors from the vehicle.

13. Disconnect both lower ball joint studs from the lower control arms.

14. Remove both lower engine splash shields. Remove the ground cable at the transaxle.

15. Using a modified halfshaft seal protector tool J–34754 or equivalent, install 1 on each halfshaft to protect the seal from damage and the joint from possible failure. Remove both halfshafts from the transaxle and support the halfshafts to the body to prevent CV-joint damage. Take care not to damage the halfshaft boots.

16. Remove the torsional and lateral strut from the transaxle.

17. Remove the left side stabilizer link pin bolt.

18. Remove the rack and pinion heat shield and electrical connector, if equipped.

19. Disconnect the speedometer wire from the transaxle. Remove the starter motor.

20. Remove the transaxle converter cover and matchmark the converter to the flywheel for assembly.

21. Remove the bolt holding the wiring harness to the transaxle case and position aside.

22. Remove the bolts holding the power steering lines to the frame.

23. Position and secure a transmission jack under the transaxle. Remove the remaining transaxle-to-engine bolts.

24. Make sure the torque converter does not fall out and remove the transaxle from the vehicle.

NOTE: The transaxle cooler and lines should be flushed any time the transaxle is removed for overhaul or to replace the pump, case or converter.

To install:

25. Put a small amount of grease on the pilot hub of the converter and make sure the converter is properly engaged with the pump.

26. Raise the transaxle to the engine while guiding the right side halfshaft into the transaxle.

27. Install the lower transaxle mounting bolts, tighten to 55 ft. lbs. (75 Nm) and remove the jack.

28. Align the converter with the marks made on the flywheel and install the bolts hand-tight.

29. Torque the converter bolts to 46 ft. lbs. (61 Nm). Retorque the first bolt after the others.

30. Install the starter assembly. Install both halfshafts.

31. Install the converter cover, oil cooler lines and cover. Install the sub-frame assembly. Install the lower engine mount retaining bolts and the transaxle mount nuts.

32. Install the right and left ball joints. Install the power steering rack, heat shield and cooler lines to the frame.

33. Install the right and left inner fender splash shields. Install the tire assemblies.

34. Lower the vehicle. Connect all electrical leads. Install the upper transaxle mount bolts, tighten to 55 ft. lbs. (75 Nm).

35. Attach the crossover pipe to the exhaust manifold. Connect the EGR tube to the crossover.

36. Connect the TV cable and the shift cable. Install the air cleaner and inlet tube.

37. Remove the engine support tool. Connect the negative battery cable.

Turbo Hydro–Matic 4T60–E

NOTE: Special tools needed for this procedure: engine support fixture J–28467A, oil cooler and line flusher J–35944A, oil cooler and line flusher adapter J–36462 and axle seal protector J–37292B.

1. Disconnect the negative battery cable and remove the air cleaner.

2. Remove the engine torque strut from the engine.

3. Disconnect the shift control cable and remove the bracket from the transaxle case lever.

4. Disconnect the TCC switch connector and vacuum hose.

5. Remove the upper transaxle mounting bolts and install engine support fixture tool J–28467A.

6. Raise the vehicle and support safely. Remove the front tire assemblies and engine splash shields.

7. Remove the pinch bolts from the controls arms and steering shaft.

8. Remove the stabilizer shaft nuts and brackets from the frame. Separate the stabilizer from the control arm.

9. Use a 7/16 inch drill bit to drill through the 2 spot welds located between the front and rear holes of the left front stabilizer shaft mounting.

10. Remove the front and rear transaxle mounting nuts. Disconnect the power steering cooler line bolts.

11. Disconnect the engine wiring harness from the frame.

12. Remove the right frame-to-left frame retaining bolt. Position jackstands under the frame for support.

13. Loosen the 2 right frame mounts and discard bolts. Remove the 2 left frame bolts from the frame.

14. Remove the left frame with the help of an assistant.

15. Disconnect the right lower ball joint from the steering knuckle.

16. Remove the transaxle support bracket bolts from the transaxle.

17. Disconnect the power steering cooler line support and remove the torque converter cover.

18. Remove the starter motor and torque converter bolts.

19. Remove the transaxle mount bolts and mount from the case.

20. Disconnect all electrical connectors from the transaxle.

21. Remove both halfshafts from the transaxle and install the protective covers J–37292B, or equivalent.

22. Install a suitable transaxle jack.

23. Disconnect the oil cooler lines and plug openings.

24. Remove the remaining transaxle bolts and transaxle. Remove slowly to check for components not disconnected or hanging up.

To install:

25. Place the transaxle on the jack and move into position. Install the front bolt and torque to 55 ft. lbs. (75 Nm).

26. Connect the cooler lines and remove the transaxle jack.

27. Connect all electrical, vacuum and cable connections to the lower portion of the transaxle.

28. Install the halfshafts into the transaxle and make sure they are seated properly.

29. Install the transaxle mount and torque to 41 ft. lbs. (55 Nm).

30. Install the torque converter bolts and torque to 47 ft. lbs. (63 Nm). Retorque again using same pattern.

31. Install the starter motor, converter cover, power steering cooler line and transaxle support bracket.

32. Install the pinch bolts to the control arms. Install the right and left frame assembly and torque the bolts to 40 ft. lbs. (54 Nm).

33. Install the jackstands and the remainder of the right and left frame bolts.

34. Install the transaxle rear nuts and torque to 24 ft. lbs. (33 Nm).

35. Install the stabilizer bar bolts and torque to 30 ft. lbs. (44 Nm).

36. Install the steering shaft pinch bolt.

37. Install the engine splash shields, front wheels and remove the engine support fixture.

38. Install the upper transaxle bolts and ground wires. Torque bolts to 55 ft. lbs. (75 Nm).

39. Install the engine torque strut and air cleaner.

40. Connect the battery cable, refill the transaxle fluid, start the engine and check for leaks.

SHIFT LINKAGE ADJUSTMENTS

1. Disconnect the negative battery cable.

2. Lift up the locking button at the shift cable bracket on the transaxle.

3. Place the transaxle shift lever in the **N** position. This position can be found by rotating the selector shaft/shift lever clockwise from **P** through **R** to **N**.

4. Place the shift control inside the vehicle to the **N** position.

5. Push down the locking button at the cable bracket and connect the negative battery cable.

THROTTLE LINKAGE ADJUSTMENTS

1. Disconnect the negative battery cable.

2. Pull on the upper end of the TV cable. It should travel a short distance with light resistance caused by a small spring on the TV lever.

3. The cable should go to the 0 position when the upper end of the cable is released.

4. Verify that the TV cable is installed properly in the throttle lever and the slider is in the non-adjusted position.

5. With the engine not running, rotate the throttle lever to the full travel position (throttle body stop).

6. Depress and hold the adjustment button, pull the cable conduit out until the slider hits against the adjustment and release the button.

7. Repeat the adjustment.

PARK/LOCK CONTROL CABLE ADJUSTMENTS

1. Disconnect the negative battery cable.

2. With the shift lever in the **P** position and the key in the **LOCK** position, make sure the shifter cannot be moved to another position. The key should be removable from the column.

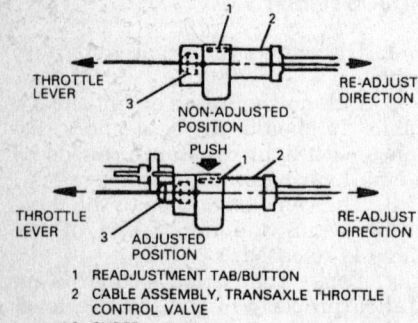

1. Readjustment button
2. Fitting
3. Slider against fitting in full non-adjusted position
4. Conduit
5. Slider
6. To throttle lever

8470M106

TV cable adjustment

THROTTLE LEVER

NON-ADJUSTED POSITION

RE-ADJUST DIRECTION

PUSH

THROTTLE LEVER

ADJUSTED POSITION

RE-ADJUST DIRECTION

1 READJUSTMENT TAB/BUTTON
2 CABLE ASSEMBLY, TRANSAXLE THROTTLE CONTROL VALVE
3 SLIDER

8569y004

TV cable assembly — 1994-96 2.2L engine

3. With the key in the **RUN** position and the shifter in the **N** position, the key should NOT turn to the **LOCK** position.

4. Adjust the cable by pulling up the cable connector lock at the shifter mechanism. If the key cannot be removed in the **P** position, snap the connector lock button to the up position and move the cable connector nose rearward until the key can be removed from the ignition.

5. Snap the lock button down and recheck operation and connect the negative battery cable.

DRIVE AXLE

Halfshaft

REMOVAL AND INSTALLATION

Vehicles equipped with a manual transaxle use an intermediate shaft connecting the transaxle assembly and the right halfshaft. The right halfshaft inner CV–joint uses a female spline that will be installed over the intermediate axle shaft.

NOTE: Do not attempt to move the vehicle with the with the drive axle(s) removed from the vehicle. Wheel(s) could fall off, dropping vehicle to the ground and cause personal injury or damage to the vehicle.

1. With the weight of the vehicle on the tires, loosen the hub nut 1 revolution.
2. Raise and safely support the vehicle.
3. Remove the tire and wheel assembly.
4. Remove the brake caliper and rotor assembly. Do not separate the brake hose from the caliper and tie aside using wire.
5. If equipped with ABS, remove the ABS sensor mounting bolt and position the sensor aside.
6. Remove the hub/bearing to strut housing bolts. Pull the hub/bearing out of the strut bracket.
7. Remove the right halfshaft from the transaxle using removal tool J–33008 or equivalent and the extension tool J–29794 or equivalent.
8. If equipped with 3T40 transaxle, separate the halfshaft from the transaxle assembly using removal tool J–33008 or equivalent and the extension tool J–29794 or equivalent.
9. If equipped with 4T60 or 4T60–E transaxles, using the frame for leverage, separate the drive axle from the transaxle assembly using a prybar in the groove provided on the inner joint.
10. Remove the hub nut, if not already done. Pull the axle and hub assembly through the strut housing. Using a spindle remover tool J–28733 or equivalent, remove the halfshaft from the hub and bearing.
To install:
11. Install tool J–37292–A or equivalent, to the right side of the transaxle in a position so it can be

removed after axle is installed, approximately between 5 and 7 o'clock position.
12. Install the axle assembly into the transaxle and remove tool J–37292–A or equivalent,.
13. Properly position the ABS sensor and install the retainer bolt, if removed.
14. Loosely secure the bearing to knuckle bolts.
15. Seat the axle into the transaxle using prybar in the groove provided on the inner joint. Pry against the frame or lower control arm.
16. Verify that the snapring is seated by tapping on the inner groove. Also grasp the inner housing and pull outward. If correctly seated, the axle will remain in place. Do not pull on the shaft.
17. Install the hub and bearing assembly to the shaft using new drive axle nut and washer. Tighten the drive axle nut but do not torque.
18. Install the brake rotor ad caliper assembly. Install the tire and wheel.
19. Lower the vehicle. With the weight of the vehicle on the suspension, tighten the axle nut to 184 ft. lbs. (250 Nm).
20. Inspect the transaxle fluid and add as required. Pump the brakes until a firm pedal is obtained. Test drive the vehicle.

Intermediate Shaft

REMOVAL AND INSTALLATION

Manual Transaxle

NOTE: Use care when removing the halfshaft. Tri-pot joints can be damaged if the halfshaft is over-extended. It is important to handle the halfshaft in a manner to prevent overextending.

1. Disconnect the negative battery cable.
2. Raise and support the vehicle safely. Drain the transaxle fluid.
3. Remove the right wheel and tire.
4. Position a drain pan under the transaxle.
5. Remove the right halfshaft assembly from the vehicle.
6. Remove the housing-to-bracket bolts, bracket and housing-to-transaxle bolts.
7. Carefully disengage the intermediate shaft from the transaxle and remove the shaft.

1. Axle shaft
2. 60 ft. lbs. (80 Nm)
3. Disc
4. Brake caliper
5. J 28733-A
6. Knuckle and strut assy
7. Splines
8. 184 ft. lbs. (250 Nm)

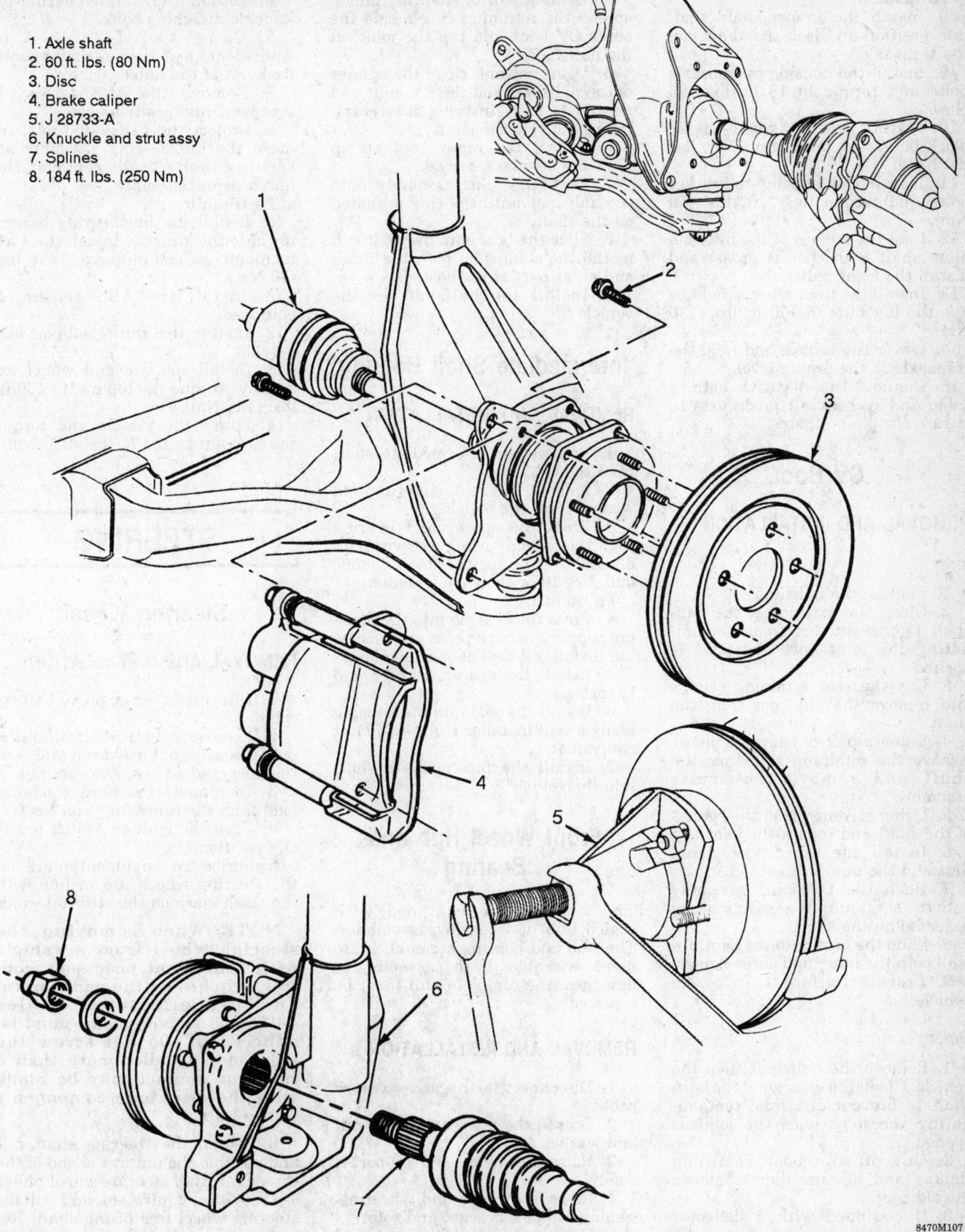

Removing the drive axle from the hub

8470M107

To install:

8. Install the intermediate shaft into position and lock the shaft into the transaxle.

9. Install the housing-to-transaxle bolts and torque to 18 ft. lbs. (25 Nm).

10. Install the bracket-to-engine block bolts and torque to 37 ft. lbs. (50 Nm).

11. Install the housing-to-bracket bolts and torque to 37 ft. lbs. (50 Nm).

12. Coat the splines of the intermediate shaft with chassis grease and install the right halfshaft.

13. Install the front wheels and torque the lug nuts to 100 ft. lbs. (136 Nm).

14. Lower the vehicle and refill the transaxle to the proper level.

15. Connect the negative battery cable and recheck all procedures to ensure complete repair.

CV Boot

REMOVAL AND INSTALLATION

Inner

1. Remove the halfshaft.

2. Clean the exterior of the halfshaft to prevent dirt from contaminating the joint once the joint is opened.

3. Cut the seal retaining clamps and remove the old boot from the shaft.

4. Using a pair of snapring pliers, remove the retaining ring from the shaft and remove the spider assembly.

5. Using solvent, clean the splines of the shaft and repack the joint.

6. Install the inner boot clamp first and the new boot second.

7. Push the CV joint assembly onto the shaft until the retaining ring is seated on the shaft.

8. Slide the boot onto the joint. Install both the inner and outer clamps.

9. Install halfshaft into the vehicle.

Outer

1. Remove the halfshaft from the vehicle. Clean the exterior of the halfshaft to prevent dirt from contaminating the joint once the joint is opened.

2. Cut off the boot retaining clamps and discard them. Remove the old boot.

3. If equipped with a deflector ring, use a brass drift and carefully tap it off.

4. Using a pair of snapring pliers, spread the retaining ring inside the outer CV joint and tap the joint off the halfshaft.

5. Using solvent, clean the splines of the halfshaft and the CV joint and repack the joint. Install a new retaining ring inside the joint.

6. Install the inner boot clamp first, the new boot second.

7. Push the joint assembly onto the halfshaft until the ring is seated on the shaft.

8. Slide the boot onto the joint and install the clamps on both the inner and outer part of the boot.

9. Install the halfshaft in the vehicle.

Intermediate Shaft Bearing

REMOVAL AND INSTALLATION

1. Remove the intermediate shaft from the vehicle.

2. Remove the seal, snapring and washer from the housing.

3. Press the spacer and bearing from the housing using a driver handle and bearing remover tools J–8592 and J–8810 or their equivalents.

To install:

4. Press the bearing into the housing support, using a press and a bearing installer J–36379 or equivalent.

5. Install the spacer, washer and snapring.

6. Install the seal into the housing using a seal installer tool J–23771 or equivalent.

7. Install the intermediate shaft into the vehicle.

Front Wheel Hub and Bearing

The vehicles are equipped with sealed hub and bearing assemblies. The hub and bearing assemblies are non-serviceable. If the assembly is damaged, the complete unit must be replaced.

REMOVAL AND INSTALLATION

1. Disconnect the negative battery cable.

2. Loosen the drive axle shaft nut and washer 1 turn.

3. Raise the vehicle and support it safely.

4. Remove the tire and wheel assembly, caliper, bracket and rotor.

5. Remove the halfshaft nut and washer.

6. Loosen the 4 hub/bearing-to-knuckle attaching bolts.

7. Using tool J–28733–A or equivalent, push the halfshaft splines back out of the hub/bearing.

8. Remove the ABS sensor, if equipped, and position aside.

9. Protect the halfshaft boots, remove the hub/bearing assembly attaching bolts and remove the hub/bearing assembly.

To install:

10. Install the hub/bearing assembly onto the knuckle. Install the 4 attaching bolts and torque to 52 ft. lbs. (70 Nm).

11. Install the ABS sensor, if equipped.

12. Install the rotor, caliper and bracket.

13. Install the tire and wheel assembly. Torque the lug nut to 100 ft. lbs. (135 Nm).

14. Lower the vehicle and torque the hub nut to 184 ft. lbs. (250 Nm).

STEERING

Steering Wheel

REMOVAL AND INSTALLATION

1. Disconnect the negative battery cable.

2. Remove the screws holding the pad, if equipped. Push down and turn the horn pad and remove retainer.

3. Disconnect the horn electrical lead from the cancelling cam tower.

4. Turn the ignition switch to the **ON** position.

5. Scribe an alignment mark on the steering wheel hub in line with the slash mark on the steering shaft.

NOTE: When removing the steering wheel from a vehicle with redundant accessory control switches on the pad, careful and proper use of puller J–1859–03 or equivalent must be adhered to. Do not screw the bolts of the puller more than 5 turns or contact may be made with the electronic components in the hub.

6. Loosen the steering shaft nut and position the nut at the end of the threads. Install steering wheel puller J–1859–03 or equivalent, and pull the steering wheel free of the shaft. Remove the steering wheel nut and the steering wheel.

Steering Column

REMOVAL AND INSTALLATION

To install:

7. Align the matchmarks on the wheel hub and shaft and install the steering wheel. Tighten the steering shaft nut to 30 ft. lbs. (41 Nm).

8. Connect the horn electrical lead and install the horn pad.

9. Connect the negative battery cable.

Steering Column

REMOVAL AND INSTALLATION

NOTE: The steering column has energy absorbing properties that are vulnerable to damage. Do not hammer on the end of the steering shaft or drop the column. Protect the shaft from impact action while the column is out of the vehicle.

1. Disconnect the negative battery cable.

2. Remove the lower left hand trim panel below the steering column.

3. Push the top of the intermediate shaft seal down for access to the intermediate shaft seal coupling.

4. Remove the upper shaft coupling pinch bolt.

5. Disconnect the shift indicator cable end and casing from the column.

NOTE: If equipped with park lock, disconnect the park lock cable from the column.

6. Disconnect the shift cable from the ball stud on the shift lever.

7. Remove the lower column bolts first and then remove the upper bolts. Lower the column to the seat.

8. Disconnect the electrical connectors and remove the column from the vehicle.

To install:

9. Install the column into the vehicle and loosely install the column bolts. Install the upper shaft pinch bolt and tighten it to 35 ft. lbs. (48 Nm).

10. Connect the electrical connector and all the shift cables. Connect the park lock cable, if equipped.

11. Tighten the steering column mounting bolts to 18 ft. lbs. (25 Nm).

12. Reposition the intermediate shaft seal and install the trim panel.

13. Connect the negative battery cable.

Power Rack and Pinion

REMOVAL AND INSTALLATION

1. Disconnect the negative battery cable. Remove the air cleaner assembly.

2. Raise and safely support the vehicle.

3. If equipped with 3.4L engine, disconnect the front exhaust pipe at the exhaust manifold.

4. Remove both front tire and wheel assemblies.

NOTE: Failure to disconnect the intermediate shaft from the rack and pinion stub shaft can result in damage to the steering gear or intermediate shaft. This damage can cause loss of steering control which could result in personal injury.

5. Remove the intermediate shaft lower pinch bolt at the steering gear. Remove the intermediate shaft from the stub shaft.

6. Disconnect the electrical lead at the power steering idle switch.

7. Separate the tie rod ends from the knuckle assembly.

8. Support the frame at center rear using appropriate equipment. Remove the sub-frame mounting bolts and lower the rear of the sub-frame approximately 4 in.

9. Remove the steering rack heat shield. Disconnect the pressure lines at the steering rack.

10. Remove the steering rack mounting bolts, remove the rack and pinion through the left wheel opening.

To install:

11. Install the rack and pinion through the left wheel opening. Tighten the mounting bolts to 59 ft. lbs. (81 Nm).

12. Connect the pressure lines, tighten the fittings to 20 ft. lbs. (27 Nm).

13. Install the rack heat shield, tighten the retaining bolts to 53 inch lbs. (6 Nm).

14. Raise the frame assembly and align the steering gear stub shaft to the intermediate steering shaft. Install the frame retaining bolts and secure frame in place. Remove the support at the frame.

15. Connect the electrical lead to the power steering idle switch. Attach the intermediate shaft to the stub shaft, tighten the pinch bolt to 35 ft. lbs. (48 Nm).

16. Install the intermediate steering shaft pinch bolt at the steering gear and tighten to 35 ft. lbs. (47 Nm).

17. Install the exhaust pipe and converter assembly to the exhaust manifold, if removed.

18. Connect the tie rod ends to the steering knuckle and secure.

19. Install both wheel assemblies, tighten lug nuts to 100 ft. lbs. (136 Nm) and lower the vehicle.

20. Install the air cleaner. Connect the negative battery cable. Fill and bleed the power steering system.

21. Inspect and adjust the front suspension toe setting as required.

RACK BEARING PRELOAD ADJUSTMENT

1. Disconnect the negative battery cable.

2. Raise and safely support the vehicle. Center the steering wheel.

3. Loosen the adjuster plug locknut and turn clockwise until it bottoms in the housing, then back off 50–70 degrees (1 flat).

4. Tighten the locknut to the adjuster plug to 50 ft. lbs. (70 Nm), while holding the adjuster plug stationary. Make sure the steering does not bind.

5. Connect the negative battery cable.

Power Steering Pump

REMOVAL AND INSTALLATION

2.2L Engine

1. Disconnect the negative battery cable.

2. Remove the serpentine drive belt.

3. Install a suitable drain pan below the vehicle to catch draining fluid.

4. Disconnect the pressure pipe from the power steering pump.

5. Remove the hose clamp and disconnect the return hose from the reservoir.

6. Remove the pump mounting bolts, access to the bolts may be obtained through the holes in the pulley.

7. Remove the rear power steering pump mounting bolt and remove the pump.

To install:

8. Install the power steering pump to the vehicle.

9. Install the front power steering pump mounting bolts and tighten to 25 ft. lbs. (34 Nm).

10. Install the rear power steering pump mounting bolt and tighten to 22 ft. lbs. (30 Nm).

11. Connect the return hose to the reservoir and install the hose clamp.

12. Connect the power steering pressure pipe to the power steering pump.

13. Install the serpentine drive belt and refill the power steering fluid to the proper level.

14. Properly bleed the power steering system and connect the negative battery cable.

2.5L Engine

1. Disconnect the negative battery cable.

2. Raise and safely support the vehicle.

3. Remove the pressure and return hoses from the pump and drain the fluid.

4. Lower the vehicle, remove the ECM heat shield and serpentine belt.

5. Remove the pump mounting bolts and pump.

To install:

6. Install the pump and tighten the bolts to 20 ft. lbs. (27 Nm).

7. Install the serpentine belt, ECM heat shield. Raise and safely support the vehicle.

8. Install the inlet and outlet hoses and lower the vehicle.

9. Refill the pump with power steering fluid and bleed the system. Connect the negative battery cable.

3.1L and 3.8L Engines

1. Disconnect the negative cable from the battery.

2. Remove the pressure and return hoses from the pump and drain the system into an appropriate container.

3. Cap the fittings at the pump.

4. Remove the serpentine belt.

5. Locate the pump attaching bolts through the pulley and remove the bolts.

6. Remove the pump assembly.

To install:

7. Install the pump and torque the mounting bolts to 25 ft. lbs. (34 Nm) for the 3.1L engines or 20 ft. lbs. (27 Nm), in sequence, top bolt first, bottom bolt second, for the 3.8L engine.

8. Reconnect the hoses to the pump and install the serpentine belt.

9. Refill the power steering pump reservoir and bleed the system. Connect the negative battery cable.

3.4L Engine

1. Disconnect the negative battery cable.

2. Remove the air cleaner assembly and the coolant recovery reservoir.

3. Siphon as much fluid from the reservoir as possible. Power steering fluid will damage the secondary timing belt if contact is made.

4. Remove the serpentine drive belt from the engine. Remove the steering line bracket from the cover.

5. Disconnect the lines from the power steering pump. Plug the lines and the connections at the pump housing to prevent dirt from entering.

6. Remove the pump mounting bolts and remove the pump.

To install:

7. Connect the power steering lines at the pump.

8. Install the power steering pump to mounting bracket and tighten attaching bolts to 25 ft. lbs. (34 Nm).

9. Install the serpentine belt, coolant recovery tank and air cleaner assembly.

10. Fill the reservoir with fluid and bleed the system. Inspect the power steering system for leaks.

BELT ADJUSTMENT

Serpentine belt tension is maintained by the tensioner and is not adjustable.

SYSTEM BLEEDING

NOTE: Automatic transmission fluid is not compatible with the seals and hoses of the power steering system. Under no circumstances should automatic transmission fluid be used in place of power steering fluid in this system.

1. With the engine turned **OFF**, turn the wheels all the way to the left.

2. Fill the reservoir with power steering fluid until the level is at the FULL COLD mark on the reservoir.

3. Raise the front wheels off the ground.

4. Turn the steering way from side to side without touching the stops. Keep the fluid level and the FULL COLD mark.

5. Start the engine. With the engine at idle, check the fluid level and add as required to bring fluid to FULL COLD.

6. Continue to run the vehicle and allow to idle for 3 minutes. Recheck the fluid level and add as required.

Tie Rod Ends

REMOVAL AND INSTALLATION

Outer

1. Disconnect the negative battery cable.

2. Remove the cotter pin and hex slotted nut from the outer tie rod assembly.

3. Loosen the jam nut and remove the tie rod from the steering knuckle using a steering linkage removing tool J–35917 or equivalent.

4. Holding the inner tie rod stationary, count number of turns to remove the outer tie rod.

To install:

5. Lubricate the inner rod threads with anti-seize compound and install the outer tie rod the same amount of turns that it took to remove.

6. Install the outer tie rod-to-knuckle and install the slotted nut. Torque the nut to 35 ft. lbs. (50 Nm) and to 45 ft. lbs. (60 Nm) maximum to align the cotter pin slot. Do not back off to align the cotter pin.

7. Install a new cotter pin and bend over. Torque the jam nut to 50 ft. lbs. (70 Nm) and connect the negative battery cable.

Inner

1. Disconnect the negative battery cable.

2. Remove the rack and pinion assembly from the vehicle.

3. Remove the outer tie rod end.

4. Remove the jam nut, boot clamps and boot. Use side cutters to cut the boot clamps.

5. Remove the shock dampener from the inner tie rod and slide back on the rack.

NOTE: Do not let the rack slide out of the rack housing while the tie rods are moved.

6. Place wrenches on the flats of the rack and inner tie rod assemblies.

7. Rotate the housing counter-clockwise until the inner rod separates from the rack.

To install:

8. Install the inner tie rod end onto the rack and torque to 70 ft. lbs. (95 Nm).

9. Support the rack assembly in a vise.

10. Stake both sides of the inner tie rod housing to the flats on the rack.

11. Slide the shock dampener over the housing until it engages.

12. Install the boot and new boot clamps. Do not tighten the clamps at this time.

13. Apply grease to the inner tie rod, housing and boot.

14. Align the breather tube with the boot, making sure it is not twisted.

15. Crimp the boot clamps with keystone clamp pliers, tool J–22610 or equivalent.

16. Install the jam nut and outer tie rod end.

17. Install the rack and pinion assembly into the vehicle.

BRAKES

Master Cylinder

REMOVAL AND INSTALLATION

NOTE: On vehicles equipped with ABS, to help avoid personal injury due to a retained load on the ABS Hydraulic Modulator assembly, the gear tension relief function of the TECH I Scan tool must be performed prior to removal of the brake control and modulator assembly.

1. If equipped with Anti-lock Brakes, depressurize the ABS brake system as follows:

a. With the ignition key **OFF**, firmly apply and release the brake pedal a minimum of 40 times.

b. A noticeable change in the pedal feel will occur when the accumulator is completely discharged (a hard pedal).

c. Do not turn the ignition key **ON** after depressurizing the system.

2. Using the TECH I Scan tool, perform the gear tension relief function. Remove the ABS hydraulic modulator assembly, if equipped with ABS brakes.

3. Disconnect the electrical harness connector from the fluid level sensor on the master cylinder.

4. Using a flare nut wrench, remove the brake lines from the master cylinder. Plug the lines to prevent fluid loss and contamination.

5. Remove the 2 master cylinder-to-brake power booster retaining nuts and remove master cylinder.

To install:

6. Install the master cylinder and torque the retaining nuts to 20 ft. lbs. (27 Nm).

7. Install the brake lines and torque to 15 ft. lbs. (20 Nm), using a flare nut wrench.

8. Connect the fluid level sensor electrical wire.

9. Install the ABS hydraulic modulator assembly, if removed.

10. Fill the master cylinder to the proper level with new brake fluid meeting DOT 3 specification.

11. Bleed the hydraulic system and recheck the fluid level. Do not move the vehicle until a firm brake pedal is obtained.

Proportioning Valve

REMOVAL AND INSTALLATION

The proportioning valves are an integral part of the master cylinder assembly. On some models equipped with anti-lock brakes, there is a remote proportioning valve located in the rear of the vehicle. This valve is not serviceable and must be replaced as a complete unit.

1. Depressurize the ABS brake system as follows:

a. With the ignition key **OFF**, firmly apply and release the brake pedal a minimum of 40 times.

b. A noticeable change in the pedal feel will occur when the accumulator is completely discharged (a hard pedal).

c. Do not turn the ignition key **ON** after depressurizing the system.

2. Disconnect the negative battery cable.

NOTE: On vehicles equipped with ABS, to help avoid personal injury due to a retained load on the ABS VI hydraulic modulator assembly, the gear tension relief function of the TECH I Scan tool must be performed prior to removal of the brake control and modulator assembly.

3. Remove the ABS hydraulic modulator assembly, if equipped with ABS brakes.

4. Remove the proportioning valve cap assemblies located on the left upper side of the master cylinder body. It may be necessary to remove the reservoir to accomplish this.

5. Remove the proportioning valve O-rings and springs. Remove the proportioning valve pistons using needle-nose pliers. Take care not to damage or scratch the piston stems during removal.

6. Remove the proportioning valve seals from the pistons. Clean all parts with denatured alcohol and dry with unlubricated compressed air. Inspect all components for corrosion

and deformation and replace as required.

To install:

7. Lubricate new O-ring and proportioner valve seals with silicone grease normally supplied in the repair kit. Lubricate stem of proportioning valve piston.

8. Install new seals on proportioning valve pistons with the seal lip facing upward toward cap assembly. Install pistons into the master cylinder body.

9. Install springs in master cylinder body. Install new O-rings into the proportioning valve caps and install caps in place tightened to 20 ft. lbs. (27 Nm).

10. Install the reservoir, if removed.

11. Install the ABS modulator assembly, if removed.

12. Depress the brake pedal. If the pedal feels spongy, bleeding of the brake system is required.

Power Brake Booster

REMOVAL AND INSTALLATION

1. Disconnect the negative battery cable.

2. From inside the engine compartment, remove the secondary dash panels. Remove the interior sound panels around the booster assembly.

3. Remove the booster grommet bolt and grommet.

4. Remove the master cylinder from the power booster.

5. Scribe a mark on the front and rear booster covers in case the 2 covers get separated during removal.

NOTE: When disconnecting the pushrod from the brake pedal, the brake pedal must be kept stationary or damage to the brake switch may result.

6. Disconnect the brake pushrod from the brake pedal.

7. Unlock the booster from the front of the dash as follows.

a. Install a booster holding tool J–22805–01 to the master cylinder mounting studs.

b. Torque the stud nuts to 28 ft. lbs. (38 Nm).

c. Use a prybar to pry the locking tab on the booster out of the locking notch on the mounting flange.

d. At the same time, turn the booster counterclockwise with a large wrench on the booster holding tool.

e. Do not attempt to remove the booster until the pushrod has been disconnected from the brake pedal.

To install:

8. Lubricate the inside and outside diameters of the grommet and front housing seal with silicone grease before installation.

9. Install the booster by turning the booster holding tool clockwise until the locking flanges are engaged. Make sure the locking tab is fully seated to prevent rotation of the booster.

10. Install the booster pushrod to the brake pedal.

11. Install the master cylinder, booster grommet and secondary dash panel.

12. Connect the negative battery cable and bleed the system, if fluid pipes were disconnected from the master cylinder.

Brake Caliper

REMOVAL AND INSTALLATION

Front

1. Remove ⅔ of the brake fluid from the brake reservoir using a proper tool and dispose of fluid in a correct manner.

2. Raise and support the vehicle safely.

3. Mark the relationship of the wheel-to-hub and bearing assembly.

4. Remove the tire and wheel. Install 2 lug nuts to retain the rotor.

5. If the caliper is going to be removed, disconnect and plug the brake hose.

6. Remove the caliper mounting bolts and pull the caliper from the mounting bracket and rotor. Support the caliper with wire if not removing.

To install:

7. Inspect the bolt boots and support bushings for cuts or damage, replace if necessary. Inspect the bolts and bushings for corrosion, replace if any corrosion is found. Do not attempt to polish away the corrosion.

8. Install the caliper over the rotor into the mounting bracket. Make sure the bolt boots are in place.

9. Lubricate the entire shaft of the mounting bolts and cavities with silicone grease.

10. Install the mounting bolts and torque to 79 ft. lbs. (107 Nm).

11. Install the brake hose, using new copper washers and torque to 32 ft. lbs. (44 Nm).

12. Remove the 2 wheel lugs, install the wheels and torque the lug nuts to 100 ft. lbs. (136 Nm).

13. Lower the vehicle.

14. Fill the master cylinder and bleed the front brake calipers.

15. Check for hydraulic leaks. Pump the brake pedal a few times before moving the vehicle.

Rear

1. Remove ⅔ of the brake fluid from the reservoir with a syringe.

2. Raise and support the vehicle safely.

3. Remove the rear wheel assembly and install 2 lug nuts to retain the rotor.

4. Remove the brake shield assembly.

5. Loosen the tension on the parking brake cable at the equalizer.

6. Remove the parking cable and return spring from the lever.

7. Hold the cable lever and remove the lock nut, lever and seal.

8. Push the piston into the caliper bore using 2 adjustable pliers over the inboard pad tabs.

NOTE: Do not allow pliers to contact the actuator screw. Protect the piston so the contact surface does not get damaged.

9. Reinstall the lever seal with the sealing bead against the caliper housing, lever and locknut.

10. Remove and plug the brake hose inlet fitting only if the caliper is going to be removed from the vehicle.

11. Remove the bolt and bracket to gain access to the upper mounting bolt.

12. Remove the caliper mounting bolts, caliper and hang from the suspension with a piece of wire to prevent brake hose damage.

To install:

13. Inspect all brake parts for damage and deterioration. Replace any parts, if necessary.

14. Push the caliper sleeves inward. Install the caliper to the adapter bracket.

15. Install the caliper-to-mounting bracket bolts. Torque the mounting bolts to 92 ft. lbs. (125 Nm).

16. Install the bracket and bolt after the mounting bolts have been torqued.

17. Install the brake hose inlet with new copper washers, if removed. Torque the hose bolt to 32 ft. lbs. (44 Nm).

18. Remove the locknut, lever and seal. Lubricate the lever seal and lever shaft.

19. Install the seal and lever with the lever facing down.

20. Hold the lever back against the stop and torque the lock nut to 35 ft. lbs. (47 Nm).

21. Install the return spring and parking brake cable and adjust.

22. Install the brake shield and rear wheel assembly. Torque the lug nuts to 100 ft. lbs. (136 Nm).

23. Lower the vehicle.

24. Fill the brake reservoir with DOT 3 brake fluid.

25. Bleed the brake caliper, if removed.

26. Inspect the brake system for fluid leaks.

27. Pump the brakes until a firm pedal is achieved, prior to moving the vehicle. This will seat the brake pads against the rotors.

Disc Brake Pads

REMOVAL AND INSTALLATION

Front

1. Disconnect the negative battery cable.

2. Raise and support the vehicle safely.

3. Remove the wheel and tire assembly.

4. Remove the 2 caliper mounting bolts, caliper and hang from the suspension with a piece of wire. Do not hang by the brake hose.

5. Using a prybar, lift the outboard pad retaining spring to clear the center lug.

6. Remove the inboard pad by unsnapping from the pistons.

To install:

7. Remove about ⅔ of the fluid from the brake reservoir with a syringe.

8. Bottom the pistons in the caliper bore using a C-clamp and the old inboard brake pad.

9. Install the new inboard brake pad. Make sure both inboard pad tabs are inside the piston cavity.

10. Install the outboard pad by snapping the pad retainer spring over the housing center lug and into the housing slot.

11. Make sure both pads remain free of grease or oil. The wear sensor should be at the trailing edge of the pad during rotation.

12. Install the caliper assembly, wheels assembly and lower the vehicle.

13. Fill the master cylinder to the FULL mark and pump the brakes until a firm pedal is obtained.

14. Connect the negative battery cable.

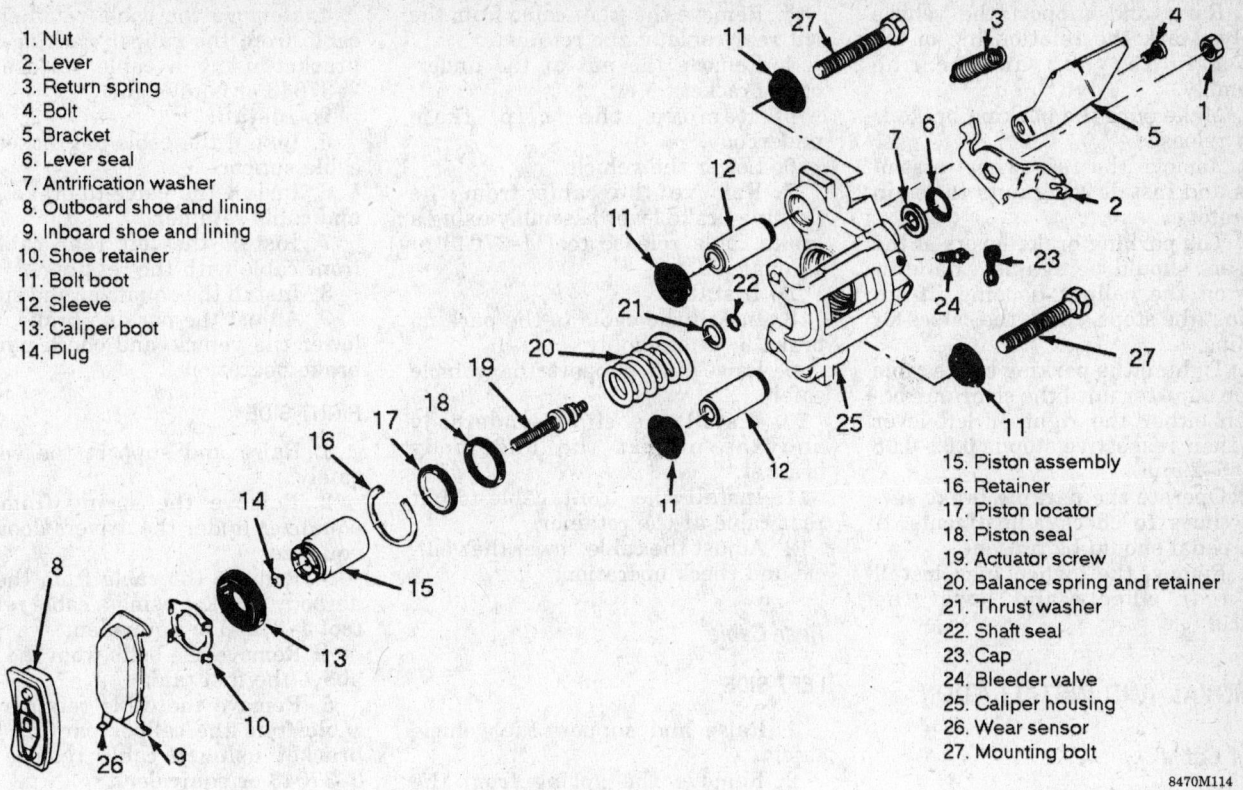

1. Nut
2. Lever
3. Return spring
4. Bolt
5. Bracket
6. Lever seal
7. Antrification washer
8. Outboard shoe and lining
9. Inboard shoe and lining
10. Shoe retainer
11. Bolt boot
12. Sleeve
13. Caliper boot
14. Plug

15. Piston assembly
16. Retainer
17. Piston locator
18. Piston seal
19. Actuator screw
20. Balance spring and retainer
21. Thrust washer
22. Shaft seal
23. Cap
24. Bleeder valve
25. Caliper housing
26. Wear sensor
27. Mounting bolt

8470M114

Rear brake caliper assembly

Rear

1. Raise and support the vehicle safely.
2. Remove the rear wheel assemblies.
3. Remove the rear caliper and hang by the suspension with a piece of wire to prevent brake hose damage.
4. Using a prybar, disengage the buttons on the outboard pad from the holes in the caliper housing.
5. Press in on the edge of the inboard pad and tilt outward to release the pad from the pad retainer.
6. Remove the plug from the end of the caliper piston using a small prybar.
To install:

NOTE: Do not allow pliers to contact the actuator screw. Protect the piston so the contact surface does not get damaged.

7. Bottom the piston into the caliper bore by positioning a twelve inch adjustable pliers over the caliper housing and piston surface.
8. Lubricate a new plug and install it into the end of the piston.
9. Install the inboard brake pad. Engage the pad edge in the retainer tabs closest to the caliper bridge. Press down and snap the tabs at the

open side of the caliper. The wear sensor should be at the leading edge of the pad during wheel rotation. The back of the pad must lay flat against the piston. The button on the back of the pad must engage the D-shaped notch in the piston.

NOTE: If the piston will not align or retract into the bore, turn the piston clockwise using a piston turning tool J–7624 or equivalent.

10. Install the outboard brake pad. Snap the pad retainer spring into the slots in the caliper housing. The back of the pad must lie flat against the caliper.
11. Install the caliper onto the mounting bracket.
12. Apply force to the brake pedal until a firm pedal is obtained, prior to moving the vehicle. This will seat the brake pads against the rotors.
13. Install the rear wheels and torque the lug nuts to 100 ft. lbs. (136 Nm).
14. Lower the vehicle and check for fluid leaks.

Brake Rotor

REMOVAL AND INSTALLATION

1. Raise and support the vehicle safely.
2. Remove the wheel and tire assembly.
3. Remove the brake caliper and support with a wire to the body.
4. Slide the rotor off the hub assembly.
To install:
5. Install the brake rotor over the hub assembly.
6. Install the brake caliper.
7. Install the wheel and tire assembly. Torque the lug nuts to 100 ft. lbs. (136 Nm).
8. Lower the vehicle. Pump the brakes until a firm pedal is obtained, prior to moving the vehicle.

Parking Brake Cable

ADJUSTMENT

1. Apply the parking brake pedal 3 times with heavy force.
2. Do not apply the main brake pedal during this step. Fully apply and release the parking brake 3 times.

3. Raise and support the vehicle safely. Mark the relationship of the wheel to the hub and bearing assembly.

4. Make sure the parking brake is fully released.

5. Remove the rear wheel assemblies and install 2 lug nuts to retain the rotors.

6. The parking brake levers at the calipers should be against the lever stop on the caliper housing. If not against the stops, check the cables for binding.

7. Tighten the parking brake cable at the adjuster until the clearance between either the right or left lever and their respective stop is 0.02–0.08 in.(0.5–2.mm).

8. Operate the parking brake several times to check adjustments. A firm pedal should be present.

9. Remove the 2 wheel lugs, install the rear wheels and lower the vehicle.

REMOVAL AND INSTALLATION

Front Cable

1. Raise and support the vehicle safely.

2. Loosen the equalizer under the driver's side door.

3. Remove the front cable from the left rear cable at the retainer.

4. Remove the nut at the underbody bracket.

5. Remove the clip from underbody.

6. Lower the vehicle.

7. Remove the cable from the parking brake lever assembly using a brake cable release tool J–37043 or equivalent.

To install:

8. Install the cable to the parking brake lever assembly.

9. Raise and support the vehicle safely.

10. Install the clip-to-underbody and the nut at the underbody bracket.

11. Install the front cable-to-left rear cable at the retainer.

12. Adjust the cable, lower the vehicle and check operation.

Rear Cable

LEFT SIDE

1. Raise and support the vehicle safely.

2. Remove the spring from the equalizer under the drivers door and equalizer.

3. Remove the left rear cable from the front cable at the retainer.

4. Remove the cable retainer and cable from the caliper parking lever bracket using a cable release tool J–37043 or equivalent.

To install:

5. Install the cable-to-bracket and cable support.

6. Install the cable-to-brake lever and cable retainer.

7. Install the left rear cable-to-front cable with the retainer.

8. Install the equalizer and spring.

9. Adjust the parking brake cable, lower the vehicle and check parking brake operation.

RIGHT SIDE

1. Raise and support the vehicle safely.

2. Remove the spring from the equalizer under the drivers door and equalizer.

3. Remove the cable from the underbody bracket using a cable release tool J–37043 or equivalent.

4. Remove the bolts from the clips above the fuel tank.

5. Remove the cable retainer and cable from the caliper parking lever bracket using a cable release tool J–37043 or equivalent.

To install:

6. Position the cable above the fuel tank.

7. Install the cable-to-bracket and cable support.

8. Install the cable-to-brake lever and cable retainer.

9. Install the clips above the fuel tank.

10. Install the cable-to-underbody brackets.

11. Install the equalizer and spring.

12. Adjust the parking brake, lower the vehicle and check operation.

Brake System Bleeding

STANDARD SYSTEM

1. Fill the master cylinder reservoir with brake fluid and keep the reservoir at least half full during the bleeding operation.

2. If the master cylinder has air in the bore, it must be removed before bleeding the calipers. Bleed the master cylinder as follows:

   a. Fill the reservoir with clean brake fluid. Do not allow brake fluid to contact painted surfaces, it will damage the finish.

   b. Loosen the brake tubes at the master cylinder and slowly depress the brake pedal. While holding the brake pedal to the floor, tighten the brake tubes. Wait 15 seconds and

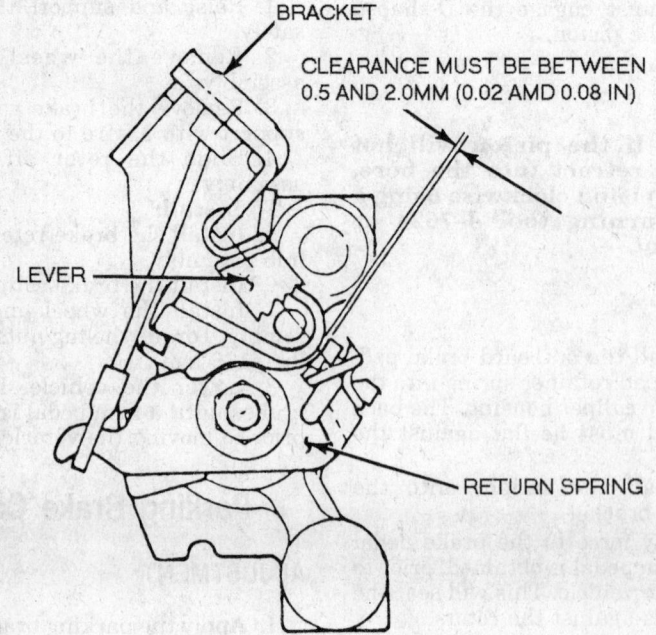

BRACKET

CLEARANCE MUST BE BETWEEN 0.5 AND 2.0MM (0.02 AMD 0.08 IN)

LEVER

RETURN SPRING

8470M115

Parking brake adjustment

repeat until all air is removed from the master cylinder.

3. Bleed the brakes in the following order:
- Right rear caliper
- Left front caliper
- Left rear caliper
- Right front caliper

4. Install a box end wrench over the bleeder valve and connect a clear tube onto the valve. Place the other end of the tube into a container of new brake fluid. The end of the tube must be submerged in brake fluid.

5. Depress the brake pedal slowly 1 time and hold. Loosen the bleeder valve to purge the air from the caliper. Close the valve and release the pedal. Wait 15 seconds. Repeat the procedure until all air is removed from the brake fluid. It may take 10 repetitions or more to completely purge the system of air.

6. Do not pump the brake pedal rapidly; this causes the secondary master cylinder piston to push to the end of the bore and makes bleeding difficult.

7. After the calipers have been bled, check the brake pedal and system for proper operation.

8. Repeat the bleeding operation if a spongy pedal is felt and fill the reservoir to the MAX line.

ANTI-LOCK BRAKE SYSTEM (ABS)

1992–94

If pressure bleeding the system, the equipment must be of the diaphragm type. It must have a rubber diaphragm between the air supply and the brake fluid to prevent air, moisture and other contaminants from entering the system. Follow the specific instructions that are supplied with the pressure bleeder.

------ CAUTION ------
Use only clean DOT 3 brake fluid from a sealed container in the anti-lock brake system. Any other type of fluid may cause severe damage to the internal components causing brake failure and personal injury. Prior to bleeding the brakes, the front and the rear displacement cylinder pistons must be returned to the top most position.

1. Position the front and the rear displacement cylinder pistons at the top most position as follows:
   a. Using a Tech I or T–100 (CAMS), enter the manual control

function and apply the front and rear motors. Be sure the relay is ON.
   b. If Tech I or T–100 (CAMS) is not available, bleed the front brakes. Start the engine and allow to run for at least 10 seconds. This will cause the ABS system to initialize itself and return the front and the rear displacement cylinders to the top position.
   c. At this point, the entire brake system should be bled again.

2. Clean and remove the reservoir cover.

3. Inspect the fluid level in the reservoir and add as required to correct level.

4. Prime the ABS modulator and master cylinder assembly as follows:
   a. Attach bleeder hose to the rearward bleeder valve and submerge the opposite end of hose in container partially filled with clean brake fluid.
   b. Slowly open the rearward bleeder valve ½ turn. Depress the brake pedal until fluid begins to flow.
   c. Close the valve and release the brake pedal. Repeat this procedure for forward bleeder valve until fluids begins to flow.

5. Remove the reservoir cover and inspect the fluid level and add fluid as required.

6. Bleed the wheels in the following sequence:
- Right rear
- Left rear
- Right front
- Left front

7. Raise and support the vehicle safely.

8. Bleed the wheel in the sequence listed above by attaching a clean hose to the bleeder valve and submerge the other end into a container partially filled with brake fluid.

9. Open the valve and slowly depress the brake pedal.

10. Tap lightly on the brake caliper with a rubber mallet to dislodge the air bubbles.

11. Close the valve and release the brake pedal. Wait 5 seconds and repeat until all air is removed.

12. Repeat Steps 5–8 until all wheels are bled. Lower the vehicle.

13. Remove the reservoir cover and inspect the fluid level. Add brake fluid as required to correct the level.

Anti-Lock Brake System Service

PRECAUTIONS

Failure to observe the following precautions may result in system damage.
- The brake system uses a hydraulic accumulator which, when fully charged, contains brake fluid at high pressure. Before disconnecting any hydraulic lines, hoses or fittings, be sure the accumulator is fully depressurized.
- Never disassemble any component of the Anti-Lock Brake System (ABS) which is designated non-serviceable; the component must be replaced as an assembly.
- Replace all components included in repair kits used to service the system.
- When filling the master cylinder, always use Delco Supreme 11 brake fluid or equivalent, which meets DOT-3 specifications; petroleum–based fluid will destroy the rubber parts.
- Avoid spilling brake fluid on the vehicles painted surfaces, wiring, cables or electrical connectors. Brake fluid will damage paint and electrical connections.

Powermaster III Unit

REMOVAL AND INSTALLATION

1. Depressurize the ABS brake system as follows:
   a. With the ignition key **OFF**, firmly apply and release the brake pedal a minimum or 40 times.
   b. A noticeable change in the pedal feel will occur when the accumulator is completely discharged (a hard pedal).
   c. Do not turn the ignition key **ON** after depressurizing the system.

2. Disconnect the negative battery cable.

3. Disconnect the 3 Powermaster III electrical connectors and move out of the way.

4. Remove and plug the 3 metal brake lines using flare nut wrenches. Plug the lines to prevent fluid loss and contamination.

5. Remove the hair pin clip from inside the vehicle at the brake pedal.

6. Remove the 2 ABS unit-to-cowl retaining nuts.

7. Remove the ABS unit. Make sure none of the electrical connectors are still connected.

To install:

8. Lightly lubricate the entire outer surface of the pushrod with silicone grease.

9. Position the ABS unit into the vehicle. Loosely install the retaining nuts and pushrod.

10. Install the pushrod hair pin clip and torque the 2 retaining nuts to 15–25 ft. lbs. (20–34 Nm).

11. Install the 3 brake pipes using flare nut wrenches. Torque the pipes to 11 ft. lbs. (20 Nm).

12. Install the ABS unit electrical connectors.

13. Adjust the stoplight switch.

14. Bleed the ABS system. Reconnect the negative battery cable.

ABS Hydraulic Modulator and Master Cylinder Assembly

REMOVAL AND INSTALLATION

1992–96

--- **CAUTION** ---

To avoid personal injury, due to a retained load on the modulator assembly, the gear tension relief function of the Tech I Scan tool must be performed prior to removal of the brake control and motor assembly.

1. Using Tech I, perform the gear reduction tension relief procedure.
2. Remove the air cleaner assembly.
3. If equipped 3.1L or 3.4L engine, disconnect the upper fuel lines and set aside.
4. Disconnect the 2 solenoid electrical connectors and the fluid level sensor connector.
5. Disconnect the 6-pin motor pack electrical connector.
6. Place a shop cloth on top of the motor pack to catch any dripping fluid. Disconnect the 4 brake lines at the modulator assembly. Plug the

open lines to prevent loss of brake fluid.

7. Raise and safely support the vehicle. Remove the lower modulator assembly attaching bolt. Lower the vehicle. It may be necessary to remove the vacuum check valve from the booster to gain access to the nut nearest the valve.

8. Remove the upper modulator assembly bolts and remove the assembly from the vehicle.

To install:

9. Install the modulator assembly to the vehicle. Install the bolts and tighten the bolts to 20 ft. lbs. (27 Nm).

10. Install the lower modulator assembly bolt and tighten to 20 ft. lbs. (27 Nm).

11. Connect the brake lines to the modulator assembly and tighten to 24 ft. lbs. (32 Nm).

12. Connect the electrical connectors to the modulator assembly.

13. Attach the upper fuel lines, if removed.

14. Install the air cleaner assembly. Bleed the brake system.

Sensor

The front sensor is serviceable only as an assembly. Do not attempt to

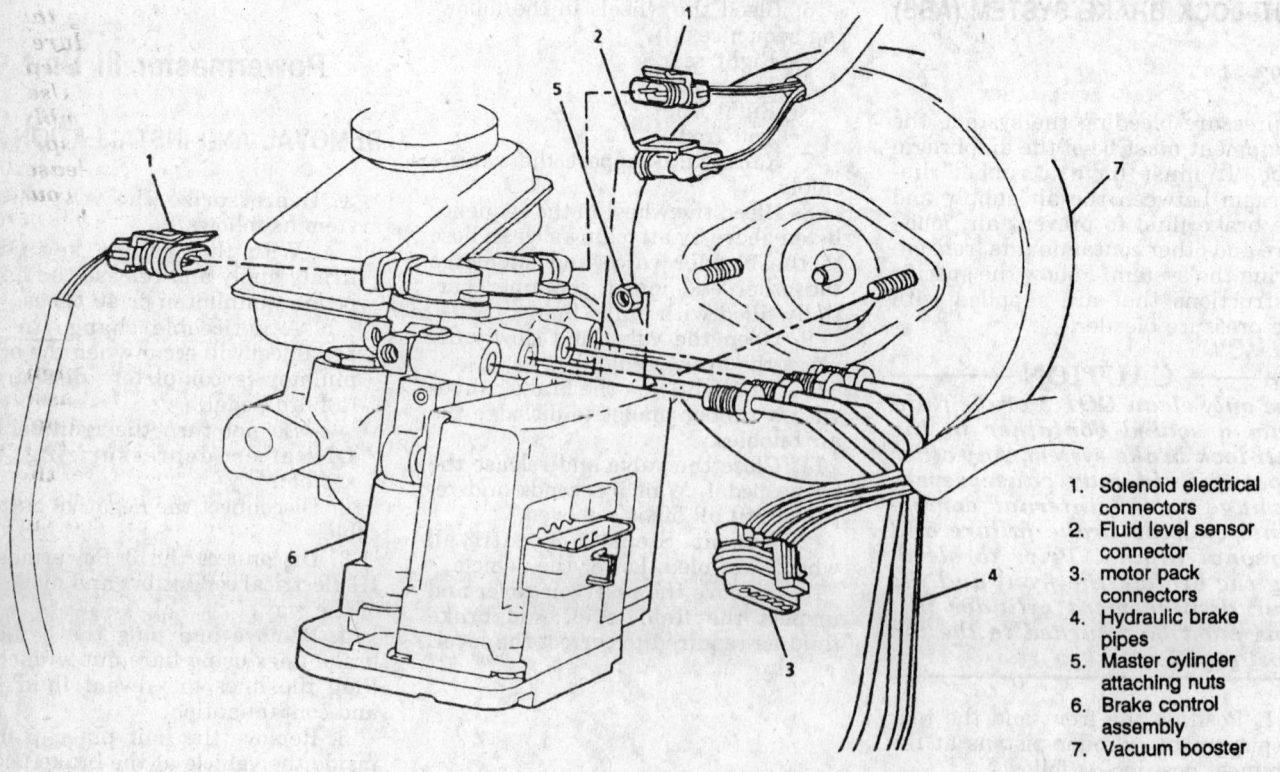

1. Solenoid electrical connectors
2. Fluid level sensor connector
3. motor pack connectors
4. Hydraulic brake pipes
5. Master cylinder attaching nuts
6. Brake control assembly
7. Vacuum booster

8569M001

ABS hydraulic modulator assembly — 1992–96 vehicles

service the sensor harness as it is part of the sensor.

REMOVAL AND INSTALLATION

Front

1. Raise and support the vehicle safely and disconnect the negative battery cable.
2. Disconnect the wiring harness connector from the sensor.
3. Remove the 2 front wheel speed sensor bolts, the 1 connector bracket bolt and remove the speed sensor.

To install:
4. Position the speed sensor and install the 2 front wheel speed sensor bolts and tighten to 52 ft. lbs. (70 Nm). Install the 1 bracket bolt and tighten to 89 inch lbs. (10 Nm).
5. Inspect the air gap. Proper air gap should be between 0.19–0.68 in. (0.48–1.73mm). If the air gap is not correct, look for damaged or misaligned components that would effect the air gap.
6. Install the sensor connector to the wiring harness. Install the Connector Position Assurance (CPA) locking pin.
7. Route the wire to avoid contact with suspension components.
8. Lower the vehicle.

Rear

The rear wheel speed sensors and rings are an integral part of the hub and bearing assemblies. Should a speed sensor or ring require replacement, the entire hub and bearing assembly must be replaced.

Electronic Brake Control Module (EBCM)

REMOVAL AND INSTALLATION

1992–96

1. Disconnect the negative battery cable.
2. Raise and safely support the vehicle. Remove the left front tire and wheel assembly. Remove the screws retaining the inner fender.
3. Remove the screws retaining the Electromagnetic Compatibility (EMC) shield. Slide the shield back on the harness ensuring not to damage harness.
4. Remove the screws retaining the EBCM and remove from it's mounting bracket.
5. Disconnect the electrical connector from the module.

To install:
6. Connect the electrical harness connector to the module.
7. Install the module onto it's mounting bracket insuring it's back guide pin is in it's groove. Secure EBCM using the retainer screws tightened to 14 inch lbs. (2.0 Nm).
8. Inspect the EMC shield and replace if damaged. Install EMC shield and tighten retainers to 13 inch lbs. (1.5 Nm).
9. Install the inner fender and secure in place.
10. Install the left front tire and wheel assembly. Lower the vehicle.
11. Connect the negative battery cable.

FRONT SUSPENSION

MacPherson Strut/Knuckle

REMOVAL AND INSTALLATION

———— CAUTION ————
Do not remove the strut cartridge nut without compressing the coil spring first. Use care to support the strut assembly adequately. Never remove the center strut nuts unless the spring is compressed with a MacPherson strut spring compressor tool J–26584 or equivalent.

1. Disconnect the negative battery cable.
2. Loosen the cover plate bolts.
3. Loosen the wheel nuts. Raise and safely support the vehicle.
4. Remove the tire and wheel assembly. Remove the brake caliper and bracket assembly, hang the caliper aside. Do not hang the caliper by the brake lines.
5. Remove the brake rotor. Remove the hub and bearing attaching bolts.
6. Remove the halfshaft. Remove the tie rod attaching nut. Using tool J–35917 or equivalent, separate the tie rod from the steering knuckle.
7. Remove the lower ball joint attaching nut and separate the lower ball from the lower control arm.
8. Remove the hub and bearing attaching bolts and hub assembly.
9. Remove the cover plate bolts and remove the strut from the vehicle.

To install:
10. Install the strut mount cover plate, tighten the nuts after lowering the vehicle. Install the lower ball joint and torque to specifications. Install new cotter pin.
11. Install the tie rod and torque to 40 ft. lbs. (54 Nm) to align the cotter pin hole. Install new cotter pin.
12. Install the halfshaft and install the hub and bearing-to-knuckle attaching bolts and tighten to 52 ft. lbs. (70 Nm).
13. Install the brake rotor and caliper assembly.
14. Install the wheel assembly, tighten the wheel lug nuts to 100 ft. lbs. (136 Nm).
15. Lower the vehicle, tighten the strut cover bolts to 17 ft. lbs. (24 Nm) and tighten the wheel nuts.
16. Connect the negative battery cable.

Strut Cartridge

REPLACEMENT

The front MacPherson strut assembly does not have to be removed from the vehicle to remove the strut cartridge.

———— CAUTION ————
Do not remove the strut cartridge nut without compressing the coil spring first. This procedure must be followed because it keeps the coil spring compressed. Use care to support the strut assembly adequately because the coil spring is under heavy load, if released too quickly personal injury could result. Never remove the center strut nuts unless the spring is compressed with a MacPherson strut spring compressor tool J–26584 or equivalent.

NOTE: The vehicle weight can be used when the strut assembly is still in the vehicle and only the strut cartridge is going to be replaced. Do not service the the strut cartridge unless the weight of the vehicle is on the suspension. The weight of the vehicle keeps the spring compressed.

1. Disconnect the negative battery cable.
2. Scribe the strut mount cover plate-to-body to ensure proper camber adjustment.
3. Remove the 3 strut mount cover plate retaining nuts and cover.
4. Remove the strut shaft nut using a No. 50 Torx® bit.

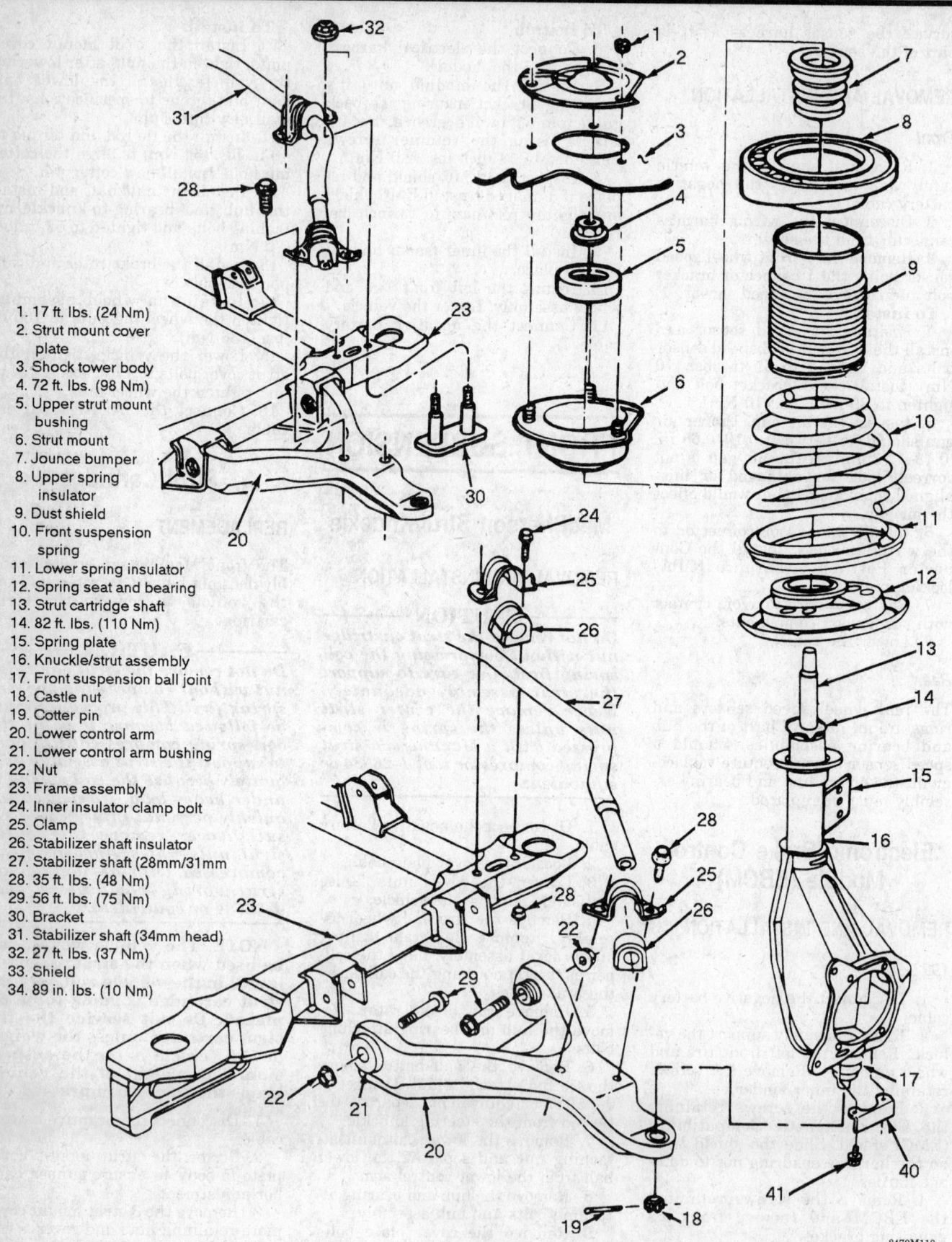

1. 17 ft. lbs. (24 Nm)
2. Strut mount cover plate
3. Shock tower body
4. 72 ft. lbs. (98 Nm)
5. Upper strut mount bushing
6. Strut mount
7. Jounce bumper
8. Upper spring insulator
9. Dust shield
10. Front suspension spring
11. Lower spring insulator
12. Spring seat and bearing
13. Strut cartridge shaft
14. 82 ft. lbs. (110 Nm)
15. Spring plate
16. Knuckle/strut assembly
17. Front suspension ball joint
18. Castle nut
19. Cotter pin
20. Lower control arm
21. Lower control arm bushing
22. Nut
23. Frame assembly
24. Inner insulator clamp bolt
25. Clamp
26. Stabilizer shaft insulator
27. Stabilizer shaft (28mm/31mm)
28. 35 ft. lbs. (48 Nm)
29. 56 ft. lbs. (75 Nm)
30. Bracket
31. Stabilizer shaft (34mm head)
32. 27 ft. lbs. (37 Nm)
33. Shield
34. 89 in. lbs. (10 Nm)

Front suspension

8470M118

5. Remove the strut mount bushing by prying with a prybar.

6. Remove the jounce bumper retainer using a jounce bumper spanner wrench tool J–35670 or equivalent. Remove the jounce bumper by attaching the strut extension rod tool J–35668 or equivalent. Compress the shaft down into the cartridge. Remove the extension rod and pull out the jounce bumper.

7. Remove the strut cartridge closure nut by attaching the strut extension rod and re-extending the shaft. Remove the extension rod and unscrew the closure nut using a strut cap nut wrench J–35671 or equivalent.

8. Remove the strut cartridge and oil from the strut tube using a suction device.

To install:

9. Install the self contained replacement cartridge using the strut cap nut wrench J–35671 or equivalent. The cartridge does not need oil added unless specified. If oil is not supplied with the cartridge, add the specified amount of hydraulic jack oil.

10. Install the jounce bumper and retainer.

11. Install the strut mount bushing. Use a soap solution to lubricate the bushing during installation.

12. Install the strut shaft nut and torque to 72 ft. lbs. (98 Nm).

13. Align the scribed marks from the strut cover-to-body. Install the strut cover plate and nuts. Torque the nuts to 17 ft. lbs. (24 Nm).

14. Connect the negative battery cable and check for proper suspension operation.

Coil Springs

REMOVAL AND INSTALLATION

1. Remove the MacPherson strut assembly.

2. Mount the strut assembly in a strut compressing tool J–34013–A and J–34013–88 or equivalent. Compress the spring using the forcing screw. Release the spring tension enough to remove the spring insulator.

3. Using a Torx® bit and a strut shaft nut remover tool J–35669 or equivalent, remove the strut shaft nut. Make sure there is no spring tension on the shaft.

4. Release all spring tension and remove the spring and insulator. Remove any component needed to perform repair.

To install:

5. Inspect all components for wear and damage.

6. Install the spring seat and bearing.

7. Install the lower spring insulator. The lower spring coil end must be visible between the step and the first retention tab of the insulator.

8. Install the spring, dust shield and jounce bumper.

9. Install the upper spring insulator. The upper spring coil end must be between the step and location mark on the insulator.

10. Install the jounce bumper retainer-to-strut mount using a jounce bumper spanner tool J–35670 or equivalent.

11. Align the strut cartridge shaft with a strut extension rod tool J–35668 or equivalent.

12. Install the strut mount and the upper strut mount bushing.

13. Compress the strut assembly using the strut spring compressor tool J–34013–A and J–34013–88 or equivalent.

14. Install the shaft nut using the strut rod installer and Torx® bit. Torque the shaft nut to 72 ft. lbs. (98 Nm).

15. Install the MacPherson strut assembly into vehicle.

Lower Ball Joint

INSPECTION

1. Raise and safely support the vehicle, allowing the front suspension to hang freely.

2. Grasp and shake the wheel at the top and bottom to feel if there is any in and out movement.

3. Replace the ball joint if any movement is detected.

4. When the ball joint is disconnected from the knuckle, check for any looseness or if the ball joint can be twisted freely in the socket by hand.

REMOVAL AND INSTALLATION

1. Raise and safely support the vehicle.

2. Remove the wheel assembly.

3. Remove the ball joint heat shield retaining nuts and remove the heat shield.

4. Remove the ball joint cotter pin and nut.

5. Loosen, but do not remove, the stabilizer bar bushing bolts.

6. Using tool J–35917 or equivalent, remove the ball joint from the lower control arm.

7. Using an ⅛ in. drill bit, make a pilot hole in each of the rivets retaining the ball joint to the lower control arm. Using a ½ in. drill bit, drill the rivets out and remove the ball joint.

To install:

8. Install the ball joint to the lower control arm, install the retaining nut hand-tight.

9. Install the ball joint to the steering knuckle. Install the 4 ball joint retaining nuts and bolts, supplied with the replacement joint.

10. Tighten the stabilizer bushing bar bushing bolts to 35 ft. lbs. (48 Nm). Tighten the ball joint retaining nut to 63 ft. lbs. (85 Nm).

NOTE: Once torque specification has been obtained, tighten nut as little as possible to align cotter pin holes. Do not at any time loosen the ball joint nut to align it when installing the cotter pin.

11. Install a new cotter pin and bend against nut flats to lock in place.

12. Install the ball joint heat shield and tighten the retaining bolts to 89 inch lbs. (10 Nm).

13. Install tire and wheel assembly and lower the vehicle.

Lower Control Arms

REMOVAL AND INSTALLATION

1. Raise and safely support the vehicle.

2. Remove the tire and wheel assembly from the vehicle. If equipped with 3.4L engine, remove the splash shield from the vehicle.

3. Remove the stabilizer shaft-to-lower control arm bolts. Remove the ball joint retaining nut and cotter pin.

4. Using tool J–35917 or equivalent, separate the ball joint from the control arm.

5. Remove the lower control arm-to-frame attaching nuts and bolts. Remove the lower control arm from the vehicle.

To install:

6. Install the lower control arm to the frame and pivot it to the ball joint.

7. Tighten the lower control arm bolts to 56 ft. lbs. (75 Nm). Tighten the ball joint nut to specifications and install a new cotter pin.

8. Install the stabilizer shaft to the lower control arm, tighten the bolts to 35 ft. lbs. (48 Nm). Install the splash shield, if removed.

9. Install the tire and wheel assembly and lower the vehicle. Tighten the wheel nuts to 100 ft. lbs. (136 Nm).

Sway Bar

REMOVAL AND INSTALLATION

1. Disconnect the negative battery cable.
2. Raise and support the vehicle safely.
3. Remove the front wheel.
4. Move the steering shaft dust seal for access to the pinch bolt.
5. Remove the pinch bolt from the lower intermediate steering shaft.
6. Loosen all the stabilizer insulator clamp attaching nuts and bolts.
7. Place a jackstand under the center of the rear frame crossmember.
8. Loosen the 2 front frame-to-body bolts (4 turns only).
9. Remove the 2 rear frame-to-body bolts and lower the rear of the frame just enough to gain access to remove the stabilizer shaft.
10. Remove the insulators and clamps from the frame and control arms. Pull the stabilizer shaft rearward, swing down and remove from the left side of the vehicle.

To install:

11. Install the stabilizer shaft through the left side of the vehicle.
12. Coat the new insulators with rubber lubricant.
13. Loosely install the clamps-to-control arms and clamps-to-frame.
14. Raise the frame into position while guiding the steering gear into place.
15. Install new frame-to-body bolts and torque to 103 ft. lbs. (140 Nm).
16. Remove the frame jackstand.
17. Torque the stabilizer clamps-to-frame and control arms to 35 ft. lbs. (47 Nm).
18. Install the steering gear pinch bolt and dust seal.
19. Install the front wheels and torque the lug nuts to 100 ft. lbs. (136 Nm).
20. Check for completion of repair and lower the vehicle.
21. Connect the negative battery cable.

Front Wheel Bearings

The hub and bearing assemblies are not serviced independently. If the assembly is damaged, the complete unit must be replaced. Refer to the "Drive Axle" section for the procedure.

REAR SUSPENSION

The rear suspension features a lightweight composite fiberglass mono-leaf transverse spring. Each wheel is mounted to a tri-link independent suspension system. The 3 links consist of an inverted U–channel trailing arm and tubular front and rear rods.

MacPherson Strut

REMOVAL AND INSTALLATION

1. Disconnect the negative battery cable.
2. Raise and support the vehicle safely.
3. Remove the rear wheel assembly.
4. Scribe the strut-to-knuckle for proper installation.
5. Remove the auxiliary spring, if equipped.
6. Remove the jack pad.
7. Install a rear leaf spring compressor tool J–35778 or equivalent.
8. Fully compress the spring but do not remove the retention plates or the spring.
9. Remove the 2 strut-to-body bolts.
10. Remove the brake hose from the strut.
11. Remove the strut and auxiliary spring upper bracket from the knuckle.

To install:

12. Position the strut to the body and knuckle bracket.
13. Install the strut-to-body bolts and torque to 34 ft. lbs. (46 Nm).
14. Install the strut to the knuckle, align the scribe marks and torque the bolts to 133 ft. lbs. (180 Nm).
15. Install the brake hose bracket and remove the spring compressing tool.
16. Install the jack pad and torque the bolts to 18 ft. lbs. (25 Nm).
17. Install the auxiliary spring, if equipped.
18. Install the wheel and torque the lug nuts to 100 ft. lbs. (136 Nm).

19. Lower the vehicle and connect the negative battery cable.

NOTE: The rear strut assembly is not serviceable. The assembly is replaced as a complete unit.

Transverse Spring Assembly

REMOVAL AND INSTALLATION

— CAUTION —

Do not disconnect any rear suspension components until the transverse spring has been compressed using a rear spring compressor tool J–35778 or equivalent. Failure to follow this procedure may result in personal injury.

NOTE: Do not use any corrosive cleaning agents, silicone lubricants, engine degreasers, solvents, etc. on or near the fiberglass rear transverse spring. These materials may cause extensive spring damage.

1. Disconnect the negative battery cable.
2. Raise the vehicle and support it safely.
3. Remove the jack pad in the middle of the spring. Remove the exhaust system, if equipped with dual exhaust.
4. Remove the spring retention plates and the right trailing arm at the knuckle. Remove the ABS electrical harness, if equipped.
5. Separate the rear leaf spring compressor tool J–35778 or equivalent, from the center shank and hang the center shank of the tool at the spring center.

NOTE: Attach the center shank of the compressor from the front side of the vehicle only.

6. Install the compressor body to the center shank and spring. Important, always center the spring on the rollers of the spring compressor.
7. Fully compress the spring using the spring compressor tool J–35778 or equivalent.
8. Slide the spring to the left side. It may be necessary to pry the spring to the left using a prybar against the right knuckle. When prying, do not damage any components.
9. Relax the spring to provide removal clearance from the right side and remove the spring.

To install:

10. Using the spring compressor tool, compress the spring and install it through the left knuckle. Slide towards the left side as far as possible and raise the right side of the spring as far as possible.

11. Compress the spring fully and install it into right knuckle.

NOTE: The rear spring retention plates are designed with tabs on 1 end. The tabs must be aligned with the support assembly to prevent damage to the fuel tank.

12. Center the spring to align the holes for the spring retention plate bolts.

13. Install the spring retention plates and bolts. Do not tighten at this time.

14. Position the trailing arm and install the bolt. Torque the bolt to 192 ft. lbs. (260 Nm).

15. Install the ABS electrical harness, if equipped.

16. Remove the spring compressor tool J–35778. Torque the spring retention plate bolts to 15 ft. lbs. (20 Nm).

17. Install the jack pads and torque the bolts to 18 ft. lbs. (25 Nm).

18. Install the exhaust system. Install the wheels and torque the lug nuts to 100 ft. lbs. (136 Nm).

19. Lower the vehicle and connect the negative battery cable.

Knuckle Assembly

REMOVAL AND INSTALLATION

1. Disconnect the negative battery cable.

2. Raise and support the vehicle safely.

3. Remove the rear wheels and scribe the strut-to-knuckle.

4. Remove the jack pad and install the rear leaf spring compressor tool J–35778 or equivalent.

5. Fully compress the spring but do not remove the spring or retention plates.

6. Remove the auxiliary spring, if equipped. If not equipped, remove the rod-to-knuckle bolt.

7. Remove the front rod-to-knuckle.

8. Remove the brake hose bracket, caliper and rotor. Do not leave the caliper hang by the brake hose.

9. Remove the hub and bearing assembly, trailing arm and the strut/upper auxiliary spring bracket

from the knuckle. Remove the knuckle.

To install:

10. Install the knuckle and position it to the strut/upper auxiliary spring bracket. Hand start the bolts, but do not tighten.

11. Install the front rod and trailing arm-to-knuckle. Hand-tighten the bolts.

12. Torque the trailing arm bolt and nut to 192 ft. lbs. (260 Nm).

13. Install the hub/bearing assembly and torque the bolts to 52 ft. lbs. (70 Nm).

14. Install the rotor and caliper.

15. Align the scribe marks to ensure proper alignment. Torque the strut-to-knuckle attaching bolts to 133 ft. lbs. (180 Nm).

16. Remove the rear leaf spring compressor.

17. Install the jack pad, auxiliary spring, if equipped, and rod-to-knuckle bolt. Apply thread locking compound to the knuckle bolts.

18. Torque the rod-to-knuckle bolts to 66 ft. lbs. (90 Nm), + 90 degree turn.

19. Install the rear wheels and torque the lug nuts to 100 ft. lbs. (136 Nm).

20. Check for completion of repair, lower the vehicle and connect the negative battery cable.

Tri-Link Suspension Assembly

REMOVAL AND INSTALLATION

Trailing Arm

1. Raise and support the vehicle safely.

2. Remove the trailing arm-to-knuckle nut and bolt.

3. Remove the trailing arm-to-body nut, bolt and arm.

To install:

4. Install the trailing arm, bolts and nuts.

5. Torque the arm-to-knuckle bolt to 192 ft. lbs. (260 Nm) and the arm-to-body bolt to 48 ft. lbs. (65 Nm).

6. Lower the vehicle and recheck all repair procedures.

Rear Rod

1. Raise and support the vehicle safely.

2. Remove the rear wheels.

3. Remove the auxiliary spring, if equipped. If not equipped, remove the rod-to-knuckle bolt.

4. Remove the lower auxiliary spring bracket at the rod, if equipped.

5. Scribe the toe adjusting cam, remove the rod-to-crossmember bolt and rod.

To install:

6. Install the rod, push the bolt through the rod bushing and install the adjusting cam in its original location. Do not tighten at this time.

7. Install the lower auxiliary spring bracket-to-rod, if equipped. Torque the nut to 133 ft. lbs. (180 Nm).

8. Install the rod-to-knuckle with thread locking compound. Do not tighten.

9. Install the rear wheels and lower the vehicle.

10. Torque the rod-to-crossmember bolt to 66 ft. lbs. (90 Nm), + 120 degree turn.

11. Adjust the rear toe.

Front Rod

1. Raise and support the vehicle safely.

2. Remove the rear wheels.

3. Remove the rod-to-knuckle bolt and exhaust pipe heat shield.

4. Lower and support the fuel tank just enough for access to the bolt at the frame.

5. Remove the rod-to-frame bolt and rod.

To install:

6. Install the rod, bolt and nut. Do not tighten at this time.

7. Apply thread locking compound to the rod-to-knuckle bolt.

8. Torque the rod-to-frame and rod-to-knuckle bolts to 66 ft. lbs. (90 Nm), + 120 degrees turn.

9. Reposition the fuel tank.

10. Install the exhaust pipe heat shield, rear wheels and lower the vehicle.

Stabilizer Shaft

REMOVAL AND INSTALLATION

1. Disconnect the negative battery cable.

2. Raise and support the vehicle safely.

3. Remove the right and left stabilizer shaft link bolts and open the brackets to remove the insulators.

4. Remove the right and left strut-to-knuckle-to-stabilizer shaft nuts. Do not remove the strut-to-knuckle bolts.

5. Remove the stabilizer shaft by prying the shaft on 1 side for clearance at the strut.

To install:

6. Install the stabilizer shaft by prying the shaft on 1 side for clearance at the strut.

7. Install the insulator brackets-to-stabilizer shaft-to-knuckle bolts. Do not tighten at this time.

8. Install the right and left stabilizer shaft link bolts.

9. Torque the link bolts to 40 ft. lbs. (54 Nm) and the knuckle bolts to 133 ft. lbs. (180 Nm).

10. Connect the negative battery cable and lower the vehicle. Check the rear wheel toe setting.

Rear Wheel Bearings

The hub and bearing assemblies are sealed units and are non-serviceable. If the assembly is damaged, the complete unit must be replaced.

REMOVAL AND INSTALLATION

1. Disconnect the negative battery cable.

2. Raise and support the vehicle safely.

3. Remove the rear wheel, caliper, bracket and rotor.

4. Loosen the 4 hub/bearing-to-knuckle attaching bolts.

5. Remove the hub/bearing assembly.

To install:

6. Install the hub/bearing assembly onto the knuckle. Install the 4 attaching bolts and torque to 52 ft. lbs. (70 Nm).

7. Install the rotor, caliper and bracket.

8. Install the rear wheel and torque the lug nut to 100 ft. lbs. (135 Nm).

9. Lower the vehicle and connect the negative battery cable.

GM-CADILLAC (RWD)
Rear Wheel Drive
CADILLAC—Brougham, Fleetwood Brougham

18

FIRING ORDERS

NOTE: To avoid confusion, always replace spark plugs and wires one at a time.

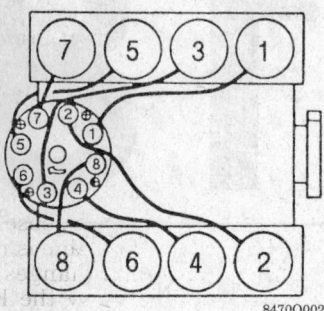

8470O002

5.0L (VIN E) and 5.7L (VIN 7)
Engines
Engine Firing Order:
1–8–4–3–6–5–7–2
Distributor Rotation: Clockwise

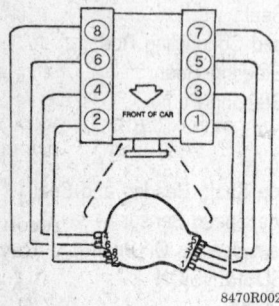

8470R002

5.7L (VIN P) Engine
Engine Firing Order:
1–8–4–3–6–5–7–2
Distributor Rotates with
Camshaft

ENGINE ELECTRICAL

NOTE: Disconnecting the negative battery cable on some vehicles may interfere with the functions of the on board computer systems and may require the computer to undergo a relearning process.

Distributor

All vehicles use a High Energy Ignition (HEI) distributor with Electronic Spark Timing (EST). The 5.0L (VIN E) and 5.7L (TBI) engines use an ex-

ternally mounted ignition coil. The 5.7L (VIN P) engine utilizes the new Opti-Spark distributor ignition system, which consists of a distributor assembly, control circuitry and an external coil. In the Opti-Spark system, all ignition timing is controlled by the ECM based on signals from the distributor's internally mounted optical camshaft position sensor. There is no way to bypass the ECM control or to adjust/set ignition timing on this system.

REMOVAL

5.7L Engine Except (VIN P)

1. Disconnect the negative battery cable. If necessary, remove the air cleaner assembly.
2. On the 5.0L (VIN E) and 5.7L engines, disconnect the wiring harness connectors at the side of the distributor cap.
3. Remove the distributor cap with spark plug wires attached and position it aside. If necessary to remove the spark plug wires, be sure to tag all wires before disconnection.
4. Remove the distributor assembly retaining bolt.
5. Note and mark the position of the rotor. Pull the distributor upward until the rotor stops turning and again note and mark the position of the rotor. Remove the distributor assembly from the vehicle.

5.7L (VIN P) Engine

1. Be sure the ignition is in the OFF or LOCK position, then disconnect the negative battery cable.
2. Disengage the wiring harness from the engine cooling fan assembly, then remove the cooling fan from the vehicle.
3. Remove the block drain plug and the knock sensor, then drain the engine cooling system.

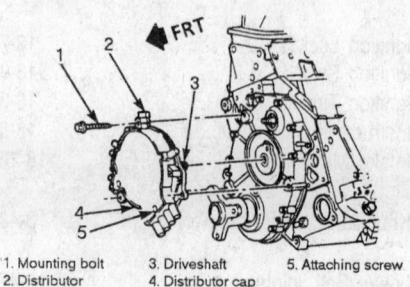

1. Mounting bolt 3. Driveshaft 5. Attaching screw
2. Distributor 4. Distributor cap

8470Q004

Distributor installation — 5.7L (VIN P) engine

4. Remove the air intake duct and the air cleaner assembly.
5. Remove the coolant and heater hoses from the water pump assembly and the throttle body.
6. Unplug the wiring harness from the Engine Coolant Temperature (ECT) sensor, then reposition the ignition coil and bracket.
7. Remove the water pump assembly.
8. Remove the serpentine drive belt from the vehicle.
9. If not done already to remove the pump or the belt, raise and safely support the vehicle for access.
10. Remove the torsional damper bolts, then remove the damper from the crankshaft hub.
11. Disconnect the spark plug wires from the distributor. Be sure to twist each boot ½ turn and pull only on the boot to remove each wire. The wire numbers should be molded into the distributor housing. If not, be sure to tag the wires before disconnection.
12. Unplug the 4-terminal ECM connector from the distributor.
13. Remove the distributor mounting bolts and pull the distributor forward until the driveshaft disengages from the engine. Mark the top of the shaft for alignment during reassembly.

INSTALLATION

Timing Not Disturbed

EXCEPT 5.7L (VIN P) ENGINE

1. To install the distributor, position the rotor in the last position as marked and lower the assembly into the distributor bore of the engine. On TBI vehicles, the distributor will install easier if it is tilted toward the driver's side of the vehicle and then slid into place. When the distributor rotor stops turning and the unit is seated, the rotor should be pointing to the first position marked.
2. Tighten the distributor retaining bolt.
3. Install the distributor cap. Connect all required electrical connections.
4. If removed, install the air cleaner assembly.
5. Connect the negative battery cable and check the ignition timing.

5.7L (VIN P) ENGINE

1. Align the match mark made on the distributor shaft, install the distributor to the engine. Tighten the distributor bolts to 8 ft. lbs. (11 Nm).

2. Install the 4-terminal ECM connector and the spark plug wires to the distributor.

3. Position the crankshaft damper to the hub, then install the damper bolts and tighten to 60 ft. lbs. (81 Nm).

4. Install the serpentine drive belt.

5. Install the water pump assembly and engage the ECT wiring harness.

6. Reposition the ignition coil and bracket, then install the coolant and heater hoses.

7. Install the air cleaner assembly and air intake duct.

8. Install the engine block drain plug and the knock sensor.

9. Install the right cooling fan assembly, then connect the wiring harness.

10. Connect the negative battery cable and fill the engine cooling system.

11. Start and run the engine, then check for leaks.

Timing Disturbed

EXCEPT 5.7L (VIN P) ENGINE

1. If the engine has been accidently cranked with the distributor out, remove the No. 1 spark plug. Place a finger over the No. 1 spark plug hole and crank the engine slowly until a compression build up can be felt in that cylinder.

2. Carefully align the timing mark on the crankshaft pulley to the **O** mark on the timing indicator of the engine. Turn the distributor rotor to point between the No. 1 and No. 8 spark plug towers on the distributor cap.

3. Lower the assembly into the distributor bore of the engine. When the distributor rotor stops turning and the unit is seated, the rotor should be pointing to No. 1 cylinder segment of the distributor cap.

4. Tighten the distributor retaining bolt.

5. Install the distributor cap. Install the spark plug wires. Connect all required electrical connections.

6. If removed, install the air cleaner assembly.

7. Connect the negative battery cable and check the ignition timing.

Ignition Timing

ADJUSTMENT

NOTE: Always refer to the timing specifications listed on the Emission Control Information Label.

Except 5.7L (VIN P) Engines

1. Connect a timing light and tachometer to the engine. Some tachometers currently available are not compatible with the HEI ignition system. Be sure to connect the timing light to the No. 1 spark plug wire and to connect the tachometer according to the tools instructions.

2. Start the engine and operate until normal operating temperature is reached and the chock is fully opened.

3. Turn all accessories **OFF** and with the engine running, ground the diagnostic terminal of the ALDL connector using a jumper.

4. Check the ignition timing at the specified rpm. If the ignition timing is not within specification, loosen the distributor clamp bolt and rotate the

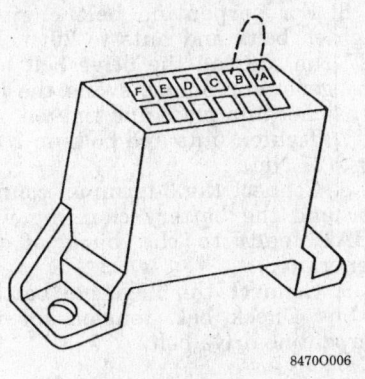

84700006

ALDL connector

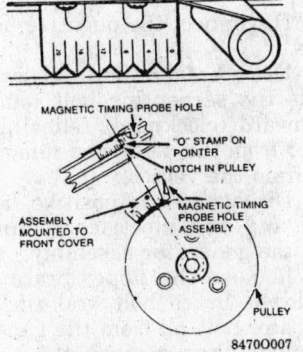

MAGNETIC TIMING PROBE HOLE

"O" STAMP ON POINTER

NOTCH IN PULLEY

MAGNETIC TIMING PROBE HOLE ASSEMBLY

ASSEMBLY MOUNTED TO FRONT COVER

PULLEY

84700007

Typical timing mark location

distributor gradually until the specified timing is obtained.

5. Tighten the distributor clamp bolt making sure the distributor does not change position. Recheck the ignition timing.

6. With the engine still running, remove the jumper from the ALDL terminal.

7. Make fuel system adjustments, as required.

8. Turn the engine **OFF**. Remove the tachometer and timing light.

5.7L (VIN P) Engine

On the 5.7L (VIN P) engine, base timing is preset when the engine is manufactured. All timing changes are then controlled directly by the ECM based on information from the ignition and knock sensor systems. No adjustments are necessary or possible.

Generator

PRECAUTIONS

Several precautions must be observed with generator equipped vehicles to avoid damage to the unit.

• If the battery is removed for any reason, make sure it is reconnected with the correct polarity. Reversing the battery connections may result in damage to the 1-way rectifiers.

• When utilizing a booster battery as a starting aid, always connect the positive to positive terminals and the negative terminal from the booster battery to a good engine ground on the vehicle being started.

• Never use a fast charger as a booster to start vehicles.

• Disconnect the battery cables when charging the battery with a fast charger.

• Never attempt to polarize the generator.

• Do not use test lights of more than 12 volts when checking diode continuity.

• Never operate the generator with the output terminal disconnected.

• Do not short across or ground any of the generator terminals.

• The polarity of the battery, generator and regulator must be matched and considered before making any electrical connections within the system.

• Never separate the generator on an open circuit. Make sure all connections within the circuit are clean and tight.

• Disconnect the battery ground terminal when performing any service on electrical components.

• Disconnect the battery if arc welding is to be done on the vehicle.

BELT TENSION ADJUSTMENT

5.0L (VIN E) and 5.7L Engines

NOTE: Serpentine belts are automatically adjusted by the tensioner on the engine. If the belt is loose, check the condition of the belt and tensioner. The tensioner should place enough tension on the belt so it can only be twisted 90 degrees at it's longest run.

1. Run the engine for about 10 minutes and shut the engine **OFF**.
2. Using belt tension gauge J-23600-B or equivalent, check the belt tension between 2 pulleys and record the reading.
3. Remove the gauge. Run the engine for about 30 seconds and shut the engine **OFF**.
4. Check the belt tension between the same 2 pulleys and record the reading.

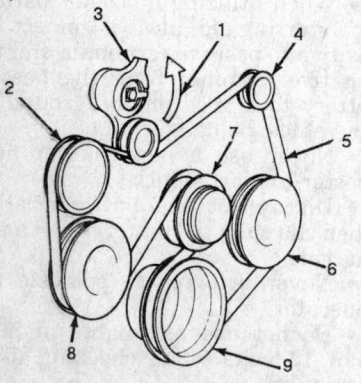

1. Rotate tensioner in direction shown to install or remove belt
2. A/C compressor
3. Belt tensioner
4. Generator assembly pulley
5. Serpentine belt
6. P/S pump pulley
7. Water pump pulley
8. Air pump pulley
9. Crankshaft pulley

84700008

Serpentine accessory drivebelt

5. Remove the gauge. Run the engine for about 30 seconds and shut the engine **OFF**.
6. Check the belt tension between the same 2 pulleys and record the reading.
7. Take the average of the 3 recorded readings. The belt tension should be 99–121 lbs. (440–538 N).
8. If the drive belt is not worn and the drive tensioner is operating normally but the tension is still below specification, replace the belt tensioner.

REMOVAL AND INSTALLATION

Except 5.7L (VIN P) Engines

1. Disconnect the negative battery cable.
2. Disconnect the 3-terminal connector and the battery charging wire (BAT lead) from the back of the generator.
3. With V-Belts, loosen the bolt holding the slotted adjusting bracket to the generator and remove the belt.
4. With serpentine belts, loosen and rotate the tensioner to release the drive belt.
To install:
5. Position the ground strap and generator in place.
6. For serpentine belt engines, tighten bolts and nuts to 20 ft. lbs. (27 Nm), install the drive belt over the generator pulley, swing the belt tensioner into place and tighten.
7. Tighten nuts and bolts to 20 ft. lbs. (27 Nm).
8. Connect the 3-terminal connector and the battery charging wire (BAT lead) to the back of the generator.
9. Connect the negative battery cable. Check belt tension for the serpentine drive belt.

5.7 (VIN P) Engine

1. Disconnect the negative battery cable.
2. Use a breaker bar and socket to rotate the serpentine belt tensioner downward (clockwise) relieving tensioner from the belt, then remove the belt from the vehicle.
3. Disengage the positive battery wire and the electrical connector from the generator assembly.
4. Remove the upper brace bolts, the lower brace bolt and the front generator bolt all from the generator assembly, then remove the nut retaining the upper brace to the top of

the engine and remove the upper brace from the vehicle.
5. Remove the generator from the accessory mounting bracket and from the vehicle.
To install:
6. Position the generator to the engine and accessory mounting bracket.
7. Install the upper brace and tighten the retaining nut to 24 ft. lbs. (33 Nm), then install the generator and brace bolts. Tighten the rear upper brace and front generator bolts to 37 ft. lbs. (50 Nm) and tighten the rear lower brace bolt to 18 ft. lbs. (25 Nm).
8. Engage the electrical connector and the battery positive wire to the generator assembly.
9. Install the serpentine drive belt.
10. Connect the negative battery cable.

Starter

REMOVAL AND INSTALLATION

5.0L (VIN E) and 5.7L Engines

1. Disconnect the negative battery cable.
2. Raise and support the vehicle safely.
3. Remove front support attaching bolt, nut and bracket.
4. Disconnect and tag the wiring at the solenoid.
5. Disconnect the exhaust pipe from the left manifold and loosen the pipe from the right manifold.
6. Remove the starter mounting bolts, lower the starter and, if equipped, remove the shims. Inspect the flywheel teeth for damage.
To install:
7. Position the starter in the vehicle. If shims were removed, they must be installed in their original location to assure proper drive pinion to flywheel engagement.
8. Check the pinion to flywheel clearance. A 0.020 inch (0.5 mm) gauge should just fit between the center end of a flywheel tooth and the pinion gear. Add shims, if necessary.
9. Tighten the starter mounting bolts to 35 ft. lbs. (47 Nm).
10. Connect the electrical connections to the starter solenoid and the exhaust pipes to the manifolds.
11. Install the front starter bracket. Tighten the bolt to 18 ft. lbs. (24 Nm) and the nut to 71 inch lbs. (8 Nm).
12. Lower the vehicle and connect the negative battery cable.

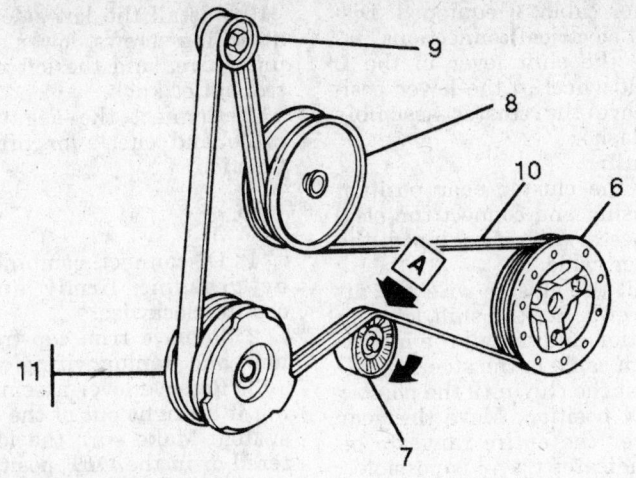

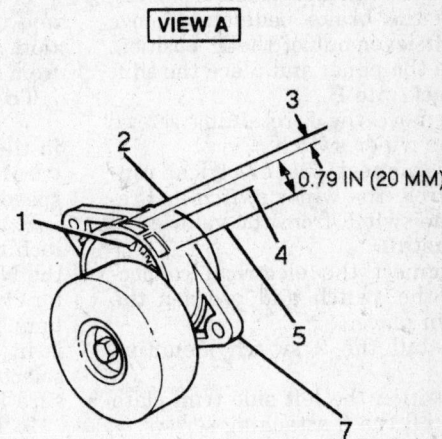

1. Indicator mark
2. Reading for replacing belt in service
3. Defective parts check range
4. Maximum tolerance belt reading
5. Minimum tolerance belt reading
6. Balancer assembly, crankshaft
7. Tensioner assembly, drive belt
8. Pump assembly, power steering
9. Generator assembly
10. Compressor assembly, air conditioning
11. Pulley, drive belt idler

8470Q008

Serpentine drive belt and tensioner — 5.7L (VIN P) engine

CHASSIS ELECTRICAL

Air Bag

DISARMING

1. Align the steering wheel so the wheels are pointing in the straight-ahead position.
2. Turn the ignition switch to the **LOCK** position.
3. Remove the SIR or AIR BAG fuse from the fuse block.
4. Remove the Connector Position Assurance (CPA) device, then disengage the yellow 2-way SIR wire harness connector at the base of the steering column.
   To enable system:
5. Turn the ignition switch to the **LOCK** position.
6. Engage the yellow 2-way connector at the base of the steering column, then install the CPA device.
7. Reinstall the SIR or AIR BAG fuse.
8. Turn the ignition switch to the **RUN** position.

9. Verify the SIR indicator light flashes 7–9 times, if not, inspect system for malfunction.

Heater Blower Motor

REMOVAL AND INSTALLATION

1. Disconnect the negative battery cable.
2. Disconnect the electrical connector from the blower motor assembly. Disconnect the blower motor cooling tube.
3. Remove the blower motor retaining screws and remove the blower motor assembly from the air conditioning module.
4. Installation is the reverse of the removal procedure.

Windshield Wiper Motor

REMOVAL AND INSTALLATION

1. Disconnect the negative battery cable.
2. Remove the cowl screen.
3. Reach through the opening and disengage the transmission drive link from the wiper crank arm by loosening the nuts.

4. Disconnect the electrical wiring and washer hoses.
5. Remove the bolts that secure the wiper/washer unit to the bulkhead.
6. Remove the entire assembly.
   To install:
7. Be sure the wiper crank arm is in the park position and install the assembly with the attaching bolts.
8. Connect the electrical wiring and the washer hoses.
9. Reach through the opening and engage the transmission drive link to the wiper crank arm. Tighten the retaining nuts.
10. Install the cowl screen and connect the negative battery cable.

Windshield Wiper Switch

REMOVAL AND INSTALLATION

1992

1. Disconnect the negative battery cable.
2. With an Allen wrench, loosen the screw on the bottom of the left climate control outlet door knob and remove the knob.
3. Remove the lower steering column cover and the 2 retaining screws.

4. Remove the 6 retaining screws from the trim panel and remove the panel. To facilitate panel removal, depress the brake pedal and move the shift lever out of the **P** position. Remove the panel and place the shift lever back into **P**.

5. Remove the 2 retaining screws from the wiper switch.

6. Disconnect the electrical connector from the wiper switch and remove the switch from the vehicle.

To install:

7. Connect the electrical connection to the switch and position the switch in place.

8. Install the 2 switch mounting screws.

9. Position the left side trim plate and install the 6 attaching screws.

10. Install the outlet grille directional knob and secure with the attaching screws. Attach the lower column cover and screws.

11. Connect the negative battery cable.

1993–96

1. Disconnect turn signal lever by grasping firmly and turning counterclockwise.

2. Remove trim cap from the column and unplug wiring connector.

3. Remove turn signal lever assembly by pulling it straight out of the turn signal switch. Make sure the lever is centered or in the **OFF** position.

To install:

4. Connect the lever assembly by pushing into the turn signal switch and turning clockwise.

5. Plug in wiring connector and install trim cover.

Instrument Cluster

REMOVAL AND INSTALLATION

1. Disconnect the negative battery cable.

2. Remove the left side trim panel by removing the left climate control outlet knob, the lower steering column cover and the left side trim panel attaching screws.

3. To ease removal of the trim panel, depress the brake pedal and move the shift lever from the **P** position.

4. With the shift lever in the **P** position, remove the shift indicator cable and clip from the steering column.

5. Remove the cluster assembly retaining screws. Carefully pull the cluster outward and disengage the

speedometer cable, if equipped. Disconnect all electrical connections.

6. Place the shift lever in the **L** and the tilt wheel in the lower position. Remove the cluster assembly from the dash.

To install:

7. Hold the cluster near position in the housing and connect the electrical connector and, if equipped, the speedometer cable.

8. Install the cluster with the attaching screws. Set the shift lever in the **N** position and install the indicator clip with cable to the steering column. Adjust the clip until the pointer is in the **N** position. Move the gear selector over the entire range to be sure full indicator travel is possible.

9. Install the left side trim plate, attaching screws, lower steering column cover and the left climate control outlet knob.

10. Connect the negative battery cable.

Headlight Switch

REMOVAL AND INSTALLATION

1992

1. Disconnect the negative battery cable.

2. Remove the left side trim panel by removing the left climate control outlet knob, the lower steering column cover and the left side trim panel attaching screws.

3. Remove the screws securing the headlight switch to the instrument panel.

4. Remove the cruise control switch retaining screws, if equipped, and pull the switch forward slightly to better access the headlight switch.

5. Disconnect the 2 piece connector from the headlight switch.

6. Remove the switch rod by depressing the retaining button while pulling the switch rod from the switch. Disconnect the twilight sentinel wiring, if equipped.

7. Remove the switch by unthreading the retaining nut from the front of the lens housing.

To install:

8. Thread the switch onto the lens housing and install the rod into the switch. Connect the twilight sentinel wiring, if equipped and attach the 2 piece electrical connector to the headlight switch.

9. Install the 3 screws securing the headlight switch to the instrument panel. Reposition and install the cruise control switch, if applicable.

10. Install the left side trim plate, attaching screws, lower steering column cover and the left climate control outlet knob.

11. Connect the negative battery cable and check for proper switch function.

1993–96

1. Disconnect combination lever by grasping firmly and turning counterclockwise.

2. Remove trim cap from the column and unplug wiring connector.

3. Remove lever assembly by pulling it straight out of the turn signal switch. Make sure the lever is centered or in the **OFF** position.

To install:

4. Connect the lever assembly by pushing into the combination switch and turning clockwise.

5. Plug in wiring connector and install trim cover.

Dimmer Switch

REMOVAL AND INSTALLATION

1. Disconnect negative battery cable and set the ignition in the **LOCK** position.

2. Remove left sound insulator and the lower column cover as necessary to access the steering column.

3. Remove 2 nuts securing steering column to upper mounting bracket.

4. Carefully lower and support the steering column.

5. Remove the 2 screws securing the ignition switch and the dimmer switch. Disconnect electrical connection and remove the dimmer switch.

To install:

6. Install the switch to the steering column with the actuator rod in place and adjust the dimmer switch.

7. Connect the switch electrical connection. Raise the steering column into position and attach the securing nut.

8. Install the left sound insulator and the lower steering column cover as necessary.

9. Connect the negative battery cable and check switch operation.

ADJUSTMENT

1. Depress the switch slightly to insert alignment tool ($^3/_{32}$ inch drill bit) through the locating hole.

2. Loosen the adjustment screws attaching the dimmer switch mounting bracket.

3. Slide the dimmer switch firmly against the actuator arm to remove all lash and tighten both adjusting screws.

Turn Signal Switch

REMOVAL AND INSTALLATION

1. Disconnect the negative battery cable.
2. Remove the steering wheel.
3. Remove the ignition lock cylinder.
4. Remove the hazard switch and screw from the column.
5. Unscrew and remove the tilt column lever, if applicable.
6. Remove the turn signal lever by pulling outward and off the column.
7. Remove the lock housing cover and screws.
8. Remove the lower column cover and fuse panel cover to gain access to the switch electrical connector.
9. Disconnect the electrical harness connector and the wiring protector.
10. Remove the turn signal switch mounting screws. If the switch is known to be bad, cut the wires and discard the switch. Tape the connector of the new switch to the old wires, and pull the new harness down through the steering column while removing the old wires. If the original switch is to be reused, wrap tape around the connector and pull the harness up through the column. It may be helpful to attach a length of mechanic's wire to the harness connector before pulling it up through the column to assist with installation.
11. After freeing the switch wiring protector from its mounting, pull the turn signal switch straight up and remove the switch, switch harness and the connector from the column.
To install:
12. Pull the switch harness connector through the column, either with the old switch wires or the length of mechanic's wire which was attached to the old connector during removal.
13. Install the switch and attaching screws to the column.
14. Connect the electrical harness connector and the wiring protector.
15. Install the lock housing cover and screws. Install the hazard switch to the column.
16. Install the turn signal and tilt column levers, as applicable.
17. Install the ignition lock cylinder and the steering wheel.

18. Connect the negative battery cable and check switch operation.

Ignition Lock

REMOVAL AND INSTALLATION

1992

1. Disconnect the negative battery cable.
2. Remove the steering wheel.
3. Remove the spacers, the steering shaft bumper, and the plastic retainer, as applicable.
4. Install a suitable lock plate tool onto the steering shaft. Tighten the tool to compress the lock plate and the spring. Remove the lock retainer.
5. Remove the lock plate, carrier assembly and the upper bearing spring from the upper steering shaft.
6. Insert the key into the ignition switch and turn the ignition switch to the **RUN** position.
7. Remove the key warning buzzer switch and retaining clip.
8. Remove the ignition cylinder retaining screw located inside the lock housing cover.
9. Remove the lock cylinder from the column.
To install:
10. Install the lock cylinder to the steering column and install the lock cylinder retaining screws.
11. Install the key warning buzzer and retaining clip, with the cylinder still in the run position.
12. Install the upper bearing spring, the carrier assembly and the lock plate, from the upper steering shaft.
13. Using a suitable lock plate tool, compress the lock plate and the spring and install the lock retainer.
14. Install the plastic retainer, the steering shaft bumper and the spacers, as applicable.
15. Install the steering wheel.
16. Connect the negative battery cable.

1993–96

------ **CAUTION** ------
When performing service on or around SIR components or wiring, follow the procedures to disable the SIR system. Failure to follow procedures could result in possible air bag deployment, personal injury or unneeded SIR system repairs.

1. Turn steering wheel so the tires are pointing straight-ahead.

2. Turn ignition switch to **LOCK**.
3. Remove "AIR BAG" fuse from the fuse block.
4. Remove the left sound insulator and unplug the Connector Position Assurance (CPA) and yellow 2-way connector, located near the base of the steering column.
5. Disconnect the negative battery cable.
6. Remove the steering wheel.
7. Remove the spacers, the steering shaft bumper and the plastic retainer, as applicable.
8. Install a suitable lock plate tool onto the steering shaft. Tighten the tool to compress the lock plate and the spring. Remove the lock retainer.
9. Remove the lock plate, carrier assembly and the upper bearing spring from the upper steering shaft.
10. Insert the key into the ignition switch and turn the ignition switch to the **RUN** position.

NOTE: With "AIR BAG" fuse removed and ignition switch in "RUN" position, the "AIR BAG" lamp on the instrument panel cluster will light. This is normal and does not indicate an SIR fault.

11. Remove the key warning buzzer switch and retaining clip.
12. Remove the ignition cylinder retaining screw located inside the lock housing cover.
13. Remove the lock cylinder from the column.
To install:
14. Install the lock cylinder to the steering column and install the lock cylinder retaining screws.
15. Install the key warning buzzer and retaining clip, with the cylinder still in the **RUN** position.
16. Install the upper bearing spring, the carrier assembly and the lock plate, from the upper steering shaft.
17. Using a suitable lock plate tool, compress the lock plate and the spring and install the lock retainer.
18. Install the plastic retainer, the steering shaft bumper and the spacers, as applicable.
19. Turn the ignition to **LOCK**.
20. Connect the negative battery cable.
21. Connect the Connector Position Assurance (CPA) and yellow 2-way connector at the base of the steering column.
22. Reinstall "AIR BAG" fuse.
23. Turn ignition switch to **"RUN"** and verify that the "AIR BAG" lamp flashes 7 times and turns OFF.
24. Install the steering wheel.

Ignition Switch

REMOVAL AND INSTALLATION

1. Disconnect negative battery cable and set the ignition in the **LOCK** position.

2. Remove left sound insulator and the lower column cover as necessary to access the steering column.

3. Remove 2 nuts securing steering column to upper mounting bracket.

4. Carefully lower and support the steering column.

5. Remove the 2 screws securing the ignition switch and the dimmer switch. Disconnect electrical connection and remove the ignition switch.

To install:

6. Install the dimmer and ignition switches to the steering column and connect the ignition switch electrical connection. Adjust the dimmer switch as necessary.

7. Assemble the ignition switch on the actuator rod and adjust it to the **LOCK** position.

8. If equipped with a standard column, hold the switch actuating rod stationary with while moving the switch toward the bottom of the column until it reaches the end of its travel, which is the **ACC** position. Back off 2 detents to the right, which is the **OFF/UNLOCK** position, then with the key also in the **OFF/UNLOCK** position, tighten the switch mounting screws to 35 inch lbs.

9. If equipped with a tilt wheel, hold the switch actuating rod stationary with one hand while moving the switch toward the upper end of column until it reaches the end of its travel, which is the **ACC** position. Back off 1 detent and with the key in **LOCK** position, tighten the switch mounting screws to 35 inch lbs.

10. Raise the steering column into position and attach the securing nuts.

11. Install the left sound insulator and the lower steering column support, as necessary.

12. Connect the negative battery cable and check that the starting system will only start in the **P** and **N** positions.

Brake Light Switch

ADJUSTMENT

1. Place the brake light switch clip in the bore on the pedal assembly bracket.

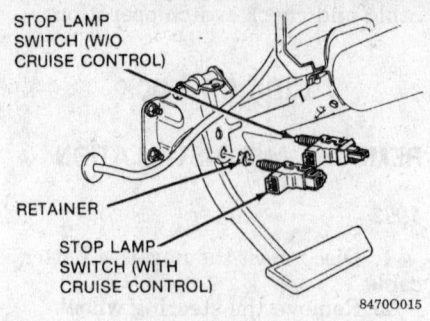

STOP LAMP SWITCH (W/O CRUISE CONTROL)

RETAINER

STOP LAMP SWITCH (WITH CRUISE CONTROL)

84700015

Brake light switch

2. With the brake pedal depressed, insert the switch well into the clip. Clicks can be heard as the threaded portion of the switch is pushed through the clip towards the brake pedal.

3. Pull the brake pedal rearward just enough to reach the normal released position. The switch will move in the clip automatically adjusting the switch. There should be free-play between the pedal and switch bodies when the pedal is pulled toward the released direction from the unapplied position.

4. When the switch is properly adjusted, no clicks should be heard and the brake lights should not remain ON when the pedal is pulled upward. Nominal actuation of stop lamp contacts is at $5/16$ in.$11/16$in. (7.5-17mm) of pedal travel measured at the centerline of the brake pedal pad.

5. Finish installation and verify that the brake lights operate correctly.

6. If necessary, repeat step 3 and adjust the switch within the clip to correct the adjustment.

REMOVAL AND INSTALLATION

NOTE: The cruise control release switch and the brake light switch are adjusted or replaced in the same manner.

1. Disconnect the negative battery cable. Remove the left sound insulator and the lower steering column cover, as required.

2. Disconnect the wire harness connector from the switch. Remove the switch from the clip and then remove the clip from the bracket.

To install:

3. Place the clip in its bore on the bracket.

4. With the brake pedal depressed, insert the switch into the clip and depress the switch body. Clicks can be heard as the threaded portion of the switch is pushed through the clip towards the brake pedal.

5. Adjust the switch, connect the negative battery cable and check for proper switch operation.

6. Install the left sound insulator and the lower steering column cover, as necessary.

Neutral Safety Switch

The vehicles incorporate a mechanical neutral start system. This system relies on a mechanical block, rather than the starter safety switch to prevent starting the engine in other than **P** or **N** positions.

The mechanical block is achieved by a cast in finger added to the switch actuator rod, which interferes with the bowl plate in all shift positions except **P** or **N**. This interference prevents rotation of the lock cylinder into the **START** position.

In either **P** or **N**, this finger passes through the bowl plate slots allowing the lock cylinder full rotational travel into the **START** position.

Fuses, Circuit Breakers and Relays

LOCATION

Fusible links

Fusible links are used to prevent major wire harness damage in the event of a short circuit or an overload condition in the wiring circuits which are normally not fused, due to carrying high amperage loads or because of their locations within the wiring harness. Each fusible link is of a fixed valve for a specific electrical load and should a link fail, the cause of the failure must be determined and repaired prior to installing a new fusible link of the same value.

Circuit Breakers

Various circuit breakers are located under the instrument panel. In order to gain access these components, it may be necessary to first remove the under dash padding. Circuit breakers function by creating an open circuit if a short or overload condition occurs within the circuit which might damage other components.

Circuit breakers of 2 types can be found in these vehicles. The standard breaker is used, which will continue to cycle open and closed until the high current is removed. Also used is the Positive Temperature Coefficient (PTC) type breaker which will not reset until the circuit is manually opened by removing voltage from its terminals. The PTC breaker should reset within a few seconds after the open circuit condition is manually created.

Fuse Panel

The fuse panel is located on the left side of the vehicle. It is under the instrument panel assembly. In order to gain access to the fuse panel, it may be necessary to first remove the under dash padding.

Relays

All vehicles use a combination of the following electrical relays in order to function properly.

Air Condition Compressor Control Relay — located on the left side of the firewall in the engine compartment.

Brake Modulator Pump Motor Relay — incorporated in the electronic brake modulator located in left hand front of the engine compartment, ahead of the engine.

Brake Modulator Solenoid Relay — incorporated into the electronic brake modulator located in left hand front of the engine compartment, ahead of the engine.

Defogger Relay — located in the accessory relay panel under the left side dash panel, to the left of the fuse block.

Door Lock Relay — attached to the lower right shroud panel behind the kick panel.

Electronic Level Control Relay — located in the accessory relay panel under the left side dash panel, to the left of the fuse block.

Fuel Pump Relay — located in the accessory relay panel under the left side dash panel, to the left of the fuse block.

Horn Relay — located in the convenience center, under the left side of the dash panel, to the left of the steering column.

Moon Roof Relay — located in the center of the windshield header, to the right of the moon roof actuator assembly.

Over-voltage Protection Relay — located on the ABS harness near the EBCM under the glove box.

Power Antenna Relay — located in the accessory relay panel under the left side of the dash panel, to the left of the fuse box.

Reverse Light Relay — located in the accessory relay panel under

the left side of the dash panel, to the left of the fuse box.

Starter Interrupt Relay — located in the accessory relay panel under the left side of the dash panel, to the left of the fuse box.

Theft Deterrent Relay — located behind the left side of the instrument panel to the right of the steering column.

Wiper/Washer Park and Pulse Relays — incorporated into the wiper/washer assembly on the firewall in the engine compartment.

Computers

LOCATION

Electronic Control Module (ECM) — located on the right side of the vehicle. It is positioned in front of the right kick panel. In order to gain access to the assembly, the trim panel and, if necessary, the glove box must first be removed.

Electronic Brake Control Module (EBCM) — located under the right side of the dash. In order to gain access to the module, the trim panel must first be removed.

Flashers

LOCATION

Turn Signal — located at the base of the steering column to the right of the steering column support. In order to gain access to the turn signal flasher, it may be necessary to first remove the under dash padding.

Hazard Flasher — located in the fuse block. It is positioned on the lower right corner of the fuse block assembly. In order to gain access, it may be necessary to first remove the under dash padding.

Cruise Control

ADJUSTMENT

Cruise Control Brake Release Switch

If equipped with cruise control, an electric switch and in some cases a vacuum switch is mounted on the pedal support to disengage the cruise control when vehicle braking occurs.

1. Hold the brake pedal depressed and install a switch or valve into the retainer on the brake pedal support. Clicks can be heard as the threaded portion of the switch is pushed

through the retainer. Press the switch or valve body until it bottoms on the retainer.

2. Pull the brake pedal slowly back to the fully rearward position against the pedal stop. This action will move the switch or valve assembly rearward in the retainer and into adjustment.

3. Release the brake pedal and pull back again to assure proper adjustment.

4. The switch should now be properly adjusted. The cruise control switch contacts must now be open at $1/8–1/2$ in. (3.5–12.5mm) of brake pedal travel measure at the center-line of the brake pedal pad.

5. If equipped, the vacuum release valve assembly must open at $1–5/16$ in. (27–33mm) of brake pedal travel measured at the center-line of the brake pedal pad.

Servo Cable Adjustment

Adjust the servo blade by installing the cable attaching rod and nut to the servo blade hole which offers the minimum cable slack.

ENGINE COOLING

Radiator

REMOVAL AND INSTALLATION

1. Disconnect the negative battery cable. Drain the cooling system into a suitable container.

2. Disconnect the top and bottom radiator hoses from the radiator. Remove the reservoir hose from the radiator filler neck.

3. Disconnect and plug the transmission fluid cooler lines. Disconnect and plug the oil cooler lines, if equipped.

4. Remove the bolts retaining the engine compartment support rod to the radiator core support. Loosen each anchor bolt and position the support rods aside.

5. Remove the fan shroud retaining bolts. On 1993–96 models without VO8 heavy duty cooling, remove the twin electric cooling fans and position the fan shroud assembly aside.

6. Remove the radiator core support cover retaining bolts. Remove the radiator core support cover.

7. Carefully lift the radiator assembly upward and out of the vehicle.

To install:

8. Lower the radiator into place making sure it is properly seated on the insulator.

9. Install the radiator core support cover and electric fans, if equipped.

10. Position the fan shroud in place and install the retaining bolts.

11. Position the engine compartment support rods to the radiator core support. Tighten the support bar bolts to 22 ft. lbs. (30 Nm).

12. Install the engine oil cooler lines, if applicable, and the transmission oil cooler lines. Tighten the fittings to 20 ft. lbs. (27 Nm).

13. Install the top, bottom and reservoir hoses and tighten the clamps to 26 inch lbs. (3 Nm).

14. Connect the negative battery cable and refill the cooling system with the proper type and quantity of coolant mixture.

Heater Core

REMOVAL AND INSTALLATION

1. Disconnect the negative battery cable and partially drain the cooling system so the coolant level falls below the heater inlet and outlet hoses.

2. Disconnect the tag the electrical connectors form the blower motor, compressor cycling switch, power module and radio lead-in connections. Position the wiring harness aside.

3. Remove the 2 screws holding the compressor cycling switch to the module. Remove the black insulation, loosen the 2 hose clamps and carefully remove the switch. Remove the right windshield washer nozzle.

4. Remove the 3 retaining screws and the right secondary air inlet screen. Partially remove the rubber molding above the plenum (1 screw on the right side).

5. Remove the remaining screws and remove the primary inlet screen. Remove the blower motor.

6. Remove the screws securing the case cover. Remove the cover. Remove the heater hoses and clamps from the heater core outlets.

7. Remove the screw and the retainer holding the heater core to the frame at the top of the assembly.

8. With the temperature door in the **MAX/HOT** position, reach through the temperature housing and push the lower forward corner of the heater core away from the housing.

9. Rotate the core parallel to the housing. This will cause the core to snap out of the lower clamp. Remove the heater core from the assembly. The core cannot be removed in a vertical direction due to the configuration of the components.

To install:

10. If sealer was used on the case cover, be sure to completely remove the old sealer and replace before installation.

11. Install the heater core into the vehicle and push down firmly to seat the core into the bottom clip. Install the heater core to the frame with the screw and retainer.

12. Connect the heater hoses to the core outlets and secure with hose clamps.

13. Install the case cover and attaching screws. Install the blower motor.

14. Install the primary and secondary inlet screens and the rubber molding.

15. Connect the right windshield washer nozzle.

16. Install the 2 screws on the compressor cycling switch. Apply black insulation, install the 2 hose clamps and install the switch.

17. Connect the wiring harness connectors to the blower motor, compressor cycling switch, power module and the radio lead-in connections. Properly reposition the wiring harness.

18. Connect the negative battery cable and refill the cooling system.

Water Pump

REMOVAL AND INSTALLATION

1993 Except 5.7L (VIN P) Engine

1. Disconnect the negative battery cable and drain the cooling system.

2. Disconnect the lower radiator hose, the bypass hose and the heater hose from the water pump, as applicable.

3. Disconnect the engine compartment support rods from the radiator core support, loosen the anchor bolt and push rods out of the way.

4. Remove the fan shroud screws and the fan shroud.

5. If without electric fans, disconnect the 4 nuts attaching the fan assembly to the water pump hub.

6. Pull the fan and clutch assembly forward, then up and remove from the vehicle. Remove the spacer if equipped. Support the assembly in a vertical position to prevent damage to the clutch.

7. Remove the serpentine drive belt or all drive belts, as applicable.

8. Remove the water pump pulley.

9. Remove accessory brackets, as necessary and position the accessories aside.

10. Remove the water pump retaining bolts and remove the water pump from the engine. Discard the old pump gasket.

To install:

11. Clean the cylinder block and pump gasket mating surfaces.

12. Install a new gasket and thin bead of sealer to the water pump.

13. Install the water pump to the vehicle and secure with the mounting bolts. Tighten the pump-to-block bolts to 22 ft. lbs. (30 Nm) and on 1992 engines, the pump-to-front cover bolts to 10 ft. lbs. (14 Nm).

14. Install the accessory brackets with the accessories, as applicable.

15. Install all hoses and tighten the clamps to 27 inch lbs. (3 Nm).

16. Install the water pump pulley and the serpentine drive belt, if applicable.

17. Inspect the fan assembly and replace as necessary. Install the fan and clutch assembly, be sure to install the spacer, if equipped. Tighten the nuts to 18 ft. lbs. (24 Nm).

— CAUTION —

It is essential that the fan assembly remain in proper balance. Balance cannot be assured once a fan assembly has been bent or damaged. A fan that is not in proper balance could fail and fly apart during use creating an extremely dangerous situation.

18. Install the fan shroud and screws. Position the engine compartment support rods and tighten the bolts to 22 ft. lbs. (30 Nm).

19. Connect the negative battery cable and refill the cooling system with the correct mixture of antifreeze and water. Start the engine and check for leaks.

5.7L (VIN P) Engine

1. Disconnect the negative battery cable.

2. Disengage the wiring harness from the cooling fan assembly, then remove the assembly from the vehicle.

3. Drain the engine cooling system, removing the block drain plug and the knock sensor to assure proper draining. Reinstall the drain plug and knock sensor, as soon as the system is empty.

4. Disconnect the upper and lower radiator hoses from the water pump assembly.

1. Water pump assembly
2. Water pump gasket
3. Shaft coupling
4. Water pump cover bolt,
   33 LB FT (45 NM)
5. Water pump bolt,
   31 LB FT (42 NM)

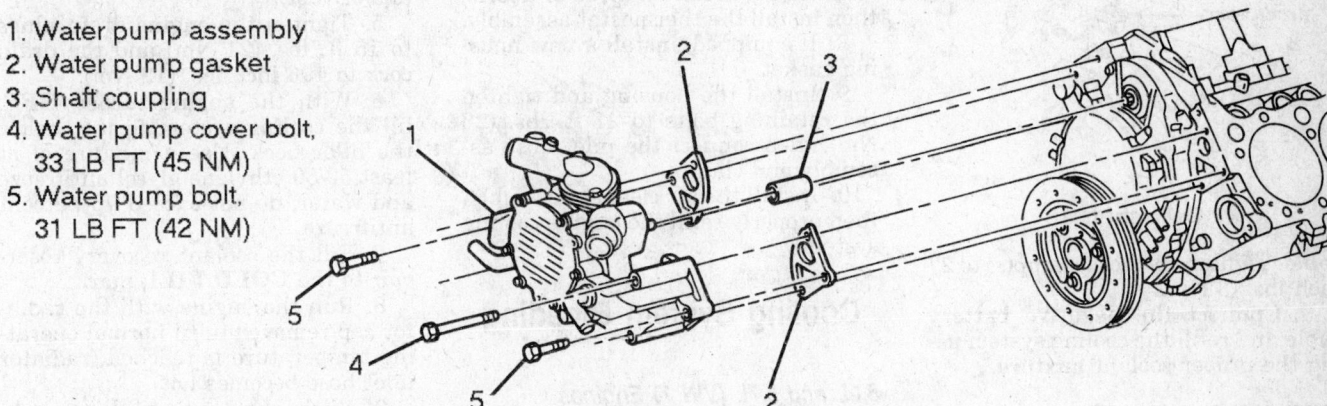

Water pump assembly removal and installation — 5.7L (VIN P) engine

8470Q020

5. Remove the heater hose assemblies from the water pump and from the throttle body.

6. Disengage the coolant sensor wiring harness, then reposition the ignition coil and bracket assembly.

7. Remove the shorter water pump retaining bolt from the center of each pump mating flange, then remove the longer pump bolts from either side of the center bolts.

8. Carefully remove the water pump assembly and gaskets along with the pump shaft coupling.

To install:

9. Thoroughly clean the gasket mating surfaces of any remaining gasket material.

10. Install the water pump shaft coupling along with the water pump and gaskets.

11. Install the longer pump bolts and tighten 33 ft. lbs. (45 Nm), then install the shorter bolts and tighten to 31 ft. lbs. (42 Nm).

12. Reposition the ignition coil and bracket assembly.

13. Engage the coolant sensor electrical connector.

14. Install the heater and radiator hoses to the throttle body and water pump, as applicable.

15. Install the air cleaner and intake duct assemblies.

16. Install the engine cooling fan assembly and engage the wiring harness connector.

17. Connect the negative battery cable and properly fill the engine cooling system.

Thermostat

REMOVAL AND INSTALLATION

1992 5.0L and 5.7L (VIN E) Engines

1. Disconnect the negative battery cable. Drain the cooling system to a level below the thermostat housing.

2. Remove the radiator hose from the thermostat housing on the 5.0L engine, remove the clamp on the coolant bypass hose.

3. Remove the thermostat housing retaining bolts. Remove the thermostat housing assembly from the engine.

4. Remove the thermostat and discard the gasket.

To install:

5. Install the thermostat into the intake manifold with the arrow or marking pointing up.

6. Install a new gasket and the thermostat housing onto the manifold. Tighten the thermostat housing bolts to 21 ft. lbs. (28 Nm).

7. Connect the radiator inlet hose and the coolant bypass hose, as applicable. Tighten the hose clamp(s) to 27 inch lbs. (3 Nm).

8. Connect the negative battery cable and refill the cooling system using the proper coolant mixture.

1993–96 5.7L (VIN 7) Engine

1. Disconnect the negative battery cable.

2. Raise and support vehicle properly.

3. Open coolant drain valve, located on the radiator bypass hose, and allow cooling system to drain.

4. Remove radiator outlet hose and clamp from thermostat cover assembly located on the right lower corner of the engine.

5. Remove thermostat cover assembly and remove thermostat, discard old gasket.

To install:

6. Install the thermostat and new rubber gasket into the housing with the arrow or marking pointing up.

7. Install thermostat cover assembly and tighten retaining bolts to 24 ft.lbs. (33 Nm).

8. Connect the radiator inlet hose and the coolant bypass hose, as appli-

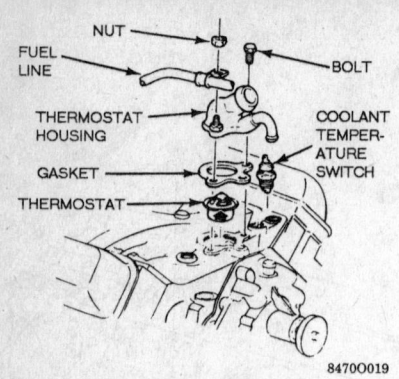

Thermostat 1992

cable. Tighten the hose clamp(s) to 27 inch lbs. (3 Nm).

9. Connect the negative battery cable and refill the cooling system using the proper coolant mixture.

5.7L (VIN P) ENGINE

1. Open the radiator drain cock and allow the engine coolant to drain to a level just below the thermostat housing, then close the drain and tighten to 106 inch lbs. (12 Nm).

2. Remove the air cleaner assembly.

3. Disconnect the inlet hose and clamp from the thermostat assembly.

4. Remove the thermostat housing bolts, then remove the housing.

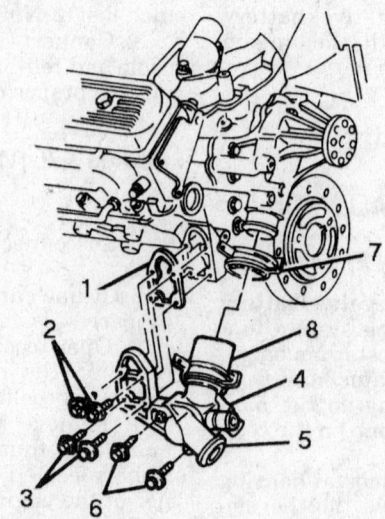

1. Gasket
2. Engine coolant thermostat housing bolt/screw
3. Engine coolant thermostat at housing bolt/screw
4. Engine coolant thermostat housing assembly
5. Engine coolant thermostat cover assembly
6. Engine coolant thermostat 24 ft. lbs. (33 NM) bolt/screw
7. Water pump inlet hose clamp
8. Water (hose) outlet

Thermostat 1992–93

5. If equipped, remove the housing gasket.

6. Remove the thermostat assembly.

To install:

7. Make sure the flange mating surfaces are clean and free of debris, then install the thermostat assembly.

8. If equipped, install a new housing gasket.

9. Install the housing and tighten the retaining bolts to 21 ft. lbs. (28 Nm), then connect the inlet hose assembly and clamp.

10. Install the air cleaner assembly, then properly refill the engine cooling system.

Cooling System Bleeding

5.0L and 5.7L (VIN 7) Engines

1. With the engine **OFF** and completely cool, remove the radiator cap to relieve all pressure.

2. Position a suitable container under the vehicle. Drain the coolant by opening the radiator drain cock located on the bottom right of the radiator and remove the 2 block drain plugs located on either side of the engine block.

3. Dispose of used coolant properly. Close the radiator drain cock

and reinstall the engine block drain plugs.

4. Fill the cooling system with water and run the engine until the thermostat opens. Repeat Steps 1–4 until drained fluid is free of coolant and/or rust.

5. Tighten the engine drain plugs to 15 ft. lbs. (21 Nm) and the drain cock to 106 inch lbs. (12 Nm).

6. With the engine turned **OFF**, fill the cooling system to just below the filler neck. Use a mixture of at least 50/50 ethylene glycol antifreeze and water; do not exceed 70 percent antifreeze.

7. Fill the coolant recovery reservoir to the **COLD FILL** mark.

8. Run the engine with the radiator cap removed until normal operating temperature is reached (radiator inlet hose becomes hot).

9. With the engine idling, add coolant to the radiator until it reaches the bottom of the filler neck.

10. Install the radiator cap, with the arrows on the cap aligned with the coolant reservoir hose.

5.7L (VIN P) Engine

1. Make sure the vehicle is parked or supported on a level surface with the pressure cap removed. Drain the engine cooling system by opening the radiator drain cock, then opening the air bleed vents on the thermostat housing and the heater outlet hose pipe. To assure the system is fully drained, remove the engine block drain plug and the engine knock sensor from either side of the block.

2. Once the system is completely drained, close the drain cock and install the knock sensor. cover the threads of the drain plug with sealer, then install the plug into the block. The drain plug should be tightened to 15 ft. lbs. (21 Nm), while the knock sensor should be tightened to 14 ft. lbs. (19 Nm).

3. After the repair or service has been completed, fill the cooling system with a solution which is at least 50 percent ethylene glycol antifreeze and the balance water. Do not use a solution that exceeds 70 percent antifreeze. Continue filling the radiator until the level is just below the filler neck.

4. Once the system is filled, close the air bleeds, taking care not to overtighten and damage the brass valves.

5. Install the pressure cap, then start and run the engine to check for leaks.

FUEL SYSTEM

Fuel System Service Precautions

Safety is the most important factor when performing any type of maintenance, but even more so when performing fuel system maintenance. Failure to conduct maintenance and repairs in a safe manner may result in serious personal injury or death. Maintenance and testing of the vehicle's fuel system components can be accomplished safely and effectively by adhering to the following rules and guidelines.

• To avoid the possibility of fire and personal injury, always disconnect the negative battery cable unless the repair or test procedure requires that battery voltage be applied.

• Always relieve the fuel system pressure prior to disconnecting any fuel system component (injector, fuel rail, pressure regulator, etc.), fitting or fuel line connection. Exercise extreme caution whenever relieving fuel system pressure to avoid exposing skin, face and eyes to fuel spray. Under pressure, fuel may penetrate the skin or any part of the body that it contacts.

• Always place a shop towel or cloth around the fitting or connection prior to loosening to absorb any excess fuel due to spillage. Ensure that all fuel spillage, should it occur, is quickly removed from engine surfaces. Ensure that all fuel soaked cloths or towels are deposited into a suitable waste container.

• Always keep a dry chemical (Class B) fire extinguisher near the work area.

• Do not allow fuel spray or fuel vapors to come into contact with a spark or open flame.

• Always use a backup wrench when loosening and tightening fuel line connection fittings. This will prevent unnecessary stress and torsion to fuel line piping. Always follow the proper torque specifications.

• Always replace worn fuel fitting O-rings with new. Do not substitute fuel hose or equivalent where fuel pipe is installed.

RELIEVING FUEL SYSTEM PRESSURE

5.0L (VIN E) and 5.7L TBI Engines

1. Release the fuel vapor pressure in the fuel tank by removing the fuel tank cap.
2. Ensure the engine is cold and disconnect the negative battery cable.
3. The internal constant bleed feature to throttle body injection relieves the fuel pump system pressure when the engine is not running. Therefore, no further action is required.

Except 5.7L TBI Engines

1. Disconnect the negative battery cable to prevent fuel discharge if the key is accidentally turned to the **RUN** position.
2. Loosen the fuel filler cap to relieve the tank pressure and do not tighten until service has been completed.
3. Connect J–34730–1 fuel pressure gauge or equivalent, to the fuel pressure valve. Wrap a shop cloth around the fitting while connecting the gauge to avoid spillage.
4. Place the end of the bleed hose into a suitable container and open the valve to relieve the fuel system pressure.

Fuel Tank

REMOVAL AND INSTALLATION

5.0L (VIN E) and 5.7L Engines

1. Disconnect the negative battery cable and relieve fuel system pressure.
2. Drain the fuel tank, raise and support the vehicle safely. To help avoid the possibility of the vehicle falling off the hoist, provide additional support at the opposite end of the vehicle from where the work is to take place.

NOTE: If a nylon fuel line becomes kinked and cannot be straightened or becomes otherwise damaged, it must be replaced.

3. Disconnect the quick-connect fuel pipe fittings from the fuel pump assembly as follows:
   a. Grip both ends of 1 pipe connection and twist ¼ turn in each direction to loosen dirt.
   b. While wearing safety glasses, use compressed air to blow dirt out of the fittings.
   c. Disconnect the fitting by squeezing the plastic tabs of the male connector and pulling the fitting apart.
4. Clean and disconnect the vapor hose connection at the fuel pump assembly. Disconnect the fuel pump assembly electrical connectors.
5. Support the fuel tank with the aid of an assistant and remove the fuel tank retaining strap, nuts, bolts and straps. Lower the fuel tank from the vehicle.
To install:
6. Raise and support the fuel tank in position and install the retaining straps. Tighten the front retaining strap bolts to 26 ft. lbs. (35 Nm) and the rear strap nuts to 10 ft. lbs. (13 Nm).
7. Connect the vapor hose and the fuel pump assembly electrical connector.
8. Install the quick-connect fuel pipe fittings to the fuel pump assembly as follows:
   a. Apply a few drops of clean engine oil to the male ends of the fittings to ensure proper reconnection and prevent leaks.
   b. Push the connectors together until the retaining tabs/fingers snap into place.
   c. Gently pull on both ends of each connected fitting to assure the connection is secure.
9. Lower the vehicle, fill the fuel tank and connect the negative battery cable.
10. Turn the ignition switch to the **ON** position for 2 seconds, **OFF** for 5 seconds, then to the **ON** position and check for fuel leaks.

Fuel Filter

REMOVAL AND INSTALLATION

5.0L (VIN E) and 5.7L Engines

1. Disconnect the negative battery cable and properly relieve the fuel system pressure.
2. Raise and support the vehicle safely.
3. Grasp the fuel filter and one of the fuel line fittings. Twist the quick connect assembly about a ¼ turn in each direction to loosen any dirt within the fitting.
4. Grasp the fuel filter and the other fuel line fitting. Twist the quick connect assembly about a ¼ turn in each direction to loosen any dirt within the fitting.
5. Clean the areas surrounding the fuel line fittings. If compressed air is used, be sure to wear safety

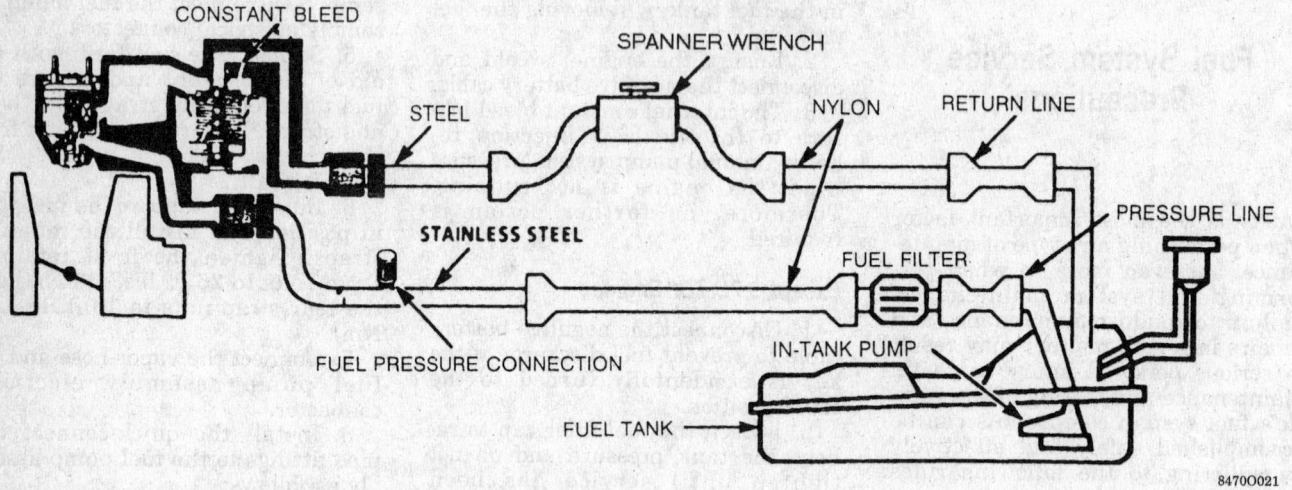

Fuel line pressure connector locations 5.0L (VIN E) and 5.7L engines

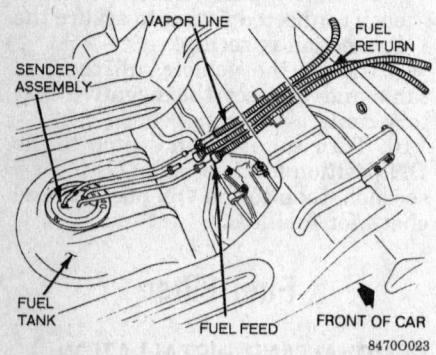

Rear fuel lines at sender

glasses to prevent eye injury from flying dirt.

6. Squeeze the plastic tabs of the male connectors and pull the connections apart.

7. Remove the fuel filter bracket retaining bolt. Remove the fuel filter from its mounting.

To install:

8. Prior to installation, apply a few drops of clean engine oil to both tube ends of the filter.

NOTE: The application of clean engine oil will ensure proper reconnection and prevent a possible fuel leak. During normal operation the O-ring that is located in the connector will swell and may prevent proper reconnection if not lubricated. If the new filter is nicked, scratched or damaged during installation, it must be replaced.

9. Remove the protective caps from the new filter and install the new plastic connector retainers on the filter inlet and outlet pipes, in the same manner as the old filter.

10. Install the quick connect fittings onto the filter, after applying oil, by pushing the connectors together causing the retaining tabs/fingers to snap into place.

11. Gently tug on both ends of each connection to ensure that the connection is secure.

12. Install the fuel filter into the bracket on the frame and install the attaching bolt. Tighten the bolt to 88 inch lbs. (10 Nm).

13. Connect the negative battery cable and tighten the fuel filler cap.

14. Turn the ignition switch to the **ON** position for 2 seconds, **OFF** for 5 seconds, then to the **ON** position and check for fuel leaks.

Electric Fuel Pump

PRESSURE TESTING

5.0L (VIN E) and 5.7L (VIN 7) Engines

When the ignition switch is turned ON, the ECM will turn the in-tank fuel pump ON. It will remain ON as long as the engine is cranking or running and the ECM is receiving ignition reference pulses. If there are no reference pulses, the ECM will shut the fuel pump OFF within 2 seconds after the key is turned ON. The pump will deliver fuel to the TBI unit at a pressure controlled by the internal regulator to approximately 9–13 psi. Excess fuel is then returned to the fuel tank.

While the engine is stopped, the fuel pump can be activated by applying battery voltage to the fuel pump test terminal located near the passenger side cowl of the engine compartment.

NOTE: The fuel pressure should be recorded while the fuel pump is operating. Fuel pump pressure will drop immediately after the fuel pump stops running due to a controlled bleed within the fuel system. The fuel pump test location is on the right side of the engine compartment.

1. Turn the ignition **OFF** and relieve fuel system pressure by removing fuel filler cap.
2. Locate the engine compartment fuel feed quick-connect fitting. Uncouple the fuel supply flexible hose as follows:
    a. Grasp both ends of the fitting and twist female end ¼ turn in each direction to loosen any dirt in fitting.
    b. Wearing proper safety glasses, use compressed air to blow dirt out of the quick-connect fitting.
3. Separate the male and female leads of the connector by inserting tool into female end of the connector to release the male end.
4. Install a fuel pressure gauge between both ends of the connector. Be sure to always lubricate the male end with a few drops of engine oil to ensure proper connection and prevent a fuel leak.
5. Apply battery voltage to the fuel pump test connector.
6. The fuel pressure should be 9–13 psi.

5.7L (VIN P) Engine

1. Relieve fuel system pressure and check that there is an adequate quantity of fuel in the tank.
2. Install a fuel pressure gauge to the underhood pressure connector fitting.
3. Make sure the ignition switch has been in the **OFF** position for at least 10 seconds and that all accessories are **OFF**.
4. Turn the ignition switch **ON** and the pump will run for about 2 seconds. Note the system pressure with the pump running, it should be the pressure should be 40–47 psi.

NOTE: The ignition switch may have to be cycled to ON more than once to obtain maximum pressure. It is also normal for the pressure to drop slightly when the pump first stops, but it should then hold steady.

5. If fuel pressure is not as specified, verify that fuel pump operation is heard in the tank.
6. If fuel pump operation is not heard, inspect the fuel pump relay and wiring.
7. If fuel pump operation is heard, inspect filter and lines for restriction.
8. Start the engine and make sure the pressure decreases about 3–10 psi at idle.
9. If fuel pressure does not decrease, inspect pressure regulator and vacuum hose.
10. Disconnect the fuel pressure gauge.

REMOVAL AND INSTALLATION

1. Disconnect the negative battery cable and properly relieve the fuel system pressure.
2. Drain the fuel tank. Raise and support the vehicle safely.
3. Remove the fuel tank and fuel pump assembly from the vehicle.
4. Using tool J–24187, J–36608 or equivalent fuel pump assembly spanner wrench, remove the fuel pump assembly retaining cam, the fuel pump assembly and the O-ring gasket from the tank. Discard the O-ring gasket.
To install:
5. Clean and inspect the assembly. Take care not to damage the O-ring sealing surface. Replace assembly components as necessary.

NOTE: Care should be taken when installing the fuel pump assembly into the fuel tank. Do not fold or twist the fuel pump strainer, as this will restrict fuel flow. Also, be sure the fuel pump strainer does not interfere with the full travel of the float arm.

6. Position a new O-ring gasket in place on the fuel tank. Using the spanner wrench, install the fuel pump assembly and the retainer cam onto the fuel tank.
7. Install the fuel tank and fuel pump assembly onto the vehicle.
8. Lower the vehicle, fill the fuel tank and connect the negative battery cable.
9. Turn the ignition switch to the **ON** position for 2 seconds, **OFF** for 5 seconds, then to the **ON** position and check for fuel leaks.

Fuel Injection

IDLE SPEED ADJUSTMENT

The idle speed and mixture are electronically controlled by the Electronic Control Module (ECM). All adjustments are preset at the factory and do not need periodic attention. Some replacement throttle body units are equipped with a idle stop screw to allow adjustment of the minimum idle speed. The only time the idle speed should need adjustment is when the throttle body assembly has been replaced.

1. Block the drive wheels and apply the parking brake. Remove the air cleaner assembly and/or air duct.
2. Connect a scan tool to the ALDL connector and select the field service mode. Turn the ignition **ON** and leave the engine **OFF**. Wait at least 45 seconds, this will allow the Idle Air Control (IAC) pintle to seat in the throttle body.
3. With the ignition switch in the **ON** position, the engine **OFF** and the scan tool in field service mode, disconnect the IAC valve electrical connector and the distributor set-timing connector.
4. Connect a tachometer to the engine to monitor the engine speed.
5. Place the transmission in the **P** or **N** position and start the engine.
6. Run the engine until it reaches normal operating temperature or closed loop operation as indicated by the scan tool. It may be necessary to hold the throttle open slightly in order to maintain idle.
7. The idle speed should be 450–500 rpm, be sure the throttle and, if applicable, the cruise control cables do not hold the throttle open. If not as specified, remove the idle speed stop screw plug and adjust as necessary.
8. Turn the ignition **OFF** and reconnect the IAC valve electrical connector and the distributor set-timing connector.
9. Reset the Idle Air Control (IAC) valve pintle position.
10. Connect the air cleaner assembly, check and clear all ECM trouble codes.

IAC VALVE PINTLE ADJUSTMENT

Idle speed is controlled by the ECM through voltage pulses sent to the Idle Air Control (IAC) motor windings. Based on the number of voltage pulses received, the motor will move the IAC pintle in or out allowing more or less air through the throttle body.

NOTE: If installing a new IAC valve measure and adjust the valve accordingly. If reinstalling a used IAC valve, do not push or pull on the pintle to adjust pintle length or damage to the IAC worm gear might occur. The valve is preset at the factory and will self adjust when the following procedure is performed.

1. On a new IAC valve only, measure the distance between the tip of the pintle and the valve mounting surface. If greater than 1.10 inch (28mm), use light finger pressure to slowly retract the pintle. The force required to retract a new IAC valve will not damage the valve.
2. Install the IAC valve and gasket.
3. Connect the IAC valve wire connector.
4. Reset the IAC valve pintle position as follows:
   a. Depress the accelerator pedal slightly.
   b. Start the engine and run for 5 seconds. Turn the ignition **OFF** for 10 seconds.
   c. Restart the vehicle and check for proper idle operation.

IDLE MIXTURE ADJUSTMENT

The idle mixture is controlled by the ECM, therefore no service adjustments are necessary. The ECM will change the air/fuel ratio by controlling the fuel injectors, based on oxygen sensor and various other outputs. A 14.7:1 ratio is required for efficient catalytic converter operation.

Fuel Injector

REMOVAL AND INSTALLATION

Except 5.7L (VIN P) Engine

1. Disconnect the negative battery cable and properly relieve the fuel system pressure.
2. Remove the air cleaner assembly and extension. Disconnect the electrical connectors to the fuel injectors.
3. Remove the fuel meter cover retaining screws. Remove the fuel meter cover assembly.

4. Remove the fuel meter outlet passage gasket and the pressure regulator dust seal.

NOTE: If the fuel meter cover gasket is stuck to the fuel meter body, leave it in place. If it is stuck to the fuel meter cover, remove it and place it on the fuel meter body.

5. With the fuel meter cover gasket in place on the fuel meter body, use a proper pry tool and fulcrum to carefully pry out the fuel injector.
6. Remove and discard the small O-ring from the nozzle end of the fuel injector.
7. Remove and discard the fuel meter cover gasket. Remove and discard the large O-ring and fuel injector washer from the top of the injector cavity.

To install:

8. Be sure to replace fuel injectors with an identical part. Injectors from other models may fit, but are calibrated for different flow rates.

NOTE: When installing the injectors, install the fuel injector washer and large O-ring before the injector, to be sure the O-ring is properly seated. Reversing these procedures could result in a fuel leak and possible engine fire.

9. Lubricate the new upper (large) O-ring with engine oil and install. Be sure the ring is properly seated and flush with the top of the fuel meter body.
10. Lubricate the new lower (small) O-ring with engine oil and install on the end of the injector by pushing the O-ring far enough to contact the filter.
11. Install the fuel injector by aligning the raised lug on the injector base with the notch in the fuel meter body cavity. Push down on the injector until it is fully seated. The electrical terminals of the injector should be parallel with the throttle shaft.
12. Install the new pressure regulator dust seal, fuel meter outlet gasket and cover gasket.
13. Install the fuel meter cover assembly. Coat the fuel meter cover attaching screws with appropriate thread-locking compound. Install and tighten the screws to 27 inch lbs. (3.0 Nm).
14. Connect the electrical connectors to the fuel injectors and install the air cleaner assembly.
15. Connect the negative battery cable and tighten the fuel filler cap.

5.7L (VIN P) Engine

1. Make sure the ignition is in the **OFF** position, then disconnect the negative battery cable.
2. Properly relieve the fuel system pressure.
3. Disengage the quick-connect fittings at the fuel rail feed and return pipes as follows:
   a. Slide the rubber dust cover from the fitting.
   b. Grasp both ends of a connection and twist ¼ turn in each direction to loosen any dirt. Repeat for other fitting.
   c. While wearing safety glasses, use compressed air to blow out dirt from the fitting.
   d. Insert a fuel line separator tool, into the female connector, then push inward to release the male connector.
   e. Repeat for the other fitting.
4. Disconnect the vacuum line at the pressure regulator, then as necessary, tag and disconnect any remaining vacuum lines which must be removed to access the fuel rail and engine fuel pipes.
5. Remove the fuel injector wiring harness from the routing clips of the fuel rail, then remove the fuel pipe attaching bolt and disengage the injector electrical connectors.
6. Remove the fuel rail attaching bolts and carefully remove the fuel rail assembly along with the injectors, from the top of the intake.
7. Rotate the injector retaining clip to the release position and remove the injector from the fuel rail assembly.
8. Remove and discard the O-ring seals from either side of the injector.
9. Remove and discard the injector retaining clip.

To install:

10. Lubricate the new injector O-rings with clean engine oil and install onto the injector.

NOTE: Always replace injectors using an identical part number as inscribed on top of the old injector.

11. Connect a new retainer clip onto the fuel injector and install the injector to the fuel rail assembly. Rotate the injector retaining clip to the lock position.
12. Install the fuel rail assembly to the intake manifold. Tighten the attaching bolts to 15 ft. lbs. (20 Nm).
13. Rotate the fuel injectors as necessary to avoid stretching the wire harnesses, then engage the injector electrical connections.

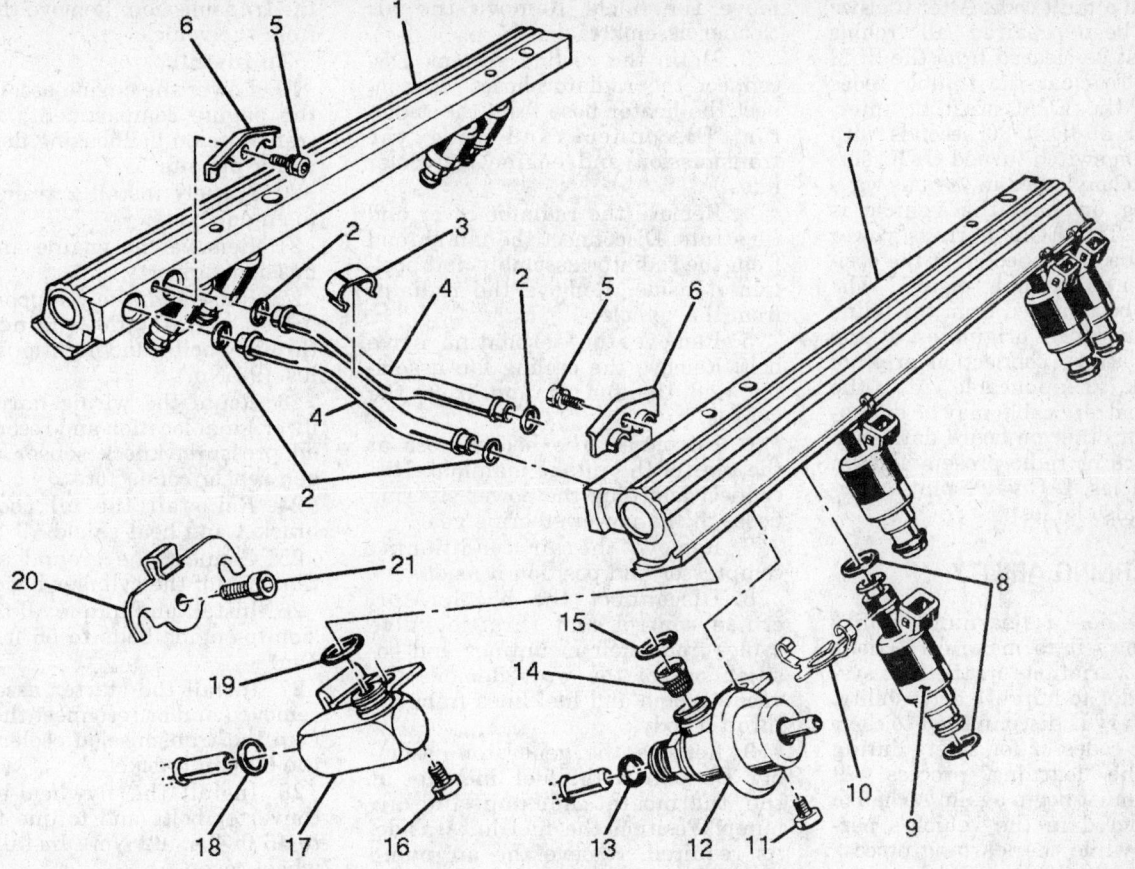

1. LH MFI fuel rail assembly
2. Fuel crossover tube o-ring
3. Fuel crossover tube clip
4. Fuel crossover tube
5. Crossover tube retainer attaching screw
6. Fuel crossover tube retainer
7. RH MFI Fuel rail assembly
8. Fuel injector o-ring
9. MFI fuel injector assembly
10. Injector retainer clip
11. Pressure regulator attaching screw
12. Fuel pressure regulator assembly
13. Fuel outlet tube o-ring
14. Filter screen (if equipped)
15. Fuel inlet fitting o-ring
16. Fuel inlet assembly attaching screw
17. Fuel inlet assembly
18. Fuel in let tube o-ring
19. Fuel inlet assembly o-ring
20. Fuel tube retainer assembly
21. Fuel tube retainer assembly attaching screw

8470Q026

Exploded view of the fuel rail assembly — 5.7L (VIN P) engine

14. Install the fuel pipe retaining nut, then position the wiring harness into the routing clips at the fuel rail.

15. Connect the vacuum lines to the intake, as necessary, then connect the vacuum line to the pressure regulator.

16. Apply a few drops of clean engine oil to the male ends of the fuel line quick-connect fittings. Engage the fittings by pushing the connectors together until the retaining tabs snap into place. Pull gently on both sides of each fitting to be sure the connection is secure. When secure, slide the dust covers over the fittings.

17. Tighten the fuel filler cap and connect the negative battery cable.

18. Turn the ignition **ON** for 2 seconds, **OFF** for 10 seconds, then **ON** again and inspect the system for leaks.

EMISSION CONTROLS

Emission Warning Lamps

RESETTING

A service engine soon light, located on the instrument panel, alerts the driver that the vehicle should be taken for service as soon as possible. If the light remains ON, the self-diagnostic system has detected a problem and stored a fault code. After the system has been repaired, all trouble codes must be cleared from the ECM memory. To clear the trouble codes power to the ECM must be interrupted for at least 30 seconds with the ignition switch turned **OFF**. This may be accomplished in various ways depending on how the vehicle is equipped. The ECM harness power feed may be disconnected at the positive battery terminal "pigtail." The fuse may be removed from the inline fuseholder which originates at the positive battery connection or from fuse block, as applicable. Also, the negative battery cable may be disconnected, but other on-board data such as the clock or radio presets and, on some vehicles, IAC valve pintle position may also be lost.

ECM LEARNING ABILITY

The ECM has a "learning" ability which allows it to make corrections for minor variations in the fuel system, in order to improve driveability. If the battery is disconnected to clear diagnostic codes or for safety during repairs, the "learning" process will reset and must begin again. A change may be noted in the vehicle's performance while the learning process occurs. To "teach" the vehicle, make sure the engine is at normal operating temperature, then drive the vehicle at part throttle, with moderate acceleration and idle conditions, until normal performance returns.

ENGINE MECHANICAL

NOTE: Disconnecting the negative battery cable on some vehicles may interfere with the functions of the on board computer systems and may require the computer to undergo a relearning process.

Engine Assembly

REMOVAL AND INSTALLATION

5.0L (VIN E) and 5.7L Engines

1. Disconnect the battery cables and properly relieve fuel system pressure.
2. Mark the hood hinge outline for proper reassembly alignment and remove the hood. Remove the air cleaner assembly.
3. Drain the cooling system. Disconnect the radiator hoses. Disconnect the heater hose from the radiator. Disconnect and plug the transmission and engine oil cooler lines.
4. Remove the radiator cover and tie struts. Disconnect the fan shroud from the radiator assembly and position it aside. Remove the radiator from the vehicle.
5. Remove the serpentine drive belt. Remove the cooling fan assembly and the fan shroud from the vehicle.
6. Disconnect the heater hose at the rear of the intake manifold. Disconnect and plug the power steering hoses at the power steering gear.
7. Remove the air conditioning compressor and position it aside.
8. Disconnect the accelerator, cruise control and throttle valve cables from their mountings and position out of the way. Remove the vacuum pipe and fuel lines from the throttle body.
9. Remove the generator assembly. Disconnect the fuel line clips at the thermostat housing and air pump. Position the fuel lines aside. As required, remove the air pump assembly.
10. Disconnect and plug all required electrical connectors. Remove the distributor cap. Remove the negative battery cable from the cylinder head.
11. Raise and support the vehicle safely. Disconnect the the crossover pipe at both manifolds.
12. Disconnect the starter electrical connectors and the positive battery cable. If necessary, remove the starter retaining bolts and remove the starter from the vehicle.
13. Remove the flywheel cover. Remove the torque converter to flywheel retaining bolts. Remove the motor mount through bolts.
14. Disconnect the transmission oil cooler lines at the clip on the oil pan. Disconnect the oil pressure, knock and oxygen sensor connectors. Remove the oil cooler hose shield.
15. Remove the ground wires from the rear of the cylinder head at both sides.
16. Remove the transmission to engine retaining bolts. Lower the vehicle.
17. Install the lifting equipment to the engine. Support the transmission properly.
18. Raise the engine slightly and pull it forward to disengage it from the transmission. Remove the engine from the vehicle.

To install:

19. Lower the engine assembly into the engine compartment; align the transmission bellhousing dowels and motor mounts.
20. Loosely install 2 transmission-to-engine bolts.
21. Remove the engine and transmission supports.
22. Raise and safely support the vehicle, install the engine mount through bolts and tighten to 70 ft. lbs. (95 Nm).
23. Route the wiring harness into its original location and reconnect the oil pressure, knock sensor and oxygen sensor connectors.
24. Reinstall the oil cooler line bracket and heat shield.
25. Connect the ground straps to the back of the cylinder heads.
26. Install and torque all transmission-to-engine bolts to 55 ft. lbs. (75 Nm).
27. Install the starter assembly, if removed and/or reconnect the wiring. Clip the transmission cooler lines to the oil pan bracket.
28. Install the flywheel-to-torque converter bolts and torque the bolts to 45 ft. lbs. (62 Nm). Install the flywheel cover.
29. Reconnect the exhaust and exhaust hangers. Tighten the crossover pipe bolts to 15 ft. lbs. (20 Nm).
30. Lower the vehicle.
31. Install heater hose to the right rear of intake manifold. Reconnect the throttle cable brackets and cables.
32. Install the distributor cap and coil wires.
33. Install the generator with wiring, but leave the rear brace disconnected. Connect the negative battery cable at the cylinder head.
34. Unplug and connect the power steering lines at the power steering gear.
35. Route the fuel lines and connect at the throttle body. Install the fuel line clips at the thermostat housing and the AIR pump.
36. Connect the rear generator brace. Connect all vacuum hoses to the throttle body. Connect all electrical connections to the intake manifold and the throttle body.
37. Connect the AIR hose from the diverter valve to the converter.
38. Install the fan and fan shroud assembly.
39. Install the radiator assembly. Connect the transmission and oil cooler lines.

40. Connect the the heater hose to the radiator tank and the radiator hoses.

41. Install the radiator cover and secure the fan shroud. Install the radiator tie struts.

42. Install the air conditioning compressor and serpentine belt. Install the air cleaner assembly.

43. Fill the cooling system and connect the battery cables.

44. Check all fluid levels, start engine and inspect for leaks.

45. Align the marks made earlier and install the hood assembly.

Engine Mounts

REMOVAL AND INSTALLATION

—————— **WARNING** ——————

Never raise the engine using a jack under the oil pan, crankshaft pulley or any sheetmetal. Because there only is a small clearance between the oil pan and the oil pump screen, if the pan is bent even slightly, damage could occur to the pump screen and pickup unit.

1. Disconnect the negative battery cable.

2. Remove the engine mount through bolt and nut.

3. Using a suitable lifting device, carefully raise the front of the engine far enough to remove the engine mount retaining bolts and the engine mount. Watch the clearance between the rear of the engine and the cowl panel.

4. Remove the engine mount nuts, bolts and the engine mount.

5. Installation is the reverse of the removal procedure. Tighten the engine mount bolts to 35 ft. lbs. (47 Nm) and the mount through bolts to 70 ft. lbs. (95 Nm).

Cylinder Head

REMOVAL AND INSTALLATION

5.0L (VIN E) and 5.7L (VIN 7) Engines

1. Disconnect the negative battery cable and properly relieve the fuel system pressure. Drain the radiator.

2. Remove the intake manifold.

3. Remove the valve covers, rocker assemblies and pushrods. Note the location of the valve train components so they can be reassembled in the proper location.

4. Remove the exhaust manifolds.

5. Remove the diverter valve.

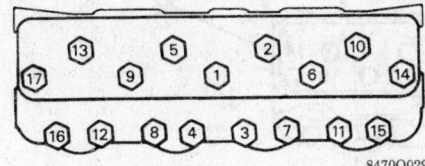

Cylinder head torque sequence 5.7L engines

6. As required, remove one stud at the front of the cylinder head attaching the the generator/power steering pump bracket and/or the air pump/air conditioning compressor bracket.

7. Remove the the cylinder head bolts. Remove the cylinder head and place on 2 blocks of wood to prevent damage. Remove and discard the old gasket.

To install:

8. Position the new cylinder head gasket in place on the block over the dowl pins with the proper side up. Do not use any sealer on a composition gasket.

9. Install the cylinder head in on the dowl pins over the gasket.

10. Coat the threads of the cylinder head bolts with sealing compound, GM part 1052080 or equivalent. Install the bolts finger-tight. The intermediate length bolts go in positions 14 and 17. Tighten the bolts with 3 passes in the proper sequence to 70 ft. lbs. (95 Nm).

11. Install the accessory brackets, as required.

12. Install the exhaust manifolds and the diverter valve.

13. Install the intake manifold.

14. Install and adjust the rocker arm and pushrod assemblies. Install the valve covers.

15. Connect the negative battery cable, tighten the fuel filler cap and fill the cooling system.

5.7L (VIN P) Engine

LEFT SIDE

1. Disconnect the negative battery cable, then raise and support the vehicle safely.

2. Drain the engine cooling system, then disconnect the crossover pipe from the exhaust manifold.

3. Lower the vehicle.

4. Remove the intake manifold assembly.

5. Disconnect the secondary air injection hose from the check valve assembly.

6. Disconnect the coolant air bleed pipe and bolt from the left cylinder head assembly using a backup wrench on the pipe fitting.

7. Remove the ignition coil assembly.

8. Remove the left exhaust manifold assembly.

9. Remove the spark plug wire harness assembly from the clips, then disconnect the harness from the spark plugs and remove the plugs from the left cylinder head.

10. Disengage the coolant temperature sensor connector.

11. Remove the left rocker arm cover.

12. Loosen the rocker arm nuts, then remove the arms and pushrods, either tagging or arranging the components to assure installation in their original locations.

13. Remove the cylinder head bolts, then remove the cylinder head and old gasket from the block.

To install:

14. Thoroughly clean the gasket mating surfaces of any remaining gasket material, then position a new cylinder head gasket on the block with the yellow tab facing upwards.

15. Install the cylinder head over the locator pins and the new gasket.

16. Coat the cylinder head bolts with a sealing compound, then install the bolts finger-tight.

17. Torque the bolts using 3 passes of the proper sequence until all bolts have been torqued to 65 ft. lbs. (88 Nm).

18. Install the pushrods and rocker arms, making sure they are in the proper locations, then adjust the valve lash.

19. Install the left rocker arm cover and tighten the retaining bolts to 100 inch lbs. (11 Nm).

20. Install the spark plugs and tighten to 11 ft. lbs. (15 Nm), then install the wiring harness assembly and secure the assembly to the clips.

21. Install the left exhaust manifold assembly.

22. Install the ignition coil assembly and tighten the bolts to 24 ft. lbs. (33 Nm).

23. Connect the engine coolant air bleed pipe and bolt to the left cylinder head assembly using a backup wrench on the pipe fitting in order to prevent component damage. Tighten the bolt to 30 ft. lbs. (40 Nm).

24. Install the secondary air injector hose to the check valve assembly.

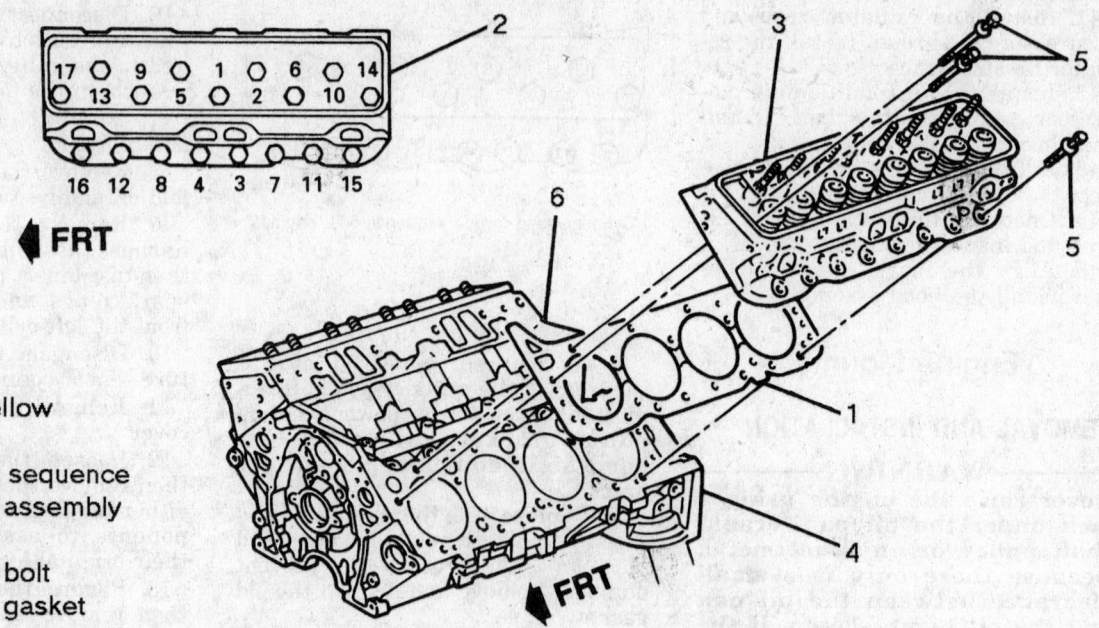

1. Gasket tab (yellow side up)
2. Bolt tightening sequence
3. Cylinder head assembly
4. Engine block
5. Cylinder head bolt
6. Cylinder head gasket

8470Q030

Cylinder head installation and bolt torque sequence — 5.7L (VIN P) engine

25. Install the intake manifold assembly.

26. Raise and support the vehicle safely, then connect the crossover pipe to the exhaust manifold.

27. Lower the vehicle and fill the engine cooling system.

28. Connect then negative battery cable.

RIGHT SIDE

1. Disconnect the negative battery cable.

2. Raise and support the vehicle safely, then drain the engine cooling system.

3. Remove the serpentine drive belt and the belt tensioner assembly.

4. Remove the transmission fluid level indicator tube assembly bracket from the transmission housing.

5. Remove the air conditioning compressor rear brace bolt from the engine block, then disengage the compressor connector.

6. Remove the front compressor mounting bolts, then position the compressor aside taking care not to kink or damage the lines.

7. Remove the right exhaust manifold assembly.

8. Lower the vehicle.

9. Remove the generator assembly.

10. Remove the right rocker arm cover.

11. Remove the intake manifold assembly.

12. Remove the coolant air bleed pipe bolt from the left cylinder head assembly.

13. Disconnect the lower radiator hose and the heater hose from the water pump assembly, then position the hoses aside.

14. Remove the coolant air bleed pipe hose from the radiator.

15. Remove the power steering pump assembly.

16. Remove the engine accessory bracket bolts, then remove the bracket assembly.

17. Disconnect the wire harness assembly from the spark plugs, then remove the plugs from the right cylinder head.

18. Loosen the rocker arm nuts, then remove the arms and pushrods, either tagging or arranging the components to assure installation in their original locations.

19. Remove the cylinder head bolts, then remove the cylinder head and old gasket from the block. If necessary, carefully remove the coolant air bleed pipe bolt and pipe assembly from the cylinder head.

To install:

20. If removed, loosely install the coolant air bleed pipe bolt and pipe to the cylinder head.

21. Thoroughly clean the gasket mating surfaces of any remaining gasket material, then position a new cylinder head gasket on the block with the yellow tab facing upwards.

22. Install the cylinder head over the locator pins and the new gasket.

23. Coat the cylinder head bolts with a sealing compound, then install the bolts finger-tight.

24. Torque the bolts using 3 passes of the proper sequence until all bolts have been torqued to 65 ft. lbs. (88 Nm).

25. If loosened, tighten the coolant air bleed pipe bolt to 30 ft. lbs. (40 Nm).

26. Install the pushrods and rocker arms, making sure they are in the proper locations, then adjust the valve lash.

27. Install the spark plugs and tighten to 11 ft. lbs. (15 Nm), then install the wiring harness assembly to the plugs.

28. Install the engine accessory bracket and tighten the retaining bolts to 31 ft. lbs. (42 Nm).

29. Install the right rocker arm cover and tighten the retaining bolts to 100 inch lbs. (11 Nm).

30. Install the generator assembly.
31. Install the power steering pump assembly.
32. Connect the coolant air bleed pipe hose to the radiator, then connect the heater hose and the lower radiator hose to the water pump.
33. Connect the coolant air bleed pipe bolt to the left cylinder head and tighten to 30 ft. lbs. (41 Nm) while using a backup wrench to prevent component damage.
34. Install the intake manifold assembly.
35. Raise and support the vehicle safely.
36. Install the right exhaust manifold assembly.
37. Position the compressor and install the front mounting bolts, then engage the electrical connector. Install the rear compressor brace bolt and tighten to 24 ft. lbs. (33 Nm).
38. Install the transmission fluid level indicator tube assembly to the transmission housing.
39. Install the serpentine drive belt, then lower the vehicle.
40. Fill the engine cooling system, then connect the negative battery cable.

Valve Lifters

REMOVAL AND INSTALLATION

1. Disconnect the negative battery cable and properly relieve the fuel system pressure. Drain the radiator.
2. Remove the intake manifold.
3. Remove the valve covers.
4. Remove the rocker arms and pushrod assemblies. Mark all valve train components, so they may be installed into there original positions.
5. Remove the lifter retainer bolts and remove the lifter retainer and restrictor. Using the proper valve lifter removal tool, remove the valve lifters. If the same lifters are to be reinstalled, position or mark the lifters so they will be installed in their original locations.
To install:
6. Coat the lifters with Molykote® or equivalent.
7. Install the lifters. If the old lifters are being reinstalled, be sure to place them in their original bores.
8. Install the valve lifter restrictor, the lifter retainer and the retainer bolts. Tighten the bolts to 12 ft. lbs. (16 Nm) for other engines.
9. Install the intake manifold.
10. Install the pushrod and rocker arm assemblies and adjust as applicable. Install the valve covers.

11. Connect the negative battery cable, tighten the fuel filler cap and fill the cooling system.

Valve Lash

ADJUSTMENT

5.0L (VIN E) and 5.7L Engines

The valve lifters on these engines should not require periodic adjustment. Any time the rocker arms are removed valve lash must be set upon reinstallation.
1. Disconnect the negative battery cable and remove the valve covers.
2. Tighten the rocker arm nuts, as necessary, until rocker arm lash is eliminated.
3. Adjust the valves when the lifter is on the base circle of the camshaft lobe. To do this, crank or slowly turn the engine until the mark on the vibration damper alines with the center or **0** mark on the timing tab, which is fastened to the crankcase front cover. Ensure the engine is in the No. 1 firing position.

NOTE: This may be determined by placing a finger on the No. 1 valve as the mark on the damper comes near the 0 mark on the crankcase front cover. If the valves move as the mark comes up to the timing tab, the engine is in the No. 6 firing position and should be turned 1 full turn to reach the No. 1 firing position.

4. With the engine in the No. 1 firing position, adjust the following valves. Exhaust — 1, 3, 4, 8; Intake — 1, 2, 5, 7.
5. Back out adjusting nut until lash is felt at the pushrod, then turn in adjusting nut until all lash is removed. This can be determined by rotating pushrod while turning the ad-

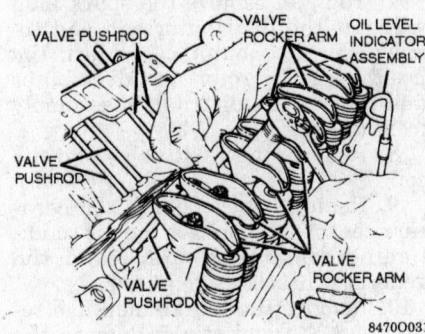

Valve adjustment procedure

justing nut. When the pushrod stops turning, turn in the adjusting nut ¾–1¼ additional turns.
6. Crank or slowly turn the engine one revolution until the pointer, **0** mark and the vibration damper mark are again in alignment. This is the No. 6 firing position.
7. With the engine in this position, repeat the above procedure, adjusting the following valves: Exhaust — 2, 5, 6, 7; Intake — 3, 4, 6, 8.
8. Install the valve covers.
9. Start the engine, check and adjust the minimum idle speed, as required.

Rocker Arms

REMOVAL AND INSTALLATION

5.0L (VIN E) and 5.7L (VIN 7) Engines

1. Disconnect the negative battery cable. Remove the air cleaner assembly.
2. Disconnect the computer command control harness from the intake manifold and oxygen sensor.
3. Disconnect the power brake vacuum pipe and disconnect the AIR hose at the manifold check valve. Tag and remove the spark plug wires.
4. Disconnect the wiring harnesses from the valve covers. Remove the crankcase air inlet hose and connector.
5. Remove the EGR valve solenoid bracket. Remove the PCV valve and hose from the valve cover.
6. Relieve fuel system pressure and disconnect the fuel lines, as required. Remove the generator rear support bracket and wire harness.
7. Remove the valve cover retaining bolts and washers. Remove the valve covers from the engine and discard the gaskets.
8. Remove the rocker arm nuts, rocker arm balls and rocker arms, marking each component to ensure they are installed in their original location.
To install:
9. If installing new rocker arms or balls, coat their bearing surfaces with Molykote® or equivalent. Install all used components in their original locations.
10. Install the rockers arms, balls and adjusting nuts. Tighten the nuts until all lash is eliminated and properly adjust the valves.
11. Thoroughly clean the cylinder head and valve cover mating surfaces. Install the new gaskets and the valve covers to the cylinder heads.

12. Install the valve cover washers and retaining bolts. Tighten the bolts to 95 inch lbs. (11 Nm).

13. If removed, connect the fuel lines and tighten the fuel filler cap. Install the generator rear support bracket and wire harness.

14. Install the PCV valve and hose, and the air inlet hose and connector to the appropriate valve covers. Install the EGR valve solenoid bracket.

15. Connect the wiring harnesses to the valve covers and connect the spark plug wires.

16. Connect the AIR hose to the manifold check valve and connect the power brake vacuum pipe.

17. Connect the computer command control harness to the intake manifold and oxygen sensor.

18. Install the air cleaner assembly and connect the negative battery cable.

5.7L (VIN P) Engine

1. Disconnect the negative battery cable.

2. Remove the left valve cover:

a. Remove the brake booster vacuum hose.

b. Remove the secondary AIR injection hose from the pump to check valve assembly.

c. Remove the valve cover retaining bolts, then remove the cover and gasket.

3. Remove the right valve cover:

a. Raise and support the vehicle safely, then remove the serpentine drive belt.

b. Remove the transmission fluid level indicator tube assembly from the bracket on the transmission housing.

c. Lower the vehicle, then remove the crankcase vent hose.

d. Remove the generator and rear generator brace.

e. Remove the valve cover retaining bolts, then remove the cover and gasket.

4. Remove the valve rocker arm nuts and balls, then remove the rocker arms and pushrods. Tag or arrange all valve train components to assure installation in their original locations.

To install:

5. Coat the bearing surfaces of the rocker arms, balls and pushrods with prelube.

6. Install the pushrods, making sure they are properly seated in the lifter sockets, then install the rocker arms, balls and nuts. If components are being reused, be sure they are installed in their original locations.

7. Adjust the valve lash.

8. Install the valve covers and gaskets, then tighten the retainers to 100 inch lbs. (11 Nm).

9. Install the components which were removed to access the valve covers in the reverse order of removal.

10. Connect the negative battery cable.

Intake Manifold

REMOVAL AND INSTALLATION

5.0L (VIN E) and 5.7L (VIN 7) Engines

1. Disconnect the negative battery cable and properly relieve the fuel system pressure.

2. Remove the air cleaner assembly and drain the radiator fluid into a suitable container.

3. Remove the throttle body assembly, if necessary, as follows:

a. Disconnect all electrical connectors and remove the fuel injector wiring harness.

b. Disconnect the throttle cable, transmission control cable and the cruise control cable.

c. Tag and remove all necessary vacuum hoses. Disconnect and plug the fuel feed and return lines. Discard the old fuel line O-rings.

d. Remove the TBI attaching bolts and the TBI unit. Discard the old gasket.

4. Disconnect the computer command control harness and position it aside.

5. Remove the radiator hose at the thermostat housing and the heater hose from the rear of the intake manifold. Remove the thermostat housing and gasket, if required.

6. Disconnect the power brake vacuum pipe. Disconnect the accelerator cable and throttle valve cable retaining bracket. Disconnect the fuel line clips, as required.

7. Tag and remove the spark plug wires at the distributor cap and remove the distributor cap. Mark the position of the rotor and distributor and remove the distributor assembly from the engine.

8. Remove the EGR valve and the coil.

9. Remove the coolant temperature sensor. Disconnect the air conditioning compressor brace and the generator brace, as required.

10. Remove the intake manifold retaining bolts and studs. Remove the intake manifold from the engine. Discard the gaskets.

To install:

11. Clean the gasket and seal surfaces and position new gaskets on the cylinder heads.

12. Apply a 3/16 inch (5mm) bead of RTV sealant, part number 1052289 or equivalent on the front and rear of the cylinder block. Extend the bead of RTV sealant 1/2 inch (13mm) up each cylinder head to seal and retain the gaskets in position.

13. Install the intake manifold on the engine. Install the retaining bolts and tighten the bolts in the proper sequence to 35 ft. lbs. (47 Nm).

14. Install the compute control harness and the coolant temperature sensor.

15. Install the distributor assembly aligning the marks made earlier. Install the distributor cap and the coil.

16. Install the spark plug wires to the distributor cap. Connect the accelerator cable and throttle valve cable retaining bracket.

17. Connect the fuel line clips, as required and connect the power brake vacuum pipe.

18. Connect wires and hoses as necessary and install the EGR valve.

19. Install the thermostat housing and gasket, as required. Connect the radiator and heater hoses.

20. Connect the air conditioning compressor brace and the generator brace.

21. If removed, install the throttle body assembly. Tighten the TBI unit retaining bolts to 16 ft. lbs. (22 Nm) and be sure to install new O-rings on the fuel lines.

22. Install the air cleaner assembly and connect the negative battery cable.

23. Fill the radiator, using the proper quantity and type coolant.

24. Check and adjust the ignition timing as necessary.

5.7L (VIN P) Engine

1. Disconnect the negative battery cable and relieve the fuel system pressure.

2. Drain the engine cooling system into a suitable container.

3. Remove the throttle body air duct.

4. Disengage the wiring harness connectors from the fuel injectors. Disengage and reposition the left and right wiring harnesses.

5. Remove the accelerator cable bracket retainers, then disconnect the cable and bracket assembly from the throttle body.

6. Disconnect the secondary AIR diverter valve hoses.

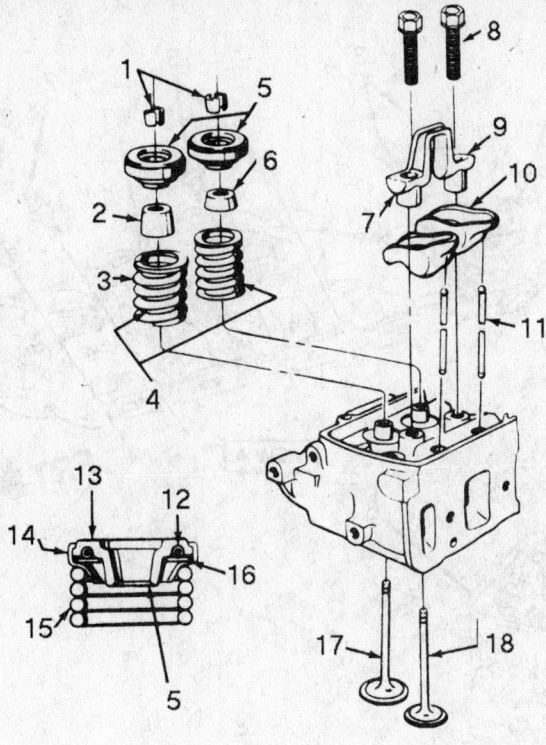

1. Valve keys
2. Intake valve seal
3. Spring
4. Dampener
5. Valve rotator
6. Exhaust valve seal
7. Identification pad
8. 22 ft. lbs. (28 NM)
9. Rocker arm pivot
10. Rocker arms
11. Push rods
12. Coil spring
13. Body
14. Collar
15. Valve spring
16. Flat washer
17. Intake valve
18. Exhaust valve

84700032

Cylinder head exploded view

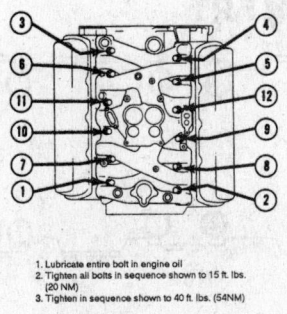

1. Lubricate entire bolt in engine oil
2. Tighten all bolts in sequence shown to 15 ft. lbs. (20 NM)
3. Tighten in sequence shown to 40 ft. lbs. (54NM)

84700033

Intake manifold torque sequence 5.0L engine

7. Disengage the fuel pipe connectors from the fuel rail assembly.

8. Remove the fuel rail bolts and disconnect the vacuum hose from the fuel pressure regulator.

9. Carefully remove the fuel rail and injector assembly from the manifold and position aside.

10. Disconnect the vacuum and crankcase vent hoses.

11. Remove the EGR solenoid assembly and the fuel EVAP canister solenoid assembly.

12. Remove the EGR valve.

13. Remove the AIR pipe from the intake and the right exhaust manifold.

14. Remove the generator rear brace.

15. Disconnect the coolant hoses from the throttle body.

16. Remove the throttle body bolts, the throttle body and gasket from the intake.

17. Remove the intake manifold bolts and studs.

18. Remove the intake manifold and discard the old gaskets.

To install:

19. Thoroughly clean the intake manifold bolts and studs. Inspect and clean all gasket mating surfaces.

20. Apply a ³/₁₆ in. (5mm) bead of RTV sealer to the front and rear of the cylinder block. Extend the bead ½ inch (13mm) up each cylinder head to seal and retain the gaskets.

21. Position the new gaskets and install the intake manifold.

22. Install the manifold bolts and studs, then tighten using 2 passes of the proper sequence. First, tighten the bolts/studs to 71 inch lbs. (8 Nm), then tighten them to 35 ft. lbs. (48 Nm).

23. Install the throttle body, gasket and retaining bolts. Tighten the throttle body bolts to 19 ft. lbs. (26 Nm).

24. Connect the coolant hoses to the throttle body, then install the generator rear brace.

25. Install the accelerator cables and bracket, then tighten the bracket bolts to 90 inch lbs. (10 Nm).

26. Install the secondary AIR pipe. Tighten the exhaust manifold fitting to 25 ft. lbs. (34 Nm) and tighten the flange-to-intake manifold bolts to 19 ft. lbs. (26 Nm).

27. Install the EGR valve, then EGR solenoid and bracket. Tighten valve nuts and the solenoid bracket nut to 16 ft. lbs. (22 Nm).

28. Install the fuel EVAP canister purge solenoid and bracket, then tighten the bolt to 53 inch lbs. (6 Nm).

29. Connect the vacuum and crankcase vent hoses.

30. Install the fuel injector and fuel rail assembly to the intake manifold, connect the fuel pressure regulator vacuum hose and install the fuel rail bolts. Tighten the bolts to 15 ft. lbs. (20 Nm). Engage the fuel pipe connections to the fuel rail assembly.

31. Connect the secondary AIR diverter valve hoses.

32. Position the left and right wiring harnesses, then engage the fuel injector electrical connectors.

33. Install the throttle body air duct.

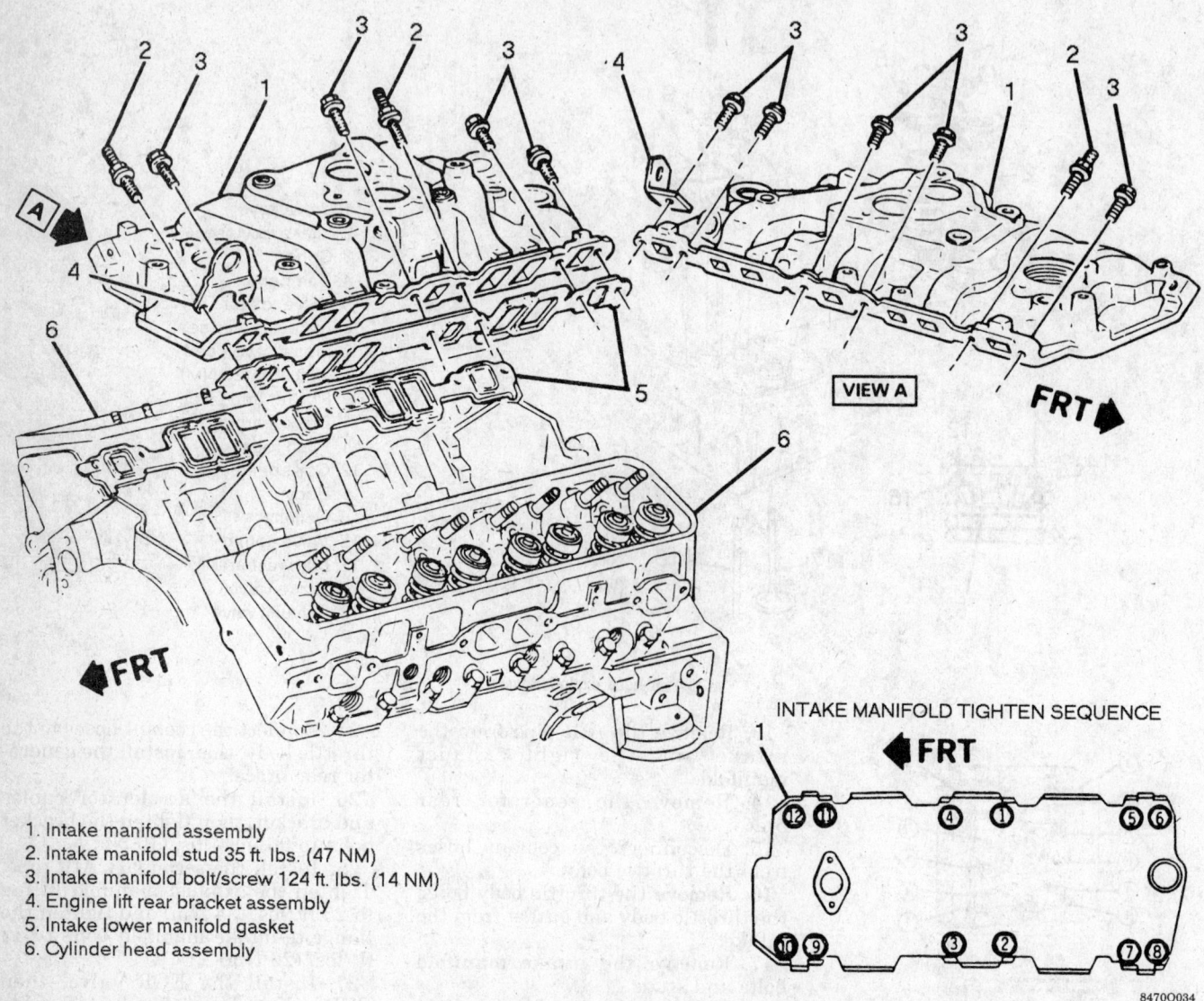

1. Intake manifold assembly
2. Intake manifold stud 35 ft. lbs. (47 NM)
3. Intake manifold bolt/screw 124 ft. lbs. (14 NM)
4. Engine lift rear bracket assembly
5. Intake lower manifold gasket
6. Cylinder head assembly

INTAKE MANIFOLD TIGHTEN SEQUENCE

84700034

Intake manifold assembly 5.7L (VIN 7) engines

34. Properly fill the engine cooling system.
35. Connect the negative battery cable.

Exhaust Manifold

REMOVAL AND INSTALLATION

5.0L (VIN E) and 5.7L Engines

LEFT SIDE

1. Disconnect the negative battery cable and remove the air cleaner assembly.

2. Raise and support the vehicle safely, remove the crossover pipe and lower the vehicle.
3. Tag and remove the spark plug wires and the wire clips.
4. Disconnect the oxygen sensor connector and disconnect the AIR hose at the check valve. Loosen or remove the generator brace, as necessary.
5. Remove the exhaust manifold retaining bolts and studs. Remove the exhaust manifold and heat shield from the engine.
   To install:
6. Clean the mating surfaces and position the manifold and heat shield to the cylinder head. Install the re-

taining bolts and studs. Tighten the bolts and studs to 25 ft. lbs. (35 Nm) and the nuts on the studs to 20 ft. lbs. (25 Nm).
7. Connect the oxygen sensor connector and connect the AIR hose to the check valve.
8. Install the spark plug wire clips and connect the spark plug wires.
9. Install and/or tighten the generator brace.
10. Raise and safely support the vehicle, install the crossover pipe and tighten the nuts to 15 ft. lbs. (20 Nm). Lower the vehicle.
11. Install the air cleaner assembly and connect the negative battery cable.

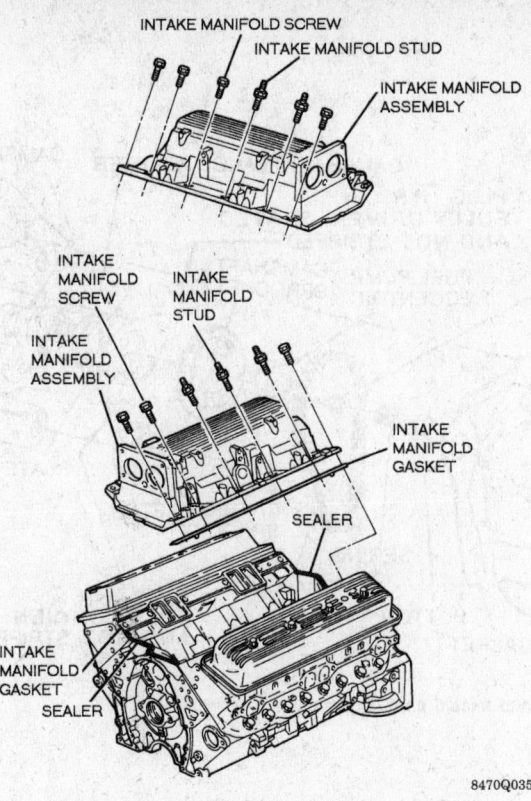

Intake manifold installation — 5.7L (VIN P) engine

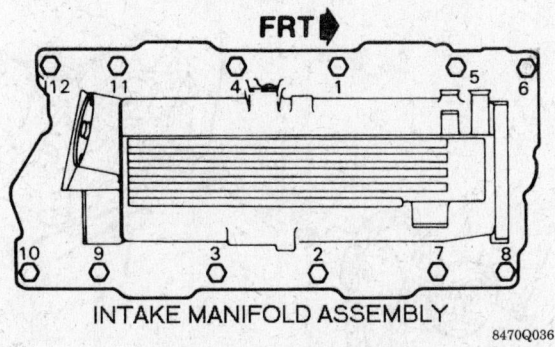

Intake manifold bolt torque sequence — 5.7L (VIN P) engine

RIGHT SIDE

1. Disconnect the negative battery cable and remove the air cleaner assembly.

2. Raise and support the vehicle safely. Disconnect the crossover pipe at both exhaust manifolds.

3. Remove the exhaust mount at the rear of the catalytic converter and remove the back 2 exhaust manifold retaining studs. Lower the vehicle.

4. Tag and disconnect the spark plug wires at the spark plugs.

5. Remove the diverter valve and AIR pipes.

6. Remove the air conditioning compressor brace.

7. Remove the remaining exhaust manifold bolts, studs and locks. Remove the exhaust manifold from the engine.

To install:

8. Clean the mating surface and position the exhaust manifold onto the cylinder head.

9. Install the 4 front manifold bolts and studs, including the flat washers and locks onto the 2 front bolts. Tighten the bolts and studs to 25 ft. lbs. (34 Nm) and the nuts on the studs to 20 ft. lbs. (25 Nm).

10. Install the diverter valve and AIR pipes. Install the air conditioning compressor brace and the spark plug wires.

11. Raise and support the vehicle safely. Install the 2 rear most manifold studs with flat washers and lock. Tighten the studs to 25 ft. lbs. (34 Nm).

12. Install the dipstick and AIR pipe brackets to the studs.

13. Install the crossover pipe to both manifolds and tighten the nuts to 15 ft. lbs. (20 Nm).

14. Install the exhaust mount at the rear of the catalytic converter and lower the vehicle.

15. Install the air cleaner assembly and connect the negative battery cable.

Timing Chain Front Cover

REMOVAL AND INSTALLATION

5.0L (VIN E) and 5.7L (VIN 7) Engines

1. Disconnect the negative battery cable and remove the serpentine drive belt.

2. Raise and support the vehicle safely.

3. Remove the vibration damper retaining bolt. Remove the crankshaft pulley bolts and the crankshaft pulley.

4. Using tool J–23523–E or equivalent harmonic balancer puller, remove the vibration damper.

5. Remove the oil pan and lower the vehicle.

6. Remove the water pump.

7. Remove the front cover retaining bolts. Remove the front cover and discard the gasket.

To install:

8. Clean the front cover and engine mating surfaces and coat the new cover gasket with gasket sealant.

9. Position the cover and the gasket over the crankshaft end.

10. Loosely install the cover to block upper retaining bolts.

NOTE: Do not force the cover over the dowels to the point where the cover flange or the dowels become distorted.

11. Tighten the bolts in a alternate pattern and evenly while pressing downward on the cover so the dowels in the block are aligned with the corresponding holes in the cover. Position the engine front cover so the dowels enter the holes in the cover without binding.

CRANK SHAFT AND CAM SPROCKETS ARE TO BE ASSEMBLED WITH "O" MARK ON CRANKSHAFT SPROCKET ALIGNED WITH TIMING NOTCH ON CAM SPROCKET.

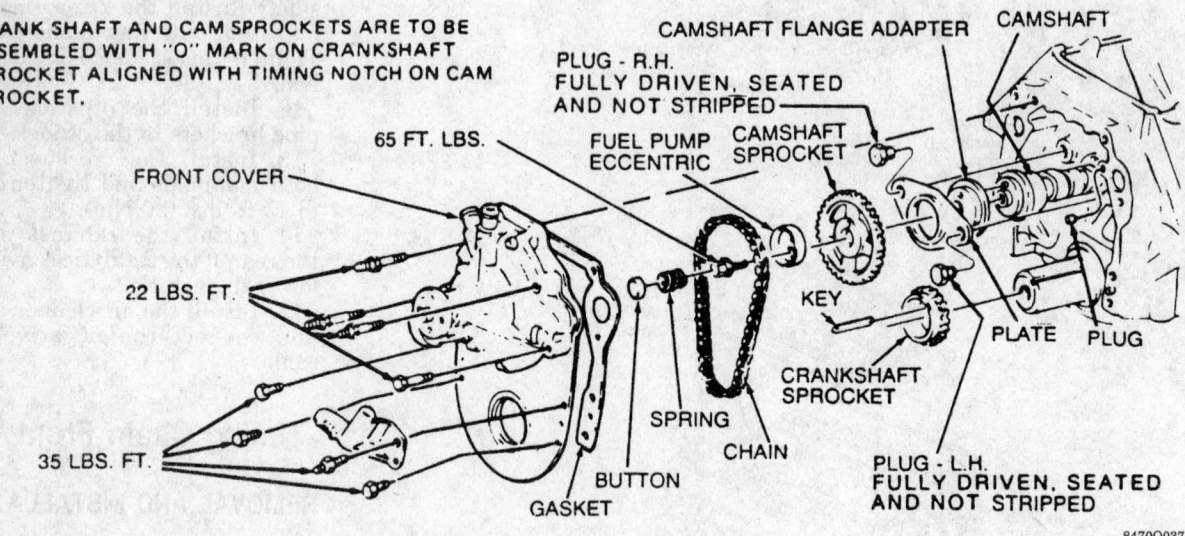

Timing chain cover and related parts 5.0L engine

1. Cylinder block assembly
2. Engine front cover assembly
3. Camshaft driven chain assembly
4. Crankshaft sprocket
5. Camshaft assembly
6. Crankshaft torsional (harmonic balancer) damper
7. Crankshaft assembly
8. Engine front cover bolt/screw 100 in. lbs. (11 NM)
9. Engine front cover gasket

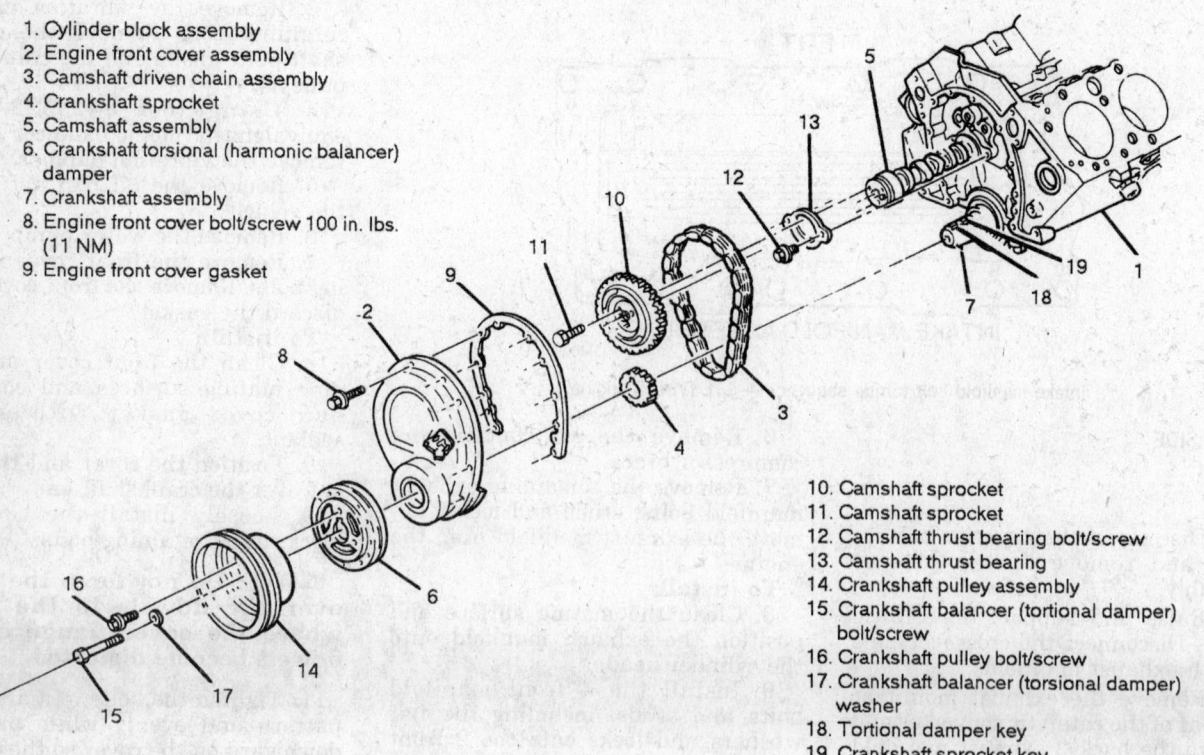

10. Camshaft sprocket
11. Camshaft sprocket
12. Camshaft thrust bearing bolt/screw
13. Camshaft thrust bearing
14. Crankshaft pulley assembly
15. Crankshaft balancer (tortional damper) bolt/screw
16. Crankshaft pulley bolt/screw
17. Crankshaft balancer (torsional damper) washer
18. Tortional damper key
19. Crankshaft sprocket key

Timing chain cover and related parts 5.7L (VIN 7) engines

12. Install the remaining cover bolts. Tighten all bolts alternately and evenly to 100 inch lbs. (11 Nm).

13. Install the water pump assembly.

14. Raise and support the vehicle safely and install the oil pan.

15. Coat the portion of the damper which contacts the front engine cover seal with oil and position the damper over the crankshaft key on the crankshaft.

16. Install the damper using J–23523–E or equivalent harmonic balancer installer. Be sure to thread the tool at least ½ inch into the crankshaft and pull the damper into position.

17. Install the crankshaft pulley and tighten the retaining bolts to 45 ft. lbs (60 Nm). Install the damper retaining bolt and tighten to 70 ft. lbs. (95 Nm).

18. Lower the vehicle and install the serpentine drive belt.

19. Connect the negative battery cable and add engine coolant.

5.7L (VIN P) Engine

1. Disconnect the negative battery cable.

2. Drain the engine oil and coolant into suitable containers.

3. Remove the throttle body air intake duct.

4. Remove the serpentine drive belt.

5. Remove the water pump assembly.

6. Remove the crankshaft balancer and hub.

   a. If not done already, raise and support the vehicle safely.

   b. Remove the crankshaft balancer retaining bolts, then remove the balancer from the hub.

   c. Matchmark the crankshaft hub to the engine front cover, then remove the hub bolt and washer.

   d. Remove the crankshaft hub using J–39046, or an equivalent hub removal/installation tool. To preserve the relationship between the hub and crankshaft, DO NOT crank the engine once the hub has been removed. If the hub is not matchmarked and installed in the original position, an engine imbalance could result.

7. Remove the distributor assembly.

8. Remove the oil pan assembly.

9. Remove the engine front cover bolts.

10. Remove the engine front cover and gasket.

To install:

11. Thoroughly clean the engine front cover and cylinder block gasket mating surfaces. Inspect the engine front cover and seals for damage, replace as necessary.

12. Using J–39087 or equivalent front cover seal protector on the water pump driveshaft install the gasket and front cover into position over the shafts and guide pins.

13. Install the engine front cover bolts and tighten to 100 inch lbs. (11 Nm).

14. Install the oil pan and gasket.

15. Install the distributor assembly.

16. Install the crankshaft hub and torsional damper assembly.

   a. Align the matchmarks made earlier and install the crankshaft hub using the hub tool. If the engine was cranked and the matchmarks were lost, set the engine to No. 1 TDC, then install the crankshaft hub with the cast arrow in the 12 o'clock position.

   b. Install the hub washer and bolt, but do not torque at this time.

   c. Install the crankshaft balancer to the hub, then tighten the crankshaft hub bolt to 75 ft. lbs. (102 Nm) and the balancer bolts to 60 ft. lbs. (81 Nm).

NOTE: If a new balancer is installed, new balancer weights of the same size must be installed in the same hole locations as the original balancer.

17. Install the water pump assembly.

18. Install the serpentine drive belt.

19. Install the throttle body air duct.

20. Properly fill the engine crankcase with clean engine oil.

21. Properly fill the engine cooling system.

22. Connect the negative battery cable, operate the engine and check for leaks.

Front Cover Oil Seal

REPLACEMENT

5.0L (VIN E) and 5.7L (VIN 7) Engines

COVER INSTALLED

1. Disconnect the negative battery cable and remove the serpentine drive belt.

2. Raise and support the vehicle safely.

1. Engine front cover assembly
2. Engine front cover gasket
3. Engine front cover bolt
4. Engine front cover locating pin

8470Q038

Timing chain front cover — 5.7L (VIN P) Engine

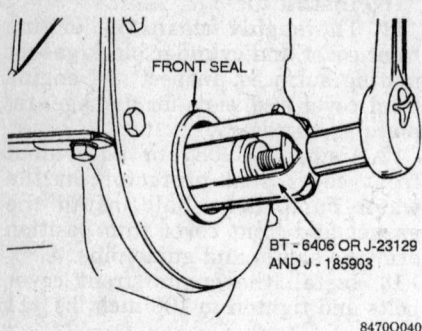

FRONT SEAL

BT - 6406 OR J-23129
AND J - 185903

84700040

Removing front oil seal

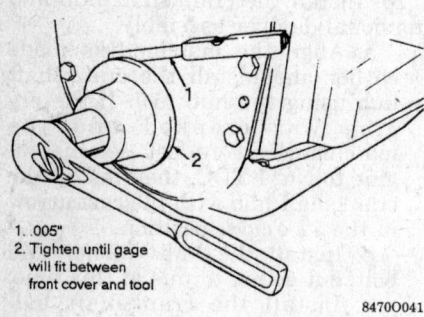

1. .005"
2. Tighten until gage
   will fit between
   front cover and tool

84700041

Installing front oil seal

3. Remove the vibration damper retaining bolt. Remove the crankshaft pulley bolts and the crankshaft pulley.

4. Using tool J–23523–E or equivalent harmonic balancer puller, remove the vibration damper.

5. Pry the old seal from the cover, with a small suitable tool. Care should be taken not to damage the cover.

To install:

6. Position the new seal so the open end of the seal faces toward the inside of the engine cover. Use tool J-35468 or equivalent to properly align and install the new oil seal.

7. Coat the portion of the damper which contacts the front engine cover seal with clean engine oil and position the damper over the crankshaft key on the crankshaft. Install the damper using J–23523–E or equivalent harmonic balancer installer. Be sure to thread the tool at least ½ inch into the crankshaft and pull the damper into position.

8. Install the crankshaft pulley and tighten the retaining bolts to 45 ft. lbs. (60 Nm). Install the damper retaining bolt and tighten to 70 ft. lbs. (95 Nm).

9. Lower the vehicle, install the serpentine drive belt and connect the negative battery cable.

COVER REMOVED

1. Remove the front cover from the engine.

2. Using a small suitable tool pry the old seal from the engine front cover and discard it. Be careful not to damage the cover when removing the seal.

3. Position the new seal so that the open end of the seal faces toward the inside of the engine cover. Support the rear of the engine cover at the seal area and use tool J-35468 or equivalent to properly align and install the new oil seal.

4. Install the front cover to the engine.

5.7L (VIN P) Engine

COVER REMOVED

In addition to the crankshaft oil seal, the 5.7L engine front cover utilizes a water pump driveshaft seal and distributor driveshaft seal. All front cover oil seals on these engines are replaced in the same manner.

1. Remove the timing chain front cover from the engine.

2. Using either a suitably sized driver or a small suitable prytool, remove oil seal from the front cover. If a driver is being used, be sure to support the cover so it is not damaged. If a prytool is used, take care not to score or damage the cover sealing surfaces.

3. Use J-35468 or equivalent to install the crankshaft seal.

4. Use J-39090 or equivalent to install the distributor shaft seal.

5. Use J-39088 or equivalent to install the water pump driveshaft seal.

6. Install the timing chain front cover to the engine.

COVER INSTALLED

The timing gear cover should be removed to install the seal properly.

Timing Chain and Sprockets

REMOVAL AND INSTALLATION

5.0L (VIN E) and 5.7L Engines

1. Disconnect the negative battery cable.

2. Remove the engine front cover and water pump assembly.

3. Rotate the engine slowly until the marks on both the camshaft sprocket and crankshaft sprocket align with the shaft centers.

4. Remove the camshaft sprocket retaining bolts. Remove the camshaft sprocket along with the timing chain.

NOTE: Do not allow the crankshaft to turn after the timing chain has been removed to prevent damage to engine parts.

5. Using a crankshaft sprocket removal tool, remove the crankshaft sprocket. Remove the crankshaft sprocket key, if required.

To install:

6. Remove the old gasket from the timing cover and engine mating surfaces.

7. Install the crankshaft key, if removed and install the crankshaft sprocket onto the crankshaft using GM tool J–5590 or equivalent gear installer.

NOTE: A new timing chain must be installed any time a new crankshaft sprocket is installed.

8. Install the timing chain with the camshaft sprocket onto the camshaft.

9. Ensure the timing marks on the crankshaft sprocket and the camshaft sprocket are aligned as close together as possible and centered with the shafts.

10. Install the bolts securing the camshaft sprocket to the camshaft and torque to 21 ft. lbs. (28 Nm).

11. Lubricate the timing chain with oil and install the engine front cover assembly.

12. Reconnect the negative battery cable, check and adjust the ignition timing as necessary.

Camshaft

REMOVAL AND INSTALLATION

5.0L (VIN E) and 5.7L Engines

1. Disconnect the negative battery cable and properly relieve the fuel system pressure.

2. Drain the cooling system. and remove the intake manifold.

3. Remove the valve covers, rocker arm assemblies, pushrods and lifters. Be sure to note the location of each component for proper installation.

4. Remove the clutch fan bolts and remove the serpentine drive belt.

5. Remove the radiator tie struts at the radiator cradle. Remove the fan shroud bolts at the top and bottom of the shroud. Push the shroud back and remove the fan clutch and water pump pulley.

6. Remove the radiator hoses from the water pump and thermostat. Remove the transmission and oil cooler lines from the radiator.

7. Remove the radiator and the fan shroud.

8. Remove the timing chain and camshaft sprocket.

9. Remove the camshaft retainer and bolts.

10. Carefully pull the camshaft partially out of the engine using the bolts as a handle. Remove the bolts from the camshaft and carefully remove the camshaft from the engine. All camshaft journals are the same diameter, so care must be used in pulling the camshaft from the bearings to prevent damage.

To install:

11. When installing a new camshaft, lubricate the camshaft lobes with Molykote® or equivalent prelube, before installing the camshaft and use new lifters.

12. Lubricate the camshaft bearing journals with clean engine oil and partially install the camshaft. Install three $5/16$-18 x 4 inch bolts in the camshaft timing gear bolt holes to serve as a handle and finish inserting the camshaft.

13. Remove the installation bolts and install the camshaft retainer and retainer bolts. Tighten the bolts to 105 inch lbs. (12 Nm).

14. Install the timing chain and engine front cover.

15. Install the valve lifters.

16. Install the fan shroud, water pump pulley and fan clutch, and the radiator. Connect all radiator hoses and lines.

17. Install the serpentine drive belt and tighten the fan clutch bolts. Secure the fan shroud top and bottom bolts. Install the radiator tie struts at the radiator cradle.

18. Install the valve rocker arms and pushrods. Adjust as necessary and install the valve rocker covers.

19. Install the intake manifold and connect the negative battery cable.

20. Tighten the fuel filler cap and add engine coolant.

Piston and Connecting Rod

POSITIONING

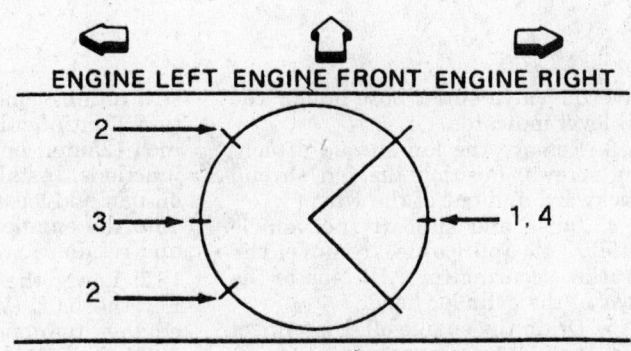

1. Oil ring spacer gap (tang in hole or slot within arc)
2. Oil ring rail gaps
3. 2nd compression ring gap
4. Top compression ring gap

84700045

Piston ring gap locations

1. Timing marks
2. Cylinder block assembly
3. Camshaft driven
   chain assembly
4. Crankshaft sprocket
5. Camshaft sprocket

84700042

Timing mark alignment

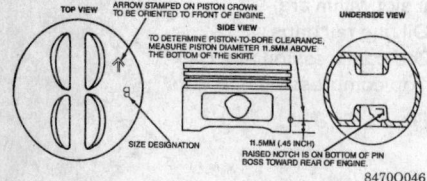

Piston positioning and identification–5.0L and 5.7L engines

84700046

ENGINE LUBRICATION

Oil Pan

REMOVAL AND INSTALLATION

1. Disconnect the negative battery cable.

2. As required remove the air cleaner assembly, the AIR pipe at the diverter valve outlet hose and/or the oil level indicator.

3. Remove the fan shroud attaching screws. Position the fan shroud backward and out of the way.

4. Raise and support the vehicle safely. If applicable, remove the bracket securing the AIR pipe to the rear of the cylinder head.

5. Drain the engine oil. Disconnect the exhaust crossover pipe and remove the flywheel cover.

6. Remove the starter assembly.

7. Using the proper jack, with a block of wood on top, place it under the crankshaft hub to support the engine. Remove both engine mount through bolts.

8. Carefully raise the front of the engine. Remove the oil pan retaining bolts, nuts and, if equipped, reinforcements.

9. Lower the oil pan enough to determine if the crankshaft throw and counterbalance are clear and remove the oil pan from the engine. If necessary turn the crankshaft slowly to create to clear the throw and weight.

To install:

10. Clean all the material from the pan and the block mating surfaces.

11. For 5.0L (VIN E) and 5.7L engines, apply a thin amount of gasket sealer only to the front cover and cylinder block junction and to the rear seal retainer and cylinder block junction. Continue the bead of sealer for 1 inch (25mm) on either side of these junctions. Install the gasket onto the oil pan and loosely install the oil pan onto the engine with the bolts, nuts and retainers.

12. Lower the engine into position. For the 5.0L (VIN E) and the 5.7L engines tighten the oil pan bolts to 100 inch lbs. (11 Nm) and the nuts to 17 ft. lbs. (23 Nm).

13. Install the engine mount through bolts and remove the engine support.

14. Install the starter assembly and, if applicable, attach the transmission oil cooler lines to the clips on the oil pan.

15. Install the flywheel cover and the exhaust crossover pipe.

16. If applicable, install the AIR pipe bracket to the rear of the cylinder head.

17. Lower the vehicle and secure the fan shroud assembly.

18. As required, install the oil level indicator, the AIR pipe at the diverter valve outlet hose and the air cleaner assembly.

19. Connect the negative battery cable and refill the engine crankcase with the proper type and amount of engine oil.

Oil Pump

REMOVAL AND INSTALLATION

1. Disconnect the negative battery cable.
2. Remove the oil pan assembly.
3. Remove the oil pump retaining bolts. Remove the oil pump with the pump driveshaft from the engine.
4. Separate the driveshaft and discard the retainer.

To install:

5. Install the new retainer to the oil pump driveshaft and install the driveshaft extension to the pump. Align the slot on the end of the driveshaft extension with the drive tang on the distributor driveshaft and install the oil pump assembly. Tighten the retaining bolt to 80 ft. lbs. (105 Nm).
6. Install the oil pan assembly.
7. Remove the oil pressure sending unit and install an oil pressure gauge.
8. Connect the negative battery cable, start the engine and ensure the oil pressure is within specification.

Rear Main Bearing Oil Seal

REMOVAL AND INSTALLATION

5.0L (VIN E) and 5.7L Engines

1. Disconnect the negative battery cable.
2. Remove the transmission assembly.
3. Remove the flywheel-to-crankshaft bolts and remove the flywheel.
4. Using the notches in the rear crankshaft seal retainer, pry the old seal out. Be careful not to nick the crankshaft sealing surface when removing the seal.

To install:

5. Coat the new seal with engine oil and install the seal onto tool J–35621 or equivalent rear main seal installer.
6. Install the tool onto the rear of the crankshaft and tighten the screws snugly to ensure the seal will be installed squarely over the crankshaft.
7. Install the seal onto the crankshaft and into the rear seal retainer by tightening the wing nut of the tool until it bottoms. Remove the tool from the retainer.
8. Reinstall the flywheel and tighten the attaching bolts to 75 ft. lbs. (100 Nm).

9. Install the transmission assembly.
10. Connect the negative battery cable, lower the vehicle and inspect the engine for oil leaks.

AUTOMATIC TRANSMISSION

Transmission Assembly

REMOVAL AND INSTALLATION

1. Disconnect the negative battery cable and position the selector lever in the **N** detent position.
2. Remove the air cleaner assembly. Disconnect the accelerator cable and detent cable, as required.
3. Remove the transmission dipstick retaining bolt and the dipstick tube.
4. Raise and support the vehicle safely.
5. Remove the floor pan reinforcement. Matchmark the driveshaft for reinstallation in its original position and remove the driveshaft.
6. Disconnect the shift linkage, speedometer cable or wire and all electrical connections or clips at the transmission.
7. Remove the flywheel cover retaining bolts and cover. Mark the flexplate and converter so they can be realigned in their original location. Remove the flexplate-to-converter bolts.
8. If necessary, remove the catalytic converter support bracket. Position a transmission jack under the transmission and remove the transmission mount to support bolt(s).
9. Slide the support rearward and remove the crossmember attaching bolts and remove the crossmember. Lower the transmission slightly on the support to gain access to the oil cooler pipes and the TV cable attachments.
10. Disconnect the transmission oil cooler pipes and the required cables. Plug all openings to prevent fluid contamination or loss.
11. Support the engine with a suitable tool and remove the transmission-to-engine bolts.
12. Install a torque converter holding tool and remove the transmission assembly from the vehicle.

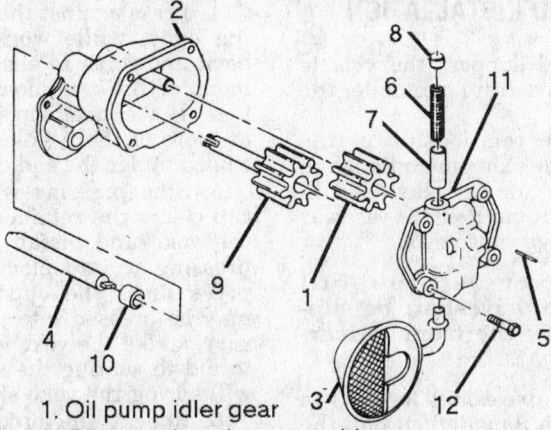

1. Oil pump idler gear
2. Oil pump housing assembly
3. Oil pump screen
4. Oil pump driveshaft assembly
5. Oil pressure relief valve pin
6. Oil pressure relief valve spring
7. Oil pressure relief valve assembly
8. Oil pressure relief valve plug
9. Oil pump driven gear
10. Oil pump driveshaft retainer
11. Oil pump cover
12. Oil pump cover bolt/screw

84700048

Oil pump assembly

To install:

13. Properly flush the transmission oil cooler and line.

14. Raise the transmission into place and remove the torque converter holding tool.

15. Install the transmission to engine bolts and tighten to 35 ft. lbs. (47 Nm).

16. Install the transmission oil cooler pipes and required cables to the transmission.

17. Install the transmission support to the frame and tighten the bolts to 41 ft. lbs. (55 Nm). Install the support-to-mount bolt(s) and tighten to 35 ft. lbs. (47 Nm). Remove the engine and transmission supports.

18. Align the marks made earlier, making sure the weld nuts on the converter are flush with the flywheel and install the converter-to-flywheel bolts. Finger-tighten 3 bolts then tighten bolts to 35 ft. lbs. (47 Nm). When finished, retighten the first bolt tightened.

19. Install the floor pan reinforcement and the catalytic converter support bracket, as required.

20. Install the flywheel cover and bolts. Tighten the bolts to 89 inch lbs. (10 Nm). Connect the shift linkage, the speedometer cable or wire and the electrical leads and retaining clips.

21. Align the marks made earlier and install the driveshaft.

22. Lower the vehicle and install the fluid filler tube with a new seal. Install the filler tube retaining bolt and the fluid indicator.

23. Connect the TV and detent cables, as required.

24. Install the air cleaner assembly and connect the negative battery cable.

25. Adjust the shift linkage and the TV cable, as necessary.

26. Check and add transmission fluid, as necessary.

SHIFT LINKAGE ADJUSTMENT

1. With the column lever and the transmission selector lever in the **N** detent, tighten the linkage rod retaining bolt to 17–22 ft. lbs. (24–32 Nm).

2. The linkage is correctly adjusted if at final vehicle inspection with the column lever raised and centered in the **N** detent, the column lever can be lowered and will engage in the column neutral notch.

3. Adjustment is unacceptable if any rotation of the column lever is required to engage the column neutral notch.

THROTTLE VALVE CABLE ADJUSTMENT

1. Remove the air cleaner assembly.

2. Depress and hold-down the metal readjustment tab at the engine end of the throttle valve cable.

3. Move the slider until it stops against the fitting. Release the readjustment tab.

4. Rotate the throttle lever to its full travel position.

5. The slider must ratchet toward the lever when the lever is rotated to its full travel position.

6. Check that the cable moves freely. The cable may function properly with a cold engine and not with a warm engine. Start the engine and run until normal operating temperature is reached.

7. Shut the engine **OFF** and check that the cable moves freely with a warm engine.

DRIVE AXLE

Driveshaft and U-Joints

REMOVAL AND INSTALLATION

1. Raise and support the vehicle safely. Position a drain pan under the transmission.

2. Mark the relationship of the driveshaft to the axle pinion flange so the driveshaft can be reinstalled in its original position. Remove the rear driveshaft flange capscrews.

NOTE: Never let the full weight of the driveshaft be supported only by the front universal joint.

3. Push the driveshaft forward to clear the pinion flange, then pull the driveshaft rearward to disengage the slip yoke from the transmission.

4. Plug the transmission to prevent fluid contamination or loss. If the bearing cups are loose, tape them together to prevent dropping and losing the bearing rollers.

5. Support the driveshaft horizontally in line with the base plate of a press but do not clamp the tube.

6. Place the U-joint so the lower ear of the shaft yoke is supported on a 1⅛ inch socket.

7. Press the lower bearing cap out of the yoke ear by placing tool

J–9522–3 or equivalent cross press, on the open horizontal bearing caps and pressing the lower bearing cap out of the yoke ear. This will shear the plastic retaining ring on the lower bearing cup. If the bearing cap is not completely removed, lift tool J–9522–3 and insert tool J–9522–5 or equivalent spacer, between the bearing cap and seal and continue pressing the U-joint out of the yoke.

8. Repeat the procedure for opposite bearing cup.

9. Remove the cross from the yoke and remove the remains of the sheared plastic retainer from the ears of the yoke.

10. If the front U-joint is also being replaced, remove in the same manner.

To install:

11. When replacing U-joints always replace the entire assembly consisting of 1 pregreased spider, 4 bearing cup assemblies with seals, needle rollers, washers, grease and 4 snaprings.

12. Install 1 bearing cap part way into 1 side of the yoke. Turn this yoke ear to the bottom.

13. Using tool J–9522–3 or equivalent cross press, seat the trunnion into the bearing cup. Install the opposite bearing cap partially and ensure that both trunnions are straight and true in the bearing cups.

14. Press against the opposite bearing cups, while working the cross back and forth to ensure free movement of the trunnions in the bearings. If the trunnion is binding, one or more of the needle bearings have tipped under the end of the trunnion.

15. Stop pressing when 1 bearing cap clears the retainer groove inside the yoke and install a snapring by pressing it into place. Continue to press until the opposite snapring may be pressed into place. If necessary, strike the yoke with a hammer to aid in seating the snaprings, this will spring the yoke slightly.

16. Repeat the procedure for the other half of the U-joint.

17. Remove any nicks, burrs, dirt or rust from the pinion yoke. Thoroughly clean the slip yoke with kerosene and dry with compressed air.

18. Pack slip yoke lubricant between the lips of the transmission extension housing seal. Lubricate the yoke with slip yoke lubricant and install onto the transmission output shaft.

19. Install the rear of the shaft, aligning the marks made earlier and install the capscrews. Tighten the capscrews to 16 ft. lbs. (21 Nm).

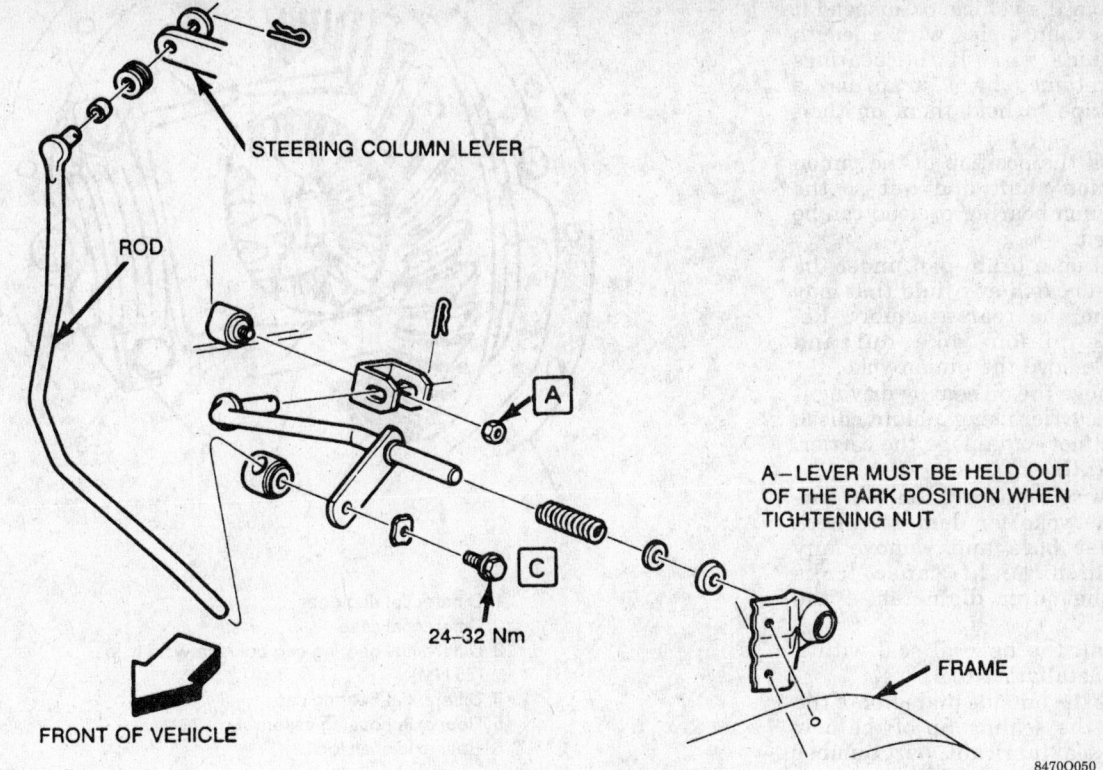

A — LEVER MUST BE HELD OUT OF THE PARK POSITION WHEN TIGHTENING NUT

STEERING COLUMN LEVER

ROD

24–32 Nm

FRONT OF VEHICLE

FRAME

84700050

Automatic transmission shift linkage adjustment

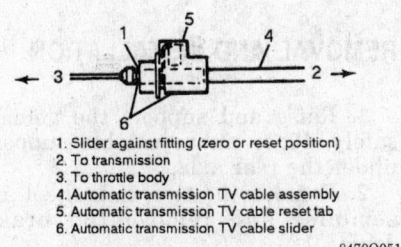

1. Slider against fitting (zero or reset position)
2. To transmission
3. To throttle body
4. Automatic transmission TV cable assembly
5. Automatic transmission TV cable reset tab
6. Automatic transmission TV cable slider

84700051

Transmission TV cable assembly

20. Remove the drainpan and lower the vehicle.

Rear Axle Shaft, Bearing and Seal

REMOVAL AND INSTALLATION

1. Raise and support the vehicle safely. Remove the wheel and tire assembly. Remove the brake drum.
2. Clean any dirt from the differential cover. Loosen the cover attaching bolts, and drain the lubricant by removing the cover.

3. Remove the pinion shaft lockbolt and remove the pinion shaft.
4. Push in on the flanged end of the axle shaft and remove the C-lock from the splined end of the axle shaft.
5. Remove the axle shaft from the housing, being cautious not to damage the oil seal.
6. Use a prybar behind the steel case of the seal to remove the oil seal from the bore. Be careful not to damage the housing.
7. Insert an axle shaft bearing puller into position behind the bearing so that the tangs on the tool engage the bearing outer race. Remove the bearing using a slide hammer.

To install:

8. Lubricate the new bearing with gear lubricant. Use bearing installer tool J–23765 or equivalent, and install the bearing so the tool bottoms out against the shoulder in the housing.
9. Lubricate the lips of the seal with gear lubricant. Position the new seal on seal installer tool J–23771 or equivalent, and position the seal into the housing bore. Tap the seal into place so it is flush with the axle tube.
10. Carefully slide the axle shaft into the housing taking care that the splines do not damage the oil seal. Continue to slide the axle into posi-

tion and engage the splines of the differential side gear.
11. Install the axle shaft C-lock on the splined end of the axle shaft in the differential. Push the shaft outward so the shaft lock seats in the counterbore of the differential side gear.
12. Install the pinion shaft through the differential case, thrust washers and pinions. Align the lockbolt hole and install the lock screw, tightening it to 20 ft. lbs. (27 Nm).
13. Clean the differential housing and cover mating surfaces and install the cover with a new gasket. Tighten the retaining bolts in a crosswise pattern to 22 ft. lbs. (30 Nm).
14. Fill the differential with lubricant flush with, or within 1/4 inch (6mm) of the filler hole.
15. Install the brake drum and install the tire and wheel assembly.
16. Lower the vehicle.

Pinion Seal

REMOVAL AND INSTALLATION

1. Raise and support the vehicle safely.
2. Mark and remove the driveshaft from the pinion yoke. Either remove the driveshaft com-

pletely from the vehicle or suspend it from the exhaust pipe with a length of mechanic's wire. If the bearings are not retained by a strap, use a piece of tape to hold them on their journals.

3. Mark the position of the pinion yoke, pinion shaft and nut so the proper pinion bearing preload can be maintained.

4. Position a drain pan under the assembly to catch any fluid that may drain from the rear assembly. Remove the pinion yoke nut and washer. Remove the pinion yoke.

5. Remove the oil seal by driving it out of the carrier using a blunt chisel. Be careful not to damage the carrier.

To install:

6. Be sure to inspect the seal surface of the yoke for damage. Check the carrier bore and remove any burrs which might cause leaks around the outer diameter of the seal.

7. Install the new oil seal with a suitable installation tool.

8. Coat the outside diameter of the yoke and the sealing lip of the new seal with seal lubricant, part number 1050169 or equivalent.

9. Install the yoke, washer and nut. Tighten the yoke nut to the position marked previously. While holding the pinion yoke tighten the nut an additional 1/16 inch beyond the alignment marks.

10. Align the marks made earlier and install the driveshaft. Check and add gear lubricant to the carrier, if necessary.

11. Lower the vehicle.

Differential Carrier

REMOVAL AND INSTALLATION

1. Raise and safely support the vehicle.

2. Remove cover and drain all axle fluid.

3. Remove the drive axles.

4. Mark the differential bearing caps **L** and **R** to make sure they will be reassembled in their original location.

5. Remove the bearing cap bolts and caps.

6. Using a suitable tool, remove the differential carrier. Be careful not to damage the gasket sealing surface when removing the unit. Place the right and left bearing outer races of the side bearing assemblies and shims in sets with the marked differ-

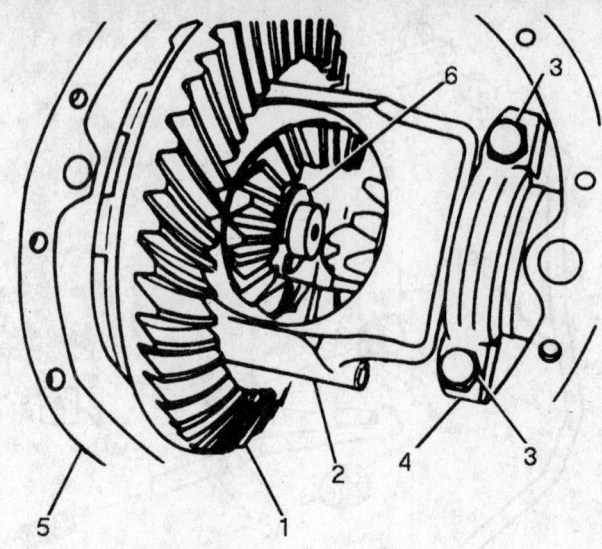

1. Differential ring gear
2. Differential case
3. Differential bearing cap bolt/screw 55 ft. lbs. (75 NM)
4. Differential bearing cap
5. Rear axle housing assembly
6. Rear axle shaft lock

84700052

Axle C-clip location

ential bearings caps so they can be reinstalled in their original positions.

To install:

7. Inspect the differential carrier housing for foreign material. Check the ring and pinion for chipped teeth, excessive wear and scoring. Check the carrier bearings visually and by feel. Clean the differential housing and replace components, as necessary.

8. Lubricate all parts with rear axle lubricant and install the differential carrier. Check the carrier bearing preload and ring and pinion backlash and adjust, as necessary. Tighten the differential bearing cap bolts to 55 ft. lbs. (75 Nm).

9. Install the axles.

10. Install the gasket to the carrier cover. Install the carrier cover and tighten the carrier cover bolts in a crosswise pattern to 22 ft. lbs. (30 Nm).

11. Add rear axle lubricant to a level flush with or within 1/4 inch (6mm) of the filler hole and install the filler plug.

12. Lower the vehicle.

Axle Housing

REMOVAL AND INSTALLATION

1. Raise and support the vehicle safely, Place an adjustable support under the rear axle.

2. Remove the tire and wheel assemblies and remove the brake drums.

3. Disconnect the shock absorbers from axle. Mark the driveshaft, disconnect it from the rear axle pinion flange and support it aside.

4. Remove the brake line junction block bolt at the axle housing. Disconnect and plug the brake lines at the junction block. If equipped with ABS, disconnect all required electrical connectors.

5. Disconnect the upper control arms from axle housing. Lower the rear axle assembly slightly and remove the springs.

6. If necessary, remove the rear axle cover and the axle shafts, the brake lines from the axle housing clips, and the backing plates.

7. Disconnect the lower control arms from the axle housing.

8. Continue lowering the rear axle assembly and remove it from the vehicle.

To install:

9. Raise the rear axle housing sufficiently and connect the upper and lower control arms. Hand tighten the bolts.

10. If applicable, install the brake backing plates, position the brake lines under the axle housing clips, install the axle shafts and install the rear axle cover.

11. Fill with axle fluid flush or to within ¼ inch of filler hole.

12. Install the coil springs.

13. Unplug and connect the brake lines to the junction block. Install the junction block retaining bolt.

14. Align the marks and install the driveshaft. Install the shock absorbers.

15. With the vehicle's weight resting on the axle, tighten the upper and lower control arm bolts to specifications.

16. Install the brake drums, tires and wheels. Remove the support from the axle housing and lower the vehicle.

17. Bleed the hydraulic brake system.

STEERING

Steering Wheel

REMOVAL AND INSTALLATION

1992

1. Disconnect the negative battery cable and turn the ignition to the **RUN** position in order to facilitate removal.

2. Remove the horn pad retaining screws. Remove the horn pad and switch.

3. Remove the horn contact wire from the plastic tower by pushing in on the wire and turning counterclockwise. The wire will spring out of the tower.

4. If applicable, remove the screws that secure the telescope locking lever assembly to the adjuster. Unscrew and remove the adjuster from the steering shaft. Remove the telescope lever from the column.

5. Scribe an alignment mark on the steering wheel hub in line with the slash mark on the steering shaft for use during installation.

6. Loosen the locknut on the steering shaft and position it flush with

the end of the shaft. Using the proper steering wheel puller, remove the wheel from its mounting on the steering shaft.

7. Remove the steering wheel removal tool, the locknut and the steering wheel from the vehicle.

To install:

8. Install the steering wheel onto the steering column, aligning the marks made during the removal procedure. The steering wheel should in no case be driven onto the column as this could seriously damage column components.

9. Install the locknut and tighten to 35 ft. lbs. (47 Nm).

10. If applicable, install the telescope lever onto the shaft. Install the telescope adjuster screw by hand. Position the locking lever and bolts along the marks made by the bolts when they were tightened and tighten the bolts to 35 inch lbs. (4 Nm). Check operation of the tilt and telescoping column. Make sure the wheel locks securely into position when the lever is all the way to the right. Adjust the slotted locking lever bolt holes, if necessary.

11. Install the horn contact into the plastic cavity, push it against the spring and twist clockwise.

12. Install the horn pad assembly and secure it with the 2 attaching screws.

13. Turn the ignition **OFF** and connect the negative battery cable.

1993–96

─────── **CAUTION** ───────
When performing service on or around SIR components or wiring, follow the procedures to disable the SIR system. Failure to follow procedures could result in possible air bag deployment, personal injury, or unneeded SIR system repairs.

1. Turn steering wheel so the tires are pointing straight–ahead.

2. Turn ignition switch to **LOCK**.

3. Remove "AIR BAG" fuse from the fuse block.

4. Remove the left sound insulator and unplug the Connector Position Assurance (CPA) and yellow 2-way connector, located near the base of the steering column.

5. Disconnect the negative battery cable.

6. Remove the SIR module assembly and personal safety, carry the module **face down** to a safe storage spot and place it **facing up**.

7. Using only tool J–1859–A or equivalent, remove the steering wheel.

NOTE: Never strike the steering shaft with a hammer, as hammering could loosen the plastic injections which maintain steering column assembly rigidity.

To install:

8. Turn the ignition to **LOCK**.

9. Align block tooth on steering wheel with block tooth on steering shaft. Install nut and tighten to 30 ft. lbs. (41 Nm).

10. Install SIR module.

11. Connect the negative battery cable.

12. Connect the Connector Position Assurance (CPA) and yellow 2-way connector at the base of the steering column.

13. Reinstall "AIR BAG" fuse.

14. Turn ignition switch to "RUN" and verify that the "AIR BAG" lamp flashes 7 times and turns OFF.

Steering Column

─────── **WARNING** ───────
When the steering column is removed from the vehicle, it is extremely susceptible to damage. Dropping the assembly on its end could collapse the steering shaft or loosen plastic injections that keep the column rigid. Leaning on the assembly could cause the jacket to bend or deform. Any of these conditions could impair the columns collapsible design.

REMOVAL AND INSTALLATION

1992

1. Disconnect the negative battery cable and lock the steering column with the wheels in the straight-ahead position.

2. Disconnect the transmission shift linkage under the hood at the lower shift lever.

3. Remove the coupling nut attaching the intermediate shaft to the steering column. Separate the shaft from the column.

4. Remove the steering column lower cover and 4 retaining screws from the instrument panel, exposing the upper support bolts.

5. If necessary, remove the lower fuse cover panel by removing 2 screws and 1 wing nut and/or remove the left air conditioning outlet duct and screw.

1. Horn lead
2. Coil wiring harness assembly
3. Inflatable restraint steering wheel module assembly
4. Steering wheel assemlby
5. Turn signal, headlamp dimmer switch, cruise control actuator, windshield wiper and windshield washer lever assembly
6. Steering column tilt wheel release lever assembly
7. Steering column assembly
8. Upper intermediate steering shaft bolt/screw
9. Pot joint coupling
10. Upper intermediate steering shaft 40 ft. lbs. nut (54 NM)
11. Upper intermediate steering shaft assembly

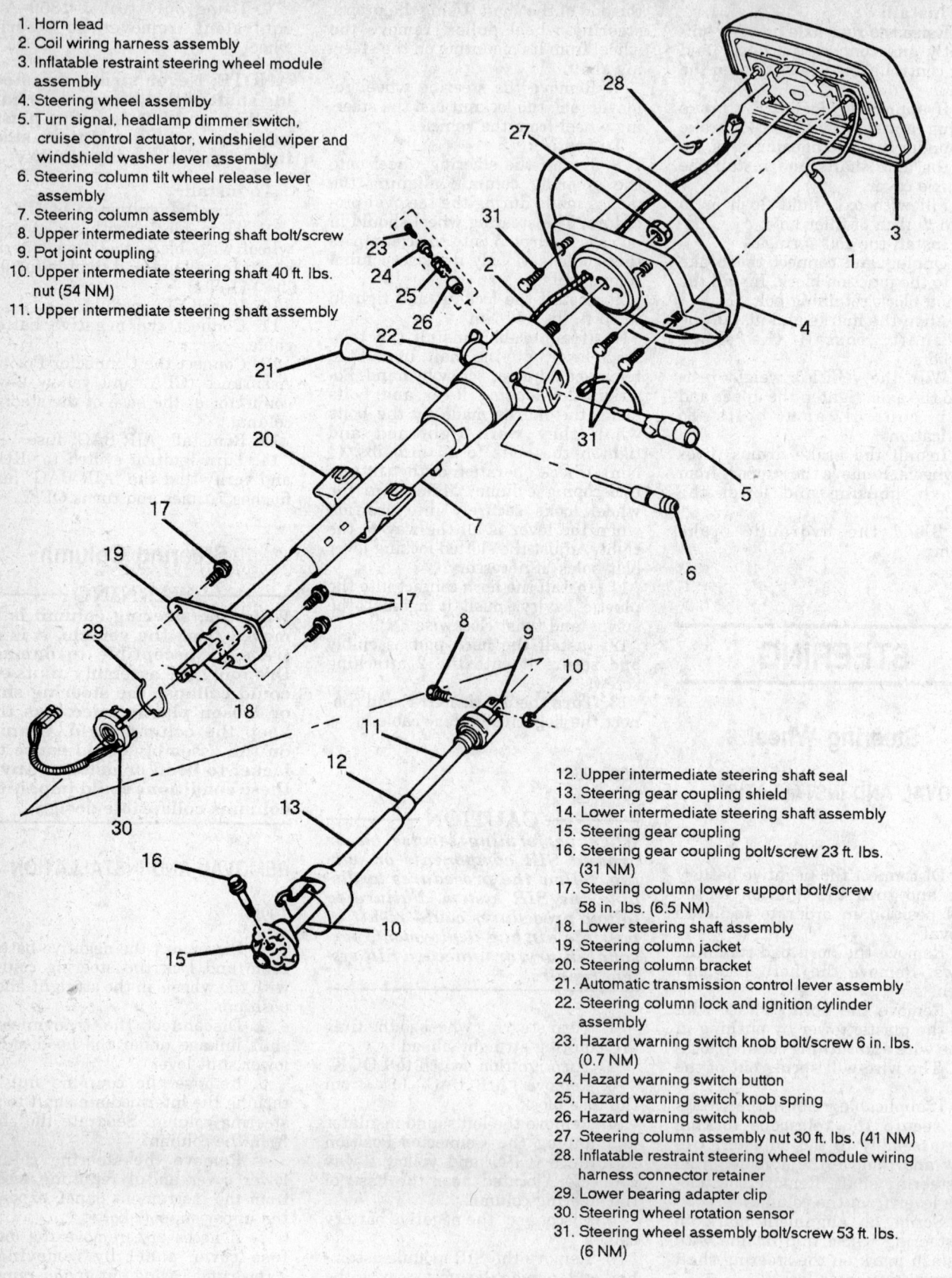

12. Upper intermediate steering shaft seal
13. Steering gear coupling shield
14. Lower intermediate steering shaft assembly
15. Steering gear coupling
16. Steering gear coupling bolt/screw 23 ft. lbs. (31 NM)
17. Steering column lower support bolt/screw 58 in. lbs. (6.5 NM)
18. Lower steering shaft assembly
19. Steering column jacket
20. Steering column bracket
21. Automatic transmission control lever assembly
22. Steering column lock and ignition cylinder assembly
23. Hazard warning switch knob bolt/screw 6 in. lbs. (0.7 NM)
24. Hazard warning switch button
25. Hazard warning switch knob spring
26. Hazard warning switch knob
27. Steering column assembly nut 30 ft. lbs. (41 NM)
28. Inflatable restraint steering wheel module wiring harness connector retainer
29. Lower bearing adapter clip
30. Steering wheel rotation sensor
31. Steering wheel assembly bolt/screw 53 ft. lbs. (6 NM)

84700055

Steering column exploded view

6. Disconnect the turn signal wiring connector. If equipped with cruise control, disconnect the harness.

7. If necessary, disconnect the park neutral switch, the parking brake release hose from the column and/or the headlight dimmer switch connector from the column.

8. Remove the clip securing the shift cable to the shift bowl.

9. Loosen bolts at the steering column upper support. Do not completely remove the upper support nuts or bolts as the steering column could bend under its own weight.

10. Move the carpet out of the way to gain access to the cowl insulator and cowl seal.

11. Remove the cowl insulator and cowl cover seal. Remove the bolts at the upper column bracket while supporting the column.

12. Carefully pull the steering column up and out of the vehicle. If the shaft hangs up in the upper coupling, secure the upper mounting bracket and free the coupling from the steering shaft. Remove the column assembly.

To install:

13. Carefully position the column in the vehicle, taking care not to damage and levers or switches. Install the upper mounting bracket nuts finger-tight.

14. Install the coupling nut securing the steering column to the intermediate shaft, finger-tight. Connect the transmission linkage to the lower shift lever.

15. Attach the clip securing the shift pointer to the shift bowl. Check and adjust alignment, as necessary.

16. Install the steering column cowl seal and finger-tighten.

17. Connect all electrical connections.

18. Tighten the upper column bracket nuts to 20 ft. lbs. (27 Nm), the cowl cover seal nuts and bolts to 35 inch lbs. (4 Nm) and the intermediate shaft coupling bolt to 52 ft. lbs. (71 Nm).

19. Install the cowl seal insulator and reposition the carpeting. If removed, install the left air conditioning outlet duct and the lower fuse cover panel.

20. Install the steering column lower cover.

21. Connect the negative battery cable.

1993–96

NOTE: The wheels of the vehicle must be straight–ahead and the ignition in the LOCK position before disconnecting the steering column assembly or intermediate steering shaft assembly. Failure to do so will cause the SIR coil assembly to become uncentered, which will cause damage to the SIR coil assembly.

1. Turn steering wheel so the tires are pointing straight–ahead.
2. Turn ignition switch to **LOCK**.
3. Remove "AIR BAG" fuse from the fuse block.
4. Remove the left sound insulator and unplug the Connector Position Assurance (CPA) and yellow 2-way connector, located near the base of the steering column.
5. Disconnect the negative battery cable.
6. Remove the SIR module assembly and personal safety, carry the module **face down** to a safe storage spot and place it **facing up**.
7. Remove brake light switch.
8. Remove the instrument panel steering column opening filler.
9. Remove the driver side knee bolster and deflector.
10. Disconnect the steering wheel rotation sensor wire connector.
11. Remove the retaining bolts from the pot joint coupling attaching the the upper intermediate steering shaft assembly to the column assembly.
12. Remove the nuts attaching the steering column bracket to the instrument panel carrier and lower the column assembly.
13. Disconnect the shift indicator cable from the column.
14. Unplug electrical connections at the base of the column.
15. Disconnect the transmission range selector rod assembly from the column.
16. Remove bolts attaching the jacket to the cowl and remove the column assembly from the vehicle.

To install:

17. Place the steering column into the vehicle. If the column is new do not remove the antirotation pin until the assembly is connected to the steering gear. Connect and tighten bolts to 23 ft. lbs. (31 Nm).
18. Connect electrical connections at the base of the column.
19. Connect the shift indicator cable to the column.
20. Attach steering column bracket nuts and tighten to 20 ft. lbs. (27 Nm).
21. Connect upper intermediate shaft to the column and tighten to 40 ft. lbs. (54 Nm).
22. Connect steering wheel rotation sensor connector.
23. Connect transmission range selector rod assembly.

24. Install SIR module.
25. Connect the negative battery cable.
26. Connect the Connector Position Assurance (CPA) and yellow 2-way connector at the base of the steering column.
27. Reinstall "AIR BAG" fuse.
28. Turn ignition switch to **"RUN"** and verify that the "AIR BAG" lamp flashes 7 times and turns OFF.

Power Steering Gear

ADJUSTMENT

NOTE: Adjust the worm bearing preload first, then proceed with the pitman shaft over-center adjustment.

Worm Thrust Bearing Preload

1. Remove the steering gear.
2. Rotate the stub shaft and drain the power steering fluid into a suitable container.
3. Mount the gear in a vise and remove the adjuster plug nut.
4. Turn the adjuster plug in (clockwise) using a suitable spanner wrench until the adjuster plug and thrust bearing are firmly bottomed in the housing. Tighten the adjuster plug to 22 ft. lbs. (30 Nm).
5. Place an index mark on the housing even with 1 of the holes in the adjuster plug.
6. Measure back counterclockwise $\frac{1}{2}$ inch (13mm) from the mark and place a 2nd mark on the housing.
7. Turn the adjuster plug counterclockwise until the hole in the adjuster plug is aligned with the 2nd mark on the housing.
8. Install the adjuster plug nut and using a suitable drift in a notch, tighten securely to 80 ft. lbs. (109 Nm). Hold the adjuster plug to maintain alignment of the marks.
9. Adjust the pitman shaft over-center if necessary. Install the steering gear.

Pitman Shaft Over-center

1. Remove the steering gear.
2. If necessary, adjust the worm bearing preload.
3. Rotate the stub shaft and drain the power steering fluid into a suitable container and loosen the adjuster locknut.
4. Turn the pitman shaft adjuster screw counterclockwise until fully extended, then turn in (clockwise) 1 full turn.

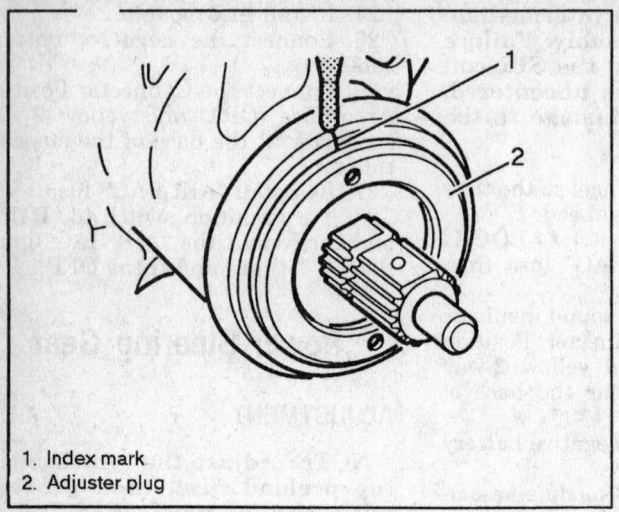

1. Index mark
2. Adjuster plug

Marking Housing Even with Adjuster Plug

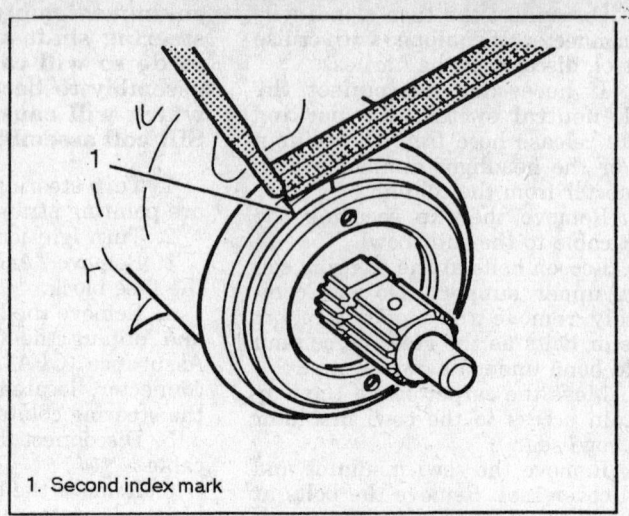

1. Second index mark

Remarking the Housing

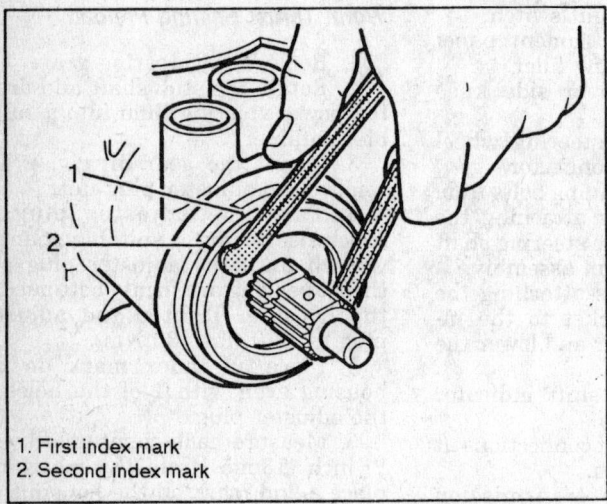

1. First index mark
2. Second index mark

Aligning the Adjuster Plug to the Second Mark

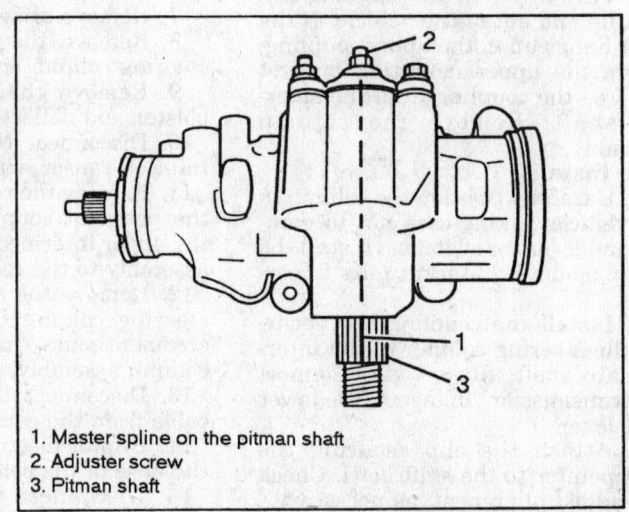

1. Master spline on the pitman shaft
2. Adjuster screw
3. Pitman shaft

Aligning Pitman Shaft Master Spline

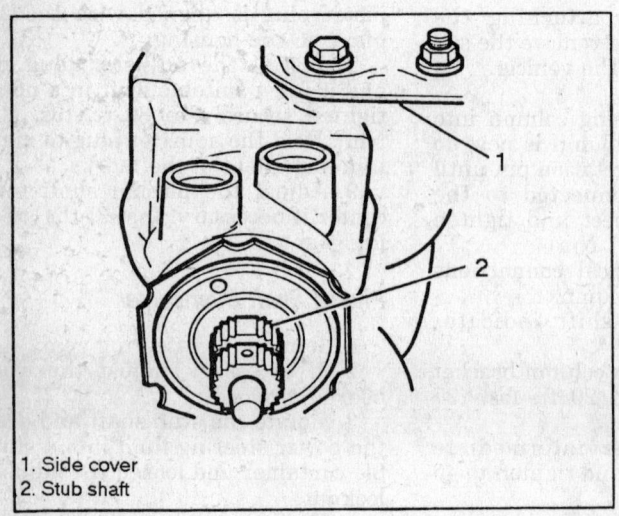

1. Side cover
2. Stub shaft

Aligning the Stub Shaft

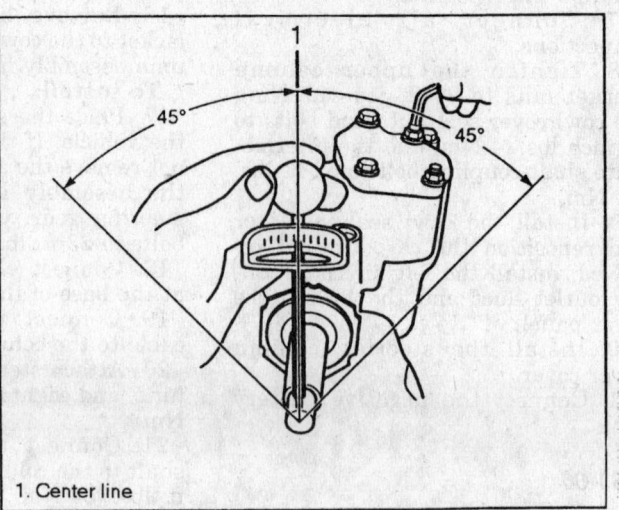

1. Center line

Checking Over-Center Rotational Torque

8470O056

Power steering gear adjustment procedure

5. Rotate the stub shaft from stop-to-stop using a 12-point socket and count the number of turns.

6. Starting at either stop, turn the stub shaft back ½ the total number of turns. This is the "Center" position of the gear. When the gear is centered, the flat on the stub shaft should face upward and be parallel with the side cover and the master spline on the pitman shaft should be in line with the adjuster screw.

7. Rotate the stub shaft 45 degrees each side of the center using a suitable torque wrench with the handle in the vertical position. The stub shaft should move smoothly and not stick or bind. Record the worm bearing preload measured on or near the center gear position, it should be in the 6–5 inch lbs. (0.7–1.7 Nm) range with the worm and ballnut installed. If the torque is outside this range, the gear assembly should be readjusted, repaired or replaced.

8. Adjust the over-center drag torque by turning the pitman shaft adjuster screw clockwise until the correct drag torque is obtained: Add 6–10 inch lbs. (0.7–1.1 Nm) of torque to the previously measured worm bearing preload torque. Tighten the adjuster locknut to 20 ft. lbs. (27 Nm), except for on 1992–93 vehicles which should be tightened 36 ft. lbs. (49 Nm). Prevent the adjuster screw from turning while tightening the adjuster locknut.

9. Install the steering gear.

REMOVAL AND INSTALLATION

1. Position a drain pan under the steering gear.

2. If necessary, remove the air cleaner snorkel.

3. Disconnect the pressure and return lines from the steering gear assembly. Plug the opening to prevent fluid contamination or loss.

4. Remove the pinch bolt from the flex coupling and disconnect the coupling from the gear.

----- **CAUTION** -----
Failure to disconnect the flexible coupling from the steering gear stub shaft may result in damage to the steering gear and or the intermediate shaft. This damage can cause the loss of steering control which could result in a vehicle crash and bodily injuries.
-----

5. Raise the vehicle and support it safely.

6. Remove the pitman arm nut and washer. Remove the pitman arm

from the steering gear using a pitman arm puller tool.

7. If necessary, partially remove the wheelhouse opening and front shield to gain access to the steering gear mounting bolts.

8. Remove the retaining bolts and washers holding the steering gear to the side rail. Lower the gear assembly from the vehicle.

To install:

9. Position the power steering gear to the frame side rail and install the bolts. Tighten the mounting bolts to 70 ft. lbs. (95 Nm). If the mounting threads are stripped, do not attempt repair, the housing must be replaced.

10. Connect the pitman arm to the shaft and install the lockwasher and nut. Tighten the pitman arm nut to 185 ft. lbs. (250 Nm).

11. If removed, install the wheelhouse opening and the front shield.

12. Lower the vehicle.

13. Unplug the pressure and return lines and install them to the steering gear. Tighten the line fittings to 20 ft. lbs. (27 Nm). Be sure the lines do not contact the wheelhousing or the lines may chafe and rupture.

14. Connect the flex coupling to the gear stub shaft, aligning the shaft. Properly seat the pinch bolt and tighten to 30 ft. lbs. (40 Nm).

15. If removed, install the air cleaner snorkel.

16. Fill and bleed the power steering system.

Power Steering Pump

REMOVAL AND INSTALLATION

5.0L (VIN E) and 5.7L Engines

1. Disconnect the negative battery cable and remove the fan assembly.

2. Remove the serpentine drive belt.

3. With a suitable puller, remove the power steering pump pulley.

4. Raise and support the vehicle safely.

5. Remove the pressure and return hoses from the pump and plug the hoses to prevent fluid contamination or loss. Remove the 3 Torx head screws an separate the pump from the bracket.

6. Remove the power steering pump from the vehicle.

To install:

7. Position the power steering pump in the vehicle and install the 3 pump torx head screws.

8. Connect the power steering pressure and return lines and tighten the fittings to 20 ft. lbs. (27 Nm).

9. Lower the vehicle and install the power steering pump pulley.

10. Install the serpentine belt and the fan assembly.

11. Connect the negative battery cable, fill and bleed the power steering system.

BELT ADJUSTMENT

5.0L (VIN E) and 5.7L Engines

The serpentine drive belt is self adjusting within the tensioner operating limits. For a drive belt and tensioner test procedure, refer to the generator belt adjusting section.

SYSTEM BLEEDING

1. Raise and support the vehicle safely.

2. With the wheels turned all the way to the left add power steering fluid to the COLD mark on the dipstick.

3. Start the engine. Check the fluid level. Add fluid as necessary to bring the level to the COLD mark on the dipstick.

4. Bleed the system by turning the steering wheel from side to side without hitting the stops.

5. Be sure to maintain the fluid level at the HOT/COLD mark on the dipstick. Fluid with air in it will have a light tan appearance. This air must be expelled from the system before normal steering action can be obtained.

6. Return the wheels to the center position. Allow the engine to run for several minutes and then turn the engine OFF.

7. Road test the vehicle and make sure the steering performs properly and there is no noise from the power steering pump.

8. Recheck the power steering fluid. Be sure the fluid level is at the HOT mark on the dipstick after the system has stabilized at its normal operating temperature.

Tie Rod Ends

REMOVAL AND INSTALLATION

1. Raise and support the vehicle safely.

2. Remove the cotter pin and castellated nut from the outer tie rod end.

3. Using the proper tool disconnect the tie rod end from the steering knuckle.

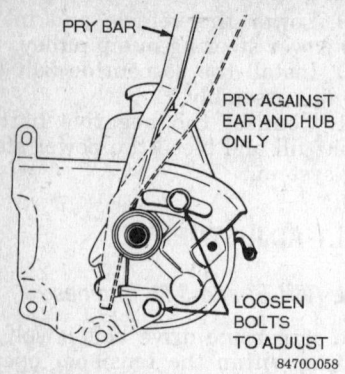

PRY BAR

PRY AGAINST
EAR AND HUB
ONLY

LOOSEN
BOLTS
TO ADJUST

84700058

Adjusting power steering belt

4. Using the proper tool remove the inner ball stud from the intermediate rod.

NOTE: When disconnecting a linkage joint no attempt should be made to disengage the joint by driving a wedge between the joint and the retained part as seal damage may result.

5. Remove the tie rod adjuster clamp bolts. Discard the nuts and bolts if the torque necessary to remove them after breakaway exceeds 80 inch lbs. (9 Nm).

6. Unscrew the tie rod end assemblies from the adjuster tube. Count the number of turns necessary to remove the tie rod from the adjuster tube to assure reassembly in the same position.

To install:

7. Lubricate the tie rod threads with chassis lube and install into the adjuster tube. Thread the tie rod ends into the adjuster tube with an equal number of turns as was necessary to remove them.

8. Be sure the threads on the ball studs and nuts are clean and free from damage. There should be no nicks on the ball stud tapers and the seals should be free of damage. Install the ball studs into the steering knuckle and the intermediate rod.

9. Install the ball stud nuts and tighten to 35 ft. lbs. (48 Nm). If necessary continue to tighten the nut just enough to align a slot in the castellated nut with a hole in the stud. Install new cotter pins.

10. Make sure the tie rod ends are in alignment with their ball studs and the adjuster clamps are properly positioned. The clamps must be between and clear of the dimples, with the bolts underneath the adjuster rod. Tighten the adjuster tube clamp bolts to 14 ft. lbs. (19 Nm).

11. Lower the vehicle, check and adjust front end alignment, as required.

BRAKES

Master Cylinder

REMOVAL AND INSTALLATION

1. Place a container under the master cylinder to catch any brake fluid leakage.

2. Disconnect the brake lines at the master cylinder. Plug the lines to prevent fluid contamination or loss.

3. Remove the nuts securing the master cylinder to the power booster.

4. Remove the master cylinder from the vehicle.

To install:

5. Position the master cylinder in the vehicle and install the attaching nuts. Tighten the nuts to 28 ft. lbs. (38 Nm).

6. Begin filling the forward chamber of the reservoir and when brake fluid appears at the outlet, unplug and connect the appropriate brake line. Repeat for the rear chamber, unplug and connect the other brake line.

7. Tighten the brake line fittings to 12 ft. lbs. (17 Nm).

8. Remove the drain pan and bleed the hydraulic brake system, as required.

Combination Valve

REMOVAL AND INSTALLATION

1. Disconnect the negative battery cable. Disconnect the electrical connector from the valve assembly.

2. Disconnect plug the brake lines at the valve. Plug the lines to prevent fluid contamination or loss.

3. Remove the valve retaining bolt(s) and remove the valve from its mounting.

4. Installation is the reverse of the removal procedure. Be sure to properly bleed the hydraulic brake system.

Power Brake Booster

REMOVAL AND INSTALLATION

1. Remove the master cylinder retaining nuts and position the assembly aside.

2. Disconnect the vacuum line from the vacuum check valve.

3. If necessary, remove the steering column lower cover inside the vehicle to access the brake pedal and the booster attaching nuts.

4. Disconnect the power booster pushrod from the brake pedal arm.

5. Remove the nuts that secure the power unit to the firewall and remove the power booster unit.

To install:

6. Position the booster to the firewall and install the attaching nuts. Tighten the nuts to 20 ft. lbs. (27 Nm).

7. Connect the power booster pushrod to the brake pedal.

8. Install the steering column lower cover, if removed.

9. Connect the vacuum line to the booster check valve.

10. Reposition the master cylinder onto the booster mounting studs and tighten the nuts to 20 ft. lbs. (27 Nm).

Brake Caliper

REMOVAL AND INSTALLATION

1. Drain ⅔ of the brake fluid from the master cylinder assembly.

2. Raise and support the vehicle safely.

3. Position a C-clamp over the inboard brake shoe tab and and the inboard caliper housing, carefully compress the piston assembly back into the caliper housing.

4. Disconnect the brake line hose at the caliper and plug the line to prevent fluid loss or contamination.

5. Remove the caliper mounting bolt and sleeves the remove the caliper assembly from its mounting bracket.

To install:

6. Lubricate the sleeves and bushings with silicone grease and install the sleeves into the caliper ears. Position the caliper over the rotor in the mounting bracket.

7. Install the mounting bolts and tighten to 38 ft. lbs. (51 Nm). Be sure there is 0.005–0.012 in. (0.13–0.30mm) of clearance between the top and bottom of the caliper and the bracket stops. If necessary, remove the caliper and file the end of the bracket stops.

8. Unplug and install the brake line hose to the caliper. Tighten the fitting to 33 ft. lbs. (45 Nm).

9. Lower the vehicle and fill the master cylinder to the proper level with clean brake fluid and bleed the hydraulic brake system.

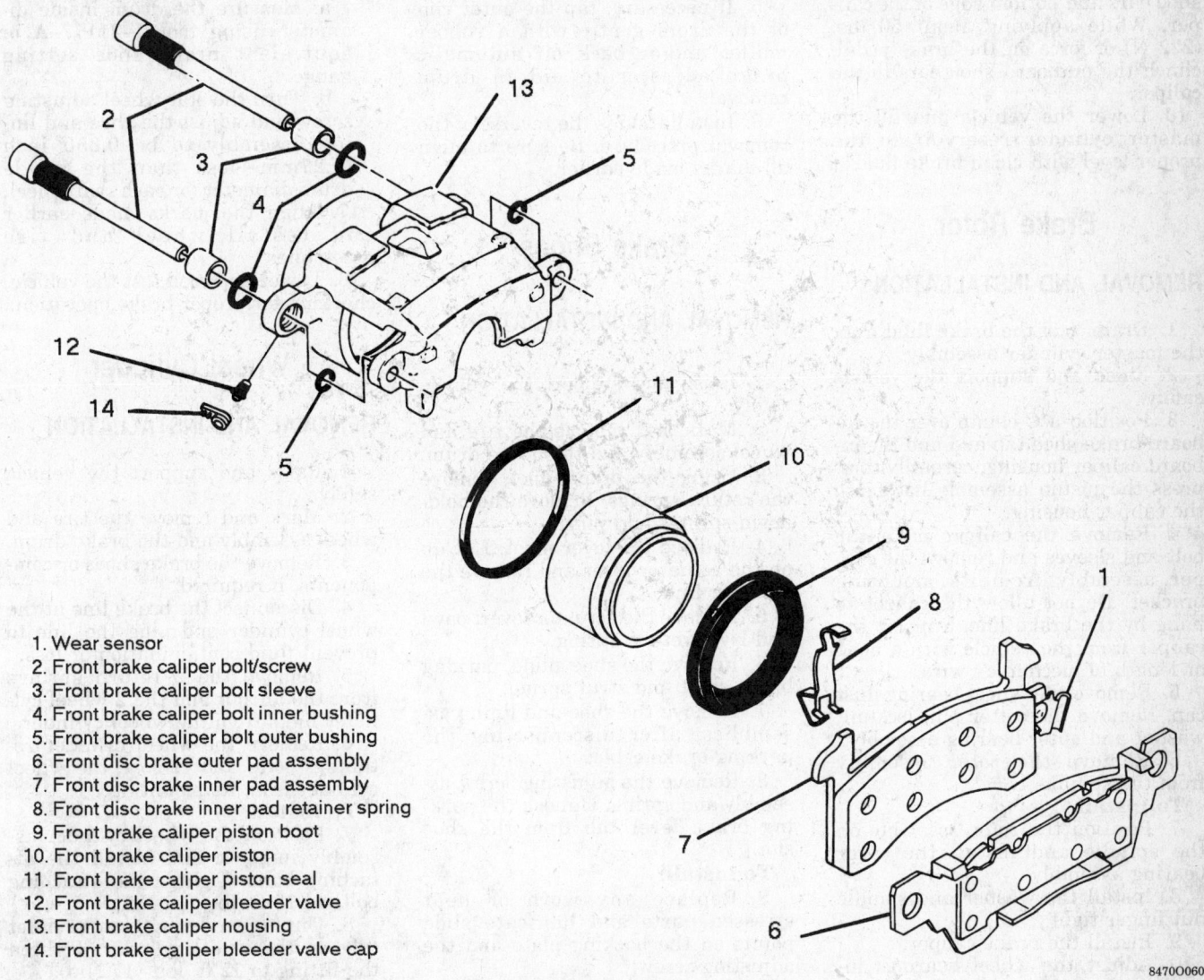

1. Wear sensor
2. Front brake caliper bolt/screw
3. Front brake caliper bolt sleeve
4. Front brake caliper bolt inner bushing
5. Front brake caliper bolt outer bushing
6. Front disc brake outer pad assembly
7. Front disc brake inner pad assembly
8. Front disc brake inner pad retainer spring
9. Front brake caliper piston boot
10. Front brake caliper piston
11. Front brake caliper piston seal
12. Front brake caliper bleeder valve
13. Front brake caliper housing
14. Front brake caliper bleeder valve cap

Front caliper assembly

84700060

Disc Brake Pads

REMOVAL AND INSTALLATION

1. Drain ⅔ of the brake fluid from the master cylinder assembly.

2. Raise and support the vehicle safely.

3. Position a C-clamp over the inboard brake shoe tab and and the inboard caliper housing, carefully compress the piston assembly back into the caliper housing.

4. Remove the caliper mounting bolt and sleeves the remove the caliper assembly from its mounting bracket. Do not allow the caliper to

hang by the brake line. Support the caliper from the vehicle with a hook or length of mechanic's wire.

5. Remove the outboard shoe and lining then remove the inboard shoe and lining.

6. Remove the bushings from the grooves in the mounting bolt holes.

To install:

7. Using silicone grease lubricate and install the new bushings into the grooves in the mounting bolt holes.

8. Lubricate and install the sleeves and into the mounting bolt holes.

9. Install the retainer spring to the inboard shoe and lining assembly. Install the shoe by snapping into

place on the piston with the wear sensor at the leading edge of the shoe during forward wheel rotation.

10. Install the outboard shoe and lining with the back of the shoe flat against the caliper and position the caliper over the rotor in the mounting bracket.

11. Install the mounting bolts and tighten to 38 ft. lbs. (51 Nm). Be sure there is 0.005–0.012 in. (0.13–0.30mm) of clearance between the top and bottom of the caliper and the bracket stops. If necessary, remove the caliper and file the end of the bracket stops.

12. Apply about 175 lbs. (778 N) of force to the brake pedal 3 times to

seat the linings. Position a pair of channel lock pliers over the brake shoe ears and bottom edge of the caliper. While applying about 50 lbs. (222 N) of force on the brake pedal, clinch the outboard shoe ears to the caliper.

13. Lower the vehicle and fill the master cylinder reservoir to the proper level with clean brake fluid.

Brake Rotor

REMOVAL AND INSTALLATION

1. Drain ⅔ of the brake fluid from the master cylinder assembly.
2. Raise and support the vehicle safely.
3. Position a C-clamp over the inboard brake shoe tab and and the inboard caliper housing, carefully compress the piston assembly back into the caliper housing.
4. Remove the caliper mounting bolt and sleeves and remove the caliper assembly from its mounting bracket. Do not allow the caliper to hang by the brake line. Support the caliper from the vehicle with a hook or length of mechanic's wire.
5. Remove the wheel bearing dust cap. Remove the cotter pin, locknut, washer and outer bearing assembly.
6. Remove the rotor assembly from the spindle.
To install:
7. Position the rotor assembly on the spindle and install the outer bearing assembly.
8. Install the washer and spindle nut finger-tight.
9. Install the brake caliper.
10. Adjust the wheel bearings install a new cotter pin and the dust cap.
11. Install the wheel cover, lower the vehicle and fill the master cylinder with to the proper level with clean brake fluid. Do not attempt to move the vehicle until the shoe linings are properly seated.

Brake Drums

REMOVAL AND INSTALLATION

1. Raise and support the vehicle safely.
2. Mark the relationship of the wheel to the axle flange for reinstallation and remove the tire and wheel assembly.
3. Mark the relationship of the drum to the axle flange for reinstallation.

4. Ensure parking brake is released and remove the drum.
5. If necessary, tap the outer rim of the drum gently with a rubber mallet and/or back off automatic brake adjuster to aid in drum removal.
6. Installation is the reverse of removal procedure. Be sure to align all marks made earlier.

Brake Shoes

REMOVAL AND INSTALLATION

1. Raise and support the vehicle safely.
2. Mark and remove the tire and wheel assembly and the brake drum.
3. Using the proper tool, remove the return springs. Remove the hold-down springs and pins.
4. Remove the lever pivot. Lift up on the actuator lever and remove the actuator link.
5. Remove the actuator lever, pawl and lever return spring.
6. Remove the shoe guide, parking brake strut and strut spring.
7. Remove the shoe and lining assemblies, after disconnecting the parking brake cable.
8. Remove the adjusting screw assembly and spring. Unhook the parking brake lever tab from the shoe slot.
To install:
9. Replace any worn or heat stressed parts and lubricate slide points on the backing plate and the adjusting screw.
10. Install the parking brake lever tab into the shoe slot and install the adjusting screw assembly and spring.
11. Attach the parking brake cable and install the shoe and lining assemblies.
12. Spread the shoes sufficiently to install the parking brake strut and strut spring. The end of the strut without the spring engages the parking brake lever and shoe. The end with the spring engages the opposite shoe and lining.
13. Install the shoe guide, the pawl, the actuator lever and the lever return spring.
14. Install the shoe hold-down pins, the lever pivot and the hold-down springs.
15. Install the actuator link on the anchor pin, then hold the actuator lever up and install the link into the lever.

16. Install the shoe return springs and adjust brake shoes as follows:
   a. Measure the drum inside diameter using tool J-21177–A or equivalent brake shoe setting gauge.
   b. Turn the star wheel adjusting screw and adjust the shoe and lining assembly to be 0.050 inch (1.27mm) less than the inside drum diameter for each rear wheel.
17. Align the marks made earlier and install wheel and tire assemblies.
18. Lower and road test the vehicle, checking for proper brake operation.

Wheel Cylinder

REMOVAL AND INSTALLATION

1. Raise and support the vehicle safely.
2. Mark and remove the tire and wheel assembly and the brake drum.
3. Remove the brake shoes or components, if required.
4. Disconnect the brake line at the wheel cylinder and plug the line to prevent fluid contamination or loss.
5. Remove the 2 return springs from the anchor and the 2 wheel cylinder links from the wheel cylinder.
6. Remove the wheel cylinder retaining bolts and remove the wheel cylinder from its mounting.
To install:
7. Position the wheel cylinder assembly in place and install the attaching bolts. Tighten the attaching bolts to 13 ft. lbs. (18 Nm).
8. Unplug and connect the inlet tube to the wheel cylinder. Tighten the fitting to 12 ft. lbs. (17 Nm).
9. Install the brake shoes or components, if removed.
10. Align the marks made earlier and install the brake drum and the wheel and tire assembly.
11. Bleed the wheel cylinder and lower the vehicle.

Parking Brake Cable

ADJUSTMENT

1. Be sure the rear brakes are properly adjusted before adjusting the parking brake. Check the parking brake linkage for the free movement of all the cables. Lubricate or replace, as necessary.
2. Depress the parking brake pedal ¼ stroke or 3 ratchet clicks.
3. Raise and support the vehicle safely.

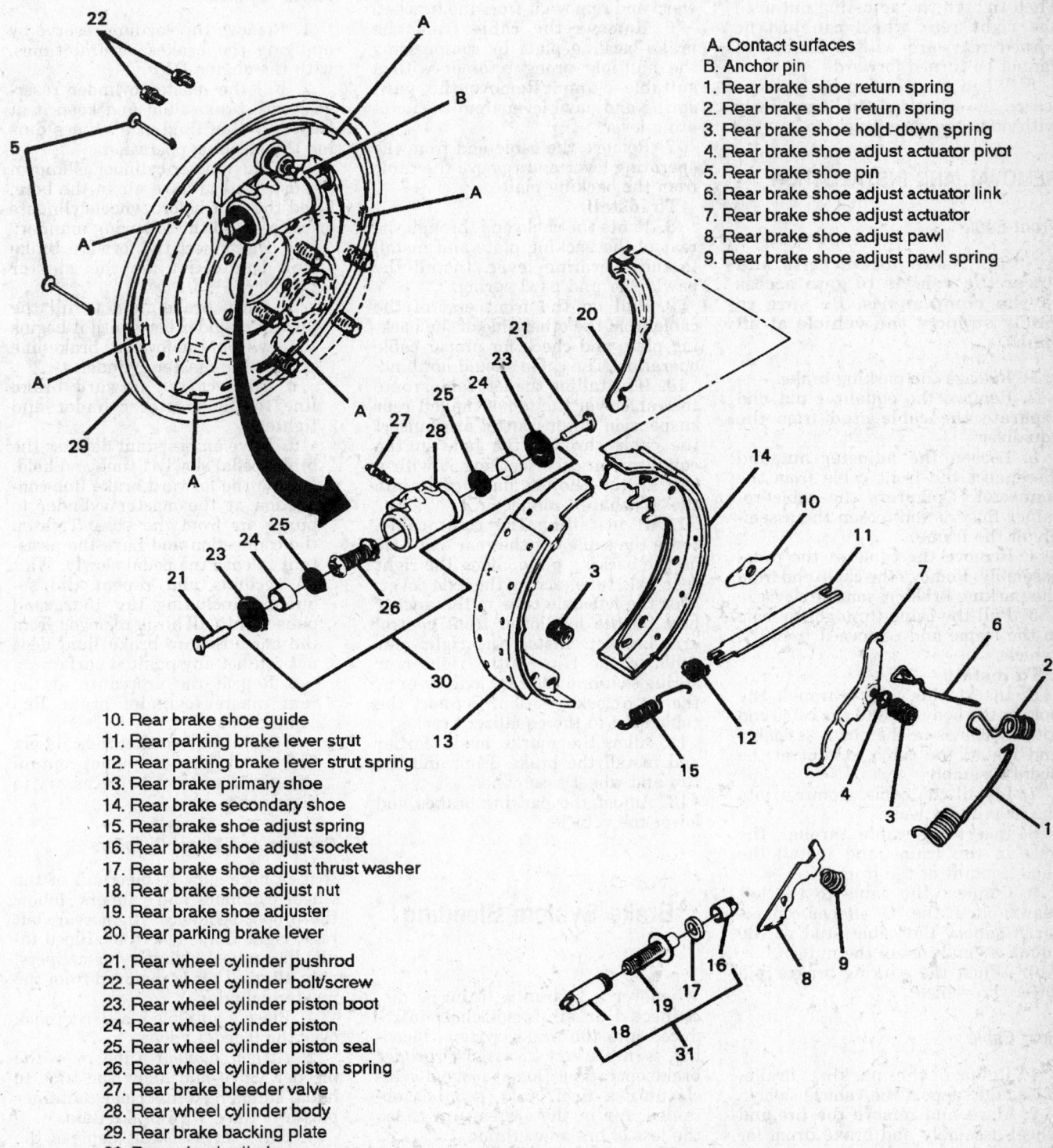

A. Contact surfaces
B. Anchor pin
1. Rear brake shoe return spring
2. Rear brake shoe return spring
3. Rear brake shoe hold-down spring
4. Rear brake shoe adjust actuator pivot
5. Rear brake shoe pin
6. Rear brake shoe adjust actuator link
7. Rear brake shoe adjust actuator
8. Rear brake shoe adjust pawl
9. Rear brake shoe adjust pawl spring

10. Rear brake shoe guide
11. Rear parking brake lever strut
12. Rear parking brake lever strut spring
13. Rear brake primary shoe
14. Rear brake secondary shoe
15. Rear brake shoe adjust spring
16. Rear brake shoe adjust socket
17. Rear brake shoe adjust thrust washer
18. Rear brake shoe adjust nut
19. Rear brake shoe adjuster
20. Rear parking brake lever

21. Rear wheel cylinder pushrod
22. Rear wheel cylinder bolt/screw
23. Rear wheel cylinder piston boot
24. Rear wheel cylinder piston
25. Rear wheel cylinder piston seal
26. Rear wheel cylinder piston spring
27. Rear brake bleeder valve
28. Rear wheel cylinder body
29. Rear brake backing plate
30. Rear wheel cylinder
31. Rear brake shoe adjuster assembly

84700061

Rear brake drum assembly

4. Before attempting to turn the adjusting nut, clean and lubricate the exposed threads of the adjusting rod. Then tighten the adjusting nut until the right rear wheel can just be turned rearward with 2 hands but cannot be turned forward.

5. When the parking brake is released the wheels should turn freely with no brake shoe drag.

REMOVAL AND INSTALLATION

Front Cable

NOTE: As required, raise and lower the vehicle to gain access to the components. Be sure to safely support the vehicle at all times.

1. Release the parking brake.
2. Remove the equalizer nut and separate the cable stud from the equalizer.
3. Loosen the adjuster nut and disconnect the front cable from the connector. Compress the cable retainer fingers and loosen the assembly at the frame.
4. Remove the cable at the pedal assembly. Remove the cable end from the parking brake assembly clevis.
5. Pull the cable through the hole in the frame and remove it from the vehicle.

To install:
6. Insert the cable through the hole in the body. Install the cable end into the clevis in the pedal assembly and install the cable conduit at the pedal assembly.
7. Install the cable grommet into the hole in the body.
8. Insert the cable through the hole in the frame and install the cable conduit at the frame.
9. Connect the cable to the left rear cable at the "C" shaped connector. Connect the cable stud at the equalizer and install the nut.
10. Adjust the parking brakes and lower the vehicle.

Rear Cable

1. Release the parking brake, raise and support the vehicle safely.
2. Mark and remove the tire and wheel assembly and brake drum for the cable being replaced.
3. Remove the equalizer nut and the retainer. If applicable, separate the equalizer from the right rear cable stud.
4. If applicable, remove the end of the left rear cable from the cable connector and equalizer.

5. If removing the right rear cable, remove the clip retaining the cable to the axle housing. Pull the cable rearward and remove it from the bracket.
6. Remove the cable from the brake backing plate by compressing the multiple prong retainer with a suitable clamp. Remove the pawl spring and pawl lever from the actuating lever.
7. Remove the cable end from the operating lever and remove the cable from the backing plate.

To install:
8. Route the cable end through the rear of the backing plate and install to the operating lever. Install the pawl lever and pawl spring.
9. Pull on the front end of the cable from the other side of the backing plate and check for proper cable operation. The cable should not bind.
10. If installing the left cable, route the cable over the top of the left rear suspension lower control arm, insert the cable through the hole in the equalizer bracket securing it with a clip. Install the left hand cable into the "C" shaped connector.
11. If installing the right cable, route the cable out the rear exit hole on the backing plate, along the right rear axle tube, across the axle cover, over the left axle tube to the anchor hole on the left lower front control arm bracket. Install the right rear cable in the clip on the right rear spring seat and the rear axle cover at the 12 o'clock position. Connect the cable stud to the equalizer bracket.
12. Align the marks made earlier and install the brake drum and the tire and wheel assemblies.
13. Adjust the parking brakes and lower the vehicle.

Brake System Bleeding

Whenever a hydraulic fitting is disconnected or air is somehow introduced into the brake system, bleeding is necessary to assure proper brake operation. Do not move a vehicle until a firm brake pedal is obtained. Air in the system can cause the loss of brake operation.

If air is introduced into the system at the master cylinder, it may be necessary to bleed the entire system. If the disconnection of a fitting or pipe is the cause for air presence in the system, then only the wheel cylinder(s) or caliper(s) served by that component need to be bled.

BLEEDING

Master Cylinder

1. Remove the vacuum reserve by applying the brakes several times, with the engine OFF.
2. Fill the master cylinder reservoir with brake fluid and keep it at least ½ full of fluid at all times during the bleeding operation.
3. If the master cylinder is known or suspected to have air in the bore, bleed the unit before wheel cylinders or calipers, in the following manner:
   a. Disconnect the forward brake line connection at the master cylinder.
   b. Allow brake fluid to fill the master cylinder bore until it begins to flow from the forward brake line port at the master cylinder.
   c. Connect the forward brake line to the master cylinder and tighten.
   d. Have an assistant depress the brake pedal slowly 1 time and hold. Loosen the forward brake line connection at the master cylinder to purge air from the bore. Tighten the connection and have the assistant release the pedal slowly. Wait 15 seconds and repeat the sequence, including the 15 second pause, until all air is removed from the bore. Ensure brake fluid does not contact any painted surface.
   e. Repeat the procedure at the rear master cylinder brake line connection.
   f. If it is known that the calipers and wheel cylinders do not contain any air, it will not be necessary to bleed them.

Calipers and Wheel Cylinders

If it is necessary to bleed all of the wheel cylinders and calipers, follow the proper sequence: Right rear, left rear, right front, left front. Bleed individual wheel cylinders or calipers, only after all air is removed from the master cylinder.

1. Place a suitable bleeder wrench over the bleeder valve.
2. Attach a clear tube over the bleeder valve and allow the tube to hang, submerged in a clear container partially filled with brake fluid.
3. Have an assistant depress the brake pedal slowly 1 time and hold. Loosen the bleeder valve to purge the air from the cylinder. Tighten the bleeder screw and have the assistant slowly release the pedal. Wait 15 seconds and repeat the sequence, including the 15 second pause, until all air is removed.

4. If necessary, repeat the sequence to remove all of the air.

NOTE: Rapid pumping of the brake pedal pushes the master cylinder secondary piston down the bore in a way that makes it difficult to bleed the rear side of the system.

5. Check for a spongy brake pedal and the red brake warning light for an indication of unbalanced pressure. Repeat the bleeding procedure to correct either of these conditions.

Anti-Lock Brake System Service

SERVICE PRECAUTIONS

Failure to observe the following precautions may result in system damage or failure which could result in bodily injury.

• Before performing electric arc welding on the vehicle, disconnect the Electronic Brake Control Module (EBCM) and the hydraulic modulator connectors.

• When performing painting work on the vehicle, do not expose the Electronic Brake Control Module (EBCM) to temperatures in excess of 185°F (85°C) for longer than 2 hours. The system may be exposed to temperatures up to 200°F (95°C) for less than 15 minutes.

• Never disconnect or connect the Electronic Brake Control Module (EBCM) or hydraulic modulator connectors with the ignition switch **ON**.

• Never disassemble any component of the Anti-Lock Brake System (ABS) which is designated non-servicable; the component must be replaced as an assembly.

• When filling the master cylinder, always use Delco Supreme 11 brake fluid or equivalent, which meets DOT-3 specifications; petroleum base fluid will destroy the rubber parts.

RELIEVING ANTI-LOCK BRAKE SYSTEM PRESSURE

When servicing and bleeding ABS components, follow normal manual or pressure bleeding procedures. Although the ABS system has the ability to increase, decrease or hold brake line pressure, the hydraulic modulator cannot increase the pressure above that which is transmitted by the master cylinder. Special service procedures for bleeding the brake system with a hydraulic modulator are not required.

BLEEDING

The hydraulic modulator valve assembly should be bled if the master cylinder reservoir fluid was low during traction control mode or valve assembly replacement. The hydraulic modulator valve assembly must be manually bled using gravity feed.

1. Fill the master cylinder reservoir with brake fluid and keep it at least $1/2$ full during bleeding operation.
2. Attach flex hose to the bleeder screw and submerge the other end in a clear container partially filled with brake fluid.
3. Open the bleeder screw and allow it to gravity bleed until all the air is purged from the system.
4. When bubbles no longer appear, close bleeder screw and remove flex hose.
5. Top off the master cylinder reservoir with fluid.

Hydraulic Modulator

REMOVAL AND INSTALLATION

1. Disconnect the negative battery cable.
2. Remove the left front radiator brace and the air cleaner intake hose.
3. Remove the ABS modulator relay cover. Disconnect the modulator 12-pin connector and ground strap.
4. Disconnect all brake line connections at the modulator assembly and plug the lines to prevent fluid contamination and loss.
5. Remove the modulator mounting nuts and remove the modulator assembly from the bracket.
6. Remove the insulators from the modulator.
   To install:
7. Install the insulators onto the modulator and position the modulator in the mounting bracket. Secure the modulator with the nuts and tighten to 8 ft. lbs. (11 Nm).
8. Unplug and connect all brake lines to the modulator. Tighten the fittings to 9 ft. lbs. (12 Nm).
9. Connect the modulator connector and ground strap. Install the ABS relay cover.
10. Install the air cleaner intake hose and the left front radiator brace.
11. Connect the negative battery cable and bleed the brake system.

Electronic Brake Control Module

REMOVAL AND INSTALLATION

1. Disconnect the negative battery cable.
2. Remove the passenger side close-out panel and remove the glove box liner.
3. Disconnect the EBCM wire harness connector and remove the EBCM from its retaining bracket.
4. Installation is the reverse of the removal procedure.

Front Wheel Speed Sensor

The speed sensor is non-adjustable, with the sensor gap set at the factory. It is mounted in the steering knuckle and a connector is located underhood near the fenderwell.

REMOVAL AND INSTALLATION

1. Disconnect the negative battery cable.
2. Disconnect the sensor connector from under the hood near the fenderwell.
3. Raise and support the vehicle safely.
4. Remove the sensor cable from the retainers.
5. Remove the sensor mounting bolt and remove the sensor from the vehicle.
   To install:
6. Route the sensor cable and install in the retainers.

NOTE: Proper installation of the wheel speed sensor cables is critical to proper operation of the ABS system. Be sure the cables are installed in the retainers. Failure to do this may result in contact with moving parts and/or the over extension of the cables, resulting in an open circuit and system failure.

7. Coat the sensor body, where it contacts the knuckle with anti-corrosion compound GM part 1052856 or equivalent and position the sensor in the knuckle. Install the retaining bolt and tighten to 9 ft. lbs. (12 Nm).
8. Lower the vehicle and connect the underhood speed sensor connector.
9. Connect the negative battery cable.

Rear Axle Speed Sensor

The rear axle speed sensor is located in the axle carrier housing. It is connected to the EBCM via a jumper harness which runs from the sensor connector to the ABS harness, under the hood, near the left fenderwell. It is non-adjustable and set at the factory.

REMOVAL AND INSTALLATION

1. Disconnect the negative battery cable. Raise and support the vehicle safely.
2. Disconnect the sensor connector and remove the sensor cable from the retainer brackets.
3. Remove the sensor mounting bolt. Remove the sensor, plastic spacer and the O-ring from the vehicle.

To install:

4. Position the O-ring, plastic spacer and the sensor in the rear axle carrier housing and install the mounting bolt. Tighten the bolt to 9 ft. lbs. (12 Nm).
5. Install the rear speed sensor cable in the retainers.

NOTE: Proper installation of the wheel speed sensor cable is critical to proper operation of the ABS system. Be sure the cables are installed in the retainers. Failure to do this may result in contact with moving parts and/or the over extension of the cable, resulting in an open circuit.

6. Connect the wheel speed sensor connector and lower the vehicle.
7. Connect the negative battery cable.

FRONT SUSPENSION

Shock Absorbers

REMOVAL AND INSTALLATION

1. Remove the top shock absorber retaining nut using a suitable socket.
2. Raise and support the vehicle safely.

NOTE: Throughout this procedure raise or lower the vehicle, as necessary to reach the components. Always support the vehicle safely.

3. Remove the 2 bottom shock absorber bolts attaching the shock absorber to the lower control arm.
4. Lower the shock absorber through the bottom of the control arm and remove the shock from the vehicle.

To install:

5. Install the retainer and grommet onto the shock and fully extend the shock absorber rod. Insert the shock up into the coil spring and guide the stem through the frame.
6. Install the grommet and retainer over the stem on top of the frame and secure with the nut. Tighten the nut to 97 inch lbs. (11 Nm). Using a suitable socket and a box wrench, tighten the nut to end of the threads, approximately 1–1/8 inch when measured from the top of the nut to the top of the shock absorber mounting stud. Do not overtighten, the rubber grommets should not mushroom out past the washers.
7. Position the lower shock absorber mount to the lower control arm and secure with the 2 bolts. Tighten the bolts to 20 ft. lbs. (27 Nm).
8. Lower the vehicle.

Coil Springs

REMOVAL AND INSTALLATION

1992

1. Raise and support the vehicle safely. Be sure the vehicle is supported so the lower control arms will hang free.
2. Remove the lower shock absorber retaining bolts and push the shock absorber up through the control arm and into the spring.
3. Secure tool J–23028–01 or equivalent lower control arm compressor, to a suitable jack. Position the tool to cradle the lower control arm inner bushings.
4. Remove the stabilizer to lower control arm attachment.
5. Raise the jack to relieve tension on the lower control arm pivot bolts. Install a safety chain around the spring and through the lower control arm as a safety precaution.
6. Remove the lower control arm rear pivot bolt first, then remove the lower control arm front pivot bolt.
7. Lower the control arm assembly from its mounting slowly. When all compression is removed from the spring, remove the spring and the safety chain.

To install:

8. Properly position the spring into the frame and lift the control arm with the tool and jack.

NOTE: The lower end of the coil must cover all or part of one inspection hole in the lower control arm. The 2nd hole must be partly or completely uncovered. Position the lower control arm into the frame and install the pivot bolts and nuts. Tighten the nuts to 92 ft. lbs. (125 Nm). The rear bolt head may be tightened instead of the nut to 114 ft. lbs. (155 Nm).

9. Install the stabilizer shaft link and tighten the nut to 13 ft. lbs. (17 Nm).
10. Install the lower shock absorber and tighten the bolts to 20 ft. lbs. (27 Nm).
11. Lower the vehicle, check and adjust the alignment, as necessary.

1993–96

1. Raise and support vehicle . Remove tire and wheel assembly.
2. Disconnect and secure front wheel sensors.
3. Remove the shock absorber and stabilizer links from the lower control arm.
4. Disconnect outer tie rod end.
5. Install spring compressor according to the directions for the particular tool and compress the spring.
6. Remove the 2 lower control arm bolts and swing the arm rearward.
7. With caution, remove compressed spring.

To install:

8. Position the spring on the lower control arm, making sure the spring insulator is in place.
9. Install spring compressor on the spring and compress . Do not compress to an overall size of 9½ inches (244 Nm) or less.
10. Pivot the lower control arm into position. Install the bolts connecting it to the frame and torque to 92 ft. lbs. (125 Nm).
11. Remove the spring compressor.
12. Connect outer tie rod end .
13. Connect stabilizer link and shock absorber to the control arm.
14. Install tire and wheel assembly and lower vehicle.

Upper Ball Joints

INSPECTION

1. Raise and support the vehicle safely using jack stands positioned

under the lower control arms as near as possible to each lower ball joint. The vehicle must not rock on the stands and the upper control arm bumpers must not contact the frame.

2. Position a dial indicator gauge against the wheel rim.

3. Grasp the front wheel and push in on the bottom of the tire while pulling out at the top, read and record the gauge.

4. Reverse the push pull procedure, read and record the gauge.

5. Horizontal deflection should not exceed 0.125 inch (3.18mm). If the horizontal deflection exceeds the specification, or if the ball joint has been disconnected from the knuckle assembly and looseness is detected or the stud can be twisted in the socket, ball joint replacement is necessary.

REMOVAL AND INSTALLATION

1. Raise and support the vehicle safely, making sure to support the lower control arm on the side which is being worked upon.

2. Mark and remove the tire and wheel assembly.

3. Remove the caliper and properly support it so the brake hose is not damaged.

4. Remove the cotter pin from the ball joint and loosen the locknut not more than 1 turn, do not remove it.

5. Using the proper ball joint separating tool, separate the ball joint stud from the steering knuckle and remove the locknut.

6. Lift the upper control arm upward and position a block of wood between the frame and the upper arm to act as a support.

7. Grind off the heads of the rivets retaining the ball joint in place and drive them out with a suitable punch.

8. Remove the ball joint from its mounting.

To install:

9. Install the new ball joint using the nut and bolt assemblies provided. Insert the bolts from the bottom with the nuts on top and tighten the nuts to 20 ft. lbs. (27 Nm).

10. Turn the ball joint stud fore and aft, remove the block of wood

11. Clean the tapered hole in the steering knuckle, if any damage or deformation is noted, the steering knuckle must be replaced.

12. Install the ball joint stud into the steering knuckle and install the castellated nut. Tighten the nut to 61 ft. lbs. (83 Nm). If necessary, tighten the nut just enough additionally to install a cotter pin. Install a new cotter pin.

13. Install the caliper assembly and lubricate the ball joint.

14. Align the marks made earlier and install the tire and wheel assembly.

15. Remove the supports and lower the vehicle.

16. Check and adjust the front end alignment, as necessary.

Lower Ball Joints

INSPECTION

The vehicle must be supported by the wheel so the weight of the vehicle will properly load the ball joints. The lower ball joint is checked for wear by visual inspection. Wear is indicated by protrusion of the ½ inch (12.7mm) diameter nipple into which the grease fitting is threaded. The round nipple projects 0.050 inch (1.27mm) beyond the surface of the ball joint cover on a new ball joint. Normal wear will result in the surface of this nipple retreating slowly inward. The stud of a worn joint will be flush with or below the cover.

Stud tightness in the knuckle can be checked by shaking the wheel. Inspect for movement at the stud end and/or the check nut torque at the knuckle boss. Looseness may indicate a bent stud or damaged hole in the knuckle. Replace all worn or damaged parts.

REMOVAL AND INSTALLATION

1. Raise and support the vehicle safely, make sure to support the lower control arm to prevent the spring from forcing it downward.

2. Mark and remove the tire and wheel assembly.

3. Remove the cotter pin from the lower ball joint. Loosen the locknut not more than 1 turn, do not remove the locknut.

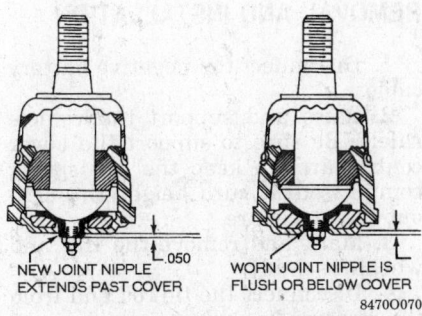

NEW JOINT NIPPLE ⌐.050
EXTENDS PAST COVER

WORN JOINT NIPPLE IS
FLUSH OR BELOW COVER

84700070

Lower ball joint visual wear indicator

4. Using the proper ball joint separator tool, separate the ball joint from the steering knuckle and remove the locknut.

5. Lift the upper control arm with the knuckle and hub assembly attached and position a block of wood between the frame and the upper arm to act as a support.

NOTE: Do not pull on the brake hose when lifting the knuckle and hub assembly as damage may occur.

6. If necessary, remove the tie rod end from the steering knuckle.

7. Using the proper ball joint removal tool press the ball joint from the lower control arm.

To install:

8. Position the new ball joint in the lower control arm and install using a suitable ball joint installation tool. Remove the block of wood.

9. Clean the tapered hole in the steering knuckle, if any damage or deformation is noted, the steering knuckle must be replaced.

10. Insert the ball joint stud into the steering knuckle and install the castellated nut. Tighten the nut to 83 ft. lbs. (113 Nm). If necessary, tighten the nut additionally to insert the new cotter pin. The maximum torque allowable is 92 ft. lbs. (125 Nm) or an additional ¹⁄₁₆ turn. Do not back off the nut to install the cotter pin.

11. If removed, install the tie rod end to the steering knuckle.

12. Align the marks made earlier and install the tire and wheel assembly.

13. Remove the supports and lower the vehicle.

14. Check and adjust the front end alignment, as necessary.

Upper Control Arms

REMOVAL AND INSTALLATION

1. Raise and support the vehicle safely, making sure to support the lower control arm.

2. Mark and remove the tire and wheel assembly.

3. Separate the upper ball joint from the steering knuckle, using the proper tools.

4. Remove the upper control arm shaft to frame bracket nuts.

5. Tape the shims exactly in the same position they were removed and label for reinstallation.

6. Remove the upper control arm assembly from the vehicle.

To install:

7. Position the new control arm attaching bolts loosely in the frame and install the control arm cross shaft on the attaching bolts.

8. Using a free running nut, tighten both nuts until the serrated bolts are reseated. Remove the free running nuts and install the locknuts.

9. Install the shims in their original location and tighten the mounting nuts to 72 ft. lbs. (98 Nm). Tighten the nut on the thinner shim pack first for improved clamping force and torque retention.

10. Clean the tapered hole in the steering knuckle, if any damage or deformation is noted, the steering knuckle must be replaced.

11. Install the ball joint stud into the steering knuckle and install the castellated nut. Tighten the nut to 61 ft. lbs. (83 Nm). If necessary, tighten the nut just enough additionally to install a cotter pin. Install a new cotter pin.

12. Align the marks made earlier and install the tire and wheel assemblies.

13. Remove the supports and lower the vehicle.

14. Check and adjust the front end alignment, as required.

Lower Control Arms

REMOVAL AND INSTALLATION

1. Raise and support the vehicle safely, making sure the lower control arms hang freely.

2. Mark and remove the tire and wheel assembly.

3. Remove the coil spring.

4. Disconnect the lower ball joint from the steering knuckle, using the proper tools.

5. Remove the lower control arm from the vehicle.

To install:

6. Position the lower control arm to the vehicle.

7. Clean the tapered hole in the steering knuckle, if any damage or deformation is noted, the steering knuckle must be replaced.

8. Install the ball joint stud into the steering knuckle and install the castellated nut. Tighten the nut to 61 ft. lbs. (83 Nm). If necessary, tighten the nut just enough additionally to install a cotter pin. Install a new cotter pin.

9. Install the coil spring.

10. Align the marks made earlier and install the tire and wheel assembly.

11. Lower the vehicle.

12. Check and adjust the front end alignment, as necessary.

Sway Bar

REMOVAL AND INSTALLATION

1. Raise and support the vehicle safely.

2. Remove the nuts, retainer and grommet from the top of each stabilizer link.

3. Remove the bolts from the mounting brackets holding the sway bar to the frame and remove the mounting brackets.

4. Remove the rubber bushings from the sway bar shaft and remove the grommets, retainers, spacers and links from the ends of the sway bar.

5. Turn the wheels of the vehicle to full stop and remove the sway bar.

To install:

6. Position the sway bar under the front frame side rails and slide the rubber bushings into place. The slit should be forward, toward the front of the vehicle. Sway bar grommets are larger than those on the shock absorbers, be sure all replacement parts are of this larger type.

7. Install the mounting brackets over the rubber bushings and secure with the attaching bolts. Tighten the bracket bolts to 24 ft. lbs. (33 Nm).

8. Install the grommets, retainers, links and spacers on the ends of the sway bar shaft. Make sure all components are properly arranged.

9. Install the grommet retainer and nut on top of the link and sway bar. Tighten the nut to 13 ft. lbs. (17 Nm).

10. Lower the vehicle.

Knuckle/Spindle Assembly

REMOVAL AND INSTALLATION

1. Disconnect the negative battery cable.

2. Raise and support the vehicle safely. Be sure to support the lower control arm to keep the coil spring compressed at curb height throughout the procedure.

3. Mark and remove the tire and wheel assembly.

4. Disconnect the tie rod end from the steering knuckle.

5. Remove the brake caliper from the mounting bracket and support

out of the way so the brake line does not kink or bend

6. Remove the brake rotor.

7. If equipped with ABS, disconnect the speed sensor cable from the bracket.

8. Remove the brake splash shield. If equipped, remove the wheel speed sensor.

9. Disconnect the upper and lower ball joints from the steering knuckle and remove the knuckle from the vehicle.

To install:

10. Position the steering knuckle in the vehicle and attach the upper and lower ball joints.

11. Tighten the upper nut to 61 ft. lbs. (83 Nm) and if necessary tighten just enough more to insert a new cotter pin. Tighten the lower nut to 83 ft. lbs. (113 Nm). If necessary, tighten the nut additionally to insert the new cotter pin. The maximum torque allowable for the lower nut is 92 ft. lbs. (125 Nm) or an additional $1/16$ turn. Do not back off either nut to install the cotter pins.

12. Install the brake splash shield.

13. If equipped with ABS, connect the speed sensor cable to the bracket and install the wheel speed sensor.

14. Install the brake rotor.

15. Install the tie rod end to the steering knuckle.

16. Install the brake caliper. Align the marks made earlier and install the tire and wheel assembly.

17. Adjust the wheel bearings install a new cotter pin and the dust cap.

18. Install the wheel cover, remove the supports and lower the vehicle.

19. Connect the negative battery cable and fill the master cylinder with to the proper level with clean brake fluid. Do not attempt to move the vehicle until the shoe linings are properly seated.

20. Check and adjust the alignment, as necessary.

Front Wheel Bearings

ADJUSTMENT

1. Raise and support the vehicle safely.

2. Remove the dust cap and cotter pin from the spindle nut. Be sure the hub is fully seated on the spindle.

3. To adjust, spin the wheel forward by hand, to fully seat the bearing and tighten the locknut nut to 12 ft. lbs. Stop the wheel.

4. Back off the nut until it is free and then tighten it finger-tight.

5. Insert the cotter pin. If the pin cannot be installed in this position, back off the nut slightly until the holes align. Make certain the pin fits tightly and will not interfere with the dust cap.

6. There should be 0.001–0.005 inch endplay when the wheel bearings are properly adjusted.

REMOVAL AND INSTALLATION

1. Raise and support the vehicle safely. Mark and remove the tire and wheel assembly.

2. Remove the brake caliper and properly support it making sure not to damage the brake line.

3. Remove the dust cap, cotter pin, locknut and washer.

4. Remove the outer wheel bearing from the hub assembly.

5. Remove the rotor taking care not to damage the spindle threads. Remove the inner bearing grease seal, bearing assembly. Discard the old seal.

6. Inner and outer bearing cups are pressed into the hub and can be removed with a suitable tool. Insert the tool and tap alternately on opposite sides of the cup to avoid cocking the cup and damaging the rotor.

To install:

7. Thoroughly clean and inspect all parts. Use a clean solvent to remove all traces of old grease and any dirt or contaminants. If any parts are worn or pitted, replace the complete bearing assembly.

8. Lubricate the spindle and the rotor bore with a thin film of high melting point wheel bearing grease to prevent rust.

9. Install the outer bearing cup using a suitable installing punch and arbor to press the cup into the rotor. Install the inner bearing cup in the same manner.

10. Pack the bearing with high melting point wheel bearing grease. Force grease in at the large end of the roller cage until grease protrudes from the small end.

11. Install the inner bearing into the bearing cup and install a new grease seal with a flat plate until the seal is flush with the rotor hub.

12. Install the rotor onto the spindle and place outer bearing into the bearing cup.

13. Install the washer and spindle finger-tight.

14. Install the brake caliper.

15. Align the marks made earlier and install the tire and wheel assembly.

16. Adjust the wheel bearings and install a new cotter pin, the dust cap and the wheel cover.

17. Lower the vehicle.

REAR SUSPENSION

Shock Absorbers

REMOVAL AND INSTALLATION

1. Raise and support the vehicle safely. Properly support the rear axle assembly.

2. If equipped with Electronic Level Control (ELC), disconnect the air line fitting(s) at the shock absorber.

3. Remove the upper shock absorber retaining bolt and nut.

4. Hold the the lower shock absorber stem steady and remove the retaining nut.

5. Remove the shock absorber from the vehicle.

To install:

6. Place the shock absorber to the vehicle and position the upper mount cross bar so the shock angles naturally toward the lower mount.

7. Install the upper retaining bolt and nut. Tighten the bolts to 20 ft. lbs. (27 Nm).

8. Guide the shock lower stud into the mounting bracket and install the nut and washer. While holding the stud to keep from rotating, tighten the nut to 65 ft. lbs. (88 Nm).

9. If equipped with ELC, connect the air line fitting(s). Turn the ignition **ON** and ground the compressor test lead with a jumper to activate the system and inflate the shocks. Do not place vehicle weight on the shocks until they have been inflated, or damage may occur.

10. Lower the vehicle.

Coil Springs

REMOVAL AND INSTALLATION

1. Raise and support the vehicle safely. Place an adjustable support under the rear axle assembly.

2. Remove the shock absorbers.

3. Remove the stabilizer shaft.

NOTE: Do not lower the axle assembly to the point at which the brake hoses become taut, as damage may result.

4. Remove the bolt that secures the brake hose junction block to the top of the rear axle housing and disconnect the brake lines from the retaining clips.

5. Remove the link from the height sensor arm.

6. Raise the axle housing slightly to relieve tension from the lower control arm bolts and remove the bolts at the axle housing.

7. Mark and remove the driveshaft from the pinion yoke and support the driveshaft to the side.

8. Remove the upper control arm pivot bolts at the rear axle housing.

9. Disconnect the left side parking brake cable at the equalizer and disconnect the cable at the frame by removing the clip. Slide the cable through the hole.

10. Disconnect the cable from the clip at the center of the rear crossmember and disconnect the cable at the "C" shaped connector which is located at the left of the frame.

11. With the rear frame rails supported, lower the axle to the point where the springs can be pried out. Be careful not to stretch the brake line or cable.

12. Remove the springs from the vehicle.

To install:

13. Tape the upper rubber insulators to the top of the springs. Position the upper end of the left rear spring coil toward the left frame side rail and the upper right end of the right spring coil toward the right frame side rail.

14. Seat the bottom of the springs on the rear axle and raise the axle, being careful to engage the axle in the upper control arms. Loosely install the nuts and pivot bolts.

15. Install the parking brake cable in clip at the center of the rear crossmember and connect the cable to the "C" shaped connector.

16. Slide the cable through the hole and connect the left parking brake cable to the equalizer and install the clips.

17. Remove support from driveshaft and install to the pinion yoke, aligning the marks made earlier.

18. Loosely install the lower control arm to the axle.

19. Install the link to the height sensor arm.

20. Install the bolt securing the brake junction block to the top of the axle housing and secure the brake lines to the clips.

21. Install the stabilizer shaft.

22. Install the shock absorbers. If equipped with Electronic Level Control (ELC), be sure to engage the system and properly inflate the shock absorbers before lowering the vehicle.

23. Check and adjust the parking brake, if necessary.

24. Remove the supports and lower the vehicle.

25. With the vehicle in the normal standing height position, tighten the upper control arm nuts to 70 ft. lbs. (95 Nm) and the lower control arm nuts to 122 ft. lbs. (165 Nm).

Upper Control Arms

REMOVAL AND INSTALLATION

NOTE: If both control arms are being replaced, replace one control arm at a time to prevent the rear axle from rolling or slipping sideways.

1. Raise and support the vehicle safely. Be sure to properly support the rear axle assembly.

2. If equipped with Electronic Level Control (ELC), remove the height sensor link retaining nut and remove the height sensor link.

3. Remove the upper control arm retaining bolts.

4. Remove the upper control arm from the vehicle.

To install:

5. Install the upper control arm to the vehicle with the flanged surface of the bushing facing inboard. Loosely install the front pivot bolt and nut then loosely install the rear pivot bolt and nut into the axle bracket.

6. Lower the vehicle with the while curb height, tighten the frame nut to 122 ft. lbs. (165 Nm) and the axle nut to 70 ft. lbs. (95 Nm).

7. If equipped with ELC, raise the vehicle and install the height sensor link to the right upper control arm with the attaching nut. Inflate the system by grounding the compressor test lead with a jumper and lower the vehicle.

Lower Control Arms

REMOVAL AND INSTALLATION

NOTE: If both control arms are being replaced, replace one control arm at a time to prevent the rear axle from rolling or slipping sideways.

1. Raise and support the vehicle safely. Be sure to properly support the rear axle assembly.

2. Disconnect the stabilizer arm bracket at the lower control arm.

3. Remove the front and rear lower control arm retaining nuts.

4. Raise the axle assembly slightly to relieve the tension on the lower control bolts.

5. Remove the lower control arm bolts and remove the control arm from the vehicle.

To install:

6. Slide the control arm into position. Be sure the stabilizer arm bracket holes are towards the rear of the frame. Install the front bolt form the outboard side and the rear bolt from the inboard side. Raise or lower the axle slightly, as necessary to ease bolt installation.

7. Connect the stabilizer shaft bracket to the lower control arm and tighten the bolts to 21 ft. lbs. (29 Nm).

8. Lower the car and with the vehicle at normal curb height, tighten the nuts to 122 ft. lbs. (165 Nm).

GM "B" BODY
Rear Wheel Drive

CHEVROLET—Caprice, Impala SS OLDSMOBILE—Custom Cruiser BUICK—Roadmaster, Estate Wagon

19

19-1

FIRING ORDERS

NOTE: To avoid confusion, always replace spark plug wires one at a time.

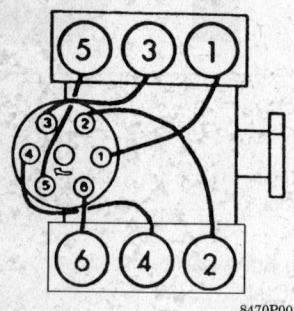

8470P001

4.3L V6 Engine
Engine Firing Order: 1–6–5–4–3–2
Distributor Rotation: Clockwise

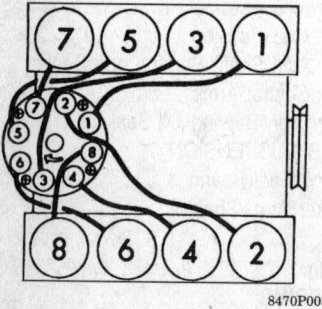

8470P003

5.0L (VIN E) and 5.7L (VIN 7) Engines
Engine Firing Order: 1–8–4–3–6–5–7–2
Distributor Rotation: Clockwise

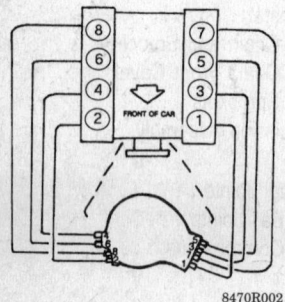

8470R002

5.7L (VIN P) Engine
Engine Firing Order:
1–8–4–3–6–5–7–2
Distributor Rotates with Camshaft

ENGINE ELECTRICAL

NOTE: Disconnecting the negative battery cable on some vehicles may interfere with the functions of the on-board computer systems and may require the computer to undergo a relearning process when the negative battery cable is reconnected.

Distributor

All 1992–93 vehicles use a Distributor Ignition (DI) system with electronic Ignition Control (IC). The major component of the DI system is the distributor assembly which consists of a cap, rotor, ignition module, pole piece with internal teeth and pickup coil. Vehicles use an externally mounted ignition coil. Spark timing changes are controlled electronically by the Engine Control Module (ECM), which monitors various engine sensors, computes the desired spark timing and signals the distributor to change the timing accordingly.

All 1994–96 vehicles, use a new distributor ignition system which was originally developed for use on the Corvette. The new system known as the Opti-Spark ignition system consists of a distributor assembly which is mounted on the front engine cover, under the water pump assembly. The system consists of a distributor assembly, control circuitry and an external coil. In the Opti-Spark system, all ignition timing is controlled by the ECM based on signals from the distributor's internally mounted optical camshaft position sensor. There is no way to bypass the ECM control or to adjust/set ignition timing on this system.

REMOVAL

1992–93 Vehicles

1. Disconnect the negative battery cable.
2. If necessary for access, remove the air cleaner assembly.
3. For the 1993 4.3L V6 engine, disconnect the accelerator lever cable, TV cable and cruise control cables, as applicable, from the accelerator lever and support assembly. Then remove the retainers and the support assembly from the intake manifold.

4. Tag and disengage the wiring harness connectors from the distributor assembly.

NOTE: Use care when releasing the connector locking tabs on the distributor assembly.

5. If equipped, disconnect the external coil wire from the distributor cap.
6. Either tag and remove the spark plug wires from the distributor cap and remove the cap from the vehicle or, if clearance allows, remove the cap with the spark plug wires attached and position it out of the way.
7. Mark the position of the rotor and the distributor housing in relation to the engine.
8. Remove the distributor holddown bolt and clamp, then pull the distributor from the engine until the rotor just stops turning. Again mark the position of rotor.
9. Tilt the distributor toward the driver's side, then remove the assembly from the vehicle. Make sure the gasket is removed with the distributor.

1994–96 Vehicles

1. Be sure the ignition is in the **OFF** or **LOCK** position, then disconnect the negative battery cable.
2. Disengage the wiring harness from the engine cooling fan assembly, then remove the cooling fan from the vehicle.
3. Remove the block drain plug and the knock sensor, then drain the engine cooling system.
4. Remove the air intake duct and the air cleaner assembly.
5. Remove the coolant and heater hoses from the water pump assembly and the throttle body.
6. Unplug the wiring harness from the Engine Coolant Temperature (ECT) sensor, then reposition the ignition coil and bracket.
7. Remove the water pump assembly.
8. Remove the serpentine drive belt from the vehicle.
9. If not done already to remove the pump or the belt, raise and safely support the vehicle for access.
10. Remove the torsional damper bolts, then remove the damper from the crankshaft hub.
11. Disconnect the spark plug wires from the distributor. Be sure to twist each boot ½ turn and pull only on the boot to remove each wire. The wire numbers should be molded into the distributor housing. If not, be sure to tag the wires before disconnection.

12. Unplug the 4-terminal ECM connector from the distributor.

13. Remove the distributor mounting bolts and pull the distributor forward until the driveshaft disengages from the engine. Mark the top of the shaft for alignment during reassembly.

INSTALLATION

Timing Not Disturbed

1992–93 VEHICLES

NOTE: To ensure correct ignition timing when the engine has not been disturbed, the distributor must be installed with the rotor in the same final position as noted during removal.

1. Make sure the gasket is positioned on the distributor assembly.
2. Align the rotor to the last mark made, tilt distributor toward the driver's side of the vehicle and slide the distributor into the engine.
3. The rotor should turn and end up at the first mark made.
4. Install the distributor hold-down bolt/clamp and tighten to 27 ft. lbs. (36 Nm), then install the distributor cap.
5. Engage all connectors or wires in the reverse order of removal.
6. Once the distributor installation has been completed, check and adjust the ignition timing.

1994–96 VEHICLES

1. With the mark made on the distributor shaft earlier on top, install the distributor to the engine. Tighten the distributor bolts to 8 ft. lbs. (11 Nm).
2. Install the 4-terminal ECM connector and the spark plug wires to the distributor.
3. Position the crankshaft damper to the hub, then install the damper bolts and tighten to 60 ft. lbs. (81 Nm).
4. Install the serpentine drive belt.
5. Install the water pump assembly and engage the ECT wiring harness.
6. Reposition the ignition coil and bracket, then install the coolant and heater hoses.
7. Install the air cleaner assembly and air intake duct.
8. Install the engine block drain plug and the knock sensor.
9. Install the cooling fan assembly, then connect the wiring harness.
10. Connect the negative battery cable and fill the engine cooling system.

11. Start and run the engine, then check for leaks.

Timing Disturbed

1992–93 VEHICLES

1. Remove the No. 1 spark plug. Place a finger over the spark plug hole and slowly rotate the engine in the normal direction of rotation, until compression is felt.
2. Align the timing mark on the crankshaft pulley to the 0 on the engine timing indicator by slowly rotating the engine in the same direction.
3. Position the rotor between No. 1 and No. 8 spark plug towers on the V8 engine or the No. 1 and No. 6 spark plug towers on the V6 engine.
4. Install the distributor, distributor cap, spark plug wiring and connectors.
5. Check the engine timing and adjust, as required.

Ignition Timing

ADJUSTMENT

When checking ignition timing NEVER pierce a secondary ignition wire. Either use a timing light with an inductive type pickup or connect an adapter between the wire and the spark plug. If the secondary wire insulation is pierced, current will eventually arc and cause engine misfiring.

NOTE: Some engines incorporate a magnetic timing probe hole for the use with electronic timing equipment. Be sure to consult the tool manufacture's instructions for the use of this equipment.

1992–93

1. Warm the engine to normal operating temperature. Make sure the air conditioning and all accessories are OFF.
2. With the engine running, disconnect the IC bypass connector located on the right side of the engine, near the air control valve. An Engine Control Module (ECM) trouble code will set when this is done.
3. Connect a timing light with the pickup lead on the No. 1 plug wire and check timing at the correct engine rpm as designated on the Vehicle Emission Information Label.
4. If the timing requires adjustment, loosen the distributor clamp bolt, the rotate the distributor, as necessary to set the timing to the

specifications noted on the information label.
5. Tighten the distributor clamp bolt to 27 ft. lbs. (36 Nm) and recheck the timing to assure it was not disturbed while tightening.
6. Once the timing has been set, turn the ignition OFF, then reconnect the IC bypass harness.
7. Clear any stored trouble codes by interrupting power to the ECM for at least 30 seconds. This can be accomplished, depending on the model, by disconnecting the ECM power feed, the ECM fuse in the fuse box or by disconnecting the negative the battery cable.

1994–96

On the 5.7L (VIN P) engine, base timing is preset when the engine is manufactured. All timing changes are then controlled directly by the ECM based on information from the ignition and knock sensor systems. No adjustments are necessary or possible.

Alternator

PRECAUTIONS

Several precautions must be observed with alternator equipped vehicles to avoid damage to the unit.

• If the battery is removed for any reason, make sure it is reconnected with the correct polarity. Reversing the battery connections may result in damage to the one-way rectifiers.
• When utilizing a booster battery as a starting aid, always connect the positive to positive terminals and the negative terminal from the booster battery to a good engine ground on the vehicle being started.
• Never use a fast charger as a booster to start vehicles.
• Disconnect the battery cables when charging the battery with a fast charger.
• Never attempt to polarize the alternator.
• Do not use test lamps of more than 12 volts when checking diode continuity.
• Do not short across or ground any of the alternator terminals.
• The polarity of the battery, alternator and regulator must be matched and considered before making any electrical connections within the system.
• Never operate the alternator on an open circuit. Make sure all connections within the circuit are clean and tight.

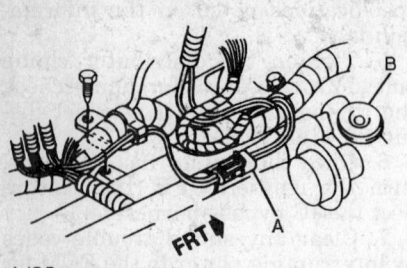

A. IC By pass connector
B. Air injection control valve assembly

8470P007

The IC bypass connector is located near the AIR control valve

• Disconnect the battery ground terminal when performing any service on electrical components.
• Disconnect the battery if arc welding is to be done on the vehicle.

BELT TENSION ADJUSTMENT

Serpentine Belts

The vehicles utilize a single, serpentine drive belt for all engine accessories. Serpentine belts are automatically adjusted by the tensioner on the engine. If the belt is loose, check the condition of the belt and tensioner. Make sure the tensioner markings are within proper operating range for belt condition (new/used). The tensioner should place enough tension on the belt so it can only be twisted 90 degrees at it's longest run.

If belt slippage occurs, while the drive belt tensioner is within its operating range, and the belt does not need replacement, check the belt tension as follows:

1. Run the engine for 10 minutes, shut OFF the engine, then using a tension gauge between any 2 pulleys, record the belt tension.
2. Run the engine for 30 seconds and repeat Step 1.
3. Once again, run the engine for 30 seconds and repeat Step 1.

1. Fixed belt length indicator
2. New belt range
3. Used belt acceptable wear range
4. Replace belt position
5. Drive belt tensioner assembly

8470P008

All serpentine drive belt tensioners have a belt length scale to help determine if the belt is stretched and in need of replacement

4. The belt tension is the average of the 3 readings. Serpentine belt tension should be 105–125 lbs. (467–556 Nm) for 1992–93 vehicles.
5. Replace the tensioner if belt length is acceptable (as measured by the tensioner scale), but the tension is below the minimum specification.

REMOVAL AND INSTALLATION

1992–93 Vehicles

1. Disconnect the negative battery cable.
2. Tag and remove the electrical connections from the alternator. If access to a connector is difficult, wait until the retainers are removed and the alternator may be repositioned, then unplug the remaining connection.
3. With V-Belts, remove the bolt holding the slotted adjusting bracket to the alternator and remove the belt.
4. With serpentine belts, rotate the tensioner to release the drive belt, then remove the belt from the alternator.
5. Remove the fasteners to release the alternator from the engine, then unplug any remaining electrical connections and remove the alternator from the engine.
To install:
6. When reinstalling, reverse the removal procedure.
7. On V-belt engines, adjust the drive belt tension before fully tightening the fasteners.
8. Tighten the upper through-bolt and rear brace bolt to 18 ft. lbs. (28 Nm). Tighten the lower through-bolt and, if applicable, rear brace nut to 37 ft. lbs. (50 Nm).
9. Install the remaining electrical connections, then connect the negative battery cable.

1994–96 5.7L (VIN P) Engine

1. Disconnect the negative battery cable.
2. Use a breaker bar and socket to rotate the serpentine belt tensioner downward (clockwise) relieving tensioner from the belt, then remove the belt from the vehicle.
3. Disengage the positive battery wire and the electrical connector from the alternator assembly.
4. Remove the upper brace bolts, the lower brace bolt and the front alternator bolt all from the alternator assembly, then remove the nut retaining the upper brace to the top of the engine and remove the upper brace from the vehicle.

5. Remove the alternator from the accessory mounting bracket and from the vehicle.
To install:
6. Position the alternator to the engine and accessory mounting bracket.
7. Install the upper brace and tighten the retaining nut to 24 ft. lbs. (33 Nm), then install the alternator and brace bolts. Tighten the rear upper brace and front alternator bolts to 37 ft. lbs. (50 Nm) and tighten the rear lower brace bolt to 18 ft. lbs. (25 Nm).
8. Engage the electrical connector and the battery positive wire to the alternator assembly.
9. Install the serpentine drive belt.
10. Connect the negative battery cable.

Starter

REMOVAL AND INSTALLATION

1. Disconnect the negative battery cable.
2. Safely raise and support the vehicle.
3. Remove the retaining nuts and bolts along with the right frame bracket.
4. If necessary on police vehicles, remove the exhaust crossover pipe for access.
5. Remove the retainers and rear starter brace from the engine and starter.
6. Remove the flywheel housing cover.
7. Remove the 2 starter mounting bolts and carefully lower the starter for access to the wiring. If present, note the position of any shims for installation purposes.
8. Tag and disconnect the wiring, then remove starter from the vehicle.
To install:
9. Position the starter and support while connecting the starter wiring as noted during removal. Be very careful not to overtighten the electrical connections and crack the solenoid cap.
10. Hold the starter in place and install the mounting bolts. If shims were removed, they must be installed in their original locations to assure proper drive pinion-to-flywheel engagement. Tighten mounting bolts to 35 ft. lbs. (47 Nm) for 1992 vehicles or to 32 ft. lbs. (43 Nm) for 1993–96 vehicles.
11. Check the flywheel-to-pinion gear clearance using a 0.20 in.

(0.5mm) gauge wire between the teeth of the flywheel and starter pinion. Add or remove shims, as necessary to achieve proper clearance.

12. Install the flywheel housing cover.

13. Install the rear brace to the starter and engine. Tighten the bolt to 18 ft. lbs. (24 Nm) and the nut to 71 inch lbs. (8 Nm).

14. Install the right frame bracket and tighten the bolts to 74 ft. lbs. (100 Nm).

15. If removed, attach exhaust crossover piper.

16. Lower vehicle and connect the negative battery cable.

CHASSIS ELECTRICAL

Air Bag

DISARMING

1. Align the steering wheel so the vehicle wheels are pointing in the straight-ahead position.

2. Turn the ignition switch to the **LOCK** position.

3. Remove the SIR or AIR BAG fuse from the fuse block.

4. Remove the Connector Position Assurance (CPA) device, then disengage the yellow 2-way SIR wire harness connector at the base of the steering column.

To enable system:

5. Turn the ignition switch to the **LOCK** position.

6. Engage the yellow 2-way connector at the base of the steering column, then install the CPA device.

7. Reinstall the SIR or AIR BAG fuse.

8. Turn the ignition switch to the **RUN** position.

9. Verify the SIR indicator light flashes 7–9 times, if not, inspect system for malfunction.

Air Bag Coil Assembly

NOTE: The coil assembly must remain centered in order to avoid accidental deployment of the air bag after any repair procedures to the internals of the steering column. There are 2 different styles of coil assemblies, 1 rotates clockwise and the other

rotates counterclockwise. An arrow on the coil indicates the proper direction of rotation.

CENTERING THE COIL

1. With the system properly disarmed and the coil partially removed from the steering column, hold the coil assembly with the clear bottom up to see the coil ribbon.

2. While holding the coil assembly, depress the lock spring and rotate the hub in the direction of the arrow until it stops. The coil should now be wound up snug against the center hub.

3. Rotate the coil assembly in the opposite direction approximately 2½ turns and release the lock spring between the locking tabs in front of the arrow.

4. Install the coil assembly onto the steering shaft.

Heater Blower Motor

REMOVAL AND INSTALLATION

Without Air Conditioning

1. Disconnect the negative battery cable.

2. Disconnect the blower motor wiring harness.

3. Remove the blower motor retaining screws and pull the blower motor and fan straight forward out of the heater module.

4. Installation is the reverse of removal. Clean and replace sealer as necessary.

With Air Conditioning

1. Disconnect the negative battery cable.

2. Remove the 4 retaining screws and remove the right side instrument panel sound insulator.

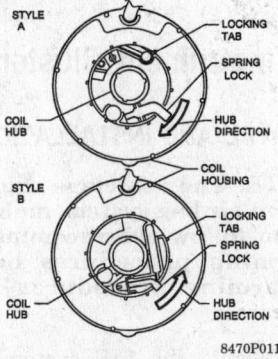

8470P011

Centering the SIR coil assembly

3. Disconnect the blower motor electrical connector.

4. Remove the right side hinge pillar trim finish panel by pulling it away from the front body hinge pillar.

5. Remove the screw from the secondary ECM bracket and swing the ECM module and bracket aside to provide access to the blower motor.

6. Remove the blower mounting screws, leaving the screw closest to the relay for last. Carefully, lower the blower motor fan assembly.

To install:

7. Align the blower motor and fan assembly, making sure the ECM module and retainer are out of the way, and carefully raise the assembly into place.

8. Insert and tighten the 3 mounting screws.

9. Swing the ECM module and bracket back into place and tighten the retaining screw to 17 inch lbs. (1.9 Nm).

10. Snap the right side hinge pillar trim finish panel into place on the front body hinge pillar.

11. Connect the blower motor electrical connector.

12. Insert the right side instrument panel sound insulator and attach the 4 retaining screws. Tighten the sound insulator retaining screws to 17 inch lbs. (1.9 Nm).

13. Connect the negative battery cable and check motor operation.

Windshield Wiper Motor

REMOVAL AND INSTALLATION

1. Disconnect the negative battery cable.

2. Raise the hood. Remove the right side wiper arm and hose. In order to keep the arm from pivoting, 2 holes are provided in the arm assembly, into which rivets or pins may be inserted to lock the arm in position.

3. Remove cowl screen. The left side must be removed first.

NOTE: The left side cowl screen must be removed before the right side cowl screen in order to prevent possible windshield damage.

4. If equipped, remove the retaining screws and the linkage access hole cover.

5. Loosen the transmission drive link-to-crank arm retainers, then disconnect link from the motor crank arm.

6. Unplug the electrical wiring and any remaining washer hoses from the motor assembly.

7. Remove the motor retaining screws, then remove the windshield wiper motor while guiding the crank arm through the hole.

To install:

8. Install the wiper motor by guiding crank arm through the hole.

9. Insert and tighten wiper motor attaching bolts to 80 inch lbs. (9 Nm).

10. Attach the electrical connectors.

11. Verify that the motor is in the **P** position, then attach the motor crank arm to the drive link. Tighten drive link nuts to 27 inch lbs. (3 Nm).

12. If equipped, install the wiper linkage access hole cover and tighten the screws to 13 inch lbs. (1.5 Nm), except for 1993–96 vehicles, on which the cover screws should be tightened to 18 inch lbs. (2 Nm).

13. Install right, then left side cowl screens.

NOTE: The right side cowl screen must be installed before the left side cowl screen in order to prevent possible windshield damage.

14. Attach the right side wiper arm and hose. If installed, remove the arm pivot prevention rivet or pin.

15. Connect the negative battery cable and check wiper motor operation.

Windshield Wiper Switch

REMOVAL AND INSTALLATION

NOTE: If equipped with an air bag, it is imperative that the disarming procedure is followed before repairs, and that the coil centering and rearming procedures are followed after repairs.

1. Disarm the air bag, if equipped, and disconnect the negative battery cable.

2. Remove the turn signal assembly.

3. If necessary, remove the SIR coil assembly from the column as follows:

  a. Remove wiring protector.

  b. Attach a length of mechanic's wire to the terminal connector in order to aid in reassembly.

  c. Carefully pull wire/harness connector through the column, leaving the wire in the column for assembly purposes.

4. Remove the lock cylinder set.

5. Remove lock housing cover screws.

6. Remove the tilt lever, if equipped, and remove the lock housing cover.

7. Remove the base plate and the dimmer switch rod actuator.

8. Disconnect and remove wiper switch actuator pivot pin.

9. Disengage the wiper switch connector from the vehicle wire harness, then remove the switch. Attach a piece of mechanic's wire to the connector to aid in reinstallation and gently pull the wire harness through column.

To install:

10. Connect the wiper switch assembly to the lock housing cover assembly

11. Attach the switch actuator pivot pin to the switch and cover.

12. Pull the wiper switch wire connector through the steering column with the mechanic's wire used during removal, then attach it to the vehicle wire harness.

13. Attach the dimmer switch rod actuator to the base plate and lubricate with lithium grease.

14. Connect base plate to the lock housing cover assembly. The bottom edge of the dimmer switch rod actuator must rest on the bend in the dimmer switch rod.

15. Position lock housing cover assembly in place and, if equipped, attach the tilt lever.

16. Starting with the housing cover screw in the 12 o'clock position, then 8 o'clock and finally 3 o'clock positions, tighten the screws to 80 inch lbs. (9 Nm).

17. Install the lock cylinder set.

18. Attach the SIR coil assembly, if necessary, by pulling wire connector through the steering column and attach the wire protector.

19. Install the turn signal assembly.

20. Be sure to center SIR coil assembly before reinstalling SIR inflator module and steering wheel.

21. Connect the negative battery cable and enable SIR system.

Instrument Cluster

REMOVAL AND INSTALLATION

NOTE: The vehicle is equipped with an air bag system, make certain to follow the recommended disarming procedures before, and arming procedures after, repairs.

1. Disable the SIR system, then disconnect the negative battery cable.

2. Remove the left side or instrument panel trim plate:

  a. Remove the steering column opening filler.

  b. Open the glove box door and carefully unsnap the right side molding from the carrier.

  c. Locate the capsule nuts attaching the steering column support bracket to the carrier. Loosen the nuts to the end of the threads, but do not remove them from the bolts. Gently lower the steering column.

  d. Remove the 6 screws attaching the trim plate to the carrier, then carefully unsnap and pull away.

3. Remove the screws attaching the cluster to the carrier.

4. Unclip the shift indicator cable from the steering column assembly.

5. Gently pull the cluster from the electrical connector and remove the cluster from the vehicle.

To install:

6. Position the cluster in the vehicle, then align and gently snap onto the connector.

7. Attach the shift indicator cable to the steering column.

8. Attach cluster to the carrier with the retaining screws and tighten to 17 inch lbs. (1.9 Nm).

9. Install the left side trim plate and, if necessary, adjust the shift indicator as follows:

  a. With the steering column in place, but the opening filler still removed, position the shift lever in the **N** gate notch.

  b. Position the guide clip on the edge of the gearshift lever bowl to centrally position the pointer on **N**. Push the guide clip onto the gearshift lever bowl. Be sure the clip is properly resting on the bowl and not the jacket.

  c. Complete installation of the trim plate assembly and steering column opening filler.

10. Connect negative battery cable and enable the SIR system.

Speedometer

REMOVAL AND INSTALLATION

NOTE: The speedometer assemblies must be replaced as a unit or sent to an authorized repair facility. No individual parts are available for replacement.

1. Disconnect the negative battery cable.

2. Remove the left sound insulator panel, then remove the screws at-

taching the steering column trim plate. Remove the trim plate from the vehicle.

3. If equipped, remove the screws attaching the left trim plate, then remove the plate.

4. If equipped, remove the knob from the trip odometer.

5. Remove the screws and the snap-in plastic fasteners attaching the speedometer lens to the cluster carrier, then carefully remove the lens.

6. Remove the screws attaching the face and adapter plates to the cluster carrier, then remove the plates.

7. Remove the screws attaching the speedometer to the carrier.

8. Carefully remove the speedometer cable from the rear of the speedometer, then remove the screw securing the speed sensor pickup to the speedometer head.

9. Pull the speedometer outward and remove from the vehicle.

To install:

NOTE: If the speedometer is being replaced, the law requires that the odometer be set to the same mileage as the proper odometer or that a label be applied to the driver's door frame to show the previous reading and the date of replacement.

10. Install the screw attaching the speed sensor pickup to the speedometer head, then carefully position the speedometer to the cluster. Connect the speedometer cable.

11. Install the screws retaining the speedometer to the cluster.

12. Install the face and adapter plates using the retaining screws.

13. Install the cluster lens and secure using the screws and the snap-in plastic fasteners.

14. If equipped, install the trip odometer knob and/or the left trim plate.

15. Install the left sound insulator panel, then install the steering column trim plate and retaining screws.

16. Connect the negative battery cable.

Headlight Switch

REMOVAL AND INSTALLATION

1. Disable the SIR system, then disconnect the negative battery cable.

NOTE: This vehicles is equipped with an air bag system. Make certain to follow the recom-

mended disarming procedure before or arming procedure after repairs.

2. Remove the left side or instrument panel trim plate:

a. Remove the steering column opening filler.

b. Open the glove box door and carefully unsnap the right side molding from the carrier.

c. Locate the capsule nuts attaching the steering column support bracket to the carrier. Loosen the nuts to the end of the threads, but do not remove them from the bolts. Gently lower the steering column.

d. Remove the 6 screws attaching the trim plate to the carrier, then carefully unsnap and pull away.

3. Remove the 3 screws attaching the switch to the instrument carrier and separate the switch from the carrier.

4. Tag and disengage the electrical connections from the switch assembly, then remove the bulb from the switch and remove the switch from the vehicle.

To install:

5. Install the bulb and the electrical connectors to the switch assembly.

6. Place switch in instrument carrier and attach using the screws.

7. Install the left side trim plate.

8. Enable SIR system and connect the negative battery cable.

Dimmer Switch

REMOVAL AND INSTALLATION

NOTE: If equipped with an air bag system, make certain to follow the recommended disarming procedure before, and rearming procedure after, repairs.

1. Disable the SIR system, if equipped, then disconnect the negative battery cable.

2. The dimmer switch is attached to the lower steering column jacket. Remove trim panels, as necessary for access to the switch. If necessary, lower the steering column assembly and/or remove the column from the vehicle to ease access to the switch.

3. Remove the nut and screw attaching the switch and bracket to the steering column jacket.

4. If equipped, remove the shift interlock solenoid assembly and bracket from the dimmer/ignition switch mounting stud.

5. Disengage the vehicle wire harness from the switch assembly and, if applicable, remove the washer head screw, then remove the switch from the steering column.

To install:

6. Position the dimmer switch to the rod and, if applicable, stud on the steering column assembly.

7. If applicable, install the solenoid and bracket.

8. Install the screw, nut and/or washer head screw(s) finger-tight.

9. Adjust the dimmer switch by placing a 3/32 in. drill bit into the hole on the switch in order to limit travel, then push the switch against the actuator rod to remove all lash. When properly adjusted, an audible click should be heard from the switch if the multifunction lever is pulled to activate the high/low beams.

10. Remove the drill bit and tighten the retainers while holding the switch in position. As applicable, tighten the washer head screw(s) and the hexagon nut to 35 inch lbs. (4.0 Nm) and the tapping screw to 22 inch lbs. (2.5 Nm).

11. Engage the vehicle wire harness to the switch assembly.

12. As applicable, install and/or raise the steering column assembly into position, then install the trim plates.

13. Connect the negative battery cable and, if equipped, properly enable the SIR system.

Turn Signal Switch

REMOVAL AND INSTALLATION

NOTE: If equipped with an air bag system, make certain to follow the recommended disarming and coil centering procedure before and after repairs.

1. Disable the Supplemental Air Restraint (SIR) air bag system, then disconnect the negative battery cable.

2. Remove the inflator module, then remove the steering wheel from the vehicle.

─────── **CAUTION** ───────

To avoid personal injury when carrying a live inflator module, make sure the bag and trim cover are pointed away. Always face the air bag assembly up, and never carry the inflator module by the wires or connector, otherwise personal injury may result if the module should deploy.

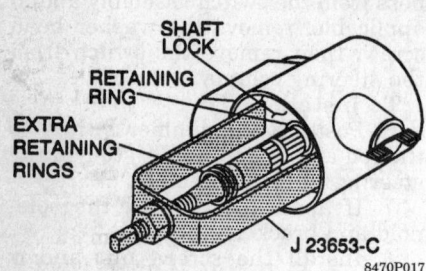

Removing the shaft lock retaining ring

8470P017

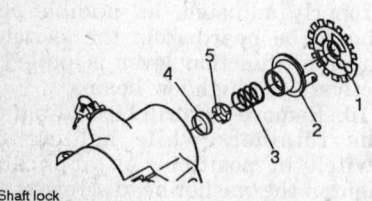

1. Shaft lock
2. Turn signal cancelling camshaft assembly
3. Upper bearing spring
4. Upper bearing inner race seat
5. Inner race

8470P018

Steering column upper shaft components

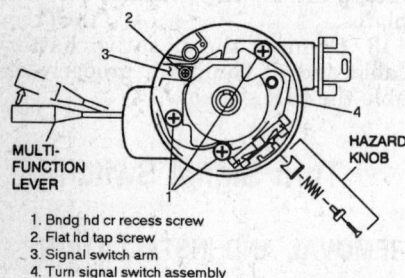

1. Bndg hd cr recess screw
2. Flat hd tap screw
3. Signal switch arm
4. Turn signal switch assembly

8470P019

Removing the hazard switch and multifunction lever in preparation for turn signal switch removal

3. Remove the coil assembly retaining ring and allow the coil assembly to hang freely.

4. Remove the wave washer.

5. Remove the shaft lock bolt guard:

a. Turn the ignition switch to the **RUN** position.

b. Rotate shaft so the blocking tooth is at 7 o'clock and bolt guard screws are accessible through large slots on lock shaft.

c. Loosen screws on lock bolt guard and remove.

d. Return ignition to the **LOCK** position.

6. Remove and discard the shaft lock retaining ring using tool J–23653–C or equivalent.

—— CAUTION ——
Use a 1/2 inch wrench to hold the shaft of tool J–23653–C or equivalent, stationary when releasing the nut. Failure to do so may cause the tool to fly off and cause personal injury.

7. Remove the shaft lock, turn signal cancelling cam, upper bearing spring, upper bearing inner race seat and inner race.

8. Turn the multifunction lever to the **RIGHT TURN** position, then remove the multifunction lever and hazard knob assembly.

9. Remove the retaining screw and signal switch arm.

10. If the signal switch is being completely removed from the column assembly, remove the wiring protector from the steering column and disengage the switch connector.

11. Remove the screws retaining the turn signal switch to the steering column, using care not to drop the screws in the column. If the switch is being completely removed from the column, attach a length of mechanic's wire to the harness connector to aid in reinstallation and gently pull wire harness through the steering column. Leave the wire in the column in order to pull the new harness into position.

To install:

12. Using the mechanic's wire, gently pull the turn switch connector through the steering column and attach switch connector to the vehicle wire harness.

13. Install the turn switch assembly and tighten the screws to 30 inch lbs. (3.4 Nm).

14. Install the signal switch arm and tighten the retaining screw to 20 inch lbs. (2.3 Nm).

15. Install the hazard knob assembly and multifunction lever.

16. Install the inner race, upper bearing race seat and upper bearing spring.

17. Lubricate turn signal cancelling cam with synthetic grease, then install the cancelling cam assembly.

18. Install shaft lock and new shaft lock retaining ring using tool J–23653–C or equivalent.

19. Install shaft lock bolt guard as follows:

a. Turn ignition switch to the **RUN** position.

b. Rotate shaft until the block tooth is at the 7 o'clock position and bolt guard screw holes are accessible though large slots on lock shaft.

c. Tighten screws on lock bolt guard until they bottom out and torque to 20 inch lbs. (2.3 Nm).

20. Install the wave washer.

21. Install and center the coil assembly and retaining ring.

22. If removed, install the wiring protector.

23. Install steering wheel, then install the SIR inflator module.

24. Connect the negative battery cable, then properly enable the SIR system.

Ignition Switch

REMOVAL AND INSTALLATION

NOTE: If equipped with an air bag system, make certain to follow the recommended disarming procedure before, and rearming procedure after, repairs.

1. Disable the SIR system, if equipped, then disconnect the negative battery cable.

2. Either lower the steering column or remove the column assembly from the vehicle, for access to the switch.

NOTE: The steering column must be supported at all times to prevent damage.

3. For 1993–96 vehicles, remove the solenoid cable assembly from the interlock solenoid assembly and bracket, then remove the assembly from the dimmer/ignition switch mounting bracket. Remove the ball joint spring, remove the washer head screw to remove the solenoid assembly, then remove the tapping screw and nut to remove the solenoid bracket.

4. Remove the washer head screw(s) from the dimmer switch assembly, then unplug the connector and remove the switch from the column.

5. Remove the ignition switch screws or the dimmer/ignition switch mounting stud, as applicable. Unplug the connector, then remove the ignition switch from the column.

To install:

6. Make sure the ignition key is in the **LOCK** or **OFF-LOCK** position, as applicable, then place the ignition switch in the proper position and install it to the steering column assembly and actuator rod:

a. For 1992 vehicles, move the switch slider to the extreme **RIGHT** position, then move the slider 1 detent to the **LEFT** (**LOCK** position). Position the switch to the column and tighten the retainers, then depress switch mechanism slightly to insert a 3/32 in. drill bit into ignition switch in order to aid with dimmer switch installation/adjustment.

b. For 1993–96 vehicles, move the switch slider to the extreme LEFT position, then move the slider 1 detent to the RIGHT (**OFF-LOCK**) position and insert a 3/32 in. drill bit into the switch hole.

7. For 1992 vehicles, install the dimmer switch to the ignition switch, then install the screws and actuator rod to the dimmer switch assembly. Properly adjust the dimmer switch, tighten the retaining screws to 35 inch lbs. (4 Nm) and remove the drill bit.

8. For 1993–96 vehicles, install the ignition/dimmer switch mounting stud and tighten to 35 inch lbs. (4 Nm), then remove the drill bit from the ignition switch and connect the switch wiring harness. Install the dimmer switch followed by the interlock solenoid and bracket, hand-tightening all fasteners. Adjust the switch assembly, then tighten the fasteners.

9. Either install and/or raise the steering column into position in the vehicle.

10. Connect the negative battery cable.

Ignition Lock Cylinder

REMOVAL AND INSTALLATION

NOTE: The vehicle is equipped with an air bag system, make certain to follow the recommended disarming and coil centering procedure before and after repairs.

1. Disable the SIR system, then disconnect the negative battery cable.

2. Remove the turn signal switch from the column and allow to hang freely from the wires.

3. If necessary, remove the SIR coil assembly from the column as follows:

a. Remove wiring protector.

b. Attach a length of mechanic's wire to the terminal connector to aid in reassembly.

c. Carefully pull wire through the column.

4. Remove the key from the lock cylinder and remove the buzzer switch assembly.

5. Reinsert the key into the lock cylinder, be sure the key is in the **LOCK** position.

6. Remove the lock cylinder retaining screw.

7. Remove the lock cylinder from the steering column.

To install:

8. Reinstall the lock cylinder set with key inserted. Install the retaining screw and tighten to 22 inch lbs. (2.5 Nm).

9. Remove the key and install the buzzer switch with retaining clip, then insert the key.

10. If removed, gently pull the coil assembly through the steering column and allow assembly to hang freely.

11. Install the turn signal switch assembly, making sure to follow proper SIR coil centering procedures.

12. Connect the negative battery cable and enable the SIR system.

Brake Light Switch

ADJUSTMENT

When properly adjusted the switch plunger will be fully depressed against the pedal assembly shank while the pedal is in the released position. If adjustment is necessary:

1. Push the switch into the retaining clip until the switch body is seated fully in the clip.

2. Pull the brake pedal up against internal pedal stop.

3. The switch will move in the retainer clip until the pedal assembly is against the stop.

4. Proper adjustment has been reached when no clicks are heard while pulling the pedal up and the brake lights do not remain ON when the pedal is released.

REMOVAL AND INSTALLATION

1. Disconnect the negative battery cable.

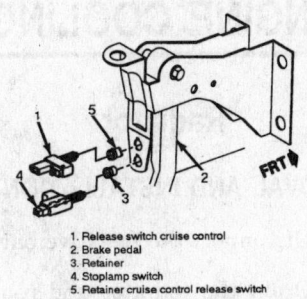

1. Release switch cruise control
2. Brake pedal
3. Retainer
4. Stoplamp switch
5. Retainer cruise control release switch

8470P020

The brake light switch and cruise control release switches are adjusted in a similar manner

2. Disengage the electrical connection from the switch.

NOTE: If equipped with cruise control, there will be 2 switches mounted on the brake pedal support. The brake light switch is normally the lower of the 2 mounted switches and does not incorporate a vacuum hose.

3. Remove the switch from the retainer clip on the brake pedal mounting bracket.

4. Installation is the reverse of the removal procedure.

Neutral Safety Switch

All steering columns use a mechanical neutral start safety system. The mechanical system relies on a block which prevents starting the engine in positions other than **P** or **N**. The mechanical block is achieved by a wedge shaped finger added to the ignition switch actuator rod. The finger will only pass through the bowl plate notches when the shift lever is in the **P** and **N** positions, which then allows the lock cylinder to rotate to the **START** position.

Fuses, Circuit Breakers and Relays

LOCATION

Fusible Links

Fusible links are used to prevent major wire harness damage in the event of a short circuit or an overload condition in the wiring circuits which are normally not fused. Each fusible link is of a fixed value for a specific electrical load and should a link fail, the cause of the failure must be determined and repaired prior to installing a new fusible link of the same value.

Circuit Breakers

Various circuit breakers are located under the instrument panel. In order to gain access to these components, it may be necessary to first remove the under dash padding.

Fuse Panel

The fuse panel is located on the left side of the vehicle. It is under the instrument panel assembly on the left front hinge pillar. Access is gained through a removable panel on the instrument panel carrier.

Relays

ABS Solenoid Valve Relay — integrated into the brake pressure modulator located in the left side of the engine compartment left of the generator.

A/C Blower Relay — integrated into the brake pressure modulator located in the left side of the engine compartment left of the generator.

A/C Blower Relay — located near the blower from under the right side of the dash.

A/C Compressor Relay located near the blower from under the right side of the dash

Antenna Relay — located under the instrument panel compartment near the convenience center.

Electronic Level Control Relay — located in the engine compartment, on the fender next to the electronic level control compressor.

Fuel Pump Relay — located on a bracket in the right side of the engine compartment.

Headlight Relay — located at the front side of the engine compartment, near the headlight.

Horn Relay — Located in the convenience center, behind the instrument panel to the left of the steering column.

Power Door Locks Relay — located behind the lower right kick panel.

Power Seat Relay — located under the right or left seat.

Rear Glass Release Relay — located in the convenience center under the dash, left of the steering column.

Tailgate Release Relay — located at the base of the left side A-pillar.

Theft Deterrent Relay — located behind the instrument panel to the left of the steering column.

Wiper Motor Relay — incorporated in the connector, on the wiper/washer assembly.

Control Modules

LOCATION

Air Bag Diagnostic Energy Reserve Module (DERM) — located behind the left side instrument panel, left of the brake pedal bracket.

Cruise Control System Module — located in the left side rear of the engine compartment next to the master cylinder.

Electronic Brake Control Module (EBCM) — located behind the

left side instrument panel, left of the brake pedal bracket.

Engine Electronic Control Module (ECM) — located behind the front right side kick panel.

Keyless Entry Control Module — mounted to left rear side under-shelf between delco-bose amplifier and left rear speaker.

Flashers

LOCATION

Turn Signal — located inside the convenience center. In order to gain access to the turn signal flasher, it may be necessary to first remove the under dash padding.

Hazard — located in the convenience center and is positioned on the lower right side corner of the fuse block assembly.

Cruise Control

ADJUSTMENT

Cruise Control Cable

1. Disconnect the negative battery cable.
2. Remove the air cleaner and resonator.
3. Lift the cable lockup to the unlocked position.
4. Pull the cable from the throttle body side until the throttle valve begins to close.
5. When the cable is at the desired position, depress the cable lock into the locked position.
6. Reinstall the air cleaner and resonator.
7. Reconnect the negative battery cable.

ENGINE COOLING

Radiator

REMOVAL AND INSTALLATION

1. Disconnect the negative battery cable.
2. Drain the radiator and remove the fan shrouds.
3. Disconnect the radiator inlet and outlet hoses from the radiator assembly.

4. Disconnect and the engine oil cooler and/or transmission fluid cooler lines from the radiator. Plug all openings to prevent system contamination or excessive fluid loss.
5. If equipped, disengage the low fluid sensor connector.
6. Disconnect the coolant reservoir hose from the radiator.
7. If applicable, disconnect the heater hoses from the radiator.
8. Remove the radiator from the vehicle.
To install:
9. Position radiator in place making sure the radiator is seated on the insulators.
10. Connect the coolant recovery hose to the filler neck.
11. If equipped, connect the transmission fluid lines to the radiator and tighten to 18 ft. lbs. (24 Nm) for 1992 vehicles or to 15 ft. lbs. (21 Nm) for 1993–96 vehicles.
12. If equipped, connect the engine oil cooler lines to the radiator and tighten to 18 ft. lbs. (24 Nm)
13. Connect the radiator inlet and outlet hoses along with their clamps to the radiator.
14. If applicable, connect the heater hoses and clamp to the radiator.
15. If equipped, connect the wiring harness to the low coolant sensor.
16. Connect the upper and lower fan shrouds.
17. Connect the negative battery cable, then add coolant and properly bleed the engine cooling system.
18. Run the engine and check system for leaks.

Heater Core

REMOVAL AND INSTALLATION

Without Air Conditioning

1. Disconnect the negative battery cable and drain the engine coolant into a suitable container.
2. Disconnect the heater hoses and clamps at the heater core inlet and outlet pipes.
3. Disconnect the blower wiring.
4. Remove the blower cover housing screws and the cover housing.
5. Remove the heater core.
To install:
6. Clean sealer from the mating flange surfaces of the heater module and blower cover housing.
7. Install heater core into the blower cover housing.
8. Apply an even ribbon of sealer completely around the flange of the blower cover housing from the edge of

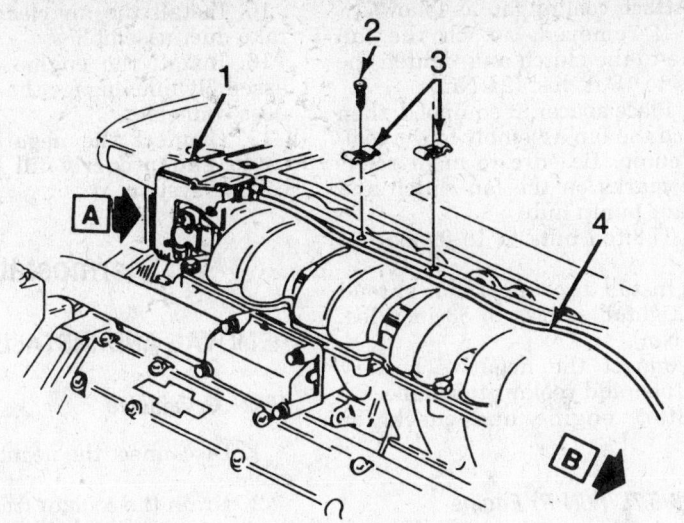

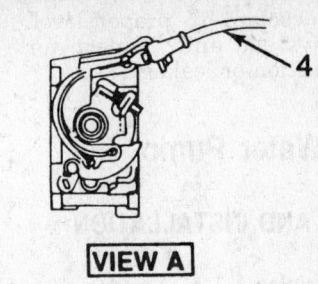

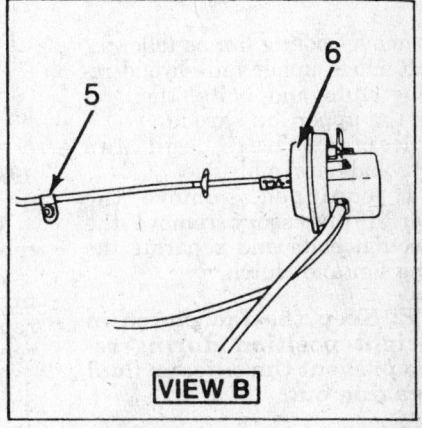

VIEW B

8569Z047

1. Throttle body linkage shield
2. Bolt
3. Cable retainer
4. Cruise control cable assembly
5. Retainer
6. Cruise control servo

Cruise control cable adjustment

the rim inward to a width that covers the mounting screw holes.

9. Install the blower cover housing to the heater module with the blower cover housing screws.

10. Connect the heater hoses at the heater core inlet and outlet pipes, using new clamps and tightening them to 15 inch lbs. (1.7 Nm).

11. Connect the blower wiring.

12. Connect the negative battery cable, add engine coolant and test system for leaks.

With Air Conditioning

1. Disconnect the negative battery cable.

2. Drain the radiator coolant into a suitable container for later use.

3. Remove the screw attaching the heater outlet pipe to the cowl panel.

4. Remove the heater inlet and outlet pipe quick connect fittings by squeezing both release tabs at the base of the heater core tube and pulling on the pipe to disengage the fitting.

5. Remove the 4 retaining screws to the right side panel insulator and pull it back until the 2 locator studs at the forward edge are disengaged. Remove the panel insulator.

6. Remove the instrument panel lower reinforcement by removing the

nut from the shroud panel stud and the screw from the instrument panel carrier.

7. Remove the 2 vacuum harness connectors at the lower evaporator case and position them out of the way.

8. Remove the right side trim panel by pulling it away from the pillar.

9. Remove the 7 lower evaporator case attaching screws.

10. Remove the lower evaporator housing.

11. Remove the heater core mounting straps and screws.

12. Remove the heater core by pulling it rearward and working the heater core tubes out of the seal.

To install:

13. Install the heater core into position, carefully guiding the heater core tubes through the seals at the cowl panel. Connect heater core mounting straps and screws.

NOTE: If installing new heater core, transfer the quick connect tabs to the tubes of the replacement core.

14. Clean old sealer from mating surfaces of the exposed flanges.

15. Place a ribbon of new sealer on the lower evaporator case mounting flanges.

16. Guide the lower evaporator case into place, taking care to avoid wiping sealer from flanges.

17. Connect lower evaporator case with attaching screws. Begin with 2 screws mounted finger-tight to hold the case in position. Install all screws and tighten evenly to compress flange.

18. Connect the vacuum harness connectors.

19. Attach the lower instrument panel reinforcement with the nut to the shroud panel and the screw to the instrument panel carrier both tightened to 89 inch lbs. (10 Nm).

20. Snap the right side pillar trim panel into place.

21. Slide the right side sound insulator into place to engage the locator studs and install the retaining screws. Tighten screws to 17 inch lbs. (1.9 Nm).

22. Connect the heater core inlet and outlet pipe quick connect fittings by aligning the tabs with the grooves in the fitting sleeve and pushing the sleeve into place on the heater core tube. Check for proper pipe installation.

23. Tighten the heater outlet pipe retaining screw to 17 inch lbs. (1.9 Nm).

24. Connect the negative battery cable.

25. Refill coolant to proper level. Operate system and inspect for proper operation or leakage.

Water Pump

REMOVAL AND INSTALLATION

1992–93 Vehicles

1. Disconnect the negative battery cable.
2. Remove cooling fan as follows:
   a. Remove upper fan shroud retaining nuts and bolts, then remove the upper fan shroud.
   b. Remove nuts and fan clutch/blade assembly.
   c. If equipped, remove the spacer. If necessary remove the connection bolts and separate the cooling fan and clutch.

NOTE: Keep the fan clutch in an upright position during repairs to prevent the silicone fluid from leaking out.

3. Relieve belt tension, then remove the serpentine belt from the water pump pulley. Remove the pulley from the hub in order to access the water pump assembly.
4. Drain the cooling system.
5. Unfasten the radiator hose.
6. Remove the bolts securing the water pump, then remove the pump from the engine.
To install:
7. Clean cylinder block and coolant pump gasket surfaces and discard old gaskets.
8. Place new gaskets on water pump and mounting bolts, then install the pump making sure the gaskets remain in position. Tighten the mounting bolts to 30 ft. lbs. (41 Nm) for 1992 vehicles or to 23 ft. lbs. (31 Nm) for 1993 vehicles.
9. If removed, position and install the air conditioning compressor and power steering brackets.
10. Fasten heater bypass and/or radiator hose to the pump, as applicable.
11. Install the water pump pulley, then install the serpentine drive belt.

——— **WARNING** ———
Inspect fan blade for bends or damage. Do not use or attempt to repair a fan blade which has been bent or damaged. It is essential that a fan blade remains in balance to prevent failure and possible injury.

12. Attach cooling fan as follows:
   a. If removed, attach the fan blade to the clutch and tighten the bolts to 18 ft. lbs. (24 Nm).
   b. Place spacer, if equipped, then attach the fan assembly to the cooling pump. Be sure to align reference marks on the fan clutch and coolant pump hub.
   c. Tighten nuts to 18 ft. lbs. (24 Nm).
   d. Install the upper fan shroud and tighten screws to 53 inch lbs. (5.8 Nm).
13. Connect the negative battery cable, then add coolant to engine.
14. Start engine and check for leaks.

1994–96 5.7L (VIN P) Engine

1. Disconnect the negative battery cable.
2. Disengage the wiring harness from the cooling fan assembly, then remove the assembly from the vehicle.
3. Drain the engine cooling system, removing the block drain plug and the knock sensor to assure proper draining. Reinstall the drain plug and knock sensor, as soon as the system is empty.
4. Disconnect the upper and lower radiator hoses from the water pump assembly.
5. Remove the heater hose assemblies from the water pump and from the throttle body.
6. Disengage the coolant sensor wiring harness, then reposition the ignition coil and bracket assembly.
7. Remove the shorter water pump retaining bolt from the center of each pump mating flange, then remove the longer pump bolts from either side of the center bolts.
8. Carefully remove the water pump assembly and gaskets along with the pump shaft coupling.
To install:
9. Thoroughly clean the gasket mating surfaces of any remaining gasket material.
10. Install the water pump shaft coupling along with the water pump and gaskets.
11. Install the longer pump bolts and tighten 33 ft. lbs. (45 Nm), then install the shorter bolts and tighten to 31 ft. lbs. (42 Nm).
12. Reposition the ignition coil and bracket assembly.
13. Engage the coolant sensor electrical connector.
14. Install the heater and radiator hoses to the throttle body and water pump, as applicable.

15. Install the air cleaner and intake duct assemblies.
16. Install the engine cooling fan assembly and engage the wiring harness connector.
17. Connect the negative battery cable and properly fill the engine cooling system.

Thermostat

REMOVAL AND INSTALLATION

1992–93 Vehicles

1. Disconnect the negative battery cable.
2. Drain the coolant from the radiator into a suitable container until the level is below the thermostat housing.
3. If necessary for access, remove the air cleaner assembly from the engine.
4. Remove the radiator inlet hose from the thermostat housing assembly.
5. Remove the thermostat housing bolts, then remove the housing and the thermostat.
6. Installation is the reverse of removal. Clean the sealing surfaces, use a new gasket and tighten the housing retaining bolts to 21 ft. lbs. (28 Nm).

1994–96 5.7L (VIN P) Engine

1. Open the radiator drain cock and allow the engine coolant to drain to a level just below the thermostat housing, then close the drain and tighten to 106 inch lbs. (12 Nm).
2. Remove the air cleaner assembly.
3. Disconnect the inlet hose and clamp from the thermostat assembly.
4. Remove the thermostat housing bolts, then remove the housing.
5. If equipped, remove the housing gasket.
6. Remove the thermostat assembly.
To install:
7. Make sure the flange mating surfaces are clean and free of debris, then install the thermostat assembly.
8. If equipped, install a new housing gasket.
9. Install the housing and tighten the retaining bolts to 21 ft. lbs. (28 Nm), then connect the inlet hose assembly and clamp.
10. Install the air cleaner assembly, then properly refill the engine cooling system.

1. Water pump assembly
2. Water pump gasket
3. Shaft coupling
4. Water pump cover bolt, 33 LB FT (45 NM)
5. Water pump bolt, 31 LB FT (42 NM)

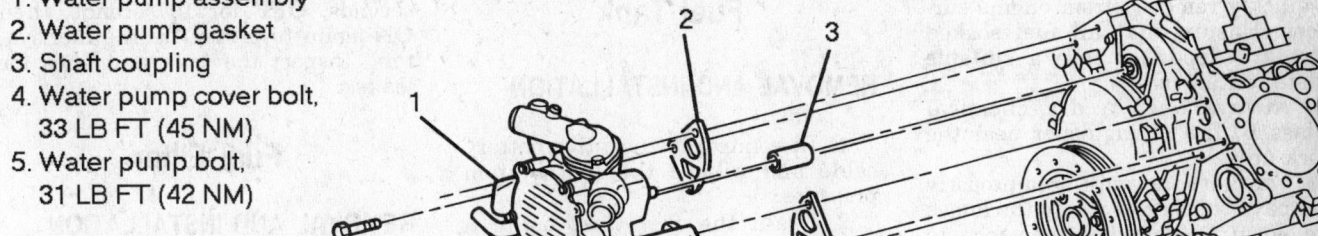

8470Q020

Water pump assembly removal and installation — 5.7L (VIN P) engine

Cooling System Bleeding

1992–93 VEHICLES

1. With the cooling system completely drained, begin adding a combination of ethylene glycol antifreeze and water to achieve a mixture of at least 50 percent, but not exceeding 70 percent antifreeze.

2. Fill the radiator up to the lower portion of the filler neck.

3. Fill the coolant recovery reservoir to the **COLD FILL** or **FULL COLD** mark, then install the coolant recovery cap.

4. Start the vehicle and run the engine with the radiator cap removed until normal engine operating temperature is reached.

5. With the engine idling, add coolant to the radiator until the level reaches the bottom of the filler neck.

6. Install the radiator cap, making sure the arrow on the cap is aligned with the coolant recovery hose.

7. Inspect the system for leaks.

1994–96 5.7L (VIN P) ENGINE

1. Make sure the vehicle is parked or supported on a level surface with the pressure cap removed. Drain the engine cooling system by opening the radiator drain cock, then opening the air bleed vents on the thermostat housing and the heater outlet hose pipe. To assure the system is fully drained, remove the engine block drain plug and the engine knock sensor from either side of the block.

2. Once the system is completely drained, close the drain cock and install the knock sensor. Cover the threads of the drain plug with sealer, then install the plug into the block. The drain plug should be tightened to 15 ft. lbs. (21 Nm), while the knock sensor should be tightened to 14 ft. lbs. (19 Nm).

3. After the repair or service has been completed, fill the cooling system with a solution which is at least 50 percent ethylene glycol antifreeze and the balance water. Do not use a solution that exceeds 70 percent antifreeze. Continue filling the radiator until the level is just below the filler neck.

4. Once the system is filled, close the air bleeds, taking care not to overtighten and damage the brass valves.

5. Install the pressure cap, then start and run the engine to check for leaks.

FUEL SYSTEM

Fuel System Service Precautions

Safety is the most important factor when performing not only fuel system maintenance, but any type of service. Failure to conduct maintenance and repairs in a safe manner may result in serious personal injury or death. Maintenance and testing of the vehicle's fuel system components can be accomplished safely and effectively by adhering to the following rules and guidelines.

• To avoid the possibility of fire and personal injury, always disconnect the negative battery cable before opening fuel system fittings, unless the repair or test procedure requires that battery voltage be applied. This will prevent excessive fuel spillage if the ignition switch is accidentally turned **ON** while fuel fittings are still disconnected.

• Always relieve the fuel system pressure prior to disconnecting any fuel system fitting or connection.

• Exercise extreme caution whenever relieving fuel system pressure to avoid exposing skin, face and eyes to fuel spray. Under pressure, fuel may penetrate the skin or any part of the body that it contacts.

• Always place a shop towel around a fitting or connection prior to loosening in order to absorb any fuel spillage. Ensure that all spilled fuel is quickly removed from engine surfaces. Ensure that all fuel soaked rags are deposited into a suitable waste container.

• Always keep a dry chemical (Class B) fire extinguisher near the work area.

• Ventilate the work area properly and pay attention to where the fumes are blown. Do not allow fuel vapors to come into contact with a source of ignition.

• Always use a backup wrench when loosening and tightening fuel line connection fittings. This will prevent unnecessary stress to fuel line piping. Always follow the proper torque specifications.

• Always replace worn fuel fitting O-rings. Do not substitute fuel hose where metal fuel pipe is normally installed.

RELIEVING FUEL SYSTEM PRESSURE

1992–93 Vehicles With TBI

1. Disconnect the negative battery cable to prevent fuel spillage if an attempt is made to start the vehicle while fittings are still disconnected.

2. Loosen the fuel filler cap to relieve tank vapor pressure and leave the cap loosened until service is completed.

NOTE: The internal constant bleed feature of the Model 220 TBI relieves fuel pump system pressure when the engine is turned OFF. Therefore, no further relief procedure is required.

3. Be sure to tighten fuel filler cap when maintenance or repairs are finished.

1994–96 Vehicles With SFI

1. Disconnect the negative battery cable to prevent fuel discharge if the key is accidentally turned to the **RUN** position.

2. Loosen the fuel filler cap to relieve the tank pressure and do not tighten until service has been completed.

3. Connect J–34730–1 fuel pressure gauge or equivalent, to the fuel pressure valve. Wrap a shop cloth

around the fitting while connecting the gauge to avoid spillage.

4. Place the end of the bleed hose into a suitable container and open the valve to relieve the fuel system pressure.

Fuel Tank

REMOVAL AND INSTALLATION

1. Disconnect the negative battery cable and relieve the fuel system pressure.

2. Drain the fuel tank using a hand operated pump and store the fuel in a safe location.

3. Raise and support the vehicle safely.

4. Disconnect lower fuel tank shield attaching screws and remove the shield.

5. Clean and disconnect vapor hose at the fuel sender, vent hose at fuel filler neck vent pipe, and fuel filler tube at fuel tank.

6. Clean and disengage the fuel feed and return line quick-connect fittings at the fuel sender assembly.

7. Disengage the fuel sender assembly electrical connector.

NOTE: Never handle the fuel sender assembly by the fuel tubes. The length of each tube is great enough to apply a damaging amount of leverage to the solder joints if mishandled.

8. For 1993–96 vehicles, remove the cross-strap attaching nut and screw, then remove the strap.

9. With the aid of an assistant, support the fuel tank and remove the fuel tank retaining straps, nuts and bolts.

10. Remove the fuel tank and place in a safe well ventilated area.

To install:

11. With the aid of an assistant, support the fuel tank in the correct position and attach the fuel tank retaining straps, nuts and bolts. Tighten front strap retaining bolts to 24 ft. lbs. (31 Nm) and rear retaining nuts to 18 ft. lbs. (24 Nm). If applicable, tighten the cross-strap attaching nut to 11 ft. lbs. (15 Nm).

12. Connect fuel filler tube, vent hose, vapor hose, and clamps.

13. Engage the fuel sender assembly electrical connector.

14. Attach the fuel feed and return pipe quick-connect fittings. Be sure to apply a few drops of clean engine oil to the male connector tube ends.

15. Connect the lower fuel tank shield and attaching screws and tighten to 18 inch lbs. (2.0 Nm).

16. Lower vehicle, add fuel and install the filler cap.

17. Connect the negative battery cable.

18. Turn the ignition **ON** for 2 seconds, **OFF** for 10 seconds, then **ON** again to pressurize the fuel system. Inspect the tank and lines for leaks.

Fuel Filter

REMOVAL AND INSTALLATION

Carbureted Engine

1. Disconnect the negative battery cable.

2. Disconnect the fuel line fitting at the fuel inlet filter nut on the carburetor.

3. Remove the fuel inlet filter nut from the carburetor.

4. Remove filter, filter check valve and spring.

5. Remove the gasket from the fuel inlet nut. Discard the gasket, filter check valve and filter.

To install:

6. Install the fuel filter spring first and then the fuel filter with the check valve facing out, into the carburetor opening.

7. Ensure that the filter assembly is installed with the check valve end facing the fuel inlet line. Ribs on the closed end of the filter prevent the filter from being installed incorrectly.

8. Install a new gasket onto the fuel line nut and tighten the nut into the carburetor opening.

9. Reconnect and tighten the fuel inlet line to the fuel nut.

10. Start the engine and inspect for leaks. Repair all fuel leaks immediately.

Fuel Injected Engine

The fuel injection system uses an in-line filter located in the fuel feed line under the hood, attached to the frame rail or on the rear crossmember of the vehicle. The high pressure fuel system used with all fuel injection systems requires special fuel lines to contain the pressure and utilizes nylon lines with quick-connect fittings.

1. Disconnect the negative battery cable and relieve fuel system pressure.

2. Raise and support the vehicle safely.

3. Remove the filter bracket attaching bolt.

4. While grasping the fuel filter and 1 of the fuel lines, twist the line approximately ¼ turn in each direction to loosen any dirt in the fitting, then use compressed air (and safety glasses) to blow dirt out of the fitting. Squeeze the plastic tabs of the male connector on the fuel lines and the pull connection apart. Repeat for the other fitting.

5. If applicable, remove the fuel feed and return line body harness clips.

6. Remove the filter.

To install:

7. Remove the protective caps from the new filter, then position the fuel filter in the original location with the arrow pointing in correct direction.

8. Install the new connector retainers on the filter inlet and outlet tubes.

9. Apply a few drops of clean engine oil to the male ends of both fuel lines connectors.

10. Push the fuel line connectors onto the fuel filter tubes until their retaining tabs snap into place.

11. Once installed, pull on both ends of the lines to verify they are secure.

12. Secure the filter and bracket to the frame trapping the return pipe and tighten the attaching bolt to 89 inch lbs. (10 Nm).

13. Lower the vehicle.

14. Reconnect the negative battery cable.

15. Turn the ignition **ON** for 2 seconds, **OFF** for 10 seconds, **ON** again to pressurize the fuel system. Inspect the tank and lines for leaks.

Mechanical Fuel Pump

PRESSURE TESTING

1. Disconnect the fuel line at the carburetor and install a rubber hose approximately 8–10 inch long over the line and attach a low-reading pressure gauge.

2. Hold the gauge up so it is approximately 16 inches. above the fuel pump. If equipped, pinch the fuel return line.

3. Start the engine and run at slow idle using the fuel in the carburetor.

4. Note the reading on the pressure gauge, if the pump is operating properly the pressure should be 5½–6½ psi constant. The pump must be replaced if pressure is too high, too low or varies greatly.

5. The fuel pump may also be checked using a vacuum gauge. Disconnect the inlet hose from the pump and connect a vacuum gauge. Crank the engine to obtain the maximum vacuum reading from the pump. The pump must be replaced if it is not able to generate a minimum of 15 Hg (51 kPa).

REMOVAL AND INSTALLATION

1. Disconnect the negative battery cable and loosen the fuel filler cap.

2. Clean all fuel feed and return pipe connections and surrounding areas to avoid contamination of the fuel system.

3. Disconnect the fuel feed and return hoses at the frame, then cap the openings to prevent contamination or leakage. Disconnect the fuel feed pipe from the outlet side of pump.

4. Remove the 2 mounting bolts.

5. Remove the fuel pump, then remove and discard the old gasket.

To install:

6. Clean the gasket sealing surfaces.

7. Install fuel pump using a new gasket, then secure using the attaching bolts.

8. Connect the fuel feed pipe to the outlet side of the pump, then tighten carefully to 22 ft. lbs. (30 Nm) using a backup wrench.

9. Uncap the fuel feed and return pipes, then install with clamps to the connecting hoses at the frame.

10. Tighten fuel filler cap and attach the negative battery cable.

11. Start the engine and check for leaks.

Electric Fuel Pump

PRESSURE TESTING

When the ignition switch is turned **ON**, the ECM will turn the in-tank fuel pump ON. It will remain in operation as long as the engine is cranking or running and the ECM is receiving ignition reference pulses. If there are no reference pulses, the ECM will shut the fuel pump OFF within 2 seconds after the key is turned **ON**. The pump will deliver fuel to the TBI unit at a pressure controlled by the internal regulator to approximately 9–13 psi. Excess fuel is then returned to the fuel tank.

TBI Systems

While the engine is stopped, the fuel pump can be activated by applying battery voltage to the fuel pump test terminal (RED wire) located near the passenger side cowl of the engine compartment.

NOTE: Fuel pressure should be noted while the fuel pump is running. Fuel pressure will drop immediately after the fuel pump stops running due to the controlled bleed in the fuel system.

1. Turn the ignition **OFF** and relieve fuel system pressure by removing fuel filler cap.

2. Locate the engine compartment fuel feed quick-connect fitting. Before disconnecting, clean the fitting to prevent system contamination:

   a. Grasp both ends of the fitting and twist female end ¼ turn in each direction to loosen any dirt in fitting.

   b. Wearing safety glasses, use compressed air to blow dirt out of the quick-connect fitting.

3. Separate the male and female leads of the connector by inserting tool into female end of the connector to release the male end.

4. Install a fuel pressure gauge between both ends of the connector. Be sure to always lubricate the male end with a few drops of engine oil to ensure proper connection and prevent a fuel leak.

5. Apply battery voltage to the fuel pump test connector.

6. The fuel pressure should be 9–13 psi.

SFI Systems

1. Relieve fuel system pressure and check that there is an adequate quantity of fuel in the tank.

2. Install a fuel pressure gauge to the underhood pressure connector fitting.

3. Make sure the ignition switch has been in the **OFF** position for at least 10 seconds and that all accessories are OFF.

4. Turn the ignition switch **ON** and the pump will run for about 2 seconds. Note the system pressure with the pump running, it should be the pressure should be 40–47 psi.

NOTE: The ignition switch may have to be cycled to ON more than once to obtain maximum pressure. It is also normal for the pressure to drop slightly when the pump first stops, but it should then hold steady.

5. If fuel pressure is not as specified, verify that fuel pump operation is heard in the tank.

6. If fuel pump operation is not heard, inspect the fuel pump relay and wiring.

7. If fuel pump operation is heard, inspect filter and lines for restriction.

8. Start the engine and make sure the pressure decreases about 3–10 psi at idle.

9. If fuel pressure does not decrease, inspect pressure regulator and vacuum hose.

10. Disconnect the fuel pressure gauge.

REMOVAL AND INSTALLATION

1. Disconnect the negative battery cable and relieve the fuel system pressure.

2. Drain the fuel tank using a suitable hand-operated pump, then raise and support the vehicle safely.

3. Remove the fuel tank.

4. Remove the fuel tank sending unit and pump assembly as follows: remove the assembly attaching nuts, retaining flag, assembly and O-ring from the tank. Discard the O-ring.

To install:

5. Install fuel sending unit in fuel tank as follows: position a new O-ring on fuel tank. Install fuel sender assembly, retaining flag, and attaching nuts to fuel tank. Tighten attaching nuts to 27 inch lbs. (3 Nm).

6. Install fuel tank.

7. Lower vehicle.

8. Turn the ignition **ON** for 2 seconds, **OFF** for 10 seconds, then **ON** again to pressurize the fuel system. Inspect the fuel system for leaks.

Fuel Injection

THROTTLE BODY INJECTION

On the 1992–93 fuel injected 4.3L, 5.0L and 5.7L engines, the EFI system centrally locates a single Model 220 Throttle Body Injection (TBI) unit on the intake manifold where air and fuel are distributed through 2 bores in the unit. Air used for combustion is controlled by 2 throttle valves which are connected to the accelerator pedal linkage through a throttle shaft and lever assembly. A special plate, located under the throttle valve, is used to aid in uniform mixture distribution. Fuel for combustion is supplied by 2 fuel injectors mounted on the TBI unit.

The metering tips of the fuel injectors are positioned directly above the throttle valve. Injector metering tips are "pulsed" or "timed" open and closed by an electronic signal received from the ECM. The ECM receives inputs from various engine sensors concerning engine operating conditions, coolant temperature, exhaust gas oxygen content, etc. Information is then used to calculate the engines fuel requirements by controlling the injector pulse openings to provide an ideal fuel/air mixture ratio.

SEQUENTIAL MULTI-PORT FUEL INJECTION

Beginning in 1994, the 4.3L and 5.7L V8 engines were equipped with a multi-port fuel injection system in which a fuel rail assembly delivered fuel to a separate injector for each cylinder. The system is called a Sequential Fuel Injection (SFI) system because the ECM pulses each individual injector to deliver fuel according to the engine firing order. Engine performance is enhanced by this close matching of fuel delivery to combustion timing.

IDLE SPEED ADJUSTMENT

The idle speed and mixture are electronically controlled by the Electronic Control Module (ECM). All adjustments are preset at the factory and do not need periodic attention. Some throttle body units are equipped with an idle stop screw to allow adjustment of the minimum idle speed if the unit is used as a replacement. The only time the idle speed should require adjustment is when the throttle body assembly has been replaced.

TBI Systems

1. Block the drive wheels and apply the parking brake. Remove the air cleaner assembly and/or air duct.

2. Connect a scan tool to the Data Link Connector (DLC) and select the field service mode. Turn the ignition **ON** and leave the engine OFF. Wait at least 45 seconds, this will allow the Idle Air Control (IAC) pintle to seat in the throttle body.

3. With the ignition switch in the **ON** position, the engine OFF and the scan tool in field service mode, disengage the IAC valve electrical connector and the distributor set-timing connector.

4. Connect a tachometer to the engine to monitor the engine speed.

5. Place the transmission in the **P** or **N** position and start the engine.

6. Run the engine until it reaches normal operating temperature or closed loop operation as indicated by the scan tool. It may be necessary to hold the throttle open slightly in order to maintain idle.

7. The idle speed should be 450–500 rpm, be sure the throttle and cruise control cables do not hold the throttle open. If not as specified, remove the idle speed stop screw plug and adjust as necessary.

8. Turn the ignition **OFF**, then reconnect the IAC valve electrical connector and the distributor set-timing connector.

9. Adjust the Idle Air Control (IAC) valve pintle position.

10. Install the air cleaner assembly, check and clear all ECM trouble codes.

SFI Systems

The idle speed and mixture are electronically controlled by the Electronic Control Module (ECM). All adjustments are preset at the factory and do not require periodic attention.

IAC VALVE PINTLE ADJUSTMENT

Idle speed is controlled by the ECM through voltage pulses sent to the Idle Air Control (IAC) motor windings. Based on the number of voltage pulses received, the motor will move the IAC pintle in or out allowing more or less air through the throttle body.

NOTE: If installing a new IAC valve measure and adjust the valve accordingly. If reinstalling a used IAC valve, do not push or pull on the pintle to adjust pintle length or damage to the worn IAC pintle threads may occur. The valve is preset at the factory and will self adjust when the following procedure is performed.

1. On new IAC valves only, measure the distance between the tip of the pintle and the valve mounting surface. If greater than 1.10 inch (28mm), use light finger pressure to slowly retract the pintle. The force required to retract a new IAC valve will not damage the valve threads.

2. Install the IAC valve and gasket.

3. Engage the IAC valve wire connector.

4. Reset the IAC valve pintle position as follows:

   a. Depress the accelerator pedal slightly.

   b. Start the engine and run for 5 seconds.

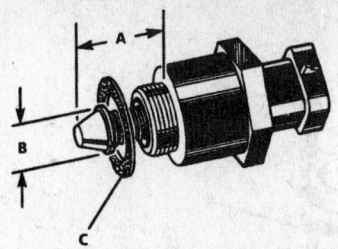

A. Distance of pintle extension
B. Diameter and shape of pintle
C. IAC valve gasket

8470P022

A new Idle Air Control (IAC) valve pintle may be adjusted by hand prior to installation

c. Turn the ignition **OFF** for 10 seconds.
d. Restart the vehicle and check for proper idle operation.

Fuel Injector

REMOVAL AND INSTALLATION

NOTE: Exercise care when removing the fuel injectors to prevent damage to the electrical connector terminals, the injector filter and the fuel nozzle. Also, since the injectors are electrical components, they should not be immersed in any type of liquid solvent or cleaner as damage may occur.

TBI Systems

1. Disconnect the negative battery cable and relieve fuel system pressure.
2. Remove the air cleaner assembly, then disengage the electrical connectors from the fuel injectors by squeezing the plastic tabs and pulling straight up.
3. Remove the fuel meter cover attaching screws, then remove the cover assembly.
4. Remove the fuel meter outlet passage gasket and pressure regulator dust seal. If, upon removal of the fuel meter assembly, the cover gasket is stuck to the fuel meter body, leave it in place. If it is stuck to the fuel meter cover, remove it from the cover and place it on the fuel meter body to protect the body in the next step.
5. With the cover gasket in place on the fuel meter body, carefully pry each injector from the throttle body using a small prytool and a smooth fulcrum. Carefully remove each injector and position aside.
6. Remove and discard the lower (small) O-rings from the injector nozzles.

7. Remove and discard the fuel meter cover gasket.
8. Remove and discard the upper (large) O-rings from top of each fuel injector cavity. If equipped, remove the steel backup washer, from the the top of each injector cavity.
To install:
9. Inspect the fuel injector filter for evidence of dirt and contamination. If present, check for presence of dirt in fuel lines and fuel tank.

NOTE: If replacements are required, ensure that the injector is replaced with an identical part. The model 220 TBI is capable of accepting other types of injectors but other injectors are calibrated for different flow rates and may cause driveability or emission problems.

10. If equipped, install the steel injector backup washer in the counterbore of the fuel meter body.
11. Lubricate new upper (large) O-ring with engine oil and install into the top of the fuel meter cavity, or if equipped, directly over the backup washer. Ensure the O-ring is seated properly and is flush with top of fuel meter body surface.
12. Lubricate new lower (small) O-ring with engine oil and push on nozzle end of injector until it seats against injector fuel filter.

NOTE: Backup washers and O-rings must be installed before the injectors or improper seating of large O-ring could cause fuel to leak.

13. Align the raised lug on each injector base with notch in fuel meter body cavity and install the injector. Push down with moderate pressure on injector until it is fully seated in fuel meter body. The electrical terminals of injector should be parallel with throttle shaft.
14. Install a new pressure regulator dust seal, fuel meter outlet gasket and fuel meter cover gasket.
15. Install the fuel meter cover.
16. Coat the threads of the fuel meter attaching screw with a suitable thread locking compound. Install and tighten the screws to 27 inch lbs. (3 Nm).
17. Engage the electrical connectors to their respective fuel injectors.
18. Tighten fuel filler cap, and reconnect the negative battery cable.
19. Turn the ignition **ON** for 2 seconds, **OFF** for 10 seconds, then **ON** again to pressurize the fuel system. Inspect the fuel system for leaks.

SFI Systems

1. Make sure the ignition is in the **OFF** position, then disconnect the negative battery cable.
2. Properly relieve the fuel system pressure.
3. Disengage the quick-connect fittings at the fuel rail feed and return pipes as follows:
   a. Slide the rubber dust cover from the fitting.
   b. Grasp both ends of a connection and twist ¼ turn in each direction to loosen any dirt. Repeat for other fitting.
   c. While wearing safety glasses, use compressed air to blow out dirt from the fitting.
   d. Insert a fuel line separator tool, into the female connector, then push inward to release the male connector.
   e. Repeat for the other fitting.
4. Disconnect the vacuum line at the pressure regulator, then as necessary, tag and disconnect any remaining vacuum lines which must be removed to access the fuel rail and engine fuel pipes.
5. Remove the fuel injector wiring harness from the routing clips of the fuel rail, then remove the fuel pipe attaching bolt and disengage the injector electrical connectors.
6. Remove the fuel rail attaching bolts and carefully remove the fuel rail assembly along with the injectors, from the top of the intake.
7. Rotate the injector retaining clip to the release position and remove the injector from the fuel rail assembly.
8. Remove and discard the O-ring seals from either side of the injector.
9. Remove and discard the injector retaining clip.
To install:
10. Lubricate the new injector O-rings with clean engine oil and install onto the injector.

NOTE: Always replace injectors using an identical part number as inscribed on top of the old injector.

11. Connect a new retainer clip onto the fuel injector and install the injector to the fuel rail assembly. Rotate the injector retaining clip to the lock position.
12. Install the fuel rail assembly to the intake manifold. Tighten the attaching bolts to 15 ft. lbs. (20 Nm).
13. Rotate the fuel injectors as necessary to avoid stretching the wire harnesses, then engage the injector electrical connections.

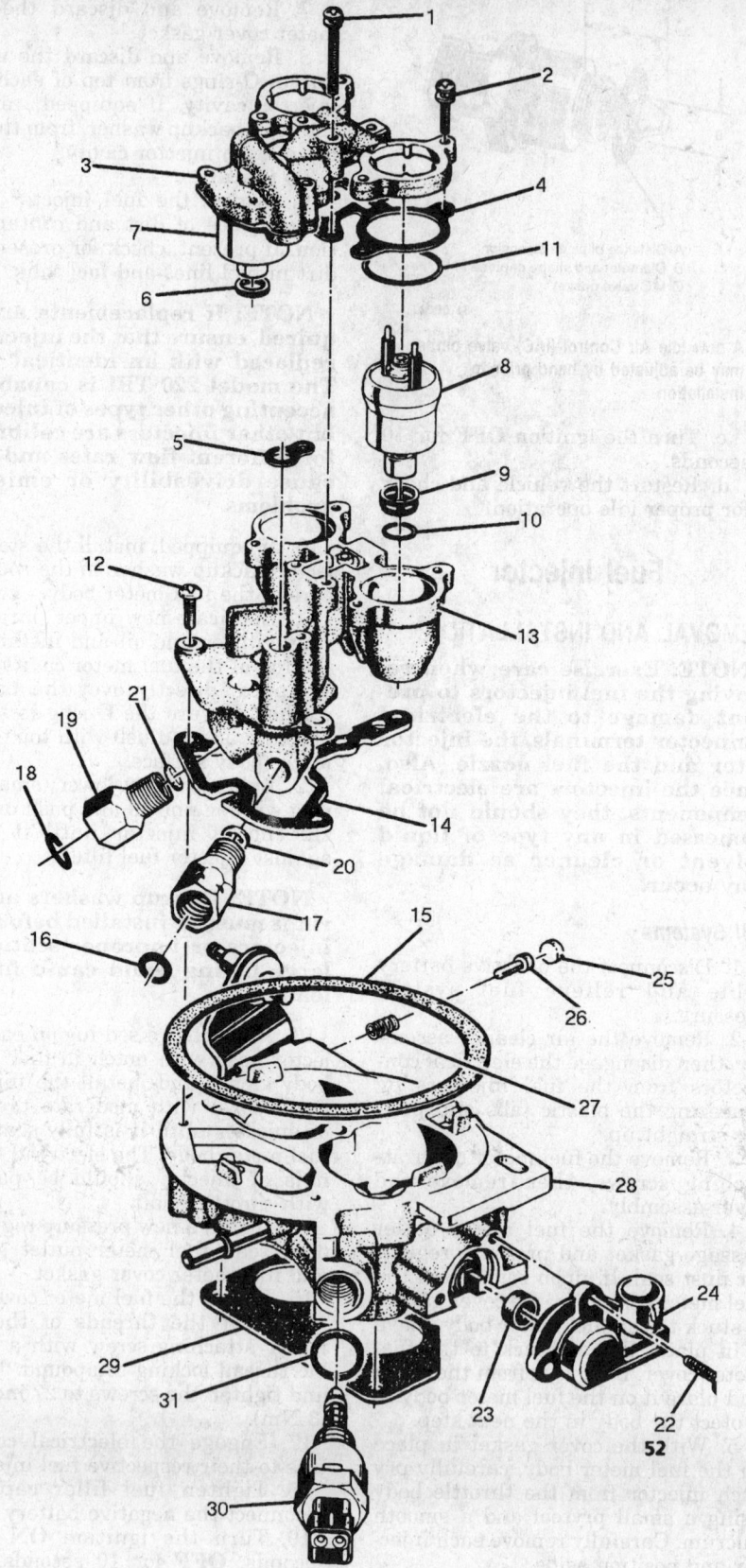

1. Fuel meter cover attaching screw-long
2. Fuel meter cover attaching screw-short
3. Fuel meter cover assembly
4. Fuel meter cover gasket
5. Fuel meter outlet gasket
6. Fuel pressure regulator seal
7. Fuel pressure regulator assembly
8. TBI fuel injector assembly
9. Fuel injector inlet filter
10. Fuel injector lower O-ring
11. Fuel injector upper O-ring
12. Fuel meter body to throttle body attaching screw
13. Fuel meter body assembly
14. Throttle body to fuel meter body gasket
15. Air cleaner gasket
16. Fuel return line gasket
17. Fuel outlet nut
18. Fuel inlet line O-ring
19. Fuel inlet nut
20. Fuel outlet nut gasket
21. Fuel inlet nut gasket
22. TP sensor attaching screw
23. TP sensor seal
24. Throttle position sensor
25. Idle stop screw plug
26. Idle stop screw
27. Idle stop screw spring
28. Throttle body assembly
29. Flange gasket
30. Idle air control assembly
31. IAC valve gasket

8470P023

Exploded view of the Model 220 TBI assembly

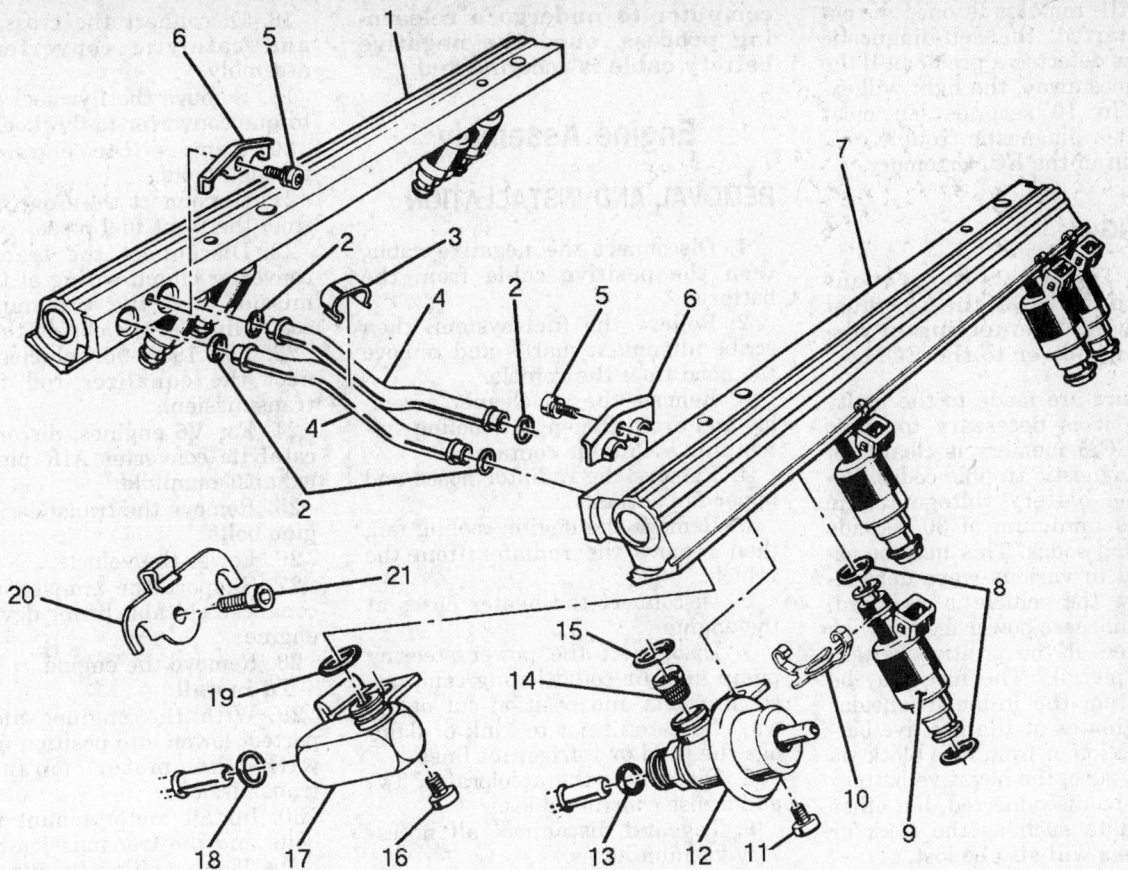

1. LH MFI fuel rail assembly
2. Fuel crossover tube o-ring
3. Fuel crossover tube clip
4. Fuel crossover tube
5. Crossover tube retainer attaching screw
6. Fuel crossover tube retainer
7. RH MFI Fuel rail assembly
8. Fuel injector o-ring
9. MFI fuel injector assembly
10. Injector retainer clip
11. Pressure regulator attaching screw
12. Fuel pressure regulator assembly
13. Fuel outlet tube o-ring
14. Filter screen (if equipped)
15. Fuel inlet fitting o-ring
16. Fuel inlet assembly attaching screw
17. Fuel inlet assembly
18. Fuel in let tube o-ring
19. Fuel inlet assembly o-ring
20. Fuel tube retainer assembly
21. Fuel tube retainer assembly attaching screw

8470Q026

Exploded view of the fuel rail assembly — 5.7L (VIN P) engine

14. Install the fuel pipe retaining nut, then position the wiring harness into the routing clips at the fuel rail.

15. Connect the vacuum lines to the intake, as necessary, then connect the vacuum line to the pressure regulator.

16. Apply a few drops of clean engine oil to the male ends of the fuel line quick-connect fittings. Engage the fittings by pushing the connectors together until the retaining tabs snap into place. Pull gently on both sides of each fitting to be sure the connection is secure. When secure, slide the dust covers over the fittings.

17. Tighten the fuel filler cap and connect the negative battery cable.

18. Turn the ignition ON for 2 seconds, OFF for 10 seconds, then ON again and inspect the system for leaks.

EMISSION CONTROLS

Emission Warning Lamps

The SERVICE ENGINE SOON Malfunction Indicator Light (MIL) located in the instrument cluster serves 2 main functions:

1. The lamp indicates to the driver when a problem has occurred and the vehicle should be taken for service as soon as reasonably possible.

2. The light may be used by technicians to monitor diagnostic trouble codes and/or open/closed loop engine operation, whenever the system is placed in the diagnostic mode.

To verify proper operation of the bulb and wiring, the lamp will illuminate when the ignition is first turned to ON, but the engine is not running. If the system is operating properly, the lamp will turn OFF once the engine is started.

If the MIL remains lit once the engine is started, the self-diagnostic system has detected a problem. If the problem goes away, the light will extinguish in 10 seconds (in most cases), but a diagnostic trouble code will remain in the ECM memory.

RESETTING

NOTE: In order to prevent damage to the ECM, the key must be OFF when connecting or disconnecting power to the ECM.

After repairs are made to the faulty system(s), it is necessary to make sure the ECM memory is cleared of any old diagnostic trouble codes. Removing the battery voltage to the ECM for a minimum of 30 seconds will clear all codes. This may be accomplished in various ways depending on how the vehicle is equipped. The ECM harness power feed may be disconnected at the positive battery terminal "pigtail." The fuse may be removed from the inline fuseholder which originates at the positive battery connection or from fuse block, as applicable. Also, the negative battery cable may be disconnected, but other on-board data such as the clock or radio presets will also be lost.

ECM LEARNING ABILITY

The ECM has a "learning" ability which allows it to make corrections for minor variations in the fuel system, in order to improve driveability. If the battery is disconnected to clear diagnostic codes or for safety during repairs, the "learning" process will reset and must begin again. A change may be noted in the vehicle's performance while the learning process begins. To "teach" the vehicle, make sure the engine is at normal operating temperature, then drive the vehicle at part throttle, with moderate acceleration and idle conditions, until normal performance returns.

ENGINE MECHANICAL

NOTE: Disconnecting the negative battery cable on some vehicles may interfere with the functions of the on-board computer systems and may require the

computer to undergo a relearning process, once the negative battery cable is reconnected.

Engine Assembly

REMOVAL AND INSTALLATION

1. Disconnect the negative cable, then the positive cable from the battery.
2. Relieve the fuel system, then scribe alignment marks and remove the hood from the vehicle.
3. Remove the air cleaner assembly and drain the engine cooling system into a suitable container.
4. Remove the radiator hoses and upper fan shroud.
5. Remove the engine cooling fan, then remove the radiator from the vehicle.
6. Disconnect the heater hoses at the engine
7. Disconnect the power steering pump and air conditioning compressor brackets and position out of the way. Be careful not to kink or damage the fluid or refrigerant lines.
8. Disconnect the accelerator, TV, and cruise control cables.
9. Tag and disconnect all necessary vacuum hoses.
10. Disconnect the ECM wiring harness, the engine wiring harness at the engine bulkhead, engine-to-bulkhead ground strap and any remaining wires between body and engine.
11. Remove the distributor assembly from the engine.
12. Remove the windshield wiper motor assembly.
13. Remove the MAP sensor, then for 1993 vehicles remove the EGR solenoid.
14. Remove the negative battery cable from the cylinder head.
15. If not done already, remove the brake pipe from the intake manifold.
16. Raise and support the vehicle safely.

----- WARNING -----
Never raise the engine using a jack under the oil pan, crankshaft pulley or any sheetmetal. Because there only is a small clearance between the oil pan and the oil pump screen, if the pan is bent even slightly, damage could occur to the pump screen and pickup unit.

17. Disconnect the battery positive cable and wires at the starter motor. Be sure to tag the wires for installation purposes.

18. Disconnect the crossover pipe and catalytic converter as an assembly.
19. Remove the flywheel cover and torque converter-to-flywheel bolts.
20. Remove the engine mount through-bolts.
21. Disconnect the front fuel hoses from the front fuel pipes.
22. Disconnect the transmission converter clutch wiring at the transmission and the transmission oil cooler lines at the clip on the oil pan.
23. For 1993–96 vehicles, disconnect the equalizer rod from the transmission.
24. For V6 engines, disconnect the catalytic converter AIR pipe at the exhaust manifold.
25. Remove the transmission-to-engine bolts.
26. Lower the vehicle.
27. Support the transmission and connect a suitable lifting device to the engine.
28. Remove the engine.
   To install:
29. With the engine safely supported, lower into position and align with the motor mounts and transmission.
30. Install motor mount through-bolts and the transmission-to-engine bolts. Tighten either the nuts to 59 ft. lbs. (80 Nm) or the through-bolts to 70 ft. lbs. (95 Nm). Tighten the transmission-to-engine bolts to 35 ft. lbs. (47 Nm).
31. Raise and support the vehicle safely.
32. If applicable, connect the AIR pipe to the exhaust manifold or the equalizer rod to the transmission.
33. Connect the transmission converter clutch wiring to the transmission and the transmission oil cooler lines to the clip on the oil pan.
34. Connect the front fuel hoses to the front fuel pipes.
35. Install the torque converter-to-flywheel bolts and the flywheel housing cover.
36. Connect the crossover pipe and catalytic converter assembly.
37. Connect the battery positive cable and wires to the starter motor.
38. Lower vehicle.
39. Connect the brake pipe to the intake manifold, then connect the negative battery cable to the cylinder head.
40. As applicable, install the EGR solenoid, the MAP sensor and the windshield wiper motor.
41. Install the distributor assembly.
42. Connect the ECM wiring harness, the engine wiring harness at

the engine bulkhead, engine to bulkhead ground straps and all other wires between body and engine.

43. Connect all vacuum hoses as noted during removal.

44. Connect the accelerator, TV and cruise control cables.

45. Connect the power steering pump and air conditioning compressor brackets.

46. Connect the heater hoses to the engine.

47. Install the engine cooling fan.

48. Install the radiator, hoses and fan shroud.

49. Install the air cleaner assembly.

50. Install the hood, aligning the marks made during removal.

51. Connect the negative battery cable, then fill and bleed the engine cooling system.

52. Inspect vehicle fluid levels, specifications and verify there are no fluid leaks.

Engine Mounts

REMOVAL AND INSTALLATION

1. Disconnect the negative battery cable.

2. As necessary to provide engine pivot/raising clearance:

   a. Remove the air intake duct assembly.

   b. Remove the radiator upper shroud.

   c. For 1992–93 vehicles, tag and disconnect the spark plug wires from the distributor cap, then remove the cap from the distributor assembly.

3. Raise and support the vehicle safely.

4. Raise the engine sufficiently to just remove the weight from the engine mount.

NOTE: Do not raise or support engine with a jack under the oil pan, crankshaft pulley or any sheetmetal. Because of the small clearance between the oil pan and oil pump screen, jacking against the oil pan may damage oil pickup assembly.

5. Remove the mount bracket bolt and nut .

6. For 1993–96 vehicles, remove the transmission fluid cooler lines from the oil pan clip.

NOTE: For 1992–93 vehicles, verify the clearance between the rear of the engine and the firewall is sufficient enough to avoid possible damage to the distributor.

7. Raise the engine sufficiently to remove the motor mounts, then remove the mount bolts and nuts. Remove the engine mount from the vehicle.

To install:

8. Position the engine mount to the frame, then secure using the bolts and/or nuts. Tighten the bolts to 33 ft. lbs. (45 Nm) and the nuts to 30 ft. lbs. (41 Nm).

9. Lower engine assembly into place, then if applicable, install the transmission fluid cooler lines to the oil pan clip.

10. Install the engine mount bracket bolt and nut. Tighten the bolt to 70 ft. lbs. (95 Nm) and/or the nut to 49 ft. lbs. (67 Nm).

11. Lower the vehicle, then install the distributor cap, radiator upper shroud and the air intake duct, as necessary.

12. Connect the negative battery cable.

Cylinder Head

REMOVAL AND INSTALLATION

1992–93 Vehicles

1. Disconnect the negative battery cable, then relieve the fuel system pressure.

2. Drain cooling system into a suitable container.

3. For 1993 vehicles, remove the cooling fan assembly.

4. Remove the intake manifold assembly from the engine.

5. Remove the exhaust manifold assemblies from the engine.

6. Remove the rocker arm cover or valve cover.

7. For 1993 4.3L engines, remove the air conditioning pressure cycling switch, then remove the electrical connectors from the wiper motor.

8. Disconnect the power steering pump, alternator, and/or air conditioning brackets, as necessary, and position aside.

9. Disconnect the ground strap and/or negative battery cable from cylinder head, as applicable.

10. Loosen cylinder head bolts gradually using at least 3 passes.

11. Clean dirt from cylinder head and adjacent area to avoid getting dirt into engine.

12. If necessary, remove rocker arm assemblies and lift out pushrods.

13. Remove cylinder head from engine.

To install:

14. Cylinder heads using a steel gasket should have both sides of the new gasket coated with a good sealer. The coating should be thin and even. Do not use sealer on composite type gaskets.

15. Place gasket over dowel pins.

16. Place cylinder head over dowel pins and gasket.

17. Coat the threads of the cylinder head bolts with sealing compound, part 1052080 or equivalent, then install the bolts finger-tight. Following the proper torque sequence, tighten the cylinder head bolts, using multiple passes, to 68 ft. lbs. (92 Nm)

18. If removed, position pushrods and attach rocker arm assemblies.

19. As applicable, connect the ground strap and/or negative battery cable to the cylinder head.

20. Attach power steering pump, alternator and/or air conditioning brackets if removed.

21. As applicable for 4.3L engines, install the AIR crossover pipe bolt and stud, then install the air conditioning pressure cycling switch, and/or engage the wiper motor electrical connectors.

22. Install the rocker arm cover or valve cover.

23. If removed, install the oil level indicator tube and/or the diverter valve.

24. Attach the intake and exhaust manifolds.

25. For 1993 vehicles, install the cooling fan assembly.

26. Connect the negative battery cable.

27. Attach the fuel filler cap, add coolant and inspect the engine for leaks.

1994–96 5.7L (VIN P) Engine

LEFT SIDE

1. Disconnect the negative battery cable, then raise and support the vehicle safely.

2. Drain the engine cooling system, then disconnect the crossover pipe from the exhaust manifold.

3. Lower the vehicle.

4. Remove the intake manifold assembly.

5. Disconnect the secondary air injection hose from the check valve assembly.

6. Disconnect the coolant air bleed pipe and bolt from the left cylinder head assembly using a backup wrench on the pipe fitting.

7. Remove the ignition coil assembly.

8. Remove the left exhaust manifold assembly.

9. Remove the spark plug wire harness assembly from the clips, then disconnect the harness from the

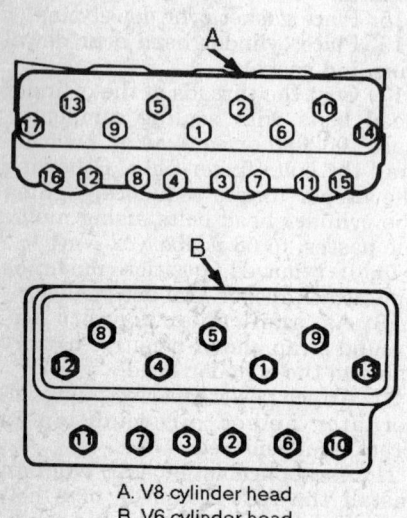

A. V8 cylinder head
B. V6 cylinder head

8470P025

Cylinder head bolt torque sequence — 4.3L (VIN Z), 5.0L (VIN E) and 5.7L (VIN 7) engines

spark plugs and remove the plugs from the left cylinder head.

10. Disengage the coolant temperature sensor connector.

11. Remove the left rocker arm cover.

12. Loosen the rocker arm nuts, then remove the arms and pushrods, either tagging or arranging the components to assure installation in their original locations.

13. Remove the cylinder head bolts, then remove the cylinder head and gasket from the block.

To install:

14. Thoroughly clean the gasket mating surfaces of any remaining gasket material, then position a new cylinder head gasket on the block with the yellow tab facing upwards.

15. Install the cylinder head over the locator pins and the new gasket.

16. Coat the cylinder head bolts with a sealing compound, then install the bolts finger-tight.

17. Torque the bolts using 3 passes of the proper sequence until all bolts have been torqued to 65 ft. lbs. (88 Nm).

18. Install the pushrods and rocker arms, making sure they are in the proper locations, then adjust the valve lash.

19. Install the left rocker arm cover and tighten the retaining bolts to 100 inch lbs. (11 Nm).

20. Install the spark plugs and tighten to 11 ft. lbs. (15 Nm), then install the wiring harness assembly and secure the assembly to the clips.

21. Install the left exhaust manifold assembly.

22. Install the ignition coil assembly and tighten the bolts to 24 ft. lbs. (33 Nm).

23. Connect the engine coolant air bleed pipe and bolt to the left cylinder head assembly using a backup wrench on the pipe fitting in order to prevent component damage. Tighten the bolt to 30 ft. lbs. (40 Nm).

24. Install the secondary air injector hose to the check valve assembly.

25. Install the intake manifold assembly.

26. Raise and support the vehicle safely, then connect the crossover pipe to the exhaust manifold.

27. Lower the vehicle and fill the engine cooling system.

28. Connect then negative battery cable.

RIGHT SIDE

1. Disconnect the negative battery cable.

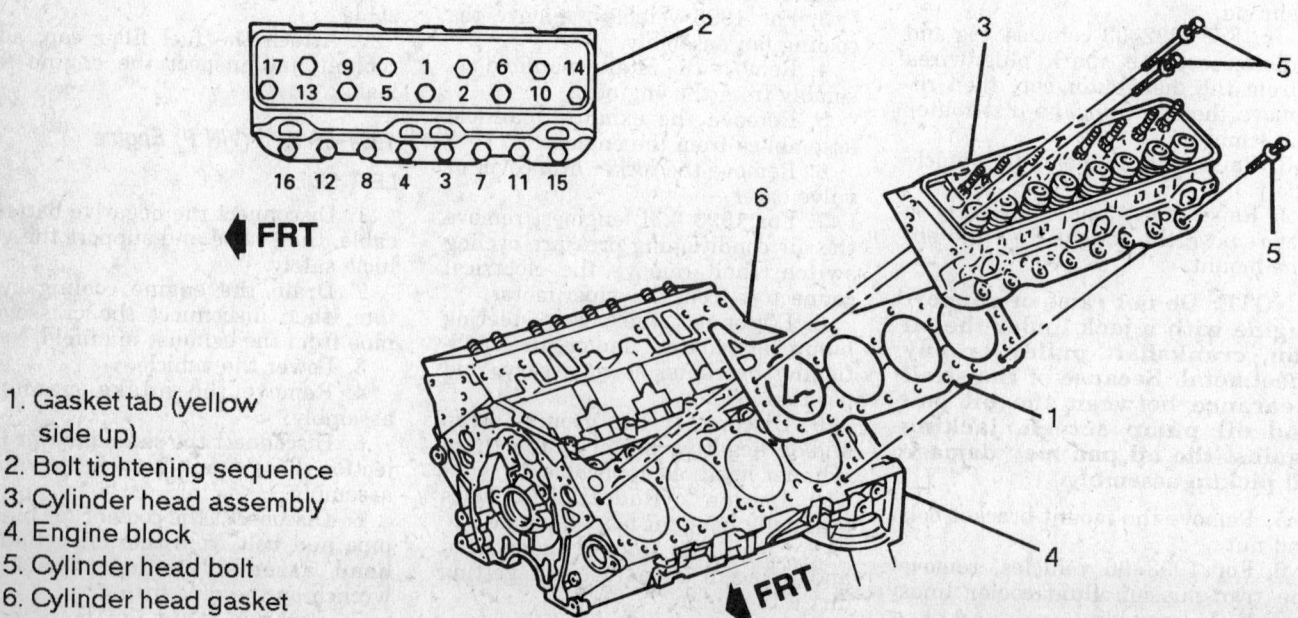

1. Gasket tab (yellow side up)
2. Bolt tightening sequence
3. Cylinder head assembly
4. Engine block
5. Cylinder head bolt
6. Cylinder head gasket

8470Q030

Cylinder head installation and bolt torque sequence — 5.7L (VIN P) engine

2. Raise and support the vehicle safely, then drain the engine cooling system.

3. Remove the serpentine drive belt and the belt tensioner assembly.

4. Remove the transmission fluid level indicator tube assembly bracket from the transmission housing.

5. Remove the air conditioning compressor rear brace bolt from the engine block, then disengage the compressor connector.

6. Remove the front compressor mounting bolts, then position the compressor aside taking care not to kink or damage the lines.

7. Remove the right exhaust manifold assembly.

8. Lower the vehicle.

9. Remove the alternator assembly.

10. Remove the right rocker arm cover.

11. Remove the intake manifold assembly.

12. Remove the coolant air bleed pipe bolt from the left cylinder head assembly.

13. Disconnect the lower radiator hose and the heater hose from the water pump assembly, then position the hoses aside.

14. Remove the coolant air bleed pipe hose from the radiator.

15. Remove the power steering pump assembly.

16. Remove the engine accessory bracket bolts, then remove the bracket assembly.

17. Disconnect the wire harness assembly from the spark plugs, then remove the plugs from the right cylinder head.

18. Loosen the rocker arm nuts, then remove the arms and pushrods, either tagging or arranging the components to assure installation in their original locations.

19. Remove the cylinder head bolts, then remove the cylinder head and gasket from the block. If necessary, carefully remove the coolant air bleed pipe bolt and pipe assembly from the cylinder head.

To install:

20. If removed, loosely install the coolant air bleed pipe bolt and pipe to the cylinder head.

21. Thoroughly clean the gasket mating surfaces of any remaining gasket material, then position a new cylinder head gasket on the block with the yellow tab facing upwards.

22. Install the cylinder head over the locator pins and the new gasket.

23. Coat the cylinder head bolts with a sealing compound, then install the bolts finger-tight.

24. Torque the bolts using 3 passes of the proper sequence until all bolts have been torqued to 65 ft. lbs. (88 Nm).

25. If loosened, tighten the coolant air bleed pipe bolt to 30 ft. lbs. (40 Nm).

26. Install the pushrods and rocker arms, making sure they are in the proper locations, then adjust the valve lash.

27. Install the spark plugs and tighten to 11 ft. lbs. (15 Nm), then install the wiring harness assembly to the plugs.

28. Install the engine accessory bracket and tighten the retaining bolts to 31 ft. lbs. (42 Nm).

29. Install the right rocker arm cover and tighten the retaining bolts to 100 inch lbs. (11 Nm).

30. Install the alternator assembly.

31. Install the power steering pump assembly.

32. Connect the coolant air bleed pipe hose to the radiator, then connect the heater hose and the lower radiator hose to the water pump.

33. Connect the coolant air bleed pipe bolt to the left cylinder head and tighten to 30 ft. lbs. (41 Nm) while using a backup wrench to prevent component damage.

34. Install the intake manifold assembly.

35. Raise and support the vehicle safely.

36. Install the right exhaust manifold assembly.

37. Position the compressor and install the front mounting bolts, then engage the electrical connector. Install the rear compressor brace bolt and tighten to 24 ft. lbs. (33 Nm).

38. Install the transmission fluid level indicator tube assembly to the transmission housing.

39. Install the serpentine drive belt, then lower the vehicle.

40. Fill the engine cooling system, then connect the negative battery cable.

Valve Lifters

REMOVAL AND INSTALLATION

1. Disconnect the negative battery cable.

2. Drain the engine cooling system.

3. Remove the intake manifold assembly.

4. Remove rocker arm covers or valve covers.

5. Remove the rocker arms and pushrods. Be sure to keep all valve train parts in order, as they must be installed in the same locations from which they were removed.

6. Remove the valve lifter retainer bolts, valve lifter retainer and/or guide.

7. Remove the valve lifters, using the a suitable valve lifter tool. If lifters are to be reinstalled, keep them in order so they may be installed in the same bores from which they were removed.

To install:

8. Coat the valve lifter rollers with Molykote®, prelube part 1052365 or equivalent.

9. Insert the valve lifters into the bores. If reinstalling used lifters, make sure they are inserted in the same location from which they were removed.

10. Install the valve lifter guide and/or retainer.

11. Tighten valve lifter retainer bolts to 12 ft. lbs. (16 Nm).

12. Install the intake manifold assembly.

13. Place the pushrods in their original positions and install the rocker arms.

14. Install the rocker arm covers or valve covers.

15. Connect the negative battery cable and add engine coolant.

Valve Lash

ADJUSTMENT

The Chevrolet 4.3L, 5.0L (VIN E) and 5.7L engines do not require any routine valve lash adjustments. However, if the rocker arms are removed, the initial valve lash must be adjusted before the engine is started. Use the following procedure for Chevrolet engines.

1. With the rocker arm covers or valve covers removed and the rocker arm assemblies loosely installed, position the engine at the No. 1 cylinder Top Dead Center (TDC) position.

2. To determine TDC, slowly turn the engine until the mark on the vibration damper aligns with the center or **0** mark on the timing tab of the front cover. At this point the engine is on the No. 1 firing position or the firing position of its opposite cyl-

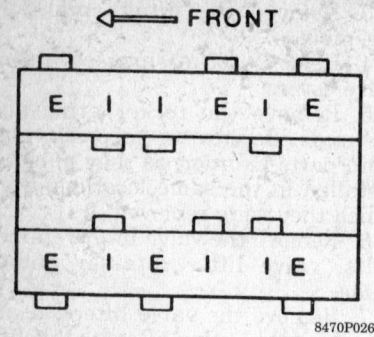

Intake and exhaust valve arrangement — 4.3L V6 engines

8470P026

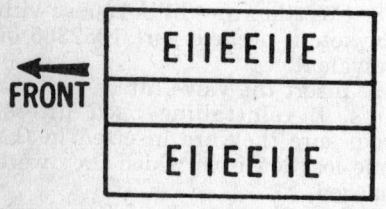

Intake and exhaust valve arrangement — V8 engines

8470P027

inder No. 6 on V8 engine or No. 4 on V6 engine.

NOTE: The firing cylinder may be determined by placing a finger on the No. 1 cylinder valve rocker arms as the mark on the damper comes near the 0 mark on the crankcase front cover. If the valve rocker arms move as the mark comes up to the timing tab, the engine is on the opposite cylinder firing position, No. 6 on V8 engine or No. 4 on V6 engine and should be turned over a complete revolution to reach the No. 1 cylinder firing position. If the engine is in the No. 1 TDC position, the valves for the No. 1 cylinder should remain closed as the timing mark approaches.

3. With the engine in the No. 1 firing position, adjust the following valves:
   a. V8 engine — Exhaust — 1, 3, 4, 8
   b. V8 engine — Intake — 1, 2, 5, 7
   c. V6 engine — Exhaust — 1, 5, 6
   d. V6 engine — Intake — 1, 2, 3

4. Adjust each valve by backing out the adjusting nut until lash is felt at the pushrod, then by tightening the adjusting nut until all lash is removed. This can be determined by rotating pushrod while turning the adjusting nut. When play has been removed, turn adjusting nut a full additional turn clockwise for V8 engines or ¾ of a turn clockwise for V6 engines. The lifter plunger will now be centered.

5. Turn the engine 1 revolution until the pointer **0** mark and the vibration damper mark are again in alignment. This is the No. 6 firing position on the V8 engine or No. 4 firing position on the V6 engine. As the timing mark approaches the pointer, the No. 1 cylinder valves should move.

6. With the engine in this position, adjust the following valves:
   a. V8 engine — Exhaust — 2, 5, 6, 7
   b. V8 engine — Intake — 3, 4, 6, 8
   c. V6 engine — Exhaust — 2, 3, 4
   d. V6 engine — Intake — 4, 5, 6

7. Install the rocker arm covers or valve covers.

8. Start the engine and check/adjust the minimum the idle speed, as required.

Rocker Arms/Shafts

REMOVAL AND INSTALLATION

4.3L (VIN Z), 5.0L (VIN E) and 5.7L (VIN 7) Engines

1. Disconnect the negative battery cable.
2. Remove the valve rocker covers.
3. Remove the rocker arm assembly; nuts, balls and rocker arms. Arrange or mark each assembly to ensure installation in original positions.
4. Remove each pushrod, if necessary, and place with the appropriate assemblies, to ensure installation in original locations.

To install:

NOTE: If new rocker arms or rocker arm balls are being installed, coat the bearing surfaces with prelube part 1052365, Molykote® or equivalent.

5. Install the pushrods. Ensure that the rods are seated properly in the lifter sockets.

6. Install the rocker arms, balls and nuts. Tighten the rocker arm nuts until all the valve lash is eliminated.

7. Adjust the valves to proper specification.

8. Install the rocker arm covers, then connect the negative battery cable.

9. Start the engine and check/adjust the minimum the idle speed, as required.

5.7L (VIN P) Engine

1. Disconnect the negative battery cable.
2. Remove the left valve cover:
   a. Remove the brake booster vacuum hose.
   b. Remove the secondary AIR injection hose from the pump to check valve assembly.
   c. Remove the valve cover retaining bolts, then remove the cover and gasket.
3. Remove the right valve cover:
   a. Raise and support the vehicle safely, then remove the serpentine drive belt.
   b. Remove the transmission fluid level indicator tube assembly from the bracket on the transmission housing.
   c. Lower the vehicle, then remove the crankcase vent hose.
   d. Remove the alternator and rear alternator brace.
   e. Remove the valve cover retaining bolts, then remove the cover and gasket.
4. Remove the valve rocker arm nuts and balls, then remove the rocker arms and pushrods. Tag or arrange all valve train components to assure installation in their original locations.

To install:

5. Coat the bearing surfaces of the rocker arms, balls and pushrods with prelube.

6. Install the pushrods, making sure they are properly seated in the lifter sockets, then install the rocker arms, balls and nuts. If components are being reused, be sure they are installed in their original locations.

7. Adjust the valve lash.

8. Install the valve covers and gaskets, then tighten the retainers to 100 inch lbs. (11 Nm).

9. Install the components which were removed to access the valve covers in the reverse order of removal.

10. Connect the negative battery cable.

Intake Manifold

REMOVAL AND INSTALLATION

4.3L (VIN Z), 5.0L (VIN E) and 5.7L (VIN 7) Engines

1. Disconnect the negative battery cable and relieve the fuel system pressure.

2. Drain the engine coolant into a suitable container and remove the air cleaner.

3. Disconnect the fuel pipes from the throttle body, and, if necessary, remove the throttle body assembly from the manifold.

4. Disconnect the ECM engine control harness and position it aside.

5. For 1993 vehicles, remove the brake tube assembly.

6. If not done already, disconnect the vacuum harness assembly.

7. Disconnect the upper radiator hose and the heater hose.

8. Except for 1993 vehicles, remove the thermostat housing and gasket.

9. Disengage all necessary electrical connections or remaining hose assemblies.

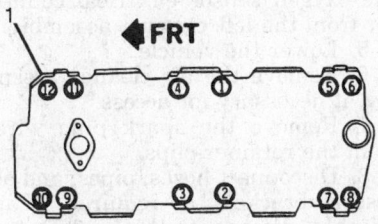

1. Intake manifold assembly

8470P030

Intake manifold torque sequence — 5.0L (VIN E) and 5.7L (VIN 7) engines

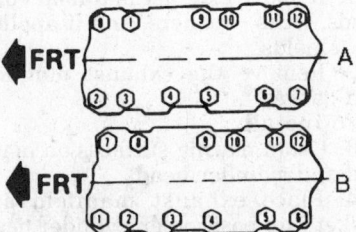

A. Initial tightening sequence
B. Final tightening sequence

8470P031

Intake manifold torque sequence — 4.3L (VIN Z) engine

10. Disconnect fuel pipe clips at AIR pump bracket and at the intake manifold.

11. Disconnect accelerator and TV cables or the accelerator control cable assembly bracket, as applicable.

12. Except for 1993 vehicles, remove the EGR valve and EGR solenoid valve.

13. Tag and remove the spark plug wires at the distributor cap, then remove the cap.

14. Mark the position of the rotor, then remove the distributor. Remove the bracket and/or coil, as required.

15. Remove the accessory mounting brackets, as required.

16. Except for 1993 vehicles, remove the coolant temperature sensor.

17. Remove the manifold bolts and studs, then remove the intake manifold. Remove and discard the intake manifold gaskets.

To install:

18. Thoroughly clean the intake manifold and cylinder block surfaces to remove any trace of gasket material or sealant.

19. Place gasket and seals on cylinder heads and block, apply a thin bead of RTV sealer, 1052289 or equivalent, to the front and rear of cylinder block. Extend the RTV bead $\frac{1}{2}$ in. up each cylinder head to seal and retain gasket.

20. Install the intake manifold, taking care not to dislodge the gaskets and seals, then install the retaining bolts and studs. Tighten the bolts and studs in proper sequence, first to 10 ft. lbs. (14 Nm) and then to 35 ft. lbs. (47 Nm).

21. Except for 1993 vehicles, install the coolant temperature sensor.

22. Attach accessory mounting brackets, if removed. Tighten compressor brace-to-manifold nut to 18 ft. lbs. (24 Nm), compressor brace-to-compressor nut to 24 ft. lbs. (32 Nm) and/or alternator to brace nut to 37 ft. lbs. (50 Nm)

23. If removed, install the bracket and/or coil.

24. Install the distributor, aligning the rotor with the mark made during removal, then install the cap and attach the wires.

25. Install the EGR valve and EGR solenoid valve, as applicable.

26. Connect the accelerator and TV cables or the accelerator control cable assembly bracket.

27. Connect the fuel pipe clips to the AIR pump bracket and intake manifold.

28. Install the wire and hose assemblies, as applicable.

29. Except for 1993 vehicles, install the thermostat housing and gasket.

30. Connect the upper radiator hose and the heater hose.

31. Connect the ECM engine control harness.

32. If removed, install the throttle body assembly.

33. Attach the fuel pipes to the TBI assembly.

34. Install the air cleaner and connect the negative battery cable.

35. Install the fuel filler cap and add engine coolant.

36. Start the engine and inspect for leaks. Check and adjust timing, as necessary.

5.7L (VIN P) engine

1. Disconnect the negative battery cable and relieve the fuel system pressure.

2. Drain the engine cooling system into a suitable container.

3. Remove the throttle body air duct.

4. Disengage the wiring harness connectors from the fuel injectors. Disengage and reposition the left and right wiring harnesses.

5. Remove the accelerator cable bracket retainers, then disconnect the cable and bracket assembly from the throttle body.

6. Disconnect the secondary AIR diverter valve hoses.

7. Disengage the fuel pipe connectors from the fuel rail assembly.

8. Remove the fuel rail bolts and disconnect the vacuum hose from the fuel pressure regulator.

9. Carefully remove the fuel rail and injector assembly from the manifold and position aside.

10. Disconnect the vacuum and crankcase vent hoses.

11. Remove the EGR solenoid assembly and the fuel EVAP canister solenoid assembly.

12. Remove the EGR valve.

13. Remove the AIR pipe from the intake and the right exhaust manifold.

14. Remove the alternator rear brace.

15. Disconnect the coolant hoses from the throttle body.

16. Remove the throttle body bolts, the throttle body and gasket from the intake.

17. Remove the intake manifold bolts and studs.

18. Remove the intake manifold and discard the old gaskets.

To install:

19. Thoroughly clean the intake manifold bolts and studs. Inspect and clean all gasket mating surfaces.

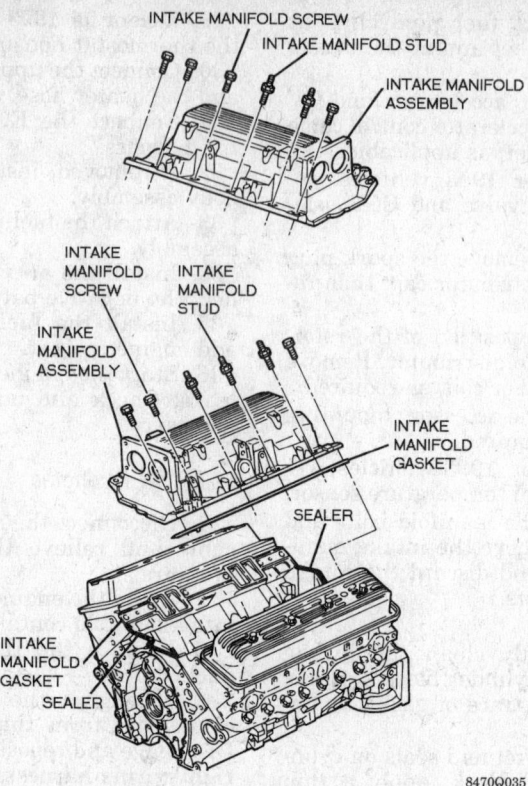

Intake manifold installation — 5.7L (VIN P) engine

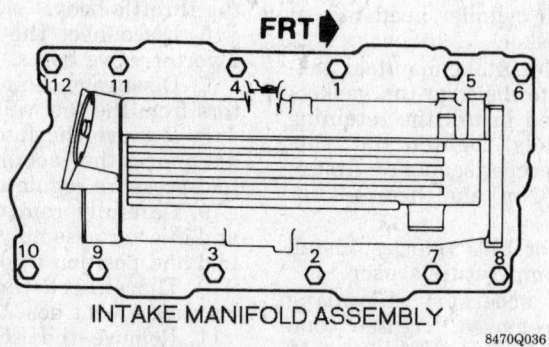

Intake manifold bolt torque sequence — 5.7L (VIN P) engine

20. Apply a 3/16 in. (5mm) bead of RTV sealer to the front and rear of the cylinder block. Extend the bead 1/2 inch (13mm) up each cylinder head to seal and retain the gaskets.

21. Position the new gaskets and install the intake manifold.

22. Install the manifold bolts and studs, then tighten using 2 passes of the proper sequence. First, tighten the bolts/studs to 71 inch lbs. (8 Nm), then tighten them to 35 ft. lbs. (48 Nm).

23. Install the throttle body, gasket and retaining bolts. Tighten the throttle body bolts to 19 ft. lbs. (26 Nm).

24. Connect the coolant hoses to the throttle body, then install the alternator rear brace.

25. Install the accelerator cables and bracket, then tighten the bracket bolts to 90 inch lbs. (10 Nm).

26. Install the secondary AIR pipe. Tighten the exhaust manifold fitting to 25 ft. lbs. (34 Nm) and tighten the flange-to-intake manifold bolts to 19 ft. lbs. (26 Nm).

27. Install the EGR valve, then EGR solenoid and bracket. Tighten valve nuts and the solenoid bracket nut to 16 ft. lbs. (22 Nm).

28. Install the fuel EVAP canister purge solenoid and bracket, then tighten the bolt to 53 inch lbs. (6 Nm).

29. Connect the vacuum and crankcase vent hoses.

30. Install the fuel injector and fuel rail assembly to the intake manifold, connect the fuel pressure regulator vacuum hose and install the fuel rail bolts. Tighten the bolts to 15 ft. lbs. (20 Nm). Engage the fuel pipe connections to the fuel rail assembly.

31. Connect the secondary AIR diverter valve hoses.

32. Position the left and right wiring harnesses, then engage the fuel injector electrical connectors.

33. Install the throttle body air duct.

34. Properly fill the engine cooling system.

35. Connect the negative battery cable.

Exhaust Manifold

REMOVAL AND INSTALLATION

1992–93 Vehicles

1. Disconnect the negative battery cable.

2. Raise and support vehicle safely.

3. Disconnect crossover pipe at the exhaust manifold.

4. For 1993 vehicles, disengage the oxygen sensor electrical connector from the left exhaust assembly.

5. Lower the vehicle.

6. Remove the air cleaner assembly, if necessary for access.

7. Remove the spark plug wires from the retainer clips.

8. Disconnect hoses, pipes, and accessory brackets, as required. If applicable, disconnect the air pipes or the hose at the check valve.

9. If necessary, remove the oil level indicator and tube.

10. For 1992 vehicles, as necessary, disengage the oxygen sensor electrical connector.

11. Remove exhaust manifold bolts, studs, locks, washers, and if applicable, shields.

12. Remove the exhaust manifold and gasket.

To install:

13. Clean mating surfaces on manifold and cylinder head.

14. Place exhaust manifold and gasket into position on cylinder head.

15. Install shields, washers, locks, studs and bolts.

16. For 1992–93 vehicles, tighten the center port bolts or studs to 26 ft. lbs. (35 Nm) and the front/rear port bolts or screws to 20 ft. lbs. (27 Nm).

17. For 1992 vehicles, connect oxygen sensor electrical connector, and/or install the oil level indicator tube, as applicable.

18. Connect any hoses, pipes and accessory brackets which were removed.

19. Install the spark plug wiring to the retaining clips and, if removed, install the air cleaner assembly.

20. Raise and support vehicle safely.

21. For 1993 vehicles, engage the oxygen sensor electrical connector.

22. Connect crossover pipe to the exhaust manifold and tighten nuts to 15 ft. lbs. (20 Nm).

23. Lower vehicle and connect the negative battery cable.

24. Start engine and check for leaks.

1994–96 5.7L (VIN P) Engine

LEFT SIDE

1. Disconnect the negative battery cable, then raise and support the vehicle safely.

2. Disconnect the exhaust crossover pipe from the manifold, then lower the vehicle.

3. Remove the brake booster vacuum hose.

4. Disconnect the secondary AIR pipe fitting from the exhaust manifold.

5. Disengage the oxygen sensor electrical connector.

6. Remove the exhaust manifold retaining bolts, then remove the heat shields, manifold and gasket.

To install:

7. Clean the gasket mating surfaces.

8. Position the gasket, then install the exhaust manifold and heat shields.

9. Install the manifold retaining bolts and tighten to 26 ft. lbs. (35 Nm).

10. Engage the oxygen sensor electrical connector.

11. Connect the secondary AIR pipe fitting to the exhaust manifold and tighten to 25 ft. lbs. (34 Nm).

12. Install the brake booster vacuum hose.

13. Raise and support the vehicle safely.

14. Connect the exhaust crossover pipe to the manifold, then lower the vehicle.

15. Connect the negative battery cable.

RIGHT SIDE

1. Disconnect the negative battery cable, then raise and support the vehicle safely.

2. Remove the exhaust crossover pipe.

3. Remove the serpentine drive belt.

4. Remove the oil level indicator and tube assembly, then disengage the oxygen sensor electrical connector.

5. Remove the 3 rear exhaust manifold retaining bolts, then lower the vehicle.

6. Disconnect the secondary AIR pipe fitting from the exhaust manifold.

7. Remove the alternator rear lower brace.

8. Remove the remaining exhaust manifold retaining bolts, then remove the heat shields, manifold and gasket.

To install:

9. Clean the gasket mating surfaces.

10. Position the gasket, then install the exhaust manifold and heat shields.

11. Install the front 3 manifold retaining bolts and tighten to 26 ft. lbs. (35 Nm).

12. Install the alternator rear lower brace.

13. Raise and support the vehicle safely.

14. Install the remaining manifold retaining bolts and tighten to 26 ft. lbs. (35 Nm).

15. Engage the oxygen sensor electrical connector.

16. Install the oil level indicator and tube assembly.

17. Install the serpentine drive belt.

18. Install the exhaust crossover pipe.

19. Lower the vehicle.

20. Connect the secondary AIR pipe fitting to the exhaust manifold and tighten to 25 ft. lbs. (34 Nm).

21. Connect the negative battery cable.

Timing Chain Front Cover

REMOVAL AND INSTALLATION

4.3L (VIN Z), 5.0L (VIN E) and 5.7L (VIN 7) Engines

1. Disconnect the negative battery cable.

2. Drain the cooling system into a suitable container, then remove the water pump assembly.

3. Remove the crankshaft pulley retaining bolts, then remove the pulley from the damper.

4. Remove the torsional damper retaining bolt, then using tool J–23523–E or equivalent, remove the torsional damper assembly.

5. Raise and safely support the vehicle.

6. Remove the oil pan assembly.

7. Remove the engine front cover retaining bolts, then remove the front cover and discard the gasket.

8. Clean the gasket mating surface.

To install:

9. Coat new engine front cover gasket with sealant and place into position on the engine front cover.

10. Position cover and gasket to the engine and loosely install the engine front cover-to-block upper attaching bolts. Tighten bolts alternately while carefully pressing downward on the engine front cover so the dowels in the block are aligned with the corresponding holes in the engine front cover. Be careful not to force the the front cover over the dowels to the point where the cover flange or dowels become distorted.

11. Install the remaining cover bolts and tighten all cover bolts alternately and evenly to 97 inch lbs. (11 Nm).

12. Install the oil pan.

13. After coating the damper-to-seal contact area with clean engine oil, install the torsional damper using J–23523–E, or equivalent. Install the pulley and tighten the pulley retaining bolts to 43 ft. lbs. (58 Nm), then tighten the damper bolt to 70 ft. lbs. (95 Nm).

14. Install the coolant pump assembly.

15. Connect the negative battery cable and add engine coolant.

5.7L (VIN P) Engine

1. Disconnect the negative battery cable.

2. Drain the engine oil and coolant into suitable containers.

3. Remove the throttle body air intake duct.

4. Remove the serpentine drive belt.

5. Remove the water pump assembly.

6. Remove the crankshaft balancer and hub.

  a. If not done already, raise and support the vehicle safely.

  b. Remove the crankshaft balancer retaining bolts, then remove the balancer from the hub.

  c. Matchmark the crankshaft hub to the engine front cover, then remove the hub bolt and washer.

  d. Remove the crankshaft hub using J–39046 or an equivalent hub removal/installation tool. To

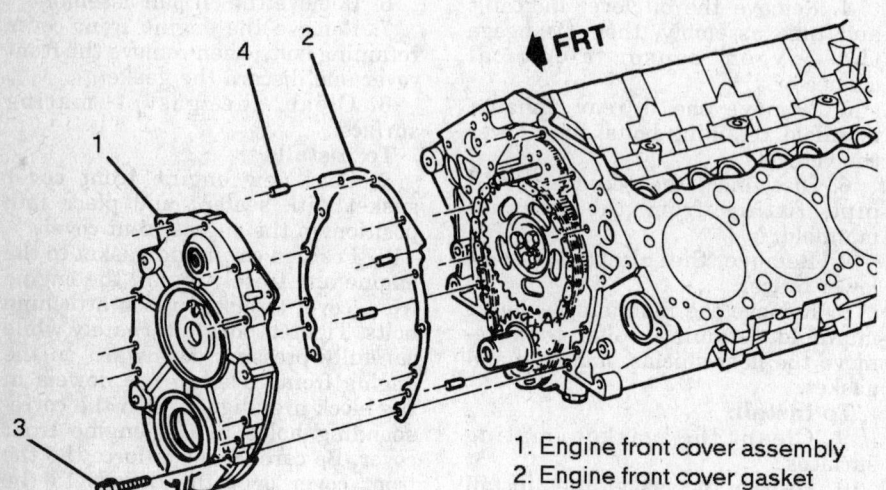

1. Engine front cover assembly
2. Engine front cover gasket
3. Engine front cover bolt
4. Engine front cover locating pin

8470Q038

Timing chain front cover — 5.7L (VIN P) Engine

preserve the relationship between the hub and crankshaft, DO NOT crank the engine over once the hub has been removed. If the hub is not matchmarked and installed in the original position, an engine imbalance could result.

7. Remove the distributor assembly.

8. Remove the oil pan assembly.

9. Remove the engine front cover bolts.

10. Remove the engine front cover and gasket.

To install:

11. Thoroughly clean the engine front cover and cylinder block gasket mating surfaces. Inspect the engine front cover and seals for damage, replace as necessary.

12. Using J–39087 or equivalent front cover seal protector on the water pump driveshaft, install the gasket and front cover into position over the shafts and guide pins.

13. Install the engine front cover bolts and tighten to 100 inch lbs. (11 Nm).

14. Install the oil pan and gasket.

15. Install the distributor assembly.

16. Install the crankshaft hub and torsional damper assembly.

   a. Align the matchmarks made earlier and install the crankshaft

hub using the hub tool. If the engine was cranked and the matchmarks were lost, set the engine to No. 1 TDC, then install the crankshaft hub with the cast arrow in the 12 o'clock position.

   b. Install the hub washer and bolt, but do not torque at this time.

   c. Install the crankshaft balancer to the hub, then tighten the crankshaft hub bolt to 75 ft. lbs. (102 Nm) and the balancer bolts to 60 ft. lbs. (81 Nm).

NOTE: If a new balancer is installed, new balancer weights of the same size must be installed in the same hole locations as the original balancer.

17. Install the water pump assembly.

18. Install the serpentine drive belt.

19. Install the throttle body air duct.

20. Properly fill the engine crankcase with clean engine oil.

21. Properly fill the engine cooling system.

22. Connect the negative battery cable, operate the engine and check for leaks.

Front Cover Oil Seal

REPLACEMENT

4.3L (VIN Z), 5.0L (VIN E) and 5.7L (VIN 7) Engines

The front cover oil seal may be replaced with the front cover either removed from or installed to the engine. If the cover is already removed, be sure to properly support the cover when driving in the new seal in order to prevent damage to the cover assembly.

1. Disconnect the negative battery cable.

2. For 1993 vehicles, remove the air cleaner assembly, then remove the radiator upper shroud, for access.

3. Remove the serpentine drive belt, then for 1993 vehicles, remove the engine cooling fan.

4. Remove the crankshaft pulley retaining bolts, then remove pulley from the damper.

5. Remove the damper retaining bolt, then using tool J–23523–E or equivalent, remove the torsional damper assembly.

6. With the torsional damper removed, carefully pry the old seal from the cover using a small prytool. Take care not to damage the front cover or the crankshaft when removing seal.

To install:

7. Position new seal with the open end toward the inside of the engine front cover and carefully drive in the new seal with tool J–35468 or equivalent.

8. After coating the damper-to-seal contact area with clean engine oil, install the torsional damper using J–23523–E or equivalent. Install the pulley and tighten the pulley retaining bolts to 43 ft. lbs. (58 Nm), then tighten the damper bolt to 70 ft. lbs. (95 Nm).

9. For 1993 vehicles, install the cooling fan assembly.

10. Install the serpentine drive belt.

11. For 1993 vehicles, install the radiator upper shroud and the air cleaner assembly.

12. Connect the negative battery cable and check cover for oil leaks.

5.7L (VIN P) Engine

In addition to the crankshaft oil seal, the 5.7L engine front cover utilizes a water pump driveshaft seal and distributor driveshaft seal. All front cover oil seals on these engines are replaced in the same manner.

1. Remove the timing chain front cover from the engine.

2. Using either a suitably sized driver or a small suitable prytool, remove oil seal from the front cover. If a driver is being used, be sure to support the cover so it is not damaged. If a prytool is used, take care not to score or damage the cover sealing surfaces.

3. Use J–35468 or equivalent to install the crankshaft seal.

4. Use J–39090 or equivalent to install the distributor shaft seal.

5. Use J–39088 or equivalent to install the water pump driveshaft seal.

6. Install the timing chain front cover to the engine.

Timing Chain and Sprockets

REMOVAL AND INSTALLATION

4.3L (VIN Z), 5.0L (VIN E) and 5.7L (VIN 7) Engines

1. Disconnect the negative battery cable.

2. Remove the engine front cover.

3. Rotate the engine until the marks on the camshaft sprocket and crankshaft sprocket are aligned with the shaft centers.

4. Remove the camshaft sprocket retaining bolts, then remove the timing chain assembly, along with the camshaft sprocket.

To install:

5. Position the camshaft sprocket in the timing chain with the timing mark located as aligned during removal, then install the timing chain under the crankshaft sprocket while installing the camshaft sprocket to the engine.

6. Verify that the timing marks on the crankshaft sprocket and the camshaft sprocket are aligned with the shaft centers, then install the

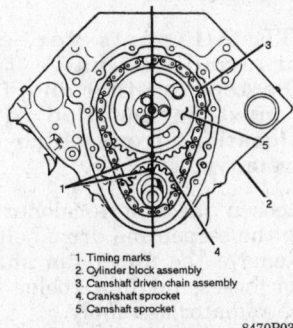

1. Timing marks
2. Cylinder block assembly
3. Camshaft driven chain assembly
4. Crankshaft sprocket
5. Camshaft sprocket

8470P034

Timing gear alignment — 4.3L (VIN Z), 5.0L (VIN E) and 5.7L (VIN 7) engines

camshaft sprocket bolts and tighten to 21 ft. lbs. (28 Nm) Lubricate the timing chain with engine oil.

7. Install the engine front cover.

8. Connect the negative battery cable.

5.7L (VIN P) Engine

1. Remove the timing chain front cover.

2. Rotate the crankshaft until the timing marks on the timing chain sprockets are aligned nearest each other. The camshaft sprocket mark should be at the 6 o'clock position while the mark on the crankshaft sprocket should be at the 12 o'clock position.

3. Remove the camshaft sprocket bolts.

4. Remove the camshaft sprocket and timing chain.

NOTE: To prevent piston or valve damage, do not turn the crankshaft after the timing chain has been removed.

5. Remove the water pump bearing retainer bolts, then remove the driveshaft assembly using J–39243 or equivalent driven gear assembly remover.

6. Remove the crankshaft sprocket using J–5825-A or equivalent crankshaft sprocket remover.

7. If necessary, remove the crankshaft key.

To install:

8. If removed, install the crankshaft key.

9. Install the crankshaft sprocket using J–5590 or an equivalent installation tool.

10. Install the water pump driveshaft assembly using J–39092 or an equivalent installer tool. Install the retainer bolts and tighten to 105 inch lbs. (12 Nm).

11. Align the timing marks and install the camshaft sprocket and timing chain. The gears of the camshaft sprocket and water pump driveshaft must mesh or damage to the thrust plate retainer could occur.

12. Install the camshaft sprocket bolts and tighten to 21 ft. lbs. (28 Nm).

13. Install a new O-ring to the water pump driven gear shaft using J–39089 or an equivalent seal installation tool.

14. Install the timing chain front cover.

Timing Sprockets

The camshaft sprocket is removed during the timing chain removal procedure. The following procedures should be followed if the crankshaft sprocket must also be removed.

REMOVAL AND INSTALLATION

4.3L (VIN Z), 5.0L (VIN E) and 5.7L (VIN 7) Engines

1. Disconnect the negative battery cable.

2. Remove the timing chain and camshaft sprocket.

3. Remove the crankshaft sprocket using tool J–5825–A or equivalent.

4. If necessary, remove crankshaft key and inspect the key/keyway for damage or wear.

To install:

5. If removed, install the crankshaft key.

6. Install the crankshaft sprocket using tool J–5590 or equivalent.

7. Install timing chain and camshaft sprocket.

8. Connect the negative battery cable.

5.7L (VIN P) Engine

1. Remove the timing chain front cover.

2. Rotate the crankshaft until the timing marks on the timing chain sprockets are aligned nearest each other. The camshaft sprocket mark should be at the 6 o'clock position while the mark on the crankshaft sprocket should be at the 12 o'clock position.

3. Remove the camshaft sprocket bolts.

4. Remove the camshaft sprocket and timing chain.

NOTE: To prevent piston or valve damage, do not turn the crankshaft after the timing chain has been removed.

5. Remove the water pump bearing retainer bolts, then remove the driveshaft assembly using J–39243 or equivalent driven gear assembly remover.

6. Remove the crankshaft sprocket using J–5825–A or equivalent crankshaft sprocket remover.

7. If necessary, remove the crankshaft key.

To install:

8. If removed, install the crankshaft key.

9. Install the crankshaft sprocket using J–5590 or an equivalent installation tool.

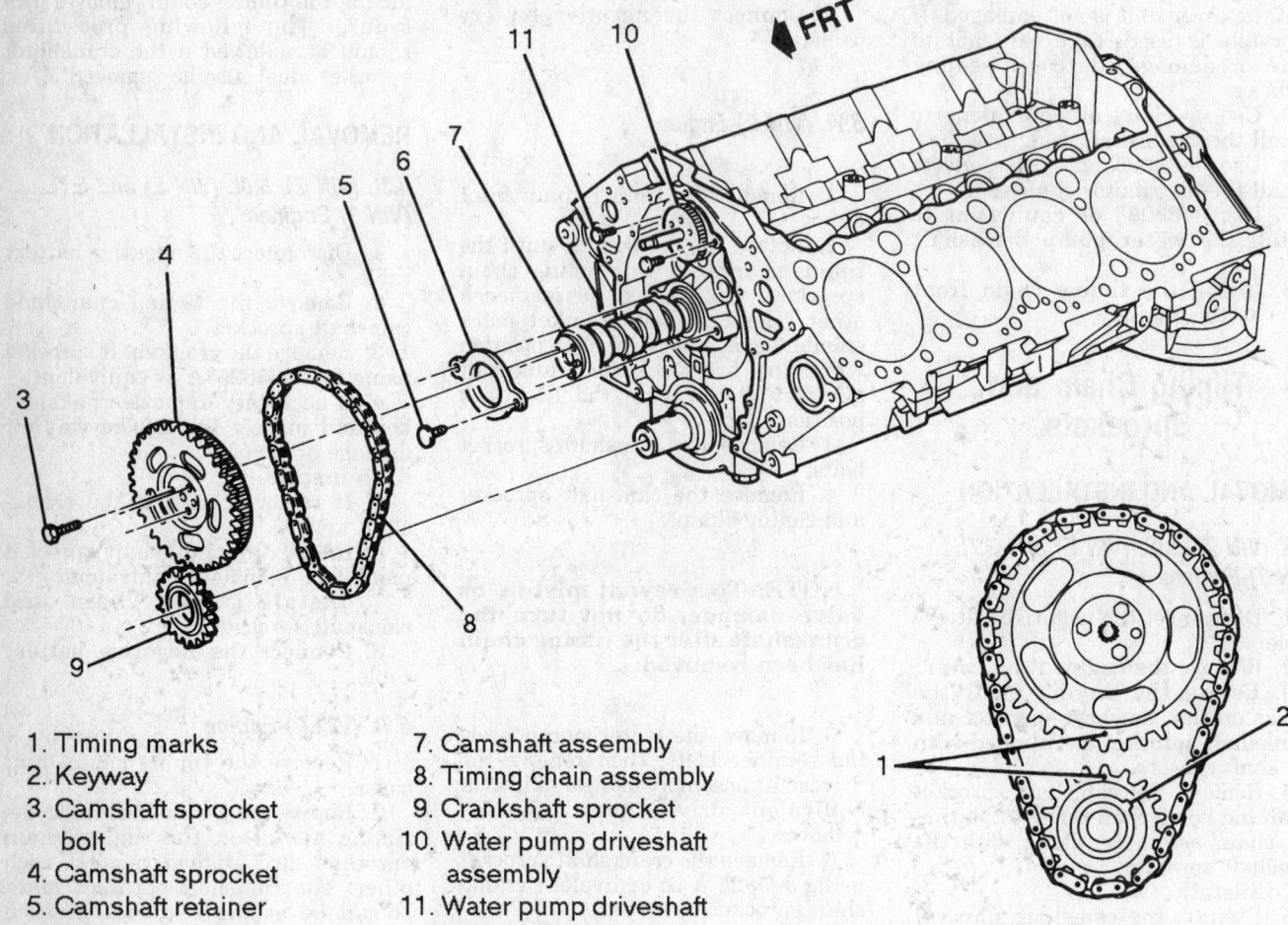

FRT

1. Timing marks
2. Keyway
3. Camshaft sprocket bolt
4. Camshaft sprocket
5. Camshaft retainer bolt
6. Camshaft retainer

7. Camshaft assembly
8. Timing chain assembly
9. Crankshaft sprocket
10. Water pump driveshaft assembly
11. Water pump driveshaft bearing retainer bolt

8470Q042

Camshaft, timing chain and sprocket alignment and installation — 5.7L (VIN P) engine

10. Install the water pump driveshaft assembly using J–39092 or an equivalent installer tool. Install the retainer bolts and tighten to 105 inch lbs. (12 Nm).

11. Align the timing marks and install the camshaft sprocket and timing chain. The gears of the camshaft sprocket and water pump driveshaft must mesh or damage to the thrust plate retainer could occur.

12. Install the camshaft sprocket bolts and tighten to 21 ft. lbs. (28 Nm).

13. Install a new O-ring to the water pump driven gear shaft using J–39089 or an equivalent seal installation tool.

14. Install the timing chain front cover.

Camshaft

REMOVAL AND INSTALLATION

4.3L (VIN Z), 5.0L (VIN E) and 5.7L (VIN 7) Engines

1. Properly discharge/recover the air conditioning system, then disconnect the negative battery cable.

2. Remove the intake manifold assembly.

3. Remove the rocker arm assemblies and pushrods.

NOTE: All parts for each rocker arm/lifter valve train must be kept together and, if reused, must be installed in the same locations from which they were removed.

4. Loosen the belt tensioner and remove the serpentine drive belt.

5. Remove the upper fan shroud, radiator hoses, oil/fluid cooler lines and the radiator assembly.

6. Remove the timing chain and camshaft sprocket.

7. Disconnect the refrigerant lines from the condenser and plug to pre-

vent system contamination, then remove the condenser from the vehicle.

8. Remove the valve lifters and arrange with the rocker arm assemblies for possible reuse, if the camshaft is not replaced.

9. Remove the camshaft retainer bolts and the camshaft retainer.

10. Install three 5/16–18 x 4 in. bolts in the camshaft bolt holes and carefully pull the camshaft from the bearings.

To install:

11. Coat camshaft lobes and journals with prelube 1052365 or equivalent.

12. Carefully slide the camshaft into the journals in the block.

13. Install the camshaft retainer and tighten the retainer bolts to 106 inch lbs. (12 Nm).

14. Install the timing chain and camshaft sprocket along with the front cover assembly.

15. Install the valve lifters. If the camshaft was replaced, use new lifters to assure durability of the camshaft lobes and lifter rollers.

16. Install the air conditioning condenser, then unplug and connect the refrigerant lines.

17. Install the radiator, oil/fluid cooler lines, radiator hoses and upper shroud assembly.

18. Install the serpentine drive belt.

19. Install the pushrods and rocker arm assemblies.

20. Install the intake manifold assembly.

21. Connect the negative battery, add coolant, and adjust valves as necessary.

22. Run the engine and check for leaks, then properly charge the air conditioning system.

5.7L (VIN P) Engine

1. Disconnect the negative battery cable.

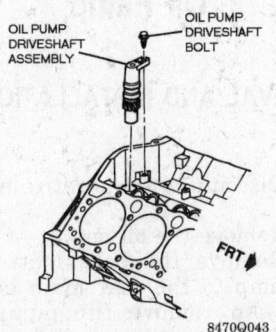

Oil pump driveshaft assembly mounting — 5.7L (VIN P) engine

2. Remove the intake manifold assembly.

3. Remove the rocker arms and pushrods.

4. Remove the bolt retaining the oil pump drive assembly, then lift the drive assembly from the rear of the block.

5. Remove the timing chain front cover, then remove the crankshaft shaft sprocket and timing chain.

6. Remove the valve lifters.

NOTE: If valve train components are to be reused, make sure they are tagged or arranged in order to assure installation in their original locations.

7. If necessary, properly discharge and recover the refrigerant from the air conditioning system.

8. Remove the air conditioning compressor and condenser hose from the condenser, then remove the receiver and dehydrator hose from the condenser. Plug all of the openings in order to prevent system contamination.

9. Remove the radiator and condenser assembly, then remove the air conditioning condenser support.

10. Remove the camshaft retainer bolts, then remove the camshaft retainer from the front of the block.

11. Install three 5/16-18 x 4 inch bolts or equivalent, in the camshaft bolt holes, then using the bolts to pull and rotate the camshaft, carefully pull the camshaft from the bearings. All camshaft journals are the same diameter and care must be used to avoid damage to the bearings.

To install:

12. If installing a new camshaft, be sure to coat all camshaft lobes with Molykote® or an equivalent prelube and to replace all lifters in order to assure camshaft durability.

13. Lubricate the camshaft journals with clean engine oil, then carefully insert the camshaft into the engine.

14. Install the camshaft retainer and tighten the bolts to 105 inch lbs. (12 Nm).

15. Install the condenser support, then install the radiator and condenser assembly.

16. Unplug the openings, then connect the condenser refrigerant lines.

17. Install the valve lifters. If reusing the camshaft and lifters, they must be installed into their original bores.

18. Install the camshaft sprocket and timing chain, then install the timing chain front cover.

19. Install the oil pump drive assembly and tighten the retaining bolt to 13 ft. lbs. (18 Nm).

20. Install the rocker arms and pushrods.

21. Install the intake manifold assembly.

22. Connect the negative battery cable, then if necessary, recharge the A/C system.

Piston and Connecting Rod

POSITIONING

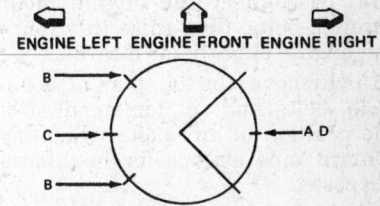

A	OIL RING SPACER GAP (TANG IN HOLE OR SLOT WITHIN ARC)
B	OIL RING RAIL GAPS
C	2ND COMPRESSION RING GAP

8470P036

Piston ring gap locations — 1992–93 engines

ENGINE LUBRICATION

Oil Pan

REMOVAL AND INSTALLATION

4.3L (VIN Z), 5.0L (VIN E) and 5.7L (VIN 7) Engines

1. Disconnect the negative battery cable and remove the air cleaner assembly.

2. For 1993 V8 engines, disengage the wiper motor electrical connector, then remove the fuse cover.

3. Remove the upper fan shroud.

4. Remove the transmission and engine oil dipsticks, then remove the distributor cap.

5. Raise and support the vehicle safely.

6. Drain the engine oil.

7. For 1992 V6 engines, disconnect the AIR converter pipe from the exhaust manifold

8. Disconnect the exhaust pipe at the manifolds, then remove the flywheel cover.

9. Disconnect the transmission fluid cooler lines at the clips on the oil pan.

10. Except for 1993 V6 engines, remove the transmission dipstick tube.

11. For 1993 V8 engines, disconnect the shift linkage from the transmission, then for all 1993 vehicles, remove the right frame brace.

12. Remove the starter motor assembly.

13. If equipped with an oil level sensor, it must be disconnected and removed to prevent possible damage to the oil level sensor, oil pump pickup screen and pipe.

14. Disconnect the engine mount through-bolts, then raise the front of the engine slightly for clearance.

15. Remove the oil pan attaching nuts, bolts and reinforcement. Note the position of any bolts which may contain pipe clamps for installation purposes.

16. Place the crankshaft timing mark to the 6 o'clock position in order to move the crankshaft throw and counterbalance aside, then raise the engine sufficiently to remove the pan. Carefully remove the oil pan and discard the old gasket.

To install:

17. Clean the gasket mating surfaces. Apply a small amount of 1052914 or equivalent sealer to the front cover and rear seal retainer-to-cylinder block junctions and continue the bead 1 in. in either direction from the radius of the cavity.

18. Install the new gasket on the oil pan, and position the oil pan in place with loosely installed nuts, bolts and reinforcement. Make sure any pipe clamps, if present, are reinstalled on the bolts from which they were removed.

19. Tighten the oil pan nuts to 17 ft. lbs. (23 Nm) and bolts to 97 inch lbs. (11 Nm).

20. Lower the engine.

21. Install the engine mount through-bolts.

22. For 1993 vehicles, install the right frame brace.

23. Install the starter motor assembly.

24. If removed, install the transmission fluid indicator tube.

25. For 1993 V8 engines, connect the shift linkage to the transmission.

26. Connect the transmission fluid cooler lines to the clips on the oil pan.

27. Install the flywheel cover, then connect the exhaust pipe to the manifolds.

28. For 1992 V6 engines, connect the AIR converter pipe to the exhaust manifold.

29. If equipped, install the oil level sensor and electrical connection.

30. Lower the vehicle.

31. Install the upper fan shroud.

32. If removed, install the transmission and oil dipsticks.

33. Install the distributor cap.

34. For 1993 V8 engines, install the fuse cover, then engage the wiper motor electrical connection.

35. Install the air cleaner assembly, then connect the negative battery cable.

36. Refill the crankcase with clean engine oil, then start the engine and check engine for leaks.

5.7L (VIN P) Engine

1. Disconnect the negative battery cable.

2. Remove the air intake duct.

3. Raise and support the vehicle safely, then drain the engine crankcase of oil.

4. Drain the engine cooling system.

5. Disengage the wiring harness connector from the oil level sensor, then remove the sensor.

6. Disconnect the exhaust crossover pipe from the exhaust manifolds, then remove the pipe hanger bolts and reposition the pipe.

7. If equipped, remove the engine oil cooler hose bracket nut from the oil pan, then remove the oil cooler bolt from the oil cooler assembly. Reposition the engine oil cooler assembly.

8. Remove the transmission fluid cooler lines from the oil pan clip and remove the torque converter cover.

9. Remove the start motor assembly.

10. Remove the engine mount through-bolts, then install a suitable engine jacking fixture and carefully raise the engine, watching the clearance between engine mounted components and the firewall.

─────── WARNING ───────
Never raise the engine using a jack under the oil pan, crankshaft pulley or any sheetmetal. Because there only is a small clearance between the oil pan and the oil pump screen, if the pan is bent even slightly, damage could occur to the pump screen and pickup unit.

11. Remove the oil pan bolts, studs and nuts, then lower the oil pan assembly along with the gasket and the pan reinforcements. If necessary, rotate the crankshaft to reposition the counterweights.

To install:

12. Thoroughly clean the gasket mating surfaces of any remaining sealer and/or gasket material.

13. Apply a small amount of RTV sealer, 1052914 or equivalent, to the front cover-cylinder block junction and to the rear seal retainer-cylinder block junction. Continue the bead of sealer for 1 inch (25mm) in either direction of the radius cavity of these junctions.

14. Install the oil pan and gasket assembly, using the reinforcements, nuts, bolts and studs.

15. Tighten the corner oil pan bolts, stud or nuts to 15 ft. lbs. (20 Nm) and the remaining bolts or studs to 100 inch lbs. (11 Nm).

16. Lower the engine, remove the jacking fixture and install the engine mount through-bolts.

17. Install the oil level sensor assembly and tighten to 16 ft. lbs. (22 Nm), then engage the wiring harness connector.

18. Install the starter motor assembly.

19. Install the torque converter cover, then secure the transmission fluid cooler lines with the oil pan clip.

20. If equipped, install the engine oil cooler bolts screw to the cooler assembly and tighten to 24 ft. lbs. (33 Nm), then install the oil cooler hose bracket nut to the oil pan.

21. Install the exhaust pipe hanger bolt, then connect the crossover pipe to the exhaust manifolds.

22. Lower the vehicle and refill the engine crankcase with clean engine oil.

23. Install the air intake duct and connect the negative battery cable.

24. Start the engine and check for leaks.

Oil Pump

REMOVAL AND INSTALLATION

1. Disconnect the negative battery cable.

2. Remove the oil pan.

3. Remove the bolt(s) attaching the pump to the rear main bearing cap, then remove the pump and driveshaft extension.

4. For the 5.7L (VIN P) engine, remove the oil pump baffle retaining nuts and remove the baffle.

To install:

NOTE: The oil pump pickup should be submerged in oil and the pump primed prior to installation. Failure to prime the pump may result in oil pump failure or internal engine damage. Also, if the pickup screen and pipe assembly was removed from the pump, they must be replaced to assure a proper interference fit.

5. If the pickup screen and pipe was removed, it should be replaced as an assembly with a new part. Using a suitable tool, install a new pickup screen and pipe to the oil pump

6. Align the slot or hexagon head on the end of the shaft extension with the drive tang or the hexagon socket on the distributor shaft.

7. For the 5.7L (VIN P) engine, position the oil pump baffle before installing the pump retaining bolt.

8. Install and tighten the oil pump bolt to 77 ft. lbs. (105 Nm) for the 4.3L, 5.0L (VIN E) and 5.7L (VIN 7) engines. For the 5.7L (VIN P) engine, install the baffle nuts and tighten to 25 ft. lbs. (34 Nm).

9. Install the oil pan assembly to the engine.

10. Connect the negative battery cable, then check engine oil level and add, as necessary.

11. Start the engine while watch the indicator light or oil pressure gauge to ensure immediate oil pump operation.

CHECKING

1. Remove the pump cover screws, then carefully remove the cover, making sure not to disturb the gears.

2. Matchmark the gear teeth for assembly purposes, then remove the gears and driveshaft assembly from the housing.

3. Remove the pressure relief valve assembly.

4. If pickup replacement is necessary, mount the housing in a soft-jawed vice, then remove the screen and tube assembly as a unit. Do not attempt to separate the screen from the tube.

5. Check the pump housing and cover for cracks, scoring, casting imperfections or damaged threads. The housing must be replaced if damage is found. Do not attempt to repair the housing.

6. Check the idler gear shaft and replace the pump assembly if it is loose in the housing.

7. Inspect the pressure relief valve assembly for scoring or sticking.

Burrs may be removed using a fine oil stone. Then check the spring for loss of tension.

8. Check the pickup screen for broken wire mesh or looseness. If the pipe is loose or has been removed, the pump screen and pipe assembly must be replaced.

9. Check gears for chipping, galling or wear.

10. Inspect the pump driven gear and driveshaft assembly for looseness or wear.

11. Install the pump components in the reverse order of removal.

12. Tighten the pump cover screws to 80 inch lbs. (9 Nm) for the 4.3L (VIN Z), 5.0L (VIN E) or the 5.7L engines.

Rear Main Bearing Oil Seal

REMOVAL AND INSTALLATION

4.3L (VIN Z), 5.0L (VIN E) and 5.7L (VIN 7 and P) Engines

1. Remove the transmission from the vehicle.

2. Remove the flywheel.

NOTE: Care should be taken when removing the seal so as not to nick the crankshaft sealing surface.

3. Using the notches provided in the rear seal retainer, pry out the seal using a suitable tool.

To install:

4. Coat new seal entirely with clean oil.

5. Install the seal on tool J–35621 or equivalent. Thread the tool into the rear of the crankshaft seal retainer. Tighten the screws snugly, this is to insure the seal will be installed squarely over the crankshaft. Tighten the tool wing nut until it bottoms.

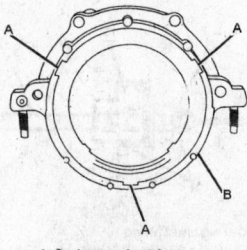

A. Seal removal notches
B. Crankshaft rear oil seal retainer

8470P038

Use the notches provided to pry the old rear main seal from the retainer — 4.3L (VIN Z), 5.0L (VIN E) and 5.7L (VIN 7) Engines

6. Remove the tool from the crankshaft seal retainer.

7. Install flywheel, making sure to align the crankshaft dowel pin with the proper locating hole in the flywheel assembly. Then install the flywheel retaining bolts and tighten to 74 ft. lbs. (100 Nm).

8. Install the transmission assembly.

AUTOMATIC TRANSMISSION

Transmission Assembly

REMOVAL AND INSTALLATION

1. Disconnect the battery negative cable and remove the air cleaner.

2. Disconnect the Throttle Valve (TV) cable at the throttle lever.

3. Remove the transmission dipstick, then remove the indicator tube from the transmission.

4. Raise and support the vehicle safely.

5. Remove the driveshaft.

6. Disconnect the shift linkage at the transmission.

7. Disengage all electrical leads at the transmission and any clips that retain the leads to the transmission case.

8. Remove the retaining bolts, then remove the flywheel cover.

9. Matchmark the flywheel and converter for installation purposes.

10. Remove and discard the torque converter-to-flywheel bolts.

11. Remove the catalytic converter support bracket.

12. Support and raise the transmission slightly using a suitable transmission jack.

13. Remove the transmission mount-to-support nut, washer, and bolt.

14. Remove the transmission support-to-frame bolts, nuts and, if used, insulators.

15. Slide the transmission support rearward.

16. Lower the transmission to gain access to the oil cooler lines and TV cable attachments.

17. Disconnect the lines and cap all openings to prevent excessive fluid loss or system contamination, then disconnect the TV cable.

18. Support the engine with a suitable tool, then and remove the transmission-to-engine bolts.

19. Install tool J–21366 or equivalent, to the torque converter or converter clutch in order to hold it in place.

20. Remove the transmission assembly from the vehicle.

To install:

21. Raise the transmission into place and remove tool J–21366.

22. Install the transmission-to-engine bolts and tighten to 35 ft. lbs. (47 Nm).

23. Unplug and install the oil cooler pipes, then connect the TV cable.

24. Install the fluid level tube using a new seal, then tighten tube retaining bolt to 35 ft. lbs. (47 Nm).

25. Install the transmission support-to-frame bolts, nuts and, if applicable, the insulators. Tighten the bolts to 25 ft. lbs. (34 Nm) and, if equipped the nuts to 30 ft. lbs. (41 Nm).

26. If removed or replaced, install the transmission mount bolts and tighten to 35 ft. lbs. (47 Nm). Install the transmission support nut and washer, then tighten to 30 ft. lbs. (41 Nm).

27. Remove the transmission jack, then position the converter by aligning it to the flywheel in the original position marked. Make sure the weld nuts on the converter are flush with the flywheel. Test the converter or clutch for freedom of movement.

28. Install and finger-tighten 3 new bolts, then tighten to 46 ft. lbs. (62 Nm). After tightening all bolts, retorque the first bolt tightened.

29. If removed, install the floor pan reinforcement.

30. Install the catalytic converter support bracket, then install the converter cover and tighten the bolts to 89 inch lbs. (10 Nm).

31. Install the shift linkage, electrical leads, retaining clips, and if equipped, speedometer cable.

32. Install the driveshaft and lower the vehicle.

33. Install the TV cable to the throttle lever, then install the fluid level indicator.

34. Install the air cleaner, then connect the negative battery cable.

35. Adjust the shift linkage and the TV cable.

36. Flush the transmission and cooler system to prevent damage to the system components.

SHIFT LINKAGE ADJUSTMENT

The shift control linkage should be set so the engine will only start in **P** or **N**. If adjustment is necessary proceed as follows:

1. Make sure the steering column attachment and all body bolts are secure as they may affect the shift linkage.

2. Position the steering column shift lever in **N**.

3. Raise and support the vehicle safely.

4. Free the control rod and swivel.

5. Set the transmission lever to the neutral detent.

6. Hold swivel flush against the equalizer lever and finger-tighten bolt against rod. No force should be exerted in either direction on the control rod or equalizer lever while tightening bolt.

7. Tighten bolt to 21 ft. lbs. (28 Nm).

8. Lower vehicle and check that adjustment was proper.

THROTTLE VALVE (TV) CABLE ADJUSTMENT

Setting of the TV cable must be done by rotating the throttle lever at the carburetor or throttle body. Do not use the accelerator pedal to rotate the throttle lever.

1. Turn the engine OFF and remove the air cleaner assembly for access.

2. Depress and hold the reset tab at the engine end of the TV cable.

3. Move the slider until it stops against the fitting, then release the reset tab.

4. Rotate the throttle lever to its full travel and watch the slider, it must move (ratchet) toward the lever

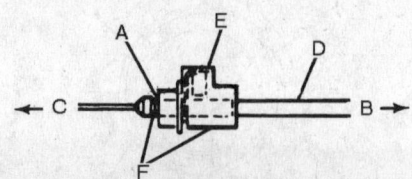

A. Slider against fitting
B. To automatic transmission assembly
C. To throttle body
D. Automatic transmission TV cable assembly
E. Automatic transmission TV cable reset tab
F. Automatic transmission TV cable

8470P040

Throttle Valve (TV) cable adjustment

when the lever is rotated to its full travel position.

NOTE: The TV cable assembly may appear to work correctly with the engine stopped and cold, but then not work when the engine is a normal operating temperature. Always check the TV cable adjustment again, after the engine has been warmed.

5. Recheck after the engine is hot and road test the vehicle.

SELECTOR/BACKUP LAMP SWITCH ADJUSTMENT

1. Block the drive wheels and place the transmission in **N**.

2. Align the actuator on the switch assembly with the hole on the shift tube.

3. Position the connector side of the switch assembly to fit into the cutout on the steering column shaft.

4. Push down on the switch assembly to lock the tangs into place in the steering shaft.

5. Move the switch assembly to the right, **LOW** gear position.

6. Place the transmission in **P**, the switch assembly will ratchet as it adjusts itself.

7. Verify the switch is adjusted properly.

DRIVE AXLE

Driveshaft

REMOVAL AND INSTALLATION

1. Raise the vehicle and support it safely.

2. Mark the relationship of the driveshaft to the differential flange.

3. Unbolt the driveshaft-to-differential flange retaining bolts, then remove the retaining straps. Tape the bearing caps in place to prevent losing the bearing rollers. Support the driveshaft to prevent excessive strain on the universal joint.

4. Position a suitable drain pan under the transmission end to catch any fluid that may leak out when the driveshaft is removed. Pull the shaft back and remove it. Be careful not to damage the splines at the transmission end.

To install:

5. Lubricate the splines with engine 1050169 or equivalent slip yoke

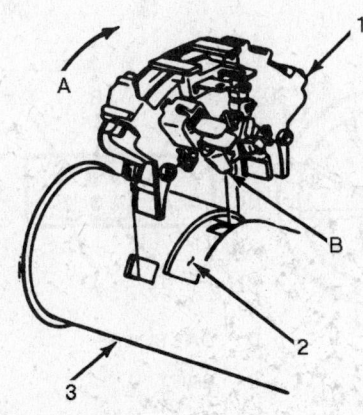

A. "Low gear" position
B. Actuator
1 Switch assembly
2. Shift tube
3. Steering column jacket

8470P041

Selector/backup lamp switch adjustment — 1992 vehicles shown — 1993–96 vehicles similar

lubricant and slide the slip yoke into place.

6. Align the driveshaft marks, then install the connect the retaining straps and tighten the bolts to 16 ft. lbs. (22 Nm).

7. Lower the vehicle.

Universal Joints

REMOVAL AND INSTALLATION

Snapring Type

1. Raise and support the vehicle safely.

2. Matchmark and remove the driveshaft.

3. Remove the snaprings from the yoke. If the snapring is difficult to remove, tap the end of the bearing cap lightly to relieve pressure from snapring.

4. Support the propeller shaft horizontally in line with the base plate of a bench vise, but never clamp the driveshaft tube.

5. Place the universal joint so the lower ear of the yoke is supported on a 1⅛ inch socket. Press 1 trunnion bearing against the socket in order to press the opposite bearing from the yoke.

6. Grasp the cap and work it out, if necessary use tool J–9522–3 and J–9522–5 or equivalents.

7. Rotate the shaft and support the other side of the yoke, then press the bearing cap from the yoke and as in previous steps.

8. Remove the trunnion from the driveshaft yoke.

9. Clean and check the condition of all parts. Use U-joint repair kits to replace all the worn parts or replace the assembly using a new U-joint.

To install:

10. Repack the bearings with chassis grease and replace the trunnion dust seals after any operation that requires disassembly of the U-joint. Be sure the lubricant reservoir at the end of the trunnion is full of lubricant. Fill the reservoirs with lubricant from the bottom.

11. Partially insert the cross into the yoke so 1 trunnion seats freely in the bearing cup, then rotate the shaft so this trunnion is on the bottom.

12. Install the opposite bearing cap part way. Be sure both trunnions are started straight into the bearing caps.

13. Press against opposite bearing caps, working the cross constantly to be sure the trunnions are free in the bearings. If binding occurs, check the needle rollers to be sure 1 or more needles have not become lodged under an end of the trunnion.

14. As soon as 1 bearing retainer groove is exposed, stop pressing and install the bearing retainer snapring.

15. Continue to press until the opposite bearing retainer can be installed. If difficulty installing the snaprings is encountered, tap the yoke with a hammer to spring the yoke ears slightly.

16. Replace the driveshaft and lower the vehicle.

Molded Retainer (Nylon Injected) Type

NOTE: Don't disassemble these joints unless replacing the complete U-joint. These factory installed joints cannot be reused and should instead be replaced by snapring type U-joints.

1. Raise and support the vehicle safely.

2. Matchmark and remove the driveshaft.

3. Support the propeller shaft horizontally in line with the base plate of a bench vise, but never clamp the driveshaft tube.

4. Place the U-joint so the lower ear of the shaft yoke is supported by a 1⅛ inch socket. Press the lower bearing cap out of the yoke ear. This

will shear the nylon injected ring retaining the lower bearing cap.

5. If the bearing cup is not completely removed, lift the cross, insert J–9522–3 and J–9522–5 or equivalent separator and spacer, then press the cap completely out.

6. Rotate the driveshaft, shear the opposite plastic retainer, and press the other bearing cup out in the same manner.

7. Remove the cross from the yoke.

NOTE: Production U-joints cannot be reassembled. There are no bearing retainer grooves in the caps. Discard all parts that were removed and substitute those in the overhaul kit.

8. If the front U-joint is being removed, separate the bearing caps from the slip yoke in the same manner.

9. Remove the sheared plastic bearing retainer from the yoke. If necessary, drive a small pin or punch through the injection holes to aid in removal.

10. Install the new snapring U-joints.

11. Install the driveshaft assembly.

12. Lower the vehicle.

Rear Axle Shaft, Bearing and Seal

REMOVAL AND INSTALLATION

1. Raise and support the vehicle safely.

2. Remove the tire and wheel assembly, then remove the brake drum.

3. Clean all dirt from the rear carrier cover, then loosen the bolts and remove the cover while draining the gear oil. Discard the old gasket.

4. Remove the shaft lock bolt from the differential case located in the housing, then withdraw the pinion gear shaft.

5. Push the flanged end of axle shaft toward center of the vehicle, then remove C-lock from the end of the shaft located in the housing.

6. Remove axle shaft from the housing. If replacement of the oil seal is not planned, be very careful not to damage the seal.

7. Remove the brake backing plate.

8. Remove seal from housing using a prybar behind the seal's steel case, being careful not to damage housing.

9. Insert an appropriately sized bearing remover into the bore and position it behind the bearing so tangs on tool engage bearing outer race. Re-

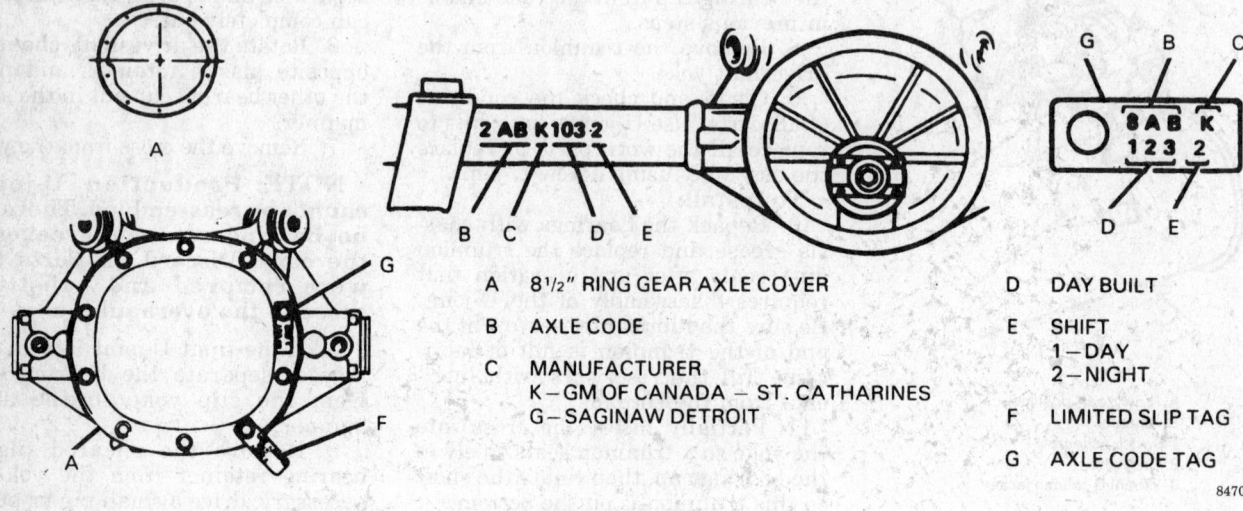

A   8½" RING GEAR AXLE COVER

B   AXLE CODE

C   MANUFACTURER
    K – GM OF CANADA – ST. CATHARINES
    G – SAGINAW DETROIT

D   DAY BUILT

E   SHIFT
    1 – DAY
    2 – NIGHT

F   LIMITED SLIP TAG

G   AXLE CODE TAG

8470P043

Rear axle identification

move the bearing, using a slide hammer.

To install:

10. Lubricate the new bearing with gear lubricant and install bearing using a suitable driver so the tool bottoms against the shoulder in the housing.

11. Lubricate seal lips with gear lubricant, then position the seal on a suitably sized driver and position seal into housing bore. Tap seal into place so it is flush with axle tube.

12. If removed, install the brake backing plate.

13. Insert the axle into the place while engaging the splines on the end of the shaft with the splines of the rear axle side gear. Be careful when inserting the axle not to damage the seal.

14. Install the C-lock on the bottom of the axle shaft and push the shaft outward so the lock seats in the counterbore of the rear axle side gear.

15. Install the rear axle pinion gear shaft through the differential case, thrust washers and pinions, align the hole in the shaft with the lock bolt hole. Install the lock bolt and tighten to 24 ft. lbs. (31 Nm) for 7½ inch ring gears or 20 ft. lbs. (27 Nm) for 8½ inch ring gear.

16. Position a new gasket, then install the carrier cover and tighten the bolt to 22 ft. lbs. (30 Nm) using a crosswise pattern.

17. Fill the rear assembly with the proper grade and type gear oil.

18. Install the brake drum, then install the tire and wheel assembly.

19. Lower the vehicle.

Pinion Seal

REMOVAL AND INSTALLATION

1. Raise and support the vehicle safely, then remove the rear tire and wheel assemblies.

2. Remove the brake drums.

3. Matchmark, then disconnect the driveshaft from the pinion yoke. Support the driveshaft assembly aside by wiring the shaft to the exhaust system or underbody.

4. Using an inch lb. torque wrench on the pinion nut, check and record combined pinion bearing, carrier bearing, axle bearing and seal preload.

5. Position a drain pan to catch any gear oil which may escape. Remove the pinion nut and washer using a suitable flange holding tool to keep the flange from rotating.

6. Slide the flange off the pinion. If necessary, use a flange puller screw and adapter.

7. Drive the oil seal from the carrier using a blunt chisel and taking care to avoid scratching the carrier bore.

To install:

8. Position the seal and install using a seal installing driver of proper size for the seal and casing.

9. Apply seal lubricant 1050169 or equivalent, to the outer diameter of the pinion yoke and to the sealing lip of the new seal.

10. Carefully install the pinion yoke and push it on as far as it will go, then install the nut and washer finger-tight.

NOTE: Never hammer the yoke into place.

11. Hold the yoke and tighten the nut gradually, rotating the pinion gear several turns after each tightening in order to set the bearing. Check the preload of the bearing assemblies each time using an inch lbs. torque wrench.

12. Tighten the pinion nut in very small increments to achieve a preload which is 3–5 inch lbs. (0.3–0.6 Nm) higher than the originally recorded torque.

13. Install the driveshaft assembly and check the rear housing fluid level.

14. Install the rear brake drums, then install the tire and wheel assemblies.

15. Lower the vehicle.

Differential Carrier

REMOVAL AND INSTALLATION

1. Raise and support the vehicle safely.

2. Remove the rear axle housing from the vehicle.

3. Remove the rear axle shafts from the housing.

4. Remove the bolts and the bearing caps, then remove the outer races and shims in sets from the assembly. Mark and/or arrange the caps, races and shims to assure installation their original locations.

NOTE: Production shims may not be reinstalled in the axle housing as they may break when they are tapped into place. Service shims, however, may be reused.

5. Carefully pry the case from the housing.

To install:

6. Position the case into the housing assembly.

7. Install the shims and outer bearing races. Select a shim 0.004 in. (0.1mm) thicker than that which was removed from the left side, then install the shim between the spacer and left bearing race. Repeat the procedure for the right shim.

8. Install the bearing caps and tighten the bolts to 55 ft. lbs. (75 Nm).

9. Check the differential ring gear-to-drive pinion gear backlash and adjust, as necessary:

   a. Rotate the case several times to seat the bearing assemblies.

   b. Mount a dial indicator to the case using the small button on the indicator stem to contact near the heel end of the tooth. Position the dial indicator so the stem is in line with gear rotation and perpendicular to the tooth angle for an accurate backlash reading.

   c. Check the backlash at 3–4 points around the ring gear. The drive gear must be held stationary when checking backlash. Lash must not vary more than 0.002 in. (0.05mm) around the gear. If lash variance is more than specification, check for burrs, uneven bolting conditions or a distorted case flange and repair, as necessary.

   d. Backlash must be adjusted to achieve a minimum lash of 0.005–0.009 in. (0.13–23mm) for all new gears.

   e. Lash may be adjusted by increasing the thickness of 1 shim and decreasing the other shim by the same amount. For each 0.001 in. (0.03mm) of desired change in backlash, transfer 0.002 in. (0.05mm) of shim thickness.

   f. To decrease backlash 0.001 in. (0.03mm), decrease the thickness of the right shim 0.002 in. (0.05mm) while increasing the thickness of the left shim by the same amount.

   g. To increase backlash 0.002 in. (0.05mm), increase the thickness of the right shim 0.004 in. (0.10mm) while decreasing the thickness of the left shim by the same amount.

10. Install the rear axle shafts to the housing assembly.

11. Install the rear axle housing to the vehicle.

12. Lower the vehicle.

Rear Axle Housing

REMOVAL AND INSTALLATION

1. Raise the vehicle and support it safely. Support the rear axle using an adjustable lifting device.

2. Disengage the ABS rear axle speed sensor connector.

3. If equipped, disconnect the automatic level sensor control link.

4. Matchmark and remove the driveshaft assembly.

5. Remove rear wheels.

6. If necessary for housing or component replacement, remove the brake drums, rear brake components, the brake backing plates and/or the axle shafts.

7. Disconnect the parking brake cables from the equalizer and the frame.

8. Disconnect the rear brake pipes from the brake hose fittings. Plug the openings to prevent system contamination or excessive fluid loss.

9. Disconnect bolt attaching the rear brake hose fitting to the housing.

10. If replacing the housing, remove rear brake pipes from the housing clips.

11. With a helper, remove rear springs and disconnect upper and lower control arms from the housing.

12. Carefully lower rear axle housing assembly.

To install:

13. Raise rear axle housing into place with a hoist.

14. With a helper to stabilize the housing, install lower and upper control arms.

15. Install the rear springs.

16. If the housing was replaced, attach the rear brake pipes to housing using retaining clips or straps.

17. Connect the rear brake fitting attaching bolt to the housing and tighten to 20 ft. lbs. (27 Nm).

18. Unplug and connect the rear brake pipes to the rear brake hose fittings and tighten to 18 ft. lbs. (24 Nm).

19. Connect the parking brake cables to the equalizer and the frame.

20. If removed, install the axle shafts, brake backing plates, rear brake components and/or the drums.

21. Install the rear wheels.

22. Align and install the driveshaft assembly.

23. If equipped, connect the automatic level control sensor link.

24. Engage the ABS rear axle speed sensor connector.

25. Fill axle housing with suitable gear oil.

26. Remove support from the housing and lower the vehicle.

27. Properly bleed the hydraulic brake system before attempting to move the vehicle.

STEERING

CAUTION

If equipped with the Supplemental Inflatable Restraint system (SIR), the system must be disabled, before working on or near any system component. Failure to do so may result in deployment of the air bag and possible personal injury.

Steering Wheel

REMOVAL AND INSTALLATION

1. Properly disable the SIR system and disconnect the negative battery cable.

2. Remove the Torx® screws from the back of the steering wheel and lift the inflator module, then disengage the SIR coil connector and retainer from the module and the horn lead from the column.

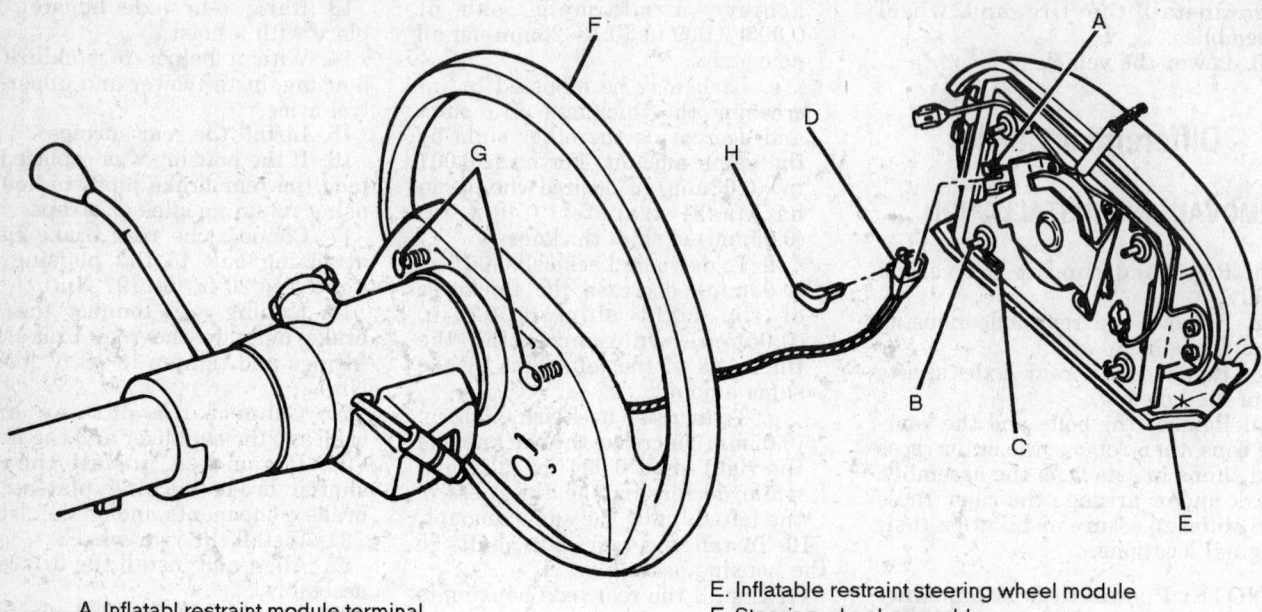

A. Inflatabl restraint module terminal
B. Inflatable restraint modul mounting post
C. Inflatable restraint module clip
D. Coil assembly terminal

E. Inflatable restraint steering wheel module
F. Steering wheel assembly
G. Steering wheel assembly bolt/screw
H. Inflatable restraint steering wheel module
   wiring harness connector retainer

8470P047

Removing the SIR inflator module

CAUTION

To avoid personal injury when carrying a live inflator module, make sure the bag and trim cover are pointed away. When placing a live inflator module on a bench or other surface, always face the bag and trim cover up and away from the surface. Never carry the inflator module by the wires or connector on the underside of the module, otherwise personal injury could result if the bag is deployed.

3. Remove the steering wheel lock nut, then remove the steering wheel and horn contact using a suitable puller.

NOTE: When attaching the wheel puller to the wheel, use care to prevent threading the side screws all the way through the wheel hub and into the coil, damaging the assembly.

To install:
4. Route the coil assembly connector through the steering wheel.
5. Install the steering wheel by aligning the block tooth on the steering wheel with the block tooth on the steering shaft within 1 female serration and install the locking nut.
6. Position the inflator module and connect the horn lead to the the

steering column, then engage the coil assembly connector to the inflator module. Install the coil connector retainer.
7. Route the coil assembly lead around the mounting post and secure under the clip.
8. Install the inflator module to the wheel and tighten the bolts to 25 inch lbs. (2.8 Nm) for 1992 vehicles or to 53 inch lbs. (60 Nm) for 1993–96 vehicles.
9. Connect the negative battery cable and properly enable the SIR system.

Steering Column

REMOVAL AND INSTALLATION

NOTE: Handle the steering column very carefully. Rapping on the end of it or leaning on it could shear off the inserts which allow the column to collapse in a crash. The wheels must be in the straight-ahead position and the key must be in the LOCK position when removing or installing the steering column in order to avoid damaging the SIR coil.

NOTE: The wheels of the vehicle must be in the straight-ahead position and the key must be in

the LOCK position when removing or installing the steering column. Failure to do so will cause the coil assembly in the steering column to become off center and possibly damage the coil or deploy the SIR module upon installation.

1. Properly disable the SIR system and disconnect the negative battery cable.
2. Remove the brake light switch.

NOTE: Failure to remove the brake light switch may cause damage to the switch or cause the switch to be thrown out of adjustment.

3. Remove the steering column opening filler and driver knee bolster.
4. Remove the bolt and nut from the joint coupler attaching the intermediate shaft to the steering column.
5. Remove the nuts attaching the steering column support bracket to the instrument panel carrier, then carefully lower the steering column.
6. Disconnect the shift indicator cable and the shift selector rod from the steering column.
7. Disengage all necessary electrical connectors.
8. Remove bolts attaching the toe plate or jacket to the cowl.

9. If the column is being replaced or internal components are to being serviced, remove the steering wheel.

10. Remove the steering column from the vehicle.

To install:

11. Place steering column in vehicle. If a service replacement column is being installed, do not remove the anti-rotation pin until after the column has been connected to the steering gear.

12. Attach the toe plate or jacket to the cowl and tighten the attaching bolts to 58 inch lbs. (6.5 Nm).

13. Engage the column electrical connectors.

14. Attach the shift indicator cable to the steering column.

15. Install the nuts attaching the column support bracket to the instrument panel carrier and tighten to 20 ft. lbs. (27 Nm).

16. Install the bolt and nut at the joint coupling attaching the upper intermediate shaft to the steering column and tighten to 40 ft. lbs. (54 Nm).

NOTE: If service replacement steering column is being installed, be sure to remove the anti-rotation pin.

17. Connect the shift selector rod and adjust the linkage.

18. Install and adjust the brake lamp switch.

19. Install the driver knee bolster and the steering column opening filler.

NOTE: If service replacement steering column is being installed be sure to; remove the hexagon locking nut, remove the coil assembly shipping cover and disengage the connector from the cover.

20. If removed, install the steering wheel.

21. Connect the negative battery cable and enable the SIR system.

Power Steering Gear

REMOVAL AND INSTALLATION

1992 vehicles

1. Disconnect the negative battery cable and lock the steering wheel in the straight-ahead position.

2. Disconnect the power steering hoses from the gear assembly. Either plug the hoses or raise and secure them to prevent excessive fluid loss.

3. Raise and support the vehicle safely.

4. Disconnect the intermediate shaft from the gear and if equipped, the ABS modulator bracket.

5. Remove the nut from the pitman arm, then separate the arm from the steering gear using J-9172 or an equivalent puller.

6. Remove steering gear mounting bolts, then remove the gear assembly.

To install:

7. Position the gear assembly to the frame and attach loosely with washers and bolts.

8. Adjust the gear to align as straight as possible with the intermediate shaft, then hold the gear in position and tighten the mounting bolts to 70 ft. lbs. (95 Nm).

9. Install the pitman arm to the steering gear using a lock washer and a new nut. Tighten the nut to 179 ft. lbs. (243 Nm).

10. Install the intermediate shaft coupling-to-gear retaining bolt and nut, then tighten to 23 ft. lbs. (31 Nm).

11. If equipped, install the ABS modulator bracket to power steering gear and tighten the nut to 18 ft. lbs. (24 Nm).

12. Lower the vehicle.

13. Connect the inlet and outlet hoses, then tighten fittings to 21 ft. lbs. (28 Nm).

14. Connect the negative battery cable and bleed the steering system.

1993–96 Vehicles

1. Disconnect the negative battery cable, then lock the steering wheel in the straight-ahead position to prevent damage to the SIR coil assembly.

2. Remove the shield from the steering gear return pipe nut, then remove the bolt from the intermediate shaft-to-gear coupling. Push the intermediate shaft rearward, disengaging the latch from the gear.

3. Remove the valve bracket nut from the gear.

4. Remove the steering linkage relay rod nut from the pitman arm.

5. Raise and support the vehicle safely.

6. Remove the nut from the pitman arm, then separate the arm from the steering gear using J-9172 or an equivalent puller.

7. Disconnect the power steering hoses from the gear assembly. Either plug the hoses or raise and secure them to prevent excessive fluid loss.

8. Remove the steering gear mounting bolts, then remove the gear assembly.

To install:

9. Position the gear to the frame and loosely install the mounting bolts.

10. Adjust the gear to align as straight as possible with the intermediate shaft, then hold the gear in position and tighten the mounting bolts to 70 ft. lbs. (95 Nm).

11. Install the power steering hose assemblies to the gear and tighten the fittings to 21 ft. lbs. (28 Nm).

12. Install the pitman arm to the steering gear using a lock washer and a new nut. Tighten the nut to 179 ft. lbs. (243 Nm).

13. Lower the vehicle, then install the steering linkage relay rod nut and tighten to 35 ft. lbs. (47 Nm).

14. Install the valve bracket nut to the gear assembly and tighten to 18 ft. lbs. (24 Nm).

15. Install the intermediate shaft coupling bolt and nut, then tighten to 40 ft. lbs. (54 Nm).

16. Position the shield, making sure the latch is seated around the gear return pipe nut.

17. Connect the negative battery cable, then properly bleed the steering system.

ADJUSTMENT

Worm Thrust Bearing Preload

1. Remove the steering gear from the vehicle, then rotate the stub shaft back and forth in order to drain any remaining fluid.

2. Remove the adjuster plug locknut from the front of the housing at the intermediator shaft coupling.

3. Use a spanner to turn the adjuster plug clockwise until the plug and thrust bearing are fully bottomed in the housing. Tighten the plug to 221 ft. lbs. (30 Nm).

4. Place an index mark on the housing even with 1 of the adjuster plug holes, then measure back ½ in. (13mm) and place a second mark on the housing.

5. Turn the adjuster plug counterclockwise until the hole in the plug is aligned with the second housing mark.

6. Hold the plug in order to maintain proper alignment while tightening the locknut to 80 ft. lbs. (109 Nm) using a drift in the notch.

7. Install the steering gear to the vehicle.

Pitman Shaft Over-Center Preload

1. Remove the steering gear from the vehicle, then rotate the stub shaft

back and forth in order to drain any remaining fluid.

2. Loosen the adjuster locknut located on top of the gear housing.

3. Turn the pitman shaft adjuster screw counterclockwise until it is fully extended, then rotate the screw clockwise 1 full turn.

4. Rotate the stub shaft from stop to stop using a 12-point socket and count the number of turns between the stops.

5. Starting from either stop, turn the shaft ½ the number of turns counted, in order to locate the center of the gear. When centered the flat on the stub shaft should face upward, parallel with the side cover and the master spline on the pitman shaft should be in line with the adjuster screw.

6. Position a torque wrench on the stub shaft with the handle in the vertical position, then rotate the stub shaft 45 degrees to each side of center. Make sure the shaft rotates smoothly and does not stick or bind. Record the worm bearing preload measured on or near center. Preload should be 6–15 inch lbs. (0.7–1.7 Nm) with the worm and ballnut installed. If outside this range, the gear must be readjusted or repaired.

7. If necessary, adjust the preload by turning the pitman shaft adjuster screw clockwise until the correct torque is obtained. Add 6–10 inch lbs. (0.7–1.1 Nm) to the previously measured bearing torque, then prevent the adjuster screw from turning while tightening the locknut to 36 ft. lbs. (49 Nm).

8. Install the steering gear to the vehicle.

Power Steering Pump

REMOVAL AND INSTALLATION

1. Disconnect the negative battery cable.

2. Loosen and remove power steering pump belt or serpentine drive belt.

3. If necessary, remove the radiator fan shroud for access.

4. Remove the power steering pump pulley using J–25034–B or equivalent puller.

5. Remove the 2 upper most pump mounting bolts, then raise and support the vehicle safely.

6. For 1993–96 vehicles, disengage the electrical connections from the pump assembly

7. Disconnect the fluid hoses from the pump, then plug the hoses to pre-

vent system contamination or excessive fluid loss.

8. Remove the remaining bolt and/or nut from the pump and carefully remove the pump from the vehicle.

To install:

9. Position pump assembly to bracket, then install the lower retaining bolt and tighten to 37 ft. lbs. (50 Nm).

10. Uncap and connect the inlet and outlet hoses.

11. For 1993–96 vehicles, engage the pressure switch connector.

12. Lower the vehicle, then install the upper pump bolts and tighten to 37 ft. lbs. (50 Nm).

13. Using a suitable pump pulley installation tool, attach the pulley to the pump assembly. Make sure the pulley hub is flush with the end of the pump shaft.

14. Install the power steering pump belt or serpentine belt.

15. Fill with fluid, bleed the system and adjust belt(s) to proper tension.

BELT TENSION ADJUSTMENT

V-Belt

Use a belt tension gauge and adjust to 112 ft. lbs. (500 Nm) on used belts or 169 ft. lbs. (750 Nm) on new belts.

Serpentine Belt

The vehicles utilize a single, serpentine drive belt for all engine accessories. Serpentine belts are automatically adjusted by the tensioner on the engine. If the belt is loose, check the condition of the belt and tensioner. Make sure the tensioner marking are within proper operating range for belt condition (new/used). The tensioner should place enough tension on the belt so it can only be twisted 90 degrees at it's longest run.

If belt slippage occurs, while the drive belt tensioner is within its operating range, and the belt does not need replacement, check the belt tension as follows:

1. Run the engine for 10 minutes, shut OFF the engine, then using a tension gauge between any 2 pulleys, record the belt tension.

2. Run the engine for 30 seconds and repeat Step 1.

3. Once again, run the engine for 30 seconds and repeat Step 1.

4. The belt tension is the average of the 3 readings. Serpentine belt tension should be 105–125 lbs. (467–556 Nm) for 1992–93 vehicles.

5. Replace the tensioner if belt length is acceptable (as measured by

the tensioner scale), but the tension is below the minimum specification.

SYSTEM BLEEDING

When the power steering system has been serviced or a fitting disconnected, air must be bled from the system by using the following procedure:

1. With the engine **OFF** and the front wheels off the ground, turn wheels all the way to the left and add power steering fluid to the FULL COLD mark on the level indicator.

2. Bleed the system by turning the wheels from side to side several times, without hitting stops. Be sure to keep the level to the FULL COLD mark.

3. Start the engine and run at fast idle momentarily, then recheck the fluid level with the engine idling. If necessary add fluid to bring the level back to the FULL COLD mark.

4. Return the wheels to the center position and continue running the engine for a few minutes. Road test to check the operation of the steering.

5. Recheck the fluid level it should now be stabilized at the FULL HOT level on the indicator.

Tie Rod Ends

REMOVAL AND INSTALLATION

NOTE: Because tie rod adjuster parts often become rusted in service it is recommend that a torque wrench be used to free the clamp nut from the bolts so the torque required can be measured. If a force in excess of 80 inch lbs. (9 Nm) is necessary to free the clamp nuts, they should be discarded and replaced with new nuts upon installation.

Inner

1. Raise and support the vehicle safely.

2. Remove the nut securing the inner ball stud to the intermediate or relay rod.

3. Remove the inner ball stud from the intermediate rod using J–24319–01 or an equivalent universal steering linkage puller.

4. Mark the tie rod end position before removing from the adjuster and note the position of the tie rod clamps for installation purposes. Loosen the clamp bolt and unscrew the end from the adjuster tube counting the number of turns necessary to remove the inner tie rod from the tube.

To install:

5. Lubricate the adjuster threads using chassis grease.

6. If installing a new tie rod, place the new and old components side-by-side, then copy the mark made during removal to the new component.

7. Thread the tie rod end into the adjuster using the same number of turns counted earlier, this should align the marks made earlier. If the marks do not align, make sure the same number of turns were used and/or the mark made on a new part was placed in the correct position.

8. Insert the inner ball stud to the intermediate rod, using J–29193 or an equivalent linkage installer to properly seat the tapers. Tighten the tool to 15 ft. lbs. (20 Nm), then remove the tool from the vehicle.

9. Install the retaining nut to the ball stud and tighten to 35 ft. lbs. (47 Nm).

10. Make sure the tie rod adjuster and clamps are properly positioned, then tighten the adjuster clamp bolt to 14 ft. lbs. (19 Nm).

11. Lower vehicle, then check and adjust vehicle toe, as necessary.

Outer

1. Raise and support the vehicle safely.

2. Remove the cotter pin from the outer tie rod ball stud, then remove the castellated nut.

3. Disconnect the tie rod end from the steering knuckle using a universal steering linkage puller.

4. Mark the tie rod end position before removing from the adjuster and note the position of the tie rod clamps for installation purposes. Loosen the clamp bolt and unscrew the end from the adjuster tube counting the number of turns necessary to remove the outer tie rod from the tube.

To install:

5. Lubricate the adjuster threads using chassis grease.

6. If installing a new tie rod, place the new and old components side-by-side, then copy the mark made during removal to the new component.

7. Thread the tie rod end into the adjuster using the same number of turns counted earlier, this should align the marks made earlier. If the marks do not align, make sure the same number of turns were used and/or the mark made on a new part was placed in the correct position.

8. Connect outer ball stud to the steering knuckle, then install the attaching nut. Tighten the nut to 35 ft. lbs. (47 Nm), then install a new cotter

pin. If after tightening a hole in the nut does not align with the stud hole, tighten the nut further, just enough to insert a cotter pin. Do not back off the specified torque to insert a cotter pin.

9. Make sure the tie rod adjuster and clamps are properly positioned, then tighten the adjuster clamp bolt to 14 ft. lbs. (19 Nm).

10. Lower vehicle, then check and adjust vehicle toe, as necessary.

BRAKES

Master Cylinder

REMOVAL AND INSTALLATION

NOTE: Be sure to clean the area where the master cylinder is mounted, before beginning removal.

1. Disconnect the brake pipes from the master cylinder assembly. Cap or plug the openings to prevent system contamination or excessive fluid loss.

2. Remove the 2 nuts attaching the master cylinder to the brake booster assembly.

3. The combination valve bracket is mounted over the master cylinder on the power brake booster studs, pull the bracket from the studs and reposition it aside.

4. Remove the master cylinder assembly from the vehicle.

To install:

5. Install the master cylinder on the power booster studs.

6. If applicable, install the combination valve bracket on the power booster studs.

7. Install the attaching nuts and tighten to 20 ft. lbs. (27 Nm).

8. Unplug the hydraulic pipes, then connect them to the master cylinder and tighten to 24 ft. lbs. (32 Nm).

9. Fill with approved brake fluid, then bleed the hydraulic brake system.

Combination Valve

REMOVAL AND INSTALLATION

1. Disconnect the negative battery cable.

2. Disconnect the hydraulic lines at the combination valve, then plug

the openings to prevent system contamination or excessive fluid loss.

3. Disengage the electrical connector from the pressure differential warning switch.

4. Remove the 2 attaching nuts from the power brake booster, then remove the combination valve bracket and valve.

To install:

5. Make sure the master cylinder is in place, then position the combination valve and bracket on the power brake booster studs.

6. Install and tighten the attaching nuts to 20 ft. lbs. (27 Nm).

7. Unplug the hydraulic lines and attach them to the combination valve. Tighten fittings to 24 ft. lbs. (32 Nm) on 1992–93 vehicles.

8. Engage the electrical connector, then connect the negative battery cable.

9. Bleed the hydraulic brake system.

Power Brake Booster

REMOVAL AND INSTALLATION

1. Disconnect the vacuum hose from the vacuum check valve.

2. Remove the 2 nuts holding the master cylinder and the combination valve bracket, to the booster. Carefully position the component(s) aside, being careful not to kink any of the hydraulic lines. It is not necessary to disconnect the brake lines if only the brake booster is being removed.

3. Loosen the 4 nuts that hold the power unit mounted on the firewall.

4. Disconnect the retainer, outer washer, pushrod assembly and inner washer, as applicable, from the brake pedal. Do not force the pushrod to the side when disconnecting.

5. For 1993–96 vehicles so equipped, remove the daytime running lamp diode.

6. Remove the 4 mounting nuts, then remove the booster assembly and gasket.

To install:

7. If removed, install the gasket over the booster studs.

8. Place the booster unit against the firewall and loosely attach nuts.

9. Connect the inner washer, pushrod assembly, outer washer, and retainer to the brake pedal. Lubricate the pedal pin before installing the inner washer.

10. For 1993–96 vehicles so equipped, install the daytime running lamp diode.

11. Tighten the power unit attaching nuts to 15 ft. lbs. (21 Nm) for 1992 vehicles or to 20 ft. lbs. (27 Nm) for 1993–96 vehicles.

12. Install the master cylinder and, if applicable, the combination valve bracket on the power booster mounting studs. Install and tighten the retaining nuts to specification.

13. Connect the hose to the vacuum check valve.

Brake Caliper

REMOVAL AND INSTALLATION

1. Remove ⅔ of the brake fluid from the master cylinder assembly.

2. Raise and support the vehicle safely.

3. Mark the relationship of the wheel to the hub for reinstallation, then remove the tire and wheel assembly.

4. Position a C-clamp over the outboard shoe and lining and the caliper housing, then slowly tighten the C-clamp in order to bottom the piston into the caliper bore.

NOTE: If removing the caliper assembly only to access other brake parts skip Step 5. If removing the caliper entirely from the vehicle, the brake system will have to be bled.

5. If removing the caliper from the vehicle for service or replacement, remove the bolt, copper washers and inlet fitting from the caliper housing. Plug the openings to prevent system contamination or excessive fluid loss and discard the used copper washers.

6. Remove the mounting bolts and the sleeves, then remove the caliper from the rotor. If the caliper is not being completely removed from the vehicle, it must be suspended from the suspension using a hook, string or wire. Never allow the caliper to hang by the brake line or damage could occur.

To install:

7. Lubricate the sleeves and bushings with silicone grease, then insert the sleeves into caliper housing.

8. Position the caliper assembly onto the rotor and knuckle assembly.

9. Insert the mounting bolts and tighten to 38 ft. lbs. (51 Nm).

10. Measure the distance between the caliper housing and the stops on the knuckle assembly. There should be 0.005–0.012 in. (0.13–0.30mm) of clearance. If necessary, remove the caliper assembly and file the ends of the stops on the knuckle to increase clearance. Excessive clearance requires replacement of the caliper and/or steering knuckle.

11. If removed for service or replacement, bolt new copper washers and the inlet fitting to the caliper housing, then tighten to 32 ft. lbs. (44 Nm).

12. Align the marks on the wheel and hub, then install the wheel assembly.

13. Lower the vehicle.

14. Fill the master cylinder to the proper level, and, if the line was disconnected, bleed the caliper.

Disc Brake Pads

REMOVAL AND INSTALLATION

1. Raise the vehicle and support it safely.

2. Remove the tire and wheel assembly.

3. Remove the caliper assembly and support it aside from the front suspension.

4. Remove the inner and outer brake pads from the caliper.

5. Remove the bushings and sleeves from the grooves in the caliper housing.

6. Remove the shoe retainer spring from the inboard pad.

To install:

7. If not done during removal, bottom the piston in the caliper bore using a large C-clamp.

8. Lift the inner edge of the piston boot and press out any trapped air.

9. Clean and then lubricate new bushings and sleeves with silicone grease, then install the bushings and sleeves into the grooves of the caliper housing.

10. Install the shoe retainer spring on the inboard pad.

11. Install the inboard pad. Be sure to seat the shoe retainer spring in the piston and check that the pad is flat against the piston. Also, the boot and inner pad must not be in contact. If necessary, reseat or reposition the boot.

NOTE: The wear sensor should be at the leading edge of the inboard pad during forward wheel rotation.

12. Install the outboard pad with the back of the pad flat against the housing.

13. Install the caliper assembly and clinch the pad tabs using a chisel or wedge tool between the tab and caliper casting, then using a brass punch to drive the tab down against the caliper.

14. Install the tire and wheel assembly, then lower the vehicle.

15. Apply the brake pedal 3 times to seat the pads and to achieve a firm brake pedal.

Brake Rotor

REMOVAL AND INSTALLATION

1. Disconnect the negative battery cable, then raise and support the vehicle safely.

2. If equipped, disconnect the ABS wheel speed sensor from the steering knuckle and secure.

3. Remove the brake caliper and position aside supported from the front suspension.

4. Remove the dust cap from the hub, then remove the cotter pin, nut and washer from the spindle. Carefully remove the hub and rotor from the spindle.

To install:

5. Position hub and rotor assembly onto the spindle.

6. Place the washer and nut on the spindle. Initially torque the hub spindle nut to 12 ft. lbs. (16 Nm) while turning the wheel forward by hand. When finished with adjustment, install a new cotter pin.

7. Attach the dust cap to the hub assembly.

8. Install the brake caliper assembly.

9. If equipped, install the ABS wheel speed sensor.

10. Lower vehicle and connect the negative battery cable.

Brake Drums

REMOVAL AND INSTALLATION

1. Raise and support the vehicle safely, then remove the rear wheel assembly.

2. Mark the relationship of the drum to the axle flange.

3. Make sure the parking brake is released and carefully slide the drum from the axle flange studs.

4. If there is difficulty removing the rotor, use a rubber mallet to tap gently on the outer rim of the drum and/or the inner drum diameter by the spindle. If necessary, remove the adjusting hole or knockout plate from the backing plate and back off the adjusting screw with a suitable tool.

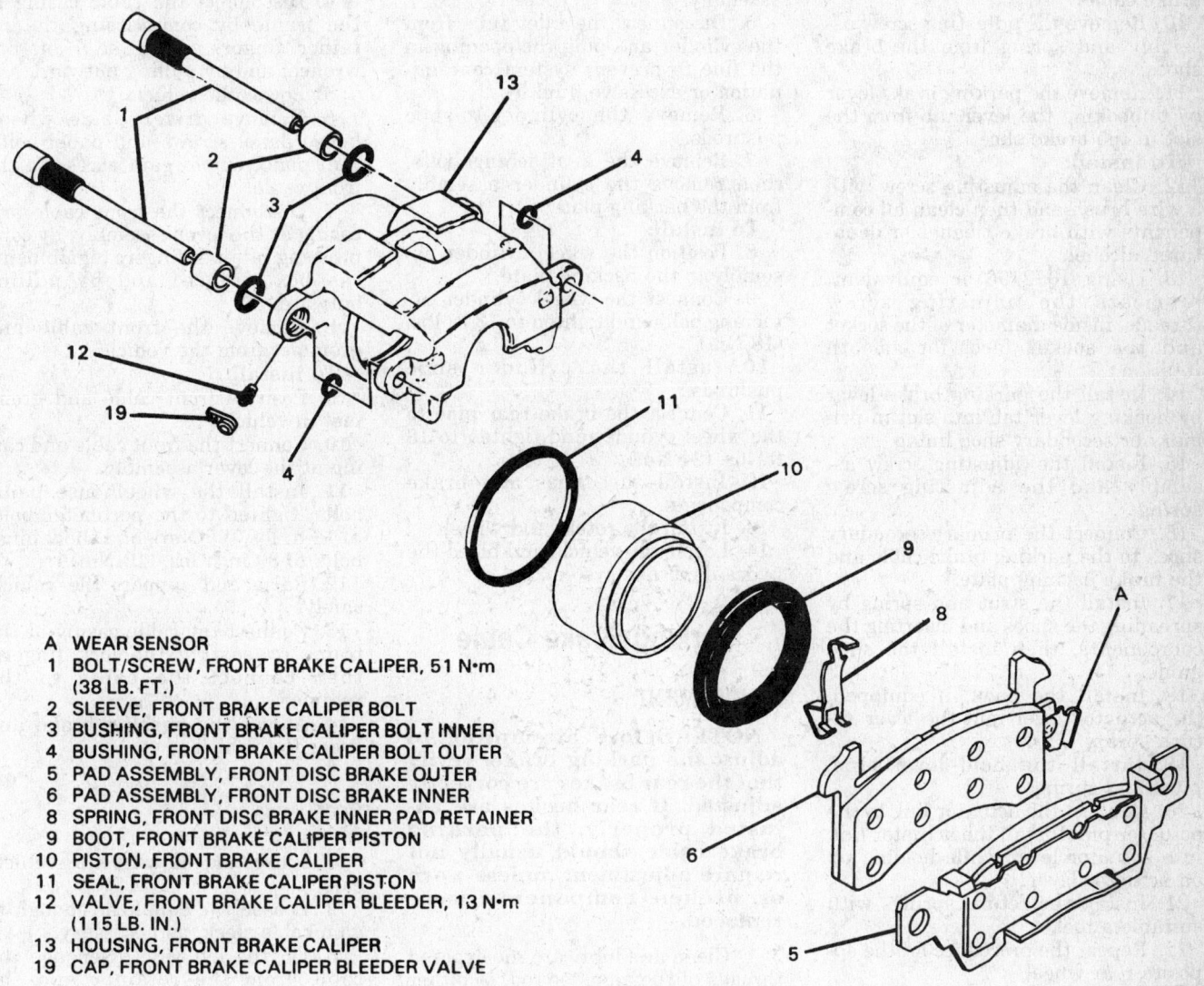

A WEAR SENSOR
1 BOLT/SCREW, FRONT BRAKE CALIPER, 51 N·m
   (38 LB. FT.)
2 SLEEVE, FRONT BRAKE CALIPER BOLT
3 BUSHING, FRONT BRAKE CALIPER BOLT INNER
4 BUSHING, FRONT BRAKE CALIPER BOLT OUTER
5 PAD ASSEMBLY, FRONT DISC BRAKE OUTER
6 PAD ASSEMBLY, FRONT DISC BRAKE INNER
8 SPRING, FRONT DISC BRAKE INNER PAD RETAINER
9 BOOT, FRONT BRAKE CALIPER PISTON
10 PISTON, FRONT BRAKE CALIPER
11 SEAL, FRONT BRAKE CALIPER PISTON
12 VALVE, FRONT BRAKE CALIPER BLEEDER, 13 N·m
   (115 LB. IN.)
13 HOUSING, FRONT BRAKE CALIPER
19 CAP, FRONT BRAKE CALIPER BLEEDER VALVE

8470P051

Exploded view of the caliper assembly

To install:

5. Adjust the brake shoes. The outside diameter of the shoe and linings should be 0.050 inch (1.27mm) less than the inside diameter of the brake drum on each wheel.

6. Position the drum on the axle flange, aligning the marks made earlier.

7. Install the rear tire and wheel assembly.

8. Adjust the parking brake, then lower vehicle.

Brake Shoes

REMOVAL AND INSTALLATION

1. Raise and support the vehicle safely.

2. Remove the tire and wheel assemblies.

3. Remove the brake drums. If the brake drum cannot be removed, try the following:

   a. Make sure the parking brake is released.

   b. Back off the parking brake cable adjustment.

   c. Remove the adjusting hole knockout plate from the backing plate and back off the adjusting screw.

   d. Use a rubber mallet to tap on the outer rim of the drum and around the inner drum diameter by the spindle.

4. Remove the return springs.

5. Remove the hold-down pins and springs.

6. Remove the actuator lever pivot.

7. Lift up on the actuator lever to remove the actuator link. Remove the lever, pawl if equipped, and lever return spring.

8. Remove the shoe guide, the parking brake strut and spring.

9. Remove the brake shoes from the backing plate and the parking brake cable.

10. Remove the adjusting screw assembly and spring from the brake shoes.

11. Remove the parking brake lever by unhooking the lever tab from the slot in the brake shoe.

To install:

12. Clean the adjusting screw with a wire brush and then clean all components with brake cleaner or denatured alcohol.

13. Using 1052196 or equivalent, lubricate the adjusting screw threads, inside diameter of the socket and the socket face, for smooth rotation.

14. Install the parking brake lever by hooking lever tab into slot in primary or secondary shoe lining.

15. Install the adjusting screw assembly and the adjusting screw spring.

16. Connect the primary/secondary shoes to the parking brake cable and the brake backing plate.

17. Install the strut and spring by spreading the shoes and inserting the components, then install the shoe guide.

18. Install the pawl, if equipped, the actuator lever and the lever return spring.

19. Install the hold-down pins, pivot and springs.

20. Connect the actuator link to the actuator pin. Install the actuator link into actuator lever while holding up on actuator lever.

21. Install the return springs with suitable a tool.

22. Repeat the procedure for the opposite rear wheel.

23. Adjust the brake shoes. The outside diameter of both shoe and linings should be 0.050 inch (1.27mm) less than the inside diameter of the brake drum on each wheel.

24. Install the drums and tires.

25. Lower the vehicle. Be sure to adjust the parking brake cable, if the parking brake adjuster was loosened to remove the drums.

Wheel Cylinder

REMOVAL AND INSTALLATION

1. Raise and support the vehicle safely.

2. Remove the wheel and brake drum.

3. Remove the brake shoes and components.

4. Clean dirt and foreign material from around wheel cylinder assembly.

5. Disconnect the inlet tube from the cylinder and plug the opening in the line to prevent system contamination or excessive fluid loss.

6. Remove the cylinder-to-shoe pushrods.

7. Remove the 2 attaching bolts, then remove the cylinder assembly from the backing plate.

To install:

8. Position the wheel cylinder assembly to the backing plate.

9. Connect the wheel cylinder attaching bolts and tighten to 13 ft. lbs. (18 Nm).

10. Install the cylinder shoe pushrods.

11. Connect the brake rear pipe to the wheel cylinder and tighten to 18 ft. lbs. (24 Nm).

12. Install the shoes and brake components.

13. Install the rotors and wheels.

14. Lower the vehicle and bleed the hydraulic brake system.

Parking Brake Cable

ADJUSTMENT

NOTE: Before attempting to adjust the parking brake, verify that the rear brakes are correctly adjusted. If rear brakes are adjusted properly, the parking brake cable should usually not require adjustment, unless worn or broken components were replaced.

1. Clean and lubricate the exposed threads of the adjuster rod, to either side of the nut.

2. Apply the parking brake 6 clicks, then raise and support the vehicle safely.

3. Tighten the adjusting nut until the right rear wheel can barely be turned backwards when using 2 hands, but locks up when attempts are made to move it forward.

4. With the parking brake disengaged the rear wheel should turn freely in either direction with no brake drag.

5. Lower the vehicle.

REMOVAL AND INSTALLATION

Front

1. Raise the vehicle and support it safely.

2. Loosen equalizer sufficiently to gain the necessary cable slack.

3. Disconnect the front cable at the retainer.

4. Disconnect the cable casing at the frame by compressing the retainer fingers, using a ½ in. box wrench, and by pulling outward.

5. Lower the vehicle.

6. Remove driver's side wheelhouse panel screws and panel bolts. Pull panel out to gain access to the front cable.

7. Disconnect the front cable and casing at the lever assembly, by compressing retainer fingers (again using the box wrench) and by pulling outward.

8. Remove the front cable and grommet from the vehicle.

To install:

9. Position front cable and grommet in vehicle.

10. Connect the front cable and casing at the lever assembly.

11. Install the wheelhouse panel bolts, tighten to the perimeter bolts to 18 ft. lbs. (25 Nm), and the 2 inner bolts to 89 inch lbs. (10 Nm).

12. Raise and support the vehicle safely.

13. Connect the cable casing at the frame by seating the lock fingers, then connect the cable to the retainer.

14. Adjust the parking brake and lower the vehicle.

Rear

1. Raise and support the vehicle safely.

2. Loosen the equalizer enough to gain cable slack, as necessary.

3. On the left side disengage the cable from the retainer and the equalizer.

4. On the right side, disconnect the cable from the equalizer. Disconnect the cable and casing at the frame by compressing the retainer fingers and pulling outward. Disconnect the cable and casing from the axle housing clips.

5. Remove the tire and wheel assembly, then remove the brake drum.

6. Remove the primary and secondary brake shoes, as necessary.

7. Disconnect the cable from the parking brake lever and remove the cable. Compress the retainer fingers and loosen the cable and casing from the backing plate.

To install:

8. Connect the cable and casing into the brake backing plate, then attach to the parking brake lever.

9. Install the brake shoes and components, as necessary.

10. Adjust the brake shoes and install the drum, then install the tire and wheel assembly.

11. On the right side, connect the cable and casing to the axle housing clips and to the frame. Then connect the cable to the equalizer.

12. On the left side connect the cable to the retainer and the equalizer.

13. Adjust the parking brake, then lower the vehicle.

Brake System Bleeding

The brake system must be bled when any brake line is disconnected or if it is suspected that there is air in the system.

NOTE: Always take extreme care to prevent fluid from touching a painted surface.

1. Clean the master cylinder of excess dirt and remove the cylinder cover and the diaphragm.

2. Fill the master cylinder to the proper level. Check the fluid level periodically during the bleeding process and replenish it, as necessary. Do not allow the master cylinder to fall below ½ full.

3. If the master cylinder is suspected or known to have air in the bore, bleed it as follows before any wheel cylinder or caliper:

   a. Disconnect the forward brake line connection at the master cylinder.

   b. Allow brake fluid to fill the master cylinder bore until it begins to flow from the forward line connector port.

   c. Connect the forward brake line to the master cylinder and tighten.

   d. Have an assistant depress the brake pedal slowly, 1 full thrust at a time and hold. Loosen the forward brake line connection at the master cylinder to purge the air from the bore, then tighten the connection and have the assistant release the brake pedal slowly. Wait 15 seconds and repeat the sequence, including the 15 second pause, until all air is removed from the bore.

   e. After all air is removed at the forward connection, repeat the procedure for the rear master cylinder connection. Both fittings should be

tightened to 24 ft. lbs. (32 Nm) after the master cylinder is bled.

NOTE: Never bleed a wheel cylinder when a drum is removed.

4. Bleed the individual wheel cylinders or calipers only after all air is removed from the master cylinder. If the master cylinder was bled, then the entire system must be bled in the proper order. The correct sequence for bleeding is to work from the brake farthest from the master cylinder to the 1 closest; (right rear, left rear, right front, left front). Bleed individual components as follows:

   a. Position the proper size box end wrench over the bleeder valve.

   b. Attach a length of clear vinyl hose to the bleeder screw of the brake to be bled. Insert the other end of the hose into a clear jar half full of clean brake fluid so the end of the hose is beneath the level of fluid.

   c. Have an assistant depress the brake pedal 1 time and hold. Loosen the bleeder valve to purge the air from the cylinder, then tighten the bleeder screw and have the assistant slowly release the pedal. Wait 15 seconds, then repeat the sequence, including the 15 second pause, until all air is removed.

NOTE: Make sure the assistant presses the brake pedal to the floor slowly. Rapid pumping of the brake pedal pushes the master cylinder secondary piston down the bore in a way that makes it difficult to bleed the rear side of the system.

5. Repeat this procedure at each of the wheels. Tighten the caliper bleeder screw to 115 inch lbs. (13 Nm) or the wheel cylinder screw to 62 inch lbs. (7 Nm) when bleeding is completed. Remember to check the master cylinder level periodically during the process. Use only fresh fluid to refill the master cylinder, not the fluid bled from the system.

6. Check the brake pedal to make sure it is free of sponginess and make sure the red BRAKE indicator lamp is OFF indicating a proper pressure balance. If necessary, repeat the entire procedure to correct either condition.

7. When the bleeding process is complete, top off the master cylinder, install its cover and diaphragm and discard the fluid bled from the brake system.

Anti-Lock Brake System Service

PRECAUTIONS

Failure to observe the following precautions may result in system damage.

• Before performing electric arc welding on the vehicle, disconnect the Electronic Brake Control Module (EBCM) and the hydraulic modulator connectors.

• When performing service on the system, pay close attention to routing, position, mounting and location of all ABS components, wiring, connectors, and clips. ABS components are extremely sensitive to Electro-Magnetic Interference (EMI).

• When performing painting work on the vehicle, do not expose the Electronic Brake Control Module (EBCM) to temperatures in excess of 185°F (85°C) for longer than 2 hours. The system may be exposed to temperatures up to 200°F (95°C) for less than 15 minutes.

• Never disconnect or connect the Electronic Brake Control Module (EBCM) or hydraulic modulator connectors with the ignition switch ON. Never disconnect the battery with the engine running.

• Never disassemble any component of the Anti-Lock Brake System (ABS) which is designated non-serviceable; the component must be replaced as an assembly.

• When filling the master cylinder, always use fresh clean Delco Supreme 11 brake fluid or equivalent, which meets DOT-3 specifications; silicone fluid, mineral oil and water will destroy the rubber parts.

Modulator Valve

REMOVAL AND INSTALLATION

———— CAUTION ————
The modulator is not repairable and no screws on the modulator may be loosened. If the screws are loosened, it will not be possible to get the brake circuits leak-tight and personal injury may result.

1. Disconnect the negative battery cable.

2. Remove the air intake duct and resonator and move the upper coolant hose aside.

3. Disconnect the canister purge line at the canister and move aside.

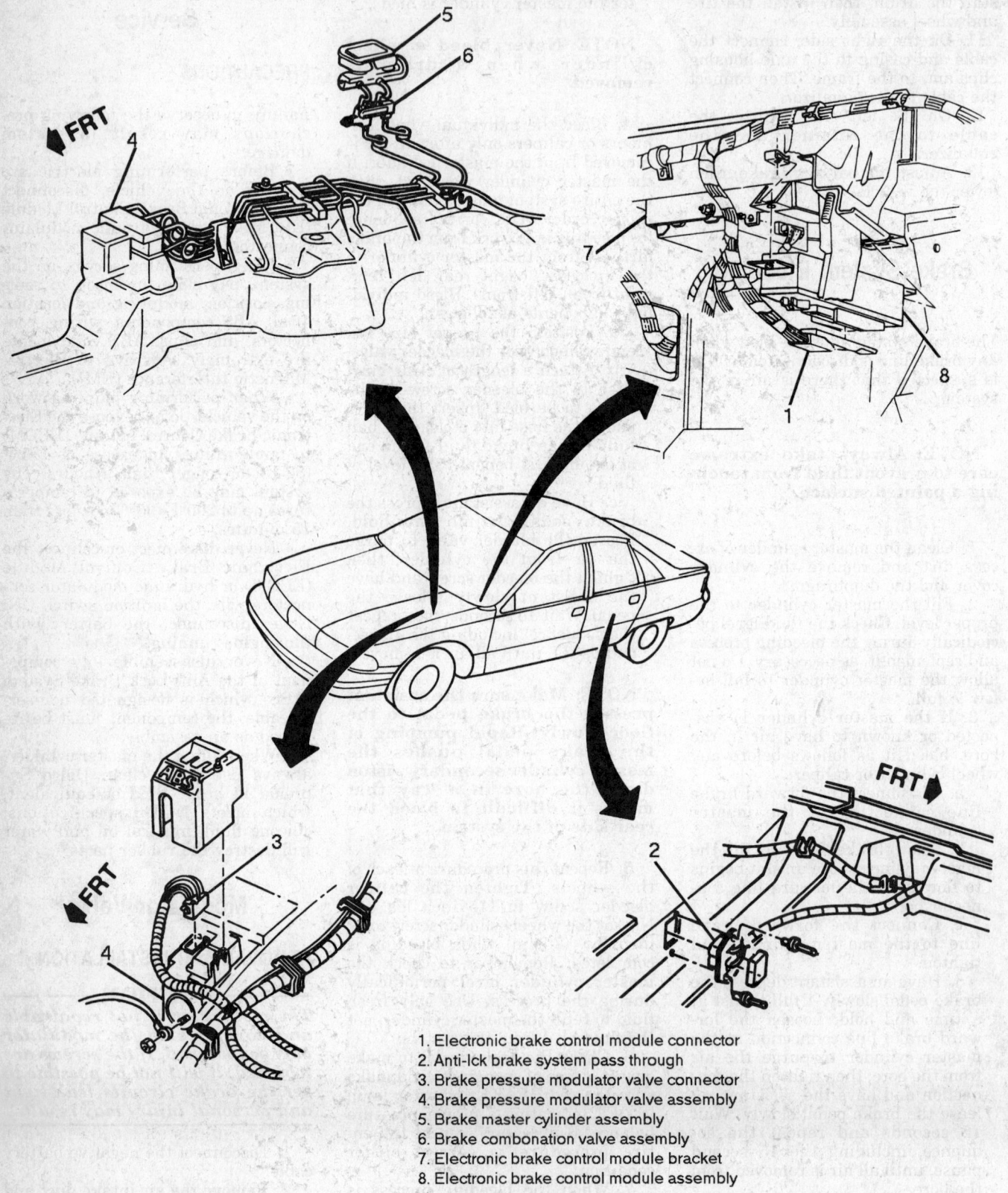

1. Electronic brake control module connector
2. Anti-lck brake system pass through
3. Brake pressure modulator valve connector
4. Brake pressure modulator valve assembly
5. Brake master cylinder assembly
6. Brake combonation valve assembly
7. Electronic brake control module bracket
8. Electronic brake control module assembly

8470P053

Anti-lock Brake System (ABS) components

4. Remove the retaining screw and remove the modulator valve cover.

5. Unlock the tab and disconnect the modulator valve electrical connector.

6. Remove the nut and disconnect the ground wire from the modulator.

7. Note the hydraulic brake pipe location then disconnect the plug the lines from the modulator to prevent fluid contamination or loss.

8. Remove the 3 nuts retaining the modulator to the bracket.

9. Remove the bracket taking care to protect the vehicle from any brake fluid spillage. If replacing the modulator assembly, remove the insulators from the modulator valve.

To install:

10. If applicable, install the insulators to the modulator valve.

11. Install the modulator valve to the bracket and tighten the 3 nuts to 89 inch lbs. (10 Nm).

12. If a new modulator is being used, remove shipping plugs from the valve openings.

13. Connect the hydraulic brake pipes to their original location in the modulator and tighten to 11 ft. lbs. (15 Nm).

--- **CAUTION** ---

If brake pipes are switched (inlet vs. outlet) wheel lockup will occur and personal injury may result.

14. Install the ground wire and nut to the modulator, tighten nut to 25 inch lbs. (2.8 Nm).

15. Install the modulator valve electrical connector.

16. Install the modulator valve cover with the retaining screw and tighten to 13 inch lbs. (1.5 Nm).

17. Connect the canister purge line to the canister.

18. Install the air intake duct and resonator and move the upper coolant hose into position.

19. Connect the negative battery cable.

20. Use only DOT 3 hydraulic brake fluid, fill and bleed the brake system.

21. Road test the vehicle.

Electronic Brake Control Module (EBCM)

The EBCM is located under the left side instrument panel, above the brake pedal, on the DERM bracket.

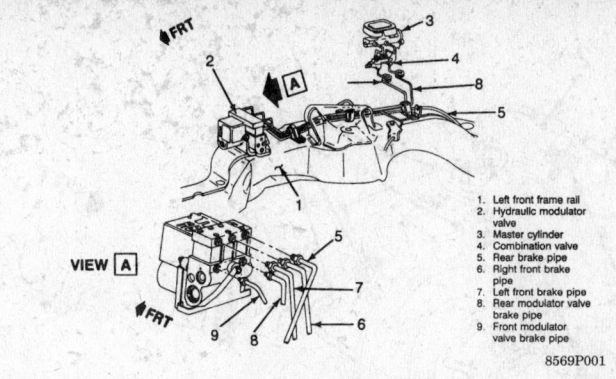

1. Left front frame rail
2. Hydraulic modulator valve
3. Master cylinder
4. Combination valve
5. Rear brake pipe
6. Right front brake pipe
7. Left front brake pipe
8. Rear modulator valve brake pipe
9. Front modulator valve brake pipe

8569P001

ABS brake line routing

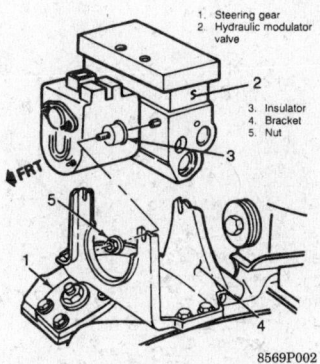

1. Steering gear
2. Hydraulic modulator valve

3. Insulator
4. Bracket
5. Nut

8569P002

ABS hydraulic modulator valve removal

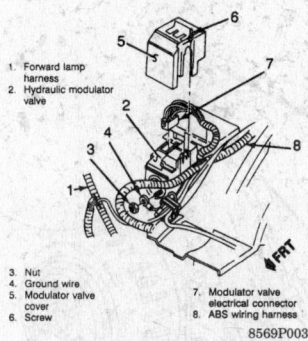

1. Forward lamp harness
2. Hydraulic modulator valve

3. Nut
4. Ground wire
5. Modulator valve cover
6. Screw
7. Modulator valve electrical connector
8. ABS wiring harness

8569P003

ABS hydraulic modulator valve electrical connections

Front Wheel Speed Sensor

REMOVAL AND INSTALLATION

1. Disconnect the negative battery cable.

2. For the right side speed sensor, unclip the connectors from the clip and separate.

3. Raise and support the vehicle safely.

4. For the left side speed sensor, with the vehicle safely supported, un-

clip the connectors from the clip and separate.

5. Remove the sensor wiring harness mounting bolt and bracket from the frame rail.

6. Remove the sensor retaining bolt and remove the sensor from the kunckle assembly.

To install:

7. Coat the steering knuckle with anti-corrosion compound 1052856 or equivalent, at the knuckle contact point.

8. Install the wheel speed sensor to the steering knuckle and tighten the sensor retaining bolt to 71 inch lbs. (8 Nm).

NOTE: Proper installation of the wheel speed sensor cables is critical to proper operation of the ABS system. Make sure the cables are installed in the retainers. Failure to do this may result in contact with moving parts and the over extension of the cables, resulting in an open circuit.

9. Connect the sensor wiring harness mounting bolt and bracket to the frame rail and tighten to 89 inch lbs. (10 Nm).

10. For the left side speed sensor, with the vehicle safely supported, attach the connectors and position them in the clip.

11. Lower the vehicle.

12. For the right side speed sensor, attach the connectors and position them in the clip.

13. Connect the negative battery cable and road test vehicle.

Rear Axle Speed Sensor

REMOVAL AND INSTALLATION

1. Disconnect the negative battery cable. Raise and support the vehicle safely.

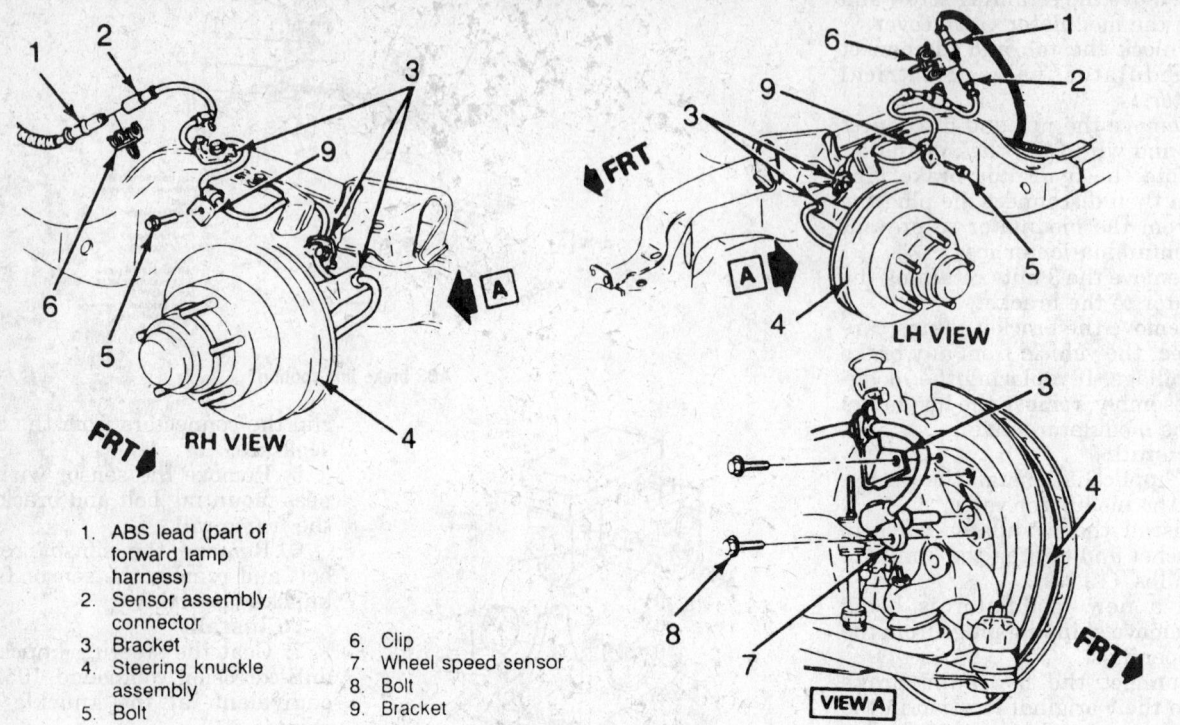

1. ABS lead (part of forward lamp harness)
2. Sensor assembly connector
3. Bracket
4. Steering knuckle assembly
5. Bolt
6. Clip
7. Wheel speed sensor
8. Bolt
9. Bracket

8569P004

ABS front wheel speed sensor

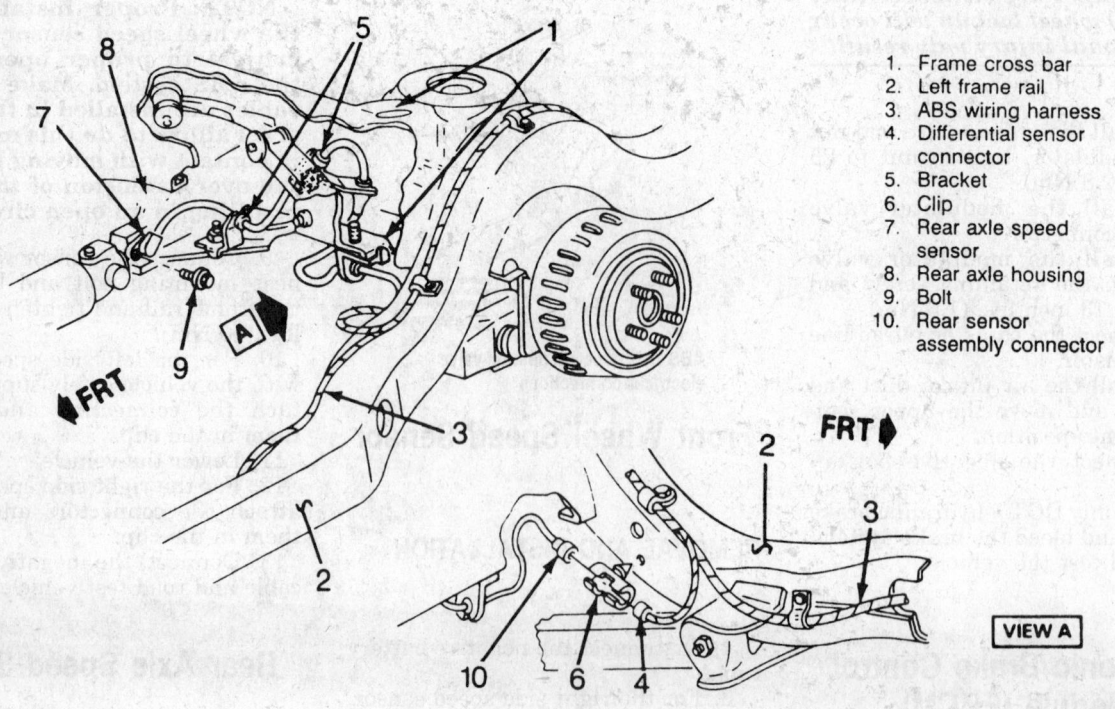

1. Frame cross bar
2. Left frame rail
3. ABS wiring harness
4. Differential sensor connector
5. Bracket
6. Clip
7. Rear axle speed sensor
8. Rear axle housing
9. Bolt
10. Rear sensor assembly connector

8569P005

ABS rear wheel speed sensor

2. Disconnect the rear sensor assembly from the differential sensor connector.

3. Remove the sensor wiring harness from the retainer brackets.

4. Remove the sensor retaining bolt and remove the speed sensor from the rear axle housing.

To install:

5. Install the sensor into the rear axle housing. The sensor is a tight fit but it must be pushed in by hand. Do not hammer the sensor into position.

6. Tighten the sensor retaining bolt to 71 inch lbs. (8 Nm).

7. Insert the sensor wiring harness into the retainer brackets.

8. Connect the rear sensor assembly to the differential sensor connector.

9. Lower the vehicle.

10. Connect the negative battery cable and road test the vehicle.

NOTE: Proper installation of the wheel speed sensor cables is critical to proper operation of the ABS system. Make sure the cables are installed in the retainers. Failure to do this may result in contact with moving parts and the over extension of the cables, resulting in an open circuit.

FRONT SUSPENSION

Shock Absorbers

REMOVAL AND INSTALLATION

1. Raise and support the vehicle safely.

2. Hold the shock absorber upper stem from turning and remove the upper nut, then remove the retainer and grommet.

3. Remove the 2 bolts and lock washers securing the shock to the lower control arm, then lower the shock from the vehicle.

To install:

4. With the lower retainer and grommet in place over the upper stem, install the fully extended shock up through the lower control arm and spring. Make sure the upper stem passes through the mounting hole in the frame bracket.

5. Install the upper rubber insulator, retainer and attaching nut over the shock, then tighten the nut to 97 inch lbs. (11 Nm).

6. Install the shock lower pivot to the lower control arm and tighten the 2 attaching bolts to 20 ft. lbs. (27 Nm).

7. Lower the vehicle.

Coil Spring

REMOVAL AND INSTALLATION

1. Raise and support the vehicle safely.

2. Remove the tire and wheel assembly from the vehicle.

3. If equipped, remove the ABS wheel speed sensor and secure aside.

4. Remove shock absorber.

5. Remove the stabilizer bar linkage nut, retainer and linkage from the lower control arm.

6. Remove the cotter pin and castellated nut, then separate the tie rod from the steering knuckle, using a suitable puller tool.

7. Compress the coil spring using a universal spring compressor tool.

8. Support the lower control arm using an adjustable lifting device, then remove the lower control arm-to-frame pivot bolts.

9. Pivot the lower control arm rearward, then carefully remove the compressor and spring.

To install:

10. Position the spring onto the lower control arm making sure the insulator is in position, then install the compressor tool and compress the spring so the control arm may be repositioned.

11. Position the control arm into the frame and install the pivot bolts (install the front bolt first, positioned from the front to the rear), but wait until the suspension is supporting the vehicle's weight before tightening the control arm fasteners to specification.

12. Remove the spring compressor tool, then install the tie rod end to the steering knuckle and tighten the nut to 35 ft. lbs. (47 Nm). Tighten the nut additionally, as necessary to align the hole, then install a new cotter pin.

13. Remove the support from the lower control arm and install the stabilizer bar linkage.

14. Install the shock absorber. Tighten the lower attaching bolts to 20 ft. lbs. (27 Nm) and the upper attaching nut to 97 inch lbs. (11 Nm).

15. If equipped, install the ABS wheel speed sensor.

16. Install the wheel and lower the vehicle.

17. Tighten the lower control arm nuts to 92 ft. lbs. (125 Nm).

Torsion Bars

REMOVAL AND INSTALLATION

1. Raise and support the vehicle safely.

2. Disconnect each side of the torsion bar by removing the nut from the link bolt, then pull the bolt from the linkage and remove the retainers, grommets and spacer.

3. Remove bracket-to-frame or body bolts and remove torsion bar, rubber bushings and brackets.

To install:

4. Position the torsion bar with the shaft identification on the right side of the vehicle and the slits in the rubber bushings facing the front of the vehicle.

5. Install the rubber insulators to the stabilizer shaft and the bracket-to-frame (or body) bolts.

6. Install the link bolts, insulators, spacers, washers and nuts. Tighten the bracket bolts to 24 ft. lbs. (33 Nm), then tighten the link bolt/nut to 13 ft. lbs. (17 Nm) for 1992 vehicles or to 18 ft. lbs. (25 Nm) for 1993–96 vehicles.

7. Lower the vehicle.

Upper Ball Joints

INSPECTION

1. Raise the vehicle and position floor stands under the left and right lower control arm as near as possible to each lower ball joint. There should be space between the upper control arm bumper and frame.

2. Position a dial indicator against the wheel rim.

3. Grasp the wheel and push in on bottom of the tire while pulling out at the top. Read the gauge, then reverse the push-pull procedure. Horizontal deflection on the dial indicator should not exceed 0.125 inch (3.18mm).

4. If the indicator exceeds 0.125 inch (3.18mm) or if the ball stud, when disconnected from the knuckle assembly, can be twisted in its socket by hand, replace the ball joint.

REMOVAL AND INSTALLATION

1. Raise and safely support the vehicle; place floor stands under the

1. Front suspension lubricant fitting
2. Front upper control arm ball stud
3. Front upper control arm assembly
4. Front upper control arm bumper assembly
5. Front shock absorber nut
6. Front shock absorber insulator retainer
7. Front shock absorber insulator
8. Front upper control arm bolt/screw
9. Front spring insulator
10. Front spring

11. Front shock absorber assembly
12. Front brake caliper bolt/screw
13. Front brake caliper housing
14. Front brake shield
15. Front brake shield gasket
16. Steering knuckle assembly

17. Steering knuckle nut
18 . Steering knuckle and hub pin
19. Front shock absorber nut
20. Front lower control arm nut
21. Front lower control arm nut
22. Steering knuckle nut
23. Front lower control arm ball
    stud assembly
24. Front wheel hub seal assembly
25. Front wheel bearing assembly
26. Front wheel bolt
27. Front brake rotor assembly
28. Front whhel outer bearing assembly
29. Front wheel bearing washer
30. Front wheel bearing lube cap
31. Front wheel bearing nut
32. Front brake shield bolt/screw
33. Spring lock washer
34. Front shock absorber bolt/screw
35. Front stavbalizer shaft bolt
36. Front stabalizer shaft insulator retainer
37. Front stabalizer shaft link insulator
38. Front lower control arm bumper nut
39. Front lower control arm assembly
40. Front lower control arm bumper assembly
41. Front lower control arm bolt
42. Front lower control arm bushing
43. Front stabalizer shaft bracket bolt
44. Front stabalizer shaft bracket
45. Front stabilizer shaft retainer spacer
46. Front stabilizer shaft assembly
47. Front stabilizer shaft insulator
48. Front stabilizer shaft nut
49. Front upper control arm shim
50. Front upper control arm pivot shaft
51. Front upper control arm nut
52. Front upper control arm pivot shaft
53. Front upper control arm bushing
54. Front upper control arm bushing
55. Front wheel bearing nut cotter pin

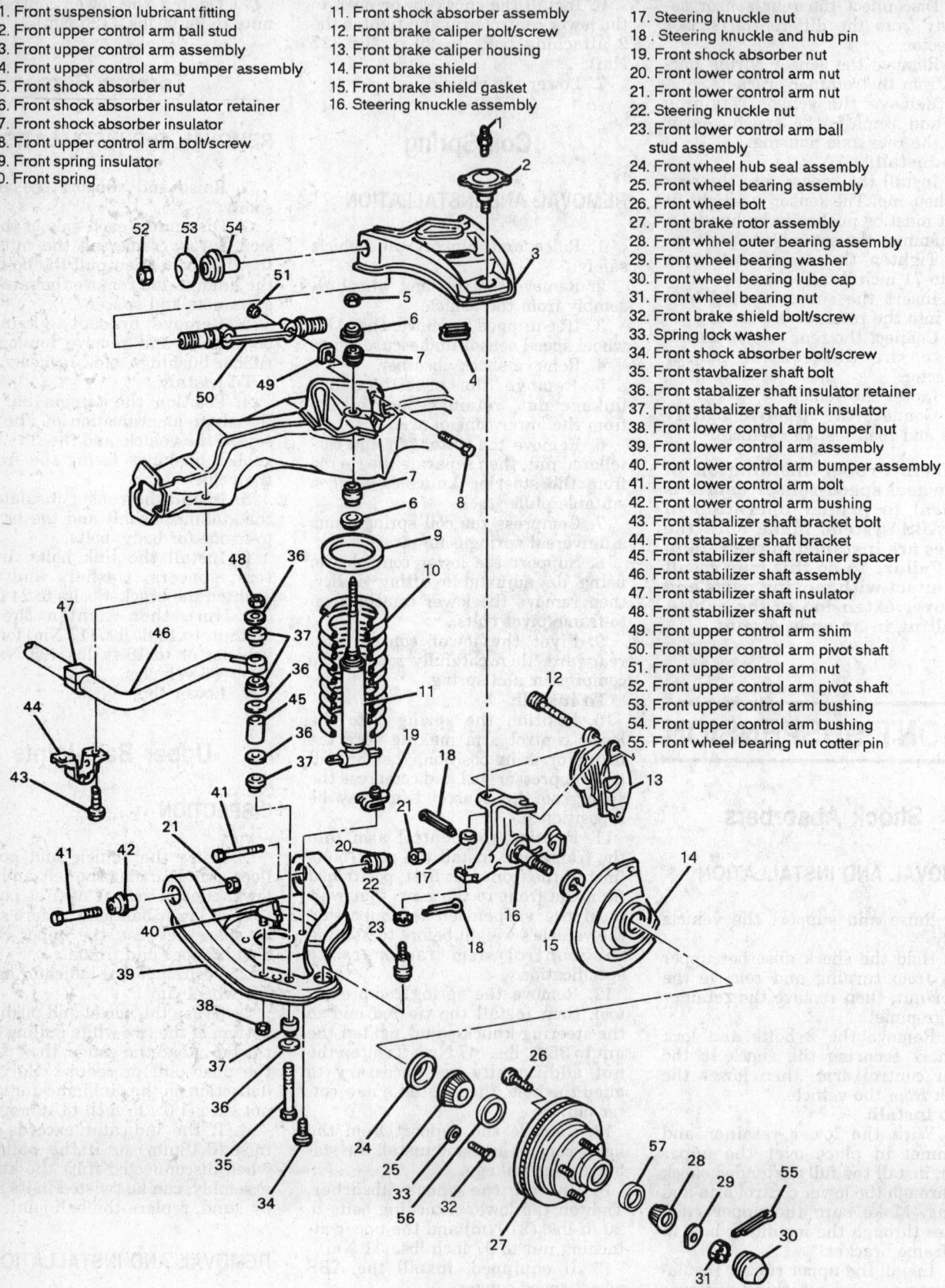

8470P056

Exploded view of the front suspension assembly — 1993-96 vehicles — 1992 similar

lower control arm between the spring seats and the ball joints.

NOTE: Leave the jack under the spring seat during removal and installation, in order to retain the coil spring and relieve spring tension from the upper control arm. The weight of the vehicle is used to relieve spring tension on the upper control arm.

2. Remove the wheel.
3. Remove the cotter pin and nut from the upper ball joint.
4. Using a ball joint separator tool, break the stud loose and pull the stud out of the knuckle. Support the steering knuckle to prevent damage to the brake line.
5. With the control arm in a raised position, use a 1/8 inch diameter bit and drill into each of the 4 rivet heads to a depth of 1/4 inch.
6. Drill off the rivet heads with a 1/2 inch diameter bit.
7. Punch out the rivets using a suitable driver or punch, then remove the ball joint.
To install:
8. Place the new ball joint in the upper control arm and secure it with 4 bolts and nuts in place of rivets. Torque the nuts to specifications provided with the ball joint kit.
9. Connect the ball joint to steering knuckle. Torque the nut to 61 ft. lbs. (83 Nm), then insert a new cotter pin. Do not back off the specified torque in order to install the cotter pin.

NOTE: When replacing the ball joints, use only high-quality replacement parts; bolts and nuts specified to be strong enough to endure the stress.

10. Attach the grease fitting and lubricate until grease appears at the seal.
11. Install the wheel and road test the vehicle.

Lower Ball Joints

INSPECTION

The lower ball joints contain a visual wear indicator and are checked in this fashion alone. The lower ball joint grease plug is threaded into the wear indicator protruding from the bottom of the ball joint housing. As long as the wear indicator extends out of the ball joint housing, the ball joint is not worn. If the tip of the wear indicator is parallel with or recessed into the ball joint housing, the ball joint is defective.

REMOVAL AND INSTALLATION

1. Raise the vehicle and support the frame safely.
2. Remove the tire and wheel assembly.
3. Place a floor jack or axle stand under the control arm spring seat.

NOTE: Leave the jack or axle stand under the spring seat during removal and installation, in order to keep the spring and control arm positioned.

4. Remove the cotter pin and nut from the ball joint stud, then using a ball joint separator, remove the ball joint from the steering knuckle.
5. With a small putty knife or similar tool, guide the control arm from the opening in the shield to a position where the ball joint is accessible.
6. Block the steering knuckle aside using a block of wood between the frame and the upper control arm.
7. Remove the grease fittings.
8. Using a suitable ball joint remover, drive the lower ball joint from the control arm.
To install:
9. Using a ball joint installer, press in a new ball joint until it bottoms on the lower control arm.

NOTE: Make sure the grease purge on the seal faces away from the brakes.

10. Assemble the suspension and torque the lower ball joint nut to 79 ft. lbs. (107 Nm) for 1992 vehicles or to 125 ft. lbs. (170 Nm) for 1993–96 vehicles. Install the cotter pin and bend it to the side, not over the top of the nut.
11. Install the ball joint fitting and lube until grease appears at the seal.
12. Install the tire and wheel assembly.
13. Check and adjust the wheel alignment, as necessary.
14. Lower and road test the vehicle.

Upper Control Arms

REMOVAL AND INSTALLATION

1. If removing the left side control ar, remove the air cleaner and resonator duct.
2. Raise and support the vehicle safely, then remove the tire and wheel assembly.

3. Place a floor jack or axle stand under the lower control arm spring seat.

NOTE: Leave the floor jack or axle stand under the spring seat during removal and installation, in order to keep the spring and control arm positioned.

4. If equipped with ABS, disconnect the wheel speed sensor and secure aside.
5. Loosen the pivot shaft-to-frame nuts and remove alignment shims. Tape the shims together and mark to assure installation in their original locations.
6. Remove the cotter pin and upper ball joint nut, then remove the ball joint from the steering knuckle, using a separator tool. Support the hub assembly to prevent damage to the brake line.
7. Remove the upper control arm shaft attaching nuts and bolts, then remove the control arm and shaft assembly.
To install:
8. Loosely install the control arm and pivot shaft assembly using the attaching bolts.
9. Install the alignment shims in the same positions from which they were removed, then install the nuts and tighten to 72 ft. lbs. (98 Nm).
10. Remove the temporary support from the hub and connect the ball joint to the steering knuckle. Tighten the upper nut to 61 ft. lbs. (83 Nm) and install a new cotter pin.
11. If equipped, install the ABS wheel speed sensor.
12. Install the tire and wheel assembly.
13. Remove the jackstands and lower the vehicle.
14. If the control arm bushings were serviced, tighten the pivot shaft end nuts to 92 ft. lbs. (125 Nm) with the vehicle weight on the suspension at normal curb height.
15. If removed, install the air cleaner and resonator.
16. Check the wheel alignment and adjust, as necessary.

Lower Control Arm

REMOVAL AND INSTALLATION

1. Raise and support the vehicle safely, then remove the tire and wheel assembly.
2. Remove the shock absorber and the front coil spring.
3. Remove the cotter pin and nut from the ball joint stud, then using a

ball joint separator, remove the ball joint from the steering knuckle.

4. Remove the lower control arm assembly from the vehicle.

To install:

5. Install the lower ball joint stud into the steering knuckle.

6. Install the coil spring, and in doing so, install the shock absorber and the lower control arm.

7. Install wheel and tire assembly.

8. Lower the vehicle, then check and adjust alignment, as necessary.

Steering Knuckle and Spindle Assembly

REMOVAL AND INSTALLATION

1. Raise and support the vehicle safely, then remove the tire and wheel assembly.

2. If equipped, disconnect the ABS wheel speed sensor.

3. Remove the brake caliper assembly and support aside.

4. Remove the dust cap, cotter pin, nut and washer from the spindle, then remove the hub and rotor assembly from the spindle.

5. Remove the rotor shield and attaching bolts from the knuckle assembly.

6. Separate the tie rod from the steering knuckle.

7. If the knuckle is to be replaced, remove the hub seal assembly.

8. Position a floor jack under the control arm near the spring seat and raise the jack until it just supports the lower control arm.

NOTE: In order to retain the spring and control arm in its original position, the jack must remain under the control arm during the complete removal and installation procedure.

9. Separate the control arm ball joints from the steering knuckle, then raise the upper control arm to free the ball stud from the knuckle.

10. Lift the steering knuckle assembly from the lower control arm and from the vehicle.

To install:

11. Install the steering knuckle onto the lower ball joint stud.

12. Lower the upper control arm ball joint stud into the steering knuckle tapered hole.

13. Install the ball joint nuts, torque the upper nut to 61 ft. lbs. (83 Nm) and the lower nut to 79 ft. lbs. (107 Nm) for 1992 vehicles or to 125 ft. lbs. (170 Nm) for 1993–96 vehicles.

14. Install the rotor splash shield and secure using the attaching bolts.

15. Install the tie rod and torque the nut to 35 ft. lbs. (47 Nm).

16. Install new cotter pins in all castellated nuts.

17. Install the rotor and hub assembly, washer and nut, then adjust the wheel bearings.

18. Install a cotter pin in wheel bearing castellated nut, then install the dust cap to the assembly.

19. Remove the support, then install the caliper assembly.

20. Install tire and wheel assembly.

21. If equipped, install ABS wheel speed sensor.

22. Remove jack assembly, then lower the vehicle.

23. Road test vehicle.

Front Wheel Bearings

ADJUSTMENT

1. Raise the vehicle so the wheel can spin freely.

2. Remove the wheel cover, dust cap, cotter pin and loosen the adjusting nut.

3. Tighten the adjusting nut to 12 ft. lbs. (16 Nm) while turning the wheel, this will seat the bearings and remove any grease or burrs which could cause play later.

4. Back off the nut until it is just loose.

5. Finger-tighten the nut and install the cotter pin through the retaining ring or castle nut.

NOTE: If the cotter pin cannot be installed, back off the nut until the slot aligns with the serrations on the nut. Do not back off the nut more than 1/4 of a turn.

6. Once adjusted, the front wheel bearings should have 0.001–0.005 inch (0.03–0.13mm) endplay.

7. When adjusted properly cut off any extra length from the cotter pin to prevent interference, then install the dust cap and wheel cover.

8. Lower the vehicle.

REMOVAL AND INSTALLATION

1. Raise and support the vehicle safely.

2. Remove the tire and wheel assembly.

3. Remove the rotor and hub assembly.

4. Pry the inner bearing seal from the hub, then remove the inner roller bearing assembly.

5. If necessary, remove the inner and outer bearing races using tool J–29117–A or a suitable brass punch inserted behind the races.

To install:

6. Using fresh solvent, clean all old grease from hub, spindle and bearing.

7. If the inner and outer races were removed, press or drive the races into the hub using a suitable sized driver.

8. Pack the bearings with a high temperature wheel bearing grease and reassemble the hub. Do not mix greases.

9. Install a new inner bearing seal using a flat plate to assure the seal is flush with the rotor.

10. Apply a thin coat of grease to the spindle, then install the rotor and hub assembly on the steering knuckle.

11. Adjust the wheel bearings, install a new cotter pin and replace the dust cap.

12. Install the caliper assembly.

13. Install the tire and wheel assembly.

14. Lower the vehicle.

REAR SUSPENSION

Shock Absorbers

REMOVAL AND INSTALLATION

1. Raise and safely support the vehicle safely, making sure to properly support the rear axle housing.

2. If equipped with adjustable shocks, disconnect the air line by turning the spring clip 90 degrees and pulling gently on air line housing.

3. Remove the upper nuts and bolts from the shock absorber at the frame.

4. Using a wrench to hold the stud in place, remove the lower nut and washer from the shock at the rear axle housing. The stud must not be allowed to turn during this operation or damage may result in the bond between the bushing and stud.

5. Remove the shock from the vehicle.

To install:

6. Install the shock absorber and loosely connect the upper frame bolts and nuts.

7. Position the stud into the bracket on the axle housing, then install the nut and washer.

8. Either tighten the upper bolts at the frame to 20 ft. lbs. (27 Nm) or the nuts at the frame to 12 ft. lbs. (16 Nm), whichever is easier. Then while holding the stud steady with a wrench, tighten the lower shock retaining nut to 48 ft. lbs. (65 Nm) for 1992 vehicles or to 50 ft. lbs. (68 Nm) for 1993–96 vehicles.

9. If equipped, connect the shock air line.

10. Remove the supports and lower the vehicle.

Coil Springs

REMOVAL AND INSTALLATION

NOTE: If both springs are to be replaced, only disconnect 1 control arm at a time in order to prevent the axle from rolling or slipping sideways.

1. Raise and support the vehicle safely, then place an adjustable support under the axle housing.

2. If equipped, disconnect the ABS rear speed sensor.

3. If equipped, disconnect the height sensor link from the upper control arm by removing the attaching nut and sliding the sensor link stud out of the hole in the upper control arm.

4. Disconnect the brake line fitting bolt at the center of the axle housing. No brake lines need to be disconnected, therefore brake bleeding should not be necessary.

5. Remove the nut and washer from the shock absorber, then disconnect the shock absorber from the axle bracket.

6. Carefully lower the axle housing sufficiently to remove the spring. Be careful not to stretch the brake hose.

7. Remove the spring, upper and lower insulator, as equipped.

To install:

8. Install the upper insulator, lower insulator, as equipped, and the rear spring to the bracket on the frame seat. Point the coil leg toward the left side of the vehicle, at a right angle from the centerline of the vehicle within 5 degrees rearward and 15 degrees forward.

NOTE: If the spring is being replaced, be sure to position the tape facing the top or spring noises could occur.

9. Raise the rear axle back into position using the adjustable lifting device.

10. Install the rear shock absorber to the bracket, and tighten the nut to 48 ft. lbs. (65 Nm) for 1992 vehicles or to 50 ft. lbs. (68 Nm) for 1993–96 vehicles.

11. Connect the rear brake line fitting bolt and tighten to 20 ft. lbs. (27 Nm).

12. If equipped, connect the height sensor link to the upper control arm and tighten the nut to 27 inch lbs. (3 Nm).

13. Remove the adjustable support from under the rear axle assembly.

14. If equipped, connect the ABS rear axle speed sensor.

15. Lower vehicle and, if necessary, adjust the height sensor.

Rear Control Arms

REMOVAL AND INSTALLATION

Upper Arm

NOTE: If both control arms are to be replaced, only remove and install 1 control arm at a time in order to prevent the axle from rolling or slipping sideways.

1. Raise and support the vehicle safely, then place a support under the axle housing.

2. If equipped, disconnect the ABS rear speed sensor.

3. If equipped, disconnect the height sensor link from the upper control arm by removing the attaching nut and sliding the sensor link stud out of the hole in the upper control arm.

4. Remove the nut and bolt at the rear axle housing.

5. Remove the nut and bolt at the frame crossmember, then disengage the upper control arm from its mounts and remove it from the vehicle.

To install:

6. Loosely attach the upper control arm to the frame crossmember using the nut and bolt.

7. Loosely attach the upper control arm to the rear axle housing using the nut and bolt.

8. Remove the jackstand from the rear axle and place supports under the tires. Lower the vehicle sufficiently so the vehicle weight rests on the tires.

9. With the weight of the vehicle on the tires, tighten the bolt at the frame crossmember to 114 ft. lbs. (155 Nm) or the nut to 91 ft. lbs. (123

Nm). Either the nut or the bolt must be tightened, torque whichever is easiest to access.

10. With the weight of the vehicle on the tires tighten either the bolt or nut at the rear axle housing, whichever is easiest to access. For 1992 vehicles, tighten the bolt to 80 ft. lbs. (108 Nm) or the nut to 70 ft. lbs. (95 Nm). For 1993–96 vehicles, tighten the bolt to 83 ft. lbs. (113 Nm) or the nut to 74 ft. lbs. (100 Nm).

11. If equipped, connect the height sensor link to the upper control arm and tighten the nut to 27 inch lbs. (3 Nm).

12. Remove the support from under the rear tires.

13. If equipped, connect the ABS rear axle speed sensor.

14. Lower vehicle and, if necessary, adjust the height sensor.

Lower Arm

NOTE: If both control arms are to be replaced, only remove and install 1 control arm at a time in order to prevent the axle from rolling or slipping sideways.

1. Raise and support the vehicle safely, then place a support under the axle housing.

2. If equipped, disconnect the stabilizer shaft bolts and washers from the control arm.

3. Remove the nut and bolt from the bracket on the rear axle assembly.

4. Remove the nut and bolt from the crossmember brace, if equipped, and from the bracket on the frame.

5. Remove the lower control arm from the vehicle.

To install:

6. Position the lower control arm to the vehicle.

7. Loosely install the nuts and bolts to the crossmember brace, if equipped, to the frame bracket, rear axle bracket and, if applicable, to the stabilizer shaft.

8. Remove the jackstand from the rear axle and place supports under the tires. Lower the vehicle sufficiently so the vehicle weight rests on the tires.

9. With the weight of the vehicle on the tires, tighten either the nut or the bolt, whichever is easiest to access. For 1992 vehicles tighten the lower control arm bolts to 74 ft. lbs. (100 Nm) or the nuts to 91 ft. lbs. (123 Nm). For 1993–96 vehicles tighten the lower control arm bolts or nuts to 91 ft. lbs. (123 Nm).

10. If applicable, tighten the stabilizer bolts to 52 ft. lbs. (29 Nm) for

1992 vehicles or to 63 ft. lbs. (85 Nm) for 1993–96 vehicles.

11. Remove the tire supports and lower the vehicle.

Rear Wheel Bearings

For all rear wheel bearing removal and installation procedures, refer to the Drive Axle section.

Rear Axle Assembly

For rear axle removal and installation procedures, refer to the Drive Axle section.

GM "F" BODY
Rear Wheel Drive
CHEVROLET—Camaro PONTIAC—Firebird

FIRING ORDERS

NOTE: To avoid confusion, always replace spark plug wires one at a time.

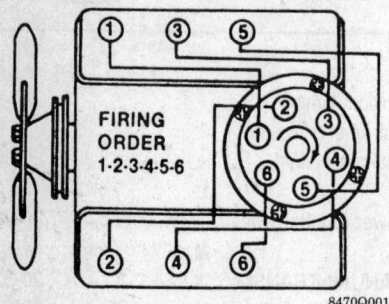

3.1L Engine
Engine Firing Order: 1–2–3–4–5–6
Distributor Rotation: Clockwise

8470Q001

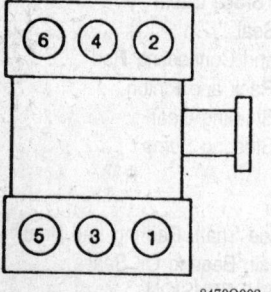

3.4L Engine
Engine Firing Order:
1–2–3–4–5–6
Distributorless Ignition System

8470Q002

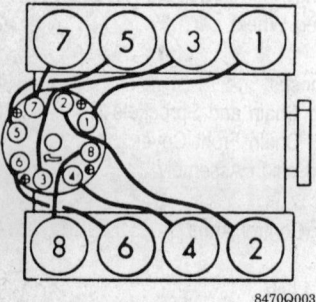

5.0L and 5.7L (VIN 8) Engines
Engine Firing Order:
1–8–4–3–6–5–7–2
Distributor Rotation: Clockwise

8470Q003

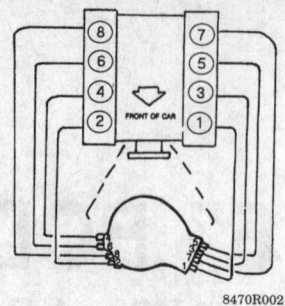

8470R002

5.7L (VIN P) Engine
Engine Firing Order:
1–8–4–3–6–5–7–2
Distributor Rotates with
Camshaft

ENGINE ELECTRICAL

NOTE: Disconnecting the negative battery cable on some vehicles may interfere with the functions of the on-board computer system and may require the computer to undergo a relearning process when the negative battery cable is reconnected.

Distributor

All engines, except the 1993–96 3.4L V6 and the 1993–96 5.7L (VIN P) engine, use a High Energy Ignition (HEI) distributor with Electronic Spark Timing (EST). The HEI system incorporates a distributor cap, rotor, ignition module, pole piece with internal teeth and pickup coil. All distributor equipped vehicles use an externally mounted ignition coil. Spark timing changes are controlled electronically by the Engine Control Module (ECM), which monitors various engine sensors, and determines the need to retard or advance spark timing, then signals the distributor to change the timing accordingly.

The 5.7L (VIN P) engine utilizes the new Opti-Spark distributor ignition system, which consists of a distributor assembly, control circuitry and an external coil. In the Opti-Spark system, all ignition timing is controlled by the ECM based on signals from the distributor's internally mounted optical camshaft position sensor. There is no way to bypass the ECM control or to adjust/set ignition timing on this system.

The 3.4L V6 engine, introduced in the 1993 F-body utilizes an Electronic Ignition (EI) system and therefore has no distributor.

REMOVAL

NOTE: When making compression checks, the ignition system can be disabled by disconnecting the "BAT" or 2-terminal connector from the distributor.

Except 5.7L (VIN P) Engine

1. Disconnect the negative battery cable.
2. Disengage the wiring harness connectors from the side of the distributor cap.

NOTE: Use care when releasing the connector locking tabs on the distributor cap.

3. If necessary for replacement, or for access, tag and remove the spark plug wires from the top of the distributor cap.
4. Remove the cap from the top of the distributor and either position it out of the way or remove it from the vehicle, as necessary.
5. Mark the position of the distributor housing and rotor in relation to the engine block.
6. Remove the distributor hold-down clamp and bolt.
7. Pull the distributor assembly up from the engine, noting the position of the rotor as the distributor gear disengages from the camshaft.

5.7L (VIN P) Engine

1. Be sure the ignition is in the OFF or LOCK position, then disconnect the negative battery cable.
2. Disengage the wiring harness from the engine cooling fan assembly, then remove the cooling fan from the vehicle.
3. Remove the block drain plug and the knock sensor, then drain the engine cooling system.
4. Remove the air intake duct and the air cleaner assembly.
5. Remove the coolant and heater hoses from the water pump assembly and the throttle body.
6. Unplug the wiring harness from the Engine Coolant Temperature (ECT) sensor, then reposition the ignition coil and bracket.
7. Remove the water pump assembly.
8. Remove the serpentine drive belt from the vehicle.
9. If not done already to remove the pump or the belt, raise and safely support the vehicle for access.

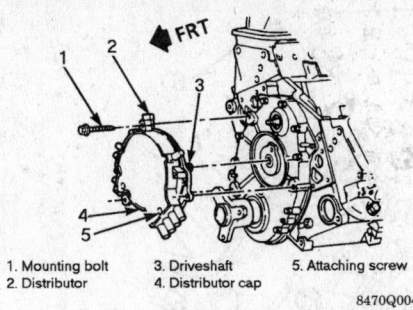

1. Mounting bolt
2. Distributor
3. Driveshaft
4. Distributor cap
5. Attaching screw

8470Q004

Distributor installation — 5.7L (VIN P) engine

10. Remove the torsional damper bolts, then remove the damper from the crankshaft hub.

11. Disconnect the spark plug wires from the distributor. Be sure to twist each boot ½ turn and pull only on the boot to remove each wire. The wire numbers should be molded into the distributor housing. If not, be sure to tag the wires before disconnection.

12. Unplug the 4-terminal ECM connector from the distributor.

13. Remove the distributor mounting bolts and pull the distributor forward until the drive shaft disengages from the engine. Mark the top of the shaft for alignment during reassembly.

INSTALLATION

Timing Not Disturbed

EXCEPT 5.7L (VIN P) ENGINE

NOTE: To ensure correct ignition timing if the engine has not been disturbed, the distributor must be installed with the rotor in the same position as when removed.

1. Install the distributor, aligning the marks that were made during the removal procedure. Once the distributor is inserted into the engine, the 1st set of matchmarks between the rotor, distributor and engine should be in alignment.

2. Install the distributor hold-down clamp and temporarily tighten the retaining bolt.

3. Install the distributor cap, then install the wires and engage the electrical connectors, as necessary.

4. Connect the negative battery cable.

5. Start the engine, then check and adjust ignition timing as necessary. Tighten the hold-down clamp bolt to 27 ft. lbs. (36 Nm) and recheck the timing.

5.7L (VIN P) ENGINE

1. With the mark made on the distributor shaft earlier on top, install the distributor to the engine. Tighten the distributor bolts to 8 ft. lbs. (11 Nm).

2. Install the 4-terminal ECM connector and the spark plug wires to the distributor.

3. Position the crankshaft damper to the hub, then install the damper bolts and tighten to 60 ft. lbs. (81 Nm).

4. Install the serpentine drive belt.

5. Install the water pump assembly and engage the ECT wiring harness.

6. Reposition the ignition coil and bracket, then install the coolant and heater hoses.

7. Install the air cleaner assembly and air intake duct.

8. Install the engine block drain plug and the knock sensor.

9. Install the right cooling fan assembly, then connect the wiring harness.

10. Connect the negative battery cable and fill the engine cooling system.

11. Start and run the engine, then check for leaks.

Timing Disturbed

EXCEPT 5.7L (VIN P) ENGINE

1. Remove the No. 1 spark plug. Place a finger over the spark plug hole and slowly rotate the engine in the normal direction of rotation, until compression is felt.

2. Place the No. 1 cylinder at TDC by aligning the timing mark on the crankshaft pulley to the **0** on the engine timing indicator by slowly rotating the engine in the same direction.

3. Position the rotor between No. 1 and No. 8 spark plug towers on the V8 engine or the No. 1 and No. 2 spark plug towers on the V6 engine.

4. Install the distributor in the engine.

5. Install the distributor hold-down clamp and temporarily tighten the retaining bolt.

6. Install the distributor cap, then install the wires and engage the electrical connectors, as necessary.

7. Connect the negative battery cable.

8. Start the engine, then check and adjust ignition timing as necessary. Tighten the hold-down clamp bolt to 27 ft. lbs. (36 Nm) and recheck the timing.

Distributorless Ignition System

The base engine (3.4L V6) of the 4th generation F-body, is equipped with a distributorless Electronic Ignition (EI) system. This system uses a "waste spark" method of spark distribution. Each cylinder is paired with it's opposite in the firing order, so a cylinder on the compression stroke fires simultaneously with it's opposing cylinder on the exhaust stroke. The cylinder on the exhaust stroke requires very little voltage to fire it's plug, so most of the available voltage is used to fire the cylinder that is on the compression stroke.

The EI system consists of a coil pack, the ignition module, a camshaft position sensor, 2 crankshaft position sensors, and the Engine Control Module (ECM). The coil pack contains 3 separate and interchangeable ignition coils (1 for each pair of cylinders) attached to the module and bracket assembly. The ignition module, mounted between the coils and the bracket, is connected to the ECM. The ignition module controls the primary circuit to the ignition coils.

REMOVAL AND INSTALLATION

Camshaft Position Sensor

The camshaft position sensor is located on top of the engine block, behind the water pump, near the lower intake manifold assembly.

1. Be sure the ignition is in the **OFF** or **LOCK** position, then disconnect the negative battery cable.

2. Disengage the wiring harness connector from the sensor.

3. Remove the sensor retaining bolt, then carefully remove the sensor from the top of the engine block. If necessary, carefully pry between alternate sides of the sensor and the engine block in order to loosen the sensor from its mounting boss. Make sure the sensor is not damaged when prying.

To install:

4. Inspect the sensor O-ring and replace, if necessary.

5. Lubricate the O-ring with clean engine oil, then install the sensor into the engine block.

6. Install the sensor retaining bolt and tighten to 17 inch lbs. (1.9 Nm).

7. Engage the sensor wiring harness, then connect the negative battery cable.

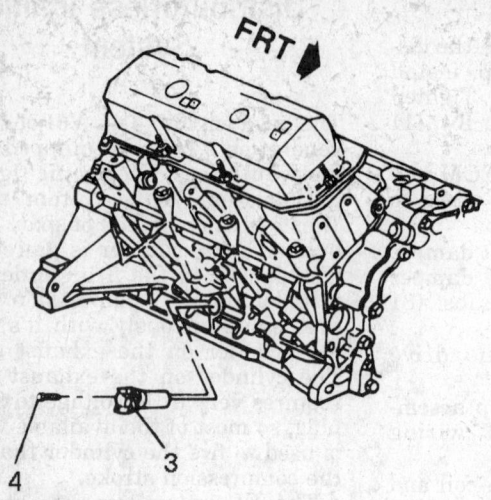

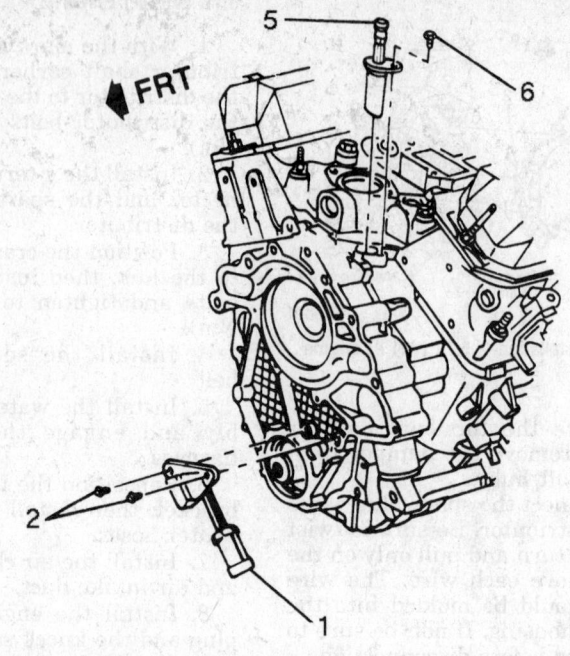

1. Sensor assembly, crankshaft position (24X signal)
2. Bolt, crankshaft position sensor
3. Sensor assembly, crankshaft position (3X signal)
4. Bolt, crankshaft position sensor
5. Sensor assembly, camshaft position
6. Bolt, camshaft position sensor

8470Q005

Ignition sensor (crankshaft/camshaft) locations — 3.4L engine

24X Signal Crankshaft Position Sensor

1. Be sure the ignition is in the **OFF** or **LOCK** position, then disconnect the negative battery cable.
2. Raise and support the vehicle safely.
3. Remove the crankshaft balancer assembly from the front of the engine:
   a. Remove the serpentine drive belt.
   b. Remove the bolt and washer from the crankshaft balancer.
   c. Remove the retaining bolts from the crankshaft pulley, then remove the pulley from the balancer.
   d. Using J–24420–B or an equivalent torsional damper remover, pull the balancer from the crankshaft.
4. Remove the sensor retaining bolts.
5. Disconnect and remove the sensor from the engine.
To install:
6. Install the sensor to the engine and tighten the retaining bolts to 17 inch lbs. (1.9 Nm).
7. Use J–29113, or an equivalent installer, to pull the balancer onto the crankshaft, then install the pulley. Tighten the balancer bolt to 58 ft.

lbs. (78 Nm), then tighten the pulley retaining bolts to 37 ft. lbs. (50 Nm).
8. Install the serpentine drive belt.
9. Lower the vehicle.
10. Connect the negative battery cable.

3X Signal Crankshaft Position Sensor

1. Be sure the ignition is in the **OFF** or **LOCK** position, then disconnect the negative battery cable.
2. Disengage the wiring harness connector from the sensor.
3. Remove the sensor retaining bolt, then carefully remove the sensor from the lower right side of the engine block.
To install:
4. Inspect the sensor O-ring and replace, if necessary.
5. Lubricate the O-ring with clean engine oil, then install the sensor into the side of the engine block.
6. Install the sensor retaining bolt and tighten to 89 inch lbs. (10 Nm).
7. Engage the sensor wiring harness, then connect the negative battery cable.

Ignition Module and Coils

1. Be sure the ignition is in the **OFF** or **LOCK** position, then disconnect the negative battery cable.

2. Tag and disconnect the spark plug wires from the ignition coils.
3. Disengage the electrical connectors from the assembly.
4. Remove the retaining nuts, then remove the ignition module and coils from the engine.
5. If necessary, remove the coils from the module and bracket:
   a. Remove the bolts retaining the coil(s) to the module and bracket assembly.
   b. Remove the ignition coil(s) and seal(s) from the assembly.
   c. Separate the module from the bracket.
To install:
6. If necessary, assemble the ignition module and coils:
   a. Position the module to the bracket.
   b. Install the seal(s), then position the coil(s) to the module and bracket assembly.
   c. Install the retaining bolts and tighten to 40 inch lbs. (4.5 Nm).
7. Install the ignition module and coil assembly to the engine.
8. Install the retaining nuts and tighten to 89 inch lbs. (10 Nm).
9. Engage the wiring harness connectors and the spark plug wires to the assembly.
10. Connect the negative battery cable.

Ignition Timing

ADJUSTMENT

1992

1. Refer to the Vehicle Emission Information label, located on the radiator support panel, for the proper timing information.

2. With the ignition **OFF**, connect the pickup lead of an inductive timing light to the No. 1 spark plug wire. Connect the timing light power leads according to the manufacturers instructions.

------ **WARNING** ------
Never pierce a secondary ignition wire in order to conduct tests or connect a timing light. A pierced wire may lead to engine misfiring and driveability problems.

3. For all 1992 vehicles, start and run the engine to normal operating temperature, then bypass the ECM spark timing system. To place the Electronic Spark Timing (EST) in the bypass mode, disengage the single wire EST bypass timing connector. This wire is tan with a black tracer that breaks from the wiring harness near the rear of the right side valve cover. Do not disconnect the 4 prong EST connector from the distributor assembly. A trouble code will set when the EST bypass connector is disengaged.

4. Run the engine to normal operating temperature, then with the engine running, disengage the EST bypass mode connector or ground the diagnostic terminal of the ALDL connector, as applicable. A trouble code will set when the EST bypass connector is disengaged.

5. Check the timing, by aiming the timing light at the timing mark and harmonic balancer. If the engine timing requires adjustment, loosen the

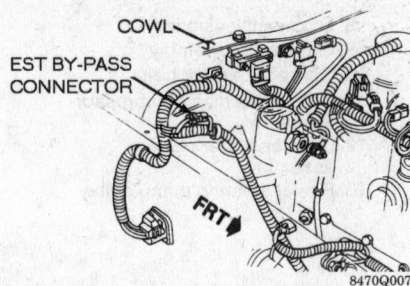

Electronic Spark Timing (EST) bypass connector location — 1992 vehicles

distributor hold-down bolt and rotate the distributor slowly in either direction, to advance or retard the engine timing, as necessary.

6. Hold the distributor in position and tighten the hold-down bolt to 27 ft. lbs. (36 Nm), then recheck the engine timing to assure the distributor was not disturbed while tightening the bolt.

7. With the engine still running, unground the diagnostic terminal or shut the engine **OFF** and reconnect the EST bypass mode connector, as applicable.

8. If necessary, with the ignition **OFF**, clear the ECM code by disconnecting the negative battery cable for at least 30 seconds.

1993–96

On the 3.4L and 5.7L (VIN P) engines, base timing is preset when the engine is manufactured. All timing changes are then controlled directly by the ECM based on information from the ignition and knock sensor systems. No adjustments are necessary or possible.

Alternator

PRECAUTIONS

Several precautions must be observed with alternator equipped vehicles to avoid damage to the unit.

• If the battery is removed for any reason, make sure it is reconnected with the correct polarity. Reversing the battery connections may result in damage to the one-way rectifiers.

• When utilizing a booster battery as a starting aid, always connect the positive to positive terminals and the negative terminal from the booster battery to a good engine ground on the vehicle being started.

• Never use a fast charger as a booster to start vehicles.

• Disconnect the battery cables when charging the battery with a fast charger.

• Never attempt to polarize the alternator.

• Do not use test lamps of more than 12 volts when checking diode continuity.

• Do not short across or ground any of the alternator terminals.

• The polarity of the battery, alternator and regulator must be matched and considered before making any electrical connections within the system.

• Never operate the alternator on an open circuit. Make sure all connec-

tions within the circuit are clean and tight.

• Disconnect the battery ground terminal when performing any service on electrical components.

• Disconnect the battery if arc welding is to be done on the vehicle.

BELT TENSION ADJUSTMENT

Serpentine belts are automatically adjusted by the tensioner on the engine. If belt slippage occurs, check the belt length scale on the drive belt tensioner for the proper installed length and replace as necessary. If the drive belt tensioner is within it's operating range and belt slippage still occurs, the tensioner may need replacement. For 1992 vehicles, check the belt tensioner as follows:

1. Run the engine for 5–10 minutes.

2. Shut OFF the engine and check the belt tension at the following locations using J–23600–B belt tension gauge or equivalent.

  a. V6 engines: If without air conditioning, check the belt tension between the tensioner and the power steering pump pulley. If with air conditioning, check the belt tension between the tensioner and the air conditioner compressor pulley.

  b. V8 engine: Check the belt tension between any 2 pulleys.

3. Run the engine for 30 seconds and recheck the belt tension.

4. Repeat Step 3. The belt tension is the average of the 3 readings.

  a. V6 engine: Belt tension should be 95–140 lbs. (422–623 N) if without air conditioning. If with air conditioning, the belt tension should be 85–110 lbs. (378–490 N).

  b. V8 engine: Belt tension should be 99–121 lbs. (440–538 N).

5. Replace the drive belt tensioner if the belt tension is below the minimum specified and if the tensioner is within it's operating range.

REMOVAL AND INSTALLATION

1992

1. Disconnect the negative battery cable.

2. Tag and disconnect the alternator wiring.

3. Using a breaker bar or breaker bar with socket, as applicable, rotate the serpentine belt tensioner to release the drive belt and remove the drive belt from the pulley.

4. Support the alternator and remove the mounting bolts, then remove the unit from the vehicle.

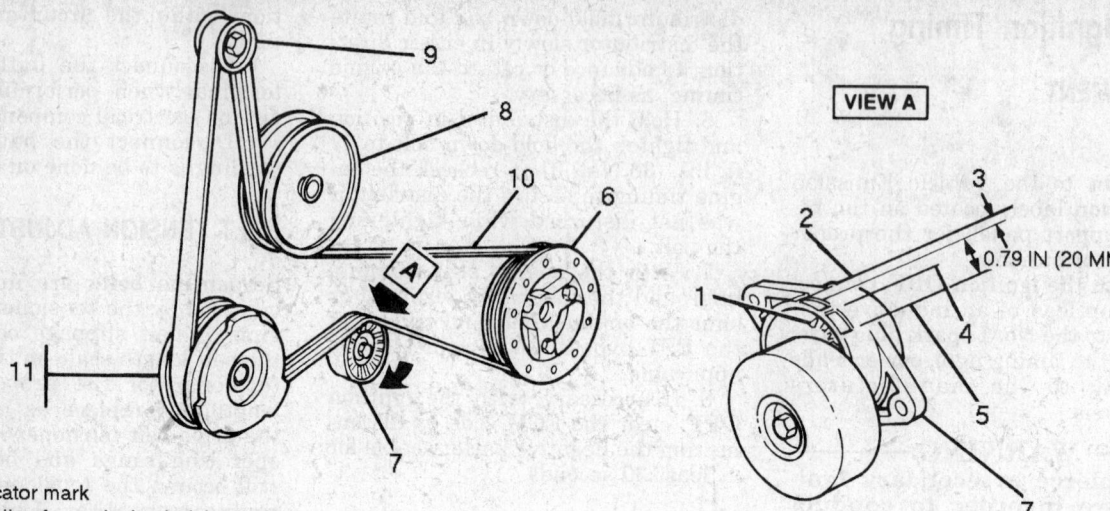

1. Indicator mark
2. Reading for replacing belt in service
3. Defective parts check range
4. Maximum tolerance belt reading
5. Minimum tolerance belt reading
6. Balancer assembly, crankshaft
7. Tensioner assembly, drive belt
8. Pump assembly, power steering
9. Generator assembly
10. Compressor assembly, air conditioning
11. Pulley, drive belt idler

8470Q008

Serpentine drive belt and tensioner — 5.7L (VIN P) engine

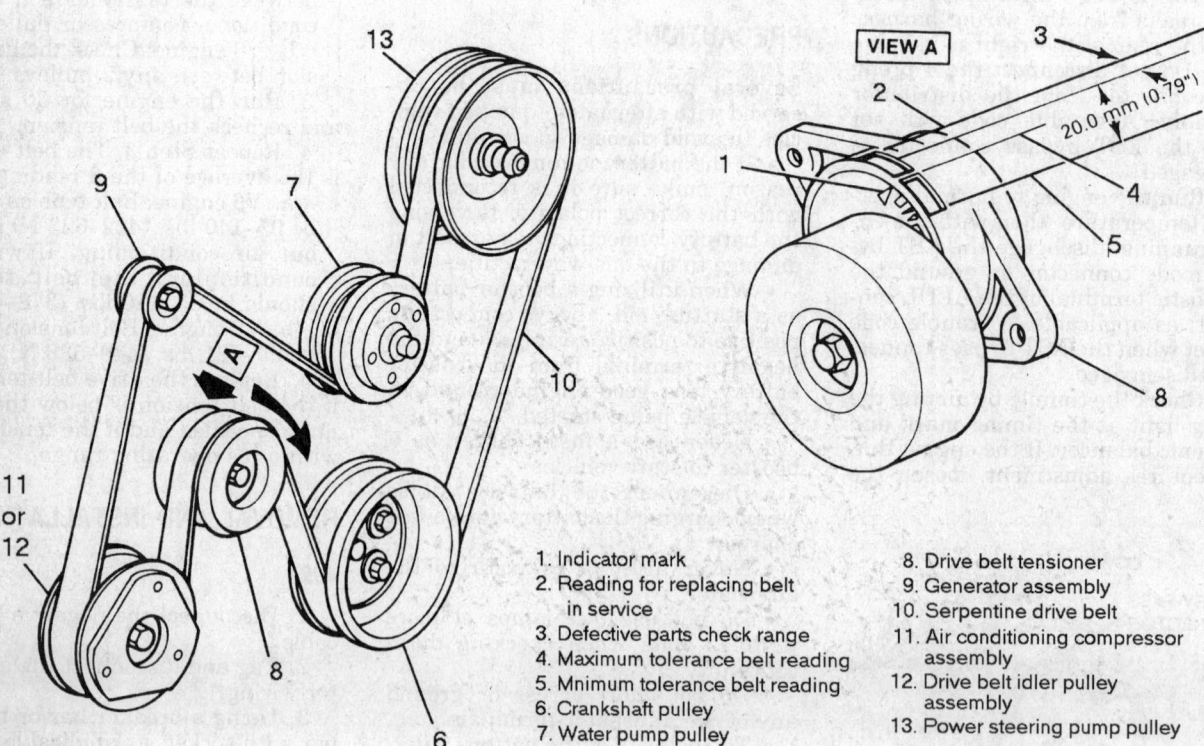

1. Indicator mark
2. Reading for replacing belt in service
3. Defective parts check range
4. Maximum tolerance belt reading
5. Mnimum tolerance belt reading
6. Crankshaft pulley
7. Water pump pulley
8. Drive belt tensioner
9. Generator assembly
10. Serpentine drive belt
11. Air conditioning compressor assembly
12. Drive belt idler pulley assembly
13. Power steering pump pulley

8470Q009

Serpentine drive belt and tensioner — 3.4L engine

To install:

5. Position the alternator in the bracket and install the mounting bolts. Tighten the rear bolt and the upper front bolt to 18 ft. lbs. (25 Nm), then tighten the lower bolt to 37 ft. lbs. (50 Nm).

6. Use the breaker bar to loosen the belt tensioner, then install the serpentine drive belt and slowly allow the tensioner to come in contact with the belt.

7. Reconnect the alternator wiring followed by the negative battery cable.

1993–96

1. Disconnect the negative battery cable.

2. Use a breaker bar and socket to rotate the serpentine belt tensioner downward (clockwise) relieving tension from the belt, then remove the belt from the vehicle. For V8 engines, it may be easier to temporarily raise and support the vehicle, then remove the belt from underneath.

3. Disengage the positive battery wire and the electrical connector from the alternator assembly.

4. For the 3.4L engine, remove the 2 rear nuts and the outer front bolt from the alternator, then remove the rear inner brace. Support the alternator, then remove the remaining front bolt and the rear brace bolt.

5. For the 5.7L engine, remove the upper brace bolts, the lower brace bolt and the front alternator bolt all from the alternator assembly, then remove the nut retaining the upper brace to the top of the engine and remove the upper brace from the vehicle.

6. Remove the alternator from the accessory mounting bracket and from the vehicle.

To install:

7. Position the alternator to the engine and accessory mounting bracket.

8. For the 5.7L engine, install the upper brace and tighten the retaining nut to 24 ft. lbs. (33 Nm), then install the alternator and brace bolts. Tighten the rear upper brace and front alternator bolts to 37 ft. lbs. (50 Nm) and tighten the rear lower brace bolt to 18 ft. lbs. (25 Nm).

9. For the 3.4L engine, install and tighten the front inner alternator bolt and the rear upper brace-to-alternator bolt. Tighten the rear brace bolt to 18 ft. lbs. (25 Nm) and the front bolt to 37 ft. lbs. (50 Nm).

10. For the 3.4L engine, install the rear inner brace, then tighten the brace-to-engine nut to 18 ft. lbs. (25 Nm). Tighten the brace-to-alternator nut and the outer front alternator bolt to 37 ft. lbs. (50 Nm).

11. Engage the electrical connector and the battery positive wire to the alternator assembly.

12. Install the serpentine drive belt.

13. Connect the negative battery cable.

Starter

REMOVAL AND INSTALLATION

1. Disconnect the negative battery cable.

2. Raise and support the vehicle safely.

3. For 1993–96 vehicles, disconnect the exhaust crossover pipe from the manifolds for access.

4. If equipped on 1992 vehicles, remove the upper support attaching bolt, nut, washer and the bracket from the side or rear of the starter motor.

5. For 1992 vehicles, remove the flywheel housing cover.

6. Remove the starter mounting bolts and lower the starter sufficiently to access the wires.

7. Tag and disconnect the wiring, then remove starter from the vehicle.

To install:

NOTE: Before tightening the starter wiring, make sure the inner nuts on the solenoids are already tightened. If they are loose, the act of tightening the outer nuts could damage the solenoid cap.

8. Raise starter sufficiently and support while connecting the starter wiring. For 1993–96 vehicles, tighten the battery terminal nut to 80 inch

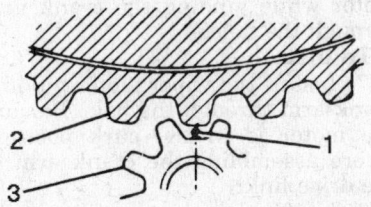

1. Insert 0.20 IN (0.5 MM) wire gage here to check
2. Flywheel assembly
3. Starter drive pinion

8470Q010

Checking flywheel-to-starter pinion clearance

lbs. (9 Nm) and the ignition terminal to 22 inch lbs. (2.5 Nm).

NOTE: If shims were removed, they must be installed in their original location to assure proper drive pinion to flywheel engagement.

9. While holding the starter in place, install the mounting bolts and shims, if equipped. Tighten mounting bolts to 35 ft. lbs. (37 Nm).

10. Check that flywheel-to-pinion clearance is 0.020 inch (0.5mm) and add or subtract shims, as necessary. If removed, install the flywheel cover.

11. If applicable, for 1992 vehicles, install the starter side or rear brace.

12. For 1993–96 vehicles, position the crossover pipe and attach it to the manifolds.

13. Lower vehicle and connect the negative battery cable.

CHASSIS ELECTRICAL

Air Bag

DISARMING

1. Turn the steering wheel to align the wheels in the straight-ahead position.

2. Turn the ignition switch to the **LOCK** position.

3. Remove the SIR or AIR BAG fuse from the fuse block.

4. Remove the left side trim panel, then remove the Connector Position Assurance (CPA) device and disengage the yellow 2-way SIR harness wire connector at the base of the steering column.

5. For vehicles equipped with a passenger side inflator module, remove the glove box door, then remove the CPA device and disengage the yellow 24-way Diagnostic Energy Reserve Module (DERM) connector.

To enable the system:

6. If not already done, turn the ignition switch to the **LOCK** position.

7. For vehicles equipped with a passenger side inflator module, engage the 24-way DERM connector and install the CPA device, then install the glove box door.

8. Engage the yellow 2-way connector and install the CPA device at the base of the steering column, install the left side trim panel.

9. Install the SIR or AIR BAG fuse to the instrument panel fuse block.

10. Turn the ignition switch to the **RUN** position.

11. Verify the SIR indicator light flashes 7–9 times and then turns OFF to signify proper system operation. If light does not flash as specified, inspect system for malfunction.

SUPPLEMENTAL INFLATABLE RESTRAINT (SIR) COIL

NOTE: After performing repairs on the internals of the steering column, the coil assembly must be centered in order to avoid coil damage or accidental air bag deployment.

Adjustment

1. Hold the coil assembly with the clear bottom up to see the coil ribbon.

2. While holding the coil assembly, depress the spring lock and rotate the hub in the direction of the arrow until it stops. The coil ribbon should now be wound snug against the center hub.

3. Rotate the coil assembly in the opposite direction approximately 2½ turns and release the lock spring between the locking tabs in front of the arrow.

4. Install the coil assembly onto the steering shaft.

Heater Blower Motor

REMOVAL AND INSTALLATION

1. Disconnect the negative battery cable. If necessary, remove the diagonal fender brace at the right rear corner of the engine compartment to gain access to the blower motor.

2. Disconnect the electrical wiring from the blower motor. If equipped

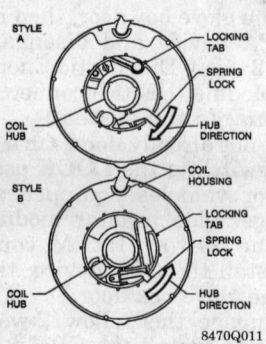

Centering the SIR steering column coil assembly

with air conditioning, remove the blower relay and bracket as an assembly and swing them aside.

3. Remove the blower motor cooling tube.

4. Remove the blower motor retaining screws.

5. Remove the blower motor and fan as an assembly from the case. Be careful not to damage the blower fan.

To install:

6. Carefully guide the blower motor and fan into position being careful not to catch the fan on any protruding parts. Install the blower motor attaching screws and attach the blower motor cooling tube.

7. Connect the blower wiring and position the blower relay and bracket assembly into place. Install the bracket retaining screws and tighten to 13 inch lbs. (1.5 Nm).

8. If removed, install the diagonal fender brace and bolts.

9. Connect the negative battery cable and check blower operation.

Windshield Wiper Motor

REMOVAL AND INSTALLATION

1992

1. Disconnect the negative battery cable.

2. Remove the left and right wiper arms.

3. Remove the cowl panel assembly or the shroud vent grille, as applicable.

4. Loosen the motor drive link to crank arm retaining bolts. Remove the drive link from the motor crank arm.

5. Disconnect the electrical wiring from the motor assembly.

6. Remove the motor retaining bolts. Remove the windshield wiper motor while guiding the crank arm through the hole.

To install:

7. Install the wiper motor guiding crank arm through the hole. Be sure the motor is in the park position before assembling the crank arm to the drive link.

8. Install the wiper motor attaching nuts and tighten to 44 inch lbs. (5 Nm). Then, connect the drive link to the crank arm and tighten the retaining bolts to 35 inch lbs. (4 Nm).

9. Install the cowl panel assembly or shroud vent grille, as applicable and install the wiper arms.

10. Connect the negative battery cable and check wiper motor operation.

1993–96

1. Operate the wipers and stop them midway through the return sweep, then disconnect the negative battery cable.

2. Remove the wiper arm and blade assemblies.

3. Remove the left cowl panel and seal, then disconnect the washer hose assembly from the cowl panel and nozzle.

4. Disengage the electrical connector from the motor assembly.

5. Remove the screw and nut attaching the left linkage to the cowl.

6. Using J–39232, or an equivalent wiper linkage separator, disconnect the socket of the right hand linkage from the ball of the left hand linkage, then remove the left linkage from the vehicle.

7. Remove the screw retaining the front of the wiper motor assembly, then carefully pull the motor free from the slots of the rear retaining bracket.

8. Using the linkage separator, disconnect the right linkage from the crank arm ball of the motor assembly, then remove the motor from the vehicle.

To install:

9. Make sure the motor crank arm is in the inner wiper position and install the motor assembly to the vehicle. The crank arm drive pin must be engaged into the cam pocket.

10. Using a wiper linkage installer, press the socket of the right linkage into engagement with the motor crank arm ball.

11. Install the motor into the rear bracket by fully pressing the locator pads into the bracket slots, then install the motor retaining screw and tighten to 7.5 ft. lbs. (10 Nm).

12. Install the left linkage assembly, without the attaching parts, and press the right linkage socket onto the left linkage ball.

13. Install the left linkage screw and nut, then tighten the fasteners to 7.5 ft. lbs. (10 Nm).

14. Engage the motor wiring harness, then install the washer hose assembly to the left cowl panel and washer nozzle.

15. Install the cowl panel and hood seal, then install the wiper arm assemblies.

16. Connect then negative battery cable and verify proper operation.

Windshield Wiper Switch

REMOVAL AND INSTALLATION

NOTE: The vehicle is equipped with a SIR air bag system, it is imperative that the disarming procedure is followed before repairs, and that the coil centering and rearming procedures are followed after repairs.

1. Disarm the SIR and disconnect the negative battery cable.
2. Remove the turn signal switch assembly, but do not disconnect or remove the wiring harness. Allow the switch assembly to hang freely from the wires unless removal is necessary for switch replacement.
3. Remove the ignition lock assembly, but do not disconnect or remove the wiring harness. Allow the lock set to hang freely from the wires, unless removal is necessary for lock cylinder replacement.
4. If not done already, remove the housing cover end cap, disconnect the electrical connectors from the multi-function lever and remove the lever by pulling toward the driver's door.
5. Remove the housing cover screws, unthread and remove the tilt lever from the column assembly.
6. Remove the lock housing cover assembly.
7. Remove the base plate and the dimmer switch rod actuator and the wiper switch actuator pivot pin.
8. For 1993–96 vehicles, remove the wire protector shield.
9. Disengage the wiper switch connector from bulkhead connector and remove the switch. Attach a piece of mechanic's wire to the connector to aid in reinstallation and gently pull the wire harness through the column. Leave the mechanic's wire routed through the column in order to pull the new switch wiring into position.

To install:
10. Connect the wiper switch to the lock housing cover assembly.
11. Attach the switch actuator pivot pin to the switch and cover.
12. Pull wiper switch wire connector through the steering column using the mechanic's wire and attach to the bulkhead harness connector. If applicable, install the wire protector shield.
13. Attach the dimmer switch rod actuator to the base plate and lubricate with lithium grease.
14. Connect base plate to lock housing cover assembly. The bottom edge of the dimmer switch rod actuator

must rest on the bend in the dimmer switch rod.
15. Position lock housing cover in place and attach the tilt lever.
16. Starting with the housing cover screw in the 12 o'clock position, then 8 o'clock and finally 3 o'clock positions, tighten the screws to 80 inch lbs. (9 Nm).
17. Install the multi-function lever and engage the lever connectors on the base plate.
18. Install the housing cover end cap.
19. Install the lock cylinder assembly.
20. Install the turn signal assembly.
21. Connect the negative battery cable and enable the SIR system.

Instrument Cluster

REMOVAL AND INSTALLATION

NOTE: The vehicle is equipped with a SIR air bag system, it is imperative that the disarming procedure is followed before repairs, and that the rearming procedure is followed after repairs.

1992

1. Disarm the SIR system and disconnect the negative battery cable.
2. Remove trimplates necessary to access the instrument cluster and lens:
   a. On the 1992 Firebird, remove the instrument panel knee bolster and the instrument panel cluster trimplate.
   b. On 1992 Camaro, remove the instrument panel knee bolster and the headlight switch knob. Remove the cluster trimplate screws and pull the cluster trimplate forward. Disconnect the electrical connectors and remove the cluster trimplate.
3. Remove the retaining screws from the instrument cluster, pull the cluster back and disconnect the electrical connectors.
4. Remove the instrument cluster. If necessary, the instrument lens screws can be removed to access individual components in the cluster.

To install:
5. If any instruments were removed for service, install instruments and the instrument cover lens onto the instrument cluster. Position the instrument cluster in front of the instrument panel and attach all electrical connections.

6. Install instrument cluster and attaching screws.
7. Install trimplates, knee bolster and headlight switch knob, as applicable.
8. Connect the negative battery cable and enable the SIR system.

1993–96

The instrument cluster on these vehicles is a non-serviceable item. If any component within the cluster malfunctions, then entire cluster must be replaced as an assembly.

1. Disarm the SIR system and disconnect the negative battery cable.
2. Remove the instrument panel upper trim panel by first disconnecting it from the lower windshield support dual lock fasteners, then by removing the panel from the carrier locating pins and dual lock fasteners.
3. Remove the bolts attaching the cluster assembly to the carrier.
4. Pull the cluster assembly forward sufficiently to disengage the electrical connectors from the rear of the assembly, then remove the cluster from the vehicle.

To install:
5. Position the cluster assembly in front of the carrier, then engage the wiring harness to the cluster.
6. Install the cluster to the carrier and secure using the attaching bolts. Tighten the bolts to 20 inch lbs. (2.2 Nm).
7. Align the instrument panel upper trim panel to the carrier locating pins, then apply pressure to the rear of the panel in order to engage the dual lock fasteners. Complete the installation of the trim panel by engaging it with the windshield support dual lock fasteners.
8. Connect the negative battery cable and enable the SIR system.

Concealed Headlights

MANUAL OPERATION

The concealed headlights used on the Firebird are electrically operated. If an electrical failure involving the headlight actuators should occur, the headlights can be operated manually. Motor knobs are located under the hood, immediately adjacent to the headlights assemblies.

To raise the headlights electrically, but without turning on the lights, turn on the parking lights and lightly press the headlight switch.

1. Hex locking nut
2. Retaining ring
3. Infl. restraint coil assembly
4. Wave washer
5. Retaining ring
6. Shaft lock
7. Turn signal cancel cam assembly
8. Upper bearing spring
9. Screw
10. Screw
11. Signal switch arm assembly
12. Turn signal switch assembly
13. Upper bearing inner race seat
14. Inner race
15. Screw
16. Buzzer switch assembly
18. Lock retaining screw
19. Lock housing cover assembly
20. Lock cylinder set
21. Dimmer switch rod actuator
22. Switch acuator pivot pin
23. Wiper switch assembly
24. Base plate
25. Cap
26. Wiring protector
27. Connector shroud
30. Steering column housing assembly
31. Bearing assembly
32. Lock bolt
33. Lock bolt spring
34. Steering wheel lock shoe
35. Steering wheel lock shoe
36. Wire protector shield
37. Drive shaft
38. Dowel pin
39. Pivot pin
40. Shoe spring
41. Release lever spring
42. Release lever pin
43. Shoe release lever
44. Switch actuator rack
45. Rack preload spring
46. Steering column housing
47. Switch actuator sector
48. Screw

50. Spring guide
51. Wheel tilt spring
52. Spring retainer
55. Steering column shaft assembly
56. Race & upper shaft assembly
57. Centering sphere
58. Joint preload spring
59. Lower steering shaft assembly
61. Support Screw
62. Support
71. Steering column housing shroud

72. Steering column jacket assembly
76. Ignition switch actuator assembly
77. Dimmer switch rod
78. Screw
79. Screw
80. Ignition switch assembly
82. Screw
83. Dimmer switch assembly
86. Lower bearing adapter
87. Bearing assembly
88. Bearing adapter retainer
89. Lower bearing adapter clip

8470Q012

Exploded view of the steering column assembly — 1993–96 vehicles — 1992 similar

Headlight Switch

REMOVAL AND INSTALLATION

1992
CAMARO

1. Disconnect the negative battery cable.
2. Remove the instrument panel knee bolster.
3. Remove the switch knob by depressing the release button on the switch from under the instrument panel.
4. Remove the retaining screws from the instrument panel cluster trimplate and pull it forward away from the instrument panel. Disengage the electrical connectors and remove the cluster trimplate.
5. Remove the retaining nut from the headlight switch and lower the switch out through the bottom of the instrument panel.
6. Disengage the electrical connectors and remove the switch.
To install:
7. Engage the electrical connectors and raise the switch up through the bottom of the instrument panel into place. Fasten the switch with the connecting nut.
8. Install the cluster trimplate and knee bolster.
9. Connect the negative battery cable.

FIREBIRD

1. Disconnect the negative battery cable.
2. Remove the instrument panel knee bolster and the instrument panel cluster trimplate.
3. Remove the headlight switch retaining screws.
4. Disengage the electrical connectors and remove the switch assembly.
To install:
5. Engage the electrical connectors and attach the switch assembly using the retaining screws. Tighten the switch retaining screws to 13 inch lbs. (1.5 Nm).
6. Install the instrument panel cluster trimplate and the knee bolster.
7. Connect the negative battery cable.

1993–96

1. Disconnect then negative battery cable.
2. For the Camaro, remove any instrument panel sound insulators or trimplates necessary to access the switch assembly.

3. Remove the switch assembly from the bezel. For the Firebird, the switch is removed from the from in front of the bezel, by pulling toward the driver's seat. For the Camaro, the switch is removed from behind the bezel, by pulling toward the firewall.
4. Disengage the wiring harness connectors from the switch assembly, then remove the switch from the vehicle.
To install:
5. Engage the wiring harness connectors to the switch assembly.
6. Install the switch into the bezel assembly. Be careful not to apply pressure to the switch knob or the thumb wheel or switch damage may occur.
7. Install any trim panels or sound insulators removed for better access.
8. Connect the negative battery cable.

Dimmer Switch

REMOVAL AND INSTALLATION

NOTE: The vehicle is equipped with a SIR air bag system, it is imperative that the disarming procedure is followed before repairs, and that the coil centering and rearming procedures are followed after repairs.

1. Properly disable the SIR system and disconnect the negative battery cable.
2. Remove the instrument panel lower trimplate.
3. Remove the steering column mounting bolts, lower and properly support the column. If access to the switch is not sufficient, remove the column from the vehicle.
4. Remove the hex tapping screw and the washer head screw securing the switch to the column.
5. Disengage the switch assembly from the actuator rod, unplug the

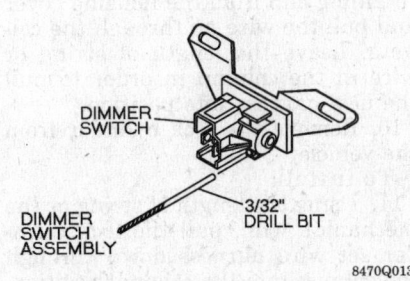

Adjusting the dimmer switch

wiring harness connector and remove the switch assembly.
To install:
6. Connect the wiring harness to the dimmer switch, then position the switch and finger-tighten the retainers.
7. Insert a 3/32 inch drill bit in the switch hole to limit travel, then push against the dimmer switch to remove all free-play.
8. Tighten the fasteners, as applicable. Tighten the retaining nut and upper retaining screw to 35 inch lbs. (4 Nm), and/or the lower retaining screw to 22 inch lbs. (2.5 Nm), then remove the drill bit.
9. Install or raise the steering column into position and install the mounting bolts.
10. Install the instrument panel lower trimplate.
11. Connect the negative battery cable and enable the SIR system.

Turn Signal Switch

REMOVAL AND INSTALLATION

NOTE: The vehicle is equipped with a SIR air bag system, it is imperative that the disarming procedure is followed before repairs, and that the coil centering and rearming procedures are followed after repairs.

1. Properly disable the SIR system. Place the ignition switch to the **LOCK** position in order to prevent uncentering of the coil assembly.
2. Disconnect the negative battery cable.
3. Properly remove and store the inflator module and the steering wheel. Either remove the column from the vehicle or lower it, as necessary for access.
4. Remove the coil assembly retaining ring. Remove the coil assembly and allow it to hang freely from the wiring.

NOTE: The coil assembly will become uncentered if the steering column is separated from the steering gear and allowed to rotate or the center spring of the coil assembly is pushed down, letting the hub rotate while the coil is removed from the steering column. In the event this should occur, follow the recommended procedure for centering of the coil in order to avoid accidental deployment of the air bag or damage to the internal components of the steering column.

5. Remove the wave washer.

6. Remove the shaft lock retaining ring using tool J–23653–C or equivalent shaft lock compressor. Discard the old ring.

7. Remove the shaft lock, turn signal canceling cam and upper bearing assembly.

8. Move the multi-function lever to the **RIGHT TURN** position. If equipped with cruise control, remove the column housing cover end cap by pulling toward the vehicle front and disengage the electrical harness connector. Remove the turn signal lever by pulling toward the driver door.

9. Remove the hazard knob retaining screw and assembly.

10. Remove the turn signal switch arm and screw.

11. Remove the turn signal switch screws.

12. Disengage the switch harness connector from the bulkhead connector and remove the wiring protector.

13. Attach a length of mechanic's wire to the switch harness in order to aid in reinstallation, then gently pull the assembly up through the housing. Leave the wire routed through the column in order to pull the new harness back into position.

14. Remove the switch and harness from the vehicle.

To install:

15. Using the mechanic's wire, pull the switch harness through the column and connect to the bulkhead connector.

16. Install the harness wiring protector.

17. Position the turn signal switch assembly and install the attaching screws. Tighten the screws to 30 inch lbs. (3.4 Nm).

18. Install the switch arm and mounting screw. Tighten the screw to 20 inch lbs. (2.3 Nm).

19. Install the hazard knob assembly and the multi-function lever.

20. Install the inner race, the upper bearing race seat, and the upper bearing spring.

21. Lubricate the friction surfaces using synthetic grease, then install the turn signal canceling cam.

22. Position the shaft lock. Install the a new shaft lock retaining ring using tool J–23653–C or equivalent. Be sure the ring is firmly seated in the groove of the shaft.

23. Install the wave washer.

24. Install the coil assembly, making sure it is properly centered.

25. Position and secure the steering column, as necessary.

26. Install the steering wheel and the inflator module.

27. Connect the negative battery cable and enable the SIR system.

Ignition Lock

REMOVAL AND INSTALLATION

NOTE: The vehicle is equipped with a SIR air bag system, it is imperative that the disarming procedure is followed before repairs, and that the coil centering and rearming procedures are followed after repairs.

1. Disable the SIR system and disconnect the negative battery cable.

2. Remove turn signal switch assembly, but do not disconnect or pull the wire harness through the column. Allow the switch assembly to hang freely from the wires.

3. If necessary, remove the coil assembly as follows:

   a. If not done already, remove the wiring protector from the vehicle.

   b. Disengage the coil terminal connector from the harness.

   c. Attach a length of mechanic's wire to the terminal connector in order to aid in reassembly.

   d. Carefully pull the wires through the column, leaving the length of mechanic's in the column for installation purposes.

4. Remove the key from the lock cylinder.

5. Remove the buzzer switch and retaining clip.

6. Reinsert the key into the lock cylinder, making sure the key is in the **LOCK** position.

7. Remove the lock set retaining screw.

8. Disengage the Pass Key wire harness connector from the bulkhead connector. If not done already, remove the wiring protector.

9. Attach a piece of string or mechanic's wire to the wire connector to aid in reassembly, disconnect the retaining clip from the housing cover and pull the wire up through the column. Leave the length of string or wire in the column in order to pull the new harness into position.

10. Remove the lock cylinder from the vehicle.

To install:

11. Using the length of string or the mechanic's wire, pull the lock cylinder set wire harness down through the column into the original position.

12. Install the lock cylinder set, snapping the wire retaining clip into the hole in the housing.

13. Engage the lock cylinder wiring connector to the bulkhead connector.

14. Install the lock cylinder retaining screw and tighten to 22 inch lbs. (2.5 Nm).

15. For 1992 vehicles, turn the key to the **RUN** position and install the buzzer switch with retaining clip, then return the key to the **LOCK** position.

16. For 1993–96 vehicles, remove the key and install the buzzer switch with retaining clip, then insert the key and leave in the **LOCK** position.

17. If removed, pull the turn signal switch wiring connector and/or the coil wiring connector through the steering column, connect the harnesses and install the wiring protector.

18. Install the turn signal switch assembly.

19. Connect the negative battery cable and enable the SIR system.

Ignition Switch

REMOVAL AND INSTALLATION

NOTE: The vehicle is equipped with a SIR air bag system, it is imperative that the disarming procedure is followed before repairs, and that the rearming procedure is followed after repairs.

1. Properly disable the SIR system and disconnect the negative battery cable.

2. Remove the instrument panel lower trimplate.

3. Remove the steering column mounting bolts, lower and properly support the column. If access to the switch is not sufficient, remove the column from the vehicle.

4. Remove the hex tapping screw and the washer head screw securing the switch to the column.

5. Disengage the switch assembly from the actuator rod, unplug the wiring harness connector and remove the switch assembly.

6. Remove the ignition switch screws or the dimmer/ignition switch mounting stud, as applicable. Unplug the connector, then remove the ignition switch from the column.

To install:

7. Verify that the key cylinder is in the ignition **OFF** and **LOCKED** position.

8. Make sure the switch slider is also in the **OFF-LOCK** position. New switches will be pinned in this position and the pin must be removed after installation or switch damage may result. To verify if a switch is in

the lock position, move the slider to the extreme right position, then move the slider 1 detent to the left.

9. Install the switch to the actuator assembly and to the steering column.

10. Install and tighten the switch mounting stud or screw, as applicable. Tighten the stud to 35 inch lbs. (4.0 Nm) or the screw to 33 inch lbs. (3.7 Nm).

11. Install and adjust the dimmer switch assembly.

12. Position the steering column and secure the column in the vehicle

13. Connect the negative battery cable and enable the SIR system.

Brake Light Switch

The brake light switch is located on the brake pedal bracket. In some applications, other switches will be located next to or above the brake light switch. On other applications, the switch may perform multiple functions such as the cruise control or torque converter clutch switch.

ADJUSTMENT

1. While depressing the brake pedal, push the switch into the retainer until fully seated.

2. Pull the brake pedal to the rear against the internal pedal stop using a force of only about 50 pounds. The brake light switch will move in the retainer giving the proper adjustment.

3. The proper adjustment is obtained when no clicks are heard when the brake pedal is pulled up and the brake lights do not stay ON when the pedal is released.

4. For 1993–96 vehicles, check for proper adjustment by measuring the point at which the switch contacts open. The switch should open at 1 in. (25.4mm) or less of brake pedal travel. This should cause lights to activate at the same time as or before the onset of braking.

REMOVAL AND INSTALLATION

1. Disconnect the negative battery cable.

2. If necessary, remove the left sound insulator panel for better access to the switch assembly.

3. Disengage the electrical connector(s) and remove the brake light switch by pulling it out of the retainer.

4. Install the replacement brake light switch by inserting it into the retainer, then engage the electrical connector(s).

5. Adjust the brake light switch and reconnect the negative battery cable.

Clutch Switch

The clutch safety switch for 1992 vehicles is located under the console trimplate. For 1993–96 vehicles, the switch is located on the brake/clutch pedal bracket assembly.

ADJUSTMENT

1992

No adjustment is necessary for these vehicles.

1993–96

1. While depressing the clutch pedal, push the switch into the retainer until fully seated.

2. Pull the clutch pedal to the rear against the internal pedal stop using a force of only about 50 pounds. The clutch safety switch will move in the retainer giving the proper adjustment.

3. The proper adjustment is obtained when no clicks are heard when the clutch pedal is pulled up and the engine will not start, unless the pedal is depressed.

REMOVAL AND INSTALLATION

1992

1. Disconnect the negative battery cable.

2. Remove the console trimplate fasteners, then remove the trimplate for access to the switch.

3. Disengage the clutch switch connector.

4. Remove the switch attaching bolt and remove the clutch switch.

5. Installation is the reverse of the removal procedure. Tighten the clutch switch retaining bolt to 19 inch lbs. (2.2 Nm).

1993–96

1. Disconnect the negative battery cable.

2. Remove the instrument panel sound insulator/driver knee bolster for better access to the switch assembly.

3. Disengage the electrical connector and remove the brake light switch by pulling it out of the retainer.

4. Install the replacement brake light switch by inserting it into the retainer, then engage the electrical connector.

5. Adjust the brake light switch and reconnect the negative battery cable.

Neutral Safety Switch

ADJUSTMENT

New switches should already be set in the N position. If the bolt holes do not align, before rotating switch, verify that the shifter is in the N position. Switch adjustment is performed with the center console removed for switch access.

1. Place the transmission shifter in the N notch in the detent plate.

2. Loosen the switch attaching bolts.

3. Insert a 0.094 in. (2.34mm) drill bit or gauge pin into the adjustment hole, then rotate the switch until the gauge pin drops to a depth of 0.59 in. (15mm).

NOTE: If the proper sized gauge pin is unavailable, a ³⁄₃₂ in. drill bit may be used.

4. Tighten the switch bolts to 18 inch lbs. (2 Nm) for 1992 vehicles or to 19 inch lbs. (2.2 Nm) for 1993–96 vehicles.

5. Remove the gauge pin and verify that the engine will only start in P or N.

REMOVAL AND INSTALLATION

1. Disconnect the negative battery cable.

2. Remove the console assembly for access to the neutral safety switch.

3. Remove the switch attaching screws, then remove the neutral safety switch from the vehicle.

To install:

4. Position shifter lever in the N position.

5. Insert carrier tang on the switch in the slot on the shifter.

6. If installing a new switch, install the retaining bolts and tighten the switch bolts to 18 inch lbs. (2 Nm) for 1992 vehicles or to 19 inch lbs. (2.2 Nm) for 1993–96 vehicles. Move the shift control lever out of the N

position to shear the factory installed plastic retaining pin.

NOTE: If installing a new switch and the holes do not align with shifter control, check that the shifter control lever is in N. Do not rotate the switch as this will shear the retaining pin. If a new switch was rotated and the pin was already broken, switch adjustment must be performed.

7. If installing an old switch, or a new switch with a sheared retaining pin, perform the switch adjustment.

8. Connect the negative battery cable and check that engine starts only in the **P** or **N** positions. If engine starts in any other position, readjust neutral switch.

9. Install center console assembly.

Fuses, Circuit Breakers and Relays

LOCATION

Fuse Panel

The fuse panel is located on the left side of the vehicle, under the instrument panel assembly. In order to gain access to the fuse panel it may be necessary to first remove the under dash padding.

Circuit Breakers

The circuit breakers are located at the fuse panel.

Relays

All vehicles use a combination of the following electrical relays:

- **Air Conditioner/Heater Blower High Speed Relay** — located near the blower module on the air conditioner module.
- **Air Conditioner Compressor Relay** — located on the left side engine cowl on the relay bracket.
- **Cooling Fan Relay** — located on the left side of the engine cowl on the relay bracket.
- **Extend Relay** — taped back to body rear harness near breakout to hatch pull-down/release unit.
- **Fog Light Relay** — located behind the left side instrument panel, near the fuse panel block.
- **Fuel Pump Relay** — located on the left side of the engine cowl on the relay bracket.
- **Hatch Release Relay** — located under the right side console, beside the gear sector.

- **Horn Relay** — located in the convenience center, behind the instrument panel to the right of the steering column.
- **Power Antenna Relay** — located behind the right side of the instrument panel lower cover near the ECM.
- **Power Door Lock Relay Assembly** — located on the left shroud near door jamb conduit.
- **Radio Amplifier Relay** — located behind the right side of the instrument panel.
- **Starter Enable Relay** — located below the left side instrument panel, on the kick panel.

Computers

LOCATION

The engine Electronic Control Module (ECM), cruise control module, PASS key theft deterrent module and the SIR Diagnostic/Energy Reserve Module (DERM) for air bag equipped vehicles are all located under the right side of the instrument panel.

Flashers

LOCATION

- **Hazard Flasher** — located in the convenience center, behind the instrument panel to the right of the steering column.
- **Turn Signal Flasher** — located in the convenience center.

Cruise Control

ADJUSTMENT

1. With the cable assembly installed in the servo bracket, install the cable assembly end onto the stud of the lever assembly. Secure the component with the retainer. It is important for 1992 5.0L (VIN E) engine, that the throttle is completely closed at this point.

2. Pull the servo assembly end of the cable toward the servo assembly without moving the lever assembly.

3. If one of the 6 holes in the servo assembly tab aligns with the cable assembly pin, connect the pin to the tab with the retainer.

4. If the tab hole does not align with the pin, move the cable assembly away from the servo assembly un-

til the next closest hole aligns. Secure the component with the retainer.

5. Do not stretch the cable assembly so as to make a particular tab hole connect to the pin, as this will prevent the engine from returning to idle.

ENGINE COOLING

Radiator

REMOVAL AND INSTALLATION

1992

1. Disconnect the negative battery cable.

2. Drain the cooling system into a suitable container.

3. Remove the radiator inlet hose and clamp.

4. Remove the intake duct, air duct bracket and air cleaner top, as equipped.

5. If equipped, remove the Mass Air Flow (MAF) sensor.

6. Remove the coolant recovery hose and the connector, then if equipped, remove the heater hose and clamp.

7. Remove the engine cooling fan. If equipped with a fan clutch, the clutch should be set aside in an upright position to prevent seal leakage.

8. If equipped with an automatic transmission, disconnect and plug the transmission cooler lines at the radiator.

9. Remove the radiator outlet hose and clamp.

10. Remove the upper radiator mount and screws, then lift the radiator straight up and out of the vehicle.

To install:

11. Install radiator and ensure that it is properly positioned in the lower cradle.

12. Install the upper radiator mount and tighten mount screws to 53 inch lbs.

13. Reconnect all hoses, install the cooling fan and refill the cooling system with the proper type and quantity of coolant.

14. Install all air intake components, including the MAF sensor, if equipped.

15. Connect the negative battery cable, then properly fill the engine cooling system.

1993–96

1. Disconnect the negative battery cable, then remove the air intake duct and air cleaner assembly.
2. Raise and support the vehicle safely, then drain the engine cooling system.
3. Disengage the cooling fan electrical connectors, then remove the fan assembly.
4. Disconnect the transmission fluid cooler lines, then plug the openings to prevent system contamination or excessive fluid loss.
5. If equipped, remove the coolant level sensor.
6. Lower the vehicle, then loosen the receiver dehydrator bracket.
7. Disconnect the lower radiator hose from the water pump assembly, then remove the upper radiator hose and the overflow tube.
8. Remove the radiator from the condenser, then carefully remove the radiator from the vehicle.
To install:
9. Install the radiator assembly into the vehicle, making sure to properly seat the radiator on the insulators, then attach the radiator to the condenser.
10. Install the overflow tube and the upper radiator hose, then connect the lower radiator hose to the water pump assembly.
11. Tighten the receiver dehydrator bracket, then raise and support the vehicle safely.
12. If equipped, install the coolant level sensor.
13. Unplug the openings, then connect the transmission fluid cooler lines.
14. Install the engine cooling fan assembly and engage the electrical connectors.
15. Lower the vehicle and install the air cleaner and intake duct assemblies.
16. Connect the negative battery cable and properly fill the engine cooling system.

Electric Cooling Fan

NOTE: Keep hands, tools and clothing away from the cooling fan. Electric cooling fans can activate whether or not the engine is running. The fan may start automatically in response to a heat sensor with the ignition in the ON position.

TESTING

1992

1. Disengage the cooling fan electrical connector from the wire harness at the cooling fan assembly.
2. Connect a 20 amp fused jumper wire from the positive terminal of the battery to 1 terminal of the cooling fan electrical connector.
3. Ground the other terminal of the cooling fan electrical connector using a jumper wire.
4. If the cooling fan does not run, the cooling fan motor must be replaced.
5. If the cooling fan runs during the test procedure but does not run during normal vehicle operation, check the coolant temperature sensor, the cooling fan relay and the ECM.

1993–96

The ECM controls secondary (5.7L engine) and/or primary cooling fans (all engines) by grounding the fan relay circuit when sensors indicate the appropriate conditions have been reached. The primary cooling fan is controlled through wire 335 (DARK GREEN) from the ECM while the secondary cooling fan on the 5.7L engine is controlled through wire 473 (DARK BLUE).

The ECM will ground the relay circuit, activating the cooling fan(s) whenever the DLC test terminals are grounded or when the coolant temperature and/or A/C refrigerant pressure sensors reach certain operating levels. If a fan does not operate when the test terminals are grounded, or when sensors indicate the appropriate operating conditions, then the fan and related circuits must be checked.

For the 3.4L engine, the ECM will activate the cooling fan if the engine is running and coolant temperature exceeds 228°F (109°C) or the A/C refrigerant pressure reaches approximately 240 psi (1655 kPa). For the 5.7L (VIN P) engine, the ECM will activate the primary cooling fan when engine coolant temperature reaches 226°F (108°C) and will activate the secondary fan when temperature reaches 230°F (110°C). The 5.7L engine will also operate cooling fans anytime the A/C is turned ON.

For both engines, terminal A (BLACK wire) of the cooling fan connector is ground, while terminal B (LIGHT BLUE wire for primary fan or BROWN wire for secondary fan) of the fan connector is the power supply from the relay.

REMOVAL AND INSTALLATION

1992

1. Disconnect the negative battery cable.
2. Remove the air cleaner top, if equipped.
3. Remove the fan harness connector from the fan motor and frame.
4. Remove the fan frame to radiator support mounting bolts, remove the bracket if necessary, and remove the fan assembly.
To install:
NOTE: It is essential that fan assemblies remain in proper balance and proper balance cannot be assured once a fan assembly has been bent or damaged. Inspect the fan assembly prior to installation and if a fan blade is bent or damaged, always replace with a new fan assembly.

5. Install the cooling fan frame and, if removed, the bracket.
6. Tighten the fan frame to radiator support bolts to 20 ft. lbs. (27 Nm).
7. Reconnect the wiring harness and, if removed, the air cleaner top.
8. Connect the negative battery cable and check fan operation.

1993–96

1. Disconnect the negative battery cable, then remove the air cleaner assembly.
2. Disengage the fan electrical connector and clips.
3. Carefully slide the engine cooling fan assembly from the radiator and retainers.
4. If necessary, remove the fan blade nut and separate the blade from the motor and bracket.
To install:
5. If removed, install the fan blade to the motor and bracket assembly, then secure using the retaining nut.
6. Install the cooling fan assembly by sliding it into position.
7. Install the clips and engage the wiring harness connector.
8. Install the air cleaner assembly and connect the negative battery cable.

Heater Core

REMOVAL AND INSTALLATION

1. Disconnect the negative battery cable. Drain the cooling system and disconnect the heater hoses.
2. Remove the right lower dash panels. Remove the instrument panel

lower trim pad and the center console.

3. Remove the retaining screws from the top, bottom and right flanges of the rear heater case. Remove the rear case from the heater module.

4. Remove the core shroud screws and, if equipped, the clamp.

5. Remove the core shroud, heater core and mounting strap as an assembly.

6. Remove the core mounting strap and remove the heater core from the core shroud. If necessary, remove the shroud seal from the shroud and/or the heater core seal.

To install:

7. If removed, install the heater core seal and/or the shroud seal.

8. Install the heater core and mounting strap to the core shroud.

9. Carefully guide both heater core tubes into position at the holes in the dash panel and install the shroud assembly to the interior of the heater module.

10. Install the clamp, if equipped, and the shroud screws.

11. Replace the rear case flange sealer with fresh sealer and install the rear case to the heater module with the mounting screws.

12. Install the center console and instrument panels.

13. Connect the heater hoses and the negative battery cable. Fill the cooling system and operate the engine to check for leaks.

Water Pump

REMOVAL AND INSTALLATION

1992

1. Disconnect the negative battery cable and drain the cooling system into a suitable container.

2. Remove the air intake duct.

3. Remove the drive belt.

4. Disconnect the radiator and heater hoses from the thermostat housing and water pump.

5. For V6 engines, remove the power steering pump bracket.

6. For V8 engines, remove the water pump pulley bolts and water pump pulley.

7. Remove the water pump retaining bolts, the water pump and gaskets.

To install:

8. Clean all gasket mating surfaces and install new gaskets.

9. For V6 engines, apply sealer to all bolt threads.

10. Install the water pump and tighten the retaining bolts as follows:
   a. V8 engines — 30 ft. lbs. (41 Nm).
   b. V6 engines — to specification.

11. Install the water pump pulley or the power steering pump bracket, as applicable. Tighten the water pump pulley bolts to 23 ft. lbs. (31 Nm).

12. Connect the thermostat and pump hoses, then install the drive belt.

13. Install the intake air duct and connect the negative battery cable.

14. Refill the cooling system with the proper type and quantity of coolant, then operate the engine and check for leaks.

3.4L Engine

1. Disconnect the negative battery cable and drain the engine cooling system.

2. Remove the air duct and disengage the electrical connector.

3. Disengage the electrical connector from the alternator, then remove the top ignition coil from the coil pack.

4. Loosen the tensioner pulley bolt, then remove the heater hose from the pump.

5. Loosen the pump pulley bolts, then remove the power steering bracket bolts.

6. Remove the serpentine drive belt, then remove the pump pulley.

7. Remove the power steering pump and bracket assembly, then position aside with the hoses intact.

8. Remove the water pump retaining bolts starting with the lower bolts and working alternately around to the top.

9. Remove the water pump assembly and gasket from the front of the engine.

To install:

10. Thoroughly clean the gasket mating surfaces of any remaining gasket material.

11. Position the water pump using a new gasket, then loosely install using the retaining bolts.

12. Tighten the water pump retaining bolts to specification, starting with the bolts that require the highest torque specification and working towards the bolts with the lowest specification.

13. Position the power steering pump and bracket assembly and loosely secure using the retaining bolts.

14. Install the water pump pulley and tighten the retaining bolts to 18 ft. lbs. (25 Nm), then install the serpentine drive belt.

15. Tighten the power steering pump bracket bolts to 23 ft. lbs. (31 Nm).

16. Install the heater hose to the pump assembly.

17. Install the top ignition coil to the coil pack.

18. Engage the electrical connector to the alternator.

19. Engage the electrical connector and install the air duct.

20. Connect the negative battery cable and refill the engine cooling system, then start the engine and check for leaks.

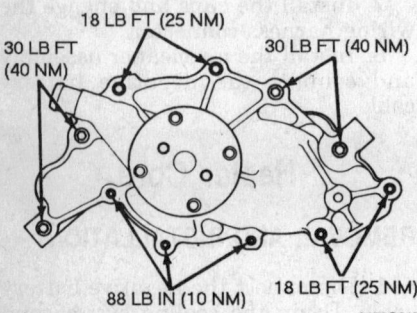

18 LB FT (25 NM)
30 LB FT (40 NM)
30 LB FT (40 NM)
88 LB IN (10 NM)
18 LB FT (25 NM)
8470Q017

Water pump assembly torque specifications — 1992 3.1L engine

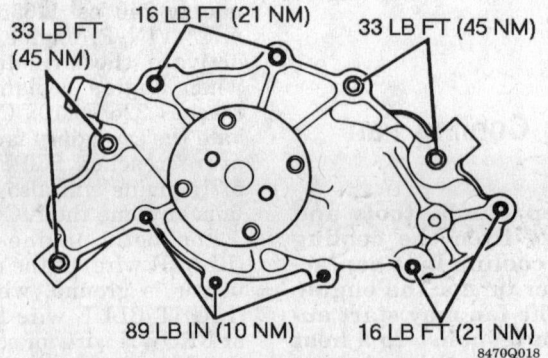

16 LB FT (21 NM)
33 LB FT (45 NM)
33 LB FT (45 NM)
89 LB IN (10 NM)
16 LB FT (21 NM)
8470Q018

Water pump assembly torque specification — 3.4L engine

5.7L (VIN P) Engine

1. Disconnect the negative battery cable.

2. Disengage the wiring harness from the cooling fan assembly, then remove the assembly from the vehicle.

3. Drain the engine cooling system, removing the block drain plug and the knock sensor to assure proper draining. Reinstall the drain plug and knock sensor, as soon as the system is empty.

4. Disconnect the upper and lower radiator hoses from the water pump assembly.

5. Remove the heater hose assemblies from the water pump and from the throttle body.

6. Disengage the coolant sensor wiring harness, then reposition the ignition coil and bracket assembly.

7. Remove the shorter water pump retaining bolt from the center of each pump mating flange, then remove the longer pump bolts from either side of the center bolts.

8. Carefully remove the water pump assembly and gaskets along with the pump shaft coupling.

To install:

9. Thoroughly clean the gasket mating surfaces of any remaining gasket material.

10. Install the water pump shaft coupling along with the water pump and gaskets.

11. Install the longer pump bolts and tighten 33 ft. lbs. (45 Nm), then install the shorter bolts and tighten to 31 ft. lbs. (42 Nm).

12. Reposition the ignition coil and bracket assembly.

13. Engage the coolant sensor electrical connector.

14. Install the heater and radiator hoses to the throttle body and water pump, as applicable.

15. Install the air cleaner and intake duct assemblies.

16. Install the engine cooling fan assembly and engage the wiring harness connector.

17. Connect the negative battery cable and properly fill the engine cooling system.

Thermostat

REMOVAL AND INSTALLATION

1992

1. Disconnect the negative battery cable.

2. Drain the cooling system to a level slightly below the thermostat.

3. Remove the air cleaner and/or intake duct, as necessary.

4. Remove the throttle body from the intake.

5. For the 3.1L engine, remove the plenum, fuel pipes and brackets.

6. Disconnect the radiator inlet hose.

7. Remove the thermostat housing retaining bolts and housing.

8. Remove the thermostat.

To install:

9. Make sure all gasket mating surfaces are clean before installation and replace the gasket as necessary. If upon removal of the thermostat housing the gasket remained attached to the housing, it is not necessary to replace the gasket.

10. Install the thermostat, then install the housing and tighten the retaining bolts as follows:

   a. 3.1L engine — 15 ft. lbs. (21 Nm).

   b. 5.0L (VIN E) TBI engine — 21 ft. lbs. (28 Nm).

   c. 5.0L (VIN F) and 5.7L (VIN 8) engines — 25 ft. lbs. (34 Nm).

11. Connect the radiator inlet hose.

12. Install the plenum, fuel lines and brackets and/or throttle body, as applicable.

13. If removed, install the air cleaner and/or intake duct.

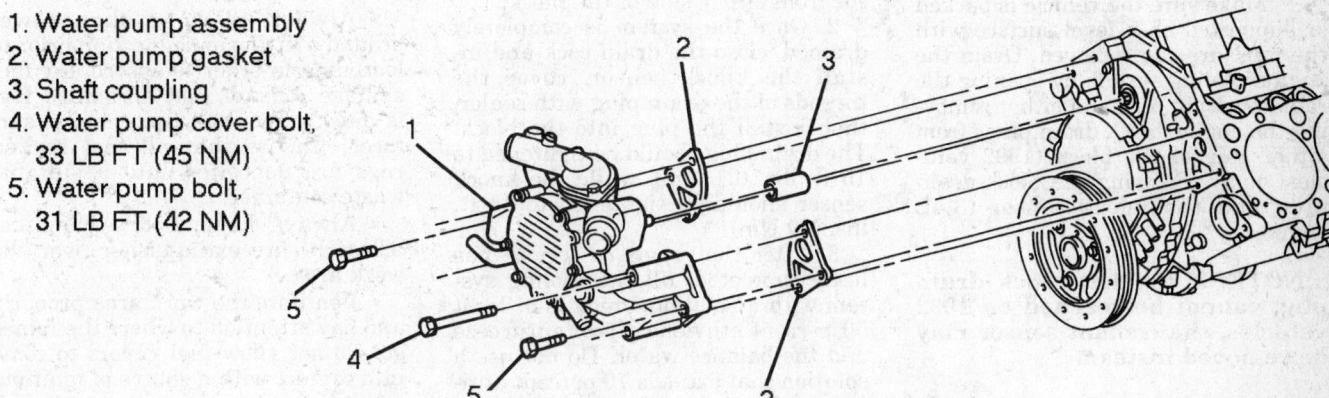

1. Water pump assembly
2. Water pump gasket
3. Shaft coupling
4. Water pump cover bolt, 33 LB FT (45 NM)
5. Water pump bolt, 31 LB FT (42 NM)

8470Q020

Water pump assembly removal and installation — 5.7L (VIN P) engine

14. Connect the negative battery cable and refill the cooling system with the proper type and quantity of coolant.

1993-96

1. Open the radiator drain cock and allow the engine coolant to drain to a level just below the thermostat housing, then close the drain and tighten to 106 inch lbs. (12 Nm).
2. Remove the air cleaner assembly.
3. Disconnect the inlet hose and clamp from the thermostat assembly.
4. Remove the thermostat housing bolts, then remove the housing.
5. If equipped, remove the housing gasket.
6. Remove the thermostat assembly.
   To install:
7. Make sure the flange mating surfaces are clean and free of debris, then install the thermostat assembly.
8. If equipped, install a new housing gasket.
9. Install the housing and tighten the retaining bolts to 21 ft. lbs. (28 Nm), then connect the inlet hose assembly and clamp.
10. Install the air cleaner assembly, then properly refill the engine cooling system.

Cooling System Bleeding

EXCEPT 5.7L (VIN P) ENGINE

1. Make sure the vehicle is parked or supported on a level surface with the pressure cap removed. Drain the engine cooling system by opening the radiator drain cock and either removing the engine block drain plugs from either side of the block (1992 vehicles) or by removing the block drain plug and the knock sensor (3.4L engine).

NOTE: If the left block drain plug cannot be reached on 1992 vehicles, the coolant sensor may be removed instead.

2. Once the system is completely drained, close the drain cock, then install the knock sensor and/or the drain plugs. The drain plugs should be tightened to 15 ft. lbs. (21 Nm), while the knock sensor should be tightened to 14 ft. lbs. (19 Nm).
3. After the repair or service has been completed, fill the cooling system with a solution which is at least 50 percent ethylene glycol antifreeze and the balance water. Do not use a solution that exceeds 70 percent antifreeze. Continue filling the radiator until the level is just below the filler neck.
4. Fill the coolant recovery reservoir to the **COLD** mark and install the reservoir cap.
5. Run the engine with the radiator cap removed until the normal operating temperature is reached.

——— CAUTION ———
Ethylene glycol in engine coolant can be flammable under some conditions. Do not spill coolant on the exhaust system or on hot engine parts.

6. With the engine idling, add coolant to the radiator until the level reaches the bottom of the filler neck.
7. Install the radiator cap. The arrows on the cap must line up with the coolant recovery reservoir hose.

5.7L (VIN P) ENGINE

1. Make sure the vehicle is parked or supported on a level surface with the pressure cap removed. Drain the engine cooling system by opening the radiator drain cock, then opening the air bleed vents on the thermostat housing and the heater outlet hose pipe. To assure the system is fully drained, remove the engine block drain plug and the engine knock sensor from either side of the block.
2. Once the system is completely drained, close the drain cock and install the knock sensor. cover the threads of the drain plug with sealer, then install the plug into the block. The drain plug should be tightened to 15 ft. lbs. (21 Nm), while the knock sensor should be tightened to 14 ft. lbs. (19 Nm).
3. After the repair or service has been completed, fill the cooling system with a solution which is at least 50 percent ethylene glycol antifreeze and the balance water. Do not use a solution that exceeds 70 percent antifreeze. Continue filling the radiator until the level is just below the filler neck.
4. Once the system is filled, close the air bleeds, taking care not to overtighten and damage the brass valves.
5. Install the pressure cap, then start and run the engine to check for leaks.

FUEL SYSTEM

Fuel System Service Precautions

Safety is the most important factor when performing not only fuel system maintenance, but any type of service. Failure to conduct maintenance and repairs in a safe manner may result in serious personal injury or death. Maintenance and testing of the vehicle's fuel system components can be accomplished safely and effectively by adhering to the following rules and guidelines.

• Always disconnect the negative battery cable before opening the fuel system fittings, unless the repair or test procedure requires that battery voltage be applied. This will prevent excessive fuel spillage if the ignition switch is accidentally turned **ON** while fuel fittings are still disconnected.
• Always relieve the fuel system pressure prior to disconnecting any fuel system fitting or connection.
• Exercise extreme caution whenever relieving fuel system pressure to avoid exposing skin, face and eyes to fuel spray. Under pressure, fuel may penetrate the skin or any part of the body that it contacts.
• Always place a shop towel around a fitting or connection prior to loosening in order to absorb any fuel spillage. Ensure that all spilled fuel is quickly removed from engine surfaces. Ensure that all fuel soaked rags are deposited into a suitable waste container.
• Always keep a dry chemical (Class B) fire extinguisher near the work area.
• Ventilate the work area properly and pay attention to where the fumes go. Do not allow fuel vapors to come into contact with a source of ignition.
• Always use a backup wrench when loosening and tightening fuel line connection fittings. This will prevent unnecessary stress to fuel line piping. Always follow the proper torque specifications.
• Always replace worn fuel fitting O-rings. Do not substitute fuel hose where metal fuel pipe is normally installed.

RELIEVING FUEL SYSTEM PRESSURE

Except TBI Engine

1. Disconnect the negative battery cable to prevent fuel discharge if the key is accidentally turned to the **RUN** position.
2. Loosen the fuel filler cap to relieve the tank pressure and do not tighten until service has been completed.
3. Connect J–34730–1 fuel pressure gauge or equivalent, to the fuel pressure valve. Wrap a shop cloth around the fitting while connecting the gauge to avoid spillage.
4. Place the end of the bleed hose into a suitable container and open the valve to relieve the fuel system pressure.

TBI Engine

1. Disconnect the negative battery cable to prevent fuel discharge if the key is accidentally turned to the **RUN** position.
2. Loosen the fuel filler cap to relieve the tank pressure and do not tighten until service has been completed.
3. Fuel system pressure is automatically relieved when the engine is turned **OFF**. No further action is necessary.

Fuel Tank

REMOVAL AND INSTALLATION

1. Disconnect the negative battery cable, relieve fuel system pressure and drain the fuel tank.
2. For 1992 vehicles, remove the fuel filler neck shield and attaching screws.
3. Raise and support vehicle safely.
4. For 1993–96 vehicles, remove the fuel filler neck shield.
5. Remove the rear axle assembly.
6. Disconnect the exhaust muffler and pipe, then remove the muffler heat shield and attaching screws.
7. Clean all fuel pipe connections and surrounding areas to prevent possible contamination of the fuel system, then disconnect the rear fuel pipe assembly and vapor return hose from the fuel sender assembly.
8. Disengage the fuel pump electrical connector.
9. With the aid of an assistant, support the fuel tank and remove the front fuel tank strap attaching bolts.

Be careful not to bend the straps, as this may damage them.
10. Remove the straps, then lower the fuel tank from the vehicle and place in a suitable work area.
   To install:
11. Hook the rear end of the fuel tank straps into the underbody bracket.
12. With the aid of an assistant, raise the fuel tank into position and support it while connecting the fuel tank straps and attaching bolts. Tighten the attaching bolts to 25 ft. lbs. (34 Nm), then engage the fuel sender assembly electrical connector.
13. Connect the fuel pipes and the vapor hoses to the fuel sender assembly.
14. Install the muffler heat shield with the attaching screws, then connect the exhaust muffler and pipe.
15. Install the rear axle assembly.
16. For 1993–96 vehicles, install the fuel filler neck shield.
17. Lower the vehicle, then for 1992 vehicles. connect the fuel filler neck shield and attaching screws.
18. Add fuel and tighten the filler cap.
19. Connect the negative battery cable.
20. Turn the ignition switch to the **ON** position for 2 seconds, **OFF** for 10 seconds, then **ON** again in order to pressurize the fuel system, then check for fuel leaks.
21. If equipped with the 3.1L (VIN T) engine, the ECM will need to relearn Idle Air Control (IAC) valve pintle position following battery reconnection.

Fuel Filter

REMOVAL AND INSTALLATION

1992

1. Disconnect the negative battery cable and relieve the fuel system pressure.
2. Raise and support the vehicle safely.
3. Clean the fuel filter line fittings before disconnecting to prevent contamination of the fuel system. Disengage the fuel lines from the fuel filter and plug the lines to prevent system contamination.
4. Remove the filter bracket retainer and slide the fuel filter from the fuel filter bracket.
   To install:
5. Check the fuel line O-rings for cuts, nicks, swelling or distortion and replace as necessary.

6. Position the replacement filter in the fuel filter bracket with the flow arrow pointing toward the engine.
7. Install the fuel filter bracket screw and and the fuel lines. Tighten the in-line fuel filter fittings to 20 ft. lbs. (27 Nm), using a backup wrench to keep the filter from turning.
8. Lower the vehicle, connect the negative battery cable and tighten the fuel filler cap.
9. Turn the ignition switch to the **ON** position for 2 seconds, **OFF** for 10 seconds, then to the **ON** position and check for fuel leaks.
10. For vehicles equipped with the 3.1L (VIN T) engine, the ECM will need to relearn Idle Air Control (IAC) valve pintle position following battery reconnection.

1993–96

1. Disconnect the negative battery cable and relieve the fuel system pressure.
2. Raise and support the vehicle safely.
3. Clean the fuel filter line fittings before disconnecting to prevent contamination of the fuel system.
4. Remove the fuel filter bracket, then Disengage the quick-connect fitting from the rear of the filter.
5. Loosen and disconnect the threaded outlet fitting from the from of the filter, then plug the lines to prevent system contamination.
6. Remove the filter from the vehicle.
   To install:
7. Position the replacement filter and install the threaded fitting, then tighten the fitting to 20 ft. lbs. (27 Nm).
8. Install the fuel filter bracket, then engage the quick-connect fitting to the rear of the filter assembly. Remember to apply a few drops of clean engine oil to the male end of the connector in order to assure proper seal.
9. Lower the vehicle, then connect the negative battery cable and tighten the fuel filler cap.
10. Turn the ignition switch to the **ON** position for 2 seconds, **OFF** for 10 seconds, then to the **ON** position and check for fuel leaks.

Electric Fuel Pump

PRESSURE TESTING

5.0L (VIN E) TBI Engine

1. Relieve fuel system pressure and check that there is an adequate quantity of fuel in the tank.

2. Ensure the ignition switch is in the **OFF** position.

3. Connect a fuel pressure gauge inline between the fuel filter outlet and the flexible filter-to-engine line.

4. Using a 10 amp fused jumper wire, apply battery voltage to the fuel pump test connector located on the passenger side of the engine compartment.

5. Fuel pump pressure will drop immediately after the fuel pump stops running due to a controlled bleed in the fuel system.

6. The fuel pressure, with the pump running, should be 9–13 psi.

7. If there is no fuel pressure, listen for pump operation in tank.

8. If pump operation is heard, inspect lines and filter for restriction.

9. If there is no restriction, replace the fuel pump.

10. If pump is not heard running, inspect the fuel pump relay and wiring.

11. Disconnect the fuel pressure gauge.

Except 5.0L (VIN E) TBI Engine

1. Relieve fuel system pressure and check that there is an adequate quantity of fuel in the tank.

2. Connect a fuel pressure gauge to the pressure connector fitting located on the end of the fuel rail assembly for all vehicles except the 5.7L (VIN P) engine. For the 5.7L (VIN P) engine, a pressure fitting is located inline shortly before the fuel rail and accumulator.

3. Make sure the ignition switch has been in the **OFF** position for at least 10 seconds and that all accessories are **OFF.**

4. Turn the ignition switch **ON** and the pump will run for about 2 seconds. Note the system pressure with the pump running, it should be the pressure should be 40–47 psi.

NOTE: The ignition switch may have to be cycled to ON more than once to obtain maximum pressure. It is also normal for the pressure to drop slightly when the pump first stops, but it should then hold steady.

5. If fuel pressure is not as specified, verify that fuel pump operation is heard in the tank.

6. If fuel pump operation is not heard, inspect the fuel pump relay and wiring.

7. If fuel pump operation is heard, inspect filter and lines for restriction.

8. Start the engine and make sure the pressure decreases about 3–10 psi at idle.

9. If fuel pressure does not decrease, inspect pressure regulator and vacuum hose.

10. Disconnect the fuel pressure gauge.

REMOVAL AND INSTALLATION

The electric fuel pump is part of the fuel sender assembly located inside the fuel tank.

1. Release the fuel pressure and disconnect the negative battery cable.

2. Drain the fuel tank, then raise and support the vehicle safely.

3. Remove the fuel tank from the vehicle.

4. Clean the area surrounding the sender assembly to prevent contamination of the fuel system.

5. Remove the fuel sender assembly from the tank as follows:

   a. For 1992 vehicles, use tool J–24187 or equivalent to remove the fuel sender retaining cam, fuel sender assembly and O-rings, from the fuel tank. Discard the old O-ring.

   b. For 1993–96 vehicles, remove the fuel sender assembly nuts and retaining ring, then carefully remove the sender assembly from the tank. Discard the old O-ring.

6. If necessary, separate the fuel pump from the sending assembly.

To install:

7. If removed, install the fuel pump to the sending unit. If the strainer was removed from the pump, the strainer must be replaced with a new component.

8. Inspect and clean the O-ring mating surfaces. Install the new O-ring in the groove around the tank opening, and if applicable, install a new O-ring on the fuel sender feed tube.

9. Install the fuel sender assembly; the fuel pump strainer must be in a horizontal position and when installed must not block the full travel of the float arm. Gently fold the fuel strainer over itself and slowly position the fuel sender assembly in the tank so the strainer is not damaged or trapped by sump walls.

10. For 1992 vehicles, install assembly retainer cam using J–24187 or equivalent.

11. For 1993–96 vehicles, install the retaining ring and nuts, then tighten the nuts to 63 inch lbs. (7 Nm).

12. Install the fuel tank assembly to the vehicle.

13. Lower the vehicle.

14. Fill the fuel tank, tighten the fuel filler cap and connect the negative battery cable.

15. Turn the ignition switch to the **ON** position for 2 seconds, **OFF** for 10 seconds, then to the **ON** position and check for fuel leaks.

16. If equipped with the 3.1L (VIN T) engine, the ECM will need to relearn Idle Air Control (IAC) valve pintle position following battery reconnection.

Fuel Injection

IDLE SPEED ADJUSTMENT

The idle speed and mixture are controlled electronically by the Engine Control Module (ECM). All adjustments are preset at the factory and do require periodic attention. Some throttle body units are equipped with a idle stop screw to allow adjustment of the minimum idle speed if the unit is used as a replacement. The only time the idle speed should need adjustment is when the throttle body assembly has been replaced.

3.1L Engine

1. Block the drive wheels and apply the parking brake.

2. Remove the air cleaner assembly, as necessary for access to the throttle body.

3. Connect a scan tool to the Data Link Connector (DLC), formerly known as the ALDL.

4. Remove the plug or cover from the idle stop screw, then back the screw up until an air gap is visible when looking downward from above the throttle body.

5. Turn the stop screw inward until it just contacts the throttle lever, then turn the screw inward 1½ additional turns.

6. Perform the idle learn procedure, then place the transmission in **P** for automatic equipped vehicles or in **N** for manual equipped vehicles and start the engine.

7. Run the engine until it reaches normal operating temperature or closed loop operation as indicated by the scan tool. It may be necessary to hold the throttle open slightly in order to maintain idle.

8. With the engine running at idle, use the scan tool to monitor IAC valve pintle counts. Counts should stabilize between 10-20, if not the procedure should be repeated.

IAC VALVE PINTLE ADJUSTMENT

Idle speed is controlled by the ECM through voltage pulses sent to the Idle Air Control (IAC) motor windings. Based on the number of voltage pulses received, the motor will move the IAC pintle in or out allowing more or less air through the throttle body. Whenever a new IAC valve is installed, the pintle must be adjusted to specification.

NOTE: If installing a new IAC valve measure and adjust the valve accordingly. If reinstalling a used IAC valve, do not push or pull on the pintle to adjust pintle length or damage to the IAC worm gear threads might occur.

1. On a new IAC valve only, measure the distance between the tip of the pintle and the valve mounting surface. If greater than 1.10 inch (28mm), use light finger pressure to slowly retract the pintle. The force required to retract a new IAC valve will not damage the valve.
2. Install the IAC valve and gasket.
3. Connect the IAC valve wire connector.
4. Except the 3.1L and 3.4L engines, reset the IAC valve pintle as follows:
   a. Depress the accelerator pedal slightly.
   b. Start the engine and run for 5 seconds.
   c. Turn the ignition **OFF** for 10 seconds.
   d. Restart the vehicle and check for proper idle operation.
5. For the 3.1L and 3.4L engines, reset the IAC valve pintle as follows:
   a. For the 3.1L engine, if the negative battery cable was disconnected install a scan tool and perform the idle learn procedure.
   b. Turn the ignition **ON** for 5 seconds, then **OFF** for 10 seconds.

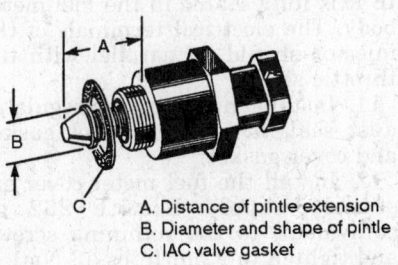

A. Distance of pintle extension
B. Diameter and shape of pintle
C. IAC valve gasket

8470Q023

Measuring the pintle position of a new IAC valve

c. Start the engine and check for proper idle operation.

IDLE LEARN PROCEDURE

Any time the battery is disconnected on vehicles equipped with the 3.1L engine, the programmed position of the IAC valve pintle is lost and replaced with a default value. To return the IAC valve pintle to the correct position, the idle learn procedure must be followed.

1. With the battery cables connected and the transmission in **P** or **N**, connect a suitable scan tool.
2. Select the IAC system, then select the Idle Learn portion of the Misc Test mode.
3. Proceed with the idle learn procedure as prompted by the scan tool.
4. The procedure should update ECM memory with the correct IAC valve pintle position and provide a stable idle speed.

Fuel Injector

REMOVAL AND INSTALLATION

3.1L Engine

1. Disconnect the negative battery cable and properly relieve the fuel system pressure.
2. Remove the air inlet duct at the throttle body and the crankcase vent pipe at the valve cover grommet.
3. Remove vacuum harness connector, throttle cable bracket bolt, throttle body attaching bolts, the throttle body and gasket. Discard the old gasket.
4. Remove the EGR transfer tube and retaining bolts.
5. Remove the air conditioning compressor-to-plenum bracket attaching hardware and bracket.
6. Remove the intake manifold plenum bolts/studs, plenum and gaskets. Discard the gaskets.
7. Clean the fuel rail assembly and surrounding connections with GM X-30A or equivalent before removal.
8. Disconnect the fuel lines at rail and discard the O-rings. Disconnect the vacuum line at the pressure regulator, then disengage the fuel injector electrical connections.
9. Disconnect the fuel rail attaching bolts and remove the assembly.

NOTE: Use care when handling the fuel rail assembly so as not to damage the injector connections or spray tips. Plug open

lines and passages to prevent dirt and other contaminants from entering. Do not immerse fuel rail in liquid cleaning solvent.

10. Rotate the fuel injector retaining clip to the release position and remove the injector. Discard the injector retainer clip and O-rings.
To install:
11. Replace all O-rings, gaskets and retainer clips which were discarded. Carefully clean all gasket mating surfaces, taking care not to score or damage them with a sharp instrument.
12. Lubricate new fuel injector O-ring seals with engine oil and install on the injector. Connect new retainer clip and install fuel injector on fuel rail, rotate injector retainer clip to the lock position.
13. Tilt the rail assembly to install the injectors and install the assembly to the intake manifold.
14. Tighten the fuel rail attaching bolts to 18 ft. lbs. (25 Nm).
15. Connect the injector electrical connectors and the vacuum line.
16. Install new O-rings on the fuel lines and connect the fuel lines. Tighten fuel line nuts to 20 ft. lbs. (27 Nm). Temporarily connect the negative battery cable, and run the fuel pump to check for leaks, then disconnect the negative battery cable.
17. Install the new plenum gaskets, the plenum and attaching bolts/studs. Tighten bolts/studs to 15 ft. lbs. (21 Nm).
18. Install the air conditioning compressor bracket and hardware. Install the EGR transfer tube and bolts, tighten bolts to 19 ft. lbs. (26 Nm).
19. Install throttle body and new gasket. Tighten the attaching bolts to 20 ft. lbs. (27 Nm).
20. Install the throttle cable bracket bolt, the vacuum harness connector, the air inlet duct and the crankcase vent pipe.
21. Connect the negative battery cable and tighten the fuel filler cap.
22. Turn the ignition switch to the **ON** position for 2 seconds, **OFF** for 10 seconds, then to the **ON** position and check for fuel leaks.
23. The ECM will need to relearn Idle Air Control (IAC) valve pintle position following battery reconnection.

3.4L Engine

1. Make sure the ignition is **OFF**, then disconnect then negative battery cable.
2. Relieve the fuel system pressure.

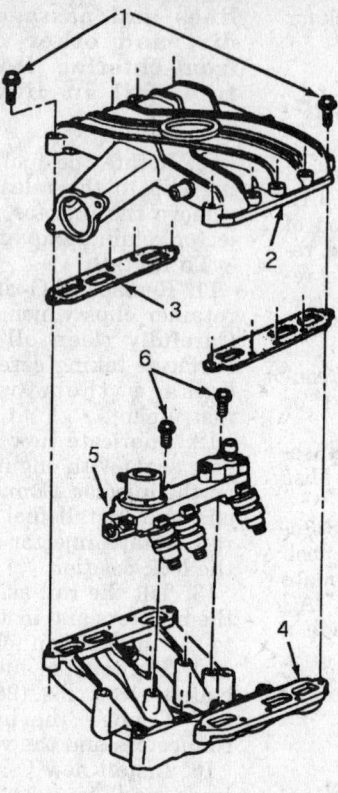

1. Plenum to manifold bolt
2. Intake plenum
3. Gasket
4. Intake manifold
5. Fuel rail assembly
6. Fuel rail attaching bolt

8470Q024

Removing the intake plenum and the fuel rail assembly — 3.1L engine

3. Disengage the quick-connect fittings from the engine fuel pipes, then remove the pipe retaining bolts. Relocate the accelerator cable from the routing clip and remove the fuel tube retainer from the fuel rail, then remove the pipes from the engine.

4. Disconnect the vacuum line harness from the fuel rail assembly.

5. Disengage the wiring harness from the fuel rail assembly, then remove the fuel rail retainers.

6. Using compressed air and safety glasses, blow any dirt which may be present out of the injector bores, then remove the fuel rail assembly.

7. Rotate the fuel injector retainer clip to the release position, then carefully remove the injector from the rail assembly.

8. Remove and discard the O-ring seals from both ends of the injector, then discard the retainer clip.

To install:

9. Lubricate the new O-rings with clean engine oil, then install them onto the injector. The lower O-ring uses a nylon collar called the O-ring backup. In order to prevent vacuum leaks and driveability problems, it is extremely important to assure that the backup O-ring is properly positioned on the injector.

10. Position a new retainer clip on the injector, then install the injector to the fuel rail assembly. Rotate the injector clip to the locked position in order to secure the injector to the rail assembly.

11. Tilt the fuel rail, as necessary to properly position the injectors, then carefully install the assembly to the intake manifold.

12. Install the fuel rail attaching bolts and tighten to 18 ft. lbs. (25 Nm).

13. Install the fuel pipes to the rail, then install the pipes to the engine. Make sure accelerator cable is properly positioned in the routing clip and that all retainers and connectors are securely fastened.

14. Rotate the injectors, as necessary, in order to avoid stretching the wire harness, then engage the harness connectors with the fuel rail assembly.

15. Install the vacuum line harness connector to the fuel rail.

16. Connect the negative battery cable, and tighten the fuel filler cap.

17. Turn the ignition switch to the **ON** position for 2 seconds, **OFF** for 10 seconds, then to the **ON** position and check for fuel leaks.

5.0L (VIN E) TBI Engine

1. Disconnect the negative battery cable and relieve the fuel system pressure.

2. Remove the air cleaner assembly.

3. Disengage the electrical connectors from the fuel injectors by squeezing the plastic tabs and pulling straight up.

4. Remove the fuel meter cover attaching screws and remove the fuel meter cover assembly.

5. Remove the fuel meter outlet passage gasket and pressure regulator dust seal. If the fuel meter cover gasket is stuck to the fuel meter body, leave it in place. If it is stuck to the fuel meter cover, remove it and place it on the fuel meter body.

6. With the fuel meter cover gasket in place to protect the fuel meter body, use a small suitable prytool and fulcrum to carefully pry out the injector.

7. Discard both injector O-rings and the fuel meter cover gasket.

To install:

NOTE: Be sure to replace the injector with an identical part. Injectors from other engines are calibrated for different flow rates. Service fuel injector packages may contain a fuel injector washer (spacer). The washer is not required for this application.

8. Lubricate a new upper (large) O-ring with engine oil and install in the fuel meter body cavity. Make sure the O-ring is seated properly and is flush with the top of the fuel meter body surface.

9. Lubricate a new lower (small) O-ring with engine oil and install on the nozzle end of the injector. Push the O-ring on far enough to contact the filter.

10. Install the injector by aligning the raised lug on the injector base with the notch in the fuel meter body cavity. Push down on the injector until it is fully seated in the fuel meter body. The electrical terminals of the injector should be parallel with the throttle shaft.

11. Install a new pressure regulator dust seal, fuel meter outlet gasket and cover gasket.

12. Install the fuel meter cover assembly. Apply Loctite 262 or equivalent, to the retaining screws and tighten to 27 inch lbs. (3 Nm).

13. Engage the electrical connectors to the fuel injectors, tighten the fuel filler cap and connect the negative battery cable.

14. Turn the ignition switch to the **ON** position for 2 seconds, **OFF** for 10 seconds, then to the **ON** position and check for fuel leaks.

15. Install the air cleaner assembly.

5.0L (VIN F) and 5.7L (VIN 8) Engines

1. Disconnect the negative battery cable and relieve the fuel system pressure.

2. Partially drain the cooling system so the coolant hoses at the throttle body can be removed.

3. Disconnect the throttle, TV and cruise control cables.

4. Disconnect the cable retaining bracket, air intake duct, vacuum hoses at the throttle body, coolant hoses and the electrical connectors from the Throttle Position Sensor (TPS) and the Idle Air Control (IAC) valve.

5. Remove the throttle body bolts and the throttle body assembly.

6. Disengage the electrical connectors from the injectors, remove the left and right electrical harness attaching nuts and move the harnesses aside.

7. Disconnect the power brake vacuum hose at the plenum and remove the runner to plenum bolt attaching the Manifold Absolute Pressure (MAP) sensor. Disconnect the MAP sensor and vacuum hoses at the plenum.

8. Remove the remaining runner to plenum bolts. Lift the plenum and disconnect the Manifold Air Temperature (MAT) sensor electrical connector. Remove the plenum and discard the plenum gaskets.

9. Remove the runner to manifold bolts, PCV valve and hose, EGR solenoid and the left and right side runners and gaskets. Discard the gaskets.

10. Disconnect the fuel feed and return lines. Discard the fuel line O-rings.

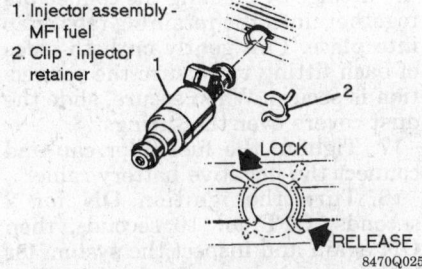

1. Injector assembly - MFI fuel
2. Clip - injector retainer

LOCK
RELEASE
8470Q025

The fuel injector retaining clip is rotated in order to lock/release the injector to/from the fuel rail

11. Remove the fuel tube bracket bolt.

12. Disconnect the vacuum line at the pressure regulator.

13. Remove the fuel rail attaching bolts and the fuel rail assembly.

14. Rotate the injector retainer clip to the release position and remove the injector. Discard the O-rings and retainer clips.

To install:

NOTE: There are 2 injector part numbers used in production for the 5.0L engine and 2 different part numbers for the 5.7L engine. Do not intermix injectors with different part numbers, as this will result in engine roughness and excessive emissions. If the entire set of injectors are being replaced, either part number listed for that specific engine may be used.

15. Lubricate new injector O-ring seals with engine oil and install on the injector.

16. Install a new retainer clip onto the injector and install the injector into the fuel rail injector socket, with the electrical connector facing outward. Rotate the injector retainer clip to the locking position.

17. Install the fuel rail assembly in the intake manifold. Install the attaching bolts to 15 ft. lbs. (20 Nm). Install the fuel tube bracket bolt and tighten to 25 ft. lbs. (34 Nm).

18. Connect the vacuum line to the pressure regulator.

19. Install new O-rings on the fuel feed and return lines and connect the fuel lines to the fuel rail. Tighten the fuel line nuts to 20 ft. lbs. (27 Nm).

20. Temporarily connect the negative battery cable. Turn the ignition switch to the **ON** position for 2 seconds, **OFF** for 10 seconds, then to the **ON** position and check for fuel leaks. Disconnect the negative battery cable.

21. Clean all plenum and runner gasket mating surfaces.

22. Install new gaskets, the runners and manifold to runner bolts to the intake manifold. Tighten the bolts to 25 ft. lbs. (34 Nm).

23. Install the EGR solenoid.

24. Install the right and left side hand runner to manifold bolts finger-tight only.

25. Support the plenum above the runners, connect the MAT sensor electrical connector and lower the plenum into position. Start a few bolts to hold the plenum in position.

26. Connect the vacuum hoses and MAP sensor.

27. Tighten all bolts to 25 ft. lbs. (34 Nm), starting in the center of the plenum/manifold and working outward.

28. Install the PCV valve and hose.

29. Connect the power brake vacuum hose to the fitting on the plenum, the left and right injector electrical harnesses, the attaching nuts and the electrical connectors to the injectors.

30. Install the throttle body with a new gasket and tighten the attaching bolts to 18 ft. lbs. (24 Nm).

31. Connect the electrical connectors to the TPS and IAC valve, coolant hoses, vacuum hoses, throttle cable bracket and the throttle, TV and cruise control cables.

32. Refill the cooling system, tighten the fuel filler cap and connect the negative battery cable.

5.7L (VIN P) Engine

1. Make sure the ignition is in the **OFF** position, then disconnect the negative battery cable.

2. Properly relieve the fuel system pressure.

3. Disengage the quick-connect fittings at the fuel rail feed and return pipes as follows:

   a. Slide the rubber dust cover from the fitting.

   b. Grasp both ends of a connection and twist ¼ turn in each direction to loosen any dirt. Repeat for other fitting.

   c. While wearing safety glasses, use compressed air to blow out dirt from the fitting.

   d. Insert a fuel line separator tool, into the female connector, then push inward to release the male connector.

   e. Repeat for the other fitting.

4. Disconnect the vacuum line at the pressure regulator, then as necessary, tag and disconnect any remaining vacuum lines which must be removed to access the fuel rail and engine fuel pipes.

5. Remove the fuel injector wiring harness from the routing clips of the fuel rail, then remove the fuel pipe attaching bolt and disengage the injector electrical connectors.

6. Remove the fuel rail attaching bolts and carefully remove the fuel rail assembly along with the injectors, from the top of the intake.

7. Rotate the injector retaining clip to the release position and remove the injector from the fuel rail assembly.

8. Remove and discard the O-ring seals from either side of the injector.

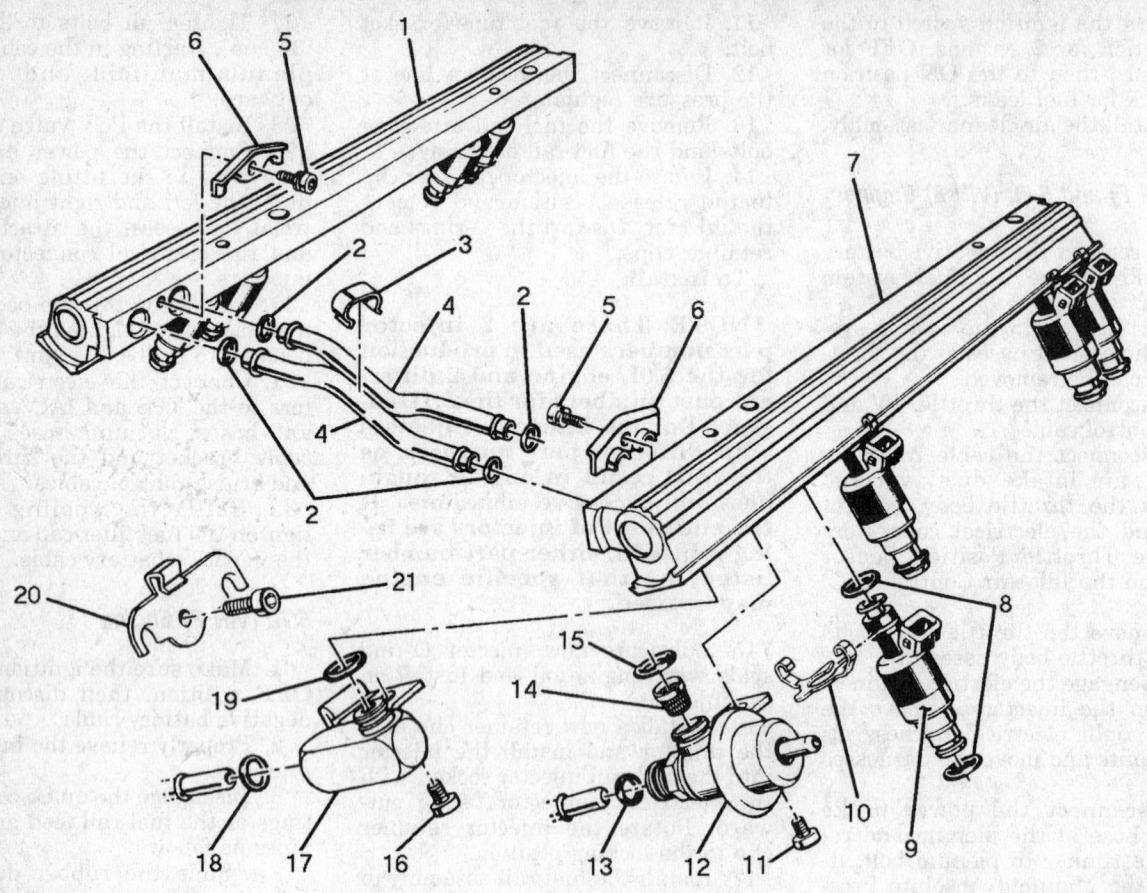

1. LH MFI fuel rail assembly
2. Fuel crossover tube o-ring
3. Fuel crossover tube clip
4. Fuel crossover tube
5. Crossover tube retainer attaching screw
6. Fuel crossover tube retainer
7. RH MFI Fuel rail assembly
8. Fuel injector o-ring
9. MFI fuel injector assembly
10. Injector retainer clip
11. Pressure regulator attaching screw
12. Fuel pressure regulator assembly
13. Fuel outlet tube o-ring
14. Filter screen (if equipped)
15. Fuel inlet fitting o-ring
16. Fuel inlet assembly attaching screw
17. Fuel inlet assembly
18. Fuel in let tube o-ring
19. Fuel inlet assembly o-ring
20. Fuel tube retainer assembly
21. Fuel tube retainer assembly attaching screw

8470Q026

Exploded view of the fuel rail assembly — 5.7L (VIN P) engine

9. Remove and discard the injector retaining clip.

To install:

10. Lubricate the new injector O-rings with clean engine oil and install onto the injector.

NOTE: Always replace injectors using an identical part number as inscribed on top of the old injector.

11. Connect a new retainer clip onto the fuel injector and install the injector to the fuel rail assembly. Rotate the injector retaining clip to the lock position.

12. Install the fuel rail assembly to the intake manifold. Tighten the attaching bolts to 15 ft. lbs. (20 Nm).

13. Rotate the fuel injectors as necessary to avoid stretching the wire harnesses, then engage the injector electrical connections.

14. Install the fuel pipe retaining nut, then position the wiring harness into the routing clips at the fuel rail.

15. Connect the vacuum lines to the intake, as necessary, then connect the vacuum line to the pressure regulator.

16. Apply a few drops of clean engine oil to the male ends of the fuel line quick-connect fittings. Engage the fittings by pushing the connectors together until the retaining tabs snap into place. Pull gently on both sides of each fitting to be sure the connection is secure. When secure, slide the dust covers over the fittings.

17. Tighten the fuel filler cap and connect the negative battery cable.

18. Turn the ignition **ON** for 2 seconds, **OFF** for 10 seconds, then **ON** again and inspect the system for leaks.

EMISSION CONTROLS

Emission Warning Lamps

The SERVICE ENGINE SOON Malfunction Indicator Light (MIL) located in the instrument cluster serves 2 main functions:

1. The lamp indicates to the driver when a problem has occurred and that the vehicle should be taken for service as soon as reasonably possible.

2. The light may be used by technicians to monitor diagnostic trouble codes and/or open/closed loop engine operation, whenever the system is placed in the diagnostic mode.

To verify proper operation of the bulb and wiring, the lamp will illuminate when the ignition is first turned to **ON**, but the engine is not running. If the system is operating properly, the lamp will turn off once the engine is started.

If the MIL remains lit once the engine is started, the self-diagnostic system has detected a problem. If the problem goes away, the light will extinguish in 10 seconds (in most cases), but a diagnostic trouble code will remain in the ECM memory.

RESETTING

NOTE: In order to prevent damage to the ECM, the ignition must always be OFF when connecting or disconnecting power to the ECM.

After repairs are made to the faulty system(s), it is necessary to make sure the ECM memory is cleared of any old diagnostic trouble codes. Removing the battery voltage to the ECM for a minimum of 30 seconds will clear all codes. This may be accomplished in various ways depending on how the vehicle is equipped. The ECM harness power feed may be disconnected at the positive battery terminal "pigtail." The fuse may be removed from the inline fuseholder which originates at the positive battery connection or from fuse block, as applicable. Also, the negative battery cable may be disconnected, but other on-board data such as the clock or radio presets and, on some vehicles, IAC valve pintle position may also be lost.

ECM LEARNING ABILITY

The ECM has a "learning" ability which allows it to make corrections for minor variations in the fuel system, in order to improve driveability. If the battery is disconnected to clear diagnostic codes or for safety during repairs, the "learning" process will reset and must begin again. A change may be noted in the vehicle's performance while the learning process occurs. To "teach" the vehicle, make sure the engine is at normal operating temperature, then drive the vehicle at part throttle, with moderate acceleration and idle conditions, until normal performance returns.

ENGINE MECHANICAL

NOTE: Disconnecting the negative battery cable on some vehicles may interfere with the functions of the on-board computer systems and may require the computer to undergo a relearning process.

Engine Assembly

REMOVAL AND INSTALLATION

3.1L Engine

1. Disconnect the negative battery cable.
2. Remove the air cleaner duct.
3. Mark the hood location on the hood supports and remove the hood.
4. Remove the serpentine belt.
5. Drain the radiator and remove the radiator hoses. Disconnect the heater hoses.
6. Remove the fan shroud, fan and radiator.
7. Disconnect the throttle linkage, including the cruise control detent cable.
8. Disconnect the air conditioning compressor and support aside.
9. Remove the power steering pump and lay aside. Remove the vacuum brake booster line.
10. Remove the distributor cap and spark plug wires.
11. Disengage the necessary electrical connections and hoses.
12. Raise and safely support the vehicle.
13. Disconnect the exhaust pipes at the exhaust manifolds.

14. Disconnect the transmission oil cooler lines at the oil pan clips.
15. Remove the flywheel cover and remove the converter bolts.
16. Disengage the starter wire connections.
17. Remove the bellhousing and the motor mount through bolts.
18. Lower the vehicle.
19. Relieve the fuel system pressure. Disconnect the fuel lines and remove the wire from the rear left engine bracket.
20. Support the transmission with a suitable jack. Attach an engine lifting device.
21. Remove the engine assembly.

To install:

22. Position the engine assembly in the vehicle.
23. Attach the motor mount to engine brackets and lower the engine in place. Remove the engine lifting device and the transmission jack.
24. Raise and support the vehicle safely.
25. Install the motor mount through bolts and tighten the nuts to 50 ft. lbs. (68 Nm). Install the bellhousing bolts and tighten to 40 ft. lbs. (54 Nm).
26. On vehicles with automatic transmission, install the converter-to-flywheel attaching bolts to 46 ft. lbs. (63 Nm).
27. Install the flywheel splash shield and tighten to 89 inch lbs. (10 Nm).
28. Connect the starter wires and the fuel lines. Connect the transmission oil cooler lines.
29. Install the exhaust pipe on the exhaust manifold.
30. Lower the vehicle.
31. Install the power steering pump and the air conditioning compressor.
32. Connect the necessary wires and hoses. Connect the fuel lines and attach the wire to the bracket at the rear left of the engine.
33. Install the radiator, fan and fan shroud. Connect the radiator and heater hoses.
34. Connect the vacuum brake booster line, the throttle linkage and cruise control cable. Install the distributor cap and spark plug wires.
35. Fill the cooling system with the proper type and amount of coolant and the crankcase with the proper type of oil to the correct level.
36. Install the serpentine belt, the air cleaner or air cleaner duct and the hood.
37. Connect the negative battery cable, tighten the fuel filler cap and start the engine and check for leaks.

3.4L Engine

1. Make sure the ignition is **OFF**, then disconnect the negative battery cable and relieve the fuel system pressure.

2. Raise and support the vehicle safely, then remove the front wheels.

3. Drain the engine cooling system and drain the crankcase of engine oil.

4. Disconnect the exhaust crossover pipe from the intermediate pipe.

5. If equipped with an automatic transmission, remove the converter cover, then remove the converter retaining bolts.

6. Remove the front facia lower deflectors from the vehicle.

7. Remove the stabilizer bar retaining bolts.

8. Remove the serpentine drive belt, then if equipped with an automatic transmission, disconnect the transmission fluid cooler lines from the radiator.

9. Disconnect the lower radiator hose from the radiator, then disconnect the heater hoses from the pipes at the engine assembly.

10. Remove the electrical ground straps from the right side of the engine block, then disengage the electrical wiring from the starter motor assembly.

11. Disengage the wiring harness connectors from the following sensor/switches:
   • Knock sensor
   • Oxygen sensor
   • Coolant temperature sensor
   • Camshaft sensor
   • Crankshaft sensors
   • Wheel speed sensors
   • Engine oil level switch
   • Fuel pump switch/engine oil pressure gauge sensor assemblies

12. Remove the right front brake line from the caliper brake hose, then plug the openings to prevent system contamination or excessive fluid loss.

13. Remove the wiring harness and the shift linkage from the transmission assembly.

14. Matchmark, then remove the driveshaft assembly.

15. Remove the torque arm from the transmission.

16. Remove the intermediate shaft from the rack and pinion assembly.

17. Remove the electrical ground straps from the left side of the frame rail.

18. Lower the vehicle sufficiently for underhood access, then remove the air intake duct.

19. Disconnect the fuel pipe assembly, then disconnect the cruise and accelerator cables from the throttle body assembly.

20. Disconnect the upper radiator hose from the intake manifold and the lower radiator hose from the front cover assembly.

21. Disengage the electrical connectors from the fan assembly, then remove the assembly from the vehicle.

22. Disconnect the brake booster vacuum hose.

23. Remove the Y brace from the right exhaust manifold assembly.

24. Remove the alternator and air conditioning compressor bracket, then position the assembly aside, taking care not to damage the components or connections.

25. Disengage and reposition the engine wiring harness connectors.

26. Remove and reposition the brake master cylinder.

27. Remove the upper bolts and nuts from the strut assemblies, then remove the right front brake line from the modulator valve assembly and clips.

28. Raise and support the vehicle safely, then position a lift table under the engine and engine frame assembly.

29. Remove the engine frame and transmission support bolts, then carefully lift the vehicle from the engine, transmission and engine frame assembly. Raise the vehicle slowly, stopping a few times to assure that all wiring and hoses are disconnected and free of the powertrain and/or vehicle.

30. Secure the strut assemblies to the frame, then, if applicable remove the transmission TV cable from the throttle body.

31. Remove the transmission assembly.

32. If equipped with a manual transmission, remove the clutch housing and clutch assembly.

33. Remove the power steering lines from the pump assembly. Plug the openings to prevent system contamination or excessive fluid loss.

34. Remove the engine mount through-bolts, then remove the engine from the engine frame.

To install:

35. Install the engine assembly to the engine frame, then install and tighten the mount through-bolts to 70 ft. lbs. (95 Nm).

36. Uncap the openings, then connect the lines to the power steering pump assembly.

37. If applicable, install the clutch housing and clutch assembly.

38. Install the transmission assembly, then if equipped with an automatic transmission, connect the TV cable to the throttle body.

39. Position the engine lift table under the vehicle, then align the strut assemblies and install the engine, transmission and engine frame to the vehicle.

40. Install the engine frame retaining bolts and tighten to 92 ft. lbs. (125 Nm), then remove the engine lift table and lower the vehicle as necessary for underhood access.

41. Install the upper strut assembly retaining bolts and nuts.

42. Install the right front brake line to the modulator valve assembly, then reposition and secure the master cylinder.

43. Engage the engine wiring harness connectors, then reposition and secure the alternator/A/C compressor bracket.

44. Install the Y brace to the right exhaust manifold assembly, then connect the brake booster vacuum hose.

45. Install the engine cooling fan assembly and engage the electrical connectors.

46. Connect the lower radiator hose to the front cover assembly and the upper radiator hose to the intake manifold assembly.

47. Connect the cruise and accelerator control cables to the throttle body assembly, then install and connect the fuel pipe assembly.

48. Raise and support the vehicle safely, then connect the electrical ground straps to the left side of the frame rail.

49. Connect the intermediate shaft to the rack and pinion assembly.

50. Install the torque arm to the transmission assembly.

51. Align the matchmarks and install the driveshaft.

52. Install the shift linkage to the transmission, then engage the transmission wiring harness.

53. Connect the right front brake line to the caliper brake hose.

54. Engage all switch and sensor electrical connectors which were disengaged to remove the engine frame and powertrain assembly.

55. Install the wiring to the starter motor wiring, then install the ground straps to the right side of the engine block.

56. Connect the heater pipes to the engine assembly and the lower radiator hose to the radiator assembly.

57. If equipped with an automatic transmission, connect the fluid cooler lines to the radiator.

58. Install the serpentine drive belt.

59. Install the stabilizer bar bolts, then install the front facia lower deflectors.

60. If equipped with an automatic transmission, install the converter retaining bolts, then install the converter cover and bolts.

61. Connect the exhaust crossover pipe assembly to the intermediate pipe.

62. Bleed the hydraulic brake system, then install the wheels and lower the vehicle.

63. Fill the engine crankcase with oil and connect the negative battery cable.

64. Properly fill the engine cooling system.

65. Install the air intake duct and bleed the power steering system.

66. Check and adjust wheel alignment, as necessary.

5.0L and 5.7L (VIN 8) Engines

1. Disconnect the negative battery cable.

2. Mark the location of the hood on the hood hinges and remove the hood.

3. Remove the air cleaner.

4. Drain the cooling system.

5. Remove the radiator hoses.

6. Disengage the electrical connectors and retaining clips at the fan, remove the fan mounting bolts and remove the fan and shroud.

7. Remove the radiator.

8. Remove the serpentine accessory drive belt.

9. Disconnect the throttle cable.

10. Remove the plenum extension screws and the plenum extension, if equipped.

11. Disconnect the spark plug wires at the distributor and remove the distributor. Remove the external coil, if equipped.

12. Disconnect the necessary vacuum hoses and wiring.

13. Disconnect the power steering and air conditioning compressors from their respective brackets and lay them aside.

14. Relieve the fuel system pressure. Disconnect the fuel lines.

15. Disconnect the negative battery cable at the engine block. Disconnect the AIR hoses and pipe.

16. Raise and safely support the vehicle.

17. Remove the exhaust pipes at the exhaust manifolds.

18. Remove the flywheel cover and remove the converter to flywheel bolts.

19. Disconnect the starter wires and remove the starter.

20. Disconnect the transmission oil cooler lines at the oil pan. Remove the motor mount through bolts.

21. Support the transmission with an adjustable lifting device and remove the crossmember bolts. Lower the transmission enough to remove the bellhousing bolts. Raise the transmission and install 2 crossmember bolts.

22. Remove the lifting device from the transmission. Lower the vehicle and Support the transmission with a suitable jack.

23. Remove the AIR/converter bracket and ground wires from the rear of the cylinder head.

24. Attach a suitable lifting device and remove the engine assembly.

To install:

25. Position the engine assembly in the vehicle.

26. Attach the motor mount to engine brackets and lower the engine into place. Attach the AIR/converter bracket and ground wires to the rear of the cylinder head.

27. Remove the engine lifting device and the transmission jack.

28. Raise and safely support the vehicle.

29. Install the motor mount through bolts and tighten to 50 ft. lbs. (68 (Nm).

30. Install the bellhousing bolts and tighten to 35 ft. lbs. (47 Nm). Tighten the transmission crossmember bolts.

31. On vehicles with automatic transmission, install the converter to flywheel bolts. Tighten the bolts to 46 ft. lbs. (63 Nm). Install the flywheel cover and connect the transmission oil cooler lines to the clip at the oil pan.

32. Connect the starter wires and install the starter.

33. Connect the exhaust pipe at the exhaust manifold.

34. Lower the vehicle and connect the AIR hoses and pipe.

35. Connect the necessary wires, hoses and the fuel lines.

36. Install the power steering pump and air conditioning compressor in their respective brackets.

37. Install the distributor and spark plug wires. Install the external coil, if equipped.

38. Install the radiator, fan and fan shroud, radiator hoses and heater hoses.

39. Engage the cooling fan electrical connectors.

40. Install the plenum extension, if equipped. Connect the throttle cable.

41. Fill the cooling system with the proper type and quantity of coolant and the crankcase with the proper type of oil to the correct level.

42. Install the air cleaner and the hood.

43. Connect the negative battery cable to the engine block, install the serpentine belt and tighten the fuel filler cap.

44. Connect the negative battery and check all fluids. Start the engine, check for leaks and check timing.

5.7L (VIN P) Engine

1. Properly discharge and recover the refrigerant from the air conditioning system.

——— **WARNING** ———
The 4th generation F-body which debuted in 1993 uses only the new R-134a refrigerant. R-134a is not compatible with the R-12 refrigerant formerly used in most automobiles. Service equipment and/or air conditioning system components may be contaminated or damaged if the 2 refrigerants and oils are mixed. Never use a recovery system which was designed for and used to service R-12 equipped vehicles on a vehicle equipped with an R-134a air conditioning system.

2. Disconnect the negative battery cable and remove the air intake duct.

3. Raise and support the vehicle safely, then remove the front wheels.

4. Drain the engine cooling system and drain the crankcase of engine oil.

5. Disconnect the exhaust crossover pipe from the intermediate pipe.

6. If equipped with an automatic transmission, remove the converter cover, then remove the converter retaining bolts.

7. Remove the front facia lower deflectors from the vehicle.

8. Remove the stabilizer bar retaining bolts.

9. Remove the serpentine drive belt.

10. Remove the secondary air injection pump.

11. Disconnect the air conditioning hose assembly from the condenser and the compressor. Plug the openings to prevent system contamination and damage.

12. If equipped, disconnect the transmission fluid cooler lines from the radiator assembly. Plug the openings to prevent system contamination or excessive fluid loss.

13. Disconnect the lower radiator hose from the radiator and the lower heater hose from the water pump.

14. Remove the electrical ground straps from the right side of the engine block, then disengage the electrical wiring from the starter motor assembly.

15. Disengage the wiring harness connectors from the following sensor/switches:
- Knock sensor
- Oxygen sensor
- Coolant temperature sensor
- Wheel speed sensors
- Engine oil level switch
- Fuel pump switch/engine oil pressure gauge sensor assemblies

16. Remove the left front brake line from the caliper brake hose, then plug the openings to prevent system contamination or excessive fluid loss.

17. Remove the wiring harness and the shift linkage from the transmission assembly.

18. Matchmark, then remove the driveshaft assembly.

19. Remove the torque arm from the transmission.

20. Remove the intermediate shaft from the rack and pinion assembly.

21. Remove the electrical ground straps from the left side of the engine block and frame rail.

22. Lower the vehicle sufficiently for underhood access, then disconnect the fuel lines from the fuel rail.

23. Disconnect the cruise and accelerator cables from the throttle body assembly.

24. Disconnect the upper radiator hose, lower radiator hose and upper heater hose from the water pump assembly.

25. Disconnect the coolant air bleed pipe hose from the radiator assembly, then disconnect the brake booster vacuum hose.

26. Remove the alternator from the engine.

27. Disengage the engine wiring harness connectors, then position the harness aside.

28. Remove the air conditioning receiver and dehydrator hose from the condenser, then remove the hose from the expansion tube. Plug the openings to prevent system contamination and damage.

29. Remove the power steering reservoir from its mounting and reposition aside.

30. Remove and reposition the brake master cylinder.

31. Remove the upper bolts and nuts from the strut assemblies, then remove the right front brake line from the modulator valve assembly and clips.

32. Raise and support the vehicle safely, then position a lift table under the engine and engine frame assembly.

33. Remove the engine frame and transmission support bolts, then carefully lift the vehicle from the en-

gine, transmission and engine frame assembly. Raise the vehicle slowly, stopping a few times to assure that all wiring and hoses are disconnected and free of the powertrain and/or vehicle.

34. Secure the strut assemblies to the frame, then if applicable, remove the transmission TV cable from the throttle body.

35. Remove the transmission assembly.

36. If equipped with a manual transmission, remove the clutch housing and clutch assembly.

37. Remove the hose assemblies from the air conditioning compressor, then loosen the retainers and remove the compressor. Plug the openings to prevent system contamination and damage.

38. Remove the power steering lines from the pump assembly. Plug the openings to prevent system contamination or excessive fluid loss.

39. Remove the engine mount through-bolts, then remove the engine from the engine frame.

To install:

40. Install the engine assembly to the engine frame, then install and tighten the mount through-bolts to 70 ft. lbs. (95 Nm).

41. Uncap the openings, then connect the lines to the power steering pump assembly.

42. Install the air conditioning compressor and retainers, then uncap the openings and install the hose assemblies to the compressor.

43. If applicable, install the clutch housing and clutch assembly.

44. Install the transmission assembly, then if equipped with an automatic transmission, connect the TV cable to the throttle body.

45. Position the engine lift table under the vehicle, then align the strut assemblies and install the engine, transmission and engine frame to the vehicle.

46. Install the engine frame retaining bolts and tighten to 92 ft. lbs. (125 Nm), then remove the engine lift table and lower the vehicle as necessary for underhood access.

47. Install the upper strut assembly retaining bolts and nuts.

48. Install the right front brake line to the modulator valve assembly and clips, then reposition and secure the master cylinder.

49. Reposition and secure the power steering reservoir.

50. Unplug the openings and install the air conditioning hose to the expansion tube, then install the re-

ceiver and dehydrator hose to the condenser.

51. Engage the engine wiring harness connectors, then install the alternator.

52. Connect the brake booster vacuum hose.

53. Connect the coolant air bleed pipe hose to the radiator assembly.

54. Connect the upper heater hose, lower radiator hose and the upper radiator hose to the water pump assembly.

55. Connect the cruise and accelerator control cables to the throttle body.

56. Connect the fuel lines to the fuel rail assembly.

57. Raise and support the vehicle safely, then install the ground straps to the left side of the engine block and the frame rail.

58. Connect the starter motor wiring.

59. Connect the intermediate shaft to the rack and pinion assembly.

60. Install the torque arm to the transmission assembly.

61. Align the matchmarks and install the driveshaft.

62. Install the shift linkage to the transmission, then engage the transmission wiring harness.

63. Connect the left front brake line to the caliper brake hose.

64. Engage all switch and sensor electrical connectors which were disengaged to remove the engine frame and powertrain assembly.

65. Connect the lower heater hose to the water pump assembly and the lower radiator hose to the radiator.

66. If applicable, connect the transmission fluid cooler lines to the radiator.

67. Unplug the openings, then connect the air conditioning hose assembly to the condenser and compressor.

68. Install the secondary air injection pump assembly.

69. Install the serpentine drive belt.

70. Install the stabilizer bar bolts, then install the front facia lower deflectors.

71. If equipped with an automatic transmission, install the converter retaining bolts, then install the converter cover and bolts.

72. Connect the exhaust crossover pipe assembly to the intermediate pipe.

73. Bleed the hydraulic brake system, then install the wheels and lower the vehicle.

74. Fill the engine crankcase with oil and connect the negative battery cable.

75. Properly fill the engine cooling system, then charge the A/C system with R-134a.

76. Install the air intake duct and bleed the power steering system.

77. Check and adjust wheel alignment, as necessary.

Engine Mounts

REMOVAL AND INSTALLATION

3.1L Engine

1. Raise and support the vehicle safely.

2. Remove the engine mount through bolts and nuts.

3. Using a suitable engine lift, safely raise the front of the engine and remove the engine mount bolts, nuts and washers from the crossmember.

NOTE: Raise the engine only enough for sufficient clearance. Check for interference between the rear of the engine and the cowl panel which could cause distributor damage.

4. Remove the engine mount.

To install:

5. Install the engine bracket and mount. Tighten the crossmember-to-mount bolts to 30 ft. lbs. (41 Nm).

6. Carefully lower the engine and install the mount through bolts and nuts. Tighten the engine mount through-bolt nuts to 50 ft. lbs. (68 Nm).

7. Connect the negative battery cable.

5.0L and 5.7L (VIN 8) Engines

1. Raise and support the vehicle safely.

2. Support the engine with a suitable jack to unload the engine mount. Remove the engine mount retaining bolt from below the frame mounting bracket.

NOTE: Do not use a jack under the oil pan, crankshaft pulley or any sheetmetal when supporting the engine. Due to the small clearance between the oil pan and the oil pump screen, jacking against the oil pan may cause it to be bent against the pump screen, resulting in a damaged oil pickup.

3. Using a suitable engine lift, raise the front of the engine and remove the engine mount and bracket

bolts and nuts. Remove the engine mount.

NOTE: Raise the engine only enough for sufficient clearance. Check for interference between the rear of the engine and the cowl panel which could cause distributor damage.

To install:

4. Install the bracket to the block and the mount to the crossmember. Tighten the mount and bracket bolts to 38 ft. lbs. (52 Nm) and the mount and bracket nuts to 30 ft. lbs. (41 Nm).

5. Carefully lower the engine and install the bracket through bolts. Tighten the through bolt nut to 50 ft. lbs. (68 Nm).

6. Lower the vehicle.

3.4L and 5.7L (VIN P) Engines

1. Raise and support the vehicle safely.

2. Disconnect the exhaust crossover pipe.

3. Remove the engine mount through-bolts and nuts.

───── WARNING ─────
Never raise the engine using a jack under the oil pan, crankshaft pulley or any sheetmetal. Because there only is a small clearance between the oil pan and the oil pump screen, if the pan is bent even slightly, damage could occur to the pump screen and pickup unit.

4. Raise the engine using a jacking fixture.

5. Remove the engine mount-to-frame bolts and/or the engine mount bracket-to-engine bolts, as necessary.

To install:

6. If removed, install the engine mount brackets and/or the engine mounts. Tighten the retaining bolts to 43 ft. lbs. (58 Nm).

7. Lower the engine, then install the mount through-bolts.

8. Tighten either the nuts to 59 ft. lbs. (80 Nm) or the through-bolts to 70 ft. lbs. (95 Nm).

9. Connect the exhaust crossover pipe.

10. Lower the vehicle.

Cylinder Head

REMOVAL AND INSTALLATION

3.1L Engine

1. Disconnect the negative battery cable.

2. Relieve the fuel system pressure and drain the engine coolant from the radiator into a suitable container.

3. Remove the intake manifold, the spark plugs and the dipstick tube with bracket.

4. Raise and support the vehicle safely. Drain the oil and remove the oil filter. Lower the vehicle.

5. Remove the exhaust manifold.

6. Remove the serpentine drive belt. Remove the air conditioning compressor with bracket and lay aside.

7. Remove the power steering pump with bracket and/or the alternator with bracket and lay aside.

8. Remove the ground cable from the rear of the cylinder head and, if equipped, remove the engine lift bracket.

9. Loosen the rocker arms and remove the pushrods.

10. Remove the cylinder head bolts and remove the cylinder heads.

To install:

11. Clean the gasket mating surfaces of all components. Be careful not to nick or scratch any surfaces as this will allow leak paths. Clean the bolt threads in the cylinder block and on the head bolts. Dirt will affect bolt torque.

12. Place the head gaskets in position over the dowel pins, with the note "This Side Up" showing.

13. Install the cylinder heads.

14. Coat the cylinder head bolts threads with GM sealer 1052080 or equivalent, and install the bolts. Tighten the bolts in the proper sequence. Tighten the head bolts in 2 steps, first tighten to 40 ft. lbs. (55 Nm), then turn each bolt in sequence an additional 1/4 turn (90 degrees).

15. Install the pushrods and loosely retain them with the rocker arms. Make sure the lower ends of the pushrods are in the lifter seats.

16. Install the power steering pump bracket with pump, the air conditioning compressor bracket with compressor and/or the alternator with bracket.

17. Install the ground cable to the rear of the cylinder head, and if equipped, the engine lift bracket.

18. Install the exhaust manifold.

19. Install the dipstick tube and bracket.

20. Adjust the valve lash.

21. Install the intake manifold.

22. Install the serpentine drive belt.

23. Install the spark plugs.

24. Fill the cooling system with the proper type and quantity of coolant.

Cylinder head bolt torque sequence — 3.1L engine

Install a new oil filter and fill the crankcase with the proper type and quantity of oil.

25. Connect the negative battery cable, tighten the fuel filler cap, start the vehicle and check for leaks.

3.4L Engine

LEFT SIDE

1. Disconnect the negative battery cable, then raise and support the vehicle safely.
2. Drain the engine cooling system, then lower the vehicle.
3. Remove the intake manifold assembly.
4. Remove the left exhaust manifold assembly.
5. Remove the oil level indicator and tube.
6. Remove the serpentine drive belt.
7. Disengage the coolant temperature sensor connector
8. Tag and disengage the wires from the spark plugs, then remove the plugs from the left cylinder head.
9. Remove the engine lift bracket.
10. Remove the wiring harness clip from the rear of the cylinder head assembly.
11. Remove the secondary air injection pipe bracket bolt.
12. Remove the power steering pump assembly and brackets, then position aside with the hoses intact. Be careful not to kink and/or damage the hydraulic lines.
13. Loosen the rocker arm assemblies so the pushrods may be removed. Arrange or tag the pushrods to assure installation in their original locations.
14. Remove the cylinder head bolts, then remove the cylinder head and gasket from the engine.
   To install:
15. Thoroughly clean the gasket mating surfaces of any remaining gasket material, then position a new cylinder head gasket on the block.

16. Install the cylinder head over the locator pins and the new gasket.
17. Coat the bolt threads with sealant, then install the bolts finger-tight. Tighten the bolts in sequence to 41 ft. lbs. (55 Nm), then still in sequence, tighten all bolts an additional 90 degrees using a torque angle meter.
18. Install the pushrods and rocker arms, then adjust the valve lash.
19. Position and secure the power steering pump assembly and brackets.
20. Install the secondary air injection pipe bracket bolt.
21. Install and tighten the spark plugs, then connect the plug wires.
22. Install the wiring harness clip to the rear of the cylinder head assembly.
23. Install the engine lift bracket, then engage the coolant temperature sensor connector.
24. Install the serpentine drive belt.
25. Install the oil level indicator and tube.
26. Install the left exhaust manifold assembly.
27. Install the intake manifold assembly.
28. Connect the negative battery cable and fill the engine cooling system.

RIGHT SIDE

1. Disconnect the negative battery cable, then raise and support the vehicle safely.
2. Drain the engine cooling system, then lower the vehicle.
3. Loosen the serpentine drive belt and remove the tensioner assembly.
4. Remove the intake manifold assembly.
5. Remove the right exhaust manifold assembly.
6. Remove the alternator and brackets.
7. Tag and disengage the wires from the spark plugs, then remove the plugs from the right cylinder head.
8. Loosen the rocker arm assemblies so the pushrods may be removed. Arrange or tag the pushrods to assure installation in their original locations.
9. Remove the cylinder head bolts, then remove the cylinder head and gasket from the engine.
   To install:
10. Thoroughly clean the gasket mating surfaces of any remaining gasket material, then position a new cylinder head gasket on the block.
11. Install the cylinder head over the locator pins and the new gasket.

12. Coat the bolt threads with sealant, then install the bolts finger-tight. Tighten the bolts in sequence to 41 ft. lbs. (55 Nm), then still in sequence, tighten all bolts an additional 90 degrees using a torque angle meter.
13. Install the pushrods and rocker arms, then adjust the valve lash.
14. Install and tighten the spark plugs, then connect the plug wires.
15. Install the alternator and brackets.
16. Install the right exhaust manifold assembly.
17. Install the intake manifold assembly.
18. Install the serpentine drive belt tensioner and verify that the belt is properly routed.
19. Refill the engine cooling system.
20. Connect the negative battery cable.

5.0L and 5.7L (VIN 8) Engines

1. Disconnect the negative battery cable.
2. Drain the cooling system and relieve the fuel system pressure.
3. Remove the serpentine drive belt and the intake manifold.
4. Remove the power steering pump and alternator bracket or the air conditioning compressor mounting bracket, as necessary.
5. Remove the exhaust manifolds, the valve rocker covers and the ground strap.
6. Remove the rocker arms and pushrods.
7. Remove the diverter valve, if equipped.
8. Remove the cylinder head bolts, cylinder head and gasket.
   To install:
9. Clean the gasket mating surfaces of all components. Be careful not to nick or scratch any surfaces as this will allow leak paths. Clean the bolt threads in the cylinder block and on the head bolts. Dirt will affect bolt torque.

NOTE: When using a steel gasket, coat both sides of the new gasket with a thin even coat of sealer. If using a composition gasket, do not use any sealer.

10. Position the head gasket over the dowel pins with the head up. Install the cylinder head over the dowel pins and gasket.
11. Coat the threads of the head bolts with GM 1052080 thread sealer or equivalent. Install the head bolts and tighten in sequence to 68 ft. lbs. (92 Nm).
12. Install the exhaust manifolds.

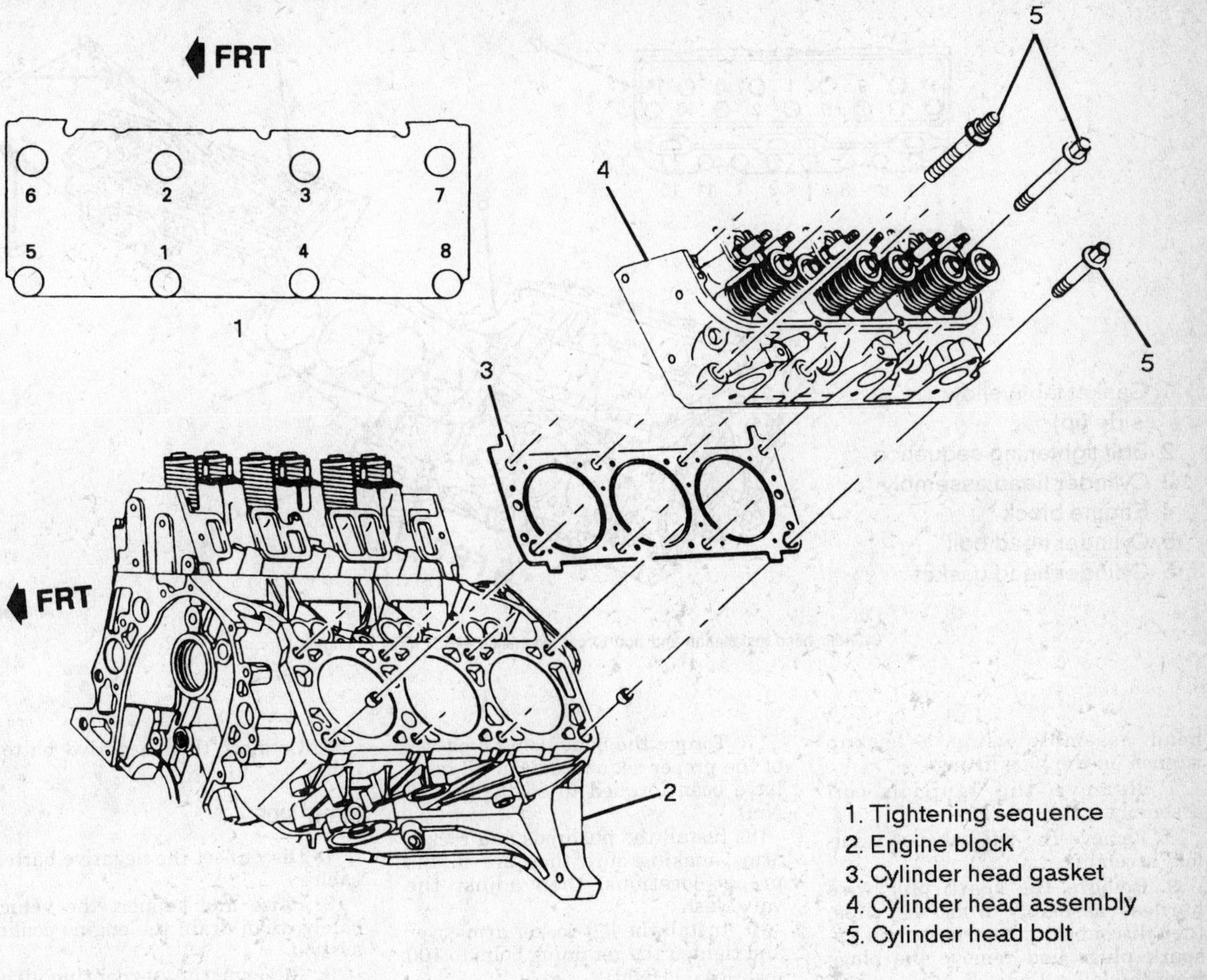

◀ FRT

1

1. Tightening sequence
2. Engine block
3. Cylinder head gasket
4. Cylinder head assembly
5. Cylinder head bolt

8470Q028

Cylinder head installation and bolt torque sequence — 3.4L engine

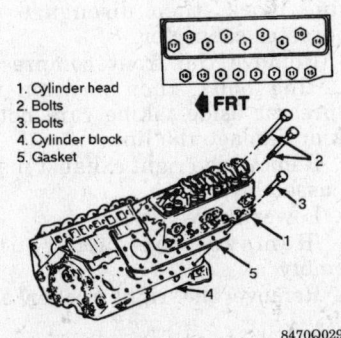

1. Cylinder head
2. Bolts
3. Bolts
4. Cylinder block
5. Gasket

◀ FRT

8470Q029

Cylinder head installation and bolt torque sequence — 5.0L and 5.7L (VIN 8) engines

13. Install the pushrods and rocker arms, then adjust the valve lash and install the valve covers.

14. Install the power steering pump and alternator bracket or air conditioning compressor mounting bracket, as necessary.

15. Connect the ground strap to the rear of the cylinder head.

16. Install the intake manifold and the serpentine drive belt.

17. Fill the cooling system with the proper type and amount of coolant.

18. Connect the negative battery cable and check fluid levels.

19. Start the engine, check for leaks and check the ignition timing.

5.7L (VIN P) Engine

LEFT SIDE

1. Disconnect the negative battery cable, then raise and support the vehicle safely.

2. Drain the engine cooling system, then disconnect the crossover pipe from the exhaust manifold.

3. Lower the vehicle.

4. Remove the intake manifold assembly.

5. Disconnect the secondary air injection hose from the check valve assembly.

6. Disconnect the coolant air bleed pipe and bolt from the left cylinder

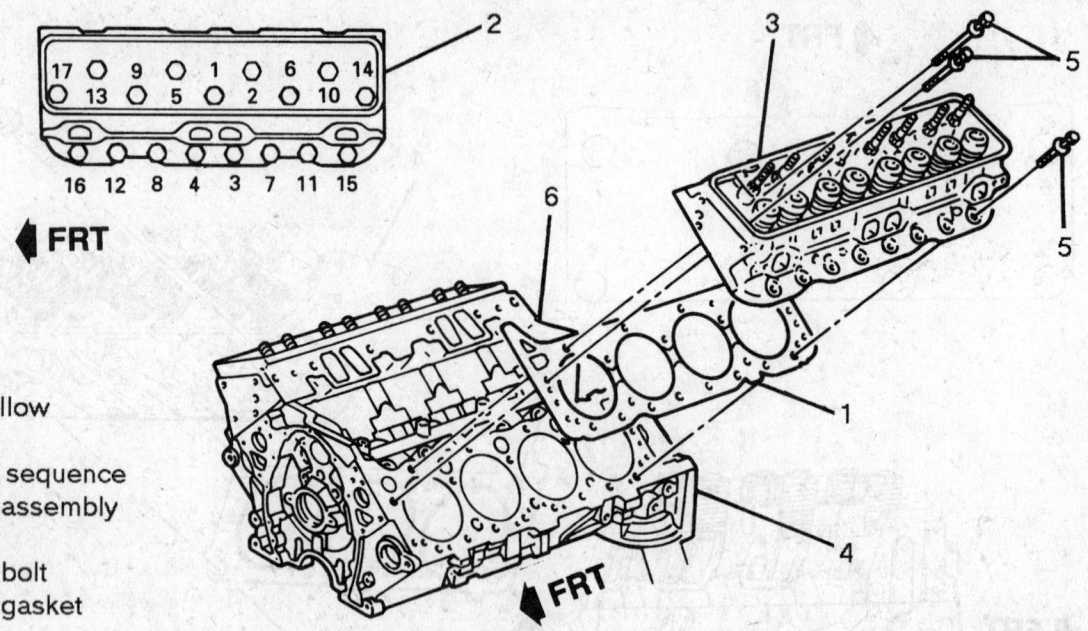

1. Gasket tab (yellow side up)
2. Bolt tightening sequence
3. Cylinder head assembly
4. Engine block
5. Cylinder head bolt
6. Cylinder head gasket

Cylinder head installation and bolt torque sequence — 5.7L (VIN P) engine

head assembly using a backup wrench on the pipe fitting.

7. Remove the ignition coil assembly.

8. Remove the left exhaust manifold assembly.

9. Remove the spark plug wire harness assembly from the clips, then disconnect the harness from the spark plugs and remove the plugs from the left cylinder head.

10. Disengage the coolant temperature sensor connector.

11. Remove the left rocker arm cover.

12. Loosen the rocker arm nuts, then remove the arms and pushrods, either tagging or arranging the components to assure installation in their original locations.

13. Remove the cylinder head bolts, then remove the cylinder head and old gasket from the block.

To install:

14. Thoroughly clean the gasket mating surfaces of any remaining gasket material, then position a new cylinder head gasket on the block with the yellow tab facing upwards.

15. Install the cylinder head over the locator pins and the new gasket.

16. Coat the cylinder head bolts with a sealing compound, then install the bolts finger-tight.

17. Torque the bolts using 3 passes of the proper sequence until all bolts have been torqued to 65 ft. lbs. (88 Nm).

18. Install the pushrods and rocker arms, making sure they are in the proper locations, then adjust the valve lash.

19. Install the left rocker arm cover and tighten the retaining bolts to 100 inch lbs. (11 Nm).

20. Install the spark plugs and tighten to 11 ft. lbs. (15 Nm), then install the wiring harness assembly and secure the assembly to the clips.

21. Install the left exhaust manifold assembly.

22. Install the ignition coil assembly and tighten the bolts to 24 ft. lbs. (33 Nm).

23. Connect the engine coolant air bleed pipe and bolt to the left cylinder head assembly using a backup wrench on the pipe fitting in order to prevent component damage. Tighten the bolt to 30 ft. lbs. (40 Nm).

24. Install the secondary air injector hose to the check valve assembly.

25. Install the intake manifold assembly.

26. Raise and support the vehicle safely, then connect the crossover pipe to the exhaust manifold.

27. Lower the vehicle and fill the engine cooling system.

28. Connect then negative battery cable.

RIGHT SIDE

1. Disconnect the negative battery cable.

2. Raise and support the vehicle safely, then drain the engine cooling system.

3. Remove the serpentine drive belt and the belt tensioner assembly.

4. Remove the transmission fluid level indicator tube assembly bracket from the transmission housing.

5. Remove the air conditioning compressor rear brace bolt from the engine block, then disengage the compressor connector.

6. Remove the front compressor mounting bolts, then position the compressor aside taking care not to kink or damage the lines.

7. Remove the right exhaust manifold assembly.

8. Lower the vehicle.

9. Remove the alternator assembly.

10. Remove the right rocker arm cover.

11. Remove the intake manifold assembly.

12. Remove the coolant air bleed pipe bolt from the left cylinder head assembly.

13. Disconnect the lower radiator hose and the heater hose from the water pump assembly, then position the hoses aside.

14. Remove the coolant air bleed pipe hose from the radiator.

15. Remove the power steering pump assembly.

16. Remove the engine accessory bracket bolts, then remove the bracket assembly.

17. Disconnect the wire harness assembly from the spark plugs, then remove the plugs from the right cylinder head.

18. Loosen the rocker arm nuts, then remove the arms and pushrods, either tagging or arranging the components to assure installation in their original locations.

19. Remove the cylinder head bolts, then remove the cylinder head and old gasket from the block. If necessary, carefully remove the coolant air bleed pipe bolt and pipe assembly from the cylinder head.

To install:

20. If removed, loosely install the coolant air bleed pipe bolt and pipe to the cylinder head.

21. Thoroughly clean the gasket mating surfaces of any remaining gasket material, then position a new cylinder head gasket on the block with the yellow tab facing upwards.

22. Install the cylinder head over the locator pins and the new gasket.

23. Coat the cylinder head bolts with a sealing compound, then install the bolts finger-tight.

24. Torque the bolts using 3 passes of the proper sequence until all bolts have been torqued to 65 ft. lbs. (88 Nm).

25. If loosened, tighten the coolant air bleed pipe bolt to 30 ft. lbs. (40 Nm).

26. Install the pushrods and rocker arms, making sure they are in the proper locations, then adjust the valve lash.

27. Install the spark plugs and tighten to 11 ft. lbs. (15 Nm), then install the wiring harness assembly to the plugs.

28. Install the engine accessory bracket and tighten the retaining bolts to 31 ft. lbs. (42 Nm).

29. Install the right rocker arm cover and tighten the retaining bolts to 100 inch lbs. (11 Nm).

30. Install the alternator assembly.

31. Install the power steering pump assembly.

32. Connect the coolant air bleed pipe hose to the radiator, then connect the heater hose and the lower radiator hose to the water pump.

33. Connect the coolant air bleed pipe bolt to the left cylinder head and tighten to 30 ft. lbs. (41 Nm) while using a backup wrench to prevent component damage.

34. Install the intake manifold assembly.

35. Raise and support the vehicle safely.

36. Install the right exhaust manifold assembly.

37. Position the compressor and install the front mounting bolts, then engage the electrical connector. Install the rear compressor brace bolt and tighten to 24 ft. lbs. (33 Nm).

38. Install the transmission fluid level indicator tube assembly to the transmission housing.

39. Install the serpentine drive belt, then lower the vehicle.

40. Fill the engine cooling system, then connect the negative battery cable.

Valve Lifters

REMOVAL AND INSTALLATION

3.1L and 3.4L Engines

1. Disconnect the negative battery cable.

2. Remove the intake manifold assembly.

3. Remove the rocker arms and pushrods. Be sure to tag or arrange all valve train components to assure installation in their original locations.

4. Remove the valve lifter assemblies from their bores. Be sure to tag or arrange the lifters for installation purposes.

To install:

NOTE: If lifters are replaced, be sure to use replacements that contain a narrow flat ground along the lower ¾ of the lifter. The flat is designed to provide additional oil to the cam lobe and lifter surfaces. Also, pay close attention to any lifter bores which may be marked indicating an oversized lifter. If an oversize lifter was used, the bore should be marked "0.25" and/or "O.S." in order to indicate that a .010 in. (0.25mm) oversize lifter was installed in that bore.

5. Coat the lifters using Molykote® or an equivalent prelube, then install the lifters into the bores. If lifters are being reused, they must be installed in their original bores.

6. Install the pushrods and the rocker arms, then adjust the valve lash.

7. Install the intake manifold.

8. Connect the negative battery cable.

5.0L and 5.7L Engines

1. Disconnect the negative battery cable.

2. Remove the intake manifold assembly.

3. Remove the valve rocker arm covers

4. Remove the rocker arms and pushrods. Be sure to tag or arrange all valve train components to assure installation in their original locations.

5. Remove the bolts securing the lifter retainer to the block, then remove the retainer.

6. Remove the valve lifter guides and lifters from the engine block. If a lifter remains stuck in a bore, use a suitable lifter removal tool, being careful not to score the lifter surface or the lifter bore. Tag or arrange the lifters and guides for installation in their original positions.

To install:

7. Coat the lifters with Molykote® or its equivalent before installation. If installing the old lifters, make certain each lifter is inserted into the same lifter bore from which it was removed.

8. Install the valve lifter guides and the lifter guide retainers, then tighten the bolts to 15 ft. lbs. (20 Nm).

9. Install the pushrods and rocker arms, then adjust the valve lash.

10. Install the valve rocker covers.

11. Install the intake manifold assembly.

12. Connect the negative battery cable.

Valve Lash

The valve lash on these engines must be adjusted whenever the rocker arm assemblies have been removed.

NOTE: These engines utilize hydraulic lifters which normally require very little maintenance or adjustment. These components are simple in design and are best maintained through regular, scheduled engine oil changes. If the engine is running well and no audible clicking sounds are heard from the valve train, there is no need to remove or disassemble the valve lifters.

ADJUSTMENT

1. Disconnect the negative battery cable.
2. Remove the valve rocker covers.
3. Tighten the nuts slowly until all lash is eliminated.
4. Adjust the valves when the lifter is on the base circle of the camshaft lobe. Slowly turn or crank the engine until the mark on the vibration damper is in the 12 o'clock position (aligned with the timing cover 0 or pointer mark, if equipped) and the engine is in the No. 1 firing position.

NOTE: The No. 1 firing position may be determined by watching the No. 1 cylinder valves as the mark on the damper approaches the 12 o'clock position. If both the intake and exhaust valves are closed as the mark comes up to the timing tab, the engine is in the No. 1 firing position. If either valve opens as the timing mark approaches the top of it's travel, the engine is in the No. 6 firing position on the V8 engine or No. 4 firing position on the V6 engine and should be turned 1 full turn to reach to No. 1 firing position.

5. With the engine in the No. 1 firing position, adjust the following valves:
   a. V8 engine — Exhaust — 1, 3, 4, 8
   b. V8 engine — Intake — 1, 2, 5, 7
   c. V6 engine — Exhaust — 1, 2, 3
   d. V6 engine — Intake — 1, 5, 6
6. Back out the rocker arm adjusting nut until lash is felt at the pushrod, then turn the adjusting nut inward until all lash is removed. This can be determined by rotating pushrod while turning the adjusting nut. When play has been removed, the pushrod will not turn. Then, tighten the adjusting nut 1 full additional turn for V8 engines or 1½ additional turns for V6 engines.
7. Slowly turn or crank the engine 1 revolution until the vibration damper mark is at 12 o'clock again and the No. 1 cylinder valves open. This is the No. 6 firing position the No. 6 firing position on V8 engines or the No. 4 firing position on V6 engines.
8. With the engine in this position, adjust the following valves:
   a. V8 engine — Exhaust — 2, 5, 6, 7

   b. V8 engine — Intake — 3, 4, 6, 8
   c. V6 engine — Exhaust — 4, 5, 6
   d. V6 engine — Intake — 2, 3, 4
9. Install the valve covers and connect the negative battery cable.
10. Start the engine and check for proper operation. For 1992 vehicles, check and adjust the timing, as required. For the 3.1L engine, check and adjust the idle speed, only if required.

Rocker Arms/Shafts

REMOVAL AND INSTALLATION

3.1L Engine

1. Disconnect the negative battery cable.
2. For left side valve cover removal proceed as follows:
   a. Remove the accessory drive belt.
   b. Remove the intake plenum and throttle body assembly.
   c. Remove the center intake manifold.
   d. Remove the transmission dipstick, if required.
   e. Remove the air management hose and air conditioning bracket, if equipped.
   f. Remove the valve cover reinforcements and nuts.
3. For right side valve cover removal proceed as follows:
   a. Remove the EGR valve adapter with the EGR valve and shield from the exhaust manifold.
   b. Remove the coil and coil mounting bracket from the cylinder head.
   c. Disconnect the crankcase vent pipe.
   d. Remove the intake plenum and throttle body assembly.
   e. Remove the center intake manifold.
   f. Disconnect the spark plug wire clips, if applicable.
   g. Remove the valve cover reinforcements and nuts.
4. Remove the valve cover by hand. Only if necessary, carefully pry until loose while being careful not to distort the sealing flange.
5. Remove the rocker arm nuts, rocker arm balls, rocker arms and pushrods. Tag or place the components in a rack for installation in the same location.
   To install:
6. Install the pushrods and rocker arm assemblies in their original positions and adjust as necessary. If new

rocker arms and/or balls are being used, coat bearing surfaces with Molykote® or its equivalent.
7. Carefully clean all gasket mating surfaces and make sure the valve cover flanges are not bent.
8. Place a ⅛ inch bead of RTV sealant 1052751 or equivalent at the intake manifold and cylinder head splitline. Install the new valve cover gasket over the studs in the manifold and cylinder head.
9. Install the valve covers, reinforcements and nuts. Tighten the nuts to 10 ft. lbs. or 120 inch lbs. (14 Nm).
10. Install components to the valve cover in reverse order of removal, as applicable.
11. Connect the negative battery cable.

3.4L Engine

1. Disconnect the negative battery cable.
2. Remove the upper intake manifold:
   a. Drain the engine cooling system and relieve the fuel system pressure, then remove the throttle body air duct.
   b. Disengage the fuel rail injector wiring harness connectors, then remove the wiring harness retaining nut and position the harness aside.
   c. Remove the accelerator cable bracket bolts, then remove the bracket and cables from the throttle body.
   d. Disengage the fuel pipe connectors, remove the pipe bracket bolts and the pipe hold-down plate bolts, then remove and reposition the fuel pipe assembly.
   e. Disconnect the coolant hoses from the throttle body.
   f. Remove the fuel rail stud, then disconnect the pressure regulator vacuum hose.
   g. Disengage the electrical connectors from the IAC valve, TP sensor, MAP sensor and EVAP canister purge solenoid.
   h. Using compressed air and safety glasses, blow any dirt which may be present out of the injector bores, then remove the fuel rail assembly.
   i. Remove the vacuum harness assembly, then remove the EGR flexible pipe bolts and reposition the pipe and gasket at the upper intake manifold assembly.
   j. Remove the bolts retaining the upper manifold, then remove the manifold and gasket from the vehicle.

1. Lower intake manifold assembly
2. Upper intake manifold gasket
3. Upper intake manifold assembly
4. Upper intake manifold bolt

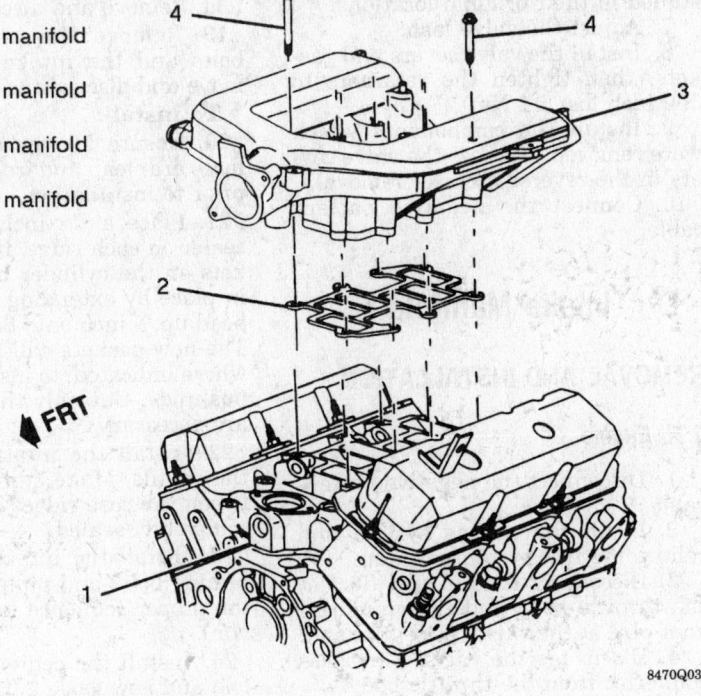

◄ FRT

8470Q032

Upper intake manifold removal — 3.4L engine

3. To remove the left valve cover:

a. Remove the PCV valve and hose assembly.

b. Remove the spark plug wire harness assembly from the clips.

c. Remove the nuts and reinforcements, then remove the valve cover and gasket.

4. To remove the right valve cover:

a. Remove the bolts, stud and EGR valve adapter along with the EGR valve assembly from the exhaust manifold.

b. Remove the crankcase vent pipe.

c. Remove the spark plug wire harness assembly from the clips.

d. Remove the nuts and reinforcements, then remove the valve cover and gasket.

5. Remove the valve rocker arm nuts and balls, then remove the rocker arms and pushrods. Tag or arrange all valve train components to assure installation in their original locations.

To install:

6. Coat the bearing surfaces of the rocker arms, balls and pushrods with prelube.

7. Install the pushrods, making sure they are properly seated in the lifter sockets, then install the rocker arms, balls and nuts. If components

are being reused, be sure they are installed in their original locations.

8. Adjust the valve lash.

9. Install the gaskets, valve covers and reinforcements. Tighten the cover retaining nuts to 89 inch lbs.

10. Install the components removed to access the valve covers in the reverse order of removal.

11. Install the upper intake manifold assembly:

a. Position the upper intake manifold and gasket, then install the retaining bolts and tighten to 18 ft. lbs. (25 Nm).

b. Install the EGR flexible pipe gasket and pipe assembly, making sure the gasket is installed with the writing TUBE SIDE facing the tube. Apply teflon sealant to the threads of the bolts, then install them and tighten to 19 ft. lbs. (26 Nm).

c. Install the vacuum harness assembly.

d. Lubricate the fuel injector O-rings using clean engine oil, then install the injectors into the manifold bore. Carefully press on the fuel rail assembly using the palms of both hands until the injectors are fully seated. Install the fuel rail retaining stud and tighten to 19 ft. lbs. (25 Nm).

e. Engage the wiring harness connectors to the IAC valve, TP sensor, MAP sensor and EVAP canister purge solenoid.

f. Connect the pressure regulator vacuum hose, then install the wiring harness retaining nut.

g. Engage the fuel pipe assembly to the fuel rail, sliding the fuel line hold-down plate over the pipe assembly. Apply teflon sealant to the hold-down plate bolt threads, then install the bolt and tighten to 18 ft. lbs. (25 Nm).

h. Install the fuel pipe bracket bolts, then position the accelerator cable bracket, bolts and cables. Tighten the cable bracket bolts to 90 inch lbs. (10 Nm), then tighten the front fuel pipe bracket bolt to 71 inch lbs. (8 Nm) and the rear bracket-to-intake bolt to 89 inch lbs. (10 Nm).

i. Engage the fuel pipe connectors.

j. Engage the fuel rail injector wiring harness connectors.

k. Connect the coolant hoses to the throttle body, then install the air duct.

l. Connect the negative battery cable and refill the engine cooling system

5.0L and 5.7L (VIN 8) Engines

1. Disconnect the negative battery cable.

2. If necessary remove the air cleaner.

3. To remove the right side valve rocker cover, perform the following:

a. Remove the EGR pipe assembly, if necessary.

b. Disconnect the electrical connections and wiring harnesses as necessary.

c. Disconnect the spark plug wires from the distributor.

d. Remove the crankcase vent hoses and valves.

e. Remove the coil and disconnect the heater hose from the throttle body, if applicable.

f. Remove the AIR control valve, check valve, pipes and hoses.

g. Remove the valve rocker cover bolts, washers and the valve rocker cover. Discard the old gasket.

4. To remove the left side valve rocker cover, perform the following:

a. Disconnect the electrical connections and the wiring harnesses, as necessary.

b. Remove the alternator and disconnect the crankcase hoses and the PCV valve.

c. Remove the valve rocker cover bolts, washers and the valve rocker cover. Discard the old gasket.

5. Remove the rocker arm balls, arms and pushrods. Tag or arrange them in a rack so they may be reinstalled in the same location.

To install:

6. Install the pushrods and rocker arm assemblies in their original positions and adjust as necessary. If new rocker arms and/or balls are being used, coat bearing surfaces with Molykote® or its equivalent.

7. Carefully clean all gasket mating surfaces and make sure the valve cover flanges are not bent.

8. Install the new valve rocker cover gasket to the cylinder head.

9. Install the valve rocker covers, washers and bolts. Tighten the bolts to 96 inch lbs. (11 Nm).

10. Install components to the valve rocker cover in reverse order of removal, as applicable.

11. Connect the negative battery cable.

5.7L (VIN P) Engine

1. Disconnect the negative battery cable.

2. Remove the left valve cover:

a. Remove the brake booster vacuum hose.

b. Remove the secondary AIR injection hose from the pump to check valve assembly.

c. Remove the valve cover retaining bolts, then remove the cover and gasket.

3. Remove the right valve cover:

a. Raise and support the vehicle safely, then remove the serpentine drive belt.

b. Remove the transmission fluid level indicator tube assembly from the bracket on the transmission housing.

c. Lower the vehicle, then remove the crankcase vent hose.

d. Remove the alternator and rear alternator brace.

e. Remove the valve cover retaining bolts, then remove the cover and gasket.

4. Remove the valve rocker arm nuts and balls, then remove the rocker arms and pushrods. Tag or arrange all valve train components to assure installation in their original locations.

To install:

5. Coat the bearing surfaces of the rocker arms, balls and pushrods with prelube.

6. Install the pushrods, making sure they are properly seated in the lifter sockets, then install the rocker

arms, balls and nuts. If components are being reused, be sure they are installed in their original locations.

7. Adjust the valve lash.

8. Install the valve covers and gaskets, then tighten the retainers to 100 inch lbs. (11 Nm).

9. Install the components which were removed to access the valve covers in the reverse order of removal.

10. Connect the negative battery cable.

Intake Manifold

REMOVAL AND INSTALLATION

3.1L Engine

1. Disconnect the negative battery cable.

2. Drain the cooling system and relieve the fuel system pressure.

3. Disconnect the air inlet duct at the throttle body and the crankcase vent pipe at the valve cover grommet.

4. Disengage the vacuum harness connector from the throttle body.

5. Remove the throttle cable bracket bolt, the throttle body attaching bolts and remove the throttle body. Discard the throttle body gasket.

6. Remove the EGR transfer tube to plenum bolts and remove the EGR transfer tube. Discard the EGR transfer tube gasket.

7. Remove the air conditioning compressor to plenum bracket attaching hardware and the bracket.

8. Remove the plenum bolts/studs and the plenum. Discard the plenum gaskets.

9. Disconnect the fuel feed and return lines at the fuel rail. Discard the fuel line O-rings.

10. Disconnect the vacuum line at the pressure regulator and the injector electrical connectors.

11. Remove the fuel rail attaching bolts and the fuel rail assembly.

12. Remove the spark plug wires and the distributor cap. Mark the distributor position and remove the hold-down bracket and the distributor.

13. If equipped, remove the air management hose and bracket.

14. Disconnect the emission canister hoses.

15. Remove the valve covers.

16. Remove the upper radiator hose at the manifold and disconnect the heater hose.

17. Disconnect the coolant switch sensors. Remove the transmission dipstick.

18. Remove the center intake manifold bolts and the center intake manifold. Remove and discard the gasket.

19. Remove the intake manifold bolts and the intake manifold. Remove and discard the gasket.

To install:

20. Ensure all gasket mating surfaces are clean and free of oil or water prior to installation.

21. Place a $3/16$ inch bead of RTV sealer on each ridge. Install new gaskets on the cylinder heads and hold in place by extending the ridge RTV bead up $1/4$ inch onto the gasket ends. The new gaskets will have to be cut, where indicated, to install behind the pushrods. Cut only those areas that are necessary.

22. Install the intake manifold on the engine. Make sure the areas between the case ridges and intake are completely sealed.

23. Install the intake manifold retaining bolts and nuts and torque in the proper sequence to 19 ft. lbs. (26 Nm).

24. Install the center intake manifold and new gasket. Tighten bolts to 15 ft. lbs. (21 Nm).

25. Install the upper radiator hose and the valve covers and connect the heater hose and the coolant switch sensors.

26. Install the distributor, distributor cap and spark plug wires. Install the air management hose and bracket, if equipped.

27. Install the fuel rail assembly in the intake manifold. Tighten the attaching bolts to 18 ft. lbs. (25 Nm). Connect the injector electrical connectors and the vacuum line to the pressure regulator.

28. Install new O-rings on the fuel feed and return lines and connect the lines to the fuel rail. Tighten the fuel line nuts to 20 ft. lbs. (27 Nm).

29. Temporarily connect the negative battery cable. Turn the ignition switch to the **ON** position for 2 seconds, **OFF** for 10 seconds, then to the **ON** position and check for fuel leaks. Disconnect the negative battery cable.

30. Install the plenum with a new gasket and install the bolts/studs. Tighten to 15 ft. lbs. (21 Nm).

31. Install the air conditioning compressor to plenum bracket and attaching hardware. Install the EGR transfer tube with a new gasket. Tighten the attaching bolts to 19 ft. lbs. (26 Nm).

32. Install the throttle body with a new gasket and tighten the retaining bolts to 20 ft. lbs. (27 Nm).

33. Install the throttle cable bracket bolts and connect the vacuum harness connector to the throttle body.

34. Connect the air inlet duct to the throttle body and the crankcase vent pipe to the valve cover grommet.

35. Install the transmission dipstick and connect the necessary wires and hoses.

36. Connect the negative battery cable.

37. Fill the cooling system with the proper type and amount of coolant. Do not install the radiator cap.

38. Let the engine run until the upper radiator hose becomes hot (thermostat open). With the engine idling, add coolant to the radiator, if necessary, until the level reaches the bottom of the filler neck. Install the radiator cap, making sure the arrows on the cap line with the overflow tube.

39. Check and adjust the timing as necessary.

3.4L Engine

1. Disconnect the negative battery cable.

2. Remove the upper intake manifold:

a. Drain the engine cooling system and relieve the fuel system pressure, then remove the throttle body air duct.

b. Disengage the fuel rail injector wiring harness connectors, then remove the wiring harness retaining nut and position the harness aside.

c. Remove the accelerator cable bracket bolts, then remove the bracket and cables from the throttle body.

d. Disengage the fuel pipe connectors, remove the pipe bracket bolts and the pipe hold-down plate bolts, then remove and reposition the fuel pipe assembly.

e. Disconnect the coolant hoses from the throttle body.

f. Remove the fuel rail stud, then disconnect the pressure regulator vacuum hose.

g. Disengage the electrical connectors from the IAC valve, TP sensor, MAP sensor and EVAP canister purge solenoid.

h. Using compressed air and safety glasses, blow any dirt which may be present out of the injector bores, then remove the fuel rail assembly.

i. Remove the vacuum harness assembly, then remove the EGR flexible pipe bolts and reposition the pipe and gasket at the upper intake manifold assembly.

j. Remove the bolts retaining the upper manifold, then remove the manifold and gasket from the vehicle.

3. To remove the left valve cover:

a. Remove the PCV valve and hose assembly.

b. Remove the spark plug wire harness assembly from the clips.

c. Remove the nuts and reinforcements, then remove the valve cover and gasket.

4. To remove the right valve cover:

a. Remove the bolts, stud and EGR valve adapter along with the EGR valve assembly from the exhaust manifold.

b. Remove the crankcase vent pipe.

c. Remove the spark plug wire harness assembly from the clips.

d. Remove the nuts and reinforcements, then remove the valve cover and gasket.

5. Disconnect the upper radiator hose and the heater hose from the intake manifold assembly.

6. Disconnect the wiring harness ground leads.

7. Remove the bolts and nuts retaining the intake manifold, then remove the intake manifold assembly and gaskets.

To install:

8. Thoroughly clean the mating surfaces of any remaining gasket material.

9. Position the intake manifold gaskets to the engine, then apply a bead of sealant at the block-to-manifold mating surfaces. The bead should be 0.08–0.012 in. (2–3mm) wide and 0.12–0.20 in. (3–5mm) thick.

10. Install the intake manifold over the gaskets, then secure using the bolts and nuts. Tighten the intake manifold fasteners to 22 ft. lbs. (30 Nm).

11. Connect the wiring harness ground leads.

12. Connect the heater and upper radiator hoses to the manifold.

13. Install the gaskets, valve covers and reinforcements. Tighten the cover retaining nuts to 89 inch lbs.

14. Install the components removed to access the valve covers in the reverse order of removal.

15. Install the upper intake manifold assembly:

a. Position the upper intake manifold and gasket, then install the retaining bolts and tighten to 18 ft. lbs. (25 Nm).

b. Install the EGR flexible pipe gasket and pipe assembly, making sure the gasket is installed with

the writing TUBE SIDE facing the tube. Apply teflon sealant to the threads of the bolts, then install them and tighten to 19 ft. lbs. (26 Nm).

c. Install the vacuum harness assembly.

d. Lubricate the fuel injector O-rings using clean engine oil, then install the injectors into the manifold bore. Carefully press on the fuel rail assembly using the palms of both hands until the injectors are fully seated. Install the fuel rail retaining stud and tighten to 19 ft. lbs. (25 Nm).

e. Engage the wiring harness connectors to the IAC valve, TP sensor, MAP sensor and EVAP canister purge solenoid.

f. Connect the pressure regulator vacuum hose, then install the wiring harness retaining nut.

g. Engage the fuel pipe assembly to the fuel rail, sliding the fuel line hold-down plate over the pipe assembly. Apply teflon sealant to the hold-down plate bolt threads, then install the bolt and tighten to 18 ft. lbs. (25 Nm).

h. Install the fuel pipe bracket bolts, then position the accelerator cable bracket, bolts and cables. Tighten the cable bracket bolts to 90 inch lbs. (10 Nm), then tighten the front fuel pipe bracket bolt to 71 inch lbs. (8 Nm) and the rear bracket-to-intake bolt to 89 inch lbs. (10 Nm).

i. Engage the fuel pipe connectors.

j. Engage the fuel rail injector wiring harness connectors.

k. Connect the coolant hoses to the throttle body, then install the air duct.

l. Connect the negative battery cable and refill the engine cooling system

5.0L (VIN E) TBI Engine

1. Disconnect the negative battery cable.

2. Drain the radiator, relieve the fuel system pressure and remove the air cleaner.

3. Disengage the electrical connectors to the IAC valve, TPS and fuel injectors. Remove the injector wiring harness. Tag and disconnect the vacuum hoses, remove the vacuum hose bracket. Disconnect all wires and hoses as necessary.

4. Disconnect the throttle, transmission control and cruise control cables. Disconnect the fuel feed and return lines and discard the O-rings.

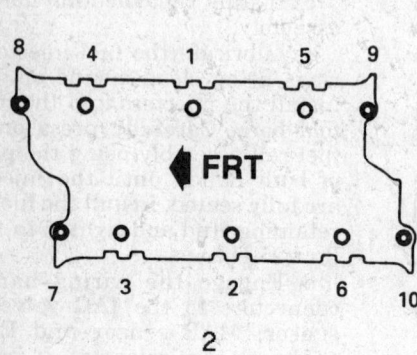

1. Apply sealant
2. Tightening sequence
3. Cylinder head assembly
4. Cylinder head stud
5. Lower intake manifold gasket
6. Lower intake manifold assembly
7. Lower intake manifold nut
8. Lower intake manifold bolt

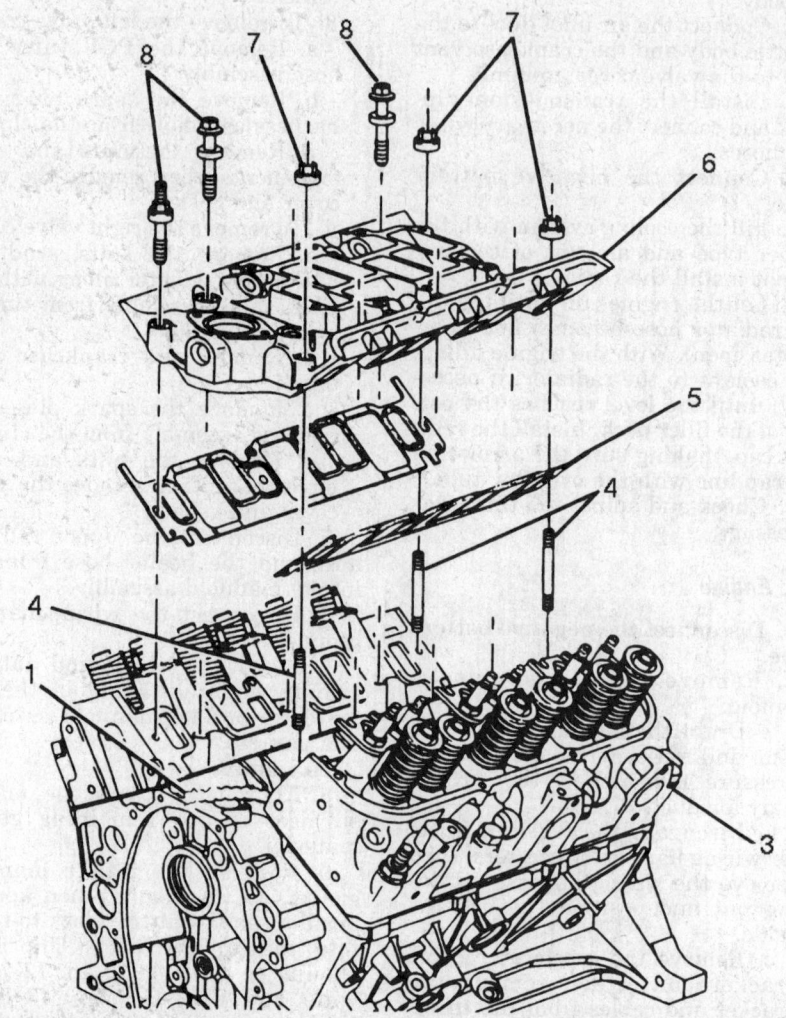

8470Q033

Intake manifold installation and bolt torque sequence — 3.4L engine shown (3.1L engine uses same torque sequence)

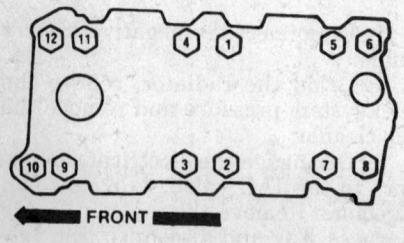

8470Q034

Intake manifold bolt torque sequence — V8 engines

5. Remove the TBI unit attaching bolts and remove the TBI unit. Discard the old gasket.

6. Disconnect the ECM engine control harness and lay aside. Disconnect the upper radiator hose and heater hose at the manifold. Remove the EGR valve and solenoid and remove the thermostat housing and gasket.

7. Disconnect the fuel line clips and lines at the cylinder head and intake manifold. Disconnect the power brake vacuum pipe at the manifold.

8. Disconnect the throttle cable bracket.

9. Disconnect and tag the spark plug wires at the distributor cap and remove the distributor cap. Mark the position of the rotor and the distributor housing and remove the distributor.

10. Remove the external coil and the coolant temperature sensor.

11. Remove the intake manifold bolts and studs and remove the intake manifold.

To install:

12. Clean all gasket mating surfaces with degreaser and remove all loose RTV.

13. Install the gaskets on the cylinder heads. Apply a 3/16 inch bead of RTV sealant on the front and rear of

the cylinder block. Extend the bead ½ inch up each cylinder head to seal and retain the intake manifold gaskets.

14. Install the intake manifold and tighten the bolts and studs in the proper 2-step sequence in order to obtain proper seal. On the first pass tighten the bolts and studs to 89 inch lbs. (10 Nm). For the final pass, tighten the bolts and studs to 35 ft. lbs. (47 Nm).

15. Install the ECM engine control harness and the coolant temperature sensor.

16. Align the rotor with the mark and install the distributor. Temporarily tighten the hold-down clamp retaining bolt. Install the distributor cap, coil and spark plug wires.

17. Install the throttle cable bracket. Connect the fuel line clips and lines to the cylinder head and intake manifold. Connect the power brake vacuum pipe at the manifold.

18. Connect any remaining wires and hoses. Install the EGR valve and solenoid, the thermostat, housing and gasket, and the heater and radiator hoses.

19. Install the throttle body unit and a new gasket. Tighten the TBI attaching bolts to 16 ft. lbs. (22 Nm).

20. Install new O-rings on the fuel lines and connect the fuel feed and return lines. Tighten the fuel line nuts to 20 ft. lbs. (27 Nm). Connect the vacuum hoses and bracket.

21. Connect the throttle, transmission control and cruise control cables, as applicable. Make sure the throttle and cruise control cables do not hold the throttle open.

22. Connect the injectors wiring harness. Connect any remaining electrical connectors.

23. Add the proper type and amount of engine coolant, tighten the fuel filler cap and connect the negative battery cable.

24. Start the engine, check for leaks, check and adjust timing as necessary. If no timing adjustment is necessary, make sure the hold-down clamp retaining bolt is tightened to specification.

5.0L (VIN F) and 5.7L (VIN 8) Engines

1. Disconnect the negative battery cable.

2. Drain the cooling system and relieve the fuel system pressure.

3. Disconnect the accelerator, TV and cruise control cables.

4. Remove the air intake duct.

5. Disconnect the heater hoses at the throttle body.

6. Disengage the electrical connections at the throttle body and the intake manifold.

7. Disconnect the vacuum hoses and vent valve assembly.

8. Disconnect the fuel lines.

9. Disconnect the vapor pipe assembly.

10. Remove the plenum extension.

11. Remove the spark plug wires from the distributor cap. Mark the position of the rotor and the distributor housing and remove the distributor.

12. Remove the throttle body attaching bolts and remove the throttle body. Discard the old gasket.

13. Disconnect the wiring harness from the fuel injectors and remove the harness from the manifold.

14. Disconnect the power brake vacuum hose at the plenum.

15. Remove the intake plenum bolts and disconnect the Manifold Absolute Pressure (MAP) sensor, if equipped.

16. Lift the plenum and disconnect the Manifold Air Temperature (MAT) sensor electrical connector, if equipped.

17. Remove the plenum and discard the plenum gaskets.

18. Remove the runner to manifold bolts, PCV valve and hose, EGR solenoid and the left and right side runners and gaskets. Discard the gaskets.

19. Remove the upper radiator hose. Remove the fuel tube bracket bolt. Disconnect the fuel feed and return lines. Discard the fuel line O-rings.

20. Disconnect the vacuum line at the pressure regulator.

21. Remove the fuel rail attaching bolts and the fuel rail assembly.

22. Remove the ignition coil.

23. Remove the intake manifold bolts and studs and remove the intake manifold.

To install:

24. Clean gasket mating surfaces on the intake manifold, block and cylinder head with engine degreaser.

25. Install the intake manifold gaskets. Apply a ³⁄₁₆ inch bead of RTV sealant to the front and rear ridges of the cylinder case. Extend the RTV bead ½ inch up each cylinder head to seal and retain the intake manifold gaskets.

26. Install the intake manifold and tighten the bolts and studs in the proper 2-step sequence in order to obtain proper seal. On the first pass tighten the bolts and studs to 89 inch lbs. (10 Nm). For the final pass,

tighten the bolts and studs to 35 ft. lbs. (47 Nm).

27. Connect the electrical wires and the upper radiator hose.

28. Install the EGR valve and pipe and the ignition coil and EGR solenoid.

29. Lubricate new injector O-ring seals with engine oil and install on the injector.

NOTE: There are 2 injector part numbers used in production for the 5.0L engine and 2 different part numbers for the 5.7L engine. If replacing injectors, do not intermix injectors with different part numbers, as this will result in engine roughness and excessive emissions.

30. Install a new retainer clip onto the injector and install the injector into the fuel rail injector socket, with the electrical connector facing outward. Rotate the injector retainer clip to the locking position.

31. Install the fuel rail assembly in the intake manifold. Install the attaching bolts to 15 ft. lbs. (20 Nm). Install the fuel tube bracket bolt and tighten to 25 ft. lbs. (34 Nm).

32. Connect the vacuum line to the pressure regulator.

33. Install new O-rings on the fuel feed and return lines and connect the fuel lines to the fuel rail. Tighten the fuel line nuts to 20 ft. lbs. (27 Nm).

34. Temporarily connect the negative battery cable. Turn the ignition switch to the ON position for 2 seconds, OFF for 10 seconds, then to the ON position and check for fuel leaks. Disconnect the negative battery cable.

35. Install new gaskets on the runners and manifold.

36. Install new gaskets, the runners and manifold to runner bolts to the intake manifold. Tighten the bolts to 25 ft. lbs. (34 Nm).

37. Install the right and left runner to manifold bolts finger-tight only.

38. Support the plenum above the runners, connect the MAT sensor electrical connector, if equipped and lower the plenum into position. Start a few bolts to hold the plenum in position.

39. Connect the vacuum hoses and MAP sensor, if equipped.

40. Tighten all bolts to 25 ft. lbs. (34 Nm), starting in the center of the plenum/manifold and working outward.

41. Install the PCV valve and hose.

42. Connect the power brake vacuum hose to the fitting on the plenum, the left and right injector electrical harnesses, the attaching nuts

and the electrical connectors to the injectors.

43. Install the throttle body with a new gasket and tighten the attaching bolts to 18 ft. lbs. (24 Nm).

44. Connect the electrical connectors to the TPS and IAC valve, coolant hoses, vacuum hoses, throttle cable bracket and the throttle, TV and cruise control cables.

45. Align the marks on the rotor and housing and install the distributor and the distributor cap. Connect the spark plug wires.

46. Install the plenum extension.

47. Install any remaining pipes, hoses, lines or electrical connections.

48. Install the air intake duct and fill the cooling system with the proper type and quantity of coolant.

49. Connect the negative battery cable, tighten the fuel filler cap and start the engine. Check for leaks, check the ignition timing and adjust as necessary.

5.7L (VIN P) Engine

1. Disconnect the negative battery cable and relieve the fuel system pressure.

2. Drain the engine cooling system into a suitable container.

3. Remove the throttle body air duct.

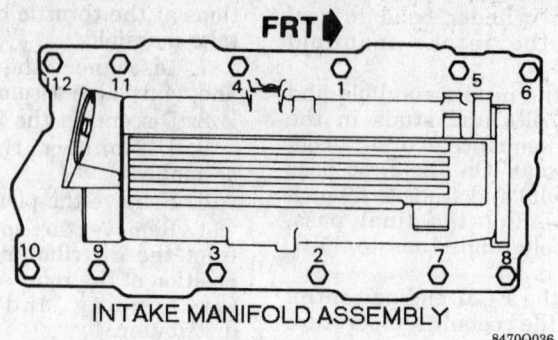

INTAKE MANIFOLD ASSEMBLY

8470Q036

Intake manifold bolt torque sequence — 5.7L (VIN P) engine

4. Disengage the wiring harness connectors from the fuel injectors. Disengage and reposition the left and right wiring harnesses.

5. Remove the accelerator cable bracket retainers, then disconnect the cable and bracket assembly from the throttle body.

6. Disconnect the secondary AIR diverter valve hoses.

7. Disengage the fuel pipe connectors from the fuel rail assembly.

8. Remove the fuel rail bolts and disconnect the vacuum hose from the fuel pressure regulator.

9. Carefully remove the fuel rail and injector assembly from the manifold and position aside.

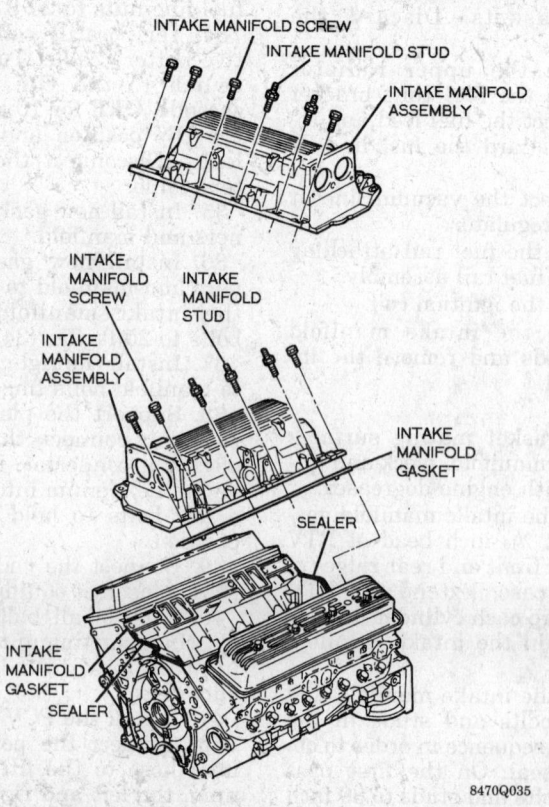

Intake manifold installation — 5.7L (VIN P) engine

8470Q035

10. Disconnect the vacuum and crankcase vent hoses.

11. Remove the EGR solenoid assembly and the fuel EVAP canister solenoid assembly.

12. Remove the EGR valve.

13. Remove the AIR pipe from the intake and the right exhaust manifold.

14. Remove the alternator rear brace.

15. Disconnect the coolant hoses from the throttle body.

16. Remove the throttle body bolts, the throttle body and gasket from the intake.

17. Remove the intake manifold bolts and studs.

18. Remove the intake manifold and discard the old gaskets.

To install:

19. Thoroughly clean the intake manifold bolts and studs. Inspect and clean all gasket mating surfaces.

20. Apply a ³/₁₆ in. (5mm) bead of RTV sealer to the front and rear of the cylinder block. Extend the bead ½ inch (13mm) up each cylinder head to seal and retain the gaskets.

21. Position the new gaskets and install the intake manifold.

22. Install the manifold bolts and studs, then tighten using 2 passes of the proper sequence. First, tighten the bolts/studs to 71 inch lbs. (8 Nm), then tighten them to 35 ft. lbs. (48 Nm).

23. Install the throttle body, gasket and retaining bolts. Tighten the throttle body bolts to 19 ft. lbs. (26 Nm).

24. Connect the coolant hoses to the throttle body, then install the alternator rear brace.

25. Install the accelerator cables and bracket, then tighten the bracket bolts to 90 inch lbs. (10 Nm).

26. Install the secondary AIR pipe. Tighten the exhaust manifold fitting to 25 ft. lbs. (34 Nm) and tighten the flange-to-intake manifold bolts to 19 ft. lbs. (26 Nm).

27. Install the EGR valve, then EGR solenoid and bracket. Tighten valve nuts and the solenoid bracket nut to 16 ft. lbs. (22 Nm).

28. Install the fuel EVAP canister purge solenoid and bracket, then tighten the bolt to 53 inch lbs. (6 Nm).

29. Connect the vacuum and crankcase vent hoses.

30. Install the fuel injector and fuel rail assembly to the intake manifold, connect the fuel pressure regulator vacuum hose and install the fuel rail bolts. Tighten the bolts to 15 ft. lbs. (20 Nm). Engage the fuel pipe connections to the fuel rail assembly.

31. Connect the secondary AIR diverter valve hoses.

32. Position the left and right wiring harnesses, then engage the fuel injector electrical connectors.

33. Install the throttle body air duct.

34. Properly fill the engine cooling system.

35. Connect the negative battery cable.

Exhaust Manifold

REMOVAL AND INSTALLATION

3.1L Engine

1. Disconnect the negative battery cable.

2. Raise and safely support the vehicle.

3. Disconnect the exhaust pipe and lower the vehicle.

4. To remove the right side manifold, disconnect the following components as applicable:

   a. Remove the throttle body air duct.

   b. Remove the serpentine drive belt.

   c. Disconnect the EGR transfer tube at the plenum and remove the EGR valve adapter with the EGR valve and shield from the exhaust manifold.

   d. Disconnect the vacuum line and the electrical connector from the diverter valve.

   e. Remove the AIR pump bolt and AIR pump with diverter valve from the lower bracket. Remove the AIR pipe from the exhaust manifold.

   f. Remove the alternator brace nuts, bolts and brace.

5. To remove the left side manifold, remove the rear power steering pump bracket.

6. Remove the exhaust manifold bolts and nuts and remove the exhaust manifold.

To install:

7. Ensure all mating surfaces are clean before installation.

8. Position the exhaust manifold and install the manifold bolts and nuts. Tighten the exhaust manifold bolts and nuts to 25 ft. lbs. (34 Nm).

9. Install components which were removed in reverse order.

10. Raise and safely support the vehicle. Disconnect the exhaust pipe and lower the vehicle.

11. Connect the negative battery cable, start the engine and check for leaks.

3.4L Engine

1. Disconnect the negative battery cable.

2. Raise and support the vehicle safely.

3. Remove the exhaust crossover pipe.

4. If removing the right manifold, remove the transmission filler tube, the A/C compressor rear bracket bolts and the 2 rear exhaust manifold bolts.

5. Lower the vehicle.

6. If removing the right manifold, remove the serpentine drive belt.

7. Disengage the oxygen sensor electrical connector.

8. If removing the right exhaust manifold:

   a. Remove the alternator from the vehicle.

   b. Disconnect the A/C compressor from the bracket and position aside, taking care not to kink or damage the refrigerant lines.

   c. Remove the alternator rear Y brace.

   d. Remove the EGR valve, adapter and flexible pipe.

9. If equipped with a manual transmission, disconnect the secondary AIR pipe assembly from the manifold.

10. Remove the manifold retaining bolts, then remove the manifold, heat shields and gasket.

To install:

11. Clean the gasket mating surfaces.

12. Position the gasket, then install the exhaust manifold and heat shields.

13. Install the manifold retaining bolts, except for the rear 2 bolts for the right manifold assembly, and tighten to 18 ft. lbs. (25 Nm).

14. If equipped with a manual transmission, secure the secondary AIR pipe assembly to the manifold.

15. If installing the right exhaust manifold:

   a. Install the EGR valve, adapter and flexible pipe.

   b. Install the alternator rear Y brace and the alternator assembly.

   c. Position and secure the compressor.

16. Engage the oxygen sensor electrical connector.

17. If installing the right manifold, install the serpentine drive belt.

18. Raise and support the vehicle safely.

19. If installing the right manifold, install the transmission filler tube, the compressor rear bracket bolts and the rear 2 manifold retaining bolts.

20. Install the crossover pipe assembly.

21. Lower the vehicle and connect the negative battery cable. If applicable, check the transmission fluid level and add as necessary.

5.0L and 5.7L (VIN 8) Engines

1. Disconnect the negative battery cable.

2. If necessary, disconnect and tag the spark plug wires, if necessary.

3. Disconnect the AIR pipes and remove the AIR valve.

4. Raise and safely support the vehicle.

5. Remove the exhaust pipes from the exhaust manifolds.

6. Lower the vehicle.

7. Remove the exhaust manifold bolts and studs and remove the exhaust manifold. Remove gasket, if equipped.

To install:

8. Make sure all mating surfaces are clean before installation. Install gasket, if equipped.

9. Install the exhaust manifold and Tighten the 4 outside exhaust manifold bolts and studs to 20 ft. lbs. (27 Nm) and the inside bolts to 26 ft. lbs. (35 Nm).

10. Raise and support the vehicle safely, connect the exhaust pipes, and lower the vehicle.

11. Install the AIR valve and connect the AIR pipes. If disconnected, reinstall the spark plug wires.

12. Connect the negative battery cable, start the engine and check for leaks.

5.7L (VIN P) Engine

LEFT SIDE

1. Disconnect the negative battery cable, then raise and support the vehicle safely.

2. Disconnect the exhaust crossover pipe from the manifold, then lower the vehicle.

3. Remove the brake booster vacuum hose.

4. Disconnect the secondary AIR pipe fitting from the exhaust manifold.

5. Disengage the oxygen sensor electrical connector.

6. Remove the exhaust manifold retaining bolts, then remove the heat shields, manifold and gasket.

To install:

7. Clean the gasket mating surfaces.

8. Position the gasket, then install the exhaust manifold and heat shields.

9. Install the manifold retaining bolts and tighten to 26 ft. lbs. (35 Nm).

10. Engage the oxygen sensor electrical connector.

11. Connect the secondary AIR pipe fitting to the exhaust manifold and tighten to 26 ft. lbs. (35 Nm).

12. Install the brake booster vacuum hose.

13. Raise and support the vehicle safely.

14. Connect the exhaust crossover pipe to the manifold, then lower the vehicle.

15. Connect the negative battery cable.

RIGHT SIDE

1. Disconnect the negative battery cable, then raise and support the vehicle safely.

2. Remove the exhaust crossover pipe.

3. Remove the serpentine drive belt.

4. Remove the oil level indicator and tube assembly, then disengage the oxygen sensor electrical connector.

5. Remove the 3 rear exhaust manifold retaining bolts, then lower the vehicle.

6. Disconnect the secondary AIR pipe fitting from the exhaust manifold.

7. Remove the alternator rear lower brace.

8. Remove the remaining exhaust manifold retaining bolts, then remove the heat shields, manifold and gasket.

To install:

9. Clean the gasket mating surfaces.

10. Position the gasket, then install the exhaust manifold and heat shields.

11. Install the front 3 manifold retaining bolts and tighten to 26 ft. lbs. (35 Nm).

12. Install the alternator rear lower brace.

13. Raise and support the vehicle safely.

14. Install the remaining manifold retaining bolts and tighten to 26 ft. lbs. (35 Nm).

15. Engage the oxygen sensor electrical connector.

16. Install the oil level indicator and tube assembly.

17. Install the serpentine drive belt.

18. Install the exhaust crossover pipe.

19. Lower the vehicle.

20. Connect the secondary AIR pipe fitting to the exhaust manifold and tighten to 25 ft. lbs. (34 Nm).

21. Connect the negative battery cable.

Timing Chain Front Cover

REMOVAL AND INSTALLATION

3.1L Engine

1. Disconnect the negative battery cable.

2. Drain the cooling system into a suitable container and remove the serpentine drive belt.

3. Disconnect the lower radiator hose at the front cover and heater hose at the water pump.

4. Raise and safely support the vehicle.

5. Drain the crankcase and remove the oil pan.

6. Lower the vehicle.

7. Remove the power steering pump with bracket and lay aside. Remove the power steering pump bracket.

8. Remove the water pump assembly.

9. Remove the vibration damper drive pulley and the damper retaining bolt. Using a suitable puller, remove the vibration damper.

10. Remove the front cover bolts and remove the front cover. Remove and discard the old gasket.

To install:

11. Ensure all gasket mating surfaces are clean before installation.

12. Install a new gasket and the engine front cover, then tighten the front cover bolts to 15 ft. lbs. (21 Nm).

13. Install a vibration damper mounting tool onto the end of the crankshaft so at least 0.2 inch of thread engagement is obtained. Pull

the vibration damper into position with the tool.

14. Install the drive pulley and the damper retaining bolt. Tighten the damper retaining bolt to 70 ft. lbs. (95 Nm).

15. Install the water pump assembly and the lower radiator hose.

16. Install the power steering pump with bracket.

17. Raise and support the vehicle safely. Install the oil pan, replacing gasket if necessary.

18. Lower the vehicles and add proper type and amount of engine oil.

19. Connect the negative battery cable and add engine coolant. Start engine and check for leaks.

3.4L Engine

1. Disconnect the negative battery cable.

2. Remove the throttle body air intake duct.

3. Remove the serpentine drive belt.

4. Remove the water pump assembly.

5. Remove the crankshaft balancer bolt and washer, then remove the pulley bolts and the pulley. Using J–24420–B, or an equivalent damper remover, pull the balancer from the end of the crankshaft assembly.

6. Remove the power steering pump and bracket assembly.

7. Remove the oil pan assembly.

8. Disconnect the lower radiator hose from the front cover assembly.

9. Remove the crankshaft sensor.

10. Remove the front cover retaining bolts, then remove the cover and gasket from the engine.

To install:

11. Thoroughly clean the mating surfaces of any remaining gasket material.

12. Coat both sides of the gasket lower tabs with sealer, then install the front cover with the gasket.

13. Install the front cover retaining bolts and tighten to 15 ft. lbs. (21 Nm).

14. Install the oil pan assembly.

15. Install the crankshaft sensor.

16. Connect the lower radiator hose to the front cover.

NOTE: If a new balancer is installed, new balancer weights of the same size must be installed in the same hole locations as the original balancer.

17. Using J–29113, or an equivalent installer tool, pull the balancer onto the end of the crankshaft. Install the crankshaft pulley and the retaining bolts, then install the

crankshaft damper bolt and washer. Tighten the damper bolt to 58 ft. lbs. (78 Nm), then tighten the pulley retaining bolts to 37 ft. lbs. (50 Nm).

18. Lower the vehicle.

19. Install the water pump assembly.

20. Install the power steering pump and bracket assembly.

21. Install the serpentine drive belt, then install the throttle body air duct.

22. Connect the negative battery cable, then refill the engine cooling system.

5.0L and 5.7L (VIN 8) Engines

1. Disconnect the negative battery cable.

2. Drain the cooling system, then remove the serpentine drive belt and pulleys.

3. Remove the water pump.

4. Remove the crankshaft pulley retaining bolts and pulley. Remove the vibration damper retaining bolt and remove the vibration damper using a suitable puller.

5. Raise and safely support the vehicle.

6. Drain the crankcase and remove the oil pan assembly.

7. Remove the front cover bolts and the timing cover. Remove and discard the old gasket.

To install:

8. Ensure all gasket mating surfaces are clean prior to installation.

9. Install a new gasket and, if necessary, a new seal. Align the front cover dowel pins and loosely install the upper cover attaching bolts.

10. Tighten the upper bolts alternately and evenly while pressing downward on the cover to align the dowels with the cover holes. Do not force the cover over the dowels to the point where the flange or dowels become distorted.

11. Install the remaining cover bolts and tighten the front cover bolts to 100 inch lbs. (11 Nm).

12. Coat the portion of the vibration damper which contacts the front cover seal with clean engine oil. Install a suitable damper installation tool fully onto the crankshaft end. Pull the damper into position using the installation tool.

13. Install the crankshaft pulley, the pulley retaining bolts and the vibration damper retaining bolt. Tighten the pulley bolts to 43 ft. lbs. (58 Nm) and the damper retaining bolt to 70 ft. lbs. (95 Nm).

14. Install the water pump.

15. Raise and safely support the vehicle. Install the oil pan assembly.

16. Lower the vehicle and add the proper type and amount of engine oil.

17. Connect the negative battery cable and add engine coolant.

18. Start the engine and check for leaks.

5.7L (VIN P) Engine

1. Disconnect the negative battery cable.

2. Drain the engine oil and coolant into suitable containers.

3. Remove the throttle body intake duct.

4. Remove the serpentine drive belt.

5. Remove the water pump assembly.

6. Remove the crankshaft balancer and hub.

a. If not done already, raise and support the vehicle safely.

b. Remove the crankshaft balancer retaining bolts, then remove the balancer from the hub.

c. Matchmark the crankshaft hub to the engine front cover, then remove the hub bolt and washer.

d. Remove the crankshaft hub using J–39046, or an equivalent hub removal/installation tool. To preserve the relationship between the hub and crankshaft, DO NOT crank the engine over once the hub has been removed. If the hub is not matchmarked and installed in the original position, an engine imbalance could result.

7. Remove the distributor assembly.

8. Remove the oil pan assembly.

9. Remove the engine front cover bolts.

10. Remove the engine front cover and gasket.

To install:

11. Thoroughly clean the engine front cover and cylinder block gasket mating surfaces. Inspect the engine front cover and seals for damage, replace as necessary.

12. Using J–39087 or equivalent front cover seal protector on the water pump driveshaft, install the gasket and front cover into position over the shafts and guide pins.

13. Install the engine front cover bolts and tighten to 100 inch lbs. (11 Nm).

14. Install the oil pan and gasket.

15. Install the distributor assembly.

16. Install the crankshaft hub and torsional damper assembly.

a. Align the matchmarks made earlier and install the crankshaft hub using the hub tool. If the engine was cranked and the

matchmarks were lost, set the engine to No. 1 TDC, then install the crankshaft hub with the cast arrow in the 12 o'clock position.

b. Install the hub washer and bolt, but do not torque at this time.

c. Install the crankshaft balancer to the hub, then tighten the crankshaft hub bolt to 75 ft. lbs. (102 Nm) and the balancer bolts to 60 ft. lbs. (81 Nm).

NOTE: If a new balancer is installed, new balancer weights of the same size must be installed in the same hole locations as the original balancer.

17. Install the water pump assembly.

18. Install the serpentine drive belt.

19. Install the throttle body air duct.

20. Properly fill the engine crankcase with clean engine oil.

21. Properly fill the engine cooling system.

22. Connect the negative battery cable, operate the engine and check for leaks.

Front Cover Oil Seal

REPLACEMENT

1992

FRONT COVER REMOVED

1. Using a suitable tool, pry the seal out from the front of the cover. Take care not to damage the cover while prying.

2. Using a suitable tool, install the new seal with the open end of the seal toward the inside of the front cover. Support the rear of the cover at the seal area while installing.

3. Inspect the sealing area of the vibration damper and crankshaft for damage or grooving, repair as necessary. Coat the area which contacts the seal with oil prior to installing. Tighten the vibration damper bolt to 70 ft. lbs. (95 Nm).

FRONT COVER INSTALLED

1. Disconnect the negative battery cable.

2. Remove the serpentine drive belt and vibration damper pulley.

3. Remove the vibration damper using a suitable puller.

4. Pry the seal out of the front cover with a suitable prying tool.

5. Using a suitable installation tool, install the new seal with the open end of the seal toward the inside of the front cover.

6. Inspect the sealing area of the vibration damper and crankshaft for damage or grooving, repair as necessary. Coat the area which contacts the seal with oil prior to installing. Tighten the vibration damper bolts to 70 ft. lbs. (95 Nm).

7. Install the serpentine drive belt and pulleys and connect the negative battery cable. Start the engine and inspect for leaks.

1993–96

In addition to the crankshaft oil seal, then 5.7L engine front cover utilizes a water pump driveshaft seal and distributor driveshaft seal. All front cover oil seals on these engines are replaced in the same manner.

1. Remove the timing chain front cover from the engine.

2. Using either a suitably sized driver or a small suitable prytool, remove oil seal from the front cover. If a driver is being used, be sure to support the cover so it is not damaged. If a prytool is used, take care not to score or damage the cover sealing surfaces.

3. For the 3.4L engine, use J–34995, or an equivalent seal installation tool to properly install the crankshaft seal to the front cover.

4. For the 5.7L engine, J–35468 or equivalent to install the crankshaft seal, J–39090 or equivalent to install the distributor shaft seal, and/or J–39088 or equivalent to install the water pump driveshaft seal.

5. Install the timing chain front cover to the engine.

Timing Chain and Sprockets

REMOVAL AND INSTALLATION

1992

1. Disconnect the negative battery cable.

2. Remove the timing chain front cover.

3. For V8 engines, turn the engine slowly until the timing marks on the camshaft and crankshaft sprockets are aligned with the shaft centers and are positioned as close together as possible. The camshaft sprocket mark should be at the 6 o'clock position while the mark on the crankshaft sprocket should be at the 12 o'clock position.

4. For V6 engines, turn the engine slowly until the engine is in the No. 1

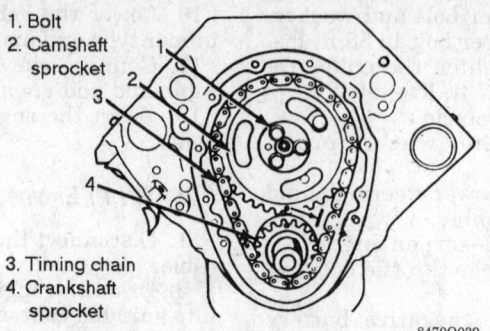

1. Bolt
2. Camshaft sprocket
3. Timing chain
4. Crankshaft sprocket

8470Q039

Timing marks should be aligned with the shaft centers, positioned as close together as possible — 1992 V8 engines

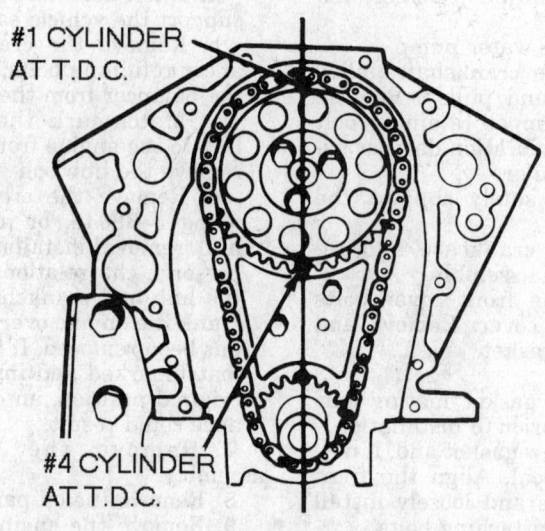

#1 CYLINDER AT T.D.C.

#4 CYLINDER AT T.D.C.

8470Q040

At the No. 1 TDC position, the sprocket timing marks should be aligned with the shaft centers, at the top most position of their travel — 1992 V6 engines

TDC position. When the engine is at No. 1 TDC the timing marks on both sprockets will be aligned with the shaft centers and in the top most positions of their travel.

NOTE: The sprocket is a tight fit on the camshaft. If the sprocket does not come off easily, strike it along the lower edge using a plastic mallet. This should dislodge the sprocket, allowing it to be removed from the shaft.

5. Remove the camshaft sprocket bolts, then remove the camshaft

sprocket along with the timing chain. If necessary, use a suitable puller and remove the crankshaft sprocket.

NOTE: Once the timing chain has been removed, do not allow the crankshaft to turn or engine components may be damaged.

To install:

6. With the timing mark facing away from the engine, install the crankshaft sprocket using a suitable installation tool. apply Molykote® or

an equivalent prelube to the thrust surface.

NOTE: The timing chains and sprockets should be replaced as an assembly. If a new chain or crankshaft sprocket is installed, replace the other parts as well.

7. Hold the camshaft sprocket vertically with the chain hanging down, then align the marks on the camshaft and crankshaft sprocket as aligned during removal. For the 3.1L engine, align the dowel in the camshaft with the dowel hole in the camshaft sprocket.
8. With the chain positioned under the crankshaft sprocket, install the camshaft sprocket to the camshaft.
9. Slowly and evenly draw the camshaft sprocket onto the camshaft using the mounting bolts and torque the bolts to 21 ft. lbs. (28 Nm).

NOTE: Do not drive the sprocket onto the camshaft, this could cause the rear camshaft core plug to be dislodged.

10. Lubricate the timing chain with clean engine oil and install the timing chain cover.
11. Connect the negative battery cable and start the engine.
12. Check and adjust the timing as necessary and inspect for leaks.

3.4L Engine

1. Remove the timing chain front cover.
2. Slowly rotate the crankshaft until the timing marks punched on the sprockets are aligned with the marks on the engine block or the timing chain damper. This should place the engine in the No. 4 TDC position.
3. Remove the bolts retaining the camshaft sprocket, then remove the camshaft sprocket along with the timing chain.
4. If necessary, use J–23444–A or an equivalent puller, to remove the crankshaft sprocket.
5. If necessary, remove the retaining bolts and the timing chain dampener.
To install:
6. If removed, use J–36812, or an equivalent installer, to draw the crankshaft sprocket into position.
7. Hold the camshaft sprocket vertically with the timing mark positioned as during removal, then place the timing chain over the sprocket. Position the chain under the crankshaft sprocket, then install the camshaft sprocket to the end of the camshaft.

8. Verify that all timing marks are properly aligned, then install the camshaft sprocket retaining bolts and tighten to 18 ft. lbs. (24 Nm).
9. If removed, install the timing chain dampener and tighten the retaining bolts to 15 ft. lbs. (21 Nm).
10. Install the timing chain front cover.

5.7L (VIN P) Engine

1. Remove the timing chain front cover.
2. Rotate the crankshaft until the timing marks on the timing chain sprockets are aligned nearest each other. The camshaft sprocket mark should be at the 6 o'clock position while the mark on the crankshaft sprocket should be at the 12 o'clock position.
3. Remove the camshaft sprocket bolts.
4. Remove the camshaft sprocket and timing chain.

NOTE: To prevent piston or valve damage, do not turn the crankshaft after the timing chain has been removed.

5. Remove the water pump bearing retainer bolts, then remove the driveshaft assembly using J–39243 or equivalent driven gear assembly remover.
6. Remove the crankshaft sprocket using J–5825–A or equivalent crankshaft sprocket remover.
7. If necessary, remove the crankshaft key.
To install:
8. If removed, install the crankshaft key.
9. Install the crankshaft sprocket using J–5590, or an equivalent installation tool.
10. Install the water pump driveshaft assembly using J–39092, or an equivalent installer tool. Install the retainer bolts and tighten to 105 inch lbs. (12 Nm).
11. Align the timing marks and install the camshaft sprocket and timing chain. The gears of the camshaft sprocket and water pump driveshaft must mesh or damage to the thrust plate retainer could occur.
12. Install the camshaft sprocket bolts and tighten to 21 ft. lbs. (28 Nm).
13. Install a new O-ring to the water pump driven gear shaft using J–39089, or an equivalent seal installation tool.
14. Install the timing chain front cover.

Camshaft

REMOVAL AND INSTALLATION

3.1L Engine

1. Disconnect the negative battery cable, then relieve fuel system pressure and drain the engine cooling system into a suitable container.
2. Remove the intake manifold and valve covers.
3. Remove the rocker arm assemblies and pushrods, then remove the valve lifters.
4. As required, remove the radiator, grille and air conditioning condenser.
5. Remove the front engine cover.
6. Remove the timing chain and sprockets. Carefully remove the camshaft.
To install:
7. Be sure to coat the camshaft lobes with GM EOS® or equivalent and the camshaft journals and lifters with clean engine oil before installation. It is recommended that all lifters be replaced to insure durability.
8. Carefully install the camshaft. Install the timing chain and sprockets.
9. Install the engine front cover. If removed, install the radiator, grille and/or air conditioning condenser.
10. Install the valve lifters, pushrods and rocker arm assemblies.
11. Install the intake manifold and valve covers.
12. Connect the negative battery cable, add engine coolant and tighten the fuel filler cap. Check and adjust engine timing as necessary.

3.4L Engine

1. Disconnect the negative battery cable.
2. Remove the intake manifold assembly.
3. Remove the bolt and clamp retaining the oil pump drive assembly, then lift the drive assembly from the rear of the block.
4. Remove the timing chain front cover, then remove the crankshaft sprocket and the timing chain.
5. Remove the valve lifters.

NOTE: If valve train components are to be reused, make sure they are tagged or arranged in order to assure installation in their original locations.

6. Properly discharge and recover the refrigerant from the air conditioning system.

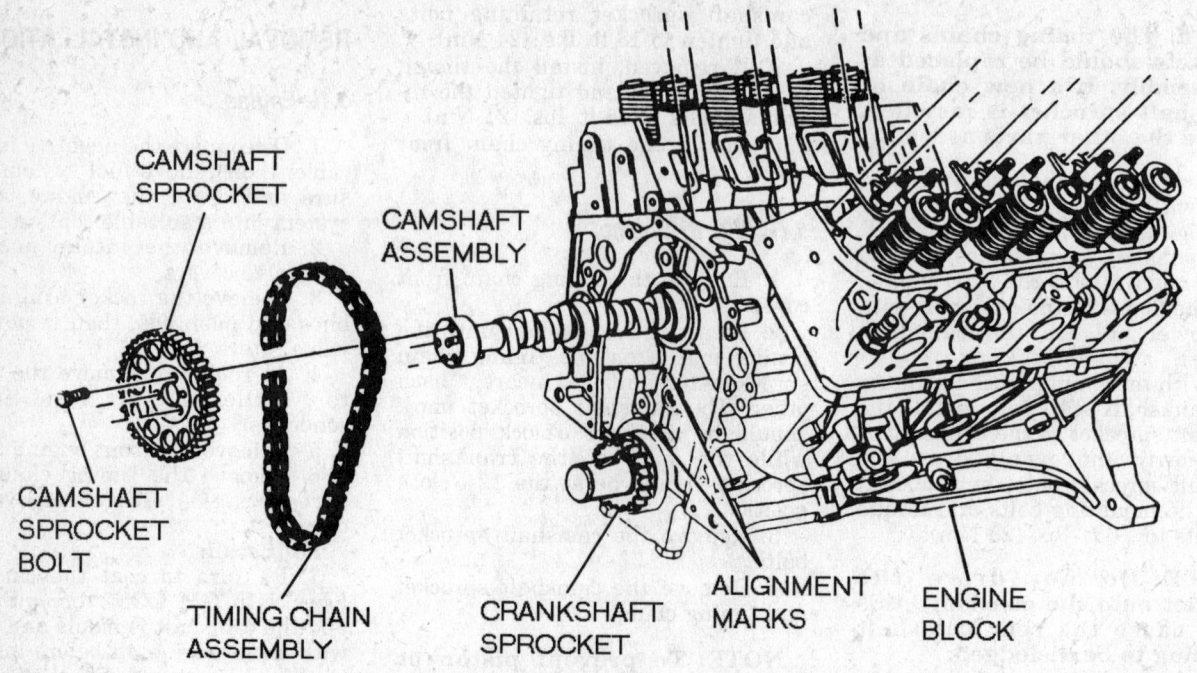

CAMSHAFT SPROCKET

CAMSHAFT ASSEMBLY

CAMSHAFT SPROCKET BOLT

TIMING CHAIN ASSEMBLY

CRANKSHAFT SPROCKET

ALIGNMENT MARKS

ENGINE BLOCK

8470Q041

Timing chain, sprocket and camshaft installation — 3.4L engine

WARNING

The 4th generation F-body which debuted in 1993 uses only the new R-134a refrigerant. R-134a is not compatible with the R-12 refrigerant formerly used in most automobiles. Service equipment and/or air conditioning system components may be contaminated or damaged if the 2 refrigerants and oils are mixed. Never use a recovery system which was designed for and used to service R-12 equipped vehicles on a vehicle equipped with an R-134a air conditioning system.

7. Remove the air conditioning compressor and condenser hose from the condenser, then remove the receiver and dehydrator hose from the condenser. Plug all of the openings in order to prevent system contamination.

8. Remove the radiator and condenser assembly, then remove the air conditioning condenser support.

9. Install three 5/16-18 x 4 inch bolts or equivalent, in the camshaft bolt holes, then using the bolts to pull and rotate the camshaft, carefully pull the camshaft from the bearings. All camshaft journals are the same

diameter and care must be used to avoid damage to the bearings.

To install:

10. If installing a new camshaft, be sure to coat all camshaft lobes with Molykote® or an equivalent prelube and to replace all lifters in order to assure camshaft durability.

11. Lubricate the camshaft journals with clean engine oil, then carefully insert the camshaft into the engine.

12. Install the condenser support, then install the radiator and condenser assembly.

13. Unplug the openings, then connect the condenser refrigerant lines.

14. Install the valve lifters. If reusing the camshaft and lifters, they must be installed into their original bores.

15. Install the camshaft sprocket and timing chain, then install the timing chain front cover.

16. Lubricate the oil pump drive gear with prelube and the assembly with clean engine oil, then install the oil pump drive assembly and tighten the clamp bolt to 25 ft. lbs. (34 Nm).

17. Install the intake manifold assembly.

18. Connect the negative battery cable, then charge the A/C system with R-134a.

5.0L and 5.7L (VIN 8) Engines

1. Disconnect the negative battery cable, relieve the fuel system pressure and drain the engine cooling system.

2. Remove the intake manifold, valve rocker covers, rocker arm assemblies and pushrods. Keep all parts in order for reinstallation.

3. Remove upper fan shroud and the serpentine drive belt. Remove all necessary wires and hoses.

4. Remove the radiator. Disconnect the transmission oil cooler lines.

5. Remove engine front cover and rotate the crankshaft slowly to align the timing marks. Remove the timing chain and the camshaft sprocket.

6. If necessary, purge the air conditioning system and remove the air conditioning condenser. Remove the grille supporting rods.

7. Remove the valve lifters.

8. Remove the camshaft retainer bolts and the camshaft retainer.

9. Install three 5/16-18 x 4 inch bolts or equivalent, in the camshaft bolt holes and carefully pull the camshaft from the bearings. All camshaft journals are the same diameter and care must be used to avoid damage to the bearings.

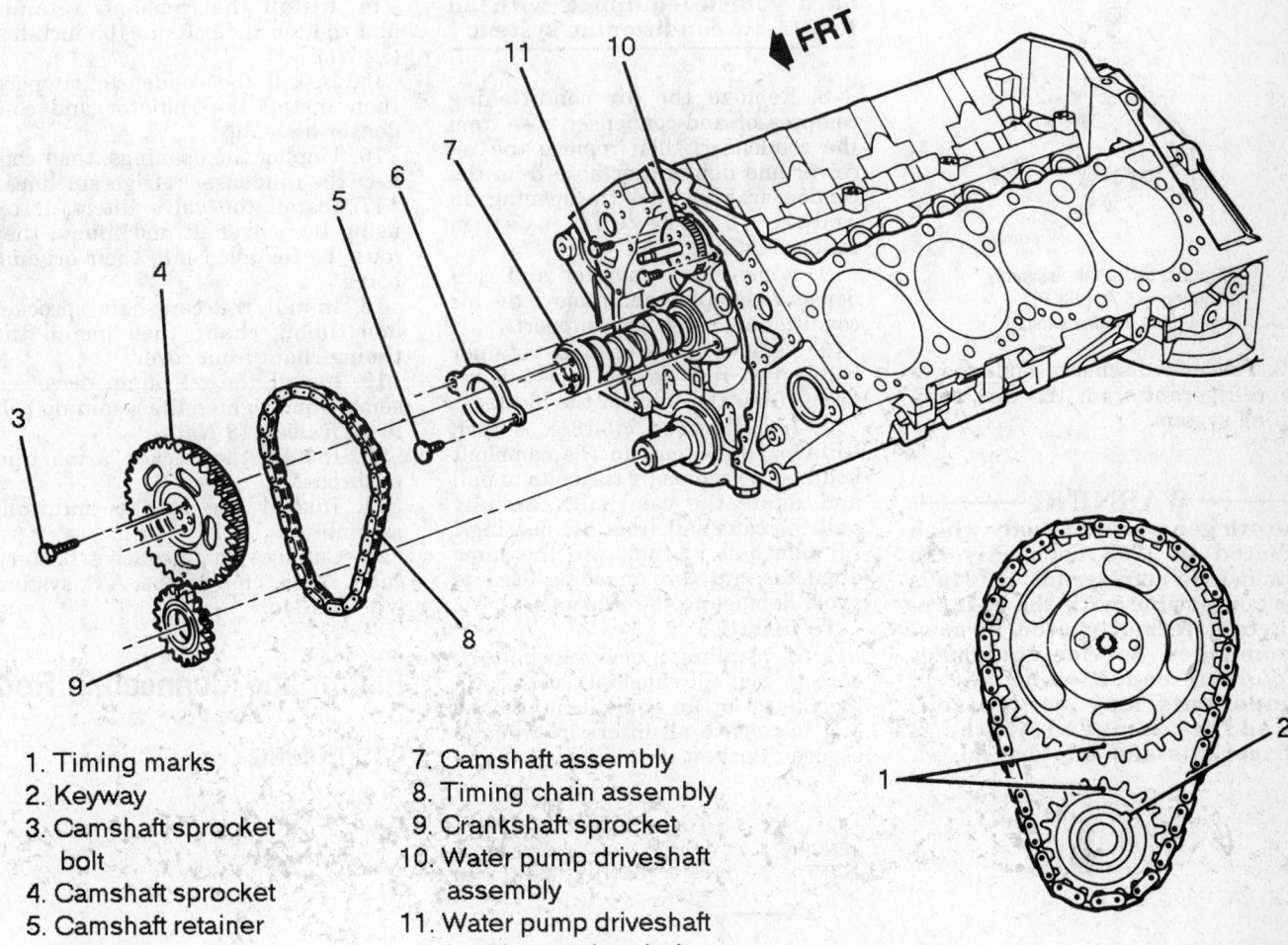

1. Timing marks
2. Keyway
3. Camshaft sprocket bolt
4. Camshaft sprocket
5. Camshaft retainer bolt
6. Camshaft retainer
7. Camshaft assembly
8. Timing chain assembly
9. Crankshaft sprocket
10. Water pump driveshaft assembly
11. Water pump driveshaft bearing retainer bolt

8470Q042

Camshaft, timing chain and sprocket alignment and installation — 5.7L (VIN P) engine

To install:

10. Lubricate the lobes of a new camshaft with Molykote®. Always lubricate the journals and lifters with a suitable engine oil, before installing the camshaft.

11. Carefully guide the camshaft into position and install the camshaft retainer. Tighten the retainer bolts to 106 inch lbs. (12 Nm).

12. Align the timing marks and install the timing chain and engine front cover assembly.

13. Install the valve lifters.

14. Install the grill support rods. Install and recharge the air conditioning condenser, if removed.

15. Install the radiator and the oil cooler lines.

16. Install the serpentine drive belt, all applicable hoses and the upper fan shroud.

17. Install the rocker arms and pushrods. Adjust as necessary.

18. Install the intake manifold and the valve rocker covers.

19. Connect any remaining wires and the negative battery cable.

20. Tighten the fuel filler cap and fill the cooling system with the proper type and amount of coolant.

5.7L (VIN P) Engine

1. Disconnect the negative battery cable.

2. Remove the intake manifold assembly.

3. Remove the rocker arms and pushrods.

4. Remove the bolt retaining the oil pump drive assembly, then lift the drive assembly from the rear of the block.

5. Remove the timing chain front cover, then remove the crankshaft shaft sprocket and timing chain.

6. Remove the valve lifters.

NOTE: If valve train components are to be reused, make sure they are tagged or arranged in order to assure installation in their original locations.

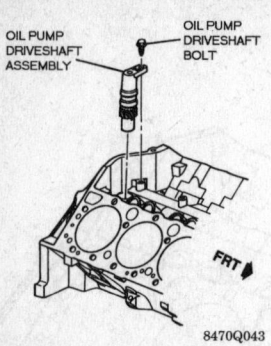

Oil pump driveshaft assembly mounting — 5.7L (VIN P) engine (3.4L engine similar)

7. Properly discharge and recover the refrigerant from the air conditioning system.

—— WARNING ——
The 4th generation F-body which debuted in 1993 uses only the new R-134a refrigerant. R-134a is not compatible with the R-12 refrigerant formerly used in most automobiles. Service equipment and/or air conditioning system components may be contaminated or damaged if the 2 refrigerants and oils are mixed.

Never use a recovery system which was designed for and used to service R-12 equipped vehicles on a vehicle equipped with an R-134a air conditioning system.

8. Remove the air conditioning compressor and condenser hose from the condenser, then remove the receiver and dehydrator hose from the condenser. Plug all of the openings in order to prevent system contamination.

9. Remove the radiator and condenser assembly, then remove the air conditioning condenser support.

10. Remove the camshaft retainer bolts, then remove the camshaft retainer from the front of the block.

11. Install three 5/16-18 x 4 inch bolts or equivalent, in the camshaft bolt holes, then using the bolts to pull and rotate the camshaft, carefully pull the camshaft from the bearings. All camshaft journals are the same diameter and care must be used to avoid damage to the bearings.

To install:

12. If installing a new camshaft, be sure to coat all camshaft lobes with Molykote® or an equivalent prelube and to replace all lifters in order to assure camshaft durability.

13. Lubricate the camshaft journals with clean engine oil, then carefully insert the camshaft into the engine.

14. Install the camshaft retainer and tighten the bolts to 105 inch lbs. (12 Nm).

15. Install the condenser support, then install the radiator and condenser assembly.

16. Unplug the openings, then connect the condenser refrigerant lines.

17. Install the valve lifters. If reusing the camshaft and lifters, they must be installed into their original bores.

18. Install the camshaft sprocket and timing chain, then install the timing chain front cover.

19. Install the oil pump drive assembly and tighten the retaining bolt to 13 ft. lbs. (18 Nm).

20. Install the rocker arms and pushrods.

21. Install the intake manifold assembly.

22. Connect the negative battery cable, then charge the A/C system with R-134a.

Piston and Connecting Rod

POSITIONING

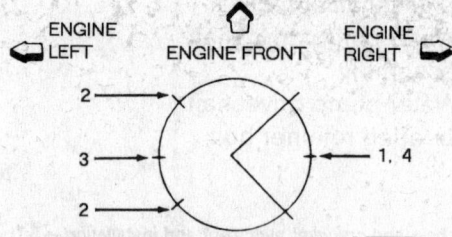

1. Oil ring spacer gap (tang in hole or slot with arc)
2. Oil ring rail gaps
3. 2nd compression ring gap
4. Top compression ring gap

Piston ring gap locations — all engines

NOTCH TO FRONT OF ENGINE

Piston and rod positioning — 3.1L and 3.4L engines

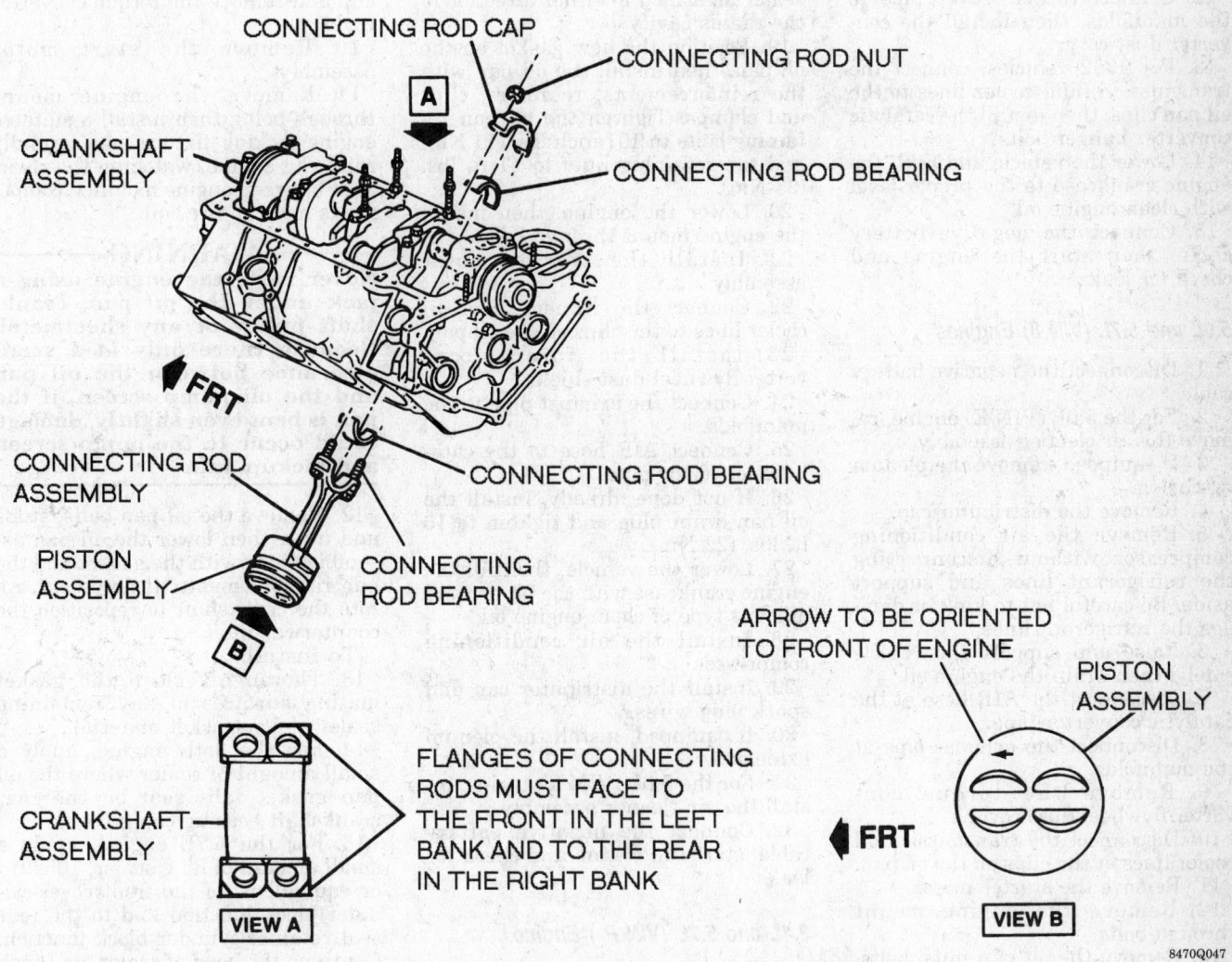

Piston and connecting rod positioning — 5.7L (VIN P) engine

8470Q047

ENGINE LUBRICATION

Oil Pan

REMOVAL AND INSTALLATION

3.1L Engine

1. Disconnect the negative battery cable.

2. Raise the vehicle and support it safely.

3. Drain the engine oil.

4. For 1992 vehicles:

    a. Remove the catalytic converter hanger bolts

    b. Disconnect the transmission fluid cooler lines from the oil pan clips.

    c. Rotate the engine slowly until the timing mark is in the 7 o'clock position. This is necessary to prevent interference from the crankshaft.

5. Remove the torque converter/flywheel dust cover.

6. Disconnect the crossover pipe from the manifolds.

7. Remove the engine mount through-bolts, then raise the engine sufficiently for clearance. Be sure to keep an eye on the clearance between engine mounted components and the firewall.

8. Remove the oil pan bolts, then remove the oil pan and gasket from the bottom of the block.

To install:

9. Thoroughly clean the mating surfaces of any remaining gasket material.

10. Position the new gasket on the oil pan, then install the oil pan and gasket. Tighten the 2 rear oil pan retaining bolts to 18 ft. lbs. (25 Nm) and the remaining bolts, nuts or studs to 89 inch lbs. (10 Nm).

11. Lower the engine into position, then install the engine mount through-bolts.

12. Connect the crossover pipe to the manifolds, then install the converter dust cover.

13. For 1992 vehicles, connect the transmission fluid cooler lines to the oil pan clips, then install the catalytic converter hanger bolts.

14. Lower the vehicle and refill the engine crankcase to the proper level with clean engine oil.

15. Connect the negative battery cable, then start the engine and check for leaks.

5.0L and 5.7L (VIN 8) Engines

1. Disconnect the negative battery cable.

2. For the 5.0L (VIN E) engine, remove the air cleaner assembly.

3. If equipped, remove the plenum extension.

4. Remove the distributor cap.

5. Remove the air conditioning compressor without disconnecting the refrigerant lines and support aside. Be careful not to kink or damage the refrigerant lines.

6. Raise and support the vehicle safely, then drain the engine oil.

7. Disconnect the AIR hose at the catalytic convertor pipe.

8. Disconnect the exhaust pipe at the manifolds.

9. Remove the torque converter/flywheel dust cover.

10. Disconnect the transmission oil cooler lines at the clips on the oil pan.

11. Remove the starter motor.

12. Remove the engine mount through-bolts.

13. Remove the oil pan nuts, bolts, reinforcements, retainers, clips and clamps.

14. Lower the oil pan enough to determine whether or not the forward crankshaft throw and counterbalance weight are in the way of pan removal. If the front of the crankshaft prohibits removal of the pan, turn the crankshaft timing mark to the 6 o'clock position.

15. Carefully raise the engine sufficiently to provide clearance for oil pan removal. Be careful to watch the clearance between the engine and firewall so as not to damage components such as the distributor.

16. Remove the oil pan and gasket from the vehicle.

To install:

17. Remove all old RTV or gasket material from the oil pan and engine block mating surfaces.

18. Apply a small amount of RTV sealer, 1052914 or equivalent, to the front cover-cylinder block junction and to the rear seal retainer-cylinder block junction. Continue the bead of sealer for 1 inch in either direction of the radius cavity.

19. Position the new gasket on the oil pan, then install the oil pan with the reinforcements, retainers, clips and clamps. Tighten the oil pan retaining bolts to 101 inch lbs. (11 Nm) and the retaining nuts to 17 ft. lbs. (23 Nm).

20. Lower the engine, then install the engine mount through bolts.

21. Install the starter motor assembly.

22. Connect the transmission oil cooler lines to the clips on the oil pan.

23. Install the torque converter/flywheel dust shield.

24. Connect the exhaust pipe to the manifolds.

25. Connect AIR hose to the catalytic convertor pipe.

26. If not done already, install the oil pan drain plug and tighten to 16 ft. lbs. (22 Nm).

27. Lower the vehicle, then fill the engine crankcase with the proper and amount type of clean engine oil.

28. Install the air conditioning compressor.

29. Install the distributor cap and spark plug wires.

30. If equipped, install the plenum extension.

31. For the 5.0L (VIN E) engine, install the air cleaner assembly.

32. Connect the negative battery cable, start the engine and check for leaks.

3.4L and 5.7L (VIN P) Engine

1. Disconnect the negative battery cable.

2. Remove the air intake duct.

3. Raise and support the vehicle safely, then drain the engine crankcase of oil.

4. For the 3.4L engine, remove the wiring harness clips from the left side of the oil pan.

5. For the 5.7L engine, drain the engine cooling system.

6. Disengage the wiring harness connector from the oil level sensor, then remove the sensor.

7. Disconnect the exhaust crossover pipe from the exhaust manifolds, then remove the pipe hanger bolts and reposition the pipe.

8. For the 5.7L engine, remove the engine oil cooler hose bracket nut from the oil pan, then remove the oil cooler bolt from the oil cooler assembly. Reposition the engine oil cooler assembly.

9. If equipped with an automatic transmission, remove the transmission fluid cooler lines from the oil pan clip and remove the torque converter cover.

10. Remove the start motor assembly.

11. Remove the engine mount through-bolts, then install a suitable engine jacking fixture and carefully raise the engine, watching the clearance between engine mounted components and the firewall.

────── WARNING ──────

Never raise the engine using a jack under the oil pan, crankshaft pulley or any sheetmetal. Because there only is a small clearance between the oil pan and the oil pump screen, if the pan is bent even slightly, damage could occur to the pump screen and pickup unit.

12. Remove the oil pan bolts, studs and nuts, then lower the oil pan assembly along with the gasket and the pan reinforcements. If necessary, rotate the crankshaft to reposition the counterweights.

To install:

13. Thoroughly clean the gasket mating surfaces of any remaining sealer and/or gasket material.

14. For the 3.4L engine, apply a small amount of sealer where the oil pan gasket tabs seat on the rear crankshaft bearing cap groove.

15. For the 5.7L engine, apply a small amount of RTV sealer, 1052914 or equivalent, to the front cover-cylinder block junction and to the rear seal retainer-cylinder block junction. Continue the bead of sealer for 1 inch (25mm) in either direction of the radius cavity of these junctions.

16. Install the oil pan and gasket assembly, using the reinforcements, nuts, bolts and studs.

17. For the 3.4L engine, tighten the front corner oil pan nuts to 24 ft. lbs. (33 Nm), the rear corner oil pan bolts to 18 ft. lbs. (25 Nm), then oil pan side rail bolts to 89 inch lbs. (10 Nm) and the oil pan studs to the 53 inch lbs. (6 Nm).

18. For the 5.7L engine, tighten corner oil pan bolts, stud or nuts to 15 ft. lbs. (20 Nm) and the remaining bolts or studs to 100 inch lbs. (11 Nm).

19. Lower the engine, remove the jacking fixture and install the engine mount through-bolts.

20. Install the oil level sensor assembly and tighten to 16 ft. lbs. (22 Nm), then engage the wiring harness connector.

21. Install the starter motor assembly.

22. If equipped with an automatic transmission, install the torque converter cover, then secure the transmission fluid cooler lines with the oil pan clip.

23. For the 5.7L engine, install the engine oil cooler bolts screw to the cooler assembly and tighten to 24 ft. lbs. (33 Nm), then install the oil cooler hose bracket nut to the oil pan.

24. Install the exhaust pipe hanger bolt, then connect the crossover pipe to the exhaust manifolds.

25. For the 3.4L engine, connect the wiring harness clips to the left side of the oil pan.

26. Lower the vehicle and refill the engine crankcase with clean engine oil.

27. Install the air intake duct and connect the negative battery cable.

28. Start the engine and check for leaks.

Oil Pump

REMOVAL AND INSTALLATION

1. Disconnect the negative battery cable.

2. Remove the oil pan assembly.

3. Remove the bolt attaching the oil pump to the rear main bearing cap.

4. For the 5.7L (VIN P) engine, remove the oil pump baffle retaining nuts and remove the baffle.

5. Remove the oil pump along with the extension shaft.

6. If necessary, remove the pickup screen and pipe as an assembly by placing the pump is a soft-jawed vice and extracting the pipe from the pump.

To install:

NOTE: The oil pump pickup should be submerged in oil and the pump primed prior to installation. Failure to prime the pump may result in oil pump failure or internal engine damage. Also, if the pickup screen and pipe assembly was removed from the pump, they must be replaced to assure a proper interference fit.

7. If the pickup screen and pipe was removed, it should be replaced as an assembly with a new part. Using a suitable tool, install a new pickup screen and pipe to the oil pump

8. Align the slot or hexagon head on the end of the shaft extension with

the drive tang or the hexagon socket on the distributor shaft.

9. For the 5.7L (VIN P) engine, position the oil pump baffle before installing the pump retaining bolt.

10. Install and tighten the oil pump bolt to 30 ft. lbs. (41 Nm) on 3.1L and 3.4L engines or to 65 ft. lbs. (88 Nm) on 5.0L and 5.7L engines. For the 5.7L (VIN P) engine, install the baffle nuts and tighten to 25 ft. lbs. (34 Nm).

11. Install the oil pan assembly.

12. Lower the vehicle and refill the crankcase with clean engine oil.

13. Connect the negative battery cable.

14. Start the engine and check oil pressure.

CHECKING

Except 3.4L Engine

1. Inspect pump housing and cover for cracks, scoring, casting imperfections and damaged threads.

2. Check idler gear shaft for play in pump body, if loose replace the oil pump assembly.

3. Check pressure regulator valve for sticking and pressure regulator spring for loss of tension.

4. Inspect the gears for chipping, galling or wear.

5. Inspect pickup screen and pipe assembly for broken wire mesh or looseness. The pickup screen and pipe are serviced as an assembly. If the assembly is removed for any reason a proper fit of the pipe to the oil pump housing cannot be assured and a new assembly must be installed.

3.4L Engine

1. Drain the oil from the pump and remove the pump cover.

2. Measure the pump gear lash using a feeler gauge. It should be 0.0037–0.0077 in. (0.094–0.195mm).

3. Measure the gear side clearance, it should be 0.003–0.004 in. (0.08–0.10mm).

4. Measure the end clearance between the gears and the pump cover. It should be 0.002–0.006 in. (0.050–0.152mm).

5. Measure the pump gear pocket depth and diameter. Depth should be 1.202–1.205 in. (30.53–30.61mm) and the diameter should be 1.504–1.506 in. (38.202–38.252mm).

6. Measure the length and diameter of the gears. Length should be 1.199–1.200 in. (30.45–30.48mm)

while the diameter should be 1.498–1.500 in. (38.05–38.10mm).

7. Lubricate all internal parts with engine oil during reassembly and install the pump gears.

NOTE: Use only original equipment gaskets. The thickness of the gasket is critical to proper functioning of the pump.

8. Install the cover and gasket and tighten the pump cover bolts to 89 inch lbs. (10 Nm).

Rear Main Bearing Oil Seal

REMOVAL AND INSTALLATION

1. Disconnect the negative battery cable.

2. Remove the transmission assembly.

3. For manual transmission vehicles, remove the clutch cover and disc assembly.

4. Remove the flywheel bolts and remove the flywheel from the vehicle.

5. Using the notches provided in the seal retainer and a small suitable tool, pry the old seal from the engine. Be careful not to nick the crankshaft sealing surface when removing the seal. If no notches are supplied in the retainer, carefully insert the prytool through the dust lip at an angle away from the crankshaft and pry outward at various points around the seal.

To install:

6. Lubricate the inside and outside of a new seal with clean engine oil.

7. Install the seal on tool J–35621 for V8 engines, J–34686 for V6 engines, or an equivalent rear main seal installer.

8. Thread the screws of the tool into the rear of the crankshaft and tighten the screws snugly to assure proper seal alignment and installation.

9. Tighten the tool wingnut until it bottoms and then remove the tool.

10. Install the flywheel, then tighten the retaining bolts to 52 ft. lbs. (74 Nm) for the 3.1 engines, 61 ft. lbs. (83 Nm) for the 3.4L engine or to 74 ft. lbs. (100 Nm) for all V8 engines.

11. If equipped with a manual transmission, install the clutch cover and disc assembly.

12. Install the transmission assembly.

13. Lower the vehicle and connect the negative battery cable.

MANUAL TRANSMISSION

Transmission Assembly

REMOVAL AND INSTALLATION

1992

1. Disconnect the negative battery cable.
2. Raise and support the vehicle safely, then drain the transmission fluid.
3. Matchmark and remove the driveshaft assembly.

NOTE: When the torque arm is disconnected from the rear axle, the pressure of the rear springs may cause the axle to twist and damage the vehicle. In order to avoid this the axle must be secured and the coil springs must removed before the torque arm is disconnected.

4. Support the left side of the rear axle using a suitable jackstand to avoid damaging the brake lines, then remove the torque arm rear attaching bolts, front torque arm outer bracket and the torque arm.
5. Disengage the speed sensor connector and the backup lamp wiring harness.
6. Remove the nuts and bolts retaining the catalytic converter hanger, then remove the hanger.
7. Support the engine using a suitable jackstand, then remove the transmission mount nuts from the support, remove the support bolts and remove the support.
8. For 1992 vehicles, carefully lower the transmission with the aid of a helper just sufficiently to remove the shift control assembly bolts, then remove the shift control assembly from the extension housing.
9. Remove the transmission-to-bellhousing bolts.
10. With the aid of a helper, remove the transmission assembly.

To install:

11. Clean the sealing surfaces of transmission-to-shifter location. Place a continuous ⅛ inch bead of RTV or equivalent on the shifter-to-transmission sealing surface.
12. Install the transmission, then tighten bellhousing bolts to 55 ft. lbs. (75 Nm).
13. For 1992 vehicles, install the shifter assembly onto the transmission and tighten the 4 retaining bolts to 13 ft. lbs. (17 Nm).
14. Install the transmission support, then tighten the support bolts to 40 ft. lbs. (54 Nm).
15. Install the transmission mount and tighten the nuts to 35 ft. lbs. (47 Nm).
16. Install the catalytic converter hanger and tighten the fasteners to 38 ft. lbs. (47 Nm).
17. Engage the backup lamp wiring harness connector and engage the speed sensor connector. If applicable, install the speedometer cable.
18. Install the torque arm, then tighten the front nuts to 30 ft. lbs. (41 Nm). Tighten the rear torque arm nuts to 98 ft. lbs. (133 Nm). Remove left rear axle support stand and, if not done already, remove the engine support.
19. Align and install the driveshaft assembly.
20. Refill the transmission with Dexron®II or equivalent transmission fluid.
21. Lower the vehicle.
22. Connect the negative battery cable.

1993–96

1. Disconnect the negative battery cable.
2. Remove the retainers, then unsnap the front floor console trimplate assembly.
3. For 6-speed vehicles, remove the transmission control lever handle bolts, then remove the handle assembly. Disconnect the clutch pedal pushrod in order to protect the slave cylinder during the procedure.
4. Raise and support the vehicle safely.
5. Drain the transmission fluid.
6. Matchmark and remove the driveshaft assembly.
7. Support the rear axle assembly using a jackstand, then remove the rear axle torque arm.
8. Remove the catalytic converter hanger assembly.
9. Disengage the wiring harness connector from the reverse lockout solenoid (6-speeds only) and from the backup lamp switch.

NOTE: Whenever the clutch slave cylinder is disconnected, the actuator pushrod must first be disconnected. If this is not done, the slave cylinder may become permanently damaged if the clutch pedal is depressed while the cylinder is disconnected.

10. For 6-speed vehicles, remove the actuator cylinder nuts. Remove the actuator cylinder and support aside using a length of mechanic's wire. Remove the actuator spacer, then pull the clutch fork downward to disengage from the release bearing.
11. Disengage the speed sensor harness connector.
12. Support the engine assembly with a jackstand, then position a transmission jack under the transmission.
13. Remove the transmission support and mount.
14. For 5-speed vehicles, lower the transmission sufficiently to reach the bolts on top of the housing which attach the transmission control assembly, then remove the bolts.
15. Remove the transmission to clutch housing retaining bolts, then with the aid of an assistant carefully lower the transmission from the vehicle. For 5-speed vehicles, the transmission control assembly must be held in position while lower the transmission. If this is not done, the control assembly could drop, causing damage to the component.

To install:

16. For 5-speed vehicles, thoroughly clean the sealant from the transmission extension housing and the control assembly. Support the control assembly to the installed position in the vehicle.
17. Raise the transmission into position, piloting the input shaft into the release bearing, clutch disc and pilot bearing, then support the transmission with a jackstand.
18. Install the transmission retaining bolts and tighten to 55 ft. lbs. (75 Nm) for 5-speed vehicles or to 26 ft. lbs. (35 Nm) for 6-speed vehicles.
19. For 5-speed vehicles, apply a continuous ⅛ in. (3mm) bead of RTV sealant around the housing-to-control assembly sealing surface. Raise the transmission, engaging the control assembly, then install the bolts and tighten to 13 ft. lbs. (17 Nm).
20. Install the transmission mount and the support. Tighten the mount bolts to 40 ft. lbs. (54 Nm), then tighten the support bolts to 43 ft. lbs. (58 Nm) and the support nuts to 35 ft. lbs. (47 Nm).
21. Remove the transmission and engine jackstands or supports.
22. For 6-speed vehicles, push the clutch fork assembly upward to engage the release bearing, then install the actuator spacer, actuator cylinder and retaining nuts. Tighten the nuts to 15 ft. lbs. (20 Nm).

23. Engage the wiring harness connectors to the speed sensor assembly, backup lamp switch, and on 6-speed vehicles, to the reverse lockout solenoid.

24. Install the catalytic converter hanger assembly.

25. Install the rear axle torque arm, then remove the support from the axle.

26. Align and install the driveshaft assembly.

27. Fill the transmission assembly using Dexron®II or equivalent transmission fluid.

28. Lower the vehicle.

29. For 6-speed vehicles, install the control lever handle and tighten the retaining bolts to 18 ft. lbs. (25 Nm), then connect the clutch actuator pushrod.

30. Install the front floor console trimplate, then connect the negative battery cable.

LINKAGE ADJUSTMENT

The M39, MK6 and MB1 5-speed manual transmissions found in the 1992 F-body and the M49 5-speed, M28 and M29 6-speed manual transmissions found in the 1993–96 F-body are designed with an internal shift mechanism. Shifter control adjustments are not necessary or possible.

CLUTCH

Clutch Assembly

REMOVAL AND INSTALLATION

1992

1. Disconnect the negative battery cable.

2. Remove the transmission assembly.

3. Remove the clutch slave cylinder and heat shield assembly from the flywheel housing.

4. Remove the housing cover and the bolts attaching the flywheel housing to the engine. Remove the housing.

5. Remove the clutch release bearing. Slide the clutch fork from the ball stud and dust boot and remove the clutch fork with spring.

6. Install tool J–33169 for V6 engines, J–5824–01 for V8 engines, or equivalent clutch alignment arbor to support the clutch assembly during removal. Locate marks or a white painted letter on the clutch housing and an **X** mark on the flywheel. If the marks are not visible, place a mark on the flywheel and clutch cover for alignment during installation.

7. Loosen the clutch-to-flywheel bolts evenly 1 turn at a time until all spring pressure is released.

8. Remove the clutch and pressure plate assembly.

To install:

9. Inspect flywheel for heat stress, cracks or other defects and repair or replace as necessary.

10. Inspect the clutch plate, disc, release bearing and fork for contamination, wear or heat stress, repair or replace as necessary.

11. Clean the pilot bearing then lubricate sparingly with machine oil.

12. Using the clutch alignment arbor, install the clutch pressure plate and disc onto the flywheel with the disc springs facing the transmission. The flywheel side is marked.

13. Align the marks on the flywheel with the mark on the pressure plate.

14. Install the pressure plate-to-flywheel bolts.

15. Alternately tighten the clutch assembly-to-flywheel bolts 1 turn at a time and then torque the bolts to 15 ft. lbs. (21 Nm) for the V6 engine or 30 ft. lbs. (40 Nm) for the V8 engine. Remove the clutch alignment tool.

16. Lubricate and install the clutch fork ball and clutch fork at the release bearing.

NOTE: If replacing the clutch fork, be sure to replace with the identical part number. Do not mix the V6 clutch fork with the V8 clutch or damage to the slave cylinder may result.

17. If removed install the dust boot.

18. Install the clutch release bearing onto the fork with the fork fingers and the retaining spring tabs installed into the release bearing grooves.

19. Install the clutch housing and torque the bolts to 35 ft. lbs. (47 Nm) for the V6 engine or 70 ft. lbs. (95 Nm) for the V8 engine.

20. Install the clutch housing cover and tighten the bolts to 53 inch lbs. (6 Nm).

21. Install the transmission, clutch slave cylinder and heat shield. Torque the slave cylinder bolts to 15 ft. lbs. (21 Nm).

22. Refill transmission with the proper type and quantity of oil. Lower the vehicle and check clutch operation.

1993–96

1. Disconnect the negative battery cable.

2. Remove the instrument panel driver knee bolster for access, then disconnect the clutch master cylinder pushrod from the clutch pedal.

3. Remove the transmission assembly.

4. For 5-speed vehicles:

   a. Remove the clutch slave cylinder actuator nuts, then support the cylinder from the vehicle using a length of mechanic's wire. Do not allow the assembly to hang by the hydraulic line or damage could occur.

   b. Remove the transmission brace nut and bolt, then remove the brace.

5. Remove the retaining bolts and the flywheel housing cover.

6. Remove the flywheel housing retaining bolts, then remove the housing from the rear of the engine.

7. Slowly and evenly loosen, then remove, the clutch pressure plate/cover bolts, then remove the pressure plate assembly along with the clutch driven disc.

To install:

8. Inspect flywheel for heat stress, cracks or other defects and repair or replace as necessary.

9. Inspect the clutch plate, disc, release bearing and fork for contamination, wear or heat stress, repair or replace as necessary.

10. Position the clutch driven disc to the flywheel, then install the pressure plate/cover assembly and finger-tighten the retaining screws.

11. Align the clutch disc with the pilot bearing and clutch pressure plate assembly using a suitable clutch alignment arbor such as J–33169 for the 5-speeds or J–38836 for 6-speeds.

12. When properly aligned, tighten the clutch pressure plate bolts to 15 ft. lbs. (20 Nm) +30 degrees of additional rotation for 5-speeds or to 22 ft. lbs. (30 Nm) for 6-speeds.

13. Install the flywheel housing assembly and tighten the retaining bolts to 75 inch lbs. (8.5 Nm).

14. For 5-speed vehicles:

   a. Install the transmission brace, then tighten the retaining nut and bolt to 37 ft. lbs. (50 Nm).

   b. Remove the support wire and install the slave cylinder, then tighten the retaining nuts to 15 ft. lbs. (10 Nm).

15. Install the transmission assembly.

16. Engage the clutch master cylinder pushrod to the clutch pedal assembly.

17. Install the driver side knee bolster.

18. Connect the negative battery cable.

PEDAL HEIGHT/FREE-PLAY ADJUSTMENT

The hydraulic clutch system locates the clutch pedal height and provides automatic clutch adjustment. No adjustment of clutch linkage or pedal position is required.

Clutch Master Cylinder

The hydraulic clutch system used on 1992 vehicles contains both a master cylinder and a slave cylinder, each of which may be serviced separately. The 1993–96 vehicles use a hydraulic system which is serviced only as an entire assembly.

REMOVAL AND INSTALLATION

1992

1. Disconnect the negative battery cable.

2. Remove the sound insulator or lower panel, as necessary, to gain access to the clutch pedal.

3. Disconnect the brake vacuum booster pushrod from the brake pedal. Remove the retainer and washer.

4. Disconnect the clutch master cylinder input rod from the pedal. Use a sharp cutting tool to cut the bushing retaining tabs.

5. Remove the clutch master cylinder-to-cowl nuts and the brake vacuum booster-to-cowl nuts.

6. Remove the hose clamp and the clutch fluid reservoir hose. Place a suitable drain pan under hose to catch the fluid leaking from the reservoir.

7. Pull the brake vacuum booster forward to gain access to the clutch master cylinder. Remove the clutch master cylinder with U-bolt from the cowl. Lower the master cylinder down to the clutch housing area.

8. Raise and safely support the vehicle.

9. Disconnect the high pressure hose and remove the clutch master cylinder.

To install:

10. Connect the high pressure hose and place the master cylinder up

near the brake vacuum booster. Lower the vehicle.

11. Install the clutch master cylinder to the cowl with the U-bolt.

12. Install a new bushing to the pedal. Install the flat end of the bushing toward the pedal.

13. Install the clutch master cylinder input rod to the pedal. Install the retainer and washer.

14. Attach the brake vacuum booster to the cowl, connect the clutch fluid reservoir hose with the hose clamp and install the clutch master cylinder-to-cowl nuts. Tighten the nuts to 115 inch lbs. (13 Nm). Tighten the brake vacuum booster-to-cowl nuts to 15 ft. lbs. (21 Nm).

15. Replace the sound insulator or lower panel as necessary.

16. Connect the brake vacuum pushrod to the brake pedal.

17. Fill and bleed the clutch hydraulic system. Connect the negative battery cable.

Clutch Slave Cylinder

The hydraulic clutch system used on 1992 vehicles contains both a master cylinder and a slave cylinder, each of which may be serviced separately. The 1993–96 vehicles use a hydraulic system which is serviced only as an entire assembly.

REMOVAL AND INSTALLATION

1992

1. Disconnect the negative battery cable.

2. Remove the sound insulator panel to gain access to the clutch pedal.

3. Disconnect the clutch master cylinder input rod from the clutch pedal. Using a sharp cutting tool, cut the bushing retaining tabs.

NOTE: If the clutch master cylinder input rod is not disconnected, permanent damage to the slave cylinder will occur in the event that the clutch pedal is depressed while the slave cylinder is disconnected.

4. Raise and safely support the vehicle.

5. Disconnect the pressure hose and catch the leaking hydraulic fluid in a suitable container.

6. Remove the slave cylinder bolts, then remove the heat shield and slave cylinder.

To install:

7. Install the actuator and heat shield. Tighten the slave cylinder bolts to 15 ft. lbs. (21 Nm).

8. Install the pressure hose and lower the vehicle.

9. Install a new clutch pedal bushing with the flat side toward the clutch pedal.

10. Connect the clutch master cylinder input rod to the clutch pedal.

11. Install the sound insulator panel, bleed the hydraulic system and connect the negative battery cable.

Clutch Master Cylinder/Slave Cylinder Assembly

The 1993–96 vehicles use a hydraulic system which is serviced only as an entire assembly.

REMOVAL AND INSTALLATION

1993–96

1. Disconnect the negative battery cable.

2. Remove the instrument panel driver knee bolster for access, then disconnect the clutch master cylinder pushrod from the clutch pedal.

3. Remove the clutch master cylinder retaining nuts, then remove the master cylinder U-bolt and clutch master cylinder from the dash panel assembly.

4. Remove the clutch master cylinder reservoir retainer, then remove the reservoir from the left hood strut bracket.

5. Raise and support the vehicle safely.

6. Remove the clutch slave cylinder nuts, then remove the cylinder from the clutch housing.

7. Remove the clutch hydraulic system from the vehicle.

To install:

8. Install the clutch slave cylinder to the clutch housing, then tighten the retaining nuts to 15 ft. lbs. (20 Nm).

9. Lower the vehicle, then position the clutch master cylinder to the dash panel. Install the U-bolt and the master cylinder nuts, then tighten the nuts to 20 ft. lbs. (27 Nm).

10. Install the master cylinder reservoir to the left hood strut bracket, then install the reservoir retainer.

11. Engage the clutch master cylinder pushrod to the clutch pedal assembly.

12. Install the instrument panel driver knee bolster.

13. Connect the negative battery cable.

Hydraulic Clutch System Bleeding

When bleeding the hydraulic clutch system always keep the reservoir filled with fresh clean brake fluid. NEVER use fluid which has been bled from a system as it may contain moisture, air or other contaminants.

1992

1. Clean all dirt and grease from the cap to make sure no foreign substances enter the system.

2. Remove the cap and diaphragm, then fill the reservoir to the top with the approved DOT 3 brake fluid. Fully loosen the bleed screw which is in the slave cylinder body next to the inlet connection.

3. At this point, bubbles of air will appear at the bleed screw outlet. When the slave cylinder is full and a steady stream of fluid comes out of the slave cylinder bleeder, tighten the bleed screw to 18 inch lbs. (2 Nm).

4. Assemble the diaphragm and cap to the reservoir. Fluid in the reservoir should be level with the step. Exert a light load of about 20 lbs. to the slave cylinder piston by pushing the clutch fork towards the cylinder and loosening the bleed screw. Maintain a constant light load. Fluid and any air that is left will be expelled through the bleed port. Tighten the bleed screw when a steady flow of fluid and no air is being expelled.

5. Fill the reservoir fluid level back to normal capacity.

6. Exert a light load to the clutch fork, but do not open the bleeder screw. The piston in the slave cylinder will move slowly down the bore. Repeat this operation 2–3 times. The fluid movement will force any air left in the system into the reservoir. The hydraulic system should now be fully bled.

7. Check the operation of the clutch hydraulic system and repeat this procedure if necessary. Check the pushrod travel at the slave cylinder to insure the minimum travel is

0.43 inch for the 3.1L engine or 0.57 in. for 5.0L and 5.7L engines.

1993–96

The sealed hydraulic system used on these vehicles should not require bleeding, unless the fluid level in the reservoir has fallen so low that air is drawn into the clutch master cylinder.

1. Loosen the clutch master cylinder retaining nuts to the ends of the U-bolt threads.

2. Clean all dirt and grease from the cap to make sure no foreign substances enter the system.

3. Remove the cap and diaphragm, then fill the reservoir with the approved DOT 3 brake fluid.

4. Wrap a piece of wire around the left hood strut bracket, making sure the wire is accessible from the underside of the vehicle. The wire will be used to support the slave cylinder once it is removed from the clutch housing.

5. Raise and support the vehicle safely.

6. Remove the clutch slave cylinder retaining nuts, then remove the slave cylinder and support it using the mechanic's wire.

7. Lower the vehicle.

8. Grasp the slave cylinder and depress the cylinder pushrod approximately 0.787 in. (20.0mm) into the slave cylinder bore and hold.

9. With the pushrod held into the slave cylinder bore, install the reservoir diaphragm and cap, then release the pushrod.

10. Hold the slave cylinder vertically with the pushrod end facing downward. The slave cylinder must be held lower than the master cylinder. Press the pushrod into the slave cylinder bore with short 0.39 in. (10mm) strokes, while watching the reservoir for air bubbles.

11. Continue depressing the pushrod with short strokes until air bubbles are no longer seen entering the reservoir.

12. Raise and support the vehicle safely.

13. Remove the slave cylinder from the mechanic's wire, then install the slave cylinder and tighten the retaining nuts to 15 ft. lbs. (20 Nm), then lower the vehicle.

14. Remove the mechanic's wire from the strut bracket.

15. Install the clutch master cylinder nuts and tighten to 20 ft. lbs. (27 Nm).

16. Check the fluid level in the clutch master cylinder reservoir and add, if necessary.

17. Check the clutch pedal for proper operation and, rebleed, as necessary.

AUTOMATIC TRANSMISSION

Transmission Assembly

REMOVAL AND INSTALLATION

1992

1. Disconnect the negative battery cable.

2. Remove the air cleaner assembly, if necessary.

3. Disconnect the Throttle Valve (TV) control cable at the throttle lever.

4. Remove the transmission oil dipstick. Unbolt and remove the dipstick tube.

5. Raise and support the vehicle safely, support the rear axle with adjustable lifting devices.

6. Remove the rear coil springs and the torque arm.

7. Mark the relationship between the driveshaft and the rear pinion flange so the driveshaft may be reinstalled in its original position. Remove the driveshaft from the vehicle.

8. Disengage the speedometer cable or speed sensor connector, along with any transmission electrical connectors and the shift linkage from the transmission.

9. Remove the flywheel cover, then mark the relationship between the torque converter and the flywheel.

10. Remove the torque converter to flywheel attaching bolts.

11. Disconnect the catalytic converter support bracket at the transmission.

12. Support the transmission with a jack, then remove the transmission mount to support nut.

13. Remove the transmission crossmember to frame bolts and, if used, insulators.

14. Lift the transmission slightly and remove the support. Slide the transmission support rearward.

15. Lower the transmission slightly. Disconnect the Throttle Valve (TV) cable from the transmis-

sion. Disconnect and plug the oil cooler lines from the transmission.

16. Support the engine with a suitable tool. Remove the transmission to engine mounting bolts.

17. Attach a torque converter holding strap and remove the transmission from the vehicle. Keep the rear of the transmission lower then the front to avoid the possibility of the torque converter disengaging from the transmission.

To install:

18. Install the transmission in the vehicle.

19. Install and tighten the transmission-to-engine bolts to 35 ft. lbs. (47 Nm).

20. Connect the TV cable and oil cooler lines to the transmission.

21. Install the crossmember. Install and tighten the transmission crossmember-to-frame bolts to 40 ft. lbs. (54 Nm) and the crossmember to transmission mount nut to 35 ft. lbs. (47 Nm).

22. Install the torque converter to the flywheel, aligning the marks that were made prior to removal and making sure the weld nuts on the converter are flush with the flywheel.

23. Finger-tighten 3 torque converter bolts. Tighten all the converter-to-flywheel bolts to 46 ft. lbs. (63 Nm), then retighten the first bolts which was tightened to specification.

24. Connect the catalytic converter support bracket.

25. Install the flywheel cover and tighten the retaining bolts to 89 inch lbs. (10 Nm).

26. Connect the speedometer cable or speed sensor, the electrical connectors and the shift linkage control.

27. Install the driveshaft, aligning the marks that were made on the driveshaft and pinion flange prior to removal.

28. Install the torque arm and the rear coil springs.

29. Lower the vehicle.

30. Install the transmission dipstick and dipstick tube. Tighten the retaining bolt to 35 ft. lbs. (47 Nm) on V8 engines or to 55 ft. lbs. (75 Nm) for V6 engines.

31. Connect the TV control cable at the throttle lever.

32. Install the air cleaner assembly, if necessary, and connect the negative battery cable.

NOTE: Transmission oil cooler flushing must be performed when a transmission is removed for service. The flushing should take place after the installation of the overhauled or replacement transmission assembly.

33. With a suitable flushing tool and fluid, flush the transmission cooler and pipes.

34. Add the proper type and amount of transmission fluid, Start the engine and check the transmission fluid level. Adjust the TV cable and shift linkage, as necessary.

1993–96

1. Disconnect the negative battery cable.

2. Disconnect the transmission Throttle Valve (TV) cable assembly from the throttle lever.

3. Raise and support the vehicle safely.

4. Matchmark the alignment of the shaft to the axle yoke, then remove the driveshaft assembly.

5. Support the transmission assembly, then remove the nut and washer attaching the support to the transmission.

6. Remove the support bolts, then remove the support from the vehicle.

7. Remove the rear axle torque arm.

8. Remove the catalytic converter hanger assembly.

9. Remove the torque converter cover bolts, then remove the cover.

10. Remove the bolts attaching the converter to the flywheel, then disengage the flywheel and converter.

11. Move the catalytic converter heat shield, as necessary for access.

12. Disconnect the automatic transmission range selector lever cable assembly.

13. Disconnect the transmission fluid cooler pipe assemblies from the transmission oil cooler pipe clips.

14. Disengage all electrical connectors from the transmission assembly.

15. Remove the bolts attaching the transmission to the engine.

16. Remove the transmission fluid level indicator assembly, then separate the transmission from the engine block.

17. Disconnect the TV cable assembly from the transmission and remove the fluid cooler lines. Plug all openings to prevent system contamination or excessive fluid loss.

18. Carefully lower the transmission from the vehicle.

To install:

19. Raise the transmission assembly into position in the vehicle, then unplug the openings and install the fluid cooler lines.

20. Connect the TV cable assembly to the transmission assembly.

21. Align the transmission with the engine block, then install the fluid level indicator assembly.

22. Install the transmission retaining bolts and tighten to 70 ft. lbs. (95 Nm) for the 3.4L engine or to 35 ft. lbs. (47 Nm) for the 5.7L engine.

23. Engage all electrical wiring harness connectors to the transmission assembly.

24. Install the fluid cooler pipe and hose assemblies to the pipe clips.

25. Connect the transmission range selector lever cable assembly.

26. Reposition the catalytic converter heat shield.

27. Position the flywheel to the torque converter, then install the bolts and tighten to 46 ft. lbs. (63 Nm).

28. Install the torque converter cover to the transmission, then tighten the retaining bolts to 89 inch lbs. (10 Nm).

29. Install the catalytic converter hanger assembly.

30. Install the rear axle torque arm.

31. Install the support to the transmission and the rail assembly. Install the support retaining screws and tighten, then install the washer and nut to the transmission. Tighten the nut to 35 ft. lbs. (47 Nm).

32. Remove the transmission jack or adjustable support from the transmission.

33. Align and install the driveshaft assembly.

34. Lower the vehicle and connect the TV cable assembly to the throttle lever.

35. Connect the negative battery cable.

SHIFT CONTROL CABLE ADJUSTMENT

1992

1. Position the floor shifter in **N**, then raise and support the vehicle safely.

2. Loosen the shift control cable attachment at the transmission shift lever.

3. Rotate the shift lever clockwise to the **P** detent, then back to the **N** detent.

4. Tighten the cable attaching nut to 11 ft. lbs. (15 Nm) while holding the lever out of **P**.

5. If applicable and necessary, tighten the shift cable bracket screws to 18 ft. lbs. (24 Nm).

6. Check cable adjustment by rotating the control lever through the detents.

1. Grommet
2. Automatic transmission range selector
   lever cable bracket
3. Automatic transmission range selector
   lever nut
4. Automatic transmission control assembly
5. Automatic transmission range selector
   lever cable assembly
6. Automatic transmission control bolt
7. Automatic transmission range selector
   lever assembly

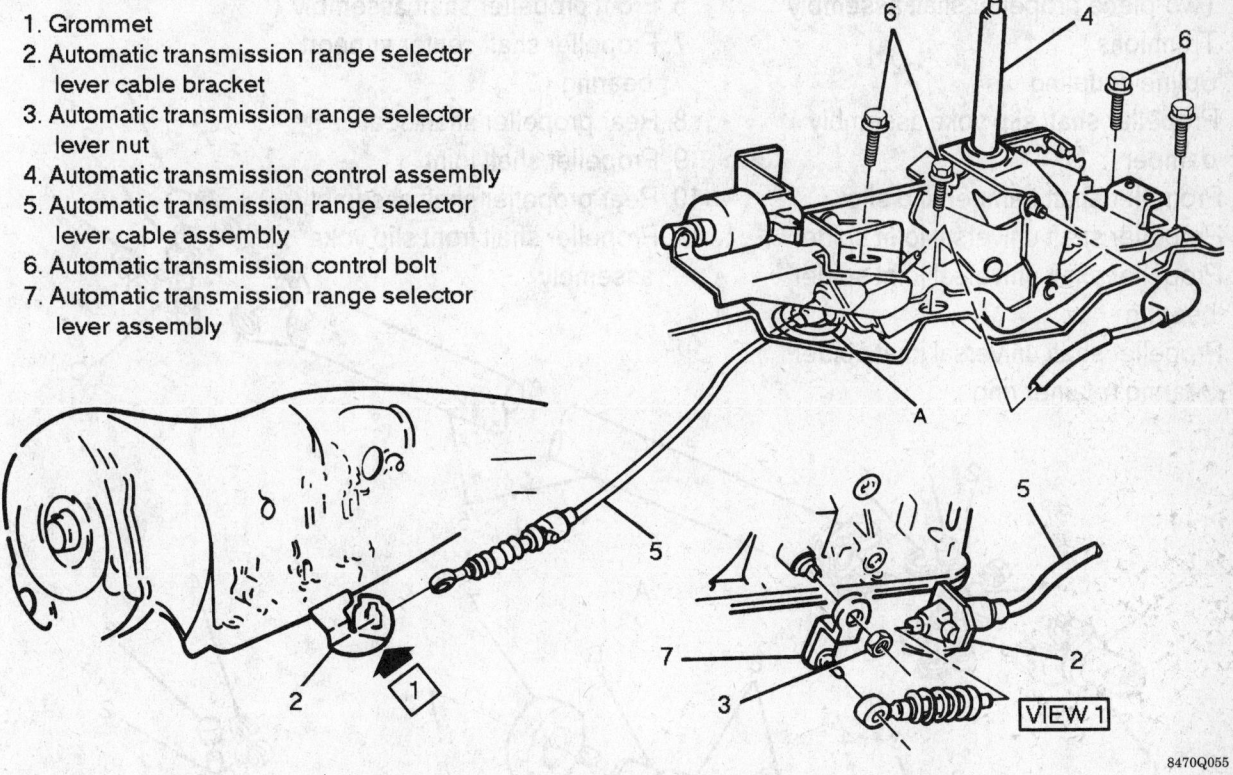

Shift control cable adjustment — 1993–96 automatic transmission vehicles

1. Position the floor shifter in **N**, then raise and support the vehicle safely.

2. Unlock the cable adjustment button by turning clockwise, then separate the shift control cable from the transmission shift lever. The cable may remain in the bracket.

3. Rotate the shift lever clockwise to the **P** detent, then rotate the lever counterclockwise back through **R** to the **N** detent.

4. With the adjustment button still in the unlocked position, connect the cable to the lever.

5. Lock the cable adjustment button by turning counterclockwise.

6. Lower the vehicle and check cable adjustment.

THROTTLE VALVE CABLE ADJUSTMENT

NOTE: Setting of the TV cable must be done by rotating the throttle lever at the throttle body. Do not use the accelerator pedal to rotate the throttle body lever.

1. Ensure the engine is **OFF**.

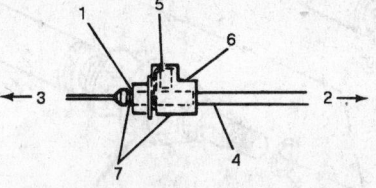

1. Slider against fitting (zero or reset position)
2. Reset direction
3. Direction of cable actuating lever
4. Automatic transmission TV cable assembly
5. Automatic transmission TV cable reset tab
6. Automatic transmission TV cable fitting
7. Automatic transmission TV cable slider

8470Q056

Throttle Valve (TV) cable adjustment

2. Depress and hold-down the metal reset tab at the engine end of the TV cable.

3. Move the slider until it stops against the fitting.

4. Release the reset tab.

5. Rotate the throttle lever to it's full travel position.

6. The slider must move (ratchet) toward the throttle when the lever is rotated to it's full travel position.

7. Ensure the cable moves freely. The cable may appear to function properly with the engine stopped and cold. Recheck after the engine is hot.

DRIVE AXLE

Driveshaft and U-Joints

REMOVAL AND INSTALLATION

1. Raise and support the vehicle safely.

2. Matchmark the rear axle pinion flange to the driveshaft assembly for installation purposes.

3. If removing a 2-piece driveshaft, remove the bolts from the center support bearing, then remove the center support bearing and washers from the torque arm assembly.

4. Remove the 4 driveshaft strap bolts at the rear of the shaft assembly, then remove the 2 retaining straps.

5. Lower the driveshaft down slightly at the rear, then carefully pull the shaft backwards and out from the transmission housing. The transmission housing should be plugged to prevent leakage. If the bearing caps are loose, tape them together to prevent dropping and losing the bearing rollers.

A. One-piece propeller shaft assembly
B. Two-piece propeller shaft assembly
C. Trunnions
D. Spline coupling
E. Propeller shaft slip yoke assembly damper
1. Propeller shaft damper and slip
2. Propeller shaft universal joint spider
3. Propeller shaft universal joint spider bearing
4. Propeller shaft universal joint spider bearing retainer ring
5. Propeller shaft assembly
6. Front propeller shaft assembly
7. Propeller shaft center support bearing
8. Rear propeller shaft seal
9. Propeller shaft joint
10. Rear propeller shaft assembly
11. Propeller shaft front slip yoke assembly

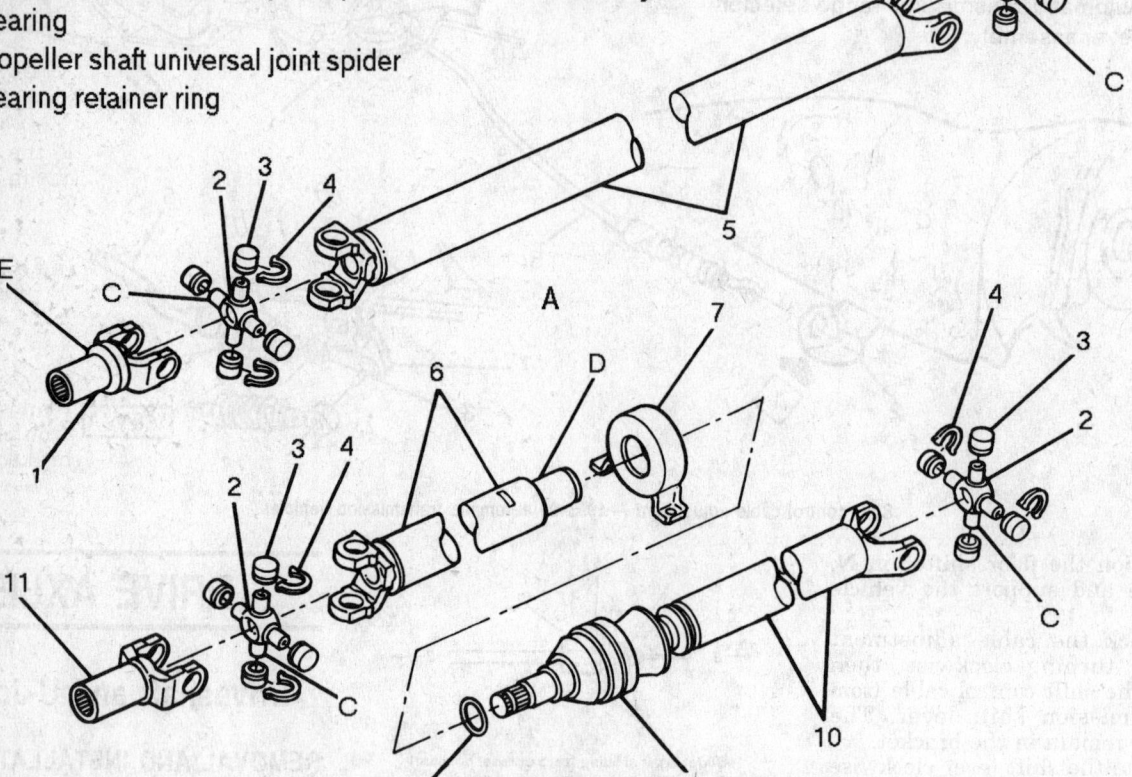

Exploded view of the 1 and 2-piece driveshaft assemblies

8470Q057

6. If necessary, separate the 2-piece driveshaft assembly:

a. Position the shaft assembly horizontally in a soft-jawed vice.

b. Screw a suitable axle shaft remover (such as J-33008) onto a slide hammer, then position the axle remover on the shaft joint between the joint bell area and the shaft assembly.

c. Use the slide hammer to drive the driveshaft halves apart.

d. Remove and discard the old shaft seal from the front of the rear shaft half.

7. The U-joints will either be the nylon injected ring type (production) or the snapring type (replacement).

To replace the U-joints proceed as applicable:

a. If equipped with the snapring type, remove the snaprings from the U-joints. If a snapring does not readily come out, tap the end of the bearing cap lightly to relieve the pressure against the snapring.

b. Support the driveshaft horizontally in line with the base plate of a press, but do not clamp the tube.

c. Support the lower ear of the universal joint with a 1⅛ inch socket.

d. Remove the lower bearing cap out of the yoke ear by placing tool J-9522-3 or equivalent U-joint

bearing separator, on the open horizontal bearing caps and pressing the lower bearing cap out of the yoke ear.

NOTE: If the U-joint is a nylon injected ring type, this will shear the nylon injector ring on the lower bearing cap. There are no bearing retainer grooves in the production bearing caps, therefore they cannot be reused. Replace nylon injected ring U-joints with external snapring type U-joints.

e. If the bearing cap is not completely removed, lift tool J-9522-3 and insert tool J-9522-5 or equivalent between the bearing cap and seal, then continue pressing the U-joint out of the yoke.

f. Repeat the procedure for the opposite side.

g. Remove the spider from the yoke.

To install:

8. When replacing U-joints always replace the entire assembly consisting of 1 pregreased spider, 4 bearing cap assemblies with seals, needle roller bearings, round and flat derlin washers, grease and 4 snaprings. Make sure the seals are in place on the bearing caps to hold the needle roller bearings in position during service. Replace U-joints as follows:

a. Install 1 bearing cap part way into 1 side of the yoke. Turn this yoke ear to the bottom.

b. Using tool J–9522–3 or equivalent, seat the trunnion into the bearing cap.

c. Install the opposite bearing cap partially onto the trunnion.

d. Ensure that both trunnions are straight and true in the bearing caps.

e. Press against the opposite bearing caps, while working the spider back and forth to ensure free movement of the trunnions in the bearings.

f. If the trunnion is binding, one or more of the needle bearings may have tipped under the end of the trunnion, stop pressing and correct the situation.

g. Stop pressing when 1 bearing cap clears the retainer groove inside the yoke.

h. Install a snapring by pressing it into place.

i. Repeat the procedure for the remaining bearing caps and U-joint.

9. If assembling and installing a 2-piece driveshaft:

a. Position a new shaft seal to the front of the rear half of the driveshaft assembly.

b. Align the 2 halves of the shaft assembly and push them together by hand until the snapring on the shaft joint engages in the shaft assembly. If the shafts can still be separated by hand, then snapring is not engaged, realign the shafts and try again.

10. Lubricate the spline with clean engine oil for 1992 vehicles or using slip yoke lubricant for 1993–96 vehicles, then install the slip yoke into the transmission.

11. Align the marks and install the rear of the driveshaft with the rear

U-joint to the pinion yoke making sure the bearing caps are properly seated.

12. Install the retaining straps and tighten the bolts evenly to 16 ft. lbs. (22 Nm).

13. If installing a 2-piece driveshaft assembly, install the washers and the center support bearing, then install the retaining bolts and tighten to 37 ft. lbs. (50 Nm).

14. Lower the vehicle.

Rear Axle Shaft, Bearing and Seal

REMOVAL AND INSTALLATION

1. Raise and support the vehicle safely.

2. Remove the rear tire and wheel assembly.

3. Remove the brake rotor or the brake drum and components, as equipped.

4. Clean the carrier cover and surrounding area to prevent dirt or contamination from entering the housing, then remove the carrier cover and drain the gear oil into a suitable container.

5. For 1993–93 vehicles, install J–39446, or an equivalent ABS exciter ring protector kit.

6. Remove the rear axle pinion shaft lockscrew and pinion shaft.

7. Push the flanged end of the axle shaft into the axle housing and remove the C-clip shaft lock from the differential case end of the shaft.

8. Remove the axle shaft from the axle housing.

9. If necessary to service the seal or bearing, use a small suitable prytool to remove the oil seal from the axle housing. Be careful not to score or damage the housing.

10. If necessary, install tool J–22813–01 or equivalent axle bearing remover, into the bore of the axle housing and position it behind the bearing, ensure the tangs of the tool engage the outer race. Remove the bearing using a slide hammer.

To install:

11. If removed, lubricate the new bearing and sealing lips with gear lubricant and install the bearing with a suitable driver so the tool bottoms against the shoulder in axle housing.

12. If removed, Position seal on suitable seal installer, then insert the seal into the housing bore. Position the seal flush with the axle tube.

13. Taking care not to damage the seal, slide the axle shaft into place so

the splines engage with the splines of the side gear.

14. Insert the shaft C-lock into the bottom end of the axle shaft and push the shaft outward so the lock seats in the counterbore of the rear axle side gear.

15. Insert the rear axle pinion gear shaft through the differential case, thrust washer and pinion gears. Align the hole in the shaft with the lockscrew hole.

16. Install the lockscrew and tighten to 27 ft. lbs. (36 Nm).

17. Clean the cover gasket mating surfaces of any remaining gasket or old sealant, then for 1992 vehicles apply a thin coat of 1052366 or equivalent, to the new gasket.

18. Install the gasket onto the carrier cover, then install the carrier cover and tighten the bolts in a crosswise pattern to 22 ft. lbs. (30 Nm) for 1992–93 vehicles.

NOTE: When refilling a limited slip differential rear axle with gear oil, 4 oz (118ml) of limited slip additive should be added.

19. Fill the differential carrier with SAE 80W-90 GL-5 gear lubricant or equivalent, then install the plug.

20. Install the rear brake assemblies and rear wheels. Lower the vehicle.

Pinion Seal

REMOVAL AND INSTALLATION

1. Raise and support the vehicle safely.

2. For 1993–96 vehicles, remove the rear tire and wheel assembly, then remove the brake rotor or the brake drum and components, as equipped.

3. Matchmark the driveshaft and pinion yoke for installation in the same position, then remove the driveshaft.

4. For 1992 vehicles, turn the rear wheels and tap the brake backing plates lightly with a soft hammer to ensure that the brakes are free

5. Use an inch-pound torque wrench to record the combined drive pinion gear inner and outer bearing, axle shaft bearing and differential nut preload.

6. Place a container under the differential to catch any fluid that may drain from the rear axle.

7. Using a yoke holding tool, keep the pinion flange from turning and remove the pinion flange nut and washer.

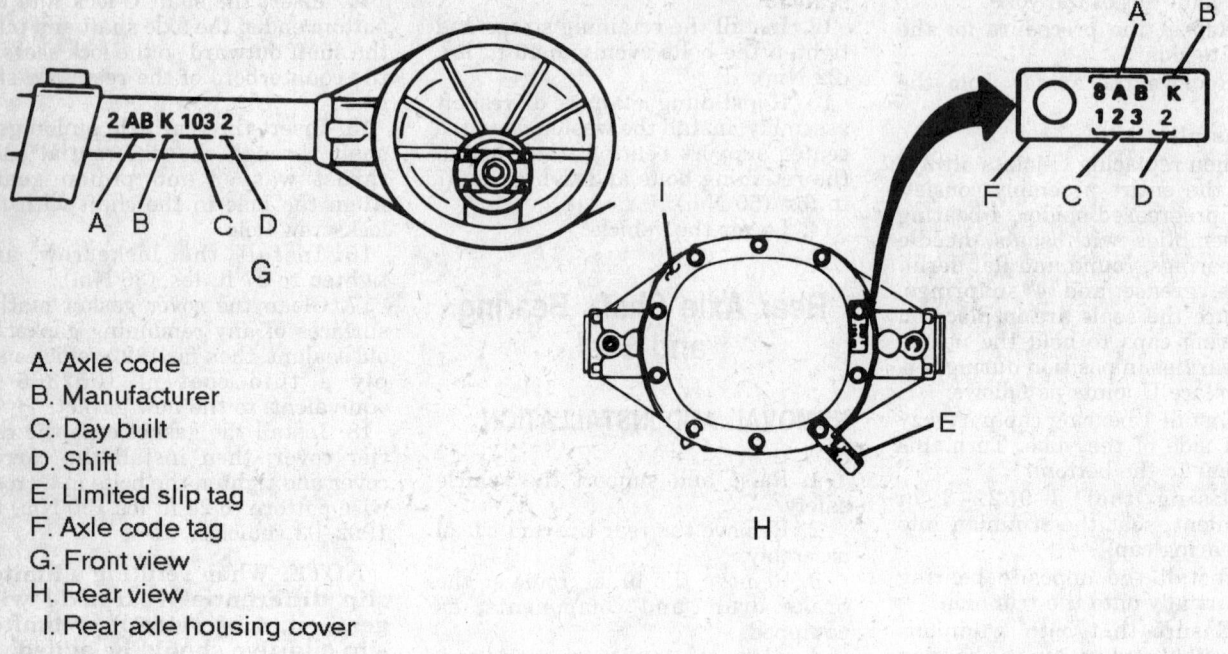

A. Axle code
B. Manufacturer
C. Day built
D. Shift
E. Limited slip tag
F. Axle code tag
G. Front view
H. Rear view
I. Rear axle housing cover

8470Q060

Standard rear axle identification

8. Using a suitable remover/adapter tool, remove the pinion yoke.

9. Use a blunt chisel to drive the pinion seal out of the carrier. Take care not to damage rear axle housing.

To install:

10. Inspect the sealing surfaces of the pinion yoke for nicks or damage and replace, as necessary. Examine the carrier bore and remove any burrs that may cause leaks around the outside of the seal.

11. Position the new seal using a suitable seal installer tool.

12. Apply a seal lubricant to the outer diameter of the pinion flange and the sealing lip of the new seal.

13. Install the pinion yoke on the drive pinion by taping with a soft-face hammer until a sufficient amount of pinion threads project through the pinion yoke.

14. Install the washer and pinion flange nut. While holding the pinion yoke, tighten the nut to achieve the preload noted earlier. Tighten the nut gradually, rotating the pinion gear several revolutions after each turn in order to set the bearings. Check the preload each time using an inch-pound torque wrench and continue the sequence until a preload is achieved which is 3-5 inch lbs.

(0.3–0.6 Nm) more than the preload noted during removal.

15. Align and install the driveshaft assembly.

16. For 1993–96 vehicles, install the brake components and drum or rotor, as applicable, then install the wheel assembly.

17. Check and add the correct lubricant, as necessary, then lower the vehicle.

Differential Carrier

REMOVAL AND INSTALLATION

1. Disconnect the negative battery cable.

2. Remove the rear axle assembly from the vehicle.

3. Remove the differential cover and drain the gear oil into a suitable container, then mount the assembly in a suitable support.

4. If not done already, remove the axle shafts from the housing.

5. For 1993–96 vehicles, remove the retaining bolts, then remove the wheel speed sensor from the top of the axle assembly.

6. Mark the differential bearing caps L and R to make sure they will be reassembled in their original locations. Remove the bearing cap bolts

and caps. Upon removal, the left and right outer races and shims should be placed in sets with the caps to assure installation in their proper locations as well.

7. Using a suitable tool, carefully pry differential carrier from the housing assembly. Be careful not to damage the gasket sealing surface when removing the unit.

To install:

8. Inspect the differential carrier housing for foreign material. Check the ring and pinion for chipped teeth, excessive wear and scoring. Check the carrier bearings visually and by feel. Clean the differential housing and replace components, as necessary.

9. Install the differential carrier into the housing assembly.

NOTE: Do not attempt to reinstall production shims as they may break when tapped into position. If service shims were already installed, they may be reused, otherwise select new shims to replace the production parts.

10. Install the shims into their respective positions. Select and install a shim for each side which is 0.004 in. (0.10mm) thicker than the shim which was removed from that side. Install the left shim followed by the

right shim, but it will be necessary to drive the right shim into position using a side bearing shim tool.

11. Install and tighten the differential bearing cap bolts to 55 ft. lbs. (75 Nm) except on Borg-Warner rear axles which should be tightened to 40 ft. lbs. (54 Nm).

12. Rotate the differential carrier a few times to seat the bearings, then mount a dial indicator set to check ring gear backlash. To assure proper measurement, position the dial indicator so the stem is in line with the gear rotation and perpendicular to the tooth angle. Measure the ring gear backlash at 3 or 4 equally spaced points:

a. Backlash tolerance is 0.005–0.009 in. (0.13–0.23mm) and cannot vary more than 0.002 in. (0.05mm).

b. High backlash is corrected by moving some shims from the opposite side of the case to the ring gear side, thus moving the ring gear closer to the pinion.

c. Low backlash is corrected by moving shims from the ring gear side of the case to the opposite side, thus moving the ring gear away from the pinion.

13. Install the rear axle shafts to the housing assembly.

14. Clean the cover gasket mating surfaces of any remaining gasket or old sealant, then for 1992 vehicles apply a thin coat of 1052366 or equivalent, to the new gasket.

15. Install the gasket onto the carrier cover, then install the carrier cover and tighten the bolts in a crosswise pattern to 22 ft. lbs. (30 Nm) for 1992–93 vehicles.

NOTE: When refilling a limited slip differential rear axle with gear oil, 4 oz (118ml) of limited slip additive should be added.

16. Fill the differential carrier with SAE 80W-90 GL-5 gear lubricant or equivalent, then install the plug.

17. For 1993–96 vehicles, install the wheel speed sensor assembly to the top of the axle housing and tighten the retaining bolt to 89 inch lbs. (10 Nm).

18. Install the rear axle assembly to the vehicle.

19. Connect the negative battery cable.

Axle Housing

REMOVAL AND INSTALLATION

1. Raise the support the vehicle safely by the frame, then position an adjustable support under the axle housing.

2. For 1993–96 vehicles, matchmark and remove the driveshaft assembly, then remove the stabilizer bar.

3. Remove the tire and wheel assemblies.

4. Disconnect the shock absorbers from the axle.

5. Remove the track bar/rear axle tie rod assembly.

6. Remove the brake line junction block bolt at the axle housing.

7. Disconnect the brake lines at the junction block, then plug all openings to prevent system contamination or excessive fluid loss. Remove the brake lines from the housing clips.

8. Remove the rear springs.

9. for 1993–96 vehicles, disconnect the parking brake assemblies from the housing assembly, then disengage the electrical connector from the wheel speed sensor.

10. For 1992 vehicles, remove the axle shafts and the brake backing plates.

11. Disconnect the torque arm and the lower control arms from the axle housing.

12. For 1992 vehicles, matchmark the driveshaft and pinion yoke, then disconnect the driveshaft and support aside.

13. With the aid of an assistant, lower the rear axle assembly and remove it from the vehicle.

To install:

14. With the aid of an assistant, raise the rear axle housing into position.

15. For 1992 vehicles, align and install the driveshaft assembly.

16. Connect the torque arm and the lower control arms to the axle.

17. For 1992 vehicles, install the brake backing plates and the axle shafts.

18. For 1993–96 vehicles, engage the wheel speed sensor connector, then install the parking brake assemblies.

19. Install the rear springs.

20. Connect the brake lines to the under axle housing clips.

21. Unplug and connect the brake lines to the junction block. Install the junction block bolt to the axle housing.

22. Install the track bar/rear axle tie rod assembly and the shock absorbers.

23. For 1993–96 vehicles, install the stabilizer shaft, then align and install the driveshaft assembly.

24. Check and add axle lubricant to the housing.

25. Install the tire and wheel assemblies.

26. With the weight of the vehicle on the axle, tighten the control arm bolts to 85 ft. lbs. (115 Nm) for 1992 vehicles or to 80 ft. lbs. (108 Nm) for 1993–96 vehicles.

27. Remove the adjustable support and lower the vehicle for access, then bleed the hydraulic brake system.

28. Completely lower the vehicle.

STEERING

Steering Wheel

REMOVAL AND INSTALLATION

—— **CAUTION** ——

The vehicle is equipped with a SIR air bag system, follow the recommended disarming procedures before performing any work on or around the system. Failure to do so may result in possible deployment of the air bag and/or personal injury.

1. Disable the Supplemental Inflatable Restraint (SIR) system.

2. Disconnect the negative battery cable.

3. Loosen the screws and on 1992 vehicles the locknuts from the back of the steering wheel using a suitable Torx® driver, then remove the inflator module from the steering wheel.

—— **CAUTION** ——

When carrying a live inflator module, ensure the bag and trim cover are pointed away from the body. Never carry the inflator module by the wires or connector on the underside of the module. This will minimize the chance of injury should the module accidentally deploy. When placing a live inflator module on a bench or other surface, always place the bag and trim cover up, away from the surface. This is necessary so a free space is provided to allow for air bag expansion in the unlikely event of accidental deployment.

4. Disengage the coil assembly connector and Connector Position Assurance (CPA) device or clip from the inflator module terminal.

5. Remove the steering wheel locking nut.

6. Using a suitable puller, remove the steering wheel and disconnect the horn contact. When attaching the steering wheel puller, use care to prevent threading the side screws all the way through the hub, into the coil, thereby damaging the SIR coil assembly.

To install:

7. Route the coil assembly connector through the steering wheel.

8. Connect the horn contact and install the steering wheel. When installing the steering wheel, align the block tooth on the steering wheel with the block tooth on the steering shaft within 1 female serration.

9. Install the steering wheel locking nut and tighten the nut to 32 ft. lbs. (43 Nm).

10. Connect the coil assembly connector and CPA device or clip to the inflator module terminal. Secure the coil assembly connector to the steering wheel by inserting the thick section of wire into the existing retainers.

11. Install the inflator module. Ensure the wiring is not exposed or trapped between the inflator module and the steering wheel. Tighten the inflator module screws to 25 inch lbs. (2.8 Nm).

12. Connect then negative battery cable and enable the SIR system.

Steering Column

REMOVAL AND INSTALLATION

1. Disable the SIR system and disconnect the negative battery cable.

2. For 1992 vehicles, remove the nut and bolt from the upper intermediate shaft coupling, then separate the coupling from the lower end of the steering column.

3. Remove the left sound insulator panel and the driver knee bolster with bracket.

4. If the column is to be repaired or replaced, remove the inflator module and the steering wheel.

5. For 1993–96 vehicles, disconnect the steering rack coupling shaft assembly:

   a. Remove the bolt attaching the assembly to the steering rack.

   b. Remove the clamp from the lower end of the protective boot,

then disengage the shaft assembly from the rack.

   c. Remove the boot from the shaft assembly.

   d. For the 5.7L engine, remove the shield from the shaft and column assemblies.

   e. Remove the bolt retaining upper end of the coupling shaft assembly to the column, then disengage the shaft assembly from the column.

6. Remove the bolts attaching the cover/toe plate to the dash, then separate the cover from the dash.

7. Disengage the electrical connectors.

8. Remove the nuts attaching the steering column support bracket to the instrument panel, then carefully lower the column.

9. If equipped with an automatic transmission, disconnect the park lock cable from the ignition switch inhibitor.

10. Remove the steering column from the vehicle. Take care when handling the column assembly, it is extremely susceptible to damage. Leaning on the column, dropping it or exposing it to shock or stress could impair the column's collapsible design.

To install:

NOTE: If a replacement steering column is being installed, do not remove the anti-rotation pin until after the steering column has been connected to the steering gear. Removing the anti-rotation pin before the steering column is connected to the steering gear may damage the SIR coil assembly.

11. Position the steering column in the vehicle.

12. Connect the park lock cable to the ignition switch inhibitor on vehicles equipped with automatic transmission.

13. Raise the column into position and install the nuts attaching the steering column support bracket to the instrument panel. Tighten the retaining nuts to 20 ft. lbs. (27 Nm) for 1992 vehicles or to 18 ft. lbs. (25 Nm) for 1993–96 vehicles.

14. For 1993–96 vehicles, install the steering rack coupling shaft assembly:

   a. Engage the shaft assembly to the column, then install the retaining bolt and tighten to 35 ft. lbs. (47 Nm).

   b. Position the boot and clamp to the shaft assembly, but do not tighten the clamp at this time.

   c. Position the shaft assembly to the body rail, then remove the clamp from the boot and place over the steering rack assembly casting.

   d. Engage the shaft assembly to the rack, then install the retaining bolt and tighten to 35 ft. lbs. (47 Nm).

   e. Make sure the shaft assembly and boot are properly installed, then for 5.7L engines position the shield and secure by pressing the shield button into the column assembly hole.

15. For 1992 vehicles install the nut and bolt to the upper intermediate shaft coupling attaching the upper intermediate shaft to the steering column. Tighten the nut to 40 ft. lbs. (54 Nm).

16. Install the bolts attaching the cover/toe plate to the dash and tighten to 37 inch lbs. (4.2 Nm) for 1992 vehicles or to 89 inch lbs. (10 Nm) for 1993–96 vehicles.

17. Engage the electrical connectors.

18. If a service replacement column is being installed, remove the anti-rotation pin, then if applicable remove the hexagon locking nut, the coil assembly shipping cover and disengage the connector from the cover.

NOTE: If SIR coil has become uncentered by turning of the steering wheel without the column connected to the steering gear, follow the proper centering procedure for the SIR coil assembly.

19. Install the steering wheel and the inflator module.

20. Install the knee bolster and bracket along with the left sound insulator panel.

21. Connect then negative battery cable and enable the SIR system.

Power Steering Gear

The 1992 vehicles are equipped with a power steering gear, which was replaced on the 1993 and later vehicles by a power rack and pinion assembly.

ADJUSTMENT

NOTE: Adjust the worm bearing preload first, then proceed with the pitman shaft over-center adjustment.

Worm Bearing Preload

1. Remove the steering gear.

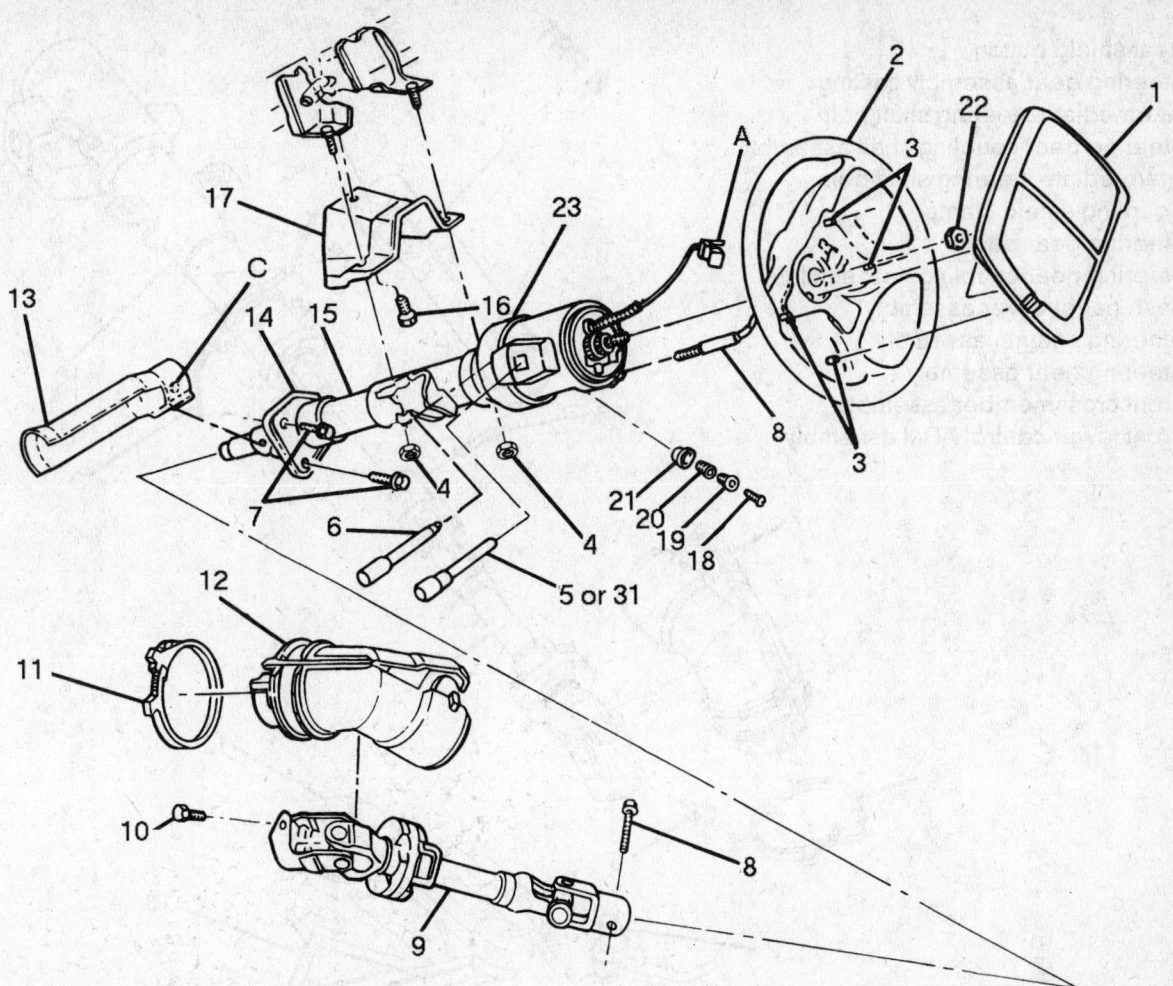

A. SIR coil assembly electrical connector
B. Horn lead
C. Steering gear coupling heat shield button
1. Inflatable restraint steering wheel module assembly
2. Steering wheel assembly
3. Steering wheel bolt/screw, 25 LB IN (2.8 NM)
4. Steering column upper support nut - 18 LB FT (25 NM)
5. Turn signal and headlamp dimmer switch and cruise control actuator and windshield wiper and windshield washer lever assembly
6. Steering column tilt wheel release lever assembly
7. Steering column bolt/screw - 89 LB IN (10 NM)
8. Intermediate steering shaft bolt/screw - 35 LB FT (47 NM)
9. Steering gear coupling shaft assembly
10. Intermediate steering shaft bolt/screw - 35 LB FT (47 NM)

11. Steering gear coupling shield clamp
12. Steering gear boot
13. Steering gear coupling heat shield
14. Steering column dash panel cover assembly
15. Steering column assembly
16. Steering column guide bolt/screw - 18 LB FT (25 NM)
17. Steering column guide
18. Hazard warning switch knob bolt/screw - 6 LB IN (0.7 NM)
19. Hazard warning switch button
20. Hazard warning switch knob spring
21. Hazard warning switch knob
22. Steering wheel nut - 32 LB FT (43 NM)
23. Steering column sealer
24. Turn signal and headlamp dimmer switch and windshield wiper and windshield washer lever assembly

8470Q062

Exploded view of the steering column mounting and outer components — 1993–96 vehicles — 1992 similar

1. Heat shield button
2. Steering gear assembly casting
3. Intermediate steering shaft bolt
4. Steering gear coupling shaft assembly
5. Intermediate steering shaft bolt
6. Coupling shield clamp
7. Steering gear boot
8. Steering gear coupling heat shield
9. Dash panel cover assembly
10. Steering column assembly
11. Steering gear assembly
12. Front crossmember assembly
13. Front lower control ARM assembly

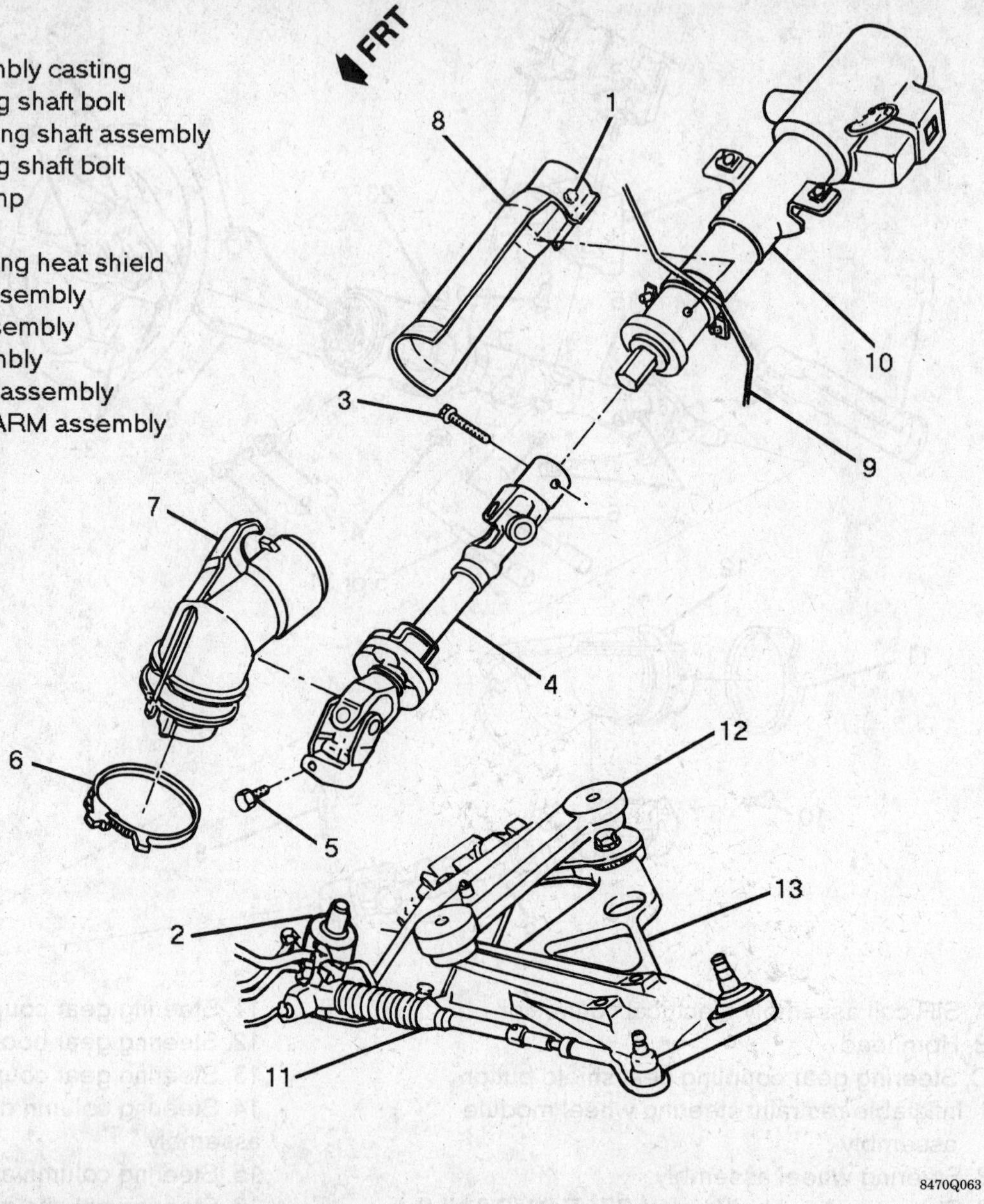

Exploded view of the steering rack coupling shaft assembly — 1993–96 vehicles

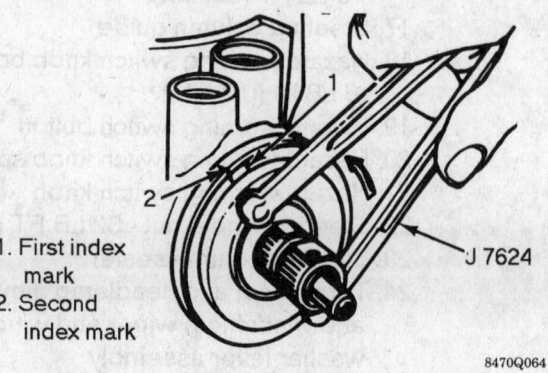

1. First index mark
2. Second index mark

Adjusting the worm bearing preload — 1992 vehicles

2. Rotate the stub shaft and drain the power steering fluid into a suitable container.

3. Mount the gear in a vise and remove the adjuster plug nut.

4. Turn the adjuster plug in (clockwise) using a suitable spanner wrench until the adjuster plug and thrust bearing are firmly bottomed in the housing. Tighten the adjuster plug to 22 ft. lbs. (30 Nm).

5. Place an index mark on the housing even with 1 of the holes in the adjuster plug.

6. Measure back counterclockwise ½ inch (13mm) from the mark and place a second mark on the housing.

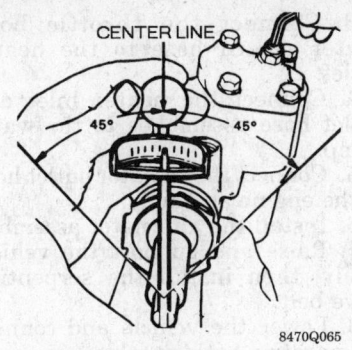

Pitman shaft over-center adjustment — 1992 vehicles

7. Turn the adjuster plug counterclockwise until the hole in the adjuster plug is aligned with the second mark on the housing.

8. Install the adjuster plug nut and using a punch in a notch, tighten securely to 80 ft. lbs. (109 Nm). Hold the adjuster plug to maintain alignment of the marks.

9. Adjust the pitman shaft over-center, if necessary. Install the steering gear.

Pitman Shaft Over-Center

1. Remove the steering gear.

2. If necessary, adjust the worm bearing preload.

3. If not done already, rotate the stub shaft and drain the power steering fluid into a suitable container.

4. Turn the pitman shaft adjuster screw counterclockwise until fully extended, then turn in 1 full turn.

5. Rotate the stub shaft from stop to stop and count the number of turns.

6. Starting at either stop, turn the stub shaft back half the total number of turns. This is the "Center" position of the gear. When the gear is centered, the flat on the stub shaft should face upward and be parallel with the side cover and the master spline on the pitman shaft should be in line with the adjuster screw.

7. Rotate the stub shaft 45 degrees each side of the center using a suitable torque wrench with the handle in the vertical position. The stub shaft should move smoothly and not stick or bind. Record the worm bearing preload measured on or near the center gear position, it should be in the 6–15 inch lbs. (0.7–1.7 Nm) range. If the torque is outside this range, the gear assembly should be readjusted, repaired or replaced.

8. Adjust the over-center drag torque by loosening the adjuster locknut and turning the pitman shaft adjuster screw clockwise until the correct drag torque is obtained: Add 6–10 inch lbs. (0.7–1.1 Nm) torque to the previously measured worm bearing preload torque. Tighten the adjuster locknut to 36 ft. lbs. (49 Nm). Keep the adjuster screw from turning while tightening the adjuster screw locknut.

9. Install the steering gear.

REMOVAL AND INSTALLATION

1. Turn the steering wheels and lock them in the straight-ahead position.

2. Disconnect the pressure hose and cooling pipe from the power steering gear. Cap and raise the lines to prevent fluid contamination or loss.

3. Remove the coupling shield and the bolt from the flexible coupling attaching the intermediate shaft to the steering gear. Gently push the shaft assembly rearward to disengage the latch from the steering gear.

4. Raise and support the vehicle safely.

5. Remove the pitman arm nut and washer. Mark the position of the pitman arm in relation to the gear pitman shaft and remove the arm from the shaft with a suitable puller.

6. Remove the bolts and washers retaining the steering gear box to the side frame rail and remove the gear box from the vehicle.

To install:

7. Position the power steering gear to the frame and loosely install the washers and bolts. Adjust the gear so it aligns as straight as possible with the intermediate shaft.

8. Tighten the steering gear mounting bolts to 73 ft. lbs. (99 Nm).

9. Align the marks on the pitman arm and gear pitman shaft and install the arm to the shaft with the washer and nut. Tighten the nut to 184 ft. lbs. (250 Nm).

10. Lower the vehicle.

11. Install the flexible coupling by aligning the flat on the flexible coupling of the intermediate shaft with the flat on the gear wormshaft. Install and tighten the coupling clamp pinch bolt to 27 ft. lbs. (36 Nm).

12. Unplug and connect the pressure hose and the cooling pipe. Tighten the line fittings to 21 ft. lbs. (28 Nm).

13. Fill and bleed the hydraulic system as necessary.

Power Rack and Pinion

The 1992 vehicles are equipped with a power steering gear, which was replaced on the 1993 and later vehicles by a power rack and pinion assembly.

ADJUSTMENT

Rack Bearing Preload

1. Raise and safely support the vehicle so the front wheels are raised and the steering wheel is centered.

2. Loosen the adjuster plug locknut.

3. Turn the adjuster plug clockwise until it bottoms, then back off 50–70 degrees (approximately 1 flat).

4. Keep the adjuster plug from turning and tighten the locknut to 55 ft. lbs. (75 Nm).

5. Inspect the steering wheel returnability to center after adjustment.

REMOVAL AND INSTALLATION

1. Disconnect the negative battery cable, then raise and support the vehicle safely.

2. Remove the tire and wheel assemblies.

3. Position a drain pan under the rack assembly, then disconnect the inlet and outlet hoses from the gear assembly. Plug all openings to prevent system contamination or excessive fluid loss.

4. Disconnect the steering linkage outer tie rods from the steering knuckles.

5. Disconnect the steering rack coupling shaft assembly from the rack.

6. Remove the nuts and bolts retaining the rack to the vehicle, then remove the rack assembly.

To install:

7. Position the rack to the crossmember, then adjust the rack so it aligns as straight as possible with the rack coupling shaft assembly. Hand-start the bolts and nuts, the using a backup wrench on the nuts, tighten the retainers to 63 ft. lbs. (85 Nm).

8. Connect the steering rack coupling shaft assembly to the rack and tighten the retaining bolt to 35 ft. lbs. (47 Nm).

9. Install the steering linkage outer tie rods to the knuckles.

10. Remove the plugs, then connect the inlet and outlet hoses to the rack assembly. Make sure the hoses are properly routed and not interfering with any other components, then

tighten the rack fittings to 21 ft. lbs. (28 Nm).

11. Install the tire and wheel assemblies, then lower the vehicle.

12. Connect the negative battery cable, then refill and bleed the power steering system.

Power Steering Pump

REMOVAL AND INSTALLATION

1992

1. Remove the serpentine drive belt by loosening the tensioner and pulling it away from the belt.

2. Remove the power steering pump pulley with a suitable puller.

3. Disconnect the hoses at the pump and cap all the openings to prevent fluid contamination or loss. Position the disconnected lines aside and in a raised position.

4. If present, remove the pump side brace, nuts and/or bolts.

5. Loosen the retaining bolts remove the power steering pump.

To install:

6. Install the pump to the front bracket and loosely install the retaining bolts.

7. If equipped, loosely install the pump side brace, nuts and/or bolts.

8. Tighten the all bolts and nuts as applicable:

   a. Side brace nuts and bolts for the 3.1L engine to 18 ft. lbs. (25 Nm).

   b. Side brace to engine nut for the 5.0L or 5.7L engines to 24 ft. lbs. (33 Nm).

   c. Side brace to pump nut for the 5.0L or 5.7L engines to 37 ft. lbs. (50 Nm).

   d. Power steering pump retaining bolts to 37 ft. lbs. (50 Nm).

9. Uncap and connect the hoses to the pump. Tighten fittings to 21 ft. lbs. (28 Nm).

10. Using a suitable pulley installation tool, install the power steering pump pulley.

11. Install the serpentine drive belt.

12. Fill and bleed the hydraulic system as necessary.

1993–96

3.4L ENGINE

1. Position a drain pan under the pump assembly.

2. Remove the serpentine drive belt.

3. Remove the front air intake duct.

4. Disconnect the inlet and outlet hose assemblies from the power steering pump. Plug the openings to prevent system contamination or excessive fluid loss.

5. Remove the pulley from the pump using a suitable puller.

6. Remove the pump support from the assembly, then remove the pump retaining bolts· and remove the assembly from the vehicle.

To install:

7. Position the pump assembly to the brace, then install the retaining bolts and tighten to 37 ft. lbs. (50 Nm).

8. Install the pump support.

9. Install the pump pulley using a suitable installer tool. Make sure the face of the pulley hub is flush with the end of the pump shaft before a load is applied to the hub.

10. Remove the plugs, then connect the inlet and outlet hose assemblies to the pump. Tighten the hose fittings to 21 ft. lbs. (28 Nm).

11. Install the front air intake duct, then install the serpentine drive belt.

12. Refill and bleed the power steering system.

5.7L ENGINE

1. Disconnect the negative battery cable, then raise and support the vehicle safely.

2. Drain the engine cooling system and remove the serpentine drive belt, then lower the vehicle.

3. Position a drain pan under the pump assembly, then remove the air intake duct.

4. Remove the alternator assembly.

5. Disconnect the radiator outlet hose from the engine.

6. Disconnect the heater inlet and outlet hose assemblies from the water pump.

7. Remove the throttle body heater return hose from the heater outlet hose assembly.

8. Remove the power steering pump assembly retaining bolts.

9. Disconnect the inlet and outlet hose assemblies from the power steering pump. Plug the openings to prevent system contamination or excessive fluid loss.

10. Remove the pump assembly from the vehicle.

To install:

11. Position the pump in the vehicle and connect the hose assemblies. Tighten the hose fittings to 21 ft. lbs. (28 Nm).

12. Install the pump assembly to the bracket and tighten the retaining bolts to 18 ft. lbs. (25 Nm).

13. Connect the throttle body heater return hose to the heater outlet.

14. Connect the heater inlet and outlet hose assemblies to the water pump.

15. Connect the radiator outlet hose to the engine assembly.

16. Install the alternator assembly.

17. Raise and support the vehicle safely, then install the serpentine drive belt.

18. Lower the vehicle and connect the negative battery cable.

19. Refill and bleed the engine cooling system.

20. Refill and bleed the power steering system.

BELT ADJUSTMENT

Serpentine belts are automatically adjusted by the tensioner on the engine. If belt slippage occurs, check the belt length scale on the drive belt tensioner for the proper installed length and replace as necessary. If the drive belt tensioner is within it's operating range and belt slippage still occurs, the tensioner may need replacement. For 1992 vehicles, check the belt tensioner as follows:

1. Run the engine for 5–10 minutes.

2. Shut OFF the engine and check the belt tension at the following locations using J-23600–B belt tension gauge or equivalent.

   a. V6 engines: If without air conditioning, check the belt tension between the tensioner and the power steering pump pulley. If with air conditioning, check the belt tension between the tensioner and the air conditioner compressor pulley.

   b. V8 engine: Check the belt tension between any 2 pulleys.

3. Run the engine for 30 seconds and recheck the belt tension.

4. Repeat Step 3. The belt tension is the average of the 3 readings.

   a. V6 engine: Belt tension should be 95–140 lbs. (422–623 N) if without air conditioning. If with air conditioning, the belt tension should be 85–110 lbs. (378–490 N).

   b. V8 engine: Belt tension should be 99–121 lbs. (440–538 N).

5. Replace the drive belt tensioner if the belt tension is below the minimum specified and if the tensioner is within it's operating range.

SYSTEM BLEEDING

1. With the engine **OFF**, raise and safely support the vehicle sufficiently

high to hold the wheels off the ground.

2. Turn the wheels all the way to the left, then add power steering fluid to the FULL COLD or C mark on the fluid level indicator.

3. Bleed the system by turning the wheels from side to side without hitting the stops. It may be necessary to continue this several times in order to bleed air from the system.

4. Start the engine and allow it to idle, then recheck the fluid level. If necessary, as fluid to bring the level to the FULL COLD or C mark.

5. Return the wheels to the center position and keep the engine running for 2–3 minutes.

6. Make sure the steering functions normally and is free from noise.

7. Road test the vehicle and recheck the fluid level ensuring the level is up to the HOT or H mark.

Tie Rod Ends

REMOVAL AND INSTALLATION

1992

1. Raise and safely support the vehicle.

2. Remove the cotter pin from the ball stud, then remove the castellated nut.

3. Disconnect the tie rod end from the steering arm relay rod (inner tie rod) or the steering knuckle (outer tie rod) with a tie rod joint separator.

4. Mark the tie rod end positions in relation to the adjuster tube for installation reference. Loosen the clamp bolts and unscrew the ends from the adjuster tubes. Count the number of turns required to remove each tie rod end from the adjuster tube. If a force of more than 80 inch lbs. (9 Nm) is required to remove the adjuster clamp fasteners after break away, the fasteners should be replaced.

To install:

5. Inspect the threads on the ball stud and castle nut for damage and the ball stud taper for nicks. Check the seal for damage. Replace components as necessary.

6. Lubricate the tie rod adjuster tube threads with chassis lube. Install the tie rod end into the tie rod adjuster tube, using the same number of turns counted during removal. This should align the marks made prior to removal of the ends from the adjuster.

7. Install the tie rod end into the steering arm relay rod or the steering knuckle, then install the castellated

nut. If necessary, a linkage installer should be used on inner tie rods to properly seat the tapers.

8. Tighten the castellated nut to 35 ft. lbs. (48 Nm) except for the inner ball attaching nut on 1992 vehicles which should be tightened to 40 ft. lbs. (54 Nm). If necessary, tighten the nut further just enough to align the slot in the nut with the hole in the stud. Do not back off the nut to align the slot and hole.

9. Install new cotter pins on all castellated nuts.

10. Position the clamp on the adjuster tube with the bolt to the bottom of the tube and the nut to the front of the vehicle. Tighten the adjuster clamp nut to 13 ft. lbs. (17 Nm).

11. Lower the vehicle, then check and adjust the toe setting as necessary.

1993–96

1. Disconnect battery ground cable.

2. Raise and support the vehicle safely.

3. Remove the tie rod cotter pin and hex slotted nut from the tie rod assembly.

4. Loosen tie rod jam nut.

5. Using tool J–24319–01, or an equivalent linkage puller, remove the tie rod from the steering knuckle.

6. Remove the tie rod from the steering rack assembly. To ease installation and give a point from which the alignment may be adjusted, scribe alignment marks on the rack assembly prior to tie rod end removal, and/or count the number of turns necessary to remove the tie rod end.

To install:

7. Install the tie rod to the steering rack assembly, but do not tighten the jam nut. Thread the tie rod end in the same number of turns and/or align it to the marks made during removal.

8. Install the tie rod to the steering knuckle and install the hex slotted nut to the tie rod stud.

9. Tighten the hex nut to 35 ft. lbs. (47 Nm), then insert a new cotter pin. If necessary tighten the nut additionally in order to insert the pin, but do not exceed a total torque of 52 ft. lbs. (70 Nm) and do not back off the original torque.

10. Check and adjust toe, as necessary.

NOTE: Make sure the rack and pinion boot is not twisted or puckered during installation or adjustment.

11. Adjust the toe by turning the inner tie rod, making sure the rack and pinion boot is not twisted or puckered during toe adjustment.

12. Tighten the jam nut against the tie rod to 50 ft. lbs. (68 Nm).

BRAKES

Master Cylinder

REMOVAL AND INSTALLATION

1992

1. Disconnect the brake lines at the master cylinder.

2. Plug the lines to prevent fluid contamination or loss.

3. Remove the 2 master cylinder attaching nuts.

4. If equipped with a manual transmission, move the clutch master cylinder reservoir and bracket aside.

5. Move the combination valve aside.

6. Remove the master cylinder.

To install:

7. Install the master cylinder, combination valve and if applicable, the clutch master cylinder with bracket.

8. Install and tighten the 2 attaching nuts to 24 ft. lbs. (33 Nm).

9. Uncap and install the brake lines to the master cylinder. Tighten the fittings to 18 ft. lbs. (24 Nm).

10. Fill the master cylinder to the proper level with clean brake fluid and bleed the brake system.

1993–96

1. Drain the brake fluid from the reservoir.

2. Disconnect the 2 brake lines from the master cylinder, then plug the openings to prevent system contamination or excessive fluid loss.

3. Remove the 2 master cylinder attaching nuts, then carefully remove the master cylinder from the vehicle. Do not allow brake fluid to come in contact with vehicle painted surfaces, wiring or electrical connections.

To install:

4. Bench bleed the master cylinder assembly:

  a. Fabricate 2 plugs for the master cylinder outlet ports. This can be accomplished using 2 pieces of ³/₁₆ in. (4.75mm) brake tubing of 2 in. (50mm) in length each, along with 2 brake tube fitting nuts, one

11 x 1.5mm and the other 12 x 1.0mm. Fashion ISO flares on 1 end of each tube, then install the nuts onto the tubes. Place approximately ½ in. (13mm) of each tube unflared end in a vise (1 tube at a time), then compress the tube end using the vise, bend the tube to a 90 degree angle, then reinstall the tube in the vise and fold the tube end against itself to form an air-tight seal.

b. Plug the master cylinder outlet ports using the plugs.

c. Place shop towels around the master cylinder assembly to absorb bled fluid, then mount the assembly in a vise. Make sure the front end of the cylinder assembly is mounted slightly lower than the rear.

d. Fill the master cylinder with clean brake fluid, then use a small tool with a smooth rounded end to stroke the primary piston about 1 in. (25mm) several times.

NOTE: The backpressure produced by plugging the outlet ports may not allow a full 1 in. (25mm) stroke.

e. Reposition the cylinder in the vise so the front end is positioned slightly higher than the rear and continue to stroke the primary piston.

f. Reposition the master cylinder so it is level in the vise, then loosen the plugs (1 at a time) and push the primary piston into the master cylinder to bleed air from the port. Tighten the plug before allowing the piston to withdraw, or air will be drawn back into the master cylinder.

g. Continue to loosen the plugs and push in the primary piston until all air is bleed from the master cylinder assembly.

5. Install the master cylinder assembly to the brake booster, then tighten the 2 attaching nuts to 32 ft. lbs. (43 Nm).

6. Install each of the brake pipe assemblies to the master cylinder 1 at a time by unplugging the brake line, then removing the fabricated plug and quickly installing the brake pipe fitting finger-tight.

7. Have an assistant depress the brake pedal to remove air at the loose brake pipe fittings, then tighten the fittings to 24 ft. lbs. (32 Nm).

8. Have the assistant quickly release and pump the brake pedal several times.

9. If the brake pedal feels firm, start the vehicle. If the pedal is still

firm with the engine running, carefully test drive the vehicle. If the pedal feels soft or spongy, bleed the entire brake system.

Combination Valve

REMOVAL AND INSTALLATION

1992

1. Disconnect the negative battery cable.

2. Disconnect the brake lines at the combination valve. Plug the openings to prevent fluid contamination or loss.

3. Disengage the electrical connector from the combination valve switch terminal.

4. Remove the 2 nuts attaching the combination valve to the booster.

5. On vehicles with a manual transmission, move the clutch master cylinder and bracket aside.

6. Remove the combination valve.

To install:

7. Install the combination valve and if applicable, the clutch master cylinder with bracket.

8. Install the 2 attaching nuts and tighten to 24 ft. lbs. (33 Nm).

9. Uncap and install the brake lines to the master cylinder, then tighten the fittings to 18 ft. lbs. (24 Nm).

10. Engage the electrical connector to the combination valve switch terminal.

11. Connect the negative battery cable and bleed the brake system.

1993–96

On these vehicles, the combination valve is attached to the ABS hydraulic modulator assembly.

1. Remove the ABS hydraulic brake modulator assembly from the vehicle, then remove the gear cover and motor pack from the assembly for access to the combination valve bolts.

2. Remove the 2 through-bolts retaining the combination valve to the modulator, then remove and discard the seals.

3. Separate the combination valve from the modulator, then remove and discard the seals.

4. Remove the transfer tubes and seals from the combination valve.

To install:

5. Lubricate the new seals with clean brake fluid, then install 2 new transfer tubes onto the combination valve assembly.

6. Lubricate the 4 new seals with clean brake fluid, then install 2 seals between the combination valve and the modulator assembly and connect the components. Install the other 2 new seals on the through-bolts, then install and tighten to 12 ft. lbs. (16 Nm).

7. Install the ABS hydraulic modulator and combination valve assembly.

Power Brake Booster

REMOVAL AND INSTALLATION

1992

1. Disconnect the negative battery cable.

2. Disconnect the vacuum hose from the vacuum check valve.

3. Remove the 2 master cylinder attaching nuts.

4. On vehicles with manual transmission, remove the clutch master cylinder bracket with the clutch master cylinder reservoir and position aside.

5. Remove the combination valve with the attached combination valve bracket and position aside.

6. Remove the master cylinder from the booster.

7. Working inside the vehicle, remove the retainer and disconnect the booster pushrod from the brake pedal. Remove the booster attaching nuts.

8. Remove the power brake booster.

To install:

9. Install the power brake booster and tighten the attaching nuts to to 24 ft. lbs. (33 Nm).

10. Connect the booster pushrod and retainer to the brake pedal.

11. Install the master cylinder, combination valve and if applicable, the clutch master cylinder reservoir and bracket to the booster mounting studs.

12. Install the 2 master cylinder attaching nuts and tighten to 24 ft. lbs. (33 Nm).

13. Connect the vacuum hose to the vacuum check valve.

14. Connect the negative battery cable and if brake lines were disconnected, bleed the hydraulic brake system.

1993–96

1. If necessary for access, disconnect the secondary AIR injection pipe from the exhaust manifold fitting, then position the pipe aside.

1. Brake pressure modulator valve assembly
2. Brake combination valve bolt
3. Brake combination valve seal
4. Brake combination valve seal
5. Brake combination valve assembly
6. Transfer tube seal
7. Transfer tube
8. Transfer tube
9. Transfer tube seal

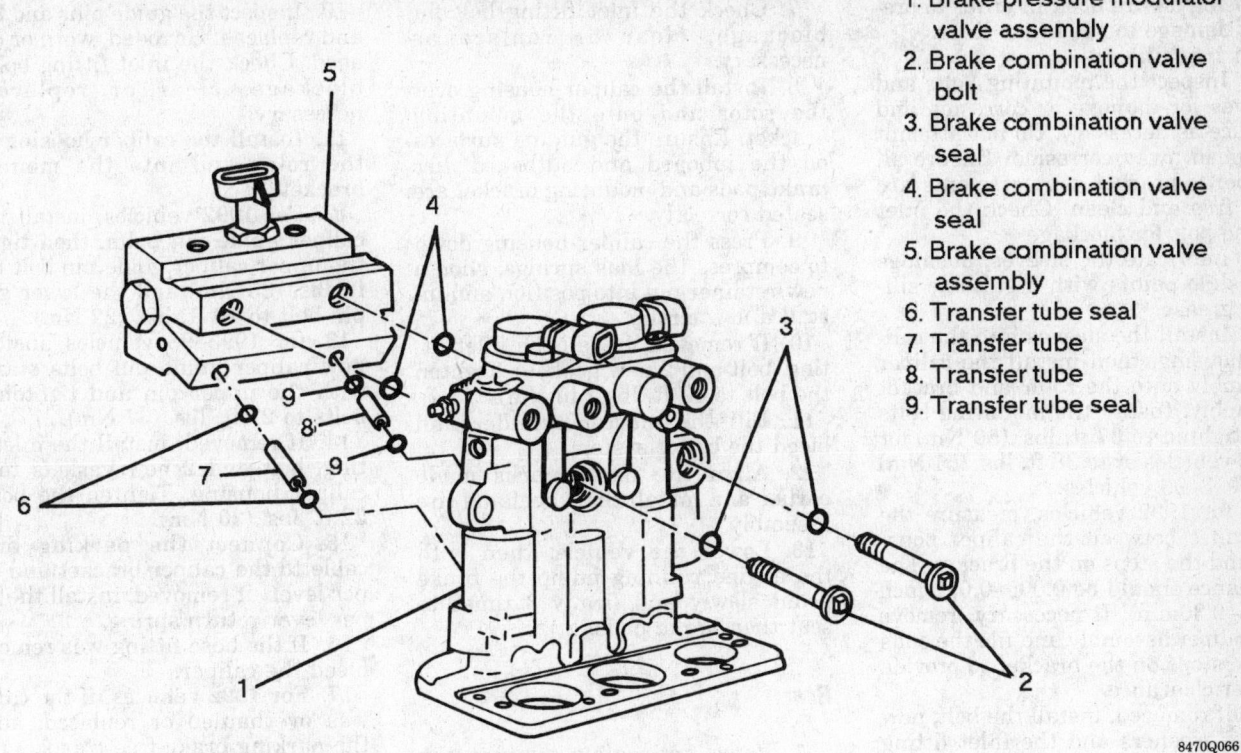

8470Q066

Exploded view of the combination valve-to-ABS modulator mounting — 1993–96 vehicles

2. Loosen the clamp, then disconnect the vacuum hose from the booster check valve.

3. Remove the nuts attaching the master cylinder assembly to the booster, then carefully move the cylinder assembly forward and toward the driver's side of the vehicle to position it aside. This will flex the pipes slightly, take care not to bend and damage the pipes.

4. Remove the lower sound insulator assembly for access to the booster mounting.

5. Remove the nuts attaching the booster to the brake pedal assembly.

6. Loosen the right brake pedal bracket nut and, on manual transmission vehicles, the 2 nuts towards the left of the assembly attaching the clutch master cylinder assembly. Then pull back on the brake pedal assembly in order to access and remove the booster-to-dash retaining nuts. The booster-to-dash retaining nuts are needed for production only and may be discarded after removal.

7. Remove the retainer and washer, then disengage the booster pushrod from the brake pedal pin. Tilt the entire booster assembly slightly to work the pushrod off the pin without putting excessive side pressure on the pushrod.

8. Remove the booster assembly from the vehicle.

To install:

9. Install the booster assembly to the vehicle.

10. Tilt the booster assembly slightly, then connect the pushrod to the brake pedal pin. From inside the vehicle, install the washer and retainer.

11. Install the booster-to-brake pedal bracket nuts and tighten to 18 ft. lbs. (25 Nm) in sequence: inboard upper, outboard lower, outboard upper and inboard lower.

12. Install the brake pedal bracket nut and tighten to 18 ft. lbs. (25 Nm), then if equipped with a manual transmission, install the clutch master cylinder retaining nuts and tighten to 20 ft. lbs. (28 Nm).

13. Reposition and install the master cylinder assembly to the booster, then tighten the retaining nuts to 32 ft. lbs. (43 Nm).

14. Install the vacuum hose along with the clamp to the booster check valve, then if disconnected, reposition and connect the AIR pipe fitting to the exhaust manifold and tighten to 25 ft. lbs. (34 Nm).

15. Install the lower sound insulator panel.

Brake Caliper

REMOVAL AND INSTALLATION

Front

SINGLE PISTON

1. Remove ⅔ of the brake fluid from the master cylinder.

2. Raise and support the vehicle safely.

3. Matchmark the relationship between the wheel and hub, then remove the wheel and tire assembly.

4. For 1993–96 vehicles, reinstall 2 of the lug nuts in order to retain the rotor.

5. Position a C-clamp over the outboard brake pad and the caliper housing, then use the C-clamp to bottom the piston into the caliper bore.

6. If completely removing the caliper from the vehicle for replacement or service, remove the bolt, copper washers and inlet fitting from the caliper housing. Plug the openings in the inlet fitting and caliper housing to prevent system contamination or excessive fluid loss.

7. Remove the mounting bolts and sleeves.

8. Remove the caliper assembly from the rotor and bracket. If the caliper is not being completely removed,

it must be suspended from the vehicle using a wire hook in order to prevent damage to the brake lines.

To install:

9. Inspect the mounting bolts and sleeves for damage or corrosion and replace as necessary. Do not attempt to polish away corrosion. Ensure all caliper-to-bracket contact points are rust free and clean. Check the inlet fitting bolt for blockage.

10. Lubricate the sleeves, bushings and slide points with a suitable silicone grease.

11. Install the sleeves into the caliper housing, then install the caliper assembly onto the rotor and bracket assembly. Install the mounting bolts and tighten to 37 ft. lbs. (50 Nm) for 1992 vehicles or to 38 ft. lbs. (51 Nm) for 1993–96 vehicles.

12. for 1992 vehicles, measure the clearance between the caliper housing and the stops on the bracket. The clearance should be 0.005–0.012 inch (0.13–0.30mm). If necessary, remove the caliper assembly and file the ends of the stops on the bracket to provide proper clearance.

13. If removed, install the bolt, new copper washers and the inlet fitting to the caliper housing. Tighten the bolt to 32 ft. lbs. (44 Nm).

14. Replace the brake fluid in the master cylinder and, if the caliper was removed, bleed the caliper.

15. Align the marks made earlier and install the wheel and tire assembly.

16. Lower the vehicle, then with the engine running pump the brake pedal slowly and firmly 3 times to seat then brake pads.

DUAL PISTON

1. Remove ⅔ of the brake fluid from the master cylinder.

2. Raise and support the vehicle safely.

3. Matchmark the relationship of the wheel and hub, then remove the wheel and tire assembly.

4. If completely removing the caliper from the vehicle for replacement or service, remove the bolt, inlet fitting and 2 gaskets from the caliper housing. Plug the openings in the caliper housing and inlet fitting to prevent system contamination or excessive fluid loss.

5. Remove the circlip and retainer pin.

6. Remove the caliper housing from the rotor and mounting bracket. If the caliper is not being completely removed, it must be suspended from the vehicle using a wire hook in order to prevent damage to the brake lines.

To install:

7. Check the inlet fitting bolt for blockage, clear or replace as necessary.

8. Install the caliper housing over the rotor and onto the mounting bracket. Ensure the guiding surfaces on the inboard and outboard disc brake pads and mounting bracket are seated correctly.

9. Press the caliper housing down to compress the bias springs, slide a new retainer pin into position and install a new circlip.

10. If removed, install the inlet fitting, bolt and 2 new gaskets. Tighten the bolt to 30 ft. lbs. (40 Nm).

11. Fill the master cylinder and bleed the brake system.

12. Align the matchmarks made earlier and install the wheel and tire assembly.

13. Lower the vehicle, then with the engine running pump the brake pedal slowly and firmly 3 times to seat then brake pads.

Rear

1. Raise and safely support the vehicle.

2. Either loosen the parking brake cable at the equalizer (for 1992) vehicles or disconnect the cable assembly at the equalizer (1993–96 vehicles).

3. Matchmark the relationship between the wheel and hub, then remove the wheel and tire assembly. Install 2 wheel nuts to retain the rotor.

4. If completely removing the caliper from the vehicle for replacement or service, remove the bolt, inlet fitting and 2 gaskets from the caliper housing. Plug the openings in the caliper housing and inlet fitting to prevent system contamination or excessive fluid loss.

5. Remove the caliper lever return spring only if it is defective. Discard the spring if the coils are opened.

6. Disconnect the parking brake cable from the caliper lever and bracket.

7. For 1993–96 vehicles, if necessary remove the vibration damper nut from the parking brake cable bracket.

8. Remove the 2 caliper guide pin bolts. For 1993–96 vehicles, discard the pins after removal.

9. Remove the caliper housing from the rotor and mounting bracket. If the caliper is not being completely removed, it must be suspended from the vehicle using a wire hook in order to prevent damage to the brake lines.

To install:

10. Inspect the guide pins and boots and replace if corroded, worn or damaged. Check the inlet fitting bolt for blockage, clear or replace as necessary.

11. Install the caliper housing over the rotor and into the mounting bracket.

12. For 1992 vehicles, install the 2 caliper guide pin bolts, then tighten the upper caliper guide pin bolt to 26 ft. lbs. (35 Nm) and the lower guide pin bolt to 16 ft. lbs. (22 Nm).

13. for 1993–96 vehicles, install 2 new caliper guide pin bolts starting with the upper pin and tighten the bolts to 27 ft. lbs. (37 Nm).

14. If removed, install the inlet fitting, bolt and 2 new gaskets to the caliper housing. Tighten the bolt to 22 ft. lbs. (30 Nm).

15. Connect the parking brake cable to the caliper bracket and caliper lever. If removed, install the caliper lever return spring.

16. If the hose fitting was removed, bleed the caliper.

17. For 1992 vehicles, if the caliper was overhauled or replaced, adjust the parking brake free travel.

18. Lower the vehicle sufficiently and cycle the parking brake.

19. Raise and safely support the vehicle.

20. Inspect the caliper parking brake levers and ensure they are against the stops on the caliper housing. If the levers are not on their stops, check the parking brake adjustment.

21. Remove the 2 nuts securing the rotor, then align the matchmarks made earlier and install the wheel assembly.

22. Lower the vehicle, then with the engine running pump the brake pedal slowly and firmly 3 times to seat then brake pads.

23. Check the hydraulic system for leaks.

Disc Brake Pads

REMOVAL AND INSTALLATION

1992 Front

SINGLE PISTON

1. Remove the caliper assembly from the rotor and mounting bracket without disconnecting the brake line, then position aside. Do not allow the caliper to hang by the brake hose, suspend it with a length of wire or a fabricated hook.

2. Remove the disc brake pads.

3. Remove the bushings from the mounting bolt holes and the pad retainer spring from the inboard pad.

To install:

4. Lubricate the bushings and sleeves with silicone grease. Install the bushings into the mounting bolt holes.

5. Install the retaining spring on the inboard pad in the correct position. Install the inboard pad into the caliper with the wear sensor at the leading edge of the pad during forward wheel rotation. Snap the retaining spring and pad into position. The pad must lay flat against the piston.

6. Install the outboard pad. The pad must lay flat against the caliper housing.

7. Install the caliper assembly to the rotor and mounting bracket.

DUAL PISTON

1. Remove the caliper assembly from the rotor and mounting bracket without disconnecting the brake line, then position aside. Do not allow the caliper to hang by the brake hose, suspend it with a length of wire or a fabricated hook.

2. Position a C-clamp or pair of pliers over the caliper housing and the center of the inboard disc brake pad. Squeeze the pliers or tighten the C-clamp until the pistons are bottomed.

3. Remove the disc brake pads.

To install:

4. Clean all residue from the mounting brackets and caliper pad contact surfaces.

5. Install the disc brake pads. The outboard disc brake pad with insulator is installed in the caliper housing. The inboard brake pad with wear sensor is pressed into the caliper pistons. Push the pads in firmly until they are flush and fully seated in the caliper housing.

6. Install the caliper assembly.

1993–96 Front

1. Remove the caliper assembly from the rotor and mounting bracket without disconnecting the brake line, then position aside. Do not allow the caliper to hang by the brake hose, suspend it with a length of wire or a fabricated hook.

2. Remove the outer pad assembly using a small prytool, if necessary, to disengage the show buttons from the caliper assembly.

3. Remove the inner pad.

To install:

4. If not done already, bottom the piston into the caliper using a large

C-clamp positioned on the housing and inside the piston well.

5. With the piston bottomed in the caliper bore, lift the inner edge of the boot next to the piston and press out any trapped air. Make sure the boot is flat.

6. Install the inner pad assembly by positioning the retainer spring into the piston. The pad must lay flat against the piston and the boot must not touch the pad. If the boot and pad are in contact, remove the pad and reposition the boot.

7. Install the outer pad assembly, making sure the back of the pad is flat against the caliper. The wear sensor should be at the trailing lower edge of the outer pad during forward wheel rotation or the outer pad has been installed on the wrong side.

8. Install the caliper assembly to the rotor and mounting bracket.

Rear

1. Remove ⅔ of the brake fluid from the master cylinder reservoir.

2. Raise and safely support the vehicle.

3. Matchmark the relationship of the wheel to the axle flange, then remove the wheel and tire assembly. Install 2 wheel nuts to retain the rotor.

4. Position a C-clamp and tighten until the piston bottoms in the base of the caliper housing. Make sure 1 end of the C-clamp rests on the inlet fitting bolt and the other against the outboard disc brake pad.

NOTE: It is not necessary to remove the parking brake caliper lever return spring to replace the disc brake pads.

5. Remove the upper caliper guide pin bolt and discard.

6. Rotate the caliper housing on the lower caliper mounting bolt. Be careful not to strain the hose or cable conduit. It may be necessary to loosen the lower caliper guide pin slightly.

7. Remove the disc brake pads and, for 1993–96 vehicles, remove and discard the shim.

To install:

8. Clean all residue from the pad guide surfaces on the mounting bracket and caliper housing. Inspect the guide pins for free movement in the mounting bracket. Replace the guide pins or boots, if they are corroded or damaged.

9. For 1993–96 vehicles, install a new shim, then install the disc brake pads. The outboard pad with insulator is installed toward the caliper

housing. The inboard pad with the wear sensor is installed nearest the caliper piston. The wear sensor must be on the leading edge with forward wheel rotation or the pad has been installed on the wrong side.

10. For 1992 vehicles, install the disc brake pads. The outboard pad with insulator is installed toward the caliper housing. The inboard pad with the wear sensor is installed nearest the caliper piston. The wear sensor must be in the trailing position with forward wheel rotation or the pad has been installed on the wrong side.

11. Rotate the caliper housing into it's operating position. The springs on the outboard brake pad must not stick through the inspection hole in the caliper housing. If the springs are sticking through the inspection hole in the caliper housing, lift the caliper housing and make the necessary corrections to the outboard brake pad positions.

12. Install a new upper caliper guide pin bolt and tighten to 26 ft. lbs. (35 Nm) for 1992 vehicles or to 27 ft. lbs. (37 Nm) for 1993–96 vehicles. Ensure that the lower caliper guide bolt is tightened to 16 ft. lbs. (22 Nm) for 1992 vehicles or to 27 ft. lbs. (37 Nm) for 1993–96 vehicles.

13. With the engine running, pump the brake pedal slowly and firmly to seat the brake pads.

14. Check the caliper parking brake levers to make sure they are against the stops on the caliper housing. If the levers are not on their stops, check the parking brake adjustment.

15. Remove the 2 wheel nuts from the rotor, then align the marks and install the wheel assembly.

16. Lower the vehicle, check the master cylinder fluid level and roadtest the vehicle.

Brake Rotor

REMOVAL AND INSTALLATION

Front

1992

1. Raise and support the vehicle safely.

2. Matchmark the relationship of the wheel and hub, then remove the wheel and tire assembly.

3. Remove the caliper assembly from the rotor and mounting bracket without disconnecting the brake line, then position aside. Do not allow the caliper to hang by the brake hose, suspend it with a length of wire or a

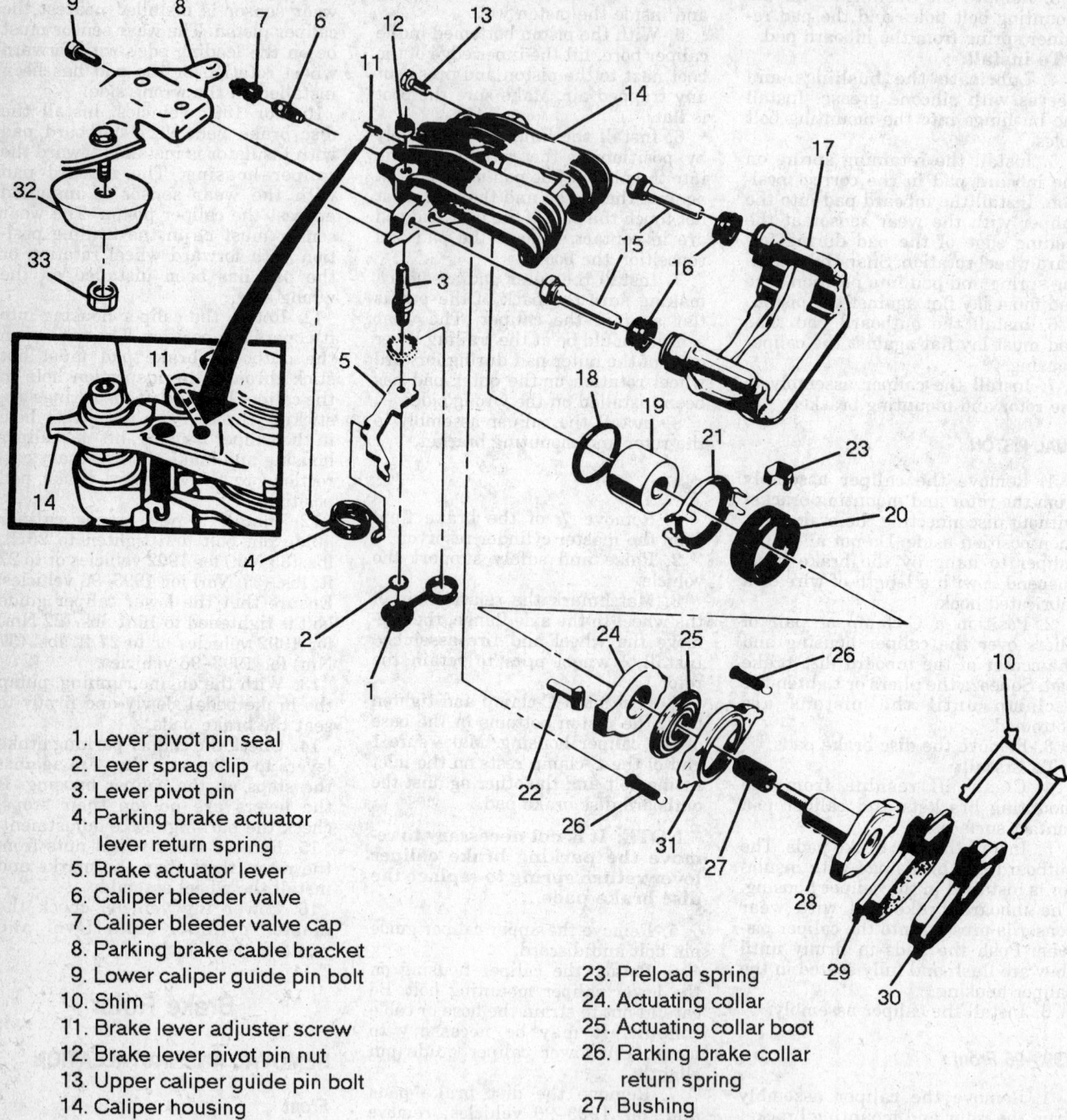

1. Lever pivot pin seal
2. Lever sprag clip
3. Lever pivot pin
4. Parking brake actuator
   lever return spring
5. Brake actuator lever
6. Caliper bleeder valve
7. Caliper bleeder valve cap
8. Parking brake cable bracket
9. Lower caliper guide pin bolt
10. Shim
11. Brake lever adjuster screw
12. Brake lever pivot pin nut
13. Upper caliper guide pin bolt
14. Caliper housing
15. Caliper guide pin
16. Caliper guide pin boot
17. Caliper anchor bracket
18. Caliper piston seal
19. Caliper piston
20. Actuating collar boot
21. Boot retainer
22. Pushrod

23. Preload spring
24. Actuating collar
25. Actuating collar boot
26. Parking brake collar
    return spring
27. Bushing
28. Clamp rod
29. Inner pad assembly
30. Outer pad assembly
31. Boot retainer
32. Brake vibration dampener
    assembly
33. Brake vibration dampener
    nut

8470Q068

Exploded view of the rear caliper assembly — 1993–96 vehicles — 1992 similar

fabricated hook. For dual piston caliper assemblies, it may be necessary to remove the caliper bracket bolts and the bracket before removing the rotor.

4. Remove the dust cap from the hub. Remove the cotter pin, nut and washer from the spindle.

5. Carefully pull the hub and rotor assembly from the spindle.

To install:

6. Check the rotor for scoring or damage. Machine or replace the rotor assembly, as necessary. If machining is required, measure the rotor and check the minimum thickness specification.

7. Install the hub and rotor assembly. Adjust the wheel bearings as follows:

a. Tighten the spindle nut to 12 ft. lbs. (16 Nm) while turning the rotor forward by hand to fully seat the bearings.

b. Back off the nut to the just loose position.

c. Hand-tighten the spindle nut. Loosen the spindle nut just enough that either hole in the spindle lines up with a slot in the nut, not more then ½ flat.

d. Install a new cotter pin and bend the ends of the pin against the nut. Cut off extra length to ensure ends will not interfere with the dust cap and install the dust cap.

e. Using a dial indicator, check the hub and rotor assembly. There should be 0.001–0.005 inch (0.03–0.13mm) endplay when properly adjusted.

8. Install caliper mounting bracket, if removed. Coat the threads of the mounting bracket bolts with suitable thread adhesive and tighten to 137 ft. lbs. (185 Nm). Recheck the torque immediately. Allow the adhesive to cure for 2 hours before moving the vehicle.

9. Install the caliper assembly.

10. Align the marks made earlier, then install the wheel and tire assembly. Lower the vehicle and check the brake fluid.

1993–96

1. Remove the caliper assembly from the rotor and mounting bracket without disconnecting the brake line, then position to hang by the brake hose, suspend it with a length of wire or a fabricated hook.

2. Slide the rotor from the hub and bearing assembly.

To install:

3. Position the rotor over the hub studs.

4. Install the caliper assembly.

Rear

1992

1. Raise and support the vehicle safely.

2. Matchmark the relationship of the wheel to the axle flange, then remove the wheel and tire assembly.

3. Remove the caliper assembly.

4. Remove the caliper mounting bracket and discard the bolts.

5. Remove the brake rotor.

To install:

6. Install the brake rotor and the mounting bracket.

7. Apply bolt adhesive to 2 new caliper mounting bracket bolts and tighten them to 70 ft. lbs. (95 Nm). Recheck the torque on both bolts immediately. Allow the bolt adhesive to dry for 2 hours before driving the vehicle.

8. Install the caliper assembly.

9. Align the marks made earlier, then install the wheel and tire assembly.

10. Lower the vehicle and test. Remember to allow the mounting bracket bolt adhesive time to cure, if removed and reinstalled.

1993–96

The rear brake rotor may be removed, without separating the caliper from the mounting bracket.

1. Raise and support the vehicle safely.

2. Matchmark the relationship of the wheel and hub, then remove the wheel and tire assembly.

3. Remove and discard the 2 bolts retaining the caliper mounting bracket, then reposition and suspend the bracket/caliper assembly from the suspension using a length of wire or a fabricated hook.

4. Remove the rotor.

To install:

5. Install the rotor.

6. Install the caliper/mounting bracket assembly using 2 new bolts. Tighten the bolts to 74 ft. lbs. (100 Nm), then recheck the torque immediately.

7. Align the marks made earlier, then install the tire and wheel assembly.

8. Lower the vehicle.

Brake Drums

REMOVAL AND INSTALLATION

1. Raise and support the vehicle safely.

2. Matchmark the relationship of the wheel to the axle flange, then remove the wheel and tire assembly.

3. Matchmark the relationship of the drum to the axle flange and remove the brake drum. If the brake drum is difficult to remove, try the following:

a. Ensure the parking brake is released.

b. Back off the parking brake cable adjustment.

c. Remove the adjusting hole cover or knockout plate from the backing plate. Back off the adjustment screw, using suitable brake adjusting tools.

d. Use a rubber mallet to tap gently on the outer rim of the drum and/or around the inner drum diameter by the spindle. Be careful not to deform the drum by excessive use of force.

To install:

4. Adjust the brake shoes. The outside diameter of the shoe and linings should be 0.050 inch (1.27mm) less than the inside diameter of the brake drum on each wheel.

5. Install the drum, aligning the marks on the drum and the axle flange.

6. Install the wheel and tire assembly, aligning the marks on the wheel and axle flange, then lower the vehicle.

Brake Shoes

REMOVAL AND INSTALLATION

1. Raise and support the vehicle safely.

2. Matchmark the relationship of the wheel to the axle flange, then remove the wheel and tire assembly.

3. Matchmark the relationship of the drum to the axle flange and remove the brake drum.

4. Remove the return springs using a suitable tool.

5. Remove the hold-down springs and pins. Remove the actuator pivot.

6. Remove the actuator link while lifting up on the actuator.

7. Remove the actuator lever and lever return spring.

8. Remove the shoe guide, parking brake strut and strut spring.

9. Remove the brake shoes and disconnect the parking brake lever from the appropriate shoe.

10. Remove the adjusting screw assembly and spring.

To install:

NOTE: Any part or spring which are of doubtful strength due to discoloration from heat, overstress or wear should be replaced. Clean the adjusting screw threads with a wire brush and check the threads for smooth rotations. Replace as necessary.

11. Install the parking brake lever on the appropriate shoe by hooking the lever tab into the slot.

12. Install the adjusting screw and spring. Lubricate the adjusting screw with suitable brake grease.

13. Clean and lubricate the contact points of the backing plate, then install the brake shoe assemblies and the parking brake cable to the backing plate.

14. Install the parking brake strut and strut spring by spreading the shoes apart. The strut end with the spring engages the parking brake lever and shoe, the other end engages the opposite shoe.

15. Install the shoe guide, actuator lever and lever return spring.

16. Install the hold-down pins, actuator pivot and springs.

17. Install the actuator link on the anchor pin. Install the actuator link into the actuator lever while holding up on the lever.

18. Install the shoe return springs and adjust the brakes. When properly adjusted, the brake shoe linings will be approximately 0.050 inch (1.27 mm) less than the inner diameter of the brake drum.

19. Align and install the brake drum, then the wheel and tire assembly.

20. Lower the vehicle.

Wheel Cylinder

REMOVAL AND INSTALLATION

1. Raise and support the vehicle safely.

2. Matchmark and remove both the tire and wheel assemblies and the brake drums.

3. Remove the brake shoes and components, as required for access to the wheel cylinder.

4. Clean the area around the wheel cylinder and brake line. Remove the brake line from the wheel cylinder and plug the brake line to prevent system contamination or excessive fluid loss.

5. For 1992 vehicles insert 2 awls, into the access slots between the wheel cylinder pilot and retainer

locking tabs, then bend both tabs away simultaneously releasing the wheel cylinder. Remove the wheel cylinder and discard the old retaining clip.

6. For 1993–96 vehicles, remove the retaining bolts, then remove the wheel cylinder from the backing plate.

To install:

7. For ease of installation hold the wheel cylinder against the backing plate by inserting a block between the wheel cylinder and the axle shaft flange.

8. For 1993–96 vehicles, install the retaining bolts and tighten to 115 inch lbs. (13 Nm).

9. For 1992 vehicles, position the wheel cylinder retainer clip so the tabs will be away from and in a horizontal position with the backing plate when installing. Press the new retaining clip over the wheel cylinder abutment and into position using a 1⅛ inch 12-point socket. Make sure the retainer tabs are properly snapped under the abutment shoulder.

10. Uncap and install the brake line, then tighten the fitting to 11 ft. lbs. (15 Nm) for 1992 vehicles or to 13 ft. lbs. (17 Nm).

11. Install the brake shoes and components.

12. Bleed the wheel cylinders.

13. Align and install the brake drums.

14. Install the wheel and tire assemblies, then lower the vehicle.

Parking Brake Cable

ADJUSTMENT

All vehicles feature a self-adjusting parking brake. The only adjustment possible on these vehicles is the brake shoe outer diameter adjustment when installing new brake components (drum brake vehicles) or parking brake free-travel (rear disc brake vehicles)

Parking Brake Free-Travel

Parking brake free-travel should only be adjusted if the caliper has been taken apart. This adjustment will not correct a condition where the caliper levers will not return to their stops.

NOTE: Disc brake pads must be new or parallel to within 0.006 inch (0.15mm). Parking brake free-travel adjustment is not valid with heavily tapered pads

and may cause caliper/parking brake binding. Replace tapered brake pads.

1. Disconnect the parking brake cable assembly and remove the actuator lever return spring.

2. Have an assistant apply a light brake pedal load, enough to stop the rotor from turning by hand. This takes up all clearances and ensures that components are correctly aligned.

3. Apply light pressure to the caliper lever.

4. Measure the free-travel between the caliper lever and the caliper housing. The free-travel must be 0.024–0.028 inch (0.6–0.7mm).

5. If the free-travel is incorrect, do the following:

a. Remove the adjuster screw.

b. Clean the thread adhesive residue from the threads.

c. Coat the threads with adhesive.

d. Screw in the adjuster screw far enough to obtain 0.024–0.028 inch (0.6–0.7mm) free-travel between the caliper lever and the caliper housing.

6. Have an assistant release the brake pedal, then apply the brake pedal firmly 3 times. Recheck the free-travel and adjust as necessary.

7. Install the actuator lever return spring and parking brake cable assembly.

REMOVAL AND INSTALLATION

Front Cable

1992

1. Remove the carpet finish molding.

2. Remove the console assembly.

3. With the parking brake lever in the down position, rotate the arm toward the front of the vehicle until a 3mm metal pin can be inserted into the hole. Insert the metal pin into the hole, locking out the self adjuster.

4. Raise and safely support the vehicle.

5. Disconnect the rear cables from the equalizer.

6. Remove the front cable from the bracket using a fabricated parking brake cable retainer compressor tool.

7. Remove the grommet from the hole.

8. Lower the vehicle.

9. Remove the barrel-shaped button from the adjuster track.

10. Remove the front cable and casing from the control assembly using a fabricated parking brake cable retainer compressor tool.

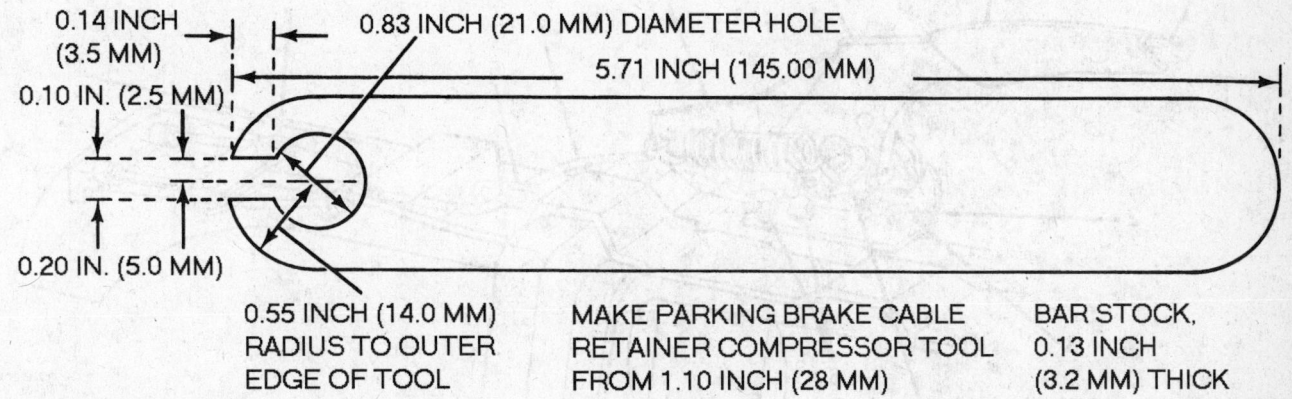

0.14 INCH (3.5 MM)

0.10 IN. (2.5 MM)

0.20 IN. (5.0 MM)

0.83 INCH (21.0 MM) DIAMETER HOLE

5.71 INCH (145.00 MM)

0.55 INCH (14.0 MM) RADIUS TO OUTER EDGE OF TOOL

MAKE PARKING BRAKE CABLE RETAINER COMPRESSOR TOOL FROM 1.10 INCH (28 MM)

BAR STOCK, 0.13 INCH (3.2 MM) THICK

8470Q070

Fabricated parking brake cable retainer compressor tool — 1992

11. Remove the front cable from the floor pan.

To install:

12. Install the cable and seat the grommet in the floor pan.

13. Connect the cable casing to the control assembly.

14. Install the barrel-shaped button into the adjuster track.

15. Raise and support the vehicle safely.

16. Connect the rear cables to the equalizer and lower the vehicle.

17. Remove the metal pin from the hole, rotate the adjuster arm toward the rear of the vehicle and cycle lever.

18. Install the console and carpet finish molding.

1993–96

1. Remove the center console assembly.

2. With the parking brake lever in the up position, remove the pretension spring.

3. With the parking brake lever in the down position, rotate the arm toward the front of the vehicle until a 3mm metal pin can be inserted into the hole. It may be necessary to first remove the remaining piece of plastic shear pin, then insert the metal pin into the hole, locking out the self adjuster.

4. Pull the parking brake lever assembly all of the way back.

5. Raise and support the vehicle safely.

6. Disconnect the rear cables from the equalizer.

7. Using J–37043 or an equivalent cable release tool, disconnect the front cable fitting from the bracket.

8. Remove the grommet from the slot in the underbody.

9. Lower the vehicle, then note the retainer tab position for installation purposes and bend back the cable retainer tab on the pulley.

10. Remove the barrel-shaped front cable fitting from the adjuster track on the pulley.

11. Remove the front cable and casing from the control assembly using the cable release tool.

12. Remove the front cable from the floor pan.

To install:

13. Install the cable and seat the grommet in the floor pan. Soapy water may be used as a lubricant to ease installation, then feed the forward end of the grommet into the slot and use a small, curved, flat-ended prybar to gently press the rearward end into the slot.

14. Connect the cable casing to the control assembly.

15. Install the barrel-shaped front cable fitting into the adjuster track on the pulley, then bend the cable retainer tab to its original position on the pulley.

16. Make sure the lever is in the down position, then raise and support the vehicle safely.

17. Connect the rear cables to the equalizer and lower the vehicle.

18. With the parking brake lever in the up position, install the pretension spring.

19. Remove the metal pin from the hole, then cycle the parking brake lever 3 times.

20. Install the center console assembly.

Rear Cable

REAR DRUM BRAKES

1. Make sure the brake lever is fully released, then raise and support the vehicle safely.

2. Pull the equalizer rearward to gain the necessary cable slack, then insert a spacer to hold the equalizer in place and remove the left and/or right cable from the equalizer.

3. Compress the retainer fingers on the casing and pull the left and/or right rear cable out of the seat belt plate or underbody bracket.

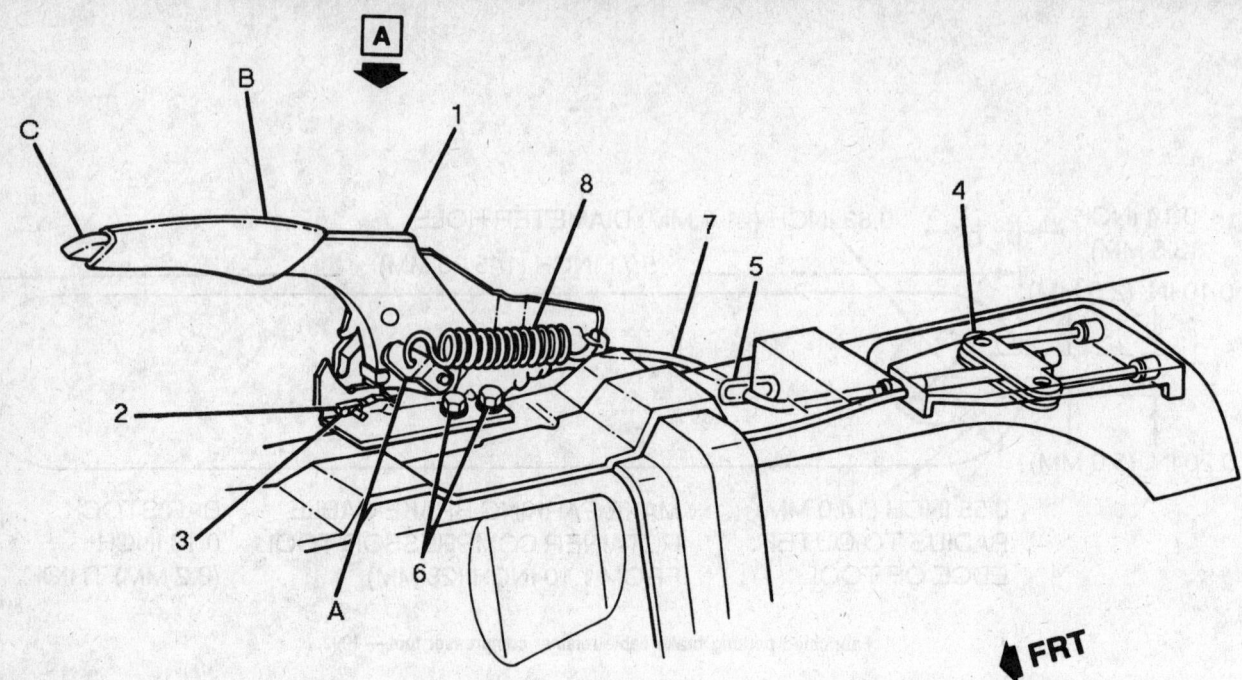

A. Adjuster arm
B. Brake lever grip
C. Brake lever release button
D. Adjust pawl
E. Adjust pawl pin
1. Parking brake lever assembly
2. Brake indiactor switch
3. Brake indicator switch bolt
4. Brake cable equalizer
5. Brake cable grommet
6. Brake lever bolt
7. Front cable assembly
8. Pretension spring

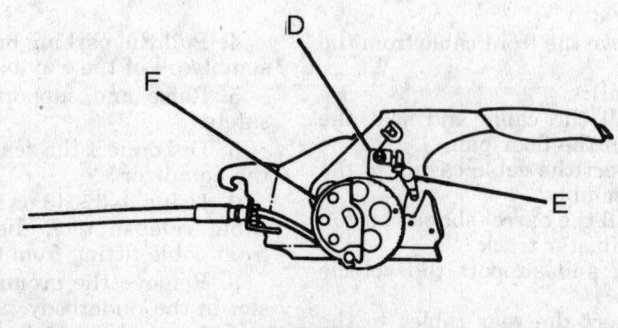

VIEW A

8470Q071

Parking brake lever assembly — 1993–96

4. For the right side on 1992 vehicles, remove the screw and clamp from the right rear cable.

5. Except for the right side on 1992 vehicles, pull the cable assembly through the guides installed on the rear axle housing.

6. Matchmark and remove the left or right wheel assemblies, as applicable.

7. Matchmark and remove the brake drum(s).

8. Disconnect the left and/or right rear cable from the brake shoe operating lever, then compress the retainer fingers and pull the left and/or right cable from the backing plate.

To install:

9. Install the left and/or right cable to the backing plate and shoe actuating lever.

10. Align the marks made earlier, then install the brake drum(s) and the wheel and tire assemblies.

11. Except for the right side on 1992 vehicles, feed the cable assembly through the guides on the rear axle housing.

12. For the right side on 1992, install the screw and clamp to the right rear cable.

13. Install the left and/or right cable into the underbody bracket or the seat belt plate and retainer.

14. Connect the left and/or right cable to the equalizer, then remove the spacer.

15. Lower the vehicle and cycle the parking brake 3 times.

REAR DISC BRAKES

1. Make sure the brake lever is fully released, then raise and support the vehicle safely.

2. Pull the equalizer rearward to gain the necessary cable slack, then insert a spacer to hold the equalizer in place and remove the left and/or right cable from the equalizer.

3. Compress the retainer fingers on the casing and pull the left and/or

right rear cable out of the seat belt plate or underbody bracket.

4. For the right side on 1992 vehicles, remove the screw and clamp from the right rear cable.

5. Except for the right side on 1992 vehicles, pull the cable assembly through the guides installed on the rear axle housing.

6. Matchmark and remove the left or right wheel assemblies, as applicable.

7. Pull all the cable slack to the caliper end of the cable by pushing forward on the caliper lever. Remove the left and/or right rear cable from the tang on the caliper lever, then release the lever.

8. Compress the retainer fingers on the cable casing and pull out of the bracket.

To install:

9. Push forward on the caliper lever, then install the left and/or right rear cable in the tang on the caliper lever and release the lever. Seat the finger retainers into the bracket.

10. Align the marks made earlier, then install the wheel assemblies.

11. Except for the right side on 1992 vehicles, feed the cable assembly through the guides on the rear axle housing.

12. For the right side on 1992, install the screw and clamp to the right rear cable.

13. Install the left and/or right cable into the underbody bracket or the seat belt plate and retainer.

14. Connect the left and/or right cable to the equalizer, then remove the spacer.

15. Lower the vehicle and cycle the parking brake 3 times.

Brake System Bleeding

NON-ABS VEHICLES (1992)

Whenever a hydraulic fitting is disconnected or air is somehow introduced into the brake system, bleeding is necessary to assure proper brake operation. Do not move a vehicle until a firm brake pedal is obtained. Air in the system can cause the loss of brake operation.

If air is introduced into the system at the master cylinder, it may be necessary to bleed the entire system. If the disconnection of a fitting or pipe is the cause for air presence in the

system, then only the wheel cylinder(s) or caliper(s) served by that component need to be bled.

1. Remove the vacuum reserve by applying the brakes several times, with the engine **OFF**.

2. Fill the master cylinder reservoir with brake fluid and keep it at least half full of fluid at all times during the bleeding operation.

3. If the master cylinder is known or suspected to have air in the bore, bleed the unit before wheel cylinders or calipers, in the following manner:

a. Disconnect the forward brake line connection at the master cylinder.

b. Allow brake fluid to fill the master cylinder bore until it begins to flow from the forward brake line port at the master cylinder.

c. Connect the forward brake line to the master cylinder and tighten.

d. Have an assistant depress the brake pedal slowly 1 time and hold. Loosen the forward brake line connection at the master cylinder to purge air from the bore. Tighten the connection and have the assistant release the pedal slowly. Wait 15 seconds and repeat the sequence, including the 15 second pause, until all air is removed from the bore. Ensure brake fluid does not contact any painted surface.

e. Repeat the procedure at the rear master cylinder brake line connection.

f. If it is known that the calipers and wheel cylinders do not contain any air, it will not be necessary to bleed them.

4. If it is necessary to bleed all of the wheel cylinders and calipers, follow the proper sequence: Right rear, left rear, right front, left front.

5. Bleed individual wheel cylinders or calipers, only after all air is removed from the master cylinder, as follows:

a. Place a suitable bleeder wrench over the bleeder valve.

b. Attach a clear tube over the bleeder valve and allow the tube to hang, submerged in a clear container partially filled with brake fluid.

c. Have an assistant depress the brake pedal slowly 1 time and hold. Loosen the bleeder valve to purge the air from the cylinder. Tighten the bleeder screw and have the assistant slowly release the pedal. Wait 15 seconds and repeat the se-

quence, including the 15 second pause, until all air is removed.

d. It may be necessary to repeat the sequence 10 or more times to remove all of the air.

NOTE: Rapid pumping of the brake pedal pushes the master cylinder secondary piston down the bore in a way that makes it difficult to bleed the rear side of the system.

6. Check the brake pedal for sponginess and the red brake warning light for an indication of unbalanced pressure. Repeat the bleeding procedure to correct either of these conditions.

Anti-Lock Brake System (ABS) Service

PRECAUTIONS

Failure to observe the following precautions may result in system damage.

• Before performing electric arc welding on the vehicle, disconnect the Electronic Brake Control Module (EBCM) and the hydraulic modulator connectors.

• When performing service on the system, pay close attention to routing, position, mounting and location of all ABS components, wiring, connectors, and clips. ABS components are extremely sensitive to Electro-Magnetic Interference (EMI).

• When performing painting work on the vehicle, do not expose the Electronic Brake Control Module (EBCM) to temperatures in excess of 185°F (85°C) for longer than 2 hours. The system may be exposed to temperatures up to 200°F (95°C) for less than 15 minutes.

• Never disconnect or connect the Electronic Brake Control Module (EBCM) or hydraulic modulator connectors with the ignition switch ON. Never disconnect the battery with the engine running.

• Never disassemble any component of the Anti-Lock Brake System (ABS) which is designated non-serviceable; the component must be replaced as an assembly.

• When filling the master cylinder, always use Delco Supreme 11 brake fluid or equivalent, which meets DOT-3 specifications; petroleum base fluid will destroy the rubber parts.

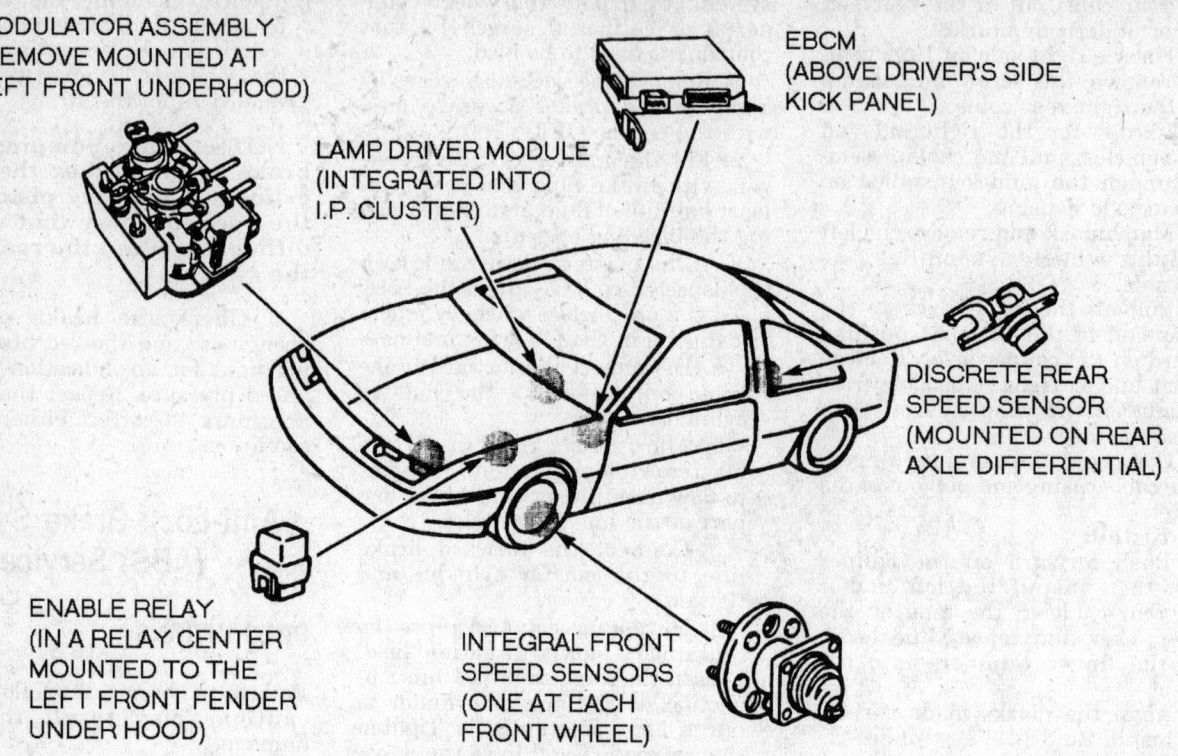

MODULATOR ASSEMBLY
(REMOVE MOUNTED AT
LEFT FRONT UNDERHOOD)

LAMP DRIVER MODULE
(INTEGRATED INTO
I.P. CLUSTER)

EBCM
(ABOVE DRIVER'S SIDE
KICK PANEL)

DISCRETE REAR
SPEED SENSOR
(MOUNTED ON REAR
AXLE DIFFERENTIAL)

ENABLE RELAY
(IN A RELAY CENTER
MOUNTED TO THE
LEFT FRONT FENDER
UNDER HOOD)

INTEGRAL FRONT
SPEED SENSORS
(ONE AT EACH
FRONT WHEEL)

8470Q072

ABS system components — 1993–96

BLEEDING THE ABS SYSTEM

1993–96 Vehicles

1. Clean the fluid reservoir cover and surrounding area to avoid system contamination, then remove the cover. Fill the reservoir to the proper level using fresh DOT 3 brake fluid from a sealed container, then reinstall the cover.

2. Prime and partially bleed the hydraulic modulator as follows:

   a. Attach a length of clear plastic hose to the rearward bleeder valve on the modulator assembly, then submerge the opposite end of the hose in a container partially filled with clean brake fluid.

   b. Open the bleeder valve slowly 1/2–3/4 turn, then have an assistant depress and hold the brake pedal until fluid begins to flow. Close the bleeder valve and release the brake pedal, then repeat until no air bubbles are present in the fluid flowing from the modulator assembly.

   c. Once air has been bleed from the rearward bleeder valve, move the length of hose to the forward bleeder and repeat the bleeding procedure to further purge the modulator assembly of air.

   d. At this point the modulator is sufficiently filled with fluid to

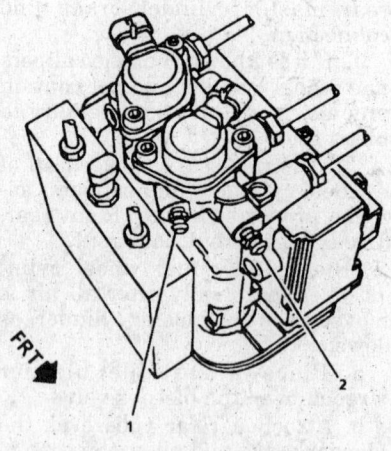

FRT

| 1 | REARWARD BLEEDER VALVE |
| 2 | FORWARD BLEEDER VALVE |

8569Q002

ABS hydraulic modulator bleeder locations

bleed the wheel cylinders and/or calipers. Once the wheel points have been bled, the modulator must be rebled to assure it is completely purged of air.

3. Remove the reservoir cover and add fresh brake fluid, as necessary to fill the reservoir to the proper level, then install the cover.

4. Raise and support the vehicle safely, then bleed the wheel points in the following sequence
   • Right rear
   • Left rear
   • Right front
   • Left front

5. Bleed each of the wheel cylinders and/or calipers as follows:

   a. Attach a length of clear plastic hose to the bleeder valve on the wheel cylinder or caliper assembly, then submerge the opposite end of the hose in a container partially filled with clean brake fluid.

   NOTE: To help free trapped air, tap lightly on the backing plate or caliper using a rubber mallet.

   b. Open the bleeder valve, then have an assistant slowly depress and hold the brake pedal. Close the bleeder valve, release the brake pedal and wait 5 seconds, then repeat the step (including the 5 second pause) until no air bubbles are present in the fluid flowing from the bleeder and a firm brake pedal is obtained.

   c. Repeat the procedure for the remaining wheel points.

6. Remove the reservoir cover and add fresh brake fluid, as necessary to fill the reservoir to the proper level, then install the cover.

7. Lower the vehicle for access, then return to the hydraulic modulator and completely purge air from the bleeder valves by repeating the modulator priming and bleeding procedure. Once the modulator is bled, tighten the bleeder valves to 80 inch lbs. (9 Nm).

8. Check and add brake fluid, as necessary.

Hydraulic Modulator Solenoid

The solenoid is mounted on top of the hydraulic modulator/motor pack assembly.

REMOVAL AND INSTALLATION

1. Disconnect the electrical connector from the hydraulic modulator solenoid.

2. Remove the hydraulic modulator solenoid bolts and the solenoid.

3. Perform the following checks:

   a. Be sure the seal is still attached to the solenoid; if not check the modulator's solenoid bore.

   b. Lubricate the seal on the new solenoid with clean brake fluid.

To install:

4. If installing a new solenoid, perform the following checks:

   a. Make sure the solenoid's lip seal is properly positioned.

   b. Position the solenoid so its electrical connector faces the same direction as the one that was removed.

   c. Firmly press the solenoid until its flange seats onto the hydraulic modulator.

5. Install the Torx® head bolts and torque to 40 inch lbs. (4.5 Nm).

6. Connect the electrical connector to the solenoid.

7. If necessary, bleed the entire system.

Hydraulic Modulator/Motor Pack Assembly

REMOVAL AND INSTALLATION

1. Using Tech 1, perform the Gear Tension Relief Sequence:

   a. Using a Tech 1 or T-100 (CAMS), select **F5: Motor Rehome**; if current DTC's are present, the motor rehome function cannot be performed.

NOTE: If DTC's are present, the vehicle must be repaired and the DTC's cleared before performing the motor rehome function.

   b. Bleed the entire brake system.

2. Remove the air cleaner duct assembly.

3. Disconnect the 2 solenoid electrical connectors.

4. Disconnect the brake pressure differential warning switch electrical connector.

5. Disconnect the 6-pin motor pack electrical connector.

6. To remove the brake tubes, perform the following procedures:

   a. Place a shop cloth on top of the motor pack to catch any dripping fluid.

   b. Be careful not to allow any brake fluid to enter the bottom of the motor pack or the electrical connectors.

   c. Using a flare tubing wrench, remove the brake tubes from the hydraulic modulator. There are 5 brake tubes: 2 to the master cylinder and 3 to the wheel brakes.

   d. Plug the brake tube openings to prevent fluid loss and contamination.

7. Remove the hydraulic modulator/motor pack assembly-to-frame rail bolt.

8. Remove the hydraulic modulator/motor pack assembly from the vehicle.

To install:

9. Install the hydraulic modulator/motor pack assembly into the vehicle and torque the bolt to 80 inch lbs. (9.0 Nm).

10. Install the 5 brake tubes to the hydraulic modulator/motor pack assembly.

11. Connect the 6-pin motor pack electrical connector.

12. Connect the brake pressure differential warning switch electrical connector.

13. Connect the 2 solenoid electrical connectors. Install the air cleaner duct connectors.

14. Bleed the entire brake system. Tighten the 2 brake combination valve tube nuts to 13 ft. lbs. (18 Nm) and the 3 hydraulic modulator tube nuts to 24 ft. lbs. (32 Nm).

Electronic Brake Control Module

REMOVAL AND INSTALLATION

1. Under the steering column, remove the lower sound insulator panel fasteners.

2. Lower the sound insulator panel and remove from the vehicle.

3. If equipped with a manual transmission, remove the left side kick panel.

4. Remove the push in (Christmas Tree) retainer attaching the EBCM bracket to the sidewall.

NOTE: If necessary, cut head off of the push in retainer to remove the EBCM bracket.

5. Remove the EBCM and EBCM bracket from its mounting place.

6. Disconnect the electrical connectors from the EBCM and remove from the vehicle.

7. In necessary, replace the destroyed retainer to insure proper retaining force when installing the new push in retainer.

To install:

8. Connect the electrical connector to the EBCM.

9. Install the EBCM and EBCM bracket into its mounting location.

10. Install the new push in (Christmas Tree) retainer attaching the EBCM bracket to the sidewall.

11. Install the EBCM bracket-to-upper instrument panel nut and torque to 18.5 ft. lbs. (25.0 Nm).

12. If equipped with a manual transmission, install the left side kick panel.

13. Install the lower sound insulator panel and fasteners.

Front Wheel Speed Sensor Assembly

REMOVAL AND INSTALLATION

The front wheel speed sensors and rings are integral with the hub and bearing assemblies. If the speed sensor or ring require replacement, the entire hub and bearing assembly must be replaced.

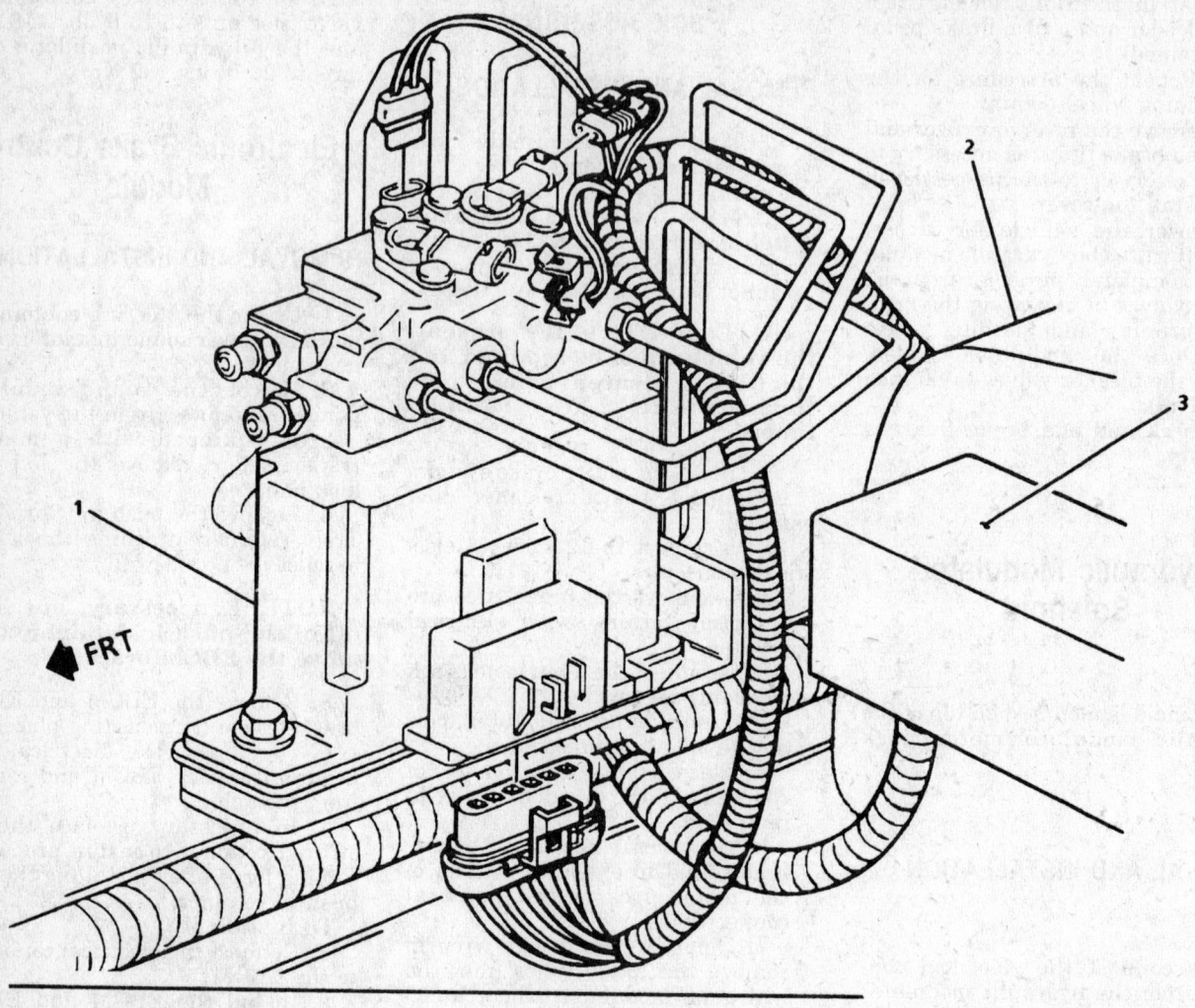

FRT

1 HYDRAULIC MODULATOR/MOTOR PACK ASSEMBLY   3 UNDERHOOD ELECTRICAL CENTER

2 LEFT HAND WHEELHOUSE

8569Q001

ABS hydraulic modulator/motor pack assembly

Rear Wheel Speed Sensor Assembly

REMOVAL AND INSTALLATION

1. Raise and safely support the vehicle.

2. Disconnect the electrical connector from the wheel speed sensor.

3. Remove the jumper harness grommet from the retainer.

4. Remove the sensor-to-differential housing bolt.

5. Remove the sensor from the differential housing.

To install:

6. Lubricate the sensor O-ring with differential oil and install the O-ring with the sensor into the differential housing.

7. Torque the sensor-to-differential housing bolt to 89 inch lbs. (10 Nm).

8. Connect the electrical connector to the wheel speed sensor.

9. Install the jumper harness grommet into the retainer.

Enable Relay

REMOVAL AND INSTALLATION

1. Remove the enable cover.

2. Disconnect the electrical connector from the enable relay.

3. Remove the enable relay from the vehicle.

4. To install, reverse the removal procedures.

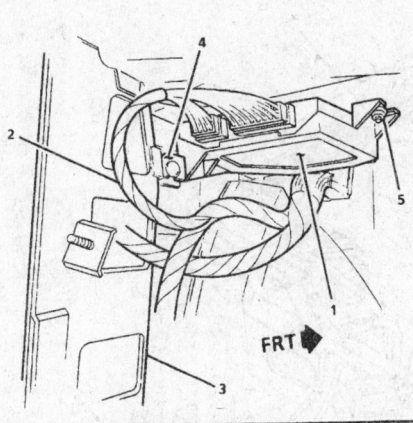

1 EBCM AND BRACKET
2 EBCM HARNESS
3 LEFT HAND KICK PANEL
4 PUSH-IN RETAINER
5 MOUNTING STUD AND NUT

8569Q003

ABS EBCM location

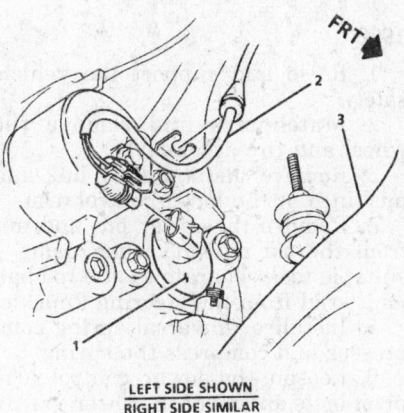

LEFT SIDE SHOWN
RIGHT SIDE SIMILAR

1 FRONT WHEEL SPEED SENSOR
2 FRONT WHEEL SPEED SENSOR JUMPER HARNESS
3 LOWER CONTROL ARM

8569Q004

ABS front wheel bearing and speed sensor assembly

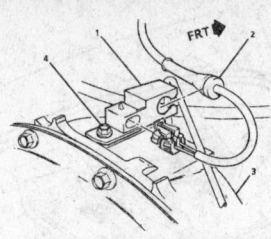

1 REAR WHEEL SPEED SENSOR
2 REAR WHEEL SPEED SENSOR JUMPER HARNESS
3 REAR AXLE HOUSING
4 REAR WHEEL SPEED SENSOR MOUNTING BOLT

8569Q005

ABS rear wheel speed sensor assembly

FRONT SUSPENSION

MacPherson Strut

REMOVAL AND INSTALLATION

1992

1. Raise and support the vehicle safely. Use a jackstand to support the lower control arm.
2. Matchmark and remove the wheel and tire assembly.
3. Remove the brake hose bracket.
4. Remove and discard the strut-to-knuckle bolts, washers and nuts.
5. Remove the cover from the upper mount assembly.
6. Remove the nut from the upper end of the strut.
7. Remove the strut and shield from the vehicle.

To install:

8. Install the strut and shield, attaching the nut to the upper end of the strut. Tighten the upper strut nut to 44 ft. lbs. (60 Nm).
9. Install the cover to the upper mount.
10. Install the new strut-to-knuckle bolts, washers and nuts. Tighten the strut-to-knuckle nuts to 125 ft. lbs. (170 Nm) followed by a 120 degree turn. Final torque must exceed 148 ft. lbs. (200 Nm).
11. Install the brake hose bracket.
12. Align the marks made earlier, then install the tire and wheel assembly.
13. Lower the vehicle and check the front end alignment.

1993–96

1. If removing the driver side strut assembly, remove the brake master cylinder retaining nuts, then carefully reposition the master cylinder

assembly, making sure not to kink or damage the hydraulic lines.
2. Remove the bolts and screws attaching the top of the strut assembly to the upper control arm support.
3. Raise and support the vehicle safely, then remove the tire and wheel assembly.
4. Remove the stabilizer shaft link.
5. Remove the nuts and bolts retaining the lower end of the strut assembly to the lower control arm.
6. Separate the lower ball stud from the steering knuckle.
7. Using chalk or paint, matchmark the location of the strut assembly lower mount location relative to the upper mount location in case the strut is to be disassembled. Do not scribe marks or the components will be damaged.
8. Remove the strut assembly from the vehicle.

To install:

9. Install the strut assembly, positioning as noted during removal, then install the bolts and nuts retaining strut to the lower control arm and tighten to 48 ft. lbs. (65 Nm).
10. Install the lower control arm ball joint to the steering knuckle.
11. Install the stabilizer shaft link assembly.
12. Install the tire and wheel assembly, then lower the vehicle.
13. Install and hand-tighten the upper strut retaining bolts and nuts, then tighten the bolts to 37 ft. lbs. (50 Nm) and the nuts to 32 ft. lbs. (43 Nm).
14. If the driver side strut was installed, reposition the brake master cylinder to the booster assembly, then install the nuts and tighten to 32 ft. lbs. (43 Nm).

Strut Cartridge Replacement

1992

The modified strut assembly used on these vehicles may not be serviced. The strut is removed separately from the coil spring and must be replaced as a single unit if damaged or worn. Likewise, the coil spring is serviced separately from the strut.

1993–96

For these vehicles, the strut and spring assembly may be removed from the vehicle, and then separated to replace either the strut unit or the

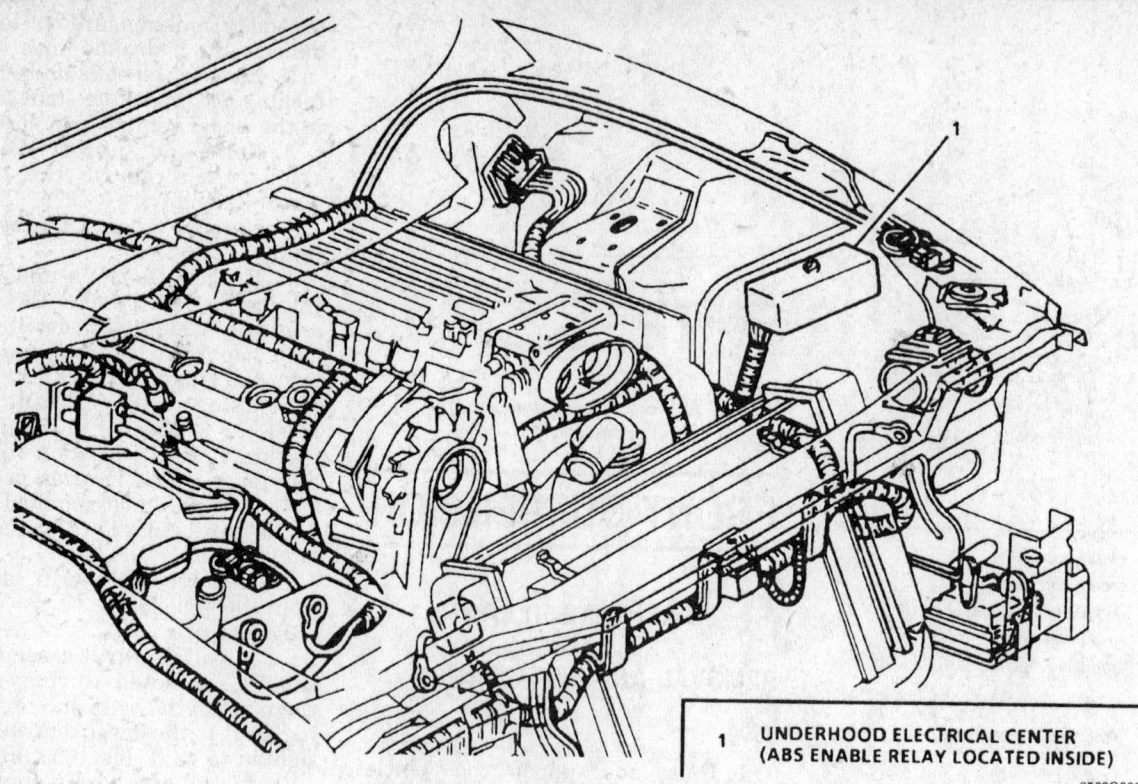

1 UNDERHOOD ELECTRICAL CENTER
(ABS ENABLE RELAY LOCATED INSIDE)

8569Q006

ABS enable relay location

spring. The unit retains the spring under great pressure and extreme care must be used when servicing the strut assembly. Do not attempt to replace the strut without a suitable spring compressor tool.

1. Position a suitable modular strut spring compressor to the work bench, then install and align any necessary supports or adapters needed to compress the modular strut assembly.

2. Install the strut assembly to the compressor tool, making sure the top of the strut assembly is properly aligned and is flat against the upper adapter in the tool fixture.

3. Secure the bottom of the strut assembly to the lower portion of the compressor and install the locking pin. The locking ears of the strut should face down and rearward in order to assure proper alignment in the tool.

4. Compress the spring assembly approximately ½ in. (13mm).

─── **CAUTION** ───
Be careful not to overcompress the spring as severe overloading could cause tool failure and result in bodily injury.

5. Using a 0.60 in. (15mm) modular strut removal set on the strut as-sembly nut, loosen the nut while holding the strut from turning. Discard the old nut once it is removed from the strut.

6. Carefully ease and release the spring tension according to the tool manufacturer's instructions. Once the spring tension is completely removed from the strut, the tool may be unlocked, then the strut and spring may be separated.

To install:

7. Position the components of the strut assembly to the compressor tool. Be sure to align the upper and lower mounts as noted during removal.

8. Once the strut components are properly secured, compress the assembly slightly, just enough to hold the strut assembly in the upper compressor adapter, but not sufficiently to load the spring.

9. Insert a strut alignment rod though the top of the strut assembly and onto the strut rod, then slowly compress the spring, making sure the threaded strut rod is properly guided into position.

10. Install a new strut assembly nut, then hold the strut rod while tightening the nut. Once the nut is tightened and the assembly is secured, carefully release the tool and remove the strut assembly.

Coil Springs

REMOVAL AND INSTALLATION

1992

1. Raise and support the vehicle safely.

2. Matchmark and remove the wheel and tire assembly.

3. Remove the stabilizer link and bushings at the lower control arm.

4. Remove the cotter pin and nut from the tie rod end, then using a suitable tool, separate the tie rod ball joint stud from the steering knuckle.

5. Install a universal spring compressor and compress the spring.

6. Loosen the lower control arm pivot bolts and pivot the lower control arm rearward.

7. Carefully remove the spring compressor and remove the spring.

To install:

8. Properly position the spring on the control arm, making sure the spring insulator is in place. The bottom of the spring is coiled helical and the top is coiled flat, with a gripper notch near the end of the wire. After assembly, the end of the spring coil must cover all or part of 1 inspection drain hole on the lower control arm. The other hole must be completely uncovered.

9. Carefully install the spring compressor and compress the spring.

NOTE: Take care not to damage the corrosion protection coating on the spring. If any of the coating is removed, it must be repaired.

10. Pivot the lower control arm forward into position in the frame.

11. Tighten the lower control arm pivot bolt/nuts to 61 ft. lbs. (83 Nm).

12. Remove the spring compressor.

13. Install the stabilizer linkage. Tighten the stabilizer link nut to 13 ft. lbs. (17 Nm).

14. Install the steering knuckle to the tie rod ball joint stud. Tighten the nut to 80 ft. lbs. (108 Nm).

15. Install a new cotter pin. If the hole in the stud does not line up with the slot in the nut, tighten the nut until it does. Do not back off the nut to install the cotter pin.

16. Align the marks made earlier, then install the wheel and tire assembly. Lower the vehicle.

1993–96

The springs on these vehicles are part of the strut assembly. In order to replace a spring, the strut assembly must be removed from the vehicle and the components must be separated using a suitable modular spring compressor tool.

Upper Ball Joints

The 1993–96 model F-body vehicles are the only of these models to utilize an upper control arm and ball joint.

INSPECTION

1. Raise the vehicle and position floor stands under the left and right lower control arm as near as possible to each lower ball joint. There should

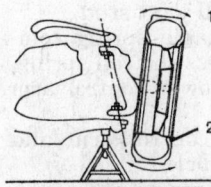

1. SUPPORT FRONT LOWER CONTROL ARM ASSEMBLY AS FAR OUTBOARD AS POSSIBLE

2. POSITION DIAL INDICATOR TO CHECK MOVEMENT AT THIS POINT

3. ROCK WHEEL AND TIRE ASSEMBLY IN AND OUT AT TOP AND BOTTOM

8470Q076

Upper ball joint inspection — 1993–96 vehicles

be space between the upper control arm bumper and frame.

2. Position a dial indicator against the wheel rim.

3. Grasp the wheel and push in on bottom of the tire while pulling out at the top. Read the gauge, then reverse the push-pull procedure. Horizontal deflection on the dial indicator should not exceed 0.125 inch (3.18mm).

4. If the indicator exceeds 0.125 inch (3.18mm) or if the ball stud, when disconnected from the knuckle assembly, can be twisted in its socket by hand, replace the ball joint.

REMOVAL AND INSTALLATION

1. Raise and support the vehicle safely; place floor stands under the strut assembly mounting location on the lower control arm.

NOTE: Leave the jack under the strut during removal and installation, in order to retain the spring assembly and lower control arm in position.

2. Matchmark and remove the tire and wheel assembly.

3. Remove the cotter pin and nut from the upper control arm ball joint stud.

4. Support the steering knuckle with a jackstand, then using a ball joint separator tool, break the stud loose and pull the stud out of the knuckle.

5. With the control arm in a raised position, use a ⅛ inch diameter bit and drill into each of the 4 rivet heads to a depth of ¼ inch (6mm).

6. Drill off the rivet heads with a ½ inch diameter bit.

7. Punch out the rivets using a suitable driver or punch, then remove the ball joint.

To install:

8. Place the new ball joint into the upper control arm and secure it with 4 bolts and nuts in place of rivets. Torque the nuts to specifications provided with the ball joint kit.

9. Remove the support from the steering knuckle, then connect the ball joint to the knuckle assembly. Torque the nut to 39 ft. lbs. (53 Nm), then insert a new cotter pin. If necessary, tighten the nut additionally in order to install the pin, but do not back off the specified torque.

NOTE: When replacing the ball joints, use only high-quality replacement parts; bolts and nuts specified to be strong enough to endure the stress.

10. Remove the floor jack from underneath the strut spring seat.

11. Install the tire and wheel assembly.

12. Lower the vehicle.

Lower Ball Joints

INSPECTION

1992

1. Visually inspect the ball joint seal for cuts and tears. Ball joints with cuts or tears in their seals must be replaced.

2. Check the ball joint when it is disconnected from the steering knuckle. If there is any looseness in the ball stud, if the ball stud can be twisted in it's socket using finger pressure or if there are any cuts or tears in the ball joint seal, replace the ball joint.

1993–96

The lower ball joints contain a visual wear indicator and are checked in this fashion alone. The lower ball joint grease plug is threaded into the wear indicator protruding from the bottom of the ball joint housing. As long as the wear indicator extends out of the ball joint housing, the ball joint is not worn. If the tip of the wear indicator is parallel with or recessed into the ball joint housing, the ball joint is defective and must be replaced.

To check if the wear indicator has receded sufficiently to necessitate ball joint replacement, make sure the vehicle is supported by the wheels in order to assure proper ball stud loading. Wipe the front suspension lubricant fitting and nipple free off dirt or grease, then observe the round nipple. If it is difficult to gauge the nipple by sight, scrape a small tool or fingernail across the cover to see if it has receded.

REMOVAL AND INSTALLATION

1. Raise and support the vehicle safely. Support the lower control arm under the spring seat or strut/spring assembly mount using a suitable jack which must remain in position throughout the procedure to retain the spring and control arm position.

2. Matchmark and remove the wheel and tire assembly.

3. For 1993–96 vehicles, use a ball joint separator to loosen the ball stud in the steering knuckle before the cotter pin and nut is removed.

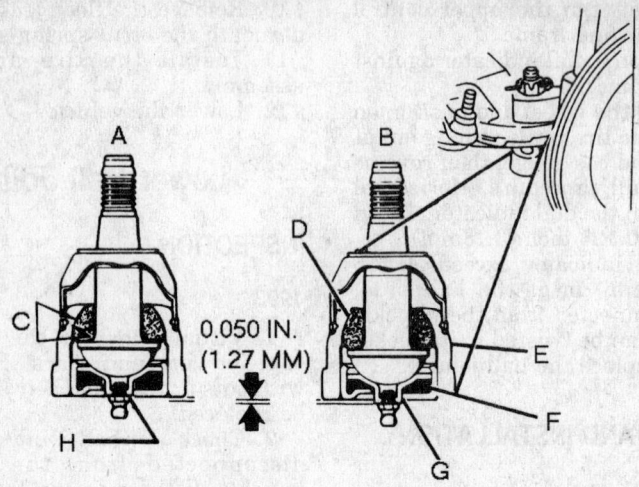

A. Worn
B. New
C. Wear surfaces
D. Sintered iron bearing
E. Housing socket
F. Rubber pressure ring
G. Wear indicator shoulder
   (out when new)

H. When lower control arm
   ball stud assembly wear
   causes wear indicator
   shoulder to be below
   surface, replacement is
   needed

0.050 IN.
(1.27 MM)

8470Q077

Lower ball joint inspection — 1993–96 vehicles

4. Remove the cotter pin and loosen the lower ball joint nut.

5. For 1992 vehicles, after the cotter pin and nut have been removed, use a ball joint separator to disconnect the lower control arm from the steering knuckle, then remove the grease fittings.

6. Using suitable ball joint removal tools, press the ball joint from the lower control arm.

To install:

7. Position the new ball joint into the lower control arm and press into place using suitable ball joint installation tools. If the ball joint cannot press firmly into position, either the ball joint is defective or the lower control arm must be replaced.

NOTE: When installing a new ball joint on 1992 vehicles, be sure to position the purge vent on the rubber boot facing inward.

8. Connect the ball joint to the steering knuckle, then install the ball stud nut and tighten to 80 ft. lbs. (108 Nm) for 1992 vehicles or to 81 ft. lbs. (110 Nm) for 1993–96 vehicles. Then, if necessary, tighten the nut just sufficiently to align the nut slot with the stud hold and install a cotter pin. Do not back off the torque value to align the slot and hole.

9. For 1992 vehicles, install and lubricate the ball joint fitting until grease appears at the seal.

10. Remove the jackstand from under the lower control arm.

11. Align the marks made earlier, then install the wheel and tire assembly.

12. Lower the vehicle, then check and adjust the front end alignment, as necessary.

Upper Control Arms

The 1993–96 model F-body vehicles are the only of these models to utilize an upper control arm and ball joint.

REMOVAL AND INSTALLATION

1. If removing the driver side strut assembly, remove the brake master cylinder retaining nuts, then carefully reposition the master cylinder assembly, making sure not to kink or damage the hydraulic lines.

2. Remove the bolts and screws attaching the top of the strut assembly to the upper control arm support.

3. Raise and support the vehicle safely, then remove the tire and wheel assembly.

4. Remove the stabilizer shaft link.

5. Remove the nuts and bolts retaining the lower end of the strut assembly to the lower control arm.

6. Separate the upper ball stud from the steering knuckle.

7. Remove the steering knuckle from the upper control arm assembly. Remove the upper control arm and the strut assembly from the vehicle, then support the steering knuckle using jackstands.

8. Remove the nuts and bolts attaching the control arm to the control arm support, then separate the components.

To install:

9. Install the upper control arm to the control arm support, then tighten the retaining nuts and bolts to 39 ft. lbs. (53 Nm).

10. Position the upper control arm assembly and the strut assembly in the vehicle, then install the upper ball stud to the steering knuckle.

11. Remove the jackstands from underneath the steering knuckle.

12. Install the lower strut assembly fasteners, then install the stabilizer link.

13. Install the upper strut assembly fasteners.

14. Install the tire and wheel assembly, then lower the vehicle.

15. If the driver side control arm installed, reposition the brake master cylinder to the booster assembly, then install the nuts and tighten to 32 ft. lbs. (43 Nm).

Lower Control Arms

REMOVAL AND INSTALLATION

1992

1. Raise and safely support the vehicle.

2. Matchmark and remove the wheel and tire assembly.

3. Remove the stabilizer link and bushings at the lower control arm.

4. Remove the cotter pin and nut from the tie rod end. Using a suitable tool, remove the steering knuckle from the tie rod ball joint stud.

5. Install a suitable spring compressor and compress the coil spring.

6. Remove the lower control arm pivot bolts.

7. Remove the control arm and spring from the vehicle.

To install:

8. Properly position the spring on the control arm, making sure the spring insulator is in place. The bottom of the spring is coiled helical and the top is coiled flat, with a gripper notch near the end of the wire. After

assembly, the end of the spring coil must cover all or part of 1 inspection drain hole. The other hole must be completely uncovered.

9. Carefully install the spring compressor and compress the spring.

NOTE: Take care not to damage the corrosion protection coating on the spring. If any of the coating is removed, it must be repaired.

10. Install the lower control arm into position in the frame.

11. Install the bolts. The front bolt installs from front to rear first. Tighten the lower control arm pivot bolt/nuts to 61 ft. lbs. (83 Nm).

12. Remove the spring compressor.

13. Install the stabilizer linkage. Tighten the stabilizer link nut to 13 ft. lbs. (17 Nm).

14. Install the steering knuckle to the tie rod ball joint stud. Tighten the nut to 80 ft. lbs. (108 Nm).

15. Install a new cotter pin. If the hole in the stud does not line up with the slot in the nut, tighten the nut until it does. Do not back off the nut to install the cotter pin.

16. Align the marks made earlier and install the wheel and tire assembly. Lower the vehicle.

1993–96

1. Raise and support the vehicle safely, then matchmark and remove the tire and wheel assembly.

2. Disconnect the steering rack outer tie rod from the steering knuckle.

3. Remove the stabilizer shaft link.

4. Remove the fasteners and disconnect the strut assembly from the lower control arm

5. Separate and remove the lower control arm ball stud from the steering knuckle.

6. Remove the control arm retaining nuts and bolts, then remove the control arm from the vehicle.

To install:

7. Position the lower control arm to the crossmember, then install and hand-tighten the retainers. Once the retainers are installed, tighten the nuts to 96 ft. lbs. (130 Nm).

8. Position the lower control arm assembly to the steering knuckle and hand start the nut, then tighten the nut to 81 ft. lbs. (110 Nm) and install a new cotter pin. If necessary, tighten the nut further in order to align a slot with the stud hole, but do not back off from the torque specification.

9. Position the strut assembly to the lower control arm and secure using the lower strut fasteners.

10. Install the stabilizer shaft link.

11. Connect the steering rack tie rod to the steering knuckle assembly.

12. Align the matchmarks made earlier, then install the tire and wheel assembly.

13. Lower the vehicle, then check and adjust the alignment, as necessary.

Sway Bar/Stabilizer Shaft

REMOVAL AND INSTALLATION

1992

1. Raise and support the vehicle safely.

2. Remove each side of the sway bar linkage by removing the nut from the link bolt, pulling the bolt from the linkage and remove the retainers, grommets and spacer.

3. Remove the bracket-to-frame or body bolts and remove the sway bar, rubber bushings and brackets. Remove the lower structure brace if equipped.

To install:

4. Reverse of the removal procedure. Install the sway bar with the identification tag on the right side of the vehicle. The rubber bushings should be positioned squarely in the bracket with the slit in the bushings facing the front of the vehicle.

5. Tighten the sway bar link nut/bolt to 16 ft. lbs. (22 Nm) on all vehicles except 1992, for these vehicles tighten the link nut/bolt to 13 ft. lbs. (17 Nm) unless the vehicle is equipped with the ride and handling suspension system. For 1992 vehicles equipped with the ride and handling suspension system, tighten the link nut/bolt to 18 ft. lbs. (24 Nm).

6. Tighten the bracket bolts on all vehicles to 39 ft. lbs. (53 Nm).

1993–96

1. Raise and support the vehicle safely.

2. Remove the nut retaining the stabilizer shaft link to the lower control arm, then remove the link assembly and sleeve.

3. Remove the bolts and clamps retaining the stabilizer shaft to the side rail brackets.

4. Remove the sway bar/stabilizer shaft and insulators from the vehicle.

5. If necessary, remove the retaining bolts and the shaft brackets from the side rails.

To install:

6. If removed, install the brackets to the side rails and tighten the retaining bolts to 41 ft. lbs. (55 Nm).

7. Position the insulators over the shaft, making sure each insulator slit is facing the front of the vehicle.

8. Position the shaft and install the clamps. Tighten the clamp retaining bolts to 41 ft. lbs. (55 Nm).

9. Install the link sleeve between the control arm and the stabilizer shaft, then install the link assembly through the lower control arm, up through the sleeve to the stabilizer shaft. Install the retaining nut and tighten to 17 ft. lbs. (23 Nm).

10. Lower the vehicle.

Steering Knuckle/Spindle Assembly

REMOVAL AND INSTALLATION

1992

1. Raise and safely support the vehicle.

2. Matchmark and remove the tire and wheel assembly.

3. Remove the caliper mounting bolts and remove the caliper. Support the caliper with mechanic's wire, do not let the caliper hang by the brake hose.

4. Remove the dust cap from the hub and remove the cotter pin, nut and washer from the spindle. Remove the hub and rotor assembly from the spindle. Remove the splash shield.

5. Remove the outer wheel bearing assembly from the hub. Using a suitable tool, pry out the inner bearing lip seal and remove the inner wheel bearing assembly.

6. Using a suitable tool, disconnect the tie rod from the spindle.

7. Support the lower control arm. Using a suitable tool, disconnect the ball joint from the spindle.

8. Remove and discard 2 bolts, washers and nuts attaching the strut to the spindle and remove the spindle.

To install:

9. Position the spindle to the strut. Install new strut-to-spindle bolts, washers and nuts to the strut. Tighten the 2 nuts to 125 ft. lbs. (170 Nm) followed by an additional 120 degree turn. The final torque must exceed 148 ft. lbs. (200 Nm).

10. Connect the ball joint stud and nut to the spindle. Tighten the castle nut to 83 ft. lbs. (113 Nm) and install a new cotter pin. If the hole in the stud does not line up with the slot in

the castellated nut, continue to tighten the nut just enough to allow insertion of the cotter pin. Do not back off the nut to insert the cotter pin.

11. Connect the tie rod. Tighten the castellated nut to 35 ft. lbs. (47 Nm). If the hole in the stud does not line up with a slot in the castellated nut, continue to tighten the nut just enough to allow insertion of the cotter pin. Do not back off the nut to insert the cotter.

12. Install the splash shield.

13. Clean and inspect the wheel bearings, replace the bearings and races as necessary.

14. Install the inner wheel bearing assemblies.

15. Install the hub and rotor assembly.

16. Place the outer bearing in the outer bearing cup and install the washer and nut. Adjust the wheel bearings, install a new cotter pin and install the bearing dust cap.

17. Install the caliper to the steering knuckle. Tighten the caliper mounting bolts to 38 ft. lbs. (51 Nm).

18. Align the marks made earlier and install the wheel and tire assembly.

19. Lower the vehicle and check the brake fluid level.

1993–96

1. Disconnect the negative battery cable, then raise and support the vehicle safely.

2. Matchmark and remove the wheel assembly.

3. Remove the brake caliper with the brake hose attached and support aside using a hook or wire.

4. Remove the brake rotor.

5. Disengage the wheel speed sensor electrical connector.

6. If necessary, remove the front wheel hub and bearing assembly.

7. Disconnect the steering rack outer tie rod from the steering knuckle.

8. Remove the stabilizer shaft link assembly.

9. Remove the strut assembly lower fasteners.

10. Separate and remove the lower ball stud from the steering knuckle.

11. Separate and remove the upper ball stud from the steering knuckle.

12. Remove the steering knuckle from the vehicle.

To install:

13. Install the steering knuckle to the vehicle.

14. Install the upper ball stud and control arm to the steering knuckle.

15. Install the lower ball stud and control arm to the steering knuckle.

16. Position the strut assembly to the lower control arm and install the fasteners.

17. Install the stabilizer link.

18. Connect the steering rack tie rod to the steering knuckle.

19. If removed, install the wheel hub and bearing assembly.

20. Engage the wheel speed sensor electrical connector.

21. Install the brake rotor.

22. Remove the support and install the caliper assembly.

23. Align and install the wheel assembly.

24. Lower the vehicle and connect the negative battery cable.

25. Check and adjust vehicle toe, as necessary.

Front Wheel Bearings

ADJUSTMENT

1992

1. Raise and safely support the vehicle.

2. Remove the wheel cover or center cap to expose the rotor dust cap.

3. Remove the dust cap from the hub.

4. Remove the cotter pin from the spindle nut.

5. Tighten the spindle nut to 12 ft. lbs. (16 Nm) while turning the wheel forward by hand to fully seat the bearings. This will remove any grease or burrs which could cause excessive wheel bearing play later.

6. Back off the nut to the just loose position.

7. Hand-tighten the spindle nut. Loosen the spindle nut just enough that either hole in the spindle lines up with a slot in the nut, not more than ½ flat.

8. Install a new cotter pin. Bend the ends of the cotter pin against the nut and cut off the extra length to ensure the ends will not interfere with the dust cap.

9. Using a dial indicator, check the hub assembly. There should be 0.001–0.005 inch (0.03–0.13mm) end-play when properly adjusted.

10. Install the dust cap on the hub. Install the wheel cover or center cap.

11. Lower the vehicle.

1993–96

The wheel hub and bearing assembly used on these vehicles is a sealed, non-serviceable unit. No wheel bear-ing adjustments are necessary or possible.

REMOVAL AND INSTALLATION

1992

1. Raise and support the vehicle safely.

2. Matchmark and remove the wheel and tire assembly.

3. Remove the caliper assembly.

4. Remove the dust cap from the hub. Remove the cotter pin, nut and washer from the spindle.

5. Remove the hub and rotor assembly.

6. Remove the outer bearing assembly from the hub. The inner bearing assembly will remain in the hub and may be removed by prying out the inner seal with a suitable tool. Discard the seal after removal.

7. Remove the old bearing races from the hub with a suitable brass drift inserted behind the races in a recessed slot.

8. Clean all parts in clean solvent and air dry. Remove all old grease from the entire assembly. Do not mix greases as mixing may change grease properties and result in poor performance. Do not spin the bearing with compressed air while drying or the bearing may be damaged.

To install:

9. Inspect the bearings for cracked cages and worn or pitted rollers. Check the bearing races for cracks, scores or pitting condition. Replace as necessary.

10. If the races were removed, drive or press the races into the hub.

11. Apply a thin film of high temperature wheel bearing grease to the spindle at the outer bearing seat and at the inner bearing seat, shoulder and seal seat.

12. Put a small quantity of grease inboard of each bearing cup in the hub.

13. Pack the wheel bearings using a suitable bearing packer. If a bearing packer is not available, the bearings can be packed by hand. If hand packing is used, it is extremely important to work the grease thoroughly into the bearings between the rollers, cone and cage.

14. Place the inner bearing cone and roller assembly in the hub. Put an additional quantity of grease outboard of the bearing.

15. Install a new grease seal using a suitable tool until the seal is flush with the hub. Lubricate the seal lip with a thin layer of grease.

16. Carefully install the hub and rotor assembly. Place the outer bear-

ing assembly in the outer bearing race. Install the washer and nut and tighten to 12 ft. lbs. (16 Nm).

17. Install caliper assembly, align the marks made earlier, then install the wheel and tire assembly.

18. Adjust the wheel bearings and install the dust cap and the wheel cover or center cap as applicable. Lower the vehicle.

1993–96

1. Disconnect the negative battery cable, then raise and support the vehicle safely.

2. Matchmark and remove the tire and wheel assembly.

3. Remove the brake caliper with the brake hose attached and support aside using a hook or wire.

4. Remove the brake rotor.

5. Disengage the wheel speed sensor electrical connector.

6. Remove the 4 bolts retaining the hub and bearing assembly to the steering knuckle, then remove the assembly from the vehicle.

To install:

7. Position the hub and bearing assembly to the steering knuckle, then install the retaining bolts and tighten to 63 ft. lbs. (86 Nm).

8. Make sure the wheel speed sensor connector is properly routed in the wire bracket or system damage may occur, then engage the connector to the speed sensor.

9. Install the brake rotor.

10. Remove the support and install the caliper assembly.

11. Align and install the wheel assembly.

12. Lower the vehicle and connect the negative battery cable.

REAR SUSPENSION

Shock Absorbers

REMOVAL AND INSTALLATION

1. For 1993–96 vehicles, fold down the seatback frame assembly, then remove the quarter trim panel and pull the folding carpet back.

2. Raise and support the vehicle safely at height which will allow access to both the upper and lower shock mounts. The rear axle must be supported with a jackstand to prevent damage to the rear suspension once the shocks are disconnected.

3. For 1992 vehicles, pull back the carpet in the rear hatch.

4. Remove the upper shock attaching nut, upper washer and grommet.

5. Remove the lower shock mounting nut from the rear axle.

6. Lower the shock absorber from the vehicle along with the remaining grommet and washer.

To install:

7. For 1992 vehicles, position the shock absorber through the body mounting hold, with the lower of the upper shock grommet and washers in place.

8. Position the shock to the rear axle assembly.

9. For 1993–96 vehicles, install the lower shock absorber mounting nut and tighten to 66 ft. lbs. (90 Nm), then position the lower pair of grommet and washer to the top of the shock and guide the shock through the underbody pan assembly.

10. With the shock properly positioned through the body mounting hole, install the upper grommet and washer over the end of the shock, then install the upper shock absorber mounting nut and tighten to 13 ft. lbs. (17 Nm).

11. Tighten the lower attaching nut to 66 ft. lbs. (90 Nm).

12. Remove the rear axle support and lower the vehicle.

13. Reposition the carpeting and trim panels, as applicable.

Coil Springs

REMOVAL AND INSTALLATION

1992

1. Raise and support the vehicle safely so the rear axle hangs freely, then install an adjustable lifting device supporting the rear axle.

2. Remove the track bar mounting bolt at the axle assembly and loosen the track bar bolt at the body brace.

3. Disconnect the rear brake hose clip at the underbody to allow additional brake line play to lower axle.

4. Disconnect the right and left shock absorber lower attaching nuts.

5. Carefully lower the rear axle sufficiently to remove the coil springs and, if necessary, the insulators. Make certain that at no time is the rear axle suspended by the brake lines as damage to the hydraulic brake system may occur.

To install:

6. Position the springs and insulators properly in the spring seats. Be sure the spring is seated in the same

position as before removal and raise the axle into place.

7. Install the shock absorbers to the rear axle. Tighten the shock mounting nuts to 66 ft. lbs. (90 Nm).

8. Clean and install the track bar mounting bolt and nut and the axle.

9. Tighten the track bar mounting nut at the axle to 76 ft. lbs. (103 Nm). Tighten the track bar bracket nut to 61 ft. lbs. (83 Nm).

10. Connect the rear brake line clip to the underbody.

11. Remove the adjustable lifting device and lower the vehicle.

1993–96

1. Raise and support the vehicle safely so the rear axle hangs freely, then install an adjustable lifting device supporting the rear axle.

2. Disconnect the right and left shock absorber lower attaching nuts, then free the shock absorbers from the rear axle assembly.

3. Carefully lower the rear axle sufficiently to remove the upper insulators and coil springs. Make certain that at no time is the rear axle suspended by the brake lines as damage to the hydraulic brake system may occur.

To install:

4. Position the coil springs to the rear axle assembly. Be careful not to chip or damage the spring protective coatings. Should the coatings become chipped or damaged, do not used the spring until it has been replaced.

5. Position the upper insulators on the springs, then carefully raise the rear axle into position.

6. Connect the shock absorbers to the rear axle assembly, then tighten the retaining nuts to 66 ft. lbs. (90 Nm).

7. Remove the adjustable lifting device from the rear axle.

8. Lower the vehicle.

Rear Control Arms

REMOVAL AND INSTALLATION

NOTE: If both control arms are being replaced, remove and replace 1 control arm at a time to prevent the axle from rolling or slipping sideways and thus making replacement difficult or damaging components.

1. Raise and support the vehicle safely, using an adjustable jack to support the rear axle at the curb height position.

2. Remove the control arm-to-axle housing bolt and control arm-to-underbody bolt.

3. Remove the control arm assembly from the vehicle.

To install:

4. Position the control arm to the vehicle, then install the retaining nuts and bolts. The control arm-to-axle bolts should be installed from the inboard side outward.

5. With the suspension at its curb height position, tighten the control arm bolts to 80 ft. lbs. (108 Nm) for 1992 vehicles. The nuts for 1993–96 vehicles should be tightened to 60 ft. lbs. (82 Nm).

6. Remove the supports and lower the vehicle.

Track Bar (Rear Axle Tie Rod Assembly)

REMOVAL AND INSTALLATION

1992

1. Raise and support the vehicle safely, making sure the rear axle is supported at curb height.

2. Remove the track bar mounting bolts and nuts at the spring seat and the body bracket.

3. Remove the track bar from the vehicle.

To install:

4. Position the track bar in the body bracket and loosely install the retainer.

5. Thoroughly clean the track bar-to-spring seat bolt, then position the track bar to the spring seat and install the retainer.

6. Tighten the bar-to-spring seat nut and bolt to 76 ft. lbs. (103 Nm).

7. Tighten the bar-to-body bracket nut and bolt to 61 ft. lbs. (83 Nm).

8. Remove the rear axle support and lower the vehicle.

1993–96

1. Raise and support the vehicle safely, then position a support to hold the rear axle at its normal curb height position.

2. Remove the bolt and nut attaching the track bar to the rear axle.

3. Remove the bolts and nuts attaching the track bar to the underbody brackets.

4. Remove the track bar and the brace from the vehicle.

To install:

5. Position the brace to the right underbody bracket, then hand-tighten 1 bolt and nut to retain it.

6. Position the track bar to the right underbody bracket then hand-tighten the other bolt and screw to retain it.

7. Install the remaining underbody bracket bolts, then tighten the bolts to 35 ft. lbs. (47 Nm) and the nuts to 75 ft. lbs. (102 Nm).

8. Install the bolt and nut retaining the track bar to the rear axle, then tighten to 75 ft. lbs. (102 Nm).

9. Remove the rear axle support, then lower the vehicle.

Torque Arm

REMOVAL AND INSTALLATION

1992

1. In order to prevent spring pressure from rotating the rear axle and causing vehicle damage, remove the rear coil springs.

2. Remove the rear torque arm attaching bolts.

3. Remove the front torque arm outer bracket, then remove the torque arm from the vehicle.

To install:

4. Position the torque arm to the vehicle and loosely install the rear attaching bolts.

5. Install the front torque arm bracket and tighten the nuts to 30 ft. lbs. (41 Nm) for 1992 vehicles.

6. Tighten the torque arm rear nuts to 98 ft. lbs. (133 Nm).

7. Install the coil springs.

1993–96

1. Raise and support the vehicle safely, then position an adjustable lifting device under the rear axle assembly.

2. If equipped with a 2-piece driveshaft assembly, disconnect the torque arm from the driveshaft assembly.

3. Remove the bolts, nuts and washers attaching the torque arm to the rear axle housing.

4. Remove the bolts and nuts attaching the torque arm to the transmission.

5. Remove the torque arm-to-transmission bracket assemblies, then remove the torque arm from the vehicle.

To install:

6. Position the inner bracket assembly to the transmission, then install the outer bracket to the inner bracket and loosely install the fasteners.

7. Insert the torque arm into the inner and outer brackets, then tighten the fasteners. Tighten the nuts to 30 ft. lbs. (41 Nm), the bolts which thread through or into the transmission housing to 37 ft. lbs. (50 Nm) and the outer bracket-to-inner bracket bolt to 20 ft. lbs. (27 Nm).

8. Position the torque arm to the rear axle, then install the fasteners. Tighten the bolts to 96 ft. lbs. (130 Nm) and the nuts to 97 ft. lbs. (132 Nm).

9. If equipped with a 2-piece driveshaft assembly, connect the torque arm to the driveshaft.

10. Remove the rear axle support, then lower the vehicle.

GM "Y" BODY
Rear Wheel Drive
CHEVROLET—Corvette

21

FIRING ORDERS

NOTE: To avoid confusion, always replace spark plug wires one at a time.

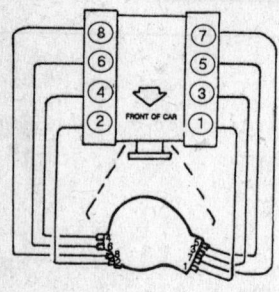

8470R002

5.7L (VIN P) Engine
Engine Firing Order:
1-8-4-3-6-5-7-2
Distributor Rotates with
Camshaft

8470R003

5.7L (VIN J) Engine
Engine Firing Order:
1-8-4-3-6-5-7-2
Distributorless Ignition System

ENGINE ELECTRICAL

NOTE: Disconnecting the negative battery cable on some vehicles may interfere with the functions of the on-board computer system and may require the computer to undergo a relearning process when the negative battery cable is reconnected.

Distributor

The 5.7 (VIN P) introduced for 1992 utilizes a front engine mounted distributor assembly.

REMOVAL

5.7 (VIN P) Engine

NOTE: The ignition system may be disabled for compression checks by removing the "BAT" terminal and the 4-terminal connector from the distributor.

1. Disconnect the negative battery cable, then unplug the Intake Air Temperature (IAT) sensor harness connector.
2. Remove the air intake duct and the serpentine drive belt.
3. Drain the engine coolant into a suitable container and remove the coolant hoses from the water pump assembly.
4. Unplug the wiring harness from the Engine Coolant Temperature (ECT) sensor and remove the water pump assembly.
5. Remove the crankshaft torsional damper as follows:
   a. Raise and safely support the vehicle or lower the vehicle, as necessary.
   b. Position a suitable drain pan and remove the power steering fluid cooler. Disconnect the line from the steering gear.
   c. Remove the motor mount nuts, then carefully raise the engine sufficiently to gain tool access to the damper.
   d. Remove the torsional damper bolts, then remove the damper from the hub.
6. Remove the belt tensioner from the engine.
7. Disconnect the spark plug wires from the distributor. Be sure to twist each boot ½ turn and pull only on the boot to remove each wire. The wire numbers should be molded into the distributor housing. If not, be sure to tag the wires before disconnection.
8. Unplug the 4-terminal ECM connector from the distributor.
9. Remove the distributor mounting bolts and pull the distributor forward until the driveshaft disengages from the engine. Mark the top of the shaft for alignment during reassembly.

INSTALLATION

Timing Not Disturbed

NOTE: To ensure correct ignition timing the distributor must be installed with the rotor in the same position as it was removed.

5.7L (VIN P) ENGINE

1. With the mark made on the distributor shaft earlier on top, install the distributor to the engine. Tighten the distributor bolts to 8 ft. lbs. (11 Nm).
2. Install the ECM connector and the spark plug wires to the distributor.
3. Install the belt tensioner.
4. Install the torsional damper as follows:
   a. Raise and support the vehicle safely or lower the vehicle, as necessary.
   b. Position the damper to the hub and install the damper bolts. Tighten the bolts to 60 ft. lbs. (81 Nm).
   c. Connect the power steering line to the gear, then lower the engine and install the power steering fluid cooler.
   d. Install the motor mount nuts and tighten to 40 ft. lbs. (54 Nm).
5. Install the water pump assembly, the ECT wiring harness and the coolant hoses.
6. Install the serpentine drive belt and the air intake duct.
7. Install the IAT sensor connector.
8. Connect the negative battery cable, fill the engine to the proper level with coolant and bleed the power steering system, as necessary.

Distributorless Ignition System

REMOVAL AND INSTALLATION

Crankshaft Sensor

1. Disconnect the battery negative cable.
2. Raise and support vehicle safely
3. Unplug the crankshaft sensor electrical connector.
4. Remove the crankshaft sensor mounting bolt, crankshaft sensor and, if applicable, the sensor shim.
   To install:
5. Coat crankshaft sensor O-ring with clean engine oil.
6. Install the sensor shim (if equipped), sensor and mounting bolt. Torque the crankshaft sensor bolt to 71 inch lbs. (8 Nm).

7. Install the wiring harness connector to the sensor terminal.

8. Lower the vehicle and connect the battery negative cable.

Ignition Module

NOTE: Before removing the ignition module, refer to the manufacturer's instructions provided with the replacement component.

1. Disconnect the battery negative cable.

2. Separate the intake plenum assembly from the top of the engine.

3. Unplug the electrical connectors from the ignition module.

4. Remove the mounting bolts, then the separate the ignition module from the underside of the intake plenum.

To install:

5. Apply a suitable dielectric grease to the back of the ignition module.

6. Position the module to the plenum and tighten the 4 mounting bolts to 89 inch lbs. (10 Nm).

7. Engage the electrical connectors nearest the front of the engine to the module.

8. Install the intake plenum assembly.

9. Connect the negative battery cable.

Ignition Coil Pack

1. Disconnect the battery negative cable.

2. Remove the intake plenum assembly.

3. Tag and disconnect the spark plug wires from the ignition coil pack.

4. Remove the 2 mounting bolts, then remove the coil pack from the ignition housing.

5. Installation is the reverse of the removal procedure.

6. Torque mounting bolts to 40 inch lbs. (4.5 Nm).

Ignition Housing

1. Disconnect battery negative cable.

2. Remove intake plenum assembly.

3. Tag and disconnect the electrical connectors and spark plug wires.

4. Remove the 4 ignition housing bracket mounting bolts.

5. Remove the ignition coil mounting bolts. Note the position of each coil and remove the coils from the ignition housing. Remove the ignition housing from the bracket.

To install:

6. Install the ignition housing on the bracket and install the 4 seals packaged with the new housing.

7. Install the coils in their proper position on the housing and tighten the coil retaining bolts to 40 inch lbs. (4.5 Nm).

8. Install the ignition housing bracket to the engine and tighten the bracket bolts as follows: M6–16 bolts to 89 inch lbs. (10 Nm); M8–20 bolts to 19 ft. lbs. (26 Nm).

9. Engage the electrical connectors and the spark plug wires.

10. Install the intake plenum assembly.

11. Connect the negative battery cable.

Ignition Timing

For the 5.7L (VIN J and VIN P) engines the base engine timing is preset at the factory. The ECM then controls engine timing based on signals from the optical camshaft position sensor (VIN P) or the from crankshaft position sensor (VIN J). No adjustments are necessary or possible.

Alternator

PRECAUTIONS

Several precautions must be observed with alternator equipped vehicles to avoid damage to the unit.

- If the battery is removed for any reason, make sure it is reconnected with the correct polarity. Reversing the battery connections may result in damage to the one-way rectifiers.
- When utilizing a booster battery as a starting aid, always connect the positive to positive terminals and the negative terminal from the booster battery to a good engine ground on the vehicle being started.
- Never use a fast charger as a booster to start vehicles.
- Disconnect the battery cables when charging the battery with a fast charger.
- Never attempt to polarize the alternator.
- Do not use test lamps of more than 12 volts when checking diode continuity.
- Do not short across or ground any of the alternator terminals.
- The polarity of the battery, alternator and regulator must be matched and considered before making any electrical connections within the system.
- Never operate the alternator on an open circuit. Make sure all connections within the circuit are clean and tight.
- Disconnect the battery ground terminal when performing any service on electrical components.
- Disconnect the battery if arc welding is to be done on the vehicle.

BELT TENSION ADJUSTMENT

A single serpentine belt is used to drive all accessories. Belt tension is maintained by a spring loaded tensioner which has the ability to maintain belt tension over a broad range of belt lengths. There is an indicator to make sure the tensioner and belt are adjusted to within their operating ranges.

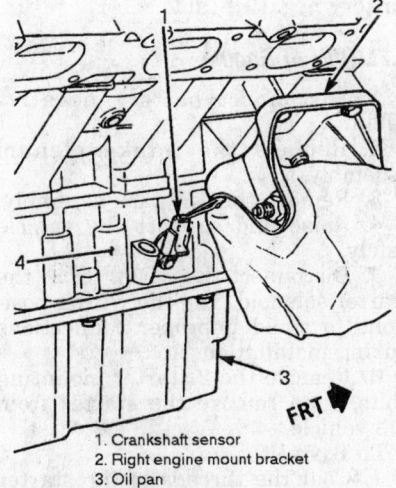

1. Crankshaft sensor
2. Right engine mount bracket
3. Oil pan
4. Engine block

8470R004

Crankshaft position sensor location — 5.7L (VIN J) engine

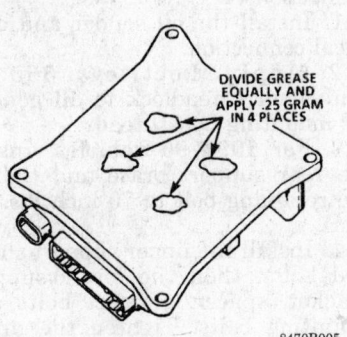

DIVIDE GREASE EQUALLY AND APPLY .25 GRAM IN 4 PLACES

8470R005

Ignition module dielectric grease application — 5.7L (VIN J) engine

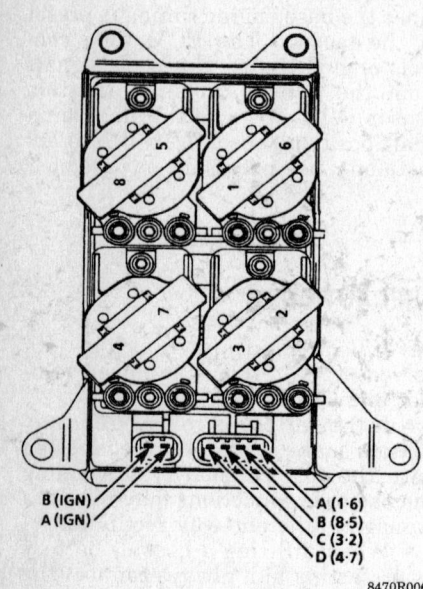

B (IGN)
A (IGN)
A (1·6)
B (8·5)
C (3·2)
D (4·7)

8470R006

Ignition housing and coil packs — 5.7L (VIN J) engine

Belt inspection may reveal cracks in the belt ribs. These cracks will not impair belt performance. A belt should be replaced if belt slip occurs or if sections of the belt ribs are missing.

The belt tensioner can be pulled up to free the belt with the use of a ½ inch drive ratchet or breaker bar. Always disconnect the negative battery cable before servicing any of the belt driven accessories or components adjacent to the belt.

REMOVAL AND INSTALLATION

5.7L (VIN P) Engine

1. Disconnect the negative battery cable.
2. If necessary, remove the air intake duct.
3. Disconnect the regulator connector and the battery lead from the back of the alternator.
4. Use a ½ breaker bar to rotate the tensioner clockwise (loosening belt tension) and remove the serpentine drive belt.
5. Remove the rear alternator mounting bolt, nut and bracket.
6. Remove the alternator mounting bolts. Remove the upper or lower brackets, as necessary and remove the alternator from the vehicle.

To install:

7. Position the alternator in the vehicle and install the lower mounting bolt and bracket. Be sure the bolt is finger-tight only at this time.
8. Install the alternator upper mounting bolt and bracket, but do not tighten at this time.
9. Install the rear alternator bracket, bolt and/or nut.
10. Tighten the lower and upper mounting bolts to 37 ft. lbs. (50 Nm), the rear bracket bolt to 17 ft. lbs. (23 Nm) and, if applicable, the rear bracket nut to 24 ft. lbs. (33 Nm).
11. Install the serpentine drive belt.
12. Install the regulator harness connector and the battery lead to the back of the alternator. Be careful not to overtighten the battery lead nut.
13. Install the air intake duct, if removed, and connect the negative battery cable.

5.7L (VIN J) ENGINE

1. Disconnect the negative battery cable.
2. Remove the air intake duct and the throttle body extension.
3. Remove the serpentine drive belt.
4. Remove the alternator lower mounting bolt, noting the length for installation purposes.
5. Remove the lower support bracket bolts, noting the lengths for installation purposes.
6. Remove the upper support bolts (noting the length) and remove the shield.
7. For 1993–96 vehicles, remove the rear support brace.
8. Unplug the oil sender electrical connector, then remove the sender.
9. Disconnect the alternator electrical connections and remove the alternator from the vehicle.

To install:

10. Position the alternator in the vehicle and engage the electrical connections.
11. Install the oil sender and electrical connection.
12. Apply Loctite® 565 or equivalent threadlock to all generator mounting bolt threads.
13. For 1993–96 vehicles, install the rear support brace and tighten the retaining bolt to 70 inch lbs. (23 Nm).
14. Install the upper support shield and bolts, then the lower support bracket, spacer, support bolts and mounting bolts. Tighten the upper shield and lower mounting bolts to 38 ft. lbs. (52 Nm) and the lower support bracket bolts to 19 ft. lbs. (26 Nm).
15. Install the serpentine drive belt, then install the throttle body extension and tighten the bolts to 53 inch lbs. (6 Nm).
16. Install the air intake duct, then connect the negative battery cable.

Starter

REMOVAL AND INSTALLATION

5.7L (VIN P) Engine

1. Disconnect the negative battery cable.
2. Raise and support the vehicle safely.
3. Disconnect the wiring from the starter solenoid. Tag the wiring positions to avoid improper connections during installation.
4. Loosen the 2 starter mounting bolts, support the starter and remove the bolts. Lower the starter from the vehicle and if equipped, remove the shims, noting their locations for installation purposes.

To install:

5. Position the shims and starter into the vehicle and insert the mounting bolts. Tighten the bolts to 34 ft. lbs. (47 Nm) and replace sealer to the front of the motor. The sealer must be applied after the motor is installed.
6. Check that flywheel-to-pinion clearance is 0.020 inch (0.5mm) and add or subtract shims, if necessary.
7. Connect the start wiring.
8. Lower vehicle and connect the battery negative cable.

5.7L (VIN J) Engine

1. Disconnect battery negative cable.
2. Remove the intake plenum assembly.
3. Remove the coil pack assembly.
4. Raise and support the vehicle safely.
5. Disconnect the wiring from the starter solenoid. Tag the wiring positions to avoid improper connections during installation.
6. Remove the 2 starter mounting bolts, then remove the starter from the vehicle.

To install:

7. Coat the threads of the starter mounting bolts with Loctite® 262 or equivalent threadlock.
8. Position the starter in the vehicle and install the mounting bolts. Tighten the starter mounting bolts to 38 ft. lbs. (52 Nm).
9. Connect the starter wiring and lower the vehicle.
10. Install the coil pack assembly.

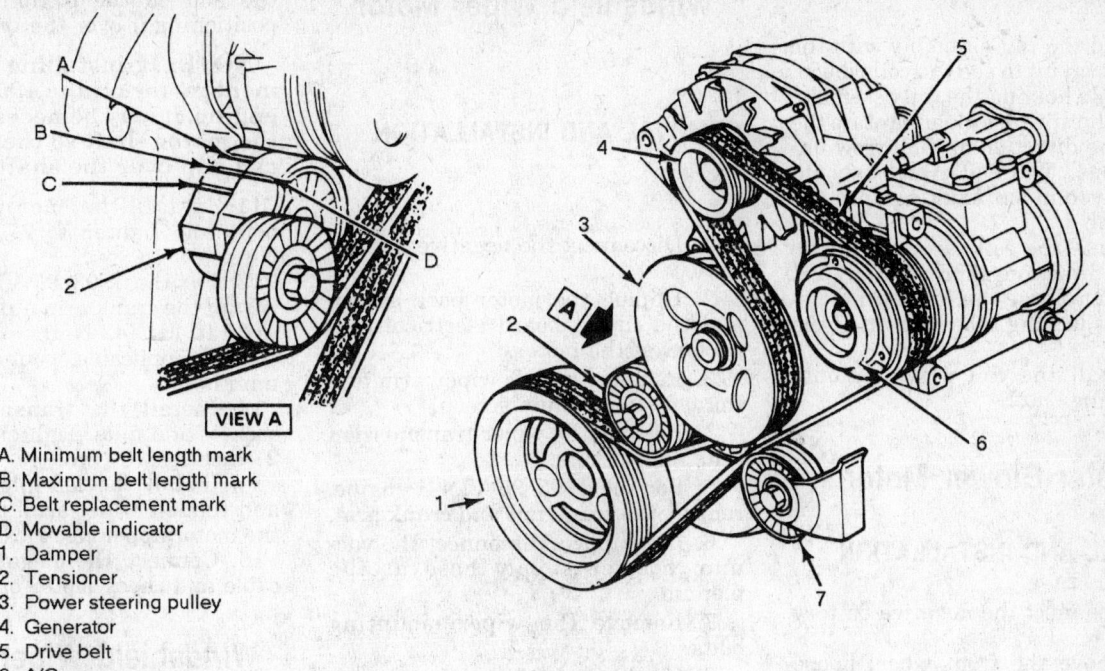

A. Minimum belt length mark
B. Maximum belt length mark
C. Belt replacement mark
D. Movable indicator
1. Damper
2. Tensioner
3. Power steering pulley
4. Generator
5. Drive belt
6. A/C compressor
7. Idler pulley

8470R008

Serpentine drive belt and tensioner — 5.7L (VIN P) engine

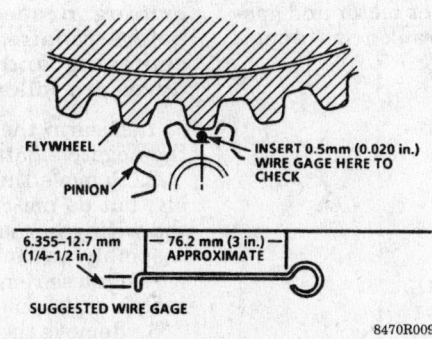

8470R009

Check flywheel to starter pinion clearance using a wire gauge — 5.7L (VIN P) engine

11. Install the intake plenum assembly.
12. Connect the negative battery cable.

CHASSIS ELECTRICAL

Air Bag

DISARMING

1. Turn the steering wheel to align the wheels in the straight-ahead position.
2. Turn the ignition switch to the **LOCK** position.

3. Remove the AIR BAG fuse from the fuse block.
4. Remove the left side lower trim panel, then unplug the Connector Position Assurance (CPA) device and the yellow 2-way SIR harness wire connector at the base of the steering column.

To enable system:
5. Turn the ignition switch to the **LOCK** position.
6. Engage the yellow 2-way connector and the CPA device at the base of the steering column.
7. Install the left side lower trim panel, then install the SIR fuse to the fuse block.
8. Turn the ignition switch to the **RUN** position.
9. Verify the SIR indicator light flashes 7–9 times and then turns OFF. If not, inspect system for malfunction.

SUPPLEMENTAL INFLATABLE RESTRAINT (SIR) COIL

NOTE: After performing repairs on the internals of the steering column, the coil assembly must be centered in order to avoid coil damage or accidental air bag deployment.

Adjustment

1. Hold the coil assembly with the clear bottom up to see the coil ribbon.

2. While holding the coil assembly, depress the spring lock and rotate the hub in the direction of the arrow until it stops. The coil ribbon should now be wound up snug against the center hub.

3. Rotate the coil assembly in the opposite direction approximately 2½ turns and release the lock spring between the locking tabs in front of the arrow.

4. Install the coil assembly onto the steering shaft.

Heater Blower Motor

REMOVAL AND INSTALLATION

1. Disconnect the negative battery cable.

2. Remove the front wheel house rear panel and seal.

3. Disconnect the motor electrical connectors.

4. Remove the blower motor cooling tube.

5. Remove the motor and fan.

6. Installation is the reverse of the removal procedure.

Windshield Wiper Motor

REMOVAL AND INSTALLATION

1. Disconnect the negative battery cable.

2. Unplug the motor park switch and the circuit board electrical connectors at the motor.

3. Remove the left wiper arm and the left side plenum screen.

4. Remove the wiper transmission nuts and sockets.

5. For the 1993–96 VIN J engine, remove the crank nut and crank arm.

6. If equipped, disconnect the vacuum booster supply hose at the plenum.

7. Remove the wiper mounting bolts.

8. Unplug any remaining motor electrical connectors while removing wiper motor assembly.

To install:

9. Connect the wiper motor electrical connector.

10. Install the wiper motor and gasket by guiding the crank arm through

the hole in the plenum panel and positioning it over the transmission.

NOTE: If installing a replacement motor on the 1993–96 VIN J engine, it may be necessary to file the motor shaft so the crank arm can slip over the shaft.

11. Install the motor mounting bolts and tighten to 27 inch lbs. (3 Nm).

12. For the 1993–96 VIN J engine, Install the crank arm nut and tighten to 30 ft. lbs. (42 Nm).

13. If applicable, connect the vacuum hose.

14. Install the transmission link sockets and nuts. Tighten the nuts to 27 inch lbs. (3 Nm).

15. Install the left plenum screen and the left wiper arm, then connect the motor upper electrical connectors.

16. Connect the negative battery cable and check motor operation.

Windshield Wiper Switch

REMOVAL AND INSTALLATION

NOTE: This vehicle is equipped with a SIR air bag system, it is imperative that the disarming procedure is followed before repairs, and that the coil centering and rearming procedures are followed after repairs.

1. Disarm the SIR and disconnect the negative battery cable.

2. Remove the turn signal assembly, but do not disconnect or remove the wiring harness. Allow the switch assembly to hang freely from the wires unless removal is necessary for switch replacement.

3. Remove the ignition lock assembly, but do not disconnect or remove the wiring harness. Allow the lock set to hang freely from the wires, unless removal is necessary for lock cylinder replacement.

4. If not done already, remove the housing cover end cap, disconnect the electrical connectors from the multi-function lever and remove the lever by pulling toward the driver's door.

5. Remove the housing cover screws, unthread and remove the tilt lever from the column assembly.

6. Remove the lock housing cover assembly.

7. Remove the base plate and the dimmer switch rod actuator and the wiper switch actuator pivot pin.

8. For 1993–96 vehicles, remove the wire protector shield.

9. Disconnect wiper switch connector from vehicle wire harness and

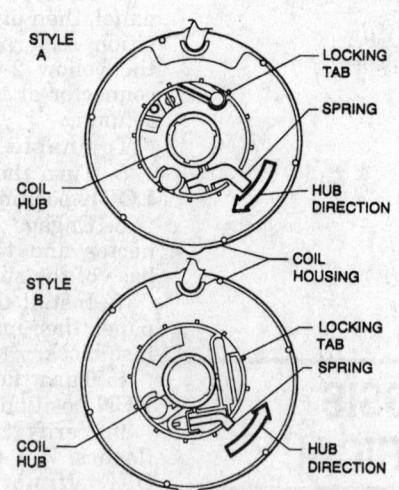

STYLE A

LOCKING TAB

SPRING

COIL HUB

HUB DIRECTION

COIL HOUSING

STYLE B

LOCKING TAB

SPRING

COIL HUB

HUB DIRECTION

PERFORM THE FOLLOWING STEPS TO CENTER COIL ASSEMBLY:
A. REMOVE COIL ASSEMBLY.
B. HOLD COIL ASSEMBLY WITH CLEAR BOTTOM UP TO SEE COIL RIBBON.
C. NOTE: THERE ARE TWO DIFFERENT STYLES OF COILS. ONE ROTATES CLOCKWISE AND THE OTHER ROTATES COUNTER-CLOCKWISE.
D. WHILE HOLDING COIL ASSEMBLY, DEPRESS SPRING LOCK TO ROTATE HUB IN DIRECTION OF ARROW UNTIL IT STOPS.
E. THE COIL RIBBON SHOULD BE WOUND UP SNUG AGAINST CENTER HUB.
F. ROTATE COIL HUB IN OPPOSITE DIRECTION APPROXIMATELY TWO AND A HALF (2-1/2) TURNS. RELEASE SPRING LOCK BETWEEN LOCKING TABS IN FRONT OF ARROW.

8470R010

Centering the SIR coil assembly

remove switch. Attach a piece of mechanic's wire to the connector to aid in reinstallation and gently pull the wire harness through the column. Leave the mechanic's wire routed through the column to pull the new switch wiring into position.

To install:

10. Connect the wiper switch to the lock housing cover assembly.

11. Attach the switch actuator pivot pin to the switch and cover.

12. Pull wiper switch wire connector through the steering column using the mechanic's wire and attach to the vehicle wire harness. If applicable, install the wire protector shield.

13. Attach the dimmer switch rod actuator to the base plate and lubricate with lithium grease.

14. Connect base plate to lock housing cover assembly. The bottom edge of the dimmer switch rod actuator must rest on the bend in the dimmer switch rod.

15. Position lock housing cover in place and attach tilt lever.

16. Starting with the housing cover screw in the 12 o'clock position, then 8 o'clock and finally 3 o'clock positions, tighten the screws to 80 inch lbs. (9 Nm).

17. Install the multi-function lever and engage the lever connectors on the base plate.

18. Install the housing cover end cap.

19. Install the lock cylinder assembly.

20. Install the turn signal assembly.

21. Connect the negative battery cable and enable the SIR system.

Instrument Cluster

PRELIMINARY PROCEDURES

Many electrical components are sensitive to static electricity discharge; in order to avoid damaging any components certain precautions should be taken:

1. To discharge personal static electricity, touch a ground point on the vehicle.

2. Personal static discharge should be performed any time you walk across the shop, slide across the seat or sit down and get up.

3. Do not touch any electric terminals on components or connectors with your fingers or any tool.

4. Always touch the component packaging to a ground before removing the component.

5. Components which may be damaged by electrostatic discharge are:

 a. The anti-lock brake system controller.

 b. The chime module.

 c. The cruise control module.

 d. The distributorless ignition system module.

 e. The electronic digital instrument clusters.

 f. The electronic control module and attributing parts.

 g. The low tire pressure warning system module.

 h. The radio assembly.

 i. The theft deterrent modules.

 j. The electronic automatic air conditioning assembly.

REMOVAL AND INSTALLATION

1. Remove the knee bolster and the lower trim panel.

2. Disable the SIR system and disconnect the negative battery cable.

3. Remove the steering column support bolts and carefully lower the steering column.

4. Remove the cluster bezel screws and the bezel.

5. If necessary for lens replacement, remove the lens screws and separate the lens from the cluster.

6. Remove the cluster mounting bolts/screws, unplug the electrical connectors and remove the cluster.

To install:

7. If removed, install the lens to the cluster.

8. Position the cluster and engage the electrical connectors.

9. Secure the cluster using the retainers and tighten to 16 inch lbs. (1.8 Nm).

10. Install the bezel and tighten the screws to 29 inch lbs. (3.3 Nm).

11. Raise the steering column and tighten the supporting bolts to 20 ft. lbs. (27 Nm).

12. Connect the negative battery cable and enable the SIR system.

13. Install the knee bolster and the lower trim panel.

Concealed Headlights

MANUAL OPERATION

The headlight doors can be opened automatically by turning the headlights switch to the ON position, then turn the switch back 1 click to the parking lights ON position and the headlight doors will stay open.

If necessary, then headlight doors may be opened manually. To open the headlight doors manually, raise the hood and turn the headlight manual control knob (located next to the headlight door) in the direction of the arrow, until the door is fully opened.

Headlight Switch

REMOVAL AND INSTALLATION

1. Disable the SIR system and disconnect the negative battery cable.

2. Remove the instrument cluster trim plate screws and reposition the trim plate to gain access to the right side of the headlight switch.

3. Remove headlight switch attaching screws and trim plate, then unplug the electrical connectors.

4. Remove the headlight switch.

5. Installation is the reverse of the removal procedure.

6. Connect the negative battery cable and properly enable the SIR system.

Dimmer Switch

REMOVAL AND INSTALLATION

1. Properly disable the SIR system and disconnect the negative battery cable.

2. Remove the instrument panel lower trim plate.

3. Remove the steering column mounting bolts, lower and properly support the column. If access to the switch is not sufficient, remove the column from the vehicle.

4. Remove the hex nut and washer head screw securing the switch to the column.

5. If equipped, remove the horn ground strap attached to the dimmer/ignition switch mounting stud.

6. If equipped, remove the cable bracket.

7. Disengage the switch assembly from the actuator rod, unplug the wiring harness connector and remove the switch assembly.

To install:

8. Position the dimmer switch and, if equipped, the cable bracket, onto the steering column. Install the nut and screw finger-tight.

9. Engage the horn ground strap and the switch wire connector.

10. Insert a $3/32$ inch drill bit in the switch hole to limit travel.

11. Push against dimmer switch to remove all free-play.

12. Tighten the switch nut and screw to 35 inch lbs. (4.0 Nm).

13. Remove the drill bit.

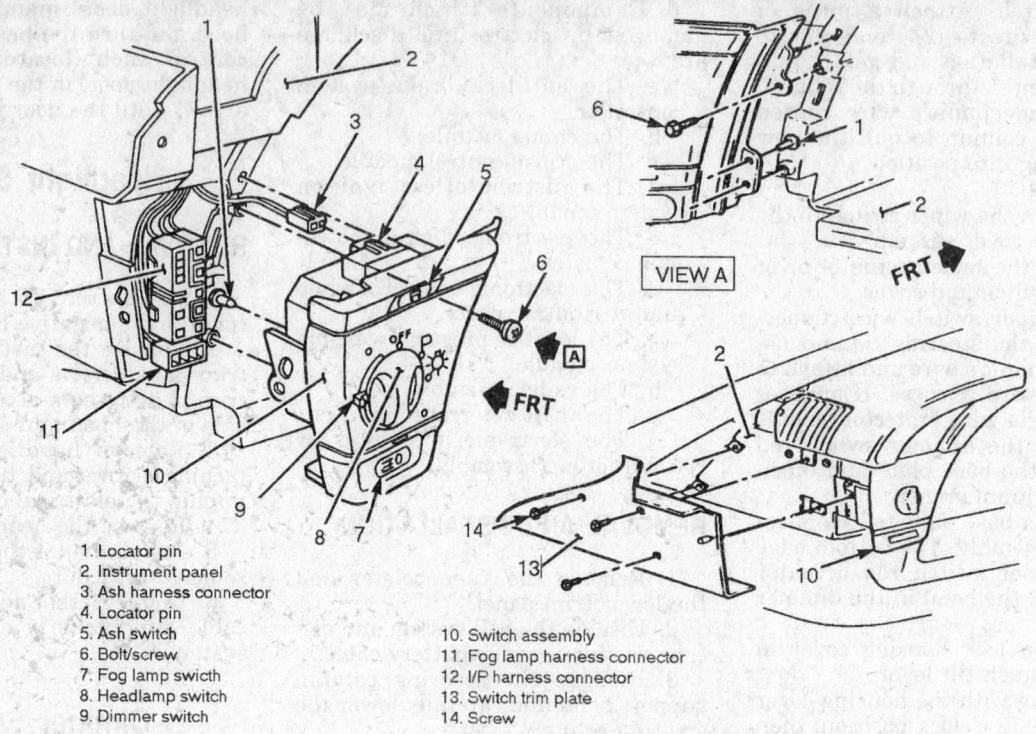

1. Locator pin
2. Instrument panel
3. Ash harness connector
4. Locator pin
5. Ash switch
6. Bolt/screw
7. Fog lamp swisch
8. Headlamp switch
9. Dimmer switch

10. Switch assembly
11. Fog lamp harness connector
12. I/P harness connector
13. Switch trim plate
14. Screw

8470R012

Headlight switch mounting

14. Install or raise the steering column into position and install the mounting bolts.

15. Install the instrument panel lower trim plate.

16. Connect the negative battery cable and enable the SIR system.

Turn Signal Switch

REMOVAL AND INSTALLATION

NOTE: This vehicle is equipped with a SIR air bag system, it is imperative that the disarming procedure is followed before repairs, and that the coil centering and rearming procedures are followed after repairs. Although it may be possible to perform this procedure with the steering column installed in the vehicle, but lowered for access, the manufacturer suggests that the column be removed.

1. Properly disable the SIR system. Place the ignition switch to the **LOCK** position in order to prevent uncentering of the coil assembly.

2. Disconnect the negative battery cable.

3. Properly remove and store the inflator module and the steering wheel. Either remove the column from the vehicle or lower it for access.

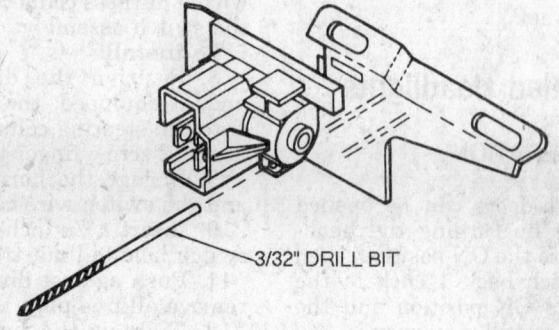

3/32" DRILL BIT

8470R013

Dimmer switch adjustment

4. Remove the coil assembly retaining ring. Remove the coil assembly and allow it to hang freely from the wiring.

NOTE: The coil assembly will become uncentered if the steering column is separated from the steering gear and allowed to rotate or the center spring of the coil assembly is pushed down, letting the hub rotate while the coil is removed from the steering column. In the event this should occur, follow the recommended procedure for recentering of the coil in order to avoid accidental deployment of the air bag or damage to the internal components of the steering column.

5. Remove the wave washer.

6. Remove the shaft lock retaining ring using tool J-23653-C or equivalent, shaft lock compressor. Discard the old ring.

7. Remove the shaft lock, turn signal canceling cam and upper bearing assembly.

8. Move the multi-function lever to the **RIGHT TURN** position. Remove the column housing cover end cap by pulling toward the vehicle front. Disconnect the electrical harness connector and remove the turn signal lever by pulling toward the driver door.

9. Remove the hazard knob retaining screw and assembly.

10. Remove the turn signal switch arm and screws.

11. Remove the turn signal switch screws.

12. Disconnect the switch harness connector from the bulkhead connector and remove the wiring protector.

13. Remove the horn pad ground wiring assembly from slot "D" of the switch connector.

14. Attach a length of mechanic's wire to the switch harness to aid in reinstallation and gently pull the assembly up through the housing. Leave the wire routed through the column in order to pull the new harness back into position.

15. Remove the switch and harness from the vehicle.

To install:

16. Connect the horn pad ground wiring assembly to slot "D" of the turn signal switch connector.

17. Using the mechanic's wire, pull the switch harness through the column and connect to the bulkhead connector.

18. Install the harness wiring protector.

19. Position the turn signal switch assembly and install the attaching screws. Tighten the screws to 30 inch lbs. (3.4 Nm).

20. Install the switch arm and mounting screws. Tighten the screws to 20 inch lbs. (2.3 Nm).

21. Install the hazard knob assembly and the multi-function lever.

22. Install the inner race, the upper bearing race seat, and the upper bearing spring.

23. Lubricate the friction surfaces using synthetic grease, then install the turn signal canceling cam.

24. Position the shaft lock. Install the a new shaft lock retaining ring using tool J–23653–C or equivalent. Be sure the ring is firmly seated in the groove of the shaft.

25. Install the wave washer.

26. Install the coil assembly, making sure it is properly centered.

27. Position and secure the steering column, as necessary.

28. Install the steering wheel and the inflator module.

29. Connect the negative battery cable and enable the SIR system.

Ignition Switch

REMOVAL AND INSTALLATION

1. Disable the SIR system and disconnect the negative battery terminal.

2. Remove the column to instrument panel trim plates and attaching nuts.

3. Loosen the steering column mounting bolts.

4. Remove the steering column mounting bolts, lower and properly support the column. If access to the switch is not sufficient, remove the column from the vehicle.

NOTE: Be sure the steering column is supported at all times in order to prevent damage to the column.

5. Remove the hex nut and washer head screw securing the dimmer switch to the column.

6. If equipped, remove the horn ground strap attached to the dimmer/ignition switch mounting stud.

7. If equipped, remove the cable bracket.

8. Disengage the switch assembly from the actuator rod, unplug the wiring harness connector and remove the dimmer switch assembly.

9. Remove the dimmer and ignition switch mounting stud.

10. Remove the ignition switch from the actuating assembly and disengage the switch wire connector.

To install:

11. Verify that the key cylinder is in the **LOCK** position.

12. Move the actuator rod hole in the switch to the **LOCK** position. New switches will be pinned in this position and the pin must be removed after installation or switch damage may result.

13. Install the switch with the rod in the hole and adjust as necessary. To verify the switch is in the lock position, move the switch slider to the extreme right position and then move the slider 1 detent to the left.

14. Install the switch mounting stud and tighten to 35 inch lbs. (4.0 Nm).

15. Install the dimmer switch assembly to the actuator rod.

16. If equipped, install the cable bracket and the horn pad ground wire.

17. Install and finger-tighten the washer head screw and the hex nut.

18. Adjust the dimmer switch and tighten the screw and nut to 35 inch lbs. (4.0 Nm).

19. Position the steering column, then engage the ignition and dimmer switch connectors. Secure the column in the vehicle

20. Connect the negative battery cable and enable the SIR system.

Ignition Lock

REMOVAL AND INSTALLATION

NOTE: This vehicle is equipped with a SIR air bag system, it is imperative that the disarming procedure is followed before repairs, and that the coil centering and rearming procedures are followed after repairs.

1. Disable the SIR system and disconnect the negative battery cable.

2. Remove turn signal switch assembly, but do not disconnect or pull the wire harness through the column. Allow the switch assembly to hang freely from the wires.

3. If necessary, remove the coil assembly as follows:

   a. Disengage the coil terminal connector from the vehicle harness. Remove the yellow connector shroud from the black connector.

   b. Remove wiring protector.

   c. Attach a length of mechanic's wire to the terminal connector to aid in reassembly.

   d. Carefully pull the wire harness through the column, leaving the mechanic's wire in the column for installation purposes.

4. Remove the key from the lock cylinder.

5. Remove the buzzer switch and clip.

6. Reinsert the key into the lock cylinder, making sure the key is in the **LOCK** position.

7. Remove the lock retaining screw.

8. Disengage the Pass Key wire harness connector from the bulkhead connector. If not done already, remove the wiring protector.

9. Attach a piece of string or mechanic's wire to the wire connector to aid in reassembly, disconnect the retaining clip from the housing cover and pull the wire up through the column. Leave the length of string or wire in the column in order to pull the new harness into position.

10. Remove the lock cylinder.

To install:

11. Using the length of string or the mechanic's wire, pull the PASS Key wire harness down through the column into the original position and engage the connector.

1. Hex locking nut
2. Retaining ring
3. Infl restraint coil assembly
4. Wave washer
5. Retaining ring
6. Shaft lock
7. Turn signal cancel cam assembly
8. Upper bearing spring
9. Bndg hd cr recess screw
10. RD wash hd screw
11. Signal switch arm assembly
12. Turn signal switch assembly
13. Upper bearing inner race seat
14. Inner race
15. Pan head soc tap screw
16. Buzzer switch assembly
18. Lock retaining screw
19. Lock housing cover assembly
20. Steering column pass key
    lock cylinder set
21. Dimmer switch rod actuator
22. Switch actuator pivot pin
23. Pivot & pulse switch assembly
24. Col housing cover end base plate
25. Col housing cover end cap
26. Wiring protector
27. Connector shroud
28. Flat head tapping screw
30. Steering column
    housing assembly
31. Bearing assembly
32. Lock bolt
33. Lock bolt spring
34. Steering wheel lock shoe
35. Steering wheel lock shoe
36. Wire protector shield
37. Drive shaft
38. Dowel pin
39. Pivot pin
40. Shoe spring
41. Release lever spring
42. Release lever pin
43. Shoe release lever
44. Switch actuator rack
45. Rack preload spring
46. Steering column housing
47. Switch actuator sector
48. Hex washer head screw
50. Spring guide
51. Wheel tilt spring
52. Spring retainer
55. Steering column shaft assembly
56. Race & upper shaft assembly
57. Centering sphere
58. Joint preload spring
59. Lower steering shaft assembly
61. Support screw

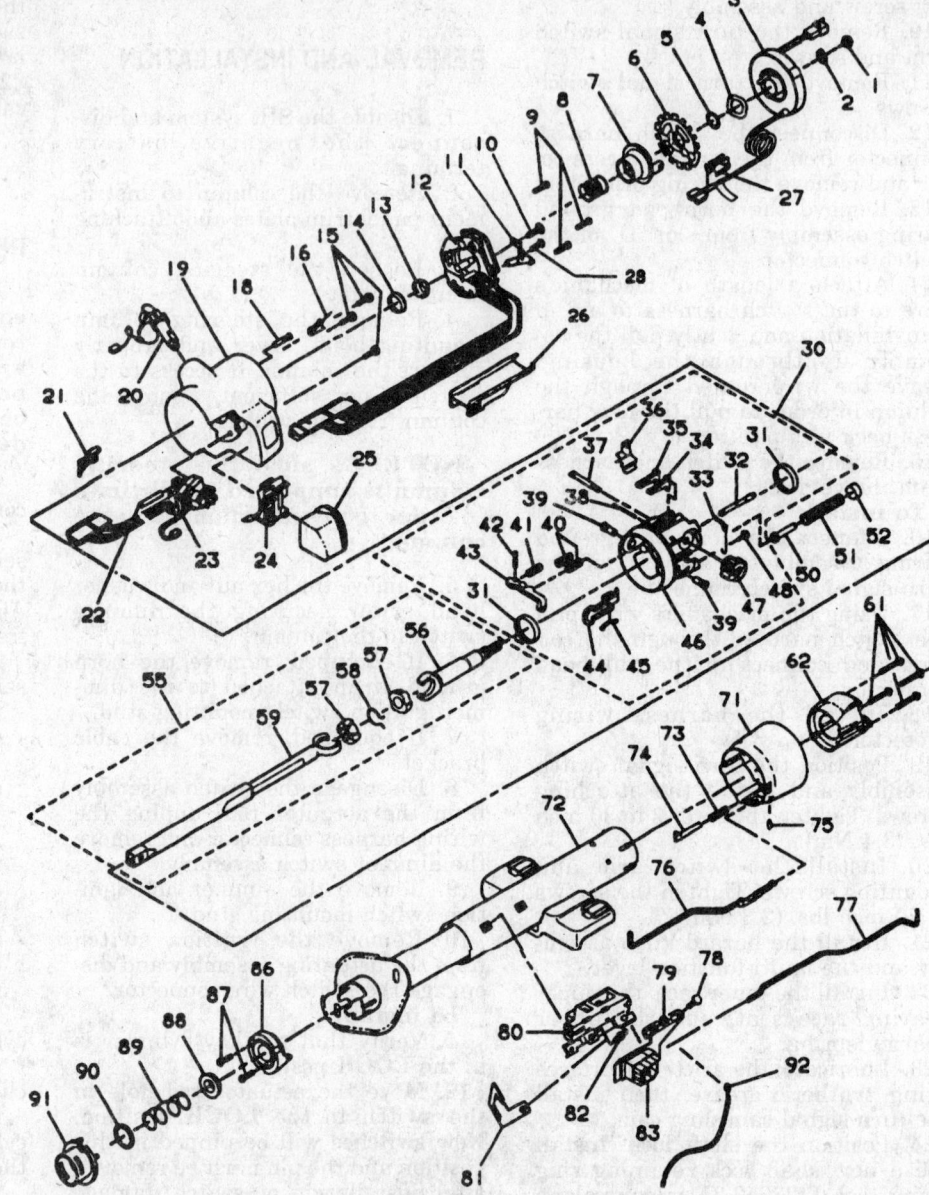

62. Steering column housing support
71. Steering column housing shroud
72. Steering column jacket assembly
73. Cable backdrive pin spring
74. Cable backdrive pin
75. Inhibitor cross pin
76. Ignition switch actuator assembly
77. Dimmer switch rod
78. Washer head screw
79. Hexagon nut
80. Ignition switch assembly

81. Cable bracket
82. Dimmer & ignition switch
    mounting stud
83. Dimmer switch assembly
86. Adapter & bearing assembly
87. Hex washer head tap screw
88. Lower bearing spring
89. Lower bearing
90. Lower spring retainer
91. Retainer
92. Horn pad wire assembly

8470R014

Exploded view of the steering column assembly

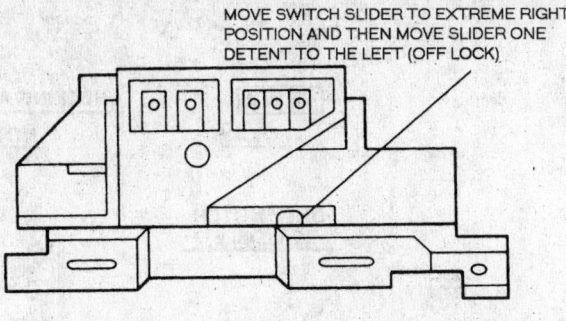

MOVE SWITCH SLIDER TO EXTREME RIGHT
POSITION AND THEN MOVE SLIDER ONE
DETENT TO THE LEFT (OFF LOCK)

8470R015

Adjusting the ignition switch assembly

12. Install the lock cylinder set. Snap the wire retaining clip into the hole in the housing.

13. Engage the lock cylinder wiring connector to the bulkhead connector.

14. Install the lock cylinder retaining screw and tighten to 22 inch lbs. (2.5 Nm).

15. Remove the key and install the buzzer switch with retaining clip, then insert the key and leave in the **LOCK** position.

16. If removed, pull the turn signal switch wiring connector and/or the coil wiring connector through the steering column, connect the harnesses and install the wiring protector.

17. Install the turn signal switch assembly.

18. Connect the negative battery cable and enable the SIR system.

Brake Light Switch

On some vehicles, the brake light switch will also perform the function of the cruise control switch. Multiple electrical connectors are found on these applications.

ADJUSTMENT

While depressing the brake pedal, insert the switch into the retainer until seated. Pull the brake pedal rearward against the pedal stop with a force of approximately 42 lbs. (187 N) until the clicking sounds are no longer heard. The switch will move in the retainer providing proper adjustment. Release the brake pedal and repeat, to ensure that no clicking sounds are heard. Check for proper brake light operation.

REMOVAL AND INSTALLATION

1. Disconnect the battery negative cable.

2. Remove the lower trim panel.

3. Disengage the electrical connector from the switch.

4. If applicable, disconnect the vacuum line from the switch.

5. Remove the retainer and the switch from the vehicle.

6. Installation is the reverse of the reverse of the removal procedure.

7. Adjust the brake light switch and check for proper operation.

Clutch Switch

REMOVAL AND INSTALLATION

1. Disconnect the negative battery cable.

2. Remove the sound insulator panel from under the dash.

3. Remove the clip retainer from the actuating rod at the clutch pedal.

4. Remove the bolt, switch and rod from the clutch bracket.

5. Disengage the wire connector from the switch, then remove the switch assembly.

To install:

6. Install the electrical wiring harness to the switch connector.

7. Position the switch, aligning the actuating rod with the hole in the clutch pedal, then install the bolt.

8. Insert the rod into the bracket and secure with the retainer.

9. Install the sound insulator panel under the dash.

10. Connect the negative battery cable and check for proper switch operation.

Neutral Safety Switch

ADJUSTMENT

Switch adjustment is performed with the center console removed for switch access.

1. Place the transmission shifter in the **N** notch in the detent plate.

2. Loosen the switch attaching nuts.

3. Insert a 0.094 in. (2.34mm) drill bit or gauge pin into the adjustment hole, then rotate the switch until the gauge pin drops to a depth of 0.59 in. (15mm).

NOTE: If the proper sized gauge pin is unavailable, a 3/32 in. drill bit may be used.

4. Tighten the switch nuts to 26 inch lbs. (3 Nm).

5. Remove the gauge pin and verify that the engine will only start in **P** or **N**.

REMOVAL AND INSTALLATION

1. Disconnect negative battery cable.

2. Remove the shifter knob assembly.

3. Remove the console assembly.

4. Remove the neutral switch mounting nuts.

5. Remove the switch and the gauge pin.

To install:

6. Position shifter lever in the **N** position.

7. Insert carrier tang on the switch in the slot on the shifter.

8. If installing a new switch, install the mounting nuts and tighten the mounting nuts to 26 inch lbs. (3 Nm). Move the shift control lever out of the **N** position to shear the factory installed plastic retaining pin.

NOTE: If installing a new switch and the holes do not align with shifter control, check that the shifter control lever is in N. Do not rotate the switch as this will shear the retaining pin. If a new switch was rotated and the pin was already broken, switch adjustment must be performed.

9. If installing an old switch or a new switch with a sheared retaining pin, perform switch adjustment.

10. Connect the negative battery cable and check that engine starts only in the **P** or **N** positions. If engine starts in any other position, readjust neutral switch.

11. Install console and shifter knob assembly.

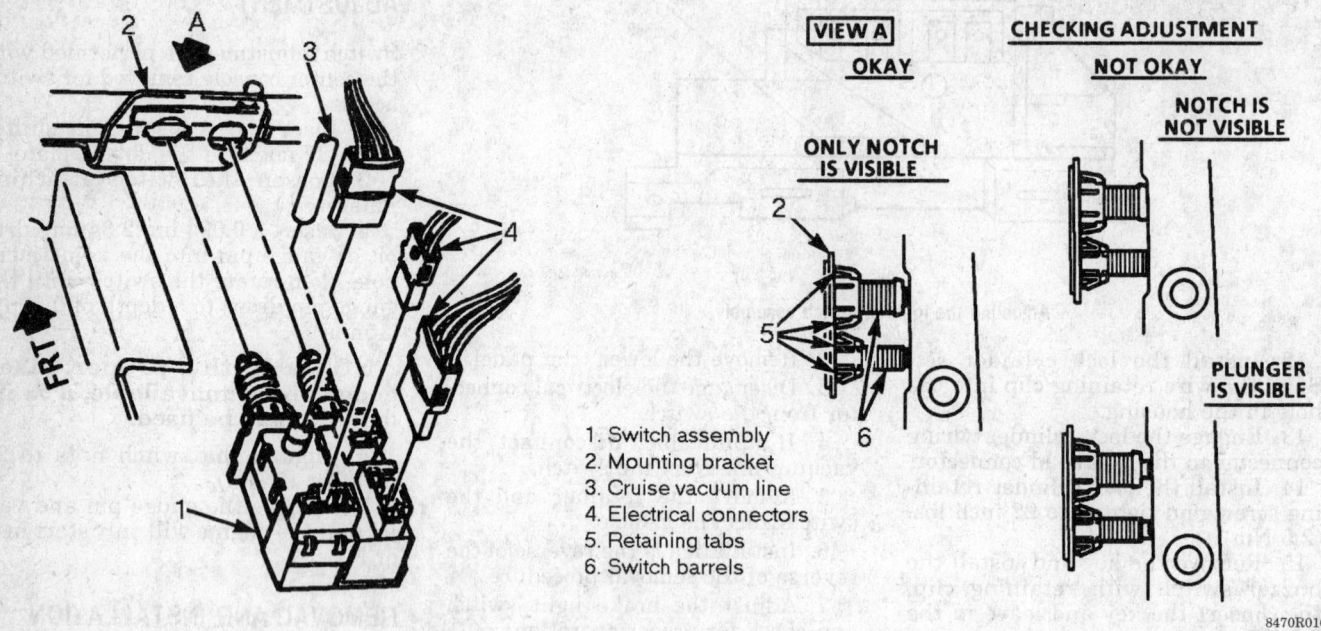

1. Switch assembly
2. Mounting bracket
3. Cruise vacuum line
4. Electrical connectors
5. Retaining tabs
6. Switch barrels

8470R016

Adjusting the brake light/cruise control switch — 1993–96 vehicles

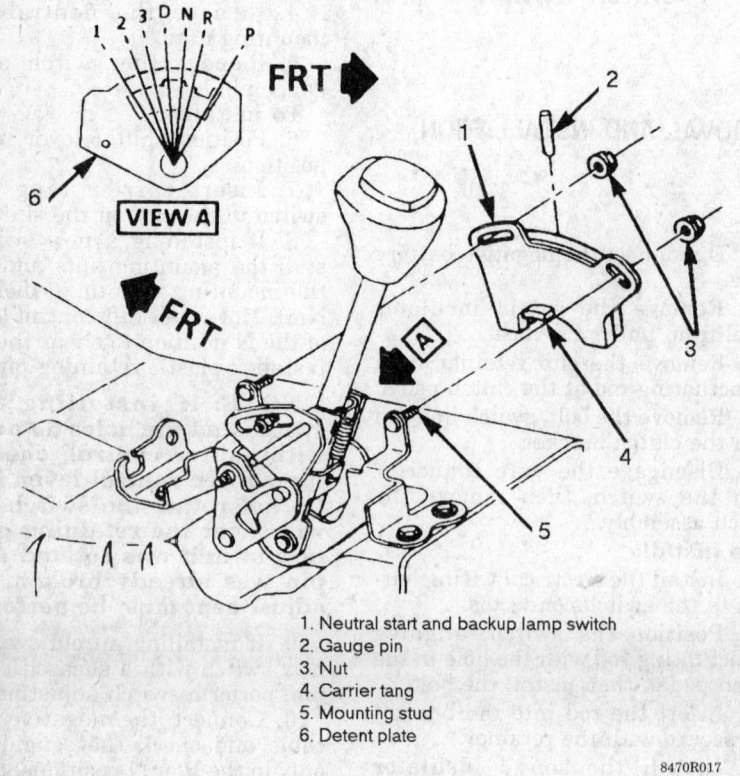

1. Neutral start and backup lamp switch
2. Gauge pin
3. Nut
4. Carrier tang
5. Mounting stud
6. Detent plate

8470R017

Adjusting the neutral safety/backup light switch

Fuses, Circuit Breakers and Relays

LOCATION

Fusible Links

Fusible links are located in various positions, including at the jump start junction block. Fusible links, which are normally not fused, are used to prevent wire harness damage in the event of a short circuit or an overload condition. Each fusible link is a fixed valve for a specific electrical load. Should a link fail, the cause of the failure must be determined and repaired prior to installing a new fusible link of the same value.

Circuit Breakers

There are 3 styles of circuit breakers used. A standard heat activated circuit breaker is used which will cycle open and closed until the overload condition is corrected. A mechanical type breaker and a solid state design called a Positive Temperature Coefficient (PTC) circuit breaker, both will not reset until the current source is removed for a few seconds. Various circuit breakers are located throughout the vehicle and the fuse block.

Fuse Block

The main fuse block assembly is located behind the far right side of the instrument panel. The 2 auxiliary fuse blocks are found below the right of the instrument panel, next to the radio receiver box.

Relays

ABS ACTIVE Indicator Relay — located under the left side of the cargo compartment.

ABS Pump Motor Relay — located under the corner of the rear floor on the ABS modulator assembly, in the storage compartment.

ABS Valve Solenoid Relay — located under the corner of the rear floor on the ABS modulator assembly, in the storage compartment.

Air Conditioning Clutch Relay — located in the left side of the engine compartment, in front of the battery.

Air Pump Relay — located in the left hand front of the engine compartment, on top of the air pump.

Amplifier Relay — located behind the left side of the instrument panel, to the right of the instrument cluster.

Blower Relays (High and Low) — located in the left side of the engine compartment, on the wheelhouse.

Cruise Control Cut-Off Relay — located below the instrument panel, left of the steering column.

Deck Lid Release Relay — located on the right front of the cargo compartment.

Delayed Accessory Bus (DAB) Relay — located below the left side of the instrument panel.

Dome Lamp Relay — located on the multi-use relay bracket to the bottom right side of the instrument panel.

Engine Cooling Fan Relays (Primary and Secondary) — located in the front of the engine compartment on the left side of the radiator shroud.

Fuel Pump Relays — located below the right side of the instrument panel, left of the glove compartment on the multi-use relay bracket. The 5.7L (VIN J) engine uses a second relay located below the left side of the instrument panel.

Fog Lamp Relay — located on the multi-use relay bracket to the bottom right side of the instrument panel.

Hatch Release Relay — located in the rear of the cargo compartment, on the end panel.

Horn Relay — located on the multi-use relay bracket to the bottom right of the instrument panel.

Power Antenna Relay (Convertible and Coupe) — located on the left side of the cargo compartment above the rear of the wheel house.

Rear Defogger Relay — located on the multi-use relay bracket to the bottom right of the instrument panel.

Secondary Injector Relays (VIN J) — located rear of the left hand front wheelhouse, in front of the battery and behind the battery near the left hand door hinges.

Starter Enable Relay — located below the left side of the instrument panel, left of the steering column.

Shift-Up Relay — located in the left hand middle of the engine compartment, near the frame rail.

Computers

LOCATION

Electronic Brake Control Module (EBCM) — located under the left corner of the cargo compartment, behind the driver's seat.

Central Control Module (CCM) — located behind the middle of the instrument panel.

Diagnostic Energy Reserve Module (DERM) — located in the middle of the instrument panel, in front of and below the CCM.

Electronic Control Module (ECM) 1992 — located in the engine compartment, above the battery.

Select Ride Control Module (SRCM) — located rear of the cargo compartment, under the cargo deck.

Flashers

LOCATION

Turn Signal — located below the left side of the instrument panel, to the left of the steering column.

Hazard Flasher — Located near the radio on the right side of the instrument panel.

Cruise Control

ADJUSTMENT

Servo Linkage

1. With the cruise control cable installed into the servo bracket, pull the servo assembly end of the cable toward the servo without moving the throttle lever.

2. If 1 out of the 5 holes in the servo assembly tab aligns with the cable pin, push the pin through the hole and connect the pin to the tab with the retainer.

3. If the tab holes do not align with the pin, move the cable away from the servo assembly until the next closest tab hole aligns and connect the pin to the tab with the retainer.

ENGINE COOLING

Radiator

REMOVAL AND INSTALLATION

1992 Vehicles

5.7L (VIN P) ENGINE

1. Disconnect battery negative cable.

2. Drain the engine coolant into a suitable container.

3. Remove the air cleaner assembly.

4. Unplug the electrical connectors from the cooling fan relays.

5. Remove the bolts attaching the accumulator bracket to the radiator upper support.

6. Remove the fan shroud-to-upper support attaching bolts.

7. Remove the rubber access plug from the top of the radiator.

8. Remove the radiator air bleed hose.

9. Remove the nuts and bolts attaching the upper support to the front side member.

10. Remove the screws attaching the upper support to the lower support.

11. Remove upper support.

12. Remove the radiator upper and lower hose clamps, then the hoses.

13. Disconnect and plug the transmission oil cooler lines from the radiator, if equipped.

14. Remove the radiator from the vehicle.

To install:

15. Install the radiator.

16. Connect transmission cooler lines to the radiator, if equipped, and tighten the fittings to 20 ft. lbs. (27 Nm).

17. Install the upper and lower radiator hoses.

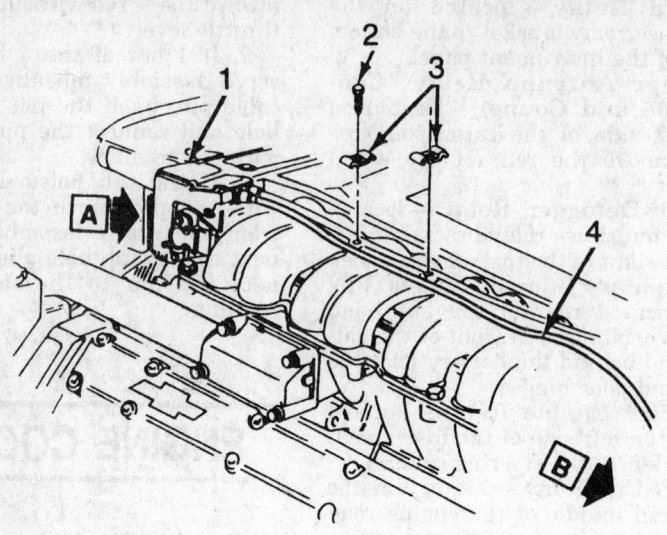

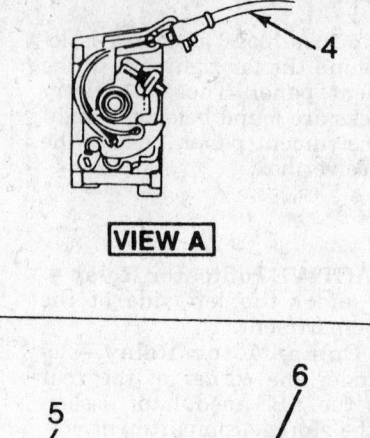

1. Throttle body linkage shield
2. Bolt
3. Cable retainer
4. Cruise control cable assembly
5. Retainer
6. Cruise control servo

Cruise control cable routing and adjustment — 5.7L (VIN J) engine

18. Install upper support. Torque the upper support to front side member nuts and bolts to 18 ft. lbs. (25 Nm).

19. Connect cooling fan electrical connectors to the cooling fan relays.

20. Install fan shroud to upper support attaching screws. Tighten the screws to 80 inch lbs. (9 Nm).

21. Install the accumulator bracket to upper support attaching bolts. Torque bolts to 80 inch lbs. (9 Nm).

22. Connect the radiator air bleed hose.

23. Install access plug and the air cleaner assembly.

24. Connect the negative battery cable.

25. Fill cooling system with the proper type and quantity of antifreeze and check for leaks.

5.7L (VIN J) ENGINE

1. Disconnect battery negative cable.

2. Drain the engine coolant into a suitable container.

3. Remove the air cleaner assembly and remove the radiator upper air deflector.

4. Disconnect the electrical connectors from the cooling fan relays.

5. Remove the bolts attaching the accumulator bracket to the radiator upper support.

6. Remove the fan shroud to upper support attaching bolts.

7. Remove the rubber access plug from the top of the radiator.

8. Remove the radiator air bleed hose.

9. Remove the nuts and bolts attaching the upper support to the front side member.

10. Remove the bolt retaining oil cooler lines to the oil cooler.

11. Remove the seal retainers and seal from the oil cooler and air conditioning lines

12. Remove the air pump assembly.

13. Remove the air pump bracket at the rear and loosen the front bolt.

14. Remove the air pump intake duct.

15. Remove the screws attaching the upper support to the lower support and Remove upper support from the vehicle.

16. Remove the radiator upper and lower hoses and clamp.

17. Remove the radiator from the vehicle.

To install:
18. Install the radiator.

19. Install the upper and lower radiator hoses.

20. Install upper support. Torque the upper support to front side member nuts and bolts to 18 ft. lbs. (25 Nm).

21. Install the air pump intake duct, retaining brackets and the air pump assembly.

22. Connect the cooling fan relay electrical connectors.

23. Install fan shroud to upper support attaching screws. Tighten the screws to 80 inch lbs. (9 Nm).

24. Install the accumulator bracket to upper support attaching bolts. Torque the bolts to 80 inch lbs. (9 Nm).

25. Install the seal retainers and seal onto the oil cooler and air conditioning line.

26. Install the bolt retaining the oil cooler lines to the oil cooler. Tighten the bolt to 89 inch lbs. (10 Nm).

27. Connect the radiator air bleed hose.

28. Install the rubber access plug on the radiator support, the upper air deflector and the air cleaner assembly.

29. Connect the negative battery cable.

30. Fill cooling system with the proper type and quantity of antifreeze and check for leaks.

1993–96 Vehicles

1. Disconnect battery negative cable.

2. Drain the engine coolant into a suitable container.

3. Remove the air cleaner and air duct assembly.

4. Remove the bleed hose from the radiator.

5. If equipped, disconnect the automatic transmission fluid cooler lines.

6. Remove the screws retaining the fan relays, then remove the relays from the vehicle.

7. Unplug the electrical connectors from the air pump and horn.

8. Remove the AIR pump.

9. Remove the bolts retaining the shroud to the upper support, then remove the bolts/screws retaining the upper support to the lower support.

10. Remove upper support from the vehicle.

11. Remove the radiator upper and lower hose clamps, then the disconnect the hoses from the radiator.

12. Remove the radiator from the vehicle.

To install:

13. Install the radiator.

14. Connect and secure the inlet/outlet hoses to the radiator.

15. Install upper support to the vehicle and secure using the screws attaching the upper support to the lower support. Tighten the screws to 80 inch lbs. (9 Nm).

16. Install the nuts and bolts retaining the support to the shroud and tighten to 18 ft. lbs. (25 Nm).

17. Install the AIR pump and tighten the bolts to 89 inch lbs. (10 Nm).

18. Engage the electrical connectors to the AIR pump and horn.

19. Install the fan relays and tighten the retaining screws to 80 inch lbs. (9 Nm).

20. If equipped, connect the transmission fluid cooler lines.

21. Connect the radiator bleed hose.

22. Install the air cleaner and duct assembly.

23. Connect the negative battery cable.

24. Fill cooling system with the proper type and quantity of antifreeze and check for leaks.

Electric Cooling Fans

REMOVAL AND INSTALLATION

5.7L (VIN P) Engines

Although this procedure is for both the primary (left) and auxiliary (right) fans, the primary fan does not need to be removed if only the auxiliary fan requires service.

1992 VEHICLES

1. Disconnect battery negative cable and remove the air intake duct assembly.

2. Disconnect the electrical connector from the primary cooling fan.

3. Remove the screws attaching the fan assembly to the fan shroud.

4. Remove the primary fan assembly from the vehicle.

5. Remove the auxiliary fan upper right mounting bolt.

6. Raise and safely support the vehicle.

7. Disconnect the auxiliary cooling fan electrical connector from the fan motor.

8. Remove remaining auxiliary cooling fan mounting bolts and remove the auxiliary cooling fan from the vehicle.

To install:

9. Install the auxiliary cooling fan assembly and tighten the retaining bolts to 89 inch lbs. (10 Nm).

10. Connect the auxiliary fan electrical connector and lower the vehicle.

11. Install the remaining bolt attaching the upper right of the fan assembly to the fan shroud.

12. Install the primary fan assembly and tighten the bolts to 89 inch lbs. (10 Nm).

13. Engage the electrical connector to the fan motor.

14. Install the air intake duct and connect the negative battery cable.

1993–96 VEHICLES

1. Disconnect battery negative cable.

2. If removing the primary (left) fan assembly, remove the radiator upper support from the vehicle:

a. Drain the engine coolant into a suitable container.

b. Remove the air cleaner and air duct assembly.

c. Remove the bleed hose from the radiator.

d. If equipped, disconnect the automatic transmission fluid cooler lines.

e. Remove the screws retaining the fan relays, then remove the relays from the vehicle.

f. Unplug the electrical connectors from the air pump and horn.

g. Remove the AIR pump.

h. Remove the bolts retaining the shroud to the upper support, then remove the bolts/screws retaining the upper support to the lower support.

i. Remove upper support from the vehicle.

j. If not done already, remove the shroud upper retaining bolts.

3. If removing the auxiliary (right) fan, remove the upper bolts retaining the assembly to the shroud.

4. Raise and support the vehicle safely.

5. Remove the bolts retaining the impact bar, then remove the impact bar from the vehicle.

6. Unplug the fan motor electrical connectors.

7. Remove the bolts retaining the auxiliary (right) fan assembly to the shroud, then remove the assembly from the vehicle. If necessary separate the fan blade and motor for replacement purposes.

8. If removing the primary (left) fan assembly, remove the fan shroud with the assembly still attached. With the shroud out of the vehicle, remove the assembly from the shroud. If necessary, separate the fan blade and motor for replacement purposes.

To install:

9. If separated, assemble the fan blade(s) and motor(s) for installation.

10. If removed, install the primary (left) fan assembly to the shroud and tighten the retaining bolts to 89 inch lbs. (10 Nm), then install the shroud to the vehicle. Tighten the shroud and lower mounting bolts to 80 inch lbs. (9 Nm).

11. Install the auxiliary (right) fan assembly to the shroud and tighten the retaining bolts to 89 inch lbs. (10 Nm).

12. Engage the electrical connectors to the fan assemblies.

13. Install the impact bar and tighten the retainers to 20 ft. lbs. (27 Nm), then lower the vehicle.

14. If only the auxiliary (right) fan was removed, install the upper bolts retaining the fan to the shroud and tighten to 89 inch lbs. (10 Nm).

15. If the primary (left) fan assembly was removed, install the radiator upper support.

a. Install upper support to the vehicle and secure using the screws attaching the upper support to the lower support. Tighten the screws to 80 inch lbs. (9 Nm).

b. Install the nuts and bolts retaining the support to the shroud and tighten to 18 ft. lbs. (25 Nm).

c. Install the AIR pump and tighten the bolts to 89 inch lbs. (10 Nm).

d. Engage the electrical connectors to the AIR pump and horn.

e. Install the fan relays and tighten the retaining screws to 80 inch lbs. (9 Nm).

f. If equipped, connect the transmission fluid cooler lines.

g. Connect the radiator bleed hose.

h. Install the air cleaner and duct assembly.

i. Install the shroud upper radiator bolts and tighten to 80 inch lbs. (9 Nm).

16. Connect the negative battery cable.

17. If drained, fill cooling system with the proper type and quantity of antifreeze and check for leaks.

5.7L (VIN J) Engine

Although this procedure is for both the primary and auxiliary fans, either fan assembly can be removed and serviced without removing the other.

1. Disconnect the negative battery cable.

2. If removing the auxiliary (right) fan assembly, remove the bolt retaining the upper right of the auxiliary fan assembly to the fan shroud.

3. Raise and support the vehicle safely.

4. Unplug the electrical connector from the auxiliary fan motor.

5. Remove the bolts retaining the auxiliary fan assembly to the fan shroud, then remove the assembly from the vehicle.

6. If removing the primary (left) fan assembly, lower the vehicle and drain the engine coolant into a suitable container.

7. Remove the cleaner and intake duct assembly.

8. Remove the hoses and clamps from the coolant outlets, the radiator inlet and the bypass inlet pipe.

9. Remove the hose and inlet pipe assembly from the vehicle.

10. Unplug the electrical connector from the fan motor.

11. Remove the screws retaining the fan motor to the motor support and remove the bolt retaining the air conditioning discharge line clamp to the crossmember.

12. Remove the bolts retaining the fan assembly to the fan shroud, remove the end cap from the power steering pump pulley and remove the primary fan assembly from the vehicle.

To install:

13. If removed, install the primary fan assembly and tighten the bolts to 89 inch lbs. (10 Nm).

14. Install the screws retaining the motor to the motor support and tighten to 89 inch lbs. (10 Nm).

15. Engage the electrical connector to the primary fan motor.

16. Install the bolt retaining the air conditioning discharge line clamp to the crossmember and install the end cap to the power steering pump pulley.

17. Install the hose and inlet pipe assembly. Connect the hoses and clamps to the coolant outlets, the radiator inlet and the bypass inlet pipe.

18. Install the air cleaner and intake duct assembly

19. If the auxiliary fan assembly was removed, raise and support the vehicle safely.

20. Install the auxiliary fan assembly to the vehicle and tighten the fan-to-fan shroud bolts to 89 inch lbs. (10 Nm).

21. Engage the electrical connector to the auxiliary fan motor and lower the vehicle.

22. Install the upper right bolt retaining the assembly to the fan shroud.

23. Connect the negative battery cable.

24. If drained, fill the cooling system with the proper type and amount of coolant and check the system for leaks.

Heater Core

REMOVAL AND INSTALLATION

1. Properly disable the SIR air bag system and disconnect the battery negative cable.

2. Remove the instrument panel upper trim pad as follows:

a. Remove the lower right trim panel.

b. Remove the fuse box cover and side trim panel.

c. Remove the glove compartment.

d. Remove the right outer air outlet and center air outlet.

e. Remove the console trim plate and accessory trim plate.

f. Remove the windshield defroster grill.

g. Remove the left outer air outlet.

h. Remove the dash pad retaining bolts/screws and the pad by pulling rearward and upward.

3. Drain the engine coolant into a suitable container. Disconnect the in-vehicle temperature sensor aspirator hose.

4. Disconnect the in-vehicle temperature sensor electrical connector.

5. Remove the floor heat deflector attaching screws, right side knee bolster brace and the floor heat deflector.

6. Disconnect the relays from the multi-use relay bracket.

7. Loosen the nuts attaching the wiring harness retainer to the radio receiver, then slide the wiring harness retainer from the receiver.

8. Remove the harnesses from the wiring harness retainer, then remove the wiring harness retainer.

9. Remove the carrier nuts from the right side pillar, the multi-use relay bracket and the passenger knee bolster brace attachments.

10. Unclip the side window defroster duct clip, then remove the duct hose from the knee bolster brace.

11. Pull the carrier back, then remove the passenger knee bolster brace. Disconnect the electrical connectors from the radio receiver.

12. Remove the multi-use relay bracket and disconnect the cruise control module electrical connector.

13. Remove the screws attaching the side window defroster duct to the rear of the heater case. Remove the fuse block from the carrier.

14. Disconnect the vacuum hose from the actuator, then remove the vacuum line retainer tape from the heater. Remove the harness from the retainer clip, mounted on the bottom of the rear heater case.

15. Disconnect the side window defroster duct (center) extension, in the heater case. Remove the rear heater case attaching screws, then the rear heater case half.

16. Remove the high fill reservoir. Disconnect the heater hoses from the heater core. Remove the heater core from the case.

To install:

17. Install the heater core into the case. Connect the heater hoses to the heater core. Install the high fill reservoir, then the rear heater case.

18. Install the side window defroster duct extension. Install the harnesses to the retainer clip on the bottom rear of the heater case.

19. Install the vacuum line and tape onto the retainer. Connect the vacuum hose to the actuator. Install the fuse block to the carrier.

20. Install the side window defroster duct screws to the rear of the heater case. Connect the radio receiver and cruise control module electrical connectors.

21. Install the multi-use relay bracket, the knee bolster brace and attachments. Install the carrier to pillar attachment, then the wiring harness retainer, harness retainer to the radio receiver and the relays to the multi-use relay bracket.

22. Install the floor heat deflector, the right side knee bolster brace and then the floor heat deflector screws. Connect the in-vehicle temperature sensor electrical connectors and the aspirator hose.

23. Install the upper instrument pad assembly in the reverse order of removal. Connect the negative battery cable and enable the SIR system. Properly fill the engine cooling system and check for leaks.

Water Pump

REMOVAL AND INSTALLATION

5.7L (VIN P) Engine

1. Disconnect the negative battery cable.
2. Unplug the IAT electrical connection.
3. Remove the air cleaner and air intake duct assembly.
4. Drain the cooling system into a suitable container. Remove the knock sensors from the lower left and right side of the block to assure proper draining.
5. Remove the upper and lower radiator hoses and the heater hose from the water pump. For 1993–96 vehicles, remove the throttle body hose from the tee fitting.
6. Unplug the coolant sensor electrical connection and remove the sensor wire harness from the retainer on the front of the coolant pump.
7. Use a box wrench or socket on the tensioner pulley bolt to rotate the tensioner and relieve belt tension, then remove the serpentine drive belt from the alternator pulley. This should create sufficient room to work, if additional room is necessary, the belt can be completely removed.
8. Remove the 6 bolts securing the water pump flanges to the engine block, then remove the water pump from the vehicle.
9. Remove and discard the old gaskets from the mating surfaces.
10. If replacing the pump, remove the coolant sensor from the old pump.
   To install:
11. If replacing the pump, install the coolant sensor on the new pump and tighten to 17 ft. lbs. (23 Nm).
12. Thoroughly clean all gasket mating surfaces and apply a light coat of grease to the seals and splines before assembling the coupling to the water pump. The white band on the coupling should be positioned towards the engine.

13. Install the new gaskets with the tabs up, the coolant pump with the drive coupling and the mounting bolts. Tighten the bolts to 30 ft. lbs. (41 Nm).
14. Install the serpentine drive belt.
15. Install the coolant sensor wire harness to the retainer on the front of the pump, then engage the sensor electrical connection.
16. Connect the heater hose and the upper and lower radiator hoses to the water pump.
17. For 1993–96 vehicles, install the throttle body hose at the tee.
18. If removed, install the knock sensors.
19. Open the bleed valves on the thermostat housing and the throttle body. Fill the cooling system through the radiator surge tank until a solid stream of coolant comes out of the bleeds.
20. Close all bleeds and continue to fill the surge tank until the coolant is level at the base of the surge tank neck.
21. Install the radiator pressure cap and check the coolant recovery reservoir for the proper level of coolant, add as necessary.
22. Install the air cleaner and intake duct assembly.
23. Engage the IAT electrical connection and clean any excess coolant from the engine compartment.
24. Connect the negative battery cable, start the engine and check for leaks.
25. If the low coolant indicator lamp is lit, the engine must be cycled from cold to normal operating temperature and back to cold 3 times. If the lamp does not go out after this and coolant is at the proper level, the indicator system must be repaired.

5.7L (VIN J) Engine

1. Disconnect the negative battery cable.
2. Drain engine coolant into a suitable container.
3. Remove the air cleaner and intake duct assembly.
4. Remove the screws attaching the throttle body extension to the throttle body, then remove the throttle body extension and gasket.
5. Remove clamps and hoses from the coolant outlets, radiator inlet and inlet pipe.
6. Remove the inlet pipe assembly and hose from the vehicle.

7. Except for 1993–96 vehicles:
   a. Loosen the coolant pump pulley attaching bolts, then rotate the belt tensioner.
   b. Remove the bolts from the pulley, then the pulley from the vehicle.
   c. Release the belt tensioner, then remove the belt from the vehicle. Remove the belt tensioner bolt and remove the tensioner.
8. For 1993–96 vehicles, remove the serpentine drive belt, then remove the tensioner retaining bolt and remove the tensioner from the pump. It is not necessary to remove the water pump pulley.
9. Remove the engine hose clamp, then the hose from the water pump.
10. Remove the alternator lower bracket mounting bolts, then remove the bracket from the vehicle.
11. Remove the water pump attaching bolts (noting the position and size of each bolt) and remove the bolt attaching the air conditioning compressor to the water pump. Remove the water pump from the vehicle.
   To install:
12. Thoroughly clean the pump and front cover sealing surfaces.
13. Install the water pump, new gasket and bolts, finger-tight only.
14. Install and finger-tighten the bolt attaching air conditioning compressor to the pump.
15. Torque air conditioning compressor bolt and water pump attaching bolts to 20 ft. lbs. (26 Nm).
16. Install engine hose and clamp.
17. Apply Loctite® 565 to the bolt threads, then install the alternator mounting bolts. Torque the bolts to 39 ft. lbs. (52 Nm) and the bracket bolts to 20 ft. lbs. (26 Nm).
18. Install the belt tensioner and tighten the retaining bolt to 45 ft. lbs. (60 Nm).
19. Install the serpentine drive belt.
20. Except for 1993–96 vehicles, rotate the tensioner and install the water pump pulley. Torque water pump pulley bolts to 89 inch lbs. (10 Nm).
21. Install the hose and inlet pipe assembly.
22. Install throttle body extension and gasket. Torque bolts to 53 inch lbs. (6 Nm).
23. Install air cleaner and intake duct assembly, then connect the negative battery cable.
24. Refill the cooling system with the proper type and quantity of antifreeze and inspect the system for leaks.

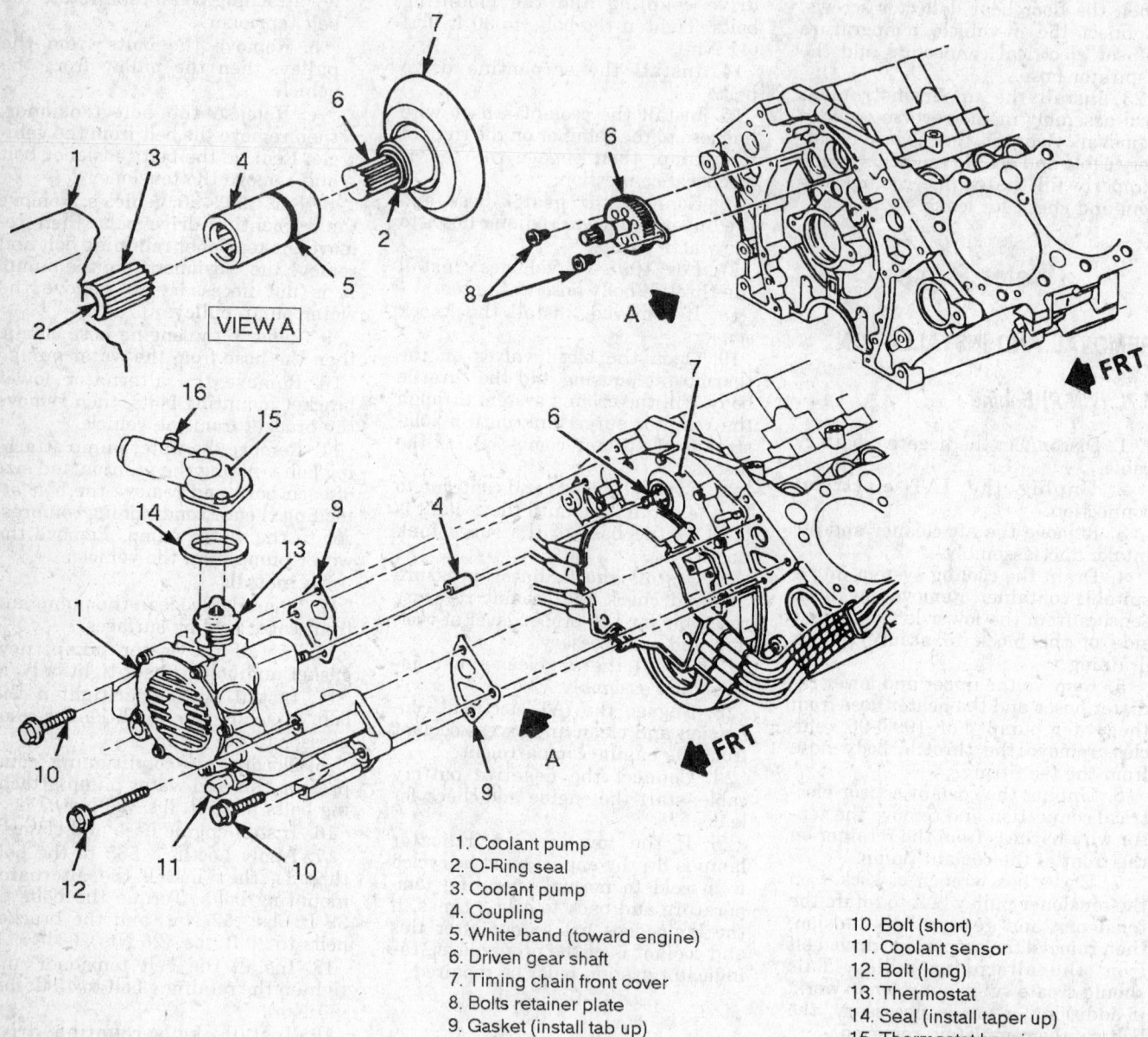

VIEW A

1. Coolant pump
2. O-Ring seal
3. Coolant pump
4. Coupling
5. White band (toward engine)
6. Driven gear shaft
7. Timing chain front cover
8. Bolts retainer plate
9. Gasket (install tab up)
10. Bolt (short)
11. Coolant sensor
12. Bolt (long)
13. Thermostat
14. Seal (install taper up)
15. Thermostat housing

8470R021

Exploded view of the water pump mounting — 5.7L (VIN P) engine

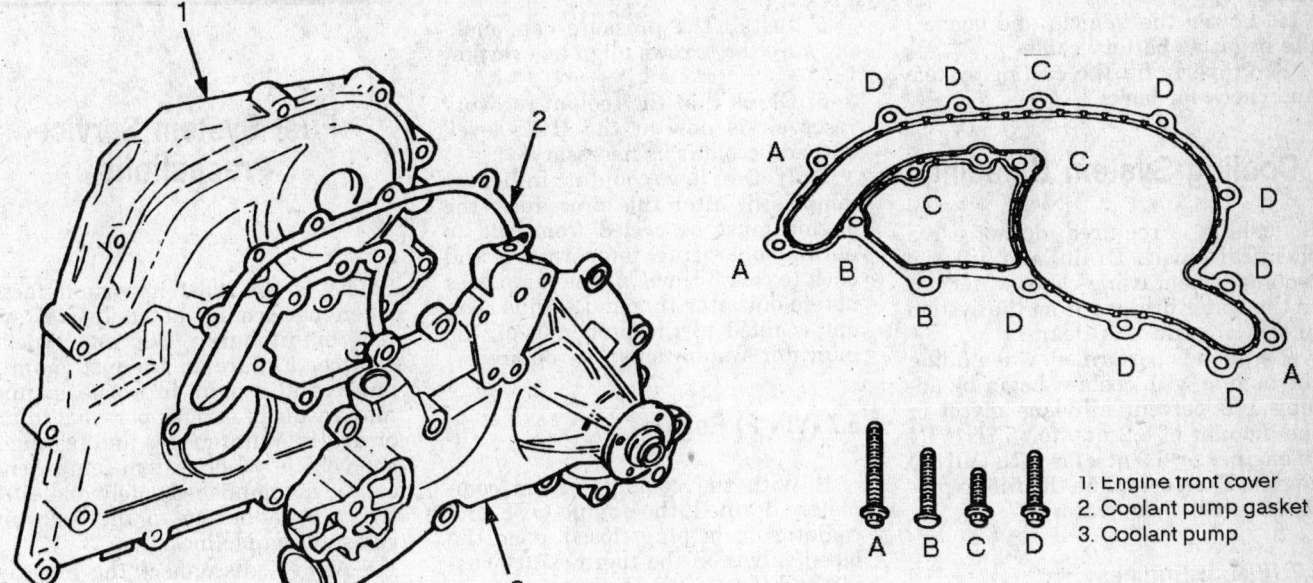

1. Engine front cover
2. Coolant pump gasket
3. Coolant pump

8470R022

Water pump assembly mounting — 5.7L (VIN J) engine

Thermostat

REMOVAL AND INSTALLATION

5.7L (VIN P) Engine

1. Disconnect the negative battery cable.
2. Unplug the IAT electrical connection.
3. Remove the air cleaner and intake duct assembly.
4. Drain the cooling system into a suitable container. Only drain the system to a level below the thermostat housing.
5. Disconnect the radiator hose from the thermostat housing inlet of the water pump.
6. Remove the thermostat housing bolts and housing.
7. Remove the thermostat and seal.
   To install:
8. Thoroughly clean the thermostat housing and water pump sealing surfaces.
9. Install the thermostat, seal (with the taper up) and the housing to the water pump. Tighten the bolts to 8 ft. lbs. (10 Nm).
10. Connect the radiator hose to the thermostat inlet on the water pump.
11. Open the bleed valves on the thermostat housing and the throttle body. Fill the cooling system through the radiator surge tank until a solid stream of coolant comes out of the bleeder.
12. Close all bleeds and continue to fill the surge tank until the coolant is level at the base of the surge tank neck.
13. Install the pressure cap and check the coolant recovery reservoir for the proper level of coolant, add as necessary.
14. Install the air cleaner and intake duct assembly.
15. Engage the IAT electrical connection and clean any excess coolant from the engine compartment.
16. Connect the negative battery cable, start the engine and check for leaks.

5.7L (VIN J) Engine

1. Disconnect the negative battery cable.
2. Drain the engine coolant into a suitable container.

NOTE: A large amount of engine coolant will remain in the VIN J engine after coolant has drained through the radiator draincock. Much of this coolant will drain from the thermostat housing when the 2-piece housing is separated.

3. Raise and support the vehicle safely.
4. Remove the bolts attaching the thermostat housing assembly brackets to the front side member.
5. Remove the clamps securing the thermostat radiator hose, radiator bypass hose and engine hose.
6. Remove the quick-connect fittings at the heater hose-thermostat housing junction.
7. Remove the thermostat housing assembly from the vehicle.
8. Remove the housing bolts, then remove the thermostat and seal from the housing.
   To install:
9. Thoroughly clean all gasket mating surfaces.
10. Install the thermostat, seal and housing. Be sure the seal is installed with the taper towards the radiator and remains seated in housing groove when assembling the housing sections.
11. Tighten the thermostat housing bolts to 18 ft. lbs. (25 Nm).
12. Install the quick-connect fittings at the heater hose-thermostat housing junction.
13. Install the clamps to the radiator outlet hose, radiator bypass hose and the engine hose. Tighten the clamps to 35 inch lbs. (4 Nm).

14. Install the bolts retaining the housing bracket to the front side member and tighten to 18 ft. lbs. (25 Nm).

15. Lower the vehicle and connect the negative battery cable.

16. Properly fill the cooling system and check for leaks.

Cooling System Bleeding

If flushing is required, do not use a chemical flush. Drain and fill the cooling system using clean water until the water drained from the system in this procedure is clear.

If a flush is performed, when filling the engine with coolant begin by adding 100 percent ethylene glycol in the amount of 8.2 qts. for 5.7L (VIN P) engines or 6.9 qts. for 5.7L (VIN J) engine. Then complete the filling procedure with clean water.

5.7 (VIN J) Engines

1. With the cooling system completely drained, the engine **OFF** and radiator drain plug closed, begin adding antifreeze. Use a final mixture of 50 percent ethylene glycol antifreeze and 50 percent water for system refill.

NOTE: To completely drain the engine cooling system on the VIN J engine, the thermostat must be removed from the housing. The thermostat housing should temporarily be installed, without the thermostat, if system flushing is to be performed, but the thermostat must be installed before the system is filled coolant.

2. Slowly fill the cooling system through the opening in the high fill surge tank until the level is even with the base of the fill neck. Also, be sure the coolant recovery reservoir is filled to the **COLD** mark.

3. Run the engine with the pressure cap removed until normal operating temperature is reached and the upper radiator hose becomes hot.

NOTE: The coolant temperature gauge must be monitored during the running of the engine and at no time should the engine temperature be allowed to reach the 260°F mark or the engine HOT light be allowed to come ON. If this should occur, the engine should be turned OFF immediately and allowed to cool down to 80°F (27°C) before continuing with the bleeding process.

4. With the engine idling, add coolant until the level reaches the bottom of the high fill reservoir filler neck.

5. Install the pressure cap, making sure the arrows align he overflow tube.

6. Check that the coolant recovery reservoir is now at the **HOT** level, and add coolant as necessary.

7. If the low coolant indicator lamp is lit after this procedure, the engine must be cycled from cold to normal operating temperature and back to cold 3 times. If the lamp does not go out after this and engine coolant is filled to the proper level, the indicator system must be repaired.

5.7 (VIN P) Engine

1. With the cooling system completely drained, the engine **OFF** and radiator drain plug closed, open the bleed valves on the thermostat housing and the throttle body.

NOTE: To completely drain the engine cooling system on the VIN P engine, the knock sensors must be removed from the lower left and right sides of the block. The sensors should then be reinstalled before filling the engine with coolant.

2. Begin adding antifreeze. Use a final mixture of 50 percent ethylene glycol antifreeze and 50 percent water for system refills. Fill the cooling system through the radiator surge tank until a solid stream of coolant comes out of the bleeders.

3. Close all bleeds and continue to fill the surge tank until the coolant is level at the base of the surge tank neck.

4. Install the pressure cap and check the coolant recovery reservoir for the proper level of coolant, add as necessary. If removed, install the air cleaner and intake duct assembly.

5. Clean any excess coolant from the engine compartment.

6. Connect the negative battery cable, start the engine and check for leaks.

7. Run the engine at normal operating temperature and make sure the coolant remains at the proper level.

8. If the low coolant indicator lamp is lit after this procedure, the engine must be cycled from cold to normal operating temperature and back to cold 3 times. If the lamp does not go out after this and engine coolant is filled to the proper level, the indicator system must be repaired.

FUEL SYSTEM

Fuel System Service Precautions

Safety is the most important factor when performing not only fuel system maintenance, but any type of service. Failure to conduct maintenance and repairs in a safe manner may result in serious personal injury or death. Maintenance and testing of the vehicle's fuel system components can be accomplished safely and effectively by adhering to the following rules and guidelines.

• Always disconnect the negative battery cable before opening the fuel system fittings, unless the repair or test procedure requires that battery voltage be applied. This will prevent excessive fuel spillage if the ignition switch is accidentally turned **ON** while fuel fittings are still disconnected.

• Always relieve the fuel system pressure prior to disconnecting any fuel system fitting or connection.

• Exercise extreme caution whenever relieving fuel system pressure to avoid exposing skin, face and eyes to fuel spray. Under pressure, fuel may penetrate the skin or any part of the body that it contacts.

• Always place a shop towel around a fitting or connection prior to loosening in order to absorb any fuel spillage. Ensure that all spilled fuel is quickly removed from engine surfaces. Ensure that all fuel soaked rags are deposited into a suitable waste container.

• Always keep a dry chemical (Class B) fire extinguisher near the work area.

• Ventilate the work area properly and pay attention to where the fumes go. Do not allow fuel vapors to come into contact with a source of ignition.

• Always use a backup wrench when loosening and tightening fuel line connection fittings. This will prevent unnecessary stress to fuel line piping. Always follow the proper torque specifications.

• Always replace worn fuel fitting O-rings. Do not substitute fuel hose where metal fuel pipe is normally installed.

RELIEVING FUEL SYSTEM PRESSURE

1. Disconnect the negative battery cable.
2. Loosen the fuel filler cap to relieve the tank pressure.
3. Wrap a shop towel around the fuel pressure valve fitting (located on the side or end of the fuel rail assembly) to catch any fuel spray and connect J–34730–1 or an equivalent fuel gauge.
4. Install the bleed hose into a suitable container, then open the valve to bleed the fuel system pressure.
5. Close the valve and disconnect the fuel gauge. Drain any remaining fuel from the gauge into the bleed container.

Fuel Tank

REMOVAL AND INSTALLATION

NOTE: Ensure an approved dry chemical (Class B) fire extinguisher is near the work area. For safety, additional vehicle supports should be added to the end of the vehicle opposite the work area to keep the vehicle stable on the lift.

1. Disconnect the negative battery cable and properly relieve fuel system pressure.
2. Drain the fuel tank into an approved container using a hand-operated fuel pump.
3. Remove the 4 screws attaching the fuel door bezel, then remove the bezel and the filler cap.
4. Lift the filler neck housing and disconnect the the drain hose from the nipple.
5. Reinstall the filler cap to prevent dirt from entering and remove the filler neck housing.
6. Unplug the fuel sender electrical connector at the tank.
7. Thoroughly clean the surrounding areas to prevent fuel system contamination, then disconnect the fuel hoses from the sender assembly.
8. Remove the license plate and all rear lamps to provide access, then remove the carriage bolts securing the fascia to the impact bar.
9. Raise and support the vehicle safely.
10. Remove the spare tire and tire carrier from the frame.
11. With the aid of an assistant, remove the mufflers as an assembly from the converter.

12. Remove the canister splash shield, if equipped, and both rear inner fender braces at the frame.
13. Remove both rear wheel house liner panels.
14. Remove the antenna ground strap and clip at the antenna base and frame.
15. Disconnect the fuel vapor pipes from the canister or the bottom of the tank, then remove the canister.
16. Remove both fuel tank cables from the stabilizer shaft supports.
17. Remove the 2 bottom fascia-to-energy absorbing pad attaching screws.
18. Remove the marker lamps and spare tire light.
19. Remove the 4 nuts attaching each side of the fascia to the horizontal body retainer. Then remove the 5 nuts securing each side of the outer body retainer to the fascia.
20. Remove 6 side impact bar bolts and loosen the front 2 bolts, 1 on each side. With the aid of an assistant, support the impact bar, and remove the front bar bolts. Remove the impact bar and fuel tank assembly, then separate the fuel tank.
21. If the tank is being replaced, transfer the cables, vapor connections and hoses, fuel sender assembly, and/or fuel connector, as required and applicable.

To install:
22. Install the fuel tank to the impact bar assembly and tighten the strap bolts to 11 ft. lbs. (15 Nm) and the strap nuts to 40 inch lbs. (4.5 Nm). Install the impact bar assembly to the vehicle and tighten the 8 bolts to 37 ft. lbs. (50 Nm).
23. Install rear and side fascia to the body retainer using the attaching nuts. Tighten the nuts to 53 inch lbs. (6 Nm).
24. Install the marker lights and the spare tire light sockets.
25. Attach screws to the edge of the fascia and impact bar.
26. Attach the fuel tank cables to the stabilizer shaft supports. Tighten the cable attaching nuts to 18 ft. lbs. (25 Nm).
27. Install the 2 carriage bolts securing the fascia to the impact bar, then install the antenna ground strap and clip.
28. Install both inner fender panels, then the braces to the frame.
29. Connect the vapor hoses to the canister or the bottom of the tank, then install the canister and, if equipped, the canister splash shield.
30. With the aid of an assistant, install the muffler assembly to the rear of the converter.

31. Install the spare tire and carrier to the frame.
32. Lower the vehicle and install all rear lamps.
33. Install the license plate.
34. Connect all lines and electrical connections to the fuel sender assembly.
35. Refill the fuel tank, tighten the fuel filler cap and connect the negative battery cable.
36. Turn the ignition **ON** for 2 seconds, **OFF** for 10 seconds, then **ON** again and inspect the system for leaks.
37. Install the drain hose, seal and fuel filler door bezel.

Fuel Filter

REMOVAL AND INSTALLATION

1992 Vehicles

1. Disconnect the battery negative cable and properly relieve the fuel system pressure.
2. Raise and support the vehicle safely.
3. Clean the filter connections and surrounding areas to prevent fuel system contamination, disconnect the fuel pipes from the filter and drain any remaining fuel into a suitable container.
4. Remove the fuel filter attaching screw and remove the filter from the vehicle.

To install:
5. Loosely install the fuel filter to the rail with the attaching screw.
6. Inspect the fuel line O-rings and replace as necessary. Connect the fuel lines to the fuel filter and tighten to 20 ft. lbs. (27 Nm). Use a backup wrench to prevent the filter from turning.
7. Tighten the fuel filter attaching screw to 53 inch lbs. (6 Nm).
8. If equipped, install the fuel filter shield and attaching screws.
9. Lower the vehicle, tighten the fuel filler cap and connect the negative battery cable.
10. Turn the ignition **ON** for 2 seconds, **OFF** for 10 seconds, then **ON** again and inspect the system for leaks.

1993–96 Vehicles

1. Disconnect the battery negative cable and properly relieve the fuel system pressure.
2. Remove the fuel pipe retaining nut from the evaporator case.
3. Raise and support the vehicle safely.

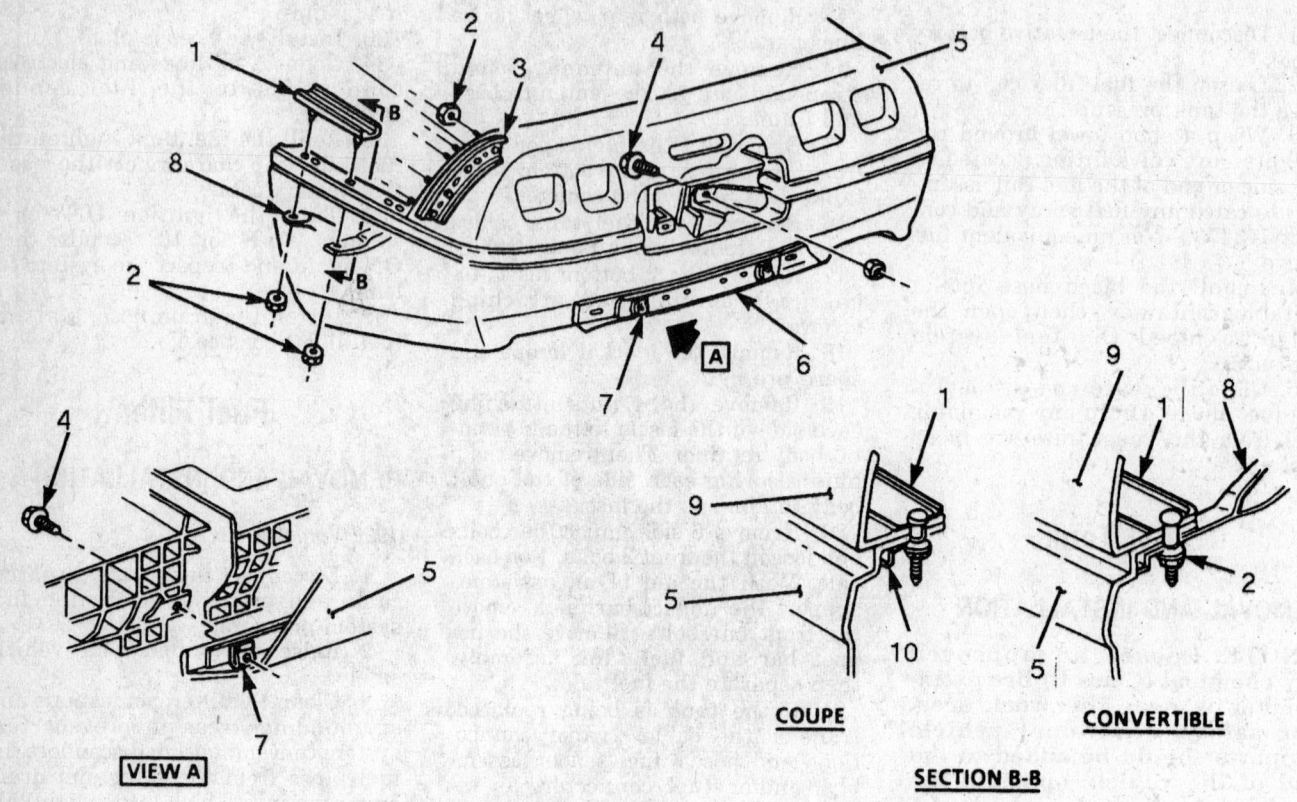

VIEW A

COUPE

CONVERTIBLE

SECTION B-B

1. Fascia side retainer
2. Nut
3. Fascia outer retainer LH
4. Bolt
5. Rear bumper fascia
6. Fascia lower reinforcement
7. J nut
8. Fascia support LH
9. Upper rear body panel
10. Fascia upper retainer LH

8470R023

Rear fascia-to-lower body mounting

4. For convertibles, remove the underbody brace.

5. Remove the 3 nuts retaining the fuel pipes to the chassis.

6. Clean the filter connections and surrounding areas to prevent fuel system contamination.

7. Disconnect the inlet pipe from the filter, drain any remaining fuel from the line and reposition the line for access to the filter.

8. Hold the pipe outlet nut and remove the filter by turning to unthread it from the fitting.

To install:

9. Check the fuel pipe O-rings for cuts, nicks, swelling or distortion and replace, if damaged.

10. Install the fuel filter onto the fuel outlet pipe nut.

11. Connect the fuel inlet pipe to the filter and tighten the fitting to 20 ft. lbs. (27 Nm).

12. Install the 3 chassis-to-fuel pipe retaining nuts.

13. For convertibles, install the underbody brace, tighten the retaining nuts to 20 ft. lbs. (27 Nm) and the retaining bolts to 47 ft. lbs. (63 Nm).

14. Lower the vehicle and install the fuel pipe retaining nut to the evaporator case.

15. Tighten the fuel filler cap and connect the negative battery cable.

16. Turn the ignition **ON** for 2 seconds, **OFF** for 10 seconds, then

ON again and inspect the system for leaks.

Electric Fuel Pump

PRESSURE TESTING

1. Properly relieve fuel system pressure.

2. With ignition **OFF**, install J–34730–1 or an equivalent fuel pressure gauge, to the fuel rail pressure connection.

3. For the VIN J engine, test the primary fuel pump by removing the secondary fuel pump fuse **FP2** or test

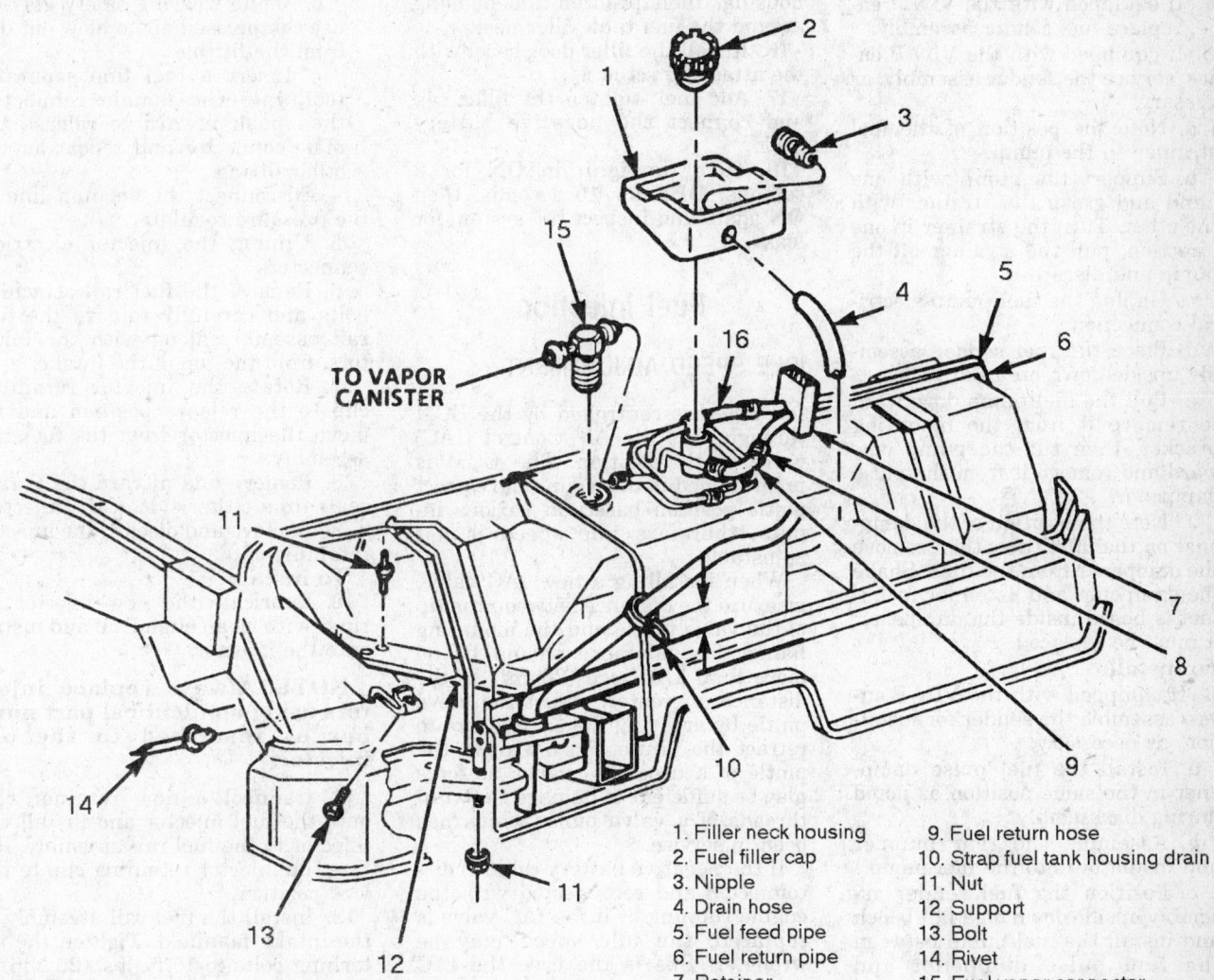

TO VAPOR CANISTER

1. Filler neck housing
2. Fuel filler cap
3. Nipple
4. Drain hose
5. Fuel feed pipe
6. Fuel return pipe
7. Retainer
8. Clamp
9. Fuel return hose
10. Strap fuel tank housing drain
11. Nut
12. Support
13. Bolt
14. Rivet
15. Fuel vapor connector
16. Fuel feed hose

8470R024

Fuel tank assembly

the secondary fuel pump by removing the primary fuel pump fuse **FP1**.

4. Turn the ignition switch **ON,** but with the engine not running. The fuel pump will operate for 2 seconds and then turn **OFF.** It may be necessary to cycle the ignition a few times to build system pressure. If this is necessary, make sure the ignition remains **OFF** for at least 10 seconds between cycles.

5. With the pump running, fuel pressure should be 41–47 psi, if equipped with the VIN P engine or 48–55 psi, if equipped with the VIN J engine.

6. When the pump stops, the pressure may vary slightly, but then

should hold steady with little or no pressure drop.

7. Start the engine and the pressure should drop approximately 3–10 psi.

REMOVAL AND INSTALLATION

NOTE: Vehicles equipped with the 5.7L (VIN J) engine use a fuel sender assembly which is equipped with 2 fuel pumps. The strainers and pumps are not serviced separately from the sender and, if 1 component is damaged, the sender assembly must be replaced as a unit.

1. Disconnect the negative battery cable.

2. Properly relieve the fuel system pressure and drain the fuel tank.

3. Remove the 4 filler door bezel attaching screws, then remove the filler door bezel.

4. Lift the fuel tank filler neck housing and disconnect the drain hose from the nipple. Remove filler neck housing.

5. Clean the area around all fuel fittings to prevent system contamination, then disconnect and plug the fuel pipes and fuel vapor pipe.

6. Unplug the sending unit electrical connector, remove the attaching

bolts and remove the sending unit assembly from the vehicle.

7. If equipped with the VIN J engine, replace fuel sender assembly.

8. If equipped with the VIN P engines, service the sender assembly, as necessary:

a. Note the position of the fuel strainer on the pump.

b. Support the pump with one hand and grasp the strainer with the other. Turn the strainer in one direction, pull the strainer off the pump and discard it.

c. Unplug the fuel pump electrical connection.

d. Place the fuel sender assembly upside down on a flat bench.

e. Pull the fuel pump downward to remove it from the mounting bracket, then tilt the pump outward and remove it from the pulse dampener.

f. Note the position of the dampener on the inlet tube, then remove the dampener from the tube. Shake the dampener and listen for fuel, if fuel is heard inside the dampener, it must be replaced.

To install:

9. If equipped with the VIN P engines, assemble the sender for installation, as necessary:

a. Install the fuel pulse dampener in the same position as noted during disassembly.

b. Assemble the rear bumper and insulator onto the fuel pump.

c. Position the fuel sender assembly upside down on a flat bench and install the fuel pump between the fuel pulse dampener and mounting bracket.

d. Engage the pump electrical connector.

e. Install the new fuel strainer into the same position as noted during disassembly. Push on the outer edge of ferrule until fully seated.

10. Position a new gasket on the fuel tank with the notch facing forward in the right corner of the fuel tank.

11. Carefully fold the strainer to allow it to fit through the opening in the tank. Make sure the strainer unfolds in the tank and lower the fuel sender assembly into position.

12. Install the fuel sender assembly attaching screws and tighten alternately and evenly to 45 inch lbs. (5 Nm).

13. Engage the fuel sender assembly electrical connector.

14. Connect all sender assembly fuel and vapor hoses.

15. Connect the fuel drain hose to the nipple on the rubber filler neck housing, then position the housing around the fuel tank filler neck.

16. Install the filler door bezel with the attaching screws.

17. Add fuel, tighten the filler cap and connect the negative battery cable.

18. Turn the ignition **ON** for 2 seconds, **OFF** for 10 seconds, then **ON** again and inspect the system for leaks.

Fuel Injection

IDLE SPEED ADJUSTMENT

Idle speed is controlled by the ECM through the Idle Air Control (IAC) valve pintle position. The ECM is programmed to determine the correct pintle position based on various inputs, therefore idle speed is not adjustable.

When installing a new IAC valve, measure the distance between the tip of the valve pintle and the mounting flange. The distance should be no more than 1.10 inch (28mm). If the distance is greater, adjust the valve pintle by applying finger pressure to retract the pintle. Do not push the pintle of a used IAC valve, as force may be sufficient to damage the worn threads of a valve pintle which has been in service.

If the negative battery cable is disconnected and reconnected with the engine running or if the IAC valve is replaced, the idle speed may be wrong. If this is the case the IAC valve may be reset as follows:

1. Depress the accelerator pedal slightly.

2. Start the engine and run for 5 seconds.

3. Turn the ignition **OFF** for 10 seconds.

4. Restart the vehicle and check for proper idle operation.

Fuel Injector

REMOVAL AND INSTALLATION

5.7L (VIN P) Engine

1. Disconnect the negative battery cable and properly relieve fuel system pressure.

2. Remove the fuel rail cover.

3. Disengage the quick-connect fittings at the fuel rail feed and return pipes as follows:

a. Grasp both ends of a connection and twist ¼ turn in each direction to loosen any dirt. Repeat for other fitting.

b. While wearing safety glasses, use compressed air to blow out dirt from the fitting.

c. Insert a fuel line separator tool, into the female connector, then push inward to release the male connector and repeat for the other fitting.

4. Disconnect the vacuum line at the pressure regulator.

5. Unplug the injector electrical connectors.

6. Remove the fuel rail attaching bolts and carefully remove the fuel rail assembly along with the injectors, from the top of the intake.

7. Rotate the injector retaining clip to the release position and remove the injector from the fuel rail assembly.

8. Remove and discard the O-ring seals from either side of the injector.

9. Remove and discard the injector retaining clip.

To install:

10. Lubricate the new injector O-rings with clean engine oil and install onto the injector.

NOTE: Always replace injectors using an identical part number as inscribed in the old injector.

11. Connect a new retainer clip onto the fuel injector and install the injector to the fuel rail assembly. Rotate the injector retaining clip to the lock position.

12. Install the fuel rail assembly to the intake manifold. Tighten the attaching bolts to 15 ft. lbs. (20 Nm).

13. Rotate the fuel injectors as necessary to avoid stretching the wire harnesses and connect the injector electrical connections.

14. Connect the vacuum line to the pressure regulator.

15. Apply a few drops of clean engine oil to the male ends of the fuel line quick-connect fittings. Engage the fittings by pushing the connectors together until the retaining tabs snap into place. Pull gently on both sides of each fitting to be sure the connection is secure.

16. Tighten the fuel filler cap and connect the negative battery cable.

17. Turn the ignition **ON** for 2 seconds, **OFF** for 10 seconds, then **ON** again and inspect the system for leaks.

5.7L (VIN J) Engine

1. Disconnect the negative battery cable and properly relieve fuel system pressure.

2. Drain the cooling system into a suitable container.

3. Remove the intake plenum assembly.

4. If not done already when removing the intake plenum, disconnect the fuel feed and return lines from the fuel rail. Remove and discard the old O-rings from the fittings. Disconnect the vacuum line to the pressure regulator.

5. Unplug the fuel injector wire connectors.

6. Remove the bolts securing the fuel rail to the injector housing.

7. Carefully remove the fuel rails making sure not to damage the injector connector terminals or spray tips. Remove the spacers, if equipped. Note the routing of the vacuum hoses around the fuel rail before removing the rail.

8. Remove the injector retaining clip, then remove the injector.

9. Remove and discard the injector O-ring seals.

To install:

10. Lubricate new injector O-rings with engine oil and install the injector with retaining clip onto fuel rail. Make sure the injector wire connection is facing outward and push the injector onto the rail sufficiently to engage the clip with the machined slots on the rail socket.

NOTE: Each injector is calibrated for a specific flow rate and must be replaced with an identical part number.

11. Install the fuel rail into the injector housing, routing the vacuum lines in their previous positions around the rail.

12. If equipped, be sure the spacers are properly positioned under the rail mounting bracket.

13. Install the fuel rail bolts and tighten to 20 ft. lbs. (26 Nm).

14. Engage the injector electrical connectors, turning the injectors if necessary to avoid stretching the wire harnesses.

15. Install new O-rings to the fuel feed and return pipes.

16. Connect the fuel feed and return lines with the retaining bolts tightened to 13 ft. lbs. (18 Nm). Temporarily connect the negative battery cable and turn the ignition switch **ON** for 2 seconds, then **OFF** for 10 seconds. Cycle the ignition once again to assure proper system pressure, then disconnect the battery negative cable and inspect the fuel system for leaks.

17. Install the plenum assembly. It may be necessary to disconnect the fuel lines for proper installation; if so

be sure to relieve the system pressure before disconnecting any fuel fitting.

18. Tighten the fuel filler cap and connect the negative battery terminal.

19. Properly refill the engine cooling system.

EMISSION CONTROLS

Emission Warning Lamps

The SERVICE ENGINE SOON emission warning lamp located on the instrument panel has 2 main functions:

1. The lamp indicates to the driver that a problem has occurred and the vehicle should be taken for service as soon as reasonably possible.

2. The light may be used by technicians to monitor diagnostic trouble codes and/or open/closed loop engine operation, whenever the system is placed in the diagnostic modes.

To verify proper operation of the bulb and wiring, the lamp will illuminate when the ignition is first turned **ON**, but the engine is not running. If the system is operating properly, the lamp will turn **OFF** once the engine is started.

If the SERVICE ENGINE SOON lamp remains lit once the engine is started, the self-diagnostic system has detected a problem. If the problem goes away, the light will extinguish in 10 seconds (in most cases), but a diagnostic trouble code will remain in the ECM memory.

RESETTING

NOTE: In order to prevent damage to the ECM, the key must be OFF when connecting or disconnecting power to the ECM.

After repairs are made to the faulty system(s), it is necessary to make sure the ECM memory is cleared of any old diagnostic trouble codes. Removing the battery voltage to the ECM for a minimum of 30 seconds will clear all codes. This may be accomplished in various ways depending on how the vehicle is equipped. The ECM harness power feed may be disconnected at the positive battery terminal "pigtail." The fuse may be removed from the inline fuseholder which originates at the positive battery connection or from fuse block, as

applicable. Also, the negative battery cable may be disconnected, but other on-board data such as the clock or radio presets will also be lost.

ECM LEARNING ABILITY

The ECM has a "learning" ability which allows it to make corrections for minor variations in the fuel system, in order to improve driveability. If the battery is disconnected to clear diagnostic codes or for safety during repairs, the "learning" process will reset and must begin again. A change may be noted in the vehicle's performance while the learning process begins. To "teach" the vehicle, make sure the engine is at normal operating temperature, then drive the vehicle at part throttle, with moderate acceleration and idle conditions, until normal performance returns.

ENGINE MECHANICAL

NOTE: Disconnecting the negative battery cable on some vehicles may interfere with the functions of the on board computer systems and may require the computer to undergo a relearning process.

Engine Assembly

REMOVAL AND INSTALLATION

5.7L (VIN P) Engine

1. Disconnect the negative battery cable and properly relieve fuel system pressure.

2. Drain the coolant into a suitable container.

3. Remove the air intake duct.

4. Unplug the electrical harness and vacuum connections from the top of the engine.

5. Disconnect the upper radiator, radiator hose and heater hoses from the pump, then remove the throttle body coolant hose from the radiator tee and from the right side of the throttle body.

6. Remove the power steering pump and support aside.

7. Remove the alternator and support aside.

8. Remove the left wheel well center panel. Remove the serpentine drive belt.

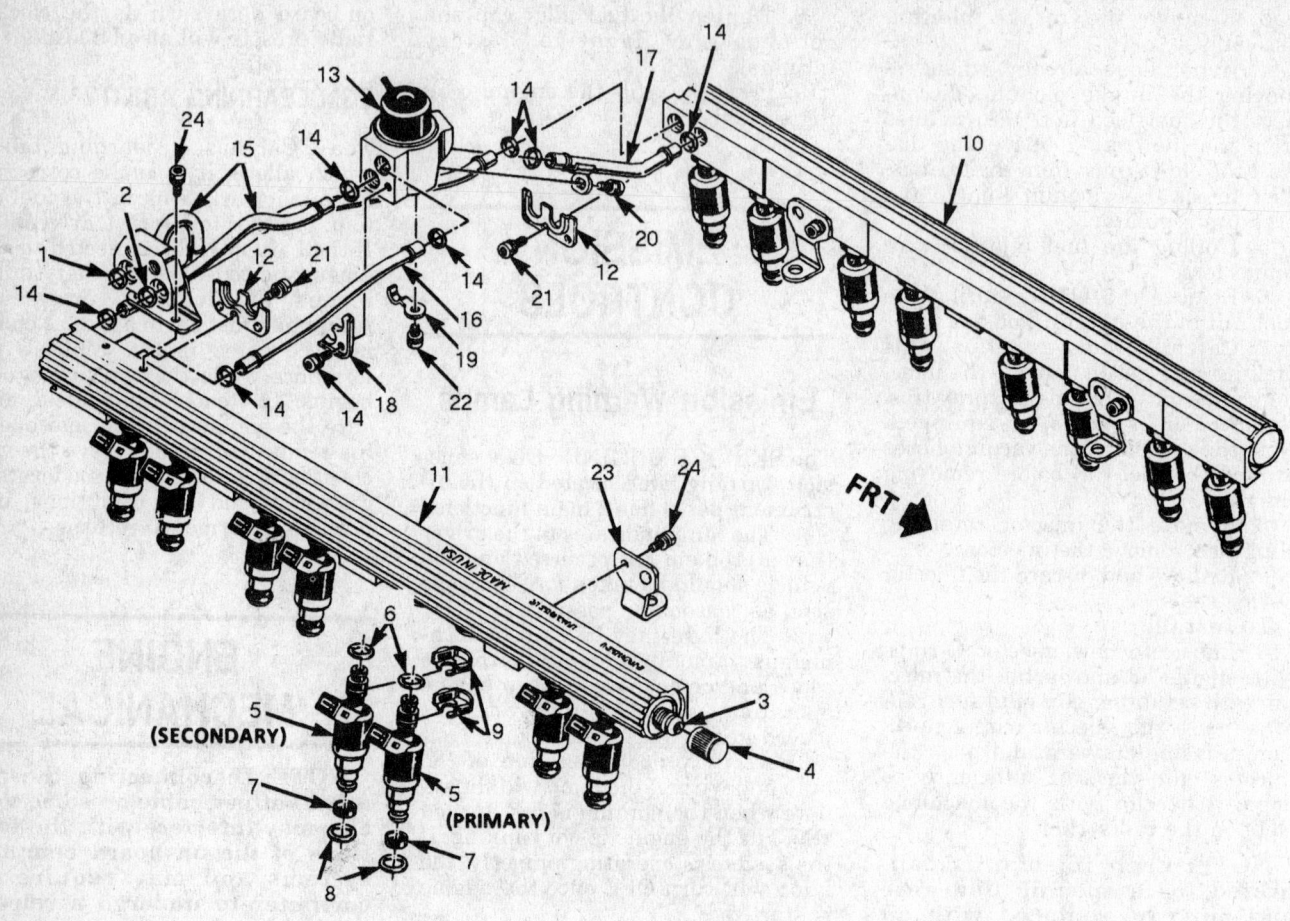

1. O-Ring fuel inlet line
2. O-Ring fuel return line
3. Connection assembly fuel pressure
4. Cap fuel pressure connection assembly
5. Injector assembly fuel: P-Primary, S-Secondary
6. O-Ring upper injector (black)
7. Backup O-Ring
8. O-Ring lower injector (brown)
9. Clip injector retainer
10. Rail assembly fuel (lh)
11. Rail assembly fuel (rh)
12. Retainer crossover tube

13. Regulator assembly fuel pressure
14. Seal O-Ring
15. Tube assembly fuel inlet and outlet
16. Tube fuel return (rh)
17. Tube fuel return (lh)
18. Retainer regulator tube
19. Retainer fuel inlet tube
20. Screw fuel return tube retainer attaching
21. Screw crossover tube retainer attaching
22. Screw fuel inlet tube retainer attaching
23. Bracket fuel rail mounting
24. Screw bracket attaching

8470R027

Exploded view of the fuel rail assembly — 5.7L (VIN J) engine

9. Remove the air conditioning compressor from the bracket and position aside.

10. Unplug the electrical connector and remove the cover from the wiper motor.

11. Disconnect the AIR diverter valve hose.

12. Disconnect and plug the fuel lines at the fuel rail.

13. Remove the hoses from the power steering fluid reservoir. Plug the openings to prevent system contamination or excessive fluid loss.

14. Disconnect the accelerator cable from the throttle body.

15. Raise and support the vehicle safely.

16. Remove the starter motor.

17. Remove the left and right catalytic converters, then remove the exhaust pipe and muffler assembly.

18. Remove the transmission.

19. If equipped with a manual transmission, remove the clutch cover and plate, then remove the flywheel.

20. Remove the ground leads from the rear of the engine, then disengage the electrical connectors from the oil level, knock, oil temperature and coolant temperature sensors.

21. Remove the nuts from the engine mount studs, then lower the vehicle.

22. Install a suitable lifting device and carefully remove the engine from the vehicle.

To install:

23. Lower the engine into position in the vehicle.

24. Remove the lifting device from the engine, then raise and support the vehicle safely.

25. Install the nuts on the engine mount studs.

26. Engage the sensor electrical connectors and then connect the ground leads to the rear of the engine.

27. If equipped with a manual transmission, install the flywheel, then install the clutch cover and plate.

28. Install the transmission.

29. Install the right and left catalytic converters, then install the exhaust pipe and muffler assembly.

30. Install the starter and lower the vehicle.

31. Connect the accelerator cable to the throttle body, then unplug the openings and install the hose to the power steering reservoir.

32. Unplug and connect the fuel lines to the fuel rail.

33. Connect the AIR diverter valve hose.

34. Install the electrical connector and cover to the wiper motor.

35. Install the air conditioning compressor.

36. Install the serpentine drive belt, then install the left wheel well center panel.

37. Install the alternator and the power steering pump.

38. Connect the coolant hose to the right side of the throttle body and connect the throttle body hose to the radiator tee. Connect the heater and radiator hoses.

39. Engage the electrical harness and all vacuum connections to the top of the engine.

40. Install the air intake duct and properly fill the engine cooling system.

41. Check all fluid levels, connect the negative battery cable and tighten the fuel filler cap.

42. Reset the CHANGE OIL indicator:

   a. Turn the ignition **ON** but do not start the engine.

   b. Depress the ENG MET button on the trip monitor, then within 5 seconds, depress the button a 2nd time. Within another 5 seconds, depress and hold the GAUGES button.

   c. While holding the GAUGES button and watch the CHANGE OIL light, it should begin to flash. Continue to hold the gauges button until the flashing stops and the light goes out indicating that the indicator is reset.

   d. If the indicator does not reset, turn the ignition **OFF** and restart the procedure.

43. Check and adjust the ASR control cables, as necessary.

44. Start the engine and check for leaks, then bleed the power steering system.

5.7L (VIN J) Engine

1. Disconnect the battery negative cable and properly relieve fuel system pressure.

2. Raise and support the vehicle safely.

3. Drain engine coolant into a suitable container and drain the engine oil.

4. Remove the complete exhaust system assembly, then remove the driveshaft.

5. Position a suitable transmission support stand under transmission and remove the transmission support beam.

6. Remove transmission from the vehicle.

7. Remove the clutch actuator cylinder, left side converter shield and clutch housing cover, then remove the clutch cover and disc.

8. Install a suitable engine lift hook to rear of engine.

9. Remove the AIR tube center section from the AIR hose and oil pan.

10. Unplug the oxygen sensor electrical connector.

11. Remove the power steering lower hose from the oil cooler.

12. Remove the negative battery cable from the cylinder case.

13. Remove the nuts attaching the engine mounts to the driveline and suspension frame, then lower the vehicle.

14. Remove the air cleaner assembly and air duct.

15. Disconnect the engine oil cooler lines from the oil filter housing.

16. Raise the rear of the engine.

17. Disconnect the fuel lines from the fuel rail.

18. Remove the evaporator housing panel and the resistor.

19. Remove the bolts attaching the right bulkhead connector.

20. Remove the engine right side wiring harness.

21. Remove the instrument panel right lower sound insulator pan.

22. Disengage the bulkhead wiring harness connectors from under the dash.

23. Remove the air bleed hose from the plenum.

24. Remove the radiator upper and lower hoses, then disconnect the power steering pump vacuum line(s).

25. Properly discharge and recover the air conditioning system.

26. Remove the air conditioning suction and discharge line flange from the compressor, then remove the air conditioning compressor-to-accumulator line from the accumulator.

27. Remove the air conditioning accumulator and position aside.

28. Remove the air conditioning accumulator bracket from the vehicle.

29. Disconnect and plug the power steering pressure line at the power steering gear.

30. Disconnect the throttle body linkage shield, then remove the throttle body cable to plenum retainer.

31. Disconnect the accelerator and cruise control cable or the control cable from the throttle body.

32. Install a suitable engine lift hook to front of the engine.

33. Remove the ECM from the ECM bracket, then disconnect ECM harness connector.

34. Remove the left front fender attaching bolts, shims and seal. Remove the left fender.

35. Disconnect the positive cable from the battery, remove the battery hold-down clamp, and remove the battery from the vehicle.

36. Disengage the engine left side bulkhead block electrical connector.

37. Disconnect the engine wiring harness fusible links at the junction block.

38. Disengage the engine harness connectors from the following:
   Secondary injector modules
   Positive battery cable at junction block
   Differential pressure switch vacuum and electrical connectors
   Air conditioning cutout relay
   Air conditioning high blower relay
   Transmission shift solenoid relay
   Fuel pump fuse
   Forward light link connector
   Positive battery lead
   Air conditioning blower resistor
   Air conditioning pressure sensors
   Air conditioning cooling fan switch
   Windshield washer pump
   Low coolant sensor
   Blower motor
   ESC knock sensor
   ESC knock sensor relay

39. Disconnect hoses from the vacuum pump, then tag and disconnect the front and rear vacuum connections.

40. Reposition engine harness aside and remove the braided ground strap from the left side frame rail.

41. Reposition the positive battery cable aside and remove the left side plenum panel screen.

42. Disconnect the brake booster vacuum hose.

43. Remove the windshield wiper motor from the vehicle.

44. Remove the MAP sensor and the MAP sensor bracket from the plenum.

45. Disconnect the AIR hose from the left exhaust manifold.

46. Using an engine lifting device, carefully remove the engine from the vehicle.

47. Transfer the following parts to the new engine, as necessary:
   Oil level indicator tube
   The exhaust manifolds
   The converter heat shields
   The wire pack heat shields
   Engine mounts

To install:

48. Install the engine mounts to the drivetrain and to the suspension frame, finger-tighten only at this time.

49. Position the engine into the vehicle using the lifting device.

50. Install the engine mount/bracket bolts, then remove the the lifting device and lifting brackets.

51. Connect the AIR hose to the left exhaust manifold.

52. Install the MAP sensor and bracket to the plenum.

53. Install the wiper motor.

54. Install the left side plenum panel screen.

55. Route the left side wiring harness into position, then install the braided ground strap to the frame rail.

56. Install the left side bulkhead block connector.

57. Engage the engine harness fusible links and relays.

58. Install the battery and hold-down clamp.

59. Connect the battery positive cable to the battery, then install the left front fender.

60. Install the ECM to the ECM bracket, then engage the wiring harness electrical connector.

61. Remove the front engine lift hook, then connect power brake booster vacuum hose to the plenum.

62. Connect the cruise control and throttle cables or the control cable to the throttle body. Adjust the cables or the ASR cable adjuster, as applicable.

63. Install the cable shield, then install cable retainers to the plenum.

64. Connect the power steering pressure line to the power steering gear.

65. Connect the engine oil cooler lines to the engine.

66. Install the accumulator bracket and then install the accumulator.

67. Connect the air conditioning lines.

68. Attach the vacuum line(s) to the power steering pump.

69. Connect the radiator upper and lower hoses.

70. Connect the air bleed hose to the plenum.

71. Install the bulkhead wire connector to the bulkhead.

72. Engage the evaporator housing panel resistor connector.

73. Install the hose onto the vacuum pump, then install the front and rear vacuum connections.

74. Engage the engine harness connectors to the following:
   Air conditioning blower resistor
   Air conditioning pressure sensor
   Air conditioning cooling fan
   Windshield washer pump
   Low coolant sensor
   Blower motor
   ESC knock sensor
   ESC knock sensor relay
   Differential pressure switch

75. Connect the fuel lines to the fuel rail.

76. Install the engine right side wiring harness under the dash.

77. Install the instrument panel right sound insulator panel.

78. Raise and support the vehicle safely, then tighten the engine/bracket bolts and nuts to 40 ft. lbs. (54 Nm).

79. Install the power steering hose to power steering oil cooler.

80. Install the oxygen sensor wire connectors.

81. Connect the AIR tube center section to the AIR hose and oil pan.

82. Connect the negative battery cable to the engine and suitably support the engine, then remove the rear engine lift hook.

83. Install the clutch cover and disc, then install the clutch housing to the cylinder block and install the housing cover.

84. Install the left side converter shield to the housing, then position the actuator cylinder and install the retaining nuts.

85. Install the transmission and support beam.

86. Install the driveshaft.

87. Install the complete exhaust system assembly.

88. Lower the vehicle and add the proper type and amount of engine oil.

89. Tighten the fuel filler cap and connect the negative battery cable.

90. Properly fill the engine cooling system and check for leaks.

91. Recharge the air conditioning system.

92. If equipped, reset the CHANGE OIL indicator:

   a. Turn the ignition **ON** but do not start the engine.

   b. Depress the ENG MET button on the trip monitor, then within 5 seconds, depress the button a 2nd time. Within another 5 seconds, depress and hold the GAUGES button.

   c. While holding the GAUGES button and watch the CHANGE OIL light, it should begin to flash. Continue to hold the gauges button until the flashing stops and the light goes out indicating that the indicator is reset.

d. If the indicator does not reset, turn the ignition **OFF** and restart the procedure.

Engine Mounts

REMOVAL AND INSTALLATION

5.7L (VIN P) Engine

1. Disconnect the negative battery cable.
2. Raise and support the vehicle safely.
3. Remove the engine mount nuts from both sides.
4. Disconnect the catalytic converters from the exhaust manifolds and reposition.

NOTE: When raising and supporting the engine, NEVER place a jack under the oil pan, crankshaft pulley or any sheetmetal. There is a minimal clearance between the oil pan and the pump screen. Jacking against the pan could cause sufficient deformation to damage the oil pickup unit.

5. Raise the engine with a lifting device, sufficiently for the mount studs to clear the crossmembers.
6. Remove the engine mount through-bolt and nut.
7. Remove the engine mounts, heat shield, and any spacers, if present.
8. Remove the engine bracket bolts and remove the bracket.
   To install:
9. Install the engine bracket and bolts. Tighten the bolts to 41 ft. lbs. (56 Nm).
10. Install the engine mounts, heat shield and spacers.
11. Install the engine mount through bolt and nut.
12. Lower the engine and remove the lifting device, then tighten the mount nuts to 40 ft. lbs. (54 Nm) and the through-bolt to 77 ft. lbs. (105 Nm).
13. Install the catalytic converters and nuts to the exhaust manifolds. Tighten the nuts to 15 ft. lbs. (21 Nm).
14. Lower the vehicle and connect the negative battery cable.

5.7L (VIN J) Engine

1. Disconnect the battery negative cable.
2. Remove the exhaust manifold.

3. Remove the nut attaching the engine mount to the drivetrain and suspension frame.
4. Support and raise the engine just sufficiently for engine mount removal clearance.
5. Remove the engine mount/bracket nut and bolt from the bracket.
6. Remove the engine mount and heat shield from the vehicle.
7. Remove the bolts attaching the bracket to the cylinder case, then remove the bracket from the vehicle.
   To install:
8. Install the engine mount bracket to the cylinder case and install the retaining bolts. Tighten the bolts to 38 ft. lbs. (52 Nm).
9. Install the engine mount and heat shield onto the vehicle using with the engine mount/bracket bolt and nut. Tighten the nut to 40 ft. lbs. (54 Nm).
10. Lower the engine into position and install the nut retaining the mount to the drivetrain and suspension frame. Tighten the nut to 40 ft. lbs. (54 Nm).
11. Install the exhaust manifold.
12. Connect the negative battery cable.

Cylinder Head

REMOVAL AND INSTALLATION

5.7L (VIN P) Engine

RIGHT SIDE

1. Disconnect the negative battery cable and properly relieve the fuel system pressure.
2. Raise and support the vehicle safely.
3. Disconnect the catalytic converter.
4. Drain the engine cooling system, then lower the vehicle.

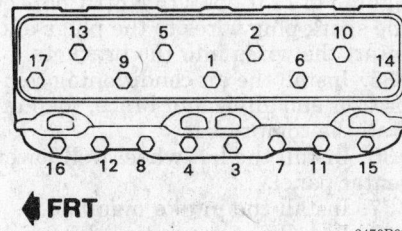

8470R029

Cylinder head bolt torque sequence — 5.7L (VIN P) engines

5. Remove the lower radiator and heater hoses from the water pump.
6. Disconnect the power steering pump reservoir from the cylinder head and reposition aside.
7. Remove the coil and bracket assembly.
8. Remove the intake manifold.
9. Remove the spark plug wires from the clips, then remove the front wire bracket.
10. Remove the oil level indicator tube.
11. Disconnect the spark plug wires from the plugs, then remove the spark plugs from the cylinder head.
12. Remove the right exhaust manifold.
13. Using a backup wrench on the pipe fitting, disconnect the coolant air bleed pipe from the left cylinder head.
14. Remove the right valve rocker cover, then remove the rocker arm and pushrod assemblies.
15. Remove the cylinder head bolts.
16. Remove the cylinder head along with the coolant air bleed pipe, then remove the head gasket.
17. If necessary, remove the coolant air bleed pipe from the cylinder head.
    To install:
18. Thoroughly clean the cylinder head and cylinder case mating surfaces. Make sure both surfaces are free of any foreign matter, nicks or scratches. The threads in both the bolts holes and on the bolts must be clean and free of old sealer.
19. If removed, install the coolant air bleed pipe to the cylinder head, finger-tight.
20. Position the new gasket in place on the cylinder case with the yellow tab facing up. Install the cylinder head over the dowel pins and gasket.
21. Coat the bolts with 1052080, or an equivalent sealant. Install and tighten the cylinder head bolts, using 3 passes of the proper sequence, to 65 ft. lbs. (88 Nm).
22. Install the rocker arm and pushrod assemblies.
23. Install the valve rocker cover and tighten the bolts to 75 inch lbs. (8 Nm) for 1992 vehicles or to 100 inch lbs. (11 Nm) for 1993–96 vehicles.
24. Connect the coolant air bleed pipe to the left cylinder head and torque the pipe to both cylinder heads. Using a backup wrench, tighten the coolant air bleed pipe to 30 ft. lbs. (41 Nm).
25. Install the right exhaust manifold.
26. Install the spark plugs and tighten to 11 ft. lbs. (15 Nm).

27. Connect the spark plug wires to the plugs, then install the oil level indicator tube.

28. Install the front wire bracket, then connect the spark plug wire harness assembly to the wire bracket.

29. Install the intake manifold.

30. Install the coil and bracket assembly.

31. Position and secure the power steering pump reservoir.

32. Install the lower radiator and heater hoses to the water pump.

33. Raise and support the vehicle safely.

34. Connect the catalytic converter, then lower the vehicle.

35. Properly fill the cooling system.

36. Tighten the fuel filler cap and connect the negative battery cable.

LEFT SIDE

1. Disconnect the negative battery cable and properly relieve the fuel system pressure.

2. Raise and support the vehicle safely.

3. Disconnect the catalytic converter.

4. Drain the engine cooling system, then lower the vehicle.

5. Remove the upper radiator hose.

6. Remove the serpentine drive belt.

7. Remove the intake manifold.

8. Remove the left wheel well lower center panel.

9. Disconnect the air conditioning compressor from the bracket and position aside. Use care not to kink or damage the refrigerant lines. Remove the compressor and alternator brace.

10. Remove the spark plug wire bracket, disconnect the wires from the spark plugs and remove the spark plugs from the cylinder head.

11. Remove the left exhaust manifold.

12. Remove the remaining alternator brace, then remove the alternator.

13. Disconnect the AIR diverter valve hose.

14. Remove the left valve rocker cover.

15. Remove the drive belt idler pulley, then remove the drive belt tensioner.

16. Disconnect the power steering lines from the pump, then remove the pump. Plug the openings to prevent system contamination or excessive fluid loss.

17. Remove the spark plug and coil wires from the distributor.

18. Remove the accessory mounting bracket.

19. Remove the rocker arm and pushrod assemblies.

20. Disconnect the coolant air bleed pipe from the cylinder head.

21. Remove the cylinder head bolts, then remove the cylinder head and gasket.

To install:

22. Thoroughly clean the cylinder head and cylinder case mating surfaces. Make sure both surfaces are free of any foreign matter, nicks or scratches. The threads in both the bolts holes and on the bolts must be clean and free of old sealer.

23. Position the new gasket in place on the cylinder case with the yellow tab facing up. Install the cylinder head over the dowel pins and gasket.

24. Coat the bolts with 1052080, or an equivalent sealant. Install and tighten the cylinder head bolts, using 3 passes of the proper sequence, to 65 ft. lbs. (88 Nm).

25. Connect the coolant air bleed pipe to the cylinder head and tighten to 30 ft. lbs. (41 Nm).

26. Install the rocker arm and pushrod assemblies.

27. Install the accessory mounting bracket and bolts. Tighten the bolts to 25 ft. lbs. (34 Nm) for 1992 vehicles or to 31 ft. lbs. (42 Nm) for 1993–96 vehicles.

28. Connect the spark plug and coil wires to the distributor.

29. Install the power steering pump, then remove the plugs from the openings and connect the lines.

30. Install the drive belt tensioner, then install the idler pulley. Tighten the tensioner and pulley bolts to 24 ft. lbs. (33 Nm).

31. Install the left valve rocker cover and bolts. Tighten the bolts to 75 inch lbs. (8 Nm) for 1992 vehicles or to 100 inch lbs. (11 Nm) for 1993–96 vehicles.

32. Connect the AIR diverter valve hose and install the alternator lower brace.

33. Install the left exhaust manifold.

34. Install the spark plugs and tighten to 11 ft. lbs. (15 Nm). Connect the spark plug wires to the plugs and insert the wires into the brackets.

35. Install the air conditioning compressor and alternator brace, then install the compressor.

36. Install the left wheel well lower center panel.

37. Install the intake manifold.

38. Install the serpentine drive belt and the upper radiator hose.

39. Raise and safely support the vehicle, then connect the catalytic converter and lower the vehicle.

40. Properly fill the engine cooling system.

41. Tighten the fuel filler cap and connect the negative battery cable.

42. Bleed the power steering system.

5.7L (VIN J) Engine

RIGHT SIDE

1. Disconnect the negative battery cable and properly relieve fuel system pressure.

2. Drain engine coolant into a suitable container.

3. Remove the intake plenum assembly.

4. Remove the right injector housing.

5. Remove the right bank valve lifters.

6. Remove the alternator assembly.

7. Disconnect the right exhaust manifold from the cylinder head. It is not necessary to completely remove the exhaust manifold from the vehicle for cylinder head removal.

8. If raised, lower the vehicle for underhood access.

9. Remove the vacuum hose from secondary port throttle valve actuator.

10. Remove the access plug from the right cylinder head.

11. Remove the top bolt attaching the right secondary timing chain fixed guide.

12. Remove cylinder head bolts, then remove the cylinder head and gasket from the vehicle.

To install:

13. Thoroughly clean the cylinder head and cylinder case mating surfaces. Make sure both surfaces are free of any foreign matter, nicks or scratches. The threads in both the bolts holes and on the bolts must be clean and free of old sealer.

NOTE: Cylinder head gaskets are not interchangeable between cylinder banks.

14. Install the cylinder head locating dowels into block, if loosened or removed, then position the new gasket in place on the cylinder case.

15. Install the cylinder head over the dowels. Coat bolt threads and washers with clean engine oil and insert.

16. Tighten the cylinder head bolts in sequence as follows:

   1st pass—45 ft. lbs. (60 Nm)
   2nd pass—74 ft. lbs. (100 Nm)
   3rd pass—118 ft. lbs. (160 Nm)

17. Apply Loctite® 262 to the fixed guide top bolt threads, install the bolt and tighten to 19 ft. lbs. (26 Nm).

18. Install the access plug into the cylinder head and torque to 15 ft. lbs. (20 Nm).

19. Connect the vacuum hose to the actuator.

20. Raise and support vehicle, drain the engine oil.

21. Install the exhaust manifold.

22. If still supported, lower the vehicle for underhood access.

23. Install the alternator.

24. Install valve lifters.

25. Install the right injector housing assembly.

26. Install the plenum assembly.

27. Fill the engine crankcase with the proper type and amount of engine oil.

28. Tighten the fuel filler cap and properly refill the cooling system.

29. Connect the negative battery cable.

30. If equipped, reset the CHANGE OIL indicator:

a. Turn the ignition **ON** but do not start the engine.

b. Depress the ENG MET button on the trip monitor, then within 5 seconds, depress the button a 2nd time. Within another 5 seconds, depress and hold the GAUGES button.

c. While holding the GAUGES button and watch the CHANGE OIL light, it should begin to flash. Continue to hold the gauges button until the flashing stops and the light goes out indicating that the indicator is reset.

d. If the indicator does not reset, turn the ignition **OFF** and restart the procedure.

LEFT SIDE

1. Disconnect the negative battery cable and properly relieve fuel system pressure.

2. Drain engine coolant into a suitable container.

3. Remove the intake plenum assembly.

4. Remove the left injector housing.

5. Remove the vacuum hose from the secondary port throttle valve actuator.

6. Remove the power brake booster assembly.

7. Remove the left bank valve lifters.

8. Remove the AIR control valve hoses, then disengage the electrical connector.

9. Remove the camshaft position sensor.

10. Disconnect the left exhaust manifold from the cylinder head. It is not necessary to completely remove

the exhaust manifold from the vehicle for cylinder head removal.

11. Remove the access plug from the left cylinder head.

12. Remove the bolt attaching the left secondary timing chain guide.

13. Remove the cylinder head bolts. Remove the cylinder head and gasket from the vehicle.

To install:

14. Thoroughly clean the cylinder head and cylinder case mating surfaces. Make sure both surfaces are free of any foreign matter, nicks or scratches. The threads in both the bolts holes and on the bolts must be clean and free of old sealer.

NOTE: Cylinder head gaskets are not interchangeable between cylinder banks.

15. Install the cylinder head locating dowels into block, if loosened or removed, then position the new gasket in place on the cylinder case.

16. Install the cylinder head over the dowels. Coat bolt threads and washers with clean engine oil and insert.

17. Tighten the cylinder head bolts in sequence as follows:

1st pass—45 ft. lbs. (60 Nm)
2nd pass—74 ft. lbs. (100 Nm)
3rd pass—118 ft. lbs. (160 Nm)

18. Apply Loctite® 262 to the fixed guide bolt threads, install the bolt and tighten to 19 ft. lbs. (26 Nm).

19. Install the access plug into the cylinder head and torque to 15 ft. lbs. (20 Nm).

20. Connect the vacuum hose to the actuator.

21. Raise and support vehicle, drain the engine oil and lower the vehicle.

22. Install the exhaust manifold.

23. Install the camshaft position sensor.

24. Connect the AIR control valve hoses and electrical connector.

25. Install the valve lifters.

26. Install the left injector housing assembly.

27. Install the plenum assembly.

28. Fill the engine crankcase with the proper type and amount of engine oil.

29. Tighten the fuel filler cap and properly refill the cooling system.

30. Connect the negative battery cable.

31. If equipped, reset the CHANGE OIL indicator:

a. Turn the ignition **ON** but do not start the engine.

b. Depress the ENG MET button on the trip monitor, then within 5 seconds, depress the button a 2nd time. Within another 5 seconds, de-

press and hold the GAUGES button.

c. While holding the GAUGES button and watch the CHANGE OIL light, it should begin to flash. Continue to hold the gauges button until the flashing stops and the light goes out indicating that the indicator is reset.

d. If the indicator does not reset, turn the ignition **OFF** and restart the procedure.

Valve Lifters

REMOVAL AND INSTALLATION

5.7L (VIN P) Engines

1. Disconnect the negative battery cable and properly relieve fuel system pressure.

2. Drain the engine cooling system into a suitable container.

3. Remove the intake manifold assembly.

4. Remove the valve rocker covers.

5. Remove the rocker arms and pushrod assemblies. Be sure to tag or arrange all parts in order to assure installation in their original locations.

6. Remove the valve lifter guide (restrictor) retainer bolts, then remove the retainer.

7. Remove the valve lifter guide (restrictor) and valve lifter assemblies. If necessary a valve lifter tool should be used to remove lifters which are stuck in their bores.

8. If lifters are to be reused, place the lifters in a rack so they may be installed in their original bores.

To install:

9. Coat the lifter rollers with 1052365 or equivalent prelube, and install the lifters to the bores. If old lifters are being reused, make sure they are installed into the same bores from which they were removed.

10. Install the valve lifter guides (restrictors), retainer and bolts. Tighten the bolts to 15 ft. lbs. (20 Nm).

11. Install the rocker arm and pushrod assemblies.

12. Install the valve rocker covers.

13. Install the intake manifold.

14. Tighten the fuel filler cap and connect the negative battery cable.

15. Properly fill the engine cooling system.

5.7L (VIN J) Engine

1. Disconnect the negative battery cable.

2. Remove the camshaft covers.

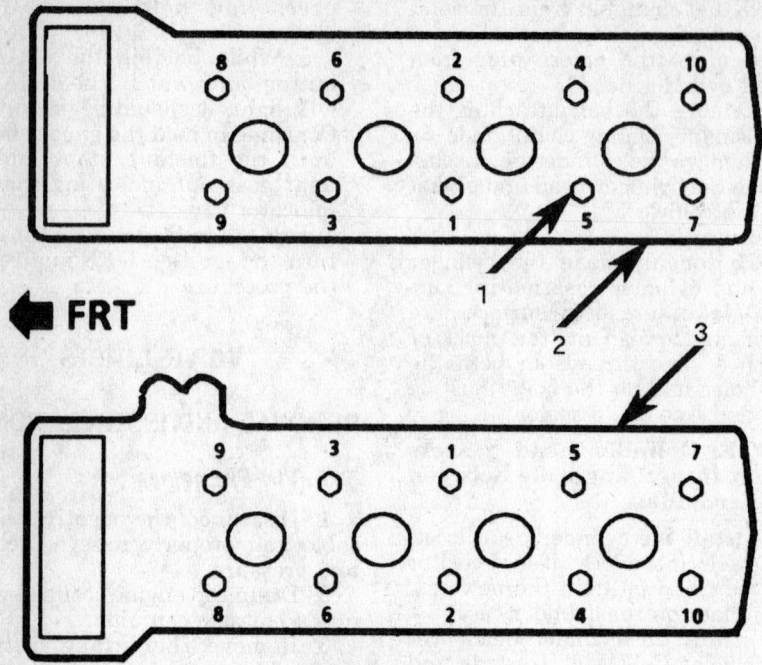

1. Cylinder head bolt
2. Cylinder head RH
3. Cylinder head LH

8470R030

Cylinder head torque sequence — 5.7L (VIN J) engine

3. Remove the camshafts.
4. Remove lifters from bores.

NOTE: If lifters are to be re-used, be sure to retain them in proper order so each lifter can be reinstalled in its original bore.

5. Installation is the reverse of the removal procedure. Lubricate lifter bores with clean engine oil.
6. Lifters should be replaced as sets with a camshaft. If new lifters are being used, be sure to pre-oil them.

Valve Lash

ADJUSTMENT

5.7L (VIN P) Engine

The valve lash on the VIN P engine is adjusted whenever the rocker arm assemblies have been removed.

NOTE: The 5.7L (VIN P) engine utilize hydraulic lifters which normally require very little maintenance or adjustment. These components are simple in design and are best maintained through regular, scheduled engine oil changes. If the engine is running well and no audible

clicking sounds are heard from the valve train, there is no need to remove or disassemble the valve lifters.

1. Disconnect the negative battery cable.
2. Remove the valve rocker covers.
3. Tighten the nuts slowly until all lash is eliminated.
4. Adjust the valves when the lifter is on the base circle of the camshaft lobe. Slowly turn or crank the engine until the mark on the vibration damper is in the 12 o'clock position (aligned with the timing cover mark, if equipped) and the engine is in the No. 1 firing position.

NOTE: The No. 1 firing position may be determined by watching the No. 1 cylinder valves as the mark on the damper approaches the 12 o'clock position. If both the intake and exhaust valves are closed as the mark comes up to the timing tab, the engine is in the No. 1 firing position. If either valve opens as the timing mark approaches the top of it's travel, the engine is in No. 6 firing position and should be turned over 1 full revolution in order to reach the No. 1 firing position.

5. With the engine in the No. 1 firing position, adjust the following valves:
- Exhaust — 1, 3, 4, 8
- Intake — 1, 2, 5, 7
6. Back out the rocker arm adjusting nut until lash is felt at the pushrod, then turn the adjusting nut inward until all lash is removed. This can be determined by rotating pushrod while turning the adjusting nut. When play has been removed, the pushrod will not turn. Then, tighten the adjusting nut 1 full additional turn.
7. Slowly turn or crank the engine 1 revolution until the vibration damper mark is at 12 o'clock again and the No. 1 cylinder valves open. This is the No. 6 firing position.
8. With the engine in this position, adjust the following valves:
- Exhaust — 2, 5, 6, 7
- Intake — 3, 4, 6, 8
9. Install the valve rocker arm covers.
10. Connect the battery negative cable.

5.7L (VIN J) Engine

This engine is equipped with hydraulic lifters which are installed in bores directly below the camshaft lobes. The lifters maintain 0 lash between the camshaft lobes and the valve stem. The lifter and installation position is non-adjustable, therefore upon failure, the lifter assembly must be replaced.

Rocker Arms

REMOVAL AND INSTALLATION

5.7L (VIN P) Engine

1. Disconnect the negative battery cable.
2. Remove the right valve rocker cover as follows:
   a. Remove the fuel rail cover and the fuel rail bolts.
   b. Disconnect the fuel pressure regulator vacuum hose.
   c. Remove the fuel injector and rail assembly from the manifold and reposition.
   d. Remove the fuel rail cover studs and position the wiring harness aside.
   e. Remove the AIR pipe and check valve from the intake and exhaust manifolds.
   f. Disconnect the crankcase vent hose.

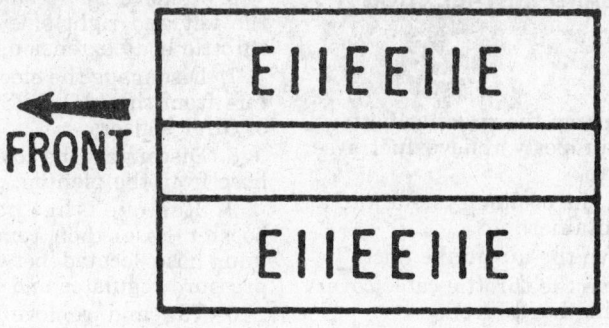

```
E I I E E I I E

E I I E E I I E
```

FRONT ←

8470R033

Valve arrangement — 5.7L (VIN P) engine

g. Remove the valve rocker cover bolts, cover and gasket. Replace the gasket as necessary.

3. Remove the left rocker arm cover as follows:

a. If not done already, remove the fuel rail cover.

b. Remove the alternator brace bolts, then remove the brace.

c. Remove the remaining alternator bolts and position the alternator aside.

d. Disconnect the AIR diverter valve hose from the check valve.

e. Position the wiring harness aside.

f. Remove the valve rocker cover bolts, cover and gasket. Replace the gasket as necessary.

4. Remove the rocker arm nuts, rocker arm balls, rocker arms and pushrods. If the valve train components are to be reused, mark or arrange the assemblies in a rack to assure installation in their original locations.

To install:

5. Coat the bearing surfaces of the rocker arms and rocker arm balls with 1052365 or equivalent pre-lube, prior to installation.

6. Install the pushrods making certain they seat in the lifter sockets.

7. Install the rocker arms, rocker arm balls and rocker arm nuts in their original positions.

8. Tighten the rocker arm nuts until all lash is eliminated.

9. Adjust the valve lash.

10. Thoroughly clean the gasket mating surfaces and install the valve rocker arm covers in the reverse order of removal. Tighten the valve rocker cover bolts to 75 inch lbs. (8 Nm) for 1992 vehicles or to 100 inch lbs. (11 Nm) for 1993–96 vehicles. For the right valve cover, be sure to tighten the AIR pipe-to-exhaust manifold fitting to 25 ft. lbs. (34 Nm).

11. Connect the battery negative cable, start the engine and inspect for leaks.

5.7L (VIN J) Engine

This engine utilizes an overhead cam design, thus eliminating the need for any rocker arm assembly. This design improves and smoothes engine operation.

Intake Manifold

REMOVAL AND INSTALLATION

5.7L (VIN P) Engine

1. Disconnect the negative battery cable.

2. Drain engine coolant into a suitable container.

3. Remove the throttle body air duct.

4. Remove the fuel rail covers.

5. Disengage the wiring harness connectors from the fuel injectors. Disengage and reposition the left and right wiring harnesses.

6. Remove the accelerator cable bracket, then disconnect the cables from the throttle body.

7. Disconnect the AIR diverter valve hoses.

8. Remove the electrical ground strap from the intake manifold.

9. Remove the fuel rail bolts and disconnect the vacuum hose from the fuel pressure regulator.

10. Carefully remove the fuel rail and injector assembly from the manifold and position aside. Be careful not to damage the fuel lines.

11. Disconnect the vacuum and crankcase vent hoses.

12. Remove the EGR solenoid assembly and the fuel EVAP canister solenoid assembly.

13. Remove the EGR valve.

14. Remove the AIR pipe from the intake and the right exhaust manifold.

15. Remove the alternator brace.

16. Disconnect the coolant hoses from the throttle body.

17. Remove the throttle body bolts, the throttle body and gasket.

18. Remove the intake manifold bolts and studs.

19. Remove the intake manifold and gaskets.

To install:

20. Thoroughly clean the intake manifold bolts and studs. Inspect and clean all gasket mating surfaces.

21. Apply a ³/₁₆ in. (5mm) bead of RTV sealer to the front and rear of the cylinder block. Extend the bead ½ inch (13mm) up each cylinder head to seal and retain the gaskets.

22. Position the new gaskets and install the intake manifold.

23. Install the manifold bolts and studs, then tighten using 2 passes of the proper sequence. First, tighten the bolts/studs to 71 inch lbs. (8 Nm), then tighten them to 35 ft. lbs. (48 Nm).

24. Install the throttle body, gasket and retaining bolts. Tighten the throttle body bolts to 19 ft. lbs. (26 Nm).

25. Connect the coolant hoses to the throttle body.

26. Install the alternator brace.

27. Install the accelerator cables and bracket. Tighten the bracket bolts to 90 inch lbs. (10 Nm).

28. Install the AIR pipe. Tighten the exhaust manifold fitting and the bracket-to-cylinder head bolt to 25 ft. lbs. (34 Nm) and tighten the flange-to-intake manifold bolts to 19 ft. lbs. (26 Nm).

29. Install the EGR valve, then EGR solenoid and bracket. Tighten valve bolts to 16 ft. lbs. (22 Nm) and the solenoid bracket nut to 25 ft. lbs. (34 Nm).

30. Install the fuel EVAP canister purge solenoid and bracket, then tighten the nut to 25 ft. lbs. (34 Nm) for 1992 vehicles or to 15 ft. lbs. (20 Nm) for 1993–96 vehicles.

31. Connect the vacuum and crankcase vent hoses.

32. Install the fuel injector and fuel rail assembly to the intake manifold, connect the fuel pressure regulator vacuum hose and install the fuel rail bolts. Tighten the bolts to 15 ft. lbs. (20 Nm).

33. Connect the electrical ground strap to the intake manifold.

34. Connect the AIR diverter valve hoses.

35. Position the left and right wiring harnesses, then engage the fuel injector electrical connectors.

36. Install the throttle body air duct.

37. Install the fuel rail covers.

38. Properly fill the engine cooling system.

39. Connect the negative battery cable, then adjust the ASR accelerator and cruise control cables, as necessary.

Intake Plenum Assembly

The 5.7L (VIN J) engine does not utilize an intake manifold assembly like the other 5.7L Corvette engines. Instead it uses an intake plenum mated to a right and left fuel injector housing.

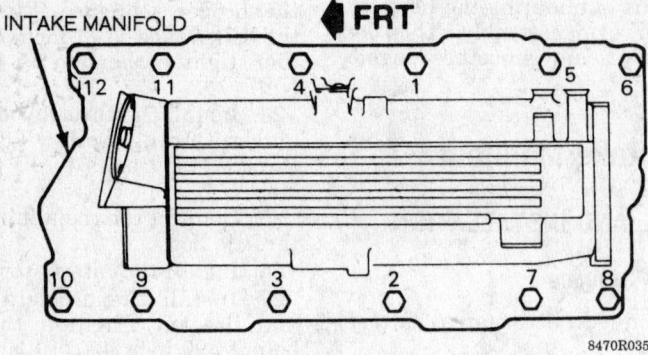

Intake manifold bolt torque sequence — 5.7L (VIN P) engine

1. Sealer
2. Intake manifold
3. Bolt
4. Stud
5. Gasket

REMOVAL AND INSTALLATION

1. Disconnect the negative battery cable and properly relieve fuel system pressure.

2. Drain the cooling system into a suitable container.

3. Remove the air intake duct.

4. Remove the throttle cable cover and attaching hardware.

5. Remove the throttle and cruise control cables or the ASR control cable from the throttle body. Remove the cable hold-down clamp(s) and set the cables aside.

6. Remove the fresh air hose from the left and right side of the of the throttle body extension.

7. Disengage the electrical connectors from the IAC, TPS and the IAT or MAT sensors.

8. Disconnect the coolant air bleed hose from the plenum.

9. Remove the power brake booster hose, then remove the vacuum hose located between the fuel pressure regulator and the plenum.

10. Tag and remove the left and right vacuum hoses at the mid-plenum.

11. Tag and remove the MAP sensor vacuum hose.

12. Disconnect the fuel lines from the fuel rail assembly and discard the O-rings.

13. Remove the plenum assembly attaching bolts.

14. Remove the EVAP purge solenoid/PCV dual hose fitting from the plenum.

15. Remove the EVAP purge canister hose from the plenum.

16. For 1993–96 vehicles, remove the upper EGR pipe bolts, then remove the pipe.

17. Lift the plenum and disengage the ignition module electrical connections, then remove the plenum assembly and discard the gaskets.

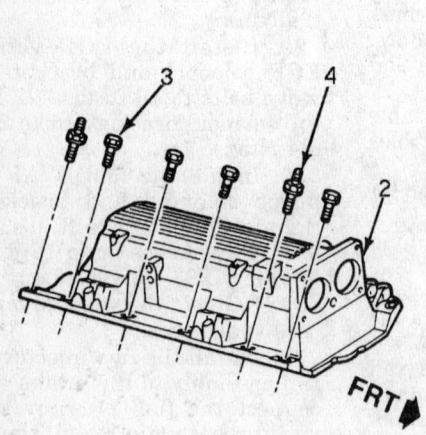

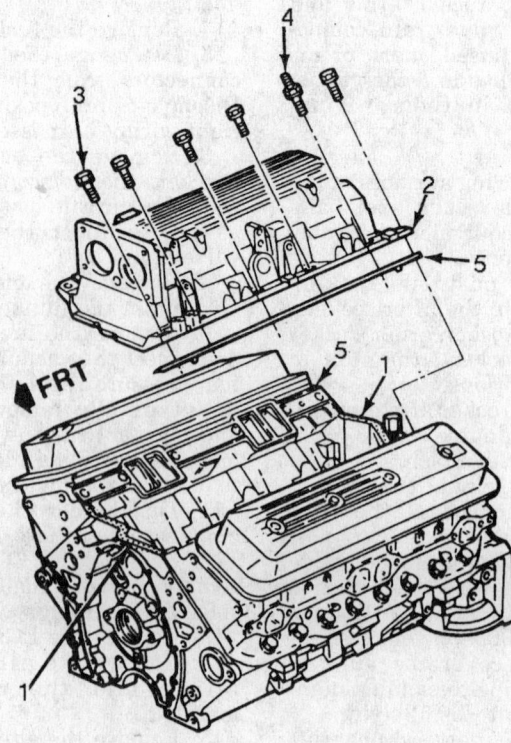

Intake manifold installation — 5.7L (VIN P) engine

18. Cover the intake ports to prevent dirt or other contaminants from entering.

To install:

19. If the plenum is being replaced, transfer the MAP sensor and bracket, the throttle body, the throttle body extension and the ignition module to the new plenum.

20. Remove the tape or other cover from the intake ports and position the plenum assembly on the injector housings with the MAP sensor over the fuel pressure regulator. Engage the electrical connectors to the ignition module and MAP sensor, then install the MAP sensor vacuum hose.

21. Make sure the remaining vacuum hoses and electrical connectors are accessible, then position the new plenum gaskets between the plenum and injector housing, Install the plenum attaching bolts and tighten the bolts in their proper torque sequence to 20 ft. lbs. (26 Nm).

22. Install the vacuum hoses to mid-plenum.

23. Install new O-rings, then reconnect the fuel lines to the fuel rail assembly. Tighten the fuel line fittings to 20 ft. lbs. (26 Nm).

24. Install the vacuum hose between the pressure regulator and the plenum.

25. Connect the power brake booster vacuum hose to the plenum.

26. Install the fresh air hose onto the left and right side of the throttle body extension.

27. Install the EVAP purge solenoid/PCV hose fitting to the plenum, then install the EVAP canister connection to the rear right side.

28. Engage the wiring harness connectors to the TPS, IAC and IAT or MAT sensors.

29. Install the screws retaining the cable hold-down clamps to the plenum and tighten to 18 inch lbs. (2 Nm).

30. Install the coolant air bleed hose to the plenum.

31. Connect the throttle and cruise control cables or the ASR control cable to the throttle. Make sure the cables do not hold the throttle open and adjust, as necessary.

32. Install the cable shield, screw and nuts to the throttle body.

33. For 1993–96 vehicles, connect the upper EGR pipe. Tighten the screw and nuts to 27 inch lbs. (3 Nm), then tighten the EGR pipe bolts to 89 inch lbs. (10 Nm).

34. Install the air intake duct, tighten the fuel filler cap and connect the negative battery terminal.

35. Properly refill the engine cooling system, then start the engine and check for leaks.

Injector Housing Assembly

The 5.7L (VIN J) engine does not utilize an intake manifold assembly like the other 5.7L Corvette engines. Instead it uses an intake plenum mated to a right and left fuel injector housing.

REMOVAL AND INSTALLATION

Right Side

1. Disconnect the negative battery cable and properly relieve fuel system pressure.

2. Drain the cooling system into a suitable container.

3. Remove the intake plenum assembly.

4. Disengage the electrical connectors from the fuel injectors.

5. Remove the bolts attaching the fuel rail assembly to the injector housing.

6. Remove the injectors from the housing and remove the fuel rail assembly from the vehicle.

7. Disconnect the hose from the right coolant outlet pipe.

8. Remove the oil pressure sensor from the oil filter housing.

9. Remove the bolt attaching the coolant outlet pipe to the injector housing. Remove the outlet pipe and gasket from the vehicle.

10. Remove the PCV grommet from the injector housing.

11. Remove the clamp and ventilation hose from the injector housing.

12. Remove the bolt attaching the alternator rear support bracket to the alternator.

13. Remove the screws attaching the alternator rear support bracket and right side ventilation pipe to the injector housing.

14. Remove the ventilation pipe and bracket from the vehicle.

15. Remove the injector housing attaching bolts, then remove the injector housing and gasket from the vehicle.

To install:

16. Thoroughly clean all gasket mating surfaces and position the a new housing gasket.

17. Install the injector housing, rear alternator bracket, right ventilation pipe and the housing bolts. Be sure the spark plug wire harness retainer is secured to the injector housing rear bolt and tighten the fasteners to 19 ft. lbs. (26 Nm).

18. Install the ventilation hose.

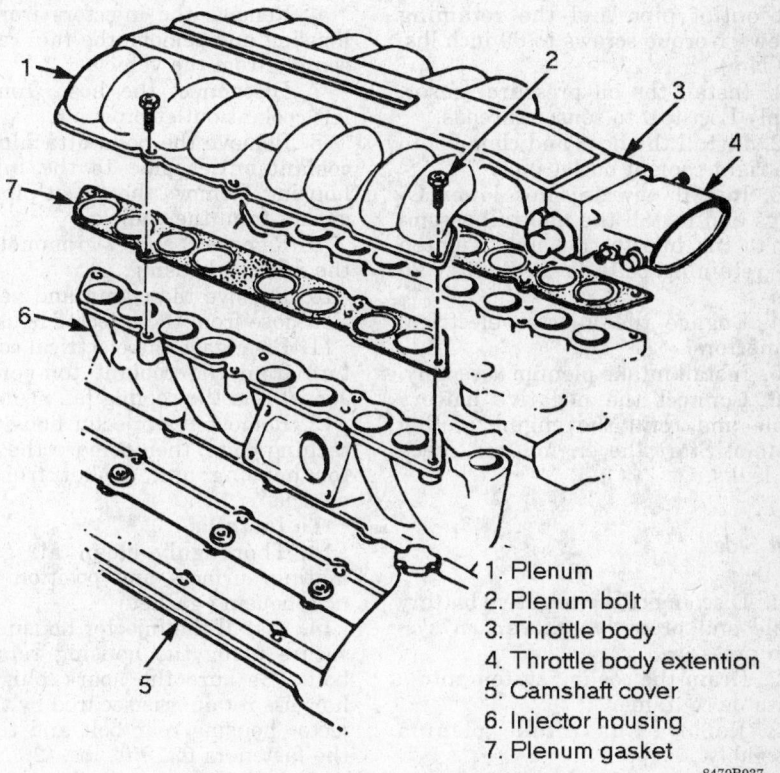

1. Plenum
2. Plenum bolt
3. Throttle body
4. Throttle body extention
5. Camshaft cover
6. Injector housing
7. Plenum gasket

8470R037

Intake plenum installation — 5.7L (VIN J) engine

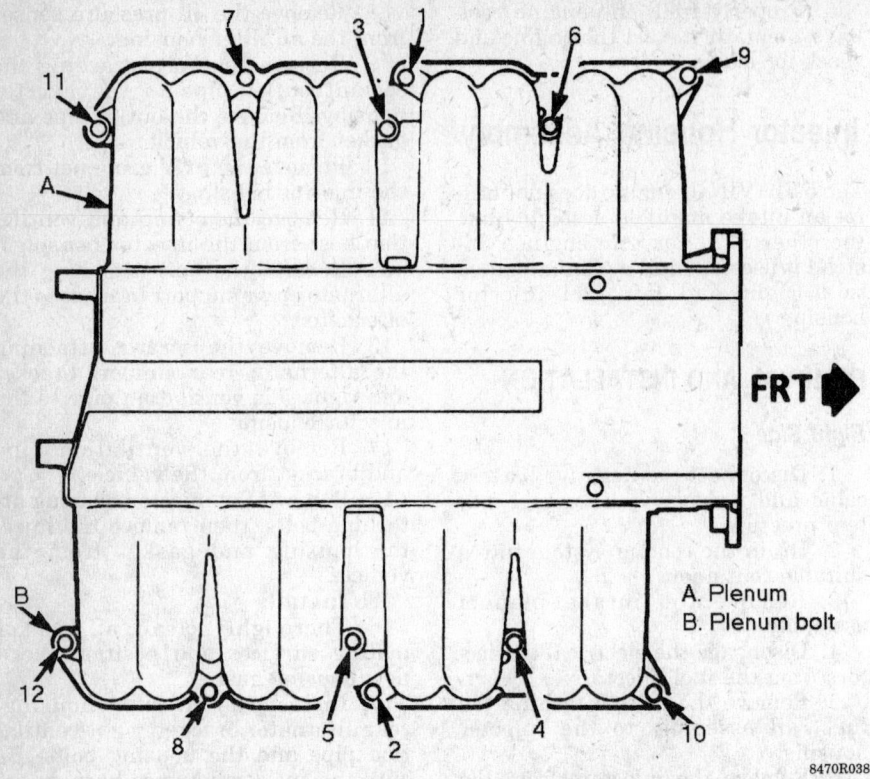

Intake plenum bolt torque sequence — 5.7L (VIN J) engine

8470R038

A. Plenum
B. Plenum bolt

FRT ▶

16. Install PCV grommet into the injector housing.

17. Engage the electrical connectors to the coolant temperature sensor and the cooling fan switch.

18. Install a new gasket, the coolant outlet pipe and the retaining screws. Torque screws to 89 inch lbs. (10 Nm).

19. Install the hose and clamp onto the left coolant outlet pipe.

20. Install new injector lower O-rings and install the fuel rail assembly to the injector housing. Tighten the retaining bolts to 19 ft. lbs. (26 Nm).

21. Engage the injector electrical connectors.

22. Install intake plenum assembly.

23. Connect the negative battery cable and refill the engine cooling system. Start the engine and check for leaks.

Exhaust Manifold

REMOVAL AND INSTALLATION

5.7L (VIN P) Engine

RIGHT SIDE

1. Disconnect the negative battery cable.

2. Raise and support the vehicle safely.

3. For convertibles, if necessary for access, remove the underbody crossbrace.

4. Remove the nuts and disconnect the catalytic converter from the exhaust manifold. For 1993–96 vehicles, it may be necessary to loosen and remove the entire exhaust assembly.

5. Lower the vehicle.

6. Remove the fuel rail covers and disengage the fuel injector electrical connectors.

7. Remove the vacuum hose from the fuel pressure regulator.

8. Remove the fuel rail bolts, then remove the fuel injector/rail assembly from the intake manifold and position aside. Be careful not to damage the fuel lines.

9. Disconnect the spark plug wires from the plugs, then disconnect the wire clips from the supports. If necessary for clearance, or to prevent the possibility of breakage during manifold removal, remove the spark plugs.

10. Remove the front spark plug bracket and bolt.

11. Remove the oil level indicator and guide tube.

12. Remove the AIR pipe, gasket and check valve as an assembly from

19. Install PCV grommet into the injector housing.

20. Install a new gasket, the coolant outlet pipe and the retaining screws. Torque screws to 89 inch lbs. (10 Nm).

21. Install the oil pressure sensor. Apply Loctite® to sensor threads.

22. Install the hose and clamp onto the right coolant outlet pipe.

23. Install new injector lower O-rings and install the fuel rail assembly to the injector housing. Tighten the retaining bolts to 19 ft. lbs. (26 Nm).

24. Engage the injector electrical connectors.

25. Install intake plenum assembly.

26. Connect the negative battery cable and refill the engine cooling system. Start the engine and check for leaks.

Left Side

1. Disconnect the negative battery cable and properly relieve fuel system pressure.

2. Drain the cooling system into a suitable container.

3. Remove the intake plenum assembly.

4. Disengage the electrical connectors from the fuel injectors.

5. Remove the screws attaching the fuel rail assembly to the injector housing.

6. Remove the injectors from the housing and remove the fuel rail assembly from the vehicle.

7. Disconnect the hose from the left coolant outlet pipe.

8. Remove the bolts attaching the coolant outlet pipe to the injector housing. Remove the outlet pipe and gasket from the vehicle.

9. Remove the PCV grommet from the injector housing.

10. Remove the clamp and ventilation hose from the injector housing.

11. Disengage the electrical connectors from the coolant temperature sensor and the cooling fan switch.

12. Remove the injector housing attaching bolts, then remove the injector housing and gasket from the vehicle.

To install:

13. Thoroughly clean all gasket mating surfaces and position the a new housing gasket.

14. Install the injector housing and secure using the housing retaining bolts. Be sure the spark plug wire harness retainer is secured by the injector housing rear bolt and tighten the fasteners to 19 ft. lbs. (26 Nm).

15. Install the ventilation hose and clamp.

the intake manifold, exhaust manifolds and the cylinder head.

13. Remove the exhaust manifold studs and bolts.

14. Remove the heat shields, exhaust manifold and gasket.

To install:

15. Thoroughly clean the manifold and cylinder head gasket mating surfaces.

16. Install the exhaust manifold gasket, manifold and heat shields.

17. Install the exhaust manifold studs and bolts. Tighten the fasteners to 26 ft. lbs. (35 Nm).

18. Install the AIR pipe, gasket and check valve assembly with the retaining bolts. Tighten the AIR pipe-to-exhaust manifold fitting and the bracket bolt to 25 ft. lbs. (34 Nm) and tighten the pipe flange bolts to 19 ft. lbs. (26 Nm).

19. Apply 1052080 or equivalent, sealer to the oil level indicator guide tube ½ inch (13mm) below the bead. Install the level indicator and guide tube into the block.

20. Install the front spark plug bracket and bolt. Tighten to 108 inch lbs. (12 Nm).

21. If removed, install the spark plugs and tighten to 11 ft. lbs. (15 Nm).

22. Install the spark plug wires and clips.

23. Install the fuel injectors and fuel rail assembly to the intake manifold. Tighten the fuel rail bolts to 15 ft. lbs. (20 Nm).

24. Connect the fuel pressure regulator vacuum hose.

25. Engage the wiring harness connectors to the fuel injectors.

26. Install the fuel rail covers.

27. Raise and support the vehicle safely.

28. If removed, install the exhaust assembly.

29. Connect the catalytic converter and nuts to the exhaust manifold.

30. Tighten catalytic converter nuts to 15 ft. lbs. (21 Nm).

31. If removed on a convertible, install the the underbody crossbrace.

32. Lower the vehicle.

33. Connect the negative battery cable.

LEFT SIDE

1. Disconnect the negative battery cable.

2. Raise and support the vehicle safely.

3. For convertibles, if necessary for access, remove the underbody crossbrace.

4. Remove the nuts and disconnect the catalytic converter from the exhaust manifold. For 1993–96 vehi-

cles, it may be necessary to loosen and remove the entire exhaust assembly.

5. Lower the vehicle.

6. Remove the air intake duct and the serpentine drive belt.

7. For 1993–96 vehicles, remove the ASR adjuster assembly from the wheel well center panel and reposition out of the way.

8. For 1992 vehicles, remove the left wheel well center panel.

9. Remove the mounting bolts and reposition the alternator and the A/C compressor.

10. Remove the AIR pipe, check valve and hose as an assembly from the exhaust manifold.

11. Remove the spark plug wires from the plugs and the clips from the supports, then position the wires aside.

12. For 1992 vehicles, remove the accessory braces.

13. Remove the spark plug wire supports. If necessary for clearance, or to prevent the possibility of breakage during manifold removal, remove the spark plugs.

14. Remove the exhaust manifold studs and bolts.

15. Remove the heat shields, exhaust manifold and gasket.

To install:

16. Thoroughly clean the manifold and cylinder head gasket mating surfaces.

17. Install the exhaust manifold gasket, manifold and heat shields.

18. Install the exhaust manifold studs and bolts. Tighten the fasteners to 26 ft. lbs. (35 Nm).

19. Install the spark plug wire supports and tighten to 108 inch lbs. (12 Nm).

20. If removed, install the spark plugs and tighten to 11 ft. lbs. (15 Nm).

21. For 1992 vehicles, install the accessory braces to the manifold.

22. Connect the spark plug wires and clips.

23. Install the AIR pipe, check valve and hose assembly. Tighten the AIR pipe-to-exhaust manifold fitting and the bracket bolt to 25 ft. lbs. (34 Nm).

24. Reposition and the install the air conditioning compressor and alternator.

25. For 1992 vehicles, install the left wheel well center panel.

26. Install the serpentine drive belt and the air intake duct.

27. For 1993–96 vehicles, install the ASR adjuster assembly, then check and adjust the control cable, as necessary.

28. Raise and support the vehicle safely.

29. If removed, install the exhaust assembly.

30. Connect the catalytic converter and nuts to the exhaust manifold.

31. Tighten catalytic converter nuts to 15 ft. lbs. (21 Nm).

32. If removed on a convertible, install the the underbody crossbrace.

33. Lower the vehicle.

34. Connect the negative battery cable.

5.7L (VIN J) Engine

Until mid-1992, the Corvette ZR-1 engine (VIN J) was equipped with an exhaust manifold/catalytic converter assembly. During the 1992 model year, a 2 piece unit was introduced into production cars so the catalytic converter could be separated from the manifold.

RIGHT SIDE

1. Disconnect the negative battery cable, then raise and support the vehicle safely.

2. Remove the right tire and wheel assembly, then remove the wheel house lower rear and center panels.

3. For vehicles up until early 1992, remove the center stud nut.

4. For late 1992 and later vehicles, remove the manifold outer heat shields.

5. Disconnect the exhaust system assembly from the catalytic converter.

6. If equipped, remove the engine block heat shield.

7. For late 1992 and later vehicles, disconnect the catalytic converter from the manifold.

8. Disengage the oxygen sensor wiring harness connector.

9. For early 1992 vehicles, or as applicable, disconnect the AIR hose from the manifold and remove the catalytic converter heat shields.

10. Remove the rear exhaust manifold bolts, spacers and nut.

11. For 1993–96 vehicles, disconnect the lower EGR pipe from the manifold.

12. Lower the vehicle.

13. Disconnect the AIR check valve and hose from the manifold.

14. Remove the retaining bolt, then remove the oil level indicator and guide tube from the vehicle.

15. Remove the remaining exhaust manifold attaching bolts and spacers.

16. Remove the exhaust manifold and gasket from the vehicle. If the manifold is being replaced, transfer the oxygen sensor and heat shields to the new manifold, as necessary.

To install:

17. Thoroughly clean the manifold and cylinder head gasket mating surfaces.

18. Install the gasket and manifold to the engine using the front and center manifold bolts and spacers.

19. Install the oil level indicator and guide tube, then tighten the manifold bolts to 18 ft. lbs. (24 Nm).

20. Install the AIR check valve and hose.

21. Raise and support the vehicle safely.

22. Install the rear manifold bolts, spacers and nut. Tighten the bolts and nut to 18 ft. lbs. (24 Nm).

23. For early 1992 vehicles, or as applicable, install the catalytic converter heat shields and connect the AIR hose to the manifold.

24. Install the wiring harness connector to the oxygen sensor.

25. For late 1992 and later vehicles, connect the catalytic converter and bolts to the manifold. Tighten the bolts to 17 ft. lbs. (23 Nm).

26. If equipped, install the engine block heat shield.

27. Connect the exhaust system assembly.

28. For late 1992 and later vehicles, install the manifold outer heat shields.

29. For 1993–96 vehicles, install the lower EGR pipe to the manifold.

30. Lower the vehicle sufficiently for access.

31. For vehicles up until early 1992, install the center stud nut and tighten to 18 ft. lbs. (24 Nm) for 1992 vehicles.

32. Install the wheelhouse lower rear and center panels.

33. Install the tire and wheel assembly, then lower the vehicle completely.

34. Connect the negative battery cable.

LEFT SIDE

1. Disconnect the negative battery cable, then raise and support the vehicle safely.

2. Remove the right tire and wheel assembly, then remove the wheel house lower rear and center panels.

3. Disconnect the exhaust assembly from the catalytic converter.

4. Remove the left floor pan heat shield, the left heat shield from the frame and the engine block heat shield.

5. Disengage the converter oxygen sensor electrical connector.

6. Disconnect the AIR check valves, hoses and pipes from the manifold.

7. For vehicles up until early 1992, remove the screws attaching the converter heat shields, then remove the heat shield from the vehicle.

8. For late 1992 and later vehicles, remove the manifold outer heat shield and remove the catalytic converter from the exhaust manifold.

9. Remove the exhaust manifold bolts, spacers and nut.

10. If applicable, remove the center stud nut.

11. Remove the manifold and gasket from the vehicle.

To install:

12. Thoroughly clean the manifold and cylinder head gasket mating surfaces.

13. Install the gasket and manifold to the engine.

14. Install the manifold bolts, spacer, nut, and if applicable, center stud nut. Tighten the bolts and nut(s) to 18 ft. lbs. (24 Nm).

15. For late 1992 and later vehicles, install the catalytic converter and bolts to the manifold. Tighten to 17 ft. lbs. (23 Nm) and install the manifold outer heat shield. Install the AIR check valve, hoses and pipe.

16. For vehicles up until early 1992, install the converter heat shields and retainers.

17. Engage the oxygen sensor wiring harness connector.

18. Install the engine block heat shield, the left side heat shield to the frame and the floor pan heat shield.

19. Install the exhaust system assembly to the catalytic converter.

20. Install the wheelhouse lower rear and center panels, then install the tire and wheel assembly.

21. Lower the vehicle and connect the negative battery cable.

Timing Chain Front Cover

REMOVAL AND INSTALLATION

5.7L (VIN P) Engine

1. Disconnect the negative battery cable.

2. Drain the engine oil and coolant into suitable containers.

3. Remove the throttle body air intake duct.

4. Remove the serpentine drive belt.

5. Remove the water pump assembly.

6. Remove the crankshaft balancer and hub.

   a. If not done already, raise and support the vehicle safely, then remove the motor mount nuts.

   b. Remove the power steering fluid cooler, then raise the engine sufficiently for tool access to the crankshaft balancer.

NOTE: When raising and supporting the engine, NEVER place a jack under the oil pan, crankshaft pulley or any sheetmetal. There is a minimal clearance between the oil pan and the pump screen. Jacking against the pan could cause sufficient deformation to damage the oil pickup unit.

   c. Remove the balancer bolts, then remove the balancer from the hub.

   d. Disconnect the power steering line from the steering gear.

   e. Matchmark the crankshaft hub to the engine front cover, then remove the hub bolt and washer.

   f. Remove the crankshaft hub using J–39046, or an equivalent hub removal/installation tool. To preserve the relationship between the hub and crankshaft, DO NOT crank the engine over once the hub has been removed. If the hub is not matchmarked and installed in the original position, an engine imbalance could result.

7. Remove the distributor assembly.

8. Remove the oil pan assembly.

9. Remove the engine front cover bolts.

10. Remove the engine front cover and gasket.

To install:

11. Thoroughly clean the engine front cover and cylinder block gasket mating surfaces. Inspect the engine front cover and seals for damage, replace as necessary.

12. Using J–39087 or equivalent shaft gear front cover seal protector, on the water pump driveshaft, install the gasket and front cover into position over the shafts and guide pins.

13. Install the engine front cover bolts and tighten to 100 inch lbs. (11 Nm).

14. Install the oil pan and gasket.

15. Install the distributor assembly.

16. Install the and the torsional damper.

   a. Align the matchmarks made earlier and install the crankshaft hub. If the engine was cranked and the matchmarks were lost, set the engine to No. 1 TDC, then install the crankshaft hub with the cast arrow in the 12 o'clock position.

   b. Install the hub washer and bolt, but do not torque at this time.

c. Raise the engine, as necessary for access, then install the crankshaft balancer assembly. Tighten the crankshaft hub bolt to 75 ft. lbs. (102 Nm) and the balancer bolts to 60 ft. lbs. (81 Nm).

NOTE: If a new balancer is installed, new balancer weights of the same size must be installed in the same hole locations as the original balancer.

d. Install the power steering line to the gear, then lower the engine into position.

e. Install the power steering fluid cooler.

f. Install the motor mount nuts and tighten to 40 ft. lbs. (50 Nm).

17. Install the water pump assembly.

18. Install the serpentine drive belt and the throttle body air duct.

19. Properly fill the engine crankcase with oil.

20. Tighten the fuel filler cap and properly fill the engine cooling system.

21. Connect the negative battery cable, operate the engine and check for leaks.

22. Bleed the power steering hydraulic system, as necessary.

23. If equipped, reset the CHANGE OIL indicator:

a. Turn the ignition **ON** but do not start the engine.

b. Depress the ENG MET button on the trip monitor, then within 5 seconds, depress the button a 2nd time. Within another 5 seconds, depress and hold the GAUGES button.

c. While holding the GAUGES button and watch the CHANGE OIL light, it should begin to flash. Continue to hold the gauges button until the flashing stops and the light goes out indicating that the indicator is reset.

d. If the indicator does not reset, turn the ignition **OFF** and restart the procedure.

5.7L (VIN J) Engine

1. Disconnect the negative battery cable and drain the engine coolant into a suitable container.

2. Remove the water pump assembly.

3. Remove the air conditioning compressor as follows:

a. Properly discharge and recover the air conditioning system.

b. Remove the throttle body.

c. Remove the serpentine drive belt.

1. Damper
2. Bolt
3. Washer
4. Hub
5. Bolt
6. Weight

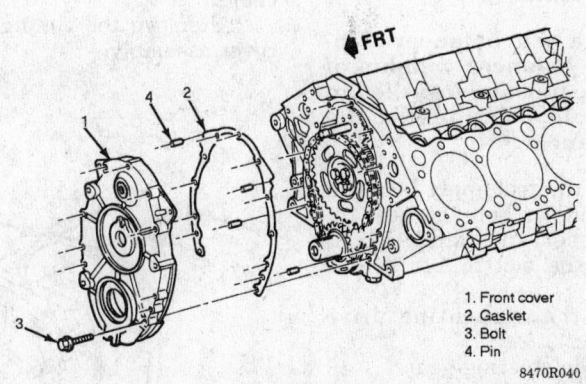

Exploded view of the crankshaft balancer and hub assembly — 5.7L (VIN P) engine

1. Front cover
2. Gasket
3. Bolt
4. Pin

Timing chain front cover and gasket installation — 5.7L (VIN P) engine

d. Remove the engine oil temperature sensor.

e. Remove the alternator.

f. Remove the refrigerant hose from the A/C compressor, then immediately cap or plug the openings to prevent system contamination and damage.

g. Remove the compressor mounting bolts and electrical connection.

h. Remove the compressor from the vehicle.

4. Remove the steering gear for access to the damper.

5. Remove the bolt and washer attaching the torsional damper to the crankshaft.

6. Using tool J–24420–C, or an equivalent torsional damper puller, remove the damper from the crankshaft.

7. Remove the drift key, from the crankshaft.

8. Remove the nuts and/or bolts attaching the front cover to the engine.

9. Remove the front cover and gasket from the vehicle. If necessary, remove the old seal from the front cover

using J–29077–A or an equivalent oil seal remover.

To install:

10. Thoroughly clean the cylinder case, front cover and water pump sealing surfaces.

11. Apply Loctite® 262 to the stud threads and Loctite® 565 to the bolt threads.

12. Install a new cover gasket and the cover, nuts and bolts.

13. If removed, install a new front cover oil seal using J–37309 or equivalent front cover seal installer.

14. Tighten the front cover attaching bolts to 19 inch lbs. (26 Nm) and the stud nuts to 21 ft. lbs. (28 Nm).

15. Install the water pump assembly.

16. Install the air conditioning compressor in the reverse order of the removal procedure. Replace the refrigerant line seal washers and coat the new washers with 525 refrigerant oil prior to assembly. When installed, properly evacuate and charge the A/C system.

17. Install the key to the crankshaft and, then install the torsional damper using J–38463, or an equivalent torsional damper installer. Check for proper key seating during installation.

NOTE: If a new balancer is installed, new balancer weights of the same size must be installed in the same hole locations as the original balancer.

18. Remove the tool apply Loctite® 262 to the damper bolt threads. Install the washer and damper bolt, then tighten the bolt to 148 ft. lbs. (200 Nm).

19. Install the serpentine drive belt.

20. Install the steering gear.

21. Connect the negative battery cable, properly fill the engine cooling system and check for leaks.

22. If the engine oil was changed, and if equipped, reset the CHANGE OIL indicator:

   a. Turn the ignition **ON** but do not start the engine.

   b. Depress the ENG MET button on the trip monitor, then within 5 seconds, depress the button a 2nd time. Within another 5 seconds, depress and hold the GAUGES button.

   c. While holding the GAUGES button and watch the CHANGE OIL light, it should begin to flash. Continue to hold the gauges button until the flashing stops and the light goes out indicating that the indicator is reset.

   d. If the indicator does not reset, turn the ignition **OFF** and restart the procedure.

Front Cover Oil Seal

REPLACEMENT

5.7L (VIN P) Engine

1. Disconnect the battery negative cable.

2. Remove the engine front cover.

3. Using a suitable tool, remove the crankshaft, distributor shaft and/or water pump driven gear shaft seals, as necessary.

4. As applicable; use tool J–35468 or equivalent aligner and installer, to install the crankshaft seal, tool J–39090 or equivalent, to install the distributor shaft seal and/or tool J–39088 or equivalent, to install the water pump shaft seal.

5. Install the engine front cover.

6. Connect the negative battery cable.

5.7L (VIN J) Engine

1. Disconnect the battery negative cable.

2. Remove the timing chain front cover assembly.

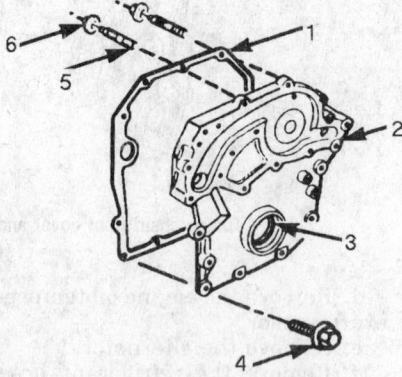

1. Engine front cover gasket
2. Engine front cover
3. Engine front cover seal
4. Engine front cover bolt
5. Engine front cover stud
6. Engine front cover stud nut

8470R041

Timing chain front cover and gasket installation — 5.7L (VIN J) engine

3. Remove the seal from the front cover using J–29077–A or equivalent seal remover tool.

4. Thoroughly clean the cylinder case, front cover and water pump sealing surfaces.

5. Apply Loctite® 262 to studs and Loctite® 565 to the bolt threads.

6. Install a new cover gasket and the cover, nuts and bolts.

7. Install the new seal coated with engine oil using tool J–37309 or equivalent.

NOTE: Do not remove seal installing tool J–37309, until the front cover bolts are torqued.

8. Tighten the front cover attaching bolts to 19 inch lbs. (26 Nm) and the stud nuts to 21 ft. lbs. (28 Nm).

9. Complete the front cover installation procedure and connect the negative battery cable.

Timing Chain and Sprockets

REMOVAL AND INSTALLATION

5.7L (VIN P) Engine

1. Disconnect the negative battery cable.

2. Remove the timing chain front cover.

3. Rotate the crankshaft until the timing marks on the timing chain sprockets are aligned nearest each other. The camshaft sprocket mark should be at the 6 o'clock position while the mark on the crankshaft sprocket should be at the 12 o'clock position.

4. Remove the camshaft sprocket bolts.

5. Remove the camshaft sprocket and timing chain.

NOTE: To prevent piston or valve damage, do not turn the crankshaft after the timing chain has been removed.

6. Remove the water pump bearing retainer bolts, then remove the driveshaft assembly using J–39243 or equivalent driven gear assembly remover.

7. Remove the crankshaft sprocket using J–5825–A or equivalent crankshaft sprocket remover.

8. If necessary, remove the crankshaft key.

To install:

9. If removed, install the crankshaft key.

10. Install the crankshaft sprocket using a suitable installation tool.

11. Install the water pump driveshaft assembly using a suitable tool. Install the retainer bolts and tighten to 108 inch lbs. (12 Nm).

12. Align the timing marks and install the camshaft sprocket and timing chain. The gears of the camshaft sprocket and water pump driveshaft must mesh or damage to the thrust plate retainer could occur.

13. Install the camshaft sprocket bolts and tighten to 21 ft. lbs. (28 Nm).

14. Install a new O-ring to the water pump driven gear shaft using a suitable seal installation tool.

15. Install the timing chain front cover and connect the negative battery cable.

5.7L (VIN J) Engine

PRIMARY TIMING CHAIN AND CRANKSHAFT SPROCKET

1. Disconnect battery negative cable.

2. Remove the timing chain front cover assembly.

3. Remove the left and right intake camshafts.

4. Remove the bolts attaching the primary chain guide to the oil pump, then remove the guide from the vehicle.

5. Remove the idler sprocket assembly attaching bolts, then disengage the primary timing chain from the idler and crankshaft sprockets. Remove the chain from the vehicle.

6. Using the crankshaft torsional damper puller along with J–38211 or equivalent sprocket tool, remove the crankshaft sprocket. Note which side of the sprocket faces forward for installation purposes.

7. Remove the key and oil pump seal seat from the crankshaft.

To install:

8. Inspect the primary chain guide for excessive wear. Wear groove should not exceed a depth of 0.040 inch (1.0mm). If necessary, replace wear strip.

9. Install oil pump seal seat and key onto the crankshaft.

10. Install the crankshaft sprocket using J–38132 or equivalent sprocket installer. Make sure sprocket is installed with same side to the front as noted during removal, this should be the wide shoulder.

11. Engage the primary chain onto the idler and crankshaft sprocket.

12. Apply Loctite® 262 or equivalent, to the idler sprocket assembly bolts and tighten to 19 ft. lbs. (26 Nm).

13. Apply Loctite® 262 or equivalent, to the primary chain

guide bolts. Install the guide and bolts. Push the guide so the slack is removed from the chain and tighten the bolts to 89 inch lbs. (10 Nm).

NOTE: When installing guide, do not use any leverage tools, finger pressure is sufficient.

14. Install the left and right intake camshafts.

15. Install the timing chain front cover.

16. Connect the negative battery cable.

SECONDARY TIMING CHAINS AND IDLER SPROCKET ASSEMBLY

1. Disconnect battery negative cable.

2. Remove the camshafts.

3. Remove the primary timing chain and crankshaft sprocket.

4. Disengage the left and right secondary chains from the idler sprocket.

5. Remove the idler sprocket assembly.

6. Remove the left and right secondary chains from the vehicle.

To install:

7. Inspect chains and sprockets for abnormal wear or damage. If abnormal wear or damage is present on either the secondary timing chain, cam

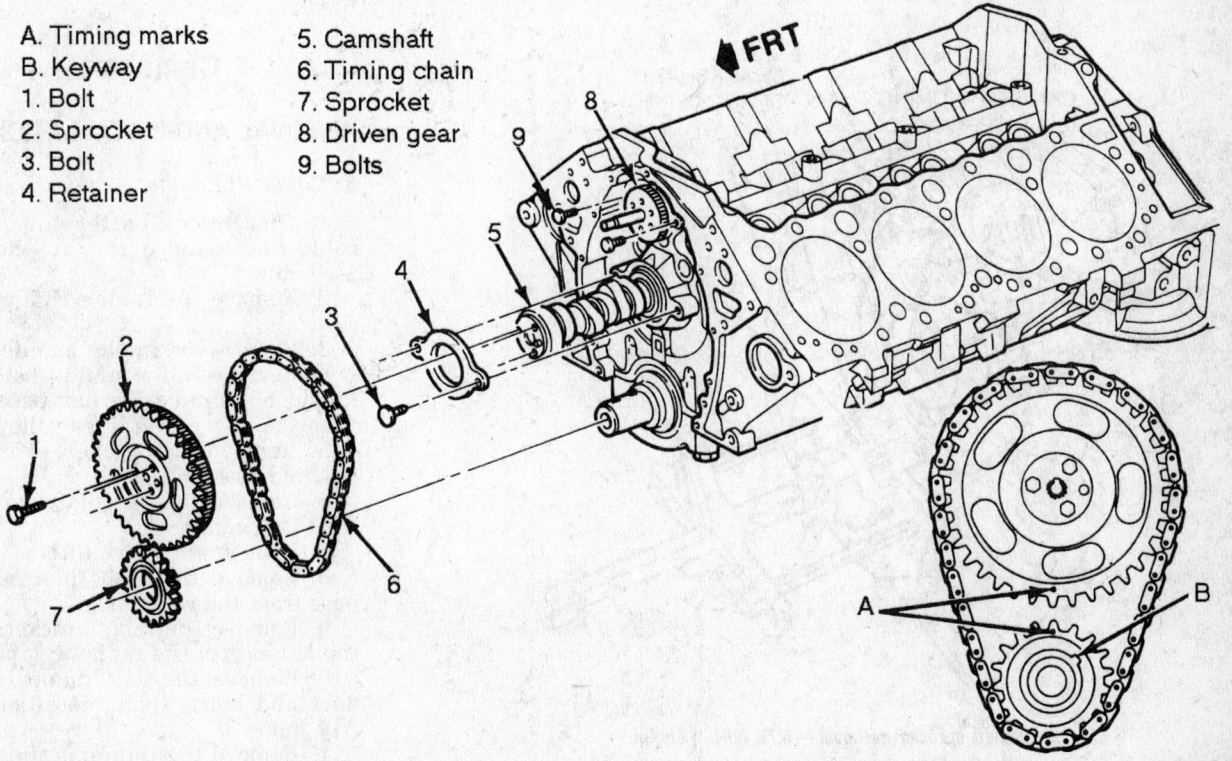

A. Timing marks
B. Keyway
1. Bolt
2. Sprocket
3. Bolt
4. Retainer
5. Camshaft
6. Timing chain
7. Sprocket
8. Driven gear
9. Bolts

8470R046

Exploded view of the timing chain and gear assembly — 5.7L (VIN P) engine

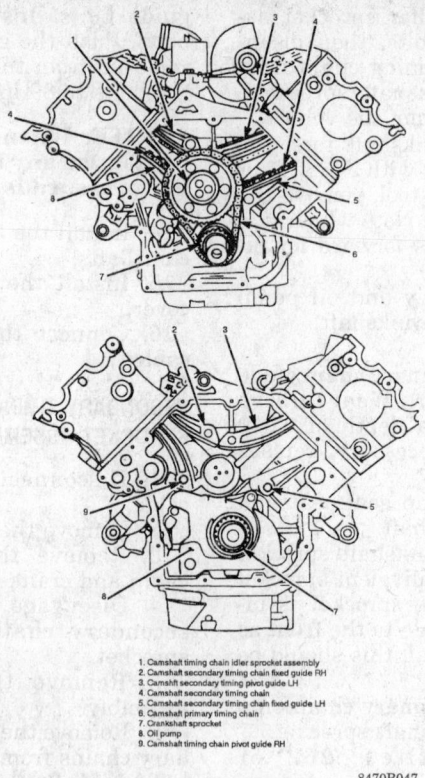

1. Camshaft timing chain idler sprocket assembly
2. Camshaft secondary timing chain fixed guide RH
3. Camshaft secondary timing pivot guide LH
4. Camshaft secondary timing chain
5. Camshaft secondary timing chain fixed guide LH
6. Camshaft primary timing chain
7. Crankshaft sprocket
8. Oil pump
9. Camshaft timing chain pivot guide RH

8470R047

Primary and secondary timing chain assembly — 5.7L (VIN J) engine

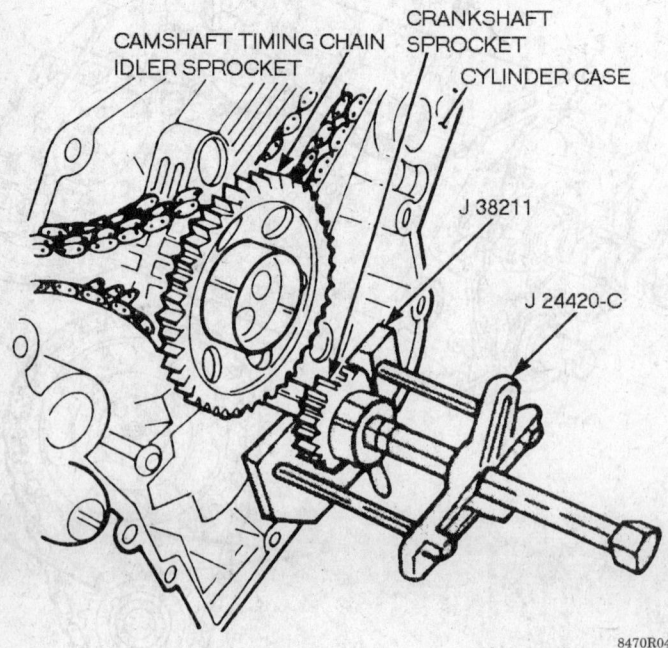

CAMSHAFT TIMING CHAIN IDLER SPROCKET

CRANKSHAFT SPROCKET

CYLINDER CASE

J 38211

J 24420-C

8470R048

Crankshaft sprocket removal — 5.7L (VIN J) engine

sprockets or idler sprockets, the entire assembly must be replaced.

8. Inspect the idler sprocket shaft bearings for wear or damage. If necessary, replace idler sprocket shaft bearings as follows:

a. Remove the idler sprocket screw, washer and shaft.

b. Using tool J–37328 or equivalent, remove bearings from idler sprocket.

c. When installing bearings, ensure the manufacture's name and part Nos. are visible from either end of the sprocket assembly.

d. Using a press, carefully push in the bearings until they are flush with idler sprocket. Apply minimum pressure to obtain a fit 0.0–1.3mm below the surface.

9. Install the shorter (inner) secondary chain through the right head and install J–38099 or equivalent timing chain retaining tool.

10. Locate the right chain onto the rear idler sprocket.

11. Install the longer (outer) secondary chain through the left head and install J–38099 or equivalent timing chain retaining tool.

12. Locate the left chain onto the middle idler sprocket.

13. Install the primary timing chain.

14. Install the camshafts.

15. Connect the negative battery cable.

Camshaft

REMOVAL AND INSTALLATION

5.7L (VIN P) Engine

1. Disconnect battery negative cable and remove the air cleaner assembly.

2. Remove the timing chain front cover.

3. Remove the intake manifold.

4. Remove the retaining bolt and lift the oil pump driveshaft assembly from the rear of the lifter valley.

5. Remove the rocker arm and pushrod assemblies.

6. Remove the camshaft sprocket from the engine.

7. Remove the valve lifters.

8. Remove the high fill reservoir hose from the radiator.

9. Remove the relay bracket from the left side of the radiator support.

10. Remove the AIR pump intake duct and bolts, then reposition the AIR pump.

11. Remove the retaining nuts and screws, then remove the upper radiator support.

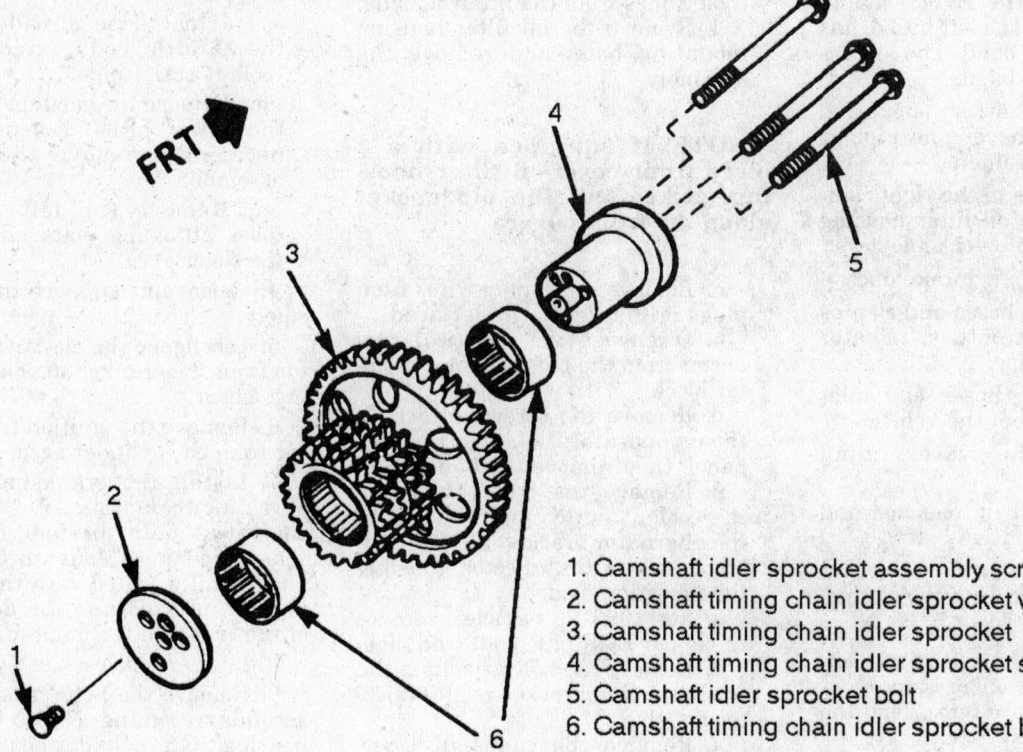

1. Camshaft timing chain idler sprocket
2. Cylinder case
J 38132
3. Camshaft secondary timing chain fixed guide - LH
4. Oil pump seal seat
5. Crankshaft   6. Crankshaft sprocket

8470R049

Installing the crankshaft sprocket — 5.7L (VIN J) engine

12. Remove the radiator.
13. Raise and support the vehicle safely.
14. Unplug the cooling fan electrical connector.
15. Remove the lower fan shroud bolts and lower the vehicle.
16. Remove the fan shroud and fan assembly.
17. Disconnect the A/C condenser line bracket at the front crossmember.
18. Raise the front of the engine with a suitable lifting device.

NOTE: When raising and supporting the engine, NEVER place a jack under the oil pan, crankshaft pulley or any sheetmetal.

There is a minimal clearance between the oil pan and the pump screen. Jacking against the pan could cause sufficient deformation to damage the oil pickup unit.

19. Remove the camshaft retainer bolts and retainer.
20. Install three $^5/_{16}$–18 x 4 inch bolts into the camshaft bolt holes.
21. Using the bolts, carefully rotate the camshaft and pull from the bearings. All camshaft journals are the same diameter so care must be used to avoid damaging the bearings. Remove the camshaft from the vehicle.
To install:
22. Inspect the camshaft and bearings, replace as necessary.
23. If installing a new camshaft, coat the lobes with Molykote® or equivalent pre-lube and be sure to replace all lifters to assure camshaft durability.
24. Lubricate all camshaft journals with clean engine oil and carefully insert the camshaft into the engine block.
25. Install the camshaft retainer and tighten the bolts to 108 inch lbs. (12 Nm).
26. Lower the front of the engine and connect the A/C condenser line bracket to the front crossmember.

27. Install the fan and shroud assembly.
28. Raise and support the vehicle safely, then install the lower fan shroud bolts.
29. Engage the cooling fan electrical connections and lower the vehicle.
30. Install the radiator, followed by the upper radiator support, nuts and screws.
31. Install the AIR pump, bolts and intake duct.
32. Install the relay bracket to the left side of the radiator support.
33. Connect the high fill reservoir hose to the radiator.
34. Install the valve lifters.
35. Install the camshaft sprocket.
36. Install the valve rocker arm and pushrod assemblies.
37. Install the oil pump driveshaft assembly and bolt. Tighten the bolt to 13 ft. lbs. (18 Nm).
38. Install the intake manifold.
39. Install the timing chain front cover.
40. Install the air cleaner assembly and connect the negative battery cable.

5.7L (VIN J) Engine

The VIN J engine utilizes 4 overhead camshafts. Certain shafts will have identifying bands between the first

FRT

1. Camshaft idler sprocket assembly screw
2. Camshaft timing chain idler sprocket washer
3. Camshaft timing chain idler sprocket
4. Camshaft timing chain idler sprocket shaft
5. Camshaft idler sprocket bolt
6. Camshaft timing chain idler sprocket bearing

8470R050

Timing chain idler sprocket assembly — 5.7L (VIN J) engine

FRT

A. Camshaft sensor reluctor disc
1. Camshaft secondary timing chain
2. Plenum
3. Intake camshaft LH
4. Exhaust camshaft LH

8470R051

Left cylinder head camshaft assembly — 5.7L (VIN J) engine

journal and lobe to distinguish between the right and left, intake and exhaust camshafts. The right intake has 1 flat band. The right exhaust has 1 raised band. The left intake has 1 flat and 1 raised band. The left exhaust has 2 raised bands.

1. Disconnect battery negative cable and drain the engine coolant into a suitable container.

2. To gain access to the right camshafts, remove the oil filter housing and right camshaft cover as follows:

a. Remove the air intake duct.

b. Remove the hoses and clamps from the coolant outlets, radiator inlet and inlet pipe.

c. Remove the hoses and inlet pipe assembly from the vehicle.

d. Remove the water pump pulley.

e. Release the belt tensioner and remove the serpentine belt.

f. Remove the retaining bolt and the belt tensioner from the engine.

g. Remove the oil filter.

h. Disengage the electrical connectors from the oil pressure sensor, oil temperature sensor and the low oil pressure switch.

i. Remove the oil pressure sensor from the oil filter housing.

j. Remove the alternator bracket from the oil filter housing.

k. Disconnect and plug the oil cooler lines from the filter housing.

l. Remove the oil filter housing mounting bolts and remove the assembly.

NOTE: If equipped with a 1 piece front cover/oil filter housing gasket, cut the old gasket along the front cover.

m. Remove spark plug wires from plugs in the right cylinder head.

n. Disengage the electrical connector from the blower motor resistor block.

o. Remove the screws attaching the evaporator housing quarter panel, then remove the panel.

p. Remove the bolts attaching the coolant outlet pipe bracket to the alternator bracket and the coolant outlet to the injector housing, then position aside.

q. For 1993–96 vehicles, remove the upper EGR pipe bolts and pipe.

r. Remove the bolt attaching the fresh air pipe bracket to the injector housing.

s. Remove the camshaft cover attaching bolts and the camshaft cover.

3. To gain access to the left camshafts, remove the air conditioning compressor and left valve cover as follows:

a. Properly discharge the air conditioning system.

b. Remove the throttle body assembly and the serpentine drive belt.

c. Remove the engine oil temperature sensor.

d. Remove the alternator assembly.

e. Remove the refrigerant hose from the A/C compressor, then immediately cap or plug the openings to prevent system contamination and damage.

f. Remove the compressor mounting bolts and electrical connection.

g. Remove the compressor from the vehicle.

h. Remove the power steering pump from the engine.

i. Remove the spark plug wires from the plugs in the left cylinder head.

j. Remove the ventilation breather pipe from the camshaft cover.

k. Remove the throttle and cruise control cable or control cable hold-down clamps from the plenum.

l. If not done already, remove the throttle body extension and coolant outlet pipe.

m. Remove the vacuum hose from the power brake booster and, if necessary, remove the booster assembly.

n. Remove the left camshaft cover attaching bolts and remove the cover.

4. Raise and support the vehicle safely.

5. Disengage the electrical connector from the crankshaft ignition timing sensor.

6. Remove the ignition timing sensor from the cylinder case.

7. Install the crankshaft timing slot locator tool J–38098 or equivalent, into the ignition timing sensor opening. Make sure the tool head is fully seated with the indicating pin inserted into the deep notch of the crankshaft timing disc.

8. Lower vehicle.

9. Remove the bolts attaching the secondary timing chain tensioner housing to the cylinder head, then remove the housing, O-ring and tensioner from the cylinder case.

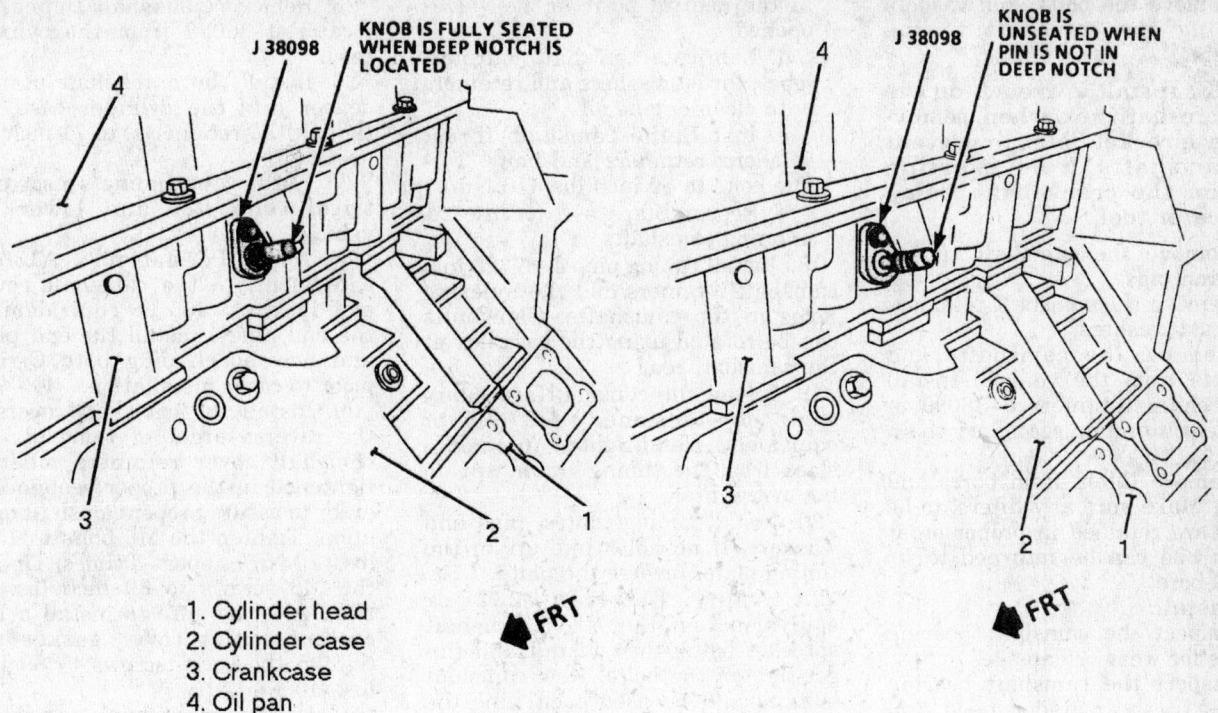

1. Cylinder head
2. Cylinder case
3. Crankcase
4. Oil pan

FRT

8470R052

Crankshaft timing slot locator tool — 5.7L (VIN J) engine

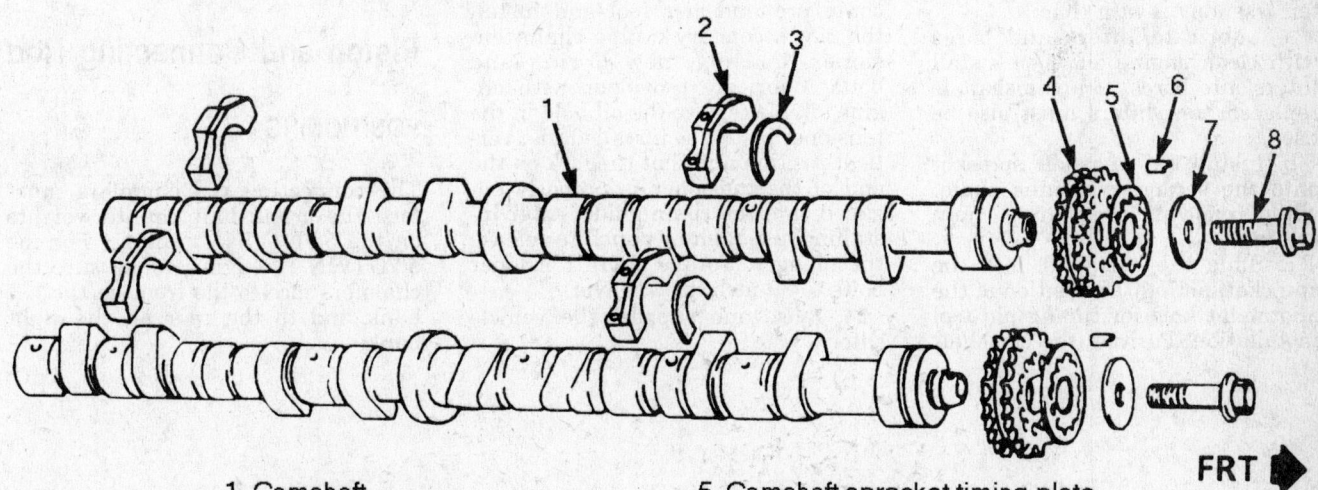

1. Camshaft
2. Camshaft retainer
3. Camshaft thrust washer
4. Camshaft sprocket

5. Camshaft sprocket timing plate
6. Camshaft sprocket pin
7. Camshaft sprocket washer
8. Camshaft sprocket bolt

FRT

8470R053

Cylinder head camshaft assembly — 5.7L (VIN J) engine

10. Remove the bolts and washers attaching the camshaft to the sprockets.

NOTE: Install a wrench on the rear camshaft hex when removing the sprocket bolts, to prevent the camshafts from exerting force on the crankshaft timing slot locator tool.

11. Remove the camshaft timing plates and pins.
12. Remove the camshaft retainers and thrust washers.
13. Remove the camshafts and sprockets from the vehicle. Install timing chain retainers J–38099 or equivalent, to retain secondary chain loops.
14. Remove lifters from bores and inspect. Make sure any lifters, to be reused, are retained in proper order so each one can be returned to its original bore.
To install:
15. Inspect the camshaft bearing journals for wear or damage.
16. Inspect the camshaft bearing surfaces in the cylinder head and camshaft cover for wear or damage.

NOTE: The camshaft cover and cylinder head must be replaced as a set if excessive wear or damage to the bearing surfaces is found.

17. Install the each camshaft and lifter assembly, 1 at a time:
    a. Lubricate lifters and bores with clean engine oil, then install lifters into bores. If a camshaft is replaced, new lifters must also be used.
    b. Install the camshaft sprocket onto the secondary timing chain, while removing the timing chain retainer.
    c. Slide the camshaft into the sprocket, noting the position of the alignment hole for timing pin tool installation. Position the camshaft

in the neutral position, no valves opened.
    d. Lubricate camshaft journals, lobes, thrust washers and retainers with clean engine oil.
    e. Install the camshaft thrust washers, retainers and bolts. Torque bolts to 89 inch lbs. (10 Nm).
    f. Repeat Steps a–e for the remaining camshafts.
18. Install timing pins J–37326 into camshaft retainers and the indexing holes in the camshafts. Camshafts can be rotated using the cast hex at the camshaft rear.
19. Install the camshaft secondary chain pre-tensioner, J–37305 or equivalent. Hand-tighten to remove slack from the timing chain, but do not overtighten.
20. Install timing plates, pins and washers. If no holes line up on the timing plate, reverse the plate.
21. Apply Loctite® 262 or equivalent, on the NEW camshaft sprocket bolts, then install and finger-tighten the bolts. New camshaft bolts should be used each time the camshaft is removed. Tighten the bolts to 18 ft. lbs. (25 Nm) and turn 80–85 degrees using a torque angle meter. A backup wrench should be used on the rear camshaft hex to prevent damaging the timing pins.
22. Remove timing pins J–37326.
23. Remove the secondary timing chain pre-tensioner tool and install the new secondary timing chain tensioner, housing, new O-ring and bolts. Lubricate tensioner with engine oil. Make sure the oil hole in the tensioner piston be installed in a vertical position and that the fork on the end of the tensioner is properly engaged onto the chain guide. After installing, use a blunt punch to release the plunger. Torque chain tensioner bolts to 89 inch lbs. (10 Nm).
24. Raise and support the vehicle safely.

25. Remove crankshaft timing slot locator J–38098 from the cylinder case.
26. Install the crankshaft position sensor into the cylinder case and tighten the retainer(s) to 71 inch lbs. (8 Nm).
27. Engage the timing sensor electrical connector and lower the vehicle.
28. Apply Permabond® A136 or equivalent, to the camshaft covers and Loctite® 565 or equivalent, to the end plugs. Install the end plugs and new spark plug bore O-rings prior to cover installation.
29. Install the camshaft covers in the reverse order of removal. The camshaft cover retainers must be tightened in the proper sequence in order to assure proper camshaft operation. Tighten the M8 bolts to 15 ft. lbs. (20 Nm), repeat 3 times. Tighten the M6 screws to 89 inch lbs. (10 Nm). Also, be sure to install a new coolant outlet cover gasket and tighten the cover screws to 89 inch lbs. (10 Nm).
30. For the right bank camshafts, install oil filter housing assembly.
31. For the left bank camshafts, install the air conditioning compressor assembly.
32. Reconnect the battery negative cable and properly fill the engine cooling system.

Piston and Connecting Rod

POSITIONING

The connecting rod chamfers must face the crankshaft counterweights on the 5.7L (VIN J) engine. For the 5.7L (VIN P) engine, make sure the chamfers face to the front on the left bank and to the rear on the right bank.

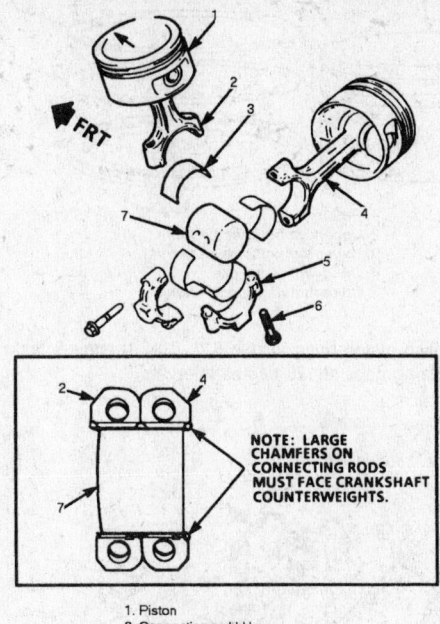

NOTE: LARGE CHAMFERS ON CONNECTING RODS MUST FACE CRANKSHAFT COUNTERWEIGHTS.

1. Piston
2. Connecting rod LH
3. Connecting rod bearing
4. Connecting rod RH
5. Connecting rod bearing cap
6. Connecting rod bearing cap bolt
7. Crankshaft

8470R059

5.7L (VIN J) engine piston assembly — 5.7L (VIN P) engine similar

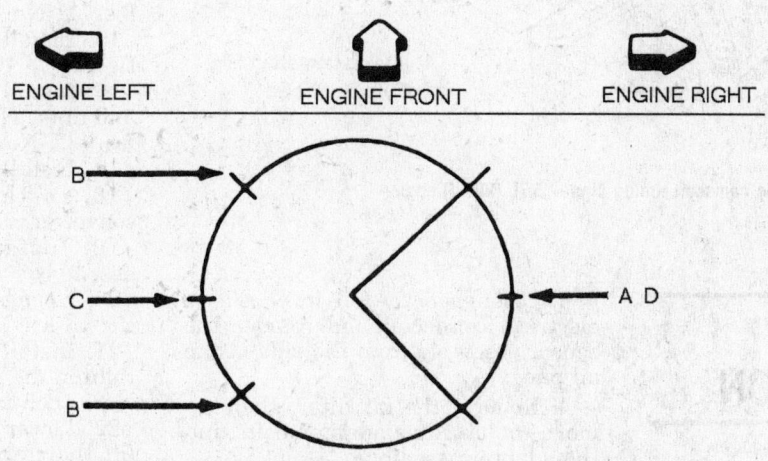

ENGINE LEFT   ENGINE FRONT   ENGINE RIGHT

A. Oil ring spacer gap
B. Oil ring rail gaps
C. 2nd compression ring gap
D. Top compression ring gap

8470R060

Engine ring gap locations — 5.7L (VIN P) engine

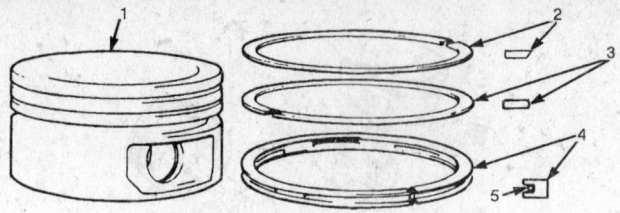

1. Piston
2. Upper compression piston ring
3. Lower compression piston ring
4. Oil control piston ring
5. Oil control ring spring w/spacer

8470R061

When installing piston rings for the 5.7L (VIN J) engine, make sure to position the ring gaps at 120 degree intervals

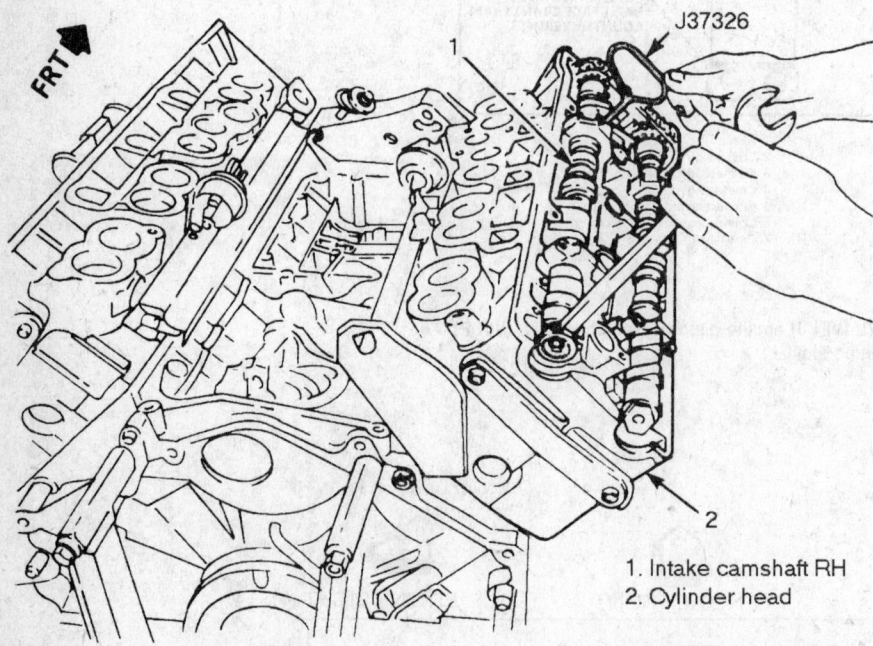

J37326

FRT

1. Intake camshaft RH
2. Cylinder head

8470R054

Installing the camshaft timing pins — 5.7L (VIN J) engine

ENGINE LUBRICATION

Oil Pan

REMOVAL AND INSTALLATION

5.7L (VIN P) Engine

1. Disconnect the negative battery cable.
2. Raise and support the vehicle safely, then drain the engine oil.
3. Disengage the oil level sensor electrical connector and remove the sensor assembly from the side of the oil pan.
4. Remove the oil filter, then remove the oil filter adapter bolts and the adapter assembly.
5. Remove the starter motor assembly.
6. Remove the left catalytic converter.
7. Remove the flywheel cover.
8. Remove the knock sensor retaining nuts and shields.
9. Remove the oil pan bolts, nuts and studs. Be sure to note the location of stud bolts.

10. Remove the oil pan, reinforcements and gasket.

To install:

11. Thoroughly clean all gasket mating surfaces and apply a small amount of 1052914 or equivalent sealer, to the front cover and cylinder block junction and the rear seal retainer and cylinder block junction. Extend the bead of sealer approximately 1 inch (25mm) in either direction of these junctions.
12. Install the gasket onto the oil pan and reinforcements.
13. Install the gasket, pan and reinforcement assembly to the cylinder block with the bolts, studs and nuts.
14. Tighten the corner bolts or stud and nuts to 17 ft. lbs. (23 Nm) on 1992 vehicles or to 15 ft. lbs. (20 Nm) for 1993–96 vehicles. Tighten the remainder of the bolts and studs to 8 ft. lbs. (11 Nm).
15. Install the oil level sensor and tighten to 16 ft. lbs. (22 Nm).
16. Install the knock sensor shields and nuts. Tighten the nuts to 75 inch lbs. (8.5 Nm).
17. Install the flywheel cover.
18. Install the left catalytic converter.
19. Install the starter motor assembly.
20. Engage the wiring harness to the oil level sensor terminal.
21. Install the oil filter adapter and tighten the retainers to 17 ft. lbs. (23 Nm), then install the oil filter.
22. Lower the vehicle and properly fill the crankcase with clean engine oil.
23. Connect the negative battery cable.
24. Reset the CHANGE OIL indicator:
   a. Turn the ignition **ON** but do not start the engine.
   b. Depress the ENG MET button on the trip monitor, then within 5 seconds, depress the button a 2nd time. Within another 5 seconds, de-

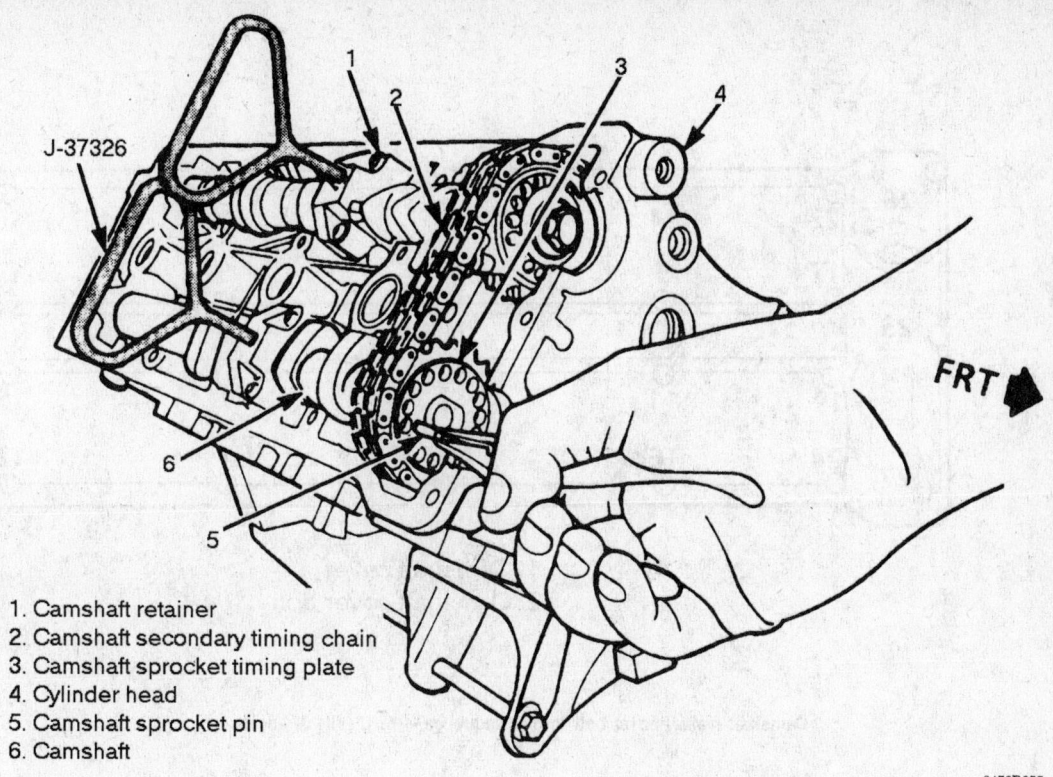

J-37326

FRT

1. Camshaft retainer
2. Camshaft secondary timing chain
3. Camshaft sprocket timing plate
4. Cylinder head
5. Camshaft sprocket pin
6. Camshaft

8470R055

Installing the camshaft sprocket pin — 5.7L (VIN J) engine

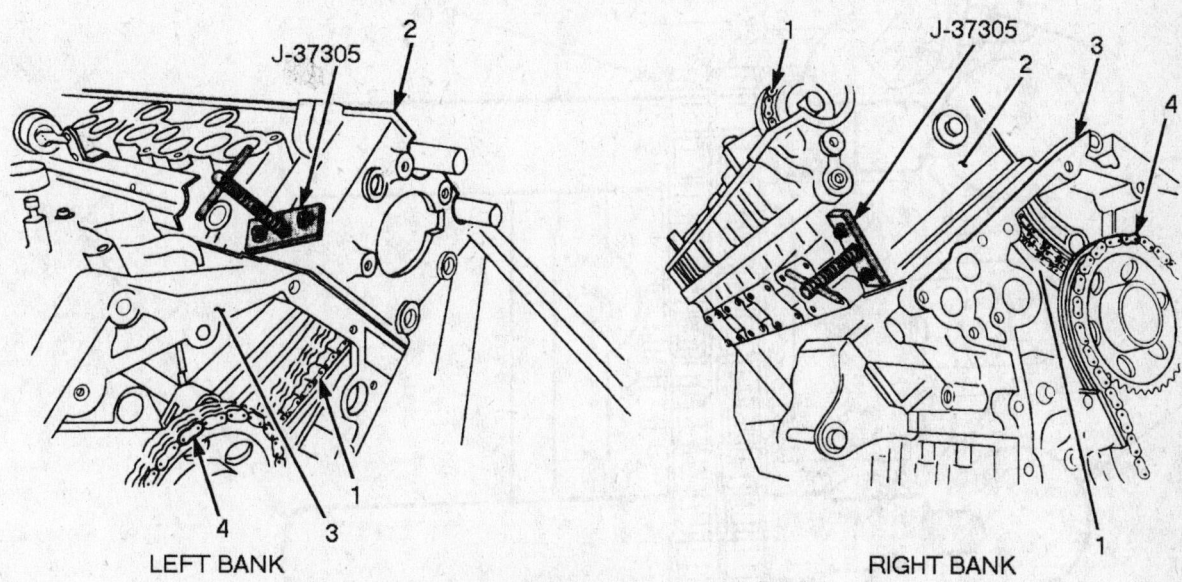

J-37305

LEFT BANK

J-37305

RIGHT BANK

1. Camshaft secondary timing chain
2. Cylinder head
3. Cylinder case
4. Camshaft primary timing chain

8470R056

Secondary timing chain pre-tensioner tool — 5.7L (VIN J) engine

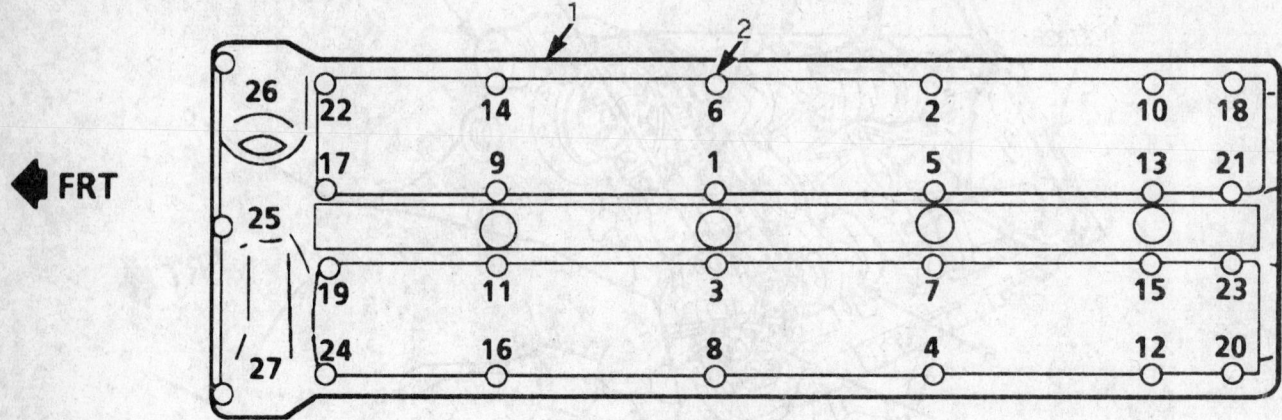

1. Camshaft cover
2. Camshaft cover bolt

8470R057

Camshaft (valve) cover bolt torque sequence — 5.7L (VIN J) engine

J-38099

1. Cylinder head
2. Camshaft secondary timing chain
3. Valve lifter

8470R058

Secondary timing chain retainers — 5.7L (VIN J) engine

press and hold the GAUGES button.

c. While holding the GAUGES button and watch the CHANGE OIL light, it should begin to flash. Continue to hold the gauges button until the flashing stops and the light goes out indicating that the indicator is reset.

d. If the indicator does not reset, turn the ignition **OFF** and restart the procedure.

5.7L (VIN J) Engine

1. Disconnect negative battery cable and remove the oil lever indicator from the guide tube.
2. Raise and support the vehicle safely, then drain the engine oil.
3. Remove the clutch housing cover attaching bolts, then remove the cover from the vehicle.
4. If equipped, remove the left and right wiring harness heat shields from the oil pan.
5. Disconnect the low oil sensor connection and remove the sensor from the pan.
6. Remove the bolts attaching the AIR pipe bracket to the oil pan, then remove the left and right converter heat shields.
7. Remove the nuts attaching the engine mounts at the front crossmember rear brace on the left and right sides. Remove the bolts attaching the front crossmember to the rear braces.
8. Remove the bolts attaching the left front crossmember rear brace to the left front side member, then remove the brace from the vehicle.
9. Remove the bolts attaching the right front crossmember rear brace to the right front side member, then remove the brace from the vehicle.
10. Remove the bolts attaching the oil pan and crankcase. Remove the oil pan and gasket from the vehicle.

To install:

11. Apply Loctite® 242 to the oil pan screw threads.
12. Install the oil pan and new gasket to the engine crankcase. Tighten the oil pan front screws to 106 inch lbs. (12 Nm). Tighten the oil pan bolts to 23 ft. lbs. (31 Nm).
13. Install the front crossmember rear braces and bolts retaining the braces to the front crossmember bolts. Finger-tighten the bolts.
14. Install the bolts retaining the left front crossmember rear brace to the left front side member, finger-tight.
15. Install the bolts retaining the right front crossmember rear brace to

the left front side member, finger-tight.
16. Tighten the left and right front crossmember rear brace to front crossmember bolts to 59 ft. lbs. (80 Nm), then tighten the left and right front crossmember rear brace to front side member bolts to 46 ft. lbs. (62 Nm).
17. Install the nuts retaining the engine mounts to the front crossmember and tighten to 40 ft. lbs. (54 Nm).
18. Install the converter heat shields and screws.
19. Install the bolts retaining the AIR pipe bracket to the oil pan and tighten to 89 inch lbs. (10 Nm).
20. Install the oil level sensor in the pan and tighten to 18 ft. lbs. (25 Nm), then engage the wiring harness to the sensor.
21. Install the left and right wiring harness heat shields, if equipped, and tighten the bolts to 89 inch lbs. (10 Nm).
22. Install the clutch housing cover and tighten the bolts to 80 inch lbs. (9 Nm).
23. Lower the vehicle and insert the oil level indicator into the guide tube.
24. Properly fill the crankcase with clean engine oil.
25. Connect the negative battery cable.
26. If equipped, reset the CHANGE OIL indicator:

a. Turn the ignition **ON** but do not start the engine.

b. Depress the ENG MET button on the trip monitor, then within 5 seconds, depress the button a 2nd time. Within another 5 seconds, depress and hold the GAUGES button.

c. While holding the GAUGES button and watch the CHANGE OIL light, it should begin to flash. Continue to hold the gauges button until the flashing stops and the light goes out indicating that the indicator is reset.

d. If the indicator does not reset, turn the ignition **OFF** and restart the procedure.

Oil Pump

REMOVAL AND INSTALLATION

5.7L (VIN P) Engine

1. Disconnect the negative battery cable.
2. Raise and support the vehicle safely.
3. Drain the engine oil and remove the oil pan.

4. Remove the oil pan baffle nuts.
5. Support the oil pump by hand and remove the bolt attaching the oil pump to the main bearing cap.
6. Carefully remove the baffle, the oil pump assembly, driveshaft and retainer.

To install:

NOTE: **The oil pump pickup should be submerged in oil and the pump primed prior to installation. Failure to prime the pump may result in oil pump failure or internal engine damage. Also, if the pickup screen and pipe assembly was removed from the pump, they must be replaced to assure a proper interference fit.**

7. Install the oil pump assembly, shaft and retainer, aligning the slot on the top of the pump driveshaft with the drive tang on the lower end of the distributor driveshaft.
8. Install the oil pan baffle, then install the bolt to the main bearing cap, followed by the baffle nuts. Tighten the retaining bolt to 65 ft. lbs. (88 Nm) and the baffle nuts to 25 ft. lbs. (34 Nm).
9. Install the oil pan and lower the vehicle.
10. Properly fill the engine crankcase with clean engine oil.
11. Connect the negative battery cable.
12. If equipped, reset the CHANGE OIL indicator:

a. Turn the ignition **ON** but do not start the engine.

b. Depress the ENG MET button on the trip monitor, then within 5 seconds, depress the button a 2nd time. Within another 5 seconds, depress and hold the GAUGES button.

c. While holding the GAUGES button and watch the CHANGE OIL light, it should begin to flash. Continue to hold the gauges button until the flashing stops and the light goes out indicating that the indicator is reset.

d. If the indicator does not reset, turn the ignition **OFF** and restart the procedure.

5.7L (VIN J) Engine

1. Disconnect battery negative cable.
2. Remove the primary timing chain and crankshaft sprocket.
3. Remove bolts attaching the oil pump to the cylinder case, then remove the oil pump from the vehicle.
4. Remove O-rings from crankshaft and, if applicable, the oil pump.

5. For 1993–96 vehicles, remove the oil pickup seal.

To install:

6. Install new O-rings onto the crankshaft and oil pump, as applicable.

7. If applicable, install the oil pickup assembly seal.

8. Apply Loctite® 262 to the oil pump bolts and install them along with the oil pump, finger-tight.

NOTE: Make sure the 2 flats of the pump drive gear are aligned with the 2 flats on the crankshaft. Do not force pump onto crankshaft.

9. Using oil pump aligning tool J–38135 or equivalent pump aligner/seal installer, align oil pump on the crankshaft. Tighten the oil pump bolts to 19 ft. lbs. (26 Nm).

10. Install a new oil pump shaft seal using tools J–38135 and J–38463 or equivalent aligner and seal installer.

NOTE: Install a new oil pump shaft seal whenever the pump is removed from the vehicle.

11. Install the primary timing chain and crankshaft sprocket.

12. Connect the negative battery cable.

Rear Main Bearing Oil Seal

REMOVAL AND INSTALLATION

5.7L (VIN P) Engine

1. Disconnect the negative battery cable.

2. Remove the transmission assembly.

3. For manual transmission vehicles, remove the clutch cover and disc assembly.

4. Remove the flywheel bolts and remove the flywheel from the vehicle.

5. Using the notches provided in the seal retainer and a small suitable tool, pry the old seal from the engine. Be careful not to nick the crankshaft sealing surface when removing the seal.

To install:

6. Lubricate the inside and outside of a new seal with clean engine oil.

7. Install the seal on tool J–35621 or equivalent rear main seal installer.

8. Thread the screws of the tool into the rear of the crankshaft and tighten the screws snugly to assure proper seal alignment and installation.

9. Tighten the tool wingnut until it bottoms and then remove the tool.

10. Install the flywheel and tighten the bolts to 74 ft. lbs. (100 Nm).

11. If equipped, install the clutch cover and disc assembly.

12. Install the transmission assembly.

13. Lower the vehicle and connect the negative battery cable.

5.7L (VIN J) Engine

1. Disconnect battery negative cable.

2. Remove transmission assembly.

3. Remove the clutch cover and disc assembly.

4. Remove the flywheel bolts and flywheel.

5. Remove the screws attaching the crankshaft rear main oil seal/housing assembly to the cylinder case.

6. Remove the retaining screws, then remove the seal/housing assembly from the engine.

7. Remove the seal from the housing.

To install:

8. Lubricate the seal lip with engine oil.

9. Install seal into housing using crankshaft rear seal tool J–37312 or equivalent. Make sure the seal is installed 1.0–1.5mm below the housing surface.

10. Install the housing and tighten the bolts to 89 inch lbs. (10 Nm).

11. Apply Loctite® 242 or equivalent, to the bolts threads, then install the flywheel and tighten the bolts to 74 ft. lbs. (100 Nm).

12. Install the clutch cover and disc assembly.

13. Install the transmission assembly.

14. Connect the negative battery cable.

MANUAL TRANSMISSION

Transmission Assembly

REMOVAL AND INSTALLATION

1992 Vehicles

1. Disconnect the negative battery cable.

2. Remove the center air outlet.

3. Remove the console and accessory trim plates.

4. Remove the control lever button.

5. Remove the shift lever knob assembly.

6. Remove the center console trim plate.

7. Remove the shift lever snapring.

8. Remove the shifter retainer nuts.

9. Raise and safely support the vehicle.

10. Remove the complete exhaust assembly.

11. Remove the driveshaft.

12. Support the transmission with a suitable jack.

13. Remove the driveline support beam.

14. Disengage the electrical connectors from the speed sensor, backup lamp switch and shift solenoid.

15. Remove the transmission to clutch housing attaching bolts.

16. Remove the transmission assembly from the vehicle.

To install:

17. Install transmission assembly into the vehicle.

18. Install and torque the transmission to clutch housing bolts to 37 ft. lbs. (50 Nm). Make sure to torque the bolts using the proper crisscross sequence, starting at the top right bolt.

19. Engage the wiring harness connectors to the speed sensor, backup lamp switch and shift solenoid.

20. Install the driveline support beam.

21. Tighten the driveline support beam to differential bolts to 60 ft. lbs. (80 Nm) and the driveline support beam to transmission bolts to 37 ft. lbs. (50 Nm).

22. Install the driveshaft assembly.

23. Remove the transmission support jack.

24. Check transmission oil level and add if necessary.

NOTE: In a horizontal position, the transmission should be filled to the point of overflow.

25. Install the exhaust system.

26. Lower the vehicle.

27. Install the shifter and console assembly.

28. Install the center air outlet.

29. Connect the negative battery cable.

1993–96 Vehicles

1. Disconnect the negative battery cable.

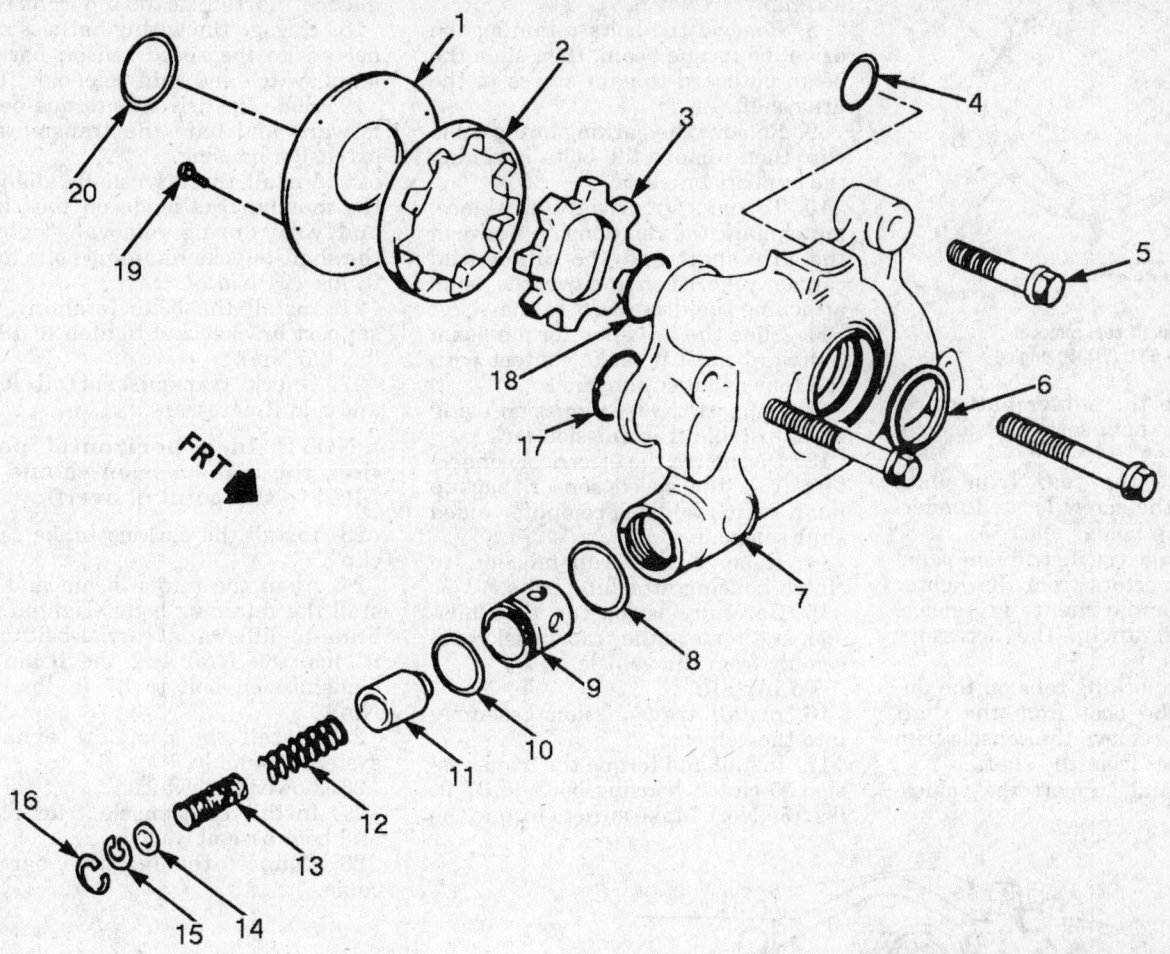

FRT

NOTE: CHAMFER ON INNER GEAR MUST FACE TO THE REAR (TOWARD ENGINE) SO AS TO ACCOMMODATE CRANKSHAFT O-RING 20.

1. Oil pump plate
2. Outer gear
3. Inner gear
4. Oil pump body o-ring
5. Oil pump bolt
6. Oil pump crankshaft seal
7. Oil pump body
8. Oil pressure regulation valve o-ring
9. Oil pressure regulation valve housing
10. Oil pressure regulation valve o-ring
11. Oil pressure regulation valve
12. Oil pressure regulation valve outer spring
13. Oil pressure regulation valve inner spring
14. Oil pressure regulation valve stop
15. Oil pressure regulation valve retainer
16. Oil pressure regulation valve retainer
17. Oil filter feed return o-ring
18 Oil filter feed return o-ring
19. Oil pump plate screw
20. Oil pump crankshaft o-ring

8470R062

Exploded view of the oil pump assembly — 5.7L (VIN J) engine

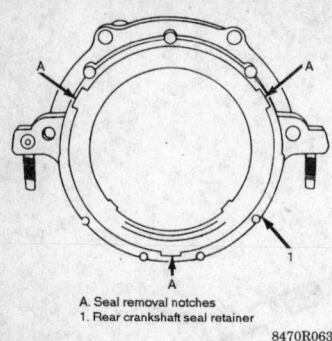

A. Seal removal notches
1. Rear crankshaft seal retainer

8470R063

Rear crankshaft seal removal locations — 5.7L (VIN P) engine

2. Remove the shifter button, retainer, shift knob, set screw and reverse inhibitor.

3. Remove the rear trim plate screws and the screw located underneath the cup holder mat.

4. Disengage the instrument panel harness connectors from the lighter and rear compartment lid release switch, then unclip the accessory plug harness.

5. Pry the locking tabs on the underside of the boot from the shaft groove, then remove the console trim plate and boot from the shaft.

6. Raise and support the vehicle safely.

7. Remove the complete exhaust assembly.

8. Remove the bolts retaining the driveline torque beam, then slide the beam outboard to gain access to the driveshaft.

9. Remove the parking brake cable clip, then remove the bolts retaining the support bracket.

10. To maintain drivetrain balance, matchmark the relationship between the driveshaft and the differential carrier yoke, then remove the bolts attaching the driveshaft to the yoke.

11. Slide the driveline torque beam rearward until it make contact with the rear exhaust hanger.

12. Support the transmission using an adjustable transmission jack.

13. Disengage the electrical connectors from the speed sensor, backup lamp switch and the computer aided shift solenoid.

14. Remove the transmission to clutch housing attaching bolts.

15. Carefully lower the transmission and remove the transmission assembly from the vehicle.

To install:

16. Install transmission assembly into the vehicle.

17. Install and torque the transmission to clutch housing bolts to 37 ft. lbs. (50 Nm). Make sure to torque the bolts using the proper crisscross sequence, starting at the top right bolt.

18. Engage the wiring harness connectors to the speed sensor, backup lamp switch and shift solenoid.

19. Slide the driveline torque beam forward and onto the transmission extension housing.

20. Install the driveshaft, aligning the matchmarks made on the shaft and yoke during removal. Tighten the shaft-to-yoke retaining bolts to 18 ft. lbs. (24 Nm).

21. Install the bolts retaining the support bracket and tighten to 18 ft. lbs. (25 Nm).

22. Check transmission oil level and add if necessary.

NOTE: In a horizontal position, the transmission should be filled to the point of overflow.

23. Install the parking brake cable clip.

24. Align the torque beam and install the retaining bolts. Tighten the beam-to-differential carrier bolt to 60 ft. lbs. (80 Nm) and the beam-to-transmission bolt to 37 ft. lbs. (50 Nm).

25. Install the complete exhaust system assembly.

26. Lower the vehicle.

27. Install the console trim plate and boot assembly.

28. Connect the negative battery cable.

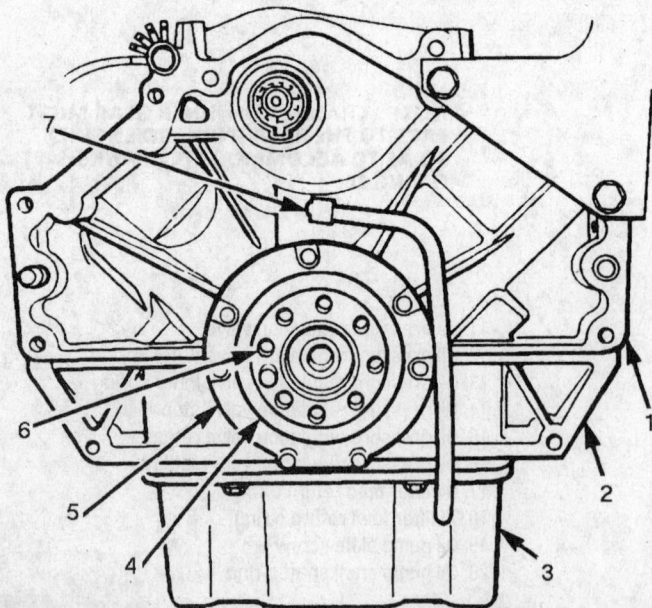

1. Cylinder case
2. Crankcase
3. Oil pan
4. Crankcase rear seal
5. Rear oil seal housing
6. Crankshaft
7. Cylinder case "vee" drain

8470R064

Rear main bearing/crankshaft oil seal — 5.7L (VIN J) engine

CLUTCH

Clutch Assembly

REMOVAL AND INSTALLATION

1. Disconnect the negative battery cable, then raise and support the vehicle safely.

2. Remove the complete exhaust system.

3. Remove the transmission assembly.

4. Except for the VIN J engine, disconnect the ground wire attached to the left clutch housing stud.

5. Remove the nuts attaching the clutch slave cylinder to the housing and support the cylinder to the side. Do not allow the cylinder to hang freely.

6. Except for the VIN J and 1993–96 VIN P engines, remove the starter assembly.

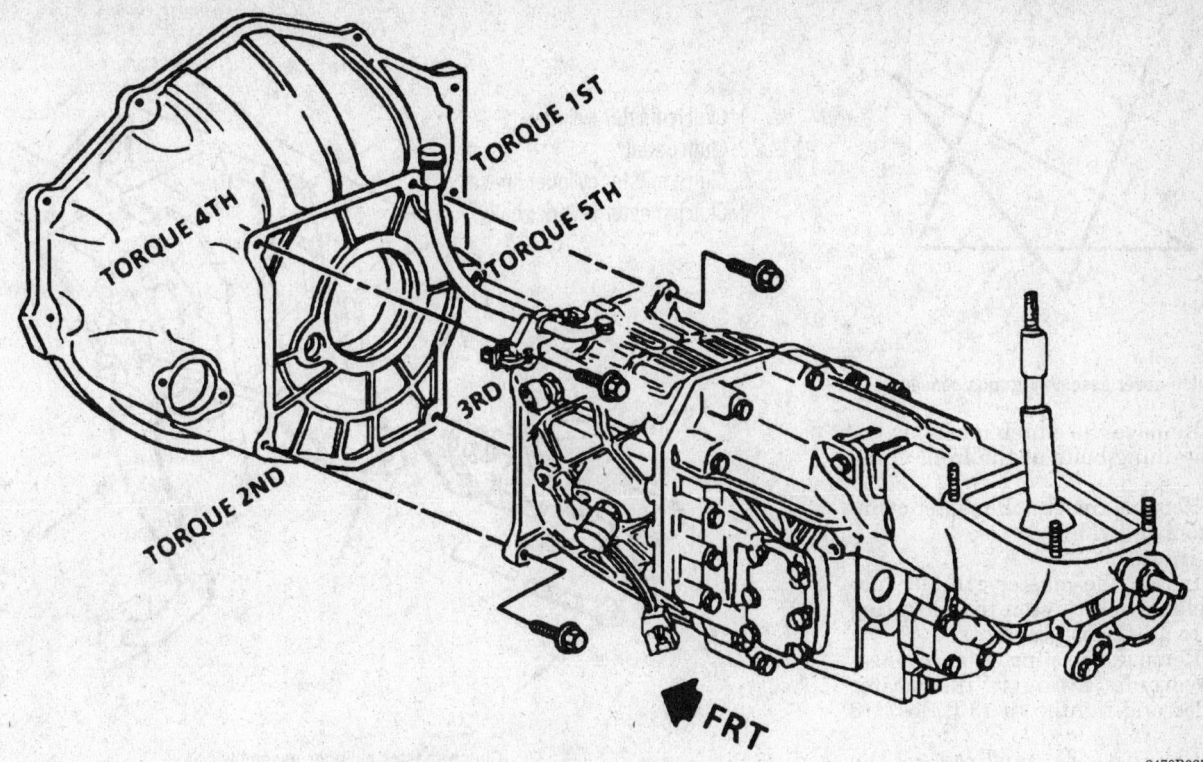

Transmission-to-clutch housing torque sequence

8470R065

7. For the VIN J engine, remove the nut retaining the left converter shield to the housing.

8. Remove the clutch housing cover.

9. Remove the bolts retaining the housing to the engine block and, if applicable on the 5.7L (VIN J) engine, the right side converter heat shield.

10. Remove the housing by aligning the fork onto the 2 flats of the release bearing and push the fork away from the bearing with a twisting motion. Remove the clutch housing and, for 5.7L (VIN P) engines with magnesium housings, the aluminum spacers.

NOTE: Excessive clutch wear may require removal of the ball stud locking screw and loosening of the ball stud to disengage the fork and housing.

11. Mark the alignment of the clutch cover and flywheel for installation purposes.

12. Loosen the clutch cover bolts evenly, 1 turn at a time until spring pressure is released. Failure to properly release spring pressure may result in damage to the clutch cover assembly and the flywheel.

13. Remove the clutch plate and disc assembly.

To install:

14. Inspect flywheel, clutch plate and disc for heat stress, cracks or worn parts and replace as necessary.

15. Install the clutch assembly using a suitable universal clutch disc alignment tool.

16. Make sure the marks made earlier are in alignment, then install the cover assembly-to-flywheel bolts. Tighten the bolts in the proper sequence, 1 turn at a time, until spring pressure is properly attained and the bolts are tightened to 30 ft. lbs. (41 Nm).

17. Position the clutch housing to the engine block and engage the fork onto the release bearing. If equipped, be sure the aluminum spacer is in position.

18. Verify the housing is properly positioned on the 2 engine dowel pins and, for the 5.7L (VIN J) engine, that the right converter heat shield is installed.

19. Tighten the clutch housing bolts to 37 ft. lbs. (50 Nm) and the ball stud to 33 ft. lbs. (45 Nm). Tighten the ball stud locking screw to 20 ft. lbs. (27 Nm) for 1992 vehicles, to 11 ft. lbs. (15 Nm) for 1993–96 VIN P engines or to 16 ft. lbs. (22 Nm) for 1993–96 VIN J engines, as applicable.

20. If equipped, install the ground harness connection to the housing.

21. Install the housing cover and tighten the bolts to 80 inch lbs. (9 Nm).

22. For the VIN J engine, install the left heat shield and tighten the retaining nut to 12 inch lbs. (1.4 Nm).

23. Install the clutch slave cylinder and tighten the retaining nuts to 19 ft. lbs. (25 Nm).

24. Install the transmission assembly.

25. Install the exhaust system and lower the vehicle.

26. Connect the battery negative cable and check clutch for proper operation.

Clutch Master Cylinder

REMOVAL AND INSTALLATION

1. Disconnect the negative battery cable, then remove the battery from the vehicle.

2. Remove the sound insulator panel from under the dash.

3. Disconnect the pushrod retaining clip and pushrod at the clutch pedal.

4. Disconnect and plug the hydraulic line at the clutch master cylinder.

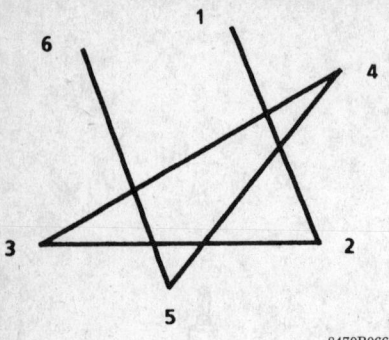

Clutch cover assembly torque sequence

8470R066

1. Clutch master cylinder
2. Cluth pedal
3. Clutch master cylinder spacer
4. Clutch master cylinder bolt

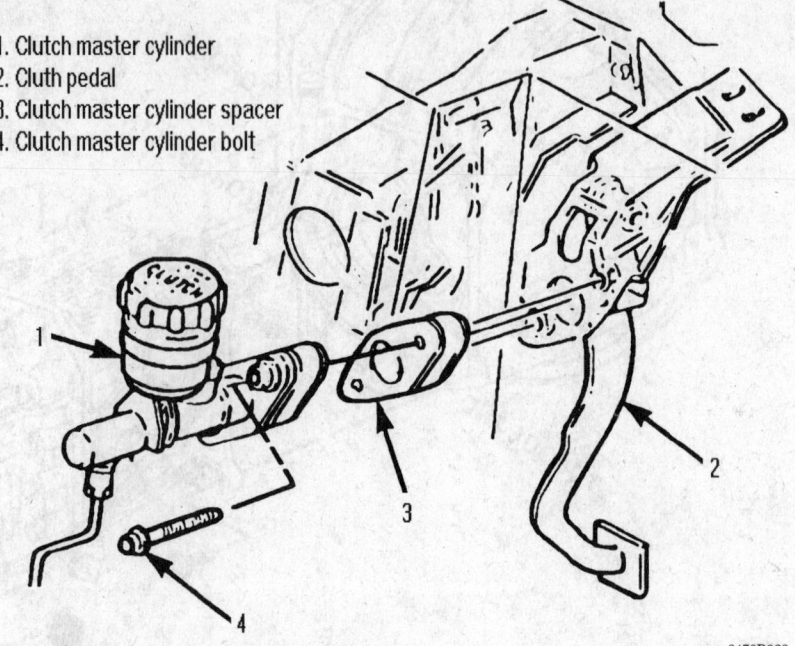

8470R068

Clutch master cylinder assembly

5. Remove the clutch master cylinder retaining bolts at the front of the dash.

6. Remove the clutch master cylinder from the vehicle.

To install:

7. Install the master cylinder into the vehicle and tighten the mounting bolts to 12 ft. lbs. (17 Nm).

8. Remove the plug, then connect the hydraulic fitting to the master cylinder and tighten to 13 ft. lbs. (18 Nm).

9. Connect the pushrod to the pedal and install the retaining clip.

10. Install the under dash hush panel.

11. Bleed the system, as required.

12. Install the battery and connect the positive, followed by the battery negative cables.

Clutch Slave/Actuator Cylinder

REMOVAL AND INSTALLATION

1. Raise and support the vehicle safely.

2. Remove the actuator cylinder stud nuts.

3. Note the position of the hydraulic line and disconnect the line from the retaining clip.

4. Remove the actuator and pushrod assembly from the clutch housing.

NOTE: Do not allow the slave cylinder to hang freely from the hydraulic line.

5. Disconnect and plug the hydraulic line at the actuator cylinder.

To install:

6. Remove the plug, then connect the hydraulic line to the actuator cylinder. Tighten the fitting to 13 ft. lbs. (18 Nm).

7. Install the pushrod and actuator assembly. Tighten the stud nuts to 19 ft. lbs. (25 Nm).

8. Place the hydraulic line in its original position in the retaining clip.

9. Bleed the system, as required.

Hydraulic Clutch System Bleeding

1. Disconnect the negative battery cable and remove the ECM from the mounting bracket to access the master cylinder for filling. Fill the master cylinder reservoir with the proper grade and type of fresh brake fluid or hydraulic clutch fluid.

2. Prior to bleeding the actuator, most of the air can be removed as follows:

   a. Remove the master cylinder cap and moisture barrier.

   b. Install the master cylinder cover.

   c. Lightly stroke the clutch pedal to release trapped air through the master cylinder.

   d. Remove the master cylinder cap and install the moisture barrier.

   e. Install the master cylinder cap.

3. Raise and support the vehicle safely.

4. Remove the actuator cylinder attaching stud nuts.

5. Remove the pushrod and actuator cylinder from the clutch housing and the hydraulic line from the retaining clip.

6. Lower cylinder slightly for access and disconnect the hydraulic hose fitting from the actuator cylinder.

7. Remove the bleed screw dust cap.

8. Position a drain pan or attach a clear plastic hose.

9. Support the slave cylinder in a horizontal position, with the bleeder screw vertical.

10. Fully depress the clutch pedal and open the bleeder screw.

11. Close the bleed screw and release the clutch pedal.

12. Repeat Steps 11 and 12 until all the air is expelled from the system. Check the fluid reservoir and replenish, as required during the procedure. Make sure the reservoir is kept sufficiently full to prevent air from being drawn into the system.

13. Tighten the bleeder screw and install the dust cover.

14. Install the hydraulic line into the retaining clip, position the actua-

tor cylinder and tighten the stud nuts to 19 ft. lbs. (25 Nm).
15. Lower the vehicle.
16. Install the ECM and connect the negative battery cable.

AUTOMATIC TRANSMISSION

Transmission Assembly

REMOVAL AND INSTALLATION

The engine must be supported before removing the transmission assembly in order to prevent the vapor blow pipe located across the rear of the engine from contacting the dash panel.
1. Disconnect the negative battery cable and remove the transmission fluid level indicator.
2. Disconnect the TV cable at the throttle lever or the adjuster assembly.
3. Raise and support the vehicle safely.
4. If equipped, remove the upper and lower underbody braces.
5. Remove the complete exhaust system.
6. Support the transmission with a suitable jack.
7. Remove the driveline support beam.
8. Matchmark and remove the driveshaft.
9. Disengage the speedometer electrical connector, then disconnect the shift control cable and the remaining electrical leads from the transmission.
10. Remove the torque converter cover and mark the relationship of the converter to the flywheel, then remove the converter-to-flywheel bolts.
11. Disconnect the oil cooler pipes at the transmission. Plug the openings to prevent system contamination or excessive fluid loss.
12. Disconnect the TV cable at the transmission.
13. Remove the transmission-to-engine mounting bolts and fasten the torque converter to the transmission using a converter restraining tool or a length of wire.

14. Carefully move the transmission rearward, downward and out from under the vehicle. If interference is encountered with cables, cooler lines, etc., remove the component(s) before finally lowering the transmission.

To install:
15. Flush the transmission oil cooler lines using J–35944 or an equivalent transmission cooler and line flushing tool.
16. Install a converter restraint tool to hold the torque converter in place.
17. Support the transmission with a suitable jack, then raise the transmission into position and remove the torque converter holding tool.
18. Install and tighten the transmission to engine bolts to 35 ft. lbs. (47 Nm).
19. Connect the TV cable to the transmission.
20. Remove the plugs, then connect the oil cooler pipes to the transmission.
21. Align the marks made during removal and start the torque converter to flywheel bolts by hand. Tighten the bolts to 46 ft. lbs. (62 Nm).
22. Install converter cover and torque screws to 89 inch lbs. (10 Nm).
23. Engage the electrical connectors to the transmission.
24. Connect the shift control cable.
25. Engage the speedometer electrical connector.
26. Align the marks made earlier and install the driveshaft, then the driveline support beam.
27. Install the exhaust system and, if equipped, the underbody braces.
28. Lower the vehicle and install the oil level indicator.
29. Connect the TV cable to the throttle lever or to the adjuster assembly.
30. Connect the negative battery cable.
31. Check and add the proper type and amount of transmission fluid.
32. Because the driveline support beam was removed, check clearance between the air intake duct and the throttle body. If the air duct becomes dislodged from the throttle body, a driveability problem could occur.

SHIFT LINKAGE ADJUSTMENT

1. Disconnect the negative battery cable.

2. Place the control lever in the **N** position.
3. Raise and support the vehicle safely.
4. Loosen the cable attachment at the shift lever.
5. Rotate the shift lever clockwise to **P** detent and then back to **N**.
6. Tighten the cable attachment to 15 ft. lbs. (20 Nm).

NOTE: The lever must be be held out of the P position when tightening the nut.

7. Lower the vehicle.
8. Check the cable adjustment by rotating the control lever through the detents.
9. Connect the battery negative cable.

THROTTLE LINKAGE ADJUSTMENT

Beginning in 1992, the Acceleration Slip Regulation (ASR) system was added to all Corvettes. This required a cable adjuster assembly which has the ability to extend cables slightly, according to commands from the control module. This extension allows the throttle close regardless of accelerator pedal position. The adjuster does not have the ability to apply throttle, it can only release it.
The cable adjuster assembly must be adjusted each time the throttle and/or TV cables are disconnect. On some models, the TV cable is also attached to a servo. The cable may be adjusted BEFORE cable adjuster assembly adjustment.

TV Cable Servo Linkage Adjustment

1. Make sure the TV cable is installed into servo bracket.
2. Pull servo assembly end of cable toward servo without moving the throttle lever.
3. If 1 out of the 5 holes in the servo assembly tab aligns with the cable pin, push pin through hole and connect pin to tab with retainer.
4. If the tab holes does not align with the pin, move the cable away from the servo assembly until the next closest tab hole aligns and connect the pin to the tab with the retainer.
5. Perform the adjustment procedure for the ASR accelerator and cruise control adjuster assembly.

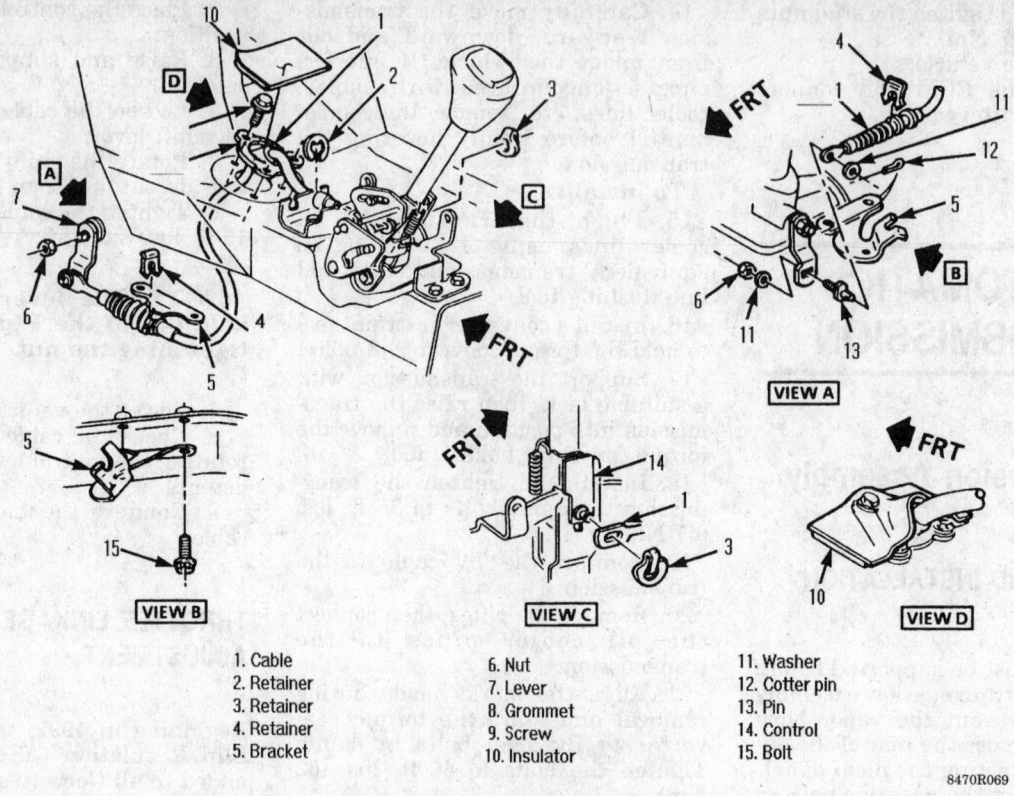

1. Cable
2. Retainer
3. Retainer
4. Retainer
5. Bracket
6. Nut
7. Lever
8. Grommet
9. Screw
10. Insulator
11. Washer
12. Cotter pin
13. Pin
14. Control
15. Bolt

8470R069

Automatic transmission shifter cable

DRIVE AXLE

Driveshaft and U-Joints

REMOVAL AND INSTALLATION

1. Raise and support the vehicle safely.
2. If equipped, remove the upper and lower underbody braces.
3. Remove the complete exhaust system as an assembly.
4. Support the transmission, then remove the bolts, washers and nuts attaching the driveline support beam at the axle and/or transmission to gain necessary clearance.
5. Mark relationship of shaft to the pinion yoke and disconnect the rear universal joint by removing trunnion bearing straps. Tape bearing cups to trunnion to prevent dropping and loss of roller bearings.
6. Place a suitable drain pan under the transmission for oil leakage, slide the slip yoke from the transmission and remove the driveshaft from the vehicle.

7. If necessary, remove the universal joints:
   a. Remove the snaprings. If a snapring does not readily come out, tap the end of the bearing cap lightly to relieve pressure against the ring.
   b. Place the driveshaft horizontally in line with the base plate of a press, but do not clamp the tube.
   c. Support the lower ear of the universal joint with a 1⅛ inch socket.
   d. Press the lower bearing cap out from the yoke using a pusher on the upper bearing cup.
   e. Rotate the driveshaft, then remove the opposite bearing cup.
   f. Remove the universal joint from the yoke.
To install:
8. If removed, install the U-joints:
   a. Install one bearing cap partially into 1 side of the yoke, then turn this side to the bottom.
   b. Install the joint into the yoke so the trunnion seats freely in the bearing cap.
   c. Install the opposite bearing cap partially into the yoke, verifying the trunnions are straight and true in the bearing caps.
   d. Press against the opposite bearing caps, while working the joint in order to verify that the

joint is not binding and turns freely. If the joint begins to bind, there is probably 1 or more needle bearings out of place and tipped under the trunnion.
   e. When 1 bearing cap snapring retainer groove clears the inside of the yoke, stop pressing and install a snapring into place.
   f. Continue to press the opposite side until a snapring can be inserted. If difficulty is encountered, strike the yoke firmly with a hammer to slightly spring the yoke ears.
   g. Assemble the other half of the joint in the same manner.
9. Slide the driveshaft slip yoke into the transmission extension.
10. Align the marks made during removal and install the rear of the driveshaft to the pinion yoke. If no marks were made or the driveshaft is being replaced, align the black paint dot on the driveshaft as close to 180 degrees opposite the yellow paint dot on the axle pinion yoke.
11. Install the propeller shaft retainers and bolts. Tighten the bolts to 18 ft. lbs. (24 Nm).
12. If removed, install and align driveline support beam as follows:
   a. To ensure proper alignment of the driveline, a clearance of 1.53–2.00 in. (39–51mm) must be

maintained between the top of the beam to the underbody and a clearance of 0.86–1.34 in. (22–34mm) from the passenger side of the beam to the side wall.

b. Take the measurements directly above and to the right of the driveshaft yoke.

c. Apply sealer to the support sealing surfaces at the transmission extension, the differential carrier and the driveline support.

d. Install the washers, bolts and nuts then tighten the bolts at the carrier to 60 ft. lbs. (80 Nm) and the transmission bolts to 37 ft. lbs. (50 Nm).

e. Remove the transmission support.

13. Install the exhaust system assembly.

14. If equipped, install the upper and lower underbody braces.

15. Lower the vehicle.

Rear Axle Shaft, Bearing and Seal

REMOVAL AND INSTALLATION

1. Raise and support the vehicle safely, making sure the rear suspension hangs freely.

NOTE: Do not support the vehicle by means of the differential or the transverse leaf springs.

2. Remove the rear transverse leaf spring from the knuckle as follows:

a. Remove 1 rear wheel assembly.

b. Install tool J–33432 or equivalent transverse leaf compressor, onto the rear transverse spring and compress the spring.

c. Remove the cotter pin, nut, rubber grommets and bolt attaching the spring to the knuckle.

d. Carefully release and remove spring compressor.

3. Remove the cotter pin, nut and washer from the tie rod outer socket at knuckle. Using a suitable linkage puller, disconnect the outer tie rod from the knuckle.

4. Disconnect the spindle rod bracket at the differential carrier.

5. Remove the axle shaft universal joint straps at the both the spindle and yoke shaft ends.

6. Remove the shaft by supporting the shaft and pushing out on the knuckle assembly.

7. If necessary, remove rear axle yoke, oil seal and bearing as follows:

a. If equipped, remove the upper and lower underbody braces.

b. Remove the exhaust assembly.

c. Support the rear differential, then remove the differential carrier outer support bolts.

d. Remove the carrier cover and drain the gear oil into a suitable container.

e. Remove the snapring from the axle shaft yoke and remove the yoke.

f. If only replacing the seal, pry the axle shaft yoke seal out using a suitable tool. Be careful not to damage the yoke shaft bearing assembly.

g. If the seal cannot be removed in this manner or the bearing assembly is to be replaced as well, remove the differential assembly.

h. Using tools J–34171 for the 7.875 inch axle (automatic transmission) or J–35509 for the 8.5 inch axle (manual transmission), and driver handle J–8592 or equivalents, and a hammer, remove the seal and bearing assembly. Discard the seal and bearing.

To install:

8. If removed, install a new rear axle shaft bearing and seal as follows:

a. If installing a new bearing, clean the seal bore using a standard metal cleaning solvent.

b. Install a new rear axle bearing assembly. Use tools J–34172 for the 7.875 inch axle (automatic transmission) or J–35510 for the 8.5 inch axle (manual transmission) with driver handle J–8592 or equivalents, and a hammer.

c. Lubricate bearings with a suitable hypoid lubricant.

d. Apply a light coat of hypoid lubricant on the lip of the axle shaft seal.

e. Install axle shaft seal using tools J–26938 for 7.875 in. axle or J–35511 for 8.5 in. axle and driver J–8592 or equivalents.

f. If removed, install the differential assembly.

g. Install the axle yoke shaft and snapring into the differential carrier.

h. If a new yoke shaft is installed, yoke shaft end play should be checked and adjusted, if necessary by using snaprings of varying thickness. Endplay should be 0.0005–0.0085 inch (0.013–0.216mm).

i. Apply a continuous ¼ inch bead of sealant to the mating surfaces, then install the differential carrier cover, with gasket, to the carrier. Tighten the bolts to specifi-

cation using the proper torque sequence.

j. Install the carrier outer support retaining bolts and tighten to 60 ft. lbs. (80 Nm).

k. Remove the differential support and install the exhaust assembly or connect the crossover pipe, as applicable.

l. If applicable, install the underbody upper and lower braces.

9. Install the axle assembly shaft into the differential and spindle yoke.

10. Install the shaft U-joint retainers and tighten the bolts to 26 ft. lbs. (35 Nm).

11. Connect the spindle rod bracket to the differential carrier and tighten the spindle rod bracket bolts to 60 ft. lbs. (80 Nm).

12. Install the tie rod outer axle socket to the knuckle. Install the washer and nut, tighten the end nut to 33 ft. lbs. (45 Nm), then replace the cotter pin.

13. Using a suitable compression tool, connect the leaf spring to the knuckle and install the bolt, grommets and nut. Tighten the nut and align the slot in the nut with the hole in the bolt, then insert a new cotter pin.

14. Lower the vehicle.

Rear Wheel Hub and Bearings

REMOVAL AND INSTALLATION

1. Disconnect the negative battery cable, then raise and support the vehicle safely.

2. Remove the tire and wheel assembly.

3. Remove the wheel speed sensor.

4. Remove the brake caliper and parking brake assembly, then remove the rotor.

5. Remove the wheel hub mounting bolts.

6. Remove the cotter pin, wheel nut retainer, spindle nut and washer.

7. Remove the wheel hub and bearing, caliper mounting plate and wheel spindle washer from the vehicle.

To install:

8. Inspect the wheel hub and bearing seal, replace if necessary. Also inspect the wheel spindle washer and replace, if damaged or excessively worn.

9. Install the wheel hub and bearing, caliper mounting plate and the wheel spindle washer. The washer flat should firmly seat against the shoulder of the wheel spindle. The lip

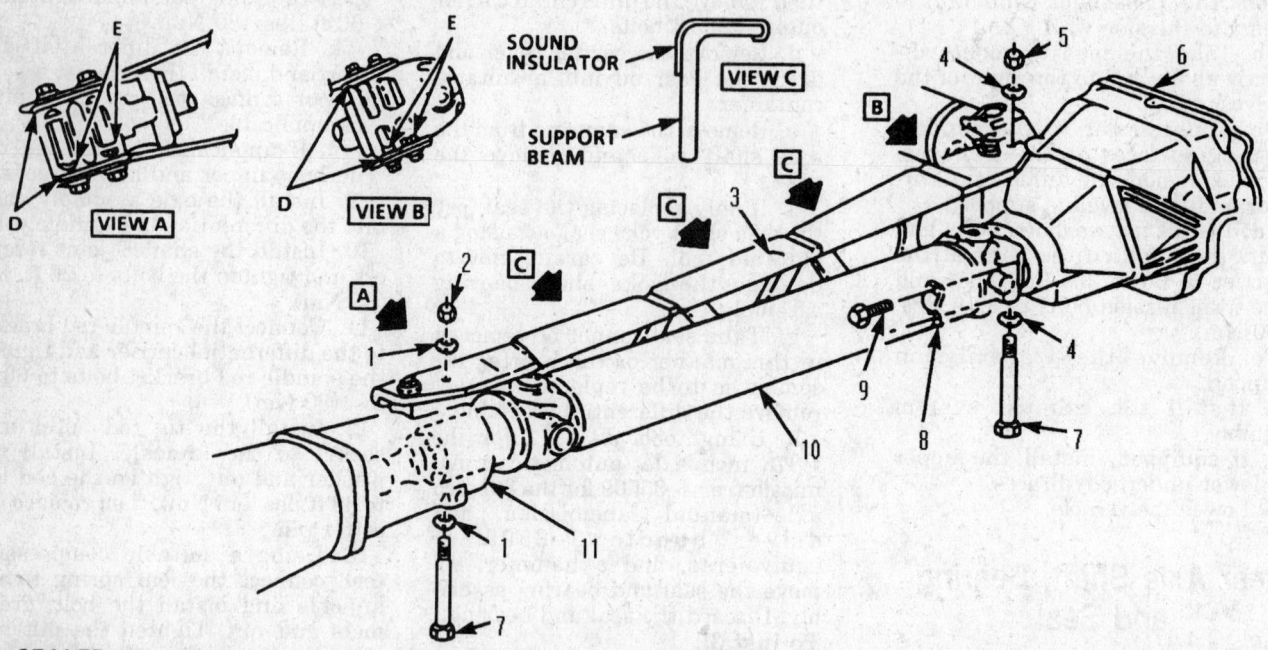

SEALER

APPLY A BEAD OF SEALER AROUND THE TOP AND BOTTOM MATING SURFACES OF DRIVELINE TO AXLE AND TRANSMISSION EXTENSION AT POINTS D AND ALSO TO THE CAVITY AROUND THE BOLTS AT POINTS E. USE URETHANE IN CAULKING KIT (P/N 963067) OR EQUIVALENT.

INSULATOR

REMOVE INSULATOR WITH FLAT BLADE SCRAPER AND CLEAN SURFACE. INSTALL INSULATOR BY REMOVING THE BACKING ON THE INSULATOR AND PRESSING THE INSULATOR AS SHOWN IN VIEW C TO OBTAIN ADHESION TO SUPPORT BEAM. TRIM OFF ANY OVERHANG.

1. Driveline support front washer
2. Self-locking nut
3. Driveline support
4. Washer

5. Hex self-locking nut
6. Rear axle carrier
7. Hex bolt
8. Propeller shaft retainer

9. Propeller bolt
10. Propeller shaft
11. Transmission extention housing

Driveshaft support beam alignment

of the washer should face the wheel spindle splines prior to hub and bearing installation.

10. Install the wheel hub mounting bolts and tighten to 66 ft. lbs. (90 Nm).

11. Install the washer and spindle nut, then tighten the nut to 164 ft. lbs. (223 Nm). The vehicle should not rest on the tires or move until the spindle nut is tightened.

12. Install the wheel retainer and a new cotter pin.

13. Install the brake rotor, then install the caliper and parking brake assembly.

14. Install the wheel speed sensor, then install the wheel and tire assembly.

15. Lower the vehicle and connect the negative battery cable.

Rear Wheel Axle Shaft Spindle

REMOVAL AND INSTALLATION

1. Disconnect the negative battery cable, then raise and support the vehicle safely.

NOTE: Do not support the vehicle by means of the differential or the transverse leaf springs.

2. Remove the tire and wheel assembly.

3. Remove the wheel speed sensor.

4. Remove the cotter pin, wheel nut retainer, spindle nut and washer.

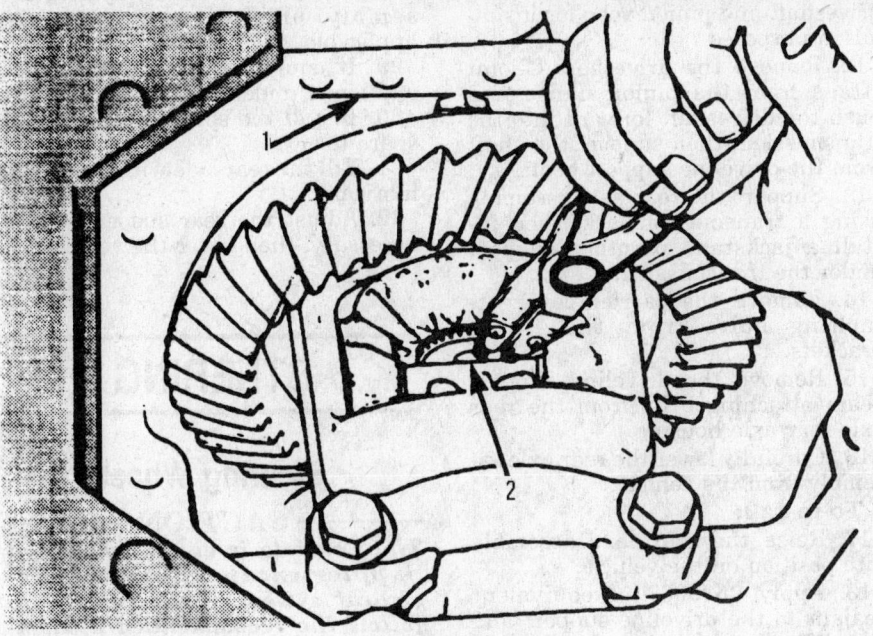

1. Differential carrier
2. Yoke shaft snap ring

8470R073

Removing the yoke shafts

5. Remove the axle shaft.

6. Remove the wheel spindle from the wheel hub and bearing.

7. Remove the wheel spindle washer from the spindle.

To install:

8. Inspect the spindle washer and replace, if necessary. Install the spindle washer onto the wheel spindle with the flat portion seated firmly against the shoulder of the spindle. The lip of the washer should face the spindle splines.

9. Install the spindle through the wheel hub and bearing.

10. Install the axle shaft.

11. Install the washer and spindle nut, tighten the nut to 164 ft. lbs. (223 Nm). The vehicle should not move or rest on the tires until the nut is tightened.

12. Install the wheel speed sensor.

13. Install the tire and wheel assembly.

14. Lower the vehicle and connect the negative battery cable.

Pinion Seal

REMOVAL AND INSTALLATION

1. Raise and safely support the vehicle.

2. If equipped, remove the upper and lower underbody braces.

3. Remove the exhaust assembly.

4. Remove the driveline support beam and driveshaft.

5. Remove the pinion yoke nut using a suitable tool to hold the yoke, then remove the yoke from the carrier.

6. Inspect the yoke seal area for wear, replace the yoke if necessary.

7. Carefully pry the pinion yoke seal from the differential housing using a small suitable tool. Be careful not to damage the pinion threads.

To install:

8. Clean the seal bore of the differential carrier.

9. Use J–34163 for the 7.875 inch axle (automatic transmission), J–35503 for the 8.5 inch axle (manual transmission), or an equivalent pinion seal installation tool, to install the new seal into the carrier bore.

10. Install the pinion yoke and tighten the nut while using a suitable tool to hold the pinion yoke. Tighten the pinion nut to 200 ft. lbs. (271 Nm) for an automatic transmission or 250 ft. lbs. (339 Nm) for a manual transmission.

11. Install the driveshaft and the driveline support beam.

12. Install the exhaust assembly or crossover pipe, as applicable.

13. If equipped, install the upper and lower underbody braces.

14. Check and fill the differential, as necessary.

15. Lower the vehicle.

Differential Assembly

REMOVAL AND INSTALLATION

1. Disconnect the negative battery cable.

2. Remove the rear axle assembly.

3. Remove the differential cover and drain the gear oil into a suitable container, then mount the assembly in a suitable support.

4. Remove the snaprings from each axle shaft yoke in the differential carrier. Mark each snapring to indicate which side it was removed from. The snaprings come in several different sizes.

5. Remove the axle shaft yokes.

6. Remove the differential bearing caps, noting the matched letters stamped on the caps and carrier.

7. Mount the carrier housing spreader tools J–24385–01 and J–24385–20 or equivalents, to the carrier housing and install a dial indicator set.

8. Measure the carrier spread using the dial indicator mounted to the assembly.

9. Spread the case, but do not exceed 0.010 inch (0.25mm) of spread.

10. Use 2 prybars to carefully pry the carrier assembly from the case. Be sure to avoid damage to any machined surfaces and tag the bearing cups to indicate from which side they were removed.

11. Remove the spreader after the assembly has been removed.

To install:

12. With the spreader mounted to carrier, spread the carrier, but not exceeding 0.010 in. (0.25mm) of spread then remove the dial set.

13. Lubricate and assemble the bearing cups to the differential bearing.

14. Install the differential assembly into the carrier and seat the differential assembly into the cross bore of the carrier. If necessary, use a rawhide or heavy duty plastic hammer to seat the differential.

15. Install the bearing caps and bolts, make sure the letters stamped on the caps and carrier assembly coincide in both direction and letter.

16. Tighten the cap bolts to 45 ft. lbs. (60 Nm) for the 7.875 inch axle (automatic transmission) or to 63 ft.

lbs. (85 Nm) for the 8.5 inch axle (manual transmission).

17. Measure the ring gear backlash at 3 equally spaced points:

 a. Backlash tolerance is 0.006–0.009 in. (0.15–0.23mm) and cannot vary more than 0.0010–0.0015 in. (0.03–0.04mm).

 b. High backlash is corrected by moving some shims from the opposite side of the case to the ring gear side, thus moving the ring gear closer to the pinion.

 c. Low backlash is corrected by moving shims from the ring gear side of the case to the opposite side, thus moving the ring gear away from the pinion.

18. Install axle shaft yokes and snaprings, ensuring snaprings are installed on the side from which they were removed.

19. Apply a continuous ¼ inch bead of 1052914 or equivalent sealant, to the mating surfaces and install the carrier cover with gasket onto the carrier. Tighten the bolts to specification, following the proper sequence.

20. Install the rear axle housing assembly into vehicle.

21. Lower the vehicle and connect the negative battery cable.

Rear Axle Housing

There are 2 Corvette differential assemblies, a Dana model 36 with a 7.875 inch ring gear used with an automatic transmission and a Dana model 44 with a 8.5 inch ring gear used with a manual transmission.

REMOVAL AND INSTALLATION

1. Raise and support the vehicle safely.

2. Remove the spare tire, then remove tire cover by disengaging the support hooks.

3. If equipped, remove the upper and lower underbody braces.

4. Remove the exhaust assembly.

5. Remove the transverse leaf springs from vehicle.

6. If necessary, remove exhaust hangers.

7. Remove the spindle support rod, bolts and mounting bracket from the carrier.

8. Remove both tie rod ends from knuckles.

9. Remove the axle universal joint straps from differential yokes.

10. Support the axle shaft and push the wheel and tire assembly outward to disengage joints from differential yokes.

11. Scribe alignment marks on driveshaft and pinion yoke for installation purposes.

12. Remove the driveshaft U-joint straps from the pinion flange and push the driveshaft forward into the transmission, then support the shaft from the driveline support beam.

13. Support the rear axle assembly using a transmission jack, then install a jackstand or other support under the transmission.

14. Remove the carrier cover attaching bolts from the frame brackets.

15. Remove the driveline support beam attaching bolts from the rear axle rear axle housing.

16. Carefully lower the rear axle assembly from the vehicle.

To install:

17. Raise the rear axle assembly into position on the vehicle.

18. Apply 9636067 or equivalent sealant to the driveline support and the differential carrier, then install the driveline support bolts at the front of the carrier cover.

19. To ensure proper alignment of the driveline, a clearance of 1.53–2.00 in. (39–51mm) must be maintained between the top of the beam to the underbody and a clearance of 0.86–1.34 in. (22–34mm) from the passenger side of the beam to the side wall. Take the measurements directly above and to the right of the driveshaft yoke and adjust if necessary, then tighten the bolts to 60 ft. lbs. (80 Nm).

20. Install the differential carrier cover-to-frame bracket bolts and tighten to 89 ft. lbs. (120 Nm).

21. Align the marks on driveshaft and yoke, and install the driveshaft. Tighten the U-joint strap bolts to 18 ft. lbs. (24 Nm).

22. Install wheel axle shaft joints into the yokes.

23. Install axle shaft U-joint retainers onto the yoke shafts, then tighten the retainers to 26 ft. lbs. (35 Nm).

24. Install tie rod ends into knuckle. Install the washers and nuts, then tighten the tie rod nut to 33 ft. lbs. (45 Nm) to align slot in nut with hole in stud. Install a new cotter pin.

25. Install the spindle support rod mounting bracket onto the carrier and tighten the bolts to 60 ft. lbs. (80 Nm).

26. Install the transverse leaf spring.

27. If removed, install the exhaust system hangers and nuts, tighten the nuts to 13 ft. lbs. (17 Nm).

28. Install the exhaust system assembly or crossover pipe, as applicable.

29. If equipped, install the upper and lower underbody braces.

30. Install the spare tire cover and spare tire.

31. Fill the rear axle with a suitable lubricant.

32. Adjust the rear suspension, as necessary, then lower the vehicle.

STEERING

Steering Wheel

CAUTION

The Corvette is equipped with a Supplemental Inflatable Restraint system, make certain to follow the recommended disarming procedure before and the coil centering and SIR enabling procedures, after repairs.

REMOVAL AND INSTALLATION

1. Properly disable the SIR system and disconnect the negative battery cable.

2. Remove screws from the back of the steering wheel attaching the inflator module.

3. Remove the inflator module from the steering wheel.

4. Disengage the Connector Pin Assurance (CPA) device and unplug the SIR electrical connector at the inflator module.

5. Remove the steering wheel attaching nut and disengage the horn connector. Mark the relationship of the steering wheel to the column splines for installation purposes.

NOTE: To avoid damaging the SIR coil, do not use any steering wheel puller other than those recommended.

6. Using steering wheel puller tool J-1859-03 and puller screws J-38720, or equivalents, remove the steering wheel. If the steering wheel does not come off easily, proceed as follows:

 a. With the puller installed and the side screws threaded to the shoulder, tighten the puller center screw snugly against the steering shaft.

 b. Back out each side screw 1 revolution from the fully threaded position.

MODEL 36 AND 44 COVER BEAM TO CARRIER TIGHTENING SEQUENCE

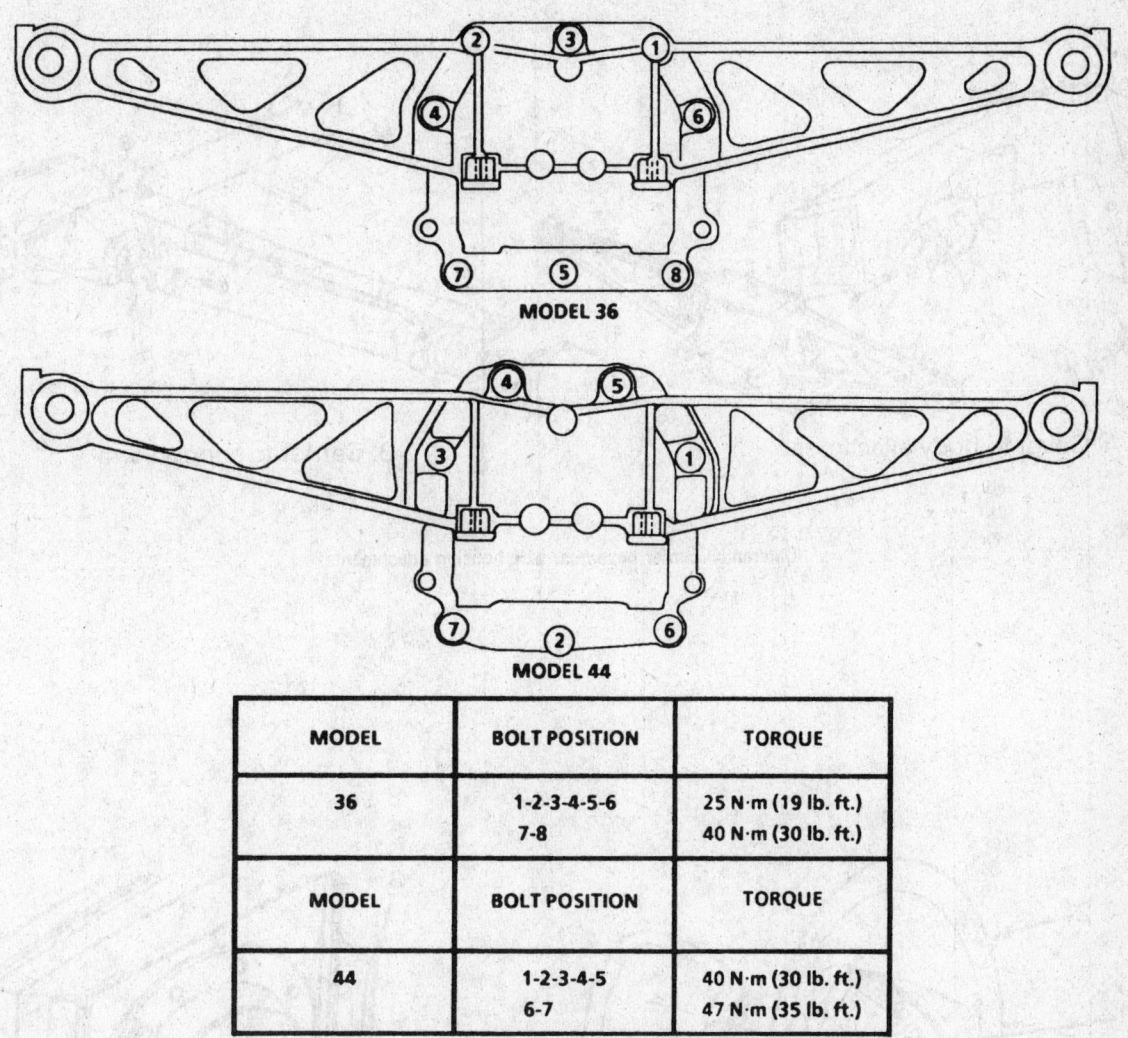

MODEL 36

MODEL 44

MODEL	BOLT POSITION	TORQUE
36	1-2-3-4-5-6	25 N·m (19 lb. ft.)
	7-8	40 N·m (30 lb. ft.)

MODEL	BOLT POSITION	TORQUE
44	1-2-3-4-5	40 N·m (30 lb. ft.)
	6-7	47 N·m (35 lb. ft.)

8470R077

Differential carrier cover torque specification and sequence — Dana model 36 (automatic transmission) and Dana model 44 (manual transmission)

c. Retighten the puller center screw.

d. Alternately tighten each side screw ¼ turn. Tightening the screws more than ¼ turn at a time could result in damage to the steering wheel.

e. Remove the steering wheel from the vehicle.

To install:

7. Engage the horn connector, then install the steering wheel to the column aligning the marks made earlier.

8. Install a new steering wheel retaining nut and tighten the new nut to 30 ft. lbs. (41 Nm).

9. Make sure the ignition is **OFF** and the negative battery cable is disconnected, the engage the SIR coil electrical connector to the inflator module. Install the CPA device to retain the connection.

10. Position the inflator module onto the steering wheel and install the module retaining screws. Except for 1993–96 vehicles, make sure to use new retaining screws. Tighten the screws to 87 inch lbs. (9.7 Nm).

11. Connect the negative battery cable and properly enable the SIR system.

Steering Column

REMOVAL AND INSTALLATION

1. Properly disable the SIR system.

2. Disconnect battery negative cable.

3. Verify the steering wheel and vehicle wheels are straight-ahead and the ignition key is in the **LOCKED** position, then remove the steering wheel.

4. Remove the intermediate shaft upper bolt.

5. Remove the driver's side knee bolster.

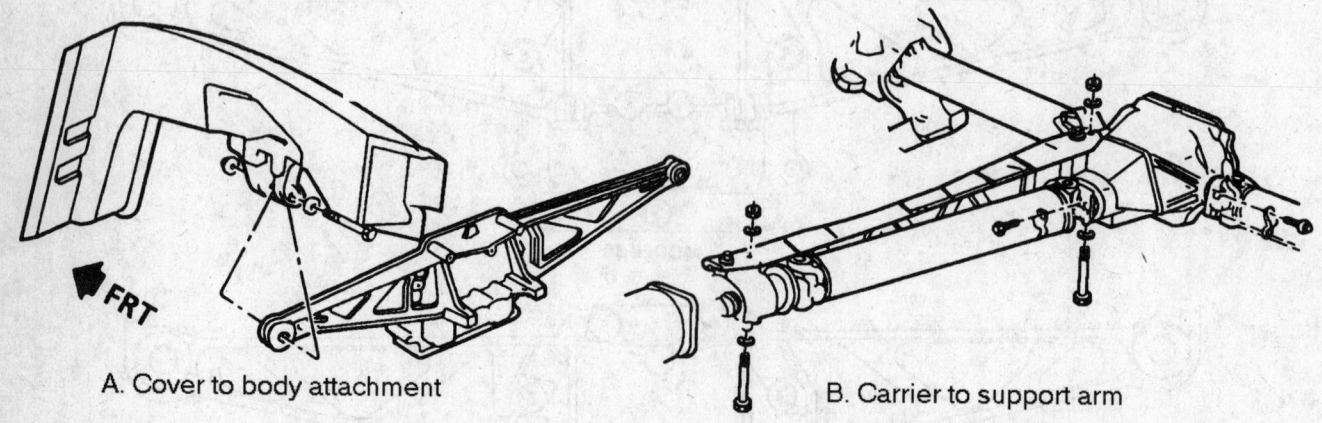

A. Cover to body attachment

B. Carrier to support arm

8470R078

Differential carrier cover/rear axle housing attachments

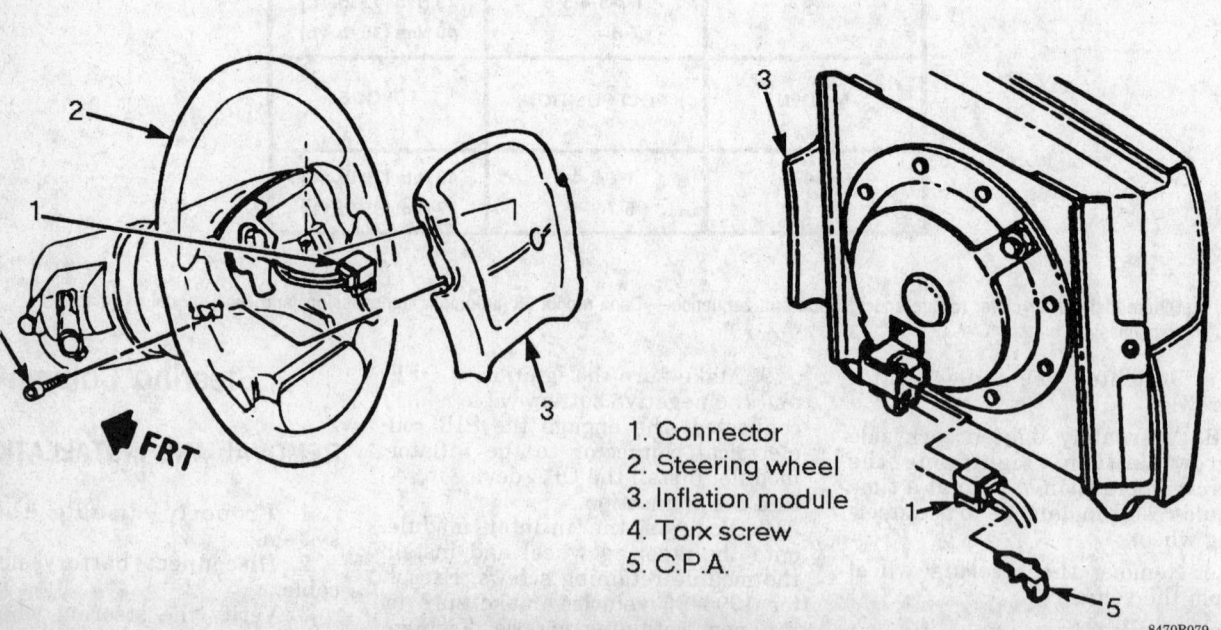

1. Connector
2. Steering wheel
3. Inflation module
4. Torx screw
5. C.P.A.

8470R079

SIR inflator module removal and installation

6. Remove the tilt lever.

7. Remove the nuts from the lower support plate and the capsule bolts from the reinforcement assembly. For vehicles equipped with automatic transmission, the bolts must also be removed from the upper support plate and cable backdrive assembly.

8. Disengage the electrical connectors from the steering column.

9. Remove the sound insulator from the steering column lower support bracket.

10. Remove the accelerator pedal bracket nuts.

11. Remove the steering column assembly from the vehicle.

To install:

12. Inspect the steering column to lower cowl gasket for tears. If damaged, the gasket must be replaced tears could allow carbon monoxide into the vehicle resulting in possible serious injuries or death.

13. Position steering column assembly into the vehicle and insert the lower steering shaft assembly into the U-joint of the intermediate shaft. Loosely install the shaft upper bolt.

14. Loosely attach the steering column and upper support plate to the instrument panel reinforcement assembly with the capsule bolts, and on automatic transmission vehicles, with the cable backdrive.

15. Loosely attach the steering column nuts to the support plate studs.

16. Tighten the intermediate shaft bolt to 26 ft. lbs. (34 Nm).

17. Tighten the lower support plate nuts to 10 ft. lbs. (14 Nm) and then tighten the capsule to reinforcement bolts to 20 ft. lbs. (27 Nm). The lower support plate nuts must be tightened first to prevent damage to the column assembly.

18. Engage all electrical connectors to the steering column, except the SIR connector.

19. Install the driver's side knee bolster.

20. Install the sound insulator bracket to lower column support.

21. Install the accelerator pedal bracket nuts and tighten to 71 inch lbs. (8 Nm).

22. Install the steering wheel and the inflator module assembly.

23. Connect the negative battery cable and properly enable the SIR system.

Power Rack and Pinion

ADJUSTMENT

Rack Bearing Preload

1. Raise and safely support the vehicle so the front wheels are raised and the steering wheel is centered.

2. Loosen the adjuster plug locknut.

3. Turn the adjuster plug clockwise until it bottoms, then back off 50–70 degrees.

4. Keep the adjuster plug from turning and tighten the locknut to 50 ft. lbs. (70 Nm), except for 1993–96 vehicles which should be tightened to 55 ft. lbs. (75 Nm).

5. Inspect the steering wheel returnability to center after adjustment.

REMOVAL AND INSTALLATION

1. Disconnect the negative battery cable and position a drain pan under the vehicle to catch fluid.

2. For 1993–96 VIN P engines, remove the air intake duct, then remove the serpentine drive belt and the drive belt idler pulley.

3. Remove the power steering gear inlet hose assembly from the steering gear.

4. Remove the power steering gear outlet hose assembly from the steering gear.

NOTE: If equipped with a power steering fluid cooling pipe, disconnect fluid cooling pipe outlet hose from the fluid cooling pipe.

5. Remove the steering gear coupling shield.

6. Disconnect the intermediate shaft from the power steering gear and lower steering shaft, then position aside.

7. Raise and support the vehicle safely.

8. Remove the front tire and wheel assemblies.

9. Remove both outer tie rods from the knuckles using a suitable puller.

10. If equipped, remove the power steering cooler assembly.

11. Remove the stabilizer shaft.

12. Remove the steering gear to frame attaching clamp nuts, then remove the bolts and clamp from the vehicle.

13. Remove the power steering gear attaching attaching nut and bolt.

14. Remove the power steering gear from the vehicle.

15. If necessary, remove the outer tie rods, rack and pinion boots, and the inner tie rods from the power steering gear.

To install:

16. If removed, install the inner tie rods, boots and outer tie rods.

17. Install the power steering gear, nuts and bolts. Torque the attaching nut to 30 ft. lbs. (40 Nm). Torque the steering gear clamp nuts to 18 ft. lbs. (25 Nm).

18. Install the stabilizer shaft and, if applicable, the power steering cooler assembly.

19. Install both outer tie rods to the steering knuckle.

20. Install tire and wheel assemblies, then lower the vehicle.

21. Install the intermediate shaft and the steering gear coupling shield.

22. Install the power steering gear outlet hose assembly to the power steering gear. Tighten fitting to 21 ft. lbs. (28 Nm).

23. Install the power steering gear inlet hose assembly to the power steering gear. Tighten the fitting to 21 ft. lbs. (28 Nm).

24. For 1993–96 VIN P engines, install the drive belt idler pulley and the serpentine drive belt, then install the air intake duct.

25. Remove the drain and fill the power steering reservoir.

26. Connect the negative battery cable, bleed the system and check for proper operation.

Power Steering Pump

REMOVAL AND INSTALLATION

5.7L (VIN P) Engine

1. Disconnect the negative battery cable and place a drain pan under the vehicle to catch fluid.

2. Remove the air intake duct, then remove the serpentine drive belt.

3. Remove the steering pump pulley hub cap, then remove the pulley using J–25034–B or an equivalent puller tool.

4. For 1993–96 vehicles, remove the serpentine drive belt idler pulley.

5. Disconnect the gear inlet hose assembly from the pump. For 1993–96 vehicles, remove the pump inlet pipe mounting bolts, then disconnect the pipe assembly from the pump.

6. For 1992 vehicles. disconnect the reservoir hose and clamp from the pump.

7. Remove the power steering pump mounting bolts.

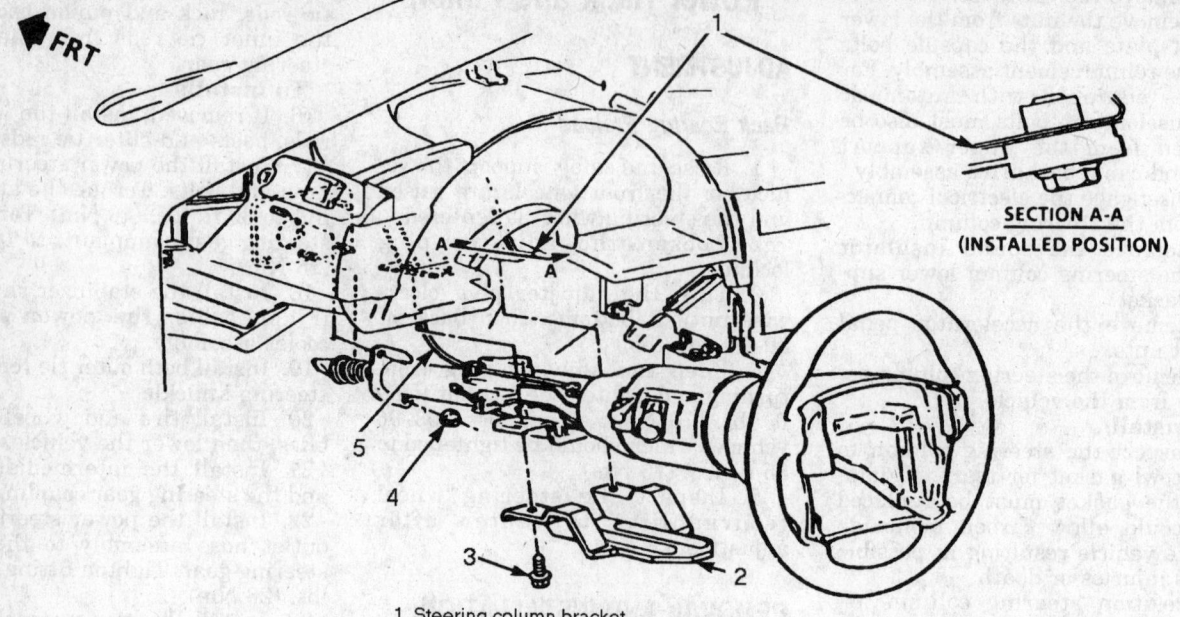

1. Steering column bracket
2. Steering column lower support bracket
3. Steering column capsule bolt
4. Lower support plate nut
5. Cable backdrive (automatic only)

8470R081

Steering column mounting

8. Remove the power steering pump and front bracket.

To install:

9. Install the power steering pump and front bracket with the mounting bolts. Tighten the bolts to 18 ft. lbs. (25 Nm).

10. For 1992 vehicles, connect the power steering pump reservoir hose and clamp to the pump. Tighten the clamp to 22 inch lbs. (2.5 Nm).

11. For 1993–96 vehicles, install the pump inlet pipe to the pump, then install the mounting bolts and tighten to 24 ft. lbs. (33 Nm).

12. Connect the power steering gear inlet hose assembly to the power steering pump and tighten the fitting to 21 ft. lbs. (28 Nm).

13. For 1993–96 vehicles, install the serpentine drive belt idler pulley.

14. Using J–25033–B, or an equivalent installation tool, install the power steering pump pulley so the front of the pulley hub is flush with the front of the pump shaft.

15. Install the hub cap to the pulley.

16. Install the serpentine drive belt, then install the intake air duct.

17. Connect the negative battery cable and remove the drain pan.

18. Refill the power steering reservoir and properly bleed the system.

5.7L (VIN J) ENGINE

1. Disconnect the negative battery cable and remove the air intake duct.

2. Drain the engine cooling system into a suitable container.

3. Drain and appropriately discard the power steering fluid.

4. Remove the serpentine drive belt.

5. Remove the left coolant outlet cover and hose.

6. Disconnect the vacuum hose retainer from the pump reservoir, then remove the vacuum hose(s) and set aside.

7. For 1992 vehicles:

a. Remove the power steering pump bracket-to-cylinder head bolts.

b. Remove the pump bracket to air conditioning compressor bolt.

c. Remove the cooler assembly outlet hose from the reservoir.

d. Disconnect the power steering gear inlet pipe from the power steering pump, then remove the power steering pump assembly from the vehicle.

e. As necessary, remove the pump pulley using tool J–25034–B or equivalent puller. Remove the reservoir hose from the pump. Remove the power steering pump-to-

mounting bracket bolts and remove the pump and/or reservoir from the bracket.

8. For 1993–96 vehicles:

a. Remove the bolts retaining the compressor hose clip to the crossmember.

b. Remove the pulley hub cap and separate the pulley from the pump using J–25034–B or an equivalent puller.

c. Remove the crankcase vent inlet pipe from the power steering pump bracket.

d. Remove the crankcase vent inlet hose from the throttle body extension.

e. Remove the compressor-to-power steering pump bracket bolt.

f. Remove the gear inlet pipe from the pump, then remove the outlet hose from the cooler assembly.

g. Remove the power steering pump bracket-to-cylinder head bolts, then remove the pump from the vehicle.

h. As necessary, remove the fluid reservoir hose from the assembly, remove the pump-to-mounting bracket bolts and remove the pump and/or reservoir from the mounting bracket.

To install:

9. If replacing the pump, do not use a pump with the letter **R** on the back of the pump housing.

10. If removed, install the reservoir and/or pump to the bracket. Apply Loctite® 565 or equivalent, to the pump-to-bracket mounting bolts and install. Tighten the bolts to 19 ft. lbs. (26 Nm).

11. If removed, connect the pump reservoir hose to the pump and tighten the clamp screw to 22 inch lbs. (2.5 Nm).

12. For 1993–96 vehicles:

a. Install the pump assembly to the vehicle. Coat the bolt threads with Loctite® 565 or equivalent, then install the bolts and tighten 19 ft. lbs. (26 Nm).

b. Connect the outlet hose to the cooler assembly. Tighten the clamp screw to 22 inch lbs. (2.5 Nm).

c. Connect the power steering gear inlet pipe to the pump, then tighten the fitting to 21 ft. lbs. (28 Nm).

d. Install the compressor-to-power steering pump bracket bolt and tighten to 19 ft. lbs. (26 Nm).

e. Install the crankcase vent inlet hose to the throttle body extension and to the power steering pump bracket.

f. Install the pump pulley using J–25033–B or equivalent installation tool, then install the hub cap.

g. Install the bolt retaining the compressor hose clip to the crossmember.

13. For 1992 vehicles:

a. If removed, install the power steering pump pulley using a suitable installation tool.

b. Position the pump assembly onto the engine.

c. Connect the gear inlet pipe to the pump and tighten the fitting to 21 ft. lbs. (28 Nm).

d. Install the cooler assembly outlet hose to the reservoir and tighten the hose clamp screw to 22 inch lbs. (2.5 Nm).

e. Install the A/C compressor to power steering pump bracket bolt and tighten to 19 ft. lbs. (26 Nm).

f. Apply a coat of Loctite® 565 to the pump bracket-to-cylinder head bolts, install and tighten the bolts to 19 ft. lbs. (26 Nm).

14. Install the vacuum hose(s) and connect the retainer to the power steering pump reservoir. Tighten the screws to 13 inch lbs. (1.5 Nm).

15. Install the left coolant outlet cover and hose.

16. Install the serpentine drive belt.

17. Install the air intake duct and connect the negative battery cable.

18. Refill the power steering reservoir.

19. Properly fill the engine cooling system.

20. Bleed the power steering system.

System Bleeding

1. With the engine **OFF** and wheels off the ground, turn the steering wheel all the way to the left. Add power steering fluid to the **COLD** mark on the fluid level indicator.

2. Bleed the system by turning the wheels from side-to-side without reaching the stop at either end. It may be necessary to turn the wheel from side-to-side several times. Be sure to keep the fluid full.

3. Start the engine. With engine idling, recheck the fluid level. If necessary add fluid to bring the fluid up to the **COLD** mark.

4. Return the wheels to the center position. Lower the front wheels to the ground and continue to run for 2–3 minutes.

5. Road test the vehicle to make sure the steering functions normally and without noise.

6. Check for fluid leakage. Check to make sure the fluid level is at the **HOT** mark after system is stabilized at its normal operating temperature.

Tie Rod Ends

REMOVAL AND INSTALLATION

1. Disconnect battery ground cable.

2. Raise and support the vehicle safely.

3. Remove the tie rod cotter pin and hex slotted nut from the tie rod assembly.

4. Loosen tie rod jam nut.

5. Using tool J–24319–01 or equivalent linkage puller, remove the tie rod from the steering knuckle.

6. Remove the tie rod from the steering rack assembly. To ease installation and give a point from which the alignment may be adjusted, scribe alignment marks on the rack assembly prior to tie rod end removal, and/or count the number of turns necessary to remove the tie rod end.

To install:

7. Install the tie rod to the steering rack assembly, but do not tighten the jam nut. Thread the tie rod end in the same number of turns and/or align it to the marks made during removal.

8. Install the tie rod to the steering knuckle and install the hex slotted nut to the tie rod stud.

9. Tighten the hex nut to 35 ft. lbs. (47 Nm), then insert a new cotter pin. If necessary tighten the nut additionally in order to insert the pin, but do not exceed a total torque of 52 ft. lbs. (70 Nm) and do not back off the original torque.

10. Check and adjust toe, as necessary.

NOTE: Make sure the rack and pinion boot is not twisted or puckered during installation or adjustment.

11. Adjust the toe by turning the inner tie rod, making sure the rack and pinion boot is not twisted or puckered during toe adjustment.

12. Tighten the jam nut against the tie rod to 50 ft. lbs. (68 Nm).

BRAKES

Master Cylinder

REMOVAL AND INSTALLATION

1. Disconnect the negative battery cable.

2. Unplug the electrical connector from the warning switch and, if equipped, the fluid level warning switch assemblies.

3. Disconnect the hydraulic brake lines at the master cylinder. Plug the openings to prevent fluid contamination or loss.

4. If equipped, disconnect the master cylinder prime pipe from the reservoir.

5. Remove the retaining nuts holding the cylinder to the brake booster assembly.

6. Reposition the battery cable and cruise control cable.

7. Remove the master cylinder assembly from the brake booster.

To install:

8. Position the master cylinder assembly to the power booster.

9. Clip the battery and cruise control cables into position.

10. Install the master cylinder retaining nuts and tighten to 13 ft. lbs. (18 Nm).

11. Remove the plugs, then connect the hydraulic brake lines to the

master cylinder and tighten the fittings to 13 ft. lbs. (18 Nm).

12. If equipped, connect the master cylinder prime pipe.

13. Engage the electrical connections to the warning switch assemblies.

14. Fill the master cylinder and properly bleed the hydraulic brake system.

15. Connect the negative battery cable.

Proportioning Valve

REMOVAL AND INSTALLATION

1. Disconnect the negative battery cable.

2. Remove the master cylinder assembly from the vehicle.

3. Remove the warning switch assembly from the master cylinder.

4. Remove the end plug and O-ring from the master cylinder.

5. Remove the electrical bias spring, then remove the proportioning valve assembly along with the O-ring and spacer.

NOTE: If necessary, gently tap the cylinder body against a piece of wood to dislodge the proportioning valve assembly.

6. Do not disassemble the proportioning valve, it is serviced only as an assembly. Also, do not clean the proportioning valve with any solution as the internal components are lubricated with a special grease.

To install:

7. Lubricate the valve and cylinder bore with clean brake fluid, then install the valve into the master cylinder and bottom it into the bore. The proportioning valve should be installed with the capped end first.

8. Install a new O-ring over the end plug, then install the spring followed by the end plug.

9. Tighten the proportioning valve end plug to 18 ft. lbs. (25 Nm).

10. Install the warning switch assembly, hand-tighten only.

11. Install the master cylinder assembly to the vehicle.

12. Connect the negative battery cable and properly bleed the hydraulic brake system.

Power Brake Booster

REMOVAL AND INSTALLATION

1. Disconnect the negative battery cable.

2. Remove the ECM, then remove the ECM housing bracket attaching bolt.

3. Remove the cruise control cable from the cruise control servo and the servo mounting bracket.

4. Disengage the pressure differential sensor electrical connector and the vacuum hose.

5. Disengage the master cylinder warning switch electrical connector, then remove the nuts attaching the master cylinder to the power booster assembly.

6. Reposition the master cylinder assembly, cruise control cable and the battery cable aside. Be careful not to damage the hydraulic lines.

7. Remove the power booster vacuum check valve from the power booster assembly.

8. Remove the instrument panel left sound insulator.

9. Remove the input pushrod assembly retaining ring and washer from the brake pedal.

10. For the VIN P engine, remove the nuts and washers from the tie rods.

11. Remove the power booster assembly attaching nuts and washers, then remove the power booster with seals and the ECM bracket attached, while disengaging the input pushrod assembly.

To install:

12. Install the seals, ECM bracket and power booster assembly to the brake pedal bracket. Have an assistant engage the pushrod assembly onto the brake pedal while installing the booster.

13. Install the booster assembly retaining nuts and tighten to 15 ft. lbs. (21 Nm).

14. Install the washer and retaining clip to the brake pedal, then install the left sound insulator.

15. Connect the vacuum check valve to the power booster assembly.

16. Position the master cylinder, cruise control cable bracket and the battery cable clip, then install the retaining nuts and tighten to 13 ft. lbs. (18 Nm).

17. Engage the master cylinder warning switch electrical connector.

18. Engage the pressure differential sensor electrical connection and vacuum hose.

19. Connect the cruise control cable to the servo and the mounting bracket.

20. Install the ECM housing bracket bolt and tighten to 18 ft. lbs. (25 Nm).

21. Install the ECM.

22. Connect the negative battery cable.

Brake Caliper

REMOVAL AND INSTALLATION

Front

1. Disconnect the negative battery cable and remove ⅔ of the brake fluid from the master cylinder reservoir.

2. Raise and support the vehicle safely.

3. Mark the relationship between the wheel and axle flange, then remove the tire and wheel assembly.

4. Install 2 wheel nuts to retain the brake rotor.

5. Depress the caliper pistons into the caliper bores in order to provide clearance between the pads and the rotor.

6. If the caliper is being completely removed from the vehicle for service, disconnect the brake line fitting at the caliper by removing the bolt, 2 gaskets and then the brake hose inlet fitting. Plug all openings to prevent fluid contamination or loss.

NOTE: Do not allow the fluid to come into contact with the front transverse spring as damage to the spring may occur.

7. Remove the circlip and the retainer pin, then the caliper housing from the rotor and the caliper mounting bracket. Remove the caliper from the vehicle or if the brake line is still attached, support the caliper from the control arm with a suitable hook or length of mechanic's wire.

To install:

8. Install the caliper over the brake rotor and into the caliper mounting bracket. Make sure the shoe lining guiding surfaces are correctly seated in the bracket.

NOTE: There are 2 sets of retainer pins in most repair kits. One set is for base calipers and the other is for heavy duty calipers. Make certain the correct retainer pins are installed.

9. Compress the bias springs by applying pressure to the mounting bracket, then install the new retainer pin and circlip.

10. If removed, connect the brake hose inlet fitting, 2 new gaskets and the inlet fitting bolt. Tighten the bolt to 30 ft. lbs. (40 Nm).

11. If the inlet fitting was removed, properly bleed the hydraulic brake system.

12. Remove the wheel nuts retaining the rotor, align the marks made earlier and install the tire and wheel assembly.

13. Lower the vehicle and check the brake fluid; add as necessary.

14. Connect the negative battery cable, start the engine and pump the brake pedal slowly and firmly 3 times to seat the shoe and lining assemblies.

Rear

1. Disengage the parking brake automatic adjuster as follows:

   a. Remove the drivers seat cushion.

   b. Remove the parking brake lever cover and screws.

   c. Using a suitable offset tool, disengage and hold the drive pawl from the drive sector.

   d. Insert a nail or drift through the hole in the anchor plate to retain the drive pawl in the disengaged position.

   e. Move the parking brake lever until it aligns with the lock pawl.

   f. Depress the button on the lever and move the lever to the down position.

   g. Verify the anchor plate is against the stud on the parking brake lever, if not as specified, repeat the procedure.

2. Raise and support the vehicle safely.

3. Mark the relationship between the wheel and axle flange, then remove the tire and wheel assembly.

4. Install 2 wheel nuts to retain the brake rotor.

5. If the caliper is being completely removed from the vehicle for service or replacement, disconnect the brake line fitting at the caliper by removing the bolt, 2 gaskets and the brake hose inlet fitting. Plug all openings to prevent fluid contamination or loss.

NOTE: Do not remove the lever return spring unless the parking brake cable automatic adjuster has been properly disabled.

6. Remove the lever return spring. Discard the spring if the coils are opened.

7. Disconnect the brake cable from the lever and bracket.

8. Remove the 2 guide pins bolts and discard.

9. Remove the caliper housing from the brake rotor and caliper mounting bracket.

To install:

10. Inspect the guide pins for free movement and replace the pins or boots if damaged or corroded.

11. Install the caliper over the brake rotor and into the mounting bracket.

12. Install 2 new guide pin bolts. Tighten the upper bolt to 26 ft. lbs. (35 Nm) and the lower bolt to 16 ft. lbs. (22 Nm).

13. Install the cable to the bracket and parking brake lever, then install the lever return spring.

14. If removed, connect the brake line fitting, 2 new gaskets and the inlet fitting bolt. Tighten the bolt to 30 ft. lbs. (40 Nm).

15. If the inlet fitting was removed, properly bleed the hydraulic brake system.

16. Enable the parking brake automatic adjuster in the reverse order of the disable procedure and make sure the levers are against the stops on the caliper housing.

17. Remove the 2 nuts securing the rotor to the hub, align the marks made earlier and install the tire and wheel assembly.

18. Lower the vehicle and check the brake fluid level.

19. Connect the negative battery cable, start the engine and pump the brake pedal slowly and firmly 3 times

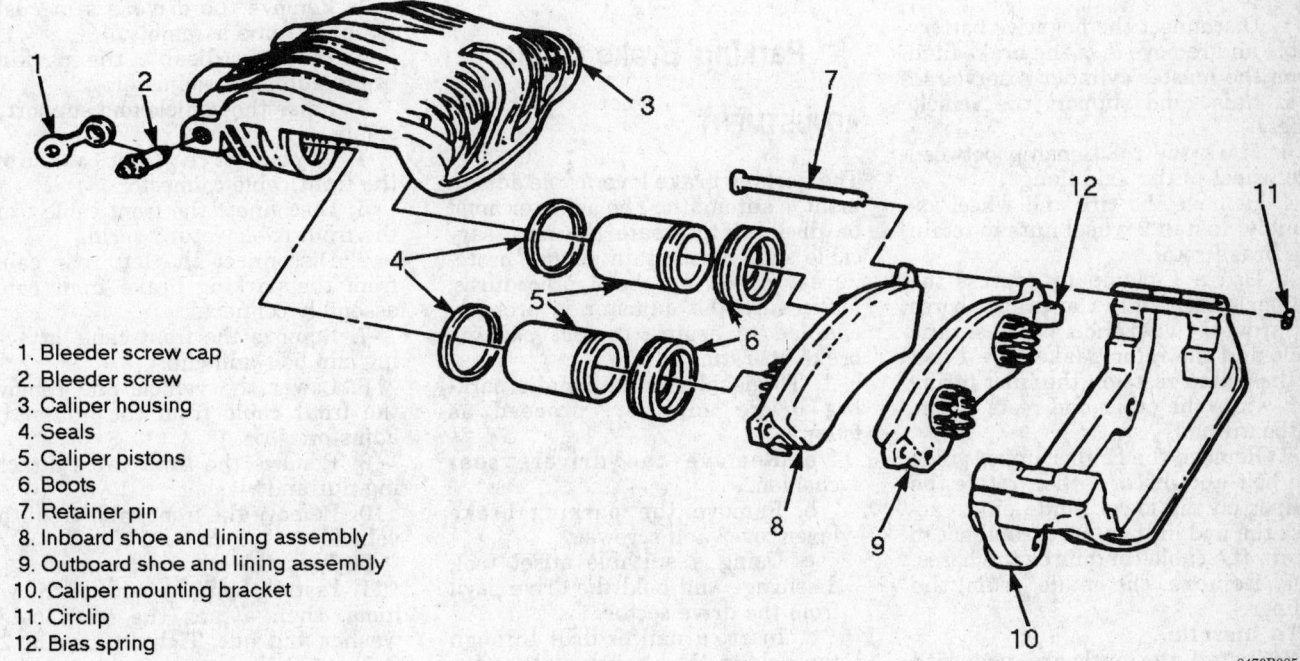

1. Bleeder screw cap
2. Bleeder screw
3. Caliper housing
4. Seals
5. Caliper pistons
6. Boots
7. Retainer pin
8. Inboard shoe and lining assembly
9. Outboard shoe and lining assembly
10. Caliper mounting bracket
11. Circlip
12. Bias spring

8470R085

Exploded view of the front caliper assembly

to seat the shoe and lining assemblies.

Disc Brake Pads

REMOVAL AND INSTALLATION

Front

1. Disconnect the negative battery cable.
2. Remove the caliper from the mounting bracket but do not disconnect the brake hose and inlet fitting assembly.
3. Suspend the caliper from the upper control arm with wire to avoid damage to the brake hose.
4. Remove the pad and lining assemblies from the caliper.
   To install:
5. Clean all residue from the pad and lining assembly guiding surfaces on the caliper housing and the mounting bracket.
6. Install the outboard pad with the insulator to the caliper housing and the inboard pad with the wear sensor into the caliper pistons. Press the pads firmly until they are they are fully seated.
7. Remove the support and install the caliper to the mounting bracket.
8. Connect the negative battery cable.

Rear

1. Disconnect the negative battery cable and remove ⅔ of the brake fluid from the master cylinder reservoirs.
2. Raise and support the vehicle safely.
3. Mark the relationship between the wheel to the axle flange.
4. Remove the tire and wheel assembly. Install 2 wheel nuts to retain the brake rotor.
5. Use a C-clamp to depress the caliper pistons into the caliper bores to provide clearance between the pads and the rotor. Make sure 1 end of the clamp rests on the inlet fitting bolt while the other end rests on the outboard pad.
6. Remove the caliper upper guide pin bolt and discard, then rotate the caliper on the lower guide pin to access the pad linings. Be careful not to strain the cable conduit or the hoses.
7. Remove the pads from the caliper.
   To install:
8. Install the outboard pad with the insulator to the caliper housing and the inboard pad with the wear sensor nearest the caliper pistons. The wear sensor must be in the trail-

ing position during forward wheel rotation. Press the pads firmly until they are they are fully seated.
9. Rotate the caliper housing into position, then install a new upper guide pin bolt and tighten 26 ft. lbs. (35 Nm).
10. Remove the wheel nuts securing the rotor to the hub and install the tire and wheel assembly.
11. Lower the vehicle and fill the master cylinder to the proper level with clean brake fluid.
12. Connect the negative battery cable, start the engine and pump the brake pedal slowly and firmly 3 times to seat the shoe and lining assemblies.

Brake Rotor

REMOVAL AND INSTALLATION

Front and Rear

1. Disconnect battery negative cable.
2. Remove the caliper assembly. Either completely remove the assembly from the vehicle or suspend the assembly using a length of mechanic's wire.
3. Remove the rotor from the vehicle.
4. Installation is the reverse of removal.

Parking Brake Cable

ADJUSTMENT

The parking brake lever/cable adjustment is automatic. The adjuster must be disabled to create the necessary cable slack for certain service procedures. Following these procedures, make sure the adjuster is properly enabled to assure correct parking brake operation.
1. To disable the automatic parking brake adjuster, proceed as follows:
   a. Remove the drivers seat cushion.
   b. Remove the parking brake lever cover and screws.
   c. Using a suitable offset tool, disengage and hold the drive pawl from the drive sector.
   d. Insert a nail or drift through the hole in the anchor plate to retain the drive pawl in the disengaged position.
   e. Move the parking brake lever until it aligns with the lock pawl.

f. Depress the button on the lever and move the lever to the down position.
   g. Verify the anchor plate is against the stud on the parking brake lever, if not as specified, repeat the procedure.
2. To enable the automatic parking brake adjuster, proceed as follows:
   a. Remove the nail or drift pin from the anchor plate.
   b. Apply and release the parking brake 3 times.
   c. Pull up on the parking brake lever. Proper adjustment will result in the lever moving 3–5 ratchet clicks with a force of 61 lbs. (270 N).
   d. Release the parking brake, there should be no rear brake drag and no gap between the caliper housings and caliper parking brake levers. It may be necessary to remove the tire and wheel assemblies to see the caliper housings and levers.
   e. If removed, install the wheel and tire assembly.
   f. Install the parking brake lever cover and screws.
   g. Install the driver's seat cushion.

REMOVAL AND INSTALLATION

Front Cable

1. Remove the driver's seat cushion and frame assembly.
2. Properly disable the parking brake automatic adjuster.
3. Raise the vehicle and support it safely.
4. Disconnect the front cable from the front cable connector.
5. Disconnect the front cable from the front cable return spring.
6. Disconnect the left rear cable from the parking brake front cable assembly connector.
7. Remove the front cable attaching clip bolt and clip.
8. Lower the vehicle and remove the front cable from the automatic adjuster.
9. Remove the front cable attaching nut and washer.
10. Remove the front cable from the vehicle.
    To install:
11. Install the front cable to the vehicle, then attach the front cable washer and nut. Tighten the nut 24 ft. lbs. (33 Nm).
12. Connect the front cable to the automatic adjuster.
13. Raise and support the vehicle safely.

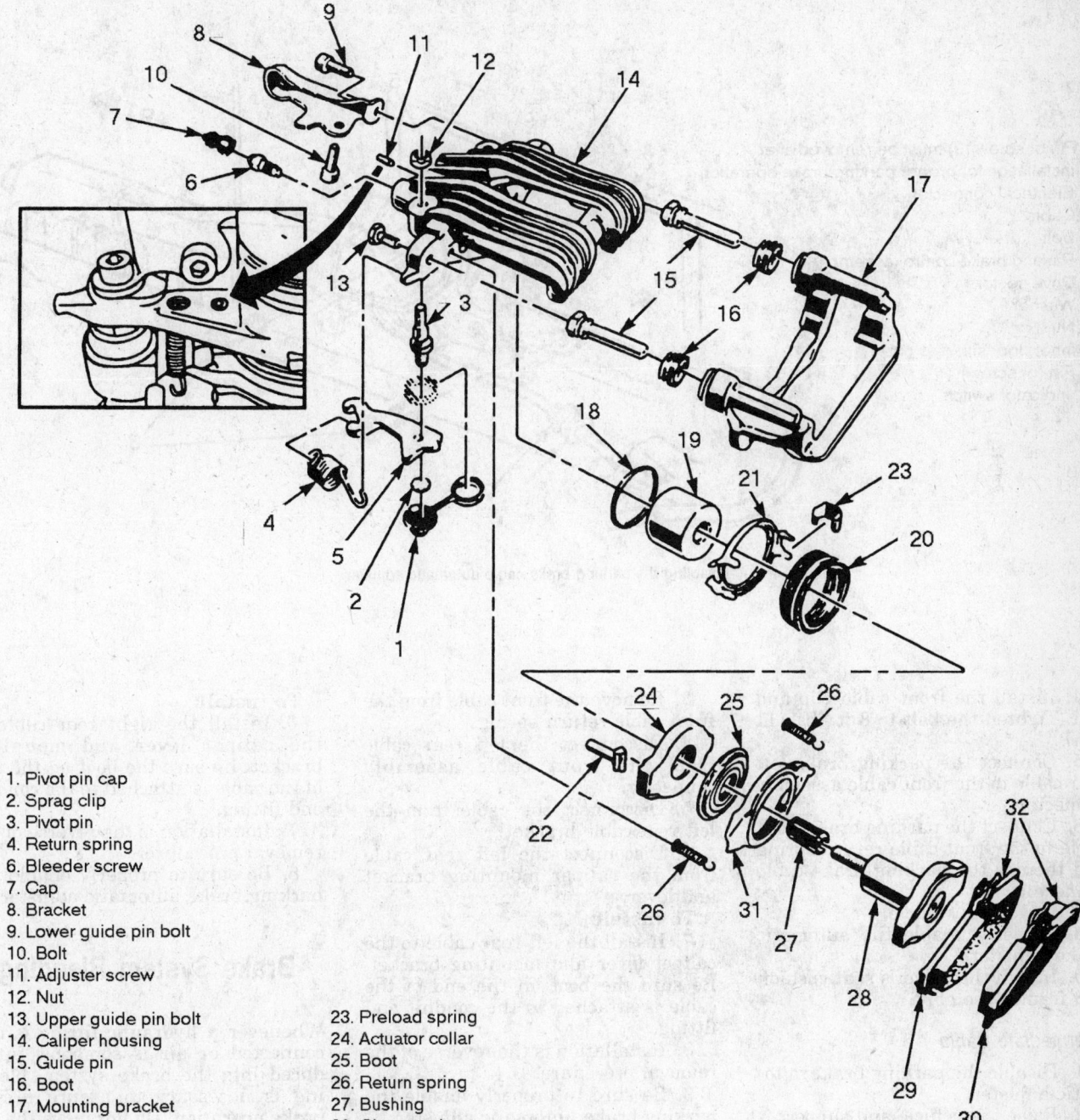

1. Pivot pin cap
2. Sprag clip
3. Pivot pin
4. Return spring
6. Bleeder screw
7. Cap
8. Bracket
9. Lower guide pin bolt
10. Bolt
11. Adjuster screw
12. Nut
13. Upper guide pin bolt
14. Caliper housing
15. Guide pin
16. Boot
17. Mounting bracket
18. Piston seal
19. Piston
20. Boot
21. Retainer
22. Pushrod

23. Preload spring
24. Actuator collar
25. Boot
26. Return spring
27. Bushing
28. Clamp rod
29. Inboard shoe and lining assembly
30. Outboard shoe and lining assembly
31. Retainer
32. Spring

8470R086

Exploded view of the rear caliper assembly

A. Pin or screw (9) must be removed after installation for proper parking brake operation
1. Electrical connector
2. Cable
3. Bolt
4. Parking brake control assembly
5. Drive sector
6. Washer
7. Nut
8. Inner door sill
9. Pin (or screw)
10. Indicator switch

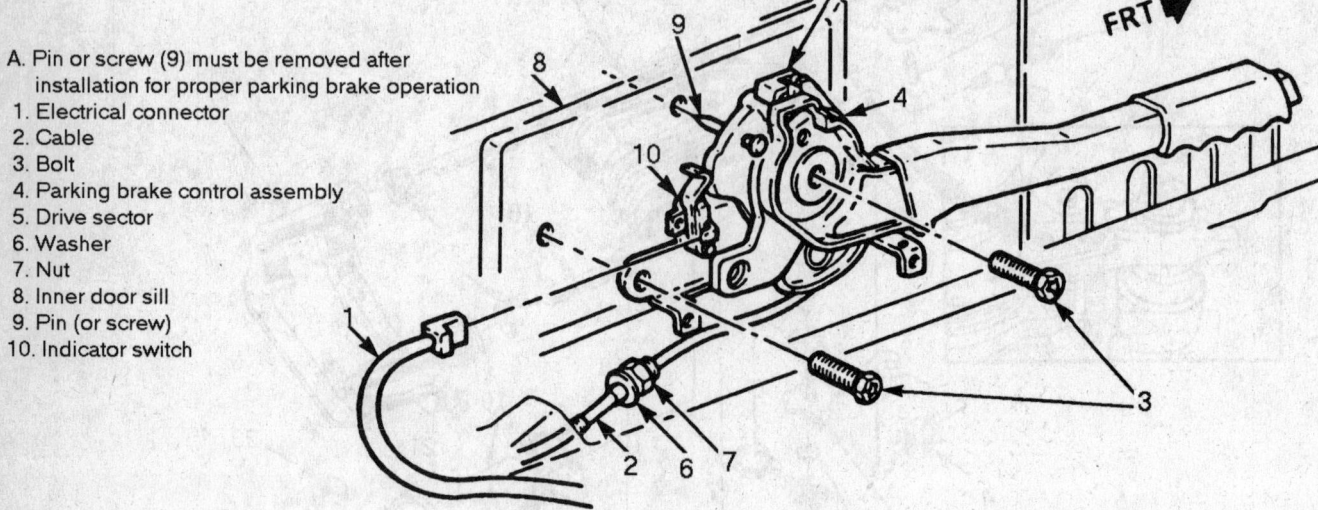

8470R087

Disabling the parking brake cable automatic adjuster

14. Install the front cable clip and bolt. Tighten the bolt to 8 ft. lbs. (11 Nm).

15. Connect the parking brake left rear cable to the front cable assembly connector.

16. Connect the parking brake front cable to the front cable return spring and then to the parking brake cable connector.

17. Lower the vehicle.

18. Properly enable the automatic brake adjuster.

19. Install the driver's seat cushion and frame assembly.

Intermediate Cable

1. Disable the parking brake automatic adjuster.

2. Raise the vehicle and support it safely.

3. Disconnect the parking brake intermediate cable from the cable connectors and front cable guide.

4. Installation is the reverse of the removal procedure.

Rear Cable

LEFT

1. Disable the automatic parking brake adjuster.

2. Raise and support the vehicle safely, then remove the tire and wheel assembly.

3. Remove the front cable from the front cable return spring.

4. Disconnect the left rear cable from the front cable assembly connector.

5. Disconnect the cable from the left rear cable bracket.

6. Disconnect the left rear cable from the caliper mounting bracket and lever.

To install:

7. Install the left rear cable to the caliper lever and mounting bracket. Be sure the boot on the end of the cable is attached to the conduit end fitting.

8. Installation is the reverse of the removal procedure.

9. Be sure to properly enable the parking brake automatic adjuster.

RIGHT

1. Disable the parking brake automatic adjuster.

2. Raise the vehicle and support it safely, then remove the tire and wheel assembly.

3. Disconnect the right rear cable from the intermediate cable.

4. Disconnect the right rear cable from the right rear cable bracket.

5. Disconnect the right rear cable from the caliper mounting bracket and lever.

To install:

6. Install the right rear cable to the caliper lever and mounting bracket. Be sure the boot on the end of the cable is attached to the conduit end fitting.

7. Installation is the reverse of the removal procedure.

8. Be sure to properly enable the parking brake automatic adjuster.

Brake System Bleeding

Whenever a hydraulic fitting is disconnected or air is somehow introduced into the brake system, bleeding is necessary to assure proper brake operation. Do not move the vehicle until a firm brake pedal is obtained. Air in the system can cause the loss of brake operation.

If air is introduced into the system at the master cylinder, it may be necessary to bled the entire system. If the disconnection of a fitting or pipe is the cause for air presence in the system, then only the caliper(s) served by that component need to be bled.

1. Fill the master cylinder reservoir with brake fluid and keep it at least ½ full of fluid at all times during the bleeding operation.

2. Deplete the brake vacuum reserve by applying and releasing the brakes several times while the engine is **OFF**.

3. If the entire system must be bled, the master cylinder prime pipe must first be bled at the hydraulic modulator located in the left rear storage compartment.

   a. Open the left rear storage compartment, then remove the sound insulator pad.

   b. Remove the cap from the modulator bleed screw, then position a box wrench and a short piece of clear tube over the screw.

   c. Position a container and rags to protect the vehicle interior from the brake fluid. Open the bleed screw and allow fluid to flow until all air is removed.

   d. Tighten the bleed screw to 106 inch lbs. (12 Nm) and remove the tubing. Wipe the screw off and make sure it has properly sealed.

   e. Install the sound insulator pad, making sure it covers the entire modulator valve or excessive noise may be heard when the system is operating. Close the rear compartment.

4. If the master cylinder is known or suspected to have air in the bore, bleed the unit before bleeding the calipers, in the following manner:

   a. Disconnect the forward (blind end) brake line connection at the master cylinder.

   b. Allow brake fluid to fill the master cylinder piston bore until it begins to flow from the forward pipe connector port at the master cylinder.

   c. Connect the forward brake line to the master cylinder and tighten.

   d. Have an assistant depress the brake pedal slowly 1 time and hold. Loosen the forward brake line connection at the master cylinder to purge air from the bore. Tighten the connection and have the assistant release the pedal slowly. Wait 15 seconds and repeat the sequence, including the 15 second pause, until all air is removed from the bore. Make sure brake fluid does not contact any painted surface.

   e. Repeat the procedure at the rear master cylinder brake line connection.

   f. If it is known that the calipers do not contain any air, it will not be necessary to bleed them.

5. If it is necessary to bleed all of the calipers, follow the proper sequence: right rear, left rear, right front, left front.

6. After all air is removed from the master cylinder, bleed the individual calipers as follows:

   a. Place a suitable sized box wrench over the bleeder valve.

   b. Attach a clear tube over the bleeder valve and allow the tube to hang, submerged in a clear container partially filled with brake fluid.

   c. Have an assistant depress the brake pedal slowly 1 time and hold. Loosen the bleeder valve to purge the air from the cylinder. Tighten the bleeder screw and have the assistant slowly release the pedal. Wait 15 seconds and repeat the sequence, including the 15 second pause, until all air is removed.

   d. It may be necessary to repeat the sequence 10 or more times to remove all of the air.

NOTE: Rapid pumping of the brake pedal pushes the master cylinder secondary piston down the bore in a way that makes it difficult to bleed the system.

7. Check the brake pedal for sponginess and the brake warning light for an indication of unbalanced pressure. Repeat the bleeding procedure to correct either of these conditions.

Anti-Lock Brake System Service

PRECAUTIONS

Failure to observe the following precautions may result in system damage.

• Before performing electric arc welding on the vehicle, disconnect the Electronic Brake Control Module (EBCM) and the hydraulic modulator connectors.

• When performing painting work on the vehicle, do not expose the Electronic Brake Control Module (EBCM) to temperatures in excess of 185°F (85°C) for longer than 2 hrs. The system may be exposed to temperatures up to 200°F (95°C) for less than 15 min.

• Always note the routing, position, mounting and location of all system components. Speed sensor wiring, routing and retention is especially important to help prevent false signals due to electrical noise picked up by the wiring.

• Never disconnect or connect the Electronic Brake Control Module (EBCM) or hydraulic modulator connectors with the ignition switch ON.

• Never disassemble any component of the Anti-Lock Brake System (ABS) which is designated non-serviceable; the component must be replaced as an assembly.

• When filling the master cylinder, always use Delco Supreme 11 brake fluid or equivalent, which meets DOT-3 specifications; incorrect fluid will destroy the rubber parts.

Modulator Valve

REMOVAL AND INSTALLATION

1. Disconnect the negative battery cable. Remove the storage compartment door and frame, then remove the sound insulator pad.

2. Disconnect the wire harness with selective ride control module, if equipped.

3. Release the retaining clip and remove the wiring harness connector from the Electronic Brake Control Module (EBCM), then remove the EBCM from the vehicle.

4. Disconnect the brake lines from the modulator valve and note the location for reinstallation purposes. Plug the lines to prevent fluid contamination or loss.

5. Raise and support the vehicle safely, remove the modulator valve bracket to underbody cover attaching bolts, then lower the vehicle.

6. Remove the modulator valve assembly.

To install:

7. If the modulator valve is being replaced, transfer the ground wire, valve bracket and relays to the new valve.

8. Install the modulator valve assembly. Raise and support the vehicle safely, then install the modulator valve bracket to the underbody cover attaching bolts.

9. Tighten the bolts to 86 inch lbs. (10 Nm), then lower the vehicle. Unplug and install the brake lines in their original location, then tighten the fittings to 13 ft. lbs. (18 Nm).

NOTE: It is extremely important that all brake lines are correctly attached or wheel lock up could occur causing personal injury to the vehicle operator.

10. Install the EBCM. Connect the wiring harness with selective ride control module, if equipped. Connect the negative battery cable and properly bleed the hydraulic brake system.

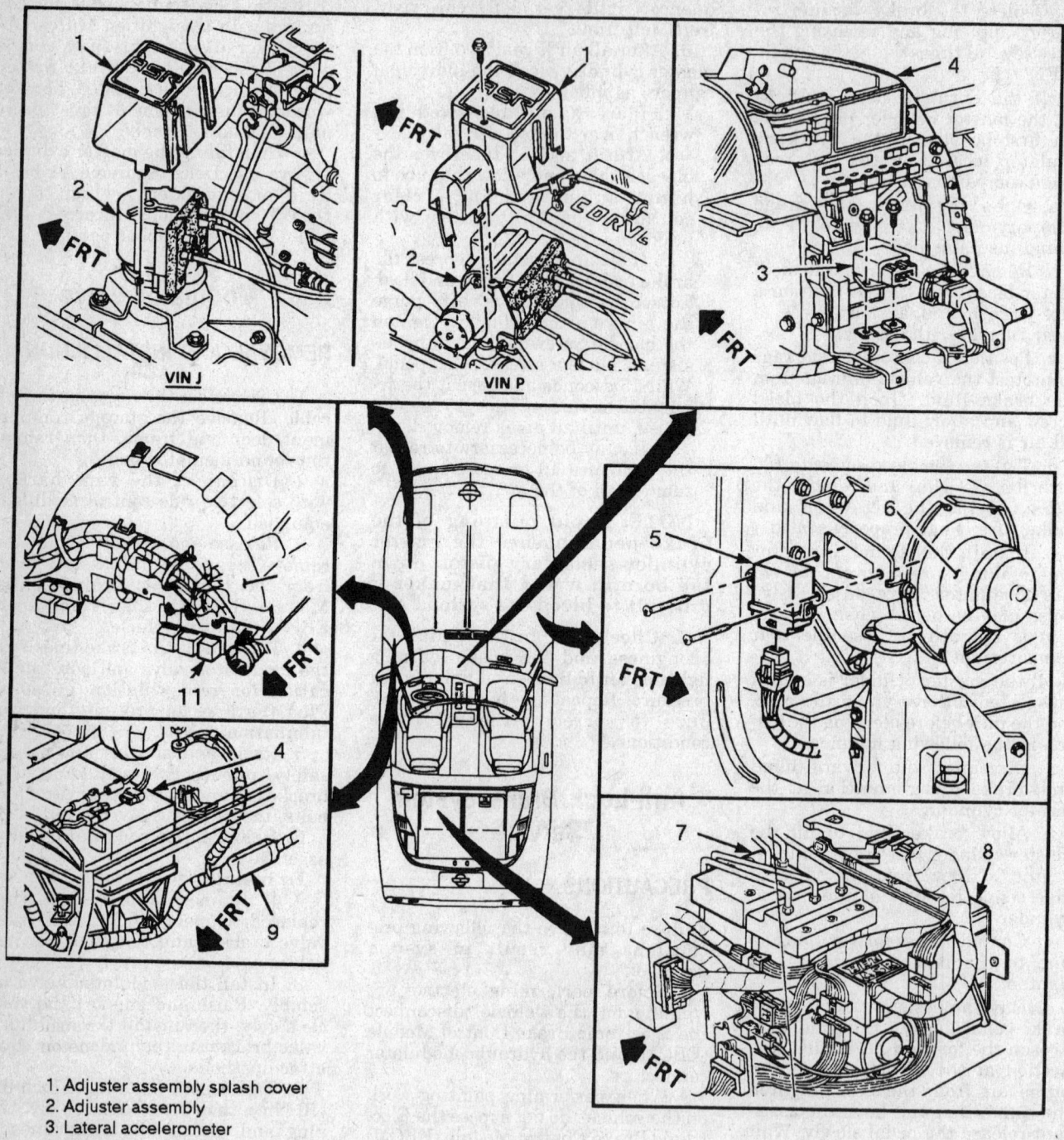

1. Adjuster assembly splash cover
2. Adjuster assembly
3. Lateral accelerometer
4. I/P carrier
5. TPS module
6. Blower motor
7. Modulator valve
8. Electronic brake control module (EBCM)
9. Brake fluid level isolation diode
10. Battery
11. Cruise control cut off relay

8470R088

Anti-lock Brake System (ABS) and Acceleration Slip Regulation (ASR) system components

11. Install the sound insulator pad, the rear storage compartment door and frame assembly. Check for proper system operation.

Lateral Accelerometer

REMOVAL AND INSTALLATION

1. Disconnect the negative battery cable.

2. Remove the console and accessory trim plates.

3. Remove the radio assembly.

4. Push on the spring to release and disconnect the ABS/ASR wiring harness connector from the lateral accelerometer.

5. Remove the lateral accelerometer attaching screws from the carrier assembly and remove the accelerometer from the vehicle.

6. Installation is the reverse of the removal procedures.

Wheel Speed Sensor

REMOVAL AND INSTALLATION

The front wheel speed sensors are part of the wheel hub assembly and cannot be replaced separately.

Rear Wheel

1. Disconnect the negative battery cable. Raise and safely support the vehicle. Remove the wheel and tire assembly.

2. Disconnect the sensor wiring harness from the ABS wiring harness connector. Unclip the connectors from the bracket and separate.

3. Remove the bracket and bolt from the knuckle.

4. Remove the sensor wiring harness with the grommets from the bracket. Note the position of the grommets and the harness routing for insulation purposes.

5. Remove the wheel speed sensor attaching bolt, then remove the speed sensor from the knuckle.

To install:

6. Clean all sealant from the sensor and the sensor mounting in the knuckle.

7. Apply 12345489 or equivalent anti-corrosion sealer, to the speed sensor and install the sensor into the knuckle. The sensor is tight fit and must be installed by hand. Do not hammer the sensor into position.

8. Install the sensor retaining bolt and tighten to 86 inch lbs. (10 Nm).

9. Install the sensor wiring harness with grommets into the brackets, make sure the grommets and routing is the same as what was noted during removal.

10. Install the bracket and bolt to knuckle, tighten the bolt to 86 inch lbs. (10 Nm).

11. Connect the sensor wiring harness connector to the wiring harness connector. Make sure the connection is tight, then snap the connectors into the bracket.

12. Install the wheel and tire assembly, then lower the vehicle. Connect the negative battery cable and check for proper system operation.

Electronic Brake Control Module

REMOVAL AND INSTALLATION

1. Disconnect the negative battery cable.

2. For Coupes, open the left rear storage compartment. For Convertibles, remove the storage compartment frame and covers.

3. Remove the sound insulator pad.

4. Release the retaining clips and disconnect the wiring harness from the EBCM.

5. Remove the EBCM retaining nut, then remove the control module from the vehicle.

6. Installation is the reverse of the removal.

FRONT SUSPENSION

Shock Absorbers

REMOVAL AND INSTALLATION

Without Selective Ride Control

1. Raise and support the vehicle safely.

2. Remove the tire and wheel assemblies.

3. Disconnect the shock absorber from the lower control arm and the shock tower. If necessary, remove the front wheelhouse lower center panel to access the upper mount nut.

4. Remove the insulator and retainers from the shock absorber and the shock absorber from the vehicle.

5. Installation is the reverse of the removal procedure. Tighten the upper and lower mount nuts to 19 ft. lbs. (26 Nm).

With Selective Ride Control

1. Disconnect the negative battery cable.

2. Raise and safely support vehicle, then remove the tire and wheel assemblies.

3. Safely support the lower control arm with a jackstand.

4. Remove the actuator retaining clip, then remove the actuator from the cup retainer. Note the position of the actuator electrical leads for installation purposes.

5. Remove the shock absorber upper mounting nuts.

6. Remove the cup retainer, then the upper insulator retainer and insulator.

7. Remove the shock absorber lower mounting bolts, nuts, then compress the shock absorber and remove it from the vehicle. If necessary, remove the lower insulator from the shock.

To install:

8. If removed, install the lower insulator to the shock absorber, compress the shock and install into the vehicle.

9. Install the shock absorber lower mounting nuts and bolts, then tighten the bolts to 19 ft. lbs. (26 Nm).

10. Install the upper insulator and retainer, then install the cup assembly retainer.

11. Install the upper mounting nut and tighten the 31 ft. lbs. (42 Nm). The selector gear should be at least 0.178 inch (4.5mm) above the top of the cup assembly retainer.

12. Install and properly seat the actuator retaining clip onto the cup assembly retainer. Make sure the ends of the actuator clip protrude outward from the retainer.

13. Install the actuator onto the cup assembly retainer with the electrical leads in the same position as noted earlier. Verify that there is at least 0.315 inch (8mm) of clearance between the front wheelhouse lower center panel and the actuator electrical leads.

NOTE: Very little effort is required to snap the actuator onto the retainer, do not force it into position.

14. Remove the jackstand, then install the tire and wheel assembly.

15. Lower the vehicle and connect the negative battery cable.

Transverse Spring

REMOVAL AND INSTALLATION

1. Raise and support the vehicle safely. Position the supports so the front suspension hangs freely.
2. Remove both front tire and wheel assemblies.

NOTE: Do not use corrosive cleaning agents, engine degreasers or solvents near the fiberglass front spring, or extensive damage could occur to the spring assembly.

3. Disconnect both shock absorbers from the lower control arms, then disconnect the stabilizer shaft links from both lower control arms.
4. Disengage the wheel speed sensor electrical connectors, then remove the speed sensor wire from the bracket.
5. Remove the spring protectors.
6. Compress the front leaf springs using tool J–33432 and adapters J–33432–88 or a suitable equivalent tool, then compress the spring.
7. Disconnect the lower control arms from the steering knuckles by separating the ball joints from the knuckle bores.
8. Remove the spring retainer nuts and retainers, then carefully release the spring compression and remove the tools.
9. With the aid of an assistant, pull both lower control arms downward to release the spring ends from the lower control arms.
10. Remove the spring and retainer shims from the vehicle. Use care not to scratch or damage the spring and note the number, types (color) and positions of the shims.
To install:
11. Lubricate the spring pads with an appropriate lubricant.
12. Carefully install the retainer shims and the spring. Be careful not to scratch the spring and be sure to use the correct number and type of shims.
13. With the aid of an assistant, pull both lower control arms downward while seating the spring ends into the lower control arms.
14. Using the J–33432 and J–33432–88 or equivalents, compress the spring.
15. Install the retainers and hand-tighten the retainer nuts. Install both lower control arm ball joints into the steering knuckles. The ball joints must be positioned so the cotter pins can be inserted from the rear to the front of the vehicle.

16. Install both lower control arm ball stud washers and nuts. Tighten the hex nut to 50 ft. lbs. (68 Nm), then insert a new cotter pin. If necessary tighten the nut additionally in order to insert the pin, but do not exceed a total torque of 88 ft. lbs. (120 Nm) and do not back off the original torque.
17. Install the cotter pins from the rear to the front of the vehicle.
18. Release and remove the spring compression tools.
19. Install both spring protectors and tighten the bolts to 18 ft. lbs. (25 Nm).
20. Install the wheel speed sensor connector, cable and/or bracket, as applicable.
21. Install the stabilizer shaft links, bolts and nuts to the lower control arm. Make sure the link bolts are properly positioning, then hand-tighten the nuts.
22. Connect both shock absorbers to the lower control arms and tighten the lower mounting nuts to 19 ft. lbs. (26 Nm).
23. Use jackstands to hold the suspension at proper trim height, then tighten the spring retainer nuts to 46 ft. lbs. (63 Nm) and the stabilizer shaft link nuts to 33 ft. lbs. (45 Nm).
24. Remove the jackstand supports, then install the tire and wheel assemblies.
25. Lower the vehicle, check and adjust the front end alignment, as necessary.

Upper Ball Joints

INSPECTION

NOTE: Anytime the ball joint is separated from the knuckle, it should be checked for looseness. If it is loose or can be twisted in the socket by hand, the ball joint must be replaced.

1. Raise and safely support the vehicle with jackstands under the left and right lower control arms, as far outboard and nearest to the ball joint as possible.
2. Make sure the vehicle is stable and does not rock on the stands.
3. Position a dial indicator against the wheel rim.
4. Grasp the front tire and push in on the bottom while pulling out at the top. Read the dial indicator, then reverse the push-pull procedure.
5. Horizontal deflection on the dial indicator must not exceed 0.125 in. (3.18mm).

6. The ball joint must be replaced if deflection is greater than indicated.

REMOVAL AND INSTALLATION

1. Raise and support the vehicle safely.
2. Safely support the lower control arm with a jackstand.
3. Remove the tire and wheel assemblies.
4. Using J–33436 or equivalent ball joint removal tool, separate the ball joint from the knuckle.
5. Remove the upper ball joint from the control arm as follows:
   a. Center punch the rivet.
   b. Drill a pilot hole, then drill the rivet head.
   c. Punch out the rivet.
To install:
6. Install a new ball joint into the upper control arm and position so the cotter pin can be installed from the rear to the front of the vehicle.
7. Install and tighten the mounting nuts to 13 ft. lbs. (18 Nm).
8. Position the ball stud into the steering knuckle, then install the upper ball joint stud washer and nut. Tighten the upper control arm ball stud nut to 33 ft. lbs. (45 Nm). Tighten the nut additionally as necessary to insert the cotter pin but do not exceed 63 ft. lbs. (85 Nm).
9. Install a new cotter pin from the rear to the front of the vehicle.
10. Remove the jackstand and lubricate the ball joint.
11. Install the tire and wheel assembly, then lower the vehicle.

Lower Ball Joints

INSPECTION

1. With the weight of the vehicle properly loading the ball joints, check the wear indicators on the bottom of the lower ball joints.
2. The wear indicator (lower grease fitting shoulder) should protrude 0.050 in. (1.27mm) when new.
3. When the wear indicator shoulder retreats below the surface, the ball joint must be replaced.

REMOVAL AND INSTALLATION

1. Raise and support the vehicle safely.
2. Safely support the lower control arm with a jackstand.
3. Remove the tire and wheel assembly.

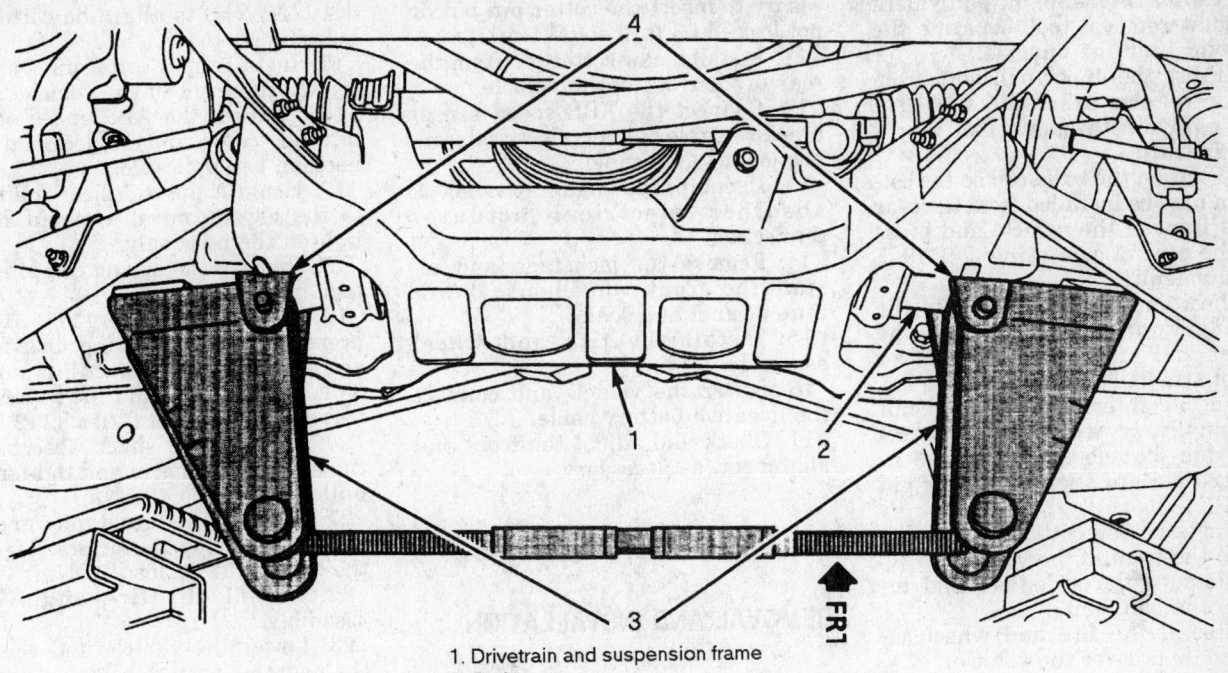

1. Drivetrain and suspension frame
2. Spring
3. Tool J-33432
4. Tool adapters J33432-88

8470R090

Transverse spring compression tool

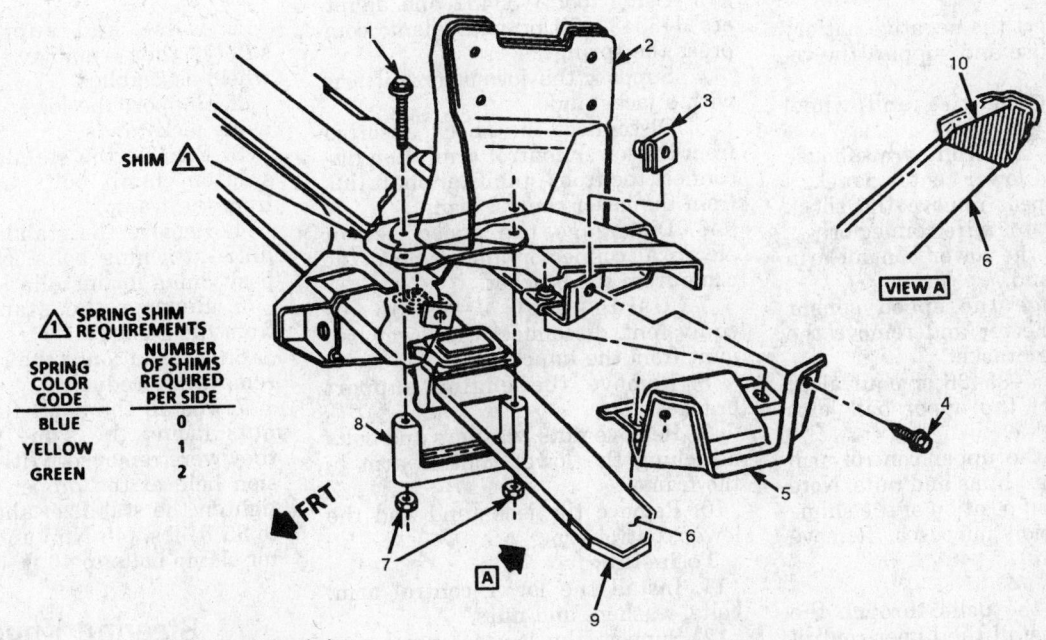

⚠ SPRING SHIM REQUIREMENTS	
SPRING COLOR CODE	NUMBER OF SHIMS REQUIRED PER SIDE
BLUE	0
YELLOW	1
GREEN	2

1. Spring retainer bolt
2. Drivetrain and suspension frame
3. Multi-thread "U" nut
4. Spring protector to frame bolt 25 n-m (18 lb. ft.)
5. Spring protector

6. Front transverse spring
7. Spring retainer nut
8. Front spring retainer
9. Spring pad
10. Apply rubber lubricant

8470R091

Front transverse spring and shim installation

4. Using J–33436 or equivalent ball joint removal tool, separate the ball joint from the knuckle.

5. Press the upper ball joint from the control arm using tool J–9519–E or an equivalent removal tool.

To install:

6. Position the ball stud so the cotter pin may be installed from the rear to the front of the vehicle and press into the control arm using J–9519–E or equivalent.

7. Position the ball joint into the steering knuckle, then install the washer and nut. Tighten the lower control arm ball stud nut to 50 ft. lbs. (68 Nm). Tighten the ball stud nut additionally, as necessary to insert a cotter pin, but do not exceed 88 ft. lbs. (120 Nm) to align the cotter pin holes.

8. Install a new cotter pin from the rear to the front of the vehicle.

9. Remove the jackstand and lubricate the ball joint.

10. Install the tire and wheel assembly, then lower the vehicle.

Upper Control Arms

REMOVAL AND INSTALLATION

1. Disconnect the negative battery cable, then raise and support the vehicle safely.

2. Remove the tire and wheel assembly.

3. Remove the front wheelhouse panel seal and lower center panel.

4. If equipped, remove the shock absorber actuator wire connector.

5. Support the lower control arm with a jackstand.

6. Disengage the speed sensor electrical connector and remove the cable from the bracket.

7. Use tool J–33436 or equivalent and disconnect the upper ball joint from the knuckle.

8. Remove the upper control arm attaching bolts, shims and nuts. Note the number and position of the shims for reinstallation purposes. Remove the control arm.

To install:

9. Position the bolts through the frame, then install the upper control arm and shims. Place the shims in the locations noted during removal. Install and tighten the control arm nuts to 37 ft. lbs. (50 Nm).

10. Position the ball stud into the steering knuckle, then install the upper ball joint stud washer and nut. Tighten the upper control arm ball stud nut to 33 ft. lbs. (45 Nm). Tighten the nut additionally as nec-

essary to insert the cotter pin but do not exceed 63 ft. lbs. (85 Nm).

11. Install a new cotter pin from the rear to the front of the vehicle.

12. Connect the ABS speed sensor bracket, cable and/or electrical connection, as applicable.

13. If equipped, engage the shock absorber electrical actuator connection.

14. Remove the jackstand and install the front wheelhouse lower center panel and seal.

15. Install the tire and wheel assembly.

16. Lower the vehicle and connect the negative battery cable.

17. Check and adjust the front end alignment, as necessary.

Lower Control Arms

REMOVAL AND INSTALLATION

1. Disconnect the negative battery cable, then raise and support the vehicle safely.

2. Remove the tire and wheel assembly, then remove both spring protectors.

3. Using tool J–33432 and adapters J–33432–88 or equivalent, compress the spring.

4. Support the lower control arm with a jackstand.

5. Disconnect the shock absorber from the lower control arm, then disconnect the front stabilizer shaft link from the lower control arm.

6. Disengage the speed sensor electrical connector and remove the cable from the bracket.

7. Using tool J–33436 or equivalent, disconnect the lower ball joint from the knuckle.

8. Remove the engine support bracket.

9. Remove nuts, washers and bolts attaching the lower control arm to the frame.

10. Remove the jackstand and the lower control arm.

To install:

11. Install the lower control arm, bolts, washers and nuts.

12. Support the lower control arm with a jackstand.

13. Install the engine support bracket.

14. Position the ball joint into the steering knuckle, then install the washer and nut. Tighten the lower control arm ball stud nut to 50 ft. lbs. (68 Nm). Tighten the ball stud nut additionally, as necessary to insert a cotter pin, but do not exceed 88 ft.

lbs. (120 Nm) to align the cotter pin holes.

15. Install a new cotter pin from the rear to the front of the vehicle.

16. Connect the ABS speed sensor bracket, cable and/or electrical connection, as applicable.

17. Connect the stabilizer shaft link to the lower control arm but hand-tighten the nuts only.

18. Remove the spring compression tool and adapters.

19. Hold the suspension at the proper trim height using jackstands and tighten the stabilizer link nuts to 35 ft. lbs. (48 Nm) and the lower control arm bolts to 82 ft. lbs. (112 Nm).

20. Connect the shock absorber to the lower control arm and tighten the nuts to 19 ft. lbs. (26 Nm).

21. Remove the jackstands and install both spring protectors. Tighten the bolts to 18 ft. lbs. (25 Nm).

22. Install the tire and wheel assembly.

23. Lower the vehicle and connect the negative battery cable.

Stabilizer Shaft

REMOVAL AND INSTALLATION

1. Raise and support vehicle safely, then remove the tire and wheel assemblies.

2. Support the lower control arms using jackstands.

3. Remove the stabilizer shaft insulator clamp bolts and brackets from the frame.

4. Remove the stabilizer shaft-to-links attaching bolts. Note the bolt positioning for installation purposes.

5. Remove the stabilizer shaft from the vehicle.

6. Installation is the reverse of the removal procedure.

7. Install the shaft link bolts and nuts facing the same positions as they were removed. With the suspension held at the proper trim height, tighten the stabilizer shaft link nuts to 35 ft. lbs. (48 Nm) and the insulator clamp bolts to 40 ft. lbs. (54 Nm).

Steering Knuckle

REMOVAL AND INSTALLATION

1. Disconnect the negative battery cable, then raise and support the vehicle safely.

2. Remove the tire and wheel assembly.

3. Remove the brake caliper and rotor. Support the caliper from the

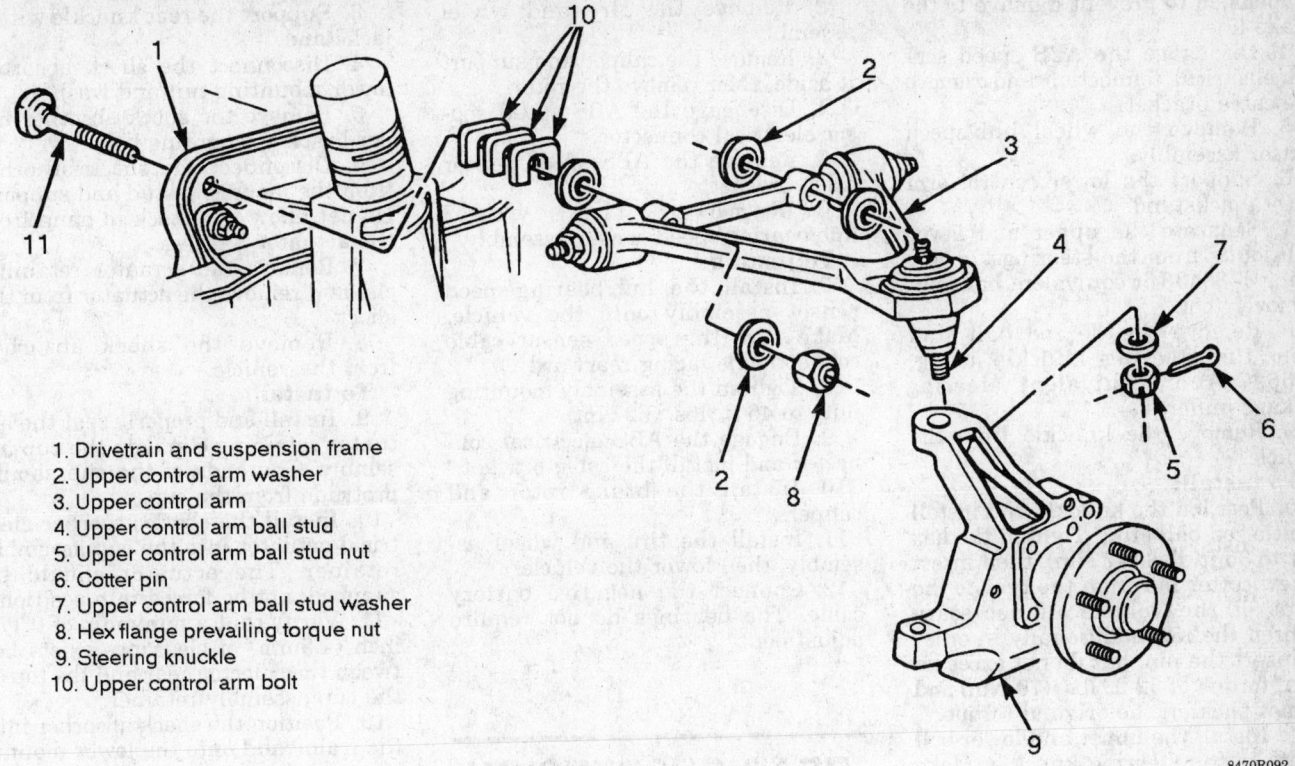

1. Drivetrain and suspension frame
2. Upper control arm washer
3. Upper control arm
4. Upper control arm ball stud
5. Upper control arm ball stud nut
6. Cotter pin
7. Upper control arm ball stud washer
8. Hex flange prevailing torque nut
9. Steering knuckle
10. Upper control arm bolt

8470R092

Upper control arm assembly

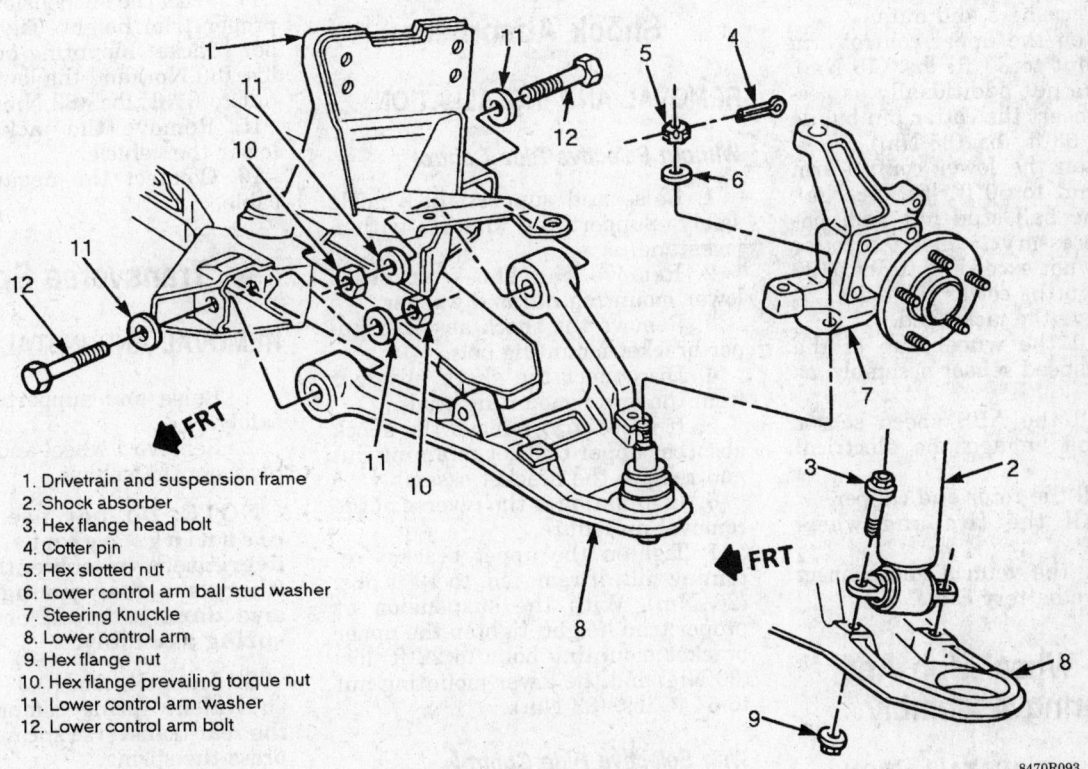

1. Drivetrain and suspension frame
2. Shock absorber
3. Hex flange head bolt
4. Cotter pin
5. Hex slotted nut
6. Lower control arm ball stud washer
7. Steering knuckle
8. Lower control arm
9. Hex flange nut
10. Hex flange prevailing torque nut
11. Lower control arm washer
12. Lower control arm bolt

8470R093

Lower control arm assembly

suspension to prevent damage to the brake line.

4. Disengage the ABS speed sensor electrical connection and remove the cable bracket.

5. Remove the wheel hub/speed sensor assembly.

6. Support the lower control arm with a jackstand.

7. Separate the upper and lower ball joints from the steering knuckle using J–33436 or equivalent ball joint remover tool.

8. Remove the tie rod ball stud from the steering knuckle using, J–6627–A or equivalent steering linkage puller.

9. Remove the knuckle from the vehicle.

To install:

10. Position the knuckle and install the tie rod ball stud. Tighten the hex nut to 35 ft. lbs. (47 Nm), then insert a new cotter pin from the rear to the front of the vehicle. If necessary tighten the nut additionally in order to insert the pin, but do not exceed a total torque of 52 ft. lbs. (70 Nm) and do not back off the original torque.

11. Install the upper and lower ball joints to the steering knuckle. Make sure the studs are positioned so cotter pins may be installed from the rear to the front of the vehicle, then install the washers and nuts.

12. Tighten the upper control arm ball stud nut to 33 ft. lbs. (45 Nm). Tighten the nut additionally as necessary to insert the cotter pin but do not exceed 63 ft. lbs. (85 Nm).

13. Tighten the lower control arm ball stud nut to 50 ft. lbs. (68 Nm). Tighten the ball stud nut additionally, as necessary to insert a cotter pin, but do not exceed 88 ft. lbs. (120 Nm) to align the cotter pin holes.

14. Remove the jackstand.

15. Install the wheel hub or the wheel hub/speed sensor assembly, as applicable.

16. Install the ABS speed sensor bracket and engage the electrical connection.

17. Install the rotor and caliper.

18. Install the tire and wheel assembly.

19. Lower the vehicle and connect the negative battery cable.

Front Wheel Hub And Bearing Assembly

REMOVAL AND INSTALLATION

1. Disconnect the negative battery cable, then raise and support the vehicle safely.

2. Remove the tire and wheel assembly.

3. Remove the caliper and support it aside, then remove the rotor.

4. Disengage the ABS speed sensor electrical connector.

5. Remove the ABS speed sensor cable bracket.

6. Remove the wheel hub/bearing/speed sensor assembly.

To install:

7. Install the hub/bearing/speed sensor assembly onto the vehicle. Make sure the speed sensor cable connection is facing rearward.

8. Tighten the assembly mounting nuts to 46 ft. lbs. (62 Nm).

9. Engage the ABS electrical connector and install the cable bracket.

10. Install the brake rotor and caliper.

11. Install the tire and wheel assembly, then lower the vehicle.

12. Connect the negative battery cable. The bearings do not require adjustment.

REAR SUSPENSION

Shock Absorbers

REMOVAL AND INSTALLATION

Without Selective Ride Control

1. Raise and support the vehicle safely. Support the knuckle with a jackstand.

2. Remove the shock absorber lower mounting nut and washer.

3. Remove the shock absorber upper bracket mounting bolt.

4. Disconnect the shock absorber from the lower mounting stud.

5. If necessary, remove the shock absorber upper bracket retaining nut and remove the bracket assembly.

6. Installation is the reverse of the removal procedure.

7. Tighten the upper bracket retaining nut, if removed, to 19 ft. lbs. (26 Nm). With the suspension at proper trim height, tighten the upper bracket mounting bolts to 22 ft. lbs. (30 Nm) and the lower mounting nut to 61 ft. lbs. (83 Nm).

With Selective Ride Control

1. Disconnect the negative battery cable.

2. Raise and support the vehicle safely.

3. Support the rear knuckle with a jackstand.

4. Disconnect the shock absorber lower mounting nut and washer.

5. Remove the shock absorber upper bracket mounting bolt.

6. Disconnect the shock absorber from the mounting stud and support. Do not allow the shock to hang from the actuator harness.

7. Remove the actuator retaining clip and remove the actuator from the shock.

8. Remove the shock absorber from the vehicle.

To install:

9. Install and properly seat the actuator retaining clip onto the cup assembly. The ends of the clip should protrude from the cup.

10. Install the shock absorber electrical actuator into the cup assembly retainer. The actuator should be snapped, not be forced into position.

11. Verify that a minimum of 0.178 inch (4.5mm) of clearance exists between the selector gear and the top of the cup assembly retainer.

12. Position the shock absorber into the frame and onto the lower mounting stud.

13. Install the shock absorber upper bracket mounting bolt.

14. With the suspension held at the proper trim height. Tighten the upper bracket mounting bolts to 22 ft. lbs. (30 Nm) and the lower mounting nut to 61 ft. lbs. (83 Nm).

15. Remove the jackstands and lower the vehicle.

16. Connect the negative battery cable.

Transverse Spring

REMOVAL AND INSTALLATION

1. Raise and support the vehicle safely.

2. Remove 1 wheel and tire assembly from the vehicle.

NOTE: Do not use corrosive cleaning agents, engine degreasers or solvents near the fiberglass rear spring or extensive damage could occur to the spring assembly.

3. Install tool J–33432 or equivalent spring compressor, onto the rear transverse spring, then compress the spring.

4. Remove the cotter pins, retaining nuts, insulators and spring bolts attaching the spring to the knuckles.

5. Carefully release and remove the spring compression tool.

6. Remove the rear spring anchor plate bolts, then the anchor plate, spacers and insulator from the vehicle. Note the spacer positioning for installation purposes.

7. Remove the transverse spring from the vehicle.

To install:

8. Position the spring in the vehicle. Take care not to scratch the spring during installation.

9. Position the spacers as noted during removal, then install the insulators and anchor plates onto the differential carrier.

10. Install the anchor plate bolts and tighten to 37 ft. lbs. (50 Nm).

11. Install the spring compression tool and compress the spring.

12. Position the spring to the knuckles and install the spring bolts, insulators and nuts. Tighten the nuts until slot in nut aligns with hole in bolt and install a new cotter pin.

13. Carefully release and remove the spring compression tool.

14. Install the tire and wheel assembly.

15. Remove the jackstands and lower the vehicle.

Rear Control Arms

REMOVAL AND INSTALLATION

1. Raise and support the vehicle safely.

2. Remove the control arm nut, bolt and washers at the knuckle.

3. Remove control arm nut and bolt at the bracket.

4. Remove the control arm from the vehicle.

5. Installation is the reverse of the removal procedure.

6. With the suspension held at the proper trim height, tighten the bracket bolt to 63 ft. lbs. (85 Nm) and the knuckle nut to 140 ft. lbs. (190 Nm).

Spindle/Support Rod

REMOVAL AND INSTALLATION

1. Raise and support vehicle safely.

2. Scribe alignment marks on the wheel spindle/support rod adjustment bolt and the spindle/support rod bracket so they can be installed in the same position.

3. Remove the adjustment bolt, cam and nut, then separate the spindle/support rod from the bracket.

4. Remove the spindle/support bolt, washer and nut at the knuckle, then remove the spindle/support rod from the vehicle.

5. Installation is the reverse of the removal procedure. Be sure to align the marks made during removal.

6. With the suspension held at the proper trim height, tighten the spindle/support rod-to-knuckle nut to 107 ft. lbs. (145 Nm), then tighten the spindle/support rod adjustment nut to 186 ft. lbs. (253 Nm).

7. Check and adjust the rear suspension alignment, as necessary.

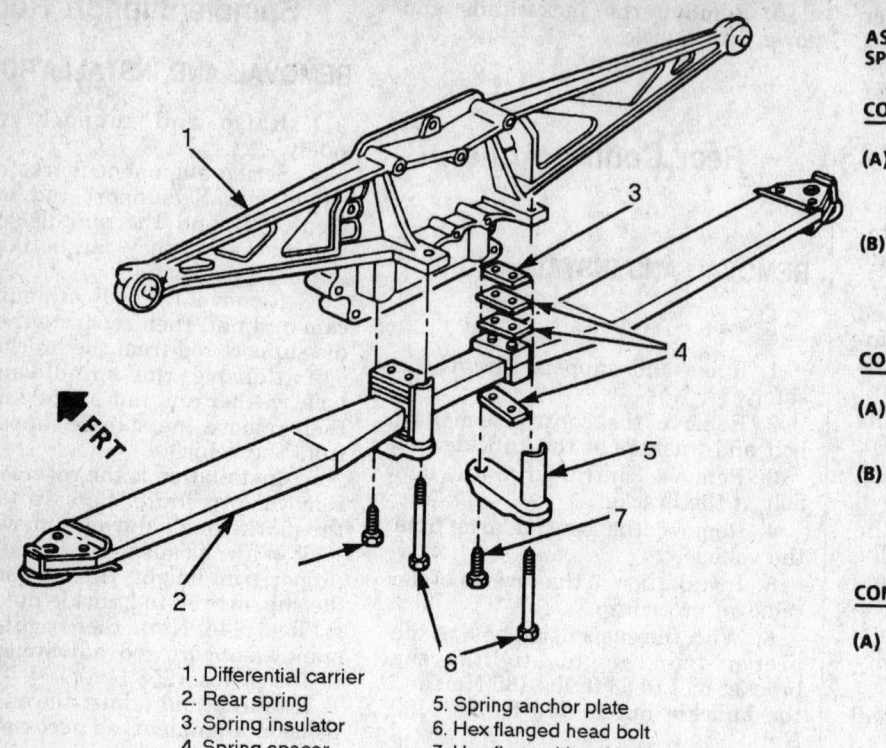

1. Differential carrier
2. Rear spring
3. Spring insulator
4. Spring spacer
5. Spring anchor plate
6. Hex flanged head bolt
7. Hex flanged head bolt

ASSEMBLE SPRING
SPACERS AS FOLLOWS:

COUPE WITH FE1

(A) SPRING (YELLOW CODE)
   1-14044572 ABOVE SPRING
   1-14048950 BELOW SPRING
   1-14044572 BELOW SPRING
(B) SPRING (GREEN CODE)
   1-14044572 ABOVE SPRING
   1-14048950 ABOVE SPRING
   1-14044572 BELOW SPRING

COUPE WITH FE7

(A) SPRING (YELLOW CODE)
   1-14084056 ABOVE SPRING
   2-14048950 BELOW SPRING
(B) SPRING (GREEN CODE)
   1-14084056 ABOVE SPRING
   1-14048950 ABOVE SPRING
   1-14048950 BELOW SPRING

CONVERTIBLE

(A) SPRING (YELLOW CODE ONLY)
   2-14044572 ABOVE SPRING
   1-14093185 ABOVE SPRING
   1-14084056 BELOW SPRING

8470R094

Rear transverse spring and shim installation. Do not add extra shims to raise the trim height or the spring will be overstressed

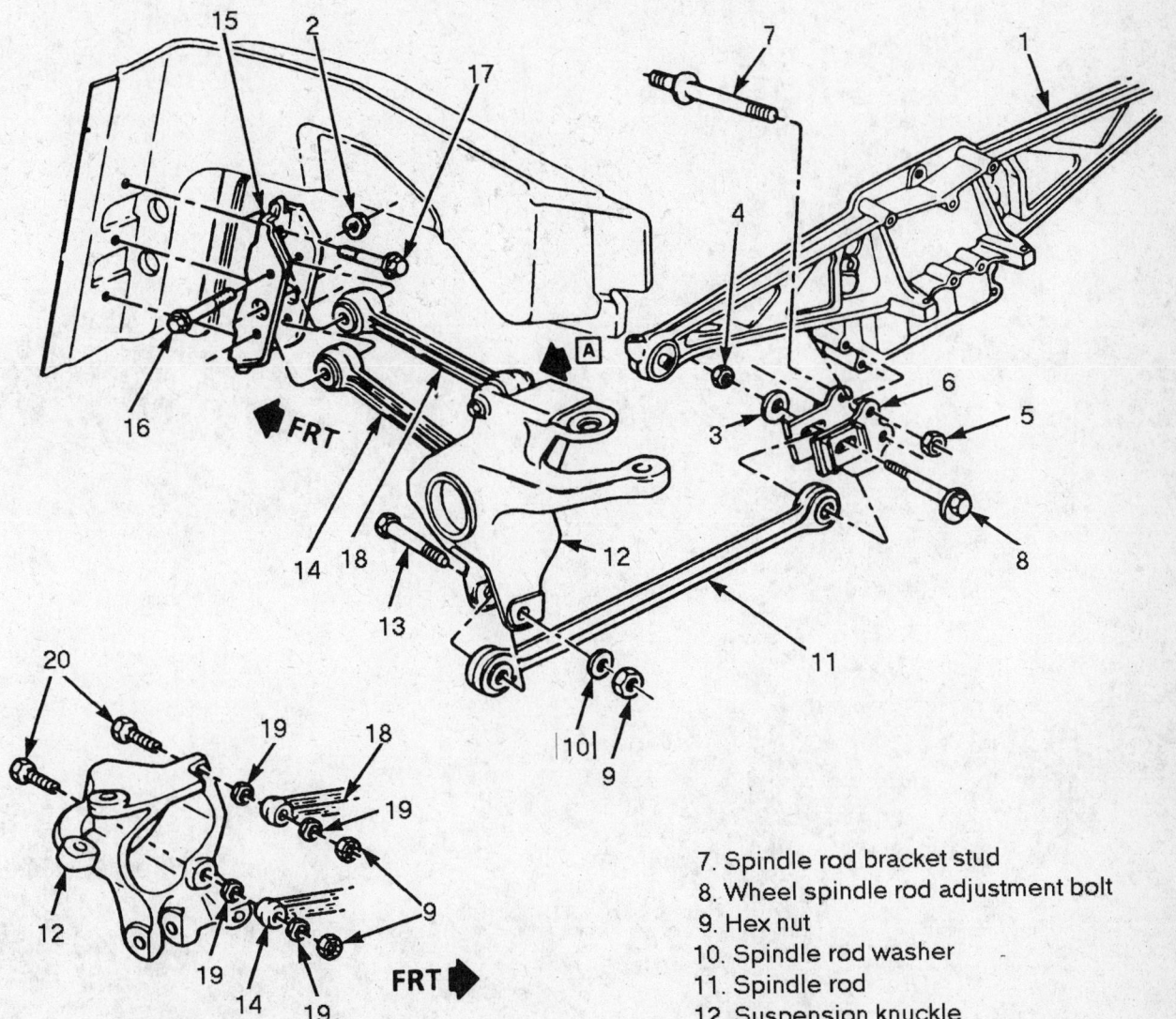

1. Differential carrier
2. Hex nut
3. Spindle rod adjustment cam
4. Spindle rod adjustment nut
5. Hex nut
6. Spindle rod bracket

7. Spindle rod bracket stud
8. Wheel spindle rod adjustment bolt
9. Hex nut
10. Spindle rod washer
11. Spindle rod
12. Suspension knuckle
13. Hex bolt
14. Wheel spindle lower control rod
15. Spindle control rod bracket
16. Wheel spindle rod bolt
17. Hex bolt
18. Wheel spindle upper control rod
19. Spindle rod washer
20. Spindle rod bolt

8470R095

Exploded view of the rear suspension assembly

SATURN
Front Wheel Drive
SATURN—SC, SC1, SC2, SL, SL1, SL2, SW1, SW2

FIRING ORDERS

NOTE: To avoid confusion, always replace spark plug wires one at a time.

8470N001

1.9L Engines
Engine Firing Order: 1-3-4-2
Distributorless Ignition System

ENGINE ELECTRICAL

NOTE: Disconnecting the negative battery cable on some vehicles may interfere with the functions of the on-board computer systems and may require the computer to undergo a relearning process, once the negative battery cable is reconnected.

Electronic Ignition System

NOTE: The 1.9L engine is equipped with a distributorless Electronic Ignition (EI) system. Besides the Powertrain Control Module (PCM), which regulates ignition timing under normal operating conditions, the 2 major components of the EI system are an EI module/coil pack and a crankshaft position sensor.

REMOVAL AND INSTALLATION

Ignition Module and Coils

1. Properly disable the SIR system, if equipped, and disconnect the negative battery cable.
2. Tag and disconnect the spark plug wires from the EI unit. The unit is on the front of the transaxle bellhousing.
3. Disengage the electrical connectors from the ignition module.
4. Remove the 4 retaining bolts, then remove the EI unit from the vehicle.
5. If necessary, the 2 coils may be removed from the unit at this time by using a pair of needle-nose pliers to squeeze the retaining tabs while pulling the coils upward.

To install:

6. If removed, install the coils over the retaining tabs on the ignition module.
7. Run a 6 x 1.0mm tap through the module mounting holes to remove remaining thread sealant residue and verify that the module and bellhousing mating surfaces are clean and free from grit or dirt.
8. Always use new module mounting bolts. Install the ignition module/coil assembly using the new mounting bolts with the factory applied yellow sealant and tighten the bolts to 71 inch lbs. (8 Nm). Be careful when tightening the mounting bolts, verify that each bolt head is properly seated on the module unit when tightened.
9. Engage the electrical connectors and spark plug wires to the module unit.
10. Connect the negative battery cable and, if equipped, properly enable the SIR system.
11. Start the engine and check operation.

Crankshaft Position Sensor

1. Disconnect the negative battery cable.
2. Raise the vehicle and support safely.
3. Disengage the electrical connector from the sensor located at the lower rear of the engine block.
4. Remove the retaining bolt from the sensor flange, then remove the sensor from the engine block.
5. Lubricate the sensor O-ring with clean engine oil and install in the reverse of removal. Tighten the sensor retaining bolt to 80 inch lbs. (9 Nm).

Ignition Timing

ADJUSTMENT

There is no conventional distributor for the EI system. Instead, timing is controlled by the Powertrain Control Module (PCM) through the EI module. The PCM has the ability to advance or retard ignition timing, as necessary for optimal engine performance. No timing adjustments are necessary or possible.

Alternator

PRECAUTIONS

Several precautions must be observed with alternator equipped vehicles to avoid damage to the unit.

• If the battery is removed for any reason, make sure it is reconnected with the correct polarity. Reversing the battery connections may result in damage to the one-way rectifiers.
• When utilizing a booster battery as a starting aid, always connect the positive to positive terminals and the negative terminal from the booster battery to a good engine ground on the vehicle being started.
• Never use a fast charger as a booster to start vehicles.
• Disconnect the battery cables when charging the battery with a fast charger.
• Never attempt to polarize the alternator.
• Do not use test lamps of more than 12 volts when checking diode continuity.
• Do not short across or ground any of the alternator terminals.
• The polarity of the battery, alternator and regulator must be matched and considered before making any electrical connections within the system.
• Never operate the alternator on an open circuit. Make sure all connections within the circuit are clean and tight.
• Disconnect the battery ground terminal when performing any service on electrical components.
• Disconnect the battery if arc welding is to be done on the vehicle.

BELT TENSION ADJUSTMENT

The belt is automatically adjusted using a spring loaded automatic tensioner. The marking on the tensioner arm must fall within the operating range (2 marks) on the tensioner body. If the tensioner falls outside the operating range, the serpentine drive belt must be replaced.

REMOVAL AND INSTALLATION

1. Disconnect the negative battery cable and remove the serpentine drive belt.

2. Remove the power steering pump assembly; this must be done in order to access the alternator attaching bolts.

3. Remove the alternator splash shield attaching bolt from the rear of the alternator, then unclip the shield from the alternator.

4. Disengage the alternator electrical connections.

5. Remove the upper and lower alternator attaching bolts.

NOTE: The alternator attaching bolts can usually be reached from under the hood. If difficulty is encountered loosening the lower mounting bolt, remove the vehicle passenger side tire and splash shield. With these components removed, the alternator may be removed through the wheelwell.

6. Lift the alternator through the opening between the shock tower and the intake manifold and remove the alternator from the vehicle.

To install:

7. Position the alternator in the vehicle and install the lower attaching bolt.

NOTE: Always use a new wiring harness-to-alternator fastener to assure proper electrical contact.

8. Install the upper attaching bolt and the 2 wiring harness connectors.

9. Tighten the alternator attaching bolts to 27 ft. lbs. (37 Nm), then tighten the alternator positive terminal fastener to 89 inch lbs. (10 Nm).

10. If removed, install the vehicle passenger's side tire and splash shield.

11. Install the alternator splash shield and tighten the fastener bolt to 89 inch lbs. (10 Nm).

12. Install the power steering pump assembly.

13. Connect the negative battery cable.

Serpentine Drive Belt

REMOVAL AND INSTALLATION

1. Depress the tensioner arm using Snap-On® tool S-8190A, or an equivalent ⁹⁄₁₆ in. (14mm) wrench.

2. Remove the belt from the idler or air conditioning compressor pulley.

3. Remove the drive belt from the vehicle.

To install:

4. Route the belt around the pulleys, except for the front cover idler or air conditioning compressor pulley.

5. Depress the tensioner arm and slip the belt over the idler or air conditioning compressor pulley. Make sure the belt ribs are properly aligned on the pulleys.

6. If the tensioner idler pulley retaining bolt is loose, remove the bolt and apply Loctite® 242 or equivalent to the bolt threads. Install the bolt and tighten to 22 ft. lbs. (30 Nm).

Starter

REMOVAL AND INSTALLATION

1. Disconnect the negative battery cable.

2. Remove the air inlet tube and fresh air hose. For the DOHC engine, the resonator must be lifted for disengagement from the engine support bracket.

3. Remove the upper starter bolts using the access hole provided next to the intake manifold support bracket. If necessary, remove the intake support bracket to provide better access and tool swing.

4. Raise and support the vehicle safely.

5. Remove the starter shield pin by pulling on it with pliers. Lift upward and carefully release the shield from the solenoid.

——— WARNING ———
It is very important that the solenoid electrical connection nuts and studs are sprayed with penetrating oil prior to removal in order to avoid damage to the solenoid end cap.

6. Carefully loosen the retainers and disengage the starter electrical connectors. Be sure to tag the connections to assure proper installation.

7. Remove the lower starter bolt.

8. Remove the rear starter support bracket attaching bolt.

9. Rotate the starter until the bracket misses the axle shaft support bracket. Pull the starter rearward and toward the left side of the vehicle to remove.

To install:

10. If removed, or if the starter is being replaced, install the rear starter support bracket to the starter. Tighten the bracket nuts to 80 inch lbs. (9 Nm).

11. Guide the starter and bracket assembly into the bellhousing, then rotate the assembly until the lower bolt hole in the starter nose aligns.

12. Verify that the bracket is properly aligned, then loosely install the bracket and housing bolts.

13. If necessary, raise or lower the vehicle for access, then install the upper bolt.

14. Torque the starter mounting bolts to 27 ft. lbs. (37 Nm) and the bracket bolt to 22 ft. lbs. (30 Nm).

15. Install the electrical connectors and wiring nuts. Be careful not to overtighten the nuts and crack the solenoid end cap. Tighten the starter positive terminal to 89 inch lbs. (10 Nm) and the solenoid terminal to 44 inch lbs. (5 Nm).

16. Install the shield and push pin, making sure the pin is positioned for possible future removal.

17. Lower the vehicle, as necessary, and if removed, install the intake manifold support bracket.

18. Install the air intake tube and fresh air hose. For the DOHC engine, verify the resonator button is properly located in the service bracket.

19. Connect the negative battery cable.

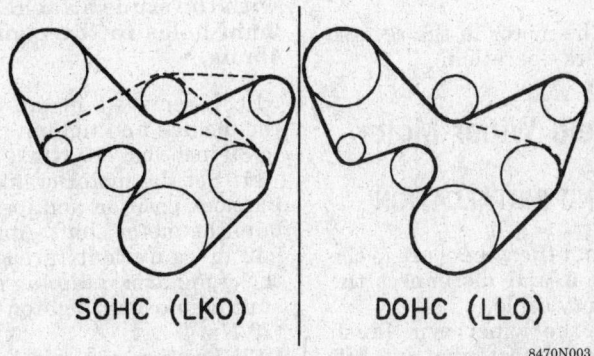

SOHC (LKO)   DOHC (LLO)

8470N003

Accessory drive belt routing

CHASSIS ELECTRICAL

Air Bag

DISARMING

1. Align the steering wheel so the vehicle wheels are pointing in the straight-ahead position.
2. Turn the ignition switch to the **OFF** position.
3. Remove the SIR fuse from the top left of the Instrument Panel Junction Block (IPJB).
4. Remove the Connector Position Assurance (CPA) device, then disengage the yellow 2-way SIR harness wire connector at the base of the steering column.
To enable system:
5. Verify that the ignition switch is in the **OFF** position.
6. Engage the yellow 2-way connector at the base of the steering column and install the CPA.
7. Install the SIR fuse.
8. Turn the ignition switch to the **RUN** position.
9. Verify the SIR indicator light flashes 7–9 times and then turns **OFF** to signify proper system operation. If light does not flash as specified, inspect system for malfunction.

Heater Blower Motor

REMOVAL AND INSTALLATION

1. Disconnect the negative battery cable.
2. Disconnect the blower motor connectors under the glove compartment.
3. Remove the blower motor mounting screws and motor assembly.
4. Install the motor in the reverse order and check operation.

Windshield Wiper Motor

REMOVAL AND INSTALLATION

1. Verify that the wipers are in the **PARK** position and disconnect the negative battery cable.
2. Remove the wiper arm finish cap and wiper arm fastening nut. Lift the blade away from the windshield

and remove. Repeat for the other blade.
3. Remove the cowl trim panel fasteners at the windshield edge of the panel, then open the hood and remove the remaining fasteners. Carefully remove the cowl trim panel. If equipped with cowl mounted washer nozzles, disconnect the washer hoses from the nozzles.
4. Remove the 2 instrument panel top cover screw caps and screws. Carefully remove the cover by lifting at the rear edge to disengage the retaining clips and sliding the panel out of the windshield clips.
5. Remove the retaining screws and unsnap the windshield defroster duct from the heating and air conditioning mode valve assembly.
6. Except for SC vehicles, remove the defroster nozzle by rotating the front up and away from the windshield, exposing the wiper module fasteners. On Coupes, the windshield rake angle prevents nozzle removal.
7. Remove the wiper module fasteners and reposition the module in order to disconnect the wiring from the motor and module frame. Carefully remove the wiper module and motor assembly making sure not to contact or damage the windshield.
8. If necessary, remove the crank arm nut and disconnect the arm from the motor shaft, then remove the wiper motor attaching screws and remove the motor from the module.
To install:
9. Verify that the motor is in the **PARK** position. If necessary, temporarily connect the motor wiring and the negative battery cable, turn the wiper control ON then OFF and the motor will move to the correct position.

NOTE: If replacing the wiper module on early 1992 vehicles, the center fastening studs nuts must be removed from the instrument panel cover. To install the new module, which should come with the studs attached, open the 9mm holes in the center cowl to 15mm.

10. If removed, install the motor to the module and tighten the retainers to 89 inch lbs. (10 Nm).
11. Set the motor crank arm to the 9 o'clock position and install the arm onto the motor shaft. Apply Loctite® 242 or equivalent thread sealant to the crank arm retaining nut, then install the nut and tighten to 21 ft. lbs. (28 Nm).
12. Position the wiper module assembly into the vehicle and connect

the wiring to the wiper motor and to the module frame.
13. Install the module retaining bolts and tighten to 89 inch lbs. (10 Nm).
14. Install the cowl trim panel and, if applicable, connect the washer hoses to the nozzles.
15. Install the wiper arm assemblies using new nuts (torque retention of the old nuts may be insufficient) and tighten the nuts to 21 ft. lbs. (28 Nm).
16. If removed, rotate the windshield defroster nozzle onto the mode valve assembly.
17. Install the screws fastening the defroster duct and make sure the duct is snapped on both sides of the heating and air conditioning module.
18. Install the instrument panel top cover and screws. Insert the panel cover screw caps.
19. Connect the negative battery cable and verify proper system operation.

Liftgate Window Wiper Motor

REMOVAL AND INSTALLATION

1. Make sure the wiper is in the **PARK** position, then disconnect the negative battery cable.
2. Remove the rear wiper arm finish cap, then remove the retaining nut.
3. Lift the wiper blade away from the liftgate window and remove the blade/arm assembly.
4. Remove the rear wiper pivot bushing.
5. Raise the liftgate, then remove the wedge blocks from either end of the liftgate assembly.
6. Remove the lower fasteners from the liftgate lower trim panel, by pushing in of each center pin approximately 1/8 inch until it clicks, then remove the fastener.
7. Insert a small prybar into the hole in the lower trim panel (located near the wiper pivot on the pivot hump) so the tool sits on top of the pivot. Lift up on the tool handle to disengage the trim panel upper clips, then remove the trim panel.
8. Remove the fasteners and pivot nut from the rear wiper module, then disconnect the washer hose from the module check valve.
9. Disconnect the wiring from the module, then remove the module from the liftgate.

To install:

10. Position the wiper module to the liftgate, then connect the washer hose to the check valve and the wiring to the module terminals.

11. Install the module fasteners and tighten to 89 inch lbs. (10 Nm).

12. Install the grommet, washer and nut on the wiper module pivot shaft, then tighten the nut to 119 inch lbs. (14 Nm).

13. Align the upper clips on the lower trim panel to the liftgate slots, then install the panel by pushing at the clip locations.

14. Reset the trim panel push-in fasteners by spreading the center pin tabs and moving the pin so it sits approximately ¼ in. out of the fastener. Insert the fasteners into the bottom of the liftgate lower trim panel and push the center pin until flush.

15. Install the liftgate wedge blocks.

16. Install the rear wiper pivot bushing.

17. Position the arm onto the pivot shaft with the blade horizontal to the liftgate glass lower edge, then install the retaining nut and tighten to 159 inch lbs. (18 Nm).

18. Install the finish cap over the retaining nut.

19. Connect the negative battery cable, then check for proper motor operation.

Instrument Cluster Assembly

REMOVAL AND INSTALLATION

1. Properly disable the SIR system, if equipped, and disconnect the negative battery cable.

2. Remove the 2 instrument panel top cover screw caps and screws. Carefully remove the cover by lifting at the rear edge to disengage the retaining clips and by sliding the panel out of the windshield clips.

3. Carefully remove the center radio finish panel/air outlet assembly by pulling outward at the clip locations. Start at the bottom and move upward. Do not use tools that might damage the trim panel. For 1993–95 vehicles so equipped, remove and disconnect the traction control/fog lamp switch.

4. Open the glove box, then remove the 4 cluster trim panel attaching screws.

5. Carefully pull the cluster trim panel upward/outward to disengage it from the retainers, then remove

the CPA devices and disengage the electrical connectors from the instrument panel lighting and rear window defogger switches. Remove the panel from the vehicle.

6. Remove the instrument cluster retaining screws, then pull the cluster out far enough to unplug the electrical connectors. Disengage the connectors by depressing the retainer legs, then remove the cluster assembly from the vehicle.

To install:

7. Position the cluster assembly in the vehicle, then engage electrical connectors.

8. Verify that the connectors for the cluster trim panel lighting and rear window defogger switches are properly positioned and secure the instrument cluster assembly using the retaining screws.

9. Position the cluster trim panel and engage the electrical connectors to the panel lighting and the rear defogger switches, then install the CPA devices.

10. Install the cluster trim panel into the retainers, then install and tighten the retaining screws.

11. For 1993–95 vehicles so equipped, engage the traction control/fog lamp connector.

12. Install the the center radio finish panel/air outlet assembly by pushing inward at the clip locations.

13. Install the rear of the instrument panel top cover into the windshield clips and snap the panel into position. Install the 2 upper panel cover screws and screw caps.

14. Connect the negative battery cable and, if equipped, properly enable the SIR system.

Concealed Headlights

OPERATION

If equipped with concealed headlights, the headlight doors can be opened automatically by turning the headlight switch to the ON position. Turning the switch back 1 click to the parking lights ON position or 2 clicks to the lights OFF position will leave the doors open. To close the headlight doors turn the switch 1 final click to the headlight closed position.

A headlight manual control knob is located next to each headlight door to open the doors without the aid of the electric motor. To manually open the door, raise the hood and turn the control knob in the direction of the arrow until the door is fully opened.

Combination Switch

REMOVAL AND INSTALLATION

1. Properly disable the SIR system, if equipped, and disconnect the negative battery cable.

2. Remove the steering wheel.

3. Remove the 2 retaining screws and the upper steering column cover from the steering column.

4. Remove the ignition lock bezel, then remove the 2 retaining screws and the lower steering column cover.

5. Disconnect the velcro fasteners, then remove the left and right lower trim panel extensions by pulling them each out of the 2 upper fasteners.

6. Carefully remove the center radio finish panel/air outlet assembly by pulling outward at the clip locations. Start at the bottom and move upward. Do not use tools that might damage the trim panel. For 1993–95 vehicles, so equipped, disconnect the wiring from the traction control/fog lamp switch.

7. If necessary, remove the trim panel extension strip by pulling out at the fastener location.

8. Remove the 2 instrument panel top cover screw caps and screws. Carefully remove the cover by lifting at the rear edge to disengage the retaining clips and by sliding the panel out of the windshield clips.

9. Remove the 4 cluster trim panel attaching screws. Carefully pull the cluster trim panel upward/outward to disengage it from the retainers.

10. Remove the CPA devices, then disengage the electrical connectors from the instrument panel lighting and rear window defogger switches. Remove the cluster trim panel from the vehicle.

11. Remove the 6 screws attaching the steering column opening filler, then carefully remove the assembly. Protect the console from the damage when removing the assembly.

12. Remove the CPA device and disconnect the wires from the lever control switch.

13. Remove the retaining bolts and remove the combination switch assembly from the steering column.

To install:

14. Install the combination switch aligning the bottom locating holes on the ignition module, then install the retaining bolts. Tighten the lower mounting bolt first to assure proper location and seating, then engage the switch electrical connectors and insert the CPA device.

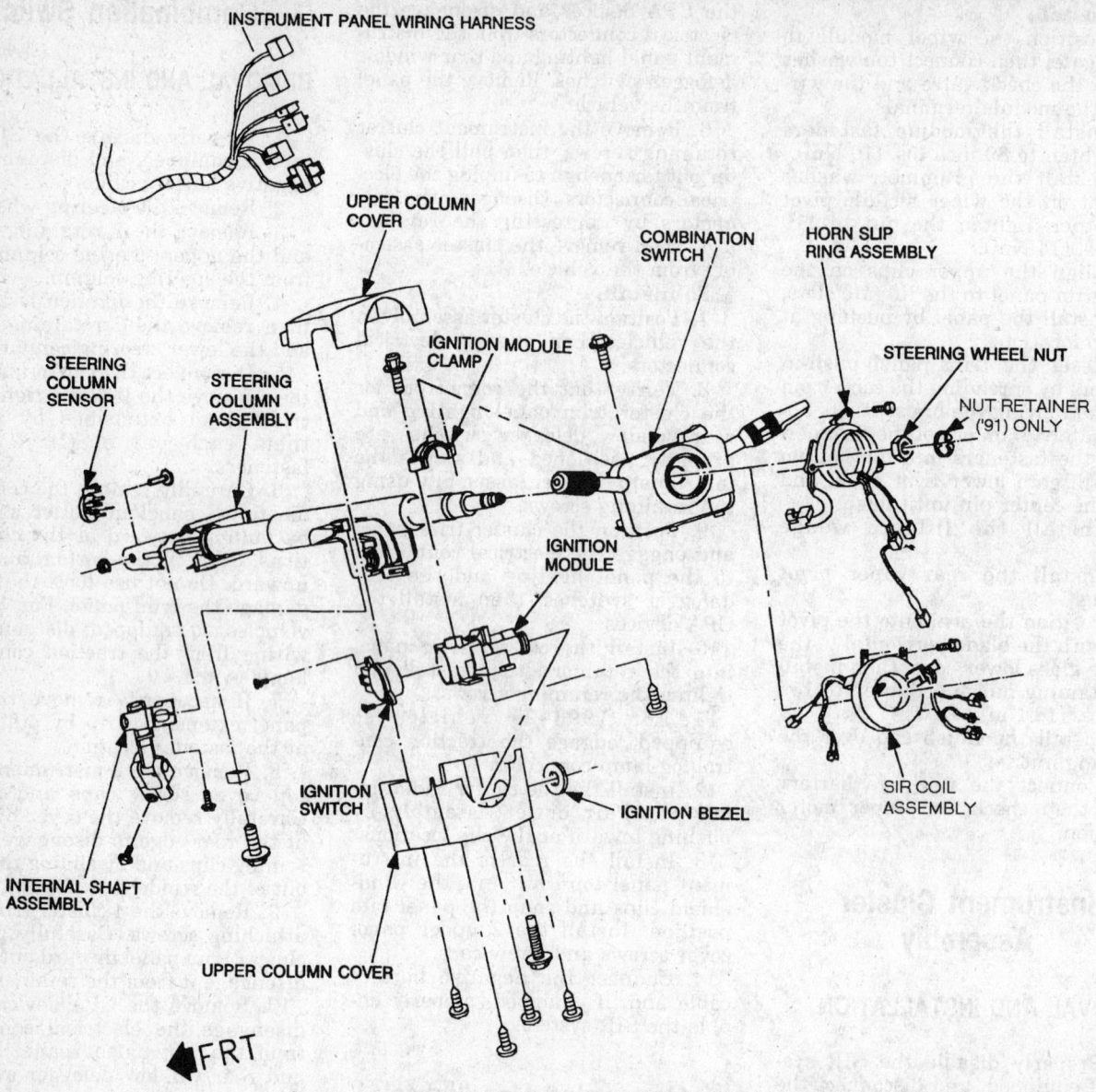

INSTRUMENT PANEL WIRING HARNESS

UPPER COLUMN COVER

COMBINATION SWITCH

HORN SLIP RING ASSEMBLY

STEERING COLUMN SENSOR

STEERING COLUMN ASSEMBLY

IGNITION MODULE CLAMP

STEERING WHEEL NUT

NUT RETAINER ('91) ONLY

IGNITION MODULE

INTERNAL SHAFT ASSEMBLY

IGNITION SWITCH

IGNITION BEZEL

SIR COIL ASSEMBLY

UPPER COLUMN COVER

FRT

8470N005

Exploded view of the steering column assembly

15. Install the steering column opening filler and attaching screws.

16. Position the cluster trim panel, engage the electrical connectors to the panel lighting and the rear defogger switches, then install the CPA devices. Install the cluster trim panel into the retainers, then install and tighten the retaining screws

17. Install the rear of the instrument panel top cover into the windshield clips and snap the panel into position. If necessary, replace the 6 rearward clips. Install the upper panel cover screws and screw caps.

18. For 1993–95 vehicles so equipped, engage the traction control/fog lamp connector.

19. Install the trim panel extension strip and push the center radio finish panel/air outlet assembly into the clip locations.

20. Install the lower left and right trim panel extensions.

21. Install the steering column covers and the ignition bezel.

22. Install the steering wheel.

23. Connect the negative battery cable and, if equipped, properly enable the SIR system.

Dimmer Switch (Instrument Panel Rheostat)

An instrument panel dimmer switch is mounted in the instrument cluster trim panel, to the lower left of the cluster. The headlight dimmer switch is part of the combination switch assembly mounted on the steering column, under the steering wheel.

REMOVAL AND INSTALLATION

1. Properly disable the SIR system, if equipped, and disconnect the negative battery cable.

2. Remove the 2 instrument panel top cover screw caps and screws. Carefully remove the cover by lifting at the rear edge to disengage the retaining clips and by sliding the panel out of the windshield clips.

3. Carefully remove the center radio finish panel/air outlet assembly by pulling outward at the clip locations. Start at the bottom and move upward. Do not use tools that might damage the trim panel. For 1993–95 vehicles so equipped, remove and disconnect the traction control/fog lamp switch.

4. Open the glove box, then remove the 4 cluster trim panel attaching screws.

5. Carefully pull the cluster trim panel upward/outward to disengage it from the retainers.

6. Remove the CPA device and disengage the electrical connector from the instrument panel dimmer switch.

7. Remove the retaining bolt and instrument panel dimmer switch from the cluster trim panel.

To install:

8. Install the instrument panel dimmer switch to the cluster trim panel and tighten the retaining bolt.

9. Engage the dimmer switch electrical connector and install the CPA device.

10. Verify that the connectors for the cluster trim panel lighting and rear window defogger switches are properly positioned and secure the instrument cluster assembly using the retaining screws.

11. Install the cluster trim panel into the retainers, then install and tighten the retaining screws.

12. For 1993–95 vehicles so equipped, engage the traction control/fog lamp connector.

13. Install the the center radio finish panel/air outlet assembly by pushing inward at the clip locations.

14. Install the rear of the instrument panel top cover into the windshield clips and snap the panel into position. Install the 2 upper panel cover screws and screw caps.

15. Connect the negative battery cable and, if equipped, properly enable the SIR system.

Ignition Switch

REMOVAL AND INSTALLATION

1. Properly disable the SIR system, if equipped, and disconnect the negative battery cable.

2. Remove the steering wheel.

3. Remove the combination switch.

4. Remove the 2 screws retaining the combination switch connector.

5. Remove the 2 retaining screws, then disconnect the ignition switch from the ignition module and remove the switch from the vehicle.

To install:

6. Install the combination switch and retaining bolts. Tighten the lower mounting bolt first to assure proper location and seating.

7. Install the bolts retaining the combination switch connector, then engage the switch electrical connectors and insert the CPA device.

8. Install the ignition switch and retaining bolts to the ignition module.

9. Install the steering column opening filler and attaching screws.

10. Position the cluster trim panel, engage the electrical connectors to the panel lighting and the rear defogger switches, then install the CPA devices. Install the cluster trim panel into the retainers, then install and tighten the retaining screws

11. Install the rear of the instrument panel top cover into the windshield clips and snap the panel into position. If necessary, replace the 6 rearward clips. Install the upper panel cover screws and screw caps.

12. For 1993–95 vehicles so equipped, engage the traction control/fog lamp connector.

13. Install the trim panel extension strip and push the center radio finish panel/air outlet assembly into the clip locations.

14. Install the lower left and right trim panel extensions.

15. Install the steering column covers and the ignition bezel.

16. Install the steering wheel.

17. Connect the negative battery cable and, if equipped, properly enable the SIR system.

Ignition Lock Assembly

REMOVAL AND INSTALLATION

1. Properly disable the SIR system, if equipped, and disconnect the negative battery cable.

2. Remove the steering column from the vehicle.

3. Position the steering column in a vise at the upper bracket.

NOTE: Always wear the proper eye protection when using drills, chisels and punches.

4. Using a center punch, mark the center of the shear bolts on the ignition lock assembly.

5. Remove the left shear bolt from the ignition module and column:

a. Tap the chisel to create a divet on the side of the bolt.

b. Turn the chisel and tap bolt at the divet on an angle in order to drive the bolt counterclockwise.

c. Continue to tap the chisel and drive the bolt counterclockwise until the bolt is sufficiently loosened or removed.

6. Remove the right shear bolt from the ignition module and column in the same manner as the left bolt was removed.

7. Remove the ignition lock module from the steering column.

To install:

8. Using new shear bolts, install the ignition lock assembly to the steering column. Torque the bolts until the heads break off.

9. Install the steering column into the vehicle.

10. Connect the negative battery cable and, if equipped, properly enable the SIR system.

Brake Light Switch

ADJUSTMENT CHECK

1. View the brake light switch and bracket from the side while pulling the pedal upward using a moderate force of about 20 lbs. If then switch and/or bracket moves, perform switch adjustment.

2. Release the pedal and inspect the green switch plunger located in the center of the switch assembly. There should be 0.03–0.05 in. (0.8–1.2mm) or less of the plunger visible between the switch and the brake pedal actuator pad. If so, the switch is correctly adjusted. The height of the plunger rounded crown is equivalent to 0.04 in. (1mm).

3. If more the 0.05 in. (1.2mm) of plunger is visible, the switch adjustment procedure must be performed.

ADJUSTMENT

1. Loosen the brake light switch mounting nut sufficiently to allow the switch to move forward and rearward in the adjustment slot.

2. Insert SA-9303BR, or an equivalent 0.03–0.05 in. (0.8–1.2mm) adjustment gauge between the switch and the brake pedal switch actuator pad. SA-9303BR is equipped with a slot in the gauge for the switch

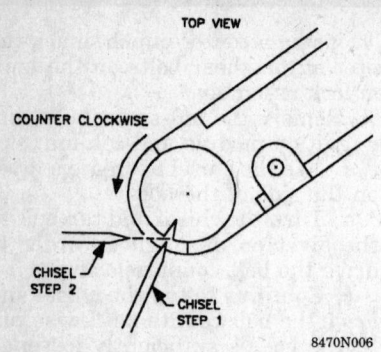

8470N006

Using a chisel to remove the shear bolts from the ignition module and steering column

plunger to protrude through, if a slotted gauge is not available, be careful to make sure the switch is not cocked when adjusted.

3. While pulling upward on the brake pedal with moderate force, push the switch assembly downward, against the gauge.

NOTE: The switch must be held while tightening the mounting nut, in order to prevent the switch from rotating out of alignment.

4. Hold the switch in position and make sure it remains perpendicular to the actuator pad, then tighten the switch retaining but to 89 inch lbs. (10 Nm).

5. Release the brake pedal, then with the gauge still in position, tap the gauge side-to-side and to see if it swings freely. If the gauge sticks or does not swing freely, restart the adjustment procedure.

6. Pull up on the brake pedal with a very light force or about 2 lbs. and tap the gauge from side-to-side. If the gauge swings freely with a light upward force, restart the adjustment procedure.

7. Perform the switch adjustment check to determine if the switch is in the proper position.

REMOVAL AND INSTALLATION

1. Disconnect the negative battery cable, then disengage the brake switch electrical connector.
2. Remove the retaining nut, then remove the switch from the mounting bracket.
3. Install the switch. There should be a tab on the switch which fits into a slotted hole and keeps the switch parallel to the brake pedal.

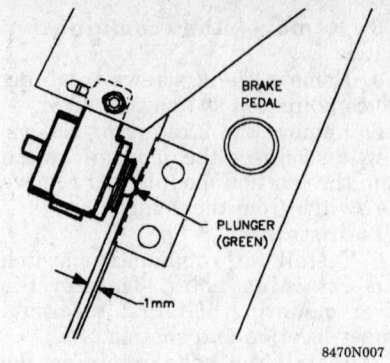

8470N007

Checking brake light switch adjustment

4. Adjust the switch and tighten the retaining bolt to 89 inch lbs. (10 Nm).
5. Connect the wiring and the negative battery cable.
6. Verify proper switch operation. Brake lights should come ON and, if equipped, the cruise control should shut OFF when the brake pedal is depressed.

Clutch Switch

ADJUSTMENT

1. Check the switch with the clutch depressed. The switch contacts should be open (no continuity). When the clutch is released the contacts will close and there should be continuity.
2. If adjustment is necessary, loosen the bolt and slide the switch towards or away from the brake pedal.
3. The plunger should protrude approximately 0.039 in. (1mm) with the clutch pedal released.
4. When the switch is properly adjusted, tighten the retaining bolt to 89 inch lbs. (10 Nm).

REMOVAL AND INSTALLATION

1. Disconnect the negative battery cable, then disengage the clutch switch electrical connector.
2. Remove the retaining bolt and switch.
3. Install the switch. There is a tab on the switch which fits into a slotted hole a keeps the switch parallel to the clutch pedal.
4. Adjust the switch and tighten the retaining bolt to 89 inch lbs. (10 Nm).
5. Connect the wiring and the negative battery cable.

6. Verify proper switch operation. The engine should not start unless the clutch pedal is depressed. If equipped, the cruise control should shut OFF when the clutch pedal is depressed.

Neutral Safety/Selector Switch

ADJUSTMENT

1. Place the transaxle selector in **D**.
2. Locate the gear selector switch mounted on the side of the transaxle housing and disengage the switch connector.
3. Use an ohmmeter or continuity tester to check for continuity across the switch terminals.
4. If no continuity exists, loosen the bolts and rotate the switch to achieve continuity.
5. Tighten the switch bolts to 124 inch lbs. (14 Nm) and recheck continuity.

REMOVAL AND INSTALLATION

1. Disconnect the negative battery cable.
2. Remove the air induction tube. For the DOHC engine, remove the air filter box. Lift the resonator upward to disengage it from the support bracket.
3. Disengage the electrical connectors from the switch, then disconnect the shifter cable from the control lever.
4. Remove the retaining nut from the control lever shaft. Note the position of the manual lever, then remove.
5. Remove the 2 switch-to-transaxle housing retaining bolts, then remove the switch.
   To install:
6. Install the switch to the transaxle and loosely install the retaining bolts.
7. Position the lever as noted and install the nut. Tighten the nut to 97 inch lbs. (11 Nm).
8. Adjust the switch and tighten the retaining bolts.
9. Install the shift cable to the control lever and adjust as necessary.
10. Engage the switch electrical connectors, then install the air induction tube.
11. Connect the negative battery cable and verify proper switch operation.

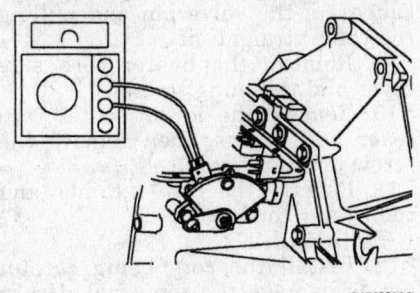

8470N008

Adjusting the neutral safety switch

Fuses, Circuit Breakers and Relays

LOCATION

Underhood Junction Block

The block is located next to the battery on the left inner fender. It houses maxifuses, minifuses, relays and 1 circuit breaker. There are two 30 amp maxifuses for the ignition and 1 each for the battery, ABS and cooling fan. The circuit breaker is a 20 amp unit for the power windows and/or sunroof.

The horn, air conditioning control, cooling fan and automatic transaxle relays are located in the underhood junction block.

Instrument Panel Junction Block

The block is located under the instrument panel, behind the center console. It houses minifuses and relays. The relays for the power window, fuel pump, flasher, rear defogger and blower motor are located in the block.

Computers

LOCATION

ABS Electronic Brake Control Module (EBCM) — located on the carrier assembly behind the left kickpanel. The EBCM is on the bracket behind the PCM in the carrier assembly.

Cruise Control Module — located on the steering column support bracket, above the accelerator pedal.

Powertrain Control Module (PCM) — located on the carrier assembly behind the left kickpanel. The PCM container the Engine Controller (EC) for all vehicles and the Transaxle Controller (TC) for vehicles with automatic transaxles.

Flashers

LOCATION

The turn signal/hazard flasher unit is located in the instrument panel junction block, under the instrument panel and behind the center console.

Cruise Control

ADJUSTMENT

NOTE: The cable and adjuster are not repairable or replaceable. Do not attempt to remove the cable and adjuster from the cruise control module or damage to the module could result.

1. Disconnect the air intake tube at the throttle body.
2. Observe the position of the throttle blade.
3. Adjust the cable by pulling forward and turning the ring on the adjuster, located at the module, until the throttle blade is fully closed.
4. Loosen the adjuster ½ turn to allow approximately 0.040–0.079 in. (1–2mm) of slack in the cable.
5. Connect the air intake tube and check for proper operation.

ENGINE COOLING

Radiator

REMOVAL AND INSTALLATION

1. Disconnect the negative battery cable and drain the engine coolant.
2. Remove the air intake ducts and for the DOHC engine, remove the air cleaner housing.
3. If necessary, unplug the temperature sensor connector.
4. Remove the upper radiator hose and, if equipped with an automatic transaxle, disconnect the upper transaxle cooler line. Plug the openings to prevent fluid contamination or loss.
5. Remove the electric cooling fan assembly.
6. Remove the lower radiator hose.
7. Raise and support the vehicle safely.
8. Remove the lower splash shield, then if applicable, disconnect and plug the lower transaxle cooler line.
9. Remove the 4 condenser bracket-to-radiator bolts. Wire the

condenser to the frame assembly so it stays in place, then lower the vehicle.
10. Remove the upper radiator nuts and brackets. If equipped the air conditioning, remove the upper radiator seal.
11. Remove the radiator from the vehicle.
   To install:
12. Install the radiator into the vehicle.
13. Install the upper seal, if applicable, then install the brackets and retaining nuts. Be sure the L-shaped brackets do not pinch the radiator locating pins and the radiator moves freely in the grommets.
14. Raise and support the vehicle safely.
15. Install the condenser bracket bolts, and if applicable, install the lower transaxle cooler line.
16. Install the lower splash shield and lower the vehicle.
17. Install the lower radiator hose with the clamp tangs positioned at 1 o'clock.
18. Install the cooling fan assembly.
19. For vehicles with an automatic transaxle, connect the upper transaxle cooler line at a 35 degree angle inward from vertical and hold in position while tightening.
20. Install the upper radiator hose with the clamp tangs at 12 o'clock.
21. For the DOHC engine, install the air cleaner housing.
22. Install the intake air ducts and connect the air temperature sensor connector.
23. Close the radiator drain plug and install the cylinder block drain plug. Tighten the block plug to 26 ft. lbs. (35 Nm).
24. Connect the negative battery cable and properly fill the engine cooling system.

Electric Cooling Fan

TESTING

When conducting tests on the electric cooling fan and circuit use of a high impedance Digital Volt Ohm Meter (DVOM) is necessary.

Cooling Fan Inoperative Test

1. Check the 30 amp cooling fan maxifuse (maxifuse No. 6, labeled COOL FAN) in the underhood junction block.
2. If the fuse is OK, unplug the cooling fan motor connector and connect a DVOM from terminal B (BLK/RED) wire to ground.

3. Unplug the A/C compressor connector, then start the engine and turn the air conditioning ON:

a. If there is voltage at the B wire, check for open at terminal A (BLK) wire to ground which would prevent circuit completion and keep an otherwise good motor from operating. If there is no open and voltage is present, the motor must be faulty. Repair the open wire or replace the faulty motor, as applicable.

b. If there is no voltage at the B wire, turn the ignition **OFF** and with the DVOM still connected to terminal B, unplug the PCM connector. Install a jumper wire between the PCM connector terminal J2A03 (DRK GRN/WHT) wire and ground. If there is no voltage at the connector with the ignition switch **ON**, the fan relay is faulty. If there is voltage, the PCM is bad.

4. The fan motor may also be checked by jumping 12 volts to the cooling fan motor connector. The motor should run while voltage is applied.

Cooling Fan Constantly On Test

1. Disconnect the negative battery cable and remove the cooling fan relay from the underhood junction block. Connect the negative battery cable and inspect the motor to see if it still operates.

2. If the motor operates with the relay removed, a short to power exists in the BLK/RED wire from the underhood junction block to the fan motor.

3. If the fan does not operate with the relay removed, substitute a new relay and watch for operation. If the fan operates with a new relay, check the DRK GRN/WHT wire for a short to ground and repair. If a short does not exist, yet the fan operates, the PCM is likely to be at fault.

REMOVAL AND INSTALLATION

1. Disconnect the negative battery cable.

2. If equipped with the DOHC engine, remove the air intake ducts and unplug the temperature sensor connector.

3. Disengage the fan motor electrical connector.

4. Remove the top fan motor assembly bolts.

5. It may be necessary to loosen the top automatic transaxle cooler line, if equipped with air conditioning, and position it aside.

6. Lift the fan assembly off the lower mounting brackets. Move the assembly to the left and rotate counterclockwise (as pictured standing in front of the vehicle) lifting the right side up past the radiator hose, then remove the assembly from the vehicle.

7. If necessary, remove the retaining nut (while holding the fan), then remove the fan blade from the shaft and remove the motor from the housing.

To install:

8. If removed, install the motor and fan blade. Torque the fan nut to 27–44 inch lbs. (3–5 Nm).

9. Install the assembly with the lower left corner 1st. Rotate the assembly clockwise to place the lower left mount under the radiator hose and position the assembly onto the mounting brackets.

10. Install the upper retaining bolts.

11. If disconnected, install and tighten the transaxle oil cooler line. Position the transaxle cooler line 35 degrees inward from vertical and hold while tightening.

12. Engage the fan motor electrical connector.

13. If removed, install the intake air ducts and the temperature sensor connector.

14. Connect the negative battery cable.

Heater Core

REMOVAL AND INSTALLATION

1. Disconnect the negative battery cable and drain the engine coolant.

2. Raise and safely support the vehicle safely.

3. Move the heater core clamps up the hoses and off the fittings, then lower the vehicle.

4. For the DOHC engine, remove the air cleaner housing cover and disconnect the air induction hose at the intake manifold. For the SOHC engine, remove the air cleaner housing.

5. Remove the hoses from the heater core.

6. Remove the left and right lower trim panel extensions by disconnecting the velcro and pulling them out of the upper retaining clips.

7. Remove the retaining screws and lower the heater duct straight down. Carefully slide the duct to the side and out.

8. Push down on the cable and lift the plastic tab to release the temperature cable hold-down clip, then disconnect the temperature cable by squeezing the valve pin and pulling the cable straight off.

9. Remove the heater core side cover and retaining screws.

10. Remove the lower heater core cover and screws, then remove the screw and pipe clamp.

11. Remove the core retainer and the heater core.

To install:

12. Install the core being careful not to damage the pipe seal. Use a coating of petroleum jelly to ease installation of the pipes through the cowl.

13. Install the heater core retainer, pipe clamp, lower and side covers.

14. Push the temperature cable over the pin and snap the cable hold-down clip over the cable holder.

15. Slide the heater duct in sideways and raise into position being careful not to damage the rear floor heater seal.

16. Install the left and right trim panel extensions.

17. Raise and support the vehicle safely.

18. Install the heater hoses and position the tangs on the clamps away from the opposite hose.

19. Close the radiator drain plug and install the cylinder block drain plug. Tighten the block plug to 26 ft. lbs. (35 Nm).

20. Lower the vehicle and replace the air cleaner housing components, as applicable.

21. Connect the negative battery cable and properly fill the engine cooling system.

Water Pump

REMOVAL AND INSTALLATION

1. Disconnect the negative battery cable and drain the engine coolant.

2. Remove the serpentine drive belt.

3. If pump access is desired from the top, remove the air conditioning compressor bolts and position the compressor aside with the refrigerant lines intact. Be careful not to kink or damage the lines.

4. Raise the vehicle and support safely. Remove the right front tire and inner wheelwell splash shield.

5. Spray the water pump hub with a penetrating oil to loosen corrosion on the pulley and prevent damage during pump removal.

6. A 1 inch (25.4mm) block of wood may be wedged between the pump pulley and crankshaft to hold the pul-

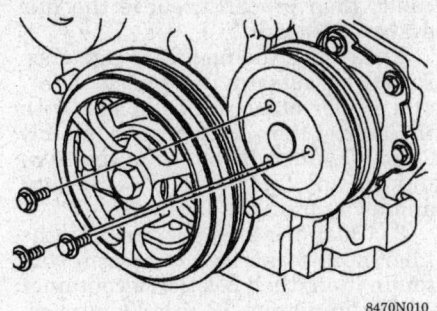

8470N010

Water pump pulley removal

ley while loosening the retaining bolts. Remove the water pump pulley bolts and allow the pulley to hang freely on the hub.

7. Move the pulley outward or remove, as necessary, for access to the flange bolts.

8. Remove the 6 water pump flange bolts, then carefully pull the pump and pulley assembly away from the engine and remove the assembly from the vehicle. If necessary, a gasket scrapper may be inserted under the flange to help loosen the seal, but be careful not to damage the aluminum block sealing surface.

To install:

9. Thoroughly clean the gasket mating surface of all old gasket material. Apply a small amount of sealant at the outer edges of the bolt holes to hold that gasket in place, then position the gasket onto the water pump assembly.

10. If removed, position the pulley onto the pump hub.

11. Install the pump assembly with the small bump located next to 1 of the attaching bolts in the 11 o'clock position. Install the bolts and tighten the bolts in a criss-cross sequence (beginning with the upper left bolt) to 22 ft. lbs. (30 Nm).

12. If the pump hub exposed through the pulley is rusty, clean it with a wire brush and apply a thin coat of primer to prevent the pulley from rusting onto the hub. Install the bolts retaining the pulley to the pump hub and tighten to 19 ft. lbs. (25 Nm).

13. Install the serpentine drive belt, splash shield and tire.

14. If raised, lower the vehicle.

15. If repositioned, install the air conditioning compressor.

16. Close the radiator drain plug and install the cylinder block drain plug. Tighten the block plug to 26 ft. lbs. (35 Nm).

17. Connect the negative battery cable and properly fill the engine cooling system.

Thermostat

REMOVAL AND INSTALLATION

1. Drain the engine cooling system.

2. Disconnect the lower radiator hose at the thermostat housing.

3. Remove the 2 bolts at the water inlet housing, then remove the housing, thermostat and O-ring assembly.

4. Remove the thermostat from the housing using the tool provided with the replacement thermostat element.

To install:

NOTE: The thermostat will not function correctly if it has been contacted by oil. If oil is found in the cooling system, the thermostat cartridge must be replaced and the cooling system must be flushed.

5. Install the replacement thermostat using the tool provided. Make sure the element's retaining tangs are properly seated in the 2 legs and the element piston is correctly positioned in the inlet housing.

6. Install a new O-ring and position the housing assembly to the engine. Tighten the retaining bolts to 22 ft. lbs. (30 Nm).

7. Close the radiator drain plug and install the cylinder block drain plug. Tighten the block plug to 26 ft. lbs. (35 Nm).

8. Install the hose to the inlet housing.

9. Connect the negative battery cable and properly fill the engine cooling system.

Cooling System Bleeding

The Saturn cooling system uses a pressure coolant surge tank and an inlet side thermostat. Coolant is added through the pressure cap in the surge tank and fills the engine cylinder block, cylinder head, heater core and hoses and the radiator. The system therefore, does not require any bleeding.

DRAINING ENGINE COOLING SYSTEM

1. With the engine cool and the vehicle parked on a level surface, re-move the surge tank pressure cap and position a drain pan with a minimum 2 gallon capacity below the engine and radiator.

2. Unscrew the drain plug on the radiator and carefully pry the plug out of the housing. If necessary for replacement, pinch the housing tabs closed and remove the housing from the radiator by pulling straight out.

3. Remove the cylinder block drain plug located at the right front of the engine below the thermostat housing and allow the coolant to drain from the openings.

REFILLING ENGINE COOLING SYSTEM

1. If removed, install the drain plug housing into the radiator by pinching the tabs and inserting into the hole. Once the housing is in the hole, release the tabs and push the housing until it snaps into place. Be careful not to push the housing through the hole into the radiator.

2. Install the radiator drain plug into the housing and tighten.

3. Install the engine drain plug and tighten to 26 ft. lbs. (35 Nm).

4. Fill the system through the surge tank with a non-phosphate low silicate base ethylene glycol-based coolant mixed to the manufacturer's instructions. The coolant should be recommended for use in aluminum engines.

5. Start the engine and check for leaks.

6. Fill the surge tank to the cold line after the engine has run for 2–3 minutes and install the pressure cap.

FUEL SYSTEM

Fuel System Service Precaution

Safety is the most important factor when performing not only fuel system maintenance, but any type of service. Failure to conduct maintenance and repairs in a safe manner may result in serious personal injury or death. Maintenance and testing of the vehicle's fuel system components can be accomplished safely and effectively by adhering to the following rules and guidelines.

• To avoid the possibility of fire and personal injury, always disconnect the negative battery cable before opening the fuel system fittings, unless the repair or test procedure requires that battery voltage be applied. This will prevent excessive fuel spillage if the ignition switch is accidentally turned **ON** while fuel fittings are still disconnected.

• Always relieve the fuel system pressure prior to disconnecting any fuel system fitting or connection.

• Exercise extreme caution whenever relieving fuel system pressure to avoid exposing skin, face and eyes to fuel spray. Under pressure, fuel may penetrate the skin or any part of the body that it contacts.

• Always place a shop towel around a fitting or connection prior to loosening in order to absorb any fuel spillage. Ensure that all spilled fuel is quickly removed from engine surfaces. Ensure that all fuel soaked rags are deposited into a suitable waste container.

• Always keep a dry chemical (Class B) fire extinguisher near the work area.

• Ventilate the work area properly and pay attention to where the fumes go. Do not allow fuel vapors to come into contact with a source of ignition.

• Always use a backup wrench when loosening and tightening fuel line connection fittings. This will prevent unnecessary stress to fuel line piping. Always follow the proper torque specifications.

• Always replace worn fuel fitting O-rings. Do not substitute fuel hose where metal fuel pipe is normally installed.

RELIEVING FUEL SYSTEM PRESSURE

1. Unless battery voltage is needed for testing, disconnect the negative battery cable.
2. Remove the air cleaner or air intake duct, as applicable.
3. Wrap a shop rag around the fuel test port fitting at the rear of the engine, remove the cap and connect pressure gauge tool SA9127E or equivalent.
4. Install the bleed hose into an approved container and open the valve to bleed the system pressure.
5. After the system pressure is bled, remove the gauge from the pressure test port and recap it.

Relieving fuel system pressure — DOHC engine shown, SOHC engine similar

6. Install the air cleaner or intake duct, unless the procedure requires its removal.

7. After repairs are completed, connect the negative battery cable and prime the fuel system as follows:

a. Turn the ignition **ON** for 5 seconds and then **OFF** for 10 seconds.

b. Repeat the ON/OFF cycle 2 more times.

c. Crank the engine until it starts.

d. If it does not start, repeat Steps a–d

e. Run the engine and check for leaks.

Fuel Tank

REMOVAL AND INSTALLATION

To prevent excessive fuel spillage, whenever the tank is removed from the vehicle it should be no more than ³⁄₄ full. Removal of the fuel pump module assembly requires the removal of the fuel tank. Most vehicles will be equipped with a fuel tank inlet check ball, if equipped, the ball must be knocked into the tank in order to allow fuel tank draining. If the ball is knocked into the tank, the fuel pump module must be removed so the ball may be reinserted into the inlet, from inside the tank.

If the fuel tank is to be replaced , a new filler neck should be installed which contains a check ball. The inlet check ball should then be removed and discarded.

─────── **CAUTION** ───────
The following procedure will produce a small fuel spill and fumes. Make sure there is proper ventilation and be sure to take the appropriate fire safety precautions.

1. Disconnect the negative battery cable, then properly relieve the fuel system pressure.

2. Remove the fuel filler cap, then raise and support the vehicle safely at a comfortable working height, with the rear of the vehicle approximately 28 in. (711mm) higher than the front to keep any fuel in the tank forward and away from the fill hose.

3. Clean the area surrounding the filler neck to avoid fuel system contamination, then position a container with a minimum 12 in. (300mm) diameter opening under the filler neck to catch any escaping fuel. Loosen the filler neck clamp at the rear of the fuel tank, wrap a shop rag around the neck tube and carefully remove the tube from the tank.

4. If equipped with a tank inlet check ball and the fuel tank must be drained, the check ball must be dislodged. Use the large round end of a ¹⁄₂ in. drive ratchet extension (which is at least 18 in. long) to push the check ball into the fuel tank.

NOTE: Once the check ball has been knocked into the fuel tank, the tank must be removed from the vehicle and the pump module must be removed from the tank in order to reinstall the check ball.

5. If necessary, use a pump or siphon and a length of clean hose to drain the fuel tank into an approved container.

6. Remove the filler neck bracket fastener at the left side of the rear frame rail, then loosen the fuel vent hose retaining clamp at the tank.

NOTE: It is easier to remove hoses from the tank than to pull them from the steel vent and fill tubes.

7. Disengage the fuel pressure and return line quick-connects by pinching the 2 plastic tangs together, then grasp both ends of 1 fuel line connection and twist ¹⁄₄ turn in each direction while pulling them apart. Disconnect the fuel vent hose by holding the line and by pushing on the rubber connector with a small open end wrench.

NOTE: Do not allow the fuel tank retaining straps to become bent during tank removal or strap damage may occur. Always use an assistant when removing the fuel tank to prevent damage.

8. With the aid of an assistant, remove the 2 support strap fasteners at the rear of the tank, then lower the tank and support panel approxi-

mately 8 in. (203mm). Reach upward and unplug the electrical connector from the top of the tank, then remove the tank from the vehicle.

9. If the check ball was removed or fuel pump module replacement/service is necessary, remove the fuel pump module from the tank.

To install:

10. If removed, install the tank inlet check ball and/or install the fuel pump assembly.

11. With the aid of an assistant, position the tank so the wires can be connected to the module, install the module electrical connector, then secure the tank in place using the retaining straps. Tighten the strap bolts to 35 ft. lbs. (47 Nm).

12. Loosely install the filler tube, vent lines and clamps. Align the fill neck and tank so the fender will not be deflected or pushed outward by the hose. When everything is properly positioned, install the fill neck tube and bracket fastener. Vent lines should be installed into the rubber boot until the tube white marks align with the side of the boot.

13. Tighten the clamps to 18 inch lbs. (2 Nm) and tighten the fill neck bracket fastener to 53 inch lbs. (6 Nm). If the clamps must be replaced, original equipment or equivalent parts must be used, because the original parts are designed to prevent hose damage.

14. Lubricate the male ends of the fuel supply and return quick-connect fittings with a few drops of clean engine oil. Push the connectors together until the retaining tabs snap into place, then pull on opposite ends of each connection to verify the connection is secure.

15. Carefully lower the vehicle, then install the fuel filler cap and connect the negative battery cable.

16. Prime the fuel system and check for leaks:

   a. Turn the ignition for 5 seconds, then OFF for 10 seconds.

   b. Repeat the ON/OFF cycle 2 more times.

   c. Crank the engine until it starts.

   d. If the engine does not readily start, repeat Steps a–d.

   e. Run the engine and check for leaks.

Fuel Filter

REMOVAL AND INSTALLATION

1. Disconnect the negative battery cable.

2. Remove the air intake duct, and for the DOHC engine, disconnect the fresh air inlet hose from the camshaft cover.

3. Properly relieve the fuel system pressure.

4. Disconnect the large underhood fuel line connection located near the intake manifold support brace on the left side of the vehicle using the tool supplied with the replacement filter, SA9157E or equivalent. It may be necessary to clean the female end of the quick-connect fittings by spraying them with penetrating oil prior to disconnection.

5. Raise and support the vehicle safely.

6. Disengage the quick-connect at the fuel filter inlet by pinching the 2 plastic tangs together and pulling on the supply line.

7. Loosen the fuel filter band clamp nut, but do not completely remove.

8. Carefully push or pull the filter out of the assembly and discard the filter in an appropriate container.

To install:

9. If the band clamp was removed, clip the fuel return and vapor lines in place and install 2 new band clamp nuts. Make sure all lines are in place and will not interfere with or be damaged by filter installation and tighten the bracket nuts to 27 inch lbs. (3 Nm).

10. Clean the female end of the filter inlet quick-connect fitting by holding the line facing downward while spraying penetrating oil up into the fitting. Be careful not to bend of kink the line.

11. If not already installed, insert a new snap lock retainer into the female end of the filter inlet quick-connect fitting.

12. Route the filter's nylon outlet line through the band clamp under the A/C suction hose and engine wiring. Insert the filter far enough into the band clamp to connect the outlet line to the engine fuel line attachment. Lubricate the male end of the connector with clean engine oil, snap the connector together and pull on the line to verify proper fitting.

13. Make sure the fuel lines are properly routed and are not contacting other lines, hoses or wiring. Position the filter in the band clamp assembly with the filter's upper edge located ¼ inch (6.35mm) from the top of the band clamp.

14. Lubricate the male end of the fuel supply line with clean engine oil. Snap the line to the fuel filter and pull back to verify the fitting is se-

cure. Tighten the band clamp nut to 89 inch lbs. (10 Nm).

15. Lower the vehicle and install the air inlet tube and/or intake duct, as applicable.

16. Connect the negative battery cable and prime the fuel system.

17. Run the engine and check for leaks.

Electric Fuel Pump

NOTE: In order to assure proper test readings, the vehicle battery must always be charged to a minimum of 12 volts during testing.

PRESSURE TESTING

Pump Pressure Test

A trouble Code 44 or 45 could indicate pressure regulator or system pressure problems. The pump pressure test may be used to determine if the fuel pump is delivering fuel at the proper pressure or if the pump must be replaced.

—————— **CAUTION** ——————
The following procedure will produce a small fuel spill and fumes. Make sure there is proper ventilation and be sure to take the appropriate fire safety precautions.
————————————————

1. Remove the air intake duct for access.

2. Locate the pressure test port on the fuel supply line, below and behind the EGR valve. Properly relieve any residual system pressure using a gauge attached to the pressure test port, then remove the fuel gauge from the test port and install the port cap.

3. Disconnect the fuel supply hose from the metal line, then connect the fuel gauge to the supply hose using a suitable adapter. Make sure the gauge is capable of reading 0–100 psi (0–690 kPa).

4. Verify that the fuel gauge shutoff valve is closed, then turn the ignition switch **ON** without starting the engine to run the fuel pump and build pressure in the system. The pump will only run for about 2 seconds without the engine running. Bleed the air out of the gauge line and cycle the fuel pump again as required to fully bleed the gauge and establish an accurate pressure reading.

5. Once maximum pressure has been achieved, allow the reading to stabilize for 30 seconds. Normal pump pressure is 58–94 psi (400–650 kPa). Allow the gauge to sit undis-

turbed for 5 minutes after the pump stops running, pressure should leak down no more than 6–8 psi (41–55 kPa) from the maximum stabilized reading. This is a fuel pump delivery pressure test only (non-regulated pressure) and the results will differ from the system pressure test.

6. Bleed off the fuel system pressure and repeat the test a minimum of 2 additional times to be certain of accurate results.

7. Install the bleed hose into an approved container, then bleed the fuel system pressure and remove the gauge from the line. Lubricate the male end of the fitting with clean engine oil and reconnect the fuel line.

System Pressure Test

CAUTION
The following procedure will produce a small fuel spill and fumes. Make sure there is proper ventilation and be sure to take the appropriate fire safety precautions.

1. Remove the air cleaner or air intake tube assembly for access, then connect fuel pressure gauge SA9127E or an equivalent gauge capable of 0–100 psi (0–690 kPa) to the fuel system test port.

2. Close the fuel gauge shut-off valve. Turn the ignition switch **ON** to run the fuel pump and build pressure in the system, then turn the ignition **OFF** again. The pump will only run for about 2 seconds without the engine running. Bleed the air out of the gauge line and cycle the fuel pump again as required to fully bleed the gauge.

3. Start and run the engine, then check for the proper fuel pressure. The fuel pressure should read as follows:

a. SOHC at idle and 3000 rpm — 26–31 psi.

b. DOHC at idle — 31–36 psi.

c. DOHC at idle with the vacuum line disconnected from the pressure regulator — pressure should drop 6–10 psi.

d. DOHC key ON engine OFF — 38–44 psi.

4. Replace the pressure regulator if the pressure reading does not change when the vacuum line is disconnected.

5. Shut the ignition **OFF** and allow the system to leak down. After

about 5 minutes with the pump not running, pressure should leak down no more than 6–8 psi (41–55 kPa).

6. If pressure readings are low check the following:

a. Check for bent or pinched lines.

b. Check for proper fuel pump pressure.

c. Check the fuel pump for flow.

d. Replace the fuel filter with a known clean component.

e. Substitute a known good fuel pressure regulator.

7. If pressure readings are high check the following:

a. Inspect for a restricted fuel return lines.

b. Substitute a known good fuel pressure regulator.

REMOVAL AND INSTALLATION

The fuel pump module is located in the fuel tank. The tank must be removed to access the module pump/sender assembly.

1. Disconnect the negative battery cable and properly relieve fuel system pressure.

2. Drain the fuel from the tank into a suitable container and remove the tank from the vehicle.

3. Clean the area surrounding the fuel pump module and spray the cam lockring tangs with a suitable penetrating oil to loosen the fitting.

4. Using SA9156E, or an equivalent fuel module lockring removal tool, and a ½ inch breaker bar of approximately 18 in. (457mm) in length, remove the pump unit locking ring from the tank. Attempting to use a 12 in. or shorter breaker bar may cause lockring damage.

5. Lift and tilt the unit out at a 45 degree angle, being careful not to bend the sending unit filter and float arm. Remove and discard the unit-to-tank O-ring.

6. The sending unit is the only portion of the module that may be serviced. The filter may be cleaned with mineral spirits, but must be replaced as an assembly with the module if damaged. If necessary, remove the sending unit from the module as follows:

a. Unplug the 2 electrical connections using needle-nose pliers or by pressing down the locking tab and pulling the connectors from the terminal.

b. Using a small suitable tool, push in on the sender assembly attaching tang, then lift upward and remove the sender.

c. Late 1992 and all 1993–95 vehicles use a brass float instead of plastic. Some floats may be serviced, check with a parts supplier for availability to determine if the vehicle's float may be replaced. If serviceable, use a ¼ in. flat-tipped prytool to carefully pry the float from the wire loop. Do not bend the float arm or deform the wire loop.

To install:

7. If removed, pinch a new float onto the float arm wire loop and/or install the sending unit to the pump module by positioning the tang in the locator slot and snapping the unit into place. Connect the 2 sending unit electrical connectors to their terminals.

8. If applicable, carefully install the fuel tank inlet check ball from inside the fuel tank by reaching through the tank module mount opening and gently pushing the ball into position.

9. Clean any debris from the O-ring mating surface and position a new O-ring onto the tank.

10. Carefully insert the pump module into the tank at a 45 degree angle to prevent sending unit and float damage. The filter and flow arm must be directed toward the front of the tank.

11. Align the pump locator tabs with the fuel tank slots, then install the cam lockring using the ring service tool.

12. Install the fuel tank assembly.

13. Lower the vehicle, connect the negative battery cable and fill the fuel tank.

14. Prime the fuel system, start the engine and check for leaks.

Fuel Injection

IDLE SPEED ADJUSTMENT

The Saturn Powertrain Control Module (PCM) directly controls idle speed using the Idle Air Control (IAC) valve. Under normal circumstances and routine maintenance, tampering with the idle stop screw should NEVER occur. The screw is not used to set a engine idle speed per se, instead it is used to set the minimum position from which the PCM can use the IAC valve to control idle speed.

NOTE: The minimum idle speed adjustment is preset at the factory and requires no periodic adjustments. Adjustments should be performed ONLY when the throttle body has been replaced and/or proper idle speed cannot be obtained. The engine should be at normal operating temperature, the A/C and cooling fans should be OFF when making adjustments.

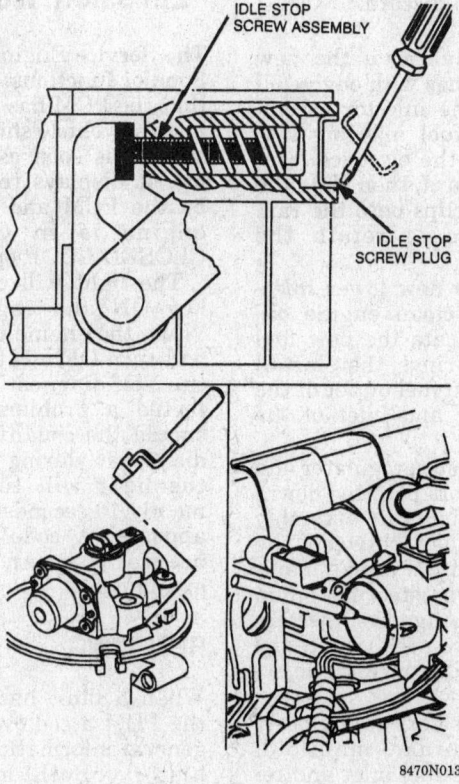

Installing the IAC connector to the valve terminals at the throttle body

Connecting the Saturn diagnostic tool to the ALDL

1. Before making any adjustments, clean the throttle body bore with a shop towel and carburetor cleaner that does not contain methyl ethyl keytone. Then check the idle speed to be sure adjustment is necessary. Proper idle speeds are as follows:
   SOHC with manual or automatic transaxle in N — 700–800 rpm
   SOHC with automatic transaxle in D — 600–700 rpm
   SOHC with automatic transaxle in D and A/C ON — 725–825 rpm
   DOHC with manual transaxle in N — 800–900 rpm

IDLE STOP SCREW ASSEMBLY

IDLE STOP SCREW PLUG

Removing the idle screw plug and installing the IAC air plug

DOHC with automatic transaxle in D — 700–800 rpm
DOHC with automatic transaxle in D and A/C ON — 725–825 rpm

2. If adjustment is necessary, block the wheels and apply the parking brake.

3. The IAC pintle must be properly seated in the throttle body. Connect the IAC tester SA9195E or equivalent, to the IAC valve at the throttle body. The Saturn PDT or an equivalent scan tool may attached to the ALDL and used instead of the IAC tester.

4. Remove the idle stop screw plug by piercing it with an awl and applying leverage for SOHC engines. On DOHC engines, remove the idle stop screw cover.

5. Insert the IAC air plug in the throttle body; use SA9196E for TBI or SA9106E for MFI or equivalent.

6. Connect the Saturn Portable Diagnostic Tool (PDT) or equivalent to the Assembly Line Diagnostic Link (ALDL), start the engine and check the minimum idle speed for proper setting. The minimum idle speed should be 450–650 rpm for all engines.

7. If not within specification adjust the idle screw to obtain an minimum idle speed of 500–600 rpm.

8. Turn the ignition **OFF**, then reinstall the IAC electrical connector.

9. Using the Saturn PDT or equivalent scan tool, check the TP sensor voltage. Do not replace the TP sensor unless setting is not between 0.35–0.70 volts.

10. Remove the IAC air plug and install the idle stop plug or cover.

11. Start the engine and check for proper idle operation.

12. Shut the engine **OFF** and remove the PDT or scan tool.

IDLE MIXTURE ADJUSTMENT

The idle mixture is controlled by the Powertrain Control Module (PCM) and is not adjustable.

Fuel Injector

REMOVAL AND INSTALLATION

Throttle Body Injection (TBI)

1. Disconnect the negative battery cable.
2. Remove the air cleaner assembly.
3. Properly relieve fuel system pressure.

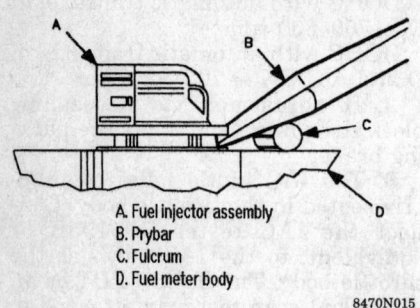

A. Fuel injector assembly
B. Prybar
C. Fulcrum
D. Fuel meter body

8470N015

Removing the fuel injector — TBI engine

4. Remove the electrical connector from the injector terminal.

5. Remove the injector retaining screw and bracket.

6. Using a smooth, round fulcrum and prybar, carefully pry the injector out of the throttle body. Make sure the electrical connector and injector nozzle are protected from damage.

To install:

7. Remove the upper and lower O-rings and inspect the injector for dirt or contamination. The injector may be cleaned using safety glasses and compressed air, but the screen may not be removed from the injector. If injector replacement is necessary, be sure to use an identical part.

8. Install new O-rings and lubricate with clean engine oil. Be sure the upper O-ring is in the groove on the injector and the lower ring is properly installed in the fuel meter body cavity.

9. Install the injector, pushing it straight into the injector cavity with the electrical connector facing toward the fuel pressure regulator.

10. Install the retaining bracket. Coat the screw with Loctite® 242 or equivalent, then install and tighten the screw to 35 inch lbs. (3 Nm).

11. Engage the wiring harness to the injector connector, then connect the negative battery cable.

12. Prime the fuel system, start the engine and check for leaks.

13. Shut the engine **OFF** and install the air cleaner assembly.

Multi-Port Fuel Injection (MFI)

1. Disconnect the negative battery cable.

2. Remove the air intake tube with resonator and fresh air tube.

3. Properly relieve fuel system pressure.

4. Remove the fuel line bracket bolt, then disconnect the fuel pressure and return lines. Be sure to use a $^{15}\!/_{16}$ in. (24mm) backup wrench to prevent inlet port or bracket damage. If necessary, remove the fuel line bolts and rotate the rail slightly for wrench access. Remove the old O-rings from the lines with a suitable tool and discard.

5. Disconnect the pressure regulator vacuum hose.

6. Remove the throttle cable bracket bolts, then disconnect the cable from the throttle lever. Lay the cable over the intake manifold.

7. Remove the wiring harness connectors from the fuel injector terminals and remove the fuel rail retaining bolts.

8. Remove the fuel rail assembly by carefully pulling the rail back and upward to pull the injectors from the manifold ports. Be careful not to damage the injector spray tips and electrical connectors. Rotate the rail so the injectors point downward, then lift the rail end opposite of the fuel connections to remove the rail from between the camshaft cover and intake manifold.

9. Make sure the rails and injectors are clean and free of dirt. If injector removal is required, slide the injector retaining clip off the injector and pull the injector from the fuel rail. Remove the old injector O-rings with a suitable seal removal tool or brass seal pick and discard.

To install:

10. If removed, lubricate the new upper injector O-rings with engine oil and install onto the injector assemblies. Install the fuel injectors into the fuel rail, with the electrical connectors facing upward, then slide the injector retaining clips onto the rail. Engage the clips to retain the injectors.

11. Lubricate the new lower injector O-rings with clean engine oil, then install. Lubricate the new fuel inlet and return O-rings, then install the O-rings into the fuel outlet of the pressure regulator and inlet of the fuel rail.

12. With the pressure regulator end first and the injectors pointing downward, guide the fuel rail assembly through the passage between the camshaft cover and the intake manifold from the power steering pump side of the engine. Align the injectors with their respective ports, rotate the fuel rail and carefully push the injectors into the port.

13. Verify the injectors are properly seated in the intake manifold. Loosely connect the fuel inlet and return lines to the rail assembly, then install the fuel rail retaining bolts and tighten to 22 ft. lbs. (30 Nm).

14. Engage the wiring harness connectors to the fuel injector terminals.

15. Connect the PCV valve hose to the camshaft cover, and the vacuum line to the pressure regulator, making sure they are properly seated.

16. Install the throttle cable bracket bolts and tighten to 19 ft. lbs. (25 Nm), then connect the throttle cable.

17. Using a backup wrench, tighten the fuel inlet and return line fittings to 133 inch lbs. (15 Nm).

18. Install the fuel line bracket bolt and tighten to 106 inch lbs. (12 Nm).

19. Connect the negative battery cable, then prime the fuel system by cycling the ignition key **ON** and **OFF**.

20. Start the engine and check for leaks.

21. Shut the engine **OFF**, then install the air intake tube and resonator assembly.

EMISSION CONTROLS

Emission Warning Lamps

The Service Engine Soon light serves 3 major functions. It informs a driver that the PCM has detected a problem and the vehicle should be taken in for service as soon as reasonably possible. It displays trouble codes stored by the PCM and it indicates if the engine is in OPEN LOOP or CLOSED LOOP operation.

The light will come ON with the key ON and engine not running. When the engine is started, the light will turn OFF. If the light stays ON, the self-diagnostic system has detected a problem. In most cases, should the condition causing a fault disappear during vehicle operation, the light will turn OFF approximately 10 seconds after the fault disappears. A code will be stored in memory even if the light extinguishes.

RESETTING

When a fault has been detected by the PCM a code will set in 2 places, general information and malfunction history. Both memories can be cleared with the use of the Saturn PDT or an equivalent scan tool. If no scan tool is available, general information can be cleared if the A and B terminals are of the ALDL are grounded 3 times in 5 seconds with the ignition **ON**. General information will also clear if the problem is absent for 50 ignition ON/OFF cycles or if the battery supply to the PCM is interrupted. Malfunction history can only be cleared with aid of a scan tool.

ECM LEARNING ABILITY

The PCM has a "learning" ability which allows it to make corrections for minor variations in the fuel system, in order to improve driveability. If the battery is disconnected to clear diagnostic codes or for safety during repairs, the "learning" process will reset and must begin again. A change may be noted in the vehicle's performance while the learning process begins. The following steps must be performed in order to assure the PCM will properly relearn smooth engine operation:

1. Start and warm the engine until it is at normal operating temperature.
2. Drive the vehicle at part throttle, with moderate acceleration and idle conditions, until normal performance returns.
3. Park the vehicle and engage the parking brake, but leave the engine running.
4. Place the transaxle in **D** if equipped with an automatic transaxle or **N** if the vehicle is equipped with a manual transaxle.
5. Allow the engine to continue idling for about 2 minutes, until the idle stabilizes. The engine must still be at normal operating temperature.

ENGINE MECHANICAL

NOTE: Disconnecting the negative battery cable on some vehicles may interfere with the functions of the on-board computer systems and may require the computer to undergo a relearning process, once the negative battery cable is reconnected.

Engine Assembly

REMOVAL AND INSTALLATION

NOTE: The manufacturer recommends that the engine and transaxle be removed as a complete unit. Instead of lifting the assembly from the vehicle, the engine cradle should be disconnected from the spaceframe and the powertrain should be lowered from the vehicle.

1. Properly disable the SIR system, if equipped.
2. Disconnect the negative and then the positive battery cable.
3. Drain the engine cooling system from the engine block and radiator drain plugs.
4. Properly relieve the fuel system pressure.
5. Unplug and label the following electrical connectors and vacuum lines:
   a. The 2 coolant temperature sensors.
   b. Oxygen sensor and clip at the transaxle front mount bracket.
   c. Idle Air Control (IAC) valve.
   d. The 2 ignition coil module connectors.
   e. Throttle Position Sensor (TPS).
   f. Manifold Absolute Pressure (MAP) sensor.
   g. Exhaust Gas Recirculation (EGR) solenoid.
   h. Brake booster vacuum hose from the booster or intake manifold.
   i. Disengage the 2 ground connectors from the transaxle attachment studs at the rear side of the cylinder block.
   j. Fuel injector electrical connector(s).
6. Disconnect the following automatic or manual transaxle electrical connectors. If access to any of the wires is difficult, wait until the vehicle is safely raised and supported, then unplug the connections from underneath the vehicle:
   a. The 3 neutral safety switch connectors.
   b. Valve body actuator connection.
   c. Turbine speed sensor.
   d. Temperature sensor.
   e. For manual transaxles only, the reverse light switch.
   f. The 2 gear shift (PRNDL switch) connectors.
7. Disconnect the accelerator cable assembly.
8. Using service tool SA9157E or equivalent, disconnect the fuel sup-

ply and return lines at the connectors. Plug the lines to prevent fuel contamination or loss. The lines may be tied to the master cylinder lines to help prevent fuel spillage and to keep them out of the way.

9. Disconnect the upper radiator hose and the cylinder head outlet and the de-aeration hose at the engine.
10. If equipped with A/C, remove serpentine drive belt, then remove the air conditioning compressor from its brackets with the hoses attached. Support the compressor from the front crossbar.

NOTE: It is not necessary to discharge the A/C compressor during engine removal, but be careful not to kink, damage or rupture the refrigerant lines.

11. If equipped, disconnect the automatic transaxle cooler lines at the transaxle by pinching the plastic connector tabs and carefully pulling back on the lines. Plug the openings to prevent fluid loss or contamination.
12. Disconnect the automatic transaxle shifter cable or the manual shifter cables from the transaxle.

NOTE: On manual transaxle vehicles, position a block of wood under the clutch pedal to prevent accidental actuation of the slave cylinder while it is removed from the transaxle.

13. If equipped with manual transaxles, remove the 2 hydraulic slave cylinder retaining nuts from the clutch housing studs, then slide the cylinder and bracket assembly from the studs. Rotate the clutch actuator ¼ turn counterclockwise while pushing toward the housing to disengage the bayonet connector and remove it from the clutch housing. Support the clutch hydraulic system to the battery tray; being sure not to kink or pinch the hydraulic lines.
14. Using a length of an appropriate wire, tie the radiator, condenser and fan to the front crossbar. Route the wire around the 2 fan shroud supports and the crossbar.
15. Raise and support the front end of the vehicle safely.
16. Remove the front wheels and remove the fasteners connecting the side and front fender shields to the cradle.
17. Remove the brake caliper bracket attaching bolts (2 on each side) and hang the caliper assemblies from the shock tower springs using wire. Do not hang the assembly by the brake hose or damage to the brake hydraulic system may occur. The spring and shock assemblies will

remain with the body when the powertrain is lowered.

18. Disconnect the struts from the knuckles on each side of the vehicle (2 bolts per side). This will allow the knuckle and hub assembly to remain with the powertrain cradle when lowered. The stabilizer bar will remain attached to the cradle and the lower control arms.

19. Disconnect the lower radiator and heater return hoses from the engine. Disconnect the heater inlet hose at the front of the dash or the engine.

20. Disengage the steering shaft and pressure switch connectors at the gear, as applicable.

21. Disconnect the front exhaust pipe at the manifold, catalytic converter and powertrain stiffening bracket.

22. If equipped with an automatic transaxle, remove the flywheel cover, then remove the torque converter bolts.

23. Remove the alternator and starter shields.

24. Label and unplug the remaining electrical and vacuum connectors from the following components:

a. Remove the wires from the starter solenoid and the battery feed.

b. The alternator field and battery feed connectors.

c. Oil pressure sensor.

d. Knock sensor.

e. Crankshaft position sensor.

f. If equipped, the EVO solenoid.

g. Vehicle speed sensor.

h. Canister purge solenoid.

i. Powertrain Control Module (PCM) and Oxygen sensor.

j. If equipped, the ABS wheel sensor connector grounds.

25. Unclip the brake lines from the rear side of the cradle.

26. Carefully remove the electrical harness from the engine and transaxle, then lay the electrical harness on top of the underhood junction block and battery cover.

27. With a torque axis mount system, place a 1 inch x 1 inch x 2 inch long block of wood between the torque strut and cradle to ease removal and installation of the torque engine mount. Remove the 3 right side upper engine torque axis-to-front cover nuts and the 2 mount-to-midrail bracket nuts, allowing the powertrain to rest on the block of wood.

NOTE: Placing a block of wood under the torque axis mount prior to removing the upper mount will allow the engine to rest on the wood, thus preventing the engine from shifting. If the

engine is not to be removed from the cradle, this will allow you to install the engine and the upper mount without jacking or raising the engine.

28. Place a powertrain support dolly under the cradle. Use two 4 inch x 4 inch x 36 inch pieces of wood to support the cradle on the dolly.

29. Remove the 2 right side front engine mount, torque strut brackets-to-cradle nuts.

30. Remove the 4 cradle attaching bolts and carefully lower the complete powertrain assembly from the vehicle. Verify that all necessary components are disconnected and free before complete removal.

31. Attach the 2 washers located between the cradle and body, to the cradle. They must be repositioned and installed during cradle installation.

32. Tag and disconnect the spark plug wires at the ignition module.

33. If applicable, remove the power steering pump and bracket. Support the assembly, in an upright position, from the cradle or the steering gear.

34. Install a suitable engine lifting device to the service support brackets.

35. Remove the front mount assembly and disconnect the motion restrictor bracket, if applicable.

36. Place a 1/2 inch x 1 inch x 3 inch block of wood under the axle shaft, then remove the starter support bracket bolt, intake manifold support brace (on DOHC engines), and 3 axle shaft bracket support bolts. Allow the bracket to rotate rearward. Lift the engine slightly for clearance, as necessary.

37. Place a 4 inch x 4 inch x 6 inch long block of wood under the transaxle housing for support. Then remove the engine strut bracket and torque strut from the front of the engine as an assembly. Lift the engine slightly as necessary for removal.

38. Remove the 4 transaxle attaching bolts/studs and separate the assembly. Manual transaxles will require the engine to be moved about 4 inches (100mm) forward in the cradle to disengage the input shaft.

39. Carefully lift the engine off the cradle.

To install:

40. If installing a manual transaxle, align the yellow dot on the clutch pressure plate near the mark on the flywheel. Use SA9145T or an equivalent clutch alignment tool to align the disk and input shaft, then tighten the pressure plate bolts to 19 ft. lbs. (25 Nm).

41. If installing an automatic transaxle, the yellow dot on the torque converter must be in the 6 o'clock position when the first flexplate-to-torque converter bolt is tightened.

42. Position the engine on the cradle aligning it with the transaxle using 2 threaded 10mm x 6 in. guide pins in the lower attachment holes. When aligned, remove the pins and install the 4 transaxle attaching bolts along with the stiffening bracket fastener. Tighten the lower bolts to 96 ft. lbs. (130 Nm) and the upper bolts to 66 ft. lbs. (90 Nm) and the stiffening bracket to powertrain fastener to 40 ft. lbs. (54 Nm). If applicable, remove the 4 inch x 4 inch x 6 inch block of wood from under the transaxle housing.

43. Install the front engine mount assembly to the engine and tighten to 41 ft. lbs. (55 Nm).

44. If removed, install the engine mount torque strut-to-cradle bracket and tighten the engine fasteners to 52 ft. lbs. (70 Nm). Hand-tighten the cradle fasteners, but do not torque until the upper midrail mount is installed.

45. Install the 1 inch x 1 inch x 2 inch long block of wood between the torque strut and cradle to ease installation of the torque mount.

46. Attach the axle shaft and starter bracket. Tighten the axle shaft bracket fasteners to 41 ft. lbs. (55 Nm) and the starter bracket to 80 inch lbs. (9 Nm).

47. Position the powertrain and cradle assembly onto the dolly, using the 2 wooden boards to support and protect the cradle assembly.

48. Carefully lift the powertrain and cradle into position. Make sure the radiator grommets are correctly aligned and that the 2 washers are reinstalled between the cradle and body at each rear cradle attachment position. If necessary, use two 9/16 in. x 18 in. long guide pins in the forward cradle holes (located next to the attaching holes) to help align the cradle. Tighten the cradle to body fasteners to 151 ft. lbs. (205 Nm).

49. Attach the brake lines to the cradle and install the steering shaft U-joint. Tighten the U-joint bolt to 35 ft. lbs. (47 Nm).

50. Position the electrical harness around the engine, then install and/or connect the following components or connectors, as applicable:

a. Starter solenoid connector and tighten to 44 inch lbs. (5 Nm).

b. Alternator and starter battery connectors and tighten to 89 inch lbs. (10 Nm).

c. Oil pressure sensor, tighten to 26 ft. lbs. (35 Nm), and connector.

d. Knock sensor and tighten to 133 inch lbs. (15 Nm), and connector.

e. Crankshaft position sensor and tighten to 80 inch lbs. (9 Nm), and connector.

f. Canister purge valve and tighten to 22 ft. lbs. (30 Nm) and connector/hoses.

g. Wiring harness PCM ground and tighten to 89 inch lbs. (10 Nm).

h. Wiring harness to the transaxle case/engine block and tighten to 18 ft. lbs. (25 Nm).

i. If equipped, the EVO solenoid.

j. Vehicle speed sensor.

k. Power steering pressure switch.

l. If equipped, the ABS wheel speed sensors.

51. Install the engine stiffening bracket bolts, as applicable and tighten to 35 ft. lbs. (47 Nm).

52. Install new gaskets and the exhaust front pipe. Tighten the pipe-to-manifold fasteners to 23 ft. lbs. (31 Nm), the pipe-to-stiffener bracket fasteners to 35 ft. lbs. (47 Nm), the pipe-to-support bracket fasteners to 23 ft. lbs. (31 Nm) and the pipe-to-catalytic converter fasteners to 35 ft. lbs. (48 Nm).

53. Connect the heater, lower radiator and coolant fill hoses, then remove the radiator assembly support wires.

54. Install the cylinder block drain plug and tighten to 27 ft. lbs. (36 Nm), then close the radiator drain.

55. Install the knuckle-to-strut attachment bolts, tighten the bolts to 148 ft. lbs. (200 Nm).

56. Install the brake caliper assemblies and tighten the bolts to 81 ft. lbs. (110 Nm).

57. Install the shift cables using new retainers.

58. Remove the supports and carefully lower the vehicle sufficiently to gain underhood access, then reposition the supports under the vehicle.

59. If equipped with a manual transaxle, install the hydraulic clutch slave cylinder, damper and shift cables, then tighten the fasteners to 19 ft. lbs. (25 Nm). Remove the wooden block from underneath the clutch pedal.

60. If equipped, install the automatic transaxle cooler lines and/or the air conditioning compressor assembly. Tighten the compressor to front bracket bolts to 35 ft. lbs. (47 Nm) and the compressor to rear bracket bolts to 22 ft. lbs. (30 Nm).

61. If removed, install the serpentine drive belt, making sure the belt is properly aligned in the grooves.

62. If equipped with a torque axis mount system, install the 2 engine mount-to-midrail bracket nuts and tighten to 52 ft. lbs. (70 Nm). Next install the 3 mount-to-front cover nuts, tighten them uniformly to 52 ft. lbs. (70 Nm) in order to prevent front cover damage. Finally, remove the block of wood from under the torque strut.

63. For 1992–93 vehicles, tighten the strut bracket-to-cradle nuts to 52 ft. lbs. (70 Nm).

64. If equipped with an automatic transaxle, install the torque converter-to-flexplate bolts and tighten the bolts to 52 ft. lbs. (70 Nm). Install the dust cover and tighten to 89 inch lbs. (10 Nm).

65. Install the tires and splash shields, tightening the lug nuts to 103 ft. lbs. (140 Nm). Remove the supports and carefully lower the vehicle to the ground.

66. Attach the following electrical and vacuum connections:

a. Coolant temperature sensors.

b. Oxygen sensor.

c. IAC valve.

d. Fuel injector connector(s).

e. The 2 ignition coil module connectors.

f. TPS connector.

g. MAP sensor.

h. EGR solenoid.

i. If equipped, the A/C compressor.

j. The brake booster hose to the intake manifold or booster.

k. The ground connectors to the transaxle attachment studs located at the rear side of the block, above the starter.

67. Attach the following transaxle connectors, as applicable:

a. The 3 neutral safety switch connectors.

b. Valve body actuator connector.

c. Turbine speed sensor.

d. On manual transaxles, the reverse light switch.

e. The temperature sensor.

f. The 2 gear shift (PRNDL switch) connectors.

68. Install the accelerator cable, then apply a drop of clean engine oil to the male ends of the fuel line connectors and attach the line quick-connect fittings. Make sure the lines are not kinked or damaged.

69. Install the upper radiator and de-aeration hoses, verify proper alignment of the radiator L-bracket fasteners.

NOTE: Check the upper cooling module grommets for binding or misalignment. The module retaining pins must be centered in the grommets supported by the brackets. If the grommets are pinched, loosen the brackets and reposition them. It is extremely important that the cooling module be able to move freely.

70. Install the air induction system, PCV valve and fresh air hoses.

71. Connect the battery cables and tighten to 151 inch lbs. (17 Nm).

72. If equipped, enable the SIR system.

73. Fill the engine cooling system, then check all engine and transaxle fluids, add or fill as necessary.

74. Prime the fuel system by cycling the ignition **ON** for 5 seconds and **OFF** for 10 seconds a few times without cranking the engine. Start the engine and check for leaks.

Engine Mounts

REMOVAL AND INSTALLATION

The engine mount system consists of 2 groups of interconnected components. The first group is the engine mount which bolts to the top of the front cover and to the top of the midrail bracket. The midrail bracket bolts to the mid-frame rail and supports the engine mount.

The second engine mount group consists of the engine strut which in fastened to 2 brackets, 1 mounted to the engine and the other to the cradle.

1. Properly disable the SIR system, if equipped and disconnect the negative battery cable.

2. Remove the 2 engine mount-to-midrail bracket nuts.

3. Raise and support the vehicle safely.

4. Unless only removing the engine mount, remove the right wheel, then remove the inner splash shield.

5. Position a suitable floor jack and a block of wood under the engine oil pan, then raise the powertrain slightly to unload the mount.

6. If removing the midrail bracket and/or the engine mount:

a. Remove the 3 engine mount-to-engine front cover nuts, then remove the engine mount.

b. If the engine midrail bracket removal is required, remove the 4 midrail bracket-to-midrail bolts (from the bracket side of the assembly), then remove the 3 midrail-to-bracket bolts (from the rail side of the assembly) and remove the bracket from the vehicle.

7. If removing the engine strut and/or the strut brackets:

a. Loosen the 2 strut bracket-to-cradle nuts, located under the cradle.

b. Remove the strut-to-engine bracket and strut-to-cradle bracket bolts.

c. If removing the engine strut bracket, remove the 4 bracket-to-engine bolts.

d. If removing the cradle strut bracket, remove the 2 bracket-to-engine nuts.

e. Remove the strut brackets, and/or the engine strut from the vehicle. In order free the strut and/or the cradle bracket, the floor jack must be used to raise the engine slightly for clearance.

To install:

8. If removed, install the engine strut and/or strut bracket:

a. If removed, position the strut bracket to the engine, then install the 4 retaining bolts and tighten to 40 ft. lbs. (54 Nm).

b. If removed, position the engine strut and/or the cradle bracket, then lower the jack slightly to align the fasteners and holes.

c. Loosely install the cradle bracket fasteners, then install the strut-to-bracket bolts. Tighten the strut bolts to 52 ft. lbs. (70 Nm).

d. Fully lower the powertrain and tighten the cradle fasteners to 37 ft. lbs. (50 Nm).

9. If removed, install the midrail bracket and/or engine mount:

a. If the powertrain was lowered to install the engine strut or brackets, raise it again slightly to install the engine mount.

b. If removed, position the bracket to the midrail and hand-tighten all 7 retaining bolts. After all bolts are sufficiently threaded and tightened by hand, tighten all bolts to 24 ft. lbs. (32 Nm).

c. Position the engine mount to the front cover and install the 3 nuts. Tighten the nuts to 37 ft. lbs. (50 Nm).

d. Carefully lower the powertrain, guiding the mount over the midrail studs to prevent thread damage. Remove the jack and the block of wood.

e. Install the 2 mount-to-bracket nuts and tighten to 37 ft. lbs. (50 Nm).

10. Install the inner splash shield followed by the wheel assembly.

11. Lower the vehicle and connect the negative battery cable.

12. If equipped, properly enable the SIR system.

Cylinder Head

REMOVAL AND INSTALLATION

NOTE: Remove the cylinder head when the engine is cold. Warpage may result if removed hot.

1. Disconnect the negative battery cable and properly drain the engine coolant.

2. Remove the air cleaner assembly and air inlet duct. For SOHC engines, disconnect the PCV valve and fresh air hose. For DOHC engines, disconnect the camshaft cover air hose at the cover.

3. Disconnect the accelerator cable from the throttle body and the bracket from the intake manifold.

4. Properly relieve the fuel system pressure.

5. Label and disengage the electrical connectors from the cylinder head assembly. Long nose pliers are neces-

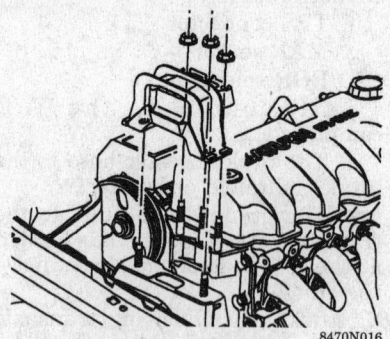

8470N016

Removing the engine mount from the midrail bracket and front cover studs

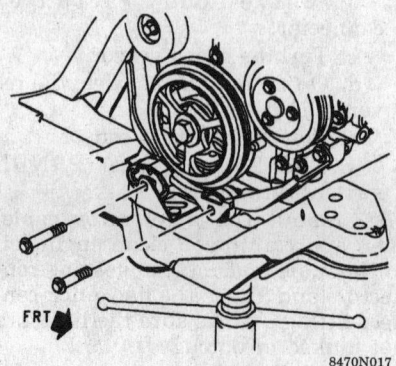

8470N017

Removing the 2 strut to bracket bolts

sary to unplug the coolant temperature sensor connectors. Position the electrical harness over the underhood junction block.

6. Label and disconnect all necessary vacuum hoses from the area around the cylinder head assembly.

7. Disconnect the upper radiator hose at the cylinder head outlet, the heater hose at the intake manifold and the deareation hose next to the TBI assembly or at the intake manifold.

8. Remove the bolt which retains the fuel lines to the intake manifold assembly. Disconnect the fuel feed and return lines from the fuel rail and pressure regulator or from the throttle body, as applicable. For SOHC engines, remove the lower intake manifold support bracket stud. For DOHC engines, remove the upper intake manifold support bracket bolt.

9. With a torque axis mount system, unclip the lower splash shield. Place a 1 inch x 1 inch x 2 inch block of wood between the torque strut and cradle prior to mount removal. This will hold the engine in position eliminating the need for jacking to install the mount. Then, remove the 3 right side upper engine mount-to-engine front cover nuts and the 2 mount-to-midrail bracket nuts allowing the engine to rest on the block of wood.

10. Remove the serpentine drive belt and belt tensioner. It is not necessary to remove the water pump pulley, however, fit will be necessary to remove the idler pulley to access the engine front cover while the engine is still in the vehicle.

11. For SOHC engines, disconnect the deareation line at the cylinder head water outlet and from the support bracket.

12. Remove the camshaft cover, then inspect the cover silicone insulators for cracks or deterioration and replace as necessary. Be sure to cover the valve train area in order to prevent foreign debris from entering the engine.

13. If equipped, remove the power steering pump bracket attaching bolts and position the assembly next to the right side front of the dash panel, away from the intake manifold and cylinder head. It is not necessary to remove the water pump pulley.

14. If equipped, remove the 3 air conditioning compressor front bracket bolts attached to the cylinder head and block, then remove the rear bracket bolts from the compressor. Do not discharge the system or disconnect the refrigerant lines. Support

Intake Side				
8	4	1	5	9
7	3	2	6	10
Exhaust Side				

8470N018

Cylinder head torque sequence

the compressor aside from the vehicle front support bar.

15. Raise and support vehicle safely, then drain the engine oil.

16. Remove the right side tire and splash shield.

17. For DOHC engines, remove the intake manifold support brace bolt attached to the intake manifold next to the alternator.

18. Remove the crankshaft damper/pulley assembly. Use a strap wrench or a block of wood wedged between the pulley spoke and the rear lower side of the front cover to hold the assembly while removing the bolt. Then use a 3 jaw puller on the

jaw slots cast into the pulley and remove the assembly.

19. Disconnect the front exhaust pipe from the manifold.

20. Install crankshaft gear retainer tool SA9104E or equivalent to hold the gear in position, then properly remove the engine front cover. After the cover is loosened and moved approximately 1 in. (25.4mm) from the engine, the timing gear tool should be removed.

NOTE: Do not attempt to loosen the front cover without using a gear service tool which is designed to prevent damage to the timing chain guide. The tool is also used during installation to align the oil pump gerotor. The crankshaft gear service tool must be installed with the flat side toward the sprocket.

21. Rotate the crankshaft clockwise so the crankshaft gear timing mark and keyway align with the main bearing cap split line. This will set the engine to 90 degrees off top dead center and make sure pistons will not contact the valves upon assembly.

22. Remove the timing chain, tensioner, guides, camshaft sprocket(s) and chain. Use a $\frac{7}{8}$ in. (21mm) wrench to hold the camshaft when removing the sprocket bolts.

23. For the SOHC engine, remove the throttle body assembly and cover the intake manifold opening.

24. Use a 6-point socket to remove the 10 cylinder head bolts in several passes of the proper sequence (the reverse of the torque sequence). Failure to follow the proper sequence, or removal of the head when hot, could result in head warpage or cracking. Also, the use of a 12-point socket on the cylinder head bolts may round the bolt heads.

25. Lift the cylinder head from the dowels. Be careful not to damage the sealing surfaces if prying is necessary to remove the head from the block.

26. If necessary, remove the intake manifold or the exhaust manifold by loosening the mounting nuts in the proper sequence. If any cylinder head studs come out, the threads should be cleaned, the studs carefully installed and then tightened to 106 inch lbs. (12 Nm).

To install:

27. If removed, install the intake manifold and/or the exhaust manifold and new gasket(s). Tighten the fasteners to specification using the proper torque sequence.

28. Clean the gasket mating surfaces. Be careful not to damage the aluminum components. Make sure the block bolt holes are clean of any residual sealer, oil or foreign matter.

29. Inspect the top of the cylinder block for excessive warpage. Transverse warpage must not exceed 0.002 in (0.05mm), while longitudinal warpage must not exceed 0.004 in. (0.10mm).

30. Check that the cylinder liners are flush or do not deviate more than 0.0005 in. (0.013mm) from the deck.

31. Make sure the crankshaft is positioned at 90 degrees past TDC to prevent valve or piston damage.

NOTE: Replacement head gaskets on 1992 vehicles, are equipped with a 0.157 in. (4mm) orifice, where a cylinder block orifice plug is installed. The oil gallery plug is no longer required, and may be removed using a slide hammer and screw puller when the gasket is replaced.

32. Install the cylinder head gasket and carefully guide the head into place over the dowels.

33. If the head bolts or the block were replaced, install the bolts and tighten in sequence to 48 ft. lbs. (65 Nm) to insure proper clamp load, then remove the bolts.

34. Coat the cylinder head bolts with clean engine oil and thread the

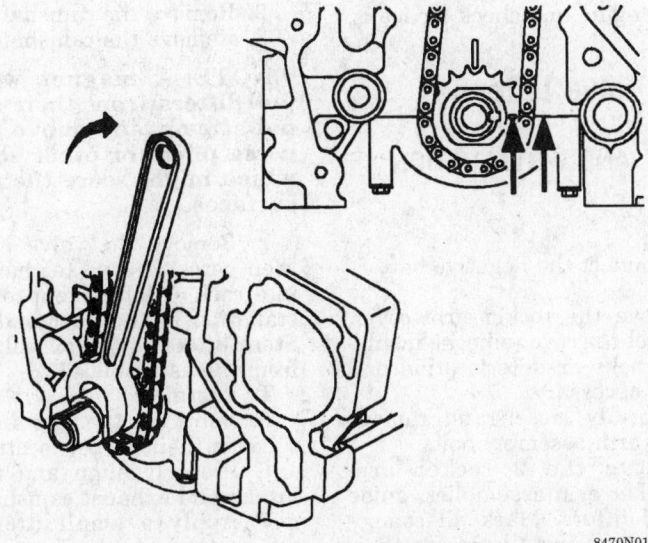

8470N019

Align the crankshaft gear timing mark and keyway with the bearing cap split line to set the engine 90 degrees past TDC

bolts by hand until finger-tight. Tighten the bolts in sequence to 22 ft. lbs. (30 Nm).

35. Tighten the cylinder head bolts again, in sequence to 33 ft. lbs. (45 Nm) for SOHC engines or to 37 ft. lbs. (50 Nm) for DOHC engines. Install Snap-On® tool 360 or equivalent torque angle gauge and calibrate the gauge to 0, then tighten each cylinder head bolt an additional 90 degrees, in sequence.

36. Align the camshaft(s) to TDC, then rotate the crankshaft counterclockwise 90 degrees, also to TDC. Install the timing chain, sprockets, guides and tensioner.

37. Install the front cover assembly and connect the exhaust manifold to the exhaust pipe.

38. Install the crankshaft damper/pulley assembly and tighten the bolt to 159 ft. lbs. (215 Nm).

39. For DOHC vehicles, install the intake manifold support brace bolts next to the alternator, then tighten the bracket-to-block bolt to 33 ft. lbs. (45 Nm) and tighten the bracket-to-manifold bolt to 22 ft. lbs. (30 Nm).

40. Apply a small drop of RTV across the cylinder head and front cover T-joints. Inspect the old camshaft cover gasket and replace if damaged. Install the gasket and the camshaft cover. Tighten the fasteners uniformly to 22 ft. lbs. (30 Nm) for SOHC vehicles or in proper sequence to 89 inch lbs. (10 Nm) for DOHC vehicles.

41. Install the drive belt tensioner and tighten the bolt to 22 ft. lbs. (30 Nm). Install the idler pulley and tighten the fasteners to 33 ft. lbs. (45 Nm).

42. If not done during removal, drain the engine oil. Change the filter, then install the drain plug and tighten to 26 ft. lbs. (35 Nm).

43. If removed, verify the gaps on all spark plugs and install. Tighten to 20 ft. lbs. (27 Nm).

44. For SOHC engines applicable, install a new gasket and the TBI assembly. Tighten the assembly retainers to 24 ft. lbs. (33 Nm).

45. If equipped, install the power steering pump assembly to the bracket, then tighten the bolts to 22 ft. lbs. (30 Nm).

46. If equipped, install the air conditioning compressor and bolts. Tighten the rear bracket bolts to 19 ft. lbs. (25 Nm), then tighten the front bracket bolts to 35 ft. lbs. (47 Nm).

47. Install the serpentine drive belt making sure the belt is properly aligned on the pulleys.

48. With a torque axis mounting, install the 2 mount-to-midrail bracket nuts and tighten to 52 ft. lbs. (70 Nm). Then, install the 3 upper mount-to-engine front cover nuts and tighten them uniformly to 52 ft. lbs. (70 Nm). Remove the support block of wood after the assembly is installed.

49. Install the splash shield, then install the wheel assembly.

50. Position the wiring harness and engage all wire connectors.

51. Install all vacuum hoses disconnected during removal.

52. If removed, install the accelerator cable bracket and tighten the fastener to 19 ft. lbs. (25 Nm). Connect the cable, then verify that it is properly routed and not binding.

53. Install all coolant hoses which were disconnected during removal.

54. For the SOHC engine, install the intake manifold support bracket and/or fasteners. Tighten the manifold fasteners to 21 ft. lbs. (28 Nm) and the block fasteners to 22 ft. lbs. (30 Nm).

55. Connect the fuel feed and return lines to the throttle body and tighten the fittings to 19 ft. lbs. (25 Nm) or to the fuel rail and pressure regulator and tighten the fittings to 133 inch lbs. (15 Nm). Install fuel bracket retaining bolts, as applicable.

56. Install the air cleaner and intake duct assembly.

57. Add engine oil and properly fill the engine cooling system.

58. Connect the negative battery cable.

59. Prime the fuel system, then start the engine and check for leaks.

Valve Lifters

REMOVAL AND INSTALLATION

SOHC Engine

1. Disconnect the negative battery cable.

2. Remove the rocker arm cover, then inspect the cover silicone insulators for cracks or deterioration and replace as necessary.

3. Uniformly loosen and remove the rocker arm assembly bolts.

4. Remove the 2 rocker arm shafts, rocker arm assemblies, guide plates and lifters. Mark all components to assure installation in their original locations.

To install:

5. Oil the lifters, then install them into the cylinder head bores.

6. Rotate the lifters until the flats are parallel with the intake and ex-

haust sides of cylinder head, then install the guide plates. Make sure the plates are properly seated with the retaining spring slot upwards and the lifters fitted squarely into the guide plate.

7. Install the rocker arm shaft assemblies. Make sure the rocker arm tangs are squarely seated on the lifter and the retaining spring is positioned in the guide plate slot. The retaining springs should be snapped onto the rocker arm shafts between the No. 1–2 and the No. 3–4 cylinder rocker arms.

NOTE: During installation, a flat piece of cardboard or a ratchet extension bar may be positioned on top of the rocker arm shaft assemblies to align the arms on both the valves and lifters.

8. Torque the rocker arm bolts to 19 ft. lbs. (25 Nm) in a uniform sequence.

9. Apply a small drop of RTV to each cylinder head and front cover T-joint. Inspect the rocker arm cover gasket and replace if necessary. Install the gasket and rocker arm cover, then tighten the fasteners uniformly to 22 ft. lbs. (30 Nm).

10. Connect the negative battery cable, start the engine and check for leaks.

DOHC Engine

1. Disconnect the negative battery cable.

2. Remove the camshaft cover.

3. Remove the camshafts.

NOTE: A magnet will easily pull lifters from their bores. Do not attempt to remove the lifters using pliers or other sharp tools which might score the machined surfaces.

4. Remove the valve lifters from their bores. Be sure to place all lifters in a rack or label them to assure installation in their original locations. Store lifters so the oil will not drain from the assemblies.

To install:

5. Lubricate the lifters and install them in their proper locations.

6. Properly align and install the intake and exhaust camshafts.

7. Apply a small drop of RTV across the cylinder head and front cover T-joints. Inspect the old camshaft cover gasket and replace if damaged. Install the gasket and the camshaft cover. Tighten the fasteners in the proper sequence to 89 inch lbs. (10 Nm).

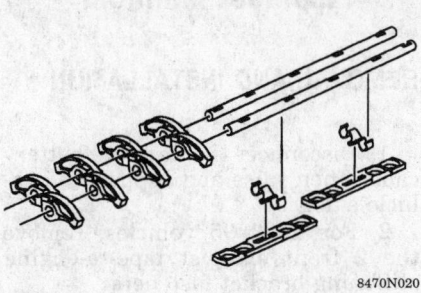

Lifter guide plate positioning — SOHC engine

8. Connect the negative battery cable, start the engine and check for leaks.

Valve Lash

ADJUSTMENT

All Saturn engines are equipped with hydraulic valve lifters which are designed to maintain zero lash. No periodic adjustments are needed or possible.

Rocker Arms/Shafts

The SOHC engine, is the only Saturn engine which utilizes rocker arms.

REMOVAL AND INSTALLATION

1. Disconnect the negative battery cable.
2. Remove the rocker arm cover, then inspect the cover silicone insulators for cracks or deterioration and replace as necessary.
3. Uniformly remove the rocker arm shaft bolts, then remove the 2 rocker arm shafts. The shafts may be unsnapped from the lifter guide plates in order to leave the guide plates and lifters in the engine.
4. If necessary, disassemble the rocker arms from the shafts.
   To install:
5. If removed, oil the rocker arm shafts, then install the arms onto the shafts.
6. Snap 1 end of each lifter guide plate retaining spring onto the rocker arm shaft between the No. 1–2 and the No. 3–4 cylinder rocker arms.

NOTE: During installation, a flat piece of cardboard or a ratchet extension bar may be positioned on top of the rocker

arm shaft assemblies to align the arms on both the valves and lifters.

7. Install the rocker arm shaft assemblies. To prevent valve or piston damage, be sure the rocker arm tangs are squarely seated on the lifters and the retaining springs are positioned in the guide plate slots.
8. Verify the proper position and seating of all rocker components, then tighten the 5 rocker arm bolts on each shaft to 19 ft. lbs. (25 Nm) in a uniform sequence.
9. Apply a small drop of RTV to each cylinder head and front cover T-joint. Inspect the rocker arm cover gasket and replace if necessary. Install the gasket and rocker arm cover, then tighten the fasteners uniformly to 22 ft. lbs. (30 Nm).
10. Connect the negative battery cable, start the engine and check for leaks.

Intake Manifold

REMOVAL AND INSTALLATION

SOHC Engine

1. Disconnect the negative battery cable and drain the engine coolant.
2. Remove the air cleaner and the fresh air tube at the rocker cover. Remove the PCV tube and hose.
3. Properly relieve the fuel system pressure at the test port, then disconnect the fuel supply and return lines at the connectors using service tool SA9157E or equivalent. Plug the lines to prevent system contamination or excessive fuel spillage.
4. Disconnect the throttle cable from the throttle body, then remove the throttle cable bracket attaching nuts and position the assembly aside.
5. Label and disconnect the following wiring from the following throttle

Upper Side			
8	4	1	5
7	3	2	6	9
Lower Side			

8470N021

Intake manifold torque sequence — SOHC engine

body and intake manifold components:
- Fuel injector
- Idle Air Control (IAC) valve
- Throttle Position (TP) sensor
- Exhaust Gas Recirculation (EGR) valve
- Manifold Absolute Pressure (MAP) sensor

6. Position the wiring harness away from the manifold onto the fuel relay.
7. Tag and disconnect the vacuum hoses from the TBI tube module assembly and from the brake booster.
8. Remove the heater hose from the manifold and the de-aeration line from the cylinder head, then remove the 2 clamps and position the line on the coolant bottle.
9. Remove the intake manifold support bracket bolt located next to the starter and attached to the block. If necessary, the bolt can be removed from below the vehicle.
10. Remove the serpentine drive belt, then remove the power steering pump from the bracket and support the pump next to the right side dash panel sufficiently away from the intake manifold and cylinder head.
11. Remove the manifold retaining nuts, then remove the manifold and throttle body assembly. If necessary the lower manifold nuts can be accessed from under the vehicle.
    To install:
12. Thoroughly clean all gasket mating surfaces. Be careful not to damage or score the aluminum surface. If replaced, use Loctite® 290 or equivalent to seal a new PCV valve inlet tube into the manifold.
13. Position the new gasket, then install the manifold and retaining nuts. Tighten the nuts in sequence to 22 ft. lbs. (30 Nm).
14. Install the power steering pump and tighten the fasteners to 27 ft. lbs. (38 Nm).
15. Install the serpentine drive belt.
16. Connect the heater hose, then install the de-aeration line and clamps.
17. Install the manifold support bracket bolt and tighten to 22 ft. lbs. (30 Nm).
18. Connect the fuel supply and return lines to the TBI unit, then tighten the fittings to 19 ft. lbs. (25 Nm).
19. Reposition the wiring harness, then connect the wiring and vacuum hoses to their original locations. The harness leads to the TPS and EGR solenoid must be routed between the No. 3 and 4 intake manifold runners.

20. Install the air cleaner and fresh air tubes, then install the PCV valve hose.

21. Connect the negative battery cable and properly fill the engine cooling system.

22. Prime the fuel system, start the engine and check for leaks.

DOHC Engine

1. Disconnect the negative battery cable and drain the engine coolant.

2. Remove the air inlet tube and resonator, then remove the PCV tube.

3. Properly relieve the fuel system pressure at the test port.

4. Remove the fuel line bracket bolt and disconnect the lines from the fuel rail. Disconnect the fuel lines from the connectors using service tool SA9157E or equivalent. Plug the openings to prevent fuel system contamination or excessive fuel spillage.

5. Disconnect the throttle cable from the throttle body, then remove the cable bracket assembly and position aside.

6. Label and disconnect the following wiring from the following throttle body and intake manifold components:
- Fuel injectors
- Idle Air Control (IAC) valve
- Throttle Position (TP) sensor
- Manifold Absolute Pressure (MAP) sensor

7. Disconnect the heater and de-aeration hoses from the intake manifold, then disconnect the vacuum hose from the EGR solenoid.

8. Position the wiring harness over the brake master cylinder, then remove the intake manifold support bracket bolt attached to the manifold next to the brake master cylinder.

9. Remove the serpentine drive belt. Remove the power steering pump assembly with the support bracket, then remove the upper pump bracket attachment bolts and

position the pump away from the manifold and cylinder head, near the right dash panel. Remove the lower power steering pump bracket brace.

10. Remove the 3 upper intake manifold attachment nuts, then raise and support the vehicle safely.

11. Remove the lower power steering unit support bracket. Remove the intake manifold support bracket bolt located next to the alternator, then loosen the lower bracket bolt and rotate the bracket out of the way.

12. Disconnect the canister purge solenoid and brake booster vacuum hoses.

13. Remove the intake manifold attaching stud and lower the vehicle.

14. Remove the intake manifold assembly, then remove and discard the old gasket.

To install:

15. Thoroughly clean the gasket mating surfaces. Be careful not to score or damage the aluminum sealing surfaces. If installing a new coolant de-aeration tube elbow into the manifold, use Loctite® 290 or equivalent to assure proper seal.

16. Position the new gasket, then install the intake manifold and retaining nuts. Torque the nuts in sequence to 22 ft. lbs. (30 Nm).

17. Install the power steering pump and brackets. Tighten the fasteners to 28 ft. lbs. (38 Nm).

18. Install the serpentine drive belt making sure the belt is properly aligned on the pulleys.

19. Connect the heater hose and de-aeration line to the manifold.

20. Position the manifold support brackets and install the retainers. Tighten the right bracket-to-block retainer to 41 ft. lbs. (55 Nm), then tighten the left block retainer and the support bracket-to-intake manifold bolts to 22 ft. lbs. (30 Nm).

21. Lubricate the male fuel supply and return connect fittings, then install.

22. Connect the throttle cable to the throttle body and install the support bracket. Tighten the bracket retaining bolts to 19 ft. lbs. (25 Nm). Verify that the cable locking tangs are fully engaged when assembled.

23. Position the wiring harness, then engage all electrical connectors and vacuum hoses in their original locations.

24. Install the PCV hose, the air inlet tube and resonator.

25. Connect the negative battery cable and properly fill the engine cooling system.

26. Prime the fuel system, start the engine and check for leaks.

Exhaust Manifold

REMOVAL AND INSTALLATION

1. Disconnect the negative battery cable, then raise and support the vehicle safely.

2. For 1993–95 vehicles, remove the 2 front exhaust pipe-to-engine stiffening bracket fasteners.

3. Remove the pipe-to-manifold nuts and lower the pipe slightly, then remove the old gasket and discard.

4. Lower the vehicle.

5. If equipped, remove the the air conditioning compressor and bracket and support to the side. Do not disconnect the refrigerant lines.

6. Unplug the oxygen sensor connector. If necessary, use a 19mm, 6-point, crows foot to remove the oxygen sensor.

7. Remove the manifold retaining nuts and remove the manifold. Remove and discard the old gasket.

To install:

8. Thoroughly clean the gasket mating surfaces, be careful not to score or damage the aluminum surface.

9. Install the new gasket with the smooth side facing the manifold, then install the manifold and attaching nuts. Tighten the nuts in sequence to 16 ft. lbs. (22 Nm) for the SOHC engine or to 23 ft. lbs. (31 Nm) for the DOHC engine.

10. If replacing the oxygen sensor, coat the threads with nickel based anti-seize compound and tighten to 18 ft. lbs. (25 Nm). Install the wiring harness to the oxygen sensor electrical connector.

11. Install the air conditioning compressor and brackets. Tighten all fasteners except the front bracket-to-compressor fasteners to 19 ft. lbs. (25 Nm). Tighten the front bracket to compressor fasteners to 40 ft. lbs. (54 Nm).

12. Raise and support the vehicle safely, then install a new gasket onto the studs between the pipe and manifold.

13. Connect the pipe and manifold, then tighten the fasteners in a crosswise pattern to 23 ft. lbs. (31 Nm).

14. For 1993–95 vehicles, install the clamp-to-front exhaust pipe and support bracket, then tighten the fasteners to 44 ft. lbs. (60 Nm).

15. Lower the vehicle, then connect the negative battery cable.

16. Start the engine and check for leaks.

Upper Side		
5	2	3
7	4	1	6
Lower Side		

8470N022

Intake manifold torque sequence — DOHC engine

Upper Side			
8	4	1	5
7	3	2	6
Lower Side			

8470N023

Exhaust manifold torque sequence — SOHC engine

Upper Side		
	2	3
4	1	5
Lower Side		

8470N024

Exhaust manifold torque sequence — DOHC engine

Timing Chain Front Cover

REMOVAL AND INSTALLATION

1. Disconnect the negative battery cable and drain the engine oil.

2. Raise and support the vehicle safely, then remove the right wheel and splash shield.

3. With a torque axis mount system, place a 1 inch x 1 inch x 2 inch block of wood between the torque strut and cradle prior to mount removal. This will hold the engine in position eliminating the need for jacking to install the mount. Then,

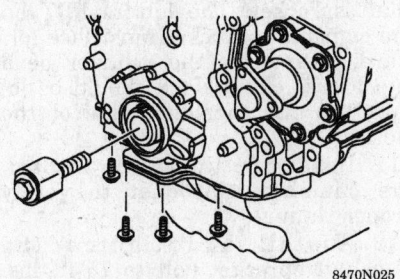

8470N025

SA9104E, or an equivalent timing sprocket retainer must be used when separating the front cover in order to prevent timing chain and guide damage

remove the 3 right side upper engine mount-to-engine front cover nuts and the 2 mount-to-midrail bracket nuts allowing the engine to rest on the block of wood.

4. Remove the serpentine drive belt and belt tensioner. It is not necessary to remove the water pump pulley, however the idler pulley must be removed to access the engine front cover.

5. Using a strap wrench or a piece of wood wedged between the damper spoke and the lower side of the engine front cover, hold the damper and remove the bolt. Using a suitable 3 jaw puller and the slots cast into the damper, pull the crankshaft damper/pulley assembly from the crankshaft.

6. Remove the power steering pump and position the assembly aside.

7. Remove the rocker or camshaft cover. Be sure to protect the valve train assemblies from foreign debris or dirt.

8. Install the special tool SA9104E or equivalent to make sure the crankshaft timing sprocket is held firmly in place and to prevent guide damage. Install with the flat side towards the crankshaft sprocket.

9. Remove the front 4 oil pan bolts, then using a suitable RTV cutting tool, cut the front seal away from the front cover.

10. Spray the 2 dowel pin holes with penetrating oil to facilitate front cover removal from the dowel pins.

11. Remove the front cover bolts. For DOHC vehicles, 1 bolt is located above the serpentine drive belt idler pulley, under the torque axis mount flange.

12. Using a small suitable tool, carefully pry the cover away from the cylinder block at the pry locations tabs which are provided. Once the cover has been loosened and moved approximately 1 in. (25.4mm), remove the crankshaft gear retaining tool, then remove the cover from the vehicle. Remove and discard the 2 oil gallery transfer seals.

To install:

13. Make sure the oil galleys are clear. Carefully clean the gasket mating surfaces with a scraper or wire brush and carburetor solvent, brake clean or alcohol. Use a 3/16 in. drill bit and tap handle to clean the front cover holes. The non-tapped front cover holes may be cleaned using a 3/8 in. drill bit.

NOTE: If the engine front cover casting or assembly is replaced, the 3 torque axis mount

studs should also be replaced. Tighten the studs to 133 inch lbs. (15 Nm).

14. If removed, install the oil pump and cover to the front cover. Be sure to pack the pump with petroleum jelly to assure proper priming. Also, if removed, install a new front seal and/or oil pressure and suction seals.

15. Apply a 0.16 inch (4mm) bead of RTV sealer on the along the vertical sealing surfaces of the front cover to the inside of the bolt holes and a 0.08 in. (2mm) bead to the front of the oil pan. For DOHC engines, apply a thin bead around the 2 inner cover bolt holes. Be sure to assemble the front cover to the engine within 3 minutes of application.

16. In order to properly align the oil pump gerotor, install the crankshaft gear retaining tool and position the front cover to the engine. Install the bolts, then tighten the perimeter bolts starting at the center and working outwards on both sides to 19 ft. lbs. (25 Nm) for the perimeter and upper center bolts.

17. Install and tighten the front cover lower center bolt to 89 inch lbs. (10 Nm), then install the 4 oil pan front bolts and tighten to 80 inch lbs. (9 Nm).

18. After front cover installation, spray 6–12 squirts of oil though the front oil seal drain back hole to verify it is not plugged.

19. Apply a thin film of RTV between the damper/pulley assembly flange and washer only, the washer and bolt head flange are designed to prevent oil leakage.

20. Remove the crankshaft retaining tool and position the crankshaft damper/pulley assembly, then secure as accomplished during removal while tightening the bolt to 159 ft. lbs. (215 Nm).

21. Apply a small drop of RTV across the cylinder head and front cover T-joints. Inspect the old camshaft cover gasket and replace if damaged. Install the gasket and the camshaft cover. Tighten the fasteners uniformly to 22 ft. lbs. (30 Nm) for SOHC vehicles or in proper sequence to 89 inch lbs. (10 Nm) for DOHC vehicles.

22. Install the power steering pump assembly.

23. If removed, install the idler pulley and tighten the retainer to 33 ft. lbs. (45 Nm).

24. Install the belt tensioner and the serpentine drive belt.

25. With a torque axis mounting, install the 2 mount-to-midrail bracket nuts and tighten to 52 ft. lbs.

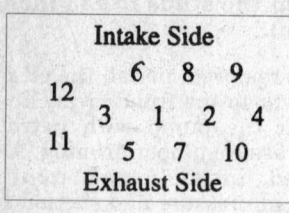

```
          Intake Side
        6   8   9
   12
        3   1   2   4
   11
        5   7   10
          Exhaust Side
```

8470N026

Camshaft cover torque sequence — DOHC engine

(70 Nm). Then, install the 3 upper mount-to-engine front cover nuts and tighten them uniformly to 52 ft. lbs. (70 Nm). Remove the support block of wood after the assembly is installed.

26. Install the splash shield and the wheel assembly, then lower the vehicle.

27. Properly fill the engine crankcase and connect the negative battery cable.

28. Start the engine and check for leaks.

Front Cover Oil Seal

REPLACEMENT

With Front Cover Installed

1. Disconnect the negative battery cable and drain the engine oil.

2. Raise the vehicle and support safely, then remove the right wheel and splash shield.

3. Remove the serpentine drive belt from the crankshaft damper/pulley.

4. Using a strap wrench or a piece of wood wedged between the damper spoke and the lower side of the engine front cover, hold the damper and remove the bolt. With a suitable 3 jaw puller and the slots cast into the damper, pull the crankshaft damper/pulley assembly from the crankshaft.

5. Use a small suitable tool to pry the oil seal from the front cover. Be very careful not to damage the front cover or crankshaft.

6. Clean the seal bore and oil drain back passage.

To install:

7. Make sure the oil drain back is free of RTV or debris. Position the oil seal and thread the service seal installer tool, SA9104E or equivalent, onto the end of the crankshaft. Use the tool to draw the seal into position.

Never tap on the seal or the seal install with a hammer.

8. Apply a thin film of clean engine oil to the new seal lip.

9. Position the crankshaft damper/pulley assembly, then secure as accomplished during removal while tightening the bolt to 159 ft. lbs. (215 Nm).

10. Install the serpentine drive belt.

11. Install the splash shield and the wheel assembly, then lower the vehicle.

12. Properly fill the engine crankcase and connect the negative battery cable.

13. Start the engine and check for leaks.

With Front Cover Removed

1. Use a suitable prytool to carefully pry the front oil seal from the front cover. Be careful not to damage the front cover or crankshaft.

2. Clean the seal bore and oil drain back passage.

3. Place the engine front cover on the base of a suitable arbor press. Support the cover in order to prevent deformation or damage.

4. Position the seal to the front cover and place tool SA9104E, or equivalent installation tool, over the seal.

5. Press the seal into the engine front cover approximately 0.04 inch (1mm) further into the engine front cover than the factory seal removed earlier.

6. Install the timing chain front cover to the vehicle.

Timing Chain and Sprockets

REMOVAL AND INSTALLATION

SOHC Engine

1. Disconnect the negative battery cable.

2. Remove the timing chain front cover.

NOTE: When removing the timing chain and sprockets, the crankshaft should be positioned 90 degrees past TDC to make sure the pistons will not contact the valves upon assembly.

3. Carefully rotate the crankshaft clockwise from TDC (timing mark at 12 o'clock) so the timing mark and keyway on the crankshaft sprocket align with the main bearing cap split line to the right of the crankshaft.

4. Remove the timing guides and tensioner.

5. Remove the camshaft sprocket bolt, using a ⅞ in. (21mm) wrench to hold the camshaft. Then remove the timing chain and camshaft sprocket. If necessary, remove the crankshaft sprocket.

To install:

6. Inspect the chain for wear and damage. Check the inside diameter of the chain, it should be no more than 16.77 in. (426mm). Inspect the chain guides for wear or cracks and the timing gears for teeth or key wear. Replace components as necessary.

7. Verify that the crankshaft is positioned 90 degrees clockwise past TDC by checking that the keyway and timing mark are at 3 o'clock, parallel with the main bearing cap split line.

8. Bring the camshaft up to the No. 1 TDC by loosely installing the sprocket and rotating the sprocket and crankshaft in the clockwise direction until the timing pin can be installed. The camshaft contains wrench flats to assist in turning the shaft. The dowel pin should be at 12 o'clock when No. 1 is at TDC and a timing pin (³⁄₁₆ in. drill bit) should then install at about the 8 o'clock position.

9. With the camshaft at No. 1 TDC, rotate the crankshaft counterclockwise 90 degrees up to the No. 1 cylinder TDC position. The gear keyway and timing mark should be at 12 o'clock, aligned with the block timing mark. Remove the camshaft sprocket and timing pin so the chain can be installed.

10. Position the chain over the camshaft sprocket and under the crankshaft sprocket, then slide the camshaft sprocket into position. Install the timing chain and sprockets so the 1 silver link plate aligns with the pip mark on the top of the camshaft sprocket and the other aligns with the downward tooth at the 6 o'clock position on the crankshaft sprocket. The letters FRT on the camshaft sprocket must face forward, away from the cylinder head and excess chain slack should be located on the tensioner side of the block.

11. Install the timing pin through the camshaft sprocket to verify proper timing.

12. Install and tighten the camshaft sprocket bolt to 75 ft. lbs. (102 Nm). Again, use an wrench on the camshaft wrench flats to hold the shaft in position while tightening the bolt. Do not allow the camshaft re-

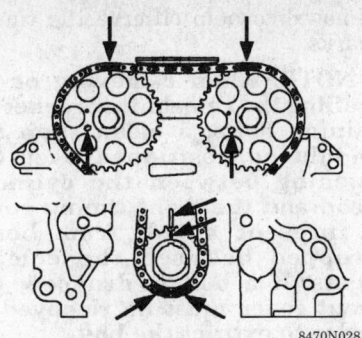

Timing chain and sprocket alignment marks — DOHC engine

8470N028

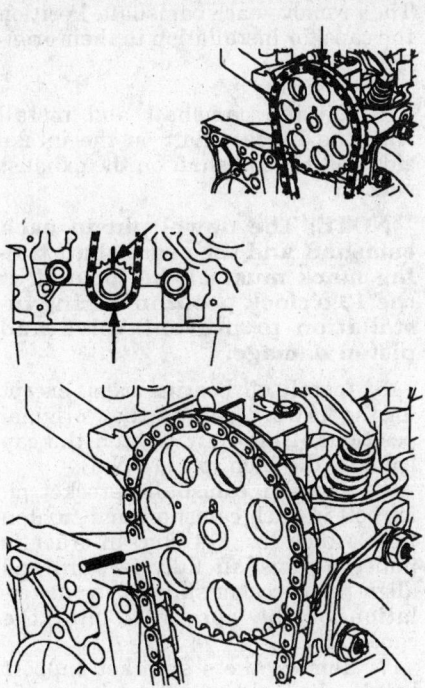

8470N027

Timing chain and sprocket alignment marks — SOHC engine

taining bolt to torque against the timing pin or cylinder head damage will result.

13. Install the fixed chain guides, the word FRONT on the fixed guide must be facing outward. Install the fixed guide first and verify the chain is snug against the guide, then install the pivot guide. Tighten the bolts to 19 ft. lbs. (26 Nm) and verify that the pivot guide moves freely.

14. Retract the tensioner plunger and pin the ratchet lever using a $\frac{1}{8}$ in. No. 31 drill bit inserted in the alignment hole. Install the tensioner and tighten the bolts to 168 inch lbs. (19 Nm), then remove the drill bit.

15. Verify the proper positioning of all timing marks, then remove all alignment pins.

16. Install the timing chain front cover.

17. Connect the negative battery cable.

18. Start the engine and check for leaks.

DOHC Engine

1. Disconnect the negative battery cable.

2. Remove the timing chain front cover.

NOTE: When removing the timing chain and sprockets, the crankshaft should be positioned 90 degrees past TDC to make sure the pistons will not contact the valves upon assembly.

3. Carefully rotate the crankshaft clockwise from TDC (timing mark at 12 o'clock) so the timing mark and keyway on the crankshaft sprocket align with the main bearing cap split line to the right of the crankshaft.

4. Remove the timing guides and tensioner.

5. Remove the camshaft sprocket bolts, using a $\frac{7}{8}$ in. (21mm) wrench to hold the camshaft from turning. Then remove the timing chain and camshaft sprockets. If necessary, remove the crankshaft sprocket.

To install:

6. Inspect the chain for wear and damage. Check the inside diameter of the chain, it should be no more than 23.15 in. (588mm). Inspect the chain guides for wear or cracks and the timing gears for teeth or key wear. Replace components as necessary.

7. If removed, install the crankshaft sprocket, then verify that the crankshaft is positioned 90 degrees clockwise past TDC. The crankshaft timing mark and keyway should be at the 3 o'clock position, aligned with the main bearing cap split line. This will position the pistons downward in order to prevent possible valve or piston damage.

8. Install the camshaft gears, retaining bolts and washers. Make sure the letters FRT on the gears face forward, away from the cylinder block. Use the wrench flats provided on the camshafts to hold the shaft and tighten the bolts to 75 ft. lbs. (102 Nm).

9. Bring the camshafts up to No. 1 TDC; the timing mark should be at 12 o'clock and the letters FRT should

be between 1 and 3 o'clock. Install a $\frac{3}{16}$ in. drill bit into the hole in each sprocket at about 8 o'clock. Turn the sprockets slightly, as necessary to verify insert the pins into the hole and verify proper timing.

10. Rotate the crankshaft counterclockwise up to the No. 1 TDC position (keyway and timing mark at 12 o'clock, aligned with the block timing mark).

11. Position the timing chain over the camshaft sprockets so the 2 silver link plates align with the pip marks on the top center of the camshaft sprockets, then position the chain under the crankshaft sprocket so the other 2 plates align on either side of the downward tooth (at 6 o'clock position) on the crankshaft sprocket. Excess chain slack should be located on the tensioner side of the cylinder block.

12. Verify that the crankshaft pip mark aligns with the cylinder block mark at 12 o'clock and that the timing pin holes are aligned at about the 8 o'clock position. Remove the timing pins from the camshaft sprockets.

13. Install the timing chain fixed guide to the right of the block face toward the water pump. Tighten the bolts to 21 ft. lbs. (28 Nm) and verify the chain is snug against the guide.

14. Install the pivoting chain guide and check for clearance between the block and head. Tighten the bolt to 19 ft. lbs. (26 Nm) and verify that the guide pivots freely.

15. Retract the tensioner plunger and pin the ratchet lever using a $\frac{1}{8}$ in. No. 31 drill bit inserted in the alignment hole. Install the tensioner and tighten the bolts to 168 inch lbs. (19 Nm), then remove the drill bit allowing the tensioner to extend.

16. Make sure all alignment pins are removed.

17. Install the timing chain front cover.

18. Connect the negative battery cable, then start the engine and check for leaks.

Camshaft

REMOVAL AND INSTALLATION

SOHC Engine

1. Disconnect the negative battery cable.

2. Remove the timing chain front cover.

3. Remove the timing chain and camshaft sprocket.

4. Remove the rocker arm and shaft assemblies.

5. Remove the lifters and tag or arrange to assure assembly in their original locations.

6. Remove the battery cover and battery.

7. Drive the camshaft plug (located on the battery side of the cylinder head) inward, then remove it from the cylinder head with a magnet.

8. Carefully pull the camshaft from the rear of the cylinder head though the oversized camshaft plug hole.

To install:

9. Lubricate the camshaft and install into the rear of the cylinder head.

10. Coat a new rear cylinder head plug with Loctite® 242 or equivalent and install it using a standard bushing driver.

11. Install the battery and tighten the battery hold-down nut and screw to 80 inch lbs. (9 Nm). Connect only the positive battery cable, at this time.

12. Install the valve lifters into their original bores. If a new camshaft was installed, the lifters must be replaced to assure camshaft life.

13. Install the rocker arm shaft assemblies.

14. Install the timing chain and camshaft sprocket.

15. Install the timing chain front cover.

16. Connect the negative battery cable, then start the engine and check for leaks.

DOHC Engine

1. Disconnect the negative battery cable and remove the serpentine drive belt.

2. Disconnect the spark plug wires from the plugs, remove the EGR valve solenoid attachment screw and remove the PCV fresh air hose.

3. Remove the camshaft cover, then inspect the cover silicone insulators for cracks or deterioration and replace as necessary.

4. Turn the crankshaft until the mark on the crankshaft pulley is in alignment with the front cover pointer at the damper's 12 o'clock position and No. 1 cylinder is at TDC of the compression stroke. Both camshaft dowel pins will be at the 12 o'clock position and the timing pin holes will be aligned when the No. 1 cylinder is at TDC. If necessary, the right wheel and splash shield may be

removed to help observe the timing marks.

NOTE: When removing or installing the camshaft sprocket retaining bolts, a clean shop rag should be positioned over the opening between the cylinder head and the front timing cover to prevent a bolt from being dropped between the components. If a bolt is dropped, the front cover must be removed in order to extract the bolt.

5. Carefully remove each camshaft sprocket's retaining bolts and washers. Use a 7/8 in. (21mm) open end wrench to hold each camshaft from turning while removing the bolts.

6. Position the front angled support fixture in front of the camshaft sprockets.

7. Attach the camshaft sprocket adapters to the end of each camshaft using the pilot bolts, but do not tighten the bolts. The support fixture rests between the sprockets and the sprocket adapters.

8. Remove the upper timing chain guide and both front camshaft bearing caps.

9. Secure the support fixture using the 3/8 in. bolts/blocks and align the 2 holes in each camshaft sprocket, adapter and the front support fixture. Install the 4 nuts, but do not tighten. The steel blocks should be installed against the rearward side of the camshaft sprocket. Tighten the sprocket pilot bolts to 19 ft. lbs. (25 Nm) while holding the camshafts from turning with an open end wrench.

10. Move each camshaft sprocket off the end of the camshaft by rocking the sprocket forward at the 3 and 9 o'clock positions or by carefully prying between the end of the camshaft and the sprocket. Then tighten the 4 nuts and bolts with blocks from the side of the support fixture to 19 ft. lbs. (25 Nm).

11. Install the 2 bolts retaining the support fixture to the engine front cover and tighten the bolts to 89 inch lbs. (10 Nm). Then remove each camshaft sprocket pilot bolt while holding the camshafts with a wrench.

12. Carefully pry between the sprocket and the end of the camshaft to move the camshaft rearward. Pry only sufficiently to remove its end from inside the sprocket pilot otherwise camshaft or lifter damage may occur.

13. Uniformly loosen and remove the remaining camshaft bearing cap bolts. To prevent bolt/cap damage, do not use power tools, but instead make

several passes using a hand ratchet. Then remove each camshaft. Position the caps for installation in their original locations.

To install:

14. Oil the camshaft and install with the IN camshaft on the intake side and EX camshaft on the exhaust side.

NOTE: The dowel pin in each camshaft and the crankshaft timing mark must all be located at the 12 o'clock position during installation to prevent valve and piston damage.

15. Install all bearing caps, except for the forward pair, in their original positions. Uniformly tighten the cap bolts to 124 inch lbs. (14 Nm).

16. Install 1 camshaft sprocket pilot bolt in each camshaft and tighten to 124 inch lbs. (14 Nm) in order to pull the camshaft fully forward and align the sprocket support for installation of the sprockets onto the camshafts.

17. Remove the 4 sprocket support bolt/blocks and nuts. The torque axis mount system requires the fixture to remain in place longer.

18. Verify that the camshafts are fully positioned forward and install the 2 forward bearing caps and the upper chain guide. The caps are marked E1 or I1 for exhaust or intake and must be positioned with their arrows pointing towards the sprockets. Tighten the cap bolts to 124 inch lbs. (14 Nm).

19. Make sure the camshaft dowel pin aligns with the slot in each camshaft sprocket. If necessary, rotate the camshaft slightly (1–2 degrees), then move each sprocket from the adapter onto the end of the camshaft. Fully seat each sprocket on the end of each camshaft.

20. Remove the 2 sprocket pilot bolts and adapters while using a wrench on the camshaft flats to assure the camshafts cannot move.

21. Remove the support angled fixture.

22. Install the camshaft sprocket retaining bolts and washers. Hold the camshafts and tighten the bolts to 76 ft. lbs. (103 Nm).

23. Verify all visible timing marks and holes are in alignment. If necessary, turn the crankshaft clockwise until the mark on the crankshaft pulley aligns with the mark on the front cover. Insert 3/16 in. drill bits through the camshaft sprocket alignment holes, into the cylinder head. If the alignment pins cannot be inserted, turn the crankshaft 360 degrees clockwise and repeat. If the pins can-

not be inserted within 1–2 degrees of either TDC position, the camshafts are not properly timed. Do not start the engine until the camshafts are timed.

24. Apply a small drop of RTV across the cylinder head and front cover T-joints. Inspect the old camshaft cover gasket and replace if damaged. Install the gasket and the camshaft cover. Tighten the fasteners in proper sequence to 89 inch lbs. (10 Nm).

25. Install the right splash shield and wheel, if removed to observe the timing marks.

26. Install the PCV and fresh air hoses, the EGR valve solenoid attaching screw and the spark plug wires.

27. Install the serpentine drive belt and connect the negative battery cable.

28. Start the engine and check for leaks.

Piston and Connecting Rod

POSITIONING

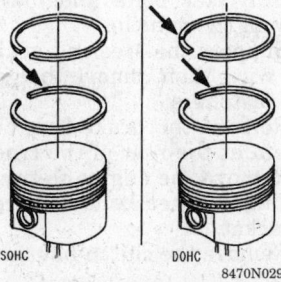

8470N029

Only the top ring on the DOHC engine and the second ring on both engines have pip marks. The top ring on the SOHC engine can be installed with either side up.

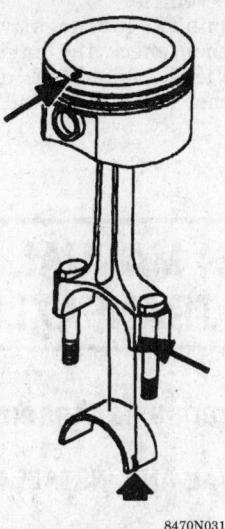

8470N031

Piston and connecting rod positioning — align the mark on top of the piston with the front of the engine. Assemble the connecting rod to the piston with the bearing tang slots directed toward the exhaust manifold side.

ENGINE LUBRICATION

Oil Pan

REMOVAL AND INSTALLATION

1. Raise and support the vehicle safely, then drain the engine oil.

2. Remove the front exhaust pipe.

3. Remove the right wheel and splash shield, then loosen the 4 front motor mount-to-block or motor-to-front cover bolts. Back the bolts out about ½ inch (12mm).

4. Remove all the oil pan bolts. For vehicles with a manual transaxle, an 8mm flex socket may be used to access the rear oil pan bolts next to the flywheel.

5. Using SA9123E, or an equivalent RTV cutter tool, separate the oil pan from the engine. Drive the tool around the pan to shear the RTV seam, then tap the pan sideways with a rubber mallet to loosen.

6. Pry the engine mount away from the engine as necessary and remove the oil pan.

To install:

7. Carefully clean the gasket mating surfaces with a scraper and solvent.

8. Apply a 0.16 inch (4mm) bead of RTV sealer to the pan flange, towards the inside of the bolt holes.

9. Install the oil pan within 3 minutes and tighten the bolts to 80 inch lbs. (9 Nm).

10. Tighten the front mount-to-block bolts to 52 ft. lbs. (70 Nm) or the mount-to-front cover bolts to 37 ft. lbs. (50 Nm).

11. Install the right splash shield and wheel.

12. Install the exhaust pipe. Tighten the pipe-to-manifold nuts in a crosswise pattern to 23 ft. lbs. (31 Nm) and the pipe-to-converter bolts to 33 ft. lbs. (45 Nm).

13. Lower the vehicle and properly fill the engine crankcase.

14. Start the engine and check for leaks.

Oil Pump

REMOVAL AND INSTALLATION

1. Disconnect the negative battery cable and drain the engine oil.

2. Remove the timing chain front cover which contains the oil pump assembly.

3. Remove the oil pump cover Torx® bolts using a suitable impact driver. Because the pump cover screws are coated with a sealant to prevent oil leakage, they must be replaced when removed.

4. Remove the drive rotor and driven rotor.

5. If necessary, remove the relief valve using tool SA9103E or equivalent, to pull the valve from the bore. Because the puller jaws will damage the relief valve sealing seat, the valve cannot be used again when removed.

To install:

6. If removed, install a new relief valve into the cover bore. Coat the valve with clean engine oil and tap it into the bore using a hammer and SA9103E or an equivalent installer tool.

NOTE: Whenever the oil pump is installed, the assembly must be packed with petroleum jelly in order to prime the pump.

7. Install the drive and driven rotors into the pump with the chamfer toward the front oil seal.

8. Make sure the front cover bolt holes are clean, then install the pump body cover and secure using new bolts that are coated with sealant to prevent oil leakage. Tighten the bolts to 97 inch lbs. (11 Nm).

9. Install the timing chain cover and oil pump assembly to the front of the engine.

10. Properly fill the engine crankcase, then start the engine and check for leaks.

CHECKING

1. With the timing chain front cover and the oil pump body cover removed, use a feeler gauge to measure the clearance between the driven rotor and pump body. Clearance should not exceed 0.0042 in. (0.105mm).

2. Use a feeler gauge and measure the clearance between the both rotor tips. Clearance should not exceed 0.006 in. (0.150mm).

3. Using Plastigage®, install the pump cover to measure the gerotor assembly-to-cover clearance. Clearance should not exceed 0.005 in. (0.128mm).

Rear Main Bearing Oil Seal

REMOVAL AND INSTALLATION

Both engines use a 1-piece round seal.

1. Disconnect the negative battery cable.

2. Remove the transaxle assembly from the vehicle.

3. Remove the flywheel assembly.

4. Use the pry tangs provided in the carrier to remove the seal with a small prybar. Be careful not to damage the crankshaft oil seal lip contact surface.

To install:

5. Clean the carrier and crankshaft with solvent and shop rag to prevent damage during installation. Check for scores or damage to the sealing surfaces.

6. Oil the seal install using a seal installer SA9121E or equivalent. The tool is designed to prevent seal lip from rolling during installation and will seat the seal 0.04 inch (1mm) lower than the factory seal. Never tap on the seal or seal installer with a hammer.

7. Install the flywheel assembly.

8. Install the transaxle assembly into the vehicle.

9. Connect the negative battery cable, then check the engine crankcase oil level and add, as necessary.

10. Start the engine and check for leaks.

MANUAL TRANSAXLE

Transaxle Assembly

REMOVAL AND INSTALLATION

1. Properly disable the SIR system, if equipped and disconnect the negative battery cable.

2. Remove the 2 air inlet duct fasteners, disengage the air temperature sensor connector and remove the air inlet duct. For the DOHC engine, loosen the flex tube-to-air box clamp, remove the 3 air box fasteners and remove the air box.

3. Remove the transaxle strut-to-cradle bracket through bolt located on the radiator side of the transaxle. Loosen the transaxle strut-to-transaxle bracket fasteners, then position the transaxle strut out of the way.

4. Disengage the backup light switch and vehicle speed sensor electrical connectors from the transaxle. Remove the vent tube retaining clip.

5. Remove the 2 ground terminals from the top 2 clutch housing studs, then unclip the oxygen sensor wire from the clutch housing.

6. Remove the top 2 clutch housing studs.

7. Remove the 4 EI coil to clutch housing bolts, then wire the coil to the cylinder head coolant outlet. Discard the old coil retaining bolts and replace with new coated fasteners upon installation.

8. Remove the shifter cables from the shift arms and clutch housing, taking care not to damage the cable boot.

--- **WARNING** ---
Do not use power tools when loosening and removing the slave cylinder. The use of a power tool to remove the slave cylinder could result in breaking off the hydraulic line.

---

9. Rotate the clutch slave cylinder 1/4 turn counterclockwise while pushing into the clutch housing, then remove the cylinder from the housing. Remove the 2 clutch hydraulic damper-to-clutch housing bolts, then wire the hydraulic assembly to the battery tray.

10. Wire the radiator to the upper radiator support in order to hold the assembly in place when the cradle is removed.

11. Install SA9105E or an equivalent engine support bar assembly.

12. Raise and support the vehicle safely, then remove the drain plug from the lower center of the housing and drain the transaxle fluid.

13. Remove the front wheels and engine splash shields from the vehicle. For coupes, remove the left and right lower facia braces.

14. Remove the front engine strut cradle bracket-to-cradle nuts from below the cradle.

15. Remove the transaxle mount-to-cradle nut from under the cradle.

16. Remove the front exhaust pipe nuts at the manifold, then disconnect the pipe from the support bracket.

17. Remove the front pipe to catalytic converter bolts and lower the pipe from the vehicle.

18. Support the steering gear with safety wire, then remove the gear-to-cradle fasteners.

19. Remove the brake line bracket push pin at the rear of the cradle.

20. Remove the engine-to-transaxle stiffening bracket bolts and remove the bracket.

21. Remove the clutch housing dust cover.

22. Remove and discard the cotter pins from the lower ball joints. Back the ball joint nut until the top of the nut is even with the top of the threads.

23. Use tool SA9132S to separate the lower control arm ball joint from the steering knuckle, then pull down on the lower control arm and remove the nut. Do not use a wedge tool or seal damage may occur.

NOTE: The outer CV-joint for vehicles equipped with ABS contains a speed sensor ring. Use of an incorrect tool to separate the control arm from the knuckle may result in damage and loss of the ABS system.

24. Use a prybar to separate the left side axle from the transaxle. Only remove the axle sufficiently to install SA91112T or an equivalent seal protector around the axle and into the seal to prevent the seal from being cut by the shaft spline.

25. Position two 4 inch x 4 inch x 36 inch pieces of wood onto a powertrain support dolly, then position the dolly under the vehicle.

26. Remove the 4 cradle-to-body bolts, then carefully lower the cradle from the vehicle with the support dolly. Tape or wire the 2 large washers from the rear cradle-to-body attachments in position to prevent loss.

27. Support the transaxle securely with a suitable jack.

28. Remove the 2 bottom clutch housing-to-engine bolts and install a guide bolt into the bottom rear clutch housing bolt hole from the side of the engine block.

29. Carefully separate the transaxle from the engine enough to clear the intermediate shaft and lower the transaxle from the vehicle.

To install:

30. Place the transaxle assembly securely onto the jack and position under the vehicle.

31. Install axle seal protectors into seals on both sides, then place the transaxle in any gear.

32. Raise the transaxle into the vehicle guiding the unit onto the intermediate shaft. While guiding the transaxle onto the shaft, rotate the shaft back and forth to align the splines. When aligned, continue to rotate the intermediate shaft until the input shaft splines are aligned with the clutch.

33. Verify that the intermediate shaft splines are aligned with the differential side gear spline and the input shaft splines are aligned with the clutch disc splines, then install the 2 lower clutch housing-to-engine bolts and tighten to 96 ft. lbs. (130 Nm). The bolts should not be used to draw the transaxle to the engine.

34. Install the left side axle into the transaxle and remove the seal protectors. Lower the transaxle jack.

35. Clean and lubricate the ball joint threads, then raise the cradle up on the support dolly and place the ball joints into the knuckles.

36. Verify the correct positioning of the lower control arm bar studs to the knuckles, the cooling module support bushings, the engine strut bracket and the transaxle mount.

37. Insert 9/16 in. round steel rods into the cradle-to-body alignment holes near the front cradle-to-body fastener holes. Guide the cradle into position making sure all mount studs are properly guided into their holes.

38. Make sure the washers are in place, then install the 2 rear cradle to body bolts. Verify proper cradle positioning and install the 2 front cradle bolts. Tighten the 4 cradle bolts to 151 ft. lbs. (205 Nm).

39. Remove the support dolly and lower the vehicle sufficiently for underhood access. Remove the engine support bar assembly.

40. Install the transaxle strut, and if removed, the transaxle bracket-to-transaxle bolts. Tighten the fasteners to 40 ft. lbs. (54 Nm). Install the remaining transaxle strut fasteners, as applicable, and tighten to 52 ft. lbs. (70 Nm).

41. Remove the radiator assembly support wire.

42. Use a 6 x 1.0mm tap to clean the sealant from the ignition module mounting holes in the transaxle. Install the ignition module and the new bolts with sealant. Use extreme caution to assure proper bolt installation. Tighten the bolts to 71 inch lbs. (8 Nm) and verify that the bolt heads are properly seated on the ignition module.

43. Install the 2 top clutch housing-to-engine studs and tighten to 66 ft. lbs. (90 Nm). Connect the 2 ground terminals to the studs and tighten to 18 ft. lbs. (25 Nm).

44. Engage the vehicle speed sensor and backup light switch electrical connectors to the transaxle.

45. Install the vent hose clip and the oxygen sensor wire clip to the housing.

46. Connect the shift control cables to the shift arms and the clutch housing, then install the cable retainers.

47. Remove the support wire from the battery tray, position the damper, then install the 2 slave cylinder-to-clutch housing nuts and tighten to 18 ft. lbs. (25 Nm). Push the actuator into the clutch housing and rotate 1/4 turn clockwise, then install the retaining clip. Check that the master cylinder at the front of dash connection is locked in place.

48. For DOHC engines, install the air box and tighten the fasteners to 89 inch lbs. (10 Nm). Connect the flex tube to the air box, align the arrows and tighten the clamp to 18 inch lbs. (2 Nm).

49. Install the air inlet duct and fasteners, then engage the air temperature sensor electrical connector.

50. Raise and support the vehicle safely.

51. Install the transaxle mount-to-cradle fastener and tighten to 52 ft. lbs. (70 Nm), then install the 2 engine strut cradle bracket-to-cradle fasteners to 52 ft. lbs. (70 Nm).

52. Remove the steering gear support wire and position the gear to the cradle. Install the gear bolts and nuts, then tighten the fasteners to 40 ft. lbs. (54 Nm). Connect the brake line and retainer to the cradle.

53. Install the clutch housing dust cover and tighten the fasteners to 89 inch lbs. (10 Nm).

54. Install the powertrain stiffening bracket and tighten the retainers to 35 ft. lbs. (47 Nm).

55. Position the front exhaust pipe into the vehicle, then install the gasket and the manifold retaining nuts. Tighten the nuts in a crosswise pattern to 23 ft. lbs. (31 Nm). Install the front pipe to the catalytic converter and tighten the bolts to 33 ft. lbs. (45 Nm). Finally, install the front pipe to the transaxle support bracket and tighten the fasteners to 23 ft. lbs. (31 Nm).

NOTE: If the converter flange threads are damaged use the Saturn 21010753 converter fastener kit in place of the self tapping screws in order to provide proper clamp load and prevent exhaust leaks.

56. Install the nuts onto the ball joint studs and tighten to 55 ft. lbs. (75 Nm). Continue to tighten the nuts as necessary and install new cotter pin.

57. Install the center and both wheel splash shields.

58. For coupes, install the right left lower facia braces and J-nuts. Tighten the fasteners to 89 inch lbs. (10 Nm).

59. If not done already, install the transaxle drain plug and tighten to 40 ft. lbs. (45 Nm). For 1992 vehicles, the drain plug seal should be replaced each time the plug is removed.

60. Install the tire and wheel assemblies, then lower the vehicle.

61. Connect the negative battery cable and fill the transaxle with automatic transaxle fluid, Dexron® IIE or equivalent.

62. If equipped, properly enable the SIR system.

63. Check the vehicle alignment and adjust as necessary.

CLUTCH

Clutch Assembly

REMOVAL AND INSTALLATION

1. Properly disable the SIR system, if equipped, and disconnect the negative battery cable.
2. Remove the transaxle from the vehicle.
3. Unsnap the release fork from the ball stud, then remove the fork and bearing from the vehicle. Slide the bearing from the fork.

NOTE: The release bearing is packed with grease and should not be washed with solvent.

4. Remove the pressure plate-to-flywheel bolts using a progressive criss-cross pattern to slowly release spring pressure and prevent cover warpage, then remove the pressure plate and clutch disc.
5. Inspect the flywheel for scores, warpage or burnt spots. Repair or replace as necessary.
To install:
6. If removed, install the flywheel and tighten the bolts in a criss-cross sequence to 59 ft. lbs. (80 Nm).
7. Install the clutch disc and pressure plate with the yellow dot on the pressure plate aligned as close as possible to the mark on the flywheel. The clutch disc is labeled FLYWHEEL SIDE in order to help correctly position the disc.
8. Install clutch alignment tool SA9145T or equivalent, in the clutch disc and push in until it bottoms out in the crankshaft, then start the pressure plate bolts.
9. Tighten the pressure plate bolts using multiple passes of a crisscross sequence to 18 ft. lbs. (25 Nm), then remove the alignment tool.
10. Lube the fork pivot point with high temperature grease, then install the release bearing to the fork. Do not lube the release bearing or bearing quill.
11. Snap the fork and bearing assembly onto the ball stud.
12. Lube the splines of the input shaft lightly with a high temperature grease.
13. Install the transaxle assembly.

14. Connect the negative battery cable and if equipped, properly enable the SIR system.

PEDAL HEIGHT/FREE-PLAY ADJUSTMENT

The hydraulic clutch release system is adjusted automatically. No periodic adjustment is necessary or possible.

Clutch Master and Slave Cylinder Assembly

REMOVAL AND INSTALLATION

NOTE: The master cylinder, pipes and slave cylinder are part of a complete fluid filled and bled assembly that must be replaced as a single unit.

1. Block the clutch pedal to prevent it from being depressed while the slave cylinder is remove from the transaxle.
2. Remove the air intake duct.
3. Check to make sure the hydraulic system has sufficient fluid and, add if necessary.
4. Rotate the slave cylinder about ¼ turn counterclockwise while pushing toward the bellhousing in order to

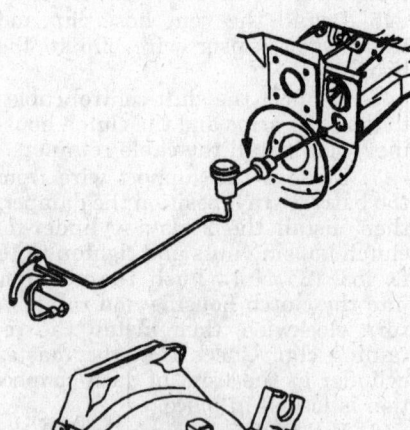
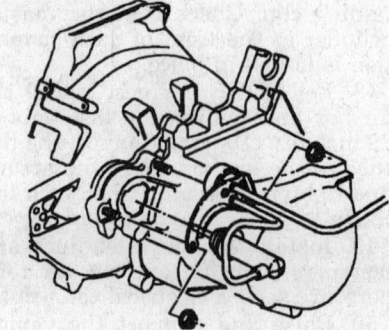

8470N035

Hydraulic clutch release system installation — removal is in the opposite direction

disengage the bayonet connector and remove the cylinder from the clutch housing. Remove the slave cylinder bracket retaining nuts and pull the assembly from the studs.
5. Remove the master cylinder pushrod retaining clip and disconnect the pushrod from the clutch pedal.
6. Turn the clutch cylinder about ⅛ turn clockwise and remove from the instrument panel.
To install:
7. Position the master cylinder to the dash with the reservoir leaning toward the driver's fender. Install and turn about ⅛ turn counterclockwise to lock in position.
8. Slide the slave cylinder onto the clutch housing studs, install the nuts and tighten to 18 ft. lbs. (25 Nm).

NOTE: When installing a new assembly, the plastic retainer straps should remain in place on the slave cylinder to ensure the actuator rod seats on the release fork pocket upon installation. If reinstalling an assembly, be sure to position a new plastic retainer strap onto the end of the pushrod and attach the straps to the cylinder.

9. Insert the slave cylinder into the housing with the hydraulic line facing downward and rotate about ¼ turn clockwise while pushing into the housing.
10. Lube the clutch pedal pin with silicone grease, then connect the pushrod to the clutch pedal and install the retaining clip.
11. Install the air inlet duct assembly and connect the negative battery cable.
12. Remove the block from behind the clutch pedal and if equipped, properly enable the SIR system.
13. Start the engine and check the pedal for proper operation.

Hydraulic Clutch System Bleeding

The clutch hydraulic assembly is serviced as a complete unit which has been filled with fluid and bled of air at the factory. The unit does not require periodic checking. The system is full when the reservoir is half full.

Only DOT 3 brake fluid should be added to the system. If fluid levels drop, inspect the system, including the slave cylinder, for leakage. A slight wetting of the slave cylinder surface is normal.

Although the slave cylinder assembly contains a bleeding screw, the manufacturer warns that the system should NOT be bleed using the bleeder. The screw is used only during the original factory fluid fill.

AUTOMATIC TRANSAXLE

Transaxle Assembly

REMOVAL AND INSTALLATION

1. Properly disable the SIR system, if equipped and disconnect the negative battery cable.

2. Remove the 2 air inlet duct fasteners, disengage the air temperature sensor connector and remove the air inlet duct. For the DOHC engine, loosen the flex tube to air box clamp, remove the 3 air box fasteners and remove the air box.

3. Remove the transaxle strut-to-cradle bracket through bolt located on the radiator side of the transaxle.

4. Disengage the wiring harness connectors from the vehicle and turbine speed sensor, transaxle temperature sensor, selector switch and actuator connector from the transaxle.

5. Remove the 2 ground terminals from the top 2 converter housing studs.

6. Remove the ground wire from the neutral (selector) switch and unclip the oxygen sensor wire retainer from the converter housing.

7. Remove the top 2 converter housing studs.

8. Remove the 4 EI coil to converter housing bolts, then wire the coil to the cylinder head coolant outlet. Discard the old coil retaining bolts and replace with new bolts upon installation.

9. Wire the radiator to the upper radiator support in order to hold the assembly in place when the cradle is removed.

10. Install SA9105E or an equivalent engine support bar assembly.

11. Raise and support the vehicle safely.

12. Remove the drain plug from the transaxle housing and drain the transaxle fluid. The drain plug is on the lower cowl side of the housing and is inserted from the engine side of the vehicle.

13. Remove the front wheels and engine splash shields from the vehicle. For coupes, remove the left and right lower facia braces.

14. Remove the front engine strut cradle bracket-to-cradle nuts from below the cradle.

15. Remove the transaxle mount-to-cradle nut from under the cradle.

16. Remove and discard the cotter pin from the lower ball joints. Back the ball joint nut until the top of the nut is even with the top of the threads.

17. Use tool SA9132S to separate the lower control arm ball joint from the steering knuckle then remove the nut. Do not use a wedge tool or seal damage may occur.

NOTE: The outer CV-joint for vehicles equipped with ABS contains a speed sensor ring. Use of an incorrect tool to separate the control arm from the knuckle may result in damage and loss of the ABS system.

18. Remove the front exhaust pipe nuts at the manifold, then disconnect the pipe from the support bracket.

19. Remove the front pipe-to-catalytic converter bolts and lower the pipe from the vehicle.

20. Remove the engine-to-transaxle stiffening bracket bolts and remove the bracket.

21. Remove the steering rack-to-cradle bolts and wire the gear for support when the cradle is removed.

22. Remove the brake line from the retainer at the rear of the cradle.

23. Remove the torque converter dust cover, then remove the converter-to-flywheel bolts.

24. Position two 4 inch x 4 inch x 36 inch pieces of wood onto a powertrain support dolly and position the dolly under the vehicle.

25. Remove the 4 cradle-to-body bolts and carefully lower the cradle from the vehicle with the support dolly. Tape or wire the 2 large washers from the rear cradle-to-body attachments in position to prevent loss.

26. Squeeze the plastic tabs at the transaxle cooler line connectors and pull the lines out of the connectors. The plastic retainer should remain on the lines. Connect 1 end of a ⅜ in. rubber hose over each cooler line to prevent fluid contamination or loss.

27. If necessary for the transaxle to clear the body, lower the vehicle enough to adjust the engine support assembly and lower the transaxle side of the assembly until the valve body cover clears the frame.

28. Raise and support the vehicle safely, then support the transaxle securely with a suitable jack.

29. Use a prybar to separate the left side axle from the transaxle. Remove the axle sufficiently to install SA91112T or an equivalent seal protector around the axle and into the seal to prevent the seal from being cut by the shaft spline.

30. Remove the 2 bottom converter housing-to-engine bolts and lower the transaxle sufficiently to reach the shifter cable.

31. Separate the transaxle only sufficiently enough to install an axle seal protector on the remaining engaged axle.

32. Disconnect the transaxle shifter cable, then squeeze the retaining tabs to release the cable from the converter housing.

33. Carefully lower the transaxle from the vehicle. Use SA9165T or an equivalent transaxle cooler cleaning tool to clean the cooler and lines.

To install:

34. Place the transaxle assembly securely onto the jack and position under the vehicle. Install axle seal protectors into seals on both sides.

35. Raise the transaxle sufficiently, then connect the shifter cable to the gear selector lever and to the converter housing.

36. Raise the transaxle into the vehicle and verify that the intermediate shaft splines line up with the differential side gear splines, then install the 2 lower clutch housing-to-engine bolts and tighten to 96 ft. lbs. (130 Nm). The bolts should not be used to draw the transaxle to the engine.

37. Make sure the axle seal protectors are installed into the transaxle. Carefully install the axles to the transaxle, after the splines clear the seal, but before the axle snaps into place remove the seal protector. Push the axle all of the way into the transaxle and install the snapring. Remove the transaxle jack.

38. Clean and lubricate the ball joint threads, then raise the cradle up on the support dolly and place the ball joints into the knuckles. Verify the correct positioning of the lower control arm bar studs to the knuckles, the cooling module support bushings, the engine strut bracket and the transaxle mount.

39. Insert ⁹⁄₁₆ in. round steel rods into the cradle-to-body alignment holes near the front cradle to body fastener holes. Guide the cradle into

position making sure all mount studs are properly guided into their holes.

NOTE: The 1992 cradle differs slightly from the 1993–95 cradles in terms of height, bolt length and shim thickness. If replacing parts, be sure to use the proper fasteners. The 1993–95 cradle may be used on 1992 vehicles, provided the shorter fasteners are used.

40. Make sure the washers are in place, then install the 2 rear cradle to body bolts. Verify proper cradle positioning and install the 2 front cradle bolts, then tighten the 4 cradle bolts to 151 ft. lbs. (205 Nm).

41. Remove the support dolly and lower the vehicle sufficiently for underhood access. Remove the engine support bar assembly.

42. For 1992–93 vehicles, install the transaxle strut-to-cradle bracket through bolt and nut, then tighten the fasteners to 52 ft. lbs. (70 Nm). If removed, install the strut cradle bracket-to-cradle bolt and also tighten to 52 ft. lbs. (70 Nm).

43. Remove the radiator assembly support wire.

44. Use a 6 x 1.0mm tap to clean the sealant from the ignition module mounting holes in the transaxle. Install the ignition module, then secure using the new bolts with sealant. Use extreme caution to assure proper bolt installation. Tighten the bolts to 71 inch lbs. (8 Nm) and verify that the bolt heads are properly seated on the ignition module.

45. Install the 2 top converter housing to engine studs and tighten to 66 ft. lbs. (90 Nm). Connect the 2 ground terminals to the studs and tighten to 19 ft. lbs. (25 Nm).

46. Engage the actuator circuit connector and tighten to 22 inch lbs. (2.5 Nm). Engage the wiring harness connectors to the vehicle and turbine speed sensors, the transaxle oil temperature sensor and the selector switch connectors.

47. Connect the ground wire to the neutral (selector) switch and clip the oxygen sensor wire to the converter housing.

48. Unplug the transaxle cooler lines and press them into the transaxle connectors until they bottom out.

49. Adjust the shifter cable, then for DOHC vehicles, install the air box and tighten the fasteners to 89 inch lbs. (10 Nm). Connect the flex tube to the air box, align the arrows and tighten the clamp to 18 inch lbs. (2 Nm).

50. Install the air inlet duct and fasteners, then engage the air temperature sensor electrical connector.

51. Raise and support the vehicle safely.

52. Install the transaxle mount-to-cradle nut and the transaxle strut cradle bracket-to-cradle nut, then tighten the nuts to 52 ft. lbs. (70 Nm).

53. Install the 2 engine strut cradle bracket-to-cradle fasteners from under the cradle and tighten to 52 ft. lbs. (72 Nm).

54. If applicable, install the nuts to the front transaxle-to-cradle studs and tighten to 35 ft. lbs. (48 Nm).

55. Remove the steering gear support wire and position the gear to the cradle. Install the gear bolts and nuts, then tighten the fasteners to 40 ft. lbs. (54 Nm).

56. Connect the brake line to the cradle retainer.

57. Install the torque converter-to-flexplate bolts and tighten to 52 ft. lbs. (70 Nm). Install the converter housing dust cover and tighten the bolts to 89 inch lbs. (10 Nm).

58. Install the powertrain stiffening bracket and tighten the bracket bolts to 35 ft. lbs. (47 Nm).

59. Position the exhaust manifold front pipe into the vehicle, then install the gasket and manifold retaining nuts. Tighten the nuts in a crosswise pattern to 23 ft. lbs. (31 Nm). Install the front pipe to the catalytic converter and tighten the bolts to 33 ft. lbs. (45 Nm). Finally, install the front pipe to the transaxle support bracket and tighten the fasteners to 23 ft. lbs. (31 Nm).

NOTE: If the converter flange threads are damaged use the Saturn 21010753 converter fastener kit in place of the self tapping screws in order to provide proper clamp load and prevent exhaust leaks.

60. Install the nuts onto the ball joint studs and tighten to 55 ft. lbs. (75 Nm). Continue to tighten the nuts as necessary and install a new cotter pin.

61. Install the center and both wheel splash shields.

62. For coupes, install the right left lower facia braces and J-nuts. Tighten the fasteners to 89 inch lbs. (10 Nm).

63. Install the tire and wheel assemblies, then lower the vehicle.

64. Connect the negative battery cable and fill the transaxle with Dexron® II or equivalent fluid.

65. Properly enable the SIR system, if equipped.

66. Warm the engine and check the transaxle fluid. Check and adjust vehicle alignment, as necessary.

SHIFT CABLE ADJUSTMENT

This procedure begins with the shift cable disconnected from the transaxle lever, but routed through the converter housing.

1. Place the transaxle in the **P** position.

2. Place the transaxle shift lever in the **P** position.

3. Release the cable adjustment lock tab by lifting upward with a small prybar.

4. Connect the cable to the shift transaxle lever and install the retainer.

5. Move the cable housing back and forth in the adjuster to note endplay, then center the cable housing in the middle of the endplay and press in the lock tab.

6. Check operation.

PARK LOCK CABLE ADJUSTMENT

1. Remove the front ashtray for access to the cable. If necessary, remove the center console assembly for additional access.

2. FTurn the ignition switch to **ON**.

3. Place the shifter in **P** and make sure the brake pedal is released.

4. If adjusting a new cable, depress the lock on the cable end fitting and remove the adjustment clip (the clip is designed to leave the appropriate gap.)

5. If adjusting a cable which does not have an adjustment clip, secure the end of the cable to provide a 0.05 inch (1.25mm) gap between the cable end and the park lock connector.

6. Verify proper adjustment by the following:

    a. With the ignition **OFF**, the lever should not shift out of **P**.

    b. Turn the ignition to the **ON** position and the lever should shift.

    c. With the lever out of **P** and the ignition **OFF**, the key cannot be removed from the ignition.

    d. With the lever out of **P** and the ignition **OFF**, the lever should shift into **P**.

    e. With the ignition **OFF** and the lever in **P**, remove the key.

7. Repeat the adjustment procedure if any of the conditions are incorrect.

8. Install the ashtray and/or console assembly when properly adjusted.

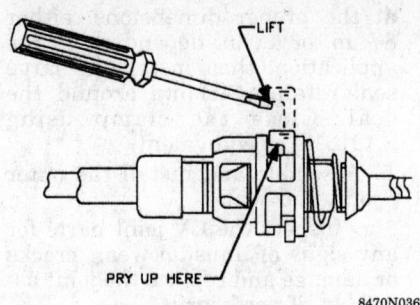

Shifter cable adjustment

A properly adjusted park lock cable will have a 0.05 in. (1.25mm) gap between the cable end and the park lock connector

DRIVE AXLE

Halfshaft

REMOVAL AND INSTALLATION

1. Remove the wheel cover or center cap, then loosen the halfshaft nut while an assistant depresses the brake pedal.
2. Raise and support the vehicle safely.
3. Remove the corresponding wheel and splash shield.
4. If removing the left side axle, drain the transaxle fluid into a suitable container.
5. Remove the halfshaft nut and washer.
6. Remove and discard the cotter pin from the lower control arm ball joint for the axle being removed. Back the ball joint nut until the top of the nut is even with the top of the threads.
7. Use tool SA9132S to separate the lower control arm ball joint from the steering knuckle, then remove

the nut. Do not use a wedge tool or seal damage may occur.

NOTE: The outer CV-joint for vehicles equipped with ABS contains a speed sensor ring. Use of an incorrect tool to separate the control arm from the knuckle may result in damage and loss of the ABS system.

8. Remove the tie rod cotter pin and castle nut, then separate the tie rod end from the knuckle using a tie rod separator SA91100C or equivalent. Do not use a wedge-type tool.
9. Place a cloth over the sway bar to protect the surface, then position a prybar over the cloth with which to apply leverage to the knuckle and separate the lower control arm ball joint. Position a cloth at the prybar contact point with the cradle, then push down on the bar and separate the ball joint from the knuckle. Make sure the knuckle does not contact and damage the ball stud seal.
10. While pulling the knuckle/strut assembly away from the halfshaft, pull the end of the halfshaft from the wheel hub. If difficulty is encountered, tap on the end of the halfshaft using a block of wood and a hammer. Support the halfshaft assembly using a length of mechanic's wire or with a jack stand.
11. If removing the right halfshaft, disconnect the halfshaft from the intermediate shaft by tapping the inner joint with a hammer using a block of wood positioned to cushion the joint from the blows. Remove the halfshaft from the vehicle.
12. If removing the left halfshaft, disconnect the halfshaft by inserting a large prybar into the space between the inner joint and transaxle. Pry the halfshaft from the transaxle being careful not to contact and damage the transaxle oil seal. Remove the halfshaft from the vehicle.

To install:

13. If installing the left side halfshaft, install SA91112T or equivalent transaxle seal protector. Install the halfshaft into the transaxle, after the splines have safely passed the transaxle oil seal, remove the seal protector and fully seat the halfshaft.
14. If installing the right side halfshaft, insert the shaft onto the intermediate shaft and push firmly to engage the circlip.
15. Insert the outer end of the halfshaft into the wheel hub. Be careful not to damage the CV-joint boot.
16. Thoroughly clean and lubricate the ball joint stud threads of the lower control arm and tie rod end.

17. Install the lower control arm ball stud and install the nut, but do not tighten at this time.
18. Install the tie rod end and nut. Tighten the nut to 33 ft. lbs. (45 Nm) and install a new cotter pin. If necessary, tighten the nut additionally, but do not back off to insert the cotter pin.
19. Tighten the lower control arm ball stud nut to 55 ft. lbs. (75 Nm), tighten additionally if necessary and install a new cotter pin.
20. Install the washer and a new halfshaft nut, then tighten the nut to 145 ft. lbs. (200 Nm).
21. Install the inner splash shield and wheel.
22. Lower the vehicle and, if necessary, properly fill the transaxle.
23. Check and adjust the alignment, as necessary.

CV-Boot

REMOVAL AND INSTALLATION

1. Using soft metal or wood to protect the shaft, clamp the halfshaft to a workbench in a vise.
2. Remove and service the CV-joint from the end of the halfshaft, as follows:

  a. If the halfshaft has a damaged deflector ring, use a brass drift and hammer to remove the damaged component from the CV outer race.

  b. Either cut the outer seal retaining clamps using a side cutter or use a hammer and chisel to disengage the outer band from the inner band at the retaining peg on both the large and small seal clamps, then discard the clamps.

  c. Separate the joint seal from the CV-joint race at the large diameter, then slide the seal away from the joint, along the halfshaft. Wipe any excess grease from the CV inner race.

  d. Use a suitable pair of snapring pliers to spread the ears of the inner race retaining ring, then remove the CV-joint assembly from the shaft.

  e. Remove the seal from the halfshaft.

  f. If necessary, disassemble the CV-joint. Use a brass drift and gently tap on the cage until it is cocked and the first ball may be removed. Repeat this to remove the remaining balls. When the balls are removed, pivot the cage and inner race at a 90 degree angle to the center line of outer race. Cage windows should align with the lands of

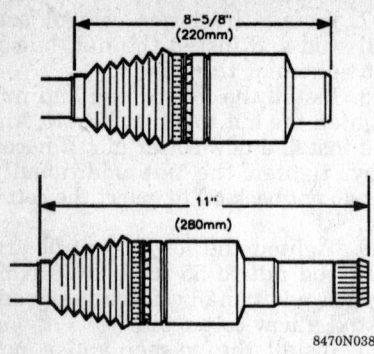

The tri-pot seal must be shaped to the proper dimension

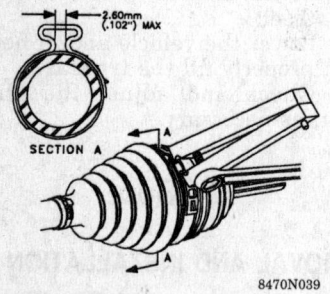

When a seal clamp is crimped, check dimension A (the inner gap between the walls of the crimp) — CV-joint large seal clamp shown

the outer race, then lift the cage and inner race. Rotate the inner race up and out of the cage. Thoroughly clean and de grease all CV-joint parts and allow to dry before assembly.

3. Remove and service the tri-pot joint and joint seal from the half-shaft's other end, as follows:

a. Cut the eared seal retaining clamp on the tri-pot seal using a side cutter, then discard the clamp.

b. Remove and discard the earless clamp using a small flat blade chisel or other suitable tool.

c. Separate the seal from the tri-pot housing at the large diameter, then slide the seal away from the joint along the halfshaft. Wipe away excess grease from the face of the tri-pot spider and the inside of the housing.

d. Remove the tri-pot housing from the spider and shaft.

e. Spread the spacer ring using SA9198C, or equivalent, and slide the spacer ring along with the tri-pot spider, back on the axle towards the repositioned seal.

f. Carefully remove the spider retaining ring from the halfshaft groove, and slide the spider assembly off the shaft. Use care not to

loose the tri-pot balls and needle rollers which may separate from the spider trunnions.

g. Remove the seal from the axle shaft.

h. Thoroughly clean and de grease the housing and allow to dry prior to assembly.

To install:

4. Install the tri-pot joint and seal:

a. Inspect the tri-pot joint components for unusual wear, cracks or damage and replace, as necessary. Clean the shaft; if rust is present in the seal mounting grooves, use a wire brush.

b. Install the small seal retaining clamp on the neck of the seal, but do not crimp.

c. Slide the seal onto the shaft and locate the neck of the seal on the halfshaft seal groove

d. Crimp the retaining clamp using SA9203C or equivalent. Measure the dimension or section A (gap between the clamp walls within the crimp) and recrimp, if necessary. Dimension A should be no more than 0.085 in. (2.15mm).

e. Install the spacer ring on the shaft and position it beyond the retaining groove, then install the spider, also past the retaining groove. Be sure the counterbored surface of the tri-pot spider faces the end of the shaft after installation.

f. Using SA9198C, or an equivalent tool, install the retaining ring to the halfshaft ring groove, then slide the tri-pot spider towards the end of the shaft and seat the spacer ring in the axle groove.

g. Place about ½ of the grease from the overhaul kit inside the seal and use the remainder to re-pack the tri-pot housing.

h. Install the convolute retainer (also supplied with the overhaul kit) over the seal. The retainer must be in position when the joint is assembled or seal damage may result.

i. Position the retaining clamp around the large diameter of the seal, the slide the tri-pot housing over the tri-pot assembly on the shaft.

j. Slide the large diameter of the seal over the outside of the tri-pot housing and locate the seal lip in the housing groove. The seal must not be dimpled or stretched. If necessary, carefully insert a thin, flat and blunt tool between the large seal opening and outer race to equalize pressure, then shape the seal by hand and remove the tool.

k. Position the tri-pot assembly at the proper dimensions, either 8⅝ in. or 11 in. depending on the application, then install the large seal retaining clamp around the seal. Close the clamp using SA9161C or equivalent.

5. Assemble and install the outer CV-joint and seal:

a. Inspect the CV-joint parts for any signs of unusual wear, cracks or damage and replace the joint assembly, if necessary.

b. If necessary, assemble the CV-joint for installation purposes. Put a light coat of grease on the inner and outer race grooves, then insert and rotate the inner race into the cage. Install the cage and inner race into the outer race with the windows of the cage aligned with the lines of the outer race. Use a brass drift to gently cock the cage/race and install the balls. If removed, install the race retaining ring into the inner race.

c. Pack the assembled joint using the premeasured amount of grease from the service kit.

d. Install the small retaining clamp on the neck of the new seal, then slide the seal onto the shaft and locate the seal neck in the shaft seal groove.

e. Crimp the seal retaining ring using SA9203C, or an equivalent crimping tool. A proper crimp will share the same dimensions of the tri-pot seal retaining ring crimp. The gap between the inner walls of the crimp should be no more than 0.085 in. (2.15mm).

f. Place about ½ of the provided grease inside the seal, then repack the CV-joint using the remaining grease.

g. Position the large seal retaining clamp around the seal.

h. Make sure the retaining ring side of the inner race is facing the halfshaft, then push the CV-joint onto the shaft until the ring is seated in the shaft groove.

i. Slide the seal large diameter over the outside of the CV-joint race and locate the lip of the seal in the housing groove. The seal must not be dimpled or stretched. If necessary, carefully insert a thin, flat and blunt tool between the large seal opening and outer race to equalize pressure, then shape the seal by hand and remove the tool.

j. Crimp the retaining clamp using the SA9203C or equivalent. The proper crimp gap dimension should be no larger than 0.102 in.

(2.6mm). Recrimp if necessary to achieve the proper dimension.

k. If removed, position the deflecting ring at the CV-joint outer race. Use SA9160C or equivalent along with a M20 x 1.5 nut to tighten the tool until the deflector bottoms against the shoulder of the CV-joint outer race.

6. Remove the shaft assembly from the vise and install in the vehicle.

Front Wheel Knuckle/Hub and Bearings

REMOVAL AND INSTALLATION

1. If equipped with ABS, disconnect the negative battery cable.

2. Loosen the front halfshaft nut, while an assistant depresses the brake pedal, then raise and support the vehicle safely.

3. Remove the wheel assembly.

4. Remove the brake caliper mounting bracket bolts and suspend the assembly from the strut spring with wire.

5. Loosen the strut-to-knuckle bolts, but do not remove at this time.

6. Remove the rotor, axle nut and washer.

7. Remove and discard the cotter pin from the lower control arm ball joint. Back the ball joint nut until the top of the nut is even with the top of the threads.

8. Use tool SA9132S to separate the lower control arm ball joint from the steering knuckle, then remove the nut. Do not use a wedge tool or seal damage may occur.

NOTE: The outer CV-joint for vehicles equipped with ABS contains a speed sensor ring. Use of an incorrect tool to separate the control arm from the knuckle may result in damage and loss of the ABS system.

9. Remove the tie rod cotter pin and castle nut, then separate the tie rod end from the knuckle using a tie rod separator SA91100C or equivalent. Do not use a wedge-type tool.

10. If equipped, disengage the ABS wheel speed sensor electrical connector.

11. Suspend the halfshaft from the body with wire, then remove the 2 knuckle-to-strut fasteners and remove the knuckle/hub assembly from the vehicle. If difficulty is encountered, position a block of wood on the end of the halfshaft and tap on the

wood with a hammer to free the hub assembly.

12. If necessary, disassemble the knuckle hub assembly as follows:

a. If equipped, remove the ABS wheel speed sensor from the knuckle.

NOTE: Any time the hub or bearing is separated from the steering knuckle, a new bearing must be used upon assembly.

b. Install wheel bearing removing tools SA9159S or equivalent, to the knuckle and secure the assembly in a vice.

c. Hold the hub driver with a wrench and tighten the hub driver screw to remove the hub. If the inner bearing race is pulled out with the hub, remove the race with a bearing race remover.

d. Remove the assembly from the vice and separate the wheel hub removal tool from the knuckle.

e. Remove the bearing retainer snapring.

f. Position the knuckle in a shop press on a knuckle support tube and press the bearing from the knuckle with a suitable small driver.

To install:

13. If necessary, assemble the knuckle hub assembly as follows:

a. Use a suitable large driver and press in the new bearing until seats.

b. Use the small driver and the knuckle support tube to press in the hub assembly. The small driver must be used to support the bearing inner race with its small (pilot) side facing towards the press and away from the bearing.

c. Install the bearing retainer snapring.

d. If equipped, install the ABS wheel speed sensor into the knuckle and tighten the fastener to 6 ft. lbs. (8 Nm).

NOTE: Service knuckles may not have holes for brake dust shield mounting. The dust shield is no longer required and does not have to be reinstalled. Also, should the shield become damaged it may be removed, there is no need to repair or replace it. But, should a shield be removed and discarded, the shield should also be removed from the opposite side to maintain balance/symmetry.

14. Thoroughly clean and lubricate the ball joint stud threads of the lower control arm and tie rod end. Install the knuckle/hub assembly

onto the axle shaft. Then install the washer with a new nut, but do not tighten the nut at this time.

15. Install the lower control arm ball stud through the knuckle bore and install the nut, but do not tighten at this time.

16. Install the steering knuckle-to-strut fasteners, but do not tighten at this time.

17. Install the tie rod end and nut, then tighten the nut to 33 ft. lbs. (45 Nm) and install a new cotter pin. If necessary, tighten the nut additionally, do not back off to insert the cotter pin.

18. Push inward on the bottom of the strut and tighten the knuckle fasteners to 148 ft. lbs. (200 Nm).

19. Tighten the lower control arm ball stud nut to 55 ft. lbs. (75 Nm), tighten additionally if necessary and install a new cotter pin.

20. Install the rotor onto the hub, then install the caliper mount bracket onto the knuckle. Tighten the mount bracket assembly bolts to 81 ft. lbs. (110 Nm).

21. If equipped, engage the ABS electrical connector to the wheel speed sensor.

22. While an assistant depresses the brake pedal, tighten the halfshaft nut to 148 ft. lbs. (200 Nm).

23. Install the wheel assembly and lower the vehicle.

24. Connect the negative battery cable, check and adjust the alignment, as necessary.

STEERING

Steering Wheel

REMOVAL AND INSTALLATION

Without Air Bag

1. Disconnect the negative battery cable.

2. Remove the horn pad by pulling on the edge of the pad firmly, disconnect the wires and remove the horn pad from the vehicle.

3. Remove the clip on the end of the steering column shaft, then remove the wheel retaining nut.

4. Note the position of the steering wheel locating notch for reassembly purposes.

5. Install a suitable steering wheel puller and remove the wheel from the steering column.

To install:

6. Route the wires through the wheel and position the steering wheel making sure to properly align the locating notch. If the locating notch is not properly positioned, any attempt to install the steering wheel will damage the wheel and column beyond repair.

7. Install a new steering wheel nut and tighten to 30 ft. lbs. (40 Nm), then install a new clip on the end of the column.

8. Connect the wires to the horn pad and press the pad firmly into position on the wheel.

9. Connect the negative battery cable.

With Air Bag

— **CAUTION** —

When the vehicle is equipped with a Supplemental Inflatable Restraint (SIR) system, follow the recommended disarming procedures before performing any work on or around the system. Failure to do so may result in possible deployment of the air bag and/or personal injury.

1. Properly disable the SIR system and disconnect the negative battery cable.

2. Loosen the 4 fasteners from the back of the steering wheel and lift the inflator module from the wheel.

3. Remove the CPA device and unplug the wiring harness from the module, then remove the inflator module from the steering wheel.

— **CAUTION** —

When carrying a live inflator module, ensure the bag and trim cover are pointed away from the body. Never carry the inflator module by the wires or connector on the underside of the module. This will minimize the chance of injury should the module accidentally deploy. When placing a live inflator module on a bench or other surface, always place the bag and trim cover up, away from the surface. This is necessary so a free space is provided to allow for air bag expansion in the unlikely event of accidental deployment.

4. Unplug the horn connector and, if equipped, unplug the cruise control switch connector.

5. Remove the clip steering wheel retaining nut.

6. Note the position of the steering wheel locating notch for reassembly purposes.

7. Install a suitable steering wheel puller and remove the steering wheel from the steering column while extracting the wiring from the wheel.

8. Install a yellow retaining tab into the SIR coil assembly to keep it from rotating. If a retaining tab is not available, tape the coil in position to prevent coil damage.

To install:

9. Route the SIR wire and other electrical connections through the wheel, then position the steering wheel making sure to properly align the locating notch. If the locating notch is not properly positioned, any attempt to install the steering wheel will damage the wheel and column beyond repair.

10. Remove the yellow retaining tab or the tape from the SIR coil assembly.

11. Install a new steering wheel nut and tighten to 30 ft. lbs. (40 Nm).

12. Connect the wiring harness to the horn and, if equipped, to the cruise control switch.

13. Position the inflator module and connect the SIR wiring harness, then seat the module on the steering wheel.

14. Secure the module using NEW fasteners, then tighten the new fasteners to 89 inch lbs. (10 Nm).

15. Connect the negative battery cable and enable the SIR system. Check for proper system function by watching the AIR BAG indicator lamp.

Steering Column

REMOVAL AND INSTALLATION

1. Properly disable the SIR system, if equipped, and disconnect the negative battery cable.

2. Remove the steering wheel.

3. Remove the 2 retaining screws and the upper column cover from the steering column.

4. Remove the ignition lock bezel, then remove the 2 retaining screws and remove the lower column cover.

5. Disconnect the velcro fasteners, then remove the left and right lower trim panel extensions by pulling them out of the 2 upper fasteners on each side.

6. Carefully remove the center radio finish panel/air outlet assembly by pulling outward at the clip locations. Start at the bottom and move upward. Do not use tools that might damage the trim panel. For 1993–95 vehicles, so equipped, disconnect the

wiring from the traction control/fog lamp switch.

7. If necessary, remove the trim panel extension strip by pulling out at the fastener location.

8. Remove the 2 instrument panel top cover screw caps and screws. Carefully remove the cover by lifting at the rear edge to disengage the retaining clips and by sliding the panel out of the windshield clips.

9. Remove the 4 cluster trim panel attaching screws. Carefully pull the cluster trim panel upward/outward to disengage it from the retainers.

10. Remove the CPA devices, then disengage the electrical connectors from the instrument panel lighting and rear window defogger switches. Remove the cluster trim panel from the vehicle.

11. Remove the 6 screws attaching the steering column opening filler, then carefully remove the assembly. Protect the console from the damage when removing the assembly.

12. Remove the CPA device and disconnect the wires from the lever control switch, then remove the switch from the column.

13. Remove the 2 retaining screws, then remove the switch connector.

14. Remove the 2 retaining screws, disconnect the ignition switch from the ignition module and remove the switch from the vehicle.

15. Remove the 2 upper steering column bolts and carefully lower the column onto the seat.

16. Remove the upper bolt from the intermediate shaft and disconnect the shaft from the column.

17. For coupes, unplug the hand wheel sensor electrical connector.

18. Remove the 2 lower bolts and disconnect the column at the hinge point. Verify that all wires are removed from the column and carefully remove the column from the vehicle.

To install:

19. Install the steering column into the vehicle and position at the hinge point.

20. Connect the intermediate shaft, install the bolt and tighten to 33 ft. lbs. (45 Nm).

21. For coupes, engage the hand wheel sensor electrical connector.

22. Position column component wires as necessary, then raise the column into place and install the upper column bolts. Tighten the steering column fasteners to 26 ft. lbs. (35 Nm).

23. Install the combination switch and retaining bolts. Tighten the lower mounting bolt first to assure proper location and seating.

24. Install the bolts retaining the combination switch connector, then connect the switch electrical connectors and insert the CPA.

25. Install the ignition switch and retaining bolts to the ignition module.

26. Install the steering column opening filler and attaching screws.

27. Position the cluster trim panel in the vehicle. Engage the electrical connectors to the panel lighting and the rear defogger switches, then install the CPA devices.

28. Install the cluster trim panel into the retainers, then install and tighten the retaining screws

29. Install the rear of the instrument panel top cover into the windshield clips and snap the panel into position. If necessary, replace the 6 rearward clips. Install the upper panel cover screws and screw caps.

30. For 1993–95 vehicles so equipped, engage the traction control/fog lamp connector.

31. Install the trim panel extension strip and push the center radio finish panel/air outlet assembly into the clip locations.

32. Install the lower left and right trim panel extensions.

33. Install the steering column covers and the ignition bezel.

34. Install the steering wheel.

35. Connect the negative battery cable and, if equipped, properly enable the SIR system.

Manual Rack and Pinion

REMOVAL AND INSTALLATION

1. Disconnect the negative battery cable, then raise and support the vehicle safely.

2. Remove the front tires and the left inner splash shield.

3. Remove and discard the tie rod cotter pins, then remove the castle nuts. Disconnect the tie rod ends using SA91100C or an equivalent separator tool. Do not use a wedge-type tool or seal damage may occur.

4. Loosen the intermediate shaft cover from the steering gear and move up enough to access the pinch bolt. Remove the pinch bolt.

5. Remove the steering gear-to-cradle fasteners, then remove the gear through the left fenderwell.

To install:

6. Install the steering gear and torque the steering gear retainers to 37 ft. lbs. (50 Nm). Be sure to use new nuts because the torque retention of the old nuts may be insufficient.

7. Position the intermediate steering shaft to the gear and tighten the pinch bolt to 35 ft. lbs. (47 Nm).

8. Thoroughly clean and lubricate the threads of the tie rod ends, then install the ends into the steering knuckles. Install the castle nuts and tighten to 33 ft. lbs. (45 Nm), then install new cotter pins. If necessary, tighten the nut additionally to install the pin, but do not back off the torque specification.

9. Install the left inner splash shield and install the front wheels.

10. Lower the vehicle and connect the negative battery cable.

11. Check alignment and adjust vehicle toe, as necessary.

ADJUSTMENT

Steering gear bearing preload adjustment is the same for both manual and power rack and pinion units.

Power Rack and Pinion

REMOVAL AND INSTALLATION

1. Disconnect the negative battery cable, then raise and support the vehicle safely.

2. Remove both front tires and the left inner splash shield.

3. Remove and discard the tie rod cotter pins, then remove the castle nuts. Disconnect the tie rod ends using SA91100C or an equivalent separator tool. Do not use a wedge-type tool or seal damage may occur.

4. Loosen the intermediate shaft cover from the steering gear and move up enough to access the pinch bolt. Remove the pinch bolt.

5. Place a suitable container under the steering assembly. Disconnect the pressure and return lines at the steering gear and allow the system to drain.

6. Remove the steering gear-to-cradle fasteners, then remove the gear through the left fenderwell.

To install:

7. Install the steering gear and tighten the steering gear fasteners to 37 ft. lbs. (50 Nm). Be sure to use new nuts because the torque retention of the old nuts may be insufficient.

8. Position the intermediate steering shaft to the gear and tighten the pinch bolt to 35 ft. lbs. (47 Nm).

9. Connect the pressure and return hoses, then tighten the fittings to 20 ft. lbs. (27.5 Nm).

10. Thoroughly clean and lubricate the threads of the tie rod ends, then install the ends into the steering

knuckles. Install the castle nuts and tighten to 33 ft. lbs. (45 Nm), then install new cotter pins. If necessary, tighten the nut additionally to install the pin, do not back off.

11. Install the left inner splash shield and install the front wheels.

12. Lower the vehicle and connect the negative battery cable.

13. Check alignment and adjust vehicle toe, as necessary.

14. Bleed the power steering system.

ADJUSTMENT

1. Center the steering wheel, then raise and support the vehicle safely.

2. Loosen the locknut on the steering gear adjuster plug, then turn the adjuster plug clockwise until it bottoms in the gear housing.

3. Tighten the plug to 106 inch lbs. (12 Nm).

4. Back off the adjuster plug 50–70 degrees (about 1 nut flat).

5. While holding the plug steady, tighten the locknut with a crows foot wrench to 52 ft. lbs. (70 Nm).

6. Check the steering for returnability, binding or difficulty in turning.

Power Steering Pump

REMOVAL AND INSTALLATION

1. Disconnect the negative battery cable.

2. Remove the pump reservoir fill cap.

3. Raise and support the vehicle safely.

4. Place a suitable container under the power steering hoses, then remove the hoses from the steering gear and allow the system to drain.

NOTE: Once the hoses have been removed from the steering gear, do not rotate the steering wheel or additional fluid will be forced from the gear.

5. Lower the vehicle sufficiently for underhood access, if desired. Use a box end wrench to relieve the spring tension from the accessory drive belt tensioner and remove the serpentine belt from the steering pump pulley.

6. For DOHC engines, remove the pump-to-intake and pump-to-block fasteners and brackets.

7. Remove the 3 pump to block bolts and raise the pump sufficiently for access, then disconnect the electrical connector from the pump.

BACK OFF 50° TO 70° (APPROX. ONE FLAT)

8470N041

Adjusting steering gear bearing preload

8. Remove the pump, with the hoses connected, from the vehicle. If necessary, remove the pressure and return hoses from the pump.

To install:

9. If removed, install new O-ring seals, then install the pressure and return hoses. Tighten the fittings to 20 ft. lbs. (27.5 Nm).

10. Position the pump to the block and engage the electrical connector. Install the 3 retaining bolts and tighten the bolts to 28 ft. lbs. (38 Nm).

11. For DOHC engines, install the pump-to-intake and pump-to-block brackets and fasteners. Tighten the fasteners to 22 ft. lbs. (30 Nm).

12. Install the drive belt to the steering pump pulley.

13. If lowered, raise and support the vehicle safely. Connect the pressure and return hoses to the steering gear, then tighten the fittings to 20 ft. lbs. (27.5 Nm). Route the return hose, then the pressure hose into the retaining clip.

14. Lower the vehicle and fill the power steering reservoir with clean fluid.

15. Connect the negative battery cable and bleed the power steering system.

BELT ADJUSTMENT

The serpentine drive belt is automatically adjusted by a self-tensioning device. Periodic adjustments are not needed or possible.

SYSTEM BLEEDING

1. Raise and support the vehicle safely.

2. Turn the steering wheels all the way to the left and fill the reservoir to the FULL mark.

3. Bleed the system by turning the wheels from side-to-side without hit-

ting the stops. It may take several cycles to bleed the system.

4. Keep the reservoir to the FULL mark during the procedure.

5. Start the engine and check the fluid level with the engine idling. If necessary, add to bring the level to the FULL mark.

6. Return the wheels to the center position, then lower the vehicle and allow it to idle for 2–3 minutes.

7. Road test the vehicle and check for proper operation. Recheck the fluid level and make sure it is at or slightly above the full mark after the system has stabilized at normal operating temperature.

Tie Rod Ends

REMOVAL AND INSTALLATION

Outer

1. Raise and support the vehicle safely.

2. Remove the front wheel and if necessary, remove the splash shield.

3. Remove the cotter pin and nut from the tie rod end.

4. Separate the tie rod end from the knuckle with separator tool SA91100C or equivalent. Do not use a wedge-type tool or the seal may be damaged.

5. Mark the threaded portion of the steering arm for installation purposes.

6. Loosen the tie rod jam nut and thread the tie rod end off the steering shaft. Count the number of turns necessary to remove the end for installation purposes.

To install:

7. Clean the threads and grease before installation. Be sure to only lubricate the threaded portion of the stud.

8. Install the tie rod end using the same number of turns as counted during removal. Align the tie rod end to the marked location.

9. Install the tie rod to the knuckle. Install the castle nut and tighten to 33 ft. lbs. (45 Nm), then install a new cotter pin. If necessary, tighten the nut additionally, do not back off to insert the cotter pin.

10. Tighten the tie rod jam nut to 74 ft. lbs. (100 Nm).

11. Install the splash shield, if removed, then install the wheel assembly.

12. Lower the vehicle, check and adjust toe as necessary.

Inner

1. Remove the rack and pinion assembly from the vehicle.

2. Place the assembly in a holding fixture, being careful not to damage the components, then loosen the outer tie rod jam nut.

3. Unthread the outer tie rod from the inner tie rod. Count the number of turns necessary or mark for realignment.

4. Remove the outer tie rod jam nut, then remove the steering gear boot.

5. Slide the shock damper toward the steering gear and off the inner tie rod.

6. Remove the inner tie rod assembly from the steering gear. To prevent damage, place a shop cloth over the gear teeth and hold the teeth with a suitable open end wrench. If removing the right inner tie rod, the left side boot must be removed to access the teeth.

To install:

7. Remove the old Loctite® from the rack and inner tie rod threads. Then, apply an even coat of Loctite® 262 to the inner tie rod threads.

8. If removed, slide the shock damper onto the steering gear.

9. Properly hold the gear teeth and install the inner tie rod assembly onto the steering gear. Tighten the inner rod to 70 ft. lbs. (95 Nm).

10. Slide the shock damper up against the inner tie rod assembly and install the steering boot onto the gear.

11. Thread the outer tie rod jam nut onto the inner tie rod, then install the outer tie rod to the assembly. Use the same number or turns or align the marks made earlier and tighten the jam nut to 74 ft. lbs. (100 Nm).

12. Install the rack and pinion assembly to the vehicle.

13. Align the front end and bleed the power steering system, as necessary.

BRAKES

Master Cylinder

REMOVAL AND INSTALLATION

Without Anti-Lock Brakes

1. Disconnect the negative battery cable, then disengage the fluid level

connector from the side of the reservoir.

2. Remove the hydraulic pipes fittings from the master cylinder using a suitable wrench. Plug the openings to prevent system contamination or excessive fluid loss.

3. Remove the 2 master cylinder retaining nuts and remove the master cylinder from the vehicle.

To install:

4. Install the master cylinder onto the brake booster studs, then install the retaining nuts and tighten to 20 ft. lbs. (27 Nm).

5. Unplug the openings, then connect the hydraulic brake pipes to the master cylinder and tighten the fittings to 18 ft. lbs. (24 Nm).

6. Engage the wiring harness connector to the brake fluid level sensor terminal.

7. Connect the negative battery cable.

8. Properly bleed the hydraulic brake system.

With Anti-Lock Brakes

The master cylinder for ABS equipped vehicles is attached to, and removed with, the ABS control assembly.

Proportioning/Combination Valve

The valves located in the master cylinder assembly can be removed and replaced.

REMOVAL AND INSTALLATION

Although the removal and installation procedures differ between ABS and non-ABS master cylinders, the same basic component is used on both systems. The overhaul procedure is virtually the same.

1. Remove the master cylinder or the ABS control assembly, as applicable.

2. Wipe the reservoir cap with a clean cloth. Remove the cap and inspect both the cap and diaphragm for cuts, nicks, cracks or deformation and replace as necessary.

3. Empty reservoir of brake fluid.

—————— **WARNING** ——————
Do not allow brake fluid to spill on or come in contact with the vehicle's finish as it will remove the paint. In case of a spill, immediately flush the area with water.

4. For ABS units, remove the master cylinder from the control assembly.

5. Remove the brake fluid level sensor from the bottom side of the cylinder reservoir.

6. Place the master cylinder in a suitable vise and drive out the reservoir spring pins. Use a 1/8 inch punch to drive the pins, then pull the reservoir from the cylinder body.

7. Remove and discard the old reservoir O-rings from the grooves in the reservoir bayonets or from the master cylinder bores.

8. Insert a wooden dowel into the rear of the cylinder body and depress the primary piston while removing the retainer clip from the end of the cylinder.

9. Use low pressure, non-lubricated compressed air in the forward top brake fluid output port to help release the primary piston assembly and the secondary piston, seals, spring and spring retainer.

To install:

10. Clean all parts in denatured alcohol and dry with low pressure, non-lubricated compressed air.

11. Inspect the pistons and seals for nicks, cuts, cracks, wear or corrosion and replace all worn of damaged parts.

12. Check the master cylinder bore for scoring or corrosion and replace if damage is found. Do not hone the master cylinder bore and allow no abrasives to come into contact with the bore.

13. Lubricate the seals and the master cylinder bore with clean brake fluid.

14. Install the spring into the cylinder bore.

15. Install the secondary piston assembly into the bore.

16. Install the primary piston assembly into the bore.

17. Depress the primary piston assembly with a wooden dowel and install the retainer clip.

18. Lubricate the new reservoir O-rings using clean brake fluid, then install the new O-rings into the reservoir bayonet grooves. Press the reservoir straight onto the cylinder body by hand, then carefully drive in the reservoir retention spring pins.

19. Install the level sensor into the lower side of the reservoir.

20. For ABS equipped vehicles, install the master cylinder to the ABS control assembly.

21. Install the master cylinder or the ABS control assembly into the vehicle, as applicable.

22. Properly bleed the hydraulic brake system.

Power Brake Booster

Brake boosters and pushpins are matched sets. the boosters are measured during manufacture and mated with a pushpin of appropriate length. Boosters and pushpins are therefore not interchangeable, do not attempt to use an incorrect pushpin on a booster.

REMOVAL AND INSTALLATION

1. Disconnect the negative battery cable and remove the air cleaner assembly.

2. On ABS equipped vehicles, remove the battery, battery box and tray.

3. Remove the master cylinder-to-booster nuts and reposition the master cylinder in order to allow booster removal. Be careful not to bend the brake lines.

4. Disconnect the vacuum line at the check valve.

5. From under the dash, remove the booster pushrod retainer and washer, then remove the rod from the brake pedal pin.

6. Remove the 4 retaining nuts and remove the booster from the vehicle.

To install:

7. Position the booster in the vehicle, but do not install the fasteners at this time.

8. Connect the booster pushrod to the brake pedal pin with the retainer and washer, then tighten the 4 booster retaining nuts to 20 ft. lbs. (27 Nm).

9. Connect the vacuum line to the check valve.

10. Reposition the master cylinder to the brake booster studs and tighten the retaining nuts to 20 ft. lbs. (27 Nm).

11. If removed, install the battery tray, battery and cover box.

12. Install the air cleaner assembly.

13. Connect the negative battery cable.

14. Check and adjust the brake light switch, as necessary.

Brake Caliper

REMOVAL AND INSTALLATION

Front

1. Raise and support the vehicle safely, then remove the front wheel.

2. Disconnect the brake hose from the caliper. Plug the openings to prevent system contamination or excessive fluid loss.

3. Remove the lock pin and guide pin from the caliper and support.

4. Remove the caliper from the support, being careful not to damage the pin boots. Remove the pin boots from the caliper support and inspect for damage.

To install:

5. Make sure the piston is bottomed in the bore. If necessary bottom the piston by hand or using a C-clamp.

6. If removed, install the brake pads to the caliper support.

7. Lubricate the pin boots and guide pins with silicone grease. If removed, install the pin boots into the caliper support, using the pin to assure that the boot passes all the way through the support.

8. Position the caliper onto the support and over the brake pads, then lubricate the non-threaded portion of the guide and lock pins with silicone grease. Install the pins and tighten to 27 ft. lbs. (36 Nm).

9. Make sure the brake line is properly routed with loop to the rear, then install the brake hose with new washers. Tighten the fitting to 36 ft. lbs. (49 Nm).

10. Properly bleed the hydraulic brake system.

11. Install the wheel, remove the supports and carefully lower the vehicle.

Rear

1. Raise and support the vehicle safely, then remove the rear wheel.

2. Disconnect the brake hose from the caliper. Plug the openings to prevent system contamination or excessive fluid loss.

3. Slip the end of the parking cable off the parking brake lever, then remove the cable outer housing from the cable bracket with SA9151BR or an equivalent cable release tool.

4. Remove the lock pin and guide pin.

5. Remove the caliper from the support, being careful not to damage the pin boots. If necessary, remove the pin boots from the caliper support.

To install:

6. Make sure the piston is bottomed in the bore. Do not compress the piston using a C-clamp; instead the piston must be rotated into the caliper on it's threads using a piston driver tool.

7. If removed, install the brake pads to the caliper support.

8. Lubricate the pin boots and guide pins with silicone grease. If removed, install the pin boots into the caliper support, using the pin to assure that the boot passes all the way through the support.

9. Position the caliper, then lubricate the non-threaded portion of the guide and lock pins. Install the pins and tighten to 27 ft. lbs. (36 Nm).

10. Install the brake hose using new washers, then tighten the fitting to 36 ft. lbs. (49 Nm).

11. Connect the parking brake cable.

12. Properly bleed the hydraulic brake system.

13. Install the wheel assembly and lower the vehicle.

Disc Brake Pads

REMOVAL AND INSTALLATION

Front

NOTE: Always replace the brake pads in sets, both front or both rear axle assemblies.

1. Raise and support the vehicle safely and remove the front wheels.

2. Remove the caliper lower lock pins.

NOTE: The lower caliper lock pin may be removed in order to allow pivoting of the caliper upward, away from the brake pads. Be very careful not to pivot the caliper so far as to stretch or damage the brake line. To avoid the possibility of brake line damage, remove the upper guide pin and support the caliper assembly aside.

3. Either pivot the caliper up on the guide pin or remove the upper guide pin and support the caliper from the strut using a coat hanger or length of wire.

4. Remove the 2 brake pads and the pad clips from the caliper support. Discard the old pad clips.

5. Check the caliper pins, pin boots and the piston boot for deterioration or damage.

To install:

6. By hand or using a C-clamp, bottom the piston all the way into the caliper bore.

7. Carefully lift the inner edge of the piston boot by hand to release any trapped air.

8. Install new pad clips into the caliper support.

9. Install the inner and outer brake pads into the support. If installed, remove the temporary support wire from the caliper.

10. Pivot or place the caliper body on the support and upper guide pin into position. Compress the boots by hand as the caliper is positioned onto the support.

11. Lubricate the smooth ends of the removed pin(s) with silicone grease, then install the pin(s) and tighten to 27 ft. lbs. (36 Nm). Do not get grease on the pin threads.

12. Install the wheels, then lower the vehicle.

13. Prior to operating the vehicle, depress the brake pedal a few times until the brake pads are seated against the rotor.

Rear

NOTE: Always replace the brake pads in sets, both front or both rear axle assemblies.

1. Raise and support the vehicle safely, then remove the rear wheels.

2. Remove the caliper lock and guide pins.

3. Remove the caliper from the support, being careful not to damage the pin boots and suspend the caliper from a wire.

4. Remove the brake pads from the support.

To install:

5. Using SA91110NE or an equivalent piston driver tool, bottom the piston by rotating it clockwise into the caliper bore; do not use a C-clamp to press the piston into the bore.

6. Align the piston slots so they are perpendicular to the brake pads.

7. Carefully lift the inner edge of the piston boot to release any trapped air. The boot must lay flat below the level of the piston face.

8. Install new pad clips into the caliper support.

9. Install the inner and outer brake pads into the clips on the support. The pad with the wear sensor should be located outboard. The piston indentation slots should be positioned to correctly accept the brake pads.

10. Position the caliper body onto the support. Lubricate the non-threaded portion of the guide and lock pins, then install the pins and tighten to 27 ft. lbs. (36 Nm).

11. Check the position of the pad clips. If necessary, use a small suitable tool to re-seat or center the pad clips on the support. Repeat the procedure for the opposite side brake pads.

12. Install the rear wheel assemblies and lower the vehicle.

13. Prior to operating the vehicle, depress the brake pedal a few times until the brake pads are seated against the rotor.

Brake Rotor

REMOVAL AND INSTALLATION

1. Raise and support the vehicle safely, then remove the wheel assembly.

2. Remove the brake caliper from the support bracket and hang it from the suspension with wire to prevent brake line damage.

3. Remove the 2 caliper support brackets-to-knuckle mounting bolts.

4. Remove the rotor from the vehicle. If it is difficult to remove the rotor from the hub, insert two M8 x 1.25 self tapping bolts into the holes provided on the rotor and drive it from the hub.

To install:

5. Install the rotor over the hub and bearing assembly.

6. Install the caliper support bracket, then tighten the bolts to 81 ft. lbs. (110 Nm) for front caliper brackets or to 63 ft. lbs. (85 Nm) for rear caliper brackets.

7. Unwire and install the caliper.

8. Install the wheel assembly and lower the vehicle.

Brake Drums

REMOVAL AND INSTALLATION

1. Release the parking brake, then raise and support the vehicle safely.

2. Remove the rear wheel and remove the brake drum.

3. If necessary, turn the star wheel of the brake adjuster assembly to loosen the brake shoes and allow for drum removal.

Brake Shoes

REMOVAL AND INSTALLATION

NOTE: Brake shoes must be replaced as axle sets.

1. Raise and support the vehicle, then remove the wheels and brake drums.

2. Remove the lower return and adjuster springs using a universal brake spring remover. Do not over ex-

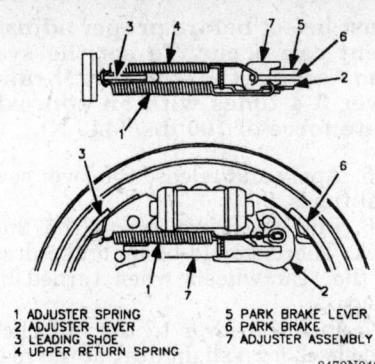

1 ADJUSTER SPRING	5 PARK BRAKE LEVER
2 ADJUSTER LEVER	6 PARK BRAKE
3 LEADING SHOE	7 ADJUSTER ASSEMBLY
4 UPPER RETURN SPRING	

8470N046

Rear brake shoe and adjuster installation

tend the springs or they will damaged and will need to be replaced.

3. Compress the leading brake shoe hold-down cup and spring while removing the pin from the rear of the backing plate. Release spring compression, then remove the hold-down cup and spring.

4. Pull the leading shoe towards the front of the vehicle and remove the adjuster assembly and lever. It may be necessary to turn the adjuster star wheel to shorten the adjuster's length.

5. Remove the leading shoe by twisting the shoe out of engagement with the upper return spring.

6. Remove the upper return spring from the park brake shoe, then remove the park brake shoe hold-down cup, spring and pin assembly.

7. Push the park brake shoe lever into the cable spring while disengaging the cable from the end lever and remove the parking brake shoe, lever and cable spring from the vehicle.

8. Remove the retainer and wave washer, then remove the park brake lever from the shoe.

9. Disassemble the brake adjuster socket, screw and nut, then clean the components in denatured alcohol. Inspect the assembly, making sure the screw threads smoothly into the adjusting nut over the full threaded length.

10. Inspect the wheel cylinder for signs of leakage and for cut or damaged boots. Do not attempt to repair a damaged cylinder, the assembly must be replaced.

To install:

11. Lubricate the adjuster assembly, the 6 backing plate raised shoe contact pads, the brake lever pin and surfaces which contact brake shoe webs with brake lubricant.

12. Install the park brake lever onto the pin on the brake shoe and secure with the wave washer and re-

tainer clip. Crimp the ends of the retainer to secure the brake lever.

13. Install the cable spring into the cage on the park brake lever, then install the cable through the spring and onto the lever.

14. Install the park brake shoe using the hold-down cup assembly; use a universal spring cup remover/installer tool. Make sure the shoe is correctly engaged into the wheel cylinder (top) and the anchor (bottom).

15. Install the long straight end of the upper return spring into the back hole in the park brake shoe, position the other brake shoe and install the other end of the spring into the back of the leading shoe.

16. Pull the lead shoe toward the front of the vehicle and install the adjuster between the park and leading brake shoes. Verify that the adjuster notches properly engage the brake shoe notches and that the shoe is properly aligned in the wheel cylinder and anchor.

17. Install the adjuster lever and adjuster spring. Make sure the notch on the lever engages the pin on the park shoe and the notch on the adjusting socket. The lower leg of the lever should engage the teeth of the star wheel adjuster assembly.

18. Secure the leading brake shoe using the hold-down cup assembly.

19. Install the adjuster spring to the upper side of the brake shoes with the short end to the lead shoe and the long end to the adjuster lever. Then install the lower return spring into the lower holes of the shoes.

20. Verify the correct location of all brake components, if necessary, use the other side brake assembly for comparison.

21. Using a suitable drum clearance gauge, measure the inner diameter of the brake drum and adjust the outside diameter of the brake shoes to 0.02 inch (0.50mm) less than the inner diameter of the drum.

22. Repeat the procedure for the opposite brake shoes and install the brake drums.

23. If the wheel cylinders have been replaced, bleed the hydraulic brake system.

24. Install the rear wheels and lower the vehicle.

25. Apply and release the brake pedal 20 times to allow the adjuster to properly position the brake shoes.

26. Check and adjust the parking brake cable, as necessary.

Wheel Cylinder

REMOVAL AND INSTALLATION

1. Raise and support the vehicle safely, then remove the wheel.
2. Remove the brake drum and shoes, as necessary for access to the cylinder.
3. Remove the bleeder valve and cap.
4. Disconnect the hydraulic brake line using a suitable wrench. Plug the line to prevent system contamination or excessive fluid loss.
5. Remove the wheel cylinder retaining bolts and remove the cylinder.

To install:

6. Install the cylinder to the backing plate, then tighten the retainers to 89 inch lbs. (10 Nm).
7. Connect the hydraulic brake line using new washers and tighten the fastener to 36 ft. lbs. (49 Nm).
8. Install the bleeder valve and cap, tighten the valve to 66 inch lbs. (7.5 Nm).
9. Install the brake shoes and drum. Be sure to properly bleed the hydraulic brake system.
10. Install the wheel assembly and lower the vehicle.

Parking Brake Cable

ADJUSTMENT

NOTE: If equipped with rear drum brakes that have been serviced, before performing parking brake adjustment procedures, apply and release the brake pedal 20 times. This allows the adjuster to position the brake shoes and prevents premature wear of the brake linings due to improper park brake adjustment.

Access to the parking brake cable adjuster may be obtained through the rear ashtray opening on the center console.

1. Remove the rear ashtray from the console. A thin stiff plastic card works well to help free the ashtray.
2. Raise and support the vehicle so the rear wheels are free to turn.
3. Pull the parking brake lever up to the 3rd click.
4. Tighten the parking brake adjuster until a light brake drag is at both rear wheels when turned by hand.

NOTE: If any of the parking brake components were replaced, the parking brake system

must be set before proper adjustment can occur. To set the system, apply the parking brake lever 3–4 times with an approximate force of 100 lbs. (445 N).

5. Apply and release the lever several times.
6. Pull the lever up to the 2nd click. There should be no brake drag at the rear wheels when turned by hand.
7. Pull the lever to the 3rd click and check for a slight drag at the rear wheels.
8. Pull the lever to the 4th click and verify the rear wheels are locked or under heavy drag.
9. Loosen or tighten the adjuster nut as necessary until these conditions are met.
10. If both rear wheels do exhibit similar drag check for damage to/incorrect installation of the drum brake components, park brake cables and/or park brake lever assembly. If any damage is found, make repairs, then return to Step 3.
11. Lower the vehicle.

REMOVAL AND INSTALLATION

1. Disconnect the negative battery cable.

Parking brake cable tie strap

Type A parking brake equalizers must be installed with the cable entry holes facing downward

2. Remove the shift knob for manual transaxles or tape the release button to the in position for automatic transaxles.
3. Remove the liner from the rear storage tray and remove the 2 screws.
4. Remove the 2 side screws at the front of the console.
5. Apply the parking brake and remove the trim plate below the parking brake handle.
6. Remove the ashtrays and disconnect the front ashtray light.
7. If equipped, remove the power window/mirror switch by pushing the switch forward and lifting the rear edge of the assembly. Unplug the electrical connectors and remove the switch from the console.
8. Remove the side panels by disconnecting the bottom velcro fasteners and pulling the panels from the upper snaps. Lift the rear of the console and press out the seat belt bezels, then remove the console.
9. Remove the adjuster nut and, if present, the spring from the threaded rod, then remove the cables from the equalizer assembly.
10. Using SA9151BR or an equivalent release tool, remove the brake cable from the console bracket.

NOTE: Before removing the cable from the vehicle, tie a piece of wire or string to the console end of the cable. After removal, the string can be used to pull the new cable through the floor pan and into position.

11. Remove the rear seat cushion.
12. Raise the rear of the vehicle and support safely, then remove the rear wheels.
13. Remove the park brake grommet/cable assembly from the floor pan. Then remove the trailing arm/park cable-to-body fasteners.
14. If equipped with a cable retaining tie strap, cut and remove the strap.
15. If equipped with drum brakes, proceed as follows:
   a. Remove the brake drum.
   b. Remove the lower return spring and the adjuster spring.
   c. Remove the park brake shoe hold-down cup assembly.
   d. Pull the park brake shoe towards the rear of the vehicle and remove the adjuster assembly.
   e. Disconnect the upper return spring from the park brake shoe.
   f. Remove the park brake cable from the park brake lever, by pushing the lever into the cable spring, while disengaging the cable end from the lever.

g. Remove the park brake cable spring.

h. Use SA9151BR or an equivalent cable release tool and remove the cable from the backing plate.

16. If equipped with disc brakes, proceed as follows:

a. Remove the nut securing the cable to the floor pan stud.

b. Use SA9151BR or an equivalent cable release tool and remove the cable from the caliper lever.

17. Remove the cable from the vehicle.

To install:

18. If equipped with disc brakes, proceed as follows:

a. Install the park brake cable into the caliper bracket.

b. Attach the cable to the caliper park brake lever.

c. Install the trailing arm/park brake cable-to-body fasteners, then tighten the fasteners to 89 ft. lbs. (120 Nm).

d. Install the cable bracket to the floor pan stud. Install the nut and tighten to 25 inch lbs. (2.8 Nm).

19. If equipped with drum brakes, proceed as follows:

a. Install the cable through the brake backing plate and correctly seat the retaining fingers.

b. Install the cable spring onto the cable, then install the cable end into the actuator lever.

c. Connect the short end of the upper return spring to the leading brake shoe, then connect the other end of the spring to the park shoe.

d. Pull the park brake shoe toward the vehicle's rear and install the adjuster assembly between the shoes, then install the adjuster lever.

e. Install the adjuster spring with the short end into the leading shoe and the other end into the adjuster lever.

f. Install the lower return spring, then install the park shoe hold-down cup assembly.

g. Adjust the brake shoe outer diameter to 0.02 inch (0.50mm) less than the inner diameter of the brake drum, then install the brake drum.

h. Install the trailing arm/park brake cable-to-body fasteners, then tighten the fasteners to 89 ft. lbs. (120 Nm).

20. Pull the cable into the vehicle with the wire or string positioned during disassembly.

21. Install the grommet into the floor pan.

22. Install a park brake cable tie strap.

23. Install the rear wheels.

24. Install the cables into the console bracket, then attach the cables to the equalizer. Refer to the appropriate illustration for equalizers of the first production design, the cable entry holes (rounded outer side of the equalizer) must face downward. For the seconds design, the cable entry holes may face up or down.

25. Install the cable and equalizer assembly onto the threaded rod, then install the adjusting nut.

26. For rear drum vehicles, apply and release the brake pedal 20 times to allow the drum brake adjuster to position the shown.

27. Adjust the parking brake; refer to the procedure later in this section.

28. Install the center console and the rear seat cushion.

29. Lower the vehicle to the ground.

30. Connect the negative battery cable.

Brake System Bleeding

EXCEPT ANTI-LOCK BRAKES

Make sure the master cylinder is at least 1/2 full with clean DOT 3 brake fluid at all times during the procedure.

1. The master cylinder must be bled first if it is suspected to contain air. Bleed the master cylinder as follows:

a. Loosen the front upper brake line at the master cylinder and allow the fluid to flow from the front port.

b. Connect the line and tighten to 24 ft. lbs. (32 Nm).

c. Loosen the front line 1/4 turn, then have an assistant depress the brake pedal slowly (1 time) until fluid is seen flowing from the fitting and hold. Tighten the fitting, then have the assistant release the brake pedal. Repeat until all air is removed from the front (secondary) master cylinder bore.

d. Tighten the brake line to 24 ft. lbs. (32 Nm) when finished.

e. Repeat Steps a–d for the rear upper brake line fitting in order to

bleed air from the rear (primary) master cylinder bore.

2. If a pipe or fitting was the only hydraulic line disconnected, then only the caliper(s) or wheel cylinder(s) affected by that line must be bled. If the master cylinder required bleeding, then all calipers and wheel cylinders must be bled in the proper sequence:

a. Right rear
b. Left front
c. Left rear
d. Right front

NOTE: Calipers may be tapped lightly using a rubber mallet in order to help free trapped air.

3. Bleed the individual calipers or wheel cylinders as follows:

a. Place a suitable wrench over the bleeder screw and attach a clear plastic hose over the screw end.

b. Submerge the other end in a transparent container of brake fluid.

c. Loosen the bleed screw, then have an assistant apply the brake pedal slowly and hold. Tighten the bleed screw to 97 inch lbs. (11 Nm) and release the brake pedal. Repeat the sequence until all air is expelled from the caliper or cylinder.

d. Tighten the bleed screw to 97 inch lbs. (11 Nm) when finished.

4. Check the pedal for a hard feeling with the engine not running. If the pedal is soft, repeat the bleeding procedure until a firm pedal is obtained.

Anti-Lock Brake System Service

RELIEVING ANTI-LOCK BRAKE SYSTEM PRESSURE

The Saturn anti-lock brake system does not operate under abnormally high hydraulic pressures that would necessitate relieving system pressure. However, if pressure relief is desired to minimize the possibility of fluid spray when servicing lines or fittings, connect 1 end of a thin plastic tube to the bleeder screw on the ABS control unit (modulator) and place the other end into a suitable container, then slowly loosen the bleeder 1/2–3/4 of a turn until the pressure is released.

Anti-lock Brake System Bleeding

NOTE: Prior to bleeding the rear brakes, the rear displacement cylinder pistons must be returned to the top most or HOME position. To return the pistons to HOME, use a Scan tool to perform special test, RUN ABS PISTONS UP-HOME. This test will run the piston to the top of their travel.

1. Fill the master cylinder with clean brake fluid and keep the reservoir at least ½ full during the bleeding operation.

2. Prime the control assembly as follows:

    a. Attach a clear tube to the rear bleeder valve and allow the tube to hang in a transparent container of clean brake fluid.

    b. Slowly open the valve ½–¾ of a turn, then have an assistant depress and hold the brake pedal.

    c. Continue to hold the brake pedal until fluid begins to flow from the valve, then close the valve and release the pedal.

    d. Tighten the valve to 62 inch lbs. (7 Nm).

    e. Repeat the procedure at the front bleeder valve.

3. Once fluid flows from both control assembly valves, the master cylinder and modulator are sufficiently filled with fluid in order to bleed the system, but they may not be completely purged of air. To assure that the unit is free of air bleed the calipers to remove air from the assemblies lowest points, then return and bleed the control assembly again.

4. Bleed the calipers in the proper order:

    a. Right rear
    b. Left rear
    c. Right front
    d. Left front

NOTE: If when performing the bleed procedure on the rear calipers, brake fluid does not come out of the bleeder, the rear displacement pistons may not be at the home or top position.

5. Bleed each caliper, in the proper order, as follows:

    a. Attach a clear tube to the caliper bleeder valve and allow the tube to hang in a transparent container of clean brake fluid.

    b. Open the valve ½–¾ of a turn, then have an assistant slowly depress and hold the brake pedal.

    c. Watch for air bubbles as the fluid begins to flow from the valve, then close the valve and release the pedal.

    d. Wait 5 seconds and repeat the procedure until the pedal feels firm and no air is present in the brake line.

    e. Tighten the valve to 97 inch lbs. (11 Nm).

6. Bleed the control assembly from the 2 valves in the same fashion as the calipers are bled. Tighten the bleeder valves to 62 inch lbs. (7 Nm) when finished.

7. Check the pedal for excessive travel with the engine OFF and then with the engine running. If pedal feel is firm go to Step 11.

8. If the pedal feel is not firm, use a Scan tool to run the ABS motors up and down 2 times, then make sure the pistons are run up to the HOME position.

9. Start the engine, let the engine run for 2 seconds after the ABS light goes out then turn the engine OFF. Repeat the ignition cycle 9 more times.

10. Re-bleed the entire system.

11. With the engine running and brake applied, check the system for leaks.

12. Road test the vehicle and make several normal, non-ABS stops. Then make 1–2 ABS stops from a higher speed (about 50 MPH).

13. After road testing the vehicle it is recommended that the entire system be bled and inspected 1 final time.

Electronic Brake Control Module (EBCM)

REMOVAL AND INSTALLATION

The EBCM is located under the instrument panel, to the left of the steering column. The module is outboard of the Powertrain Control Module (PCM) and closest to the left kick panel.

NOTE: If replacing the EBCM with a service replacement, the EE PROM of the new module must be programmed by the Saturn Service Stall or equivalent system.

1. Disconnect the negative battery cable.

2. Remove the CPA connector locking pin and disconnect the 2-way connector from the EBCM.

3. Disconnect the 32-way electrical connector from the EBCM.

4. Turn the module retaining screw ¼ turn and remove the module by pulling downward. Be careful not to snag the wiring.

To install:

5. Position the EBCM into the bracket, taking care not to snag the wiring.

6. Seat the retaining screw by pushing upward 2 clicks.

7. Connect the wiring and insert the CPA locking pin onto the 2-way connector.

8. If necessary, program the EE PROM.

ABS Solenoid Valve

REMOVAL AND INSTALLATION

The valves are located on top of the ABS control assembly mounted to the power brake booster. The valves are directly outboard of the master cylinder. There are 2 different valve types which can be identified by an 8 digit number etched on top of the valve and referenced in the Saturn parts catalog. Always be sure to use the correct replacement type.

1. Disconnect the negative battery cable, then clean the dirt from the solenoid valve surrounding area.

2. Disconnect the electrical connector from the valve.

3. Remove the 2 retainers and remove the solenoid.

4. Verify the O-ring remained in the valve groove and was lifted up from the modulator bore, if equipped with the type A solenoids. If using a type B solenoid or if the type A O-ring remained in the bore, carefully extract the valve lip seal or O-ring from the modulator.

To install:

5. Lubricate the valve O-ring or lip seal with clean brake fluid and install onto the valve. O-rings should be installed into the groove provided on the solenoid. Lip seals should be inserted over the bottom of the valve with the lip or cupped side of the seal facing upward, toward the solenoid top.

6. Position the solenoid into the modulator and push downward until the valve flange is fully seated. Install the 2 screws and tighten to 45 inch lbs. (5 Nm).

7. Connect the electrical connector to the valve and connect the negative battery cable.

8. Properly bleed the anti-lock brake system.

ABS Control Assembly

The ABS control assembly consists of the solenoid valves, master cylinder and hydraulic modulator.

REMOVAL AND INSTALLATION

———— CAUTION ————

The ABS modulator pistons are normally in the HOME or top position. In this position the modulator drive gears are under spring tension and will turn during disassembly if not unloaded. The sudden rotation of gears and release of tension could cause injury if done without care. It is recommended that the pistons be run down and the tension released prior to removing the brake control assembly if the unit is to be disassembled.

1. If removing the unit for disassembly, connect the Saturn Portable Diagnostic Tool (PDT) or an equivalent scan tool and perform the RUN ABS MOTORS, PISTONS DOWN-REL test to run the modulator pistons down and release spring tension.
2. Disconnect the negative battery cable, then remove the battery box and battery from the vehicle.
3. Disconnect the 2 electrical connectors from the solenoids and the brake fluid level sensor electrical connector from the fluid reservoir.
4. Remove the CPA locking pin from the motor pack 6-way connector and disengage the connector from the bottom of the motor pack.
5. Label and disconnect the brake lines from the control assembly using a suitable wrench. Plug the lines to prevent fluid contamination or loss.
6. Remove the 2 brake control assembly-to-brake booster retaining nuts and remove the assembly.
7. If necessary, disassemble the unit as follows:
   a. Remove the 6 gear cover screws and the cover.
   b. Mark the location of the modulator drive gears for reassembly. Insert a small prybar between the holes in the gears to keep them from moving and remove the 3 gear to driveshaft retaining nuts. Remove the gears from the modulator.
   c. Remove the 4 motor pack-to-modulator screws and separate the motor pack from the modulator.
   d. Remove the 2 modulator-to-master cylinder through-bolts and

separate the master cylinder from the assembly.
   e. Remove the 2 transfer tubes and O-rings from the master cylinder and modulator.
   f. Remove the through-bolt O-rings from the master cylinder and modulator.
To install:
8. If necessary, assemble the ABS control unit as follows:
   a. Lubricate the new transfer tube O-rings with clean brake fluid. Press the new tubes and O-rings into the modulator by hand until fully bottomed.
   b. Lubricate the new through-bolt O-rings with clean fluid and install the rings into the master cylinder and modulator.
   c. Install the master cylinder onto the modulator, press the transfer tubes into position on the master cylinder.
   d. Install the through-bolts and tighten to 146 inch lbs. (16.5 Nm).
   e. Position the drive gears onto the driveshafts as noted earlier. Hold the gears from turning and tighten the retaining nuts to 75 inch lbs. (8.5 Nm).
   f. Hold the modulator upside down with the gears facing you and carefully rotate each gear counterclockwise until movement stops. This will position the pistons close to the TOP or HOME position and simplify the bleeding procedure.
   g. Position the motor pack to the modulator aligning the gears and install the 4 motor pack retaining screws. Tighten the screws to 40 inch lbs. (4.5 Nm).
   h. Install the gear cover onto the modulator assembly with the 6 retaining screws, then tighten the screws to 20 inch lbs. (2.25 Nm).
9. Position the control assembly onto the brake booster studs, install the retaining nuts and tighten to 20 ft. lbs. (27 Nm).
10. Position the brake lines into the control assembly as originally noted and tighten the fittings to 18 ft. lbs. (24 Nm). From the front of the master cylinder moving back the lines are: LF, RR, LR and RF.
11. Connect the 6-way connector and insert the CPA locking pin. Connect the brake fluid level and 2 solenoid valve electrical connectors.
12. Connect the negative battery cable.
13. If the ABS pistons were run down for unit disassembly, connect the scan tool and perform the RUN ABS MOTORS, PISTONS UP-HOME

test to restore tension to the modulator gears before moving the vehicle.
14. Properly bleed the ABS system.

FRONT SUSPENSION

MacPherson Strut

REMOVAL AND INSTALLATION

———— CAUTION ————

The MacPherson strut is under extreme spring pressure. Do not remove the strut shaft center support nut from the top of the shaft assembly without using an approved spring compressor. Personal injury may result if this caution is not followed.

1. If equipped with ABS, disconnect the negative battery cable, then raise and support the vehicle safely.
2. Remove the front wheel.
3. If equipped, note the ABS wiring position for assembly purposes, disconnect the ABS wiring harness from the strut wiring bracket. If the strut is being replaced, drill the rivet head retaining the ABS wiring bracket to the strut and remove the bracket.
4. Loosen the 2 steering knuckle-to-strut housing bolts, but do not remove them at this time.
5. Lower the vehicle sufficiently and remove the 3 upper strut-to-body nuts.
6. Place a rag over the CV-joint seal to protect it from damage, then remove the 2 steering knuckle-to-strut housing bolts.
7. Remove the strut assembly from the vehicle.
To install:
8. Position the strut to the vehicle, then install 3 new upper mount nuts and tighten to 21 ft. lbs. (29 Nm). New nuts must be used because the torque retention of the old nuts may be insufficient.
9. Install the knuckle bolts, also using new nuts. Push the bottom of the strut inward while tightening the fasteners to 148 ft. lbs. (200 Nm).
10. If the strut was replaced, install the ABS wiring bracket to the strut using a new rivet.
11. If applicable, connect the ABS wiring to the bracket.
12. Install the wheel assembly and lower the vehicle.

13. Connect the negative battery cable.

14. Check and adjust the alignment as necessary.

Strut Cartridge Replacement

1. Mount the strut in a suitable spring compressor/holding fixture such as SA9155S or equivalent. Fasten the strut using a strut/knuckle bolt and nut through the lower strut mounting hole.

2. Compress the spring sufficiently to completely unload the upper strut mount.

3. Remove the strut shaft nut while holding the strut stationary with a Torx® head socket wrench.

4. Carefully release the spring compressor and tilt the strut assembly outward in the fixture.

5. Remove the upper mount assembly and inspect the rubber for cracks or deterioration. Rotate the support bearing by hand and check for smooth operation.

6. Remove the spring from the strut and inspect the spring for damage.

7. Remove the dust shield assembly and inspect for cracks or deterioration.

8. Remove the strut from the compressor, then extend and retract the strut shaft, checking for smooth, even resistance.

9. Position the new strut shaft into the mounting and secure using the knuckle fastener in the lower mounting hole.

10. Tilt the strut outward slightly and extend it to the limit of its travel.

11. Install the dust shield assembly onto the strut, then install the spring.

12. Install the spring isolator and the strut mount to the top of the assembly.

13. Tilt the assembly back into the fixture and compress the spring while guiding the shaft through the upper strut mount assembly. Compress until the washer and shaft nut can be installed to the end of the shaft, but do not over compress and damage the spring.

14. Tighten the shaft to the nut using a Torx® head socket wrench and a torque wrench, while holding the nut steady with an open end wrench. Tighten the fastener to 37 ft. lbs. (50 Nm).

15. Release the spring compressor tool and remove the strut from the fixture.

Lower Ball Joints

INSPECTION

Raise and safely support the vehicle until the front wheel is clear of the floor. Try to rock the wheel up and down. If any play is felt, have an assistant rock the wheel while observing the lower ball joint. If any movement is seen between the steering knuckle and control arm, the ball joint is bad. If not, any wheel play indicates wheel bearing wear.

REMOVAL AND INSTALLATION

The lower ball joint is an integral part of the lower control arm. If the ball joint needs replacement, the entire lower arm must be replaced as an assembly.

Lower Control Arms

REMOVAL AND INSTALLATION

1. Raise and support the vehicle safely.

2. Remove the wheel and splash shield.

3. Remove and discard the cotter pin from the lower control arm ball joint. Back the ball joint nut until the top of the nut is even with the top of the threads.

4. Use tool SA9132S to separate the lower control arm ball joint from the steering knuckle, then remove the nut. Do not use a wedge tool or seal damage may occur.

NOTE: The outer CV-joint for vehicles equipped with ABS contains a speed sensor ring. Use of an incorrect tool to separate the control arm from the knuckle may result in damage and loss of the ABS system.

5. Remove the control arm-to-cradle bolt.

6. Remove the sway bar-to-control arm nut, then remove the control arm from the vehicle.

To install:

7. Position the control arm and install the arm onto the sway bar without the fastener, then place the end of the arm into the cradle. Install the cradle nut and bolt. Tighten the cradle bolt to 92 ft. lbs. (125 Nm), then tighten the cradle nut to 74 ft. lbs. (100 Nm).

8. Install the sway bar nut and tighten to 106 ft. lbs. (144 Nm).

9. Thoroughly clean and lubricate the ball joint stud threads, then install the lower control arm ball stud into the steering knuckle. Install the nut and tighten the lower control arm ball stud nut to 55 ft. lbs. (75 Nm). Tighten the nut additionally if necessary and install a new cotter pin, but do not back off the original torque specification.

10. Install the splash shield and the wheel assembly.

11. Lower the vehicle, check and adjust the alignment as necessary.

Tension Strut (Swaybar)

REMOVAL AND INSTALLATION

1. Place the steering in the unlocked position, then raise and support the vehicle safely.

2. Remove the left wheel and splash shield.

3. Remove and discard the cotter pin from the left lower control arm ball joint. Back the ball joint nut until the top of the nut is even with the top of the threads.

4. Use tool SA9132S to separate the lower control arm ball joint from the steering knuckle, then remove the nut. Do not use a wedge tool or seal damage may occur.

NOTE: The outer CV-joint for vehicles equipped with ABS contains a speed sensor ring. Use of an incorrect tool to separate the control arm from the knuckle may result in damage and loss of the ABS system.

5. Remove the left lower control arm-to-cradle fastener.

6. Turn the steering wheel to the left for access to and remove of the right tension strut nut and washer.

7. Remove both tension strut-to-cradle mounting brackets. If a cradle nut is damaged or broken loose from the cradle, replace the nut as follows:

  a. If the nut is damaged but not broken loose and the bolt can be removed, distort the bolt threads sufficiently to lock the bolt into the nut. Insert the bolt and tighten with an air impact wrench. Continue to turn the bolt until the nut breaks free of the cradle.

  b. If the nut was already broken loose and the bolt could not be extracted or if the bolt was used to break the nut loose, cut the bolt head off.

  c. Retrieve the bolt shank and nut from the cradle cavity.

  d. Install a new bolt 21010823 and nut 21006321 or equivalents.

8. Remove the tension strut with the left control arm from the vehicle. If necessary, remove the nut and the left control arm from the strut.

To install:

9. If removed, position the left control arm to the strut, but do not tighten the fastener at this time.

10. Install the strut mounting bushings onto the strut with the bushings slits facing the front of the vehicle.

11. Position the right end of the strut into the right control arm still on the vehicle, then position the left control arm into the cradle. Do not install fasteners at this time.

12. Using new bolts or a suitable threadlock such as Loctite® 242, install the mounting brackets and tighten the bolts to 103 ft. lbs. (140 Nm). Then tighten the fasteners a second time to 103 ft. lbs. (140 Nm).

13. Temporarily install the left wheel assembly onto the vehicle and with an assistant, push the bottom of the left wheel into the vehicle in order to facilitate lower control arm-to-cradle bolt installation.

14. Tighten the lower control arm cradle bolt to 92 ft. lbs. (125 Nm), then tighten the nut to 74 ft. lbs. (100 Nm).

15. Install new nuts onto the right and left tension strut-to-control arm studs. Tighten the right nut, then left nut to 106 ft. lbs. (144 Nm).

16. Thoroughly clean and lubricate the left ball joint stud threads, then install the left lower control arm ball stud into the left steering knuckle. Install the nut and tighten the stud nut to 55 ft. lbs. (75 Nm), tighten additionally if necessary and install a new cotter pin.

17. If not done already, remove the wheel, then install the splash shield and reinstall wheel assembly.

18. Lower the vehicle, check and adjust the alignment as necessary.

REAR SUSPENSION

MacPherson Strut

REMOVAL AND INSTALLATION

CAUTION

The MacPherson strut is under extreme spring pressure. Do not remove the strut shaft center support nut from the top of the shaft assembly without using an approved spring compressor. Personal injury may result if this caution is not followed.

1. On coupes, remove the rear seat cushion bottom, left or right rocker panel interior moldings and left or right rear sail interior panels.

2. On sedans, remove the left or right C-pillar interior moulding.

3. Fold down the rear seat backs and remove the rear seat side bolsters from the vehicle.

4. On coupes, remove the rear deck package shelf screws attaching the shelf to the side of the cargo area.

5. Remove the speaker grills and fasteners from the shelf, then remove the seatbelt bezel and separate the seat belts from the shelf. Remove the rear package shelf carpeting.

6. If equipped with ABS, disconnect the negative battery cable.

7. Raise and support the vehicle safely, then remove the appropriate rear wheel.

8. If equipped, unplug the ABS wiring from the strut wiring bracket. If the strut is being replaced, drill the rivet head retaining the ABS wiring bracket to the strut and remove the bracket.

9. Loosen the 2 strut-to-knuckle bolts; but do not remove at this time.

10. Lower the vehicle sufficiently and place a floor jack under the rear knuckle, then raise the jack enough to support the knuckle.

11. Remove and discard the 3 upper strut-to-body nuts.

12. Slowly raise the hoist, lowering the strut from the bottom.

13. Remove the strut to knuckle bolts and remove the strut assembly from the vehicle.

To install:

14. Install 3 new strut-to-body upper mount nuts and tighten to 21 ft. lbs. (29 Nm). New nuts must be used because the torque retention of the old nuts may be insufficient.

15. Install the knuckle bolts with new nuts, then push the bottom of the strut inward and tighten the fasteners to 148 ft. lbs. (200 Nm).

16. If the strut was replaced, install the ABS wiring bracket to the strut using a new rivet.

17. If applicable, connect the ABS wiring to the bracket.

18. Install the wheel assembly and lower the vehicle.

19. Install the interior components.

20. Connect the negative battery cable, then check and adjust the rear alignment as necessary.

Strut Cartridge Replacement

1. Mount the strut in a suitable spring compressor/holding fixture such as SA9155S or equivalent. Fasten the strut using a strut/knuckle bolt and nut through the lower strut mounting hole.

2. Compress the spring sufficiently to completely unload the upper strut mount.

3. Remove the strut shaft nut while holding the strut stationary with a Torx® head socket wrench.

4. Carefully release the spring compressor and tilt the strut assembly outward in the fixture.

5. Remove the upper spring support and inspect the rubber for cracks or deterioration.

6. Remove the spring from the strut and inspect the spring for damage.

7. Remove the dust shield assembly and inspect for cracks or deterioration.

8. Remove the strut from the compressor, then extend and retract the strut shaft, checking for smooth, even resistance.

9. Position the new strut into the mounting and secure using the knuckle fastener in the lower mounting hole.

10. Tilt the strut outward slightly and extend it to the limit of its travel.

11. Install the dust shield assembly onto the strut, then install the spring.

12. Install the upper strut mount to the top of the assembly.

13. Tilt the assembly back into the fixture and compress the spring while guiding the shaft through the upper strut mount assembly. Compress until the washer and shaft nut can be installed to the end of the shaft, but do not over compress and damage the spring.

14. Tighten the shaft to the nut using a Torx® head socket wrench and a torque wrench, while holding the nut steady with an open end wrench. Tighten the fastener to 37 ft. lbs. (50 Nm).

15. Release the spring compressor tool and remove the strut from the fixture.

Rear Control Arms

REMOVAL AND INSTALLATION

Lateral Links

If the front lateral link is to be replaced, the fuel tank must first be removed.

1. Raise and support the vehicle safely, then remove the rear wheel(s).
2. If removing the front lateral link, remove the fuel tank.
3. Remove the lateral link-to-knuckle bolt, then remove the crossmember bolt.
4. Remove the link from the vehicle.

To install:

5. Install the link into the crossmember using the fastener, but do not tighten at this time.
6. Install the link to the knuckle with the knuckle-to-link bolt, but do not tighten at this time.
7. Tighten the crossmember bolt, as applicable. Tighten the front link bolt to 126 ft. lbs. (170 Nm) or the rear link bolt to 89 ft. lbs. (120 Nm). Then tighten the knuckle bolt to 122 ft. lbs. (165 Nm).
8. If the front lateral link was removed, install the fuel tank.
9. Install the rear wheel(s) and lower the vehicle, then check and adjust the rear alignment as necessary.

Trailing Arm

1. Raise and support the vehicle safely, then remove the rear wheels.
2. Remove the trailing arm-to-knuckle nut.
3. Remove the trailing arm-to-body bolts.
4. Slide the trailing arm from the knuckle.

To install:

5. Install the trailing arm into the knuckle and torque the nut to 74 ft. lbs. (100 Nm).
6. Position the arm to the body, install and tighten the body bolts to 89 ft. lbs. (120 Nm).
7. Install the rear wheels and lower the vehicle.
8. Check and adjust the rear alignment, as necessary.

Rear Wheel Hub/Bearing Assembly

Unlike the Saturn front wheel bearings, which may be removed from the hub for replacement, the rear wheel hub and bearing assembly is not serviceable. If damaged or worn, the hub and bearing assembly must be replaced as a unit.

REMOVAL AND INSTALLATION

1. If equipped with ABS, disconnect the negative battery cable.
2. Raise and support the vehicle safely, then remove the rear wheel.
3. If equipped, unplug the ABS speed sensor connector.
4. On disc brake equipped models, remove the caliper assembly-to-knuckle mounting bolts and support it with a wire from the strut, then remove the rotor.
5. On drum brake equipped models, remove the brake drum.
6. Remove the 4 hub/bearing-to-knuckle bolts, then remove the assembly from the vehicle.

To install:

7. Install the brake backing plate, hub/bearing assembly and retaining bolts. Tighten the bolts to 63 ft. lbs. (85 Nm).
8. Install the brake drum or rotor and caliper assembly. If applicable, tighten the caliper retaining bolts to 63 ft. lbs. (85 Nm).
9. If equipped, engage the ABS speed sensor connector.
10. Install the wheel assembly and lower the vehicle. If applicable, connect the negative battery cable.

ADJUSTMENT

The rear hub/bearing assembly is a sealed assembly, requiring no periodic maintenance. No adjustments are necessary or possible.

Rear Knuckle Assembly

REMOVAL AND INSTALLATION

1. Raise and support the vehicle safely.
2. Remove the hub/bearing assembly.
3. If equipped with rear drum brakes, suspend the brake assembly clear of the knuckle.
4. Loosen the lateral link-to-knuckle and strut-to-knuckle bolts, but do not remove at this time.
5. Remove the trailing arm knuckle nut and body bolts.
6. Slide the trailing arm out of the knuckle.
7. Remove the lateral link and remove the strut-to-knuckle bolts, then remove the knuckle from the vehicle.

To install:

8. Place the knuckle in the strut and install the bolts, but do not tighten at this time.
9. Loosely install the lateral links and trailing arm.
10. Tighten the trailing arm-to-body bolts to 89 ft. lbs. (120 Nm), trailing arm-to-knuckle nut to 74 ft. lbs. (100 Nm) and the lateral link-to-knuckle bolts to 122 ft. lbs. (165 Nm). Push inward on the bottom of the strut and tighten the strut-to-knuckle bolts to 148 ft. lbs. (200 Nm).
11. Install the hub/bearing assembly.
12. Lower the vehicle, then check and adjust the rear alignment as necessary.

Rear Crossmember Assembly

REMOVAL AND INSTALLATION

1. Raise and support the vehicle safely.
2. Remove the left and right trailing arms.
3. Remove the left and right lateral link bolts and disconnect the links from the knuckles.
4. Unsnap the brake line fasteners and disconnect the crossbody brake line from the crossmember.
5. If equipped, remove the left and right stabilizer bar-to-link fasteners.
6. Note the position and routing of all rear brake lines for installation purposes, then disconnect the left and right lines from their junction brackets. Plug the lines to prevent system contamination or excessive fluid loss.
7. Remove the left and right brake hose-to-crossmember securing clips. Remove the brake line longitudinal fastener. Carefully pull the right rear brake line out of the crossmember from the left side of the vehicle.
8. If equipped with ABS, disconnect the left and right ABS speed sensor harness-to-crossmember fasteners.
9. Place a suitable support under the rear crossmember to prevent the member from falling when disconnected. Add additional supports to the front of the vehicle to make sure the vehicle does not become unbalanced and fall from the lift when the crossmember is removed.
10. Note the size and location of all bolts, then remove the 4 crossmember-to-body attaching bolts and carefully lower the crossmember from the vehicle.

To install:

11. Position the crossmember into the vehicle and align the member to the body using ⅜ inch rods at the alignment holes near the crossmember-to-body fastener holes.

12. Install the crossmember to the body using 4 new bolts of the proper size and specification. Position the bolts as noted during removal, then tighten the bolts to 89 ft. lbs. (120 Nm).

13. Position the trailing arms with bushings into the knuckles and install the nuts, but do not tighten the nuts at this time.

14. Install the trailing arms to the body and tighten the bolts to 89 ft. lbs. (120 Nm).

15. Install the lateral links to the knuckles with the link bolts, but do not tighten at this time.

16. Tighten the trailing arm fastener nuts to 74 ft. lbs. (100 Nm), then tighten the lateral link knuckle fasteners to 122 ft. lbs. (165 Nm).

17. If equipped, install the stabilizer bar to the links with fasteners and tighten to 30 ft. lbs. (40 Nm).

18. Position all brake lines as noted earlier, then attach the left and right brake lines to the crossmember with the securing clips. Install the left and right brake lines into their respective junction brackets. Install the brake line longitudinal fastener.

19. If equipped with ABS, connect the speed sensor harness-to-crossmember fasteners and tighten to 53 inch lbs. (6 Nm).

20. Properly bleed the hydraulic brake system.

21. Install the rear wheel assemblies and lower the vehicle.

22. Check and adjust the rear alignment as necessary.

Specifications

23

LASER/STEALTH/SUMMIT/TALON

VEHICLE IDENTIFICATION CHART

Code	Liters	Cu. In. (cc)	Cyl.	Fuel Sys.	Eng. Mfg.
A	1.5	90 (1468)	4	MFI	Mitsubishi
B	1.8	107 (1753)	4	MFI	Mitsubishi
T	1.8	107 (1755)	4	MFI	Mitsubishi
C	1.8	112 (1834)	4	MFI	Mitsubishi
D	1.8	112 (1834)	4	MFI	Mitsubishi
E	2.0	122 (1999)	4	MFI	Mitsubishi
F	2.0	122 (1999)	4	MFI Turbo	Mitsubishi
R	2.0	122 (1999)	4	MFI	Mitsubishi
U	2.0	122 (1999)	4	MFI Turbo	Mitsubishi
Y	2.0	122 (1999)	4	MFI	Chrysler
G	2.4	146 (2350)	4	MFI	Mitsubishi
W	2.4	146 (2350)	4	MFI	Mitsubishi
B	3.0	181 (2972)	V6	MFI	Mitsubishi
C	3.0	181 (2972)	V6	MFI-TT	Mitsubishi
H	3.0	181 (2972)	V6	MFI	Mitsubishi
J	3.0	181 (2972)	V6	MFI	Mitsubishi
K	3.0	181 (2972)	V6	MFI-TT	Mitsubishi
S	3.0	181 (2972)	V6	MFI	Mitsubishi

Engine Code

Model Year	
Code	Year
N	1992
P	1993
R	1994
S	1995
T	1996

MFI - Multipoint fuel injection

TT - Twin Turbochargers

ENGINE IDENTIFICATION

Year	Model	Engine Displacement Liters (cc)	Engine Series (ID/VIN)	Fuel System	No. of Cylinders	Engine Type
1992	Summit	1.5 (1468)	A	MFI	4	SOHC
	Summit	1.8 (1834)	D	MFI	4	SOHC
	Summit Wagon	1.8 (1834)	D	MFI	4	SOHC
	Summit Wagon	2.4 (2350)	W	MFI	4	SOHC
	Talon	2.0 (1999)	R	MFI	4	DOHC
	Talon	2.0 (1999)	U	MFI Turbo	4	DOHC
	Laser	1.8 (1755)	T	MFI	4	SOHC
	Laser	2.0 (1997)	R	MFI	4	DOHC
	Laser	2.0 (1997)	U	MFI-Turbo	4	DOHC
	Stealth	3.0 (2972)	S	MFI	6	SOHC
	Stealth	3.0 (2972)	B	MFI	6	DOHC
	Stealth	3.0 (2972)	C	MFI-TT	6	DOHC
1993	Summit	1.5 (1468)	A	MFI	4	SOHC
	Summit	1.8 (1834)	C	MFI	4	SOHC
	Summit Wagon	1.8 (1834)	C	MFI	4	SOHC
	Summit Wagon	2.4 (2350)	G	MFI	4	SOHC
	Talon	1.8 (1753)	B	MFI	4	SOHC
	Talon	2.0 (1999)	E	MFI	4	DOHC

ENGINE IDENTIFICATION

Year	Model	Engine Displacement Liters (cc)	Engine Series (ID/VIN)	Fuel System	No. of Cylinders	Engine Type
	Talon	2.0 (1999)	F	MFI Turbo	4	DOHC
	Laser	1.8 (1755)	B	MFI	4	SOHC
	Laser	2.0 (1997)	E	MFI	4	DOHC
	Laser	2.0 (1997)	F	MFI-Turbo	4	DOHC
	Stealth	3.0 (2972)	H	MFI	6	SOHC
	Stealth	3.0 (2972)	J	MFI	6	DOHC
	Stealth	3.0 (2972)	K	MFI-TT	6	DOHC
1994	Summit	1.5 (1468)	A	MFI	4	SOHC
	Summit	1.8 (1834)	C	MFI	4	SOHC
	Summit Wagon	1.8 (1834)	C	MFI	4	SOHC
	Summit Wagon	2.4 (2350)	G	MFI	4	SOHC
	Talon	1.8 (1753)	B	MFI	4	SOHC
	Talon	2.0 (1999)	E	MFI	4	DOHC
	Talon	2.0 (1999)	F	MFI Turbo	4	DOHC
	Laser	1.8 (1755)	B	MFI	4	SOHC
	Laser	2.0 (1997)	E	MFI	4	DOHC
	Laser	2.0 (1997)	F	MFI-Turbo	4	DOHC
	Stealth	3.0 (2972)	H	MFI	6	SOHC
	Stealth	3.0 (2972)	J	MFI	6	DOHC
	Stealth	3.0 (2972)	K	MFI-TT	6	DOHC
1995-96	Summit	1.5 (1468)	A	MFI	4	SOHC
	Summit	1.8 (1834)	C	MFI	4	SOHC
	Summit Wagon	1.8 (1834)	C	MFI	4	SOHC
	Summit Wagon	2.4 (2350)	G	MFI	4	SOHC
	Talon	2.0 (1999)	F	MFI-Turbo	4	DOHC
	Talon	2.0 (1999)	Y	MFI	4	DOHC
	Stealth	3.0 (2972)	H	MFI	6	SOHC
	Stealth	3.0 (2972)	J	MFI	6	DOHC
	Stealth	3.0 (2972)	K	MFI-TT	6	DOHC

MFI - Multipoint fuel injection
TT - Twin Turbochargers
SOHC - Single overhead camshaft
DOHC - Double overhead camshaft

GENERAL ENGINE SPECIFICATIONS

Year	Engine ID/VIN	Engine Displacement Liters (cc)	Fuel System Type	Net Horsepower @ rpm	Net Torque @ rpm (ft. lbs.)	Bore x Stroke (In.)	Compression Ratio	Oil Pressure @ rpm
1992	A	1.5 (1468)	MFI	92@6000	93@3000	2.97x3.23	9.2:1	54@2000
	T	1.8 (1755)	MFI	92@5000	105@3500	3.17x3.39	9.0:1	42.7@2000
	D	1.8 (1834)	MFI	113@6000	116@4500	3.19x3.50	9.5:1	1
	R	2.0 (1999)	MFI	135@6000	125@5000	3.35x3.47	9.0:1	41@2000
	U	2.0 (1999)	MFI	190@6000	203@5000	3.35x3.47	7.8:1	41@2000
	W	2.4 (2350)	MFI	136@5500	145@4250	3.41x3.94	9.5:1	1
	B	3.0 (2972)	MFI	222@6000	201@4500	3.59x2.99	10.0:1	35-100@2000
	C	3.0 (2972)	MFI-TT	300@6000	307@2500	3.59x2.99	8.0:1	35-100@2000
	S	3.0 (2972)	MFI	164@5500	185@4000	3.59x2.99	8.9:1	35-100@2000

GENERAL ENGINE SPECIFICATIONS

Year	Engine ID/VIN	Engine Displacement Liters (cc)	Fuel System Type	Net Horsepower @ rpm	Net Torque @ rpm (ft. lbs.)	Bore x Stroke (in.)	Compression Ratio	Oil Pressure @ rpm
1993	A	1.5 (1468)	MFI	92@6000	93@3000	2.97x3.23	9.2:1	54@2000
	B	1.8 (1753)	MFI	92@5000	105@3500	3.17x3.39	9.0:1	41@2000
	C	1.8 (1834)	MFI	113@6000	116@4500	3.19x3.50	9.5:1	1
	E	2.0 (1999)	MFI	135@6000	125@5000	3.35x3.47	9.0:1	41@2000
	F	2.0 (1999)	MFI	190@6000	203@5000	3.35x3.47	7.8:1	41@2000
	F	3.5 (3518)	MFI	214@5800	221@2800	3.78x3.18	10.5:1	25-70@3000
	G	2.4 (2350)	MFI	136@5500	145@4250	3.41x3.94	9.5:1	1
	H	3.0 (2972)	MFI	164@5500	185@4000	3.59x2.99	8.9:1	35-100@2000
	J	3.0 (2972)	MFI	222@6000	201@4500	3.59x2.99	10.0:1	35-100@2000
	K	3.0 (2972)	MFI-TT	300@6000	307@2500	3.59x2.99	8.0:1	35-100@2000
1994	A	1.5 (1468)	MFI	92@6000	93@3000	2.97x3.23	9.2:1	54@2000
	B	1.8 (1753)	MFI	92@5000	105@3500	3.17x3.39	9.0:1	1
	C	1.8 (1834)	MFI	113@6000	116@4500	3.19x3.50	9.5:1	1
	E	2.0 (1999)	MFI	135@6000	125@5000	3.35x3.47	9.0:1	1
	F	2.0 (1999)	MFI	190@6000	203@5000	3.35x3.47	7.8:1	1
	G	2.4 (2350)	MFI	136@5500	145@4250	3.41x3.94	9.5:1	1
	H	3.0 (2972)	MFI	164@5500	185@4000	3.59x2.99	8.9:1	35-100@2000
	J	3.0 (2972)	MFI	222@6000	201@4500	3.59x2.99	10.0:1	35-100@2000
	K	3.0 (2972)	MFI-TT	320@6000	315@2500	3.59x2.99	8.0:1	35-100@2000
1995-96	A	1.5 (1468)	MFI	92@6000	93@3000	2.97x3.23	9.2:1	54@2000
	C	1.8 (1834)	MFI	113@6000	116@4500	3.19X3.50	9.5:1	1
	F	2.0 (1999)	MFI	210@6000 [3]	214@3000 [2]	3.35x3.46	8.5:1	1
	Y	2.0 (1999)	MFI	140@6000	131@4800	3.44x3.27	9.6:1	4
	G	2.4 (2350)	MFI	136@5500	145@4250	3.41x3.94	9.5:1	1
	H	3.0 (2972)	MFI	164@5500	185@4000	3.59x2.99	8.9:1	35-100@2000
	J	3.0 (2972)	MFI	222@6000	201@4500	3.59x2.99	10.0:1	35-100@2000
	K	3.0 (2972)	MFI-TT	320@6000	315@2500	3.59x2.99	8.0:1	35-100@2000

MFI - Multiport fuel injection
1 11.4 psi or more at curb idle speed
2 Automatic: 220@3000
3 Automatic: 205@6000
4 4 psi or more at curb idle speed

GASOLINE ENGINE TUNE-UP SPECIFICATIONS

Year	Engine ID/VIN	Engine Displacement Liters (cc)	Spark Plugs Gap (in.)	Ignition Timing (deg.) MT	Ignition Timing (deg.) AT	Fuel Pump (psi)	Idle Speed (rpm) MT	Idle Speed (rpm) AT	Valve Clearance In.	Valve Clearance Ex.
1992	A	1.5 (1468)	0.039-0.043	5B	5B	38	750	750	0.006	0.010
	D	1.8 (1834)	0.039-0.043	5B	5B	38	750	750	HYD	HYD
	T	1.8 (1755)	0.039-0.043	5B	5B	38	700	700	HYD	HYD
	R	2.0 (1999)	0.039-0.043	5B	5B	38	700	700	HYD	HYD
	U	2.0 (1999)	0.028-0.031	5B	5B	1	750	750	HYD	HYD
	W	2.4 (2350)	0.039-0.043	5B	5B	38	750	750	HYD	HYD
	B	3.0 (2972)	0.039-0.043	5B	5B	38	750	750	HYD	HYD
	C	3.0 (2972)	0.035	5B	5B	34	750	750	HYD	HYD
	S	3.0 (2972)	0.039-0.043	5B	5B	38	750	750	HYD	HYD

GASOLINE ENGINE TUNE-UP SPECIFICATIONS

Year	Engine ID/VIN	Engine Displacement Liters (cc)	Spark Plugs Gap (in.)	Ignition Timing (deg.) MT	Ignition Timing (deg.) AT	Fuel Pump (psi)	Idle Speed (rpm) MT	Idle Speed (rpm) AT	Valve Clearance In.	Valve Clearance Ex.
1993	A	1.5 (1468)	0.039-0.043	5B	5B	38	750	750	0.006	0.006
	B	1.8 (1753)	0.039-0.043	5B	5B	38	750	750	HYD	HYD
	C	1.8 (1834)	0.039-0.043	5B	5B	38	750	750	HYD	HYD
	E	2.0 (1999)	0.039-0.043	5B	5B	38	700	700	HYD	HYD
	F	2.0 (1999)	0.028-0.031	5B	5B	1	750	750	HYD	HYD
	G	2.4 (2350)	0.039-0.043	5B	5B	38	750	750	HYD	HYD
	H	3.0 (2972)	0.039-0.043	5B	5B	38	750	750	HYD	HYD
	J	3.0 (2972)	0.039-0.043	5B	5B	38	750	750	HYD	HYD
	K	3.0 (2972)	0.035	5B	5B	34	750	750	HYD	HYD
1994	A	1.5 (1468)	0.039-0.043	5B	5B	38 2	750	750	0.008	0.01
	B	1.8 (1753)	0.039-0.943	5B	5B	38 2	750	750	HYD	HYD
	C	1.8 (1834)	0.039-0.043	5B	5B	38 2	750	750	0.008	0.012
	E	2.0 (1999)	0.039-0.043	5B	5B	38 2	700	700	HYD	HYD
	F	2.0 (1999)	0.028-0.031	5B	5B	33 2	750	750	HYD	HYD
	G	2.4 (2350)	0.039-0.043	5B	5B	38 2	750	750	HYD	HYD
	H	3.0 (2972)	0.039-0.043	5B	5B	38	750	750	HYD	HYD
	J	3.0 (2972)	0.039-0.043	5B	5B	38	750	750	HYD	HYD
	K	3.0 (2972)	0.035	5B	5B	34	750	750	HYD	HYD
1995-96	A	1.5 (1468)	0.039-0.043	5B	5B	38 2	750	750	0.008	0.010
	C	1.8 (1834)	0.039-0.043	5B	5B	38 2	700	700	0.008	0.012
	F	2.0 (1999)	0.028-0.031	5B	5B	33 2	750	750	HYD	HYD
	Y	2.0 (1999)	0.033-0.038	3	3	38 2	700	700	HYD	HYD
	G	2.4 (2350)	0.039-0.043	5B	5B	38 2	750	750 4	HYD	HYD
	H	3.0 (2972)	0.039-0.043	5B	5B	38	750	750	HYD	HYD
	J	3.0 (2972)	0.039-0.043	5B	5B	38	750	750	HYD	HYD
	K	3.0 (2972)	0.039-0.043	5B	5B	34	750	750	HYD	HYD

NOTE: The Vehicle Emission Control Information label often reflects speicifcation changes made during production. The label figures must be used if they differ from those in this chart

HYD - Hydraulic

B - Before top dead center

1 Manual transaxle: 27
  Automatic transaxle: 33

2 Pressure at idle with vacuum applied to fuel pressure regulator

3 Basic ignition timing is not adjustable

4 Refer to underhood specifications sticker.

CAPACITIES

Year	Model	Engine ID/VIN	Engine Displacement Liters (cc)	Oil with Filter (qts.)	Transmission (pts.) 4-Spd	Transmission (pts.) 5-Spd	Transmission (pts.) Auto.	Transfer Case (pts.)	Drive Axle Front (pts.)	Drive Axle Rear (pts.)	Fuel Tank (gal.)	Cooling System (qts.)
1992	Summit	A	1.5 (1468)	3.0	3.6	3.8	13.0	-	-	-	13.2	5.3
	Summit	D	1.8 (1834)	4.0	-	3.8	13.0	-	-	-	13.2	6.3
	Summit Wagon	D	1.8 (1834)	4.0	-	3.8	13.0	1.25	-	1.5	14.5	6.3
	Summit Wagon	W	2.4 (2350)	4.1	-	4.8	13.0	1.25	-	1.5	16.0	6.8
	Talon	R	2.0 (1999)	4.6	-	4.6	13.0	-	-	-	16.0	7.6
	Talon	U	2.0 (1999)	4.8	-	1	13.0	1.25	-	1.5	16.0	7.6
	Laser	T	1.8 (1755)	4.1	-	1.9	12.8	-	-	-	16.0	6.6
	Laser	R	2.0 (1997)	4.6	-	1.9	12.8	-	-	-	16.0	7.6

CAPACITIES

Year	Model	Engine ID/VIN	Engine Displacement Liters (cc)	Oil with Filter (qts.)	Engine Transmission (pts.) 4-Spd	5-Spd	Auto.	Transfer Case (pts.)	Drive Axle Front (pts.)	Rear (pts.)	Fuel Tank (gal.)	Cooling System (qts.)
	Laser	U	2.0 (1997)	4.8	-	1	14.8	1.25	-	1.5	16.0	7.6
	Stealth	S	3.0 (2972)	4.7	-	4.8	15.8	-	-	-	19.8	8.5
	Stealth	B	3.0 (2972)	4.7	-	4.8	15.8	-	-	-	19.8	8.5
	Stealth	C	3.0 (2972)	5.2	-	2	15.8	0.58	-	2.3	19.8	8.5
1993	Summit	A	1.5 (1468)	3.0	-	3.8	13.0	-	-	-	13.2	5.3
	Summit	C	1.8 (1834)	4.0	-	3.8	13.0	-	-	-	13.2	6.3
	Summit Wagon	C	1.8 (1934)	4.0	-	3.8	13.0	1.25	-	1.5	14.5	6.3
	Summit Wagon	G	2.4 (2350)	4.1	-	4.8	13.0	1.25	-	1.5	16.0	6.8
	Talon	B	1.8 (1753)	4.1	-	3.8	13.0	-	-	-	16.0	6.6
	Talon	E	2.0 (1999)	4.6	-	4.6	13.0	-	-	-	16.0	7.6
	Talon	F	2.0 (1999)	4.8	-	1	13.0	1.25	-	1.5	16.0	7.6
	Laser	B	1.8 (1755)	4.1	-	1.9	13.2	-	-	-	16.0	6.6
	Laser	E	2.0 (1997)	4.6	-	1.9	13.2	-	-	-	16.0	7.6
	Laser	F	2.0 (1997)	4.8	-	1	15.2	1.25	-	1.5	16.0	7.6
	Stealth	H	3.0 (2972)	4.7	-	4.8	15.8	-	-	-	19.8	8.5
	Stealth	J	3.0 (2972)	4.7	-	4.8	15.8	-	-	-	19.8	8.5
	Stealth	K	3.0 (2972)	5.2	-	2	15.8	0.58	-	2.3	19.8	8.5
1994	Summit	A	1.5 (1468)	3.0	-	3.8	13.0	-	-	-	13.2	5.3
	Summit	C	1.8 (1834)	4.0	-	3.8	13.0	-	-	-	13.2	6.3
	Summit Wagon	C	1.8 (1834)	4.0	-	3.8	13.0	1.25	-	1.5	14.5	6.3
	Summit Wagon	G	2.4 (2350)	4.1	-	4.8	13.0	1.25	-	1.5	14.5	6.8
	Talon	B	1.8 (1753)	4.1	-	3.8	13.0	-	-	-	16.0	6.6
	Talon	E	2.0 (1999)	4.6	-	4.6	13.0	-	-	-	16.0	7.6
	Talon	F	2.0 (1999)	4.8	-	1	13.0	1.25	-	1.8	16.0	7.6
	Laser	B	1.8 (1755)	4.1	-	3.8	13.0	-	-	-	16.0	6.6
	Laser	E	2.0 (1997)	4.6	-	3.8	13.2	-	-	-	16.0	7.6
	Laser	F	2.0 (1997)	4.8	-	1	14.2	1.25	-	1.5	16.0	7.6
	Stealth	H	3.0 (2972)	4.7	-	4.8	15.8	-	-	-	19.8	8.5
	Stealth	J	3.0 (2972)	4.7	-	4.8	15.8	-	-	-	19.8	8.5
	Stealth	K	3.0 (2972)	5.2	-	3	15.8	0.58	-	2.3	19.8	8.5
1995-96	Summit	A	1.5 (1468)	3.7	-	3.8	13.0	-	-	-	13.2	5.3
	Summit	C	1.8 (1834)	4.2	-	3.8	13.0	-	-	-	13.2	6.3
	Summit Wagon	C	1.8 (1834)	4.0	-	3.8	13.0	1.25	-	1.5	14.5	6.3
	Summit Wagon	G	2.4 (2350)	4.5	-	4.8	13	1.25	-	1.5	14.5	6.8
	Talon	F	2.0 (1999)	5.0	-	1	14.2	1.25	-	1.8	16.0	7.4
	Talon	Y	2.0 (1999)	4.6	-	4.2	18.2	-	-	-	16.0	7.4
	Stealth	H	3.0 (2972)	4.7	-	4.8	15.8	-	-	-	19.8	8.5
	Stealth	J	3.0 (2972)	4.7	-	4.8	15.8	-	-	-	19.8	8.5
	Stealth	K	3.0 (2972)	5.2	-	3	15.8	0.58	-	2.3	19.8	8.5

1 FWD models: 4.6 pts.
  AWD models: 4.8 pts.
2 FWD models - 4.8 pts.
  AWD models - 5.0 pts.
3 6 speed manual transaxle capacity - 5.0 pts.

CAMSHAFT SPECIFICATIONS
All measurements given in inches.

Year	Engine ID/VIN	Engine Displacement Liters (cc)	Journal Diameter					Elevation		Bearing Clearance	Camshaft End Play
			1	2	3	4	5	In.	Ex.		
1992	A	1.5 (1468)	1.8110	1.8110	1.8110	1.8110	1.8110	1.5059-1.5256	1.5197-1.5394	0.0024-0.0055	NA
	T	1.8 (1755)	1.3990	1.3390	1.3390	1.3390	1.3390	1.4140	1.4140	0.0020-0.0035	0.0020-0.0059
	D	1.8 (1834)	1.7689-1.7693	1.7689-1.7693	1.7689-1.7693	1.7689-1.7693	1.7689-1.7693	1.4670-1.4880	1.4800-1.4490	0.0020-0.0035	NA
	R	2.0 (1999)	1.0217-1.0224	1.0217-1.0224	1.0217-1.0224	1.0217-1.0224	1.0217-1.0224	1.3974	1.3858	0.0020-0.0035	0.004-0.008
	U	2.0 (1999)	1.0217-1.0224	1.0217-1.0224	1.0217-1.0224	1.0217-1.0224	1.0217-1.0224	1.3974-	1.3858	0.0020-0.0035	0.004-0.008
	W	2.4 (2350)	1.7689-1.7693	1.7689-1.7693	1.7689-1.7693	1.7689-1.7693	1.7689-1.7693	1.4720	1.4752	0.0020-0.0035	NA
	S	3.0 (2972)	NA	NA	NA	NA	-	1.6240	1.6240	0.0020-0.0035	NA
	B	3.0 (2972)	NA	NA	NA	NA	-	1.3744	1.3744	0.0020-0.0035	NA
	C	3.0 (2972)	NA	NA	NA	NA	-	1.3744	1.3744	0.0020-0.0035	NA
1993	A	1.5 (1468)	1.8110	1.8110	1.8110	1.8110	1.8110	1.5059-1.5256	1.5197-1.5394	0.0024-0.0055	NA
	B	1.8 (1753)	1.3360-1.3366	1.3360-1.3366	1.3360-1.3366	1.3360-1.3366	1.3360-1.3366	1.4138	1.4138	0.0020-0.0035	0.004-0.008
	C	1.8 (1834)	1.7689-1.7693	1.7689-1.7693	1.7689-1.7693	1.7689-1.7693	1.7689-1.7693	1.4670-1.4880	1.4800-1.4490	0.0020-0.0035	NA
	E	2.0 (1999)	1.0217-1.0224	1.0217-1.0224	1.0217-1.0224	1.0217-1.0224	1.0217-1.0224	1.3974	1.3858	0.0020-0.0035	0.004-0.008
	F	2.0 (1999)	1.0217-1.0224	1.0217-1.0224	1.0217-1.0224	1.0217-1.0024	1.0217-1.0224	1.3974	1.3858	0.0020-0.0035	0.004-0.008
	G	2.4 (2350)	1.7689-1.7693	1.7689-1.7693	1.7689-1.7693	1.7689-1.7693	1.7689-1.7693	1.4720	1.4752	0.0020-0.0035	NA
	H	3.0 (2972)	NA	NA	NA	NA	-	1.6240	1.6240	0.0020-0.0035	NA
	J	3.0 (2972)	NA	NA	NA	NA	-	1.3744	1.3744	0.0020-0.0035	NA
	K	3.0 (2972)	NA	NA	NA	NA	-	1.3744	1.3744	0.0020-0.0035	NA
1994	A	1.5 (1468)	1.8110	1.8110	1.8110	1.8110	1.8110	1.5071-1.5268	1.5197-1.5394	0.0024-0.0055	NA
	B	1.8 (1753)	1.3360-1.3366	1.3360-1.3366	1.3360-1.3366	1.3360-1.3366	1.3360-1.3366	1.4138	1.4138	0.0020-0.0035	0.004-0.008
	C	1.8 (1834)	1.7689-1.7693	1.7689-1.7693	1.7689-1.7693	1.7689-1.7693	1.7689-1.7693	1.4776	1.4996	0.0020-0.0035	NA
	E	2.0 (1999)	1.0217-1.0224	1.0217-1.0224	0.0217-1.0224	1.0217-1.0224	1.0217-1.0224	1.3974-	1.3858	0.0020-0.0035	0.004-0.008

CAMSHAFT SPECIFICATIONS

All measurements given in inches.

Year	Engine ID/VIN	Engine Displacement Liters (cc)	Journal Diameter 1	2	3	4	5	Elevation In.	Ex.	Bearing Clearance	Camshaft End Play
	F	2.0 (1999)	1.0217-1.0224	1.0217-1.0224	1.0217-1.0224	1.0217-1.0224	1.0217-1.0224	1.3974	1.3858	0.0020-0.0035	0.004-0.008
	G	2.4 (2350)	1.7689-1.7693	1.7689-1.7693	1.7689-1.7693	1.7689-1.7693	1.7689-1.7693	1.4720	1.4752	0.0020-0.0035	NA
	H	3.0 (2972)	NA	NA	NA	NA	-	1.6240	1.6240	0.0020-0.0035	NA
	J	3.0 (2972)	NA	NA	NA	NA	-	1.3744	1.3744	0.0020-0.0035	NA
	K	3.0 (2972)	NA	NA	NA	NA	-	1.3744	1.3744	0.0020-0.0035	NA
1995-96	A	1.5 (1468)	1.8110	1.8110	1.8110	1.8110	1.8110	1.5071-1.5268	1.5197-1.5394	0.0024-0.0055	NA
	C	1.8 (1834)	1.7689-1.7693	1.7689-1.7693	1.7689-1.7693	1.7689-1.7693	1.7689-1.7693	1.4776	1.4996	0.0020-0.0035	NA
	F	2.0 (1999)	1.0217-1.0224	1.0217-1.0224	1.0217-1.0224	1.0217-1.0224	1.0217-1.0224	1.3974	1.3858	0.0020-0.0035	0.004-0.008
	Y	2.0 (1999)	1.0217-1.0224	1.0217-1.0224	1.0217-1.0224	1.0217-1.0224	1.0217-1.0224	0.3240	0.2760	0.0027-0.0028	0.006
	G	2.4 (2350)	1.7689-1.7693	1.7689-1.7693	1.7689-1.7693	1.7689-1.7693	1.7689-1.7693	1.4720	1.4752	0.0020-0.0035	NA
	H	3.0 (2972)	1.340	1.340	1.340	1.340	-	1.6240	1.6240	0.0020-0.0035	NA
	J	3.0 (2972)	1.020	1.020	1.020	1.020	-	1.3744	1.3744	0.0020-0.0035	NA
	K	3.0 (2972)	1.020	1.020	1.020	1.020	-	1.3744	1.3744	0.0020-0.0035	NA

NA - Not Available

CRANKSHAFT AND CONNECTING ROD SPECIFICATIONS

All measurements are given in inches.

Year	Engine ID/VIN	Engine Displacement Liters (cc)	Crankshaft Main Brg. Journal Dia.	Main Brg. Oil Clearance	Shaft End-play	Thrust on No.	Connecting Rod Journal Diameter	Oil Clearance	Side Clearance
1992	A	1.5 (1468)	1.8900	0.0008-0.0028	0.0020-0.0071	3	1.6500	0.0008-0.0024	0.0039-0.0098
	T	1.8 (1755)	2.2400	0.0008-0.0016	0.0020-0.0070	3	1.7700	0.0008-0.0020	0.0039-0.0098
	D	1.8 (1834)	1.9680	0.0008-0.0016	0.0020-0.0070	3	1.7709-1.7715	0.0008-0.0020	0.0040-0.0098
	R	2.0 (1999)	2.2430-2.2440	0.0008-0.0020	0.0020-0.0070	3	1.7709-1.7715	0.0008-0.0020	0.0040-0.0098
	U	2.0 (1999)	2.2430-2.2440	0.0008-0.0020	0.0020-0.0070	3	1.7709-1.7715	0.0008-0.0020	0.0040-0.0098
	W	2.4 (2350)	2.2430-2.2440	0.0008-0.0020	0.0020-0.0070	3	1.7709-1.7717	0.0008-0.0020	0.0039-0.0098

CRANKSHAFT AND CONNECTING ROD SPECIFICATIONS

All measurements are given in inches.

Year	Engine ID/VIN	Engine Displacement Liters (cc)	Crankshaft Main Brg. Journal Dia.	Crankshaft Main Brg. Oil Clearance	Crankshaft Shaft End-play	Crankshaft Thrust on No.	Connecting Rod Journal Diameter	Connecting Rod Oil Clearance	Connecting Rod Side Clearance
	S	3.0 (2972)	2.358	0.0008-0.0019	0.0020-0.0098	3	1.9650	0.0006-0.0018	0.0040-0.0098
	B	3.0 (2972)	2.358	0.0008-0.0019	0.0020-0.0098	3	1.9650	0.0006-0.0018	0.0040-0.0098
	C	3.0 (2972)	2.358	0.0008-0.0019	0.0020-0.0098	3	1.9650	0.0006-0.0018	0.0040-0.0098
1993	A	1.5 (1468)	1.8900	0.0008-0.0028	0.0020-0.0071	3	1.6500	0.0008-0.0024	0.0039-0.0098
	B	1.8 (1753)	2.2400	0.0008-0.0020	0.0020-0.0070	3	1.7700	0.0008-0.0020	0.0039-0.0098
	C	1.8 (1834)	1.9680	0.0008-0.0016	0.0020-0.0070	3	1.7709-1.7715	0.0008-0.0020	0.0040-0.0098
	E	2.0 (1999)	2.2430-2.2440	0.0008-0.0020	0.0020-0.0070	3	1.7709-1.7715	0.0008-0.0020	0.0040-0.0098
	F	2.0 (1999)	2.2430-2.2440	0.0008-0.0020	0.0020-0.0070	3	1.7709-1.7715	0.0008-0.0020	0.0040-0.0098
	G	2.4 (2350)	2.2430-2.2440	0.0008-0.0020	0.0020-0.0070	3	1.7709-1.7717	0.00008-0.0020	0.0039-0.0098
	H	3.0 (2972)	2.358	0.0008-0.0019	0.0020-0.0098	3	1.9650	0.0006-0.0018	0.0040-0.0098
	J	3.0 (2972)	2.358	0.0008-0.0019	0.0020-0.0098	3	1.9650	0.0006-0.0018	0.0040-0.0098
	K	3.0 (2972)	2.358	0.0008-0.0019	0.0020-0.0098	3	1.9650	0.0006-0.0018	0.0040-0.0098
1994	A	1.5 (1468)	1.8900	0.0008-0.0020	0.0020-0.0071	3	1.6500	0.0008-0.0020	0.0039-0.0098
	B	1.8 (1753)	2.2400	0.0008-0.0020	0.0020-0.0070	3	1.7700	0.0008-0.0020	0.0039-0.0098
	C	1.8 (1834)	1.9680	0.0008-0.0016	0.0020-0.0070	3	1.7709-1.7715	0.0008-0.0020	0.0040-0.0098
	E	2.0 (1999)	2.2430-2.2440	0.0008-0.0020	0.0020-0.0070	3	1.7709-1.7715	0.0008-0.0020	0.0040-0.0098
	F	2.0 (1999)	2.2430-2.2440	0.0008-0.0020	0.0020-0.0070	3	1.7709-1.7715	0.0008-0.0020	0.0040-0.0098
	G	2.4 (2350)	2.2430-2.2440	0.0008-0.0020	0.0020-0.0070	3	1.7709-1.7717	0.0008-0.0020	0.0039-0.0098
	H	3.0 (2972)	2.358	0.0008-0.0019	0.0020-0.0098	3	1.9650	0.0006-0.0018	0.0040-0.0098
	J	3.0 (2972)	2.358	0.0007-0.0014	0.0020-0.0098	3	1.9650	0.0006-0.0018	0.0040-0.0098
	K	3.0 (2972)	2.358	0.0007-0.0014	0.0020-0.0098	3	1.9650	0.0006-0.0018	0.0040-0.0098
1995-96	A	1.5 (1468)	1.8900	0.0008-0.0020	0.0020-0.0071	3	1.6500	0.0008-0.0020	0.0039-0.0098
	C	1.8 (1834)	1.9678-1.9685	0.0008-0.0016	0.0020-0.0070	3	1.7709-1.7715	0.0008-0.0020	0.0040-0.0098

CRANKSHAFT AND CONNECTING ROD SPECIFICATIONS

All measurements are given in inches.

Year	Engine ID/VIN	Engine Displacement Liters (cc)	Crankshaft				Connecting Rod		
			Main Brg. Journal Dia.	Main Brg. Oil Clearance	Shaft End-play	Thrust on No.	Journal Diameter	Oil Clearance	Side Clearance
	F	2.0 (1999)	2.2430-2.2440	0.0008-0.0016	0.0020-0.0070	3	1.7709-1.7715	0.0008-0.0020	0.0040-0.0098
	Y	2.0 (1999)	2.0469-2.0475	0.0008-0.0024	0.0035-0.0094	3	2.0075-2.0081	0.0010-0.0023	0.005-0.015
	G	2.4 (2350)	2.2430-2.2440	0.0008-0.0020	0.0020-0.0070	3	1.7709-1.7717	0.0008-0.0020	0.0039-0.0098
	H	3.0 (2972)	2.358	0.0008-0.0019	0.0020-0.0098	3	1.9650	0.0006-0.0018	0.0040-0.0098
	J	3.0 (2972)	2.358	0.0007-0.0014	0.0020-0.0098	3	1.9650	0.0009-0.0019	0.0040-0.0098
	K	3.0 (2972)	2.358	0.0007-0.0014	0.0020-0.0098	3	1.9650	0.0009-0.0019	0.0040-0.0098

VALVE SPECIFICATIONS

Year	Engine ID/VIN	Engine Displacement Liters (cc)	Seat Angle (deg.)	Face Angle (deg.)	Spring Test Pressure (lbs. @ in.)	Spring Installed Height (in.)	Stem-to-Guide Clearance (in.)		Stem Diameter (in.)	
							Intake	Exhaust	Intake	Exhaust
1992	A	1.5 (1468)	44-44.5	44-44.5	1	3	0.0008-0.0020	0.0020-0.0035	0.2585-0.2591	0.2571-0.2579
	T	1.8 (1755)	44-44.5	45-45.5	62 2	7	0.0012-0.0040	0.0020-0.0060	0.3100	0.3100
	D	1.8 (1834)	43.5-44	45-45.5	132 2	5	0.0008-0.0020	0.0020-0.0035	0.2585-0.2591	0.2571-0.2579
	R	2.0 (1999)	44-44.5	45-45.5	66 2	1.902 4	0.0008-0.0019	0.0020-0.0033	0.2585-0.2591	0.2571-0.2579
	U	2.0 (1999)	44-44.5	45-45.5	66 2	1.902 4	0.0008-0.0019	0.0020-0.0033	0.2585-0.2591	0.2571-0.2579
	W	2.4 (2350)	44-44.5	45-45.5	60 2	1.740	0.0008-0.0020	0.0012-0.0028	0.2350-0.2354	0.2343-0.2350
	S	3.0 (2972)	44-44.5	45-45.5	74 2	1.600-1.630	0.0012-0.0039	0.0020-0.0059	0.3140	0.3125
	B	3.0 (2972)	44-44.5	45-45.5	62 2	1.500-1.530	0.0008-0.0039	0.0020-0.0047	0.2600	0.2600
	C	3.0 (2972)	44-44.5	45-45.5	62 2	1.500-1.530	0.0008-0.0039	0.0020-0.0047	0.2600	0.2600
1993	A	1.5 (1468)	44-44.5	45-45.5	1	3	0.0008-0.0020	0.0020-0.0035	0.2585-0.2591	0.2571-0.2579
	B	1.8 (1753)	44-44.5	45-45.5	62 2	1.937 4	0.0012-0.0024	0.0020-0.0035	0.3100	0.3100
	C	1.8 (1934)	43.5-44	45-45.5	132 2	5	0.0008-0.0020	0.0020-0.0035	0.2585-0.2591	0.2571-0.2579
	E	2.0 (1999)	44-44.5	45-45.5	66 2	1.902 4	0.0008-0.0019	0.0020-0.0033	0.2585-0.2591	0.2571-0.2579

VALVE SPECIFICATIONS

Year	Engine ID/VIN	Engine Displacement Liters (cc)	Seat Angle (deg.)	Face Angle (deg.)	Spring Test Pressure (lbs. @ in.)	Spring Installed Height (in.)	Stem-to-Guide Clearance (in.) Intake	Stem-to-Guide Clearance (in.) Exhaust	Stem Diameter (in.) Intake	Stem Diameter (in.) Exhaust
	F	2.0 (1999)	44-44.5	45-45.5	66 [2]	1.902 [4]	0.0008-0.0019	0.0020-0.0033	0.2585-0.2591	0.2571-0.2579
	F	3.5 (3518)	45-45.5	44.5-45	[6]	1.496	0.0009-0.0026	0.0020-0.0040	0.2730-0.2737	0.2719-0.2726
	G	2.4 (2350)	44-44.5	45-45.5	60 [2]	1.740	0.0008-0.0020	0.0012-0.0028	0.2350-0.2354	0.2343-0.2350
	H	3.0 (2972)	44-44.5	45-45.5	74 [2]	1.600-1.630	0.0012-0.0039	0.0020-0.0059	0.3140	0.3125
	J	3.0 (2972)	44-44.5	45-45.5	62 [2]	1.500-1.530	0.0008-0.0039	0.0020-0.0047	0.2600	0.2600
	K	3.0 (2972)	44-44.5	45-45.5	62 [2]	1.500-1.530	0.0008-0.0039	0.0020-0.0047	0.2600	0.2600
1994	A	1.5 (1468)	44-44.5	45-45.5	[1]	[8]	0.0008-0.0020	0.0020-0.0035	0.2585-0.2591	0.2571-0.2579
	B	1.8 (1753)	44-44.5	45-45.5	68 [2]	1.937 [4]	0.0012-0.0024	0.0020-0.0035	0.3100	0.3100
	C	1.8 (1834)	43.5-44	45-45.5	132 [2]	[5]	0.0008-0.0020	0.0020-0.0035	0.2585-0.2591	0.2571-0.2579
	E	2.0 (1999)	44-44.5	45-45.5	66 [2]	1.902 [4]	0.0008-0.0019	0.0020-0.0033	0.2585-0.2591	0.2571-0.2579
	F	2.0 (1999)	44-44.5	45-45.5	66 [2]	1.902 [4]	0.0008-0.0019	0.0020-0.0033	0.2585-0.2591	0.2571-0.2579
	G	2.4 (2350)	44-44.5	45-45.5	60 [2]	1.740	0.0008-0.0020	0.0012-0.0028	0.2350-0.2354	0.2343-0.2350
	H	3.0 (2972)	44-44.5	45-45.5	74 [2]	1.600-1.630	0.0012-0.0039	0.0020-0.0059	0.3140	0.3140
	J	3.0 (2972)	44-44.5	45-45.5	53 [2]	1.500-1.530	0.0008-0.0039	0.0020-0.0047	0.2600	0.2600
	K	3.0 (2972)	44-44.5	45-45.5	53 [2]	1.500-1.530	0.0008-0.0039	0.0020-0.0047	0.2600	0.2600
1995-96	A	1.5 (1468)	44-44.5	45-45.5	[1]	[8]	0.0008-0.0020	0.0020-0.0035	0.2585-0.2591	0.2571-0.2579
	C	1.8 (1834)	43.5-44	45-45.5	132 [2]	[5]	0.0008-0.0016	0.0012-0.0024	0.2350-0.2354	0.2343-0.2350
	F	2.0 (1999)	44-44.5	45-45.5	54 [2]	1.570	0.0008-0.0019	0.0019-0.0026	0.2585-0.2591	0.2571-0.2579
	Y	2.0 (1999)	45	45-45.5	110-120	1.496	0.0019-0.0026	0.0029-0.0037	0.2336-0.2343	0.2325-0.2332
	G	2.4 (2350)	43-44	45-45.5	60 [2]	1.740	0.0008-0.0020	0.0012-0.0028	0.2350-0.2354	0.2343-0.2350
	H	3.0 (2972)	44-44.5	45-45.5	74 [2]	1.600-1.630	0.0012-0.0039	0.0020-0.0059	0.3140	0.3140
	J	3.0 (2972)	44-44.5	45-45.5	53 [2]	1.492	0.0008-0.0039	0.0020-0.0047	0.2600	0.2600
	K	3.0 (2972)	44-44.5	45-45.5	53 [2]	1.492	0.0008-0.0039	0.0020-0.0047	0.2600	0.2600

23 SPECIFICATIONS

VALVE SPECIFICATIONS

Year	Engine ID/VIN	Engine Displacement Liters (cc)	Seat Angle (deg.)	Face Angle (deg.)	Spring Test Pressure (lbs. @ in.)	Spring Installed Height (in.)	Stem-to-Guide Clearance (in.)		Stem Diameter (in.)	
							Intake	Exhaust	Intake	Exhaust

1   Intake: 51 @ Installed height
    Exhaust: 64 @ Installed height
2   At installed height
3   Free length specification: Intake 1.776-1.815
    Free length specification: Exhaust 1.803-1.843
4   Specification is for free length
5   Free length specification: 2.004
6   Intake: 201.7-218.3@1.1752
    Exhaust: 158.5-171.5@1.2390
7   Free length: 1.898-1.937
8   Both intake and exhaust: 1.57

PISTON AND RING SPECIFICATIONS
All measurements are given in inches.

Year	Engine ID/VIN	Engine Displacement Liters (cc)	Piston Clearance	Ring Gap			Ring Side Clearance		
				Top Compression	Bottom Compression	Oil Control	Top Compression	Bottom Compression	Oil Control
1992	A	1.5 (1468)	0.0008-0.0016	0.0079-0.0157	0.0079-0.0138	0.0079-0.0276	0.0012-0.0028	0.0008-0.0024	NA
	T	1.8 (1755)	0.0004-0.0012	0.0118-0.0177	0.0079-0.0138	0.0080-0.0280	0.0013-0.0033	0.0008-0.0024	NA
	D	1.8 (1834)	0.0008-0.0016	0.0098-0.0157	0.0157-0.0217	0.0079-0.0236	0.0012-0.0028	0.0008-0.0024	NA
	R	2.0 (1999)	0.0008-0.0016	0.0098-0.0157	0.0138-0.0197	0.0079-0.0276	0.0012-0.0028	0.0012-0.0028	NA
	U	2.0 (1999)	0.0012-0.0020	0.0098-0.0177	0.0138-0.0197	0.0079-0.0276	0.0012-0.0028	0.0012-0.0028	NA
	W	2.4 (2350)	0.0004-0.0012	0.0098-0.0157	0.0079-0.0157	0.0079-0.0276	0.0012-0.0028	0.0008-0.0024	NA
	S	3.0 (2972)	0.0008-0.0015	0.0120-0.0180	0.0100-0.0160	0.0120-0.0350	0.0020-0.0035	0.0008-0.0020	NA
	B	3.0 (2972)	0.0008-0.0015	0.0120-0.0180	0.0100-0.0160	0.0120-0.0350	0.0020-0.0035	0.0008-0.0020	NA
	C	3.0 (2972)	0.0008-0.0015	0.0120-0.0180	0.0100-0.0160	0.0120-0.0350	0.0020-0.0035	0.0008-0.0020	NA
1993	A	1.5 (1468)	0.0008-0.0016	0.0079-0.0157	0.0079-0.0138	0.0079-0.0276	0.0012-0.0028	0.0008-0.0024	NA
	B	1.8 (1753)	0.0004-0.0012	0.0118-0.0177	0.0079-0.0138	0.0080-0.0280	0.0018-0.0033	0.0008-0.0024	NA
	C	1.8 (1834)	0.0008-0.0016	0.0098-0.0157	0.0157-0.0217	0.0079-0.0236	0.0012-0.0028	0.0008-0.0024	NA
	E	2.0 (1999)	0.0008-0.0016	0.0098-0.0157	0.0138-0.0197	0.0079-0.0276	0.0012-0.0028	0.0012-0.0028	NA
	F	2.0 (1999)	0.0012-0.0020	0.0098-0.0177	0.0138-0.0197	0.0079-0.0276	0.0012-0.0028	0.0012-0.0028	NA
	G	2.4 (2350)	0.0004-0.0012	0.0098-0.0157	0.0079-0.0157	0.0079-0.0276	0.0012-0.0028	0.0008-0.0024	NA
	H	3.0 (2972)	0.0012-0.0020	0.0118-0.0177	0.0098-0.0157	0.0118-0.0154	0.0020-0.0035	0.0008-0.0024	NA

PISTON AND RING SPECIFICATIONS

All measurements are given in inches.

Year	Engine ID/VIN	Engine Displacement Liters (cc)	Piston Clearance	Ring Gap			Ring Side Clearance		
				Top Compression	Bottom Compression	Oil Control	Top Compression	Bottom Compression	Oil Control
	J	3.0 (2972)	0.0012-0.0020	0.0118-0.0177	0.0098-0.0157	0.0118-0.0154	0.0020-0.0035	0.0008-0.0024	NA
	K	3.0 (2972)	0.0012-0.0020	0.0118-0.0177	0.0098-0.0157	0.0118-0.0154	0.0020-0.0035	0.0008-0.0024	NA
1994	A	1.5 (1468)	0.0008-0.0016	0.0079-0.0157	0.0079-0.0138	0.0079-0.0276	0.0012-0.0028	0.0008-0.0024	NA
	B	1.8 (1753)	0.0008-0.0016	0.0118-0.0177	0.0079-0.0217	0.0079-0.0276	0.0018-0.0033	0.0008-0.0024	NA
	C	1.8 (1834)	0.0008-0.0016	0.0098-0.0157	0.0157-0.0217	0.0079-0.0236	0.0012-0.0028	0.0008-0.0024	NA
	E	2.0 (1999)	0.0008-0.0016	0.0098-0.0157	0.0177-0.0236	0.0079-0.0276	0.0012-0.0028	0.0012-0.0028	NA
	F	2.0 (1999)	0.0012-0.0020	0.0098-0.0157	0.0177-0.0236	0.0079-0.0276	0.0012-0.0028	0.0012-0.0028	NA
	G	2.4 (2350)	0.0004-0.0012	0.0098-0.0138	0.0157-0.0217	0.0039-0.0157	0.0012-0.0028	0.0012-0.0028	NA
	H	3.0 (2972)	0.0012-0.0020	0.0118-0.0177	0.0177-0.0236	0.0079-0.0236	0.0012-0.0028	0.0008-0.0024	NA
	J	3.0 (2972)	0.0012-0.0020	0.0118-0.0177	0.0177-0.0236	0.0079-0.0236	0.0012-0.0028	0.0008-0.0024	NA
	K	3.0 (2972)	0.0012-0.0020	0.0118-0.0177	0.0177-0.0236	0.0079-0.0236	0.0012-0.0028	0.0008-0.0024	NA
1995-96	A	1.5 (1468)	0.0008-0.0016	0.0079-0.0157	0.0079-0.0138	0.0079-0.0276	0.0012-0.0028	0.0008-0.0024	NA
	C	1.8 (1834)	0.0008-0.0016	0.0098-0.0157	0.0157-0.0217	0.0079-0.0236	0.0012-0.0028	0.0008-0.0024	NA
	F	2.0 (1999)	0.0012-0.0020	0.0098-0.0138	0.0157-0.0217	0.0039-0.0157	0.0012-0.0028	0.0008-0.0028	NA
	Y	2.0 (1999)	0.0005-0.0017	0.009-0.020	0.019-0.031	0.009-0.026	0.0012-0.0028	0.0012-0.0028	NA
	G	2.4 (2350)	0.0004-0.0012	0.0098-0.0138	0.0157-0.0217	0.0039-0.0157	0.0012-0.0028	0.0012-0.0028	NA
	H	3.0 (2972)	0.0012-0.0020	0.0118-0.0177	0.0177-0.0236	0.0079-0.0236	0.0012-0.0028	0.0008-0.0024	NA
	J	3.0 (2972)	0.0012-0.0020	0.0118-0.0177	0.0177-0.0236	0.0079-0.0236	0.0012-0.0028	0.0008-0.0024	NA
	K	3.0 (2972)	0.0012-0.0020	0.0118-0.0177	0.0177-0.0236	0.0079-0.0236	0.0012-0.0028	0.0008-0.0024	NA

NA - Not Available

TORQUE SPECIFICATIONS
All readings in ft. lbs.

Year	Engine ID/VIN	Engine Displacement Liters (cc)	Cylinder Head Bolts	Main Bearing Bolts	Rod Bearing Bolts	Damper Bolts	Flywheel Bolts	Crankshaft Manifold Intake	Crankshaft Manifold Exhaust	Spark Plugs	Lug Nut
1992	A	1.5 (1468)	1	47-51	36-38	51-72	94-101	11-14	11-14	15-21	65-80
	T	1.8 (1755)	51-54	37-39	24-25	80-94	94-101	13-18	18-22	15-21	87-101
	D	1.8 (1834)	2	4	15	134	72	13	13	18	65-80
	R	2.0 (1999)	65-72	47-51	36-38	94	94-101	18-22	18-22	15-21	87-101
	U	2.0 (1999)	65-72	47-51	36-38	94	94-101	18-22	18-22	15-21	87-101
	W	2.4 (2350)	2	38	38	-	98	13	13	18	65-80
	S	3.0 (2972)	76-83	58	38	108-116	55	13	13	18	87-101
	B	3.0 (2972)	76-83	58	38	108-116	55	13	13	18	87-101
	C	3.0 (2972)	3	58	38	130-137	55	9-11	22	18	87-101
1993	A	1.5 (1468)	1	47-51	36-38	51-72	94-101	11-14	11-14	15-21	65-80
	B	1.8 (1753)	51-54	37-39	24-25	80-94	94-101	13-18	18-22	15-21	87-101
	C	1.8 (1834)	2	4	15	134	72	13	13	18	65-80
	E	2.0 (1999)	65-72	47-51	36-38	94	94-101	18-22	18-22	15-21	87-101
	F	2.0 (1999)	65-72	47-51	36-38	94	94-101	18-22	18-22	15-21	87-101
	G	2.4 (2350)	2	38	38	-	98	13	13	18	65-80
	H	3.0 (2972)	76-83	58	38	108-116	55	13	13	18	87-101
	J	3.0 (2972)	76-83	58	38	108-116	55	13	13	18	87-101
	K	3.0 (2972)	3	58	38	130-137	55	9-11	22	18	87-101
1994	A	1.5 (1468)	53	38	15	51-72	94-101	11-14	11-14	15-21	65-80
	B	1.8 (1753)	51-54	37-39	24-25	80-94	94-101	13-18	18-22	15-21	65-80
	C	1.8 (1834)	2	4	15	134	72	14	11-14 5	15-21	65-80
	E	2.0 (1999)	6	4	15	94	94-101	14	18-22	15-21	65-80
	F	2.0 (1999)	6	4	15	94	94-101	14	18-22	18	65-80
	G	2.4 (2350)	6	4	15	-	98	13	18-22	18	65-80
	H	3.0 (2972)	76-83	58	38	108-116	55	13	13	18	87-101
	J	3.0 (2972)	3	58	38	130-137	55	13	22	18	87-101
	K	3.0 (2972)	3	58	38	130-137	55	13	22	18	87-101
1995-96	A	1.5 (1468)	53	38	15	62	94-101	13	13	15-21	65-80
	C	1.8 (1834)	2	4	15	134	72	14	11-14 5	15-21	65-80
	F	2.0 (1999)	6	4	15	94	94-101	14	18-22	18	65-80
	Y	2.0 (1999)	8	55	7	105	-	17	17	20	65-80
	G	2.4 (2350)	8	4	15	-	98	13	18-22	18	65-80
	H	3.0 (2972)	76-83	58	38	108-116	55	13	13	15	87-101
	J	3.0 (2972)	3	67	38	130-137	55	13	22	15	87-101
	K	3.0 (2972)	3	54	38	130-137	55	13	22	15	87-101

1 Cold: 51-54
Warm: 58-61

2 Step 1: 54 ft. lbs.
Step 2: Fully loosen
Step 3: 14 ft. lbs.
Step 4: +90 degrees
Step 5: +90 degrees

3 Step 1: 87-94 ft. lbs.
Step 2: Fully loosen
Step 3: 87-94 ft. lbs.

4 Step 1: 18 ft. lbs.
Step 2: + 90 degrees

5 Lower exhaust manifold nuts: 22 ft. lbs.

6 Step 1: 58 ft. lbs.
Step 2: Fully loosen
Step 3: 14.5 ft. lbs.
Step 4: +90 degrees
Step 5: +90 degrees

7 20 ft. lbs. +90 degrees

8 Step 1:
Bolts 1-6: 24 ft. lbs.
Bolts 7-10: 20 ft. lbs.
Step 2:
Bolts 1-6: 48 ft. lbs.
Bolts 7-10: 20 ft. lbs.
Step 3:
Bolts 1-6: 48 ft. lbs.
Bolts 7-10: 20 ft. lbs.
Step 4: +90 degrees

BRAKE SPECIFICATIONS

All measurements in inches unless noted

Year	Model			Master Cylinder Bore	Brake Disc Original Thickness	Brake Disc Minimum Thickness	Maximum Runout	Brake Drum Diameter Original Inside Diameter	Brake Drum Diameter Max. Wear Limit	Brake Drum Diameter Maximum Machine Diameter	Minimum Lining Thickness Front	Minimum Lining Thickness Rear
1992	Summit	1	F	0.813	0.510	0.449	0.006	-	-	-	0.080	-
			R	-	-	-	-	7.10	7.20	NA	-	0.040
	Summit	2	F	0.875	0.710	0.646	0.006	-	-	-	0.080	-
			R	-	-	-	-	7.10	7.20	NA	-	0.040
	Summit Wagon		F	3	0.945	0.882	0.003	-	-	-	0.080	-
			R	-	0.394	0.331	0.003	10	11	NA	-	6
	Talon/Laser		F	4	0.940	0.882	0.003	-	-	-	0.080	-
			R	-	0.390	0.331	0.003	-	-	-	-	0.080
	Stealth		F	5	0.940	0.880	0.003	-	-	-	0.080	-
			R	-	0.710	0.650	0.003	-	-	-	-	0.080
	Stealth	8	F	1.063	1.180	1.120	0.003	-	-	-	0.080	-
			R	-	0.790	0.720	0.003	-	-	-	-	0.080
1992	Summit	1	F	0.813	0.510	0.449	0.006	-	-	-	0.080	-
			R	-	-	-	-	7.10	7.20	NA	-	0.040
	Summit	2	F	0.875	0.710	0.646	0.006	-	-	-	0.080	-
			R	-	-	-	-	7.10	7.20	NA	-	0.040
	Summit Wagon		F	3	0.945	0.882	0.003	-	-	-	0.080	-
			R	-	0.394	0.331	0.003	10	11	NA	-	6
	Talon/Laser		F	4	0.940	0.882	0.003	-	-	-	0.080	-
			R	-	0.390	0.331	0.003	-	-	-	-	0.080
	Stealth		F	5	0.940	0.880	0.003	-	-	-	0.080	-
			R	-	0.710	0.650	0.003	-	-	-	-	0.080
	Stealth	8	F	1.063	1.180	1.120	0.003	-	-	-	0.080	-
			R	-	0.790	0.720	0.00	-	-	-	-	0.080
1994	Summit	1	F	0.813	0.510	0.449	0.003	-	-	-	0.080	-
			R	-	-	-	-	7.10	7.20	NA	-	0.040
	Summit	2	F	9	0.710	0.646	0.003	-	-	-	0.080	-
			R	-	0.390	0.330	0.003	8.00	8.10	NA	-	6
	Summit Wagon		F	13	0.945	0.882	0.003	-	-	-	0.080	-
			R	-	0.394	0.331	0.003	10	11	NA	-	6
	Talon/Laser		F	14	0.940	0.882	0.003	-	-	-	0.080	-
			R	-	7	12	0.003	-	-	-	-	0.080
	Stealth		F	5	0.940	0.880	0.003	-	-	-	0.080	-
			R	-	0.710	0.650	0.003	-	-	-	-	0.080
	Stealth	8	F	1.063	1.180	1.120	0.003	-	-	-	0.080	-
			R	-	0.790	0.720	0.00	-	-	-	-	0.080
1995-96	Summit	1	F	0.813	0.510	0.449	0.003	-	-	-	0.080	-
			R	-	-	-	-	7.10	7.20	NA	-	0.040
	Summit	2	F	9	0.710	0.646	0.003	-	-	-	0.080	-
			R	-	0.390	0.330	0.003	8.00	8.10	NA	-	6
	Summit Wagon		F	13	0.945	0.882	0.003	-	-	-	0.080	-
			R	-	0.394	0.331	0.003	10	11	NA	-	6
	Talon/Laser		F	14	0.940	0.882	0.003	-	-	-	0.080	-
			R	-	7	12	0.003	-	-	-	-	0.080

BRAKE SPECIFICATIONS
All measurements in inches unless noted

Year	Model			Master Cylinder Bore	Brake Disc			Brake Drum Diameter			Minimum Lining Thickness	
					Original Thickness	Minimum Thickness	Maximum Runout	Original Inside Diameter	Max. Wear Limit	Maximum Machine Diameter	Front	Rear
	Stealth		F	5	0.940	0.880	0.003	-	-	-	0.080	-
			R	-	0.710	0.650	0.003	-	-	-	-	0.080
	Stealth	8	F	1.063	1.180	1.120	0.003	-	-	-	0.080	-
			R	-	0.790	0.720	0.00	-	-	-	-	0.080

NA - Not Available
1 Hatchback
2 Sedan
3 With ABS: 0.938
  Without ABS: 1.00
4 Non-turbo without ABS: 0.875
  Non-turbo with ABS: 0.938
  FWD turbo: 0.938
  AWD turbo: 1.000
5 With ABS: 1.000
  Without ABS: 1.063
6 With drum rear brakes 0.040
  With disc rear brakes 0.080
7 FWD: 0.390
  AWD: 0.790

8 AWD Models
9 Master cylinder bore: 0.813
  With ABS: 0.938
10 8: drum: 7.992
  9" drum: 9.000
11 8" drum: 8.071
  9" drum: 9.079
12 FWD: 0.331
  AWD: 0.721
13 With ABS: 1.000
  Without ABS: 0.938
14 Non-turbocharged: 0.938
  FWD turbocharged: 0.938
  AWD turbocharged: 1.000

WHEEL ALIGNMENT

Year	Model			Caster		Camber		Toe-in (in.)	Steering Axis Inclination (deg.)
				Range (deg.)	Preferred Setting (deg.)	Range (deg.)	Preferred Setting (deg.)		
1992	Summit		F	1 13/16P-2 13/16P	2 5/16P	1/2N-1/2P	0	0	12 1/2
			R	-	-	1 3/16N-3/16N	11/16N	0	-
	Summit Wagon	1	F	1 1/2P-2 7/8P	2 3/16P	5/32N-27/32P	11/32P	0	13 13/16
			R	-	-	1N-0	1/2N	3/16P	-
	Summit Wagon	2	F	1 3/8P-2 3/4P	2 1/16P	5/32P-1 3/16P	11/16P	0	13.4375
			R	-	-	1N-0	1/2N	3/32P	-
	Laser	3	F	1 27/32P-2 27/32P	2 13/32P	1/2N-1/2P	0	0	NA
			R	-	-	1 1/6N-1/6N	2/3N	0	-
	Talon/Laser	4	F	1 29/32P-2 29/32P	2 13/32P	5/12P-7/12P	1/12P	0	NA
			R	-	-	1 1/4N-1/4N	3/4N	0	-
	Talon/Laser	5	F	1 4/5P-2 4/5P	2 3/10P	1/3N-2/3P	1/6P	0	NA
			R	-	-	2 1/16N-1 1/16N	1 9/16N	0	-
	Stealth	1	F	3 5/12P-4 5/12P	3 11/12P	1/2N-1/2P	0	0	NA
			R	-	-	1/2N-1/2P	0	0	-
	Stealth	2	F	3 5/12P-4 5/12P	3 11/12P	1/2N-1/2P	0	0	NA
			R	-	-	2/3N-1/3P	1/6N	0	-
1993	Summit		F	5/6P-2 5/6P	2 1/4P	1/2N-1/2P	0	0	12 4/5
			R	-	-	1 3/16N-3/16N	11/16N	1/8P	-
	Summit Wagon	1	F	1 1/2P-2 7/8P	2 3/16P	5/32N-27/32P	11/32P	0	13 13/16
			R	-	-	1N-0	1/2N	3/16P	-
	Summit Wagon	2	F	1 3/8P-2 3/4P	2 1/16P	5/32P-1 3/16P	11/16P	0	13.4375
			R	-	-	1N-0	1/2N	3/32P	-

WHEEL ALIGNMENT

Year	Model			Caster Range (deg.)	Caster Preferred Setting (deg.)	Camber Range (deg.)	Camber Preferred Setting (deg.)	Toe-in (in.)	Steering Axis Inclination (deg.)
	Talon/Laser	3	F	1 27/32P-2 27/32P	2 13/32P	1/2N-1/2P	0	0	NA
			R	-	-	1 1/6N-1/6N	2/3N	0	-
	Talon/Laser	4	F	1 29/32P-2 29/32P	2 13/32P	5/12N-7/12P	1/12P	0	NA
			R	-	-	1 1/4N-1/4N	3/4N	0	-
	Talon/Laser	5	F	1 4/5P-2 4/5P	2 3/10P	1/3N-2/3P	1/6P	0	NA
			R	-	-	2 1/16N-1 1/16N	1 9/16N	0	-
	Stealth		F	3 5/12P-4 5/12P	3 11/12P	1/2N-1/2P	0	0	NA
			R	-	-	1/2N-1/2P	0	0	-
	Stealth		F	3 5/12P-4 5/12P	3 11/12P	1/2N-1/2P	0	0	NA
			R	-	-	2/3N-1/3P	1/6N	0	-
1994	Summit		F	5/6P-2 5/6P	2 1/4P	1/2N-1/2P	0	0	12 4/5
			R	-	-	1 3/16N-3/16N	11/16N	1/8P	-
	Summit Wagon	1	F	1 1/2P-2 7/8P	2 3/16P	5/32N-27/32P	11/32P	0	13 13/16
			R	-	-	1N-0	1/2N	3/16P	-
	Summit Wagon	2	F	1 3/8P-2 3/4P	2 1/16P	5/32P-1 3/16P	11/16P	0	13.4375
			R	-	-	1N-0	1/2N	3/32P	-
	Talon/Laser	3	F	1 27/32P-2 27/32P	2 11/32P	1/4N-3/4P	1/4P	0	14 3/32
			R	-	-	1 1/4N-1/4N	3/4N	0	-
	Talon/Laser	4	F	1 29/32P-2 29/32P	2 13/32P	13/32N-19/32P	3/32P	0	14 11/32
			R	-	-	1 1/4N-1/4N	3/4N	0	-
	Talon/Laser	5	F	1 4/5P-2 4/5P	2 3/10P	5/16N-11/16P	3/16P	0	14 7/32
			R	-	-	2 1/16N-1 1/16N	1 9/16N	1/8P	-
	Stealth	1	F	3 1/4P-3 27/32P	3 1/2P	1/2N-1/2P	0	0	14 1/32
			R	-	-	1/2N-1/2P	0	0	-
	Stealth	2	F	3 1/4P-3 27/32P	3 1/2P	1/2N-1/2P	0	0	14 1/32
			R	-	-	2/3N-1/3P	1/6N	0	-
1995-96	Summit		F	5/6P-2 5/6P	2 1/4P	1/2N-1/2P	0	0	12 4/5
			R	-	-	1 3/16N-3/16N	11/16N	1/8P	-
	Summit Wagon	1	F	1 1/2P-2 7/8P	2 3/16P	5/32N-27/32P	11/32P	0	13 13/16
			R	-	-	1N-0	1/2N	3/16P	-
	Summit Wagon	2	F	1 3/8P-2 3/4P	2 1/16P	5/32P-1 3/16P	11/16P	0	13 7/16
			R	-	-	1N-0	1/2N	3/32P	-
	Talon	4	F	1 29/32P-2 29/32P	2 13/32P	13/32N-19/32P	3/32P	0	14 11/32
			R	-	-	1 1/4N-1/4N	3/4N	0	-
	Talon	5	F	1 4/5P-2 4/5P	2 3/10P	5/16N-11/16P	3/16P	0	14 7/32
			R	-	-	2 1/16N-1 1/16N	1 9/16N	1/8P	-
	Stealth	1	F	3 1/4P-3 27/32P	3 1/2P	1/2N-1/2P	0	0	14 1/32
			R	-	-	1/2N-1/2P	0	0	-
	Stealth	2	F	3 1/4P-3 27/32P	3 1/2P	1/2N-1/2P	0	0	14 1/32
			R	-	-	2/3N-1/3P	1/6N	0	-

F - Front
R - Rear
NA - Not Available
1 FWD Models
2 AWD Models
3 1.8L engine
4 2.0L FWD engine
5 2.0L AWD engine

ACCLAIM/DAYTONA/LEBARON/SHADOW/SPIRIT/SUNDANCE

VEHICLE IDENTIFICATION CHART

Engine Code						Model Year	
Code	Liters	Cu. In. (cc)	Cyl.	Fuel Sys.	Eng. Mfg.	Code	Year
A	2.2	135 (2212)	I4	MFI-Turbo	Chrysler	N	1992
D	2.2	135 (2212)	I4	TFI	Chrysler	P	1993
J	2.5	153 (2507)	I4	MFI-Turbo	Chrysler	R	1994
K	2.5	153 (2507)	I4	TFI	Chrysler	S	1995
V	2.5	153 (2507)	I4	MFI-M85	Chrysler	T	1996
3	3.0	181 (2972)	V6	MFI	Mitsubishi		

MFI - Multiport fuel injection
TFI - Throttle body fuel injection
TFI - Throttle body fuel injection
M85 - 85% Methanol, flexible fuel engine

ENGINE IDENTIFICATION

Year	Model	Engine Displacement Liters (cc)	Engine Series (ID/VIN)	Fuel System	No. of Cylinders	Engine Type
1992	Acclaim	2.5 (2507)	K	TFI	4	SOHC
	Acclaim	3.0 (2972)	3	MFI	6	SOHC
	Daytona	2.2 (2212)	A	MFI-Turbo	4	DOHC
	Daytona	2.5 (2507)	J	MFI-Turbo	4	SOHC
	Daytona	2.5 (2507)	K	TFI	4	SOHC
	Daytona	3.0 (2972)	3	MFI	6	SOHC
	Lebaron	2.5 (2507)	J	MFI-Turbo	4	SOHC
	Lebaron	2.5 (2507)	K	TFI	4	SOHC
	Lebaron	3.0 (2972)	3	MFI	6	SOHC
	Shadow	2.2 (2212)	D	TFI	4	SOHC
	Shadow	2.5 (2507)	J	MFI-Turbo	4	SOHC
	Shadow	2.5 (2507)	K	TFI	4	SOHC
	Shadow	3.0 (2972)	3	MFI	6	SOHC
	Spirit	2.2 (2212)	A	MFI-Turbo	4	DOHC
	Spirit	2.5 (2507)	J	MFI-Turbo	4	SOHC
	Spirit	2.5 (2507)	K	TFI	4	SOHC
	Spirit	3.0 (2972)	3	MFI	6	SOHC
	Sundance	2.2 (2212)	D	TFI	4	SOHC
	Sundance	2.5 (2507)	K	TFI	4	SOHC
	Sundance	3.0 (2972)	3	MFI	6	SOHC

ENGINE IDENTIFICATION

Year	Model	Engine Displacement Liters (cc)	Engine Series (ID/VIN)	Fuel System	No. of Cylinders	Engine Type
1993	Acclaim	2.5 (2507)	K	TFI	4	SOHC
	Acclaim	2.5 (2507)	V	MFI-M85	4	SOHC
	Acclaim	3.0 (2972)	3	MFI	6	SOHC
	Daytona	2.2 (2212)	A	MFI-Turbo	4	DOHC
	Daytona	2.5 (2507)	K	TFI	4	SOHC
	Daytona	3.0 (2972)	3	MFI	6	SOHC
	Lebaron	2.5 (2507)	K	TFI	4	SOHC
	Lebaron	3.0 (2972)	3	MFI	4	SOHC
	Shadow	2.2 (2212)	D	TFI	4	SOHC
	Shadow	2.5 (2507)	K	TFI	4	SOHC
	Shadow	3.0 (2972)	3	MFI	6	SOHC
	Spirit	2.5 (2507)	K	TFI	4	SOHC
	Spirit	2.5 (2507)	V	MFI-M85	4	SOHC
	Spirit	3.0 (2972)	3	MFI	6	SOHC
	Sundance	2.2 (2212)	D	TFI	4	SOHC
	Sundance	2.5 (2507)	K	TFI	4	SOHC
	Sundance	3.0 (2972)	3	MFI	6	SOHC
1994	Acclaim	2.5 (2507)	K	TFI	4	SOHC
	Acclaim	2.5 (2507)	V	MFI-M85	4	SOHC
	Acclaim	3.0 (2972)	3	MFI	6	SOHC
	Lebaron	3.0 (2972)	3	MFI	6	SOHC
	Shadow	2.2 (2212)	D	TFI	4	SOHC
	Shadow	2.5 (2507)	K	TFI	4	SOHC
	Shadow	3.0 (2972)	3	MFI	6	SOHC
	Spirit	2.5 (2507)	K	TFI	4	SOHC
	Spirit	2.5 (2507)	V	MFI-M85	4	SOHC
	Spirit	3.0 (2972)	3	MFI	6	SOHC
	Sundance	2.2 (2212)	D	TFI	4	SOHC
	Sundance	2.5 (2507)	K	TFI	4	SOHC
	Sundance	3.0 (2972)	3	MFI	6	SOHC
1995-96	Acclaim	2.5 (2507)	K	TFI	4	SOHC
	Acclaim	2.5 (2507)	V	MFI-M85	4	SOHC
	Acclaim	3.0 (2972)	3	MFI	6	SOHC
	Lebaron	3.0 (2972)	3	MFI	6	SOHC
	Spirit	2.5 (2507)	K	TFI	4	SOHC
	Spirit	2.5 (2507)	V	MFI-M85	4	SOHC
	Spirit	3.0 (2972)	3	MFI	6	SOHC

MFI - Multiport fuel injection
TFI - Throttle body fuel injection
SOHC - Single overhead camshaft

GENERAL ENGINE SPECIFICATIONS

Year	Engine ID/VIN	Engine Displacement Liters (cc)	Fuel System Type	Net Horsepower @ rpm	Net Torque @ rpm (ft. lbs.)	Bore x Stroke (in.)	Compression Ratio	Oil Pressure @ rpm
1992	A	2.2 (2212)	MFI-Turbo	224@6000	217@800	3.44x3.62	7.8:1	60-90@2000
	D	2.2 (2212)	TFI	93@4800	121@3200	3.44x3.62	9.5:1	60-90@2000
	J	2.5 (2507)	MFI-Turbo	①	②	3.44x4.09	7.8:1	60-90@2000
	K	2.5 (2507)	TFI	100@4800	135@2800	3.44x4.09	9.0:1	60-90@2000
	3	3.0 (2972)	MFI	141@5000	171@2800	3.59x2.99	8.9:1	35-100@2000
1993	A	2.2 (2212)	MFI-Turbo	224@6000	217@2800	3.44x3.62	7.8:1	25-80@3000
	D	2.2 (2212)	TFI	93@4800	122@3200	3.44x3.62	9.5:1	25-80@3000
	K	2.5 (2507)	TFI	100@4800	135@2800	3.44x4.09	8.9:1	25-80@3000
	V	2.5 (2507)	MFI-M85	106@4400	145@2400	3.44x4.09	9.0:1	25-80@3000
	3	3.0 (2972)	MFI	141@5000	171@2800	3.59x2.99	8.9:1	28.5@3000
1994	D	2.2 (2212)	TFI	93@4800	122@3200	3.44x3.62	9.5:1	25-80@3000
	K	2.5 (2507)	TFI	100@4800	135@2800	3.44x4.09	8.9:1	25-80@3000
	V	2.5 (2507)	MFI-M85	106@4400	145@2400	3.44x4.09	9.0:1	25-80@3000
	3	3.0 (2972)	MFI	141@5000	171@2800	3.59x2.99	8.9:1	35-75@3000
1995-96	K	2.5 (2507)	TFI	100@4800	135@2800	3.44x4.09	8.9:1	25-80@3000
	V	2.5 (2507)	MFI-M85	106@4400	145@2400	3.44x4.09	9.0:1	25-80@3000
	3	3.0 (2972)	MFI	141@5000	171@2800	3.59x2.99	8.9:1	30-80@3000

MFI - Multipoint fuel injection
TFI - Throttle body fuel injection
M85 - 85% Methanol flexible fuel engine
Automatic transaxle - 210@2400

① Manual transaxle: 150@5000
   Automatic transaxle: 152@4800
② Manual transaxle: 180@2000
   Automatic transaxle: 210@2400

GASOLINE ENGINE TUNE-UP SPECIFICATIONS

Year	Engine ID/VIN	Engine Displacement Liters (cc)	Spark Plugs Gap (in.)	Ignition Timing (deg.) MT	Ignition Timing (deg.) AT	Fuel Pump (psi)	Idle Speed (rpm) MT	Idle Speed (rpm) AT	Valve Clearance In.	Valve Clearance Ex.
1992	A	2.2 (2212)	0.035	NA	-	55	850	-	HYD	HYD
	D	2.2 (2212)	0.035	12B	12B	39	850	850	HYD	HYD
	J	2.5 (2507)	0.035	12B	12B	55	900	850	HYD	HYD
	K	2.5 (2507)	0.035	12B	12B	39	850	850	HYD	HYD
	3	3.0 (2972)	0.040	-	12B	48	-	700	HYD	HYD
1993	A	2.2 (2212)	0.035	NA	-	55	850	-	HYD	HYD
	D	2.2 (2212)	0.035	12B	12B	39	900	800	HYD	HYD
	K	2.5 (2507)	0.035	12B	12B	39	850	850	HYD	HYD
	V	2.5 (2507)	0.035	12B	12B	55	850	850	HYD	HYD
	3	3.0 (2972)	0.040	-	12B	48	-	700	HYD	HYD
1994	D	2.2 (2212)	0.035	①	①	39	850	800	HYD	HYD
	K	2.5 (2507)	0.035	①	①	39	900	850	HYD	HYD
	V	2.5 (2507)	0.035	12B	12B	55	850	850	HYD	HYD
	3	3.0 (2972)	0.035	-	①	48	-	700	HYD	HYD

GASOLINE ENGINE TUNE-UP SPECIFICATIONS

Year	Engine ID/VIN	Engine Displacement Liters (cc)	Spark Plugs Gap (in.)	Ignition Timing (deg.) MT	Ignition Timing (deg.) AT	Fuel Pump (psi)	Idle Speed (rpm) MT	Idle Speed (rpm) AT	Valve Clearance In.	Valve Clearance Ex.
1995-96	K	2.5 (2507)	0.035	-	①	39	-	850	HYD	HYD
	V	2.5 (2507)	0.035	-	①	55	-	850	HYD	HYD
	3	3.0 (2972)	0.035	-	①	48	-	700	HYD	HYD

NOTE: The Vehicle Emission Control Information label often reflects specification changes made during production. The label figures must be used if they differ from those in this chart.

B - Before top dead center

HYD - Hydraulic

NA - Not Available

① Refer to the Vehicle Emission Control Information label for correct timing specifications with a range of +/- 2 degrees

CAPACITIES

Year	Model	Engine ID/VIN	Engine Displacement Liters (cc)	Engine Oil with Filter (qts.)	Transmission (pts.) 4-Spd	Transmission (pts.) 5-Spd	Transmission (pts.) Auto.	Drive Axle Front (pts.)	Drive Axle Rear (pts.)	Fuel Tank (gal.)	Cooling System (qts.)
1992	Acclaim	K	2.5 (2507)	4.5	-	4.8	①	-	-	16.0	9.0
	Acclaim	3	3.0 (2972)	4.5	-	-	①	-	-	16.0	9.5
	Daytona	A	2.2 (2212)	4.0	-	4.8	-	-	-	14.0	9.0
	Daytona	K	2.5 (2507)	4.0	-	4.8	①	-	-	14.0	9.0
	Daytona	J	2.5 (2507)	4.0	-	4.8	①	-	-	14.0	9.0
	Daytona	3	3.0 (2972)	4.0	-	4.8	①	-	-	16.0	9.5
	Lebaron	J	2.5 (2507)	4.5	-	5.0	①	-	-	14.0	9.0
	Lebaron	K	2.5 (2507)	4.5	-	5.0	①	-	-	14.0	9.0
	Lebaron	3	3.0 (2972)	4.5	-	5.0	①	-	-	14.0	9.0
	Shadow	D	2.2 (2212)	4.0	-	4.8	①	-	-	14.0	9.0
	Shadow	K	2.5 (2507)	4.0	-	4.8	①	-	-	14.0	9.0
	Shadow	J	2.5 (2507)	4.0	-	4.8	①	-	-	14.0	9.0
	Shadow	3	3.0 (2972)	4.0	-	4.8	①	-	-	14.0	9.5
	Spirit	A	2.2 (2212)	4.0	-	4.8	-	-	-	16.0	9.0
	Spirit	K	2.5 (2507)	4.0	-	4.8	①	-	-	16.0	9.0
	Spirit	J	2.5 (2507)	4.0	-	4.8	①	-	-	16.0	9.0
	Spirit	3	3.0 (2972)	4.0	-	-	①	-	-	16.0	9.5
	Sundance	D	2.2 (2212)	4.5	-	4.8	①	-	-	14.0	9.0
	Sundance	K	2.5 (2507)	4.5	-	4.8	①	-	-	14.0	9.0
	Sundance	3	3.0 (2972)	4.5	-	4.8	①	-	-	14.0	9.0
1993	Acclaim	K	2.5 (2507)	4.5	-	4.8	①	-	-	16.0	9.0
	Acclaim	V	2.5 (2507)	4.5	-	-	①	-	-	18.0	9.0
	Acclaim	3	3.0 (2972)	4.5	-	-	①	-	-	16.0	0.5
	Daytona	A	2.2 (2212)	4.0	-	4.8	-	-	-	14.0	9.0
	Daytona	K	2.5 (2507)	4.0	-	4.8	①	-	-	14.0	9.0
	Daytona	3	3.0 (2972)	4.0	-	4.8	①	-	-	16.0	9.5
	Lebaron	K	2.5 (2507)	4.5	-	5.0	①	-	-	14.0	9.0
	Lebaron	3	3.0 (2972)	4.5	-	5.0	①	-	-	14.0	9.0

CAPACITIES

Year	Model	Engine ID/VIN	Engine Displacement Liters (cc)	Engine Oil with Filter (qts.)	Transmission (pts.)			Drive Axle		Fuel Tank (gal.)	Cooling System (qts.)
					4-Spd	5-Spd	Auto.	Front (pts.)	Rear (pts.)		
	Shadow	D	2.2 (2212)	4.0	-	4.8	①	-	-	14.0	9.0
	Shadow	K	2.5 (2507)	4.0	-	4.8	①	-	-	14.0	9.0
	Shadow	3	3.0 (2972)	4.0	-	4.8	①	-	-	14.0	9.5
	Spirit	K	2.5 (2507)	4.0	-	4.8	①	-	-	16.0	9.0
	Spirit	V	2.5 (2507)	4.0	-	-	①	-	-	18.0	9.0
	Spirit	3	3.0 (2972)	4.0	-	-	①	-	-	16.0	9.5
	Sundance	D	2.2 (2212)	4.5	-	4.8	①	-	-	14.0	9.0
	Sundance	K	2.5 (2507)	4.5	-	4.8	①	-	-	14.0	9.0
	Sundance	3	3.0 (2972)	4.5	-	4.8	①	-	-	14.0	9.0
1994	Acclaim	K	2.5 (2507)	4.5	-	4.8	①	-	-	16.0	9.0
	Acclaim	V	2.5 (2507)	4.5	-	-	①	-	-	18.0	9.0
	Acclaim	3	3.0 (2972)	4.5	-	-	①	-	-	16.0	9.5
	Lebaron	3	3.0 (2972)	4.5	-	-	①	-	-	14.0	9.5
	Shadow	D	2.2 (2212)	4.5	-	4.8	①	-	-	14.0	9.0
	Shadow	K	2.5 (2507)	4.5	-	4.8	①	-	-	14.0	9.0
	Shadow	3	3.0 (2972)	4.5	-	4.8	①	-	-	14.0	9.5
	Spirit	K	2.5 (2507)	4.5	-	4.8	①	-	-	16.0	9.0
	Spirit	V	2.5 (2507)	4.5	-	-	①	-	-	18.0	9.0
	Spirit	3	3.0 (2972)	4.5	-	-	①	-	-	16.0	9.5
	Sundance	D	2.2 (2212)	4.5	-	4.8	①	-	-	14.0	9.0
	Sundance	K	2.5 (2507)	4.5	-	4.8	①	-	-	14.0	9.0
	Sundance	3	3.0 (2972)	4.5	-	4.8	①	-	-	14.0	9.5
1995-96	Acclaim	K	2.5 (2507)	4.5	-	4.8	①	-	-	16.0	9.0
	Acclaim	V	2.5 (2507)	4.5	-	-	①	-	-	18.0	9.0
	Acclaim	3	3.0 (2972)	4.5	-	-	①	-	-	16.0	9.5
	Lebaron	3	3.0 (2972)	4.5	-	-	①	-	-	14.0	9.5
	Spirit	K	2.5 (2507)	4.5	-	4.8	①	-	-	16.0	9.0
	Spirit	V	2.5 (2507)	4.5	-	-	①	-	-	18.0	9.0
	Spirit	3	3.0 (2972)	4.5	-	-	①	-	-	16.0	9.5

① Non-fleet models: 17.8 pts.
Fleet models: 18.4 pts.
A413 with lock-up converter: 17.0 pts.
A604 transaxle: 18.2 pts.

CAMSHAFT SPECIFICATIONS
All measurements given in inches.

Year	Engine ID/VIN	Engine Displacement Liters (cc)	Journal Diameter					Elevation		Bearing Clearance	Camshaft End Play
			1	2	3	4	5	In.	Ex.		
1992	A	2.2 (2212)	1.886-1.887	1.886-1.887	1.886-1.887	1.886-1.887	1.886-1.887	NA	NA	0.0100 MAX	0.001-0.020
	D	2.2 (2212)	1.375-1.376	1.375-1.376	1.375-1.376	1.375-1.376	1.375-1.376	0.430	0.430	0.0100 MAX	0.005-0.013
	J	2.5 (2507)	1.375-1.376	1.375-1.376	1.375-1.376	1.375-1.376	1.375-1.376	0.430	0.430	0.0100 MAX	0.005-0.013
	K	2.5 (2507)	1.375-1.376	1.375-1.376	1.375-1.376	1..375-1.376	1.375-1.376	0.430	0.430	0.0100 MAX	0.005-0.013
	3	3.0 (2972)	NA	NA	NA	NA	-	①	①	0.0020-0.0035	NA
1993	A	2.2 (2212)	1.886-1.887	1.886-1.887	1.886-1.887	1.886-1.887	1.886-1.887	NA	NA	-	0.001-0.020
	D	2.2 (2212)	1.375-1.376	1.375-1.376	1.375-1.376	1.375-1.376	1.375-1.376	0.430	0.430	-	0.005-0.013
	K	2.5 (2507)	1.375-1.376	1.375-1.376	1.375-1.376	1.375-1.376	1.375-1.376	0.430	0.430	-	0.005-0.013
	V	2.5 (2507)	1.375-1.376	1.375-1.376	1.375-1.376	1.375-1.376	1.375-1.376	0.430	0.430	-	0.001-0.020
	3	3.0 (2972)	NA	NA	NA	NA	-	①	①	0.0020-0.0035	NA
1994	D	2.2 (2212)	1.395-1.396	1.395-1.396	1.395-1.396	1.395-1.396	1.395-1.396	0.430	0.430	-	0.005-0.013
	K	2.5 (2507)	1.395-1.396	1.395-1.396	1.395-1.396	1.395-1.396	1.395-1.396	0.430	0.430	-	0.005-0.013
	V	2.5 (2507)	1.375-1.376	1.375-1.376	1.375-1.376	1.375-1.376	1.375-1.376	0.430	0.430	-	0.001-0.020
	3	3.0 (2972)	NA	NA	NA	NA	-	①	①	0.0020-0.0035	NA
1995-96	K	2.5 (2507)	1.375-1.376	1.375-1.376	1.375-1.376	1.375-1.376	1.375-1.376	0.430	0.430	-	0.005-0.013
	V	2.5 (2507)	1.375-1.376	1.375-1.376	1.375-1.376	1.375-1.376	1.375-1.376	0.430	0.430	-	0.001-0.020
	3	3.0 (2972)	NA	NA	NA	NA	-	①	①	0.0020-0.0035	NA

NA - Not Available

① Intake cam lobe height: 1.6204 in.
Exhaust cam lobe height: 1.6204 in.

CRANKSHAFT AND CONNECTING ROD SPECIFICATIONS

All measurements are given in inches.

| Year | Engine ID/VIN | Engine Displacement Liters (cc) | Crankshaft | | | | Connecting Rod | | |
			Main Brg. Journal Dia.	Main Brg. Oil Clearance	Shaft End-play	Thrust on No.	Journal Diameter	Oil Clearance	Side Clearance
1992	A	2.2 (2212)	2.3620-2.3630	0.0004-0.0040	0.0020-0.0140	3	1.9680-1.9690	0.0008-0.0030	0.0050-0.0130
	D	2.2 (2212)	2.3620-2.3630	0.0004-0.0040	0.0020-0.0140	3	1.9680-1.9690	0.0008-0.0030	0.0050-0.0130
	J	2.5 (2507)	2.3620-2.3630	0.0004-0.0040	0.0020-0.0140	3	1.9680-1.9690	0.0008-0.0030	0.0050-0.0130
	K	2.5 (2507)	2.3620-2.3630	0.0004-0.0040	0.0020-0.0140	3	1.9680-1.9690	0.0008-0.0030	0.0050-0.0130
	3	3.0 (2972)	2.3610-2.3620	0.0006-0.0020	0.0020-0.0100	3	1.9680-1.9690	0.0006-0.0020	0.0040-0.0100
1993	A	2.2 (2212)	2.3620-2.3630	0.0004-0.0040	0.0020-0.0140	3	1.9680-1.9690	0.0008-0.0030	0.0050-0.0130
	D	2.2 (2212)	2.3620-2.3630	0.0004-0.0040	0.0020-0.0140	3	1.9680-1.9690	0.0008-0.0030	0.0050-0.0130
	K	2.5 (2507)	2.3620-2.3630	0.0004-0.0040	0.0020-0.0140	3	1.9680-1.9690	0.0008-0.0030	0.0050-0.0130
	V	2.5 (2507)	2.3620-2.3630	0.0004-0.0040	0.0020-0.0140	3	1.9680-1.9690	0.0008-0.0030	0.0050-0.0130
	3	3.0 (2972)	2.3610-2.3620	0.0006-0.0020	0.0020-0.0100	3	1.9680-1.9690	0.0006-0.0020	0.0040-0.0100
1994	D	2.2 (2212)	2.3620-2.3630	0.0004-0.0040	0.0020-0.0140	3	1.9680-1.9690	0.0008-0.0030	0.0050-0.0130
	K	2.5 (2507)	2.3620-2.3630	0.0004-0.0028	0.0020-0.0070	3	1.9680-1.9690	0.0008-0.0030	0.0050-0.0130
	V	2.5 (2507)	2.3620-2.3630	0.0004-0.0040	0.0020-0.0140	3	1.9680-1.9690	0.0008-0.0030	0.0050-0.0130
	3	3.0 (2972)	2.3610-2.3620	0.0006-0.0020	0.0020-0.0100	3	1.9680-1.9690	0.0006-0.0020	0.0040-0.0100
1995-96	K	2.5 (2507)	2.3620-2.3630	0.0004-0.0028	0.0020-0.0070	3	1.9680-1.9690	0.0008-0.0030	0.0050-0.0130
	V	2.5 (2507)	2.3620-2.3630	0.0004-0.0040	0.0020-0.0140	3	1.9680-1.9690	0.0008-0.0030	0.0050-0.0130
	3	3.0 (2972)	2.3610-2.3620	0.0006-0.0020	0.0020-0.0100	3	1.9680-1.9690	0.0006-0.0020	0.0040-0.0100

VALVE SPECIFICATIONS

Year	Engine ID/VIN	Engine Displacement Liters (cc)	Seat Angle (deg.)	Face Angle (deg.)	Spring Test Pressure (lbs. @ in.)	Spring Installed Height (in.)	Stem-to-Guide Clearance (in.)		Stem Diameter (in.)	
							Intake	Exhaust	Intake	Exhaust
1992	A	2.2 (2212)	45	45	225@1.34	1.65	0.0010-0.0040	0.0020-0.0040	0.2740	0.2730
	D	2.2 (2212)	45	45	114@1.65	1.65	0.0009-0.0026	0.0030-0.0047	0.3124	0.3103
	J	2.5 (2507)	45	45	114@1.65	1.65	0.0009-0.0026	0.0030-0.0047	0.3124	0.3103
	K	2.5 (2507)	45	45	114@1.65	1.65	0.0009-0.0026	0.0030-0.0047	0.3124	0.3103
	3	3.0 (2972)	44	45-45.5	73@1.59	1.99	0.0010-0.0020	0.0019-0.0030	0.3140	0.3125
1993	A	2.2 (2212)	45	45	225@1.34	1.65	0.0010-0.0040	0.0020-0.0040	0.2740	0.2730
	D	2.2 (2212)	45	45	114@1.65	1.65	0.0009-0.0026	0.0030-0.0047	0.3124	0.3103
	K	2.5 (2507)	45	45	114@1.65	1.65	0.0010-0.0030	0.0030-0.0047	0.3124	0.3103
	V	2.5 (2507)	45	45	114@1.65	1.65	0.0010-0.0030	0.0030-0.0047	0.3124	0.3103
	3	3.0 (2972)	44	45-45.5	73@1.59	1.99	0.0010-0.0020	0.0019-0.0030	0.3140	0.3125
1994	D	2.2 (2212)	45	45	114@1.65	1.65	0.0009-0.0026	0.0030-0.0047	0.3124	0.3103
	K	2.5 (2507)	45	45	114@1.65	1.65	0.0009-0.0026	0.0030-0.0047	0.3124	0.3103
	V	2.5 (2507)	45	45	114@1.65	1.65	0.0010-0.0030	0.0030-0.0047	0.3124	0.3103
	3	3.0 (2972)	44.5	45-45.5	73@1.59	1.96 [1]	0.0010-0.0020	0.0019-0.0030	0.3140	0.3125
1995-96	K	2.5 (2507)	45	45	114@1.65	1.65	0.0009-0.0026	0.0030-0.0047	0.3124	0.3103
	V	2.5 (2507)	45	45	114@1.65	1.65	0.0010-0.0030	0.0030-0.0047	0.3124	0.3103
	3	3.0 (2972)	44.5	45-45.5	73@1.59	1.59	0.0010-0.0030	0.0019-0.0030	0.3140	0.3125

[1] Free height

PISTON AND RING SPECIFICATIONS

All measurements are given in inches.

Year	Engine ID/VIN	Engine Displacement Liters (cc)	Piston Clearance	Ring Gap			Ring Side Clearance		
				Top Compression	Bottom Compression	Oil Control	Top Compression	Bottom Compression	Oil Control
1992	A	2.2 (2212)	0.0005-0.0015	0.0140-0.0390	0.0140-0.0390	0.0100-0.0390	0.0015-0.0031	0.0015-0.0037	0.0002-0.0080
	D	2.2 (2212)	0.0005-0.0015	0.0110-0.0390	0.0110-0.0390	0.0150-0.0740	0.0015-0.0031	0.0015-0.0037	0.0002-0.0080
	J	2.5 (2507)	0.0005-0.0015	0.0100-0.0200	0.0090-0.0370	0.0150-0.0740	0.0015-0.0031	0.0015-0.0037	0.0002-0.0080
	K	2.5 (2507)	0.0005-0.0015	0.0110-0.0120	0.0100-0.0160	0.0120-0.0350	0.0015-0.0031	0.0015-0.0037	0.0002-0.0080
	3	3.0 (2972)	0.0008-0.0015	0.0120-0.0180	0.0100-0.0160	0.0120-0.0350	0.0020-0.0035	0.0008-0.0020	NA
1993	A	2.2 (2212)	0.0018-0.0039	0.0140-0.0390	0.0140-0.0370	0.0100-0.0390	0.0015-0.0040	0.0015-0.0037	0.0002-0.0080
	D	2.2 (2212)	0.0005-0.0027	0.0100-0.0390	0.0110-0.0390	0.0150-0.0740	0.0015-0.0040	0.0015-0.0037	0.0002-0.0080
	K	2.5 (2507)	0.0005-0.0015	0.0110-0.0120	0.0100-0.0160	0.0120-0.0350	0.0015-0.0031	0.0015-0.0037	0.0002-0.0080
	V	2.5 (2507)	0.0006-0.0030	0.0100-0.0390	0.0090-0.0370	0.0150-0.0740	0.0016-0.0030	0.0016-0.0035	0.0002-0.0080
	3	3.0 (2972)	0.0008-0.0015	0.0120-0.0180	0.0100-0.0160	0.0120-0.0350	0.0020-0.0035	0.0008-0.0020	NA
1994	D	2.2 (2212)	0.0005-0.0027	0.0100-0.0390	0.0110-0.0390	0.0150-0.0740	0.0015-0.0040	0.0015-0.0037	0.0002-0.0080
	K	2.5 (2507)	0.0010-0.0027	0.0100-0.0390	0.0110-0.0390	0.0100-0.0740	0.0015-0.0031	0.0015-0.0037	0.0002-0.0080
	V	2.5 (2507)	0.0006-0.0030	0.0100-0.0390	0.0090-0.0370	0.0150-0.0740	0.0016-0.0030	0.0016-0.0035	0.0002-0.0080
	3	3.0 (2972)	0.0012-0.0020	0.0120-0.0180	0.0180-0.0240	0.0080-0.0240	0.0020-0.0035	0.0016-0.0033	NA
1995-96	K	2.5 (2507)	0.0005-0.0015	0.0100-0.0200	0.0110-0.0210	0.0150-0.0550	0.0015-0.0031	0.0015-0.0037	0.0002-0.0080
	V	2.5 (2507)	0.0006-0.0030	0.0100-0.0390	0.0090-0.0370	0.0150-0.0740	0.0016-0.0030	0.0016-0.0035	0.0002-0.0080
	3	3.0 (2972)	0.0012-0.0020	0.0120-0.0180	0.0180-0.0240	0.0080-0.0240	0.0020-0.0035	0.0016-0.0033	NA

NA - Not Available

TORQUE SPECIFICATIONS
All readings in ft. lbs.

Year	Engine ID/VIN	Engine Displacement Liters (cc)	Cylinder Head Bolts	Main Bearing Bolts	Rod Bearing Bolts	Crankshaft Damper Bolts	Flywheel Bolts	Manifold Intake	Manifold Exhaust	Spark Plugs	Lug Nut
1992	A	2.2 (2212)	①	②	50	80	70	17	17	20	95
	D	2.2 (2212)	①	②	③	85	70	17	17	26	95
	J	2.5 (2507)	①	②	③	85	70	17	17	26	95
	K	2.5 (2507)	①	②	③	85	70	17	17	26	95
	3	3.0 (2972)	80	60	38	112	70	17	17	20	95
1993	A	2.2 (2212)	①	②	50	80	70	17	17	20	95
	D	2.2 (2212)	①	②	③	85	70	17	17	26	95
	K	2.5 (2507)	①	②	③	85	70	17	17	26	95
	V	2.5 (2507)	①	②	③	85	70	17	17	26	95
	3	3.0 (2972)	80	60	38	112	70	17	17	20	95
1994	D	2.2 (2212)	①	②	③	85	70	17	17	20	95
	K	2.5 (2507)	①	②	③	85	70	17	17	20	95
	V	2.5 (2507)	①	②	③	85	70	17	17	26	95
	3	3.0 (2972)	80	60	38	112	70	15	16	20	95
1995-96	K	2.5 (2507)	①	②	③	85	70	17	17	20	95
	V	2.5 (2507)	①	②	③	85	70	17	17	26	95
	3	3.0 (2972)	80	60	38	112	70	15	16	20	95

① Step 1: 45 ft. lbs.
Step 2: 65 ft. lbs.
Step 3: 65 ft. lbs.
Step 4: +90 degrees
② Step 1: 30 ft. lbs.
Step 2: +90 degrees
③ Step 1: 40 ft. lbs.
Step 2: +90 degrees

BRAKE SPECIFICATIONS
All measurements in inches unless noted

Year	Model			Master Cylinder Bore	Brake Disc Original Thickness	Brake Disc Minimum Thickness	Maximum Runout	Brake Drum Diameter Original Inside Diameter	Max. Wear Limit	Maximum Machine Diameter	Minimum Lining Thickness Front	Minimum Lining Thickness Rear
1992	Acclaim			0.827	0.861	0.803	0.005	10.24	NA	NA	0.300	0.300
	Acclaim	①		-	0.856	0.797	0.005	-	-	-	-	0.280
	Daytona			0.827	0.940	0.882	0.006	10.24	NA	NA	0.300	0.300
	Daytona	④		-	0.468	0.409	0.005	-	-	-	-	0.300
	Daytona	⑤		-	0.856	0.797	0.005	-	-	-	-	0.300
	Lebaron		F	0.827	0.861	0.803	0.005	7.87	③	③	0.300	0.062
	Lebaron	④	R	-	0.468	0.409	0.005	-	-	-	-	0.280
	Lebaron	⑤	R	-	0.856	0.797	0.005	-	-	-	-	0.280
	Shadow			0.827	0.935	0.882	0.005	7.87	NA	NA	0.300	0.300
	Spirit			0.827	0.861	0.803	0.005	10.24	NA	NA	0.300	0.300
	Spirit	①		-	0.856	0.797	0.005	-	-	-	-	0.280
	Sundance			0.827	0.935	0.882	0.005	7.87	NA	NA	0.300	0.300

BRAKE SPECIFICATIONS
All measurements in inches unless noted

Year	Model			Master Cylinder Bore	Brake Disc Original Thickness	Brake Disc Minimum Thickness	Brake Disc Maximum Runout	Brake Drum Diameter Original Inside Diameter	Brake Drum Diameter Max. Wear Limit	Brake Drum Diameter Maximum Machine Diameter	Minimum Lining Thickness Front	Minimum Lining Thickness Rear
1993	Acclaim			0.827	0.861	0.803	0.005	10.24	NA	NA	0.300	0.300
	Acclaim	①		-	0.856	0.797	0.005	-	-	-	-	0.280
	Daytona			0.827	0.940	0.882	0.006	10.24	NA	NA	0.300	0.300
	Daytona	④		-	0.468	0.409	0.005	-	-	-	-	0.300
	Daytona	⑤		-	0.856	0.797	0.005	-	-	-	-	0.300
	Lebaron		F	0.827	0.861	0.803	0.005	7.87	③	③	0.300	0.062
	Lebaron	④	R	-	0.468	0.409	0.005	-	-	-	-	0.280
	Lebaron	⑤	R	-	0.856	0.797	0.005	-	-	-	-	0.280
	Shadow			0.827	0.935	0.882	0.005	7.87	NA	NA	0.300	0.280
	Shadow	①		-	0.468	0.409	0.005	-	-	-	-	0.280
	Spirit			0.827	0.861	0.803	0.004	10.24	NA	NA	0.300	0.300
	Spirit	①		-	0.856	0.797	0.005	-	-	-	-	0.280
	Sundance			0.827	0.935	0.882	0.005	-	-	-	0.300	0.280
	Sundance	①		-	0.468	0.409	0.005	-	-	-	-	0.280
1994	Acclaim			0.827	0.935	0.882	0.005	10.24	NA	NA	0.300	0.300
	Acclaim	②		-	0.468	0.409	0.005	-	-	-	-	0.280
	Lebaron		F	0.827	0.935	0.882	0.005	7.87	③	③	0.300	0.062
	Lebaron	④	R	-	0.468	0.409	0.005	-	-	-	-	0.280
	Lebaron	⑤	R	-	0.856	0.797	0.005	-	-	-	-	0.280
	Shadow			0.827	0.935	0.882	0.005	7.87	NA	NA	0.300	0.280
	Shadow	①		-	0.468	0.409	0.005	-	-	-	-	0.280
	Spirit			0.827	0.935	0.882	0.005	10.24	③	③	0.300	0.300
	Spirit	⑥		-	0.856	0.797	0.005	-	-	-	-	0.280
	Sundance			0.875	0.935	0.882	0.005	7.87	NA	NA	0.300	0.280
	Sundance	①		-	0.468	0.409	0.005	-	-	-	-	0.280
1995-96	Acclaim			0.827	0.935	0.882	0.005	10.24	NA	NA	0.300	0.300
	Acclaim	②		-	0.468	0.409	0.005	-	-	-	-	0.280
	Lebaron		F	0.827	0.935	0.882	0.005	7.87	③	③	0.300	0.062
	Lebaron	④	R	-	0.468	0.409	0.005	-	-	-	-	0.280
	Lebaron	⑤	R	-	0.856	0.797	0.005	-	-	-	-	0.280
	Spirit			0.827	0.935	0.882	0.005	10.24	③	③	0.300	0.300
	Spirit	②		-	0.468	0.409	0.005	-	-	-	-	0.280

NA - Not Available
① Rear disc.
② Optional vented rear disc brakes:
   Original thickness: 0.856
   Minimum thickness: 0.797
③ Maximum diameter is stamped on drum

④ Solid rear disc
⑤ Vented rear disc
⑥ Solid rear discs
   Original thickness: 0.468
   Minimum thickness: 0.409

WHEEL ALIGNMENT

Year	Model		Caster Range (deg.)	Caster Preferred Setting (deg.)	Camber Range (deg.)	Camber Preferred Setting (deg.)	Toe-in (in.)	Steering Axis Inclination (deg.)
1992	Acclaim	F	①	2 3/4P	1/4N-3/4P	5/16P	1/16P	12 1/2
		R	-	-	1 1/4N-1/4N	1/2N	0	-
	Daytona	F	①	2 3/4P	1/4N-3/4P	5/16P	1/16P	12 1/2
		R	-	-	1 1/4N-1/4N	1/2N	0	-
	Lebaron Sedan	F	-	2 13/16P	3/16N-13/16P	5/16P	1/16P	12 13/32
		R	-	-	1N-0	1/2N	0	-
	Lebaron Coupe	F	-	2 13/16P	3/16N-13/16P	5/16P	1/16P	13
		R	-	-	1N-0	1/2N	0	-
	Shadow	F	①	2 3/4P	1/4N-3/4P	5/16P	1/16P	12 1/2
		R	-	-	1 1/4N-1/4N	1/2N	0	-
	Spirit	F	①	2 3/4P	1/4N-3/4P	5/16P	1/16P	12 1/2
		R	-	-	1 1/4N-1/4N	1/2N	0	-
	Sundance	F	①	2 3/4P	1/4N-3/4P	5/16P	1/16P	12 1/2
		R	-	-	1 1/4N-1/4N	1/2N	0	-
1993	Acclaim	F	①	2 3/4P	1/4N-3/4P	5/16P	1/16P	12 1/2
		R	-	-	1 1/4N-1/4N	1/2N	0	-
	Daytona	F	①	2 3/4P	1/4N-3/4P	5/16P	1/16P	12 1/2
		R	-	-	1 1/4N-1/4N	1/2N	0	-
	Lebaron Sedan	F	-	2 13/16P	3/16N-13/16P	5/16P	1/16P	12 13/32
		R	-	-	1N-0	1/2N	0	-
	Lebaron Coupe	F	-	2 13/16P	3/16N-13/16P	5/16P	1/16P	13
		R	-	-	1N-0	1/2N	0	-
	Shadow	F	①	2 3/4P	1/4N-3/4P	5/16P	1/16P	12 1/2
		R	-	-	1 1/4N-1/4N	1/2N	0	-
	Spirit	F	①	2 3/4P	1/4N-3/4P	5/16P	1/16P	12 1/2
		R	-	-	1 1/4N-1/4N	1/2N	0	-
	Sundance	F	①	2 3/4P	1/4N-3/4P	5/16P	1/16P	12 1/2
		R	-	-	1 1/4N-1/4N	1/2N	0	-
1994	Acclaim	F	①	2 13/16P	3/16N-13/16P	5/16P	1/16P	12 1/2
		R	-	-	1N-0	1/2N	0	-
	Lebaron	F	-	2 13/16P	3/16N-13/16P	5/16P	1/16P	13
		R	-	-	1N-0	1/2N	0	-
	Shadow	F	①	2 13/16P	3/16N-13/16P	5/16P	1/16P	12 13/32
		R	-	-	1N-0	1/2N	0	-
	Spirit	F	①	2 3/4P	3/16N-13/16P	5/16P	1/16P	12 1/2
		R	-	-	1N-0	1/2N	0	-
	Sundance	F	①	2 13/16P	3/16N-13/16P	5/16P	1/16P	12 13/32
		R	-	-	1N-0	1/2N	0	-

WHEEL ALIGNMENT

Year	Model		Caster Range (deg.)	Caster Preferred Setting (deg.)	Camber Range (deg.)	Camber Preferred Setting (deg.)	Toe-in (in.)	Steering Axis Inclination (deg.)
1995-96	Acclaim	F	①	2 13/16P	3/16N-13/16P	5/16P	1/16P	12 1/2
		R	-	-	1N-0	1/2N	0	-
	Lebaron	F	-	2 13/16P	3/16N-13/16P	5/16P	1/16P	13
		R	-	-	1N-0	1/2N	0	-
	Spirit	F	①	2 3/4P	3/16N-13/16P	5/16P	1/16P	12 1/2
		R	-	-	1N-0	1/2N	0	-

NA - Not Available

F - Front

R - Rear

① Non-adjustable, variation should not exceed 1 1/2 degrees

DYNASTY/IMPERIAL/NEW YORKER 5TH AVENUE NEW YORKER SALON

VEHICLE IDENTIFICATION CHART

Engine Code						Model Year	
Code	Liters	Cu. In. (cc)	Cyl.	Fuel Sys.	Eng. Mfg.	Code	Year
K	2.5	153 (2507)	I4	TFI	Chrysler	N	1992
3	3.0	181 (2972)	V6	MFI	Mitsubishi	P	1993
R	3.3	201 (3300)	V6	MFI	Chrysler		
L	3.8	231 (3696)	V6	MFI	Chrysler		
K	2.5	153 (2507)	I4	TFI	Chrysler		
3	3.0	181 (2972)	V6	MFI	Mitsubishi		
R	3.3	201 (3300)	V6	MFI	Chrysler		
L	3.8	231 (3696)	V6	MFI	Chrysler		

TFI - Throttle body fuel injection

MFI - Multiport fuel injection

ENGINE IDENTIFICATION

Year	Model	Engine Displacement Liters (cc)	Engine Series (ID/VIN)	Fuel System	No. of Cylinders	Engine Type
1992	Dynasty	2.5 (2507)	K	TFI	4	SOHC
	Dynasty	3.0 (2972)	3	MFI	4	SOHC
	Dynasty	3.3 (3300)	R	MFI	6	OHV
	New Yorker	3.3 (3300)	R	MFI	6	OHV
	New Yorker	3.8 (3696)	L	MFI	6	OHV
	Imperial	3.8 (3696)	L	MFI	6	OHV
1993	Dynasty	2.5 (2507)	K	TFI	4	SOHC
	Dynasty	3.0 (2972)	3	MFI	4	SOHC
	Dynasty	3.3 (3300)	R	MFI	6	OHV
	New Yorker	3.3 (3300)	R	MFI	6	OHV
	New Yorker	3.8 (3785)	L	MFI	6	OHV
	Imperial	3.8 (3785)	L	MFI	6	OHV

TFI - Throttle body fuel injection
MFI - Multiport fuel injection
OHV - Overhead valve
SOHC - Single overhead camshaft

GENERAL ENGINE SPECIFICATIONS

Year	Engine ID/VIN	Engine Displacement Liters (cc)	Fuel System Type	Net Horsepower @ rpm	Net Torque @ rpm (ft. lbs.)	Bore x Stroke (in.)	Compression Ratio	Oil Pressure @ rpm
1992	K	2.5 (2507)	TFI	100@2800	135@2800	3.44x4.09	8.9:1	30-80@3000
	3	3.0 (2972)	MFI	141@5000	171@2000	3.59x2.99	8.9:1	30-80@3000
	R	3.3 (3300)	MFI	147@4800	183@3600	3.66x3.19	8.9:1	30-80@3000
	L	3.8 (3785)	MFI	150@4400	203@3200	3.78x3.42	9.0:1	30-80@3000
1993	K	2.5 (2507)	TFI	100@2800	135@2800	3.44x4.09	8.9:1	30-80@3000
	3	3.0 (2972)	MFI	141@5000	171@2000	3.59x2.99	8.9:1	30-80@3000
	R	3.3 (3300)	MFI	147@4800	183@3600	3.66x3.19	8.9:1	30-80@3000
	L	3.8 (3785)	MFI	150@4400	203@3200	3.78x3.42	9.0:1	30-80@3000

TFI - Throttle body fuel injection
MFI - Multiport fuel injection

GASOLINE ENGINE TUNE-UP SPECIFICATIONS

Year	Engine ID/VIN	Engine Displacement Liters (cc)	Spark Plugs Gap (in.)	Ignition Timing (deg.) MT	Ignition Timing (deg.) AT	Fuel Pump (psi)	Idle Speed (rpm) MT	Idle Speed (rpm) AT	Valve Clearance In.	Valve Clearance Ex.
1992	K	2.5 (2507)	0.035	12B	12B	39	850	850	HYD	HYD
	3	3.0 (2972)	0.040	-	12B	1	-	700	HYD	HYD
	R	3.3 (3300)	0.050	-	12B	1	-	750	HYD	HYD
	L	3.8 (3785)	0.050	-	12B	1	-	750	HYD	HYD
1993	K	2.5 (2507)	0.035	-	12B	39	-	850	HYD	HYD
	3	3.0 (2972)	0.040	-	12B	1	-	700	HYD	HYD
	R	3.3 (3300)	0.050	-	12B	1	-	750	HYD	HYD
	L	3.8 (3785)	0.050	-	12B	1	-	750-1100	HYD	HYD

NOTE: The Vehicle Emission Control Information label often reflects specification changes made during production. The label figures must be used if they differ from those in this chart
B - Before top dead center
HYD - Hydraulic
1 This reading measured with vacuum hose disconnected from fuel pressure regulator

CAPACITIES

| Year | Model | Engine ID/VIN | Engine Displacement Liters (cc) | Engine Oil with Filter (qts.) | Transmission (pts.) | | | Transfer Case (pts.) | Drive Axle | | Fuel Tank (gal.) | Cooling System (qts.) |
					4-Spd	5-Spd	Auto.		Front (pts.)	Rear (pts.)		
1992	Dynasty	K	2.5 (2507)	4.0	-	-	①	-	-	-	16.0	9.0
	Dynasty	3	3.0 (2972)	4.0	-	-	①	-	-	-	16.0	9.5
	Dynasty	R	3.3 (3300)	4.0	-	-	①	-	-	-	16.0	9.5
	New Yorker	R	3.3 (3300)	4.5	-	-	①	-	-	-	16.0	9.0
	New Yorker	L	3.8 (3785)	4.5	-	-	①	-	-	-	16.0	9.0
	Imperial	L	3.8 (3785)	4.5	-	-	①	-	-	-	16.0	9.0
1993	Dynasty	K	2.5 (2507)	4.0	-	-	①	-	-	-	16.0	9.0
	Dynasty	3	3.0 (2972)	4.0	-	-	①	-	-	-	16.0	9.5
	Dynasty	T	3.3 (3300)	4.0	-	-	①	-	-	-	16.0	9.5
	New Yorker	R	3.3 (3300)	4.5	-	-	①	-	-	-	16.0	9.0
	New Yorker	L	3.8 (3785)	4.5	-	-	①	-	-	-	16.0	9.0
	Imperial	L	3.8 (3785)	4.5	-	-	①	-	-	-	16.0	9.0

① A413 - 17.8 pts.
A413 (fleet) - 18.4 pts.
A413 (lock-up) - 17.0 pts.
A604 (electronic) - 18.2 pts.

CAMSHAFT SPECIFICATIONS

All measurements given in inches.

| Year | Engine ID/VIN | Engine Displacement Liters (cc) | Journal Diameter | | | | | Elevation | | Bearing Clearance | Camshaft End Play |
			1	2	3	4	5	In.	Ex.		
1992	K	2.5 (2507)	1.3950-1.3960	1.3950-1.3960	1.3950-1.3960	1.3950-1.3960	1.3950-1.3960	NA	NA	NA	0.005-0.020
	3	3.0 (2972)	NA	NA	NA	NA	NA	①	①	NA	NA
	R	3.3 (3300)	1.9970-1.9990	1.9800-1.9820	1.9650-1.9670	1.9490-1.9520	NA	0.400	0.400	0.0010-0.0050	0.005-0.012
	L	3.8 (3785)	1.9970-1.9990	1.9800-1.9820	1.9650-1.9670	1.9490-1.9520	NA	0.400	0.400	0.0010-0.0040	0.005-0.012
1993	K	2.5 (2507)	1.3950-1.3960	1.3950-1.3960	1.3950-1.3960	1.3950-1.3960	1.3950-1.3960	NA	NA	NA	0.005-0.020
	3	3.0 (2972)	NA	NA	NA	NA	NA	①	①	NA	NA
	R	3.3 (3300)	1.9970-1.9990	1.9800-1.9820	1.9650-1.9670	1.9490-1.9520	NA	0.400	0.400	0.0010-0.0050	0.005-0.012
	L	3.8 (3785)	1.9970-1.9990	1.9800-1.9820	1.9650-1.9670	1.9490-1.9520	NA	0.400	0.400	0.0010-0.0040	0.005-0.012

NA - Not Available
① Height of cam lobe: 1.604-1.624 in.

CRANKSHAFT AND CONNECTING ROD SPECIFICATIONS

All measurements are given in inches.

Year	Engine ID/VIN	Engine Displacement Liters (cc)	Crankshaft Main Brg. Journal Dia.	Crankshaft Main Brg. Oil Clearance	Crankshaft Shaft End-play	Crankshaft Thrust on No.	Connecting Rod Journal Diameter	Connecting Rod Oil Clearance	Connecting Rod Side Clearance
1992	K	2.5 (2507)	2.3620-2.3630	0.0004-0.0040	0.0020-0.0140	3	1.9680-1.9690	0.0008-0.0040	0.0050-0.0130
	3	3.0 (2972)	2.3610-2.3620	0.0006-0.0020	0.0020-0.0100	3	1.9680-1.9690	0.0008-0.0028	0.0040-0.0100
	R	3.3 (3300)	2.5190	0.0007-0.0022	0.0010-0.0070	2	2.2830	0.0008-0.0030	0.0050-0.0150
	L	3.8 (3785)	2.5190	0.0007-0.0022	0.0030-0.0090	2	2.2830	0.0008-0.0030	0.0050-0.0150
1993	K	2.5 (2507)	2.3620-2.3630	0.0004-0.0040	0.0020-0.0140	3	1.9680-1.9690	0.0008-0.0040	0.0050-0.0130
	3	3.0 (2972)	2.3610-2.3620	0.0006-0.0020	0.0020-0.0100	3	1.9680-1.9690	0.0008-0.0028	0.0040-0.0100
	R	3.3 (3300)	2.5190	0.0007-0.0022	0.0010-0.0070	2	2.2830	0.0008-0.0030	0.0050-0.0150
	L	3.8 (3785)	2.5190	0.0007-0.0022	0.0030-0.0090	2	2.2830	0.0008-0.0030	0.0050-0.0150

VALVE SPECIFICATIONS

Year	Engine ID/VIN	Engine Displacement Liters (cc)	Seat Angle (deg.)	Face Angle (deg.)	Spring Test Pressure (lbs. @ in.)	Spring Installed Height (in.)	Stem-to-Guide Clearance (in.) Intake	Stem-to-Guide Clearance (in.) Exhaust	Stem Diameter (in.) Intake	Stem Diameter (in.) Exhaust
1992	K	2.5 (2507)	45	45	114@1.22	1.65	0.0010-0.0030	0.0030-0.0047	0.3124	0.3103
	3	3.0 (2972)	44.5	45.5	73@1.59	1.59	0.0010-0.0020	0.0020-0.0030	0.3130-0.3140	0.3120-0.3130
	R	3.3 (3300)	45	44.5	60@1.56	1.56	0.0010-0.0030	0.0020-0.0060	0.3110-0.3120	0.3110-0.3120
	L	3.8 (3785)	45	44.5	60@1.56	1.56	0.0010-0.0030	0.0030-0.0047	0.3120-0.3130	0.3110-0.3120
1993	K	2.5 (2507)	45	45	114@1.22	1.65	0.0010-0.0030	0.0030-0.0047	0.3124	0.3103
	3	3.0 (2972)	44.5	45.5	73@1.59	1.59	0.0010-0.0020	0.0020-0.0030	0.3130-0.3140	0.3120-0.3130
	R	3.3 (3300)	45	44.5	60@1.56	1.56	0.0010-0.0030	0.0020-0.0060	0.3110-0.3120	0.3110-0.3120
	L	3.8 (3785)	45	44.5	60@1.56	1.56	0.0010-0.0030	0.0030-0.0047	0.3120-0.3130	0.3110-0.3120

PISTON AND RING SPECIFICATIONS

All measurements are given in inches.

Year	Engine ID/VIN	Engine Displacement Liters (cc)	Piston Clearance	Ring Gap			Ring Side Clearance		
				Top Compression	Bottom Compression	Oil Control	Top Compression	Bottom Compression	Oil Control
1992	K	2.5 (2507)	0.0010-0.0027	0.010-0.039	0.011-0.039	0.015-0.074	0.0015-0.0040	0.0015-0.0040	0.0002-0.0080
	3	3.0 (2972)	0.0012-0.0020	0.012-0.018	0.010-0.016	0.012-0.035	0.0020-0.0035	0.0008-0.0020	NA
	R	3.3 (3300)	0.0009-0.0022	0.012-0.022	0.012-0.022	0.010-0.040	0.0012-0.0037	0.0012-0.0037	0.0005-0.0089
	L	3.8 (3785)	0.0009-0.0022	0.012-0.022	0.012-0.022	0.010-0.040	0.0012-0.0037	0.0012-0.0037	0.0005-0.0089
1993	K	2.5 (2507)	0.0010-0.0027	0.010-0.039	0.011-0.039	0.015-0.074	0.0015-0.0040	0.0015-0.0040	0.0002-0.0080
	3	3.0 (2972)	0.0012-0.0020	0.012-0.018	0.010-0.016	0.012-0.035	0.0020-0.0035	0.0008-0.0020	NA
	R	3.3 (3300)	0.0009-0.0022	0.012-0.022	0.012-0.022	0.010-0.040	0.0012-0.0037	0.0012-0.0037	0.0005-0.0089
	L:	3.8 (3785)	0.0009-0.0022	0.012-0.022	0.012-0.022	0.010-0.040	0.0012-0.0037	0.0012-0.0037	0.0005-0.0089

NA - Not Available

TORQUE SPECIFICATIONS

All readings in ft. lbs.

Year	Engine ID/VIN	Engine Displacement Liters (cc)	Cylinder Head Bolts	Main Bearing Bolts	Rod Bearing Bolts	Crankshaft Damper Bolts	Flywheel Bolts	Manifold		Spark Plugs	Lug Nut
								Intake	Exhaust		
1992	K	2.5 (2507)	1	2	3	50	70	17	17	26	95
	3	3.0 (2972)	70	60	38	110	70	17	17	20	95
	R	3.3 (3300)	4	2	3	50	70	17	17	26	95
	L	3.8 (3785)	4	2	3	50	70	17	17	26	95
1993	K	2.5 (2507)	1	2	3	50	70	17	17	26	95
	3	3.0 (2972)	70	60	38	110	70	17	17	20	95
	R	3.3 (3300)	4	2	3	50	70	17	17	26	95
	L	3.8 (3785)	4	2	3	50	70	17	17	26	95

1 Step 1: 45 ft. lbs.
Step 2: 65 ft. lbs.
Step 3: 65 ft. lbs.
Step 4: Plus 1/4 turn
2 Step 1: 30 ft. lbs.
Step 2: Plus 1/4 turn
3 Step 1: 40 ft. lbs.
Step 2: Plus 1/4 turn

4 Step 1: 45 ft. lbs.
Step 2: 65 ft. lbs.
Step 3: 65 ft. lbs.
Step 4: Plus 1/4 turn
Torque small bolt in rear of cylinder head to 25 ft. lbs.

BRAKE SPECIFICATIONS

All measurements in inches unless noted

Year	Model		Master Cylinder Bore	Brake Disc Original Thickness	Brake Disc Minimum Thickness	Maximum Runout	Brake Drum Diameter Original Inside Diameter	Max. Wear Limit	Maximum Machine Diameter	Minimum Lining Thickness Front	Minimum Lining Thickness Rear
1992	Dynasty		0.827	0.935	0.882	0.005	8.86	NA	NA	0.300	0.300
	Dynasty 1		-	0.390	0.339	0.005	-	-	-	-	0.060
	Imperial	F	0.827	0.861	0.803	0.005	-	-	-	0.300	-
	Imperial	R	-	0.354	0.339	0.005	-	-	-	-	0.280
	New Yorker	F	0.827	0.861	0.803	0.005	-	-	-	0.300	-
	New Yorker	R	-	0.354	0.339	0.005	-	-	-	-	0.280
1993	Dynasty		0.827	0.935	0.882	0.005	8.86	NA	NA	0.300	0.300
	Dynasty 1		-	0.390	0.339	0.005	-	-	-	-	0.060
	Imperial	F	0.827	0.861	0.803	0.005	-	-	-	0.300	-
	Imperial	R	-	0.354	0.339	0.005	-	-	-	-	0.280
	New Yorker	F	0.827	0.861	0.803	0.005	-	-	-	0.300	-
	New Yorker	R	-	0.354	0.339	0.005	-	-	-	-	0.280

F - Front
R - Rear
NA - Not Available
1 Solid rear disc

WHEEL ALIGNMENT

Year	Model			Caster Range (deg.)	Caster Preferred Setting (deg.)	Camber Range (deg.)	Camber Preferred Setting (deg.)	Toe-in (in.)	Steering Axis Inclination (deg.)
1992	Dynasty	F		1	2 3/4P	1/4N-3/4P	5/16P	1/16P	12 1/2
	Dynasty	R		-	-	1 1/4N-1/4N	1/2N	0	-
	New Yorker	F	2	-	2 11/16P	3/16N-13/16P	5/16P	1/16P	12 13/32
	New Yorker	F	3	-	3P	1/4N-1/2P	1/8P	1/16P	12 13/32
	New Yorker	R		-	-	1N-0	1/2N	0	-
	Imperial	F	2	-	2 11/16P	3/16N-13/16P	5/16P	1/16P	12 13/32
	Imperial	F	3	-	3P	1/4N-1/2P	1/8P	1/16P	12 13/32
	Imperial	R		-	-	1N-0	1/2N	0	-
1993	Dynasty	F		1	2 3/4P	1/4N-3/4P	5/16P	1/16P	12 1/2
	Dynasty	R		-	-	1 1/4N-1/4N	1/2N	0	-
	New Yorker	F	2	-	2 11/16P	3/16N-13/16P	5/16P	1/16P	12 13/32
	New Yorker	F	3	-	3P	1/4N-1/2P	1/8P	1/16P	12 13/32
	New Yorker	R		-	-	1N-0	1/2N	0	-

F - Front
R - Rear
1 Non-adjustable – variation should not exceed 1 1/2 degrees
2 wo/air suspension
3 w/air suspension

CONCORDE/INTREPID/LHS/NEW YORKER/VISION

VEHICLE IDENTIFICATION CHART

		Engine Code					Model Year	
Code	Liters	Cu. In. (cc)	Cyl.	Fuel Sys.	Eng. Mfg.		Code	Year
T	3.3	201 (3300)	V6	MFI	Chrysler		P	1993
F	3.5	215 (3518)	V6	MFI	Chrysler		R	1994
T	3.3	201 (3300)	V6	MFI	Chrysler		S	1995
F	3.5	215 (3518)	V6	MFI	Chrysler		T	1996
T	3.3	201 (3300)	V6	MFI	Chrysler			
F	3.5	215 (3518)	V6	MFI	Chrysler			

MFI - Multiport fuel injection

ENGINE IDENTIFICATION

Year	Model	Engine Displacement Liters (cc)	Engine Series (ID/VIN)	Fuel System	No. of Cylinders	Engine Type
1993	Concorde	3.3 (3300)	T	MFI	6	OHV
	Concorde	3.5 (3518)	F	MFI	6	SOHC
	Intrepid	3.3 (3300)	T	MFI	6	OHV
	Intrepid	3.5 (3518)	F	MFI	6	SOHC
	Vision	3.3 (3300)	T	MFI	6	OHV
	Vision	3.5 (3518)	F	MFI	6	SOHC
1994	Concorde	3.3 (3300)	T	MFI	6	OHV
	Concorde	3.5 (3518)	F	MFI	6	SOHC
	Intrepid	3.3 (3300)	T	MFI	6	OHV
	Intrepid	3.5 (3518)	F	MFI	6	SOHC
	LHS	3.5 (3518)	F	MFI	6	SOHC
	New Yorker	3.5 (3518)	F	MFI	6	SOHC
	Vision	3.3 (3300)	T	MFI	6	OHV
	Vision	3.5 (3518)	F	MFI	6	SOHC
1995-96	Concorde	3.3 (3300)	T	MFI	6	OHV
	Concorde	3.5 (3518)	F	MFI	6	SOHC
	Intrepid	3.3 (3300)	T	MFI	6	OHV
	Intrepid	3.5 (3518)	F	MFI	6	SOHC
	LHS	3.5 (3518)	F	MFI	6	SOHC
	New Yorker	3.5 (3518)	F	MFI	6	SOHC
	Vision	3.3 (3300)	T	MFI	6	OHV
	Vision	3.5 (3518)	F	MFI	6	SOHC

MFI - Multiport fuel injection
OHV - Overhead valve
SOHC - Single overhead camshaft

GENERAL ENGINE SPECIFICATIONS

Year	Engine ID/VIN	Engine Displacement Liters (cc)	Fuel System Type	Net Horsepower @ rpm	Net Torque @ rpm (ft. lbs.)	Bore x Stroke (in.)	Compression Ratio	Oil Pressure @ rpm
1993	T	3.3 (3300)	MFI	153@5300	177@2800	3.66x3.19	8.9:1	30-80@3000
	F	3.5 (3518)	MFI	214@5800	221@2800	3.78x3.19	10.5:1	25-70@3000
1994	T	3.3 (3300)	MFI	161@5300	181@3200	3.66x3.19	8.9:1	30-80@3000
	F	3.5 (3518)	MFI	214@5800	221@3100	3.78x3.19	10.5:1	25-80@3000
1995-96	T	3.3 (3300)	MFI	161@5300	181@3200	3.66x3.19	8.9:1	30-80@2000
	F	3.5 (3518)	MFI	214@5800	221@3100	3.78x3.19	10.5:1	25-80@3000

MFI - Multiport fuel injection

GASOLINE ENGINE TUNE-UP SPECIFICATIONS

Year	Engine ID/VIN	Engine Displacement Liters (cc)	Spark Plugs Gap (in.)	Ignition Timing (deg.) MT	Ignition Timing (deg.) AT	Fuel Pump (psi)	Idle Speed (rpm) MT	Idle Speed (rpm) AT	Valve Clearance In.	Valve Clearance Ex.
1993	T	3.3 (3300)	0.048-0.053	-	1	2	-	600-840	HYD	HYD
	F	3.5 (3518)	0.048-0.053	-	1	3	-	600-840	HYD	HYD
1994	T	3.3 (3300)	0.048-0.053	-	1	2	-	600-840	HYD	HYD
	F	3.5 (3518)	0.048-0.053	-	1	3	-	600-840	HYD	HYD
1995-96	T	3.3 (3300)	0.048-0.053	-	1	2	-	600-840	HYD	HYD
	F	3.5 (3518)	0.048-0.053	-	1	3	-	600-840	HYD	HYD

NOTE: The Vehicle Emission Control Information label often reflects specification changes made during production. The label figures must be used if they differ from those in this chart
HYD - Hydraulic

1 Basic ignition timing not adjustable
2 46 psi at idle, with vacuum applied to fuel pressure regulator
3 39 psi at idle, with vacuum applied to fuel pressure regulator

CAPACITIES

Year	Model	Engine ID/VIN	Engine Displacement Liters (cc)	Engine Oil with Filter (qts.)	Transmission (pts.) 4-Spd	Transmission (pts.) 5-Spd	Transmission (pts.) Auto.	Transfer Case (pts.)	Drive Axle Front (pts.)	Drive Axle Rear (pts.)	Fuel Tank (gal.)	Cooling System (qts.)
1993	Concorde	T	3.3 (3300)	5.0	-	-	19.8	-	2.0	-	18.0	10.2
	Concorde	F	3.5 (3518)	5.5	-	-	19.8	-	2.0	-	18.0	11.8
	Intrepid	T	3.3 (3300)	5.0	-	-	19.8	-	2.0	-	18.0	10.2
	Intrepid	F	3.5 (3518)	5.5	-	-	19.8	-	2.0	-	18.0	11.8
	Vision	T	3.3 (3300)	5.0	-	-	19.8	-	2.0	-	18.0	10.2
	Vision	F	3.5 (3518)	5.5	-	-	19.8	-	2.0	-	18.0	11.8
1994	Concorde	T	3.3 (3300)	5.0	-	-	19.8	-	2.0	-	18.0	10.2
	Concorde	F	3.5 (3518)	5.5	-	-	19.8	-	2.0	-	18.0	11.8
	Intrepid	T	3.3 (3300)	5.0	-	-	19.8	-	2.0	-	18.0	10.2
	Intrepid	F	3.5 (3518)	5.5	-	-	19.8	-	2.0	-	18.0	11.8
	Vision	T	3.3 (3300)	5.0	-	-	19.8	-	2.0	-	18.0	10.2
	Vision	F	3.5 (3518)	5.5	-	-	19.8	-	2.0	-	18.0	11.8
1995-96	Concorde	T	3.3 (3300)	5.0	-	-	19.8	-	2.0	-	18.0	10.2
	Concorde	F	3.5 (3518)	5.5	-	-	19.8	-	2.0	-	18.0	11.8
	Intrepid	T	3.3 (3300)	5.0	-	-	19.8	-	2.0	-	18.0	10.2
	Intrepid	F	3.5 (3518)	5.5	-	-	19.8	-	2.0	-	18.0	11.8
	Vision	T	3.3 (3300)	5.0	-	-	19.8	-	2.0	-	18.0	10.2
	Vision	F	3.5 (3518)	5.5	-	-	19.8	-	2.0	-	18.0	11.8

CAMSHAFT SPECIFICATIONS

All measurements given in inches.

| Year | Engine ID/VIN | Engine Displacement Liters (cc) | Journal Diameter | | | | | Elevation | | Bearing Clearance | Camshaft End Play |
			1	2	3	4	5	In.	Ex.		
1993	T	3.3 (3300)	1.9970-1.9990	1.9809-1.9829	1.9659-1.9679	1.9499-1.9520	NA	0.400	0.400	0.0010-0.0030	0.005-0.012
	F	3.5 (3518)	1.6905-1.6913	1.6905-1.6913	1.6905-1.6913	1.6905-1.6913	NA	0.320	0.257	0.0030-0.0050	0.004-0.014
1994	T	3.3 (3300)	1.9970-1.9990	1.9809-1.9829	1.9659-1.9679	1.9499-1.9520	NA	0.400	0.400	0.0010-0.0030	0.005-0.012
	F	3.5 (3518)	1.6905-1.6913	1.6905-1.6913	1.6905-1.6913	1.6905-1.6913	NA	0.320	0.257	0.0030-0.0050	0.004-0.014
1995-96	T	3.3 (3300)	1.9970-1.9990	1.9809-1.9829	1.9659-1.9679	1.9499-1.9520	NA	0.400	0.400	0.0010-0.0030	0.005-0.012
	F	3.5 (3518)	1.6905-1.6913	1.6905-1.6913	1.6905-1.6913	1.6905-1.6913	NA	0.320	0.257	0.0030-0.0050	0.004-0.014

NA - Not Available

CRANKSHAFT AND CONNECTING ROD SPECIFICATIONS

All measurements are given in inches.

| Year | Engine ID/VIN | Engine Displacement Liters (cc) | Crankshaft | | | | Connecting Rod | | |
			Main Brg. Journal Dia.	Main Brg. Oil Clearance	Shaft End-play	Thrust on No.	Journal Diameter	Oil Clearance	Side Clearance
1993	T	3.3 (3300)	2.5185-2.5195	0.0007-0.0040	0.0040-0.0170	2	2.2830	0.0008-0.0030	0.0050-0.0150
	F	3.5 (3518)	2.5190-2.5200	0.0007-0.0028	0.0040-0.0170	2	2.2830	0.0008-0.0034	0.0050-0.0150
1994	T	3.3 (3300)	2.5185-2.5195	0.0007-0.0022	0.0040-0.0120	2	2.2830	0.0008-0.0030	0.0050-0.0150
	F	3.5 (3518)	2.5190-2.5200	0.0007-0.0028	0.0040-0.0120	2	2.2830	0.0008-0.0034	0.0050-0.0150
1995-96	T	3.3 (3300)	2.5185-2.5195	0.0007-0.0022	0.0040-0.0120	2	2.2830	0.0008-0.0030	0.0050-0.0150
	F	3.5 (3518)	2.5190	0.0007-0.0028	0.0040-0.0120	2	2.2830	0.0008-0.0034	0.0050-0.0150

VALVE SPECIFICATIONS

| Year | Engine ID/VIN | Engine Displacement Liters (cc) | Seat Angle (deg.) | Face Angle (deg.) | Spring Test Pressure (lbs. @ In.) | Spring Installed Height (In.) | Stem-to-Guide Clearance (in.) | | Stem Diameter (in.) | |
							Intake	Exhaust	Intake	Exhaust
1993	T	3.3 (3300)	45-45.5	44.5	1	1.539-1.598	0.0010-0.0030	0.0020-0.0060	0.3120-0.3130	0.3112-0.3119
	F	3.5 (3518)	45-45.5	44.5	2	1.496	0.0009-0.0026	0.0020-0.0040	0.2730-0.2737	0.2719-0.2726
1994	T	3.3 (3300)	45-45.5	44.5-45	1	1.622-1.681	0.0010-0.0030	0.0020-0.0060	0.3120-0.3130	0.3112-0.3119
	F	3.5 (3518)	45-45.5	44.5-45	2	1.496	0.0009-0.0026	0.0020-0.0040	0.2730-0.2737	0.2719-0.2726
1995-96	T	3.3 (3300)	45-45.5	44.5-45	1	1.622-1.681	0.0010-0.0030	0.0020-0.0060	0.3120-0.3130	0.3112-0.3119
	F	3.5 (3518)	45-45.5	44.5-45	2	1.496	0.0009-0.0026	0.0020-0.0040	0.2730-0.2737	0.2719-0.2726

1 95-100 lbs.@1.570 in. valve closed
207-229 lbs.@1.169 in. valve closed

2 Intake: 201.7-218.3 lbs.@1.1752 in.
Exhaust: 158.5-171.5 lbs.@1.239 in.

PISTON AND RING SPECIFICATIONS

All measurements are given in inches.

Year	Engine ID/VIN	Engine Displacement Liters (cc)	Piston Clearance	Ring Gap			Ring Side Clearance		
				Top Compression	Bottom Compression	Oil Control	Top Compression	Bottom Compression	Oil Control
1993	T	3.3 (3300)	0.0009-0.0022	0.012-0.022	0.012-0.022	0.010-0.040	0.0012-0.0037	0.0012-0.0037	0.0005-0.0089
	F	3.5 (3518)	0.0007-0.0020	0.012-0.018	0.012-0.022	0.010-0.030	0.0012-0.0031	0.0012-0.0031	0.0019-0.0077
1994	T	3.3 (3300)	0.0009-0.0022	0.012-0.022	0.012-0.022	0.010-0.040	0.0012-0.0037	0.0012-0.0037	0.0005-0.0089
	F	3.5 (3518)	0.0007-0.0020	0.012-0.018	0.012-0.022	0.010-0.030	0.0012-0.0031	0.0012-0.0031	0.0019-0.0077
1995-96	T	3.3 (3300)	0.0009-0.0022	0.012-0.022	0.012-0.022	0.010-0.040	0.0015-0.0033	0.0012-0.0037	0.0005-0.0089
	F	3.5 (3518)	0.0003-0.0018	0.008-0.014	0.012-0.022	0.010-0.030	0.0012-0.0031	0.0012-0.0031	0.0019-0.0077

TORQUE SPECIFICATIONS

All readings in ft. lbs.

Year	Engine ID/VIN	Engine Displacement Liters (cc)	Cylinder Head Bolts	Main Bearing Bolts	Rod Bearing Bolts	Crankshaft Damper Bolts	Flywheel Bolts	Manifold		Spark Plugs	Lug Nut
								Intake	Exhaust		
1993	T	3.3 (3300)	1	2	3	50	70	17	17	26	95
	F	3.5 (3518)	4	5	3	85	75	21	17	20	95
1994	T	3.3 (3300)	1	2	3	40	75	17	17	20	95
	F	3.5 (3518)	4	5	3	85	75	21	17	20	95
1995-96	T	3.3 (3300)	1	2	3	40	75	17	17	20	95
	F	3.5 (3518)	4	5	3	85	75	21	17	20	95

1 Step 1: 45 ft. lbs.
Step 2: 65 ft. lbs.
Step 3: 65 ft. lbs.
Step 4: Plus 1/4 turn
Torque small bolt in rear of cylinder head to 25 ft. lbs.
2 Step 1: 30 ft. lbs
Step 2: Plus 1/4 turn
3 Step 1: 40 ft. lbs.
Step 2: Plus 1/4 turn

4 Step 1: 45 ft. lbs.
Step 2: 65 ft. lbs.
Step 3: 65 ft. lbs.
Step 4: Plus 1/4 turn
Final torque should be over 90 ft. lbs.
5 Main cap bolts: 30 ft. lbs. plus 1/4 turn
Main cap tie bolts: 40 ft. lbs.

BRAKE SPECIFICATIONS

All measurements in inches unless noted

Year	Model		Master Cylinder Bore	Brake Disc			Brake Drum Diameter			Minimum Lining Thickness	
				Original Thickness	Minimum Thickness	Maximum Runout	Original Inside Diameter	Max. Wear Limit	Maximum Machine Diameter	Front	Rear
1993	Concorde	F	0.937	0.945	0.882	0.003	8.00	1	1	0.310	0.280
		R	-	0.468	0.409	0.003	-	-	-	-	0.280
	Intrepid	F	0.937	0.945	0.803	0.003	8.00	1	1	0.310	0.280
		R	-	0.945	0.803	0.003	-	-	-	-	0.280
	New Yorker	F	0.827	0.861	0.803	0.005	-	-	-	0.300	-
		R	-	0.354	0.339	0.005	-	-	-	-	0.280
	Vision		0.937	0.945	0.803	0.003	8.00	-	1	NA	0.310	0.280
1994	Concorde	F	0.937	0.945	0.882	0.003	8.00	1	1	0.310	0.280
		R	-	0.468	0.409	0.003	-	-	-	-	0.280
	Intrepid	F	0.937	0.945	0.882	0.003	8.00	1	1	0.310	0.280
		R	-	0.468	0.409	0.003	-	-	-	-	0.280

BRAKE SPECIFICATIONS

All measurements in inches unless noted

Year	Model		Master Cylinder Bore	Brake Disc Original Thickness	Brake Disc Minimum Thickness	Maximum Runout	Brake Drum Diameter Original Inside Diameter	Brake Drum Diameter Max. Wear Limit	Brake Drum Diameter Maximum Machine Diameter	Minimum Lining Thickness Front	Minimum Lining Thickness Rear
	LHS	F	0.937	0.945	0.882	0.003	-	-	-	0.310	-
		R	-	0.468	0.409	0.003	-	-	-	-	0.280
	New Yorker	F	0.937	0.945	0.882	0.003	-	-	-	0.300	-
		R	-	0.468	0.409	0.003	-	-	-	-	0.280
	Vision		0.937	2	0.882 3	0.003	8.00	1	NA	0.310	0.280
1995-96	Concorde	F	0.937	0.945	0.882	0.003	8.00	1	1	0.310	0.280
		R	-	0.468	0.409	0.003	-	-	-	-	0.280
	Intrepid	F	0.937	0.945	0.882	0.005	8.00	1	1	0.310	0.280
		R	-	0.468	0.409	0.003	-	-	-	-	0.280
	LHS	F	0.937	0.945	0.882	0.003	-	-	-	0.310	-
		R	-	0.468	0.409	0.003	-	-	-	-	0.280
	New Yorker	F	0.937	0.945	0.882	0.003	-	-	-	0.300	-
		R	-	0.468	0.409	0.003	-	-	-	-	0.280
	Vision		0.937	2	0.882 3	0.003	8.00	1	NA	0.310	0.280

F - Front
R - Rear
NA - Not Available
1 Maximum diameter is stamped on drum

2 Front disc brakes: 0.940-0.950
  Rear disc brakes: 0.458-0.478
3 Rear disc brakes: 0.409

WHEEL ALIGNMENT

Year	Model		Caster Range (deg.)	Caster Preferred Setting (deg.)	Camber Range (deg.)	Camber Preferred Setting (deg.)	Toe-in (in.)	Steering Axis Inclination (deg.)
1993	Concorde	F	2P-4P	3P	9/16N-9/16P	0	3/32P	14
		R	-	-	19/32N-13/32P	3/32N	3/64P	-
	Intrepid	F	2P-4P	3P	9/16N-9/16P	0	3/16P 1	14
		R	-	-	9/16N-7/16P	1/16N	0	-
	New Yorker	F 2	-	2 11/16P	3/16N-13/16P	5/16P	1/16P	12 13/32
		F 3	-	3P	1/4N-1/2P	1/8P	1/16P	12 13/32
		R	-	-	1N-0	1/2N	0	-
	Vision		2P-4P	3P	9/16N-9/16P	0	3/16N	14
1994	Concorde	F	2P-4P	3P	9/16N-9/16P	0	3/32P	14
		R	-	-	19/32N-13/32P	3/32N	3/64P	-
	Intrepid	F	2P-4P	3P	9/16N-9/16P	0	3/32P	14
		R	-	-	19/32N-13/32P	3/32N	3/64P	-
	LHS	F	2P-4P	3P	9/16N-9/16P	0	3/32P	14
		R	-	-	19/32N-13/32P	3/32N	3/64P	-
	New Yorker	F	2P-4P	3P	9/16N-9/16P	0	3/32P	14
		R	-	-	19/32N-13/32P	3/32N	3/64P	-
	Vision		2P-4P	3P	9/16N-9/16P 1	0 1	3/32P 1	14
1995-96	Concorde	F	2P-4P	3P	9/16N-9/16P	0	3/32P	14
		R	-	-	19/32N-13/32P	3/32N	3/64P	-
	Intrepid	F	2P-4P	3P	9/16N-9/16P	0	3/32P	14
		R	-	-	19/32N-13/32P	3/32N	3/64P	-
	LHS	F	2P-4P	3P	9/16N-9/16P	0	3/32P	14
		R	-	-	19/32N-13/32P	3/32N	3/64P	-
	New Yorker	F	2P-4P	3P	9/16N-9/16P	0	3/32P	14
		R	-	-	19/32N-13/32P	3/32N	3/64P	-
	Vision		2P-4P	3P	9/16N-9/16P	0	3/16N	14

F - Front
R - Rear

1 Non-adjustable, variation should not exceed 1 1/2 degrees
2 wo/air suspension
3 w/air suspension

ESCORT/TEMPO/TOPAZ/TRACER

VEHICLE IDENTIFICATION CHART

Engine Code						Model Year	
Code	Liters	Cu. In. (cc)	Cyl.	Fuel Sys.	Eng. Mfg.	Code	Year
8	1.8	112 (1844)	4	MFI	Mazda	N	1992
J	1.9	116 (1901)	4	MFI	Ford	P	1993
X	2.3	140 (2300)	4	MFI	Ford	R	1994
U	3.0	181 (2971)	6	MFI	Ford	S	1995
						T	1996

MFI - Multiport fuel injection

ENGINE IDENTIFICATION

Year	Model	Engine Displacement Liters (cc)	Engine Series (ID/VIN)	Fuel System	No. of Cylinders	Engine Type
1992	Escort	1.8 (1844)	8	MFI	4	DOHC
	Escort	1.9 (1901)	J	MFI	4	SOHC
	Tempo	2.3 (2300)	X	MFI	4	SOHC
	Tempo	3.0 (2971)	U	MFI	6	OHV
	Tracer	1.8 (1844)	8	MFI	4	DOHC
	Tracer ①	1.9 (1901)	J	MFI	4	SOHC
	Topaz	2.3 (2300)	X	MFI	4	SOHC
	Topaz	3.0 (2971)	U	MFI	6	OHV
1993	Escort	1.8 (1844)	8	MFI	4	DOHC
	Escort	1.9 (1901)	J	MFI	4	SOHC
	Tempo	2.3 (2300)	X	MFI	4	SOHC
	Tempo	3.0 (2971)	U	MFI	6	OHV
	Tracer	1.8 (1844)	8	MFI	4	DOHC
	Tracer ①	1.9 (1901)	J	MFI	4	SOHC
	Topaz	2.3 (2300)	X	MFI	4	SOHC
	Topaz	3.0 (2971)	U	MFI	6	OHV
1994	Escort	1.8 (1844)	8	SFI	4	DOHC
	Escort	1.9 (1901)	J	SFI	4	SOHC
	Tempo	2.3 (2300)	X	SFI	4	OHV
	Tempo	3.0 (2971)	U	SFI	6	OHV
	Tracer	1.8 (1844)	8	SFI	4	DOHC
	Tracer	1.9 (1901)	J	SFI	4	SOHC
	Topaz	2.3 (2300)	X	SFI	4	SOHC
	Topaz	3.0 (2971)	U	SFI	6	OHV
1995-96	Escort	1.8 (1844)	8	SFI	4	DOHC
	Escort	1.9 (1901)	J	SFI	4	SOHC
	Tracer	1.8 (1844)	8	SFI	4	DOHC
	Tracer	1.9 (1901)	J	SFI	4	SOHC

MFI - Multiport fuel injection
SFI - Sequential fuel injection

SOHC - Single overhead camshaft
DOHC - Double overhead camshaft

OHV - Overhead valve
① High output

GENERAL ENGINE SPECIFICATIONS

Year	Engine ID/VIN	Engine Displacement Liters (cc)	Fuel System Type	Net Horsepower @ rpm	Net Torque @ rpm (ft. lbs.)	Bore x Stroke (in.)	Compression Ratio	Oil Pressure @ rpm
1992	8	1.8 (1844)	MFI	127@6500	114@4500	3.23x3.46	9.0:1	35-65@2000
	J	1.9 (1901)	MFI	108@5200	114@4000	3.23x3.46	9.0:1	35-65@2000
	X	2.3 (2300)	MFI	98@4400	124@2200	3.70x3.30	9.0:1	55-70@2000
	U	3.0 (2971)	MFI	140@4800	160@3000	3.50x3.10	9.3:1	55-70@2000
1993	8	1.8 (1844)	MFI	127@6500	114@4500	3.23x3.46	9.0:1	35-65@2000
	J	1.9 (1901)	MFI	88@4400	108@4000	3.23x3.46	9.0:1	35-65@2000
	X	2.3 (2300)	MFI	98@4400	124@2200	3.70x3.30	9.0:1	55-70@2000
	U	3.0 (2971)	MFI	140@4800	160@3000	3.50x3.10	9.3:1	55-70@2000
1994	8	1.8 (1844)	SFI	127@6500	114@4500	3.27x3.35	9.0:1	35-65@2000
	J	1.9 (1901)	SFI	88@4400	108@4000	3.23x3.46	9.0:1	35-65@2000
	X	2.3 (2300)	SFI	98@4400	124@2200	3.68x3.30	9.0:1	55-70@2000
	U	3.0 (2971)	SFI	140@4800	160@3000	3.50x3.15	9.3:2	55-70@2500
1995-96	8	1.8 (1844)	SFI	127@6500	114@4500	3.27x3.35	9.0:1	35-65@2000
	J	1.9 (1901)	SFI	88@4400	108@4000	3.23x3.46	9.0:1	35-65@2000

MFI - Multiport fuel injection
SFI - Sequential fuel injection

GASOLINE ENGINE TUNE-UP SPECIFICATIONS

Year	Engine ID/VIN	Engine Displacement Liters (cc)	Spark Plugs Gap (in.)	Ignition Timing (deg.) MT	Ignition Timing (deg.) AT	Fuel Pump (psi)		Idle Speed (rpm) MT	Idle Speed (rpm) AT	Valve Clearance In.	Valve Clearance Ex.
1992	8	1.8 (1844)	0.041	10B	10B	64-85		750	750	HYD	HYD
	J	1.9 (1901)	0.054	10B	10B	17-35		950	950	HYD	HYD
	X	2.3 (2300)	0.054	10B	10B	45-60		975	875	HYD	HYD
	U	3.0 (2980)	0.044	10B	10B	35-45		-	625	HYD	HYD
1993	8	1.8 (1844)	0.041	10B	10B	64-85		750	750	HYD	HYD
	J	1.9 (1901)	0.054	10B	10B	17-35		950	950	HYD	HYD
	X	2.3 (2300)	0.054	10B	10B	45-60		975	875	HYD	HYD
	U	3.0 (2980)	0.044	10B	10B	35-45		-	625	HYD	HYD
1994	8	1.8 (1844)	0.041	10B	10B	31-38	②	750	750	HYD	HYD
	J	1.9 (1901)	0.054	10B	10B	30-45	②	780	780	HYD	HYD
	X	2.3 (2300)	0.054	10B	10B	45-60	②	①	①	HYD	HYD
	U	3.0 (2980)	0.044	10B	10B	30-45	②	①	①	HYD	HYD
1995-96	8	1.8 (1844)	0.041	10B	10B	31-38	②	750	750	HYD	HYD
	J	1.9 (1901)	0.054	10B	10B	30-34	②	780	780	HYD	HYD

NOTE: The Vehicle Emission Control Information label often reflects specification changes made during production. The label figures must be used if they differ from those in this chart.
B - Before top dead center
HYD - Hydraulic
① Refer to Vehicle Emission Control Information label
② Fuel pressure with engine running, pressure regulator vacuum hose connected

CAPACITIES

Year	Model	Engine ID/VIN	Engine Displacement Liters (cc)	Engine Oil with Filter (qts.)	Transmission (pts.) 4-Spd	5-Spd	Auto.	Drive Axle Front (pts.)	Rear (pts.)	Fuel Tank (gal.)	Cooling System (qts.)
1992	Escort	8	1.8 (1844)	4.0	-	7.2	13.4	①	-	13.2	7.5
	Escort	J	1.9 (1901)	4.0	-	6.2	16.6	①	-	13.0	③
	Tempo	X	2.3 (2300)	5.0	-	6.1	16.6	①	-	15.9	③
	Tempo	U	3.0 (2971)	4.5	-	6.1	16.6	①	-	15.9	②
	Tracer	8	1.8 (1844)	4.0	-	7.2	13.4	①	-	13.2	7.5
	Tracer	J	1.9 (1901)	4.0	5.0	6.2	16.6	①	-	13.0	7.5
	Topaz	X	2.3 (2300)	5.0	-	6.1	16.6	①	-	15.9	③
	Topaz	U	3.0 (2971)	4.5	-	6.1	16.6	①	-	15.9	③
1993	Escort	8	1.8 (1844)	4.0		7.2	13.4	①	-	13.2	7.5
	Escort	J	1.9 (1901)	4.0	-	6.2	16.6	①	-	13.0	③
	Tempo	X	2.3 (2300)	5.0	-	6.1	16.6	①	-	15.9	③
	Tempo	U	3.0 (2971)	4.5	-	6.1	16.6	①	-	15.9	②
	Tracer	8	1.8 (1844)	4.0	-	6.2	13.4	①	-	13.2	6.3
	Tracer	J	1.9 (1901)	4.0	5.0	6.2	16.6	①	-	13.0	6.3
	Topaz	X	2.3 (2300)	5.0	-	6.1	16.6	①	-	15.9	③
	Topaz	U	3.0 (2971)	4.5	-	6.1	16.6	①	-	15.9	③
1994	Escort	8	1.8 (1844)	4.0	-	7.2	13.4 ⑥	①	-	13.2	7.5
	Escort	J	1.9 (1901)	4.0	-	5.7	13.4 ⑥	①	-	11.9	5.3
	Tempo	X	2.3 (2300)	5.0	-	6.4	17.2 ⑥	①	-	15.9	⑤
	Tempo	U	3.0 (2971)	4.5	-	6.4	17.2 ⑥	①	-	15.9	④
	Tracer	8	1.8 (1844)	4.0	-	7.2	13.4 ⑥	①	-	13.2	6.3
	Tracer	J	1.9 (1901)	4.0	-	5.7	13.4 ⑥	①	-	11.9	5.3
	Topaz	X	2.3 (2300)	5.0	-	6.4	17.2 ⑥	①	-	15.9	⑤
	Topaz	U	3.0 (2971)	4.5	-	6.4	17.2 ⑥	①	-	15.9	④
1995-96	Escort	8	1.8 (1844)	4.0	-	7.2	13.4 ⑥	①	-	13.2	⑦
	Escort	J	1.9 (1901)	4.0	-	5.7	13.4 ⑥	①	-	11.9	⑦
	Tracer	8	1.8 (1844)	4.0	-	7.1	13.4	①	-	13.2	⑦
	Tracer	J	1.9 (1901)	4.0	-	5.7	13.4	①	-	11.9	⑦

① Included in transaxle capacity
② Manual transaxle: 7.8 qts.
   Automatic transaxle: 8.4 qts.
③ Without AC: 8.3 qts.
   Manual transaxle with AC: 7.3 qts.
   Automatic transaxle with AC: 7.8 qts.
④ Manual transaxle: 11.8 qts.
   Automatic transaxle: 7.6 qts.
⑤ Without AC: 8.3 qts.
   Manual transaxle with AC: 7.8 qts.
   Automatic transaxle with AC: 7.6 qts.
⑥ Includes torque converter
⑦ Manual transaxle: 5.3 qts.
   Automatic transaxle: 6.3 qts.

CAMSHAFT SPECIFICATIONS
All measurements given in inches.

Year	Engine ID/VIN	Engine Displacement Liters (cc)	Journal Diameter 1	2	3	4	5	Elevation In.	Ex.	Bearing Clearance	Camshaft End Play
1992	8	1.8 (1844)	1.0213-1.0222	1.0213-1.0222	1.0213-1.0222	1.0213-1.0222	1.0213-1.0222	1.7281-① 1.7360	1.7280-① 1.7360	0.0014-0.0032	③
	J	1.9 (1901)	1.8007-1.8017	1.8007-1.8017	1.8007-1.8017	1.8007-1.8017	1.8007-1.8017	0.240-0.245	0.240-0.245	0.0013-0.0033	0.002-0.006
	X	2.3 (2300)	2.006-2.008	2.006-2.008	2.006-2.008	2.006-2.008	NA	0.245-0.249	0.235-0.239	0.001-0.003	0.009
	U	3.0 (2980)	2.0074-2.0084	2.0074-2.0084	2.0074-2.0084	2.0074-2.0084	NA	0.255-0.260	0.255-0.260	0.001-0.003	0.009
1993	8	1.8 (1844)	1.0213-1.0220	1.0213-1.0220	1.0213-1.0220	1.0213-1.0220	1.0213-1.0220	1.7281-1.7360	1.7280-1.7360	0.0014-0.0032	②
	J	1.9 (1901)	1.8007-1.8017	1.8007-1.8017	1.8007-1.8017	1.8007-1.8017	1.8007-1.8017	0.240-0.245	0.240-0.245	0.0013-0.0033	0.002-0.006
	X	2.3 (2300)	2.006-2.008	2.006-2.008	2.006-2.008	2.006-2.008	NA	0.245-0.249	0.235-0.239	0.001-0.003	0.009
	U	3.0 (2980)	2.0074-2.0084	2.0074-2.0084	2.0074-2.0084	2.0074-2.0084	NA	0.255-0.260	0.255-0.260	0.001-0.003	0.009
1994	8	1.8 (1844)	1.0213-1.0222	1.0213-1.0222	1.0213-1.0222	1.0213-1.0222	1.0213-1.0222	1.7281-① 1.7360	1.7480-① 1.7560	0.0014-0.0032	0.0028-0.0075
	J	1.9 (1901)	1.8007-1.8017	1.8007-1.8017	1.8007-1.8017	1.8007-1.8017	1.8007-1.8017	0.2400-0.2450	0.2400-0.2450	0.0013-0.0033	0.0018-0.0060
	X	2.3 (2300)	2.0060-2.0080	2.0060-2.0080	2.0060-2.0080	2.0060-2.0080	2.0060-2.0080	0.2450-0.2499	0.2350-0.2390	0.0010-0.0030	0.009
	U	3.0 (2980)	2.0074-2.0084	2.0074-2.0084	2.0074-2.0084	2.0074-2.0084	2.0074-2.0084	0.2550-0.2600	0.2550-0.2600	0.001-0.003	0.001-0.005
1995-96	8	1.8 (1844)	1.0213-1.0222	1.0213-1.0222	1.0213-1.0222	1.0213-1.0222	1.0213-1.0222	1.7281-① 1.7360	1.7480-① 1.7560	0.0014-0.0032	0.0028-0.0075
	J	1.9 (1901)	1.8007-1.8017	1.8007-1.8017	1.8007-1.8017	1.8007-1.8017	1.8007-1.8017	0.2400-0.2450	0.2400-0.2450	0.0013-0.0033	0.0020-0.0060

NA - Not Available
① Figure shown indicates total lobe height
② 0.0028-0.0075 in.
③ Journal 1, right head exhaust: 1.0213-1.0220 in.
Journal 1, right head intake: 1.1801-1.1811 in.
Journal 1, left head exhaust: 1.1802-1.1809 in.
Journal 1, left head intake: 1.0213-1.0220 in.

CRANKSHAFT AND CONNECTING ROD SPECIFICATIONS
All measurements are given in inches.

Year	Engine ID/VIN	Engine Displacement Liters (cc)	Crankshaft Main Brg. Journal Dia.	Main Brg. Oil Clearance	Shaft End-play	Thrust on No.	Connecting Rod Journal Diameter	Oil Clearance	Side Clearance
1992	8	1.8 (1844)	1.9661-1.9668	0.0007-0.0014	0.0031-0.0120	4	1.7692-1.7699	0.0011-0.0027	0.0043-0.0120
	J	1.9 (1901)	2.2827-2.2835	0.0008-0.0015	0.004-0.008	3	1.8854-1.8862	0.0008-0.0015	0.004-0.011
	X	2.3 (2300)	2.2482-2.2490	0.0008-0.0015	0.004-0.008	3	2.1232-2.1240	0.0008-0.0015	0.0035-0.0105
	U	3.0 (2971)	2.5182-2.5190	0.0010-0.0014	0.004-0.008	3	2.1240	0.0010-0.0014	0.006-0.014

CRANKSHAFT AND CONNECTING ROD SPECIFICATIONS
All measurements are given in inches.

Year	Engine ID/VIN	Engine Displacement Liters (cc)	Crankshaft				Connecting Rod		
			Main Brg. Journal Dia.	Main Brg. Oil Clearance	Shaft End-play	Thrust on No.	Journal Diameter	Oil Clearance	Side Clearance
1993	8	1.8 (1844)	1.9661-1.9668	0.0007-0.0014	0.0031-0.0120	4	1.7692-1.7699	0.0011-0.0027	0.0043-0.0120
	J	1.9 (1901)	2.2827-2.2835	0.0008-0.0015	0.004-0.008	3	1.8854-1.8862	0.0008-0.0015	0.004-0.011
	X	2.3 (2300)	2.2482-2.2490	0.0008-0.0015	0.004-0.008	3	2.1232-2.1240	0.0008-0.0015	0.0035-0.0105
	U	3.0 (2971)	2.5189-2.5190	0.0010-0.0014	0.004-0.008	3	2.1240	0.0010-0.0014	0.006-0.014
1994	8	1.8 (1844)	1.9661-1.9668	0.0007-0.0014	0.0031-0.0120	4	1.7692-1.7699	0.0011-0.0030	0.0043-0.0120
	J	1.9 (1901)	2.2827-2.2835	0.0008-0.0015	0.004-0.008	3	1.7279-1.7287	0.0008-0.0015	0.004-0.011
	X	2.3 (2300)	2.2482-2.2490	0.0008-0.0015	0.004-0.008	3	2.1232-2.1240	0.0008-0.0015	0.0035-0.0105
	U	3.0 (2971)	2.5190-2.5198	0.0010-0.0014	0.004-0.008	3	2.1253-2.1261	0.0010-0.0014	0.006-0.014
1995-96	8	1.8 (1844)	1.9661-1.9668	0.0007-0.0014	0.0031-0.0120	4	1.7692-1.7699	0.0011-0.0030	0.0043-0.0120
	J	1.9 (1901)	2.2827-2.2835	0.0008-0.0015	0.0040-0.0080	3	1.7279-1.7287	0.0008-0.0015	0.0040-0.0110

VALVE SPECIFICATIONS

Year	Engine ID/VIN	Engine Displacement Liters (cc)	Seat Angle (deg.)	Face Angle (deg.)	Spring Test Pressure (lbs. @ in.)	Spring Installed Height (in.)	Stem-to-Guide Clearance (in.)		Stem Diameter (in.)	
							Intake	Exhaust	Intake	Exhaust
1992	8	1.8 (1844)	45	45	-	①	0.0010-0.0024	0.0012-0.0026	0.2350-0.2356	0.2348-0.2354
	J	1.9 (1901)	45	45	216@1.016	1.440-1.480	0.0008-0.0027	0.0018-0.0037	0.316	0.315
	X	2.3 (2300)	45	45.5	182@1.10	1.490	0.0018	0.0023	0.3415	0.3411
	U	3.0 (2971)	45	44	185@1.11	1.850	0.0001-0.0027	0.0015-0.0032	0.3126	0.3121
1993	8	1.8 (1844)	45	45	-	①	0.0010-0.0024	0.0012-0.0026	0.2350-0.2356	0.2348-0.2354
	J	1.9 (1901)	45	45	216@1.016	1.440-1.480	0.0008-0.0027	0.0018-0.0037	0.316	0.315
	X	2.3 (2300)	45	44	128-141@1.12	1.520	0.0010-0.0027	0.0015-0.0032	0.3416-0.3423	0.3411-0.3418
	U	3.0 (2971)	45	44	185@1.11	1.850	0.0001-0.0027	0.0015-0.0032	0.3126	0.3121
1994	8	1.8 (1844)	45	45	-	①	0.0010-0.0024	0.0012-0.0026	0.2350-0.2356	0.2348-0.2354
	J	1.9 (1901)	45	45.6	200@1.09	1.440-1.480	0.0008-0.0027	0.0018-0.0037	0.3159-0.3167	0.3149-0.3156
	X	2.3 (2300)	44-45	44-45	128-141@1.12	1.520	0.0018	0.0023	0.3416-0.3423	0.3411-0.3418

VALVE SPECIFICATIONS

Year	Engine ID/VIN	Engine Displacement Liters (cc)	Seat Angle (deg.)	Face Angle (deg.)	Spring Test Pressure (lbs. @ in.)	Spring Installed Height (in.)	Stem-to-Guide Clearance (in.)		Stem Diameter (in.)	
							Intake	Exhaust	Intake	Exhaust
	U	3.0 (2971)	45	44	180@1.06	1.580	0.0001-0.0027	0.0015-0.0032	0.3126-0.3129	0.3121-0.3134
1995-96	8	1.8 (1844)	45	45	-	①	0.0010-0.0024	0.0012-0.0026	0.2350-0.2356	0.2348-0.2354
	J	1.9 (1901)	45	45.6	200@1.09	1.440-1.480	0.0008-0.0027	0.0018-0.0037	0.3159-0.3167	0.3149-0.3156

① Spring height measured unloaded
Minimum length: 1.821 in.

PISTON AND RING SPECIFICATIONS
All measurements are given in inches.

Year	Engine ID/VIN	Engine Displacement Liters (cc)	Piston Clearance	Ring Gap			Ring Side Clearance		
				Top Compression	Bottom Compression	Oil Control	Top Compression	Bottom Compression	Oil Control
1992	8	1.8 (1844)	0.0015-0.0020	0.006-0.012	0.006-0.012	0.008-0.028	0.0012-0.0026	0.0012-0.0028	SNUG
	J	1.9 (1901)	0.0016-0.0024	0.010-0.020	0.010-0.020	0.016-0.055	0.0015-0.0032	0.0015-0.0035	SNUG
	X	2.3 (2300)	0.0013-0.0021	0.008-0.016	0.008-0.016	0.015-0.055	0.002-0.004	0.002-0.004	SNUG
	U	3.0 (2971)	0.0014-0.0022	0.010-0.020	0.010-0.020	0.010-0.049	0.0012-0.0031	0.0012-0.0031	SNUG
1993	8	1.8 (1844)	0.0015-0.0020	0.006-0.012	0.006-0.012	0.008-0.028	0.0012-0.0026	0.0012-0.0028	SNUG
	J	1.9 (1901)	0.0016-0.0024	0.010-0.020	0.010-0.020	0.016-0.055	0.0015-0.0032	0.0015-0.0035	SNUG
	X	2.3 (2300)	0.0013-0.0021	0.008-0.016	0.008-0.016	0.015-0.055	0.002-0.004	0.002-0.004	SNUG
	U	3.0 (2971)	0.0014-0.0022	0.010-0.020	0.010-0.020	0.010-0.049	0.0012-0.0031	0.0012-0.0031	SNUG
1994	8	1.8 (1844)	0.0015-0.0020	0.006-0.012	0.006-0.012	0.008-0.028	0.0012-0.0026	0.0012-0.0028	SNUG
	J	1.9 (1901)	0.0120-0.0280	0.010-0.030	0.010-0.030	0.016-0.066	0.0015-0.0032	0.0015-0.0035	SNUG
	X	2.3 (2300)	0.0011-0.0022	0.008-0.016	0.008-0.016	0.015-0.055	0.0020-0.0040	0.0020-0.0040	SNUG
	U	3.0 (2971)	0.0014-0.0022	0.010-0.020	0.010-0.020	0.010-0.049	0.0012-0.0031	0.0012-0.0031	SNUG
1995-96	8	1.8 (1844)	0.0015-0.0020	0.0060-0.0120	0.0060-0.0120	0.0080-0.0280	0.0012-0.0026	0.0012-0.0028	SNUG
	J	1.9 (1901)	0.0120-0.0280	0.0100-0.0300	0.0100-0.0300	0.0160-0.0660	0.0015-0.0032	0.0015-0.0035	SNUG

TORQUE SPECIFICATIONS
All readings in ft. lbs.

Year	Engine ID/VIN	Engine Displacement Liters (cc)	Cylinder Head Bolts	Main Bearing Bolts	Rod Bearing Bolts	Crankshaft Damper Bolts	Flywheel Bolts	Manifold Intake	Manifold Exhaust	Spark Plugs	Lug Nut
1992	8	1.8 (1844)	56-60	40-43	35-37	80-87	71-76	14-19	28-34	11-17	85
	J	1.9 (1901)	④	67-80	19-25	74-90	59-59	12-15	15-20	8-15	95
	X	2.3 (2300)	③	51-56	21-26	140-170	54-64	15-23	⑤	5-10	95
	U	3.0 (2971)	⑥	65-81	①	141-169	54-64	②	⑤	5-10	95
1993	8	1.8 (1844)	56-60	40-43	35-37	80-87	71-76	14-19	28-34	11-17	85
	J	1.9 (1901)	④	67-80	19-25	74-90	59-69	12-15	15-20	8-15	95
	X	2.3 (2300)	③	51-56	21-26	140-170	54-64	15-23	⑤	5-10	95
	U	3.0 (2971)	⑥	65-81	①	141-169	54-64	②	⑤	5-10	95
1994	8	1.8 (1844)	56-60	40-43	35-37	80-87	71-76	14-19	28-34	11-17	85
	J	1.9 (1901)	④	67-80	26-30	81-96	54-67	12-15	15-20	8-15	95
	X	2.3 (2300)	③	51-56	21-26	80-100	54-64	⑨	⑤	5-10	95
	U	3.0 (2971)	⑧	55-63	26	93-121	54-64	⑦	15-22	7-15	95
1995-96	8	1.8 (1844)	56-60	40-43	35-37	80-87	71-76	14-19	28-34	11-17	85
	J	1.9 (1901)	④	67-80	26-30	81-96	54-67	12-15	15-20	8-15	95

① Step 1: Tighten to 20-28 ft. lbs.
Step 2: Back off the nuts a minimum of two revolutions
Step 3: Apply final torque of 20-25 ft. lbs.

② Step 1: 11 ft. lbs.
Step 2: 18 ft. lbs.
Step 3: 24 ft. lbs.

③ Step 1: 52-59 ft. lbs.
Step 2: 70-76 ft. lbs.

④ Do no reuse cylinder head bolts. Always install new ones, as directed:
Step 1: Tighten bolts, in sequence, to 44 ft. lbs.
Step 2: Loosen all bolts approximately two turns, then retighten, in sequence, to 44 ft. lbs.
Step 3: Turn all bolts, in sequence, an additional 90 degrees
Step 4: Repeat Step 3

⑤ Step 1: 5-7 ft. lbs.
Step 2: 20-30 ft. lbs.

⑥ Step 1: 48-54 ft. lbs.
Step 2: 63-80 ft. lbs.

⑦ Step 1: 15-22 ft. lbs.
Step2 : 19-24 ft. lbs.

⑧ Step 1: 33-41 ft. lbs.
Step 2: 63-73 ft. lbs.

⑨ Step 1: 5-7 ft. lbs.
Step 2: 15-22 ft. lbs.

BRAKE SPECIFICATIONS
All measurements in inches unless noted

Year	Model		Master Cylinder Bore	Brake Disc Original Thickness	Brake Disc Minimum Thickness	Brake Disc Maximum Runout	Brake Drum Diameter Original Inside Diameter	Brake Drum Diameter Max. Wear Limit	Brake Drum Diameter Maximum Machine Diameter	Minimum Lining Thickness Front	Minimum Lining Thickness Rear
1992	Escort	②	①	0.870	0.820	0.003	9.00	9.06	9.04	0.080	0.040
	Escort	③	-	0.350	0.280	0.004	-	-	-	-	0.040
	Tempo		①	0.945	0.882	0.003	8.06	8.15	8.12	0.125	0.060
	Tracer	②	①	0.870	0.820	0.003	9.00	9.06	9.04	0.080	0.040
	Tracer	③	-	0.350	0.280	0.004	-	-	-	-	0.040
	Topaz		①	0.945	0.882	0.003	8.06	8.12	8.12	0.125	0.062
1993	Escort	②	0.875	0.870	0.820	0.004	7.87	7.95	7.91	0.080	0.040
	Escort	③	-	0.350	0.310	0.004	-	-	-	-	0.040
	Tempo		①	0.945	0.882	0.003	8.06	8.15	8.12	0.125	0.060
	Tracer	②	0.875	0.870	0.820	0.004	7.87	7.95	7.91	0.080	0.040
	Tracer	③	-	0.350	0.310	0.004	-	-	-	-	0.040
	Topaz		①	0.945	0.882	0.003	8.06	8.15	8.12	0.125	0.062
1994	Escort	②	0.875	0.870	0.790	0.004	7.87	7.95	7.91	0.080	0.040
	Escort	③	-	0.350	0.280	0.004	-	-	-	-	0.040
	Tempo		①	0.945	0.882	0.003	8.06	8.15	8.12	0.125	0.060
	Tracer	②	0.875	0.870	0.790	0.004	7.87	7.95	7.91	0.080	0.040
	Tracer	③	-	0.350	0.280	0.004	-	-	-	-	0.040
	Topaz		①	0.945	0.882	0.003	8.06	8.12	8.12	0.125	0.062

BRAKE SPECIFICATIONS
All measurements in inches unless noted

Year	Model			Master Cylinder Bore	Brake Disc Original Thickness	Brake Disc Minimum Thickness	Maximum Runout	Brake Drum Diameter Original Inside Diameter	Brake Drum Diameter Max. Wear Limit	Brake Drum Diameter Maximum Machine Diameter	Minimum Lining Thickness Front	Minimum Lining Thickness Rear
1995-96	Escort	④	F	0.875	0.870	0.790	0.004	7.87	7.95	7.91	0.080	0.040
	Escort	⑤	R	-	0.350	0.280	0.004	-	-	-	-	0.040
	Tracer	④	F	0.875	0.870	0.790	0.004	7.87	7.95	7.91	0.080	0.040
	Tracer	⑤	R	-	0.350	0.280	0.004	-	-	-	-	0.040

NOTE: Follow specifications stamped on rotor or drum if figures differ from those in this chart.
F - Front
R - Rear
① Primary bore: 1.12
   Secondary bore: 0.776
② Except rear disc
③ With rear disc

WHEEL ALIGNMENT

Year	Model		Caster Range (deg.)	Caster Preferred Setting (deg.)	Camber Range (deg.)	Camber Preferred Setting (deg.)	Toe-in (in.)	Steering Axis Inclination (deg.)
1992	Escort	LF	1 5/8P-3 1/8P	2 3/8P	3/8P-1 7/8P	1 1/8P	1/8N	14 21/32
		RF	1 5/8P-3 1/8P	2 3/8P	0-1 1/2P	3/4P	1/8N	15 3/32
		R	-	-	1 3/16N-1/2P	5/16N	3/16P	-
	Tempo	LF	1 11/16P-3 3/16P	2 7/16P	21/32P-2 5/32P	1 13/32P	3/32N	14 21/32
		RF	1 11/16P-3 3/16P	2 7/16P	7/32P-1 23/32P	31/32P	3/32N	15 3/32
	①	R	-	-	29/32N-19/32P	5/32N	0	-
	②	R	-	-	13/32P-1 3/32P	11/32P	0	-
	Tracer	LF	1 5/8P-3 1/8P	2 3/8P	3/8P-1 7/8P	1 1/8P	1/8N	14 21/32
		RF	1 5/8P-3 1/8P	2 3/8P	0-1 1/2P	3/4P	1/8N	15 3/32
		R	-	-	1 3/16N-1/2P	5/16N	3/16P	-
	Topaz	LF	1 11/16P-3 3/16P	2 7/16P	21/32P-2 5/32P	1 13/32P	3/32N	14 21/32
		RF	1 11/16P-3 3/16P	2 7/16P	7/32P-1 23/32P	31/32P	3/32N	15 3/32
	①	R	-	-	29/32N-19/32P	5/32N	0	-
	②	R	-	-	13/32P-1 3/32P	11/32P	0	-
1993	Escort	LF	1 5/8P-3 1/8P	2 3/8P	3/8P-1 7/8P	1 1/8P	1/8N	14 21/32
		RF	1 5/8P-3 1/8P	2 3/8P	0-1 1/2P	3/4P	1/8N	15 3/32
		R	-	-	1 3/16N-1/2P	5/16N	3/16P	-
	Tempo	LF	1 11/16P-3 3/16P	2 7/16P	21/32P-2 5/32P	1 13/32P	3/32N	14 21/32
		RF	1 11/16P-3 3/16P	2 7/16P	7/32P-1 23/32P	31/32P	3/32N	15 3/32
		R	-	-	29/32N-19/32P	5/32P	0	-
	Tracer	LF	1 5/8P-3 1/8P	2 3/8P	3/8P-1 7/8P	1 1/8P	1/8N	14 21/32
		RF	1 5/8P-3 1/8P	2 3/8P	0-1 1/2P	3/4P	1/8N	15 3/32
		R	-	-	1 3/16N-1/2P	5/16N	3/16P	-
	Topaz	LF	1 11/16P-3 3/16P	2 7/16P	21/32P-2 5/32P	1 13/32P	3/32N	14 21/32
		RF	1 11/16P-3 3/16P	2 7/16P	7/32P-1 23/32P	31/32P	3/32N	15 3/32
		R	-	-	29/32N-19/32P	5/32N	0	-
1994	Escort	F	1.00P-2.88P	1.94P	0.84N-0.69P	0.09N	0.09P	23.81
		R	-	-	1.09N-0.44P	0.34N	0.09P	-
	Tempo	LF	1.69P-3.19P	2.44P	0.66P-2.16P	1.41P	0.09N	14.66
		RF	1.69P-3.19P	2.44P	0.22P-1.72P	0.97P	0.09N	15.09
		R	-	-	1.31N-0.19P	0.56N	0	-
	Tracer	F	1.00P-2.88P	1.94P	0.84N-0.69P	0.09N	0.09P	23.81
		R	-	-	1.09N-0.44P	0.34N	0.09P	-

WHEEL ALIGNMENT

Year	Model		Caster Range (deg.)	Caster Preferred Setting (deg.)	Camber Range (deg.)	Camber Preferred Setting (deg.)	Toe-in (in.)	Steering Axis Inclination (deg.)
	Topaz	LF	1.69P-3.19P	2.44P	0.66P-2.16P	1.41P	0.09N	14.66
		RF	1.69P-3.19P	2.44P	0.22P-1.72P	0.97P	0.09N	15.09
		R	-	-	1.31N-0.19P	0.56N	0	-
1995-96	Escort	F	1.00P-2.84P	1.92P	0.83N-0.67P	0.08N	0.30P	12.00
		R	-	-	0.78N-0.12P	0.33N	0.30P	-
	Tracer	F	1.00P-2.84P	1.92P	0.83N-0.67P	0.08N	0.30P	12.0
		R	-	-	0.78N-0.12P	0.33N	0.30P	-

NA - Not Available
P - Positive
N - Negative
LF - Left Front
RF - Right Front

F - Front
R - Rear
① Without AWD
② With AWD

FESTIVA

VEHICLE IDENTIFICATION CHART

		Engine Code					Model Year	
Code	Liters	Cu. In. (cc)	Cyl.	Fuel Sys.	Eng. Mfg.		Code	Year
H	1.3	81 (1319)	4	MFI	Kia Motors		N	1992
							P	1993

MFI - Multiport fuel injection

ENGINE IDENTIFICATION

Year	Model	Engine Displacement Liters (cc)	Engine Series (ID/VIN)	Fuel System	No. of Cylinders	Engine Type
1992	Festiva	1.3 (1319)	H	MFI	4	SOHC
1993	Festiva	1.3 (1319)	H	MFI	4	SOHC

MFI - Multiport fuel injection
SOHC - Single overhead camshaft

23 SPECIFICATIONS

GENERAL ENGINE SPECIFICATIONS

Year	Engine ID/VIN	Engine Displacement Liters (cc)	Fuel System Type	Net Horsepower @ rpm	Net Torque @ rpm (ft. lbs.)	Bore x Stroke (in.)	Com-pression Ratio	Oil Pressure @ rpm
1992	H	1.3 (1319)	MFI	63@5000	73@3000	2.79x3.29	9.7:1	50-64@3000
1993	H	1.3 (1319)	MFI	63@5000	73@3000	2.79x3.29	9.7:1	50-64@3000

MFI - Multiport fuel injection

GASOLINE ENGINE TUNE-UP SPECIFICATIONS

Year	Engine ID/VIN	Engine Displacement Liters (cc)	Spark Plugs Gap (in.)	Ignition Timing (deg.) MT	Ignition Timing (deg.) AT	Fuel Pump (psi)	Idle Speed (rpm) MT	Idle Speed (rpm) AT	Valve Clearance In.	Valve Clearance Ex.
1992	H	1.3 (1319)	0.040	10B	10B	64-85	720	720	HYD	HYD
1993	H	1.3 (1319)	0.040	10B	10B	64-85	720	720	HYD	HYD

NOTE: The Vehicle Emission Control Information label often reflects specification changes made during production. The label figures must be used if they differ from those in this chart.
B - Before top dead center
HYD - Hydraulic

CAPACITIES

Year	Model	Engine ID/VIN	Engine Displacement Liters (cc)	Engine Oil with Filter (qts.)	Transmission (pts.) 4-Spd	Transmission (pts.) 5-Spd	Transmission (pts.) Auto.	Transfer Case (pts.)	Drive Axle Front (pts.)	Drive Axle Rear (pts.)	Fuel Tank (gal.)	Cooling System (qts.)
1992	Festiva	H	1.3 (1319)	3.6	-	5.2	11.2	-	①	-	10.0	5.3
1993	Festiva	H	1.3 (1319)	3.6	-	5.2	11.2	-	①	-	10.0	5.3

① Included in transaxle capacity

CAMSHAFT SPECIFICATIONS
All measurements given in inches.

Year	Engine ID/VIN	Engine Displacement Liters (cc)	Journal Diameter 1	2	3	4	5	Elevation In.	Elevation Ex.	Bearing Clearance	Camshaft End Play
1992	H	1.3 (1319)	1.7103-1.7112	1.7091-1.7100	1.7103-1.7112	NA	NA	1.4331-1.4371	1.4331-1.4371	①	0.002-0.007
1993	H	1.3 (1319)	1.7103-1.7112	1.7091-1.7100	1.7103-1.7112	NA	NA	1.4331-1.4371	1.4331-1.4371	①	0.002-0.007

NA - Not Available
① Front and rear journals: 0.0014-0.0030
  Center journals: 0.0026-0.0045

CRANKSHAFT AND CONNECTING ROD SPECIFICATIONS
All measurements are given in inches.

Year	Engine ID/VIN	Engine Displacement Liters (cc)	Crankshaft Main Brg. Journal Dia.	Main Brg. Oil Clearance	Shaft End-play	Thrust on No.	Connecting Rod Journal Diameter	Oil Clearance	Side Clearance
1992	H	1.3 (1319)	1.9661-1.9668	0.0009-0.0017	0.0031-0.0120	4	1.5724-1.7531	0.0011-0.0027	0.0043-0.0120
1993	H	1.3 (1319)	1.9661-1.9668	0.0009-0.0017	0.0031-0.0120	4	1.5724-1.7531	0.0011-0.0027	0.0043-0.0120

VALVE SPECIFICATIONS

Year	Engine ID/VIN	Engine Displacement Liters (cc)	Seat Angle (deg.)	Face Angle (deg.)	Spring Test Pressure (lbs. @ in.)	Spring Installed Height (in.)	Stem-to-Guide Clearance (in.)		Stem Diameter (in.)	
							Intake	Exhaust	Intake	Exhaust
1992	H	1.3 (1319)	45	45	-	①	0.008	0.008	0.2744-0.2750	0.2742-0.2748
1993	H	1.3 (1319)	45	45	-	①	0.008	0.008	0.2744-0.2750	0.2742-0.2748

① Spring height measured unloaded
Intake: 1.717 in.
Exhaust: 1.717 in.

PISTON AND RING SPECIFICATIONS
All measurements are given in inches.

Year	Engine ID/VIN	Engine Displacement Liters (cc)	Piston Clearance	Ring Gap			Ring Side Clearance		
				Top Compression	Bottom Compression	Oil Control	Top Compression	Bottom Compression	Oil Control
1992	H	1.3 (1319)	0.0015-0.0020	0.006-0.012	0.006-0.012	0.008-0.028	0.001-0.003	0.001-0.003	SNUG
1993	H	1.3 (1319)	0.0015-0.0020	0.006-0.012	0.006-0.012	0.008-0.028	0.0010-0.0030	0.0010-0.0030	SNUG

TORQUE SPECIFICATIONS
All readings in ft. lbs.

Year	Engine ID/VIN	Engine Displacement Liters (cc)	Cylinder Head Bolts	Main Bearing Bolts	Rod Bearing Bolts	Crankshaft Damper Bolts	Flywheel Bolts	Manifold		Spark Plugs	Lug Nut
								Intake	Exhaust		
1992	H	1.3 (1319)	①	40-43	②	③	71-76	14-20	12-17	10-17	85
1993	H	1.3 (1319)	①	40-43	②	③	71-76	14-20	12-17	10-17	85

① Step 1: 35-40 ft. lbs.
  Step 2: 56-60 ft. lbs.
② Step 1: 11-13 ft. lbs.
  Step 2: 22-25 ft. lbs.
③ Pulley bolts: 9-13 ft. lbs.
  Sprocket bolt: 80-87 ft. lbs.

BRAKE SPECIFICATIONS
All measurements in inches unless noted

Year	Model	Master Cylinder Bore	Brake Disc			Brake Drum Diameter			Minimum Lining Thickness	
			Original Thickness	Minimum Thickness	Maximum Runout	Original Inside Diameter	Max. Wear Limit	Maximum Machine Diameter	Front	Rear
1992	Festiva	①	NA	0.463	0.003	6.69	6.78	6.75	0.120	0.040
1993	Festiva	①	NA	0.463	0.003	6.69	6.78	6.75	0.120	0.040

NOTE: Follow specifications stamped on rotor or drum if figures differ from those in this chart.
NA - Not Available
① Primary bore: 0.75
  Secondary bore: 0.59

WHEEL ALIGNMENT

| Year | Model | | Caster | | Camber | | Toe-in (in.) | Steering Axis Inclination (deg.) |
			Range (deg.)	Preferred Setting (deg.)	Range (deg.)	Preferred Setting (deg.)		
1992	Festiva	F	5/16P-1 13/16P	1 9/16P	1/4N-1 9/16P	11/16P	5/32P	14 3/16
		R	-	-	1N-1/2P	1/4N	1/8P	-
1993	Festiva	F	5/16P-1 13/16P	1 9/16P	1/4N-1 9/16P	11/16P	5/32P	14 3/16
		R	-	-	1N-1/2P	1/4N	1/8P	-

P - Positive
N - Negative
F - Front
R - Rear

PROBE

VEHICLE IDENTIFICATION CHART

| Engine Code | | | | | | Model Year | |
Code	Liters	Cu. In. (cc)	Cyl.	Fuel Sys.	Eng. Mfg.	Code	Year
A	2.0	122 (1993)	4	MFI	Mazda	N	1992
C	2.2	133 (2189)	4	MFI	Mazda	P	1993
L ①	2.2	133 (2189)	4	MFI	Mazda	R	1994
B	2.5	153 (2501)	6	SFI	Mazda	S	1995
U	3.0	181 (2971)	6	MFI	Ford	T	1996

MFI - Multiport fuel injection
SFI - Sequential fuel injection
① Turbo

ENGINE IDENTIFICATION

Year	Model		Engine Displacement Liters (cc)	Engine Series (ID/VIN)	Fuel System	No. of Cylinders	Engine Type
1992	Probe		2.2 (2189)	C	MFI	4	SOHC
	Probe	①	2.2 (2189)	L	MFI	4	SOHC
	Probe		3.0 (2971)	U	MFI	6	OHV

ENGINE IDENTIFICATION

Year	Model	Engine Displacement Liters (cc)	Engine Series (ID/VIN)	Fuel System	No. of Cylinders	Engine Type
1993	Probe	2.0 (1993)	A	MFI	4	DOHC
	Probe	2.5 (2501)	B	MFI	6	DOHC
1994	Probe	2.0 (1993)	A	SFI	4	DOHC
	Probe	2.5 (2501)	B	SFI	6	DOHC
1995-96	Probe	2.0 (1993)	A	SFI	4	DOHC
	Probe	2.5 (2501)	B	SFI	6	DOHC

MFI - Multiport fuel injection
SFI - Sequential fuel injection
SOHC - Single overhead camshaft

DOHC - Double overhead camshaft
OHV - Overhead valve
① Turbo

GENERAL ENGINE SPECIFICATIONS

Year	Engine ID/VIN	Engine Displacement Liters (cc)	Fuel System Type	Net Horsepower @ rpm	Net Torque @ rpm (ft. lbs.)	Bore x Stroke (in.)	Compression Ratio	Oil Pressure @ rpm
1992	C	2.2 (2189)	MFI	110@4700	130@3000	3.39x3.75	8.6:1	55-65@2000
	L	2.2 (2189)	MFI	145@4300	190@3500	3.39x3.75	7.8:1	55-65@2000
	U	3.0 (2971)	MFI	140@4800	160@3000	3.50x3.10	9.3:1	55-70@2000
1993	A	2.0 (1993)	MFI	115@5500	124@3500	3.27x3.62	9.0:1	57-71@2000
	B	2.5 (2501)	MFI	164@6000	156@4000	3.33x2.92	9.2:1	49-71@2000
1994	A	2.0 (1993)	SFI	115@5500	124@3500	3.27x3.62	9.0:1	57-71@2000
	B	2.5 (2501)	SFI	164@6000	156@4000	3.33x2.92	9.2:1	49-71@3000
1995-96	A	2.0 (1993)	SFI	115@5500	124@3500	3.27x3.62	9.0:1	57-71@2000
	B	2.5 (2501)	SFI	164@6000	156@4000	3.33x2.92	9.2:1	49-71@3000

MFI - Multiport fuel injection
SFI - Sequential fuel injection

GASOLINE ENGINE TUNE-UP SPECIFICATIONS

Year	Engine ID/VIN	Engine Displacement Liters (cc)	Spark Plugs Gap (in.)	Ignition Timing (deg.) MT	Ignition Timing (deg.) AT	Fuel Pump (psi)	Idle Speed (rpm) MT	Idle Speed (rpm) AT	Valve Clearance In.	Valve Clearance Ex.
1992	C	2.2 (2189)	0.040	6B	6B	34-36	750	750	HYD	HYD
	L	2.2 (2189)	0.040	9B	9B	34-36	750	750	HYD	HYD
	U	3.0 (2980)	0.044	10B	10B	35-45	-	625	HYD	HYD
1993	A	2.0 (1993)	0.040	10B	12B	64-92	700	700	HYD	HYD
	B	2.5 (2501)	0.040	10B	10B	72-92	650	650	HYD	HYD
1994	A	2.0 (1993)	0.040	10B	12B	30-38 ①	700	700	HYD	HYD
	B	2.5 (2501)	0.040	10B	10B	30-36 ①	650	650	HYD	HYD
1995-96	A	2.0 (1993)	0.040	10B	12B	30-38 ①	700	700	HYD	HYD
	B	2.5 (2501)	0.040	10B	10B	30-36 ①	650	650	HYD	HYD

NOTE: The Vehicle Emission Control Information label often reflects specification changes made during production. The label figures must be used if they differ from those in this chart.
B - Before top dead center
HYD - Hydraulic
① Fuel pressure with engine running, pressure regulator vacuum hose connected

CAPACITIES

Year	Model	Engine ID/VIN	Engine Displacement Liters (cc)	Engine Oil with Filter (qts.)	Transmission (pts.)			Drive Axle		Fuel Tank (gal.)	Cooling System (qts.)
					4-Spd	5-Spd	Auto.	Front (pts.)	Rear (pts.)		
1992	Probe	C	2.2 (2189)	5.4	-	7.1	14.4	①	-	15.1	7.9
	Probe	L	2.2 (2189) ②	5.4	-	7.7	-	①	-	15.1	7.9
	Probe	U	3.0 (2971)	4.5	-	7.8	14.4	①	-	15.1	11.0
1993	Probe	A	2.0 (1993)	3.7	-	5.8	18.6	①	-	15.5	7.4
	Probe	B	2.5 (2501)	4.2	-	5.8	18.6	①	-	15.5	7.9
1994	Probe	A	2.0 (1993)	3.7	-	5.8	17.6 ③	①	-	15.5	7.4
	Probe	B	2.5 (2501)	4.2	-	5.8	18.6 ③	①	-	15.5	7.9
1995-96	Probe	A	2.0 (1993)	3.7	-	5.8	17.6 ③	①	-	15.5	7.4
	Probe	B	2.5 (2501)	4.2	-	5.8	14.4 ③	①	-	15.5	7.9

① Included in transaxle capacity
② Turbo
③ Includes torque converter

CAMSHAFT SPECIFICATIONS
All measurements given in inches.

Year	Engine ID/VIN	Engine Displacement Liters (cc)	Journal Diameter					Elevation		Bearing Clearance	Camshaft End Play
			1	2	3	4	5	In.	Ex.		
1992	C	2.2 (2189)	1.2575-1.2585	1.2563-1.2573	1.2563-1.2573	1.2563-1.2573	1.2575-1.2585	1.620- ② 1.630	1.640- ② 1.650	①	0.003-0.006
	L	2.2 (2189) ④	1.2575-1.2585	1.2563-1.2573	1.2563-1.2573	1.2563-1.2573	1.2575-1.2585	1.620- ② 1.630	1.640- ② 1.650	①	0.003-0.006
	U	3.0 (2980)	2.0074-2.0084	2.0074-2.0084	2.0074-2.0084	2.0074-2.0084	NA	0.255-0.260	0.255-0.260	0.001-0.003	0.009
1993	A	2.0 (1993)	1.0213-1.0222	1.0213-1.0222	1.0213-1.0222	1.0213-1.0222	1.0213-1.0222	1.6859- ② 1.6918	1.7003- ② 1.7062	③	0.003-0.008
	B	2.5 (2501)	⑤	1.0201-1.0209	1.0201-1.0209	1.0201-1.0209	1.0213-1.0220	1.7145-1.7067	1.7145-1.7067	⑥	0.002-0.004
1994	A	2.0 (1993)	1.0213-1.0222	1.0213-1.0222	1.0213-1.0222	1.0213-1.0222	1.0213-1.0222	1.6859- ② 1.6918	1.7003 ② 1.7062	0.001-0.003	0.003-0.008
	B	2.5 (2501)	⑤	1.0201-1.0209	1.0201-1.0209	1.0201-1.0209	1.0213-1.0220	1.7067- ② 1.7145	1.7067- ② 1.7145	⑥	0.002-0.004
1995-96	A	2.0 (1993)	1.0213-1.0222	1.0213-1.0222	1.0213-1.0222	1.0213-1.0222	1.0213-1.0222	1.6859- ② 1.6918	1.7003- ② 1.7062	0.001-0.003	0.0030-0.0080
	B	2.5 (2501)	⑤	1.0201-1.0209	1.0201-1.0209	1.0201-1.0209	1.0213-1.0220	1.7067- ② 1.7145	1.7067- ② 1.7145	⑥	0.0020-0.0040

NA - Not Available

① Front and rear journals: 0.0014-0.0030
  Center journals: 0.0026-0.0045
② Figure shown indicates total lobe height
③ 0.0014-0.0032 in.
④ Turbo

⑤ Journal 1, right head exhaust: 1.0213-1.0220 in.
  Journal 1, right head intake: 1.1801-1.1811 in.
  Journal 1, left head exhaust: 1.1802-1.1809 in.
  Journal 1, left head intake: 1.0213-1.0220 in.
⑥ Journals 1, 5: 0.0016-0.0032 in.
  Journals 2-4: 0.0028-0.0044 in.

CRANKSHAFT AND CONNECTING ROD SPECIFICATIONS

All measurements are given in inches.

Year	Engine ID/VIN	Engine Displacement Liters (cc)	Crankshaft				Connecting Rod		
			Main Brg. Journal Dia.	Main Brg. Oil Clearance	Shaft End-play	Thrust on No.	Journal Diameter	Oil Clearance	Side Clearance
1992	C	2.2 (2189)	2.3597- 2.3604	①	0.0031- 0.0071	3	2.0055- 2.0061	0.0011- 0.0026	0.0004- 0.0103
	L	2.2 (2189)	2.3597- 2.3604	①	0.0031- 0.0071	3	2.0055- 2.0061	0.0011- 0.0026	0.0004- 0.0103
	U	3.0 (2971)	2.5182- 2.5190	0.0010- 0.0014	0.004- 0.008	3	2.1240	0.0010- 0.0014	0.006- 0.014
1993	A	2.0 (1993)	2.2020- 2.2029	②	0.0031- 0.0118	4	1.8872- 1.8880	0.0009- 0.0026	0.004- 0.012
	B	2.5 (2501)	2.1382- 2.4292	0.0015- 0.0025	0.0032- 0.0125	4	2.0841- 2.0848	0.0009- 0.0032	0.007- 0.016
1994	A	2.0 (1993)	2.2020- 2.2029	②	0.0031- 0.0118	3	1.8872- 1.8880	0.0009- 0.0026	0.004- 0.012
	B	2.5 (2501)	2.4385- 2.4392	0.0015- 0.0025	0.0032- 0.0125	4	2.0841- 2.0848	0.0009- 0.0032	0.007- 0.016
1995-96	A	2.0 (1993)	2.2020- 2.2029	②	0.0031- 0.0118	3	1.8872- 1.8880	0.0009- 0.0026	0.0040- 0.0120
	B	2.5 (2501)	2.4385- 2.4392	0.0015- 0.0025	0.0032- 0.0125	4	2.0841- 2.0848	0.0009- 0.0032	0.0070- 0.0160

① Nos. 1-3: 0.0005-0.0023
　 No. 4: 0.0010-0.0028

② Nos. 1, 2, 4, 5: 0.0009-0.0026
　 No. 3: 0.0012-0.0026

VALVE SPECIFICATIONS

Year	Engine ID/VIN	Engine Displacement Liters (cc)	Seat Angle (deg.)	Face Angle (deg.)	Spring Test Pressure (lbs. @ in.)	Spring Installed Height (in.)	Stem-to-Guide Clearance (in.)		Stem Diameter (in.)	
							Intake	Exhaust	Intake	Exhaust
1992	C	2.2 (2189)	45	45	-	①	0.008	0.008	0.2744- 0.2750	0.2742- 0.2748
	L	2.2 (2189)	45	45	-	①	0.008	0.008	0.2744- 0.2750	0.2742- 0.2748
	U	3.0 (2971)	45	44	185@1.11	1.850	0.0001- 0.0027	0.0015- 0.0032	0.3126	0.3121
1993	A	2.0 (1993)	45	45	②	②	0.0010- 0.0024	0.0012- 0.0026	0.2350- 0.2356	0.2348- 0.2354
	B	2.5 (2501)	45	45	②	②	0.0010- 0.0023	0.0012- 0.0026	0.2351- 0.2356	0.2349- 0.2354
1994	A	2.0 (1993)	45	45	②	②	0.0010- 0.0024	0.0012- 0.0026	0.2350- 0.2356	0.2348- 0.2354
	B	2.5 (2501)	45	45	②	②	0.0010- 0.0023	0.0012- 0.0026	0.2351- 0.2356	0.2349- 0.2354

VALVE SPECIFICATIONS

Year	Engine ID/VIN	Engine Displacement Liters (cc)	Seat Angle (deg.)	Face Angle (deg.)	Spring Test Pressure (lbs. @ in.)	Spring Installed Height (in.)	Stem-to-Guide Clearance (in.) Intake	Stem-to-Guide Clearance (in.) Exhaust	Stem Diameter (in.) Intake	Stem Diameter (in.) Exhaust
1995-96	A	2.0 (1993)	45	45	②	②	0.0010-0.0024	0.0012-0.0026	0.2350-0.2356	0.2348-0.2354
	B	2.5 (2501)	45	45	②	②	0.0010-0.0023	0.0012-0.0026	0.2351-0.2356	0.2349-0.2354

① Spring height measured unloaded
  Intake: 1.949 in.
  Exhaust: 1.984 in.
② Measure spring free lenght and out-of-square.
  Maximum allowable out-of-square: 0.061
  Spring free length: 1.732

PISTON AND RING SPECIFICATIONS

All measurements are given in inches.

Year	Engine ID/VIN	Engine Displacement Liters (cc)	Piston Clearance	Ring Gap Top Compression	Ring Gap Bottom Compression	Ring Gap Oil Control	Ring Side Clearance Top Compression	Ring Side Clearance Bottom Compression	Ring Side Clearance Oil Control
1992	C	2.2 (2189)	0.0014-0.0030	0.008-0.014	0.006-0.012	0.012-0.035	0.0010-0.0030	0.0010-0.0030	SNUG
	L	2.2 (2189) ①	0.0014-0.0030	0.008-0.014	0.006-0.012	0.012-0.035	0.0010-0.0030	0.0010-0.0030	SNUG
	U	3.0 (2971)	0.0014-0.0022	0.010-0.020	0.010-0.020	0.010-0.049	0.0012-0.0031	0.0012-0.0031	SNUG
1993	A	2.0 (1993)	0.0015-0.0020	0.006-0.012	0.006-0.012	0.008-0.028	0.0014-0.0026	0.0014-0.0026	SNUG
	B	2.5 (2501)	0.0012-0.0022	0.006-0.012	0.010-0.015	0.008-0.027	0.0070-0.0130	0.0070-0.0130	SNUG
1994	A	2.0 (1993)	0.0015-0.0020	0.006-0.012	0.006-0.012	0.008-0.028	0.0014-0.0026	0.0014-0.0026	SNUG
	B	2.5 (2501)	0.0012-0.0022	0.006-0.012	0.010-0.015	0.008-0.027	0.0008-0.0026	0.0012-0.0026	SNUG
1995-96	A	2.0 (1993)	0.0015-0.0020	0.0060-0.0120	0.0060-0.0120	0.0080-0.0280	0.0014-0.0026	0.0014-0.0026	SNUG
	B	2.5 (2501)	0.0012-0.0022	0.0060-0.0120	0.0100-0.0150	0.0080-0.0270	0.0008-0.0026	0.0012-0.0026	SNUG

① Turbo

TORQUE SPECIFICATIONS
All readings in ft. lbs.

Year	Engine ID/VIN	Engine Displacement Liters (cc)	Cylinder Head Bolts	Main Bearing Bolts	Rod Bearing Bolts	Crankshaft Damper Bolts	Flywheel Bolts	Manifold Intake	Manifold Exhaust	Spark Plugs	Lug Nut
1993	C	2.2 (2189)	59-64	61-65	48-51	108-116	71-76	14-22	16-21	11-17	95
	L	2.2 (2189)	59-64	61-65	48-51	108-116	71-76	14-22	16-21	11-17	95
	U	3.0 (2971)	④	65-81	①	141-169	54-64	②	③	5-10	95
1993	A	2.0 (1993)	⑥	⑦	⑦	116-123	70-75	14-19	⑤	11-17	85
	B	2.5 (2501)	⑧	⑨	⑩	116-123	70-75	14-18	14-18	11-16	85
1994	A	2.0 (1993)	⑪	⑫	⑬	116-123	70-75	14-19	14-21	11-17	85
	B	2.5 (2501)	⑭	⑮	⑫	116-123	45-49	14-18	14-18	11-16	85
1995-96	A	2.0 (1993)	⑪	⑫	⑬	116-123	70-75	14-19	14-21	11-17	85
	B	2.5 (2501)	⑭	⑮	⑫	116-123	45-49	14-18	14-18	11-16	85

① Step 1: Tighten to 20-28 ft. lbs.
Step 2: Back off the nuts a minimum of two revolutions
Step 3: Apply final torque of 20-25 ft. lbs.

② Step 1: 11 ft. lbs.
Step 2: 18 ft. lbs.
Step 3: 24 ft. lbs.

③ Step 1: 5-7 ft. lbs.
Step 2: 20-30 ft. lbs.

④ Step 1: 48-54 ft. lbs.
Step 2: 63-80 ft. lbs.

⑤ Step 1: 12 ft. lbs.
Step 2: Rotate each bolt 85-95 degrees

⑥ Step 1: 37-50 ft. lbs.
Step 2: 62-68 ft. lbs.

⑦ Step 1: 37-50 ft. lbs.
Step 2: 58-64 ft. lbs.

⑧ Step 1: 22-26 ft. lbs.
Step 2: 33-36 ft. lbs.

⑨ Step 1: Inner bolts - 17-19 ft. lbs in two to three steps
Step 1: Outer bolts - 13-15 ft. lbs. in two to three steps
Step 2: Inner bolts 1-3: 70 degrees; Inner bolt 4: 80 degrees
Step 3: Tighten outer bolts 60 degrees
Step 4: Repeat Step 3

⑩ Step 1: 16-19 ft. lbs.
Step 2: Rotate each bolt 90 degrees
Step 3: Repeat Step 2
NOTE: Always follow the proper torque patterns

⑪ Do not reuse cylinder head bolts
Step 1: 8-10 ft. lbs.
Step 2: 13-16 ft. lbs.
Step 3: Rotate 90 degrees
Step 4: Repeat Step 3

⑫ Do not reuse main cap bolts
Step 1: 13-16 ft. lbs.
Step 2: Rotate 90 degrees

⑬ Do not reuse rod bolts
Step 1: 16-19 ft. lbs.
Step 2: Rotate 90 degrees

⑭ Do not reuse cylinder head bolts
Step 1: 10-12 ft. lbs.
Step 2: 17-19 ft. lbs.
Step 3: Rotate 90 degrees
Step 4: Repeat Step 3

⑮ Do not reuse main cap bolts
Step 1: Inner main bolts: 10-12 ft. lbs.
Step 2: Inner main bolts: 17-19 ft. lbs.
Step 3: Outer main bolts: 6-8 ft. lbs.
Step 4: Outer main bolts: 13-15 ft. lbs.
Step 5: Rotate inner bolts 75 degrees
Step 6: Rotate outer bolts 60 degrees
Step 7: Repeat Steps 5 and 6
Step 8: Outer cylinder block bolts: 14-15 ft. lbs.

BRAKE SPECIFICATIONS
All measurements in inches unless noted

Year	Model			Master Cylinder Bore	Brake Disc			Brake Drum Diameter			Minimum Lining Thickness	
					Original Thickness	Minimum Thickness	Maximum Runout	Original Inside Diameter	Max. Wear Limit	Maximum Machine Diameter	Front	Rear
1992	Probe	①	F	0.875	NA	0.863	0.004	9.00	9.89	9.06	0.120	0.040
	Probe	②	R	-	-	0.315	0.001	-	-	-	-	0.040
1993	Probe	①	F	0.937	0.940	0.890	0.004	9.00	9.89	9.06	0.040	0.040
	Probe	②	R	-	0.390	0.345	0.004	-	-	-	-	0.040
1994	Probe	①	F	0.937	0.940	0.860	0.004	9.00	9.06	9.86	0.040	0.040
	Probe	②	R	-	0.390	0.315	0.004	-	-	-	-	0.040
1995-96	Probe	①	F	0.937	0.940	0.860	0.004	9.00	9.06	9.86	0.040	0.040
	Probe	②	R	-	0.390	0.315	0.004	-	-	-	-	0.040

NOTE: Follow specifications stamped on rotor or drum if figures differ from those in this chart.

NA - Not Available

F - Front

R - Rear

① Except rear disc

② With rear disc

WHEEL ALIGNMENT

Year	Model			Caster		Camber		Toe-in (in.)	Steering Axis Inclination (deg.)
				Range (deg.)	Preferred Setting (deg.)	Range (deg.)	Preferred Setting (deg.)		
1992	Probe		F	15/16P-2 7/16P	1 11/16P	1N-1/2P	1/4N	0	12 25/32
			R	-	-	1 3/16N-5/16P	7/16N	1/8P	-
1993	Probe	①	F	2 1/4P-3 3/4P	3P	1 7/16P-1/16P	11/16N	1/8P	NA
	Probe	②	F	2 1/4P-3 3/4P	3P	1 5/8N-1/8N	7/8N	1/8P	NA
			R	-	-	1 1/6N-7/16P	5/16N	1/8P	-
1994	Probe		F	2.25P-3.75P	3.00P	1.44N-0.06P	0.69N	0.13P	15.44
	Probe GT		F	2.25P-3.75P	3.00P	1.63N-0.13N	0.88N	0.13P	15.72
	Probe		R	-	-	1.06N-0.44P	0.31N	0.13P	-
1995-96	Probe	③	F	2.03P-4.03P	3.03P	0.92N-0.08P	0.69N	0.12P	15.42
			R	-	-	1.37N-0.63P	0.37N	0.12P	-
	Probe	④	F	2.03P-4.03P	3.03P	1.90N-0.10P	0.90N	0.12P	15.74
			R	-	-	1.45N-0.55P	0.45N	0.12P	-

NA - Not Available

P - Positive

N - Negative

F - Front

R - Rear

① Except GT

② GT

③ 2.0L

④ 2.5L

CONTINENTAL/TAURUS/SABLE

VEHICLE IDENTIFICATION CHART

		Engine Code					Model Year	
Code	Liters	Cu. In. (cc)	Cyl.	Fuel Sys.	Eng. Mfg.		Code	Year
U	3.0	181 (2971)	6	MFI	Ford		N	1992
Y	3.0	182 (2980)	6	MFI	Yamaha		P	1993
P	3.2	195 (3191)	6	MFI	Yamaha		R	1994
4	3.8	232 (3802)	6	MFI	Ford		S	1995
V	4.6	280 (4593)	8	MFI	Ford		T	1996

MFI - Multiport fuel injection
SFI - Sequential fuel injection

ENGINE IDENTIFICATION

Year	Model	Engine Displacement Liters (cc)	Engine Series (ID/VIN)	Fuel System	No. of Cylinders	Engine Type
1992	Taurus	3.0 (2971)	U	MFI	6	OHV
	Taurus	3.8 (3802)	4	MFI	6	OHV
	Taurus SHO	3.0 (2980)	Y	MFI	6	DOHC
	Sable	3.0 (2971)	U	MFI	6	OHV
	Sable	3.8 (3802)	4	MFI	6	OHV
	Continental	3.8 (3801)	4	MFI	6	OHV
1993	Taurus	3.0 (2971)	U	MFI	6	OHV
	Taurus	3.8 (3802)	4	MFI	6	OHV
	Taurus SHO	3.0 (2980)	Y	MFI	6	DOHC
	Taurus SHO	3.2 (3191)	P	MFI	6	DOHC
	Sable	3.0 (2971)	U	MFI	6	OHV
	Sable	3.8 (3802)	4	MFI	6	OHV
	Continental	3.8 (3801)	4	MFI	6	OHV
1994	Taurus	3.0 (2971)	U	SFI	6	OHV
	Taurus	3.8 (3802)	4	SFI	6	OHV
	Taurus SHO	3.0 (2980)	Y	SFI	6	DOHC
	Taurus SHO	3.2 (3191)	P	SFI	6	DOHC
	Sable	3.0 (2971)	U	SFI	6	OHV
	Sable	3.8 (3802)	4	SFI	6	OHV
	Continental	3.8 (3802)	4	SFI	6	OHV
1995-96	Taurus	3.0 (2980)	U	SFI	6	OHV
	Taurus	3.8 (3802)	4	SFI	6	OHV
	Taurus SHO	3.0 (2980)	Y	SFI	6	DOHC

23 SPECIFICATIONS

ENGINE IDENTIFICATION

Year	Model	Engine Displacement Liters (cc)	Engine Series (ID/VIN)	Fuel System	No. of Cylinders	Engine Type
	Taurus SHO	3.2 (3191)	P	SFI	6	DOHC
	Sable	3.0 (2971)	U	SFI	6	OHV
	Sable	3.8 (3802)	4	SFI	6	OHV
	Continental	4.6 (4593)	V	SFI	8	DOHC

MFI - Multiport fuel injection
SFI - Sequential fuel injection
SOHC - Single overhead camshaft
DOHC - Double overhead camshaft
OHV - Overhead valve

GENERAL ENGINE SPECIFICATIONS

Year	Engine ID/VIN	Engine Displacement Liters (cc)	Fuel System Type	Net Horsepower @ rpm	Net Torque @ rpm (ft. lbs.)	Bore x Stroke (in.)	Compression Ratio	Oil Pressure @ rpm
1992	U	3.0 (2971)	MFI	140@4800	160@3000	3.50x3.10	9.3:1	55-70@2000
	Y	3.0 (2971)	MFI	220@6200	200@4800	3.50x3.15	9.8:1	40-65@2000
	4	3.8 (3802)	MFI	140@3800	215@2400	3.81x3.39	8.2:1	40-60@2000
1993	U	3.0 (2971)	MFI	140@4800	160@3000	3.50x3.10	9.3:1	55-70@2000
	Y	3.0 (2971)	MFI	220@6200	200@4800	3.50x3.15	9.8:1	40-65@2000
	P	3.2 (3191)	MFI	220@6200	215@4800	3.62x3.15	9.8:1	40-60@2000
	4	3.8 (3802)	MFI	140@3800	215@2400	3.81x3.39	8.2:1	40-60@2000
1994	U	3.0 (2971)	SFI	140@4800	160@3000	3.50x3.15	9.3:2	55-70@2500
	Y	3.0 (2971)	SFI	220@6200	200@4800	3.50x3.15	9.8:1	40-65@2000
	P	3.2 (3191)	SFI	220@6200	215@4800	3.62x3.15	9.8:1	40-60@2000
	4	3.8 (3802)	SFI	140@3800	215@2400	3.81x3.39	8.2:1	40-60@2500
1995-96	U	3.0 (2980)	SFI	140@4800	160@3000	3.50x3.15	9.3:2	55-70@2500
	Y	3.0 (2980)	SFI	220@6200	200@4800	3.50x3.15	9.8:1	40-65@2000
	P	3.2 (3191)	SFI	220@6200	215@4800	3.62x3.15	9.8:1	40-60@2000
	4	3.8 (3802)	SFI	140@3800	215@2400	3.81x3.39	9.0:1	40-60@2500
	V	4.6 (4593)	SFI	260@5750	265@4750	3.55x3.54	9.8:1	33@1500

MFI - Multiport fuel injection
SFI - Sequential fuel injection

GASOLINE ENGINE TUNE-UP SPECIFICATIONS

Year	Engine ID/VIN	Engine Displacement Liters (cc)	Spark Plugs Gap (in.)	Ignition Timing (deg.) MT	Ignition Timing (deg.) AT	Fuel Pump (psi)	Idle Speed (rpm) MT	Idle Speed (rpm) AT	Valve Clearance In.	Valve Clearance Ex.
1992	U	3.0 (2980)	0.044	10B	10B	35-45	-	625	HYD	HYD
	Y	3.0 (2980)	0.044	10B	10B	36039	800	-	0.006-0.010	0.010-0.014
	4	3.8 (3802)	0.054	10B	10B	35-45	-	550	HYD	HYD

GASOLINE ENGINE TUNE-UP SPECIFICATIONS

Year	Engine ID/VIN	Engine Displacement Liters (cc)	Spark Plugs Gap (in.)	Ignition Timing (deg.) MT	Ignition Timing (deg.) AT	Fuel Pump (psi)	Idle Speed (rpm) MT	Idle Speed (rpm) AT	Valve Clearance In.	Valve Clearance Ex.
1993	U	3.0 (2980)	0.044	10B	10B	35-45	-	625	HYD	HYD
	Y	3.0 (2980)	0.044	10B	-	36-39	800	-	0.006-0.010	0.010-0.014
	P	3.2 (3191)	0.044	-	10B	30-45	-	-	0.006-0.010	0.010-0.010
	4	3.8 (3802)	0.054	10B	10B	35-45	-	550	HYD	HYD
1994	U	3.0 (2980)	0.044	10B	10B	30-45 ②	①	①	HYD	HYD
	Y	3.0 (2980)	0.044	10B	-	28-33 ②	①	-	0.006-0.010	0.010-0.014
	P	3.2 (3191)	0.044	-	10B	28-33 ②	-	750	0.006-0.010	0.010-0.010
	4	3.8 (3802)	0.054	10B	10B	30-45 ②	①	①	HYD	HYD
1995-96	U	3.0 (2980)	0.044	10B	10B	30-45 ②	-	①	HYD	HYD
	Y	3.0 (2980)	0.044	10B	-	28-33 ② ②	①	-	0.006-0.010	0.010-0.014
	P	3.2 (3191)	0.044	-	10B	30-45 ② ②	-	800	0.006-0.010	0.010-0.014
	4	3.8 (3802)	0.054	-	10B	30-45 ②	-	①	HYD	HYD
	V	4.6 (4593)	0.054	-	10B	30-45 ②	-	①	HYD	HYD

NOTE: The Vehicle Emission Control Information label often reflects specification changes made during production. The label figures must be used if they differ from those in this chart.

B - Before top dead center

HYD - Hydraulic

① Refer to Vehicle Emission Control Information label

② Fuel pressure with engine running, pressure regulator vacuum hose connected

CAPACITIES

Year	Model	Engine ID/VIN	Engine Displacement Liters (cc)	Engine Oil with Filter (qts.)	Transmission (pts.) 4-Spd	Transmission (pts.) 5-Spd	Transmission (pts.) Auto.	Drive Axle Front (pts.)	Drive Axle Rear (pts.)	Fuel Tank (gal.)	Cooling System (qts.)
1992	Taurus	U	3.0 (2980)	5.0	-	6.2	21.8	①	-	⑤	④
	Taurus SHO	Y	3.0 (2980)	5.0	-	6.2	21.8	①	-	⑤	11.6
	Taurus	4	3.8 (3801)	4.5	-	-	25.6	①	-	⑤	12.1
	Sable	U	3.0 (2971)	5.0	-	6.2	21.8	①	-	②	④
	Sable	4	3.8 (3802)	4.5	-	-	25.6	①	-	②	④
	Continental	4	3.8 (3801)	4.5	-	-	26.2	-	-	18.4	11.1
1993	Taurus	U	3.0 (2980)	5.0	-	6.2	21.8	①	-	⑤	④
	Taurus SHO	Y	3.0 (2980)	5.0	-	6.2	21.8	①	-	⑤	11.6
	Taurus	4	3.8 (3801)	4.5	-	-	25.6	①	-	18.6	12.1
	Taurus	P	3.2 (3191)	5.0	-	-	25.6	①	-	18.6	11.2
	Sable	U	3.0 (2971)	4.5	-	-	24.5	-	①	16.0	11.0
	Sable	4	3.8 (3802)	4.5	-	-	24.5	-	①	16.0	12.1
	Continental	4	3.8 (3801)	4.5	-	-	25.6	-	-	18.4	11.1

CAPACITIES

Year	Model	Engine ID/VIN	Engine Displacement Liters (cc)	Engine Oil with Filter (qts.)	Transmission (pts.)			Drive Axle		Fuel Tank (gal.)	Cooling System (qts.)
					4-Spd	5-Spd	Auto.	Front (pts.)	Rear (pts.)		
1994	Taurus	U	3.0 (2980)	4.5	-	-	24.5 ⑫	①	-	⑤	11.0
	Taurus SHO	Y	3.0 (2980)	5.0	-	6.2	24.5 ⑫	①	-	18.4	11.6
	Taurus	4	3.8 (3801)	4.5	-	-	24.5 ⑫	①	-	⑤	12.1
	Taurus	P	3.2 (3191)	5.0	-	-	24.5 ⑫	①	-	18.4	11.4
	Sable	U	3.0 (2971)	4.5	-	-	24.5 ⑩	①	-	⑨	11.0
	Sable	4	3.8 (3802)	4.5	-	-	24.5 ⑩	①	-	⑨	12.1
	Continental	4	3.8 (3802)	4.5	-	-	24.5 ②	-	-	18.4	12.1
1995-96	Taurus	U	3.0 (2980)	4.5	-	-	24.5 ⑫	①	-	⑤	11.0
	Taurus SHO	Y	3.0 (2980)	5.0	-	6.2	24.5 ⑫	①	-	18.6	11.6
	Taurus SHO	P	3.2 (3191)	5.0	-	-	24.5 ⑫	①	-	18.6	11.4
	Taurus	4	3.8 (3802)	4.5	-	-	24.5 ⑫	①	-	⑤	12.1
	Sable	U	3.0 (2971)	4.5	-	-	24.5	①	-	⑨	11.0
	Sable	4	3.8 (3802)	4.5	-	-	24.5	①	-	⑨	12.1
	Continental	V	4.6 (4593)	6.0	-	-	26.6 ⑫	①	-	18.4	14.3

① Included in transaxle capacity
② Manual transaxle: 7.8 qts.
   Automatic transaxle: 8.4 qts.
③ Without AC: 8.3 qts.
   Manual transaxle with AC: 7.3 qts.
   Automatic transaxle with AC: 7.8 qts.
④ Wagon with AC: 11.8 qts.
   Except Wagon with AC: 11.0 qts.

⑤ Standard tank: 16.0 gals.
   Optional extended range tank: 18.6 gals.
⑥ 7.5" limited slip: 2.75 pts.
   7.50" axle: 3.0 pts.
   8.80" axle: 3.25 pts.
⑦ Turbo
⑧ Supercharged

⑨ Manual transaxle: 11.8 qts.
   Automatic transaxle: 7.6 qts.
⑩ Without AC: 8.3 qts.
   Manual transaxle with AC: 7.8 qts.
   Automatic transaxle with AC: 7.6 qts.
⑪ 7.50" axle: 3.5 pts.
   8.80" axle: 3.75 pts.

⑫ Includes torque converter
⑬ Manual transaxle: 5.3 qts.
   Automatic transaxle: 6.3 qts.
⑭ Automatic transaxle: 7.5 qts.
   Manual transaxle: 7.0 qts.
⑮ Automatic transaxle: 9.1 qts.
   Manual transaxle: 8.9 qts.

CAMSHAFT SPECIFICATIONS

All measurements given in inches.

Year	Engine ID/VIN	Engine Displacement Liters (cc)	Journal Diameter					Elevation		Bearing Clearance	Camshaft End Play
			1	2	3	4	5	In.	Ex.		
1992	U	3.0 (2980)	2.0074-2.0084	2.0074-2.0084	2.0074-2.0084	2.0074-2.0084	NA	0.255-0.260	0.255-0.260	0.2000 0.003	0.009
	Y	3.0 (2980)	1.2189-1.2195	1.2189-1.2195	1.2189-1.2195	1.2189-1.2195	1.2189-1.2195	0.335	0.315	0.0010-0.0026	0.012
	4	3.8 (3802)	2.0505-2.0515	2.0505-2.0515	2.0505-2.0515	2.0505-2.0515	2.0505-2.0515	0.240-0.245	0.241-0.245	0.001-0.003	①
1993	U	3.0 (2980)	2.0074-2.0084	2.0074-2.0084	2.0074-2.0084	2.0074-2.0084	NA	0.255-0.260	0.255-0.260	0.001-0.003	0.009
	Y	3.0 (2980)	1.2189-1.2195	1.2189-1.2195	1.2189-1.2195	1.2189-1.2195	1.2189-1.2195	0.335	0.315	0.0010-0.0026	0.012
	P	3.2 (3191)	1.2189-1.2195	1.2189-1.2195	1.2189-1.2195	1.2189-1.2195	1.2189-1.2195	0.315	0.315	0.0010-0.0026	0.012
	4	3.8 (3802)	2.0505-2.0515	2.0505-2.0515	2.0505-2.0515	2.0505-2.0515	2.0505-2.0515	0.240-0.245	0.241-0.245	0.001-0.003	①

CAMSHAFT SPECIFICATIONS

All measurements given in inches.

Year	Engine ID/VIN	Engine Displacement Liters (cc)	Journal Diameter					Elevation		Bearing Clearance	Camshaft End Play
			1	2	3	4	5	In.	Ex.		
1994	U	3.0 (2980)	2.0074-2.0084	2.0074-2.0084	2.0074-2.0084	2.0074-2.0084	2.0074-2.0084	0.2550-0.2600	0.2550-0.2600	0.001-0.003	0.001-0.005
	Y	3.0 (2980)	1.2189-1.2195	1.2189-1.2195	1.2189-1.2195	1.2189-1.2195	1.2189-1.2195	0.3550	0.3150	0.0010-0.0026	0.0012
	P	3.2 (3191)	1.2189-1.2195	1.2189-1.2195	1.2189-1.2195	1.2189-1.2195	1.2189-1.2195	0.3150	0.3150	0.0010-0.0026	0.0012
	4	3.8 (3802)	2.0505-2.0515	2.0505-2.0515	2.0505-2.0515	2.0505-2.0515	2.0505-2.0515	0.2400-0.2450	0.2540-0.2590	0.0010-0.0030	0.001-0.006
1995-96	U	3.0 (2980)	2.0074-2.0084	2.0074-2.0084	2.0074-2.0084	2.0074-2.0084	2.0074-2.0084	0.2550-0.2600	0.2550-0.2600	0.0010-0.0030	0.0010-0.0050
	Y	3.0 (2980)	1.2189-1.2195	1.2189-1.2195	1.2189-1.2195	1.2189-1.2195	1.2189-1.2195	0.3550	0.3150	0.0010-0.0026	0.0012
	P	3.2 (3191)	1.2189-1.2195	1.2189-1.2195	1.2189-1.2195	1.2189-1.2195	1.2189-1.2195	0.3150	0.3150	0.0010-0.0026	0.0012
	4	3.8 (3802)	2.0505-2.0515	2.0505-2.0515	2.0505-2.0515	2.0505-2.0515	2.0505-2.0515	0.2400-0.2450	0.2540-0.2590	0.0010-0.0030	0.0010-0.0060
	V	4.6 (4593)	1.0605-1.0615	1.0605-1.0615	1.0605-1.0615	1.0605-1.0615	1.0605-1.0615	②	0.2186	0.0010-0.0030	0.0010-0.0060

NA - Not Available

① Front and rear journals: 0.0014-0.0030
Center journals: 0.0026-0.0045

② Primary: 0.2195
Secondary: 0.2188

CRANKSHAFT AND CONNECTING ROD SPECIFICATIONS

All measurements are given in inches.

Year	Engine ID/VIN	Engine Displacement Liters (cc)	Crankshaft				Connecting Rod		
			Main Brg. Journal Dia.	Main Brg. Oil Clearance	Shaft End-play	Thrust on No.	Journal Diameter	Oil Clearance	Side Clearance
1992	U	3.0 (2971)	2.5182-2.5190	0.0010-0.0014	0.004-0.008	3	2.1240	0.0010-0.0014	0.006-0.014
	Y	3.0 (2980)	2.5187-2.5197	0.0011-0.0022	0.0008-0.0087	3	2.0463-2.0472	0.0009-0.0022	0.0063-0.0123
	4	3.8 (3802)	2.5189-2.5190	0.0010-0.0014	0.004-0.008	3	2.3103-2.3111	0.0010-0.0014	0.0047-0.0114
1993	U	3.0 (2971)	2.5189-2.5190	0.0010-0.0014	0.004-0.008	3	2.1240	0.0010-0.0014	0.006-0.014
	Y	3.0 (2980)	2.5187-2.5197	0.0011-0.0022	0.0008-0.0087	3	2.0463-2.0472	0.0009-0.0022	0.0063-0.0123
	P	3.2 (3191)	2.5187-2.5197	0.0011-0.0031	0.001-0.008	3	2.0463-2.0472	0.0009-0.0031	0.0063-0.0138
	4	3.8 (3802)	2.5189-2.5190	0.0010-0.0014	0.004-0.008	3	2.3103-2.3111	0.0010-0.0014	0.0047-0.0114

CRANKSHAFT AND CONNECTING ROD SPECIFICATIONS

All measurements are given in inches.

Year	Engine ID/VIN	Engine Displacement Liters (cc)	Crankshaft Main Brg. Journal Dia.	Crankshaft Main Brg. Oil Clearance	Crankshaft Shaft End-play	Thrust on No.	Connecting Rod Journal Diameter	Connecting Rod Oil Clearance	Connecting Rod Side Clearance
1994	U	3.0 (2971)	2.5190-2.5198	0.0010-0.0014	0.004-0.008	3	2.1253-2.1261	0.0010-0.0014	0.006-0.014
	Y	3.0 (2980)	2.5187-2.5197	0.0011-0.0022	0.0008-0.0087	3	2.0463-2.0472	0.0009-0.0031	0.0063-0.0138
	P	3.2 (3191)	2.5187-2.5197	0.0011-0.0031	0.001-0.008	3	2.0463-2.0472	0.0009-0.0031	0.0063-0.0138
	4	3.8 (3802)	2.5190-2.5198	0.0010-0.0014	0.004-0.008	3	2.3103-2.3111	0.0009-0.0027	0.0047-0.0140
1995-96	U	3.0 (2980)	2.5190-2.5198	0.0010-0.0014	0.0040-0.0080	3	2.1253-2.1261	0.0010-0.0014	0.0060-0.0140
	Y	3.0 (2980)	2.5187-2.5197	0.0011-0.0022	0.0008-0.0087	3	2.0463-2.0472	0.0009-0.0031	0.0063-0.0138
	P	3.2 (3191)	2.5187-2.5197	0.0011-0.0031	0.0010-0.0080	3	2.0463-2.0472	0.0009-0.0031	0.0063-0.0138
	4	3.8 (3802)	2.5190-2.5198	0.0010-0.0014	0.0040-0.0080	3	2.3103-2.3111	0.0009-0.0027	0.0047-0.0140
	V	4.6 (4593)	2.6567-2.6577	0.0010-0.0020	0.0051-0.0118	5	2.0859-2.0867	0.0011-0.0027	0.0059-0.0177

VALVE SPECIFICATIONS

Year	Engine ID/VIN	Engine Displacement Liters (cc)	Seat Angle (deg.)	Face Angle (deg.)	Spring Test Pressure (lbs. @ in.)	Spring Installed Height (in.)	Stem-to-Guide Clearance (in.) Intake	Stem-to-Guide Clearance (in.) Exhaust	Stem Diameter (in.) Intake	Stem Diameter (in.) Exhaust
1992	U	3.0 (2971)	45	44	185@1.11	1.850	0.0001-0.0027	0.0015-0.0032	0.3126	0.3121
	Y	3.0 (2980)	45	45.5	120@1.19	1.760	0.0010-0.0023	0.0012-0.0025	0.2346-0.2352	0.2344-0.2350
	4	3.8 (3802)	44.5	45.8	215@1.79	1.750	0.0010-0.0027	0.0015-0.0032	0.3420	0.3415
1993	U	3.0 (2971)	45	44	185@1.11	1.850	0.0001-0.0027	0.0015-0.0032	0.3126	0.3121
	Y	3.0 (2980)	45	45.5	121@1.19	1.760	0.0010-0.0023	0.0012-0.0025	0.2346-0.2352	0.2344-0.2350
	P	3.2 (3191)	45	45.5	121@1.19	1.520	0.0010-0.0023	0.0012-0.0025	0.2346-0.2352	0.2344-0.2350
	4	3.8 (3802)	44.5	45.8	215@1.79	1.750	0.0010-0.0027	0.0015-0.0032	0.3420	0.3415
1994	U	3.0 (2971)	45	44	180@1.06	1.580	0.0001-0.0027	0.0015-0.0032	0.3126-0.3129	0.3121-0.3134
	Y	3.0 (2980)	45	45.5	121@1.19	1.520	0.0010-0.0023	0.0012-0.0025	0.2346-0.2352	0.2344-0.2350

VALVE SPECIFICATIONS

Year	Engine ID/VIN	Engine Displacement Liters (cc)	Seat Angle (deg.)	Face Angle (deg.)	Spring Test Pressure (lbs. @ in.)	Spring Installed Height (in.)	Stem-to-Guide Clearance (in.)		Stem Diameter (in.)	
							Intake	Exhaust	Intake	Exhaust
	P	3.2 (3191)	45	45.5	121@1.19	1.520	0.0010-0.0023	0.0012-0.0025	0.2346-0.2352	0.2344-0.2350
	4	3.8 (3802)	44.5	45.8	220@1.18	1.970	0.0010-0.0027	0.0015-0.0032	0.3415-0.3423	0.3410-0.3418
1995-96	U	3.0 (2980)	45	44	180@1.06	1.580	0.0001-0.0027	0.0015-0.0032	0.3126-0.3129	0.3121-0.3134
	Y	3.0 (2980)	45	45.5	121@1.19	1.520	0.0010-0.0023	0.0012-0.0025	0.2346-0.2352	0.2344-0.2350
	P	3.2 (3191)	45	45.5	121@1.19	1.520	0.0010-0.0023	0.0012-0.0025	0.2346-0.2352	0.2344-0.2350
	4	3.8 (3802)	44.5	45.8	220@1.18	1.970	0.0010-0.0027	0.0015-0.0032	0.3415-0.3423	0.3410-0.3418
	V	4.6 (4593)	45	45.5	180@1.103	1.425	0.0008-0.0027	0.0018-0.0037	0.3415-0.3423	0.3410-0.3418

PISTON AND RING SPECIFICATIONS

All measurements are given in inches.

Year	Engine ID/VIN	Engine Displacement Liters (cc)	Piston Clearance	Ring Gap			Ring Side Clearance		
				Top Compression	Bottom Compression	Oil Control	Top Compression	Bottom Compression	Oil Control
1992	U	3.0 (2971)	0.0014-0.0022	0.010-0.020	0.010-0.020	0.010-0.049	0.0012-0.0031	0.0012-0.0031	SNUG
	Y	3.0 (2980)	0.0012-0.0020	0.012-0.018	0.012-0.018	0.008-0.020	0.0008-0.0024	0.0006-0.0022	0.0024-0.0059
	4	3.8 (3802)	0.0014-0.0032	0.010-0.022	0.010-0.022	0.015-0.055	0.002-0.044	0.002-0.004	SNUG
1993	U	3.0 (2971)	0.0014-0.0022	0.010-0.020	0.010-0.020	0.010-0.049	0.0012-0.0031	0.0012-0.0031	SNUG
	Y	3.0 (2980)	0.0012-0.0020	0.012-0.018	0.012-0.018	0.008-0.020	0.0008-0.0024	0.0006-0.0022	0.0024-0.0059
	P	3.2 (3191)	0.0012-0.0020	0.012-0.018	0.012-0.024	0.008-0.020	0.0016-0.0031	0.0008-0.0024	SNUG
	4	3.8 (3802)	0.0014-0.0032	0.010-0.022	0.010-0.022	0.015-0.055	0.0020-0.0040	0.0020-0.0040	SNUG
1994	U	3.0 (2971)	0.0014-0.0022	0.010-0.020	0.010-0.020	0.010-0.049	0.0012-0.0031	0.0012-0.0031	SNUG
	Y	3.0 (2980)	0.0012-0.0020	0.012-0.018	0.012-0.018	0.008-0.020	0.0008-0.0024	0.0006-0.0022	0.0024-0.0059
	P	3.2 (3191)	0.0012-0.0020	0.012-0.018	0.018-0.024	0.008-0.020	0.0016-0.0031	0.0008-0.0024	0.0024-0.0059
	4	3.8 (3802)	0.0014-0.0032	0.011-0.012	0.010-0.020	0.015-0.058	0.0016-0.0034	0.0016-0.0034	SNUG

PISTON AND RING SPECIFICATIONS

All measurements are given in inches.

Year	Engine ID/VIN	Engine Displacement Liters (cc)	Piston Clearance	Ring Gap			Ring Side Clearance		
				Top Compression	Bottom Compression	Oil Control	Top Compression	Bottom Compression	Oil Control
1995-96	U	3.0 (2980)	0.0014-0.0022	0.0100-0.0200	0.0100-0.0200	0.0100-0.0490	0.0012-0.0031	0.0012-0.0031	SNUG
	Y	3.0 (2980)	0.0012-0.0020	0.0120-0.0180	0.0120-0.0180	0.0080-0.0200	0.0008-0.0024	0.0006-0.0022	0.0024-0.0059
	P	3.2 (3191)	0.0012-0.0020	0.0120-0.0180	0.0180-0.0240	0.0080-0.0200	0.0016-0.0032	0.0008-0.0024	0.0024-0.0059
	4	3.8 (3802)	0.0014-0.0032	0.0110-0.0120	0.0100-0.0200	0.0150-0.0580	0.0016-0.0034	0.0016-0.0034	SNUG
	V	4.6 (4593)	0.0007-0.0018	0.0098-0.0200	0.0090-0.0193	0.0059-0.0260	0.0004-0.0009	0.0012-0.0031	SNUG

TORQUE SPECIFICATIONS

All readings in ft. lbs.

Year	Engine ID/VIN	Engine Displacement Liters (cc)	Cylinder Head Bolts	Main Bearing Bolts	Rod Bearing Bolts	Crankshaft Damper Bolts	Flywheel Bolts	Manifold		Spark Plugs	Lug Nut
								Intake	Exhaust		
1992	U	3.0 (2971)	⑤	65-81	①	141-169	54-64	②	③	5-10	95
	Y	3.0 (2980)	⑥	⑦	⑧	112-127	51-58	12-17	26-38	16-20	95
	4	3.8 (3802)	④	65-81	31-36	85-100	75-85	⑤	15-22	5-11	95
1993	U	3.0 (2971)	⑤	65-81	①	141-169	54-64	②	③	5-10	95
	Y	3.0 (2980)	⑥	⑦	⑧	113-126	58-64	11-16	26-38	17-19	95
	P	3.2 (3191)	⑥	⑦	⑧	112-127	58-64	11-17	26-38	16-20	95
	4	3.8 (3802)	④	65-81	31-36	85-100	75-85	⑤	15-22	5-11	95
1994	U	3.0 (2971)	⑪	55-63	26	93-121	54-64	⑨	15-22	7-15	95
	Y	3.0 (2980)	⑥	⑦	⑧	113-126	51-58	11-17	26-38	15-22	95
	P	3.2 (3191)	⑥	⑦	⑧	112-127	51-58	11-17	26-38	15-22	95
	R	3.8 (3802)	⑫	65-81	31-36	103-132	54-64	⑬	15-22	7-15	95
	4	3.8 (3802)	⑩	65-81	31-36	103-132	54-64	⑬	15-22	7-15	95
1995-96	U	3.0 (2980)	⑪	55-63	26	93-121	54-64	⑨	15-22	7-15	95
	Y	3.0 (2980)	⑥	⑦	⑧	113-126	51-58	11-17	26-38	15-22	95
	P	3.2 (3191)	⑥	⑦	⑧	112-127	51-58	11-17	26-38	15-22	95
	4	3.8 (3802)	⑩	65-81	31-36	103-132	54-64	⑬	15-22	7-15	95
	V	4.6 (4593)	⑭	⑮	⑮	114-121	54-64	⑰	13-16	7-15	95

① Step 1: Tighten to 20-28 ft. lbs.
   Step 2: Back off the nuts a minimum of two revolutions
   Step 3: Apply final torque of 20-25 ft. lbs.
② Step 1: 11 ft. lbs.
   Step 2: 18 ft. lbs.
   Step 3: 24 ft. lbs.
③ Step 1: 5-7 ft. lbs.
   Step 2: 20-30 ft. lbs.

⑧ Step 1: 22-26 ft. lbs.
   Step 2: 33-36 ft. lbs.
   Step 1: Inner bolts - 17-19 ft. lbs in two to three steps
   Step 1: Outer bolts - 13-15 ft. lbs. in two to three steps
   Step 2: Inner bolts 1-3: 70 degrees; Inner bolt 4: 80 degrees
   Step 3: Tighten outer bolts 60 degrees
   Step 4: Repeat Step 3
   Step 1: 16-19 ft. lbs.
   Step 2: Rotate each bolt 90 degrees
   Step 3: Repeat Step 2
   NOTE: Always follow the proper torque patterns

⑫ Do not reuse cylinder head bolts
   Step 1: 37 ft. lbs.
   Step 2: 45 ft. lbs.
   Step 3: 52 ft. lbs.
   Step 4: 59 ft. lbs.
   Step 5: Back off bolts two to three turns, one at a time
   Step 6: Tighten all bolts 37-44 ft. lbs.
   Step 7: Rotate bolts an additional 180-200 degrees
⑬ Step 1: 13 ft. lbs.
   Step 2: 16 ft. lbs.
   NOTE: Always follow proper torque patterns

TORQUE SPECIFICATIONS
All readings in ft. lbs.

Year	Engine ID/VIN	Engine Displacement Liters (cc)	Cylinder Head Bolts	Main Bearing Bolts	Rod Bearing Bolts	Crankshaft Damper Bolts	Flywheel Bolts	Manifold Intake	Manifold Exhaust	Spark Plugs	Lug Nut

④ Step 1: 37 ft. lbs.
  Step 2: 45 ft. lbs.
  Step 3: 52 ft. lbs.
  Step 4: 59 ft. lbs.
⑤ Step 1: 48-54 ft. lbs.
  Step 2: 63-80 ft. lbs.
⑥ Step 1: 37-50 ft. lbs.
  Step 2: 62-68 ft. lbs.
⑦ Step 1: 37-50 ft. lbs.
  Step 2: 58-64 ft. lbs.

⑨ Step 1: 15-22 ft. lbs.
  Step2 : 19-24 ft. lbs.
⑩ Do not reuse cylinder head bolts
  Step 1: 15 ft. lbs.
  Step 2: 29 ft. lbs.
  Step 3: 37 ft. lbs.
  Step 4: Loosen bolts one at a time and retorque as follows:
  Long bolts: 11-18 ft. lbs.
  Short bolts: 7-15 ft. lbs.
  Step 5: Rotate 85-95 degrees
⑪ Step 1: 33-41 ft. lbs.
  Step 2: 63-73 ft. lbs.

⑭ Step 1: 27-32 ft. lbs.
  Step 2: Rotate 85-95 degrees
  Step 3: Repeat Step 2
⑮ Step 1: Main bearing cap bolts: 6-9 ft. lbs.
  Step 2: Main bearing cap bolts, outer: 16-21 ft. lbs.
  Step 3: Main bearing cap bolts, inner: 27-32 ft. lbs.
  Step 4: Rotate main bearing cap bolts 85-95 degrees
  Step 5: Main cap adjusting screws: 4 ft. lbs. then 7.5 ft. lbs.
  Step 6: Main cap side bolts: 7 ft. lbs. then 14-17 ft. lbs.
⑯ Step 1: 5 ft. lbs.
  Step 2: 10 ft. lbs.
  Step 3: 18-25 ft. lbs.
  Step 4: Rotate 85-95 degrees
⑰ Step 1: Four inside short bolts: 9-11 ft. lbs.
  Step 2: All other bolts: 13-16 ft. lbs.
  Step 3: Rotate 85-95 degrees

BRAKE SPECIFICATIONS
All measurements in inches unless noted

Year	Model		Master Cylinder Bore	Brake Disc Original Thickness	Brake Disc Minimum Thickness	Brake Disc Maximum Runout	Brake Drum Diameter Original Inside Diameter	Brake Drum Diameter Max. Wear Limit	Brake Drum Diameter Maximum Machine Diameter	Minimum Lining Thickness Front	Minimum Lining Thickness Rear
1992	Taurus		0.875	1.024	0.974	0.003	①	NA	②	0.125	0.030
	Taurus SHO	F	0.875	NA	0.972	0.002	-	-	-	0.125	-
		R	-	-	0.900	0.002	-	-	-	-	0.123
	Sable		1.000	③	④	⑤	①	NA	②	0.125	0.030
	Continental	F	1.000	1.024	0.974	0.003	-	-	-	0.125	-
		R	-	0.944	0.890	0.002	-	-	-	-	0.123
1993	Taurus		0.875	1.024	0.974	0.003	①	NA	②	0.125	0.030
	Taurus SHO	F	0.875	NA	0.972	0.002	-	-	-	0.125	-
		R	-	-	0.900	0.002	-	-	-	-	0.123
	Sable		1.000	③	④	⑤	①	NA	②	0.125	0.030
	Continental	F	1.000	1.024	0.974	0.003	-	-	-	0.040	-
		R	-	0.550	0.500	0.002	-	-	-	-	0.123
1994	Taurus		1.000	③	④	⑤	①	NA	②	0.040	⑥
	Taurus SHO		1.000	③	④	⑤	-	-	-	0.040	0.123
	Sable		1.000	③	④	⑤	①	NA	②	0.125	0.030
	Continental	F	1.000	1.020	0.974	0.003	-	-	-	0.040	-
		R	-	0.550	0.500	0.001	-	-	-	-	0.123
1995-96	Taurus		1.000	③	④	⑤	①	NA	②	0.040	⑥
	Taurus SHO		1.000	③	④	⑤	-	-	-	0.040	0.123
	Sable		1.000	③	④	⑤	①	NA	②	0.040	⑥
	Continental	F	NA	1.020	0.974	0.003	-	-	-	0.060	-
		R	-	0.550	0.502	0.001	-	-	-	-	0.123

BRAKE SPECIFICATIONS
All measurements in inches unless noted

| Year | Model | Master Cylinder Bore | Brake Disc | | | Brake Drum Diameter | | | Minimum Lining Thickness | |
			Original Thickness	Minimum Thickness	Maximum Runout	Original Inside Diameter	Max. Wear Limit	Maximum Machine Diameter	Front	Rear

NOTE: Follow specifications stamped on rotor or drum if figures differ from those in this chart.

NA - Not Available

F - Front

R - Rear

① Sedan: 8.85
   Wagon: 9.84

② Sedan: 8.91
   Wagon: 9.90

③ Front: 0.003
   Rear: 0.002

④ Front: 1.020
   Rear: 0.940

⑤ Front: 0.974
   Rear: 0.900

⑥ With disc brakes: 0.123
   With drum brakes: 0.030

WHEEL ALIGNMENT

| Year | Model | | | Caster | | Camber | | Toe-in (in.) | Steering Axis Inclination (deg.) |
				Range (deg.)	Preferred Setting (deg.)	Range (deg.)	Preferred Setting (deg.)		
1992	Taurus	①	F	2 31/6P-5 13/16P	2 13/16P	1 1/8N-1/8P	1/2N	3/32N	15 1/2
		②	F	2 11/16P-4 11/16P	3 11/16P	1N-1/4P	3/8N	3/32N	15 1/2
			R	-	-	1 5/8N-7/32N	15/16N	1/16P	-
	Sable	①	F	2 31/6P-5 13/16P	2 13/16P	1 1/8N-1/8P	1/2N	3/32N	15 1/2
		②	F	2 11/16P-4 11/16P	3 11/16P	1N-1/4P	3/8N	3/32N	15 1/2
			R	-	-	1 5/8N-7/32N	15/16N	1/16P	-
	Continental		F	3.60P-5.20P	4.40P	1.80N-0.40N	1.10N	3/32P	15.50
			R	-	-	2.00N-0.60N	1.30N	3/32P	-
1993	Taurus	①	F	2 13/16P-5 13/16P	2 13/16P	1 1/8N-1/8P	1/2N	3/32N	15 1/2
		②	F	2 11/16P-4 11/16P	3 11/16P	1N-1/4P	3/8N	3/32N	15 1/2
			R	-	-	1 5/8N-7/32N	15/16N	1/16P	-
	Sable	①	F	2 31/6P-5 13/16P	2 13/16P	1 1/8N-1/8P	1/2N	3/32N	15 1/2
		②	F	2 11/16P-4 11/16P	3 11/16P	1N-1/4P	3/8N	3/32N	15 1/2
			R	-	-	1 5/8N-7/32N	15/16N	1/16P	-
	Continental		F	3.50P-5.50P	4.50P	1.70N-0.50N	1.10N	3/32N	15.50
			R	-	-	2.00N-0.60N	1.30N	3/32P	-
1994	Taurus	①	F	2.81P-4.81P	3.81P	1.13N-0.13P	0.50N	0.09N	15.50
			R	-	-	1.60N-0.20N	0.90N	0.06P	-
	Taurus	②	F	2.70P-4.70P	3.70P	1.00N-0.20N	0.40N	0.20N	15.50
			R	-	-	1.90N-0.10P	0.90N	0.06P	-
	Sable	①	F	2.80P-4.80P	3.80P	1.10N-0.010P	0.50N	0.20N	15.50
			R	-	-	1.60N-0.20N	0.90N	0.06P	-
	Sable	②	F	2.70P-4.70P	3.70P	1.00N-0.20N	0.40N	0.20N	15.50
			R	-	-	1.90N-0.10P	0.90N	0.06P	-
	Continental		F	3.50P-5.50P	4.50P	1.70N-0.50N	1.10N	0.20N	NA
			R	-	-	2.00N-0.60N	1.30N	0.20P	-

WHEEL ALIGNMENT

Year	Model			Caster Range (deg.)	Caster Preferred Setting (deg.)	Camber Range (deg.)	Camber Preferred Setting (deg.)	Toe-in (in.)	Steering Axis Inclination (deg.)
1995-96	Taurus	①	F	2.80P-4.80P	3.80P	1.10N-0.10P	0.50N	0.20N	15.50
			R	-	-	1.60N-0.20N	0.90N	0.06P	15.50
	Taurus	②	F	2.70P-4.70P	3.70P	1.00N-0.20N	0.40N	0.20N	15.50
			R	-	-	1.90N-0.10P	0.90N	0.06P	-
	Sable	①	F	2.80P-4.80P	3.80P	1.10N-0.10P	0.50N	0.20N	15.5
			R	-	-	1.60N-0.20N	0.90N	0.06P	-
	Sable	②	F	2.70P-4.70P	3.70P	1.00N-0.20N	0.40N	0.20N	15.5
			R	-	-	1.90N-0.10P	0.90N	0.06P	-
	Continental		F	3.50P-5.50P	4.50P	1.30N-0.10P	0.70N	0.10N	NA
			R	-	-	1.20N-0.20N	0.70N	0.10P	-

NA - Not Available
P - Positive
N - Negative

F - Front
R - Rear

① Sedan
② Wagon

COUGAR/MARK VII/MARK VIII/MUSTANG/THUNDERBIRD

VEHICLE IDENTIFICATION CHART

Engine Code							Model Year	
Code		Liters	Cu. In. (cc)	Cyl.	Fuel Sys.	Eng. Mfg.	Code	Year
M		2.3	140 (2300)	4	MFI	Ford	N	1992
4		3.8	232 (3802)	6	MFI	Ford	P	1993
R	①	3.8	232 (3802)	6	MFI	Ford	R	1994
W		4.6	280 (4593)	8	MFI	Ford	S	1995
V		4.6	280 (4593)	8	MFI	Ford	T	1996
T		5.0	302 (4949)	8	MFI	Ford		
E	②	5.0	302 (4949)	8	MFI	Ford		
D	③	5.0	302 (4949)	8	SFI	Ford		

MFI - Multiport fuel injection
SFI - Sequential fuel injection
① Supercharged
② High output
③ Special high performance

ENGINE IDENTIFICATION

Year	Model		Engine Displacement Liters (cc)	Engine Series (ID/VIN)	Fuel System	No. of Cylinders	Engine Type
1992	Mustang		2.3 (2300)	M	MFI	4	SOHC
	Mustang	①	5.0 (4949)	E	MFI	8	OHV
	Thunderbird		3.8 (3802)	4	MFI	6	OHV
	Thunderbird	②	3.8 (3802)	R	MFI	6	OHV
	Thunderbird		5.0 (4943)	T	MFI	8	OHV
	Cougar		3.8 (3802)	4	MFI	6	OHV
	Cougar		5.0 (4943)	T	MFI	8	OHV
	Mark VII		5.0 (4943)	E	MFI	8	OHV
1993	Mustang		2.3 (2300)	M	MFI	4	SOHC
	Mustang	①	5.0 (4949)	E	MFI	8	OHV
	Thunderbird		3.8 (3802)	4	MFI	6	OHV
	Thunderbird	②	3.8 (3802)	R	MFI	6	OHV
	Thunderbird		5.0 (4949)	E	MFI	8	OHV
	Cougar		3.8 (3802)	4	MFI	6	OHV
	Cougar		5.0 (4943)	T	MFI	8	OHV
	Mark VIII		4.6 (4593)	V	MFI	8	DOHC
1994	Mustang		3.8 (3802)	4	SFI	6	OHV
	Mustang	③	5.0 (4949)	D	SFI	8	OHV
	Mustang	①	5.0 (4949)	T	SFI	8	OHV
	Thunderbird		3.8 (3802)	4	SFI	6	OHV
	Thunderbird	②	3.8 (3802)	R	SFI	6	OHV
	Thunderbird		4.6 (4593)	W	SFI	8	SOHC
	Cougar		3.8 (3802)	4	SFI	6	OHV
	Cougar		4.6 (4593)	W	SFI	8	SOHC
	Mark VIII		4.6 (4593)	V	SFI	8	DOHC
1995-96	Mustang		3.8 (3802)	4	SFI	6	OHV
	Mustang	③	5.0 (4949)	D	SFI	8	OHV
	Mustang	①	5.0 (4949)	T	SFI	8	OHV
	Thunderbird		3.8 (3802)	4	SFI	6	OHV
	Thunderbird	②	3.8 (3802)	R	SFI	6	OHV
	Thunderbird		4.6 (4593)	W	SFI	8	SOHC
	Cougar		3.8 (3802)	4	SFI	6	OHV
	Cougar		4.5 (4593)	W	SFI	8	SOHC
	Mark VIII		4.6 (4593)	V	SFI	8	DOHC

MFI - Multiport fuel injection
SFI - Sequential fuel injection
SOHC - Single overhead camshaft
DOHC - Double overhead camshaft

OHV - Overhead valve
① High output
② Supercharged
③ Special performance

GENERAL ENGINE SPECIFICATIONS

Year	Engine ID/VIN		Engine Displacement Liters (cc)	Fuel System Type	Net Horsepower @ rpm	Net Torque @ rpm (ft. lbs.)	Bore x Stroke (in.)	Compression Ratio	Oil Pressure @ rpm
1992	M		2.3 (2300)	MFI	105@4600	135@2600	3.78x3.12	9.5:1	40-60@2000
	4		3.8 (3802)	MFI	140@3800	215@2400	3.81x3.39	8.2:1	40-60@2000
	R	②	3.8 (3802)	MFI	210@2000	315@2600	3.81x3.39	8.2:1	40-60@2000
	E	①	5.0 (4949)	MFI	225@4200	300@3200	4.00x3.39	9.0:1	40-60@2000
	T		5.0 (4949)	MFI	200@4000	275@3000	4.00x3.39	9.0:1	40-60@2000
1993	M		2.3 (2300)	MFI	105@4600	135@2600	3.78x3.12	9.5:1	40-60@2000
	4		3.8 (3802)	MFI	140@3800	215@2400	3.81x3.39	8.2:1	40-60@2000
	R	②	3.8 (3802)	MFI	210@2000	315@2600	3.81x3.39	8.2:1	40-60@2000
	V		4.6 (4593)	MFI	280@5500	285@4500	3.55x3.54	9.8:1	33@2000
	E	①	5.0 (4949)	MFI	235@4600	300@3200	4.00x3.39	9.0:1	40-60@2000
	T		5.0 (4949)	MFI	200@4000	275@3000	4.00x3.39	9.0:1	40-60@2000
1994	4		3.8 (3802)	SFI	140@3800	215@2400	3.81x3.39	8.2:1	40-60@2500
	R	②	3.8 (3802)	SFI	210@2000	315@2600	3.81x3.39	8.2:1	40-60@2500
	W		4.6 (4593)	SFI	③	④	3.55x3.54	9.0:1	20-45@2000
	V		4.6 (4593)	SFI	280@5500	285@4500	3.55x3.54	9.8:1	33@1500
	D	⑤	5.0 (4949)	SFI	225@4200	315@2600	4.00x3.00	9.0:1	40-60@2000
	T	①	5.0 (4949)	SFI	200@4000	275@3000	4.00x3.00	9.0:1	40-60@2000
1995-96	4		3.8 (3802)	SFI	140@3800	215@2400	3.81x3.39	9.0:1	40-60@2500
	R	②	3.8 (3802)	SFI	210@2000	315@2600	3.81x3.39	8.2:1	40-60@2500
	W		4.6 (4593)	SFI	⑥	⑦	3.55x3.54	9.0:1	20-45@2000
	V		4.6 (4593)	SFI	280@5500	285@4500	3.55x3.54	9.8:1	33@1500
	D	⑤	5.0 (4949)	SFI	225@4200	315@2600	4.00x3.00	9.0:1	40-60@2000
	T	①	5.0 (4949)	SFI	200@4000	275@3000	4.00x3.00	9.0:1	40-60@2000

MFI - Multiport fuel injection
SFI - Sequential fuel injection
① High output
② Supercharged

③ Single exhaust: 190@4200
　 Dual exhaust: 210@4600
④ Single exhaust: 260@3200
　 Dual exhaust: 270@3400

⑤ Special high performance
⑥ Single exhaust: 190@4250
　 Dual exhaust:
　 Thunderbird: 205@4500

⑦ Single exhaust: 260@3250
　 Dual exhaust:
　 Thunderbird: 265@3200

GASOLINE ENGINE TUNE-UP SPECIFICATIONS

Year	Engine ID/VIN	Engine Displacement Liters (cc)	Spark Plugs Gap (in.)	Ignition Timing (deg.) MT	Ignition Timing (deg.) AT	Fuel Pump (psi)		Idle Speed (rpm) MT	Idle Speed (rpm) AT	Valve Clearance In.	Valve Clearance Ex.
1992	M	2.3 (2300)	0.044	10B	10B	35-40		975	975	HYD	HYD
	4	3.8 (3802)	0.054	10B	10B	35-45		-	550	HYD	HYD
	R	3.8 (3802)	0.054	10B	10B	35-45		-	550	HYD	HYD
	E	5.0 (4949)	0.054	10B	10B	36-42		700	700	HYD	HYD
	T	5.0 (4949)	0.054	-	10B	35-40		-	650	HYD	HYD
1993	M	2.3 (2300)	0.044	10B	10B	35-40		975	975	HYD	HYD
	4	3.8 (3802)	0.054	10B	10B	35-45		-	550	HYD	HYD
	R	3.8 (3802)	0.054	10B	10B	35-45		-	550	HYD	HYD
	V	4.6 (4593)	0.054	-	10B	35-40		-	①	HYD	HYD
	E	5.0 (4949)	0.054	10B	10B	36-42		700	700	HYD	HYD
	T	5.0 (4949)	0.054	-	10B	35-40		-	650	HYD	HYD
1994	4	3.8 (3802)	0.054	10B	10B	30-45	②	①	①	HYD	HYD
	R	3.8 (3802)	0.054	10B	10B	30-45	②	①	①	HYD	HYD
	W	4.6 (4593)	0.054	-	10B	30-45	②	①	①	HYD	HYD
	V	4.6 (4593)	0.054	-	10B	30-45	②	-	①	HYD	HYD
	D	5.0 (4949)	0.054	10B	10B	30-45	②	①	①	HYD	HYD
	T	5.0 (4949)	0.054	10B	10B	30-45	②	①	①	HYD	HYD

GASOLINE ENGINE TUNE-UP SPECIFICATIONS

Year	Engine ID/VIN	Engine Displacement Liters (cc)	Spark Plugs Gap (in.)	Ignition Timing (deg.) MT	Ignition Timing (deg.) AT	Fuel Pump (psi)		Idle Speed (rpm) MT	Idle Speed (rpm) AT	Valve Clearance In.	Valve Clearance Ex.
1995-96	4	3.8 (3802)	0.054	-	10B	30-45	②	-	①	HYD	HYD
	R	3.8 (3802)	0.054	10B	10B	30-40	②	①	①	HYD	HYD
	W	4.6 (4593)	0.054	-	10B	30-45	②	-	①	HYD	HYD
	V	4.6 (4593)	0.054	-	10B	30-45	②	-	①	HYD	HYD
	D	5.0 (4949)	0.054	10B	10B	30-45	②	①	①	HYD	HYD
	T	5.0 (4949)	0.054	10B	10B	30-45	②	①	①	HYD	HYD

NOTE: The Vehicle Emission Control Information label often reflects specification changes made during production. The label figures must be used if they differ from those in this chart.

B - Before top dead center

HYD - Hydraulic

① Refer to Vehicle Emission Control Information label

② Fuel pressure with engine running, pressure regulator vacuum hose connected

CAPACITIES

Year	Model	Engine ID/VIN	Engine Displacement Liters (cc)	Engine Oil with Filter (qts.)	Transmission (pts.) 4-Spd	Transmission (pts.) 5-Spd	Transmission (pts.) Auto.	Drive Axle Front (pts.)	Drive Axle Rear (pts.)	Fuel Tank (gal.)	Cooling System (qts.)
1992	Mustang	M	2.3 (2300)	5.0	-	5.6	19.4	-	①	15.4	10.0
	Mustang	E	5.0 (4949)	5.0	-	5.6	24.6	-	①	15.4	14.1
	Thunderbird	4	3.8 (3802)	5.0	-	-	22.0	-	①	21.0	11.8
	Thunderbird	R	3.8 (3802) ②	5.0	-	6.3	24.0	-	①	18.8	11.8
	Thunderbird	T	5.0 (4943)	5.0	-	-	24.6	-	①	19.0	14.1
	Cougar	4	3.8 (3802)	5.0	-	-	22.0	-	3.75	21.0	11.8
	Cougar	T	5.0 (4943)	5.0	-	-	24.6	-	3.75	19.0	14.1
	Mark VII	E	5.0 (4943)	5.0	-	-	24.6	-	3.75	22.1	14.1
1993	Mustang	M	2.3 (2300)	5.0	-	5.6	19.4	-	①	15.4	10.0
	Mustang	E	5.0 (4949)	5.0	-	5.6	24.6	-	①	15.4	14.1
	Thunderbird	4	3.8 (3802)	5.0	-	-	22.0	-	①	21.0	11.8
	Thunderbird	R	3.8 (3802) ②	5.0	-	6.3	24.0	-	①	18.8	11.8
	Thunderbird	E	5.0 (4943)	5.0	-	-	24.6	-	①	19.0	14.1
	Cougar	4	3.8 (3802)	5.0	-	-	22.0	-	①	21.0	11.8
	Cougar	T	5.0 (4943)	5.0	-	-	24.6	-	①	19.0	14.1
	Mark VIII	V	4.6 (4593)	6.0	-	-	24.6	-	3.00	18.0	14.1
1994	Mustang	4	3.8 (3802)	5.0	-	5.6	25.0 ④	-	③	15.4	11.8
	Mustang	T	5.0 (4949)	5.0	-	5.6	25.0 ④	-	③	15.4	14.1
	Mustang	D	5.0 (4949)	5.0	-	5.6	24.6 ④	-	③	15.4	14.1
	Thunderbird	4	3.8 (3802)	5.0	-	-	25.0 ④	-	①	18.0	12.6
	Thunderbird	R	3.8 (3802) ②	5.0	-	6.3	25.0 ④	-	①	18.0	12.5
	Thunderbird	W	4.6 (4593)	5.0	-	-	25.0 ④	-	①	18.0	14.1
	Cougar	4	3.8 (3802)	5.0	-	-	25.0 ④	-	①	18.0	12.6
	Cougar	W	4.6 (4593)	5.0	-	-	25.0 ④	-	①	18.0	14.1
	Mark VIII	V	4.6 (4593)	6.0	-	-	25.0 ④	-	3.00	18.0	16.0
1995-96	Mustang	4	3.8 (3802)	5.0	-	5.6	27.2 ④	-	③	15.4	11.8
	Mustang	T	5.0 (4949)	5.0	-	5.6	27.2 ④	-	③	15.4	14.1
	Mustang	D	5.0 (4949)	5.0	-	5.6	27.2 ④	-	③	15.4	14.1
	Thunderbird	4	3.8 (3802)	5.0	-	-	27.2 ④	-	①	18.0	12.6
	Thunderbird	R	3.8 (3802) ②	5.0	-	6.3	27.2 ④	-	①	18.0	12.5
	Thunderbird	W	4.6 (4593)	5.0	-	-	27.2 ④	-	①	18.0	14.1

CAPACITIES

Year	Model	Engine ID/VIN	Engine Displacement Liters (cc)	Engine Oil with Filter (qts.)	Transmission (pts.)			Drive Axle		Fuel Tank (gal.)	Cooling System (qts.)
					4-Spd	5-Spd	Auto.	Front (pts.)	Rear (pts.)		
	Cougar	4	3.8 (3802)	5.0	-	-	27.2	-	①	18.0	12.6
	Cougar	W	4.6 (4593)	5.0	-	-	27.2	-	①	18.0	14.1
	Mark VIII	V	4.6 (4593)	6.0	-	-	25.0 ④	-	3.00	18.0	16.0

① 7.5" limited slip: 2.75 pts.
   7.50" axle: 3.0 pts.
   8.80" axle: 3.25 pts.
② Supercharged
③ 7.50" axle: 3.5 pts.
   8.80" axle: 3.75 pts.
④ Includes torque converter

CAMSHAFT SPECIFICATIONS
All measurements given in inches.

Year	Engine ID/VIN	Engine Displacement Liters (cc)	Journal Diameter					Elevation		Bearing Clearance	Camshaft End Play
			1	2	3	4	5	In.	Ex.		
1992	M	2.3 (2300)	1.7713-1.7720	1.7713-1.7720	1.7713-1.7720	1.7713-1.7720	1.7713-1.7720	0.2381	0.2381	0.001-0.003	0.001-0.007
	4	3.8 (3802)	2.0505-2.0515	2.0505-2.0515	2.0505-2.0515	2.0505-2.0515	2.0505-2.0515	0.240-0.245	0.241-0.245	0.001-0.003	①
	R	3.8 (3802)	2.0505-2.0515	2.0505-2.0515	2.0505-2.0515	2.0505-2.0515	2.0505-2.0515	0.240-0.245	0.241-0.245	0.001-0.003	①
	E	5.0 (4949)	2.0805-2.0815	2.0655-2.0665	2.0505-2.0515	2.0355-2.0365	2.0205-2.0515	0.2780	0.2780	0.001-0.003	0.005-0.009
	T	5.0 (4949)	2.0805-2.0815	2.0655-2.0665	2.0505-2.0515	2.0355-2.0365	2.0205-2.0515	0.2780	0.2780	0.001-0.003	0.005-0.009
1993	M	2.3 (2300)	1.7713-1.7720	1.7713-1.7720	1.7713-1.7720	1.7713-1.7720	1.7713-1.7720	0.2381 ②	0.2381 ②	0.001-0.003	0.001-0.007
	4	3.8 (3802)	2.0505-2.0515	2.0505-2.0515	2.0505-2.0515	2.0505-2.0515	2.0505-2.0515	0.240-0.245	0.241-0.245	0.001-0.003	①
	R	3.8 (3802)	2.0505-2.0515	2.0505-2.0515	2.0505-2.0515	2.0505-2.0515	2.0505-2.0515	0.240-0.245	0.241-0.259	0.001-0.003	①
	V	4.6 (4593)	1.0605-1.0615	1.0605-1.0615	1.0605-1.0615	1.0605-1.0615	1.0605-1.0615	④	0.2186	0.0010-0.0030	0.0010-0.0060
	E	5.0 (4949)	2.0805-2.0815	2.0655-2.0665	2.0505-2.0515	2.0355-2.0365	2.0205-2.0515	0.2780 ③	0.2780	0.001-0.003	0.005-0.009
	T	5.0 (4949)	2.0805-2.0815	2.0655-2.0665	2.0505-2.0515	2.0355-2.0365	2.0205-2.0515	0.2780	0.2780	0.001-0.003	0.005-0.009
1994	4	3.8 (3802)	2.0505-2.0515	2.0505-2.0515	2.0505-2.0515	2.0505-2.0515	2.0505-2.0515	0.2400-0.2450	0.2540-0.2590	0.0010-0.0030	0.001-0.006
	R	3.8 (3802)	2.0505-2.0515	2.0505-2.0515	2.0505-2.0515	2.0505-2.0515	2.0505-2.0515	0.2400-0.2450	0.2540-0.2590	0.0010-0.0030	0.001-0.006
	W	4.6 (4593)	1.0605-1.0615	1.0605-1.0615	1.0605-1.0615	1.0605-1.0615	1.0605-1.0615	0.2590	0.2590	0.0010-0.0030	0.001-0.006
	V	4.6 (4593)	1.0605-1.0615	1.0605-1.0615	1.0605-1.0615	1.0605-1.0615	1.0605-1.0615	④	0.2186	0.0010-0.0030	0.0010-0.0060
	D	5.0 (4949)	2.0805-2.0815	2.0655-2.0665	2.0505-2.0515	2.0355-2.0365	2.0205-2.0515	0.2822	0.2822	0.0010-0.0030	0.005-0.009
	T	5.0 (4949)	2.0805-2.0815	2.0655-2.0665	2.0505-2.0515	2.0355-2.0365	2.0205-2.0515	0.2780	0.2780	0.0010-0.0030	0.005-0.009

CAMSHAFT SPECIFICATIONS
All measurements given in inches.

Year	Engine ID/VIN	Engine Displacement Liters (cc)	Journal Diameter 1	2	3	4	5	Elevation In.	Ex.	Bearing Clearance	Camshaft End Play
1995-96	4	3.8 (3802)	2.0505-2.0515	2.0505-2.0515	2.0505-2.0515	2.0505-2.0515	2.0505-2.0515	0.2400-0.2450	0.2540-0.2590	0.0010-0.0030	0.0010-0.0060
	R	3.8 (3802)	2.0505-2.0515	2.0505-2.0515	2.0505-2.0515	2.0505-2.0515	2.0505-2.0515	0.2400-0.2450	0.2540-0.2590	0.0010-0.0030	0.0010-0.0060
	W	4.6 (4593)	1.0605-1.0615	1.0605-1.0615	1.0605-1.0615	1.0605-1.0615	1.0605-1.0615	0.2590	0.2590	0.0010-0.0030	0.0010-0.0060
	V	4.6 (4593)	1.0605-1.0615	1.0605-1.0615	1.0605-1.0615	1.0605-1.0615	1.0605-1.0615	④	0.2186	0.0010-0.0030	0.0010-0.0060
	D	5.0 (4949)	2.0805-2.0815	2.0655-2.0665	2.0505-2.0515	2.0355-2.0365	2.0205-2.0215	0.2822	0.2822	0.0010-0.0030	0.0050-0.0090
	T	5.0 (4949)	2.0805-2.0815	2.0655-2.0665	2.0505-2.0515	2.0355-2.0365	2.0205-2.0215	0.2780	0.2780	0.0010-0.0030	0.0050-0.0090

NA - Not Available
① Front and rear journals: 0.0014-0.0030
   Center journals: 0.0026-0.0045
② Figure shown indicates total lobe height
③ Cobra: 0.2822 lift on intake and exhaust
④ Primary: 0.2195
   Secondary: 0.2188

CRANKSHAFT AND CONNECTING ROD SPECIFICATIONS
All measurements are given in inches.

Year	Engine ID/VIN	Engine Displacement Liters (cc)	Crankshaft Main Brg. Journal Dia.	Main Brg. Oil Clearance	Shaft End-play	Thrust on No.	Connecting Rod Journal Diameter	Oil Clearance	Side Clearance
1992	M	2.3 (2295)	2.2051-2.2059	0.0008-0.0026	0.003-0.012	3	2.0462-2.0472	0.0008-0.0026	0.0035-0.0140
	4	3.8 (3802)	2.5189-2.5190	0.0010-0.0014	0.004-0.008	3	2.3103-2.3111	0.0010-0.0014	0.0047-0.0114
	R	3.8 (3801)	①	②	0.004-0.008	3	2.3103-2.3111	0.0009-0.0027	0.0047-0.0140
	E	5.0 (4949)	2.2482-2.2490	0.0004-0.0015	0.004-0.015	3	2.1228-2.1236	0.0008-0.0015	0.010-0.020
	T	5.0 (4949)	2.2482-2.2490	0.0004-0.0015	0.004-0.015	3	2.1228-2.1236	0.0008-0.0015	0.010-0.020
1993	M	2.3 (2295)	2.2051-2.2059	0.0008-0.0026	0.003-0.012	3	2.0462-2.0472	0.0008-0.0026	0.0035-0.0140
	4	3.8 (3802)	2.5189-2.5190	0.0010-0.0014	0.004-0.008	3	2.3103-2.3111	0.0010-0.0014	0.0047-0.0114
	R	3.8 (3801)	①	②	0.004-0.008	3	2.3103-2.3111	0.0009-0.0027	0.0047-0.0140
	V	4.6 (4593)	2.6567-2.6577	0.0010-0.0020	0.0051-0.0118	3	2.0859-2.0867	0.0011-0.0027	0.0047-0.0114
	E	5.0 (4949)	2.2482-2.2490	0.0004-0.0015	0.004-0.015	3	2.1228-2.1236	0.0008-0.0015	0.010-0.020
	T	5.0 (4949)	2.2482-2.2490	0.0004-0.0015	0.004-0.015	3	2.1228-2.1236	0.0008-0.0015	0.010-0.020
1994	4	3.8 (3802)	2.5190-2.5198	0.0010-0.0014	0.004-0.008	3	2.3103-2.3111	0.0009-0.0027	0.0047-0.0140
	R	3.8 (3802)	①	②	0.004-0.008	3	2.3103-2.3111	0.0009-0.0027	0.0047-0.0140

CRANKSHAFT AND CONNECTING ROD SPECIFICATIONS
All measurements are given in inches.

Year	Engine ID/VIN	Engine Displacement Liters (cc)	Crankshaft Main Brg. Journal Dia.	Crankshaft Main Brg. Oil Clearance	Crankshaft Shaft End-play	Crankshaft Thrust on No.	Connecting Rod Journal Diameter	Connecting Rod Oil Clearance	Connecting Rod Side Clearance
	W	4.6 (4593)	2.6578-2.6598	0.0011-0.0025	0.005-0.010	5	2.0874-2.0891	0.0011-0.0027	0.0006-0.0177
	V	4.6 (4593)	2.6567-2.6577	0.0010-0.0020	0.0051-0.0118	5	2.0859-2.0867	0.0011-0.0027	0.0059-0.0177
	D	5.0 (4949)	2.2482-2.2490	0.0004-0.0015	0.004-0.008	3	2.1228-2.1236	0.0008-0.0015	0.010-0.020
	T	5.0 (4949)	2.2482-2.2490	0.0004-0.0015	0.004-0.008	3	2.1228-2.1236	0.0008-0.0015	0.010-0.020
1995-96	4	3.8 (3802)	2.5190-2.5198	0.0010-0.0014	0.0040-0.0080	3	2.3103-2.3111	0.0009-0.0027	0.0047-0.0140
	R	3.8 (3802)	①	②	0.0040-0.0080	3	2.3103-2.3111	0.0009-0.0027	0.0047-0.0140
	W	4.6 (4593)	2.6578-2.6598	0.0011-0.0025	0.0050-0.0100	5	2.0874-2.0891	0.0011-0.0027	0.0006-0.0177
	V	4.6 (4593)	2.6567-2.6577	0.0010-0.0020	0.0051-0.0118	5	2.0859-2.0867	0.0011-0.0027	0.0059-0.0177
	D	5.0 (4949)	2.2482-2.2490	0.0004-0.0015	0.0040-0.0080	3	2.1228-2.1236	0.0008-0.0015	0.0100-0.0200
	T	5.0 (4949)	2.2482-2.2490	0.0004-0.0015	0.0040-0.0080	3	2.1228-2.1236	0.0008-0.0015	0.0100-0.0200

① Nos. 1-3: 2.5190-2.5198
No. 4: 2.55096-2.5104
② Nos. 1-3: 0.0005-0.0023
No. 4: 0.0010-0.0028

VALVE SPECIFICATIONS

Year	Engine ID/VIN	Engine Displacement Liters (cc)	Seat Angle (deg.)	Face Angle (deg.)	Spring Test Pressure (lbs. @ in.)	Spring Installed Height (in.)	Stem-to-Guide Clearance (in.) Intake	Stem-to-Guide Clearance (in.) Exhaust	Stem Diameter (in.) Intake	Stem Diameter (in.) Exhaust
1992	M	2.3 (2300)	45	44	128-141@1.12	1.520	0.0010-0.0027	0.0015-0.0032	0.3416-0.3423	0.3411-0.3418
	4	3.8 (3802)	44.5	45.8	215@1.79	1.750	0.0010-0.0027	0.0015-0.0032	0.3420	0.3415
	R	3.8 (3802)	44.5	45.8	220@1.18	1.650	0.0010-0.0027	0.0015-0.0032	0.3420	0.3415
	E	5.0 (4949)	45	45	①	①	0.0010-0.0027	0.0015-0.0032	0.3420	0.3420
	T	5.0 (4949)	45	45	①	②	0.0010-0.0027	0.0015-0.0032	0.3420	0.3420
1993	M	2.3 (2300)	45	44	128-141@1.12	1.520	0.0010-0.0027	0.0015-0.0032	0.3416-0.3423	0.3411-0.3418
	4	3.8 (3802)	44.5	45.8	215@1.79	1.750	0.0010-0.0027	0.0015-0.0032	0.3420	0.3415
	R	3.8 (3802)	44.5	45.8	220@1.18	1.650	0.0010-0.0027	0.0015-0.0032	0.3420	0.3415
	V	4.6 (4593)	45	45.5	180@1.103	1.575	0.0008-0.0027	0.0018-0.0037	0.3415-0.3423	0.3410-0.3418
	E	5.0 (4949)	45	44	①	②	0.0010-0.0027	0.0015-0.0032	0.3420	0.3420
	T	5.0 (4949)	45	45	①	②	0.0010-0.0027	0.0015-0.0032	0.3420	0.3420

VALVE SPECIFICATIONS

Year	Engine ID/VIN	Engine Displacement Liters (cc)	Seat Angle (deg.)	Face Angle (deg.)	Spring Test Pressure (lbs. @ in.)	Spring Installed Height (in.)	Stem-to-Guide Clearance (in.)		Stem Diameter (in.)	
							Intake	Exhaust	Intake	Exhaust
1994	4	3.8 (3802)	44.5	45.8	220@1.18	1.970	0.0010-0.0027	0.0015-0.0032	0.3415-0.3423	0.3410-0.3418
	R	3.8 (3802)	44.5	45.8	220@1.18	1.970	0.0010-0.0027	0.0015-0.0032	0.3415-0.3423	0.3410-0.3418
	W	4.6 (4593)	45	45.5	132@1.10	1.570	0.0008-0.0027	0.0018-0.0037	0.2746-0.2754	0.2736-0.2744
	V	4.6 (4593)	45	45.5	180@1.103	1.425	0.0008-0.0027	0.0018-0.0037	0.3415-0.3423	0.3410-0.3418
	T	5.0 (4949)	45	44	①	②	0.0010-0.0027	0.0015-0.0032	0.3416-0.3423	0.3411-0.3418
	D	5.0 (4949) ③	45	44	④	⑤	0.0010-0.0027	0.0015-0.0032	0.3416-0.3423	0.3411-0.3418
1995-96	4	3.8 (3802)	44.5	45.8	220@1.18	1.970	0.0010-0.0027	0.0015-0.0032	0.3415-0.3423	0.3410-0.3418
	R	3.8 (3802)	44.5	45.8	220@1.18	1.970	0.0010-0.0027	0.0015-0.0032	0.3415-0.3423	0.3410-0.3418
	W	4.6 (4593)	45	45.5	132@1.10	1..570	0.0008-0.0027	0.0018-0.0037	0.2746-0.2754	0.2736-0.2744
	V	4.6 (4593)	45	45.5	180@1.103	1.425	0.0008-0.0027	0.0018-0.0037	0.3415-0.3423	0.3410-0.3418
	T	5.0 (4949)	45	44	①	②	0.0010-0.0027	0.0015-0.0032	0.3416-0.3423	0.3411-0.3418
	D	5.0 (4949) ③	45	44	④	⑤	0.0010-0.0027	0.0015-0.0032	0.3416-0.3423	0.3411-0.3418

① Intake: 211-230@1.33 in.
   Exhaust: 200-226@1.15 in.
② Intake: 1.75-1.80 in.
   Exhaust: 1.58-1.64 in.
③ Cobra
④ Intake: 280@1.30 in.
   Exhaust: 264@1.12 in.
⑤ Intake: 1.80 in.
   Exhaust: 1.62 in.

PISTON AND RING SPECIFICATIONS
All measurements are given in inches.

Year	Engine ID/VIN	Engine Displacement Liters (cc)	Piston Clearance	Ring Gap			Ring Side Clearance		
				Top Compression	Bottom Compression	Oil Control	Top Compression	Bottom Compression	Oil Control
1992	M	2.3 (2300)	0.0024-0.0033	0.010-0.020	0.010-0.020	0.015-0.049	0.0016-0.0033	0.0016-0.0033	SNUG
	4	3.8 (3802)	0.0014-0.0032	0.010-0.022	0.010-0.022	0.015-0.055	0.002-0.044	0.002-0.004	SNUG
	R	3.8 (3802)	0.0040-0.0045	0.011-0.012	0.009-0.020	0.015-0.058	0.0016-0.0034	0.0016-0.0034	SNUG
	E	5.0 (4949)	0.0030-0.0038	0.010-0.020	0.010-0.020	0.015-0.055	0.0020-0.0040	0.0020-0.0040	SNUG
	T	5.0 (4949)	0.0030-0.0038	0.010-0.020	0.010-0.020	0.015-0.055	0.0020-0.0040	0.0020-0.0040	SNUG

PISTON AND RING SPECIFICATIONS
All measurements are given in inches.

Year	Engine ID/VIN	Engine Displacement Liters (cc)	Piston Clearance	Ring Gap			Ring Side Clearance		
				Top Compression	Bottom Compression	Oil Control	Top Compression	Bottom Compression	Oil Control
1993	M	2.3 (2300)	0.0024-0.0033	0.010-0.020	0.010-0.020	0.015-0.049	0.0016-0.0033	0.0016-0.0033	SNUG
	4	3.8 (3802)	0.0014-0.0032	0.010-0.022	0.010-0.022	0.015-0.055	0.0020-0.0040	0.0020-0.0040	SNUG
	R	3.8 (3802)	0.0040-0.0045	0.011-0.012	0.009-0.020	0.015-0.058	0.0016-0.0034	0.0016-0.0034	SNUG
	V	4.6 (4593)	0.0007-0.0018	0.0098-0.0200	0.0090-0.0130	0.0059-0.0260	0.0016-0.0035	0.0012-0.0031	SNUG
	E	5.0 (4949)	0.0030-0.0038	0.010-0.020	0.010-0.020	0.015-0.055	0.0020-0.0040	0.0020-0.0040	SNUG
	T	5.0 (4949)	0.0030-0.0038	0.010-0.020	0.010-0.020	0.015-0.055	0.0020-0.0040	0.0020-0.0040	SNUG
1994	4	3.8 (3802)	0.0014-0.0032	0.011-0.012	0.010-0.020	0.015-0.058	0.0016-0.0034	0.0016-0.0034	SNUG
	R	3.8 (3802)	0.0015-0.0032	0.011-0.012	0.009-0.020	0.015-0.058	0.0016-0.0034	0.0016-0.0034	SNUG
	W	4.6 (4593)	0.0003-0.0006	0.009-0.019	0.009-0.019	0.006-0.026	0.0016-0.0035	0.0012-0.0031	SNUG
	V	4.6 (4593)	0.0007-0.0018	0.0098-0.0200	0.0090-0.0193	0.0059-0.0260	0.0004-0.0009	0.0012-0.0031	SNUG
	D	5.0 (4949)	0.0012-0.0020	0.010-0.020	0.018-0.028	0.010-0.040	0.0020-0.0040	0.0020-0.0040	SNUG
	T	5.0 (4949)	0.0012-0.0020	0.010-0.020	0.018-0.028	0.010-0.040	0.0020-0.0040	0.0020-0.0040	SNUG
1995-96	4	3.8 (3802)	0.0014-0.0032	0.0110-0.0120	0.0100-0.0200	0.0150-0.0580	0.0016-0.0034	0.0016-0.0034	SNUG
	R	3.8 (3802)	0.0004-0.0034	0.0110-0.0120	0.0090-0.0200	0.0150-0.0580	0.0016-0.0034	0.0016-0.0034	SNUG
	W	4.6 (4593)	0.0003-0.0006	0.0090-0.0190	0.0090-0.0190	0.0060-0.0260	0.0016-0.0035	0.0012-0.0031	SNUG
	V	4.6 (4593)	0.0007-0.0018	0.0098-0.0200	0.0090-0.0193	0.0059-0.0260	0.0004-0.0009	0.0012-0.0031	SNUG
	T	5.0 (4949)	0.0012-0.0020	0.0100-0.0200	0.0180-0.0280	0.0100-0.0400	0.0020-0.0040	0.0020-0.0040	SNUG
	D	5.0 (4949)	0.0012-0.0020	0.0100-0.0200	0.0180-0.0280	0.0100-0.0400	0.0020-0.0040	0.0020-0.0040	SNUG

TORQUE SPECIFICATIONS
All readings in ft. lbs.

Year	Engine ID/VIN	Engine Displacement Liters (cc)	Cylinder Head Bolts	Main Bearing Bolts	Rod Bearing Bolts	Crankshaft Damper Bolts	Flywheel Bolts	Manifold Intake	Manifold Exhaust	Spark Plugs	Lug Nut
1992	M	2.3 (2300)	⑤	⑥	⑦	114-151	56-64	19-28	①	5-10	95
	R	3.8 (3801)	④	65-81	31-36	103-132	54-64	⑭	15-22	5-11	95
	4	3.8 (3802)	②	65-81	31-36	85-100	75-85	⑮	15-22	5-11	95
	E	5.0 (4949)	65-72	60-70	19-24	70-90	75-85	23-25	18-24	10-15	95
	T	5.0 (4949)	65-72	60-70	19-24	70-90	75-85	23-25	18-24	10-15	95
1993	M	2.3 (2300)	⑤	⑥	⑦	114-151	56-64	19-28	①	5-10	95
	R	3.8 (3801)	④	65-81	31-36	103-132	54-64	⑭	15-22	5-11	95
	4	3.8 (3802)	②	65-81	31-36	85-100	75-85	⑮	15-22	5-11	95
	V	4.6 (4593)	⑳	㉒	18-25 ㉑	114-121	54-64	㉓	15-22	7-15	95
	E	5.0 (4949)	65-72	60-70	19-24	70-90	75-85	23-25	18-24	10-15	95
	T	5.0 (4949)	65-72	60-70	19-24	70-90	75-85	23-25	18-24	10-15	95
1994	4	3.8 (3802)	⑱	65-81	31-36	103-132	54-64	⑰	15-22	7-15	95
	R	3.8 (3802)	⑲	65-81	31-36	103-132	54-64	⑯	15-22	7-15	95
	W	4.6 (4593)	⑧	⑨	⑩	114-121	54-64	15-22	15-22	7-15	95
	V	4.6 (4593)	⑧	㉔	㉕	114-121	54-64	⑬	13-16	7-15	95
	D	5.0 (4949)	⑫	60-70	19-24	110-130	75-85	⑪	26-32	10-15	95
	T	5.0 (4949)	⑫	60-70	19-24	110-130	75-85	⑪	26-32	10-15	95
1995-96	4	3.8 (3802)	⑱	65-81	31-36	103-132	54-64	⑰	15-22	7-15	95
	R	3.8 (3802)	⑲	65-81	31-36	103-132	54-64	⑯	15-22	7-15	95
	W	4.6 (4593)	⑧	⑨	⑩	114-121	54-64	15-22	15-22	7-15	95
	V	4.6 (4593)	⑧	㉔	㉕	114-121	54-64	⑬	13-16	7-15	95
	T	5.0 (4949)	⑫	60-70	19-24	110-130	75-85	⑪	26-32	10-15	95
	D	5.0 (4949)	⑫	60-70	19-24	110-130	75-85	⑪	26-32	10-15	95

① Step 1: 5-7 ft. lbs.
Step 2: 20-30 ft. lbs.

② Step 1: 37 ft. lbs.
Step 2: 45 ft. lbs.
Step 3: 52 ft. lbs.
Step 4: 59 ft. lbs.

③ Step 1: 48-54 ft. lbs.
Step 2: 63-80 ft. lbs.

④ Step 1: 37 ft. lbs.
Step 2: 45 ft. lbs.
Step 3: 52 ft. lbs.
Step 4: 59 ft. lbs.
Step 5: Back off all bolts two to three turns
Step 6: Tighten to 48-55 ft. lbs.
Step 7: Rotate bolts an additional 90-110 degrees

⑤ Step 1: 50-60 ft. lbs.
Step 2: 80-90 ft. lbs.

⑥ Step 1: 50-60 ft. lbs.
Step 2: 75-85 ft. lbs.

⑦ Step 1: 25-30 ft. lbs.
Step 2: 30-36 ft. lbs.

⑧ Do not reuse cylinder head bolts
Step 1: 25-30 ft. lbs.
Step 2: Rotate each bolt 85-95 degrees
Step 3: Repeat Step 2

⑨ Do not reuse main cap bolts
Step 1: Main bearing cap bolts: 22-25 ft. lbs.
Step 2: Rotate each bolt 85-95 degrees
Step 3: Main bearing cap adjust screws: 4 ft. lbs. then 6-8 ft. lb
Step 4: Main bearing cap side bolts: 7 ft. lbs. then 14-17 ft. lbs.

⑩ Do not reuse rod bolts
Step 1: 12 ft. lbs.
Step 2: Rotate 85-95 degrees

⑪ Step 1: 8 ft. lbs.
Step 2: 16 ft. lbs.
Step 3: 23-25 ft. lbs.

⑫ Do not reuse cylinder head bolts
Step 1: 22-35 ft. lbs.
Step 2: 44-55 ft. lbs.
Step 3: Rotate 85-95 degrees

⑬ Step 1: Four inside short bolts: 9-11 ft. lbs.
Step 2: All other bolts: 13-16 ft. lbs.
Step 3: Rotate 85-95 degrees

⑭ Supercharger to lower intake manifold bolts
M8 x 43mm bolts: 20-28 ft.lbs
M8 x 108mm bolts: 15-22 ft. lbs.
M12 bolt: 52-70 ft. lbs.
Lower intake manifold bolts
Step 1: 8 ft. lbs.
Step 2: 11 ft. lbs.

⑮ Upper intake manifold bolts
Step 1: 8 ft. lbs.
Step 2: 15 ft. lbs.
Step 3: 24 ft. lbs
Lower intake manifold bolts
Step 1: 8 ft. lbs.
Step 2: 11 ft. lbs.

⑯ Supercharger to lower intake manifold bolts
M8 x 43mm bolts: 20-28 ft.lbs
M8 x 108mm bolts: 15-22 ft. lbs.
M12 bolt: 52-70 ft. lbs.
Lower intake manifold bolts
Step 1: 13 ft. lbs.
Step 2: 16 ft. lbs.

⑰ Upper intake manifold bolts
Step 1: 8 ft. lbs.
Step 2: 15 ft. lbs.
Step 3: 24 ft. lbs
Lower intake manifold bolts
Step 1: 13 ft. lbs.
Step 2: 16 ft. lbs.

⑱ Do not reuse cylinder head bolts
Step 1: 15 ft. lbs.
Step 2: 29 ft. lbs.
Step 3: 37 ft. lbs.
Step 4: Loosen bolts one at a time and retorque as follows:
Long bolts: 11-18 ft. lbs.
Short bolts: 7-15 ft. lbs.
Step 5: Rotate 85-95 degrees

⑲ Do not reuse cylinder head bolts
Step 1: 37 ft. lbs.
Step 2: 45 ft. lbs.
Step 3: 52 ft. lbs.
Step 4: 59 ft. lbs.
Step 5: Back off bolts two to three turns, one at a time
Step 6: Tighten all bolts 37-44 ft. lbs.
Step 7: Rotate bolts an additional 180-200 degrees

⑳ 27-32 ft. lbs. plus two turns of 85-95 degrees

㉑ Plus 85-95 degrees

㉒ Step 1: Bolts 1-8, 11-18: 6-9 ft. lbs.
Step 2: Seat thrust washer
Step 3: Bolts 9-10, 19-20: 6-9 ft. lbs.
Step 4:
Bolts 1-10: 16-21 ft. lbs.
Bolts 11-20: 27-32 ft. lbs.

㉓ Tighten all bolts in numerical sequence
Tighten bolts 5, 7, 9, 11: 9-11 ft. lbs. plus 85-95 degrees
Tighten all other bolts to 13-16 ft. lbs.
Then tighten all bolts an additional 85-95 degrees

㉔ Step 1: Main bearing cap bolts: 6-9 ft. lbs.
Step 2: Main bearing cap bolts, outer: 16-21 ft. lbs.
Step 3: Main bearing cap bolts, inner: 27-32 ft. lbs.
Step 4: Rotate main bearing cap bolts 85-95 degrees
Step 5: Main cap adjusting screws: 4 ft. lbs. then 7.5 ft. lbs.
Step 6: Main cap side bolts: 7 ft. lbs. then 14-17 ft. lbs.

㉕ Step 1: 5 ft. lbs.
Step 2: 10 ft. lbs.
Step 3: 18-25 ft. lbs.
Step 4: Rotate 85-95 degrees

BRAKE SPECIFICATIONS
All measurements in inches unless noted

Year	Model			Master Cylinder Bore	Brake Disc Original Thickness	Brake Disc Minimum Thickness	Brake Disc Maximum Runout	Brake Drum Diameter Original Inside Diameter	Brake Drum Diameter Max. Wear Limit	Brake Drum Diameter Maximum Machine Diameter	Minimum Lining Thickness Front	Minimum Lining Thickness Rear
1992	Mustang	①		0.875	NA	0.810	0.003	9.00	9.89	9.06	0.125	0.030
		②		0.875	NA	0.972	0.003	9.00	9.89	9.06	0.125	0.030
	Thunderbird	④	F	0.938 ③	1.024	0.974	0.003	9.84	9.90	9.86	0.125	0.030
		⑤	R	-	0.945	0.896	0.003	-	-	-	-	0.123
	Cougar	④	F	0.938 ③	1.025	0.974	0.003	9.80	9.90	9.86	0.125	0.030
		⑤	R	-	0.710	0.657	-	-	-	-	0.123	-
	Mark VII		F	1.125	1.024	0.974	0.003	-	-	-	0.125	-
			R	-	0.944	0.890	0.002	-	-	-	-	0.123
1993	Mustang	①		0.875	NA	0.810	0.003	9.00	9.89	9.06	0.125	0.030
		②		0.875	NA	0.972	0.003	9.00	9.89	9.06	0.125	0.030
	Thunderbird	④	F	0.983 ③	1.025	0.974	0.003	9.84	9.89	9.86	0.125	0.030
		⑤	R	-	0.945	0.896	0.003	-	-	-	-	0.123
	Cougar	④	F	0.938 ③	1.025	0.974	0.003	9.80	9.89	9.86	0.125	0.030
		⑤	R	-	0.710	0.657	-	-	-	-	0.123	-
	Mark VIII		F	1.000	1.024	0.974	0.003	-	-	-	0.040	-
			R	-	0.709	0.657	0.002	-	-	-	-	0.123
1994	Mustang		F	1.060	1.030	0.970	0.002	-	-	-	0.040	-
			R	-	0.550	0.500	0.002	-	-	-	-	0.123
	Mustang	⑥	F	1.000	1.100	1.040	0.002	-	-	-	0.040	-
			R	-	0.550	0.500	0.002	-	-	-	-	0.123
	Thunderbird	④	F	0.938 ③	1.025	0.974	0.003	9.84	9.89	9.89	0.040	0.030
		⑤	R	-	0.709	0.657	0.003	-	-	-	-	0.123
	Cougar	④	F	0.938	1.025	0.974	0.003	9.80	9.89	9.89	0.040	0.030
		⑤	R	-	0.710	0.657	0.003	-	-	-	0.123	-
	Mark VIII		F	1.000	1.024	0.974	0.003	-	-	-	0.040	-
			R	-	0.709	0.657	0.002	-	-	-	-	0.123
1995-96	Mustang		F	1.060	1.030	0.970	0.002	-	-	-	0.040	-
			R	-	0.550	0.500	0.002	-	-	-	-	0.123
	Mustang	⑥	F	1.000	1.100	1.040	0.002	-	-	-	0.040	-
			R	-	0.550	0.500	0.002	-	-	-	-	0.123
	Thunderbird	④	F	0.938 ③	1.025	0.974	0.003	9.84	9.89	9.86	0.040	0.030
		⑤	R	-	0.709	0.657	0.003	-	-	-	-	0.123
	Cougar	④	F	0.938	1.025	0.974	0.003	9.80	9.89	9.89	0.040	0.030
		⑤	R	-	0.710	0.657	0.003	-	-	-	0.123	-
	Mark VIII		F	1.000	1.024	0.974	0.003	-	-	-	0.040	-
			R	-	0.709	0.657	0.002	-	-	-	-	0.123

NOTE: Follow specifications stamped on rotor or drum if figures differ from those in this chart.

NA - Not Available

F - Front

R - Rear

① Except 5.0L engine

② With 5.0L enfgine

③ Except ABS

④ Without rear disc

⑤ With rear disc

⑥ Cobra

23 SPECIFICATIONS

WHEEL ALIGNMENT

Year	Model			Caster Range (deg.)	Caster Preferred Setting (deg.)	Camber Range (deg.)	Camber Preferred Setting (deg.)	Toe-in (in.)	Steering Axis Inclination (deg.)
1992	Mustang	①		1 5/32P-2 5/8P	1 29/32P	1 1/4N-1/4P	1/2N	1/8N	15 23/32
		②		1 5/32P-2 5/8P	1 29/32P	1 3/8N-1/8P	5/8N	1/8N	15 23/32
	Thunderbird	F		4 3/4P-6 1/4P	5 1/2P	1 1/4N-1/4P	1/2N	1/4P	15 23/32
		R		-	-	1N-0	1/2N	1/16P	15 23/32
	Cougar	F		4 3/4P-6 1/4P	5 1/2P	1 1/4N-1/4P	1/2N	1/4P	15 23/32
		R		-	-	1N-0	1/2N	1/16P	15 23/32
	Mark VII			0.60P-2.70P	1.50P	0.75N-0.75P	0	3/32P	12.00
1993	Mustang	①		1 5/32P-2 5/8P	1 29/32P	1 1/4N-1/4P	1/2N	1/8N	15 23/32
		②		1 5/32P-2 5/8P	1 29/32P	1 3/8P-1/8P	5/8N	1/8N	15 23/32
		③		1 5/32P-2 21/32P	1 29/32P	1 3/8P-1/8P	5/8N	0	15 23/32
	Thunderbird	F		4 3/4P-6 1/4P	5 1/2P	1 1/4N-1/4P	1/2N	5/64P	15 23/32
		R		-	-	1N-0	1/2N	1/16P	15 23/32
	Cougar	F		4 3/4P-6 1/4P	5 1/2P	1 1/4N-1/4P	1/2N	5/64P	15 23/32
		R		-	-	1N-0	1/2N	1/16P	15 23/32
	Mark VIII	F		4.75P-6.25P	5.50P	1.25N-0.25P	0.50N	3/32P	NA
		R		-	-	1N-0	0.50N	3/64P	
1994	Mustang			2.85P-4.35P	3.60P	1.35N-0.15P	0.60N	0.12N	15.72
	Thunderbird	F		4.75P-6.75P	5.50P	1.25N-0.25P	0.50N	0.06P	-
		R		-	-	1.00N-0	0.50N	0	-
	Cougar	L		4.75P-6.75P	5.50P	1.25P-0.25P	0.50N	0	-
		R		-	-	1.00N-0	0.50N	0	-
	Mark VIII	F		4.75P-6.25P	5.50P	1.25N-0.25P	0.50N	0.07P	NA
		R		-	-	1.00N-0	0.50N	0.12P	
1995-96	Mustang	④		2.65P-4.15P	3.40P	1.35N-0.15P	0.60N	0.12N	15.72
	Mustang	②		2.65P-4.15P	3.40P	0.25N-1.25P	0.50N	0.12N	15.72
	Thunderbird	F		4.75P-6.75P	5.50P	1.25N-0.25P	0.50N	0.06P	NA
		R		-	-	1.00N-0	0.50N	0	-
	Cougar	F		4.75P-6.75P	5.50P	1.25N-0.25P	0.50N	0.06P	NA
		R		-	-	1.00N-0	0.50N	0	-
	Mark VIII	F		4.75P-6.25P	5.50P	1.25N-0.25P	0.50N	0.07P	NA
		R		-	-	1.00N-0	0.50N	0.06P	-

NA - Not Available
P - Positive
N - Negative
LF - Left Front
RF - Right Front
F - Front
R - Rear

① Except 5.0L engine - GT
② 5.0L engine - GT
③ Cobra and GT
④ All except Cobra and GT

CROWN VICTORIA/GRAND MARQUIS/TOWN CAR

VEHICLE IDENTIFICATION CHART

		Engine Code					Model Year	
Code	Liters	Cu. In. (cc)	Cyl.	Fuel Sys.	Eng. Mfg.		Code	Year
W	4.6	280 (4593)	8	MFI	Ford		N	1992
							P	1993
							R	1994
							S	1995
							T	1996

ENGINE IDENTIFICATION

Year	Model	Engine Displacement Liters (cc)	Engine Series (ID/VIN)	Fuel System	No. of Cylinders	Engine Type
1992	Crown Victoria	4.6 (4593)	W	MFI	8	SOHC
	Grand Marquis	4.6 (4593)	W	MFI	8	SOHC
	Town Car	4.6 (4593)	W	MFI	8	SOHC
1993	Crown Victoria	4.6 (4593)	W	MFI	8	SOHC
	Grand Marquis	4.6 (4593)	W	MFI	8	SOHC
	Town Car	4.6 (4593)	W	MFI	8	SOHC
1994	Crown Victoria	4.6 (4593)	W	SFI	8	SOHC
	Grand Marquis	4.6 (4593)	W	SFI	8	SOHC
	Town Car	4.6 (4593)	W	SFI	8	SOHC
1995-96	Crown Victoria	4.6 (4593)	W	SFI	8	SOHC
	Grand Marquis	4.6 (4593)	W	SFI	8	SOHC
	Town Car	4.6 (4593)	W	SFI	8	SOHC

MFI - Multiport fuel injection
SFI - Sequential fuel injection
SOHC - Single overhead camshaft

GENERAL ENGINE SPECIFICATIONS

Year	Engine ID/VIN	Engine Displacement Liters (cc)	Fuel System Type	Net Horsepower @ rpm	Net Torque @ rpm (ft. lbs.)	Bore x Stroke (in.)	Compression Ratio	Oil Pressure @ rpm
1992	W	4.6 (4593)	MFI	①	②	3.55x3.54	9.0:1	20-45@2000
1993	W	4.6 (4593)	MFI	①	②	3.55x3.54	9.0:1	20-45@2000
1994	W	4.6 (4593)	SFI	①	②	3.55x3.5.4	9.0:1	20-45@2000
1995-96	W	4.6 (4593)	SFI	210@4250	270@3250	3.55x3.54	9.0:1	20-45@2000

MFI - Multiport fuel injection
SFI - Sequential fuel injection
① Single exhaust: 190@4200
   Dual exhaust: 210@4600
② Single exhaust: 260@3200
   Dual exhaust: 270@3400

GASOLINE ENGINE TUNE-UP SPECIFICATIONS

Year	Engine ID/VIN	Engine Displacement Liters (cc)	Spark Plugs Gap (in.)	Ignition Timing (deg.) MT	AT	Fuel Pump (psi)	Idle Speed (rpm) MT	AT	Valve Clearance In.	Ex.
1992	W	4.6 (4593)	0.054	-	10B	35-40	-	560	HYD	HYD
1993	W	4.6 (4593)	0.054	-	10B	35-40	-	560	HYD	HYD
1994	W	4.6 (4593)	0.054	-	10B	30-45 ②	①	①	HYD	HYD
1995-96	W	4.6 (4593)	0.054	-	10B	30-45 ②	-	①	HYD	HYD

NOTE: The Vehicle Emission Control Information label often reflects specification changes made during production. The label figures must be used if they differ from those in this chart.

B - Before top dead center
HYD - Hydraulic
① Refer to Vehicle Emission Control Information label
② Fuel pressure with engine running, pressure regulator vacuum hose connected

CAPACITIES

Year	Model	Engine ID/VIN	Engine Displacement Liters (cc)	Engine Oil with Filter (qts.)	Transmission (pts.) 4-Spd	5-Spd	Auto.	Drive Axle Front (pts.)	Rear (pts.)	Fuel Tank (gal.)	Cooling System (qts.)
1992	Crown Victoria	W	4.6 (4593)	5.0	-	-	24.6	-	3.75	20.0	14.1
	Grand Marquis	W	4.6 (4593)	5.0	-	-	24.6	-	3.75	20.0	14.1
	Town Car	W	4.6 (4593)	5.0	-	-	24.6 ①	-	3.75	20.0	14.1
1993	Crown Victoria	W	4.6 (4593)	5.0	-	-	24.6	-	3.75	20.0	14.1
	Grand Marquis	W	4.6 (4593)	5.0	-	-	24.6	-	3.75	20.0	14.1
	Town Car	W	4.6 (4593)	5.0	-	-	27.2 ②	-	3.75	20.0	14.1
1994	Crown Victoria	W	4.6 (4593)	5.0	-	-	27.2 ②	-	3.75	20.0	14.1
	Grand Marquis	W	4.6 (4593)	5.0	-	-	27.2 ②	-	3.75	20.0	14.1
	Town Car	W	4.6 (4593)	5.0	-	-	27.2 ②	-	3.75	20.0	14.1
1995-96	Crown Victoria	W	4.6 (4593)	5.0	-	-	27.2 ②	-	3.75	20.0	14.1
	Grand Marquis	W	4.6 (4593)	5.0	-	-	27.2 ②	-	3.75	20.0	14.1
	Town Car	W	4.6 (4593)	5.0	-	-	27.2 ②	-	3.75	20.0	14.1

① AOD-E transmission: 25.8 pts.
② Includes torque converter

CAMSHAFT SPECIFICATIONS
All measurements given in inches.

Year	Engine ID/VIN	Engine Displacement Liters (cc)	Journal Diameter 1	2	3	4	5	Elevation In.	Ex.	Bearing Clearance	Camshaft End Play
1992	W	4.6 (4593)	1.605-1.0615	1.605-1.0615	1.605-1.0615	1.605-1.0615	1.605-1.0615	0.2594	0.2594	0.0010-0.0030	0.0010-0.0060
1993	W	4.6 (4593)	1.0605-1.0615	1.0605-1.0615	1.0605-1.0615	1.0605-1.0615	1.0605-1.0615	0.2594	0.2594	0.0010-0.0030	0.0010-0.0060
1994	W	4.6 (4593)	1.0605-1.0615	1.0605-1.0615	1.0605-1.0615	1.0605-1.0615	1.0605-1.0615	0.2594	0.2594	0.0010-0.0030	0.0010-0.0060
1995-96	W	4.6 (4593)	1.0605-1.0615	1.0605-1.0615	1.0605-1.0615	1.0605-1.0615	1.0605-1.0615	0.2594	0.2594	0.0010-0.0030	0.0010-0.0060

CRANKSHAFT AND CONNECTING ROD SPECIFICATIONS

All measurements are given in inches.

Year	Engine ID/VIN	Engine Displacement Liters (cc)	Crankshaft				Connecting Rod		
			Main Brg. Journal Dia.	Main Brg. Oil Clearance	Shaft End-play	Thrust on No.	Journal Diameter	Oil Clearance	Side Clearance
1992	W	4.9 (4593)	2.6578-2.6598	0.0011-0.0025	0.005-0.010	5	2.0866	0.0011-0.0027	0.006-0.019
1993	W	4.9 (4593)	2.6578-2.6598	0.0011-0.0025	0.005-0.010	5	2.0866	0.0011-0.0027	0.006-0.019
1994	W	4.6 (4593)	2.6578-2.6598	0.0011-0.0025	0.005-0.010	5	2.0874-2.0891	0.0011-0.0027	0.0006-0.0177
1995-96	W	4.6 (4593)	2.6578-2.6598	0.0011-0.0025	0.0050-0.0100	5	2.0874-2.0891	0.0011-0.0027	0.0006-0.0177

VALVE SPECIFICATIONS

Year	Engine ID/VIN	Engine Displacement Liters (cc)	Seat Angle (deg.)	Face Angle (deg.)	Spring Test Pressure (lbs. @ in.)	Spring Installed Height (in.)	Stem-to-Guide Clearance (in.)		Stem Diameter (in.)	
							Intake	Exhaust	Intake	Exhaust
1992	W	4.6 (4593)	45	45.5	180@1.103	1.575	0.0008-0.0027	0.0018-0.0037	0.2746-0.2754	0.2736-0.2744
1993	W	4.6 (4593)	45	45.5	180@1.103	1.575	0.0008-0.0027	0.0018-0.0037	0.2746-0.2754	0.2736-0.2744
1994	W	4.6 (4593)	45	45.5	180@1.103	1.575	0.0008-0.0027	0.0018-0.0037	0.2746-0.2754	0.2736-0.2744
1995-96	W	4.6 (4593)	45	45.5	180@1.103	1.575	0.0008-0.0027	0.0018-0.0037	0.2746-0.2754	0.2736-0.2744

PISTON AND RING SPECIFICATIONS

All measurements are given in inches.

Year	Engine ID/VIN	Engine Displacement Liters (cc)	Piston Clearance	Ring Gap			Ring Side Clearance		
				Top Compression	Bottom Compression	Oil Control	Top Compression	Bottom Compression	Oil Control
1992	W	4.6 (4593)	0.0007-0.0018	0.0091-0.0193	0.0091-0.0193	0.0059-0.0260	0.0016-0.0035	0.0012-0.0031	SNUG
1993	W	4.6 (4593)	0.0007-0.0018	0.0091-0.0193	0.0091-0.0193	0.0059-0.0260	0.0016-0.0035	0.0012-0.0031	SNUG
1994	W	4.6 (4593)	0.0007-0.0018	0.0091-0.0193	0.0091-0.0193	0.0059-0.0260	0.0016-0.0035	0.0012-0.0031	SNUG
1995-96	W	4.6 (4593)	0.0007-0.0018	0.0091-0.0193	0.0091-0.0193	0.0059-0.0260	0.0016-0.0035	0.0012-0.0031	SNUG

TORQUE SPECIFICATIONS
All readings in ft. lbs.

Year	Engine ID/VIN	Engine Displacement Liters (cc)	Cylinder Head Bolts	Main Bearing Bolts	Rod Bearing Bolts	Crankshaft Damper Bolts	Flywheel Bolts	Manifold Intake	Manifold Exhaust	Spark Plugs	Lug Nut
1992	W	4.6 (4593)	①	22-25 ②	12 ②	114-121	54-64	19 ③	15-22	7-15	95
1993	W	4.6 (4593)	①	22-25 ②	12 ②	114-121	54-64	19 ③	15-22	7-15	95
1994	W	4.6 (4593)	④	⑤	⑥	114-121	54-64	15-22	13-16	7-15	95
1995-96	W	4.6 (4593)	④	⑤	⑥	114-121	54-64	15-22	13-16	7-15	95

NOTE: Always follow the proper torque patterns.
① 27-32 ft. lbs. plus two turns of 85-95 degrees
② Plus 85-95 degrees
③ After assembly, retighten with engine hot
④ Do not reuse cylinder head bolts
   Step 1: 25-30 ft. lbs.
   Step 2: Rotate each bolt 85-95 degrees
   Step 3: Repeat Step 2

⑤ Step 1: Main bearing cap bolts: 22-25 ft. lbs.
   Step 2: Rotate each bolt 85-95 degrees
   Step 3: Main cap adjusting screws: 4 ft. lbs. then 6.5-8.0 ft. lbs.
   Step 4: Main cap side bolts: 7 ft. lbs. then 14-17 ft. lbs.
⑥ Step 1: 8 ft. lbs.
   Step 2: 12 ft. lbs.
   Step 3: 29-34 ft. lbs.
   Step 4: Rotate 85-95 degrees

BRAKE SPECIFICATIONS
All measurements in inches unless noted

Year	Model		Master Cylinder Bore	Brake Disc Original Thickness	Brake Disc Minimum Thickness	Brake Disc Maximum Runout	Brake Drum Diameter Original Inside Diameter	Brake Drum Diameter Max. Wear Limit	Brake Drum Diameter Maximum Machine Diameter	Minimum Lining Thickness Front	Minimum Lining Thickness Rear
1992	Crown Victoria	F	1.000	1.030	0.974	0.003	-	-	-	0.030	-
		R	-	0.500	0.440	0.003	-	-	-	-	0.030
	Grand Marquis	F	1.000	1.030	0.974	0.003	-	-	-	0.125	-
		R	-	0.500	0.440	0.003	-	-	-	-	0.123
	Town Car	F	1.000	1.024	0.974	0.003	-	-	-	0.125	-
		R	-	0.500	0.440	0.003	-	-	-	-	0.220
1993	Crown Victoria	F	1.000	1.030	0.974	0.003	-	-	-	0.030	-
		R	-	0.500	0.440	0.003	-	-	-	-	0.030
	Grand Marquis	F	1.000	1.030	0.974	0.003	-	-	-	0.125	-
		R	-	0.500	0.440	0.003	-	-	-	-	0.123
	Town Car	F	1.000	1.024	0.974	0.003	-	-	-	0.125	-
		R	-	0.500	0.440	0.003	-	-	-	-	0.003
1994	Crown Victoria	F	1.000	1.030	0.974	0.003	-	-	-	0.125	-
		R	-	0.500	0.440	0.003	-	-	-	-	0.125
	Grand Marquis	F	1.000	1.030	0.974	0.003	-	-	-	0.125	-
		R	-	0.500	0.440	0.003	-	-	-	-	0.125
	Town Car	F	1.000	1.030	0.974	0.003	-	-	-	0.125	-
		R	-	0.500	0.440	0.003	-	-	-	-	0.125
1995-96	Crown Victoria	F	1.000	1.030	0.974	0.003	-	-	-	0.125	-
		R	-	0.500	0.440	0.003	-	-	-	-	0.125
	Grand Marquis	F	1.000	1.030	0.974	0.003	-	-	-	0.125	-
		R	-	0.500	0.440	0.003	-	-	-	-	0.125
	Town Car	F	1.000	1.030	0.974	0.003	-	-	-	0.125	-
		R	-	0.500	0.440	0.003	-	-	-	-	0.125

NOTE: Follow specifications stamped on rotor if figures differ from those in this chart.
F - Front
R - Rear

WHEEL ALIGNMENT

Year	Model	Caster Range (deg.)	Caster Preferred Setting (deg.)	Camber Range (deg.)	Camber Preferred Setting (deg.)	Toe-in (in.)	Steering Axis Inclination (deg.)
1992	Crown Victoria	4.75P-6.25P	5.75P	1.25N-0.25P	0.50N	1/16P	11.00
	Grand Marquis	4.75P-6.25P	5.75P	1.25N-0.25P	0.50N	1/16P	11.00
	Town Car	5.25P-6.75P	6P	1.25N-0.25P	0.50N	1/16P	11.00
1993	Crown Victoria	4.75P-6.25P	5.75P	1.25N-0.25P	0.50N	1/16P	11.00
	Grand Marquis	4.75P-6.25P	5.75P	1.25N-0.25P	0.50N	1/16P	11.00
	Town Car	5.25P-6.75P	6P	1.25N-0.25P	0.50N	1/16P	11.00
1994	Crown Victoria	4.75P-6.25P	5.50P	1.25N-0.25P	0.50N	1/16P	11.00
	Grand Marquis	4.75P-6.25P	5.75P	1.25N-0.25P	0.50N	1/16P	11.00
	Town Car	5.25P-6.75P	6P	1.25N-0.25P	0.50N	1/16P	11.00
1995-96	Crown Victoria	4.75P-6.25P	5.50P	1.25N-0.25P	0.50N	1/16P	11.00
	Grand Marquis	4.75P-6.25P	5.75P	1.25N-0.25P	0.50N	1/16P	11.00
	Town Car	5.25P-6.75P	6P	1.25N-0.25P	0.50N	1/16P	11.00

P - Positive
N - Negative

CENTURY/CUTLASS CIERA/CUTLASS CRUISER

VEHICLE IDENTIFICATION CHART

Code	Liters	Cu. In. (cc)	Cyl.	Fuel Sys.	Eng. Mfg.
4	2.2	134 (2195)	4	MFI	BOC
M	3.1	191 (3130)	6	MFI	BOC
N	3.3	204 (3342)	6	MFI	BOC
R	2.5	151 (2474)	4	TFI	CPC

Code	Year
N	1992
P	1993
R	1994
S	1995
T	1996

MFI - Multiport fuel injection
TFI - Throttle body fuel injection
BOC - Buick/Oldsmobile/Cadillac
CPC - Chevrolet/Pontiac/Canada

ENGINE IDENTIFICATION

Year	Model	Engine Displacement Liters (cc)	Engine Series (ID/VIN)	Fuel System	No. of Cylinders	Engine Type
1992	Century	2.5 (2474)	R	TFI	4	OHV
	Century	3.3 (3342)	N	MFI	6	OHV
	Cutlass Ciera	2.5 (2474)	R	TFI	4	OHV
	Cutlass Ciera	3.3 (3342)	N	MFI	6	OHV
	Cutlass Cruiser	2.5 (2474)	R	TFI	4	OHV
	Cutlass Cruiser	3.3 (3342)	N	MFI	6	OHV
1993	Century	2.2 (2195)	4	MFI	4	OHV
	Century	3.3 (3342)	N	MFI	6	OHV
	Cutlass Ciera	2.2 (2195)	4	MFI	4	OHV
	Cutlass Ciera	3.3 (3342)	N	MFI	6	OHV
	Cutlass Cruiser	2.2 (2195)	4	MFI	4	OHV
	Cutlass Cruiser	3.3 (3342)	N	MFI	6	OHV
1994	Century	2.2 (2195)	4	MFI	4	OHV
	Century	3.1 (3130)	M	MFI	6	OHV
	Cutlass Ciera	2.2 (2195)	4	MFI	4	OHV
	Cutlass Ciera	3.1 (3130)	M	MFI	6	OHV
	Cutlass Cruiser	2.2 (2195)	4	MFI	4	OHV
	Cutlass Cruiser	3.1 (3130)	M	MFI	6	OHV
1995-96	Century	2.2 (2195)	4	MFI	4	OHV
	Century	3.1 (3130)	M	MFI	6	OHV
	Cutlass Ciera	2.2 (2195)	4	MFI	4	OHV
	Cutlass Ciera	3.1 (3130)	M	MFI	6	OHV
	Cutlass Cruiser	2.2 (2195)	4	MFI	4	OHV
	Cutlass Cruiser	3.1 (3130)	M	MFI	6	OHV

MFI - Multiport fuel injection
TFI - Throttle body fuel injection
OHV - Overhead valve

GENERAL ENGINE SPECIFICATIONS

Year	Engine ID/VIN	Engine Displacement Liters (cc)	Fuel System Type	Net Horsepower @ rpm	Net Torque @ rpm (ft. lbs.)	Bore x Stroke (in.)	Compression Ratio	Oil Pressure @ rpm
1992	R	2.5 (2474)	TFI	110@5200	135@3200	4.00x3.00	8.3:1	26@800
	N	3.3 (3342)	MFI	160@5200	185@2000	3.70x3.16	9.0:1	60@1850
1993	4	2.2 (2195)	MFI	110@5200	130@3200	3.50x3.46	9.0:1	56@3000
	N	3.3 (3342)	MFI	160@5200	185@2000	3.70x3.16	9.0:1	60@1850
1994	4	2.2 (2195)	MFI	120@5200	130@4000	3.50x3.46	9.0:1	56@3000
	M	3.1 (3130)	MFI	160@5200	185@4000	3.50x3.31	9.5:1	15@1100
1995-96	4	2.2 (2195)	MFI	120@5200	130@4000	3.50x3.46	8.85:1	56@3000
	M	3.1 (3130)	MFI	160@5200	185@4000	3.50x3.31	9.5:1	15@1100

MFI - Multiport fuel injection
TFI - Throttle body fuel injection

GASOLINE ENGINE TUNE-UP SPECIFICATIONS

Year	Engine ID/VIN	Engine Displacement Liters (cc)	Spark Plugs Gap (in.)	Ignition Timing (deg.) MT	Ignition Timing (deg.) AT	Fuel Pump (psi)	Idle Speed (rpm) MT	Idle Speed (rpm) AT	Valve Clearance In.	Valve Clearance Ex.
1992	R	2.5 (2474)	0.060	①	①	9-13	550-650 ③	550-650 ③	HYD	HYD
	N	3.3 (3342)	0.060	①	①	41-47	②	②	HYD	HYD
1993	4	2.2 (2195)	0.045	①	①	41-47	②	②	HYD	HYD
	N	3.3 (3342)	0.060	①	①	41-47	②	②	HYD	HYD
1994	4	2.2 (2195)	0.060	①	①	41-47	②	②	HYD	HYD
	M	3.1 (3130)	0.060	①	①	41-47	②	②	HYD	HYD
1995	4	2.2 (2195)	0.060	①	①	41-47 ④	②	②	HYD	HYD
	M	3.1 (3130)	0.060	①	①	41-47 ④	②	②	HYD	HYD

NOTE: The Vehicle Emission Control Information label often reflects specification changes made during production. The label figures must be used if they differ from those in this chart.

HYD - Hydraulic

① DIS Ignition System timing not adjustable

② Idle speed maintained by ECM. There is no recommended adjustment procedure

③ Idle spec is minimum air rate; Refer to manual for procedure

④ Pressure at fuel pump

CAPACITIES

Year	Model	Engine ID/VIN	Engine Displacement Liters (cc)	Engine Oil with Filter (qts.)	Transmission (pts.) 4-Spd	Transmission (pts.) 5-Spd	Transmission (pts.) Auto.	Drive Axle Front (pts.)	Drive Axle Rear (pts.)	Fuel Tank (gal.)	Cooling System (qts.)
1992	Century	R	2.5 (2474)	4.0 ①	-	-	8.0	-	-	16.5	③
	Century	N	3.3 (3342)	4.0 ①	-	-	②	-	-	16.5	9.4
	Cutlass Ciera	R	2.5 (2474)	4.0 ①	-	-	②	-	-	16.5	③
	Cutlass Ciera	N	3.3 (3342)	4.0 ①	-	-	②	-	-	16.5	9.4
	Cutlass Cruiser	R	2.5 (2474)	4.0 ①	-	-	②	-	-	16.5	③
	Cutlass Cruiser	N	3.3 (3342)	4.0 ①	-	-	②	-	-	16.5	9.4
1993	Century	4	2.2 (2195)	4.0 ①	-	-	④	-	-	16.5	8.3
	Century	N	3.3 (3342)	4.0 ①	-	-	④	-	-	16.5	10.5
	Cutlass Ciera	4	2.2 (2195)	4.0 ①	-	-	④	-	-	16.5	8.3
	Cutlass Ciera	N	3.3 (3342)	4.0 ①	-	-	④	-	-	16.5	10.5
	Cutlass Cruiser	4	2.2 (2195)	4.0 ①	-	-	④	-	-	16.5	8.3
	Cutlass Cruiser	N	3.3 (3342)	4.0 ①	-	-	④	-	-	16.5	10.5
1994	Century	4	2.2 (2195)	4.0 ①	-	-	⑤	-	-	16.5	8.7
	Century	M	3.1 (3130)	4.0 ①	-	-	⑤	-	-	16.5	11.6
	Cutlass Ciera	4	2.2 (2195)	4.0 ①	-	-	⑤	-	-	16.5	8.7
	Cutlass Ciera	M	3.1 (3130)	4.0 ①	-	-	⑤	-	-	16.5	11.6
	Cutlass Cruiser	4	2.2 (2195)	4.0 ①	-	-	⑤	-	-	16.5	8.7
	Cutlass Cruiser	M	3.1 (3130)	4.0 ①	-	-	⑤	-	-	16.5	11.6
1995-96	Century	4	2.2 (2195)	3.8 ①	-	-	⑤	-	-	16.5	8.7
	Century	M	3.1 (3130)	3.8 ①	-	-	⑤	-	-	16.5	11.6
	Cutlass Ciera	4	2.2 (2195)	3.8 ①	-	-	⑤	-	-	16.5	8.7
	Cutlass Ciera	M	3.1 (3130)	3.8 ①	-	-	⑤	-	-	16.5	11.6
	Cutlass Cruiser	4	2.2 (2195)	3.8 ①	-	-	⑤	-	-	16.5	8.7
	Cutlass Cruiser	M	3.1 (3130)	3.8 ①	-	-	⑤	-	-	16.5	11.6

CAPACITIES

Year	Model	Engine ID/VIN	Engine Displacement Liters (cc)	Engine Oil with Filter (qts.)	Transmission (pts.)			Drive Axle		Fuel Tank (gal.)	Cooling System (qts.)
					4-Spd	5-Spd	Auto.	Front (pts.)	Rear (pts.)		

① Specification is without filter replacement; Additional oil may be required

② With AT 125C: 14.0
  With AT 440-T4: 12.0

③ With std. cooling: 7.75
  With A/C: 8.00

④ 3 speed: 8.0
  4 speed: 12.0

⑤ 3 speed: 8.0
  4 speed: 14.8

CAMSHAFT SPECIFICATIONS
All measurements given in inches.

Year	Engine ID/VIN	Engine Displacement Liters (cc)	Journal Diameter 1	2	3	4	5	Elevation In.	Ex.	Bearing Clearance	Camshaft End Play
1992	R	2.5 (2474)	1.8690	1.8690	1.8690	1.8690	1.8690	0.2480	0.2480	0.0007-0.0027	0.0015-0.0050
	N	3.3 (3342)	1.7850-1.7860	1.7850-1.7860	1.7850-1.7860	1.7850-1.7860	1.7850-1.7860	0.2500	0.2550	0.0005-0.0035	NA
1993	4	2.2 (2195)	1.8670-1.8690	1.8670-1.8690	1.8670-1.8690	1.8670-1.8690	1.8670-1.8690	0.2590	0.2500	0.0010-0.0039	NA
	N	3.3 (3342)	1.7850-1.7860	1.7850-1.7860	1.7850-1.7860	1.7850-1.7860	1.7850-1.7860	0.2500	0.2550	0.0005-0.0035	NA
1994	4	2.2 (2195)	1.8680-1.8690	1.8680-1.8690	1.8680-1.8690	1.8680-1.8690	1.8680-1.8690	0.2880	0.2880	0.0010-0.0039	NA
	M	3.1 (3130)	1.8680-1.8690	1.8680-1.8690	1.8680-1.8690	1.8680-1.8690	1.8680-1.8690	0.2727	0.2727	0.0010-0.0040	NA
1995-96	4	2.2 (2195)	1.8680-1.8690	1.8680-1.8690	1.8680-1.8690	1.8680-1.8690	1.8680-1.8690	0.2880	0.2880	0.0010-0.0039	NA
	M	3.1 (3130)	1.8680-1.8690	1.8680-1.8690	1.8680-1.8690	1.8680-1.8690	1.8680-1.8690	0.2727	0.2727	0.0010-0.0040	NA

NA - Not Available

CRANKSHAFT AND CONNECTING ROD SPECIFICATIONS
All measurements are given in inches.

Year	Engine ID/VIN	Engine Displacement Liters (cc)	Crankshaft Main Brg. Journal Dia.	Main Brg. Oil Clearance	Shaft End-play	Thrust on No.	Connecting Rod Journal Diameter	Oil Clearance	Side Clearance
1992	R	2.5 (2474)	2.3000	0.0005-0.0022	0.0005-0.0100	5	2.0000	0.0005-0.0030	0.0060-0.0240
	N	3.3 (3342)	2.4988-2.4998	0.0008-0.0022	0.0030-0.0110	2	2.2487-2.2499	0.0008-0.0022	0.0030-0.0150

CRANKSHAFT AND CONNECTING ROD SPECIFICATIONS

All measurements are given in inches.

Year	Engine ID/VIN	Engine Displacement Liters (cc)	Crankshaft				Connecting Rod		
			Main Brg. Journal Dia.	Main Brg. Oil Clearance	Shaft End-play	Thrust on No.	Journal Diameter	Oil Clearance	Side Clearance
1993	4	2.2 (2195)	2.4945-2.4954	0.0006-0.0019	0.0020-0.0070	4	1.9983-1.9994	0.0010-0.0031	0.0039-0.0149
	N	3.3 (3342)	2.4988-2.4998	0.0008-0.0022	0.0030-0.0110	2	2.2487-2.2499	0.0001-0.0022	0.0030-0.0150
1994	4	2.2 (2195)	2.4945-2.4954	0.0006-0.0019	0.0020-0.0070	4	1.9983-1.9994	0.0010-0.0031	0.0039-0.0149
	M	3.1 (3130)	2.6473-2.6483	0.0012-0.0030	0.0024-0.0083	3	1.9982-1.9984	0.0011-0.0037	0.0071-0.0173
1995-96	4	2.2 (2195)	2.4945-2.4954	0.0006-0.0019	0.0020-0.0070	4	1.9983-1.9994	0.00098-0.0031	0.0039-0.0149
	M	3.1 (3130)	2.6473-2.6483	0.0012-0.0030	0.0024-0.0083	3	1.9982-1.9984	0.0011-0.0037	0.0071-0.0173

VALVE SPECIFICATIONS

Year	Engine ID/VIN	Engine Displacement Liters (cc)	Seat Angle (deg.)	Face Angle (deg.)	Spring Test Pressure (lbs. @ in.)	Spring Installed Height (in.)	Stem-to-Guide Clearance (in.)		Stem Diameter (in.)	
							Intake	Exhaust	Intake	Exhaust
1992	R	2.5 (2474)	46	45	173@1.240	1.680	0.0010-0.0028	0.0013-0.0041	NA	NA
	N	3.3 (3342)	45	45	210@1.315	1.690-1.720	0.0015-0.0035	0.0015-0.0032	NA	NA
1993	4	2.2 (2195)	46	45	215-233@1.247	1.637	0.0011-0.0026	0.0014-0.0031	NA	NA
	N	3.3 (3342)	45	45	210@1.315	1.690-1.720	0.0015-0.0035	0.0015-0.0035	NA	NA
1994	4	2.2 (2195)	46	45	220-236@1.278	1.710	0.0010-0.0027	0.0014-0.0031	NA	NA
	M	3.1 (3130)	45	45	250@1.239	1.710	0.0010-0.0027	0.0010-0.0027	NA	NA
1995-96	4	2.2 (2195)	46	45	220-236@1.278	1.710	0.0010-0.0027	0.0014-0.0031	NA	NA
	M	3.1 (3130)	45	45	250@1.239	1.710	0.0010-0.0027	0.0010-0.0027	NA	NA

NA - Not Available

PISTON AND RING SPECIFICATIONS

All measurements are given in inches.

Year	Engine ID/VIN	Engine Displacement Liters (cc)	Piston Clearance	Ring Gap			Ring Side Clearance		
				Top Compression	Bottom Compression	Oil Control	Top Compression	Bottom Compression	Oil Control
1992	R	2.5 (2474)	0.0014-0.0022	0.010-0.020	0.010-0.020	0.020-0.060	0.0020-0.0030	0.0010-0.0030	0.0150-0.0550
	N	3.3 (3342)	0.0004-0.0022 ①	0.010-0.025	0.010-0.025	0.015-0.055	0.0013-0.0031	0.0013-0.0031	0.0011-0.0081
1993	4	2.2 (2195)	0.0007-0.0017	0.010-0.020	0.010-0.020	0.010-0.050	0.0019-0.0027	0.0019-0.0027	0.0019-0.0082
	N	3.3 (3342)	0.0004-0.0022 ①	0.010-0.025	0.010-0.025	0.015-0.055	0.0013-0.0031	0.0013-0.0031	0.0110-0.0081
1994	4	2.2 (2195)	0.0007-0.0017	0.010-0.020	0.010-0.020	0.010-0.050	0.0019-0.0027	0.0019-0.0027	0.0019-0.0082
	M	3.1 (3130)	0.0013-0.0027	0.007-0.016	0.020-0.028	0.010-0.030	0.0020-0.0035	0.0020-0.0035	0.0080 MAX
1995-96	4	2.2 (2195)	0.0007-0.0017	0.010-0.020	0.010-0.020	0.010-0.050	0.0019-0.0027	0.0019-0.0027	0.0019-0.0082
	M	3.1 (3130)	0.0013-0.0027	0.007-0.016	0.020-0.028	0.010-0.030	0.0020-0.0035	0.0020-0.0035	0.0080 MAX

NA - Not Available

① Measured 44mm from top of piston

TORQUE SPECIFICATIONS

All readings in ft. lbs.

Year	Engine ID/VIN	Engine Displacement Liters (cc)	Cylinder Head Bolts	Main Bearing Bolts	Rod Bearing Bolts	Crankshaft Damper Bolts	Flywheel Bolts	Manifold		Spark Plugs	Lug Nut
								Intake	Exhaust		
1992	R	2.5 (2474)	①	65	29	162 ⑦	55	25	②	20	100
	N	3.3 (3342)	⑤	⑥	⑦	⑧	⑨	7	38	12	100
1993	4	2.2 (2195)	⑪	66	38	77	54	24	10	11	100
	N	3.3 (3342)	⑤	⑥	⑦	⑧	⑨	7	38	20	100
1994	4	2.2 (2195)	⑪	70	38	77	55	24	10	⑫	100
	M	3.1 (3130)	③	⑬	⑭	76	61	④	10	⑫	100
1995-96	4	2.2 (2195)	⑪	70	38	77	55	24	10	⑫	100
	M	3.1 (3130)	③	⑩	⑮	76	59	④	12	⑫	100

① Step 1: Tighten all head bolts to 18 ft. lbs.
  Step 2: Tighten all bolts to 26 ft. lbs., except I bolt. Retorque I bolt to 18 ft. lbs.
  Step 3: Tighten all an additional 90 degrees
② Inner bolts: 37 ft. lbs.
  Outer bolts: 28 ft. lbs.
③ Coat threads with sealer torque to 37 ft. lbs., then turn 1/4 turn (90 degrees)
④ Torque all bolts to 15 ft. lbs., Retorque to 24 ft. lbs.

⑤ Step 1: Tighten all bolts to 35 ft. lbs.
  Step 2: Turn all bolts 130 degrees
  Step 3: Rotate four center bolts an additional 30 degrees
⑥ 26 ft. lbs. plus 50 degrees
⑦ 20 ft. lbs. plus 50 degrees
⑧ 110 ft. lbs. plus 76 degrees
⑨ 11 ft. lbs. plus 50 degrees
⑩ 37 ft. lbs. plus 75 degrees

⑪ Short bolts: 43 ft. lbs. plus 90 degrees
  Long bolts: 46 ft. lbs. plus 90 degrees
⑫ New cylinder first-time installation: 21 ft. lbs.
  All others: 11 ft. lbs.
⑬ 37 ft. lbs. plus 77 degrees
⑭ Nos. 1-8: 30 ft. lbs.
  Nos. 9-10: 26 ft. lbs.
  Tighten all bolts an additional 90 degrees
⑮ 15 ft. lbs. plus 75 degrees

BRAKE SPECIFICATIONS
All measurements in inches unless noted

Year	Model		Master Cylinder Bore	Brake Disc Original Thickness	Brake Disc Minimum Thickness	Brake Disc Maximum Runout	Brake Drum Diameter Original Inside Diameter	Brake Drum Diameter Max. Wear Limit	Brake Drum Diameter Maximum Machine Diameter	Minimum Lining Thickness Front	Minimum Lining Thickness Rear
1992	Century	①	0.874	0.885	0.815	0.004	8.863	8.909	8.880	0.030	③
	Century	②	0.944	1.043	0.957	0.004	8.863	8.909	8.880	0.030	③
	Cutlass Ciera	①	0.874	0.885	0.815	0.004	8.863	8.909	8.880	0.030	③
	Cutlass Ciera	②	0.944	1.043	0.957	0.004	8.863	8.909	8.880	0.030	③
	Cutlass Cruiser		0.944	1.043	0.957	0.004	8.863	④	8.880	0.030	③
1993	Century	①	0.874	0.885	0.815	0.004	8.863	8.909	8.880	0.030	③
	Century	②	0.944	1.043	0.957	0.004	8.863	8.909	8.880	0.030	③
	Cutlass Ciera	①	0.874	0.885	0.815	0.004	8.863	8.909	8.880	0.030	③
	Cutlass Ciera	②	0.944	1.043	0.957	0.004	8.863	8.909	8.880	0.030	③
	Cutlass Cruiser		0.944	1.043	0.957	0.004	8.863	④	8.880	0.030	③
1994	Century		0.944	1.028	0.957	0.002	8.860	8.909	8.880	0.030	③
	Cutlass Ciera		0.944	1.028	0.957	0.002	8.860	8.909	8.880	0.030	③
	Cutlass Cruiser		0.944	1.028	0.957	0.002	8.860	④	8.880	0.030	③
1995-96	Century		0.944	1.028	0.957	0.002	8.863	8.909	8.880	0.030	③
	Cutlass Ciera		0.944	1.028	0.957	0.002	8.863	8.909	8.880	0.030	③
	Cutlass Cruiser		0.944	1.028	0.957	0.002	8.863	④	8.880	0.030	③

NA - Not Available

F - Front

R - Rear

① Standard

② Heavy duty and Wagon

③ 0.030 over rivet head; If bonded lining, use 0.062 from shoe

④ Use discard diameter cast into drum

WHEEL ALIGNMENT

Year	Model		Caster Range (deg.)	Caster Preferred Setting (deg.)	Camber Range (deg.)	Camber Preferred Setting (deg.)	Toe-in (in.)	Steering Axis Inclination (deg.)
1992	Century	F	11/16P-2 11/16P	1 11/16P	1/2N-1/2P	0	0	14 1/2
		R	-	-	5/16N-5/16P	0	0	-
	Cutlass Ciera	F	11/16P-2 11/16P	1 11/16P	1/2N-1/2P	0	0	14 1/2
		R	-	-	5/16N-5/16P	0	0	-
	Cutlass Cruiser	F	11/16P-2 11/16P	1 11/16P	1/2N-1/2P	0	0	14 1/2
		R	-	-	5/16N-5/16P	0	0	-
1993	Century	F	11/16P-2 11/16P	1 11/16P	1/2N-1/2P	0	0	14 1/2
		R	-	-	5/16N-5/16P	0	0	-
	Cutlass Ciera	F	11/16P-2 11/16P	1 11/16P	1/2N-1/2P	0	0	14 1/2
		R	-	-	5/16N-5/16P	0	0	-
	Cutlass Cruiser	F	11/16P-2 11/16P	1 11/16P	1/2N-1/2P	0	0	14 1/2
		R	-	-	5/16N-5/16P	0	0	-

WHEEL ALIGNMENT

Year	Model		Caster Range (deg.)	Caster Preferred Setting (deg.)	Camber Range (deg.)	Camber Preferred Setting (deg.)	Toe-in (in.)	Steering Axis Inclination (deg.)
1994	Century	F	2P-4P	3P	1/2N-1/2P	0	0	NA
		R	-	-	5/16N-5/16P	0	0	-
	Cutlass Ciera	F	2P-4P	3P	1/2N-1/2P	0	0	NA
		R	-	-	5/16N-5/16P	0	0	-
	Cutlass Cruiser	F	2P-4P	3P	1/2N-1/2P	0	0	NA
		R	-	-	5/16N-5/16P	0	0	-
1995-96	Century	F	2P-4P	3P	1/2N-1/2P	0	0	NA
		R	0-3N	1N	5/16N-5/16P	0	0	-
	Cutlass Ciera	F	2P-4P	3P	1/2N-1/2P	0	0	NA
		R	0-3N	1N	5/16N-5/16P	0	0	-
	Cutlass Cruiser	F	2P-4P	3P	1/2N-1/2P	0	0	NA
		R	0-3N	1N	5/16N-5/16P	0	0	-

NA - Not Available
F - Front
R - Rear

BONNEVILLE/DEVILLE/FLEETWOOD/LESABRE NINETY-EIGHT/EIGHTY-EIGHT/PARK AVENUE/ULTRA

VEHICLE IDENTIFICATION CHART

Engine Code						Model Year	
Code	Liters	Cu. In. (cc)	Cyl.	Fuel Sys.	Eng. Mfg.	Code	Year
1	3.8	231 (3785)	6	MFI ①	BOC	N	1992
B	4.9	300 (4917)	8	MFI	Cadillac	P	1993
K	3.8	231 (3785)	6	MFI	BOC	R	1994
L	3.8	231 (3785)	6	MFI	BOC	S	1995
						T	1996

MFI - Multiport fuel injection
BOC - Buick/Oldsmobile/Cadillac
① Supercharged engine

ENGINE IDENTIFICATION

Year	Model	Engine Displacement Liters (cc)	Engine Series (ID/VIN)	Fuel System		No. of Cylinders	Engine Type
1992	Bonneville	3.8 (3785)	L	MFI		6	OHV
	Bonneville	3.8 (3785)	1	MFI	①	6	OHV
	DeVille	4.9 (4917)	B	MFI		8	OHV
	Fleetwood	4.9 (4917)	B	MFI		8	OHV
	Fleetwood ②	4.9 (4917)	B	MFI		8	OHV
	Eighty-Eight/Royale	3.8 (3785)	L	MFI		6	OHV
	Ninety-Eight	3.8 (3785)	L	MFI		6	OHV
	Ninety-Eight	3.8 (3785)	1	MFI	①	6	OHV
	LeSabre	3.8 (3785)	L	MFI		6	OHV
	Park Avenue	3.8 (3785)	L	MFI		6	OHV
	Park Avenue Ultra	3.8 (3785)	1	MFI	①	6	OHV
1993	Bonneville	3.8 (3786)	L	MFI		6	OHV
	Bonneville	3.8 (3786)	1	MFI	①	6	OHV
	DeVille	4.9 (4917)	B	MFI		8	OHV
	Eighty-Eight/Royale	3.8 (3785)	L	MFI		6	OHV
	Ninety-Eight	3.8 (3785)	L	MFI		6	OHV
	Ninety-Eight	3.8 (3785)	1	MFI	①	6	OHV
	LeSabre	3.8 (3785)	L	MFI		6	OHV
	Park Avenue	3.8 (3785)	L	MFI		6	OHV
	Park Avenue Ultra	3.8 (3785)	1	MFI	①	6	OHV
1994	Bonneville	3.8 (3786)	L	MFI		6	OHV
	Bonneville	3.8 (3786)	1	MFI	①	6	OHV
	Eighty-Eight/Royale	3.8 (3785)	L	MFI		6	OHV
	Ninety-Eight	3.8 (3785)	L	MFI		6	OHV
	Ninety-Eight	3.8 (3785)	1	MFI	①	6	OHV
	LeSabre	3.8 (3785)	L	MFI		6	OHV
	Park Avenue	3.8 (3785)	L	MFI		6	OHV
	Park Avenue Ultra	3.8 (3785)	1	MFI	①	6	OHV
1995-96	Bonneville	3.8 (3786)	K	MFI		6	OHV
	Bonneville	3.8 (3786)	1	MFI	①	8	OHV
	Eighty-Eight/Royale	3.8 (3785)	K	MFI		6	OHV
	Eighty-Eight/LSS	3.8 (3785)	1	MFI	①	6	OHV
	Ninety-Eight	3.8 (3785)	K	MFI		6	OHV
	Ninety-Eight	3.8 (3785)	1	MFI	①	6	OHV
	LeSabre	3.8 (3785)	L	MFI		6	OHV
	Park Avenue	3.8 (3785)	L	MFI		6	OHV
	Park Avenue Ultra	3.8 (3785)	1	MFI	①	6	OHV

MFI - Multiport fuel injection

OHV - Overhead valve

① Supercharged engine

② Sixty Special

GENERAL ENGINE SPECIFICATIONS

Year	Engine ID/VIN	Engine Displacement Liters (cc)	Fuel System Type	Net Horsepower @ rpm	Net Torque @ rpm (ft. lbs.)	Bore x Stroke (in.)	Com- pression Ratio	Oil Pressure @ rpm	
1992	B	4.9 (4917)	MFI	200@4100	275@3000	3.62x3.62	9.5:1	53@2000	
	L	3.8 (3785)	MFI	170@4800	220@3200	3.80x3.40	8.5:1	60@1850	
	1	3.8 (3785)	MFI	205@4400	260@2600	3.80x3.40	8.5:1	60@1850	①
1993	B	4.9 (4917)	MFI	200@4100	275@3000	3.62x3.62	9.5:1	53@2000	
	L	3.8 (3785)	MFI	170@4800	225@3200	3.80x3.40	9.0:1	60@1850	
	1	3.8 (3785)	MFI	205@4400	260@2600	3.80x3.40	8.5:1	60@1850	①
1994	L	3.8 (3785)	MFI	170@4800	225@3200	3.80x3.40	9.0:1	60@1850	
	1	3.8 (3785)	MFI	225@5000	275@3200	3.80x3.40	9.0:1	60@1850	①
1995-96	K	3.8 (3875)	MFI	205@5200	230@4000	3.80x3.40	9.4:1	60@1850	
	1	3.8 (3875)	MFI	225@5000	275@3200	3.80x3.40	9.0:1	60@1850	①

MFI - Multiport fuel injection
① Supercharged

GASOLINE ENGINE TUNE-UP SPECIFICATIONS

Year	Engine ID/VIN	Engine Displacement Liters (cc)	Spark Plugs Gap (in.)	Ignition Timing (deg.) MT	AT	Fuel Pump (psi)		Idle Speed (rpm) MT	AT	Valve Clearance In.	Ex.
1992	B	4.9 (4917)	0.060	-	①	41-47		-	①	HYD	HYD
	L	3.8 (3785)	0.060	①	①	40-47		-	②	HYD	HYD
	1	3.8 (3785)	0.060	①	①	40-47		-	②	HYD	HYD
1993	B	4.9 (4917)	0.060	-	①	40-50		-	①	HYD	HYD
	L	3.8 (3785)	0.060	①	①	40-47		-	②	HYD	HYD
	1	3.8 (3785)	0.060	①	①	40-47		-	②	HYD	HYD
1994	L	3.8 (3785)	0.060	①	①	40-47		-	②	HYD	HYD
	1	3.8 (3785)	0.060	①	①	40-47		-	②	HYD	HYD
1995-96	K	3.8 (3785)	0.060	①	①	40-47	③	②	②	HYD	HYD
	1	3.8 (3785)	0.060	①	①	40-47	③	-	②	HYD	HYD

NOTE: The Vehicle Emission Control Information label often reflects specification changes made during production. The label figures must be used if they differ from those in this chart.
HYD - Hydraulic
① DIS Ignition System timing not adjustable
② Idle speed maintained by ECM. There is no recommended adjustment procedure
③ Pressure at fuel pump

CAPACITIES

Year	Model	Engine ID/VIN	Engine Displacement Liters (cc)	Engine Oil with Filter (qts.)	Transmission (pts.)			Drive Axle		Fuel Tank (gal.)	Cooling System (qts.)
					4-Spd	5-Spd	Auto.	Front (pts.)	Rear (pts.)		
1992	Bonneville	L	3.8 (3785)	4.0 ①	-	-	13.0	-	-	18.0	13.0
	Bonneville	1	3.8 (3785)	4.0 ①	-	-	13.0	-	-	18.0	13.0
	DeVille	B	4.9 (4917)	5.5	-	-	12.0	-	-	18.0	13.2
	Fleetwood	B	4.9 (4917)	5.5	-	-	12.0	-	-	18.0	13.2
	Eighty-Eight	L	3.8 (3785)	4.0 ①	-	-	13.0	-	-	18.0	13.0
	Ninety-Eight	L	3.8 (3785)	4.0 ①	-	-	13.0	-	-	18.0	13.0
	Ninety-Eight	1	3.8 (3785)	4.0 ①	-	-	13.0	-	-	18.0	13.0
	LeSabre	L	3.8 (3785)	4.0 ①	-	-	13.0	-	-	18.0	13.0
	Park Avenue	L	3.8 (3785)	4.0 ①	-	-	13.0	-	-	18.0	13.0
	Park Avenue Ultra	1	3.8 (3785)	4.0 ①	-	-	13.0	-	-	18.0	13.0
1993	Bonneville	L	3.8 (3785)	4.0 ①	-	-	13.0	-	-	18.0	13.0
	Bonneville	1	3.8 (3785)	4.0 ①	-	-	13.0	-	-	18.0	13.0
	DeVille	B	4.9 (4917)	5.5	-	-	13.0	-	-	18.0	12.1
	Eighty-Eight	L	3.8 (3785)	4.0 ①	-	-	13.0	-	-	18.0	13.0
	Ninety-Eight	L	3.8 (3785)	4.0 ①	-	-	13.0	-	-	18.0	13.0
	Ninety-Eight	1	3.8 (3785)	4.0 ①	-	-	13.0	-	-	18.0	13.0
	LeSabre	L	3.8 (3785)	4.0 ①	-	-	13.0	-	-	18.0	13.0
	Park Avenue	L	3.8 (3785)	4.0 ①	-	-	13.0	-	-	18.0	13.0
	Park Avenue Ultra	1	3.8 (3785)	4.0 ①	-	-	13.0	-	-	18.0	13.0
1994	Bonneville	L	3.8 (3785)	4.0 ①	-	-	13.0	-	-	18.0	13.0
	Bonneville	1	3.8 (3785)	4.0 ①	-	-	13.0	-	-	18.0	13.0
	Eighty-Eight	L	3.8 (3785)	4.0 ①	-	-	13.0	-	-	18.0	13.0
	Ninety-Eight	L	3.8 (3785)	4.0 ①	-	-	13.0	-	-	18.0	13.0
	Ninety-Eight	1	3.8 (3785)	4.0 ①	-	-	13.0	-	-	18.0	13.0
	LeSabre	L	3.8 (3785)	4.0 ①	-	-	13.0	-	-	18.0	13.0
	Park Avenue	L	3.8 (3785)	4.0 ①	-	-	13.0	-	-	18.0	13.0
	Park Avenue Ultra	1	3.8 (3785)	4.0 ①	-	-	13.0	-	-	18.0	13.0
1995-96	Bonneville	K	3.8 (3785)	3.8 ①	-	-	13.0	-	-	18.0	13.0
	Bonneville	1	3.8 (3785)	3.8 ①	-	-	13.0	-	-	18.0	13.0
	Eighty-Eight	K	3.8 (3785)	3.8 ①	-	-	13.0	-	-	18.0	13.0
	Eighty-Eight	1	3.8 (3785)	3.8 ①	-	-	13.0	-	-	18.0	13.0
	Ninety-Eight	K	3.8 (3785)	3.8 ①	-	-	13.0	-	-	18.0	13.0
	Ninety-Eight	1	3.8 (3785)	3.8 ①	-	-	13.0	-	-	18.0	13.0
	LeSabre	L	3.8 (3785)	4.0 ①	-	-	13.0	-	-	18.0	13.0
	Park Avenue	L	3.8 (3785)	4.0 ①	-	-	13.0	-	-	18.0	13.0
	Park Avenue Ultra	1	3.8 (3785)	4.0 ①	-	-	13.0	-	-	18.0	13.0

① Specification is without filter replacement; Additional oil may be required

CAMSHAFT SPECIFICATIONS

All measurements given in inches.

Year	Engine ID/VIN	Engine Displacement Liters (cc)	Journal Diameter 1	2	3	4	5	Elevation In.	Ex.	Bearing Clearance	Camshaft End Play
1992	B	4.9 (4917)	NA	NA	NA	NA	NA	0.3840	0.3960	0.0018-0.0037	NA
	L	3.8 (3785)	1.7850-1.7860	1.7850-1.7860	1.7850-1.7860	1.7850-1.7860	1.7850-1.7860	0.2500	0.2550	0.0005-0.0035	NA
	1	3.8 (3785)	1.7850-1.7860	1.7850-1.7860	1.7850-1.7860	1.7850-1.7860	1.7850-1.7860	0.2500	0.2550	0.0005-0.0035	NA
1993	B	4.9 (4917)	NA	NA	NA	NA	NA	0.0384	0.3960	0.0018-0.0037	NA
	L	3.8 (3785)	1.7850-1.7860	1.7850-1.7860	1.7850-1.7860	1.7850-1.7860	1.7850-1.7860	0.2500	0.2550	0.0005-0.0035	NA
	1	3.8 (3785)	1.7850-1.7860	1.7850-1.7860	1.7850-1.7860	1.7850-1.7860	1.7850-1.7860	0.2500	0.2550	0.0005-0.0035	NA
1994	L	3.8 (3785)	1.7850-1.7860	1.7850-1.7860	1.7850-1.7860	1.7850-1.7860	1.7850-1.7860	0.2500	0.2550	0.0005-0.0035	NA
	1	3.8 (3785)	1.7850-1.7860	1.7850-1.7860	1.7850-1.7860	1.7850-1.7860	1.7850-1.7860	0.2500	0.2550	0.0005-0.0035	NA
1995-96	K	3.8 (3785)	1.7850-1.7860	1.7850-1.7860	1.7850-1.7860	1.7850-1.7860	1.7850-1.7860	0.2500	0.2550	0.0005-0.0035	NA
	1	3.8 (3785)	1.7850-1.7860	1.7850-1.7860	1.7850-1.7860	1.7850-1.7860	1.7850-1.7860	0.2500	0.2550	0.0005-0.0035	NA

NA - Not Available

CRANKSHAFT AND CONNECTING ROD SPECIFICATIONS

All measurements are given in inches.

Year	Engine ID/VIN	Engine Displacement Liters (cc)	Crankshaft Main Brg. Journal Dia.	Main Brg. Oil Clearance	Shaft End-play	Thrust on No.	Connecting Rod Journal Diameter	Oil Clearance	Side Clearance
1992	B	4.9 (4917)	2.6350-2.6360	0.0016-0.0039	0.0010-0.0080	3	1.9270-1.9280	0.0005-0.0028	0.0080-0.0200
	L	3.8 (3785)	2.4988-2.4998	0.0008-0.0022	0.0030-0.0110	2	2.2487-2.2499	0.0003-0.0022	0.0030-0.0150
	1	3.8 (3785)	2.4988-2.4998	0.0008-0.0022	0.0030-0.0110	2	2.2487-2.2499	0.0003-0.0022	0.0030-0.0150
1993	B	4.9 (4917)	2.6350-2.6360	0.0016-0.0039	0.0010-0.0080	3	1.9270-1.9280	0.0005-0.0028	0.0080-0.0200
	L	3.8 (3785)	2.4988-2.4998	0.0008-0.0022	0.0030-0.0110	2	2.2487-2.2499	0.0001-0.0022	0.0030-0.0150
	1	3.8 (3785)	2.4988-2.4998	0.0008-0.0022	0.0030-0.0110	2	2.2487-2.2499	0.0001-0.0022	0.0030-0.0150

CRANKSHAFT AND CONNECTING ROD SPECIFICATIONS

All measurements are given in inches.

Year	Engine ID/VIN	Engine Displacement Liters (cc)	Crankshaft Main Brg. Journal Dia.	Crankshaft Main Brg. Oil Clearance	Crankshaft Shaft End-play	Thrust on No.	Connecting Rod Journal Diameter	Connecting Rod Oil Clearance	Connecting Rod Side Clearance
1994	L	3.8 (3785)	2.4988-2.4998	0.0008-0.0022	0.0030-0.0110	2	2.2487-2.2499	0.0008-0.0022	0.0030-0.0150
	1	3.8 (3785)	2.4988-2.4998	0.0008-0.0022	0.0030-0.0110	2	2.2487-2.2499	0.0008-0.0022	0.0030-0.0150
1995-96	K	3.8 (3785)	2.4988-2.4998	0.0008-0.0022	0.0030-0.0110	2	2.2487-2.2499	0.0008-0.0022	0.0030-0.0150
	1	3.8 (3785)	2.4988-2.4998	0.0008-0.0022	0.0030-0.0110	2	2.2487-2.2499	0.0008-0.0022	0.0030-0.0150

VALVE SPECIFICATIONS

Year	Engine ID/VIN	Engine Displacement Liters (cc)	Seat Angle (deg.)	Face Angle (deg.)	Spring Test Pressure (lbs. @ in.)	Spring Installed Height (in.)	Stem-to-Guide Clearance (in.) Intake	Stem-to-Guide Clearance (in.) Exhaust	Stem Diameter (in.) Intake	Stem Diameter (in.) Exhaust
1992	B	4.9 (4917)	45	44	68-76@1.730	1.730	0.0010-0.0030	0.0020-0.0040	0.3413-0.3420	0.3401-0.3408
	L	3.8 (3785)	45	45	210@1.315	1.690-1.720	0.0015-0.0035	0.0015-0.0032	NA	NA
	1	3.8 (3785)	45	45	210@1.315	1.690-1.720	0.0015-0.0035	0.0015-0.0032	NA	NA
1993	B	4.9 (4917)	45	45	68-76@1.350	1.350	0.0010-0.0030	0.0020-0.0040	0.3413-0.3420	0.3401-0.3408
	L	3.8 (3785)	45	45	210@1.315	1.690-1.720	0.0015-0.0035	0.0015-0.0032	NA	NA
	1	3.8 (3785)	45	45	210@1.315	1.690-1.720	0.0015-0.0035	0.0015-0.0032	NA	NA
1994	L	3.8 (3785)	45	45	210@1.315	1.690-1.720	0.0015-0.0035	0.0015-0.0032	NA	NA
	1	3.8 (3785)	45	45	210@1.315	1.690-1.720	0.0015-0.0035	0.0015-0.0032	NA	NA
1995-96	K	3.8 (3785)	46	45	210@1.315	1.690-1.720	0.0015-0.0035	0.0015-0.0032	NA	NA
	1	3.8 (3785)	46	45	210@1.315	1.690-1.720	0.0015-0.0035	0.0015-0.0032	NA	NA

NA - Not Available

PISTON AND RING SPECIFICATIONS

All measurements are given in inches.

| Year | Engine ID/VIN | Engine Displacement Liters (cc) | Piston Clearance | Ring Gap | | | Ring Side Clearance | | |
				Top Compression	Bottom Compression	Oil Control	Top Compression	Bottom Compression	Oil Control
1992	B	4.9 (4917)	0.0004-0.0020	0.0120-0.0220	0.0120-0.0220	0.0040-0.0200	0.0016-0.0037	0.0016-0.0037	NA
	L	3.8 (3785)	0.0004-0.0022 ①	0.010-0.025	0.010-0.025	0.015-0.055	0.0013-0.0031	0.0013-0.0031	0.0011-0.0081
	1	3.8 (3785)	0.0004-0.0022 ①	0.010-0.025	0.010-0.025	0.015-0.055	0.0013-0.0031	0.0013-0.0031	0.0011-0.0081
1993	B	4.9 (4917)	0.0004-0.0020	0.0120-0.0220	0.0120-0.0220	0.0040-0.0200	0.0016-0.0037	0.0016-0.0037	NA
	L	3.8 (3785)	0.0004-0.0022 ①	0.010-0.025	0.010-0.025	0.015-0.055	0.0013-0.0031	0.0013-0.0031	0.0110-0.0081
	1	3.8 (3785)	0.0004-0.0022 ①	0.010-0.025	0.010-0.025	0.015-0.055	0.0013-0.0031	0.0013-0.0031	0.0110-0.0081
1994	L	3.8 (3785)	0.0004-0.0022 ①	0.010-0.025	0.010-0.025	0.015-0.055	0.0013-0.0031	0.0013-0.0031	0.0110-0.0081
	1	3.8 (3785)	0.0004-0.0022 ①	0.010-0.025	0.010-0.025	0.015-0.055	0.0013-0.0031	0.0013-0.0031	0.0110-0.0081
1995-96	K	3.8 (3785)	0.0004-0.0020	0.010-0.025	0.010-0.025	0.015-0.055	0.0013-0.0031	0.0013-0.0031	0.0110-0.0081
	1	3.8 (3785)	0.0008-0.0024	0.010-0.025	0.010-0.025	0.015-0.055	0.0013-0.0031	0.0013-0.0031	0.0110-0.0081

NA - Not Available

① Measured 44mm from top of piston

TORQUE SPECIFICATIONS

All readings in ft. lbs.

| Year | Engine ID/VIN | Engine Displacement Liters (cc) | Cylinder Head Bolts | Main Bearing Bolts | Rod Bearing Bolts | Crankshaft Damper Bolts | Flywheel Bolts | Manifold | | Spark Plugs | Lug Nut |
								Intake	Exhaust		
1992	B	4.9 (4917)	⑥	85	25	70	70	⑦	16	23	100
	L	3.8 (3785)	①	④	③	④	⑤	7	38	12	100
	1	3.8 (3785)	①	④	③	④	⑤	7	38	12	100
1993	B	4.9 (4917)	⑥	85	25	70	70	⑦	16	23	100
	L	3.8 (3785)	①	②	③	④	⑤	7	38	20	100
	1	3.8 (3785)	①	②	③	④	⑤	7	38	20	100
1994	L	3.8 (3785)	①	②	③	④	⑤	7	38	11	100
	1	3.8 (3785)	①	②	③	④	⑤	7	38	11	100
1995-96	K	3.7 (3785)	①	②	③	④	⑤	11	38	11	100
	1	3.7 (3785)	①	②	③	④	⑤	11	38	11	100

① Step 1: Tighten all bolts to 35 ft. lbs.
Step 2: Turn all bolts 130 degrees
Step 3: Rotate four center bolts an additional 30 degrees

② 26 ft. lbs. plus 50 degrees
③ 20 ft. lbs. plus 50 degrees
④ 110 ft. lbs. plus 76 degrees

⑤ 11 ft. lbs. plus 50 degrees
⑥ Step 1: 38 ft. lbs.
Step 2: 68 ft. lbs.
Step 3: 90 ft. lbs.

⑦ Step 1: 8 ft. lbs.
Step 2: 12 ft. lbs.

BRAKE SPECIFICATIONS
All measurements in inches unless noted

Year	Model	Master Cylinder Bore	Brake Disc Original Thickness	Brake Disc Minimum Thickness	Brake Disc Maximum Runout	Brake Drum Diameter Original Inside Diameter	Brake Drum Diameter Max. Wear Limit	Brake Drum Diameter Maximum Machine Diameter	Minimum Lining Thickness Front	Minimum Lining Thickness Rear
1992	Bonneville	1.000	1.276	1.209	0.004	8.860	8.909	8.880	0.030	①
	DeVille	1.000	1.276	1.209	0.004	8.860	8.909	8.880	0.030	①
	Fleetwood	1.000	1.276	1.209	0.004	8.860	8.909	8.880	0.030	①
	Fleetwood ②	1.000	1.276	1.209	0.004	8.860	8.909	8.880	0.030	①
	Eighty-Eight	1.000	1.276	1.209	0.004	8.860	8.909	8.880	0.030	①
	Ninety-Eight	1.000	1.276	1.209	0.004	8.860	8.909	8.880	0.030	①
	LeSabre	1.000	1.276	1.209	0.004	8.860	8.909	8.880	0.030	①
	Park Avenue	1.000	1.276	1.209	0.004	8.860	8.909	8.880	0.030	①
1993	Bonneville	1.000	1.276	1.209	0.004	8.860	8.909	8.880	0.030	①
	DeVille	1.000	1.276	1.209	0.004	8.860	8.909	8.880	0.030	①
	Eighty-Eight	1.000	1.276	1.209	0.004	8.860	8.909	8.880	0.030	①
	Ninety-Eight	1.000	1.276	1.209	0.004	8.860	8.909	8.880	0.030	①
	LeSabre	1.000	1.276	1.209	0.004	8.860	8.909	8.880	0.030	①
	Park Avenue	1.000	1.276	1.209	0.004	8.860	8.909	8.880	0.030	①
1994	Bonneville	1.000	1.260	1.209	0.002	8.863	8.909	8.880	0.030	①
	Eighty-Eight	1.000	1.260	1.209	0.002	8.863	8.909	8.880	0.030	①
	Ninety-Eight	1.000	1.260	1.209	0.002	8.863	8.909	8.880	0.030	①
	LeSabre	1.000	1.260	1.209	0.002	8.863	8.909	8.880	0.030	①
	Park Avenue	1.000	1.260	1.209	0.002	8.863	8.909	8.880	0.030	①
1995-96	Bonneville	1.000	1.276	1.209	0.004	8.860	8.909	8.800	0.030	①
	Eighty-Eight	1.000	1.276	1.209	0.004	8.860	8.909	8.800	0.030	①
	Ninety-Eight	1.000	1.276	1.209	0.004	8.860	8.909	8.800	0.030	①
	LeSabre	1.000	1.276	1.209	0.004	8.860	8.909	8.800	0.030	①
	Park Avenue	1.000	1.276	1.209	0.004	8.860	8.909	8.800	0.030	①

NA - Not Available
F - Front
R - Rear

① 0.030 over rivet head; If bonded lining, use 0.062 from shoe
② Sixty Special

WHEEL ALIGNMENT

Year	Model		Caster Range (deg.)	Caster Preferred Setting (deg.)	Camber Range (deg.)	Camber Preferred Setting (deg.)	Toe-in (in.)	Steering Axis Inclination (deg.)
1992	Bonneville	F	2 1/2P-3 1/2P	3P	5/16N-11/16P	3/16P	0	1/2
		R	-	-	13/16N-3/16P	5/16N	3/64P	-
	DeVille	F	2.25P-3.75P	3P	1.25N-0.25P	0.50N	0	NA
	DeVille ②	F	2.25P-3.75P	3P	0.25N-1.25P	0.50P	0	NA
	DeVille	R	-	-	1.05N-0.45P	0.30N	3/32P	-
	Fleetwood ①	F	2.25P-3.75P	3P	1.25N-0.25P	0.50N	0	NA
	Fleetwood ②	F	2.25P-3.75P	3P	0.25N-1.25P	0.50P	0	NA
	Fleetwood	R	-	-	1.05N-0.45P	0.40N	3/32P	-

WHEEL ALIGNMENT

Year	Model		Caster Range (deg.)	Caster Preferred Setting (deg.)	Camber Range (deg.)	Camber Preferred Setting (deg.)	Toe-in (in.)	Steering Axis Inclination (deg.)
	Eighty-Eight	F	2 1/2P-3 1/2P	3P	5/16N-11/16P	3/16P	0	1/2
		R	-	-	13/16N-3/16P	5/16N	3/64P	-
	Ninety-Eight	F	2 1/2P-3 1/2P	3P	5/16N-11/16P	3/16P	0	1/2
		R	-	-	13/16N-3/16P	5/16N	3/64P	-
	LeSabre	F	2 1/2P-3 1/2P	3P	5/16N-11/16P	3/16P	0	1/2
		R	-	-	13/16N-3/16P	5/16N	3/64P	-
	Park Avenue	F	2 1/2P-3 1/2P	3P	5/16N-11/16P	3/16P	0	1/2
		R	-	-	13/16N-3/16P	5/16N	3/64P	-
1993	Bonneville	F	2 1/2P-3 1/2P	3P	9/16N-15/16P	3/16P	0	12 1/2
		R	-	-	1 1/16N-7/16P	5/16N	3/64P	-
	DeVille	F	2.25P-3.75P	3P	1N-0	0.05N	0	NA
	DeVille ②	F	2.25P-3.75P	3P	0-1P	0.05P	0	NA
	DeVille	R	-	-	1.05N-0.45P	0.03N	3/32P	-
	Eighty-Eight	F	2 1/2P-3 1/2P	3P	9/16N-15/16P	3/16P	0	12 1/2
		R	-	-	1 1/16N-7/16P	5/16N	3/64P	-
	Ninety-Eight	F	2 1/2P-3 1/2P	3P	9/16N-15/16P	3/16P	0	12 1/2
		R	-	-	1 1/16N-7/16P	5/16N	3/64P	-
	LeSabre	F	2 1/2P-3 1/2P	3P	9/16N-15/16P	3/16P	0	12 1/2
		R	-	-	1 1/16N-7/16P	5/16N	3/64P	-
	Park Avenue	F	2 1/2P-3 1/2P	3P	9/16N-15/16P	3/16P	0	12 1/2
		R	-	-	1 1/16N-7/16P	5/16N	3/64P	-
1994	Bonneville	F	2 1/2P-3 1/2P	3P	9/16N-15/16P	3/16P	0	NA
		R	-	-	1 1/16N-7/16P	5/16N	3/32P	-
	DeVille ③	F	2.25P-3.75P	3P	1N-0	0.50N	0	NA
	DeVille ③,②	F	2.25P-3.75P	3P	0-1P	0.05P	0	NA
	DeVille ③	R	-	-	1.05N-0.45P	0.30N	3/32P	-
	Eighty-Eight	F	2 1/2P-3 1/2P	3P	9/16N-15/16P	3/16P	0	NA
		R	-	-	1 1/16N-7/16P	5/16N	3/32P	-
	Ninety-Eight	F	2 1/2P-3 1/2P	3P	9/16N-15/16P	3/16P	0	NA
		R	-	-	1 1/16N-7/16P	5/16N	3/32P	-
	LeSabre	F	2 1/2P-3 1/2P	3P	9/16N-15/16P	3/16P	0	NA
		R	-	-	1 1/16N-7/16P	5/16N	3/32P	-
	Park Avenue	F	2 1/2P-3 1/2P	3P	9/16N-15/16P	3/16P	0	NA
		R	-	-	1 1/16N-7/16P	5/16N	3/32P	-
1995-96	Bonneville	F	2 1/2P-3 1/2P	3P	9/16N-15/16P	3/16P	0	NA
		R	-	-	1 1/16N-7/16P	5/16N	3/32P	-
	DeVille ③	F	2 1/4P-3 3/4P	3P	1N-0	1/2N	0	NA
	DeVille ③,②	F	2 1/4P-3 3/4P	3P	0-1P	3/64P	0	NA
	DeVille ③	R	-	-	1 3/64N-29/64P	1/32N	3/32P	-
	Eighty-Eight	F	2 1/2P-3 1/2P	3P	9/16N-15/16P	3/16P	0	NA
		R	-	-	1 1/16N-7/16P	5/16N	3/32P	-

WHEEL ALIGNMENT

Year	Model		Caster Range (deg.)	Caster Preferred Setting (deg.)	Camber Range (deg.)	Camber Preferred Setting (deg.)	Toe-in (in.)	Steering Axis Inclination (deg.)
	Ninety-Eight	F	2 1/2P-3 1/2P	3P	9/16N-15/16P	3/16P	0	NA
		R	-	-	1 1/16N-7/16P	5/16N	3/32P	-
	LeSabre	F	2 1/2P-3 1/2P	3P	9/16N-15/16P	3/16P	0	NA
		R	-	-	1 1/16N-7/16P	5/16N	3/32P	-
	Park Avenue	F	2 1/2P-3 1/2P	3P	9/16N-15/16P	3/16P	0	NA
		R	-	-	1 1/16N-7/16P	5/16N	3/32P	-

NA - Not Available
F - Front
R - Rear

① Sixty Special
② Right side
③ Concours

ALLANTE/DEVILLE/DEVILLE CONCOURS/ELDORADO RIVIERA/SEVILLE/TORONADO

VEHICLE IDENTIFICATION CHART

Engine Code							Model Year	
Code	Liters	Cu. In. (cc)	Cyl.	Fuel Sys.		Eng. Mfg.	Code	Year
1	3.8	231 (3785)	6	MFI	①	BOC	N	1992
8	4.5	273 (4474)	8	MFI		Cadillac	P	1993
9	4.6	279 (4573)	8	MFI		Cadillac	R	1994
B	4.9	300 (4917)	8	MFI		Cadillac	S	1995
K	3.8	231 (3785)	6	MFI		BOC	T	1996
L	3.8	231 (3785)	6	MFI		BOC		
Y	4.6	279 (4573)	8	MFI		Cadillac		

MFI - Multiport fuel injection
BOC - Buick/Oldsmobile/Cadillac
① Supercharged engine

ENGINE IDENTIFICATION

Year	Model		Engine Displacement Liters (cc)	Engine Series (ID/VIN)	Fuel System	No. of Cylinders	Engine Type
1992	Allante		4.5 (4474)	8	MFI	8	OHV
	Eldorado		4.9 (4917)	B	MFI	8	OHV
	Riviera		3.8 (3785)	L	MFI	6	OHV
	Seville		4.9 (4917)	B	MFI	8	OHV
	Seville STS		4.9 (4917)	B	MFI	8	OHV
	Toronado		3.8 (3785)	L	MFI	6	OHV
	Trofeo		3.8 (3785)	L	MFI	6	OHV
1993	Allante		4.6 (4573)	9	MFI	8	DOHC
	Eldorado	①	4.6 (4573)	Y	MFI	8	DOHC
	Eldorado	②	4.6 (4573)	9	MFI	8	DOHC
	Eldorado		4.9 (4917)	B	MFI	8	OHV
	Riviera		3.8 (3785)	L	MFI	6	OHV
	Seville STS		4.6 (4573)	9	MFI	8	DOHC
	Seville		4.9 (4917)	B	MFI	8	OHV
1994	DeVille Concours		4.6 (4573)	Y	MFI	8	DOHC
	DeVille		4.9 (4917)	B	MFI	8	OHV
	Eldorado	②	4.6 (4573)	Y	MFI	8	DOHC
	Eldorado	①	4.6 (4573)	9	MFI	8	DOHC
	Seville SLS		4.6 (4573)	Y	MFI	8	DOHC
	Seville STS		4.6 (4573)	9	MFI	8	DOHC
1995-96	DeVille Concours		4.6 (4573)	Y	MFI	8	DOHC
	DeVille		4.9 (4917)	B	MFI	8	OHV
	Eldorado	②	4.6 (4573)	Y	MFI	8	DOHC
	Eldorado	①	4.6 (4573)	9	MFI	8	DOHC
	Riviera		3.8 (3785)	1	MFI ③	6	OHV
	Riviera		3.8 (3785)	K	MFI	6	OHV
	Seville SLS		4.6 (4573)	Y	MFI	8	DOHC
	Seville STS		4.6 (4573)	9	MFI	8	DOHC

MFI - Multiport fuel injection
OHV - Overhead valve
DOHC - Double overhead camshaft
① Northstar low output (270 HP)
② Northstar high output (295 HP)
③ Supercharged engine

GENERAL ENGINE SPECIFICATIONS

Year	Engine ID/VIN	Engine Displacement Liters (cc)	Fuel System Type	Net Horsepower @ rpm	Net Torque @ rpm (ft. lbs.)	Bore x Stroke (in.)	Compression Ratio	Oil Pressure @ rpm
1992	8	4.5 (4474)	MFI	200@4400	270@3200	3.62x3.31	9.0:1	53@2000
	B	4.9 (4917)	MFI	200@4100	275@3000	3.62x3.62	9.5:1	53@2000
	L	3.8 (3785)	MFI	170@4800	220@3200	3.80x3.40	8.5:1	60@1850
1993	9	4.6 (4573)	MFI	295@6000	290@4400	3.66x3.31	10.3:1	35@2000
	B	4.9 (4917)	MFI	200@4100	275@3000	3.62x3.62	9.5:1	53@2000
	L	3.8 (3785)	MFI	170@4800	225@3200	3.80x3.40	9.0:1	60@1850
	Y	4.6 (4573)	MFI	270@5600	300@4000	3.66x3.31	10.3:1	35@2000
1994	9	4.6 (4573)	MFI	295@6000	290@4400	3.66x3.31	10.3:1	35@2000
	Y	4.6 (4573)	MFI	270@5600	300@4000	3.66x3.31	10.3:1	35@2000
	B	4.9 (4917)	MFI	200@4100	275@3000	3.62x3.62	9.5:1	53@2000

GENERAL ENGINE SPECIFICATIONS

Year	Engine ID/VIN	Engine Displacement Liters (cc)	Fuel System Type	Net Horsepower @ rpm	Net Torque @ rpm (ft. lbs.)	Bore x Stroke (in.)	Compression Ratio	Oil Pressure @ rpm
1995-96	1	3.8 (3785)	MFI ①	225@5000	275@3200	3.80x3.40	9.0:1	60@1850
	9	4.6 (4573)	MFI	300@6000	295@4400	3.66x3.31	10.3:1	35@2000
	B	4.9 (4917)	MFI	200@4100	275@3000	3.62x3.62	9.5:1	53@2000
	K	3.8 (3785)	MFI	205@5200	230@4000	3.80x3.40	9.4:1	60@1850
	Y	4.6 (4573)	MFI	275@5600	295@4400	3.66x3.31	10.3:1	35@2000

MFI - Multiport fuel injection
TFI - Throttle body fuel injection
① Supercharged engine

GASOLINE ENGINE TUNE-UP SPECIFICATIONS

Year	Engine ID/VIN	Engine Displacement Liters (cc)	Spark Plugs Gap (in.)	Ignition Timing (deg.) MT	Ignition Timing (deg.) AT	Fuel Pump (psi)	Idle Speed (rpm) MT	Idle Speed (rpm) AT	Valve Clearance In.	Valve Clearance Ex.
1992	8	4.5 (4474)	0.060	-	①	41-47	-	①	HYD	HYD
	B	4.9 (4917)	0.060	-	①	41-47	-	①	HYD	HYD
	L	3.8 (3785)	0.060	②	②	40-47	-	③	HYD	HYD
1993	9	4.6 (4573)	0.050	-	①	40-50	-	①	HYD	HYD
	B	4.9 (4917)	0.060	-	①	40-50	-	①	HYD	HYD
	L	3.8 (3785)	0.060	②	②	40-47	-	③	HYD	HYD
	Y	4.6 (4573)	0.050	-	①	40-50	-	①	HYD	HYD
1994	9	4.6 (4573)	0.050	-	①	40-50	-	①	HYD	HYD
	Y	4.6 (4573)	0.050	-	①	40-50	-	①	HYD	HYD
	B	4.9 (4917)	0.060	-	①	40-50	-	①	HYD	HYD
1995-96	1	3.8 (3785)	0.060	①	①	40-47	-	②	HYD	HYD
	9	4.6 (4573)	0.050	-	①	40-50	-	①	HYD	HYD
	B	4.9 (4917)	0.060	-	①	40-50	-	①	HYD	HYD
	K	3.8 (3785)	0.060	①	①	40-47	-	②	HYD	HYD
	Y	4.6 (4573)	0.050	-	①	40-50	-	①	HYD	HYD

NOTE: The Vehicle Emission Control Information label often reflects specification changes made during production. The label figures must be used if they differ from those in this chart.
HYD - Hydraulic
① Refer to underhood sticker
② DIS Ignition System timing is not adjustable
③ Idle speed is maintained by the ECM. There is no recommended adjustment procedure

CAPACITIES

Year	Model	Engine ID/VIN	Engine Displacement Liters (cc)	Engine Oil with Filter (qts.)	Transmission (pts.) 4-Spd	Transmission (pts.) 5-Spd	Transmission (pts.) Auto.	Drive Axle Front (pts.)	Drive Axle Rear (pts.)	Fuel Tank (gal.)	Cooling System (qts.)
1992	Allante	8	4.5 (4474)	6.5	-	-	13.0	-	-	22.0	10.8
	Eldorado	B	4.9 (4917)	5.5	-	-	12.0	-	-	18.0	12.1
	Riviera	L	3.8 (3785)	4.0 ⑤	-	-	12.0	-	-	18.0	13.0
	Seville	B	4.9 (4917)	5.5	-	-	12.0	-	-	18.0	12.1
	Seville STS	B	4.9 (4917)	5.5	-	-	12.0	-	-	18.0	12.1
	Toronado	L	3.8 (3785)	4.0 ⑤	-	-	13.0	-	-	18.0	13.0
	Trofeo	L	3.8 (3785)	4.0 ⑤	-	-	13.0	-	-	18.0	13.0

CAPACITIES

Year	Model		Engine ID/VIN	Engine Displacement Liters (cc)	Engine Oil with Filter (qts.)	Transmission (pts.) 4-Spd	5-Spd	Auto.	Drive Axle Front (pts.)	Rear (pts.)	Fuel Tank (gal.)	Cooling System (qts.)
1993	Allante		9	4.6 (4573)	7.5	-	-	16.0	-	-	22.5	12.3
	Eldorado		B	4.9 (4917)	5.5	-	-	12.0 ④	-	-	20.0	12.3
	Eldorado	①	9	4.6 (4573)	7.5	-	-	12.0 ④	-	-	20.0	12.3
	Eldorado	②	Y	4.6 (4573)	7.5	-	-	12.0 ④	-	-	20.0	12.3
	Riviera		L	3.8 (3785)	4.0 ⑤	-	-	12.0	-	-	18.0	13.0
	Seville STS		9	4.6 (4573)	7.5	-	-	12.0 ④	-	-	20.0	12.3
	Seville		B	4.9 (4917)	5.5	-	-	12.0 ④	-	-	20.0	12.3
1994	DeVille Concours		Y	4.6 (4573)	7.5	-	-	16.0	-	-	18.0	12.1
	DeVille		B	4.9 (4917)	5.5	-	-	13.0 ③	-	-	18.0	12.1
	Eldorado		Y	4.6 (4573)	7.5	-	-	16.0	-	-	20.0	12.3
	Eldorado	①	9	4.6 (4573)	7.5	-	-	16.0	-	-	20.0	12.3
	Seville SLS		Y	4.6 (4573)	7.5	-	-	16.0	-	-	20.0	12.3
	Seville STS		9	4.6 (4573)	7.5	-	-	16.0	-	-	20.0	12.3
1995-96	DeVille Concours		Y	4.6 (4573)	7.5	-	-	16.0	-	-	18.0	12.1
	DeVille		B	4.9 (4917)	5.5	-	-	13.0 ③	-	-	18.0	12.1
	Eldorado		Y	4.6 (4573)	7.5	-	-	16.0	-	-	20.0	12.3
	Eldorado	①	9	4.6 (4573)	7.5	-	-	16.0	-	-	20.0	12.3
	Riviera		K	3.8 (3785)	5.0	-	-	13.2	-	-	20.0	13.0
	Riviera		1	3.8 (3785)	5.0	-	-	13.2	-	-	20.0	13.0
	Seville SLS		Y	4.6 (4573)	7.5	-	-	16.0	-	-	20.0	12.3
	Seville STS		P	4.6 (4573)	7.5	-	-	16.0	-	-	20.0	12.3

① Touring Coupe
② Sport
③ Fluid change with filter
④ With 4T80 transaxle: 16.0 pts.
⑤ Specification is without filter replacement; Additional oil may be required

CAMSHAFT SPECIFICATIONS
All measurements given in inches.

Year	Engine ID/VIN	Engine Displacement Liters (cc)	Journal Diameter 1	2	3	4	5	Elevation In.	Ex.	Bearing Clearance	Camshaft End Play
1992	8	4.5 (4474)	NA	NA	NA	NA	NA	0.3840	0.3960	0.0018-0.0037	NA
	B	4.9 (4917)	NA	NA	NA	NA	NA	0.3840	0.3960	0.0018-0.0037	NA
	L	3.8 (3785)	1.7850-1.7860	1.7850-1.7860	1.7850-1.7860	1.7850-1.7860	1.7850-1.7860	0.250	0.255	0.0005-0.0035	NA
1993	9	4.6 (4573)	1.0610-1.0620	1.0610-1.0620	1.0610-1.0620	1.0610-1.0620	1.0610-1.0620	0.3700	0.3390	0.0020-0.0030	NA
	B	4.9 (4917)	NA	NA	NA	NA	NA	0.0384	0.3960	0.0018-0.0037	NA
	L	3.8 (3785)	1.7850-1.7860	1.7850-1.7860	1.7850-1.7860	1.7850-1.7860	1.7850-1.7860	0.250	0.255	0.0005-0.0035	NA
	Y	4.6 (4573)	1.0610-1.0620	1.0610-1.0620	1.0610-1.0620	1.0610-1.0620	1.0610-1.0620	0.3700	0.3390	0.0020-0.0030	NA
1994	9	4.6 (4573)	1.0610-1.0620	1.0610-1.0620	1.0610-1.0620	1.0610-1.0620	1.0610-1.0620	0.3700	0.3390	0.0020-0.0030	NA
	Y	4.6 (4573)	1.0610-1.0620	1.0610-1.0620	1.0610-1.0620	1.0610-1.0620	1.0610-1.0620	0.3700	0.3390	0.0020-0.0030	NA

CAMSHAFT SPECIFICATIONS
All measurements given in inches.

Year	Engine ID/VIN	Engine Displacement Liters (cc)	Journal Diameter					Elevation		Bearing Clearance	Camshaft End Play
			1	2	3	4	5	In.	Ex.		
	B	4.9 (4917)	NA	NA	NA	NA	NA	0.3840	0.3960	0.0018-0.0037	NA
1995-96	9	4.6 (4573)	1.0610-1.0620	1.0610-1.0620	1.0610-1.0620	1.0610-1.0620	1.0610-1.0620	0.3700	0.3390	0.0020-0.0030	NA
	B	4.9 (4917)	NA	NA	NA	NA	NA	0.3840	0.3960	0.0018-0.0037	NA
	K	3.8 (3785)	1.7850-1.7860	1.7850-1.7860	1.7850-1.7860	1.7850-1.7860	1.7850-1.7860	0.250	0.255	0.0005-0.0035	NA
	Y	4.6 (4573)	1.0610-1.0620	1.0610-1.0620	1.0610-1.0620	1.0610-1.0620	1.0610-1.0620	0.3700	0.3390	0.0020-0.0030	NA

NA - Not Available

CRANKSHAFT AND CONNECTING ROD SPECIFICATIONS
All measurements are given in inches.

Year	Engine ID/VIN	Engine Displacement Liters (cc)	Crankshaft				Connecting Rod		
			Main Brg. Journal Dia.	Main Brg. Oil Clearance	Shaft End-play	Thrust on No.	Journal Diameter	Oil Clearance	Side Clearance
1992	8	4.5 (4474)	2.6350-2.6360	0.0016-0.0039	0.0010-0.0070	3	1.9270-1.9280	0.0005-0.0028	0.0080-0.0200
	B	4.9 (4917)	2.6350-2.6360	0.0016-0.0039	0.0010-0.0080	3	1.9270-1.9280	0.0005-0.0028	0.0080-0.0200
	L	3.8 (3785)	2.4988-2.4998	0.0008-0.0022	0.0030-0.0110	2	2.2487-2.2499	0.0003-0.0022	0.0030-0.0150
1993	9	4.6 (4573)	2.5200	0.0005-0.0020	0.0020-0.0190	5	2.1242	0.0010-0.0030	0.0080-0.0200
	B	4.9 (4917)	2.6350-2.6360	0.0016-0.0039	0.0010-0.0080	3	1.9270-1.9280	0.0005-0.0028	0.0080-0.0200
	L	3.8 (3785)	2.4988-2.4998	0.0008-0.0022	0.0030-0.0110	2	2.2487-2.2499	0.0008-0.0022	0.0030-0.0150
	Y	4.6 (4573)	2.5200	0.0005-0.0020	0.0020-0.0190	5	2.1242	0.0010-0.0030	0.0080-0.0200
1994	9	4.6 (4573)	2.5200	0.0005-0.0020	0.0020-0.0190	5	2.1242	0.0010-0.0030	0.0080-0.0200
	B	4.9 (4917)	2.6350-2.6360	0.0016-0.0039	0.0010-0.0080	3	1.9270-1.9280	0.0005-0.0028	0.0080-0.0200
	Y	4.6 (4573)	2.5200	0.0005-0.0020	0.0020-0.0190	5	2.1242	0.0010-0.0030	0.0080-0.0200
1995-96	1	3.8 (3785)	2.4988-2.4998	0.0008-0.0022	0.0030-0.0110	2	2.2487-2.2499	0.0008-0.0022	0.0030-0.0150
	9	4.6 (4573)	2.5200	0.0005-0.0020	0.0020-0.0190	5	2.1242	0.0010-0.0030	0.0080-0.0200
	B	4.9 (4917)	2.6350-2.6360	0.0016-0.0039	0.0010-0.0080	3	1.9270-1.9280	0.0005-0.0028	0.0080-0.0200
	K	3.8 (3785)	2.4988-2.4998	0.0008-0.0022	0.0030-0.0110	2	2.2487-2.2499	0.0008-0.0022	0.0030-0.0150
	Y	4.6 (4573)	2.5200	0.0005-0.0020	0.0020-0.0190	5	2.1242	0.0010-0.0030	0.0080-0.0200

VALVE SPECIFICATIONS

Year	Engine ID/VIN	Engine Displacement Liters (cc)	Seat Angle (deg.)	Face Angle (deg.)	Spring Test Pressure (lbs. @ in.)	Spring Installed Height (in.)	Stem-to-Guide Clearance (in.)		Stem Diameter (in.)	
							Intake	Exhaust	Intake	Exhaust
1992	8	4.5 (4474)	45	44	93-103@ 1.730	1.730	0.0010-0.0030	0.0020-0.0040	0.3413-0.3420	0.3401-0.3408
	B	4.9 (4917)	45	44	68-76@ 1.730	1.730	0.0010-0.0030	0.0020-0.0040	0.3413-0.3420	0.3401-0.3408
	L	3.8 (3785)	45	45	210@1.315	1.690-1.720	0.0015-0.0035	0.0015-0.0032	NA	NA
1993	9	4.6 (4573)	46	45	53@1.190	1.190	0.0010-0.0030	0.0020-0.0040	0.2331-0.2339	0.2331-0.2339
	B	4.9 (4917)	45	45	68-76@ 1.350	1.350	0.0010-0.0030	0.0020-0.0040	0.3413-0.3420	0.3401-0.3408
	L	3.8 (3785)	45	45	210@1.315	1.690-1.720	0.0015-0.0035	0.0015-0.0032	NA	NA
	Y	4.6 (4573)	46	45	53@1.190	1.190	0.0010-0.0030	0.0020-0.0040	0.2331-0.2339	0.2331-0.2339
1994	9	4.6 (4573)	46	45	53@1.190	1.190	0.0010-0.0030	0.0020-0.0040	0.2331-0.2339	0.2331-0.2339
	B	4.9 (4917)	45	45	68-76@ 1.350	1.350	0.0010-0.0030	0.0020-0.0040	0.3413-0.3420	0.3401-0.3408
	Y	4.6 (4573)	46	45	53@1.190	1.190	0.0010-0.0030	0.0020-0.0040	0.2331-0.2339	0.2331-0.2339
1995-96	1	3.8 (3785)	45	45	210@1.315	1.690-1.720	0.0015-0.0035	0.0015-0.0032	NA	NA
	9	4.6 (4573)	46	45	53@1.190	1.190	0.0010-0.0030	0.0020-0.0040	0.2331-0.2339	0.2331-0.2339
	K	3.8 (3785)	45	45	210@1.315	1.690-1.720	0.0015-0.0035	0.0015-0.0032	NA	NA
	B	4.9 (4917)	45	45	68-76@1.350	1.350	0.0010-0.0030	0.0020-0.0040	0.3413-0.3420	0.3401-0.3408
	Y	4.6 (4573)	46	45	53@1.190	1.190	0.0010-0.0030	0.0020-0.0040	0.2331-0.2339	0.2331-0.2339

PISTON AND RING SPECIFICATIONS

All measurements are given in inches.

Year	Engine ID/VIN	Engine Displacement Liters (cc)	Piston Clearance	Ring Gap			Ring Side Clearance		
				Top Compression	Bottom Compression	Oil Control	Top Compression	Bottom Compression	Oil Control
1992	L	3.8 (3785)	0.0004-0.0022 ①	0.010-0.025	0.010-0.025	0.015-0.055	0.0013-0.0031	0.0013-0.0031	0.0011-0.0081
	8	4.5 (4474)	0.0010-0.0018	0.0150-0.0240	0.0150-0.0240	0.0100-0.0500	0.0016-0.0037	0.0016-0.0037	NA
	B	4.9 (4917)	0.0004-0.0020	0.0120-0.0220	0.0120-0.0220	0.0040-0.0200	0.0016-0.0037	0.0016-0.0037	NA
1993	L	3.8 (3785)	0.0004-0.0022 ①	0.010-0.025	0.010-0.025	0.015-0.055	0.0013-0.0031	0.0013-0.0031	0.0011-0.0081
	9	4.6 (4573)	0.0004-0.0020	0.0100-0.0160	0.0140-0.0200	0.0100-0.0300	0.0020-0.0040	0.0020-0.0040	NA
	Y	4.6 (4573)	0.0004-0.0020	0.0100-0.0160	0.0140-0.0200	0.0100-0.0300	0.0020-0.0040	0.0020-0.0040	NA
	B	4.9 (4917)	0.0004-0.0020	0.0120-0.0220	0.0120-0.0220	0.0040-0.0200	0.0016-0.0037	0.0016-0.0037	NA

PISTON AND RING SPECIFICATIONS

All measurements are given in inches.

Year	Engine ID/VIN	Engine Displacement Liters (cc)	Piston Clearance	Ring Gap — Top Compression	Ring Gap — Bottom Compression	Ring Gap — Oil Control	Ring Side Clearance — Top Compression	Ring Side Clearance — Bottom Compression	Ring Side Clearance — Oil Control
1994	9	4.6 (4573)	0.0004-0.0020	0.0100-0.0160	0.0140-0.0200	0.0100-0.0300	0.0020-0.0040	0.0020-0.0040	NA
	Y	4.6 (4573)	0.0004-0.0020	0.0100-0.0160	0.0140-0.0200	0.0100-0.0200	0.0020-0.0300	0.0020-0.0040	NA
	B	4.9 (4917)	0.0004-0.0020	0.0120-0.0220	0.0120-0.0220	0.0040-0.0200	0.0016-0.0037	0.0016-0.0037	NA
1995-96	K	3.8 (3785)	0.0004-0.0022 ①	0.010-0.025	0.010-0.025	0.015-0.055	0.0013-0.0031	0.0013-0.0031	0.0011-0.0081
	1	3.8 (3785)	0.0004-0.0022 ①	0.010-0.025	0.010-0.025	0.015-0.055	0.0013-0.0031	0.0013-0.0031	0.0011-0.0081
	9	4.6 (4573)	0.0004-0.0020	0.0100-0.0160	0.0140-0.0200	0.0100-0.0300	0.0020-0.0040	0.0020-0.0040	NA
	Y	4.6 (4573)	0.0004-0.0020	0.0100-0.0160	0.0140-0.0200	0.0100-0.0200	0.0020-0.0300	0.0020-0.0040	NA
	B	4.9 (4917)	0.0004-0.0020	0.0120-0.0220	0.0120-0.0220	0.0040-0.0200	0.0016-0.0037	0.0016-0.0037	NA

NA - Not Available
① Measured 44mm from top of piston

TORQUE SPECIFICATIONS

All readings in ft. lbs.

Year	Engine ID/VIN	Engine Displacement Liters (cc)	Cylinder Head Bolts	Main Bearing Bolts	Rod Bearing Bolts	Crankshaft Damper Bolts	Flywheel Bolts	Manifold Intake	Manifold Exhaust	Spark Plugs	Lug Nut
1992	8	4.5 (4474)	⑦	85	25	70	70	⑧	16	23	100
	B	4.9 (4917)	⑦	85	25	70	70	⑧	16	23	100
	L	3.8 (3785)	⑪	⑨	⑫	⑩	②	7	38	12	100
1993	9	4.6 (4573)	①	②	③	④	⑤	⑥	20	14	100
	B	4.9 (4917)	⑦	85	25	70	70	⑧	16	23	100
	L	3.8 (3785)	⑪	⑨	⑫	⑩	②	7	38	20	100
	Y	4.6 (4573)	①	②	③	④	⑤	⑥	20	14	100
1994	9	4.6 (4573)	①	②	③	④	⑤	⑥	20	14	100
	Y	4.6 (4573)	①	②	③	④	⑤	⑥	20	14	100
	B	4.9 (4917)	⑦	85	25	70	70	⑧	16	23	100
1995-96	1	3.8 (3785)	⑪	⑨	⑫	⑩	②	7	38	11	100
	9	4.6 (4573)	①	②	③	④	⑤	⑥	20	14	100
	B	4.9 (4917)	⑦	85	25	70	70	⑧	16	23	100
	K	3.8 (3785)	⑪	⑨	⑫	⑩	②	7	38	11	100
	Y	4.6 (4573)	①	②	③	④	⑤	⑥	20	14	100

① Step 1: 22 ft. lbs.
Step 2: Plus two turns of 90 degrees

② Step 1: 11 ft. lbs.
Step 2: Plus 50 degrees

③ Step 1: 20 ft. lbs.
Step 2: Plus 90 degrees

④ Step 1: 105 ft. lbs.
Step 2: Plus 120 degrees

⑤ Step 1: 15 ft. lbs.
Step 2: Plus 65 degrees

⑥ Step 1: 4 ft. lbs.
Step 2: Plus 120 degrees

⑦ Step 1: 38 ft. lbs.
Step 2: 68 ft. lbs.
Step 3: 90 ft. lbs.

⑧ Step 1: 8 ft. lbs.
Step 2: 12 ft. lbs.

⑨ 26 ft. lbs. plus 50 degrees

⑩ 110 ft. lbs. plus 76 degrees

⑪ Step 1: 35 ft. lbs.
Step 2: 130 degrees
Step 3: Rotate four center bolts an additional 30 degrees

⑫ 20 ft. lbs. plus 50 degrees

BRAKE SPECIFICATIONS
All measurements in inches unless noted

Year	Model		Master Cylinder Bore	Brake Disc Original Thickness	Brake Disc Minimum Thickness	Maximum Runout	Brake Drum Diameter Original Inside Diameter	Max. Wear Limit	Maximum Machine Diameter	Minimum Lining Thickness Front	Minimum Lining Thickness Rear
1992	Allante		NA	1.035	0.956	0.004	-	-	-	0.030	-
	Allante	①	NA	0.494	0.429	0.003	-	-	-	-	0.030
	Eldorado		1.000	1.260	1.209	0.002	-	-	-	0.030	-
	Eldorado	①	NA	0.433	0.374	0.002	-	-	-	-	0.030
	Riviera		1.000	1.260	1.209	0.002	-	-	-	0.030	0.030
	Riviera		1.000	0.433	0.374	0.002	-	-	-	0.030	0.030
	Seville		1.000	1.260	1.209	0.002	-	-	-	0.030	-
			NA	0.433	0.374	0.002	-	-	-	-	0.030
	Toronado		1.000	1.260	1.209	0.002	-	-	-	0.030	0.030
			1.000	0.433	0.374	0.002	-	-	-	0.030	0.030
	Trofeo		1.000	1.260	1.209	0.002	-	-	-	0.030	0.030
			1.000	0.433	0.374	0.002	-	-	-	0.030	0.030
1993	Allante		1.000	1.268	1.209	0.002	-	-	-	0.030	-
	Allante		NA	0.433	0.374	0.002	-	-	-	-	0.030
	Eldorado		1.000	1.268	1.209	0.002	-	-	-	0.030	-
	Eldorado	①	NA	0.433	0.384	0.002	-	-	-	-	0.030
	Eldorado		1.000	1.268	1.209	0.002	-	-	-	0.030	-
	Eldorado	②	NA	0.433	0.374	0.002	-	-	-	-	-
	Eldorado ETC		1.000	1.268	1.209	0.002	-	-	-	0.030	-
	Eldorado ETC	①	NA	0.433	0.374	0.002	-	-	-	-	0.030
	Riviera		1.000	1.260	1.209	0.002	-	-	-	0.030	0.030
	Riviera		1.000	0.433	0.374	0.002	-	-	-	0.030	0.030
	Seville		1.000	1.268	1.209	0.002	-	-	-	0.030	-
	Seville	①	NA	0.433	0.374	0.002	-	-	-	-	0.030
	Seville STS		1.000	1.268	1.209	0.002	-	-	-	0.030	-
	Seville STS	①	NA	0.433	0.374	0.002	-	-	-	-	0.030
1994	DeVIlle Concours		1.000	1.276	1.209	0.004	8.860	8.909	8.880	0.030	0.030
	Deville		1.000	1.276	1.209	0.004	8.860	8.909	8.880	0.030	0.030
	Eldorado		1.000	1.268	1.209	0.002	-	-	-	0.030	-
	Eldorado	①	NA	0.433	0.374	0.002	-	-	-	-	0.030
	Eldorado ETC		1.000	1.268	1.209	0.002	-	-	-	0.030	-
	Eldorado ETC	①	NA	0.433	0.374	0.002	-	-	-	-	0.030
	Seville SLS		1.000	1.268	1.209	0.002	-	-	-	0.030	-
	Seville SLS	①	NA	0.433	0.374	0.002	-	-	-	-	0.030
	Seville STS		1.000	1.268	1.209	0.002	-	-	-	0.030	-
	Seville STS	①	NA	0.433	0.374	0.002	-	-	-	-	0.030
1995-96	DeVille		1.000	1.276	1.209	0.004	8.860	8.909	8.880	0.030	0.030
	DeVille Concours		1.000	1.276	1.209	0.004	8.860	8.909	8.880	0.030	0.030
	Eldorado		1.000	1.268	1.209	0.002	-	-	-	0.030	-
	Eldorado	①	NA	0.433	0.374	0.002	-	-	-	-	0.030
	Eldorado ETC		1.000	1.268	1.209	0.002	-	-	-	0.030	-
	Eldorado ETC	①	NA	0.433	0.374	0.002	-	-	-	-	0.030
	Riviera		-	1.260	1.209	0.002	-	-	-	0.030	-
	Riviera		1.000	0.433	0.374	0.002	-	-	-	0.030	-
	Seville SLS		1.000	1.268	1.209	0.002	-	-	-	0.030	-
	Seville SLS	①	NA	0.433	0.374	0.002	-	-	-	-	0.030
	Seville STS		1.000	1.268	1.209	0.002	-	-	-	0.030	-
	Seville STS	①	NA	0.433	0.374	0.002	-	-	-	-	0.030

NA - Not Available   ① Rear disc brakes   ② Sport

WHEEL ALIGNMENT

Year	Model		Caster Range (deg.)	Caster Preferred Setting (deg.)	Camber Range (deg.)	Camber Preferred Setting (deg.)	Toe-in (in.)	Steering Axis Inclination (deg.)
1992	Allante	F	1.30P-3.30P	2.30P	0.80N-0.80P	0	3/32P	NA
		R	-	-	0.50N-0.50P	0	3/32P	-
	Eldorado	F	1.30P-3.30P	2.30P	1N-0	0.50N	3/32P	NA
	Eldorado ①	F	1.30P-3.30P	2.30P	0-1P	0.50P	3/32P	NA
		R	-	-	0.50N-0.50P	0	3/32P	-
	Riviera	F	1 5/16P-3 5/16P	2 5/16P	13/16N-13/16P	0	3/32P	13 5/16
		R	-	-	1/2N-1/2P	0	3/32P	-
	Seville	F	1.30P-3.30P	2.30P	1N-0	0.50N	3/32P	NA
	Seville ①	F	1.30P-3.30P	2.30P	0-1P	0.50P	3/32P	NA
		R	-	-	0.50N-0.50P	0	3/32P	-
	Toronado	F	1 5/16P-3 5/16P	2 5/16P	②	③	3/32P	13 5/16
		R	-	-	11/16N-5/16P	3/16N	3/32P	-
	Trofeo	F	1 5/16P-3 5/16P	2 5/16P	②	③	3/32P	13 5/16
		R	-	-	11/16N-5/16P	3/16N	3/32P	-
1993	Allante	F	1.50P-3.50P	2.50P	0.80N-0.80P	0	3/32P	NA
		R	-	-	0.50N-0.50P	0	3/32P	-
	Eldorado	F	1.50P-3.50P	2.50P	1N-0	0.50N	3/32P	NA
	Eldorado ①	F	1.50P-3.50P	2.50P	0-1P	0.50P	3/32P	NA
		R	-	-	0.50N-0.50P	0	3/32P	-
	Eldorado ETC	F	1.50P-3.50P	2.50P	1N-0	0.50N	3/32P	NA
	Eldorado ETC ①	F	1.50P-3.50P	2.50P	0-1P	0.05P	3/32P	NA
		R	-	-	0.50N-0.50P	0	3/32P	-
	Riviera	F	1 5/16P-3 5/16P	2 5/16P	13/16N-13/16P	0	3/32P	13 5/16
		R	-	-	1/2N-1/2P	0	3/32P	-
	Seville	F	1.50P-3.50P	2.50P	1N-0	0.05N	3/32P	NA
	Seville ①	F	1.50P-3.50P	2.50P	0-1P	0.05P	3/32P	NA
		R	-	-	0.50N-0.50P	0	3/32P	-
	Seville STS	F	1.50P-3.50P	2.50P	1N-0	0.05N	3/32P	NA
	Seville STS ①	F	1.50P-3.50P	2.50P	0-1P	0.50P	3/32P	NA
		R	-	-	0.50N-0.50P	0	3/32P	-
1994	DeVille	F	2.25P-3.75P	3P	1N-0	0.50N	0	NA
	DeVille ①	F	2.25P-3.75P	3P	0-1P	0.05P	0	NA
		R	-	-	1.05N-0.45P	0.30N	3/32P	-
	DeVille/Concours	F	2.25P-3.75P	3P	1N-0	0.50N	0	NA
	DeVille/Concours ①	F	2.25P-3.75P	3P	0-1P	0.05P	0	NA
		R	-	-	1.05N-0.45P	0.30N	3/32P	-
	Eldorado	F	1.50P-3.50P	2.50P	1N-0	0.50N	3/32P	NA
	Eldorado ①	F	1.50P-3.50P	2.50P	0-1P	0.50P	3/32P	NA
		R	-	-	0.05N-0.50P	0	3/32P	-
	Eldorado ETC	F	1.50P-3.50P	2.50P	1N-0	0.50N	3/32P	NA
	Eldorado ETC ①	F	1.50P-3.50P	2.50P	0-1P	0.50P	3/32P	NA
		R	-	-	0.50N-0.50P	0	3/32P	-
	Seville SLS	F	1.50P-3.50P	2.50P	1N-0	0.50N	3/32P	NA
	Seville SLS ①	F	1.50P-3.50P	2.50P	0-1P	0.50P	3/32P	NA
		R	-	-	0.05N-0.50P	0	3/32P	-
	Seville STS	F	1.50P-3.50P	2.50P	1N-0	0.50N	3/32P	NA
	Seville STS ①	F	1.50P-3.50P	2.50P	0-1P	0.50P	3/32P	NA
		R	-	-	0.05N-0.50P	0	3/32P	-

WHEEL ALIGNMENT

Year	Model			Caster Range (deg.)	Caster Preferred Setting (deg.)	Camber Range (deg.)	Camber Preferred Setting (deg.)	Toe-in (in.)	Steering Axis Inclination (deg.)
1995-96	DeVille		F	2 1/4P-3 3/4P	3P	1N-0	1/2N	0	NA
	DeVille	①	F	2 1/4P-3 3/4P	3P	0-1P	3/64P	0	NA
			R	-	-	1 3/64N-29/64P	1/32N	3/32P	-
	DeVille/Concours		F	2 1/4P-3 3/4P	3P	1N-0	1/2N	0	NA
	DeVille/Concours	①	F	2 1/4P-3 3/4P	3P	0-1P	3/64P	0	NA
			R	-	-	1 3/64N-29/64P	1/32N	3/32P	-
	Eldorado		F	1 1/2P-3 1/2P	2 1/2P	1N-0	1/2N	3/32P	NA
	Eldorado	①	F	1 1/2P-3 1/2P	2 1/2P	0-1P	1/2P	3/32P	NA
			R	-	-	3/64N-1/2P	0	3/32P	-
	Eldorado ETC		F	1 1/2P-3 1/2P	2 1/2P	1N-0	1/2N	3/32P	NA
	Eldorado ETC	①	F	1 1/2P-3 1/2P	2 1/2P	0-1P	1/2P	3/32P	NA
			R	-	-	3/64N-1/2P	0	3/32P	-
	Riviera		F	4 1/2P-6 1/2P	5 1/2P	5/64N-1 13/64P	13/64P	0	NA
			R	-	-	5/64N-13/64P	1/32N	13/64P	-
	Seville SLS		F	1 1/2P-3 1/2P	2 1/2P	1N-0	1/2N	3/32P	NA
	Seville SLS	①	F	1 1/2P-3 1/2P	2 1/2P	0-1P	1/2P	3/32P	NA
			R	-	-	3/64N-1/2P	0	3/32P	-
	Seville STS		F	1 1/2P-3 1/2P	2 1/2P	1N-0	1/2N	3/32P	NA
	Seville STS	①	F	1 1/2P-3 1/2P	2 1/2P	0-1P	1/2P	3/32P	NA
			R	-	-	3/64N-1/2P	0	3/32P	-

NA - Not Available
F - Front
R - Rear
① Right side

② Left wheel: 1N-0
   Right wheel: 0-1P
③ Left wheel: 1/2N
   Right wheel: 1/2P

CAVALIER/SUNBIRD

VEHICLE IDENTIFICATION CHART

	Engine Code				
Code	Liters	Cu. In. (cc)	Cyl.	Fuel Sys.	Eng. Mfg.
4	2.2	133 (2180)	4	MFI	CUS
D	2.3	138 (2262)	4	MFI	CUS
H	2.0	121 (1998)	4	MFI	Pontiac
T	3.1	191 (3130)	6	MFI	CPC

Model Year	
Code	Year
N	1992
P	1993
R	1994
S	1995
T	1996

CUS - Chevrolet/United States

CPC - Chevrolet/Pontiac/Canada

MFI - Multiport fuel injection

ENGINE IDENTIFICATION

Year	Model	Engine Displacement Liters (cc)	Engine Series (ID/VIN)	Fuel System	No. of Cylinders	Engine Type
1992	Sunbird	2.0 (1998)	H	MFI	4	SOHC
	Sunbird	3.1 (3130)	T	MFI	6	OHV
	Cavalier	2.2 (2180)	4	MFI	4	OHV
	Cavalier	3.1 (3130)	T	MFI	6	OHV
1993	Sunbird	2.0 (1998)	H	MFI	4	SOHC
	Sunbird	3.1 (3130)	T	MFI	6	OHV
	Cavalier	2.2 (2180)	4	MFI	4	OHV
	Cavalier	3.1 (3130)	T	MFI	6	OHV
1994	Sunbird	2.0 (1998)	H	MFI	4	SOHC
	Sunbird	3.1 (3130)	T	MFI	6	OHV
	Cavalier	2.2 (2180)	4	MFI	4	OHV
	Cavalier	3.1 (3130)	T	MFI	6	OHV
1995-96	Cavalier	2.2 (2180)	4	MFI	4	OHV
	Cavalier	2.3 (2262)	D	MFI	4	DOHC

MFI - Multiport fuel injection
OHV - Overhead valve
DOHC - Double overhead camshaft

GENERAL ENGINE SPECIFICATIONS

Year	Engine ID/VIN	Engine Displacement Liters (cc)	Fuel System Type	Net Horsepower @ rpm	Net Torque @ rpm (ft. lbs.)	Bore x Stroke (in.)	Compression Ratio	Oil Pressure @ rpm
1992	4	2.2 (2180)	TFI	95@5200	120@3200	3.50x3.46	9.0:1	63-77@1200
	H	2.0 (1998)	MFI	111@5200	125@3600	3.38x3.38	9.2:1	45@2400
	T	3.1 (3130)	MFI	140@4200	185@3200	3.50x3.31	8.5:1	8@600
1993	4	2.2 (2180)	MFI	110@5200	130@3200	3.50x3.46	9.0:1	63-77@1200
	H	2.0 (1998)	MFI	110@5200	124@3600	3.38x3.38	9.2:1	30@2000
	T	3.1 (3130)	MFI	140@4200	185@3200	3.50x3.31	8.5:1	8@600
1994	4	2.2 (2180)	MFI	110@5200	130@3200	3.50x3.46	9.0:1	63-77@1200
	H	2.0 (1998)	MFI	110@5200	124@3600	3.38x3.38	9.2:1	30@2000
	T	3.1 (3130)	MFI	140@4200	185@3200	3.50x3.31	8.5:1	8@600
1995-96	4	2.2 (2180)	MFI	120@5200	130@3200	3.50x3.46	9.0:1	63-77@1200
	D	2.3 (2262)	MFI	150@6100	145@4800	3.63x3.35	9.5:1	30@2000

TFI - Throttle body fuel injection
MFI - Multiport fuel injection

GASOLINE ENGINE TUNE-UP SPECIFICATIONS

Year	Engine ID/VIN	Engine Displacement Liters (cc)	Spark Plugs Gap (in.)	Ignition Timing (deg.) MT	Ignition Timing (deg.) AT	Fuel Pump (psi)	Idle Speed (rpm) MT	Idle Speed (rpm) AT	Valve Clearance In.	Valve Clearance Ex.
1992	4	2.2 (2180)	0.035	①	①	9-13	①	①	HYD	HYD
	H	2.0 (1998)	0.045	②	②	41-47	600	600	HYD	HYD
	T	3.1 (3130)	0.045	10B	10B	41-47	①	①	HYD	HYD
1993	4	2.2 (2180)	0.045	①	①	41-47	①	①	HYD	HYD
	H	2.0 (1998)	0.045	②	②	41-47	①	①	HYD	HYD
	T	3.1 (3130)	0.045	10B	10B	41-47	①	①	HYD	HYD
1994	4	2.2 (2180)	0.045	①	①	41-47	①	①	HYD	HYD
	H	2.0 (1998)	0.045	②	②	41-47	①	①	HYD	HYD
	T	3.1 (3130)	0.045	①	①	41-47	①	①	HYD	HYD
1995-96	4	2.2 (2180)	0.045	①	①	41-47	①	①	HYD	HYD
	D	2.3 (2262)	0.035	①	①	41-47	①	①	HYD	HYD

NOTE: The Vehicle Emission Control Information label often reflects specification changes made during production. The label figures must be used if they differ from those in this chart.

B - Before top dead center

HYD - Hydraulic

① Refer to Vehicle Emission Control Information label

② Distributorless ignition system

CAPACITIES

Year	Model	Engine ID/VIN	Engine Displacement Liters (cc)	Engine Oil with Filter (qts.)	Transmission (pts.) 4-Spd	Transmission (pts.) 5-Spd	Transmission (pts.) Auto.	Transfer Case (pts.)	Drive Axle Front (pts.)	Drive Axle Rear (pts.)	Fuel Tank (gal.)	Cooling System (qts.)
1992	Cavalier	4	2.2 (2180)	4.5	-	4.0	8.0	-	-	-	13.6	8.5
	Cavalier	T	3.1 (3130)	4.5	-	4.0	8.0 ①	-	-	-	13.6	11.0
	Sunbird	H	2.0 (1998)	4.5	-	4.0	8.0	-	-	-	15.2	11.7
	Sunbird	T	3.1 (3136)	4.5	-	4.0	8.0	-	-	-	15.2	14.2
1993	Cavalier	4	2.2 (2180)	4.5	-	4.0	8.0 ①	-	-	-	13.6	8.5
	Cavalier	T	3.1 (3130)	4.5	-	4.0	8.0 ①	-	-	-	13.6	11.0
	Sunbird	H	2.0 (1998)	4.5	-	4.0	8.0	-	-	-	13.6	11.7
	Sunbird	T	3.1 (3136)	4.5	-	4.0	8.0	-	-	-	13.6	14.2
1994	Cavalier	4	2.2 (2180)	4.5	-	4.0	8.0 ①	-	-	-	13.6	8.5
	Cavalier	T	3.1 (3130)	4.5	-	4.0	8.0 ①	-	-	-	13.6	11.0
	Sunbird	H	2.0 (1998)	4.5	-	4.0	8.0	-	-	-	15.2	10.7
	Sunbird	T	3.1 (3136)	4.5	-	4.0	8.0	-	-	-	15.2	13.7
1995-96	Cavalier	4	2.2 (2180)	4.5	-	4.0	8.0 ①	-	-	-	13.6	8.5
	Cavalier	D	2.3 (2262)	4.5	-	4.0	14.0 ①	-	-	-	13.6	10.4

① 10.0 pts. if equipped with O/D

CAMSHAFT SPECIFICATIONS

All measurements given in inches.

Year	Engine ID/VIN	Engine Displacement Liters (cc)	Journal Diameter					Elevation		Bearing Clearance	Camshaft End Play
			1	2	3	4	5	In.	Ex.		
1992	4	2.2 (2180)	1.867-1.869	1.867-1.869	1.867-1.869	1.867-1.869	1.867-1.869	0.259	0.259	0.0010-0.0039	NA
	H	2.0 (1998)	1.6706-1.6712	1.6812-1.6818	1.6911-1.6917	1.7009-1.7015	1.7100-1.7106	0.2626	0.2626	0.0011-0.0035	0.0016-0.0064
	T	3.1 (3130)	1.868-1.881	1.868-1.881	1.868-1.881	1.868-1.881	NA	0.263	0.273	0.0010-0.0039	NA
1993	4	2.2 (2180)	1.867-1.869	1.867-1.869	1.867-1.869	1.867-1.869	1.867-1.869	0.259	0.259	0.0010-0.0039	NA
	H	2.0 (1998)	1.6706-1.6712	1.6812-1.6818	1.6911-1.6917	1.7009-1.7015	1.7100-1.7106	0.2626	0.2626	0.0011-0.0035	0.0016-0.0064
	T	3.1 (3130)	1.868-1.881	1.868-1.881	1.868-1.881	1.868-1.881	NA	0.263	0.273	0.0010-0.0039	NA
1994	4	2.2 (2180)	1.867-1.869	1.867-1.869	1.867-1.869	1.867-1.869	1.867-1.869	0.259	0.259	0.0010-0.0039	NA
	H	2.0 (1998)	1.6706-1.6712	1.6812-1.6818	1.6911-1.6917	1.7009-1.7015	1.7100-1.7106	0.2626	0.2626	0.0011-0.0035	0.0016-0.0063
	T	3.1 (3130)	1.868-1.881	1.868-1.881	1.868-1.881	1.868-1.881	NA	0.263	0.273	0.0010-0.0039	NA
1995-96	4	2.2 (2180)	1.8670-1.8690	1.8670-1.8690	1.8670-1.8690	1.8670-1.8690	1.8670-1.8690	0.2880	0.2880	0.0010-0.0039	NA
	D	2.3 (2262)	1.5720-1.5730	1.3750-1.3760	1.3750-1.3760	1.3750-1.3760	1.3750-1.3760	0.3750	0.3750	0.0020-0.0040	0.0010-0.0090

NA - Not Available

CRANKSHAFT AND CONNECTING ROD SPECIFICATIONS

All measurements are given in inches.

Year	Engine ID/VIN	Engine Displacement Liters (cc)	Crankshaft				Connecting Rod		
			Main Brg. Journal Dia.	Main Brg. Oil Clearance	Shaft End-play	Thrust on No.	Journal Diameter	Oil Clearance	Side Clearance
1992	4	2.2 (2180)	2.4945-2.4954	0.0006-0.0019	0.002-0.007	4	1.9983-1.9994	0.0010-0.0030	0.0040-0.0150
	H	2.0 (1998)	2.2828-2.2833	0.0006-0.0016	0.0028-0.0118	3	1.9279-1.9287	0.0007-0.0025	0.0028-0.0095
	T	3.1 (3130)	2.6473-2.6483	0.0012-0.0030	0.002-0.008	3	1.9983-1.9994	0.0010-0.0040	0.0140-0.0270
1993	4	2.2 (2180)	2.4945-2.4954	0.0006-0.0019	0.002-0.007	4	1.9983-1.9994	0.0010-0.0030	0.0040-0.0150
	H	2.0 (1998)	2.2828-2.2833	0.0006-0.0016	0.0028-0.0118	3	1.9279-1.9287	0.0007-0.0025	0.0028-0.0095
	T	3.1 (3130)	2.6473-2.6483	0.0012-0.0030	0.002-0.008	3	1.9983-1.9994	0.0010-0.0040	0.0140-0.0270

CRANKSHAFT AND CONNECTING ROD SPECIFICATIONS

All measurements are given in inches.

Year	Engine ID/VIN	Engine Displacement Liters (cc)	Crankshaft Main Brg. Journal Dia.	Crankshaft Main Brg. Oil Clearance	Crankshaft Shaft End-play	Crankshaft Thrust on No.	Connecting Rod Journal Diameter	Connecting Rod Oil Clearance	Connecting Rod Side Clearance
1994	4	2.2 (2180)	2.4945-2.4954	0.0006-0.0019	0.002-0.007	4	1.9983-1.9994	0.0010-0.0030	0.0040-0.0150
	H	2.0 (1998)	2.2828-2.2833	0.0006-0.0016	0.0028-0.0118	3	1.9279-1.9287	0.0007-0.0025	0.0028-0.0095
	T	3.1 (3130)	2.6473-2.6483	0.0012-0.0030	0.002-0.008	3	1.9983-1.9994	0.0010-0.0040	0.0140-0.0270
1995-96	4	2.2 (2180)	2.4945-2.4954	0.0006-0.0019	0.0020-0.0070	4	1.9983-1.9994	0.0010-0.0030	0.0040-0.0150
	D	2.3 (2262)	2.0470-2.0480	0.0005-0.0023	0.0030-0.0090	3	1.8887-1.8897	0.0005-0.0020	0.0059-0.0177

VALVE SPECIFICATIONS

Year	Engine ID/VIN	Engine Displacement Liters (cc)	Seat Angle (deg.)	Face Angle (deg.)	Spring Test Pressure (lbs. @ in.)	Spring Installed Height (in.)	Stem-to-Guide Clearance (in.) Intake	Stem-to-Guide Clearance (in.) Exhaust	Stem Diameter (in.) Intake	Stem Diameter (in.) Exhaust
1992	4	2.2 (2180)	46	45	208-222@ ① 1.22	1.61 ②	0.0011-0.0026	0.0014-0.0030	NA	NA
	H	2.0 (1998)	45	46	63-71@ 1.476	1.476	0.0006-0.0017	0.0012-0.0024	0.2760-0.2755	0.2753-0.2747
	T	3.1 (3130)	46	45	90 ①	1.60 ②	0.0010-0.0027	0.0010-0.0027	NA	NA
1993	4	2.2 (2180)	46	45	225-233@ ① 1.25	1.64 ②	0.0011-0.0026	0.0014-0.0031	NA	NA
	H	2.0 (1998)	46	45	90@1.701	1.693	0.0008-0.0021	0.0014-0.0030	0.2753-0.2747	0.2760-0.2755
	T	3.1 (3130)	46	45	90 ①	1.60 ②	0.0010-0.0027	0.0010-0.0027	NA	NA
1994	4	2.2 (2180)	46	45	225-233@ ① 1.25	1.64 ②	0.0011-0.0026	0.0014-0.0031	NA	NA
	H	2.0 (1998)	45	46	63-71@ 1.476	1.476	0.0006-0.0017	0.0012-0.0024	0.2753-0.2747	0.2760-0.2755
	T	3.1 (3130)	46	45	90 ①	1.60 ②	0.0010-0.0027	0.0010-0.0027	NA	NA
1995-96	4	2.2 (2180)	46	45	225-233@ ① 1.25	1.64 ②	0.0011-0.0026	0.0014-0.0031	NA	NA
	D	2.3 (2262)	45	44	193-207@ 1.04	1.44 ②	0.0010-0.0027	0.0015-0.0032	0.2740-0.2750	0.2740-0.2750

NA - Not Available
① With valve open
② With valve closed

PISTON AND RING SPECIFICATIONS
All measurements are given in inches.

Year	Engine ID/VIN	Engine Displacement Liters (cc)	Piston Clearance	Ring Gap			Ring Side Clearance		
				Top Compression	Bottom Compression	Oil Control	Top Compression	Bottom Compression	Oil Control
1992	4	2.2 (2180)	0.0007-0.0017	0.010-0.020	0.010-0.020	0.010-0.050	0.002-0.003	0.002-0.003	0.0020-0.0082
	H	2.0 (1998)	0.0004-0.0012	0.0098-0.0177	0.0188-0.0197	NA	0.0024-0.0036	0.0019-0.0032	NA
	T	3.1 (3130)	0.0009-0.0022	0.010-0.020	0.020-0.028	0.010-0.030	0.002-0.003	0.002-0.003	0.008
1993	4	2.2 (2180)	0.0007-0.0017	0.010-0.020	0.010-0.020	0.010-0.050	0.002-0.003	0.002-0.003	0.0020-0.0082
	H	2.0 (1998)	0.0004-0.0012	0.0098-0.0177	0.0118-0.0197	NA	0.0024-0.0036	0.0019-0.0032	NA
	T	3.1 (3130)	0.0009-0.0022	0.010-0.020	0.020-0.028	0.010-0.030	0.002-0.003	0.002-0.003	0.008
1994	4	2.2 (2180)	0.0007-0.0017	0.010-0.020	0.010-0.020	0.010-0.050	0.002-0.003	0.002-0.003	0.0020-0.0082
	H	2.0 (1998)	0.0004-0.0012	0.0098-0.0177	0.0118-0.0197	NA	0.0024-0.0036	0.0019-0.0032	NA
	T	3.1 (3130)	0.0009-0.0022	0.010-0.020	0.020-0.028	0.010-0.030	0.002-0.003	0.002-0.003	0.008
1995-96	4	2.2 (2180)	0.0007-0.0017	0.010-0.020	0.010-0.020	0.010-0.050	0.0020-0.0030	0.0020-0.0030	0.0020-0.0082
	D	2.3 (2262)	0.0007-0.0020	0.014-0.024	0.016-0.026	0.016-0.055	0.0030-0.0050	0.0020-0.0030	NA

NA - Not Available

TORQUE SPECIFICATIONS
All readings in ft. lbs.

Year	Engine ID/VIN	Engine Displacement Liters (cc)	Cylinder Head Bolts	Main Bearing Bolts	Rod Bearing Bolts	Crankshaft Damper Bolts	Flywheel Bolts	Manifold		Spark Plugs	Lug Nut
								Intake	Exhaust		
1992	4	2.2 (2180)	①	77	38	85 ②	52-55	18	6-13	20	80-100
	H	2.0 (2998)	18 ⑫	44 ⑬	26 ⑬	114	48 ⑭	16	16	15	100
	T	3.1 (3130)	⑩	73	39	66-85	45-59	⑤	18	20	100
1993	4	2.2 (2180)	①	77	38	85 ②	52-55	18	6-13	20	80-100
	H	2.0 (1998)	18 ⑫	44 ⑭	26 ⑭	114	48 ⑭	16	16	15	100
	T	3.1 (3130)	⑩	73	39	66-85	45-59	⑤	18	20	100
1994	4	2.2 (2180)	①	77	38	85 ②	52-55	18	6-13	20	100
	H	2.0 (1998)	18 ⑫	44 ⑬	26 ⑬	114	48	16	16	15	100
	T	3.1 (3130)	⑩	73	39	66-85	45-59	⑤	18	20	100
1995-96	4	2.2 (2180)	①	77	38	85 ②	52-55	18	6-13	20	100
	D	2.3 (2262)	26 ④	⑥	⑦	⑧	⑨	⑪	③	17	100

23 SPECIFICATIONS

TORQUE SPECIFICATIONS
All readings in ft. lbs.

Year	Engine ID/VIN	Engine Displacement Liters (cc)	Cylinder Head Bolts	Main Bearing Bolts	Rod Bearing Bolts	Crankshaft Damper Bolts	Flywheel Bolts	Manifold Intake	Manifold Exhaust	Spark Plugs	Lug Nut

NA - Not Available

① Step 1: 41 ft. lbs.
　Step 2: Tighten an additional 45 degrees
　Step 3: Tighten an additional 45 degrees
　Step 4: Long bolts 1, 4-5, 8-9 an additional 20 degrees
　Step 4: Short bolts 2-3, 6-7, 10 an additional 10 degrees
② Center bolt spec shown; Pulley to hub bolts: 37 ft. lbs.
③ Bolts: 27 ft. lbs.
　Studs: 106 inch lbs.

④ Cylinder head bolts should be torqued 26 ft. lbs.
　Long bolts: 100 degrees
　Short bolts: 120 degrees
⑤ 15 ft. lbs., then 24 ft. lbs.
⑥ 15 ft. lbs. plus 90 degrees
⑦ 18 ft. lbs. plus 80 degrees
⑧ 74 ft. lbs. plus 90 degrees
⑨ 22 ft. lbs. plus 45 degrees
⑩ 33 ft. lbs. plus 90 degrees

⑪ Nuts: 18 ft. lbs.
　Studs: 96 inch lbs.
⑫ Plus three turns of 60 degrees;
　Plus 30-50 degrees after warm-up
⑬ Plus 45 degrees
⑭ Plus 30 degrees

BRAKE SPECIFICATIONS
All measurements in inches unless noted

Year	Model	Master Cylinder Bore	Brake Disc Original Thickness	Brake Disc Minimum Thickness	Brake Disc Maximum Runout	Brake Drum Original Inside Diameter	Brake Drum Max. Wear Limit	Brake Drum Maximum Machine Diameter	Minimum Lining Thickness Front	Minimum Lining Thickness Rear
1992	Cavalier	0.875	0.885	0.830	0.004	7.879	7.929	7.899	0.125	0.125
	Sunbird	0.874	0.806	0.736	0.002	7.880	7.929	7.900	0.030	0.030
1993	Cavalier	0.875	0.885	0.830	0.004	7.879	7.929	7.899	0.125	0.125
	Sunbird	0.874	0.806	0.736	0.002	7.874	7.929	7.899	0.030	0.030
1994	Cavalier	0.875	0.885	0.830	0.004	7.879	7.929	7.899	0.125	0.125
	Sunbird	0.874	0.806	0.736	0.002	7.874	7.929	7.899	0.030	0.030
1995-96	Cavalier	0.875	0.786	0.736	0.003	7.879	7.929	7.899	0.125	0.125

WHEEL ALIGNMENT

Year	Model		Caster Range (deg.)	Caster Preferred Setting (deg.)	Camber Range (deg.)	Camber Preferred Setting (deg.)	Toe-in (in.)	Steering Axis Inclination (deg.)
1992	Cavalier	F	11/16P-2 11/16P	1 11/16P	11/16N-11/16P	0	0	13 1/2
		R	-	-	13/16N-5/16P	1/4N	1/4P	-
	Sunbird	F	11/16P-2 11/16P	1 11/16P	11/16N-11/16P	0	0	13 1/2
		R	-	-	13/16N-5/16P	1/4N	1/4P	-
1993	Cavalier	F	5/16P-2 5/16P	1 5/16P	7/8N-9/16P	5/32N	0	13 1/2
		R	-	-	13/16N-5/16P	1/4N	1/8P	-
	Sunbird	F	5/16P-2 5/16P	1 5/16P	7/8N-9/16P	5/32N	0	13 1/2
		R	-	-	13/16N-5/16P	1/4N	1/8P	-
1994	Cavalier	F	5/16P-2 5/16P	1 5/16P	7/8N-9/16P	5/32N	0	13 1/2
		R	-	-	13/16N-5/16P	1/4N	1/8P	-
	Sunbird	F	5/16P-2 5/16P	1 5/16P	7/8N-9/16P	5/32N	0	13 1/2
		R	-	-	13/16N-5/16P	1/4N	1/8P	-
1995-96	Cavalier	F	5/16P-2 5/16P	1 5/16P	7/8N-9/16P	5/32N	0	13 1/2
		R	-	-	13/16N-5/16P	1/4N	1/8P	-

F - Front　　R - Rear

BERETTA/CORSICA

VEHICLE IDENTIFICATION CHART

		Engine Code					
Code	Liters	Cu. In. (cc)	Cyl.	Fuel Sys.	Eng. Mfg.		
4	2.2	133 (2180)	4	MFI	CUS		
A	2.3	138 (2262)	4	MFI	CUS		
M	3.1	191 (3130)	6	MFI	CPC		
T	3.1	191 (3130)	6	MFI	CPC		

	Model Year
Code	Year
N	1992
P	1993
R	1994
S	1995
T	1996

CUS - Chevrolet/United States
CPC - Chevrolet/Pontiac/Canada
MFI - Multiport fuel injection

ENGINE IDENTIFICATION

Year	Model	Engine Displacement Liters (cc)	Engine Series (ID/VIN)	Fuel System	No. of Cylinders	Engine Type
1992	Beretta	2.2 (2180)	4	TFI	4	OHV
	Beretta	2.3 (2262)	A	MFI	4	DOHC
	Beretta	3.1 (3130)	T	MFI	6	OHV
	Corsica	2.2 (2180)	4	MFI	4	OHV
	Corsica	3.1 (3130)	T	MFI	6	OHV
1993	Beretta	2.2 (2180)	4	MFI	4	OHV
	Beretta	2.3 (2262)	A	MFI	4	DOHC
	Beretta	3.1 (3130)	T	MFI	6	OHV
	Corsica	2.2 (2180)	4	MFI	4	OHV
	Corsica	3.1 (3130)	T	MFI	6	OHV
1994	Beretta	2.2 (2180)	4	MFI	4	OHV
	Beretta	2.3 (2262)	A	MFI	4	DOHC
	Beretta	3.1 (3130)	M	MFI	6	OHV
	Corsica	2.2 (2180)	4	MFI	4	OHV
	Corsica	3.1 (3130)	M	MFI	6	OHV
1995-96	Beretta	2.2 (2180)	4	MFI	4	OHV
	Beretta	3.1 (3130)	M	MFI	6	OHV
	Corsica	2.2 (2180)	4	MFI	4	OHV
	Corsica	3.1 (3130)	M	MFI	6	OHV

TFI - Throttle body fuel injection
MFI - Multiport fuel injection
OHV - Overhead valve
DOHC - Double overhead camshaft

GENERAL ENGINE SPECIFICATIONS

Year	Engine ID/VIN	Engine Displacement Liters (cc)	Fuel System Type	Net Horsepower @ rpm	Net Torque @ rpm (ft. lbs.)	Bore x Stroke (in.)	Compression Ratio	Oil Pressure @ rpm
1992	4	2.2 (2180)	TFI	95@5200	120@3200	3.50x3.46	9.0:1	63-77@1200
	A	2.3 (2262)	MFI	180@6200	160@5200	3.62x3.46	10.0:1	30@2000
	T	3.1 (3130)	MFI	140@4200	185@3200	3.50x3.31	8.5:1	8@600
1993	4	2.2 (2180)	MFI	110@5200	130@3200	3.50x3.46	9.0:1	63-77@1200
	A	2.3 (2262)	MFI	180@6200	160@5200	3.62x3.46	10.0:1	30@2000
	T	3.1 (3130)	MFI	140@4200	185@3200	3.50x3.31	8.5:1	8@600
1994	4	2.2 (2180)	MFI	110@5200	130@3200	3.50x3.46	9.0:1	63-77@1200
	A	2.3 (2262)	MFI	180@6200	160@5200	3.62x3.46	10.0:1	30@2000
	M	3.1 (3130)	MFI	155@5200	185@4000	3.50x3.31	9.6:1	15@1100
1995-96	4	2.2 (2180)	MFI	120@5200	130@3200	3.50x3.46	9.0:1	63-77@1200
	M	3.1 (3130)	MFI	155@5200	185@4000	3.50x3.31	9.6:1	15@1100

TFI - Throttle body fuel injection

MFI - Multiport fuel injection

GASOLINE ENGINE TUNE-UP SPECIFICATIONS

Year	Engine ID/VIN	Engine Displacement Liters (cc)	Spark Plugs Gap (in.)	Ignition Timing (deg.) MT	Ignition Timing (deg.) AT	Fuel Pump (psi)	Idle Speed (rpm) MT	Idle Speed (rpm) AT	Valve Clearance In.	Valve Clearance Ex.
1992	4	2.2 (2180)	0.035	①	①	9-13	①	①	HYD	HYD
	A	2.3 (2262)	0.035	①	①	41-47	①	①	HYD	HYD
	T	3.1 (3130)	0.045	10B	10B	41-47	①	①	HYD	HYD
1993	4	2.2 (2180)	0.045	①	①	41-47	①	①	HYD	HYD
	A	2.3 (2262)	0.035	①	①	41-47	①	①	HYD	HYD
	T	3.1 (3130)	0.045	①	①	41-47	①	①	HYD	HYD
1994	4	2.2 (2180)	0.045	①	①	41-47	①	①	HYD	HYD
	A	2.3 (2262)	0.035	①	①	41-47	①	①	HYD	HYD
	M	3.1 (3130)	0.045	①	①	15	①	①	HYD	HYD
1995-96	4	2.2 (2180)	0.045	①	①	41-47	①	①	HYD	HYD
	M	3.1 (3130)	0.045	①	①	15	①	①	HYD	HYD

NOTE: The Vehicle Emission Control Information label often reflects specification changes made during production. The label figures must be used if they differ from those in this chart.

B - Before top dead center

HYD - Hydraulic

① Refer to Vehicle Emission Control Information label

CAPACITIES

Year	Model	Engine ID/VIN	Engine Displacement Liters (cc)	Engine Oil with Filter (qts.)	Transmission (pts.) 4-Spd	5-Spd	Auto.	Drive Axle Front (pts.)	Rear (pts.)	Fuel Tank (gal.)	Cooling System (qts.)
1992	Beretta	G	2.2 (2180)	4.5	-	4.0	14.0 ①	-	-	15.6	9.5
	Beretta	A	2.3 (2262)	4.5	-	4.0	14.0 ①	-	-	15.6	9.5
	Beretta	T	3.1 (3130)	4.5	-	4.0	14.0 ①	-	-	15.6	②
	Corsica	G	2.2 (2180)	4.5	-	4.0	14.0 ①	-	-	15.6	9.5
	Corsica	T	3.1 (3130)	4.5	-	4.0	14.0 ①	-	-	15.6	②
1993	Beretta	4	2.2 (2180)	4.5	-	4.0	14.0 ①	-	-	15.6	9.5
	Beretta	A	2.3 (2262)	4.5	-	4.0	14.0 ①	-	-	15.6	9.5
	Beretta	T	3.1 (3130)	4.5	-	4.0	14.0 ①	-	-	15.6	②
	Corsica	4	2.2 (2180)	4.5	-	4.0	14.0 ①	-	-	15.6	9.5
	Corsica	T	3.1 (3130)	4.5	-	4.0	14.0 ①	-	-	15.6	②
1994	Beretta	4	2.2 (2180)	4.5	-	4.0	14.0 ①	-	-	15.6	9.5
	Beretta	A	2.3 (2262)	4.5	-	4.0	14.0 ①	-	-	15.6	9.5
	Beretta	M	3.1 (3130)	4.5	-	4.0	14.0 ①	-	-	15.6	②
	Corsica	4	2.2 (2180)	4.5	-	4.0	14.0 ①	-	-	15.6	9.5
	Corsica	M	3.1 (3130)	4.5	-	4.0	14.0 ①	-	-	15.6	②
1995-96	Beretta	4	2.2 (2180)	4.5	-	4.0	14.0 ①	-	-	15.6	9.5
	Beretta	M	3.1 (3130)	4.5	-	4.0	14.0 ①	-	-	15.6	②
	Corsica	4	2.2 (2180)	4.5	-	4.0	14.0 ①	-	-	15.6	9.5
	Corsica	M	3.1 (3130)	4.5	-	4.0	14.0 ①	-	-	15.6	②

① Drain and refill figure, overhaul: 16.0 pts.
② Automatic transmission: 12.4 qts.
   Manual transmission: 11.8 qts.

CAMSHAFT SPECIFICATIONS
All measurements given in inches.

Year	Engine ID/VIN	Engine Displacement Liters (cc)	Journal Diameter 1	2	3	4	5	Elevation In.	Ex.	Bearing Clearance	Camshaft End Play
1992	4	2.2 (2180)	1.867-1.869	1.867-1.869	1.867-1.869	1.867-1.869	1.867-1.869	0.259	0.259	0.0010-0.0039	NA
	A	2.3 (2262)	1.572-1.573	1.375-1.376	1.375-1.376	1.375-1.376	1.375-1.376	0.410	0.410	0.0020-0.0040	0.010-0.009
	T	3.1 (3130)	1.868-1.881	1.868-1.881	1.868-1.881	1.868-1.881	NA	0.263	0.273	0.0010-0.0039	NA
1993	4	2.2 (2180)	1.867-1.869	1.867-1.869	1.867-1.869	1.867-1.869	1.867-1.869	0.259	0.259	0.0010-0.0039	NA
	A	2.3 (2262)	1.572-1.573	1.375-1.376	1.375-1.376	1.375-1.376	1.375-1.376	0.410	0.410	0.0020-0.0040	0.0010-0.0090
	T	3.1 (3130)	1.868-1.881	1.868-1.881	1.868-1.881	1.868-1.881	NA	0.263	0.273	0.0010-0.0039	NA

CAMSHAFT SPECIFICATIONS

All measurements given in inches.

Year	Engine ID/VIN	Engine Displacement Liters (cc)	Journal Diameter					Elevation		Bearing Clearance	Camshaft End Play
			1	2	3	4	5	In.	Ex.		
1994	4	2.2 (2180)	1.867-1.869	1.867-1.869	1.867-1.869	1.867-1.869	1.867-1.869	0.259	0.259	0.0010-0.0039	NA
	A	2.3 (2262)	1.572-1.573	1.375-1.376	1.375-1.376	1.375-1.376	1.375-1.376	0.410	0.410	0.0020-0.0040	0.0010-0.0090
	M	3.1 (3130)	1.868-1.869	1.868-1.869	1.868-1.869	1.868-1.869	1.868-1.869	0.2727	0.2727	0.0010-0.0040	NA
1995-96	4	2.2 (2180)	1.8670-1.8690	1.8670-1.8690	1.8670-1.8690	1.8670-1.8690	1.8670-1.8690	0.2880	0.2880	0.0010-0.0039	NA
	M	3.1 (3130)	1.8680-1.8690	1.8680-1.8690	1.8680-1.8690	1.8680-1.8690	1.8680-1.8690	0.2727	0.2727	0.0010-0.0040	NA

NA - Not Available

CRANKSHAFT AND CONNECTING ROD SPECIFICATIONS

All measurements are given in inches.

Year	Engine ID/VIN	Engine Displacement Liters (cc)	Crankshaft				Connecting Rod		
			Main Brg. Journal Dia.	Main Brg. Oil Clearance	Shaft End-play	Thrust on No.	Journal Diameter	Oil Clearance	Side Clearance
1992	4	2.2 (2180)	2.4945-2.4954	0.0006-0.0019	0.002-0.007	4	1.9983-1.9994	0.0010-0.0030	0.0040-0.0150
	A	2.3 (2262)	2.0470-2.0480	0.0005-0.0023	0.003-0.009	3	1.8887-1.8897	0.0005-0.0020	0.0059-0.0177
	T	3.1 (3130)	2.6473-2.6483	0.0012-0.0030	0.002-0.008	3	1.9983-1.9994	0.0010-0.0040	0.0140-0.0270
1993	4	2.2 (2180)	2.4945-2.4954	0.0006-0.0019	0.002-0.007	4	1.9983-1.9994	0.0010-0.0030	0.0040-0.0150
	A	2.3 (2262)	2.0470-2.0480	0.0005-0.0023	0.003-0.009	3	1.8887-1.8897	0.0005-0.0020	0.0059-0.0177
	T	3.1 (3130)	2.6473-2.6483	0.0012-0.0030	0.002-0.008	3	1.9983-1.9994	0.0010-0.0040	0.0140-0.0270
1994	4	2.2 (2180)	2.4945-2.4954	0.0006-0.0019	0.002-0.007	4	1.9983-1.9994	0.0010-0.0030	0.0040-0.0150
	A	2.3 (2262)	2.0470-2.0480	0.0005-0.0023	0.003-0.009	3	1.8887-1.8897	0.0005-0.0020	0.0059-0.0177
	M	3.1 (3130)	2.6473-2.6483	0.0012-0.0030	0.0024-0.0083	3	1.9982-1.9984	0.0011-0.0037	0.0071-0.0173
1995-96	4	2.2 (2180)	2.4945-2.4954	0.0006-0.0019	0.0020-0.0070	4	1.9983-1.9994	0.0010-0.0030	0.0040-0.0150
	M	3.1 (3130)	2.6473-2.6483	0.0012-0.0030	0.0024-0.0083	3	1.9982-1.9984	0.0011-0.0037	0.0071-0.0173

VALVE SPECIFICATIONS

Year	Engine ID/VIN	Engine Displacement Liters (cc)	Seat Angle (deg.)	Face Angle (deg.)	Spring Test Pressure (lbs. @ in.)	Spring Installed Height (in.)	Stem-to-Guide Clearance (in.)		Stem Diameter (in.)	
							Intake	Exhaust	Intake	Exhaust
1992	4	2.2 (2180)	46	45	208-222@ ① 1.22	1.61 ②	0.0011-0.0026	0.0014-0.0030	NA	NA
	A	2.3 (2262)	45	44	193-207@ ① 1.04	1.44 ②	0.0010-0.0027	0.0015-0.0032	0.2740-0.2750	0.2740-0.2750
	R	2.5 (2475)	45	46	75@1.68	1.68	0.0010-0.0026	0.0013-0.0041	NA	NA
	T	3.1 (3130)	46	45	90 ①	1.60 ②	0.0010-0.0027	0.0010-0.0027	NA	NA
	X	3.4 (3393)	46	45	75@1.40	1.40	0.0011-0.0026	0.0014-0.0031	NA	NA
	Z	4.3 (4294)	46	45	194-206@ 1.25	1.69-1.71	0.0011-0.0027	0.0011-0.0027	NA	NA
	E	5.0 (4999)	46	45	194-206@ 1.25	③	0.0011-0.0027	0.0011-0.0027	NA	NA
	F	5.0 (4999)	46	45	194-206@ 1.25	③	0.0010-0.0027	0.0010-0.0027	NA	NA
	J	5.7 (5737)	44	45	147-166@ ④ 0.95	1.34 ⑤	0.0011-0.0027	0.0011-0.0027	NA	NA
	7	5.7 (5737)	46	45	194-206@ 1.25	1.70	0.0011-0.0027	0.0011-0.0027	NA	NA
	8	5.7 (5737)	46	45	194-206@ 1.25	③	0.0011-0.0027	0.0011-0.0027	NA	NA
1993	4	2.2 (2180)	46	45	225-233@ ① 1.25	1.64 ②	0.0011-0.0026	0.0014-0.0031	NA	NA
	A	2.3 (2262)	45	44	193-207@ ① 1.04	1.44 ②	0.0010-0.0027	0.0015-0.0032	0.2740-0.2750	0.2740-0.2750
	T	3.1 (3130)	46	45	90 ①	1.60 ②	0.0010-0.0027	0.0010-0.0027	NA	NA
	S	3.4 (3393)	46	45	190@1.20	1.61	0.0014-0.0025	0.0015-0.0029	NA	NA
	X	3.4 (3393)	46	45	75@1.40	1.40	0.0011-0.0026	0.0014-0.0031	NA	NA
	Z	4.3 (4294)	46	45	194-206@ 1.25	1.69-1.71	0.0011-0.0027	0.0011-0.0027	NA	NA
	E	5.0 (4999)	46	45	194-206@ 1.25	③	0.0011-0.0027	0.0011-0.0027	NA	NA
	J	5.7 (5737)	44	45	147-166@ ④ 0.95	1.34 ⑤	0.0012-0.0026	0.0014-0.0030	NA	NA
	P	5.7 (5737)	46	45	252-272@ 1.305	1.78	0.0011-0.0027	0.0011-0.0027	NA	NA
	7	5.7 (5737)	46	45	194-206@ 1.25	1.70	0.0011-0.0027	0.0011-0.0027	NA	NA

VALVE SPECIFICATIONS

Year	Engine ID/VIN	Engine Displacement Liters (cc)	Seat Angle (deg.)	Face Angle (deg.)	Spring Test Pressure (lbs. @ in.)	Spring Installed Height (in.)	Stem-to-Guide Clearance (in.) Intake	Stem-to-Guide Clearance (in.) Exhaust	Stem Diameter (in.) Intake	Stem Diameter (in.) Exhaust
1994	4	2.2 (2180)	46	45	225-233@ ① 1.25	1.64 ②	0.0011- 0.0026	0.0014- 0.0031	NA	NA
	A	2.3 (2262)	45	44	193-207@ ① 1.04	1.44 ②	0.0010- 0.0027	0.0015- 0.0032	0.2740- 0.2750	0.2740- 0.2750
	M	3.1 (3130)	45	45	80@1.71	1.71	0.0010- 0.0027	0.0010- 0.0027	NA	NA
	T	3.1 (3130)	46	45	90 ①	1.60 ②	0.0010- 0.0027	0.0010- 0.0027	NA	NA
	S	3.4 (3393)	46	45	190@1.20	1.61	0.0014- 0.0025	0.0015- 0.0029	NA	NA
	X	3.4 (3393)	46	45	75@1.40	1.40	0.0011- 0.0026	0.0014- 0.0031	NA	NA
	W	4.3 (4294)	46	45	187-203@ 1.27	1.70	0.0009- 0.0027	0.0009- 0.0027	NA	NA
	J	5.7 (5737)	44	45	147-166@ ④ 0.95	1.34 ⑤	0.0012- 0.0026	0.0014- 0.0030	NA	NA
	P	5.7 (5737)	46	45	187-203@ 1.27	1.70	0.0009- 0.0027	0.0009- 0.0027	NA	NA
1995-96	4	2.2 (2180)	46	45	225-233@ ① 1.25	1.64 ②	0.0011- 0.0026	0.0014- 0.0031	NA	NA
	D	2.3 (2262)	45	44	193-207@ 1.04	1.44 ②	0.0010- 0.0027	0.0015- 0.0032	0.2740- 0.2750	0.2740- 0.2750
	M	3.1 (3130)	45	45	80@1.71	1.71	0.0010- 0.0027	0.0010- 0.0027	NA	NA
	S	3.4 (3393)	46	45	190@1.20	1.61	0.0014- 0.0025	0.0015- 0.0029	NA	NA
	X	3.4 (3393)	46	45	75@1.40	1.40	0.0011- 0.0026	0.0014- 0.0031	NA	NA
	W	4.3 (4294)	46	45	187-203@ 1.27	1.70	0.0009- 0.0027	0.0009- 0.0027	NA	NA
	J	5.7 (5737)	44	45	147-166@ 0.95	1.34 ⑤	0.0012- 0.0026	0.0014- 0.0030	NA	NA
	P	5.7 (5737)	46	45	187-203@ 1.27	1.70	0.0009- 0.0027	0.0009- 0.0027	NA	NA

NA - Not Available
① 1 With valve open
② 2 With valve closed
③ 3 Intake: 1.72
    Exhaust: 1.59
④ 4 Inner spring: 75-82@0.79 in.
⑤ 5 Inner spring: 1.18 in.

PISTON AND RING SPECIFICATIONS

All measurements are given in inches.

Year	Engine ID/VIN	Engine Displacement Liters (cc)	Piston Clearance	Ring Gap			Ring Side Clearance		
				Top Compression	Bottom Compression	Oil Control	Top Compression	Bottom Compression	Oil Control
1992	4	2.2 (2180)	0.0007-0.0017	0.010-0.020	0.010-0.020	0.010-0.050	0.002-0.003	0.002-0.003	0.0020-0.0082
	A	2.3 (2262)	0.0007-0.0020	0.014-0.024	0.016-0.026	0.016-0.055	0.003-0.005	0.002-0.003	NA
	T	3.1 (3130)	0.0009-0.0022	0.010-0.020	0.020-0.028	0.010-0.030	0.002-0.003	0.002-0.003	0.008
1993	4	2.2 (2180)	0.0007-0.0017	0.010-0.020	0.010-0.020	0.010-0.050	0.002-0.003	0.002-0.003	0.0020-0.0082
	A	2.3 (2262)	0.0007-0.0020	0.014-0.024	0.016-0.026	0.016-0.055	0.003-0.005	0.002-0.003	NA
	T	3.1 (3130)	0.0009-0.0022	0.010-0.020	0.020-0.028	0.010-0.030	0.002-0.003	0.002-0.003	0.008
1994	4	2.2 (2180)	0.0007-0.0017	0.010-0.020	0.010-0.020	0.010-0.050	0.002-0.003	0.002-0.003	0.0020-0.0082
	A	2.3 (2262)	0.0007-0.0020	0.014-0.024	0.016-0.026	0.016-0.055	0.003-0.005	0.002-0.003	NA
	M	3.1 (3130)	0.0013-0.0027	0.007-0.016	0.020-0.028	0.010-0.030	0.0020-0.0035	0.0020-0.0035	0.0080 MAX
1995-96	4	2.2 (2180)	0.0007-0.0017	0.010-0.020	0.010-0.020	0.010-0.050	0.0020-0.0030	0.0020-0.0030	0.0020-0.0082
	M	3.1 (3130)	0.0013-0.0027	0.007-0.016	0.020-0.028	0.010-0.030	0.0020-0.0035	0.0020-0.0035	0.0080 MAX

NA - Not Available

TORQUE SPECIFICATIONS

All readings in ft. lbs.

Year	Engine ID/VIN	Engine Displacement Liters (cc)	Cylinder Head Bolts	Main Bearing Bolts	Rod Bearing Bolts	Crankshaft Damper Bolts	Flywheel Bolts	Manifold		Spark Plugs	Lug Nut
								Intake	Exhaust		
1992	4	2.2 (2180)	①	77	38	85 ②	52-55	18	6-13	20	80-100
	A	2.3 (2262)	26 ⑤	⑦	⑧	⑨	⑩	③	④	17	80-100
	T	3.1 (3130)	⑪	73	39	66-85	45-59	⑥	18	20	100
1993	4	2.2 (2180)	①	77	38	85 ②	52-55	18	6-13	20	80-100
	A	2.3 (2262)	26 ⑤	⑦	⑧	⑨	⑩	⑭	④	17	80-100
	T	3.1 (3130)	⑪	73	39	66-85	45-59	⑥	18	20	100
1994	4	2.2 (2180)	①	77	38	85 ②	52-55	18	6-13	20	100
	A	2.3 (2262)	26 ⑤	⑦	⑧	⑨	⑩	⑭	④	17	100
	M	3.1 (3130)	⑪	⑫	37	76	61	⑬	12	11	100
1995-96	4	2.2 (2180)	①	77	38	85 ②	52-55	18	6-13	20	100
	M	3.1 (3130)	⑪	⑫	37	76	61	⑬	12	11	100

TORQUE SPECIFICATIONS
All readings in ft. lbs.

Year	Engine ID/VIN	Engine Displacement Liters (cc)	Cylinder Head Bolts	Main Bearing Bolts	Rod Bearing Bolts	Crankshaft Damper Bolts	Flywheel Bolts	Manifold Intake	Manifold Exhaust	Spark Plugs	Lug Nut

NA - Not Available

① Step 1: 41 ft. lbs.
  Step 2: Tighten an additional 45 degrees
  Step 3: Tighten an additional 45 degrees
  Step 4: Long bolts 1, 4-5, 8-9 an additional 20 degrees
  Step 4: Short bolts 2-3, 6-7, 10 an additional 10 degrees
② Center bolt spec shown; Pulley to hub bolts: 37 ft. lbs.
③ Nuts: 37 ft. lbs.
  Studs: 96 inch lbs.

④ Bolts: 27 ft. lbs.
  Studs: 106 inch lbs.
⑤ Cylinder head bolts should be torqued 26 ft. lbs.
  Long bolts: 100 degrees
  Short bolts: 120 degrees
⑥ 15 ft. lbs., then 24 ft. lbs.
⑦ 15 ft. lbs. plus 90 degrees
⑧ 18 ft. lbs. plus 80 degrees

⑨ 74 ft. lbs. plus 90 degrees
⑩ 22 ft. lbs. plus 45 degrees
⑪ 33 ft. lbs. plus 90 degrees
⑫ 37 ft. lbs. plus 75 degrees
⑬ 115 inch lbs.
⑭ Nuts: 18 ft. lbs.
  Studs: 96 inch lbs.

BRAKE SPECIFICATIONS
All measurements in inches unless noted

Year	Model	Master Cylinder Bore	Brake Disc Original Thickness	Brake Disc Minimum Thickness	Brake Disc Maximum Runout	Brake Drum Diameter Original Inside Diameter	Brake Drum Diameter Max. Wear Limit	Brake Drum Diameter Maximum Machine Diameter	Minimum Lining Thickness Front	Minimum Lining Thickness Rear
1992	Beretta	0.945	0.885	0.830	0.004	7.879	7.929	7.899	0.940	0.940
	Corsica	0.945	0.885	0.830	0.004	7.879	7.929	7.899	0.940	0.940
1993	Beretta	0.945	0.885	0.830	0.004	7.879	7.929	7.899	0.940	0.940
	Corsica	0.945	0.885	0.830	0.004	7.879	7.929	7.899	0.940	0.940
1994	Beretta	0.945	0.885	0.830	0.004	7.879	7.929	7.899	0.940	0.940
	Corsica	0.945	0.885	0.830	0.004	7.879	7.929	7.899	0.940	0.940
1995-96	Beretta	0.945	0.885	0.830	0.004	7.879	7.929	7.899	0.940	0.940
	Corsica	0.945	0.885	0.830	0.004	7.879	7.929	7.899	0.940	0.940

WHEEL ALIGNMENT

Year	Model		Caster Range (deg.)	Caster Preferred Setting (deg.)	Camber Range (deg.)	Camber Preferred Setting (deg.)	Toe-in (in.)	Steering Axis Inclination (deg.)
1992	Beretta	F	13/32P-1 29/32P	1 5/32P	①	②	0	13 3/16
		R	-	-	7/8N-3/8P	1/4N	3/16P	-
	Corsica	F	13/32P-1 29/32P	1 5/32P	③	④	0	13 3/16
		R	-	-	7/8N-3/8P	1/4N	1/8P	-
1993	Beretta	F	3/16P-2 3/16P	1 3/16P	⑤	⑥	0	13 3/16
		R	-	-	7/8N-3/8P	1/4N	0	-
	Corsica	F	3/16P-2 3/16P	1 3/16P	⑤	⑥	0	13 3/16
		R	-	-	7/8N-3/8P	1/4N	0	-

WHEEL ALIGNMENT

Year	Model		Caster Range (deg.)	Caster Preferred Setting (deg.)	Camber Range (deg.)	Camber Preferred Setting (deg.)	Toe-in (in.)	Steering Axis Inclination (deg.)
1994	Beretta	F	3/16P-2 3/16P	1 3/16P	⑤	⑥	0	13 3/16
		R	-	-	7/8N-3/8P	1/4N	0	-
	Corsica	F	3/16P-2 3/16P	1 3/16P	⑤	⑥	0	13 3/16
		R	-	-	7/8N-3/8P	1/4N	1/8P	-
1995-96	Beretta	F	3/16P-2 3/16P	1 3/16P	⑤	⑥	0	13 3/16
		R	-	-	7/8N-3/8P	1/4N	0	-
	Corsica	F	3/16P-2 3/16P	1 3/16P	⑤	⑥	0	13 3/16
		R	-	-	7/8N-3/8P	1/4N	1/8P	-

NA - Not Available
F - Front
R - Rear

① All except sport susp.: 9/16N-13/16P
sport susp.: 13/16N-7/16P
② All except sport susp.: 1/8P
sport susp.: 3/16N

③ All except sport susp.: 9/16P-13/16P
sport susp.: 13/16N-7/16P
④ All except sport susp.: 1/8P
sport susp.: 3/16N

⑤ All except sport susp.: 11/16N-11/16P
sport susp.: 7/8N-9/16P
⑥ All except sport susp.: 0
sport susp.: 5/32N

ACHIEVA/GRAND AM/SKYLARK

VEHICLE IDENTIFICATION CHART

Code	Liters	Cu. In. (cc)	Cyl.	Fuel Sys.	Eng. Mfg.
3	2.3	138 (2261)	4	MFI	BOC
A	2.3	138 (2262)	4	MFI	BOC
D	2.3	138 (2261)	4	MFI	BOC
M	3.1	191 (3130)	6	MFI	BOC
N	3.3	204 (3342)	6	MFI	BOC

Code	Year
N	1992
P	1993
R	1994
S	1995
T	1996

MFI - Multiport fuel injection
BOC - Buick/Oldsmobile/Cadillac

ENGINE IDENTIFICATION

Year	Model	Engine Displacement Liters (cc)	Engine Series (ID/VIN)	Fuel System	No. of Cylinders	Engine Type
1992	Achieva	2.3 (2261)	3	MFI	4	DOHC
	Achieva	2.3 (2261)	A	MFI	4	DOHC
	Achieva	2.3 (2261)	D	MFI	4	DOHC
	Achieva	3.3 (3342)	N	MFI	6	OHV
	Grand Am	2.3 (2261)	3	MFI	4	SOHC
	Grand Am	2.3 (2261)	A	MFI	4	DOHC
	Grand Am	2.3 (2261)	D	MFI	4	DOHC
	Grand Am	3.3 (3342)	N	MFI	6	OHV
	Skylark	2.3 (2261)	3	MFI	4	SOHC
	Skylark	3.3 (3342)	N	MFI	6	OHV
1993	Achieva	2.3 (2261)	3	MFI	4	DOHC
	Achieva	2.3 (2261)	A	MFI	4	DOHC
	Achieva	2.3 (2261)	D	MFI	4	DOHC
	Achieva	3.3 (3342)	N	MFI	6	OHV
	Grand Am	2.3 (2261)	3	MFI	4	SOHC
	Grand Am	2.3 (2261)	A	MFI	4	DOHC
	Grand Am	2.3 (2261)	D	MFI	4	DOHC
	Grand Am	3.3 (3342)	N	MFI	6	OHV
	Skylark	2.3 (2261)	3	MFI	4	SOHC
	Skylark	3.3 (3342)	N	MFI	6	OHV
1994	Achieva	2.3 (2261)	3	MFI	4	DOHC
	Achieva	2.3 (2261)	A	MFI	4	DOHC
	Achieva	2.3 (2261)	D	MFI	4	DOHC
	Achieva	3.1 (3130)	M	MFI	6	OHV
	Grand Am	2.3 (2261)	3	MFI	4	SOHC
	Grand Am	2.3 (2261)	A	MFI	4	DOHC
	Grand Am	2.3 (2261)	D	MFI	4	DOHC
	Grand Am	3.1 (3130)	M	MFI	6	OHV
	Skylark	2.3 (2261)	3	MFI	4	SOHC
	Skylark	3.1 (3130)	M	MFI	6	OHV
1995-96	Achieva	2.3 (2261)	D	MFI	4	DOHC
	Achieva	3.1 (3130)	M	MFI	6	OHV
	Grand Am	2.3 (2261)	D	MFI	4	DOHC
	Grand Am	3.1 (3130)	M	MFI	6	OHV
	Skylark	2.3 (2261)	D	MFI	4	DOHC
	Skylark	3.1 (3130)	M	MFI	6	OHV

GENERAL ENGINE SPECIFICATIONS

Year	Engine ID/VIN	Engine Displacement Liters (cc)	Fuel System Type	Net Horsepower @ rpm	Net Torque @ rpm (ft. lbs.)	Bore x Stroke (in.)	Compression Ratio	Oil Pressure @ rpm
1992	3	2.3 (2262)	MFI	120@5200	140@3200	3.63x3.35	9.5:1	30@2000
	A	2.3 (2262)	MFI	180@6200	160@5200	3.63x3.35	10.0:1	30@2000
	D	2.3 (2262)	MFI	160@6200	155@5200	3.63x3.35	9.5:1	30@2000
	N	3.3 (3344)	MFI	160@5200	185@2000	3.70x3.16	9.0:1	60@1850
1993	3	2.3 (2262)	MFI	115@5200	140@3200	3.63x3.35	9.5:1	30@2000
	A	2.3 (2262)	MFI	175@6200	155@5200	3.63x3.35	10.0:1	30@2000
	D	2.3 (2262)	MFI	155@6000	150@4800	3.63x3.35	9.5:1	30@2000
	N	3.3 (3344)	MFI	160@5200	185@2000	3.70x3.16	9.0:1	60@1850

GENERAL ENGINE SPECIFICATIONS

Year	Engine ID/VIN	Engine Displacement Liters (cc)	Fuel System Type	Net Horsepower @ rpm	Net Torque @ rpm (ft. lbs.)	Bore x Stroke (in.)	Compression Ratio	Oil Pressure @ rpm
1994	3	2.3 (2262)	MFI	115@5200	140@3200	3.63x3.35	9.5:1	30@2000
	A	2.3 (2262)	MFI	175@6200	150@5200	3.63x3.35	10.0:1	30@2000
	D	2.3 (2262)	MFI	155@6000	150@6000	3.63x3.35	9.5:1	30@2000
	M	3.1 (3130)	MFI	160@5200	185@4000	3.50x3.31	9.5:1	15@1100
1995-96	D	2.3 (2261)	MFI	155@6000	145@4800	3.62x3.35	9.5:1	30@2000
	M	3.1 (3130)	MFI	160@5200	185@4000	3.50x3.31	9.5:1	15@1100

MFI - Multiport fuel injection

GASOLINE ENGINE TUNE-UP SPECIFICATIONS

Year	Engine ID/VIN	Engine Displacement Liters (cc)	Spark Plugs Gap (in.)	Ignition Timing (deg.) MT	Ignition Timing (deg.) AT	Fuel Pump (psi)	Idle Speed (rpm) MT	Idle Speed (rpm) AT	Valve Clearance In.	Valve Clearance Ex.
1992	3	2.3 (2262)	0.035	①	①	41-47	②	②	HYD	HYD
	A	2.3 (2262)	0.035	①	①	41-47	②	②	HYD	HYD
	D	2.3 (2262)	0.035	①	①	41-47	②	②	HYD	HYD
	N	3.3 (3344)	0.060	-	①	41-47	②	②	HYD	HYD
1993	3	2.3 (2262)	0.035	①	①	41-47	②	②	HYD	HYD
	A	2.3 (2262)	0.035	①	①	41-47	②	②	HYD	HYD
	D	2.3 (2262)	0.035	①	①	41-47	②	②	HYD	HYD
	N	3.3 (3344)	0.060	①	①	41-47	②	②	HYD	HYD
1994	3	2.3 (2262)	0.035	①	①	41-47	②	②	HYD	HYD
	A	2.3 (2262)	0.035	①	①	41-47	②	②	HYD	HYD
	D	2.3 (2262)	0.035	①	①	41-47	②	②	HYD	HYD
	M	3.1 (3130)	0.060	①	①	41-47	②	②	HYD	HYD
1995-96	D	2.3 (2262)	0.035	①	①	41-47	②	②	HYD	HYD
	M	3.1 (3130)	0.060	①	①	41-47	②	②	HYD	HYD

NOTE: The Vehicle Emission Control Information label often reflects specification changes made during production. The label figures must be used if they differ from those in this chart.
HYD - Hydraulic
① DIS Ignition System timing is not adjustable
② Idle speed is maintained by the ECM. There is no recommended adjustment procedure

CAPACITIES

Year	Model	Engine ID/VIN	Engine Displacement Liters (cc)	Engine Oil with Filter (qts.)	Transmission (pts.) 4-Spd	Transmission (pts.) 5-Spd	Transmission (pts.) Auto.	Drive Axle Front (pts.)	Drive Axle Rear (pts.)	Fuel Tank (gal.)	Cooling System (qts.)
1992	Achieva	3	2.3 (2262)	4.0 ①	-	4.0	8.0	-	-	15.2	10.4
	Achieva	A	2.3 (2262)	4.0 ①	-	4.0	8.0	-	-	15.2	10.4
	Achieva	D	2.3 (2262)	4.0 ①	-	4.0	8.0	-	-	15.2	10.4
	Achieva	N	3.3 (3344)	4.0 ①	-	4.0	8.0	-	-	15.2	10.8
	Grand Am	3	2.3 (2262)	4.0 ①	-	4.0	8.0	-	-	15.2	9.5
	Grand Am	A	2.3 (2262)	4.0 ①	-	4.0	8.0	-	-	15.2	9.5
	Grand Am	D	2.3 (2262)	4.0 ①	-	4.0	8.0	-	-	15.2	9.5
	Grand Am	N	3.3 (3344)	4.0 ①	-	-	8.0	-	-	15.2	12.7
	Skylark	3	2.3 (2262)	4.0 ①	-	4.0	8.0	-	-	15.2	9.5
	Skylark	N	3.3 (3344)	4.0 ①	-	-	8.0	-	-	15.2	12.7

CAPACITIES

Year	Model	Engine ID/VIN	Engine Displacement Liters (cc)	Engine Oil with Filter (qts.)	Transmission (pts.) 4-Spd	5-Spd	Auto.	Drive Axle Front (pts.)	Rear (pts.)	Fuel Tank (gal.)	Cooling System (qts.)
1993	Achieva	3	2.3 (2262)	4.0 ①	-	③	8.0	-	-	15.2	10.4
	Achieva	A	2.3 (2262)	4.0 ①	-	③	8.0	-	-	15.2	10.4
	Achieva	D	2.3 (2262)	4.0 ①	-	③	8.0	-	-	15.2	10.4
	Achieva	N	3.3 (3344)	4.0 ①	-	③	8.0	-	-	15.2	10.8
	Grand Am	3	2.3 (2262)	4.0 ①	-	4.0	8.0	-	-	15.2	9.5
	Grand Am	A	2.3 (2262)	4.0 ①	-	4.0	8.0	-	-	15.2	9.5
	Grand Am	D	2.3 (2262)	4.0 ①	-	4.0	8.0	-	-	15.2	9.5
	Grand Am	N	3.3 (3344)	4.0 ①	-	-	8.0	-	-	15.2	12.7
	Skylark	3	2.3 (2262)	4.0 ①	-	-	8.0	-	-	15.2	9.5
	Skylark	N	3.3 (3344)	4.0 ①	-	-	8.0	-	-	15.2	12.7
1994	Achieva	3	2.3 (2262)	4.0 ①	-	⑤	④	-	-	15.2	10.4
	Achieva	A	2.3 (2262)	4.0 ①	-	⑤	④	-	-	15.2	10.4
	Achieva	D	2.3 (2262)	4.0 ①	-	⑤	④	-	-	15.2	10.4
	Achieva	M	3.1 (3130)	4.0 ①	-	⑤	④	-	-	15.2	10.8
	Grand Am	3	2.3 (2262)	4.0 ①	-	4.0	8.0 ②	-	-	15.2	10.4
	Grand Am	A	2.3 (2262)	4.0 ①	-	4.0	8.0 ②	-	-	15.2	10.4
	Grand Am	D	2.3 (2262)	4.0 ①	-	4.0	8.0 ②	-	-	15.2	10.4
	Grand Am	M	3.1 (3130)	4.0 ①	-	4.0	8.0 ②	-	-	15.2	10.4
	Skylark	3	2.3 (2262)	4.0 ①	-	-	8.0 ②	-	-	15.2	10.4
	Skylark	M	3.1 (3130)	4.0 ①	-	-	8.0 ②	-	-	15.2	10.4
1995-96	Achieva	D	2.3 (2262)	4.0 ①	-	⑤	④	-	-	15.2	10.4
	Achieva	M	3.1 (3130)	3.8 ①	-	⑤	④	-	-	15.2	10.8
	Grand Am	D	2.3 (2262)	4.0 ①	-	4.0	8.0 ②	-	-	15.2	10.4
	Grand Am	M	3.1 (3130)	3.8 ①	-	4.0	8.0 ②	-	-	15.2	13.1
	Skylark	D	2.3 (2262)	4.0 ①	-	-	8.0 ②	-	-	15.2	10.4
	Skylark	M	3.1 (3130)	4.0 ①	-	-	8.0 ②	-	-	15.2	13.1

① Capacity is without filter replacement; Additional oil may be required
② With 4T60E transaxle: 12.0 pts.
③ With T550: 4.2
   With Isuzu: 4.0
④ 3 speed: 8.0
   4 speed: 14.8
⑤ Engine VIN code A: 4.2
   Engine VIN code 3: 4.0

CAMSHAFT SPECIFICATIONS
All measurements given in inches.

Year	Engine ID/VIN	Engine Displacement Liters (cc)	Journal Diameter 1	2	3	4	5	Elevation In.	Ex.	Bearing Clearance	Camshaft End Play
1992	3	2.3 (2262)	1.5720-1.5728	1.3751-1.3760	1.3751-1.3760	1.3751-1.3760	1.3751-1.3760	0.4100	0.4100	0.0019-0.0043	0.0009-0.0088
	A	2.3 (2262)	1.5720-1.5728	1.3751-1.3760	1.3751-1.3760	1.3751-1.3760	1.3751-1.3760	0.4100	0.4100	0.0019-0.0043	0.0009-0.0088
	D	2.3 (2262)	1.5720-1.5728	1.3751-1.3760	1.3751-1.3760	1.3751-1.3760	1.3751-1.3760	0.3750	0.3750	0.0019-0.0043	0.0009-0.0088
	N	3.3 (3344)	1.7850-1.7860	1.7850-1.7860	1.7850-1.7860	1.7850-1.7860	1.7850-1.7860	0.2500	0.2550	0.0005-0.0035	NA

CAMSHAFT SPECIFICATIONS
All measurements given in inches.

Year	Engine ID/VIN	Engine Displacement Liters (cc)	Journal Diameter 1	2	3	4	5	Elevation In.	Ex.	Bearing Clearance	Camshaft End Play
1993	3	2.3 (2262)	1.5720-1.5728	1.3751-1.3760	1.3751-1.3760	1.3751-1.3760	1.3751-1.3760	0.4100	0.4100	0.0019-0.0043	0.0009-0.0088
	A	2.3 (2262)	1.5720-1.5728	1.3751-1.3760	1.3751-1.3760	1.3751-1.3760	1.3751-1.3760	0.4100	0.4100	0.0019-0.0043	0.0009-0.0088
	D	2.3 (2262)	1.5720-1.5728	1.3751-1.3760	1.3751-1.3760	1.3751-1.3760	1.3751-1.3760	0.3750	0.3750	0.0019-0.0043	0.0009-0.0088
	N	3.3 (3344)	1.7850-1.7860	1.7850-1.7860	1.7850-1.7860	1.7850-1.7860	1.7850-1.7860	0.2500	0.2550	0.0005-0.0035	NA
1994	3	2.3 (2262)	1.5720-1.5728	1.3751-1.3760	1.3751-1.3760	1.3751-1.3760	1.3751-1.3760	0.4100	0.4100	0.0019-0.0043	0.0009-0.0088
	A	2.3 (2262)	1.5720-1.5728	1.3751-1.3760	1.3751-1.3760	1.3751-1.3760	1.3751-1.3760	0.4100	0.4100	0.0019-0.0043	0.0009-0.0088
	D	2.3 (2262)	1.5720-1.5728	1.3751-1.3760	1.3751-1.3760	1.3751-1.3760	1.3751-1.3760	0.4100	0.4100	0.0019-0.0043	0.0009-0.0088
	M	3.1 (3130)	1.8680-1.8690	1.8680-1.8690	1.8680-1.8690	1.8680-1.8690	1.8680-1.8690	0.2727	0.2727	0.0010-0.0040	NA
1995-96	D	2.3 (2262)	1.5720-1.5728	1.3751-1.3760	1.3751-1.3760	1.3751-1.3760	1.3751-1.3760	0.4100	0.4100	0.0019-0.0043	0.0009-0.0088
	M	3.1 (3130)	1.8860-1.8690	1.8860-1.8690	1.8860-1.8690	1.8860-1.8690	1.8680-1.8690	0.2727	0.2727	0.0010-0.0040	NA

NA - Not Available

CRANKSHAFT AND CONNECTING ROD SPECIFICATIONS
All measurements are given in inches.

Year	Engine ID/VIN	Engine Displacement Liters (cc)	Crankshaft Main Brg. Journal Dia.	Main Brg. Oil Clearance	Shaft End-play	Thrust on No.	Connecting Rod Journal Diameter	Oil Clearance	Side Clearance
1992	3	2.3 (2262)	2.0470-2.0480	0.0005-0.0023	0.0034-0.0095	3	1.8887-1.8897	0.0005-0.0020	0.0059-0.0177
	A	2.3 (2262)	2.0470-2.0480	0.0005-0.0023	0.0034-0.0095	3	1.8887-1.8897	0.0005-0.0020	0.0059-0.0177
	D	2.3 (2262)	2.0470-2.0480	0.0005-0.0023	0.0034-0.0095	3	1.8887-1.8897	0.0005-0.0020	0.0059-0.0177
	N	3.3 (3344)	2.4988-2.4998	0.0018-0.0030	0.0030-0.0110	2	2.2487-2.2499	0.0008-0.0022	0.0030-0.0150
1993	3	2.3 (2262)	2.0470-2.0480	0.0005-0.0023	0.0034-0.0095	3	1.8887-1.8897	0.0005-0.0020	0.0059-0.0177
	A	2.3 (2262)	2.0470-2.0480	0.0005-0.0023	0.0034-0.0095	3	1.8887-1.8897	0.0005-0.0020	0.0059-0.0177
	D	2.3 (2262)	2.0470-2.0480	0.0005-0.0023	0.0034-0.0095	3	1.8887-1.8897	0.0005-0.0020	0.0059-0.0177
	N	3.3 (3344)	2.4988-2.4998	0.0008-0.0022	0.0030-0.0110	2	2.2487-2.2499	0.0008-0.0022	0.0030-0.0150
1994	3	2.3 (2262)	2.0470-2.0480	0.0005-0.0023	0.0034-0.0095	3	1.8887-1.8897	0.0005-0.0020	0.0059-0.0177
	A	2.3 (2262)	2.0470-2.0480	0.0005-0.0023	0.0034-0.0095	3	1.8887-1.8897	0.0005-0.0020	0.0059-0.0177

CRANKSHAFT AND CONNECTING ROD SPECIFICATIONS
All measurements are given in inches.

Year	Engine ID/VIN	Engine Displacement Liters (cc)	Crankshaft				Connecting Rod		
			Main Brg. Journal Dia.	Main Brg. Oil Clearance	Shaft End-play	Thrust on No.	Journal Diameter	Oil Clearance	Side Clearance
	D	2.3 (2262)	2.0470-2.0480	0.0005-0.0023	0.0034-0.0095	3	1.8887-1.8897	0.0005-0.0020	0.0059-0.0177
	M	3.1 (3130)	2.6473-2.6483	0.0012-0.0030	0.0024-0.0083	3	1.9982-1.9984	0.0011-0.0037	0.0071-0.0173
1995-96	D	2.3 (2262)	2.0470-2.0480	0.0005-0.0023	0.0034-0.0095	3	1.8887-1.8897	0.0005-0.0020	0.0059-0.0177
	M	3.1 (3130)	2.6473-2.6483	0.0012-0.0030	0.0024-0.0083	3	1.9982-1.9984	0.0011-0.0037	0.0071-0.0173

VALVE SPECIFICATIONS

Year	Engine ID/VIN	Engine Displacement Liters (cc)	Seat Angle (deg.)	Face Angle (deg.)	Spring Test Pressure (lbs. @ in.)	Spring Installed Height (in.)	Stem-to-Guide Clearance (in.)		Stem Diameter (in.)	
							Intake	Exhaust	Intake	Exhaust
1992	3	2.3 (2262)	45	2	193-207@1.043	0.984-1.004 [1]	0.0010-0.0027	0.0015-0.0032	0.2751-0.2745	0.2740-0.2747
	A	2.3 (2262)	45	2	193-207@1.043	0.984-1.004 [1]	0.0010-0.0027	0.0015-0.0032	0.2751-0.2745	0.2740-0.2747
	D	2.3 (2262)	45	2	193-207@1.043	0.984-1.004 [1]	0.0010-0.0027	0.0015-0.0032	0.2751-0.2745	0.2740-0.2747
	N	3.3 (3344)	45	45	210@1.315	1.690-1.720	0.0015-0.0035	0.0015-0.0032	NA	NA
1993	3	2.3 (2262)	45	2	193-207@1.043	0.984-1.004 [1]	0.0010-0.0027	0.0015-0.0032	0.2751-0.2745	0.2740-0.2747
	A	2.3 (2262)	45	2	193-207@1.043	0.984-1.004 [1]	0.0010-0.0027	0.0015-0.0032	0.2751-0.2745	0.2740-0.2747
	D	2.3 (2262)	45	2	193-207@1.043	0.984-1.004 [1]	0.0010-0.0027	0.0015-0.0032	0.2751-0.2745	0.2740-0.2747
	N	3.3 (3344)	45	45	210@1.315	1.690-1.720	0.0015-0.0035	0.0015-0.0032	NA	NA
1994	3	2.3 (2262)	45	2	193-207@1.043	0.984-1.004 [1]	0.0010-0.0027	0.0015-0.0032	0.2751-0.2745	0.2740-0.2747
	A	2.3 (2262)	45	2	193-207@1.043	0.984-1.004 [1]	0.0010-0.0027	0.0015-0.0032	0.2751-0.2745	0.2740-0.2747
	D	2.3 (2262)	45	2	193-207@1.043	0.984-1.004 [1]	0.0010-0.0027	0.0015-0.0032	0.2751-0.2745	0.2740-0.2747
	M	3.1 (3136)	45	45	250@1.239	1.710	0.0010-0.0027	0.0010-0.0027	NA	NA
1995-96	D	2.3 (2262)	45	2	193-207@1.043	0.984-1.004 [1]	0.0010-0.0027	0.0015-0.0032	0.2751-0.2745	0.2740-0.2747
	M	3.1 (3136)	45	45	250@1.239	1.710	0.0010-0.0027	0.0010-0.0027	NA	NA

PISTON AND RING SPECIFICATIONS
All measurements are given in inches.

Year	Engine ID/VIN	Engine Displacement Liters (cc)	Piston Clearance	Ring Gap Top Compression	Ring Gap Bottom Compression	Ring Gap Oil Control	Ring Side Clearance Top Compression	Ring Side Clearance Bottom Compression	Ring Side Clearance Oil Control
1992	3	2.3 (2262)	0.0007-0.0020	0.0138-0.0236	0.0157-0.0256	0.0157-0.0551	0.0020-0.0039	0.0016-0.0032	NA
	A	2.3 (2262)	0.0007-0.0020	0.0138-0.0236	0.0157-0.0256	0.0157-0.0551	0.0027-0.0047	0.0016-0.0032	NA
	D	2.3 (2262)	0.0007-0.0020	0.0138-0.0236	0.0157-0.0256	0.0157-0.0551	0.0020-0.0039	0.0016-0.0032	NA
	N	3.3 (3344)	0.0004-0.0022 ①	0.0100-0.0250	0.0100-0.0250	0.0150-0.0550	0.0013-0.0031	0.0013-0.0031	0.0011-0.0081
1993	3	2.3 (2262)	0.0007-0.0020	0.0138-0.0236	0.0157-0.0256	0.0157-0.0551	0.0020-0.0039	0.0016-0.0032	NA
	A	2.3 (2262)	0.0007-0.0020	0.0138-0.0236	0.0157-0.0256	0.0157-0.0551	0.0027-0.0047	0.0016-0.0032	NA
	D	2.3 (2262)	0.0007-0.0020	0.0138-0.0236	0.0157-0.0256	0.0157-0.0551	0.0020-0.0039	0.0016-0.0032	NA
	N	3.3 (3344)	0.0004-0.0022 ①	0.0100-0.0250	0.0100-0.0250	0.0150-0.0550	0.0013-0.0031	0.0013-0.0031	0.0011-0.0081
1994	3	2.3 (2262)	0.0007-0.0020	0.0138-0.0236	0.0157-0.0256	0.0157-0.0551	0.0020-0.0039	0.0016-0.0032	NA
	A	2.3 (2262)	0.0007-0.0020	0.0138-0.0236	0.0157-0.0256	0.0157-0.0551	0.0027-0.0047	0.0016-0.0032	NA
	D	2.3 (2262)	0.0007-0.0020	0.0138-0.0236	0.0157-0.0256	0.0157-0.0551	0.0020-0.0039	0.0016-0.0032	NA
	M	3.1 (3130)	0.0013-0.0027	0.0071-0.0161	0.0200-0.0280	0.0098-0.0295	0.0020-0.0035	0.0020-0.0035	0.0080
1995-96	D	2.3 (2262)	0.0007-0.0020	0.0138-0.0236	0.0157-0.0256	0.0157-0.0551	0.0020-0.0039	0.0016-0.0032	NA
	M	3.1 (3136)	0.0013-0.0027	0.0071-0.0161	0.0200-0.0280	0.0098-0.0295	0.0020-0.0035	0.0020-0.0035	0.0080

NA - Not Available
① Measured 44mm from top of piston

TORQUE SPECIFICATIONS
All readings in ft. lbs.

Year	Engine ID/VIN	Engine Displacement Liters (cc)	Cylinder Head Bolts	Main Bearing Bolts	Rod Bearing Bolts	Crankshaft Damper Bolts	Flywheel Bolts	Manifold Intake	Manifold Exhaust	Spark Plugs	Lug Nut
1992	A	2.3 (2261)	①	②	③	④	⑤	18	31	17	100
	D	2.3 (2261)	①	②	③	④	⑤	18	31	17	100
	3	2.3 (2261)	①	②	③	④	⑤	18	31	17	100
	N	3.3 (3342)	⑧	⑨	⑩	⑪	⑫	7	38	12	100
1993	A	2.3 (2261)	⑭	②	③	⑮	⑤	18	31	16	100
	D	2.3 (2261)	⑭	②	③	⑮	⑤	18	31	16	100
	3	2.3 (2261)	20	②	③	⑮	⑤	18	31	16	100
	N	3.3 (3342)	⑧	⑨	⑩	⑪	⑫	7	38	20	100
1994	A	2.3 (2261)	⑱	②	③	⑲	⑤	19	31	16	100
	D	2.3 (2261)	⑱	②	③	⑲	⑤	19	31	16	100
	3	2.3 (2261)	⑱	②	③	⑲	⑤	19	31	16	100
	M	3.1 (3130)	⑥	⑰	⑱	76	61	⑦	10	⑯	100

TORQUE SPECIFICATIONS
All readings in ft. lbs.

Year	Engine ID/VIN	Engine Displacement Liters (cc)	Cylinder Head Bolts	Main Bearing Bolts	Rod Bearing Bolts	Crankshaft Damper Bolts	Flywheel Bolts	Manifold Intake	Manifold Exhaust	Spark Plugs	Lug Nut
1995-96	D	2.3 (2261)	⑱	②	③	⑲	⑤	19	31	16	100
	M	3.1 (3130)	⑥	⑬	⑳	76	59	⑦	12	⑯	100

NA - Not Available
① Bolts 1-6: 26 ft. lbs.
  Bolts 7-8: 15 ft. lbs.
② 15 ft. lbs. plus 90 degrees
③ 18 ft. lbs. plus 80 degrees
④ 74 ft. lbs. plus 90 degrees
⑤ 22 ft. lbs. plus 45 degrees
⑥ Coat threads with sealer torque to 37 ft. lbs.,
  then turn 1/4 turn (90 degrees)
⑦ Torque all bolts to 15 ft. lbs.,
  Retorque to 24 ft. lbs.

⑧ Step 1: Tighten all bolts to 35 ft. lbs.
  Step 2: Turn all bolts 130 degrees
  Step 3: Rotate four center bolts an
  additional 30 degrees
⑨ 26 ft. lbs. plus 50 degrees
⑩ 20 ft. lbs. plus 50 degrees
⑪ 110 ft. lbs. plus 76 degrees
⑫ 11 ft. lbs. plus 50 degrees
⑬ 37 ft. lbs. plus 75 degrees
⑭ Nos. 1-6: 18 ft. lbs. plus 90 degrees
  Nos. 7-8: 22 ft. lbs. plus 60 degrees
  Nos. 9-10: 26 ft. lbs. plus 60 degrees

⑮ 110 ft. lbs. plus 90 degrees
⑯ New cylinder first-time installation: 21 ft. lbs.
  All others: 11 ft. lbs.
⑰ 37 ft. lbs. plus 77 degrees
⑱ Nos. 1-8: 30 ft. lbs.
  Nos. 9-10: 26 ft. lbs.
  Tighten all bolts an additional 90 degrees
⑲ 129 ft. lbs. plus 90 degrees
⑳ 15 ft. lbs. plus 75 degrees

BRAKE SPECIFICATIONS
All measurements in inches unless noted

Year	Model	Master Cylinder Bore	Brake Disc Original Thickness	Brake Disc Minimum Thickness	Brake Disc Maximum Runout	Brake Drum Diameter Original Inside Diameter	Brake Drum Diameter Max. Wear Limit	Brake Drum Diameter Maximum Machine Diameter	Minimum Lining Thickness Front	Minimum Lining Thickness Rear
1992	Skylark	0.874	0.806	0.736	0.003	7.879	7.929	7.899	0.030	1
	Achieva	0.874	0.806	0.736	0.003	7.879	7.929	7.899	0.030	1
	Grand Am	0.874	0.806	0.736	0.003	7.879	7.929	7.899	0.030	1
1993	Skylark	0.874	0.806	0.736	0.003	7.874-7.890	7.929	7.899	0.030	1
	Achieva	0.874	0.806	0.736	0.003	7.874-7.890	7.929	7.899	0.030	1
	Grand Am	0.874	0.806	0.736	0.003	7.874	7.929	7.899	0.030	1
1994	Skylark	0.874	0.806	0.736	0.003	7.874-7.890	7.929	7.899	0.030	1
	Achieva	0.874	0.806	0.736	0.003	7.874-7.890	7.929	7.899	0.030	1
	Grand Am	0.874	0.806	0.736	0.003	7.874	7.929	7.899	0.030	1
1995-96	Skylark	0.874	0.806	0.736	0.003	7.874-7.890	7.929	7.899	0.030	1
	Achieva	0.874	0.806	0.736	0.003	7.874-7.890	7.929	7.899	0.030	1
	Grand Am	0.874	0.806	0.736	0.003	7.874	7.929	7.899	0.030	1

1 0.030 over rivet head; If bonded lining, use 0.062 from shoe

WHEEL ALIGNMENT

Year	Model		Caster Range (deg.)	Caster Preferred Setting (deg.)	Camber Range (deg.)	Camber Preferred Setting (deg.)	Toe-in (in.)	Steering Axis Inclination (deg.)
1992	Achieva	F	11/16P-2 11/16P	1 11/16P	11/16N-11/16P	0	0	13 3/16
		R	-	-	13/16N-5/16P	1/4N	1/8P	-
	Grand Am	F	11/16P-2 11/16P	1 11/16P	11/16N-11/16P	0	0	13 3/16
		R	-	-	13/16N-5/16P	1/4N	1/8P	-
	Skylark	F	11/16P-11/16P	1 11/16P	11/16N-11/16P	0	0	13 3/16
		R	-	-	13/16N-5/16P	1/4N	1/8P	-
1993	Achieva	F	7/16P-2 7/16P	1 7/16P	11/16N-11/16P	0	0	13 3/16
		R	-	-	1 1/16N-7/16P	1/4N	0	-
	Grand Am	F	7/16P-2 7/16P	1 7/16P	11/16N-11/16P	0	0	13 3/16
		R	-	-	13/16N-5/16P	1/4N	0	-
	Skylark	F	7/16P-2 7/16P	1 7/16P	11/16N-11/16P	0	0	13 3/16
		R	-	-	13/16N-5/16P	1/4N	0	-
1994	Achieva	F	7/16P-2 7/16P	1 7/16P	11/16N-11/16P	0	0	13 3/16
		R	-	-	7/8N-7/16P	1/4N	0	-
	Grand Am	F	7/16P-2 7/16P	1 7/16P	11/16N-11/16P	0	0	13 3/16
		R	-	-	13/16N-5/16P	1/4N	0	-
	Skylark	F	7/16P-2 7/16P	1 7/16P	11/16N-11/16P	0	0	13 3/16
		R	-	-	13/16N-7/16P	1/4N	0	-
1995-96	Achieva	F	7/16P-2 7/16P	1 7/16P	11/16N-11/16P	0	0	13 3/16
		R	-	-	7/8N-7/16P	1/4N	0	-
	Grand Am	F	7/16P-2 7/16P	1 7/16P	11/16N-11/16P	0	0	13 3/16
		R	-	-	13/16N-5/16P	1/4N	0	-
	Skylark	F	7/16P-2 7/16P	1 7/16P	11/16N-11/16P	0	0	13 3/16
		R	-	-	13/16N-7/16P	1/4N	0	-

NA - Not Available
F - Front
R - Rear

CUTLASS SUPREME/GRAND PRIX/LUMINA/REGAL

VEHICLE IDENTIFICATION CHART

Engine Code						Model Year	
Code	Liters	Cu. In. (cc)	Cyl.	Fuel Sys.	Eng. Mfg.	Code	Year
4	2.2	133 (2180)	4	MFI	CUS	N	1992
L	3.8	231 (3785)	6	MFI	BOC	P	1993
M	3.1	191 (3130)	6	MFI	BOC	R	1994
R	2.5	151 (2475)	4	TFI	CPC	S	1995
X	3.4	207 (3393)	6	MFI	CPC	T	1996
T	3.1	192 (3146)	6	MFI	CPC		

MFI - Multiport fuel injection
BOC - Buick/Oldsmobile/Cadillac
CUS - Chevrolet/United States
CPC - Chevrolet/Pontiac/Canada

ENGINE IDENTIFICATION

Year	Model	Engine Displacement Liters (cc)	Engine Series (ID/VIN)	Fuel System	No. of Cylinders	Engine Type	
1992	Cutlass Supreme	3.1 (3146)	T	MFI	6	OHV	
	Cutlass Supreme	3.4 (3392)	X	MFI	6	DOHC	①
	Grand Prix	3.1 (3136)	T	MFI	6	OHV	
	Grand Prix	3.4 (3350)	X	MFI	6	DOHC	
	Lumina	2.5 (2475)	R	TFI	4	OHV	
	Lumina	3.1 (3130)	T	MFI	6	OHV	
	Lumina	3.4 (3393)	X	MFI	6	DOHC	
	Regal	3.1 (3146)	T	MFI	6	OHV	
	Regal	3.8 (3785)	L	MFI	6	OHV	
1993	Cutlass Supreme	3.1 (3146)	T	MFI	6	OHV	
	Cutlass Supreme	3.4 (3392)	X	MFI	6	DOHC	①
	Grand Prix	3.1 (3136)	T	MFI	6	OHV	
	Grand Prix	3.4 (3350)	X	MFI	6	DOHC	
	Lumina	2.2 (2180)	4	MFI	4	OHV	
	Lumina	3.1 (3130)	T	MFI	6	OHV	
	Lumina	3.4 (3393)	X	MFI	6	DOHC	
	Regal	3.1 (3146)	T	MFI	6	OHV	
	Regal	3.8 (3785)	L	MFI	6	OHV	
1994	Cutlass Supreme	3.1 (3130)	M	MFI	6	OHV	
	Cutlass Supreme	3.4 (3392)	X	MFI	6	DOHC	①
	Grand Prix	3.1 (3136)	M	MFI	6	OHV	
	Grand Prix	3.4 (3350)	X	MFI	6	DOHC	
	Lumina	3.1 (3130)	T	MFI	6	OHV	
	Lumina	3.4 (3393)	X	MFI	6	DOHC	
	Regal	3.1 (3130)	M	MFI	6	OHV	
	Regal	3.8 (3785)	L	MFI	6	OHV	
1995-96	Cutlass Supreme	3.1 (3130)	M	MFI	6	OHV	
	Cutlass Supreme	3.4 (3392)	X	MFI	6	DOHC	①
	Grand Prix	3.1 (3136)	M	MFI	6	OHV	
	Grand Prix	3.4 (3350)	X	MFI	6	DOHC	
	Lumina	3.1 (3130)	M	MFI	6	OHV	
	Lumina	3.4 (3393)	X	MFI	6	DOHC	
	Regal	3.1 (3130)	M	MFI	6	OHV	
	Regal	3.8 (3785)	L	MFI	6	OHV	

MFI - Multiport fuel injection

OHV - Overhead valve

① Twin dual overhead camshaft

GENERAL ENGINE SPECIFICATIONS

Year	Engine ID/VIN	Engine Displacement Liters (cc)	Fuel System Type	Net Horsepower @ rpm	Net Torque @ rpm (ft. lbs.)	Bore x Stroke (in.)	Compression Ratio	Oil Pressure @ rpm
1992	R	2.5 (2475)	TFI	105@4800	135@3200	4.00x3.00	8.3:1	26@800
	T	3.1 (3146)	MFI	140@4400	185@3200	3.50x3.31	8.8:1	15@1100
	X	3.4 (3393)	MFI	210@5200	215@4000	3.62x3.31	9.25:1	15@1100
	L	3.8 (3785)	MFI	170@4800	220@3200	3.80x3.40	8.5:1	60@1850
1993	4	2.2 (2180)	MFI	110@5200	130@3200	3.50x3.46	9.0:1	63-77@1200
	T	3.1 (3146)	MFI	140@4200	185@3200	3.50x3.31	8.9:1	15@1100
	X	3.4 (3393)	MFI	210@5200	215@4000	3.62x3.31	9.25:1	15@1100
	L	3.8 (3785)	MFI	170@4800	225@3200	3.80x3.40	9.0:1	60@1850
1994	M	3.1 (3130)	MFI	160@5200	185@4000	3.50x3.31	9.5:1	15@1100
	T	3.1 (3130)	MFI	140@4200	185@3200	3.50x3.31	8.5:1	8@600
	X	3.4 (3393)	MFI	210@5200	215@4000	3.62x3.31	9.25:1	15@1100
	L	3.8 (3785)	MFI	170@4800	225@3200	3.80x3.40	9.0:1	60@1850
1995-96	M	3.1 (3130)	MFI	160@5200	185@4000	3.50x3.31	9.5:1	15@1100
	X	3.4 (3393)	MFI	210@5200	215@4000	3.62x3.31	9.25:1	15@1100
	L	3.8 (3785)	MFI	170@4800	225@3200	3.80x3.40	9.0:1	60@1850

MFI - Multiport fuel injection

TFI - Throttle body fuel injection

GASOLINE ENGINE TUNE-UP SPECIFICATIONS

Year	Engine ID/VIN	Engine Displacement Liters (cc)	Spark Plugs Gap (in.)	Ignition Timing (deg.) MT	Ignition Timing (deg.) AT	Fuel Pump (psi)	Idle Speed (rpm) MT	Idle Speed (rpm) AT	Valve Clearance In.	Valve Clearance Ex.
1992	R	2.5 (2475)	0.060	④	④	26-32	④	④	HYD	HYD
	T	3.1 (3146)	0.045	①	①	41-47	③	③	HYD	HYD
	X	3.4 (3393)	0.045	④	④	41-47	④	④	HYD	HYD
	L	3.8 (3785)	0.060	①	①	40-47	-	②	HYD	HYD
1993	4	2.2 (2180)	0.045	④	④	41-47	④	④	HYD	HYD
	T	3.1 (3146)	0.045	①	①	41-47	③	③	HYD	HYD
	X	3.4 (3393)	0.045	④	④	41-47	④	④	HYD	HYD
	L	3.8 (3785)	0.060	①	①	40-47	-	②	HYD	HYD
1994	M	3.1 (3130)	0.060	①	①	41-47	②	②	HYD	HYD
	T	3.1 (3130)	0.045	④	④	41-47	④	④	HYD	HYD
	X	3.4 (3393)	0.045	④	④	41-47	④	④	HYD	HYD
	L	3.8 (3785)	0.060	①	①	40-47	-	②	HYD	HYD
1995-96	M	3.1 (3130)	0.060	①	①	41-47	②	②	HYD	HYD
	X	3.4 (3393)	0.045	④	④	41-47	④	④	HYD	HYD
	L	3.8 (3785)	0.060	①	①	40-47	-	②	HYD	HYD

NOTE: The Vehicle Emission Control Information label often reflects specification changes made during production. The label figures must be used if they differ from those in this chart.

HYD - Hydraulic

① DIS Ignition System timing is not adjustable

② Idle speed is maintained by the ECM. There is no recommended adjustment procedure

③ Idle speed is controlled by ECM; Minimum air rate is adjusted by IAC centering; Refer to manual for procedure

④ Refer to Vehicle Emission Control Information label

CAPACITIES

Year	Model	Engine ID/VIN	Engine Displacement Liters (cc)	Engine Oil with Filter (qts.)	Transmission (pts.) 4-Spd	5-Spd	Auto.	Drive Axle Front (pts.)	Rear (pts.)	Fuel Tank (gal.)	Cooling System (qts.)
1992	Cutlass Supreme	T	3.1 (3130)	4.5	-	-	③	-	-	16.0	12.6
	Cutlass Supreme	X	3.4 (3393)	5.0	-	-	③	-	-	16.5	12.7
	Grand Prix	T	3.1 (3130)	4.5	-	-	③	-	-	16.0	12.6
	Grand Prix	X	3.4 (3393)	5.0	-	-	③	-	-	16.5	12.7
	Lumina	R	2.5 (2475)	4.5	-	-	③	-	-	16.0	9.4
	Lumina	T	3.1 (3130)	4.5	-	-	③	-	-	16.0	12.6
	Lumina	X	3.4 (3393)	5.0	-	-	③	-	-	16.5	12.7
	Regal	T	3.1 (3146)	4.0 ①	-	-	12.0	-	-	16.0	12.1
	Regal	L	3.8 (3785)	4.0 ①	-	-	12.0	-	-	16.0	11.1
1993	Cutlass Supreme	T	3.1 (3130)	4.5	-	-	③	-	-	16.0	12.6
	Cutlass Supreme	X	3.4 (3393)	5.0	-	-	③	-	-	16.5	12.7
	Grand Prix	T	3.1 (3130)	4.5	-	-	③	-	-	16.0	12.6
	Grand Prix	X	3.4 (3393)	5.0	-	-	③	-	-	16.5	12.7
	Lumina	4	2.2 (2180)	4.5	-	-	8.0 ②	-	-	16.0	9.5
	Lumina	T	3.1 (3130)	4.5	-	-	③	-	-	16.0	12.6
	Lumina	X	3.4 (3393)	5.0	-	-	③	-	-	16.5	12.7
	Regal	T	3.1 (3146)	4.0 ①	-	-	12.0	-	-	16.5	12.6
	Regal	L	3.8 (3785)	4.0 ①	-	-	12.0	-	-	16.0	11.1
1994	Cutlass Supreme	M	3.1 (3130)	4.0 ①	-	-	③	-	-	16.5	11.8
	Cutlass Supreme	X	3.4 (3393)	5.0	-	-	③	-	-	16.5	12.7
	Grand Prix	M	3.1 (3130)	4.0 ①	-	-	③	-	-	16.5	11.8
	Grand Prix	X	3.4 (3393)	5.0	-	-	③	-	-	16.5	12.7
	Lumina	T	3.1 (3130)	4.5	-	-	③	-	-	16.0	12.6
	Lumina	X	3.4 (3393)	5.0	-	-	③	-	-	16.5	12.7
	Regal	M	3.1 (3130)	4.0 ①	-	-	12.0	-	-	16.5	11.8
	Regal	L	3.8 (3785)	4.0 ①	-	-	12.0	-	-	16.5	11.1
1995-96	Cutlass Supreme	M	3.1 (3130)	4.5	-	-	③	-	-	16.0	12.6
	Cutlass Supreme	X	3.4 (3393)	5.0	-	-	③	-	-	16.5	12.7
	Grand Prix	M	3.1 (3130)	4.5	-	-	③	-	-	16.0	12.6
	Grand Prix	X	3.4 (3393)	5.0	-	-	③	-	-	16.5	12.7
	Lumina	M	3.1 (3130)	4.5	-	-	③	-	-	16.0	12.6
	Lumina	X	3.4 (3393)	5.0	-	-	③	-	-	16.5	12.7
	Regal	M	3.1 (3130)	4.0 ①	-	-	12.0	-	-	16.5	11.8
	Regal	L	3.8 (3785)	4.0 ①	-	-	12.0	-	-	16.5	11.1

① Capacity is without filter replacement; Additional oil may be required
② 10.0 pts. if equipped with O/D
③ 3T40 trans.: 8.0 pts.
4T60 trans.: 12.0 pts.
4T60E trans.: 14.8 pts.

CAMSHAFT SPECIFICATIONS

All measurements given in inches.

Year	Engine ID/VIN	Engine Displacement Liters (cc)	Journal Diameter					Elevation		Bearing Clearance	Camshaft End Play
			1	2	3	4	5	In.	Ex.		
1992	R	2.5 (2475)	1.869	1.869	1.869	NA	NA	0.398	0.398	0.0007-0.0027	0.0015-0.0050
	T	3.1 (3146)	1.8678-1.8815	1.8678-1.8815	1.8678-1.8815	1.8678-1.8815	1.8678-1.8815	0.262	0.273	0.0010-0.0040	NA
	X	3.4 (3393)	2.165-2.166	2.165-2.166	2.165-2.166	2.165-2.166	NA	0.370	0.370	0.0015-0.0035	NA
	L	3.8 (3785)	1.7850-1.7860	1.7850-1.7860	1.7850-1.7860	1.7850-1.7860	1.7850-1.7860	0.250	0.255	0.0005-0.0035	NA
1993	4	2.2 (2180)	1.867-1.869	1.867-1.869	1.867-1.869	1.867-1.869	1.867-1.869	0.259	0.259	0.0010-0.0039	NA
	T	3.1 (3146)	1.8677-1.8815	1.8677-1.8815	1.8677-1.8815	1.8677-1.8815	1.8677-1.8815	0.263	0.273	0.0010-0.0040	NA
	X	3.4 (3393)	2.165-2.166	2.165-2.166	2.165-2.166	2.165-2.166	NA	0.370	0.370	0.0015-0.0035	NA
	L	3.8 (3785)	1.7850-1.7860	1.7850-1.7860	1.7850-1.7860	1.7850-1.7860	1.7850-1.7860	0.250	0.255	0.0005-0.0035	NA
1994	M	3.1 (3130)	1.8680-1.8690	1.8680-1.8690	1.8680-1.8690	1.8680-1.8690	1.8680-1.8690	0.273	0.273	0.0010-0.0040	NA
	T	3.1 (3130)	1.868-1.881	1.868-1.881	1.868-1.881	1.868-1.881	NA	0.263	0.273	0.0010-0.0039	NA
	X	3.4 (3393)	2.165-2.166	2.165-2.166	2.165-2.166	2.165-2.166	NA	0.370	0.370	0.0015-0.0035	NA
	L	3.8 (3785)	1.7850-1.7860	1.7850-1.7860	1.7850-1.7860	1.7850-1.7860	1.7850-1.7860	0.250	0.255	0.0005-0.0035	NA
1995-96	M	3.1 (3130)	1.8680-1.8690	1.8680-1.8690	1.8680-1.8690	1.8680-1.8690	1.8680-1.8690	0.273	0.273	0.0010-0.0040	NA
	X	3.4 (3393)	2.1650-2.1660	2.1650-2.1660	2.1650-2.1660	2.1650-2.1660	NA	0.3700	0.3700	0.0015-0.0035	NA
	L	3.8 (3785)	1.7850-1.7860	1.7850-1.7860	1.7850-1.7860	1.7850-1.7860	1.7850-1.7860	0.250	0.255	0.0005-0.0035	NA

NA - Not Available

CRANKSHAFT AND CONNECTING ROD SPECIFICATIONS

All measurements are given in inches.

Year	Engine ID/VIN	Engine Displacement Liters (cc)	Crankshaft				Connecting Rod		
			Main Brg. Journal Dia.	Main Brg. Oil Clearance	Shaft End-play	Thrust on No.	Journal Diameter	Oil Clearance	Side Clearance
1992	R	2.5 (2475)	2.2995-2.3005	0.0005-0.0022	0.0035-0.0085	5	1.9995-2.0005	0.0005-0.0026	0.006-0.022
	T	3.1 (3146)	2.6473-2.6483	0.0012-0.0030	0.0024-0.0083	3	1.9983-1.9994	0.0011-0.0034	0.0140-0.0270
	X	3.4 (3393)	2.6472-2.6479	0.0013-0.0030	0.0024-0.0083	3	1.9987-1.9994	0.0011-0.0032	0.0140-0.0250
	L	3.8 (3785)	2.4988-2.4998	0.0008-0.0022	0.0030-0.0110	2	2.2487-2.2499	0.0003-0.0022	0.0030-0.0150
1993	4	2.2 (2180)	2.4945-2.4954	0.0006-0.0019	0.002-0.007	4	1.9983-1.9994	0.0010-0.0030	0.0040-0.0150
	T	3.1 (3146)	2.6473-2.6479	0.0013-0.0030	0.0024-0.0083	3	1.9987-1.9994	0.0011-0.0032	0.0071-0.0173
	X	3.4 (3393)	2.6472-2.6479	0.0013-0.0030	0.0024-0.0083	3	1.9987-1.9994	0.0011-0.0032	0.0070-0.0170
	L	3.8 (3785)	2.4988-2.4998	0.0008-0.0022	0.0030-0.0110	2	2.2487-2.2499	0.0008-0.0022	0.0030-0.0150
1994	M	3.1 (3130)	2.6473-2.6483	0.0012-0.0030	0.0024-0.0083	3	1.9982-1.9984	0.0011-0.0037	0.0071-0.0173
	T	3.1 (3130)	2.6473-2.6483	0.0012-0.0030	0.002-0.008	3	1.9983-1.9994	0.0010-0.0040	0.0140-0.0270
	X	3.4 (3393)	2.6472-2.6479	0.0013-0.0030	0.0024-0.0083	3	1.9987-1.9994	0.0011-0.0032	0.0140-0.0250
	L	3.8 (3785)	2.4988-2.4998	0.0008-0.0022	0.0030-0.0110	2	2.2487-2.2499	0.0008-0.0022	0.0030-0.0150
1995-96	M	3.1 (3130)	2.6473-2.6483	0.0012-0.0030	0.0024-0.0083	3	1.9982-1.9984	0.0011-0.0037	0.0071-0.0173
	X	3.4 (3393)	2.6472-2.6479	0.0013-0.0030	0.0024-0.0083	3	1.9987-1.9994	0.0011-0.0032	0.0140-0.0250
	L	3.8 (3785)	2.4988-2.4998	0.0008-0.0022	0.0030-0.0110	2	2.2487-2.2499	0.0008-0.0022	0.0030-0.0150

VALVE SPECIFICATIONS

Year	Engine ID/VIN	Engine Displacement Liters (cc)	Seat Angle (deg.)	Face Angle (deg.)	Spring Test Pressure (lbs. @ in.)	Spring Installed Height (in.)	Stem-to-Guide Clearance (in.)		Stem Diameter (in.)	
							Intake	Exhaust	Intake	Exhaust
1992	R	2.5 (2475)	45	46	75@1.68	1.68	0.0010-0.0026	0.0013-0.0041	NA	NA
	T	3.1 (3146)	46	45	215@1.291	1.575	0.0010-0.0027	0.0010-0.0027	NA	NA
	X	3.4 (3393)	46	45	75@1.40	1.40	0.0011-0.0026	0.0014-0.0031	NA	NA
	L	3.8 (3785)	45	45	210@1.315	1.690-1.720	0.0015-0.0035	0.0015-0.0032	NA	NA
1993	4	2.2 (2180)	46	45	225-233@ ① 1.25	1.64 ②	0.0011-0.0026	0.0014-0.0031	NA	NA
	T	3.1 (3146)	46	45	215@1.291	1.693	0.0008-0.0021	0.0014-0.0030	NA	NA
	X	3.4 (3393)	46	45	75@1.40	1.40	0.0011-0.0026	0.0014-0.0031	NA	NA
	L	3.8 (3785)	45	45	210@1.315	1.690-1.720	0.0015-0.0035	0.0015-0.0032	NA	NA
1994	M	3.1 (3130)	45	45	250@1.239	1.710	0.0001-0.0027	0.0010-0.0027	NA	NA
	T	3.1 (3130)	46	45	90 ①	1.60 ②	0.0010-0.0027	0.0010-0.0027	NA	NA
	X	3.4 (3393)	46	45	75@1.40	1.40	0.0011-0.0026	0.0014-0.0031	NA	NA
	L	3.8 (3785)	45	45	210@1.315	1.690-1.720	0.0015-0.0035	0.0015-0.0032	NA	NA
1995-96	M	3.1 (3130)	45	45	250@1.239	1.710	0.0001-0.0027	0.0010-0.0027	NA	NA
	X	3.4 (3393)	46	45	75@1.40	1.40	0.0011-0.0026	0.0014-0.0031	NA	NA
	L	3.8 (3785)	45	45	210@1.315	1.690-1.720	0.0015-0.0035	0.0015-0.0032	NA	NA

NA - Not Available

① With valve open

② With valve closed

PISTON AND RING SPECIFICATIONS

All measurements are given in inches.

Year	Engine ID/VIN	Engine Displacement Liters (cc)	Piston Clearance	Ring Gap			Ring Side Clearance		
				Top Compression	Bottom Compression	Oil Control	Top Compression	Bottom Compression	Oil Control
1992	R	2.5 (2475)	0.0014- ② 0.0022	0.010- 0.020	0.010- 0.020	0.020- 0.060	0.002- 0.003	0.001- 0.003	0.015- 0.055
	T	3.1 (3146)	0.0009- 0.0022	0.010- 0.020	0.020- 0.028	0.010- 0.030	0.0020- 0.0035	0.0020- 0.0035	0.0080 MAX
	X	3.4 (3393)	0.0009- 0.0023	0.012- 0.022	0.019- 0.029	0.010- 0.030	0.002- 0.004	0.002- 0.004	0.002- 0.008
	L	3.8 (3785)	0.0004- ① 0.0022	0.010- 0.025	0.010- 0.025	0.015- 0.055	0.0013- 0.0031	0.0013- 0.0031	0.0011- 0.0081
1993	4	2.2 (2180)	0.0007- 0.0017	0.010- 0.020	0.010- 0.020	0.010- 0.050	0.002- 0.003	0.002- 0.003	0.0020- 0.0082
	T	3.1 (3146)	0.0009- 0.0023	0.007- 0.016	0.020- 0.028	0.098- 0.030	0.0020- 0.0035	0.0020- 0.0035	0.0079 MAX
	X	3.4 (3393)	0.0009- 0.0023	0.012- 0.022	0.019- 0.029	0.010- 0.030	0.002- 0.004	0.002- 0.004	0.002- 0.008
	L	3.8 (3785)	0.0004- ① 0.0022	0.010- 0.025	0.010- 0.025	0.015- 0.055	0.0013- 0.0031	0.0013- 0.0031	0.0011- 0.0081
1994	M	3.1 (3130)	0.0013- 0.0027	0.007- 0.016	0.020- 0.028	0.010- 0.030	0.0020- 0.0035	0.0020- 0.0035	0.0080 MAX
	T	3.1 (3130)	0.0009- 0.0022	0.010- 0.020	0.020- 0.028	0.010- 0.030	0.002- 0.003	0.002- 0.003	0.008
	X	3.4 (3393)	0.0009- 0.0023	0.012- 0.022	0.019- 0.029	0.010- 0.030	0.002- 0.004	0.002- 0.004	0.002- 0.008
	L	3.8 (3785)	0.0004- ① 0.0022	0.010- 0.025	0.010- 0.025	0.015- 0.055	0.0013- 0.0031	0.0013- 0.0031	0.0011- 0.0081
1995-96	M	3.1 (3130)	0.0013- 0.0027	0.007- 0.016	0.020- 0.028	0.010- 0.030	0.0020- 0.0035	0.0020- 0.0035	0.0080 MAX
	X	3.4 (3393)	0.0009- 0.0023	0.012- 0.022	0.019- 0.029	0.010- 0.030	0.0020- 0.0040	0.0020- 0.0040	0.0020- 0.0080
	L	3.8 (3785)	0.0004- ① 0.0022	0.010- 0.025	0.010- 0.025	0.015- 0.055	0.0013- 0.0031	0.0013- 0.0031	0.0011- 0.0081

NA - Not Available

① Measured 44mm from top of piston

② Measured 1/8 inch down from piston top

TORQUE SPECIFICATIONS
All readings in ft. lbs.

Year	Engine ID/VIN	Engine Displacement Liters (cc)	Cylinder Head Bolts	Main Bearing Bolts	Rod Bearing Bolts	Crankshaft Damper Bolts	Flywheel Bolts	Manifold Intake	Manifold Exhaust	Spark Plugs	Lug Nut
1992	R	2.5 (2475)	92	70	32	200	44	29	44	15	100
	T	3.1 (3146)	(3)	73	39	76	60	(2)	18	11	100
	X	3.4 (3393)	(11)	(8)	39	78	61	18	(12)	11	100
	L	3.8 (3785)	(6)	(1)	(7)	(4)	(5)	(7)	38	12	100
1993	4	2.2 (2180)	(13)	77	38	85 (14)	52-55	18	6-13	20	80-100
	T	3.1 (3146)	(3)	(8)	37	76	52	(2)	21	11	100
	X	3.4 (3393)	(11)	(8)	39	78	61	18	(12)	11	100
	L	3.8 (3785)	(6)	(1)	(7)	(4)	(5)	(7)	38	20	100
1994	M	3.1 (3130)	(3)	(8)	(9)	76	61	(2)	10	(10)	100
	T	3.1 (3130)	(3)	(8)	37	76	52	(2)	21	11	100
	X	3.4 (3393)	(11)	(8)	39	78	61	18	(12)	11	100
	L	3.8 (3785)	(6)	(1)	(7)	(4)	(5)	(7)	38	11	100
1995-96	M	3.1 (3130)	(3)	(8)	(9)	76	61	(2)	10	(10)	100
	X	3.4 (3393)	(11)	(8)	39	78	61	18	(12)	11	100
	L	3.8 (3785)	(6)	(1)	(7)	(4)	(5)	(7)	38	11	100

(1) 26 ft. lbs. plus 50 degrees
(2) Torque all bolts to 15 ft. lbs. Retorque to 24 ft. lbs.
(3) Coat threads with sealer torque to 33 ft. lbs., then turn 1/4 turn (90 degrees)
(4) 110 ft. lbs. plus 76 degrees
(5) 11 ft. lbs., plus 50 degrees
(6) Step 1: 35 ft. lbs.
   Step 2: 130 degrees
   Step 3: Rotate four center bolts an additional 30 degrees
(7) 20 ft. lbs. plus 50 degrees
(8) 37 ft. lbs. plus 77 degrees
(9) 15 ft. lbs. plus 75 degrees

(10) New cylinder head:
   1st-time installation: 20 ft. lbs.
   All other installations: 11 ft. lbs.
(11) 37 ft. lbs. plus 90 degrees
(12) 115 inch lbs.
(13) Step 1: 41 ft. lbs.
   Step 2: Tighten an additional 45 degrees
   Step 3: Tighten an additional 45 degrees
   Step 4: Long bolts 1, 4-5, 8-9 an additional 20 degrees
   Step 4: Short bolts 2-3, 6-7, 10 an additional 10 degrees
(14) Center bolt 4   33 ft. lbs. plus 90 degrees

BRAKE SPECIFICATIONS
All measurements in inches unless noted

Year	Model		Master Cylinder Bore	Brake Disc Original Thickness	Brake Disc Minimum Thickness	Brake Disc Maximum Runout	Brake Drum Diameter Original Inside Diameter	Brake Drum Diameter Max. Wear Limit	Brake Drum Diameter Maximum Machine Diameter	Minimum Lining Thickness Front	Minimum Lining Thickness Rear
1992	Cutlass Supreme	F	0.945	1.040	0.972	0.004	-	-	-	0.030	0.030
		R	0.945	0.492	0.429	0.004	-	-	-	0.030	0.030
	Grand Prix		0.944	1.039	0.972	0.004	NA	NA	NA	0.030	NA
			NA	0.492	0.429	0.004	NA	NA	NA	NA	0.030
	Lumina		0.945	(1)	(2)	0.004	NA	NA	NA	0.030	0.030
	Regal	F	0.945	1.040	0.972	0.004	-	-	-	0.030	0.030
		R	0.945	0.492	0.429	0.004	-	-	-	0.030	0.030
1993	Cutlass Supreme	F	0.945	1.040	0.972	0.004	-	-	-	0.030	0.030
		R	0.945	0.492	0.429	0.004	-	-	-	0.030	0.030

BRAKE SPECIFICATIONS

All measurements in inches unless noted

Year	Model		Master Cylinder Bore	Brake Disc Original Thickness	Brake Disc Minimum Thickness	Maximum Runout	Brake Drum Diameter Original Inside Diameter	Max. Wear Limit	Maximum Machine Diameter	Minimum Lining Thickness Front	Rear
	Grand Prix		0.944	1.039	0.972	0.003	NA	NA	NA	0.030	NA
			NA	0.492	0.429	0.003	NA	NA	NA	NA	0.030
	Lumina		0.945	①	②	0.004	NA	NA	NA	0.030	0.030
	Regal	F	0.945	1.040	0.972	0.004	-	-	-	0.030	0.030
		R	0.945	0.492	0.429	0.004	-	-	-	0.030	0.030
1994	Cutlass Supreme	F	0.945	1.039	0.972	0.003	-	-	-	0.030	0.030
		R	0.945	0.492	0.429	0.003	-	-	-	0.030	0.030
	Grand Prix		0.944	1.039	0.972	0.004	NA	NA	NA	0.030	NA
			NA	0.492	0.429	0.004	NA	NA	NA	NA	0.030
	Lumina		0.945	①	②	0.004	NA	NA	NA	0.030	0.030
	Regal	F	0.945	1.039	0.972	0.003	-	-	-	0.030	0.030
		R	0.945	0.492	0.429	0.003	-	-	-	0.030	0.030
1995-96	Cutlass Supreme	F	1.000	1.039	0.972	0.003	-	-	-	0.030	0.030
		R	1.000	0.492	0.429	0.003	-	-	-	0.030	0.030
	Grand Prix		0.944	1.039	0.972	0.004	NA	NA	NA	0.030	NA
			NA	0.492	0.429	0.004	NA	NA	NA	NA	0.030
	Lumina		0.945	①	②	0.004	NA	NA	NA	0.030	0.030
	Regal	F	0.945	1.039	0.972	0.003	-	-	-	0.030	0.030
		R	0.945	0.492	0.429	0.003	-	-	-	0.030	0.030

F - Front
R - Rear

① Front: 1.040; Rear: 0.492
② Front: 0.972; Rear: 0.429

WHEEL ALIGNMENT

Year	Model		Caster Range (deg.)	Caster Preferred Setting (deg.)	Camber Range (deg.)	Camber Preferred Setting (deg.)	Toe-in (in.)	Steering Axis Inclination (deg.)
1992	Cutlass Supreme	F	1 1/2P-2 1/2P	2P	3/16P-1 3/16P	11/16P	0	13 3/8
		R	-	-	3/8N-5/8P	1/8P	1/16N	-
	Grand Prix	F	1 1/2P-2 1/2P	2P	3/16P-1 3/16P	11/16P	0	13 3/8
		R	-	-	3/8N-5/8P	1/8P	1/16N	-
	Lumina	F	1 1/2P-2 1/2P	2P	3/16N-1 3/16P	11/16P	0	13 13/32
		R	-	-	①	②	3/64N	-
	Regal	F	1 1/2P-2 1/2P	2P	3/16P-1 3/16P	11/16P	0	13 13/32
		R	-	-	①	②	3/64N	-
1993	Cutlass Supreme	F	1 1/2P-2 1/2P	2P	3/16P-1 3/16P	11/16P	0	13 3/8
		R	-	-	3/8N-5/8P	1/8P	1/16N	-
	Grand Prix	F	1 1/2P-2 1/2P	2P	3/16P-1 3/16P	11/16P	0	13 3/8
		R	-	-	3/8N-5/8P	1/8P	1/16N	-

WHEEL ALIGNMENT

Year	Model		Caster Range (deg.)	Caster Preferred Setting (deg.)	Camber Range (deg.)	Camber Preferred Setting (deg.)	Toe-in (in.)	Steering Axis Inclination (deg.)
	Lumina	F	1 1/2P-2 1/2P	2P	3/16P-1 3/16P	11/16P	0	13 13/32
		R	-	-	①	②	3/64N	-
	Regal	F	1 1/2P-2 1/2P	2P	3/16P-1 3/16P	11/16P	0	13 13/32
		R	-	-	①	②	3/64N	-
1994	Cutlass Supreme	F	5/16N-11/16P	3/16P	3/16P-1 3/16P	11/16P	0	NA
		R	-	-	13/32N-19/32P	3/32P	3/32N	-
	Grand Prix	F	5/16N-11/16P	3/16P	3/16P-1 3/16P	11/16P	0	NA
		R	-	-	13/32N-19/32P	3/32P	3/32N	-
	Lumina	F	1 1/2P-2 1/2P	2P	3/16P-1 3/16P	11/16P	0	13 13/32
		R	-	-	①	②	3/64N	-
	Regal	F	5/16N-11/16P	3/16P	3/16P-1 3/16P	11/16P	0	NA
		R	-	-	5/8N-5/8P	3/32P	3/32N	-
1995-96	Cutlass Supreme	F	5/16N-11/16P	3/16P	3/16P-1 3/16P	11/16P	0	NA
		R	-	-	-	-	3/32N	-
	Grand Prix	F	5/16N-11/16P	3/16P	3/16P-1 3/16P	11/16P	0	NA
		R	-	-	-	-	3/32N	-
	Lumina	F	1 1/2P-2 1/2P	2P	3/16P-1 3/16P	11/16P	0	13 13/32
		R	-	-	①	②	3/64N	-
	Regal	F	5/16N-11/16P	3/16P	3/16P-1 3/16P	11/16P	0	NA
		R	-	-	5/8N-5/8P	3/32P	3/32N	-

NA - Not Available

F - Front

R - Rear

① With 14" wheels: 3/16N-13/16P
   With 15" or 16" wheels: 13/32N-19/32P

② With 14" wheels: 5/16P
   With 15" or 16" wheels: 3/32P

BROUGHAM/FLEETWOOD BROUGHAM

VEHICLE IDENTIFICATION CHART

		Engine Code					Model Year	
Code	Liters	Cu. In. (cc)	Cyl.	Fuel Sys.	Eng. Mfg.		Code	Year
E	5.0	305 (5011)	8	TFI	Chevrolet		P	1993
7	5.7	350 (5733)	8	TFI	Chevrolet		R	1994
P	5.7	350 (5733)	8	MFI	Chevrolet		S	1995
							T	1996

MFI - Multiport fuel injection
TFI - Throttle body fuel injection

ENGINE IDENTIFICATION

Year	Model	Engine Displacement Liters (cc)	Engine Series (ID/VIN)	Fuel System	No. of Cylinders	Engine Type
1992	Brougham	5.0 (5011)	E	TFI	8	OHV
	Brougham	5.7 (5733)	7	TFI	8	OHV
1993	Fleetwood	5.7 (5733)	7	TFI	8	OHV
	Fleetwood Brougham	5.7 (5733)	7	TFI	8	OHV
1994	Fleetwood	5.7 (5733)	P	MFI	8	OHV
	Fleetwood Brougham	5.7 (5733)	P	MFI	8	OHV
1995-96	Fleetwood	5.7 (5733)	P	MFI	8	OHV
	Fleetwood Brougham	5.7 (5733)	P	MFI	8	OHV

MFI - Multiport fuel injection
TFI - Throttle body fuel injection
OHV - Overhead valve

GENERAL ENGINE SPECIFICATIONS

Year	Engine ID/VIN	Engine Displacement Liters (cc)	Fuel System Type	Net Horsepower @ rpm	Net Torque @ rpm (ft. lbs.)	Bore x Stroke (in.)	Compression Ratio	Oil Pressure @ rpm
1992	E	5.0 (5011)	TFI	170@4200	255@2400	3.74x3.48	9.3:1	18@2000
	7	5.7 (5733)	TFI	185@3800	300@2400	4.00x3.48	9.8:1	18@2000
1993	7	5.7 (5733)	TFI	185@3800	300@2400	4.00x3.48	9.8:1	18@2000
1994	P	5.7 (5733)	MFI	260@5000	330@2400	4.00x3.48	9.7:1	18@2000
1995-96	P	5.7 (5733)	MFI	260@5000	330@2400	4.00x3.48	9.7:1	18@2000

MFI - Multiport fuel injection
TFI - Throttle body fuel injection

GASOLINE ENGINE TUNE-UP SPECIFICATIONS

Year	Engine ID/VIN	Engine Displacement Liters (cc)	Spark Plugs Gap (in.)	Ignition Timing (deg.) MT	Ignition Timing (deg.) AT	Fuel Pump (psi)	Idle Speed (rpm) MT	Idle Speed (rpm) AT	Valve Clearance In.	Valve Clearance Ex.
1992	E	5.0 (5011)	0.035	-	①	9-13	-	①	HYD	HYD
	7	5.7 (5733)	0.035	-	①	9-13	-	①	HYD	HYD
1993	7	5.7 (5733)	0.035	-	①	9-13	-	①	HYD	HYD
1994	P	5.7 (5733)	0.050	-	①	41-47	-	①	HYD	HYD
1995-96	P	5.7 (5733)	0.050	-	①	41-47	-	①	HYD	HYD

NOTE: The Vehicle Emission Control Information label often reflects specification changes made during production. The label figures must be used if they differ from those in this chart.

HYD - Hydraulic

① Refer to underhood sticker

CAPACITIES

Year	Model	Engine ID/VIN	Engine Displacement Liters (cc)	Engine Oil with Filter (qts.)	Transmission (pts.) 4-Spd	Transmission (pts.) 5-Spd	Transmission (pts.) Auto.	Drive Axle Front (pts.)	Drive Axle Rear (pts.)	Fuel Tank (gal.)	Cooling System (qts.)
1992	Brougham	E	5.0 (5011)	5.0	-	-	10.0	-	4.2	25.0	16.5
	Brougham	7	5.7 (5733)	5.0	-	-	10.0	-	4.2	25.0	16.5
1993	Fleetwood	7	5.7 (5733)	5.0	-	-	10.0	-	4.2	23.0	15.7
	Fleetwood Brougham	7	5.7 (5733)	5.0	-	-	10.0	-	4.2	23.0	15.7
1994	Fleetwood	P	5.7 (5733)	5.0	-	-	10.0 ①	-	4.2	23.0	14.6
	Fleetwood Brougham	P	5.7 (5733)	5.0	-	-	10.0 ①	-	4.2	23.0	14.6
1995-96	Fleetwood	P	5.7 (5733)	5.0	-	-	10.0 ①	-	4.2	23.0	14.6
	Fleetwood Brougham	P	5.7 (5733)	5.0	-	-	10.0 ①	-	4.2	23.0	14.6

① Fluid change with filter

CAMSHAFT SPECIFICATIONS

All measurements given in inches.

Year	Engine ID/VIN	Engine Displacement Liters (cc)	Journal Diameter 1	Journal Diameter 2	Journal Diameter 3	Journal Diameter 4	Journal Diameter 5	Elevation In.	Elevation Ex.	Bearing Clearance	Camshaft End Play
1992	E	5.0 (5011)	1.8682-1.8692	1.8682-1.8692	1.8682-1.8692	1.8682-1.8692	1.8682-1.8692	0.2340	0.2570	NA	0.0040-0.0120
	7	5.7 (5733)	1.8682-1.8692	1.8682-1.8692	1.8682-1.8692	1.8682-1.8692	1.8682-1.8692	0.2570	0.2690	NA	0.0040-0.0120
1993	7	5.7 (5733)	1.8682-1.8692	1.8682-1.8692	1.8682-1.8692	1.8682-1.8692	1.8682-1.8692	0.2330	0.2560	NA	0.0040-0.0120
1994	P	5.7 (5733)	1.8677-1.8697	1.8677-1.8697	1.8677-1.8697	1.8677-1.8697	1.8677-1.8697	0.2790	0.2860	NA	0.0040-0.0120
1995-96	P	5.7 (5733)	1.8677-1.8697	1.8677-1.8697	1.8677-1.8697	1.8677-1.8697	1.8677-1.8697	0.2790	0.2860	NA	0.0040-0.0120

NA - Not Available

CRANKSHAFT AND CONNECTING ROD SPECIFICATIONS

All measurements are given in inches.

Year	Engine ID/VIN	Engine Displacement Liters (cc)	Crankshaft				Connecting Rod		
			Main Brg. Journal Dia.	Main Brg. Oil Clearance	Shaft End-play	Thrust on No.	Journal Diameter	Oil Clearance	Side Clearance
1992	E	5.0 (5011)	2.4481-2.4490 ①	0.0011-0.0020 ②	0.0010-0.0070	5	2.0893-2.0998	0.0013-0.0035	0.0060-0.0140
	7	5.7 (5733)	2.4481-2.4490 ①	0.0011-0.0020 ②	0.0010-0.0070	5	2.0893-2.0998	0.0013-0.0035	0.0060-0.0140
1993	7	5.7 (5733)	2.4481-2.9940 ①	0.0011-0.0020 ②	0.0010-0.0070	5	2.0893-2.0998	0.0013-0.0035	0.0060-0.0140
1994	P	5.7 (5733)	2.4481-2.9940 ①	0.0011-0.0020 ②	0.0010-0.0070	5	2.0893-2.0998	0.0013-0.0035	0.0060-0.0140
1995-96	P	5.7 (5733)	2.4481-2.9940 ①	0.0011-0.0020 ②	0.0010-0.0070	5	2.0893-2.0998	0.0013-0.0035	0.0060-0.0140

① No. 1: 2.4488-2.4493
No. 5: 2.4481-2.4488
② No. 1: 0.0008-0.0020
No. 5: 0.0017-0.0032

VALVE SPECIFICATIONS

Year	Engine ID/VIN	Engine Displacement Liters (cc)	Seat Angle (deg.)	Face Angle (deg.)	Spring Test Pressure (lbs. @ in.)	Spring Installed Height (in.)	Stem-to-Guide Clearance (in.)		Stem Diameter (in.)	
							Intake	Exhaust	Intake	Exhaust
1992	E	5.0 (5011)	46	45	76-84@1.700	1.719	0.0011-0.0027	0.0011-0.0027	NA	NA
	7	5.7 (5733)	46	45	76-84@1.700	1.719	0.0011-0.0027	0.0011-0.0027	NA	NA
1993	7	5.7 (5733)	46	45	76-84@1.700	1.700	0.0011-0.0027	0.0011-0.0027	NA	NA
1994	P	5.7 (5733)	46	45	76-84@1.700	1.700	0.0009-0.0027	0.0009-0.0027	NA	NA
1995-96	P	5.7 (5733)	46	45	76-84@1.700	1.700	0.0009-0.0027	0.0009-0.0027	NA	NA

NA - Not Available

PISTON AND RING SPECIFICATIONS

All measurements are given in inches.

Year	Engine ID/VIN	Engine Displacement Liters (cc)	Piston Clearance	Ring Gap			Ring Side Clearance		
				Top Compression	Bottom Compression	Oil Control	Top Compression	Bottom Compression	Oil Control
1992	E	5.0 (5011)	0.0007-0.0021	0.0100-0.0200	0.0100-0.0250	0.0150-0.0550	0.0012-0.0032	0.0012-0.0032	0.0020-0.0070
	7	5.7 (5733)	0.0007-0.0021	0.0100-0.0200	0.0100-0.0250	0.0150-0.0550	0.0012-0.0032	0.0012-0.0032	0.0020-0.0070
1993	7	5.7 (5733)	0.0005-0.0022	0.0100-0.0200	0.0180-0.0260	0.0150-0.0550	0.0012-0.0032	0.0012-0.0032	0.0020-0.0070

PISTON AND RING SPECIFICATIONS

All measurements are given in inches.

Year	Engine ID/VIN	Engine Displacement Liters (cc)	Piston Clearance	Ring Gap			Ring Side Clearance		
				Top Compression	Bottom Compression	Oil Control	Top Compression	Bottom Compression	Oil Control
1994	P	5.7 (5733)	0.0010-0.0027	0.0100-0.0200	0.0180-0.0260	0.0100-0.0300	0.0019-0.0035	0.0019-0.0035	0.0020-0.0070
1995-96	P	5.7 (5733)	0.0010-0.0027	0.0100-0.0200	0.0180-0.0260	0.0100-0.0300	0.0019-0.0035	0.0019-0.0035	0.0020-0.0070

NA - Not Available

TORQUE SPECIFICATIONS

All readings in ft. lbs.

Year	Engine ID/VIN	Engine Displacement Liters (cc)	Cylinder Head Bolts	Main Bearing Bolts	Rod Bearing Bolts	Crankshaft Damper Bolts	Flywheel Bolts	Manifold		Spark Plugs	Lug Nut
								Intake	Exhaust		
1992	E	5.0 (5011)	70	75	45	70	75	35	25	22	100
	7	5.7 (5733)	70	7	45	70	75	35	25	22	100
1993	7	5.7 (5733)	65	77	44	70	74	35	23	11	100
1994	P	5.7 (5733)	67	78	①	75	74	35	26	11	100
1995-96	P	5.7 (5733)	67	78	①	75	74	35	26	11	100

① Step 1: 20 ft. lbs.
   Step 2: Plus 50 degrees

BRAKE SPECIFICATIONS

All measurements in inches unless noted

Year	Model	Master Cylinder Bore	Brake Disc			Brake Drum Diameter			Minimum Lining Thickness	
			Original Thickness	Minimum Thickness	Maximum Runout	Original Inside Diameter	Max. Wear Limit	Maximum Machine Diameter	Front	Rear
1992	Brougham	1.125	1.032	0.965	0.004	11.00	11.09	11.06	0.030	0.030
1993	Fleetwood	1.125	1.043	0.965	0.004	11.00	11.09	11.06	0.030	0.030
	Fleetwood Broughm	1.125	1.043	0.965	0.004	11.00	11.09	11.06	0.030	0.030
1994	Fleetwood	1.125	1.043	0.965	0.004	11.00	11.09	11.06	0.030	0.030
	Fleetwood Broughm	1.125	1.043	0.965	0.004	11.00	11.09	11.06	0.030	0.030
1995-96	Fleetwood	1.125	1.043	0.965	0.004	11.00	11.09	11.06	0.030	0.030
	Fleetwood Broughm	1.125	1.043	0.965	0.004	11.00	11.09	11.06	0.030	0.030

WHEEL ALIGNMENT

Year	Model	Caster Range (deg.)	Caster Preferred Setting (deg.)	Camber Range (deg.)	Camber Preferred Setting (deg.)	Toe-in (in.)	Steering Axis Inclination (deg.)
1992	Brougham	2P-4P	3P	0.50N-0.50P	0	0	NA
1993	Fleetwood	2 1/2P-4 1/2P	3 1/2P	1N-1P	0	1/32P	NA
	Fleetwood Broughm	2 1/2P-4 1/2P	3 1/2P	1N-1P	0	1/32P	NA
1994	Fleetwood	2 1/2P-4 1/2P	3 1/2P	1N-1P	0	1/32P	NA
	Fleetwood Broughm	2 1/2P-4 1/2P	3 1/2P	1N-1P	0	1/32P	NA
1995-96	Fleetwood	2 1/2P-4 1/2P	3 1/2P	1N-1P	0	1/32P	NA
	Fleetwood Broughm	2 1/2P-4 1/2P	3 1/2P	1N-1P	0	1/32P	NA

NA - Not Available

CAPRICE/CUSTOM CRUISER/IMPALA SS
ROADMASTER/ROADMASTER ESTATE WAGON

VEHICLE IDENTIFICATION CHART

Engine Code						Model Year	
Code	Liters	Cu. In. (cc)	Cyl.	Fuel Sys.	Eng. Mfg.	Code	Year
7	5.7	350 (5737)	8	TFI	CPC	S	1995
E	5.0	305 (4999)	8	TFI	CPC	T	1996
P	5.7	350 (5737)	8	MFI	CPC	P	1993
W	4.3	265 (4294)	8	MFI	CPC	N	1992
Z	4.3	265 (4294)	6	TFI	CPC	R	1994

CPC - Chevrolet/Pontiac/Canada
MFI - Multiport fuel injection
TFI - Throttle body fuel injection

ENGINE IDENTIFICATION

Year	Model	Engine Displacement Liters (cc)	Engine Series (ID/VIN)	Fuel System	No. of Cylinders	Engine Type
1992	Caprice	4.3 (4294)	Z	TFI	6	OHV
	Caprice	5.0 (4999)	E	TFI	8	OHV
	Caprice	5.7 (5737)	7	TFI	8	OHV
	Custom Cruiser	5.0 (4998)	E	TFI	8	OHV
	Custom Cruiser	5.7 (5733)	7	TFI	8	OHV
	Roadmaster/Wagon	5.7 (5733)	7	TFI	9	OHV
1993	Caprice	4.3 (4294)	Z	TFI	6	OHV
	Caprice	5.0 (4999)	E	TFI	8	OHV
	Caprice	5.7 (5737)	7	TFI	8	OHV
	Roadmaster/Wagon	5.7 (5737)	7	TFI	8	OHV
1994	Caprice	4.3 (4294)	W	MFI	6	OHV
	Caprice	5.7 (5737)	P	MFI	8	OHV
	Impala SS	5.7 (5737)	P	MFI	8	OHV
	Roadmaster/Wagon	5.7 (5737)	P	MFI	8	OHV
1995-96	Caprice	4.3 (4294)	W	MFI	8	OHV
	Caprice	5.7 (5737)	P	MFI	8	OHV
	Impala SS	5.7 (5737)	P	MFI	8	OHV
	Roadmaster/Wagon	5.7 (5737)	P	MFI	8	OHV

TFI - Throttle body fuel injection
MFI - Multiport fuel injection
OHV - Overhead valve

GENERAL ENGINE SPECIFICATIONS

Year	Engine ID/VIN	Engine Displacement Liters (cc)	Fuel System Type	Net Horsepower @ rpm	Net Torque @ rpm (ft. lbs.)	Bore x Stroke (in.)	Compression Ratio	Oil Pressure @ rpm
1992	Z	4.3 (4294)	TFI	140@4000	225@2000	4.00x3.48	9.3:1	18@2000
	E	5.0 (4999)	MFI	170@4000	255@2400	3.74x3.48	9.3:1	18@2000
	7	5.7 (5737)	TFI	195@4200	295@2400	4.00x3.50	9.8:1	18@2000
1993	Z	4.3 (4294)	TFI	140@4000	225@2000	4.00x3.48	9.3:1	18@2000
	E	5.0 (4999)	TFI	170@4000	255@2400	3.74x3.48	9.3:1	18@2000
	7	5.7 (5737)	TFI	195@4200	295@2400	4.00x3.50	9.8:1	18@2000
1994	W	4.3 (4294)	MFI	200@5200	245@2400	3.74x3.48	9.93:1	18@2000
	P	5.7 (5737)	MFI	260@5000	330@3200	4.00x3.48	10.25:1	18@2000
1995-96	W	4.3 (4294)	MFI	200@5200	245@2400	3.74x3.48	9.93:1	18@2000
	P	5.7 (5737)	MFI	260@5000	330@3200	4.00x3.48	10.25:1	18@2000

TFI - Throttle body fuel injection
MFI - Multiport fuel injection

GASOLINE ENGINE TUNE-UP SPECIFICATIONS

Year	Engine ID/VIN	Engine Displacement Liters (cc)	Spark Plugs Gap (in.)	Ignition Timing (deg.) MT	Ignition Timing (deg.) AT	Fuel Pump (psi)	Idle Speed (rpm) MT	Idle Speed (rpm) AT	Valve Clearance In.	Valve Clearance Ex.
1992	Z	4.3 (4294)	0.035	-	①	9-13	-	①	HYD	HYD
	E	5.0 (4999)	0.035	-	-	11	-	①	HYD	HYD
	7	5.7 (5737)	0.035	-	①	9-13	-	①	HYD	HYD
1993	Z	4.3 (4294)	0.035	-	①	9-13	-	①	HYD	HYD
	E	5.0 (4999)	0.035	-	-	11	-	①	HYD	HYD
	7	5.7 (5737)	0.035	-	①	9-13	-	①	HYD	HYD
1994	W	4.3 (4294)	0.050	①	①	6-24	①	①	HYD	HYD
	P	5.7 (5737)	0.035	-	①	41-47	-	①	HYD	HYD
1995-96	W	4.3 (4294)	0.050	①	①	6-24	①	①	HYD	HYD
	P	5.7 (5737)	0.035	-	①	41-47	-	①	HYD	HYD

NOTE: The Vehicle Emission Control Information label often reflects specification changes made during production. The label figures must be used if they differ from those in this chart.

HYD - Hydraulic

① Refer to Vehicle Emission Control Information label

CAPACITIES

Year	Model	Engine ID/VIN	Engine Displacement Liters (cc)	Engine Oil with Filter (qts.)	Transmission (pts.) 4-Spd	Transmission (pts.) 5-Spd	Transmission (pts.) Auto.	Transfer Case (pts.)	Drive Axle Front (pts.)	Drive Axle Rear (pts.)	Fuel Tank (gal.)	Cooling System (qts.)
1992	Caprice	Z	4.3 (4294)	4.5	-	-	10.0	-	-	③	23.0	12.6 ①
	Caprice	E	5.0 (4999)	5.0	-	-	7.0 ②	-	-	③	24.5	16.7 ①
	Caprice	7	5.7 (5737)	5.0	-	-	7.0 ②	-	-	③	22.0	14.6 ①
	Custom Cruiser	E	5.0 (4998)	5.0	-	-	10.0	-	-	③	22.0	④
	Custom Cruiser	7	5.7 (5733)	5.0	-	-	10.0	-	-	③	22.0	⑤
	Roadmaster/Wgn	7	5.7 (5737)	5.0	-	-	10.0	-	④	④	22.0	⑤
1993	Caprice	Z	4.3 (4294)	4.5	-	-	10.0	-	-	③	23.0	12.6 ①
	Caprice	E	5.0 (4999)	5.0	-	-	7.0 ②	-	-	③	24.5	16.7 ①
	Caprice	7	5.7 (5737)	5.0	-	-	7.0 ②	-	-	③	22.0	14.6 ①
	Roadmaster/Wgn	7	5.7 (5737)	5.0	-	-	10.0	-	3.50	3.50	22.0	⑥
1994	Caprice	W	4.3 (4294)	4.5	-	-	7.0 ②	-	-	③	23.0	12.6 ①
	Caprice	P	5.7 (5737)	5.0	-	-	7.0 ②	-	-	③	22.0	14.6 ①
	Impala SS	P	5.7 (5737)	5.0	-	-	7.0 ②	-	-	③	22.0	14.6 ①
	Roadmaster/Wgn	P	5.7 (5737)	5.0	-	-	10.0	-	③	③	22.0	⑦
1995-96	Caprice	W	4.3 (4294)	4.5	-	-	7.0 ②	-	-	③	23.0	12.6 ①
	Caprice	P	5.7 (5737)	5.0	-	-	7.0 ②	-	-	③	22.0	14.6 ①
	Impala SS	P	5.7 (5737)	5.0	-	-	7.0 ②	-	-	③	22.0	14.6 ①
	Roadmaster/Wgn	P	5.7 (5737)	5.0	-	-	10.0	-	③	③	22.0	⑦

① Add 0.6 qts. for HD radiator
② 4L60 trans.: 10.0 pts.
③ With 7 5/8" ring gear: 3.50 pts.
   With 8.5" ring gear: 4.25 pts.
   With 8.75" ring gear: 5.4 pts.
④ 2.56 axle ratio-option code GM8: 2.90 pts.
   All except option GM8: 3.50 pts.
⑤ With std. cooling: 16.70
   With heavy duty/trailer pkg. cooling: 17.30
⑥ With std. cooling: 14.40
   With heavy duty cooling: 15.10
⑦ With std. cooling: 14.30
   With heavy duty cooling: 14.60

CAMSHAFT SPECIFICATIONS
All measurements given in inches.

| Year | Engine ID/VIN | Engine Displacement Liters (cc) | Journal Diameter | | | | | Elevation | | Bearing Clearance | Camshaft End Play |
			1	2	3	4	5	In.	Ex.		
1992	Z	4.3 (4294)	1.868-1.869	1.868-1.869	1.868-1.869	1.868-1.869	1.868-1.869	0.234	0.257	NA	0.004-0.012
	E	5.0 (4999)	1.8682-1.8692	1.8682-1.8692	1.8682-1.8692	1.8682-1.8692	1.8682-1.8692	0.234	0.257	NA	0.004-0.012
	7	5.7 (5737)	1.8682-1.8692	1.8682-1.8692	1.8682-1.8692	1.8682-1.8692	1.8682-1.8692	0.257	0.269	NA	0.004-0.012
1993	Z	4.3 (4294)	1.868-1.869	1.868-1.869	1.868-1.869	1.868-1.869	1.868-1.869	0.234	0.257	NA	0.004-0.012
	E	5.0 (4999)	1.8682-1.8692	1.8682-1.8692	1.8682-1.8692	1.8682-1.8692	1.8682-1.8692	0.234	0.257	NA	0.004-0.012
	7	5.7 (5737)	1.8682-1.8692	1.8682-1.8692	1.8682-1.8692	1.8682-1.8692	1.8682-1.8692	0.257	0.269	NA	0.004-0.012
1994	W	4.3 (4294)	1.8677-1.8697	1.8677-1.8697	1.8677-1.8697	1.8677-1.8697	1.8677-1.8697	0.279	0.286	NA	0.004-0.012
	P	5.7 (5737)	1.8682-1.8692	1.8682-1.8692	1.8682-1.8692	1.8682-1.8692	1.8682-1.8692	0.2980-0.3020	0.2980-0.3020	NA	0.004-0.012
1995-96	W	4.3 (4294)	1.8677-1.8697	1.8677-1.8697	1.8677-1.8697	1.8677-1.8697	1.8677-1.8697	0.2790	0.2860	NA	0.0040-0.0120
	P	5.7 (5737)	1.8682-1.8692	1.8682-1.8692	1.8682-1.8692	1.8682-1.8692	1.8682-1.8692	0.2980-0.3020	0.2980-0.3020	NA	0.0040-0.0120

NA - Not Available

CRANKSHAFT AND CONNECTING ROD SPECIFICATIONS
All measurements are given in inches.

| Year | Engine ID/VIN | Engine Displacement Liters (cc) | Crankshaft | | | | Connecting Rod | | |
			Main Brg. Journal Dia.	Main Brg. Oil Clearance	Shaft End-play	Thrust on No.	Journal Diameter	Oil Clearance	Side Clearance
1992	Z	4.3 (4294)	①	②	0.001-0.007	4	2.0983-2.0998	0.0013-0.0035	0.006-0.014
	E	5.0 (4999)	①	②	0.001-0.007	4	2.0986-2.0998	0.0013-0.0035	0.006-0.014
	7	5.7 (5737)	①	②	0.001-0.007	5	2.0986-2.0998	0.0013-0.0035	0.006-0.014
1993	Z	4.3 (4294)	①	②	0.001-0.007	4	2.0983-2.0998	0.0013-0.0035	0.006-0.014
	E	5.0 (4999)	①	②	0.001-0.007	5	2.0986-2.0998	0.0013-0.0035	0.006-0.014
	7	5.7 (5737)	①	②	0.001-0.007	5	2.0986-2.0998	0.0013-0.0035	0.006-0.014
1994	W	4.3 (4294)	③	④	0.001-0.007	4	2.0983-2.0998	0.0013-0.0035	0.006-0.014
	P	5.7 (5737)	③	④	0.002-0.006	5	2.0986-2.0998	0.0013-0.0035	0.006-0.014
1995-96	W	4.3 (4294)	③	④	0.0010-0.0070	4	2.0983-2.0998	0.0013-0.0035	0.0060-0.0140
	P	5.7 (5737)	③	④	0.0020-0.0060	5	2.0986-2.0998	0.0013-0.0035	0.0060-0.0140

CRANKSHAFT AND CONNECTING ROD SPECIFICATIONS

All measurements are given in inches.

Year	Engine ID/VIN	Engine Displacement Liters (cc)	Crankshaft Main Brg. Journal Dia.	Crankshaft Main Brg. Oil Clearance	Crankshaft Shaft End-play	Crankshaft Thrust on No.	Connecting Rod Journal Diameter	Connecting Rod Oil Clearance	Connecting Rod Side Clearance

① No. 1: 2.4484-2.4493
Nos. 2-4: 2.4481-2.4490
No. 5: 2.4479-2.4488
② No. 1: 0.0008-0.0020
Nos. 2-4: 0.0011-0.0023
No. 5: 0.0017-0.0032

③ No. 1: 2.4485-2.4491
Nos. 2-4: 2.4485-2.4491
④ No. 1: 0.0008-0.0020
Nos. 2-4: 0.0011-0.0020
No. 5: 0.0017-0.0032

VALVE SPECIFICATIONS

Year	Engine ID/VIN	Engine Displacement Liters (cc)	Seat Angle (deg.)	Face Angle (deg.)	Spring Test Pressure (lbs. @ in.)	Spring Installed Height (in.)	Stem-to-Guide Clearance (in.) Intake	Stem-to-Guide Clearance (in.) Exhaust	Stem Diameter (in.) Intake	Stem Diameter (in.) Exhaust
1992	Z	4.3 (4294)	46	45	194-206@ 1.25	1.69-1.71	0.0011-0.0027	0.0011-0.0027	NA	NA
	E	5.0 (4999)	46	45	194-206@ 1.25	①	0.0011-0.0027	0.0011-0.0027	NA	NA
	7	5.7 (5737)	46	45	194-206@ 1.25	1.70	0.0011-0.0027	0.0011-0.0027	NA	NA
1993	Z	4.3 (4294)	46	45	194-206@ 1.25	1.69-1.71	0.0011-0.0027	0.0011-0.0027	NA	NA
	E	5.0 (4999)	46	45	194-206@ 1.25	①	0.0011-0.0027	0.0011-0.0027	NA	NA
	7	5.7 (5737)	46	45	194-206@ 1.25	1.70	0.0011-0.0027	0.0011-0.0027	NA	NA
1994	W	4.3 (4294)	46	45	187-203@ 1.27	1.70	0.0009-0.0027	0.0009-0.0027	NA	NA
	P	5.7 (5737)	46	45	187-203@ 1.27	1.70	0.0009-0.0027	0.0009-0.0027	NA	NA
1995-96	W	4.3 (4294)	46	45	187-203@ 1.27	1.70	0.0009-0.0027	0.0009-0.0027	NA	NA
	P	5.7 (5737)	46	45	187-203@ 1.27	1.70	0.0009-0.0027	0.0009-0.0027	NA	NA

NA - Not Available
① Intake: 1.72
Exhaust: 1.59

PISTON AND RING SPECIFICATIONS
All measurements are given in inches.

Year	Engine ID/VIN	Engine Displacement Liters (cc)	Piston Clearance	Ring Gap			Ring Side Clearance		
				Top Compression	Bottom Compression	Oil Control	Top Compression	Bottom Compression	Oil Control
1992	Z	4.3 (4294)	0.007-0.017	0.010-0.020	0.017-0.025	0.015-0.055	0.0014-0.0032	0.0014-0.0032	0.0014-0.0032
	E	5.0 (4999)	0.007-0.017	0.010-0.020	0.010-0.025	0.015-0.055	0.0012-0.0032	0.0012-0.0032	0.0020-0.0070
	7	5.7 (5737)	0.007-0.017	0.010-0.020	0.010-0.025	0.015-0.055	0.0012-0.0032	0.0012-0.0032	0.0020-0.0070
1993	Z	4.3 (4294)	0.007-0.017	0.010-0.020	0.017-0.025	0.015-0.055	0.0014-0.0032	0.0014-0.0032	0.0014-0.0032
	E	5.0 (4999)	0.007-0.017	0.010-0.020	0.010-0.025	0.015-0.055	0.0012-0.0032	0.0012-0.0032	0.0020-0.0070
	7	5.7 (5737)	0.007-0.017	0.010-0.020	0.010-0.025	0.015-0.055	0.0012-0.0032	0.0012-0.0032	0.0020-0.0070
1994	W	4.3 (4294)	0.0010-0.0027	0.010-0.020	0.018-0.026	0.010-0.030	0.0012-0.0029	0.0012-0.0029	0.0080 MAX
	P	5.7 (5737)	0.0010-0.0027	0.010-0.020	0.018-0.026	0.010-0.030	0.0012-0.0032	0.0012-0.0032	0.0020-0.0070
1995-96	W	4.3 (4294)	0.0010-0.0027	0.010-0.020	0.018-0.026	0.010-0.030	0.0012-0.0029	0.0012-0.0029	0.0080 MAX
	P	5.7 (5737)	0.0010-0.0027	0.010-0.020	0.018-0.026	0.010-0.030	0.0012-0.0032	0.0012-0.0032	0.0020-0.0070

TORQUE SPECIFICATIONS
All readings in ft. lbs.

Year	Engine ID/VIN	Engine Displacement Liters (cc)	Cylinder Head Bolts	Main Bearing Bolts	Rod Bearing Bolts	Crankshaft Damper Bolts	Flywheel Bolts	Manifold		Spark Plugs	Lug Nut
								Intake	Exhaust		
1992	Z	4.3 (4294)	68	77	44	②	74	35	③	11	100
	E	5.0 (4999)	60-75	70-85	42-47	60	75	25-45	①	15-20	80-100
	7	5.7 (5737)	68	77	44	70	74	35	26	22	80-100
1993	Z	4.3 (4294)	68	77	44	②	74	35	③	11	100
	E	5.0 (4999)	60-75	70-85	42-47	60	75	25-45	①	15-20	80-100
	7	5.7 (5737)	68	77	44	70	74	35	26	22	80-100
1994	W	4.3 (4294)	65	78	47	60	74	④	35	11	100
	P	5.7 (5737)	65	78	47	60	74	④	35	11	100
1995-96	W	4.3 (4294)	65	78	47	60	74	④	35	11	100
	P	5.7 (5737)	65	78	47	60	74	④	35	11	100

① Outer bolts: 14-26 ft. lbs.
Inner bolts: 20-32 ft. lbs.
② Torsional damper: 70 ft. lbs.
Crankshaft pulley: 43 ft. lbs.
③ Outer bolts: 20 ft. lbs.
Inner bolts: 26 ft. lbs.
④ Step 1: 71 inch lbs.
Step 2: 35 ft. lbs.

BRAKE SPECIFICATIONS

All measurements in inches unless noted

Year	Model		Master Cylinder Bore	Brake Disc Original Thickness	Brake Disc Minimum Thickness	Brake Disc Maximum Runout	Brake Drum Diameter Original Inside Diameter	Brake Drum Diameter Max. Wear Limit	Brake Drum Diameter Maximum Machine Diameter	Minimum Lining Thickness Front	Minimum Lining Thickness Rear
1992	Caprice		1.125	1.043	0.980	0.004	11.00	11.09	11.06	0.030	0.030
	Custom Cruiser		1.250	1.043	0.965	0.004	11.00	11.09	11.06	0.030	①
	Roadmaster/Wgn		1.125	1.043	0.965	0.004	11.00	11.09	11.06	0.030	①
1993	Caprice		1.125	1.043	0.980	0.004	11.00	11.09	11.06	0.030	0.030
	Roadmaster/Wgn		1.125	1.043	0.965	0.003	11.00	11.09	11.06	0.030	①
1994	Caprice		1.125	1.043	0.980	0.004	11.00	11.09	11.06	0.030	0.030
	Impala SS		1.125	1.043	0.980	0.004	11.00	11.09	11.06	0.030	0.030
	Roadmaster ②		1.125	1.043	0.965	0.003	11.00	11.09	11.06	0.030	①
	Roadmaster ③	F	1.251	1.043	0.965	0.003	-	-	-	0.030	0.030
		R	1.251	0.787	0.728	0.004	-	-	-	0.030	0.030
1995-96	Caprice		1.125	1.043	0.980	0.004	11.00	11.09	11.06	0.030	0.030
	Impala SS		1.125	1.043	0.980	0.004	11.00	11.09	11.06	0.030	0.030
	Roadmaster ②		1.125	1.043	0.965	0.003	11.00	11.09	11.06	0.030	①
	Roadmaster ③	F	1.251	1.043	0.965	0.003	-	-	-	0.030	0.030
		R	1.251	0.787	0.728	0.004	-	-	-	0.030	0.030

F - Front
R - Rear

① 0.030 over rivet head; If bonded lining, use 0.062 from shoe
② Wagon
③ Police

WHEEL ALIGNMENT

Year	Model		Caster Range (deg.)	Caster Preferred Setting (deg.)	Camber Range (deg.)	Camber Preferred Setting (deg.)	Toe-in (in.)	Steering Axis Inclination (deg.)
1992	Caprice	F	2 1/2P-4 1/2P	3 1/2P	0-1 5/8P	13/16P	3/32P	0
		R	-	-	1/16N-1/16P	0	0	-
	Custom Cruiser		2 1/2P-4 1/2P	3 1/2P	13/16N-13/16P	0	3/32P	0
	Roadmaster/Wgn	F	2 1/2P-4 1/2P	3 1/2P	0-1 5/8P	13/16P	3/32P	-
		R	-	-	1/16N-1/16P	0	0	-
1993	Caprice		2 1/2P-4 1/2P	3 1/2P	1N-1P	0	3/32P	0
	Roadmaster/Wgn		2 1/2P-4 1/2P	3 1/2P	1N-1P	0	3/32P	0
1994	Caprice		2 1/2P-4 1/2P	3 1/2P	1N-1P	0	3/32P	0
	Impala SS		2 1/2P-4 1/2P	3 1/2P	1N-1P	0	3/32P	0
	Roadmaster/Wgn		2 1/2P-4 1/2P	3 1/2P	1N-1P	0	5/32P	NA
1994-95	Caprice		2 1/2P-4 1/2P	3 1/2P	1N-1P	0	3/32P	0
	Impala SS		2 1/2P-4 1/2P	3 1/2P	1N-1P	0	3/32P	0
	Roadmaster/Wgn		2 1/2P-4 1/2P	3 1/2P	1N-1P	0	5/32P	NA

F - Front
R - Rear

CAMARO/FIREBIRD

VEHICLE IDENTIFICATION CHART

		Engine Code					Model Year	
Code	Liters	Cu. In. (cc)	Cyl.	Fuel Sys.	Eng. Mfg.		Code	Year
T	3.1	191 (3130)	6	MFI	CPC		N	1992
S	3.4	207 (3393)	6	MFI	CPC		P	1993
E	5.0	305 (4999)	8	TFI	CPC		R	1994
F	5.0	305 (4999)	8	MFI	CPC		S	1995
8	5.7	350 (5737)	8	MFI	CPC		T	1996
P	5.7	350 (5737)	8	MFI	CPC			

MFI - Multiport fuel injection
TFI - Throttle body fuel injection
CPC - Chevrolet/Pontiac/Canada
BOC - Buick/Oldsmobile/Cadillac

ENGINE IDENTIFICATION

Year	Model	Engine Displacement Liters (cc)	Engine Series (ID/VIN)	Fuel System	No. of Cylinders	Engine Type
1992	Camaro	3.1 (3130)	T	MFI	6	OHV
	Camaro	5.0 (4999)	E	MFI	8	OHV
	Camaro	5.0 (4999)	F	TFI	8	OHV
	Camaro	5.7 (5737)	8	MFI	8	OHV
	Firebird	3.1 (3130)	T	MFI	6	OHV
	Firebird	5.0 (4999)	E	MFI	8	OHV
	Firebird	5.0 (4999)	F	TFI	8	OHV
	Firebird	5.7 (5737)	8	MFI	8	OHV
1993	Camaro	3.1 (3130)	T	MFI	6	OHV
	Camaro	3.4 (3393)	S	MFI	6	OHV
	Camaro	5.0 (4999)	E	MFI	8	OHV
	Camaro	5.7 (5737)	8	MFI	8	OHV
	Camaro	5.7 (5737)	P	MFI	8	OHV
	Firebird	3.1 (3130)	T	MFI	6	OHV
	Firebird	3.4 (3393)	S	MFI	6	OHV
	Firebird	5.0 (4999)	E	MFI	8	OHV
	Firebird	5.7 (5737)	8	MFI	8	OHV
	Firebird	5.7 (5737)	P	MFI	8	OHV
1994	Camaro	3.1 (3130)	T	MFI	6	OHV
	Camaro	3.4 (3393)	S	MFI	6	OHV
	Camaro	5.7 (5737)	P	MFI	8	OHV
	Firebird	3.1 (3130)	T	MFI	6	OHV
	Firebird	3.4 (3393)	S	MFI	6	OHV
	Firebird	5.7 (5737)	P	MFI	8	OHV
1995-96	Camaro	3.1 (3130)	T	MFI	6	OHV
	Camaro	3.4 (3393)	S	MFI	6	OHV
	Camaro	5.7 (5737)	P	MFI	8	OHV

ENGINE IDENTIFICATION

Year	Model	Engine Displacement Liters (cc)	Engine Series (ID/VIN)	Fuel System	No. of Cylinders	Engine Type
	Firebird	3.1 (3130)	T	MFI	6	OHV
	Firebird	3.4 (3393)	S	MFI	6	OHV
	Firebird	5.7 (5737)	P	MFI	8	OHV

TFI - Throttle body fuel injection
MFI - Multiport fuel injection
OHV - Overhead valve

GENERAL ENGINE SPECIFICATIONS

Year	Engine ID/VIN	Engine Displacement Liters (cc)	Fuel System Type	Net Horsepower @ rpm	Net Torque @ rpm (ft. lbs.)	Bore x Stroke (in.)	Compression Ratio	Oil Pressure @ rpm
1992	T	3.1 (3130)	MFI	140@4400	180@3600	3.50x3.31	8.5:1	8@600
	E	5.0 (4999)	TFI	170@4000	255@2400	3.74x3.48	9.3:1	18@2000
	F	5.0 (4999)	MFI	140@4000	300@3200	3.74x3.48	9.3:1	18@2000
	8	5.7 (5737)	MFI	240@4400	345@3200	4.00x.48	9.75:1	18@2000
1993	T	3.1 (3130)	MFI	140@4200	185@3200	3.50x3.31	8.5:1	8@600
	S	3.4 (3393)	MFI	160@4600	200@3600	3.62x3.31	9.0:1	15@1100
	E	5.0 (4999)	TFI	170@4000	255@2400	3.74x3.48	9.3:1	18@2000
	8	5.7 (5737)	MFI	240@4000	345@3200	4.00x3.48	9.75:1	18@2000
	P	5.7 (5737)	MFI	275@5000	325@2400	4.00x3.48	10.25:1	18@2000
1994	T	3.1 (3130)	MFI	140@4200	185@3200	3.50x3.31	8.5:1	8@600
	S	3.4 (3393)	MFI	160@4600	200@3600	3.62x3.31	9.0:1	15@1100
	P	5.7 (5737)	MFI	275@5000	325@2400	4.00x3.48	10.25:1	18@2000
1995-96	T	3.1 (3130)	MFI	140@4200	185@3200	3.50x3.31	8.5:1	8@600
	S	3.4 (3393)	MFI	160@4600	200@3600	3.62x3.31	9.0:1	15@1100
	P	5.7 (5737)	MFI	275@5000	325@2400	4.00x3.48	10.25:1	18@2000

TFI - Throttle body fuel injection
MFI - Multiport fuel injection

GASOLINE ENGINE TUNE-UP SPECIFICATIONS

Year	Engine ID/VIN	Engine Displacement Liters (cc)	Spark Plugs Gap (in.)	Ignition Timing (deg.) MT	Ignition Timing (deg.) AT	Fuel Pump (psi)	Idle Speed (rpm) MT	Idle Speed (rpm) AT	Valve Clearance In.	Valve Clearance Ex.
1992	T	3.1 (3130)	0.045	10B	10B	41-47	①	①	HYD	HYD
	E	5.0 (4999)	0.035	-	-	9-13	-	①	HYD	HYD
	F	5.0 (4999)	0.045	6B	6B	34-47	-	①	HYD	HYD
	8	5.7 (5737)	0.045	8B	8B	34-47	①	①	HYD	HYD
1993	T	3.1 (3130)	0.045	①	①	41-47	①	①	HYD	HYD
	S	3.4 (3393)	0.045	①	①	41-47	①	①	HYD	HYD
	E	5.0 (4999)	0.035	-	-	9-13	-	①	HYD	HYD
	8	5.7 (5737)	0.045	8B	8B	34-47	①	①	HYD	HYD
	P	5.7 (5737)	0.035	-	①	41-47	-	①	HYD	HYD
1994	T	3.1 (3130)	0.045	①	①	41-47	①	①	HYD	HYD
	S	3.4 (3393)	0.045	①	①	41-47	①	①	HYD	HYD
	P	5.7 (5737)	0.035	-	①	41-47	-	①	HYD	HYD

GASOLINE ENGINE TUNE-UP SPECIFICATIONS

Year	Engine ID/VIN	Engine Displacement Liters (cc)	Spark Plugs Gap (in.)	Ignition Timing (deg.) MT	Ignition Timing (deg.) AT	Fuel Pump (psi)	Idle Speed (rpm) MT	Idle Speed (rpm) AT	Valve Clearance In.	Valve Clearance Ex.
1995-96	T	3.1 (3130)	0.045	①	①	41-47	①	①	HYD	HYD
	S	3.4 (3393)	0.045	①	①	41-47	①	①	HYD	HYD
	P	5.7 (5737)	0.035	-	①	41-47	-	①	HYD	HYD

NOTE: The Vehicle Emission Control Information label often reflects specification changes made during production. The label figures must be used if they differ from those in this chart.

B - Before top dead center

HYD - Hydraulic

① Refer to Vehicle Emission Control Information label

CAPACITIES

Year	Model	Engine ID/VIN	Engine Displacement Liters (cc)	Engine Oil with Filter (qts.)	Transmission (pts.) 4-Spd	Transmission (pts.) 5-Spd	Transmission (pts.) Auto.	Drive Axle Front (pts.)	Drive Axle Rear (pts.)	Fuel Tank (gal.)	Cooling System (qts.)
1992	Camaro	T	3.1 (3136)	4.5 ⑨	-	5.9	10.0	-	3.5	15.5	14.7 ①
	Camaro	F	5.0 (5011)	4.5 ⑨	-	5.9	10.0	-	3.5	15.5	17.4 ②
	Camaro	E	5.0 (5011)	5.0 ⑨	-	5.9	10.0	-	3.5	15.5	17.9 ②
	Camaro	8	5.7 (5733)	5.0 ⑨	-	5.9	10.0	-	3.5	15.5	16.6 ③
	Firebird	T	3.1 (3136)	4.5 ⑨	-	5.9	10.0	-	3.5	15.5	14.7 ①
	Firebird	F	5.0 (5011)	4.5 ⑨	-	5.9	10.0	-	3.5	15.5	17.4 ②
	Firebird	E	5.0 (5011)	5.0 ⑨	-	5.9	10.0	-	3.5	15.5	17.9 ②
	Firebird	8	5.7 (5733)	5.0 ⑨	-	5.9	10.0	-	3.5	15.5	16.6 ③
1993	Camaro	T	3.1 (3136)	4.5 ⑨	-	5.9	10.0	-	3.5	15.5	14.7 ①
	Camaro	S	3.4 (3350)	4.5 ⑨	-	5.9	10.0	-	3.5	15.5	12.3 ⑤
	Camaro	E	5.0 (5011)	5.0 ⑨	-	5.9	10.0	-	3.5	15.5	17.9 ②
	Camaro	8	5.7 (5733)	5.0 ⑨	-	5.9	10.0	-	3.5	15.5	16.6 ③
	Camaro	P	5.7 (5733)	5.0 ⑨	-	5.9 ④	10.0	-	3.5	15.5	15.1 ⑥
	Firebird	T	3.1 (3136)	4.5 ⑨	-	5.9	10.0	-	3.5	15.5	14.7 ①
	Firebird	S	3.4 (3350)	4.5 ⑨	-	5.9	10.0	-	3.5	15.5	12.3 ⑤
	Firebird	E	5.0 (5011)	5.0 ⑨	-	5.9	10.0	-	3.5	15.5	17.9 ②
	Firebird	8	5.7 (5733)	5.0 ⑨	-	5.9	10.0	-	3.5	15.5	16.6 ③
	Firebird	P	5.7 (5733)	5.0 ⑨	-	5.9 ④	10.0	-	3.5	15.5	15.1 ⑥
1994	Camaro	T	3.1 (3136)	4.5 ⑨	-	5.9	10.0	-	3.5	15.5	14.7 ①
	Camaro	S	3.4 (3350)	4.5 ⑨	-	5.9	10.0	-	3.5	15.5	12.3 ⑦
	Camaro	P	5.7 (5733)	5.0 ⑨	-	5.9 ④	10.0	-	3.5	15.5	15.1 ⑧
	Firebird	T	3.1 (3136)	4.5 ⑨	-	5.9	10.0	-	3.5	15.5	14.7 ①
	Firebird	S	3.4 (3350)	4.5 ⑨	-	5.9	10.0	-	3.5	15.5	12.3 ⑦
	Firebird	P	5.7 (5733)	5.0 ⑨	-	5.9 ④	10.0	-	3.5	15.5	15.1 ⑧
1995-96	Camaro	T	3.1 (3136)	4.5 ⑨	-	5.9	10.0	-	3.5	15.5	14.7 ①
	Camaro	S	3.4 (3350)	4.5 ⑨	-	5.9	10.0	-	3.5	15.5	12.3 ⑦
	Camaro	P	5.7 (5733)	5.0 ⑨	-	5.9 ④	10.0	-	3.5	15.5	15.1 ⑧
	Firebird	T	3.1 (3136)	4.5 ⑨	-	5.9	10.0	-	3.5	15.5	14.7 ①
	Firebird	S	3.4 (3350)	4.5 ⑨	-	5.9	10.0	-	3.5	15.5	12.3 ⑦
	Firebird	P	5.7 (5733)	5.0 ⑨	-	5.9 ④	10.0	-	3.5	15.5	15.1 ⑧

① With AC: 14.8 qts.
② With AC: 18.0 qts.
③ With AC: 16.7 qts.
④ With 6 speed transmission: 8.0 pts.
⑤ With AC: 12.5 qts.
⑥ With AC: 15.3 qts.
⑦ With manual transmission: 12.5 qts.
⑧ With manual transmission: 15.3 qts.
⑨ With vehicle on level surface, check oil level. Add as required to fill

CAMSHAFT SPECIFICATIONS

All measurements given in inches.

Year	Engine ID/VIN	Engine Displacement Liters (cc)	Journal Diameter 1	2	3	4	5	Elevation In.	Ex.	Bearing Clearance	Camshaft End Play
1992	T	3.1 (3130)	1.868-1.881	1.868-1.881	1.868-1.881	1.868-1.881	NA	0.263	0.273	0.0010-0.0039	NA
	E	5.0 (4999)	1.8682-1.8692	1.8682-1.8692	1.8682-1.8692	1.8682-1.8692	1.8682-1.8692	0.234	0.257	NA	0.004-0.012
	F	5.0 (4999)	1.8682-1.8692	1.8682-1.8692	1.8682-1.8692	1.8682-1.8692	1.8682-1.8692	0.257	0.269	NA	0.004-0.012
	8	5.7 (5737)	1.8682-1.8692	1.8682-1.8692	1.8682-1.8692	1.8682-1.8692	1.8682-1.8692	0.273	0.284	NA	0.004-0.012
1993	T	3.1 (3130)	1.868-1.881	1.868-1.881	1.868-1.881	1.868-1.881	NA	0.263	0.273	0.0010-0.0039	NA
	S	3.4 (3393)	1.8680-1.8710	1.8680-1.8710	1.8680-1.8710	1.8680-1.8710	1.8680-1.8710	0.2626	0.2732	0.0010-0.0040	NA
	E	5.0 (4999)	1.8682-1.8692	1.8682-1.8692	1.8682-1.8692	1.8682-1.8692	1.8682-1.8692	0.234	0.257	NA	0.004-0.012
	8	5.7 (5737)	1.8682-1.8692	1.8682-1.8692	1.8682-1.8692	1.8682-1.8692	1.8682-1.8692	0.273	0.284	NA	0.004-0.012
	P	5.7 (5737)	1.8682-1.8692	1.8682-1.8692	1.8682-1.8692	1.8682-1.8692	1.8682-1.8692	0.2980-0.3020	0.2980-0.3020	NA	0.004-0.012
1994	T	3.1 (3130)	1.868-1.881	1.868-1.881	1.868-1.881	1.868-1.881	NA	0.263	0.273	0.0010-0.0039	NA
	S	3.4 (3393)	1.8680-1.8710	1.8680-1.8710	1.8680-1.8710	1.8680-1.8710	1.8680-1.8710	0.2626	0.2732	0.0010-0.0040	NA
	P	5.7 (5737)	1.8682-1.8692	1.8682-1.8692	1.8682-1.8692	1.8682-1.8692	1.8682-1.8692	0.2980-0.3020	0.2980-0.3020	NA	0.004-0.012
1995-96	T	3.1 (3130)	1.868-1.881	1.868-1.881	1.868-1.881	1.868-1.881	NA	0.263	0.273	0.0010-0.0039	NA
	S	3.4 (3393)	1.8680-1.8710	1.8680-1.8710	1.8680-1.8710	1.8680-1.8710	1.8680-1.8710	0.2626	0.2732	0.0010-0.0040	NA
	P	5.7 (5737)	1.8682-1.8692	1.8682-1.8692	1.8682-1.8692	1.8682-1.8692	1.8682-1.8692	0.2980-0.3020	0.2980-0.3020	NA	0.0040-0.0120

NA - Not Available

CRANKSHAFT AND CONNECTING ROD SPECIFICATIONS

All measurements are given in inches.

Year	Engine ID/VIN	Engine Displacement Liters (cc)	Crankshaft Main Brg. Journal Dia.	Main Brg. Oil Clearance	Shaft End-play	Thrust on No.	Connecting Rod Journal Diameter	Oil Clearance	Side Clearance
1992	T	3.1 (3130)	2.6473-2.6483	0.0012-0.0030	0.002-0.008	3	1.9983-1.9994	0.0010-0.0040	0.0140-0.0270
	E	5.0 (4999)	①	②	0.001-0.007	5	2.0986-2.0998	0.0013-0.0035	0.006-0.014
	F	5.0 (4999)	①	②	0.002-0.006	5	2.0986-2.0998	0.0018-0.0039	0.008-0.014
	8	5.7 (5737)	①	②	0.002-0.006	5	2.0986-2.0998	0.0013-0.0035	0.006-0.014

CRANKSHAFT AND CONNECTING ROD SPECIFICATIONS
All measurements are given in inches.

Year	Engine ID/VIN	Engine Displacement Liters (cc)	Crankshaft Main Brg. Journal Dia.	Crankshaft Main Brg. Oil Clearance	Crankshaft Shaft End-play	Crankshaft Thrust on No.	Connecting Rod Journal Diameter	Connecting Rod Oil Clearance	Connecting Rod Side Clearance
1993	T	3.1 (3130)	2.6473-2.6483	0.0012-0.0030	0.002-0.008	3	1.9983-1.9994	0.0010-0.0040	0.0140-0.0270
	S	3.4 (3393)	2.6473-2.6483	0.0012-0.0030	0.0024-0.0083	3	1.9987-1.9994	0.0011-0.0032	0.0070-0.0170
	E	5.0 (4999)	①	②	0.001-0.007	5	2.0986-2.0998	0.0013-0.0035	0.006-0.014
	P	5.7 (5737)	①	②	0.002-0.006	5	2.0986-2.0998	0.0013-0.0035	0.006-0.014
1994	T	3.1 (3130)	2.6473-2.6483	0.0012-0.0030	0.002-0.008	3	1.9983-1.9994	0.0010-0.0040	0.0140-0.0270
	S	3.4 (3393)	2.6473-2.6483	0.0012-0.0030	0.0024-0.0083	3	1.9987-1.9994	0.0011-0.0032	0.0070-0.0170
	P	5.7 (5737)	③	④	0.002-0.006	5	2.0986-2.0998	0.0013-0.0035	0.006-0.014
1995-96	T	3.1 (3130)	2.6473-2.6483	0.0012-0.0030	0.002-0.008	3	1.9983-1.9994	0.0010-0.0040	0.0140-0.0270
	S	3.4 (3393)	2.6473-2.6483	0.0012-0.0030	0.0024-0.0083	3	1.9987-1.9994	0.0011-0.0032	0.0070-0.0170
	P	5.7 (5737)	③	④	0.0020-0.0060	5	2.0986-2.0998	0.0013-0.0035	0.0060-0.0140

① No. 1: 2.4484-2.4493
Nos. 2-4: 2.4481-2.4490
No. 5: 2.4479-2.4488

② No. 1: 0.0008-0.0020
Nos. 2-4: 0.0011-0.0023
No. 5: 0.0017-0.0032

③ No. 1: 2.4485-2.4491
Nos. 2-4: 2.4485-2.4491

④ No. 1: 0.0008-0.0020
Nos. 2-4: 0.0011-0.0020
No. 5: 0.0017-0.0032

VALVE SPECIFICATIONS

Year	Engine ID/VIN	Engine Displacement Liters (cc)	Seat Angle (deg.)	Face Angle (deg.)	Spring Test Pressure (lbs. @ in.)	Spring Installed Height (in.)	Stem-to-Guide Clearance (in.) Intake	Stem-to-Guide Clearance (in.) Exhaust	Stem Diameter (in.) Intake	Stem Diameter (in.) Exhaust
1992	T	3.1 (3130)	46	45	90 ①	1.60 ②	0.0010-0.0027	0.0010-0.0027	NA	NA
	E	5.0 (4999)	46	45	194-206@1.25	③	0.0011-0.0027	0.0011-0.0027	NA	NA
	F	5.0 (4999)	46	45	194-206@1.25	③	0.0010-0.0027	0.0010-0.0027	NA	NA
	8	5.7 (5737)	46	45	194-206@1.25	③	0.0011-0.0027	0.0011-0.0027	NA	NA
1993	T	3.1 (3130)	46	45	90 ①	1.60 ②	0.0010-0.0027	0.0010-0.0027	NA	NA
	S	3.4 (3393)	46	45	190@1.20	1.61	0.0014-0.0025	0.0015-0.0029	NA	NA
	E	5.0 (4999)	46	45	194-206@1.25	③	0.0011-0.0027	0.0011-0.0027	NA	NA
	8	5.7 (5737)	46	45	194-206@1.25	③	0.0011-0.0027	0.0011-0.0027	NA	NA
	P	5.7 (5737)	46	45	252-272@1.305	1.78	0.0011-0.0027	0.0011-0.0027	NA	NA

VALVE SPECIFICATIONS

Year	Engine ID/VIN	Engine Displacement Liters (cc)	Seat Angle (deg.)	Face Angle (deg.)	Spring Test Pressure (lbs. @ in.)	Spring Installed Height (in.)	Stem-to-Guide Clearance (in.)		Stem Diameter (in.)	
							Intake	Exhaust	Intake	Exhaust
1994	T	3.1 (3130)	46	45	90 ①	1.60 ②	0.0010-0.0027	0.0010-0.0027	NA	NA
	S	3.4 (3393)	46	45	190@1.20	1.61	0.0014-0.0025	0.0015-0.0029	NA	NA
	P	5.7 (5737)	46	45	187-203@1.27	1.70	0.0009-0.0027	0.0009-0.0027	NA	NA
1995-96	T	3.1 (3130)	46	45	90 ①	1.60 ②	0.0010-0.0027	0.0010-0.0027	NA	NA
	S	3.4 (3393)	46	45	190@1.20	1.61	0.0014-0.0025	0.0015-0.0029	NA	NA
	P	5.7 (5737)	46	45	187-203@1.27	1.70	0.0009-0.0027	0.0009-0.0027	NA	NA

NA - Not Available
① With valve open
② With valve closed
③ Intake: 1.72
   Exhaust: 1.59

PISTON AND RING SPECIFICATIONS

All measurements are given in inches.

Year	Engine ID/VIN	Engine Displacement Liters (cc)	Piston Clearance	Ring Gap			Ring Side Clearance		
				Top Compression	Bottom Compression	Oil Control	Top Compression	Bottom Compression	Oil Control
1992	T	3.1 (3130)	0.0009-0.0022	0.010-0.020	0.020-0.028	0.010-0.030	0.002-0.003	0.002-0.003	0.008
	E	5.0 (4999)	0.007-0.017	0.010-0.020	0.010-0.025	0.015-0.055	0.0012-0.0032	0.0012-0.0032	0.0020-0.0070
	F	5.0 (4999)	0.0012-0.0032	0.010-0.020	0.010-0.025	0.015-0.055	0.0012-0.0032	0.0012-0.0032	0.0020-0.0070
	8	5.7 (5737)	0.0025-0.0035	0.010-0.020	0.010-0.025	0.015-0.055	0.0012-0.0032	0.0012-0.0032	0.0020-0.0070
1993	T	3.1 (3130)	0.0009-0.0022	0.010-0.020	0.020-0.028	0.010-0.030	0.002-0.003	0.002-0.003	0.008
	S	3.4 (3393)	0.0011-0.0024	0.007-0.016	0.019-0.029	0.010-0.030	0.0020-0.0035	0.0020-0.0035	0.0080 MAX
	E	5.0 (4999)	0.007-0.017	0.010-0.020	0.010-0.025	0.015-0.055	0.0012-0.0032	0.0012-0.0032	0.0020-0.0070
	8	5.7 (5737)	0.0025-0.0035	0.010-0.020	0.010-0.025	0.015-0.055	0.0012-0.0032	0.0012-0.0032	0.0020-0.0070
	P	5.7 (5737)	0.0010-0.0027	0.010-0.020	0.018-0.026	0.010-0.030	0.0012-0.0032	0.0012-0.0032	0.0020-0.0070
1994	T	3.1 (3130)	0.0009-0.0022	0.010-0.020	0.020-0.028	0.010-0.030	0.002-0.003	0.002-0.003	0.008
	S	3.4 (3393)	0.0011-0.0024	0.007-0.016	0.019-0.029	0.010-0.030	0.0020-0.0035	0.0020-0.0035	0.0080 MAX
	P	5.7 (5737)	0.0010-0.0027	0.010-0.020	0.018-0.026	0.010-0.030	0.0012-0.0032	0.0012-0.0032	0.0020-0.0070

PISTON AND RING SPECIFICATIONS

All measurements are given in inches.

Year	Engine ID/VIN	Engine Displacement Liters (cc)	Piston Clearance	Ring Gap			Ring Side Clearance		
				Top Compression	Bottom Compression	Oil Control	Top Compression	Bottom Compression	Oil Control
1995-96	T	3.1 (3130)	0.0009-0.0022	0.010-0.020	0.020-0.028	0.010-0.030	0.002-0.003	0.002-0.003	0.008
	S	3.4 (3393)	0.0011-0.0024	0.007-0.016	0.019-0.029	0.010-0.030	0.0020-0.0035	0.0020-0.0035	0.0080 MAX
	P	5.7 (5737)	0.0010-0.0027	0.010-0.020	0.018-0.026	0.010-0.030	0.0012-0.0032	0.0012-0.0032	0.0020-0.0070

NA - Not Available

TORQUE SPECIFICATIONS

All readings in ft. lbs.

Year	Engine ID/VIN	Engine Displacement Liters (cc)	Cylinder Head Bolts	Main Bearing Bolts	Rod Bearing Bolts	Crankshaft Damper Bolts	Flywheel Bolts	Manifold		Spark Plugs	Lug Nut
								Intake	Exhaust		
1992	T	3.1 (3130)	③	73	39	66-85	45-59	①	18	20	100
	E	5.0 (4999)	60-75	70-85	42-47	60	75	25-45	②	15-20	80-100
	F	5.0 (4999)	60-75	60-75	42-47	60	75	25-45	②	15-20	80-100
	8	5.7 (5737)	65	80	45	60	75	30	②	22	80-100
1993	T	3.1 (3130)	③	73	39	66-85	45-59	①	18	20	100
	S	3.4 (3393)	⑥	④	37	68	61	⑦	18	23	100
	E	5.0 (4999)	60-75	70-85	42-47	60	75	25-45	②	15-20	80-100
	8	5.7 (5737)	65	80	45	60	75	30	②	22	80-100
	P	5.7 (5737)	65	78	47	60	74	⑤	26	11	100
1994	T	3.1 (3130)	③	73	39	66-85	45-59	①	18	20	100
	S	3.4 (3393)	⑥	④	37	58	61	⑦	18	23	100
	P	5.7 (5737)	65	78	47	60	74	⑤	35	11	100
1995-96	T	3.1 (3130)	③	73	39	66-85	45-59	①	18	20	100
	S	3.4 (3393)	⑥	④	37	58	61	⑦	18	23	100
	P	5.7 (5737)	65	78	47	60	74	⑤	35	11	100

NA - Not Available
① 15 ft. lbs., then 24 ft. lbs.
② Outer bolts: 14-26 ft. lbs.
   Inner bolts: 20-32 ft. lbs.
③ 33 ft. lbs. plus 90 degrees
④ 37 ft. lbs. plus 75 degrees
⑤ Step 1: 71 inch lbs.
   Step 2: 35 ft. lbs.
⑥ 40 ft. lbs. plus 90 degrees
⑦ Upper manifold: 18 ft. lbs.
   Lower manifold bolt/nut: 22 ft. lbs.
   Upper manifold studs: 89 inch lbs.

BRAKE SPECIFICATIONS

All measurements in inches unless noted

Year	Model	Master Cylinder Bore	Brake Disc			Brake Drum Diameter			Minimum Lining Thickness	
			Original Thickness	Minimum Thickness	Maximum Runout	Original Inside Diameter	Max. Wear Limit	Maximum Machine Diameter	Front	Rear
1992	Camaro	①	②	③	0.005	9.50	9.59	9.56	0.030	0.030
	Firebird	①	②	③	0.005	9.50	9.59	9.56	0.030	0.030
1993	Camaro	①	②	③	0.005	9.50	9.59	9.56	0.030	0.030
	Firebird	①	②	③	0.005	9.50	9.59	9.56	0.030	0.030
1994	Camaro	①	②	③	0.005	9.50	9.59	9.56	0.030	0.030
	Firebird	①	②	③	0.005	9.50	9.59	9.56	0.030	0.030

BRAKE SPECIFICATIONS
All measurements in inches unless noted

Year	Model	Master Cylinder Bore	Brake Disc			Brake Drum Diameter			Minimum Lining Thickness	
			Original Thickness	Minimum Thickness	Maximum Runout	Original Inside Diameter	Max. Wear Limit	Maximum Machine Diameter	Front	Rear
1995-96	Camaro	①	②	③	0.005	9.50	9.59	9.56	0.030	0.030
	Firebird	①	②	③	0.005	9.50	9.59	9.56	0.030	0.030

① Rear drum: 0.945; Rear disc: 1.00
② Front: 1.043; Rear: 0.795
③ Front: 0.980; Rear: 0.744

WHEEL ALIGNMENT

Year	Model		Caster		Camber		Toe-in (in.)	Steering Axis Inclination (deg.)
			Range (deg.)	Preferred Setting (deg.)	Range (deg.)	Preferred Setting (deg.)		
1992	Camaro		4 5/16P-5 5/16P	4 13/16P	3/16N-13/16P	5/16P	0	NA
	Firebird		4 5/16P-5 5/16P	4 13/16P	3/16N-13/16P	5/16P	0	NA
1993	Camaro	F	4 3/8P-5 3/8P	4 11/16P	3/16P-1 3/16P	11/16P	0	NA
		R	-	-	9/16N-9/16P	0	0	-
	Firebird	F	4 3/8P-5 3/8P	4 11/16P	3/16P-1 3/16P	11/16P	0	NA
		R	-	-	9/16N-9/16P	0	0	-
1994	Camaro	F	4 3/8P-5 3/8P	4 11/16P	3/16P-1 3/16P	11/16P	0	NA
		R	-	-	9/16N-9/16P	0	0	-
	Firebird	F	4 3/8P-5 3/8P	4 11/16P	3/16P-1 3/16P	11/16P	0	NA
		R	-	-	9/16N-9/16P	0	0	-
1995-96	Camaro	F	4 3/8P-5 3/8P	4 11/16P	3/16P-1 3/16P	11/16P	0	NA
		R	-	-	9/16N-9/16P	0	0	-
	Firebird	F	4 3/8P-5 3/8P	4 11/16P	3/16P-1 3/16P	11/16P	0	NA
		R	-	-	9/16N-9/16P	0	0	-

NA - Not Available
F - Front
R - Rear

CORVETTE

VEHICLE IDENTIFICATION CHART

		Engine Code					Model Year	
Code	Liters	Cu. In. (cc)	Cyl.	Fuel Sys.	Eng. Mfg.		Code	Year
J	5.7	350 (5737)	8	MFI	①		N	1992
P	5.7	350 (5737)	8	MFI	CPC		P	1993
							R	1994
							S	1995
							T	1996

CPC - Chevrolet/Pontiac/Canada

MFI - Multiport fuel injection

① Manufactured by Mercury Marine

ENGINE IDENTIFICATION

Year	Model	Engine Displacement Liters (cc)	Engine Series (ID/VIN)	Fuel System	No. of Cylinders	Engine Type
1992	Corvette	5.7 (5737)	J	MFI	8	DOHC
	Corvette	5.7 (5737)	P	MFI	8	OHV
1993	Corvette	5.7 (5737)	J	MFI	8	DOHC
	Corvette	5.7 (5737)	P	MFI	8	OHV
1994	Corvette	5.7 (5737)	J	MFI	8	DOHC
	Corvette	5.7 (5737)	P	MFI	8	OHV
1995-96	Corvette	5.7 (5737)	J	MFI	8	DOHC
	Corvette	5.7 (5737)	P	MFI	8	OHV

MFI - Multiport fuel injection

OHV - Overhead valve

DOHC - Double overhead camshaft

GENERAL ENGINE SPECIFICATIONS

Year	Engine ID/VIN	Engine Displacement Liters (cc)	Fuel System Type	Net Horsepower @ rpm	Net Torque @ rpm (ft. lbs.)	Bore x Stroke (in.)	Compression Ratio	Oil Pressure @ rpm
1992	J	5.7 (5737)	MFI	375@3800	370@4800	3.90x3.66	11.0:1	40@2000
	P	5.7 (5737)	MFI	300@5000	330@4000	4.00x3.48	10.25:1	18@2000
1993	J	5.7 (5737)	MFI	375@5800	370@4800	3.90x3.66	11.0:1	40@2000
	P	5.7 (5737)	MFI	300@5000	340@3600	4.00x3.48	10.25:1	18@2000
1994	J	5.7 (5737)	MFI	375@5800	370@4800	3.90x3.66	11.0:1	40@2000
	P	5.7 (5737)	MFI	300@5000	340@3600	4.00x3.48	10.25:1	18@2000
1995-96	J	5.7 (5737)	MFI	375@5800	370@4800	3.90x3.66	11.0:1	40@2000
	P	5.7 (5737)	MFI	300@5000	340@3600	4.00x3.48	10.25:1	18@2000

MFI - Multiport fuel injection

GASOLINE ENGINE TUNE-UP SPECIFICATIONS

Year	Engine ID/VIN	Engine Displacement Liters (cc)	Spark Plugs Gap (in.)	Ignition Timing (deg.) MT	AT	Fuel Pump (psi)	Idle Speed (rpm) MT	AT	Valve Clearance In.	Ex.
1992	J	5.7 (5737)	0.035	①	①	48-55	①	①	HYD	HYD
	P	5.7 (5737)	0.035	-	①	41-47	-	①	HYD	HYD
1993	J	5.7 (5737)	0.035	①	①	48-55	①	①	HYD	HYD
	P	5.7 (5737)	0.035	-	①	41-47	-	①	HYD	HYD
1994	J	5.7 (5737)	0.035	①	①	48-55	①	①	HYD	HYD
	P	5.7 (5737)	0.035	-	①	41-47	-	①	HYD	HYD
1995-96	J	5.7 (5737)	0.035	①	①	48-55	①	①	HYD	HYD
	P	5.7 (5737)	0.035	-	①	41-47	-	①	HYD	HYD

NOTE: The Vehicle Emission Control Information label often reflects specification changes made during production. The label figures must be used if they differ from those in this chart.

HYD - Hydraulic

① Refer to Vehicle Emission Control Information label

CAPACITIES

Year	Model	Engine ID/VIN	Engine Displacement Liters (cc)	Engine Oil with Filter (qts.)	Transmission (pts.) 5-Spd	6-Spd	Auto.	Drive Axle (pts.)	Fuel Tank (gal.)	Cooling System (qts.)
1992	Corvette	J	5.7 (5737)	8.6	-	②	-	3.75	20.0	14.7
	Corvette	P	5.7 (5737)	4.5	-	②	10.0 ①	3.75	20.0	17.8
1993	Corvette	J	5.7 (5737)	8.6	-	②	-	3.75	20.0	14.7
	Corvette	P	5.7 (5737)	4.5	-	②	10.0 ①	3.75	20.0	17.8
1994	Corvette	J	5.7 (5737)	8.6	-	②	-	3.75	20.0	14.7
	Corvette	P	5.7 (5737)	4.5	-	②	10.0 ①	3.75	20.0	17.8
1995-96	Corvette	J	5.7 (5737)	8.6	-	②	-	3.75	20.0	14.7
	Corvette	P	5.7 (5737)	4.5	-	②	10.0 ①	3.75	20.0	17.8

① 440T4 trans.: 13.0 pts.
125C trans.: 8.0 pts.

② ZF 6 speed trans.: 4.4 pts.

CAMSHAFT SPECIFICATIONS
All measurements given in inches.

Year	Engine ID/VIN	Engine Displacement Liters (cc)	Journal Diameter 1	2	3	4	5	Elevation In.	Ex.	Bearing Clearance	Camshaft End Play
1992	J	5.7 (5737)	1.1400-1.1410	1.1400-1.1410	1.1400-1.1410	1.1400-1.1410	1.1400-1.1410	0.3878-0.3918	0.3878-0.3918	NA	0.006-0.014
1993	J	5.7 (5737)	1.1400-1.1410	1.1400-1.1410	1.1400-1.1410	1.1400-1.1410	1.1400-1.1410	0.3878-0.3918	0.3878-0.3918	NA	0.006-0.014
	P	5.7 (5737)	1.8682-1.8692	1.8682-1.8692	1.8682-1.8692	1.8682-1.8692	1.8682-1.8692	0.2980-0.3020	0.2980-0.3020	NA	0.004-0.012
1994	J	5.7 (5737)	1.1400-1.1410	1.1400-1.1410	1.1400-1.1410	1.1400-1.1410	1.1400-1.1410	0.3878-0.3918	0.3878-0.3918	NA	0.006-0.014
	P	5.7 (5737)	1.8682-1.8692	1.8682-1.8692	1.8682-1.8692	1.8682-1.8692	1.8682-1.8692	0.2980-0.3020	0.2980-0.3020	NA	0.004-0.012
1995-96	J	5.7 (5737)	1.1400-1.1410	1.1400-1.1410	1.1400-1.1410	1.1400-1.1410	1.1400-1.1410	0.3878-0.3918	0.3878-0.3918	NA	0.0060-0.0140
	P	5.7 (5737)	1.8682-1.8692	1.8682-1.8692	1.8682-1.8692	1.8682-1.8692	1.8682-1.8692	0.2980-0.3020	0.2980-0.3020	NA	0.0040-0.0120

NA - Not Available

CRANKSHAFT AND CONNECTING ROD SPECIFICATIONS
All measurements are given in inches.

Year	Engine ID/VIN	Engine Displacement Liters (cc)	Crankshaft				Connecting Rod		
			Main Brg. Journal Dia.	Main Brg. Oil Clearance	Shaft End-play	Thrust on No.	Journal Diameter	Oil Clearance	Side Clearance
1992	J	5.7 (5737)	2.7550-2.7560	0.0007-0.0023	0.0006-0.0010	3	2.0993-2.1000	0.0007-0.0027	0.008-0.028
1993	J	5.7 (5737)	2.7550-2.7560	0.0007-0.0023	0.0006-0.0010	3	2.0993-2.1000	0.0007-0.0027	0.008-0.028
	P	5.7 (5737)	①	②	0.002-0.006	5	2.0986-2.0998	0.0013-0.0035	0.006-0.014
1994	J	5.7 (5737)	2.7550-2.7560	0.0007-0.0023	0.0006-0.0010	3	2.0993-2.1000	0.0007-0.0027	0.008-0.028
	P	5.7 (5737)	③	④	0.002-0.006	5	2.0986-2.0998	0.0013-0.0035	0.006-0.014
1995-96	J	5.7 (5737)	2.7550-2.7560	0.0007-0.0023	0.0006-0.0010	3	2.0993-2.1000	0.0007-0.0027	0.0080-0.0280
	P	5.7 (5737)	③	④	0.0020-0.0060	5	2.0986-2.0998	0.0013-0.0035	0.0060-0.0140

① No. 1: 2.4484-2.4493
   Nos. 2-4: 2.4481-2.4490
   No. 5: 2.4479-2.4488
② No. 1: 0.0008-0.0020
   Nos. 2-4: 0.0011-0.0023
   No. 5: 0.0017-0.0032

③ No. 1: 2.4485-2.4491
   Nos. 2-4: 2.4485-2.4491
④ No. 1: 0.0008-0.0020
   Nos. 2-4: 0.0011-0.0020
   No. 5: 0.0017-0.0032

VALVE SPECIFICATIONS

Year	Engine ID/VIN	Engine Displacement Liters (cc)	Seat Angle (deg.)	Face Angle (deg.)	Spring Test Pressure (lbs. @ in.)	Spring Installed Height (in.)	Stem-to-Guide Clearance (in.)		Stem Diameter (in.)	
							Intake	Exhaust	Intake	Exhaust
1992	J	5.7 (5737)	44	45	147-166@ ① 0.95	1.34 ②	0.0011-0.0027	0.0011-0.0027	NA	NA
1993	J	5.7 (5737)	44	45	147-166@ ① 0.95	1.34 ②	0.0012-0.0026	0.0014-0.0030	NA	NA
	P	5.7 (5737)	46	45	252-272@ 1.305	1.78	0.0011-0.0027	0.0011-0.0027	NA	NA
1994	J	5.7 (5737)	44	45	147-166@ ① 0.95	1.34 ②	0.0012-0.0026	0.0014-0.0030	NA	NA
	P	5.7 (5737)	46	45	187-203@ 1.27	1.70	0.0009-0.0027	0.0009-0.0027	NA	NA
1995-96	J	5.7 (5737)	44	45	147-166@ ① 0.95	1.34 ②	0.0012-0.0026	0.0014-0.0030	NA	NA
	P	5.7 (5737)	46	45	187-203@ 1.27	1.70	0.0009-0.0027	0.0009-0.0027	NA	NA

NA - Not Available
① Inner spring: 75-82@0.79 in.
② Inner spring: 1.18 in.

PISTON AND RING SPECIFICATIONS

All measurements are given in inches.

Year	Engine ID/VIN	Engine Displacement Liters (cc)	Piston Clearance	Ring Gap			Ring Side Clearance		
				Top Compression	Bottom Compression	Oil Control	Top Compression	Bottom Compression	Oil Control
1992	J	5.7 (5737)	NA	0.016-0.026	0.031-0.039	0.012-0.024	0.002-0.003	0.002-0.003	0.001-0.002
1993	J	5.7 (5737)	NA	0.016-0.026	0.031-0.039	0.012-0.024	0.002-0.003	0.002-0.003	0.001-0.002
	P	5.7 (5737)	0.0010-0.0027	0.010-0.020	0.018-0.026	0.010-0.030	0.0012-0.0032	0.0012-0.0032	0.0020-0.0070
1994	J	5.7 (5737)	NA	0.016-0.026	0.031-0.039	0.012-0.024	0.002-0.003	0.002-0.003	0.001-0.002
	P	5.7 (5737)	0.0010-0.0027	0.010-0.020	0.018-0.026	0.010-0.030	0.0012-0.0032	0.0012-0.0032	0.0020-0.0070
1995-96	J	5.7 (5737)	NA	0.016-0.026	0.031-0.039	0.012-0.024	0.0020-0.0030	0.0020-0.0030	0.0010-0.0020
	P	5.7 (5737)	0.0010-0.0027	0.010-0.020	0.018-0.026	0.010-0.030	0.0012-0.0032	0.0012-0.0032	0.0020-0.0070

NA - Not Available

TORQUE SPECIFICATIONS

All readings in ft. lbs.

Year	Engine ID/VIN	Engine Displacement Liters (cc)	Cylinder Head Bolts	Main Bearing Bolts	Rod Bearing Bolts	Crankshaft Damper Bolts	Flywheel Bolts	Manifold		Spark Plugs	Lug Nut
								Intake	Exhaust		
1992	J	5.7 (5737)	③	②	⑤	148	66	④	①	15	100
	P	5.7 (5737)	65	68	47	70	74	35	26	NA	100
1993	J	5.7 (5737)	③	②	⑤	148	66	④	①	15	100
	P	5.7 (5737)	65	78	47	60	74	⑥	26	11	100
1994	J	5.7 (5737)	③	②	⑤	148	66	④	①	15	100
	P	5.7 (5737)	65	78	47	60	74	⑥	35	11	100
1995-96	J	5.7 (5737)	③	②	⑤	148	66	④	①	15	100
	P	5.7 (5737)	65	78	47	60	74	⑥	35	11	100

NA - Not Available

① Studs: 22 ft. lbs.
　 Bolts: 18 ft. lbs.
② Step 1: 15 ft. lbs.
　 Step 2: Inner: 65-70 degrees
　 Step 3: Outer: 50-55 degrees
③ Step 1: 45 ft. lbs.
　 Step 2: 74 ft. lbs.
　 Step 3: 118 ft. lbs.
④ Injector housing and fuel rail bolts: 20 ft. lbs.
⑤ 22 ft. lbs. plus 80-85 degrees
⑥ Step 1: 71 inch lbs.
　 Step 2: 35 ft. lbs.

BRAKE SPECIFICATIONS

All measurements in inches unless noted

Year	Model	Master Cylinder Bore	Brake Disc			Brake Drum Diameter			Minimum Lining Thickness	
			Original Thickness	Minimum Thickness	Maximum Runout	Original Inside Diameter	Max. Wear Limit	Maximum Machine Diameter	Front	Rear
1992	Corvette	NA	②	①	0.006	NA	NA	NA	0.030	0.030
1993	Corvette	NA	②	①	0.006	NA	NA	NA	0.030	0.030
1994	Corvette	NA	②	①	0.006	NA	NA	NA	0.030	0.030
1995-96	Corvette	NA	②	①	0.006	NA	NA	NA	0.030	0.030

NA - Not Available
① Heavy duty: 1.059; Std.: 0.744
② Heavy duty: 1.110; Std.: 0.795

WHEEL ALIGNMENT

Year	Model		Caster Range (deg.)	Caster Preferred Setting (deg.)	Camber Range (deg.)	Camber Preferred Setting (deg.)	Toe-in (in.)	Steering Axis Inclination (deg.)
1992	Corvette	F	5 1/2P-6 1/2P	6P	0-1P	1/2P	0	8 3/4
		R	-	-	1/2N-1/2P	0	0	-
1993	Corvette	F	5 1/2P-6 1/2P	6P	0-1P	1/2P	0	8 3/4
		R	-	-	1/2N-1/2P	0	0	-
1994	Corvette	F	5 1/2P-6 1/2P	6P	0-1P	1/2P	0	8 3/4
		R	-	-	1/2N-1/2P	0	0	-
1995-96	Corvette	F	5 1/2P-6 1/2P	6P	0-1P	1/2P	0	8 3/4
		R	-	-	1/2N-1/2P	0	0	-

SATURN

VEHICLE IDENTIFICATION CHART

		Engine Code					Model Year	
Code	Liters	Cu. In. (cc)	Cyl.	Fuel Sys.	Eng. Mfg.		Code	Year
7	1.9	116 (1901)	4	MFI	Saturn		N	1992
8	1.9	116 (1901)	4	MFI	Saturn		P	1993
9	1.9	116 (1901)	4	TFI	Saturn		R	1994
							S	1995
							T	1996

MFI - Multiport fuel injection

TFI - Throttle body fuel injection

ENGINE IDENTIFICATION

Year	Model	Engine Displacement Liters (cc)	Engine Series (ID/VIN)	Fuel System	No. of Cylinders	Engine Type
1992	Sedan	1.9 (1901)	7	MFI	4	DOHC
	Sedan	1.9 (1901)	9	TFI	4	SOHC
	Coupe	1.9 (1901)	7	MFI	4	DOHC

ENGINE IDENTIFICATION

Year	Model	Engine Displacement Liters (cc)	Engine Series (ID/VIN)	Fuel System	No. of Cylinders	Engine Type
1993	Sedan	1.9 (1901)	7	MFI	4	DOHC
	Sedan	1.9 (1901)	9	TFI	4	SOHC
	Coupe	1.9 (1901)	7	MFI	4	DOHC
	Coupe	1.9 (1901)	9	TFI	4	SOHC
	Wagon	1.9 (1901)	7	MFI	4	DOHC
	Wagon	1.9 (1901)	9	TFI	4	SOHC
1994	Sedan	1.9 (1901)	7	MFI	4	DOHC
	Sedan	1.9 (1901)	9	TFI	4	SOHC
	Coupe	1.9 (1901)	7	MFI	4	DOHC
	Coupe	1.9 (1901)	9	TFI	4	SOHC
	Wagon	1.9 (1901)	7	MFI	4	DOHC
	Wagon	1.9 (1901)	9	TFI	4	SOHC
1995-96	Sedan	1.9 (1901)	7	MFI	4	DOHC
	Sedan	1.9 (1901)	8	MFI	4	SOHC
	Coupe	1.9 (1901)	7	MFI	4	DOHC
	Coupe	1.9 (1901)	8	MFI	4	SOHC
	Wagon	1.9 (1901)	7	MFI	4	DOHC
	Wagon	1.9 (1901)	8	MFI	4	SOHC

MFI - Multiport fuel injection
TFI - Throttle body fuel injection
DOHC - Double overhead camshaft
SOHC - Single overhead camshaft

GENERAL ENGINE SPECIFICATIONS

Year	Engine ID/VIN	Engine Displacement Liters (cc)	Fuel System Type	Net Horsepower @ rpm	Net Torque @ rpm (ft. lbs.)	Bore x Stroke (in.)	Compression Ratio	Oil Pressure @ rpm
1992	7	1.9 (1901)	MFI	124@5600	122@4800	3.23x3.54	9.5:1	29@2000
	9	1.9 (1901)	TFI	85@5000	108@2400	3.23x3.54	9.3:1	36@2000
1993	7	1.9 (1901)	MFI	124@5600	122@4800	3.23x3.54	9.5:1	29@2000
	9	1.9 (1901)	TFI	85@5000	107@2400	3.23x3.54	9.3:1	36@2000
1994	7	1.9 (1901)	MFI	124@5600	122@4800	3.23x3.54	9.5:1	29@2000
	9	1.9 (1901)	TFI	85@5000	107@2400	3.23x3.54	9.3:1	36@2000
1995-96	7	1.9 (1901)	MFI	124@5600	122@4800	3.23x3.54	9.5:1	29@2000
	8	1.9 (1901)	MFI	85@5000	107@2400	3.23x3.54	9.3:1	36@2000

MFI - Multiport fuel injection
TFI - Throttle body fuel injection

GASOLINE ENGINE TUNE-UP SPECIFICATIONS

Year	Engine ID/VIN	Engine Displacement Liters (cc)	Spark Plugs Gap (in.)	Ignition Timing (deg.) MT	Ignition Timing (deg.) AT	Fuel Pump (psi)	Idle Speed (rpm) MT	Idle Speed (rpm) AT	Valve Clearance In.	Valve Clearance Ex.
1992	7	1.9 (1901)	0.040	①	①	31-36 ②	850 ③	750 ③	HYD	HYD
	9	1.9 (1901)	0.040	①	①	26-31 ②	750 ③	650 ③	HYD	HYD
1993	7	1.9 (1901)	0.040	①	①	31-36 ②	③	750 ③	HYD	HYD
	9	1.9 (1901)	0.040	①	①	26-31 ②	750 ③	650 ③	HYD	HYD
1994	7	1.9 (1901)	0.040	①	①	31-36 ②	③	750 ③	HYD	HYD
	9	1.9 (1901)	0.040	①	①	26-31 ②	③	650 ③	HYD	HYD
1995-96	7	1.9 (1901)	0.040	①	①	31-36 ②	850 ③	750 ③	HYD	HYD
	8	1.9 (1901)	0.040	①	①	26-31 ②	750 ③	650 ③	HYD	HYD

NOTE: The Vehicle Emission Control Information label often reflects specification changes made during production. The label figures must be used if they differ from those in this chart.

HYD - Hydraulic

① Engines equipped with Distributorless Ignition System (DIS). Ignition timing is not adjustable
② Pressure measured at idle
③ Idle speed measured with manual transmission in neutral; automatic transmission in drive

CAPACITIES

Year	Model	Engine ID/VIN	Engine Displacement Liters (cc)	Engine Oil with Filter (qts.)	Transmission (pts.) 4-Spd	Transmission (pts.) 5-Spd	Transmission (pts.) Auto.	Drive Axle Front (pts.)	Drive Axle Rear (pts.)	Fuel Tank (gal.)	Cooling System (qts.)
1992	Sedan	7	1.9 (1901)	4.0	-	5.2	7.5	-	-	12.8	7.0
	Sedan	9	1.9 (1901)	4.0	-	5.2	7.5	-	-	12.8	7.0
	Coupe	7	1.9 (1901)	4.0	-	5.2	7.5	-	-	12.8	7.0
1993	Wagon	7	1.9 (1901)	4.0	-	5.2	7.5	-	-	12.8	7.0
	Wagon	9	1.9 (1901)	4.0	-	5.2	7.5	-	-	12.8	7.0
	Sedan	7	1.9 (1901)	4.0	-	5.2	7.5	-	-	12.8	7.0
	Sedan	9	1.9 (1901)	4.0	-	5.2	7.5	-	-	12.8	7.0
	Coupe	7	1.9 (1901)	4.0	-	5.2	7.5	-	-	12.8	7.0
	Coupe	9	1.9 (1901)	4.0	-	5.2	7.5	-	-	12.8	7.0
1994	Wagon	7	1.9 (1901)	4.0	-	5.2	7.5 ①	-	-	12.8	7.0
	Wagon	9	1.9 (1901)	4.0	-	5.2	7.5 ①	-	-	12.8	7.0
	Sedan	7	1.9 (1901)	4.0	-	5.2	7.5 ①	-	-	12.8	7.0
	Sedan	9	1.9 (1901)	4.0	-	5.2	7.5 ①	-	-	12.8	7.0
	Coupe	7	1.9 (1901)	4.0	-	5.2	7.5 ①	-	-	12.8	7.0
	Coupe	9	1.9 (1901)	4.0	-	5.2	7.5 ①	-	-	12.8	7.0
1995-96	Sedan	7	1.9 (1901)	4.0	-	5.2	7.5 ①	-	-	12.8	7.0
	Sedan	8	1.9 (1901)	4.0	-	5.2	7.5 ①	-	-	12.8	7.0
	Coupe	7	1.9 (1901)	4.0	-	5.2	7.5 ①	-	-	12.8	7.0
	Coupe	8	1.9 (1901)	4.0	-	5.2	7.5 ①	-	-	12.8	7.0
	Wagon	7	1.9 (1901)	4.0	-	5.2	7.5 ①	-	-	12.8	7.0
	Wagon	8	1.9 (1901)	4.0	-	5.2	7.5 ①	-	-	12.8	7.0

① Overhaul

CAMSHAFT SPECIFICATIONS

All measurements given in inches.

Year	Engine ID/VIN	Engine Displacement Liters (cc)	Journal Diameter 1	2	3	4	5	Elevation In.	Ex.	Bearing Clearance	Camshaft End Play
1992	7	1.9 (1901)	1.1398-1.1406	1.1398-1.1406	1.1398-1.1406	1.1398-1.1406	1.1398-1.1406	0.3528-0.3559	0.3409-0.3441	0.0012-0.0030	0.0020-0.0080
	9	1.9 (1901)	1.7480-1.7490	1.7480-1.7490	1.7480-1.7490	1.7480-1.7490	1.7480-1.7490	0.2531-0.2556	0.2531-0.2556	0.0020-0.0040	0.0028-0.0079
1993	7	1.9 (1901)	1.1398-1.1406	1.1398-1.1406	1.1398-1.1406	1.1398-1.1406	1.1398-1.1406	0.3528-0.3559	0.3409-0.3441	0.0012-0.0030	0.0020-0.0080
	9	1.9 (1901)	1.7480-1.7490	1.7480-1.7490	1.7480-1.7490	1.7480-1.7490	1.7480-1.7490	0.2531-0.2556	0.2531-0.2556	0.0020-0.0040	0.0028-0.0079
1994	7	1.9 (1901)	1.1398-1.1406	1.1398-1.1406	1.1398-1.1406	1.1398-1.1406	1.1398-1.1406	0.3528-0.3559	0.3409-0.3441	0.0012-0.0030	0.0020-0.0080
	9	1.9 (1901)	1.7480-1.7490	1.7480-1.7490	1.7480-1.7490	1.7480-1.7490	1.7480-1.7490	0.2531-0.2556	0.2531-0.2556	0.0020-0.0040	0.0020-0.0079
1995-96	7	1.9 (1901)	1.1398-1.1406	1.1398-1.1406	1.1398-1.1406	1.1398-1.1406	1.1398-1.1406	0.3528-0.3559	0.3409-0.3441	0.0012-0.0030	0.0020-0.0080
	8	1.9 (1901)	1.7480-1.7490	1.7480-1.7490	1.7480-1.7490	1.7480-1.7490	1.7480-1.7490	0.2531-0.2556	0.2531-0.2556	0.0020-0.0079	0.0020-0.0079

CRANKSHAFT AND CONNECTING ROD SPECIFICATIONS

All measurements are given in inches.

Year	Engine ID/VIN	Engine Displacement Liters (cc)	Crankshaft Main Brg. Journal Dia.	Main Brg. Oil Clearance	Shaft End-play	Thrust on No.	Connecting Rod Journal Diameter	Oil Clearance	Side Clearance
1992	7	1.9 (1901)	2.2438-2.2444	0.0002-0.0020	0.002-0.008	3	1.8500-1.8508	0.0001-0.0021	0.0065-0.01713
	9	1.9 (1901)	2.2438-2.2444	0.0002-0.0020	0.002-0.008	3	1.8500-1.8508	0.0001-0.0021	0.0065-0.01713
1993	7	1.9 (1901)	2.2438-2.2444	0.0002-0.0020	0.002-0.008	3	1.8500-1.8508	0.0001-0.0021	0.0065-0.01713
	9	1.9 (1901)	2.2438-2.2444	0.0002-0.0020	0.002-0.008	3	1.8500-1.8508	0.0001-0.0021	0.0065-0.01713
1994	7	1.9 (1901)	2.2438-2.2444	0.0002-0.0020	0.002-0.008	3	1.8500-1.8508	0.0001-0.0021	0.0065-0.0171
	9	1.9 (1901)	2.2438-2.2444	0.0002-0.0020	0.002-0.008	3	1.8500-1.8508	0.0001-0.0021	0.0065-0.0171
1995-96	7	1.9 (1901)	2.2438-2.2444	0.0002-0.0020	0.002-0.008	3	1.8500-1.8508	0.0001-0.0021	0.0065-0.01713
	8	1.9 (1901)	2.2438-2.2444	0.0002-0.0020	0.002-0.008	3	1.8500-1.8508	0.0001-0.0021	0.0065-0.01713

VALVE SPECIFICATIONS

Year	Engine ID/VIN	Engine Displacement Liters (cc)	Seat Angle (deg.)	Face Angle (deg.)	Spring Test Pressure (lbs. @ in.)	Spring Installed Height (in.)	Stem-to-Guide Clearance (in.) Intake	Stem-to-Guide Clearance (in.) Exhaust	Stem Diameter (in.) Intake	Stem Diameter (in.) Exhaust
1992	7	1.9 (1901)	44.5-45.5	45-45.5	163-180@ 0.984	①	0.0010- 0.0025	0.0015- 0.0032	0.2736- 0.2740	0.2729- 0.2736
	9	1.9 (1901)	44.5-45.5	45-45.5	202-211@ 1.280	①	0.0010- 0.0025	0.0015- 0.0032	0.2736- 0.2741	0.2736- 0.2740
1993	7	1.9 (1901)	44.5-45.5	45-45.5	163-180@ 0.984	①	0.0010- 0.0025	0.0015- 0.0032	0.2736- 0.2740	0.2729- 0.2736
	9	1.9 (1901)	44.5-45.5	45-45.5	202-211@ 1.280	①	0.0010- 0.0025	0.0015- 0.0032	0.2736- 0.2741	0.2736- 0.2740
1994	7	1.9 (1901)	44.5-45.5	45-45.5	163-180@ 0.984	①	0.0010- 0.0025	0.0015- 0.0032	0.2736- 0.2740	0.2729- 0.2736
	9	1.9 (1901)	44.5-45.5	45-45.5	202-211@ 1.280	①	0.0010- 0.0025	0.0015- 0.0032	0.2736- 0.2741	0.2736- 0.2740
1995-96	7	1.9 (1901)	44.5-45.4	45-45.5	163-180@ 0.984	①	0.0010- 0.0025	0.0015- 0.0032	0.2736- 0.2740	0.2729- 0.2736
	8	1.9 (1901)	44.5-45.4	45-45.5	202-211@ 1.280	①	0.0010- 0.0025	0.0015- 0.0032	0.2736- 0.2741	0.2736- 0.2740

① Installed height not available
Free length SOHC: 1.8898-1.9134
Free length DOHC: 1.6100

PISTON AND RING SPECIFICATIONS
All measurements are given in inches.

Year	Engine ID/VIN	Engine Displacement Liters (cc)	Piston Clearance	Ring Gap Top Compression	Ring Gap Bottom Compression	Ring Gap Oil Control	Ring Side Clearance Top Compression	Ring Side Clearance Bottom Compression	Ring Side Clearance Oil Control
1992	7	1.9 (1901)	①	0.0098-0.0197	0.0098-0.0197	0.0098-0.0492	0.0016-0.0035	0.0012-0.0031	SNUG
	9	1.9 (1901)	①	0.0098-0.0197	0.0098-0.0197	0.0098-0.0492	0.0016-0.0035	0.0012-0.0031	SNUG
1993	7	1.9 (1901)	①	0.0098-0.0197	0.0098-0.0197	0.0098-0.0492	0.0016-0.0035	0.0012-0.0031	SNUG
	9	1.9 (1901)	①	0.0098-0.0197	0.0098-0.0197	0.0098-0.0492	0.0016-0.0035	0.0012-0.0031	SNUG
1994	7	1.9 (1901)	①	0.0098-0.0197	0.0098-0.0197	0.0098-0.0492	0.0016-0.0035	0.0012-0.0031	SNUG
	9	1.9 (1901)	①	0.0098-0.0197	0.0098-0.0197	0.0098-0.0492	0.0016-0.0035	0.0012-0.0031	SNUG
1995-96	7	1.9 (1901)	①	0.0098-0.0197	0.0098-0.0197	0.0098-0.0492	0.0016-0.0035	0.0012-0.0031	SNUG
	8	1.9 (1901)	①	0.0098-0.0197	0.0098-0.0197	0.0098-0.0492	0.0016-0.0035	0.0012-0.0031	SNUG

① Bores 1-3: 0.0002-0.0017
Bore 4: 0.0006-0.0021

TORQUE SPECIFICATIONS
All readings in ft. lbs.

Year	Engine ID/VIN	Engine Displacement Liters (cc)	Cylinder Head Bolts	Main Bearing Bolts	Rod Bearing Bolts	Crankshaft Damper Bolts	Flywheel Bolts	Manifold Intake	Manifold Exhaust	Spark Plugs	Lug Nut
1992	7	1.9 (1901)	②	37	33	159	59 ④	22 ③	23 ③	20	103
	9	1.9 (1901)	①	37	33	159	59 ④	15 ③	16 ③	20	103
1993	7	1.9 (1901)	②	37	33	159	59 ④	22 ③	23 ③	20	103
	9	1.9 (1901)	①	37	33	159	59 ④	15 ③	16 ③	20	103
1994	7	1.9 (1901)	②	37	33	159	59 ④	22 ③	22 ③	20	103
	9	1.9 (1901)	①	37	33	159	59 ④	22 ③	22 ③	20	103
1995-96	7	1.9 (1901)	②	37	33	159	59 ④	22 ③	22 ③	20	103
	8	1.9 (1901)	①	37	33	159	59 ④	22 ③	22 ③	20	103

① Step 1: 22 ft. lbs.
　Step 2: 33 ft. lbs.
　Step 3: 90 degrees
② Step 1: 22 ft. lbs.
　Step 2: 37 ft. lbs.
　Step 3: 90 degrees
③ Studs: 106 in. lbs.
④ Flexplate specification: 44 ft. lbs.

BRAKE SPECIFICATIONS
All measurements in inches unless noted

Year	Model	Master Cylinder Bore	Brake Disc Original Thickness	Brake Disc Minimum Thickness	Maximum Runout	Brake Drum Diameter Original Inside Diameter	Max. Wear Limit	Maximum Machine Diameter	Minimum Lining Thickness Front	Minimum Lining Thickness Rear
1992	Sedan	NA	①	②	0.0024	7.87	7.93	7.91	0.080	0.040
	Coupe	NA	①	②	0.0024	7.87	7.93	7.91	0.080	0.040
1993	Sedan	NA	①	②	0.0024	7.87	7.93	7.91	0.080	0.040
	Coupe	NA	①	②	0.0024	7.87	7.93	7.91	0.080	0.040
	Wagon	NA	①	②	0.0024	7.87	7.93	7.91	0.080	0.040
1994	Sedan	NA	①	②	0.0024	7.87	7.93	7.91	0.080	0.040
	Coupe	NA	①	②	0.0024	7.87	7.93	7.91	0.080	0.040
	Wagon	NA	①	②	0.0024	7.87	7.93	7.91	0.080	0.040
1995-96	Sedan	NA	①	②	0.0024	7.87	7.93	7.91	0.080	0.040
	Coupe	NA	①	②	0.0024	7.87	7.93	7.91	0.080	0.040
	Wagon	NA	①	②	0.0024	7.87	7.93	7.91	0.080	0.040

NA - Not Available
① Front: 0.710
　Rear: 0.430
② Front: 0.633
　Rear: 0.370

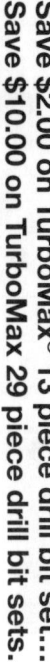

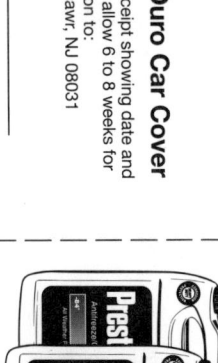

HERE'S HOW TO GET YOUR CASH

1. Purchase any of the selected quality AC products on the front of the coupon from your local AC-Delco retailer during the rebate period through December 31, 1996.
2. Circle the price of your AC product on your store receipt (dated during the rebate period) and clip the "AC" brand name and part number from each package as proof of purchase.
3. Complete this coupon and mail it with your receipts and proof of purchase to:

AC-Delco Rebate, P.O. Box 5970, Kalamazoo, MI 49003-5970
Good only in USA.

This rebate request must be received by Jan. 31, 1997.

Number of AC Spark Plugs/Glow Plugs	_____	x $ .35 = $ _____	(Excludes AC RAPIDFIRE Spark Plugs.)
Number of AC Oil Filters	_____	x $1.25 = $ _____	
Number of AC Air Filters	_____	x $1.75 = $ _____	
		TOTAL REBATE $ _____	

Name. _____

Address. _____

City. _____ State. _____ Zip. _____

Make/Model//Year of Vehicle. _____ Mileage. _____ Engine. _____ Cylinders. _____

AC Products Used _____

NOTE: Please allow up to 90 days for you rebate. Offer effective through December 31, 1996. Coupon must be received by January 31, 1997. Rebate limited to a maximum of 32 AC Spark Plugs/Glow Plugs (AC RAPIDFIRE Spark Plug is not eligible for this rebate), 4 AC Oil Filters, 4 AC Air Filters per household. Reproduction of coupon not accepted. Offer good only in U.S.A. Void where prohibited. Not available to clubs, groups or other organizations or to AC-Delco direct or indirect retailers.

Valvoline $3.00 Cash-Back Offer on DURABLEND™

To receive your Valvoline® DuraBlend™ check good for cash, complete this special order form and send it with your proof-of-purchase* to the address below. **REBATE REQUESTS MUST BE MAILED WITHIN 30 DAYS OF CASH REGISTER RECEIPT DATE.**

DuraBlend™ $3.00 Cash-Back • 400 Benigno Blvd. • Bellmawr, NJ 08031

* Proof-of-Purchase includes:

Your original dated sales receipt for Valvoline® DuraBlend™ Motor Oil; AND One of the following (check one):

_____ UPC code from bottom of one six-pack case containers of Valvoline® Semi-Synthetic DuraBlend™ Motor Oil.

_____ Tamper-proof rings from up to six 1 quart bottles of Valvoline® DuraBlend™ Motor Oil.

Rebate requests must be made on this special order form and may not be mechanically reproduced. Offer Good October 1, 1995 to December 31, 1996. Limit of one Valvoline® DuraBlend™ check per household, address or organization. Maximum rebate of $3.00 allowed. Requests in excess of the limit will not be acknowledged or returned. Offer good only in the USA and Puerto Rico. Offer void where prohibited, taxed or otherwise restricted by law. May not be used in conjunction with any other Valvoline offer. Allow 8 weeks for delivery of your Valvoline® DuraBlend™ Check. Rebate check must be cashed within 90 days of issue. (Rebate checks will not be sent to a post box number).

PLEASE COMPLETE THE FOLLOWING INFORMATION. PLEASE PRINT, NO ADDRESS LABELS ACCEPTED.

Name. _____

Address. _____ Apt.# _____

City. _____ State. _____ Zip. _____